D0931122

Collins

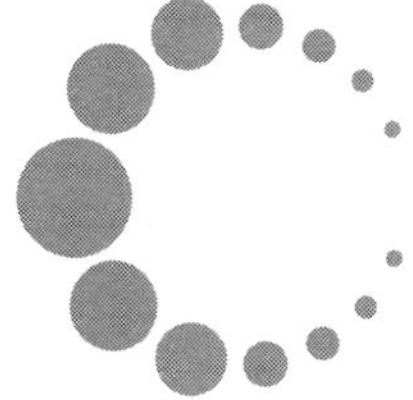

Collins English Dictionary

William Collins' dream of knowledge for all began with the publication of his first book in 1819. A self-educated mill worker, he not only enriched millions of lives, but also founded a flourishing publishing house. Today, staying true to this spirit, Collins books are packed with inspiration, innovation, and practical expertise. They place you at the centre of a world of possibility and give you exactly what you need to explore it.

Language is the key to this exploration, and at the heart of Collins Dictionaries is language as it is really used. New words, phrases, and meanings spring up every day, and all of them are captured and analysed by the Collins Word Web. Constantly updated, and with over 2.5 billion entries, this living language resource is unique to our dictionaries.

Words are tools for life. And a Collins Dictionary makes them work for you.

Collins. Do more.

Collins
English
Dictionary

HarperCollins Publishers
Westerhill Road
Bishopbriggs
Glasgow
G64 2QT

First Edition 2004

First Canadian Edition 2005

Latest Reprint 2005

UK Edition ISBN 0-00-716334-7
South African Edition ISBN 0-00-771719-9
Canadian Edition ISBN 0-00-720926-6

www.collins.co.uk

A catalogue record for this book is available from the British Library.

Designed by Mark Thomson

This edition prepared in conjunction with and typeset by Market House Books Ltd, Aylesbury, England
Printed and bound in Great Britain by Bath Press

Acknowledgements
We would like to thank those authors and publishers who kindly gave permission for copyright materialto be used in the Collins Word Web. We would also like to thank Times Newspapers Ltd for providing valuable data.

Collins

Contents

EDITORIAL STAFF

EDITORS
Sandra Anderson
Jeremy Butterfield
John Daintith
Andrew Holmes
Alan Isaacs
Jonathan Law
Cordelia Lilly
Elizabeth Martin
Cormac McKeown
Anne Stibbs
Elspeth Summers

WEBSITE RESEARCH
Mike Munro
George Davidson

SUPPLEMENT
Ian Brooke
Clare Ford
David Lindsay
Jeremy J Smith

FOR THE PUBLISHERS
Morven Dooner
Elaine Higgleton
Lorna Knight

SPECIAL CONSULTANTS

AUSTRALIAN ENGLISH
W A Krebs
Ruth Wajnryb

CANADIAN ENGLISH
James Arthurs
Fraser Sutherland

NEW ZEALAND ENGLISH
Elizabeth Gordon

SOUTH AFRICAN ENGLISH
Geoffrey Hughes

FOR ORIGINAL EDITION
JM Sinclair

SPECIALIST CONTRIBUTORS FOR PREVIOUS EDITIONS

James Barnes
Stuart Bathgate
Ephraim Borowski
David Bourke
Professor Angela M Bowey
Angus Boyd
Professor Thomas Carbery
Laurence Chizlett
Professor M Christopher
Sandra Clarke
R Cutler
Brian Russell Davis
P Donaldson
Andrew Doswell
Colonel Andrew Duncan
Major S R Elliot
Ingrid von Essen
Richard Fryer
Dr W Gratzer
Rev Canon D W Gundry
Sandra Holmes
Lloyd Humberstone
Cmdr I Johnston RN
David Kilby
Rev D Lancashire
Richard Latham
Patrick Leggatt
Bob Marsden
Bruce Martin
C H Parsons
Catherine Playford
Alexander Purdie
J P Quayle
Miranda Robertson
Christopher Sion
N J Small
Peter J Smith
Professor Stuart Sutherland
Dr Eric Taylor
Loreto Todd
M J Walker
J W Warren
Professor Yorick Wilks
Stanley White
T C Wooldridge
U Yong-ee
Catherine M Young

About the type

This dictionary is typeset in CollinsFedra, a special version of the Fedra family of types designed by Peter Bil'ak. CollinsFedra has been customized especially for Collins dictionaries; it includes both sans serif (for headwords) and serif (entries) versions, in several different weights. Its relatively large x-height and open "eye", and its basis in the tradition of humanist letterforms, make CollinsFedra both familiar and easy to read at small sizes. It has been designed to use the minimum space without sacrificing legibility, as well as including a number of characters and signs that are specific to dictionary typography. Its companion phonetic type is the first of its kind to be drawn according to the same principles as the regular typeface, rather than assembled from rotated and reflected characters from other types.

Peter Bil'ak (b. 1973, Slovakia) is a graphic and type designer living in the Netherlands. He is the author of two books, *Illegibility* and *Transparency*. As well as the Fedra family, he has designed several other typefaces including Eureka. His typotheque.com website has become a focal point for research and debate around contemporary type design.

Foreword

The best dictionaries are snapshots of the language they define at the moment they go to press. At Collins our priority is simple: to make those pictures the sharpest and most true to life available. To achieve this goal consistently, we have had to position ourselves at the very forefront of language monitoring. Collins editors have initiated an extensive reading, listening, and viewing programme, taking in all kinds of broadcasts and publications – from the *British Medical Journal* to *Viz*, from the *Sopranos* to the *Six O'clock News*.

But what keeps users of our dictionaries firmly up to speed with the latest developments in English is our close analysis of **Collins Word Web**, an unparalleled 2.5-billion-word "corpus" of lexical data. A constant flow of text is fed into it from sources around the globe – newspapers, books, websites, and even transcripts of radio and TV shows. Every month, Collins Word Web grows by 35 million words, making it the biggest such resource in the world. When we suggest an expression is growing in popularity, we can back it up with hard figures. If it appears to be shifting in meaning we can call up reams of usage examples from the real world.

It's in the discovery of new words and phrases, however, that this way of working really comes into its own. Rather than relying solely on contributors noticing the emergence of a new coinage, Collins editors are automatically alerted to it at the moment of its acceptance, however fleetingly, into the language.

This latest Collins Dictionary combines our established dictionary values with the latest technology, redefining what a dictionary can do. The entries are, of course, as sharp and up-to-the-minute as ever, but this Collins Dictionary goes further. Many thousands of definitions are augmented with relevant website addresses, every one of which can be accessed instantly through live links on the accompanying CD-rom.

Reliable information on people and places can be hard to track down when you need it most, so this dictionary includes a host of biographical and geographical entries. An extensive supplement, **Write on Target**, offers practical advice on using English to the greatest effect in real-world situations: applying for a job, writing an essay, giving a persuasive presentation, or even writing up a scientific experiment.

We have complemented this new dictionary concept with an equally innovative design. Developed to be both easy to use and easy on the eye, the new layout is refreshingly clutter-free – taking you straight to the information you need with the minimum of fuss. The understated design belies the depth of detail in the various definitions, usage notes, examples, lists, and cross-references.

An essential and comprehensive reference in its own right, this Collins Dictionary is an ideal jumping-off point for specialized exploration of the Internet's vast resources – how far you go is up to you.

Guide to the Use of the Dictionary

This dictionary is designed to be easy to use so that you can go straight to the word you want. The Guide that follows sets out the main principles on which the Dictionary is arranged and enables you to make full use of the Dictionary by showing the range of information that it contains.

Headword

All main entries, including place names, biographies, abbreviations, prefixes and suffixes, are printed in large boldface type and are listed in strict alphabetical order. This applies even if the headword consists of more than one word.

Order of entries

Words that have the same spelling but are derived from different sources (homographs) are entered separately with superscript numbers after the headwords.

> **saw**[1] (sɔː) *n* **1** any of various hand tools ...
> **saw**[2] (sɔː) *vb* the past tense of **see**[1]
> **saw**[3] (sɔː) *n* a wise saying, maxim, or proverb ...

A word with an capital initial letter, if entered separately, follows the lower-case form. For example, **Arras** follows **arras**.

Place names

If a place has more than one name, its main entry is given at the name most often used in modern English, with a cross-reference at other names. Thus, the main entry for the capital of Bavaria is at **Munich**, with a cross-reference at **München**. If a place name has no current anglicized form, its main entry is at the form of the name used in the official language of the area. Thus, the main entry is at **Brno**, with a cross-reference at **Brünn**. Historical names of importance are also given, with dates where these can be ascertained.

> **Paris**[1] ('pærɪs; *French* pari) *n* ... Ancient name: **Lutetia**
> **Volgograd** (*Russian* vəlga'grat; *English* 'vɒlgəˌgræd) *n* ...
> Former names: **Tsaritsyn** (until 1925), **Stalingrad** (1925–61)

Statistical information about places has been obtained from the most up-to-date and reliable sources available. Population figures are derived from the most recent census available, the date of which is always given.

Biographical entries

Biographical entries are entered separately from and immediately following place names of the same spelling. They are entered at the surname of the subject or at his or her title if that is the name by which he or she is better known and are grouped under one headword when the spelling of the surname (or title) is identical.

Abbreviations, acronyms, and symbols

Abbreviations, acronyms, and symbols are entered as headwords in the main alphabetical list. In line with modern practice, full stops are generally not used but it can be assumed that nearly all abbreviations are equally acceptable with or without stops.

Prefixes, suffixes, and combining forms

Prefixes (eg **in-**, **pre-**, **sub-**), suffixes (eg **-able**, **-ation**, **-ity**), and combining forms (eg **psycho-**, **-iatry**) have been entered as headwords if they are still used freely to produce new words in English.

Variant spellings

Common acceptable variant spellings of English words are given as alternative forms of the headword.

> **capitalize** *or* **capitalise** *vb* ...

US spellings

Where different, US spellings are also recorded in the headword.

> **centre** *or US* **center** *n* ...

PRONUNCIATION

Pronunciations of words in this dictionary represent those that are common in educated British English speech. They are transcribed in the International Phonetic Alphabet (IPA). A *Pronunciation Key* is printed at the end of this Guide. The pronunciation is normally given in brackets immediately after the headword.

> **abase** (ə'beɪs) *vb* **abases, abasing, abased** (*tr*) **1** to humble ...

The stress pattern is marked by the symbols ' for primary stress and ˌ for secondary stress. The stress mark precedes the syllable to which it applies.

Variant pronunciations

When a headword has an acceptable variant pronunciation or stress pattern, the variant is given by repeating only the syllable or syllables that change.

> **economic** (ˌiːkə'nɒmɪk, ˌɛkə-) *adj* **1** of or relating to ...

Pronunciations with different parts of speech

When two or more parts of speech of a word have different pronunciations, the pronunciations are shown in brackets before the relevant group of senses.

> **record** *n* ('rɛkɔːd) **1** an account in permanent form, ...
> ▷ *vb* (rɪ'kɔːd) (*mainly tr*) **18** to set down in some permanent form ...

Pronunciation of individual senses

If one sense of a headword is pronounced differently from the other senses, the pronunciation is given in brackets after the sense number.

> **conjure** (ˈkʌndʒə) *vb* **conjures, conjuring, conjured**
> 1 *(intr)* to practise conjuring 2 *(intr)* to call upon supposed supernatural forces by spells and incantations
> 3 (kənˈdʒʊə) *(tr)* to appeal earnestly to: *I conjure you to help me*

PARTS OF SPEECH

A part-of-speech label in italics precedes the sense or senses relating to that part of speech.

Standard parts of speech

The standard parts of speech, with the abbreviations used, are as follows: adjective (*adj*), adverb (*adv*), conjunction (*conj*), interjection (*interj*), noun (*n*), preposition (*prep*), pronoun (*pron*), verb (*vb*).

Less traditional parts of speech

Some less traditional parts of speech have been used in this dictionary:

determiner this denotes such words as *the, a, some, any, that, this,* as well as the numerals, and possessives such as *my* and *your.* Many determiners can have a pronoun function without change of meaning:

> **some** *determiner* ... **2a** an unknown or unspecified quantity or amount of: *there's some rice on the table; he owns some horses*
> **2b** *(as pron; functioning as sing or pl): we'll buy some ...*

sentence connector this description replaces the traditional classification of certain words, such as *therefore* and *however*, as adverbs or conjunctions. These words link sentences together rather in the manner of conjunctions; however, they are not confined to the first position in a clause as conjunctions are.

sentence substitute sentence substitutes are words such as *yes, no, perhaps, definitely*, and *maybe*. They can stand alone as meaningful utterances.

GRAMMATICAL INFORMATION

Grammatical information is provided in brackets and typically in italics to distinguish it from other types of information.

Adjectives and determiners

Some adjectives and determiners are restricted by usage to a particular position relative to the nouns they qualify. This is indicated by the following labels:

postpositive (used predicatively or after the noun, but not before it):

> **ablaze** *adj (postpositive), adv* **1** on fire; burning ...

immediately postpositive (always used immediately following the noun qualified and never used predicatively):

> **galore** *determiner (immediately postpositive)* in great numbers or quantity: *there were daffodils galore in the park* ...

prenominal (used before the noun, and never used predicatively):

> **chief** ... *adj* 4 *(prenominal)* **4a** most important; principal ...

Intensifiers

Adjectives and adverbs that perform an exclusively intensifying function, with no addition of meaning, are described as (intensifier) without further explanation.

> **blooming** *adv, adj Brit inf* (intensifier): *a blooming genius; blooming painful*

Conjunctions

Conjunctions are divided into two classes, marked by the following labels:

coordinating coordinating conjunctions connect words, phrases, or clauses that perform an identical function and are not dependent on each other. They include *and, but,* and *or.*

subordinating subordinating conjunctions introduce clauses that are dependent on a main clause in a complex sentence. They include *where, until,* and *if.*

Some conjunctions, such as *while* and *whereas*, can function as either coordinating or subordinating conjunctions.

Singular and plural labelling of nouns

Headwords and senses that are apparently plural in form but that take a singular verb, etc, are marked *(functioning as sing)*:

> **physics** *n (functioning as sing)* 1 the branch of science ...

Headwords and senses that appear to be singular, such as collective nouns, but that take a plural verb, etc, are marked *(functioning as pl)*:

> **cattle** *n (functioning as pl)* 1 bovid mammals of the tribe *Bovini* ...

Headwords and senses that may take either a singular or a plural verb, etc, are marked *(functioning as sing or pl)*:

> **bellows** *n (functioning as sing or pl)* 1 Also: **pair of bellows** an instrument consisting of an air chamber ...

Modifiers

A noun that is commonly used as if it were an adjective is labelled *modifier*. If the sense of the modifier can be understood from the sense of the noun, the modifier is shown without further explanation, with an example to illustrate its use. Otherwise its meaning and/or usage is explained separately.

> **key**[1] *n* ... 8 *(modifier)* of great importance: *a key issue*

Verbs

The principal parts given are: 3rd person singular of the present tense; present participle; past tense; past participle if different from the past tense.

Intransitive and transitive verbs

When a sense of a verb *(vb)* is restricted to transitive use, it is labelled *(tr)*; if it is intransitive only, it is labelled *(intr)*. If all the senses of a verb are transitive or all are intransitive, the appropriate label appears before the first numbered sense and is not repeated.
Absence of a label is significant: it indicates that the sense may be used both transitively and intransitively.
If nearly all the senses of a verb are transitive, the label *(mainly tr)* appears immediately before the first numbered sense. This indicates that, unless otherwise labelled, any given sense of the verb is transitive. Similarly, all the senses of a verb may be labelled *(mainly intr)*.

Copulas

A verb that takes a complement is labelled *(copula)*.

> **seem** *vb (may take an infinitive)* 1 *(copula)* to appear to the mind or eye; look: *the car seems to be running well* ...

Phrasal verbs

Verbal constructions consisting of a verb and a prepositional or an adverbial particle are given headword status if the meaning of the phrasal verb cannot be deduced from the separate meanings of the verb and the particle.
Phrasal verbs are labelled to show four possible distinctions:
a transitive verb with an adverbial particle *(tr, adv)*; a transitive verb with a prepositional particle *(tr, prep)*; an intransitive verb with an adverbial particle *(intr, adv)*; an intransitive verb with a prepositional particle:

> **turn on** ... 4 *(tr, adv) inf* to produce (charm, tears, etc) suddenly or automatically
> **take for** *vb (tr, prep) inf* to consider or suppose to be, esp mistakenly: *the fake coins were taken for genuine; who do you take me for?*
> **break off** ... 3 *(intr, adv)* to stop abruptly: *he broke off in the middle of his speech*
> **turn on** ... 2 *(intr, prep)* to depend or hinge on: *the success of the party turns on you*

The absence of a label is significant. If there is no label *(tr)* or *(intr)*, the verb may be used either transitively or intransitively. If there is no label *(adv)* or *(prep)*, the particle may be either adverbial or prepositional.

Any noun, adjective, or modifier formed from a phrasal verb is entered under the phrasal-verb headword. In some cases, where the noun or adjective is more common than the verb, the phrasal verb is entered after the noun or adjective form:

> **breakaway** *n* **1a** loss or withdrawal of a group of members from an association, club, etc **1b** (*as modifier*): *a breakaway faction* ... *vb* **break away** (*intr, adv*) **3** (often foll by *from*) to leave hastily or escape **4** to withdraw or secede

RESTRICTIVE LABELS

If a particular sense is restricted as to appropriateness, connotation, subject field, etc, an italic label is placed immediately before the relevant definition:

> **hang on** *vb (intr)* ... **5** *(adv) inf* to wait: *hang on for a few minutes*

If a label applies to all senses of one part of speech, it is placed immediately after the part-of-speech label.

> **assured** *adj* ... *n* **4** *chiefly Brit* **4a** the beneficiary under a life assurance policy **4b** the person whose life is insured ...

If a label applies to all senses of a headword, it is placed immediately after the pronunciation (or inflections).

> **con**[1] *inf* ... *n* **1a** short for confidence trick **1b** (*as modifier*): *con man* ... *vb* **cons, conning, conned** **2** *(tr)* to swindle ...

Usage labels

sl (slang) refers to words or senses that are informal and restricted in context, for example, to members of a particular social or cultural group. Slang words are inappropriate in formal speech or writing.
inf (informal) applies to words or senses that may be widely used, especially in conversation, letter-writing, etc, but that are not common in formal writing. Such words are subject to fewer contextual restrictions than slang words.
taboo indicates words that are not acceptable in polite use.
offens (offensive) indicates that a word might be regarded as offensive by the person described or referred to, even if the speaker uses the word without any malicious intention.
derog (derogatory) implies that the connotations of a word are unpleasant with intent on the part of the speaker or writer.
not standard indicates words or senses that are frequently encountered but widely regarded as incorrect.
arch (archaic) denotes a word or sense that is no longer in common use but that may be found in literary works or used to impart a historical colour to contemporary writing.
obs (obsolete) denotes a word or sense that is no longer in use. In specialist or technical fields the label often implies that the term has been superseded.

The word 'formerly' is placed in brackets before a sense when the practice, concept, etc, being described, rather than the word itself, is obsolete or out-of-date.

A number of other usage labels, such as *ironic*, *facetious*, and *euphemistic*, are used where appropriate.

Further help on usage is provided in usage notes after certain entries.

Subject-field labels

A number of italic labels are used to indicate that a word or sense is used in a particular specialist or technical field.

MEANING

The meaning of each headword in this dictionary is explained in one or more definitions, together with information about context and typical use.

Order of senses

As a general rule, where a headword has more than one sense, the first sense given is the one most common in current usage.

> **complexion** *n* **1** the colour and general appearance of a person's skin, esp of the face **2** aspect or nature: *the general complexion of a nation's finances* **3** *obs* temperament ...

Where the lexicographers consider that a current sense is the 'core meaning' in that it illuminates the meaning of other senses, the core meaning may be placed first.

> **competition** *n* **1** the act of competing **2** a contest in which a winner is selected from among two or more entrants **3** a series of games, sports events, etc **4** the opposition offered by competitors ...

Subsequent senses are arranged so as to give a coherent account of the meaning of a headword. If a word is used as more than one part of speech, all the senses of each part of speech are grouped together in a single block. Within a part-of-speech block, closely related senses are grouped together; technical senses generally follow general senses; archaic and obsolete sense follow technical senses; idioms and fixed phrases are generally placed last.

Scientific and technical definitions

Units, physical quantities, formulas, etc. In accordance with the recommendations of the International Standards Organization, all scientific measurements are expressed in SI units (*Système International d'Unités*). Measurements and quantities in more traditional units are often given as well as SI units. The entries for chemical compounds give the systematic names as well as the more familiar popular names.

RELATED ADJECTIVES

Certain nouns, especially of Germanic origin, have related adjectives that are derived from Latin or French. For example, **mural** (from Latin) is an adjective related in meaning to **wall**. Such adjectives are shown in a number of cases after the sense (or part-of-speech block) to which they are related.

> **wall** *n* 1a a vertical construction made of stone, brick, wood, etc ... *related adj* **mural** ...

IDIOMS

Fixed noun phrases, such as **dark horse**, and certain other idioms are given full headword status. Other idioms are placed under the key word of the idiom, as a separate sense, generally at the end of the appropriate part-of-speech block.

> **ground¹** *n* ... 17 **break new ground** to do something that has not been done before ...

ETYMOLOGIES

Etymologies are within square brackets and appear after the definition. They are given for all headwords except those that are derivative forms (consisting of a base word and a suffix or prefix), compound words, inflected forms, and proper names.

Many headwords, such as **enlighten** and **prepossess**, consist of a prefix and a base word and are not accompanied by etymologies since the essential etymological information is shown for the component parts, all of which are entered in the Dictionary as headwords in their own right.

The purpose of the etymologies is to trace briefly the history of the word back from the present day, through its first recorded appearance in English, to its origin, often in some source language other than English. The etymologies show the history of the word both in English (wherever there has been significant change in form or sense) and in its pre-English source languages.

Words printed in SMALL CAPITALS refer to other headwords where relevant or additional information, either in the definition or in the etymology, may be found.

Dating

The etymology records the first known occurrence (a written citation) of a word in English. Words first appearing in the language during the Middle English period or later are dated by century, abbreviated c.

> **mantis** ... [c17 NL, from Gk: prophet, alluding to its praying posture]

This indicates that there is a written citation for **mantis** in the seventeenth century. The absence of a New Latin or Greek form in the etymology means that the form of the word was the same in those languages as in English.

Old English

Native words from Old English are not dated, written records of Old English being scarce, but are simply identified as being of Old English origin.

DERIVED WORDS

Words derived from a base word by the addition of suffixes such as *-ly*, *-ness*, etc, are entered in boldface type immediately after the etymology or after the last definition if there is no etymology. They are preceded by the icon >. The meanings of such words may be deduced from the meanings of the suffix and the headword.

USAGE NOTES

A brief note introduced by the label USAGE has been added after entries in order to comment on matters of usage.

WEBSITE ADDRESSES

Many entries include helpful or interesting urls relating to them. A guide to internet safety follows.

▷ www.anglosaxon.net

PANEL ENTRIES

Throughout the dictionary there are a number of panel entries containing further useful information relating to a variety of topics:

BINARY PREFIXES

In 1998 the International Electrotechnical Commission approved the following prefixes for the powers of 2:

kibi-	**Ki-**	2^{10} = 1 024
mebi-	**Mi-**	2^{20} = 1 048 576
gibi-	**Gi-**	2^{30} = 1 073 741 824
tebi-	**Ti-**	2^{40} = 1 099 511 627 776
pebi-	**Pi-**	2^{50} = 1 125 899 906 842 624
exbi-	**Ei-**	2^{60} = 1 152 921 504 606 846 976

▷ http://whatis.techtarget.com/definition/0,,sid9_gci825099,00.html

Using the Internet safely

This section offers advice chiefly to parents concerned with the online safety of their children. Hints and tips for safe surfing are provided as is a list of websites dealing with this subject in more detail.

The Internet contains an inconceivably large amount of information, much of it free, on a vast range of topics. It does not belong to and is not controlled by any single organization, government, or nation. Although the absence of centralized control is occasionally lamented as anarchic, the lack of a top-down structure provides many benefits.

The Internet offers the chance for anyone with a computer and a modem to communicate with and learn from any person, group, or organization similarly equipped. Libraries, museums, art galleries, governments, universities, research institutes, and many other bodies provide open access to their data and links to the online resources of other organizations.

This availability of information and the unparalleled potential for communication and the spread of ideas provides Internet users with incalculable benefits, but there are downsides. As the Internet is unregulated and decentralized there is no quality-control mechanism; the only barrier preventing someone from setting up a website is technical ability. There is much of little merit on the Internet.

More worrying is the potential for criminal misuse. The Internet's accessibility and inclusiveness is exploited by those who wish to disseminate hate or obscenity or to take advantage of the vulnerable or gullible. As 70 per cent of UK households with school-age children are online it is important that parents and carers are aware of the potential dangers as well as the benefits.

Tips for safe use of the Internet and chatrooms

- Find out as much as possible about the Internet, chatrooms, instant messaging, and email. A number of websites dealing with the concerns of parents are listed at the bottom of this section.
- Make Internet surfing a family event as often as possible.
- Limit the amount of time your children spend online. Encourage them to maintain their other interests and hobbies.
- Keep the computer in a family room so that you can check how long your children have been using the Internet.
- Make sure your child doesn't give out personal details, phone numbers, addresses, or any other information that could be used to identify him or her, such as information about your family or the school he or she goes to.

- Make sure that any chatroom used by your child is monitored to prevent publication of offensive material or personal contact details.
- Online contacts should not be taken at face value. They may not be what they seem.
- Warn children never to arrange to meet someone only ever previously met on the Internet without first telling you. Accompany your child to any meetings and make sure they are held in a public place.
- Children should not accept files from people they don't know and trust offline, since the files could contain viruses or self-extracting software which could reveal personal information to the sender.
- Video-conferencing and webcams allow the transmission of voice and live images. Children should be discouraged from using this technology unsupervised and with people they don't know and trust offline.
- Talk with your children if they are made uncomfortable or feel threatened by anything they see online.
- Warn your children never to respond directly to anything they find disturbing. Encourage them to log off and report what they found to an adult.
- Discuss with your children news stories concerning the dangers of chatrooms and the Internet. The website www.chatdanger.com has a number of such reports.
- Consider using Internet filtering software and child-friendly search engines. Use your browser's controls, as some offer varying degrees of security for each family member.
- Investigate your Internet Service Provider's (ISP) child-protection services. Do they filter out spam (unwanted email), for instance?
- Investigate Internet safety in greater detail at the following websites:

  - www.chatdanger.com
  - http://safety.ngfl.gov.uk
  - www.childnet-int.org/links/index.html
  - www.internetcrimeforum.org.uk/chatwise_streetwise.html
  - www.nspcc.org.uk/html/home/needadvice/
  - helpyourchildsurfinsafety.htm

Pronunciation Key

The symbols used in the pronunciation transcriptions are those of the International Phonetic Alphabet. The following consonant symbols have their usual English values: *b, d, f, h, k, l, m, n, p, r, s, t, v, w, z*. The remaining symbols and their interpretations are listed below.

English Sounds

ɑː	as in *father* ('fɑːðə), *alms* (ɑːmz), *clerk* (klɑːk), *heart* (hɑːt), *sergeant* ('sɑːdʒənt)
æ	as in *act* (ækt), *Caedmon* ('kædmən), *plait* (plæt)
aɪ	as in *dive* (daɪv), *aisle* (aɪl), *guy* (gaɪ), *might* (maɪt), *rye* (raɪ)
aɪə	as in *fire* ('faɪə), *buyer* ('baɪə), *liar* ('laɪə), *tyre* ('taɪə)
aʊ	as in *out* (aʊt), *bough* (baʊ), *crowd* (kraʊd), *slouch* (slaʊtʃ)
aʊə	as in *flour* ('flaʊə), *cower* ('kaʊə), *flower* ('flaʊə), *sour* ('saʊə)
ɛ	as in *bet* (bɛt), *bury* ('bɛrɪ), *heifer* ('hɛfə), *said* (sɛd), *says* (sɛz)
eɪ	as in *paid* (peɪd), *day* (deɪ), *deign* (deɪn), *gauge* (geɪdʒ), *grey* (greɪ), *neigh* (neɪ)
ɛə	as in *bear* (bɛə), *dare* (dɛə), *prayer* (prɛə), *stairs* (stɛəz), *where* (wɛə)
g	as in *get* (gɛt), *give* (gɪv), *ghoul* (guːl), *guard* (gɑːd), *examine* (ɪg'zæmɪn)
ɪ	as in *pretty* ('prɪtɪ), *build* (bɪld), *busy* ('bɪzɪ), *nymph* (nɪmf), *pocket* ('pɒkɪt), *sieve* (sɪv), *women* ('wɪmɪn)
iː	as in *see* (siː), *aesthete* ('iːsθiːt), *evil* ('iːvᵊl), *magazine* (ˌmægə'ziːn), *receive* (rɪ'siːv), *siege* (siːdʒ)
ɪə	as in *fear* (fɪə), *beer* (bɪə), *mere* (mɪə), *tier* (tɪə)
j	as in *yes* (jɛs), *onion* ('ʌnjən), *vignette* (vɪ'njɛt)
ɒ	as in *pot* (pɒt), *botch* (bɒtʃ), *sorry* ('sɒrɪ)
əʊ	as in *note* (nəʊt), *beau* (bəʊ), *dough* (dəʊ), *hoe* (həʊ), *slow* (sləʊ), *yeoman* ('jəʊmən)
ɔː	as in *thaw* (θɔː), *broad* (brɔːd), *drawer* ('drɔːə), *fault* (fɔːlt), *halt* (hɔːlt), *organ* ('ɔːgən)
ɔɪ	as in *void* (vɔɪd), *boy* (bɔɪ), *destroy* (dɪ'strɔɪ)
ʊ	as in *pull* (pʊl), *good* (gʊd), *should* (ʃʊd), *woman* ('wʊmən)
uː	as in *zoo* (zuː), *do* (duː), *queue* (kjuː), *shoe* (ʃuː), *spew* (spjuː), *true* (truː), *you* (juː)
ʊə	as in *poor* (pʊə), *skewer* (skjʊə), *sure* (ʃʊə)
ə	as in *potter* ('pɒtə), *alone* (ə'ləʊn), *furious* ('fjʊərɪəs), *nation* ('neɪʃən), *the* (ðə)
ɜː	as in *fern* (fɜːn), *burn* (bɜːn), *fir* (fɜː), *learn* (lɜːn), *term* (tɜːm), *worm* (wɜːm)
ʌ	as in *cut* (kʌt), *flood* (flʌd), *rough* (rʌf), *son* (sʌn)

ʃ as in *ship* (ʃɪp), *election* (ɪˈlɛkʃən), *machine* (məˈʃiːn), *mission* (ˈmɪʃən), *pressure* (ˈprɛʃə), *schedule* (ˈʃɛdjuːl), *sugar* (ˈʃʊgə)

ʒ as in *treasure* (ˈtrɛʒə), *azure* (ˈæʒə), *closure* (ˈkləʊʒə), *evasion* (ɪˈveɪʒən)

tʃ as in *chew* (tʃuː), *nature* (ˈneɪtʃə)

dʒ as in *jaw* (dʒɔː), *adjective* (ˈædʒɪktɪv), *lodge* (lɒdʒ), *soldier* (ˈsəʊldʒə), *usage* (ˈjuːsɪdʒ)

θ as in *thin* (θɪn), *strength* (strɛŋθ), *three* (θriː)

ð as in *these* (ðiːz), *bathe* (beɪð), *lather* (ˈlɑːðə)

ŋ as in *sing* (sɪŋ), *finger* (ˈfɪŋgə), *sling* (slɪŋ)

ᵊ indicates that the following consonant (l or n) is syllabic, as in *bundle* (ˈbʌndᵊl), *button* (ˈbʌtᵊn)

Foreign Sounds

The symbols above are also used to represent foreign sounds where these are similar to English sounds. However, certain common foreign sounds require symbols with markedly different values, as follows:

a *a* in French *ami*, German *Mann*, Italian *pasta*: a sound between English (æ) and (ɑː), similar to the vowel in Northern English *cat* or London *cut*

ɑ *a* in French *bas*: a sound made with the tongue position similar to that of English (ɑː), but shorter

e *é* in French *été*, *eh* in German *sehr*, *e* in Italian *che*: a sound similar to the first part of the English diphthong (eɪ) in *day* or to the Scottish vowel in *day*

i *i* in French *il*, German *Idee*, Spanish *filo*, Italian *signore*: a sound made with a tongue position similar to that of English (iː), but shorter

ɔ *o* in Italian *no*, French *bonne*, German *Sonne*: a vowel resembling English (ɒ), but with a higher tongue position and more rounding of the lips

o *o* in French *rose*, German *so*, Italian *voce*: a sound between English (ɔː) and (uː) with closely rounded lips, similar to the Scottish vowel in *so*

u *ou* in French *genou*, *u* in German *kulant*, Spanish *puna*: a sound made with a tongue position similar to that of English (uː), but shorter

y *u* in French *tu*, *ü* in German *über* or *fünf*: a sound made with a tongue position similar to that of English (iː), but with closely rounded lips

ø *eu* in French *deux*, *ö* in German *schön*: a sound made with the tongue position of (e), but with closely rounded lips

œ *œu* in French *œuf*, *ö* in German *zwölf*: a sound made with a tongue position similar to that of English (ɛ), but with

	open rounded lips
˜	above a vowel indicates nasalization, as in French *un* (œ̃), *bon* (bɔ̃), *vin* (vɛ̃), *blanc* (blɑ̃)
χ	*ch* in Scottish *loch*, German *Buch*, *j* in Spanish *Juan*
ç	*ch* in German *ich*: a (j) sound as in *yes*, said without voice; similar to the first sound in *huge*
β	*b* in Spanish *Habana*: a voiced fricative sound similar to (v), but made by the two lips
ʎ	*ll* in Spanish *llamar*, *gl* in Italian *consiglio*: similar to the (lj) sequence in *million*, but with the tongue tip lowered and the sounds said simultaneously
ɥ	*u* in French *lui*: a short (y)
ɲ	*gn* in French *vigne*, Italian *gnocchi*, ñ in Spanish *España*: similar to the (nj) sequence in *onion*, but with the tongue tip lowered and the two sounds said simultaneously
ɣ	*g* in Spanish *luego*: a weak (g) made with voiced friction

Length

The symbol ː denotes length and is shown together with certain vowel symbols when the vowels are typically long.

Stress

Three grades of stress are shown in the transcriptions by the presence or absence of marks placed immediately *before* the affected syllable. Primary or strong stress is shown by ˈ, while secondary or weak stress is shown by ˌ. Unstressed syllables are not marked. In *photographic* (ˌfəʊtəˈɡræfɪk), for example, the first syllable carries secondary stress and the third primary stress, while the second and fourth are unstressed.

Notes

(i) Though words like *castle*, *path*, and *fast* are shown as pronounced with an /ɑː/ sound, many speakers use an /æ/. Such variations are acceptable and are to be assumed by the reader.
(ii) The letter 'r' in some positions is not sounded in the speech of Southern England and elsewhere. However, many speakers in other areas do sound the 'r' in such positions with varying degrees of distinctness. Again such variations are to be assumed, and in such words as *fern*, *fear*, and *arm* the reader will sound or not sound the 'r' according to his or her speech habits.
(iii) Though the widely received pronunciation of words like *which* and *why* is with a simple /w/ sound and is so shown in the dictionary, many speakers in Scotland and elsewhere preserve an aspirated sound: /hw/. Once again this variation is to be assumed.

Abbreviations

abbrev	**abbreviation**
Abor	**Aboriginal**
adj	**adjective**
adv	**adverb(ial)**
Afrik	**Afrikaans**
Amerind	**American Indian**
anat	**anatomy**
approx	**approximate(ly)**
Ar	**Arabic**
arch	**archaic**
archaeol	**archaeology**
archit	**architecture**
astrol	**astrology**
astron	**astronomy**
Austral	**Australian**
biol	**biology**
bot	**botany**
Brit	**Britain; British**
c	**century (eg c14 = 14th century)**
°C	**degrees Celsius**
Canad	**Canadian**
cap	**capital**
Cf	**compare**
chem	**chemistry**
comp	**comparative**
conj	**conjunction**
derog	**derogatory**
dim	**diminutive**
Du	**Dutch**
E	**east(ern); (in etymologies) English**
econ	**economics**
eg	**for example**
esp	**especially**
est	**estimate**
F	**French**
fem	**feminine**
foll	**followed**
ft	**foot** *or* **feet**
G	**German**
geog	**geography**
geol	**geology**
geom	**geometry**
Gk	**Greek**
Gmc	**Germanic**
Heb	**Hebrew**
ie	**that is**
imit	**of imitative origin**
in	**inch(es)**
inf	**informal**
infl	**influence(d)**
interj	**interjection**
intr	**intransitive**
It	**Italian**
km	**kilometre(s)**
L	**Late; Latin**
lit	**literally**
LL	**Late Latin**
m	**metre(s)**
M	**Middle**
masc	**masculine**
maths	**mathematics**
med	**medicine**
Med	**(in etymologies) Medieval**
MHG	**Middle High German**
mil	**military**
mod	**modern**
myth	**mythology**
n	**noun**
N	**north(ern)**
naut	**nautical**
NE	**northeast(ern)**
NL	**New Latin**
no	**number**
NW	**northwest(ern)**
NZ	**New Zealand**
O	**old**
obs	**obsolete**
offens	**offensive**
OHG	**Old High German**
ON	**Old Norse**
orig	**originally**
photog	**photography**
pl	**plural**
pop	**population**
Port	**Portuguese**
poss	**possibly**
p.p.	**past participle**
prep	**preposition(al)**
prob	**probably**
pron	**pronoun**
psychol	**psychology**
pt	**point**
p.t.	**past tense**
rel	**related**
S	**south(ern)**
S African	**South African**
Sansk	**Sanskrit**
Scand	**Scandinavian**
Scot	**Scottish; Scots**
SE	**southeast(ern)**
sing	**singular**
sl	**slang**
Sp	**Spanish**
sq	**square**
sup	**superlative**
SW	**southwest(ern)**
theol	**theology**
tr	**transitive**
ult	**ultimately**
US	**United States**
usu	**usually**
var	**variant**
vb	**verb**
vol	**volume**
W	**west(ern)**
wt	**weight**
Zool	**Zoology**
?	**(in etymologies) indicates a query**

a *or* **A** (eɪ) *n, pl* **a's, A's,** *or* **As 1** the first letter and first vowel of the English alphabet **2** any of several speech sounds represented by this letter, as in *take, bag,* or *calm* **3** Also called: **alpha** the first in a series, esp the highest mark **4 from A to Z** from start to finish

a[1] (ə; *emphatic* eɪ) *determiner* (*indefinite article;* used before an initial consonant ▷ Cf **an**[1]) **1** used preceding a singular countable noun, not previously specified: *a dog; a great pity* **2** used preceding a noun or determiner of quantity: *a dozen eggs; a great many; to read a lot* **3** (preceded by *once, twice, several times,* etc) each or every; per: *once a day* **4** a certain; one: *a Mr Jones called* **5** (preceded by *not*) any at all: *not a hope* ▷ Cf **the**[1]

USAGE See at **an**[1]

a[2] *symbol for:* **1** acceleration **2** are(s) (metric measure of area) **3** atto-

A *symbol for:* **1** *music* **1a** the sixth note of the scale of C major **1b** the major or minor key having this note as its tonic **2** a human blood type of the ABO group, containing the A antigen **3** (in Britain) a major arterial road **4** ampere(s) **5** absolute (temperature) **6** area **7** (*in combination*) atomic: *an A-bomb; an A-plant* **8a** a person whose job is in top management, or who holds a senior administrative or professional position **8b** (*as modifier*): *an A worker* ▷ See also **occupation groupings**

Å *symbol for* angstrom unit

A. *abbrev for:* **1** acre(s) **2** America(n) **3** answer

a-[1] *or before a vowel* **an-** *prefix* not; without; opposite to: *atonal; asocial* [from Gk *a-, an-* not, without]

a-[2] *prefix* **1** on; in; towards: *aground; aback* **2** in the state of: *afloat; asleep*

A1, A-1, *or* **A-one** (ˈeɪˈwʌn) *adj* **1** physically fit **2** *inf* first class; excellent **3** (of a vessel) in first-class condition

A2 *n Brit* an advanced level of a subject taken for the General Certificate of Education, forming the second part of an A-level course, after the AS level

A4 *n* a standard paper size, 297 × 210 mm

AA *abbrev for:* **1** Advertising Association **2** Alcoholics Anonymous **3** anti-aircraft **4** (in Britain) Automobile Association

AAA *abbrev for:* **1** *Brit* Amateur Athletic Association **2** Automobile Association of America **3** Automobile Association of Australia

Aachen (ˈɑːkən; *German* ˈaːxən) *n* a city and spa in W Germany, in North Rhine-Westphalia: the northern capital of Charlemagne's empire. Pop: 243 600 (1999 est). French name: **Aix-la-Chapelle**

Aalborg *or* **Ålborg** (*Danish* ˈɔlbɔr) *n* a city and port in Denmark, in N Jutland. Pop: 161 161 (2000 est)

Aalesund (*Norwegian* ˈoːləsun) *n* a variant spelling of **Ålesund**

Aalto (*Finnish* ˈɑːltɔ) *n* **Alvar** (ˈalvar) 1898–1976, Finnish architect and furniture designer, noted particularly for his public and industrial buildings, in which wood is much used. He invented bent plywood furniture (1932)

A & E *abbrev for* Accident and Emergency department (in hospitals)

A & R *abbrev for* artists and repertoire

AAP *abbrev for:* **1** Australian Associated Press **2** (in the US) affirmative action programme

▷ http://aap.com.au

Aarau (*German* ˈaːrau) *n* a town in N Switzerland, capital of Aargau canton: capital of the Helvetic Republic from 1798 to 1803. Pop: 15 881 (1990)

aardvark (ˈɑːdˌvɑːk) *n* a nocturnal burrowing African mammal that has long ears and snout and feeds on termites. Also called: **ant bear** [C19 from obs. Afrik., from *aarde* earth + *varken* pig]

aardwolf (ˈɑːdˌwʊlf) *n, pl* **aardwolves** a nocturnal mammal of the hyena family that inhabits the plains of southern Africa and feeds on termites and insect larvae [c19 from Afrik., from *aarde* earth + *wolf* wolf]

Aargau (*German* 'a:rgau) *n* a canton in N Switzerland. Capital: Aarau. Pop: 540 600 (2000 est). Area: 1404 sq km (542 sq miles). French name: **Argovie**

Aarhus *or* **Århus** (*Danish* 'ɔrhu:s) *n* a city and port in Denmark, in E Jutland. Pop: 284 846 (2000 est)

Aaron ('ɛərən) *n Old Testament* the first high priest of the Israelites, brother of Moses (Exodus 4:14)

Aaron's beard *n* another name for **rose of Sharon**

Aaron's rod *n* a widespread Eurasian plant having tall erect spikes of yellow flowers

A'asia *abbrev for* Australasia

AB *abbrev for:* **1** Also: **a.b.** able-bodied seaman **2** Alberta **3** (in the US) Bachelor of Arts ▷ **4** *symbol for* a human blood type of the ABO group, containing both the A antigen and the B antigen

ab-[1] *prefix* away from; opposite to: *abnormal* [from L *ab* away from]

ab-[2] *prefix* a cgs unit of measurement in the electromagnetic system: *abampere, abvolt* [from ABSOLUTE]

aba ('æbə) *n* **1** a type of cloth from Syria, made of goat or camel hair **2** a sleeveless outer garment of such cloth [from Ar.]

abaca ('æbəkə) *n* **1** a Philippine plant, the source of Manila hemp **2** another name for **Manila hemp** [via Sp. from Tagalog *abaká*]

aback (ə'bæk) *adv* **taken aback a** startled or disconcerted **b** *naut* (of a vessel or sail) having the wind against the forward side so as to prevent forward motion [OE *on bæc* to the back]

abacus ('æbəkəs) *n, pl* **abaci** (-ˌsaɪ) *or* **abacuses 1** a counting device that consists of a frame holding rods on which a number of beads are free to move **2** *archit* the flat upper part of the capital of a column [c16 from L, from Gk *abax* board covered with sand, from Heb. *ābhāq* dust]

Abaddon (ə'bædᵊn) *n* **1** the Devil (Revelation 9:11) **2** (in rabbinical literature) a part of Gehenna; Hell [Heb., lit.: destruction]

abaft (ə'bɑ:ft) *naut* ▷ *adv, adj* (*postpositive*) **1** closer to the stern than to another place on a vessel ▷ *prep* **2** behind; aft of [c13 *on baft; baft* from OE *beæftan*, from *be* by + *æftan* behind]

Abakan (*Russian* aba'kan) *n* a city in S central Russia, capital of the Khakass Republic, at the confluence of the Yenisei and Abakan Rivers. Pop: 169 000 (1999 est)

abalone (ˌæbə'ləʊnɪ) *n* an edible marine mollusc having an ear-shaped shell perforated with a row of respiratory holes and lined with mother-of-pearl. Also called: **ear shell** [c19 from American Sp. *abulón*]

abandon (ə'bændən) *vb* (*tr*) **1** to forsake completely; desert; leave behind **2** to give up completely: *to abandon hope* **3** to give up (something begun) before completion: *the game was abandoned* **4** to surrender (oneself) to emotion without restraint **5** to give (insured property that has suffered partial loss or damage) to the insurers in order that a claim for a total loss may be made ▷ *n* **6** freedom from inhibitions, restraint, or worry: *she danced with abandon* [c14 *abandounen* (vb), from OF, from *a bandon* under one's control, from *a* at, to + *bandon* control] > **a'bandonment** *n*

abandoned (ə'bændənd) *adj* **1** deserted: *an abandoned hut* **2** forsaken: *an abandoned child* **3** uninhibited

abase (ə'beɪs) *vb* **abases, abasing, abased** (*tr*) **1** to humble or belittle (oneself, etc) **2** to lower or reduce, as in rank [c15 *abessen*, from OF *abaissier* to make low. See BASE[2]] > **a'basement** *n*

abash (ə'bæʃ) *vb* (*tr; usually passive*) to cause to feel ill at ease, embarrassed, or confused [c14 from OF *esbair* to be astonished, from *es-* out + *bair* to gape]

abashed (ə'bæʃt) *adj* embarrassed or confused; ashamed > **abashedly** (ə'bæʃɪdlɪ) *adv* > **a'bashment** *n*

abate (ə'beɪt) *vb* **abates, abating, abated 1** to make or become less in amount, intensity, degree, etc **2** (*tr*) *law* **2a** to suppress or terminate (a nuisance) **2b** to suspend or extinguish (a claim or action) **2c** to annul (a writ) **3** (*intr*) *law* (of a writ, etc) to become null and void [c14 from OF *abatre* to beat down] > **a'batement** *n*

abatis *or* **abattis** ('æbətɪs) *n* **1** a rampart of felled trees with their branches outwards **2** a barbed-wire entanglement before a position [c18 from F, from *abattre* to fell]

abattoir ('æbəˌtwɑ:) *n* another name for **slaughterhouse** [c19 F, from *abattre* to fell]

Abba ('æbə) *n* **1** *New Testament* father (used of God) **2** a title given to bishops and patriarchs in the Syrian, Coptic, and Ethiopian Churches [from Aramaic] **3** Swedish pop group (1972–82): comprised Benny Andersson (born 1946), Agnetha Faltskog (born 1950), Anni-Frid Lyngstad (born 1945), and Bjorn Ulvaeus (born 1945); numerous hit singles included "Waterloo" (1974), "Dancing Queen" (1977), and "The Winner Takes It All" (1980)

abbacy ('æbəsɪ) *n, pl* **abbacies** the office, term of office, or jurisdiction of an abbot or abbess [c15 from Church L *abbātia*, from *abbāt-* ABBOT]

Abbado (ə'bɑ:dəʊ) *n* **Claudio** born 1933, Italian conductor; principal conductor of the London Symphony Orchestra (1979–88); director of the Vienna State Opera (1986–91), and the Berlin Philharmonic (1989–2001)

abbatial (ə'beɪʃəl) *adj* of an abbot, abbess, or abbey [c17 from Church L *abbātiālis*, from *abbāt-* ABBOT]

abbé ('æbeɪ) *n* **1** a French abbot **2** a title used in addressing any other French cleric, such as a priest

Abbe ('æbɪ; *German* 'a:bə) *n* **Ernst** 1840–1905, German physicist, noted for his work in optics and the microscope condenser known as the **Abbe condenser**

abbed (æbd) *adj inf* displaying well-developed abdominal muscles

abbess ('æbɪs) *n* the female superior of a convent [c13 from OF, from Church L *abbātissa*]

Abbevillian (æb'vɪlɪən) *archaeol* ▷ *n* **1** the period represented by Lower Palaeolithic European sites containing the earliest hand axes ▷ *adj* **2** of this period [c20 after *Abbeville*, N France, where the stone tools were discovered]

abbey ('æbɪ) *n* **1** a building inhabited by a community of monks or nuns **2** a church built in conjunction with such a building **3** a community of monks or nuns [c13 via OF *abeie* from Church L *abbātia* ABBACY]

abbot ('æbət) *n* the superior of an abbey of monks [OE *abbod*, from Church L *abbāt-* (stem of *abbas*), ult. from Aramaic *abbā* father] > **'abbotship** *or* **'abbotcy** *n*

abbreviate (ə'bri:vɪˌeɪt) *vb* **abbreviates, abbreviating, abbreviated** (*tr*) **1** to shorten (a word or phrase) by contraction or omission of some letters or words **2** to cut short; curtail [c15 from p.p. of LL *abbreviāre*, from L *brevis* brief]

abbreviation (əˌbri:vɪ'eɪʃən) *n* **1** a shortened or contracted form of a word or phrase **2** the process or result of abbreviating

ABBREVIATIONS WITH NUMBERS

1-to-1 a marketing concept involving personalisation in relationships with customers

9/11 September 11th, 2001

24/7 twenty-four hours a day, seven days a week

24/7/365 twenty-four hours a day, seven days a week, 365 days a year

2G second generation: a system for mobile phones characterized by digital technology, Internet access, and a short-message service
3G third generation: a system for mobile phones allowing fast connection, Internet access, digital photography, graphics transmission and display, and other advanced features
A2O apples to oranges: denoting a comparison between dissimilar things.
B2A business-to-anyone: denoting a desperate or ill-conceived business concept
B2B business-to-business: denoting an Internet communication channel between a company and its employers
B2B2C business-to-business-to-consumer: denoting an Internet communication channel connecting one company to another and then to consumers
B2C business-to-consumer: denoting an Internet communication channel between a business and consumers
B2E business-to-employee: denoting trade between commercial organizations rather than between businesses and private customers
B2G business-to-government: denoting commercial relationships between business and the government
C2B consumer-to-business: denoting the use of the Internet by consumers to dictate the prices that they are willing to pay to businesses for products, in a similar fashion to a reverse auction
C2C consumer-to-consumer: denoting the online sale and purchase of goods between private individuals, as in online auctions and through websites such as eBay
D2D developer-to-developer: denoting a collaboration between software developers
E2E 1 exchange-to-exchange: denoting an Internet communication channel between two websites that act as exchanges for goods or services 2 end-to-end: denoting complete solutions provided by a company to enable other companies to run online businesses
F2F flesh-to-flesh: denoting actually meeting someone rather than chatting online
M2M manufacturer-to-manufacturer: denoting an Internet communication channel that enables manufacturers to coordinate their business processes
MP3 MPEG-1 Audio Layer-3: tradename for software created by the Motion Picture Experts Group that enables files to be compressed quickly to 10% or less of their original size for storage on disk or hard drive or esp. for transfer across the Internet
O3 business shorthand for Out of Office
P2P peer-to-peer: (of a computer network) designed so that computers can send information directly to one another without passing through a centralized server
PP2P personal peer-to-peer: denoting direct transmission of information between personal digital assistants and digital telephones
R2I resistance to interrogation: a method of training soldiers to endure interrogation and torture techniques
S2R send to receive: an instruction used in Internet chatrooms to indicate that a person should send a photo of himself or herself to receive a photo in return
V2V voice-to-voice: to speak to someone rather than exchanging e-mail
W3 the world wide web
W3C World Wide Web Consortium: an organization that exists to develop the potential of the Internet
Y2K the year 2000 AD, esp. in reference to the millennium bug

ABC[1] *n* 1 *(pl in US)* the rudiments of a subject 2 an alphabetical guide 3 *(often pl in US)* the alphabet

ABC[2] *abbrev for:* 1 American Broadcasting Company 2 Australian Broadcasting Corporation
▷ www.abc.net.au

Abdias (æb'daɪəs) *n Bible* the Douay form of **Obadiah**

abdicate ('æbdɪˌkeɪt) *vb* **abdicates, abdicating, abdicated** to renounce (a throne, rights, etc), esp formally [C16 from L *abdicāre* to disclaim] > ˌ**abdi'cation** *n* > '**abdiˌcator** *n*

abdomen ('æbdəmən) *n* 1 the region of the body of a vertebrate that contains the viscera other than the heart and lungs 2 the front or surface of this region; belly 3 (in arthropods) the posterior part of the body behind the thorax [C16 from L; from ?] > **abdominal** (æb'dɒmɪnᵊl) *adj*

abduct (æb'dʌkt) *vb (tr)* 1 to remove (a person) by force or cunning; kidnap 2 (of certain muscles) to pull (a leg, arm, etc) away from the median axis of the body [C19 from L *abdūcere* to lead away] > **ab'duction** *n* > **ab'ductor** *n*

Abdul-Hamid II (ˌæbdʊl'hæmɪd) *n* 1842–1918, sultan of Turkey (1876–1909), deposed by the Young Turks, noted for his brutal suppression of the Armenian revolt (1894–96)

abeam (ə'bi:m) *adv, adj (postpositive)* at right angles to the length of a vessel or aircraft [C19 A-[2] + BEAM]

abed (ə'bɛd) *adv arch* in bed

Abednego (ə'bɛdnɪˌgəʊ) *n Old Testament* one of Daniel's three companions who, together with Shadrach and Meshach, was miraculously saved from destruction in Nebuchadnezzar's fiery furnace (Daniel 3:12–30)

Abel ('eɪbᵊl) *n Old Testament* the second son of Adam and Eve, a shepherd, murdered by his brother Cain (Genesis 4:1–8)

Abelard ('æbəˌlɑ:d) *n* **Peter** French name *Pierre Abélard*. 1079–1142, French scholastic philosopher and theologian whose works include *Historia Calamitatum* and *Sic et Non* (1121). His love for Hëloïse is recorded in their correspondence

Abeokuta (ˌæbɪəʊ'ku:tə) *n* a town in W Nigeria, capital of Ogun state. Pop: 427 400 (1996 est)

Aberdare (ˌæbə'dɛə) *n* a town in South Wales, in Rhondda, Cynon, Taff county borough. Pop: 29 040 (1991)

Aberdeen[1] (ˌæbə'di:n) *n* 1 a city in NE Scotland, on the North Sea: centre for processing North Sea oil and gas; university (1494). Pop: 217 260 (1996 est) 2 **City of** a council area in NE Scotland, established in 1996. Pop: 212 125 (2001). Area: 186 sq km (72 sq miles) > **Aberdonian** (ˌæbə'dəʊnɪən) *n, adj*

Aberdeen[2] (ˌæbə'di:n) *n* **George Hamilton-Gordon,** 4th Earl of. 1784–1860, British statesman. He was foreign secretary under Wellington (1828) and Peel (1841–46); became prime minister of a coalition ministry in 1852 but was compelled to resign after mismanagement of the Crimean War (1855)

Aberdeen Angus *n* a black hornless breed of beef cattle originating in Scotland

Aberdeenshire (ˌæbə'di:nʃɪə, -ʃə) *n* a council area and historical county of N Scotland, on the North Sea: became part of Grampian Region in 1975 but reinstated as an independent unitary authority (with adjusted borders) in 1996: rises to the Grampian and Cairngorm Mountains in the SW: chiefly agricultural (esp sheep and stock raising). Administrative centre: Aberdeen. Pop: 226 871 (2001). Area 6319 sq km (2439 sq miles)

Aberfan (ˌæbə'væn) *n* a coal-mining village in S Wales, in Merthyr Tydfil county borough: scene of a disaster in 1966 when a slag heap collapsed onto part of the village killing 144 people (including 116 children)

aberrant (æ'bɛrənt) *adj* 1 deviating from the normal or usual type 2 behaving in an abnormal or untypical way 3 deviating from morality [rare before C19 from L *aberrāre* to wander away] > **ab'errance** *or* **ab'errancy** *n*

aberration (ˌæbəˈreɪʃən) *n* **1** deviation from what is normal, expected, or usual **2** departure from truth, morality, etc **3** a lapse in control of one's mental faculties **4** *optics* a defect in a lens or mirror that causes either a distorted image or one with coloured fringes **5** *astron* the apparent displacement of a celestial body due to the motion of the observer with the earth

Aberystwyth (ˌæbəˈrɪstwɪθ) *n* a resort and university town in Wales, in Ceredigion on Cardigan Bay. Pop: 11 154 (1991)

abet (əˈbɛt) *vb* **abets, abetting, abetted** (*tr*) to assist or encourage, esp in wrongdoing [C14 from OF *abeter* to lure on, from *beter* to bait] > **a'betment** *n* > **a'better** *or* (*esp Law*) **a'bettor** *n*

abeyance (əˈbeɪəns) *n* **1** (usually preceded by *in* or *into*) a state of being suspended or put aside temporarily **2** (usually preceded by *in*) *law* an indeterminate state of ownership [C16–17: from Anglo-F, from OF *abeance* expectation, lit. a gaping after]

ABH *abbrev for* actual bodily harm

abhor (əbˈhɔː) *vb* **abhors, abhorring, abhorred** (*tr*) to detest vehemently; find repugnant [C15 from L *abhorrēre*, from *ab-* away from + *horrēre* to shudder] > **ab'horrer** *n*

abhorrence (əbˈhɒrəns) *n* **1** a feeling of extreme loathing or aversion **2** a person or thing that is loathsome

abhorrent (əbˈhɒrənt) *adj* **1** repugnant; loathsome **2** (when *postpositive*, foll by *of*) feeling extreme aversion (for): *abhorrent of vulgarity* **3** (usually *postpositive* and foll by *to*) conflicting (with): *abhorrent to common sense*

Abia (æbˈiːa) *n* a state of SE Nigeria. Capital: Umuahia. Pop: 2 569 362 (1995 est). Area (including Imo state): 11 850 sq km (4575 sq miles)

abide (əˈbaɪd) *vb* **abides, abiding, abode** *or* **abided** **1** (*tr*) to tolerate; put up with **2** (*tr*) to accept or submit to **3** (*intr*; foll by *by*) **3a** to comply (with): *to abide by the decision* **3b** to remain faithful (to): *to abide by your promise* **4** (*intr*) to remain or continue **5** (*intr*) *arch* to dwell **6** (*tr*) *arch* to await in expectation [OE *ābīdan*, from *a-* (intensive) + *bīdan* to wait] > **a'bider** *n*

abiding (əˈbaɪdɪŋ) *adj* permanent; enduring: *an abiding belief*

Abidjan (ˌæbɪˈdʒɑːn; *French* abidʒɑ̃) *n* a port in the Côte d'Ivoire, on the Gulf of Guinea: the legislative capital (Yamoussoukro became the administrative capital in 1983). Pop: 2 797 000 (1995 est)

Abigail (ˈæbɪˌgeɪl) *n* *Old Testament* the woman who brought provisions to David and his followers and subsequently became his wife (I Samuel 25:1–42)

ability (əˈbɪlɪtɪ) *n, pl* **abilities** **1** possession of necessary skill, competence, or power **2** considerable proficiency; natural capability: *a man of ability* **3** (*pl*) special talents [C14 from OF from L *habilitās* aptitude, from *habilis* ABLE]

Abingdon (ˈæbɪŋdən) *n* a market town in S England, in Oxfordshire. Pop: 35 234 (1991)

ab initio *Latin* (æb ɪˈnɪʃɪˌəʊ) from the start; from scratch: *ab initio courses*

abiogenesis (ˌeɪbaɪəʊˈdʒɛnɪsɪs) *n* **1** Also called: **autogenesis** the hypothetical process by which living organisms first arose on earth from matter **2** another name for **spontaneous generation** [C19 NL, from A-¹ + BIO- + GENESIS]

abiotrophy (ˌeɪbaɪəʊˈtrəʊfɪ) *n* the progressive degeneration of tissues, cells, etc [C20 from Gk A-¹ + BIO- + TROPHY] > **ˌabio'trophic** *adj*

abject (ˈæbdʒɛkt) *adj* **1** utterly wretched or hopeless **2** forlorn; dejected **3** submissive: *an abject apology* **4** contemptible; despicable: *an abject liar* [C14 (in the sense: rejected, cast out): from L *abjectus* thrown away, from *abjicere*, from *ab-* away + *jacere* to throw] > **ab'jection** *n* > **'abjectly** *adv* > **'abjectness** *n*

abjure (əbˈdʒʊə) *vb* **abjures, abjuring, abjured** (*tr*) **1** to renounce or retract, esp formally or under oath **2** to abstain from [C15 from OF *abjurer* or L *abjurāre* to deny on oath] > **ˌabju'ration** *n* > **ab'jurer** *n*

Abkhazia (æbˈkɑːzɪə) *n* an administrative division of NW Georgia, between the Black Sea and the Caucasus Mountains: a subtropical region, with mountains rising over 3900 m (13 000 ft); Abkhazian separatists seized control of the region in 1993. Capital: Sukhumi. Pop: 516 600 (1993 est). Area: 8600 sq km (3320 sq miles). Also called: **Abkhaz Autonomous Republic**

ablation (æbˈleɪʃən) *n* **1** the surgical removal of an organ, structure, or part **2** the melting or wearing away of a part, such as the heat shield of a space re-entry vehicle on passing through the earth's atmosphere **3** the wearing away of a rock or glacier [C15 from LL *ablatiōn-*, from L *auferre* to carry away] > **ablate** (æbˈleɪt) *vb*

ablative (ˈæblətɪv) *grammar* ▷ *adj* **1** (in certain inflected languages such as Latin) denoting a case of nouns, pronouns, and adjectives indicating the agent, or the instrument, manner, or place of the action ▷ *n* **2** the ablative case or a speech element in it

ablaut (ˈæblaʊt) *n* *linguistics* vowel gradation, esp in Indo-European languages. See **gradation** (sense 5) [G, coined 1819 by Jakob Grimm from *ab* off + *Laut* sound]

ablaze (əˈbleɪz) *adj* (*postpositive*), *adv* **1** on fire; burning **2** brightly illuminated **3** emotionally aroused

able (ˈeɪbᵊl) *adj* **1** (*postpositive*) having the necessary power, resources, skill, opportunity, etc, to do something **2** capable; talented **3** *law* competent or authorized [C14 ult. from L *habilis* easy to hold, manageable, from *habēre* to have + *-ilis* -ILE]

-able *suffix forming adjectives* **1** capable of or deserving of (being acted upon as indicated): *enjoyable; washable* **2** inclined to; able to; causing: *comfortable; variable* [via OF from L *-ābilis, -ībilis*, forms of *-bilis*, adjectival suffix] > **-ably** *suffix forming adverbs* > **-ability** *suffix forming nouns*

able-bodied *adj* physically strong and healthy; robust

able-bodied seaman *n* a seaman, esp one in the merchant navy, who has been trained in certain skills. Also: **able seaman** Abbrev: **AB, a.b.**

abled (ˈeɪbᵊld) *adj* having a range of physical powers as specified (esp in **less abled, differently abled**)

ableism (ˈeɪbᵊlˌɪzəm) *n* discrimination against disabled or handicapped people

able rating *n* (esp in the Royal Navy) a rating who is qualified to perform certain duties of seamanship

abloom (əˈbluːm) *adj* (*postpositive*) in flower; blooming

ablution (əˈbluːʃən) *n* **1** the ritual washing of a priest's hands or of sacred vessels **2** (*often pl*) the act of washing: *perform one's ablutions* **3** (*pl*) *mil inf* a washing place [C14 ult. from L *ablŭere* to wash away] > **ab'lutionary** *adj*

ably (ˈeɪblɪ) *adv* in a competent or skilful manner

ABM *abbrev for* antiballistic missile

abnegate (ˈæbnɪˌgeɪt) *vb* **abnegates, abnegating, abnegated** (*tr*) to deny to oneself; renounce [C17 from L *abnegāre* to deny] > **ˌabne'gation** *n* > **'abneˌgator** *n*

abnormal (æbˈnɔːməl) *adj* **1** not normal; deviating from the usual or typical **2** concerned with abnormal behaviour: *abnormal psychology* **3** *inf* odd; strange [C19 AB-¹ + NORMAL, replacing earlier *anormal* from Med. L *anormalus*, a blend of LL *anōmalus* ANOMALOUS + L *abnormis* departing from a rule] > **ab'normally** *adv*

abnormality (ˌæbnɔːˈmælɪtɪ) *n, pl* **abnormalities** **1** an abnormal feature, event, etc **2** a physical malformation **3** deviation from the usual

Abo (ˈæbəʊ) *n, pl* **Abos** (*sometimes not cap*) *Austral inf, often derog* short for **Aborigine** (sense 1)

Åbo (ˈoːbuː) *n* the Swedish name for **Turku**

aboard (əˈbɔːd) *adv, adj* (*postpositive*), *prep* **1** on, in, onto, or into (a ship, train, etc) **2** *naut* alongside **3** **all aboard!** a warning to passengers to board a vehicle, ship, etc

abode¹ (əˈbəʊd) *n* a place in which one lives; one's home [C17 n formed from ABIDE]

abode[2] (ə'bəʊd) *vb* a past tense and past participle of abide

abolish (ə'bɒlɪʃ) *vb (tr)* to do away with (laws, regulations, customs, etc) [c15 from OF, ult. from L *abolēre* to destroy] > **a'bolishable** *adj* > **a'bolisher** *n* > **a'bolishment** *n*

abolition (ˌæbə'lɪʃən) *n* **1** the act of abolishing or the state of being abolished; annulment **2** *(often cap)* (in British territories) the ending of the slave trade (1807) or of slavery (1833) **3** *(often cap)* (in the US) the emancipation of slaves, by the Emancipation Proclamation (1863, ratified 1865) [c16 from L *abolitio*, from *abolēre* to destroy] > **ˌabo'litionary** *adj* > **ˌabo'litionism** *n* > **ˌabo'litionist** *n, adj*

abomasum (ˌæbə'meɪsəm) *n* the fourth and last compartment of the stomach of ruminants [c18 NL, from AB-[1] + *omāsum* bullock's tripe]

A-bomb *n* short for **atomic bomb**

abominable (ə'bɒmɪnəbᵊl) *adj* **1** offensive; loathsome; detestable **2** *inf* very bad or inferior: *abominable workmanship* [c14 from L, from *abōminārī* to ABOMINATE] > **a'bominably** *adv*

abominable snowman *n* a large manlike or apelike creature alleged to inhabit the Himalayas. Also called: **yeti** [translation of Tibetan *metohkangmi*, from *metoh* foul + *kangmi* snowman]

abominate (ə'bɒmɪˌneɪt) *vb* **abominates, abominating, abominated** *(tr)* to dislike intensely; detest [c17 from L *abōminārī* to regard as an ill omen, from *ab-* away from + *ōmin-*, from OMEN] > **a'bomiˌnator** *n*

abomination (əˌbɒmɪ'neɪʃən) *n* **1** a person or thing that is disgusting or loathsome **2** an action that is vicious, vile, etc **3** intense loathing or disgust

aboriginal (ˌæbə'rɪdʒɪnᵊl) *adj* existing in a place from the earliest known period; indigenous > **ˌabo'riginally** *adv*

Aboriginal (ˌæbə'rɪdʒɪnᵊl) *adj* **1** of, relating to, or characteristic of the native peoples of Australia ▷ *n* **2** another word for **Aborigine** (sense 1) > **ˌAboˌrigi'nality** *n*

aborigine (ˌæbə'rɪdʒɪnɪ) *n* an original inhabitant of a country or region [c16 back formation from *aborigines*, from L: inhabitants of Latium in pre-Roman times, associated in folk etymology with *ab origine* from the beginning]

Aborigine (ˌæbə'rɪdʒɪnɪ) *n* **1** Also called: **native Australian, Aboriginal** a member of a dark-skinned hunting and gathering people who were living in Australia when European settlers arrived **2** any of the languages of this people

abort (ə'bɔːt) *vb* **1** to undergo or cause (a woman) to undergo the termination of pregnancy before the fetus is viable **2** *(tr)* to cause (a fetus) to be expelled from the womb before it is viable **3** *(intr)* to fail to come to completion **4** *(tr)* to stop the development of; cause to be abandoned **5** *(intr)* to give birth to a dead or nonviable fetus **6** (of a space flight or other undertaking) to fail or terminate prematurely **7** *(intr)* (of an organism or part of an organism) to fail to develop into the mature form ▷ *n* **8** the premature termination or failure of (a space flight, etc) [c16 from L *abortāre*, from *aborīrī* to miscarry, from *ab-* wrongly + *orīrī* to be born]

abortifacient (əˌbɔːtɪ'feɪʃənt) *adj* **1** causing abortion ▷ *n* **2** a drug or agent that causes abortion

abortion (ə'bɔːʃən) *n* **1** an operation or other procedure to terminate pregnancy before the fetus is viable **2** the premature termination of pregnancy by spontaneous or induced expulsion of a nonviable fetus from the uterus **3** an aborted fetus **4** a failure to develop to completion or maturity **5** a person or thing that is deformed

abortionist (ə'bɔːʃənɪst) *n* a person who performs abortions, esp illegally

abortion pill *n* a drug, such as mifepristone (Mifegyne), used to terminate a pregnancy in its earliest stage

abortive (ə'bɔːtɪv) *adj* **1** failing to achieve a purpose; fruitless **2** (of organisms) imperfectly developed **3** causing abortion

ABO system *n* a system for classifying human blood on the basis of the presence or absence of two antigens on the red cell membrane: there are four such blood types (A, B, AB, and O)

Aboukir Bay *or* **Abukir Bay** (ˌæbuː'kɪə) *n* a bay on the N coast of Egypt, where the Nile enters the Mediterranean: site of the Battle of the Nile (1798), in which Nelson defeated the French fleet. Arabic name: **Abu Qîr** (abu'kiːr)

aboulia (ə'buːlɪə, -'bjuː-) *n* a variant spelling of **abulia**

abound (ə'baʊnd) *vb (intr)* **1** to exist or occur in abundance **2** (foll by *with* or *in*) to be plentifully supplied (with): *the fields abound in corn* [c14 via OF from L *abundāre* to overflow, from *undāre* to flow, from *unda* wave]

about (ə'baʊt) *prep* **1** relating to; concerning **2** near or close to **3** carried on: *I haven't any money about me* **4** on every side of **5** active in or engaged in ▷ *adv* **6** near in number, time, degree, etc: *about 50 years old* **7** nearby **8** here and there: *walk about to keep warm* **9** all around; on every side **10** in or to the opposite direction **11** in rotation or revolution: *turn and turn about* **12** used in informal phrases to indicate understatement: *it's about time you stopped* **13** *arch* around **14** **about to** **14a** on the point of; intending to: *she was about to jump* **14b** *(with a negative)* determined not to: *nobody is about to miss it* ▷ *adj* **15** *(predicative)* active; astir after sleep: *up and about* **16** *(predicative)* in existence, current, or in circulation: *there aren't many about nowadays* [OE *abūtan, onbūtan*, from ON + *būtan* outside]

about turn *or US* **about face** *sentence substitute* **1** a military command to a formation of men to reverse the direction in which they are facing ▷ *n* **about-turn** *or US* **about-face** **2** a complete change of opinion, direction, etc ▷ *vb* **about-turn** *or US* **about-face** **3** *(intr)* to perform an about-turn

Aa

above (ə'bʌv) *prep* **1** on top of or higher than; over **2** greater than in quantity or degree: *above average* **3** superior to or prior to: *to place honour above wealth* **4** too high-minded for: *above petty gossiping* **5** too respected for; beyond: *above suspicion* **6** too difficult to be understood by: *the talk was above me* **7** louder or higher than (other noise) **8** in preference to **9** north of **10** upstream from **11** **above all** most of all; especially **12** **above and beyond** in addition to ▷ *adv* **13** in or to a higher place: *the sky above* **14a** in a previous place (in something written) **14b** *(in combination): the above-mentioned clause* **15** higher in rank or position **16** in or concerned with heaven ▷ *n* **17** **the above** something previously mentioned ▷ *adj* **18** appearing in a previous place (in something written) [OE *abufan*, from *a-* on + *bufan* above]

above board *adj* (**aboveboard** *when prenominal*), *adv* in the open; without dishonesty, concealment, or fraud

above-the-line *adj* **1** denoting entries printed above the horizontal line on a company's profit-and-loss account separating the entries that show how the profit (or loss) was made from the entries showing how the profit is to be distributed **2** (of an advertising campaign) employing an advertising agency to use the press, television, radio, cinema, and posters **3** (in national accounts) denoting transactions concerned with revenue shown above a horizontal line that separates them from capital transactions. Compare **below-the-line**

abracadabra (ˌæbrəkə'dæbrə) *interj* **1** a spoken formula, used esp by conjurors ▷ *n* **2** a word used in incantations, etc, considered to possess magic powers **3** gibberish [c17 magical word used in certain Gnostic writings, ? rel. to Gk *Abraxas*, a Gnostic deity]

abrade (ə'breɪd) *vb* **abrades, abrading, abraded** *(tr)* to scrape away or wear down by friction [c17 from L *abrādere*, from AB-^{1} + *rādere* to scrape] > **a'brader** *n*

Abraham ('eɪbrəˌhæm, -həm) *n* **1** *Old Testament* the first of the patriarchs, the father of Isaac and the founder of the Hebrew people (Genesis 11–25) **2 Abraham's bosom** the place where the just repose after death (Luke 16:22)

abranchiate (ə'bræŋkɪɪt, -ˌeɪt) *or* **abranchial** *adj zool* having no gills [c19 A-^{1} + BRANCHIATE]

abrasion (ə'breɪʒən) *n* **1** the process of scraping or wearing down by friction **2** a scraped area or spot; graze **3** *geog* the effect of mechanical erosion of rock, esp a river bed, by rock fragments scratching and scraping it [c17 from Med. L *abrāsiōn-*, from L *abrādere* to ABRADE]

abrasive (ə'breɪsɪv) *n* **1** a substance or material such as sandpaper, pumice, or emery, used for cleaning, smoothing, or polishing ▷ *adj* **2** causing abrasion; rough **3** irritating in manner or personality

abreaction (ˌæbrɪ'ækʃən) *n psychoanal* the release and expression of emotional tension associated with repressed ideas by bringing those ideas into consciousness

abreast (ə'brɛst) *adj (postpositive)* **1** alongside each other and facing in the same direction **2** (foll by *of* or *with*) up to date (with)

abridge (ə'brɪdʒ) *vb* **abridges, abridging, abridged** *(tr)* **1** to reduce the length of (a written work) by condensing **2** to curtail [c14 via OF *abregier* from LL *abbreviāre* to shorten] > **a'bridgable** *or* **a'bridgeable** *adj* > **a'bridger** *n*

abridgment *or* **abridgement** (ə'brɪdʒmənt) *n* **1** a shortened version of a written work **2** the act of abridging or state of being abridged

abroad (ə'brɔːd) *adv, adj (postpositive)* **1** to or in a foreign country or countries **2** (of rumours, etc) in general circulation **3** out in the open **4** over a wide area [c13 from A-^{2} + BROAD]

abrogate ('æbrəʊˌgeɪt) *vb* **abrogates, abrogating, abrogated** *(tr)* to cancel or revoke formally or officially [c16 from L *abrogātus* repealed, from AB-^{1} + *rogāre* to propose (a law)] > ˌ**abro'gation** *n* > '**abroˌgator** *n*

> USAGE *Abrogate* is sometimes confused with *arrogate*. These words have almost opposite meanings, *abrogate* meaning 'to get rid of' and *arrogate* meaning 'to acquire unjustifiably', as in *the State arrogated to itself more powers*. To use *abrogate* in this kind of context is incorrect, though it does occasionally happen. *Abrogate* is about four times more common in the Bank of English than *arrogate*, so the error may be due to people tending to associate this meaning mistakenly with the word they know better. The mistake does not seem to occur the other way round

abrupt (ə'brʌpt) *adj* **1** sudden; unexpected **2** brusque or brief in speech, manner, etc **3** (of a style of writing or speaking) disconnected **4** precipitous; steep **5** *bot* truncate **6** *geol* (of strata) cropping out suddenly [c16 from L *abruptus* broken off, from AB-^{1} + *rumpere* to break] > **ab'ruptly** *adv* > **ab'ruptness** *n*

Abruzzi (*Italian* a'bruttsi) *or* **Abruzzo** (*Italian* a'bruttso) *n* a region of S central Italy, between the Apennines and the Adriatic: separated from the former administrative region **Abruzzi e Molise** in 1965. Capital: Aquila. Pop: 1 279 016 (2000 est). Area: 10 794 sq km (4210 sq miles)

abs (æbz) *pl n inf* abdominal muscles

Absalom ('æbsələm) *n Old Testament* the third son of David, who rebelled against his father and was eventually killed by Joab (II Samuel 15–18)

ABS brake *n* another name for **antilock brake** [from G *Antiblockiersystem*]

abscess ('æbsɛs) *n* **1** a localized collection of pus formed as the product of inflammation and usually caused by bacteria ▷ *vb* **2** *(intr)* to form such a collection of pus [c16 from L *abscessus*, from *abscēdere* to go away] > '**abscessed** *adj*

abscissa (æb'sɪsə) *n, pl* **abscissas** *or* **abscissae** (-'sɪsiː) the horizontal or *x*-coordinate of a point in a two-dimensional system of Cartesian coordinates. It is the distance from the *y*-axis measured parallel to the *x*-axis ▷ Cf **ordinate** [c17 NL, orig. *linea abscissa* a cut-off line]

abscission (æb'sɪʒən) *n* **1** the separation of leaves, branches, flowers, and bark from plants **2** the act of cutting off [c17 from L, from AB-^{1} + *scissiō* a cleaving]

abscond (əb'skɒnd) *vb (intr)* to run away secretly, esp to avoid prosecution or punishment [c16 from L *abscondere*, from *abs-* AB-^{1} + *condere* to stow] > **ab'sconder** *n*

abseil ('æbsaɪl) *mountaineering* ▷ *vb (intr)* **1** to descend a steep slope or vertical drop by a rope secured from above and coiled around one's body ▷ *n* **2** an instance or the technique of abseiling [c20 from G *abseilen*, from *ab-* down + *Seil* rope]

absence ('æbsəns) *n* **1** the state of being away **2** the time during which a person or thing is away **3** the fact of being without something; lack [c14 via OF from L *absentia*, from *absēns* a being away]

absent *adj* ('æbsənt) **1** away or not present **2** lacking **3** inattentive ▷ *vb* (æb'sɛnt) **4** *(tr)* to remove (oneself) or keep away [c14 from L *absent-*, from *abesse* to be away]

absentee (ˌæbsən'tiː) *n* **a** a person who is absent **b** (*as modifier*): *an absentee landlord*

absenteeism (ˌæbsən'tiːɪzəm) *n* persistent absence from work, school, etc

absent-minded *adj* preoccupied; forgetful > ˌ**absent-'mindedly** *adv* > ˌ**absent-'mindedness** *n*

absinthe *or* **absinth** ('æbsɪnθ) *n* **1** a potent green alcoholic drink, originally having high wormwood content **2** another name for **wormwood** (the plant) [c15 via F and L from Gk *apsinthion* wormwood]

absolute ('æbsəˌluːt) *adj* **1** complete; perfect **2** free from limitations, restrictions, or exceptions **3** despotic: *an absolute ruler* **4** undoubted; certain: *the absolute truth* **5** not dependent on, conditioned by, or relative to anything else; independent: *absolute humidity; absolute units* **6** pure; unmixed: *absolute alcohol* **7** (of a grammatical construction) syntactically independent of the main clause, as for example the construction *Joking apart* in the sentence *Joking apart, we'd better leave now* **8** *grammar* (of a transitive verb) used without a direct object, as the verb *intimidate* in the sentence *His intentions are good, but his rough manner tends to intimidate* **9** *grammar* (of an adjective) used as a noun, as for instance *young* and *aged* in the sentence *The young care little for the aged* ▷ *n* **10** something that is absolute [c14 from L *absolūtus* unconditional, from *absolvere*. See ABSOLVE]

Absolute ('æbsəˌluːt) *n (sometimes not cap) Philosophy* **1** the ultimate basis of reality **2** that which is totally unconditioned, unrestricted, pure, perfect, or complete

absolutely (ˌæbsə'luːtlɪ) *adv* **1** in an absolute manner, esp completely or perfectly ▷ *sentence substitute* **2** yes; certainly

absolute magnitude *n* the magnitude a given star would have if it were 10 parsecs (32.6 light years) from earth

absolute majority *n* a number of votes totalling over 50 per cent, such as the total number of votes or seats obtained by a party that beats the combined opposition

absolute pitch *n* **1** Also called: **perfect pitch** the ability to identify the pitch of a note, or to sing a given note, without reference to one previously sounded **2** the exact pitch of a note determined by vibration per second

absolute temperature *n* another name for **thermodynamic temperature**

absolute value *n* **1** the positive real number equal to a given real but disregarding its sign: written $|x|$. Where x is positive, $|x| = x = |-x|$ **2** Also called: **modulus** a measure of the magnitude of a complex number

absolute zero *n* the lowest temperature theoretically attainable, at which the particles constituting matter would be at rest: equivalent to −273.15°C or −459.67°F

absolution (ˌæbsəˈluːʃən) *n* **1** the act of absolving or the state of being absolved; release from guilt, obligation, or punishment **2** *Christianity* **2a** a formal remission of sin pronounced by a priest in the sacrament of penance **2b** the form of words granting such a remission [c12 from L *absolūtiōn-* acquittal, from *absolvere* to ABSOLVE]

absolutism (ˈæbsəluːˌtɪzəm) *n* the principle or practice of a political system in which unrestricted power is vested in a monarch, dictator, etc; despotism > **absoˈlutist** *n, adj*

absolve (əbˈzɒlv) *vb* **absolves, absolving, absolved** (*tr*) **1** (usually foll by *from*) to release from blame, sin, obligation, or responsibility **2** to pronounce not guilty [c15 from L *absolvere*, from AB-[1] + *solvere* to make loose] > **abˈsolver** *n*

absorb (əbˈsɔːb) *vb* (*tr*) **1** to soak or suck up (liquids) **2** to engage or occupy (the interest or time) of (someone) **3** to receive or take in (the energy of an impact) **4** *physics* to take in (all or part of incident radiated energy) and retain it **5** to take in or assimilate; incorporate **6** to pay for as part of a commercial transaction: *the distributor absorbed the cost of transport* **7** *chem* to cause to undergo a process in which one substance permeates into or is dissolved by a liquid or solid: *porous solids absorb water* [c15 via OF from L *absorbēre*, from AB-[1] + *sorbēre* to suck] > **abˌsorbaˈbility** *n* > **abˈsorbable** *adj*

absorbed (əbˈsɔːbd) *adj* engrossed; deeply interested

absorbed dose *n* the amount of energy transferred by radiation to a unit mass of absorbing material

absorbent (əbˈsɔːbənt) *adj* **1** able to absorb ▷ *n* **2** a substance that absorbs > **abˈsorbency** *n*

absorbing (əbˈsɔːbɪŋ) *adj* occupying one's interest or attention > **abˈsorbingly** *adv*

absorptance (əbˈsɔːptəns) *or* **absorption factor** *n physics* the ability of an object to absorb radiation, measured as the ratio of absorbed flux to incident flux [c20 from ABSORPTION + -ANCE]

absorption (əbˈsɔːpʃən) *n* **1** the process of absorbing or the state of being absorbed **2** *physiol* **2a** normal assimilation by the tissues of the products of digestion **2b** the passage of a gas, fluid, drug, etc, through the mucous membranes or skin [c16 from L *absorptiōn-*, from *absorbēre* to ABSORB] > **abˈsorptive** *adj*

absorption spectrum *n* the characteristic pattern of dark lines or bands that occurs when electromagnetic radiation is passed through an absorbing medium into a spectroscope. See also **emission spectrum**

abstain (əbˈsteɪn) *vb* (*intr*; usually foll by *from*) **1** to choose to refrain **2** to refrain from voting, esp in a committee, legislature, etc [c14 via OF from L *abstinēre*, from *abs-* AB-[1] + *tenēre* to hold] > **abˈstainer** *n*

abstemious (əbˈstiːmɪəs) *adj* sparing, esp in the consumption of alcohol or food [c17 from L *abstēmius*, from *abs-* AB-[1] + *tēm-*, from *tēmētum* intoxicating drink] > **abˈstemiously** *adv* > **abˈstemiousness** *n*

abstention (əbˈstɛnʃən) *n* **1** the act of refraining or abstaining **2** the act of withholding one's vote [c16 from LL *abstentiōn*; see ABSTAIN]

abstinence (ˈæbstɪnəns) *n* the act or practice of refraining from some action or from the use of something, esp alcohol [c13 via OF from L *abstinentia*, from *abstinēre* to ABSTAIN] > **ˈabstinent** *adj*

abstract *adj* (ˈæbstrækt) **1** having no reference to material objects or specific examples **2** not applied or practical; theoretical **3** hard to understand **4** denoting art characterized by geometric, formalized, or otherwise nonrepresentational qualities ▷ *n* (ˈæbstrækt) **5** a condensed version of a piece of writing, speech, etc; summary **6** an abstract term or idea **7** an abstract painting, sculpture, etc **8 in the abstract** without reference to specific circumstances ▷ *vb* (æbˈstrækt) (*tr*) **9** to regard theoretically **10** to form a general idea of (something) by abstraction **11** (ˈæbstrækt) (*also intr*) to summarize **12** to remove or extract [c14 (in the sense: extracted): from L *abstractus* drawn off, from *abs-* AB-[1] + *trahere* to draw]

abstracted (æbˈstræktɪd) *adj* **1** lost in thought; preoccupied **2** taken out or separated > **abˈstractedly** *adv*

abstract expressionism *n* a school of painting in the 1940s that combined the spontaneity of expressionism with abstract forms in apparently random compositions

▷ www.artlex.com/ArtLex/a/abstractexpr.htm

▷ www. wwar.com/categories/Artists/Masters

abstraction (æbˈstrækʃən) *n* **1** preoccupation **2** the process of formulating generalized concepts by extracting common qualities from specific examples **3** a concept formulated in this way: *good and evil are abstractions* **4** an abstract painting, sculpture, etc > **abˈstractive** *adj*

abstract noun *n* a noun that refers to an abstract concept, as for example *peace, joy*, etc

abstract term *n* in traditional logic, the name of an attribute of many individuals: *humanity is an abstract term*

abstruse (əbˈstruːs) *adj* not easy to understand [c16 from L *abstrūsus*, from *abs-* AB-[1] + *trūdere* to thrust] > **abˈstrusely** *adv* > **abˈstruseness** *n*

absurd (əbˈsɜːd) *adj* **1** at variance with reason; manifestly false **2** ludicrous; ridiculous [c16 via F from L *absurdus*, from AB-[1] (intensive) + *surdus* dull-sounding] > **abˈsurdity** *or* **abˈsurdness** *n* > **abˈsurdly** *adv*

ABTA (ˈæbtə) *n acronym for* Association of British Travel Agents

Abu Dhabi (ˈæbuː ˈdɑːbɪ) *n* a sheikdom (emirate) of SE Arabia, on the S coast of the Persian Gulf: the chief sheikdom and capital of the United Arab Emirates, consisting principally of the port of Abu Dhabi and a desert hinterland; contains major oilfields. Pop: 1 186 000 (2001 est). Area: 67 350 sq km (25 998 sq miles)

▷ www.uae.org.ae/tourist/index.htm

Abuja (əˈbuːdʒə) *n* the federal capital of Nigeria, in the centre of the country. Pop: 350 100 (1996 est)

Abukir Bay (ˌæbuːˈkɪə) *n* a variant spelling of **Aboukir Bay**

abulia *or* **aboulia** (əˈbuːlɪə, -ˈbjuː-) *n psychiatry* a pathological inability to take decisions [c19 NL, from Gk *aboulia* lack of resolution, from A-[1] + *boulē* will]

abundance (əˈbʌndəns) *n* **1** a copious supply; great amount **2** fullness or benevolence: *from the abundance of my heart* **3** degree of plentifulness: *the abundance of uranium-235 in natural uranium* **4** Also: **abondance** a call in solo whist undertaking to make nine tricks **5** affluence [c14 via OF from L, from *abundāre* to ABOUND]

abundant (əˈbʌndənt) *adj* **1** existing in plentiful supply **2** (*postpositive*; foll by *in*) having a plentiful supply (of) [c14 from L *abundant-*, p.p. of *abundāre* to ABOUND] > **aˈbundantly** *adv*

abuse *vb* (əˈbjuːz) **abuses, abusing, abused** (*tr*) **1** to use incorrectly or improperly; misuse **2** to maltreat, esp physically or sexually **3** to speak insultingly or cruelly to ▷ *n* (əˈbjuːs) **4** improper, incorrect, or excessive use **5** maltreatment of a person; injury **6** insulting or coarse speech **7** an evil, unjust, or corrupt practice **8** See **child abuse 9** *arch* a deception [c14 (vb): via OF from L *abūsus*, p.p. of *abūtī* to misuse, from AB-[1] + *ūtī* to USE] > **aˈbuser** *n*

Abu Simbel (ˌæbuː ˈsɪmbᵊl) *n* a former village in S Egypt: site of two temples of Rameses II, which were moved to higher ground (1966–67) before the area behind the Aswan High Dam was flooded. Also called: **Ipsambul**

abusive (əˈbjuːsɪv) *adj* **1** characterized by insulting or coarse language **2** characterized by maltreatment **3** incorrectly used > **a'busively** *adv* > **a'busiveness** *n*

abut (ə'bʌt) *vb* **abuts, abutting, abutted** (usually foll by *on, upon,* or *against*) to adjoin, touch, or border on (something) at one end [c15 from OF *abouter* to join at the ends; infl. by *abuter* to touch at an end]

abutment (ə'bʌtmənt) *or* **abuttal** (ə'bʌtᵊl) *n* **1** the state or process of abutting **2a** something that abuts **2b** the thing on which something abuts **2c** the point of junction between them **3** a construction that supports the end of a bridge

abutter (ə'bʌtə) *n property law* the owner of adjoining property

abuzz (ə'bʌz) *adj (postpositive)* humming, as with conversation, activity, etc; buzzing

Abydos (ə'baɪdəs) *n* **1** an ancient town in central Egypt: site of many temples and tombs **2** an ancient Greek colony on the Asiatic side of the Dardanelles (Hellespont): scene of the legend of Hero and Leander

abysm (ə'bɪzəm) *n* an archaic word for **abyss** [c13 via OF from Med. L *abysmus* ABYSS]

abysmal (ə'bɪzməl) *adj* **1** immeasurable; very great **2** *inf* extremely bad > **a'bysmally** *adv*

abyss (ə'bɪs) *n* **1** a very deep gorge or chasm **2** anything that appears to be endless or immeasurably deep, such as time, despair, or shame **3** hell [c16 via LL from Gk *abussos* bottomless, from A-^{1} + *bussos* depth]

abyssal (ə'bɪsəl) *adj* **1** of or relating to an abyss **2** of or belonging to the ocean depths, esp below 2000 metres (6500 ft): *abyssal zone*

Abyssinia (,æbɪ'sɪnɪə) *n* a former name for **Ethiopia** > **,Abys'sinian** *adj, n*

ac *the Internet domain name for* Ascension Island

Ac *the chemical symbol for* actinium

AC *abbrev for:* **1** Air Corps **2** alternating current ▷ Cf **DC** **3** ante Christum [L: before Christ] **4** athletic club **5** Companion of the Order of Australia

a/c *book-keeping abbrev for:* **1** account **2** account current

acacia (ə'keɪʃə) *n* **1** a tropical or subtropical shrub or tree, having small yellow or white flowers in dense influorescences. In Australia, the term is applied esp to the wattle **2** **false acacia** another name for **locust** (senses 2, 3) **3** **gum acacia** another name for **gum arabic** [c16 from L, from Gk *akakia*, ? rel. to *akē* point]

academe ('ækə,diːm) *n literary* any place of learning, such as a college or university [c16 first used by Shakespeare in *Love's Labour's Lost* (1594); see ACADEMY]

academic (,ækə'dɛmɪk) *adj* **1** belonging or relating to a place of learning, esp a college, university, or academy **2** of purely theoretical or speculative interest **3** (esp of pupils) having an aptitude for study **4** excessively concerned with intellectual matters **5** conforming to set rules and traditions: *an academic painter* **6** relating to studies such as languages and pure science rather than technical, applied, or professional studies ▷ *n* **7** a member of a college or university > **,aca'demically** *adv*

academician (ə,kædə'mɪʃən) *n* a member of an academy (senses 1, 2)

academy (ə'kædəmɪ) *n, pl* **academies** **1** an institution or society for the advancement of literature, art, or science **2** a school for training in a particular skill or profession: *a military academy* **3** a secondary school, esp in Scotland: now only used as part of a name [c16 via L from Gk *akadēmeia* the grove where Plato taught, named after the legendary hero *Akadēmos*] > **,aca'demical** *adj*

Academy Award *n* the official name for an **Oscar**

Acadia (ə'keɪdɪə) *n* **1a** the Atlantic Provinces of Canada **1b** the French-speaking areas of these provinces **2** (formerly) a French colony in the present-day Atlantic Provinces: ceded to Britain in 1713 ▷ French name **Acadie** (akadi) > **A'cadian** *adj, n*

acanthus (ə'kænθəs) *n, pl* **acanthuses** *or* **acanthi** (-θaɪ) **1** a shrub or herbaceous plant, native to the Mediterranean region but widely cultivated as an ornamental plant, having large spiny leaves and spikes of white or purplish flowers **2** a carved ornament based on the leaves of the acanthus plant, esp as used on the capital of a Corinthian column [c17 NL, from Gk *akanthos*, from *akantha* thorn, spine]

a cappella (ɑː kə'pɛlə) *adj, adv music* without instrumental accompaniment [It.: lit., according to (the style of the) chapel]

Acapulco (,ækə'pʊlkəʊ; *Spanish* aka'pulko) *n* a port and resort in SW Mexico, in Guerrero state. Pop: 619 253 (2000 est). Official name: **Acapulco de Juárez** (*Spanish* de 'xwares)

acariasis (,ækə'raɪəsɪs) *n* infestation with mites or ticks [c19 NL: see ACARID, -IASIS]

acarid ('ækərɪd) *or* **acaridan** (ə'kærɪdᵊn) *n* any of an order of small arachnids that includes the ticks and mites [c19 from Gk *akari* a small thing, mite]

acarpous (eɪ'kɑːpəs) *adj* (of plants) producing no fruit [from Gk *akarpos*, from A-^{1} + *karpos* fruit]

ACAS *or* **Acas** ('eɪkæs) *n* (in Britain) *acronym for* Advisory Conciliation and Arbitration Service
▷ www.acas.org.uk

acc. *grammar abbrev for:* accusative

accede (æk'siːd) *vb* **accedes, acceding, acceded** (*intr;* usually foll by *to*) **1** to assent or give one's consent **2** to enter upon or attain (to an office, right, etc): *the prince acceded to the throne* **3** *international law* to become a party (to an agreement between nations, etc) [c15 from L *accēdere*, from *ad-* to + *cēdere* to yield] > **ac'cedence** *n*

accelerando (æk,sɛlə'rændəʊ) *adj, adv music* (to be performed) with increasing speed [It.]

accelerate (æk'sɛlə,reɪt) *vb* **accelerates, accelerating, accelerated** **1** to go, occur, or cause to go or occur more quickly; speed up **2** (*tr*) to cause to happen sooner than expected **3** (*tr*) to increase the velocity of (a body, reaction, etc) [c16 from L *accelerātus*, from *accelerāre*, from *ad-* (intensive) + *celerāre* to hasten, from *celer* swift] > **ac'celerative** *adj*

acceleration (æk,sɛlə'reɪʃən) *n* **1** the act of accelerating or the state of being accelerated **2** the rate of increase of speed or the rate of change of velocity **3** the power to accelerate

acceleration of free fall *n* the acceleration of a body falling freely in a vacuum in the earth's gravitational field. Symbol: *g* Also called: **acceleration due to gravity**

accelerator (æk'sɛlə,reɪtə) *n* **1** a device for increasing speed, esp a pedal for controlling the fuel intake in a motor vehicle; throttle **2** *physics* a machine for increasing the kinetic energy of subatomic particles or atomic nuclei **3** Also: **accelerant** *chem* a substance that increases the speed of a chemical reaction; catalyst

accelerometer (æk,sɛlə'rɒmɪtə) *n* an instrument for measuring acceleration, esp of an aircraft or rocket

accent *n* ('æksənt) **1** the characteristic mode of pronunciation of a person or group, esp one that betrays social or geographical origin **2** the relative prominence of a spoken or sung syllable, esp with regard to stress or pitch **3** a mark (such as ', ,, ´, or `) used in writing to indicate the stress or prominence of a syllable **4** any of various marks or symbols conventionally used in writing certain languages to indicate the quality of a vowel. See **acute** (sense 8), **grave**^{2} (sense 5), **circumflex** **5** rhythmic stress in verse or prose **6** *music* **6a** stress placed on certain notes in a piece of music, indicated by a symbol printed over the note concerned **6b** the rhythmic pulse of a piece or passage, usually represented as the stress on the first beat of each bar **7** a distinctive characteristic of anything, such as taste, pattern, style, etc **8** particular attention or emphasis: *an accent on learning* **9** a strongly contrasting detail ▷ *vb* (æk'sɛnt) (*tr*) **10** to mark with an accent in writing, speech, music, etc **11** to lay particular emphasis or stress on [c14 via OF from L *accentus*, from *ad-* to + *cantus* chant]

accentor (æk'sɛntə) *n* a small sparrow-like songbird, which inhabits mainly mountainous regions of Europe and Asia. See also **hedge sparrow**

accentual (æk'sɛntʃʊəl) *adj* **1** of, relating to, or having accents; rhythmic **2** *prosody* of or relating to verse based on the number of stresses in a line > **ac'centually** *adv*

accentuate (æk'sɛntʃʊˌeɪt) *vb* **accentuates, accentuating, accentuated** (*tr*) to stress or emphasize > **acˌcentu'ation** *n*

accept (ək'sɛpt) *vb* (*mainly tr*) **1** to take or receive (something offered) **2** to give an affirmative reply to **3** to take on the responsibilities, duties, etc, of: *he accepted office* **4** to tolerate **5** to consider as true or believe in (a philosophy, theory, etc) **6** (*may take a clause as object*) to be willing to believe: *you must accept that he lied* **7** to receive with approval or admit, as into a community, group, etc **8** *commerce* to agree to pay (a bill, draft, etc) **9** to receive as adequate or valid [c14 from L *acceptāre*, from *ad-* to + *capere* to take] > **ac'cepter** *n*

acceptable (ək'sɛptəbᵊl) *adj* **1** satisfactory; adequate **2** pleasing; welcome **3** tolerable > **acˌcepta'bility** *or* **ac'ceptableness** *n* > **ac'ceptably** *adv*

acceptance (ək'sɛptəns) *n* **1** the act of accepting or the state of being accepted or acceptable **2** favourable reception **3** (often foll by *of*) belief (in) or assent (to) **4** *commerce* a formal agreement by a debtor to pay a draft, bill, etc **5** (*pl*) *Austral inf* a list of horses accepted as starters in a race

acceptation (ˌæksɛp'teɪʃən) *n* the accepted meaning, as of a word, phrase, etc

accepted (ək'sɛptɪd) *adj* commonly approved or recognized; customary; established

acceptor (ək'sɛptə) *n* **1** *commerce* the person or organization on which a draft or bill of exchange is drawn **2** *electronics* an impurity, such as gallium, added to a semiconductor material to increase its p-type semiconductivity

access ('æksɛs) *n* **1** the act of approaching or entering **2** the condition of allowing entry, esp (of a building, etc) entry by prams, wheelchairs, etc **3** the right or privilege to approach, enter, or make use of something **4** a way or means of approach or entry **5** the opportunity or right to see or approach someone: *my ex-wife sabotages my access to the children* **6** (*modifier*) designating programmes made by the general public: *access television* **7** a sudden outburst or attack, as of rage or disease ▷ *vb* (*tr*) **8** *computing* **8a** to obtain or retrieve (information) from a storage device **8b** to place (information) in a storage device **9** to gain access to; make accessible or available [c14 from OF or from L *accessus*, from *accēdere* to ACCEDE]

accessible (ək'sɛsəbᵊl) *adj* **1** easy to approach, enter, or use **2** **accessible to** likely to be affected by **3** obtainable; available > **acˌcessi'bility** *n*

accession (ək'sɛʃən) *n* **1** the act of attaining to an office, right, condition, etc **2** an increase due to an addition **3** an addition, as to a collection **4** *property law* an addition to land or property by natural increase or improvement **5** *international law* the formal acceptance of a convention or treaty **6** agreement ▷ *vb* **7** (*tr*) to make a record of (additions to a collection) > **ac'cessional** *adj*

accessory (ək'sɛsərɪ) *n, pl* **accessories** **1** a supplementary part or object, as of a car, appliance, etc **2** (*often pl*) a small accompanying item of dress, esp of women's dress **3** (formerly) a person involved in a crime although absent during its commission ▷ *adj* **4** supplementary; additional **5** assisting in or having knowledge of an act, esp a crime [c17 from LL *accessōrius*: see ACCESS] > **accessorial** (ˌæksɛ'sɔːrɪəl) *adj* > **ac'cessorily** *adv*

access road *n* a road giving entry to a region or, esp, a motorway

access time *n computing* the time required to retrieve a piece of stored information

acciaccatura (əˌtʃækə'tʊərə) *n, pl* **acciaccaturas** *or* **acciaccature** (-reɪ) a small grace note melodically adjacent to a principal note and played simultaneously with or immediately before it [c18 It.: lit., a crushing sound]

accidence ('æksɪdəns) *n* the part of grammar concerned with changes in the form of words for the expression of tense, person, case, number, etc [c15 from L *accidentia* accidental matters, from *accidere* to happen. See ACCIDENT]

accident ('æksɪdənt) *n* **1** an unforeseen event or one without an apparent cause **2** anything that occurs unintentionally or by chance: *I met him by accident* **3** a misfortune or mishap, esp one causing injury or death **4** *geol* a surface irregularity in a natural formation [c14 via OF from L *accident-*, from the p.p. of *accidere* to happen, from *ad-* to + *cadere* to fall]

accidental (ˌæksɪ'dɛntᵊl) *adj* **1** occurring by chance, unexpectedly, or unintentionally **2** nonessential; incidental **3** *music* denoting sharps, flats, or naturals that are not in the key signature of a piece ▷ *n* **4** an incidental or supplementary circumstance, factor, or attribute **5** *music* a symbol denoting a sharp, flat, or natural that is not a part of the key signature > ˌ**acci'dentally** *adv*

accident-prone *adj* liable to become involved in accidents

accidie ('æksɪdɪ) *or* **acedia** *n* spiritual sloth; apathy; indifference [in use c13 to c16 and revived c19 via LL from Gk *akēdia*, from A-¹ + *kēdos* care]

accipiter (æk'sɪpɪtə) *n* any of a genus of hawks having short rounded wings and a long tail [c19 NL, from L: hawk] > **ac'cipitrine** *adj*

acclaim (ə'kleɪm) *vb* **1** (*tr*) to acknowledge publicly the excellence of (a person, act, etc) **2** to applaud **3** (*tr*) to acknowledge publicly: *they acclaimed him king* ▷ *n* **4** an enthusiastic expression of approval, etc [c17 from L *acclāmāre*, from *ad-* to + *clamāre* to shout] > **ac'claimer** *n*

Aa

acclamation (ˌæklə'meɪʃən) *n* **1** an enthusiastic reception or exhibition of welcome, approval, etc **2** an expression of approval with shouts or applause **3** *Canad* an instance of electing or being elected without opposition > **acclamatory** (ə'klæmətərɪ) *adj*

acclimatize *or* **acclimatise** (ə'klaɪməˌtaɪz) *vb* **acclimatizes, acclimatizing, acclimatized** *or* **acclimatises, acclimatising, acclimatised** to adapt or become accustomed to a new climate or environment > **ac'climaˌtizable** *or* **ac'climaˌtisable** *adj* > **acˌclimati'zation** *or* **acˌclimati'sation** *n*

acclivity (ə'klɪvɪtɪ) *n, pl* **acclivities** an upward slope, esp of the ground ▷ Cf **declivity** [c17 from L, from *acclīvis* sloping up] > **ac'clivitous** *adj*

accolade ('ækəˌleɪd) *n* **1** strong praise or approval **2** an award or honour **3** the ceremonial gesture used to confer knighthood, a touch on the shoulder with a sword **4** a rare word for **brace** (sense 6) [c17 via F & It. from Vulgar L *accollāre* (unattested) to hug; rel. to L *collum* neck]

accommodate (ə'kɒməˌdeɪt) *vb* **accommodates, accommodating, accommodated** **1** (*tr*) to supply or provide, esp with lodging **2** (*tr*) to oblige or do a favour for **3** to adapt **4** (*tr*) to bring into harmony **5** (*tr*) to allow room for **6** (*tr*) to lend money to [c16 from L *accommodāre*, from *ad-* to + *commodus* having the proper measure]

accommodating (ə'kɒməˌdeɪtɪŋ) *adj* willing to help; kind; obliging

accommodation (əˌkɒmə'deɪʃən) *n* **1** lodging or board and lodging **2** adjustment, as of differences or to new circumstances; settlement or reconciliation **3** something fulfilling a need, want, etc **4** *physiol* the automatic or voluntary adjustment of the shape of the lens of the eye for far or near vision **5** willingness to help or oblige **6** *commerce* a loan

accommodation address *n* an address on letters, etc, to a person or business that does not wish or is not able to receive post at a permanent or actual address

accommodation ladder *n naut* a flight of stairs or a ladder for lowering over the side of a ship for access to and from a small boat, pier, etc

accompaniment (əˈkʌmpənɪmənt) *n* **1** something that accompanies or is served or used with something else **2** *music* a subordinate or supporting part for an instrument, voices, or an orchestra

accompanist (əˈkʌmpənɪst) *n* a person who plays a musical accompaniment for another performer

accompany (əˈkʌmpənɪ) *vb* **accompanies, accompanying, accompanied** **1** (*tr*) to go along with, so as to be in company with **2** (*tr; foll by with*) to supplement **3** (*tr*) to occur or be associated with **4** to provide a musical accompaniment for (a soloist, etc) [c15 from OF *accompaignier*, from *compaing* COMPANION[1]]

accomplice (əˈkɒmplɪs, əˈkʌm-) *n* a person who has helped another in committing a crime [c15 from *a complice*, interpreted as one word, from OF, from LL *complex* partner, from L *complicāre* to COMPLICATE]

accomplish (əˈkɒmplɪʃ, əˈkʌm-) *vb* (*tr*) **1** to manage to do; achieve **2** to complete [c14 from OF *acomplir*, ult. from L *complēre* to fill up. See COMPLETE]

accomplished (əˈkɒmplɪʃt, əˈkʌm-) *adj* **1** successfully completed; achieved **2** expert; proficient

accomplishment (əˈkɒmplɪʃmənt, əˈkʌm-) *n* **1** the act of achieving **2** something successfully completed **3** (*often pl*) skill or talent **4** (*often pl*) social grace and poise

accord (əˈkɔːd) *n* **1** agreement; accordance (esp in **in accord with**) **2** concurrence of opinion **3** **with one accord** unanimously **4** pleasing relationship between sounds, colours, etc **5** **of one's own accord** voluntarily ▹ *vb* **6** to be or cause to be in harmony or agreement **7** (*tr*) to grant; bestow [c12 via OF from L *ad-* to + *cord-*, stem of *cor* heart]

accordance (əˈkɔːdəns) *n* conformity; agreement; accord (esp in **in accordance with**)

according (əˈkɔːdɪŋ) *adj* **1** (foll by *to*) in proportion **2** (foll by *to*) as stated (by) **3** (foll by *to*) in conformity (with) **4** (foll by *as*) depending (on whether)

accordingly (əˈkɔːdɪŋlɪ) *adv* **1** in an appropriate manner; suitably ▹ *sentence connector* **2** consequently

accordion (əˈkɔːdɪən) *n* **1** a portable box-shaped instrument consisting of metallic reeds that are made to vibrate by air from a set of bellows controlled by the player's hands. Notes are produced by means of studlike keys **2** short for **piano accordion** [c19 from G, from *Akkord* harmony] > **acˈcordionist** *n*

accordion pleats *pl n* tiny knife pleats

accost (əˈkɒst) *vb* (*tr*) to approach, stop, and speak to (a person), as to ask a question, solicit sexually, etc [c16 from LL *accostāre*, from L *costa* side, rib] > **acˈcostable** *adj*

accouchement *French* (akuʃmɑ̃) *n* childbirth or the period of confinement [c19 from *accoucher* to put to bed. See COUCH]

account (əˈkaʊnt) *n* **1** a verbal or written report, description, or narration of some occurrence, event, etc **2** an explanation of conduct, esp one made to someone in authority **3** basis; consideration: *on this account* **4** importance, consequence, or value: *of little account* **5** assessment; judgment **6** profit or advantage: *to good account* **7** part or behalf (only in **on one's** *or* **someone's account**) **8** *finance* **8a** a business relationship between a bank, department store, etc, and a depositor, customer, or client permitting the latter certain banking or credit services **8b** the sum of money deposited at a bank **8c** the amount of credit available to the holder of an account **8d** a record of these **9** a statement of monetary transactions with the resulting balance **10a** a regular client or customer **10b** an area of business assigned to another: *they transferred their publicity account to a new agent* **11** **call** (*or* **bring**) **to account** **11a** to insist on explanation **11b** to reprimand **11c** to hold responsible **12** **give a good** (**bad**, etc) **account of oneself** to perform well (badly, etc) **13** **on account** **13a** on credit **13b** Also: **to account** as partial payment **14** **on account of** (*prep*) because of **15** **take account of** *or* **take into account** to take into consideration; allow for **16** **settle** *or* **square accounts with** **16a** to pay or receive a balance due **16b** to get revenge on (someone) **17** See **bank account** ▹ *vb* **18** (*tr*) to consider or reckon: *he accounts himself poor* [c13 from OF *acont*, from *conter* to COUNT[1]]

> USAGE The phrase *on account of* can provide a useful alternative to *because of* in writing. It occurs relatively infrequently in spoken language, where it is sometimes followed by a clause, as in ...*on account of I don't do drugs*. This use is considered nonstandard

accountable (əˈkaʊntəbəl) *adj* **1** responsible to someone or for some action **2** able to be explained > **acˌcountaˈbility** *n* > **acˈcountably** *adv*

accountancy (əˈkaʊntənsɪ) *n* the profession or business of an accountant

accountant (əˈkaʊntənt) *n* a person concerned with the maintenance and audit of business accounts

account executive *n* an executive in an advertising agency or public relations firm who manages a client's account

account for *vb* (*intr, prep*) **1** to give reasons for (an event, act, etc) **2** to make or provide a reckoning of (expenditure, etc) **3** to be responsible for destroying or putting (people, aircraft, etc) out of action

accounting (əˈkaʊntɪŋ) *n* **a** the skill or practice of maintaining and auditing accounts and preparing reports on the assets, liabilities, etc, of a business **b** (*as modifier*): *an accounting period*

accoutre *or US* **accouter** (əˈkuːtə) *vb* **accoutres, accoutring, accoutred** *or US* **accouters, accoutering, accoutered** (*tr; usually passive*) to provide with equipment or dress, esp military [c16 from OF *accoustrer*, ult. rel. to L *consuere* to sew together]

accoutrement (əˈkuːtrəmənt, əˈkuːtə-) *or US* **accouterment** (əˈkuːtərmənt) *n* **1** equipment worn by soldiers in addition to their clothing and weapons **2** (*usually pl*) clothing, equipment, etc; trappings: *the correct accoutrements for any sport*

Accra (əˈkrɑː) *n* the capital of Ghana, a port on the Gulf of Guinea: built on the site of three 17th-century trading fortresses founded by the English, Dutch, and Danish. Pop: 1 446 000 (1998 est)

accredit (əˈkrɛdɪt) *vb* (*tr*) **1** to ascribe or attribute **2** to give official recognition to **3** to certify as meeting required standards **4** (often foll by *at* or *to*) **4a** to send (an envoy, etc) with official credentials **4b** to appoint (someone) as an envoy, etc **5** to believe [c17 from F *accréditer*, from *mettre à crédit* to put to CREDIT] > **acˌcrediˈtation** *n*

accredited (əˈkrɛdɪtɪd) *adj* **1** officially authorized; recognized **2** (of milk, cattle, etc) certified as free from disease; meeting certain standards

accrete (əˈkriːt) *vb* **accretes, accreting, accreted** **1** to grow or cause to grow together **2** to make or become bigger, as by addition [c18 back formation from ACCRETION]

accretion (əˈkriːʃən) *n* **1** any gradual increase in size, as through growth or external addition **2** something added, esp extraneously, to cause growth or an increase in size **3** the growing together of normally separate plant or animal parts [c17 from L *accretiō* increase, from *accrēscere*. See ACCRUE] > **acˈcretive** *adj*

accrual (əˈkruːəl) *n* **1** the act of accruing **2** something that has accrued **3** *accounting* a charge incurred in one accounting period that has not been paid by the end of it

accrue (ə'kru:) *vb* **accrues, accruing, accrued** (*intr*) **1** to increase by growth or addition, esp (of capital) to increase by periodic addition of interest **2** (often foll by *to*) to fall naturally (to) [c15 from OF *accreue*, ult. from L *accrēscere*, from *ad-* to, in addition + *crēscere* to grow]

acct *book-keeping abbrev for* account

acculturate (ə'kʌltʃə,reɪt) *vb* **acculturates, acculturating, acculturated** (of a cultural or social group) to assimilate the cultural traits of another group [c20 from AD- + CULTURE + -ATE[1]] > **ac,cultur'ation** *n*

accumulate (ə'kju:mjʊ,leɪt) *vb* **accumulates, accumulating, accumulated** to gather or become gathered together in an increasing quantity; collect [c16 from L *accumulāre* to heap up, from *cumulus* a heap] > **ac'cumulable** *adj* > **ac'cumulative** *adj*

accumulation (ə,kju:mjʊ'leɪʃən) *n* **1** the act or process of collecting together or becoming collected **2** something that has been collected, gathered, heaped, etc **3** *finance* the continuous growth of capital by retention of interest or earnings

accumulator (ə'kju:mjʊ,leɪtə) *n* **1** Also called: **battery, storage battery** a rechargeable device for storing electrical energy in the form of chemical energy **2** *horse racing, Brit* a collective bet on successive races, with both stake and winnings being carried forward to accumulate progressively **3** a register in a calculator or computer used for holding the results of a computation or data transfer

accuracy ('ækjʊrəsɪ) *n, pl* **accuracies** faithful measurement or representation of the truth; correctness; precision

accurate ('ækjərɪt) *adj* **1** faithfully representing or describing the truth **2** showing a negligible or permissible deviation from a standard: *an accurate ruler* **3** without error; precise **4** *maths* (of a number) correctly represented to a specified number of decimal places or significant figures [c16 from L *accūrāre* to perform with care, from *cūra* care] > **'accurately** *adv*

accursed (ə'kɜ:sɪd, ə'kɜ:st) *or* **accurst** (ə'kɜ:st) *adj* **1** under or subject to a curse **2** (*prenominal*) hateful; detestable [OE *ācursod*, p.p. of *ācursian* to put under a CURSE] > **accursedly** (ə'kɜ:sɪdlɪ) *adv* > **ac'cursedness** *n*

accusation (,ækjʊ'zeɪʃən) *n* **1** an allegation that a person is guilty of some fault or crime **2** a formal charge brought against a person

accusative (ə'kju:zətɪv) *adj* **1** *grammar* denoting a case of nouns, pronouns, and adjectives in inflected languages that is used to identify the direct object of a finite verb, of certain prepositions, and for certain other purposes **2** another word for **accusatorial** ▷ *n* **3** *grammar* the accusative case or a speech element in it [c15 from L; in grammar, from *cāsus accūsātīvus* accusative case, a mistaken translation of Gk *ptōsis aitiatikē* the case indicating causation. See ACCUSE] > **accusatival** (ə,kju:zə'taɪvəl) *adj* > **ac'cusatively** *adv*

accusatorial (ə,kju:zə'tɔ:rɪəl) *or* **accusatory** (ə'kju:zətərɪ) *adj* **1** containing or implying blame or strong criticism **2** *law* denoting a legal system in which the defendant is prosecuted before a judge in public ▷ Cf **inquisitorial**

accuse (ə'kju:z) *vb* **accuses, accusing, accused** to charge (a person or persons) with some fault, offence, crime, etc [c13 via OF from L *accūsāre* to call to account, from *ad-* to + *causa* lawsuit] > **ac'cuser** *n* > **ac'cusing** *adj* > **ac'cusingly** *adv*

accused (ə'kju:zd) *n* (preceded by *the*) *law* the defendant or defendants on a criminal charge

accustom (ə'kʌstəm) *vb* (*tr*; usually foll by *to*) to make (oneself) familiar (with) or used (to), as by habit or experience [c15 from OF *acostumer*, from *costume* CUSTOM]

accustomed (ə'kʌstəmd) *adj* **1** usual; customary **2** (*postpositive*; foll by *to*) used (to) **3** (*postpositive*; foll by *to*) in the habit (of): *accustomed to walking*

AC/DC *adj inf* (of a person) bisexual [c20 humorous reference to electrical apparatus that is adaptable for ALTERNATING CURRENT and DIRECT CURRENT]

ace (eɪs) *n* **1** any die, domino, or any of four playing cards with one spot **2** a single spot or pip on a playing card, die, etc **3** *tennis* a winning serve that the opponent fails to reach **4** a fighter pilot accredited with destroying several enemy aircraft **5** *inf* an expert: *an ace at driving* **6** **an ace up one's sleeve** a hidden and powerful advantage ▷ *adj* **7** *inf* superb; excellent [c13 via OF from L *as* a unit]

-acea *suffix forming plural proper nouns* denoting animals belonging to a class or order: *Crustacea* (class); *Cetacea* (order) [NL, from L, neuter pl of *-āceus* -ACEOUS]

-aceae *suffix forming plural proper nouns* denoting plants belonging to a family: *Liliaceae* [NL, from L, fem pl of *-āceus* -ACEOUS]

acedia (ə'si:dɪə) *n* another word for **accidie**

Aceh ('a:tʃəɪ) *n* a special region of N Indonesia, in N Sumatra; mountainous with rain forests; scene of separatist conflict since the later 1990s. Capital: Banda Aceh. Pop: 3 930 905 (2000). Area: 55 392 sq km (21 381 sq miles)

ACE inhibitor *n* any one of a class of drugs, including captopril, enalapril, and ramipril that cause the arteries to widen by preventing the synthesis of angiotensin: used to treat high blood pressure and heart failure [c20 from *a(ngiotensin-)c(onverting) e(nzyme) inhibitor*]

-aceous *suffix forming adjectives* relating to, having the nature of, or resembling: *herbaceous* [NL, from L *-āceus* of a certain kind; rel. to *-āc*, *-āx*, adjectival suffix]

acephalous (ə'sɛfələs) *adj* having no head or one that is reduced and indistinct, as certain insect larvae [c18 via Med. L from Gk *akephalos*. See A-[1], -CEPHALIC]

acer ('eɪsə) *n* any tree or shrub of the genus *Acer*, often cultivated for their brightly coloured foliage. See also **maple**

Aa

acerbate ('æsə,beɪt) *vb* **acerbates, acerbating, acerbated** (*tr*) **1** to embitter or exasperate **2** to make sour or bitter [c18 from L *acerbāre* to make sour]

acerbic (ə'sɜ:bɪk) *adj* harsh, bitter, or astringent; sour [c17 from L *acerbus* sour, bitter]

acerbity (ə'sɜ:bɪtɪ) *n, pl* **acerbities** **1** vitriolic or embittered speech, temper, etc **2** sourness or bitterness of taste

acetabulum (,æsɪ'tæbjʊləm) *n, pl* **acetabula** (-lə) the deep cuplike cavity on the side of the hipbone that receives the head of the thighbone [L: vinegar cup, hence a cuplike cavity, from *acētum* vinegar + *-abulum*, suffix denoting a container]

acetal ('æsɪ,tæl) *n* **1** a type of organic compound formed by addition of an alcohol to an aldehyde or ketone **2** a colourless pleasant-smelling volatile liquid used in perfumes. Formula: $CH_3CH(OC_2H_5)_2$. Systematic name: **diethoxyethane** [c19 from G *Azetal*, from ACETO- + ALCOHOL]

acetaldehyde (,æsɪ'tældɪ,haɪd) *n* a colourless volatile pungent liquid, used in the manufacture of organic compounds and as a solvent. Formula: CH_3CHO. Systematic name: **ethanal**

acetanilide (,æsɪ'tænɪ,laɪd) *n* a white crystalline powder used in the manufacture of dyes and as an analgesic in medicine. Formula: $C_6H_5NH(COCH_3)$. Systematic names: **N-phenylethanamide, phenylacetamide** [c19 from ACETO- + ANILINE + -IDE]

acetate ('æsɪ,teɪt) *n* **1** any salt or ester of acetic acid. Systematic name: **ethanoate** **2** short for **acetate rayon** *or* **cellulose acetate** **3** an audio disc with an acetate lacquer coating: used for demonstration purposes, etc [c19 from ACETIC + -ATE[1]]

acetate rayon *n* a synthetic textile fibre made from cellulose acetate

acetic (ə'si:tɪk) *adj* of, containing, producing, or derived from acetic acid or vinegar [c19 from L *acētum* vinegar]

acetic acid *n* a colourless pungent liquid widely used in the manufacture of plastics, pharmaceuticals, dyes, etc Formula: CH_3COOH. Systematic name: **ethanoic acid** See also **vinegar**

acetify (ə'sɛtɪ,faɪ) *vb* **acetifies, acetifying, acetified** to become or cause to become acetic acid or vinegar > **a,cetifi'cation** *n*

aceto- *or before a vowel* **acet-** *combining form* containing an acetyl group or derived from acetic acid: *acetone* [from L *acētum* vinegar]

acetone ('æsɪ,təʊn) *n* a colourless volatile pungent liquid used in the manufacture of chemicals and as a solvent for paints, varnishes, and lacquers. Formula: CH_3COCH_3. Systematic name: **propanone** [c19 from G *Azeton*, from ACETO- + -ONE]

acetous ('æsɪtəs) *or* **acetose** ('æsɪ,təʊs) *adj* **1** producing or resembling acetic acid or vinegar **2** tasting like vinegar [c18 from LL *acētōsus* vinegary, from *acētum* vinegar]

acetyl ('æsɪ,taɪl, ə'si:taɪl) *n* (*modifier*) of or containing the monovalent group CH_3CO- [c19 from ACET(IC) + -YL]

acetylcholine (,æsɪtaɪl'kəʊli:n, -lɪn) *n* a chemical substance secreted at the ends of many nerve fibres, responsible for the transmission of nervous impulses

acetylene (ə'sɛtɪ,li:n) *n* **1** a colourless soluble flammable gas used in the manufacture of organic chemicals and in cutting and welding metals. Formula: C_2H_2. Systematic name: **ethyne** **2** another name for **alkyne**

acetylene series *n* another name for **alkyne series**

acetylsalicylic acid (,æsɪtaɪl,sælɪ'sɪlɪk) *n* the chemical name for **aspirin**

Achaea (ə'ki:ə) *or* **Achaia** (ə'kaɪə) *n* **1** a department of Greece, in the N Peloponnese. Capital: Patras. Pop: 300 078 (1991). Area: 3209 sq km (1239 sq miles). Modern Greek name: **Akhaïa** **2** a province of ancient Greece, in the N Peloponnese on the Gulf of Corinth: enlarged as a Roman province in 27 BC.

Achaean (ə'ki:ən) *or* **Achaian** (ə'kaɪən) *n* **1** a member of a principal Greek tribe in the Mycenaean era ▷ *adj* **2** of or relating to the Achaeans

Achates (ə'keɪti:z) *n* **1** *classical myth* Aeneas' faithful companion in Virgil's *Aeneid* **2** a loyal friend

ache (eɪk) *vb* **aches, aching, ached** (*intr*) **1** to feel, suffer, or be the source of a continuous dull pain **2** to suffer mental anguish ▷ *n* **3** a continuous dull pain [OE *ācan* (vb), *æce* (n), ME *aken* (vb), *ache* (n)] > **'aching** *adj*

Achebe (ə'tʃeɪbɪ) *n* **Chinua** born 1930, Nigerian novelist. His works include *Things Fall Apart* (1958), *A Man of the People* (1966), *Anthills of the Savannah* (1987), and *Another Africa* (1998)

Achelous (,ækɪ'ləʊəs) *n* *classical myth* a river god who changed into a snake and a bull while fighting Hercules but was defeated when Hercules broke off one of his horns

achene (ə'ki:n) *n* a dry one-seeded indehiscent fruit with the seed distinct from the fruit wall [c19 from NL *achaenium* that which does not open, from A-[1] + Gk *khainein* to yawn]

Acheron ('ækə,rɒn) *n* *Greek myth* **1** one of the rivers in Hades over which the souls of the dead were ferried by Charon ▷ Cf **Styx** **2** the underworld or Hades

Acheson ('ætʃɪsən) *n* **Dean** (**Gooderham**) 1893–1971, US lawyer and statesman: secretary of state (1949–53) under President Truman

Acheulian *or* **Acheulean** (ə'ʃu:lɪən) *archaeol* ▷ *n* **1** (in Europe) the period in the Lower Palaeolithic following the Abbevillian, represented by the use of soft hammerstones in hand-axe production **2** (in Africa) the period represented by every stage of hand-axe development ▷ *adj* **3** of or relating to this period [c20 after *St Acheul*, town in N France]

achieve (ə'tʃi:v) *vb* **achieves, achieving, achieved** (*tr*) **1** to bring to a successful conclusion **2** to gain as by hard work or effort: *to achieve success* [c14 from OF *achever* to bring to an end, from *a chef* to a head] > **a'chievable** *adj* > **a'chiever** *n*

achievement (ə'tʃi:vmənt) *n* **1** something that has been accomplished, esp by hard work, ability, or heroism **2** successful completion; accomplishment

achillea (,ækɪ'li:ə) *n* any of several cultivated varieties of yarrow [NL, from Gk *akhilleios* plant used medicinally by ACHILLES]

Achilles (ə'kɪli:z) *n* *Greek myth* Greek hero, the son of Peleus and the sea goddess Thetis: in the *Iliad* the foremost of the Greek warriors at the siege of Troy. While he was a baby his mother plunged him into the river Styx making his body invulnerable except for the heel by which she held him. After slaying Hector, he was killed by Paris who wounded him in the heel > **Achillean** (,ækɪ'li:ən) *adj*

Achilles heel *n* a small but fatal weakness

Achilles tendon *n* the fibrous cord that connects the muscles of the calf to the heelbone

Achill Island ('ækɪl) *n* an island in the Republic of Ireland, off the W coast of Co. Mayo. Area: 148 sq km (57 sq miles). Pop: 2853 (1991)

Achitophel (ə'kɪtə,fɛl) *n* *Bible* the Douay spelling of **Ahithophel**

achromat ('ækrə,mæt) *or* **achromatic lens** *n* a lens designed to reduce chromatic aberration

achromatic (,ækrə'mætɪk) *adj* **1** without colour **2** capable of reflecting or refracting light without chromatic aberration **3** *music* involving no sharps or flats > **,achro'matically** *adv* > **achromatism** (ə'krəʊmə,tɪzəm) *or* **achromaticity** (ə,krəʊmə'tɪsɪtɪ) *n*

acid ('æsɪd) *n* **1** any substance that dissociates in water to yield a sour corrosive solution containing hydrogen ions, and turning litmus red **2** a sour-tasting substance **3** a slang name for **LSD** ▷ *adj* **4** *chem* **4a** of, derived from, or containing acid **4b** being or having the properties of an acid **5** sharp or sour in taste **6** cutting, sharp, or hurtful in speech, manner, etc [c17 from F *acide* or L *acidus*, from *acēre* to be sour] > **'acidly** *adv* > **'acidness** *n*

acid-fast *adj* (of bacteria and tissues) resistant to decolorization by mineral acids after staining

Acid House *or* **Acid** *n* a dance music dominated by beat and bass line, created with synthesizers and digital sampling; popular in the late 1980s [c20 from ACID (LSD) + HOUSE (MUSIC)]

acidic (ə'sɪdɪk) *adj* another word for **acid**

acidify (ə'sɪdɪ,faɪ) *vb* **acidifies, acidifying, acidified** to convert into or become acid > **a'cidi,fiable** *adj* > **a,cidifi'cation** *n*

acidity (ə'sɪdɪtɪ) *n, pl* **acidities** **1** the quality or state of being acid **2** the amount of acid present in a solution

acidosis (,æsɪ'dəʊsɪs) *n* a condition characterized by an abnormal increase in the acidity of the blood > **acidotic** (,æsɪ'dɒtɪk) *adj*

acid rain *n* rain containing pollutants, chiefly sulphur dioxide and nitrogen oxide, released into the atmosphere by burning coal or oil

acid rock *n* rock music characterized by bizarre amplified instrumental effects [c20 from ACID (LSD)]

acid test *n* a rigorous and conclusive test to establish worth or value [c19 from the testing of gold with nitric acid]

acidulate (ə'sɪdjʊ,leɪt) *vb* **acidulates, acidulating, acidulated** (*tr*) to make slightly acid or sour [c18 ACIDULOUS + -ATE[1]] > **a,cidu'lation** *n*

acidulous (ə'sɪdjʊləs) *or* **acidulent** *adj* **1** rather sour **2** sharp or sour in speech, manner, etc; acid [c18 from L *acidulus* sourish, dim. of *acidus* sour]

acinus ('æsɪnəs) *n, pl* **acini** (-,naɪ) **1** *anat* any of the terminal saclike portions of a compound gland **2** *bot* any of the small drupes that make up the fruit of the raspberry, etc **3** *bot, obs* a collection of berries, such as a bunch of grapes [c18 NL, from L: grape, berry]

Acis ('eɪsɪs) *n Greek myth* a Sicilian shepherd and the lover of the nymph Galatea. In jealousy, Polyphemus crushed him with a huge rock, and his blood was turned by Galatea into a river

ack-ack ('æk,æk) *n mil* **a** anti-aircraft fire **b** *(as modifier)*: *ack-ack guns* [c20 British Army World War I phonetic alphabet for AA, abbrev of *anti-aircraft*]

acknowledge (ək'nɒlɪdʒ) *vb* **acknowledges, acknowledging, acknowledged** *(tr)* **1** *(may take a clause as object)* to recognize or admit the existence, truth, or reality of **2** to indicate recognition or awareness of, as by a greeting, glance, etc **3** to express appreciation or thanks for **4** to make the receipt of known: *to acknowledge a letter* **5** to recognize, esp in legal form, the authority, rights, or claims of [c15 prob. from earlier *knowledge*, on the model of OE *oncnāwan*, ME *aknowen* to confess, recognize] > **ac'knowledgeable** *adj*

acknowledgment *or* **acknowledgement** (ək'nɒlɪdʒmənt) *n* **1** the act of acknowledging or state of being acknowledged **2** something done or given as an expression of thanks **3** *(pl)* an author's statement acknowledging his or her use of the works of other authors

ACL *abbrev for* anterior cruciate ligament

aclinic line (ə'klɪnɪk) *n* another name for **magnetic equator** [c19 *aclinic*, from Gk *aklinēs* not bending, from A-[1] + *klinein* to bend]

acme ('ækmɪ) *n* the culminating point, as of achievement or excellence [c16 from Gk *akmē*]

acne ('æknɪ) *n* a chronic skin disease common in adolescence, characterized by pustules on the face [c19 NL, from a misreading of Gk *akmē* eruption on the face. See ACME]

acolyte ('ækə,laɪt) *n* **1** a follower or attendant **2** *Christianity* an officer who assists a priest [c16 via OF & Med. L from Gk *akolouthos* a follower]

Aconcagua (*Spanish* akon'kaɣwa) *n* a mountain in W Argentina: the highest peak in the Andes and in the W Hemisphere. Height: 6960 m (22 835 ft)

aconite ('ækə,naɪt) *n* **1** any of a genus of N temperate plants, such as monkshood and wolfsbane, many of which are poisonous ▷ Cf **winter aconite** **2** the dried poisonous root of many of these plants, sometimes used as an antipyretic [c16 via OF or L from Gk *akoniton* aconite] > **aconitic** (,ækə'nɪtɪk) *adj*

Açôres (ə'sorəʃ) *n* the Portuguese name for (the) **Azores**

acorn ('eɪkɔːn) *n* the fruit of an oak tree, consisting of a smooth thick-walled nut in a woody scaly cuplike base [c16 var. (infl. by *corn*) of OE *æcern* the fruit of a tree, acorn]

acoustic (ə'kuːstɪk) *or* **acoustical** *adj* **1** of or related to sound, hearing, or acoustics **2** designed to respond to or absorb sound: *an acoustic tile* **3** (of a musical instrument or recording) without electronic amplification: *an acoustic guitar* [c17 from Gk *akoustikos*, from *akouein* to hear] > **a'coustically** *adv*

acoustics (ə'kuːstɪks) *n* **1** *(functioning as sing)* the scientific study of sound and sound waves **2** *(functioning as pl)* the characteristics of a room, auditorium, etc, that determine the fidelity with which sound can be heard within it

acoustic shock *n* a condition characterized by dizziness and partial hearing loss suffered by some people exposed to sudden loud noises over telephone or radio headsets; associated esp with workers in call centres

ACP *abbrev for* African Caribbean Pacific: a group of 71 former European colonies

acquaint (ə'kweɪnt) *vb (tr)* (foll by *with* or *of*) to make (a person) familiar (with) [c13 via OF & Med. L from L *accognitus*, from *accognōscere* to know perfectly, from *ad-* (intensive) + *cognōscere* to know]

acquaintance (ə'kweɪntəns) *n* **1** a person whom one knows but who is not a close friend **2** knowledge of a person or thing, esp when slight **3** **make the acquaintance of** to come into social contact with **4** those persons collectively whom one knows > **ac'quaintanceship** *n*

acquaintance violence *n* impulsive aggressive behaviour towards someone with whom the attacker has been in contact

acquainted (ə'kweɪntɪd) *adj (postpositive)* **1** (sometimes foll by *with*) on terms of familiarity but not intimacy **2** (foll by *with*) familiar (with)

acquiesce (,ækwɪ'ɛs) *vb* **acquiesces, acquiescing, acquiesced** *(intr; often foll by in or to)* to comply (with); assent (to) without protest [c17 from L *acquiēscere*, from *ad-* at + *quiēscere* to rest, from *quiēs* QUIET] > **,acqui'escence** *n* > **,acqui'escent** *adj*

acquire (ə'kwaɪə) *vb* **acquires, acquiring, acquired** *(tr)* to get or gain (something, such as an object, trait, or ability) [c15 via OF from L *acquīrere*, from *ad-* in addition + *quaerere* to get, seek] > **ac'quirable** *adj* > **ac'quirement** *n*

acquired behaviour *n psychol* the behaviour of an organism resulting from the effects of the environment

acquired characteristic *n* a characteristic of an organism that results from the effects of the environment and cannot be inherited

acquired immune deficiency syndrome *or* **acquired immunodeficiency syndrome** *n* the full name for **AIDS**

acquired immunity *n* the immmunity produced by exposure of an organism to antigens, which stimulates the production of antibodies

acquired taste *n* **1** a liking for something at first considered unpleasant **2** the thing liked

acquisition (,ækwɪ'zɪʃən) *n* **1** the act of acquiring or gaining possession **2** something acquired **3** a person or thing of special merit added to a group [c14 from L *acquīsītiōn-*, from *acquīrere* to ACQUIRE]

Aa

acquisitive (ə'kwɪzɪtɪv) *adj* inclined or eager to acquire things, esp material possessions > **ac'quisitively** *adv* > **ac'quisitiveness** *n*

acquit (ə'kwɪt) *vb* **acquits, acquitting, acquitted** *(tr)* **1** (foll by *of*) **1a** to free or release (from a charge of crime) **1b** to pronounce not guilty **2** (foll by *of*) to free or relieve (from an obligation, duty, etc) **3** to repay or settle (a debt or obligation) **4** to conduct (oneself) [c13 from OF *aquiter*, from *quiter* to release, QUIT] > **ac'quittal** *n* > **ac'quitter** *n*

acquittance (ə'kwɪtəns) *n* **1** a release from or settlement of a debt, etc **2** a record of this, such as a receipt

acre ('eɪkə) *n* **1** a unit of area used in certain English-speaking countries, equal to 4840 square yards or 4046.86 square metres **2** *(pl)* **2a** land, esp a large area **2b** *inf* a large amount **3** **farm the long acre** *NZ* to graze stock on the grass along a highway [OE *æcer* field, acre]

Acre *n* **1** ('ɑːkrə) a state of W Brazil: mostly unexplored tropical forests; acquired from Bolivia in 1903. Capital: Rio Branco. Pop: 557 337 (2000 est). Area: 152 589 sq km (58 899 sq miles) **2** ('eɪkə, 'ɑːkə) a city and port in N Israel, strategically situated on the **Bay of Acre** in the E Mediterranean: taken and retaken during the Crusades (1104, 1187, 1191, 1291), taken by the Turks (1517), by Egypt (1832), and by the Turks again (1839). Pop: 40 500 (1989 est). Old Testament name: **Accho** (ɑː'kəʊ) Arabic name: **'Akka** (ɑː'kɑː) Hebrew name: **'Akko** (ɑː'kəʊ)

acreage ('eɪkərɪdʒ) *n* **1** land area in acres ▷ *adj* **2** *Austral* of or relating to a large residential block of land, esp in a rural area

acrid ('ækrɪd) *adj* **1** unpleasantly pungent or sharp to the smell or taste **2** sharp or caustic, esp in speech or nature [c18 from L *ācer* sharp, sour; prob. infl. by ACID] > **acridity**

(ə'krɪdɪtɪ) *or* '**acridness** *n* > '**acridly** *adv*
acridine ('ækrɪˌdiːn) *n* a colourless crystalline solid used in the manufacture of dyes
acriflavine (ˌækrɪ'fleɪvɪn) *n* a brownish or orange-red powder used in medicine as an antiseptic [c20 from ACRIDINE + FLAVIN]
acriflavine hydrochloride *n* a red crystalline substance obtained from acriflavine and used as an antiseptic
Acrilan ('ækrɪˌlæn) *n trademark* an acrylic fibre or fabric, characterized by strength and resistance to creasing and used for clothing, carpets, etc
acrimony ('ækrɪmənɪ) *n, pl* **acrimonies** bitterness or sharpness of manner, speech, temper, etc [c16 from L *ācrimōnia*, from *ācer* sharp, sour] > **acrimonious** (ˌækrɪ'məʊnɪəs) *adj*
acro- *combining form* **1** denoting something at a height, top, beginning, or end: *acropolis* **2** denoting an extremity of the human body: *acromegaly* [from Gk *akros* extreme, topmost]
acrobat ('ækrəˌbæt) *n* **1** an entertainer who performs acts that require skill, agility, and coordination, such as swinging from a trapeze or walking a tightrope **2** a person noted for his or her frequent and rapid changes of position or allegiance [c19 via F from Gk *akrobatēs*, one who walks on tiptoe, from ACRO- + *bat-*, from *bainein* to walk] > ˌ**acro'batic** *adj* > ˌ**acro'batically** *adv*
acrobatics (ˌækrə'bætɪks) *pl n* **1** the skills or feats of an acrobat **2** any activity requiring agility and skill: *mental acrobatics*
acrogen ('ækrədʒən) *n* any flowerless plant, such as a fern or moss, in which growth occurs from the tip of the main stem > **acrogenous** (ə'krɒdʒɪnəs) *adj*
acrolect ('ækrəˌlɛkt) *n linguistics* the best level of spoken English developed in a Caribbean territory, considered to be the standard variety of English in that country [c20 from ACRO- + Gk *lektos* speech] > ˌ**acro'lectal** *adj*
acromegaly (ˌækrəʊ'mɛgəlɪ) *n* a chronic disease characterized by enlargement of the bones of the head, hands, and feet, and swelling and enlargement of soft tissue. It is caused by excessive secretion of growth hormone by the pituitary gland [c19 from F *acromégalie*, from ACRO- + Gk *megal-*, stem of *megas* big] > **acromegalic** (ˌækrəʊmɪ'gælɪk) *adj, n*
acronym ('ækrənɪm) *n* a pronounceable name made from a series of initial letters or parts of a group of words; for example, UNESCO for the *United Nations Educational, Scientific, and Cultural Organization* [c20 from ACRO- + -ONYM]
acrophobia (ˌækrə'fəʊbɪə) *n* abnormal fear or dread of being at a great height [c19 from ACRO- + -PHOBIA] > ˌ**acro'phobic** *adj, n*
acropolis (ə'krɒpəlɪs) *n* the citadel of an ancient Greek city [c17 from Gk, from ACRO- + *polis* city]
Acropolis (ə'krɒpəlɪs) *n* the citadel of Athens on which the Parthenon and the Erechtheum stand
across (ə'krɒs) *prep* **1** from one side to the other side of **2** on or at the other side of **3** so as to transcend the boundaries or barriers of: *across religious divisions* ▷ *adv* **4** from one side to the other **5** on or to the other side [c13 *on croice, acros*, from OF *a croix* crosswise]
across-the-board *adj* (**across the board** *when postpositive*) (of salary increases, taxation cuts, etc) affecting all levels or classes equally
acrostic (ə'krɒstɪk) *n* a number of lines of writing, such as a poem, certain letters of which form a word, proverb, etc. A **single acrostic** is formed by the initial letters of the lines, a **double acrostic** by the initial and final letters, and a **triple acrostic** by the initial, middle, and final letters [c16 via F from Gk, from ACRO- + *stikhos* line of verse]
acrylic (ə'krɪlɪk) *adj* **1** of, derived from, or concerned with acrylic acid ▷ *n* **2** short for **acrylic fibre, acrylic resin** [c20 from L *ācer* sharp + *olēre* to smell + -IC]
acrylic acid *n* a colourless corrosive pungent liquid, used in the manufacture of acrylic resins. Formula: CH_2: CHCOOH. Systematic name: **propenoic acid**
acrylic fibre *n* a man-made fibre used in blankets, knitwear, etc
acrylic resin *n* any of a group of polymers of acrylic acid, its esters, or amides, used as synthetic rubbers, paints, and as plastics such as Perspex
act (ækt) *n* **1** something done or performed **2** the performance of some physical or mental process; action **3** (*cap. when part of a name*) the formally codified result of deliberation by a legislative body **4** (*often pl*) a formal written record of transactions, proceedings, etc, as of a society, committee, or legislative body **5** a major division of a dramatic work **6a** a short performance of skill, a comic sketch, dance, etc **6b** those giving such a performance **7** an assumed attitude or pose, esp one intended to impress **8** **get in on the act** *inf* to become involved in a profitable situation in order to share in the benefit **9** **get one's act together** *inf* to organize oneself ▷ *vb* **10** (*intr*) to do something **11** (*intr*) to operate; react: *his mind acted quickly* **12** to perform (a part or role) in a play, etc **13** (*tr*) to present (a play, etc) on stage **14** (*intr; usually foll by for or as*) to be a substitute (for) **15** (*intr; foll by as*) to serve the function or purpose (of) **16** (*intr*) to conduct oneself or behave (as if one were): *she usually acts like a lady* **17** (*intr*) to behave in an unnatural or affected way **18** (*copula*) to play the part of: *to act the fool* **19** (*copula*) to behave in a manner appropriate to: *to act one's age* ▷ See also **act on, act up** [c14 from L *actus* a doing, & *actum* a thing done, from the p.p. of *agere* to do] > '**actable** *adj* > ˌ**acta'bility** *n*
ACT **1** *abbrev for* Australian Capital Territory **2** *abbrev for* (formerly, in Britain) advance corporation tax ▷ **3** (ækt) *n* (in New Zealand) *acronym for* Association of Consumers and Taxpayers: a small political party of the far right
Actaeon (æk'tiːən, 'æktɪən) *n Greek myth* a hunter of Boeotia who, having accidentally seen Artemis bathing, was turned into a stag and torn apart by his own hounds
ACTH *n* adrenocorticotrophic hormone; a hormone, secreted by the anterior lobe of the pituitary gland, that stimulates growth of the adrenal gland. It is used in treating rheumatoid arthritis, allergic and skin diseases, etc
acting ('æktɪŋ) *adj* (*prenominal*) **1** taking on duties temporarily, esp as a substitute for another **2** performing the duties of though not yet holding the rank of: *acting lieutenant* **3** operating or functioning **4** intended for stage performance; provided with directions for actors: *an acting version of "Hedda Gabler"* ▷ *n* **5** the art or profession of an actor
▷ www.linksnorth.com/acting
▷ www.myactingagent.com
▷ www.caryn.com/acting
actinia (æk'tɪnɪə) *n, pl* **actiniae** (-'tɪnɪˌiː) *or* **actinias** a sea anemone common in rock pools [c18 NL, lit.: things having a radial structure]
actinic (æk'tɪnɪk) *adj* (of radiation) producing a photochemical effect [c19 from ACTINO- + -IC] > **ac'tinically** *adv* > '**actinˌism** *n*
actinide series ('æktɪˌnaɪd) *n* a series of 15 radioactive elements with increasing atomic numbers from actinium to lawrencium
actinium (æk'tɪnɪəm) *n* a radioactive element of the actinide series, occurring as a decay product of uranium. It is used in neutron production. Symbol: Ac; atomic no.: 89; half-life of most stable isotope, ^{227}Ac: 22 years [c19 NL, from ACTINO- + -IUM]
actino- *or before a vowel* **actin-** *combining form* **1** indicating a radial structure: *actinomorphic* **2** indicating radioactivity or radiation: *actinometer* [from Gk, from *aktis* ray]

actinoid (ˈæktɪˌnɔɪd) *adj* having a radiate form, as a sea anemone or starfish

actinometer (ˌæktɪˈnɒmɪtə) *n* an instrument for measuring the intensity of radiation, esp of the sun's rays

actinomycin (ˌæktɪnəʊˈmaɪsɪn) *n* any of several toxic antibiotics obtained from soil bacteria, used in treating some cancers

actinozoan (ˌæktɪnəʊˈzəʊən) *n, adj* another word for **anthozoan**

action (ˈækʃən) *n* **1** the state or process of doing something or being active **2** something done, such as an act or deed **3** movement or posture during some physical activity **4** activity, force, or energy: *a man of action* **5** (*usually pl*) conduct or behaviour **6** *law* a legal proceeding brought by one party against another; lawsuit **7** the operating mechanism, esp in a piano, gun, watch, etc **8** the force applied to a body **9** the way in which something operates or works **10** **out of action** not functioning **11** the events that form the plot of a story, play, or other composition **12** *mil* **12a** a minor engagement **12b** fighting at sea or on land: *he saw action in the war* **13** *inf* the profits of an enterprise or transaction (esp in **a piece of the action**) **14** *sl* the main activity, esp social activity **15** short for **industrial action** ▷ *vb* (*tr*) **16** to put into effect; take action concerning ▷ *sentence substitute* **17** a command given by a film director to indicate that filming is to begin [C14 *accioun*, ult. from L *āctiōn-*, from *agere* to do]

actionable (ˈækʃənəbᵊl) *adj law* affording grounds for legal action > ˈ**actionably** *adv*

action committee *or* **group** *n* a committee or group formed to pursue an end, usually political, using petitions, marches, etc

action painting *n* a development of abstract expressionism characterized by accidental effects of thrown, smeared, dripped, or spattered paint. Also called: **tachisme**

action replay *n* the rerunning of a small section of a television film or tape of a match or other sporting contest, often in slow motion

action stations *pl n* **1** *mil* the positions taken up by individuals in preparation for or during a battle ▷ *sentence substitute* **2** a command to take up such positions **3** *inf* a warning to get ready for something

Actium (ˈæktɪəm) *n* a town of ancient Greece that overlooked the naval battle in 31 BC at which Octavian's fleet under Agrippa defeated that of Mark Antony and Cleopatra

activate (ˈæktɪˌveɪt) *vb* **activates, activating, activated** (*tr*) **1** to make active or capable of action **2** *physics* to make radioactive **3** *chem* to increase the rate of (a reaction) **4** to purify (sewage) by aeration **5** *US mil* to mobilize or organize (a unit) > ˌ**actiˈvation** *n* > ˈ**actiˌvator** *n*

activated carbon *n* a highly adsorptive form of carbon used to remove colour or impurities from liquids and gases

activated sludge *n* a mass of aerated precipitated sewage added to untreated sewage to bring about purification by hastening decomposition by microorganisms

active (ˈæktɪv) *adj* **1** moving, working, or doing something **2** busy or involved: *an active life* **3** physically energetic **4** effective: *an active ingredient* **5** *grammar* denoting a voice of verbs used to indicate that the subject of a sentence is performing the action or causing the event or process described by the verb, as *kicked* in *The boy kicked the football* **6** being fully engaged in military service **7** (of a volcano) erupting periodically; not extinct **8** *astron* (of the sun) exhibiting a large number of sunspots, solar flares, etc, and a marked variation in intensity and frequency of radio emission ▷ *n* **9** *grammar* **9a** the active voice **9b** an active verb [C14 from L *āctīvus*. See ACT, -IVE] > ˈ**actively** *adv* > ˈ**activeness** *n*

active list *n mil* a list of officers available for full duty

active matrix *n computing* **a** a liquid crystal display in which each pixel is individually controlled to provide a sharp image at a wide viewing angle; it is used in laptop and notebook computing **b** (*as modifier*): *an active-matrix screen*

activism (ˈæktɪˌvɪzəm) *n* a policy of taking direct and often militant action to achieve an end, esp a political or social one > ˈ**activist** *n*

activity (ækˈtɪvɪtɪ) *n, pl* **activities** **1** the state or quality of being active **2** lively action or movement **3** any specific action, pursuit, etc: *recreational activities* **4** the number of disintegrations of a radioactive substance in a given unit of time **5** *chem* a measure of the ability of a substance to take part in a chemical reaction

act of God *n law* a sudden and inevitable occurrence caused by natural forces, such as a flood or earthquake

act on *or* **upon** *vb* (*intr, prep*) **1** to regulate one's behaviour in accordance with (advice, information, etc) **2** to have an effect on (illness, a part of the body, etc)

actor (ˈæktə) *or* (*fem*) **actress** (ˈæktrɪs) *n* a person who acts in a play, film, broadcast, etc

> USAGE The use of *actress* is now very much on the decline, and women who work in the profession invariably prefer to be referred to as *actors*

actual (ˈæktʃʊəl) *adj* **1** existing in reality or as a matter of fact **2** real or genuine **3** existing at the present time; current ▷ See also **actuals** [C14 *actuel* existing, from LL, from L *āctus* ACT]

> USAGE In writing, it is best to avoid the excessive use of *actual* and *actually*, unless they really add something to the meaning of the sentence. In a sentence such as *he did actually go to the play but did not enjoy it*, the word *actually* is only necessary if there was any doubt about his going. An alternative here would be *in the end*

Aa

actual bodily harm *n criminal law* injury caused by one person to another that is less serious than grievous bodily harm. Abbrev: **ABH**

actuality (ˌæktʃʊˈælɪtɪ) *n, pl* **actualities** **1** true existence; reality **2** (*sometimes pl*) a fact or condition that is real

actualize *or* **actualise** (ˈæktʃʊəˌlaɪz) *vb* **actualizes, actualizing, actualized** *or* **actualises, actualising, actualised** (*tr*) **1** to make actual or real **2** to represent realistically > ˌ**actualiˈzation** *or* ˌ**actualiˈsation** *n*

actually (ˈæktʃʊəlɪ) *adv* **1a** as an actual fact; really **1b** (*as sentence modifier*): *actually, I haven't seen him* **2** at present

actuals (ˈæktʃʊəlz) *pl n commerce* commodities that can be purchased and used, as opposed to those bought and sold in a futures market. Also called: **physicals**

actuary (ˈæktʃʊərɪ) *n, pl* **actuaries** a person qualified to calculate commercial risks and probabilities involving uncertain future events, esp in such contexts as life assurance [C16 (meaning: registrar): from L *āctuārius* one who keeps accounts, from *actum* public business, & *acta* documents] > **actuarial** (ˌæktʃʊˈɛərɪəl) *adj*

actuate (ˈæktʃʊˌeɪt) *vb* **actuates, actuating, actuated** (*tr*) **1** to put into action or mechanical motion **2** to motivate: *actuated by unworthy desires* [C16 from Med. L *actuātus*, from *actuāre* to incite to action, from L *āctus* ACT] > ˌ**actuˈation** *n* > ˈ**actuˌator** *n*

act up *vb* (*intr, adv*) *inf* to behave in a troublesome way: *the engine began to act up*

acuity (əˈkjuːɪtɪ) *n* keenness or acuteness, esp in vision or thought [C15 from OF, from L *acūtus* ACUTE]

aculeus (əˈkjuːlɪəs) *n* **1** a prickle, such as the thorn of a rose **2** a sting [C19 from L, dim. of *acus* needle] > **aˈculeate** *adj*

acumen (ˈækjʊˌmɛn, əˈkjuːmən) *n* the ability to judge

well; insight [c16 from L: sharpness, from *acuere* to sharpen] > **a'cuminous** *adj*

acuminate *adj* (ə'kju:mɪnɪt) **1** narrowing to a sharp point, as some types of leaf ▷ *vb* (ə'kju:mɪˌneɪt), **acuminates, acuminating, acuminated 2** *(tr)* to make pointed or sharp [c17 from L *acūmināre* to sharpen] > **aˌcumi'nation** *n*

acupoint ('ækjʊˌpɔɪnt) *n* any of the specific points on the body into which a needle is inserted in acupuncture or onto which pressure is applied in shiatsu [c19 from ACU(PUNCTURE) + POINT]

acupressure ('ækjʊˌprɛʃə) *n* another name for **shiatsu** [c19 from ACU(PUNCTURE) + PRESSURE]

acupuncture ('ækjʊˌpʌŋktʃə) *n* the insertion of the tips of needles into the skin at specific points for the purpose of treating various disorders by stimulating nerve impulses [c17 from L *acus* needle + PUNCTURE] > **'acuˌpuncturist** *n*

acute (ə'kju:t) *adj* **1** penetrating in perception or insight **2** sensitive to details; keen **3** of extreme importance; crucial **4** sharp or severe; intense **5** having a sharp end or point **6** *maths* (of an angle) less than 90° **7** (of a disease) **7a** arising suddenly and manifesting intense severity **7b** of relatively short duration **8** *phonetics* of or relating to an accent (´) placed over vowels, denoting that the vowel is pronounced with higher musical pitch (as in ancient Greek) or with certain special quality (as in French) **9** (of a hospital, hospital bed, or ward) intended to accommodate short-term patients with acute illnesses ▷ *n* **10** an acute accent [c14 from L *acūtus*, p.p. of *acuere* to sharpen, from *acus* needle] > **a'cutely** *adv* > **a'cuteness** *n*

acute accent *n* the diacritical mark (´), used in some languages to indicate that the vowel over which it is placed has a special quality (as in French *été*) or that it receives the strongest stress in the word (as in Spanish *hablé*)

acute dose *n* a fatal dose of radiation

ad (æd) *n inf* short for **advertisement**

AD *or* **A.D.** (indicating years numbered from the supposed year of the birth of Christ) *abbrev for* anno Domini: *70* AD [L: in the year of the Lord]

> USAGE In strict usage, AD should be only employed with specific years: *he died in 1621* AD. In practice, it is often used with centuries, for clarity, and to mirror BC. Formerly the practice was to write AD preceding the date (AD *1621*), and it is also strictly correct to omit *in* when AD is used, since this is already contained in the meaning of the Latin *anno Domini* (in the year of Our Lord), but nowadays this rule is not observed. BC is used with both specific dates and indications of the period: *Heraclitus was born about 540* BC; *the battle took place in the 4th century* BC

ad- *prefix* **1** to; towards: *adsorb* **2** near; next to: *adrenal* [from L: towards. As a prefix in words of L origin, *ad-* became *ac-*, *af-*, *ag-*, *al-*, *an-*, *acq-*, *ar-*, *as-*, and *at-* before *c*, *f*, *g*, *l*, *n*, *q*, *r*, *s*, and *t*, and became *a-* before *gn*, *sc*, *sp*, *st*]

adage ('ædɪdʒ) *n* a traditional saying that is accepted by many as true; proverb [c16 via OF from L *adagium*; rel. to *āio* I say]

adagio (ə'dɑ:dʒɪˌəʊ) *music* ▷ *adj, adv* **1** (to be performed) slowly ▷ *n, pl* **adagios 2** a movement or piece to be performed slowly [c18 It., from *ad* at + *agio* ease]

Adam¹ ('ædəm) *n* **1** *Bible* the first man, created by God (Genesis 2–3) **2 not know (someone) from Adam** to have no knowledge of or acquaintance with someone **3 Adam's ale** *or* **wine** water

Adam² *n* **1** (*French* adã) **Adolphe** 1803–56, French composer, best known for his romantic ballet *Giselle* (1841) **2** ('ædəm) **Robert** 1728–92, Scottish architect and furniture designer. Assisted by his brother, **James**, 1730–94, he emulated the harmony of classical and Italian Renaissance architecture ▷ *adj* **3** in the neoclassical style made popular by Robert Adam

adamant ('ædəmənt) *adj* **1** unshakable in determination, purpose, etc; inflexible **2** unbreakable; impenetrable ▷ *n* **3** any extremely hard substance **4** a legendary stone said to be impenetrable [OE: from L *adamas*, from Gk, lit.: unconquerable, from A-¹ + *daman* to conquer] > **ˌada'mantine** *adj*

Adams¹ ('ædəmz) *n* a mountain in SW Washington, in the Cascade Range. Height: 3751 m (12 307 ft)

Adams² ('ædəmz) *n* **1 Gerry**, full name *Gerrard Adams*. born 1948, Northern Ireland politician; president of Sinn Féin from 1983: negotiated the Irish Republican Army ceasefires in 1994–96 and 1997 **2 Henry (Brooks)** 1838–1918, US historian and writer. His works include *Mont Saint Michel et Chartres* (1913) and his autobiography *The Education of Henry Adams* (1918) **3 John** 1735–1826, second president of the US (1797–1801); US ambassador to Great Britain (1785–88); helped draft the Declaration of Independence (1776) **4 John Coolidge** born 1947, US composer; works include the operas *Nixon in China* (1987) and *The Death of Klinghoffer* (1991) **5 John Couch** 1819–92, British astronomer who deduced the existence and position of the planet Neptune **6 John Quincey** son of John Adams. 1767–1848, sixth president of the US (1825–29); secretary of state (1817–25) **7 Samuel** 1722–1803, US revolutionary leader; one of the organizers of the Boston Tea Party; a signatory of the Declaration of Independence

Adam's apple *n* the visible projection of the thyroid cartilage of the larynx at the front of the neck

Adana ('ædənə) *n* a city in S Turkey, capital of Adana province. Pop: 1 066 544 (1995 est). Also called: **Seyhan**

adapt (ə'dæpt) *vb* **1** (often foll by *to*) to adjust (someone or something) to different conditions **2** *(tr)* to fit, change, or modify to suit a new or different purpose [c17 from L *adaptāre*, from *ad-* to + *aptāre* to fit] > **a'daptable** *adj* > **aˌdapta'bility** *n* > **a'daptive** *adj*

adaptation (ˌædæp'teɪʃən) *n* **1** the act or process of adapting or the state of being adapted **2** something that is produced by adapting something else **3** something that is changed or modified to suit new conditions **4** *biol* a modification in organisms that makes them better suited to survive and reproduce in a particular environment

adaptogen (ə'dæptəˌdʒən) *n* (in complementary medicine) a substance that regulates the body's systems and increases resistance to stress

adaptor *or* **adapter** (ə'dæptə) *n* **1** a person or thing that adapts **2** any device for connecting two parts, esp ones that are of different sizes **3a** a plug used to connect an electrical device to a mains supply when they have different types of terminals **3b** a device used to connect several electrical appliances to a single socket

ADC *abbrev for:* **1** aide-de-camp **2** analogue-digital converter

add (æd) *vb* **1** to combine (two or more numbers or quantities) by addition **2** *(tr; foll by to)* to increase (a number or quantity) by another number or quantity using addition **3** *(tr; often foll by to)* to join (something) to something else in order to increase the size, effect, or scope: *to add insult to injury* **4** *(intr; foll by to)* to have an extra and increased effect (on) **5** *(tr)* to say or write further **6** *(tr; foll by in)* to include ▷ See also **add up** [c14 from L *addere*, from *ad-* to + *-dere*, *dare* to put]

ADD *abbrev for* attention deficit disorder

Addams ('ædəmz) *n* **Jane** 1860–1935, US social reformer, feminist, and pacifist, who founded Hull House, a social settlement in Chicago: Nobel peace prize 1931

addax ('ædæks) *n* a large light-coloured antelope having ribbed loosely spiralled horns and inhabiting desert regions in N Africa [c17 L, from an unidentified ancient N African language]

addend ('ædɛnd) *n* any of a set of numbers that is to be added [c20 short for ADDENDUM]

addendum (ə'dɛndəm) *n, pl* **addenda** (-də) **1** something added; an addition **2** a supplement or appendix to a book, magazine, etc [c18 from L, gerundive of *addere* to ADD]

adder ('ædə) *n* **1** Also called: **viper** a common viper that is widely distributed in Europe, including Britain, and Asia and is dark grey with a black zigzag pattern along the back **2** any of various similar venomous or nonvenomous snakes ▷ See also **death adder, puff adder** [OE *nǣdre* snake; in ME *a naddre* was mistaken for *an addre*]

adder's-tongue *n* any of several ferns that grow in the N hemisphere and have a narrow spore-bearing body that sticks out like a spike from the leaf

addict *vb* (ə'dɪkt) **1** (*tr; usually passive;* often foll by *to*) to cause (someone or oneself) to become dependent (on something, esp a narcotic drug) ▷ *n* ('ædɪkt) **2** a person who is addicted, esp to narcotic drugs **3** *inf* a person devoted to something: *a jazz addict* [c16 (as adj and as vb; n use c20): from L *addictus* given over, from *addīcere*, from *ad-* to + *dīcere* to say] > **ad'diction** *n* > **ad'dictive** *adj*
▷ www.addictionsearch.com
▷ www.adpana.com
▷ www.alcoholicsanonymous.org

Addington ('ædɪŋtən) *n* **Henry,** 1st Viscount Sidmouth. 1757–1844, British statesman; prime minister (1801–04) and Home Secretary (1812–21)

Addis Ababa ('ædɪs 'æbəbə) *n* the capital of Ethiopia, on a central plateau 2400 m (8000 ft) above sea level: founded in 1887; became capital in 1896. Pop: 2 316 400 (1994 est)
▷ www.tourethio.com/capital

Addison ('ædɪsən) *n* **Joseph** 1672–1719, English essayist and poet who, with Richard Steele, founded *The Spectator* (1711–14) and contributed most of its essays, including the *de Coverley Papers*

Addison's disease *n* a disease characterized by bronzing of the skin, anaemia, and extreme weakness, caused by underactivity of the adrenal glands [c19 after Thomas *Addison* (1793–1860), E physician who identified it]

addition (ə'dɪʃən) *n* **1** the act, process, or result of adding **2** a person or thing that is added or acquired **3** a mathematical operation in which the sum of two numbers or quantities is calculated. Usually indicated by the symbol + **4** *obs* a title **5** **in addition** (*adv*) also; as well **6** **in addition to** (*prep*) besides; as well as [c15 from L *additiōn-*, from *addere* to ADD]

additional (ə'dɪʃənəl) *adj* added or supplementary > **ad'ditionally** *adv*

additionality (ə,dɪʃə'nælɪtɪ) *n* **1** (in Britain) the principle that money raised by the National Lottery should be spent only on projects that would not otherwise be funded by government spending **2** (in the European Union) the principle that the EU contributes to the funding of a project in a member country provided that the member country also contributes

Additional Member System *n* a system of voting in which people vote separately for a candidate and a party. Parties are allocated extra seats if the number of constituencies they win does not reflect their overall share of the vote. See also **proportional representation**

additive ('ædɪtɪv) *adj* **1** characterized or produced by addition ▷ *n* **2** any substance added to something to improve it, prevent deterioration, etc **3** short for **food additive** [c17 from LL *additīvus*, from *addere* to ADD]

addle ('ædəl) *vb* **addles, addling, addled** **1** to make or become confused or muddled **2** to make or become rotten ▷ *adj* **3** (*in combination*) indicating a confused or muddled state: *addle-brained* [c18 (vb), back formation from *addled*, from c13 *addle* rotten, from OE *adela* filth]

add-on *n* a feature that can be added to a standard model or package to give increased benefits

address (ə'drɛs) *n* **1** the conventional form by which the location of a building is described **2** the written form of this, as on a letter or parcel **3** the place at which someone lives **4** a speech or written communication, esp one of a formal nature **5** skilfulness or tact **6** *arch* manner of speaking **7** *computing* a number giving the location of a piece of stored information **8** (*usually pl*) expressions of affection made by a man in courting a woman ▷ *vb* (*tr*) **9** to mark (a letter, etc) with an address **10** to speak to, refer to in speaking, or deliver a speech to **11** (used reflexively; foll by *to*) **11a** to speak or write to **11b** to apply oneself to: *he addressed himself to the task* **12** to direct (a message, warning, etc) to the attention of **13** to adopt a position facing (the ball in golf, etc) [c14 (in the sense: to make right, adorn) and c15 (in the modern sense: to direct words): via OF from Vulgar L *addrictiāre* (unattested), from L *ad-* to + *dīrectus* DIRECT] > **ad'dresser** *or* **ad'dressor** *n*

address bar *n computing* the space provided (on a browser) for showing the addresses of websites

addressee (,ædrɛ'siː) *n* a person or organization to whom a letter, etc, is addressed

adduce (ə'djuːs) *vb* **adduces, adducing, adduced** (*tr*) to cite (reasons, examples, etc) as evidence or proof [c15 from L *addūcere* to lead to] > **ad'ducent** *adj* > **ad'ducible** *adj* > **adduction** (ə'dʌkʃən) *n*

adduct (ə'dʌkt) *vb* (*tr*) **1** (of a muscle) to draw or pull (a leg, arm, etc) towards the median axis of the body ▷ *n* **2** *chem* a compound formed by direct combination of two or more different compounds or elements [c19 from L *addūcere*; see ADDUCE] > **ad'duction** *n* > **ad'ductor** *n*

add up *vb* (*adv*) **1** to find the sum (of) **2** (*intr*) to result in a correct total **3** (*intr*) *inf* to make sense **4** (*intr;* foll by *to*) to amount to

Aa

-ade *suffix forming nouns* a sweetened drink made of various fruits: *lemonade* [from F, from L *-āta* made of, fem p.p. of verbs ending in *-āre*]

Adelaide ('ædɪ,leɪd) *n* the capital of South Australia: **Port Adelaide,** 11 km (7 miles) away on St. Vincent Gulf, handles the bulk of exports. Pop: 1 081 000 (1995 est)

Aden ('eɪdən) *n* **1** the main port and commercial capital of Yemen, on the N coast of the **Gulf of Aden**, an arm of the Indian Ocean at the entrance to the Red Sea: capital of South Yemen until 1990: formerly an important port of call on shipping routes to the East. Pop: 562 000 (1995 est) **2** a former British colony and protectorate on the S coast of the Arabian Peninsula: became part of South Yemen in 1967, now part of Yemen. Area: 195 sq km (75 sq miles)

Adenauer (*German* 'aːdənauər) *n* **Konrad** ('kɔnraːt) 1876–1967, German statesman; chancellor of West Germany (1949–63)

adenine ('ædənɪn) *n* a purine base present in all living organisms as a constituent of the nucleic acids DNA and RNA

adeno- *or before a vowel* **aden-** *combining form* gland or glandular: *adenoid; adenology* [NL, from Gk *adēn* gland]

adenoidal (,ædɪ'nɔɪdəl) *adj* **1** having the nasal tones or impaired breathing of one with enlarged adenoids **2** of adenoids

adenoids ('ædɪ,nɔɪdz) *pl n* a mass of lymphoid tissue at the back of the throat behind the uvula: when enlarged it often restricts nasal breathing, esp in young children [c19 : from Gk *adenoeidēs*. See ADENO-, -OID]

adenoma (,ædɪ'nəʊmə) *n, pl* **adenomas** *or* **adenomata** (-mətə) **1** a tumour occurring in glandular tissue **2** a tumour having a glandlike structure

adenopathy (,ædɪ'nɒpəθɪ) *n pathol* **1** enlargement of the lymph nodes **2** enlargement of a gland

adenosine (æ'dɛnə,si:n) *n biochem* a compound formed by the condensation of adenine and ribose. It is present in all living cells in a combined form. See also **ADP**[1], **AMP, ATP** [c20 a blend of ADENINE + RIBOSE]

adept *adj* (ə'dɛpt) **1** proficient in something requiring skill or manual dexterity **2** expert ▷ *n* ('ædɛpt) **3** a person who is skilled or proficient in something [c17 from Med. L *adeptus*, from L *adipiscī*, from *ad-* to + *apiscī* to attain] > **a'deptness** *n*

adequate ('ædɪkwɪt) *adj* able to fulfil a need without being abundant, outstanding, etc [c17 from L *adaequāre*, from *ad-* to + *aequus* EQUAL] > **adequacy** ('ædɪkwəsɪ) *n* > **'adequately** *adv*

à deux *French* (a dø) *adj, adv* of or for two persons

ADFA *abbrev for* Australian Defence Force Academy

ADH *abbrev for* antidiuretic hormone. See **vasopressin**

ADHD *abbrev for* attention deficit hyperactivity disorder

adhere (əd'hɪə) *vb* **adheres, adhering, adhered** (*intr*) **1** (usually foll by *to*) to stick or hold fast **2** (foll by *to*) to be devoted (to a political party, religion, etc) **3** (foll by *to*) to follow exactly [c16 via Med. L, from L *adhaerēre* to stick to]

USAGE See at **adhesion**

adherent (əd'hɪərənt) *n* **1** (usually foll by *of*) a supporter or follower ▷ *adj* **2** sticking, holding fast, or attached > **ad'herence** *n*

adhesion (əd'hi:ʒən) *n* **1** the quality or condition of sticking together or holding fast **2** ability to make firm contact without slipping **3** attachment, as to a political party, cause, etc **4** an attraction or repulsion between the molecules of unlike substances in contact **5** *pathol* abnormal union of structures or parts [c17 from L *adhaesiōn-* a sticking. See ADHERE]

USAGE *Adhesion* is preferred when talking about sticking or holding fast in a physical sense. *Adherence* is preferred when talking about attachment to principles, rules, values, etc

adhesive (əd'hi:sɪv) *adj* **1** able or designed to adhere: *adhesive tape* **2** tenacious or clinging ▷ *n* **3** a substance used for sticking, such as glue or paste > **ad'hesively** *adv* > **ad'hesiveness** *n*

ad hoc (æd 'hɒk) *adj, adv* for a particular purpose only: *an ad hoc committee* [L, lit.: to this]

ad hominem *Latin* (æd 'hɒmɪ,nɛm) *adj, adv* directed against a person rather than his or her arguments [lit.: to the man]

adiabatic (,ædɪə'bætɪk) *adj* **1** (of a thermodynamic process) taking place without loss or gain of heat ▷ *n* **2** a curve on a graph representing the changes in a system undergoing an adiabatic process [c19 from Gk, from A-[1] + *diabatos* passable]

adieu (ə'dju:) *sentence substitute, n, pl* **adieus** *or* **adieux** (ə'dju:z) goodbye [c14 from OF, from *a* to + *dieu* God]

ad infinitum (æd ,ɪnfɪ'naɪtəm) *adv* without end; endlessly; to infinity. Abbrev: **ad inf** [L]

ad interim (æd 'ɪntərɪm) *adj, adv* for the meantime: *ad interim measures*. Abbrev: **ad int** [L]

adipocere (,ædɪpəʊ'sɪə) *n* a waxlike fatty substance sometimes formed during the decomposition of corpses [c19 from NL *adiposus* fat + F *cire* wax]

adipose ('ædɪ,pəʊs) *adj* **1** of, resembling, or containing fat; fatty ▷ *n* **2** animal fat [c18 from NL *adiposus*, from L *adeps* fat]

Adirondack Mountains (,ædɪ'rɒndæk) *or* **Adirondacks** *pl n* a mountain range in NE New York State. Highest peak: Mount Marcy, 1629 m (5344 ft)

adit ('ædɪt) *n* an almost horizontal shaft into a mine, for access or drainage [c17 from L *aditus*, from *adīre*, from *ad-* towards + *īre* to go]

adj. *abbrev for* adjective

adjacent (ə'dʒeɪsᵊnt) *adj* being near or close, esp having a common boundary; contiguous [c15 from L *adjacēre*, from *ad-* near + *jacēre* to lie] > **ad'jacently** *adv*

adjacent angles *pl n* two angles having the same vertex and a side in common

adjective ('ædʒɪktɪv) *n* **1a** a word imputing a characteristic to a noun or pronoun **1b** (*as modifier*): *an adjective phrase*. Abbrev: **adj** ▷ *adj* **2** additional or dependent [c14 from LL, from L from *adjicere*, from *ad-* to + *jacere* to throw] > **adjectival** (,ædʒɪk'taɪvᵊl) *adj*

adjoin (ə'dʒɔɪn) *vb* **1** to be next to (an area of land, etc) **2** (*tr*; foll by *to*) to join; attach [c14 via OF from L, from *ad-* to + *jungere* to join]

adjoining (ə'dʒɔɪnɪŋ) *adj* being in contact; connected or neighbouring

adjourn (ə'dʒɜ:n) *vb* **1** (*intr*) (of a court, etc) to close at the end of a session **2** to postpone or be postponed, esp temporarily **3** (*tr*) to put off (a problem, discussion, etc) for later consideration **4** (*intr*) *inf* to move elsewhere: *let's adjourn to the kitchen* [c14 from OF *ajourner* to defer to an arranged day, from *a-* to + *jour* day, from LL *diurnum*, from L *diēs* day] > **ad'journment** *n*

adjudge (ə'dʒʌdʒ) *vb* **adjudges, adjudging, adjudged** (*tr*; *usually passive*) **1** to pronounce formally; declare **2a** to judge **2b** to decree: *he was adjudged bankrupt* **2c** to award (costs, damages, etc) **3** *arch* to condemn [c14 via OF from L *adjūdicāre*. See ADJUDICATE]

adjudicate (ə'dʒu:dɪ,keɪt) *vb* **adjudicates, adjudicating, adjudicated** **1** (when *intr*, usually foll by *upon*) to give a decision (on), esp a formal or binding one **2** (*intr*) to serve as a judge or arbiter, as in a competition [c18 from L *adjūdicāre*, from *ad-* to + *jūdicāre* to judge, from *jūdex* judge] > **ad,judi'cation** *n* > **adjudicative** (ə'dʒu:dɪkətɪv) *adj* > **ad'judi,cator** *n*

adjunct ('ædʒʌŋkt) *n* **1** something incidental or not essential that is added to something else **2** a person who is subordinate to another **3** *grammar* **3a** part of a sentence other than the subject or the predicate **3b** a modifier ▷ *adj* **4** added or connected in a secondary position [c16 from L *adjunctus*, p.p. of *adjungere* to ADJOIN] > **adjunctive** (ə'dʒʌŋktɪv) *adj* > **'adjunctly** *adv*

adjure (ə'dʒʊə) *vb* **adjures, adjuring, adjured** (*tr*) **1** to command, often by exacting an oath **2** to appeal earnestly to [c14 from L *adjūrāre*, from *ad-* to + *jūrāre* to swear, from *jūs* oath] > **adjuration** (,ædʒʊə'reɪʃən) *n* > **ad'juratory** *adj* > **ad'jurer** *or* **ad'juror** *n*

adjust (ə'dʒʌst) *vb* **1** (*tr*) to alter slightly, esp to achieve accuracy **2** to adapt, as to a new environment, etc **3** (*tr*) to put into order **4** (*tr*) *insurance* to determine the amount payable in settlement of (a claim) [c17 from OF *adjuster*, from *ad-* to + *juste* right, JUST] > **ad'justable** *adj* > **ad'juster** *n*

adjustment (ə'dʒʌstmənt) *n* **1** the act of adjusting or state of being adjusted **2** a control for regulating

adjutant ('ædʒətənt) *n* an officer who acts as administrative assistant to a superior officer [c17 from L *adjūtāre* to AID] > **'adjutancy** *n*

adjutant bird *or* **stork** *n* either of two large carrion-eating storks which are similar to the marabou and occur in S and SE Asia [so called for its supposedly military gait]

adjutant general *n, pl* **adjutants general** **1** *Brit army* a member of the Army Board responsible for personnel and administrative functions **2** *US army* the adjutant of a military unit with general staff

adjuvant ('ædʒəvənt) *adj* **1** aiding or assisting ▷ *n* **2** something that aids or assists; auxiliary [c17 from L *adjuvāre*, from *juvāre* to help]

Adler *n* **1** (*German* 'a:dlər) **Alfred** ('alfre:t) 1870–1937, Austrian psychiatrist, noted for his descriptions of overcompensation and inferiority feelings **2** ('ædlə) **Larry**, full name *Lawrence Cecil Adler*. 1914–2001, US harmonica player

Adlerian (æd'lɪərɪən) *adj* of or relating to the work of Alfred Adler

ad-lib (æd'lɪb) *vb* **ad-libs, ad-libbing, ad-libbed** **1** to improvise and deliver spontaneously (a speech, etc) ▷ *adj* (**ad lib** *when predicative*) **2** improvised ▷ *adv* **ad lib** **3** spontaneously; freely ▷ *n* **4** an improvised performance, often humorous [c18 short for L *ad libitum*, lit.: according to pleasure]

ad libitum (ˌæd ˈlɪbɪtəm) *adv, adj music* at the performer's discretion [L.: see AD-LIB]

Adm. *abbrev for* Admiral

adman (ˈædˌmæn) *n, pl* **admen** *inf* a man who works in advertising

admass (ˈædmæs) *n* the section of the public that is susceptible to advertising, etc, and the processes involved in influencing them [c20 from AD + MASS]

admeasure (ædˈmɛʒə) *vb* **admeasures, admeasuring, admeasured** to measure out (land, etc) as a share; apportion [c14 *amesuren*, from OF, from *mesurer* to MEASURE; the modern form derives from AD- + MEASURE]

Admetus (ædˈmiːtəs) *n Greek myth* a king of Thessaly, one of the Argonauts, who was married to Alcestis

admin (ˈædmɪn) *n inf* short for **administration**

administer (ədˈmɪnɪstə) *vb* (*mainly tr*) **1** (*also intr*) to direct or control (the affairs of a business, etc) **2** to dispense: *administer justice* **3** (when *intr*, foll by *to*) to give or apply (medicine, etc) **4** to supervise the taking of (an oath, etc) **5** to manage (an estate, property, etc) [c14 *amynistre* via OF from L, from *ad-* to + *ministrāre* to MINISTER]

administrate (ədˈmɪnɪˌstreɪt) *vb* **administrates, administrating, administrated** to manage or direct (the affairs of a business, institution, etc)

administration (ədˌmɪnɪˈstreɪʃən) *n* **1** management of the affairs of an organization, such as a business or institution **2** the duties of an administrator **3** the body of people who administer an organization **4** the conduct of the affairs of government **5** term of office: used of governments, etc **6** the government as a whole **7** (*often cap*) *chiefly US* the political executive, esp of the US **8** *property law* **8a** the conduct or disposal of the estate of a deceased person **8b** the management by a trustee of an estate **9a** the administering of something, such as a sacrament or medical treatment **9b** the thing that is administered > **adˈministrative** *adj* > **adˈministratively** *adv*

administration order *n law* **1** an order by a court appointing a person to manage a company that is in financial difficulty **2** an order by a court for the administration of the estate of a debtor who has been ordered by the court to pay money that he owes

administrator (ədˈmɪnɪˌstreɪtə) *n* **1** a person who administers the affairs of an organization, official body, etc **2** *property law* a person authorized to manage an estate **3** a person who manages a computer system

admirable (ˈædmərəbᵊl) *adj* deserving or inspiring admiration; excellent > **ˈadmirably** *adv*

admiral (ˈædmərəl) *n* **1** the supreme commander of a fleet or navy **2** Also called: **admiral of the fleet, fleet admiral** a naval officer of the highest rank **3** a senior naval officer entitled to fly his own flag. See also **rear admiral, vice admiral** **4** *chiefly Brit* the master of a fishing fleet **5** any of various brightly coloured butterflies, esp the red admiral or white admiral [c13 *amyral*, from OF *amiral* emir, & from Med. L *admīrālis* (spelling prob. infl. by *admīrābilis* admirable); both from Ar. *amīr* emir, commander, esp in *amīr-al* commander of] > **ˈadmiralship** *n*

admiralty (ˈædmərəltɪ) *n, pl* **admiralties** **1** the office or jurisdiction of an admiral **2** jurisdiction over naval affairs

Admiralty Board *n* **the** (formerly) a department of the British Ministry of Defence, responsible for the administration of the Royal Navy

Admiralty House *n* the official residence of the Governor General of Australia, in Sydney

Admiralty Islands *pl n* a group of about 40 volcanic and coral islands in the SW Pacific, part of Papua New Guinea, in the Bismarck Archipelago: main island: Manus. Pop: 35 200 (1995). Area: about 2000 sq km (800 sq miles). Also called: **Admiralties**

Admiralty Range *n* a mountain range in Antarctica, on the coast of Victoria Land, northwest of the Ross Sea

admiration (ˌædməˈreɪʃən) *n* **1** pleasurable contemplation or surprise **2** a person or thing that is admired

admire (ədˈmaɪə) *vb* **admires, admiring, admired** (*tr*) **1** to regard with esteem, approval, or pleased surprise **2** *arch* to wonder at [c16 from L *admīrārī*, from *ad-* to, at + *mīrārī* to wonder] > **adˈmirer** *n* > **adˈmiring** *adj* > **adˈmiringly** *adv*

admissible (ədˈmɪsəbᵊl) *adj* **1** able or deserving to be considered or allowed **2** deserving to be allowed to enter **3** *law* (esp of evidence) capable of being admitted in a court of law > **adˌmissiˈbility** *n*

admission (ədˈmɪʃən) *n* **1** permission to enter or the right to enter **2** the price charged for entrance **3** acceptance for a position, etc **4** a confession, as of a crime, etc **5** an acknowledgment of the truth of something [c15 from L *admissiōn-*, from *admittere* to ADMIT] > **adˈmissive** *adj*

admit (ədˈmɪt) *vb* **admits, admitting, admitted** (*mainly tr*) **1** (*may take a clause as object*) to confess or acknowledge (a crime, mistake, etc) **2** (*may take a clause as object*) to concede (the truth of something) **3** to allow to enter **4** (foll by *to*) to allow participation (in) or the right to be part (of) **5** (when *intr*, foll by *of*) to allow (of) [c14 from L *admittere*, from *ad-* to + *mittere* to send]

admittance (ədˈmɪtᵊns) *n* **1** the right or authority to enter **2** the act of giving entrance **3** *electricity* the reciprocal of impedance

admittedly (ədˈmɪtɪdlɪ) *adv* (*sentence modifier*) willingly conceded: *admittedly I am afraid*

admix (ədˈmɪks) *vb* (*tr*) *rare* to mix or blend [c16 back formation from obs. *admixt*, from L *admiscēre* to mix with]

Aa

admixture (ədˈmɪkstʃə) *n* **1** a less common word for **mixture** **2** an ingredient

admonish (ədˈmɒnɪʃ) *vb* (*tr*) **1** to reprove firmly but not harshly **2** to warn; caution [c14 via OF from Vulgar L *admonestāre* (unattested), from L *admonēre*, from *monēre* to advise] > **adˈmonishment** *n* > **admonition** (ˌædməˈnɪʃən) *n* > **adˈmonitory** *adj*

ad nauseam (æd ˈnɔːzɪˌæm) *adv* to a disgusting extent [L: to (the point of) nausea]

USAGE This phrase is quite often misspelt as *ad nauseum*

ado (əˈduː) *n* bustling activity; fuss; bother; delay (esp in **without more ado, with much ado**) [c14 from *at do* a to-do, from ON *at* to (marking the infinitive) + DO[1]]

ADO *Austral abbrev for* accumulated day off

adobe (əˈdəʊbɪ) *n* **1** a sun-dried brick used for building **2** a building constructed of such bricks **3** the clayey material from which such bricks are made [c19 from Sp.]

adolescence (ˌædəˈlɛsəns) *n* the period in human development that occurs between the beginning of puberty and adulthood [c15 via OF from L, from *adolēscere* to grow up]

adolescent (ˌædəˈlɛsᵊnt) *adj* **1** of or relating to adolescence **2** *inf* behaving in an immature way ▷ *n* **3** an adolescent person

Adonai (ˌædɒˈnaɪ, -ˈneɪaɪ) *n judaism* a name for God [c15 from Heb.: lord; cf. ADONIS]

Adonis (əˈdəʊnɪs) *n* **1** *Greek myth* a handsome youth loved by Aphrodite **2** a handsome young man [c16 from L via Gk from Phoenician *adōni* my lord; rel. to Heb. *Adonai* Lord]

adopt (əˈdɒpt) *vb* (*tr*) **1** *law* to take (another's child) as one's own child **2** to choose and follow (a plan, method, etc) **3** to take over (an idea, etc) as if it were one's own

4 to assume: *to adopt a title* 5 to accept (a report, etc) [c16 from L *adoptāre*, from *optāre* to choose] > ˌ**adop'tee** *n* > **a'doption** *n*

adopted (ə'dɒptɪd) *adj* having been adopted

adoptive (ə'dɒptɪv) *adj* 1 acquired or related by adoption: *an adoptive father* ▷ Cf **adopted** 2 of or relating to adoption

adorable (ə'dɔːrəbᵊl) *adj* 1 very attractive; lovable 2 *becoming rare* deserving adoration > **a'dorably** *adv*

adoration (ˌædə'reɪʃən) *n* 1 deep love or esteem 2 the act of worshipping

adore (ə'dɔː) *vb* **adores, adoring, adored** 1 (*tr*) to love intensely or deeply 2 to worship (a god) with religious rites 3 (*tr*) *inf* to like very much [c15 via F from L *adōrāre*, from *ad-* to + *ōrāre* to pray] > **a'dorer** *n* > **a'doring** *adj* > **a'doringly** *adv*

adorn (ə'dɔːn) *vb* (*tr*) 1 to decorate 2 to increase the beauty, distinction, etc, of [c14 via OF from L *adōrnāre*, from *ōrnāre* to furnish] > **a'dornment** *n*

Adowa ('ɑːdʊˌwɑː) *n* a variant spelling of **Aduwa**

ADP *n biochem* adenosine diphosphate; a substance derived from ATP with the liberation of energy that is then used in the performance of muscular work

Adrastus (ə'dræstəs) *n Greek myth* a king of Argos and leader of the Seven against Thebes of whom he was the sole survivor

ad rem *Latin* (æd 'rɛm) *adj, adv* to the point; without digression [L, lit.; to the matter]

adrenal (ə'driːnᵊl) *adj* 1 on or near the kidneys 2 of or relating to the adrenal glands or their secretions ▷ *n* 3 an adrenal gland [c19 from AD- (near) + RENAL]

adrenal gland *n* an endocrine gland at the anterior end of each kidney. It secretes adrenaline. Also called: **suprarenal gland**

adrenaline *or* **adrenalin** (ə'drɛnəlɪn) *n* a hormone that is secreted by the adrenal medulla in response to stress and increases heart rate, pulse rate, and blood pressure. It is extracted from animals or synthesized for medical use. US name: **epinephrine**

adrenalized *or* **adrenalised** (ə'driːnəlaɪzd) *adj* tense or highly charged: *adrenalized with excitement*

Adrian IV *n* original name *Nicholas Breakspear*. ?1100–59, the only English pope (1154–59)

Adrianople (ˌeɪdrɪə'nəʊpᵊl) *or* **Adrianopolis** (ˌeɪdrɪə'nɒpəlɪs) *n* former names of **Edirne**

Adriatic (ˌeɪdrɪ'ætɪk) *adj* 1 of or relating to the Adriatic Sea, or to the inhabitants of its coast or islands ▷ *n* 2 **the** short for the **Adriatic Sea**

Adriatic Sea *n* an arm of the Mediterranean between Italy and the Balkan Peninsula

adrift (ə'drɪft) *adj* (*postpositive*), *adv* 1 floating without steering or mooring; drifting 2 without purpose; aimless 3 *inf* off course

adroit (ə'drɔɪt) *adj* 1 skilful or dexterous 2 quick in thought or reaction [c17 from F *à droit* rightly] > **a'droitly** *adv* > **a'droitness** *n*

adsorb (əd'sɔːb) *vb* to undergo or cause to undergo a process in which a substance, usually a gas, accumulates on the surface of a solid forming a thin film [c19 AD- + *-sorb* as in ABSORB] > **ad'sorbable** *adj* > **ad'sorbent** *adj* > **ad'sorption** *n*

adsorbate (əd'sɔːbeɪt) *n* a substance that has been or is to be adsorbed

ADT (in the US and Canada) *abbrev for* Atlantic Daylight Time

adulate ('ædjʊˌleɪt) *vb* **adulates, adulating, adulated** (*tr*) to flatter or praise obsequiously [c17 back formation from c15 *adulation*, from L *adūlāri* to flatter] > **'aduˌlator** *n*

adulation (ˌædjʊ'leɪʃən) *n* obsequious flattery or praise; extreme admiration

adulatory (ˌædjʊ'leɪtərɪ, 'ædjʊˌleɪtərɪ) *adj* expressing praise, esp obsequiously; flattering

adult ('ædʌlt, ə'dʌlt) *adj* 1 having reached maturity; fully developed 2 of or intended for mature people: *adult education* 3 suitable only for adults because of being pornographic ▷ *n* 4 a person who has attained maturity 5 a mature fully grown animal or plant 6 *law* a person who has attained the age of legal majority [c16 from L *adultus*, from *adolēscere* to grow up] > **a'dulthood** *n*

adulterant (ə'dʌltərənt) *n* 1 a substance that adulterates ▷ *adj* 2 adulterating

adulterate *vb* (ə'dʌltəˌreɪt), **adulterates, adulterating, adulterated** 1 (*tr*) to debase by adding inferior material: *to adulterate milk with water* ▷ *adj* (ə'dʌltərɪt) 2 debased or impure [c16 from L *adulterāre* to corrupt, commit adultery, prob. from *alter* another] > **aˌdulter'ation** *n* > **a'dulterˌator** *n*

adulterer (ə'dʌltərə) *or* (*fem*) **adulteress** *n* a person who has committed adultery [c16 orig. also *adulter*, from L *adulter*, back formation from *adulterāre* to ADULTERATE]

adulterous (ə'dʌltərəs) *adj* of, characterized by, or inclined to adultery > **a'dulterously** *adv*

adultery (ə'dʌltərɪ) *n, pl* **adulteries** voluntary sexual intercourse between a married man or woman and a partner other than the legal spouse [c15 *adulterie*, altered from c14 *avoutrie*, via OF from L *adulterium*, from *adulter*, back formation from *adulterāre*. See ADULTERATE]

adumbrate ('ædʌmˌbreɪt) *vb* **adumbrates, adumbrating, adumbrated** (*tr*) 1 to outline; give a faint indication of 2 to foreshadow 3 to obscure [c16 from L *adumbrāre* to cast a shadow on, from *umbra* shadow] > ˌ**adum'bration** *n* > **adumbrative** (æd'ʌmbrətɪv) *adj*

Aduwa *or* **Adowa** ('ɑːdʊˌwɑː) *n* a town in N Ethiopia: Emperor Menelik II defeated the Italians here in 1896. Pop: 17 476 (1989 est). Italian name: **Adua** (a'dua)

adv. *abbrev for:* 1 adverb 2 adverbial

ad valorem (æd və'lɔːrəm) *adj, adv* (of taxes) in proportion to the estimated value of the goods taxed. Abbrev: **ad val., a.v., A/V** [from L]

advance (əd'vɑːns) *vb* **advances, advancing, advanced** 1 to go or bring forward in position 2 (foll by *on*) to move (towards) in a threatening manner 3 (*tr*) to present for consideration 4 to improve; further 5 (*tr*) to cause (an event) to occur earlier 6 (*tr*) to supply (money, goods, etc) beforehand, either for a loan or as an initial payment 7 to increase (a price, etc) or (of a price, etc) to be increased 8 (*intr*) to be promoted ▷ *n* 9 forward movement; progress in time or space 10 improvement; progress in development 11 *commerce* 11a the supplying of commodities or funds before receipt of an agreed consideration 11b the commodities or funds supplied in this manner 12 Also called: **advance payment** a money payment made before it is legally due: *this is an advance on your salary* 13 a loan of money 14 an increase in price, etc 15 **in advance** 15a beforehand: *payment in advance* 15b (foll by *of*) ahead in time or development: *ideas in advance of the time* 16 (*modifier*) forward in position or time: *advance booking* ▷ See also **advances** [c15 *advauncen*, altered from c13 *avauncen*, via OF from L *abante*, from *ab-* away + *ante* before] > **ad'vancer** *n*

advanced (əd'vɑːnst) *adj* 1 being ahead in development, knowledge, progress, etc 2 having reached a comparatively late stage: *a man of advanced age* 3 ahead of the times

advanced gas-cooled reactor *n* a nuclear reactor using carbon dioxide as the coolant, and ceramic uranium dioxide cased in stainless steel as the fuel. Abbrev: **AGR**

advance directive *n* another name for **living will**

Advanced level *n* a formal name for **A level**

advanced skills teacher *n Brit education* a teacher who has achieved high standards of classroom practice and success and who, after passing a national assessment, is paid to share his or her skills and experience with other teachers. Abbreviation: **AST**

advancement (əd'vɑːnsmənt) *n* 1 promotion in rank,

status, etc **2** a less common word for **advance** (senses 9, 10)

advances (əd'vɑːnsɪz) *pl n* (*sometimes sing; often foll by to or towards*) overtures made in an attempt to become friendly, etc

advantage (əd'vɑːntɪdʒ) *n* **1** (*often foll by over or of*) a more favourable position; superiority **2** benefit or profit (esp in **to one's advantage**) **3** *tennis* the point scored after deuce **4** **take advantage of** **4a** to make good use of **4b** to impose upon the weakness, good nature, etc, of **4c** to seduce **5** **to advantage** to good effect ▷ *vb* **advantages, advantaging, advantaged** **6** (*tr*) to put in a better position; favour [C14 *avantage* (later altered to *advantage*), from OF *avant* before, from L *abante* from before. See ADVANCE]

advantageous (ˌædvən'teɪdʒəs) *adj* producing advantage > ˌ**advan'tageously** *adv*

advection (əd'vɛkʃən) *n* the transference of heat energy in a horizontal stream of gas, esp of air [C20 from L *advectiō*, from *advehere*, from *ad-* to + *vehere* to carry]

advent ('ædvɛnt, -vənt) *n* an arrival or coming, esp one which is awaited [C12 from L *adventus*, from *advenīre*, from *ad-* to + *venīre* to come]

Advent ('ædvɛnt) *n* the season including the four Sundays preceding Christmas

Advent calendar *n* a large card with small numbered doors for children to open on each of the days of Advent, revealing pictures beneath them

Adventist ('ædvɛntɪst) *n* a member of a Christian group that holds that the Second Coming of Christ is imminent

adventitious (ˌædvɛn'tɪʃəs) *adj* **1** added or appearing accidentally **2** (of a plant or animal part) developing in an abnormal position [C17 from L *adventīcius* coming from outside, from *adventus* a coming] > ˌ**adven'titiously** *adv*

adventure (əd'vɛntʃə) *n* **1** a risky undertaking of unknown outcome **2** an exciting or unexpected event or course of events **3** a hazardous financial operation ▷ *vb* **adventures, adventuring, adventured** **4** to take a risk or put at risk **5** (*intr; foll by into, on, or upon*) to dare to enter (into a place, dangerous activity, etc) **6** to dare to say (something): *he adventured his opinion* [C13 *aventure* (later altered to *adventure*), via OF ult. from L *advenīre* to happen to (someone), arrive]

adventure playground *n Brit* a playground for children that contains building materials, etc, used to build with, climb on, etc

adventurer (əd'vɛntʃərə) *or* (*fem*) **adventuress** *n* **1** a person who seeks adventure, esp one who seeks success or money through daring exploits **2** a person who seeks money or power by unscrupulous means **3** a speculator

adventure tourism *n Austral and NZ* tourism involving activities that are physically challenging

adventurism (əd'vɛntʃəˌrɪzəm) *n* recklessness, esp in politics and finance > **ad'venturist** *n*

adventurous (əd'vɛntʃərəs) *adj* **1** Also: **adventuresome** daring or enterprising **2** dangerous; involving risk

adverb ('ædˌvɜːb) *n* **a** a word or group of words that serves to modify a whole sentence, a verb, another adverb, or an adjective; for example, *easily*, *very*, and *happily* respectively in the sentence *They could easily envy the very happily married couple* **b** (*as modifier*): *an adverb marker*. Abbrev: **adv** [C15–C16 from L *adverbium* adverb, lit.: added word] > **ad'verbial** *adj*

adversarial (ˌædvɜː'sɛərɪəl) *adj* (of political parties) hostile to and opposing each other on party lines; antagonistic

adversary ('ædvəsərɪ) *n, pl* **adversaries** **1** a person or group that is hostile to someone **2** an opposing contestant in a sport [C14 from L *adversārius*, from *adversus* against]

adversative (əd'vɜːsətɪv) *grammar* ▷ *adj* **1** (of a word, phrase, or clause) implying opposition. *But* and *although* are adversative conjunctions ▷ *n* **2** an adversative word or speech element

adverse ('ædvɜːs) *adj* **1** antagonistic; hostile: *adverse criticism* **2** unfavourable to one's interests: *adverse circumstances* **3** contrary or opposite: *adverse winds* [C14 from L *adversus*, from *advertere*, from *ad-* towards + *vertere* to turn] > **ad'versely** *adv* > **ad'verseness** *n*

> USAGE The construction *adverse to* is sometimes mistakenly used instead of *averse to*. In the following example *averse* is correct, and *adverse* would be wrong: *...not averse to a little self-promotion*

adversity (əd'vɜːsɪtɪ) *n, pl* **adversities** **1** distress; affliction; hardship **2** an unfortunate event

advert[1] (əd'vɜːt) *vb* (*intr; foll by to*) to draw attention (to) [C15 from L *advertere* to turn one's attention to]

advert[2] ('ædvɜːt) *n Brit inf* short for **advertisement**

advertise *or US* (*sometimes*) **advertize** ('ædvəˌtaɪz) *vb* **advertises, advertising, advertised** *or US* (*sometimes*) **advertizes, advertizing, advertized** **1** to present or praise (goods, a service, etc) to the public, esp in order to encourage sales **2** to make (a vacancy, article for sale, etc) publicly known: *to advertise a job* **3** (*intr; foll by for*) to make a public request (for): *she advertised for a cook* [C15 from OF *avertir*, ult. from L *advertere* to turn one's attention to. See ADVERSE] > '**adverˌtiser** *or US* (*sometimes*) '**adverˌtizer** *n*

advertisement *or US* (*sometimes*) **advertizement** (əd'vɜːtɪsmənt) *n* any public notice, as a printed display in a newspaper, short film on television, etc, designed to sell goods, publicize an event, etc

advertising *or US* (*sometimes*) **advertizing** ('ædvəˌtaɪzɪŋ) *n* **1** the promotion of goods or services for sale through impersonal media such as television **2** the business that specializes in creating such publicity **3** advertisements collectively

Advertising Standards Authority *n* (in Britain) an independent body set up by the advertising industry to ensure that all advertisements comply with the British Code of Advertising Practice. Abbrev: **ASA**

advertorial (ˌædvɜː'tɔːrɪəl) *n* **1** advertising presented under the guise of editorial material ▷ *adj* **2** presented in such a manner [C20 from blend of ADVERT[2] + EDITORIAL]

advice (əd'vaɪs) *n* **1** recommendation as to appropriate choice of action **2** (*sometimes pl*) formal notification of facts [C13 *avis* (later *advise*), via OF from Vulgar L, from L *ad* to + *vīsum* view]

advisable (əd'vaɪzəbᵊl) *adj* worthy of recommendation; prudent > **ad'visably** *adv* > **adˌvisa'bility** *or* **ad'visableness** *n*

advise (əd'vaɪz) *vb* **advises, advising, advised** (*when tr, may take a clause as object or an infinitive*) **1** to offer advice (to a person or persons): *he advised caution* **2** (*tr*; sometimes foll by *of*) to inform or notify **3** (*intr; foll by with*) *chiefly US, obs. in Britain.* to consult [C14 via OF from Vulgar L *advīsāre* (unattested), from L *ad-* to + *vidēre* to see]

advised (əd'vaɪzd) *adj* resulting from deliberation. See also **ill-advised, well-advised** > **advisedly** (əd'vaɪzɪdlɪ) *adv*

adviser *or* **advisor** (əd'vaɪzə) *n* **1** a person who advises **2** *education* a person responsible for advising students on career guidance, etc **3** *Brit education* a subject specialist who advises on current teaching methods and facilities

advisory (əd'vaɪzərɪ) *adj* **1** empowered to make recommendations: *an advisory body* ▷ *n, pl* **advisories** **2** a statement issued to give advice, recommendations, or a warning: *a travel advisory* **3** a person or organization with an advisory function: *the Prime Minister's media advisory*

advocaat ('ædvəʊˌkɑː) *n* a liqueur having a raw egg base [C20 Du.]

advocacy ('ædvəkəsɪ) *n, pl* **advocacies** active support, esp of a cause: *passionate advocacy of federalism*

advocate *vb* ('ædvəˌkeɪt), **advocates, advocating, advocated** **1** (*tr; may take a clause as object*) to support or recommend publicly ▷ *n* ('ædvəkɪt) **2** a person who upholds or defends a cause **3** a person who intercedes on behalf of another **4** a person who pleads his or her client's cause in a court of law **5** *Scots law* the usual word for **barrister** [C14 via OF from L *advocātus* legal witness, from *advocāre*, from *vocāre* to call]

advowson (əd'vaʊzᵊn) *n English ecclesiastical law* the right of presentation to a vacant benefice [C13 via OF from L *advocātiōn-*, from *advocāre* to summon]

advt *abbrev for* advertisement

Adygei Republic *or* **Adygea** (ˌɑːdɪ'geɪə; *Russian* adɪ'gɛja) *n* a constituent republic of SW Russia, bordering on the Caucasus Mountains: chiefly agricultural but with some mineral resources. Capital: Maikop. Pop: 449 000 (2000 est). Area: 7600 sq km (2934 sq miles)

adze *or US* **adz** (ædz) *n* a hand tool with a steel blade attached at right angles to a wooden handle, used for dressing timber [OE *adesa*]

Adzhar Autonomous Republic (ə'dʒɑː) *or* **Adzharia** (ə'dʒɑːrɪə) *n* an administrative division of SW Georgia, on the Black Sea: part of Turkey from the 17th century until 1878; mostly mountainous, reaching 2805 m (9350 ft), with a subtropical coastal strip. Capital: Batumi. Pop: 386 700 (1993 est). Area: 3000 sq km (1160 sq miles)

AEA (in Britain) *abbrev for* Atomic Energy Authority

AEC (in the US) *abbrev for* Atomic Energy Commission

aedes (eɪ'iːdiːz) *n* a mosquito of tropical and subtropical regions which transmits yellow fever [C20 NL, from Gk *aēdēs* unpleasant, from A-[1] + *ēdos* pleasant]

aedile *or US (sometimes)* **edile** ('iːdaɪl) *n* a magistrate of ancient Rome in charge of public works, games, buildings, and roads [C16 from L *aedīlis*, from *aedēs* a building]

Aeëtes (iː'iːtiːz) *n Greek myth* a king of Colchis, father of Medea and keeper of the Golden Fleece

Aegean (iː'dʒiːən) *adj* of or relating to the Aegean Sea or Islands

Aegean Islands *pl n* the islands of the Aegean Sea, including the Cyclades, Dodecanese, Euboea, and Sporades. The majority are under Greek administration

Aegean Sea *n* an arm of the Mediterranean between Greece and Turkey

Aegeus (iː'dʒiːuːs, 'iːdʒɪəs) *n Greek myth* an Athenian king and father of Theseus

Aegina (iː'dʒaɪnə) *n* **1** an island in the Aegean Sea, in the Saronic Gulf. Area: 85 sq km (33 sq miles) **2** a town on the coast of this island: a city-state of ancient Greece **3 Gulf of** another name for the **Saronic Gulf** Greek name: **Aiyina**

Aegir ('iːdʒɪə) *n Norse myth* the god of the sea

aegis *or US (sometimes)* **egis** ('iːdʒɪs) *n* **1** sponsorship or protection (esp in **under the aegis of**) **2** *Greek myth* the shield of Zeus [C18 from L, from Gk *aigis* shield of Zeus]

Aegisthus (iː'dʒɪsθəs) *n Greek myth* a cousin to and the murderer of Agamemnon, whose wife Clytemnestra he had seduced. He usurped the kingship of Mycenae until Orestes, Agamemnon's son, returned home and killed him

Aegospotami (ˌiːgəs'pɒtəˌmaɪ) *n* a river of ancient Thrace that flowed into the Hellespont. At its mouth the Spartan fleet under Lysander defeated the Athenians in 405 BC, ending the Peloponnesian War

aegrotat ('aɪgrəʊˌtæt, 'iː-) *n* **1** (in British and certain other universities, and, sometimes, schools) a certificate allowing a candidate to pass an examination although he has missed all or part of it through illness **2** a degree or other qualification obtained in such circumstances [C19 L, lit.: he is ill]

Ælfric ('ælfrɪk) *n* called *Grammaticus*. ?955–?1020, English abbot, writer, and grammarian

-aemia, -haemia, *or US* **-emia, -hemia** *n combining form* denoting blood, esp a specified condition of the blood in diseases: *leukaemia* [NL, from Gk, from *haima* blood]

Aeneas (ɪ'niːəs) *n classical myth* a Trojan prince, the son of Anchises and Aphrodite, who escaped the sack of Troy and sailed to Italy via Carthage and Sicily. After seven years, he and his followers established themselves near the site of the future Rome

Aeneid (ɪ'niːɪd) *n* an epic poem in Latin by Virgil relating the experiences of Aeneas after the fall of Troy

aeolian harp (iː'əʊlɪən) *n* a stringed instrument that produces a musical sound when wind passes over the strings. Also called: **wind harp** [after AEOLUS]

Aeolian Islands *pl n* another name for the **Lipari Islands**

Aeolis ('iːəlɪs) *or* **Aeolia** (iː'əʊlɪə) *n* the ancient name for the coastal region of NW Asia Minor, including the island of Lesbos, settled by the Aeolian Greeks (about 1000 BC)

aeolotropic (ˌiːələʊ'trɒpɪk) *adj* a less common word for **anisotropic** [C19 from Gk *aiolos* fickle + -TROPIC] > **aeolotropy** (ˌiːə'lɒtrəpɪ) *n*

Aeolus ('iːələs, iː'əʊləs) *n Greek myth* **1** the god of the winds **2** the founding king of the Aeolians in Thessaly

aeon *or esp US* **eon** ('iːən, 'iːɒn) *n* **1** an immeasurably long period of time **2** *astron* a period of one thousand million years [C17 from Gk *aiōn* an infinitely long time]

aerate ('ɛəreɪt) *vb* **aerates, aerating, aerated** (*tr*) **1** to charge (a liquid) with a gas, as in the manufacture of effervescent drink **2** to expose to the action or circulation of the air > **aer'ation** *n* > **'aerator** *n*

aeri- *combining form* a variant of **aero-**

aerial ('ɛərɪəl) *adj* **1** of or resembling air **2** existing, moving, or operating in the air: *aerial cable car* **3** ethereal; light and delicate **4** imaginary **5** extending high into the air **6** of or relating to aircraft: *aerial combat* ▷ *n* **7** Also called: **antenna** the part of a radio or television system by means of which radio waves are transmitted or received [C17 via L from Gk *aērios*, from *aēr* air]

aerialist ('ɛərɪəlɪst) *n* a trapeze artist or tightrope walker

aerial top dressing *n* the process of spreading lime, fertilizer, etc over farmland from an aeroplane

aerie ('ɛərɪ) *n* a variant spelling (esp US) of **eyrie**

aeriform ('ɛərɪˌfɔːm) *adj* **1** having the form of air; gaseous **2** unsubstantial

aero ('ɛərəʊ) *n* (*modifier*) of or relating to aircraft or aeronautics: *an aero engine*

aero-, aeri-, *or before a vowel* **aer-** *combining form* **1** denoting air, atmosphere, or gas: *aerodynamics* **2** denoting aircraft: *aeronautics* [ult. from Gk *aēr* air]

aerobatics (ˌɛərəʊ'bætɪks) *n* (*functioning as sing or pl*) spectacular or dangerous manoeuvres, such as loops or rolls, performed in an aircraft or glider [C20 from AERO- + (ACRO)BATICS]

aerobe ('ɛərəʊb) *or* **aerobium** (ɛə'rəʊbɪəm) *n, pl* **aerobes** *or* **aerobia** (-'əʊbɪə) an organism that requires oxygen for respiration [C19 from AERO- + Gk *bios* life]

aerobic (ɛə'rəʊbɪk) *adj* **1** (of an organism or process) depending on oxygen **2** of or relating to aerobes **3** designed for or relating to aerobics: *aerobic shoes; aerobic dances*

aerobics (ɛə'rəʊbɪks) *n* (*functioning as sing*) any system of exercises designed to increase the amount of oxygen in the blood

aerodrome ('ɛərəˌdrəʊm) *n* a landing area that is smaller than an airport

aerodynamic braking *n* **1** the use of aerodynamic drag to slow spacecraft re-entering the atmosphere **2** the use of airbrakes to retard flying vehicles or objects **3** the use of a parachute or reversed thrust to decelerate an aircraft before landing

aerodynamics (ˌɛərəʊdaɪ'næmɪks) *n* (*functioning as sing*) the study of the dynamics of gases, esp of the forces acting on a body passing through air > ˌ**aerody'namic** *adj*

> ˌaerodyˈnamically *adv* > ˌaerodyˈnamicist *n*
aero engine *n* an engine for powering an aircraft
aerofoil (ˈɛərəʊˌfɔɪl) *n* a cross section of a wing, rotor blade, etc
aerogram *or* **aerogramme** (ˈɛərəˌgræm) *n* an airmail letter written on a single sheet of lightweight paper that folds and is sealed to form an envelope. Also called: **air letter**
aerolite (ˈɛərəˌlaɪt) *n* a stony meteorite consisting of silicate minerals
aerology (ɛəˈrɒlədʒɪ) *n* the study of the atmosphere, particularly its upper layers > **aerological** (ˌɛərəˈlɒdʒɪkᵊl) *adj* > **aerˈologist** *n*
aeromechanics (ˌɛərəʊmɪˈkænɪks) *n (functioning as sing)* the mechanics of gases, esp air > ˌ**aeromeˈchanical** *adj*
aeronautics (ˌɛərəˈnɔːtɪks) *n (functioning as sing)* the study or practice of all aspects of flight through the air > ˌ**aeroˈnautical** *adj*
▷ www.sae.org/technology/aerospace.htm
▷ www.aeronautics.ru/links.htm
aeropause (ˈɛərəˌpɔːz) *n* the region of the upper atmosphere above which aircraft cannot fly
aeroplane (ˈɛərəˌpleɪn) *or US* **airplane** (ˈɛəˌpleɪn) *n* a heavier-than-air powered flying vehicle with fixed wings [c19 from F *aéroplane*, from AERO- + Gk *-planos* wandering]
aerosol (ˈɛərəˌsɒl) *n* **1** a colloidal dispersion of solid or liquid particles in a gas **2** a substance, such as a paint or insecticide, dispensed from a small metal container by a propellant under pressure **3** Also called: **air spray** such a substance together with its container [c20 from AERO- + SOL(UTION)]
aerospace (ˈɛərəˌspeɪs) *n* **1** the atmosphere and space beyond **2** *(modifier)* of rockets, missiles, space vehicles, etc: *the aerospace industry*
▷ www.airspacemag.com
▷ www.janes.com/aerospace/civil/
aerostat (ˈɛərəˌstæt) *n* a lighter-than-air craft, such as a balloon [c18 from F *aérostat*, from AERO- + Gk *-statos* standing] > ˌ**aeroˈstatic** *adj*
aerostatics (ˌɛərəˈstætɪks) *n (functioning as sing)* **1** the study of gases in equilibrium and bodies held in equilibrium in gases ▷ Cf **aerodynamics** **2** the study of lighter-than-air craft, such as balloons
aerugo (ɪˈruːgəʊ) *n* (esp of old bronze) another name for **verdigris** [c18 from L, from *aes* copper, bronze] > **aeruginous** (ɪˈruːdʒɪnəs) *adj*
aery (ˈɛərɪ) *n, pl* **aeries** a variant of **eyrie**
Aeschylus (ˈiːskələs) *n* ?525–?456 BC, Greek dramatist, regarded as the father of Greek tragedy. Seven of his plays are extant, including *Seven Against Thebes*, *The Persians*, *Prometheus Bound*, and the trilogy of the *Oresteia*
Aesculapius (ˌiːskjʊˈleɪpɪəs) *n* the Roman god of medicine or healing. Greek counterpart: **Asclepius** > ˌ**Aescuˈlapian** *adj*
Aesir (ˈeɪsɪə) *pl n* the chief gods of Norse mythology dwelling in Asgard [ON, lit.: gods]
Aesop (ˈiːsɒp) *n* ?620–564 BC, Greek author of fables in which animals are given human characters and used to satirize human failings
aesthesia *or US* **esthesia** (iːsˈθiːzɪə) *n* the normal ability to experience sensation [c20 back formation from ANAESTHESIA]
aesthete *or US* **esthete** (ˈiːsθiːt) *n* a person who has or who affects a highly developed appreciation of beauty [c19 back formation from AESTHETICS]
aesthetic (iːsˈθɛtɪk, ɪs-) *or US (sometimes)* **esthetic** *adj* also **aesthetical** *or US (sometimes)* **esthetical** **1** connected with aesthetics **2a** relating to pure beauty rather than to other considerations **2b** artistic: *an aesthetic consideration* ▷ *n* **3** a principle of taste or style adopted by a particular person, group, or culture: *the Bauhaus aesthetic of functional modernity* [c19 from Gk *aisthētikos*, from *aisthanesthai* to perceive, feel] > **aesˈthetically** *or US (sometimes)* **esˈthetically** *adv* > **aesˈthetiˌcism** *or US (sometimes)* **esˈthetiˌcism** *n*
aesthetic labour *n* workers employed by a company for their appearance or accent, with the aim of promoting the company's image
aesthetics *or US (sometimes)* **esthetics** (iːsˈθɛtɪks) *n (functioning as sing)* **1** the branch of philosophy concerned with the study of such concepts as beauty, taste, etc **2** the study of the rules and principles of art
aestival *or US* **estival** (iːˈstaɪvᵊl) *adj rare* of or occurring in summer [c14 from F, from LL *aestīvālis*, from L *aestās* summer]
aestivate *or US* **estivate** (ˈiːstɪˌveɪt) *vb* **aestivates, aestivating, aestivated** *or US* **estivates, estivating, estivated** *(intr)* **1** to pass the summer **2** (of animals) to pass the summer or dry season in a dormant condition [c17 from L, from *aestīvāre*, from *aestās* summer] > ˌ**aestiˈvation** *or US* ˌ**estiˈvation** *n*
aet. *or* **aetat.** *abbrev for* aetatis [L: at the age of]
Æthelbert (ˈæθəlˌbɜːt) *n* a variant of **Ethelbert**
Æthelred (ˈæθəlˌrɛd) *n* a variant of **Ethelred**
aether (ˈiːθə) *n* a variant spelling of **ether** (senses 3, 4)
aetiology *or* **etiology** (ˌiːtɪˈɒlədʒɪ) *n, pl* **aetiologies** *or* **etiologies** **1** the philosophy or study of causation **2** the study of the causes of diseases **3** the cause of a disease [c16 from LL *aetologia*, from Gk *aitiologia*, from *aitia* cause] > ˌ**aetioˈlogical** *or* ˌ**etioˈlogical** *adj* > ˌ**aetioˈlogically** *or* ˌ**etioˈlogically** *adv* > ˌ**aetiˈologist** *or* ˌ**etiˈologist** *n*
Aetna (ˈɛtnə) *n* the Latin name for Mount **Etna**
Aetolia (iːˈtəʊlɪə) *n* a mountainous region forming (with the region of Acarnania) a department of W central Greece, north of the Gulf of Patras: a powerful federal state in the 3rd century BC. Chief city: Missolonghi. Pop (with Acarnania): 228 180 (1991). Area: 5461 sq km (2108 sq miles)
a.f. *abbrev for* audio frequency
afar (əˈfɑː) *adv* **1** at, from, or to a great distance ▷ *n* **2** a great distance (esp in **from afar**) [c14 *a fer*, altered from earlier *on fer* & *of fer*; see A-², FAR]
Afars and the Issas (ˈɑːfɑːz, ˈiːsɑːs) *n* **Territory of the** a former name (1967–77) of **Djibouti**
AFC *abbrev for:* **1** Air Force Cross **2** Association Football Club **3** automatic frequency control
afeard *or* **afeared** (əˈfɪəd) *adj (postpositive)* an archaic or dialect word for **afraid** [OE *āfǣred*, from *afǣran* to frighten]
affable (ˈæfəbᵊl) *adj* **1** showing warmth and friendliness **2** easy to converse with; approachable [c16 from L *affābilis*, from *affārī*, from *ad-* to + *fārī* to speak] > ˌ**affaˈbility** *n* > ˈ**affably** *adv*
affair (əˈfɛə) *n* **1** a thing to be done or attended to; matter **2** an event or happening: *a strange affair* **3** *(qualified by an adjective or descriptive phrase)* something previously specified: *our house is a tumbledown affair* **4** a sexual relationship between two people who are not married to each other [c13 from OF, from *à faire* to do]
affairs (əˈfɛəz) *pl n* **1** personal or business interests **2** matters of public interest: *current affairs*
affect¹ *vb* (əˈfɛkt).*(tr)* **1** to act upon or influence, esp in an adverse way **2** to move or disturb emotionally or mentally **3** (of pain, disease, etc) to attack ▷ *n* (ˈæfɛkt) **4** *psychol* the emotion associated with an idea or set of ideas [c17 from L *affectus*, p.p. of *afficere*, from *ad-* to + *facere* to do]

USAGE See at **effect**

affect² (əˈfɛkt) *vb (mainly tr)* **1** to put on an appearance or show of: *to affect ignorance* **2** to imitate or assume, esp pretentiously **3** to have or use by preference **4** to adopt the character, manner, etc, of **5** to incline habitually towards [c15 from L *affectāre* to strive after; rel. to *afficere* to AFFECT¹]
affectation (ˌæfɛkˈteɪʃən) *n* **1** an assumed manner of

Aa

speech, dress, or behaviour, esp one that is intended to impress others **2** (often foll by *of*) deliberate pretence [c16 from L *affectātiōn-*, from *affectāre*; see AFFECT[2]]

affected[1] (ə'fɛktɪd) *adj* (*usually postpositive*) **1** deeply moved, esp by sorrow or grief **2** changed, esp detrimentally [c17 from AFFECT[1]]

affected[2] (ə'fɛktɪd) *adj* **1** behaving, speaking, etc, in an assumed way, esp in order to impress others **2** feigned: *affected indifference* [c16 from AFFECT[2]] > **af'fectedly** *adv*

affecting (ə'fɛktɪŋ) *adj* evoking feelings of pity; moving > **af'fectingly** *adv*

affection (ə'fɛkʃən) *n* **1** a feeling of fondness or tenderness for a person or thing **2** (*often pl*) emotion, feeling, or sentiment: *to play on a person's affections* **3** *pathol* any disease or pathological condition **4** the act of affecting or the state of being affected [c13 from L *affectiōn-*, from *afficere* to AFFECT[1]] > **af'fectional** *adj*

affectionate (ə'fɛkʃənɪt) *adj* having or displaying tender feelings, affection, or warmth > **af'fectionately** *adv*

affective (ə'fɛktɪv) *adj* concerned with the emotions or affection > **affectivity** (ˌæfɛk'tɪvɪtɪ) *n*

affective disorder *n* any mental disorder, such as depression or mania, that is characterized by abnormal disturbances of mood

affectless ('æfɛktˌlɪs, ə'fɛktlɪs) *adj* **a** showing no emotion or concern for others **b** not giving rise to any emotion or feeling: *an affectless novel* [c20 from AFFECT[1] (sense 4) + -LESS]

afferent ('æfərənt) *adj* bringing or directing inwards to a part or an organ of the body, esp towards the brain or spinal cord [c19 from L *afferre*, from *ad-* to + *ferre* to carry]

affiance (ə'faɪəns) *vb* **affiances, affiancing, affianced** (*tr*) to bind (a person or oneself) in a promise of marriage; betroth [c14 via OF from Med. L *affīdāre* to trust (oneself) to, from *fīdāre* to trust]

affidavit (ˌæfɪ'deɪvɪt) *n law* a declaration in writing made upon oath before a person authorized to administer oaths [c17 from Med. L, lit.: he declares on oath, from *affīdare*; see AFFIANCE]

affiliate *vb* (ə'fɪlɪˌeɪt), **affiliates, affiliating, affiliated** **1** (*tr*; foll by *to* or *with*) to receive into close connection or association (with a larger body, group, organization, etc) **2** (foll by *with*) to associate (oneself) or be associated, esp as a subordinate or subsidiary ▷ *n* (ə'fɪlɪɪt) **3a** a person or organization that is affiliated with another **3b** (*as modifier*): *an affiliate member* [c18 from Med. L *affīliātus* adopted as a son, from *affīliare*, from L *filius* son] > **afˌfili'ation** *n*

affiliation order *n law* an order that a man adjudged to be the father of an illegitimate child shall contribute towards the child's maintenance

affine ('æfaɪn) *adj maths* denoting transformations which preserve collinearity, esp those of translation, rotation, and reflection [c16 from F: see AFFINITY]

affinity (ə'fɪnɪtɪ) *n*, *pl* **affinities** **1** a natural liking, taste, or inclination for a person or thing **2** the person or thing so liked **3** a close similarity in appearance or quality **4** relationship by marriage **5** similarity in structure, form, etc, between different animals, plants, or languages **6** *chem* chemical attraction **7** *immunol* a measure of the degree of interaction between an antigen and an antibody [c14 via OF from L *affīnitāt-*, from *affīnis* bordering on, related] > **af'finitive** *adj*

affinity card *n* a credit card issued by a bank or credit-card company, which donates a small percentage of the money spent using the card to a specified charity

affirm (ə'fɜːm) *vb* (*mainly tr*) **1** (*may take a clause as object*) to declare to be true **2** to uphold, confirm, or ratify **3** (*intr*) *law* to make an affirmation [c14 via OF from L *affirmāre*, from *ad-* to + *firmāre* to make FIRM[1]] > **af'firmer** *or* **af'firmant** *n*

affirmation (ˌæfə'meɪʃən) *n* **1** the act of affirming or the state of being affirmed **2** a statement of the truth of something; assertion **3** *law* a solemn declaration permitted on grounds of conscientious objection to taking an oath

affirmative (ə'fɜːmətɪv) *adj* **1** confirming or asserting something as true or valid **2** indicating agreement or assent **3** *logic* (of a categorical proposition) affirming the satisfaction by the subject of the predicate, as in the proposition *some men are married* ▷ *n* **4** a positive assertion **5** a word or phrase stating agreement or assent, such as *yes*: *to answer in the affirmative* ▷ *sentence substitute* **6** *mil, etc* a signal codeword used to express assent or confirmation > **af'firmatively** *adv*

affix *vb* (ə'fɪks) (*tr*; usually foll by *to* or *on*) **1** to attach, fasten, join, or stick **2** to add or append: *to affix a signature to a document* **3** to attach or attribute (guilt, blame, etc) ▷ *n* ('æfɪks) **4** a linguistic element added to a word or root to produce a derived or inflected form, as *-ment* in *establishment*. See also **prefix, suffix, infix** **5** something fastened or attached [c15 from Med. L *affixāre*, from *ad-* to + *fixāre* to FIX] > **affixture** (ə'fɪkstʃə) *n*

afflatus (ə'fleɪtəs) *n* an impulse of creative power or inspiration considered to be of divine origin [c17 L, from *afflātus*, from *afflāre*, from *flāre* to blow]

afflict (ə'flɪkt) *vb* (*tr*) to cause suffering or unhappiness to; distress greatly [c14 from L *afflictus*, p.p. of *afflīgere* to knock against, from *flīgere* to strike] > **af'flictive** *adj*

affliction (ə'flɪkʃən) *n* **1** a condition of great distress or suffering **2** something responsible for physical or mental suffering

affluence ('æflʊəns) *n* **1** an abundant supply of money, goods, or property; wealth **2** *rare* abundance or profusion

affluent ('æflʊənt) *adj* **1** rich; wealthy **2** abundant; copious **3** flowing freely ▷ *n* **4** *arch* a tributary stream [c15 from L *affluent-*, present participle of *affluere*, from *fluere* to flow]

affluential (ˌæflʊ'ɛnʃəl) *n* an affluent person who does not display his or her wealth in the form of material possessions

affluent society *n* a society in which the material benefits of prosperity are widely available

afflux ('æflʌks) *n* a flowing towards a point: *an afflux of blood to the head* [c17 from L *affluxus*, from *fluxus* FLUX]

afford (ə'fɔːd) *vb* **1** (preceded by *can, could*, etc) to be able to do or spare something, esp without incurring financial difficulties or without risk of undesirable consequences **2** to give, yield, or supply [OE *geforthian* to further, promote, from *forth* FORTH] > **af'fordable** *adj* > **afˌforda'bility** *n*

afforest (ə'fɒrɪst) *vb* (*tr*) to plant trees on [c15 from Med. L *afforestāre*, from *forestis* FOREST] > **afˌforest'ation** *n*

affranchise (ə'fræntʃaɪz) *vb* **affranchises, affranchising, affranchised** (*tr*) to release from servitude or an obligation [c15 from OF *afranchir*] > **af'franchisement** *n*

affray (ə'freɪ) *n* a fight, noisy quarrel, or disturbance between two or more persons in a public place [c14 via OF from Vulgar L *exfridāre* (unattested) to break the peace]

affricate ('æfrɪkɪt) *n* a composite speech sound consisting of a stop and a fricative articulated at the same point, such as the sound written *ch*, as in *chair* [c19 from L *affricāre*, from *fricāre* to rub]

affright (ə'fraɪt) *arch or poetic* ▷ *vb* **1** (*tr*) to frighten ▷ *n* **2** a sudden terror [OE *āfyrhtan*, from *a-* + *fyrhtan* to FRIGHT]

affront (ə'frʌnt) *n* **1** a deliberate insult ▷ *vb* (*tr*) **2** to insult, esp openly **3** to offend the pride or dignity of [c14 from OF *afronter* to strike in the face, from L *ad frontem* to the face]

Afg. *or* **Afgh.** *abbrev for* Afghanistan

afghan ('æfgæn, -gən) *n* **1** a knitted or crocheted wool blanket or shawl, esp one with a geometric pattern **2** a sheepskin coat, often embroidered [from AFGHANISTAN]

Afghan ('æfgæn) *or* **Afghani** (æf'gænɪ) *n* **1** a native, citizen, or inhabitant of Afghanistan **2** another name for **Pashto** (the language) ▷ *adj* **3** denoting Afghanistan, its people, or their language

Afghan hound *n* a tall graceful breed of hound with a long silky coat

Afghanistan (æfˈgænɪˌstɑːn, -ˌstæn) *n* a republic in central Asia: became independent in 1919; occupied by Soviet troops, 1979–89; controlled by mujaheddin forces from 1992 until 1996 when Taliban forces seized power; in the US-led 'war against terrorism' (2001) the Taliban were overthrown and replaced by an interim administration; generally arid and mountainous, with the Hindu Kush range rising over 7500 m (25 000 ft) and fertile valleys of the Amu Darya, Helmand, and Kabul Rivers. Official languages: Pashto and Dari (Persian), Tajik also widely spoken. Religion: Muslim. Currency: afghani. Capital: Kabul. Pop: 26 813 000 (2001 est). Area: 657 500 sq km (250 000 sq miles)
▷ www.afghanistan.org

aficionado (əˌfɪʃjəˈnɑːdəʊ) *n, pl* **aficionados** **1** an ardent supporter or devotee: *a jazz aficionado* **2** a devotee of bullfighting [Sp., from *aficionar*, from *aficion* AFFECTION]

afield (əˈfiːld) *adv, adj (postpositive)* **1** away from one's usual surroundings or home (esp in **far afield**) **2** off the subject (esp in **far afield**) **3** in or to the field

afire (əˈfaɪə) *adv, adj (postpositive)* **1** on fire **2** intensely interested or passionate: *he was afire with enthusiasm for the new plan*

AFIS *n* Automated Fingerprint Identification System: a computer system that scans fingerprints from crime scenes and compares them with millions of others around the world

AFK *computing abbrev for* away from keyboard

AFL *abbrev for* Australian Football League: the national body for Australian Rules football

aflame (əˈfleɪm) *adv, adj (postpositive)* **1** in flames **2** deeply aroused, as with passion: *he was aflame with desire*

aflatoxin (ˌæfləˈtɒksɪn) *n* a toxin produced by a fungus growing on peanuts, maize, etc, causing liver disease (esp cancer) in man [c20 from L name of fungus *A(spergillus) fla(vus)* + TOXIN]

afloat (əˈfləʊt) *adj (postpositive), adv* **1** floating **2** aboard ship; at sea **3** covered with water **4** aimlessly drifting **5** in circulation: *nasty rumours were afloat* **6** free of debt

aflutter (əˈflʌtə) *adj (postpositive), adv* in or into a nervous or excited state

AFM *abbrev for* Air Force Medal

afoot (əˈfʊt) *adj (postpositive), adv* **1** in operation; astir: *mischief was afoot* **2** on or by foot

afore (əˈfɔː) *adv, prep, conj* an archaic or dialect word for **before**

aforementioned (əˈfɔːˌmɛnʃənd) *adj (usually prenominal)* (chiefly in legal documents) stated or mentioned before

aforesaid (əˈfɔːˌsɛd) *adj (usually prenominal)* (chiefly in legal documents) spoken of or referred to previously

aforethought (əˈfɔːˌθɔːt) *adj (immediately postpositive)* premeditated (esp in **malice aforethought**)

a fortiori (ˈeɪ ˌfɔːtɪˈɔːraɪ) *adv* for similar but more convincing reasons [L]

afp *abbrev for* alpha-fetoprotein

afraid (əˈfreɪd) *adj (postpositive)* **1** (often foll by *of*) feeling fear or apprehension **2** reluctant (to do something), as through fear or timidity **3** (often foll by *that*; used to lessen the effect of an unpleasant statement) regretful: *I'm afraid that I shall have to tell you to go* [c14 *affraied*, p.p. of AFFRAY (*obs.*) to frighten]

afreet *or* **afrit** (ˈæfriːt, əˈfriːt) *n Arabian myth* a powerful evil demon [c19 from Ar. *'ifrīt*]

afresh (əˈfrɛʃ) *adv* once more; again; anew

Afric (ˈæfrɪk) *adj* **1** of African descent and native to a place outside sub-Saharan Africa ▷ *n* **2** an Afric person [c20 by analogy with INDIC]

Africa (ˈæfrɪkə) *n* the second largest of the continents, on the Mediterranean in the north, the Atlantic in the west, and the Red Sea, Gulf of Aden, and Indian Ocean in the east. The Sahara desert divides the continent unequally into North Africa (an early centre of civilization, in close contact with Europe and W Asia, now inhabited chiefly by Arabs) and Africa south of the Sahara (relatively isolated from the rest of the world until the 19th century and inhabited chiefly by Negroid peoples). It was colonized mainly in the 18th and 19th centuries by Europeans and now comprises independent nations. The largest lake is Lake Victoria and the chief rivers are the Nile, Niger, Congo, and Zambezi. Pop: 755 919 000 (1998 est). Area: about 30 300 000 sq km (11 700 000 sq miles)

African (ˈæfrɪkən) *adj* **1** denoting or relating to Africa or any of its peoples, languages, nations, etc ▷ *n* **2** a native or inhabitant of any of the countries of Africa **3** a member or descendant of any of the peoples of Africa, esp a Black

Africana (ˌæfrɪˈkɑːnə) *pl n* objects of cultural or historical interest of southern African origin

African-American *or* **Afro-American** *n* **1** an American of African descent ▷ *adj* **2** of or relating to Americans of African descent

African-Canadian *n* **1** a Canadian of African descent ▷ *adj* **2** of or relating to Canadians of African descent

Africander *or* **Afrikander** (ˌæfrɪˈkændə) *n* a breed of hump-backed beef cattle originally raised in southern Africa [c19 from South African Du., formed on the model of *Hollander*]

African National Congress *n* a political party, founded in 1912 in South Africa as an African nationalist movement and banned from 1960 until 1990 because of its opposition to apartheid. In 1994 the ANC won South Africa's first multiracial elections. Abbrev: **ANC**

African violet *n* a tropical African plant cultivated as a house plant, with violet, white, or pink flowers and hairy leaves

Afrikaans (ˌæfrɪˈkɑːns, -ˈkɑːnz) *n* one of the official languages of the Republic of South Africa, closely related to Dutch. Sometimes called: **South African Dutch** [c20 from Du.: African]

Afrikaner (ˌæfrɪˈkɑːnə) *n* a White native of the Republic of South Africa whose mother tongue is Afrikaans. See also **Boer**

afrit (ˈæfriːt, əˈfriːt) *n* a variant spelling of **afreet**

Afro (ˈæfrəʊ) *n, pl* **Afros** a hairstyle in which the hair is shaped into a wide frizzy bush [c20 independent use of AFRO-]

Afro- *combining form* indicating Africa or African: *Afro-Asiatic*

Afro-American *n, adj* another word for **African-American**

Afro-Caribbean *adj* **1** denoting or relating to Caribbean people of African descent or their culture ▷ *n* **2** a Caribbean of African descent

Afro-pessimism *n* the belief that the provision of aid to African countries is futile

afrormosia (ˌæfrɔːˈməʊzɪə) *n* a hard teaklike wood obtained from a genus of tropical African trees [c20 from AFRO- + *Ormosia* (genus name)]

aft (ɑːft) *adv, adj chiefly naut* towards or at the stern or rear: *the aft deck; aft of the engines* [c17 ? shortened from earlier ABAFT]

after (ˈɑːftə) *prep* **1** following in time; in succession to: *after dinner* **2** following; behind **3** in pursuit or search of: *he's only after money* **4** concerning: *to inquire after his health* **5** considering: *after what you have done, you shouldn't complain* **6** next in excellence or importance to **7** in imitation of; in the manner of **8** in accordance with or in conformity to: *a man after her own heart* **9** with a name derived from **10** US past (the hour of): *twenty after three* **11** **after all** **11a** in spite of everything: *it's only a game after all* **11b** in spite of expectations, efforts, etc **12** **after you** please go, enter, etc, before me ▷ *adv* **13** at a later time; afterwards **14** coming afterwards **15** *naut* further aft ▷ *conj* **16** (*subordinating*) at a time later than that at which ▷ *adj* **17** *naut* further aft: *the after cabin* [OE *æfter*]

afterbirth (ˈɑːftəˌbɜːθ) *n* the placenta and fetal membranes expelled from the uterus after the birth of the offspring

afterburner (ˈɑːftəˌbɜːnə) *n* **1** a device in the exhaust system of an internal-combustion engine for removing dangerous exhaust gases **2** a device in an aircraft jet engine to produce extra thrust by igniting additional fuel

aftercare (ˈɑːftəˌkɛə) *n* **1** support services by a welfare agency for a person discharged from a hospital, prison, etc **2** *med* the care of a patient after a serious illness or operation **3** any system of maintenance or upkeep of an appliance or product: *contact-lens aftercare*

afterdamp (ˈɑːftəˌdæmp) *n* a poisonous gas, consisting mainly of carbon monoxide, formed after the explosion of firedamp in coal mines

aftereffect (ˈɑːftərɪˌfɛkt) *n* any result occurring some time after its cause

afterglow (ˈɑːftəˌgləʊ) *n* **1** the glow left after a light has disappeared, such as that sometimes seen after sunset **2** the glow of an incandescent metal after the source of heat has been removed

afterimage (ˈɑːftərˌɪmɪdʒ) *n* a sustained or renewed sensation, esp visual, after the original stimulus has ceased

afterlife (ˈɑːftəˌlaɪf) *n* life after death or at a later time in a person's lifetime

aftermath (ˈɑːftəˌmæθ) *n* **1** signs or results of an event or occurrence considered collectively: *the aftermath of war* **2** *agriculture* a second crop of grass from land that has already yielded one crop earlier in the same year [C16 AFTER + *math* a mowing, from OE *mæth*]

aftermost (ˈɑːftəˌməʊst) *adj* closer or closest to the rear or (in a vessel) the stern; last

afternoon (ˌɑːftəˈnuːn) *n* **1a** the period between noon and evening **1b** (*as modifier*): *afternoon tea* **2** a later part: *the afternoon of life*

afternoons (ˌɑːftəˈnuːnz) *adv Inf* during the afternoon, esp regularly

afterpains (ˈɑːftəˌpeɪnz) *pl n* cramplike pains caused by contraction of the uterus after childbirth

afters (ˈɑːftəz) *n* (*functioning as sing or pl*) *Brit inf* dessert; sweet

aftershave lotion (ˈɑːftəʃeɪv) *n* a lotion, usually perfumed, for application to the face after shaving. Often shortened to **aftershave**

aftertaste (ˈɑːftəˌteɪst) *n* **1** a taste that lingers on after eating or drinking **2** a lingering impression or sensation

afterthought (ˈɑːftəˌθɔːt) *n* **1** a comment, reply, etc, that occurs to one after the opportunity to deliver it has passed **2** an addition to something already completed

afterwards (ˈɑːftəwədz) *or* **afterward** *adv* after an earlier event or time [OE *æfterweard, æfteweard*, from AFT + WARD]

Ag *the chemical symbol for* silver [from L *argentum*]

AG *abbrev for*: **1** Adjutant General **2** Attorney General

aga *or* **agha** (ˈɑːgə) *n* (in the Ottoman Empire) a title of respect, often used with the title of a senior position [C17 Turkish, lit.: lord]

Agadir (ˌægəˈdɪə) *n* a port in SW Morocco, which became the centre of an international crisis (1911), when a gunboat arrived to protect German interests. Britain issued a strong warning to Germany but the French negotiated and war was averted. In 1960 the town was virtually destroyed by an earthquake, about 10 000 people being killed. Pop: 155 244 (1994)

again (əˈgɛn, əˈgeɪn) *adv* **1** another or a second time: *he had to start again* **2** once more in a previously experienced state or condition: *he is ill again* **3** in addition to the original amount, quantity, etc (esp in **as much again; half as much again**) **4** (*sentence modifier*) on the other hand **5** besides; also **6** *arch* in reply; back: *he answered again* **7** **again and again** continuously; repeatedly ▷ *sentence connector* **8** moreover; furthermore [OE *ongegn* opposite to, from A-² + *gegn* straight]

against (əˈgɛnst, əˈgeɪnst) *prep* **1** opposed to; in conflict or disagreement with **2** standing or leaning beside: *a ladder against the wall* **3** coming in contact with **4** in contrast to: *silhouettes are outlines against a light background* **5** having an unfavourable effect on: *the system works against small companies* **6** as a protection from: *a safeguard against contaminated water* **7** in exchange for or in return for **8** *now rare* in preparation for: *he gave them warm clothing against their journey* **9** **as against** as opposed to or as compared with [C12 *ageines*, from *again, ageyn*, etc AGAIN + *-es*, genitive ending]

Aga Khan (ˈɑːgə ˈkɑːn) *n* the hereditary title of the head of the Ismaili Islamic sect

Aga Khan IV *n* Prince **Karim** (kəˈriːm) born 1936, spiritual leader of the Ismaili sect of Muslims from 1957

Agamemnon (ˌægəˈmɛmnɒn) *n Greek myth* a king of Mycenae who led the Greeks at the siege of Troy. On his return home he was murdered by his wife Clytemnestra and her lover Aegisthus. See also **Menelaus**

agamic (əˈgæmɪk) *adj* asexual; occurring or reproducing without fertilization [C19 from Gk *agamos* unmarried, from A-¹ + *gamos* marriage]

agamogenesis (ˌægəməʊˈdʒɛnɪsɪs) *n* asexual reproduction, such as fission or parthenogenesis [C19 AGAMIC + GENESIS]

Agaña (əˈgɑːnjə) *n* the capital of the Pacific island of Guam, on its W coast. Pop: 2000 (1995 est)

agapanthus (ˌægəˈpænθəs) *n* a South African plant with blue funnel-shaped flowers, widely cultivated for ornament [C19 NL, from Gk *agape* love + *anthos* flower]

agape (əˈgeɪp) *adj* (*postpositive*) **1** (esp of the mouth) wide open **2** very surprised, expectant, or eager [C17 A-² + GAPE]

Agape (ˈægəpɪ) *n* **1** Christian love, esp as contrasted with erotic love; charity **2** a communal meal in the early Church in commemoration of the Last Supper [C17 Gk *agapē* love]

agar (ˈeɪgə) *n* a gelatinous carbohydrate obtained from seaweeds, used as a culture medium for bacteria, as a laxative, a thickening agent (**E406**) in food, etc Also called: **agar-agar** [C19 Malay]

agaric (ˈægərɪk) *n* a fungus having gills on the underside of the cap. The group includes the edible mushrooms and poisonous forms such as the fly agaric [C16 via L from Gk *agarikon*]

Agartala (ˈʌgətəˌlɑː) *n* a city in NE India, capital of the state of Tripura. Pop: 157 636 (1991)

Agassi (ˈægəsɪ) *n* **Andre** (ˈɑːndreɪ) born 1970, US tennis player: won the Wimbledon men's singles in 1992 and the US Open in 1994 and 1999

agate¹ (ˈægɪt) *n* **1** an impure form of quartz consisting of a variegated, usually banded chalcedony, used as a gemstone and in making pestles and mortars **2** a playing marble of this quartz or resembling it [C16 via F from L, from Gk *akhatēs*]

agate² (əˈgeɪt) *adv Northern English dialect* on the way [C16 A-² + GATE³]

agave (əˈgeɪvɪ) *n* a plant native to tropical America, with tall flower stalks rising from a massive rosette of leaves. Some species are the source of fibres such as sisal [C18 NL, from Gk *agauē*, fem. of *agauos* illustrious]

age (eɪdʒ) *n* **1** the period of time that a person, animal, or plant has lived or is expected to live **2** the period of existence of an object, material, group, etc: *the age of this table is 200 years* **3a** a period or state of human life: *he should know better at his age* **3b** (*as modifier*): *age group* **4** the latter part of life **5a** a period of history marked by some feature or characteristic **5b** (*cap. when part of a name*): *the Middle Ages* **6** generation: *the Edwardian age* **7** *geol, palaeontol* **7a** a period of the earth's history distinguished by special characteristics: *the age of reptiles* **7b** a subdivision of an epoch **8** (*often pl*) *inf* a relatively long time: *I've been waiting ages* **9** *psychol* the level in years that a person has reached in any area of development, compared with the normal level for his chronological age **10 of age** adult and legally responsible for one's actions (usually at 18 years) ▷ *vb* **ages, ageing** *or* **aging, aged 11** to become or cause to become old or aged **12** (*intr*) to begin to seem older: *to have aged a lot in the past year* **13** *brewing* to mature or cause to mature [c13 via OF from Vulgar L, from L *aetās*]

-age *suffix forming nouns* **1** indicating a collection, set, or group: *baggage* **2** indicating a process or action or the result of an action: *breakage* **3** indicating a state or relationship: *bondage* **4** indicating a house or place: *orphanage* **5** indicating a charge or fee: *postage* **6** indicating a rate: *dosage* [from OF, from LL *-āticum* belonging to]

aged (ˈeɪdʒɪd) *adj* **1a** advanced in years; old **1b** (*as collective n;* preceded by *the*): *the aged* **2** of, connected with, or characteristic of old age **3** (eɪdʒd) (*postpositive*) having the age of: *a woman aged twenty*

Agee (ˈeɪdʒiː) *n* **James** 1909–55, US novelist, poet, and film critic. His works include the autobiographical novel *A Death in the Family* (1957)

ageing *or* **aging** (ˈeɪdʒɪŋ) *n* **1** the process of growing old or developing the appearance of old age ▷ *adj* **2** becoming or appearing older: *an ageing car* **3** giving the appearance of elderliness: *that dress is really ageing*

ageism *or* **agism** (ˈeɪdʒɪzəm) *n* discrimination against people on the grounds of age; specifically, discrimination against the elderly > **ˈageist** *or* **ˈagist** *adj*

ageless (ˈeɪdʒlɪs) *adj* **1** apparently never growing old **2** timeless; eternal: *an ageless quality*

agency (ˈeɪdʒənsɪ) *n, pl* **agencies 1** a business or other organization providing a specific service: *an employment agency* **2** the place where an agent conducts business **3** the business, duties, or functions of an agent **4** action, power, or operation: *the agency of fate* [c17 from Med. L *agentia*, from L *agere* to do]

agenda (əˈdʒɛndə) *n* **1** (*functioning as sing*) Also: **agendum** a schedule or list of items to be attended to **2** (*functioning as pl*) Also: **agendas, agendums** matters to be attended to, as at a meeting [c17 L, lit.: things to be done, from *agere* to do]

agent (ˈeɪdʒənt) *n* **1** a person who acts on behalf of another person, business, government, etc **2** a person or thing that acts or has the power to act **3** a substance or organism that exerts some force or effect: *a chemical agent* **4** the means by which something occurs or is achieved **5** a person representing a business concern, esp a travelling salesman [c15 from L *agent-*, noun use of the present participle of *agere* to do] > **agential** (eɪˈdʒɛnʃəl) *adj*

agent-general *n, pl* **agents-general** a representative in London of a Canadian province or an Australian state

Agent Orange *n* a highly poisonous herbicide used as a spray for defoliation and crop destruction, esp by US forces during the Vietnam War [c20 named after the identifying colour stripe on its container]

agent provocateur *French* (aʒɑ̃ prɔvɔkatœr) *n, pl* ***agents provocateurs*** (aʒɑ̃ prɔvɔkatœr) a secret agent employed to provoke suspected persons to commit illegal acts and so be discredited or liable to punishment

age of consent *n* **1** the age at which a person, esp a female, is considered legally competent to consent to marriage or sexual intercourse **2** the age at which a person can enter into a legally binding contract

Age of Reason *n* (usually preceded by *the*) the 18th century in W Europe. See also **Enlightenment**

age-old *or* **age-long** *adj* very old or of long duration; ancient

age-proof *adj* **1** not adversely affected by a person's age: *an age-proof career* ▷ *vb* **2** to make (something) age-proof

ageratum (ˌædʒəˈreɪtəm) *n* a tropical American plant with thick clusters of purplish-blue flowers [c16 NL, via L from Gk *agēraton* that does not age, from A-[1] + *gērat-*, stem of *gēras* old age]

agglomerate *vb* (əˈglɒməˌreɪt), **agglomerates, agglomerating, agglomerated 1** to form or be formed into a mass or cluster ▷ *n* (əˈglɒmərɪt, -ˌreɪt) **2** a confused mass **3** a rock consisting of angular fragments of volcanic lava ▷ *adj* (əˈglɒmərɪt, -ˌreɪt) **4** formed into a mass [c17 from L *agglomerāre*, from *glomerāre* to wind into a ball] > **agˌglomerˈation** *n* > **agˈglomerative** *adj*

agglutinate (əˈgluːtɪˌneɪt) *vb* **agglutinates, agglutinating, agglutinated 1** to adhere or cause to adhere, as with glue **2** *linguistics* to combine or be combined by agglutination **3** (*tr*) to cause (bacteria, red blood cells, etc) to clump together [c16 from L *agglūtināre* to glue to, from *gluten* glue] > **agˈglutinable** *adj* > **agˈglutinant** *adj*

agglutination (əˌgluːtɪˈneɪʃən) *n* **1** the act or process of agglutinating **2** a united mass of parts **3** *chem* the formation of clumps of particles in a suspension **4** *immunol* the formation of a mass of particles, such as red blood cells, by the action of antibodies **5** *linguistics* the building up of words from component morphemes in such a way that these undergo little or no change of form or meaning

aggrandize *or* **aggrandise** (əˈgrændaɪz) *vb* **aggrandizes, aggrandizing, aggrandized** *or* **aggrandises, aggrandising, aggrandised** (*tr*) **1** to increase the power, wealth, prestige, scope, etc, of **2** to cause (something) to seem greater [c17 from OF *aggrandiss-*, stem of *aggrandir*, from L *grandis* GRAND] > **aggrandizement** *or* **aggrandisement** (əˈgrændɪzmənt) *n* > **ˈaggranˌdizer** *or* **ˈaggranˌdiser** *n*

Aa

aggravate (ˈægrəˌveɪt) *vb* **aggravates, aggravating, aggravated** (*tr*) **1** to make (a disease, situation, problem, etc) worse **2** *inf* to annoy [c16 from L *aggravāre* to make heavier, from *gravis* heavy] > **ˈaggraˌvating** *adj* > **ˌaggraˈvation** *n*

aggravated (ˈægrəˌveɪtɪd) *adj law* (of a criminal offence) made more serious by its circumstances

aggravated trespass *n law* an offence in which a trespasser in the open air attempts to interfere with a lawful activity, such as hunting

aggregate *adj* (ˈægrɪgɪt) **1** formed of separate units collected into a whole **2** (of fruits and flowers) composed of a dense cluster of florets ▷ *n* (ˈægrɪgɪt, -ˌgeɪt) **3** a sum or assemblage of many separate units **4** *geol* a rock, such as granite, consisting of a mixture of minerals **5** the sand and stone mixed with cement and water to make concrete **6 in the aggregate** taken as a whole ▷ *vb* (ˈægrɪˌgeɪt) **7** to combine or be combined into a body, etc **8** (*tr*) to amount to (a number) [c16 from L *aggregāre* to add to a flock or herd, from *grex* flock] > **ˌaggreˈgation** *n* > **aggregative** (ˈægrɪˌgeɪtɪv) *adj*

aggregator (ˈægrɪˌgeɪtə) *n* **1** a business organization that collates the details of an individual's financial affairs so that the information can be presented on a single website **2** a firm that brings together a large group of consumers on whose behalf it negotiates reduced rates for good or services, esp in the energy sector

aggress (əˈgrɛs) *vb* (*intr*) to attack first or begin a quarrel [c16 from Med. L *aggressāre*, from L *aggredī* to attack] > **aggressor** (əˈgrɛsə) *n*

aggression (əˈgrɛʃən) *n* **1** an attack or harmful action, esp an unprovoked attack by one country against another **2** any offensive activity, practice, etc **3** *psychol* a hostile or destructive mental attitude [C17 from L *aggression-*, from *aggredi* to attack]

aggressive (ə'grɛsɪv) *adj* **1** quarrelsome or belligerent **2** assertive; vigorous > **ag'gressively** *adv* > **ag'gressiveness** *n*

aggressive accountancy *n euphemistic* dishonest or deliberately misleading accounting practices

aggrieve (ə'gri:v) *vb* **aggrieves, aggrieving, aggrieved** (*tr*) **1** (*often impersonal or passive*) to grieve; distress; afflict **2** to injure unjustly, esp by infringing a person's legal rights [C14 *agreven*, via OF from L *aggravāre* to AGGRAVATE]

aggrieved (ə'gri:vd) *adj* feeling resentment at having been treated unjustly > **aggrievedly** (ə'gri:vɪdlɪ) *adv*

aggro ('ægrəʊ) *n Brit sl* aggressive behaviour [C20 from AGGRAVATION]

aghast (ə'gɑ:st) *adj* (*postpositive*) overcome with amazement or horror [C13 *agast*, from OE *gæstan* to frighten]

agile ('ædʒaɪl) *adj* **1** quick in movement; nimble **2** mentally quick or acute [C15 from L *agilis*, from *agere* to do, act] > **'agilely** *adv* > **agility** (ə'dʒɪlɪtɪ) *n*

agin (ə'gɪn) *prep inf or dialect* against [C19 from obs. *again* AGAINST]

Agincourt ('ædʒɪn,kɔ:t; *French* aʒɛ̃kur) *n* a battle fought in 1415 near the village of Azincourt, N France: a decisive victory for English longbowmen under Henry V over French forces vastly superior in number

agio ('ædʒɪəʊ) *n, pl* **agios a** the difference between the nominal and actual values of a currency **b** the charge payable for conversion of the less valuable currency [C17 from It., lit.: ease]

agitate ('ædʒɪ,teɪt) *vb* **agitates, agitating, agitated 1** (*tr*) to excite, disturb, or trouble (a person, the mind or feelings) **2** (*tr*) to shake, stir, or disturb **3** (*intr*; often foll by *for* or *against*) to attempt to stir up public opinion for or against something [C16 from L *agitātus*, from *agitāre* to set into motion, from *agere* to act] > **'agi,tated** *adj* > **'agi,tatedly** *adv* > **,agi'tation** *n*

agitato (,ædʒɪ'tɑ:təʊ) *adj, adv music* (to be performed) in an agitated manner

agitator ('ædʒɪ,teɪtə) *n* **1** a person who agitates for or against a cause, etc **2** a device for mixing or shaking

agitprop ('ædʒɪt,prɒp) *n* **a** any promotion, as in the arts, of political propaganda, esp of a Communist nature **b** (*as modifier*): *agitprop theatre* [C20 short for Russian *Agitpropbyuro*]

Aglaia (ə'glaɪə) *n Greek myth* one of the three Graces [Gk: splendour, from *aglaos* splendid]

agleam (ə'gli:m) *adj* (*postpositive*) glowing; gleaming

aglet ('æglɪt) *or* **aiglet** *n* **1** a metal sheath or tag at the end of a shoelace, ribbon, etc **2** a variant spelling of **aiguillette** [C15 from OF *aiguillette* a small needle]

agley (ə'gleɪ, ə'gli:, ə'glaɪ) *or* **aglee** (ə'gli:) *adv, adj Scot.* awry; askew [from *gley* squint]

aglitter (ə'glɪtə) *adj* (*postpositive*) sparkling; glittering

aglow (ə'gləʊ) *adj* (*postpositive*) glowing

aglu *or* **agloo** ('æglu:) *n Canad* a breathing hole made in ice by a seal [C19 from Inuktitut]

AGM *abbrev for* annual general meeting

agnail ('æg,neɪl) *n* another name for **hangnail**

agnate ('ægneɪt) *adj* **1** related by descent from a common male ancestor **2** related in any way ▷ *n* **3** a male or female descendant by male links from a common male ancestor [C16 from L *agnātus* born in addition, from *agnāscī*, from *ad-* in addition + *gnāscī* to be born]

Agnes ('ægnɪs) *n* **Saint** ?292–?304 AD, Christian child martyr under Diocletian. Feast day: Jan. 21

Agnesi (*Italian* aɲ'ɲezi) *n* **Maria Gaetana** 1718–99, Italian mathematician and philosopher, noted for her work on differential calculus. See **witch of Agnesi**

Agni ('ʌgnɪ) *n Hinduism* the god of fire, one of the three chief deities of the Vedas [Sansk.: fire]

agnostic (æg'nɒstɪk) *n* **1** a person who holds that knowledge of a Supreme Being, ultimate cause, etc, is impossible ▷ Cf **atheist, theist 2** a person who claims, with respect to any particular question, that the answer cannot be known with certainty ▷ *adj* **3** of or relating to agnostics [C19 coined 1869 by T. H. Huxley from A-[1] + GNOSTIC] > **ag'nosti,cism** *n*

Agnus Dei ('ægnʊs 'deɪɪ) *n* **1** the figure of a lamb bearing a cross or banner, emblematic of Christ **2** a chant beginning with these words or a translation of them, forming part of the Roman Catholic Mass [L: Lamb of God]

ago (ə'gəʊ) *adv* in the past: *five years ago; long ago* [C14 *ago*, from OE *āgān* to pass away]

> USAGE The use of *ago* with *since*, as in *it's ten years ago since he wrote that novel*, is redundant. It should be replaced in writing by *it's ten years since he wrote that novel*, or *it's ten years ago that he wrote that novel*

agog (ə'gɒg) *adj* (*postpositive*) eager or curious [C15 ?from OF *en gogues* in merriments]

-agogue *or esp US* **-agog** *n combining form* indicating a person or thing that leads or incites to action: *demagogue* [via LL from Gk *agōgos*, from *agein* to lead] > **-agogic** *adj combining form* > **-agogy** *n combining form*

agonic (ə'gɒnɪk) *adj* forming no angle [C19 from Gk *agōnos*, from A-[1] + *gōnia* angle]

agonic line *n* an imaginary line on the surface of the earth connecting points of zero magnetic declination

agonize *or* **agonise** ('ægə,naɪz) *vb* **agonizes, agonizing, agonized** *or* **agonises, agonising, agonised 1** to suffer or cause to suffer agony **2** (*intr*) to struggle; strive [C16 via Med. L from Gk *agōnizesthai* to contend for a prize, from *agōn* contest] > **'ago,nizingly** *or* **'ago,nisingly** *adv*

agony ('ægənɪ) *n, pl* **agonies 1** acute physical or mental pain; anguish **2** the suffering or struggle preceding death [C14 via LL from Gk *agōnia* struggle, from *agōn* contest]

agony aunt *n* (*sometimes cap*) a person who replies to readers' letters in an agony column

agony column *n* **1** a newspaper or magazine feature offering sympathetic advice to readers on their personal problems **2** *inf* a newspaper or magazine column devoted to advertisements relating esp to personal problems

agora ('ægərə) *n, pl* **agorae** (-ri:, -raɪ) *or* **agoras** (*often cap*) **a** the marketplace in Athens, used for popular meetings in ancient Greece **b** the meeting itself [from Gk, from *agorein* to gather]

agoraphobia (,ægərə'fəʊbɪə) *n* a pathological fear of being in public spaces > **,agora'phobic** *adj, n*

agouti (ə'gu:tɪ) *n, pl* **agoutis** *or* **agouties** a rodent of Central and South America and the Caribbean. Agoutis are agile and long-legged, with hooflike claws, and are valued for their meat [C18 via F & Sp. from Guarani]

AGR *abbrev for* advanced gas-cooled reactor

Agra ('ɑ:grə) *n* a city in N India, in W Uttar Pradesh on the Jumna River: a capital of the Mogul empire until 1658; famous for its Mogul architecture, esp the Taj Mahal. Pop: 899 195 (1991)

Agram ('a:gram) *n* the German name for **Zagreb**

agrarian (ə'grɛərɪən) *adj* **1** of or relating to land or its cultivation **2** of or relating to rural or agricultural matters ▷ *n* **3** a person who favours the redistribution of landed property [C16 from L *agrārius*, from *ager* field, land] > **a'grarian,ism** *n*

agree (ə'gri:) *vb* **agrees, agreeing, agreed** (*mainly intr*) **1** (often foll by *with*) to be of the same opinion **2** (*also tr*; when *intr*, often foll by *to*; when *tr*, *takes a clause as object or an infinitive*) to give assent; consent **3** (*also tr*; when *intr*, foll by *on* or *about*; when *tr*, *may take a clause as object*) to come to terms (about) **4** (foll by *with*) to be similar or consistent; harmonize **5** (foll by *with*) to be agreeable or suitable (to one's health, etc) **6** (*tr; takes a clause as object*) to concede: *they agreed that the price was too high* **7** *grammar* to undergo agreement [C14 from OF *agreer*, from *a gre* at will or pleasure]

agreeable (əˈgrɪəbᵊl) *adj* **1** pleasing; pleasant **2** prepared to consent **3** (foll by *to* or *with*) in keeping **4** (foll by *to*) to one's liking > **aˈgreeableness** *n* > **aˈgreeably** *adv*

agreed (əˈgriːd) *adj* **1** determined by common consent: *the agreed price* ▷ *sentence substitute* **2** an expression of consent or agreement

agreement (əˈgriːmənt) *n* **1** the act of agreeing **2** a settlement, esp one that is legally enforceable **3** a contract or document containing such a settlement **4** the state of being of the same opinion **5** the state of being similar or consistent **6** *grammar* the determination of the inflectional form of one word by some grammatical feature, such as number or gender, of another word [C14 from OF]

agribusiness (ˈægrɪˌbɪznɪs) *n* the various businesses that process and distribute farm products [C20 from AGRI(CULTURE) + BUSINESS]

Agricola (əˈgrɪkələ) *n* **Gnaeus Julius** (ˈniːəs ˈdʒuːlɪəs) 40–93 AD, Roman general; governor of Britain who advanced Roman rule north to the Firth of Forth

agriculture (ˈægrɪˌkʌltʃə) *n* the science or occupation of cultivating land and rearing crops and livestock; farming [C17 from L *agricultūra*, from *ager* field, land + *cultūra* CULTURE] > ˌ**agriˈcultural** *adj* > ˌ**agriˈculturist** *or* ˌ**agriˈculturalist** *n*
▷ www.vlib.org/Agriculture.html
▷ www.agnic.org
▷ www.fao.org

Agrigento (*Italian* agriˈdʒɛnto) *n* a town in Italy, in SW Sicily: site of six Greek temples. Pop: 56 372 (1990). Former name (until 1927): **Girgenti** (gɜːˈgɛntɪ)

agrimony (ˈægrɪmənɪ) *n* **1** any of various plants of the rose family, which have compound leaves, long spikes of small yellow flowers, and bristly burlike fruits **2** any of several other plants, such as hemp agrimony [C15 via OF from L, from Gk *argemōnē* poppy]

Agrippa (əˈgrɪpə) *n* **Marcus Vipsanius** (ˈmɑːkəs vɪpˈseɪnɪəs) 63–12 BC, Roman general: chief adviser and later son-in-law of Augustus

Agrippina (ˌægrɪˈpiːnə) *n* **1** called *the Elder*. *c*. 14 BC–33 AD, Roman matron: granddaughter of Augustus, wife of Germanicus, mother of Caligula and Agrippina the Younger **2** called *the Younger*. 15–59 AD, mother of Nero, who put her to death after he became emperor

agri-tourism *n* tourist activity in rural areas as a way of improving the economic viability of small farms and agricultural communities [C20 from AGRI(CULTURE) + TOURISM]

agro- *combining form* denoting fields, soil, or agriculture: *agrobiology* [from Gk *agros* field]

agrobiology (ˌægrəʊbaɪˈɒlədʒɪ) *n* the science of plant growth and nutrition in relation to agriculture

agroforestry (ˌægrəʊˈfɒrɪstrɪ) *n* a method of farming integrating herbaceous and tree crops

agronomics (ˌægrəˈnɒmɪks) *n* (*functioning as sing*) the branch of economics dealing with the distribution, management, and productivity of land > ˌ**agroˈnomic** *adj*

agronomy (əˈgrɒnəmɪ) *n* the science of cultivation of land, soil management, and crop production > **aˈgronomist** *n*

agrostemma (ˌægrəʊˈstɛmə) *n* any cultivated variety of corncockle [NL, from Gk *agros* field + *stemma* wreath]

aground (əˈgraʊnd) *adv, adj* (*postpositive*) on or onto the ground or bottom, as in shallow water

agterskot (ˈaxtəˌskɒt) *n* (in South Africa) the final payment to a farmer for crops ▷ Cf **voorskot** [C20 Afrikaans *agter* after + *skot* shot, payment]

Aguascalientes (*Spanish* aɣwaskaˈljentes) *n* **1** a state in central Mexico. Pop: 943 506 (2000). Area: 5471 sq km (2112 sq miles) **2** a city in central Mexico, capital of Aguascalientes state, about 1900 m (6200 ft) above sea level, with hot springs. Pop: 594 056 (2000 est)

ague (ˈeɪgjuː) *n* **1** a fever with successive stages of fever and chills, esp when caused by malaria **2** a fit of shivering [C14 from OF (*fievre*) *ague* acute fever; see ACUTE] > ˈ**aguish** *adj*

ah (ɑː) *interj* an exclamation expressing pleasure, pain, sympathy, etc, according to the intonation of the speaker

AH (indicating years in the Muslim system of dating, numbered from the Hegira (622 AD)) *abbrev for* anno Hegirae [L]

aha (ɑːˈhɑː) *interj* an exclamation expressing triumph, surprise, etc, according to the intonation of the speaker

Ahab (ˈeɪhæb) *n Old Testament* the king of Israel from approximately 869 to 850 BC and husband of Jezebel: rebuked by Elijah (I Kings 16:29–22:40)

aha moment *n inf* an instant at which the solution to a problem becomes clear

Ahasuerus (əˌhæzjuːˈɪərəs) *n Old Testament* a king of ancient Persia and husband of Esther, generally identified with Xerxes

ahead (əˈhɛd) *adj* **1** (*postpositive*) in front; in advance ▷ *adv* **2** at or in the front; before **3** forwards: *go straight ahead* **4 ahead of 4a** in front of; at a further advanced position than **4b** *stock exchange* in anticipation of: *the share price rose ahead of the annual figures* **5 be ahead** *inf* to have an advantage; be winning **6 get ahead** to attain success

ahem (əˈhɛm) *interj* a clearing of the throat, used to attract attention, express doubt, etc

Ahern (əˈhɜːn) *n* **Bertie** born 1951, Irish politician; leader of the Fianna Fáil party from 1994; prime minister of the Republic of Ireland from 1997

ahimsa (ɑːˈhɪmsɑː) *n* (in Hindu, Buddhist, and Jainist philosophy) the law of reverence for, and nonviolence to, every form of life [Sansk., from *a* without + *himsā* injury]

Ahithophel (əˈhɪθəˌfɛl) *or* **Achitophel** *n Old Testament* a member of David's council, who became one of Absalom's advisers in his rebellion and hanged himself when his advice was overruled (II Samuel 15:12–17:23)

Ahmedabad *or* **Ahmadabad** (ˈɑːmədəˌbɑːd) *n* a city in W India, in Gujarat: famous for its mosque. Pop: 2 872 865 (1991)

Ahmednagar *or* **Ahmadnagar** (ˌɑːmədˈnʌgə) *n* a city in W India, in Maharashtra: formerly one of the kingdoms of Deccan. Pop: 181 015 (1991)

ahoy (əˈhɔɪ) *interj naut* a hail used to call a ship or to attract attention

Ahriman (ˈɑːrɪmən) *n Zoroastrianism* the supreme evil spirit and diabolical opponent of Ormazd

Ahura Mazda (əˈhʊərə ˈmæzdə) *n Zoroastrianism* another name for **Ormazd**

Ahvenanmaa (ˈɑhvɛnɑmmɑː) *n* the Finnish name for the **Åland Islands**

Ahwaz (ɑːˈwɑːz) *or* **Ahvaz** (ɑːˈvɑːz) *n* a town in SW Iran, on the Karun River. Pop: 804 980 (1996)

ai (ˈɑːɪ) *n, pl* **ais** another name for **three-toed sloth** (see **sloth** (sense 1)) [C17 from Port., from Tupi]

AI *abbrev for:* **1** Amnesty International **2** artificial insemination **3** artificial intelligence

aid (eɪd) *vb* **1** to give support to (someone to do something); help or assist **2** (*tr*) to assist financially ▷ *n* **3** assistance; help; support **4** a person, device, etc, that helps or assists **5** *mountaineering* a device such as a piton when used as a direct help in the ascent **6** (in medieval Europe) a feudal payment made to the king or any lord by his vassals on certain occasions such as the knighting of an eldest son [C15 via OF *aidier* from L *adjūtāre*, from *juvāre* to help] > ˈ**aider** *n*

Aid *or* **-aid** *n combining form* denoting a charitable

Aa

organization or function that raises money for a cause: *Band Aid; Ferryaid*

Aidan ('eɪdᵊn) *n* **Saint** died 651 AD, Irish missionary in Northumbria, who founded the monastery at Lindisfarne (635). Feast day: Aug. 31

aide (eɪd) *n* **1** an assistant **2** short for **aide-de-camp**

aide-de-camp *or* **aid-de-camp** ('eɪd də 'kɒŋ) *n, pl* **aides-de-camp** *or* **aids-de-camp** a military officer serving as personal assistant to a senior. Abbrev: **ADC** [C17 from F: camp assistant]

aide-mémoire ('eɪdmɛm'wɑː) *n, pl* **aides-mémoire** ('eɪdzmɛm'wɑː) **1** a note serving as a reminder **2** a summarized diplomatic communication [F, from *aider* to help + *mémoire* memory]

AIDS *or* **Aids** (eɪdz) *n acronym for* acquired immune (*or* immuno-) deficiency syndrome: a condition, caused by a virus, in which the body loses its ability to resist infection. AIDS is transmitted by sexual intercourse, through infected blood and blood products, and through the placenta

▷ www.aids.org

▷ www.amfar.org

AIDS-related complex *n* See **ARC**

AIF (formerly) *abbrev for* Australian Imperial Force

aiglet ('eɪglɪt) *n* a variant of **aglet**

aigrette *or* **aigret** ('eɪgrɛt) *n* **1** a long plume worn on hats or as a headdress, esp one of long egret feathers **2** an ornament in imitation of a plume of feathers [C17 from F; see EGRET]

aiguille (eɪ'gwiːl) *n* **1** a rock mass or peak shaped like a needle **2** an instrument for boring holes in rocks or masonry [C19 F, lit.: needle]

aiguillette (ˌeɪgwɪ'lɛt) *n* **1** an ornamentation worn by certain military officers, consisting of cords with metal tips **2** a variant of **aglet** [C19 F; see AGLET]

AIH *abbrev for* artificial insemination (by) husband

aikido (aɪ'kiːdəʊ) *n* a Japanese system of self-defence employing similar principles to judo, but including blows from the hands and feet [from Japanese, from *ai* to join, receive + *ki* spirit, force + *do* way]

ail (eɪl) *vb* **1** (*tr*) to trouble; afflict **2** (*intr*) to feel unwell [OE *eglan*, from *egle* painful]

ailanthus (eɪ'lænθəs) *n, pl* **ailanthuses** an E Asian deciduous tree having pinnate leaves, small greenish flowers, and winged fruits. Also called: **tree of heaven** [C19 NL, from native name in the Moluccas in the Indian and Pacific Oceans]

aileron ('eɪlərɒn) *n* a flap hinged to the trailing edge of an aircraft wing to provide lateral control [C20 from F, dim. of *aile* wing]

ailing ('eɪlɪŋ) *adj* unwell or unsuccessful, esp over a long period

ailment ('eɪlmənt) *n* a slight but often persistent illness

aim (eɪm) *vb* **1** to point (a weapon, missile, etc) or direct (a blow) at a particular person or object **2** (*tr*) to direct (satire, criticism, etc) at a person, object, etc **3** (*intr;* foll by *at* or an infinitive) to propose or intend **4** (*intr;* often foll by *at* or *for*) to direct one's efforts or strive (towards) ▷ *n* **5** the action of directing something at an object **6** the direction in which something is pointed: *to take aim* **7** the object at which something is aimed **8** intention; purpose [C14 via OF *aesmer* from L *aestimāre* to ESTIMATE]

AIM *abbrev for* (in Britain) Alternative Investment Market

aimless ('eɪmlɪs) *adj* having no purpose or direction > '**aimlessly** *adv* > '**aimlessness** *n*

Ain (*French* ɛ̃) *n* **1** a department in E central France, in Rhône-Alpes region. Capital: Bourg. Pop: 515 270 (1999). Area: 5785 sq km (2256 sq miles) **2** a river in E France, rising in the Jura Mountains and flowing south to the Rhône. Length: 190 km (118 miles)

ain't (eɪnt) *not standard contraction of* am not, is not, are not, have not, *or* has not: *I ain't seen it*

A into G *NZ sl abbrev for* arse into gear (esp in the phrase **get your A into G**)

Aintree ('eɪntrɪ) *n* a suburb of Liverpool, in Merseyside: site of the racecourse over which the Grand National steeplechase has been run since 1839

Ainu ('aɪnuː) *n* **1** (*pl* **Ainus** *or* **Ainu**) a member of the aboriginal people of Japan **2** the language of this people, sometimes tentatively associated with Altaic, still spoken in parts of Hokkaido [Ainu: man]

air (ɛə) *n* **1** the mixture of gases that forms the earth's atmosphere. It consists chiefly of nitrogen, oxygen, argon, and carbon dioxide **2** the space above and around the earth; sky. Related adj: **aerial** **3** breeze; slight wind **4** public expression; utterance **5** a distinctive quality: *an air of mystery* **6** a person's distinctive appearance, manner, or bearing **7** *music* a simple tune for either vocal or instrumental performance **8** transportation in aircraft (esp in **by air**) **9** an archaic word for **breath** (senses 1–3) **10** **in the air** **10a** in circulation; current **10b** unsettled **11** **into thin air** leaving no trace behind **12** **on** (*or* **off**) **the air** (not) in the act of broadcasting or (not) being broadcast on radio or television **13** **take the air** to go out of doors, as for a short walk **14** **up in the air** **14a** uncertain **14b** *inf* agitated or excited **15** (*modifier*) *Astrol.* of or relating to a group of three signs of the zodiac, Gemini, Libra, and Aquarius ▷ *vb* **16** to expose or be exposed to the air so as to cool or freshen **17** to expose or be exposed to warm or heated air so as to dry: *to air linen* **18** (*tr*) to make known publicly: *to air one's opinions* **19** (*intr*) (of a television or radio programme) to be broadcast ▷ See also **airs** [C13 via OF & L from Gk *aēr* the lower atmosphere]

Aïr ('ɑːɪə) *n* a mountainous region of N central Niger, in the Sahara, rising to 1500 m (5000 ft): a former native kingdom. Area: about 77 700 sq km (30 000 sq miles). Also called: **Asben, Azbine**

air bag *n* a safety device in a car, consisting of a bag that inflates automatically in an accident and prevents the passengers from being thrown forwards

air base *n* a centre from which military aircraft operate

air bladder *n* **1** an air-filled sac, lying above the alimentary canal in bony fishes, that regulates buoyancy at different depths by a variation in the pressure of the air **2** any air-filled sac, such as one in seaweeds

airborne ('ɛəˌbɔːn) *adj* **1** conveyed by or through the air **2** (of aircraft) flying; in the air

air brake *n* **1** a brake operated by compressed air, esp in heavy vehicles and trains **2** an articulated flap or small parachute for reducing the speed of an aircraft

airbrick ('ɛəˌbrɪk) *n chiefly Brit* a brick with holes in it, put into the wall of a building for ventilation

airbrush ('ɛəˌbrʌʃ) *n* **1** an atomizer for spraying paint or varnish by means of compressed air ▷ *vb* (*tr*) **2** to paint or varnish (something) by using an airbrush **3** to improve the image of (a person or thing) by concealing defects beneath a bland exterior: *an airbrushed version of the government's record*

airbrush out *vb* (*tr, adverb*) to remove evidence of (someone or something from photographs, books, or history)

air chief marshal *n* a senior officer of the Royal Air Force and certain other air forces, of equivalent rank to admiral in the Royal Navy

air cleaner *n* a filter that prevents dust and other particles from entering the air intake of an internal-combustion engine. Also called: **air filter**

Air Command *n Canad* the Canadian air force

air commodore *n* a senior officer of the Royal Air Force and certain other air forces, of equivalent rank to brigadier in the Army

air conditioning *n* a system or process for controlling the temperature and sometimes the humidity of the air

in a house, etc > 'air-con,dition *vb (tr)* > **air conditioner** *n*
air-cool *vb (tr)* to cool (an engine) by a flow of air ▹ Cf **water-cool**
aircraft ('ɛə,krɑːft) *n, pl* **aircraft** any machine capable of flying by means of buoyancy or aerodynamic forces, such as a glider, helicopter, or aeroplane
▹ www.aerospaceweb.org/aircraft/index.shtml
aircraft carrier *n* a warship with an extensive flat deck for the launch and landing of aircraft
aircraftman ('ɛə,krɑːftmən) *n, pl* **aircraftmen** a serviceman of the most junior rank in the Royal Air Force > '**aircraft,woman** *fem n*
air curtain *n* an air stream across a doorway to exclude draughts, etc
air cushion *n* **1** an inflatable cushion **2** the pocket of air that supports a hovercraft
Airdrie ('ɛədrɪ; *Scot* 'erdrɪ) *n* a town in W central Scotland, in North Lanarkshire, E of Glasgow: manufacturing and pharmaceutical industries. Pop: 36 998 (1991)
airdrop ('ɛə,drɒp) *n* **1** a delivery of supplies, troops, etc, from an aircraft by parachute ▹ *vb* **airdrops, airdropping, airdropped 2** *(tr)* to deliver (supplies, etc) by an airdrop
Aire (ɛə) *n* a river in N England rising in the Pennines and flowing southeast to the Ouse. Length: 112 km (70 miles)
Airedale ('ɛə,deɪl) *n* a large rough-haired tan-coloured breed of terrier with a black saddle-shaped patch covering most of the back. Also called: **Airedale terrier** [C19 from district in Yorkshire]
air engine *n* **1** an engine that uses the expansion of heated air to drive a piston **2** a small engine that uses compressed air to drive a piston
airfield ('ɛə,fiːld) *n* a landing and taking-off area for aircraft
air filter *n* another name for **air cleaner**
airfoil ('ɛə,fɔɪl) *n* the US and Canad name for **aerofoil**
air force *n* **a** the branch of a nation's armed services primarily responsible for air warfare **b** *(as modifier): an air-force base*
airframe ('ɛə,freɪm) *n* the body of an aircraft, excluding its engines
air guitar *n* an imaginary guitar played while miming to rock music
air gun *n* a gun discharged by means of compressed air
airhead ('ɛə,hɛd) *n sl* a stupid or simple-minded person; idiot [C20 from AIR + HEAD]
air hole *n* **1** a hole that allows the passage of air, esp for ventilation **2** a section of open water in a frozen surface
air hostess *n* a stewardess on an airliner
airily ('ɛərɪlɪ) *adv* **1** in a jaunty or high-spirited manner **2** in a light or delicate manner
airiness ('ɛərɪnɪs) *n* **1** the quality or condition of being fresh, light, or breezy **2** gaiety
airing ('ɛərɪŋ) *n* **1a** exposure to air or warmth, as for drying or ventilation **1b** *(as modifier): airing cupboard* **2** an excursion in the open air **3** exposure to public debate
airless ('ɛəlɪs) *adj* **1** lacking fresh air; stuffy or sultry **2** devoid of air > '**airlessness** *n*
air letter *n* another name for **aerogram**
airlift ('ɛə,lɪft) *n* **1** the transportation by air of passengers, troops, cargo, etc, esp when other routes are blocked ▹ *vb* **2** *(tr)* to transport by an airlift
airline ('ɛə,laɪn) *n* **1a** a system or organization that provides scheduled flights for passengers or cargo **1b** *(as modifier): an airline pilot* **2** a hose or tube carrying air under pressure
▹ http://routesinternational.com/air.htm
▹ http://airlines.afriqonline.com
airliner ('ɛə,laɪnə) *n* a large passenger aircraft
▹ www.airliners.net/info
airlock ('ɛə,lɒk) *n* **1** a bubble in a pipe causing an obstruction **2** an airtight chamber with regulated air pressure used to gain access to a space that has air under pressure
airmail ('ɛə,meɪl) *n* **1** the system of conveying mail by aircraft **2** mail conveyed by aircraft ▹ *adj* **3** of or for airmail
airman ('ɛəmən) *n, pl* **airmen** a man who serves in his country's air force > '**air,woman** *fem n*
air marshal *n* **1** a senior Royal Air Force officer of equivalent rank to a vice admiral in the Royal Navy **2** a Royal Australian Air Force officer of the highest rank **3** a Royal New Zealand Air Force officer of the highest rank when chief of defence forces
air mass *n* a large body of air having characteristics of temperature, moisture, and pressure that are approximately uniform horizontally
Air Miles *pl n trademark* points awarded by certain companies to purchasers of flight tickets and some other products that may be used to pay for other flights
air miss *n* a situation in which two aircraft pass very close to one another in the air; near miss
airplane ('ɛə,pleɪn) *n* the US and Canad name for **aeroplane**
airplay ('ɛə,pleɪ) *n* (of recorded music) radio exposure
air pocket *n* a localized region of low air density or a descending air current, causing an aircraft to suffer an abrupt decrease in height
airport ('ɛə,pɔːt) *n* a landing and taking-off area for civil aircraft, usually with runways and aircraft maintenance and passenger facilities
▹ http://routesinternational.com/airports.htm
▹ www.internationalairportguide.com
air power *n* the strength of a nation's air force
air pump *n* a device for pumping air into or out of something
air rage *n* aggressive behaviour by an airline passenger that endangers the safety of the crew or other passengers
air raid *n* **a** an attack by hostile aircraft or missiles **b** *(as modifier): an air-raid shelter*
air-raid warden *n* a member of a civil defence organization responsible for enforcing regulations, etc, during an air attack
air rifle *n* a rifle discharged by compressed air
airs (ɛəz) *pl n* affected manners intended to impress others: *to give oneself airs; put on airs*
air sac *n* any of the membranous air-filled extensions of the lungs of birds, which increase the efficiency of respiration
airscrew ('ɛə,skruː) *n Brit* an aircraft propeller
air-sea rescue *n* an air rescue at sea
air shaft *n* a shaft for ventilation, esp in a mine or tunnel
airship ('ɛə,ʃɪp) *n* a lighter-than-air self-propelled craft. Also called: **dirigible**
▹ http://spot.colorado.edu/~dziadeck/airship.html
airshow ('ɛə,ʃəʊ) *n* an occasion when an air base is open to the public and a flying display and, usually, static exhibitions are held
airsick ('ɛə,sɪk) *adj* nauseated from travelling in an aircraft
airside ('ɛə,saɪd) *n* the part of an airport nearest the aircraft, the boundary of which is the security check, customs, passport control, etc Cf **landside** (sense 1)
airspace ('ɛə,speɪs) *n* the atmosphere above the earth or part of the earth, esp the atmosphere above a particular country
airspeed ('ɛə,spiːd) *n* the speed of an aircraft relative to the air in which it moves
airstrip ('ɛə,strɪp) *n* a cleared area for the landing and taking-off of aircraft; runway. Also called: **landing strip**
air terminal *n Brit* a building in a city from which air passengers are taken to an airport

airtight (ˈɛəˌtaɪt) *adj* 1 not permitting the passage of air 2 having no weak points; rigid or unassailable
air-to-air *adj* operating between aircraft in flight
air-traffic control *n* an organization that determines the altitude, speed, and direction at which planes fly in a given area, giving instructions to pilots by radio
> **air-traffic controller** *n*
airtsy-mairtsy (ˈɛətsɪˈmɛətsɪ) *adj Midlands English dialect* affected; effeminate
air vice-marshal *n* 1 a senior Royal Air Force officer of equivalent rank to a rear admiral in the Royal Navy 2 a Royal Australian Air Force officer of the second highest rank 3 a Royal New Zealand Air Force officer of the highest rank
airwaves (ˈɛəˌweɪvz) *pl n inf* radio waves used in radio and television broadcasting
airway (ˈɛəˌweɪ) *n* 1 an air route, esp one that is fully equipped with navigational aids, etc 2 a passage for ventilation, esp in a mine 3 a passage down which air travels from the nose or mouth to the lungs 4 *med* a tubelike device inserted via the throat to keep open the airway of an unconscious patient
air waybill *n* a document made out by the consigner of goods by air freight giving details of the goods and the name of the consignee
airworthy (ˈɛəˌwɜːðɪ) *adj* (of an aircraft) safe to fly
airy (ˈɛərɪ) *adj* **airier, airiest** 1 abounding in fresh air 2 spacious or uncluttered 3 nonchalant 4 visionary; fanciful: *airy promises* 5 of or relating to air 6 weightless and insubstantial 7 light and graceful in movement 8 high up in the air
AIS *abbrev for* Australian Institute of Sport
Aisha *or* **Ayesha** (ˈɑːiːʃɑː) *n* ?613–678 AD, the favourite wife of Mohammed.
aisle (aɪl) *n* 1 a passageway separating seating areas in a theatre, church, etc 2 a lateral division in a church flanking the nave or chancel [C14 *ele* (later *aile, aisle*, through confusion with *isle*), via OF from L *āla* wing]
> **aisled** *adj*
Aisne (eɪn; *French* ɛn) *n* 1 a department of NE France, in Picardy region. Capital: Laon. Pop: 535 842 (1999). Area: 7428 sq km (2897 sq miles) 2 a river in N France, rising in the Argonne Forest and flowing northwest and west to the River Oise: scene of a major Allied offensive in 1918 which turned the tide finally against Germany in World War I. Length: 282 km (175 miles)
ait (eɪt) *or* **eyot** *n dialect* an islet, esp in a river [OE *ȳgett* small island, from *ieg* ISLAND]
aitch (eɪtʃ) *n* the letter *h* or the sound represented by it [C16 a phonetic spelling]
aitchbone (ˈeɪtʃˌbəʊn) *n* 1 the rump bone in cattle 2 a cut of beef from or including the rump bone [C15 *hach-boon*, altered from earlier *nache-bone* (*a nache* mistaken for *an ache, an aitch*); *nache* buttock, via OF from LL *natica*, from L *natis* buttock]
Aitken (ˈeɪtkɪn) *n* 1 **Robert Grant** 1864–1951, US astronomer who discovered over three thousand double stars 2 **William Maxwell** See **Beaverbrook**
Aix-en-Provence (*French* ɛksɑ̃prɔvɑ̃s) *n* a city and spa in SE France: the medieval capital of Provence. Pop: 134 222 (1999). Also called: **Aix**
Aix-la-Chapelle (*French* ɛkslaʃapɛl) *n* the French name for **Aachen**
Aix-les-Bains (*French* ɛksləbɛ̃) *n* a town in E France: a resort with sulphurous springs. Pop: 24 830 (1990)
Aíyina (ˈɛjina) *n* transliteration of the Modern Greek name for **Aegina**
Ajaccio (əˈdʒætsɪˌəʊ, -ˈdʒeɪ-) *n* the capital of Corsica, a port on the W coast. Pop: 55 279 (1990 est)
ajar (əˈdʒɑː) *adj (postpositive), adv* (esp of a door) slightly open [C18 altered form of obs. *on char*, lit.: on the turn; from OE *cierran* to turn]
Ajax (ˈeɪdʒæks) *n Greek myth* 1 the son of Telamon; a Greek hero of the Trojan War who killed himself in vexation when Achilles' armour was given to Odysseus 2 called *Ajax the Lesser*, a Locrian king, a swift-footed Greek hero of the Trojan War
Ajmer (ʌdʒˈmɪə) *n* a city in NW India, in Rajasthan: textile centre. Pop: 402 700 (1991)
AK *abbrev for:* 1 Alaska 2 Knight of the Order of Australia
AK-47 *n trademark* a type of Kalashnikov
a.k.a. *or* **AKA** *abbrev for:* also known as
Akabusi (ækəˈbuːsɪ) *n* **Kriss** born 1959, British athlete; won gold medals in the 400 m hurdles in the Commonwealth Games (1990) and European Games (1990)
Akbar (ˈækbɑː) *n* called *Akbar the Great*. 1542–1605, Mogul emperor of India (1556–1605), who extended the Mogul empire to include N India
akene (əˈkiːn) *n* a variant spelling of **achene**
Akhaïa (aˈxaːja) *n* transliteration of the modern Greek name for **Achaea**
Akhenaten *or* **Akhenaton** (ˌækəˈnɑːtᵊn) *n* original name *Amenhotep IV*. died ?1358 BC, king of Egypt, of the 18th dynasty; he moved his capital from Thebes to Tell El Amarna and introduced the cult of Aten
Akhmatova (*Russian* axˈmatəvə) *n* **Anna** (ˈannə) pseudonym of *Anna Gorenko* 1889–1966, Russian poet: noted for her concise and intensely personal lyrics
Akihito (ˌækɪˈhiːtəʊ) *n* born 1933, Emperor of Japan from 1989
akimbo (əˈkɪmbəʊ) *adj, adv* (**with**) **arms akimbo** with hands on hips and elbows out [C15 *in kenebowe*, lit.: in keen bow, that is, in a sharp curve]
akin (əˈkɪn) *adj (postpositive)* 1 related by blood 2 (often foll by *to*) having similar characteristics, properties, etc
Akkad (ˈækæd) *n* 1 a city on the Euphrates in N Babylonia, the centre of a major empire and civilization (2360–2180 BC). Ancient name: **Agade** (əˈgɑːdɪ, əˈgeɪdɪ) 2 an ancient region lying north of Babylon, from which the Akkadian language and culture is named
Akkadian *or* **Accadian** (əˈkædɪən) *n* 1 a member of an ancient Semitic people who lived in Mesopotamia in the third millennium BC 2 the extinct language of this people
Akkerman (*Russian* akɪrˈman) *n* the former name (until 1946) of **Byelgorod-Dnestrovski**
Akmola *or* **Aqmola** (ækˈməʊlə; *Kazakh* ɑkmɔˈlɑ) *n* the former name (1994–98) of **Astana**
Aktyubinsk (*Russian* akˈtjubinsk) *n* the former name (until 1991) of **Aqtöbe**
Akure (əˈkuːre) *n* a city in SW Nigeria, capital of Ondo state: agricultural trade centre. Pop: 162 300 (1996 est)
Al *the chemical symbol for* aluminium
AL *abbrev for:* 1 Alabama 2 Anglo-Latin 3 (in the US and Canada) American League (of baseball teams) 4 international car registration for Albania
-al¹ *suffix forming adjectives* of; related to: *functional; sectional; tonal* [from L *-ālis*]
-al² *suffix forming nouns* the act or process of doing what is indicated by the verb stem: *renewal* [via OF *-aille, -ail*, from L *-ālia*, neuter pl used as substantive, from *-ālis* -AL¹]
-al³ *suffix forming nouns* 1 (*not used systematically*) indicating any aldehyde: *ethanal* 2 indicating a pharmaceutical product: *phenobarbital* [shortened from ALDEHYDE]
ala (ˈeɪlə) *n, pl* **alae** (ˈeɪliː) 1 *zool* a wing or flat winglike process or structure 2 *bot* a winglike part, such as one of the wings of a sycamore seed [C18 from L *āla* a wing]
à la (ɑː lɑː) *prep* 1 in the manner or style of 2 as prepared in (a particular place) or by or for (a particular person) [C17 from F, short for *à la mode de* in the style of]
Ala. *abbrev for* Alabama
Alabama (ˌæləˈbæmə) *n* 1 a state of the southeastern US, on the Gulf of Mexico: consists of coastal and W lowlands crossed by the Tombigbee, Black Warrior, and Alabama Rivers, with parts of the Tennessee Valley and

Cumberland Plateau in the north; noted for producing cotton and white marble. Capital: Montgomery. Pop: 4 447 100 (2000). Area: 131 333 sq km (50 708 sq miles). Abbreviations: **Ala.** *or* (with zip code) **AL** **2** a river in Alabama, flowing southwest to the Mobile and Tensaw Rivers. Length: 507 km (315 miles) > ˌ**Ala'bamian** *adj*

alabaster ('æləˌbɑːstə) *n* **1** a fine-grained usually white, opaque, or translucent variety of gypsum **2** a variety of hard semitranslucent calcite ▷ *adj* **3** of or resembling alabaster [c14 from OF *alabastre*, from L *alabaster*, from Gk *alabastros*] > ˌ**ala'bastrine** *adj*

à la carte (ɑː lɑː 'kɑːt) *adj, adv* (of a menu) having dishes listed separately and individually priced ▷ Cf **table d'hôte** [c19 from F, lit.: according to the card]

alack (ə'læk) *or* **alackaday** (ə'lækəˌdeɪ) *interj* an archaic or poetic word for **alas** [c15 from *a* ah! + *lack* loss, LACK]

alacrity (ə'lækrɪtɪ) *n* liveliness or briskness [c15 from L, from *alacer* lively]

Ala Dağ *or* **Ala Dagh** (*Turkish* ɑ'lɑ dɑː) *n* **1** the E part of the Taurus Mountains, in SE Turkey, rising over 3600 m (12 000 ft) **2** a mountain range in E Turkey, rising over 3300 m (11 000 ft) **3** a mountain range in NE Turkey, rising over 3000 m (10 000 ft)

Alagez *or* **Alagöz** (ɑlɑ'gœz) *n* the Turkish name for (Mount) **Aragats**

Alagna (ə'lænja) *n* **Roberto** born 1963, Italian opera singer, born in France; a lyric tenor, he is married to the soprano Angela Gheorghiu

Alagoas (*Portuguese* ala'goːaʃ) *n* a state in NE Brazil, on the Atlantic coast. Capital: Maceió. Pop: 2 817 903 (2000). Area: 30 776 sq km (11 031 sq miles)

Alai (ɑː'laɪ) *n* a mountain range in central Asia, in SW Kyrgyzstan, running from the Tian Shan range in China into Tajikistan. Average height: 4800 m (16 000 ft), rising over 5850 m (19 500 ft)

Alain-Fournier (*French* alɛ̃furnje) *n* real name *Henri-Alban Fournier* 1886–1914, French novelist; author of *Le Grand Meaulnes* (1913; translated as *The Lost Domain*, 1959)

Alamein ('æləˌmeɪn) *n* See **El Alamein**

Alamo ('æləˌməʊ) *n* **the** a mission in San Antonio, Texas, the site of a siege and massacre in 1836 by Mexican forces under Santa Anna of a handful of American rebels fighting for Texan independence from Mexico

à la mode (ɑː lɑː 'məʊd) *adj* **1** fashionable in style, design, etc **2** (of meats) braised with vegetables in wine [c17 from F: according to the fashion]

Alanbrooke ('ælənˌbrʊk) *n* **Alan Francis Brooke**, 1st Viscount. 1883–1963, British field marshal; chief of Imperial General Staff (1941–46)

Åland Islands ('ɑːlənd, 'ɔːlənd; *Swedish* 'oːland) *pl n* a group of over 6000 islands under Finnish administration, in the Gulf of Bothnia. Capital: Mariehamn. Pop: 24 847 (1992). Finnish name: **Ahvenanmaa**

Al-Anon ('æləˌnɒn) *n* an association for the families and friends of alcoholics to give mutual support

alar ('eɪlə) *adj* relating to, resembling, or having wings or alae [c19 from L *āla* a wing]

Alar ('eɪlɑː) *n* *trademark* a chemical sprayed on cultivated apple trees in certain countries to increase fruit set; daminozide

Alarcón (*Spanish* alar'kon) *n* **Pedro Antonio de** ('peðro an'tonjo de) 1833–91, Spanish novelist and short-story writer, noted for his humorous sketches of rural life, esp in *The Three-Cornered Hat* (1874)

Alaric ('ælərɪk) *n* ?370–410 AD, king of the Visigoths, who served under the Roman emperor Theodosius I but later invaded Greece and Italy, capturing Rome in 410

alarm (ə'lɑːm) *vb* (*tr*) **1** to fill with apprehension, anxiety, or fear **2** to warn about danger; alert **3** to fit or activate a burglar alarm on (a house, car, etc) ▷ *n* **4** fear or terror aroused by awareness of danger **5** apprehension or uneasiness **6** a noise, signal, etc, warning of danger **7** any device that transmits such a warning: *a burglar alarm* **8a** the device in an alarm clock that triggers off the bell or buzzer **8b** short for **alarm clock** **9** *arch* a call to arms [c14 from OF *alarme*, from OIt. *all'arme* to arms; see ARM²] > **a'larming** *adj*

alarm clock *n* a clock with a mechanism that sounds at a set time: used esp for waking a person up

alarmist (ə'lɑːmɪst) *n* **1** a person who alarms or attempts to alarm others needlessly **2** a person who is easily alarmed ▷ *adj* **3** characteristic of an alarmist

alarum (ə'lærəm, -'lɑːr-) *n* **1** *arch* an alarm, esp a call to arms **2** (used as a stage direction, esp in Elizabethan drama) a loud disturbance or conflict (esp in **alarums and excursions**) [c15 var. of ALARM]

alas (ə'læs) *sentence connector* **1** unfortunately; regrettably: *there were, alas, none left* ▷ *interj* **2** *arch* an exclamation of grief or alarm [c13 from OF *ha las!* oh wretched!; *las* from L *lassus* weary]

Alas. *abbrev for* Alaska

Alaska (ə'læskə) *n* **1** the largest state of the US, in the extreme northwest of North America: the aboriginal inhabitants are Inuit; the earliest White settlements were made by the Russians; it was purchased by the US from Russia in 1867. It is mostly mountainous and volcanic, rising over 6000 m (20 000 ft), with the Yukon basin in the central region; large areas are covered by tundra; it has important mineral resources (chiefly coal, oil, and natural gas). Capital: Juneau. Pop: 626 932 (2000). Area: 1 530 694 sq km (591 004 sq miles). Abbreviations: **Alas.** *or* (with zip code) **AK** **2** **Gulf of** the N part of the Pacific, between the Alaska Peninsula and the Alexander Archipelago > **A'laskan** *adj, n*

Alaska Highway *n* a road extending from Dawson Creek, British Columbia, to Fairbanks, Alaska: built by the US Army (1942). Length: 2452 km (1523 miles). Originally called: **Alcan Highway**

Alaska Peninsula *n* an extension of the mainland of SW Alaska between the Pacific and the Bering Sea, ending in the Aleutian Islands. Length: about 644 km (400 miles)

Alaska Range *n* a mountain range in S central Alaska. Highest peak: Mount McKinley, 6194 m (20 320 ft)

alate ('eɪleɪt) *adj* having wings or winglike extensions [c17 from L, from *āla* wing]

alb (ælb) *n* *Christianity* a long white linen vestment with sleeves worn by priests and others [OE *albe*, from Med. L *alba* (*vestis*) white (clothing)]

Alb. *abbrev for* Albania(n)

Alba (*Spanish* 'alβa) *n* See (Duke of) **Alva**

albacore ('ælbəˌkɔː) *n* a tunny found mainly in warm regions of the Atlantic and Pacific. It has very long pectoral fins and is a valued food fish [c16 from Port., from Ar.]

Alba Longa ('ælbə 'lɒŋgə) *n* a city of ancient Latium, southeast of modern Rome: the legendary birthplace of Romulus and Remus

Alban ('ɔːlbən) *n* **Saint** 3rd century AD, the first English martyr. He was beheaded by the Romans on the site on which St Alban's Abbey now stands, for admitting his conversion to Christianity. Feast day: June 17

Albania (æl'beɪnɪə) *n* a republic in SE Europe, on the Balkan Peninsula: became independent in 1912 after more than four centuries of Turkish rule; established as a republic (1946) under Communist rule; multiparty constitution adopted in 1991. It is generally mountainous, rising over 2700 m (9000 ft), with extensive forests. Language: Albanian. Religion: Muslim majority. Currency: lek. Capital: Tirana. Pop: 3 091 000 (2001 est). Area: 28 749 sq km (11 100 sq miles) ▷ www.instat.gov.al

Albany ('ɔːlbənɪ) *n* **1** a city in E New York State, on the Hudson River: the state capital. Pop: 195 658 (2000) **2** a river in central Canada, flowing east and northeast to

Aa

James Bay. Length: 982 km (610 miles)

albatross ('ælbə,trɒs) *n* **1** a large bird of cool southern oceans, with long narrow wings and a powerful gliding flight. See also **wandering albatross** **2** a constant and inescapable burden or handicap **3** *golf* a score of three strokes under par for a hole [c17 from Port. *alcatraz* pelican, from Ar., from *al* the + *ghattās* white-tailed sea eagle; infl. by L *albus* white: c20 in sense 2, from Coleridge's poem *The Rime of the Ancient Mariner* (1798)]

albedo (æl'bi:dəʊ) *n* the ratio of the intensity of light reflected from an object, such as a planet, to that of the light it receives from the sun [c19 from Church L: whiteness, from L *albus* white]

Albee ('ɔ:lbi:) *n* **Edward** born 1928, US dramatist. His plays include *Who's Afraid of Virginia Woolf?* (1962), *Seascape* (1975), *Marriage Play* (1986), *Three Tall Women* (1990), and *Goat* (2004)

albeit (ɔ:l'bi:ɪt) *conj* even though [c14 *al be it*, that is, although it be (that)]

Albemarle Sound ('ælbə,mɑ:l) *n* an inlet of the Atlantic in NE North Carolina. Length: about 96 km (60 miles)

Alberich (*German* 'albərɪç) *n* (in medieval German legend) the king of the dwarfs and guardian of the treasures of the Nibelungs

Albers ('ælbəz) *n* **Josef** 1888–1976, US painter, designer, and poet, born in Germany. His works include a series of abstract paintings entitled *Homage to the Square*

albert ('ælbət) *n* a kind of watch chain usually attached to a waistcoat [c19 after Prince ALBERT, who was presented with one by the jewellers of Birmingham in 1845]

Albert[1] ('ælbət) *n* **Lake** a lake in E Africa, between the Democratic Republic of Congo (formerly Zaïre) and Uganda in the great Rift Valley, 660 m (2200 ft) above sea level: a source of the Nile, fed by the Victoria Nile, which leaves as the Albert Nile. Area: 5345 sq.km (2064 sq miles). Former name: **Lake Mobutu**

Albert[2] ('ælbət) *n* **Prince** full name *Albert Francis Charles Augustus Emmanuel of Saxe-Coburg-Gotha* 1819–61, Prince Consort of Queen Victoria of Great Britain and Ireland

Albert I *n* **1** *c.* 1255–1308, king of Germany (1298–1308) **2** 1875–1934, king of the Belgians (1909–34) **3** called *Albert the Bear c.* 1100–70, German military leader: first margrave of Brandenburg

Alberta (æl'bɜ:tə) *n* a province of W Canada: mostly prairie, with the Rocky Mountains in the southwest. Capital: Edmonton. Pop: 3 064 200 (2001 est). Area: 661 188 sq km (255 285 sq miles). Abbreviations: **Alta, AB**
> **Al'bertan** *adj, n*
▷ www.gov.ab.ca
▷ www.discoveralberta.com

Alberta clipper *n meteorol* (in Canada) an area of low pressure that forms in winter near the Rocky Mountains

Albert Edward *n* a mountain in SE New Guinea, in the Owen Stanley Range. Height: 3993 m (13 100 ft)

Alberti (*Italian* al'bɛrti) *n* **Leon Battista** (le'ɔn bat'tista) 1404–72, Italian Renaissance architect, painter, writer, and musician; among his architectural designs are the façades of Sta. Maria Novella at Florence and S. Francesco at Rimini

Albertus Magnus (æl'bɜ:təs 'mægnəs) *n* **Saint** original name *Albert, Count von Böllstadt*. ?1193–1280, German scholastic philosopher; teacher of Thomas Aquinas and commentator on Aristotle. Feast day: Nov. 15

albescent (æl'bɛsᵊnt) *adj* shading into or becoming white [c19 from L *albēscere*, from *albus* white]
> **al'bescence** *n*

Albi (*French* albi) *n* a town in S France: connected with the Albigensian heresy and the crusade against it. Pop: 48 700 (1990)

Albigenses (,ælbɪ'dʒɛnsi:z) *pl n* members of a Manichean sect that flourished in S France from the 11th to the 13th century [from Med. L: inhabitants of ALBI] > ,**Albi'gensian** *adj* > ,**Albi'gensian,ism** *n*

albino (æl'bi:nəʊ) *n, pl* **albinos** **1** a person with congenital absence of pigmentation in the skin, eyes, and hair **2** any animal or plant that is deficient in pigment [c18 via Port. & Sp. from L *albus* white]
> **albinism** ('ælbɪ,nɪzəm) *n* > **albinotic** (,ælbɪ'nɒtɪk) *adj*

Albinoni (*Italian* albi'no:ni) *n* **Tomaso** (to'ma:zo) 1671–1750, Italian composer and violinist. He wrote concertos and over 50 operas

Albinus (æl'bi:nəs) *n* another name for **Alcuin**

Albion ('ælbɪən) *n arch or poetic* Britain or England [c13 from Latin, of Celtic origin]

albite ('ælbaɪt) *n* a white, bluish-green, or reddish-grey feldspar mineral used in the manufacture of glass and as a gemstone [c19 from L *albus* white]

Ålborg (*Danish* 'ɔlbɔr) *n* a variant spelling of **Aalborg**

album ('ælbəm) *n* **1** a book or binder consisting of blank pages, for keeping photographs, stamps, autographs, etc **2** one or more long-playing CDs, cassettes, or records released as a single item **3** a booklike holder containing sleeves for gramophone records **4** *chiefly Brit* an anthology [c17 from L: blank tablet, from *albus* white]

albumen ('ælbjʊmɪn) *n* **1** the white of an egg; the nutritive substance that surrounds the yolk **2** a variant spelling of **albumin** [c16 from L: white of an egg, from *albus* white]

albumin *or* **albumen** ('ælbjʊmɪn) *n* any of a group of simple water-soluble proteins that are found in blood plasma, egg white, etc [c19 from ALBUMEN + -IN]
> **al'buminous** *adj*

albuminoid (æl'bju:mɪ,nɔɪd) *adj* **1** resembling albumin ▷ *n* **2** another name for **scleroprotein**

albuminuria (æl,bju:mɪ'njʊərɪə) *n* the presence of albumin in the urine. Also called: **proteinuria**

Albuquerque[1] ('ælbə,kɜ:kɪ) *n* a city in central New Mexico, on the Rio Grande. Pop: 448 607 (2000)

Albuquerque[2] ('ælbə,kɜ:kɪ; *Portuguese* ɑlbu'kɛrkə) *n* **Afonso de** (ə'fõsu də:) 1453–1515, Portuguese navigator who established Portuguese colonies in the East by conquering Goa, Ceylon, Malacca, and Ormuz

Albury-Wodonga ('ɔ:bərɪ, -brɪ wə'dɒŋgə) *n* an urban growth centre in SE Australia, in S central New South Wales, on the Murray River: commercial centre of an agricultural region. Pop: 63 610 (1991)

Alcaeus (æl'sɪəs) *n* 7th century BC, Greek lyric poet who wrote hymns, love songs, and political odes

Alcaic (æl'keɪɪk) *adj* **1** of a metre used by Alcaeus, consisting of a strophe of four lines each with four feet ▷ *n* **2** (*usually pl*) verse written in the Alcaic form [c17 from LL *Alcaicus* of ALCAEUS]

alcalde (æl'kældɪ) *or* **alcade** (æl'keɪd) *n* (in Spain and Spanish America) the mayor or chief magistrate in a town [c17 from Sp., from Ar. *al-qāḍī* the judge]

Alcan Highway ('ælkæn) *n* original name of the **Alaska Highway**

Alcatraz ('ælkə,træz) *n* an island in W California, in San Francisco Bay: a federal prison until 1963

alcazar (,ælkə'zɑ:; *Spanish* al'kaθar) *n* any of various palaces or fortresses built in Spain by the Moors [c17 from Sp., from Ar. *al-qasr* the castle]

Alcazar de San Juan ('ælkə,zɑ:; *Spanish* al'kaθar) *n* a town in S central Spain: associated with Cervantes and Don Quixote. Pop: 25 679 (1991)

Alcestis (æl'sɛstɪs) *n Greek myth* the wife of king Admetus of Thessaly. To save his life, she died in his place, but was rescued from Hades by Hercules

alchemist ('ælkəmɪst) *n* a person who practises alchemy

alchemize *or* **alchemise** ('ælkə,maɪz) *vb* **alchemizes, alchemizing, alchemized** *or* **alchemises, alchemising, alchemised** (*tr*) to alter (an element, metal, etc) by alchemy

alchemy ('ælkəmɪ) *n, pl* **alchemies** **1** the pseudoscientific predecessor of chemistry that sought a method of transmuting base metals into gold, and an elixir to prolong life indefinitely **2** a power like that of alchemy: *her beauty had a potent alchemy* [c14 *alkamye*, via OF from Med. L, from Ar., from *al* the + *kīmiyā'* transmutation, from LGk *khēmeia* the art of transmutation] > **alchemic** (æl'kɛmɪk) *or* **al'chemical** *adj*

alcheringa (ˌæltʃə'rɪŋgə) *n* another name for **Dreamtime** [from Abor., lit.: dream time]

Alchevsk (æl'tʃɛvsk) *n* a city in the E Ukraine. Pop: 120 900 (1998 est). Former name (until 1992): **Kommunarsk**

Alcibiades (ˌælsɪ'baɪəˌdiːz) *n* 450–404 BC, Athenian statesman and general in the Peloponnesian War: brilliant, courageous, and unstable, he defected to the Spartans in 415, but returned and led the Athenian victories at Abydos (411) and Cyzicus (410)

Alcides (æl'saɪdiːz) *n* another name for **Hercules** (sense 1)

Alcinoüs (æl'sɪnəʊəs) *n* (in Homer's *Odyssey*) a Phaeacian king at whose court the shipwrecked Odysseus told of his wanderings. See also **Nausicaä**

ALCM *abbrev for* air-launched cruise missile: a type of cruise missile that can be launched from an aircraft

Alcock ('ɔːlkɒk) *n* Sir **John William** 1892–1919, English aviator who with A.W. Brown made the first nonstop flight across the Atlantic (1919)

alcohol ('ælkəˌhɒl) *n* **1** a colourless flammable liquid, the active principle of intoxicating drinks, produced by the fermentation of sugars. Formula: C_2H_5OH. Also called: **ethanol, ethyl alcohol** **2** a drink or drinks containing this substance **3** *chem* any one of a class of organic compounds that contain one or more hydroxyl groups bound to carbon atoms that are not part of an aromatic ring ▷ Cf **phenol** (sense 2) [c16 via NL from Med. L, from Ar. *al-kuhl* powdered antimony]

alcohol-free *adj* **1** (of beer or wine) containing only a trace of alcohol ▷ Cf **low-alcohol** **2** (of a period of time) during which no alcoholic drink is consumed: *there should be one or two alcohol-free days per week*

alcoholic (ˌælkə'hɒlɪk) *n* **1** a person affected by alcoholism ▷ *adj* **2** of, relating to, containing, or resulting from alcohol

▷ www.ias.org.uk

▷ www.alcoholconcern.org.uk

Alcoholics Anonymous *n* an association of alcoholics who try, esp by mutual assistance, to overcome alcoholism

alcoholism ('ælkəhɒˌlɪzəm) *n* a condition in which dependence on alcohol harms a person's health, family life, etc

alcoholize *or* **alcoholise** ('ælkəhɒˌlaɪz) *vb* **alcoholizes, alcoholizing, alcoholized** *or* **alcoholises, alcoholising, alcoholised** (*tr*) to turn into alcoholic drink, as by fermenting or mixing with alcohol > **ˌalcoˌholi'zation** *or* **ˌalcoˌholi'sation** *n*

alcool ('ælkuːl) *n* a form of pure grain spirit distilled in Quebec [alcohol]

alcopop ('ælkəʊˌpɒp) *n inf* an alcoholic drink that tastes like a soft drink [c20 from ALCO(HOL) + POP[1] (sense 11)]

Alcoran *or* **Alkoran** (ˌælkɒ'rɑːn) *n* another name for the **Koran** > **ˌAlco'ranic** *or* **ˌAlko'ranic** *adj*

Alcott ('ɔːlkət) *n* **Louisa May** 1832–88, US novelist, noted for her children's books, esp *Little Women* (1869)

alcove ('ælkəʊv) *n* **1** a recess or niche in the wall of a room, as for a bed, books, etc **2** any recessed usually vaulted area, as in a garden wall **3** any covered or secluded spot [c17 from F, from Sp. *alcoba*, from Ar. *al-qubbah* the vault]

Alcuin ('ælkwɪn) *or* **Albinus** *n* 735–804 AD, English scholar and theologian; friend and adviser of Charlemagne

Aldabra (æl'dæbrə) *n* an island group in the Indian Ocean: part of the British Indian Ocean Territory (1965–76); now administratively part of the Seychelles

Aldan (*Russian* al'dan) *n* a river in E Russia in the SE Sakha Republic, rising in the **Aldan Mountains** and flowing north and west to the Lena River. Length: about 2700 km (1700 miles)

Aldeburgh ('ɔːlbərə) *n* a small resort in SE England, in Suffolk: site of an annual music festival established in 1948 by Benjamin Britten. Pop: 2654 (1991)

aldehyde ('ældɪˌhaɪd) *n* **1** any organic compound containing the group -CHO. Aldehydes are oxidized to carboxylic acids **2** (*modifier*) consisting of, containing, or concerned with the group -CHO [c19 from NL *al(cohol) dehyd(rogenātum)* dehydrogenated alcohol] > **aldehydic** (ˌældə'hɪdɪk) *adj*

al dente (ˌæl 'dɛntɪ) *adj* (of pasta) still firm after cooking [It., lit: to the tooth]

alder ('ɔːldə) *n* **1** a shrub or tree of the birch family, having toothed leaves and conelike fruits. The wood is used for bridges, etc, because it resists underwater rot **2** any of several similar trees or shrubs [OE *alor*]

alderman ('ɔːldəmən) *n, pl* **aldermen** **1** (in England and Wales until 1974) one of the senior members of a local council, elected by other councillors **2** (in the US, Canada, Australia, etc) a member of the governing body of a municipality **3** *history* a variant spelling of **ealdorman** [OE *aldormann*, from *ealdor* chief (comp. of *eald* OLD) + *mann* MAN] > **aldermanic** (ˌɔːldə'mænɪk) *adj*

Aldermaston ('ɔːldəˌmɑːstən) *n* a village in S England, in West Berkshire unitary authority, Berkshire, SW of Reading: site of the Atomic Weapons Research Establishment and starting point of the Aldermaston marches (1958–63), organized by the Campaign for Nuclear Disarmament. Pop: 2157 (1987 est)

Alderney ('ɔːldənɪ) *n* **1** one of the Channel Islands, in the English Channel: separated from the French coast by a dangerous tidal channel (the **Race of Alderney**). Pop: 2147 (1996) Area: 8 sq km (3 sq miles). French name: **Aurigny** **2** an early, but now extinct, breed of dairy cattle originating from the island of Alderney

Aldershot ('ɔːldəʃɒt) *n* a town in S England, in Hampshire: site of a large military camp. Pop: 51 356 (1991)

Aldington ('ɔːldɪŋtən) *n* **Richard** 1892–1962, English poet, novelist, and biographer. His novels include *Death of a Hero* (1929) and *The Colonel's Daughter* (1931), which reflect postwar disillusion following World War I

Aldis lamp ('ɔːldɪs) *n* a portable signalling lamp [c20 after its inventor A.C.W. *Aldis*]

Aldiss ('ɔːldɪs) *n* **Brian W(ilson)** born 1925, British novelist, best known for his science fiction. His works include *Non-Stop* (1958), *Enemies of the System* (1978), *The Helliconia Trilogy* (1983–86), *Forgotten Life* (1988), and *The Detached Retina* (1995)

Aldridge-Brownhills ('ɔːldrɪdʒ'braʊnˌhɪlz) *n* a town in central England, in Walsall unitary authority, West Midlands: formed by the amalgamation of neighbouring towns in 1966. Pop: 37 444 (1991)

aldrin ('ɔːldrɪn) *n* a poisonous crystalline solid, mostly $C_{12}H_8Cl_6$, used as an insecticide [c20 after K. *Alder* (1902–58), G chemist]

Aldrin ('ɔːldrɪn) *n* **Edwin Eugene Jr.**, known as *Buzz*, born 1930, US astronaut; the second man to set foot on the moon on July 20, 1969, during the Apollo 11 flight

Aldus Manutius ('ɔːldəs mə'njuːʃɪəs) *n* 1450–1515, Italian printer, noted for his fine editions of the classics. He introduced italic type

ale (eɪl) *n* **1** a beer fermented in an open vessel using yeasts that rise to the top of the brew. Compare **beer, lager** **2** (formerly) an alcoholic drink made by fermenting a cereal, esp barley, but differing from beer by being unflavoured by hops **3** *chiefly Brit* another word

Aa

for **beer** [OE *alu, ealu*; rel. to ON *öl*]
aleatory (ˈeɪlɪətərɪ) *or* **aleatoric** (ˌeɪlɪəˈtɒrɪk) *adj* **1** dependent on chance **2** (esp of a musical composition) involving elements chosen at random by the performer [c17 from L, from *āleātor* gambler, from *ālea* game of chance]
Alecto (əˈlɛktəʊ) *n Greek myth* one of the three Furies; the others are Megaera and Tisiphone
alee (əˈliː) *adv, adj (postpositive) naut* on or towards the lee: *with the helm alee*
alehouse (ˈeɪlˌhaʊs) *n* **1** *arch* a place where ale was sold; tavern **2** *inf* a pub
Aleichem (ɑːˈleɪçɛm) *n* **Sholom,** real name *Solomon Rabinowitz.* 1859–1916, US Jewish writer, born in Russia. His works include *Tevye the Milkman*, which was adapted for the stage musical *Fiddler on the Roof*
Aleixandre (*Spanish* aleˈsandre) *n* **Vicente** (Viˈθente) 1898–1984, Spanish poet, whose collections include *La destrucción o el amor* (1935; Destruction or Love): Nobel prize for literature 1977
Aleksandropol (*Russian* alɪksanˈdrɔpəlj) *n* the former name (from 1837 until after the Revolution) of **Leninakan**
Aleksandrovsk (*Russian* alɪkˈsandrəfsk) *n* the former name (until 1921) of **Zaporozhye**
Alembert, d' (*French* dalɑ̃bɛr) *n* **Jean Le Rond** (ʒɑ̃ lə rɔ̃) 1717–83, French mathematician, physicist, and rationalist philosopher, noted for his contribution to Newtonian physics in *Traité de dynamique* (1743) and for his collaboration with Diderot in editing the *Encyclopédie*
alembic (əˈlɛmbɪk) *n* **1** an obsolete type of retort used for distillation **2** anything that distils or purifies [c14 from Med. L, from Ar. *al-anbīq* the still, from Gk *ambix* cup]
Alençon (*French* alɑ̃sɔ̃) *n* a town in NW France: early lace-manufacturing centre. Pop: 31 140 (1990)
aleph (ˈɑːlɪf; *Hebrew* ˈalɛf) *n* the first letter in the Hebrew alphabet [Heb.: ox]
aleph-null *or* **aleph-zero** *n* the smallest infinite cardinal number; the cardinal number of the set of positive integers
Aleppo (əˈlɛpəʊ) *n* an ancient city in NW Syria: industrial and commercial centre. Pop: 1 582 930 (1994). French name: **Alep** (alɛp) Arabic name: **Haleb** (ˈhalɛp)
alert (əˈlɜːt) *adj (usually postpositive)* **1** vigilantly attentive: *alert to the problems* **2** brisk, nimble, or lively ▷ *n* **3** an alarm or warning **4** the period during which such a warning remains in effect **5** **on the alert** **5a** on guard against danger, attack, etc **5b** watchful; ready ▷ *vb (tr)* **6** to warn or signal (troops, police, etc) to prepare for action **7** to warn of danger, an attack, etc [c17 from It. *all'erta* on the watch, from *erta* lookout post] > **aˈlertly** *adv* > **aˈlertness** *n*
Alessandria (*Italian* alesˈsandrja) *n* a town in NW Italy, in Piedmont. Pop: 93 866 (1990)
Ålesund *or* **Aalesund** (*Norwegian* ˈoːləsun) *n* a port and market town in W Norway, on an island between Bergen and Trondheim: fishing and sealing fleets. Pop: 35 862 (1990)
aleurone layer (əˈlʊərən) *or* **aleuron layer** (əˈlʊərɒn) *n* the outer protein-rich layer of certain seeds, esp of cereal grains [c19 from Gk *aleuron* flour]
Aleut (æˈluːt) *n* **1** a member of a people inhabiting the Aleutian Islands and SW Alaska, related to the Inuit **2** the language of this people, related to Inuktitut [from Russian *aleút*, prob. of native origin] > **Aleutian** (əˈluːʃən) *n, adj*
Aleutian Islands, *pl n* a chain of over 150 volcanic islands, extending southwestwards from the Alaska Peninsula between the N Pacific and the Bering Sea
A level *n* (in Britain) **1a** a public examination in a subject taken for the General Certificate of Education (**GCE**), usually at the age of 17–18 **1b** the course leading to this examination **1c** *(as modifier)*: *A-level maths* **2** a pass in a particular subject at A level: *she has three A levels*
A2 level *n* (British Education) **a** the second part of an A-level course, taken after the AS level examination **b** the examination at the end of this
alewife (ˈeɪlˌwaɪf) *n, pl* **alewives** a North American fish similar to the herring [c19 ?from F *alose* shad]
Alexander (ˌælɪgˈzɑːndə) *n* **Harold** (**Rupert Leofric George**), Earl Alexander of Tunis. 1891–1969, British field marshal in World War II, who organized the retreat from Dunkirk and commanded in North Africa (1943) and Sicily and Italy (1944–45); governor general of Canada (1946–52); British minister of defence (1952–54)
Alexander I *n* **1** *c.* 1080–1124, king of Scotland (1107–24), son of Malcolm III **2** 1777–1825, tsar of Russia (1801–25), who helped defeat Napoleon and formed the Holy Alliance (1815)
Alexander II *n* **1** 1198–1249, king of Scotland (1214–49), son of William (the Lion) **2** 1818–81, tsar of Russia (1855–81), son of Nicholas I, who emancipated the serfs (1861). He was assassinated by the Nihilists
Alexander III *n* **1** 1241–86, king of Scotland (1249–86), son of Alexander II **2** original name *Orlando Bandinelli.* died 1181, pope (1159–81), who excommunicated Barbarossa **3** 1845–94, tsar of Russia (1881–94), son of Alexander II
Alexander VI *n* original name *Rodrigo Borgia* 1431–1503, pope (1492–1503): noted for his extravagance and immorality as well as for his patronage of the arts; father of Cesare and Lucrezia Borgia, with whom he is said to have committed incest
Alexander Archipelago (ˌælɪgˈzɑːndə) *n* a group of over 1000 islands along the coast of SE Alaska
Alexander I Island *n* an island of Antarctica, west of Palmer Land, in the Bellingshausen Sea. Length: about 378 km (235 miles)
Alexander Nevski (ˈnɛvskɪ, ˈnɛf-; *Russian* ˈnjɛfskij) *n* **Saint** ?1220–63, Russian prince and military leader, who defeated the Swedes at the River Neva (1240) and the Teutonic knights at Lake Peipus (1242)
Alexander technique *n* a technique for developing awareness of one's posture and movement in order to improve it [c20 named after Frederick Matthias *Alexander* (d. 1955), Australian actor who originated it]
Alexander the Great *n* 356–323 BC, king of Macedon, who conquered Greece (336), Egypt (331), and the Persian Empire (328), and founded Alexandria
Alexandra (ˌælɪgˈzɑːndrə) *n* **1** 1844–1925, queen consort of Edward VII of Great Britain and Ireland **2** 1872–1918, the wife of Nicholas II of Russia; her misrule while Nicholas was supreme commander of the Russian forces during World War I precipitated the Russian Revolution
Alexandretta (ˌælɪgzɑːnˈdrɛtə) *n* the former name of **Iskenderun** *n*
Alexandria (ˌælɪgˈzændrɪə, -ˈzɑːn-) *n* the chief port of Egypt, on the Nile Delta: cultural centre of ancient times, founded by Alexander the Great (332 BC). Pop: 3 328 196 (1996). Arabic name: **El Iskandariyah** > ˌ**Alexˈandrian** *adj*,
Alexandrine (ˌælɪgˈzændraɪn) *n* **1** a line of verse having six iambic feet, usually with a caesura after the third foot ▷ *adj* **2** of or written in Alexandrines [c16 from F, from *Alexandre*, 15th-cent. poem in this metre]
alexandrite (ˌælɪgˈzændraɪt) *n* a variety of chrysoberyl used as a gemstone. It appears green in sunlight, but red in artificial light [c19 after ALEXANDER I of Russia; see -ITE[1]]
Alexandroúpolis (*Greek* alɛksanˈðrupɔlis) *n* a port in NE Greece, in W Thrace. Pop: 39 283 (1991 est). Former name (until the end of World War I): **Dedéagach**
alexia (əˈlɛksɪə) *n* a disorder of the central nervous system characterized by impaired ability to read [c19 from NL, from A-[1] + Gk *lexis* speech]
Alexis Mikhailovich (əˈlɛksɪs mɪˈkaɪləˌvɪtʃ) *n* 1629–76,

tsar of Russia (1645–76); father of Peter the Great
alfalfa (æl'fælfə) *n* a leguminous plant of Europe and Asia, widely cultivated for forage. Also called: **lucerne** [c19 from Sp., from Ar. *al-fasfasah*]
al Fayed (æl 'faɪjəd) *n* **Mohamed** born 1933, Egyptian-born businessman; owner of the Harrods department store from 1985 and of the Ritz Hotel, Paris, from 1979: his son **Dodi Fayed** (1956–97) died in the same Paris car crash as Diana, Princess of Wales
Alfonso VI (*Spanish* al'fonso) *n* died 1109, king of Léon (1065–1109) and of Castile (1072–1109). He appointed his vassal, the Spanish hero El Cid, ruler of Valencia
Alfonso XIII (*Spanish* al'fonso) *n* 1886–1941, king of Spain (1886–1931), who was forced to abdicate on the establishment of the republic in 1931
Alfred the Great ('ælfrɪd) *n* 849–99, king of Wessex (871–99) and overlord of England, who defeated the Danes and encouraged learning and writing in English
alfresco (æl'frɛskəʊ) *adj, adv* in the open air [c18 from It.: in the cool]
Alfvén (al'ven) *n* **Hannes Olaf Gösta** ('hannɛs 'u:laf 'jøsta) 1908–95, Swedish physicist, noted for his research on magnetohydrodynamics; shared the Nobel prize for physics in 1970
Alg. *abbrev for* Algeria(n)
algae ('ældʒi:) *pl n, sing* **alga** ('ælgə) unicellular or multicellular organisms formerly classified as plants, occurring in water or moist ground, that have chlorophyll but lack true stems, roots, and leaves [c16 from L, pl of *alga* seaweed, from ?] > **algal** ('ælgəl) *or* **algoid** ('ælgɔɪd) *adj*
Algarve (æl'gɑ:v) *n* **the** an area in the south of Portugal, on the Atlantic; it approximately corresponds to the administrative district of Faro: fishing and tourism important
algebra ('ældʒɪbrə) *n* **1** a branch of mathematics in which arithmetical operations and relationships are generalized by using symbols to represent numbers **2** any abstract calculus, a formal language in which functions and operations can be defined and their properties studied [c14 from Med. L, from Ar. *al-jabr* the bone-setting, mathematical reduction] > **algebraic** (ˌældʒɪ'breɪɪk) *or* ˌ**alge'braical** *adj* > **algebraist** (ˌældʒɪ'breɪɪst) *n*
Algeciras (ˌældʒɪ'sɪrəs; *Spanish* alxe'θiras) *n* a port and resort in SW Spain, on the Strait of Gibraltar: scene of a conference of the Great Powers in 1906. Pop: 101 972 (1998 est)
Algeria (æl'dʒɪərɪə) *n* a republic in NW Africa, on the Mediterranean: became independent in 1962, after more than a century of French rule; one-party constitution adopted in 1976; religious extremists led a campaign of violence from 1988 until 2000; consists chiefly of the N Sahara, with the Atlas Mountains in the north, and contains rich deposits of oil and natural gas. Official language: Arabic; French also widely spoken, and Berber. Religion: Muslim. Currency: dinar. Capital: Algiers. Pop: 30 821 000 (2001 est). Area: about 2 382 800 sq km (920 000 sq miles). French name: **Algérie** (alʒeri) > **Al'gerian** *or* **Algerine** ('ældʒəˌri:n) *adj, n*
▹ www.gouvernement.dz
▹ www.algeria-tourism.org
-algia *n combining form* denoting pain in the part specified: *neuralgia; odontalgia* [from Gk *algos* pain] > **-algic** *adj combining form*
algid ('ældʒɪd) *adj med* chilly or cold [c17 from L *algidus*, from *algēre* to be cold] > **al'gidity** *n*
Algiers (æl'dʒɪəz) *n* the capital of Algeria, an ancient port on the Mediterranean; until 1830 a centre of piracy. Pop: 1 519 570 (1998). Arabic name: **Al-Jezair** (ˌældʒɛ'zɑ:ɪə) French name: **Alger** (alʒe)
alginate ('ældʒɪˌneɪt) *n* a salt or ester of alginic acid
alginic acid (æl'dʒɪnɪk) *n* a white or yellowish powdery substance having hydrophilic properties. Extracted from kelp, it is used mainly in the food and textile industries
Algol ('ælgɒl) *n* a computer-programming language designed for mathematical and scientific purposes [c20 *alg(orithmic) o(riented) l(anguage)*]
algolagnia (ˌælgə'lægnɪə) *n* sexual pleasure got from suffering or inflicting pain [ML, from Gk *algos* pain + *lagneiā* lust]
Algonquian (æl'gɒŋkɪən, -kwɪ-) *or* **Algonkian** *n* **1** a widespread family of North American Indian languages **2** (*pl* **Algonquians** *or* **Algonquian**) a member of any of the North American Indian peoples that speak any of these languages ▹ *adj* **3** denoting or relating to this linguistic family or its speakers
Algonquin (æl'gɒŋkɪn, -kwɪn) *or* **Algonkin** (æl'gɒŋkɪn) *n* **1** (*pl* **Algonquins, Algonquin** *or* **Algonkins, Algonkin**) a member of a North American Indian people formerly living along the St Lawrence and Ottawa Rivers in Canada **2** the language of this people, a dialect of Ojibwa ▹ *n, adj* **3** a variant of **Algonquian** [c17 from Canad F., earlier written as *Algoumequin*; perhaps rel. to Micmac *algoomaking* at the fish-spearing place]
algorism ('ælgəˌrɪzəm) *n* **1** the Arabic or decimal system of counting **2** the skill of computation **3** an algorithm [c13 from OF, from Med. L, from Ar., from the name of abu-Ja'far Mohammed ibn-Mūsa *al-Khuwārizmi*, 9th-cent. Persian mathematician]
algorithm ('ælgəˌrɪðəm) *n* **1** a logical arithmetical or computational procedure that if correctly applied ensures the solution of a problem **2** *logic, maths* a recursive procedure whereby an infinite sequence of terms can be generated ▹ Also called: **algorism** [c17 changed from ALGORISM, infl. by Gk *arithmos* number] > ˌ**algo'rithmic** *adj*
Algren ('ɔ:lgrən) *n* **Nelson** 1909–81, US novelist. His novels, mostly set in Chicago, include *Never Come Morning* (1942) and *The Man with the Golden Arm* (1949)
Alhambra (æl'hæmbrə) *n* a citadel and palace in Granada, Spain, built for the Moorish kings during the 13th and 14th centuries: noted for its rich ornamentation > **Alhambresque** (ˌælhæm'brɛsk) *adj*
Al Hijrah *or* **Al Hijra** (æl 'hɪdʒrə) *n* an annual Muslim festival marking the beginning of the Muslim year. It commemorates Mohammed's move from Mecca to Medina. See also **Hegira** [from Ar. *hijrah* emigration or flight]
Al Hufuf *or* **Al Hofuf** (æl hʊ'fu:f) *n* a town in E Saudi Arabia: a trading centre with nearby oilfields and oases. Pop: 225 847 (1992)
Ali ('ɑ:li:) *n* **1** ?600–661 AD, fourth caliph of Islam (656–61 AD), considered the first caliph by the Shiites: cousin and son-in-law of Mohammed **2** **Mehemet** See **Mehemet Ali** **3** **Muhammad** See **Muhammad Ali**
alias ('eɪlɪəs) *adv* **1** at another time or place known as or named: *Dylan, alias Zimmerman* ▹ *n, pl* **aliases** **2** an assumed name [c16 from L *aliās* (adv) otherwise, from *alius* other]
aliasing ('eɪlɪəsɪŋ) *n radio & TV* the error in a vision or sound signal arising from limitations in the system that generates or processes the signal
alibi ('ælɪˌbaɪ) *n, pl* **alibis** **1** *law* **1a** a defence by an accused person that he or she was elsewhere at the time the crime was committed **1b** the evidence given to prove this **2** *inf* an excuse ▹ *vb* **alibis, alibiing, alibied** **3** (*tr*) to provide with an alibi [c18 from L *alibī* elsewhere, from *alius* other + *-bī* as in *ubī* where]
Alicante (ˌælɪ'kæntɪ) *n* a port in SE Spain: commercial centre. Pop: 272 432 (1998 est)
Alice ('ælɪs) *or* **the Alice** *n Austral sl* short for **Alice Springs**
Alice band *n* an ornamental band worn across the front of the hair to hold it back from the face

Aa

Alice-in-Wonderland *adj* fantastic; irrational [c20 alluding to the absurdities of Wonderland in Lewis Carroll's book]
Alice Springs *n* a town in central Australia, in the Northern Territory, in the Macdonnell Ranges. Pop: 24 852 (1994). Former name (until 1931): **Stuart**
alicyclic (ˌælɪˈsaɪklɪk, -ˈsɪk-) *adj* (of an organic compound) having essentially aliphatic properties, in spite of the presence of a ring of carbon atoms [c19 from ALI(PHATIC) + CYCLIC]
alidade (ˈælɪˌdeɪd) *or* **alidad** (ˈælɪˌdæd) *n* **1** a surveying instrument used for drawing lines of sight on a distant object and taking angular measurements **2** the upper rotatable part of a theodolite [c15 from F, from Med. L, from Ar. *al-ʿidāda* the revolving radius of a circle]
alien (ˈeɪlɪən) *n* **1** a person owing allegiance to a country other than that in which he lives **2** any being or thing foreign to its environment **3** (in science fiction) a being from another world ▷ *adj* **4** unnaturalized; foreign **5** having foreign allegiance: *alien territory* **6** unfamiliar: *an alien quality* **7** (*postpositive*; foll by *to*) repugnant or opposed (to): *war is alien to his philosophy* **8** (in science fiction) of or from another world [c14 from L *aliēnus* foreign, from *alius* other]
alienable (ˈeɪlɪənəbᵊl) *adj law* (of property) transferable to another owner > ˌ**alienaˈbility** *n*
alienate (ˈeɪlɪəˌneɪt) *vb* **alienates, alienating, alienated** (*tr*) **1** to cause (a friend, etc) to become unfriendly or hostile **2** to turn away: *to alienate the affections of a person* **3** *law* to transfer the ownership of (property, etc) to another person > ˌ**alienˈation** *n* > ˈ**alienˌator** *n*
alienee (ˌeɪlɪəˈniː) *n law* a person to whom a transfer of property is made
alienist (ˈeɪlɪənɪst) *n US* a psychiatrist who specializes in the legal aspects of mental illness
alienor (ˈeɪlɪənə) *n law* a person who transfers property to another
aliform (ˈælɪˌfɔːm) *adj* wing-shaped [c19 from NL *āliformis*, from L *āla* a wing]
Aligarh (ˌɑːlɪˈgɜː, ˌælɪ-) *n* a city in N India, in W Uttar Pradesh, with a famous Muslim university (1920). Pop: 480 520 (1991)
alight[1] (əˈlaɪt) *vb* **alights, alighting, alighted** *or* **alit** (*intr*) **1** (usually foll by *from*) to step out (of): *to alight from a taxi* **2** to come to rest; land: *a thrush alighted on the wall* [OE *ālīhtan*, from A-[2] + *līhtan* to make less heavy]
alight[2] (əˈlaɪt) *adj* (*postpositive*), *adv* **1** burning; on fire **2** illuminated [OE, from *ālīhtan* to light up]
align (əˈlaɪn) *vb* **1** to place or become placed in a line **2** to bring (components or parts) into proper coordination or relation **3** (*tr*; usually foll by *with*) to bring (a person, country, etc) into agreement with the policy, etc, of another [c17 from OF, from *à ligne* into line]
alignment (əˈlaɪnmənt) *n* **1** arrangement in a straight line **2** the line or lines formed in this manner **3** alliance with a party, cause, etc **4** proper coordination or relation of components **5** a ground plan of a railway, road, etc
alike (əˈlaɪk) *adj* (*postpositive*) **1** possessing the same or similar characteristics: *they all look alike* ▷ *adv* **2** in the same or a similar manner or degree: *they walk alike* [OE *gelīc*]
aliment (ˈælɪmənt) *n* something that nourishes or sustains the body or mind [c15 from L *alimentum* food, from *alere* to nourish] > ˌ**aliˈmental** *adj*
alimentary (ˌælɪˈmɛntərɪ) *adj* **1** of or relating to nutrition **2** providing sustenance or nourishment
alimentary canal *or* **tract** *n* the tubular passage extending from the mouth to the anus, through which food is passed and digested
alimentation (ˌælɪmɛnˈteɪʃən) *n* **1** nourishment **2** sustenance; support
alimony (ˈælɪmənɪ) *n law* (formerly) an allowance paid under a court order by one spouse to another when they are separated but not divorced. See also **maintenance** [c17 from L, from *alere* to nourish]
A-line (ˈeɪˌlaɪn) *adj* (of garments) flaring out slightly from the waist or shoulders
Ali Pasha (ˈɑːliː ˈpɑːʃə) *n* known as *the Lion of Janina*. 1741–1822, Turkish pasha and ruler of Albania (1787–1820), who was deposed and assassinated after intriguing against Turkey
aliphatic (ˌælɪˈfætɪk) *adj* (of an organic compound) not aromatic, esp having an open chain structure [c19 from Gk *aleiphat-*, *aleiphar* oil]
aliquant (ˈælɪkwənt) *adj maths* of or signifying a quantity or number that is not an exact divisor of a given quantity or number: *5 is an aliquant part of 12* [c17 from NL, from L *aliquantus* somewhat, a certain quantity of]
aliquot (ˈælɪˌkwɒt) *adj maths* **1** of or signifying an exact divisor of a quantity or number: *3 is an aliquot part of 12* ▷ *vb* **2** to divide or be divided into aliquots [c16 from L: several, a few]
A list *n* **a** the most socially desirable category **b** (*as modifier*): *an A-list event* ▷ Cf **B list**
alit (əˈlɪt) *vb* a rare past tense and past participle of **alight**[1]
aliterate (eɪˈlɪtərɪt) *n* **1** a person who is able to read but disinclined to do so ▷ *adj* **2** of or relating to aliterates
alive (əˈlaɪv) *adj* (*postpositive*) **1** living; having life **2** in existence; active: *they kept hope alive* **3** (*immediately postpositive*) now living: *the happiest woman alive* **4** full of life; lively **5** (usually foll by *with*) animated: *a face alive with emotion* **6** (foll by *to*) aware (of); sensitive (to) **7** (foll by *with*) teeming (with): *the mattress was alive with fleas* **8** *electronics* another word for **live**[2] (sense 11) [OE *on līfe* in LIFE]
alizarin (əˈlɪzərɪn) *n* a brownish-yellow powder or orange-red crystalline solid used as a dye [c19 prob. from F, from Ar. *al-ʿaṣārah* the juice, from *ʿasara* to squeeze]
alkali (ˈælkəˌlaɪ) *n*, *pl* **alkalis** *or* **alkalies** **1** *chem* a soluble base or a solution of a base **2** a soluble mineral salt that occurs in arid soils [c14 from Med. L, from Ar. *al-qili* the ashes (of saltwort)]
alkali metal *n* any of the monovalent metals lithium, sodium, potassium, rubidium, caesium, and francium
alkaline (ˈælkəˌlaɪn) *adj* having the properties of or containing an alkali > **alkalinity** (ˌælkəˈlɪnɪtɪ) *n*
alkaline earth *n* **1** Also called: **alkaline earth metal, alkaline earth element** any of the divalent electropositive metals beryllium, magnesium, calcium, strontium, barium, and radium **2** an oxide of one of the alkaline earth metals
alkalize *or* **alkalise** (ˈælkəˌlaɪz) *vb* **alkalizes, alkalizing, alkalized** *or* **alkalises, alkalising, alkalised** (*tr*) to make alkaline > ˈ**alkaˌlizable** *or* ˈ**alkaˌlisable** *adj*
alkaloid (ˈælkəˌlɔɪd) *n* any of a group of nitrogenous compounds found in plants. Many are poisonous and some are used as drugs
alkane (ˈælkeɪn) *n* any saturated aliphatic hydrocarbon with the general formula C_nH_{2n+2}. Former name: **paraffin**
alkane series *n* a homologous series of saturated hydrocarbons starting with methane and having the general formula C_nH_{2n+2}. Also called: **methane series**
alkanet (ˈælkəˌnɛt) *n* **1** a European plant, the roots of which yield a red dye **2** the dye obtained [c14 from Sp., from Med. L, from Ar. *al* the + *hinnā'* henna]
alkene (ˈælkiːn) *n* any unsaturated aliphatic hydrocarbon with the general formula C_nH_{2n}. Former name: **olefine**
alkene series *n* a homologous series of unsaturated hydrocarbons starting with ethylene (ethene) and having the general formula C_nH_{2n}. Also called: **ethylene series, ethene series**

Alkmaar (*Dutch* 'alkma:r) *n* a city in the W Netherlands, in North Holland. Pop: 92 962 (1994)
Alkoran *or* **Alcoran** (ˌælkɒ'rɑ:n) *n* a less common name for the **Koran**
alky *or* **alkie** ('ælkɪ) *n sl* a heavy drinker or alcoholic
alkyd resin ('ælkɪd) *n* any of several synthetic resins made from a dicarboxylic acid, used in paints and adhesives
alkyl ('ælkɪl) *n* (*modifier*) of or containing the monovalent group C_nH_{2n+1}: *alkyl radical* [c19 from G, from *Alk(ohol)* ALCOHOL + -YL]
alkylating agent ('ælkɪˌleɪtɪŋ) *n* any cytotoxic drug containing alkyl groups that acts by damaging DNA; widely used in chemotherapy
alkyne ('ælkaɪn) *n* any unsaturated aliphatic hydrocarbon with the general formula C_nH_{2n-2}
alkyne series *n* a homologous series of unsaturated hydrocarbons starting with acetylene (ethyne) and having the general formula C_nH_{2n-2}. Also called: **acetylene series**
all (ɔ:l) *determiner* **1a** the whole quantity or amount of; everyone of a class: *all the rice; all men are mortal* **1b** (*as pronoun; functioning as sing or pl*): *all of it is nice; all are welcome* **1c** (*in combination with a noun used as a modifier*): *an all-night sitting; an all-ticket match* **2** the greatest possible: *in all earnestness* **3** any whatever: *beyond all doubt* **4 all along** all the time **5 all but** nearly: *all but dead* **6 all of** no less or smaller than: *she's all of thirteen years* **7 all over** **7a** finished **7b** everywhere (in, on, etc): *all over England* **7c** *inf* typically (in **that's me** (**him,** etc) **all over**) **7d** unduly effusive towards **8 all in all 8a** everything considered: *all in all, it was a great success* **8b** the object of one's attention: *you are my all in all* **9 all the** (foll by a comp. adj or adv) so much (more or less) than otherwise: *we must work all the faster now* **10 all too** definitely but regrettably: *it's all too true* **11 at all 11a** (*used with a negative or in a question*) in any way or to any degree: *I didn't know that at all* **11b** anyway: *I'm surprised you came at all* **12 be all for** *inf* to be strongly in favour of **13 for all 13a** in so far as: *for all anyone knows, he was a baron* **13b** notwithstanding: *for all my pushing, I still couldn't move it* **14 for all that** in spite of that: *he was a nice man for all that* **15 in all** altogether: *there were five in all* ▷ *adv* **16** (in scores of games) apiece; each: *the score was three all* **17** completely: *all alone* ▷ *n* **18** (preceded by *my, his,* etc) (one's) complete effort or interest: *to give your all* **19** totality or whole [OE *eall*]
all- *combining form* a variant of **allo-** before a vowel
alla breve ('ælə 'breɪvɪ) *music* ▷ *adj, adv* **1** with two beats to the bar instead of four, i.e. twice as fast as written ▷ *n* **2** (formerly) a time of two or four minims to the bar. Symbol: ¢ [c19 It., lit.: according to the breve]
Allah ('ælə) *n* the name of God in Islam [c16 from Ar., from *al* the + *Ilāh* god]
Allahabad (ˌæləhə'bæd, -'bɑ:d) *n* a city in N India, in SE Uttar Pradesh at the confluence of the Ganges and Jumna Rivers: Hindu pilgrimage centre. Pop: 792 858 (1991)
all-American *adj US* **1** representative of the whole of the United States **2** composed exclusively of American members **3** (of a person) typically American
allantoin (ˌælən'təʊɪn) *n* a substance derived from the secretions of snails and contained in some plants, used in skin care products and valued for its soothing properties [c19 from ALLANTOIS]
allantois (ˌælən'təʊɪs, ə'læntɔɪs) *n* a membranous sac growing out of the ventral surface of the hind gut of embryonic reptiles, birds, and mammals [c17 NL, from Gk *allantoeidēs* sausage-shaped] > **allantoic** (ˌælən'təʊɪk) *adj*
allay (ə'leɪ) *vb* **1** to relieve (pain, grief, etc) or be relieved **2** (*tr*) to reduce (fear, anger, etc) [OE *ālecgan* to put down]
All Blacks *pl n* **the** the international Rugby Union football team of New Zealand [so named because of the players' black strip]
all clear *n* **1** a signal indicating that some danger, such as an air raid, is over **2** permission to proceed
all-dayer (ˌɔ:l'deɪə) *n* an entertainment, such as a pop concert or film screening, that lasts all day
all-dressed *adj Canad* (of a hot dog, hamburger, etc) served with all available garnishes
allegation (ˌælɪ'geɪʃən) *n* **1** the act of alleging **2** an unproved assertion, esp an accusation
allege (ə'lɛdʒ) *vb* **alleges, alleging, alleged** (*tr; may take a clause as object*) **1** to state without or before proof: *he alleged malpractice* **2** to put forward (an argument or plea) for or against an accusation, claim, etc [c14 *aleggen*, ult. from L *allēgāre* to dispatch on a mission, from *lēx* law]
alleged (ə'lɛdʒd) *adj* (*prenominal*) **1** stated to be such: *the alleged murderer* **2** dubious: *an alleged miracle*
allegedly (ə'lɛdʒɪdlɪ) *adv* **1** reportedly; supposedly: *payments allegedly made to a former colleague* **2** (*sentence modifier*) it is alleged that ▷ *interj* **3** an exclamation expressing disbelief or scepticism.

> USAGE In recent years it has become common for speakers to include *allegedly* in statements that are controversial or possibly even defamatory. The implication is that, by saying *allegedly*, the speaker is distancing himself or herself from the controversy and even protecting himself or herself from possible prosecution. However, the effect created may be deliberate. The use of *allegedly* can be a signal that, although the statement may seem outrageous, it is in fact true: *He was drunk at work. Allegedly*. Conversely, it is also possible to use *allegedly* as an expression of ironic scepticism: *He's a hard worker. Allegedly*

Allegheny Mountains (ˌælɪ'geɪnɪ) *or* **Alleghenies** *pl n* a mountain range in Pennsylvania, Maryland, Virginia, and West Virginia: part of the Appalachian system; rising from 600 m (2000 ft) to over 1440 m (4800 ft)
allegiance (ə'li:dʒəns) *n* **1** loyalty, as of a subject to his or her sovereign **2** (in feudal society) the obligations of a vassal to his liege lord [c14 from OF, from *lige* LIEGE]
allegorical (ˌælɪ'gɒrɪkəl) *or* **allegoric** *adj* used in, containing, or characteristic of allegory
allegorize *or* **allegorise** ('ælɪgəˌraɪz) *vb* **allegorizes, allegorizing, allegorized** *or* **allegorises, allegorising, allegorised** **1** to transform (a story, fable, etc) into or compose in the form of allegory **2** (*tr*) to interpret allegorically > **ˌallegori'zation** *or* **ˌallegori'sation** *n*
allegory ('ælɪgərɪ) *n, pl* **allegories** **1** a poem, play, picture, etc, in which the apparent meaning of the characters and events is used to symbolize a moral or spiritual meaning **2** use of such symbolism **3** anything used as a symbol [c14 from OF, from L, from Gk, from *allēgorein* to speak figuratively, from *allos* other + *agoreuein* to make a speech in public] > **'allegorist** *n*
allegretto (ˌælɪ'grɛtəʊ) *music* ▷ *adj, adv* **1** (to be performed) fairly quickly or briskly ▷ *n, pl* **allegrettos** **2** a piece or passage to be performed in this manner [c19 dim. of ALLEGRO]
Allegri (*Italian* al'legrɪ) *n* **Gregorio** 1582–1652, Italian composer and singer. His compositions include a *Miserere* for nine voices
allegro (ə'leɪgrəʊ, -'lɛg-) *music* ▷ *adj, adv* **1** (to be performed) in a brisk lively manner ▷ *n, pl* **allegros** **2** a piece or passage to be performed in this manner [c17 from It.: cheerful, from L *alacer* brisk, lively]
allele (ə'li:l) *n* any of two or more variants of a gene that are responsible for alternative characteristics, such as smooth or wrinkled seeds in peas. Also called: **allelomorph** (ə'li:ləˌmɔ:f) [c20 from G *Allel*, from

Aa

Allelomorph, from Gk *allēl-* one another + *morphē* form]

alleluia (ˌælɪˈluːjə) *interj* praise the Lord! Used in liturgical contexts in place of *hallelujah* [c14 via Med. L from Heb. *hallelūyāh*]

allemande (ˈælɪmænd) *n* **1** the first movement of the classical suite, composed in a moderate tempo **2** any of several German dances **3** a figure in country dancing or square dancing by which couples change position in the set [c17 from F *danse allemande* German dance]

Allen[1] (ˈælən) *n* **1 Bog of** a region of peat bogs in central Ireland, west of Dublin. Area: over 10 sq km (3.75 sq miles) **2 Lough** a lake in Ireland, in county Leitrim

Allen[2] (ˈælən) *n* **1 Ethan** 1738–89, American soldier during the War of Independence who led the Green Mountain Boys of Vermont **2 Sir Thomas** born 1944, British operatic baritone **3 Woody** real name *Allen Stewart Konigsberg*. born 1935, US film comedian, screenwriter, and director. His films as an actor and director include *Annie Hall* (1977), *Manhattan* (1979), *Hannah and Her Sisters* (1986), *Bullets over Broadway* (1994), and *Hollywood Ending* (2002)

Allenby (ˈælənbɪ) *n* **Edmund Henry Hynman**, 1st Viscount. 1861–1936, British field marshal who captured Palestine and Syria from the Turks in 1918; high commissioner in Egypt (1919–25)

Allende (*Spanish* aˈʎende) *n* **1 Isabel** born 1942, Chilean writer, born in Peru; her works include *Eva Luna* (1989) and *Daughter of Fortune* (1999) **2** her uncle, **Salvador** (salβaˈðor) 1908–73, Chilean Marxist politician; president of Chile from 1970 until 1973, when the army seized power and he was killed

allergen (ˈæləˌdʒɛn) *n* any substance capable of inducing an allergy > ˌ**allerˈgenic** *adj*

allergic (əˈlɜːdʒɪk) *adj* **1** of, having, or caused by an allergy **2** (*postpositive; foll by to*) *inf* having an aversion (to): *allergic to work*

allergist (ˈælədʒɪst) *n* a physician skilled in the treatment of allergies

allergy (ˈælədʒɪ) *n, pl* **allergies 1** a hypersensitivity to a substance that causes the body to react to any contact with it. Hay fever is an allergic reaction to pollen **2** *inf* an aversion [c20 from G *Allergie* (indicating a changed reaction), from Gk *allos* other + *ergon* activity]
▷ www.aafa.org

alleviate (əˈliːvɪˌeɪt) *vb* **alleviates, alleviating, alleviated** (*tr*) to make (pain, sorrow, etc) easier to bear; lessen [c15 from LL, from L *levis* light] > **alˌleviˈation** *n* > **alˈleviˌator** *n*
USAGE See at **ameliorate**

alley[1] (ˈælɪ) *n* **1** a narrow passage, esp one between or behind buildings **2** See **bowling alley 3** *tennis, chiefly US* the space between the singles and doubles sidelines **4** a walk in a garden, esp one lined with trees **5 up** (*or* **down**) **one's alley** *sl* suited to one's abilities or interests [c14 from OF, from *aler* to go, ult. from L *ambulāre* to walk]

alley[2] (ˈælɪ) *n* a large playing marble [c18 shortened and changed from ALABASTER]

alleyway (ˈælɪˌweɪ) *n* a narrow passage; alley

All Fools' Day *n* another name for **April Fools' Day** (see **April fool**)

all found *adj* (of charges for accommodation) inclusive of meals, heating, etc

all hail *sentence substitute* an archaic greeting or salutation [c14, lit.: all health (to someone)]

Allhallows (ˌɔːlˈhæləʊz) *n* a less common term for **All Saints' Day**

alliaceous (ˌælɪˈeɪʃəs) *adj* **1** of or relating to *Allium*, a genus of plants that have a strong smell and often have bulbs. The genus occurs in the N hemisphere and includes onion and garlic **2** tasting or smelling like garlic or onions **3** of, relating to, or belonging to the *Alliaceae*, a family of flowering plants that includes the genus *Allium* [c18 from L *allium* garlic]

alliance (əˈlaɪəns) *n* **1** the act of allying or state of being allied; union **2** a formal agreement, esp a military one, between two or more countries **3** the countries involved **4** a union between families through marriage **5** affinity or correspondence in characteristics **6** *bot* a taxonomic category consisting of a group of related families [c13 from OF, from *alier* to ALLY]

allied (əˈlaɪd, ˈælaɪd) *adj* **1** joined, as by treaty or marriage; united **2** of the same type or class

Allied (ˈælaɪd) *adj* of or relating to the Allies

Allier (*French* alje) *n* **1** a department of central France, in Auvergne region. Capital: Moulins. Pop: 344 721 (1999). Area: 7382 sq km (2879 sq miles) **2** a river in S central France, rising in the Cévennes and flowing north to the Loire. Length: over 403 km (250 miles)

Allies (ˈælaɪz) *pl n* **1** (in World War I) the powers of the Triple Entente (France, Russia, and Britain) together with the nations allied with them **2** (in World War II) the countries that fought against the Axis and Japan, esp Britain and the Commonwealth countries, the US, the Soviet Union, China, Poland, and France

alligator (ˈælɪˌgeɪtə) *n* **1** a large crocodilian of the southern US, having powerful jaws but differing from the crocodiles in having a shorter and broader snout **2** a similar but smaller species occurring in China **3** any of various tools or machines having adjustable toothed jaws [c17 from Sp. *el lagarto* the lizard, from L *lacerta*]

alligator pear *n* another name for **avocado**

all-important *adj* crucial; vital

all in *adj* **1** (*postpositive*) *inf* completely exhausted ▷ *adv, adj* (**all-in** *when prenominal*) **2** with all expenses included: *one hundred pounds a week all in* **3** (of wrestling) in freestyle

Allingham (ˈælɪŋəm) *n* **Margery** 1904–66, British author of detective stories, featuring Albert Campion. Her works include *Tiger in the Smoke* (1952) and *The Mind Readers* (1965)

alliterate (əˈlɪtəˌreɪt) *vb* **alliterates, alliterating, alliterated 1** to contain or cause to contain alliteration **2** (*intr*) to speak or write using alliteration

alliteration (əˌlɪtəˈreɪʃən) *n* the use of the same consonant (**consonantal alliteration**) or of a vowel (**vocalic alliteration**), at the beginning of each word or stressed syllable in a line of verse, as in *around the rock the ragged rascal ran* [c17 from L *litera* letter] > **alˈliterative** *adj*

allium (ˈælɪəm) *n* any plant of the genus *Allium*, such as the onion, garlic, shallot, leek, and chive: family *Alliaceae* [c19 from L: garlic]

all-nighter (ˌɔːlˈnaɪtə) *n* an entertainment, such as a pop concert or film screening, that lasts all night

allo- *or before a vowel* **all-** *combining form* indicating difference, variation, or opposition: *allopathy; allomorph* [from Gk *allos* other, different]

Alloa (ˈæləʊə) *n* a town in E central Scotland, the administrative centre of Clackmannanshire. Pop: 18 842 (1991)

allocate (ˈæləˌkeɪt) *vb* **allocates, allocating, allocated** (*tr*) **1** to assign for a particular purpose **2** a less common word for **locate** (sense 2) [c17 from Med. L, from L *locus* a place] > ˈ**alloˌcatable** *adj* > ˌ**alloˈcation** *n*

allocution (ˌæləˈkjuːʃən) *n rhetoric* a formal or authoritative speech or address [c17 from LL *allocūtiō*, from L *alloquī* to address]

allomerism (əˈlɒməˌrɪzəm) *n* similarity of crystalline structure in substances of different chemical composition > **allomeric** (ˌæləˈmɛrɪk) *or* **alˈlomerous** *adj*

allomorph (ˈæləˌmɔːf) *n* **1** *linguistics* any of the representations of a single morpheme. For example, the final (s) and (z) sounds of *bets* and *beds* are allomorphs **2** any of the different crystalline forms of a chemical compound, such as a mineral > ˌ**alloˈmorphic** *adj*

allopath (ˈæləˌpæθ) *or* **allopathist** (əˈlɒpəθɪst) *n* a person who practises or is skilled in allopathy

allopathy (əˈlɒpəθɪ) *n* the orthodox medical method of treating disease, by inducing a condition different from

or opposed to the cause of the disease ▷ Cf **homeopathy** > **allopathic** (ˌæləˈpæθɪk) *adj*
allophone (ˈæləˌfəʊn) *n* **1** any of several speech sounds regarded as variants of the same phoneme. In English the aspirated initial (p) in *pot* and the unaspirated (p) in *spot* are allophones of the phoneme /p/ **2** *Canad* a Canadian whose native language is neither French nor English > **allophonic** (ˌæləˈfɒnɪk) *adj*
All-Ordinaries Index *n* an index of share prices on the Australian Stock Exchange giving a weighted arithmetic average of 245 ordinary shares
allot (əˈlɒt) *vb* **allots, allotting, allotted** (*tr*) **1** to assign or distribute (shares, etc) **2** to designate for a particular purpose; apportion: *we allotted two hours to the case* [c16 from OF, from *lot* portion]
allotment (əˈlɒtmənt) *n* **1** the act of allotting **2** a portion or amount allotted **3** *Brit* a small piece of land rented by an individual for cultivation
allotrope (ˈæləˌtrəʊp) *n* any of two or more physical forms in which an element can exist
allotropy (əˈlɒtrəpɪ) *or* **allotropism** *n* the existence of an element in two or more physical forms > **allotropic** (ˌæləˈtrɒpɪk) *adj*
all-out *inf* ▷ *adj* **1** using one's maximum powers: *an all-out effort* ▷ *adv* **all out** **2** to one's maximum capacity: *he went all out*
allow (əˈlaʊ) *vb* **1** (*tr*) to permit (to do something) **2** (*tr*) to set aside: *five hours were allowed to do the job* **3** (*tr*) to let enter or stay: *they don't allow dogs* **4** (*tr*) to acknowledge (a point, claim, etc) **5** (*tr*) to let have: *he was allowed few visitors* **6** (*intr*; foll by *for*) to take into account **7** (*intr*; often foll by *of*) to permit: *a question that allows of only one reply* **8** (*tr*; *may take a clause as object*) *US dialect* to assert; maintain [c14 from OF, from LL *allaudāre* to extol, infl. by Med. L *allocāre* to assign] > **alˈlowable** *adj* > **alˈlowably** *adv*
allowance (əˈlaʊəns) *n* **1** an amount of something, esp money or food, given at regular intervals **2** a discount, as in consideration for something given in part exchange; rebate **3** (in Britain) an amount of a person's income that is not subject to income tax **4** a portion set aside to cover special expenses **5** admission; concession **6** the act of allowing; toleration **7** **make allowances** (*or* **allowance**) (usually foll by *for*) **7a** to take mitigating circumstances into account **7b** to allow (for) ▷ *vb* **allowances, allowancing, allowanced** (*tr*) **8** to supply (something) in limited amounts
Alloway (ˈæləˌweɪ) *n* a village in Scotland, in South Ayrshire, S of Ayr: birthplace of Robert Burns
allowedly (əˈlaʊɪdlɪ) *adv* (*sentence modifier*) by general admission or agreement; admittedly
alloy *n* (ˈælɔɪ, əˈlɔɪ) **1** a metallic material, such as steel, consisting of a mixture of two or more metals or of metallic with nonmetallic elements **2** something that impairs the quality of the thing to which it is added ▷ *vb* (əˈlɔɪ) (*tr*) **3** to add (one metal or element to another) to obtain a substance with a desired property **4** to debase (a pure substance) by mixing with an inferior element **5** to diminish or impair [c16 from OF *aloi* a mixture, from *aloier* to combine, from L *alligāre*]
all-points bulletin *n* (in the US) an alert broadcast to all police officers within an area, instructing the arrest of a suspect
all-purpose *adj* useful for many things
all right *adj* (*postpositive except in slang use*), *adv* **1** adequate; satisfactory **2** unharmed; safe **3** **all-right** *US sl* acceptable; reliable ▷ *sentence substitute* **4** very well: used to express assent ▷ *adv* **5** satisfactorily: *the car goes all right* **6** without doubt ▷ Also: **alright**

USAGE See at **alright**

all-round *adj* **1** efficient in all respects, esp in sport: *an all-round player* **2** comprehensive; many-sided: *an all-round education*
all-rounder *n* a versatile person, esp in a sport
All Saints' Day *n* a Christian festival celebrated on Nov. 1 to honour all the saints
all-singing all-dancing *adj* having every desirable feature possible: *an all-singing all-dancing computer*
All Souls' Day *n* *RC Church* a day of prayer (Nov. 2) for the dead in purgatory
allspice (ˈɔːlˌspaɪs) *n* **1** a tropical American tree, having small white flowers and aromatic berries **2** the seeds of this berry used as a spice, having a flavour said to resemble a mixture of cinnamon, cloves, and nutmeg ▷ Also called: **pimento**
all-star *adj* (*prenominal*) consisting of star performers
all-time *adj* (*prenominal*) *inf* unsurpassed
all told *adv* (*sentence modifier*) in all: *we were seven all told*
allude (əˈluːd) *vb* **alludes, alluding, alluded** (*intr*; foll by *to*) **1** to refer indirectly **2** (loosely) to mention [c16 from L *allūdere*, from *lūdere* to sport, from *lūdus* a game]

USAGE See at **elude**

allure (əˈlʊə) *vb* **allures, alluring, allured** **1** (*tr*) to entice or tempt (someone); attract ▷ *n* **2** attractiveness; appeal [c15 from OF *alurer*, from *lure* bait] > **alˈlurement** *n* > **alˈluring** *adj*
allusion (əˈluːʒən) *n* **1** the act of alluding **2** a passing reference [c16 from LL *allūsiō*, from L *allūdere* to sport with]
allusive (əˈluːsɪv) *adj* containing or full of allusions > **alˈlusiveness** *n*
alluvial (əˈluːvɪəl) *adj* **1** of or relating to alluvium ▷ *n* **2** another name for **alluvium**
alluvion (əˈluːvɪən) *n* **1a** the wash of the sea or a river **1b** a flood **1c** sediment; alluvium **2** *law* the gradual formation of new land, as by the recession of the sea [c16 from L *alluviō* an overflowing, from *luere* to wash]
alluvium (əˈluːvɪəm) *n*, *pl* **alluviums** *or* **alluvia** (-vɪə) a fine-grained fertile soil consisting of mud, silt, and sand deposited by flowing water [c17 from L; see ALLUVION]
ally *vb* (əˈlaɪ) **allies, allying, allied** (usually foll by *to* or *with*) **1** to unite or be united, esp formally, as by treaty **2** (*tr*; *usually passive*) to be related, as through being similar ▷ *n* (ˈælaɪ), *pl* **allies** **3** a country, person, or group allied with another **4** a plant, animal, etc, closely related to another in characteristics or form [c14 from OF *alier* to join, from L *ligāre* to bind]
allyl resin (ˈælɪl) *n* any of several thermosetting synthetic resins, containing the CH_2:$CHCH_2$– group, used as adhesives [c19 from L *allium* garlic + -YL]
Alma-Ata (*Russian* alˈmaaˈta) *n* the former name of **Almaty**
Almada (*Portuguese* alˈmaːdə) *n* a town in S central Portugal, on the S bank of the Tagus estuary opposite Lisbon: statue of Christ 110 m (360 ft) high, erected 1959. Pop: 153 189 (1991)
Al Madinah (ˌæl mæˈdiːnə) *n* the Arabic name for **Medina**
alma mater (ˈælmə ˈmɑːtə, ˈmeɪtə) *n* (*often caps.*) one's school, college, or university [c17 from L: bountiful mother]
almanac (ˈɔːlməˌnæk) *n* a yearly calendar giving statistical information, such as the phases of the moon, tides, anniversaries, etc Also (archaic): **almanack** [c14 from Med. L *almanachus*, ?from LGk *almenikhiaka*]
almandine (ˈælməndɪn) *n* a deep violet-red garnet [c17 from F, from Med. L, from *Alabanda*, ancient city of Asia Minor where these stones were cut]
Al Mansûrah (ˌæl mænˈsʊərə) *n* a variant of **El Mansûra**
Al Marj (æl ˈmɑːdʒ) *n* an ancient town in N Libya: founded in about 550 BC. Pop: 25 166 (latest est). Italian name: **Barce**
Alma-Tadema (ˈælməˈtædɪmə) *n* Sir **Lawrence** 1836–1912, Dutch-English painter of studies of Greek and Roman life
Almaty (ælˈmɑːtɪ) *n* a city in SE Kazakhstan; capital of

Aa

Kazakhstan (1991–97): an important trading centre. Pop: 1 129 400 (1999). Former name (until 1927): **Verny** Also called: **Alma-Ata**

almighty (ɔːl'maɪtɪ) *adj* 1 omnipotent 2 *inf* (intensifier): *an almighty row* ▷ *adv* 3 *inf* (intensifier): *an almighty loud bang*

Almighty (ɔːl'maɪtɪ) *n* **the** another name for **God**

Almodóvar (*Spanish* almɔ'ðoβar) *n* **Pedro** born 1949, Spanish film director. His provocative black comedies include *Dark Habits* (1983), *Women on the Verge of a Nervous Breakdown* (1988), *The Flower of My Secret* (1995), and *Talk to Her* (2002)

almond ('ɑːmənd) *n* 1 a small widely cultivated rosaceous tree that is native to W Asia and has pink flowers and an edible nutlike seed 2 the seed, which has a yellowish-brown shell 3 (*modifier*) made of or containing almonds: *almond cake* [c13 from OF *almande*, ult. from Gk *amugdalē*]

almond-eyed *adj* having narrow oval eyes

almoner ('ɑːmənə) *n* 1 *Brit* a former name for a trained hospital social worker 2 (formerly) a person who distributes charity on behalf of a household or institution [c13 from OF, from *almosne* alms, ult. from LL *eleēmosyna*]

almost ('ɔːlməʊst) *adv* very nearly

alms (ɑːmz) *pl n* charitable donations of money or goods to the poor or needy [OE *ælmysse*, from LL, from Gk *eleēmosunē* pity]

almshouse ('ɑːmz,haʊs) *n Brit history* a privately supported house offering accommodation to the aged or needy

almucantar *or* **almacantar** (,ælmə'kæntə) *n* 1 a circle on the celestial sphere parallel to the horizon 2 an instrument for measuring altitudes [c14 from F, from Ar. *almukantarāt* sundial]

aloe ('æləʊ) *n, pl* **aloes** 1 any plant of the genus *Aloe*, chiefly native to southern Africa, with fleshy spiny-toothed leaves and red or yellow flowers 2 **American aloe** Also called: **century plant** a tropical American agave which blooms only once in 10 to 30 years [c14 from L *aloē*, from Gk]

aloes ('æləʊz) *n* (*functioning as sing*) a bitter purgative drug made from the leaves of several species of aloe. Also called: **bitter aloes**

aloe vera ('vɪərə) *n* juice obtained from the leaves of a liliaceous plant, *Aloe vera*, the leaves of which yield a juice used as an emollient in skin and hair preparations

aloft (ə'lɒft) *adv, adj* (*postpositive*) 1 in or into a high or higher place 2 *naut* in or into the rigging of a vessel [c12 from ON *ā lopt* in the air]

alone (ə'ləʊn) *adj* (*postpositive*), *adv* 1 apart from another or others 2 without anyone or anything else: *one man alone could lift it* 3 without equal: *he stands alone in the field of microbiology* 4 to the exclusion of others: *she alone believed him* 5 **leave** *or* **let alone** to refrain from annoying or interfering with 6 **leave well alone** to refrain from interfering with something that is satisfactory 7 **let alone** not to mention; much less: *he can't afford beer, let alone whisky* [OE *al one*, lit.: all (entirely) one]

along (ə'lɒŋ) *prep* 1 over or for the length of: *along the road* ▷ *adv* 2 continuing over the length of some specified thing 3 together with some specified person or people: *he'd like to come along* 4 forward: *the horse trotted along* 5 to a more advanced state: *he got the work moving along* 6 **along with** together with: *consider the advantages along with the disadvantages* [OE *andlang*, from *and-* against + *lang* LONG[1]]

USAGE See at **plus**

alongshore (ə,lɒŋ'ʃɔː) *adv, adj* (*postpositive*) close to, by, or along a shore

alongside (ə'lɒŋ,saɪd) *prep* 1 (often foll by *of*) close beside: *alongside the quay* ▷ *adv* 2 near the side of something: *come alongside*

aloof (ə'luːf) *adj* distant, unsympathetic, or supercilious in manner [c16 from A-[1] + *loof*, var. of LUFF] > **a'loofly** *adv* > **a'loofness** *n*

alopecia (,ælə'piːʃɪə) *n* baldness [c14 from L, from Gk *alōpekia*, orig.: mange in foxes]

aloud (ə'laʊd) *adv, adj* (*postpositive*) 1 in a normal voice 2 in a spoken voice; not silently

Aloysius (,æləʊ'ɪʃəs) *n* **Saint** full name *Aloysius Luigi Gonzaga*. 1568–91, Italian Jesuit who died nursing plague victims; the patron saint of youth. Feast day: June 21

alp (ælp) *n* 1 (in the European Alps) an area of pasture above the valley bottom but below the mountain peaks 2 a high mountain 3 **the Alps** a high mountain range in S central Europe [c16 from L *Alpes*]

ALP *abbrev for* Australian Labor Party

alpaca (æl'pækə) *n* 1 a domesticated South American mammal related to the llama, with dark shaggy hair 2 the cloth made from the wool of this animal 3 a glossy fabric simulating this [c18 via Sp. from Aymara *allpaca*]

alpenhorn ('ælpən,hɔːn) *n* another name for **alphorn**

alpenstock ('ælpən,stɒk) *n* a stout stick with an iron tip used by hikers, mountain climbers, etc [c19 from G, from *Alpen* Alps + *Stock* STICK[1]]

Alpes-de-Haute-Provence (*French* alpdəotprɔvɑ̃s) *n* a department of SE France in Provence-Alpes-Côte-d'Azur region. Capital: Digne. Pop: 139 561 (1999). Area: 6988 sq km (2725 sq miles). Former name: **Basses-Alpes**

Alpes Maritimes (*French* alp maritim) *n* a department of the SE corner of France in Provence-Alpes-Côte-d'Azur region. Capital: Nice. Pop: 1 011 326 (1999). Area: 4298 sq km (1676 sq miles)

alpha ('ælfə) *n* 1 the first letter in the Greek alphabet (Α, α) 2 *Brit* the highest grade or mark, as in an examination 3 (*modifier*) 3a involving helium nuclei 3b denoting an isomeric or allotropic form of a substance [via L from Gk, of Phoenician origin]

alpha and omega *n* the first and last, a phrase used in Revelation 1:8 to signify God's eternity

alphabet ('ælfə,bɛt) *n* 1 a set of letters or other signs used in a writing system, each letter or sign being used to represent one or sometimes more than one phoneme in the language being transcribed 2 any set of characters, esp one representing sounds of speech 3 basic principles or rudiments [c15 from LL, from the first two letters of the Gk alphabet; see ALPHA, BETA]

▷ www.omniglot.com/writing/atoz.htm

alphabetical (,ælfə'bɛtɪkᵊl) *or* **alphabetic** *adj* 1 in the conventional order of the letters of an alphabet 2 of or expressed by an alphabet > **,alpha'betically** *adv*

alphabetize *or* **alphabetise** ('ælfəbə,taɪz) *vb* **alphabetizes, alphabetizing, alphabetized** *or* **alphabetises, alphabetising, alphabetised** (*tr*) 1 to arrange in conventional alphabetical order 2 to express by an alphabet > **,alphabeti'zation** *or* **,alphabeti'sation** *n*

alpha-blocker *n* any of a class of drugs that prevent the stimulation of alpha adrenoreceptors, a type of receptor in the sympathetic nervous system, by adrenaline and noradrenaline and that therefore cause widening of blood vessels: used in the treatment of high blood pressure

alpha decay *n* the radioactive decay process resulting in emission of alpha particles

alpha-fetoprotein (,ælfə,fiːtəʊ'prəʊtiːn) *n* a protein that forms in the liver of the human fetus; excessive quantities in the amniotic fluid may indicate spina bifida in the fetus; low levels may point to Down's syndrome. Abbrev: **afp**

alpha-hydroxy acid *n* a type of organic acid, commonly used in skin-care preparations, that has a hydroxyl group attached to the carbon atom next to the carbon atom carrying the carboxyl group

alpha male *n* the dominant male animal or person in a group

alphanumeric (ˌælfənjuːˈmɛrɪk) *or* **alphameric** *adj* (of a character set or file of data) consisting of alphabetical and numerical symbols

alpha particle *n* a helium nucleus, containing two neutrons and two protons, emitted during some radioactive transformations

alpha ray *n* ionizing radiation consisting of a stream of alpha particles

alpha rhythm *or* **wave** *n physiol* the normal bursts of electrical activity from the cerebral cortex of a person at rest. See also **brain wave**

alpha stock *n* any of the most active securities on the London stock exchange of which there are between 100 and 200

Alpheus (ælˈfiːəs) *n Greek myth* a river god, lover of the nymph Arethusa. She changed into a spring to evade him, but he changed into a river and mingled with her

alphorn (ˈælpˌhɔːn) *or* **alpenhorn** *n* a wind instrument used in the Swiss Alps, made from a very long tube of wood [c19 from G: Alps horn]

alpine (ˈælpaɪn) *adj* **1** of or relating to high mountains **2** (of plants) growing on mountains, esp above the limit for tree growth **3** connected with mountaineering **4** *skiing* of racing events on steep prepared slopes, such as the slalom and downhill ▷ Cf **nordic** ▷ *n* **5** a plant grown in or native to high altitudes

alpinist (ˈælpɪnɪst) *n* a mountain climber

Alps (ælps) *pl n* **1** a mountain range in S central Europe, extending over 1000 km (650 miles) from the Mediterranean coast of France and NW Italy through Switzerland, N Italy, and Austria to Slovenia. Highest peak: Mont Blanc, 4807 m (15 771 ft) **2** a range of mountains in the NW quadrant of the moon, which is cut in two by a straight fracture, the **Alpine Valley**

al-Qaeda *or* **al-Qaida** (ælˈkaɪdə, ælkɑːˈiːdə) *n* a loosely-knit militant Islamic organization led and funded by Osama bin Laden, by whom it was established in the late 1980s from Arab volunteers who had fought the Soviet troops previously based in Afghanistan; known or believed to be behind a number of operations against Western, especially US, interests, including bomb attacks on two US embassies in Africa in 1998 and the destruction of the World Trade Center in New York in 2001 [c20 from Arabic *al-qa'ida* the base]

already (ɔːlˈrɛdɪ) *adv* **1** by or before a stated or implied time: *he is already here* **2** at a time earlier than expected: *is it ten o'clock already?*

alright (ɔːlˈraɪt) *adv, sentence substitute, adj* a variant spelling of **all right**

> USAGE The single-word form *alright* is still considered by many people to be wrong or less acceptable than *all right*. This is borne out by the data in the Bank of English, which suggests that the two-word form is about twenty times commoner than the alternative spelling

Alsace (ælˈsæs; *French* alzas) *n* a region and former province of NE France, between the Vosges mountains and the Rhine: famous for its wines. Area: 8280 sq km (3196 sq miles). Ancient name: **Alsatia** German name: **Elsass**

Alsace-Lorraine *n* an area of NE France, comprising the modern regions of Alsace and Lorraine: under German rule 1871–1919 and 1940–44. Area: 14 522 sq km (5607 sq miles). German name: **Elsass-Lothringen**

Alsatia (ælˈseɪʃə) *n* **1** the ancient name for **Alsace** **2** an area around Whitefriars, London, in the 17th century, which was a sanctuary for criminals and debtors

Alsatian (ælˈseɪʃən) *n* **1** Also called: **German shepherd (dog)** a large wolflike breed of dog often used as a guard dog and by the police **2** a native or inhabitant of Alsace ▷ *adj* **3** of or relating to Alsace or its inhabitants

also (ˈɔːlsəʊ) *adv* **1** (*sentence modifier*) in addition; as well; too ▷ *sentence connector* **2** besides; moreover [OE *alswā*; see ALL, SO[1]]

also-ran *n* **1** a contestant, horse, etc, failing to finish among the first three **2** a loser

alstroemeria (ˌælstrəʊˈmɪərɪə) *n* any of several plants with fleshy roots and brightly coloured flowers in summer, esp the Peruvian lily [c18 NL, after Claude *Alstroemer* (1736–96), Swedish naturalist]

Alta. *abbrev for* Alberta

Altaic (ælˈteɪɪk) *n* **1** a postulated family of languages of Asia and SE Europe, including the Turkic, Tungusic, and Mongolic subfamilies. See also **Ural-Altaic** ▷ *adj* **2** denoting or relating to this linguistic family or its speakers

Altai Mountains (ɑːlˈtaɪ) *pl n* a mountain system of central Asia, in W Mongolia, W China, and S Russia. Highest peak: Belukha, 4506 m (14 783 ft)

Altai Republic *n* another name for **Gorno-Altai Republic**

Altamira (*Spanish* altaˈmira) *n* a cave in N Spain, SW of Santander, noted for Old Stone Age wall drawings

altar (ˈɔːltə) *n* **1** a raised place or structure where sacrifices are offered and religious rites performed **2** (in Christian churches) the communion table **3** a step in the wall of a dry dock [OE, ult. from L *altus* high]

altar boy *n RC Church, Church of England* a boy serving as an acolyte

altarpiece (ˈɔːltəˌpiːs) *n* a work of art set above and behind an altar; a reredos

altazimuth (ælˈtæzɪməθ) *n* an instrument for measuring the altitude and azimuth of a celestial body [c19 from ALT(ITUDE) + AZIMUTH]

altazimuth mounting *n* a telescope mounting that allows motion of the telescope about a vertical axis (in altitude) and a horizontal axis (in azimuth)

Altdorf (*German* ˈaltdɔrf) *n* a town in central Switzerland, capital of Uri canton: setting of the William Tell legend. Pop: 8150 (1990)

alter (ˈɔːltə) *vb* **1** to make or become different in some respect; change **2** (*tr*) *inf, chiefly US* a euphemistic word for **castrate** or **spay** [c14 from OF, ult. from L *alter* other] > ˈ**alterable** *adj*

alteration (ˌɔːltəˈreɪʃən) *n* **1** a change or modification **2** the act of altering

alterative (ˈɔːltərətɪv) *adj* **1** likely or able to produce alteration **2** *obsolete* (of a drug) able to restore health ▷ *n* **3** such a drug

altercate (ˈɔːltəˌkeɪt) *vb* **altercates, altercating, altercated** (*intr*) to argue, esp heatedly; dispute [c16 from L *altercārī* to quarrel with another, from *alter* other]

altercation (ˌɔːltəˈkeɪʃən) *n* an angry or heated discussion or quarrel; argument

alter ego (ˈæltər ˈiːgəʊ, ˈɛgəʊ) *n* **1** a second self **2** a very close friend [L: other self]

alternate *vb* (ˈɔːltəˌneɪt) **alternates, alternating, alternated** **1** (often foll by *with*) to occur or cause to occur by turns: *day and night alternate* **2** (*intr*; often foll by *between*) to swing repeatedly from one condition, action, etc, to another **3** (*tr*) to interchange regularly or in succession **4** (*intr*) (of an electric current, voltage, etc) to reverse direction or sign at regular intervals ▷ *adj* (ɔːlˈtɜːnɪt) **5** occurring by turns: *alternate feelings of love and hate* **6** every other or second one of a series: *he came on alternate days* **7** being a second choice; alternative **8** *bot* (of leaves, etc) arranged singly at different heights on either side of the stem ▷ *n* (ˈɔːltənɪt, ɔːlˈtɜːnɪt) **9** *US & Canad* a person who substitutes for another; stand-in [c16 from L *alternāre* to do one thing and then another, ult. from *alter* other] > ˌ**alterˈnation** *n*

alternate angles *pl n* two angles at opposite ends and on opposite sides of a transversal cutting two lines

alternately (ɔːlˈtɜːnɪtlɪ) *adv* in an alternating sequence or position

alternating current *n* an electric current that

Aa

periodically reverses direction. Abbrev: **AC**

alternation of generations *n* the occurrence in the life cycle of many plants and lower animals of alternating sexual and asexual reproductive forms

alternative (ɔːlˈtɜːnətɪv) *n* **1** a possibility of choice, esp between two things **2** either of such choices: *we took the alternative of walking* ▷ *adj* **3** presenting a choice, esp between two possibilities only **4** (of two things) mutually exclusive **5** denoting a lifestyle, culture, art form, etc, that is regarded as preferable to that of contemporary society because it is less conventional, materialistic, or institutionalized > **alˈternatively** *adv*

alternative curriculum *n Brit education* any course of study offered as an alternative to the National Curriculum

alternative energy *n* a form of energy derived from a natural source, such as the sun, wind, tides, or waves. Also called: **renewable energy**

Alternative Investment Market *n* a market on the London Stock Exchange for small companies that want to avoid the expenses of a main-market listing. Abbrev: **AIM**

alternative medicine *n* the treatment or alleviation of disease by techniques such as osteopathy and acupuncture, sometimes allied with attention to a person's general wellbeing. Also called: **complementary medicine**

▷ www.amfoundation.org
▷ www.pitt.edu/cbw/altm.html
▷ www.sumeria.net/health.htm
▷ www.yuthog.org

alternative society *n* a group of people who agree in rejecting the traditional values of the society around them

Alternative Vote *n (modifier)* of or relating to a system of voting in which voters list the candidates in order of preference. If no candidate obtains more than 50% of first-preference votes, the votes for the bottom candidate are redistributed according to the voters' next preference. See **proportional representation**

alternator (ˈɔːltəˌneɪtə) *n* an electrical machine that generates an alternating current

althaea *or US* **althea** (ælˈθiːə) *n* any Eurasian plant of the genus *Althaea*, such as the hollyhock, having tall spikes of showy flowers [c17 from L, from Gk *althaia* marsh mallow]

althorn (ˈæltˌhɔːn) *n* a valved brass musical instrument belonging to the saxhorn family

Althorp House (ˈɔːlθɔːp, -θrʌp) *n* a mansion in Northamptonshire: seat of the Earls Spencer since 1508; originally a medieval house; altered (1787) to its present neoclassical style by Henry Holland. Diana, Princess of Wales is buried on Round Oval Island in the centre of the ornamental lake in Althorp Park

although (ɔːlˈðəʊ) *conj (subordinating)* even though: *although she was ill, she worked hard*

altimeter (ælˈtɪmɪtə, ˈæltɪˌmiːtə) *n* an instrument that indicates height above sea level, esp one based on an aneroid barometer and fitted to an aircraft [c19 from L *altus* high + -METER]

Altiplano (*Spanish* altiˈplano) *n* a plateau of the Andes, covering two thirds of Bolivia and extending into S Peru: contains Lake Titicaca. Height: 3000 m (10 000 ft) to 3900 m (13 000 ft)

altitude (ˈæltɪˌtjuːd) *n* **1** the vertical height of an object, esp above sea level **2** *geom* the perpendicular distance from the vertex to the base of a geometrical figure or solid **3** Also called: **elevation** *astron, navigation* the angular distance of a celestial body from the horizon **4** *surveying* the angle of elevation of a point above the horizontal plane of the observer **5** *(often pl)* a high place or region [c14 from L *altus* high, deep]

alto (ˈæltəʊ) *n, pl* **altos 1** (in choral singing) short for contralto **2** the highest adult male voice; countertenor **3** a singer with such a voice **4** a flute, saxophone, etc, that is the third or fourth highest instrument in its group ▷ *adj* **5** denoting such an instrument [c18 from It.: high, from L *altus*]

alto clef *n* the clef that establishes middle C as being on the third line of the staff

altocumulus (ˌæltəʊˈkjuːmjʊləs) *n, pl* **altocumuli** (-laɪ) a globular cloud at an intermediate height of about 2400 to 6000 m (8000 to 20 000 ft)

altogether (ˌɔːltəˈgɛðə, ˈɔːltəˌgɛðə) *adv* **1** with everything included: *altogether he owed me sixty pounds* **2** completely; utterly: *altogether mad* **3** on the whole: *altogether it was very good* ▷ *n* **4** **in the altogether** *inf* naked.

> USAGE The single-word form *altogether* is frequently written by mistake instead of two separate words. As the examples in the entry show, *altogether* is an adverb, and should not be confused with *all together*, meaning 'everyone together'. Thus: *altogether there were six or seven families sharing the flat's facilities* means 'in total', as against *there were six or seven families all together in one flat*, meaning 'all crowded in together'

altoist (ˈæltəʊɪst) *n* a person who plays the alto saxophone

altostratus (ˌæltəʊˈstreɪtəs, -ˈstrɑː-) *n, pl* **altostrati** (-taɪ) a layer cloud at an intermediate height of about 2400 to 6000 m (8000 to 20 000 ft)

altricial (ælˈtrɪʃəl) *adj* **1** denoting birds whose young, after hatching, are naked, blind, and dependent on the parents for food ▷ *n* **2** an altricial bird ▷ Cf **precocial** [c19 from NL, from L *altrix* a nurse]

Altrincham (ˈɔːltrɪŋəm) *n* a residential town in NW England, in Trafford unitary authority, Greater Manchester. Pop: 40 042 (1991)

altruism (ˈæltruːˌɪzəm) *n* unselfish concern for the welfare of others [c19 from F, from It. *altrui* others, from L] > **ˈaltruist** *n* > **ˌaltruˈistic** *adj* > **ˌaltruˈistically** *adv*

ALU *computing abbrev for* arithmetical and logical unit

alum (ˈæləm) *n* **1** a colourless soluble hydrated double sulphate of aluminium and potassium used in manufacturing and in medicine. Formula: $K_2SO_4.Al_2(SO_4)_3.24H_2O$ **2** any of a group of similar hydrated double sulphates of a monovalent metal or group and a trivalent metal [c14 from OF, from L *alūmen*]

alumina (əˈluːmɪnə) *n* another name for **aluminium oxide** [c18 from NL, pl of L *alūmen* ALUM]

aluminium (ˌæljʊˈmɪnɪəm) *or US & Canad* **aluminum** (əˈluːmɪnəm) *n* a light malleable silvery-white metallic element that resists corrosion; the third most abundant element in the earth's crust, occurring as a compound, principally in bauxite. Symbol: Al; atomic no.: 13; atomic wt.: 26.981

aluminium oxide *n* a powder occurring naturally as corundum and used in the production of aluminium, abrasives, glass, and ceramics. Formula: Al_2O_3. Also called: **alumina**

aluminize *or* **aluminise** (əˈluːmɪˌnaɪz) *vb* **aluminizes, aluminizing, aluminized** *or* **aluminises, aluminising, aluminised** *(tr)* to cover with aluminium or aluminium paint

aluminous (əˈluːmɪnəs) *adj* resembling aluminium

alumnus (əˈlʌmnəs) *or (fem)* **alumna** (əˈlʌmnə) *n, pl* **alumni** (-naɪ) *or* **alumnae** (-niː) *chiefly US & Canad* a graduate of a school, college, etc [c17 from L: nursling, pupil, from *alere* to nourish]

Alva *or* **Alba** (ˈælvə; *Spanish* ˈalβa) *n* **Duke of,** title of *Fernando Alvarez de Toledo*. 1508–82, Spanish general and statesman who suppressed the Protestant revolt in the Netherlands (1567–72) and conquered Portugal (1580)

Alvarez (ˈælvərɛz) *n* **Luis Walter** 1911–88, US physicist. He made (with Felix Bloch) the first measurement of the neutron's magnetic moment (1939). Nobel prize for physics 1968

alveolar (æl'vɪələ, ˌælvɪ'əʊlə) *adj* **1** *anat* of an alveolus **2** denoting the part of the jawbone containing the roots of the teeth **3** (of a consonant) articulated with the tongue in contact with the part of the jawbone immediately behind the upper teeth ▷ *n* **4** an alveolar consonant, such as *t*, *d*, and *s* in English

alveolate (æl'vɪəlɪt, -ˌleɪt) *adj* having many small cavities [c19 from LL *alveolātus* hollowed, from L: ALVEOLUS] > ˌ**alveo'lation** *n*

alveolus (æl'vɪələs) *n, pl* **alveoli** (-ˌlaɪ) any small pit, cavity, or saclike dilation, such as a honeycomb cell, a tooth socket, or the tiny air sacs in the lungs [c18 from L: a little hollow, dim. of *alveus*]

always ('ɔːlweɪz) *adv* **1** without exception; every time: *he always arrives on time* **2** continually; repeatedly **3** in any case: *you could always take a day off work* ▷ Also (archaic): **alway** [c13 *alles weiss*, from OE *ealne weg*, lit.: all the way]

Alwyn ('ɔːlwɪn) *n* **William** 1905–85, British composer. His works include the oratorio *The Marriage of Heaven and Hell* (1936) and the *Suite of Scottish dances* (1946)

alyssum ('ælɪsəm) *n* a widely cultivated herbaceous garden plant, having clusters of small yellow or white flowers [c16 from NL, from Gk *alusson*, from *alussos* (adj) curing rabies]

Alzheimer's disease ('ælts,haɪməz) *n* a disorder of the brain resulting in progressive decline and eventual dementia. Often shortened to **Alzheimer's** [c20 after A. *Alzheimer* (1864–1915), G physician who first identified it]
▷ www.zarcrom.com/users/yeartorem
▷ www.alz.org

am (æm; *unstressed* əm) *vb* (used with I) a form of the present tense of **be** [OE *eam*]

Am *the chemical symbol for* americium

AM *abbrev for:* **1** Also: **am** amplitude modulation **2** Assembly Member (of the National Assembly of Wales) **3** *US* Master of Arts **4** Member of the Order of Australia

Am. *abbrev for* America(n)

a.m., A.M., am, *or* **AM** (indicating the period from midnight to midday) *abbrev for* ante meridiem [L: before noon]

amabokoboko (ama'bɒkɒbɒkɒ) *pl n* *S. African* an African name for the **Springbok** rugby team [c20 from Nguni *ama*, a plural prefix + *bokoboko*, from *bok* a diminutive of SPRINGBOK]

amadoda (ama'dɔːdə) *pl n* *S African* grown men [from Nguni *ama*, a plural prefix + *doda* men]

amadou ('æməˌduː) *n* a spongy substance got from some fungi, used (formerly) as tinder, a styptic, and by fishermen to dry flies [c18 from F, from Provençal: lover, from L *amāre* to love (because easily set alight)]

amah ('ɑːmə) *n* (in the East, esp formerly) a nurse or maidservant [c19 from Port. *ama* nurse]

amain (ə'meɪn) *adv* *arch or poetic* with great strength or haste [c16 from A-[2] + MAIN[1]]

amakwerekwere (ˌama'kwerɪ'kwerɪ) *pl n* *S African inf* a term used by Blacks to refer to foreign Africans [c20 from ?]

Amalfi (ə'mælfɪ) *n* a town in Italy: a major Mediterranean port from the 10th to the 18th century, now a resort

amalgam (ə'mælgəm) *n* **1** an alloy of mercury with another metal, esp silver: *dental amalgam* **2** a blend or combination [c15 from Med. L *amalgama*, from ?]

amalgamate (ə'mælgəˌmeɪt) *vb* **amalgamates, amalgamating, amalgamated** **1** to combine or cause to combine; unite **2** to alloy (a metal) with mercury

amalgamation (əˌmælgə'meɪʃən) *n* **1** the process of amalgamating **2** the state of being amalgamated **3** a method of extracting precious metals by treatment with mercury **4** a merger

amandla (a'mɑːndlə) *n* *S African* a political slogan calling for power to the Black population [c20 Nguni, lit.: power]

amanuensis (əˌmænjʊ'ɛnsɪs) *n, pl* **amanuenses** (-siːz) a person employed to take dictation or to copy manuscripts [c17 from L, from *servus ā manū* slave at hand (that is, handwriting)]

Amanullah Khan (ˌæmə'nʊlə kɑːn) *n* 1892–1960, emir (1919–26) and king (1926–29) of Afghanistan; he obtained Afghan independence from Britain (1919)

Amapá (*Portuguese* ˌəmə'pɑː) *n* a state of N Brazil, on the Amazon delta. Capital: Macapá. Pop: 475 843 (2000). Area: 143 716 sq km (55 489 sq miles)

amaranth ('æməˌrænθ) *n* **1** *poetic* an imaginary flower that never fades **2** any of numerous plants having tassel-like heads of small green, red, or purple flowers **3** a synthetic red food colouring (**E123**), used in packet soups, cake mixes, etc [c17 from L *amarantus*, from Gk, from A-[1] + *marainein* to fade]

amaretto (ˌæmə'rɛtəʊ) *n* an Italian liqueur with a flavour of almonds [c20 from It. *amaro* bitter]

amaryllis (ˌæmə'rɪlɪs) *n* **1** a plant native to southern Africa having large lily-like reddish or white flowers **2** any of several related plants esp hippeastrum [c18 from NL, from L: after *Amaryllis*, Gk conventional name for a shepherdess]

amass (ə'mæs) *vb* **1** (*tr*) to accumulate or collect (esp riches, etc) **2** to gather in a heap [c15 from OF, from *masse* MASS] > **a'masser** *n*

amateur ('æmətə) *n* **1** a person who engages in an activity, esp a sport, as a pastime rather than for gain **2** a person unskilled in a subject or activity **3** a person who is fond of or admires something **4** (*modifier*) of or for amateurs: *an amateur event* ▷ *adj* **5** not professional or expert: *an amateur approach* [c18 from F, from L *amātor* lover, from *amāre* to love] > '**amateurism** *n*

amateurish ('æmətərɪʃ) *adj* lacking professional skill or expertise > '**amateurishly** *adv*

Aa

Amati *n* **1** (*Italian* a'maːti) a family of Italian violin makers, active in Cremona in the 16th and 17th centuries, esp **Nicolò** (niko'lɔ), 1596–1684, who taught Guarneri and Stradivari **2** (ə'mɑːtɪ) (*pl* **Amatis**) a violin or other stringed instrument made by any member of this family

amative ('æmətɪv) *adj* a rare word for **amorous** [c17 from Med. L, from L *amāre* to love]

amatory ('æmətərɪ) *or* **amatorial** (ˌæmə'tɔːrɪəl) *adj* of, relating to, or inciting sexual love or desire [c16 from L *amātōrius*, from *amāre* to love]

amaurosis (ˌæmɔː'rəʊsɪs) *n* blindness, esp when occurring without observable damage to the eye [c17 via NL from Gk: darkening, from *amauroun* to dim] > **amaurotic** (ˌæmɔː'rɒtɪk) *adj*

amaze (ə'meɪz) *vb* **amazes, amazing, amazed** (*tr*) **1** to fill with incredulity or surprise; astonish ▷ *n* **2** an archaic word for **amazement** [OE *āmasian*]

amazement (ə'meɪzmənt) *n* incredulity or great astonishment; complete wonder

amazing (ə'meɪzɪŋ) *adj* causing wonder or astonishment: *amazing feats* > **a'mazingly** *adv*

Amazon[1] ('æməzᵊn) *n* **1** *Greek myth* one of a race of women warriors of Scythia near the Black Sea **2** (*often not cap*) any tall, strong, or aggressive woman [c14 via L from Gk *Amazōn*, from ?] > **Amazonian** (ˌæmə'zəʊnɪən) *adj*

Amazon[2] ('æməzᵊn) *n* a river in South America, rising in the Peruvian Andes and flowing east through N Brazil to the Atlantic: in volume, the largest river in the world; navigable for 3700 km (2300 miles). Length: over 6440 km (4000 miles). Area of basin: over 5 827 500 sq km (2 250 000 sq miles)

Amazonas (ˌæmə'zəʊnəs) *n* a state of W Brazil, consisting of the central Amazon basin: vast areas of unexplored tropical rainforest. Capital: Manaus. Pop: 2 840 889 (2000). Area: 1 542 277 sq km (595 474 sq miles)

Amazonia (æmə'zəʊnɪə) *n* the land around the Amazon river

Ambala (əm'bɑːlə) *n* a city in N India, in Haryana: site of archaeological remains of a prehistoric Indian civilization: grain, cotton, food processing. Pop: 119 338 (1991)

ambassador (æm'bæsədə) *n* **1** a diplomat of the highest rank, accredited as permanent representative to another country **2 ambassador extraordinary** a diplomat of the highest rank sent on a special mission **3 ambassador plenipotentiary** a diplomat of the first rank with treaty-signing powers **4 ambassador-at-large** *US* an ambassador with special duties who may be sent to more than one government **5** an authorized representative or messenger [C14 from OF, from It., from OProvençal *ambaisador*, from *ambaisa* (unattested) mission, errand] > **am'bassadress** *fem n* > **ambassadorial** (æm,bæsə'dɔːrɪəl) *adj* > **am'bassador,ship** *n*

amber ('æmbə) *n* **1** a yellow translucent fossil resin derived from extinct coniferous trees and often containing trapped insects **2a** a brownish-yellow colour **2b** (*as adj*): *an amber dress* **3** an amber traffic light used as a warning between red and green [C14 from Med. L *ambar*, from Ar. *'anbar* ambergris]

amber gambler *n Brit inf* a driver who races through traffic lights when they are at amber

ambergris ('æmbə,griːs, -grɪs) *n* a waxy substance secreted by the intestinal tract of the sperm whale and often found floating in the sea: used in the manufacture of some perfumes [C15 from OF *ambre gris* grey amber]

amberjack ('æmbə,dʒæk) *n* any of several large fishes occurring in tropical and subtropical Atlantic waters [C19 from AMBER + JACK]

ambi- *combining form* indicating both: *ambidextrous; ambivalence* [from L: round, on both sides, both, from *ambo* both]

ambidextrous (,æmbɪ'dɛkstrəs) *adj* **1** equally expert with each hand **2** *inf* skilled or adept **3** underhanded > **ambidexterity** (,æmbɪdɛk'stɛrɪtɪ) *or* **,ambi'dextrousness** *n*

ambience *or* **ambiance** ('æmbɪəns) *n* the atmosphere of a place [C19 from F, from *ambiant* surrounding]

ambient ('æmbɪənt) *adj* **1** surrounding **2** creating a relaxing atmosphere: *ambient music* [C16 from L *ambiēns* going round, from AMBI- + *īre* to go]

ambiguity (,æmbɪ'gjuːɪtɪ) *n, pl* **ambiguities** **1** the possibility of interpreting an expression in more than one way **2** an instance or example of this, as in the sentence *they are cooking apples* **3** vagueness or uncertainty of meaning

ambiguous (æm'bɪgjʊəs) *adj* **1** having more than one possible interpretation **2** difficult to understand; obscure [C16 from L *ambiguus* going here and there, uncertain, from *ambigere* to go around] > **am'biguously** *adv* > **am'biguousness** *n*

ambisexual (,æmbɪ'sɛksjʊəl) *or* **ambosexual** *adj biol* relating to or affecting both the male and female sexes

ambit ('æmbɪt) *n* **1** scope or extent **2** limits or boundary [C16 from L *ambitus* a going round, from *ambīre* to go round]

ambition (æm'bɪʃən) *n* **1** strong desire for success or distinction **2** something so desired; goal [C14 from OF, from L *ambitiō* a going round (of candidates), from *ambīre* to go round]

ambitious (æm'bɪʃəs) *adj* **1** having a strong desire for success or achievement **2** necessitating extraordinary effort or ability: *an ambitious project* **3** (often foll by *of*) having a great desire (for something or to do something) > **am'bitiousness** *n*

ambivalence (æm'bɪvələns) *or* **ambivalency** *n* the coexistence of two opposed and conflicting emotions, etc > **am'bivalent** *adj*

amble ('æmbᵊl) *vb* **ambles, ambling, ambled** (*intr*) **1** to walk at a leisurely relaxed pace **2** (of a horse) to move, lifting both legs on one side together **3** to ride a horse at an amble ▷ *n* **4** a leisurely motion in walking **5** a leisurely walk **6** the ambling gait of a horse [C14 from OF, from L *ambulāre* to walk]

Ambler ('æmblə) *n* **Eric** 1909–1998, English novelist. His thrillers include *The Mask of Dimitrios* (1939), *Journey into Fear* (1940), *A Kind of Anger* (1964), and *Doctor Frigo* (1974)

Ambleside ('æmbᵊl,saɪd) *n* a town in NW England, in Cumbria: a tourist centre for the Lake District. Pop: 2905 (1991)

amblyopia (,æmblɪ'əʊpɪə) *n* impaired vision with no discernible damage to the eye or optic nerve [C18 NL, from Gk *ambluōpia*, from *amblus* dull, dim + *ōps* eye] > **amblyopic** (,æmblɪ'ɒpɪk) *adj*

ambo ('æmbəʊ) *n pl* **ambos** *Austral informal* **1** an ambulance driver **2** an ambulance

Amboina (æm'bɔɪnə) *n* **1** an island in Indonesia, in the Moluccas. Capital: Amboina. Area: 1000 sq km (386 sq miles) **2** Also called: **Ambon** ('ɑːmbɔːn) a port in the Moluccas, the capital of Amboina island

Amboise (*French* ɑ̃bwaz) *n* a town in NW central France, on the River Loire: famous castle, a former royal residence. Pop: 11 415 (latest est)

amboyna *or* **amboina** (æm'bɔɪnə) *n* the mottled curly-grained wood of an Indonesian tree, used in making furniture

Ambrose ('æmbrəʊz) *n* **1 Saint** ?340–397 AD, bishop of Milan; built up the secular power of the early Christian Church; also wrote music and Latin hymns. Feast day: Dec. 7 or April 4 **2 Curtly** ('kɜːtlɪ) born 1963, Antiguan cricketer; played for the West Indies 1987–2000

ambrosia (æm'brəʊzɪə) *n* **1** *classical myth* the food of the gods, said to bestow immortality ▷ Cf **nectar** (sense 2) **2** anything particularly delightful to taste or smell **3** another name for **beebread** [C16 via L from Gk: immortality, from A-[1] + *brotos* mortal] > **am'brosial** *or* **am'brosian** *adj*

ambry ('æmbrɪ) *or* **aumbry** ('ɔːmbrɪ) *n, pl* **ambries** *or* **aumbries** **1** a recessed cupboard in the wall of a church near the altar, used to store sacred vessels, etc **2** *obs* a small cupboard [C14 from OF *almarie*, ult. from L *armārium* chest for storage, from *arma* arms]

ambulance ('æmbjʊləns) *n* a motor vehicle designed to carry sick or injured people [C19 from F, based on (*hôpital*) *ambulant* mobile or field (hospital), from L *ambulāre* to walk]

ambulance chaser *n sl* a lawyer who seeks to encourage and profit from the lawsuits of accident victims > **ambulance chasing** *n*

ambulance stocks *pl n* high-performance stocks and shares recommended by a broker to a dissatisfied client to improve their relationship

ambulant ('æmbjʊlənt) *adj* **1** moving about from place to place **2** *med* another word for **ambulatory** (sense 3)

ambulate ('æmbjʊ,leɪt) *vb* **ambulates, ambulating, ambulated** (*intr*) to wander about or move from place to place [C17 from L *ambulāre* to walk] > **,ambu'lation** *n*

ambulatory ('æmbjʊlətərɪ) *adj* **1** of or designed for walking **2** changing position; not fixed **3** Also: **ambulant** able to walk ▷ *n, pl* **ambulatories** **4** a place for walking, such as an aisle or a cloister

ambuscade (,æmbə'skeɪd) *n* **1** an ambush ▷ *vb* **ambuscades, ambuscading, ambuscaded** **2** to ambush or lie in ambush [C16 from F, from OIt. *imboscata*, prob. of Gmc origin; cf. AMBUSH]

ambush ('æmbʊʃ) *n* **1** the act of waiting in a concealed position in order to launch a surprise attack **2** a surprise attack from such a position **3** the concealed position from which such an attack is launched **4** the person or persons waiting to launch such an attack ▷ *vb* **5** to lie in wait (for) **6** (*tr*) to attack suddenly from a concealed position [c14 from OF *embuschier* to position in ambush, from *em-* IM- + *-buschier*, from *busche* piece of firewood, prob. of Gmc origin]

ameba (əˈmiːbə) *n, pl* **amebae** (-biː) *or* **amebas** the usual US spelling of **amoeba** > **aˈmebic** *adj*

ameer (əˈmɪə) *n* a variant spelling of **emir**

ameliorate (əˈmiːljəˌreɪt) *vb* **ameliorates, ameliorating, ameliorated** to make or become better [c18 from F *améliorer* to improve, from OF, from *meillor* better, from L *melior*] > **aˌmelioˈration** *n* > **aˈmeliorative** *adj* > **aˈmelioˌrator** *n*

USAGE *Ameliorate* is sometimes confused with *alleviate*. *Ameliorate* comes ultimately from the Latin for 'better', and means 'to improve'. The nouns it typically goes with are *condition*, and *situation*. *Alleviate* means 'to lessen', and frequently occurs with *poverty*, *suffering*, *pain*, *symptoms*, and *effects*. Occasionally *ameliorate* is used with *effects* and *poverty* where the other verb may be more appropriate

amen (ˌeɪˈmɛn, ˌɑːˈmɛn) *sentence substitute* **1** so be it!: a term used at the end of a prayer ▷ *n* **2** the use of the word *amen* [c13 via LL via Gk from Heb. *āmēn* certainly]

Amen (ˈɑːmən) *n Egyptian myth* a local Theban god, having a ram's head and symbolizing life and fertility, identified by the Egyptians with the national deity Amen-Ra

amenable (əˈmiːnəbᵊl) *adj* **1** likely to listen, cooperate, etc **2** accountable to some authority; answerable **3** capable of being tested, judged, etc [c16 from Anglo-F, from OF, from L *mināre* to drive (cattle), from *minārī* to threaten] > **aˌmenaˈbility** *or* **aˈmenableness** *n* > **aˈmenably** *adv*

amend (əˈmɛnd) *vb* (*tr*) **1** to improve; change for the better **2** to correct **3** to alter or revise (legislation, etc) by formal procedure [c13 from OF, from L *ēmendāre* to EMEND] > **aˈmendable** *adj* > **aˈmender** *n*

amendment (əˈmɛndmənt) *n* **1** correction **2** an addition or alteration to a document, etc

amends (əˈmɛndz) *n* (*functioning as sing*) recompense or compensation for some injury, insult, etc: *to make amends* [c13 from OF, from *amende* compensation, from *amender* to EMEND]

Amenhotep III (ˌæmɛnˈhəʊtɛp) *or* **Amenhotpe III** (ˌæmɛnˈhɒtpɪ) *n* Greek name *Amenophis*. ?1411–?1375 BC, Egyptian pharaoh who expanded Egypt's influence by peaceful diplomacy and erected many famous buildings

amenity (əˈmiːnɪtɪ) *n, pl* **amenities** **1** (*often pl*) a useful or pleasant facility: *a swimming pool was one of the amenities* **2** the fact or condition of being agreeable **3** (*usually pl*) a social courtesy [c14 from L, from *amoenus* agreeable]

amenorrhoea *or esp US* **amenorrhea** (æˌmɛnəˈrɪə, eɪ-) *n* abnormal absence of menstruation [c19 from A-¹ + MENO- + -RRHOEA]

Amen-Ra (ˌɑːmənˈrɑː) *n Egyptian myth* the sun-god; the principal deity during the period of Theban hegemony

ament (ˈæmənt) *n* another name for **catkin.** Also called: **amentum** (əˈmɛntəm) [c18 from L *āmentum* thong] > ˌ**amenˈtaceous** *adj*

amentia (əˈmɛnʃə) *n* severe mental deficiency, usually congenital [c14 from L: insanity, from *āmēns* mad, from *mēns* mind]

Amer. *abbrev for* America(n)

amerce (əˈmɜːs) *vb* **amerces, amercing, amerced** (*tr*) *obs* **1** *law* to punish by a fine **2** to punish with any arbitrary penalty [c14 from Anglo-F, from OF *à merci* at the mercy; see MERCY] > **aˈmercement** *n*

America (əˈmɛrɪkə) *n* **1** short for the **United States of America** **2** Also called: **the Americas** the American continent, including North, South, and Central America [c16 from *Americus*, Latin form of *Amerigo*; after Amerigo Vespucci (?1454–1512), Florentine navigator in the New World]

American (əˈmɛrɪkən) *adj* **1** of or relating to the United States of America, its inhabitants, or their form of English **2** of or relating to the American continent ▷ *n* **3** a native or citizen of the US **4** a native or inhabitant of any country of North, Central, or South America **5** the English language as spoken or written in the United States

Americana (əˌmɛrɪˈkɑːnə) *pl n* objects, such as documents, relics, etc, relating to America

American aloe *n* See **aloe** (sense 2)

American Civil War *n* See **Civil War** (sense 2)

American Dream *n* **the** the notion that the American social, economic, and political system makes success possible for every individual

American football *n* **1** a team game similar to rugby, with 11 players on each side **2** the oval-shaped inflated ball used in this game
▷ www.nfl.com

American Indian *n* **1** Also called: **Indian, Amerindian, Native American** a member of any of the indigenous peoples of America, typically having straight black hair and a yellow-to-brown skin ▷ *adj* **2** Also called: **Amerindian** of or relating to any of these peoples, their languages, or their cultures

Americanism (əˈmɛrɪkəˌnɪzəm) *n* **1** a custom, linguistic usage, or other feature peculiar to or characteristic of the United States **2** loyalty to the United States

Americanize *or* **Americanise** (əˈmɛrɪkəˌnaɪz) *vb* **Americanizes, Americanizing, Americanized** *or* **Americanises, Americanising, Americanised** to make or become American in outlook, attitudes, etc > **Aˌmericaniˈzation** *or* **Aˌmericaniˈsation** *n*

American Revolution *n* the usual US term for **War of American Independence**

Aa

American Samoa *n* the part of Samoa administered by the US Capital: Pago Pago. Pop: 58 000 (2001 est). Area: 197 sq km (76 sq miles)

americium (ˌæməˈrɪsɪəm) *n* a white metallic transuranic element artificially produced from plutonium. It is used as an alpha-particle source. Symbol: Am; atomic no.: 95; half-life of most stable isotope, ^{243}Am: 7.4 × 10³ years [c20 from AMERICA (where it was first produced) + -IUM]

Amerigo Vespucci (*Italian* ameˈriːgo vesˈputtʃi) *n* See **Vespucci**

Amerindian (ˌæməˈrɪndɪən) *n also* **Amerind** (ˈæmərɪnd), *adj* another word for **American Indian** > ˌ**Amerˈindic** *adj*

amethyst (ˈæmɪθɪst) *n* **1** a purple or violet variety of quartz used as a gemstone **2** a purple variety of sapphire **3a** the purple colour of amethyst **3b** (*as adj*): *amethyst shadow* [c13 from OF, from L, from Gk *amethustos*, lit.: not drunken, from A-¹ + *methuein* to make drunk; from the belief that the stone could prevent intoxication] > **amethystine** (ˌæmɪˈθɪstaɪn) *adj*

Amex (ˈæmɛks) *n acronym for* **1** *trademark* American Express **2** American Stock Exchange

AMF *abbrev for* Australian Military Forces

Amhara (æmˈhɑːrə) *n* **1** a region of NW Ethiopia: formerly a kingdom **2** an inhabitant of the former kingdom of Amhara

Amharic (æmˈhærɪk) *n* **1** the official language of Ethiopia ▷ *adj* **2** denoting this language

Amherst (ˈæmhɜːst) *n* **Jeffrey,** 1st Baron Amherst. 1717–97, British general who defeated the French in Canada (1758–60): governor general of British North America (1761–63)

amiable (ˈeɪmɪəbᵊl) *adj* having or displaying a pleasant or agreeable nature; friendly [c14 from OF, from LL *amīcābilis* AMICABLE] > ˌ**amiaˈbility** *or* ˈ**amiableness** *n* > ˈ**amiably** *adv*

amianthus (ˌæmɪˈænθəs) *n* any of the fine silky varieties of asbestos [C17 from L *amiantus*, from Gk *amiantos* unsullied, from A-[1] + *miainein* to pollute]

amicable (ˈæmɪkəbᵊl) *adj* characterized by friendliness: *an amicable agreement* [C15 from LL *amīcābilis*, from L *amīcus* friend] > ˌ**amicaˈbility** *or* ˈ**amicableness** *n* > ˈ**amicably** *adv*

amice (ˈæmɪs) *n Christianity* a rectangular piece of white linen worn by priests around the neck and shoulders under the alb or, formerly, on the head [C15 from OF, from L *amictus* cloak]

amicus curiae (æˈmiːkʊs ˈkjʊərɪˌiː) *n, pl* **amici curiae** (æˈmiːkaɪ) *law* a person, not directly engaged in a case, who advises the court [L, lit.: friend of the court]

amid (əˈmɪd) *or* **amidst** *prep* in the middle of; among [OE *on middan* in the middle]

amide (ˈæmaɪd) *n* **1** any organic compound containing the group -CONR$_2$, where R denotes a hydrogen atom or a hydrocarbon group **2** (*modifier*) containing the group -CONR$_2$: *amide group or radical* **3** an inorganic compound containing the NH_2^- ion and having the general formula $M(NH_2)_x$, where M is a metal atom [C19 from AM(MONIA) + -IDE]

amidships (əˈmɪdʃɪps) *adv, adj* (*postpositive*) *naut* at, near, or towards the centre of a vessel

Amiens (ˈæmɪənz; *French* amjɛ̃) *n* a city in N France: its Gothic cathedral is the largest church in France. Pop: 135 501 (1999)

amigo (æˈmiːɡəʊ, ə-) *n, pl* **amigos** a friend; comrade [Sp., from L *amicus*]

Amin[1] (æˈmiːn, ɑː-) *n* **Lake** a former official name for (Lake) **Edward**

Amin[2] (æˈmiːn, ɑː-) *n* **Idi** (ˈiːdiː) 1925–2003, Ugandan soldier; dictator and head of state (1971–79). Notorious for his brutality, he was overthrown and exiled

amine (əˈmiːn, ˈæmɪn) *n* an organic base formed by replacing one or more of the hydrogen atoms of ammonia by hydrocarbon groups [C19 from AM(MONIUM) + -INE[2]]

amino (əˈmiːnəʊ) *n* (*modifier*) of or containing the group of atoms -NH$_2$: *amino radical*

amino acid *n* **1** any of a group of organic compounds containing one or more amino groups, -NH$_2$, and one or more carboxyl groups, -COOH **2** any of a group of organic nitrogenous compounds that form the component molecules of proteins

amino resin *n* a thermosetting synthetic resin used as an adhesive and coating for paper and textiles

amir (əˈmɪə) *n* a variant spelling of **emir** [C19 from Ar., var. of EMIR] > **aˈmirate** *n*

Amis (ˈeɪmɪs) *n* **1** Sir **Kingsley** 1922–95, British novelist and poet, noted for his novels *Lucky Jim* (1954), *Jake's Thing* (1978), *Stanley and the Women* (1984), *The Old Devils* (1986), and *The Folks that Live on the Hill* (1990) **2** his son, **Martin** born 1949, British novelist. His works include *The Rachel Papers* (1974), *Money* (1984), *London Fields* (1989), *The Information* (1994), and *Yellow Dog* (2003)

Amish (ˈæmɪʃ, ˈɑː-) *adj* of a US and Canadian Mennonite sect [C19 from G *Amisch*, after Jakob *Amman*, 17th-cent. Swiss Mennonite bishop]

amiss (əˈmɪs) *adv* **1** in an incorrect or defective manner **2 take (something) amiss** to be annoyed or offended by (something) ▹ *adj* **3** (*postpositive*) wrong or faulty [C13 *a mis*, from *mis* wrong]

amitosis (ˌæmɪˈtəʊsɪs) *n* a form of cell division in which the nucleus and cytoplasm divide without the formation of chromosomes [C20 from A-[1] + MITOSIS] > **amitotic** (ˌæmɪˈtɒtɪk) *adj*

amity (ˈæmɪtɪ) *n, pl* **amities** friendship; cordiality [C15 from OF *amité*, ult. from L *amīcus* friend]

Amman (əˈmɑːn) *n* the capital of Jordan, northeast of the Dead Sea: ancient capital of the Ammonites, rebuilt by Ptolemy in the 3rd century BC. Pop: 969 598 (1994). Ancient names: **Rabbath Ammon, Philadelphia** ▹ www.access2arabia.com/moga

ammeter (ˈæmˌmiːtə) *n* an instrument for measuring an electric current in amperes [C19 AM(PERE) + -METER]

ammo (ˈæməʊ) *n inf* short for **ammunition**

Ammon[1] (ˈæmən) *n Old Testament* the ancestor of the Ammonites

Ammon[2] (ˈæmən) *n myth* the classical name of the Egyptian god Amen, identified by the Greeks with Zeus and by the Romans with Jupiter

ammonia (əˈməʊnɪə) *n* **1** a colourless pungent gas used in the manufacture of fertilizers and as a refrigerant and solvent. Formula: NH_3 **2** a solution of ammonia in water, containing ammonium hydroxide [C18 from NL, from L (*sal*) *ammōniacus* (sal) AMMONIAC]

ammoniac (əˈməʊnɪˌæk) *n* a gum resin obtained from the stems of an Asian plant and formerly used as a stimulant, perfume, and in porcelain cement. Also called: **gum ammoniac** [C14 from L, from Gk *ammōniakos* belonging to Ammon (apparently the gum resin was extracted from plants found in Libya near the temple of Ammon)]

ammoniacal (ˌæməˈnaɪəkᵊl) *adj* of, containing, or resembling ammonia

ammoniate (əˈməʊnɪˌeɪt) *vb* **ammoniates, ammoniating, ammoniated** to unite or treat with ammonia > **amˌmoniˈation** *n*

ammonify (əˈmɒnɪˌfaɪ) *vb* **ammonifies, ammonifying, ammonified** to treat or impregnate with ammonia or a compound of ammonia > **amˌmonifiˈcation** *n*

ammonite (ˈæməˌnaɪt) *n* **1** any extinct marine cephalopod mollusc of the order *Ammonoidea*, which were common in Mesozoic times and generally had a coiled partitioned shell **2** the shell of any of these animals, commonly occurring as a fossil [C18 from L *cornū Ammōnis*, lit.: horn of Ammon]

ammonium (əˈməʊnɪəm) *n* (*modifier*) of or containing the monovalent group NH_4– or the ion NH_4^+: *ammonium compounds*

ammonium chloride *n* a white soluble crystalline solid used as an electrolyte in dry batteries. Formula: NH_4Cl. Also called: **sal ammoniac**

ammonium hydroxide *n* a compound existing in solution when ammonia is dissolved in water. Formula: NH_4OH

ammonium sulphate *n* a white soluble crystalline solid used mainly as a fertilizer and in water purification. Formula: $(NH_4)_2SO_4$

ammunition (ˌæmjʊˈnɪʃən) *n* **1** any projectiles, such as bullets, rockets, etc, that can be discharged from a weapon **2** bombs, missiles, chemicals, etc, capable of use as weapons **3** any means of defence or attack, as in an argument [C17 from obs. F *amunition*, by mistaken division from earlier *la munition*; see MUNITION]

amnesia (æmˈniːzjə, -ʒjə, -zɪə) *n* a defect in memory, esp one resulting from a pathological cause [C19 via NL from Gk: forgetfulness, prob. from *amnēstia* oblivion] > **amnesiac** (æmˈniːzɪˌæk) *or* **amnesic** (æmˈniːsɪk, -zɪk) *adj, n*

amnesty (ˈæmnɪstɪ) *n, pl* **amnesties** **1** a general pardon, esp for offences against a government **2** a period during which a law is suspended to allow offenders to admit their crime without fear of prosecution ▹ *vb* **amnesties, amnestying, amnestied** **3** (*tr*) to overlook or forget (an offence) [C16 from L *amnēstia*, from Gk: oblivion, from A-[1] + *-mnēstos*, from *mnasthai* to remember]

Amnesty International *n* an international organization that works to secure the release of people imprisoned for their beliefs, to ban the use of torture, and to abolish the death penalty. Abbrev: **AI**

amnio (ˈæmnɪəʊ) *n* short for **amniocentesis**

amniocentesis (ˌæmnɪəʊsɛnˈtiːsɪs) *n, pl* **amniocenteses**

(-si:z) removal of amniotic fluid for diagnostic purposes by the insertion into the womb of a hollow needle [C20 from AMNION + *centesis* from Gk *kentēsis* from *kentein* to prick]

amnion ('æmnɪən) *n, pl* **amnions** *or* **amnia** (-nɪə) the innermost of two membranes enclosing an embryonic reptile, bird, or mammal [C17 via NL from Gk: a little lamb, from *amnos* a lamb] > **amniotic** (ˌæmnɪ'ɒtɪk) *adj*

amniotic fluid *n* the fluid surrounding the fetus in the womb

amoeba *or US* **ameba** (ə'mi:bə) *n, pl* **amoebae** (-bi:) *or* **amoebas** *or US* **amebae** (-bi:) *or* **amebas** any of a phylum of protozoans able to change shape because of the movements of cell processes. They live in fresh water or soil or as parasites in man and animals [C19 from NL, from Gk, from *ameibein* to change, exchange] > **a'moebic** *or US* **a'mebic** *adj*

amok (ə'mʌk, ə'mɒk) *or* **amuck** (ə'mʌk) *n* **1** a state of murderous frenzy ▷ *adv* **2** **run amok** to run about as with a frenzied desire to kill [C17 from Malay *amoq* furious assault]

among (ə'mʌŋ) *or* **amongst** *prep* **1** in the midst of: *he lived among the Indians* **2** to each of: *divide the reward among yourselves* **3** in the group, class, or number of: *among the greatest writers* **4** taken out of (a group): *he is one among many* **5** with one another within a group: *decide it among yourselves* **6** in the general opinion or practice of: *accepted among experts* [OE *amang*, contracted from *on gemang* in the group of, from ON + *gemang* crowd]

USAGE See at **between**

amontillado (əˌmɒntɪ'lɑ:dəʊ) *n* a medium-dry sherry [C19 from Sp. *vino amontillado* wine of *Montilla*, town in Spain]

amoral (ˌeɪ'mɒrəl) *adj* **1** having no moral quality; nonmoral **2** without moral standards or principles > **amorality** (ˌeɪmɒ'rælɪtɪ) *n*

USAGE *Amoral* is sometimes confused with *immoral*. The *a-* at the beginning of the word means 'without' or 'lacking', so the word is properly used of people who have no moral code, or about places or situations where moral considerations do not apply: *the film was violent and amoral*. In contrast *immoral* should be used to talk about the breaking of moral rules, as in: *drug dealing is the most immoral and evil of all human activities*

amorist ('æmərɪst) *n* a lover or a writer about love

amoroso (ˌæmə'rəʊsəʊ) *adj, adv* **1** *music* (to be played) tenderly ▷ *n* **2** a rich sweet sherry [from It. & Sp.: AMOROUS]

amorous ('æmərəs) *adj* **1** inclined towards or displaying love or desire **2** in love **3** of or relating to love [C14 from OF, from Med. L, from L *amor* love] > **'amorously** *adv* > **'amorousness** *n*

amorphous (ə'mɔ:fəs) *adj* **1** lacking a definite shape **2** of no recognizable character or type **3** (of rocks, etc) not having a crystalline structure [C18 from NL, from Gk, from A-[1] + *morphē* shape] > **a'morphism** *n* > **a'morphousness** *n*

amortize *or* **amortise** (ə'mɔ:taɪz) *vb* **amortizes, amortizing, amortized** *or* **amortises, amortising, amortised** (*tr*) **1** *finance* to liquidate (a debt, mortgage, etc) by payments or by periodic transfers to a sinking fund **2** to write off (a wasting asset) by transfers to a sinking fund **3** *property law* (formerly) to transfer (lands, etc) in mortmain [C14 from Med. L, from OF *amortir* to reduce to the point of death, ult. from L *ad* to + *mors* death] > **aˌmorti'zation** *or* **aˌmorti'sation** *n*

Amos ('eɪmɒs) *n Old Testament* **1** a Hebrew prophet of the 8th century BC **2** the book containing his oracles

amount (ə'maʊnt) *n* **1** extent; quantity **2** the total of two or more quantities **3** the full value or significance of something **4** a principal sum plus the interest on it, as in a loan ▷ *vb* **5** (*intr*; usually foll by *to*) to be equal or add up [C13 from OF *amonter* to go up, from *amont* upwards, from *a* to + *mont* mountain (from L *mōns*)]

USAGE The use of a plural noun after *amount of* (*the amount of people; the amount of goods*) should be avoided: *the number of people; the number of goods* is more appropriate

amount of substance *n* a measure of the number of entities (atoms, molecules, ions, electrons, etc) present in a substance, expressed in moles

amour *French* (amur) *n* a love affair, esp a secret or illicit one [C13 from OF, from L *amor* love]

amour-propre *French* (amurprɔprə) *n* self-respect

Amoy (ə'mɔɪ) *n* **1** a port in SE China, in Fujian province on **Amoy Island**, at the mouth of the Jiu-long River opposite Taiwan: one of the first treaty ports opened to European trade (1842) Pop: 368 786 (1990 est). Modern Chinese name: **Xiamen** **2** the dialect of Chinese spoken in Amoy, Taiwan, and elsewhere: a Min dialect

amp (æmp) *n* **1** an ampere **2** *inf* an amplifier

AMP *n biochem* adenosine monophosphate; a substance produced by hydrolysis of ATP with the liberation of energy. The cyclic form (**cyclic AMP**) acts as a messenger in many hormone-induced biochemical reactions

ampelopsis (ˌæmpɪ'lɒpsɪs) *n* any of a genus of woody climbing plants of tropical and subtropical Asia and America [C19 from NL, from Gk *ampelos* grapevine]

amperage ('æmpərɪdʒ) *n* the strength of an electric current measured in amperes

ampere ('æmpɛə) *n* **1** the basic SI unit of electric current; the constant current that, when maintained in two parallel conductors of infinite length and negligible cross section placed 1 metre apart in free space, produces a force of 2×10^{-7} newton per metre between them **2** a former unit of electric current (**international ampere**); the current that, when passed through a solution of silver nitrate, deposits silver at the rate of 0.001118 gram per second ▷ Abbrev: **amp** Symbol: A [C19 after A. M. AMPÈRE]

Ampère ('æmpɛə; *French* ɑ̃pɛr) *n* **André Mari** (ɑ̃dre mari) 1775–1836, French physicist and mathematician, who made major discoveries in the fields of magnetism and electricity

ampere-turn *n* a unit of magnetomotive force; the magnetomotive force produced by a current of 1 ampere passing through one complete turn of a coil

ampersand ('æmpəˌsænd) *n* the character (&), meaning *and*: *John Brown & Co* [C19 shortened from *and per se and*, that is, the symbol & by itself (represents) *and*]

amphetamine (æm'fɛtəˌmi:n) *n* a synthetic colourless liquid used medicinally as the white crystalline sulphate, mainly for its stimulant action on the central nervous system [C20 from A(LPHA) + M(ETHYL) + PH(ENYL) + ET(HYL) + AMINE]

amphi- *prefix* **1** on both sides; at both ends; of both kinds: *amphipod; amphibious* **2** around: *amphibole* [from Gk]

amphibian (æm'fɪbɪən) *n* **1** any cold-blooded vertebrate of the class *Amphibia*, typically living on land but breeding in water. The class includes newts, frogs, and toads **2** an aircraft able to land and take off from both water and land **3** any vehicle able to travel on both water and land ▷ *adj* **4** another word for **amphibious** **5** of or belonging to the class *Amphibia*

amphibious (æm'fɪbɪəs) *adj* **1** able to live both on land and in the water, as frogs, etc **2** designed for operation on or from both water and land **3** relating to military forces and operations launched from the sea against an enemy shore **4** having a dual or mixed nature [C17 from Gk *amphibios*, lit.: having a double life, from AMPHI- + *bios* life] > **am'phibiousness** *n*

amphibole ('æmfɪˌbəʊl) *n* any of a large group of minerals consisting of the silicates of calcium, iron, magnesium, sodium, and aluminium, which are

Aa

common constituents of igneous rocks [c17 from F, from Gk *amphibolos* uncertain; so called from the large number of varieties in the group]

amphibology (ˌæmfɪˈbɒlədʒɪ) *or* **amphiboly** (æmˈfɪbəlɪ) *n, pl* **amphibologies** *or* **amphibolies** ambiguity of expression, esp when due to a grammatical construction, as in *save rags and waste paper* [c14 from LL, ult. from Gk *amphibolos* ambiguous]

amphimixis (ˌæmfɪˈmɪksɪs) *n, pl* **amphimixes** (-ˈmɪksiːz) true sexual reproduction by the fusion of gametes from two organisms [c19 from AMPHI- + Gk *mixis* a blending] > **amphimictic** (ˌæmfɪˈmɪktɪk) *adj*

amphioxus (ˌæmfɪˈɒksəs) *n, pl* **amphioxi** (-ˈɒksaɪ) *or* **amphioxuses** another name for the **lancelet** [c19 from NL, from AMPHI- + Gk *oxus* sharp]

amphipod (ˈæmfɪˌpɒd) *n* **1** any marine or freshwater crustacean of the order *Amphipoda*, such as the sand hoppers, in which the body is laterally compressed ▷ *adj* **2** of or belonging to the *Amphipoda*

amphiprostyle (æmˈfɪprəˌstaɪl) *adj* **1** (esp of a classical temple) having a set of columns at both ends but not at the sides ▷ *n* **2** a temple of this kind

amphisbaena (æmfɪsˈbiːnə) *n, pl* **amphisbaenae** (-niː) *or* **amphisbaenas** **1** a genus of wormlike lizards of tropical America **2** *classical myth* a fabulous serpent with a head at each end [c16 from L, from Gk *amphisbaina*, from *amphis* both ways + *bainein* to go]

amphitheatre *or US* **amphitheater** (ˈæmfɪˌθɪətə) *n* **1** a building, usually circular or oval, in which tiers of seats rise from a central open arena **2** a place where contests are held **3** any level circular area of ground surrounded by higher ground **4** a gallery in a theatre **5** a lecture room in which seats are tiered away from a central area

Amphitrite (ˌæmfɪˈtraɪtɪ) *n Greek myth* a sea goddess, wife of Poseidon and mother of Triton

amphora (ˈæmfərə) *n, pl* **amphorae** (-fəˌriː) *or* **amphoras** a Greek or Roman two-handled narrow-necked jar for oil, etc [c17 from L, from Gk, from AMPHI- + *phoreus* bearer, from *pherein* to bear]

amphoteric (ˌæmfəˈtɛrɪk) *adj chem* able to function as either a base or an acid [c19 from Gk *amphoteros* each of two (from *amphō* both) + -IC]

ampicillin (ˌæmpɪˈsɪlɪn) *n* a form of penicillin used to treat various infections

ample (ˈæmpᵊl) *adj* **1** more than sufficient: *an ample helping* **2** large: *of ample proportions* [c15 from OF, from L *amplus* spacious] > **ˈampleness** *n*

amplification (ˌæmplɪfɪˈkeɪʃən) *n* **1** the act or result of amplifying **2** material added to a statement, story, etc, to expand or clarify it **3** a statement, story, etc, with such additional material **4** *electronics* the increase in strength of an electrical signal by means of an amplifier

amplifier (ˈæmplɪˌfaɪə) *n* **1** an electronic device used to increase the strength of the current fed into it, esp one for the amplification of sound signals in a radio, record player, etc **2** *photog* an additional lens for altering focal length **3** a person or thing that amplifies

amplify (ˈæmplɪˌfaɪ) *vb* **amplifies, amplifying, amplified** **1** (*tr*) to increase in size, extent, effect, etc, as by the addition of extra material **2** *electronics* to produce amplification of (electrical signals) **3** (*intr*) to expand a speech, narrative, etc [c15 from OF, ult. from L *amplificāre* to enlarge, from *amplus* spacious + *facere* to make]

amplitude (ˈæmplɪˌtjuːd) *n* **1** greatness of extent; magnitude **2** abundance **3** breadth or scope, as of the mind **4** *astron* the angular distance along the horizon measured from true east or west to the point of intersection of the vertical circle passing through a celestial body **5** *physics* the maximum displacement from the zero or mean position of a periodic motion [c16 from L, from *amplus* spacious]

amplitude modulation *n* one of the principal methods of transmitting information using radio waves, the relevant signal being superimposed onto a radio-frequency carrier wave. The frequency of the carrier wave remains unchanged but its amplitude is varied in accordance with the amplitude of the input signal ▷ Cf **frequency modulation**

amply (ˈæmplɪ) *adv* fully; generously

ampoule (ˈæmpuːl, -pjuːl) *or esp US* **ampule** *n med* a small glass vessel in which liquids for injection are hermetically sealed [c19 from F, from L: see AMPULLA]

ampulla (æmˈpʊlə) *n, pl* **ampullae** (-ˈpʊliː) **1** *anat* the dilated end part of certain ducts or canals **2** *Christianity* **2a** a vessel for the wine and water used at the Eucharist **2b** a small flask for consecrated oil **3** a Roman two-handled bottle for oil, wine, or perfume [c16 from L, dim. of AMPHORA]

amputate (ˈæmpjʊˌteɪt) *vb* **amputates, amputating, amputated** *surgery* to remove (all or part of a limb) [c17 from L, from *am-* around + *putāre* to trim, prune] > **ˌampuˈtation** *n*

amputee (ˌæmpjʊˈtiː) *n* a person who has had a limb amputated

Amritsar (æmˈrɪtsə) *n* a city in India, in NW Punjab: centre of the Sikh religion; site of a massacre in 1919 of unarmed supporters of Indian self-government by British troops; in 1984 the Golden Temple, fortified by Sikhs, was attacked by Indian troops with the loss of many Sikh lives. Pop: 708 835 (1991)

Amsterdam (ˌæmstəˈdæm; *Dutch* ɑmstərˈdɑm) *n* the commercial capital of the Netherlands, a major industrial centre and port on the IJsselmeer, connected with the North Sea by canal: built on about 100 islands within a network of canals. Pop: 727 053 (1999 est) ▷ www.visitamsterdam.nl

amu *abbrev for* atomic mass unit

amuck (əˈmʌk) *n, adv* a variant spelling of **amok**

Amu Darya (*Russian* aˈmu darjˈja) *n* a river in central Asia, rising in the Pamirs and flowing northwest through the Hindu Kush and across Turkmenistan and Uzbekistan to its delta in the Aral Sea: forms much of the N border of Afghanistan and is important for irrigation. Length: 2400 km (1500 miles). Ancient name: **Oxus**

amulet (ˈæmjʊlɪt) *n* a trinket or piece of jewellery worn as a protection against evil; charm [c17 from L *amulētum*, from ?]

Amundsen (*Norwegian* ˈaːmunsən) *n* **Roald** (ˈrɔald) 1872–1928, Norwegian explorer and navigator, who was the first man to reach the South Pole (1911)

Amundsen Sea (ˈɑːmʊndsən) *n* a part of the South Pacific Ocean, in Antarctica off Byrd Land

Amur (əˈmʊə) *n* a river in NE Asia, rising in N Mongolia as the Argun and flowing southeast, then northeast to the Sea of Okhotsk: forms the boundary between Manchuria and Russia. Length: about 4350 km (2700 miles). Modern Chinese name: **Heilong Jiang**

amuse (əˈmjuːz) *vb* **amuses, amusing, amused** (*tr*) **1** to entertain; divert **2** to cause to laugh or smile [c15 from OF *amuser* to cause to be idle, from *muser* to MUSE¹]

amusement (əˈmjuːzmənt) *n* **1** something that amuses, such as a game or pastime **2** a mechanical device used for entertainment, as at a fair **3** the act of amusing or the state or quality of being amused

amusement arcade *n Brit* a covered area having coin-operated game machines

amusing (əˈmjuːzɪŋ) *adj* entertaining; causing a smile or laugh > **aˈmusingly** *adv*

amygdalin (əˈmɪgdəlɪn) *n* a white soluble bitter-tasting glycoside extracted from bitter almonds and stored fruit [c17 from Gk: ALMOND + -IN]

amyl (ˈæmɪl) *n* (*modifier*) (no longer in technical usage) of or containing any of eight isomeric forms of the monovalent group C_5H_{11}–: *amyl group or radical* [c19 from L: AMYLUM]

amylaceous (ˌæmɪˈleɪʃəs) *adj* of or resembling starch

amyl alcohol *n* **1** any of eight isomeric alcohols with the general formula $C_5H_{11}OH$ **2** a mixture of these alcohols, used in preparing amyl nitrite

amylase (ˈæmɪˌleɪz) *n* any of several enzymes that hydrolyse starch and glycogen to simple sugars, such as glucose

amyl nitrite *n* an ester of amyl alcohol and nitrous acid used as a vasodilator, esp to treat angina

amyloid (ˈæmɪˌlɔɪd) *n* **1** any substance resembling starch ▷ *adj* **2** starchlike

amylopsin (ˌæmɪˈlɒpsɪn) *n* an enzyme of the pancreatic juice that converts starch into sugar; pancreatic amylase [C19 from AMYL + (PE)PSIN]

amylum (ˈæmɪləm) *n* another name for **starch** (senses 1,2) [L, from Gk *amulon* fine meal, starch]

amyotrophic lateral sclerosis (ˌæmɪəʊˈtrəʊfɪk) *n* a form of motor neurone disease in which degeneration of motor tracts in the spinal cord causes progressive muscular paralysis starting in the limbs. Also called: **Lou Gehrig's disease**

Amytal (ˈæmɪˌtæl) *n trademark* sodium amytal, a barbiturate used as a sedative and hypnotic

an[1] (æn; *unstressed* ən) *determiner* (*indefinite article*) a form of **a**[1], used before an initial vowel sound: *an old car; an elf; an hour* [OE *ān* ONE]

> USAGE *An* was formerly often used before words beginning with a pronounced *h* that were unstressed on the first syllable, as in *an hotel; an historic meeting*. Sometimes the initial *h* was not pronounced. This usage is neither more nor less correct than using *a*, and is now considerably less common even in written sources, though some newspapers recommend it as part of their house style. The Bank of English shows that *a* is hugely more common with *hotel*, and at least twice as common with *heroic*, *historian*, *historical*, and *horrendous*. *Habitual* and *horrific* are used almost as much with *an* as with *a*, while *historic* seems equally at home with either

an[2] *or* **an'** (æn; *unstressed* ən) *conj* (*subordinating*) an obsolete or dialect word for **if** See **and** (sense 8)

An (ɑːn) *n myth* the Sumerian sky god. Babylonian counterpart: **Anu**

AN *abbrev for* Anglo-Norman

an- *or before a consonant* **a-** *prefix* not; without: *anaphrodisiac* [from Gk]

-an, -ean, *or* **-ian** *suffix* **1** (*forming adjectives and nouns*) belonging to; coming from; typical of; adhering to: *European; Elizabethan; Christian* **2** (*forming nouns*) a person who specializes or is expert in: *dietitian* [from L *-ānus*, suffix of adjectives]

ana- *or before a vowel* **an-** *prefix* **1** up; upwards: *anadromous* **2** again: *anagram* **3** back; backwards: *anapaest* [from Gk *ana*]

-ana *or* **-iana** *suffix forming nouns* denoting a collection of objects or information relating to a particular individual, subject or place: *Victoriana, Americana* [NL, from L *-āna*, lit.: matters relating to, neuter pl of *-ānus*; see -AN]

Anabaptist (ˌænəˈbæptɪst) *n* **1** a member of any of various Protestant movements, esp of the 16th century, that rejected infant baptism, insisted that adults be rebaptized, and sought to establish Christian communism ▷ *adj* **2** of these sects or their doctrines [C16 from Ecclesiastical L, from *anabaptīzāre* to baptize again, from LGk *anabaptizein*] > ˌ**Ana**ˈ**baptism** *n*

anabas (ˈænəˌbæs) *n* any of several freshwater fishes, esp the climbing perch, that can travel on land [C19 from NL, from Gk *anabainein* to go up]

anabasis (əˈnæbəsɪs) *n, pl* **anabases** (-ˌsiːz) **1** the march of Cyrus the Younger from Sardis to Cunaxa in Babylonia in 401 BC, described by Xenophon in his *Anabasis* **2** any military expedition, esp one from the coast to the interior [C18 from Gk: a going up, from *anabainein* to go up]

anabatic (ˌænəˈbætɪk) *adj meteorol* (of air currents) rising upwards [C19 from Gk *anabatikos* relating to ascents, from *anabainein* to go up]

anabiosis (ˌænəbaɪˈəʊsɪs) *n* the ability to return to life after apparent death; suspended animation [C19 via NL from Gk, from *anabioein* to come back to life] > **anabiotic** (ˌænəbaɪˈɒtɪk) *adj*

anabolic steroid *n* any of a group of synthetic steroid hormones (androgens) used to stimulate muscle and bone growth for athletic or therapeutic purposes

anabolism (əˈnæbəˌlɪzəm) *n* a metabolic process in which complex molecules are synthesized from simpler ones with the storage of energy; constructive metabolism [C19 from ANA- + (META)BOLISM] > **anabolic** (ˌænəˈbɒlɪk) *adj*

anachronism (əˈnækrəˌnɪzəm) *n* **1** the representation of an event, person, or thing in a historical context in which it could not have occurred or existed **2** a person or thing that belongs or seems to belong to another time [C17 from L, from Gk *anakhronismos* a mistake in chronology, from ANA- + *khronos* time] > **a**ˌ**nachro**ˈ**nistic** *adj* > **a**ˌ**nachro**ˈ**nistically** *adv*

anacoluthon (ˌænəkəˈluːθɒn) *n, pl* **anacolutha** (-θə) a construction that involves the change from one grammatical sequence to another within a single sentence [C18 from LL, from Gk, from *anakolouthos* not consistent, from AN- + *akolouthos* following]

anaconda (ˌænəˈkɒndə) *n* a very large nonvenomous arboreal and semiaquatic snake of tropical South America, which kills its prey by constriction [C18 prob. changed from Sinhalese *henakandayā* whip snake; orig. referring to a snake of Sri Lanka]

Anacreon (əˈnækrɪˌɒn, -ən) *n* ?572–?488 BC, Greek lyric poet, noted for his short songs celebrating love and wine

anacrusis (ˌænəˈkruːsɪs) *n, pl* **anacruses** (-siːz) **1** *prosody* one or more unstressed syllables at the beginning of a line of verse **2** *music* an unstressed note or group of notes immediately preceding the strong first beat of the first bar [C19 from Gk, from *anakrouein* to strike up, from ANA- + *krouein* to strike]

anadromous (əˈnædrəməs) *adj* (of fishes such as the salmon) migrating up rivers from the sea in order to breed [C18 from Gk *anadromos* running upwards]

Anadyr (*Russian* aˈnadirj) *n* **1** a town in Russia, in NE Siberia at the mouth of the Anadyr River. Pop: 6586 (1993 est) **2** a mountain range in Russia, in NE Siberia, rising over 1500 m (5000 ft) **3** a river in Russia, rising in mountains on the Arctic Circle, south of the Anadyr Range, and flowing east to the Gulf of Anadyr. Length: 725 km (450 miles) **4** **Gulf of** an inlet of the Bering Sea, off the coast of NE Russia

anaemia *or US* **anemia** (əˈniːmɪə) *n* a deficiency in the number of red blood cells or in their haemoglobin content, resulting in pallor and lack of energy [C19 from NL, from Gk *anaimia* lack of blood, from AN- + *haima* blood]

anaemic *or US* **anemic** (əˈniːmɪk) *adj* **1** relating to or suffering from anaemia **2** pale and sickly looking; lacking vitality

anaerobe (æˈnɛərəʊb, ˈænərəʊb) *or* **anaerobium** (ˌænɛəˈrəʊbɪəm) *n, pl* **anaerobes** *or* **anaerobia** (-ˈəʊbɪə) an organism that does not require, or requires the absence of, oxygen for respiration

anaerobic (ˌænɛəˈrəʊbɪk) *adj* **1** (of an organism or process) requiring the absence of or not dependent on the presence of oxygen **2** of or relating to anaerobes > ˌ**anaer**ˈ**obically** *adv*

anaesthesia *or US* **anesthesia** (ˌænɪsˈθiːzɪə) *n* **1** loss of bodily sensation, esp of touch, as the result of nerve damage or other abnormality **2** loss of sensation, esp of pain, induced by drugs: called **general anaesthesia** when consciousness is lost and **local anaesthesia** when only a specific area of the body is involved [C19 from NL, from Gk *anaisthēsia* absence of sensation]

anaesthetic *or US* **anesthetic** (ˌænɪsˈθɛtɪk) *n* **1** a substance that causes anaesthesia ▷ *adj* **2** causing or characterized by anaesthesia

anaesthetics (ˌænɪsˈθɛtɪks) *n* (*functioning as sing*) the science of anaesthesia and its application. US name: **anesthesiology**

anaesthetist (əˈniːsθətɪst) *n* **1** *Brit* a doctor specializing in the administration of anaesthetics. US name: **anesthesiologist** **2** *US* See **anesthetist**

anaesthetize, anaesthetise, *or US* **anesthetize** (əˈniːsθəˌtaɪz) *vb* **anaesthetizes, anaesthetizing, anaesthetized** *or* **anaesthetises, anaesthetising, anaesthetised** *or US* **anesthetizes, anesthetizing, anesthetized** (*tr*) to render insensible to pain by administering an anaesthetic > **aˌnaesthetiˈzation, aˌnaesthetiˈsation,** *or US* **aˌnestheti'zation** *n*

anaglyph (ˈænəˌɡlɪf) *n* **1** *photog* a stereoscopic picture consisting of two images of the same object, taken from slightly different angles, in two complementary colours. When viewed through coloured spectacles, the images merge to produce a stereoscopic sensation **2** anything cut to stand in low relief, such as a cameo [C17 from Gk *anagluphē* carved in low relief, from ANA- + *gluphē* carving, from *gluphein* to carve] > ˌ**anaˈglyphic** *adj*

Anaglypta (ˌænəˈɡlɪptə) *n trademark* a type of thick embossed wallpaper designed to be painted [C19 from Gk *anagluptos*; see ANAGLYPH]

anagram (ˈænəˌɡræm) *n* a word or phrase the letters of which can be rearranged into another word or phrase [C16 from NL, from Gk, from *anagrammatizein* to transpose letters, from ANA- + *gramma* a letter] > **anagrammatic** (ˌænəɡrəˈmætɪk) *or* ˌ**anagramˈmatical** *adj*

anagrammatize *or* **anagrammatise** (ˌænəˈɡræməˌtaɪz) *vb* **anagrammatizes, anagrammatizing, anagrammatized** *or* **anagrammatises, anagrammatising, anagrammatised** to arrange into an anagram

anal (ˈeɪnᵊl) *adj* **1** of or near the anus **2** *psychoanal* relating to a stage of psychosexual development during which the child's interest is concentrated on the anal region and excremental functions [C18 from NL *ānālis*; see ANUS] > ˈ**anally** *adv*

analects (ˈænəˌlɛkts) *or* **analecta** (ˌænəˈlɛktə) *pl n* selected literary passages from one or more works [C17 via L from Gk, from *analegein* to collect up, from *legein* to gather]

analeptic (ˌænᵊˈlɛptɪk) *adj* **1** (of a drug, etc) stimulating the central nervous system ▷ *n* **2** (formerly) a restorative remedy or drug **3** any drug, such as doxapram, that stimulates the central nervous system [C17 from NL, from Gk *analēptikos* stimulating, from *analambanein* to take up]

anal fin *n* an unpaired fin between the anus and tail fin in fishes that maintains equilibrium

analgesia (ˌænᵊlˈdʒiːzɪə) *or* **analgia** (ænˈældʒɪə) *n* **a** inability to feel pain **b** the relief of pain [C18 via NL from Gk: insensibility, from AN- + *algēsis* sense of pain]

analgesic (ˌænᵊlˈdʒiːzɪk) *adj* **1** of or causing analgesia ▷ *n* **2** a substance that produces analgesia

analog (ˈænəˌlɒɡ) *n* a variant spelling of **analogue**

> USAGE The spelling *analog* is a US variant of *analogue* in all its senses, and is also the generally preferred spelling in the computer industry

analog computer *n* a computer that performs arithmetical operations using a variable physical quantity, such as mechanical movement or voltage, to represent numbers

analogize *or* **analogise** (əˈnæləˌdʒaɪz) *vb* **analogizes, analogizing, analogized** *or* **analogises, analogising, analogised** **1** (*intr*) to make use of analogy, as in argument **2** (*tr*) to make analogous or reveal analogy in

analogous (əˈnæləɡəs) *adj* **1** similar or corresponding in some respect **2** *biol* (of organs and parts) having the same function but different evolutionary origin **3** *linguistics* formed by analogy: *an analogous plural* [C17 from L, from Gk *analogos* proportionate, from ANA- + *logos* speech, ratio]

> USAGE The use of *with* after *analogous*, though occasionally found, should be avoided: *swimming has no event that is analogous to* (not *with*) *the 100 metres in athletics*. In this word the *g* is pronounced as in *gate*

analogue *or US* (*sometimes*) **analog** (ˈænᵊˌlɒɡ) *n* **1a** a physical object or quantity used to measure or represent another quantity **1b** (*as modifier*): *analogue watch; analogue recording* **2** something analogous to something else **3** *biol* an analogous part or organ.

> USAGE See at **analog**

analogue recording *n* a sound recording process in which an audio input is converted into an analogous electrical waveform

analogy (əˈnælədʒɪ) *n, pl* **analogies** **1** agreement or similarity, esp in a limited number of features **2** a comparison made to show such a similarity: *an analogy between an atom and the solar system* **3** *biol* the relationship between analogous organs or parts **4** *logic, maths, philosophy* a form of reasoning in which a similarity between two or more things is inferred from a known similarity between them in other respects **5** *linguistics* imitation of existing models or regular patterns in the formation of words, etc: *a child may use "sheeps" as the plural of "sheep" by analogy with "cat," "cats," etc* [C16 from Gk *analogia* correspondence, from *analogos* ANALOGOUS] > **analogical** (ˌænəˈlɒdʒɪkᵊl) *adj*

anal retentive *psychoanal* ▷ *n* **1** a person who exhibits anal personality traits, such as orderliness, meanness, stubbornness, etc ▷ *adj* **anal-retentive** **2** exhibiting anal personality traits, such as orderliness, meanness, stubbornness, etc

analysand (əˈnælɪˌsænd) *n* any person who is undergoing psychoanalysis [C20 from ANALYSE + *-and*, on the model of *multiplicand*]

analyse *or US* **analyze** (ˈænᵊˌlaɪz) *vb* **analyses, analysing, analysed** *or US* **analyzes, analyzing, analyzed** (*tr*) **1** to examine in detail in order to discover meaning, essential features, etc **2** to break down into components or essential features **3** to make a mathematical, chemical, etc, analysis of **4** another word for **psychoanalyse** [C17 back formation from ANALYSIS] > ˈ**anaˌlyser** *or US* ˈ**anaˌlyzer** *n*

analysis (əˈnælɪsɪs) *n, pl* **analyses** (-ˌsiːz) **1** the division of a physical or abstract whole into its constituent parts to examine or determine their relationship **2** a statement of the results of this **3** short for **psychoanalysis** **4** *chem* **4a** the decomposition of a substance in order to determine the kinds of constituents present (**qualitative analysis**) or the amount of each constituent (**quantitative analysis**) **4b** the result obtained by such a determination **5** *linguistics* the use of word order together with word function to express syntactic relations in a language, as opposed to the use of inflections **6** *maths* the branch of mathematics principally concerned with the properties of functions **7** **in the last, final,** *or* **ultimate analysis** after everything has been given due consideration [C16 from NL, from Gk *analusis*, lit.: a dissolving, from ANA- + *luein* to loosen]

analysis of variance *n statistics* a technique for analysing the total variation of a set of observations as measured by the variance of the observations multiplied by their number

analyst ('ænəlɪst) *n* **1** a person who analyses or is skilled in analysis **2** short for **psychoanalyst**

analytic (ˌænə'lɪtɪk) *or* **analytical** *adj* **1** relating to analysis **2** capable of or given to analysing: *an analytic mind* **3** *linguistics* denoting languages characterized by analysis **4** *logic* (of a proposition) true or false by virtue of the meanings of the words alone: *all spinsters are unmarried* is analytically true [C16 via LL from Gk *analutikos*, from *analuein* to dissolve, break down] > ˌ**ana'lytically** *adv* > **analyticity** (ˌænəlɪ'tɪsɪtɪ) *n*

analytical geometry *n* the branch of geometry that uses algebraic notation to locate a point; coordinate geometry

analytic philosophy *n* See **philosophical analysis**

Anambra (ə'næmbrə) *n* a state of S Nigeria, formed in 1976 from part of East-Central State. Capital: Enugu. Pop: 3 094 783 (1995 est). Area: 4844 sq km (1870 sq miles)

Ananda (ə'nændə) *n* 5th century BC, the first cousin, favourite disciple, and personal attendant of the Buddha

anandrous (æn'ændrəs) *adj* (of flowers) having no stamens [C19 from Gk *anandros* lacking males, from AN- + *anēr* man]

Ananias (ˌænə'naɪəs) *n* **1** *New Testament* a Jewish Christian of Jerusalem who was struck dead for lying (Acts 5) **2** a liar

anapaest *or* **anapest** ('ænəpɛst, -piːst) *n prosody* a metrical foot of three syllables, the first two short, the last long (˘˘¯) [C17 via L from Gk *anapaistos* reversed, from *ana-* back + *paiein* to strike] > ˌ**ana'paestic** *or* ˌ**ana'pestic** *adj*

anaphora (ə'næfərə) *n* **1** *grammar* the use of a word such as a pronoun to avoid repetition, as for example *one* in *He offered me a drink but I didn't want one* **2** *rhetoric* the repetition of a word or phrase at the beginning of successive clauses [C16 via L from Gk: repetition, from ANA- + *pherein* to bear]

anaphrodisiac (ˌænæfrə'dɪzɪˌæk) *adj* **1** tending to lessen sexual desire ▷ *n* **2** an anaphrodisiac drug

anaphylactic shock *n* a severe, sometimes fatal, reaction to a substance to which a person has an extreme sensitivity, often involving respiratory difficulty and circulation failure

anaphylaxis (ˌænəfɪ'læksɪs) *n* extreme sensitivity to an injected antigen following a previous injection [C20 from ANA- + (PRO)PHYLAXIS]
▷ www.anaphylaxis.org

anaplasmosis (ˌænəplæz'məʊsɪs) *n vet science* another name for **gallsickness**

anaptyxis (ˌænæp'tɪksɪs) *n, pl* **anaptyxes** (-'tɪksiːz) the insertion of a short vowel between consonants in order to make a word more easily pronounceable [C19 via NL from Gk *anaptuxis*, from *anaptussein* to unfold, from ANA- + *ptussein* to fold]

Anapurna (ˌænə'pʊənə) *n* a variant spelling of **Annapurna**

anarchism ('ænəˌkɪzəm) *n* **1** *political theory* a doctrine advocating the abolition of government **2** the principles or practice of anarchists

anarchist ('ænəkɪst) *n* **1** a person who advocates a society based on voluntary cooperation and the abolition of government **2** a person who causes disorder or upheaval

anarchy ('ænəkɪ) *n* **1** general lawlessness and disorder, esp when thought to result from an absence or failure of government **2** the absence of government **3** the absence of any guiding or uniting principle; chaos **4** political anarchism [C16 from Med. L, from Gk, from *anarkhos* without a ruler, from AN- + *arkh-* leader, from *arkhein* to rule] > **anarchic** (æn'ɑːkɪk) *or* **an'archical** *adj*

Anastasia (ˌænə'stɑːzɪə, -'steɪ-) *n* **Grand Duchess** 1901–?18, daughter of Tsar Nicholas II, believed to have been executed by the Bolsheviks in 1918, although several women subsequently claimed to be her

anastigmat (æ'næstɪgmæt, ˌænə'stɪgmæt) *n* a lens system designed to be free of astigmatism [C19 from AN- + ASTIGMATIC] > ˌ**anastig'matic** *adj*

anastomose (ə'næstəˌməʊz) *vb* **anastomoses, anastomosing, anastomosed** to join (two parts of a blood vessel, etc) by anastomosis

anastomosis (əˌnæstə'məʊsɪs) *n, pl* **anastomoses** (-siːz) **1** a natural connection between two tubular structures, such as blood vessels **2** the union of two hollow parts that are normally separate [C16 via NL from Gk: opening, from *anastomoun* to equip with a mouth, from *stoma* mouth]

anastrophe (ə'næstrəfɪ) *n rhetoric* another term for **inversion** (sense 3) [C16 from Gk, from *anastrephein* to invert]

anathema (ə'næθəmə) *n, pl* **anathemas** **1** a detested person or thing: *he is anathema to me* **2** a formal ecclesiastical excommunication, or denunciation of a doctrine **3** the person or thing so cursed **4** a strong curse [C16 via Church L from Gk: something accursed, from *anatithenai* to dedicate, from ANA- + *tithenai* to set]

anathematize *or* **anathematise** (ə'næθɪməˌtaɪz) *vb* **anathematizes, anathematizing, anathematized** *or* **anathematises, anathematising, anathematised** to pronounce an anathema (upon a person, etc); curse

Anatolia (ˌænə'təʊlɪə) *n* the Asian part of Turkey, occupying the peninsula between the Black Sea, the Mediterranean, and the Aegean: consists of a plateau, largely mountainous, with salt lakes in the interior. Historical name: **Asia Minor** > ˌ**Ana'tolian** *adj, n*

anatomical (ˌænə'tɒmɪkᵊl) *adj* of anatomy

anatomist (ə'nætəmɪst) *n* an expert in anatomy

anatomize *or* **anatomise** (ə'nætəˌmaɪz) *vb* **anatomizes, anatomizing, anatomized** *or* **anatomises, anatomising, anatomised** (*tr*) **1** to dissect (an animal or plant) **2** to examine in minute detail

Aa

anatomy (ə'nætəmɪ) *n, pl* **anatomies** **1** the science concerned with the physical structure of animals and plants **2** the physical structure of an animal or plant or any of its parts **3** a book or treatise on this subject **4** dissection of an animal or plant **5** any detailed analysis: *the anatomy of a crime* **6** *inf* the human body [C14 from L, from Gk *anatomē*, from ANA- + *temnein* to cut]
▷ http://omni.ac.uk/subject-listing/QS4.html
▷ www.bartleby.com/107

anatto (ə'nætəʊ) *n, pl* **anattos** a variant spelling of **annatto**

Anaxagoras (ˌænæk'sægərəs) *n* ?500–428 BC, Greek philosopher who maintained that all things were composed of minute particles arranged by an eternal intelligence

Anaximander (əˌnæksɪ'mændə) *n* 611–547 BC, Greek philosopher, astronomer, and mathematician who believed the first principle of the world to be the Infinite

ANC *abbrev for* African National Congress
▷ www.anc.org.za

-ance *or* **-ancy** *suffix forming nouns* indicating an action, state or condition, or quality: *resemblance; tenancy* [via OF from L *-antia*]

ancestor ('ænsɛstə) *n* **1** a person from whom another is directly descended; forefather **2** an early animal or plant from which a later type has evolved **3** a person or thing regarded as a forerunner: *the ancestor of the modern camera* [C13 from OF, from LL *antecēssor* one who goes before, from L *antecēdere*] > '**ancestress** *fem n*

ancestral (æn'sɛstrəl) *adj* of or inherited from ancestors

ancestry ('ænsɛstrɪ) *n, pl* **ancestries** **1** lineage or descent, esp when noble or distinguished **2** ancestors collectively

Anchises (æn'kaɪsiːz) *n classical myth* a Trojan prince and father of Aeneas. In the *Aeneid*, he is rescued by his son at the fall of Troy and dies in Sicily

anchor ('æŋkə) *n* **1** a device attached to a vessel by a cable and dropped overboard so as to grip the bottom and restrict movement **2** an object used to hold something else firmly in place: *the rock provided an anchor for the rope* **3** a source of stability or security **4** short for **anchorman** *or* **anchorwoman** **5** **cast, come to,** *or* **drop anchor** to anchor a vessel **6** **ride at anchor** to be anchored ▹ *vb* **7** to use an anchor to hold (a vessel) in one place **8** to fasten or be fastened securely; fix or become fixed firmly ▹ See also **anchors** [OE *ancor*, from L, from Gk *ankura*]

anchorage ('æŋkərɪdʒ) *n* **1** the act of anchoring **2** any place where a vessel is anchored **3** a place designated for vessels to anchor **4** a fee imposed for anchoring **5** anything used as an anchor **6** a source of security or strength

Anchorage ('æŋkərɪdʒ) *n* the largest city in Alaska, a port in the south, at the head of Cook Inlet. Pop: 260 283 (2000)

anchor ice *n Canad* ice that forms at the bottom of a lake or river

anchorite ('æŋkə,raɪt) *n* a person who lives in seclusion, esp a religious recluse; hermit [c15 from Med. L, from LL, from Gk, from *anakhōrein* to retire, from *khōra* a space] > **'anchoress** *fem n*

anchorman ('æŋkəmæn) *n, pl* **anchormen** **1** *sport* the last person in a team to compete, esp in a relay race **2** (in broadcasting) a person in a central studio who links up and maintains contact with various outside camera units, reporters, etc > **'anchor,woman** ('æŋkəwʊmən) *fem n*

anchors ('æŋkəz) *pl n* *sl* the brakes of a motor vehicle: *he rammed on the anchors*

anchovy ('æntʃəvɪ) *n, pl* **anchovies** *or* **anchovy** any of various small marine food fishes which have a salty taste and are often tinned or made into a paste or essence [c16 from Sp. *anchova*, ? ult. from Gk *aphuē* small fish]

anchusa (æŋ'kju:sə) *n* any of several Eurasian plants having rough hairy stems and leaves and blue flowers [c18 from L]

anchylose ('æŋkɪ,ləʊz) *vb* a former spelling of **ankylose**

ancien régime *French* (ɑ̃sjɛ̃ reʒim) *n, pl* ***anciens régimes*** (ɑ̃sjɛ̃ reʒim). the political and social system of France before the Revolution of 1789 [lit.: old regime]

ancient ('eɪnʃənt) *adj* **1** dating from very long ago: *ancient ruins* **2** very old **3** of the far past, esp before the collapse of the Western Roman Empire (476 AD) ▹ *n* **4** (*often pl*) a member of a civilized nation in the ancient world, esp a Greek or Roman **5** (*often pl*) one of the classical authors of Greek or Roman antiquity **6** *arch* an old man [c14 from OF *ancien*, from Vulgar L *anteanus* (unattested), from L *ante* before] > **'ancientness** *n*

ancient lights *n (usually functioning as sing)* the legal right to receive, by a particular window or windows, adequate and unobstructed daylight

anciently ('eɪnʃəntlɪ) *adv* in ancient times

Ancient of Days *n* a name for God, originating in the Authorized Version of the Old Testament (Daniel 7:9)

ancillary (æn'sɪlərɪ) *adj* **1** subsidiary **2** auxiliary; supplementary: *ancillary services* ▹ *n, pl* **ancillaries** **3** a subsidiary or auxiliary thing or person [c17 from L *ancillāris* concerning maidservants, ult. from *ancūla* female servant]

Ancohuma (,æŋkəʊ'u:mə) *n* one of the two peaks of Mount **Sorata**

ancon ('æŋkɒn) *or* **ancone** ('æŋkəʊn) *n, pl* **ancones** (æŋ'kəʊni:z) *architect* a projecting bracket or console supporting a cornice [c18 from Gk *ankōn* a bend]

Ancona (*Italian* aŋ'ko:na) *n* a port in central Italy, on the Adriatic, capital of the Marches: founded by Greeks from Syracuse in about 390 BC. Pop: 100 597 (1994 est)

-ancy *suffix forming nouns* a variant of **-ance,** indicating condition or quality: *poignancy*

ancylostomiasis (,ænsɪ,lɒstə'maɪəsɪs) *or* **ankylostomiasis** (,æŋkɪ,lɒstə'maɪəsɪs) *n* infestation of the intestine with blood-sucking hookworms; hookworm disease [from NL, ult. from Gk *ankulos* hooked + *stoma* mouth]

and (ænd; *unstressed* ənd, ən) *conj (coordinating)* **1** in addition to: *boys and girls* **2** as a consequence: *he fell down and cut his knee* **3** afterwards: *we pay and go through that door* **4** plus: *two and two equals four* **5** used to give emphasis or indicate repetition or continuity: *it rained and rained* **6** used to express a contrast between instances of what is named: *there are jobs and jobs* **7** *inf* used in place of *to* in infinitives after verbs such as *try, go,* and *come*: *try and see it my way* **8** an obsolete word for **if**: *and it please you* [OE *and*]

> USAGE The use of *and* instead of *to* after *try* and *wait* is typical of spoken language, but should be avoided in any writing which is not informal: *We must try to prevent* (not *try and prevent*) *this happening*

-and *or* **-end** *suffix forming nouns* indicating a person or thing that is to be dealt with in a specified way: *dividend; multiplicand* [from L gerundives ending in *-andus, -endus*]

Andalusia (,ændə'lu:zɪə) *n* a region of S Spain, on the Mediterranean and the Atlantic, with the Sierra Morena in the north, the Sierra Nevada in the southeast, and the Guadalquivir River flowing over fertile lands between them; a centre of Moorish civilization; it became an autonomous region in 1981. Area: about 87 280 sq km (33 700 sq miles). Spanish name: **Andalucía** (andalu'θia)

Andaman and Nicobar Islands ('ændəmən, 'nɪkəʊ,bɑ:) *pl n* a territory of India, in the E Bay of Bengal, consisting of two groups of over 200 islands. Capital: Port Blair. Pop: 356 265 (2001). Area: 8140 sq km (3143 sq miles)

Andaman Islands *pl n* a group of islands in the E Bay of Bengal, part of the Indian territory of the Andaman and Nicobar Islands. Area: 6408 sq km (2474 sq miles). Pop: 240 089 (1991 est)

Andaman Sea *n* part of the Bay of Bengal, between the Andaman and Nicobar Islands and the Malay Peninsula

andante (æn'dæntɪ) *music* ▹ *adj, adv* **1** (to be performed) at a moderately slow tempo ▹ *n* **2** a passage or piece to be performed in this manner [c18 from It., from *andare* to walk, from L *ambulāre*]

andantino (,ændæn'ti:nəʊ) *music* ▹ *adj, adv* **1** (to be performed) slightly faster or slower than andante ▹ *n, pl* **andantinos** **2** a passage or piece to be performed in this manner [c19 dim. of ANDANTE]

AND circuit *or* **gate** (ænd) *n* *computing* a logic circuit that has a high-voltage output signal if and only if all input signals are at a high voltage simultaneously ▹ Cf **NAND circuit, NOR circuit, OR circuit** [c20 from similarity of operation of *and* in logical conjunctions]

Andersen ('ændəsᵊn) *n* **Hans Christian** 1805–75, Danish author of fairy tales, including *The Ugly Duckling, The Tin Soldier,* and *The Snow Queen*

Andersen Nexø ('anərsen) *n* See (Martin Andersen) **Nexø**

Anderson[1] ('ændəsᵊn) *n* a river in N Canada, in the Northwest Territories, rising in lakes north of Great Bear Lake and flowing west and north to the Beaufort Sea. Length: about 580 km (360 miles)

Anderson[2] ('ændəsᵊn) *n* **1** **Carl David** 1905–91, US physicist, who discovered the positron in cosmic rays (1932): Nobel prize for physics 1936 **2** **Elizabeth Garrett** 1836–1917, English physician and feminist: a campaigner for the admission of women to the professions **3** **John** 1893–1962, Australian philosopher, born in Scotland, whose theories are expounded in

Studies in Empirical Philosophy (1962) 4 **Lindsay (Gordon)** 1923–94, British film and theatre director: his films include *This Sporting Life* (1963), *If* (1968), *O Lucky Man!* (1973), and *The Whales of August* (1987) 5 **Marian** 1902–93, US contralto, the first Black permanent member of the Metropolitan Opera Company, New York 6 **Philip Warren** born 1923, US physicist, noted for his work on solid-state physics. Nobel prize for physics 1977 7 **Sherwood** 1874–1941, US novelist and short-story writer, best known for *Winesburg Ohio* (1919), a collection of short stories illustrating small-town life

Andes ('ændi:z) *pl n* a major mountain system of South America, extending for about 7250 km (4500 miles) along the entire W coast, with several parallel ranges or cordilleras and many volcanic peaks: rich in minerals, including gold, silver, copper, iron ore, and nitrates. Average height: 3900 m (13 000 ft). Highest peak: Aconcagua, 6960 m (22 835 ft)

Andhra Pradesh ('ændrə prɑ:'dɛʃ) *n* a state of SE India, on the Bay of Bengal: formed in 1953 from parts of Madras and Hyderabad states. Capital: Hyderabad. Pop: 75 727 541 (2001). Area: about 275 068 sq km (106 204 sq miles)

andiron ('ænd,aɪən) *n* either of a pair of metal stands for supporting logs in a hearth; firedog [c14 from OF *andier*, from ?; infl. by IRON]

Andong ('æn'dʊŋ) *n* a port in E China, in Liaoning province at the mouth of the Yalu River. Pop: 188 452 (1995). Also called: **Tan-tung**

and/or *conj (coordinating)* used to join terms when either one or the other or both is indicated: *passports and/or other means of identification.*

> USAGE Many people think that *and/or* is only acceptable in legal and commercial contexts. In other contexts, it is better to use *or both*: *many drinkers lose their jobs or their driving licences or both* (not *their jobs and/or their driving licences*)

Andorra (æn'dɔ:rə) *n* a mountainous principality in SW Europe, between France and Spain: according to tradition, given independence by Charlemagne in the 9th century for helping to fight the Moors; placed under the joint sovereignty of the Comte de Foix and the Spanish bishop of Urgel in 1278; under the joint overlordship of the French head of state and the bishop of Urgel from the 16th century; adopted a constitution reducing the powers of the overlords in 1993. Languages: Catalan (official), French, and Spanish. Religion: Roman Catholic. Currency: euro. Capital: Andorra la Vella. Pop: 66 900 (2001 est). Area: 464 sq km (179 sq miles). Official name: **Principat d'Andorra** > **An'dorran** *adj, n*
▷ www.andorra.ad

Andorra la Vella (*Spanish* an'dɔrra la 'beʎa) *n* the capital of Andorra, situated in the west of the principality. Pop: 21 189 (2000 est). French name: **Andorre la Vieille** (ɑ̃dɔr la vjɛj)

Andrássy (æn'dræsɪ; *Hungarian* 'ɔndra:ʃi) *n* Count **Gyula** ('djulɔ) 1823–90, Hungarian statesman; the first prime minister of Hungary under the Dual Monarchy of Austria-Hungary (1867)

Andrea del Sarto (*Italian* an'drea del 'sarto) *n* See **Sarto**

Andreanof Islands (,ændrɪ'ɑ:nɒf) *pl n* a group of islands in the central Aleutian Islands, Alaska. Area: 3710 sq km (1432 sq miles)

Andrew ('ændru:) *n* **Saint** *New Testament* one of the twelve apostles of Jesus; the brother of Peter; patron saint of Scotland. Feast day: Nov. 30

Andrewes ('ændru:z) *n* **Lancelot** 1555–1626, English bishop and theologian

Andrews ('ændru:z) *n* **Thomas** 1813–85, Irish physical chemist, noted for his work on the liquefaction of gases

Andrić (*Serbo-Croat* 'andritʃ) *n* **Ivo** ('i:vɔ) 1892–1975, Bosnian novelist; author of *The Bridge on the Drina* (1945): Nobel prize for literature 1961

andro- *or before a vowel* **andr-** *combining form* 1 male; masculine: *androsterone* 2 (in botany) stamen or anther: *androecium* [from Gk *anēr* (genitive *andros*) man]

Androcles ('ændrə,kli:z) *or* **Androclus** ('ændrəkləs) *n* (in Roman legend) a slave whose life was spared in the arena by a lion from whose paw he had once extracted a thorn

androecium (æn'dri:sɪəm) *n, pl* **androecia** (-sɪə) the stamens of a flowering plant collectively [c19 from NL, from ANDRO- + Gk *oikion* a little house]

androgen ('ændrədʒən) *n* any of several steroids that promote development of male sexual characteristics > **androgenic** (,ændrə'dʒɛnɪk) *adj*

androgyne ('ændrə,dʒaɪn) *n* another word for **hermaphrodite** [c17 from OF, via L from Gk *androgunos*, from *anēr* man + *gunē* woman]

androgynous (æn'drɒdʒɪnəs) *adj* 1 *bot* having male and female flowers in the same inflorescence, as cuckoo pint 2 having male and female characteristics; hermaphrodite > **an'drogyny** *n*

android ('ændrɔɪd) *n* 1 (in science fiction) a robot resembling a human being ▷ *adj* 2 resembling a human being [c18 from LGk *androeidēs* manlike; see ANDRO-, -OID]

andrology (æn'drɒlədʒɪ) *n* the branch of medicine concerned with diseases in men, esp of the reproductive organs [c20 from ANDRO- + -LOGY] > **an'drologist** *n*

Andromache (æn'drɒməkɪ) *n* *Greek myth* the wife of Hector

Andromeda (æn'drɒmɪdə) *n* *Greek myth* the wife of Perseus, who saved her from a sea monster

Andropov[1] (æn'drɒpɒv; *Russian* ən'drɔ:pəf) *n* a former name (1984–91) for **Rybinsk**

Andropov[2] (æn'drɒpɒv; *Russian* ən'drɔ:pəf) *n* **Yuri Vladimirovich** 1914–84, Soviet statesman; president of the Soviet Union (1983–84)

Andros ('ændrəs) *n* 1 an island in the Aegean Sea, the northernmost of the Cyclades: long famous for wine. Capital: Andros. Pop: 8155 (1990). Area: about 311 sq km (120 sq miles) 2 an island in the N Caribbean, the largest of the Bahamas. Pop: 8177 (1990). Area: 4144 sq km (1600 sq miles)

androsterone (æn'drɒstə,rəʊn) *n* an androgenic steroid hormone produced in the testes

-androus *adj combining form* (in botany) indicating number or type of stamens: *diandrous* [from NL, from Gk *-andros*, from *anēr* man]

Andvari (æn'dwɑ:rɪ) *n* *Norse myth* a dwarf who possessed a treasure hoard, which was robbed by Loki

ane (eɪn) *determiner, pron, n* a Scottish word for **one**

-ane *suffix forming nouns* indicating a hydrocarbon of the alkane series: *hexane* [coined to replace *-ene*, *-ine*, and *-one*]

anecdotage ('ænɪk,dəʊtɪdʒ) *n* *humorous* garrulous old age [from ANECDOTE + -AGE, with play on *dotage*]

anecdote ('ænɪk,dəʊt) *n* a short usually amusing account of an incident [c17 from Med. L, from Gk *anekdotos* unpublished, from AN- + *ekdotos* published] > ,**anec'dotal** *or* ,**anec'dotic** *adj* > ,**anec'dotalist** *or* '**anec,dotist** *n*

anechoic (,ænɪ'kəʊɪk) *adj* having a low degree of reverberation: *an anechoic recording studio*

Aneirin (ə'naɪərɪn) *n* 6th century AD, Welsh poet. His *Y Gododdin*, preserved in *The Book of Aneirin* (?1250), is one of the earliest surviving Welsh poems

anemia (ə'ni:mɪə) *n* the usual US spelling of **anaemia** > **anemic** (ə'ni:mɪk) *adj*

anemo- *combining form* indicating wind: *anemometer; anemophilous* [from Gk *anemos* wind]

anemograph (ə'nɛməʊ,grɑ:f) *n* a self-recording anemometer

anemometer (,ænɪ'mɒmɪtə) *n* an instrument for

Aa

recording the speed and often the direction of winds. Also called: **wind gauge** > ˌ**ane'mometry** *n* > **anemometric** (ˌænɪməʊ'mɛtrɪk) *adj*

anemone (ə'nɛmənɪ) *n* any woodland plant of the genus *Anemone* of N temperate regions, such as the white-flowered **wood anemone** or **windflower**. Some cultivated anemones have coloured flowers [C16 via L from Gk: windflower, from *anemos* wind]

anemophilous (ˌænɪ'mɒfɪləs) *adj* (of flowering plants such as grasses) pollinated by the wind > ˌ**ane'mophily** *n*

anent (ə'nɛnt) *prep arch or Scot* **1** lying against; alongside **2** concerning; about [OE *on efen*, lit.: on even (ground)]

aneroid barometer ('ænəˌrɔɪd) *n* a device for measuring atmospheric pressure without the use of fluids. It consists of a partially evacuated chamber, the lid of which is displaced by variations in air pressure. This displacement is magnified by levers and made to operate a pointer [C19 *aneroid*, from F, from AN- + Gk *nēros* wet + -OID]

anesthesia (ˌænɪs'θiːzɪə) *n* the usual US spelling of **anaesthesia**

anesthesiologist (ˌænɪsˌθiːzɪ'ɒlədʒɪst) *n* the US name for an **anaesthetist**

anesthesiology (ˌænɪsˌθiːzɪ'ɒlədʒɪ) *n* the US name for **anaesthetics**

anesthetic (ˌænɪs'θɛtɪk) *n, adj* the usual US spelling of **anaesthetic**

anesthetist (ə'nɛsθətɪst) *n* (in the US) a person qualified to administer anaesthesia, often a nurse or someone other than a physician

Aneto (*Spanish* a'neto) *n* **Pico de** ('piko de) a mountain in N Spain, near the French border: the highest in the Pyrenees. Height: 3404 m (11 168 ft)

aneurysm *or* **aneurism** ('ænjəˌrɪzəm) *n* a sac formed by abnormal dilation of the weakened wall of a blood vessel [C15 from Gk *aneurusma*, from *aneurunein* to dilate]

anew (ə'njuː) *adv* **1** once more **2** in a different way; afresh [OE *of nīwe*; see OF, NEW]

Anfinsen ('ænfɪnsən) *n* **Christian Boehmer** 1916–95, US biochemist, noted for his research on the structure of enzymes. Nobel prize for chemistry 1972

Angara (*Russian* anga'ra) *n* a river in S Russia, in Siberia, flowing from Lake Baikal north and west to the Yenisei River: important for hydroelectric power. Length: 1840 km (1150 miles)

angary ('æŋgərɪ) *n law* the right of a belligerent state to use the property of a neutral state or to destroy it subject to payment of compensation to the owners [C19 from F, from LL *angaria* enforced service, from Gk *angaros* courier]

angel ('eɪndʒəl) *n* **1** one of a class of spiritual beings attendant upon God. In medieval angelology they are divided by rank into nine orders **2** a divine messenger from God **3** a guardian spirit **4** a conventional representation of any of these beings, depicted in human form with wings **5** *inf* a person who is kind, pure, or beautiful **6** *inf* an investor, esp in a theatrical production **7** Also called: **angel-noble** a former English gold coin with a representation of the archangel Michael on it **8** *inf* an unexplained signal on a radar screen [OE, from LL *angelus*, from Gk *angelos* messenger]

angel cake *or esp US* **angel food cake** *n* a very light sponge cake made without egg yolks

angel dust *n* a slang name for **PCP**

Angel Falls *n* a waterfall in SE Venezuela, on the Caroní River. Height (probably the highest in the world): 979 m (3211 ft)

angelfish ('eɪndʒəlˌfɪʃ) *n, pl* **angelfish** *or* **angelfishes** **1** any of various small tropical marine fishes which have a deep flattened brightly coloured body **2** a South American freshwater fish having a compressed body and large dorsal and anal fins: a popular aquarium fish **3** a shark with flattened pectoral fins

angelic (æn'dʒɛlɪk) *adj* **1** of or relating to angels **2** Also: **angelical** resembling an angel in beauty, purity, etc > **an'gelically** *adv*

angelica (æn'dʒɛlɪkə) *n* **1** an umbelliferous plant, the aromatic seeds, leaves, and stems of which are used in medicine and cookery **2** the candied stems of this plant, used for decorating and flavouring sweet dishes [C16 from Med. L (*herba*) *angelica* angelic (herb)]

Angelico (*Italian* an'dʒɛːliko) *n* **Fra** (fra), original name *Guido di Pietro;* monastic name *Fra Giovanni da Fiesole.* ?1400–55, Italian fresco painter and Dominican friar

Angell ('eɪndʒəl) *n* Sir **Norman,** real name *Ralph Norman Angell Lane.* 1874–1967, English writer, pacifist, and economist, noted for his work on the economic futility of war, *The Great Illusion* (1910): Nobel peace prize 1933

Angel of the North *n* the UK's largest sculpture (wingspan 53 m), by Anthony Gormley, erected in 1997 on the outskirts of Gateshead

Angelou ('ændʒəluː) *n* **Maya,** real name *Marguerite Johnson.* born 1928, US Black novelist, poet, and dramatist. Her works include the autobiographical novel *I Know Why the Caged Bird Sings* (1970) and its sequels

Angelus ('ændʒɪləs) *n RC Church* **1** a series of prayers recited in the morning, at midday, and in the evening **2** the bell (**Angelus bell**) signalling the times of these prayers [C17 L, from *Angelus domini nuntiavit Mariae* the angel of the Lord brought tidings to Mary]

anger ('æŋgə) *n* **1** a feeling of great annoyance or antagonism as the result of some real or supposed grievance; rage; wrath ▷ *vb* (*tr*) **2** to make angry; enrage [C12 from ON *angr* grief]

Angers (*French* ɑ̃ʒe) *n* a city in W France, on the River Maine. Pop: 151 279 (1999)

Angevin ('ændʒɪvɪn) *n* **1** a native or inhabitant of Anjou **2** *history* a member of the Plantagenet royal line, esp one of the kings of England from Henry II to John (1154–1216) ▷ *adj* **3** of Anjou or its inhabitants **4** of the Plantagenet kings of England between 1154 and 1216

angina (æn'dʒaɪnə) *n* **1** any disease marked by painful attacks of spasmodic choking **2** Also called: **angina pectoris** ('pɛktərɪs) a sudden intense pain in the chest, caused by momentary lack of adequate blood supply to the heart muscle [C16 from L: quinsy, from Gk *ankhonē* a strangling]

angio- *or before a vowel* **angi-** *combining form* indicating a blood or lymph vessel; seed vessel [from Gk *angeion* vessel]

angioma (ˌændʒɪ'əʊmə) *n, pl* **angiomas** *or* **angiomata** (-mətə) a tumour consisting of a mass of blood vessels or a mass of lymphatic vessels

angioplasty ('ændʒɪəˌplæstɪ) *n* a surgical technique for restoring normal blood flow through an artery narrowed or blocked by atherosclerosis, either by inserting a balloon into it or by using a laser beam ▷ www.ptca.org

angiosperm ('ændʒɪəˌspɜːm) *n* any seed-bearing plant in which the ovules are enclosed in an ovary which develops into the fruit after fertilization; any flowering plant ▷ Cf **gymnosperm** > ˌ**angio'spermous** *adj*

Angkor ('æŋkɔː) *n* a large area of ruins in NW Cambodia, containing **Angkor Thom** (tɔːm), the capital of the former Khmer Empire, and **Angkor Wat** (wɒt), a three-storey temple, which were overgrown with dense jungle from the 14th to 19th centuries

angle[1] ('æŋgᵊl) *n* **1** the space between two straight lines or two planes that extend from a common point **2** the shape formed by two such lines or planes **3** the extent to which one such line or plane diverges from the other, measured in degrees or radians **4** a recess; corner **5** point of view: *look at the question from another angle* **6** See **angle iron** ▷ *vb* **angles, angling, angled** **7** to move in or bend into angles or an angle **8** (*tr*) to produce (an article, statement, etc) with a particular point of view **9** (*tr*) to present or place at an angle **10** (*intr*) to turn in a different direction [c14 from F, from OL *angulus* corner]

angle² ('æŋgᵊl) *vb* **angles, angling, angled** (*intr*) **1** to fish with a hook and line **2** (often foll by *for*) to attempt to get: *he angled for a compliment* ▷ *n* **3** *obs* a fish-hook [OE *angul* fish-hook]

Angle ('æŋgᵊl) *n* a member of a people from N Germany who invaded and settled large parts of E and N England in the 5th and 6th centuries AD [from L *Anglus*, of Gmc origin, an inhabitant of *Angul*, a district in Schleswig, a name identical with OE *angul* hook, ANGLE², referring to its shape] > '**Anglian** *adj, n*

angledug ('æŋgᵊl,dʌg) *n Southwestern English dialect* an earthworm. Also: **angletwitch**

angle iron *n* an iron or a steel structural bar that has an L-shaped cross section. Also called: **angle, angle bar**

angle of incidence *n* **1** the angle that a line or beam of radiation makes with a line perpendicular to the surface at the point of incidence **2** the angle between the chord line of an aircraft wing or tailplane and the aircraft's longitudinal axis

angle of reflection *n* the angle that a beam of reflected radiation makes with the normal to a surface at the point of reflection

angle of refraction *n* the angle that a refracted beam of radiation makes with the normal to the surface between two media at the point of refraction

angle of repose *n* the maximum angle to the horizontal at which rock, soil, etc, will remain without sliding

angler ('æŋglə) *n* **1** a person who fishes with a hook and line **2** Also called: **angler fish** any of various spiny-finned fishes which live at the bottom of the sea and typically have a long movable dorsal fin with which they lure their prey

Anglesey ('æŋgᵊlsɪ) *n* an island and county of N Wales, formerly part of Gwynedd (1974–96), separated from the mainland by the Menai Strait. Administrative centre: Llangefni. Pop: 66 828 (2001). Area: 720 sq km (278 sq miles). Welsh name: **Ynys Môn**

Anglia ('æŋglɪə) *n* a Latin name for **England**

Anglican ('æŋglɪkən) *adj* **1** denoting or relating to the Church of England or one of the churches in communion with it ▷ *n* **2** a member of the Anglican Church [c17 from Med. L, from *Anglicus* English, from L *Anglī* the Angles] > '**Anglican,ism** *n*

▷ www.anglicancommunion.org/

Anglicism ('æŋglɪ,sɪzəm) *n* **1** a word, or idiom peculiar to the English language, esp as spoken in England **2** an English mannerism, custom, etc **3** the fact of being English

anglicize *or* **anglicise** ('æŋglɪ,saɪz) *vb* **anglicizes, anglicizing, anglicized** *or* **anglicises, anglicising, anglicised** (*sometimes cap*) to make or become English in outlook, form, etc

angling ('æŋglɪŋ) *n* the art or sport of catching fish with a baited hook or other lure, such as a fly; fishing

▷ www.cips-fips.org

Anglo ('æŋgləʊ) *n*, *pl* **Anglos 1** *US* a White inhabitant of the US who is not of Latin extraction **2** *Canad* an English-speaking Canadian, esp one of Anglo-Celtic origin; an Anglo-Canadian

Anglo- *combining form* denoting English or England: *Anglo-Saxon* [from Med. L *Anglii*]

Anglo-American *adj* **1** of relations between England and the United States ▷ *n* **2** *chiefly US* an inhabitant of the United States who was or whose ancestors were born in England

Anglo-Catholic *adj* **1** of or relating to a group within the Anglican Church that emphasizes the Catholic elements in its teaching and practice ▷ *n* **2** a member of this group > ,**Anglo-Ca'tholi,cism** *n*

Anglo-Egyptian Sudan *n* the former name (1899–1956) of the **Sudan**

Anglo-French *adj* **1** of England and France **2** of Anglo-French ▷ *n* **3** the Norman-French language of medieval England

Anglo-Indian *adj* **1** of England and India **2** denoting or relating to Anglo-Indians **3** (of a word) introduced into English from an Indian language ▷ *n* **4** a person of mixed English and Indian descent **5** an English person who lives or has lived for a long time in India

Anglomania (,æŋgləʊ'meɪnɪə) *n* excessive respect for English customs, etc > ,**Anglo'mani,ac** *n*

Anglo-Norman *adj* **1** relating to the Norman conquerors of England, their society, or their language ▷ *n* **2** a Norman inhabitant of England after 1066 **3** the Anglo-French language

Anglophile ('æŋgləʊfɪl, -,faɪl) *or* **Anglophil** *n* a person having admiration for England or the English

Anglophobe ('æŋgləʊ,fəʊb) *n* **1** a person who hates or fears England or its people **2** *Canad* a person who hates or fears Canadian Anglophones

Anglophone ('æŋglə,fəʊn) (*often not cap*) ▷ *n* **1** a person who speaks English ▷ *adj* **2** speaking English

Anglo-Saxon *n* **1** a member of any of the West Germanic tribes that settled in Britain from the 5th century AD **2** the language of these tribes. See **Old English 3** any White person whose native language is English **4** *inf* plain blunt English ▷ *adj* **5** forming part of the Germanic element in Modern English: *"forget" is an Anglo-Saxon word* **6** of the Anglo-Saxons or the Old English language **7** of the White Protestant culture of Britain, Australia, and the US

Angola (æŋ'gəʊlə) *n* a republic in SW Africa, on the Atlantic: includes the enclave of Cabinda, north of the River Congo; a Portuguese possession from 1575 until its independence in 1975; multiparty constitution adopted in 1991; factional violence. It consists of a narrow coastal plain with a large fertile plateau in the east. Currency: kwanza. Religion: Christian majority. Capital: Luanda. Pop: 10 366 000 (2001 est). Area: 1 246 693 sq km (481 351 sq miles) > **An'golan** *adj, n*

▷ www.angola.org

▷ www.angola.org.uk/prov_tourism.html

angophora (æŋ'gɒfərə) *n* any of various trees related to the eucalyptus and native to E Australia [New Latin, from Greek *angeion* vessel + *phoreus* bearer]

angora (æŋ'gɔːrə) *n* (*sometimes cap*) **1** the long soft hair of the Angora goat or the fur of the Angora rabbit **2** yarn, cloth, or clothing made from this hair or fur **3** (*as modifier*): *an angora sweater* ▷ See also **mohair** [from *Angora*, former name of Ankara, in Turkey]

Angora goat (æŋ'gɔːrə) *n* a breed of domestic goat with long soft hair

Angora rabbit *n* a breed of rabbit with long silky fur

Angostura (*Spanish* aŋgɔs'tura) *n* the former name (1764–1846) for **Ciudad Bolívar**

angostura bark (,æŋgə'stjʊərə) *n* the bitter aromatic bark of certain South American trees, formerly used to reduce fever [c18 from ANGOSTURA]

angostura bitters *pl n* (*often cap*) *trademark* a bitter aromatic tonic, used as a flavouring in alcoholic drinks

angry ('æŋgrɪ) *adj* **angrier, angriest 1** feeling or expressing annoyance, animosity, or resentment **2** suggestive of anger: *angry clouds* **3** severely inflamed: *an angry sore* > '**angrily** *adv*

USAGE It was formerly considered incorrect by some people to talk about being *angry at* a person. The evidence suggests that *with* is still more common, but *at* appears more often in American sources

angst (æŋst) *n* an acute but nonspecific sense of anxiety or remorse [G]

angstrom ('æŋstrəm) *n* a unit of length equal to 10^{-10} metre, used principally to express the wavelengths of electromagnetic radiations. Symbol: Å or A. Also called: **angstrom unit** [c20 after Anders J. ÅNGSTRÖM]

Aa

Ångström ('æŋstrəm; *Swedish* 'ɔŋstrœm) *n* **Anders Jonas** ('andərs 'ju:nas) 1814–74, Swedish physicist, noted for his work on spectroscopy and solar physics

Anguilla (æŋ'gwɪlə) *n* an island in the Caribbean, in the Leeward Islands: part of the British associated state of St Kitts-Nevis-Anguilla from 1967 until 1980, when it reverted to the status of a British dependency and is now a UK Overseas Territory. Pop: 8960 (1992). Area: 90 sq km (35 sq miles)

anguine ('æŋgwɪn) *adj* of or similar to a snake [c17 from L *anguīnus*, from *anguis* snake]

anguish ('æŋgwɪʃ) *n* **1** extreme pain or misery; mental or physical torture; agony ▷ *vb* **2** to afflict or be afflicted with anguish [c13 from OF *angoisse* a strangling, from L, from *angustus* narrow] > '**anguished** *adj*

angular ('æŋgjʊlə) *adj* **1** lean or bony **2** awkward or stiff **3** having an angle or angles **4** placed at an angle **5** measured by an angle or by the rate at which an angle changes; *angular momentum; angular velocity* [c15 from L *angulāris*, from *angulus* ANGLE[1]]

angularity (,æŋgjʊ'lærɪtɪ) *n, pl* **angularities** **1** the condition of being angular **2** an angular shape

Angus ('æŋgəs) *n* a council area of E Scotland on the North Sea: the historical county of Angus became part of Tayside region in 1975; reinstated as a unitary authority (excluding City of Dundee) in 1996. Administrative centre: Forfar. Pop: 108 400 (2001). Area: 2181 sq km (842 sq miles)

Angus Og (əʊg) *n Irish myth* the god of love and beauty

Anhalt (*German* 'anhalt) *n* a former duchy and state of central E Germany, now part of the state of Saxony-Anhalt: part of East Germany until 1990

anhedral (æn'hi:drəl) *n* the downward inclination of an aircraft wing in relation to the lateral axis

Anhui *or* **Anhwei** ('æn'weɪ) *n* a province of E China, crossed by the Yangtze River. Capital: Hefei. Pop: 59 860 000 (2000). Area: 139 860 sq km (54 000 sq miles)

anhydride (æn'haɪdraɪd) *n* **1** a compound that has been formed from another compound by dehydration **2** a compound that forms an acid or base when added to water [c19 from ANHYDR(OUS) + -IDE]

anhydrous (æn'haɪdrəs) *adj* containing no water, esp no water of crystallization [c19 from Gk *anudros*; see AN-, HYDRO-]

Aniakchak (,ænɪ'æktʃæk) *n* an active volcanic crater in SW Alaska, on the Alaska Peninsula: the largest explosion crater in the world. Height: 1347 m (4420 ft). Diameter: 9 km (6 miles)

anil ('ænɪl) *n* a leguminous West Indian shrub which is a source of indigo. Also called: **indigo** [c16 from Port., from Ar. *an-nīl*, the indigo]

aniline ('ænɪlɪn, -,li:n) *n* a colourless oily poisonous liquid used in the manufacture of dyes, plastics, and explosives. Formula: $C_6H_5NH_2$

aniline dye *n* any synthetic dye originally made from aniline, obtained from coal tar

anima ('ænɪmə) *n* (in Jungian psychology) **a** the feminine principle as present in the male unconscious **b** the inner personality [L: air, breath, spirit, fem of ANIMUS]

animadversion (,ænɪmæd'vɜ:ʃən) *n* criticism or censure

animadvert (,ænɪmæd'vɜ:t) *vb* (*intr*) **1** (usually foll by *on* or *upon*) to comment with strong criticism (upon); make censorious remarks (about) **2** to make an observation or comment [c16 from L *animadvertere* to notice, from *animus* mind + *advertere* to turn to]

animal ('ænɪməl) *n* **1** *zool* any living organism characterized by voluntary movement, the possession of specialized sense organs enabling rapid response to stimuli, and the ingestion of complex organic substances **2** any mammal, esp except man **3** a brutish person **4** *facetious* a person or thing (esp in **no such animal**) ▷ *adj* **5** of, relating to, or derived from animals **6** of or relating to physical needs or desires; carnal; sensual [c14 from L, from *animālis* (adj) living, breathing; see ANIMA]

▷ www.biosis.org.uk/free_resources/classifn/classifn.html
▷ http://animaldiversity.ummz.umich.edu/index.html
▷ www.a25.com/animals.html
▷ www.itis.usda.gov

animalcule (,ænɪ'mælkju:l) *n* a microscopic animal such as an amoeba or rotifer [c16 from NL *animalculum* a small animal] > ,**ani'malcular** *adj*

animal husbandry *n* the science of breeding, rearing, and caring for farm animals

animalism ('ænɪmə,lɪzəm) *n* **1** preoccupation with physical matters; sensuality **2** the doctrine that man lacks a spiritual nature **3** a mode of behaviour typical of animals

animality (,ænɪ'mælɪtɪ) *n* **1** the animal side of man, as opposed to the intellectual or spiritual **2** the characteristics of an animal

animalize *or* **animalise** ('ænɪmə,laɪz) *vb* **animalizes, animalizing, animalized** *or* **animalises, animalising, animalised** (*tr*) to rouse to brutality or sensuality or make brutal or sensual > ,**animali'zation** *or* ,**animali'sation** *n*

animal magnetism *n* **1** the quality of being attractive, esp to members of the opposite sex **2** *obs* hypnotism

animal rights *pl n* **a** the rights of animals to be protected from exploitation and abuse by humans **b** (*as modifier*): *the animal-rights lobby*

animal spirits *pl n* boisterous exuberance [from a vital force once supposed to be dispatched by the brain to all points of the body]

animate *vb* ('ænɪ,meɪt), **animates, animating, animated** (*tr*) **1** to give life to or cause to come alive **2** to make energetic or lively **3** to encourage or inspire **4** to impart motion to **5** to record on film or video tape so as to give movement to ▷ *adj* ('ænɪmɪt) **6** having life **7** spirited or lively [c16 from L *animāre* to make alive, from *anima* breath, spirit] > '**ani,matedly** *adv*

animated cartoon *n* a film produced by photographing a series of gradually changing drawings, etc, which give the illusion of movement when the series is projected rapidly

▷ www.cliphoto.com/disney.htm
▷ www.artie.com/
▷ www.aaascreensavers.com/cartoonscreensavers.phtml

animation (,ænɪ'meɪʃən) *n* **1** vivacity **2** the condition of being alive **3** the techniques used in the production of animated cartoons

animato (,ænɪ'mɑ:təʊ) *adj, adv music* lively; animated [It.]

animatronics (,ænɪmə'trɒnɪks) *n* (*functioning as sing*) a branch of film and theatre technology that combines traditional puppetry techniques with electronics to create lifelike animated effects [c20 from ANIMA(TION) + (ELEC)TRONICS]

▷ www.animatronics.org
▷ www.howstuffworks.com/animatronic.htm

animé ('ænɪ,meɪ, -mɪ) *n* any of various resins, esp that obtained from a tropical American leguminous tree [F: from ?]

animism ('ænɪ,mɪzəm) *n* **1** the belief that natural objects have desires and intentions **2** (in the philosophies of Plato and Pythagoras) the hypothesis that there is an immaterial force that animates the universe [c19 from L *anima* vital breath, spirit] > **animistic** (,ænɪ'mɪstɪk) *adj*

▷ www.wikipedia.org/wiki/Animism

animosity (,ænɪ'mɒsɪtɪ) *n, pl* **animosities** a powerful and active dislike or hostility [c15 from LL *animōsitās*, from ANIMUS]

animus ('ænɪməs) *n* **1** intense dislike; hatred; animosity

2 motive or purpose 3 (in Jungian psychology) the masculine principle present in the female unconscious [C19 from L: mind, spirit]

anion ('æn,aɪən) *n* a negatively charged ion; an ion that is attracted to the anode during electrolysis ▷ Cf **cation** [C19 from ANA- + ION] > **anionic** (,ænaɪ'ɒnɪk) *adj*

anise ('ænɪs) *n* a Mediterranean umbelliferous plant having clusters of small yellowish-white flowers and liquorice-flavoured seeds [C13 from OF *anis*, via L from Gk *anison*]

aniseed ('ænɪ,siːd) *n* the liquorice-flavoured aromatic seeds of the anise plant, used medicinally for expelling intestinal gas and in cookery

anisette (,ænɪ'zɛt, -'sɛt) *n* a liquorice-flavoured liqueur made from aniseed [C19 from F]

anisotropic (æn,aɪsəʊ'trɒpɪk) *adj* 1 having different physical properties in different directions: *anisotropic crystals* 2 (of a plant) responding unequally to an external stimulus in different parts > **an,iso'tropically** *adv* > **anisotropy** (,ænaɪ'sɒtrəpɪ) *n*

Anjou (*French* ɑ̃ʒu) *n* a former province of W France, in the Loire valley: a medieval countship from the 10th century, belonging to the English crown from 1154 until 1204; annexed by France in 1480. Related adj: **Angevin**

Ankara ('æŋkərə) *n* the capital of Turkey: an ancient city in the Anatolian highlands: first a capital in the 3rd century BC, in the Celtic kingdom of Galatia. Pop: 2 984 099 (1997). Ancient name: **Ancyra** Former name (until 1930): **Angora**
▷ www.visitturkeynow.com/cities/c_ankara.htm

ankh (æŋk) *n* a tau cross with a loop on the top, symbolizing eternal life: often appearing in Egyptian personal names, such as Tutankhamen [from Egyptian *'nh* life, soul]

Anking ('ɑːn'kɪŋ) *n* a variant transliteration of the Chinese name for **Anqing**

ankle ('æŋkᵊl) *n* 1 the joint connecting the leg and the foot 2 the part of the leg just above the foot [C14 from ON]

ankle biter *n Austral sl* a child

anklebone ('æŋkᵊl,bəʊn) *n* the nontechnical name for **talus**[1]

anklet ('æŋklɪt) *n* an ornamental chain worn around the ankle

ankylose *or* **anchylose** ('æŋkɪ,ləʊz) *vb* **ankyloses, ankylosing, ankylosed** *or* **anchyloses, anchylosing, anchylosed** (of bones in a joint, etc) to fuse or stiffen by ankylosis

ankylosis *or* **anchylosis** (,æŋkɪ'ləʊsɪs) *n* abnormal adhesion or immobility of the bones in a joint, as by a fibrous growth of tissues within the joint [C18 from NL, from Gk *ankuloun* to crook] > **ankylotic** *or* **anchylotic** (,æŋkɪ'lɒtɪk) *adj*

anna ('ænə) *n* a former Indian coin, worth one sixteenth of a rupee [C18 from Hindi *ānā*]

Annaba ('ænəbə) *n* a port in NE Algeria: site of the Roman city of Hippo Regius. Pop: 348 554 (1998). Former name: **Bône**

annals ('ænᵊlz) *pl n* 1 yearly records of events 2 history in general 3 regular reports of the work of a society, learned body, etc [C16 from L (*librī*) *annālēs* yearly (books), from *annus* year] > **'annalist** *n* > **,annal'istic** *adj*

Annan ('ænæn) *n* **Kofi** ('kəʊfɪ) born 1938, Ghanaian international civil servant; secretary-general of the United Nations from 1997: Nobel peace prize 2001 with the UN

Annapolis (ə'næpəlɪs) *n* the capital of Maryland, near the mouth of the Severn River on Chesapeake Bay: site of the US Naval Academy. Pop: 33 187 (1990)

Annapolis Royal *n* a town in SE Canada in W Nova Scotia on an arm of the Bay of Fundy: the first settlement in Canada (1605). Pop: 633 (1991). Former name (until 1710): **Port Royal**

Annapurna *or* **Anapurna** (,ænə'pʊənə) *n* a massif of the Himalayas, in Nepal. Highest peak: 8078 m (26 502 ft)

Ann Arbor (æn 'ɑːbə) *n* a city in SE Michigan: seat of the University of Michigan. Pop: 114 024 (2000)

annates ('æneɪts, -əts) *pl n RC Church* the first year's revenue of a see, etc, paid to the pope [C16 from F, from Med. L *annāta*, from L *annus* year]

annatto *or* **anatto** (ə'nætəʊ) *n, pl* **annattos** *or* **anattos** 1 a small tropical American tree having pulpy seeds that yield a dye 2 the yellowish-red dye obtained from the seeds of this tree, used for colouring fabrics, butter, varnish, etc [from Carib]

Anne (æn) *n* 1 **Queen** 1665–1714, queen of Great Britain and Ireland (1702–14), daughter of James II, and the last of the Stuart monarchs 2 **Saint** (in Christian tradition) the mother of the Virgin Mary. Feast day: July 26 or 25

anneal (ə'niːl) *vb* 1 to temper or toughen (something) by heat treatment to remove internal stress, crystal defects, and dislocations 2 (*tr*) to toughen or strengthen (the will, determination, etc) ▷ *n* 3 an act of annealing [OE *onǣlan*, from ON + *ǣlan* to burn, from *āl* fire] > **an'nealer** *n*

Anne Boleyn *n* See (Anne) **Boleyn**

Annecy (*French* ansi) *n* 1 a city and resort in E France, on Lake Annecy. Pop: 51 143 (1990) 2 **Lake** a lake in E France, in the Alps

annelid ('ænəlɪd) *n* 1 a worm in which the body is divided into segments both externally and internally, as the earthworms ▷ *adj* 2 of such worms [C19 from NL *Annelida*, from OF, ult. from L *ānulus* ring] > **annelidan** (ə'nɛlɪdən) *n, adj*

Anne of Austria *n* 1601–66, wife of Louis XIII of France and daughter of Philip III of Spain: regent of France (1643–61) for her son Louis XIV

Anne of Cleves (kliːvz) *n* 1515–57, the fourth wife of Henry VIII of England: their marriage (1540) was annulled after six months

annex *vb* (æ'nɛks). (*tr*) 1 to join or add, esp to something larger 2 to add (territory) by conquest or occupation 3 to add or append as a condition, etc 4 to appropriate without permission ▷ *n* ('ænɛks) 5 a variant spelling (esp US) of **annexe** [C14 from Med. L, from L *annectere* to attach to, from *nectere* to join] > **an'nexable** *adj* > **,annex'ation** *n*

annexe *or esp US* **annex** ('ænɛks) *n* 1a an extension to a main building 1b a building used as an addition to a main one nearby 2 something added, esp a supplement to a document

Annigoni (*Italian* anni'goːni) *n* **Pietro** ('pjɛːtro) 1910–88, Italian painter; noted esp for his portraits of President Kennedy (1961) and Queen Elizabeth II (1955 and 1970)

annihilate (ə'naɪə,leɪt) *vb* **annihilates, annihilating, annihilated** (*tr*) 1 to destroy completely; extinguish 2 *inf* to defeat totally, as in argument [C16 from LL, from L *nihil* nothing] > **an,nihi'lation** *n* > **an'nihi,lator** *n*

anniversary (,ænɪ'vɜːsərɪ) *n, pl* **anniversaries** 1 the date on which an event occurred in some previous year: *a wedding anniversary* 2 the celebration of this ▷ *adj* 3 of or relating to an anniversary [C13 from L *anniversārius* returning every year, from *annus* year + *vertere* to turn]

anno Domini ('ænəʊ 'dɒmɪ,naɪ, -,niː) 1 the full form of AD ▷ *n* 2 *inf* advancing old age [L: in the year of our Lord]

annotate ('ænəʊ,teɪt, 'ænə,teɪt) *vb* **annotates, annotating, annotated** to supply (a written work) with critical or explanatory notes [C18 from L *annotāre*, from *nota* mark] > **'anno,tative** *adj* > **'anno,tator** *n*

annotation (,ænəʊ'teɪʃən, ,ænə'teɪʃən) *n* 1 the act of annotating 2 a note added in explanation, etc, esp of some literary work

announce (ə'naʊns) *vb* **announces, announcing, announced** 1 (*tr; may take a clause as object*) to make known publicly 2 (*tr*) to declare the arrival of: *to announce a guest*

3 (*tr; may take a clause as object*) to presage: *the dark clouds announced rain* 4 (*intr*) to work as an announcer, as on radio or television [C15 from OF, from L *annuntiāre*, from *nuntius* messenger]

announcement (əˈnaʊnsmənt) *n* 1 a public statement 2 a brief item or advertisement, as in a newspaper 3 a formal printed or written invitation 4 the act of announcing

announcer (əˈnaʊnsə) *n* a person who announces, esp one who reads the news, etc, on radio or television

annoy (əˈnɔɪ) *vb* 1 to irritate or displease 2 to harass with repeated attacks [C13 from OF, from LL *inodiāre* to make hateful, from L *in odiō (esse)* (to be) hated, from *odium* hatred] > **anˈnoyer** *n* > **anˈnoying** *adj* > **anˈnoyingly** *adv*

annoyance (əˈnɔɪəns) *n* 1 the feeling of being annoyed 2 the act of annoying 3 a person or thing that annoys

annual (ˈænjʊəl) *adj* 1 occurring, done, etc, once a year or every year; yearly: *an annual income* 2 lasting for a year: *an annual subscription* ▷ *n* 3 a plant that completes its life cycle in less than one year 4 a book, magazine, etc, published once every year [C14 from LL, from L *annuus* yearly, from *annus* year] > **ˈannually** *adv*

annual general meeting *n* the statutory meeting of the directors and shareholders of a company or of the members of a society, held once every financial year. Abbrev: **AGM**

annualize *or* **annualise** (ˈænjʊəˌlaɪz) *vb* **annualizes, annualizing, annualized** *or* **annualises, annualising, annualised** (*tr*) to convert (a rate of interest) to an annual rate when it is quoted for a period less than a year: *an annualized percentage rate*

annual percentage rate *n* the annual equivalent of a rate of interest when the rate is quoted more frequently than annually, usually monthly. Abbrev: **APR**

annual ring *n* a ring indicating one year's growth, seen in the transverse section of stems and roots of woody plants. Also called: **tree ring**

annuitant (əˈnjuːɪtənt) *n* a person in receipt of or entitled to an annuity

annuity (əˈnjuːɪtɪ) *n, pl* **annuities** a fixed sum payable at specified intervals over a period, such as the recipient's life, or in perpetuity, in return for a premium paid either in instalments or in a single payment [C15 from F, from Med. L *annuitās*, from L *annuus* ANNUAL]

annul (əˈnʌl) *vb* **annuls, annulling, annulled** (*tr*) to make (something, esp a law or marriage) void; abolish [C14 from OF, from LL *adnullāre* to bring to nothing, from L *nullus* not any] > **anˈnullable** *adj*

annular (ˈænjʊlə) *adj* ring-shaped [C16 from L *annulāris*, from *annulus, ānulus* ring]

annular eclipse *n* an eclipse of the sun in which the moon does not cover the entire disc of the sun, so that a ring of sunlight surrounds the shadow of the moon

annular ligament *n anat* any of various ligaments that encircle a part, such as the wrist

annulate (ˈænjʊlɪt, -ˌleɪt) *adj* having, composed of, or marked with rings [C19 from L *ānulātus*, from *ānulus* a ring] > **ˌannuˈlation** *n*

annulet (ˈænjʊlɪt) *n* 1 *archit* a moulding in the form of a ring 2 *heraldry* a ring-shaped device on a shield 3 a little ring [C16 from L *ānulus* ring + -ET]

annulment (əˈnʌlmənt) *n* 1 a formal invalidation, as of a marriage, judicial proceeding, etc 2 the act of annulling

annulus (ˈænjʊləs) *n, pl* **annuli** (-ˌlaɪ) *or* **annuluses** 1 the area between two concentric circles 2 a ring-shaped part [C16 from L, var. of *ānulus* ring]

annunciate (əˈnʌnsɪˌeɪt, -ʃɪ-) *vb* **annunciates, annunciating, annunciated** (*tr*) a less common word for **announce** [C16 from Med L from L *annuntiāre*; see ANNOUNCE]

Annunciation (əˌnʌnsɪˈeɪʃən) *n* 1 **the** the announcement of the Incarnation by the angel Gabriel to the Virgin Mary (Luke 1:26–38) 2 Also called: **Annunciation Day** the festival commemorating this, on March 25 (Lady Day)

annunciator (əˈnʌnsɪˌeɪtə) *n* 1 a device that gives a visual indication as to which of a number of electric circuits has operated, such as an indicator showing in which room a bell has been rung 2 a device giving an audible signal indicating the position of a train 3 an announcer

annus horribilis (ˈænʊs hɒˈriːbɪlɪs) *n* a terrible year [C20 from L, modelled on ANNUS MIRABILIS, first used by Elizabeth II of the year 1992]

annus mirabilis (ˈænʊs mɪˈræbɪlɪs) *n, pl* **anni mirabiles** (ˈænaɪ mɪˈræbɪliːz) a year of wonders, catastrophes, or other notable events [L: wonderful year]

anoa (əˈnəʊə) *n* the smallest of the cattle tribe, having small straight horns and inhabiting the island of Celebes in Indonesia [from a native name in Celebes]

anode (ˈænəʊd) *n* 1 the positive electrode in an electrolytic cell or in an electronic valve 2 the negative terminal of a primary cell ▷ Cf **cathode** [C19 from Gk *anodos* a way up, from *hodos* a way; alluding to the movement of the current] > **anodal** (eɪˈnəʊdᵊl) *or* **anodic** (əˈnɒdɪk) *adj*

anodize *or* **anodise** (ˈænəˌdaɪz) *vb* **anodizes, anodizing, anodized** *or* **anodises, anodising, anodised** to coat (a metal, such as aluminium) with a protective oxide film by electrolysis

anodyne (ˈænəˌdaɪn) *n* 1 a drug that relieves pain 2 anything that alleviates mental distress ▷ *adj* 3 capable of relieving pain or distress [C16 from L, from Gk *anōdunos* painless, from AN- + *odunē* pain]

anoint (əˈnɔɪnt) *vb* (*tr*) 1 to smear or rub over with oil 2 to apply oil to as a sign of consecration or sanctification [C14 from OF, from L *inunguere*, from IN-² + *unguere* to smear with oil] > **aˈnointer** *n* > **aˈnointment** *n*

anointing of the sick *n RC Church* a sacrament in which a person who is seriously ill or dying is anointed by a priest with consecrated oil. Former name: **extreme unction**

anomalistic (əˌnɒməˈlɪstɪk) *adj* 1 *astron* 1a (of a month) measured between successive perigees of the moon 1b (of a year) between successive perihelia of the earth 2 anomalous

anomalous (əˈnɒmələs) *adj* deviating from the normal or usual order, type, etc [C17 from LL, from Gk *anōmalos* uneven, inconsistent, from AN- + *homalos* even, from *homos* one and the same] > **aˈnomalousness** *n*

anomaly (əˈnɒməlɪ) *n, pl* **anomalies** 1 something anomalous 2 deviation from the normal; irregularity 3 *astron* the angle between a planet, the sun, and the previous perihelion of the planet

anomie *or* **anomy** (ˈænəʊmɪ) *n sociol* lack of social or moral standards in an individual or society [from Gk *anomia* lawlessness, from A-¹ + *nomos* law] > **anomic** (əˈnɒmɪk) *adj*

anon (əˈnɒn) *adv arch. or literary* 1 soon 2 **ever and anon** now and then [OE *on āne*, lit.: in one, that is, immediately]

anon. *abbrev for* anonymous

anonym (ˈænənɪm) *n* 1 a less common word for **pseudonym** 2 an anonymous person or publication

anonymize *or* **anonymise** (əˈnɒnɪˌmaɪz) *vb* **anonymizes, anonymizing, anonymized** *or* **anonymises, anonymising, anonymised** (*tr*) to carry out or organize in such a way as to preserve anonymity: *anonymized AIDS screening*

anonymous (əˈnɒnɪməs) *adj* 1 from or by a person, author, etc, whose name is unknown or withheld 2 having no known name 3 lacking individual characteristics 4 (*often cap*) denoting an organization which provides help to applicants who remain anonymous: *Alcoholics Anonymous* [c17 via LL from Gk *anōnumos*, from AN- + *onoma* name] > **anonymity** (ˌænəˈnɪmɪtɪ) *n*

anopheles (əˈnɒfɪˌliːz) *n, pl* **anopheles** any of various mosquitoes constituting the genus *Anopheles*, some species of which transmit the malaria parasite to man [c19 via NL from Gk *anōphelēs* useless, from AN- + *ōphelein* to help]

anorak (ˈænəˌræk) *n* **1** a warm waterproof hip-length jacket usually with a hood **2** *inf* a boring or socially inept person [from Inuktitut *ánorâq*]

anorexia (ˌænɒˈrɛksɪə) *n* **1** loss of appetite **2** Also called: **anorexia nervosa** (nɜːˈvəʊsə) a disorder characterized by fear of becoming fat and refusal of food, leading to debility and even death [c17 via NL from Gk, from AN- + *orexis* appetite] > ˌ**anoˈrectic** *or* ˌ**anoˈrexic** *adj, n*

anosmia (ænˈɒzmɪə, -ˈɒs-) *n* loss of the sense of smell [c19 from NL, from AN- + Gk *osmē* smell] > **anosmatic** (ˌænɒzˈmætɪk) *or* **anˈosmic** *adj*

another (əˈnʌðə) *determiner* **1a** one more: *another chance* **1b** *(as pron): help yourself to another* **2a** a different: *another era from ours* **2b** *(as pron): to try one, then another* **3a** a different example of the same sort **3b** *(as pron): we got rid of one, but I think this is another* [c14 orig. *an other*]

A.N. Other *n Brit* an unnamed person: used in team lists, etc, to indicate a place that remains to be filled

Anouilh (*French* anuj) *n* **Jean** (ʒɑ̃) 1910–87, French dramatist, noted for his reinterpretations of Greek myths: his works include *Eurydice* (1942), *Antigone* (1944), and *Becket* (1959)

anoxia (ænˈɒksɪə) *n* lack or deficiency of oxygen [c20 from AN- + OX(YGEN) + -IA] > **anˈoxic** *adj*

Anqing (ˈɑːnˈtʃɪŋ) *or* **Anking** *n* a city in E China, in SW Anhui province on the Yangtze River: famous seven-storeyed pagoda. Pop: 356 920 (1999 est)

Anschluss (ˈænʃlʊs) *n* a political or economic union, esp the annexation of Austria by Nazi Germany (1938) [G, from *anschliessen* to join]

Anselm (ˈænsɛlm) *n* **Saint** 1033–1109, Italian Benedictine monk; archbishop of Canterbury (1093–1109): one of the founders of scholasticism; author of *Cur Deus Homo?* (*Why did God become Man?*). Feast day: Aug. 21

anserine (ˈænsəˌraɪn) *adj* of or resembling a goose [c19 from L *anserīnus*, from *anser* goose]

Ansermet (*French* ɑ̃sɛrmɛ) *n* **Ernest** (ɛrnɛst) 1883–1969, Swiss orchestral conductor; principal conductor of Diaghilev's Ballet Russe

answer (ˈɑːnsə) *n* **1** a reply, either spoken or written, as to a question, request, letter, or article **2** a reaction or response: *drunkenness was his answer to disappointment* **3** a solution, esp of a mathematical problem ▷ *vb* **4** (*when tr, may take a clause as object*) to reply or respond (to) by word or act: *to answer a question; to answer the door* **5** (*tr*) to reply correctly to; solve: *I could answer only three questions* **6** (*intr;* usually foll by *to*) to respond or react: *the steering answers to the slightest touch* **7a** (when *intr*, often foll by *for*) to meet the requirements (of); be satisfactory (for): *this will answer his needs* **7b** to be responsible (to a person or for a thing) **8** (when *intr*, foll by *to*) to match or correspond (esp in **answer** (*or* **answer to**) **the description**) **9** (*tr*) to give a defence or refutation of (a charge) or in (an argument) [OE *andswaru* an answer; see SWEAR]

answerable (ˈɑːnsərəbᵊl) *adj* **1** (*postpositive;* foll by *for* or *to*) responsible or accountable: *answerable to one's boss* **2** able to be answered

answer back *vb* (*adv*) to reply rudely to (a person, esp someone in authority) when one is expected to remain silent

answering machine *n* a device by which a telephone call is answered automatically and the caller leaves a recorded message. In full: **telephone answering machine** Also called: **answerphone**

ant (ænt) *n* **1** a small social insect of a widely distributed hymenopterous family, typically living in highly organized colonies of winged males, wingless sterile females (workers), and fertile females (queens). Related adj: **formic 2 white ant** another name for a **termite** [OE *ǣmette*]

-ant *suffix forming adjectives and nouns* causing or performing an action or existing in a certain condition: *pleasant; deodorant; servant* [from L *-ant*, ending of present participles of the first conjugation]

antacid (æntˈæsɪd) *n* **1** a substance used to neutralize acidity, esp in the stomach ▷ *adj* **2** having the properties of this substance

Antaeus (ænˈtiːəs) *n Greek myth* an African giant who was invincible as long as he touched the ground, but was lifted into the air by Hercules and crushed to death

antagonism (ænˈtægəˌnɪzəm) *n* **1** openly expressed and usually mutual opposition **2** the inhibiting or nullifying action of one substance or organism on another

antagonist (ænˈtægənɪst) *n* **1** an opponent or adversary **2** any muscle that opposes the action of another **3** a drug that counteracts the effects of another drug > **anˌtagoˈnistic** *adj* > **anˌtagoˈnistically** *adv*

antagonize *or* **antagonise** (ænˈtægəˌnaɪz) *vb* **antagonizes, antagonizing, antagonized** *or* **antagonises, antagonising, antagonised** (*tr*) **1** to make hostile; annoy or irritate **2** to act in opposition to or counteract [c17 from Gk, from ANTI- + *agōnizesthai* to strive, from *agōn* contest] > **anˌtagoniˈzation** *or* **anˌtagoniˈsation** *n*

Antakiya (ˌæntɑːˈkiːjə) *n* the Arabic name for **Antioch**

Antakya (ɑnˈtɑkjɑ) *n* the Turkish name for **Antioch**

antalkali (æntˈælkəˌlaɪ) *n, pl* **antalkalis** *or* **antalkalies** a substance that neutralizes alkalis

Antananarivo (ˌæntəˌnænəˈriːvəʊ) *n* the capital of Madagascar, on the central plateau: founded in the 17th century by a Hova chief; university (1961). Pop: 1 052 835 (1993). Former name: **Tananarive**
▷ www.embassy.org/madagascar/points.html

Antarctic (æntˈɑːktɪk) *n* **1 the** Also called: **Antarctic Zone** Antarctica and the surrounding waters. *adj* **2** of or relating to the south polar regions [c14 via Latin from Greek *antarktikos;* see ANTI-, ARCTIC]

Antarctica (æntˈɑːktɪkə) *n* a continent around the South Pole: consists of an ice-covered plateau, 1800–3000 m (6000 ft to 10 000 ft) above sea level, and mountain ranges rising to 4500 m (15 000 ft) with some volcanic peaks; average temperatures all below freezing and human settlement is confined to research stations

Antarctic Archipelago *n* the former name of the **Palmer Archipelago**

Antarctic Circle *n* the imaginary circle around the earth, parallel to the equator, at latitude 66° 32′ S; it marks the southernmost point at which the Sun appears above the level of the horizon on the winter solstice

Antarctic Ocean *n* the sea surrounding Antarctica, consisting of the most southerly parts of the Pacific, Atlantic, and Indian Oceans. Also called: **Southern Ocean**

Antarctic Peninsula *n* the largest peninsula of Antarctica, between the Weddell Sea and the Pacific: consists of Graham Land in the north and the Palmer Peninsula in the south. Former name (until 1964): **Palmer Peninsula**

ant bear *n* another name for **aardvark**

ante (ˈæntɪ) *n* **1** the gaming stake put up before the deal in poker by the players **2** *inf* a sum of money representing a person's share, as in a syndicate **3 up the ante** *inf* to increase the costs, risks, or considerations involved in taking an action or reaching a conclusion ▷ *vb* **antes, anteing, anted** *or* **anteed 4** to place (one's stake) in poker **5** (usually foll by *up*) *inf* to pay

ante- *prefix* before in time or position: *antedate; antechamber* [from L]
anteater ('ænt,iːtə) *n* any of several toothless mammals having a long tubular snout used for eating termites
antebellum (,æntɪ'bɛləm) *adj* of or during the period before a war, esp the American Civil War [L *ante bellum*, lit.: before the war]
antecede (,æntɪ'siːd) *vb* **antecedes, anteceding, anteceded** (*tr*) to go before; precede [C17 from L *antecēdere*, from *cēdere* to go]
antecedent (,æntɪ'siːdᵊnt) *n* **1** an event, etc, that happens before another **2** *grammar* a word or phrase to which a pronoun refers. In "People who live in glass houses shouldn't throw stones," *people* is the antecedent of *who* **3** *logic* the first hypothetical clause in a conditional statement ▷ *adj* **4** preceding in time or order; prior > ,**ante'cedence** *n*
antecedents (,æntɪ'siːdᵊnts) *pl n* **1** ancestry **2** a person's past history
antechamber ('æntɪ,tʃeɪmbə) *n* an anteroom [C17 from OF, from It. *anticamera*; see ANTE-, CHAMBER]
antedate ('æntɪ,deɪt) *vb* (*tr*) **1** to be or occur at an earlier date than **2** to affix or assign a date to (a document, event, etc) that is earlier than the actual date **3** to cause to occur sooner ▷ *n* **4** an earlier date
antediluvian (,æntɪdɪ'luːvɪən) *adj* **1** of the ages before the biblical Flood **2** old-fashioned ▷ *n* **3** an antediluvian person or thing [C17 from ANTE- + L *dīluvium* flood]
antelope ('æntɪ,ləʊp) *n, pl* **antelopes** *or* **antelope** any of a group of mammals of Africa and Asia. They are typically graceful, having long legs and horns, and include the gazelles, springbok, impala, and dik-diks [C15 from OF, from Med. L, from LGk *antholops* a legendary beast]
antemeridian (,æntɪmə'rɪdɪən) *adj* before noon; in the morning [C17 from L]
ante meridiem ('æntɪ mə'rɪdɪəm) the full form of **a.m.** [L, from ANTE- + *merīdiēs* midday]
antenatal (,æntɪ'neɪtᵊl) *adj* occurring or present before birth; during pregnancy
antenna (æn'tɛnə) *n* **1** (*pl* **antennae** (-niː)) one of a pair of mobile appendages on the heads of insects, crustaceans, etc, that often respond to touch and taste but may be specialized for swimming **2** (*pl* **antennas**) an aerial [C17 from L: sail yard, from ?] > **an'tennal** *or* **an'tennary** *adj*
antenuptial contract (,æntɪ'nʌpʃəl) *n* (in South Africa) a marriage contract effected prior to the wedding giving each partner control over his or her property
antependium (,æntɪ'pɛndɪəm) *n, pl* **antependia** (-dɪə) a covering hung over the front of an altar [C17 from Med. L, from L ANTE- + *pendēre* to hang]
antepenult (,æntɪpɪ'nʌlt) *n* the third last syllable in a word [C16 shortened from L (*syllaba*) *antepaenultima*; see ANTE-, PENULT]
antepenultimate (,æntɪpɪ'nʌltɪmɪt) *adj* **1** third from last ▷ *n* **2** anything that is third from last
ante-post *adj Brit* (of a bet) placed before the runners in a race are confirmed
anterior (æn'tɪərɪə) *adj* **1** at or towards the front **2** earlier **3** *zool* of or near the head end **4** *bot* (of part of a flower or leaf) farthest away from the main stem [C17 from L, comp. of *ante* before]
anterior cruciate ligament *n* a ligament in the knee that is often torn or sprained in sports injuries
anteroom ('æntɪ,ruːm, -,rʊm) *n* a room giving entrance to a larger room, often used as a waiting room
anthelion (æn'θiːlɪən) *n, pl* **anthelia** (-lɪə) **1** a faint halo sometimes seen in high altitude regions around a shadow cast onto fog **2** a white spot occasionally appearing at the same height as and opposite to the sun [C17 from LGk, from *anthēlios* opposite the sun, from ANTE- + *hēlios* sun]
anthelmintic (,ænθɛl'mɪntɪk) *or* **anthelminthic** (,ænθɛl'mɪnθɪk) *or* **antihelminthic** (æntIhel'mInθIk) *n med* another name for **vermifuge**
anthem ('ænθəm) *n* **1** a song of loyalty: *a national anthem* **2** a musical composition for a choir, usually set to words from the Bible **3** a religious chant sung antiphonally [OE *antemne*, from LL *antiphōna* ANTIPHON]
anthemis (æn'θiːmɪs) *n* any of several cultivated varieties of camomile [NL, from L, from Gk *anthos* flower]
anther ('ænθə) *n* the terminal part of a stamen consisting of usually two lobes each containing two sacs in which the pollen matures [C18 from NL, from L, from Gk *anthēros* flowery, from *anthos* flower]
antheridium (,ænθə'rɪdɪəm) *n, pl* **antheridia** (-ɪə) the male sex organ of algae, fungi, bryophytes, ferns, etc [C19 from NL, dim. of *anthēra* ANTHER]
ant hill *n* a mound of soil, leaves, etc, near the entrance of an ants' or termites' nest, deposited there by the ants or termites while constructing the nest
anthologize *or* **anthologise** (æn'θɒlə,dʒaɪz) *vb* **anthologizes, anthologizing, anthologized** *or* **anthologises, anthologising, anthologised** to compile or put into an anthology
anthology (æn'θɒlədʒɪ) *n, pl* **anthologies** **1** a collection of literary passages by various authors **2** any printed collection of literary pieces, songs, etc [C17 from Med. L, from Gk, lit.: a flower gathering, from *anthos* flower + *legein* to collect] > **an'thologist** *n*
Anthony ('æntənɪ) *n* **Saint** ?251–?356 AD, Egyptian hermit, commonly regarded as the founder of Christian monasticism. Feast day: Jan. 17
Anthony of Padua *n* **Saint** 1195–1231, Franciscan friar, who preached in France and Italy. Feast day: June 13
anthozoan (,ænθə'zəʊən) *n* **1** any of the sessile marine coelenterates of the class *Anthozoa*, including corals and sea anemones, in which the body is in the form of a polyp ▷ *adj* also: **actinozoan** **2** of or relating to these
anthracene ('ænθrə,siːn) *n* a colourless crystalline solid, used in the manufacture of chemicals and as crystals in scintillation counters [C19 from ANTHRAX + -ENE]
anthracite ('ænθrə,saɪt) *n* a hard coal that burns slowly with a nonluminous flame giving out intense heat. Also called: **hard coal** [C19 from L, from Gk *anthrakitēs* coal-like, from *anthrax* coal] > **anthracitic** (,ænθrə'sɪtɪk) *adj*
anthracosis (,ænθrə'kəʊsɪs) *n* a lung disease due to inhalation of coal dust
anthrax ('ænθræks) *n, pl* **anthraces** (-θrə,siːz) **1** a highly infectious and often fatal disease of herbivores, esp cattle and sheep, which can be transmitted to humans **2** a pustule caused by this disease [C19 from LL, from Gk: carbuncle]
anthropic principle *n astron* the cosmological theory that the presence of life in the universe limits the ways in which the very early universe could have evolved
anthropo- *combining form* indicating man or human: *anthropology* [from Gk *anthrōpos*]
anthropocentric (,ænθrəpəʊ'sɛntrɪk) *adj* regarding humans as the central factor in the universe
anthropogenesis (,ænθrəpəʊ'dʒɛnɪsɪs) *or* **anthropogeny** (,ænθrə'pɒdʒɪnɪ) *n* the study of the origins of humans
anthropoid ('ænθrə,pɔɪd) *adj* **1** resembling humans **2** resembling an ape; apelike ▷ *n* **3** any primate of the suborder *Anthropoidea*, including monkeys, apes, and humans
anthropoid ape *n* any of a group of primates having no tail, elongated arms, and a highly developed brain, including gibbons, orang-utans, chimpanzees, and gorillas
anthropology (,ænθrə'pɒlədʒɪ) *n* the study of human beings, their origins, institutions, religious beliefs,

social relationships, etc > ˌ**anthropoˈlogical** *adj* > ˌ**anthroˈpologist** *n*
▷ http://vlib.anthrotech.com/
▷ www.sosig.ac.uk/ethnology_ethnography_anthropology/
▷ www.rai.anthropology.org.uk

anthropometry (ˌænθrəˈpɒmɪtrɪ) *n* the comparative study of sizes and proportions of the human body > ˌ**anthropoˈmetric** *or* ˌ**anthropoˈmetrical** *adj*

anthropomorphic (ˌænθrəpəˈmɔːfɪk) *adj* **1** of or relating to anthropomorphism **2** resembling the human form > ˈ**anthropoˌmorph** *n* > ˌ**anthropoˈmorphically** *adv*

anthropomorphism (ˌænθrəpəˈmɔːfɪzəm) *n* the attribution of human form or behaviour to a deity, animal, etc

anthropomorphous (ˌænθrəpəˈmɔːfəs) *adj* **1** shaped like a human being **2** another word for **anthropomorphic**

anthropophagi (ˌænθrəˈpɒfəˌgaɪ) *pl n, sing* **anthropophagus** (-gəs) cannibals [c16 from L, from Gk *anthrōpophagos;* see ANTHROPO-, -PHAGE]

anthroposophy (ˌænθrəˈpɒsəfɪ) *n* the spiritual and mystical teachings of Rudolph Steiner, based on the belief that creative activities are psychologically valuable, esp for educational and therapeutic purposes > ˌ**anthropoˈsophic** *adj*

anti (ˈæntɪ) *inf* ▷ *adj* **1** opposed to a party, policy, attitude, etc ▷ *n* **2** an opponent

anti- *prefix* **1** against; opposing: *anticlerical* **2** opposite to: *anticlimax* **3** rival; false: *antipope* **4** counteracting or neutralizing: *antifreeze; antihistamine* **5** designating the antiparticle of the particle specified: *antineutron* [from Gk *anti*]

anti-aircraft (ˌæntɪˈɛəkrɑːft) *n* (*modifier*) of or relating to defence against aircraft attack: *anti-aircraft batteries*

anti-apartheid *adj* opposed to a policy of racial segregation

antiar (ˈæntɪˌɑː) *n* another name for **upas** (senses 1, 2) [from Javanese]

anti-atom (ˌæntɪˈætəm) *n* an atom composed of antiparticles, in which the nucleus contains antiprotons with orbiting positrons

antiballistic missile (ˌæntɪbəˈlɪstɪk) *n* a ballistic missile designed to destroy another ballistic missile in flight

Antibes (*French* ɑ̃tib) *n* a port and resort in SE France, on the Mediterranean: an important Roman town. Pop: 60 000 (latest est)

antibiosis (ˌæntɪbaɪˈəʊsɪs) *n* an association between two organisms, esp microorganisms, that is harmful to one of them

antibiotic (ˌæntɪbaɪˈɒtɪk) *n* **1** any of various chemical substances, such as penicillin, produced by microorganisms, esp fungi, or made synthetically, and capable of destroying microorganisms, esp bacteria ▷ *adj* **2** of or relating to antibiotics

antibody (ˈæntɪˌbɒdɪ) *n, pl* **antibodies** any of various proteins produced in the blood in response to an antigen. By becoming attached to antigens on infectious organisms antibodies can render them harmless

antic (ˈæntɪk) *arch* ▷ *n* **1** an actor in a ludicrous or grotesque part; clown ▷ *adj* **2** fantastic; grotesque ▷ See also **antics** [c16 from It. *antico* something grotesque (from its application to fantastic carvings found in ruins of ancient Rome)]

anticathode (ˌæntɪˈkæθəʊd) *n* the target electrode for the stream of electrons in a vacuum tube, esp an X-ray tube

Antichrist (ˈæntɪˌkraɪst) *n* **1** *Bible* the antagonist of Christ, expected by early Christians to appear and reign over the world until overthrown at Christ's Second Coming **2** (*sometimes not cap*) an enemy of Christ or Christianity

anticipant (ænˈtɪsɪpənt) *adj* **1** operating in advance ▷ *n* **2** a person who anticipates

anticipate (ænˈtɪsɪˌpeɪt) *vb* **anticipates, anticipating, anticipated** (*mainly tr*) **1** (*may take a clause as object*) to foresee and act in advance of; forestall: *I anticipated his punch* **2** (*also intr*) to mention (something) before its proper time: *don't anticipate the climax of the story* **3** (*may take a clause as object*) to regard as likely; expect **4** to make use of in advance of possession: *he anticipated his salary in buying a leather jacket* [c16 from L *anticipāre* to take before, from *anti-* ANTE- + *capere* to take] > **anˈticiˌpator** *n* > **anˈticiˌpatory** *or* **anˈticipative** *adj*

> USAGE Some people consider that the use of *anticipate* to mean *expect* should be avoided. However, the Bank of English shows that this usage is well established. Moreover, the use of *anticipate* adds a suggestion of being prepared for the event referred to. The most common expressions associated with this use are clauses beginning with *that* and *problems*. This use is also markedly commoner in American sources than in British ones

anticipation (ænˌtɪsɪˈpeɪʃən) *n* **1** the act of anticipating; expectation, premonition, or foresight **2** *music* an unstressed, usually short note introduced before a downbeat

anticlerical (ˌæntɪˈklɛrɪkᵊl) *adj* **1** opposed to the power and influence of the clergy, esp in politics ▷ *n* **2** a supporter of an anticlerical party > ˌ**antiˈclericalism** *n*

anticlimax (ˌæntɪˈklaɪmæks) *n* **1** a disappointing or ineffective conclusion to a series of events, etc **2** a sudden change from a serious subject to one that is disappointing or ludicrous > **anticlimactic** (ˌæntɪklaɪˈmæktɪk) *adj*

anticline (ˈæntɪˌklaɪn) *n* a formation of stratified rock raised up, by folding, into a broad arch so that the strata slope down on both sides from a common crest > ˌ**antiˈclinal** *adj*

Aa

anticlockwise (ˌæntɪˈklɒkˌwaɪz) *adv, adj* in the opposite direction to the rotation of the hands of a clock. US equivalent: **counterclockwise**

anticoagulant (ˌæntɪkəʊˈægjʊlənt) *adj* **1** acting to prevent or retard coagulation, esp of blood ▷ *n* **2** an agent that prevents or retards coagulation

anti-Communist *adj* opposed to Communism or its principles

anticonvulsant (ˌæntɪkənˈvʌlsənt) *n* **1** any of a class of drugs used to prevent or abolish convulsions ▷ *adj* **2** of or relating to such drugs

Anticosti (ˌæntɪˈkɒstɪ) *n* an island of E Canada, in the Gulf of St Lawrence; part of Quebec. Area: 7881 sq km (3043 sq miles)

antics (ˈæntɪks) *pl n* absurd acts or postures

anticyclone (ˌæntɪˈsaɪkləʊn) *n* *meteorol* a body of moving air of higher pressure than the surrounding air, in which the pressure decreases away from the centre. Also called: **high** > **anticyclonic** (ˌæntɪsaɪˈklɒnɪk) *adj*

antidazzle mirror (ˌæntɪˈdæzᵊl) *n* a rear-view mirror for road vehicles that only partially reflects headlights behind

antidepressant (ˌæntɪdɪˈprɛsᵊnt) *n* **1** any of a class of drugs used to alleviate depression ▷ *adj* **2** of this class of drugs

antidiuretic hormone (ˌæntɪˌdaɪjʊˈrɛtɪk) *n* another name for **vasopressin.** Abbrev: **ADH**

antidote (ˈæntɪˌdəʊt) *n* **1** *med* a drug or agent that counteracts or neutralizes the effects of a poison **2** anything that counteracts or relieves a harmful condition [c15 from L, from Gk *antidoton* something given as a countermeasure, from ANTI- + *didonai* to give] > ˌ**antiˈdotal** *adj*

antiemetic (ˌæntɪɪˈmɛtɪk) *adj* **1** preventing vomiting

▷ *n* **2** any antiemetic drug, such as promethazine

antifreeze (ˈæntɪˌfriːz) *n* a liquid, usually ethylene glycol (ethanediol), added to water to lower its freezing point, esp for use in an internal-combustion engine

antifungal (ˌæntɪˈfʌŋgᵊl) *adj* **1** inhibiting the growth of fungi **2** (of a drug) possessing antifungal activity and therefore used to treat fungal infections ▷ Also: **antimycotic**

antigen (ˈæntɪdʒən, -ˌdʒɛn) *n* a substance, usually a toxin produced by a bacterium, that stimulates the production of antibodies [C20 from ANTI(BODY) + -GEN]

anti-globalization *or* **anti-globalisation** *n* the political belief that the process of globalization should be halted and practices that do not cause environmental damage should be encouraged

Antigone (ænˈtɪgənɪ) *n Greek myth* daughter of Oedipus and Jocasta, who was condemned to death for cremating the body of her brother Polynices in defiance of an edict of her uncle, King Creon of Thebes

Antigua (ænˈtiːgə) *n* an island in the Caribbean, one of the Leeward Islands: a British colony, with its dependency Barbuda, until 1967, when it became a British associated state; it became independent in 1981 as part of the state of Antigua and Barbuda. Area: 279 sq km (108 sq miles) > **Anˈtiguan** *adj, n*

Antigua and Barbuda *n* a state in the Caribbean, comprising the islands of Antigua, Barbuda, and Redonda: gained independence in 1981: a member of the Commonwealth. Official language: English. Religion: Christian majority. Currency: East Caribbean dollar. Capital: St John's. Pop: 71 500 (2001 est). Area: 442 sq km (171 sq miles)

▷ www.antiguagov.com

▷ www.antigua-barbuda.org

antihero (ˈæntɪˌhɪərəʊ) *n, pl* **antiheroes** a central character in a novel, play, etc, who lacks the traditional heroic virtues

antihistamine (ˌæntɪˈhɪstəˌmiːn, -mɪn) *n* any drug that neutralizes the effects of histamine, used esp in the treatment of allergies

antihydrogen (ˌæntɪˈhaɪdrɪdʒən) *n* hydrogen in which the nucleus is an antiproton with an orbiting positron

anti-inflammatory *adj* **1** reducing inflammation ▷ *n, pl* **anti-inflammatories** **2** any anti-inflammatory drug, such as cortisone, aspirin, or ibuprofen

anti-inflationary *adj* (of an economic policy) designed to reduce or counteract the effects of inflation

antiknock (ˌæntɪˈnɒk) *n* a compound, such as lead tetraethyl, added to petrol to reduce knocking in the engine

Anti-Lebanon *n* a mountain range running north and south between Syria and Lebanon, east of the Lebanon Mountains. Highest peak: Mount Hermon, 2814 m (9232 ft)

Antilles (ænˈtɪliːz) *pl n* **the** a group of islands in the Caribbean consisting of the **Greater Antilles** and the **Lesser Antilles**

antilock brake (ˈæntɪˌlɒk) *n* a brake fitted to some road vehicles that prevents skidding and improves control by sensing and compensating for overbraking. Also called: **ABS brake**

antilogarithm (ˌæntɪˈlɒgəˌrɪðəm) *n* a number whose logarithm to a given base is a given number: *100 is the antilogarithm of 2 to base 10*. Often shortened to **antilog** > **ˌantiˌlogaˈrithmic** *adj*

antilogy (ænˈtɪlədʒɪ) *n, pl* **antilogies** a contradiction in terms [C17 from Gk *antilogia*]

antimacassar (ˌæntɪməˈkæsə) *n* a cloth covering the back and arms of chairs, etc, to prevent soiling [C19 from ANTI- + MACASSAR (OIL)]

antimagnetic (ˌæntɪmægˈnɛtɪk) *adj* of a material that does not acquire permanent magnetism when exposed to a magnetic field

antimalarial (ˌæntɪməˈlɛərɪəl) *adj* **1** effective in the treatment of malaria ▷ *n* **2** an antimalarial drug or agent

antimasque (ˈæntɪˌmɑːsk) *n* a comic dance, presented between the acts of a masque

antimatter (ˈæntɪˌmætə) *n* a form of matter composed of antiparticles, such as antihydrogen, consisting of antiprotons and positrons

antimetabolite (ˌæntɪmɪˈtæbəˌlaɪt) *n* any drug that acts by disrupting the normal growth of a cell. Antimetabolites, e.g. some sulfonamide drugs, are used in cancer treatment

antimissile (ˌæntɪˈmɪsaɪl) *adj* **1** relating to defensive measures against missile attack: *an antimissile system* ▷ *n* **2** Also called: **antimissile missile** a defensive missile used to intercept and destroy attacking missiles

antimony (ˈæntɪmənɪ) *n* a toxic metallic element that exists in two allotropic forms and is added to alloys to increase their strength and hardness. Symbol: Sb; atomic no.: 51; atomic wt.: 121.75 [C15 from Med. L *antimōnium*, from ?] > **antimonial** (ˌæntɪˈməʊnɪəl) *adj*

antimuon (ˌæntɪˈmjuːɒn) *n* the antiparticle of a muon

antimycotic (ˌæntɪmaɪˈkɒtɪk) *adj* another word for **antifungal**

anti-Nazi *adj* opposed to Nazism or its principles

antinoise (ˈæntɪˌnɔɪz) *n* sound generated so that it is out of phase with a noise, such as that made by an engine, in order to reduce the noise level by interference

antinomian (ˌæntɪˈnəʊmɪən) *adj* **1** relating to the doctrine that by faith a Christian is released from the obligation of adhering to any moral law ▷ *n* **2** a member of a Christian sect holding such a doctrine > **ˌantiˈnomianism** *n*

antinomy (ænˈtɪnəmɪ) *n, pl* **antinomies** **1** opposition of one law, principle, or rule to another **2** *philosophy* contradiction existing between two apparently indubitable propositions [C16 from L, from Gk: conflict between laws, from ANTI- + *nomos* law] > **antinomic** (ˌæntɪˈnɒmɪk) *adj*

antinovel (ˈæntɪˌnɒvᵊl) *n* a type of prose fiction in which conventional or traditional novelistic elements are rejected

antinuclear (ˌæntɪˈnjuːklɪə) *adj* opposed to nuclear weapons or nuclear power

Antioch (ˈæntɪˌɒk) *n* a city in S Turkey, on the Orontes River: ancient commercial centre and capital of Syria (300–64 BC); early centre of Christianity. Pop: 137 200 (1994 est). Arabic name: **Antakiya** Turkish name: **Antakya**

Antiochus III (ænˈtaɪəkəs) *n* known as *Antiochus the Great*. 242–187 BC, king of Syria (223–187), who greatly extended the Seleucid empire but was forced (190) to surrender most of Asia Minor to the Romans

Antiochus IV *n* ?215–164 BC, Seleucid king of Syria (175–164), who attacked the Jews and provoked the revolt of the Maccabees

antioxidant (ˌæntɪˈɒksɪdənt) *n* **1** any substance that retards deterioration by oxidation, esp of fats, oils, foods, or rubber **2** *biol* a substance, such as vitamin C, vitamin E, or beta carotene, that counteracts the damaging effects of oxidation in a living organism

antiparticle (ˈæntɪˌpɑːtɪkᵊl) *n* any of a group of elementary particles that have the same mass as their corresponding particle but have a charge of equal magnitude but opposite sign. When a particle collides with its antiparticle mutual annihilation occurs

antipasto (ˌæntɪˈpɑːstəʊ, -ˈpæs-) *n, pl* **antipastos** a course of hors d'oeuvres in an Italian meal [It.: before food]

antipathetic (ænˌtɪpəˈθɛtɪk, ˌæntɪpə-) *or* **antipathetical** *adj* (often foll by *to*) having or arousing a strong aversion

antipathy (ænˈtɪpəθɪ) *n, pl* **antipathies** **1** a feeling of dislike or hostility **2** the object of such a feeling [C17 from L, from Gk, from ANTI- + *patheia* feeling]

antipersonnel (ˌæntɪˌpɜːsəˈnɛl) *adj* (of weapons, etc) designed to cause casualties to personnel rather than to destroy equipment

antiperspirant (ˌæntɪˈpɜːspərənt) *n* **1** a substance applied to the skin to reduce or prevent perspiration ▷ *adj* **2** reducing perspiration

antiphlogistic (ˌæntɪfləˈdʒɪstɪk) *adj* **1** of or relating to the prevention or alleviation of inflammation ▷ *n* **2** an antiphlogistic drug

antiphon (ˈæntɪfən) *n* **1** a short passage, usually from the Bible, recited or sung as a response after certain parts of a liturgical service **2** a psalm, hymn, etc, chanted or sung in alternate parts **3** any response [C15 from LL *antiphōna* sung responses, from LGk, pl of *antiphōnon* (something) responsive, from ANTI- + *phōnē* sound] > **antiphonal** (ænˈtɪfənəl) *adj*

antiphonary (ænˈtɪfənərɪ) *n, pl* **antiphonaries** a bound collection of antiphons

antiphony (ænˈtɪfənɪ) *n, pl* **antiphonies** **1** antiphonal singing **2** any musical or other sound effect that answers or echoes another

antipode (ˈæntɪpəʊd) *n* the exact or direct opposite > **antipodal** (ænˈtɪpədᵊl) *adj*

antipodes (ænˈtɪpəˌdiːz) *pl n* **1** either or both of two places that are situated diametrically opposite one another on the earth's surface **2** the people who live there **3** (*often cap*) **the** Australia and New Zealand [C16 via LL from Gk, pl of *antipous* having the feet opposite, from ANTI- + *pous* foot] > **antipodean** (ænˌtɪpəˈdiːən) *adj*

Antipodes Islands *pl n* **the** a group of small uninhabited islands in the South Pacific, southeast of and belonging to New Zealand. Area: 62 sq km (24 sq miles)

antipope (ˈæntɪˌpəʊp) *n* a rival pope elected in opposition to one who has been canonically chosen

anti-Protestant *adj* opposed to Protestantism

antipsychotic (ˌæntɪsaɪˈkɒtɪk) *adj* **1** preventing or treating psychosis ▷ *n* **2** any antipsychotic drug, such as chlorpromazine: used to treat such conditions as schizophrenia

antipyretic (ˌæntɪpaɪˈrɛtɪk) *adj* **1** preventing or alleviating fever ▷ *n* **2** an antipyretic remedy or drug >**antipyresis** ˌæntɪpaɪˈriːsɪs) *n*

antiquarian (ˌæntɪˈkwɛərɪən) *adj* **1** concerned with the study of antiquities or antiques ▷ *n* **2** a less common name for **antiquary** > ˌ**antiˈquarianism** *n*

antiquark (ˈæntɪˌkwɑːk) *n* the antiparticle of a quark

antiquary (ˈæntɪkwərɪ) *n, pl* **antiquaries** a person who collects, deals in, or studies antiques or ancient works of art. Also called: **antiquarian**

antiquate (ˈæntɪˌkweɪt) *vb* **antiquates, antiquating, antiquated** (*tr*) to make obsolete or old-fashioned [C15 from L *antīquāre* to make old, from *antīquus* ancient]

antiquated (ˈæntɪˌkweɪtɪd) *adj* **1** outmoded; obsolete: *antiquated safety procedures* **2** aged; ancient > ˈ**antiˌquatedness** *n*

antique (ænˈtiːk) *n* **1a** a decorative object, piece of furniture, or other work of art created in an earlier period, that is valued for its beauty, workmanship, and age **1b** (*as modifier*): *an antique shop* **2** any object made in an earlier period **3** **the** the style of ancient art, esp Greek or Roman ▷ *adj* **4** made in or in the style of an earlier period **5** of or belonging to the distant past, esp of ancient Greece or Rome **6** *inf* old-fashioned **7** *arch* aged or venerable ▷ *vb* **antiques, antiquing, antiqued** **8** (*tr*) to give an antique appearance to [C16 from L *antīquus* ancient, from *ante* before]

▷ www.antiqueweb.com
▷ http://antiquerestorers.com
▷ www.pbs.org/wgbh/pages/roadshow/speak/index.htm

antiquities (ænˈtɪkwɪtɪz) *pl n* remains or relics, such as statues, buildings, or coins, that date from ancient times

antiquity (ænˈtɪkwɪtɪ) *n, pl* **antiquities** **1** the quality of being ancient: *a vase of great antiquity* **2** the far distant past, esp preceding the Middle Ages **3** the people of ancient times collectively

antiracism (ˌæntɪˈreɪsɪzəm) *n* the policy of challenging racism and promoting racial tolerance > ˌ**antiˈracist** *n, adj*

anti-riot *adj* designed for or employed in controlling crowds: *anti-riot police*

anti-roll bar *n* a crosswise rubber-mounted bar in the suspension of a motor vehicle, which counteracts the movement downwards on one side when cornering

antirrhinum (ˌæntɪˈraɪnəm) *n* any plant of the genus *Antirrhinum*, esp the snapdragon, which has two-lipped flowers of various colours [C16 via L from Gk *antirrhinon*, from ANTI- (imitating) + *rhis* nose]

Antisana (*Spanish* antiˈsana) *n* a volcano in N central Ecuador, in the Andes. Height: 5756 m (18 885 ft)

antiscorbutic (ˌæntɪskɔːˈbjuːtɪk) *adj* **1** preventing or curing scurvy ▷ *n* **2** an antiscorbutic agent

anti-Semite *n* a person who persecutes or discriminates against Jews > ˌ**anti-Seˈmitic** *adj* > ˌ**anti-ˈSemitism** *n*

antisepsis (ˌæntɪˈsɛpsɪs) *n* **1** destruction of undesirable microorganisms, such as those that cause disease or putrefaction **2** the state of being free from such microorganisms

antiseptic (ˌæntɪˈsɛptɪk) *adj* **1** of or producing antisepsis **2** entirely free from contamination **3** *inf* lacking spirit or excitement ▷ *n* **4** an antiseptic agent > ˌ**antiˈseptically** *adv*

antiserum (ˌæntɪˈsɪərəm) *n, pl* **antiserums** *or* **antisera** (-rə) blood serum containing antibodies against a specific antigen, used to treat or provide immunity to a disease

anti-site *n* a website through which people can express their contempt for a particular person, organization, pop group, etc

antisocial (ˌæntɪˈsəʊʃəl) *adj* **1** avoiding the company of other people; unsociable **2** contrary or injurious to the interests of society in general

antispasmodic (ˌæntɪspæzˈmɒdɪk) *adj* **1** preventing or arresting spasms ▷ *n* **2** an antispasmodic drug

antistatic (ˌæntɪˈstætɪk) *adj* (of a substance, textile, etc) retaining sufficient moisture to provide a conducting path, thus avoiding the effects of static electricity

antistrophe (ænˈtɪstrəfɪ) *n* (in ancient Greek drama) **a** the second of two movements made by a chorus during the performance of a choral ode **b** the second part of a choral ode sung during this movement ▷ See **strophe** [C17 via LL from Gk *antistrophē* an answering turn, from ANTI- + *strophē* a turning] > **antistrophically** (ˌæntɪˈstrɒfɪkəlɪ) *adv*

antitank (ˌæntɪˈtæŋk) *adj* designed to immobilize or destroy armoured vehicles

antithesis (ænˈtɪθɪsɪs) *n, pl* **antitheses** (-ˌsiːz) **1** the exact opposite **2** contrast or opposition **3** *rhetoric* the juxtaposition of contrasting ideas or words to produce an effect of balance, such as *my words fly up, my thoughts remain below* [C15 via L from Gk: a setting against, from ANTI- + *tithenai* to place] > **antithetical** (ˌæntɪˈθɛtɪkᵊl) *adj*

antitoxin (ˌæntɪˈtɒksɪn) *n* **1** an antibody that neutralizes a toxin **2** blood serum that contains a specific antibody > ˌ**antiˈtoxic** *adj*

antitrades (ˈæntɪˌtreɪdz) *pl n* winds in the upper atmosphere blowing in the opposite direction from and above the trade winds

antitrust (ˌæntɪˈtrʌst) *n* (*modifier*) *chiefly US* regulating or opposing trusts, monopolies, cartels, or similar organizations

antitussive (ˌæntɪˈtʌsɪv) *n* **1** any of a class of drugs used to suppress or alleviate coughing ▷ *adj* **2** of or relating to such drugs [from ANTI- + L *tussis* a cough]

antitype (ˈæntɪˌtaɪp) *n* **1** a person or thing that is

Aa

foreshadowed or represented by a type or symbol **2** an opposite type > **antitypical** (ˌæntɪˈtɪpɪkᵊl) *adj*
antivenin (ˌæntɪˈvɛnɪn) *or* **antivenene** (ˌæntɪvɪˈniːn) *n* an antitoxin that counteracts a specific venom, esp snake venom [C19 from ANTI- + VEN(OM) + -IN]
antiviral (ˌæntɪˈvaɪrəl) *adj* **1** inhibiting the growth of viruses ▷ *n* **2** any antiviral drug
antler (ˈæntlə) *n* one of a pair of bony outgrowths on the heads of male deer and some related species of either sex [C14 from OF *antoillier*] > **ˈantlered** *adj*
antlion (ˈæntˌlaɪən) *n* **1** any of various insects which resemble dragonflies and are most common in tropical regions **2** the larva of this insect, which buries itself in the sand to await its prey
Antoinette (*French* ɑ̃twanɛt) *n* See **Marie Antoinette**
Antonello da Messina (ˌæntəˈnɛləʊ) *n* ?1430–?79, Italian painter, born in Sicily. His paintings include *St Jerome in His Study* and *Portrait of a Man*
Antonescu (ˌæntɒˈnɛskjuː) *n* **Ion** 1882–1946, Romanian general and statesman; appointed prime minister (1940) by King Carol II. He was executed for war crimes
Antonine Wall (ˈæntənaɪn) *n* a Roman frontier defence work across S Scotland, extending between the River Clyde and the Firth of Forth. It was built in 142 AD on the orders of Antoninus Pius (86–161 AD), emperor of Rome (138–161)
Antoninus (ˌæntəˈnaɪnəs) *n* See **Marcus Aurelius Antoninus**
Antoninus Pius *n* 86–161 AD, emperor of Rome (138–161); adopted son and successor of Hadrian
Antonioni (ˌæntəʊnɪˈəʊnɪ) *n* **Michelangelo** (mikeˈlandʒelo) born 1912, Italian film director; his films include *L'Avventura* (1959), *La Notte* (1961), *Blow-Up* (1966), *Zabriskie Point* (1970), and *Beyond the Clouds* (1995)
antonomasia (ˌæntənəˈmeɪzɪə) *n* **1** the substitution of a title or epithet for a proper name, such as *his highness* **2** the use of a proper name for an idea: *he is a Daniel come to judgment* [C16 via L from Gk, from *antonomazein* to name differently, from *onoma* name]
Antony (ˈæntənɪ) *n* **Mark** Latin name *Marcus Antonius.* ?83–30 BC, Roman general who served under Julius Caesar in the Gallic wars and became a member of the second triumvirate (43). He defeated Brutus and Cassius at Philippi (42) but having repudiated his wife for Cleopatra, queen of Egypt, he was defeated by his brother-in-law Octavian (Augustus) at Actium (31)
antonym (ˈæntənɪm) *n* a word that means the opposite of another [C19 from Gk, from ANTI- + *onoma* name] > **antonymous** (ænˈtɒnɪməs) *adj*
Antrim (ˈæntrɪm) *n* **1** a historical county of NE Northern Ireland, famous for the Giant's Causeway on the N coast: in 1973 it was replaced for administrative purposes by the districts of Antrim, Ballymena, Ballymoney, Carrickfergus, Larne, Moyle, Newtownabbey, and parts of Belfast and Lisburn. Area: 3100 sq km (1200 sq miles) **2** a district of Northern Ireland, in Co. Antrim. Pop: 48 366 (2001). Area: 415 sq km (160 sq miles)
antrum (ˈæntrəm) *n, pl* **antra** (-trə) *anat* a natural cavity, hollow, or sinus, esp in a bone [C14 from L: cave, from Gk *antron*] > **ˈantral** *adj*
Antung (ˈænˈtʊŋ) *n* a variant transliteration of the Chinese name for **Andong**
antwackie (ˈæntwækɪ) *adj Northern English dialect* old-fashioned
Antwerp (ˈæntwɜːp) *n* **1** a province of N Belgium. Pop: 1 643 972 (2000 est). Area: 2859 sq km (1104 sq miles) **2** a port in N Belgium, capital of Antwerp province, on the River Scheldt: a major European port. Pop: 446 525 (2000 est). Flemish name: **Antwerpen** (ˈɑntwɛrpə) French name: **Anvers**
Anu (ˈɑːnuː) *n Babylonian myth* the sky god
ANU *abbrev for* Australian National University
Anubis (əˈnjuːbɪs) *n Egyptian myth* a deity, a son of Osiris, who conducted the dead to judgment. He is represented as having a jackal's head and was identified by the Greeks with Hermes
Anuradhapura (əˈnʊərədəˌpʊərə, ˌʌnʊˈrɑːdə-) *n* a town in Sri Lanka: ancient capital of Ceylon; site of the sacred bo tree and place of pilgrimage for Buddhists. Pop: 42 600 (1995 est)
anuresis (ˌænjʊˈriːsɪs) *n* inability to urinate [C20 NL, from AN- + Gk *ouresis* urination]
anus (ˈeɪnəs) *n* the excretory opening at the end of the alimentary canal [C16 from L]
Anvers (ɑ̃vɛr) *n* the French name for **Antwerp**
anvil (ˈænvɪl) *n* **1** a heavy iron or steel block on which metals are hammered during forging **2** any part having a similar shape or function, such as the lower part of a telegraph key **3** *anat* the nontechnical name for **incus** [OE *anfealt*]
anxiety (æŋˈzaɪɪtɪ) *n, pl* **anxieties** **1** a state of uneasiness or tension caused by apprehension of possible misfortune, danger, etc **2** intense desire; eagerness **3** *psychol* a state of intense apprehension, common in mental illness or after a very distressing experience [C16 from L *anxietas*]
anxiety disorder *n* any of various mental disorders characterized by extreme anxiety
anxious (ˈæŋkʃəs, ˈæŋʃəs) *adj* **1** worried and tense because of possible misfortune, danger, etc **2** causing anxiety; worrying; distressing: *an anxious time* **3** intensely desirous: *anxious for promotion* [C17 from L *anxius*; rel. to L *angere* to torment] > **ˈanxiously** *adv* > **ˈanxiousness** *n*
any (ˈɛnɪ) *determiner* **1a** one, some, or several, as specified, no matter how much, what kind, etc: *you may take any clothes you like* **1b** (*as pron; functioning as sing or pl*): *take any you like* **2** (*usually used with a negative*) **2a** even the smallest amount or even one: *I can't stand any noise* **2b** (*as pron; functioning as sing or pl*): *don't give her any* **3** whatever or whichever: *any dictionary will do* **4** an indefinite or unlimited (amount or number): *any number of friends* ▷ *adv* **5** (*usually used with a negative*) (foll by a comp. adj) to even the smallest extent: *it isn't any worse* [OE *ǣnig*]
Anyang (ˈɑːnˈjɑːŋ) *n* a town in E China, in Henan province: archaeological site and capital of the Shang dynasty. Pop: 527 982 (1999 est)
anybody (ˈɛnɪˌbɒdɪ) *pron* **1** any person; anyone **2** (*usually used with a negative or a question*) a person of any importance: *he isn't anybody* ▷ *n, pl* **anybodies** **3** (often preceded by *just*) any person at random
anyhow (ˈɛnɪˌhaʊ) *adv* **1** in any case **2** by any means whatever **3** carelessly
any more *or esp US* **anymore** (ˌɛnɪˈmɔː) *adv* any longer; still; nowadays
anyone (ˈɛnɪˌwʌn) *pron* **1** any person; anybody **2** (*used with a negative or a question*) a person of any importance: *is he anyone?* **3** (often preceded by *just*) any person at random
anyplace (ˈɛnɪˌpleɪs) *adv US & Canad inf* anywhere
anything (ˈɛnɪˌθɪŋ) *pron* **1** any object, event, action, etc, whatever: *anything might happen* ▷ *n* **2** a thing of any kind: *have you anything to declare?* ▷ *adv* **3** in any way: *he wasn't anything like his father* **4** **anything but** not in the least: *she was anything but happy* **5** **like anything** (intensifier): *he ran like anything*
anyway (ˈɛnɪˌweɪ) *adv* **1** in any case; at any rate; nevertheless **2** in a careless manner **3** Usually **any way** in any manner
anywhere (ˈɛnɪˌwɛə) *adv* **1** in, at, or to any place **2** **get anywhere** to be successful
anywise (ˈɛnɪˌwaɪz) *adv chiefly US* in any way
ANZ *abbrev for* Australian and New Zealand Banking Group
ANZAAS (ˈænzəs, -zæs) *n acronym for* Australian and New

Zealand Association for the Advancement of Science
▷ www.usyd.edu.au/pharmacology/anzaas

Anzac ('ænzæk) *n* **1** (in World War I) a soldier serving with the Australian and New Zealand Army Corps **2** (now) any Australian or New Zealand soldier **3** the Anzac landing at Gallipoli in 1915
▷ www.anzacs.net
▷ www.awm.gov.au

Anzac Day *n* April 25, a public holiday in Australia and New Zealand commemorating the Anzac landing at Gallipoli in 1915

Anzio ('ænzɪˌəʊ; *Italian* 'antsjo) *n* a port and resort on the W coast of Italy: site of Allied landings in World War II. Pop: 32 383 (1991 est)

ANZUS ('ænzəs) *n acronym for* Australia, New Zealand, and the United States, with reference to the security alliance between them
▷ www.australianpolitics.com/foreign/anzus

AO *abbrev for* Officer of the Order of Australia

A/O *or* **a/o** (accounting, etc) *abbrev for* account of

AOB *or* **a.o.b.** *abbrev for* any other business

AOC *abbrev for* appellation d'origine contrôlée: the highest French wine classification; indicates that the wine meets strict requirements concerning area of production, strength, etc Cf **VDQS, vin de pays**

AONB (in England, Wales, and Northern Ireland) *abbrev for* area of outstanding natural beauty: an area officially designated as requiring protection to conserve and enhance its natural beauty

Aorangi-Mount Cook (ˌeɪəʊ'ræŋgɪ) *n* the official name for Mount **Cook**

aorist ('eɪərɪst, 'ɛərɪst) *n grammar* a tense of the verb, esp in classical Greek, indicating past action without reference to whether the action involved was momentary or continuous [c16 from Gk *aoristos* not limited, from A-¹ + *horistos*, from *horizein* to define]

aorta (eɪ'ɔːtə) *n, pl* **aortas** *or* **aortae** (-tiː) the main vessel in the arterial network, which conveys oxygen-rich blood from the heart [c16 from NL, from Gk *aortē*, lit.: something lifted, from *aeirein* to raise] > **a'ortic** *or* **a'ortal** *adj*

Aosta (*Italian* a'ɔsta) *n* a town in NW Italy, capital of Valle d'Aosta region: Roman remains. Pop: 36 339 (1990)

Aotearoa (ˌæɒˌtɪəˌrɔːə) *n* the Maori name for **New Zealand** [from Maori *ao tea roa* Land of the Long White Cloud]

aoudad ('ɑːʊˌdæd) *n* a wild mountain sheep of N Africa. Also called: **Barbary sheep** [from F, from Berber *audad*]

ap (æp) son of: occurring as part of some surnames of Welsh origin: *ap Thomas* [from Welsh *mab* son]

apace (ə'peɪs) *adv* quickly; rapidly [c14 prob. from OF *à pas*, at a (good) pace]

apache (ə'pæʃ) *n* a Parisian gangster or ruffian [from F: APACHE]

Apache (ə'pætʃɪ) *n* **1** (*pl* **Apaches** *or* **Apache**) a member of a North American Indian people inhabiting the southwestern US and N Mexico **2** the language of this people [from Mexican Sp.]

apanage ('æpənɪdʒ) *n* a variant spelling of **appanage**

apart (ə'pɑːt) *adj (postpositive), adv* **1** to or in pieces: *he had the television apart* **2** placed or kept separately or for a particular purpose, etc; aside (esp in **set** *or* **put apart**) **3** separate in time, place, or position: *he stood apart from the group* **4** not being taken into account: *these difficulties apart, the project ran smoothly* **5** individual; distinct: *a race apart* **6** separately or independently: *considered apart, his reasoning was faulty* **7** **apart from** (*prep*) besides ▷ See also **take apart, tell apart** [c14 from OF *a part* at (the) side]

apartheid (ə'pɑːthaɪt, -heɪt) *n* (formerly, in South Africa) the government policy of racial segregation; officially renounced in 1992 [c20 Afrik., from *apart* APART + *-heid* -HOOD]
▷ www.apartheidmuseum.org
▷ http://racerelations.about.com/cs/apartheid

apartment (ə'pɑːtmənt) *n* **1** (*often pl*) any room in a building, usually one of several forming a suite, used as living accommodation, offices, etc **2a** another name (esp US and Canad) for **flat²** **2b** (*as modifier*): *apartment house* [c17 from F *appartement*, from It., from *appartare* to separate]

apathetic (ˌæpə'θɛtɪk) *adj* having or showing little or no emotion or interest [c18 from APATHY + PATHETIC]
> ˌ**apa'thetically** *adv*

apathy ('æpəθɪ) *n* **1** absence of interest in or enthusiasm for things generally considered interesting or moving **2** absence of emotion [c17 from L, from Gk *apatheia*, from A-¹ + *pathos* feeling]

apatite ('æpəˌtaɪt) *n* a common naturally occurring mineral consisting basically of calcium fluorophosphate. It is a source of phosphorus and is used in fertilizers [c19 from G *Apatit*, from Gk *apatē* deceit; from its misleading similarity to other minerals]

APB (in the US) *abbrev for* all-points bulletin

ape (eɪp) *n* **1** any of various primates in which the tail is very short or absent. See also **great ape** **2** (not in technical use) any monkey **3** an imitator; mimic ▷ *vb* **apes, aping, aped** **4** (*tr*) to imitate [OE *apa*]
> '**apeˌlike** *adj*

APEC ('eɪpɛk) *n acronym or abbreviation for* **1** (in Canada) Atlantic Provinces Economic Council **2** Asian-Pacific Economic Cooperation Group
▷ www.apecsec.org.sg/apec.html

Apeldoorn ('æpəlˌdɔːn; *Dutch* 'aːpəldoːrn) *n* a town in the Netherlands, in central Gelderland province: nearby is the summer residence of the Dutch royal family. Pop: 152 860 (1999 est)

Apelles (ə'pɛliːz) *n* 4th century BC, Greek painter of mythological subjects, none of whose work survives, his fame resting on the testimony of Pliny and other writers

apeman ('eɪpˌmæn) *n, pl* **apemen** any of various extinct apelike primates thought to have been the forerunners of modern man

Apennines ('æpəˌnaɪnz) *pl n* **1** a mountain range in Italy, extending over 1250 km (800 miles) from the northwest to the southernmost tip of the peninsula. Highest peak: Monte Corno, 2912 m (9554 ft) **2** a mountain range lying in the N quadrants of the moon, extending over 950 km along the SE border of the Mare Imbrium and rising to 6200 m

aperçu *French* (apɛrsy) *n* **1** an outline **2** an insight [from *apercevoir* to PERCEIVE]

aperient (ə'pɪərɪənt) *med* ▷ *adj* **1** laxative ▷ *n* **2** a mild laxative [c17 from L *aperīre* to open]

aperiodic (ˌeɪpɪərɪ'ɒdɪk) *adj* **1** not periodic; not occurring at regular intervals **2** *physics* **2a** (of a system or instrument) being damped sufficiently to reach equilibrium without oscillation **2b** (of an oscillation or vibration) not having a regular period **2c** (of an electrical circuit) not having a measurable resonant frequency > **aperiodicity** (ˌeɪpɪərɪə'dɪsɪtɪ) *n*

apéritif (əˌpɛrɪ'tiːf) *n* an alcoholic drink before a meal to whet the appetite [c19 from F, from Med. L, from L *aperīre* to open]

aperture ('æpətʃə) *n* **1** a hole; opening **2** *physics* a usually circular and often variable opening in an optical instrument or device that controls the quantity of radiation entering or leaving it [c15 from LL *apertūra* opening, from *aperīre* to open]

apetalous (eɪ'pɛtələs) *adj* (of flowering plants) having no petals [c18 from NL; see A-¹, PETAL]

apex ('eɪpɛks) *n, pl* **apexes** *or* **apices** **1** the highest point; vertex **2** the pointed end or tip of something **3** a high point, as of a career [c17 from L: point]

APEX ('eɪpɛks) *n acronym for:* **1** Advance Purchase Excursion, a reduced airline or long-distance rail fare

Aa

that must be paid a specified number of days in advance **2** Association of Professional, Executive, Clerical, and Computer Staff

Apex Club ('eɪpɛks) *n* (in Australia) an association of business and professional men to promote community welfare > **Apexian** (eɪ'pɛksɪən) *adj, n*

apgar score *or* **rating** ('æpgɑ:) *n* a system for determining the condition of an infant at birth by allotting a maximum of 2 points to each of the following: heart rate, breathing effort, muscle tone, response to stimulation, and colour [C20 after V. *Apgar* (1909–74), US anaesthetist]

aphaeresis *or* **apheresis** (ə'fɪərɪsɪs) *n* the omission of a letter or syllable at the beginning of a word [C17 via LL from Gk, from *aphairein* to remove]

aphasia (ə'feɪzɪə) *n* a disorder of the central nervous system characterized by loss of the ability to communicate, esp in speech [C19 via NL from Gk, from A-[1] + *-phasia*, from *phanai* to speak]

aphelion (æp'hi:lɪən, ə'fi:-) *n, pl* **aphelia** (-lɪə) the point in its orbit when a planet or comet is at its greatest distance from the sun [C17 from NL *aphēlium*, from AP(O)- + Gk *hēlios* sun]

apheresis (ə'fɪərɪsɪs) *n* **1** the omission of a letter or syllable at the beginning of a word **2** a method of collecting blood from donors that enables its different components, such as the platelets or plasma, to be separated out [C17 from Gk *aphairein* to remove]

aphesis ('æfɪsɪs) *n* the gradual disappearance of an unstressed vowel at the beginning of a word, as in *squire* from *esquire* [C19 from Gk, from *aphienai* to set free] > **aphetic** (ə'fɛtɪk) *adj*

aphid ('eɪfɪd) *n* any of the small homopterous insects of the family Aphididae, which feed by sucking the juices from plants [C19 from *aphides*, pl. of APHIS]

aphis ('eɪfɪs) *n, pl* **aphides** ('eɪfɪˌdi:z) any of a genus of aphids, such as the blackfly [C18 from NL (coined by Linnaeus for obscure reasons)]

aphonia (ə'fəʊnɪə) *or* **aphony** ('æfənɪ) *n* loss of voice caused by damage to the vocal tract [C18 NL, from Gk, from A-[1] + *phōnē* sound]

aphorism ('æfəˌrɪzəm) *n* a short pithy saying expressing a general truth; maxim [C16 from LL, from Gk *aphorismos*, from *aphorizein* to define] > **'aphorist** *n* > **ˌapho'ristic** *adj*

aphrodisiac (ˌæfrə'dɪzɪæk) *n* **1** a drug, food, etc, that excites sexual desire ▷ *adj* **2** exciting sexual desire [C18 from Gk, from *aphrodisios* belonging to *Aphrodite*, goddess of love]

Aphrodite (ˌæfrə'daɪtɪ) *n Greek myth* the goddess of love and beauty, daughter of Zeus. Roman counterpart: **Venus** Also called: **Cytherea**

aphyllous (ə'fɪləs) *adj* (of plants) having no leaves [C19 from NL, from Gk A-[1] + *phullon* leaf]

▷ www.go-samoa.com/apia.html

apian ('eɪpɪən) *adj* of, relating to, or resembling bees [C19 from L *apiānus*, from *apis* bee]

apiarist ('eɪpɪərɪst) *n* a person who studies or keeps bees

apiary ('eɪpɪərɪ) *n, pl* **apiaries** a place where bees are kept [C17 from L *apiārium*, from *apis* bee]

apical ('æpɪkᵊl, 'eɪ-) *adj* of, at, or being the apex [C19 from NL *apicālis*] > **'apically** *adv*

apices ('æpɪˌsi:z, 'eɪ-) *n* a plural of **apex**

apiculture ('eɪpɪˌkʌltʃə) *n* the breeding and care of bees [C19 from L *apis* bee + CULTURE] > **ˌapi'cultural** *adj* > **ˌapi'culturist** *n*

apiece (ə'pi:s) *adv* (*postpositive*) for, to, or from each one: *they were given two apples apiece*

Apis ('ɑ:pɪs) *n* (in ancient Egypt) a sacred bull worshipped at Memphis

apish ('eɪpɪʃ) *adj* **1** stupid; foolish **2** resembling an ape **3** slavishly imitative > **'apishly** *adv* > **'apishness** *n*

aplanatic (ˌæplə'nætɪk) *adj* (of a lens or mirror) free from spherical aberration [C18 from Gk *aplanetos* free from error, from A-[1] + *planaein* to wander]

aplenty (ə'plɛntɪ) *adj* (*postpositive*), *adv* in plenty

aplomb (ə'plɒm) *n* equanimity, self-confidence, or self-possession [C18 from F: uprightness, from *à plomb* according to the plumb line]

apnoea *or US* **apnea** (æp'nɪə) *n* a temporary inability to breathe [C18 from NL, from Gk *apnoia*, from A-[1] + *pnein* to breathe]

Apo ('ɑ:pəʊ) *n* the highest mountain in the Philippines, on SE Mindanao: active volcano with three peaks. Height: 2954 m (9690 ft)

apo- *or* **ap-** *prefix* **1** away from; off: *apogee* **2** separation of: *apocarpous* [from Gk *apo* away, off]

Apoc. *abbrev for:* **1** Apocalypse **2** Apocrypha *or* Apocryphal

apocalypse (ə'pɒkəlɪps) *n* **1** a prophetic disclosure or revelation **2** an event of great importance, violence, etc, like the events described in the Apocalypse [C13 from LL *apocalypsis*, from Gk, from APO- + *kaluptein* to hide] > **aˌpoca'lyptic** *adj*

Apocalypse (ə'pɒkəlɪps) *n Bible* another name for the Book of Revelation

apocarpous (ˌæpə'kɑ:pəs) *adj* (of the ovaries of flowering plants) consisting of separate carpels [C19 from NL, from Gk APO- + *karpos* fruit]

apochromat (ˌæpə'krəʊmæt) *or* **apochromatic lens** (ˌæpəkrə'mætɪk) *n* a lens system designed to bring trichromatic light to a single focus and reduce chromatic aberration

apocope (ə'pɒkəpɪ) *n* omission of the final sound or sounds of a word [C16 via LL from Gk, from *apokoptein* to cut off]

apocrine ('æpəkraɪn, -krɪn) *adj* losing cellular tissue in the process of secreting, as in mammary glands ▷ Cf **eccrine** [C20 from APO- + *-crine*, from Gk *krinein* to separate]

Apocrypha (ə'pɒkrɪfə) *n* **the** (*functioning as sing or pl*) the 14 books included as an appendix to the Old Testament in the Septuagint and the Vulgate but not in the Hebrew canon [C14 via LL *apocrypha* (*scripta*) hidden (writings), from Gk, from *apokruptein* to hide away]

▷ www.sacred-texts.com/chr/apo/

apocryphal (ə'pɒkrɪfəl) *adj* **1** of questionable authenticity **2** (*sometimes cap*) of or like the Apocrypha **3** untrue; counterfeit

apodal ('æpədᵊl) *or* **apodous** ('æpədəs) *adj* without feet; having no pelvic fins [C18 from Gk A-[1] + *pous* foot]

apodosis (ə'pɒdəsɪs) *n, pl* **apodoses** (-ˌsi:z) *Logic, grammar.* the consequent of a conditional statement, as *I won't go* in *if it rains I won't go* [C17 via LL from Gk, from *apodidonai* to give back]

apogee ('æpəˌdʒi:) *n* **1** the point in its orbit around the earth when the moon or an artificial satellite is at its greatest distance from the earth **2** the highest point [C17 from NL, from Gk, from *apogaios* away from the earth] > **ˌapo'gean** *adj*

apolitical (ˌeɪpə'lɪtɪkᵊl) *adj* politically neutral; without political attitudes, content, or bias

Apollinaire (*French* apɔlinɛr) *n* **Guillaume** (gijom), real name *Wilhelm Apollinaris de Kostrowitzki*. 1880–1918, French poet, novelist, and dramatist, regarded as a precursor of surrealism; author of *Alcoöls* (1913) and *Calligrammes* (1918)

Apollo (ə'pɒləʊ) *n classical myth* the god of light, poetry, music, healing, and prophecy: son of Zeus and Leto

Apollyon (ə'pɒljən) *n* the destroyer, a name given to the Devil (Revelation 9:11) [C14 via LL from Gk, from *apollunai* to destroy totally]

apologetic (əˌpɒlə'dʒɛtɪk) *adj* **1** expressing or anxious to make apology; contrite **2** defending in speech or writing > **aˌpolo'getically** *adv*

apologetics (əˌpɒlə'dʒɛtɪks) *n* (*functioning as sing*) **1** the branch of theology concerned with the rational justification of Christianity **2** a defensive method of argument

apologia (ˌæpəˈləʊdʒɪə) *n* a formal written defence of a cause or one's beliefs or conduct
apologist (əˈpɒlədʒɪst) *n* a person who offers a defence by argument
apologize *or* **apologise** (əˈpɒləˌdʒaɪz) *vb* **apologizes, apologizing, apologized** *or* **apologises, apologising, apologised** (*intr*) **1** to express or make an apology; acknowledge faults **2** to make a formal defence
apologue (ˈæpəˌlɒg) *n* an allegory or moral fable [C17 from L, from Gk *apologos*]
apology (əˈpɒlədʒɪ) *n, pl* **apologies 1** a verbal or written expression of regret or contrition for a fault or failing **2** a poor substitute **3** another word for **apologia** [C16 from OF, from LL, from Gk: a verbal defence, from APO- + *logos* speech]
apophthegm *or* **apothegm** (ˈæpəˌθɛm) *n* a short remark containing some general or generally accepted truth; maxim [C16 from Gk *apophthegma*, from *apophthengesthai* to speak frankly]
apoplectic (ˌæpəˈplɛktɪk) *adj* **1** of apoplexy **2** *inf* furious > ˌ**apoˈplectically** *adv*
apoplexy (ˈæpəˌplɛksɪ) *n* sudden loss of consciousness, often followed by paralysis, caused by rupture or occlusion of a blood vessel in the brain [C14 from OF *apoplexie*, from LL, from Gk, from *apoplēssein* to cripple by a stroke]
aport (əˈpɔːt) *adv, adj* (*postpositive*) *naut* on or towards the port side: *with the helm aport*
apostasy (əˈpɒstəsɪ) *n, pl* **apostasies** abandonment of one's religious faith, party, a cause, etc [C14 from Church L *apostasia*, from Gk *apostasis* desertion]
apostate (əˈpɒsteɪt, -tɪt) *n* **1** a person who abandons his or her religion, party, etc ▷ *adj* **2** guilty of apostasy > **apostatical** (ˌæpəˈstætɪkᵊl) *adj*
apostatize *or* **apostatise** (əˈpɒstəˌtaɪz) *vb* **apostatizes, apostatizing, apostatized** *or* **apostatises, apostatising, apostatised** (*intr*) to abandon one's belief, faith, or allegiance
a posteriori (eɪ pɒsˌtɛrɪˈɔːraɪ, -rɪ; ɑː) *adj logic* **1** relating to inductive reasoning from particular facts to a general principle **2** derived from or requiring evidence for its validation; empirical [C18 from L, lit.: from the latter]
apostle (əˈpɒsᵊl) *n* **1** (*often cap*) one of the 12 disciples chosen by Christ to preach his gospel **2** any prominent Christian missionary, esp one who first converts a people **3** an ardent early supporter of a cause, movement, etc [OE *apostol*, from Church L, from Gk *apostolos* a messenger]
Apostles' Creed *n* a concise statement of Christian beliefs dating from about 500 AD, traditionally ascribed to the Apostles
apostolate (əˈpɒstəlɪt, -ˌleɪt) *n* the office, authority, or mission of an apostle
apostolic (ˌæpəˈstɒlɪk) *adj* **1** of or relating to the Apostles or their teachings or practice **2** of or relating to the pope as successor of the Apostles > ˌ**aposˈtolical** *adj*
Apostolic See (ˌæpəˈstɒlɪk) *n* the see of the pope
Apostolic succession *n* the doctrine that the authority of Christian bishops derives from the Apostles through an unbroken line of consecration
apostrophe[1] (əˈpɒstrəfɪ) *n* the punctuation mark ' used to indicate the omission of a letter or number, such as *he's* for *he has* or *he is*, also used in English to form the possessive, as in *John's father* [C17 from LL, from Gk *apostrophos* mark of elision, from *apostrephein* to turn away]
apostrophe[2] (əˈpɒstrəfɪ) *n rhetoric* a digression from a discourse, esp an address to an imaginary or absent person or a personification [C16 from L *apostrophē*, from Gk: a turning away]
apostrophize *or* **apostrophise** (əˈpɒstrəˌfaɪz) *vb* **apostrophizes, apostrophizing, apostrophized** *or* **apostrophises, apostrophising, apostrophised** *rhetoric* (*tr*) to address an apostrophe to
apothecaries' measure *n* a system of liquid volume measure used in pharmacy in which 20 fluid ounces equal 1 pint
apothecaries' weight *n* a system of weights formerly used in pharmacy based on the Troy ounce
apothecary (əˈpɒθɪkərɪ) *n, pl* **apothecaries 1** an archaic word for **pharmacist 2** *law* a chemist licensed by the Society of Apothecaries of London to prescribe, prepare, and sell drugs [C14 from OF, from LL, from Gk *apothēkē* storehouse]
apothegm (ˈæpəˌθɛm) *n* a variant spelling of **apophthegm**
apothem (ˈæpəˌθɛm) *n* the perpendicular from the centre of a regular polygon to any of its sides [C20 from APO- + Gk *thema*, from *tithenai* to place]
apotheosis (əˌpɒθɪˈəʊsɪs) *n, pl* **apotheoses** (-siːz) **1** elevation to the rank of a god; deification **2** glorification of a person or thing **3** a glorified ideal **4** the best or greatest time or event: *the apotheosis of De Niro's career* [C17 via LL from Gk: deification]
apotheosize *or* **apotheosise** (əˈpɒθɪəˌsaɪz) *vb* **apotheosizes, apotheosizing, apotheosized** *or* **apotheosises, apotheosising, apotheosised** (*tr*) **1** to deify **2** to glorify or idealize
appal *or US* **appall** (əˈpɔːl) *vb* **appals, appalling, appalled** *or US* **appalls, appalling, appalled** (*tr*) to fill with horror; shock or dismay [C14 from OF *appalir* to turn pale]
Appalachia (ˌæpəˈleɪtʃɪə) *n* a highland region of the eastern US, containing the Appalachian Mountains, extending from Pennsylvania to Alabama > ˌ**Appaˈlachian** *adj*
Appalachian Mountains *or* **Appalachians** *pl n* a mountain system of E North America, extending from Quebec province in Canada to central Alabama in the US: contains rich deposits of anthracite, bitumen, and iron ore. Highest peak: Mount Mitchell, 2038 m (6684 ft)
appalling (əˈpɔːlɪŋ) *adj* **1** causing dismay, horror, or revulsion **2** *inf* very bad > **apˈpallingly** *adv*
Appaloosa (ˌæpəˈluːsə) *n* a breed of horse, originally from America, having a spotted rump [C19 ?from *Palouse*, river in Idaho]
appanage *or* **apanage** (ˈæpənɪdʒ) *n* **1** land or other provision granted by a king for the support of esp a younger son **2** a customary accompaniment or perquisite, as to a job or position [C17 from OF, from Med. L, from *appānāre* to provide for, from L *pānis* bread]
apparatchik (ˌæpəˈrɑːtʃɪk) *n* **1** a member of a Communist Party organization **2** a bureaucrat in any organization [C20 from Russian, from *apparat* apparatus, instrument + *-chik*, suffix denoting agent]
apparatus (ˌæpəˈreɪtəs, -ˈrɑːtəs) *n, pl* **apparatus** *or* **apparatuses 1** a collection of equipment used for a particular purpose **2** a machine having a specific function: *breathing apparatus* **3** the means by which something operates; organization **4** *anat* any group of organs having a specific function [C17 from L, from *apparāre* to make ready]
apparel (əˈpærəl) *n* **1** *arch* clothing **2** *naut* a vessel's gear and equipment ▷ *vb* **apparels, apparelling, apparelled** *or US* **apparels, appareling, appareled 3** (*tr*) *arch* to clothe, adorn, etc [C13 from OF *apareillier* to make ready, from Vulgar L *appariculāre* (unattested), from L *parāre* to prepare]
apparent (əˈpærənt) *adj* **1** readily seen or understood; obvious **2** (*usually prenominal*) seeming, as opposed to real: *his apparent innocence* **3** *physics* as observed but ignoring such factors as the motion of the observer, etc [C14 from L *appārēns*, from *appārēre* to APPEAR]
apparently (əˈpærəntlɪ, əˈpɛər-) *adv* (*sentence modifier*) it appears that; as far as one knows; seemingly
apparent magnitude *n* See **magnitude** (sense 4)

Aa

apparition (ˌæpəˈrɪʃən) *n* **1** an appearance, esp of a ghost or ghostlike figure **2** the figure so appearing; spectre **3** the act of appearing [C15 from LL *appāritiō*, from L *appārēre* to APPEAR]

appassionato (əˌpæsjəˈnɑːtəʊ) *adj, adv music* (to be performed) with passion [It.]

appeal (əˈpiːl) *n* **1** a request for relief, aid, etc **2** the power to attract, please, stimulate, or interest **3** an application or resort to another authority, esp a higher one, as for a decision **4** *law* **4a** the judicial review by a superior court of the decision of a lower tribunal **4b** a request for such review **5** *cricket* a request to the umpire to declare a batsman out ▷ *vb* **6** (*intr*) to make an earnest request **7** (*intr*) to attract, please, stimulate, or interest **8** *law* to apply to a superior court to review (a case or issue decided by a lower tribunal) **9** (*intr*) to resort (to), as for a decision **10** (*intr*) *cricket* to ask the umpire to declare a batsman out **11** (*intr*) to challenge the umpire's or referee's decision [C14 from OF *appeler*, from L *appellāre* to entreat, from *pellere* to drive] > **apˈpealable** *adj* > **apˈpealer** *n* > **apˈpealing** *adj* > **apˈpealingly** *adv*

appear (əˈpɪə) *vb* (*intr*) **1** to come into sight **2** (*copula; may take an infinitive*) to seem: *the evidence appears to support you* **3** to be plain or clear, as after further evidence, etc: *it appears you were correct after all* **4** to develop; occur: *faults appeared during testing* **5** to be published: *his biography appeared last month* **6** to perform: *he has appeared in many London productions* **7** to be present in court before a magistrate or judge: *he appeared on two charges of theft* [C13 from OF *aparoir*, from L *appārēre* to become visible, attend upon, from *pārēre* to appear]

appearance (əˈpɪərəns) *n* **1** the act or an instance of appearing **2** the outward aspect of a person or thing **3** an outward show; pretence: *he gave an appearance of working hard* **4** **keep up appearances** to maintain the public impression of wellbeing or normality **5** **put in** *or* **make an appearance** to attend briefly, as out of politeness **6** **to all appearances** apparently

appearance money *n* money paid by a promoter of an event to a particular celebrity in order to ensure that the celebrity takes part in the event

appease (əˈpiːz) *vb* **appeases, appeasing, appeased** (*tr*) **1** to calm or pacify, esp by acceding to the demands of **2** to satisfy or quell (a thirst, etc) [C16 from OF *apaisier*, from *pais* peace, from L *pax*] > **apˈpeaser** *n*

appeasement (əˈpiːzmənt) *n* **1** the policy of acceding to the demands of a potentially hostile nation in the hope of maintaining peace **2** the act of appeasing

Appel (*Dutch* ˈɑpəl) *n* **Karel** (ˈkaːrəl) born 1921, Dutch abstract expressionist painter

appellant (əˈpɛlənt) *n* **1** a person who appeals **2** *law* the party who appeals to a higher court from the decision of a lower tribunal ▷ *adj* **3** *law* another word for **appellate** [C14 from OF; see APPEAL]

appellate (əˈpɛlɪt) *adj law* **1** of appeals **2** (of a tribunal) having jurisdiction to review cases on appeal [C18 from L *appellātus* summoned, from *appellāre* to APPEAL]

appellation (ˌæpɪˈleɪʃən) *n* **1** a name or title **2** the act of naming

appellative (əˈpɛlətɪv) *n* **1** a name or title **2** *grammar* another word for **common noun** ▷ *adj* **3** of or relating to a name **4** (of a proper noun) used as a common noun

append (əˈpɛnd) *vb* (*tr*) **1** to add as a supplement: *to append a footnote* **2** to attach; hang on [C15 from LL *appendere* to hang (something) from, from L *pendere* to hang]

appendage (əˈpɛndɪdʒ) *n* an ancillary or secondary part attached to a main part; adjunct, such as an organ that projects from the trunk of an animal

appendant (əˈpɛndənt) *adj* **1** attached or added **2** attendant or associated as an accompaniment or result ▷ *n* **3** a person or thing attached or added

appendicectomy (əˌpɛndɪˈsɛktəmɪ) *or esp US & Canad* **appendectomy** (ˌæpənˈdɛktəmɪ) *n, pl* **appendicectomies** *or* **appendectomies** surgical removal of any appendage, esp the vermiform appendix

appendicitis (əˌpɛndɪˈsaɪtɪs) *n* inflammation of the vermiform appendix

appendix (əˈpɛndɪks) *n, pl* **appendices** (-dɪˌsiːz) *or* **appendixes** **1** a body of separate additional material at the end of a book, etc **2** any part that is dependent or supplementary **3** *anat* See **vermiform appendix** [C16 from L: an appendage, from *appendere* to APPEND]

Appenzell (*German* apənˈtsɛl, ˈapəntsɛl) *n* **1** a canton of NE Switzerland, divided in 1597 into the Protestant demicanton of **Appenzell Outer Rhodes** and the Catholic demicanton of **Appenzell Inner Rhodes.** Capitals: Herisau and Appenzell. Pop: 54 104 and 14 750 (1996 est) respectively. Areas: 243 sq km (94 sq miles) and 171 sq km (66 sq miles) respectively **2** a town in NE Switzerland, capital of Appenzell Inner Rhodes demicanton. Pop: 5157 (1990)

apperceive (ˌæpəˈsiːv) *vb* **apperceives, apperceiving, apperceived** (*tr*) **1** to be aware of perceiving **2** *psychol* to comprehend by assimilating (a perception) to ideas already in the mind [C19 from OF, from L *percipere* to PERCEIVE]

apperception (ˌæpəˈsɛpʃən) *n* **1** *psychol* the attainment of full awareness of a sensation or idea **2** the act of apperceiving > ˌ**apperˈceptive** *adj*

appertain (ˌæpəˈteɪn) *vb* (*intr;* usually foll by *to*) to belong (to) as a part, function, right, etc; relate (to) or be connected (with) [C14 from OF *apertenir*, from LL, from L AD- + *pertinēre* to PERTAIN]

appetence (ˈæpɪtəns) *or* **appetency** *n, pl* **appetences** *or* **appetencies** **1** a craving or desire **2** an attraction or affinity [C17 from L *appetentia*, from *appetere* to crave]

appetite (ˈæpɪˌtaɪt) *n* **1** a desire for food or drink **2** a desire to satisfy a bodily craving, as for sexual pleasure **3** (usually foll by *for*) a liking or willingness: *a great appetite for work* [C14 from OF *apetit*, from L, from *appetere* to desire ardently] > **appetitive** (əˈpɛtɪtɪv) *adj*

appetizer *or* **appetiser** (ˈæpɪˌtaɪzə) *n* **1** a small amount of food or drink taken to stimulate the appetite **2** any stimulating foretaste

appetizing *or* **appetising** (ˈæpɪˌtaɪzɪŋ) *adj* pleasing or stimulating to the appetite; delicious; tasty

Appian Way (ˈæpɪən) *n* a Roman road in Italy, extending from Rome to Brindisi: begun in 312 BC by Appius Claudius Caecus. Length: about 560 km (350 miles)

applaud (əˈplɔːd) *vb* **1** to indicate approval of (a person, performance, etc) by clapping the hands **2** (*usually tr*) to express approval or praise of: *I applaud your decision* [C15 from L *applaudere*, from *plaudere* to beat, applaud]

applause (əˈplɔːz) *n* appreciation or praise, esp as shown by clapping the hands

apple (ˈæpᵊl) *n* **1** a rosaceous tree, widely cultivated in temperate regions in many varieties. See also **crab apple** **2** the fruit of this tree, having red, yellow, or green skin and crisp whitish flesh **3** the wood of this tree **4** any of several unrelated trees that have fruit similar to the apple **5** **apple of one's eye** a person or thing that is very much loved [OE *æppel*]

appledrain (ˈæpᵊlˌdreɪn) *n Southwestern English dialect* a wasp

apple green *n* **a** a bright light green **b** (*as adj*): *an apple-green carpet*

Apple Isle *n* **the** *Austral inf* Tasmania > **Apple Islander** *n*

apple-pie bed *n Brit* a bed made with the sheets folded so as to prevent the person from entering it

apple-pie order *n inf* perfect order or condition

applet (ˈæplɪt) *n computing* a computer program that runs within a page on the World Wide Web [C20 from APP(LICATION) + -LET]

Appleton (ˈæpᵊltən) *n* Sir **Edward** (**Victor**) 1892–1965,

English physicist, noted particularly for his research on the ionosphere: Nobel prize for physics 1947

appliance (ə'plaɪəns) *n* 1 a machine or device, esp an electrical one used domestically 2 any piece of equipment having a specific function 3 another name for a **fire engine**

applicable ('æplɪkəbᵊl, ə'plɪkə-) *adj* being appropriate or relevant; able to be applied; fitting > ,**applica'bility** *n* > '**applicably** *adv*

applicant ('æplɪkənt) *n* a person who applies, as for a job, grant, support, etc; candidate [c15 from L *applicāns*, from *applicāre* to APPLY]

application (,æplɪ'keɪʃən) *n* 1 the act of applying to a particular use 2 relevance or value: *the practical applications of space technology* 3 the act of asking for something 4 a written request, as for a job, etc 5 diligent effort: *a job requiring application* 6 something, such as a lotion, that is applied, esp to the skin

applicator ('æplɪ,keɪtə) *n* a device, such as a spatula or rod, for applying a medicine, glue, etc

applicatory ('æplɪkətərɪ) *adj* suitable for application

applied (ə'plaɪd) *adj* put to practical use: *applied mathematics* ▷ Cf **pure** (sense 5)

appliqué (æ'pli:keɪ) *n* 1 a decoration of one material sewn or fixed onto another 2 the practice of decorating in this way ▷ *vb* **appliqués, appliquéing, appliquéd** 3 (*tr*) to sew or fix (a decoration) on as an appliqué [c18 from F, lit.: applied]

apply (ə'plaɪ) *vb* **applies, applying, applied** 1 (*tr*) to put to practical use; employ 2 (*intr*) to be relevant or appropriate 3 (*tr*) to cause to come into contact with 4 (*intr*; often foll by *for*) to put in an application or request 5 (*tr*; often foll by *to*) to devote (oneself or one's efforts) with diligence 6 (*tr*) to bring into use: *the police only applied the law to aliens* [c14 from OF *aplier*, from L *applicāre* to attach to] > **ap'plier** *n*

appoggiatura (ə,pɒdʒə'tʊərə) *n, pl* **appoggiaturas** *or* **appoggiature** (-reɪ) *music* an ornament consisting of a nonharmonic note preceding a harmonic one either before or on the stress [c18 from It., lit.: a propping]

appoint (ə'pɔɪnt) *vb* (*mainly tr*) 1 (*also intr*) to assign officially, as to a position, responsibility, etc 2 to establish by agreement or decree 3 to prescribe: *laws appointed by tribunal* 4 *property law* to nominate (a person) to take an interest in property 5 to equip with usual features; furnish: *a well-appointed hotel* [c14 from OF *apointer* to put into a good state] > **appoin'tee** *n* > **ap'pointer** *n*

appointive (ə'pɔɪntɪv) *adj chiefly US* filled by appointment: *an appointive position*

appointment (ə'pɔɪntmənt) *n* 1 an arrangement to meet a person or be at a place at a certain time 2 the act of placing in a job or position 3 the person who receives such a job 4 the job or position to which such a person is appointed 5 (*usually pl*) a fixture or fitting

appointment television *n* televison programmes that people set aside time to watch

apportion (ə'pɔ:ʃən) *vb* (*tr*) to divide, distribute, or assign shares of; allot proportionally > **ap'portionable** *adj* > **ap'portionment** *n*

appose (ə'pəʊz) *vb* **apposes, apposing, apposed** (*tr*) 1 to place side by side or near to each other 2 (usually foll by *to*) to place (something) near or against another thing [c16 from OF *apposer*, from *poser* to put, from L *pōnere*] > **ap'posable** *adj*

apposite ('æpəzɪt) *adj* appropriate; apt [c17 from L *appositus*, from *appōnere*, from *pōnere* to put] > '**appositely** *adv* > '**appositeness** *n*

apposition (,æpə'zɪʃən) *n* 1 a putting into juxtaposition 2 a grammatical construction in which a word, esp a noun, is placed after another to modify its meaning > ,**appo'sitional** *adj*

appositive (ə'pɒzɪtɪv) *grammar* ▷ *adj* 1 in, of, or relating to apposition ▷ *n* 2 an appositive word or phrase > **ap'positively** *adv*

appraisal (ə'preɪzᵊl) *or* **appraisement** *n* 1 an assessment of the worth or quality of a person or thing 2 a valuation

appraise (ə'preɪz) *vb* **appraises, appraising, appraised** (*tr*) 1 to assess the worth, value, or quality of 2 to make a valuation of, as for taxation [c15 from OF, from *prisier* to PRIZE²] > **ap'praisable** *adj* > **ap'praiser** *n*

> USAGE *Appraise* is sometimes used where *apprise* is meant: *both patients had been fully apprised* (not *appraised*) *of the situation*. This may well be due to the fact that *appraise* is considerably more common, and that people therefore tend to associate this meaning mistakenly with a word they know better

appreciable (ə'pri:ʃəbᵊl) *adj* sufficient to be easily measured or noticed > **ap'preciably** *adv*

appreciate (ə'pri:ʃɪ,eɪt, -sɪ-) *vb* **appreciates, appreciating, appreciated** (*mainly tr*) 1 to feel thankful or grateful for 2 (*may take a clause as object*) to take sufficient account of: *to appreciate a problem* 3 to value highly 4 (*usually intr*) to increase in value [c17 from Med. L *appretiāre* to value, from L *pretium* PRICE] > **ap'preci,ator** *n*

appreciation (ə,pri:ʃɪ'eɪʃən, -sɪ-) *n* 1 thanks or gratitude 2 assessment of the true worth of persons or things 3 perceptive recognition of qualities, as in art 4 an increase in value 5 a review of a book, etc, esp when favourable

appreciative (ə'pri:ʃɪətɪv) *or* **appreciatory** *adj* feeling or expressing appreciation > **ap'preciatively** *adv* > **ap'preciativeness** *n*

apprehend (,æprɪ'hɛnd) *vb* 1 (*tr*) to arrest and escort into custody 2 to grasp mentally; understand 3 to await with fear or anxiety [c14 from L *apprehendere* to hold]

apprehensible (,æprɪ'hɛnsɪbᵊl) *adj* capable of being comprehended or grasped mentally > ,**appre,hensi'bility** *n*

apprehension (,æprɪ'hɛnʃən) *n* 1 anxiety over what may happen 2 the act of arresting 3 understanding 4 a notion or conception

apprehensive (,æprɪ'hɛnsɪv) *adj* 1 fearful or anxious 2 (*usually postpositive* and foll by *of*) *Arch* intelligent, perceptive > ,**appre'hensively** *adv* > ,**appre'hensiveness** *n*

apprentice (ə'prɛntɪs) *n* 1 someone who works for a skilled or qualified person in order to learn a trade, esp for a recognized period 2 any beginner or novice ▷ *vb* **apprentices, apprenticing, apprenticed** 3 (*tr*) to take, place, or bind as an apprentice [c14 from OF *aprentis*, from *aprendre* to learn, from L *apprehendere* to APPREHEND] > **ap'prenticeship** *n*

apprise *or* **apprize** (ə'praɪz) *vb* **apprises, apprising, apprised** *or* **apprizes, apprizing, apprized** (*tr*; often foll by *of*) to make aware; inform [c17 from F *appris*, from *apprendre* to teach; learn]

> USAGE See at **appraise**

appro ('æprəʊ) *n* an informal shortening of **approval**: *on appro*

approach (ə'prəʊtʃ) *vb* 1 to come nearer in position, time, quality, character, etc, to (someone or something) 2 (*tr*) to make a proposal or suggestion to 3 (*tr*) to begin to deal with ▷ *n* 4 the act of drawing close or closer 5 a close approximation 6 the way or means of entering or leaving 7 (*often pl*) an overture to a person 8 a means adopted in tackling a problem, job of work, etc 9 Also called: **approach path** the course followed by an aircraft preparing for landing 10 Also called: **approach shot** *golf* a shot made to or towards the green after a tee shot [c14 from OF *aprochier*, from LL *appropiāre* to draw near, from L *prope* near] > **ap'proachable** *adj* > **ap,proacha'bility** *n*

approbation (,æprə'beɪʃən) *n* 1 commendation; praise 2 official recognition > '**appro,bative** *or* '**appro,batory** *adj*

Aa

appropriate *adj* (əˈprəʊprɪɪt) **1** right or suitable; fitting ▷ *vb* (əˈprəʊprɪˌeɪt), **appropriates, appropriating, appropriated** (*tr*) **2** to take for one's own use, esp illegally **3** to put aside (funds, etc) for a particular purpose or person [c15 from LL *appropriāre* to make one's own, from L *proprius* one's own] > **apˈpropriately** *adv* > **apˈpropriateness** *n* > **apˈpropriˌator** *n*
appropriation (əˌprəʊprɪˈeɪʃən) *n* **1** the act of setting apart or taking for one's own use **2** a sum of money set apart for a specific purpose
approval (əˈpruːvᵊl) *n* **1** the act of approving **2** formal agreement **3** a favourable opinion **4 on approval** (of articles for sale) for examination with an option to buy or return
approve (əˈpruːv) *vb* **approves, approving, approved** **1** (when *intr*, often foll by *of*) to consider fair, good, or right **2** (*tr*) to authorize or sanction [c14 from OF *aprover*, from L *approbāre* to approve, from *probāre* to test, PROVE]
approved school *n* (in Britain) a former name for **community home**
approx. *abbrev for* approximate(ly)
approximate *adj* (əˈprɒksɪmɪt) **1** almost accurate or exact **2** inexact; rough; loose **3** much alike; almost the same **4** near; close together ▷ *vb* (əˈprɒksɪˌmeɪt), **approximates, approximating, approximated** **5** (usually foll by *to*) to come or bring near or close; be almost the same (as) **6** *maths* to find an expression for (some quantity) accurate to a specified degree [c15 from LL *approximāre*, from L *proximus* nearest]
approximately (əˈprɒksɪmɪtlɪ) *adv* close to; around; roughly or in the region of
approximation (əˌprɒksɪˈmeɪʃən) *n* **1** the process or result of making a rough calculation, estimate, or guess **2** an imprecise or unreliable record or version **3** *maths* an inexact number, relationship, or theory that is sufficiently accurate for a specific purpose
appurtenance (əˈpɜːtɪnəns) *n* **1** a less significant thing or part **2** (*pl*) accessories **3** *property law* a minor right, interest, or privilege [c14 from Anglo-F *apurtenance*, from OF *apartenance*, from *apartenir* to APPERTAIN]
APR *abbrev for* annual percentage rate
Apr. *abbrev for* April
apraxia (əˈpræksɪə) *n* a disorder of the central nervous system characterized by impaired ability to carry out certain purposeful muscular movements [c19 via NL from Gk: inactivity, from A-¹ + *praxis* action]
après-ski (ˌæpreɪˈskiː) *n* **a** social activity following a day's skiing **b** (*as modifier*): *an après-ski outfit* [F, lit.: after ski]
apricot (ˈeɪprɪˌkɒt) *n* **1** a tree native to Africa and W Asia, but widely cultivated for its edible fruit **2** the yellow juicy fruit of this tree, which resembles a small peach [c16 from Port., from Ar., from LGk, from L *praecox* early-ripening]
April (ˈeɪprəl) *n* the fourth month of the year, consisting of 30 days [c14 from L *Aprīlis*]
April fool *n* a victim of a practical joke performed on the first of April (**April Fools' Day** *or* **All Fools' Day**)
a priori (eɪ praɪˈɔːraɪ, ɑː prɪˈɔːrɪ) *adj* **1** *logic* relating to or involving deductive reasoning from a general principle to the expected facts or effects **2** known to be true independently of experience of the subject matter [c18 from L, lit.: from the previous] > **apriority** (ˌeɪpraɪˈɒrɪtɪ) *n*
apron (ˈeɪprən) *n* **1** a protective or sometimes decorative garment worn over the front of the body and tied around the waist **2** the part of a stage extending in front of the curtain **3** a hard-surfaced area in front of an aircraft hangar, terminal building, etc **4** a continuous conveyor belt composed of metal slats **5** a protective plate screening the operator of a machine, artillery piece, etc **6** *geol* a sheet of sand, gravel, etc, deposited at the front of a moraine **7** another name for **skirt** (sense 3) **8 tied to someone's apron strings** dominated by someone, esp a mother or wife ▷ *vb* **9** (*tr*) to protect or provide with an apron [c16 mistaken division of *a napron*, from OF, from L *mappa* napkin]
apron stage *n* a stage that projects into the auditorium so that the audience sits on three sides of it
apropos (ˌæprəˈpəʊ) *adj* **1** appropriate ▷ *adv* **2** appropriately **3** by the way; incidentally **4 apropos of** (*prep*) in respect of [c17 from F *à propos* to the purpose]
apse (æps) *n* a domed or vaulted semicircular or polygonal recess, esp at the east end of a church. Also called: **apsis** [c19 from L *apsis*, from Gk: a fitting together, from *haptein* to fasten] > **ˈapsidal** *adj*
apsis (ˈæpsɪs) *n, pl* **apsides** (æpˈsaɪdiːz) either of two points lying at the extremities of an eccentric orbit of a planet, satellite, etc Also called: **apse** [c17 via L from Gk; see APSE] > **apsidal** (ˈæpsɪdᵊl) *adj*
apt (æpt) *adj* **1** suitable; appropriate **2** (*postpositive*; foll by an infinitive) having a tendency (to behave as specified) **3** having the ability to learn and understand easily [c14 from L *aptus* fitting, from *apere* to fasten] > **ˈaptly** *adv* > **ˈaptness** *n*
APT *abbrev for* Advanced Passenger Train
apterous (ˈæptərəs) *adj* **1** (of insects) without wings, as silverfish **2** without winglike expansions, as some seeds and fruits [c18 from Gk, from A-¹ + *pteron* wing] > **ˈapterˌism** *n*
apteryx (ˈæptərɪks) *n* another name for **kiwi** (the bird) [c19 from NL; see APTEROUS]
aptitude (ˈæptɪˌtjuːd) *n* **1** inherent or acquired ability **2** ease in learning or understanding **3** the quality of being apt [c15 via OF from LL, from L *aptus* APT]
Apuleius (ˌæpjʊˈliːəs) *n* **Lucius** (ˈluːsɪəs) 2nd century AD, Roman writer, noted for his romance *The Golden Ass*
Apulia (əˈpjuːljə) *n* a region of SE Italy, on the Adriatic. Capital: Bari. Pop: 4 085 239 (2000 est). Area: 19 223 sq km (7422 sq miles). Italian name: **Puglia**
Aqaba *or* **Akaba** (ˈækəbə) *n* the only port in Jordan, in the southwest, on the **Gulf of Aqaba**. Pop: 46 090 (1990 est)
Aqtöbe (ækˈtjuːbɪ; *Kazakh* aktøˈbe) *n* an industrial city in W Kazakhstan. Pop: 258 900 (1995 est). Former name (until 1991): **Aktyubinsk**
aqua (ˈækwə) *n, pl* **aquae** (ˈækwiː) *or* **aquas** **1** water: used in compound names of certain liquid substances or solutions of substances in water ▷ *n, adj* **2** short for **aquamarine** (the colour) [L: water]
aquaculture (ˈækwəˌkʌltʃə) *or* **aquiculture** *n* the cultivation of freshwater and marine organisms for human consumption or use
aquaerobics *or* **aquarobics** (ˌækwəˈrəʊbɪks) *n* (*functioning as sing*) the practice of exercising to music in a swimming pool [c20 from L *aqua* water + AEROBICS]
aqua fortis (ˈfɔːtɪs) *n* an obsolete name for **nitric acid** [c17 from L, lit.: strong water]
aqualung (ˈækwəˌlʌŋ) *n* breathing apparatus used by divers, etc, consisting of a mouthpiece attached to air cylinders strapped to the back
aquamarine (ˌækwəməˈriːn) *n* **1** a pale greenish-blue transparent variety of beryl used as a gemstone **2a** a pale blue to greenish-blue colour **2b** (*as adj*): *an aquamarine dress* [c19 from NL, from L: sea water (referring to the gem's colour)]
aquanaut (ˈækwənɔːt) *n* a person who works, swims, or dives underwater [c20 from AQUA + *-naut*, as in ASTRONAUT]
aquaplane (ˈækwəˌpleɪn) *n* **1** a board on which a person stands and is towed by a motorboat ▷ *vb* **aquaplanes, aquaplaning, aquaplaned** (*intr*) **2** to ride on an aquaplane **3** (of a motor vehicle travelling at high speeds on wet roads) to rise up onto a thin film of water so that contact with the road is lost
aqua regia (ˈriːdʒɪə) *n* a mixture of nitric acid and

hydrochloric acid [c17 from NL: royal water; referring to its use in dissolving gold, the royal metal]
aquarist ('ækwərɪst) *n* **1** the curator of an aquarium **2** a person who studies aquatic life
aquarium (ə'kwɛərɪəm) *n, pl* **aquariums** *or* **aquaria** (-rɪə) **1** a tank, bowl, or pool in which aquatic animals and plants are kept for pleasure, study, or exhibition **2** a building housing a collection of aquatic life, as for exhibition [c19 from L *aquārius* relating to water, on the model of VIVARIUM]
Aquarius (ə'kwɛərɪəs) *n, Latin genitive* **Aquarii** (ə'kwɛərɪ,aɪ) **1** *astron* a S constellation **2** *astrol* also called: the **Water Carrier** the eleventh sign of the zodiac. The sun is in this sign between about Jan. 20 and Feb. 18 [L]
aquatic (ə'kwætɪk) *adj* **1** growing, living, or found in water **2** *sport* performed in or on water ▷ *n* **3** a marine or freshwater animal or plant [c15 from L *aquāticus*, from *aqua* water]
aquatics (ə'kwætɪks) *pl n* sports or pastimes performed in or on the water
aquatint ('ækwə,tɪnt) *n* **1** a technique of etching copper with acid to produce an effect resembling watercolour **2** an etching made in this way ▷ *vb* **3** (*tr*) to etch (a block, etc) in aquatint [c18 from It. *acqua tinta* dyed water]
aquavit ('ækwə,vɪt) *n* a grain- or potato-based spirit flavoured with aromatic seeds. Also called: **akvavit** [of Scandinavian origin: see AQUA VITAE]
aqua vitae ('vi:taɪ, 'vaɪti:) *n* an archaic name for **brandy** [Med. L: water of life]
aqueduct ('ækwɪ,dʌkt) *n* **1** a conduit used to convey water over a long distance **2** a structure, often a bridge, that carries such a conduit or a canal across a valley or river **3** a channel or conduit in the body [c16 from L *aquaeductus*, from *aqua* water + *dūcere* to convey]
aqueous ('eɪkwɪəs) *adj* **1** of, like, or containing water **2** dissolved in water: *aqueous ammonia* **3** (of rocks, etc) formed from material laid down in water [c17 from Med. L *aqueus*, from L *aqua* water]
aqueous humour *n physiol* the watery fluid within the eyeball between the cornea and the lens
aquiculture ('eɪkwɪ,kʌltʃə, 'ækwɪ-) *n* **1** another name for **hydroponics** **2** a variant of **aquaculture** > **'aqui,culturist** *n* > **'aqui,cultural** *adj*
aquifer ('ækwɪfə) *n* a porous deposit or rock, such as a sandstone, containing water that can be used to supply wells
Aquila('ækwɪlə; *Italian* 'a:kwila) *or* **l'Aquila** *n* a city in central Italy, capital of Abruzzi region. Pop: 67 820 (1990). Official name: **Aquila degli Abruzzi** ('deʎʎi a'bruttsi)
aquilegia (,ækwɪ'li:dʒɪə) *n* another name for **columbine** [c19 from Med. L, from ?]
aquiline ('ækwɪ,laɪn) *adj* **1** (of a nose) having the curved shape of an eagle's beak **2** of or like an eagle [c17 from L, from *aquila* eagle]
Aquinas (ə'kwaɪnəs) *n* **Saint Thomas** 1225–74, Italian theologian, scholastic philosopher, and Dominican friar, whose works include *Summa contra Gentiles* (1259–64) and *Summa Theologiae* (1267–73), the first attempt at a comprehensive theological system. Feast day: Jan. 28. See also **Thomism**
Aquino (ə'ki:nəʊ) *n* **Corazón,** known as *Cory*. born 1933, Philippine stateswoman: president (1986–92)
Aquitaine (,ækwɪ'teɪn; *French* akitɛn) *n* a region of SW France, on the Bay of Biscay: a former Roman province and medieval duchy. It is generally flat in the west, rising to the slopes of the Massif Central in the northeast and the Pyrenees in the south; mainly agricultural. Ancient name: **Aquitania** (,ækwɪ'teɪnɪə)
Ar *the chemical symbol for* argon
Ar. *abbrev for:* **1** Arabia(n) **2** Also: **Ar** Arabic
-ar *suffix forming adjectives* of; belonging to; like: *linear; polar; minuscular; solar* [via OF *-er* from L *-āris*]
ARA *abbrev for:* **1** (in Britain) Associate of the Royal Academy **2** (in New Zealand) Auckland Regional Authority
Arab ('ærəb) *n* **1** a member of a Semitic people originally inhabiting Arabia **2** a lively intelligent breed of horse, used for riding **3** (*modifier*) of or relating to the Arabs [c14 from L, from Gk *Araps*, from Ar. *'Arab*]
arabesque (,ærə'bɛsk) *n* **1** *ballet* a classical position in which the dancer has one leg raised behind **2** *music* a piece or movement with a highly ornamented melody **3** *arts* a type of curvilinear decoration in painting, metalwork, etc, with intricate intertwining designs [c18 from F, from It. *arabesco* in the Arabic style]
Arabia (ə'reɪbɪə) *n* a great peninsula of SW Asia, between the Red Sea and the Persian Gulf: consists chiefly of a desert plateau, with mountains rising over 3000 m (10 000 ft) in the west and scattered oases; includes the present-day countries of Saudi Arabia, Yemen, Oman, Bahrain, Qatar, Kuwait, and the United Arab Emirates. Area: about 2 600 000 sq km (1 000 000 sq miles)
Arabian (ə'reɪbɪən) *adj* **1** of or relating to Arabia or the Arabs ▷ *n* **2** another word for **Arab**
Arabian camel *n* a domesticated camel with one hump on its back, used as a beast of burden in the deserts of N Africa and SW Asia
Arabian Desert *n* **1** a desert in E Egypt, between the Nile, the Gulf of Suez, and the Red Sea: mountainous parts rise over 1800 m (6000 ft). Area: about 220 000 sq km (85 000 sq miles) **2** a desert, mainly in Saudi Arabia, forming the desert area of the Arabian Peninsula, esp in the north. Area: about 2 330 000 sq km (900 000 sq miles)
Arabian Sea *n* the NW part of the Indian Ocean, between Arabia and India
Arabic ('ærəbɪk) *n* **1** the Semitic language of the Arabs, which has its own alphabet and is spoken in Algeria, Egypt, Iraq, Jordan, Saudi Arabia, Syria, Tunisia, etc ▷ *adj* **2** denoting or relating to this language, any of the peoples that speak it, or the countries in which it is spoken

Arabic Alphabet

alif	ا
bā	ب
tā	ت
thā	ث
jīm	ج
ḥā	ح
khā	خ
dāl	د
dhāl	ذ
rā	ر
zā	ز
sīn	س
shīn	ش
ṣād	ص
ḍād	ض
ṭā	ط
ẓā	ظ
`ain	ع
ghain	غ
fā	ف
qāf	ق
kāf	ك
lām	ل
mīm	م
nūn	ن

hā ه
wāw و
yā ي

arabica bean (əˈræbɪkə) *n* a high-quality coffee bean, obtained from the tree *Coffea arabica*
Arabic numeral *n* one of the numbers 0, 1, 2, 3, 4, 5, 6, 7, 8, 9 ▷ Cf **Roman numerals**
arabis (ˈærəbɪs) *n* any of several trailing plants having pink or white flowers in spring. Also called: **rock cress** [c16 from Med. L, from Gk *arabis*, ult. from *Arābios* Arabian, prob. from growing in sandy or stony soil]
Arabist (ˈærəbɪst) *n* a student of Arabic culture, language, history, etc
arable (ˈærəbᵊl) *adj* **1** (of land) being or capable of being tilled for the production of crops **2** of, relating to, or using such land [c15 from L *arābilis*, from *arāre* to plough]
Araby (ˈærəbɪ) *n* an archaic or poetic name for **Arabia**
Aracajú (*Portuguese* arəkəˈʒu) *n* a port in E Brazil, capital of Sergipe state. Pop: 460 898 (2000)
Arachne (əˈræknɪ) *n Greek myth* a maiden changed into a spider for having presumptuously challenged Athena to a weaving contest [from Gk *arakhnē* spider]
arachnid (əˈræknɪd) *n* any of a class of arthropods characterized by simple eyes and four pairs of legs, including the spiders, scorpions, and ticks [c19 from NL *Arachnida*, from Gk *arakhnē* spider] > **aˈrachnidan** *adj, n*
arachnoid (əˈræknɔɪd) *n* **1** the middle one of three membranes that cover the brain and spinal cord ▷ *adj* **2** of or relating to this membrane **3** *bot* consisting of or covered with soft fine hairs or fibres
arachnophobia (əˌræknəˈfəʊbɪə) *n* an abnormal fear of spiders [c20 from Gk *arakhnē* spider + -PHOBIA]
Arafat *n* **Yasser** (ˈjæsə) born 1929, Palestinian leader; cofounder of Al Fatah (1956), leader from 1968 of the Palestine Liberation Organization, president of the Palestinian National Authority from 1996: signed a peace agreement with Israel (1993); Nobel peace prize 1994 with Shimon Peres and Yitzhak Rabin
Arafura Sea (ˌærəˈfʊərə) *n* a part of the W Pacific Ocean, between N Australia and SW New Guinea
Aragats (*Russian* ˌaraˈgats) *n* **Mount** a volcanic mountain in NW Armenia. Height: 4090 m (13 419 ft). Turkish name: **Alagez**
Aragon¹ (ˈærəgən) *n* an autonomous region of NE Spain: independent kingdom from the 11th century until 1479, when it was united with Castile to form modern Spain. Pop: 1 189 909 (2000 est). Area: 47 609 sq km (18 382 sq miles) > **Aragonese** (ˌærəgəˈniːz) *n, adj*
Aragon² (*French* aragɔ̃) *n* **Louis** (lwi) 1897–1982, French poet, essayist, and novelist; an early surrealist, later a committed Communist. His works include the verse collections *Le Crève-Coeur* (1941) and *Les Yeux d'Elsa* (1942) and the series of novels *Le Monde réel* (1933–51)
Araguaia *or* **Araguaya** (ˌɑːrəˈgwaɪə) *n* a river in central Brazil, rising in S central Mato Grosso state and flowing north. Length: over 1771 km (1100 miles)
arak (ˈærək) *n* a variant spelling of **arrack**
Arakan Yoma (ˌɑːrɑːˈkɑːn ˈjəʊmɑː) *n* a mountain range in Myanmar, between the Irrawaddy River and the W coast: forms a barrier between Myanmar and India; teak forests
Araks (aˈraks) *n* the Russian name for the **Aras**
Araldite (ˈærəldaɪt) *n trademark* an epoxy resin used as a glue for mending glass, plastic, and china
Aral Sea (ˈærəl) *n* a lake in Kazakhstan and Uzbekistan, east of the Caspian Sea, formerly the fourth largest lake in the world: shallow and saline, now badly polluted; use of its source waters for irrigation led to a loss of over 50% of its area between 1967 and 1997. Area (including salt flats): about 64 750 sq km (25 000 sq miles). Also called: **Lake Aral**
Aram (ˈɛəræm, -rəm) *n* the biblical name for ancient Syria > **Aramaean** *or* **Aramean** (ˌærəˈmiːən) *adj, n*
Aramaic (ˌærəˈmeɪɪk) *n* **1** an ancient Semitic language of the Middle East, still spoken in parts of Syria and the Lebanon ▷ *adj* **2** of, relating to, or using this language
Aran Islands (ˈærən) *pl n* a group of three islands in the Atlantic, off the W coast of the Republic of Ireland: Aranmore or Inishmore (the largest), Inishmaan, and Inisheer. Pop: 1000 (latest est). Area: 46 sq km (18 sq miles)
Ararat (ˈærəˌræt) *n* an extinct volcanic mountain massif in E Turkey: two main peaks; **Great Ararat** 5155 m (16 916 ft), said to be the resting place of Noah's Ark after the Flood (Genesis 8:4), and **Little Ararat** 3914 m (12 843 ft)
Aras (æˈræs) *n* a river rising in mountains in Turkish Armenia and flowing east to the Caspian Sea: forms part of the E border of Turkey and the N border of Iran. Length: about 1100 km (660 miles). Ancient name: **Araxes** Russian name: **Araks**
Araucania (ˌærɔːˈkeɪnɪə; *Spanish* arauˈkanja) *n* a region of central Chile, inhabited by Araucanian Indians > ˌ**Arauˈcanian** *adj, n*
araucaria (ˌærɔːˈkɛərɪə) *n* any of a group of coniferous trees of South America, Australia, and Polynesia, such as the monkey puzzle [c19 from NL (*arbor*) *Araucaria* (tree) from *Arauco*, a province in Chile]
arbalest *or* **arbalist** (ˈɑːbəlɪst) *n* a large medieval crossbow, usually cocked by mechanical means [c11 from OF, from LL *arcuballista*, from L *arcus* bow + BALLISTA]
Arbela (ɑːˈbiːlə) *n* an ancient city in Assyria, near which the **Battle of Arbela** took place (331 BC), in which Alexander the Great defeated the Persians. Modern name: **Erbil**
Arber (ˈɑːbə) *n* **Werner** born 1929, Swiss microbiologist, noted for his work on restriction enzymes. Nobel prize for physiology or medicine 1978
arbiter (ˈɑːbɪtə) *n* **1** a person empowered to judge in a dispute; referee **2** a person having control of something [c15 from L, from ?] > ˈ**arbitress** *fem n*
arbitrament (ɑːˈbɪtrəmənt) *n* **1** the decision or award made by an arbitrator upon a disputed matter **2** another word for **arbitration**
arbitrary (ˈɑːbɪtrərɪ) *adj* **1** founded on or subject to personal whims, prejudices, etc **2** not absolute **3** (of a government, ruler, etc) despotic or dictatorial **4** *law* (esp of a penalty) within the court's discretion [c15 from L *arbitrārius* arranged through arbitration] > ˈ**arbitrarily** *adv* > ˈ**arbitrariness** *n*
arbitrate (ˈɑːbɪˌtreɪt) *vb* **arbitrates, arbitrating, arbitrated 1** to achieve a settlement between parties **2** to submit to or settle by arbitration [c16 from L *arbitrāri* to give judgment] > ˈ**arbiˌtrator** *n*
arbitration (ˌɑːbɪˈtreɪʃən) *n* the hearing and determination of a dispute, esp an industrial one, by an impartial referee selected or agreed upon by the parties concerned
Arblay, d' (ˈdɑːbleɪ; *French* darblɛ) *n* **Madame** the married name of (Fanny) **Burney**
arbor¹ (ˈɑːbə) *n* the US spelling of **arbour**
arbor² (ˈɑːbə) *n* **1** a rotating shaft in a machine on which a milling cutter or grinding wheel is fitted **2** a rotating shaft [c17 from L: tree]
arboraceous (ˌɑːbəˈreɪʃəs) *adj literary* **1** resembling a tree **2** wooded
arboreal (ɑːˈbɔːrɪəl) *adj* **1** of or resembling a tree **2** living in or among trees
arborescent (ˌɑːbəˈrɛsᵊnt) *adj* having the shape or characteristics of a tree > ˌ**arboˈrescence** *n*
arboretum (ˌɑːbəˈriːtəm) *n, pl* **arboreta** (-tə) *or* **arboretums** a place where trees or shrubs are cultivated [c19 from L, from *arbor* tree]
arboriculture (ˈɑːbərɪˌkʌltʃə) *n* the cultivation of trees or shrubs > ˌ**arboriˈculturist** *n*

arborio rice (ɑːˈbɔːrɪəʊ) *n* a variety of round-grain rice used for making risotto [c20 after *Arborio*, a town in N Italy]
arbor vitae (ˈɑːbɔː ˈviːtaɪ, ˈvaɪtiː) *n* any of several Asian and North American evergreen coniferous trees having tiny scalelike leaves and egglike cones [c17 from NL, lit.: tree of life]
arbour (ˈɑːbə) *n* a leafy glade or bower shaded by trees, vines, shrubs, etc [c14 *erber*, from OF, from L *herba* grass]
Arbroath (ɑːˈbrəʊθ) *n* a port and resort in E Scotland, in Angus: scene of the barons of Scotland's declaration of independence to Pope John XXII in 1320. Pop: 23 474 (1991)
Arbus (ˈɑːbəs) *n* **Diane,** original name *Diane Nemerov.* 1923–71, US photographer, noted esp for her portraits of vagrants, dwarfs, transvestites, etc
Arbuthnot (ɑːˈbʌθnɒt) *n* **John** 1667–1735, Scottish physician and satirist: author of *The History of John Bull* (1712) and, with others, of the *Memoirs of Martinus Scriblerus* (1741)
arbutus (ɑːˈbjuːtəs) *n, pl* **arbutuses** any of a genus of shrubs having clusters of white or pinkish flowers, broad evergreen leaves, and strawberry-like berries [c16 from L; rel. to *arbor* tree]
arc (ɑːk) *n* **1** something curved in shape **2** part of an unbroken curved line **3** a luminous discharge that occurs when an electric current flows between two electrodes separated by a small gap **4** *maths* a section of a curve, graph, or geometric figure ▷ *vb* **arcs, arcing, arced** *or* **arcs, arcking, arcked 5** (*intr*) to form an arc ▷ *adj* **6** *maths* specifying an inverse trigonometric function: *arcsin, arccos, arctan* [c14 from OF, from L *arcus* bow, arch]
ARC *abbrev for* AIDS-related complex: a condition in which a person infected with the AIDS virus suffers from relatively mild symptoms, such as loss of weight, fever, etc
arcade (ɑːˈkeɪd) *n* **1** a set of arches and their supporting columns **2** a covered and sometimes arched passageway, usually with shops on one or both sides [c18 from F, from It. *arcata*, from L *arcus* bow, arch]
Arcadia (ɑːˈkeɪdɪə) *n* **1** a department of Greece, in the central Peloponnese. Capital: Tripolis. Pop: 105 309 (1991). Area: 4367 sq km (1686 sq miles) **2** Also called (poetic): **Arcady** (ˈɑːkədɪ) the traditional idealized rural setting of Greek and Roman bucolic poetry and later in the literature of the Renaissance
Arcadian (ɑːˈkeɪdɪən) *adj* **1** of the idealized Arcadia of pastoral poetry **2** rustic or bucolic ▷ *n* **3** a person who leads a quiet simple rural life > **Arˈcadianism** *n*
arcane (ɑːˈkeɪn) *adj* requiring secret knowledge to be understood; esoteric [c16 from L *arcānus* secret, from *arcēre* to keep safe]
arcanum (ɑːˈkeɪnəm) *n, pl* **arcana** (-nə) (*sometimes pl*) a secret or mystery [c16 from L; see ARCANE]
Arc de Triomphe (ˈɑːk də ˈtriːəʊmf; *French* ark də trijɔ̃f) *n* the triumphal arch in Paris begun by Napoleon I to commemorate his victories of 1805–6 and completed in 1836
arch¹ (ɑːtʃ) *n* **1** a curved structure that spans an opening **2** Also called: **archway** a structure in the form of an arch that serves as a gateway **3** something curved like an arch **4** any of various parts or structures of the body having a curved or archlike outline, such as the raised vault formed by the tarsal and metatarsal bones (**arch of the foot**) ▷ *vb* **5** (*tr*) to span (an opening) with an arch **6** to form or cause to form an arch or a curve resembling that of an arch **7** (*tr*) to span or extend over [c14 from OF *arche*, from L *arcus* bow, ARC]
arch² (ɑːtʃ) *adj* **1** (*prenominal*) chief; principal; leading **2** (*prenominal*) expert: *an arch criminal* **3** knowing or superior; coyly playful: *an arch look* [c16 independent use of ARCH-] > **ˈarchly** *adv* > **ˈarchness** *n*
arch. *abbrev for:* **1** archaic **2** archaism
arch- *or* **archi-** *combining form* **1** chief; principal: *archbishop* **2** eminent above all others of the same kind: *archenemy* [ult. from Gk *arkhi-*, from *arkhein* to rule]
-arch *n combining form* leader; ruler; chief: *patriarch; monarch* [from Gk *-arkhēs*, from *arkhein* to rule]
archaean (ɑːˈkɪən) *n* any member of the *Archaea*, a domain of prokaryotic microorganisms, distinguished from bacteria on molecular phylogenetic grounds and often found in hostile environments, such as volcanic vents and hot springs
Archaean *or esp US* **Archean** (ɑːˈkiːən) *adj* of the metamorphosed rocks formed in the early Precambrian era
archaeology *or* **archeology** (ˌɑːkɪˈɒlədʒɪ) *n* the study of man's past by scientific analysis of the material remains of his cultures [c17 from LL, from Gk *arkhaiologia* study of what is ancient, from *arkhē* beginning]
> **archaeological** *or* **archeological** (ˌɑːkɪəˈlɒdʒɪkᵊl) *adj*
> **ˌarchaeˈologist** *or* **ˌarcheˈologist** *n*
▷ www.britac.ac.uk/portal/bysection.asp?section=H7
▷ http://ads.ahds.ac.uk/catalogue
▷ http://archnet.asu.edu/
▷ www.serve.com/archaeology
archaeopteryx (ˌɑːkɪˈɒptərɪks) *n* any of several extinct primitive birds which occurred in Jurassic times and had teeth, a long tail, and well-developed wings [c19 from Gk *arkhaios* ancient + *pterux* winged creature]
archaic (ɑːˈkeɪɪk) *adj* **1** belonging to or characteristic of a much earlier period **2** out of date; antiquated **3** (of vocabulary, etc) characteristic of an earlier period of a language [c19 from F, from Gk *arkhaïkos*, from *arkhaios* ancient, from *arkhē* beginning, from *arkhein* to begin]
> **arˈchaically** *adv*
archaism (ˈɑːkeɪˌɪzəm) *n* **1** the adoption or imitation of archaic words or style **2** an archaic word, style, etc [c17 from NL, from Gk, from *arkhaizein* to model one's style upon that of ancient writers; see ARCHAIC] > **ˈarchaist** *n* > **ˌarchaˈistic** *adj*
archangel (ˈɑːkˌeɪndʒəl) *n* a principal angel
> **archangelic** (ˌɑːkænˈdʒɛlɪk) *adj*
Archangel (ˈɑːkˌeɪndʒəl) *n* a port in NW Russia, on the Dvina River: major centre for the timber trade and White Sea fisheries. Pop: 366 200 (1999 est). Russian name: **Arkhangelsk**
archbishop (ˈɑːtʃˈbɪʃəp) *n* a bishop of the highest rank. Abbrev: **abp, Abp, Arch., Archbp**
archbishopric (ˈɑːtʃˈbɪʃəprɪk) *n* the rank, office, or jurisdiction of an archbishop
archdeacon (ˈɑːtʃˈdiːkən) *n* **1** an Anglican clergyman ranking just below a bishop **2** a clergyman of similar rank in other Churches > **ˈarchˈdeaconry** *n*
archdiocese (ˌɑːtʃˈdaɪəˌsiːs) *n* the diocese of an archbishop > **archdiocesan** (ˌɑːtʃdaɪˈɒsɪsᵊn) *adj*
archducal (ˈɑːtʃˈdjuːkᵊl) *adj* of or relating to an archduke, archduchess, or archduchy
archduchess (ˈɑːtʃˈdʌtʃɪs) *n* **1** the wife or widow of an archduke **2** (since 1453) a princess of the Austrian imperial family
archduchy (ˈɑːtʃˈdʌtʃɪ) *n, pl* **archduchies** the territory ruled by an archduke or archduchess
archduke (ˈɑːtʃˈdjuːk) *n* a chief duke, esp (since 1453) a prince of the Austrian imperial dynasty
Archean (ɑːˈkiːən) *adj* a variant spelling (esp US) of **Archaean**
archegonium (ˌɑːkɪˈɡəʊnɪəm) *n, pl* **archegonia** (-nɪə) a female sex organ, occurring in mosses, ferns, etc [c19 from NL, from Gk, from *arkhe-* chief, first + *gonos* seed, race]
archenemy (ˈɑːtʃˈɛnɪmɪ) *n, pl* **archenemies 1** a chief enemy **2** (*often cap; preceded by the*) the devil
archeology (ˌɑːkɪˈɒlədʒɪ) *n* a variant of **archaeology**
archer (ˈɑːtʃə) *n* a person skilled in the use of a bow and arrow [c13 from OF, from LL, from L *arcus* bow]

Archer[1] ('ɑːtʃə) *n* **the** the constellation Sagittarius

Archer[2] ('ɑːtʃə) *n* **1 Frederick Scott** 1813–57, British inventor and sculptor. He developed (1851) the wet collodion photographic process, enabling multiple copies of pictures to be made **2 William** 1856–1924, Scottish critic and dramatist: made the first English translations of Ibsen

archerfish ('ɑːtʃə,fɪʃ) *n, pl* **archerfish** *or* **archerfishes** a freshwater fish, related to the perch, of SE Asia and Australia, that catches insects by spitting water at them

archery ('ɑːtʃərɪ) *n* **1** the art or sport of shooting with bows and arrows **2** archers or their weapons collectively

▷ www.archery.org

archetype ('ɑːkɪ,taɪp) *n* **1** a perfect or typical specimen **2** an original model; prototype **3** *psychoanal* one of the inherited mental images postulated by Jung **4** a recurring symbol or motif in literature, etc [c17 from L *archetypum* an original, from Gk, from *arkhetupos* first-moulded; see ARCH-, -TYPE] > ,**arche'typal** *adj*

archfiend (,ɑːtʃ'fiːnd) *n* (*often cap*) **the** the devil; Satan

archidiaconal (,ɑːkɪdaɪ'ækənᵊl) *adj* of or relating to an archdeacon or his or her office > ,**archidi'aconate** *n*

archiepiscopal (,ɑːkɪɪ'pɪskəpᵊl) *adj* of or associated with an archbishop > ,**archie'piscopate** *n*

archil ('ɑːtʃɪl) *n* a variant of **orchil**

archimandrite (,ɑːkɪ'mændraɪt) *n Greek Orthodox Church* the head of a monastery [c16 from LL, from LGk *arkhimandritēs*, from ARCHI- + *mandra* monastery]

Archimedes(,ɑːkɪ'miːdiːz) *n* ?287–212 BC, Greek mathematician and physicist of Syracuse, noted for his work in geometry, hydrostatics, and mechanics

Archimedes' principle *n* a law of physics stating that the apparent loss in weight of a body immersed in a fluid is equal to the weight of the displaced fluid

Archimedes' screw *or* **Archimedean screw** *n* an ancient water-lifting device using a spiral passage in an inclined cylinder

archipelago (,ɑːkɪ'pɛlə,gəʊ) *n, pl* **archipelagos** *or* **archipelagoes 1** a group of islands **2** a sea studded with islands [c16 (meaning: the Aegean Sea): from It., from L *pelagus*, from Gk, from ARCH- + *pelagos* sea] > **archipelagic** (,ɑːkɪpə'lædʒɪk) *adj*

architect ('ɑːkɪ,tɛkt) *n* **1** a person qualified to design buildings and to supervise their erection **2** a person similarly qualified in another form of construction: *a naval architect* **3** any planner or creator [c16 from F, from L, from Gk *arkhitektōn* director of works, from ARCHI- + *tektōn* workman; rel. to *tekhnē* art, skill]

architectonic (,ɑːkɪtɛk'tɒnɪk) *adj* **1** denoting, relating to, or having architectural qualities **2** *metaphysics* of the systematic classification of knowledge [c16 from LL *architectonicus* concerning architecture; see ARCHITECT]

architectonics (,ɑːkɪtɛk'tɒnɪks) *n* (*functioning as sing*) **1** the science of architecture **2** *metaphysics* the scientific classification of knowledge

architecture ('ɑːkɪ,tɛktʃə) *n* **1** the art and science of designing and superintending the erection of buildings, etc **2** a style of building or structure **3** buildings or structures collectively **4** the structure or design of anything > ,**archi'tectural** *adj*

▷ www.architecture.com
▷ www.architectureweek.com
▷ http://architecture.about.com
▷ www.bluffton.edu/~sullivanm/index

architrave ('ɑːkɪ,treɪv) *n archit* **1** the lowest part of an entablature that bears on the columns **2** a moulding around a doorway, window opening, etc [c16 via F from It., from ARCHI- + *trave* beam, from L *trabs*]

archive ('ɑːkaɪv) *n* (*often pl*) **1** a collection of records of an institution, family, etc **2** a place where such records are kept **3** *computing* data transferred to a tape or disk for long-term storage rather than frequent use ▷ *vb* **4** (*tr*) to store (documents, data, etc) in an archive or other repository [c17 from LL, from Gk *arkheion* repository of official records, from *arkhē* government] > **ar'chival** *adj*

archivist ('ɑːkɪvɪst) *n* a person in charge of archives

archon ('ɑːkɒn) *n* (in ancient Athens) one of the nine chief magistrates [c17 from Gk *arkhōn* ruler, from *arkhein* to rule] > **'archon,ship** *n*

archpriest ('ɑːtʃ'priːst) *n* **1** (formerly) a chief assistant to a bishop **2** a senior priest

archway ('ɑːtʃ,weɪ) *n* a passageway or entrance under an arch or arches

-archy *n combining form* government; rule: *anarchy; monarchy* [from Gk *-arkhia*; see -ARCH]

arc light *n* a light source in which an arc between two electrodes produces intense white illumination. Also called: **arc lamp**

arctic ('ɑːktɪk) *adj* **1** of or relating to the Arctic **2** *inf* cold; freezing ▷ *n* **3** (*modifier*) suitable for conditions of extreme cold: *arctic clothing* [c14 from L *arcticus*, from Gk *arktikos* northern, lit.: pertaining to (the constellation of) the Bear, from *arktos* bear]

Arctic ('ɑːktɪk) *n* **1 the** Also called: **Arctic Zone** the regions north of the Arctic Circle ▷ *adj* **2** of or relating to the regions north of the Arctic Circle

Arctic Circle *n* the imaginary circle round the earth, parallel to the equator, at latitude 66° 32′ N; it marks the northernmost point at which the Sun appears above the level of the horizon on the winter solstice

arctic hare *n* a large hare of the Canadian Arctic whose fur is white in winter

Arctic Ocean *n* the ocean surrounding the North Pole, north of the Arctic Circle. Area: about 14 100 000 sq km (5 440 000 sq miles)

arctic willow *n* a low-growing shrub of the tundra

Arcturus (ɑːk'tjʊərəs) *n* the brightest star in the constellation Boötes: a red giant [c14 from L, from Gk *Arktouros*, from *arktos* bear + *ouros* guard, keeper]

arcuate ('ɑːkjʊɪt) *adj* shaped or bent like an arc or bow [c17 from L *arcuāre*, from *arcus* ARC]

arc welding *n* a technique in which metal is welded by heat generated by an electric arc > **arc welder** *n*

-ard *or* **-art** *suffix forming nouns* indicating a person who does something, esp to excess: *braggart; drunkard* [via OF, of Gmc origin]

Ardèche (*French* ardɛʃ) *n* a department of S France, in Rhône-Alpes region. Capital: Privas. Pop: 286 023 (1999). Area: 5556 sq km (2167 sq miles)

Arden[1] ('ɑːdᵊn) *n* **Forest of** a region of N Warwickshire, part of a former forest: scene of Shakespeare's *As You Like It*

Arden[2] ('ɑːdᵊn) *n* **John** born 1930, British dramatist and novelist. His plays include *Serjeant Musgrave's Dance* (1959) and *The Workhouse Donkey* (1963); novels include *Silence Among the Weapons* (1982): he often works in collaboration with his wife Margaretta D'Arcy

Ardennes (ɑː'dɛn; *French* ardɛn) *n* **1** a department of NE France, in Champagne-Ardenne region. Capital: Mézières. Pop: 290 130 (1999). Area: 5253 sq km (2049 sq miles) **2 the** a wooded plateau in SE Belgium, Luxembourg, and NE France: scene of heavy fighting in both World Wars

ardent ('ɑːdᵊnt) *adj* **1** expressive of or characterized by intense desire or emotion **2** intensely enthusiastic; eager **3** glowing or shining: *ardent eyes* **4 ardent spirits** alcoholic drinks [c14 from L *ārdēre* to burn] > **'ardency** *n* > **'ardently** *adv*

ardour *or US* **ardor** ('ɑːdə) *n* **1** feelings of great intensity and warmth **2** eagerness; zeal [c14 from OF, from L *ārdor*, from *ārdēre* to burn]

Ards (ɑːdz) *n* a district of Northern Ireland, in Co. Down. Pop: 73 244 (2001). Area: 368 sq km (142 sq miles)

arduous ('ɑːdjuːəs) *adj* **1** difficult to accomplish; strenuous **2** hard to endure; harsh **3** steep or difficult: *an arduous track* [c16 from L *arduus* steep, difficult]

> 'arduously *adv* > 'arduousness *n*

are[1] (ɑː; *unstressed* ə) *vb* the plural form of the present tense of **be** and the singular form used with *you* [OE *aron*, second person pl of *bēon* to BE]

are[2] (ɑː) *n* a unit of area equal to 100 square metres [c19 from F, from L *ārea* piece of ground; see AREA]

area ('ɛərɪə) *n* **1** any flat, curved, or irregular expanse of a surface **2a** the extent of a two-dimensional surface: *the area of a triangle* **2b** the two-dimensional extent of a plane or surface: *the area of a sphere* **3** a section or part **4** region; district **5a** a geographical division of administrative responsibility **5b** (*as modifier*): *area manager* **6** a part or section, as of a building, town, etc, having some specified function: *reception area; commercial area* **7** the range or scope of anything **8** a subject field or field of study **9** Also called: **areaway** a sunken area, usually enclosed, giving light, air, and sometimes access to a cellar basement [c16 from L: level ground, threshing-floor; rel. to *ārēre* to be dry] > 'areal *adj*
▷ www.naic.edu

arena (ə'riːnə) *n* **1** an enclosure or platform, usually surrounded by seats, in which sports events, entertainments, etc, take place: *a boxing arena* **2** the central area of an ancient Roman amphitheatre, in which gladiatorial contests were held **3** a sphere of intense activity: *the political arena* [c17 from L *harēna* sand, place where sand was strewn for the combats]

arenaceous (ˌærɪ'neɪʃəs) *adj* **1** (of sedimentary rocks) composed of sand **2** (of plants) growing in a sandy soil [c17 from L *harēnāceus* sandy, from *harēna* sand]

Arendt ('ɛərənt) *n* **Hannah** 1906–75, US political philosopher, born in Germany. Her publications include *The Origins of Totalitarianism* (1951) and *Eichmann in Jerusalem* (1961)

aren't (ɑːnt) **1** *contraction of* are not **2** *inf, chiefly Brit* (used in interrogative sentences) *contraction of* am not

areola (ə'rɪələ) *n, pl* **areolae** (-ˌliː) *or* **areolas** *anat* any small circular area, such as the pigmented ring around the human nipple [c17 from L: dim. of AREA] > **a'reolar** *or* **areolate** (ə'rɪəlɪt, -ˌleɪt) *adj*

areole ('ærɪəʊl) *n* **1** *biol* a space outlined on a surface, such as an area between veins on a leaf **2** a sunken area on a cactus from which spines, hairs, etc, arise > 'areoˌlate *adj*

Areopagus (ˌærɪ'ɒpəgəs) *n* **1a** the hill to the northwest of the Acropolis in Athens **1b** (in ancient Athens) the judicial council whose members (Areopagites) met on this hill **2** *literary* any high court [via Latin from Greek *Areiopagus*, contracted from *Areios pagos*, hill of Ares]

Arequipa (ˌærɪ'kiːpə; *Spanish* are'kipa) *n* a city in S Peru, at an altitude of 2250 m (7500 ft): founded in 1540 on the site of an Inca city. Pop: 710 103 (1998 est)

Ares ('ɛəriːz) *n Greek myth* the god of war, born of Zeus and Hera. Roman counterpart: **Mars**

arête (ə'reɪt, ə'rɛt) *n* a sharp ridge that separates glacial valleys [c19 from F: fishbone, ridge, from L *arista* ear of corn, fishbone]

Arethusa (ˌærɪ'θjuːzə) *n Greek myth* a nymph who was changed into a spring on the island of Ortygia to escape the amorous advances of the river god Alpheus

Arezzo (ə'rɛtsəʊ; *Italian* a'rettso) *n* a city in central Italy, in E Tuscany. Pop: 91 527 (1990). Ancient Latin name: **Arretium**

Arg. *abbrev for* Argentina

argal ('ɑːgəl) *n* another name for **argol**

argali ('ɑːgəlɪ) *or* **argal** *n, pl* **argali** *or* **argals** a wild sheep, with massive horns in the male, inhabiting semidesert regions in central Asia [c18 from Mongolian]

argent ('ɑːdʒənt) *n* **a** an archaic or poetic word for **silver** **b** (*as adj; often postpositive, esp in heraldry*): *a bend argent* [c15 from OF, from L]

Argenteuil (*French* arʒɑ̃tœj) *n* a suburb of Paris, France, with a convent (656) that became famous when Héloïse was abbess (12th century). Pop: 93 096 (1990)

argentiferous (ˌɑːdʒən'tɪfərəs) *adj* containing or bearing silver

Argentina (ˌɑːdʒən'tiːnə) *n* a republic in southern South America: colonized by the Spanish from 1516 onwards; gained independence in 1816 and became a republic in 1852; ruled by military dictatorships for much of the 20th century; civilian rule restored in 1983; consists chiefly of subtropical plains and forests (the Chaco) in the north, temperate plains (the pampas) in the central parts, the Andes in the west, and an infertile plain extending to Tierra del Fuego in the south (Patagonia); an important meat producer. Language: Spanish. Religion: Roman Catholic. Currency: peso. Capital: Buenos Aires. Pop: 37 487 000 (2001 est). Area: 2 776 653 sq km (1 072 067 sq miles). Also called: **the Argentine**
▷ www.nic.ar
▷ www.turismo.gov.ar

argentine ('ɑːdʒənˌtaɪn) *adj* **1** of or resembling silver ▷ *n* **2** a small marine fish characterized by a long silvery body

Argentine ('ɑːdʒənˌtiːn, -ˌtaɪn) *n* **1** **the** another name for ▷ **Argentina** **2** a native or inhabitant of Argentina. *adj* **3** of or relating to Argentina ▷ Also (for senses 2, 3) **Argentinian** (ˌɑːdʒən'tɪnɪən)

Argerich (ˌɑːgəritʃ) *n* **Martha** born 1941, Argentinian concert pianist

argillaceous (ˌɑːdʒɪ'leɪʃəs) *adj* (of sedimentary rocks) composed of very fine-grained material, such as clay [c18 from L *argilla* white clay, from Gk, from *argos* white]

Argive ('ɑːdʒaɪv, -gaɪv) *adj* **1** of or relating to Argos **2** a literary word for **Greek** ▷ *n* **3** an ancient Greek, esp one from Argos

Argo ('ɑːgəʊ) *n Greek myth* the ship in which Jason sailed in search of the Golden Fleece

argol ('ɑːgɒl) *or* **argal** ('ɑːgəl) *n* crude potassium hydrogentartrate [c14 from Anglo-F *argoil*, from ?]

Argolis ('ɑːgəlɪs) *n* **1** a department and ancient region of Greece, in the NE Peloponnese. Capital: Nauplion. Pop: 97 636 (1991). Area: 2261 sq km (873 sq miles) **2** **Gulf of** an inlet of the Aegean Sea, in the E Peloponnese

Aa

argon ('ɑːgɒn) *n* an unreactive colourless odourless element of the rare gas series that forms almost 1 per cent of the atmosphere. It is used in electric lights. Symbol: Ar; atomic no.: 18; atomic wt.: 39.95 [c19 from Gk, from *argos* inactive, from A-[1] + *ergon* work]

Argonaut ('ɑːgəˌnɔːt) *n* **1** *Greek myth* one of the heroes who sailed with Jason in quest of the Golden Fleece **2** a person who took part in the Californian gold rush of 1849 **3** (*not cap*) another name for the **paper nautilus** [c16 from Gk *Argonautēs*, from *Argō* the name of Jason's ship + *nautēs* sailor] > ˌArgo'nautic *adj*

Argonne ('ɑːgɒn; *French* argɔn) *n* **the** a wooded region of NE France: scene of major battles in both World Wars

Argos ('ɑːgɒs, -gəs) *n* an ancient city in SE Greece, in the NE Peloponnese: one of the oldest Greek cities, it dominated the Peloponnese in the 7th century BC. Pop: 22 000 (1995 est)

argosy ('ɑːgəsɪ) *n, pl* **argosies** *arch or poetic* a large abundantly laden merchant ship, or a fleet of such ships [c16 from It. *Ragusea* (*nave*) (ship) of Ragusa]

argot ('ɑːgəʊ) *n* slang or jargon peculiar to a particular group, esp (formerly) a group of thieves [c19 from F, from ?]

Argovie (argɔvi) *n* the French name for **Aargau**

arguable ('ɑːgjʊəbᵊl) *adj* **1** capable of being disputed **2** plausible; reasonable > 'arguably *adv*

argue ('ɑːgjuː) *vb* **argues, arguing, argued** **1** (*intr*) to quarrel; wrangle **2** (*intr; often foll by for or against*) to present supporting or opposing reasons or cases in a dispute **3** (*tr; may take a clause as object*) to try to prove by presenting reasons **4** (*tr; often passive*) to debate or discuss

5 (*tr*) to persuade 6 (*tr*) to suggest: *her looks argue despair* [C14 from OF *arguer* to assert, from L *arguere* to make clear, accuse] > 'arguer *n*

argufy ('ɑːgjʊˌfaɪ) *vb* **argufies, argufying, argufied** *facetious or dialect* to argue or quarrel, esp over something trivial

argument ('ɑːgjʊmənt) *n* 1 a quarrel; altercation 2 a discussion in which reasons are put forward; debate 3 (*sometimes pl*) a point or series of reasons presented to support or oppose a proposition 4 a summary of the plot or subject of a book, etc 5 *logic* 5a a process of reasoning in which the conclusion can be shown to be true or false 5b the middle term of a syllogism 6 *maths* another name for **independent variable** of a function

argumentation (ˌɑːgjʊmɛnˈteɪʃən) *n* 1 the process of reasoning methodically 2 argument; debate

argumentative (ˌɑːgjʊˈmɛntətɪv) *adj* 1 given to arguing 2 characterized by argument; controversial

Argus ('ɑːgəs) *n* 1 *Greek myth* a giant with a hundred eyes who was made guardian of the heifer Io 2 a vigilant person

Argus-eyed *adj* observant; vigilant

argy-bargy *or* **argie-bargie** ('ɑːdʒɪˈbɑːdʒɪ) *n, pl* **argy-bargies** *Brit inf* a wrangling argument or verbal dispute [C19 from Scot., from dialect *argle*, prob. from ARGUE]

Argyll and Bute (ɑːˈgaɪl) *n* a council area in W Scotland on the Atlantic Ocean: in 1975 the historical counties of Argyllshire and Bute became part of Strathclyde region; in 1996 they were reinstated as a single unitary authority. Argyll and Bute is mountainous and includes the islands of Bute, Mull, Islay, and Jura. Administrative centre: Lochgilphead. Pop: 91 306 (2001). Area: 6930 sq km (2676 sq miles)

Argyllshire (ɑːˈgaɪlʃɪə, -ʃə) *n* (until 1975) a county of W Scotland, part of Strathclyde region (1975–96), now part of Argyll and Bute

Århus (*Danish* ˈɔrhuːs) *n* a variant spelling of **Aarhus**

aria ('ɑːrɪə) *n* an elaborate accompanied song for solo voice from a cantata, opera, or oratorio [C18 from It.: tune, AIR]

Ariadne (ˌærɪˈædnɪ) *n Greek myth* daughter of Minos and Pasiphaë: she gave Theseus the thread with which he found his way out of the Minotaur's labyrinth

Arian ('ɛərɪən) *adj* 1 of or relating to Arius or to Arianism ▷ *n* 2 an adherent of Arianism

-arian *suffix forming nouns* indicating a person or thing that advocates, believes, or is associated with something: *vegetarian; librarian* [from L *-ārius* -ARY + -AN]

Arianism ('ɛərɪəˌnɪzəm) *n* the doctrine of Arius, declared heretical, which asserted that Christ was not of one substance with the Father

Arica (əˈriːkə; *Spanish* aˈrika) *n* a port in extreme N Chile: awarded to Chile in 1929 after the lengthy Tacna-Arica dispute with Peru; outlet for Bolivian and Peruvian trade. Pop: 178 547 (1999 est). See also **Tacna-Arica**

arid ('ærɪd) *adj* 1 having little or no rain; dry 2 devoid of interest [C17 from L *āridus*, from *ārēre* to be dry] > **aridity** (əˈrɪdɪtɪ) *or* 'aridness *n*

arid zone *n* either of the zones of latitude 15–30° N and S, with low rainfall and desert or semidesert terrain

Ariège (*French* arjɛʒ) *n* a department of SW France, in Midi-Pyrénées region. Capital: Foix. Pop: 137 205 (1999). Area: 4903 sq km (1912 sq miles)

Aries ('ɛəriːz) *n, Latin genitive* **Arietis** (əˈraɪɪtɪs) 1 *astron* a N constellation 2 *astrol* Also called: the **Ram** the first sign of the zodiac. The sun is in this sign between about March 21 and April 19 [C14 from L: ram]

aright (əˈraɪt) *adv* correctly; rightly; properly

aril ('ærɪl) *n* an additional covering formed on certain seeds, such as those of the yew and nutmeg, after fertilization [C18 from NL, from Med. L *arilli* raisins, pips of grapes] > 'arilˌlate *adj*

Arimathea *or* **Arimathaea** (ˌærɪməˈθiːə) *n* a town in ancient Palestine: location unknown

Ariminum (əˈrɪmɪnəm) *n* the ancient name of **Rimini**

arioso (ˌɑːrɪˈəʊzəʊ) *n, pl* **ariosos** *or* **ariosi** (-siː) *music* a recitative with the lyrical quality of an aria [C18 from It., from ARIA]

Ariosto (*Italian* aˈrjɔsto) *n* **Ludovico** (ludoˈviːko) 1474–1533, Italian poet, famous for his romantic epic *Orlando Furioso* (1516)

arise (əˈraɪz) *vb* **arises, arising, arose, arisen** (əˈrɪzᵊn) (*intr*) 1 to come into being; originate 2 (foll by *from*) to proceed as a consequence 3 to get or stand up, as from a sitting or lying position 4 to come into notice 5 to ascend [OE *ārīsan*]

aristo ('ærɪstəʊ, əˈrɪstəʊ) *n, pl* **aristos** *inf* short for **aristocrat**

aristocracy (ˌærɪˈstɒkrəsɪ) *n, pl* **aristocracies** 1 a privileged class of people usually of high birth; the nobility 2 such a class as the ruling body of a state 3 government by such a class 4 a state governed by such a class 5 a class of people considered to be outstanding in a sphere of activity [C16 from LL, from Gk *aristokratia* rule by the best-born, from *aristos* best; see -CRACY]

aristocrat ('ærɪstəˌkræt) *n* 1 a member of the aristocracy 2 a person who has the manners or qualities of a member of a privileged class 3 a supporter of aristocracy as a form of government

aristocratic (ˌærɪstəˈkrætɪk) *adj* 1 relating to or characteristic of aristocracy or an aristocrat 2 elegant or stylish in appearance and behaviour > ˌ**aristo'cratically** *adv*

Aristophanes (ˌærɪˈstɒfəˌniːz) *n* ?448–?380 BC, Greek comic dramatist, who satirized leading contemporary figures such as Socrates and Euripides. Eleven of his plays are extant, including *The Clouds, The Frogs, The Birds*, and *Lysistrata*

Aristotelian (ˌærɪstəˈtiːlɪən) *adj* 1 of or relating to Aristotle or to his philosophy ▷ *n* 2 a follower of Aristotle

Aristotelian logic *n* 1 traditional logic, esp relying on the theory of syllogism 2 the logical method of Aristotle, esp as developed in the Middle Ages

Aristotle ('ærɪˌstɒtᵊl) *n* 384–322 BC, Greek philosopher; pupil of Plato, tutor of Alexander the Great, and founder of the Peripatetic school at Athens; author of works on logic, ethics, politics, poetics, rhetoric, biology, zoology, and metaphysics. His works influenced Muslim philosophy and science and medieval scholastic philosophy

arithmetic *n* (əˈrɪθmətɪk) 1 the branch of mathematics concerned with numerical calculations, such as addition, subtraction, multiplication, and division 2 calculations involving numerical operations 3 knowledge of or skill in using arithmetic ▷ *adj* (ˌærɪθˈmɛtɪk) *also* **arithmetical** 4 of, relating to, or using arithmetic [C13 from L, from Gk *arithmētikē*, from *arithmein* to count, from *arithmos* number] > ˌ**arith'metically** *adv* > aˌ**rithme'tician** *n*

arithmetic mean *n* the average value of a set of terms or quantities, expressed as their sum divided by their number: *the arithmetic mean of 3, 4, and 8 is 5*. Also called: **average**

arithmetic progression *n* a sequence, each term of which differs from the succeeding term by a constant amount, such as 3,6,9,12

-arium *suffix forming nouns* indicating a place for or associated with something: *aquarium; solarium* [from L *-ārium*, neuter of *-ārius* -ARY]

Arius ('ɛərɪəs) *n* ?250–336 AD, Greek Christian theologian, originator of the doctrine of Arianism

Ariz. *abbrev for* Arizona

Arizona (ˌærɪˈzəʊnə) *n* a state of the southwestern US: consists of the Colorado plateau in the northeast, including the Grand Canyon, divided from desert in the southwest by mountains rising over 3750 m (12 500 ft). Capital: Phoenix. Pop: 5 130 632 (2000). Area: 293 750 sq km (113 417 sq miles). Abbreviations: **Ariz** *or* (with zip code) **AZ**

Arjuna (ˈɑːdʒʊnə) *n Hindu myth* the most important of the five princes in the *Mahabharata*. Krishna served as his charioteer in the battle with the Kauravas

ark (ɑːk) *n* **1** the vessel that Noah built which survived the Flood (Genesis 6–9) **2** a place or thing offering shelter or protection **3** *dialect* a box [OE *arc*, from L *arca* box, chest]

Ark (ɑːk) *n judaism* **1** Also called: **Holy Ark** the cupboard in a synagogue in which the Torah scrolls are kept **2** Also called: **Ark of the Covenant** the most sacred symbol of God's presence among the Hebrew people, carried in their journey from Sinai to the Promised Land (Canaan)

Ark. *abbrev for* Arkansas

Arkansas *n* **1** (ˈɑːkənˌsɔː) a state of the southern US: mountainous in the north and west, with the alluvial plain of the Mississippi in the east; has the only diamond mine in the US; the chief US producer of bauxite. Capital: Little Rock. Pop: 2 673 400 (2000). Area: 134 537 sq km (51 945 sq miles). Abbreviations: **Ark** *or* (with zip code) **AR** **2** (ɑːˈkænzəs) a river in the S central US, rising in central Colorado and flowing east and southeast to join the Mississippi in Arkansas. Length: 2335 km (1450 miles) > **Arkansan** (ɑːˈkænzən) *n, adj*

Arkhangelsk (arˈxangɪljsk) *n* the Russian name for **Archangel**

Arkwright (ˈɑːkraɪt) *n* Sir **Richard** 1732–92, English cotton manufacturer: inventor of the spinning frame (1769) which produced cotton thread strong enough to be used as a warp

Arles (ɑːlz; *French* arl) *n* **1** a city in SE France, on the Rhône: Roman amphitheatre. Pop: 52 590 (1990) **2** **Kingdom of** a kingdom in SE France which had dissolved by 1378: known as the Kingdom of Burgundy until about 1200

Arlington (ˈɑːlɪŋtən) *n* a county of N Virginia: site of **Arlington National Cemetery**

Arlon (*French* arlɔ̃) *n* a town in SE Belgium, capital of Luxembourg province. Pop: 17 000 (1991 est)

arm¹ (ɑːm) *n* **1** (in man) either of the upper limbs from the shoulder to the wrist. Related adj: **brachial** **2** the part of either of the upper limbs from the elbow to the wrist; forearm **3a** the corresponding limb of any other vertebrate **3b** an armlike appendage of some invertebrates **4** an object that covers or supports the human arm, esp the sleeve of a garment or the side of a chair, etc **5** anything considered to resemble an arm in appearance, function, etc: *an arm of the sea; the arm of a record player* **6** an administrative subdivision of an organization: *an arm of the government* **7** power; authority: *the arm of the law* **8** **arm in arm** with arms linked **9** **at arm's length** at a distance **10** **in the arms of Morpheus** sleeping **11** **with open arms** with great warmth and hospitality [OE]

arm² (ɑːm) *vb* **1** to equip with weapons as a preparation for war **2** (*tr*) to provide (a person or thing) with something that strengthens, protects, or increases efficiency **3a** (*tr*) to activate (a fuse) so that it will explode at the required time **3b** to prepare (an explosive device) for use by introducing a detonator, etc ▷ *n* **4** (*usually pl*) a weapon, esp a firearm [c14 from OF *armes*, from L *arma* arms, equipment]

Arm. *abbrev for:* Armenia(n)

ARM. *abbrev for:* adjustable rate mortgage

armada (ɑːˈmɑːdə) *n* **1** a large number of ships or aircraft **2** (*cap.*) **the** Also called: **Spanish Armada** the great fleet sent by Philip II of Spain against England in 1588 [c16 from Sp., from Med. L *armāta* fleet, armed forces, from L *armāre* to provide with arms]

armadillo (ˌɑːməˈdɪləʊ) *n, pl* **armadillos** a burrowing mammal of Central and South America with a covering of strong horny plates over most of the body [c16 from Sp., dim. of *armado* armed (man), from L *armātus* armed; cf. ARMADA]

Armageddon (ˌɑːməˈɡɛdᵊn) *n* **1** *New Testament* the final battle between good and evil at the end of the world **2** a catastrophic and extremely destructive conflict [c19 from LL, from Gk, from Heb. *har megiddōn*, mountain district of *Megiddo* (in N Palestine)]

Armagh (ɑːˈmɑː) *n* **1** a historical county of S Northern Ireland: in 1973 it was replaced for administrative purposes by the districts of Armagh and Craigavon. Area: 1326 sq km (512 sq miles) **2** a district in Northern Ireland, in Co. Armagh. Pop: 54 263 (2001). Area: 667 sq km (258 sq miles) **3** a town in S Northern Ireland, in Armagh district, Co. Armagh: seat of Roman Catholic and Protestant archbishops. Pop: 14 640 (1991)

Armalite (ˈɑːməlaɪt) *n trademark* a lightweight high-velocity rifle of various calibres, capable of automatic and semiautomatic operation [c20 from *Armalite* Division, Fairchild Engine and Airplane Company, manufacturers]

armament (ˈɑːməmənt) *n* **1** (*often pl*) the weapon equipment of a military vehicle, ship, or aircraft **2** a military force raised and armed ready for war **3** preparation for war [c17 from L *armāmenta* utensils, from *armāre* to equip]

Armani (ɑːˈmɑːnɪ; *Italian* arˈmaːni) *n* **Giorgio** born 1936, Italian fashion designer, noted for his restrained classical style

armature (ˈɑːmətjʊə) *n* **1** a revolving structure in an electric motor or generator, wound with the coils that carry the current **2** any part of an electric machine or device that moves under the influence of a magnetic field or within which an electromotive force is induced **3** Also called: **keeper** a soft iron or steel bar placed across the poles of a magnet to close the magnetic circuit **4** *sculpture* a framework to support the clay or other material used in modelling **5** the protective outer covering of an animal or plant [c15 from L *armātūra* armour, equipment, from *armāre* to furnish with equipment]

armchair (ˈɑːmˌtʃɛə) *n* **1** a chair, esp an upholstered one, that has side supports for the arms or elbows **2** (*modifier*) taking or involving no active part: *an armchair strategist*

armed¹ (ɑːmd) *adj* **1** equipped with or supported by arms, armour, etc **2** prepared for conflict or any difficulty **3** (of an explosive device) prepared for use **4** (of plants) having the protection of thorns, spines, etc

armed² (ɑːmd) *adj* **a** having an arm or arms **b** (*in combination*): *long-armed; one-armed*

armed forces *pl n* the military forces of a nation or nations, including the army, navy, air force, etc

armed response unit *n* a unit of police officers who are trained to use firearms in situations where unarmed police officers would be in danger

armed response vehicle *n* a police vehicle carrying armed officers who are trained to respond to incidents involving firearms

Armenia (ɑːˈmiːnɪə) *n* **1** a republic in NW Asia: originally part of the historic Armenian kingdom; acquired by Russia in 1828; became the Armenian Soviet Socialist Republic in 1936; gained independence in 1991. It is mountainous, rising over 4000 m (13 000 ft). Language: Armenian. Religion: Christian (Armenian Apostolic) majority. Currency: dram. Capital: Yerevan. Pop: 3 807 000 (2001 est). Area: 29 800 sq km (11 490 sq miles) **2** a former kingdom in W Asia, between the Black Sea and the Caspian Sea, south of Georgia **3** a town in central Colombia: centre of a coffee-growing district. Pop: 283 842 (1997 est) > **Arˈmenian** *adj, n*
▷ www.armenia.com

Armentières ('ɑːmən,tɪəz; *French* armɑ̃tjɛr) *n* a town in N France: site of battles in both World Wars. Pop: 26 240 (1990)

armful ('ɑːmfʊl) *n, pl* **armfuls** the amount that can be held by one or both arms

armhole ('ɑːm,həʊl) *n* the opening in an article of clothing through which the arm passes

Armidale ('ɑːmɪ,deɪl) *n* a town in Australia, in NE New South Wales: a centre for tourism. Pop: 21 606 (1991 est)

armillary sphere (ɑː'mɪlərɪ) *n* a model of the celestial sphere formerly used in fixing the positions of heavenly bodies

Arminian (ɑː'mɪnɪən) *adj* denoting, relating to, or believing in the Protestant doctrines of Jacobus Arminius, which rejected absolute predestination and stressed free will in man > **Ar'minian,ism** *n*

armistice ('ɑːmɪstɪs) *n* an agreement between opposing armies to suspend hostilities; truce [c18 from NL, from L *arma* arms + *sistere* to stop]

Armistice Day ('ɑːmɪstɪs) *n* the anniversary of the signing of the armistice that ended World War I, on Nov 11, 1918. See also **Remembrance Sunday**

Armitage ('ɑːmətɪdʒ) *n* **Simon** (**Robert**) born 1963, British poet and writer, whose collections include *Zoom!* (1989), *Killing Time* (1999), and *Universal Home Doctor* (2002)

armlet ('ɑːmlɪt) *n* **1** a small arm, as of a lake **2** a band or bracelet worn round the arm

armoire (ɑːm'wɑː) *n* a large cabinet, originally used for storing weapons [c16 from F, from OF *armaire*, from L *armārium* chest, closet; see AMBRY]

armorial (ɑː'mɔːrɪəl) *adj* of or relating to heraldry or heraldic arms

armour *or US* **armor** ('ɑːmə) *n* **1** any defensive covering, esp that of metal, chain mail, etc, worn by medieval warriors **2** the protective metal plates on a tank, warship, etc **3** *mil* armoured fighting vehicles in general **4** any protective covering, such as the shell of certain animals **5** heraldic insignia; arms ▹ *vb* **6** (*tr*) to equip or cover with armour [c13 from OF *armure*, from L *armātūra* armour, equipment]

armoured *or US* **armored** ('ɑːməd) *adj* **1** having a protective covering **2** comprising units making use of armoured vehicles: *an armoured brigade*

armourer *or US* **armorer** ('ɑːmərə) *n* **1** a person who makes or mends arms and armour **2** a person employed in the maintenance of small arms and weapons in a military unit

armour plate *n* a tough heavy steel often hardened on the surface, used for protecting warships, tanks, vehicles, etc

armoury *or US* **armory** ('ɑːmərɪ) *n, pl* **armouries** *or* **armories** **1** a secure place for the storage of weapons **2** armour generally; military supplies **3** *Canad* a building in which troops drill **4** resources, such as arguments, on which to draw: *a few choice terms from her armoury of invective*

armpit ('ɑːm,pɪt) *n* **1** the small depression beneath the arm where it joins the shoulder. Technical name: **axilla** **2** *sl* an extremely unpleasant place: *the armpit of the Middle West*

armrest ('ɑːm,rɛst) *n* the part of a chair, sofa, etc, that supports the arm. Sometimes shortened to **arm**

arms (ɑːmz) *pl n* **1** weapons collectively. See also **small arms** **2** military exploits: *prowess in arms* **3** the official heraldic symbols of a family, state, etc **4** **bear arms** **4a** to carry weapons **4b** to serve in the armed forces **4c** to have a coat of arms **5** **in** *or* **under arms** armed and prepared for war **6** **lay down one's arms** to stop fighting; surrender **7** **take** (**up**) **arms** to prepare to fight **8** **up in arms** indignant; prepared to protest strongly [c13 from OF, from L *arma*; see ARM[2]]

Armstrong ('ɑːm,strɒŋ) *n* **1** **Edwin Howard** 1890–1954, US electrical engineer; invented the superheterodyne radio receiver and the FM radio **2** (**Daniel**) **Louis**, known as *Satchmo*. 1900–71, US jazz trumpeter, bandleader, and singer **3** **Gillian** born 1950, Australian film director; her films include *My Brilliant Career* (1978), *Little Women* (1994), and *Charlotte Gray* (2001) **4** **Neil** (**Alden**) born 1930, US astronaut; commanded Apollo 11 on the first manned lunar landing during which he became the first man to set foot on the moon on July 20, 1969

arm wrestling *n* a contest of strength in which two people rest the elbow of one arm on a flat surface, grasp each other's hand, and try to force their opponent's forearm down flat

army ('ɑːmɪ) *n, pl* **armies** **1** the military land forces of a nation **2** a military unit usually consisting of two or more corps with supporting arms and services **3** (*modifier*) of or characteristic of an army **4** any large body of people united for some specific purpose **5** a large number of people, animals, etc [c14 from OF, from Med. L *armāta* armed forces]

▹ www.army.mod.uk
▹ www.army.dnd.ca
▹ www.army.mil.nz
▹ www.army.gov.au
▹ www.mil.za

army ant *n* any of various tropical American predatory ants which travel in vast hordes preying on other animals. Also called: **legionary ant**

army worm *n* a type of caterpillar which travels in vast hordes and is a serious pest of cereal crops

Arnaud ('ɑːnəʊ; *French* arno) *n* **Yvonne** 1892–1958, French actress, who was well-known on the London stage and in British films. A theatre in Guildford is named after her

Arne (ɑːn) *n* **Thomas** (**Augustine**) 1710–78, English composer, noted for his setting of Shakespearean songs and for his song *Rule Britannia*

Arnhem ('ɑːnəm) *n* a city in the E Netherlands, capital of Gelderland province, on the Rhine: site of a World War II battle. Pop: 137 222 (1999 est)

Arnhem Land *n* a region of N Australia in the N Northern Territory, large areas of which are reserved for native Australians

arnica ('ɑːnɪkə) *n* **1** any of a genus of N temperate or arctic plants having yellow flowers **2** the tincture of the dried flower heads of any of these plants, used in treating bruises [c18 from NL, from ?]

Arnim (*German* 'arnɪm) *n* **Achim von** ('axɪm fɔn) 1781–1831, German romantic poet. He published, with Clemens Brentano, the collection of folk songs, *Des Knaben Wunderhorn* (1805–08)

Arno ('ɑːnəʊ) *n* a river in central Italy, rising in the Apennines and flowing through Florence to the Ligurian Sea. Length: about 240 km (150 miles)

Arnold[1] ('ɑːnəld) *n* a town in N central England, in S Nottinghamshire. Pop: 37 646 (1991)

Arnold[2] ('ɑːnəld) *n* **1** Sir **Malcolm** born 1921, English composer, esp of orchestral works in a traditional idiom **2** **Matthew** 1822–88, English poet, essayist, and literary critic, noted particularly for his poems *Sohrab and Rustum* (1853) and *Dover Beach* (1867), and for his *Essays in Criticism* (1865) and *Culture and Anarchy* (1869) **3** his father, **Thomas** 1795–1842, English historian and educationalist, headmaster of Rugby School, noted for his reforms in public-school education

aroha ('ɑːrɒhə) *n* NZ love, compassion, or affectionate regard [Maori]

aroid ('ærɔɪd, 'ɛər-) *adj* of or relating to a plant family that includes the arum, calla, and anthurium [c19 from ARUM + -OID]

aroint thee *or* **ye** (ə'rɔɪnt) *sentence substitute arch* away! begone! [c17 from ?]

aroma (ə'rəʊmə) *n* **1** a distinctive usually pleasant smell, esp of spices, wines, and plants **2** a subtle pervasive quality or atmosphere [c18 via L from Gk: spice]

aromatherapy (əˌrəʊməˈθɛrəpɪ) *n* the use of fragrant essential oils as a treatment in alternative medicine to relieve tension and cure certain minor ailments > **aˌromaˈtherapist** *n*

aromatic (ˌærəˈmætɪk) *adj* **1** having a distinctive, usually fragrant smell **2** (of an organic compound) having an unsaturated ring, esp containing a benzene ring ▷ Cf **aliphatic** ▷ *n* **3** something, such as a plant or drug, giving off a fragrant smell > ˌ**aroˈmatically** *adv* > **aˌromaˈticity** *n*

aromatize *or* **aromatise** (əˈrəʊməˌtaɪz) *vb* **aromatizes, aromatizing, aromatized** *or* **aromatises, aromatising, aromatised** (*tr*) to make aromatic > **aˌromatiˈzation** *or* **aˌromatiˈsation** *n*

arose (əˈrəʊz) *vb* the past tense of **arise**

around (əˈraʊnd) *prep* **1** situated at various points in: *a lot of shelves around the house* **2** from place to place in: *driving around Ireland* **3** somewhere in or near **4** approximately in: *it happened around 1957* ▷ *adv* **5** surrounding, encircling, or enclosing: *a 'band around her head* **6** in all directions from a point of reference: *he owns the land for ten miles around* **7** in the vicinity, esp restlessly but idly: *to stand around* **8** in no particular place or direction: *dotted around* **9** *inf* (of people) active and prominent in a particular area or profession **10** *inf* present in some place (the exact location being unknown or unspecified) **11** *inf* in circulation; available: *that type of phone has been around for some years now* **12** *inf* to many places, so as to have gained considerable experience, often of a worldly or social nature: *I've been around* [c17 (rare earlier): from A-² + ROUND]

> USAGE In American English, *around* is usually used instead of *round* in adverbial and prepositional senses, except in a few fixed phrases such as *all year round*. The use of *around* in adverbial senses is less common in British English

arouse (əˈraʊz) *vb* **arouses, arousing, aroused 1** (*tr*) to evoke or elicit (a reaction, emotion, or response) **2** to awaken from sleep > **aˈrousal** *n* > **aˈrouser** *n*

Arp (*French* arp) *n* **Jean** (ʒɑ̃) or **Hans** (hans) 1887–1966, Alsatian sculptor, painter, and poet, cofounder of the Dada movement in Zürich, noted particularly for his abstract organic sculptures based on natural forms

arpeggio (ɑːˈpɛdʒɪəʊ) *n, pl* **arpeggios** a chord whose notes are played or sung in rapid succession rather than simultaneously [c18 from It., from *arpeggiare* to perform on the harp, from *arpa* HARP]

arquebus (ˈɑːkwɪbəs) *or* **harquebus** *n* a portable long-barrelled gun dating from the 15th century [c16 via OF from MDu. *hakebusse*, lit.: hook gun, from the shape of the butt, from *hake* hook + *busse* box, gun, from LL *busis* box]

arr. *abbrev for*: **1** arranged (by) **2** arrival

arrack *or* **arak** (ˈærək) *n* a coarse spirit distilled in various Eastern countries from grain, rice, sugar cane, etc [c17 from Ar. *'araq* sweat, sweet juice, liquor]

arraign (əˈreɪn) *vb* (*tr*) **1** to bring (a prisoner) before a court to answer an indictment **2** to call to account; accuse [c14 from OF, from Vulgar L *ratiōnāre* (unattested) to talk, argue, from L *ratiō* a reasoning] > **arˈraigner** *n* > **arˈraignment** *n*

Arran (ˈærən) *n* an island off the SW coast of Scotland, in the Firth of Clyde. Pop: 4000 (latest est). Area: 427 sq km (165 sq miles)

arrange (əˈreɪndʒ) *vb* **arranges, arranging, arranged 1** (*tr*) to put into a proper or systematic order **2** (*tr; may take a clause as object or an infinitive*) to arrive at an agreement about **3** (when *intr*, often foll by *for*; when *tr*, *may take a clause as object or an infinitive*) to make plans or preparations in advance (for something): *we arranged for her to be met* **4** (*tr*) to adapt (a musical composition) for performance in a different way, esp on different instruments **5** (*intr; often foll by with*) to come to an agreement [c14 from OF *arangier*, from A-² + *rangier* to put in a row, RANGE] > **arˈrangeable** *adj* > **arˈranger** *n*

arrangement (əˈreɪndʒmənt) *n* **1** the act of arranging or being arranged **2** the form in which things are arranged **3** a thing composed of various ordered parts: *a flower arrangement* **4** (*often pl*) a preparation **5** an understanding **6** an adaptation of a piece of music for performance in a different way, esp on different instruments

arrant (ˈærənt) *adj* utter; out-and-out: *an arrant fool* [c14 var. of ERRANT (wandering, vagabond)] > ˈ**arrantly** *adv*

arras (ˈærəs) *n* a wall hanging, esp of tapestry

Arras (ˈærəs; *French* arɑs) *n* a town in N France: formerly famous for tapestry; severely damaged in both World Wars. Pop: 42 715 (1990)

Arrau (əˈraʊ) *n* **Claudio** 1903–91, Chilean pianist

array (əˈreɪ) *n* **1** an impressive display or collection **2** an orderly arrangement, esp of troops in battle order **3** *poetic* rich clothing **4** *maths* a set of numbers or symbols arranged in rows and columns, as in a determinant or matrix **5** *law* a panel of jurors **6** *computing* a regular data structure in which elements may be located by reference to index numbers ▷ *vb* (*tr*) **7** to dress in rich attire **8** to arrange in order (esp troops for battle) **9** *law* to draw up (a panel of jurors) [c13 from OF, from *arayer* to arrange, of Gmc origin] > **arˈrayal** *n*

arrears (əˈrɪəz) *n* (*sometimes sing*) **1** Also called: **arrearage** something outstanding or owed **2 in arrears** *or* **arrear** late in paying a debt or meeting an obligation [c18 from obs. *arrear* (adv) behindhand, from OF, from Med. L *adretrō*, from L *ad* to + *retrō* backwards]

arrest (əˈrɛst) *vb* (*tr*) **1** to deprive (a person) of liberty by taking him or her into custody, esp under lawful authority **2** to seize (a ship) under lawful authority **3** to slow or stop the development of (a disease, growth, etc) **4** to catch and hold (one's attention, etc) ▷ *n* **5** the act of taking a person into custody, esp under lawful authority **6** the act of seizing and holding a ship under lawful authority **7** the state of being held: *under arrest* **8** the slowing or stopping of something: *a cardiac arrest* [c14 from OF, from Vulgar L *arrestāre* (unattested), from L *ad* at, to + *restāre* to stand firm, stop]

arresting (əˈrɛstɪŋ) *adj* attracting attention; striking > **arˈrestingly** *adv*

Arretium (æˈriːtɪəm, -ˈrɛt-) *n* the ancient Latin name of **Arezzo** > **Arretine** (ˈærɪˌtaɪn) *adj*

arrhythmia (əˈrɪðmɪə) *n* any variation from the normal rhythm in the heartbeat [c19 NL, from Gk *arrhuthmia*, from A-¹ + *rhuthmos* RHYTHM]

arrière-pensée *French* (arjɛrpɑ̃se) *n* an unrevealed thought or intention [c19 lit.: behind thought]

Ar Rimal (ɑːr rɪˈmɑːl) *n* another name for **Rub' al Khali**

arris (ˈærɪs) *n, pl* **arris** *or* **arrises** a sharp edge at the meeting of two surfaces at an angle with one another [c17 from OF *areste* beard of grain, sharp ridge; see ARÊTE]

arrish (ˈærɪʃ) *n Southwest English dialect* corn stubble [Old English *ersc*]

arrival (əˈraɪvᵊl) *n* **1** the act or time of arriving **2** a person or thing that arrives or has arrived

arrive (əˈraɪv) *vb* **arrives, arriving, arrived** (*intr*) **1** to come to a certain place during or after a journey **2** to reach: *to arrive at a decision* **3** to occur eventually: *the moment arrived when pretence was useless* **4** *inf* (of a baby) to be born **5** *inf* to attain success [c13 from OF, from Vulgar L *arrīpāre* (unattested) to land, reach the bank, from L *ad* to + *rīpa* river bank]

arrivederci *Italian* (arriveˈdertʃi) *sentence substitute* goodbye

arriviste (ˌæriːˈviːst) *n* a person who is unscrupulously ambitious [F: see ARRIVE, -IST]

arrogant (ˈærəgənt) *adj* having or showing an

Aa

exaggerated opinion of one's own importance, merit, ability, etc: *an arrogant assumption* [c14 from L *arrogāre* to claim as one's own; see ARROGATE] > **'arrogance** *n* > **'arrogantly** *adv*

arrogate ('ærə,geɪt) *vb* **arrogates, arrogating, arrogated** (*tr*) **1** to claim or appropriate for oneself without justification **2** to attribute or assign to another without justification [c16 from L *arrogāre*, from *rogāre* to ask] > **,arro'gation** *n* > **arrogative** (ə'rɒgətɪv) *adj*

arrondissement (*French* arɔ̃dismɑ̃) *n* (in France) **1** the largest subdivision of a department **2** a municipal district of large cities, esp Paris [c19 from *arrondir* to make round]

arrow ('ærəʊ) *n* **1** a long slender pointed weapon, usually having feathers fastened at the end as a balance, that is shot from a bow **2** any of various things that resemble an arrow in shape, function, or speed [OE *arwe*]

arrowhead ('ærəʊ,hɛd) *n* **1** the pointed tip of an arrow, often removable from the shaft **2** something that resembles the head of an arrow in shape **3** an aquatic herbaceous plant having arrow-shaped leaves

arrowroot ('ærəʊ,ru:t) *n* **1** a white-flowered West Indian plant, whose rhizomes yield an easily digestible starch **2** the starch obtained from this plant

arroyo (ə'rɔɪəʊ) *n, pl* **arroyos** *chiefly southwestern US* a steep-sided stream bed that is usually dry except after heavy rain [c19 from Sp.]

Arroyo (ə'rɔɪjəʊ) *n* **Gloria Macapagal** born 1948, Filipino stateswoman; president of the Philippines from 2001; vice-president (1998–2001)

arse (ɑ:s) *or US & Canad* **ass** *n sl* **1** the buttocks **2** the anus **3** a stupid person; fool ▹ Also called (for senses 2, 3): **arsehole**, (US & Canad) **asshole** [OE]

arsenal ('ɑ:sənᵊl) *n* **1** a store for arms, ammunition, and other military items **2** a workshop that produces munitions **3** a store of anything regarded as weapons [c16 from It. *arsenale* dockyard, from Ar., from *dār* house + *sinā'ah* manufacture]

arsenate ('ɑ:sə,neɪt, -nɪt) *n* a salt or ester of arsenic acid

arsenic *n* ('ɑ:snɪk) **1** a toxic metalloid element used in transistors, lead-based alloys, and high-temperature brasses. Symbol: As; atomic no.: 33; atomic wt.: 74.92 **2** a nontechnical name for **arsenic trioxide** (As_2O_3), used as rat poison and an insecticide ▹ *adj* (ɑ:'sɛnɪk) **3** of or containing arsenic, esp in the pentavalent state; designating an arsenic(V) compound [c14 from L, from Gk *arsenikon* yellow arsenic ore, from Syriac *zarnīg* (infl. by Gk *arsenikos* virile)]

arsenic acid *n* a white poisonous soluble crystalline solid used in the manufacture of insecticides

arsenical (ɑ:'sɛnɪkᵊl) *adj* **1** of or containing arsenic ▹ *n* **2** a drug or insecticide containing arsenic

arsenious (ɑ:'si:nɪəs) *or* **arsenous** ('ɑ:sɪnəs) *adj* of or containing arsenic in the trivalent state; designating an arsenic(III) compound

arson ('ɑ:sᵊn) *n criminal law* the act of intentionally or recklessly setting fire to property for some improper reason [c17 from OF, from Med. L *ārsiō*, from L *ārdēre* to burn] > **'arsonist** *n*

art¹ (ɑ:t) *n* **1a** the creation of works of beauty or other special significance **1b** (*as modifier*): *an art movement* **2** the exercise of human skill (as distinguished from *nature*) **3** imaginative skill as applied to representations of the natural world or figments of the imagination **4a** works of art collectively, esp of the visual arts **4b** (*as modifier*): *an art gallery* **5** any branch of the visual arts, esp painting **6a** any field using the techniques of art to display artistic qualities **6b** (*as modifier*): *art film* **7** method, facility, or knack: *the art of threading a needle* **8** skill governing a particular human activity: *the art of government* **9** cunning **10** **get something down to a fine art** to become highly proficient at something through practice ▹ See also **arts** [c13 from OF, from L *ars* craftsmanship]

art² (ɑ:t) *vb arch* (used with the pronoun *thou*) a singular form of the present tense of **be** [OE *eart*, part of *bēon* to BE]

-art *suffix forming nouns* a variant of **-ard**

Artaud (*French* arto) *n* **Antonin** (ɑ̃tɔnɛ̃) 1896–1948, French stage director and dramatist, whose concept of the theatre of cruelty is expounded in *Manifeste du théâtre de la cruauté* (1932) and *Le Théâtre et son double* (1938)

Artaxerxes II (,ɑ:tə'zɜ:ksi:z) *n* died ?358 BC, king of Persia (?404–?358). He defeated his brother Cyrus the Younger at Cunaxa (401)

Art Deco ('dɛkəʊ) *n* a style of interior decoration, architecture, etc, at its height in the 1930s and characterized by geometrical shapes [c20 from *art décoratif*, after the *Exposition des arts décoratifs* held in Paris in 1925]
▹ www.art-deco.com
▹ www.artcyclopedia.com/history/art-deco.htm
▹ www.adsw.org/resource/websites.htm

art director *n* a person responsible for the sets and costumes in a film

artefact *or* **artifact** ('ɑ:tɪ,fækt) *n* **1** something made or given shape by man, such as a tool or a work of art, esp an object of archaeological interest **2** anything man-made, such as a spurious experimental result **3** *cytology* a structure seen in dead tissue that is not normally present in the living tissue [c19 from L *arte factum*, from *ars* skill + *facere* to make]

artel (ɑ:'tɛl) *n* (in the former Soviet Union) a cooperative union or organization, esp of producers, such as peasants [from Russian *artel'*, from It. *artieri* artisans, from *arte* work, from L *ars* ART¹]

Artemis ('ɑ:tɪmɪs) *n Greek myth* the virgin goddess of the hunt and the moon: the twin sister of Apollo. Roman counterpart: **Diana**. Also called: **Cynthia**

arterial (ɑ:'tɪərɪəl) *adj* **1** of or affecting an artery or arteries **2** denoting or relating to the bright red reoxygenated blood that circulates in the arteries **3** being a major route, esp one with many minor branches > **ar'terially** *adv*

arterialize *or* **arterialise** (ɑ:'tɪərɪə,laɪz) *vb* **arterializes, arterializing, arterialized** *or* **arterialises, arterialising, arterialised** (*tr*) **1** to change (venous blood) into arterial blood by replenishing the depleted oxygen **2** to provide with arteries > **ar,teriali'zation** *or* **ar,teriali'sation** *n*

arteriole (ɑ:'tɪərɪ,əʊl) *n anat* any of the small subdivisions of an artery that form thin-walled vessels ending in capillaries [c19 from NL, from L *artēria* ARTERY]

arteriosclerosis (ɑ:,tɪərɪəʊsklɪə'rəʊsɪs) *n, pl* **arterioscleroses** (-si:z) a thickening and loss of elasticity of the walls of the arteries. Nontechnical name: **hardening of the arteries** > **arteriosclerotic** (ɑ:,tɪərɪəʊsklɪə'rɒtɪk) *adj*

artery ('ɑ:tərɪ) *n, pl* **arteries** **1** any of the tubular thick-walled muscular vessels that convey oxygenated blood from the heart to various parts of the body ▹ Cf **pulmonary artery, vein** **2** a major road or means of communication [c14 from L *artēria*, rel. to Gk *aortē* the great artery, AORTA]

artesian well (ɑ:'ti:zɪən) *n* a well sunk through impermeable strata into strata receiving water from an area at a higher altitude than that of the well, so the water is forced to flow upwards [c19 from F, from OF *Arteis* Artois, old province, where such wells were common]

Artex ('ɑ:tɛks) *n trademark* a textured coating for walls and ceilings

art form *n* **1** an accepted mode of artistic composition, such as the sonnet, symphony, etc **2** a recognized medium of artistic expression

artful ('ɑ:tfʊl) *adj* **1** cunning or tricky **2** skilful in achieving a desired end > **'artfully** *adv* > **'artfulness** *n*

art house *n* **1** a cinema that specializes in showing films that are not part of the commercial mainstream ▷ *adj* **2** of or relating to such films or a cinema that specializes in showing them

arthralgia (ɑːˈθrældʒə) *n pathol* pain in a joint

arthritis (ɑːˈθraɪtɪs) *n* inflammation of a joint or joints characterized by pain and stiffness of the affected parts [C16 via L from Gk *arthron* joint + -ITIS] > **arthritic** (ɑːˈθrɪtɪk) *adj, n*

arthropod (ˈɑːθrəˌpɒd) *n* an invertebrate having jointed limbs, a segmented body, and an exoskeleton made of chitin, as the crustaceans, insects, arachnids, and centipedes [C19 from NL, from Gk *arthron* joint + *-podus* footed, from *pous* foot]

Arthur (ˈɑːθə) *n* **1** a legendary king of the Britons in the sixth century AD, who led Celtic resistance against the Saxons: possibly based on a historical figure; represented as leader of the Knights of the Round Table at Camelot **2 Chester Alan** 1830–86, 21st president of the US (1881–85)

Arthurian (ɑːˈθjʊərɪən) *adj* of or relating to King Arthur and his Knights of the Round Table

artic (ɑːˈtɪk) *n inf* short for **articulated lorry**

artichoke (ˈɑːtɪˌtʃəʊk) *n* **1** Also called: **globe artichoke** a thistle-like Eurasian plant, cultivated for its large edible flower head **2** the unopened flower head of this plant, which can be cooked and eaten **3** See **Jerusalem artichoke** [C16 from It., from OSp., from Ar. *al-kharshūf*]

article (ˈɑːtɪkᵊl) *n* **1** one of a class of objects; item **2** an unspecified or previously named thing, esp a small object **3** a written composition on a subject, often being one of several found in a magazine, newspaper, etc **4** *grammar* a kind of determiner, occurring in many languages including English, that lacks independent meaning. See also **definite article, indefinite article** **5** a clause or section in a written document **6** (*often cap*) *Christianity.* See **Thirty-nine Articles** ▷ *vb* **articles, articling, articled** (*tr*) **7** to bind by a written contract, esp one that governs a period of training: *an articled clerk* [C13 from OF, from L *articulus* small joint, from *artus* joint]

articular (ɑːˈtɪkjʊlə) *adj* of or relating to joints or to the structural components in a joint [C15 from L *articulāris* concerning the joints, from *articulus* small joint]

articulate *adj* (ɑːˈtɪkjʊlɪt) **1** able to express oneself fluently and coherently **2** having the power of speech **3** distinct, clear, or definite: *an articulate document* **4** *zool* (of arthropods and higher vertebrates) possessing joints or jointed segments ▷ *vb* (ɑːˈtɪkjʊˌleɪt) **articulates, articulating, articulated** **5** to speak or enunciate (words, syllables, etc) clearly and distinctly **6** (*tr*) to express coherently in words **7** (*intr*) *zool* to be jointed or form a joint [C16 from L *articulāre* to divide into joints] > **arˈticulately** *adv* > **arˈticulateness** *n* > **arˈticuˌlator** *n*

articulated lorry *n* a large lorry made in two separate sections, a tractor and a trailer, connected by a pivoted bar

articulation (ɑːˌtɪkjʊˈleɪʃən) *n* **1** the act or process of speaking or expressing in words **2a** the process of articulating a speech sound **2b** the sound so produced, esp a consonant **3** the act or the state of being jointed together **4** *zool* **4a** a joint such as that between bones or arthropod segments **4b** the way in which jointed parts are connected **5** *bot* the part of a plant at which natural separation occurs

artifact (ˈɑːtɪˌfækt) *n* a variant spelling of **artefact**

artifice (ˈɑːtɪfɪs) *n* **1** a clever expedient **2** crafty or subtle deception **3** skill; cleverness **4** a skilfully contrived device [C16 from OF, from L *artificium* skill, from *artifex* one possessed of a specific skill, from *ars* skill + *-fex*, from *facere* to make]

artificer (ɑːˈtɪfɪsə) *n* **1** a skilled craftsman **2** a clever or inventive designer **3** a serviceman trained in mechanics

artificial (ˌɑːtɪˈfɪʃəl) *adj* **1** produced by man; not occurring naturally **2** made in imitation of a natural product: *artificial cream* **3** pretended; insincere **4** lacking in spontaneity; affected: *an artificial laugh* [C14 from L *artificiālis* belonging to art, from *artificium* skill, ARTIFICE] > **artificiality** (ˌɑːtɪˌfɪʃɪˈælɪtɪ) *n* > ˌ**artiˈficially** *adv*

artificial daylight *n physics* artificial light having approximately the same spectral characteristics as natural daylight

artificial disintegration *n physics* radioactive transformation of a substance by bombardment with high-energy particles, such as alpha particles or neutrons

artificial insemination *n* introduction of spermatozoa into the vagina or uterus by means other than sexual union

artificial intelligence *n* the ability of a machine, such as a computer, to imitate intelligent human behaviour. Abbrev: **AI**

artificial respiration *n* **1** any of various methods of restarting breathing after it has stopped **2** any method of maintaining respiration, as by use of an iron lung

artillery (ɑːˈtɪlərɪ) *n* **1** guns, cannon, mortars, etc, of calibre greater than 20mm **2** troops or military units specializing in using such guns **3** the science dealing with the use of guns [C14 from OF, from *artillier* to equip with weapons, from ?]
▷ www.geocities.com/brit_artillery/field_guns

artiodactyl (ˌɑːtɪəʊˈdæktɪl) *n* an ungulate with an even number of toes, as pigs, camels, deer, cattle, etc [C19 from Gk *artios* even-numbered + *daktulos* finger] > ˌ**artioˈdactylous** *adj*

artisan (ˈɑːtɪˌzæn, ˌɑːtɪˈzæn) *n* a skilled workman; craftsman [C16 from F, from OIt. *artigiano*, from *arte* ART[1]] > **artisanal** (ɑːˈtɪzənᵊl, ˈɑːtɪzənᵊl) *adj*

artist (ˈɑːtɪst) *n* **1** a person who practises or is skilled in an art, esp painting, drawing, or sculpture **2** a person who displays in his or her work qualities required in art, such as sensibility and imagination **3** a person whose profession requires artistic expertise **4** a person skilled in some task or occupation **5** *sl* a person devoted to or proficient in something: *a con artist; a booze artist* > **arˈtistic** *adj* > **arˈtistically** *adv*

artiste (ɑːˈtiːst) *n* **1** an entertainer, such as a singer or dancer **2** a person who is highly skilled in some occupation: *a hair artiste* [F]

artistry (ˈɑːtɪstrɪ) *n* **1** artistic workmanship, ability, or quality **2** artistic pursuits **3** great skill

artless (ˈɑːtlɪs) *adj* **1** free from deceit; ingenuous: *an artless remark* **2** natural; unpretentious **3** without art or skill > ˈ**artlessly** *adv*

Art Nouveau (ɑː nuːˈvəʊ; *French* ar nuvo) *n* a style of art and architecture of the 1890s, characterized by sinuous outlines and stylized natural forms [F, lit.: new art]
▷ http://kubos.org/AN/en
▷ www.artchive.com/artchive/art_nouveau.htm

art paper *n* a high-quality type of paper having a smooth coating of china clay or similar substance on it

arts (ɑːts) *pl n* **1a the** imaginative, creative, and nonscientific branches of knowledge considered collectively, esp as studied academically **1b** (*as modifier*): *an arts degree* **2** See **fine art** **3** cunning actions or schemes

Arts and Crafts *pl n* decorative handicraft and design, esp that of the **Arts and Crafts movement**, in late nineteenth-century Britain, which sought to revive medieval craftsmanship

art union *n Austral* an officially approved lottery for prizes other than cash (formerly works of art)

arty (ˈɑːtɪ) *adj* **artier, artiest** *inf* having an affected interest in artists or art > ˈ**artiness** *n*

Aruba (əˈruːbə; *Dutch* ɑˈryːbaː) *n* an island in the Caribbean, off the NW coast of Venezuela, a dependency of the Netherlands with special status; part of the

Aa

Netherlands Antilles until 1986. Chief town: Oranjestad. Pop: 97 200 (2001 est). Area: about 181 sq km (70 sq miles)

arugula (əˈruːgjʊlə) *n* a Mediterranean plant of the mustard family with yellowish-white flowers and pungent leaves that are used as a salad; rocket. See also **rocket²** (sense 1) [c20 from N It. dialect]

Aru Islands (ˈɑːruː) *pl n* a group of islands in Indonesia, in the SW Moluccas. Area: about 8500 sq km (3300 sq miles)

arum (ˈɛərəm) *n* **1** any of various aroid plants of Europe and the Mediterranean region, having arrow-shaped leaves and a typically white spathe, such as the cuckoopint **2 arum lily** another name for **calla** (sense 1) [c16 from L, var. of *aros* wake-robin, from Gk *aron*]

Arunachal Pradesh (ˌɑːrəˈnɑːkəl prəˈdɛʃ) *n* a state in NE India, formed in 1986 from the former Union Territory. Capital: Itanagar. Pop: 1 091 117 (2001). Area: 83 743 sq km (32 648 sq miles). Former name (until 1972): **North East Frontier Agency**

Arundel (ˈærəndəl) *n* a town in S England, in West Sussex: 11th-century castle. Pop: 3033 (1991)

arvo (ˈɑːvəʊ) *n Austral inf* afternoon

-ary *suffix* **1** *(forming adjectives)* of; related to; belonging to: *cautionary* **2** *(forming nouns)* a person or thing connected with: *missionary; aviary* [from L *-ārius, -āria, -ārium*]

Aryan (ˈɛərɪən) *n* **1** (in Nazi ideology) a Caucasian of non-Jewish descent **2** a member of any of the peoples supposedly descended from the Indo-Europeans ▷ *adj* **3** of or characteristic of an Aryan or Aryans ▷ *adj, n* **4** *arch* Indo-European [c19 from Sansk. *ārya* of noble birth]

as¹ (æz; *unstressed* əz) *conj (subordinating)* **1** (often preceded by *just*) while; when: *he caught me as I was leaving* **2** in the way that: *dancing as only she can* **3** that which; what: *I did as I was told* **4** (of) which fact, event, etc (referring to the previous statement): *to become wise, as we all know, is not easy* **5 as it were** in a way; as if it were really so **6** since; seeing that **7** in the same way that: *he died of cancer, as his father had done* **8** for instance: *capital cities, as London* ▷ *adv, conj* **9 a** used to indicate identity of extent, amount, etc: *she is as heavy as her sister* **9b** used with this sense after a noun phrase introduced by *the same: the same height as her sister* ▷ *prep* **10** in the role of; being: *as his friend, I am probably biased* **11 as for** *or* **to** with reference to: *as for my past, I'm not telling you anything* **12 as if** *or* **though** as it would be if: *he talked as if he knew all about it* **13 as (it) is** in the existing state of affairs **14 as was** in a previous state [OE *alswā* likewise]

USAGE See at **like**

as² (æs) *n* **1** an ancient Roman unit of weight approximately equal to 1 pound troy (373 grams) **2** a copper coin of ancient Rome [c17 from L *ās* unity]

As *symbol for:* **1** altostratus **2** *chem* arsenic

AS *abbrev for:* **1** Also: **A.S.** Anglo-Saxon **2** antisubmarine

ASA *abbrev for:* **1** (in Britain) Amateur Swimming Association **2** (in Britain) Advertising Standards Authority **3** (in the US) American Standards Association

ASA/BS *abbrev* an obsolete expression of the speed of a photographic film, replaced by the ISO rating [c20 from *American Standards Association/British Standard*]

asafoetida *or* **asafetida** (ˌæsəˈfɛtɪdə) *n* a bitter resin with an unpleasant onion-like smell, obtained from the roots of some umbelliferous plants: formerly used as a carminative, antispasmodic, and expectorant [c14 from Med. L, from *asa* gum (cf. Persian *azā* mastic) + L *foetidus* evil-smelling]

a.s.a.p. *abbrev for* as soon as possible

Asben (æsˈbɛn) *n* another name for **Aïr** (region of the Sahara)

asbestos (æsˈbɛstɒs) *n* **a** any of the fibrous amphibole minerals that are incombustible and resistant to chemicals. It was formerly widely used in the form of fabric or board as a heat-resistant structural material **b** *(as modifier): asbestos matting* [c14 via L from Gk: from *asbestos* inextinguishable, from A-¹ + *sbennunai* to extinguish]

asbestosis (ˌæsbɛsˈtəʊsɪs) *n* inflammation of the lungs resulting from chronic inhalation of asbestos particles

Ascanius (æˈskeɪnɪəs) *n Roman myth* the son of Aeneas and Creusa; founder of Alba Longa, mother city of Rome. Also called: **Iulus**

ascarid (ˈæskərɪd) *n* a parasitic nematode worm such as the common roundworm of man and pigs [c14 from NL, from Gk *askarides*, pl. of *askaris*]

ascend (əˈsɛnd) *vb* **1** to go or move up (a ladder, hill, slope, etc) **2** *(intr)* to slope or incline upwards **3** *(intr)* to rise to a higher point, level, etc **4** to trace (a genealogy, etc) back in time **5** to sing or play (a scale, etc) from the lower to higher notes **6 ascend the throne** to become king or queen [c14 from L *ascendere*, from *scandere*]

ascendancy, ascendency (əˈsɛndənsɪ) *or* **ascendance, ascendence** *n* the condition of being dominant

ascendant *or* **ascendent** (əˈsɛndənt) *adj* **1** proceeding upwards; rising **2** dominant or influential ▷ *n* **3** a position or condition of dominance **4** *astrol (sometimes cap)* **4a** a point on the ecliptic that rises on the eastern horizon at a particular moment **4b** the sign of the zodiac containing this point **5 in the ascendant** increasing in influence, etc

ascender (əˈsɛndə) *n* **1** *printing* the part of certain lower-case letters, such as *b* or *h*, that extends above the body of the letter **2** a person or thing that ascends

ascension (əˈsɛnʃən) *n* the act of ascending > **asˈcensional** *adj*

Ascension¹ (əˈsɛnʃən) *n Bible* the passing of Jesus Christ from earth into heaven (Acts 1:9)

Ascension² (əˈsɛnʃən) *n* an island in the S Atlantic, northwest of St Helena: uninhabited until claimed by Britain in 1815. Pop: 1117 (1993). Area: 88 sq km (34 sq miles)

Ascension Day *n* the 40th day after Easter, when the Ascension of Christ into heaven is celebrated

ascent (əˈsɛnt) *n* **1** the act of ascending; upward movement **2** an upward slope **3** movement back through time (esp in **line of ascent**)

ascertain (ˌæsəˈteɪn) *vb (tr)* **1** to determine definitely **2** *arch* to make certain [c15 from OF *acertener* to make certain] > ˌ**ascerˈtainable** *adj* > ˌ**ascerˈtainment** *n*

ascetic (əˈsɛtɪk) *n* **1** a person who practises great self-denial and abstains from worldly comforts and pleasures, esp for religious reasons ▷ *adj also* **ascetical** **2** rigidly abstinent or abstemious **3** of or relating to ascetics or asceticism [c17 from Gk *askētikos*, from *askētēs*, from *askein* to exercise] > **asˈcetically** *adv* > **aˈsceti͵cism** *n*

Asch (æʃ) *n* **Sholem** (ˈʃəʊləm) 1880–1957, US writer, born in Poland, who wrote in Yiddish. His works include biblical novels

Aschaffenburg (*German* aˈʃafənbʊrk) *n* a city in Germany, on the River Main in Bavaria: seat of the Imperial Diet (1447); ceded to Bavaria in 1814. Pop: 62 050 (latest est)

Ascham (ˈæskəm) *n* **Roger** ?1515–68, English humanist writer and classical scholar: tutor to Queen Elizabeth I

ascidian (əˈsɪdɪən) *n* any of a class of minute marine invertebrate animals, such as the sea squirt, the adults of which are degenerate and sedentary

ascidium (əˈsɪdɪəm) *n, pl* **ascidia** (-ˈsɪdɪə) part of a plant that is shaped like a pitcher, such as the modified leaf of the pitcher plant [c18 from NL, from Gk *askidion* a little bag, from *askos* bag]

Asclepius (əˈskliːpɪəs) *n Greek myth* a god of healing; son of Apollo. Roman counterpart: **Aesculapius** (ˌiːskjʊˈleɪpɪəs)

ascomycete (ˌæskəmaɪˈsiːt) *n* any of a phylum of fungi in which the spores (ascospores) are formed inside a club-shaped cell (ascus). The group includes yeast, penicillium, and certain mildews > ˌ**ascomyˈcetous** *adj*

ascorbic acid (əˈskɔːbɪk) *n* a white crystalline vitamin present in plants, esp citrus fruits, tomatoes, and green vegetables. A deficiency in the human diet of leads to scurvy. Also called: **vitamin C**

Ascot (ˈæskət) *n* a town in S England, in Bracknell Forest unitary authority, Berkshire: noted for its horse-race meetings, esp **Royal Ascot**, a four-day meeting held in June. Pop: 13 500 (latest est)

ascribe (əˈskraɪb) *vb* **ascribes, ascribing, ascribed** (*tr*) **1** to credit or assign, as to a particular origin or period **2** to consider as belonging to: *to ascribe beauty to youth* [c15 from L *ascrībere* to enrol, from *ad* in addition + *scrībere* to write] > **asˈcribable** *adj*

USAGE *Ascribe* is sometimes used where *subscribe* is meant: *I do not subscribe* (not *ascribe*) *to this view of music*

ascription (əˈskrɪpʃən) *n* **1** the act of ascribing **2** a statement ascribing something to someone [c16 from L *ascrīptiō*, from *ascrībere* to ASCRIBE]

asdic (ˈæzdɪk) *n* an early form of **sonar** [c20 from *A(nti-)S(ubmarine) D(etection) I(nvestigation) C(ommittee)*]

-ase *suffix forming nouns* indicating an enzyme: *oxidase* [from DIASTASE]

ASEAN (ˈæsɪˌæn) *n acronym for* Association of South-East Asian Nations

▷ www.aseansec.org

asepsis (əˈsɛpsɪs, eɪ-) *n* **1** the state of being free from living pathogenic organisms **2** the methods of achieving a germ-free condition > **aˈseptic** *adj*

asexual (eɪˈsɛksjʊəl) *adj* **1** having no apparent sex or sex organs **2** (of reproduction) not involving the fusion of male and female gametes. Cf: **sexual** (sense 2) > ˌ**asexuˈality** *n* > **aˈsexually** *adv*

Asgard (ˈæsgɑːd) *or* **Asgarth** (ˈæsgɑːθ) *n Norse myth* the dwelling place of the principal gods, the Aesir

ash[1] (æʃ) *n* **1** the residue formed when matter is burnt **2** fine particles of lava thrown out by an erupting volcano **3** a light silvery-grey colour ▷ See also **ashes** [OE *æsce*]

ash[2] (æʃ) *n* **1** a tree having compound leaves, clusters of small greenish flowers, and winged seeds **2** the wood of this tree, used for tool handles, etc **3** any of several trees resembling the ash, such as the mountain ash **4** *Austral* any of various eucalypts [OE *æsc*]

ash[3] (æʃ) *n* the digraph æ, as in Old English, representing a vowel approximately like that of the *a* in Modern English *hat*

ASH (æʃ) *n* (in Britain) *acronym for* Action on Smoking and Health

ashamed (əˈʃeɪmd) *adj* (*usually postpositive*) **1** overcome with shame or remorse **2** (foll by *of*) suffering from feelings of shame in relation to (a person or deed) **3** (foll by *to*) unwilling through fear of humiliation, shame, etc [OE *āscamod*, p.p. of *āscamian* to shame, from *scamu* SHAME] > **ashamedly** (əˈʃeɪmɪdlɪ) *adv*

Ashanti (əˈʃæntɪ) *n* **1** an administrative region of central Ghana: former native kingdom, suppressed by the British in 1900 after four wars. Capital: Kumasi. Pop: 2 485 766 (1991 est). Area: 24 390 sq km (9417 sq miles) **2** (*pl* **-ti -tis**) a native or inhabitant of Ashanti

A shares *pl n* ordinary shares in a company which carry restricted voting rights

ash can *n* a US word for **dustbin**. Also called: **garbage can, ash bin, trash can**

Ashcroft (ˈæʃkrɒft) *n* Dame **Peggy** 1907–91, English stage and film actress

Ashdod (ˈæʃdɒd) *n* a town in central Israel, on the Mediterranean coast: an important city in the Philistine Empire, with its artificial harbour (1961) it is now a major port. Pop: 155 800 (1999 est)

Ashe (æʃ) *n* **Arthur** (**Robert**) 1943–93, US tennis player: US champion 1968; Wimbledon champion 1975

ashen[1] (ˈæʃən) *adj* **1** drained of colour **2** consisting of or resembling ashes **3** of a pale greyish colour

ashen[2] (ˈæʃən) *adj* of, relating to, or made from the ash tree or its timber

Asher (ˈæʃə) *n* the son of Jacob and ancestor of one of the 12 tribes of Israel

ashes (ˈæʃɪz) *pl n* **1** ruins or remains, as after burning **2** the remains of a human body after cremation

Ashes (ˈæʃɪz) *pl n* **the** a cremated cricket stump constituting a trophy competed for by England and Australia in test cricket since 1882 [from a mock obituary of English cricket after a great Australian victory]

Ashford (ˈæʃfəd) *n* a market town in SE England, in central Kent. Pop: 52 002 (1991)

Ashkenazi (ˌæʃkəˈnɑːzɪ) *n, pl* **Ashkenazim** (-zɪm) **1** (*modifier*) of or relating to the Jews of Germany and E Europe **2** a Jew of German or E European descent ▷ Cf **Sephardi** [c19 LHeb., from Heb. *Ashkenaz*, the son of Gomer (Genesis 10:3; I Chronicles 1:6)]

Ashkenazy (ˌæʃkəˈnɑːzɪ) *n* **Vladimir** born 1937, Soviet-born Icelandic pianist and conductor

Ashkhabad (*Russian* aʃxaˈbat) *or* **Ashgabat** (ˈɑːʃgəbæt; *Turkmen* ɑʃgɑˈbɑt) *n* the capital of Turkmenistan. Pop: 605 000 (1999 est)

ashlar *or* **ashler** (ˈæʃlə) *n* **1** a square block of hewn stone for use in building **2** a thin dressed stone with straight edges, used to face a wall **3** masonry made of ashlar [c14 from OF *aisselier* crossbeam, from *ais* board, from L *axis* axletree]

Ashley (ˈæʃlɪ) *n* **1 Jack**, Baron. born 1922, British Labour politician and campaigner for the deaf and disabled **2 Laura** 1925–85, British designer, who built up a successful chain of retail stores selling dresses and fabrics based on traditional English patterns

ashore (əˈʃɔː) *adv* **1** towards or onto land from the water ▷ *adj* (*postpositive*), *adv* **2** on land: *a day ashore before sailing*

ashram (ˈæʃrəm) *n* a religious retreat or community where a Hindu holy man lives [from Sansk. *āśrama*, from *ā-* near + *śrama* religious exertion]

Ashton (ˈæʃtən) *n* Sir **Frederick** 1906–88, British ballet dancer and choreographer. His ballets include *Façade* (1931), to music by Walton, *La Fille mal gardée* (1960), *The Dream* (1964), and *A Month in the Country* (1976)

Ashton-under-Lyne (laɪn) *n* a town in NW England, in Tameside unitary authority, Greater Manchester. Pop: 43 906 (1991)

Ashtoreth (ˈæʃtəˌrɛθ) *n Old Testament* an ancient Semitic fertility goddess, identified with Astarte and Ishtar

ashtray (ˈæʃˌtreɪ) *n* a receptacle for tobacco ash, cigarette butts, etc

Ashur (ˈæʃʊə) *n* a variant spelling of **Assur**

Ash Wednesday *n* the first day of Lent, named from the Christian custom of sprinkling ashes on penitents' heads

ashy (ˈæʃɪ) *adj* **ashier, ashiest 1** of a pale greyish colour; ashen **2** consisting of, covered with, or resembling ash

'Asi (ˈæsɪ) *n* the Arabic name for the **Orontes**

Asia (ˈeɪʃə, ˈeɪʒə) *n* the largest of the continents, bordering on the Arctic Ocean, the Pacific Ocean, the Indian Ocean, and the Mediterranean and Red Seas in the west. It includes the large peninsulas of Asia Minor, India, Arabia, and Indochina and the island groups of Japan, Indonesia, the Philippines, and Ceylon (Sri Lanka); contains the mountain ranges of the Hindu Kush, Himalayas, Pamirs, Tian Shan, Urals, and Caucasus, the great plateaus of India, Iran, and Tibet, vast plains and deserts, and the valleys of many large rivers including the Mekong, Irrawaddy, Indus, Ganges, Tigris, and Euphrates. Pop: 3 589 233 000 (1998 est). Area:

44 391 162 sq km (17 139 445 sq miles)
asiago (ˌæzɪˈɑːgəʊ) *n* either of two varieties (ripened or fresh) of a cow's-milk cheese produced in NE Italy [Italian]
Asia Minor *n* the historical name for **Anatolia**
Asian (ˈeɪʃən, ˈeɪʒən) *adj* **1** of or relating to Asia or to any of its peoples or languages **2** *Brit* of or relating to natives of the Indian subcontinent or their descendants, esp when living in Britain ▷ *n* **3** a native or inhabitant of Asia or a descendant of one **4** *Brit* a native of the Indian subcontinent or a descendant of one
Asian flu *n* a type of influenza caused by a virus which apparently originated in China in 1957
Asian pear *n* a variety of pear, apple-shaped with crisp juicy flesh
Asiatic (ˌeɪʃɪˈætɪk, -zɪ-) *n, adj* another word for **Asian**
Asiatic cholera *n* another name for **cholera**
aside (əˈsaɪd) *adv* **1** on or to one side **2** out of hearing; in or into seclusion **3** away from oneself: *he threw the book aside* **4** out of mind or consideration: *he put aside all fears* **5** in or into reserve: *to put aside money for old age* ▷ *n* **6** something spoken by an actor, intended to be heard by the audience, but not by the others on stage **7** any confidential statement spoken in undertones **8** an incidental remark, note, etc
A-side *n* the side of a gramophone record regarded as more important
Asimov (ˈæzɪmɒf) *n* **Isaac** 1920–92, US writer and biochemist, born in Russia. His science-fiction works include *Foundation Trilogy* (1951–53; sequel 1982) and the collection of stories *I, Robot* (1950)
asinine (ˈæsɪˌnaɪn) *adj* **1** obstinate or stupid **2** resembling an ass [c16 from L *asinīnus*, from *asinus* ASS[1]] > **ˈasiˌninely** *adv* > **asininity** (ˌæsɪˈnɪnɪtɪ) *n*
ASIO *abbrev for* Australian Security Intelligence Organization
Asir (æˈsɪə) *n* a region of SW Saudi Arabia, in the Southern Province on the Red Sea: under Turkish rule until 1933. Area: 81 000 sq km (31 000 sq miles)
ask (ɑːsk) *vb* **1** (often foll by *about*) to put a question (to); request an answer (from) **2** (*tr*) to inquire about: *she asked the way* **3** (*tr*) to direct or put (a question) **4** (*may take a clause as object or an infinitive*; often foll by *for*) to make a request or demand: *they asked for a deposit* **5** (*tr*) to demand or expect (esp in **ask a lot of, ask too much of**) **6** (*tr*) Also: **ask out, ask over** to request (a person) politely to come or go to a place: *he asked her to the party* **7 a big** *or* **tough ask** *Austral & NZ inf* a task that is difficult to fulfil [OE *āscian*] > **ˈasker** *n*
Ask (ɑːsk) *n Norse myth* the first man, created by the gods from an ash tree
ask after *vb* (*prep*) to make inquiries about the health of (someone): *he asked after her mother*
askance (əˈskæns) *or* **askant** (əˈskænt) *adv* **1** with an oblique glance **2** with doubt or mistrust [c16 from ?]
askew (əˈskjuː) *adv, adj* at an oblique angle; towards one side; awry
Askey (ˈæskɪ) *n* **Arthur** 1900–82, British comedian
ask for *vb* (*prep*) **1** to try to obtain by requesting **2** (*intr*) *inf* to behave in a provocative manner that is regarded as inviting (trouble, etc): *you're asking for it*
asking price *n* the price suggested by a seller but usually considered to be subject to bargaining
Askja (ˈɑːskjə) *n* a volcano in E central Iceland: active in 1961; largest crater in Iceland. Height: 1510 m (4954 ft). Area of crater: 88 sq km (34 sq miles)
ASL *abbrev for* American Sign Language. See **Ameslan**
aslant (əˈslɑːnt) *adv* **1** at a slant ▷ *prep* **2** at a slant across or athwart
asleep (əˈsliːp) *adj* (*postpositive*) **1** in or into a state of sleep **2** in or into a dormant or inactive state **3** (of limbs) numb; lacking sensation **4** *euphemistic* dead
ASLEF (ˈæzlɛf) *n* (in Britain) *acronym for* Associated Society of Locomotive Engineers and Firemen
AS level *n Brit* **1a** a public examination taken for the General Certificate of Education, with a smaller course content than an A level: since 2000 taken either as the first part of a full A level or as a qualification in its own right **1b** the course leading to this examination **1c** (*as modifier*): *AS-level English* **2** a pass in a subject at AS level: *I've got three AS levels*
ASM *abbrev for*: **1** air-to-surface missile **2** *theatre* assistant stage manager
Asmara (æsˈmɑːrə) *n* the capital of Eritrea; cathedral (1922); Grand Mosque (1937); university (1958). Pop: 431 000 (1995 est)
Asnières (*French* anjɛr) *n* a suburb of Paris, France, on the Seine. Pop: 72 250 (1990)
Aso (ˈɑːsəʊ) *n* a group of five volcanic cones in Japan on central Kyushu, one of which, Naka-dake, has the largest crater in the world, between 16 km (10 miles) and 24 km (15 miles) in diameter. Highest cone: 1592 m (5223 ft). Also called: **Asosan** (ˌɑːsəʊˈsɑːn)
asocial (eɪˈsəʊʃəl) *adj* **1** avoiding contact **2** unconcerned about the welfare of others **3** hostile to society
asp (æsp) *n* **1** the venomous snake that caused the death of Cleopatra **2** Also called: **asp viper** a viper that occurs in S Europe and is very similar to but smaller than the adder **3 horned asp** another name for **horned viper** [c15 from L *aspis*, from Gk]
asparagus (əˈspærəgəs) *n* **1** a plant of the lily family, having small scaly or needle-like leaves **2** the succulent young shoots, which may be cooked and eaten **3 asparagus fern** a fernlike species of asparagus, native to southern Africa [c15 from L, from Gk *asparagos*, from ?]
aspartame (əˈspɑːˌteɪm) *n* an artificial sweetener produced from a nonessential amino acid [c20 from *aspart(ic acid)* + *(phenyl)a(lanine) m(ethyl) e(ster)*]
aspect (ˈæspɛkt) *n* **1** appearance to the eye; visual effect **2** a distinct feature or element in a problem, situation, etc; facet **3** the way in which a problem, idea, etc, may be considered **4** a facial expression: *a severe aspect* **5** a position facing a particular direction: *the southern aspect of a house* **6** a view in a certain direction **7** *astrol* any of several specific angular distances between two planets **8** *grammar* a category of verbal inflections that expresses such features as the continuity, repetition, or completedness of the action described [c14 from L *aspectus* a sight, from *ad-* to, at + *specere* to look]
aspect ratio *n* **1** the ratio of width to height of a picture on a television or cinema screen **2** *aeronautics* the ratio of the span of a wing to its mean chord
aspen (ˈæspən) *n* a kind of poplar tree in which the leaves are attached to the stem by long flattened stalks so that they quiver in the wind [OE *æspe*]
aspendicitis (əˌspɛndɪˈsaɪtɪs) *n jocular* an inability to control the amount one spends [c20 from a blend of SPEND and APPENDICITIS]
Asperger's syndrome (ˈæspəgəz) *n* a form of autism in which the sufferer has limited but obsessive interests and has difficulty relating to other people [c20 after Hans *Asperger* (20th century), Austrian physician who first described it]
asperity (æˈspɛrɪtɪ) *n, pl* **asperities 1** roughness or sharpness of temper **2** roughness or harshness of a surface, sound, etc **3** *physics* the elongated compressed region of contact between two surfaces caused by the normal force [c16 from L *asperitās*, from *asper* rough]
asperse (əˈspɜːs) *vb* **asperses, aspersing, aspersed** (*tr*) to spread false rumours about; defame [c15 from L *aspersus*, from *aspergere* to sprinkle] > **asˈperser** *n* > **asˈpersive** *adj*
aspersion (əˈspɜːʃən) *n* **1** a disparaging or malicious remark (esp in **cast aspersions (on)**) **2** the act of defaming
asphalt (ˈæsfælt) *n* **1** any of several black semisolid substances composed of bitumen and inert mineral

matter. They occur naturally and as a residue from petroleum distillation **2** a mixture of this substance with gravel, used in road-surfacing and roofing materials **3** (*modifier*) containing or surfaced with asphalt ▷ *vb* **4** (*tr*) to cover with asphalt [c14 from LL *aspaltus*, from Gk *asphaltos*, prob. from A-[1] + *sphallein* to cause to fall; referring to its use as a binding agent] > **as'phaltic** *adj*

asphodel ('æsfəˌdɛl) *n* **1** any of various S European plants of the lily family having clusters of white or yellow flowers **2** an unidentified flower of Greek legend said to cover the Elysian fields [c16 from L *asphodelus*, from Gk *asphodelos*, from ?]

asphyxia (æs'fɪksɪə) *n* lack of oxygen in the blood due to restricted respiration; suffocation [c18 from NL, from Gk *asphuxia* a stopping of the pulse, from A-[1] + *sphuxis* pulse, from *sphuzein* to throb] > **as'phyxial** *adj* > **as'phyxiant** *adj*

asphyxiate (æs'fɪksɪˌeɪt) *vb* **asphyxiates, asphyxiating, asphyxiated** to cause asphyxia in or undergo asphyxia; smother; suffocate > **asˌphyxi'ation** *n* > **as'phyxiˌator** *n*

aspic ('æspɪk) *n* a savoury jelly based on meat or fish stock, used as a relish or as a mould for meat, vegetables, etc [c18 from F: aspic (jelly), asp]

aspidistra (ˌæspɪ'dɪstrə) *n* a popular house plant of the lily family with long tough evergreen leaves [c19 from NL, from Gk *aspis* shield, on the model of *Tupistra*, genus of liliaceous plants]

aspirant ('æspɪrənt) *n* **1** a person who aspires, as to a high position ▷ *adj* **2** aspiring

aspirate *vb* ('æspɪˌreɪt), **aspirates, aspirating, aspirated** (*tr*) **1** *phonetics* **1a** to articulate (a stop) with some force, so that breath escapes audibly **1b** to pronounce (a word or syllable) with an initial *h* **2** to remove by inhalation or suction, esp to suck (air or fluid) from a body cavity **3** to supply air to (an internal-combustion engine) ▷ *n* ('æspɪrɪt) **4** *phonetics* **4a** a stop pronounced with an audible release of breath **4b** the glottal fricative represented in English and several other languages as *h* ▷ *adj* ('æspɪrɪt) **5** *phonetics* (of a stop) pronounced with a forceful expulsion of breath

aspiration (ˌæspɪ'reɪʃən) *n* **1** strong desire to achieve something, such as success **2** the aim of such desire **3** the act of breathing **4** *phonetics* **4a** the pronunciation of an aspirated consonant **4b** an aspirated consonant **5** *med* **5a** the sucking of fluid or foreign matter into the air passages of the body **5b** the removal of air or fluid from the body by suction > **ˌaspi'rational** *adj* > **aspiratory** (ə'spaɪrətərɪ) *adj*

aspirator ('æspɪˌreɪtə) *n* a device employing suction, such as a jet pump or one for removing fluids from a body cavity

aspire (ə'spaɪə) *vb* **aspires, aspiring, aspired** (*intr*) **1** (usually foll by *to* or *after*) to yearn (for), desire, or hope (to do or be something): *to aspire to be a great leader* **2** to rise to a great height [c15 from L *aspīrāre* to breathe upon, from *spīrāre* to breathe] > **as'piring** *adj*

aspirin ('æsprɪn) *n, pl* **aspirin** *or* **aspirins** **1** a white crystalline compound widely used in the form of tablets to relieve pain and fever, and to prevent strokes. Chemical name: **acetylsalicylic acid** **2** a tablet of aspirin [c19 from G, from *A(cetyl)* + *Spir(säure)* spiraeic acid (modern salicylic acid) + -IN]

Aspirin ('æsprɪn) *n* (in Canada) a trademark for **aspirin**

aspro ('æsprəʊ) *n, pl* **-pros** *Austral inf* an associate professor at an academic institution [c20 from AS(SOCIATE) + PRO(FESSOR)]

asquint (ə'skwɪnt) *adv, adj* (*postpositive*) with a glance from the corner of the eye, esp a furtive one [c13 ?from Du. *schuinte* slant, from ?]

Asquith ('æskwɪθ) *n* **Herbert Henry,** 1st Earl of Oxford and Asquith. 1852–1928, British statesman; prime minister (1908–16); leader of the Liberal Party (1908–26)

ass[1] (æs) *n* **1** a mammal related to the horse. It is hardy and sure-footed, having longer ears than the horse **2** (not in technical use) the donkey **3** a foolish or ridiculously pompous person [OE *assa*, prob. from OIrish *asan*, from L *asinus*; rel. to Gk *onos* ass]

ass[2] (æs) *n* the usual US and Canad word for **arse** [OE *ærs*]

Assad ('asat) *n* **1** **Hafiz al** ('hafɪz æl) 1928–2000, Syrian statesman and general; president of Syria from 1971 **2** his son, **Bashar al** (bæʃəæl) born 1965, Syrian statesman; president of Syria from 2000

assagai ('æsəˌgaɪ) *n, pl* **assagais** a variant spelling of **assegai**

assai (æ'saɪ) *adv music* (usually preceded by a musical direction) very: *allegro assai* [It.: enough]

assail (ə'seɪl) *vb* (*tr*) **1** to attack violently; assault **2** to criticize or ridicule vehemently **3** to beset or disturb: *his mind was assailed by doubts* **4** to encounter with the intention of mastering [c13 from OF *asalir*, from L *assilīre*, from *salīre* to leap] > **as'sailable** *adj* > **as'sailer** *n*

assailant (ə'seɪlənt) *n* a person who attacks another, either physically or verbally

Assam (æ'sæm) *n* **1** a state of NE India, situated in the central Brahmaputra valley: tropical forest, with the heaviest rainfall in the world; produces large quantities of tea. Capital: Dispur. Pop: 26 638 407 (2001 est). Area: 78 438 sq km (30 673 sq miles) **2** a high-quality black tea grown in the state of Assam > **ˌAssa'mese** *adj, n*

assassin (ə'sæsɪn) *n* a murderer, esp one who kills a prominent political figure [c16 from Med. L *assassīnus*, from Ar. *hashshāshīn*, pl. of *hashshāsh* one who eats HASHISH]

assassinate (ə'sæsɪˌneɪt) *vb* **assassinates, assassinating, assassinated** (*tr*) **1** to murder (a political figure) **2** to ruin or harm (a person's reputation, etc) by slander > **asˌsassi'nation** *n*

assault (ə'sɔːlt) *n* **1** a violent attack, either physical or verbal **2** *law* an act that threatens violence to another **3a** the culmination of a military attack **3b** (*as modifier*): *assault troops* **4** rape or attempted rape ▷ *vb* (*tr*) **5** to make an assault upon **6** to rape or attempt to rape [c13 from OF *asaut*, from Vulgar L, from *assalīre* (unattested) to leap upon; see ASSAIL] > **as'saultive** *adj*

Aa

assault and battery *n criminal law* a threat of attack to another person followed by actual attack

assault course *n* an obstacle course designed to give soldiers practice in negotiating hazards

assay *vb* (ə'seɪ) **1** to subject (a substance, such as silver or gold) to chemical analysis, as in the determination of the amount of impurity **2** (*tr*) to attempt (something or to do something) ▷ *n* (ə'seɪ, 'æseɪ) **3a** an analysis, esp a determination of the amount of metal in an ore or the amounts of impurities in a precious metal **3b** (*as modifier*): *an assay office* **4** a substance undergoing an analysis **5** a written report on the results of an analysis **6** a test [c14 from OF *assai*; see ESSAY] > **as'sayer** *n*

assegai *or* **assagai** ('æsəˌgaɪ) *n, pl* **assegais** *or* **assagais** **1** a southern African tree, the wood of which is used for making spears **2** a sharp light spear [c17 from Port. *azagaia*, from Ar. *az zaghāyah*, from *al* the + *zaghāyah* assegai, from Berber]

assemblage (ə'sɛmblɪdʒ) *n* **1** a number of things or persons assembled together **2** the act of assembling or the state of being assembled **3** (ˌæsəm'blɑːʒ) a three-dimensional work of art that combines various objects

assemble (ə'sɛmbᵊl) *vb* **assembles, assembling, assembled** **1** to come or bring together; collect or congregate **2** to fit or join together (the parts of something, such as a machine) [c13 from OF *assembler*, from Vulgar L *assimulāre* (unattested) to bring together, from L *simul* together]

assembler (ə'sɛmblə) *n* **1** a person or thing that assembles **2** a computer program that converts a program written in assembly language into machine code ▷ Cf **compiler** 3 another name for **assembly language**

assembly (əˈsɛmblɪ) *n, pl* **assemblies** 1 a number of people gathered together, esp for a formal meeting held at regular intervals 2 the act of assembling or the state of being assembled 3 the process of putting together a number of parts to make a machine 4 *mil* a signal for personnel to assemble

Assembly (əˈsɛmblɪ) *n, pl* **Assemblies** the lower chamber in various state legislatures, esp in Australia and America. See also **House of Assembly, legislative assembly**

assembly language *n computing* a low-level programming language that allows a programmer complete control of the machine code to be generated

assembly line *n* a sequence of machines, tools, operations, workers, etc, in a factory, arranged so that at each stage a further process is carried out

Assen (*Dutch* ˈɑsə) *n* a city in the N Netherlands, capital of Drenthe province. Pop: 52 268 (1994)

assent (əˈsɛnt) *n* 1 agreement, as to a statement, proposal, etc 2 compliance ▷ *vb* (*intr; usually foll by* to) 3 to agree or express agreement [C13 from OF *assenter*, from L *assentīrī*, from *sentīre* to think]

assert (əˈsɜːt) *vb* (*tr*) 1 to insist upon (rights, etc) 2 (*may take a clause as object*) to state to be true; declare 3 to put (oneself) forward in an insistent manner [C17 from L *asserere* to join to oneself, from *serere* to join] > **asˈserter** *or* **asˈsertor** *n*

assertion (əˈsɜːʃən) *n* 1 a positive statement, usually made without evidence 2 the act of asserting

assertion sign *n* a sign ⊢ used in symbolic logic to introduce the conclusion of a valid argument: often read as "therefore"

assertive (əˈsɜːtɪv) *adj* 1 confident and direct in dealing with others 2 given to making assertions; dogmatic or aggressive > **asˈsertively** *adv* > **asˈsertiveness** *n*

assess (əˈsɛs) *vb* (*tr*) 1 to evaluate 2 (foll by *at*) to estimate the value of (income, property, etc) for taxation purposes 3 to determine the amount of (a fine, tax, etc) 4 to impose a tax, fine, etc, on (a person or property) [C15 from OF *assesser*, from L *assidēre* to sit beside, from *sedēre* to sit] > **asˈsessable** *adj*

assessment (əˈsɛsmənt) *n* 1 the act of assessing, esp (in Britain) the evaluation of a student's achievement on a course 2 an amount determined as payable 3 a valuation set on taxable property, etc 4 evaluation; estimation

assessment tests *pl n Brit education* nationally standardized tests for pupil assessment based on attainment targets in the National Curriculum. Formal name: **standard assessment tasks, SATs**

assessor (əˈsɛsə) *n* 1 a person who evaluates the merits of something 2 a person who values property for taxation 3 a person who estimates the value of damage to property for insurance purposes 4 a person with technical expertise called in to advise a court > **assessorial** (ˌæsɛˈsɔːrɪəl) *adj*

asset (ˈæsɛt) *n* anything valuable or useful [C19 back formation from ASSETS]

assets (ˈæsɛts) *pl n* 1 *accounting* the property and claims against debtors that are shown balanced against liabilities 2 *law* the property available to an executor for settling a deceased person's estate 3 any property owned by a person or firm [C16 from OF *asez* enough, from Vulgar L *ad satis* (unattested) from L *ad* up to + *satis* enough]

asset-stripping *n commerce* the practice of taking over a failing company at a low price and then selling the assets piecemeal > **ˈasset-ˌstripper** *n*

asset value *n* the value of a share in a company calculated by dividing the difference between the total of its assets and its liabilities by the number of ordinary shares issued

asseverate (əˈsɛvəˌreɪt) *vb* **asseverates, asseverating, asseverated** (*tr*) to declare solemnly [C18 from L *asseverāre* to do (something) earnestly, from *sevērus* SEVERE] > **asˌseverˈation** *n*

Asshur (ˈæʃʊə) *n* a variant spelling of **Assur**

assibilate (əˈsɪbɪˌleɪt) *vb* **assibilates, assibilating, assibilated** (*tr*) *phonetics* to pronounce (a speech sound) with or as a sibilant [C19 from LL *assībilāre* to hiss at, from *sībilāre* to hiss] > **asˌsibiˈlation** *n*

assiduity (ˌæsɪˈdjuːɪtɪ) *n, pl* **assiduities** 1 constant and close application 2 (*often pl*) devoted attention

assiduous (əˈsɪdjʊəs) *adj* 1 hard-working; persevering 2 undertaken with perseverance and care [C16 from L, from *assidēre* to sit beside, from *sedēre* to sit] > **asˈsiduousness** *n*

assign (əˈsaɪn) *vb* (*mainly tr*) 1 to select for and appoint to a post, etc 2 to give out or allot (a task, problem, etc) 3 to set apart (a place, person, time, etc) for a particular function or event: *to assign a day for the meeting* 4 to attribute to a specified cause, origin, or source 5 to transfer (one's right, interest, or title to property) to someone else ▷ *n* 6 *law* a person to whom property is assigned; assignee [C14 from OF, from L *assignāre*, from *signāre* to mark out] > **asˈsignable** *adj* > **asˈsigner** *or* **ˌassignˈor** *n*

assignation (ˌæsɪgˈneɪʃən) *n* 1 a secret or forbidden arrangement to meet, esp one between lovers 2 the act of assigning; assignment [C14 from OF, from L *assignātiō* a marking out]

assignee (ˌæsaɪˈniː) *n law* a person to whom some right, interest, or property is transferred

assignment (əˈsaɪnmənt) *n* 1 something that has been assigned, such as a mission or task 2 a position or post to which a person is assigned 3 the act of assigning or state of being assigned 4 *law* 4a the transfer to another of a right, interest, or title to property 4b the document effecting such a transfer

assimilate (əˈsɪmɪˌleɪt) *vb* **assimilates, assimilating, assimilated** 1 (*tr*) to learn (information, etc) and understand it thoroughly 2 (*tr*) to absorb (food) 3 (*intr*) to become absorbed, incorporated, or learned and understood 4 (usually foll by *into* or *with*) to adjust or become adjusted: *the new immigrants assimilated easily* 5 (usually foll by *to* or *with*) to become or cause to become similar 6 (usually foll by *to*) *phonetics* to change (a consonant) or (of a consonant) to be changed into another under the influence of one adjacent to it [C15 from L *assimilāre* to make one thing like another, from *similis* like, SIMILAR] > **asˈsimilable** *adj* > **asˌsimiˈlation** *n* > **asˈsimilative** *or* **asˈsimilatory** *adj* > **asˈsimiˌlator** *n*

Assiniboine (əˈsɪnɪˌbɔɪn) *n* a river in W Canada, rising in E Saskatchewan and flowing southeast and east to the Red River at Winnipeg. Length: over 860 km (500 miles)

Assisi (*Italian* asˈsiːzi) *n* a town in central Italy, in Umbria: birthplace of St Francis, who founded the Franciscan religious order here in 1208. Pop: 24 790 (1990)

assist (əˈsɪst) *vb* 1 to give help or support to (a person, cause, etc) 2 to work or act as an assistant or subordinate to (another) ▷ *n* 3 *US* the act of helping [C15 from F, from L *assistere* to stand by, from *sistere* to cause to stand, from *stāre* to stand] > **asˈsister** *n*

assistance (əˈsɪstəns) *n* 1 help; support 2 the act of assisting 3 *Brit inf* See **national assistance**

assistant (əˈsɪstənt) *n* 1a a person who assists, esp in a subordinate position 1b (*as modifier*): *assistant manager* 2 See **shop assistant**

assistant referee *n soccer* the official name for **linesman** (sense 1)

assisted living (əˈsɪstɪd) *n* a a living environment for elderly people, in which personal and medical care are supplied **b** (*as modifier*): *private assisted-living apartments*

assize (ə'saɪz) *n Scots law* **a** trial by a jury **b** a jury [C13 from OF *assise* session, from *asseoir* to seat, from L *assidēre* to sit beside]

assizes (ə'saɪzɪz) *pl n* (formerly in England and Wales) the sessions of the principal court in each county, exercising civil and criminal jurisdiction: replaced in 1971 by crown courts

assoc. *abbrev for:* **1** associate(d) **2** association

associate *vb* (ə'səʊʃɪˌeɪt, -sɪ-) (usually foll by *with*) **associates, associating, associated 1** (*tr*) to link or connect in the mind or imagination **2** (*intr*) to mix socially: *to associate with writers* **3** (*intr*) to form or join an association, group, etc **4** (*tr; usually passive*) to consider in conjunction: *rainfall is associated with humidity* **5** (*tr*) to bring (a person, esp oneself) into friendship, partnership, etc **6** (*tr; often passive*) to express agreement (with): *Bertrand Russell was associated with the CND movement* ▷ *n* (ə'səʊʃɪɪt, -sɪ-) **7** a person joined with another or others in an enterprise, business, etc **8** a companion or friend **9** something that usually accompanies another thing **10** a person having a subordinate position in or admitted to only partial membership of an institution, association, etc ▷ *adj* (ə'səʊʃɪɪt, -sɪ-) (*prenominal*) **11** joined with another or others in an enterprise, business, etc: *an associate director* **12** having partial rights or subordinate status: *an associate member* **13** accompanying; concomitant [C14 from L *associāre* to ally with, from *sociāre* to join, from *socius* an ally] > **as'sociable** *adj* > **as'sociˌator** *n* > **as'sociateˌship** *n*

association (əˌsəʊsɪ'eɪʃən, -ʃɪ-) *n* **1** a group of people having a common purpose or interest; a society or club **2** the act of associating or the state of being associated **3** friendship or companionship: *their association will not last* **4** a mental connection of ideas, feelings, or sensations **5** *chem* the formation of groups of molecules and ions held together by weak chemical bonds **6** *ecology* a group of similar plants that grow in a uniform environment

association football *n* a more formal name for **soccer**

associative (ə'səʊʃɪətɪv, -sɪ-) *adj* **1** of, relating to, or causing association or union **2** *maths, logic* **2a** of an operation, such as multiplication or addition, in which the answer is the same regardless of the way in which the elements are grouped: $(2 \times 3) \times 4 = 2 \times (3 \times 4)$ **2b** referring to this property: *the associative laws of arithmetic*

assonance ('æsənəns) *n* **1** the use of the same vowel sound with different consonants or the same consonant with different vowels, as in a line of verse. Examples are *time* and *light* or *mystery* and *mastery* **2** partial correspondence [C18 from F, from L *assonāre* to sound, from *sonāre* to sound] > **'assonant** *adj, n*

assort (ə'sɔːt) *vb* **1** (*tr*) to arrange or distribute into groups of the same type; classify **2** (*intr;* usually foll by *with*) to fit or fall into a class or group **3** (*tr*) to supply with an assortment of merchandise **4** (*tr*) to put in the same category as others [C15 from OF *assorter*, from *sorte* SORT] > **as'sortative** *adj*

assorted (ə'sɔːtɪd) *adj* **1** consisting of various kinds mixed together **2** classified: *assorted categories* **3** matched (esp in **well-assorted, ill-assorted**)

assortment (ə'sɔːtmənt) *n* **1** a collection or group of various things or sorts **2** the act of assorting

ASSR (formerly) *abbrev for* Autonomous Soviet Socialist Republic

asst *abbrev for* assistant

assuage (ə'sweɪdʒ) *vb* **assuages, assuaging, assuaged** (*tr*) **1** to soothe, moderate, or relieve (grief, pain, etc) **2** to give relief to (thirst, etc) **3** to pacify; calm [C14 from OF, from Vulgar L *assuāviāre* (unattested) to sweeten, from L *suāvis* pleasant] > **as'suagement** *n* > **as'suager** *n*

Assuan *or* **Assouan** (ɑːs'wɑːn) *n* variant spellings of Aswan

assume (ə'sjuːm) *vb* **assumes, assuming, assumed** (*tr*) **1** (*may take a clause as object*) to take for granted; suppose **2** to undertake or take on or over (a position, responsibility, etc): *to assume office* **3** to pretend to; feign: *he assumed indifference* **4** to take or put on; adopt: *the problem assumed gigantic proportions* **5** to appropriate or usurp (power, control, etc) [C15 from L *assūmere* to take up, from *sūmere* to take up, from SUB- + *emere* to take] > **as'sumable** *adj* > **as'sumer** *n*

assumed (ə'sjuːmd) *adj* **1** false; fictitious: *an assumed name* **2** taken for granted **3** usurped

assuming (ə'sjuːmɪŋ) *adj* **1** expecting too much; presumptuous ▷ *conj* **2** (often foll by *that*) if it is assumed or taken for granted

assumption (ə'sʌmpʃən) *n* **1** the act of taking something for granted or something that is taken for granted **2** an assuming of power or possession **3** presumption **4** *logic* a statement that is used as the premise of a particular argument but may not be otherwise accepted [C13 from L *assūmptiō* a taking up, from *assūmere* to ASSUME] > **as'sumptive** *adj*

Assumption (ə'sʌmpʃən) *n Christianity* **1** the taking up of the Virgin Mary (body and soul) into heaven when her earthly life was ended **2** the feast commemorating this

Assur, Asur ('æsə), **Asshur,** *or* **Ashur** ('æʃʊə) *n* **1** the supreme national god of the ancient Assyrians, chiefly a war god, whose symbol was an archer within a winged disc **2** one of the chief cities of ancient Assyria, on the River Tigris about 100 km (60 miles) downstream from the present-day city of Mosul

assurance (ə'ʃʊərəns) *n* **1** a statement, assertion, etc, intended to inspire confidence **2** a promise or pledge of support **3** freedom from doubt; certainty **4** forwardness; impudence **5** *chiefly Brit* insurance providing for certainties such as death as contrasted with fire

Aa

assure (ə'ʃʊə) *vb* **assures, assuring, assured** (*tr; may take a clause as object*) **1** to convince: *to assure a person of one's love* **2** to promise; guarantee **3** to state positively **4** to make (an event) certain **5** *chiefly Brit* to insure against loss, esp of life [C14 from OF, from Med. L *assēcūrāre* to secure or make sure, from *sēcūrus* SECURE] > **as'surer** *n*

assured (ə'ʃʊəd) *adj* **1** sure; guaranteed **2** self-assured **3** *chiefly Brit* insured ▷ *n* **4** *chiefly Brit* **4a** the beneficiary under a life assurance policy **4b** the person whose life is insured > **assuredly** (ə'ʃʊərɪdlɪ) *adv*

asswipe ('æsˌwaɪp) *n US sl* a despicable or stupid person [C20 orig.: toilet paper, from ASS[2] + WIPE]

Assyria (ə'sɪrɪə) *n* an ancient kingdom of N Mesopotamia: it established an empire that stretched from Egypt to the Persian Gulf, reaching its greatest extent between 721 and 633 BC. Its chief cities were Assur and Nineveh > **A'ssyrian** *adj, n*

▷ www.allempires.com/empires/assyria

AST *abbrev for* Atlantic Standard Time

Astaire (ə'stɛə) *n* **Fred,** real name *Frederick Austerlitz.* 1899–1987, US dancer, singer, and actor, whose films include *Top Hat* (1935), *Swing Time* (1936), and *The Band Wagon* (1953)

Astana (æ'stænə) *n* the capital of Kazakhstan, in the N of the country; replaced Almaty as a capital in 1997; an important railway junction. Pop: 313 000 (1999 est). Former names: **Akmolinsk** (until 1961), **Tselinograd** (1961–94), **Akmola** (1994–98)

Astanga yoga *or* **Ashtanga** (æ'ʃtæŋgə) *n* a revived ancient form of yoga that involves a fast and powerful series of movements

Astarte (æ'stɑːtɪ) *n* a fertility goddess worshipped by the Phoenicians: identified with Ashtoreth of the Hebrews and Ishtar of the Babylonians and Assyrians

astatic (æ'stætɪk, eɪ-) *adj* **1** not static; unstable **2** *physics*

having no tendency to assume any particular position or orientation [c19 from Gk *astatos* unsteady]
> a'**statically** *adv*

astatine ('æstəˌtiːn) *n* a radioactive element that occurs naturally in minute amounts and is artificially produced by bombarding bismuth with alpha particles. Symbol: At; atomic no.: 85; half-life of most stable isotope, ^{210}At: 8.1 hours [c20 from Gk *astatos* unstable]

Astbury ('æstbərɪ) *n* **John** 1688–1743, English potter; earliest of the great Staffordshire potters

aster ('æstə) *n* **1** a plant having white, blue, purple, or pink daisy-like flowers **2 China aster** a related Chinese plant widely cultivated for its showy brightly coloured flowers [c18 from NL, from L *aster* star, from Gk]

-aster *suffix forming nouns* a person or thing that is inferior to what is specified: *poetaster* [from L]

asterisk ('æstərɪsk) *n* **1** a star-shaped character (*) used in printing or writing to indicate a cross-reference to a footnote, an omission, etc ▷ *vb* **2** (*tr*) to mark with an asterisk [c17 from LL *asteriscus* a small star, from Gk, from *astēr* star]

asterism ('æstəˌrɪzəm) *n* **1** three asterisks arranged in a triangle (⁎*⁎ or *⁎*), to draw attention to the text that follows **2** a cluster of stars or a constellation [c16 from Gk *asterismos* arrangement of constellations, from *astēr* star]

astern (ə'stɜːn) *adv, adj* (*postpositive*) *naut* **1** at or towards the stern **2** with the stern first: *full speed astern!* **3** aft of the stern of a vessel

asteroid ('æstəˌrɔɪd) *n* **1** Also called: **minor planet, planetoid** any of numerous small celestial bodies that move around the sun mainly between the orbits of Mars and Jupiter **2** a starfish ▷ *adj* Also ˌ**aste'roidal** **3** of a starfish **4** shaped like a star [c19 from Gk *asteroeidēs* starlike, from *astēr* a star]

asthenia (æs'θiːnɪə) *n* *pathol* an abnormal loss of strength; debility [c19 via NL from Gk *astheneia* weakness, from A-^{1} + *sthenos* strength]

asthenic (æs'θɛnɪk) *adj* **1** of or having asthenia; weak **2** referring to a physique characterized by long limbs and a small trunk ▷ *n* **3** a person with long limbs and a small trunk

asthma ('æsmə) *n* a respiratory disorder, often of allergic origin, characterized by difficulty in breathing [c14 from Gk: laborious breathing, from *azein* to breathe hard]

asthmatic (æs'mætɪk) *adj* **1** of or having asthma ▷ *n* **2** a person who has asthma > **asth'matically** *adv*

Asti ('æstɪ) *n* a town in NW Italy: famous for its sparkling wine (**Asti spumante** (spuː'mæntɪ)). Pop: 74 649 (1990)

astigmatic (ˌæstɪg'mætɪk) *adj* relating to or affected with astigmatism [c19 from A-^{1} + Gk *stigmat-*, *stigma* spot, focus] > ˌ**astig'matically** *adv*

astigmatism (ə'stɪgməˌtɪzəm) *or* **astigmia** (ə'stɪgmɪə) *n* **1** a defect of a lens resulting in the formation of distorted images, caused by light rays not meeting at a single focal point **2** faulty vision resulting from defective curvature of the cornea or lens of the eye

astilbe (ə'stɪlbɪ) *n* any perennial plant of the genus *Astilbe*, cultivated for its spikes of ornamental pink or white flowers [c19 NL, from Gk A-^{1} + *stilbē*, from *stilbein* to glitter; referring to its inconspicuous individual flowers]

astir (ə'stɜː) *adj* (*postpositive*) **1** awake and out of bed **2** in motion; on the move

Astolat ('æstəʊˌlæt) *n* a town in Arthurian legend: location unknown

Aston ('æstən) *n* **Francis William** 1877–1945, English physicist and chemist, who developed the first mass spectrograph, using it to investigate the isotopic structures of elements: Nobel prize for chemistry 1922

astonish (ə'stɒnɪʃ) *vb* (*tr*) to fill with amazement; surprise greatly [c15 from earlier *astonyen*, from OF, from Vulgar L *extonāre* (unattested) to strike with thunder, from L *tonāre* to thunder]

astonishing (ə'stɒnɪʃɪŋ) *adj* causing great surprise or amazement; astounding > **a'stonishingly** *adv*

astonishment (ə'stɒnɪʃmənt) *n* **1** extreme surprise; amazement **2** a cause of amazement

Astor ('æstə) *n* **1 John Jacob,** 1st Baron Astor of Hever. 1886–1971, British proprietor of *The Times* (1922–66) **2 Nancy** (**Witcher**), Viscountess, original name *Nancy Langhorne*. 1879–1964, British Conservative politician, born in the US; the first woman to sit in the British House of Commons

astound (ə'staʊnd) *vb* (*tr*) to overwhelm with amazement; bewilder [c17 from *astoned* amazed, from OF, from *estoner* to ASTONISH]

astounding (ə'staʊndɪŋ) *adj* causing amazement and wonder; bewildering > **a'stoundingly** *adv*

astraddle (ə'stræd^{ə}l) *adj* **1** (*postpositive*) with a leg on either side of something ▷ *prep* **2** astride

astragal ('æstrəg^{ə}l) *n* **1** *archit* Also called: **bead** a small convex moulding, usually with a semicircular cross section **2** *anat* the ankle or anklebone [c17 from L, from Gk *astragalos* anklebone, hence, small round moulding]

astragalus (æ'strægələs) *n, pl* **astragali** (-ˌlaɪ) *anat* another name for **talus^1** [c16 via NL from L: ASTRAGAL]

astrakhan (ˌæstrə'kæn) *n* **1** a fur, usually black or grey, made of the closely curled wool of lambs from Astrakhan **2** a cloth with curled pile resembling this **3** (*modifier*) made of such fur or cloth

Astrakhan (ˌæstrə'kæn, -'kɑːn; *Russian* 'astrəxənj) *n* a city in SE Russia, on the delta of the Volga River, 21 m (70 ft) below sea level. Pop: 488 000 (1999 est)

astral ('æstrəl) *adj* **1** relating to or resembling the stars **2** *theosophy* relating to a supposed supersensible substance taking the form of an aura discernible to certain gifted individuals [c17 from LL *astrālis*, from L *astrum* star, from Gk *astron*]

astray (ə'streɪ) *adj* (*postpositive*), *adv* **1** out of the correct path or direction **2** out of the right or expected way [c13 from OF, from *estraier* to STRAY]

astride (ə'straɪd) *adj* (*postpositive*) **1** with a leg on either side **2** with the legs far apart ▷ *prep* **3** with a leg on either side of **4** with a part on both sides of; spanning

astringent (ə'strɪndʒənt) *adj* **1** severe; harsh **2** sharp or invigorating **3** causing contraction of body tissues, checking blood flow; styptic ▷ *n* **4** an astringent drug or lotion [c16 from L *astringēns* drawing together]
> **as'tringency** *n* > **as'tringently** *adv*

astro- *combining form* indicating a star or star-shaped structure: *astrology* [from Gk, from *astron* star]

astrobiology (ˌæstrəʊbaɪ'ɒlədʒɪ) *n* the branch of biology that investigates the possibility of life elsewhere in the universe

astrochemistry (ˌæstrəʊ'kɛmɪstrɪ) *n* the study of the chemistry of celestial bodies and space

astrodome ('æstrəˌdəʊm) *n* a transparent dome on the top of an aircraft, through which observations can be made

astrol. *abbrev for:* **1** astrological **2** astrology

astrolabe ('æstrəˌleɪb) *n* an instrument used by early astronomers to measure the altitude of stars and planets and also as a navigational aid [c13 via OF & Med. L from Gk, from *astrolabos*, from *astron* star + *lambanein* to take]

astrology (ə'strɒlədʒɪ) *n* **1** the study of the motions and relative positions of the planets, sun, and moon, interpreted in terms of human characteristics and activities **2** primitive astronomy [c14 from OF, from L *astrologia*, from Gk, from *astrologos* (orig.: astronomer); see ASTRO-, -LOGY] > **as'trologer** *or* **as'trologist** *n*
> **astrological** (ˌæstrə'lɒdʒɪk^{ə}l) *adj*
▷ www.astrology-numerology.com/

astron. *abbrev for:* **1** astronomer **2** astronomical **3** astronomy

astronaut ('æstrəˌnɔːt) *n* a person trained for travelling in space. See also **cosmonaut** [c20 from ASTRO- + *-naut*, from Gk *nautēs* sailor, on the model of *aeronaut*]

astronautics (ˌæstrə'nɔːtɪks) *n (functioning as sing)* the science and technology of space flight > ˌ**astro'nautical** *adj*

▷ www.spaceref.com/Directory/Astronautics
▷ www.sti.nasa.gov/scan/astronautics.html

Astronomer Royal *n* an honorary title awarded to an eminent British astronomer: until 1972, the Astronomer Royal was also director of the Royal Greenwich Observatory

astronomical (ˌæstrə'nɒmɪkᵊl) *or* **astronomic** *adj* **1** enormously large **2** of or relating to astronomy > ˌ**astro'nomically** *adv*

astronomical clock *n* **1** a complex clock showing astronomical phenomena, such as the phases of the moon **2** any clock showing sidereal time used in observatories

astronomical unit *n* a unit of distance used in astronomy equal to the mean distance between the earth and the sun. 1 astronomical unit is equivalent to 1.495×10^{11} metres

astronomy (ə'strɒnəmɪ) *n* the scientific study of the individual celestial bodies (excluding the earth) and of the universe as a whole [c13 from OF, from L *astronomia*, from Gk; see ASTRO-, -NOMY] > **as'tronomer** *n*

▷ www.astronomy.net
▷ www.astronomytoday.com
▷ www.astronomynow.com
▷ www.popastro.com/home.htm
▷ www.bbc.co.uk/science/space
▷ www.rog.nmm.ac.uk

astrophysics (ˌæstrəʊ'fɪzɪks) *n (functioning as sing)* the branch of physics concerned with the physical and chemical properties of the celestial bodies > ˌ**astro'physicist** *n*

astrotourist ('æstrəʊˌtʊərɪst) *n* a person who pays to travels into space as a form of recreation > ˌ**astro'tourism** *n*

Astroturf ('æstrəʊˌtɜːf) *n trademark* a type of grasslike artificial surface used for playing fields and lawns [c20 from *Astro(dome)* the baseball stadium in Texas where it was first used + *turf*]

Asturias[1] (æ'stʊərɪˌæs) *n* a region and former kingdom of NW Spain, consisting of a coastal plain and the Cantabrian Mountains: a Christian stronghold against the Moors (8th to 13th centuries); rich mineral resources

Asturias[2] (æ'stʊərɪˌæs) *n* **Miguel Ángel** 1899–1974, Guatemalan novelist and poet. His novels include *El Señor Presidente* (1946). Nobel prize for literature 1967

astute (ə'stjuːt) *adj* having insight or acumen; perceptive; shrewd [c17 from L *astūtus* cunning, from *astus* (n) cleverness] > **as'tutely** *adv* > **as'tuteness** *n*

Asunción (*Spanish* asun'sjon) *n* the capital and chief port of Paraguay, on the Paraguay River, 1530 km (950 miles) from the Atlantic. Pop: 502 426 (1992)

asunder (ə'sʌndə) *adv, adj (postpositive)* in or into parts or pieces; apart: *to tear asunder* [OE *on sundran* apart]

Asur ('æsə) *n* a variant spelling of **Assur**

Aswan Assuan, *or* **Assouan** (ɑːs'wɑːn) *n* an ancient town in SE Egypt, on the Nile, just below the First Cataract. Pop: 219 017 (1996 est). Ancient name: **Syene**

Aswan High Dam *n* a dam on the Nile forming a reservoir (Lake Nasser) extending 480 km (300 miles) from the First to the Third Cataracts: opened in 1971, it was built 6 km (4 miles) upstream from the old **Aswan Dam** (built in 1902 and twice raised) Height of dam: 109 m (365 ft)

asylum (ə'saɪləm) *n* **1** shelter; refuge; sanctuary **2** a safe or inviolable place of refuge, esp as formerly offered by the Christian Church **3** *international law* refuge afforded to a person whose extradition is sought by a foreign government: *political asylum* **4** an institution for the care or confinement of individuals, esp (formerly) a mental hospital [c15 via L from Gk *asulon* refuge, from A-[1] + *sulon* right of seizure]

asylum shopper *n* a migrant who passes through several countries before applying for asylum in a country that appears to be the most accommodating

asymmetric (ˌæsɪ'mɛtrɪk, ˌeɪ-) *or* **asymmetrical** *adj* **1** not symmetrical; lacking symmetry; misproportioned **2** *logic, maths* (of a relation) never holding between a pair of values *x* and *y* when it holds between *y* and *x*, as in *John is the father of David* > ˌ**asym'metrically** *adv*

asymmetric bars *pl n gymnastics* **a** *(functioning as pl)* a pair of wooden or fibreglass bars placed parallel to each other but set at different heights, for various exercises **b** *(functioning as sing)* an event in a gymnastic competition in which competitors exercise on such bars

asymmetry (æ'sɪmɪtrɪ, eɪ-) *n* lack or absence of symmetry

asymptomatic (ˌeɪsɪmptə'mætɪk) *adj* not showing any symptoms of disease

asymptote ('æsɪmˌtəʊt) *n* a straight line that is closely approached by a curve so that the distance between them decreases to zero as the distance from the origin increases to infinity [c17 from Gk *asumptōtos* not falling together, from A-[1] + SYN- + *ptōtos* inclined to fall, from *piptein* to fall] > **asymptotic** (ˌæsɪm'tɒtɪk) *or* ˌ**asymp'totical** *adj*

asystole (ə'sɪstəlɪ) *n pathol* the absence of heartbeat; cardiac arrest > **asystolic** (ˌæsɪs'tɒlɪk) *adj*

at (æt) *prep* **1** used to indicate location or position: *are they at the table?* **2** towards; in the direction of: *looking at television* **3** used to indicate position in time: *come at three o'clock* **4** engaged in; in a state of (being): *children at play* **5** (in expressions concerned with habitual activity) during the passing of: *he used to work at night* **6** for; in exchange for: *it's selling at four pounds* **7** used to indicate the object of an emotion: *shocked at his behaviour* **8 where it's at** *sl* the real place of action [OE *æt*]

At *the chemical symbol for* astatine

AT *Brit education abbrev for:* attainment target

at. *abbrev for:* **1** atmosphere (unit of pressure) **2** atomic

Atacama Desert (*Spanish* ata'kama) *n* a desert region along the W coast of South America, mainly in N Chile: a major source of nitrates. Area: about 80 000 sq km (31 000 sq miles)

Atahualpa (ˌætə'wɑːlpə) *or* **Atabalipa** (ˌætə'bɑːlɪpə) *n* ?1500–33, the last Inca emperor of Peru (1525–33), who was put to death by the Spanish under Pizarro

Atalanta (ˌætə'læntə) *n Greek myth* a maiden who agreed to marry any man who could defeat her in a running race. She lost to Hippomenes when she paused to pick up three golden apples that he had deliberately dropped

ataractic (ˌætə'ræktɪk) *or* **ataraxic** (ˌætə'ræksɪk) *adj* **1** able to calm or tranquillize ▷ *n* **2** *obsolete* an ataractic drug

ataraxia (ˌætə'ræksɪə) *or* **ataraxy** ('ætəˌræksɪ) *n* calmness or peace of mind; emotional tranquillity [c17 from Gk: serenity, from A-[1] + *tarassein* to trouble]

Atatürk ('ætəˌtɜːk) *n* **Kemal** (kɛ'mɑːl), real name *Mustafa Kemal*. 1881–1938, Turkish general and statesman; founder of the Turkish republic and president of Turkey (1923–38), who westernized and secularized the country

atavism ('ætəˌvɪzəm) *n* **1** the recurrence in a plant or animal of certain primitive characteristics that were present in an ancestor but have not occurred in intermediate generations **2** reversion to a former type [c19 from F, from L *atavus* strictly: great-grandfather's grandfather, prob. from *atta* daddy + *avus* grandfather] > ˌ**ata'vistic** *adj*

ataxia (ə'tæksɪə) *or* **ataxy** (ə'tæksɪ) *n pathol* lack of

Aa

muscular coordination [c17 via NL from Gk: lack of coordination, from A-[1] + -*taxia*, from *tassein* to put in order] > **a'taxic** *adj*

ATB *abbrev for:* **1** Advanced Technology Bomber **2** *text messaging abbrev for* all the best

Atbara ('ætbərə, æt'bɑː-) *n* **1** a town in NE Sudan. Pop: 73 000 (latest est) **2** a river in NE Africa, rising in N Ethiopia and flowing through E Sudan to the Nile at Atbara. Length: over 800 km (500 miles)

ATC *abbrev for:* **1** air-traffic control **2** (in Britain) Air Training Corps

ate (ɛt, eɪt) *vb* the past tense of **eat**

Ate ('eɪtɪ, 'ɑːtɪ) *n Greek myth* a goddess who makes men blind so that they will blunder into rash acts [c16 via L from Gk *atē* a rash impulse]

-ate[1] *suffix* **1** (*forming adjectives*) having the appearance or characteristics of: *fortunate* **2** (*forming nouns*) a chemical compound, esp a salt or ester of an acid: *carbonate* **3** (*forming nouns*) the product of a process: *condensate* **4** forming verbs from nouns and adjectives: *hyphenate* [from L -*ātus*, p.p. ending of verbs ending in -*āre*]

-ate[2] *suffix forming nouns* denoting office, rank, or a group having a certain function: *episcopate* [from L -*ātus*, suffix of collective nouns]

atelier ('ætəl,jeɪ) *n* an artist's studio or workshop [c17 from OF, from *astele* chip of wood, from L *astula* splinter, from *assis* board]

a tempo (ɑː 'tɛmpəʊ) *music* ▷ *adj, adv* **1** to the original tempo ▷ *n* **2** a passage thus marked ▷ Also: **tempo primo** [It.: in (the original) time]

Aten *or* **Aton** ('ɑːtᵊn) *n* (in ancient Egypt) the solar disc worshipped as the sole god in the reign of Akhenaten

Atget (*French* adʒe) *n* (**Jean**) **Eugène Auguste** 1856–1927, French photographer, noted for his pictures of Parisian life

Athabaska *or* **Athabasca** (,æθə'bæskə) *n* **1 Lake** a lake in W Canada, in NW Saskatchewan and NE Alberta. Area: about 7770 sq km (3000 sq miles) **2** a river in W Canada, rising in the Rocky Mountains and flowing northeast to Lake Athabaska. Length: 1230 km (765 miles)

athame ('ɑːθæmeɪ) *n* (in Wicca) a witch's ceremonial knife, usually with a black handle, used in rituals rather than for cutting or carving

Athanasian Creed (,æθə'neɪʃən) *n Christianity* a profession of faith widely used in the Western Church which, though formerly attributed to Athanasius, probably originated in Gaul between 381 and 428 AD

Athanasius (,æθə'neɪʃəs) *n* **Saint** ?296–373 AD, patriarch of Alexandria who championed Christian orthodoxy against Arianism. Feast day: May 2

Athapascan, Athapaskan (,æθə'pæskən) *or* **Athabascan, Athabaskan** (,æθə'bæskən) *n* a group of North American Indian languages including Apache and Navaho [from Cree *athapaskaaw* scattered grass]

atheism ('eɪθɪ,ɪzəm) *n* rejection of belief in God or gods [c16 from F, from Gk *atheos* godless, from A-[1] + *theos* god] > **'atheist** *n, adj* > **,athe'istic** *adj*

Athelstan ('æθəlstən) *n* ?895–939 AD, king of Wessex and Mercia (924–939 AD), who extended his kingdom to include most of England

athematic (,æθɪ'mætɪk) *adj* **1** *music* not based on themes **2** *linguistics* (of verbs) having a suffix attached with no intervening vowel

Athena (ə'θiːnə) *or* **Athene** (ə'θiːnɪ) *n Greek myth* a virgin goddess of wisdom, practical skills, and prudent warfare. She was born, fully armed, from the head of Zeus. Also called: **Pallas Athena, Pallas.** Roman counterpart: **Minerva**

athenaeum *or US* **atheneum** (,æθɪ'niːəm) *n* **1** an institution for the promotion of learning **2** a building containing a reading room or library [c18 from LL, from Gk *Athēnaion* temple of Athene, frequented by poets]

Athenian (ə'θiːnɪən) *n* **1** a native or inhabitant of Athens ▷ *adj* **2** of or relating to Athens

Athens ('æθɪnz) *n* the capital of Greece, in the southeast near the Saronic Gulf: became capital after independence in 1834; ancient city-state, most powerful in the 5th century BC; contains the hill citadel of the Acropolis. Pop: 772 072 (1991). Greek name: **Athinai** (a'θinɛ)

▷ www.cityofathens.gr/et/en/index.html

atherosclerosis (,æθərəʊsklɪə'rəʊsɪs) *n, pl* **atheroscleroses** (-siːz) a degenerative disease of the arteries characterized by thickening of the arterial walls, caused by deposits of fatty material [c20 from NL, from Gk *athērōma* tumour full of grainy matter + SCLEROSIS] > **atherosclerotic** (,æθərəʊsklɪə'rɒtɪk) *adj*

athirst (ə'θɜːst) *adj* (*postpositive*) **1** (often foll by *for*) having an eager desire; longing **2** *arch* thirsty

athlete ('æθliːt) *n* **1** a person trained to compete in sports or exercises **2** a person who has a natural aptitude for physical activities **3** *chiefly Brit* a competitor in track and field events [c18 from L via Gk, from *athlein* to compete for a prize, from *athlos* a contest]

athlete's foot *n* a fungal infection of the skin of the foot, esp between the toes and on the soles

athletic (æθ'lɛtɪk) *adj* **1** physically fit or strong **2** of, relating to, or suitable for an athlete or for athletics > **ath'letically** *adv* > **ath'leticism** *n*

athletics (æθ'lɛtɪks) *n* (*functioning as sing or pl*) **1** *chiefly Brit* **1a** track and field events **1b** (*as modifier*): *an athletics meeting in Rome* **2** sports or exercises engaged in by athletes

▷ www.iaaf.org

athletic support *n* a more formal term for **jockstrap**

at-home *n* **1** a social gathering in a person's home **2** another name for **open day**

-athon *suffix forming nouns* a variant of **-thon**

Athos ('æθɒs, 'eɪ-) *n* **Mount** a mountain in NE Greece, in Macedonia Central region: site of the Monastic Republic of Mount Athos, autonomous since 1927 and inhabited by Greek Orthodox Basilian monks in 20 monasteries founded in the 10th century. Pop: 1557 (1991)

athwart (ə'θwɔːt) *adv* **1** transversely; from one side to another ▷ *prep* **2** across the path or line of (esp a ship) **3** in opposition to; against [c15 from A-[2] + THWART]

-atic *suffix forming adjectives* of the nature of the thing specified: *problematic* [from F, from Gk -*atikos*]

atigi ('ætəgɪ, ə'tiːgɪ) *n* a type of parka worn by the Inuit in Canada.

-ation *suffix forming nouns* indicating an action, process, state, condition, or result: *arbitration; hibernation* [from L -*ātiōn*-, suffix of abstract nouns]

-ative *suffix forming adjectives* of, relating to, or tending to: *authoritative; informative* [from L -*ātīvus*]

ATK *abbrev for* **1** antitank **2** *computing* at the keyboard

Atkins ('ætkɪnz) *n* **Robert C** 1930–2003, US physician, cardiologist, and nutritionist. An advocate of complementary medicine, he devised a widely-used diet (the **Atkins diet**) based on controlled intake of carbohydrates for weight management and disease prevention

Atkinson ('ætkɪnsᵊn) *n* Sir **Harry Albert** 1831–92, New Zealand statesman, born in England: prime minister of New Zealand (1876–77; 1883–84; 1887–91)

Atlanta (æt'læntə) *n* a city in N Georgia: the state capital. Pop: 416 474 (2000)

Atlantean (,ætlæn'tiːən) *adj literary* of, relating to, or like Atlas; extremely strong

Atlantic (ət'læntɪk) *n* **1 the** short for the **Atlantic Ocean** ▷ *adj* **2** of, relating to, or bordering the Atlantic Ocean **3** of or relating to Atlas or the Atlas Mountains [c15 from L, from Gk (*pelagos*) *Atlantikos* (the sea) of Atlas (so called because it lay beyond the Atlas Mountains)]

Atlantic City *n* a resort in SE New Jersey on Absecon

Beach, an island on the Atlantic coast. Pop: 37 986 (1990)

Atlantic Intracoastal Waterway *n* a system of inland and coastal waterways along the Atlantic coast of the US from Cape Cod to Florida Bay. Length: 2495 km (1550 miles)

Atlanticism (ət'læntɪˌsɪzəm) *n* advocacy of close cooperation in military, political, and economic matters between Western Europe, esp the UK, and the US > **At'lanticist** *n*

Atlantic Ocean *n* the world's second largest ocean, bounded in the north by the Arctic, in the south by the Antarctic, in the west by North and South America, and in the east by Europe and Africa. Greatest depth: 9220 m (30 246 ft). Area: about 81 585 000 sq km (31 500 000 sq miles)

Atlantic Provinces *pl n* **the** certain of the Canadian provinces with coasts facing the Gulf of St Lawrence or the Atlantic: New Brunswick, Nova Scotia, Prince Edward Island, and Newfoundland

Atlantis (ət'læntɪs) *n* (in ancient legend) a continent said to have sunk beneath the Atlantic west of Gibraltar

atlas ('ætləs) *n* **1** a collection of maps, usually in book form **2** a book of charts, graphs, etc: *an anatomical atlas* **3** *anat* the first cervical vertebra, supporting the skull in man **4** (*pl* **atlantes**) *archit* another name for **telamon** [c16 via L from Gk; first applied to maps from depictions of Atlas supporting the heavens in 16th-cent. books of maps]

Atlas ('ætləs) *n Greek myth* **1** a Titan compelled to support the sky on his shoulders as punishment for rebelling against Zeus **2** a US intercontinental ballistic missile, also used in launching spacecraft

Atlas Mountains *pl n* a mountain system of N Africa, between the Mediterranean and the Sahara. Highest peak: Mount Toubkal, 4165 m (13 664 ft)

Atli ('ɑːtlɪ) *n Norse legend* a king of the Huns who married Gudrun for her inheritance and was slain by her after he killed her brothers

ATM *abbrev for* automated teller machine

atm. *abbrev for* atmosphere (unit of pressure)

atman ('ɑːtmən) *n Hinduism* **1** the personal soul or self **2** Brahman considered as the Universal Soul [from Sansk. *ātman* breath]

atmolysis (æt'mɒlɪsɪs) *n, pl* **atmolyses** (-ˌsiːz) the separation of gases by differential diffusion through a porous substance

atmosphere ('ætməsˌfɪə) *n* **1** the gaseous envelope surrounding the earth or any other celestial body **2** the air or climate in a particular place **3** a general pervasive feeling or mood **4** the prevailing tone or mood of a novel, symphony, painting, etc **5** any local gaseous environment or medium: *an inert atmosphere* **6** Abbrev: **at., atm.** a unit of pressure; the pressure that will support a column of mercury 760 mm high at 0°C at sea level > **atmospheric** (ˌætməs'fɛrɪk) *adj.* > ˌ**atmos'pherically** *adv.*

atmospheric pressure *n* the pressure exerted by the atmosphere at the earth's surface. It has an average value of 1 atmosphere

atmospherics (ˌætməs'fɛrɪks) *pl n* radio interference, heard as crackling or hissing in receivers, caused by electrical disturbance

at. no. *abbrev for* atomic number

ATO *abbrev for* Australian Tax Office

atoll ('ætɒl) *n* a circular coral reef or string of coral islands surrounding a lagoon [c17 from *atollon*, native name in the Maldive Islands]

atom ('ætəm) *n* **1a** the smallest quantity of an element that can take part in a chemical reaction **1b** this entity as a source of nuclear energy: *the power of the atom* **2** the hypothetical indivisible particle of matter postulated by certain ancient philosophers **3** a very small amount or quantity: *to smash something to atoms* [c16 via OF & L, from Gk, from *atomos* (adj) that cannot be divided, from A-[1] + *temnein* to cut]

atomic (ə'tɒmɪk) *adj* **1** of, using, or characterized by atomic bombs or atomic energy: *atomic warfare* **2** of or comprising atoms: *atomic hydrogen* > **a'tomically** *adv*

atomic bomb *or* **atom bomb** *n* a type of bomb in which the energy is provided by nuclear fission. Also called: **A-bomb, fission bomb** Cf **fusion bomb**

atomic clock *n* an extremely accurate clock in which an electrical oscillator is controlled by the natural vibrations of an atomic or molecular system such as caesium or ammonia

atomic energy *n* another name for **nuclear energy**

atomicity (ˌætə'mɪsɪtɪ) *n* **1** the state of being made up of atoms **2** the number of atoms in the molecules of an element **3** a less common name for **valency**

atomic mass unit *n* a unit of mass used to express atomic and molecular weights that is equal to one-twelfth of the mass of an atom of carbon-12. Abbrev: **amu**

atomic number *n* the number of protons in the nucleus of an atom of an element. Abbrev: **at. no.**

atomic pile *n* the original name for a **nuclear reactor**

atomic sentence *n logic* a sentence consisting of one predicate and a finite number of terms: *"it is raining" is an atomic sentence*

atomic structure *n* the concept of an atom as a central positively charged nucleus consisting of protons and neutrons surrounded by a number of electrons. The number of electrons is equal to the number of protons: the whole entity is thus electrically neutral

atomic theory *n* **1** any theory in which matter is regarded as consisting of atoms **2** the current concept of the atom as an entity with a definite structure. See **atomic structure**

atomic weight *n* the former name for **relative atomic mass** Abbrev: **at. wt.**

Aa

atomize *or* **atomise** ('ætəˌmaɪz) *vb* **atomizes, atomizing, atomized** *or* **atomises, atomising, atomised** **1** to separate or be separated into free atoms **2** to reduce (a liquid or solid) to fine particles or spray or (of a liquid or solid) to be reduced in this way **3** (*tr*) to destroy by weapons, esp nuclear weapons

atomizer *or* **atomiser** ('ætəˌmaɪzə) *n* a device for reducing a liquid to a fine spray, such as a bottle with a fine outlet used to spray perfumes

atom smasher *n physics* the nontechnical name for **accelerator** (sense 2)

atomy ('ætəmɪ) *n, pl* **atomies** *arch* a minute particle or creature [c16 from L *atomi* atoms, used as sing]

Aton ('ɑːtᵊn) *n* a variant spelling of **Aten**

atonal (eɪ'təʊnᵊl) *adj music* having no established key

atonality (ˌeɪtəʊ'nælɪtɪ) *n* **1** absence of or disregard for an established musical key in a composition **2** the principles of composition embodying this

atone (ə'təʊn) *vb* **atones, atoning, atoned** (*intr*; foll by *for*) to make amends or reparation (for a crime, sin, etc) [c16 back formation from ATONEMENT] > **a'toner** *n*

atonement (ə'təʊnmənt) *n* **1** satisfaction, reparation, or expiation given for an injury or wrong **2** (*often cap*) *Christian theology* **2a** the reconciliation of man with God through the sacrificial death of Christ **2b** the sufferings and death of Christ [c16 from ME *at onement* in harmony]

atonic (eɪ'tɒnɪk, æ-) *adj* **1** (of a syllable, word, etc) carrying no stress; unaccented **2** lacking body or muscle tone ▷ *n* **3** an unaccented or unstressed syllable, word, etc [c18 from L, from Gk *atonos* lacking tone]

atop (ə'tɒp) *adv* **1** on top; at the top ▷ *prep* **2** on top of; at the top of

-ator *suffix forming nouns* a person or thing that performs a certain action: *agitator; radiator* [from L *-ātor*]

-atory *suffix forming adjectives* of, relating to, characterized by, or serving to: *circulatory; explanatory* [from L *-ātōrius*]

ATP *n* adenosine triphosphate; a substance found in all plant and animal cells. It is the major source of energy for cellular reactions

atrabilious (ˌætrəˈbɪlɪəs) *or* **atrabiliar** *adj rare* irritable or gloomy [c17 from L *ātra bīlis* black bile, from *āter* black + *bīlis* BILE[1]] > ˌatraˈ**biliousness** *n*

atrazine (ˈætrəziːn) *n* a white crystalline compound widely used as a weedkiller. Formula: $C_8H_{14}N_5Cl$ [c20 from A(MINO) *tr(i)azine*]

Atreus (ˈeɪtrɪˌuːs, ˈeɪtrɪəs) *n Greek myth* a king of Mycenae, son of Pelops, father of Agamemnon and Menelaus, and member of the family known as the **Atreids** (ˈeɪtrɪɪdz)

atrium (ˈeɪtrɪəm, ˈɑː-) *n, pl* **atria** (ˈeɪtrɪə, ˈɑː-) **1** the open main court of a Roman house **2** a central often glass-roofed hall that extends through several storeys in a building, such as a shopping centre or hotel **3** a court in front of an early Christian or medieval church **4** *anat* a cavity or chamber in the body, esp the upper chamber of each half of the heart [c17 from L; rel. to *āter* black] > ˈ**atrial** *adj*

atrocious (əˈtrəʊʃəs) *adj* **1** extremely cruel or wicked: *atrocious deeds* **2** horrifying or shocking **3** *inf* very bad: *atrocious writing* [c17 from L *ātrōx* dreadful, from *āter* black] > aˈ**trociousness** *n*

atrocity (əˈtrɒsɪtɪ) *n, pl* **atrocities** **1** behaviour or an action that is wicked or ruthless **2** the fact or quality of being atrocious **3** (*usually pl*) acts of extreme cruelty

atrophy (ˈætrəfɪ) *n, pl* **atrophies** **1** a wasting away of an organ or part, or a failure to grow to normal size **2** any degeneration or diminution ▷ *vb* **atrophies, atrophying, atrophied** **3** to waste away or cause to waste away [c17 from LL, from Gk, from *atrophos* ill-fed, from A-[1] + *-trophos*, from *trephein* to feed] > **atrophic** (əˈtrɒfɪk) *adj*

atropine (ˈætrəˌpiːn) *n* a poisonous alkaloid obtained from the deadly nightshade, used to speed a slow heart rate [c19 from NL *atropa* deadly nightshade, from Gk *atropos* unchangeable, inflexible]

Atropos (ˈætrəˌpɒs) *n Greek myth* the one of the three Fates who severs the thread of life [Gk, from *atropos* that may not be turned, from A-[1] + *-tropos* from *trepein* to turn]

attach (əˈtætʃ) *vb* (*mainly tr*) **1** to join, fasten, or connect **2** (*reflexive or passive*) to become associated with or join **3** (*intr; foll by to*) to be connected (with): *responsibility attaches to the job* **4** to attribute or ascribe **5** to include or append: *a proviso is attached to the contract* **6** (*usually passive*) *Mil.* to place on temporary duty with another unit **7** to appoint officially **8** *law* to arrest or take (a person, property, etc) with lawful authority [c14 from OF *atachier* to fasten, changed from *estachier* to fasten with a stake] > atˈ**tachable** *adj* > atˈ**tacher** *n*

attaché (əˈtæʃeɪ) *n* a specialist attached to a diplomatic mission: *military attaché* [c19 from F: someone attached (to a mission)]

attaché case *n* a small flat rectangular briefcase used for carrying documents, papers, etc

attached (əˈtætʃt) *adj* **1** (foll by *to*) fond (of) **2** married, engaged, or associated in an exclusive sexual relationship

attachment (əˈtætʃmənt) *n* **1** a fastening **2** (often foll by *to*) affection or regard (for) **3** an object to be attached: *an attachment for an electric drill* **4** the act of attaching or the state of being attached **5a** the lawful seizure of property and placing of it under control of a court **5b** a writ authorizing such seizure

attack (əˈtæk) *vb* **1** to launch a physical assault (against) with or without weapons **2** (*intr*) to take the initiative in a game, sport, etc **3** (*tr*) to criticize or abuse vehemently **4** (*tr*) to turn one's mind or energies to (a job, problem, etc) **5** (*tr*) to begin to injure or affect adversely: *rust attacked the metal* ▷ *n* **6** the act or an instance of attacking **7** strong criticism or abuse **8** an offensive move in a game, sport, etc **9** **the attack** *ball games* the players in a team whose main role is to attack the opponents **10** commencement of a task, etc **11** any sudden and usually severe manifestation of a disease or disorder: *a heart attack* **12** *music* **12a** decisiveness in beginning a passage, movement, or piece **12b** (in electronic instruments) the time between the start of a note and its maximum volume [c16 from F, from OIt. *attaccare* to attack, attach, from *estaccare* to attach] > atˈ**tacker** *n*

attain (əˈteɪn) *vb* **1** (*tr*) to achieve or accomplish (a task, aim, etc) **2** (*tr*) to reach in space or time **3** (*intr; often foll by to*) to arrive (at) with effort or exertion [c14 from OF, from L *attingere* to reach, from *tangere* to touch] > atˈ**tainable** *adj* > atˌtainaˈ**bility** *or* atˈ**tainableness** *n*

attainder (əˈteɪndə) *n* (formerly) the extinction of a person's civil rights resulting from a sentence of death or outlawry on conviction for treason or felony [c15 from Anglo-F *attaindre* to convict, from OF *ateindre* to ATTAIN]

attainment (əˈteɪnmənt) *n* an achievement or the act of achieving; accomplishment

attainment target *n Brit education* a general defined level of ability that a pupil is expected to achieve in every subject at each key stage in the National Curriculum. Abbrev: **AT**

attaint (əˈteɪnt) *vb* (*tr*) *arch* **1** to pass judgment of death or outlawry upon (a person) **2** (of sickness) to affect or strike (somebody) ▷ *n* **3** a less common word for **attainder** [c14 from OF *ateint* convicted, from *ateindre* to ATTAIN]

attar (ˈætə), **otto** (ˈɒtəʊ), *or* **ottar** (ˈɒtə) *n* an essential oil from flowers, esp the damask rose: *attar of roses* [c18 from Persian, from *ʻitr* perfume, from Ar.]

attempt (əˈtɛmpt) *vb* (*tr*) **1** to make an effort (to do something) or to achieve (something); try **2** to try to surmount (an obstacle) **3** to try to climb ▷ *n* **4** an endeavour to achieve something; effort **5** a result of an attempt or endeavour **6** an attack, esp with the intention to kill [c14 from OF, from L *attemptāre* to strive after, from *tentāre* to try] > atˈ**temptable** *adj*

Attenborough (ˈætᵊnbᵊrə) *n* **1** Sir **David** born 1926, British naturalist and broadcaster; noted esp for his TV series *Life on Earth* (1978), *The Living Planet* (1983), *The Life of Birds* (1998), and *The Life of Mammals* (2003) **2** his brother, **Richard,** Baron Attenborough. born 1923, British film actor, director, and producer; his films include *Gandhi* (1982), *Cry Freedom* (1987), and *Shadowlands* (1993)

attend (əˈtɛnd) *vb* **1** to be present at (an event, etc) **2** (when *intr*, foll by *to*) to give care (to); minister (to) **3** (when *intr*, foll by *to*) to pay attention **4** (*tr; often passive*) to accompany or follow: *a high temperature attended by a severe cough* **5** (*intr;* foll by *on* or *upon*) to follow as a consequence (of) **6** (*intr;* foll by *to*) to apply oneself: *to attend to the garden* **7** (*tr*) to escort or accompany **8** (*intr;* foll by *on* or *upon*) to provide for the needs (of): *to attend on a guest* [c13 from OF, from L *attendere* to stretch towards, from *tendere* to extend]

attendance (əˈtɛndəns) *n* **1** the act or state of attending **2** the number of persons present

attendant (əˈtɛndənt) *n* **1** a person who accompanies or waits upon another **2** a person employed to assist, guide, or provide a service for others **3** a person who is present ▷ *adj* **4** being in attendance **5** associated: *attendant problems*

attendee (əˌtɛnˈdiː) *n* a person who is present at a specified event

attention (əˈtɛnʃən) *n* **1** concentrated direction of the mind, esp to a problem or task **2** consideration, notice, or observation **3** detailed care or special treatment: *to pay attention to one's appearance* **4** (*usually pl*) an act of courtesy or gallantry indicating affection or love **5** the motionless position of formal military alertness, an upright position with legs and heels together ▷ *sentence substitute* **6** the order to be alert or to adopt a position of formal military alertness [c14 from L, from *attendere* to apply the mind to]

attention deficit disorder *n* a disorder, particularly of children, characterized by excessive activity and inability to concentrate on one task for any length of time. Abbrev: **ADD**

attention deficit hyperactivity disorder *n* a form of attention deficit disorder in which hyperactivity is a prominent symptom. Abbreviation: **ADHD**

attentive (ə'tɛntɪv) *adj* 1 paying attention; listening carefully 2 (*postpositive; often foll by to*) careful to fulfil the needs or wants (of) > **at'tentively** *adv* > **at'tentiveness** *n*

attenuate *vb* (ə'tɛnjʊˌeɪt) **attenuates, attenuating, attenuated** 1 to weaken or become weak 2 to make or become thin or fine; extend ▷ *adj* (ə'tɛnjʊɪt, -ˌeɪt) 3 weakened or reduced 4 *bot* tapering [C16 from L *attenuāre* to weaken, from *tenuis* thin] > **atˌtenu'ation** *n*

attercop ('ætəkɒp) *n arch or dialect* 1 a spider 2 an ill-natured person [Old English *attorcoppa*, from *ātor* poison and possibly *cop* head]

attest (ə'tɛst) *vb* 1 (*tr*) to affirm the correctness or truth of 2 (when *intr*, usually foll by *to*) to witness (an act, event, etc) or bear witness (to an act, event, etc) 3 (*tr*) to make evident; demonstrate 4 (*tr*) to provide evidence for [C16 from L, from *testārī* to bear witness, from *testis* a witness] > **at'testable** *adj* > **at'testant, at'tester** *or esp in legal usage* **at'testor** *n* > **attestation** (ˌætɛ'steɪʃən) *n*

attested (ə'tɛstɪd) *adj Brit* (of cattle, etc) certified to be free from a disease, esp from tuberculosis

attic ('ætɪk) *n* 1 a space or room within the roof of a house 2 *archit* a storey or low wall above the cornice of a classical façade [C18 special use of ATTIC, from use of Attic-style pilasters on façade of top storey]

Attic ('ætɪk) *adj* 1 of or relating to Attica, its inhabitants, or the dialect of Greek spoken there 2 (*often not cap*) classically elegant, simple, or pure ▷ *n* 3 the dialect of Ancient Greek spoken and written in Athens

Attica ('ætɪkə) *n* a region and department of E central Greece: in ancient times the territory of Athens. Capital: Athens. Pop: 3 764 348 (2001). Area: 14 157 sq km (5466 sq miles)

Atticism ('ætɪˌsɪzəm) *n* 1 the idiom or character of the Attic dialect of Ancient Greek 2 an elegant, simple expression

Attic salt *or* **wit** *n* refined incisive wit

Attila (ə'tɪlə) *n* ?406–453 AD, king of the Huns, who devastated much of the Roman Empire, invaded Gaul in 451 AD, but was defeated by the Romans and Visigoths at Châlons-sur-Marne

attire (ə'taɪə) *vb* **attires, attiring, attired** 1 (*tr*) to dress, esp in fine elegant clothes; array ▷ *n* 2 clothes or garments, esp if fine or decorative [C13 from OF *atirier* to put in order, from *tire* row]

attitude ('ætɪˌtjuːd) *n* 1 the way a person views something or tends to behave towards it, often in an evaluative way 2 a theatrical pose created for effect (esp in **strike an attitude**) 3 a position of the body indicating mood or emotion 4 *inf* a hostile manner: *don't give me attitude, my girl* 5 the orientation of an aircraft's axes or a spacecraft in relation to some plane or the direction of motion [C17 from F, from It. *attitudine* disposition, from LL *aptitūdō* fitness, from L *aptus* APT] > **ˌatti'tudinal** *adj*

attitudinize *or* **attitudinise** (ˌætɪ'tjuːdɪˌnaɪz) *vb* **attitudinizes, attitudinizing, attitudinized** *or* **attitudinises, attitudinising, attitudinised** (*intr*) to adopt a pose or opinion for effect; strike an attitude

Attlee ('ætlɪ) *n* **Clement Richard,** 1st Earl Attlee. 1883–1967, British statesman; prime minister (1945–51); leader of the Labour party (1935–55). His government instituted the welfare state, with extensive nationalization

attn *abbrev for* attention

atto- *prefix* denoting 10^{-18}: *attotesla*. Symbol: a [from Norwegian & Danish *atten* eighteen]

attolaser ('æəʊˌleɪzə) *n* a high-power laser capable of producing pulses with a duration measured in attoseconds

attorney (ə'tɜːnɪ) *n* 1 a person legally appointed or empowered to act for another 2 *US* a lawyer qualified to represent clients in legal proceedings [C14 from OF, from *atourner* to direct to, from *tourner* to TURN] > **at'torneyˌship** *n*

attorney-at-law *n, pl* **attorneys-at-law** *law, now chiefly US* a lawyer

attorney general *n, pl* **attorneys general** *or* **attorney generals** a chief law officer and senior legal adviser of some national, provincial, and state governments

attract (ə'trækt) *vb* (*mainly tr*) 1 to draw (notice, a crowd of observers, etc) to oneself (esp in **attract attention**) 2 (*also intr*) to exert a force on (a body) that tends to oppose a separation: *the gravitational pull of the earth attracts objects to it* 3 to possess some property that pulls or draws (something) towards itself 4 (*also intr*) to exert a pleasing or fascinating influence (upon) [C15 from L *attrahere* to draw towards, from *trahere* to pull] > **at'tractable** *adj* > **at'tractor** *n*

attraction (ə'trækʃən) *n* 1 the act or quality of attracting 2 a person or thing that attracts or is intended to attract 3 a force by which one object attracts another: *magnetic attraction*

attractive (ə'træktɪv) *adj* 1 appealing to the senses or mind through beauty, form, character, etc 2 arousing interest: *an attractive opportunity* 3 possessing the ability to draw or pull: *an attractive force* > **at'tractively** *adv*

attrib. *abbrev for:* 1 attribute 2 attributive

attribute *vb* (ə'trɪbjuːt). **attributes, attributing, attributed** 1 (*tr; usually foll by to*) to regard as belonging (to), produced (by), or resulting (from): *to attribute a painting to Picasso* ▷ *n* ('ætrɪˌbjuːt) 2 a property, quality, or feature belonging to or representative of a person or thing 3 an object accepted as belonging to a particular office or position 4 *grammar* 4a an adjective or adjectival phrase 4b an attributive adjective 5 *logic* the property or feature that is affirmed or denied concerning the subject of a proposition [C15 from L *attribuere* to associate with, from *tribuere* to give] > **at'tributable** *adj* > **attribution** (ˌætrɪ'bjuːʃən) *n*

attributive (ə'trɪbjʊtɪv) *adj* 1 relating to an attribute 2 *grammar* (of an adjective or adjectival phrase) preceding the noun modified ▷ Cf **predicative** 3 *philosophy* relative to an understood domain, as *small* in *that elephant is small*

attrition (ə'trɪʃən) *n* 1 the act of wearing away or the state of being worn away, as by friction 2 constant wearing down to weaken or destroy (often in **war of attrition**) 3 *geog* the grinding down of rock particles by friction 4 *theol* sorrow for sin arising from fear of damnation, esp as contrasted with contrition [C14 from LL *attrītiō* a rubbing against something, from L *atterere* to weaken, from *terere* to rub]

Attu ('ætuː) *n* the westernmost of the Aleutian Islands, off the coast of SW Alaska: largest of the Near Islands

attune (ə'tjuːn) *vb* **attunes, attuning, attuned** (*tr*) to adjust or accustom (a person or thing); acclimatize

ATV *abbrev for* all-terrain vehicle

at. vol. *abbrev for* atomic volume

Atwood ('ætwʊd) *n* **Margaret** (**Eleanor**) born 1939, Canadian poet and novelist. Her novels include *The Handmaid's Tale* (1986), *Alias Grace* (1996), the Booker Prize-winning *The Blind Assassin* (2000), and *Oryx and Crake* (2003)

at. wt. *abbrev for* atomic weight

atypical (eɪ'tɪpɪkᵊl) *adj* not typical; deviating from or not conforming to type > **a'typically** *adv*

Au *the chemical symbol for* gold [from NL *aurum*]

aubade (əʊ'bɑːd) *n* a poem or short musical piece appropriate to or greeting the dawn [C19 F, from

OProvençal *aubada* (unattested), *auba* dawn, ult. from L *albus* white]

Aube (*French* ob) *n* **1** a department of N central France, in Champagne-Ardenne region. Capital: Troyes. Pop: 292 131 (1999). Area: 6026 sq km (2350 sq miles) **2** a river in N central France, flowing northwest to the Seine. Length: about 225 km (140 miles)

aubergine ('əʊbəˌʒiːn) *n* **1** *chiefly Brit* a tropical Old World plant widely cultivated for its egg-shaped typically dark purple fruit. US, Canad, and Austral name: **eggplant** **2** the fruit of this plant, which is cooked and eaten as a vegetable **3a** a dark purple colour **3b** (*as adj*): *an aubergine dress* [c18 from F, from Catalan *alberginia*, from Ar. *al-bādindjān*, ult. from Sansk. *vatin-ganah*, from ?]

Aubrey ('ɔːbrɪ) *n* **John** 1626–97, English antiquary and author, noted for his vivid biographies of his contemporaries, *Brief Lives* (edited 1898)

aubrietia, aubrieta, *or* **aubretia** (ɔː'briːʃə) *n* a trailing purple-flowered plant native to European mountains but widely planted in rock gardens [c19 from NL, after Claude *Aubriet*, 18th-cent. F painter of flowers and animals]

auburn ('ɔːbᵊn) *n* **a** a moderate reddish-brown colour **b** (*as adj*): *auburn hair* [c15 (orig. meaning: blond): from OF *alborne* blond, from Med. L, from L *albus* white]

Aubusson (*French* obysɔ̃) *n* **1** a town in central France, in the Creuse department: a centre for flat-woven carpets and for tapestries since the 16th century. Pop: 5000 (latest est) ▷ *adj* **2** denoting or relating to these carpets or tapestries

▷ www.ville-aubusson.com

Auckland ('ɔːklənd) *n* the chief port of New Zealand, in the northern part of North Island: former capital of New Zealand (1840–65). Pop (urban area): 381 800 (1999 est)

▷ www.aucklandcity.govt.nz
▷ www.aucklandnz.com

Auckland Islands *pl n* a group of six uninhabited islands, south of New Zealand. Area: 611 sq km (234 sq miles)

au courant *French* (o kurɑ̃) *adj* up-to-date, esp in knowledge of current affairs [lit.: in the current]

auction ('ɔːkʃən) *n* **1** a public sale of goods or property in which prospective purchasers bid until the highest price is reached **2** the competitive calls made in bridge before play begins ▷ *vb* **3** (*tr*; *often foll by off*) to sell by auction [c16 from L *auctiō* an increasing, from *augēre* to increase]

auction bridge *n* a variety of bridge in which all the tricks made score towards game

auctioneer (ˌɔːkʃə'nɪə) *n* **1** a person who conducts an auction ▷ *vb* **2** (*tr*) to sell by auction

auctorial (ɔːk'tɔːrɪəl) *adj* of or relating to an author [c19 from L *auctor* AUTHOR]

audacious (ɔː'deɪʃəs) *adj* **1** recklessly bold or daring **2** impudent or presumptuous [c16 from L *audāx* bold, from *audēre* to dare] > **au'daciousness** *or* **audacity** (ɔː'dæsɪtɪ) *n*

Aude (*French* od) *n* a department of S France on the Gulf of Lions, in Languedoc-Roussillon region. Capital: Carcassonne. Pop: 309 770 (1999). Area: 6342 sq km (2473 sq miles)

Auden ('ɔːdᵊn) *n* **W**(**ystan**) **H**(**ugh**) 1907–73, US poet, dramatist, critic, and librettist, born in Britain; noted for his lyric and satirical poems and for plays written in collaboration with Christopher Isherwood

audible ('ɔːdɪbᵊl) *adj* perceptible to the hearing; loud enough to be heard [c16 from LL, from L *audīre* to hear] > ˌ**audi'bility** *or* '**audibleness** *n* > '**audibly** *adv*

audience ('ɔːdɪəns) *n* **1** a group of spectators or listeners, esp at a concert or play **2** the people reached by a book, film, or radio or television programme **3** the devotees or followers of a public entertainer, etc **4** a formal interview with a monarch or head of state [c14 from OF, from L *audientia* a hearing, from *audīre* to hear]

audio ('ɔːdɪəʊ) *n* (*modifier*) **1** of or relating to sound or hearing: *audio frequency* **2** relating to or employed in the transmission or reproduction of sound [c20 from L *audīre* to hear]

audio book *n* a reading of a book recorded on tape

audio frequency *n* a frequency in the range 20 hertz to 20 000 hertz. A sound wave of this frequency would be audible to the human ear

audiology (ˌɔːdɪ'ɒlədʒɪ) *n* the scientific study of hearing, often including the treatment of persons with hearing defects > ˌ**audi'ologist** *n*

audiometer (ˌɔːdɪ'ɒmɪtə) *n* an instrument for testing hearing > ˌ**audi'ometrist** *n* > ˌ**audi'ometry** *n*

audiophile ('ɔːdɪəʊˌfaɪl) *n* a person who has a great interest in high-fidelity sound reproduction

audiotypist ('ɔːdɪəʊˌtaɪpɪst) *n* a typist trained to type from a dictating machine > '**audio**ˌ**typing** *n*

audiovisual (ˌɔːdɪəʊ'vɪʒʊəl) *adj* (esp of teaching aids) involving or directed at both hearing and sight > ˌ**audio'visually** *adv*

audit ('ɔːdɪt) *n* **1a** an inspection, correction, and verification of business accounts, conducted by an independent qualified accountant **1b** (*as modifier*): *audit report* **2** *US* an audited account **3** any thoroughgoing examination or check ▷ *vb* **audits, auditing, audited** **4** to inspect, correct, and certify (accounts, etc) [c15 from L *audītus* a hearing, from *audīre* to hear]

audition (ɔː'dɪʃən) *n* **1** a test at which a performer or musician is asked to demonstrate his ability for a particular role, etc **2** the act or power of hearing ▷ *vb* **3** to judge by means of or be tested in an audition [c16 from L *audītiō* a hearing, from *audīre* to hear]

auditor ('ɔːdɪtə) *n* **1** a person qualified to audit accounts **2** a person who hears or listens [c14 from OF, from L *audītor* a hearer] > ˌ**audi'torial** *adj*

Auditor General *n* (in Canada) an officer appointed by the Governor General to audit the accounts of the Federal Government and report to Parliament

auditorium (ˌɔːdɪ'tɔːrɪəm) *n, pl* **auditoriums** *or* **auditoria** (-'tɔːrɪə) **1** the area of a concert hall, theatre, etc, in which the audience sits **2** *US & Canad* a building for public meetings [c17 from L: a judicial examination]

auditory ('ɔːdɪtərɪ) *adj* of or relating to hearing or the sense of hearing [c14 from L *audītōrius* relating to hearing, from *audīre* to hear]

Audubon ('ɔːdəˌbɒn) *n* **John James** 1785–1851, US naturalist and artist, noted particularly for his paintings of birds in *Birds of America* (1827–38)

Auerbach ('aʊəˌbɑːk) *n* **Frank** (**Helmuth**) born 1931, British painter, born in Germany, noted esp for his use of impasto

au fait *French* (o fɛ) *adj* fully informed; in touch or expert [c18 lit.: to the point]

au fond *French* (o fɔ̃) *adv* fundamentally; essentially [lit.: at the bottom]

auf Wiedersehen *German* (auf 'viːdərzeːən) *sentence substitute*. goodbye, until we see each other again

Aug. *abbrev for* August

Augean (ɔː'dʒiːən) *adj* extremely dirty or corrupt [c16 from *Augeas*, in Gk myth., king whose filthy stables Hercules cleaned in one day]

augend ('ɔːdʒɛnd, ɔː'dʒɛnd) *n* a number to which another number, the addend, is added [from L *augendum*, from *augēre* to increase]

auger ('ɔːgə) *n* **1** a hand tool with a bit shaped like a corkscrew, for boring holes in wood **2** a larger tool of the same kind for boring holes in the ground [c15 *an augur*, mistaken division of *a nauger*, from OE *nafugār* nave (of a wheel) spear, from *nafu* NAVE² + *gār* spear]

aught *or* **ought** (ɔːt) (*used with a negative or in conditional or interrogative sentences or clauses*) *arch or literary* ▷ *pron* **1** anything whatever (esp in **for aught I know**) ▷ *adv* **2** *dialect* to any degree [OE *āwiht*, from *ā* ever, + *wiht* thing]

augment (ɔːgˈmɛnt) *vb* to make or become greater in number, strength, etc [c15 from LL, from *augmentum* growth, from L *augēre* to increase] > **augˈmentable** *adj* > **augˈmenter** *n*

augmentation (ˌɔːgmɛnˈteɪʃən) *n* **1** the act of augmenting or the state of being augmented **2** the amount by which something is increased

augmentative (ɔːgˈmɛntətɪv) *adj* **1** tending or able to augment **2** *grammar* denoting an affix that may be added to a word to convey the meaning *large* or *great*: for example, the suffix *-ote* in Spanish, where *hombre* means man and *hombrote* big man

augmented (ɔːgˈmɛntɪd) *adj* **1** *music* (of an interval) increased from being perfect or major by the raising of the higher note or the dropping of the lower note by one semitone: *C to G sharp is an augmented fifth* **2** having been increased, esp in number: *an augmented orchestra*

au gratin (*French* o gratɛ̃) *adj* covered and cooked with browned breadcrumbs and sometimes cheese [F, lit.: with the grating]

Augsburg (*German* ˈauksbʊrk) *n* a city in S Germany, in Bavaria: founded by the Romans in 14 BC; site of the diet that produced the **Peace of Augsburg** (1555), which ended the struggles between Lutherans and Catholics in the Holy Roman Empire and established the principle that each ruler should determine the form of worship in his lands. Pop: 254 400 (1999 est). Roman name: **Augusta Vindelicorum** (aʊˈguːstə vɪnˈdɛlɪˌkəʊrəm)

augur (ˈɔːgə) *n* **1** (in ancient Rome) a religious official who observed and interpreted omens and signs **2** any prophet or soothsayer ▷ *vb* **3** to predict (some future event), as from signs or omens **4** (*tr; may take a clause as object*) to be an omen (of) **5** (*intr*) to foreshadow future events: *this augurs well for us* [c14 from L: a diviner, ?from *augēre* to increase] > **augural** (ˈɔːgjʊrəl) *adj*

augury (ˈɔːgjʊrɪ) *n, pl* **auguries** **1** the art of or a rite conducted by an augur **2** a sign or portent; omen

august (ɔːˈgʌst) *adj* **1** dignified or imposing **2** of noble birth or high rank: *an august lineage* [c17 from L *augustus*; rel. to *augēre* to increase] > **auˈgustness** *n*

August (ˈɔːgəst) *n* the eighth month of the year, consisting of 31 days [OE, from L, after the emperor AUGUSTUS]

Augusta (ɔːˈgʌstə) *n* **1** a town in the US, in Georgia. Pop: 44 639 (1990) **2** a port in S Italy, in E Sicily. Pop: 38 900 (latest est) **3** a city in the US, in Maine: the state capital; founded (1628) as a trading post; timber industry. Pop: 21 325 (1990)

Augustan (ɔːˈgʌstən) *adj* **1** characteristic of or relating to the Roman emperor Augustus Caesar, his period, or the poets writing during his reign **2** of or characteristic of any literary period noted for refinement and classicism, esp the 18th century in England ▷ *n* **3** an author in an Augustan Age

Augustine (ɔːˈgʌstɪn) *n* **1** **Saint** 354–430 AD, one of the Fathers of the Christian Church; bishop of Hippo in North Africa (396–430), who profoundly influenced both Catholic and Protestant theology. His most famous works are *Confessions*, a spiritual autobiography, and *De Civitate Dei*, a vindication of the Christian Church. Feast day: Aug. 28 **2** **Saint** died 604 AD, Roman monk, sent to Britain (597 AD) to convert the Anglo-Saxons to Christianity and to establish the authority of the Roman See over the native Celtic Church; became the first archbishop of Canterbury (601–604). Feast day: May 26 or 27 **3** a member of an Augustinian order

Augustinian (ˌɔːgəˈstɪnɪən) *adj* **1** of Saint Augustine of Hippo, his doctrines, or the Christian religious orders founded on his doctrines ▷ *n* **2** a member of any of several religious orders that are governed by the rule of Saint Augustine **3** a person who follows the doctrines of Saint Augustine

Augustus (ɔːˈgʌstəs) *n* original name *Gaius Octavianus*; after his adoption by Julius Caesar (44 BC) known as *Gaius Julius Caesar Octavianus*. 63 BC–14 AD, Roman statesman, a member of the second triumvirate (43 BC). After defeating Mark Antony at Actium (31 BC), he became first emperor of Rome, adopting the title Augustus (27 BC)

auk (ɔːk) *n* **1** a diving bird of northern oceans having a heavy body, short tail, narrow wings, and a black-and-white plumage. See also **great auk, razorbill** **2** **little auk** a small short-billed auk, abundant in Arctic regions [c17 from ON *ālka*]

au lait (əʊ ˈleɪ) *adj* prepared or served with milk [F, lit.: with milk]

auld (ɔːld) *adj* a Scottish word for **old** [OE *āld*]

auld lang syne (ˈɔːld læŋ ˈsaɪn) *n* times past, esp those remembered with nostalgia [Scot., lit.: old long since]

Auld Reekie (ˈriːkɪ) *n Scot* a nickname for **Edinburgh** [literally: Old Smoky]

Aulis (ˈɔːlɪs) *n* an ancient town in E central Greece, in Boeotia: traditionally the harbour from which the Greeks sailed at the beginning of the Trojan war

aumbry (ˈɔːmbrɪ) *n, pl* **aumbries** a variant of **ambry**

au naturel *French* (o natyrɛl) *adj, adv* **1** naked; nude **2** uncooked or plainly cooked [lit.: in (a) natural (condition)]

Aung San Suu Kyi (ˈaʊŋ ˈsæn ˈsuː ˈkiː) *n* born 1945, Burmese politician; cofounder (1988) and general secretary (1988–91; 1995–) of the National League for Democracy: Nobel peace prize 1991

aunt (ɑːnt) *n* (*often cap, esp as a term of address*) **1** a sister of one's father or mother **2** the wife of one's uncle **3** a term of address used by children for a female friend of the parents **4** **my (sainted) aunt!** an exclamation of surprise [c13 from OF, from L *amita* a father's sister]

auntie *or* **aunty** (ˈɑːntɪ) *n, pl* **aunties** a familiar or diminutive word for **aunt**

Auntie *or* **Aunty** (ˈɑːntɪ) *n* **1** *Brit inf* the BBC **2** *Austral inf* the Australian Broadcasting Association

Aunt Sally (ˈsælɪ) *n, pl* **Aunt Sallies** *Brit* **1** a figure of an old woman used in fairgrounds and fêtes as a target **2** any person who is a target for insults or criticism

Aunty (ˈɑːntɪ) *n Austral* an informal name for the **Australian Broadcasting Association**

au pair (əʊ ˈpɛə) *n* **a** a young foreigner, usually a girl, who undertakes housework in exchange for board and lodging, esp in order to learn the language **b** (*as modifier*): *an au pair girl* [c20 from F: on an equal footing]

aura (ˈɔːrə) *n, pl* **auras** *or* **aurae** (ˈɔːriː) **1** a distinctive air or quality considered to be characteristic of a person or thing **2** any invisible emanation, esp surrounding a person or object **3** *pathol* strange sensations, such as noises in the ears or flashes of light, that immediately precede an attack, esp of epilepsy [c18 via L from Gk: breeze]

aural (ˈɔːrəl) *adj* of or relating to the sense or organs of hearing; auricular [c19 from L *auris* ear] > **ˈaurally** *adv*

> USAGE *Aural* is sometimes mistakenly used for *oral*. Your *oral skills* are your proficiency in talking about events and situations; your *aural skills* relate to your ability to hear sounds and melodies

aureate (ˈɔːrɪɪt) *adj* **1** covered with gold; gilded **2** (of a style of writing or speaking) excessively elaborate [c15 from LL, from L *aureus* golden, from *aurum* gold]

Aurelian (ɔːˈriːlɪən) *n* Latin name *Lucius Domitius Aurelianus*. ?212–275 AD, Roman emperor (270–275), who conquered Palmyra (273) and restored political unity to the Roman Empire

Aurelius (ɔːˈriːlɪəs) *n* See **Marcus Aurelius Antoninus**

aureole (ˈɔːrɪˌəʊl) *or* **aureola** (ɔːˈriːələ) *n* **1** a border of light or radiance enveloping the head of a figure represented as holy **2** a less common word for **halo**

Aa

3 another name for **corona** (sense 2) [c13 from OF, from Med. L (*corōna*) *aureola* golden (crown), from L, from *aurum* gold]

au revoir *French* (o rəvwar) *sentence substitute* goodbye [lit.: to the seeing again]

auric ('ɔːrɪk) *adj* of or containing gold, esp in the trivalent state; designating a gold(III) compound [c19 from L *aurum* gold]

Auric (*French* ɔrik) *n* **Georges** (ʒɔrʒ) 1899–1983, French composer; one of *les Six*. His works include ballet and film music

auricle ('ɔːrɪkᵊl) *n* **1** the upper chamber of the heart; atrium **2** Also called: **pinna** *anat* the external part of the ear **3** *biol* an ear-shaped part or appendage [c17 from L *auricula* the external ear, from *auris* ear] > '**auricled** *adj*

auricula (ɔː'rɪkjʊlə) *n pl* **-lae** (-ˌliː) *or* **-las 1** Also called: **bear's-ear** a widely cultivated alpine primrose, *Primula auricula*, with leaves shaped like a bear's ear **2** another word for **auricle** (sense 3) [c17 from New Latin, from Latin: external ear; see AURICLE]

auricular (ɔː'rɪkjʊlə) *adj* **1** of, relating to, or received by the sense or organs of hearing; aural **2** shaped like an ear **3** of or relating to an auricle of the heart

auriferous (ɔː'rɪfərəs) *adj* (of rock) containing gold; gold-bearing [c18 from L, from *aurum* gold + *ferre* to bear]

Aurignacian (ˌɔːrɪg'neɪʃən) *adj* of or produced during a flint culture of the Upper Palaeolithic type characterized by the use of bone and antler tools, and also by cave art [c20 after *Aurignac*, France, near the cave where remains were discovered]

Auriol (*French* ɔrjɔl) *n* **Vincent** (vɛ̃sɑ̃) 1884–1966, French statesman; president of the Fourth Republic (1947–54)

aurochs ('ɔːrɒks) *n, pl* **aurochs** a recently extinct member of the cattle tribe that inhabited forests in N Africa, Europe, and SW Asia. Also called: **urus** [c18 from G, from OHG *ūrohso*, from *ūro* bison + *ohso* ox]

aurora (ɔː'rɔːrə) *n, pl* **auroras** *or* **aurorae** (-riː) **1** an atmospheric phenomenon consisting of bands, curtains, or streamers of light, that move across the sky **2** *poetic* the dawn [c14 from L: dawn] > **au'roral** *adj*

Aurora[1] (ɔː'rɔːrə) *n* **1** the Roman goddess of the dawn. Greek counterpart: **Eos 2** the dawn or rise of something

Aurora[2] (ɔː'rɔːrə) *n* another name for **Maewo**

aurora australis (ɒ'streɪlɪs) *n* (*sometimes cap*) the aurora seen around the South Pole. Also called: **southern lights** [NL: southern aurora]

aurora borealis (ˌbɔːrɪ'eɪlɪs) *n* (*sometimes cap*) the aurora seen around the North Pole. Also called: **northern lights** [c17 NL: northern aurora]

aurous ('ɔːrəs) *adj* of or containing gold, esp in the monovalent state; designating a gold(I) compound [c19 from F *aureux*, LL *aurōsus* gold-coloured, from L *aurum* gold]

Aus. *abbrev for:* **1** Australia(n) **2** Austria(n)

Auschwitz (*German* 'aʊʃvɪts) *n* an industrial town in S Poland; site of a Nazi concentration camp during World War II. Pop: 45 400 (latest est). Polish name: **Oświęcim**

auscultation (ˌɔːskəl'teɪʃən) *n* **1** the diagnostic technique in medicine of listening to the various internal sounds made by the body, usually with the aid of a stethoscope **2** the act of listening [c19 from L, from *auscultāre* to listen attentively; rel. to L *auris* ear] > '**auscul,tate** *vb* > **auscultatory** (ɔː'skʌltətərɪ) *adj*

auspice ('ɔːspɪs) *n* **1** (*usually pl*) patronage (esp in **under the auspices of**) **2** (*often pl*) an omen, esp one that is favourable [c16 from L *auspicium* augury from birds]

auspicious (ɔː'spɪʃəs) *adj* **1** favourable or propitious **2** *arch* fortunate > **aus'piciously** *adv* > **aus'piciousness** *n*

Aussie ('ɒzɪ) *n, adj inf* Australian

Aussie battler *n Austral sl* an Australian working-class person. Also called: **little Aussie battler**

Aust. *abbrev for:* **1** Australia(n) **2** Austria(n)

Austen ('ɒstɪn, 'ɔː-) *n* **Jane** 1775–1817, English novelist, noted particularly for the insight and delicate irony of her portrayal of middle-class families. Her completed novels are *Sense and Sensibility* (1811), *Pride and Prejudice* (1813), *Mansfield Park* (1814), *Emma* (1816), *Northanger Abbey* (1818), and *Persuasion* (1818)

austere (ɒ'stɪə) *adj* **1** stern or severe in attitude or manner **2** grave, sober, or serious **3** self-disciplined, abstemious, or ascetic: *an austere life* **4** severely simple or plain: *an austere design* [c14 from OF, from L *austērus* sour, from Gk *austēros* astringent; rel. to Gk *hauein* to dry] > **aus'terely** *adv*

austerity (ɒ'stɛrɪtɪ) *n, pl* **austerities 1** the state or quality of being austere **2** (*often pl*) an austere habit, practice, or act **3a** reduced availability of luxuries and consumer goods **3b** (*as modifier*): *an austerity budget*

Austerlitz ('ɔːstəlɪts) *n* a town in the Czech Republic, in Moravia: site of Napoleon's victory over the Russian and Austrian armies in 1805. Pop: 4747 (latest est). Czech name: **Slavkov**

Austin[1] ('ɒstɪn'('ɒstɪn) *n* a city in central Texas, on the Colorado River: state capital since 1845. Pop: 656 462 (2000)

Austin[2] ('ɒstɪn, 'ɔː-) *n* **1 Herbert,** 1st Baron. 1866–1941, British automobile engineer, who founded the Austin Motor Company **2 John** 1790–1859, British jurist, whose book *The Province of Jurisprudence Determined* (1832) greatly influenced legal theory and the English legal system **3 J(ohn) L(angshaw)** ('læŋʃɔː) 1911–60, English philosopher, whose lectures *Sense and Sensibilia* and *How to do Things with Words* were published posthumously in 1962

austral[1] ('ɔːstrəl) *adj* of or coming from the south: *austral winds* [c14 from L *austrālis*, from *auster* the south wind]

austral[2] (aʊ'strɑːl) *n, pl* **australes** (-'strɑːlɛs) a former monetary unit of Argentina [from Sp.; see AUSTRAL[1]]

Austral. *abbrev for:* **1** Australasia **2** Australia(n)

Australasia (ˌɒstrə'leɪzɪə) *n* **1** Australia, New Zealand, and neighbouring islands in the S Pacific Ocean **2** (loosely) the whole of Oceania > **ˌAustra'lasian** *adj*

Australia (ɒ'streɪlɪə) *n* a country and the smallest continent, situated between the Indian Ocean and the Pacific: a former British colony, now an independent member of the Commonwealth, constitutional links with Britain formally abolished in 1986; consists chiefly of a low plateau, mostly arid in the west, with the basin of the Murray River and the Great Dividing Range in the east and the Great Barrier Reef off the NE coast. Official language: English. Religion: Christian majority. Currency: dollar. Capital: Canberra. Pop: 19 358 000 (2001 est). Area: 7 682 300 sq km (2 966 150 sq miles) > **Aus'tralian** *adj, n*

▷ www.gov.au

▷ www.australia.com

Australiana (ɒˌstreɪlɪ'ɑːnə) *pl n* objects, books, documents, etc relating to Australia and its history and culture

Australian Alps *pl n* a mountain range in SE Australia, in E Victoria and SE New South Wales. Highest peak: Mount Kosciusko, 2195 m (7316 ft)

Australian Antarctic Territory *n* the area of Antarctica, other than Adélie Land, that is administered by Australia, lying south of latitude 60°S and between longitudes 45°E and 160°E

Australian Capital Territory *n* a territory of SE Australia, within New South Wales: consists of two exclaves, one containing Canberra, the capital of Australia, and one at Jervis Bay. Pop: 310 170 (1999 est). Area: 2432 sq km (939 sq miles). Former name: **Federal Capital Territory**

Australian cattle dog *n* a compact strongly-built dog of a breed with pricked ears and a smooth bluish-grey coat, often used for controlling and moving cattle

Australian Rules *n* (*functioning as sing*) a game resembling

rugby, played in Australia between teams of 18 men each on an oval pitch, with a ball resembling a large rugby ball. Players attempt to kick the ball between posts (without crossbars) at either end of the pitch
▷ www.afl.com.au

Australian salute *n Austral inf* a movement of the hand and arm made to brush flies away from one's face

Australian silky terrier *n* a small compact variety of terrier with pricked ears and a long straight silky coat

Austral Islands ('ɔːstrəl) *pl n* another name for the **Tubuai Islands**

Australoid ('ɒstrəˌlɔɪd) *adj* **1** denoting, relating to, or belonging to a racial group that includes the native Australians and certain other peoples of southern Asia and the Pacific islands ▷ *n* **2** any member of this racial group

australopithecine (ˌɒstrələʊ'pɪθɪˌsiːn) *n* any of various extinct apelike primates whose remains have been found in southern and E Africa. Some species are estimated to be over 4.5 million years old [c20 from NL, from L *austrālis* southern + Gk *pithēkos* ape]

Australorp ('ɒstrəˌlɔːp) *n* a heavy black breed of domestic fowl laying brown eggs [shortened from *Austral(ian Black) Orp(ington)*]

Austrasia (ɒ'streɪʒə, -ʃə) *n* the eastern region of the kingdom of the Merovingian Franks that had its capital at Metz and lasted from 511 AD until 814 AD It covered the area now comprising NE France, Belgium, and western Germany

Austria ('ɒstrɪə) *n* a republic in central Europe: ruled by the Hapsburgs from 1282 to 1918; formed a dual monarchy with Hungary in 1867 and became a republic in 1919; a member of the European Union; contains part of the Alps, the Danube basin in the east, and extensive forests. Official language: German. Religion: Roman Catholic majority. Currency: euro. Capital: Vienna. Pop: 8 069 000 (2001 est). Area: 83 849 sq km (32 374 sq miles). German name: **Österreich** > **'Austrian** *adj, n*
▷ www.austria.org
▷ www.austria-tourism.at

Austrian blind *n* a window blind consisting of rows of vertically gathered fabric that may be drawn up to form a series of ruches

Austro-[1] ('ɒstrəʊ) *combining form* southern: *Austro-Asiatic* [from L *auster* the south wind]

Austro-[2] ('ɒstrəʊ) *combining form* Austrian: *Austro-Hungarian*

Austronesia (ˌɒstrəʊ'niːʒə, -ʃə) *n* the islands of the central and S Pacific, including Indonesia, Melanesia, Micronesia, and Polynesia > **ˌAustro'nesian** *adj, n*

AUT (in Britain) *abbrev for* Association of University Teachers

autarchy ('ɔːtɑːkɪ) *n, pl* **autarchies** unlimited rule; autocracy [c17 from Gk *autarkhia*, from *autarkhos* autocratic] > **au'tarchic** *or* **au'tarchical** *adj*

autarky ('ɔːtɑːkɪ) *n, pl* **autarkies** (esp of a political unit) a system or policy of economic self-sufficiency [c17 from Gk *autarkeia*, from *autarkēs* self-sufficient, from AUTO- + *arkein* to suffice] > **au'tarkic** *adj* > **'autarkist** *n*

auteur (ɔː'tɜː) *n* a director whose creative influence on a film is so great as to be considered its author [F: author] > **au'teurism** *n* > **au'teurist** *n*

authentic (ɔː'θɛntɪk) *adj* **1** of undisputed origin or authorship; genuine **2** trustworthy; reliable: *an authentic account* **3** (of a deed, etc) duly executed **4** *music* **4a** using period instruments and historically researched scores and playing techniques **4b** (*in combination*): *an authentic-instrument performance* **5** *music* commencing on the perfect and ending an octave higher ▷ Cf **plagal** [c14 from LL *authenticus* coming from the author, from Gk, from *authentēs* one who acts independently, from AUTO- + *hentēs* a doer] > **au'thentically** *adv* > **authenticity** (ˌɔːθɛn'tɪsɪtɪ) *n*

authenticate (ɔː'θɛntɪˌkeɪt) *vb* **authenticates, authenticating, authenticated** (*tr*) **1** to establish as genuine or valid **2** to give authority or legal validity to > **auˌthenti'cation** *n* > **au'thentiˌcator** *n*

author ('ɔːθə) *n* **1** a person who composes a book, article, or other written work. Related adj: **auctorial** **2** a person who writes books as a profession; writer **3** an originator or creator: *the author of this plan* ▷ *vb* (*tr*) **4** to write or originate [c14 from OF, from L *auctor* author, from *augēre* to increase] > **authorial** (ɔː'θɔːrɪəl) *adj*

authoring ('ɔːθərɪŋ) *n computing* **a** the creation of documents, esp multimedia documents **b** (*as modifier*): *an authoring tool*

authoritarian (ɔːˌθɒrɪ'tɛərɪən) *adj* **1** favouring or characterized by strict obedience to authority **2** favouring or relating to government by a small elite **3** dictatorial; domineering ▷ *n* **4** a person who favours or practises authoritarian policies

authoritative (ɔː'θɒrɪtətɪv) *adj* **1** recognized or accepted as being true or reliable **2** commanding: *an authoritative manner* **3** possessing or supported by authority; official > **au'thoritatively** *adv* > **au'thoritativeness** *n*

authority (ɔː'θɒrɪtɪ) *n, pl* **authorities** **1** the power or right to control, judge, or prohibit the actions of others **2** (*often pl*) a person or group of people having this power, such as a government, police force, etc **3** a position that commands such a power or right (often in **in authority**) **4** such a power or right delegated: *she has his authority* **5** the ability to influence or control others **6** an expert or an authoritative written work in a particular field **7** evidence or testimony **8** confidence resulting from great expertise **9** (*cap. when part of a name*) a public board or corporation exercising governmental authority: *Advertising Standards Authority* [c14 from OF, from L, from *auctor* author]

authorize *or* **authorise** ('ɔːθəˌraɪz) *vb* **authorizes, authorizing, authorized** *or* **authorises, authorising, authorised** (*tr*) **1** to confer authority upon (someone to do something) **2** to permit (someone to do or be something) with official sanction > **ˌauthori'zation** *or* **ˌauthori'sation** *n*

Authorized Version *n* **the** an English translation of the Bible published in 1611 under James I. Also called: **King James Version**

authorship ('ɔːθəʃɪp) *n* **1** the origin or originator of a written work, plan, etc **2** the profession of writing books

autism ('ɔːtɪzəm) *n psychiatry* abnormal self-absorption, usually affecting children, characterized by lack of response to people and limited ability to communicate [c20 from Gk *autos* self + -ISM] > **au'tistic** *adj*

auto ('ɔːtəʊ) *n, pl* **autos** *US & Canad inf* **a** short for **automobile** **b** (*as modifier*): *auto parts*

auto- *or sometimes before a vowel* **aut-** *combining form* **1** self; same; of or by the same one: *autobiography* **2** self-caused: *autohypnosis* **3** self-propelling: *automobile* [from Gk *autos* self]

autobahn ('ɔːtəˌbɑːn) *n* a motorway in German-speaking countries [c20 from G from *Auto* car + *Bahn* road, track]

autobiography (ˌɔːtəʊbaɪ'ɒgrəfɪ) *n, pl* **autobiographies** an account of a person's life written or otherwise recorded by that person > **ˌautobi'ographer** *n* > **autobiographical** (ˌɔːtəˌbaɪə'græfɪkᵊl) *adj*

autocephalous (ˌɔːtəʊ'sɛfələs) *adj* (of an Eastern Christian Church) governed by its own national synods and appointing its own patriarchs or prelates

autochthon (ɔː'tɒkθən) *n, pl* **autochthons** *or* **autochthones** (-θəˌniːz) **1** (*often pl*) one of the earliest known inhabitants of any country **2** an animal or plant that is native to a particular region [c17 from Gk *autokhthōn* from the earth itself, from AUTO- + *khthōn* the earth] > **au'tochthonous** *adj*

Aa

autoclave ('ɔːtəˌkleɪv) *n* **1** a strong sealed vessel used for chemical reactions at high pressure **2** an apparatus for sterilizing objects (esp surgical instruments) by means of steam under pressure [c19 from F AUTO- + *-clave*, from L *clāvis* key]

autocracy (ɔː'tɒkrəsɪ) *n, pl* **autocracies** **1** government by an individual with unrestricted authority **2** a country, society, etc, ruled by an autocrat

autocrat ('ɔːtəˌkræt) *n* **1** a ruler who possesses absolute and unrestricted authority **2** a domineering or dictatorial person > **ˌauto'cratic** *adj* > **ˌauto'cratically** *adv*

autocross ('ɔːtəʊˌkrɒs) *n* a motor sport in which cars race over a half-mile circuit of rough grass

Autocue ('ɔːtəʊˌkjuː) *n trademark* an electronic television prompting device whereby a script, unseen by the audience, is displayed for the speaker

auto-da-fé (ˌɔːtəʊdə'feɪ) *n, pl* **autos-da-fé** **1** *history* a ceremony of the Spanish Inquisition including the pronouncement and execution of sentences passed on sinners or heretics **2** the burning to death of people condemned as heretics by the Inquisition [c18 from Port., lit.: act of the faith]

autoeroticism (ˌɔːtəʊɪ'rɒtɪˌsɪzəm) *or* **autoerotism** (ˌɔːtəʊ'ɛrəˌtɪzəm) *n psychol* the arousal and use of one's own body as a sexual object > **ˌautoe'rotic** *adj*

autoexposure (ˌɔːtəʊɪk'spəʊʒə) *n* another name for **automatic exposure**

autofocus ('ɔːtəʊˌfəʊkəs) *n* another name for **automatic focus**

autogamy (ɔː'tɒgəmɪ) *n* self-fertilization

autogenic training (ˌɔːtəʊ'dʒɛnɪk) *n* a technique for reducing stress through mental exercises. Also called: **autogenics**

autogenous (ɔː'tɒdʒɪnəs) *adj* **1** originating within the body **2** self-produced **3** denoting a weld in which the filler metal and the parent metal are of similar composition > **au'togenously** *adv*

autogiro *or* **autogyro** (ˌɔːtəʊ'dʒaɪrəʊ) *n, pl* **autogiros** *or* **autogyros** a self-propelled aircraft supported in flight mainly by unpowered rotating horizontal blades [c20 orig. a trademark]

autograph ('ɔːtəˌgrɑːf) *n* **1a** a handwritten signature, esp that of a famous person **1b** (*as modifier*): *an autograph album* **2** a person's handwriting **3a** a book, document, etc, handwritten by its author **3b** (*as modifier*): *an autograph letter* ▷ *vb* (*tr*) **4** to write one's signature on or in; sign **5** to write with one's own hand > **autographic** (ˌɔːtə'græfɪk) *adj* > **ˌauto'graphically** *adv*

autohypnosis (ˌɔːtəʊhɪp'nəʊsɪs) *n psychol* the process or result of self-induced hypnosis

autoimmune (ˌɔːtəʊɪ'mjuːn) *adj* (of a disease) caused by the action of antibodies produced against substances normally present in the body > **ˌautoim'munity** *n*

autointoxication (ˌɔːtəʊɪnˌtɒksɪ'keɪʃən) *n* self-poisoning caused by toxic products originating within the body

autologous (ɔː'tɒləgəs) *adj* (of a tissue graft, blood transfusion, etc) originating from the recipient rather than from a donor

Autolycus (ɔːtɒlɪkəs) *n Greek myth* a thief who stole cattle from his neighbour Sisyphus and prevented him from recognizing them by making them invisible

autolysis (ɔː'tɒlɪsɪs) *n* the destruction of cells and tissues of an organism by enzymes produced by the cells themselves > **autolytic** (ˌɔːtə'lɪtɪk) *adj*

automat ('ɔːtəˌmæt) *n* another name, esp US, for **vending machine**

automate ('ɔːtəˌmeɪt) *vb* **automates, automating, automated** to make (a manufacturing process, factory, etc) automatic, or (of a manufacturing process, etc) to be made automatic

automated teller machine *n* a computerized cash dispenser. Abbrev: **ATM**

automatic (ˌɔːtə'mætɪk) *adj* **1** performed from force of habit or without conscious thought: *an automatic smile* **2a** (of a device, mechanism, etc) able to activate, move, or regulate itself **2b** (of an act or process) performed by such automatic equipment **3** (of the action of a muscle, etc) involuntary or reflex **4** occurring as a necessary consequence: *promotion is automatic after a year* **5** (of a firearm) utilizing some of the force of each explosion to eject the empty shell, replace it with a new one, and fire continuously until release of the trigger ▷ *n* **6** an automatic firearm **7** a motor vehicle having automatic transmission **8** a machine that operates automatically [c18 from Gk *automatos* acting independently] > **ˌauto'matically** *adv*

automatic door *n* a self-opening door

automatic exposure *n* the automatic adjustment of the lens aperture and shutter speed of a camera by a control mechanism. Also called: **autoexposure**

automatic focus *n* **a** a system in a camera that automatically adjusts the lens so that the object being photographed is in focus **b** (*as modifier*): *automatic-focus lens*. Also called: **autofocus**

automatic gain control *n* a control of a radio receiver which adjusts the magnitude of the input so that the output (or volume) remains approximately constant

automatic pilot *n* **1** a device that automatically maintains an aircraft on a preset course **2** *inf* a state of mind in which a person performs familiar tasks automatically: *I was on automatic pilot all day* ▷ Also called: **autopilot**

automatic transmission *n* a transmission system in a motor vehicle in which the gears change automatically

automation (ˌɔːtə'meɪʃən) *n* **1** the use of methods for controlling industrial processes automatically, esp by electronically controlled systems **2** the extent to which a process is so controlled

automatism (ɔː'tɒməˌtɪzəm) *n* **1** the state or quality of being automatic; mechanical or involuntary action **2** *psychol* the performance of actions, such as sleepwalking, without conscious knowledge or control > **au'tomatist** *n*

automatize *or* **automatise** (ɔː'tɒməˌtaɪz) *vb* **automatizes, automatizing, automatized** *or* **automatises, automatising, automatised** to make (a process, etc) automatic or (of a process, etc) to be made automatic > **auˌtomati'zation** *or* **auˌtomati'sation** *n*

automaton (ɔː'tɒmətᵊn) *n, pl* **automatons** *or* **automata** **1** a mechanical device operating under its own hidden power **2** a person who acts mechanically [c17 from L, from Gk, from *automatos* spontaneous]

automobile ('ɔːtəməˌbiːl) *n* another word (esp US) for **car** (sense 1) > **ˌautomo'bilist** *n*
▷ www.fisita.com
▷ www.uscar.org/links.htm

automobilia (ˌɔːtəmə'biːlɪə) *pl n* items connected with cars and motoring that are of interest to the collector

automotive (ˌɔːtə'məʊtɪv) *adj* **1** relating to motor vehicles **2** self-propelling

autonomic (ˌɔːtə'nɒmɪk) *adj* **1** occurring involuntarily or spontaneously **2** of or relating to the autonomic nervous system **3** Also: **autonomous** (of plant movements) occurring as a result of internal stimuli > **ˌauto'nomically** *adv*

autonomic nervous system *n* the section of the nervous system of vertebrates that controls the involuntary actions of the smooth muscles, heart, and glands

autonomics (ˌɔːtə'nɒmɪks) *n* (*functioning as sing*) *electronics* the study of self-regulating systems for process control

autonomous (ɔː'tɒnəməs) *adj* **1** (of a community, country, etc) possessing a large degree of self-government **2** of or relating to an autonomous community **3** independent of others **4** *biol* existing as an organism independent of other organisms or parts [c19 from Gk *autonomos* living under one's own laws, from AUTO- + *nomos* law] > **au'tonomously** *adv*

autonomy (ɔː'tɒnəmɪ) *n, pl* **autonomies** 1 the right or state of self-government, esp when limited 2 a state or individual possessing autonomy 3 freedom to determine one's own actions, behaviour, etc 4 *philosophy* the doctrine that the individual human will is, or ought to be, governed only by its own principles and laws [c17 from Gk *autonomia* freedom to live by one's own laws]

autopilot (ˌɔːtə'paɪlət) *n* short for **automatic pilot**

autopsy ('ɔːtəpsɪ, ɔː'tɒp-) *n, pl* **autopsies** 1 Also called: **postmortem examination** dissection and examination of a dead body to determine the cause of death 2 an eyewitness observation 3 any critical analysis [c17 from NL, from Gk: seeing with one's own eyes, from AUTO- + *opsis* sight]

auto-repeat *computing n* 1 a feature of computer keys whereby a character is generated repeatedly as long as the user holds down the key in question ▷ *vb (intr)* 2 (of a computer key) to go on automatically regenerating a character

autoroute ('ɔːtəʊˌruːt) *n* a motorway in French-speaking countries [c20 from F from *auto* car + *route* road]

autostrada ('ɔːtəʊˌstrɑːdə) *n* a motorway in Italian-speaking countries [c20 from It. from *auto* car + *strada* road]

autosuggestion (ˌɔːtəʊsə'dʒɛstʃən) *n* a process of suggestion in which the person unconsciously supplies the means of influencing his own behaviour or beliefs

autotelic (ˌɔːtəʊ'tɛlɪk) *adj* being or having an end or justification in itself [c20 from AUTO- + Gk *telos* end]

autotomy (ɔː'tɒtəmɪ) *n, pl* **autotomies** the casting off by an animal of a part of its body, to facilitate escape when attacked > **autotomic** (ˌɔːtə'tɒmɪk) *adj*

autotrophic (ˌɔːtə'trɒfɪk) *adj* (of organisms such as green plants) capable of manufacturing complex organic nutritive compounds from simple inorganic sources, using energy from the sun > **'autoˌtroph** *n*

autumn ('ɔːtəm) *n* 1 (*sometimes cap*) 1a Also called (esp US): **fall** the season of the year between summer and winter, astronomically from the September equinox to the December solstice in the N hemisphere and from the March equinox to the June solstice in the S hemisphere 1b (*as modifier*): *autumn leaves* 2 a period of late maturity, esp one followed by a decline [c14 from L *autumnus*] > **autumnal** (ɔː'tʌmnᵊl) *adj*

autumn crocus *n* a plant of the lily family having pink or purplish autumn flowers, found in Europe and N Africa

Auvergne (əʊ'vɛən, əʊ'vɜːn; *French* ovɛrɲ) *n* a region of S central France: largely mountainous, rising over 1800 m (6000 ft)

auxanometer (ˌɔːksə'nɒmɪtə) *n* an instrument that measures the linear growth of plant shoots [c19 from Gk *auxanein* to increase + -METER]

Aux Cayes (əʊ 'keɪ; *French* o kaj) *n* the former name of **Les Cayes**

Auxerre (*French* ozɛr, oksɛr) *n* a town in central France, capital of the Yonne department; Gothic cathedral. Pop: 40 600 (1990)

auxiliaries (ɔːg'zɪljərɪz, -'zɪlə-) *pl n* foreign troops serving another nation; mercenaries

auxiliary (ɔːg'zɪljərɪ, -'zɪlə-) *adj* 1 secondary or supplementary 2 supporting ▷ *n, pl* **auxiliaries** 3 a person or thing that supports or supplements 4 *naut* 4a a sailing vessel with an engine 4b the engine of such a vessel [c17 from L, from *auxilium* help, from *augēre* to increase, strengthen]

auxiliary rotor *n* the tail rotor of a helicopter, used for directional and rotary control

auxiliary verb *n* a verb used to indicate the tense, voice, or mood of another verb where this is not indicated by inflection, such as English *will* in *he will go*

auxin ('ɔːksɪn) *n* a plant hormone that promotes growth [c20 from Gk *auxein* to grow]

AV *abbrev for* Authorized Version (of the Bible)

av. *abbrev for* average

Av. *or* **av.** *abbrev for* avenue

a.v. *or* **A/V** *abbrev for* ad valorem

avadavat (ˌævədə'væt) *or* **amadavat** (ˌæmədə'væt) *n* either of two Asian weaverbirds having a red plumage: often kept as cagebirds [c18 from *Ahmadabad*, Indian city from which these birds were brought to Europe]

avail (ə'veɪl) *vb* 1 to be of use, advantage, profit, or assistance (to) 2 **avail oneself of** to make use of to one's advantage ▷ *n* 3 use or advantage (esp in **of no avail, to little avail**) [c13 *availen*, from OF *valoir*, from L *valēre* to be strong]

available (ə'veɪləbᵊl) *adj* 1 obtainable or accessible; capable of being made use of 2 *arch* advantageous > **aˌvaila'bility** *or* **a'vailableness** *n* > **a'vailably** *adv*

avalanche ('ævəˌlɑːntʃ) *n* 1a a fall of large masses of snow and ice down a mountain 1b a fall of rocks, sand, etc 2 a sudden or overwhelming appearance of a large quantity of things ▷ *vb* **avalanches, avalanching, avalanched** 3 to come down overwhelmingly (upon) [c18 from F, by mistaken division from *la valanche*, from *valanche*, from dialect *lavantse*]

Avalon ('ævəˌlɒn) *n* *Celtic myth* an island paradise in the western seas: in Arthurian legend it is where King Arthur was taken after he was mortally wounded [from Med L *insula avallonis* island of Avalon, from O Welsh *aballon* apple]

avant- ('ævɒŋ) *prefix* of or belonging to the avant-garde of a specified field

avant-garde (ˌævɒŋ'gɑːd) *n* 1 those artists, writers, musicians, etc, whose techniques and ideas are in advance of those generally accepted ▷ *adj* 2 of such artists, etc, their ideas, or techniques [from F: VANGUARD]

avarice ('ævərɪs) *n* extreme greed for riches [c13 from OF, from L, from *avārus* covetous, from *avēre* to crave] > **avaricious** (ˌævə'rɪʃəs) *adj*

avast (ə'vɑːst) *sentence substitute naut* stop! cease! [c17 ?from Du. *hou'vast* hold fast]

avatar ('ævəˌtɑː) *n* 1 *Hinduism* the manifestation of a deity in human or animal form 2 a visible manifestation of an abstract concept [c18 from Sansk. *avatāra* a going down, from *ava* down + *tarati* he passes over]

avaunt (ə'vɔːnt) *sentence substitute arch* go away! depart! [c15 from OF *avant!* forward! from LL *ab ante* forward, from L *ab* from + *ante* before]

avdp. *abbrev for* avoirdupois

ave ('ɑːvɪ, 'ɑːveɪ) *sentence substitute* welcome or farewell [L]

Ave¹ ('ɑːvɪ) *n* *RC Church* short for **Ave Maria**: see **Hail Mary** [c13 from L: hail!]

Ave² *or* **ave** *abbrev for* avenue

Avebury ('eɪvbərɪ) *n* a village in Wiltshire, site of an extensive neolithic stone circle

Aveiro (*Portuguese* ə'veːiru) *n* a port in N central Portugal, on the **Aveiro lagoon**: ancient Roman town; linked by canal with the Atlantic Ocean. Pop: 35 250 (1991). Ancient name: **Talabriga** (ˌtælə'briːgə)

Ave Maria (mə'riːə) *n* another name for **Hail Mary** [c14 from med L: hail, Mary!]

avenge (ə'vɛndʒ) *vb* **avenges, avenging, avenged** (*usually tr*) to inflict a punishment in retaliation for (harm, injury, etc) done to (a person or persons): *to avenge a crime; to avenge a murdered friend* [c14 from OF, from *vengier*, from L *vindicāre*; see VENGEANCE, VINDICATE] > **a'venger** *n*

USAGE The use of *avenge* with *oneself* was formerly considered incorrect, but is now acceptable and relatively common: *one of*

Aa

those writers who avenged themselves on somebody in print

avens ('ævɪnz) *n, pl* **avens** (*functioning as sing*) **1** any of a genus of plants, such as **water avens,** which has a purple calyx and orange-pink flowers **2** **mountain avens** either of two trailing evergreen white-flowered shrubs that grow on mountains in N temperate regions and in the Arctic [c15 from OF, from Med. L *avencia* variety of clover]

Aventine ('ævɪn,taɪn, -tɪn) *n* one of the seven hills on which Rome was built

aventurine (ə'vɛntjʊrɪn) *or* **avanturine** (ə'væntjʊrɪn) *n* **1** a dark-coloured glass, usually green or brown, spangled with fine particles of gold, copper, or some other metal **2** a variety of quartz containing red or greenish particles of iron oxide or mica [c19 from F, from It., from *avventura* chance; so named because usually found by accident]

avenue ('ævɪnju:) *n* **1a** a broad street, often lined with trees **1b** (*cap. as part of a street name*) a road, esp in a built-up area **2** a main approach road, as to a country house **3** a way bordered by two rows of trees **4** a line of approach: *explore every avenue* [c17 from F, from *avenir* to come to, from L, from *venīre* to come]

aver (ə'vɜ:) *vb* **avers, averring, averred** (*tr*) **1** to state positively **2** *law* to allege as a fact or prove to be true [c14 from OF, from Med. L *advērāre*, from L *vērus* true] > **a'verment** *n*

average ('ævərɪdʒ, 'ævrɪdʒ) *n* **1** the typical or normal amount, quality, degree, etc: *above average in intelligence* **2** Also called: **arithmetic mean** the result obtained by adding the numbers or quantities in a set and dividing the total by the number of members in the set: *the average of 3, 4, and 8 is 5* **3** a similar mean for continuously variable ratios, such as speed **4** *maritime law* **4a** a loss incurred or damage suffered by a ship or its cargo at sea **4b** the equitable apportionment of such loss among the interested parties **5** **on** (**the** *or* **an**) **average** usually; typically ▷ *adj* **6** usual or typical **7** mediocre or inferior: *his performance was only average* **8** constituting a numerical average: *an average speed* **9** approximately typical of a range of values: *the average contents of a matchbox* ▷ *vb* **averages, averaging, averaged** **10** (*tr*) to obtain or estimate a numerical average of **11** (*tr*) to assess the general quality of **12** (*tr*) to perform or receive a typical number of: *to average eight hours' work a day* **13** (*tr*) to divide up proportionately **14** to amount to or be on average: *the children averaged 15 years of age* [c15 *averay* loss arising from damage to ships, from OIt. *avaria*, ult. from Ar. *awār* damage, blemish] > **'averagely** *adv*

Averno (*Italian* a'vɛrno) *n* a crater lake in Italy, near Naples: in ancient times regarded as an entrance to hell. Latin name: **Avernus** (ə'vɜ:nəs) [from Latin, from Greek *aornos* without birds, from A-[1] + *ornis* bird; referring to the legend that the lake's sulphurous exhalations killed birds]

Averroës (ə'vɛrəʊ,i:z) *n* Arabic name *ibn-Rushd*. 1126–88, Arab philosopher and physician in Spain, noted particularly for his attempts to reconcile Aristotelian philosophy with Islamic religion, which profoundly influenced Christian scholasticism

averse (ə'vɜ:s) *adj* (*postpositive;* usually foll by *to*) opposed, disinclined, or loath [c16 from L, from *āvertere* to turn from, from *vertere* to turn] > **a'versely** *adv* > **a'verseness** *n*

USAGE See at **adverse**

aversion (ə'vɜ:ʃən) *n* **1** (usually foll by *to* or *for*) extreme dislike or disinclination **2** a person or thing that arouses this: *he is my pet aversion*

aversion therapy *n psychiatry* a way of suppressing an undesirable habit, such as smoking, by associating an unpleasant effect, such as an electric shock, with the habit

avert (ə'vɜ:t) *vb* (*tr*) **1** to turn away or aside: *to avert one's gaze* **2** to ward off: *to avert danger* [c15 from OF, from L *āvertere;* see AVERSE] > **a'vertible** *or* **a'vertable** *adj*

Avesta (ə'vɛstə) *n* a collection of sacred writings of Zoroastrianism, including the Songs of Zoroaster

Avestan (ə'vɛstən) *n* **1** the earliest recorded form of the Iranian language, formerly called **Zend** ▷ *adj* **2** of the Avesta or its language

Aveyron (*French* avɛrɔ̃) *n* a department of S France in Midi-Pyrénées region. Capital: Rodez. Pop: 263 808 (1999). Area: 8771 sq km (3421 sq miles)

avian ('eɪvɪən) *adj* of, relating to, or resembling a bird [c19 from L *avis* bird]

aviary ('eɪvjərɪ) *n, pl* **aviaries** a large enclosure in which birds are kept [c16 from L, from *aviārius* concerning birds, from *avis* bird]

aviation (,eɪvɪ'eɪʃən) *n* **1** the art or science of flying aircraft **2** the design, production, and maintenance of aircraft [c19 from F, from L *avis* bird]

▷ www.icao.int

aviator ('eɪvɪ,eɪtə) *n old-fashioned* the pilot of an aeroplane or airship; flyer > **'avi,atrix** *or* **'avi,atress** *fem n*

Avicenna (,ævɪ'sɛnə) *n* Arabic name *ibn-Sina*. 980–1037, Arab philosopher and physician whose philosophical writings, which combined Aristotelianism with neo-Platonist ideas, greatly influenced scholasticism, and whose medical work Qanun was the greatest single influence on medieval medicine

avid ('ævɪd) *adj* **1** very keen; enthusiastic: *an avid reader* **2** (*postpositive;* often foll by *for* or *of*) eager (for): *avid for revenge* [c18 from L, from *avēre* to long for] > **avidity** (ə'vɪdɪtɪ) *n* > **'avidly** *adv*

Aviemore (,ævɪ'mɔ:) *n* a winter sports resort in Scotland, in Moray between the Monadhliath and Cairngorm Mountains. Pop: 2214 (1991)

avifauna (,eɪvɪ'fɔ:nə) *n* all the birds in a particular region > **,avi'faunal** *adj*

Avignon (*French* aviɲɔ̃) *n* a city in SE France, on the Rhône: seat of the papacy (1309–77); famous 12th-century bridge, now partly destroyed. Pop: 181 136 (1990)

Ávila (*Spanish* 'aβila) *n* a city in central Spain: 11th-century granite walls and Romanesque cathedral. Pop: 45 092 (1988 est)

avionics (,eɪvɪ'ɒnɪks) *n* **1** (*functioning as sing.*) the science and technology of electronics applied to aeronautics **2** (*functioning as pl*) the electronic circuits and devices of an aerospace vehicle [c20 from *avi(ation electr)onics*] > **,avi'onic** *adj*

avitaminosis (æ,vɪtəmɪn'əʊsɪs) *n, pl* **avitaminoses** (-si:z) any disease caused by a vitamin deficiency in the diet

Avlona (æv'ləʊnə) *n* the ancient name for **Vlorë**

avocado (,ævə'kɑ:dəʊ) *n, pl* **avocados** **1** a pear-shaped fruit having a leathery green or blackish skin, a large stony seed, and a greenish-yellow edible pulp **2** the tropical American tree that bears this fruit **3a** a dull greenish colour **3b** (*as adj*): *an avocado bathroom suite* ▷ Also called (for senses 1 & 2): **avocado pear, alligator pear** [c17 from Sp. *aguacate*, from Nahuatl *ahuacatl* testicle, alluding to the shape of the fruit]

avocation (,ævə'keɪʃən) *n* **1** *formal* a minor occupation undertaken as a diversion **2** *not standard* a person's regular job [c17 from L, from *āvocāre* to distract, from *vocāre* to call]

avocet ('ævə,sɛt) *n* a long-legged shore bird having black-and-white plumage and a long slender upward-curving bill [c18 from F, from It. *avocetta*, from ?]

Avogadro (,ævə'gɑ:drəʊ; *Italian* avo'ga:dro) *n* **Amedeo** (ame'dɛ:o), *Conte di Quaregna*. 1776–1856, Italian physicist, noted for his work on gases

Avogadro constant *or* **number** *n* the number of atoms or molecules in a mole of a substance, equal to 6.02252×10^{23} per mole

Avogadro's law *or* **hypothesis** *n* the principle that equal volumes of all gases contain the same number of molecules at the same temperature and pressure

avoid (əˈvɔɪd) *vb* (*tr*) **1** to keep out of the way of **2** to refrain from doing **3** to prevent from happening: *to avoid damage to machinery* **4** *law* to invalidate; quash [c14 from Anglo-F, from OF *esvuidier*, from *vuidier* to empty] > **aˈvoidable** *adj* > **aˈvoidably** *adv* > **aˈvoidance** *n* > **aˈvoider** *n*

avoirdupois *or* **avoirdupois weight** (ˌævədəˈpɔɪz) *n* a system of weights used in many English-speaking countries. It is based on the pound, which contains 16 ounces or 7000 grains [c14 from OF *aver de peis* goods of weight]

Avon[1] (ˈeɪvᵊn) *n* **1** a former county of SW England, created in 1974 from areas of N Somerset and S Gloucestershire: replaced in 1996 by the unitary authorities of Bath and North East Somerset (Somerset), North Somerset (Somerset), South Gloucestershire (Gloucestershire), and Bristol **2** a river in central England, rising in Northamptonshire and flowing southwest through Stratford-on-Avon to the River Severn at Tewkesbury. Length: 154 km (96 miles) **3** a river in SW England, rising in Gloucestershire and flowing south and west through Bristol to the Severn estuary at **Avonmouth.** Length: 120 km (75 miles) **4** a river in S England, rising in Wiltshire and flowing south to the English Channel. Length: about 96 km (60 miles)

Avon[2] (ˈeɪvᵊn) *n* **Earl of** title of (Anthony) **Eden**

avouch (əˈvaʊtʃ) *vb* (*tr*) *arch* **1** to vouch for; guarantee **2** to acknowledge **3** to assert [c16 from OF *avochier* to summon, call on, from L *advocāre*; see ADVOCATE] > **aˈvouchment** *n*

avow (əˈvaʊ) *vb* (*tr*) **1** to state or affirm **2** to admit openly [c13 from OF *avouer* to confess, from L *advocāre* to appeal to, call upon] > **aˈvowal** *n* > **aˈvowed** *adj* > **avowedly** (əˈvaʊɪdlɪ) *adv* > **aˈvower** *n*

avuncular (əˈvʌŋkjʊlə) *adj* **1** of or concerned with an uncle **2** resembling an uncle; friendly [c19 from L *avunculus* (maternal) uncle, dim. of *avus* grandfather]

AWACS *or* **Awacs** (ˈeɪwæks) *n acronym for* Airborne Warning and Control System

await (əˈweɪt) *vb* **1** (*tr*) to wait for **2** (*tr*) to be in store for **3** (*intr*) to wait, esp with expectation

awake (əˈweɪk) *vb* **awakes, awaking, awoke** *or* **awaked, awoken** *or* **awaked 1** to emerge or rouse from sleep **2** to become or cause to become alert **3** (usually foll by *to*) to become or make aware (of) **4** Also: **awaken** (*tr*) to arouse (feelings, etc) or cause to remember (memories, etc) ▷ *adj* (*postpositive*) **5** not sleeping **6** (sometimes foll by *to*) lively or alert [OE *awacian, awacan*]

USAGE See at **wake**

award (əˈwɔːd) *vb* (*tr*) **1** to give (something due), esp as a reward for merit: *to award prizes* **2** *law* to declare to be entitled, as by decision of a court or an arbitrator ▷ *n* **3** something awarded, such as a prize or medal **4** *Austral & NZ* the amount of an **award wage** (esp in **above award**) **5** *law* **5a** the decision of an arbitrator **5b** a grant made by a court of law [c14 from Anglo-F *awarder*, from OF *eswarder* to decide after investigation, from *es-* EX-[1] + *warder* to observe] > **aˈwarder** *n*

award wage *n* (in Australia and New Zealand) statutory minimum pay for a particular group of workers. Sometimes shortened to **award**

aware (əˈwɛə) *adj* **1** (*postpositive; foll by of*) having knowledge: *aware of his error* **2** informed of current developments: *politically aware* [OE *gewær*] > **aˈwareness** *n*

awash (əˈwɒʃ) *adv, adj* (*postpositive*) *naut* **1** level with the surface of the sea **2** washed over by the waves

away (əˈweɪ) *adv* **1** from a particular place: *to swim away* **2** in or to another, a usual, or a proper place: *to put toys away* **3** apart; at a distance: *to keep away from strangers* **4** out of existence: *the music faded away* **5** indicating motion, displacement, transfer, etc, from a normal or proper place: *to turn one's head away* **6** indicating activity that is wasteful or designed to get rid of something: *to sleep away the hours* **7** continuously: *laughing away* **8 away with** a command for a person to go or be removed: *away with him to prison!* ▷ *adj* (*usually postpositive*) **9** not present: *away from school* **10** distant: *he is a good way away* **11** having started; released: *he was away before sunrise* **12** (*also prenominal*) *sport* played on an opponent's ground ▷ *n* **13** *sport* a game played or won at an opponent's ground ▷ *sentence substitute* **14** an expression of dismissal [OE *on weg* on way]

awayday (əˈweɪˌdeɪ) *n* a day trip taken for pleasure, relaxation, etc; day excursion [c20 from *awayday ticket*, name applied to some special-rate railway day returns]

away goal *n* a goal scored by a team playing away from its home ground. Away goals count for more than home goals in certain competitions

awe (ɔː) *n* **1** overwhelming wonder, respect, or dread **2** *arch* power to inspire fear or reverence ▷ *vb* **awes, awing, awed 3** (*tr*) to inspire with reverence or dread [c13 from ON *agi*]

aweigh (əˈweɪ) *adj* (*postpositive*) *naut* (of an anchor) no longer hooked into the bottom; hanging by its rope or chain

awe-inspiring *adj* causing or worthy of admiration or respect; amazing or magnificent

awesome (ˈɔːsəm) *adj* **1** inspiring or displaying awe **2** *sl* excellent or outstanding > **ˈawesomely** *adv* > **ˈawesomeness** *n*

awestruck *or* **awe-stricken** *adj* overcome or filled with awe

awful (ˈɔːfʊl) *adj* **1** very bad; unpleasant **2** *arch* inspiring reverence or dread **3** *arch* overcome with awe ▷ *adv* **4** *not standard* (intensifier): *an awful cold day* [c13 see AWE, -FUL] > **ˈawfulness** *n*

awfully (ˈɔːfəlɪ) *adv* **1** in an unpleasant, bad, or reprehensible manner **2** *inf* (intensifier): *I'm awfully keen to come* **3** *arch* so as to express or inspire awe

awhile (əˈwaɪl) *adv* for a brief period.

USAGE *Awhile* written as a single word can only be used with a verb, and is most common after verbs such as *linger*, *rest*, and *pause*. It is quite commonly written by mistake where the meaning intended is 'for a period of time', and where *while* is being used as a noun: *I thought about that for a while* (not *awhile*)

awkward (ˈɔːkwəd) *adj* **1** lacking dexterity, proficiency, or skill; clumsy **2** ungainly or inelegant in movements or posture **3** unwieldy; difficult to use **4** embarrassing: *an awkward moment* **5** embarrassed: *he felt awkward about leaving* **6** difficult to deal with; requiring tact: *an awkward customer* **7** deliberately unhelpful **8** dangerous or difficult [c14 *awk*, from ON *öfugr* turned the wrong way round + -WARD] > **ˈawkwardly** *adv* > **ˈawkwardness** *n*

awl (ɔːl) *n* a pointed hand tool with a fluted blade used for piercing wood, leather, etc [OE *ǣl*]

awn (ɔːn) *n* any of the bristles growing from the spikelets of certain grasses, including cereals [OE *agen* ear of grain] > **awned** *adj*

awning (ˈɔːnɪŋ) *n* a roof of canvas or other material supported by a frame to provide protection from the weather, esp one placed over a doorway or part of a deck of a ship [c17 from ?]

awoke (əˈwəʊk) *vb* a past tense and (now rare or dialectal) past participle of **awake**

AWOL (ˈeɪwɒl) *or* **A.W.O.L.** *adj mil* absent without leave but without intending to desert

awry (əˈraɪ) *adv, adj* (*postpositive*) **1** with a slant or twist to one side; askew **2** away from the appropriate or right course; amiss [c14 *on wry*; see A-[2], WRY]

AWS *abbrev for* automatic warning system: a train safety

Aa

system that gives audible warnings about the signals being passed, and can apply the brakes automatically if necessary

aw-shucks (ˌɔːˈʃʌks) *adj (prenominal)* seeming to be modest, self-deprecating, or shy: *don't be fooled by his aw-shucks attitude* [c20 from the US interjection *aw shucks*, an expression of modesty or diffidence]

axe *or US* **ax** (æks) *n, pl* **axes** **1** a hand tool with one side of its head forged and sharpened to a cutting edge, used for felling trees, splitting timber, etc **2** **an axe to grind** **2a** an ulterior motive **2b** a grievance **2c** a pet subject **3** **the axe** *inf* **3a** dismissal, esp from employment (esp in **get the axe**) **3b** *Brit* severe cutting down of expenditure, esp in a public service ▷ *vb* **axes, axing, axed** *(tr)* **4** to chop or trim with an axe **5** *inf* to dismiss (employees), restrict (expenditure or services), or terminate (a project, etc) [OE *æx*]

axel (ˈæksəl) *n skating* a jump of one and a half, two and a half, or three and a half turns, taking off from the forward outside edge of one skate and landing on the backward outside edge of the other [c20 after *Axel* Paulsen (d. 1938), Norwegian skater]

axeman (ˈæksmən) *n, pl* **axemen** **1** a man who wields an axe, esp to cut down trees **2** a person who makes cuts in expenditure or services, esp on behalf of another: *the chancellor's axeman*

axes¹ (ˈæksiːz) *n* the plural of **axis¹**

axes² (ˈæksɪz) *n* the plural of **axe**

axial (ˈæksɪəl) *adj* **1** forming or characteristic of an axis **2** situated in, on, or along an axis > ˌ**axiˈality** *n* > ˈ**axially** *adv*

axil (ˈæksɪl) *n* the upper angle between a branch or leafstalk and the stem from which it grows [c18 from L *axilla* armpit]

axilla (ækˈsɪlə) *n, pl* **axillae** (-liː) **1** the technical name for the **armpit** **2** the area under a bird's wing corresponding to the armpit [c17 from L: armpit]

axillary (ækˈsɪlərɪ) *adj* **1** of, relating to, or near the armpit **2** *bot* growing in or related to the axil ▷ *n, pl* **axillaries** **3** *(usually pl)* Also called: **axillar** (ækˈsɪlə) one of the feathers growing from the axilla of a bird's wing

axiom (ˈæksɪəm) *n* **1** a generally accepted proposition or principle, sanctioned by experience **2** a universally established principle or law that is not a necessary truth **3** a self-evident statement **4** *logic, maths* a statement that is stipulated to be true for the purpose of a chain of reasoning [c15 from L *axiōma* a principle, from Gk, from *axioun* to consider worthy, from *axios* worthy]

axiomatic (ˌæksɪəˈmætɪk) *adj* **1** self-evident **2** containing maxims; aphoristic > ˌ**axioˈmatically** *adv*

axis¹ (ˈæksɪs) *n, pl* **axes** **1** a real or imaginary line about which a body, such as an aircraft, can rotate or about which an object, form, composition, or geometrical construction is symmetrical **2** one of two or three reference lines used in coordinate geometry to locate a point in a plane or in space **3** *anat* the second cervical vertebra **4** *bot* the main central part of a plant, typically consisting of the stem and root **5** an alliance between a number of states to coordinate their foreign policy **6** Also called: **principal axis** *optics* the line of symmetry of an optical system, such as the line passing through the centre of a lens [c14 from L: axletree, earth's axis; rel. to Gk *axōn* axis]

axis² (ˈæksɪs) *n, pl* **axises** a S Asian deer with a reddish-brown white-spotted coat and slender antlers [c18 from L: Indian wild animal, from ?]

Axis (ˈæksɪs) *n* **a** **the** the alliance (1936) of Nazi Germany and Fascist Italy, later joined by Japan and other countries, and lasting until their defeat in World War II **b** *(as modifier): the Axis powers*

axle (ˈæksəl) *n* a bar or shaft on which a wheel, pair of wheels, or other rotating member revolves [c17 from ON *öxull*]

axletree (ˈæksəlˌtriː) *n* a bar fixed across the underpart of a wagon or carriage that has rounded ends on which the wheels revolve

Axminster carpet (ˈæksˌmɪnstə) *n* a type of patterned carpet with a cut pile. Often shortened to **Axminster** [after *Axminster* in Devon]

axolotl (ˌæksəˈlɒtᵊl) *n* an aquatic salamander of N America, such as the **Mexican axolotl**, in which the larval form (including external gills) is retained throughout life under natural conditions [c18 from Nahuatl, from *atl* water + *xolotl* servant, doll]

axon (ˈæksɒn) *n* the long threadlike extension of a nerve cell that conducts nerve impulses from the cell body [c19 via NL from Gk: axis, axle, vertebra]

ay¹ *or* **aye** (eɪ) *adv arch, poetic* always

ay² (aɪ) *sentence substitute, n* a variant spelling of **aye**

Ayacucho (*Spanish* ajaˈkutʃo) *n* a city in SE Peru: nearby is the site of the battle (1824) that won independence for Peru. Pop: 118 960 (1998 est)

ayah (ˈaɪə) *n* (in parts of the former British Empire) a native maidservant or nursemaid [c18 from Hindi *āyā*, from Port. *aia*, from L *avia* grandmother]

ayatollah (ˌaɪəˈtɒlə) *n* one of a class of Shiite religious leaders in Iran [via Persian from Ar., from *aya* creation + ALLAH]

Ayckbourn (ˈeɪkbɔːn) *n* Sir **Alan** born 1939, English dramatist. His plays include *Absurd Person Singular* (1973), the trilogy *The Norman Conquests* (1974), *A Chorus of Disapproval* (1985), and *House and Garden* (2000)

Aycliffe (ˈeɪklɪf) *n* a town in Co. Durham: founded as a new town in 1947. Pop: 40 000 (latest est)

Aydin (ˈaɪdɪn) *n* a town in SW Turkey: an ancient city of Lydia. Pop: 133 757 (1997). Ancient name: **Tralles**

aye *or* **ay** (aɪ) *sentence substitute* **1** yes: archaic or dialectal except in voting by voice ▷ *n* **2a** a person who votes in the affirmative **2b** an affirmative vote ▷ Cf **nay** [c16 prob. from pron I, expressing assent]

aye-aye (ˈaɪˌaɪ) *n* a rare nocturnal arboreal primate of Madagascar related to the lemurs. It has long bony fingers and rodent-like incisor teeth [c18 from F, from Malagasy *aiay*, prob. imit.]

Ayer (ɛə) *n* Sir **Alfred Jules** 1910–89, English positivist philosopher, noted particularly for his antimetaphysical work *Language, Truth, and Logic* (1936)

Ayers Rock (ɛəz) *n* the former name of **Uluru**

Ayesha (ˈɑːiːˌʃɑː) *n* a variant spelling of **Aisha**

Ayia Napa (ˌaɪjəˈnæpə) *n* a coastal resort in SE Cyprus. Pop,: 9 500 (2004 est)

Aykroyd (ˈeɪkˌrɔɪd) *n* **Dan** born 1952, Canadian film actor and screenwriter, best known for the television show *Saturday Night Live* (1975–80) and the films *The Blues Brothers* (1980), *Ghostbusters* (1984), and *Driving Miss Daisy* (1989)

Aylesbury (ˈeɪlzbərɪ, -brɪ) *n* a town in SE central England, administrative centre of Buckinghamshire. Pop: 58 058 (1991)

Aylward (ˈeɪlwəd) *n* **Gladys** 1903–70, English missionary in China

Aymara (ˌaɪməˈrɑː) *n* **1** *(pl* **-ras** *or* **-ra**) a member of a S American Indian people of Bolivia and Peru **2** the language of this people [from Sp. *aimará*, from Amerind]

Ayodha (ɑːɪˈjəʊdjɑː) *n* an ancient town in N India, in Uttar Pradesh state: as the birthplace of Rama it is sacred to Hindus; also a Buddhist centre. Also called: **Awadh** (əˈwɒd), **Oudh** (aʊd)

Ayr (ɛə) *n* a port in SW Scotland, in South Ayrshire. Pop: 47 962 (1991)

Ayrshire (ˈɛəʃɪə, -ʃə) *n* **1** a historical county of SW Scotland, formerly part of Strathclyde region (1975–96), now divided into the council areas of North Ayrshire, South Ayrshire, and East Ayrshire **2** any one of a hardy breed of brown-and-white dairy cattle

Ayub Khan (aɪˈjuːb ˈkɑːn) *n* **Mohammed** 1907–74, Pakistani field marshal; president of Pakistan (1958–69)

Ayutthaya (ɑːˈjuːtəjə) *n* a city in S Thailand, on the Chao Phraya River: capital of the country until 1767; noted for its canals and ruins. Pop: 61 185 (1990). Also called: **Ayudhya** (ɑːˈjuːdjə), **Ayuthia** (ɑːˈjuːθɪə)

AZ *abbrev for* Arizona

azalea (əˈzeɪljə) *n* an ericaceous plant cultivated for its showy pink or purple flowers [c18 via NL from Gk, from *azaleos* dry; from its supposed preference for a dry situation]

Azaña (*Spanish* aˈθaɲa) *n* **Manuel** (maˈnwel) 1880–1940, Spanish statesman; president of the Spanish Republic (1936–39) until overthrown by Franco

Azania (əˈzɑːnɪə, əˈzɑːnjə) *n* another name (used esp by many Black political activists) for **South Africa** [perhaps from Arabic *Adzan* East Africa] > **Aˈzanian** *n, adj*

Azbine (æzˈbiːn) *n* another name for **Aïr**

azeotrope (əˈziːəˌtrəʊp) *n* a mixture of liquids that boils at a constant temperature, at a given pressure, without change of composition [c20 from A-[1] + *zeo-*, from Gk *zein* to boil + -TROPE] > **azeotropic** (ˌeɪzɪəˈtrɒpɪk) *adj*

Azerbaijan (ˌæzəbaɪˈdʒɑːn) *n* **1** a republic in NW Asia: the region was acquired by Russia from Persia in the early 19th century; became the Azerbaijan Soviet Socialist Republic in 1936 and gained independence in 1991; consists of dry subtropical steppes around the Aras and Kura rivers, surrounded by the Caucasus; contains the extensive Baku oilfields. Language: Azerbaijani. Religion: Shiite Muslim. Currency: manat. Capital: Baku. Pop: 8 105 000 (2001 est). Area: 86 600 sq km (33 430 sq miles) **2** a mountainous region of NW Iran, separated from the republic of Azerbaijan by the Aras River: divided administratively into **Eastern Azerbaijan** and **Western Azerbaijan**. Capitals: Tabriz and Rezaiyeh. Pop: 5 562 926 (1991) > ˌ**Azerbaiˈjani** *adj, n*

azerty *or* **AZERTY keyboard** (əˈzɜːtɪ) *n* a common European version of typewriter keyboard layout with the characters a, z, e, r, t, and y positioned at the top left of the keyboard

azide (ˈeɪzaɪd) *n* **a** an acyl derivative or salt of hydrazoic acid, used as a coating to enhance electron emission **b** (*as modifier*): *an azide group or radical*

Azikiwe (ˌɑːziːˈkiːweɪ) *n* **Nnamdi** (ᵊnˈnæmdɪ) 1904–96, Nigerian statesman; first president of Nigeria (1963–66)

Azilian (əˈzɪlɪən) *n* **1** a Palaeolithic culture of Spain and SW France that can be dated to the 10th millennium BC, characterized by flat bone harpoons and schematically painted pebbles ▹ *adj* **2** of or relating to this culture [c19 after Mas d'*Azil*, France, where artefacts were found]

azimuth (ˈæzɪməθ) *n* **1** *astron, navigation* the angular distance usually measured clockwise from the south point of the horizon in astronomy or from the north point in navigation to the intersection with the horizon of the vertical circle passing through a celestial body **2** *surveying* the horizontal angle of a bearing clockwise from north [c14 from OF *azimut*, from Ar. *as-sumūt*, pl. of *as-samt* the path, from L *semita* path] > **azimuthal** (ˌæzɪˈmʌθəl) *adj*

azine (ˈeɪziːn) *n* an organic compound having a six-membered ring with at least one nitrogen atom, the other atoms in the ring being carbon atoms

azo (ˈeɪzəʊ, ˈæ-) *adj* of, consisting of, or containing the divalent group -N:N-: *an azo group or radical*. See also **diazo** [from F *azote* nitrogen, from Gk *azōos* lifeless]

azoic (əˈzəʊɪk) *adj* without life; characteristic of the ages that have left no evidence of life in the form of organic remains [c19 from Gk *azōos* lifeless]

Azores (əˈzɔːz) *pl n* **the** three groups of volcanic islands in the N Atlantic, since 1976 an autonomous region of Portugal. Capital: Ponta Delgada (on São Miguel). Pop: 242 073 (2001). Area: 2335 sq km (901 sq miles). Portuguese name: **Açôres**

Azorín (*Spanish* aθoˈrin) *n* real name *José Martínez Ruiz*. 1874–1967, Spanish writer: noted for his stories of the Spanish countryside

Azov (ˈɑːzɒv) *n* **Sea of** a shallow arm of the Black Sea, to which it is connected by the Kerch Strait: almost entirely landlocked; fed chiefly by the River Don. Area: about 37 500 sq km (14 500 sq miles)

AZT *abbrev for* azidothymidine: another name for **zidovudine**

Aztec (ˈæztɛk) *n* **1** a member of a Mexican Indian people who established a great empire, centred on the valley of Mexico, that was overthrown by Cortés in the early 16th century **2** the language of the Aztecs. See also **Nahuatl** ▹ *adj* Also **Aztecan** **3** of, relating to, or characteristic of the Aztecs, their civilization, or their language [c18 from Sp., from Nahuatl *Aztecatl*, from *Aztlan*, their traditional place of origin, lit.: near the cranes]

▹ www.aztecempire.com

▹ www.indians.org/welker/aztec.html

azure (ˈæʒə, ˈeɪ-) *n* **1** a deep blue similar to the colour of a clear blue sky **2** *poetic* a clear blue sky ▹ *adj* **3** of the colour azure **4** (*usually postpositive*) *heraldry* of the colour blue [c14 from OF, from OSp., from Ar. *lāzaward* lapis lazuli, from Persian *lāzhuward*]

azurite (ˈæʒʊˌraɪt) *n* a deep blue mineral consisting of hydrated basic copper carbonate. It is used as an ore of copper and as a gemstone

azygous (ˈæzɪgəs) *adj* *biol* developing or occurring singly [c17 via NL from Gk *azugos*, from A-[1] + *zugon* YOKE]

Bb

b *or* **B** (biː) *n, pl* **b's, B's,** *or* **Bs** **1** the second letter of the English alphabet **2** a speech sound represented by this letter **3** Also: **beta** the second in a series, class, or rank

B *symbol for:* **1** *music* **1a** the seventh note of the scale of C major **1b** the major or minor key having this note as its tonic **2** the less important of two things **3** a human blood type of the ABO group, containing the B antigen **4** (in Britain) a secondary road **5** *chem* boron **6** magnetic flux density **7** *chess* bishop **8** (on Brit pencils, signifying degree of softness of lead) black **9** Also: **b** *physics* bel **10** *physics* baryon number **11a** a person whose job is in middle management, or who holds an intermediate administrative or professional position **11b** (*as modifer*): *a B worker* ▷ See also **occupation groupings**

b. *abbrev for:* **1** born **2** *cricket* bowled

B. *abbrev for* (on maps, etc) bay

B- (of US military aircraft) *abbrev for* bomber

Ba[1] *the chemical symbol for* barium

Ba[2] (bɑː) *n Egyptian myth* the soul, represented as a bird with a human head

BA *abbrev for:* **1** Bachelor of Arts **2** British Academy **3** British Airways **4** British Association (for the Advancement of Science) **5** British Association screw thread

▷ www.britac.ac.uk/index.asp

baa (bɑː) *vb* **baas, baaing, baaed** **1** (*intr*) to make the cry of a sheep; bleat ▷ *n* **2** the cry made by sheep

BAA *abbrev for* British Airports Authority

Baader-Meinhof Gang (*German* ˈbaːdər ˈmainhoːf) *n* **the** a group of West German guerrillas dedicated to the violent overthrow of capitalist society. Also called: **Red Army Faction** [C20 named after its leading members, Andreas *Baader* (1943–77) and Ulrike *Meinhof* (1934–76)]

Baal (bɑːl) *n* **1** any of several ancient Semitic fertility gods **2** *Phoenician myth* the sun god and supreme national deity **3** (*sometimes not cap*) any false god or idol [from Heb. *bá'al* lord, master]

Baalbek (ˈbɑːlbɛk) *n* a town in E Lebanon: an important city in Phoenician and Roman times; extensive ruins. Pop: 15 600 (1995 est). Ancient name: **Heliopolis**

Baal Shem Tov *or* **Baal Shem Tob** (bɑːl ˈʃɛm tɒv, ˈʃɑːm) *n* original name *Israel ben Eliezer* ?1700–60, Jewish religious leader, teacher, and healer in Poland: founder of modern Hasidism

baas (bɑːs) *n* a South African word for **boss**[1] (sense 1): used by Africans and Coloured people in addressing European managers or overseers [C17 from Afrik., from MDu. *baes* master]

baaskap *or* **baasskap** (ˈbɑːsˌkap) *n* (*sometimes cap*) (in South Africa) control by Whites of non-Whites [from Afrik., from BAAS + *-skap* -SHIP]

Bab (bɑːb) *n* **the.** title of *Mirza Ali Mohammed* 1819–50, Persian religious leader: founded Babism; executed as a heretic of Islam [from Persian *bāb* gate, from Arabic]

baba (ˈbɑːbɑː) *n* a small cake, usually soaked in rum (**rum baba**) [C19 from F, from Polish, lit.: old woman]

babalas (ˈbabalas) *n S African* a hangover [from Zulu *ibhabhalasi*]

Babar (ˈbɑːbə) *n* a variant spelling of **Baber**

Babbage (ˈbæbɪdʒ) *n* **Charles** 1792–1871, English mathematician and inventor, who built a calculating machine that anticipated the modern electronic computer

babbitt (ˈbæbɪt) *vb* (*tr*) to line (a bearing) or face (a surface) with Babbitt metal

Babbitt (ˈbæbɪt) *n US derog* a narrow-minded and complacent member of the middle class [C20 after George *Babbitt*, central character in the novel *Babbitt* (1922) by Sinclair Lewis] > **ˈBabbittry** *n*

Babbitt metal *n* any of a number of alloys originally

based on tin, antimony, and copper but now often including lead: used esp in bearings [c19 after Isaac *Babbitt* (1799–1862), US inventor]

babble ('bæbᵊl) *vb* **babbles, babbling, babbled** 1 to utter (words, sounds, etc) in an incoherent jumble 2 (*intr*) to talk foolishly, incessantly, or irrelevantly 3 (*tr*) to disclose (secrets, etc) carelessly 4 (*intr*) (of streams, birds, etc) to make a low murmuring sound ▷ *n* 5 incoherent or foolish speech 6 a murmuring sound [c13 prob. imit.]

babbler ('bæblə) *n* 1 a person or thing that babbles 2 any of various birds of the Old World tropics and subtropics having an incessant song

babbling brook *n Austral sl* a cook [rhyming slang]

babe (beɪb) *n* 1 a baby 2 *inf* a naive or gullible person 3 *sl* a girl or young woman, esp an attractive one

Babel[1] ('beɪbᵊl) *n* 1 *Old Testament* Also called: **Tower of Babel** a tower presumptuously intended to reach from earth to heaven, the building of which was frustrated when Jehovah confused the language of the builders (Genesis 11:1–10) 2 (*often not cap*) 2a a confusion of noises or voices 2b a scene of noise and confusion [from Heb. *Bābhēl*, from Akkadian *Bāb-ilu*, lit.: gate of God]

Babel[2] (*Russian* 'babɪl) *n* **Issak Emmanuilovich** (i'sak imənu'iləvitʃ) 1894–1941, Russian short-story writer, whose works include *Stories from Odessa* (1924) and *Red Cavalry* (1926)

Bab el Mandeb ('bæb ɛl 'mændɛb) *n* a strait between SW Arabia and E Africa, connecting the Red Sea with the Gulf of Aden

Baber, Babar, *or* **Babur** ('bɑːbə) *n* original name *Zahir ud-Din Mohammed* 1483–1530, founder of the Mogul Empire: conquered India in 1526

Babeuf (*French* babœf) *n* **François Noël** (frɑ̃swa nɔɛl) 1760–97, French political agitator: plotted unsuccessfully to destroy the Directory and establish a communistic system

Babington ('bæbɪŋtən) *n* **Anthony** 1561–86, English conspirator, executed for organizing an unsuccessful plot (1586) to assassinate Elizabeth I and place Mary, Queen of Scots, on the English throne

babirusa (ˌbɑːbɪ'ruːsə) *n* a wild pig of Indonesia. It has an almost hairless wrinkled skin and enormous curved canine teeth [c17 from Malay, from *bābī* hog + *rūsa* deer]

Babism ('bɑːbɪzəm) *n* a pantheistic Persian religious sect, founded in 1844, forbidding polygamy, concubinage, begging, trading in slaves, and indulgence in alcohol and drugs [c19 from the BAB]
▷ http://i-cias.com/cgi-bin/eo-direct.pl?babism.htm

baboon (bə'buːn) *n* any of several medium-sized Old World monkeys. They have an elongated muzzle, large teeth, and a fairly long tail [c14 *babewyn* gargoyle, later, baboon, from OF]

babu ('bɑːbuː) *n* (in India) 1 a form of address more or less equivalent to *Mr* 2 (formerly) an Indian clerk who could write English [Hindi, lit.: father]

Babur ('bɑːbə) *n* a variant spelling of **Baber**

babushka (bə'buːʃkə) *n* 1 a headscarf tied under the chin, worn by Russian peasant women 2 (in Russia) an old woman [Russian: grandmother, from *baba* old woman]

baby ('beɪbɪ) *n, pl* **babies** 1a a newborn child; infant 1b (*as modifier*): *baby food* 2 an unborn child; fetus 3 the youngest or smallest of a family or group 4 a newborn or recently born animal 5 *usually derog* an immature person 6 *sl* a young woman or sweetheart 7 a project of personal concern 8 **be left holding the baby** to be left with the responsibility ▷ *adj* 9 (*prenominal*) comparatively small of its type: *a baby car* ▷ *vb* **babies, babying, babied** 10 (*tr*) to treat with love and attention 11 to treat (someone) like a baby; pamper or overprotect [c14 prob. childish reduplication] > '**babyˌhood** *n* > '**babyish** *adj*

baby bond *n Brit* a sum of money invested shortly after the birth of a child, the returns of which may not be collected until the child reaches adulthood

baby bonus *n Canad inf* Family Allowance

baby boomer *n* a person born during a **baby boom,** a sharp increase in the birth rate, esp (in Britain and the US) one born during the years 1945–55

baby broker *n* an adoption service, esp on the Internet

baby buggy *n* 1 *Brit trademark* a child's pushchair 2 *US & Canad inf* a small pram

baby carriage *n* the US and Canad name for **pram**[1]

Babylon ('bæbɪlən) *n* 1 the chief city of ancient Mesopotamia: first settled around 3000 BC. See also **Hanging Gardens of Babylon** 2 *derog* (in Protestant polemic) the Roman Catholic Church, regarded as the seat of luxury and corruption 3 *derog* any society or group in a society considered as corrupt or as a place of exile by another society or group, esp White Britain as viewed by some West Indians [via Latin and Greek from Hebrew *Bābhel*; see BABEL] > **Babylonian** (ˌbæbɪ'ləʊnɪən) *adj, n*

Babylonia (ˌbæbɪ'ləʊnɪə) *n* the southern kingdom of ancient Mesopotamia: a great empire from about 2200–538 BC, when it was conquered by the Persians
▷ http://ragz-international.com/babylonia.htm
▷ www.bible-history.com/babylonia

baby-sit *vb* **baby-sits, baby-sitting, baby-sat** (*intr*) to act or work as a baby-sitter > '**baby-ˌsitting** *n, adj*

baby-sitter *n* a person who takes care of a child or children while the parents are out

baby snatcher *n inf* 1 a person who steals a baby from its pram 2 someone who marries or has an affair with a much younger person

baby wipe *n* a disposable moistened medicated paper towel used for cleaning babies

Bacău ('bækaʊ) *n* a city in E Romania on the River Bistrila: oil refining, textiles, paper. Pop: 209 689 (1997 est)

baccalaureate (ˌbækə'lɔːrɪɪt) *n* the university degree of Bachelor of Arts [c17 from Med. L *baccalaureātus*, from *baccalaureus* advanced student from *baccalārius* BACHELOR]

baccarat ('bækəˌrɑː, ˌbækə'rɑː) *n* a card game in which two or more punters gamble against the banker [c19 from F *baccara* from ?]

baccate ('bækeɪt) *adj bot* 1 like a berry 2 bearing berries [c19 from L *bāca* berry]

Bacchae ('bækiː) *pl n* the priestesses or female devotees of Bacchus [L, from Gk *Bakkhai*, plural of *Bakkhē* priestess of BACCHUS]

bacchanal ('bækənᵊl) *n* 1 a follower of Bacchus 2 a drunken and riotous celebration 3 a participant in such a celebration ▷ *adj* 4 of or relating to Bacchus [c16 from L *Bacchānālis*]

bacchanalia (ˌbækə'neɪlɪə) *pl n* 1 (*often cap*) orgiastic rites associated with Bacchus 2 any drunken revelry > ˌ**baccha'nalian** *adj, n*

bacchant ('bækənt) *or* (*fem*) **bacchante** (bə'kæntɪ) *n, pl* **bacchants** *or* **bacchantes** (bə'kæntɪz) 1 a priest, priestess, or votary of Bacchus 2 a drunken reveller [c17 from L *bacchāns*, from *bacchārī* to celebrate the BACCHANALIA]

Bacchic ('bækɪk) *adj* 1 of or relating to Bacchus 2 (*often not cap*) riotously drunk

Bacchus ('bækəs) *n* (in ancient Greece and Rome) a god of wine and giver of ecstasy, identified with Dionysus [c15 from L, from Gk *Bakkhos*; related to L *bāca* small round fruit, berry]

baccy ('bækɪ) *n* a Brit informal name for **tobacco**

bach (bætʃ) NZ ▷ *n* 1 a seaside, bush, or country cottage ▷ *vb* 2 a variant spelling of **batch**[2]

Bach (*German* bax) *n* 1 **Johann Christian** (jo'han 'krɪstjan), 11th son of J. S. Bach. 1735–82, German composer, called *the English Bach*, resident in London from 1762 2 **Johann**

Bb

Christoph ('krɪstɔf) 1642–1703, German composer: wrote oratorios, cantatas, and motets, some of which were falsely attributed to J. S. Bach, of whom he was a distant relative **3** **Johann Sebastian** (ze'bastjan) 1685–1750, German composer: church organist at Arnstadt (1703–07) and Mühlhausen (1707–08); court organist at Weimar (1708–17); musical director for Prince Leopold of Köthen (1717–28); musical director for the city of Leipzig (1728–50). His output was enormous and displays great vigour and invention within the northern European polyphonic tradition. His works include nearly 200 cantatas and oratorios, settings of the *Passion according to St John* (1723) and *St Matthew* (1729), the six *Brandenburg Concertos* (1720–21), the 48 preludes and fugues of the *Well-tempered Clavier* (completed 1744), and the *Mass in B Minor* (1733–38) **4** **Karl** (*or* **Carl**) **Philipp Emanuel** (karl 'fi:lɪp e'ma:nuɛl), 3rd son of J. S. Bach. 1714–88, German composer, chiefly of symphonies, keyboard sonatas, and church music **5** **Wilhelm Friedemann** ('vɪlhɛlm 'fri:dəman), eldest son of J. S. Bach. 1710–84, German composer: wrote nine symphonies and much keyboard and religious music

bachelor ('bætʃələ, 'bætʃlə) *n* **1a** an unmarried man **1b** (*as modifier*): *a bachelor flat* **2** a person who holds the degree of Bachelor of Arts, Bachelor of Education, Bachelor of Science, etc **3** (in the Middle Ages) a young knight serving a great noble **4** **bachelor seal** a young male seal that has not yet mated [C13 from OF *bacheler* youth, squire, from Vulgar L *baccalāris* (unattested) farm worker] > **'bachelor,hood** *n*

bachelor apartment *n Canad* a flat consisting of one room that is used as a sitting room and bedroom, as well as a kitchenette and a bathroom

bachelor girl *n* a young unmarried woman, esp one who is self-supporting

Bachelor of Arts *n* **1** a degree conferred on a person who has successfully completed undergraduate studies in the liberal arts or humanities **2** a person who holds this degree

Bachelor of Science *n* **1** a degree conferred on a person who has successfully completed undergraduate studies in a science **2** a person who holds this degree

bachelor's-buttons *n* (*functioning as sing or pl*) any of various plants with button-like flower heads

Bach flower remedy (ba:x) *n trademark* an alternative medicine consisting of a distillation from various flowers, supposed to counteract negative states of mind and restore emotional balance [C20 after Dr E. *Bach* (1886–1936), homeopath who developed this system]

bacillary (bə'sɪlərɪ) *or* **bacillar** (bə'sɪlə) *adj* **1** of, relating to, or caused by bacilli **2** Also: **bacilliform** (bə'sɪlɪ,fɔ:m) shaped like a short rod

bacillus (bə'sɪləs) *n, pl* **bacilli** (-'sɪlaɪ) **1** any rod-shaped bacterium **2** any of various rodlike spore-producing bacteria constituting the family Bacillaceae [C19 from L, from *baculum* walking stick]

back (bæk) *n* **1** the posterior part of the human body, from the neck to the pelvis **2** the corresponding or upper part of an animal **3** the spinal column **4** the part or side of an object opposite the front **5** the part or side of anything less often seen or used **6** the part or side of anything that is furthest from the front or from a spectator: *the back of the stage* **7** something that supports, covers, or strengthens the rear of an object **8** *ball games* **8a** a mainly defensive player behind a forward **8b** the position of such a player **9** the part of a book to which the pages are glued or that joins the covers **10** **at the back of one's mind** not in one's conscious thoughts **11** **back of Bourke** *Austral* a remote or backward place **12** **behind one's back** secretly or deceitfully **13** **break one's back** to overwork or work very hard **14** **break the back of** to complete the greatest or hardest part of (a task) **15** **get off someone's back** *inf* to stop criticizing or pestering someone **16** **put one's back into** to devote all one's strength to (a task) **17** **put** (*or* **get**) **someone's back up** to annoy someone **18** **the back of beyond** a very remote place **19** **turn one's back on** **19a** to turn away from in anger or contempt **19b** to refuse to help; abandon ▷ *vb* (*mainly tr*) **20** (*also intr*) to move or cause to move backwards **21** **back water** to reverse the direction of a boat, esp to push the oars of a rowing boat **22** to provide support, money, or encouragement for (a person, enterprise, etc) **23** to bet on the success of: *to back a horse* **24** to provide with a back, backing, or lining **25** to provide with a musical accompaniment **26** to countersign or endorse **27** (*intr; foll by on or onto*) to have the back facing (towards): *the house backs onto a river* **28** (*intr*) (of the wind) to change direction anticlockwise ▷ Cf **veer** (sense 3) ▷ *adj* (*prenominal*) **29** situated behind: *a back lane* **30** of the past: *back issues of a magazine* **31** owing from an earlier date: *back rent* **32** remote: *a back road* **33** *phonetics* of or denoting a vowel articulated with the tongue retracted towards the soft palate, as for the vowels in English *hard, fall, hot, full, fool* ▷ *adv* **34** at, to, or towards the rear; behind **35** in, to, or towards the original starting point, place, or condition: *to go back home; put the book back* **36** in or into the past: *to look back on one's childhood* **37** in reply, repayment, or retaliation: *to hit someone back* **38** in check: *the dam holds back the water* **39** in concealment; in reserve: *to keep something back* **40** **back and forth** to and fro **41** **back to front** **41a** in reverse **41b** in disorder ▷ See also **back down, back off, back out, back up** [OE *bæc*]

back bacon *n* lean bacon from the back of a pig's loin

backbencher ('bæk'bɛntʃə) *n Brit, Austral, NZ, etc* a Member of Parliament who does not hold office in the government or opposition

backbite ('bæk,baɪt) *vb* **backbites, backbiting, backbit; backbitten** *or* **backbit** to talk spitefully about (an absent person) > **'back,biter** *n*

backboard ('bæk,bɔ:d) *n* **1** a board that is placed behind something to form or support its back **2** a board worn to straighten or support the back, as after surgery **3** (in basketball) a flat upright surface supported on a high frame, under which the basket is attached

back boiler *n* a tank or series of pipes at the back of a fireplace for heating water

backbone ('bæk,bəʊn) *n* **1** a nontechnical name for **spinal column** **2** something that resembles the spinal column in function, position, or appearance **3** strength of character; courage

backbreaking ('bæk,breɪkɪŋ) *adj* exhausting

backburn ('bæk,bɜ:n) *Austral & NZ* ▷ *vb* **1** (*tr*) to clear (an area of scrub, bush, etc) by creating a new fire that burns in the opposite direction to the line of advancing fire ▷ *n* **2** the act or result of backburning

back-calculate *vb* **back-calculates, back-calculating, back-calculated** to estimate (the probable amount of alcohol in a person's blood) at an earlier time than that at which the blood test was taken, based on an average rate at which alcohol leaves the bloodstream: used to determine whether a driver had more than the legal limit of alcohol at the time of an accident > **'back-,calcu'lation** *n*

back catalogue *n* the recordings that a musician has made in the past, as distinct from his or her current recording: *favourites from his back catalogue*

backchat ('bæk,tʃæt) *n inf* the act of answering back, esp impudently

backcloth ('bæk,klɒθ) *n* a painted curtain at the back of a stage set. Also called: **backdrop**

backcomb ('bæk,kəʊm) *vb* to comb the under layers of (the hair) towards the roots to give more bulk to a hairstyle. Also: **tease**

back country *n Austral & NZ* land remote from settled areas

backdate (ˌbækˈdeɪt) *vb* **backdates, backdating, backdated** (*tr*) to make effective from an earlier date

back door *n* **1** a door at the rear or side of a building **2a** a means of entry to a job, etc, that is secret or obtained through influence **2b** (*as modifier*): *a backdoor way of making firms pay more*

back down *vb* **1** (*intr, adv*) to withdraw an earlier claim ▷ *n* **backdown 2** abandonment of an earlier claim

backed (bækt) *adj* **a** having a back or backing **b** (*in combination*): *high-backed; black-backed*

backer (ˈbækə) *n* **1** a person who gives financial or other support **2** a person who bets on a competitor or contestant

backfield (ˈbækˌfiːld) *n American football* **1** (usually preceded by *the*) the quarterback and running backs in a team **2** the area behind the line of scrimmage from which the backfield begin each play

backfill (ˈbækˌfɪl) *vb* (*tr*) to refill an excavated trench, esp (in archaeology) at the end of an investigation

backfire (ˌbækˈfaɪə) *vb* **backfires, backfiring, backfired** (*intr*) **1** (of an internal-combustion engine) to emit a loud noise as a result of an explosion in the exhaust system **2** to fail to have the desired effect, and, instead, recoil upon the originator **3** to start a controlled fire in order to halt an advancing forest or prairie fire by creating a barren area ▷ *n* **4** (in an internal-combustion engine) an explosion of unburnt gases in the exhaust system **5** a controlled fire started to create a barren area that will halt an advancing forest or prairie fire

back formation *n* **1** the invention of a new word on the assumption that a familiar word is derived from it. The verbs *edit* and *burgle* in English were so created from *editor* and *burglar* **2** a word formed by this process

backgammon (ˈbækˌgæmən) *n* **1** a game for two people played on a board with pieces moved according to throws of the dice **2** the most complete form of win in this game [C17 BACK + *gammon*, var. of GAME[1]]
▷ www.worldbackgammonfederation.com

background (ˈbækˌgraʊnd) *n* **1** the part of a scene furthest from the viewer **2a** an inconspicuous or unobtrusive position (esp in **in the background**) **2b** (*as modifier*): *a background influence* **3** the plane or ground in a picture upon which all other planes or forms appear superimposed **4** a person's social class, education, or experience **5a** the circumstances that lead up to or help to explain something **5b** (*as modifier*): *background information* **6a** a low level of sound, lighting, etc, whose purpose is to be an unobtrusive accompaniment to something else **6b** (*as modifier*): *background music* **7** Also called: **background radiation** *physics* low-intensity radiation from small amounts of radioisotopes in soil, air, etc **8** *electronics* unwanted effects, such as noise, occurring in a measuring instrument, electronic device, etc

backhand (ˈbækˌhænd) *n* **1** *tennis, etc* a stroke made across the body with the back of the hand facing the direction of the stroke **2** the side on which backhand strokes are made **3** handwriting slanting to the left ▷ *adv* **4** with a backhand stroke

backhanded (ˌbækˈhændɪd) *adj* **1** (of a blow, shot, etc) performed with the arm moving across the body **2** double-edged; equivocal: *a backhanded compliment* **3** (of handwriting) slanting to the left ▷ *adv* **4** in a backhanded manner

backhander (ˈbækˌhændə) *n* **1** a backhanded stroke or blow **2** *inf* an indirect attack **3** *sl* a bribe

backie (ˈbækɪ) *n Brit inf* a ride on the back of someone's bicycle

backing (ˈbækɪŋ) *n* **1** support **2** a body of supporters **3** something that forms, protects, or strengthens the back of something **4** musical accompaniment, esp for a pop singer **5** *meteorol* an anticlockwise change in wind direction

backing dog *n NZ & Austral* a dog that moves a flock of sheep in yards or trucks by jumping on their backs

backlash (ˈbækˌlæʃ) *n* **1** a sudden and adverse reaction **2** a reaction or recoil between interacting worn or badly fitting parts in a mechanism **3** the excessive play between such parts

backlog (ˈbækˌlɒg) *n* an accumulation of uncompleted work, unsold stock, etc, to be dealt with

back marker *n* a competitor who is at the back of a field in a race

back matter *n* the parts of a book, such as the index and appendices, that follow the text

backmost (ˈbækˌməʊst) *adj* furthest back

back number *n* **1** an issue of a newspaper, magazine, etc, that appeared on a previous date **2** *inf* a person or thing considered to be old-fashioned

back off *vb* (*adv*) *Inf* **1** (*intr*) to retreat **2** (*tr*) to abandon (an intention, objective, etc)

back office *n* **a** the administrative and support staff of a financial institution or other business **b** (*as modifier*): *back-office operations*

back out *vb* (*intr, adv; often foll by of*) to withdraw (from an agreement, etc)

backpack (ˈbækˌpæk) *n* **1** a rucksack **2** a pack carried on the back of an astronaut, containing oxygen cylinders, etc ▷ *vb* (*intr*) **3** to travel about with a backpack

back passage *n* the rectum

back-pedal *vb* **back-pedals, back-pedalling, back-pedalled** *or US* **back-pedals, back-pedaling, back-pedaled** (*intr*) **1** to turn the pedals of a bicycle backwards **2** to retract or modify a previous opinion, principle, etc

back projection *n* a method of projecting pictures onto a translucent screen so that they are viewed from the opposite side, used esp in films to create the illusion that the actors in the foreground are moving

Back River *n* a river in N Canada, flowing northeast through Nunavut to the Arctic Ocean. Length: about 966 km (600 miles)

Bb

back room *n* **a** a place where important and usually secret research or planning is done **b** (*as modifier*): *back-room boys*

Backs (bæks) *pl n* **the** the grounds between the River Cam and certain Cambridge colleges

back seat *n* **1** a seat at the back, esp of a vehicle **2** *inf* a subordinate or inconspicuous position (esp in **take a back seat**)

back-seat driver *n inf* **1** a passenger in a car who offers unwanted advice to the driver **2** a person who offers advice on or tries to direct matters that are not his or her concern

backsheesh (ˈbækʃiːʃ) *n* a variant spelling of **baksheesh**

back shift *n Brit* **1** a group of workers who work a shift from late afternoon to midnight in an industry or occupation where a day or a night shift is also worked **2** the period worked ▷ US and Canad name: **swing shift**

backside (ˌbækˈsaɪd) *n inf* the buttocks

backslide (ˌbækˈslaɪd) *vb* **backslides, backsliding, backslid** (*intr*) to relapse into former bad habits > **ˌbackˈslider** *n*

backspace (ˈbækˌspeɪs) *vb* **backspaces, backspacing, backspaced** to move (a typewriter carriage, etc) backwards

backspin (ˈbækˌspɪn) *n sport* a backward spin imparted to a ball to reduce its speed at impact

back-stabbing *n* actions or remarks that are treacherous and likely to cause harm to a person, esp a friend or colleague

backstage (ˌbækˈsteɪdʒ) *adv* **1** behind the part of the theatre in view of the audience **2** towards the rear of the stage ▷ *adj* **3** situated backstage **4** *inf* away from public view

backstairs (ˌbækˈstɛəz) *pl n* **1** a secondary staircase in a house, esp one originally for the use of servants ▷ *adj* 2 Also: **backstair** underhand: *backstairs gossip*

backstay ('bæk,steɪ) *n naut* a stay leading aft from the upper mast to the deck or stern

back story *n* the events which take place before, and which help to bring about, the events portrayed in a film

backstreet ('bæk,stri:t) *n* 1 a street in a town remote from the main roads 2 (*modifier*) denoting illicit activities regarded as likely to take place in such a street: *a backstreet abortion*

backstroke ('bæk,strəʊk) *n swimming* a stroke performed on the back, using backward circular strokes of each arm and flipper movements of the feet. Also called: **back crawl**

back-to-back *adj* (*usually postpositive*) 1 facing in opposite directions, often with the backs touching 2 *chiefly Brit* (of urban houses) built so that their backs are joined or separated only by a narrow alley

backtrack ('bæk,træk) *vb* (*intr*) 1 to return by the same route by which one has come 2 to retract or reverse one's opinion, policy, etc

back up *vb* (*adv*) 1 (*tr*) to support 2 (*intr*) *cricket* (of a nonstriking batsman) to move down the wicket in readiness for a run as a ball is bowled 3 (of water) to accumulate 4 (of traffic) to become jammed behind an accident or other obstruction 5 *computing* to make a copy of (a data file), esp as a security copy 6 (*intr*; usually foll by *on*) *Austral* to repeat an action immediately ▷ *n* **backup** 7 a support or reinforcement 8a a substitute 8b (*as modifier*): *a backup copy* 9 the overflow from a blocked drain or pipe

backward ('bækwəd) *adj* 1 (*usually prenominal*) directed towards the rear: *a backward glance* 2 retarded in physical, material, or intellectual development 3a conservative or reactionary 3b (*in combination*): *backward-looking* 4 reluctant or bashful: *a backward lover* ▷ *adv* 5 a variant of **backwards** > '**backwardness** *n*

backwardation (,bækwə'deɪʃən) *n* 1 the difference between the spot price for a commodity, including rent and interest, and the forward price 2 (formerly, on the Stock Exchange) postponement of delivery by a seller of securities until the next settlement period

backwards ('bækwədz) *or* **backward** *adv* 1 towards the rear 2 with the back foremost 3 in the reverse of usual order or direction 4 to or towards the past 5 into a worse state 6 towards the point of origin 7 **bend, lean,** *or* **fall over backwards** *inf* to make a special effort, esp in order to please

backwash ('bæk,wɒʃ) *n* 1 water washed backwards by the motion of oars or other propelling devices 2 the backward flow of air set up by aircraft engines 3 a repercussion

backwater ('bæk,wɔ:tə) *n* 1 a body of stagnant water connected to a river 2 an isolated or backward place or condition

backwoods ('bækwʊdz) *pl n* 1 partially cleared, sparsely populated forests 2 any remote sparsely populated place 3 (*modifier*) of or like the backwoods 4 (*modifier*) uncouth; rustic > '**back,woodsman** *n*

backword ('bæk,wɜ:d) *n dialect* a failure to keep a promise

back yard *n* 1 a yard at the back of a house, etc 2 **in one's own back yard** 2a close at hand 2b involving or implicating one

baclava ('bɑ:klə,vɑ:) *n* a variant spelling of **baklava**

Bacolod (bə'kɒləd) *n* a town in the Philippines, on the NW coast of Negros Island. Pop: 429 076 (2000)

bacon ('beɪkən) *n* 1 meat from the back and sides of a pig, dried, salted, and usually smoked 2 **bring home the bacon** *inf* 2a to achieve success 2b to provide material support 3 **save (someone's) bacon** *Brit inf* to help (someone) to escape from danger [C12 from OF *bacon*, from OHG *bahho*, rel. to OSaxon *baco*; see BACK[1]]

Bacon ('beɪkən) *n* 1 **Francis**, Baron Verulam, Viscount St. Albans. 1561–1626, English philosopher, statesman, and essayist; described the inductive method of reasoning: his works include *Essays* (1625), *The Advancement of Learning* (1605), and *Novum Organum* (1620) 2 **Francis** 1909–92, British painter, born in Dublin, noted for his distorted, richly coloured human figures, dogs, and carcasses 3 **Roger** ?1214–92, English Franciscan monk, scholar, and scientist: stressed the importance of experiment, demonstrated that air is required for combustion, and first used lenses to correct vision. His *Opus Majus* (1266) is a compendium of all the sciences of his age

Baconian (beɪ'kəʊnɪən) *adj* 1 of or relating to Francis Bacon, the philosopher, or his inductive method of reasoning ▷ *n* 2 a follower of Bacon's philosophy 3 one who believes that plays attributed to Shakespeare were written by Bacon

BACS (bæks) *n acronym for* Bankers Automated Clearing System; a method of making payments direct to a creditor's bank without using a cheque

bacteria (bæk'tɪərɪə) *pl n, sing* **bacterium** a very large group of microorganisms comprising one of the three domains of living organisms. They are prokaryotic, unicellular, and either free-living in soil or water or parasites of plants and animals [C19 NL, from Gk *baktērion*, from *baktron* rod, staff] > **bac'terial** *adj* > **bac'terially** *adv*

> USAGE *Bacteria* is a plural noun, so the usage *a bacteria* is incorrect, though not uncommonly encountered, particularly in the media

bactericide (bæk'tɪərɪ,saɪd) *n* a substance able to destroy bacteria > **bac,teri'cidal** *adj*

bacterio-, bacteri-, *or sometimes before a vowel* **bacter-** *combining form* indicating bacteria or an action or condition relating to bacteria: *bacteriology; bactericide*

bacteriology (bæk,tɪərɪ'ɒlədʒɪ) *n* the study of bacteria > **bacteriological** (bæk,tɪərɪə'lɒdʒɪkᵊl) *adj* > **bac,teri'ologist** *n*

bacteriophage (bæk'tɪərɪə,feɪdʒ) *n* a virus that is parasitic in a bacterium and multiplies within its host, which is destroyed when the new viruses are released. Often shortened to: **phage** > **bacteriophagic** (bæk,tɪərɪə'fædʒɪk) *adj* > **bacteriophagous** (bæk,tɪərɪ'ɒfəgəs) *adj*

bacterium (bæk'tɪərɪəm) *n* the singular of **bacteria**

> USAGE See at **bacteria**

Bactria ('bæktrɪə) *n* an ancient country of SW Asia, between the Hindu Kush mountains and the Oxus River: forms the present Balkh region in N Afghanistan > '**Bactrian** *adj, n*

Bactrian camel *n* a two-humped camel, used in the cold deserts of central Asia

bad[1] (bæd) *adj* **worse, worst** 1 not good; of poor quality; inadequate 2 (often foll by *at*) lacking skill or talent; incompetent 3 (often foll by *for*) harmful 4 immoral; evil 5 naughty; mischievous 6 rotten; decayed: *a bad egg* 7 severe; intense: *a bad headache* 8 incorrect; faulty: *bad pronunciation* 9 ill or in pain (esp in **feel bad**) 10 sorry or upset (esp in **feel bad about**) 11 unfavourable; distressing: *bad news* 12 offensive; unpleasant: *bad language; bad temper* 13 not valid or sound: *a bad cheque* 14 not recoverable: *a bad debt* 15 (**badder, baddest**) *sl* good; excellent 16 **go bad** to putrefy; spoil 17 **in a bad way** *inf* 17a seriously ill 17b in trouble 18 **make the best of a bad job** to manage as well as possible in unfavourable circumstances 19 **not bad** *or* **not so bad** *inf* passable; fairly good 20 **too bad** *inf* (often used dismissively) regrettable ▷ *n* 21 unfortunate or unpleasant events (often in **take the bad with the good**) 22 an immoral or degenerate state (often in **go to the**

bad) **23** the debit side of an account: *£200 to the bad* **24 go from bad to worse** to deteriorate even more ▷ *adv* **25** *not standard* badly: *to want something bad* [c13 prob. from *bæd-*, as the first element of OE *bǣddel* hermaphrodite] > **'baddish** *adj* > **'badness** *n*

bad² (bæd) *vb* a variant spelling of **bade**

Badajoz ('bædə,hɒz; *Spanish* ba'ðaxoθ) *n* a city in SW Spain: strategically positioned near the frontier with Portugal. Pop: 134 710 (1998 est)

Badalona (*Spanish* baða'lona) *n* a port in NE Spain: an industrial suburb of Barcelona. Pop: 209 606 (1995 est)

bad blood *n* a feeling of intense hatred or hostility; enmity

baddie *or* **baddy** ('bædɪ) *n, pl* **baddies** *inf* a bad character in a film, etc, esp an opponent of the hero

bade (bæd, beɪd) *or* **bad** *vb past tense of* **bid**

Baden ('bɑːdən) *n* a former state of West Germany, now part of Baden-Württemberg

Baden-Baden *n* a spa in SW Germany, in Baden-Württemberg. Pop: 52 520 (1991)

Baden-Powell ('beɪdᵊn'pəʊəl, -'paʊəl) *n* **Robert Stephenson Smyth** (smɪθ, smaɪθ), 1st Baron Baden-Powell. 1857–1941, British general, noted for his defence of Mafeking (1899–1900) in the Boer War; founder of the Boy Scouts (1908) and (with his sister Agnes) the Girl Guides (1910)

Baden-Württemberg (*German* 'baːdən'vyrtəmbɛrk) *n* a state of SW Germany; formerly in West Germany. Capital: Stuttgart. Pop: 10 475 900 (2000 est). Area: 35 742 sq km (13 800 sq miles)

Bader ('bɑːdə) *n* Sir **Douglas** 1910–82, British fighter pilot. Despite losing both legs after a flying accident (1931), he became a national hero as a pilot in World War II

badge (bædʒ) *n* **1** a distinguishing emblem or mark worn to signify membership, employment, achievement, etc **2** any revealing feature or mark [c14 from OF *bage*]

badger ('bædʒə) *n* **1** any of various stocky omnivorous mammals occurring in Europe, Asia, and N America. They are large burrowing animals, with strong claws and a thick coat striped black and white on the head ▷ *vb* **2** (*tr*) to pester or harass [c16 var. of *badgeard*, prob. from BADGE (from the white mark on its forehead) + -ARD]

Bad Godesberg (*German* baːt 'goːdəsbɛrk) *n* the official name for **Godesberg**

bad hair day *n inf* **1** a day on which one's hair is untidy and unmanageable **2** a day of mishaps and general irritation

badinage ('bædɪ,nɑːʒ) *n* playful or frivolous repartee or banter [c17 from F, from *badiner* to jest]

badlands ('bæd,lændz) *pl n* any deeply eroded barren area

Bad Lands *pl n* a deeply eroded barren region of SW South Dakota and NW Nebraska

badly ('bædlɪ) *adv* **worse, worst** **1** poorly; defectively; inadequately **2** unfavourably; unsuccessfully: *our scheme worked out badly* **3** severely; gravely: *badly hurt* **4** incorrectly or inaccurately: *to speak German badly* **5** improperly; wickedly: *to behave badly* **6** cruelly: *to treat badly* **7** very much (esp in **need badly, want badly**) **8** regretfully: *he felt badly about it* **9 badly off** poor

badminton ('bædmɪntən) *n* **1** a game played with rackets and a shuttlecock which is hit back and forth across a high net **2** Also called: **badminton cup** a long drink of claret with soda water and sugar [from *Badminton* House, Glos]

▷ www.intbadfed.org

Badminton ('bædmɪntən) *n* a village in SW England, in South Gloucestershire unitary authority, Gloucestershire: site of Badminton House, seat of the Duke of Beaufort; annual horse trials

bad-mouth *vb* (*tr*) *sl, chiefly US & Canad* to speak unfavourably about

bad-tempered *adj* angry; irritable

bad trot *n Austral sl* a period of ill fortune

Baedeker ('beɪdɪkə) *n* any of a series of travel guidebooks issued by the German publisher Karl Baedeker (1801–59) or his firm

Baez ('baɪɛz) *n* **Joan** born 1941, US rock and folk singer and songwriter, noted for the pure quality of her voice and for her committed pacifist and protest songs

BAF *abbrev for* British Athletics Federation

baffies ('bæfɪz) *pl n Scot dialect* slippers

Baffin Bay ('bæfɪn) *n* part of the Northwest Passage, situated between Baffin Island and Greenland [named after William *Baffin*, 17th-century English navigator]

Baffin Island *n* the largest island of the Canadian Arctic, between Greenland and Hudson Bay. Area: 476 560 sq km (184 000 sq miles)

baffle ('bæfᵊl) *vb* **baffles, baffling, baffled** (*tr*) **1** to perplex; bewilder; puzzle **2** to frustrate (plans, efforts, etc) **3** to check, restrain, or regulate (the flow of a fluid or the emission of sound or light) ▷ *n* **4** Also called: **baffle board, baffle plate** a plate or mechanical device to restrain or regulate the flow of fluid, light, or sound, esp in a loudspeaker or microphone [c16 ?from Scot. dialect *bachlen* to condemn publicly] > **'bafflement** *n* > **'baffler** *n* > **'baffling** *adj* > **'bafflingly** *adv*

BAFTA ('bæftə) *n acronym for* British Academy of Film and Television Arts

▷ www.bafta.org

▷ www.bafta.com

bag (bæg) *n* **1** a flexible container with an opening at one end **2** Also: **bagful** the contents of or amount contained in such a container **3** a piece of portable luggage **4** short for **handbag** **5** anything that sags, or is shaped like a bag, such as a loose fold of skin under the eyes **6** any pouch or sac forming part of the body of an animal **7** the quantity of quarry taken in a single hunting trip or by a single hunter **8** *derog sl* an ugly or bad-tempered woman or girl (often in **old bag**) **9 bag and baggage** *inf* **9a** with all one's belongings **9b** entirely **10 bag of bones** a lean creature **11 in the bag** *sl* almost assured of succeeding or being obtained **12 rough as bags** *Austral sl* **12a** uncouth **12b** shoddy ▷ *vb* **bags, bagging, bagged** **13** (*tr*) to put into a bag **14** to bulge or cause to bulge **15** (*tr*) to capture or kill, as in hunting **16** (*tr*) to catch, seize, or steal **17** (*intr*) to hang loosely; sag **18** (*tr*) *Brit & Austral inf* to secure the right to do or to have: *he bagged the best chair* **19** (*tr*) to achieve or accomplish: *she bagged seven birdies.* ▷ See also **bags** [c13 prob. from ON *baggi*]

Bb

bagasse (bə'gæs) *n* the dry pulp remaining after the extraction of juice from sugar cane or similar plants: used as fuel, for making fibreboard, etc [c19 from F, from Sp. *bagazo* dregs]

bagatelle (,bægə'tɛl) *n* **1** something of little value **2** a board game in which balls are struck into holes, with pins as obstacles **3** a short light piece of music [c17 from F, from It. *bagattella*, from (dialect) *bagatta* a little possession]

Bagdad (bæg'dæd) *n* a variant spelling of **Baghdad**

Bagehot ('bædʒət) *n* **Walter** 1826–77, English economist and journalist: editor of *The Economist*; author of *The English Constitution* (1867), *Physics and Politics* (1872), and *Lombard Street* (1873)

bagel *or* **beigel** ('beɪgᵊl) *n* a hard ring-shaped bread roll [c20 from Yiddish *beygel*]

baggage ('bægɪdʒ) *n* **1** suitcases, bags, etc, packed for a journey; luggage **2** an army's portable equipment **3** *inf, old-fashioned* **3a** a pert young woman **3b** an immoral woman **4** *Irish inf* a cantankerous old woman **5** *inf* previous knowledge and experience that a person may use or be influenced by in new circumstances: *cultural* *baggage* [c15 from OF *bagage*, from *bague* a bundle]

baggy ('bægɪ) *adj* **baggier, baggiest** (of clothes) hanging loosely; puffed out > '**baggily** *adv* > '**bagginess** *n*

baggy green *n Austral inf* **1** the Australian Test cricket cap **2 don** *or* **wear the baggy green** to represent Australia at Test cricket

Baghdad *or* **Bagdad** (bæg'dæd) *n* the capital of Iraq, on the River Tigris: capital of the Abbasid Caliphate (762–1258). Pop: 4 478 000 (1995 est)
▹ www.iraqioasis.com/baghdad.html

bag lady *n* a homeless woman who wanders city streets with all her possessions in shopping bags

bagman ('bægmən) *n, pl* **bagmen 1** *Brit inf* a travelling salesman **2** *sl, chiefly US* a person who collects or distributes money for racketeers **3** *Austral* a tramp or swagman, esp one on horseback **4** *inf, chiefly Canad* a person who solicits money for a political party

bagnio ('bɑːnjəʊ) *n, pl* **bagnios 1** a brothel **2** *obs* an oriental prison for slaves **3** *obs* an Italian or Turkish bathhouse [c16 from It. *bagno*, from L *balneum* bath]

Bagnold ('bægnəʊld) *n* **Enid** (**Algerine**) 1889–1981, British novelist and playwright; her works include the novel *National Velvet* (1935) and the play *The Chalk Garden* (1955)

bagpipes ('bæg,paɪps) *pl n* any of a family of musical wind instruments in which sounds are produced in reed pipes by air from a bag inflated either by the player's mouth or by arm-operated bellows

Bagram ('bægrəm) *n* an air base in NE Afghanistan, near Kabul; now under the control of US forces

bags (bægz) *pl n* **1** *inf* a lot **2** *Brit inf* trousers ▹ *interj* **3** Also: **bags I** *children's sl, Brit & Austral* an indication of the desire to do, be, or have something

baguette *or* **baguet** (bæ'gɛt) *n* **1** a narrow French stick loaf **2** a small gem cut as a long rectangle **3** *archit* a small moulding having a semicircular cross section [c18 from F, from It. *bacchetta* a little stick, from *bacchio* rod]

Baguio ('bægɪ,əʊ) *n* a city in the N Philippines, on N Luzon: summer capital of the Republic. Pop: 252 386 (2000)

bah (bɑː, bæ) *interj* an expression of contempt or disgust

Bahá'í (bə'hɑːɪ) *n* **1** an adherent of the Bahá'í Faith ▹ *adj* **2** of or relating to the Bahá'í Faith [from Persian *bahā'ī*, lit.: of glory]
▹ http://www.bahai.org/
▹ http://bahai-library.org/

Bahá'í Faith *or* **Bahá'í** *n* a religious system founded in 1863, based on Babism and emphasizing the value of all religions and the spiritual unity of mankind

Bahá'ism (bə'hɑː,ɪzəm) *n* another name, not in Bahá'í use, for the **Bahá'í Faith**

Bahamas (bə'hɑːməz) *or* **Bahama Islands** *pl n* **the** a group of over 700 coral islands (about 20 of which are inhabited) in the Caribbean: a British colony from 1783 until 1964; an independent nation within the Commonwealth from 1973. Language: English. Currency: Bahamian dollar. Capital: Nassau. Pop: 298 000 (2001 est). Area: 13 939 sq km (5381 sq miles) > **Bahamian** (bə'heɪmɪən, -'hɑː-) *adj, n*
▹ www.bahamas.com
▹ www.bahamas.gv.bs
▹ www.bahamas.de

Bahawalpur (,bæhə'wɒlpə) *n* an industrial city in Pakistan: cotton, soap. Pop (urban area): 403 408 (1998)

Bahia (bə'hiːə; *Portuguese* bə'iːə) *n* **1** a state of E Brazil, on the Atlantic coast. Capital: Salvador. Pop: 13 066 764 (2000). Area: about 562 000 sq km (217 000 sq miles) **2** the former name of **San Salvador**

Bahía Blanca (*Spanish* ba'ia 'blanka) *n* a port in E Argentina. Pop: 281 161 (1999 est)

Bahia de los Cochinos (ba'ia de los ko'tʃinos) *n* the Spanish name for the **Bay of Pigs**

Bahrain *or* **Bahrein** (bɑː'reɪn) *n* an independent sheikhdom on the Persian Gulf, consisting of several islands: under British protection until the declaration of independence in 1971. It has large oil reserves. Language: Arabic. Religion: Muslim. Currency: dinar. Capital: Manama. Pop: 701 000 (2001 est). Area: 678 sq km (262 sq miles) > **Bah'raini** *or* **Bah'reini** *adj, n*
▹ www.bahrain.gov.bh
▹ www.bahraintourism.com

Baikal (baɪ'kɑːl, -'kæl) *n* **Lake** a lake in Russia, in SE Siberia: the largest freshwater lake in Eurasia and the deepest in the world. Greatest depth: over 1500 m (5000 ft) Area: about 33 670 sq km (13 000 sq miles)

Baikonur (baɪ'kəʊnə) *n* a launching site for spacecraft in central Kazakhstan; formerly the centre for the Soviet space programme, now leased from Kazakhstan by Russia

bail[1] (beɪl) *law* ▹ *n* **1** a sum of money by which a person is bound to take responsibility for the appearance in court of another person or himself, forfeited if the person fails to appear **2** the person or persons so binding themselves; surety **3** the system permitting release of a person from custody where such security has been taken: *he was released on bail* **4 jump bail** *or* (*formal*) **forfeit bail** to fail to appear in court to answer to a charge **5 stand** *or* **go bail** to act as surety (for someone) ▹ *vb* (*tr*) **6** (often foll by *out*) to release or obtain the release of (a person) from custody, security having been made [c14 from OF: custody, from *baillier* to hand over, from L *bāiulāre* to carry burdens]

bail[2] *or* **bale** (beɪl) *vb* **bails, bailing, bailed** *or* **bales, baling, baled** (often foll by *out*) to remove (water) from (a boat). See also **bail out** [c13 from OF *baille* bucket, from L *bāiulus* carrier] > '**bailer** *or* '**baler** *n*

bail[3] (beɪl) *n* **1** *cricket* either of two small wooden bars across the tops of the stumps **2** a partition between stalls in a stable or barn **3** *Austral & NZ* a framework in a cowshed used to secure the head of a cow during milking **4** a movable bar on a typewriter that holds the paper against the platen ▹ *vb* **5** See **bail up** [c18 from OF *baile* stake, fortification, prob. from L *baculum* stick]

bail[4] *or* **bale** (beɪl) *n* the semicircular handle of a kettle, bucket, etc [c15 prob. of Scand. origin]

bailey ('beɪlɪ) *n* the outermost wall or court of a castle [c13 from OF *baille* enclosed court, from *bailler* to enclose]

Bailey ('beɪlɪ) *n* **1 David** born 1938, English photographer **2 Nathan** *or* **Nathaniel** died 1742, English lexicographer: compiler of *An Universal Etymological English Dictionary* (1721–27)

Bailey bridge ('beɪlɪ) *n* a temporary bridge made of prefabricated steel parts that can be rapidly assembled [c20 after Sir Donald Coleman *Bailey* (1901–85), its Brit designer]

bailie ('beɪlɪ) *n* (in Scotland) a municipal magistrate [c13 from OF *bailli*, from earlier *baillif* BAILIFF]

bailiff ('beɪlɪf) *n* **1** *Brit* the agent of a landlord or landowner **2** a sheriff's officer who serves writs and summonses, makes arrests, and ensures that the sentences of the court are carried out **3** *chiefly Brit* (formerly) a high official having judicial powers **4** *chiefly US* an official having custody of prisoners appearing in court [c13 from OF *baillif*, from *bail* custody; see BAIL[1]]

bailiwick ('beɪlɪwɪk) *n* **1** *law* the area over which a bailiff has jurisdiction **2** a person's special field of interest [c15 from BAILIE + WICK[2]]

bail out *or* **bale out** *vb* (*adv*) **1** (*intr*) to make an emergency parachute jump from an aircraft **2** (*tr*) *inf* to help (a person, organization, etc) out of a predicament

bail up *vb* (*adv*) **1** *Austral & NZ* to confine (a cow) or (of a cow) to be confined by the head in a bail. See **bail**[3] (sense 3) **2** (*tr*) *Austral* (of a bushranger) to hold under guard in order to rob **3** (*intr*) *Austral* to submit to robbery without offering resistance **4** (*tr*) *Austral inf* to accost or detain, esp in conversation

Bainbridge ('beɪn,brɪdʒ) *n* Dame **Beryl** born 1934, British novelist and playwright. Novels include *The Dressmaker* (1973), *Injury Time* (1977), *Master Georgie* (1998), and *According to Queeney* (2001)

bain-marie *French* (bɛ̃mari) *n, pl* ***bains-marie*** (bɛ̃mari) a vessel for holding hot water, in which sauces and other dishes are gently cooked or kept warm [c19 from F, from Med. L *balneum Mariae*, lit.: bath of Mary, inaccurate translation of Med. Gk *kaminos Marios*, lit.: furnace of *Miriam*, alleged author of a treatise on alchemy]

Bairam (baɪ'ræm, 'baɪræm) *n* either of two Muslim festivals, one (**Lesser Bairam**) at the end of Ramadan, the other (**Greater Bairam**) at the end of the Islamic year [from Turkish *bayrām*]

Baird (bɛəd) *n* **John Logie** ('ləʊgɪ) 1888–1946, Scottish engineer: inventor of a 240-line mechanically scanned system of television, replaced in 1935 by a 405-line electrically scanned system

bairn (bɛən) *n Scot & N English* a child [OE *bearn*]

bait[1] (beɪt) *n* **1** something edible fixed to a hook or in a trap to attract fish or animals **2** an enticement; temptation **3** a variant spelling of **bate**[3] **4** *arch* a short stop for refreshment during a journey ▷ *vb* **5** *(tr)* to put a piece of food on or in (a hook or trap) **6** *(tr)* to persecute or tease **7** *(tr)* to entice; tempt **8** *(tr)* to set dogs upon (a bear, etc) **9** *(intr) arch* to stop for rest and refreshment during a journey [c13 from ON *beita* to hunt]

> USAGE The phrase *with bated breath* is sometimes wrongly spelled *with baited breath*. The correct spelling may be more easily recalled if it is remembered that *bated* in this phrase is related to *abate*

bait[2] (beɪt) *vb* a variant spelling of **bate**[2]

baize (beɪz) *n* a woollen fabric resembling felt, usually green, used mainly for the tops of billiard tables [c16 from OF *baies*, pl. of *baie* baize, from *bai* reddish brown, BAY[5]]

Baja California Norte ('nɔ:teɪ) *n* a state of NW Mexico, in the N part of the Lower California peninsula. Capital: Mexicali. Pop: 2 487 700 (2000). Area: about 71 500 sq km (27 600 sq miles)

Baja California Sur *n* a state of NW Mexico, in the S part of the Lower California peninsula. Capital: La Paz. Pop: 423 516 (2000). Area: 73 475 sq km (28 363 sq miles)

bake (beɪk) *vb* **bakes, baking, baked** **1** *(tr)* to cook by dry heat as in an oven **2** *(intr)* to cook bread, pastry, etc **3** to make or become hardened by heat **4** *(intr) inf* to be extremely hot ▷ *n* **5** a batch of things baked at one time **6** *Caribbean* a small flat fried cake [OE *bacan*]

bakeapple ('beɪk,æpᵊl) *n Canad* the fruit of the cloudberry

baked Alaska (ə'læskə) *n* a dessert made of cake and ice cream covered with meringue and cooked very quickly

baked beans *pl n* haricot beans, baked and tinned in tomato sauce

Bakelite ('beɪkə,laɪt) *n trademark* any one of a class of thermosetting resins used as electric insulators and for making plastic ware, etc [c20 after L. H. *Baekeland* (1863–1944), Belgian-born US inventor]

baker ('beɪkə) *n* a person whose business or employment is to make or sell bread, cakes, etc

Baker ('beɪkə) *n* **1** Sir **Benjamin** 1840–1907, British engineer who, with Sir John Fowler, designed and constructed much of the London underground railway, the Forth Railway Bridge, and the first Aswan Dam **2** **Chet**, full name *Chesney H. Baker*. 1929–88, US jazz trumpeter and singer **3** Dame **Janet** born 1933, British mezzo-soprano **4** Sir **Samuel White** 1821–93, British explorer: discovered Lake Albert (1864)

baker's dozen *n* thirteen [c16 from the bakers' former practice of giving thirteen rolls where twelve were requested, to protect themselves against accusations of giving light weight]

bakery ('beɪkərɪ) *n, pl* **bakeries** **1** a room or building equipped for baking **2** a shop in which bread, cakes, etc, are sold

Bakewell ('beɪkwɛl) *n* **Robert** 1725–95, English agriculturist; radically improved livestock breeding, esp of cattle and sheep

Bakhtaran (,bæktə'rɑ:n, -'ræn) *n* a city in W Iran, in the valley of the Qareh Su: oil refinery. Pop: 692 986 (1996). Former name (until 1987): **Kermanshah**

baking powder *n* a powdered mixture that contains sodium bicarbonate and one or more acidic compounds, such as cream of tartar: used in baking as a raising agent

bakkie ('bʌki:) *n S African* a small truck with an open body and low sides [c20 from Afrik. *bak* container]

baklava *or* **baclava** ('bɑ:klə,vɑ:) *n* a rich cake consisting of thin layers of pastry filled with nuts and honey [from Turkish]

baksheesh *or* **backsheesh** ('bækʃi:ʃ) *n* (in some Eastern countries, esp formerly) money given as a tip, a present, or alms [c17 from Persian *bakhshīsh*, from *bakhshīdan* to give]

Bakst (*Russian* bakst) *n* **Leon Nikolayevich** (lɪ'ɔn nika'lajɪvitʃ) 1866–1924, Russian painter and stage designer, noted particularly for his richly coloured sets for Diaghilev's *Ballet Russe* (1909–21)

Baku (*Russian* ba'ku) *n* the capital of Azerbaijan, a port on the Caspian Sea: important for its extensive oilfields. Pop: 1 727 200 (1997 est)
▷ www.baku.com

Bakunin (*Russian* ba'kunin) *n* **Mikhail** (mixa'il) 1814–76, Russian anarchist and writer: a prominent member of the First International, expelled from it after conflicts with Marx

Bala ('bælə) *n* **Lake** a narrow lake in Gwynedd: the largest natural lake in Wales. Length: 6 km (4 miles)

Balaam ('beɪlæm) *n Old Testament* a Mesopotamian diviner who, when summoned to curse the Israelites, prophesied future glories for them instead, after being reproached by his ass (Numbers 22–23)

Balaclava *or* **Balaclava helmet** (,bælə'klɑ:və) *n (often not caps)* a close-fitting woollen hood that covers the ears and neck, as originally worn by soldiers in the Crimean War [c19 from BALAKLAVA]

Balakirev (*Russian* ba'lakirɪf) *n* **Mily Alexeyevich** ('milij alɪk'sjejɪvitʃ) 1837–1910, Russian composer, whose works include two symphonic poems, two symphonies, and many arrangements of Russian folk songs

Balaklava *or* **Balaclava** (,bælə'klɑ:və; *Russian* bəla'klavə) *n* a small port in the Ukraine, in S Crimea: scene of an inconclusive battle (1854), which included the charge of the Light Brigade, during the Crimean War

balalaika (,bælə'laɪkə) *n* a Russian plucked musical instrument, usually having a triangular body and three strings [c18 from Russian]

balance ('bæləns) *n* **1** a weighing device, generally consisting of a horizontal beam pivoted at its centre, from the ends of which two pans are suspended. The substance to be weighed is placed in one pan and weights are placed in the other until the beam returns to the horizontal **2** a state of equilibrium **3** something that brings about such a state **4** equilibrium of the body; steadiness: *to lose one's balance* **5** emotional stability **6** harmony in the parts of a whole **7** the act of weighing factors, quantities, etc, against each other **8** the power to influence or control: *the balance of power* **9** something that remains: *the balance of what you owe* **10** *accounting* **10a** equality of debit and credit totals in an account **10b** a difference between such totals **11** **in the balance** in an uncertain or undecided condition **12** **on balance** after weighing up all the factors **13** **strike a balance** to make a compromise ▷ *vb* **balances, balancing, balanced** **14** *(tr)* to weigh in or as if in a balance **15** *(intr)* to be or come into equilibrium **16** (*tr*) to bring into or hold in equilibrium **17** (*tr*) to compare the relative weight, importance, etc, of **18** (*tr*) to be equal to **19** (*tr*) to arrange so as to create a state of harmony **20** (*tr*) *accounting* **20a** to compare the credit and debit totals of (an account) **20b** to equalize the credit and debit totals of (an account) by making certain entries **20c** to settle or adjust (an account) by paying any money due **21** (*intr*) (of a balance sheet, etc) to have the debit and credit totals equal [c13 from OF, from Vulgar L *bilancia* (unattested), from LL *bilanx* having two scales, from BI- + *lanx* scale] > **'balanceable** *adj* > **'balancer** *n*

Balance ('bæləns) *n* **the** the constellation Libra, the seventh sign of the zodiac

balance of payments *n* the difference over a given time between total payments to foreign nations and total receipts from foreign nations

balance of power *n* the distribution of power among countries so that no one nation can seriously threaten another

balance of trade *n* the difference in value between total exports and total imports of goods

balance sheet *n* a statement that shows the financial position of a business by listing the asset balances and the claims on such assets

balance wheel *n* a wheel oscillating against the hairspring of a timepiece, regulating its beat

Balanchine ('bælənˌtʃiːn, ˌbælən'tʃiːn) *n* **George** 1904–83, US choreographer, born in Russia

balata ('bælətə) *n* **1** a tropical American tree, yielding a latex-like sap **2** a rubber-like gum obtained from this sap: a substitute for gutta-percha [from American Sp., of Carib origin]

Balaton (*Hungarian* 'bɔlɔton) *n* **Lake** a large shallow lake in W Hungary. Area: 689 sq km (266 sq miles)

Balboa¹ (bæl'bəʊə; *Spanish* bal'βoa) *n* **Vasco Núñez de** ('basko 'nuɲeθ de) ?1475–1519, Spanish explorer, who discovered the Pacific Ocean in 1513

Balboa² (bæl'bəʊə; *Spanish* bal'βoa) *n* a port in Panama at the Pacific end of the Panama Canal: the administrative centre of the former Canal Zone. Pop: 2750 (1990)

Balcon ('bɔːlkən) *n* Sir **Michael** 1896–1977, British film producer; his films made at Ealing Studios include the comedies *Kind Hearts and Coronets* (1949) and *The Lavender Hill Mob* (1951)

balcony ('bælkənɪ) *n, pl* **balconies 1** a platform projecting from a building with a balustrade along its outer edge, often with access from a door or window **2** a gallery in a theatre, above the dress circle **3** *US & Canad* any circle in a theatre [c17 from It. *balcone*, prob. from OHG *balko* beam] > **'balconied** *adj*

bald (bɔːld) *adj* **1** having no hair or fur, esp (of a man) having no hair on the scalp **2** lacking natural growth or covering **3** plain or blunt: *a bald statement* **4** bare or unadorned **5** Also: **baldfaced** (of birds and animals) having white markings on the head and face **6** (of a tyre) having a worn tread [c14 *ballede* (lit.: having a white spot)] > **'baldish** *adj* > **'baldly** *adv* > **'baldness** *n*

baldachin *or* **baldaquin** ('bɔːldəkɪn) *n* **1** a richly ornamented brocade **2** a canopy over an altar, shrine, or throne or carried in Christian religious processions over an object of veneration [OE *baldekin*, from It. *baldacchino*, lit.: stuff from Baghdad]

bald eagle *n* a large eagle of North America, having a white head and tail. It is the US national bird

Balder ('bɔːldə) *n* *Norse myth* a god, son of Odin and Frigg, noted for his beauty and sweet nature. He was killed by a bough of mistletoe thrown by the blind god Höd, misled by the malicious Loki

balderdash ('bɔːldəˌdæʃ) *n* stupid or illogical talk; senseless rubbish [c16 from ?]

balding ('bɔːldɪŋ) *adj* somewhat bald or becoming bald

baldric ('bɔːldrɪk) *n* a sash or belt worn over the right shoulder to the left hip for carrying a sword, etc [c13 from OF *baudrei*, of Frankish origin]

Baldwin ('bɔːldwɪn) *n* **1** **James Arthur** 1924–87, US Black writer, whose works include the novel *Go Tell it on the Mountain* (1954) **2** **Stanley**, 1st Earl Baldwin of Bewdley. 1867–1947, British Conservative statesman: prime minister (1923–24, 1924–29, 1935–37)

Baldwin I *n* 1058–1118, crusader and first king of Jerusalem (1100–18), who captured Acre (1104), Beirut (1109), and Sidon (1110)

baldy ('bɔːldɪ) *inf* ▷ *adj* **1** bald ▷ *n, pl* **baldies 2** a bald person

bale¹ (beɪl) *n* **1** a large bundle, package, or carton of goods bound by ropes, wires, etc, for storage or transportation **2** *US* 500 pounds of cotton ▷ *vb* **bales, baling, baled 3** to make (hay, etc) or put (goods) into a bale or bales [c14 prob. from OF *bale*, from OHG *balla* BALL¹]

bale² (beɪl) *n* *arch* **1** evil; injury **2** woe; suffering; pain [OE *bealu*]

bale³ (beɪl) *vb* a variant spelling of **bail²**

bale⁴ (beɪl) *n* a variant spelling of **bail⁴**

Bâle (bɑl) *n* the French name for **Basel**

Balearic Islands (ˌbælɪ'ærɪk) *pl n* a group of islands in the W Mediterranean, consisting of Majorca, Minorca, Ibiza, Formentera, Cabrera, and 11 islets: a province of Spain. Capital: Palma, on Majorca. Pop: 845 630 (2000 est). Area: 5012 sq km (1935 sq miles). Spanish name: **Baleares** (bale'ares)

baleen (bə'liːn) *n* whalebone [c14 from L *bālaena* whale]

baleen whale *n* another name for **whalebone whale**

baleful ('beɪlfʊl) *adj* harmful, menacing, or vindictive > **'balefully** *adv* > **'balefulness** *n*

Balenciaga (*Spanish* balen'θjaɣa) *n* **Cristobal** (kris'toβal) 1895–1972, Spanish couturier

baler ('beɪlə) *n* a machine for making bales of hay, etc Also called: **baling machine**

Balfour ('bælfɔː, -fə, -fʊə) *n* **Arthur James**, 1st Earl of Balfour. 1848–1930, British Conservative statesman: prime minister (1902–05); foreign secretary (1916–19)

Bali ('bɑːlɪ) *n* an island in Indonesia, east of Java: mountainous, rising over 3000 m (10 000 ft). Capital: Denpasar. Pop: 2 902 200 (1995 est). Area: 5558 sq km (2146 sq miles) > ˌ**Bali'nese** *adj, n*

Balikpapan (ˌbɑːlɪk'pɑːpɑːn) *n* a city in Indonesia, on the SE coast of Borneo. Pop: 416 200 (1995 est)

Baliol *or* **Balliol** ('beɪlɪəl) *n* **1** **Edward** ?1283–1364, king of Scotland (1332, 1333–56) **2** his father, **John** 1249–1315, king of Scotland (1292–96): defeated and imprisoned by Edward I of England (1296)

balk *or* **baulk** (bɔːk, bɔːlk) *vb* **1** (*intr*; usually foll by *at*) to stop short; jib: *the horse balked at the jump* **2** (*intr*; foll by *at*) to recoil: *he balked at the idea of murder* **3** (*tr*) to thwart, check, or foil: *he was balked in his plans* ▷ *n* **4** a roughly squared heavy timber beam **5** a timber tie beam of a roof **6** an unploughed ridge between furrows **7** an obstacle; hindrance; disappointment **8** *baseball* an illegal motion by a pitcher ▷ See also **baulk** [OE *balca*]

Balkan ('bɔːlkən) *adj* of, denoting, or relating to the Balkan States or their inhabitants, the Balkan Peninsula, or the Balkan Mountains

Balkan Mountains *pl n* a mountain range extending across Bulgaria from the Black Sea to the eastern border. Highest peak: Mount Botev, 2376 m (7793 ft)

Balkan Peninsula *n* a large peninsula in SE Europe, between the Adriatic and Aegean Seas

Balkan States *pl n* the countries of the Balkan Peninsula: the former Yugoslavian Republics, Romania, Bulgaria, Albania, Greece, and the European part of Turkey. Also called: **the Balkans**

Balkh (bɑːlk) *n* a region of N Afghanistan, corresponding to ancient Bactria. Chief town: Mazar-i-Sharif

Balkhash (*Russian* bal'xaʃ) *n* **Lake** a salt lake in SE

Kazakhstan: fed by the Ili River. Area: about 18 000 sq km (7000 sq miles)

balky *or* **baulky** ('bɔːkɪ, 'bɔːlkɪ) *adj* **balkier, balkiest** *or* **baulkier, baulkiest** inclined to stop abruptly and unexpectedly: *a balky horse*

ball[1] (bɔːl) *n* **1** a spherical or nearly spherical body or mass **2** a round or roundish body, of a size and composition suitable for any of various games **3** a ball propelled in a particular way: *a high ball* **4** any rudimentary game with a ball: *to play ball* **5** a single delivery of the ball in cricket and other games **6a** a solid nonexplosive projectile for a firearm, cannon, etc **6b** such projectiles collectively **7** any more or less rounded part: *the ball of the foot* **8 ball of muscle** *Austral* a very strong, fit person **9 have the ball at one's feet** to have the chance of doing something **10 keep the ball rolling** to maintain the progress of a project, plan, etc **11 on the ball** *inf* alert; informed **12 play ball** *inf* to cooperate **13 set** *or* **start the ball rolling** to initiate an action, discussion, etc ▷ *vb* **14** to make, form, wind, gather, etc, into a ball or balls ▷ See also **balls, balls-up** [c13 from ON *böllr*]

ball[2] (bɔːl) *n* **1** a social function for dancing, esp one that is lavish or formal **2** *inf* a very enjoyable time (esp in **have a ball**) [c17 from F *bal* (n), from OF *baller* (vb), from LL *ballāre* to dance]

Ball (bɔːl) *n* **John** died 1381, English priest: executed as one of the leaders of the Peasants' Revolt (1381)

ballad ('bæləd) *n* **1** a narrative song with a recurrent refrain **2** a narrative poem in short stanzas of popular origin **3** a slow sentimental song, esp a pop song [c15 from OF *balade*, from OProvençal *balada* song accompanying a dance]

ballade (bæ'lɑːd) *n* **1** *prosody* a verse form consisting of three stanzas and an envoy, all ending with the same line **2** *music* an instrumental composition based on or intended to evoke a narrative

balladeer (ˌbælə'dɪə) *n* a singer of ballads

Ballance ('bæləns) *n* **John** 1839–93, New Zealand statesman, born in Northern Ireland: prime minister of New Zealand (1891–93)

ball-and-socket joint *n anat* a joint in which a rounded head fits into a rounded cavity, allowing a wide range of movement

Ballarat ('bæləˌræt, ˌbælə'ræt) *n* a town in SE Australia, in S central Victoria: originally the centre of a gold-mining region. Pop: 64 980 (1991). See also **Eureka Stockade**

Ballard ('bælɑːd) *n* **J(ames) G(raham)** born 1930, British novelist, born in China; his books include *Crash* (1973), *The Unlimited Dream Company* (1979), *Empire of the Sun* (1984), *Cocaine Nights* (1996), and *Super-Cannes* (2000)

ballast ('bæləst) *n* **1** any heavy material used to stabilize a vessel, esp one that is not carrying cargo **2** crushed rock, broken stone, etc, used for the foundation of a road or railway track or in making concrete **3** anything that provides stability or weight **4** *electronics* a device for maintaining the current in a circuit ▷ *vb (tr)* **5** to give stability or weight to [c16 prob. from Low G]

ball bearing *n* **1** a bearing consisting of steel balls rolling between a metal sleeve fitted over the rotating shaft and an outer sleeve held in the bearing housing, so reducing friction **2** a metal ball, esp one used in such a bearing

ball boy *or (fem)* **ball girl** *n* (esp in tennis) a person who retrieves balls that go out of play

ballbreaker ('bɔːlˌbreɪkə) *n sl* someone, esp a woman, whose behaviour may be regarded as threatening a man's sense of power [c20 from BALLS (in the sense: testicles) + BREAKER]

ball cock *n* a device for regulating the flow of a liquid into a tank, cistern, etc, consisting of a floating ball mounted at one end of an arm and a valve on the other end that opens and closes as the ball falls and rises

ballerina (ˌbælə'riːnə) *n* a female ballet dancer [c18 from It., fem of *ballerino* dancing master, from *ballare* to dance]

ballet ('bæleɪ, bæ'leɪ) *n* **1** a classical style of expressive dancing based on precise conventional steps **2** a theatrical representation of a story or theme performed by ballet dancers **3** a troupe of ballet dancers **4** music written for a ballet [c17 from F, from It. *balletto*, lit.: a little dance, from *ballare* to dance] > **balletic** (bæ'lɛtɪk) *adj*

▷ www.ballet.co.uk

▷ www.culturekiosque.com/dance

balletomane ('bælɪtəʊˌmeɪn) *n* a ballet enthusiast

balletomania (ˌbælɪtəʊ'meɪnɪə) *n* passionate enthusiasm for ballet

ball game *n* **1** any game played with a ball **2** *US & Canad* a game of baseball **3** *inf* a situation; state of affairs (esp in **a whole new ball game**)

ballicatter (ˌbælɪ'kætə) *n* (in Newfoundland) ice that forms along a shore from waves and freezing spray

Balliol ('beɪlɪəl) *n* See **Baliol**

ballista (bə'lɪstə) *n, pl* **ballistae** (-tiː) an ancient catapult for hurling stones, etc [c16 from L, ult. from Gk *ballein* to throw]

ballistic (bə'lɪstɪk) *adj* **1** of or relating to ballistics **2** denoting or relating to the flight of projectiles moving under their own momentum and the force of gravity **3** (of a measurement or measuring instrument) depending on a brief impulse or current that causes a movement related to the quantity to be measured: *a ballistic pendulum* **4 go ballistic** *inf* to become enraged or frenziedly violent > **bal'listically** *adv*

ballistic missile *n* a missile that has no wings or fins and that follows a ballistic trajectory when its propulsive power is discontinued

ballistics (bə'lɪstɪks) *n (functioning as sing)* **1** the study of the flight dynamics of projectiles **2** the study of the effects of firing on firearms and their projectiles

ball lightning *n meteorol* a luminous ball occasionally seen during electrical storms

ballocks ('bɒləks) *pl n, interj* a variant spelling of **bollocks**

ball of fire *n inf* a very lively person

balloon (bə'luːn) *n* **1** an inflatable rubber bag used as a plaything or party decoration **2** a large bag inflated with a lighter-than-air gas, designed to rise and float in the atmosphere. It may have a basket or gondola for carrying passengers, etc **3** an outline containing the words or thoughts of a character in a cartoon **4** a large rounded brandy glass **5** *commerce* **5a** a large sum paid as an irregular instalment of a loan repayment **5b** *(as modifier)*: *a balloon loan* **6** *surgery* **6a** an inflatable plastic tube used for dilating obstructed blood vessels or parts of the alimentary canal **6b** *(as modifier)*: *balloon angioplasty* **7 go down like a lead balloon** to prove unsuccessful or unpopular; fail: *the suggestion that the chairman should get a 77% pay rise went down like a lead balloon* **8 when the balloon goes up** *inf* when the action starts ▷ *vb* **9** *(intr)* to go up or fly in a balloon **10** to inflate or be inflated: *the wind ballooned the sails* **11** *(intr)* to increase or expand significantly and rapidly: *losses ballooned to £278 million* **12** *(tr) Brit* to propel (a ball) high into the air [c16 (in the sense: ball, ball game): from It. dialect *ballone*] > **bal'loonist** *n* > **bal'loon-ˌlike** *adj*

▷ www.fai.org/ballooning

balloon loan *n* a loan in respect of which interest and capital are paid off in instalments at irregular intervals

balloon payment *n* a large payment that concludes a series of smaller payments, for example in order to repay a loan

ballot ('bælət) *n* **1** the practice of selecting a representative, course of action, etc, by submitting the options to a vote of all qualified persons **2** an instance of voting, usually in secret **3** a list of candidates standing

Bb

for office **4** the number of votes cast in an election ▷ *vb* **ballots, balloting, balloted** **5** to vote or elicit a vote from: *we balloted the members on this issue* **6** (*tr*; usually foll by *for*) to vote for or decide on by lot or ballot [c16 from It. *ballotta*, lit.: a little ball]

ballot box *n* a box into which ballot papers are dropped after voting

ballotini (ˌbæləˈtiːnɪ) *pl n* small glass beads used in reflective paints [c20 from Italian *ballotini* small balls]

ballot paper *n* a paper used for voting

ballpark (ˈbɔːlˌpɑːk) *n* **1** *US & Canad* a stadium used for baseball games **2** *inf* **2a** approximate range: *in the right ballpark* **2b** (*as modifier*): *a ballpark figure* **3** *inf* a situation; state of affairs: *it's a whole new ballpark*

ball-peen hammer *n* a hammer with one end of the head rounded for beating metal

ballpoint *or* **ballpoint pen** (ˈbɔːlˌpɔɪnt) *n* a pen having a small ball bearing as a writing point

ballroom (ˈbɔːlˌruːm, -ˌrʊm) *n* a large hall for dancing

ballroom dancing *n* social dancing, popular since the beginning of the 20th century, to dances in conventional rhythms (**ballroom dances**)
▷ www.ballroomdancers.com
▷ www.dancesport.uk.com

balls (bɔːlz) *sl* ▷ *pl n* **1** the testicles **2** nonsense; rubbish **3** courage; determination ▷ *interj* **4** an exclamation of disagreement, contempt, etc

balls-up *sl* ▷ *n* **1** something botched or muddled ▷ *vb* **balls up** **2** (*tr, adv*) to muddle or botch

ballsy (ˈbɔːlzɪ) *adj* **ballsier, ballsiest** *sl, chiefly US* showing courage or determination; bold [c20 from BALLS (sense 3) + -Y[1]] > ˈ**ballsiness** *n*

bally (ˈbælɪ) *adj, adv* (intensifier) *Brit sl* a euphemistic word for **bloody** (sense 5)

ballyhoo (ˌbælɪˈhuː) *inf* ▷ *n* **1** a noisy, confused, or nonsensical situation **2** sensational or blatant advertising or publicity ▷ *vb* **ballyhoos, ballyhooing, ballyhooed** **3** (*tr*) *chiefly US* to advertise by sensational or blatant methods [c19 from ?]

Ballymena (ˌbælɪˈmiːnə) *n* a district in central Northern Ireland, in Co. Antrim. Pop: 58 610 (2001). Area: 634 sq km (247 sq miles)

Ballymoney (ˌbælɪˈmʌnɪ) *n* a district in N Northern Ireland, in Co. Antrim. Pop: 26 894 (2001). Area: 417 sq km (161 sq miles)

balm (bɑːm) *n* **1** any of various oily aromatic substances obtained from certain tropical trees and used for healing and soothing. See also **balsam** (sense 1) **2** any plant yielding such a substance, esp the balm of Gilead **3** something comforting or soothing **4** Also called: **lemon balm** an aromatic Eurasian plant, having clusters of small fragrant white flowers **5** a pleasant odour [c13 from OF *basme*, from L *balsamum* BALSAM]

Balmain (*French* balmɛ̃) *n* **Pierre Alexandre** (pjɛr alɛksɑ̃drə) 1914–82, French couturier

Balmain bug (ˈbælmeɪn) *n* a flattish edible Australian shellfish, *Ibacus peronii*, similar to the Moreton Bay bug [named after *Balmain*, a suburb of Sydney, Australia]

balm of Gilead (ˈɡɪlɪˌæd) *n* **1** any of several trees of Africa and W Asia that yield a fragrant oily resin **2** the resin exuded by these trees **3** a North American poplar tree **4** a fragrant resin obtained from the balsam fir

Balmoral[1] (bælˈmɒrəl) *n* (*sometimes not cap*) **1** a laced walking shoe **2** a Scottish brimless hat usually with a cockade and plume [from BALMORAL Castle]

Balmoral[2] (bælˈmɒrəl) *n* a castle in NE Scotland, in SW Aberdeenshire: a private residence of the British sovereign

balmy (ˈbɑːmɪ) *adj* **balmier, balmiest** **1** (of weather) mild and pleasant **2** having the qualities of balm; fragrant or soothing **3** a variant spelling of **barmy** > ˈ**balmily** *adv* > ˈ**balminess** *n*

balneology (ˌbælnɪˈɒlədʒɪ) *n* the branch of medical science concerned with the therapeutic value of baths, esp with natural mineral waters [c19 from L *balneum* bath] > **balneological** (ˌbælnɪəˈlɒdʒɪkəl) *adj* > ˌ**balneˈologist** *n*

baloney *or* **boloney** (bəˈləʊnɪ) *n inf* foolish talk; nonsense [c20 from *Bologna* (sausage)]

BALPA (ˈbælpə) *n acronym for* British Airline Pilots' Association

balsa (ˈbɔːlsə) *n* **1** a tree of tropical America **2** Also called: **balsawood** the very light wood of this tree, used for making rafts, etc **3** a light raft [c18 from Sp.: raft]

balsam (ˈbɔːlsəm) *n* **1** any of various fragrant oleoresins, such as balm, obtained from any of several trees and shrubs and used as a base for medicines and perfumes **2** any of various similar substances used as ointments **3** any of certain aromatic resinous turpentines. See **Canada balsam** **4** any plant yielding balsam **5** Also called: **busy Lizzie** any of several plants of the genus *Impatiens* **6** anything healing or soothing [c15 from L *balsamum*, from Gk *balsamon*, from Heb. *bāśām* spice] > **balsamic** (bɔːlˈsæmɪk) *adj*

balsam fir *n* a fir tree of NE North America, that yields Canada balsam

Balthazar (ˈbælθəˌzɑː, bælˈθæzə) *n* one of the Magi, the others being Caspar and Melchior

Balthus (*French* baltys) *n* real name *Balthasar Klossowski de Rola*. 1908–2001, French painter of Polish descent, noted esp for his paintings of adolescent girls

balti (ˈbɔːltɪ, ˈbæltɪ) *n* **a** a spicy Indian dish, stewed until most of the liquid has evaporated, and served in a woklike pot **b** (*as modifier*): *a balti house* [c20 from ?]

Baltic (ˈbɔːltɪk) *adj* **1** denoting or relating to the Baltic Sea or the Baltic states **2** of or characteristic of Baltic as a group of languages ▷ *n* **3** a branch of the Indo-European family of languages consisting of Lithuanian, Latvian, and Old Prussian **4** Also called: **Baltic Exchange** a freight-chartering market in the City of London, which formerly also dealt in some commodities

Baltics (ˈbɔːltɪks) *pl n* **the** another name for the **Baltic States**

Baltic Sea *n* a sea in N Europe, connected with the North Sea by the Skaggerak, Kattegat, and Öresund; shallow, with low salinity and small tides

Baltic Shield *n* the wide area of ancient rock in Scandinavia. Also called: **Scandinavian Shield.** See **shield** (sense 6)

Baltic States *pl n* the republics of Estonia, Latvia, and Lithuania, which became constituent republics of the former Soviet Union in 1940, regaining their independence in 1991. Sometimes shortened to: **the Baltics**

Baltimore[1] (ˈbɔːltɪˌmɔː) *n* a port in N Maryland, on Chesapeake Bay. Pop: 651 154 (2000)

Baltimore[2] (ˈbɔːltɪˌmɔː) *n* **1** **David** born 1938, US molecular biologist: shared the Nobel prize for physiology or medicine (1975) for his discovery of reverse transcriptase **2** **Lord** See (Sir George) **Calvert**

Baluchistan (bəˈluːtʃɪˌstɑːn, -ˌstæn) *or* **Balochistan** (bəˈlɒtʃɪˌstɑːn, -ˌstæn) *n* **1** a mountainous region of SW Asia, in SW Pakistan and SE Iran **2** a province of SW Pakistan: a former territory of British India (until 1947). Capital: Quetta. Pop: 6 511 000 (1998)

baluster (ˈbæləstə) *n* any of a set of posts supporting a rail or coping [c17 from F *balustre*, from It. *balaustro* pillar resembling a pomegranate flower, ult. from Gk *balaustion*]

balustrade (ˈbæləˌstreɪd) *n* an ornamental rail or coping with its supporting set of balusters [c17 from F, from *balustre* BALUSTER]

Balzac (ˈbælzæk; *French* balzak) *n* **Honoré de** (ɔnɔre də) 1799–1850, French novelist: author of a collection of novels under the general title *La Comédie humaine*, including *Eugénie Grandet* (1833), *Le Père Goriot* (1834), and *La Cousine Bette* (1846)

Bamako (ˌbæməˈkəʊ) *n* the capital of Mali, in the south, on the River Niger. Pop: 809 552 (1996 est)

Bamberg (ˈbæmbɜːɡ; *German* ˈbambɛrk) *n* a town in S Germany, in N Bavaria: seat of independent prince-bishops of the Holy Roman Empire (1007–1802). Pop: 70 690 (1991)

bambino (bæmˈbiːnəʊ) *n, pl* **bambinos** *or* **bambini** (-niː) *inf* a young child, esp Italian [c18 from It.]

bamboo (bæmˈbuː) *n* **1** a tall treelike tropical or semitropical grass having hollow stems with ringed joints **2** the stem, used for building, poles, and furniture [c16 prob. from Malay *bambu*]

bamboo network *n* a network of close-knit Chinese entrepreneurs with large corporate empires in southeast Asia

bamboozle (bæmˈbuːzᵊl) *vb* **bamboozles, bamboozling, bamboozled** (*tr*) *inf* **1** to cheat; mislead **2** to confuse [c18 from ?] > **bamˈboozlement** *n* > **bamˈboozler** *n*

ban (bæn) *vb* **bans, banning, banned 1** (*tr*) to prohibit, esp officially, from action, display, entrance, sale, etc; forbid ▷ *n* **2** an official prohibition or interdiction **3** a public proclamation, esp of outlawry **4** *arch* a curse; imprecation [OE *bannan* to proclaim]

Banaba (bəˈnɑːbə) *n* an island in the SW Pacific, in the Republic of Kiribati. Phosphates were mined by Britain (1900–79). Area: about 5 sq km (2 sq miles). Pop: 284 (1990). Also called: **Ocean Island** > **Baˈnaban** *adj, n*

banal (bəˈnɑːl) *adj* lacking force or originality; trite; commonplace [c18 from OF: relating to compulsory feudal service, hence common to all, commonplace] > **banality** (bəˈnælɪtɪ) *n* > **baˈnally** *adv*

banana (bəˈnɑːnə) *n* **1** any of several tropical and subtropical treelike plants, esp a widely cultivated species having hanging clusters of edible fruit **2** the crescent-shaped fruit of any of these plants [c16 from Sp. or Port., of African origin]

banana prawn *n Austral* a prawn of the genus *Penaeus*, fished commercially in tropical waters of N Australia

banana republic *n inf & derog* a small country, esp in Central America, that is politically unstable and has an economy dominated by foreign interest, usually dependent on one export

banana skin *n* **1** the soft outer covering of a banana **2** *inf* something unforeseen that causes an obvious and embarrassing mistake [sense 2 from the common slapstick joke of slipping on a banana skin]

Banaras (bəˈnɑːrəz) *n* a variant spelling of **Benares**

Banat (ˈbænɪt, ˈbɑːnɪt) *n* a fertile plain extending through Hungary, Romania, and Serbia

Banbridge (ˈbænbrɪdʒ) *n* a district in S Northern Ireland, in Co. Down. Pop: 41 392 (2001). Area: 442 sq km (170 sq miles)

Banbury (ˈbænbərɪ) *n* a town in central England, in N Oxfordshire: telecommunications, financial services. Pop: 39 906 (1991)

bancassurance (ˈbæŋkəʃʊərəns) *n* the selling of insurance products by a bank to its customers [from French *banc* bank + *assurance* assurance]

band¹ (bænd) *n* **1** a company of people having a common purpose; group: *a band of outlaws* **2** a group of musicians playing either brass and percussion instruments only (**brass band**) or brass, woodwind, and percussion instruments (**concert band** or **military band**) **3** a group of musicians who play popular music, jazz, etc, often for dancing **4** *Canad* a formally recognized group of Indians on a reserve ▷ *vb* **5** (usually foll by *together*) to unite; assemble [c15 from F *bande*, prob. from OProvençal *banda*, of Gmc origin]

band² (bænd) *n* **1** a thin flat strip of some material, used esp to encircle objects and hold them together: *a rubber band* **2a** a strip of fabric or other material used as an ornament or to reinforce clothing **2b** (*in combination*): *waistband; hatband* **3** a stripe of contrasting colour or texture **4** a driving belt in machinery **5** a range of values that are close or related in number, degree, or quality **6** *physics* a range of frequencies or wavelengths between two limits **7** short for **energy band 8** *computing* one or more tracks on a magnetic disk or drum **9** *anat* any structure resembling a ribbon or cord that connects, encircles, or binds different parts **10** *archit* a strip of flat panelling, such as a fascia, usually attached to a wall **11** either of a pair of hanging extensions of the collar, forming part of academic, legal, or (formerly) clerical dress ▷ *vb* (*tr*) **12** to fasten or mark with a band [c15 from OF *bende*, of Gmc origin]

Banda (ˈbændə) *n* **Hastings Kamuzu** (kæˈmuːzuː) 1906–97, Malawi statesman. As first prime minister of Nyasaland (from 1963), he led his country to independence (1964) as Malawi: president (1966–94)

Banda Aceh (ˈbændə ˈɑːtʃeɪ) *n* a city in N Indonesia, in N Sumatra; the capital of Aceh region. Pop: 143 360 (1995 est)

bandage (ˈbændɪdʒ) *n* **1** a piece of material used to dress a wound, bind a broken limb, etc ▷ *vb* **bandages, bandaging, bandaged 2** to cover or bind with a bandage [c16 from F, from *bande* strip, BAND²]

bandanna *or* **bandana** (bænˈdænə) *n* a large silk or cotton handkerchief or neckerchief [c18 from Hindi *bāndhnū* tie-dyeing]

Bandaranaike (ˌbændərəˈnaɪɪkə) *n* **1 Chandrika** See Chandrika **Kumaratunga 2 Sirimavo** (ˌsɪrɪˈmɑːvəʊ) 1916–2000, prime minister of Sri Lanka, formerly Ceylon (1960–65; 1970–77; 1994–2000); the world's first woman prime minister **3** her husband, **Solomon** 1899–1959, prime minister of Ceylon (1956–59); assassinated

Bandar Seri Begawan (ˈbɑːndɑː ˈsɛrɪ bəˈɡɑːwən) *n* the capital of Brunei. Pop: 21 484 (1991). Former name: **Brunei**

▷ www.municipal-bsb.gov.bn

Banda Sea *n* a part of the Pacific in Indonesia, between Sulawesi and New Guinea

B & B *abbrev for* bed and breakfast

bandbox (ˈbændˌbɒks) *n* a lightweight usually cylindrical box for small articles, esp hats

bandeau (ˈbændəʊ) *n, pl* **bandeaux** (-dəʊz) a narrow band of ribbon, velvet, etc, worn round the head [c18 from F, from OF *bandel* a little BAND²]

banderole *or* **banderol** (ˈbændəˌrəʊl) *n* **1** a long narrow flag, usually with forked ends, esp one attached to the mast of a ship **2** a ribbon-like scroll or sculptured band bearing an inscription [c16 from OF, from It. *banderuola*, lit.: a little banner]

bandicoot (ˈbændɪˌkuːt) *n* **1** an agile terrestrial marsupial of Australia and New Guinea with a long pointed muzzle and a long tail **2 bandicoot rat** Also called: **mole rat** any of three burrowing rats of S and SE Asia [c18 from Telugu *pandikokku*]

banding (ˈbændɪŋ) *n Brit* the practice of putting schoolchildren into ability groups to ensure a balanced intake to secondary school

bandit (ˈbændɪt) *n, pl* **bandits** *or* **banditti** (bænˈdɪtɪ) a robber, esp a member of an armed gang [c16 from It. *bandito*, from *bandire* to proscribe, from *bando* edict] > **ˈbanditry** *n*

Bandjarmasin *or* **Bandjermasin** (ˌbændʒəˈmɑːsɪn) *n* variant spellings of **Banjarmasin**

bandmaster (ˈbændˌmɑːstə) *n* the conductor of a band

Band of Hope *n* a society devoted to abstinence from alcohol

bandolier *or* **bandoleer** (ˌbændəˈlɪə) *n* a soldier's broad shoulder belt having small pockets or loops for cartridges [c16 from OF *bandouliere*]

band-pass filter *n* **1** *electronics* a filter that transmits only currents having frequencies within specified

Bb

limits **2** an optical device for transmitting waves of predetermined wavelengths

B & S *n Austral inf* a dance held for young people in country areas, usually in a field or barn [abbreviation for BACHELOR AND SPINSTER]

band saw *n* a power-operated saw consisting of an endless toothed metal band running over and driven by two wheels

bandsman ('bændzmən) *n, pl* **bandsmen** a player in a musical band, esp a brass or military band

bandstand ('bænd,stænd) *n* a platform for a band, usually out of doors and roofed

band theory *n* the theory that electrons in solids have a range of energies falling into allowed bands, between which are forbidden bands

Bandung ('bændʊŋ) *n* a city in Indonesia, in SW Java. Pop: 2 356 120 (1995 est)

bandwagon ('bænd,wægən) *n* **1** *US* a wagon for the band in a parade **2** **jump, climb,** *or* **get on the bandwagon** to join or support a party or movement that seems assured of success

bandwidth ('bænd,wɪdθ) *n* the range of frequencies within a given waveband used for a particular radio transmission

bandy ('bændɪ) *adj* **bandier, bandiest 1** Also: **bandy-legged** having legs curved outwards at the knees **2** (of legs) curved thus ▷ *vb* **bandies, bandying, bandied** (*tr*) **3** to exchange (words) in a heated or hostile manner **4** to give and receive (blows) **5** (often foll by *about*) to circulate (a name, rumour, etc) [c16 prob. from OF *bander* to hit the ball back and forth at tennis]

bane (beɪn) *n* **1** a person or thing that causes misery or distress (esp in **bane of one's life**) **2** something that causes death or destruction **3a** a fatal poison **3b** (*in combination*): *ratsbane* **4** *arch* ruin or distress [OE *bana*] > **'baneful** *adj*

baneberry ('beɪnbərɪ) *n, pl* **baneberries 1** Also called: **herb Christopher** (Brit) a plant which has small white flowers and red or white poisonous berries **2** the berry

Banff (bæmf) *n* **1** a town in NE Scotland, in Aberdeenshire. Pop: 6230 (1991) **2** a town in Canada, in SW Alberta, in the Rocky Mountains: surrounded by **Banff National Park** Pop: 5700 (1991)

Banffshire ('bæmf,ʃɪə, -ʃə) *n* (until 1975) a county of NE Scotland: formerly (1975–96) part of Grampian region, now part of Aberdeenshire

bang¹ (bæŋ) *n* **1** a short loud explosive noise, as of the report of a gun **2** a hard blow or knock, esp a noisy one **3** *sl* an injection of heroin or other narcotic **4** *taboo sl* an act of sexual intercourse **5** **with a bang** successfully: *the party went with a bang* ▷ *vb* **6** to hit or knock, esp with a loud noise **7** to move noisily or clumsily: *to bang about the house* **8** to close (a door, window, etc) or (of a door, etc) be closed noisily; slam **9** (*tr*) to cause to move by hitting vigorously: *he banged the ball over the fence* **10** to make or cause to make a loud noise, as of an explosion **11** *taboo sl* to have sexual intercourse (with) **12** (*intr*) *sl* to inject heroin, etc **13** **bang one's head against a brick wall** to try to achieve something impossible ▷ *adv* **14** with a sudden impact or effect: *the car drove bang into a lamppost* **15** precisely: *bang in the middle* **16** **go bang** to burst, shut, etc, with a loud noise [c16 from ON *bang, banga* hammer]

bang² (bæŋ) *n* **1** (*usually pl*) a section of hair cut straight across the forehead ▷ *vb* (*tr*) **2** to cut (the hair) in such a style **3** to dock (the tail of a horse, etc) [c19 prob. short for *bangtail* short tail]

Bangalore (,bæŋgə'lɔː) *n* a city in S India, capital of Karnataka state: printing, textiles, pharmaceuticals. Pop: 2 660 088 (1991)

banger ('bæŋə) *n Brit* **1** *sl* a sausage **2** *inf* an old decrepit car **3** a firework that explodes loudly

Bangka *or* **Banka** ('bæŋkə) *n* an island in Indonesia, separated from Sumatra by the **Bangka Strait** Chief town: Pangkalpinang. Area: about 11 914 sq km (4600 sq miles)

Bangkok ('bæŋkɒk, bæŋ'kɒk) *n* the capital and chief port of Thailand, on the Chao Phraya River: became a royal city and the capital in 1782. Pop: 6 320 174 (1999 est). Thai name: **Krung Thep** ('krʊŋ 'teɪp)

▷ www.tourismthailand.org

▷ www.guidetothailand.com/bangkok-thailand

Bangla ('bæŋglə) *n* another name for **Bengali** (sense 2)

Bangladesh (,bɑːŋglə'dɛʃ, ,bæŋ-) *n* a republic in S Asia: formerly the Eastern Province of Pakistan; became independent in 1971 after civil war and the defeat of Pakistan by India; consists of the plains and vast deltas of the Ganges and Brahmaputra Rivers; prone to flooding: economy based on jute and jute products (over 70 per cent of world production); a member of the Commonwealth. Language: Bengali. Religion: Muslim. Currency: taka. Capital: Dhaka. Pop: 131 270 000 (2001 est). Area: 142 797 sq km (55 126 sq miles) > ,**Bangla'deshi** *adj, n*

▷ www.bangladeshgov.org

▷ www.bangladesh.com

bangle ('bæŋgᵊl) *n* a bracelet, usually without a clasp, often worn round the arm or sometimes round the ankle [c19 from Hindi *bangrī*]

bang on *adj, adv Brit inf* **1** with absolute accuracy **2** excellent or excellently

Bangor ('bæŋgɔː, -gə) *n* **1** a university town in NW Wales, in Gwynedd, on the Menai Strait. Pop: 12 330 (1991) **2** a town in SE Northern Ireland, in North Down district, Co. Down, on Belfast Lough. Pop: 52 437 (1991)

bangtail ('bæŋ,teɪl) *n* **1** a horse's tail cut straight across but not through the bone **2** a horse with a tail cut in this way [c19 from *bangtail* short tail]

Bangui (*French* bɑ̃gi) *n* the capital of the Central African Republic, in the south part, on the Ubangi River. Pop: 553 000 (1995 est)

Bangweulu (,bæŋwɪ'uːlʊ) *n* **Lake** a shallow lake in NE Zambia, discovered by David Livingstone, who died there in 1873. Area: about 9850 sq km (3800 sq miles), including swamps

banian ('bænjən) *n* a variant spelling of **banyan**

banish ('bænɪʃ) *vb* (*tr*) **1** to expel from a place, esp by an official decree as a punishment **2** to drive away: *to banish gloom* [c14 from OF *banir*, of Gmc origin] > **'banishment** *n*

banisters *or* **bannisters** ('bænɪstəz) *pl n* the railing and supporting balusters on a staircase; balustrade [c17 altered from BALUSTER]

Banja Luka (*Serbo-Croat* 'baːnjaː ,luːka) *n* a city in NW Bosnia-Herzegovina, on the Vrbas River: scene of battles between the Austrians and Turks in 1527, 1688, and 1737; besieged by Serb forces (1992–95). Pop: 160 000 (1997 est)

Banjarmasin, Banjermasin, Bandjarmasin, *or* **Bandjermasin** (,bændʒə'mɑːsɪn) *n* a port in Indonesia, in SW Borneo. Pop: 534 600 (1995 est)

banjo ('bændʒəʊ) *n, pl* **banjos** *or* **banjoes** a stringed musical instrument with a long neck and a circular drumlike body overlaid with parchment, plucked with the fingers or a plectrum [c18 var. (US Southern pronunciation) of earlier *bandore*, ult. from Gk *pandora*] > **'banjoist** *n*

Banjul (bæn'dʒuːl) *n* the capital of The Gambia, a port at the mouth of the Gambia River. Pop: 42 407 (1993). Former name (until 1973): **Bathurst**

bank¹ (bæŋk) *n* **1** an institution offering certain financial services, such as the safekeeping of money and lending of money at interest **2** the building used by such an institution **3** a small container used at home for keeping money **4** the funds held by a banker or dealer in some gambling games **5** (in various games) **5a** the stock, as of money, etc, on which players may draw **5b** the player holding this stock **6** any supply, store, or reserve: *a data bank* ▷ *vb* **7** (*tr*) to deposit (cash, cheques, etc) in a bank **8** (*intr*) to transact business with a bank **9** (*intr*) to engage in banking ▷ See also **bank on** [c15 prob. from It. *banca* bench, moneychanger's table, of Gmc origin]

bank[2] (bæŋk) *n* **1** a long raised mass, esp of earth; ridge **2** a slope, as of a hill **3** the sloping side of any hollow in the ground, esp when bordering a river **4** the ground beside a river or canal **5a** an elevated section of the bed of a sea, lake, or river **5b** (*in combination*): *sandbank* **6** the face of a body of ore in a mine **7** the lateral inclination of an aircraft about its longitudinal axis during a turn **8** a bend on a road, athletics track, etc, having the outside built higher than the inside to reduce the effects of centrifugal force on vehicles, runners, etc, rounding it at speed. Also called: **camber, superelevation** ▷ *vb* **9** (when *tr*, often foll by *up*) to form into a bank or mound **10** (*tr*) to border or enclose (a road, etc) with a bank **11** (*tr*; sometimes foll by *up*) to cover (a fire) with ashes, fresh fuel, etc, so that it will burn slowly **12** to cause (an aircraft) to tip laterally about its longitudinal axis or (of an aircraft) to tip in this way, esp while turning [c12 of Scand. origin]

bank[3] (bæŋk) *n* **1** an arrangement of similar objects in a row or in tiers: *a bank of dials* **2** a tier of oars in a galley ▷ *vb* **3** (*tr*) to arrange in a bank [c17 from OF *banc* bench, of Gmc origin]

Banka ('bæŋkə) *n* a variant spelling of **Bangka**

bankable ('bæŋkəbᵊl) *adj* **1** appropriate for receipt by a bank **2** dependable or reliable: *a bankable promise* **3** (esp of a star) likely to ensure the financial success of a film > ˌ**banka'bility** *n*

bank account *n* **1** an account created by the deposit of money at a bank by a customer **2** the amount credited to a depositor at a bank

bank bill *n* **1** Also called: **bank draft** a bill of exchange drawn by one bank on another **2** *US* a banknote

bankbook ('bæŋkˌbʊk) *n* a book held by depositors at certain banks, in which the bank enters a record of deposits, withdrawals, and earned interest. Also called: **passbook**

bank card *or* **banker's card** *n* any plastic card issued by a bank, such as a cash card or cheque card

bank draft *n* a cheque drawn by a bank on itself, which is bought by a person to pay a supplier unwilling to accept a normal cheque. Also called: **banker's cheque**

banker[1] ('bæŋkə) *n* **1** a person who owns or is an executive in a bank **2** an official or player in charge of the bank in various games **3** a result that has been forecast identically in a series of entries on a football pool coupon **4** a person or thing that appears certain to win or be successful

banker[2] ('bæŋkə) *n Austral & NZ inf* a stream almost overflowing its banks (esp in **run a banker**)

banker's order *n* another name for **standing order** (sense 1)

Bankhead ('bæŋkˌhɛd) *n* **Tallulah** (**Brockman**) 1902–68, US stage and film actress; her successes included the plays *The Little Foxes* (1939) and *The Skin of Our Teeth* (1942)

bank holiday *n* (in Britain) any of several weekdays on which banks are closed by law and which are observed as national holidays

banking ('bæŋkɪŋ) *n* the business engaged in by a bank

bank manager *n* a person who directs the business of a local branch of a bank

banknote ('bæŋkˌnəʊt) *n* a promissory note, esp one issued by a central bank, serving as money

Bank of England *n* the central bank of the United Kingdom, which acts as banker to the government and the commercial banks
▷ www.bankofengland.co.uk

bank on *vb* (*intr, prep*) to expect or rely with confidence on: *you can bank on him*

bankroll ('bæŋkˌrəʊl) *chiefly US & Canad* ▷ *n* **1** a roll of currency notes **2** the financial resources of a person, organization, etc ▷ *vb* **3** (*tr*) *sl* to provide the capital for

bankrupt ('bæŋkrʌpt, -rəpt) *n* **1** a person adjudged insolvent by a court, his or her property being administered for the benefit of creditors **2** any person unable to discharge all his or her debts **3** a person whose resources in a certain field are exhausted: *a spiritual bankrupt* ▷ *adj* **4** adjudged insolvent **5** financially ruined **6** depleted in resources: *spiritually bankrupt* **7** (foll by *of*) *Brit* lacking: *bankrupt of intelligence* ▷ *vb* **8** (*tr*) to make bankrupt [c16 from OF *banqueroute*, from OIt. *bancarotta*, from *banca* BANK[1] + *rotta* broken, from L *ruptus*] > '**bankruptcy** *n*

Banks (bæŋks) *n* **1** **Iain** (**Menzies**) born 1954, Scottish novelist and science fiction writer. His novels include *The Wasp Factory* (1984), *The Crow Road* (1992), and *Dead Air* (2002); science-fiction (under the name Iain M. Banks) includes *Look to Windward* (2000) **2** Sir **Joseph** 1743–1820, British botanist and explorer: circumnavigated the world with James Cook (1768–71)

banksia ('bæŋksɪə) *n* any shrub or tree of the Australian genus *Banksia*, having dense cylindrical heads of flowers that are often red or yellowish [c19 NL, after Sir Joseph BANKS]

Banks Island *n* **1** an island of N Canada, in the Northwest Territories: the westernmost island of the Arctic Archipelago. Area: about 67 340 sq km (26 000 sq miles) **2** an island of W Canada, off British Columbia. Length: about 72 km (45 miles)

bank statement *n* a statement of transactions in a bank account, esp one of a series sent at regular intervals to the depositor

banner ('bænə) *n* **1** a long strip of material displaying a slogan, advertisement, etc **2** a placard carried in a procession or demonstration **3** something that represents a belief or principle **4** the flag of a nation, army, etc **5** Also called: **banner headline** a large headline in a newspaper, etc, extending across the page **6** an advertisement, often animated, that extends across the top of a web page [c13 from OF *baniere*, of Gmc origin] > '**bannered** *adj*

banner ad *n* **1** a banner advertising a product **2** an advert along the top of a page of a website

Bannister ('bænɪstə) *n* Sir **Roger** (**Gilbert**) born 1929, British athlete and doctor: first man to run a mile in under four minutes (1954)

bannisters ('bænɪstəz) *pl n* a variant spelling of **banisters**

bannock ('bænək) *n* a round flat cake originating in Scotland, made from oatmeal or barley and baked on a griddle [OE *bannuc*]

Bannockburn ('bænəkˌbɜːn) *n* a village in central Scotland, south of Stirling: nearby is the site of a victory (1314) of the Scots, led by Robert the Bruce, over the English. Pop: 2675 (1991)

banns *or* **bans** (bænz) *pl n* **1** the public declaration of an intended marriage, usually on three successive Sundays in the parish churches of the betrothed **2** **forbid the banns** to raise an objection to a marriage announced in this way [c14 pl of *bann* proclamation]

banquet ('bæŋkwɪt) *n* **1** a sumptuous meal; feast **2** a ceremonial meal for many people ▷ *vb* **banquets, banqueting, banqueted** **3** (*intr*) to hold or take part in a banquet **4** (*tr*) to entertain (a person) with a banquet [c15 from OF, from It. *banchetto*, from *banco* a table, of Gmc origin] > '**banqueter** *n*

banquette (bæŋ'kɛt) *n* **1** an upholstered bench **2** (formerly) a raised part behind a parapet [c17 from F, from Provençal *banqueta*, lit.: a little bench]

banshee ('bænʃiː, bæn'ʃiː) *n* (in Irish folklore) a female spirit whose wailing warns of impending death [c18 from Irish Gaelic *bean sídhe*, lit.: woman of the fairy mound]

Bb

Banstead (ˈbænˌstɛd) *n* a town in S England, in NE Surrey: a dormitory town for London. Pop: 37 245 (1991)

bantam (ˈbæntəm) *n* **1** any of various very small breeds of domestic fowl **2** a small but aggressive person **3** *boxing* short for **bantamweight** **4** *Canad* an age level between 13 and 15 in amateur sport [c18 after *Bantam*, village in Java, said to be the original home of this fowl]

bantamweight (ˈbæntəmˌweɪt) *n* **1a** a professional boxer weighing 112–118 pounds (51–53.5 kg) **1b** an amateur boxer weighing 51–54 kg (112–119 pounds) **2** an amateur wrestler weighing usually 52–57 kg (115–126 pounds)

banter (ˈbæntə) *vb* **1** to speak or tease lightly or jokingly ▷ *n* **2** teasing or joking language or repartee [c17 from ?] > ˈ**banterer** *n*

Banting (ˈbæntɪŋ) *n* Sir **Frederick Grant** 1891–1941, Canadian physiologist: discovered the insulin treatment for diabetes with Best and Macleod (1922) and shared the Nobel prize for physiology or medicine with Macleod (1923)

Bantock (ˈbæntɒk) *n* Sir **Granville** 1868–1946, British composer. His works include the *Hebridean Symphony* (1915), five ballets, and three operas

Bantu (ˈbɑːntʊ) *n* **1** a group of languages of Africa, including most of the principal languages spoken from the equator to the Cape of Good Hope **2** (*pl* **Bantu** *or* **Bantus**) *Derog.* a Black speaker of a Bantu language ▷ *adj* **3** of or relating to this group of peoples or their languages [c19 from Bantu *Ba-ntu* people]

USAGE This term is now generally avoided because of its use in the era of apartheid

Bantustan (ˈbɑːntʊˌstɑːn) *n* *derog* (formerly, in South Africa) an area reserved for occupation by a Black African people, with limited self-government; abolished in 1993. Official name: **homeland** [from BANTU + Hindi *-stan* country of]

banyan *or* **banian** (ˈbænjən) *n* **1** an Indian tree with aerial roots that grow down into the soil forming additional trunks **2** a member of the Hindu merchant caste of India **3** a loose-fitting shirt, or robe, worn originally in India [c16 from Hindi *baniyā*, from Sansk. *vānija* merchant]

Banyana banyana (bəˈnjɑːnə bəˈnjɑːnə) *pl n* the South Africa women's national soccer team [c20 from Nguni *banyana* the girls]

banzai (ˈbɑːnzaɪ, bɑːnˈzaɪ) *interj* a patriotic cheer, battle cry, or salutation [Japanese: lit.: (may you live for) ten thousand years]

baobab (ˈbeɪəʊˌbæb) *n* a tree native to Africa, that has a very thick trunk, angular branches, and a gourdlike fruit with an edible pulp [c17 prob. from a native African word]

Baoding (ˈbaʊˈdɪŋ), **Paoting**, *or* **Pao-ting** *n* a city in NE China, in N Hebei province. Pop: 570 167 (1999 est). Former name: **Ch'ing-yüan** *or* **Tsingyuan**

BAOR *abbrev for* British Army of the Rhine

Baotou (ˈbaʊˈtuː) *or* **Paotow** *n* an industrial city in N China, in the central Inner Mongolia AR on the Yellow River. Pop: 1 092 819 (1999 est)

bap (bæp) *n* *Brit* a large soft bread roll [from ?]

baptism (ˈbæpˌtɪzəm) *n* a Christian religious rite consisting of immersion in or sprinkling with water as a sign that the subject is cleansed from sin and constituted as a member of the Church > **bap'tismal** *adj* > **bap'tismally** *adv*

baptism of fire *n* **1** a soldier's first experience of battle **2** any initiating ordeal

Baptist (ˈbæptɪst) *n* **1** a member of any of various Christian sects that affirm the necessity of baptism (usually of adults and by immersion) **2** **the Baptist** John the Baptist, the cousin and forerunner of Jesus, whom he baptized ▷ *adj* **3** denoting or characteristic of any Christian sect of Baptists
▷ www.baptist.org/
▷ www.baptist.org.uk/
▷ http://baptist.org.au/
▷ www.baptist.org.nz/
▷ www.baptist.org.nz/

baptistry *or* **baptistery** (ˈbæptɪstrɪ) *n*, *pl* **baptistries** *or* **baptisteries** **1** a part of a Christian church in which baptisms are carried out **2** a tank in a Baptist church in which baptisms are carried out

baptize *or* **baptise** (bæpˈtaɪz) *vb* **baptizes, baptizing, baptized** *or* **baptises, baptising, baptised** **1** *Christianity* to immerse (a person) in water or sprinkle water on (a person) as part of the rite of baptism **2** (*tr*) to give a name to; christen [c13 from LL *baptīzāre*, from Gk, from *baptein* to bathe, dip]

bar[1] (bɑː) *n* **1** a rigid usually straight length of metal, wood, etc, used esp as a barrier or as a structural part: *a bar of a gate* **2** a solid usually rectangular block of any material: *a bar of soap* **3** anything that obstructs or prevents **4** an offshore ridge of sand, mud, or shingle across the mouth of a river, bay, or harbour **5** a counter or room where alcoholic drinks are served **6** a counter, room, or establishment where a particular range of goods, food, services, etc, are sold: *a coffee bar; a heel bar* **7** a narrow band or stripe, as of colour or light **8** a heating element in an electric fire **9** See **Bar** **10** the place in a court of law where the accused stands during his or her trial **11** a particular court of law **12** *Brit* (in Parliament) the boundary where nonmembers wishing to address either House appear and where persons are arraigned **13** a plea showing that a plaintiff has no cause of action **14** anything referred to as an authority or tribunal: *the bar of decency* **15** *music* a group of beats that is repeated with a consistent rhythm throughout a piece of music. The number of beats in the bar is indicated by the time signature. Also called: **measure** **16a** *Brit* insignia added to a decoration indicating a second award **16b** *US* a strip of metal worn with uniform, esp to signify rank or as an award for service **17** *football, etc* See **crossbar** **18** *gymnastics* See **horizontal bar** **19** *heraldry* a narrow horizontal line across a shield **20** **behind bars** in prison **21** **won't have a bar of** *Austral & NZ inf* cannot tolerate; dislikes ▷ *vb* **bars, barring, barred** (*tr*) **22** to secure with a bar: *to bar the door* **23** to shut in or out with or as if with barriers: *to bar the entrances* **24** to obstruct: *the fallen tree barred the road* **25** (usually foll by *from*) to prohibit; forbid: *to bar a couple from meeting* **26** (usually foll by *from*) to keep out; exclude: *to bar a person from membership* **27** to mark with a bar or bars **28** *law* to prevent or halt (an action) by showing that the plaintiff has no cause ▷ *prep* **29** except for **30** **bar none** without exception [c12 from OF *barre*, from Vulgar L *barra* (unattested) bar, rod, from ?]

bar[2] (bɑː) *n* a cgs unit of pressure equal to 10^6 dynes per square centimetre [c20 from Gk *baros* weight]

Bar (bɑː) *n* **the** **1** (in England and elsewhere) barristers collectively **2** *US* the legal profession collectively **3** **be called to the Bar** *Brit* to become a barrister **4** **be called within the Bar** *Brit* to be appointed as a Queen's Counsel

bar. *abbrev for*: **1** barometric **2** barrel **3** barrister

Barabbas (bəˈræbəs) *n* *New Testament* a condemned robber who was released at the Passover instead of Jesus (Matthew 27:16)

barachois (ˌbærəˈʃwɑː) *n* (in the Atlantic Provinces of Canada) a shallow lagoon formed by a sand bar [F]

Barak (ˈbærək) *n* **Ehud** (ɛˈhʊd) born 1942, Israeli Labour politician, prime minister (1999–2001)

Baranof Island (ˈbærənəf) *n* an island off SE Alaska, in the western part of the Alexander Archipelago. Area: 4162 sq km (1607 sq miles)

barathea (ˌbærəˈθɪə) *n* a fabric made of silk and wool or cotton and rayon [c19 from ?]

barb[1] (bɑːb) *n* **1** a point facing in the opposite direction to the main point of a fish-hook, harpoon, etc, intended to make extraction difficult **2** any of various pointed parts **3** a cutting remark **4** any of the hairlike filaments that form the vane of a feather **5** a beardlike growth, hair, or projection ▷ *vb* **6** (*tr*) to provide with a barb or barbs [c14 from OF *barbe* beard, point, from L *barba* beard] > **barbed** *adj*

barb² (bɑːb) *n* a breed of horse of North African origin, similar to the Arab but less spirited [c17 from F *barbe*, from It. *barbero* a Barbary (horse)]

Barbados (bɑːˈbeɪdəʊs, -dəʊz, -dɒs) *n* an island in the Caribbean, in the E Lesser Antilles: a British colony from 1628 to 1966, now an independent state within the Commonwealth. Language: English. Currency: Barbados dollar. Capital: Bridgetown. Pop: 269 000 (2001). Area: 430 sq km (166 sq miles) > **Barˈbadian** *adj, n*
▷ www.barbados.gov.bb
▷ www.barbados.org

barbarian (bɑːˈbɛərɪən) *n* **1** a member of a primitive or uncivilized people **2** a coarse or uncultured person **3** a vicious person ▷ *adj* **4** of an uncivilized culture **5** uncultured or brutal [c16 see BARBAROUS]

barbaric (bɑːˈbærɪk) *adj* **1** of or characteristic of barbarians **2** primitive; unrestrained **3** brutal [c15 from L *barbaricus* outlandish; see BARBAROUS] > **barˈbarically** *adv*

barbarism (ˈbɑːbəˌrɪzəm) *n* **1** a brutal, coarse, or ignorant act **2** the condition of being backward, coarse, or ignorant **3** a substandard word or expression; solecism **4** any act or object that offends against accepted taste [c16 from L *barbarismus* error of speech, from Gk *barbarismos*, from *barbaros* BARBAROUS]

barbarity (bɑːˈbærɪtɪ) *n, pl* **barbarities 1** the state of being barbaric or barbarous **2** a vicious act

barbarize *or* **barbarise** (ˈbɑːbəˌraɪz) *vb* **barbarizes, barbarizing, barbarized** *or* **barbarises, barbarising, barbarised 1** to make or become barbarous **2** to use barbarisms in (language) > **ˌbarbariˈzation** *or* **ˌbarbariˈsation** *n*

Barbarossa (ˌbɑːbəˈrɒsə) *n* **1** the nickname of the Holy Roman Emperor **Frederick I** See **Frederick Barbarossa 2** real name *Khair ed-Din*. *c*. 1465–1546, Turkish pirate and admiral: conquered Tunis for the Ottomans (1534)

barbarous (ˈbɑːbərəs) *adj* **1** uncivilized; primitive **2** brutal or cruel **3** lacking refinement [c15 via L from Gk *barbaros* barbarian, non-Greek, imit. of incomprehensible speech] > **ˈbarbarously** *adv* > **ˈbarbarousness** *n*

Barbary (ˈbɑːbərɪ) *n* a region of N Africa, extending from W Egypt to the Atlantic and including the former **Barbary States** of Tripolitania, Tunisia, Algeria, and Morocco

Barbary ape *n* a tailless macaque that inhabits NW Africa and Gibraltar

Barbary Coast *n* **the** the Mediterranean coast of North Africa: a centre of piracy against European shipping from the 16th to the 19th centuries

barbate (ˈbɑːbeɪt) *adj biol* having tufts of long hairs; bearded [c19 from L *barba* a beard]

barbecue (ˈbɑːbɪˌkjuː) *n* **1** a meal cooked out of doors over an open fire **2** a grill or fireplace used in barbecuing **3** the food so cooked **4** a party or picnic at which barbecued food is served ▷ *vb* **barbecues, barbecuing, barbecued** (*tr*) **5** to cook (meat, fish, etc) on a grill, usually over charcoal and often with a highly seasoned sauce [c17 from American Sp. *barbacoa*: frame made of sticks]

barbed wire *n* strong wire with sharply pointed barbs at close intervals

barbel (ˈbɑːbᵊl) *n* **1** any of several slender tactile spines or bristles that hang from the jaws of certain fishes, such as the carp **2** any of several European cyprinid fishes that resemble the carp [c14 from OF, from LL from L *barba* beard]

barbell (ˈbɑːˌbɛl) *n* a long metal rod to which heavy discs are attached at each end for weightlifting

barber (ˈbɑːbə) *n* **1** a person whose business is cutting men's hair and shaving beards ▷ *vb* (*tr*) **2** to cut the hair of [c13 from OF *barbeor*, from *barbe* beard, from L *barba*]

Barber (ˈbɑːbə) *n* **Samuel** 1910–81, US composer: his works include an *Adagio for Strings*, adapted from the second movement of his string quartet No. 1 (1936) and the opera *Vanessa* (1958)

Barbera (bɑːˈbeɪrə) *n* **Joseph** ▷ See **(William) Hanna**

barberry (ˈbɑːbərɪ) *n, pl* **barberries** any spiny shrub of the widely distributed genus *Berberis*, having clusters of yellow flowers and orange or red berries [c15 from OF *berberis*, from Ar. *barbāris*]

barbershop (ˈbɑːbəˌʃɒp) *n* **1** *now chiefly US* the premises of a barber **2** (*modifier*) denoting a type of close four-part harmony for male voices: *a barbershop quartet*
▷ www.soundsofpgh.org/barbershop.html
▷ www.harmonize.com/bbshop
▷ www.singers.com/barbershop

barber's pole *n* a barber's sign consisting of a pole painted with red-and-white spiral stripes

barbican (ˈbɑːbɪkən) *n* **1** a walled outwork to protect a gate or drawbridge of a fortification **2** a watchtower projecting from a fortification [c13 from OF *barbacane*, from Med. L, from ?]

Barbican (ˈbɑːbɪkən) *n* **the** a building complex in the City of London: includes residential developments and the Barbican Arts Centre (completed 1982) housing concert and exhibition halls, theatres, cinemas, etc
▷ www.barbican.org.uk/home.asp

barbicel (ˈbɑːbɪˌsɛl) *n ornithol* any of the minute hooks on the barbules of feathers that interlock with those of adjacent barbules [c19 from NL *barbicella*, lit.: a small beard]

Barbirolli (ˌbɑːbəˈrɒlɪ) *n* Sir **John** 1899–1970, English conductor of the Hallé Orchestra (1943–68)

barbiturate (bɑːˈbɪtjʊrɪt, -ˌreɪt) *n* a derivative of barbituric acid, such as phenobarbitol, used in medicine as a sedative, hypnotic, or anticonvulsant

barbituric acid (ˌbɑːbɪˈtjʊərɪk) *n* a white crystalline solid used in the preparation of barbiturate drugs [c19 partial translation of G *Barbitursäure*]

Barbour jacket *or* **Barbour** (ˈbɑːbə) *n trademark* a hard-wearing waterproof waxed jacket

Barbuda (bɑːˈbuːdə) *n* a coral island in the E Caribbean, in the Leeward Islands: part of the independent state of Antigua and Barbuda. Area: 160 sq km (62 sq miles)

barbule (ˈbɑːbjuːl) *n ornithol* any of the minute hairs that project from a barb and in some feathers interlock [c19 from L *barbula* a little beard]

Barbusse (*French* barbys) *n* **Henri** (ãri) 1873–1935, French novelist and poet. His novels include *L'Enfer* (1908) and *Le Feu* (1916), reflecting the horror of World War I

barcarole *or* **barcarolle** (ˈbɑːkəˌrəʊl, -ˌrɒl; ˌbɑːkəˈrəʊl) *n* **1** a Venetian boat song **2** an instrumental composition resembling this [c18 from F, from It. *barcarola*, from *barcaruolo* boatman, from *barca* boat]

Barce (ˈbartʃe) *or* **Barca** (ˈbarka) *n* the Italian name for **Al Marj**

Barcelona (ˌbɑːsɪˈləʊnə) *n* the chief port of Spain, on the NE Mediterranean coast: seat of the Republican government during the Civil War (1936–39); the commercial capital of Spain. Pop: 1 505 581 (1998 est). Ancient name: **Barcino** (bɑːˈsiːnəʊ)

bar chart *n* another term for **bar graph**

Barclay de Tolly (ˈbɑːklɪ də ˈtɒlɪ; *Russian* barˈklai də ˈtɔlj) *n* Prince **Mikhail** (mixaˈil) 1761–1818, Russian field marshal: commander in chief against Napoleon in 1812

bar code *n commerce* a machine-readable arrangement of numbers and parallel lines printed on a package, which can be electronically scanned at a checkout to register the price of the goods and to activate computer stock checking and reordering. Also called: **Universal Product Code, UPC**

Barcoo River (bɑːˈkuː) *n* a river in E central Australia, in SW Queensland: joins with the Thomson River to form Cooper Creek

bard[1] (bɑːd) *n* **1a** (formerly) one of an ancient Celtic order of poets **1b** a poet who wins a verse competition at a Welsh eisteddfod **2** *arch or literary* any poet [C14 from Scot. Gaelic] > ˈ**bardic** *adj*

bard[2] (bɑːd) *n* **1** a piece of bacon or pork fat placed on meat during roasting to prevent drying out ▷ *vb (tr)* **2** to place a bard on [C15 from OF *barde*, from OIt. *barda*, from Ar. *barda'ah* packsaddle]

Bard (bɑːd) *n* **the** an epithet of (William) **Shakespeare**

Bardeen (ˌbɑːˈdiːn) *n* **John** 1908–91, US physicist and electrical engineer, noted for his research on electrical conduction in solids; shared Nobel prize for physics 1956 for research on semiconductors leading to the invention of the transistor; shared Nobel prize for physics 1972 for contributions to the theory of superconductivity

bardie (ˈbɑːdɪ) *n* **1** an edible white wood-boring grub of Australia **2 starve the bardies!** *Austral* an exclamation of surprise or protest [from Abor.]

bardo (ˈbɑːdəʊ) *n (often capital)* (in Tibetan Buddhism) the state of the soul between its death and its rebirth [Tibetan *bardo* between two]

Bardot (*French* bardo) *n* **Brigitte** (briʒit) born 1934, French film actress

bare[1] (bɛə) *adj* **1** unclothed: used esp of a part of the body **2** without the natural, conventional, or usual covering **3** lacking appropriate furnishings, etc **4** unembellished; simple: *the bare facts* **5** *(prenominal)* just sufficient: *the bare minimum* **6 with one's bare hands** without a weapon or tool ▷ *vb* **bares, baring, bared 7** *(tr)* to make bare; uncover [OE *bær*] > ˈ**bareness** *n*

bare[2] (bɛə) *vb arch* a past tense of **bear**[1]

bareback (ˈbɛəˌbæk) *or* **barebacked** *adj, adv* (of horse-riding) without a saddle

barefaced (ˈbɛəˌfeɪst) *adj* unconcealed or shameless: *a barefaced lie* > **barefacedly** (ˈbɛəˌfeɪsɪdlɪ) *adv* > ˈ**bareˌfacedness** *n*

barefoot (ˈbɛəˌfʊt) *or* **barefooted** *adj, adv* **1** with the feet uncovered ▷ *adj* **2** denoting a worker with basic training sent to help people in remote rural areas, esp of developing countries: *barefoot doctor*

bareheaded (ˌbɛəˈhɛdɪd) *adj, adv* with the head uncovered

Bareilly (bəˈreɪlɪ) *n* a city in N India, in N central Uttar Pradesh. Pop: 587 211 (1991)

bare-knuckle *adj* **1** without boxing gloves: *a bare-knuckle fighter* **2** aggressive; without civilized restraint: *a bare-knuckle confrontation*

barely (ˈbɛəlɪ) *adv* **1** only just: *barely enough* **2** *inf* not quite: *barely old enough* **3** scantily: *barely furnished* **4** *arch* openly.

USAGE See at **scarcely**

Barenboim (ˈbærənˌbɔɪm) *n* **Daniel** born 1942, Israeli concert pianist and conductor, born in Argentina

Barents Sea (ˈbærənts) *n* a part of the Arctic Ocean, bounded by Norway, Russia, and the islands of Novaya Zemlya, Spitsbergen, and Franz Josef Land [named after Willem *Barents* (1550–97) Dutch navigator and explorer]

barf (bɑːf) *vb (intr) sl* to vomit [C20 prob. imit.]

bargain (ˈbɑːgɪn) *n* **1** an agreement establishing what each party will give, receive, or perform in a transaction **2** something acquired or received in such an agreement **3a** something bought or offered at a low price **3b** *(as modifier)*: *a bargain price* **4 into the bargain** in excess; besides **5 make** *or* **strike a bargain** to agree on terms ▷ *vb* **6** *(intr)* to negotiate the terms of an agreement, transaction, etc **7** *(tr)* to exchange, as in a bargain **8** to arrive at (an agreement or settlement) [C14 from OF *bargaigne*, from *bargaignier* to trade, of Gmc origin] > ˈ**bargainer** *n*

bargain away *vb (tr, adv)* to lose (rights, etc) in return for something valueless

bargain for *vb (intr, prep)* to expect; anticipate: *he got more than he bargained for*

bargain on *vb (intr, prep)* to rely or depend on (something): *he bargained on her support*

barge (bɑːdʒ) *n* **1** a vessel, usually flat-bottomed and with or without its own power, used for transporting freight, esp on canals **2** a vessel, often decorated, used in pageants, etc **3** *Navy* a boat allocated to a flag officer, used esp for ceremonial occasions ▷ *vb* **barges, barging, barged 4** *(intr; foll by into) inf* to bump (into) **5** *inf* to push (someone or one's way) violently **6** *(intr; foll by into or in) inf* to interrupt rudely or clumsily: *to barge into a conversation* [C13 from OF, from Med. L *barga*, prob. from LL *barca* a small boat]

bargeboard (ˈbɑːdʒˌbɔːd) *n* a board, often decorated, along the gable end of a roof

bargee (bɑːˈdʒiː) *n* a person employed on or in charge of a barge

bargepole (ˈbɑːdʒˌpəʊl) *n* **1** a long pole used to propel a barge **2 not touch with a bargepole** *inf* to refuse to have anything to do with

bar graph *n* a graph consisting of vertical or horizontal bars whose lengths are proportional to amounts or quantities

Bari (ˈbɑːrɪ) *n* a port in SE Italy, capital of Apulia, on the Adriatic coast. Pop: 331 848 (2000 est)

bariatrics (ˌbærɪˈætrɪks) *n (functioning as sing)* the branch of medicine concerned with the treatment of obese people [C20 from Gk *barōs* weight + -IATRICS]

Baring (ˈbɛərɪŋ) *n* **Evelyn**, 1st Earl of Cromer. 1841–1917, English administrator. As consul general in Egypt with plenipotentiary powers, he controlled the Egyptian government from 1883 to 1907

barite (ˈbɛəraɪt) *n* the usual US and Canad name for **barytes** [C18 from BAR(IUM) + -ITE[1]]

baritone (ˈbærɪˌtəʊn) *n* **1** the second lowest adult male voice **2** a singer with such a voice **3** the second lowest instrument in the families of the saxophone, horn, oboe, etc ▷ *adj* **4** relating to or denoting a baritone [C17 from It., from Gk, from *barus* heavy, low + *tonos* TONE]

barium (ˈbɛərɪəm) *n* a soft silvery-white metallic element of the alkaline earth group. Symbol: Ba; atomic no.: 56; atomic wt.: 137.34 [C19 from BAR(YTA) + -IUM]

barium meal *n* a preparation of barium sulphate, which is opaque to X-rays, swallowed by a patient before X-ray examination of the upper part of the alimentary canal

bark[1] (bɑːk) *n* **1** the loud abrupt usually harsh cry of a dog or certain other animals **2** a similar sound, such as one made by a person, gun, etc **3 his** *(or* **her***)* **bark is worse than his** *(or* **her***)* **bite** he *(or* she) is bad-tempered but harmless ▷ *vb* **4** *(intr)* (of a dog, etc) to make its typical cry **5** *(intr)* (of a person, gun, etc) to make a similar loud harsh sound **6** to say or shout in a brusque or angry tone: *he barked an order* **7 bark up the wrong tree** *inf* to misdirect one's attention, efforts, etc; be mistaken [OE *beorcan*]

bark[2] (bɑːk) *n* **1** a protective layer of dead corky cells on the outside of the stems of woody plants **2** any of several varieties of this, used in tanning, dyeing, or in medicine ▷ *vb (tr)* **3** to scrape or rub off skin, as in an injury **4** to remove the bark or a circle of bark from (a tree) **5** to tan (leather), principally by the tannins in barks [C13 from ON *börkr*]

bark[3] (bɑːk) *n* a variant spelling of **barque**

barkentine (ˈbɑːkənˌtiːn) *n* the usual US and Canad spelling of **barquentine**

barker (ˈbɑːkə) *n* **1** an animal or person that barks **2** a person at a fair booth, etc, who loudly addresses passers-by to attract customers

Barker (ˈbɑːkə) *n* **1 George (Granville)** 1913–91, British poet: author of *Calamiterror* (1937) and *The True Confession of*

George Barker (1950) **2 Howard** born 1946, British playwright: his plays include *Claw* (1975), *The Castle* (1985), and *13 Objects* (2003) **3 Ronnie**, full name *Ronald William George Barker*. born 1929, British comedian: known esp for his partnership with Ronnie Corbett (born 1930) in the TV series *The Two Ronnies* (1971–85)

barking ('bɑːkɪŋ) *sl* ▷ *adj* **1** mad; crazy ▷ *adv* **2** (intensifier): *barking mad*

Barking and Dagenham ('bɑːkɪŋ) *n* a borough of E Greater London. Pop: 163 944 (2001). Area: 34 sq km (13 sq miles)

Bar Kochba, Bar Kokhba, *or* **Bar Kosba** (bɑː 'kɒxbə, 'kɒs-) *n* **Simeon** died 135 AD. Jewish leader who led an unsuccessful revolt against the Romans in Palestine

Barletta (*Italian* bar'letta) *n* a port in SE Italy, in Apulia. Pop: 88 750 (1990)

barley ('bɑːlɪ) *n* **1** any of various annual temperate grasses that have dense bristly flower spikes and are widely cultivated for grain and forage **2** the grain of any of these grasses, used in making beer and whisky and for soups, puddings, etc [OE *bærlīc* (adj); rel. to *bere* barley]

barleycorn ('bɑːlɪˌkɔːn) *n* **1** a grain of barley, or barley itself **2** an obsolete unit of length equal to one third of an inch

barley sugar *n* a brittle clear amber-coloured sweet

barley water *n* a drink made from an infusion of barley

barm (bɑːm) *n* **1** the yeasty froth on fermenting malt liquors **2** an archaic or dialect word for **yeast** [OE *bearm*]

barmaid ('bɑːˌmeɪd) *n* a woman who serves in a pub

barman ('bɑːmən) *n, pl* **barmen** a man who serves in a pub

Barmecide ('bɑːmɪˌsaɪd) *adj* lavish in imagination only; illusory; sham: *a Barmecide feast* [c18 from a prince in the *Arabian Nights' Entertainment* who served empty plates to beggars, alleging that they held sumptuous food]

Bar Mitzvah (bɑː 'mɪtsvə) (*sometimes not caps.*) *Judaism* ▷ *adj* **1** (of a Jewish boy) having assumed full religious obligations, being at least thirteen years old ▷ *n* **2** the occasion or celebration of this **3** the boy himself [Heb.: son of the law]

barmy ('bɑːmɪ) *adj* **barmier, barmiest** *sl* insane [c16 orig., full of BARM, hence frothing, excited]

barn[1] (bɑːn) *n* **1** a large farm outbuilding, chiefly for storing grain, etc, but also for livestock **2** *US & Canad* a large shed for railroad cars, trucks, etc **3** any large building, esp an unattractive one **4** (*modifier*) relating to a system of poultry farming in which birds are allowed to move freely within a barn: *barn eggs* [OE *beren*, from *bere* barley + *ærn* room]

barn[2] (bɑːn) *n* a unit of nuclear cross section equal to 10^{-28} square metres. Symbol: b [c20 from BARN[1]; so called because of the relatively large cross section]

Barnabas ('bɑːnəbəs) *n* **Saint** *New Testament* original name *Joseph*. a Cypriot Levite who supported Saint Paul in his apostolic work (Acts 4:36,37). Feast day: June 11

barnacle ('bɑːnək^əl) *n* **1** any of various marine crustaceans that, as adults, live attached to rocks, ship bottoms, etc **2** a person or thing that is difficult to get rid of [c16 from earlier *bernak*, from OF *bernac*, from LL, from ?] > **'barnacled** *adj*

barnacle goose *n* a N European goose that has a black-and-white head and body [c13 *bernekke*: it was formerly believed that the goose developed from a shellfish]

Barnard ('bɑːnɑːd) *n* **1 Christiaan** (**Neethling**) 1923–2001, South African surgeon, who performed the first human heart transplant (1967) **2 Edward Emerson** 1857–1923, US astronomer: noted for his discovery of the fifth satellite of Jupiter and his discovery of comets, nebulae, and a red dwarf (1916)

Barnardo (bə'nɑːdəʊ, bɑː-) *n* Dr **Thomas John** 1845–1905, British philanthropist, who founded homes for destitute children

Barnaul (*Russian* bərna'ul) *n* a city in S Russia, on the River Ob. Pop: 586 200 (1999 est)

barn dance *n* **1** *Brit* a progressive round country dance **2** *Brit* a disco or party held in a barn **3** *US & Canad* a party with hoedown music and square-dancing

Barnet ('bɑːnɪt) *n* a borough of N Greater London: scene of a Yorkist victory (1471) in the Wars of the Roses. Pop: 314 561 (2001). Area: 89 sq km (34 sq miles)

barney ('bɑːnɪ) *inf* ▷ *n* **1** a noisy fight or argument ▷ *vb* **2** (*intr*) *chiefly Austral & NZ* to argue or quarrel [c19 from ?]

barn owl *n* an owl with a pale brown and white plumage and a heart-shaped face

Barnsley ('bɑːnzlɪ) *n* **1** an industrial town in N England, in Barnsley unitary authority, South Yorkshire. Pop: 75 120 (1991) **2** a unitary authority in N England, in South Yorkshire. Pop: 218 062 (2001). Area: 329 sq km (127 sq miles)

Barnstaple ('bɑːnstəp^əl) *n* a town in SW England, in Devon, on the estuary of the River Taw: tourism, agriculture. Pop: 27 691 (1991)

barnstorm ('bɑːnˌstɔːm) *vb* (*intr*) **1** to tour rural districts putting on shows **2** *chiefly US & Canad* to tour rural districts making speeches in a political campaign > **'barnˌstorming** *n, adj*

Barnum ('bɑːnəm) *n* **P**(**hineas**) **T**(**aylor**) 1810–91, US showman, who created The Greatest Show on Earth (1871) and, with J. A. Bailey, founded the Barnum and Bailey Circus (1881)

barnyard ('bɑːnˌjɑːd) *n* **1** a yard adjoining a barn **2** (*modifier*) characteristic of a barnyard **3** (*modifier*) crude or earthy

baro- *combining form* indicating weight or pressure: *barometer* [from Gk *baros* weight]

baroceptor ('bærəʊˌsɛptə) *n* another name for **baroreceptor**

Baroda (bə'rəʊdə) *n* **1** a former state of W India, part of Gujarat since 1960 **2** the former name (until 1976) of **Vadodara**

Bb

barogram ('bærəˌɡræm) *n meteorol* the record of atmospheric pressure traced by a barograph or similar instrument

barograph ('bærəˌɡrɑːf) *n meteorol* a self-recording aneroid barometer > **barographic** (ˌbærə'ɡræfɪk) *adj*

Baroja (*Spanish* ba'roxa) *n* **Pio** ('pio) 1872–1956, Spanish Basque novelist, who wrote nearly 100 novels, including a series of twenty-two under the general title *Memorias de un Hombre de Acción* (1944–49)

barometer (bə'rɒmɪtə) *n* **1** an instrument for measuring atmospheric pressure, usually to determine altitude or weather changes **2** anything that shows change > **barometric** (ˌbærə'mɛtrɪk) *or* **ˌbaro'metrical** *adj* > **ba'rometry** *n*

baron ('bærən) *n* **1** a member of a specific rank of nobility, esp the lowest rank in the British Isles **2** (in Europe from the Middle Ages) originally any tenant-in-chief of a king or other overlord **3** a powerful businessman or financier: *a press baron* [c12 from OF, of Gmc origin]

baronage ('bærənɪdʒ) *n* **1** barons collectively **2** the rank or dignity of a baron

Baron-Cohen (ˌbærən'kəʊən) *n* **Sacha** born 1970, British television comedian, best known for his creation of the character Ali G

baroness ('bærənɪs) *n* **1** the wife or widow of a baron **2** a woman holding the rank of baron

baronet ('bærənɪt, -ˌnɛt) *n* (in Britain) a commoner who holds the lowest hereditary title of honour, ranking below a baron. Abbrev: **Bart, Bt** > **'baronetage** *n* > **'baronetcy** *n*

baronial (bə'rəʊnɪəl) *adj* of, relating to, or befitting a baron or barons

baron of beef *n* a cut of beef consisting of a double sirloin joined at the backbone

barony ('bærənɪ) *n, pl* **baronies 1a** the domain of a baron **1b** (in Ireland) a division of a county **1c** (in Scotland) a large estate or manor **2** the rank or dignity of a baron

baroque (bə'rɒk, bə'rəʊk) *n (often cap)* **1** a style of architecture and decorative art in Europe from the late 16th to the early 18th century, characterized by extensive ornamentation **2** a 17th-century style of music characterized by extensive use of ornamentation **3** any ornate or heavily ornamented style ▷ *adj* **4** denoting, in, or relating to the baroque **5** (of pearls) irregularly shaped [c18 from F, from Port. *barroco* a rough or imperfectly shaped pearl]

▷ witcombe.sbc.edu/ARTHbaroque.html
▷ www.artlex.com/ArtLex/b/baroque.html
▷ www.baroquemusic.org
▷ classicalmus.hispeed.com/baroque.html
▷ www.baroque-music.co.uk

baroreceptor ('bærəʊrɪˌsɛptə) *or* **baroceptor** *n* a collection of sensory nerve endings, principally in the carotid sinuses and the aortic arch, that monitor blood-pressure changes in the body

baroscope ('bærəˌskəʊp) *n* any instrument for measuring atmospheric pressure > **baroscopic** (ˌbærə'skɒpɪk) *adj*

barouche (bə'ruːʃ) *n* a four-wheeled horse-drawn carriage, popular in the 19th century, having a retractable hood over the rear half [c19 from G (dialect) *Barutsche*, from It. *baroccio*, from LL *birotus*, from BI- + *rota* wheel]

Barozzi (*Italian* ba'rottsi) *n* See (Giacomo Barozzi da) **Vignola**

barperson ('bɑːˌpɜːsᵊn) *n, pl* **barpersons** a person who serves in a pub: used esp in advertisements

barque (bɑːk) *n* **1** a sailing ship of three or more masts having the foremasts rigged square and the aftermast rigged fore-and-aft **2** *poetic* any boat [c15 from OF, from OProvençal *barca*]

barquentine *or* **barquantine** ('bɑːkənˌtiːn) *n* a sailing ship of three or more masts rigged square on the foremast and fore-and-aft on the others [c17 from BARQUE + (BRIG)ANTINE]

Barquisimeto (*Spanish* barkisi'meto) *n* a city in NW Venezuela. Pop: 875 790 (2000 est)

barra ('bærə) *n Austral inf* a barramundi

Barra ('bærə) *n* an island in NW Scotland, in the Outer Hebrides: fishing, crofting, tourism. Pop: 1200 (latest est)

barrack[1] ('bærək) *vb* to house (soldiers, etc) in barracks

barrack[2] ('bærək) *vb Brit, Austral, & NZ inf* **1** to criticize loudly or shout against (a team, speaker, etc); jeer **2** (*intr; foll by for*) to shout support (for) [c19 from Irish: to boast]

barrack-room lawyer *n* a person who freely offers opinions, esp in legal matters, that he or she is unqualified to give

barracks ('bærəks) *pl n* (*sometimes sing; when pl, sometimes functions as sing*) **1** a building or group of buildings used to accommodate military personnel **2** any large building used for housing people, esp temporarily **3** a large and bleak building [c17 from F *baraque*, from OCatalan *barraca* hut, from ?]

barracouta (ˌbærə'kuːtə) *n* a large predatory Pacific fish [c17 var. of BARRACUDA]

barracuda (ˌbærə'kjuːdə) *n, pl* **barracuda** *or* **barracudas** a predatory marine mostly tropical fish, which attacks man [c17 from American Sp., from ?]

barrage ('bærɑːʒ) *n* **1** *mil* the firing of artillery to saturate an area, either to protect against an attack or to support an advance **2** an overwhelming and continuous delivery of something, as questions **3** a construction across a watercourse, esp one to increase the depth [c19 from F, from *barrer* to obstruct; see BAR[1]]

barrage balloon *n* one of a number of tethered balloons with cables or net suspended from them, used to deter low-flying air attack

barramundi (ˌbærə'mʌndɪ) *n, pl* **barramundis, barramundies,** *or* **barramundi** a large edible Australian estuary fish of the perch family [from Abor.]

Barranquilla (*Spanish* barran'kiʎa) *n* a port in N Colombia, on the Magdalena River. Pop: 1 223 260 (1999 est)

barratry *or* **barretry** ('bærətrɪ) *n* **1** *criminal law* (formerly) the vexatious stirring up of quarrels or bringing of lawsuits **2** *maritime law* a fraudulent practice committed by the master or crew of a ship to the prejudice of the owner **3** the purchase or sale of public or Church offices [c15 from OF *baraterie* deception, from *barater* to BARTER] > '**barratrous** *or* '**barretrous** *adj* > '**barrator** *n*

Barrault (*French* baro) *n* **Jean-Louis** (ʒɑ̃lwi) 1910–94, French actor and director, noted particularly as a mime

barre *French* (bar) *n* a rail at hip height used for ballet practice and leg exercises [lit.: bar]

barrel ('bærəl) *n* **1** a cylindrical container usually bulging outwards in the middle and held together by metal hoops **2** Also called: **barrelful** the amount that a barrel can hold **3** a unit of capacity of varying amount in different industries **4** a thing shaped like a barrel, esp a tubular part of a machine **5** the tube through which the projectile of a firearm is discharged **6** the trunk of a four-legged animal: *the barrel of a horse* **7 over a barrel** *inf* powerless **8 scrape the barrel** *inf* to be forced to use one's last and weakest resource ▷ *vb* **barrels, barrelling, barrelled** *or US* **barrels, barreling, barreled 9** (*tr*) to put into a barrel or barrels **10** (*intr; foll by along, etc*) *inf* to travel or move very fast [c14 from OF *baril*, ?from *barre* BAR[1]]

barrel-chested *adj* having a large rounded chest

barrel organ *n* an instrument consisting of a cylinder turned by a handle and having pins on it that interrupt the air flow to certain pipes or pluck strings, thereby playing tunes

barrel roll *n* a flight manoeuvre in which an aircraft rolls about its longitudinal axis while following a spiral course in line with the direction of flight

barrel vault *n archit* a vault in the form of a half cylinder

barren ('bærən) *adj* **1** incapable of producing offspring, seed, or fruit; sterile **2** unable to support the growth of crops, etc: *barren land* **3** lacking in stimulation; dull **4** not producing worthwhile results; unprofitable: *a barren period* **5** (foll by *of*) devoid (of): *barren of wit* **6** (of rock strata) having no fossils [c13 from OF *brahain*, from ?] > '**barrenness** *n*

Barren Lands *pl n* **the** a region of tundra in N Canada, extending westwards from Hudson Bay: sparsely inhabited, chiefly by Inuit. Also called: **Barren Grounds**

barricade (ˌbærɪ'keɪd, 'bærɪˌkeɪd) *n* **1** a barrier for defence, esp one erected hastily, as during street fighting ▷ *vb* **barricades, barricading, barricaded** (*tr*) **2** to erect a barricade across (an entrance, etc) or at points of access to (a room, district, etc) [c17 from OF, from *barriquer* to barricade, from *barrique* a barrel, from Sp. *barrica*, from *barril* BARREL]

Barrie ('bærɪ) *n* Sir **James Matthew** 1860–1937, Scottish dramatist and novelist, noted particularly for his popular children's play *Peter Pan* (1904)

barrier ('bærɪə) *n* **1** anything serving to obstruct passage or to maintain separation, such as a fence or gate **2** anything that prevents progress **3** anything that separates or hinders union: *a language barrier* [c14 from OF *barriere*, from *barre* BAR[1]]

barrier cream *n* a cream used to protect the skin, esp the hands

barrier-nurse *vb* (*tr*) to tend (infectious patients) in isolation, to prevent the spread of infection > **barrier nursing** *n*

barrier reef *n* a long narrow coral reef near the shore, separated from it by deep water

barring ('bɑːrɪŋ) *prep* unless (something) occurs; except for

barrister ('bærɪstə) *n* **1** Also called: **barrister-at-law** (in England) a lawyer who has been called to the bar and is qualified to plead in the higher courts ▷ Cf **solicitor** **2** (in Canada) a lawyer who pleads in court **3** *US* a less common word for **lawyer** [c16 from BAR[1]]

barrow[1] ('bærəʊ) *n* **1** See **wheelbarrow, handbarrow** **2** Also called: **barrowful** the amount contained in or on a barrow **3** *chiefly Brit* a handcart with a canvas roof, used esp by street vendors [OE *bearwe*]

barrow[2] ('bærəʊ) *n* a heap of earth placed over one or more prehistoric tombs, often surrounded by ditches [OE *beorg*]

Barrow ('bærəʊ) *n* **1** a river in SE Ireland, rising in the Slieve Bloom Mountains and flowing south to Waterford Harbour. Length: about 193 km (120 miles) **2** See **Barrow-in-Furness** and **Barrow Point**

barrow boy *n Brit* a man who sells his wares from a barrow; street vendor

Barrow-in-Furness *n* an industrial town in NW England, in S Cumbria. Pop: 48 947 (1991)

Barrow Point *n* the northernmost tip of Alaska, on the Arctic Ocean

barry *or* **Barry Crocker** ('bærɪ) *n Austral sl* a mistake or blunder; a disappointing performance [rhyming slang for SHOCKER]

Barry ('bærɪ) *n* **John,** real name *John Barry Prendergast.* born 1933, British composer of film scores, including several for films in the James Bond series

Barry[1] ('bærɪ) *n* a port in SE Wales, in Vale of Glamorgan county borough on the Bristol Channel. Pop: 49 887 (1991)

Barry[2] *n* **1** ('bærɪ) Sir **Charles** 1795–1860, English architect: designer of the Houses of Parliament in London **2** (*French* bari) **Comtesse du** See **du Barry** **3** **John,** real name *John Barry Prendergast.* born 1933, British composer of film scores, including several for films in the James Bond series

Barrymore ('bærɪˌmɔː) *n* a US family of actors, esp **Ethel** (1879–1959), **John** (1882–1942), and **Lionel** (1878–1954)

Barry Mountains *pl n* a mountain range in SE Australia, in E Victoria: part of the Australian Alps

bar sinister *n* **1** (not in heraldic usage) another name for **bend sinister** **2** the condition or stigma of being of illegitimate birth

Bart (bɑːt) *n* **Lionel** 1930–99, British composer and playwright. His musicals include *Oliver!* (1960)

Bart. *abbrev for* Baronet

bartender ('bɑːˌtɛndə) *n* another name (esp US and Canad) for **barman** or **barmaid**

barter ('bɑːtə) *vb* **1** to trade (goods, services, etc) in exchange for other goods, services, etc, rather than for money **2** (*intr*) to haggle over such an exchange; bargain ▷ *n* **3** trade by the exchange of goods [c15 from OF *barater* to cheat]

Barth *n* **1** (*German* bart) **Heinrich** 1821–65, German explorer: author of *Travels and Discoveries in North and Central Africa* (1857–58) **2** (bɑːθ) **John** (**Simmons**) born 1930, US novelist; his novels include *The Sot-Weed Factor* (1960), *Giles Goat-Boy* (1966), and *Once Upon a Time* (1994) **3** (*German* bart) **Karl** 1886–1968, Swiss Protestant theologian. He stressed man's dependence on divine grace in such works as *Commentary on Romans* (1919)

Barthes (*French* bart) *n* **Roland** 1915–80, French writer and critic, who applied structuralist theory to literature and popular culture: his books include *Mythologies* (1957) and *Elements of Semiology* (1964)

Bartholdi (*French* bartɔldɪ) *n* **Frédéric August** 1834–1904, French sculptor and architect, who designed (1884) the Statue of Liberty

Bartholomew (bɑːˈθɒləˌmjuː) *n* **Saint** *New Testament* one of the twelve apostles (Matthew 10:3). Feast day: Aug. 24 or June 11

bartizan ('bɑːtɪzən, ˌbɑːtɪ'zæn) *n* a small turret projecting from a wall, parapet, or tower [c19 var. of *bertisene*, erroneously for *bretising*, from *bretasce* parapet; see BRATTICE] > **bartizaned** ('bɑːtɪzənd, ˌbɑːtɪ'zænd) *adj*

Bartók ('bɑːtɒk; *Hungarian* 'bɔrtoːk) *n* **Béla** ('beːlɔ) 1881–1945, Hungarian composer, pianist, and collector of folk songs, by which his music was deeply influenced. His works include six string quartets, three piano concertos, several piano pieces including *Mikrokosmos* (1926–37), ballets (including *The Miraculous Mandarin*, 1919), and the opera *Bluebeard's Castle* (produced 1918)

Bartoli (*Italian* ba'tolɪ) *n* **Cecilia** born 1966, Italian mezzo-soprano, noted for her performances in Mozart and Rossini operas

Bartolommeo (*Italian* bartolom'meo) *n* **Fra** original name *Baccio della Porta.* 1472–1517, Italian painter of the Florentine school, noted for his austere religious works

Barton ('bɑːtᵊn) *n* **1** Sir **Derek** (**Harold Richard**) 1918–98, British organic chemist: shared the Nobel prize for chemistry (1969) for his work on conformational analysis **2** Sir **Edmund** 1849–1920, Australian statesman; first prime minister of Australia (1901–03) **3** **Elizabeth,** known as the *Maid of Kent.* ?1506–34, English nun, who claimed the gift of prophecy. Her criticism of Henry VIII's attempt to annul his first marriage led to her execution **4** **John** (**Bernard Adie**) born 1928, British theatre director, noted esp for his productions of Shakespeare

Baruch ('bɛərʊk, 'bɑː-) *n Bible* **a** a disciple of Jeremiah (Jeremiah 32–36) **b** the book of the Apocrypha said to have been written by him

baryon ('bærɪˌɒn) *n* any of a class of elementary particles that have a mass greater than or equal to that of the proton. Baryons are either nucleons or hyperons. The **baryon number** is the number of baryons in a system minus the number of antibaryons [c20 from Gk *barus* heavy + -ON] > ˌ**bary'onic** *adj*

baryta (bə'raɪtə) *n* another name for barium oxide or barium hydroxide [c19 NL, from Gk *barutēs* weight, from *barus* heavy]

barytes (bə'raɪtiːz) *n* a colourless or white mineral occurring in sedimentary rocks and with sulphide ores: a source of barium [c18 from Gk *barus* heavy + *-itēs* -ITE[1]]

basal ('beɪsᵊl) *adj* **1** at, of, or constituting a base **2** of or constituting a basis; fundamental

basal metabolism *n* the amount of energy required by an individual in the resting state, for such functions as breathing and blood circulation

basalt ('bæsɔːlt) *n* **1** a dark basic igneous rock: the most common volcanic rock **2** a form of black unglazed pottery resembling basalt [c18 from LL *basaltēs*, var. of *basanītēs*, from Gk *basanitēs* touchstone] > **ba'saltic** *adj*

bascule ('bæskjuːl) *n* **1** a bridge with a movable section hinged about a horizontal axis and counterbalanced by a weight **2** a movable roadway forming part of such a bridge [c17 from F: seesaw, from *bas* low + *cul* rump]

base[1] (beɪs) *n* **1** the bottom or supporting part of anything **2** the fundamental principle or part **3a** a centre of operations, organization, or supply **3b** (*as modifier*): *base camp* **4** starting point: *the new discovery became the base for further research* **5** the main ingredient of a mixture: *to use rice as a base in cookery* **6** a chemical compound that combines with an acid to form a salt and water. A solution of a base in water turns litmus paper blue and produces hydroxyl ions **7** a medium such as oil or water in which the pigment is dispersed in paints, inks, etc **8** *biochem* any of the nitrogen constituents of nucleic acids: adenine, thymine (in DNA), uracil (in RNA), guanine or cytosine **9** *biol* the point of attachment of an organ or part **10** the bottommost layer or part of anything **11** *archit* the part of a column between the pedestal and the shaft **12** the lower side or face of a geometric construction **13** *maths* the number of units in a counting system that is equivalent to one in the next higher counting place: *10 is the base of the decimal system* **14** *maths* the number that when raised to a certain power has a logarithm (based on that number) equal to that power: *the logarithm to the base 10 of 1000 is 3* **15** *linguistics* a root or stem **16** *electronics* the region in a transistor between the emitter and collector **17** a starting or finishing point in any of various games ▷ *vb* **bases, basing, based 18** (*tr*; foll by *on* or *upon*) to use as a basis (for); found (on) **19** (often foll by *at* or *in*) to station, post, or place (a person or oneself) [C14 from OF, from L *basis* pedestal; see BASIS]

base² (beɪs) *adj* **1** devoid of honour or morality; contemptible **2** of inferior quality or value **3** debased; alloyed; counterfeit: *base currency* **4** *English history* (of land tenure) held by villein or other ignoble service **5** *arch* born of humble parents **6** *arch* illegitimate [C14 from OF *bas*, from LL *bassus* of low height] > **'baseness** *n*

baseball ('beɪs,bɔːl) *n* **1** a team game with nine players on each side, played on a field with four bases connected to form a diamond. The object is to score runs by batting the ball and running round the bases **2** the hard rawhide-covered ball used in this game
▷ www.majorleaguebaseball.com
▷ www.baseball-links.com

baseball cap *n* a close-fitting thin cap with a deep peak

baseborn ('beɪs,bɔːn) *adj arch* **1** born of humble parents **2** illegitimate

base hospital *n Austral* a hospital serving a large rural area

Basel ('bɑːzᵊl) *n* a variant spelling of **Basle**

baseless ('beɪslɪs) *adj* not based on fact; unfounded > **'baselessness** *n*

baseline ('beɪs,laɪn) *n* **1** *surveying* a measured line through a survey area from which triangulations are made **2** a line at each end of a tennis court that marks the limit of play

basement ('beɪsmənt) *n* **1a** a partly or wholly underground storey of a building, esp one used for habitation rather than storage **1b** (*as modifier*): *a basement flat* **2** the foundation of a wall or building

base metal *n* any of certain common metals, such as copper and lead, as distinct from precious metals

basenji (bə'sɛndʒɪ) *n* a small African breed of dog that is unable to bark [C20 from Bantu]

base rate *n* **1** *Brit* the rate of interest used by individual commercial banks as a basis for their lending rates **2** *Brit inf* the rate at which the Bank of England lends to the discount houses, which effectively controls the interest rates charged throughout the banking system **3** *statistics* the average number of times an event occurs divided by the average number of times on which it might occur

bases¹ ('beɪsiːz) *n* the plural of **basis**

bases² ('beɪsɪz) *n* the plural of **base**

base unit *n physics* any of the fundamental units in a system of measurement. The base SI units are the metre, kilogram, second, ampere, kelvin, candela, and mole

bash (bæʃ) *inf* ▷ *vb* **1** (*tr*) to strike violently or crushingly **2** (*tr*; often foll by *in*, *down*, etc) to smash, break, etc, with a crashing blow **3** (*intr*; foll by *into*) to crash (into); collide (with) **4** to dent or be dented ▷ *n* **5** a heavy blow **6** a party **7 have a bash** *inf* to make an attempt [C17 from ?]

bashful ('bæʃfʊl) *adj* **1** shy or modest; diffident **2** indicating or characterized by shyness or modesty [C16 from *bash*, short for ABASH + -FUL] > **'bashfully** *adv* > **'bashfulness** *n*

-bashing *n and adj combining form inf or sl* **a** indicating a malicious attack on members of a particular group: *union-bashing* **b** indicating any of various other activities: *Bible-bashing* > **-basher** *n combining form*

Bashkir Republic *n* a constituent republic of E central Russia, in the S Urals: established as the first Soviet autonomous republic in 1919; rich mineral resources. Capital: Ufa. Pop: 4 117 000 (2000 est). Area: 143 600 sq km (55 430 sq miles). Also called: **Bashkiria** (bæʃ'kɪərɪə), **Bashkortostan** (bæʃ'kɔːtɔ,stɑːn; *Russian* baʃkɔrtɔ'stɑːn)

basho ('bæʃəʊ) *n, pl* **basho** a grand tournament in sumo wrestling [C20 from Japanese, lit.: place]

Basho (bɑː'ʃɔː) *n* full name **Matsuo Basho**, originally *Matsuo Munefusa*. 1644–94, Japanese poet and travel writer, noted esp for his haiku

basic ('beɪsɪk) *adj* **1** of, relating to, or forming a base or basis; fundamental **2** elementary or simple: *a few basic facts* **3** excluding additions or extras: *basic pay* **4** *chem* of, denoting, or containing a base; alkaline **5** *metallurgy* of or made by a process in which the furnace or converter is made of a basic material, such as magnesium oxide **6** (of such igneous rocks as basalt) containing between 52 and 45 per cent silica ▷ *n* **7** (*usually pl*) a fundamental principle, fact, etc

BASIC *or* **Basic** ('beɪsɪk) *n* a computer programming language that uses common English terms [C20 *b(eginner's) a(ll-purpose) s(ymbolic) i(nstruction) c(ode)*]

basically ('beɪsɪklɪ) *adv* **1** in a fundamental or elementary manner; essentially: *strident and basically unpleasant* **2** (*sentence modifier*) in essence; in summary; put simply: *basically we had underestimated mother nature*

Basic Curriculum *n Brit education* the National Curriculum plus religious education

basic English *n* a simplified form of English with a vocabulary of approximately 850 common words, intended as an international language

basic industry *n* an industry which is highly important in a nation's economy

basicity (beɪ'sɪsɪtɪ) *n chem* **a** the state of being a base **b** the number of molecules of acid required to neutralize one molecule of a given base

basic rate *n* the standard or lowest level on a scale of money payable, esp in taxation

basic slag *n* a slag produced in steel-making, containing calcium phosphate

basic wage *n* **1** a person's wage excluding overtime, bonuses, etc **2** *Austral* the statutory minimum wage for any worker

basidiomycete (bæ,sɪdɪəʊmaɪ'siːt) *n* any of a class of fungi, including puffballs and rusts, which produce spores at the tips of slender projecting stalks [C19 see BASIS, -MYCETE] > **ba,sidiomy'cetous** *adj*

Basie ('beɪsɪ) *n* **William**, known as *Count Basie*. 1904–84, US jazz pianist, bandleader, and composer: associated particularly with the polished phrasing and style of big-band jazz

basil ('bæzᵊl) *n* a Eurasian plant having spikes of small white flowers and aromatic leaves used as herbs for seasoning. Also called: **sweet basil** [C15 from OF *basile*, from LL, from Gk *basilikos* royal]

Basil ('bæzᵊl) *n* **Saint**, called *the Great*, ?329–379 AD, Greek patriarch: an opponent of Arianism and one of the founders of monasticism. Feast day: Jan 2, June 14, or Jan 1

Basilan (bə'siːlɑːn, bæ'siːlæn) *n* **1** a group of islands in the Philippines, SW of Mindanao **2** the main island of this group, separated from Mindanao by the **Basilan Strait** Area: 1282 sq km (495 sq miles) **3** a city on Basilan Island. Pop: 201 407 (1980)

basilar ('bæsɪlə) *adj chiefly anat* of or at a base. Also: **basilary** ('bæsɪlərɪ, -sɪlrɪ) [C16 from NL *basilaris*]

Basildon ('bæzɪldən) *n* a town in SE England, in S Essex: designated a new town in 1955. Pop: 100 924 (1991)

basilect ('beɪsɪ,lɛkt) *n linguistics* the level of spoken

English developed from Creole speech in a Caribbean territory, considered to be of the lowest social status [c20 from Gk *basi* bottom + *lektos* speech] > ˌ**basi'lectal** *adj*

basilica (bəˈzɪlɪkə) *n* **1** a Roman building, used for public administration, having a large rectangular central nave with an aisle on each side and an apse at the end **2** a Christian church of similar design **3** a Roman Catholic church having special ceremonial rights [c16 from L, from Gk, from *basilikē oikia* the king's house] > **ba'silican** *or* **ba'silic** *adj*

Basilicata (*Italian* baziliˈkata) *n* a region of S Italy, between the Tyrrhenian Sea and the Gulf of Taranto. Capital: Potenza. Pop: 606 183 (2000 est). Area: 9985 sq km (3855 sq miles)

basilisk (ˈbæzɪˌlɪsk) *n* **1** (in classical legend) a serpent that could kill by its breath or glance **2** a small semiaquatic lizard of tropical America. The males have an inflatable head crest, used in display [c14 from L *basiliscus*, from Gk *basiliskos* royal child]

basin (ˈbeɪsᵊn) *n* **1** a round container open and wide at the top with sides sloping inwards towards the bottom **2** Also called: **basinful** the amount a basin will hold **3** a washbasin or sink **4** any partially enclosed or sheltered area where vessels may be moored **5** the catchment area of a particular river and its tributaries **6** a depression in the earth's surface **7** *geol* a part of the earth's surface consisting of rock strata that slope down to a common centre [c13 from OF *bacin*, from LL *bacchīnon*]

Basingstoke (ˈbeɪzɪŋˌstəʊk) *n* a town in S England, in N Hampshire. Pop: 77 837 (1991)

basis (ˈbeɪsɪs) *n, pl* **bases** (-siːz) **1** something that underlies, supports, or is essential to something else, esp an idea **2** a principle on which something depends or from which something has issued [c14 via L from Gk: step]

basis point *n* a measure used for describing interest rates, equal to one hundredth of a percentage point (0.01%)

bask (bɑːsk) *vb* (*intr*; usually foll by *in*) **1** to lie in or be exposed to pleasant warmth, esp that of the sun **2** to flourish or feel secure under some benevolent influence or favourable condition [c14 from ON *bathask* to BATHE]

basket (ˈbɑːskɪt) *n* **1** a container made of interwoven strips of pliable materials, such as cane, and often carried by a handle **2** Also called: **basketful** the amount a basket will hold **3** something resembling such a container, such as the structure suspended from a balloon **4** *basketball* **4a** the hoop fixed to the backboard, through which a player must throw the ball to score points **4b** a point or points scored in this way **5** a group of similar or related things: *a basket of currencies* **6** the list of items an Internet shopper chooses to buy at one time from a website: *add these items to your basket* **7** *inf* a euphemism for **bastard** (senses 1–3) [c13 prob. from OF *baskot* (unattested), from L *bascauda* wickerwork holder]

basketball (ˈbɑːskɪtˌbɔːl) *n* **1** a game played by two teams of five men (or six women), usually on an indoor court. Points are scored by throwing the ball through an elevated horizontal hoop **2** the ball used in this game

▹ www.basketball.com

▹ www.nba.com

basket case *n sl* **1** *chiefly US & Canad* a person who has had both arms and both legs amputated **2** a person who is suffering from extreme nervous strain; nervous wreck **3a** someone or something that is incapable of functioning effectively **3b** (*as modifier*): *a basket-case economy*

basket chair *n* a chair made of wickerwork

basketry (ˈbɑːskɪtrɪ) *n* **1** the art or practice of making baskets **2** baskets collectively

basket weave *n* a weave of yarns, resembling that of a basket

basketweaver (ˈbɑːskɪtˌwiːvə) *n Austral derog sl* a person who advocates simple, natural, and unsophisticated living

basketwork (ˈbɑːskɪtˌwɜːk) *n* another word for **wickerwork**

basking shark *n* a very large plankton-eating shark, often floating at the sea surface

Basle (bɑːl) *or* **Basel** (ˈbɑːzᵊl) *n* **1** a canton of NW Switzerland, divided into the demicantons of **Basle-Landschaft** and **Basle-Stadt**. Pops.: 258 600 and 188 500 (2000 est) Areas: 427 sq km (165 sq miles) and 36 sq km (14 sq miles) respectively **2** a city in NW Switzerland, capital of Basle canton, on the Rhine: oldest university in Switzerland. Pop: 174 007 (1996 est). French name: **Bâle**

basmati rice (bəzˈmætɪ) *n* a variety of long-grain rice with slender aromatic grains, used for savoury dishes [from Hindi, lit.: aromatic]

basophil (ˈbeɪsəfɪl) *or* **basophile** *adj Also* **basophilic** (ˌbeɪsəˈfɪlɪk) **1** (of cells or cell contents) easily stained by basic dyes ▹ *n* **2** a basophil cell, esp a leucocyte [c19 from Gk; see BASIS, -PHILE]

Basotho-Qwaqwa (bəˈsuːtuːˈkwɑːkwə, -ˈsəʊtəʊ-) *n* (formerly) a Bantu homeland in South Africa; reintegrated into South Africa in 1994. Also called: **Qwaqwa** Former name (until 1972): **Basotho-Ba-Borwa**

basque (bæsk) *n* a type of tight-fitting bodice for women [from F, from BASQUE]

Basque (bæsk, bɑːsk) *n* **1** a member of a people living around the W Pyrenees in France and Spain **2** the language of this people, of no known relationship with any other language ▹ *adj* **3** of or relating to this people or their language [c19 from F, from L *Vascō* a Basque]

Basque Provinces *n* an autonomous region of N Spain, comprising the provinces of Álava, Guipúzcoa, and Viscaya: inhabited mainly by Basques, who retained virtual autonomy from the 9th to the 19th century. Pop: 2 098 596 (2000 est). Area: about 7250 sq km (2800 sq miles)

Basra, Basrah (ˈbæzrə), **Busra,** *or* **Busrah** (ˈbʌsrə) *n* a port in SE Iraq, on the Shatt-al-Arab. Pop: 406 296 (1987)

bas-relief (ˌbɑːrɪˈliːf, ˈbæsrɪˌliːf) *n* sculpture in low relief, in which the forms project slightly from the background [c17 from F, from It. *basso rilievo* low relief]

Bas-Rhin (*French* barɛ̃) *n* a department of NE France in Alsace region. Capital: Strasbourg. Pop: 1 026 120 (1999). Area: 4793 sq km (1869 sq miles)

bass¹ (beɪs) *n* **1** the lowest adult male voice **2** a singer with such a voice **3** **the bass** the lowest part in a piece of harmony **4** *inf* short for **bass guitar, double bass** **5a** the low-frequency component of an electrical audio signal, esp in a record player or tape recorder **5b** the knob controlling this ▹ *adj* **6** relating to or denoting the bass [c15 *bas* BASE¹; modern spelling infl. by BASSO]

bass² (bæs) *n* **1** any of various sea perches **2** a European spiny-finned freshwater fish **3** any of various predatory North American freshwater fishes [c15 from BASE², infl. by It. *basso* low]

bass clef (beɪs) *n* the clef that establishes F a fifth below middle C on the fourth line of the staff

bass drum (beɪs) *n* a large drum of low pitch

Bassein (bɑːˈseɪn) *n* a city in Myanmar, on the Irrawaddy delta: a port on the **Bassein River** (the westernmost distributary of the Irrawaddy) Pop: 183 900 (1993 est)

Basse-Normandie (*French* basnɔrmɑ̃di) *n* a region of NW France, on the English Channel: consists of the Cherbourg peninsula in the west rising to the Normandy hills in the east; mainly agricultural

Bassenthwaite (ˈbæsᵊnˌθweɪt) *n* a lake in NW England, in Cumbria near Keswick. Length: 6 km (4 miles)

Basses-Alpes (*French* basalp) *n* the former name for **Alpes-de-Haute-Provence**

Bb

Basses-Pyrénées (*French* baspirene) *pl n* the former name for **Pyrénées** (Atlantiques)

basset (ˈbæsɪt) *n* a smooth-haired breed of hound with short legs and long ears. Also: **basset hound** [c17 from F, from *basset* short, from *bas* low]

Basseterre (bæsˈtɛə; *French* bastɛr) *n* a port in the Caribbean, on St Kitts in the Leeward Islands: the capital of St Kitts-Nevis. Pop: 12 605 (1994 est)
▷ www.geographia.com/stkitts-nevis/knpnto2.htm

Basse-Terre (ˈbæsˈtɛə; *French* bastɛr) *n* **1** a mountainous island in the Caribbean, in the Leeward Islands, comprising part of Guadeloupe. Area: 848 sq km (327 sq miles) **2** a port in W Guadeloupe, on Basse-Terre Island: the capital of the French Overseas Department of Guadeloupe. Pop: 12 549 (1999)

basset horn *n* an obsolete woodwind instrument [c19 prob. from G *Bassetthorn*, from It. *bassetto*, dim. of BASSO + HORN]

bass guitar (beɪs) *n* a guitar that has the same pitch and tuning as a double bass, usually electrically amplified

bassinet (ˌbæsɪˈnɛt) *n* a wickerwork or wooden cradle or pram, usually hooded [c19 from F: little basin; associated in folk etymology with F *barcelonnette* a little cradle]

bassist (ˈbeɪsɪst) *n* a player of a double bass or bass guitar

basso (ˈbæsəʊ) *n, pl* **bassos** *or* **bassi** (-sɪ) (esp in operatic or solo singing) a singer with a bass voice [c19 from It., from LL *bassus* low; see BASE[2]]

bassoon (bəˈsuːn) *n* **1** a woodwind instrument, the tenor of the oboe family **2** an orchestral musician who plays a bassoon [c18 from F *basson*, from It., from *basso* deep] > **basˈsoonist** *n*

basso rilievo (*Italian* ˈbasso riˈljɛːvo) *n, pl* **basso rilievos** Italian name for **bas-relief**

Bass Strait (bæs) *n* a channel between mainland Australia and Tasmania, linking the Indian Ocean and the Tasman Sea

bass viol (beɪs) *n* **1** another name for **viola da gamba** **2** *US* a less common name for **double bass** (sense 1)

bast (bæst) *n* **1** fibrous material obtained from the phloem of jute, flax, etc, used for making rope, matting, etc **2** *bot* another name for **phloem** [OE *bæst*]

bastard (ˈbɑːstəd, ˈbæs-) *n* **1** *inf, offens* an obnoxious or despicable person **2** *inf* a person, esp a man: *lucky bastard* **3** *inf* something extremely difficult or unpleasant **4** *arch or offens* a person born of parents not married to each other **5** something irregular, abnormal, or inferior **6** a hybrid, esp an accidental or inferior one ▷ *adj (prenominal)* **7** *arch or offens* illegitimate by birth **8** irregular, abnormal, or inferior **9** resembling a specified thing, but not actually being such: *a bastard cedar* **10** counterfeit; spurious **11** hybrid [c13 from OF *bastart*, ?from *fils de bast* son of the packsaddle] > ˈ**bastardy** *n*

bastardize *or* **bastardise** (ˈbɑːstəˌdaɪz, ˈbæs-) *vb* **bastardizes, bastardizing, bastardized** *or* **bastardises, bastardising, bastardised** *(tr)* **1** to debase **2** *arch* to declare illegitimate

baste[1] (beɪst) *vb* **bastes, basting, basted** *(tr)* to sew with loose temporary stitches [c14 from OF *bastir* to build, of Gmc origin] > ˈ**basting** *n*

baste[2] (beɪst) *vb* **bastes, basting, basted** *(tr)* to moisten (meat) during cooking with hot fat and the juices produced [c15 from ?]

baste[3] (beɪst) *vb* **bastes, basting, basted** *(tr)* to beat thoroughly; thrash [c16 prob. from ON *beysta*]

Bastia (ˈbɑːstjə) *n* a port in NE Corsica: the main commercial and industrial town of the island: capital of Haute-Corse department. Pop: 38 728 (1990)

Bastille (bæˈstiːl) *n* a fortress in Paris: a prison until its destruction in 1789, at the beginning of the French Revolution [c14 from OF *bastile* fortress, from OProvençal *bastida*, from *bastir* to build]

bastinado (ˌbæstɪˈneɪdəʊ) *n, pl* **bastinadoes** **1** punishment or torture in which the soles of the feet are beaten with a stick ▷ *vb* **bastinadoes, bastinadoing, bastinadoed** **2** *(tr)* to beat (a person) thus [c16 from Sp. *bastonada*, from *baston* stick]

bastion (ˈbæstɪən) *n* **1** a projecting part of a fortification, designed to permit fire to the flanks along the the face of the wall **2** any fortified place **3** a thing or person regarded as defending a principle, etc [c16 from F, from earlier *bastillon* bastion, from *bastille* BASTILLE]

Bastogne (bæˈstəʊn; *French* bastɔŋ) *n* a town in SE Belgium: of strategic importance to Allied defences during the Battle of the Bulge; besieged by the Germans during the winter of 1944–45. Pop: 7000 (1991 est)

Basutoland (bəˈsuːtəʊˌlænd) *n* the former name (until 1966) of **Lesotho**

bat[1] (bæt) *n* **1** any of various types of club with a handle, used to hit the ball in certain sports, such as cricket **2** a flat round club with a short handle used by a man on the ground to guide the pilot of an aircraft when taxiing **3** *cricket* short for **batsman** **4** *inf* a blow from a stick **5** *sl* speed; pace: *they went at a fair bat* **6** **carry one's bat** *cricket* (of an opening batsman) to reach the end of an innings without being dismissed **7** **off one's own bat** **7a** of one's own accord **7b** by one's own unaided efforts ▷ *vb* **bats, batting, batted** **8** *(tr)* to strike with or as if with a bat **9** *(intr) cricket, etc* (of a player or a team) to take a turn at batting [OE *batt* club, prob. of Celtic origin]

bat[2] (bæt) *n* **1** a nocturnal mouselike animal flying with a pair of membranous wings **2** *sl* an irritating or eccentric woman **3** **blind as a bat** having extremely poor eyesight **4** **have bats in the** (*or* **one's**) **belfry** *inf* to be mad or eccentric [c14 *bakke*, prob. of Scand. origin]

bat[3] (bæt) *vb* **bats, batting, batted** *(tr)* **1** to wink or flutter (one's eyelids) **2** **not bat an eye** (*or* **eyelid**) *inf* to show no surprise or concern [c17 prob. var. of BATE[2]]

Bataan (bəˈtæn, -ˈtɑːn) *n* a peninsula in the Philippines, in W Luzon: scene of the surrender of US and Philippine forces to the Japanese during World War II, later retaken by American forces

Batangas (bəˈtæŋgæs) *n* a port in the Philippines, in SW Luzon. Pop: 190 627 (1994 est)

Batan Islands (bəˈtɑːn) *pl n* a group of islands in the Philippines, north of Luzon. Capital: Basco. Pop: 12 091 (latest est). Area: 197 sq km (76 sq miles)

Batavia (bəˈteɪvɪə) *n* **1** an ancient district of the Netherlands, on an island at the mouth of the Rhine **2** an archaic or literary name for **Holland**[1] **3** a former name for **Jakarta** > **Baˈtavian** *adj, n*

batch[1] (bætʃ) *n* **1** a group or set of usually similar objects or people, esp if sent off, handled, or arriving at the same time **2** the bread, cakes, etc, produced at one baking **3** the amount of a material needed for an operation ▷ *vb* **4** to group (items) for efficient processing **5** to handle by batch processing [c15 *bache*; rel. to OE *bacan* to BAKE]

batch[2] *or* **bach** (bætʃ) *vb (intr) Austral & NZ inf* **1** (of a man) to do his own cooking and housekeeping **2** to live alone

batch processing *n* a system by which the computer programs of a number of individual users are submitted as a single batch

bate[1] (beɪt) *vb* **bates, bating, bated** **1** another word for **abate** **2** **with bated breath** in suspense or fear

bate[2] (beɪt) *vb* **bates, bating, bated** *(intr)* (of a hawk) to jump violently from a perch or the falconer's fist, often hanging from the leash while struggling to escape [c13 from OF *batre* to beat]

bate[3] (beɪt) *n Brit sl* a bad temper or rage [c19 from BAIT[1], alluding to the mood of a person who is being baited]

bateau (bæˈtəʊ) *n, pl* **bateaux** (-ˈtəʊz) a light flat-bottomed boat used on rivers in Canada and the northern US [c18 from F: boat]

bateleur eagle (ˈbætələː) *n* an African short-tailed bird of prey [c19 from F *bateleur* juggler]

Bates (beɪts) *n* **1** Sir **Alan** (**Arthur**) 1934–2003, British film and stage actor. His films include *A Kind of Loving* (1962), *Women in Love* (1969), *The Go-Between* (1971), and *The Cherry Orchard* (1999) **2** **H**(**erbert**) **E**(**rnest**) 1905–74, English writer of short stories and novels, which include *The Darling Buds of May* (1958), *A Moment in Time* (1964), and *The Triple Echo* (1970)

bath (bɑːθ) *n, pl* **baths** (bɑːðz) **1** a large container used for washing the body **2** the act or an instance of washing in such a container **3** the amount of liquid contained in a bath **4** (*usually pl*) a place having baths or a swimming pool for public use **5a** a vessel in which something is immersed to maintain it at a constant temperature, to process it photographically, etc, or to lubricate it **5b** the liquid used in such a vessel ▷ *vb* **6** *Brit* to wash in a bath [OE *bæth*]

Bath (bɑːθ) *n* a city in SW England, in Bath and North East Somerset unitary authority, Somerset, on the River Avon: famous for its hot springs; a fashionable spa in the 18th century; Roman remains, notably the baths; university (1966). Pop: 85 202 (1991). Latin name: **Aquae Sulis** (ˈækwiːˈsuːlɪs)

Bath and North East Somerset (ˈsʌməsɛt) *n* a unitary authority in SW England, in Somerset; formerly (1974–96) part of the county of Avon. Pop: 169 045 (2001). Area: 351 sq km (136 sq miles)

Bath bun (bɑːθ) *n Brit* a sweet bun containing spices and dried fruit

Bath chair *n* a wheelchair for invalids

bath cube *n* a cube of soluble scented material for use in a bath

bathe (beɪð) *vb* **bathes, bathing, bathed** **1** (*intr*) to swim in a body of open water, esp for pleasure **2** (*tr*) to apply liquid to (skin, a wound, etc) in order to cleanse or soothe **3** to immerse or be immersed in a liquid **4** *chiefly US & Canad* to wash in a bath **5** (*tr; often passive*) to suffuse ▷ *n* **6** *Brit* a swim in a body of open water [OE *bathian*] > ˈ**bather** *n*

bathers (ˈbeɪðəz) *pl n Austral & S Wales* a swimming costume

bathhouse (ˈbɑːθˌhaʊs) *n* a building containing baths, esp for public use

bathing cap (ˈbeɪðɪŋ) *n* a tight rubber cap worn by a swimmer to keep the hair dry

bathing costume (ˈbeɪðɪŋ) *n* another name for **swimming costume**

bathing machine (ˈbeɪðɪŋ) *n* a small hut, on wheels so that it could be pulled to the sea, used in the 18th and 19th centuries for bathers to change their clothes

bathing suit (ˈbeɪðɪŋ) *n* a garment worn for bathing, esp an old-fashioned one that covers much of the body

batho- *combining form* a variant of **bathy-**

batholith (ˌbæθəlɪθ) *or* **batholite** (ˈbæθəˌlaɪt) *n* a very large irregular-shaped mass of igneous rock, esp granite, formed from an intrusion of magma at great depth, esp one exposed after erosion of less resistant overlying rocks > ˌ**bathoˈlithic** *or* **batholitic** (ˌbæθəˈlɪtɪk) *adj*

Bath Oliver (ˈɒlɪvə) *n Brit* a kind of unsweetened biscuit [c19 after William *Oliver* (1695–1764), a physician at Bath]

bathometer (bəˈθɒmɪtə) *n* an instrument for measuring the depth of water > **bathometric** (ˌbæθəˈmɛtrɪk) *adj* > **baˈthometry** *n*

bathos (ˈbeɪθɒs) *n* **1** a sudden ludicrous descent from exalted to ordinary matters or style in speech or writing **2** insincere or excessive pathos [c18 from Gk: depth] > **baˈthetic** *adj*

bathrobe (ˈbɑːθˌrəʊb) *n* **1** a loose-fitting garment of towelling, for wear before or after a bath or swimming **2** *US & Canad* a dressing gown

bathroom (ˈbɑːθˌruːm, -ˌrʊm) *n* **1** a room containing a bath or shower and usually a washbasin and lavatory **2** *US & Canad* another name for **lavatory**

bath salts *pl n* soluble scented salts for use in a bath

Bathsheba (bæθˈʃiːbə, ˈbæθʃɪbə) *n Old Testament* the wife of Uriah, who committed adultery with David and later married him and became the mother of his son Solomon (II Samuel 11–12)

bathtub (ˈbɑːθˌtʌb) *n* a bath, esp one not permanently fixed

bathtub race *n Canad* a sailing race between bathtubs fitted with outboard motors

Bathurst (ˈbæθəst) *n* **1** a city in SE Australia, in E New South Wales: scene of a gold rush in 1851. Pop: 24 682 (1991) **2** a port in E Canada, in NE New Brunswick: rich mineral resources discovered in 1953. Pop: 15 890 (1991) **3** the former name (until 1973) of **Banjul**

bathy- *or* **batho-** *combining form* indicating depth: *bathysphere* [from Gk *bathus* deep]

bathyscaph (ˈbæθɪˌskæf), **bathyscaphe** (ˈbæθɪˌskeɪf, -ˌskæf), *or* **bathyscape** (ˈbæθɪˌskæp) *n* a submersible vessel with an observation capsule underneath, capable of reaching ocean depths of over 10 000 metres [c20 from BATHY- + Gk *skaphē* light boat]

bathysphere (ˈbæθɪˌsfɪə) *n* a strong steel deep-sea diving sphere, lowered by cable

batik (ˈbætɪk) *n* **a** a process of printing fabric in which parts not to be dyed are covered by wax **b** fabric printed in this way [c19 via Malay from Javanese: painted]
▷ www.batikguild.org.uk

Batista (*Spanish* baˈtista) *n* **Fulgencio** (fulˈxenθjo), full name *Batista y Zaldívar*. 1901–73, Cuban military leader and dictator: president of Cuba (1940–44, 1952–59); overthrown by Fidel Castro

batiste (bæˈtiːst) *n* a fine plain-weave cotton [c17 from F, prob. after *Baptiste* of Cambrai, 13th-cent. F weaver, its reputed inventor]

Batley (ˈbætlɪ) *n* a town in N England, in Kirklees unitary authority, West Yorkshire. Pop: 48 030 (1991)

batman (ˈbætmən) *n, pl* **batmen** an officer's servant in the armed forces [c18 from OF *bat, bast*, from Med. L *bastum* packsaddle]

baton (ˈbætən) *n* **1** a thin stick used by the conductor of an orchestra, choir, etc **2** *athletics* a short bar carried by a competitor in a relay race and transferred to the next runner at the end of each stage **3** a long stick with a knob on one end, carried, twirled, and thrown up and down by a drum major or majorette, esp at the head of a parade **4** a police truncheon (esp in **baton charge**) **5** a staff or club carried as a symbol of authority [c16 from F *bâton*, from LL *bastum* rod]

Baton Rouge (ˈbætᵊn ˈruːʒ) *n* the capital of Louisiana, in the SE part on the Mississippi River. Pop: 227 818 (2000)

baton round *n* the official name for **plastic bullet**

batrachian (bəˈtreɪkɪən) *n* **1** any amphibian, esp a frog or toad ▷ *adj* **2** of or relating to the frogs and toads [c19 from NL *Batrachia*, from Gk *batrakhos* frog]

bats (bæts) *adj inf* mad or eccentric

batsman (ˈbætsmən) *n, pl* **batsmen** **1** *cricket, etc* **1a** a person who bats or whose turn it is to bat **1b** a player who specializes in batting **2** a person on the ground who uses bats to guide the pilot of an aircraft when taxiing

battalion (bəˈtæljən) *n* **1** a military unit comprised of three or more companies or formations of similar size **2** (*usually pl*) any large array [c16 from F *bataillon*, from OIt., from *battaglia* company of soldiers, BATTLE]

batten[1] (ˈbætᵊn) *n* **1** a sawn strip of wood used in building to cover joints, support lathing, etc **2** a long narrow board used for flooring **3** a lath used for holding a tarpaulin along the side of a hatch on a ship **4** *theatre* **4a** a row of lights **4b** the bar supporting them ▷ *vb* **5** (*tr*) to furnish or strengthen with battens **6** **batten down the hatches** **6a** to use battens in securing a tarpaulin over a hatch on a ship **6b** to prepare for

Bb

action, a crisis, etc [c15 from F *bâton* stick; see BATON]

batten[2] ('bæt°n) *vb* (*intr*) (usually foll by *on*) to thrive, esp at the expense of someone else [c16 prob. from ON *batna* to improve]

Batten ('bæt°n) *n* **Jean** 1909–82, New Zealand aviator: the first woman to fly single-handed from Australia to Britain (1935)

batter[1] ('bætə) *vb* **1** to hit (someone or something) repeatedly using heavy blows, as with a club **2** (*tr; often passive*) to damage or injure, as by blows, heavy wear, etc **3** (*tr*) to subject (a person, esp a close relative) to repeated physical violence [c14 *bateren*, prob. from *batten* to BAT[1]] > **'batterer** *n* > **'battering** *n*

batter[2] ('bætə) *n* a mixture of flour, eggs, and milk, used to make cakes, pancakes, etc, and to coat certain foods before frying [c15 *bater*, prob. from *bateren* to BATTER[1]]

batter[3] ('bætə) *n baseball, etc* a player who bats

batter[4] ('bætə) *n* **1** the slope of the face of a wall that recedes gradually backwards and upwards ▷ *vb* **2** (*intr*) to have such a slope [c16 (vb: to incline): from ?]

battered[1] ('bætəd) *adj* subjected to persistent physical violence, esp by a close relative living in the house: *a battered baby*

battered[2] ('bætəd) *adj* coated in batter: *battered cod and chips*

battering ram *n* (esp formerly) a large beam used to break down fortifications

Battersea ('bætəsɪ) *n* a district in London, in Wandsworth: noted for its dogs' home, power station (being developed into a leisure centre), and park

battery ('bætərɪ) *n, pl* **batteries** **1** two or more primary cells connected, usually in series, to provide a source of electric current **2** another name for **accumulator** (sense 1) **3** a number of similar things occurring together: *a battery of questions* **4** *criminal law* unlawful beating or wounding of a person or mere touching in a hostile or offensive manner **5** a fortified structure on which artillery is mounted **6** a group of guns, missile launchers, etc, operated as a single entity **7** a small unit of artillery **8** *chiefly Brit* **8a** a large group of cages for intensive rearing of poultry and other farm animals **8b** (*as modifier*): *battery hens* **9** *baseball* the pitcher and the catcher considered together [c16 from OF *batterie* beating, from *battre* to beat, from L *battuere*]

batting ('bætɪŋ) *n* **1** cotton or woollen wadding used in quilts, etc **2** the action of a person or team that hits with a bat

battle ('bæt°l) *n* **1** a fight between large armed forces; military or naval engagement **2** conflict; struggle **3** **do, give,** *or* **join battle** to engage in conflict or competition ▷ *vb* **battles, battling, battled** **4** (when *intr*, often foll by *against, for,* or *with*) to fight in or as if in military combat; contend (with): *shop stewards battling to improve conditions at work* **5** to struggle: *he battled through the crowd* **6** (*intr*) *Austral* to scrape a living [c13 from OF *bataile*, from LL *battālia* exercises performed by soldiers, from *battuere* to beat] > **'battler** *n*

Battle[1] ('bæt°l) *n* a town in SE England, in East Sussex: site of the Battle of Hastings (1066); medieval abbey. Pop: 5234 (1991)

Battle[2] ('bæt°l) *n* **Kathleen** born 1948, US opera singer: a coloratura soprano, she made her professional debut in 1972 and sang with New York City's Metropolitan Opera (1977–94)

battle-axe *n* **1** (formerly) a large broad-headed axe **2** *inf* an argumentative domineering woman

battle-axe block *n Austral* a block of land behind another, with access from the street through a narrow drive

battle cruiser *n* a high-speed warship of battleship size but with lighter armour

battle cry *n* **1** a shout uttered by soldiers going into battle **2** a slogan used to rally the supporters of a campaign, movement, etc

battledore ('bæt°l,dɔː) *n* **1** Also called: **battledore and shuttlecock** an ancient racket game **2** a light racket used in this game **3** (formerly) a wooden utensil used for beating clothes, in baking, etc [c15 *batyldoure*, ?from OProvençal *batedor* beater, from OF *battre* to beat]

battledress ('bæt°l,drɛs) *n* the ordinary uniform of a soldier

battle fatigue *n psychol* mental disorder, characterized by anxiety and depression, caused by the stress of warfare. Also: **combat fatigue**

battlefield ('bæt°l,fiːld) *or* **battleground** ('bæt°l,graʊnd) *n* the place where a battle is fought

battlement ('bæt°lmənt) *n* a parapet or wall with indentations or embrasures, originally for shooting through [c14 from OF *batailles*, pl. of *bataille* BATTLE] > **'battlemented** *adj*

battle royal *n* **1** a fight, esp with fists or cudgels, involving more than two combatants; melee **2** a long violent argument

battleship ('bæt°lʃɪp) *n* a heavily armoured warship of the largest type

batty ('bætɪ) *adj* **battier, battiest** *sl* **1** insane; crazy **2** odd; eccentric [c20 from BAT[2]]

Batum (bɑː'tuːm) *or* **Batumi** (bɑː'tuːmɪ) *n* a city in Georgia: capital of the Adzhar Autonomous Republic; a major Black Sea port. Pop: 137 100 (1997 est)

batwoman ('bætwʊmən) *n, pl* **batwomen** a female servant in any of the armed forces

bauble ('bɔːb°l) *n* **1** a trinket of little value **2** (formerly) a mock staff of office carried by a jester [c14 from OF *baubel* plaything, from ?]

Bauchi ('baʊtʃɪ) *n* **1** a state of N Nigeria: formed in 1976 from part of North-Eastern State; tin mining. Capital: Bauchi. Pop: 4 801 569 (1995 est). Area: 64 605 sq km (24 944 sq miles) **2** a town in N central Nigeria, capital of Bauchi state. Pop: 76 070 (1991 est)

baud (bɔːd) *n* a unit used to measure the speed of electronic code transmissions [after J. M. E. *Baudot* (1845-1903), F inventor]

Baudelaire (*French* bodlɛr) *n* **Charles Pierre** (ʃarl pjɛr) 1821–67, French poet, noted for his macabre imagery; author of *Les fleurs du mal* (1857)

Baudouin I (*French* bodwɛ̃) *n* 1930–93, king of Belgium (1951–93)

Baudrillard (*French* bodrijɑr) *n* **Jean** born 1929, French sociologist and theorist of postmodernism; his books include *Seduction* (1979), *America* (1986), and *The Spirit of Terrorism* (2002)

bauera ('baʊərə) *n* a small evergreen Australian shrub with pink or purple flowers [c19 after Franz & Ferdinand *Bauer*, 19th-cent. Austrian botanical artists]

Bauhaus ('baʊ,haʊs) *n* a German school of functionalist architecture and applied arts founded in 1919 [G, lit.: building house]
▷ www.cs.umb.edu/
▷ http://alilley/bauhaus.html

bauhinia (bɔː'hɪnɪə, bəʊ-) *n* any climbing or shrubby leguminous plant of tropical and warm regions, cultivated for ornament [c18 NL, after Jean & Gaspard *Bauhin*, 16th-cent. F herbalists]

baulk (bɔːk; *usually for sense 1* bɔːlk) *n* **1** Also: **balk** *billiards* the space between the baulk line and the bottom cushion **2** *archaeol* a strip of earth left between excavation trenches for the study of the complete stratigraphy of a site ▷ *vb, n* **3** a variant spelling of **balk**

baulk line *or* **balk line** *n billiards* a straight line across a billiard table behind which the cue balls are placed at the start of a game. Also: **string line**

baulky ('bɔːkɪ, 'bɔːlkɪ) *adj* a variant of **balky**

Bautzen ('baʊtsən) *n* a city in E Germany, in Saxony: site of an indecisive battle in 1813 between Napoleon's army and an allied army of Russians and Prussians. Pop: 52 390 (latest est)

bauxite ('bɔːksaɪt) *n* an amorphous claylike substance consisting of hydrated alumina with iron and other impurities: the chief source of aluminium [c19 from F, from (*Les*) *Baux* in southern France, where orig. found]

Bavaria (bəvɛərɪə) *n* a state of S Germany: a former duchy and kingdom; mainly wooded highland, with the Alps in the south. Capital: Munich. Pop: 12 014 700 (1996 est). Area: 70 531 sq km (27232 sq miles) > **Ba'varian** *adj, n*

bawd (bɔːd) *n arch* **1** a person who runs a brothel, esp a woman **2** a prostitute [c14 from OF *baude*, fem. of *baud* merry]

bawdy ('bɔːdɪ) *adj* **bawdier, bawdiest 1** (of language, plays, etc) containing references to sex, esp to be humorous ▷ *n* **2** obscenity or eroticism in writing or drama > **'bawdily** *adv* > **'bawdiness** *n* > **bawdry** ('bɔːdrɪ) *n*

bawdyhouse ('bɔːdɪ,haʊs) *n* an archaic word for **brothel**

bawl (bɔːl) *vb* **1** (*intr*) to utter long loud cries, as from pain or frustration; wail **2** to shout loudly, as in anger ▷ *n* **3** a loud shout or cry [c15 imit.] > **'bawler** *n* > **'bawling** *n*

bawl out *vb* (*tr, adv*) *inf* to scold loudly

Bax (bæks) *n* Sir **Arnold** (**Edward Trevor**) 1883–1953, English composer of romantic works, often based on Celtic legends, including the tone poem *Tintagel* (1917)

Baxter ('bækstə) *n* **1 James** (**Keir**) 1926–72, New Zealand lyric poet. His works include *The Fallen House* (1953) and *In Fires of No Return* (1958) **2 Richard** 1615–91, English Puritan divine and devotional writer: prominent in church affairs during the Restoration

bay[1] (beɪ) *n* **1** a wide semicircular indentation of a shoreline, esp between two headlands **2** an extension of lowland into hills that partly surround it [c14 from OF *baie*, ?from OF *baer* to gape, from Med. L *batāre* to yawn]

bay[2] (beɪ) *n* **1** an alcove or recess in a wall **2** any partly enclosed compartment **3** See **bay window 4** an area off a road in which vehicles may park or unload **5** a compartment in an aircraft: *the bomb bay* **6** *naut* a compartment in the forward part of a ship between decks, often used as the ship's hospital **7** *Brit* a tracked recess in the platform of a railway station, esp one forming the terminus of a branch line [c14 from OF *baee* gap, from *baer* to gape; see BAY[1]]

bay[3] (beɪ) *n* **1** a deep howl, esp of a hound on the scent **2 at bay 2a** forced to turn and face attackers: *a deer at bay* **2b** at a distance **3 bring to bay** to force into a position from which retreat is impossible ▷ *vb* **4** (*intr*) to howl (at) in deep prolonged tones **5** (*tr*) to utter in a loud prolonged tone **6** (*tr*) to hold at bay [c13 from OF, imit.]

bay[4] (beɪ) *n* **1** a Mediterranean laurel. See **laurel** (sense 1) **2** any of several magnolias. See **sweet bay 3** any of certain other trees or shrubs, esp bayberry **4** (*pl*) a wreath of bay leaves [c14 from OF *baie* laurel berry, from L *bāca* berry]

bay[5] (beɪ) *n, adj* **1** (of) a reddish-brown colour ▷ *n* **2** an animal of this colour [c14 from OF *bai*, from L *badius*]

Bayamón (*Spanish* baja'mon) *n* a city in NE central Puerto Rico, south of San Juan. Pop: 203 499 (2000)

bayberry ('beɪbərɪ) *or* **bay** *n, pl* **bayberries 1** any of several North American aromatic shrubs or small trees that bear grey waxy berries **2** a tropical American tree that yields an oil used in making bay rum **3** the fruit of any of these plants

Bayern ('baiərn) *n* the German name for **Bavaria**

Bayeux (*French* bajø) *n* a town in NW France, on the River Aure: its museum houses the Bayeux tapestry and there is a 13th-century cathedral: dairy foods, plastic. Pop: 14 704 (1990)
▷ http://hastings1066.com/baythumb.shtml
▷ www.historylearningsite.co.uk/bayeaux_tapestry.htm

bay leaf *n* a leaf, usually dried, of the Mediterranean laurel, used in cooking to flavour soups and stews

Baylis ('beɪlɪs) *n* **1 Lillian Mary** 1874–1937, British theatre manager: founded the Old Vic (1912) and the Sadler's Wells company for opera and ballet (1931) **2 Trevor** (**Graham**) born 1937, British inventor of the clockwork radio (1992)

Bay of Pigs *n* a bay on the SW coast of Cuba: scene of an unsuccessful invasion of Cuba by US-backed troops (April 17, 1961). Spanish name: **Bahia de los Cochinos**

bayonet ('beɪənɪt) *n* **1** a blade for stabbing that can be attached to the muzzle of a firearm **2** a type of fastening in which a cylindrical member is inserted into a socket against spring pressure and turned so that pins on its side engage in slots in the socket ▷ *vb* **bayonets, bayoneting, bayoneted** *or* **bayonets, bayonetting, bayonetted 3** (*tr*) to stab or kill with a bayonet [c17 from F *baïonnette*, from BAYONNE]

Bayonne (*French* bajɔn) *n* a port in SW France: a commercial centre for the Basque region. Pop: 41 846 (1990)

bayou ('baɪjuː) *n* (in the southern US) a sluggish marshy tributary of a lake or river [c18 from Louisiana F, from Amerind *bayuk*]

Bayreuth (*German* bai'rɔyt) *n* a city in E Germany, in NE Bavaria: home and burial place of Richard Wagner; annual festivals of his music. Pop: 72 780 (1991)

bay rum *n* an aromatic liquid, used in medicines and cosmetics, originally obtained from the bayberry tree

bay window *n* a window projecting from a wall and forming an alcove of a room

bazaar *or* **bazar** (bə'zɑː) *n* **1** (esp in the Orient) a market area, esp a street of small stalls **2** a sale in aid of charity, esp of second-hand or handmade articles **3** a shop where a variety of goods is sold [c16 from Persian *bāzār*]

bazooka (bə'zuːkə) *n* a portable tubular rocket-launcher, used by infantrymen as a short-range antitank weapon [c20 after a comic pipe instrument]

BB *abbrev for:* **1** Boys' Brigade **2** (on British pencils, signifying degrees of softness of lead) double black

B2B *abbrev for* business-to-business; denoting trade between commercial organizations rather than between businesses and private customers ▷ Cf **B2C, B2E**

BBC *abbrev for* British Broadcasting Corporation
▷ www.bbc.co.uk

BBL *text messaging abbrev for* be back later

BBQ *abbrev for* barbecue

BBS *text messaging abbrev for* be back soon

BC *abbrev for:* **1** (indicating years numbered back from the supposed year of the birth of Christ) before Christ. Also: **B.C. 2** British Columbia.

USAGE See at **AD**

BCE *abbrev for:* **1** Before Common Era (used, esp by non-Christians, in numbering years BC) **2** *Brit* Board of Customs and Excise

BCG *abbrev for* Bacillus Calmette-Guérin (antituberculosis vaccine)

BCNU *text messaging abbrev for* be seeing you

BCNZ *abbrev for* (the former) Broadcasting Corporation of New Zealand

B complex *n* short for **vitamin B complex**

B.C.S. (in the US and Canada) *abbrev for* Bachelor of Computer Science

BD *abbrev for* Bachelor of Divinity

bdellium ('dɛlɪəm) *n* **1** any of several African or W Asian trees that yield a gum resin **2** the aromatic gum resin produced by any of these trees [c16 from L, from Gk *bdellion*, ? from Heb. *bĕdhōlah*]

BDS *abbrev for* Bachelor of Dental Surgery

be (biː; *unstressed* bɪ) *vb present sing 1st person* **am**; *2nd person* **are**; *3rd person* **is**, *present pl* **are**, *past sing 1st person* **was**; *2nd person* **were**; *3rd person* **was**, *past pl* **were**, *present participle* **being**, *past participle* **been** (*intr*) **1** to have presence in perceived reality; exist; live: *I think, therefore I am* **2** (*used in* *the perfect tenses only*) to pay a visit; go: *have you been to Spain?* **3** to take place: *my birthday was last Thursday* **4** (*copula*) used as a linking verb between the subject of a sentence and its noun or adjective complement. In this case *be* expresses relationship of equivalence or identity (*John is a man; John is a musician*) or specifies an attribute (*honey is sweet; Susan is angry*). It is also used with an adverbial complement to indicate a relationship in space or time (*Bill is at the office; the party is on Saturday*) **5** (*takes a present participle*) forms the progressive present tense: *the man is running* **6** (*takes a past participle*) forms the passive voice of all transitive verbs: *a good film is being shown on television tonight* **7** (*takes an infinitive*) expresses intention, expectation, or obligation: *the president is to arrive at 9.30* [OE *bēon*]

Be *the chemical symbol for* beryllium

BE *abbrev for:* **1** bill of exchange **2** Bachelor of Education **3** Bachelor of Engineering

be- *prefix forming transitive verbs* **1** (*from nouns*) to surround or cover: *befog* **2** (*from nouns*) to affect completely: *bedazzle* **3** (*from nouns*) to consider as or cause to be: *befriend* **4** (*from nouns*) to provide or cover with: *bejewel* **5** (*from verbs*) at, for, against, on, or over: *bewail; berate* [OE *be-, bi-*, unstressed var. of *bī* BY]

beach (biːtʃ) *n* **1** an area of sand or shingle sloping down to a sea or lake, esp the area between the high- and low-water marks on a seacoast ▷ *vb* **2** to run or haul (a boat) onto a beach [C16 perhaps rel. to OE *bæce* river]

beachcomber (ˈbiːtʃˌkəʊmə) *n* **1** a person who searches shore debris for anything of worth **2** a long high wave rolling onto a beach

beachhead (ˈbiːtʃˌhɛd) *n mil* an area on a beach that has been captured from the enemy and on which troops and equipment are landed

Beachy Head (ˈbiːtʃɪ) *n* a headland in East Sussex, on the English Channel, having chalk cliffs 171 m (570 ft) high

beacon (ˈbiːkən) *n* **1** a signal fire or light on a hill, tower, etc, esp formerly as a warning of invasion **2** a hill on which such fires were lit **3** a lighthouse, signalling buoy, etc **4** short for **radio beacon** **5** a radio or other signal marking a flight course in air navigation **6** short for **Belisha beacon** **7** a person or thing that serves as a guide, inspiration, or warning [OE *beacen* sign]

beacon school *n Brit* a notably successful school whose methods and practices are brought to the attention of the education service as a whole in order that they may be adopted by other schools

Beaconsfield[1] (ˈbɛkənzˌfiːld, ˈbiːk-) *n* a town in SE England, in Buckinghamshire: a residential centre for London. Pop: 12 292 (1991)

Beaconsfield[2] (ˈbɛkənzˌfiːld, ˈbiːk-) *n* **1st Earl of** title of (Benjamin) **Disraeli**

beacon status *n Brit* a ranking awarded by the government to an organization, rendering it eligible for extra funding, and aimed at encouraging organizations to share good practice with each other

bead (biːd) *n* **1** a small pierced usually spherical piece of glass, wood, plastic, etc, which may be strung with others to form a necklace, etc **2** **tell one's beads** to pray with a rosary **3** a small drop of moisture **4** a small bubble in or on a liquid **5** a small metallic knob acting as the sight of a firearm **6** **to draw** *or* **hold a bead on** to aim a rifle or pistol at **7** *archit, furniture* a small convex moulding having a semicircular cross section ▷ *vb* **8** (*tr*) to decorate with beads **9** to form into beads or drops [OE *bed* prayer] > ˈ**beaded** *adj*

beading (ˈbiːdɪŋ) *n* **1** another name for **bead** (sense 7) **2** Also called: **beadwork** (ˈbiːdˌwɜːk) a narrow strip of some material used for edging or ornamentation

beadle (ˈbiːdᵊl) *n* **1** *Brit* (formerly) a minor parish official who acted as an usher and kept order **2** *Judaism* a synagogue attendant **3** *Scot* a church official who attends the minister **4** an official in certain British institutions [OE *bydel*] > ˈ**beadleship** *n*

beadsman *or* **bedesman** (ˈbiːdzmən) *n, pl* **beadsmen** *or* **bedesmen** *arch* **1** a person who prays for another's soul, esp one paid or fed for doing so **2** a person kept in an almshouse

beady (ˈbiːdɪ) *adj* **beadier, beadiest** **1** small, round, and glittering (esp in **beady eyes**) **2** resembling or covered with beads > ˈ**beadiness** *n*

beagle (ˈbiːgᵊl) *n* **1** a small sturdy breed of hound **2** *arch* a spy ▷ *vb* **beagles, beagling, beagled** **3** (*intr*) to hunt with beagles [C15 from ?]

Beaglehole (ˈbiːgᵊlˌhəʊl) *n* **John** 1901–71, New Zealand historian and author. His works include *Exploration of the Pacific* (1934) and *The Journals of James Cook* (1955)

beak[1] (biːk) *n* **1** the projecting jaws of a bird, covered with a horny sheath **2** any beaklike mouthpart in other animals **3** *sl* a person's nose **4** any projecting part, such as the pouring lip of a bucket **5** *naut* another word for **ram** (sense 5) [C13 from OF *bec*, from L *beccus*, of Gaulish origin] > **beaked** *adj* > ˈ**beaky** *adj*

beak[2] (biːk) *n* a Brit slang word for **judge, magistrate, headmaster,** or **schoolmaster** [C19 orig. thieves' jargon]

beaker (ˈbiːkə) *n* **1** a cup usually having a wide mouth **2** a cylindrical flat-bottomed container used in laboratories, usually made of glass and having a pouring lip [C14 from ON *bikarr*]

Beaker folk (ˈbiːkə) *n* a prehistoric people inhabiting Europe and Britain during the second millennium BC [after beakers found among their remains]

Beale (biːl) *n* **Dorothea** 1831–1906, British schoolmistress, a champion of women's education and suffrage. As principal of Cheltenham Ladies' College (1858–1906) she introduced important reforms

be-all and end-all *n inf* the ultimate aim or justification

beam (biːm) *n* **1** a long thick piece of wood, metal, etc, esp one used as a horizontal structural member **2** the breadth of a ship or boat taken at its widest part **3** a ray or column of light, as from a beacon **4** a broad smile **5** one of two cylindrical rollers on a loom, which hold the warp threads and the finished work **6** the main stem of a deer's antler **7** the central shaft of a plough to which all the main parts are attached **8** a narrow unidirectional flow of electromagnetic radiation or particles: *an electron beam* **9** the horizontal centrally pivoted bar in a balance **10** **beam in one's eye** a fault or grave error greater in oneself than in another person **11** **broad in the beam** *inf* having wide hips **12** **off (the) beam** **12a** not following a radio beam to maintain a course **12b** *inf* mistaken or irrelevant **13** **on the beam** **13a** following a radio beam to maintain a course **13b** *inf* correct, relevant, or appropriate ▷ *vb* **14** to send out or radiate **15** (*tr*) to divert or aim (a radio signal, light, etc) in a certain direction: *to beam a programme to Tokyo* **16** (*intr*) to smile broadly [OE] > ˈ**beaming** *adj*

beam-ends *pl n* **1** **on her beam-ends** (of a vessel) heeled over through an angle of 90° **2** **on one's beam-ends** out of resources; destitute

bean (biːn) *n* **1** any of various leguminous plants producing edible seeds in pods **2** any of various other plants whose seeds are produced in pods or podlike fruits **3** the seed or pod of any of these plants **4** any of various beanlike seeds, as coffee **5** *US & Canad sl* another word for **head** **6** **full of beans** *inf* full of energy and vitality **7** **not have a bean** *sl* to be without money [OE *bēan*]

beanbag (ˈbiːnˌbæg) *n* **1** a small cloth bag filled with dried beans and thrown in games **2** a very large cushion filled with foam rubber or polystyrene granules and used as a seat

beanbag gun *n* a gun that fires a fabric bag containing lead shot, designed to stun or knock the target to the ground

bean counter *n inf* an accountant

bean curd *n* another name for **tofu**
beanfeast ('bi:n,fi:st) *n Brit inf* 1 an annual dinner given by employers to employees 2 any festive or merry occasion
beanie *or* **beany** ('bi:nɪ) *n, pl* **beanies** a round close-fitting hat resembling a skullcap
beano ('bi:nəʊ) *n, pl* **beanos** *Brit sl* a celebration, party, or other enjoyable time
beanpole ('bi:n,pəʊl) *n* 1 a tall stick used to support bean plants 2 *sl* a tall thin person
bean sprout *n* the sprout of a newly germinated mung bean, eaten esp in Chinese dishes
beanstalk ('bi:n,stɔ:k) *n* the stem of a bean plant
bear[1] (bɛə) *vb* **bears, bearing, bore, borne** (*mainly tr*) 1 to support or hold up 2 to bring: *to bear gifts* 3 to accept or assume the responsibility of: *to bear an expense* 4 (**born** in passive use except when followed by *by*) to give birth to: *to bear children* 5 (*also intr*) to produce as by natural growth: *to bear fruit* 6 to tolerate or endure 7 to admit of; sustain: *his story does not bear scrutiny* 8 to hold in the mind: *to bear a grudge* 9 to show or be marked with: *he still bears the scars* 10 to render or supply (esp in **bear witness**) 11 to conduct (oneself, the body, etc) 12 to have, be, or stand in (relation or comparison): *his account bears no relation to the facts* 13 (*intr*) to move or lie in a specified direction 14 **bear a hand** to give assistance 15 **bring to bear** to bring into operation or effect ▷ See also **bear down, bear on,** etc [OE *beran*]
bear[2] (bɛə) *n, pl* **bears** *or* **bear** 1 a plantigrade mammal typically having a large head, a long shaggy coat, and strong claws 2 any of various bearlike animals, such as the koala 3 a clumsy, churlish, or ill-mannered person 4 a teddy bear 5 *stock exchange* 5a a speculator who sells in anticipation of falling prices to make a profit on repurchase 5b (*as modifier*): *a bear market* ▷ Cf **bull**[1] (sense 4) ▷ *vb* **bears, bearing, beared** 6 (*tr*) to lower or attempt to lower the price or prices of (a stock market or a security) by speculative selling [OE *bera*]
Bear (bɛə) *n* **the** 1 the English name for either Ursa Major (Great Bear) or Ursa Minor (Little Bear) 2 an informal name for **Russia**
bearable ('bɛərəbᵊl) *adj* endurable; tolerable
bear-baiting *n* (formerly) an entertainment in which dogs attacked a chained bear
beard (bɪəd) *n* 1 the hair growing on the lower parts of a man's face 2 any similar growth in animals 3 a tuft of long bristles in the spikelets of such grasses as barley; awn 4 a barb, as on a fish-hook ▷ *vb* (*tr*) 5 to oppose boldly or impertinently [OE *beard*] > '**bearded** *adj*
bearded dragon *n* 1 a large Australian lizard, *Amphibolurus barbatus*, with an erectile frill around the neck. Also called: **bearded lizard, jew lizard** 2 another name for **frill-necked lizard**
beardless ('bɪədlɪs) *adj* 1 without a beard 2 too young to grow a beard; immature
bear down *vb* (*intr, adv;* often foll by *on* or *upon*) 1 to press or weigh down 2 to approach in a determined or threatening manner
Beardsley ('bɪədzlɪ) *n* **Aubrey (Vincent)** 1872–98, English illustrator: noted for his stylized black-and-white illustrations, esp those for Oscar Wilde's *Salome* and Pope's *Rape of the Lock*
beard-stroking *n* 1 deep thought: *the response involved much beard-stroking* ▷ *adj* 2 boringly intellectual: *a beard-stroking bore*
beardy ('bɪədɪ) *adj* **beardier, beardiest** 1 wearing a beard ▷ *n, pl* **beardies** 2 a person who has a beard
bearer ('bɛərə) *n* 1 a person or thing that bears, presents, or upholds 2 a person who presents a note or bill for payment 3 (in Africa, India, etc, formerly) a native porter or servant 4 (*modifier*) *Finance.* payable to the person in possession: *bearer bonds*
bear garden *n* 1 (formerly) a place where bear-baiting took place 2 a place or scene of tumult
bear hug *n* 1 a wrestling hold in which the arms are locked tightly round an opponent's chest and arms 2 any similar tight embrace 3 *commerce* an approach to the board of one company by another to indicate that an offer is to be made for their shares
bearing ('bɛərɪŋ) *n* 1 a support for a rotating or reciprocating mechanical part 2 (foll by *on* or *upon*) relevance (to): *it has no bearing on this problem* 3 a person's general social conduct 4 the act, period, or capability of producing fruit or young 5 anything that carries weight or acts as a support 6 the angular direction of a point or course measured from a known position 7 (*usually pl*) the position, as of a ship, fixed with reference to two or more known points 8 (*usually pl*) a sense of one's relative position; orientation (esp in **lose, get,** *or* **take one's bearings**) 9 *heraldry* 9a a device on a heraldic shield 9b another name for **coat of arms**
bearing rein *n chiefly Brit* a rein from the bit to the saddle, designed to keep the horse's head in the desired position
bearish ('bɛərɪʃ) *adj* 1 like a bear; rough; clumsy; churlish 2 *stock exchange* causing, expecting, or characterized by a fall in prices: *a bearish feel to the market* > '**bearishness** *n*
bear on *vb* (*intr, prep*) 1 to be relevant to; relate to 2 to be burdensome to or afflict
bear out *vb* (*tr, adv*) to show to be true or truthful; confirm: *the witness will bear me out*
bear paw ▷ *n Canad* a type of small round snowshoe
bear raid *n* an attempt to force down the price of a security or commodity by sustained selling
bearskin ('bɛə,skɪn) *n* 1 the pelt of a bear, esp when used as a rug 2 a tall helmet of black fur worn by certain British Army regiments
bear up *vb* (*intr, adv*) to endure cheerfully
bear with *vb* (*intr, prep*) to be patient with
beast (bi:st) *n* 1 any animal other than man, esp a large wild quadruped 2 savage nature or characteristics: *the beast in man* 3 a brutal, uncivilized, or filthy person [C13 from OF *beste*, from L *bestia*, from ?]
beastly ('bi:stlɪ) *adj* **beastlier, beastliest** 1 *inf* unpleasant; disagreeable 2 *obs* of or like a beast; bestial ▷ *adv* 3 *inf* (intensifier): *the weather is so beastly hot* > '**beastliness** *n*
beast of burden *n* an animal, such as a donkey or ox, used for carrying loads
beast of prey *n* any animal that hunts other animals for food
beat (bi:t) *vb* **beats, beating, beat; beaten** *or* **beat** 1 (when *intr*, often foll by *against, on,* etc) to strike with or as if with a series of violent blows 2 (*tr*) to punish by striking; flog 3 to move up and down; flap: *the bird beat its wings heavily* 4 (*intr*) to throb rhythmically; pulsate 5 (*tr;* sometimes foll by *up*) *Cookery.* to stir or whisk vigorously 6 (*tr;* sometimes foll by *out*) to shape, thin, or flatten (metal) by repeated blows 7 (*tr*) *music* to indicate (time) by one's hand, baton, etc, or by a metronome 8 (when *tr*, sometimes foll by *out*) to produce (a sound or signal) by or as if by striking a drum 9 to overcome; defeat 10 (*tr*) to form (a path, track, etc) by repeatedly walking or riding over it 11 (*tr*) to arrive, achieve, or finish before (someone or something) 12 (*tr;* often foll by *back, down, off,* etc) to drive, push, or thrust 13 to scour (woodlands or undergrowth) so as to rouse game for shooting 14 (*tr*) *sl* to puzzle or baffle: *it beats me* 15 (*intr*) *naut* to steer a sailing vessel as close as possible to the direction from which the wind is blowing 16 **beat a retreat** to withdraw in haste 17 **beat it** *sl* (*often imperative*) to go away 18 **beat the bounds** *Brit* (formerly) to define the boundaries of a parish by making a procession around them and hitting the ground with rods 19 **can you beat it** *or* **that?** *sl* an expression of surprise ▷ *n* 20 a stroke or

Bb

blow **21** the sound made by a stroke or blow **22** a regular throb **23a** an assigned or habitual round or route, as of a policeman **23b** (*as modifier*): *beat police officers* **24** the basic rhythmic unit in a piece of music **25a** pop or rock music characterized by a heavy rhythmic beat **25b** (*as modifier*): *a beat group* **26** *physics* one of the regular pulses produced by combining two sounds or electrical signals that have similar frequencies **27** *prosody* the accent or stress in a metrical foot **28** (*modifier*) (*often cap*) of, characterized by, or relating to the Beat Generation ▷ *adj* **29** (*postpositive*) *sl* totally exhausted ▷ See also **beat down, beat up** [OE *bēatan*] > **'beatable** *adj*

beatbox ('bi:t,bɒks) *n* another name for **drum machine**

beat down *vb* (*adv*) **1** (*tr*) *inf* to force or persuade (a seller) to accept a lower price **2** (*intr*) (of the sun) to shine intensely

beaten ('bi:tᵊn) *adj* **1** defeated or baffled **2** shaped or made thin by hammering: *beaten gold* **3** much travelled; well trodden **4 off the beaten track 4a** in unfamiliar territory **4b** out of the ordinary; unusual **5** (of food) mixed by beating; whipped **6** tired out; exhausted

beater ('bi:tə) *n* **1** a person who beats or hammers: *a panel beater* **2** a device used for beating: *a carpet beater* **3** a person who rouses wild game

Beat Generation *n* (*functioning as sing or pl*) **1** members of the generation that came to maturity in the 1950s, whose rejection of the social and political systems of the West was expressed through contempt for regular work, possessions, traditional dress, etc **2** a group of US writers, notably Jack Kerouac, Allen Ginsberg, and William Burroughs, who emerged in the 1950s

beatific (,bi:ə'tɪfɪk) *adj* **1** displaying great happiness, calmness, etc **2** of or conferring a state of celestial happiness [C17 from LL *beātificus*, from L *beātus*, from *beāre* to bless + *facere* to make] > **,bea'tifically** *adv*

beatify (bɪ'ætɪ,faɪ) *vb* **beatifies, beatifying, beatified** (*tr*) **1** *RC Church* (of the pope) to declare formally that (a deceased person) showed a heroic degree of holiness in life and is worthy of veneration: the first step towards canonization **2** to make extremely happy [C16 from OF *beatifier*; see BEATIFIC] > **beatification** (bɪ,ætɪfɪ'keɪʃən) *n*

beating ('bi:tɪŋ) *n* **1** a whipping or thrashing **2** a defeat or setback **3 take some** *or* **a lot of beating** to be difficult to improve upon

beatitude (bɪ'ætɪ,tju:d) *n* **1** supreme blessedness or happiness **2** an honorific title of the Eastern Christian Church, applied to those of patriarchal rank [C15 from L *beātitūdō*, from *beātus* blessed; see BEATIFIC]

Beatitude (bɪ'ætɪ,tju:d) *n Christianity* any of eight sayings of Jesus in the Sermon on the Mount (Matthew 5:3–11) in which he declares that the poor, the meek, etc, will, in various ways, receive the blessings of heaven

Beatles ('bi:tᵊlz) *pl n* **the** British rock group (1961–70): comprised John Lennon, Paul McCartney, George Harrison (1943–2001), and Ringo Starr (real name *Richard Starkey*, born 1940). See also (John Winston Ono) **Lennon,** (Paul) **McCartney**

beatnik ('bi:tnɪk) *n* **1** a member of the Beat Generation (sense 1) **2** *inf* any person with long hair and shabby clothes [C20 from BEAT (n) + -NIK]

Beaton ('bi:tᵊn) *n* Sir **Cecil** (**Walter Hardy**) 1904–80, British photographer, noted esp for his society portraits

Beatrix ('bi:ətrɪks) *n* full name *Beatrix Wilhelmina Armgard*. born 1938, queen of the Netherlands from 1980

Beatty ('bi:tɪ) *n* **1 David,** 1st Earl Beatty. 1871–1936, British admiral of the fleet in World War I **2 Warren,** full name *Henry Warren Beatty*. born 1937, US film actor and director: his films include *Bonnie and Clyde* (1967), *Heaven Can Wait* (1978), *Reds* (1981, also directed), *Bugsy* (1991), and *Bulworth* (1998, also wrote and directed)

beat up *inf* ▷ *vb* **1** (*tr, adv*) to strike or kick repeatedly, so as to inflict severe physical damage ▷ *adj* **beat-up 2** worn-out; dilapidated

beau (bəʊ) *n, pl* **beaux** (bəʊ, bəʊz) *or* **beaus** (bəʊz) **1** a man who is greatly concerned with his clothes and appearance; dandy **2** *chiefly US* a boyfriend; sweetheart [C17 from F, from OF *biau*, from L *bellus* handsome]

Beaufort ('bəʊfət) *n* **1 Henry** ?1374–1447, English cardinal, half-brother of Henry IV; chancellor (1403–04, 1413–17, 1424–26) **2** Lady **Margaret,** Countess of Richmond and Derby. ?1443–1509, mother of Henry VII. She helped to found two Cambridge colleges and was a patron of Caxton

Beaufort scale *n meteorol* an international scale of wind velocities from 0 (calm) to 12 (hurricane) (0 to 17 in the US) [C19 after Sir Francis *Beaufort* (1774–1857), Brit admiral and hydrographer who devised it]

Beaufort Sea *n* part of the Arctic Ocean off the N coast of North America

beau geste *French* (bo ʒɛst) *n, pl* ***beaux gestes*** (bo ʒɛst). a noble or gracious gesture or act [lit.: beautiful gesture]

Beauharnais (*French* boarnɛ) *n* **1 Alexandre** (alɛksɑ̃dr), Vicomte de. 1760–94, French general, who served in the War of American Independence and the French Revolutionary wars; first husband of Empress Joséphine: guillotined **2** his son, **Eugène de** (øʒɛn də) 1781–1824, viceroy of Italy (1805–14) for his stepfather Napoleon I **3** (**Eugénie**) (øʒeni) **Hortense de** (ɔrtɑ̃s də) 1783–1837, queen of Holland (1806–10) as wife of Louis Bonaparte; daughter of Alexandre Beauharnais and sister of Eugène: mother of Napoleon III **4 Joséphine de** (ʒozefin də). See (Empress) **Josephine**

beaujolais ('bəʊʒə,leɪ) *n* (*sometimes cap*) a popular fresh-tasting red or white wine from southern Burgundy in France

Beaulieu ('bju:lɪ) *n* a village in S England, in Hampshire: site of Palace House, seat of Lord Montagu and once the gatehouse of the ruined 13th-century abbey; the National Motor Museum is in its grounds. Pop: 1200 (latest est)

Beaumarchais (*French* bomarʃɛ) *n* **Pierre Augustin Caron de** (pjɛr ogystɛ̃ karɔ̃ də) 1732–99, French dramatist, noted for his comedies *The Barber of Seville* (1775) and *The Marriage of Figaro* (1784)

Beaumaris (bəʊ'mærɪs) *n* a resort in N Wales, on the island of Anglesey: 13th-century castle. Pop: 1561 (1991)

beau monde ('bəʊ 'mɒnd) *n* the world of fashion and society [C18 F, lit.: fine world]

Beaumont[1] ('bəʊmɒnt) *n* a city in SE Texas. Pop: 113 866 (2000)

Beaumont[2] ('bəʊmɒnt) *n* **Francis** 1584–1616, English dramatist, who collaborated with John Fletcher on plays including *The Knight of the Burning Pestle* (1607) and *The Maid's Tragedy* (1611)

Beaune (bəʊn) *n* **1** a city in E France, near Dijon: an important trading centre for Burgundy wines. Pop: 22 170 (1990) **2** a wine produced in this district

beaut (bju:t) *sl, chiefly Austral & NZ* ▷ *n* **1** an outstanding person or thing ▷ *adj, interj* **2** excellent ▷ *interj* **4** Also: **you beaut!** an exclamation of joy or pleasure

beauteous ('bju:tɪəs) *adj* a poetic word for **beautiful** > **'beauteousness** *n*

beautician (bju:'tɪʃən) *n* a person who works in or manages a beauty salon

beautiful ('bju:tɪfʊl) *adj* **1** possessing beauty; aesthetically pleasing **2** highly enjoyable; very pleasant > **'beautifully** *adv*

beautify ('bju:tɪ,faɪ) *vb* **beautifies, beautifying, beautified** to make or become beautiful > **beautification** (,bju:tɪfɪ'keɪʃən) *n* > **'beauti,fier** *n*

beauty ('bju:tɪ) *n, pl* **beauties 1** the combination of all the qualities of a person or thing that delight the senses and mind **2** a very attractive woman **3** *inf* an outstanding example of its kind **4** *inf* an advantageous feature: *one beauty of the job is the short hours* ▷ *interj* **5** (NZ 'bju:dɪ) *Austral & NZ sl* an expression of approval or

Beaufort Scale

Beaufort number	Wind force	Speed (kph)	Speed (knots)	Characteristics
0	Calm	less than 1	less than 1	smoke goes straight up; sea like a mirror
1	Light air	1-5	1-3	smoke blows in the wind; sea ripples, but without foam crests
2	Light breeze	6-11	4-6	wind felt on the face; leaves rustle; small wavelets; wave crests have a glassy appearance and do not break
3	Gentle breeze	12-19	7-10	light flag flutters; leaves in constant motion; large wavelets; wave crests begin to break; scattered white horses
4	Moderate breeze	20-28	11-16	dust and loose paper blown about; small branches move; small waves, becoming larger; white horses fairly frequent
5	Fresh	29-38	17-21	small tress sway; moderate waves; white horses frequent
6	Strong	39-49	22-27	hard to use umbrellas; large waves begin to form; white foam crests more extensive
7	Near gale	50-61	28-33	hard to walk into; whole trees in motion; sea heaps up; white foam from breaking waves begins to be blown along the direction of the wind
8	Gale	62-74	34-40	twigs break off trees; moderately high waves; edges of crests begin to break into spindrift; foam is blown along the direction of the wind
9	Strong gale	75-88	41-47	slates lost; high waves; crests of waves begin to topple, tumble and roll over; spray may affect visibility
10	Storm	89-102	48-55	trees uprooted; considerable structural damage; very high waves; the surface of the sea takes on a white appearance; visibility affected
11	Violent storm	103-117	56-63	widespread damage; exceptionally high waves (small and medium-size ships might be lost to view behind the waves); visibility affected
12	Hurricane	118 and over	64 and over	violent, massive damage; the air is filled with foam and spray; visibility very seriously affected

▷ www.crh.noaa.gov/lot/webpage/beaufort/
▷ www.met-office.gov.uk/education/historic/beaufort.html
▷ www.bom.gov.au/lam/glossary/beaufort.shtml

agreement [c13 from OF *biauté*, from *biau* beautiful; see BEAU]

beauty queen *n* an attractive young woman, esp one who has won a beauty contest

beauty salon *or* **parlour** *n* an establishment providing services such as hairdressing, facial treatment, and massage

beauty sleep *n inf* sleep, esp sleep before midnight

beauty spot *n* **1** a place of outstanding beauty **2** a mole or other similar natural mark on the skin **3** (esp in the 18th century) a small dark-coloured patch or spot worn on a lady's face as an adornment

Beauvais (*French* bovɛ) *n* a market town in N France, 64 km (40 miles) northwest of Paris. Pop: 56 280 (1990)

Beauvoir (*French* bovwar) *n* **Simone de** (simɔn də) 1908–86, French existentialist novelist and feminist, whose works include *Le sang des autres* (1944), *Le deuxième sexe* (1949), and *Les mandarins* (1954)

beaux (bəʊ, bəʊz) *n* a plural of **beau**

beaux-arts (bəʊˈzɑː) *pl n* **1** another word for **fine art**

2 (*modifier*) relating to the classical decorative style, esp that of the École des Beaux-Arts in Paris: *beaux-arts influences* [F]

beaver[1] (ˈbiːvə) *n* **1** a large amphibious rodent of Europe, Asia, and North America. It has soft brown fur, a broad flat hairless tail, and webbed hind feet, and constructs complex dams and houses (lodges) in rivers **2** its fur **3** a tall hat of beaver fur worn during the 19th century **4** a woollen napped cloth resembling beaver fur **5** *obs* a full beard **6** a bearded man **7** (*modifier*) made of beaver fur or similar material ▹ *vb* **8** (*intr*; usually foll by *away*) to work industriously or steadily [OE *beofor*]

beaver[2] (ˈbiːvə) *n* a movable piece on a medieval helmet used to protect the lower face [c15 from OF *baviere*, from *baver* to dribble]

Beaverbrook (ˈbiːvəˌbrʊk) *n* **1st Baron**, title of *William Maxwell Aitken*. 1879–1964, British newspaper proprietor and Conservative politician, born in Canada, whose newspapers included the *Daily Express*; minister of information (1918); minister of aircraft production (1940–41)

beaver fever *n Canad* an infectious disease caused by drinking water that has been contaminated by wildlife

Beaver Tail *n trademark* a flat oval doughnut served fried and sugared

Bebington (ˈbɛbɪŋtən) *n* a town in NW England, in Wirral unitary authority, Merseyside: docks and chemical works. Pop: 60 148 (1991)

bebop (ˈbiːbɒp) *n* the full name for **bop** (sense 1) [c20 imit. of the rhythm] > **ˈbebopper** *n*

becalmed (bɪˈkɑːmd) *adj* (of a sailing boat or ship) motionless through lack of wind

became (bɪˈkeɪm) *vb* the past tense of **become**

because (bɪˈkɒz, -ˈkəz) *conj* **1** (*subordinating*) on account of the fact that; since: *because it's so cold we'll go home* **2 because of** (*prep*) on account of: *I lost my job because of her* [c14 *bi cause*, from *bi* BY + CAUSE]

USAGE See at **account, reason**

béchamel sauce (ˌbeɪʃəˈmɛl) *n* a thick white sauce flavoured with onion and seasonings [c18 after the Marquis of *Béchamel*, its F inventor]

Béchar (*French* beʃar) *n* a city in NW Algeria: an oasis. Pop: 131 010 (1998). Former name: **Colomb-Béchar**

bêche-de-mer (ˌbɛʃdəˈmɛə) *n, pl* **bêches-de-mer** (ˌbɛʃdəˈmɛə) *or* **bêche-de-mer** another name for **trepang** [c19 quasi-F, from earlier E *biche de mer*, from Port. *bicho do mar* worm of the sea]

Bechet (ˈbɛʃeɪ) *n* **Sidney (Joseph)** 1897–1959, US jazz soprano saxophonist and clarinettist

Bechstein (*German* ˈbɛçʃtaɪn) *n* **Karl** 1826–1900, German piano maker; founder (1853) of the Bechstein company of piano manufacturers in Berlin

Bechuana (bɛˈtʃwɑːnə; ˌbɛkjʊˈɑːnə) *n, pl* **Bechuana** *or* **Bechuanas** a former name for a Bantu of Botswana

Bechuanaland (bɛˈtʃwɑːnəˌlænd, ˌbɛtʃʊˈɑːnəˌlænd, ˌbɛkjʊ-) *n* the former name (until 1966) of **Botswana**

beck[1] (bɛk) *n* **1** a nod, wave, or other gesture **2 at (someone's) beck and call** subject to (someone's) slightest whim [c14 short for *becnen* to BECKON]

beck[2] (bɛk) *n* (in N England) a stream [OE *becc*]

Beckenbauer (ˈbɛkənˌbaʊə) *n* **Franz** born 1945, German footballer: team captain when West Germany won the World Cup (1974): manager of West Germany (1984–90), coaching the team to success in the 1990 World Cup

Becker (ˈbɛkə) *n* **Boris** (ˈbɒrɪs) born 1967, German tennis player: Wimbledon champion 1985, 1986, and 1989: the youngest man ever to win Wimbledon

Becket (ˈbɛkɪt) *n* **Saint Thomas à** 1118–70, English prelate; chancellor (1155–62) to Henry II; archbishop of Canterbury (1162–70): murdered following his opposition to Henry's attempts to control the clergy. Feast day: Dec. 29 or July 7

Beckett (ˈbɛkɪt) *n* **1 Margaret Mary** born 1943, British politician; deputy leader of the Labour Party (1992–94); leader of the House of Commons (1998–2001); secretary of state for environment, food, and rural affairs (2001–) **2 Samuel (Barclay)** 1906–89, Irish dramatist and novelist writing in French and English, whose works portray the human condition as insignificant or absurd in a bleak universe. They include the plays *En attendant Godot* (*Waiting for Godot*, 1952), *Fin de partie* (*Endgame*, 1957), and *Not I* (1973) and the novel *Malone meurt* (*Malone Dies*, 1951): Nobel prize for literature 1969

Beckford (ˈbɛkfəd) *n* **William** 1759–1844, English writer and dilettante; author of the oriental romance *Vathek* (1787)

Beckham (ˈbɛkəm) *n* **David** born 1975, British footballer; captain of England from 2000: married to the pop singer Victoria Beckham ("Posh Spice" of the Spice Girls)

Beckmann (*German* ˈbɛkman) *n* **1 Ernst Otto** (ɛrnst ˈɔːto) 1853–1923, German chemist: devised the Beckmann thermometer, used for measuring small temperature changes in liquids **2 Max** (maks) 1884–1950, German expressionist painter

beckon (ˈbɛkən) *vb* **1** to summon with a gesture of the hand or head **2** to entice or lure ▹ *n* **3** a summoning gesture [OE *bīecnan*, from *bēacen* sign] > **ˈbeckoner** *n* > **ˈbeckoning** *adj, n*

becloud (bɪˈklaʊd) *vb* (*tr*) **1** to cover or obscure with a cloud **2** to confuse or muddle

become (bɪˈkʌm) *vb* **becomes, becoming, became, become** (*mainly intr*) **1** (*copula*) to come to be; develop or grow into: *he became a monster* **2** (foll by *of*; *usually used in a question*) to happen (to): *what became of him?* **3** (*tr*) to suit: *that dress becomes you* **4** (*tr*) to be appropriate; to befit: *it ill becomes you to complain* [OE *becuman* to happen]

becoming (bɪˈkʌmɪŋ) *adj* suitable; appropriate > **beˈcomingly** *adv* > **beˈcomingness** *n*

becquerel (ˌbɛkəˈrɛl) *n* the SI unit of activity of a radioactive source [after A. H. BECQUEREL]

Becquerel (*French* bɛkrɛl) *n* **Antoine Henri** (ɑ̃twan ɑ̃ri) 1852–1908, French physicist, who discovered the photographic action of the rays emitted by uranium salts and so instigated the study of radioactivity: Nobel prize for physics 1903

BECTU (ˈbɜktuː) *n* (in Britain) *abbrev or acronym for* Broadcasting, Entertainment, Cinematograph and Theatre Union

bed (bɛd) *n* **1** a piece of furniture on which to sleep **2** the mattress and bedclothes: *an unmade bed* **3** sleep or rest: *time for bed* **4** any place in which a person or animal sleeps or rests **5** *med* a unit of potential occupancy in a hospital or residential institution **6** *inf* sexual intercourse **7** a plot of ground in which plants are grown **8** the bottom of a river, lake, or sea **9** a part of this used for cultivation of a plant or animal: *oyster beds* **10** any underlying structure or part **11** a layer of rock, esp sedimentary rock **12 go to bed 12a** (often foll by *with*) to have sexual intercourse (with) **12b** *journalism, printing* (of a newspaper, etc) to go to press; start printing **13 in bed with** *inf* cooperating closely with (another person, organization, government, etc), esp covertly **14 put to bed** *journalism* to finalize work on (a newspaper, etc) so that it is ready to go to press **15 take to one's bed** to remain in bed, esp because of illness ▹ *vb* **beds, bedding, bedded 16** (usually foll by *down*) to go to or put into a place to sleep or rest **17** (*tr*) to have sexual intercourse with **18** (*tr*) to place firmly into position; embed **19** *geol* to form or be arranged in a distinct layer; stratify **20** (*tr*; often foll by *out*) to plant in a bed of soil [OE *bedd*]

BEd *abbrev for* Bachelor of Education

bed and board *n* sleeping accommodation and meals

bed and breakfast *n chiefly Brit* **1** (in a hotel, boarding house, etc) overnight accommodation and breakfast

2 the selling of shares after hours one evening on a stock exchange and buying them back the next morning, in order to establish a loss for capital-gains tax purposes

bedaub (bɪˈdɔːb) *vb* (*tr*) **1** to smear all over with something thick, sticky, or dirty **2** to ornament in a gaudy or vulgar fashion

bedazzle (bɪˈdæzᵊl) *vb* **bedazzles, bedazzling, bedazzled** (*tr*) to dazzle or confuse, as with brilliance > **beˈdazzlement** *n*

bed bath *n* another name for **blanket bath**

bed-blocking *n Brit* the use of hospital beds by elderly patients who cannot leave hospital because they have no place in a residential care home > **ˈbed-ˌblocker** *n*

bedbug (ˈbɛdˌbʌg) *n* any of several bloodsucking wingless insects of temperate regions, infesting dirty houses

bedchamber (ˈbɛdˌtʃeɪmbə) *n* an archaic word for **bedroom**

bedclothes (ˈbɛdˌkləʊðz) *pl n* sheets, blankets, and other coverings for a bed

beddable (ˈbɛdəbᵊl) *adj* sexually attractive

bedding (ˈbɛdɪŋ) *n* **1** bedclothes, sometimes considered with a mattress **2** litter, such as straw, for animals **3** a foundation, such as mortar under a brick **4** the stratification of rocks

bedding plant *n* an immature plant that may be planted out in a garden bed

Beddoes (ˈbɛdəʊz) *n* **Thomas Lovell** 1803–49, British poet, noted for his macabre imagery, esp in *Death's Jest-Book* (1850)

Bede (biːd) *n* **Saint**, known as *the Venerable Bede*. ?673–735 AD, English monk, scholar, historian, and theologian, noted for his Latin *Ecclesiastical History of the English People* (731) Feast day: May 27 or 25. Latin name: **Baeda**

bedeck (bɪˈdɛk) *vb* (*tr*) to cover with decorations; adorn

bedevil (bɪˈdɛvᵊl) *vb* **bedevils, bedevilling, bedevilled** *or US* **bedevils, bedeviling, bedeviled** (*tr*) **1** to harass or torment **2** to throw into confusion **3** to possess, as with a devil > **beˈdevilment** *n*

bedew (bɪˈdjuː) *vb* (*tr*) to wet as with dew

bedfellow (ˈbɛdˌfɛləʊ) *n* **1** a person with whom one shares a bed **2** a temporary ally or associate

Bedford¹ (ˈbɛdfəd) *n* **1** a town in SE central England, administrative centre of Bedfordshire, on the River Ouse. Pop: 73 917 (1991) **2** short for **Bedfordshire**

Bedford² (ˈbɛdfəd) *n* **1** **David** born 1937, British composer, influenced by rock music **2** **Duke of**, title of *John of Lancaster*. 1389–1435, son of Henry IV of England: protector of England and regent of France (1422–35)

Bedfordshire (ˈbɛdfədˌʃɪə, -ʃə) *n* a county of S central England: mainly low-lying, with the Chiltern Hills in the south: the geographical county includes Luton, which became a separate unitary authority in 1997. Administrative centre: Bedford. Pop (excluding Luton): 381 571 (2001). Area (excluding Luton): 1192 sq km (460 sq miles). Abbreviation: **Beds**

bedight (bɪˈdaɪt) *arch* ▷ *vb* **bedights, bedighting, bedight** *or* **bedighted** **1** (*tr*) to array or adorn ▷ *adj* **2** (*p.p.*) adorned or bedecked [C14 from DIGHT]

bedim (bɪˈdɪm) *vb* **bedims, bedimming, bedimmed** (*tr*) to make dim or obscure

Bedivere (ˈbɛdɪˌvɪə) *n* **Sir** (in Arthurian legend) a knight who took the dying King Arthur to the barge in which he was carried to Avalon

bedizen (bɪˈdaɪzᵊn, -ˈdɪzᵊn) *vb* (*tr*) *arch* to dress or decorate gaudily or tastelessly [C17 from BE- + obs. *dizen* to dress up, from ?] > **beˈdizenment** *n*

bed jacket *n* a woman's short upper garment worn over a nightgown when sitting up in bed

bedlam (ˈbɛdləm) *n* **1** a noisy confused situation **2** *arch* a madhouse [C13 *bedlem, bethlem*, from Hospital of St Mary of *Bethlehem* in London]

bed linen *n* sheets, pillowcases, etc, for a bed

Bedloe's Island (ˈbɛdləʊz) *or* **Bedloe Island** *n* the former name (until 1956) of **Liberty Island**

Bedouin *or* **Beduin** (ˈbɛdʊɪn) *n* **1** (*pl* **Bedouins, Bedouin** *or* **Beduins, Beduin**) a nomadic Arab tribesman of the deserts of Arabia, Jordan, and Syria **2** a wanderer ▷ *adj* **3** of or relating to the Bedouins **4** wandering [C14 from OF *beduin*, from Ar. *badāwi*, pl. of *badwi*, from *badw* desert]

bedpan (ˈbɛdˌpæn) *n* a vessel used by a bedridden patient to collect faeces and urine

bedraggle (bɪˈdrægᵊl) *vb* **bedraggles, bedraggling, bedraggled** (*tr*) to make (hair, clothing, etc) limp, untidy, or dirty, as with rain or mud

bedraggled (bɪˈdrægᵊld) *adj* (of hair, clothing, etc) limp, untidy, or dirty, as with rain or mud

bedridden (ˈbɛdˌrɪdᵊn) *adj* confined to bed because of illness, esp for a long or indefinite period [OE *bedreda*]

bedrock (ˈbɛdˌrɒk) *n* **1** the solid rock beneath the surface soil, etc **2** basic principles or facts **3** the lowest point, level, or layer

bedroll (ˈbɛdˌrəʊl) *n* a portable roll of bedding

bedroom (ˈbɛdˌruːm, -ˌrʊm) *n* **1** a room used for sleeping **2** (*modifier*) containing references to sex: *a bedroom comedy*

Beds (bɛdz) *abbrev for* Bedfordshire

bedside (ˈbɛdˌsaɪd) *n* **a** the space beside a bed, esp a sickbed **b** (*as modifier*): *a bedside lamp*

bedsit (ˈbɛdˌsɪt) *n* a furnished sitting room containing sleeping accommodation. Also called: **bedsitting room, bedsitter**

bedsore (ˈbɛdˌsɔː) *n* a chronic ulcer on the skin of a bedridden person, caused by prolonged pressure

bedspread (ˈbɛdˌsprɛd) *n* a top cover on a bed

bedstead (ˈbɛdˌstɛd) *n* the framework of a bed

bedstraw (ˈbɛdˌstrɔː) *n* any of numerous plants which have small white or yellow flowers and prickly or hairy fruits: some species formerly used as straw for beds

bedtime (ˈbɛdˌtaɪm) *n* **a** the time when one usually goes to bed **b** (*as modifier*): *a bedtime story*

bed-wetting *n* the act of urinating in bed

Bedworth (ˈbɛdwəθ) *n* a town in central England, in N Warwickshire. Pop: 31 932 (1991)

bee¹ (biː) *n* **1** any of various four-winged insects that collect nectar and pollen and make honey and wax **2** **busy bee** a person who is industrious or has many things to do **3** **have a bee in one's bonnet** to be obsessed with an idea [OE *bīo*]

bee² (biː) *n chiefly US* a social gathering for a specific purpose, as to carry out a communal task: *quilting bee*. [?from dialect *bean* neighbourly help, from OE *bēn* boon]

Beeb (biːb) *n* **the** an informal name for the **BBC**

beebread (ˈbiːˌbrɛd) *n* a mixture of pollen and nectar prepared by worker bees and fed to the larvae. Also called: **ambrosia**

beech (biːtʃ) *n* **1** a European tree having smooth greyish bark **2** a similar tree of temperate Australasia and South America **3** the hard wood of either of these trees **4** See **copper beech** [OE *bēce*] > **ˈbeechen** *or* **ˈbeechy** *adj*

Beecham (ˈbiːtʃəm) *n* Sir **Thomas** 1879–1961, English conductor who did much to promote the works of Delius, Sibelius, and Richard Strauss

Beecher Stowe *n* See (Harriet Elizabeth Beecher) **Stowe**

beechnut (ˈbiːtʃˌnʌt) *n* the small brown triangular edible nut of the beech tree, collectively often termed **beech mast**

bee-eater *n* any of various insectivorous birds of the Old World tropics and subtropics

beef (biːf) *n* **1** the flesh of various bovine animals, esp the cow, when killed for eating **2** (*pl* **beeves**) an adult ox, etc, reared for its meat **3** *inf* human flesh, esp when muscular **4** (*pl* **beefs**) *sl* a complaint ▷ *vb* **5** (*intr*) *sl* to complain, esp repeatedly **6** (*tr*; *often foll by up*) *inf* to strengthen; reinforce [C13 from OF *boef*, from L *bōs* ox]

beefburger (ˈbiːfˌbɜːgə) *n* a flat fried cake of minced beef

Bb

often served in a bread roll; hamburger
beefcake ('bi:f,keɪk) *n sl* men displayed for their muscular bodies, esp in photographs
beefeater ('bi:f,i:tə) *n* a nickname applied to the Yeomen of the Guard, and the Yeomen Warders at the Tower of London
beef road *n Austral* a road used for transporting cattle
beefsteak ('bi:f,steɪk) *n* a lean piece of beef that can be grilled, fried, etc
beef tea *n* a drink made by boiling pieces of lean beef
beef tomato *n* a very large fleshy variety of tomato. Also called: **beefsteak tomato**
beefy ('bi:fɪ) *adj* **beefier, beefiest** 1 like beef 2 *inf* muscular; brawny > '**beefiness** *n*
beehive ('bi:,haɪv) *n* 1 a man-made receptacle used to house a swarm of bees 2 a dome-shaped structure 3 a place where busy people are assembled 4 **the Beehive** the dome-shaped building which houses Parliament in Wellington, New Zealand
beekeeper ('bi:,ki:pə) *n* a person who keeps bees for their honey > '**bee,keeping** *n*
beeline ('bi:,laɪn) *n* the most direct route between two places (esp in **make a beeline for**)
Beelzebub (bɪ'ɛlzɪ,bʌb) *n* Satan or any devil [OE *Belzebub*, ult. from Heb. *bá'al zebūb*, lit.: lord of flies]
bee moth *n* any of various moths whose larvae live in the nests of bees or wasps, feeding on nest materials and host larvae
been (bi:n, bɪn) *vb* the past participle of **be**
beep (bi:p) *n* 1 a short high-pitched sound, as made by a car horn or by electronic apparatus ▷ *vb* 2 to make or cause to make such a noise [c20 imit.] > '**beeper** *n*
beer (bɪə) *n* 1 an alcoholic drink brewed from malt, sugar, hops, and water 2 a slightly fermented drink made from the roots or leaves of certain plants: *ginger beer* 3 (*modifier*) relating to beer: *beer glass* 4 (*modifier*) in which beer is drunk, esp (of licensed premises) having a licence to sell beer but not spirits: *beer house; beer garden* [OE *beor*]
▷ www.realbeer.com
▷ www.howstuffworks.com/beer.htm
▷ www.beerinfo.com/vlib
▷ www.camra.org.uk
▷ www.history-of-beer.com
beer and skittles *n* (*functioning as sing*) *inf* enjoyment or pleasure
Beerbohm ('bɪəbəʊm) *n* Sir (**Henry**) **Max(imilian)** 1872–1956, English critic, wit, and caricaturist, whose works include *Zuleika Dobson* (1911), a satire on Oxford undergraduates
beer parlour *or* **parlor** *n Canad* a room in a tavern, hotel, etc in which beer is served
Beersheba (bɪə'ʃi:bə) *n* a town in S Israel: commercial centre of the Negev. In biblical times it marked the southern limit of Palestine. Pop: 163 700 (1999 est)
beery ('bɪərɪ) *adj* **beerier, beeriest** 1 smelling or tasting of beer 2 given to drinking beer > '**beerily** *adv* > '**beeriness** *n*
bee's knees *n* **the** (*functioning as sing*) *inf* an excellent or ideally suitable person or thing
beestings, biestings, *or US* **beastings** ('bi:stɪŋz) *n* (*functioning as sing*) the first milk secreted by a cow or similar animal after giving birth; colostrum [OE *bӯsting*]
beeswax ('bi:z,wæks) *n* 1 a wax secreted by honeybees for constructing honeycombs 2 this wax after refining, used in polishes, etc
beeswing ('bi:z,wɪŋ) *n* a light filmy crust of tartar that forms in some wines after long keeping in the bottle
beet (bi:t) *n* 1 a plant of a genus widely cultivated in such varieties as the sugar beet, mangelwurzel, and beetroot 2 the leaves of any of several varieties of this plant, cooked and eaten as a vegetable 3 **red beet** the US name for **beetroot** [OE *bēte*, from L *bēta*]
Beethoven ('beɪt,həʊvᵊn) *n* **Ludwig van** ('lu:tvɪç fan) 1770–1827, German composer, who greatly extended the form and scope of symphonic and chamber music, bridging the classical and romantic traditions. His works include nine symphonies, 32 piano sonatas, 16 string quartets, five piano concertos, a violin concerto, two masses, the opera *Fidelio* (1805), and choral music
beetle[1] ('bi:tᵊl) *n* 1 an insect having biting mouthparts and forewings modified to form shell-like protective casings 2 a game in which the players draw or assemble a beetle-shaped form ▷ *vb* **beetles, beetling, beetled** (*intr*; foll by *along, off*, etc) 3 *inf* to scuttle or scurry; hurry [OE *bitela*]
beetle[2] ('bi:tᵊl) *n* 1 a heavy hand tool for pounding or beating 2 a machine used to finish cloth by stamping it with wooden hammers [OE *bīetel*, from *bēatan* to BEAT]
beetle[3] ('bi:tᵊl) *vb* **beetles, beetling, beetled** 1 (*intr*) to overhang; jut ▷ *adj* 2 overhanging; prominent [c14 ? rel. to BEETLE[1]] > '**beetling** *adj*
beetle-browed *adj* having bushy or overhanging eyebrows
Beeton ('bi:tᵊn) *n* **Isabella Mary**, known as *Mrs Beeton*. 1836–65, British cookery writer, author of *The Book of Household Management* (1861)
beetroot ('bi:t,ru:t) *n* a variety of the beet plant that has a bulbous dark red root that may be eaten as a vegetable, in salads, or pickled
beet sugar *n* the sucrose obtained from sugar beet, identical in composition to cane sugar
beeves (bi:vz) *n arch* the plural of **beef** (sense 2)
BEF *abbrev for* British Expeditionary Force, the British armies that served in France and Belgium 1914–18 and in France 1939–40
befall (bɪ'fɔ:l) *vb* **befalls, befalling, befell, befallen** *arch or literary* 1 (*intr*) to take place 2 (*tr*) to happen to 3 (*intr*; usually foll by *to*) to be due, as by right [OE *befeallan*; see BE-, FALL]
befit (bɪ'fɪt) *vb* **befits, befitting, befitted** (*tr*) to be appropriate to or suitable for [c15 from BE- + FIT[1]] > **be'fitting** *adj* > **be'fittingly** *adv*
befog (bɪ'fɒg) *vb* **befogs, befogging, befogged** (*tr*) 1 to surround with fog 2 to make confused
before (bɪ'fɔ:) *conj* (*subordinating*) 1 earlier than the time when 2 rather than: *he'll resign before he agrees to it* ▷ *prep* 3 preceding in space or time; in front of; ahead of: *standing before the altar* 4 in the presence of: *to be brought before a judge* 5 in preference to: *to put friendship before money* ▷ *adv* 6 at an earlier time; previously 7 in front [OE *beforan*]
beforehand (bɪ'fɔ:,hænd) *adj* (*postpositive*), *adv* early; in advance; in anticipation
befoul (bɪ'faʊl) *vb* (*tr*) to make dirty or foul
befriend (bɪ'frɛnd) *vb* (*tr*) to be a friend to; assist; favour
befuddle (bɪ'fʌdᵊl) *vb* **befuddles, befuddling, befuddled** (*tr*) 1 to confuse 2 to make stupid with drink > **be'fuddlement** *n*
beg (bɛg) *vb* **begs, begging, begged** 1 (when *intr*, often foll by *for*) to solicit (for money, food, etc), esp in the street 2 to ask formally, humbly, or earnestly: *I beg forgiveness; I beg to differ* 3 (*intr*) (of a dog) to sit up with forepaws raised expectantly 4 **beg the question** 4a to evade the issue 4b to put forward an argument that assumes the very point it is supposed to establish or that depends on some other questionable assumption 4c to suggest that a question needs to be asked: *the firm's success begs the question: why aren't more companies doing the same?* 5 **go begging** to be unwanted or unused ▷ See also **beg off** [c13 prob. from OE *bedecian*]

USAGE The use of *beg the question* to mean that a question needs to be asked is considered by some people to be incorrect

began (bɪ'gæn) *vb* the past tense of **begin**
beget (bɪ'gɛt) *vb* **begets, begetting, begot** *or* **begat;**

begotten *or* **begot** (*tr*) 1 to father 2 to cause or create [OE *begietan;* see BE-, GET] > **be'getter** *n*

beggar ('bɛgə) *n* 1 a person who begs, esp one who lives by begging 2 a person who has no money or resources; pauper 3 *chiefly Brit* a fellow: *lucky beggar!* ▷ *vb* (*tr*) 4 to be beyond the resources of (esp in **beggar description**) 5 to impoverish > **'beggardom** *n*

beggarly ('bɛgəlɪ) *adj* meanly inadequate; very poor > **'beggarliness** *n*

beggar-my-neighbour *n* a card game in which one player tries to win all the cards of the other player

beggary ('bɛgərɪ) *n* extreme poverty or need

begin (bɪ'gɪn) *vb* **begins, beginning, began, begun** 1 to start or cause to start (something or to do something) 2 to bring or come into being; arise or originate 3 to start to say or speak 4 (*with a negative*) to have the least capacity (to do something): *he couldn't begin to compete* 5 **to begin with** in the first place [OE *beginnan*]

Begin ('bɛgɪn) *n* **Menachem** (mə'nɑːkɪm) 1913–92, Israeli statesman, born in Poland. In Palestine after 1942, he became a leader of the militant Zionists; prime minister of Israel (1977–83); Nobel peace prize jointly with Sadat 1978. In 1979 he concluded the Camp David treaty with Anwar Sadat of Egypt

beginner (bɪ'gɪnə) *n* a person who has just started to do or learn something; novice

beginning (bɪ'gɪnɪŋ) *n* 1 a start; commencement 2 (*often pl*) a first or early part or stage 3 the place where or time when something starts 4 an origin; source

begird (bɪ'gɜːd) *vb* **begirds, begirding, begirt** *or* **begirded** (*tr*) *poetic* 1 to surround; gird around 2 to bind [OE *begierdan;* see BE-, GIRD[1]]

beg off *vb* (*intr, adv*) to ask to be released from an engagement, obligation, etc

begone (bɪ'gɒn) *sentence substitute* go away! [C14 from BE (imperative) + GONE]

begonia (bɪ'gəʊnjə) *n* a plant of warm and tropical regions, having ornamental leaves and waxy flowers [C18 NL, after Michel *Bégon* (1638–1710), F patron of science]

begorra (bɪ'gɔːrə) *interj* an emphatic exclamation, regarded as characteristic of Irishmen [C19 from *by God!*]

begot (bɪ'gɒt) *vb* a past tense and past participle of **beget**

begotten (bɪ'gɒtᵊn) *vb* a past participle of **beget**

begrime (bɪ'graɪm) *vb* **begrimes, begriming, begrimed** (*tr*) to make dirty; soil

begrudge (bɪ'grʌdʒ) *vb* **begrudges, begrudging, begrudged** (*tr*) 1 to give, admit, or allow unwillingly or with a bad grace 2 to envy (someone) the possession of (something) > **be'grudgingly** *adv*

beguile (bɪ'gaɪl) *vb* **beguiles, beguiling, beguiled** (*tr*) 1 to charm; fascinate 2 to delude; influence by slyness 3 (often foll by *of* or *out of*) to cheat (someone) of 4 to pass pleasantly; while away > **be'guilement** *n* > **be'guiler** *n* > **be'guiling** *adj* > **be'guilingly** *adv*

beguine (bɪ'giːn) *n* 1 a dance of South American origin in bolero rhythm 2 a piece of music in the rhythm of this dance [C20 from Louisiana F, from F *béguin* flirtation]

begum ('beɪgəm) *n* (in certain Muslim countries) a woman of high rank [C18 from Urdu *begam*, from Turkish *begim;* see BEY]

begun (bɪ'gʌn) *vb* the past participle of **begin**

behalf (bɪ'hɑːf) *n* interest, part, benefit, or respect (only in **on (someone's) behalf, on** *or US & Canad* **in behalf of, in this** (*or* **that**) **behalf**) [OE *be halfe*, from *be* by + *halfe* side]

> USAGE *On behalf of* is sometimes wrongly used where *on the part of* is intended. The distinction is that *on behalf of someone* means 'for someone's benefit' or 'representing someone', while *on the part of someone* can be roughly paraphrased as 'by someone'. So, the following example is incorrect: *...another act of apparent negligence, this time not on behalf of the company itself, but on behalf of its banker,* when what is meant is that there was negligence by the company and its bankers

Behan ('biːən) *n* **Brendan** 1923–64, Irish writer, noted esp for his plays *The Quare Fellow* (1954) and *The Hostage* (1958) and for an account of his detention as a member of the Irish Republican Army, *Borstal Boy* (1958)

behave (bɪ'heɪv) *vb* **behaves, behaving, behaved** 1 (*intr*) to act or function in a specified or usual way 2 to conduct (oneself) in a specified way: *he behaved badly* 3 to conduct (oneself) properly or as desired [C15 see BE-, HAVE]

behaviour *or US* **behavior** (bɪ'heɪvjə) *n* 1 manner of behaving 2 **on one's best behaviour** behaving with careful good manners 3 *psychol* the response of an organism to a stimulus 4 the reaction or functioning of a machine, etc, under normal or specified circumstances [C15 from BEHAVE; infl. by ME *havior*, from OF *havoir*, from L *habēre* to have] > **be'havioural** *or US* **be'havioral** *adj*

behavioural science *n* the scientific study of the behaviour of organisms

behaviourism *or US* **behaviorism** (bɪ'heɪvjə,rɪzəm) *n* a school of psychology that regards objective observation of the behaviour of organisms as the only valid subject for study > **be'haviourist** *or US* **be'haviorist** *adj, n* > **be,haviour'istic** *or US* **be,havior'istic** *adj*

behaviour therapy *n* any of various means of treating psychological disorders, such as aversion therapy, that depend on the patient systematically learning new behaviour

behead (bɪ'hɛd) *vb* (*tr*) to remove the head from [OE *behēafdian*, from BE- + *heafod* HEAD]

beheld (bɪ'hɛld) *vb* the past tense and past participle of **behold**

behemoth (bɪ'hiːmɒθ) *n* 1 *Bible* a gigantic beast described in Job 40:15 2 a huge or monstrous person or thing [C14 from Heb. *bĕhēmōth*, pl. of *bĕhēmāh* beast]

Bb

behest (bɪ'hɛst) *n* an order or earnest request [OE *behǣs*, from *behātan;* see BE-, HEST]

behind (bɪ'haɪnd) *prep* 1 in or to a position further back than 2 in the past in relation to: *I've got the exams behind me now* 3 late according to: *running behind schedule* 4 concerning the circumstances surrounding: *the reasons behind his departure* 5 supporting: *I'm right behind you in your application* ▷ *adv* 6 in or to a position further back; following 7 remaining after someone's departure: *he left his books behind* 8 in debt; in arrears: *to fall behind with payments* ▷ *adj* 9 (*postpositive*) in a position further back ▷ *n* 10 *inf* the buttocks 11 *Australian rules football* a score of one point made by kicking the ball over the **behind line** between a goalpost and one of the smaller outer posts (**behind posts**) [OE *behindan*]

behindhand (bɪ'haɪnd,hænd) *adj* (*postpositive*), *adv* 1 remiss in fulfilling an obligation 2 in arrears 3 backward 4 late

Behistun (,beɪhɪ'stuːn), **Bisitun**, *or* **Bisutun** *n* a village in W Iran by the ancient road from Ecbatana to Babylon. On a nearby cliff is an inscription by Darius in Old Persian, Elamite, and Babylonian describing his enthronement

Behn (bɛn) *n* **Aphra** ('æfrə) 1640–89, English dramatist and novelist, best known for her play *The Rover* (1678) and her novel *Oroonoko* (1688)

behold (bɪ'həʊld) *vb* **beholds, beholding, beheld** (*often imperative*) *arch or literary* to look (at); observe [OE *bihealdan;* see BE-, HOLD[1]] > **be'holder** *n*

beholden (bɪ'həʊldᵊn) *adj* indebted; obliged [OE *behealden*, p.p. of *behealdan* to BEHOLD]

behoof (bɪ'huːf) *n, pl* **behooves** *rare* advantage or profit [OE *behōf;* see BEHOVE]

behove (bɪ'həʊv) *vb* **behoves, behoving, behoved** (*tr;*

impersonal) arch to be necessary or fitting for: *it behoves me to arrest you* [OE *behōfian*]

> **USAGE** The mistaken form *behoven* is occasionally used where *beholden* is intended, especially in writing done in a rush, or in speech. *Behove* only ever really occurs in the structure 'it behoves somebody to...', with *ill* often modifying the verb

Behrens ('bɛərənz; *German* 'be:rəns) *n* **Peter** 1868–1940, German architect

Behring *n* **1** (*German* 'be:rɪŋ) **Emil (Adolf) von** ('e:mi:l fɔn) 1854–1917, German bacteriologist, who discovered diphtheria and tetanus antitoxins: Nobel prize for physiology or medicine 1901 **2** ('bɛrɪŋ, 'bɛər-). See (Vitus) **Bering**

Beiderbecke ('baɪdə,bɛk) *n* **Leon Bismarcke,** known as *Bix.* 1903–31, US jazz cornettist, composer, and pianist

beige (beɪʒ) *n* **1a** a very light brown, sometimes with a yellowish tinge **1b** (*as adj*): *beige gloves* **2** a fabric made of undyed or unbleached wool [c19 from OF, from ?]

Beijing ('beɪ'dʒɪŋ) *n* the capital of the People's Republic of China, in the northeast in central Hebei province: dates back to the 12th century BC; consists of two central walled cities, the Outer City (containing the commercial quarter) and the Inner City, which contains the Imperial City, within which is the Purple or Forbidden City; three universities. Pop: 6 633 929 (1999 est). Former English name: **Peking**

▹ www.beijing.gov.cn

being ('bi:ɪŋ) *n* **1** the state or fact of existing; existence **2** essential nature; self **3** something that exists or is thought to exist: *a being from outer space* **4** a person; human being

Beira ('baɪərə) *n* a port in E Mozambique: terminus of a transcontinental railway from Lobito, Angola, through the Democratic Republic of Congo (formerly Zaïre), Zambia, and Zimbabwe. Pop: 298 847 (1991 est)

Beirut *or* **Beyrouth** (,beɪ'ru:t) *n* the capital of Lebanon, a port on the Mediterranean: part of the Ottoman Empire from the 16th century until 1918; four universities (Lebanese, American, French, and Arab). Pop: 1 500 000 (1998 est)

▹ www.middleeast.com/beirut.htm

bejabers (bɪ'dʒeɪbəz) *or* **bejabbers** (bɪ'dʒæbəz) *interj* an exclamation of surprise, emphasis, etc, regarded as characteristic of Irishmen [c19 from *by Jesus!*]

bejewel (bɪ'dʒu:əl) *vb* **bejewels, bejewelling, bejewelled** *or US* **bejewels, bejeweling, bejeweled** (*tr*) to decorate as with jewels

Bekaa *or* **Beqaa** (bɪ'kɑ:) *n* a broad valley in central Lebanon, between the Lebanon and Anti-Lebanon Mountains. Ancient name: **Coelesyria** (,si:li:'sɪrɪə)

bel (bɛl) *n* a unit for comparing two power levels, equal to the logarithm to the base ten of the ratio of the two powers [c20 after A. G. BELL]

Bel (beɪl) *n* (in Babylonian and Assyrian mythology) the god of the earth

belabour *or US* **belabor** (bɪ'leɪbə) *vb* (*tr*) **1** to beat severely; thrash **2** to attack verbally

Belarus ('bɛlə,rʌs, -,rʊs), **Byelorussia,** *or* **Belorussia** (,bjɛləʊ'rʌʃə, ,bɛl-) *n* a republic in E Europe; part of the medieval Lithuanian and Polish empires before occupied by Russia; a Soviet republic (1919–91); in 1997 formed a close political and economic union with Russia: mainly low-lying and forested. Languages: Belarussian; Russian. Religion: believers are mostly Christian. Currency: rouble. Capital: Minsk. Pop: 9 986 000 (2001 est). Area: 207 600 sq km (80 134 sq miles). Also called: **Byelorussian Republic, Bielorussia, White Russia**

▹ www.president.gov.by

▹ www.belarustourist.minsk.by

Belarussian *or* **Belarusian** (,bɛləʊ'rʌʃən) *adj* **1** of, relating to, or characteristic of Belarus, its people, or their language ▹ *n* **2** the official language of Belarus **3** a native or inhabitant of Belarus. Also: **Belorussian, Byelorussian, Bielorussian**

belated (bɪ'leɪtɪd) *adj* late or too late: *belated greetings* > **be'latedly** *adv* > **be'latedness** *n*

Belau (bə'laʊ) *n* **Republic of** a republic comprising a group of islands in the W Pacific, in the W Caroline Islands; administratively part of the UN Trust Territory of the Pacific Islands 1947–87; entered into an agreement of free association with the US (1980); became fully independent in 1994. Chief island: Babelthuap. Capital: Koror. Pop: 19 700 (2001 est). Area: 476 sq km (184 sq miles). Former names: **Pelew Islands, Palau Islands** (until 1981)

▹ www.palaunet.com/palmap1.htm

belay *vb* (bɪ'leɪ) **belays, belaying, belayed** **1** *naut* to secure (a line) to a pin, cleat, or bitt **2** (*usually imperative*) *naut* to stop **3** ('bi:,leɪ) *mountaineering* to secure (a climber) by means of a belay ▹ *n* ('bi:l,eɪ) **4** *mountaineering* the attachment of a climber to a mountain by securing a rope round a rock, piton, etc, to safeguard the party in the event of a fall [OE *belecgan*]

belaying pin *n naut* a cylindrical metal or wooden pin used for belaying

bel canto ('bɛl 'kæntəʊ) *n music* a style of singing characterized by beauty of tone rather than dramatic power [It., lit.: beautiful singing]

belch (bɛltʃ) *vb* **1** (*usually intr*) to expel wind from the stomach noisily through the mouth **2** to expel or be expelled forcefully from inside: *smoke belching from factory chimneys* ▹ *n* **3** an act of belching [OE *bialcan*]

beldam *or* **beldame** ('bɛldəm) *n arch* an old woman [c15 from *bel-* grand (as in *grandmother*), from OF *bel* beautiful, + *dam* mother]

beleaguer (bɪ'li:gə) *vb* (*tr*) **1** to lay siege to **2** to harass [c16 from BE- + obs. *leaguer* a siege]

Belém (*Portuguese* bə'lẽi) *n* a port in N Brazil, the capital of Pará state, on the Pará River: major trading centre for the Amazon basin. Pop: 1 271 615 (2000)

belemnite ('bɛləm,naɪt) *n* **1** an extinct marine mollusc related to the cuttlefish **2** its long pointed conical internal shell: a common fossil [c17 from Gk *belemnon* dart]

Belfast ('bɛlfɑ:st, bɛl'fɑ:st) *n* **1** the capital of Northern Ireland, a port on Belfast Lough in Belfast district, Co. Antrim and Co. Down: became the centre of Irish Protestantism and of the linen industry in the 17th century; seat of the Northern Ireland assembly and executive. Pop: 279 237 (1991) **2** a district of W Northern Ireland, in Co. Antrim and Co. Down. Pop: 277 391 (2001). Area: 115 sq km (44 sq miles)

Belfort (*French* bɛlfɔr) *n* **1** **Territoire de** (tɛritwar də) a department of E France, now in Franche-Comté region: the only part of Alsace remaining to France after 1871. Capital: Belfort. Pop: 137 408 (1999). Area: 608 sq km (237 sq miles) **2** a fortress town in E France: strategically situated in the **Belfort Gap** between the Vosges and the Jura mountains. Pop: 50 125 (1990)

belfry ('bɛlfrɪ) *n, pl* **belfries** **1** the part of a tower or steeple in which bells are hung **2** a tower or steeple [c13 from OF *berfrei*, of Gmc origin]

Belg. *or* **Bel.** *abbrev for:* **1** Belgian **2** Belgium

Belgaum (bɛl'gaʊm) *n* a city in India, in Karnataka: cotton, furniture, leather. Pop: 326 399 (1991)

Belgian ('bɛldʒən) *n* **1** a native or inhabitant of Belgium ▹ *adj* **2** of or relating to Belgium, the Belgians, or their languages

Belgian Congo *n* a former name (1908–60) of (Democratic Republic of) **Congo** (sense 1)

Belgian hare *n* a large red domestic rabbit

Belgium ('bɛldʒəm) *n* a federal kingdom in NW Europe:

at various times under the rulers of Burgundy, Spain, Austria, France, and the Netherlands before becoming an independent kingdom in 1830. It formed the Benelux customs union with the Netherlands and Luxembourg in 1947 and was a founder member of the EEC (now the EU). It consists chiefly of a low-lying region of sand, woods, and heath (the Campine) in the north and west, and a fertile undulating central plain rising to the Ardennes Mountains in the southeast. Languages: French, Flemish (Dutch), German. Religion: Roman Catholic majority. Currency: euro. Capital: Brussels. Pop: 10 268 000 (2001 est). Area: 30 513 sq km (11 778 sq miles)
▷ www.belgium.be
▷ www.visitbelgium.com

Belgorod-Dnestrovski *or* **Byelgorod-Dnestrovski** (*Russian* 'bjɛlgərət-dnjɪ'strɔfskij) *n* a port in the SW Ukraine, on the Dniester estuary: belonged to Romania from 1918 until 1940; under Soviet rule (1944–91). Pop: 56 800 (1991 est). Romanian name: **Cetatea Albă** Former name (until 1946): **Akkerman**

Belgrade (bɛl'greɪd, 'bɛlgreɪd) *n* the capital of the Union of Serbia and Montenegro and of Serbia, in the E part at the confluence of the Danube and Sava Rivers: became the capital of Serbia in 1878 and of Yugoslavia in 1929. Pop: 1 194 878 (1991). Serbo-Croat name: **Beograd**
▷ www.beograd.org.yu
▷ www.belgradetourism.org.yu

Belgravia (bɛl'greɪvɪə) *n* a fashionable residential district of W central London, around Belgrave Square

Belial ('bi:lɪəl) *n* the devil or Satan [c13 from Heb. *bəlīyya'al*, from *bəlīy* without + *ya'al* worth]

belie (bɪ'laɪ) *vb* **belies, belying, belied** (*tr*) **1** to show to be untrue **2** to misrepresent; disguise the nature of **3** to fail to justify; disappoint [OE *belēogan*; see BE-, LIE[1]]

belief (bɪ'li:f) *n* **1** a principle, etc, accepted as true, esp without proof **2** opinion; conviction **3** religious faith **4** trust or confidence, as in a person's abilities, etc

believe (bɪ'li:v) *vb* **believes, believing, believed 1** (*tr; may take a clause as object*) to accept (a statement or opinion) as true: *I believe God exists* **2** (*tr*) to accept the statement or opinion of (a person) as true **3** (*intr; foll by in*) to be convinced of the truth or existence (of): *to believe in fairies* **4** (*intr*) to have religious faith **5** (when *tr, takes a clause as object*) to think, assume, or suppose **6** (*tr*) to think that someone is able to do (a particular action): *I wouldn't have believed it of him* [OE *beliefan*] > **be'lievable** *adj* > **be'liever** *n*

belike (bɪ'laɪk) *adv arch* perhaps; maybe

Belisarius (,bɛlɪ'sɑ:rɪəs) *n* ?505–565 AD, Byzantine general under Justinian I. He recovered North Africa from the Vandals and Italy from the Ostrogoths and led forces against the Persians

Belisha beacon (bə'li:ʃə) *n Brit* a flashing orange globe on a post, indicating a pedestrian crossing on a road [c20 after L. Hore-*Belisha* (1893–1957), Brit politician]

belittle (bɪ'lɪtᵊl) *vb* **belittles, belittling, belittled** (*tr*) **1** to consider or speak of (something) as less important than it really is **2** to make small; dwarf > **be'littlement** *n* > **be'littler** *n*

Belitung (bɪ'li:tʊŋ) *n* another name for **Billiton**

Belize (bə'li:z) *n* a state in Central America, on the Caribbean Sea: site of a Mayan civilization until the 9th century AD; colonized by the British from 1638; granted internal self-government in 1964; became an independent state within the Commonwealth in 1981. Official language: English; Carib and Spanish are also spoken. Currency: Belize dollar. Capital: Belmopan. Pop: 247 000 (2001 est). Area: 22 965 sq km (8867 sq miles). Former name (until 1973): **British Honduras** > **Be'lizean** *adj, n*
▷ www.belize.gov.bz
▷ www.travelbelize.org

Belize City *n* a port and the largest city in Belize, on the Caribbean coast: capital until 1973, when it was abandoned as hurricane-prone. Pop: 48 655 (1994)

bell[1] (bɛl) *n* **1** a hollow, usually metal, cup-shaped instrument that emits a ringing sound when struck **2** the sound made by such an instrument, as for marking the beginning or end of a period of time **3** an electrical device that rings or buzzes as a signal **4** something shaped like a bell, as the tube of certain musical wind instruments, or the corolla of certain flowers **5** *naut* a signal rung on a ship's bell to count the number of half-hour intervals during each of six four-hour watches reckoned from midnight **6** *Brit sl* a telephone call **7 bell, book, and candle 7a** instruments used formerly in excommunications and other ecclesiastical rites **7b** *inf* the solemn ritual ratification of such acts **8 beat** *or* **knock seven bells out of** *Brit inf* to give a severe beating to **9 ring a bell** to sound familiar; recall something previously experienced **10 sound as a bell** in perfect condition ▷ *vb* **11** to be or cause to be shaped like a bell **12** (*tr*) to attach a bell or bells to [OE *belle*]

bell[2] (bɛl) *n* **1** a bellowing or baying cry, esp that of a stag in rut ▷ *vb* **2** to utter (such a cry) [OE *bellan*]

Bell (bɛl) *n* **1 Acton, Currer** ('kʌrə), and **Ellis** pen names of the sisters Anne, Charlotte, and Emily **Brontë 2 Alexander Graham** 1847–1922, US scientist, born in Scotland, who invented the telephone (1876) **3 Sir Francis Henry Dillon** 1851–1936, New Zealand statesman; prime minister of New Zealand (1925) **4 Gertrude** (**Margaret Lowthian**) 1868–1926, British traveller, writer, and diplomat; secretary to the British High Commissioner in Baghdad (1917–26) **5 Joshua** born 1967, US violinist **6** (**Susan**) **Jocelyn**, married name *Jocelyn Burnell*, born 1943, British radio astronomer, who discovered the first pulsar **7 Vanessa**, original name *Vanessa Stephen*. 1879–1961, British painter; a member of the Bloomsbury group, sister of Virginia Woolf and wife of the art critic Clive Bell (1881–1964)

Bb

belladonna (,bɛlə'dɒnə) *n* **1** either of two alkaloid drugs obtained from the leaves and roots of the deadly nightshade **2** another name for **deadly nightshade** [c16 from It., lit.: beautiful lady; supposed to refer to its use as a cosmetic]

Bellarmine ('bɛlɑ:,mi:n) *n* **Saint Robert** 1542–1621, Italian Jesuit theologian and cardinal; an important influence during the Counter-Reformation

Bellay (*French* bɛlɛ) *n* **Joachim du** (ʒɔaʃɛ̃ dy) 1522–60, French poet, a member of the Pléiade

bellbird ('bɛl,bɜ:d) *n* **1** any of several tropical American birds having a bell-like call **2** either of two other birds with a bell-like call: an Australian flycatcher (**crested bellbird**) or a New Zealand honeyeater

bell-bottoms *pl n* trousers that flare from the knee > **'bell-,bottomed** *adj*

bellboy ('bɛl,bɔɪ) *n chiefly US & Canad* a porter or page in a hotel, club, etc. Also called: **bellhop**

bell buoy *n* a navigational buoy with a bell which strikes when the waves move the buoy

belle (bɛl) *n* **1** a beautiful woman **2** the most attractive woman at a function, etc (esp in **belle of the ball**) [c17 from F, fem of BEAU]

Belleau Wood ('bɛləʊ; *French* bɛlo) *n* a forest in N France: site of a battle (1918) in which the US Marines halted a German advance on Paris

belle époque *French* (bɛl epɔk) *n* the period of comfortable well-established life before World War I [lit.: fine period]

Belle Isle *n* an island in the Atlantic, at the N entrance to the **Strait of Belle Isle**, between Labrador and Newfoundland. Area: about 39 sq km (15 sq miles)

Bellerophon (bə'lɛrə,fɒn) *n Greek myth* a hero of Corinth who performed many deeds with the help of the winged horse Pegasus, notably the killing of the Chimera

belles-lettres (*French* bɛllɛtrə) *n* (*functioning as sing*) literary works, esp essays and poetry, valued for their aesthetic content [c17 from F: fine letters] > **bel'letrist** *n*

bellflower ('bɛl,flauə) *n* another name for **campanula**

bellfounder ('bɛl,faundə) *n* a foundry worker who casts bells

bellicose ('bɛlɪ,kəus, -,kəuz) *adj* warlike; aggressive; ready to fight [c15 from L *bellicōsus*, from *bellum* war] > **bellicosity** (,bɛlɪ'kɒsɪtɪ) *n*

belligerati (bɪ,lɪdʒə'rɑːtɪ) *pl n* intellectuals, such as writers, who advocate war or imperialism [c20 from bellig(erent) + *-ati* as in LITERATI]

belligerence (bɪ'lɪdʒərəns) *n* the act or quality of being belligerent or warlike; aggressiveness

belligerency (bɪ'lɪdʒərənsɪ) *n* the state of being at war

belligerent (bɪ'lɪdʒərənt) *adj* **1** marked by readiness to fight or argue; aggressive **2** relating to or engaged in a war ▷ *n* **3** a person or country engaged in war [c16 from L *belliger*, from *bellum* war + *gerere* to wage]

Bellingshausen Sea ('bɛlɪŋz,hauzᵊn) *n* an area of the S Pacific Ocean off the coast of Antarctica [named after Fabian Gottlieb *Bellingshausen* (1778–1852), Russian explorer]

Bellini (*Italian* bel'lini) *n* **1** **Giovanni** (dʒo'vanni) ?1430–1516, Italian painter of the Venetian school, noted for his altarpieces, landscapes, and Madonnas. His father **Jacopo** (?1400–70) and his brother **Gentile** (?1429–1507) were also painters **2** **Vincenzo** (vin'tʃɛntso) 1801–35, Italian composer of operas, esp *La Sonnambula* (1831) and *Norma* (1831)

Bellinzona (*Italian* bellin'tsona) *n* a town in SE central Switzerland, capital of Ticino canton. Pop: 35 860 (1990)

bell jar *n* a bell-shaped glass cover to protect flower arrangements, etc, or to cover apparatus in experiments. Also called: **bell glass**

bellman ('bɛlmən) *n, pl* **bellmen** a man who rings a bell; (formerly) a town crier

bell metal *n* an alloy of copper and tin, with some zinc and lead, used in casting bells

Belloc ('bɛlɒk) *n* **Hilaire** ('hɪlɛə, hɪ'lɛə) 1870–1953, British poet, essayist, and historian, born in France, noted particularly for his verse for children in *The Bad Child's Book of Beasts* (1896) and *Cautionary Tales* (1907)

bellow ('bɛləu) *vb* **1** (*intr*) to make a loud deep cry like that of a bull; roar **2** to shout (something) unrestrainedly, as in anger or pain ▷ *n* **3** the characteristic noise of a bull **4** a loud deep sound, as of pain or anger [c14 prob. from OE *bylgan*]

Bellow ('bɛləu) *n* **Saul** born 1915, US novelist, born in Canada. His works include *Dangling Man* (1944), *The Adventures of Angie March* (1954), *Herzog* (1964), *Humboldt's Gift* (1975), *The Dean's December* (1981), and *Ravelstein* (2000): Nobel prize for literature 1976

bellows ('bɛləuz) *n* (*functioning as sing or pl*) **1** Also: **pair of bellows** an instrument consisting of an air chamber with flexible sides that is used to create a stream of air, as for producing a draught for a fire or for sounding organ pipes **2** a flexible corrugated part, as that connecting the lens system of some cameras to the body [c16 from pl of OE *belig* BELLY]

bell pull *n* a handle, rope, or cord pulled to operate a doorbell or servant's bell

bell push *n* a button pressed to operate an electric bell

bell-ringer *n* a person who rings church bells or musical handbells > **'bell-,ringing** *n*

bells and whistles *pl n* additional features or accessories which are nonessential but very attractive [c20 from the bells and whistles which used to decorate fairground organs]

bell tent *n* a cone-shaped tent having a single central supporting pole

bellwether ('bɛl,wɛðə) *n* **1** a sheep that is used to lead the herd, often bearing a bell **2** a leader, esp a person who is followed blindly

belly ('bɛlɪ) *n, pl* **bellies** **1** the lower or front part of the body of a vertebrate, containing the intestines and other organs; abdomen **2** the stomach, esp when regarded as the seat of gluttony **3** a part that bulges deeply: *the belly of a sail* **4** the inside or interior cavity of something **5** the front, lower, or inner part of something **6** the surface of a stringed musical instrument over which the strings are stretched **7** *Austral & NZ* the wool from a sheep's belly **8** *arch* the womb **9** **go belly up** *inf* to die, fail, or come to an end ▷ *vb* **bellies, bellying, bellied** **10** to swell out or cause to swell out; bulge [OE *belig*]

bellyache ('bɛlɪ,eɪk) *n* **1** an informal term for **stomachache** ▷ *vb* **bellyaches, bellyaching, bellyached** **2** (*intr*) *sl* to complain repeatedly > **'belly,acher** *n*

bellyband ('bɛlɪ,bænd) *n* a strap around the belly of a draught animal, holding the shafts of a vehicle

bellybutton ('bɛlɪ,bʌtᵊn) *n* an informal name for the **navel**. Also called: **tummy button**

belly dance *n* **1** a sensuous dance of Middle Eastern origin, performed by women, with undulating movements of the abdomen ▷ *vb* **belly-dance, belly-dances, belly-dancing, belly-danced** **2** (*intr*) to dance thus > **belly dancer** *n*

belly flop *n* **1** a dive into water in which the body lands horizontally ▷ *vb* **belly-flop, belly-flops, belly-flopping, belly-flopped** **2** (*intr*) to perform a belly flop

bellyful ('bɛlɪ,fʊl) *n* **1** as much as one wants or can eat **2** *sl* more than one can tolerate

belly landing *n* the landing of an aircraft on its fuselage without use of its landing gear

belly laugh *n* a loud deep hearty laugh

Belmopan (,bɛlmə'pæn) *n* (since 1973) the capital of Belize, about 50 miles inland: founded in 1970. Pop: 6490 (1996 est)

▷ www.travel-belize.com/belmopan.htm

Belo Horizonte (*Portuguese* 'bɛːlori'zõːntə) *n* a city in SE Brazil, the capital of Minas Gerais state. Pop: 2 229 697 (2000)

belong (bɪ'lɒŋ) *vb* (*intr*) **1** (foll by *to*) to be the property or possession (of) **2** (foll by *to*) to be bound (to) by ties of affection, allegiance, etc **3** (foll by *to, under, with*, etc) to be classified (with): *this plant belongs to the daisy family* **4** (foll by *to*) to be a part or adjunct (of) **5** to have a proper or usual place **6** *inf* to be acceptable, esp socially [c14 *belongen*, from BE- (intensive) + *longen*, from OE *langian* to belong]

belonging (bɪ'lɒŋɪŋ) *n* secure relationship; affinity (esp in **a sense of belonging**)

belongings (bɪ'lɒŋɪŋz) *pl n* (*sometimes sing*) the things that a person owns or has with him or her

Belorussia (,bjɛləu'rʌʃə, ,bɛl-) *n* a variant spelling of **Belarus** > **,Belo'russian** *n, adj*

Belostok (bjɪla'stɔk) *n* transliteration of the Russian name for **Białystok**

beloved (bɪ'lʌvɪd, -'lʌvd) *adj* **1** dearly loved ▷ *n* **2** a person who is dearly loved

Belovo (*Russian* 'bjɛləvə) *n* a variant spelling of **Byelovo**

below (bɪ'ləu) *prep* **1** at or to a position lower than; under **2** less than **3** south of **4** downstream of **5** unworthy of; beneath ▷ *adv* **6** at or to a lower position **7** at a later place (in something written) **8** *arch* on earth or in hell [c14 *biloghe*, from *bi* BY + *looghe* LOW[1]]

below-the-line *adj* **1** denoting the entries printed below the horizontal line on a company's profit-and-loss account that show how any profit is to be distributed **2** (of an advertising campaign) employing sales promotions, direct marketing, in-store exhibitions and displays, trade shows, sponsorship, and merchandising that do not involve an advertising agency **3** (in national accounts) below the horizontal line separating revenue from capital transactions ▷ Cf **above-the-line**

Bel Paese (ˈbɛl pɑːˈeɪzɪ) *n* a mild creamy Italian cheese [from It., lit.: beautiful country]
Belsen (ˈbɛlsᵊn; *German* ˈbɛlzən) *n* a village in NE Germany: with Bergen, the site of a Nazi concentration camp (1943–45)
Belshazzar (bɛlˈʃæzə) *n* 6th century BC, the son of Nabonidus, coregent of Babylon with his father for eight years: referred to as king and son of Nebuchadnezzar in the Old Testament (Daniel 5:1, 17; 8:1); described as having received a divine message of doom written on a wall at a banquet (**Belshazzar's Feast**)
belt (bɛlt) *n* **1** a band of cloth, leather, etc, worn, usually around the waist, to support clothing, carry weapons, etc, or as decoration **2** a belt worn to show rank (as by a knight), to mark expertise (as in judo), or awarded as a prize (as in boxing) **3** a narrow band, circle, or stripe, as of colour **4** an area where a specific thing is found; zone: *a belt of high pressure* **5** See **seat belt** **6** a band of flexible material between rotating shafts or pulleys to transfer motion or transmit goods: *a fan belt; a conveyer belt* **7** *inf* a sharp blow **8** **below the belt** **8a** *boxing* below the waist **8b** *inf* in an unscrupulous or cowardly way **9** **tighten one's belt** to take measures to reduce expenditure **10** **under one's belt** **10a** in one's stomach **10b** as part of one's experience: *he had a degree under his belt* ▷ *vb* **11** (*tr*) to fasten or attach with or as if with a belt **12** (*tr*) to hit with a belt **13** (*tr*) *sl* to give a sharp blow; punch **14** (*intr*; often foll by *along*) *sl* to move very fast, esp in a car **15** (*tr*) *rare* to encircle [OE, from L *balteus*] > ˈ**belted** *adj*
belt-and-braces *adj* providing double security, in case one security measure should fail: *a belt-and-braces policy*
Beltane (ˈbɛlteɪn, -tən) *n* an ancient Celtic festival with a sacrificial bonfire on May Day [c15 from Scot. Gaelic *bealltainn*]
belter (ˈbɛltə) *n sl* **1** an event, person, quality, etc, that is admirable, outstanding, or thrilling: *a real belter of a match* **2a** a rousing or spirited popular song that is sung loudly and enthusiastically **2b** a person who sings popular songs in a loud and spirited manner
belting (ˈbɛltɪŋ) *n* **1** material for belts **2** belts collectively **3** *inf* a beating
belt man *n Austral & NZ* (formerly) the member of a beach life-saving team who swam out wearing a belt with a line attached
belt out *vb* (*tr, adv*) *inf* to sing or emit sound loudly
belt up *vb* (*adv*) **1** *sl* to stop talking: often imperative **2** to fasten with a belt
beluga (bɪˈluːgə) *n* **1** a large white sturgeon of the Black and Caspian Seas: a source of caviar and isinglass **2** another name for **white whale** [c18 from Russian *byeluga*, from *byely* white]
belvedere (ˈbɛlvɪˌdɪə, ˌbɛlvɪˈdɪə) *n* a building, such as a summerhouse, sited to command a fine view [c16 from It.: beautiful sight]
Bembo[1] (*Italian* ˈbɛmbo) *n* **Pietro** (ˈpjɛːtro) 1470–1547, Italian scholar, poet, and cardinal (1539). His treatise *Prose della volgar lingua* (1525) helped to establish a standard form of literary Italian
bemire (bɪˈmaɪə) *vb* **bemires, bemiring, bemired** (*tr*) **1** to soil as with mire **2** (*usually passive*) to stick fast in mire
bemoan (bɪˈməʊn) *vb* to mourn; lament (esp in **bemoan one's fate**) [OE *bemǣnan*; see BE-, MOAN]
bemuse (bɪˈmjuːz) *vb* **bemuses, bemusing, bemused** (*tr*) to confuse; bewilder
bemused (bɪˈmjuːzd) *adj* preoccupied; lost in thought
ben[1] (bɛn) *Scot* ▷ *n* **1** an inner room in a cottage ▷ *prep, adv* **2** in; within; inside ▷ Cf **but**[2] [OE *binnan*, from BE- + *innan* inside]
ben[2] (bɛn) *n Scot, Irish* a mountain peak: *Ben Lomond* [c18 from Gaelic *beinn*, from *beann*]
Benares (bɪˈnɑːrɪz) *or* **Banaras** *n* the former name of **Varanasi**
Ben Bella (bɛn ˈbɛlə) *n* **Mohammed Ahmed** (ˈɑːmɪd) born 1916, Algerian statesman: first prime minister (1962–65) and president (1963–65) of independent Algeria: overthrown and imprisoned (1965–80)
Benbow (ˈbɛnbəʊ) *n* **John** 1653–1702, English admiral, noted esp for his heroic death during the War of the Spanish Succession
bench (bɛntʃ) *n* **1** a long seat for more than one person, usually lacking a back **2** a plain stout worktable **3** **the bench** (*sometimes cap*) **3a** a judge or magistrate sitting in court **3b** judges or magistrates collectively **4** a ledge in a mine or quarry from which work is carried out **5** (in a gymnasium) a low table, which may be inclined, used for various exercises **6** a platform on which dogs, etc, are exhibited at shows **7** *NZ, old-fashioned.* a natural feature of terrain used by sheep for shelter ▷ *vb* (*tr*) **8** to provide with benches **9** to exhibit (a dog, etc) at a show **10** *US & Canad, sports* to take (a player) out of a game, often for disciplinary reasons [OE *benc*]
bencher (ˈbɛntʃə) *n* (*often pl*) *Brit* **1** a member of the governing body of one of the Inns of Court **2** See **backbencher**
benchmark (ˈbɛntʃˌmɑːk) *n* **1** a mark on a stone post or other permanent feature, used as a reference point in surveying **2** a criterion by which to measure something; reference point ▷ *vb* **3** to measure or test against a benchmark: *the firm benchmarked its pay against that in industry*
bench press *n* a weight-training exercise in which a person lies on a bench and pushes a barbell upwards with both hands from chest level until the arms are straight, then lowers it again
bench test *n* the critical evaluation of a new or repaired component, device, apparatus, etc, prior to installation to ensure that it is in perfect condition
bench warrant *n* a warrant issued by a judge or court directing that an offender be apprehended
bend[1] (bɛnd) *vb* **bends, bending, bent** **1** to form or cause to form a curve **2** to turn or cause to turn from a particular direction: *the road bends left* **3** (*intr*; often foll by *down*, etc) to incline the body; stoop; bow **4** to submit or cause to submit: *to bend before superior force* **5** (*tr*) to turn or direct (one's eyes, steps, attention, etc) **6** (*tr*) *naut* to attach or fasten, as a sail to a boom **7** **bend (someone's) ear** to speak at length to an unwilling listener, esp to voice one's troubles **8** **bend the rules** *inf* to ignore rules or change them to suit one's own convenience ▷ *n* **9** a curved part **10** *naut* a knot in a line for joining it to another or to an object **11** the act of bending **12** **round the bend** *Brit sl* mad [OE *bendan*] > ˈ**bendable** *adj* > ˈ**bendy** *adj*

Bb

bend[2] (bɛnd) *n heraldry* a diagonal line traversing a shield [OE *bend* BAND[2]]
bender (ˈbɛndə) *n inf* **1** a drinking bout **2** a makeshift shelter constructed by placing tarpaulin or plastic sheeting over bent saplings or woven branches
Bendigo (ˈbɛndɪˌgəʊ) *n* a city in SE Australia, in central Victoria: founded in 1851 after the discovery of gold. Pop: 57 427 (1991)
bends (bɛndz) *pl n* (*functioning as sing or pl*) **the** a nontechnical name for **decompression sickness**
bend sinister *n heraldry* a diagonal line bisecting a shield from the top right to the bottom left, typically indicating a bastard line
beneath (bɪˈniːθ) *prep* **1** below, esp if covered, protected, or obscured by **2** not as great or good as would be demanded by: *beneath his dignity* ▷ *adv* **3** below; underneath [OE *beneothan*, from BE- + *neothan* low]
benedicite (ˌbɛnɪˈdaɪsɪtɪ) *n* (esp in Christian religious orders) a blessing or grace [c13 from L, from *benedīcere*, from *bene* well + *dīcere* to speak]
Benedict (ˈbɛnɪˌdɪkt) *n* **Saint** ?480–?547 AD, Italian monk: founded the Benedictine order at Monte Cassino in Italy

in about 540 AD. His *Regula Monachorum* became the basis of the rule of all Western Christian monastic orders. Feast day: July 11 or March 14

Benedict XV *n* original name *Giacomo della Chiesa*. 1854–1922, pope (1914–22); noted for his repeated attempts to end World War I and for his organization of war relief

Benedictine *n* **1** (ˌbɛnɪˈdɪktɪn, -taɪn) a monk or nun who is a member of the order of Saint Benedict **2** (ˌbɛnɪˈdɪktiːn) a greenish-yellow liqueur first made at the Benedictine monastery at Fécamp in France in about 1510 ▷ *adj* (ˌbɛnɪˈdɪktɪn, -taɪn) **3** of or relating to Saint Benedict or his order

benediction (ˌbɛnɪˈdɪkʃən) *n* **1** an invocation of divine blessing **2** a Roman Catholic service in which the congregation is blessed with the sacrament **3** the state of being blessed [c15 from L *benedictio*, from *benedīcere* to bless; see BENEDICITE] > ˌ**beneˈdictory** *adj*

Benedictus (ˌbɛnɪˈdɪktəs) *n* (*sometimes not cap*) *Christianity* **1** a canticle beginning *Benedictus qui venit in nomine Domini* in Latin and *Blessed is he that cometh in the name of the Lord* in English **2** a canticle beginning *Benedictus Dominus Deus Israel* in Latin and *Blessed be the Lord God of Israel* in English

benefaction (ˌbɛnɪˈfækʃən) *n* **1** the act of doing good, esp by giving a donation to charity **2** the donation or help given [c17 from LL *benefactiō*, from L *bene* well + *facere* to do]

benefactor (ˈbɛnɪˌfæktə, ˌbɛnɪˈfæk-) *n* a person who supports or helps a person, institution, etc, esp by giving money > ˈ**beneˌfactress** *fem n*

benefice (ˈbɛnɪfɪs) *n* **1** *Christianity* an endowed Church office yielding an income to its holder; a Church living **2** the property or revenue attached to such an office [c14 from OF, from L *beneficium* benefit, from *bene* well + *facere* to do] > ˈ**beneficed** *adj*

beneficent (bɪˈnɛfɪsᵊnt) *adj* charitable; generous [c17 from L *beneficus*; see BENEFICE] > **beˈneficence** *n*

beneficial (ˌbɛnɪˈfɪʃəl) *adj* **1** (sometimes foll by *to*) advantageous **2** *law* entitling a person to receive the profits or proceeds of property [c15 from LL *beneficiālis*, from L *beneficium* kindness]

beneficiary (ˌbɛnɪˈfɪʃərɪ) *n, pl* **beneficiaries 1** a person who gains or benefits **2** *law* a person entitled to receive funds or other property under a trust, will, etc **3** the holder of a benefice **4** NZ a person who receives government assistance: *social security beneficiary* ▷ *adj* **5** of or relating to a benefice

benefit (ˈbɛnɪfɪt) *n* **1** something that improves or promotes **2** advantage or sake **3** (*sometimes pl*) a payment or series of payments made by an institution or government to a person who is ill, unemployed, etc **4** a theatrical performance, sports event, etc, to raise money for a charity ▷ *vb* **benefits, benefiting, benefited** *or US* **benefits, benefitting, benefitted 5** to do or receive good; profit [c14 from Anglo-F *benfet*, from L *benefactum*, from *bene facere* to do well]

benefit in kind *n* a non-pecuniary benefit, such as a company car or medical insurance, given to an employee

benefit of clergy *n* *Christianity* **1** sanction by the church: *marriage without benefit of clergy* **2** (in the Middle Ages) a privilege that placed the clergy outside the jurisdiction of secular courts

benefit society *n* a US term for **friendly society**

Benelux (ˈbɛnɪˌlʌks) *n* **1** the customs union formed by Belgium, the Netherlands, and Luxembourg in 1948; became an economic union in 1960 **2** these countries collectively

Beneš (*Czech* ˈbɛnɛʃ) *n* **Eduard** (ˈeːduart) 1884–1948, Czech statesman; president of Czechoslovakia (1935–38; 1946–48) and of its government in exile (1939–45)

Benevento (ˌbɛnəˈvɛntəʊ) *n* a city in S Italy, in N Campania: at various times under Samnite, Roman, Lombard, Saracen, Norman, and papal rule. Pop: 64 690 (1990). Ancient name: **Beneventum** (ˌbɛnəˈvɛntʊm)

benevolence (bɪˈnɛvələns) *n* **1** inclination to do good; charity **2** an act of kindness

benevolent (bɪˈnɛvələnt) *adj* **1** intending or showing goodwill; kindly; friendly **2** doing good rather than making profit; charitable: *a benevolent organization* [c15 from L *benevolēns*, from *bene* well + *velle* to wish]

Benfleet (ˈbɛnˌfliːt) *n* a town in SE England, in S Essex on an inlet of the Thames estuary. Pop: 49 701 (1991)

BEng *abbrev for* Bachelor of Engineering

Bengal (bɛnˈgɔːl, bɛŋ-) *n* **1** a former province of NE India, in the great deltas of the Ganges and Brahmaputra Rivers: in 1947 divided into West Bengal (belonging to India) and East Bengal (Bangladesh) **2 Bay of** a wide arm of the Indian Ocean, between India and Myanmar **3** a breed of medium-large cat with a spotted or marbled coat

Bengali (bɛnˈgɔːlɪ, bɛŋ-) *n* **1** a member of a people living chiefly in Bangladesh and in West Bengal **2** Also called: **Bangla** their language ▷ *adj* **3** of or relating to Bengal, the Bengalis, or their language

Bengal light *n* a firework or flare that burns with a bright blue light, formerly used as a signal

Bengbu (ˈbɛŋˈbuː), **Pengpu**, *or* **Pang-fou** *n* a city in E China, in Anhui province. Pop: 506 239 (1999 est)

Benghazi *or* **Bengasi** (bɛnˈgɑːzɪ) *n* a port in N Libya, on the Gulf of Sidra: centre of Italian colonization (1911–42); scene of much fighting in World War II. Pop: 650 000 (1995 est). Ancient names: **Hesperides, Berenice** (bɛrəˈnaɪsɪ)

Benguela (bɛŋˈgwɛlə) *n* a port in W Angola: founded in 1617; a terminus (with Lobito) of the railway that runs from Beira in Mozambique through the Copper Belt of Zambia and Zimbabwe. Pop: 41 000 (latest est)

Ben-Gurion (bɛnˈgʊərɪən) *n* **David**, original name *David Gruen*. 1886–1973, Israeli socialist statesman, born in Poland; first prime minister of Israel (1948–53, 1955–63)

Beni (*Spanish* ˈbeni) *n* a river in N Bolivia, rising in the E Cordillera of the Andes and flowing north to the Marmoré River. Length: over 1600 km (1000 miles)

Benidorm (ˈbɛnɪdɔːm) *n* a coastal resort in W Spain, on the Costa Blanca

benighted (bɪˈnaɪtɪd) *adj* **1** lacking cultural, moral, or intellectual enlightenment **2** *arch* overtaken by night > **beˈnightedness** *n*

benign (bɪˈnaɪn) *adj* **1** showing kindliness; genial **2** (of soil, climate, etc) mild; gentle **3** favourable; propitious **4** *pathol* (of a tumour, etc) not malignant [c14 from OF *benigne*, from L *benignus*, from *bene* well + *gignere* to produce] > **beˈnignly** *adv*

benignant (bɪˈnɪgnənt) *adj* **1** kind; gracious **2** a less common word for **benign** (senses 3, 4) > **beˈnignancy** *n*

benignity (bɪˈnɪgnɪtɪ) *n, pl* **benignities 1** the quality of being benign **2** a kind or gracious act

Beni Hasan (ˈbɛnɪ hæˈsɑːn) *n* a village in central Egypt, on the Nile, with cliff-cut tombs dating from 2000 BC

Benin (bɛˈniːn) *n* **1** a republic in W Africa, on the **Bight of Benin**, a section of the Gulf of Guinea: in the early 19th century a powerful kingdom, famed for its women warriors; became a French colony in 1893, gaining independence in 1960. It consists chiefly of coastal lagoons and swamps in the south, a fertile plain and marshes in the centre, and the Atakora Mountains in the northwest. Official language: French. Religion: animist majority. Currency: franc. Capital: Porto Novo (the government is based in Cotonou) Pop: 6 591 000 (2001 est). Area: 112 622 sq km (43 474 sq miles). Former name (until 1975): **Dahomey 2** a former kingdom of W Africa, powerful from the 14th to the 17th centuries: now a province of S Nigeria: noted for its bronzes > **Beˌniˈnese** *or* **Beninois** (ˌbɛniːˈnwɑː) *adj, n*
▷ www.benintourisme.com

Benin City *n* a city in S Nigeria, capital of Edo state: former capital of the kingdom of Benin. Pop: 229 400 (1996 est)

benison ('bɛnɪzᵊn, -sᵊn) *n arch* a blessing [c13 from OF *beneison*, from L *benedictiō* BENEDICTION]

Benjamin[1] ('bɛndʒəmɪn) *n* **1** *Old Testament* **1a** the youngest and best-loved son of Jacob and Rachel (Genesis 35:16–18; 42:4) **1b** the tribe descended from this patriarch **1c** the territory of this tribe, northwest of the Dead Sea **2** *arch* a youngest and favourite son

Benjamin[2] ('bɛndʒəmɪn) *n* **1 Arthur** 1893–1960, Australian composer. In addition to *Jamaican Rumba* (1938), he wrote five operas and a harmonica concerto (1953) **2** (*German* 'beːniamin) **Walter** ('valtər) 1892–1940, German critic and cultural theorist

Ben Lomond (bɛn 'ləʊmənd) *n* **1** a mountain in W central Scotland, on the E side of Loch Lomond. Height: 973 m (3192 ft) **2** a mountain in NE Tasmania. Height: 1527 m (5010 ft) **3** a mountain in SE Australia, in NE New South Wales. Height: 1520 m (4986 ft)

Bennett ('bɛnɪt) *n* **1 Alan** born 1934, British actor and playwright. His plays include *Forty Years On* (1968), *The Old Country* (1977), *The Madness of George III* (1991), and the monologues for television *Talking Heads* (1987, 1998) **2** (**Enoch**) **Arnold** 1867–1931, British novelist, noted for *The Old Wives' Tale* (1908), *Clayhanger* (1910), and other works set in the Staffordshire Potteries **3 James Gordon** 1837–1931, US newspaper editor, born in Scotland. He founded (1835) the *New York Herald* and introduced techniques of modern news reporting **4 Jill** 1931–90, British actress **5 Richard Bedford**, 1st Viscount. 1870–1947, Canadian Conservative statesman; prime minister (1930–35) **6** Sir **Richard Rodney** born 1936, British composer, noted for film music and his operas *The Mines of Sulphur* (1965) and *Victory* (1970)

Ben Nevis (bɛn 'nɛvɪs) *n* a mountain in W Scotland, in the Grampian mountains: highest peak in Great Britain. Height: 1343 m (4406 ft)

Bennington ('bɛnɪŋtən) *n* a town in SW Vermont: the site of a British defeat (1777) in the War of American Independence. Pop: 16 451 (1990)

Benny ('bɛnɪ) *n* **Jack**, real name *Benjamin Kubelsky*. 1894–1974, US comedian

Benoît de Sainte-Maure (*French* bənwa də sɛ̃t mɔr) *n* 12th-century French trouvère: author of the *Roman de Troie*, which contains the episode of Troilus and Cressida

Benoni (bɪ'nəʊnɪ) *n* a city in NE South Africa: gold mines. Pop: 365 467 (1996)

bent[1] (bɛnt) *adj* **1** not straight; curved **2** (foll by *on*) resolved (to); determined (to) **3** *sl* **3a** dishonest; corrupt **3b** (of goods) stolen **3c** crazy **3d** sexually deviant ▷ *n* **4** personal inclination or aptitude **5** capacity of endurance (esp in **to the top of one's bent**)

bent[2] (bɛnt) *n* **1** short for **bent grass** **2** *arch* any stiff grass or sedge **3** *arch or dialect* heath or moorland [OE *bionot*]

bent grass *n* a perennial grass which has a spreading panicle of tiny flowers sometimes planted for hay or in lawns

Bentham ('bɛnθəm) *n* **Jeremy** 1748–1832, British philosopher and jurist: a founder of utilitarianism. His works include *A Fragment on Government* (1776) and *Introduction to the Principles of Morals and Legislation* (1789)

Benthamism ('bɛnθəmɪzəm) *n* the utilitarian philosophy of Jeremy Bentham, which holds that the ultimate goal of society should be to promote the greatest happiness of the greatest number > **'Benthamite** *n, adj*

benthos ('bɛnθɒs) *n* the animals and plants living at the bottom of a sea or lake [c19 from Gk: depth; rel. to *bathus* deep] > **'benthic** *adj*

Bentinck ('bɛntɪŋk) *n* Lord **William Cavendish** 1774–1839, British statesman, governor general of Bengal (1828–35)

Bentley ('bɛntlɪ) *n* **Edmund Clerihew** 1875–1956, English journalist, noted for his invention of the clerihew

bento *or* **bento box** ('bɛntəʊ) *n, pl* **bentos** a thin box, made of plastic or lacquered wood, divided into compartments, which contain small separate dishes comprising a Japanese meal, esp lunch [from Japanese *bentō* box lunch]

bentonite ('bɛntəˌnaɪt) *n* a clay that swells as it absorbs water: used as a filler in various industries [after Fort *Benton*, Montana, USA, where found]

bentwood ('bɛntˌwʊd) *n* **a** wood bent in moulds after being heated by steaming, used mainly for furniture **b** (*as modifier*): *a bentwood chair*

Benue ('bɛnʊˌeɪ) *n* **1** a state of SE Nigeria, formed in 1976 from part of Benue-Plateau state. Capital: Makurdi. Pop: 3 108 754 (1995 est). Area: 34 059 sq km (13 150 sq miles) **2** a river in W Africa, rising in N Cameroon and flowing west across Nigeria: chief tributary of the River Niger. Length: 1400 km (870 miles)

benumb (bɪ'nʌm) *vb* (*tr*) **1** to make numb or powerless; deaden, as by cold **2** (*usually passive*) to stupefy (the mind, senses, will, etc)

Benxi ('bɛn'ʃiː), **Penchi**, *or* **Penki** *n* an industrial city in SE China, in S Liaoning province. Pop: 827 203 (1999 est)

Benz (bɛnz; *German* bɛnts) *n* **Karl** (**Friedrich**) (karl) 1844–1929, German engineer; designed and built the first car to be driven by an internal- combustion engine (1885)

Benzedrine ('bɛnzɪˌdriːn, -drɪn) *n* a trademark for **amphetamine**

benzene ('bɛnziːn) *n* a colourless flammable poisonous liquid used in the manufacture of styrene, phenol, etc, as a solvent for fats, resins, etc, and as an insecticide. Formula: C_6H_6

benzene ring *n* the hexagonal ring of bonded carbon atoms in the benzene molecule

benzine ('bɛnziːn, bɛn'ziːn) *or* **benzin** ('bɛnzɪn) *n* a volatile mixture of the lighter hydrocarbon constituents of petroleum

Bb

benzo- *or* **benz-** *combining form* **1** indicating a fused benzene ring **2** indicating derivation from benzene or benzoic acid or the presence of phenyl groups [from BENZOIN]

benzoate ('bɛnzəʊˌeɪt, -ɪt) *n* a salt or ester of benzoic acid

benzocaine ('bɛnzəʊˌkeɪn) *n* a white crystalline ester used as a local anaesthetic

benzodiazepine (ˌbɛnzəʊdaɪ'eɪzəˌpiːn) *n* any of a group of chemical compounds that are used as minor tranquillizers, such as diazepam (Valium) and chlordiazepoxide (Librium) [c20 from BENZO- + DI-[1] + AZ(O)- + EP(OXY)- + -INE[2]]

benzoic (bɛn'zəʊɪk) *adj* of, containing, or derived from benzoic acid or benzoin

benzoic acid *n* a white crystalline solid occurring in many natural resins, used in plasticizers and dyes and as a food preservative (**E210**)

benzoin ('bɛnzɔɪn, -zəʊɪn) *n* a gum resin containing benzoic acid, obtained from various tropical Asian trees and used in ointments, perfume, etc [c16 from F *benjoin*, from OCatalan *benjui*, from Ar. *lubān jāwī*, lit.: frankincense of Java]

benzol *or* **benzole** ('bɛnzɒl) *n* **1** a crude form of benzene obtained from coal tar or coal gas and used as a fuel **2** an obsolete name for **benzene**

Beograd (bɛ'ɔgrad) *n* the Serbo-Croat name for **Belgrade**

Beothuk (bɪ'ɒθʊk) *n* a member of an extinct Native Canadian people formerly living in Newfoundland.

bequeath (bɪ'kwiːð, -'kwiːθ) *vb* (*tr*) **1** *law* to dispose of (property) by will **2** to hand down; pass on [OE *becwethan*] > **be'queathal** *n*

bequest (bɪ'kwɛst) *n* **1** the act of bequeathing **2** something that is bequeathed: *a bequest to the University*

of Victoria [C14 BE- + OE -*cwiss* degree]
Berar (bɛ'rɑː) *n* a region of W central India: part of Maharashtra state since 1956; important for cotton growing
berate (bɪ'reɪt) *vb* **berates, berating, berated** (*tr*) to scold harshly
Berber ('bɜːbə) *n* **1** a member of a Caucasoid Muslim people of N Africa **2** the language of this people ▷ *adj* **3** of or relating to this people or their language
Berbera ('bɜːbərə) *n* a port in N Somalia, on the Gulf of Aden. Pop: 70 000 (latest est)
berberis ('bɜːbərɪs) *n* any of a genus of mainly N temperate shrubs. See **barberry** [C19 from Med. L, from ?]
berceuse (*French* bɛrsøz) *n* **1** a lullaby **2** an instrumental piece suggestive of this [C19 from F: lullaby]
Berchtesgaden (*German* 'bɛrçtəsgaːdən) *n* a town in Germany, in SE Bavaria: site of the fortified mountain retreat of Adolf Hitler. Pop: 7865 (1992 est)
bereave (bɪ'riːv) *vb* **bereaves, bereaving, bereaved** (*tr*) (usually foll by *of*) to deprive (of) something or someone valued, esp through death [OE *bereafian*]
bereaved (bɪ'riːvd) *adj* having been deprived of something or someone valued, esp through death
bereavement (bɪ'riːvmənt) *n* **1** the condition having been deprived of something or someone valued, esp through death **2** a death
bereft (bɪ'rɛft) *adj* (usually foll by *of*) deprived; parted (from): *bereft of hope*
beret ('bɛreɪ) *n* a round close-fitting brimless cap [C19 from F *béret*, from OProvençal *berret*]
Berezina (*Russian* bɪrɪzi'na) *n* a river in Belarus, rising in the north and flowing south to the River Dnieper: linked with the River Dvina and the Baltic Sea by the **Berezina Canal**. Length: 563 km (350 miles)
Berezniki (*Russian* bɪrɪzni'ki) *n* a city in E Russia: chemical industries. Pop: 182 200 (1999 est)
berg[1] (bɜːg) *n* short for **iceberg**
berg[2] (bɜːg) *n* a South African word for **mountain**
Berg (bɜːg; *German* bɛrk) *n* **1** **Alban** (**Maria Johannes**) ('albaːn) 1885–1935, Austrian composer: a pupil of Schoenberg. His works include the operas *Wozzeck* (1921) and *Lulu* (1935), a violin concerto (1935), chamber works, and songs **2** **Paul** born 1926, US molecular biologist, the first to identify transfer RNA (1956): Nobel prize for chemistry 1980
Bergamo (*Italian* 'bɛrgamo) *n* a walled city in N Italy, in Lombardy. Pop: 117 837 (2000 est)
bergamot ('bɜːgəˌmɒt) *n* **1** a small Asian tree having sour pear-shaped fruit **2** **essence of bergamot** a fragrant essential oil extracted from the fruit rind of this plant, used in perfumery and some teas (including Earl Grey) **3** a Mediterranean mint that yields a similar oil [C17 from F *bergamote*, from It. *bergamotta*, of Turkic origin]
Bergen *n* **1** (*Norwegian* 'bærgən) a port in SW Norway: chief city in medieval times. Pop: 229 496 (2000 est) **2** ('bɛrxən) the Flemish name for **Mons**
Bergerac (*French* bɛrʒərak) *n* See **Cyrano de Bergerac**
bergie ('bɜːgiː) *n* *S African inf* a vagabond, esp one living on the slopes of Table Mountain in SW South Africa [from Afrik. *berg* mountain]
Bergius (*German* 'bɛrgjʊs) *n* **Friedrich** (**Karl Rudolph**) ('friːdrɪç) 1884–1949, German chemist, who invented a process for producing oil by high-pressure hydrogenation of coal: Nobel prize for chemistry 1931
Bergman ('bɜːgmən) *n* **1** (**Ernst**) **Ingmar** ('ɪŋmar) born 1918, Swedish film and stage director, whose films include *The Seventh Seal* (1956), *Wild Strawberries* (1957), *Persona* (1966), *Scenes from a Marriage* (1974), *Autumn Sonata* (1978), and *Fanny and Alexander* (1982) **2** **Ingrid** 1915–82, Swedish film and stage actress, working in Hollywood 1938–48; noted for her leading roles in many films, including *Casablanca* (1942), *For Whom the Bell Tolls* (1943), *Anastasia* (1956), and *The Inn of the Sixth Happiness* (1958)
bergschrund ('bɛrkʃrʊnt) *n* a crevasse at the head of a glacier [C19 G: mountain crack]
Bergson ('bɜːgsᵊn; *French* bɛrksɔn) *n* **Henri Louis** (ɑ̃ri lwi) 1859–1941, French philosopher, who sought to bridge the gap between metaphysics and science. His main works are *Memory and Matter*(1896, trans. 1911) and *Creative Evolution*(1907, trans. 1911): Nobel prize for literature 1927
bergwind ('bɜːxvənt) *n* a hot dry wind in South Africa blowing from the plateau down to the coast
Beria ('bɛrɪə; *Russian* 'bjerijə) *n* **Lavrenti Pavlovich** (la'vrjentij 'pavləvitʃ) 1899–1953, Soviet chief of secret police; arrested and executed shortly after Stalin's death
beriberi (ˌbɛrɪ'bɛrɪ) *n* a disease, endemic in E and S Asia, caused by dietary deficiency of thiamine (vitamin B_1) [C19 from Sinhalese, by reduplication from *beri* weakness]
Bering *or* **Behring** ('bɛrɪŋ, 'bɛər-; *Danish* 'beːreŋ) *n* **Vitus** ('viːtʊs) 1681–1741, Danish navigator, who explored the N Pacific for the Russians and discovered Bering Island and the Bering Strait
Bering Sea *n* a part of the N Pacific Ocean, between NE Siberia and Alaska. Area: about 2 275 000 sq km (878 000 sq miles)
Bering Strait *n* a strait between Alaska and Russia, connecting the Bering Sea and the Arctic Ocean
berk *or* **burk** (bɜːk) *n* *Brit sl* a stupid person; fool [C20 shortened from *Berkeley* or *Berkshire Hunt*, rhyming slang for *cunt*]
Berkeley[1] ('bɜːklɪ) *n* a city in W California, on San Francisco Bay: seat of the University of California. Pop: 102 743 (2000)
Berkeley[2] *n* **1** ('bɜːklɪ) **Busby** real name *William Berkeley Enos*. 1895–1976, US dance director, noted esp for his elaborate choreography in film musicals **2** ('bɑːklɪ) **George** 1685–1753, Irish philosopher and Anglican bishop, whose system of subjective idealism was expounded in his works *A Treatise concerning the Principles of Human Knowledge* (1710) and *Three Dialogues between Hylas and Philonous* (1713). He also wrote *Essay towards a New Theory of Vision* (1709) **3** ('bɑːklɪ) Sir **Lennox** (**Randal Francis**) 1903–89, British composer; his works include four symphonies, four operas, and the *Serenade for Strings* (1939)
berkelium (bɜː'kiːlɪəm, 'bɜːklɪəm) *n* a radioactive transuranic element produced by bombardment of americium. Symbol: Bk; atomic no.: 97; half-life of most stable isotope, ^{247}Bk: 1400 years [C20 after BERKELEY[1], where it was discovered]
berko ('bɜːkəʊ) *adj* *Austral sl* berserk
Berks (bɑːks) *abbrev for* Berkshire
Berkshire ('bɑːkʃɪə, -ʃə) *n* **1** a historic county of S England: since reorganization in 1974 the River Thames has marked the N boundary while the **Berkshire Downs** occupy central parts; the county council was replaced by six unitary authorities in 1998. Area: 1259 sq km (486 sq miles). Abbreviation: **Berks** **2** a rare breed of pork and bacon pig having a black body and white points
berley *or* **burley** ('bɜːlɪ) *Austral* ▷ *n* **1** bait scattered on water to attract fish **2** *sl* rubbish, nonsense ▷ *vb* (*tr*) **3** to scatter (bait) on water **4** to hurry (someone); urge on [from ?]
berlin (bə'lɪn, 'bɜːlɪn) *n* **1** (*sometimes cap*) Also called: **berlin wool** a fine wool yarn used for tapestry work, etc **2** a four-wheeled two-seated covered carriage, popular in the 18th century [after BERLIN[1]]
Berlin[1] (bɜː'lɪn; *German* bɛr'liːn) *n* the capital of Germany (1871–1945 and from 1990), formerly divided (1945–90) into the eastern sector, capital of East Germany, and the western sectors, which formed an exclave in East German territory closely affiliated with West Germany: a wall dividing the sectors was built in 1961 by the East

German authorities to stop the flow of refugees from east to west; demolition of the wall began in 1989 and the city was formally reunited in 1990: formerly (1618–1871) the capital of Brandenburg and Prussia. Pop: 3 392 900 (1999 est) > **Ber'liner** *n*
▹ www.btm.de
▹ www.dailysoft.com/berlinwall
▹ www.newseum.org/berlinwall

Berlin² (bɜː'lɪn) *n* **1 Irving** original name *Israel Baline*, 1888–1989, US composer and writer of lyrics, born in Russia. His musical comedies include *Annie Get Your Gun* (1946); his most popular song is *White Christmas* **2 Sir Isaiah** 1909–97, British philosopher, born in Latvia, historian, and diplomat. His books include *Historical Inevitability* (1954) and *The Magus of the North* (1993)

Berlioz ('bɛəlɪˌəʊz; *French* bɛrljoz) *n* **Hector (Louis)** (ɛktɔr) 1803–69, French composer, regarded as a pioneer of modern orchestration. His works include the cantata *La Damnation de Faust* (1846), the operas *Les Troyens* (1856–59) and *Béatrice et Bénédict* (1860–62), the *Symphonie fantastique* (1830), and the oratorio *L'Enfance du Christ* (1854)

Berlusconi (*Italian* ˌberlʊs'konɪ) *n* **Silvio** ('silvjo) born 1936, Italian politician and media tycoon: prime minister of Italy (1994, from 2001)

berm *or* **berme** (bɜːm) *n* **1** a narrow path or ledge as at the edge of a slope, road, or canal **2** *mil* a man-made ridge of sand or earth, used as an obstacle to tanks **3** *NZ* the grass verge of a suburban street, usually kept mown [c18 from F *berme*, from Du. *berm*]

Bermejo (*Spanish* ber'mexo) *n* a river in Argentina, rising in the northwest and flowing southeast to the Paraguay River. Length: about 1600 km (1000 miles)

Bermuda (bə'mjuːdə) *n* a UK Overseas Territory consisting of a group of over 150 coral islands (**the Bermudas**) in the NW Atlantic: discovered in about 1503, colonized by the British by 1612, although not acquired by the British crown until 1684. Capital: Hamilton. Pop: 63 500 (2001 est) Area: 53 sq km (20 sq miles) > **Ber'mudan** *or* **Ber'mudian** *n, adj*

Bermuda shorts *pl n* close-fitting shorts that come down to the knees

Bermuda Triangle *n* an area in the Atlantic Ocean bounded by Bermuda, Puerto Rico, and Florida where ships and aeroplanes are alleged to have disappeared mysteriously

Bern (bɜːn; *German* bɛrn) *n* **1** the capital of Switzerland, in the W part, on the Aar River: entered the Swiss confederation in 1353 and became the capital in 1848. Pop: 123 254 (1999 est) **2** a canton of Switzerland, between the French frontier and the Bernese Alps. Capital: Bern. Pop: 943 400 (2000 est). Area: 6884 sq km (2658 sq miles). French name: **Berne** (bɛrn)
▹ www.berne.ch
▹ www.tripadvisor.com/Tourism-g188052-Bern-Vacations.html

Bernadette of Lourdes (ˌbɜːnə'dɛt) *n* **Saint** original name *Marie Bernarde Soubirous*. 1844–79, French peasant girl born in Lourdes, whose visions of the Virgin Mary led to the establishment of Lourdes as a centre of pilgrimage, esp for the sick or crippled. Feast day: Feb. 18

Bernadotte *n* **1** (*Swedish* 'bɛrnadɔt) **Folke** ('fɔlke), Count. 1895–1948, Swedish diplomat, noted for his work with the Red Cross during World War II and as United Nations mediator in Palestine (1948). He was assassinated by Jewish terrorists **2** ('bɜːnəˌdɒt; *French* bɛrnadɔt) **Jean Baptiste Jules** (ʒɑ̃ batist ʒyl) 1764–1844, French marshal under Napoleon; king of Norway and Sweden (1818–44) as Charles XIV

Bernard *n* **1** (*French* bɛrnar) **Claude** (klod) 1813–78, French physiologist, noted for his research on the action of secretions of the alimentary canal and the glycogenic function of the liver **2** ('bɜːnəd) **Saint**, known as *Bernard of Menthon* and the *Apostle of the Alps*. 923–1008, French monk who founded hospices in the Alpine passes. Feast day: Aug. 20

Bernard of Clairvaux *n* **Saint** ?1090–1153, French abbot and theologian, who founded the stricter branch of the Cistercians in 1115

Bernese Alps *or* **Oberland** ('bɜːniːz) *n* a mountain range in SW Switzerland, the N central part of the Alps. Highest peak: Finsteraarhorn, 4274 m (14 022 ft)

Bernhardt ('bɜːnhɑːt; *French* bɛrnar) *n* **Sarah** original name *Rosine Bernard*. 1844–1923, French actress, regarded as one of the greatest tragic actresses of all time

Bernina (bə'niːnə; *Italian* ber'nina) *n* **Piz** a mountain in SE Switzerland, the highest peak of the **Bernina Alps** in the S Rhaetian Alps. Height: 4049 m (13 284 ft)

Bernina Pass *n* a pass in the Alps between SE Switzerland and N Italy, east of Piz Bernina. Height: 2323 m (7622 ft)

Bernini (*Italian* ber'nini) *n* **Gian Lorenzo** (dʒan lo'rɛntso) 1598–1680, Italian painter, architect, and sculptor: the greatest exponent of the Italian baroque

Bernoulli *or* **Bernouilli** (*French* bɛrnuji; *German* bɛr'nʊli) *n* **1 Daniel** (danjɛl), son of Jean Bernoulli. 1700–82, Swiss mathematician and physicist, who developed an early form of the kinetic theory of gases and stated the principle of conservation of energy in fluid dynamics **2 Jacques** (ʒɑk) *or* **Jakob** ('jaːkɔp) 1654–1705, Swiss mathematician, noted for his work on calculus and the theory of probability **3** his brother, **Jean** (ʒɑ̃) *or* **Johann** (jo'han) 1667–1748, Swiss mathematician who developed the calculus of variations

Bernstein ('bɜːnstaɪn, -stiːn) *n* **Leonard** 1918–90, US conductor and composer, whose works include *The Age of Anxiety* (1949), the score of the musical *West Side Story* (1957), and *Mass* (1971)

berretta (bɪ'rɛtə) *n* a variant spelling of **biretta**

berry ('bɛrɪ) *n, pl* **berries 1** any of various small edible fruits such as the blackberry and strawberry **2** *bot* a fruit with two or more seeds and a fleshy pericarp, such as the grape or gooseberry **3** any of various seeds or dried kernels, such as a coffee bean **4** the egg of a lobster, crayfish, or similar animal ▹ *vb* **berries, berrying, berried** (*intr*) **5** to bear or produce berries **6** to gather or look for berries [OE *berie*]

Berry *n* **1** ('bɛrɪ) **Chuck**, full name *Charles Edward Berry*. born 1926, US rock-and-roll guitarist, singer, and songwriter. His frequently covered songs include "Maybellene" (1955), "Roll over Beethoven" (1956), "Johnny B. Goode" (1958), "Memphis, Tennessee" (1959), and "Promised Land" (1964) **2** (*French* bɛri) **Jean de France** (ʒɑ̃ də frɑ̃s), Duc de. 1340–1416, French prince, son of King John II; coregent (1380–88) for Charles VI and a famous patron of the arts

berserk (bə'zɜːk, -'sɜːk) *adj* **1** frenziedly violent or destructive (esp in **go berserk**) ▹ *n* **2** Also called: **berserker** one of a class of ancient Norse warriors who fought frenziedly [c19 Icelandic *berserkr*, from *björn* bear + *serkr* shirt]

berth (bɜːθ) *n* **1** a bed or bunk in a vessel or train **2** *naut* a place assigned to a ship at a mooring **3** *naut* sufficient room for a ship to manoeuvre **4 give a wide berth to** to keep clear of **5** *inf* a job, esp as a member of a ship's crew ▹ *vb* **6** (*tr*) *naut* to assign a berth to (a vessel) **7** *naut* to dock (a vessel) **8** (*tr*) to provide with a sleeping place **9** (*intr*) *naut* to pick up a mooring in an anchorage [c17 prob. from BEAR¹ + -TH¹]

bertha ('bɜːθə) *n* a wide deep collar, often of lace, usually to cover a low neckline [c19 from F *berthe*, from *Berthe*, 8th-cent. Frankish queen]

Bertolucci (*Italian* berto'luttʃi) *n* **Bernardo** (ber'nardo) born 1940, Italian film director: his films include *The Spider's Stratagem* (1970), *The Conformist* (1970), *1900* (1976), *The Last Emperor* (1987), *The Sheltering Sky* (1990), and *Besieged* (1999)

Bb

Berwick ('bɛrɪk) *n* **James Fitzjames**, Duke of Berwick. 1670–1734, marshal of France and illegitimate son of James II of England. He led French forces during the War of the Spanish Succession (1701–14)

Berwickshire ('bɛrɪkʃɪə, -ʃə) *n* (until 1975) a county of SE Scotland: part of the Borders region from 1975 to 1996, now part of Scottish Borders council area

Berwick-upon-Tweed (twiːd) *n* a town in N England, in N Northumberland at the mouth of the Tweed: much involved in border disputes between England and Scotland between the 12th and 16th centuries; neutral territory 1551–1885. Pop: 13 544 (1991). Also called: **Berwick**

beryl ('bɛrɪl) *n* a green, blue, yellow, pink, or white hard mineral consisting of beryllium aluminium silicate in hexagonal crystalline form. Emerald and aquamarine are transparent varieties [C13 from OF, from L, from Gk *bērullos*] > '**beryline** *adj*

beryllium (bɛ'rɪlɪəm) *n* a corrosion-resistant toxic silvery-white metallic element used mainly in X-ray windows and alloys. Symbol: Be; atomic no.: 4; atomic wt.: 9.012 [C19 from L, from Gk *bērullos*]

Berzelius (bə'ziːlɪəs; *Swedish* bær'seːlius) *n* Baron **Jöns Jakob** ('jœns 'jaːkɔp) 1779–1848, Swedish chemist, who invented the present system of chemical symbols and formulas, discovered several elements, and determined the atomic and molecular weight of many substances

Besançon (*French* bəzɑ̃sɔ̃) *n* a city in E France, on the Doubs River: university (1422). Pop: 117 304 (1999)

Besant ('bɛzᵊnt, bɪ'zænt) *n* **Annie**, *née* **Wood**. 1847–1933, British theosophist, writer, and political reformer in England and India

beseech (bɪ'siːtʃ) *vb* **beseeches, beseeching, besought** *or* **beseeched** (*tr*) to ask (someone) earnestly (to do something or for something); beg [C12 see BE-, SEEK]

beseem (bɪ'siːm) *vb arch* to be suitable for or worthy of

beset (bɪ'sɛt) *vb* **besets, besetting, beset** (*tr*) **1** (esp of dangers or temptations) to trouble or harass constantly **2** to surround or attack from all sides **3** *arch* to cover with, esp with jewels

besetting (bɪ'sɛtɪŋ) *adj* tempting, harassing, or assailing (esp in **besetting sin**)

beside (bɪ'saɪd) *prep* **1** next to; at, by, or to the side of **2** as compared with **3** away from; wide of **4** *arch* besides **5 beside oneself** (*postpositive; often foll by* with) overwhelmed; overwrought: *beside oneself with grief* ▷ *adv* **6** at, by, to, or along the side of something or someone [OE *be sīdan*; see BY, SIDE]

> USAGE There is occasional confusion between *beside* as a preposition, which can mean 'next to', and *besides*, which means 'in addition to'. The following sentence, taken from the Bank of English, illustrates the mistake: *beside all these considerations, trees are beautiful – or most of them are.* Conversely, the following is correct: *but that is beside* (not *besides*) *the point*

besides (bɪ'saɪdz) *prep* **1** apart from; even considering ▷ *sentence connector* **2** anyway; moreover ▷ *adv* **3** as well

besiege (bɪ'siːdʒ) *vb* **besieges, besieging, besieged** (*tr*) **1** to surround (a fortified area) with military forces to bring about its surrender **2** to crowd round; hem in **3** to overwhelm, as with requests > **be'sieger** *n*

besmear (bɪ'smɪə) *vb* (*tr*) **1** to smear over; daub **2** to sully; defile (often in **besmear (a person's) reputation**)

besmirch (bɪ'smɜːtʃ) *vb* (*tr*) **1** to make dirty; soil **2** to reduce the brightness of **3** to sully (often in **besmirch (a person's) name**)

besom[1] ('biːzəm) *n* a broom, esp one made of a bundle of twigs tied to a handle [OE *besma*]

besom[2] ('bɪzəm) *n Scot & N English dialect* a derogatory term for a **woman** [?from OE *bysen* example; rel. to ON *bysn* wonder]

besotted (bɪ'sɒtɪd) *adj* **1** stupefied with drink **2** infatuated; doting **3** foolish; muddled

besought (bɪ'sɔːt) *vb* a past tense and past participle of **beseech**

bespangle (bɪ'spæŋgᵊl) *vb* **bespangles, bespangling, bespangled** (*tr*) to cover or adorn with or as if with spangles

bespatter (bɪ'spætə) *vb* (*tr*) **1** to splash, as with dirty water **2** to defile; besmirch

bespeak (bɪ'spiːk) *vb* **bespeaks, bespeaking, bespoke; bespoken** *or* **bespoke** (*tr*) **1** to engage or ask for in advance **2** to indicate or suggest: *this act bespeaks kindness* **3** *poetic* to address

bespectacled (bɪ'spɛktəkᵊld) *adj* wearing spectacles

bespoke (bɪ'spəʊk) *adj chiefly Brit* **1** (esp of a suit, jacket, etc) made to the customer's specifications **2** making or selling such suits, jackets, etc: *a bespoke tailor*

besprinkle (bɪ'sprɪŋkᵊl) *vb* **besprinkles, besprinkling, besprinkled** (*tr*) to sprinkle all over with liquid, powder, etc

Bessarabia (ˌbɛsə'reɪbɪə) *n* a region in E Europe, mostly in Moldova and the Ukraine: long disputed by the Turks and Russians; a province of Romania from 1918 until 1940. Area: about 44 300 sq km (17 100 sq miles)

Bessel ('bɛsᵊl) *n* **Friedrich Wilhelm** ('friːdrɪç 'vɪlhɛlm) 1784–1846, German astronomer and mathematician. He made the first authenticated measurement of a star's distance (1841) and systematized a series of mathematical functions used in physics

Bessemer process ('bɛsɪmə) *n* (formerly) a process for producing steel by blowing air through molten pig iron in a **Bessemer converter** (a refractory-lined furnace): impurities are removed and the carbon content is controlled [C19 after Sir Henry *Bessemer* (1813–98), E engineer]

best (bɛst) *adj* **1** the superlative of **good** **2** most excellent of a particular group, category, etc **3** most suitable, desirable, etc **4 the best part of** most of ▷ *adv* **5** the superlative of **well**[1] **6** in a manner surpassing all others; most excellently, attractively, etc ▷ *n* **7 the best** the most outstanding or excellent person, thing, or group in a category **8** the utmost effort **9** a winning majority **10** Also: **all the best** best wishes **11** a person's smartest outfit of clothing **12 at best 12a** in the most favourable interpretation **12b** under the most favourable conditions **13 for the best 13a** for an ultimately good outcome **13b** with good intentions **14 get** *or* **have the best of** to defeat or outwit **15 give (someone) the best** to concede (someone's) superiority **16 make the best of** to cope as well as possible with ▷ *vb* **17** (*tr*) to gain the advantage over or defeat: *I had bested him at chess* [OE *betst*]

Best (bɛst) *n* **1 Charles Herbert** 1899–1978, Canadian physiologist: associated with Banting and Macleod in their discovery of insulin in 1922 **2 George** born 1946, Northern Ireland footballer

bestead (bɪ'stɛd) *arch* ▷ *vb* **besteads, besteading, besteaded; besteaded** *or* **bestead** **1** (*tr*) to help; avail ▷ *adj also* **bested** **2** placed; situated [C13 see BE-, STEAD]

bestial ('bɛstɪəl) *adj* **1** brutal or savage **2** sexually depraved **3** lacking in refinement; brutish **4** of or relating to a beast [C14 from LL *bestiālis*, from L *bestia* BEAST]

bestiality (ˌbɛstɪ'ælɪtɪ) *n, pl* **bestialities** **1** bestial behaviour **2** sexual activity between a person and an animal

bestialize *or* **bestialise** ('bɛstɪəˌlaɪz) *vb* **bestializes, bestializing, bestialized** *or* **bestialises, bestialising, bestialised** (*tr*) to make bestial or brutal

bestiary ('bɛstɪərɪ) *n, pl* **bestiaries** a moralizing medieval collection of descriptions of real and mythical animals

bestir (bɪ'stɜː) *vb* **bestirs, bestirring, bestirred** (*tr*) to cause (oneself) to become active; rouse

best man *n* the male attendant of the bridegroom at a wedding

bestow (bɪˈstəʊ) *vb (tr)* **1** to present (a gift) or confer (an honour) **2** *arch* to apply (energy, resources, etc) **3** *arch* to house (a person) or store (goods) > **beˈstowal** *n*

best practice *n* the recognized methods of correctly running businesses or providing services

bestrew (bɪˈstruː) *vb* **bestrews, bestrewing, bestrewed; bestrewn** *or* **bestrewed** *(tr)* to scatter or lie scattered over (a surface)

bestride (bɪˈstraɪd) *vb* **bestrides, bestriding, bestrode** *or (arch)* **bestrid; bestridden** *or (arch)* **bestrid** *(tr)* **1** to have or put a leg on either side of **2** to extend across; span **3** to stride over or across

bestseller (ˌbɛstˈsɛlə) *n* **1** a book or other product that has sold in great numbers **2** the author of one or more such books, etc > ˌ**bestˈselling** *adj*

bet (bɛt) *n* **1** an agreement between two parties that a sum of money or other stake will be paid by the loser to the party who correctly predicts the outcome of an event **2** the stake risked **3** the predicted result in such an agreement **4** a person, event, etc, considered as likely to succeed or occur **5** a course of action (esp in **one's best bet**) **6** *inf* an opinion: *my bet is that you've been up to no good* ▷ *vb* **bets, betting, bet** *or* **betted 7** (when *intr* foll by *on* or *against*) to make or place a bet with (a person or persons) **8** *(tr)* to stake (money, etc) in a bet **9** *(tr; may take a clause as object) inf* to predict (a certain outcome) **10 you bet** *inf* of course; naturally [C16 prob. short for ABET]

beta (ˈbiːtə) *n* **1** the second letter in the Greek alphabet (Β or β) **2** the second in a group or series [from Gk *bēta*, from Heb.; see BETH]

beta-blocker *n* any of a class of drugs, such as propranolol, that decrease the contraction and speed of the heart: used in the treatment of high blood pressure and angina

betacarotene (ˌbiːtəˈkærəˌtiːn) *n* the most important form of the plant pigment carotene, which occurs in milk, vegetables, and other foods and, when eaten by man and animals, is converted in the body to vitamin A

beta coefficient *n stock exchange* a measure of the extent to which a particular security rises or falls in value in response to market movements

beta decay *n* the radioactive change in an atomic nucleus accompanying the emission of an electron

betake (bɪˈteɪk) *vb* **betakes, betaking, betook, betaken** *(tr)* **1 betake oneself** to go; move **2** *arch* to apply (oneself) to

beta particle *n* a high-speed electron or positron emitted by a nucleus during radioactive decay or nuclear fission

beta ray *n* a stream of beta particles

beta rhythm *or* **wave** *n physiol* the normal electrical activity of the cerebral cortex

beta stock *n* any of the second rank of active securities on the London stock exchange, of which there are about 500. Continuous display of prices by market makers is required but not immediate publication of transactions

betatron (ˈbiːtəˌtrɒn) *n* a type of particle accelerator for producing high-energy beams of electrons by magnetic induction

betel (ˈbiːtᵊl) *n* an Asian climbing plant, the leaves of which are chewed by the peoples of SE Asia [C16 from Port., from Malayalam *vettila*]

betel nut *n* the seed of the betel palm, chewed with betel leaves and lime by people in S and SE Asia as a digestive stimulant and narcotic

betel palm *n* a tropical Asian feather palm

bête noire *French* (bɛt nwar) *n, pl* ***bêtes noires*** (bɛt nwar). a person or thing that one particularly dislikes or dreads [lit.: black beast]

beth (bɛt) *n* the second letter of the Hebrew alphabet [from Heb. *bēth-*, *bayith* house]

Bethany (ˈbɛθənɪ) *n* a village in the West Bank, near Jerusalem at the foot of the Mount of Olives: in the New Testament, the home of Lazarus and the lodging place of Jesus during Holy Week

Bethe (ˈbeɪtə) *n* **Hans Albrecht** (hans ˈalbrɛçt) born 1906, US physicist, born in Germany; noted for his research on astrophysics and nuclear physics: Nobel prize for physics 1967

Bethel (ˈbɛθəl) *n* **1** an ancient town in the West Bank, near Jerusalem: in the Old Testament, the place where the dream of Jacob occurred (Genesis 28:19) **2** a chapel of any of certain Nonconformist Christian sects **3** a seamen's chapel [C17 from Hebrew *bēth 'Ēl* house of God]

Bethesda (bəˈθɛzdə) *n* **1** *New Testament* a pool in Jerusalem reputed to have healing powers, where a paralytic was healed by Jesus (John 5:2) **2** a chapel of any of certain Nonconformist Christian sects

bethink (bɪˈθɪŋk) *vb* **bethinks, bethinking, bethought** *arch or dialect* **1** to cause (oneself) to consider or meditate **2** *(tr; often foll by of)* to remind (oneself)

Bethlehem (ˈbɛθlɪˌhɛm, -lɪəm) *n* a town in the West Bank, near Jerusalem: birthplace of Jesus and early home of King David

Bethmann Hollweg (*German* ˈbeːtman ˈhɔlveːk) *n* **Theobald von** (ˈteːobalt fɔn) 1856–1921, chancellor of Germany (1909–17)

Bethsaida (bɛθˈseɪdə) *n* a ruined town in N Israel, near the N shore of the Sea of Galilee

betide (bɪˈtaɪd) *vb* **betides, betiding, betided** to happen or happen to (often in **woe betide (someone)**) [C13 from BE- + obs. *tide* to happen]

betimes (bɪˈtaɪmz) *adv arch* **1** in good time; early **2** soon [C14 *bitimes*; see BY, TIME]

Betjeman (ˈbɛtʃəmən) *n* Sir **John** 1906–84, English poet, noted for his nostalgic and humorous verse and essays and for his concern for the preservation of historic buildings, esp of the Victorian era. Poet laureate (1972–84)

betoken (bɪˈtəʊkən) *vb (tr)* **1** to indicate; signify **2** to portend; augur

betony (ˈbɛtənɪ) *n, pl* **betonies 1** a Eurasian plant with a spike of reddish-purple flowers, formerly used in medicine and dyeing **2** any of several related plants [C14 from OF, from L]

betray (bɪˈtreɪ) *vb (tr)* **1** to hand over or expose (one's nation, friend, etc) treacherously to an enemy **2** to disclose (a secret, confidence, etc) treacherously **3** to break (a promise) or be disloyal to (a person's trust) **4** to show signs of; indicate **5** to reveal unintentionally: *his grin betrayed his satisfaction* [C13 from BE- + *trayen*, from OF, from L *trādere* to hand over] > **beˈtrayal** *n* > **beˈtrayer** *n*

betroth (bɪˈtrəʊð) *vb (tr) arch* to promise to marry or to give in marriage [C14 *betreuthen*, from BE- + *treuthe* TROTH, TRUTH]

betrothal (bɪˈtrəʊðəl) *n* **1** engagement to be married **2** a mutual promise to marry

betrothed (bɪˈtrəʊðd) *adj* **1** engaged to be married ▷ *n* **2** the person to whom one is engaged; fiancé or fiancée

better (ˈbɛtə) *adj* **1** the comparative of **good 2** more excellent than others **3** more suitable, advantageous, attractive, etc **4** improved or fully recovered in health **5 better off** in more favourable circumstances, esp financially **6 the better part of** a large part of ▷ *adv* **7** the comparative of **well**[1] **8** in a more excellent manner; more advantageously, attractively, etc **9** in or to a greater degree or extent; more **10 had better** would be wise, sensible, etc, to: *I had better be off* **11 think better of 11a** to change one's mind about (a course of action, etc) after reconsideration **11b** to rate more highly ▷ *n* **12 the better** something that is the more excellent, useful, etc, of two such things **13** *(usually pl)* a person who is superior, esp in social standing or ability **14 for the better** by way of improvement **15 get the better of**

to defeat, outwit, or surpass ▹ *vb* **16** to make or become better **17** (*tr*) to improve upon; surpass [OE *betera*]

better half *n humorous* one's spouse

betterment ('bɛtəmənt) *n* **1** a change for the better; improvement **2** *property law* an improvement effected on real property that enhances the value of the property

betting shop *n* (in Britain) a licensed bookmaker's premises not on a racecourse

between (bɪ'twi:n) *prep* **1** at a point or in a region intermediate to two other points in space, times, degrees, etc **2** in combination; together: *between them, they saved enough money to buy a car* **3** confined or restricted to: *between you and me* **4** indicating a reciprocal relation or comparison **5** indicating two or more alternatives ▹ *adv also* **in between 6** between one specified thing and another [OE *betwēonum;* see TWO, TWAIN]

> USAGE After *distribute* and words with a similar meaning, *among* should be used rather than *between*: *this enterprise issued shares which were distributed among its workers*

betweentimes (bɪ'twi:n,taɪmz) *or* **betweenwhiles** *adv* between other activities; during intervals

betwixt (bɪ'twɪkst) *prep, adv* **1** *arch* another word for **between 2 betwixt and between** in an intermediate or indecisive position [OE *betwix*]

Betws-y-Coed (,bɛtsɪ'kɔɪd) *n* a village in N Wales, in Conwy county borough, on the River Conwy: noted for its scenery. Pop: 2860 (1991)

Beulah ('bju:lə) *n Old Testament* the land of Israel (Isaiah 62:4) [Heb., lit.: married woman]

Beuthen ('bɔytən) *n* the German name for **Bytom**

BeV (in the US) *abbrev for* gigaelectronvolts (GeV) [c20 from *b(illion) e(lectron) v(olts)*]

Bevan ('bɛvən) *n* **Aneurin** (ə'naɪərɪn), known as *Nye*. 1897–1960, British Labour statesman, born in Wales: noted for his oratory. As minister of health (1945–51) he introduced the National Health Service (1948)

bevel ('bɛvəl) *n* **1** Also called: **cant** a surface that meets another at an angle other than a right angle ▹ *vb* **bevels, bevelling, bevelled** *or US* **bevels, beveling, beveled 2** (*intr*) to be inclined; slope **3** (*tr*) to cut a bevel on (a piece of timber, etc) [c16 from OF, from *baer* to gape; see BAY[1]]

bevel gear *n* a gear having teeth cut into a conical surface. Two such gears mesh together to transmit power between two shafts at an angle

bevel square *n* a tool with an adjustable arm that can be set to mark out an angle

beverage ('bɛvərɪdʒ, 'bɛvrɪdʒ) *n* any drink, usually other than water [c13 from OF *bevrage*, from *beivre* to drink, from L *bibere*]

beverage room *n Canad* another name for **beer parlour**

Beveridge ('bɛvərɪdʒ) *n* **William Henry**, 1st Baron Beveridge. 1879–1963, British economist, whose *Report on Social Insurance and Allied Services* (1942) formed the basis of social-security legislation in Britain

Beverley ('bɛvəlɪ) *n* a market town in NE England, the administrative centre of the East Riding of Yorkshire. Pop: 23 632 (1991)

Beverly Hills ('bɛvəlɪ) *n* a city in SW California, near Los Angeles: famous as the home of film stars. Pop: 31 970 (1990)

Bevin ('bɛvɪn) *n* **Ernest** 1881–1951, British Labour statesman and trade unionist, who was largely responsible for the creation of the Transport and General Workers' Union (1922): minister of labour (1940–45); foreign secretary (1945–51)

bevvy ('bɛvɪ) *n, pl* **bevvies** *dialect* **1** a drink, esp an alcoholic one **2** a session of drinking [prob. from OF *bevee, buvee* drinking]

bevy ('bɛvɪ) *n, pl* **bevies 1** a flock of quails **2** a group, esp of girls [c15 from ?]

bewail (bɪ'weɪl) *vb* to express great sorrow over (a person or thing); lament > **be'wailer** *n*

beware (bɪ'wɛə) *vb* (*usually used in the imperative or infinitive; often foll by of*) to be cautious or wary (of); be on one's guard (against) [c13 *be war*, from BE (imperative) + *war* WARY]

Bewick ('bju:ɪk) *n* **Thomas** 1753–1828, English wood engraver; his best-known works are *Chillingham Bull* (1789), a large woodcut, *Aesop's Fables* (1818), and his *History of British Birds* (1797–1804)

bewilder (bɪ'wɪldə) *vb* (*tr*) to confuse utterly; puzzle [c17 see BE-, WILDER] > **be'wildering** *adj* > **be'wilderingly** *adv* > **be'wilderment** *n*

bewitch (bɪ'wɪtʃ) *vb* (*tr*) **1** to attract and fascinate **2** to cast a spell over [c13 *bewicchen;* see BE-, WITCH[1]] > **be'witching** *adj*

bewray (bɪ'reɪ) *vb* (*tr*) an obsolete word for **betray** [c13 from BE- + OE *wrēgan* to accuse]

Bexhill (-on-Sea) (,bɛks'hɪl) *n* a resort in S England, in East Sussex on the English Channel. Pop: 38 905 (1991)

Bexley ('bɛkslɪ) *n* a borough of SE Greater London. Pop: 218 307 (2001). Area: 61 sq km (23 sq miles)

bey (beɪ) *n* **1** (in the Ottoman Empire) a title given to provincial governors **2** (in modern Turkey) a title of address, corresponding to *Mr* ▹ Also called: **beg** [c16 Turkish: lord]

Beyoğlu ('beɪɔ:lu:) *n* a district of Istanbul, north of the Golden Horn: the European quarter. Former name: **Pera**

beyond (bɪ'jɒnd) *prep* **1** at or to a point on the other side of; at or to the further side of: *beyond those hills* **2** outside the limits or scope of ▹ *adv* **3** at or to the other or far side of something **4** outside the limits of something ▹ *n* **5 the beyond** the unknown, esp life after death in certain religious beliefs [OE *begeondan;* see BY, YONDER]

Beyrouth (beɪ'ru:t, 'beɪru:t) *n* a variant spelling of **Beirut**

Beza (*French* bəza) *or* **de Bèze** (*French* də bɛz) *n* **Théodore** (teodɔr)1519–1605, French Calvinist theologian and scholar, who lived in Switzerland. He succeeded Calvin as leader of the Swiss Protestants

bezel ('bɛzəl) *n* **1** the sloping face adjacent to the working edge of a cutting tool **2** the upper oblique faces of a cut gem **3** a grooved ring or part holding a gem, watch crystal, etc **4** a retaining outer rim used in vehicle instruments such as tachometers and speedometers **5** a small indicator light used in vehicle instrument panels [c17 prob. from F *biseau*]

Béziers (*French* bezje) *n* a city in S France: scene of a massacre (1209) during the Albigensian Crusade. It is a centre of the wine trade. Pop: 70 996 (1990)

bezique (bɪ'zi:k) *n* **1** a card game for two or more players using two packs with nothing below a seven **2** (in this game) the queen of spades and jack of diamonds declared together [c19 from F *bésigue*, from ?]

Bezwada ('beɪz,wɑ:də) *n* the former name of **Vijayawada**

B/F *or* **b/f** *book-keeping abbrev for* brought forward

BFN *text messaging abbrev for* bye for now

BFPO *abbrev for* British Forces Post Office

Bhagalpur ('bɑ:gəl,pʊə) *n* a city in India, in Bihar: agriculture, textiles, university (1960). Pop: 253 225 (1991)

bhaji ('bɑ:dʒɪ) *n, pl* **bhaji, bhajis,** *or* **bhajia** ('bɑ:dʒɪə) an Indian savoury made of chopped vegetables mixed in a spiced batter and deep-fried [Hindi *bhājī* fried vegetables]

bhang *or* **bang** (bæŋ) *n* a preparation of the leaves and flower tops of Indian hemp having psychoactive properties: much used in India [c16 from Hindi *bhāng*]

bhangra ('bæŋgrə) *n* a type of Asian pop music that combines elements of traditional Punjabi music with Western pop [c20 from Hindi]

▹ http://preview.bhangraomega.com

bharal *or* **burhel** ('bʌrəl) *n* a wild Himalayan sheep with a bluish-grey coat [Hindi]

Bharat ('bʌrʌt) *n* transliteration of the Hindi name for **India**

Bhaskar ('bʌsˌkɑː) *n* **Sanjeev** ('sændʒiːv) born 1964, British actor and writer of Asian origin, known for the TV comedy series *Goodness Gracious Me* (1998) and *The Kumars at No. 42* (2001–02)
Bhatpara (bɑːt'pɑːrə) *n* a city in NE India, in West Bengal on the Hooghly River: jute and cotton mills. Pop: 304 952 (1991)
Bhavnagar ('bɑːvnəgə) *n* a port in W India, in S Gujarat. Pop: 402 338 (1991)
bhindi ('bɪndɪ) *n* the okra as used in Indian cooking [Hindi]
Bhopal (bəʊ'pɑːl) *n* a city in central India, the capital of Madhya Pradesh state and of the former state of Bhopal: site of a poisonous gas leak from a US-owned factory, which killed over 2000 people in 1984. Pop: 1 062 771 (1991)
bhp *abbrev for* brake horsepower
BHP *Austral abbrev for* Broken Hill Proprietary
Bhubaneswar (ˌbʊbə'neɪʃwə) *n* an ancient city in E India, the capital of Orissa state: many temples built between the 7th and 16th centuries. Pop: 411 542 (1991)
bhuna ('buːnə) *n* an Indian dish or sauce in which spices are dry roasted in a pan and then combined with a moistening agent such as yogurt or water [from Urdu]
Bhutan (buː'tɑːn) *n* a kingdom in central Asia: disputed by Tibet, China, India, and Britain since the 18th century, the conflict now being chiefly between China and India (which is responsible for Bhutan's external affairs); contains inaccessible stretches of the E Himalayas in the north. Official language: Dzongka; Nepali is also spoken. Official religion: Mahayana Buddhist. Currencies: ngultrum and Indian rupee. Capital: Thimbu. Pop: 692 000 (2001 est). Area: about 46 600 sq km (18 000 sq miles) > ˌ**Bhutan'ese** *n, adj*
▹ www.bhutan.gov.bt
▹ www.tourism.gov.bt
Bi *the chemical symbol for* bismuth
bi- *or sometimes before a vowel* **bin-** *combining form* **1** two; having two: *bifocal* **2** occurring every two; lasting for two: *biennial* **3** on both sides, directions, etc: *bilateral* **4** occurring twice during: *biweekly* **5a** denoting a compound containing two identical cyclic hydrocarbon systems: *biphenyl* **5b** (rare in technical usage) indicating an acid salt of a dibasic acid: *sodium bicarbonate* **5c** (not in technical usage) equivalent of **di-**¹ (sense 2) [from L, from *bis* TWICE]
Biafra (bɪ'æfrə) *n* **1** a region of E Nigeria, formerly a local government region: seceded as an independent republic (1967–70) during the Civil War, but defeated by Nigerian government forces **2 Bight of** former name (until 1975) of (the Bight of) **Bonny** > **Bi'afran** *adj, n*
Biak (biː'jɑːk) *n* an island in Indonesia, north of West Irian: the largest of the Schouten Islands. Area: 2455 sq km (948 sq miles)
Białystok (*Polish* bja'wɪstɔk) *n* a city in E Poland: belonged to Prussia (1795–1807) and to Russia (1807–1919). Pop: 283 937 (1999 est). Russian name: **Belostock**
biannual (baɪ'ænjʊəl) *adj* occurring twice a year ▹ Cf **biennial** > **bi'annually** *adv*

> USAGE An event which is *biannual* will occur four times as often as one which is *biennial*. In order to make your message simpler, it may be clearer to spell out exactly what you intend, by saying *six-monthly*

Biarritz ('bɪərɪts, bɪə'rɪts; *French* bjarits) *n* a town in SW France, on the Bay of Biscay: famous resort, patronized by Napoleon III and by Queen Victoria and Edward VII of Great Britain and Ireland. Pop: 28 890 (1990)
bias ('baɪəs) *n* **1** mental tendency or inclination, esp irrational preference or prejudice **2** a diagonal line or cut across the weave of a fabric **3** *electronics* the voltage applied to an electrode of a transistor or valve to establish suitable working conditions **4** *bowls* **4a** a bulge or weight inside one side of a bowl **4b** the curved course of such a bowl **5** *statistics* a latent influence that disturbs an analysis ▹ *adv* **6** obliquely; diagonally ▹ *vb* **biases, biasing, biased** *or* **biasses, biassing, biassed** **7** (*tr; usually passive*) to cause to have a bias; prejudice; influence [c16 from OF *biais*] > '**biased** *or* '**biassed** *adj*
bias binding *n* a strip of material cut on the bias, used for binding hems or for decoration
biathlon (baɪ'æθlən, -lɒn) *n sport* a contest in which skiers with rifles shoot at four targets along a 20-kilometre (12.5-mile) cross-country course
biaxial (baɪ'æksɪəl) *adj* (esp of a crystal) having two axes
bib (bɪb) *n* **1** a piece of cloth or plastic worn, esp by babies, to protect their clothes while eating **2** the upper front part of some aprons, dungarees, etc **3** Also called: **pout, whiting pout** a light brown European marine gadoid food fish with a barbel on its lower jaw **4 stick one's bib in** *Austral inf* to interfere ▹ *vb* **bibs, bibbing, bibbed** **5** *arch* to drink (something) [c14 *bibben* to drink, prob. from L *bibere*]
bib and tucker *n inf* an outfit of clothes
bibcock ('bɪbˌkɒk) *or* **bib** *n* a tap with a nozzle bent downwards fed from a horizontal pipe
bibelot ('bɪbləʊ) *n* an attractive or curious trinket [c19 from F, from OF *beubelet*]
Bible ('baɪbᵊl) *n* **1a the** the sacred writings of the Christian religion, comprising the Old and New Testaments **1b** (*as modifier*): *a Bible reading* **2** (*often not cap*) the sacred writings of a religion **3** (*usually not cap*) a book regarded as authoritative [c13 from OF, from Med. L *biblia* books, from Gk, dim. of *biblos* papyrus]
▹ http://unbound.biola.edu/
▹ www.yallop.org/synopsis/
▹ www.bible-history.com/
Bible Belt *n* those states of the S US where Protestant fundamentalism is dominant
Bible-thumper *n sl* an enthusiastic or aggressive exponent of the Bible. Also: **Bible-basher** > '**Bible-ˌthumping** *n, adj*
biblical ('bɪblɪkᵊl) *adj* **1** of or referring to the Bible **2** resembling the Bible in written style
Biblicist ('bɪblɪsɪst) *or* **Biblist** *n* **1** a biblical scholar **2** a person who takes the Bible literally
biblio- *combining form* indicating book or books: *bibliography* [from Gk *biblion* book]
bibliography (ˌbɪblɪ'ɒgrəfɪ) *n, pl* **bibliographies** **1** a list of books on a subject or by a particular author **2** a list of sources used in a book, thesis, etc **3a** the study of the history, classification, etc, of literary material **3b** a work on this subject > ˌ**bibli'ographer** *n* > **bibliographic** (ˌbɪblɪəʊ'græfɪk) *or* ˌ**biblio'graphical** *adj*
bibliomancy ('bɪblɪəʊˌmænsɪ) *n* prediction of the future by interpreting a passage chosen at random from a book, esp the Bible
bibliomania (ˌbɪblɪəʊ'meɪnɪə) *n* extreme fondness for books > ˌ**biblio'maniˌac** *n, adj*
bibliophile ('bɪblɪəˌfaɪl) *or* **bibliophil** ('bɪblɪəfɪl) *n* a person who collects or is fond of books > **bibliophilism** (ˌbɪblɪ'ɒfɪˌlɪzəm) *n* > ˌ**bibli'ophily** *n*
bibliopole ('bɪblɪəʊˌpəʊl) *or* **bibliopolist** (ˌbɪblɪ'ɒpəlɪst) *n* a dealer in books, esp rare or decorative ones [c18 from L, from Gk, from BIBLIO- + *pōlein* to sell] > ˌ**bibli'opoly** *n*
bibulous ('bɪbjʊləs) *adj* addicted to alcohol [c17 from L *bibulus*, from *bibere* to drink] > '**bibulously** *adv* > '**bibulousness** *n*
bicameral (baɪ'kæmərəl) *adj* (of a legislature) consisting of two chambers [c19 from BI- + L *camera* CHAMBER] > **bi'cameralˌism** *n*
bicarb ('baɪkɑːb) *n* short for **bicarbonate of soda**
bicarbonate (baɪ'kɑːbənɪt, -ˌneɪt) *n* a salt of carbonic acid
bicarbonate of soda *n* sodium bicarbonate, esp as

Bb

medicine or a raising agent in baking

bice (baɪs) *n* **1** Also called: **bice blue** medium blue **2** Also called: **bice green** a yellowish green [c14 from OF *bis* dark grey, from ?]

bicentenary (ˌbaɪsɛnˈtiːnərɪ) *or US* **bicentennial** (ˌbaɪsɛnˈtɛnɪəl) *adj* **1** marking a 200th anniversary **2** occurring every 200 years **3** lasting 200 years ▷ *n, pl* **bicentenaries 4** a 200th anniversary

bicephalous (baɪˈsɛfələs) *adj* **1** *biol* having two heads **2** crescent-shaped

biceps (ˈbaɪsɛps) *n, pl* **biceps** *anat* any muscle having two heads or origins, esp the muscle that flexes the forearm [c17 from L, from BI- + *caput* head]

bichloride (baɪˈklɔːraɪd) *n* another name for **dichloride**

bichloride of mercury *n* another name for **mercuric chloride**

bichromate (baɪˈkrəʊˌmeɪt, -mɪt) *n* another name for **dichromate**

bicker (ˈbɪkə) *vb (intr)* **1** to argue over petty matters; squabble **2** *poetic* **2a** (esp of a stream) to run quickly **2b** to flicker; glitter ▷ *n* **3** a squabble [c13 from ?] > ˈ**bickerer** *n*

bicolour (ˈbaɪˌkʌlə), **bicoloured** *or US* **bicolor, bicolored** *adj* two-coloured

biconcave (baɪˈkɒnkeɪv, ˌbaɪkɒnˈkeɪv) *adj* (of a lens) having concave faces on both sides

biconditional (ˌbaɪkənˈdɪʃənᵊl) *n* **1** *logic, maths* a relation, taken as meaning *if and only if*, between two propositions which are either both true or both false and such that each implies the other **2** *logic* a logical connective between two propositions whose truth table is true only if both propositions are true or both false ▷ Also called (esp sense 1): **equivalence**

biconvex (baɪˈkɒnvɛks, ˌbaɪkɒnˈvɛks) *adj* (of a lens) having convex faces on both sides

bicuspid (baɪˈkʌspɪd) *or* **bicuspidate** (baɪˈkʌspɪˌdeɪt) *adj* **1** having two cusps or points ▷ *n* **2** a bicuspid tooth; premolar

bicycle (ˈbaɪsɪkᵊl) *n* **1** a vehicle with a tubular metal frame mounted on two spoked wheels, one behind the other. The rider sits on a saddle, propels the vehicle by means of pedals, and steers with handlebars on the front wheel. Often shortened to **bike** (*inf*), **cycle** ▷ *vb* **bicycles, bicycling, bicycled 2** (*intr*) to ride a bicycle > ˈ**bicyclist** *or* ˈ**bicycler** *n*
▷ www.ibike.org

bicycle clip *n* one of a pair of clips worn around the ankles by cyclists to keep the trousers tight and out of the chain

bid (bɪd) *vb* **bids, bidding, bad, bade,** *or* (esp for senses 1, 2, 5, 6) **bid; bidden** *or* (esp for senses 1, 2, 5, 6) **bid 1** (often foll by *for* or *against*) to offer (an amount) in attempting to buy something **2** *commerce* to respond to an offer by a seller stating (the more favourable terms) on which one is willing to make a purchase **3** (*tr*) to say (a greeting, etc): *to bid farewell* **4** to order; command: *do as you are bid!* **5** (*intr;* usually foll by *for*) to attempt to attain power, etc **6** *bridge, etc* to declare before play how many tricks one expects to make **7 bid defiance** to resist boldly **8 bid fair** to seem probable ▷ *n* **9a** an offer of a specified amount **9b** the price offered **10a** the quoting by a seller of a price **10b** the price quoted **11** *commerce* **11a** a statement by a buyer, in response to an offer by a seller, of the more favourable terms that would be acceptable **11b** the price or other terms so stated **12** an attempt, esp to attain power **13** *bridge* **13a** the number of tricks a player undertakes to make **13b** a player's turn to make a bid ▷ See also **bid up** [OE *biddan*] > ˈ**bidder** *n*

Bida (ˈbaɪdɑː) *or* **El Beda** (ɛl ˈbeɪdɑː) *n* the former name of **Doha**

biddable (ˈbɪdəbᵊl) *adj* **1** having sufficient value to be bid on, as a hand at bridge **2** docile; obedient > ˈ**biddableness** *n*

bidding (ˈbɪdɪŋ) *n* **1** an order; command **2** an invitation; summons **3** bids or the act of making bids

biddy[1] (ˈbɪdɪ) *n, pl* **biddies** a dialect word for **chicken** or **hen** [c17 ? imit. of calling chickens]

biddy[2] (ˈbɪdɪ) *n, pl* **biddies** *inf* a woman, esp an old gossipy one [c18 from pet form of *Bridget*]

biddy-biddy (ˈbɪdɪˌbɪdɪ) *n, pl* **biddy-biddies 1** a low-growing rosaceous plant of New Zealand, having prickly burs **2** the burs of this plant ▷ Also: **bidgee-widgee** (ˈbɪdʒɪˌwɪdʒɪ) [from Maori *piripiri*]

bide (baɪd) *vb* **bides, biding, bided** *or* **bode, bided 1** (*intr*) *arch or dialect* to continue in a certain place or state; stay **2** (*tr*) *arch or dialect* to tolerate; endure **3 bide one's time** to wait patiently for an opportunity [OE *bīdan*]

bidentate (baɪˈdɛnˌteɪt) *adj* having two teeth or toothlike parts or processes

bidet (ˈbiːdeɪ) *n* a small low basin for washing the genital area [c17 from F: small horse]

bid up *vb (adv)* to increase the market price of (a commodity) by making artificial bids

Biel (biːl) *n* **1** a town in NW Switzerland, on Lake Biel. Pop: 52 197 (1994). French name: **Bienne 2 Lake** a lake in NW Switzerland: remains of lake dwellings were discovered here in the 19th century. Area: 39 sq km (15 sq miles) German name: **Bielersee** (ˈbiːləzeː)

Bielefeld (*German* ˈbiːləfɛlt) *n* a city in Germany, in NE North Rhine-Westphalia: food, textiles. Pop: 321 600 (1999 est)

Bielsko-Biała (*Polish* ˈbjɛlskɔˈbjawa) *n* a town in S Poland: created in 1951 by the union of Bielsko and Biala Krakowska; a leading textile centre since the 16th century. Pop: 180 307 (1999 est)

Bien Hoa (ˈbjɛn ˈhəʊə) *n* a town in S Vietnam: a former capital of Cambodia. Pop: 273 879 (1992 est)

Bienne (bjɛn) *n* the French name for **Biel**

biennial (baɪˈɛnɪəl) *adj* **1** occurring every two years **2** lasting two years ▷ Cf **biannual** ▷ *n* **3** a plant that completes its life cycle within two years **4** an event that takes place every two years > biˈ**ennially** *adv*

bier (bɪə) *n* a platform or stand on which a corpse or a coffin containing a corpse rests before burial [OE *bǣr;* rel. to *beran* to BEAR[1]]

Bierce (bɪəs) *n* **Ambrose** (**Gwinett**) 1842–?1914, US journalist and author of humorous sketches, horror stories, and tales of the supernatural: he disappeared during a mission in Mexico (1913)

biestings (ˈbiːstɪŋz) *n* a variant spelling of **beestings**

biff (bɪf) *sl* ▷ *n* **1** a blow with the fist ▷ *vb* **2** (*tr*) to give (someone) such a blow [c20 prob. imit.]

biffo (ˈbɪfəʊ) *Austral slang* ▷ *n* **1** fighting or aggressive behaviour: *he enjoys a bit of biffo now and then* ▷ *adj* **2** aggressive; pugnacious

bifid (ˈbaɪfɪd) *adj* divided into two lobes by a median cleft [c17 from L, from BI- + *-fidus*, from *findere* to split] > biˈ**fidity** *n* > ˈ**bifidly** *adv*

bifocal (baɪˈfəʊkᵊl) *adj* **1** *optics* having two different focuses **2** relating to a compound lens permitting near and distant vision

bifocals (baɪˈfəʊkᵊlz) *pl n* a pair of spectacles with bifocal lenses

BIFU (in Britain) *abbrev for* Banking, Insurance and Finance Union

bifurcate *vb* (ˈbaɪfəˌkeɪt), **bifurcates, bifurcating, bifurcated 1** to fork or divide into two branches ▷ *adj* (ˈbaɪfəˌkeɪt, -kɪt) **2** forked or divided into two branches [c17 from Med. L, from L, from BI- + *furca* fork] > ˌ**bifurˈcation** *n*

big (bɪg) *adj* **bigger, biggest 1** of great or considerable size, height, weight, number, power, or capacity **2** having great significance; important **3** important through having power, influence, wealth, authority, etc **4** *inf* considerable in extent or intensity (esp in **in a big way**) **5a** elder: *my big brother* **5b** grown-up

6a generous; magnanimous: *that's very big of you* **6b** (*in combination*): *big-hearted* **7** extravagant; boastful: *big talk* **8 too big for one's boots** *or* **breeches** conceited; unduly self-confident **9** in an advanced stage of pregnancy (esp in **big with child**) ▷ *adv inf* **10** boastfully; pretentiously (esp in **talk big**) **11** in an exceptional way; well: *his talk went over big* **12** on a grand scale (esp in **think big**) ▷ See also **big up** [c13 ?from ON] > **'bigness** *n*

bigamy ('bɪgəmɪ) *n, pl* **bigamies** the crime of marrying a person while still legally married to someone else [c13 via F from Med. L; see BI-, -GAMY] > **'bigamist** *n* > **'bigamous** *adj*

Big Apple *n* **the** *inf* New York City [c20 probably from US jazzmen's earlier use to mean any big, esp northern, city; of obscure origin]

Big Bang *n* the reorganization of the London Stock Exchange that took effect in October 1986 when operations became fully computerized, fixed commissions were abolished, and the functions of jobbers and brokers were merged

big-bang theory *n* a cosmological theory postulating that all the matter of the universe was hurled in all directions by a cataclysmic explosion and that the universe is still expanding ▷ Cf **steady-state theory**

Big Brother *n* a person, organization, etc, that exercises total dictatorial control [c20 from George Orwell's novel *1984* (1949)]

big business *n* large commercial organizations collectively, esp when considered as exploitative or socially harmful

Big C *n* **the** a euphemism for **cancer** (senses 1 and 2)

big deal *interj Sl.* an exclamation of scorn, derision, etc, used esp to belittle a claim or offer

big dipper *n* (in amusement parks) a narrow railway with open carriages that run swiftly over a route of sharp curves and steep inclines

big end *n Brit* the larger end of a connecting rod in an internal-combustion engine

big game *n* large animals that are hunted or fished for sport

big gun *n inf* an important person

bighead ('bɪg,hɛd) *n inf* a conceited person > **,big'headed** *adj* > **,big'headedness** *n*

big hitter ▷ *n* **1** a sportsperson who is capable of hitting the ball long or hard **2** *inf* an influential and important person: *one of the government's big hitters*

bighorn ('bɪg,hɔ:n) *n, pl* **bighorns** *or* **bighorn** a large wild sheep inhabiting mountainous regions in North America

bight (baɪt) *n* **1** a wide indentation of a shoreline, or the body of water bounded by such a curve **2** the slack middle part of an extended rope **3** a curve or loop in a rope [OE *byht*; see BOW[2]]

Bight *n* **the** *Austral inf* the major indentation of the S coast of Australia, from Cape Pasley in W Australia to the Eyre Peninsula in S Australia. In full: **the Great Australian Bight**

Big Mac (mæk) *n trademark* two hamburgers served with salad and dressing on a soft bread roll

bigmouth ('bɪg,maʊθ) *n sl* a noisy, indiscreet, or boastful person > **'big-,mouthed** *adj*

big name *n inf* **a** a famous person **b** (*as modifier*): *a big-name performer*

big noise *n Brit inf* an important person: *a big noise in the oil industry*

bignonia (bɪg'nəʊnɪə) *n* a tropical American climbing shrub cultivated for its trumpet-shaped yellow or reddish flowers [c19 from NL, after the Abbé Jean-Paul *Bignon* (1662–1743)]

big-note *vb* **big-notes, big-noting, big-noted** (*tr*) *Austral inf* to boast about (oneself)

bigot ('bɪgət) *n* a person who is intolerant, esp regarding religion, politics, or race [c16 from OF: name applied contemptuously to the Normans by the French, from ?] > **'bigoted** *adj* > **'bigotry** *n*

big shot *n inf* an important person

Big Smoke *n* **the** *inf* a large city, esp London

big stick *n inf* force or the threat of force

big tent *n* **a** a political approach in which a party claims to be open to a wide spectrum of constituents and groups **b** (*as modifier*): *big-tent politics*

big time *n inf* **a the** the highest level of a profession, esp entertainment **b** (*as modifier*): *a big-time comedian* > **'big-'timer** *n*

big top *n inf* **1** the main tent of a circus **2** the circus itself

big up *vb* **bigs, bigging, bigged** (*tr, adv*) *sl, chiefly Caribbean* to make important, prominent, or famous: *we'll do our best to big you up*

bigwig ('bɪg,wɪg) *n inf* an important person

Bihar (bɪ'hɑ:) *n* a state of NE India: consists of part of the Ganges plain; important for rice: lost the S to the new state of Jharkand in 2000. Capital: Patna. Pop: 82 878 796 (2001). Area: 99 225 sq km (38 301 sq miles)

Biisk (*Russian* bijsk) *n* a variant spelling of **Biysk**

Bijapur (bɪ'dʒɑ:pʊə) *n* an ancient city in W India, in N Mysore: capital of a former kingdom, which fell at the end of the 17th century: cotton. Pop: 186 939 (1991)

bijou ('bi:ʒu:) *n, pl* **bijoux** (-ʒu:z) **1** something small and delicately worked **2** (*modifier*) *often ironic* small but tasteful: *a bijou residence* [c19 from F, from Breton *bizou* finger ring, from *biz* finger]

bijugate ('baɪdʒʊ,geɪt, baɪ'dʒu:geɪt) *or* **bijugous** *adj* (of compound leaves) having two pairs of leaflets

Bikaner ('bi:kə,nɪə) *n* a walled city in NW India, in Rajasthan: capital of the former state of Bikaner, on the edge of the Thar Desert. Pop: 416 289 (1991)

bike (baɪk) *n* **1** *inf* short for **bicycle** or **motorcycle** **2** *sl* a promiscuous woman **3 get off one's bike** *Austral & NZ sl* to lose one's self-control ▷ *vb* **bikes, biking, biked** **4** (*intr*) *inf* to ride a cycle

biker ('baɪkə) *n* a member of a motorcycle gang. Also called (Austral and NZ): **bikie**

biker jacket *n* a short, close-fitting leather jacket with zips and studs, often worn by motorcyclists

bikini (bɪ'ki:nɪ) *n* a woman's very brief two-piece swimming costume [c20 after *Bikini* atoll, from a comparison between the obvious and powerful effect of the atom-bomb test and the effect (on men) of women wearing bikinis]

Bikini (bɪ'ki:nɪ) *n* an atoll in the N Pacific; one of the Marshall Islands: site of a US atomic-bomb test in 1946

Biko ('bi:kəʊ) *n* **Steven Bantu**, known as *Steve*. 1946–77, Black South African civil rights leader: founder of the South African Students Organization. His death in police custody caused worldwide concern

bilabial (baɪ'leɪbɪəl) *adj* **1** of or denoting a speech sound articulated using both lips: *(p) is a bilabial stop* ▷ *n* **2** a bilabial speech sound

bilabiate (baɪ'leɪbɪ,eɪt, -ɪt) *adj bot* divided into two lips: *the snapdragon has a bilabiate corolla*

bilateral (baɪ'lætərəl) *adj* **1** having or involving two sides **2** affecting or undertaken by two parties; mutual **3** having identical sides or parts on each side of an axis; symmetrical

bilateral symmetry *n* symmetry in one plane only ▷ Cf **radial symmetry**

Bilbao (bɪl'bɑ:əʊ; *Spanish* bil'βau) *n* a port in N Spain, on the Bay of Biscay: the largest city in the Basque Provinces: famous since medieval times for the production of iron and steel goods: modern buildings include the Guggenheim Art Museum (1997). Pop: 358 467 (1998 est)

bilberry ('bɪlbərɪ) *n, pl* **bilberries** **1** any of several shrubs, of the genus *Vaccinium*, having edible blue or blackish berries **2** the fruit of any of these plants [c16 prob. of Scand. origin]

Bb

bilboes ('bɪlbəʊz) *pl n* a long iron bar with sliding shackles, for the ankles of a prisoner [C16 ?from *Bilbao*, Spain]

Bildungsroman *German* ('bɪldʊŋsroma:n) *n* a novel about a person's formative years [lit.: education novel]

bile (baɪl) *n* **1** a bitter greenish to golden brown alkaline fluid secreted by the liver and stored in the gall bladder. It aids digestion of fats **2** a health disorder due to faulty secretion of bile **3** irritability or peevishness [C17 from F, from L *bīlis*]

bilge (bɪldʒ) *n* **1** *naut* the parts of a vessel's hull where the sides curve inwards to form the bottom **2** (*often pl*) the parts of a vessel between the lowermost floorboards and the bottom **3** Also called: **bilge water** the dirty water that collects in a vessel's bilge **4** *inf* silly rubbish; nonsense **5** the widest part of a cask ▷ *vb* **bilges, bilging, bilged 6** (*intr*) *naut* (of a vessel) to take in water at the bilge **7** (*tr*) *naut* to damage (a vessel) in the bilge [C16 prob. var. of BULGE]

bilharzia (bɪl'hɑ:tsɪə) *n* **1** another name for a **schistosome 2** another name for **schistosomiasis** [C19 NL, after Theodor *Bilharz* (1825–62), G parasitologist who discovered schistosomes]

bilharziasis (ˌbɪlhɑ:'tsaɪəsɪs) *or* **bilharziosis** (bɪlˌhɑ:tsɪ'əʊsɪs) *n* another name for **schistosomiasis**

biliary ('bɪlɪərɪ) *adj* of or relating to bile, to the ducts that convey bile, or to the gall bladder

bilingual (baɪ'lɪŋgwəl) *adj* **1** able to speak two languages, esp with fluency **2** expressed in two languages ▷ *n* **3** a bilingual person > **bi'lingual,ism** *n*

bilious ('bɪlɪəs) *adj* **1** of or relating to bile **2** affected with or denoting any disorder related to secretion of bile **3** *inf* bad-tempered; irritable [C16 from L *bīliōsus* full of BILE] > **'biliousness** *n*

bilk (bɪlk) *vb* (*tr*) **1** to balk; thwart **2** (often foll by *of*) to cheat or deceive, esp to avoid making payment to **3** to escape from; elude ▷ *n* **4** a swindle or cheat **5** a person who swindles or cheats [C17 ? var. of BALK] > **'bilker** *n*

bill[1] (bɪl) *n* **1** money owed for goods or services supplied **2** a statement of money owed **3** *chiefly Brit* such an account for food and drink in a restaurant, hotel, etc **4** any list of items, events, etc, such as a theatre programme **5** a statute in draft, before it becomes law **6** a printed notice or advertisement **7** *US & Canad* a piece of paper money; note **8** an obsolete name for **promissory note 9** See **bill of exchange, bill of fare** ▷ *vb* (*tr*) **10** to send or present an account for payment to (a person) **11** to enter (items, goods, etc) on an account or statement **12** to advertise by posters **13** to schedule as a future programme [C14 from Anglo-L *billa*, alteration of LL *bulla* document, BULL[3]]

bill[2] (bɪl) *n* **1** the projecting jaws of a bird, covered with a horny sheath; beak **2** any beaklike mouthpart in other animals **3** a narrow promontory ▷ *vb* (*intr*) (esp in **bill and coo**) **4** (of birds, esp doves) to touch bills together **5** (of lovers) to kiss and whisper amorously [OE *bile*]

bill[3] (bɪl) *n* **1** a pike or halberd with a narrow hooked blade **2** short for **billhook** [OE *bill* sword]

billabong ('bɪləˌbɒŋ) *n Austral* **1** a backwater channel that forms a lagoon or pool **2** a branch of a river running to a dead end [C19 from Abor., from *billa* river + *bong* dead]

billboard ('bɪlˌbɔ:d) *n chiefly US & Canad* another name for **hoarding** [C19 from BILL[1] + BOARD]

billet[1] ('bɪlɪt) *n* **1** accommodation, esp for a soldier, in civilian lodgings **2** the official requisition for such lodgings **3** a space or berth in a ship **4** *inf* a job ▷ *vb* **5** (*tr*) to assign a lodging to (a soldier) **6** to lodge or be lodged [C15 from OF *billette*, from *bulle* a document; see BULL[3]]

billet[2] ('bɪlɪt) *n* **1** a chunk of wood, esp for fuel **2** a small bar of iron or steel [C15 from OF *billette* a little log, from *bille* log]

billet-doux (ˌbɪlɪ'du:) *n, pl* **billets-doux** (ˌbɪlɪ'du:z) *Old-fashioned or jocular.* a love letter [C17 from F, lit.: a sweet letter]

billhook ('bɪlˌhʊk) *n* a tool with a curved blade terminating in a hook, used for pruning, chopping, etc Also called: **bill**

billiard ('bɪljəd) *n* (*modifier*) of or relating to billiards: *a billiard table; a billiard cue*

billiards ('bɪljədz) *n* (*functioning as sing*) any of various games in which long cues are used to drive balls on a rectangular table covered with a smooth cloth and having raised cushioned edges [C16 from OF *billard* curved stick, from *bille* log; see BILLET[2]]
▷ http://moveto/wbfsuperstars

billing ('bɪlɪŋ) *n* **1** *theatre* the relative importance of a performer or act as reflected in the prominence given in programmes, advertisements, etc **2** *chiefly US & Canad* public notice or advertising

billingsgate ('bɪlɪŋzˌgeɪt) *n* obscene or abusive language [C17 after BILLINGSGATE, notorious for such language]

Billingsgate ('bɪlɪŋzˌgeɪt) *n* the largest fish market in London, on the N bank of the River Thames; moved to new site on the Isle of Dogs in 1982

Billings method ('bɪlɪŋz) *n* a natural method of birth control that involves examining the colour and viscosity of the cervical mucus to discover when ovulation is occurring [C20 after Drs John and Evelyn *Billings*]

billion ('bɪljən) *n, pl* **billions** *or* **billion 1** one thousand million: written as 1 000 000 000 or 10^9 **2** (formerly, in Britain) one million million: written as 1 000 000 000 000 or 10^{12}. US word: **trillion 3** (*often pl*) any exceptionally large number ▷ *determiner* **4** (preceded by *a* or a cardinal number) amounting to a billion [C17 from F, from BI- + *-llion* as in *million*] > **'billionth** *adj, n*

USAGE The meaning of 'one thousand million' is now the established one in the UK as well as in the US, contrary to older British usage

billionaire (ˌbɪljə'nɛə) *n* a person whose wealth exceeds a billion monetary units of his or her country

Billiton ('bɪlɪtɒn, bɪ'li:tɒn) *n* an island of Indonesia, in the Java Sea between Borneo and Sumatra. Chief town: Tandjungpandan. Area: 4833 sq km (1866 sq miles). Also called: **Belitung**

bill of attainder *n* (formerly) a legislative act finding a person guilty without trial of treason or felony and declaring him or her attainted

bill of exchange *n* (now chiefly in foreign transactions) a document, usually negotiable, instructing a third party to pay a stated sum at a designated future date or on demand

bill of fare *n* another name for **menu**

bill of health *n* **1** a certificate that attests to the health of a ship's company **2 clean bill of health** *inf* **2a** a good report of one's physical condition **2b** a favourable account of a person's or a company's financial position

bill of lading *n* (in foreign trade) a document containing full particulars of goods shipped

bill of quantities *n* a document drawn up by a quantity surveyor providing details of the prices, dimensions, etc, of the materials required to build a large structure, such as a factory

Bill of Rights *n* **1** an English statute of 1689 guaranteeing the rights and liberty of the individual subject **2** the first ten amendments to the US Constitution which guarantee the liberty of the individual **3** (*usually not caps*) any charter of basic human rights

bill of sale *n law* a deed transferring personal property

billow ('bɪləʊ) *n* **1** a large sea wave **2** a swelling or surging mass, as of smoke or sound **3** a large atmospheric wave, usually in the lee of a hill ▷ *vb* **4** to rise up, swell out, or cause to rise up or swell out [C16 from ON *bylgja*] > **'billowing** *adj, n* > **'billowy** *adj* > **'billowiness** *n*

billposter ('bɪl,pəʊstə) *or* **billsticker** *n* a person who sticks advertising posters to walls, etc > **'bill,posting** *or* **'bill,sticking** *n*

billy ('bɪlɪ) *or* **billycan** ('bɪlɪ,kæn) *n, pl* **billies** *or* **billycans** **1** a metal can or pot for boiling water, etc, over a campfire **2** *Austral & NZ (as modifier): billy-tea* **3** **boil the billy** *Austral & NZ inf* to make tea [C19 from Scot. *billypot* cooking vessel]

billy goat *n* a male goat

Billy No-Mates *n slang* a person with no friends

Billy the Kid *n* nickname of *William H. Bonney*. 1859–81, US outlaw

bilobate (baɪ'ləʊ,beɪt) *or* **bilobed** ('baɪ,ləʊbd) *adj* divided into or having two lobes

biltong ('bɪl,tɒŋ) *n S African* strips of meat dried and cured in the sun [C19 Afrik., from Du. *bil* buttock + *tong* TONGUE]

BIM *abbrev for* British Institute of Management

bimanous ('bɪmənəs, baɪ'meɪ-) *adj* (of man and the higher primates) having two hands distinct in form and function from the feet [C19 from NL, from BI- + L *manus* hand]

bimanual (,baɪ'mænjʊəl) *adj* using both hands

bimbo ('bɪmbəʊ) *n, pl* **bimbos** *derog sl* **1** an attractive but empty-headed young person, esp a woman **2** a fellow; a foolish or stupid person [C20 from It.: little child, perhaps via Polari]

bimetallic (,baɪmɪ'tælɪk) *adj* **1** consisting of two metals **2** of or based on bimetallism

bimetallic strip *n* strips of two metals that expand differently welded together for use in a thermostat

bimetallism (baɪ'mɛtə,lɪzəm) *n* the use of two metals, esp gold and silver, in fixed relative values as the standard of value and currency > **bi'metallist** *n*

bimonthly (baɪ'mʌnθlɪ) *adj, adv* **1** every two months **2** twice a month ▷ *n, pl* **bimonthlies** **3** a periodical published every two months

bimorph ('baɪmɔːf) *or* **bimorph cell** *n electronics* two piezoelectric crystals cemented together so that their movement converts electrical signals into mechanical energy or vice versa: used in record player pick-ups and loudspeakers

bin (bɪn) *n* **1** a large container for storing something in bulk, such as coal, grain, or bottled wine **2** Also called: **bread bin** a small container for bread **3** Also called: **dustbin, rubbish bin** a container for rubbish, etc ▷ *vb* **bins, binning, binned** (*tr*) **4** to store in a bin **5** to put in a wastepaper bin [OE *binne* basket]

binary ('baɪnərɪ) *adj* **1** composed of or involving two; dual **2** *maths, computers* of or expressed in binary notation or binary code **3** (of a compound or molecule) containing atoms of two different elements ▷ *n, pl* **binaries** **4** something composed of two parts **5** *astron* See **binary star** [C16 from LL *bīnārius*; see BI-]

Binary Prefixes

In 1998 the International Electrotechnical Commission approved the following prefixes for the powers of 2:

kibi-	Ki-	2^{10}	1 024
mebi-	Mi-	2^{20}	1 048 576
gibi-	Gi-	2^{30}	1 073 741 824
tebi-	Ti-	2^{40}	1 099 511 627 776
pebi-	Pi-	2^{50}	1 125 899 906 842 624
exbi-	Ei-	2^{60}	1 152 921 504 606 846 976

▷ http://whatis.techtarget.com/definition/0,,sid9_gci825099.00.html

binary code *n computing* the representation of each one of a set of numbers, letters, etc, as a unique group of bits

binary notation *or* **system** *n* a number system having a base of two, numbers being expressed by sequences of the digits 0 and 1: used in computing, as 0 and 1 can be represented electrically as *off* and *on*

binary number *n* a number expressed in binary notation

binary star *n* a double star system containing two associated stars revolving around a common centre of gravity in different orbits

binary weapon *n* a chemical weapon containing two substances separately that mix to produce a lethal agent when the projectile is fired

binate ('baɪ,neɪt) *adj bot* occurring in two parts or in pairs: *binate leaves* [C19 from NL *bīnātus*, prob. from L *combīnātus* united] > **'bi,nately** *adv*

binaural (baɪ'nɔːrəl, bɪn'ɔːrəl) *adj* **1** relating to, having, or hearing with both ears **2** employing two separate channels for recording or transmitting sound

Binchy ('bɪntʃɪ) *n* **Maeve** (meɪ'ɪv) born 1940, Irish novelist and journalist; her bestselling novels include *Circle of Friends* (1990) and *Quentins* (2002)

bind (baɪnd) *vb* **binds, binding, bound** **1** to make or become fast or secure with or as if with a tie or band **2** (*tr*; often foll by *up*) to encircle or enclose with a band: *to bind the hair* **3** (*tr*) to place (someone) under obligation; oblige **4** (*tr*) to impose legal obligations or duties upon (a person) **5** (*tr*) to make (a bargain, agreement, etc) irrevocable; seal **6** (*tr*) to restrain or confine with or as if with ties, as of responsibility or loyalty **7** (*tr*) to place under certain constraints; govern **8** (*tr*; often foll by *up*) to bandage **9** to cohere or cause to cohere: *egg binds fat and flour* **10** to make or become compact, stiff, or hard: *frost binds the earth* **11** (*tr*) to enclose and fasten (the pages of a book) between covers **12** (*tr*) to provide (a garment, hem, etc) with a border or edging **13** (*tr*; sometimes foll by *out* or *over*) to employ as an apprentice; indenture **14** (*intr*) *sl* to complain ▷ *n* **15** something that binds **16** *inf* a difficult or annoying situation **17** a situation in which freedom of action is restricted ▷ See also **bind over** [OE *bindan*]

binder ('baɪndə) *n* **1** a firm cover or folder for holding loose sheets of paper together **2** a material used to bind separate particles together **3** a person who binds books; bookbinder **4** something used to fasten or tie, such as rope or twine **5** Also called: **reaper binder** *obs* a machine for cutting grain and binding it into sheaves **6** an informal agreement giving insurance coverage pending formal issue of a policy

bindery ('baɪndərɪ) *n, pl* **binderies** a place in which books are bound

bindi-eye ('bɪndɪ,aɪ) *n Austral* **1** any of various small weedy Australian herbaceous plants with burlike fruits **2** any bur or prickle [C20 ?from Abor.]

binding ('baɪndɪŋ) *n* **1** anything that binds or fastens **2** the covering within which the pages of a book are bound **3** the tape used for binding hems, etc ▷ *adj* **4** imposing an obligation or duty **5** causing hindrance; restrictive

bind over *vb* (*tr, adv*) to place (a person) under a legal obligation, such as one to keep the peace

bindweed ('baɪnd,wiːd) *n* any of various plants that twine around a support. See also **convolvulus**

bine (baɪn) *n* the climbing or twining stem of any of various plants, such as the woodbine [C19 var. of BIND]

Binet-Simon scale ('biːneɪ'saɪmən) *n psychol* a test used to determine the mental age of subjects. Also called: **Binet scale** *or* **test** [C20 after Alfred *Binet* (1857–1911) + Théodore *Simon* (1873–1961), F psychologists]

binge (bɪndʒ) *inf* ▷ *n* **1** a bout of excessive drinking or eating **2** excessive indulgence in anything: *a shopping binge* ▷ *vb* **binges, bingeing** *or* **binging, binged** **3** (*intr*) to indulge in a binge [c19 prob. dial. *binge* to soak]

Bingen ('bɪŋən) *n* a town in W Germany on the Rhine: wine trade and tourist centre. Pop: 23 141 (latest est)

bingo ('bɪŋgəʊ) *n, pl* **bingos** a gambling game, usually played with several people, in which random numbers are called out and the players cover the numbers on their individual cards. The first to cover a given arrangement of numbers is the winner [c19 ?from *bing,* imit. of a bell ringing to mark the win]

bin Laden (ˌbɪn'lɑːdən) *n* **Osama** (ʊ'sɑːmə) born 1957, Saudi-born leader of the al-Qaida terrorist network: presumed architect of the terrorist attacks on New York and Washington of September 11 2001

binman ('bɪnˌmæn, 'bɪnmən) *n, pl* **binmen** *inf* another name for **dustman**

binnacle ('bɪnəkᵊl) *n* a housing for a ship's compass [c17 changed from c15 *bitakle,* from Port. from LL *habitāculum* dwelling-place, from L *habitāre* to inhabit]

binocular (bɪ'nɒkjʊlə, baɪ-) *adj* involving, relating to, seeing with or intended for both eyes: *binocular vision* [c18 from BI- + L *oculus* eye]

binoculars (bɪ'nɒkjʊləz, baɪ-) *pl n* an optical instrument for use with both eyes, consisting of two small telescopes joined together

binomial (baɪ'nəʊmɪəl) *n* **1** a mathematical expression consisting of two terms, such as $3x + 2y$ **2** a two-part taxonomic name for an animal or plant indicating genus and species ▷ *adj* **3** referring to two names or terms [c16 from Med. L, from BI- + L *nōmen* name] > **bi'nomially** *adv*

binomial distribution *n* a statistical distribution giving the probability of obtaining a specified number of independent trials of an experiment, with a constant probability of success in each

binomial theorem *n* a general mathematical formula that expresses any power of a binomial without multiplying out, as in $(x+a)^n=x^n+nx^{n-1}a+n(n-1)/2$ $[x^{n-2}a^2...+a^n.]$

bint (bɪnt) *n sl* a derogatory term for **girl** or **woman** [c19 from Ar., lit.: daughter]

binturong ('bɪntjʊˌrɒŋ, bɪn'tjʊərɒŋ) *n* a long-bodied short-legged arboreal SE Asian mammal having shaggy black hair [from Malay]

Binyon ('bɪnjən) *n* (**Robert**) **Laurence** 1869–1943, British poet and art historian, best known for his elegiac war poems "For the Fallen" (1914) and "The Burning of the Leaves" (1944)

bio- *or before a vowel* **bi-** *combining form* **1** indicating or involving life or living organisms: *biogenesis* **2** indicating a human life or career: *biography* [from Gk *bios* life]

bioassay (ˌbaɪəʊ'æseɪ) *n* **1** a method of determining the concentration or effect of a drug, etc, by comparing its effect on living organisms with that of a standard preparation ▷ *vb (tr)* **2** to subject to a bioassay

bioastronautics (ˌbaɪəʊˌæstrə'nɔːtɪks) *n (functioning as sing)* the study of the effects of space flight on living organisms

bioastronomy (ˌbaɪəʊə'strɒnəmɪ) *n* the branch of astronomy concerned with the search for life on other planets

Bío-Bío (*Spanish* 'biːo'biːo) *n* a river in central Chile, rising in the Andes and flowing northwest to the Pacific. Length: about 390 km (240 miles)

biochemical oxygen demand *n* a measure of the organic pollution of water; the number of milligrams of oxygen per litre of water absorbed in a given period. Abbrev: **BOD**

biochemistry (ˌbaɪəʊ'kɛmɪstrɪ) *n* the study of the chemical compounds, reactions, etc, in living organisms > **biochemical** (ˌbaɪəʊ'kɛmɪkᵊl) *adj* > ˌ**bio'chemist** *n*

▷ http://restools.sdsc.edu/
▷ www.geocities.com/peterroberts.geo/biology.htm

biochip ('baɪəʊˌtʃɪp) *n* a small glass or silicon plate containing an array of biochemical molecules or structures, used as a biosensor or in gene sequencing

biocide ('baɪəˌsaɪd) *n* a chemical capable of killing living organisms > ˌ**bio'cidal** *adj*

biocoenosis *or US* **biocenosis** (ˌbaɪəʊsɪ'nəʊsɪs) *n* the relationships between animals and plants subsisting together [c19 NL from BIO- + Gk *koinōsis* sharing]

biocomputing (ˌbaɪəʊˌkəm'pjuːtɪŋ) *n* the application of computing to problems in biology, biochemistry, and genetics

biodata ('baɪəʊˌdeɪtə, -ˌdɑːtə) *n* information regarding an individual's education and work history, esp in the context of a selection process [c20 from BIO(GRAPHICAL) + DATA]

biodegradable (ˌbaɪəʊdɪ'greɪdəbᵊl) *adj* (of sewage, packaging, etc) capable of being decomposed by bacteria or other biological means > **biodegradability** (ˌbaɪəʊdɪˌgreɪdə'bɪlɪtɪ) *n*

biodiesel ('baɪəʊˌdiːzᵊl) *n* a biofuel intended for use in diesel engines

biodiversity (ˌbaɪəʊdaɪ'vɜːsɪtɪ) *n* the existence of a wide variety of plant and animal species in their natural environments, the maintaining of which is the aim of conservationists concerned about the indiscriminate destruction of rainforests and other habitats

▷ www.biosis.org.uk/zrdocs/zooinfo/biodiv.htm
▷ www.eti.uva.nl
▷ www.biodiv.org

bioengineering (ˌbaɪəʊˌɛndʒɪ'nɪərɪŋ) *n* **1** the design and manufacture of aids, such as artificial limbs, to rectify defective body functions **2** the design, manufacture, and maintenance of engineering equipment used in biosynthetic processes > ˌ**bioˌengi'neer** *n*

bioethics (ˌbaɪəʊ'ɛθɪks) *n (functioning as sing)* the study of ethical problems arising from scientific advances, esp in biology and medicine

biofeedback (ˌbaɪəʊ'fiːdˌbæk) *n physiol, psychol* the technique of recording and presenting (usually visually) the activity of an autonomic function, such as the rate of heartbeat, in order to teach control of it

biofuel ('baɪəʊˌfjʊəl) *n* a substance of biological origin that is used as a fuel

biog. *abbrev for:* **1** biographical **2** biography

biogenesis (ˌbaɪəʊ'dʒɛnɪsɪs) *n* the principle that a living organism must originate from a parent organism similar to itself > ˌ**bioge'netic** *or* ˌ**bioge'netical** *adj*

biogenic (ˌbaɪəʊ'dʒɛnɪk) *adj* produced or originating from a living organism

biography (baɪ'ɒgrəfɪ) *n, pl* **biographies** **1** an account of a person's life by another **2** such accounts collectively > **bi'ographer** *n* > **biographical** (ˌbaɪə'græfɪkᵊl) *adj*

Finding Biographical Information On the Internet

Make sure that websites are up to date and that hyperlinks have been maintained and do not produce error messages. Although there are a large number of sites produced by enthusiastic individuals, the comprehensiveness and up-to-dateness of such sources cannot always be relied upon. Before using a site remember to check the 'Last Updated' and 'About this site' information.

Reference

A number of websites offer online versions of fairly recently published encyclopedias and encyclopedic dictionaries with biographical content.
The 5th edition of the Collins English Dictionary,

which contains over 5000 biographical entries covering both contemporary and historical figures, is available through subscription at
▹ www.xrefer.com.

All 32 volumes of the Encyclopedia Britannica can be accessed through subscription at
▹ www.britannica.com.

The sixth edition of the US-published Columbia Encyclopedia contains thousands of biographies which are thematically arranged into 140 different sections. The content of the website is free and the biographical entries can be found at
▹ www.bartleby.com/65/ao.html

Another free online source is
▹ www.s9.com/biograph.
This American website contains brief biographies of over 28,000 people from ancient history to the present day.

Obituaries
BBC World News has a useful archive of notable individuals who have died since January 1999. This information is available at
▹ http://news.bbc.co.uk/1/hi/world/1739105.stm

News
▹ http://news.google.com
This popular search engine provides access to '4500 news sources updated continuously'. Key in a name and relevant reports will be shown and ranked chronologically.

Individuals
One way of finding information concerning a specific individual is to use Google's directory of people at
▹ http://directory.google.com/Top/Society/People.
This page has a list of professions – composers, film directors, inventors, celebrities, etc – which link to websites dedicated to or run by specific individuals in those fields.

bioindustry (ˈbaɪəʊˌɪndəstrɪ) *n pl* **bioindustries** an industry that makes use of biotechnology and other advanced life science methodologies in the creation or alteration of life forms or processes

bioinformatics (ˌbaɪəʊˌɪnfəˈmætɪks) *n (functioning as sing)* the branch of information science concerned with large databases of biochemical or pharmaceutical information

Bioko (baɪˈəʊkəʊ) *n* an island in the Gulf of Guinea, off the coast of Cameroon: part of Equatorial Guinea. Capital: Malabo. Area: 2017 sq km (786 sq miles). Former names: **Fernando Po** (until 1973), **Macías Nguema** (1973–79)

biol. *abbrev for:* **1** biological **2** biology

biological (ˌbaɪəˈlɒdʒɪkᵊl) *adj* **1** of or relating to biology **2** (of a detergent) containing enzymes for removing stains of organic origin from items to be washed ▹ *n* **3** *(usually pl)* a drug derived from a living organism

biological clock *n* **1** an inherent periodicity in the physiological processes of living organisms that is independent of external periodicity **2** the hypothetical mechanism responsible for this ▹ See also **circadian**

biological control *n* the control of destructive organisms by the use of other organisms, such as the natural predators of the pests

biological warfare *n* the use of living organisms or their toxic products to induce death or incapacity in humans
▹ www.howstuffworks.com/biochem_war.htm

biology (baɪˈɒlədʒɪ) *n* **1** the study of living organisms **2** the animal and plant life of a particular region > **biˈologist** *n*
▹ http://mcb.harvard.edu/BioLinks
▹ http://biology-online.org/
▹ http://cellbiol.com/
▹ www.webref.org/biology/biology.htm

bioluminescence (ˌbaɪəʊˌluːmɪˈnɛsəns) *n* the production of light by living organisms, such as the firefly > **ˌbioˌlumiˈnescent** *adj*

biomass (ˈbaɪəʊˌmæs) *n* the total number of living organisms in a given area, expressed in terms of living or dry weight per unit area

biomathematics (ˌbaɪəʊˌmæθəˈmætɪks, -ˌmæθˈmæt-) *n (functioning as sing)* the study of the application of mathematics to biology

biomechanics (ˌbaɪəʊmɪˈkænɪks) *n (functioning as sing)* the study of the mechanics of the movement of living organisms

biomedical (ˌbaɪəʊˈmɛdɪkᵊl) *adj* of or relating to biology and medicine or biomedicine

biomedicine (ˌbaɪəʊˈmɛdɪsɪn) *n* **1** the medical and biological study of the effects of unusual environmental stress, esp in connection with space travel **2** the study of herbal remedies

biometric (ˌbaɪəʊˈmɛtrɪk) *adj* relating to the digital scanning of the physiological or behavioural characteristics of individuals as a means of identification: *biometric fingerprinting*

biometry (baɪˈɒmɪtrɪ) *or* **biometrics** (ˌbaɪəˈmɛtrɪks) *n (functioning as sing)* the analysis of biological data using statistical methods > **ˌbioˈmetric** *adj*

biomorph (ˈbaɪəʊˌmɔːf) *n* a set of two-dimensional branching biomorphic images that can be used to illustrate evolutionary concepts

biomorphic (ˌbaɪəʊˈmɔːfɪk) *adj* having the form of a living organism

bionic (baɪˈɒnɪk) *adj* **1** of or relating to bionics **2** (in science fiction) having physiological functions augmented by electronic equipment

bionics (baɪˈɒnɪks) *n (functioning as sing)* **1** the study of certain biological functions that are applicable to the development of electronic equipment designed to operate similarly **2** the replacement of limbs or body parts by artificial limbs or parts that are electronically or mechanically powered

bionomics (ˌbaɪəˈnɒmɪks) *n (functioning as sing)* a less common name for **ecology** [C19 from BIO- + *nomics* on pattern of ECONOMICS] > **ˌbioˈnomic** *adj* > **bionomist** (baɪˈɒnəmɪst) *n*

bio-organism *n* a dangerous fast-proliferating organism that could be used as the basis of a biological weapon

biophysics (ˌbaɪəʊˈfɪzɪks) *n (functioning as sing)* the physics of biological processes and the application of the methods used in physics to biology > **ˌbioˈphysical** *adj* > **ˌbioˈphysically** *adv* > **biophysicist** (ˌbaɪəʊˈfɪzɪsɪst) *n*

biopic (ˈbaɪəʊˌpɪk) *n inf* a film based on the life of a famous person [C20 from *bio(graphical)* + *pic(ture)*]

bioprospecting (ˌbaɪəʊˈprɒspɛktɪŋ) *n* searching for plant or animal species for use as a source of commercially exploitable products, such as medicinal drugs

biopsy (ˈbaɪɒpsɪ) *n, pl* **biopsies** examination, esp under a microscope, of tissue from a living body to determine the cause or extent of a disease [C20 from BIO- + Gk *opsis* sight]

biorhythm (ˈbaɪəʊˌrɪðəm) *n* a cyclically recurring pattern of physiological states, believed by some to affect a person's physical, emotional, and mental states and behaviour

bioscope (ˈbaɪəˌskəʊp) *n* **1** a kind of early film projector

2 a South African word for **cinema**

bioscopy (baɪˈɒskəpɪ) *n, pl* **bioscopies** examination of a body to determine whether it is alive

biosensor (ˌbaɪəʊˈsɛnsə) *n* a device for detecting the presence of a specific chemical compound by its effect on enzymes, antibodies, or other biological substances

-biosis *n combining form* indicating a specified mode of life [NL, from Gk *biōsis;* see BIO-, -OSIS] > **-biotic** *adj combining form*

biosphere (ˈbaɪəˌsfɪə) *n* the part of the earth's surface and atmosphere inhabited by living things

biosurgery (ˈbaɪəʊˌsɜːdʒərɪ) *n* the use of live sterile maggots to treat patients with infected wounds

biosynthesis (ˌbaɪəʊˈsɪnθɪsɪs) *n* the formation of complex compounds from simple substances by living organisms > **biosynthetic** (ˌbaɪəʊsɪnˈθɛtɪk) *adj* > ˌ**biosynˈthetically** *adv*

biotech (ˈbaɪəʊˌtɛk) *n* **a** short for **biotechnology b** (*as modifier*): *a biotech company*

biotechnology (ˌbaɪəʊtɛkˈnɒlədʒɪ) *n* the use of microorganisms for beneficial effect, as in the processing of waste matter or (using genetic engineering) to produce antibiotics, hormones, vaccines, etc
▷ www.cato.com/biotech
▷ www.academicinfo.net/biotechmeta.html
▷ www.bio.com

biotic (baɪˈɒtɪk) *adj* of or relating to living organisms [C17 from Gk *biotikos,* from *bios* life]

biotin (ˈbaɪətɪn) *n* a vitamin of the B complex, abundant in egg yolk and liver [C20 from Gk *biotē* life, way of life + -IN]

bipartisan (ˌbaɪpɑːtɪˈzæn, baɪˈpɑːtɪˌzæn) *adj* consisting of or supported by two political parties > ˌ**bipartiˈsanship** *n*

bipartite (baɪˈpɑːtaɪt) *adj* **1** consisting of or having two parts **2** affecting or made by two parties **3** *bot* (esp of some leaves) divided into two parts almost to the base > **biˈpartitely** *adv* > **bipartition** (ˌbaɪpɑːˈtɪʃən) *n*

biped (ˈbaɪpɛd) *n* **1** any animal with two feet ▷ *adj also* **bipedal** (baɪˈpiːdᵊl, -ˈpɛdᵊl) **2** having two feet

bipinnate (baɪˈpɪneɪt) *adj* (of pinnate leaves) having the leaflets themselves divided into smaller leaflets > **biˈpinnately** *adv*

biplane (ˈbaɪˌpleɪn) *n* a type of aeroplane having two sets of wings, one above the other

bipolar (baɪˈpəʊlə) *adj* **1** having two poles: *a bipolar dynamo* **2** of or relating to the North and South Poles **3** having or characterized by two opposed opinions, etc **4** (of a transistor) utilizing both majority and minority charge carriers > ˌ**bipoˈlarity** *n*

biprism (ˈbaɪˌprɪzəm) *n physics* a prism that has a highly obtuse angle to facilitate beam splitting

biquadratic (ˌbaɪkwɒˈdrætɪk) *maths* ▷ *adj* **1** of or relating to the fourth power ▷ *n* **2** a biquadratic equation, such as $x^4 + x + 6 = 0$

biracial (baɪˈreɪʃəl) *adj* of or for members of two races > **biˈracialism** *n*

birch (bɜːtʃ) *n* **1** any catkin-bearing tree or shrub having thin peeling bark ▷ See also **silver birch 2** the hard close-grained wood of any of these trees **3 the birch** a bundle of birch twigs or a birch rod used, esp formerly, for flogging offenders ▷ *adj* **4** consisting or made of birch ▷ *vb* **5** (*tr*) to flog with a birch [OE *bierce*] > ˈ**birchen** *adj*

birchbark biting (ˈbɜːtʃˌbɑːk) *n* a Native Canadian craft in which designs are bitten onto bark from birch trees

bird (bɜːd) *n* **1** any warm-blooded egg-laying vertebrate, characterized by a body covering of feathers and forelimbs modified as wings **2** *inf* a person, as in **rare bird, odd bird, clever bird 3** *sl, chiefly Brit* a girl or young woman **4** *sl* prison or a term in prison (esp in **do bird**) **5 a bird in the hand** something definite or certain **6 birds of a feather** people with the same characteristics, ideas, interests, etc **7 get the bird** *inf* **7a** to be fired or dismissed **7b** (esp of a public performer) to be hissed at **8 kill two birds with one stone** to accomplish two things with one action **9** (**strictly**) **for the birds** *inf* deserving of disdain or contempt; not important [OE *bridd,* from ?]

birdbath (ˈbɜːdˌbɑːθ) *n* a small basin or trough for birds to bathe in, usually in a garden

bird-brained *adj inf* silly; stupid

birdcage (ˈbɜːdˌkeɪdʒ) *n* **1** a wire or wicker cage for captive birds **2** *Austral & NZ* an area on a racecourse where horses parade before a race **3** *NZ inf* a second-hand car dealer's yard

bird call *n* **1** the characteristic call or song of a bird **2** an imitation of this

birdie (ˈbɜːdɪ) *n* **1** *golf* a score of one stroke under par for a hole **2** *inf* a bird, esp a small bird ▷ *vb* **3** (*tr*) *golf* to play (a hole) in one stroke under par

birding (ˈbɜːdɪŋ) *n* another name for **bird-watching**

birdlime (ˈbɜːdˌlaɪm) *n* **1** a sticky substance smeared on twigs to catch small birds ▷ *vb* **birdlimes, birdliming, birdlimed 2** (*tr*) to smear (twigs) with birdlime to catch (small birds)

bird-nesting *or* **birds'-nesting** *n* searching for birds' nests as a hobby, often to steal the eggs

bird of paradise *n* **1** any of various songbirds of New Guinea and neighbouring regions, the males having brilliantly coloured plumage **2 bird-of-paradise flower** any of various plants native to tropical southern Africa and South America that have purple bracts and large orange or yellow flowers resembling birds' heads

bird of passage *n* **1** a bird that migrates seasonally **2** a transient person

bird of prey *n* a bird, such as a hawk or owl, that hunts other animals for food

birdseed (ˈbɜːdˌsiːd) *n* a mixture of various kinds of seeds for feeding cagebirds

bird's-eye *adj* **1a** seen or photographed from high above **1b** summarizing (esp in **bird's-eye view**) **2** having markings resembling birds' eyes

bird's-eye chilli *n* a small red hot-tasting chilli

bird's-foot *or* **bird-foot** *n, pl* **bird's-foots** *or* **bird-foots** any of various plants whose flowers, leaves, or pods resemble a bird's foot or claw

birdshot (ˈbɜːdˌʃɒt) *n* small pellets designed for shooting birds

bird strike *n* a collision of an aircraft with a bird

bird table *n* a table or platform in the open on which food for birds may be placed

bird-watcher *n* a person who identifies and studies wild birds in their natural surroundings > ˈ**bird-ˌwatching** *n*
▷ www.birder.com
▷ www.birdwatching.com

birefringence (ˌbaɪrɪˈfrɪndʒəns) *n* another name for **double refraction** > ˌ**bireˈfringent** *adj*

bireme (ˈbaɪriːm) *n* an ancient galley having two banks of oars [C17 from L, from BI- + *-rēmus* oar]

biretta *or* **berretta** (bɪˈrɛtə) *n RC Church* a stiff square clerical cap [C16 from It. *berretta,* from OProvençal, from LL *birrus* hooded cape]

Birgitta (bɪəˈgɪtə) *n* **Saint** ▷ See (Saint) **Bridget** (sense 2)

Birkbeck (ˈbɜːkˌbɛk) *n* **George** 1776–1841, British educationalist, who helped to establish vocational training for working men: founder and first president of the London Mechanics Institute (1824), which later became Birkbeck College

Birkenhead¹ (ˌbɜːkənˈhɛd) *n* a port in NW England, in Wirral unitary authority, Merseyside: former shipbuilding centre. Pop: 93 087 (1991)

Birkenhead² (ˈbɜːkənˌhɛd) *n* **Frederick Edwin Smith,** 1st Earl of, known as *F. E. Smith.* 1872–1930, British Conservative statesman, lawyer, and orator

birl (bɜːl) *vb* **1** *Scot* to spin; twirl **2** *US & Canad* to cause (a floating log) to spin using the feet while standing on it, esp as a sport among lumberjacks ▷ *n* **3** a variant spelling of **burl²** [c18 prob. imit. & infl. by WHIRL & HURL]

Birmingham (ˈbɜːmɪŋəm) *n* **1** an industrial city in central England, in Birmingham unitary authority, in the West Midlands: the second largest city in Great Britain; two cathedrals; three universities (1900, 1966, 1992). Pop: 965 928 (1994 est). Related adjective: **Brummie** **2** a unitary authority in central England, in the West Midlands. Pop: 977 091 (2001). Area: 283 sq km (109 sq miles) **3** (ˈbɜːmɪŋˌhæm) an industrial city in N central Alabama: rich local deposits of coal, iron ore, and other minerals. Pop: 242 820 (2000)

Biro (ˈbaɪrəʊ) *n, pl* **Biros** *trademark, Brit* a kind of ballpoint [c20 after Laszlo *Bíró* (1900–85), its Hungarian inventor]

Birobidzhan *or* **Birobijan** (*Russian* birəbidˈʒan) *n* **1** a city in SE Russia: capital of the Jewish Autonomous Region. Pop: 82 000 (1994) **2** another name for the **Jewish Autonomous Region**

birth (bɜːθ) *n* **1** the process of bearing young; childbirth **2** the act or fact of being born; nativity **3** the coming into existence of something; origin **4** ancestry; lineage: *of high birth* **5** natural or inherited talent: *an artist by birth* **6 give birth (to)** **6a** to bear (offspring) **6b** to produce or originate (an idea, plan, etc) ▷ *vb* **7** (*tr*) *rare* to bear or bring forth (a child) [c12 from ON *byrth*]

birth certificate *n* an official form giving details of the time and place of a person's birth

birth control *n* limitation of child-bearing by means of contraception

birthday (ˈbɜːθˌdeɪ) *n* **1a** an anniversary of the day of one's birth **1b** (*as modifier*): *birthday present* **2** the day on which a person was born

birthing ball *n* a large soft rubber ball used by women during childbirth to give support and to aid pain relief

birthing centre (ˈbɜːθɪŋ) *n* a private maternity hospital

birthing pool *n* a large bath in which a woman can give birth

birthmark (ˈbɜːθˌmɑːk) *n* a blemish on the skin formed before birth; naevus

birth mother *n* the woman who gives birth to a child, regardless of whether she is the genetic mother or subsequently brings up the child

birthplace (ˈbɜːθˌpleɪs) *n* the place where someone was born or where something originated

birth rate *n* the ratio of live births in a specified area, group, etc, to population, usually expressed per 1000 population per year

birthright (ˈbɜːθˌraɪt) *n* **1** privileges or possessions that a person has or is believed to be entitled to as soon as he is born **2** the privileges or possessions of a first-born son **3** inheritance

birthstone (ˈbɜːθˌstəʊn) *n* a precious or semiprecious stone associated with a month or sign of the zodiac and thought to bring luck if worn by a person born in that month or under that sign

Birtwistle (ˈbɜːtˌwɪsəl) *n* Sir **Harrison** born 1934, English composer, whose works include the operas *Punch and Judy* (1967), *The Mask of Orpheus* (1984), *Gawain* (1991), and *Exody* (1998)

biryani *or* **biriani** (ˌbɪrɪˈɑːnɪ) *n* an Indian dish made with rice, highly flavoured and coloured, mixed with meat or fish [from Urdu]

Bisayas (biˈsajas) *pl n* the Spanish name for the **Visayan Islands**

Biscay (ˈbɪskeɪ, -kɪ) *n* **Bay of** a large bay of the Atlantic Ocean between W France and N Spain: notorious for storms

biscuit (ˈbɪskɪt) *n* **1** *Brit* a small flat dry sweet or plain cake of many varieties. US and Canad word: **cookie** **2a** a pale brown or yellowish-grey colour **2b** (*as adj*): *biscuit gloves* **3** Also called: **bisque** earthenware or porcelain that has been fired but not glazed **4 take the biscuit** *Brit* to be regarded (by the speaker) as most surprising [c14 from OF, from (*pain*) *bescuit* twice-cooked (bread), from *bes* twice + *cuire* to cook]

▷ www.nicecupofteaandasitdown.com
▷ www.biscuit.org.uk
▷ www.gourmetsleuth.com

bise (biːz) *n* a cold dry northerly wind in Switzerland and parts of France and Italy [c14 from OF, of Gmc origin]

bisect (baɪˈsɛkt) *vb* **1** (*tr*) *maths* to divide into two equal parts **2** to cut or split into two [c17 BI- + *-sect*, from L *secāre* to cut] > **bisection** (baɪˈsɛkʃən) *n*

bisector (baɪˈsɛktə) *n maths* a straight line or plane that bisects an angle, etc

bisexual (baɪˈsɛksjʊəl) *adj* **1** sexually attracted by both men and women **2** showing characteristics of both sexes **3** of or relating to both sexes ▷ *n* **4** a bisexual organism; a hermaphrodite **5** a bisexual person > **bisexuality** (ˌbaɪsɛksjʊˈælɪtɪ) *n*

Bishkek (bɪʃˈkɛk) *n* the capital of Kyrgyzstan. Pop: 619 000 (1999 est). Also called: **Pishpek.** Former name (1926–91): **Frunze**

Bisho (ˈbɪʃəʊ) *n* a new town in S S Africa, on the Buffalo River adjacent to King Williams Town; the capital of Eastern Cape, it was formerly the capital of the Ciskei Bantustan: it is the centre of a sheep and cattle ranching area with various industries

bishop (ˈbɪʃəp) *n* **1** a clergyman having spiritual and administrative powers over a diocese. See also **suffragan** Related adj: **episcopal** **2** a chesspiece, capable of moving diagonally **3** mulled wine, usually port, spiced with oranges, cloves, etc [OE *biscop*, from LL, from Gk *episkopos*, from EPI- + *skopos* watcher]

Bishop Auckland *n* a town in N England, in central Durham: seat of the bishops of Durham since the 12th century: light industries. Pop: 23 154 (1991)

bishopric (ˈbɪʃəprɪk) *n* the see, diocese, or office of a bishop

Bisitun (ˌbiːsɪˈtuːn) *n* another name for **Behistun**

Bisk (*Russian* bijsk) *n* a variant spelling of **Biysk**

Biskra (ˈbɪskrɑː) *n* a town and oasis in NE Algeria, in the Sahara. Pop: 170 956 (1998)

Bisley (ˈbɪzlɪ) *n* a village in SE England, in Surrey: annual meetings of the National Rifle Association

Bismarck¹ (ˈbɪzmɑːk) *n* a city in North Dakota, on the Missouri River: the state capital. Pop: 49 256 (1990)

Bismarck² (*German* ˈbɪsmark) *n* Prince **Otto (Eduard Leopold) von** (ˈɔto fɔn), called *the Iron Chancellor*. 1815–98, German statesman; prime minister of Prussia (1862–90). Under his leadership Prussia defeated Austria and France, and Germany was united. In 1871 he became the first chancellor of the German Reich

Bismarck Archipelago *n* a group of over 200 islands in the SW Pacific, northeast of New Guinea: part of Papua New Guinea. Main islands: New Britain, New Ireland, Lavongai, and the Admiralty Islands. Chief town: Rabaul, on New Britain. Pop: 424 000 (1995 est). Area: 49 658 sq km (19 173 sq miles)

bismuth (ˈbɪzməθ) *n* a brittle pinkish-white crystalline metallic element. It is widely used in alloys; its compounds are used in medicines. Symbol: Bi; atomic no.: 83; atomic wt.: 208.98 [c17 from NL *bisemūtum*, from G *Wismut*, from ?]

bison (ˈbaɪsᵊn) *n, pl* **bison** **1** Also called: **American bison, buffalo** a member of the cattle tribe, formerly widely distributed over the prairies of W North America, with a massive head, shaggy forequarters, and a humped back **2** Also called: **wisent, European bison** a closely related and similar animal formerly widespread in Europe [c14 from L *bisōn*, of Gmc origin]

bisque¹ (bɪsk) *n* a thick rich soup made from shellfish [c17 from F]

bisque² (bɪsk) *n* **1a** a pink to yellowish tan colour **1b** (*as*

Bb

adj): *a bisque tablecloth* **2** *ceramics* another name for **biscuit** (sense 3) [C20 shortened from BISCUIT]

bisque[3] (bɪsk) *n tennis, golf, croquet* an extra point, stroke, or turn allowed to an inferior player, usually taken when desired [C17 from F, from ?]

Bissau (bɪˈsaʊ) *or* **Bissão** (*Portuguese* biˈsəʊ) *n* the capital of Guinea-Bissau, a port on the Atlantic: until 1974 the capital of Portuguese Guinea. Pop: 274 000 (1999 est)

bistable (ˌbaɪˈsteɪbᵊl) *adj* **1** (of an electrical circuit switch, etc) having two stable states ▷ *n* **2** *computing* another name for **flip-flop** (sense 2)

bistort (ˈbɪstɔːt) *n* **1** Also called: **snakeweed** a Eurasian plant having leaf stipules fused to form a tube around the stem and a spike of small pink flowers **2** Also called: **snakeroot** a related plant of W North America, with oval clusters of pink or white flowers **3** any of several similar plants [C16 from F, from L *bis* twice + *tortus* from *torquēre* to twist]

bistoury (ˈbɪstərɪ) *n, pl* **bistouries** a long narrow-bladed surgical knife [C15 from OF *bistorie* dagger, from ?]

bistre *or US* **bister** (ˈbɪstə) *n* **1** a transparent water-soluble brownish-yellow pigment made by boiling the soot of wood **2a** a yellowish-brown to dark brown colour **2b** (*as adj*): *bistre paint* [C18 from F, from ?]

bistro (ˈbiːstrəʊ) *n, pl* **bistros** a small restaurant [F: ?from Russian *bistro* fast]

bisulphate (baɪˈsʌlˌfeɪt) *n* a salt or ester of sulphuric acid containing the monovalent group $-HSO_4$ or the ion HSO_4^-. Systematic name: **hydrogensulphate**

bisulphide (baɪˈsʌlfaɪd) *n* another name for **disulphide**

Bisutun (ˌbiːsʊˈtuːn) *n* another name for **Behistun**

bit[1] (bɪt) *n* **1** a small piece, portion, or quantity **2** a short time or distance **3** *US & Canad inf* the value of an eighth of a dollar: spoken of only in units of two: *two bits* **4** any small coin **5** short for **bit part** **6** **a bit** rather; somewhat: *a bit dreary* **7** **a bit of** **7a** rather: *a bit of a dope* **7b** a considerable amount: *it takes quite a bit of time* **8** **bit by bit** gradually **9** **do one's bit** to make one's expected contribution [OE *bite* action of biting; see BITE]

bit[2] (bɪt) *n* **1** a metal mouthpiece on a bridle for controlling a horse **2** anything that restrains or curbs **3** a cutting or drilling tool, part, or head in a brace, drill, etc **4** the part of a key that engages the levers of a lock **5** the mouthpiece of a smoker's pipe ▷ *vb* **bits, bitting, bitted** (*tr*) **6** to put a bit in the mouth of (a horse) **7** to restrain; curb [OE *bita*; rel. to OE *bītan* to BITE]

bit[3] (bɪt) *vb* the past tense of **bite**

bit[4] (bɪt) *n maths, computers* **1** a single digit of binary notation, represented either by 0 or by 1 **2** the smallest unit of information, indicating the presence or absence of a single feature [C20 from B(INARY + DIG)IT]

bitch (bɪtʃ) *n* **1** a female dog or other female canine animal, such as a wolf **2** *sl, derog* a malicious, spiteful, or coarse woman **3** *inf* a difficult situation or problem ▷ *vb inf* **4** (*intr*) to complain; grumble **5** to behave (towards) in a spiteful manner **6** (*tr*; often foll by *up*) to botch; bungle [OE *bicce*]

bitchin' (ˈbɪtʃɪn) *or* **bitching** (ˈbɪtʃɪŋ) *US sl* ▷ *adj* **1** wonderful or excellent ▷ *adv* **2** extremely: *bitchin' good*

bitchy (ˈbɪtʃɪ) *adj* **bitchier, bitchiest** *sl* of or like a bitch; malicious; snide > ˈ**bitchiness** *n*

bite (baɪt) *vb* **bites, biting, bit, bitten** **1** to grip, cut off, or tear as with the teeth or jaws **2** (of animals, insects, etc) to injure by puncturing or tearing (the skin or flesh) with the teeth, fangs, etc **3** (*tr*) to cut or penetrate, as with a knife **4** (of corrosive material such as acid) to eat away or into **5** to smart or cause to smart; sting **6** (*intr*) *angling* (of a fish) to take or attempt to take the bait or lure **7** to take firm hold (of) or act effectively (upon) **8** (*tr*) *sl* to annoy or worry: *what's biting her?* **9** (*tr*; often foll by *for*) *Austral & NZ sl* to ask (for); scrounge from **10** **bite the dust** **10a** to fall down dead **10b** to be rejected: *another good idea bites the dust* ▷ *n* **11** the act of biting **12** a thing or amount bitten off **13** a wound, bruise, or sting inflicted by biting **14** *angling* an attempt by a fish to take the bait or lure **15** a light meal; snack **16** a cutting, stinging, or smarting sensation **17** *dentistry* the angle or manner of contact between the upper and lower teeth **18** **put the bite on** *sl* to cadge or borrow from [OE *bītan*] > ˈ**biter** *n*

Bithynia (bɪˈθɪnɪə) *n* an ancient country on the Black Sea in NW Asia Minor

biting (ˈbaɪtɪŋ) *adj* **1** piercing; keen: *a biting wind* **2** sarcastic; incisive > ˈ**bitingly** *adv*

bitmap (ˈbɪtˌmæp) *computing* ▷ *n* **1** a picture created on a visual display unit where each pixel corresponds to one or more bits in memory, the number of bits per pixel determining the number of available colours ▷ *vb* **bitmaps, bitmapping, bitmapped** **2** (*tr*) to create a bitmap of

bitmap font *n computing* a font format in which letters and symbols are stored as a pattern of dots. Compare **outline font**

Bitolj (*Serbo-Croat* ˈbitolj) *or* **Bitola** (ˈbiːtəʊlə) *n* a city in SW Macedonia: under Turkish rule from 1382 until 1913 when it was taken by the Serbs. Pop: 75 386 (1994)

bit part *n* a very small acting role with few lines to speak

bitstream (ˈbɪtˌstriːm) *n computing* a sequence of digital data transmitted electronically

bitt (bɪt) *naut* ▷ *n* **1** one of a pair of strong posts on the deck of a ship for securing mooring and other lines **2** another word for **bollard** (sense 1) ▷ *vb* **3** (*tr*) to secure (a line) by means of a bitt [C14 prob. from ON]

bitten (ˈbɪtᵊn) *vb* the past participle of **bite**

bitter (ˈbɪtə) *adj* **1** having or denoting an unpalatable harsh taste, as the peel of an orange **2** showing or caused by strong unrelenting hostility or resentment **3** difficult or unpleasant to accept or admit: *a bitter blow* **4** cutting; sarcastic: *bitter words* **5** bitingly cold: *a bitter night* ▷ *adv* **6** very; extremely (esp in **bitter cold**) ▷ *n* **7** a thing that is bitter **8** *Brit* beer with a slightly bitter taste [OE *biter*; rel. to *bītan* to BITE] > ˈ**bitterly** *adv* > ˈ**bitterness** *n*

bitter end *n* **1** *naut* the end of a line, chain, or cable **2** **to the bitter end** **2a** until the finish of a task, etc, however unpleasant or difficult **2b** until final defeat or death [C19 ?from BITT]

Bitter Lakes *pl n* two lakes, the **Great Bitter Lake** and **Little Bitter Lake** in NE Egypt: part of the Suez Canal

bittern (ˈbɪtən) *n* a wading bird related and similar to the herons but with shorter legs and neck and a booming call [C14 from OF *butor*, ?from L *būtiō* bittern + *taurus* bull]

bitters (ˈbɪtəz) *pl n* **1** bitter-tasting spirits of varying alcoholic content flavoured with plant extracts **2** a similar liquid containing a bitter-tasting substance, used as a tonic

bittersweet (ˈbɪtəˌswiːt) *n* **1** any of several North American woody climbing plants having orange capsules that open to expose scarlet-coated seeds **2** another name for **woody nightshade** ▷ *adj* **3** tasting of or being a mixture of bitterness and sweetness **4** pleasant but tinged with sadness

bitty (ˈbɪtɪ) *adj* **bittier, bittiest** **1** lacking unity; disjointed **2** containing bits, sediment, etc > ˈ**bittiness** *n*

bitumen (ˈbɪtjʊmɪn) *n* **1** any of various viscous or solid impure mixtures of hydrocarbons that occur naturally in asphalt, tar, mineral waxes, etc: used as a road surfacing and roofing material **2** **the bitumen** *Austral & NZ inf* any road with a bitumen surface [C15 from L *bitūmen*] > **bituminous** (bɪˈtjuːmɪnəs) *adj*

bituminize *or* **bituminise** (bɪˈtjuːmɪˌnaɪz) *vb* **bituminizes, bituminizing, bituminized** *or* **bituminises, bituminising, bituminised** (*tr*) to treat with or convert into bitumen

bituminous coal *n* a soft black coal that burns with a smoky yellow flame

bivalent (baɪˈveɪlənt, ˈbɪvə-) *adj* **1** *chem* another word for **divalent** **2** (of homologous chromosomes) associated together in pairs > **biˈvalency** *n*

bivalve (ˈbaɪˌvælv) *n* **1** a marine or freshwater mollusc, having a laterally compressed body, a shell consisting of two hinged valves, and gills for respiration. The group includes clams, cockles, oysters, and mussels ▷ *adj* **2** of or relating to these molluscs ▷ Also: **lamellibranch**

bivouac (ˈbɪvʊˌæk, ˈbɪvwæk) *n* **1** a temporary encampment, as used by soldiers, mountaineers, etc ▷ *vb* **bivouacs, bivouacking, bivouacked** **2** (*intr*) to make such an encampment [c18 from F *bivuac*, prob. from Swiss G *Beiwacht*, lit.: BY + WATCH]

biweekly (baɪˈwiːklɪ) *adj, adv* **1** every two weeks **2** twice a week. See **bi-** ▷ *n, pl* **biweeklies** **3** a periodical published every two weeks

biyearly (baɪˈjɪəlɪ) *adj, adv* **1** every two years; biennial or biennially **2** twice a year; biannual or biannually. See **bi-**

Biysk, Biisk, *or* **Bisk** (*Russian* bijsk) *n* a city in SW Russia, at the foot of the Altai Mountains. Pop: 225 700 (1999 est)

biz (bɪz) *n inf* short for **business**

bizarre (bɪˈzɑː) *adj* odd or unusual, esp in an interesting or amusing way [c17 from F, from It. *bizzarro* capricious, from ?] > **biˈzarreness** *n*

Bizerte (bɪˈzɜːtə; *French* bizɛrt) *or* **Bizerta** *n* a port in N Tunisia, on the Mediterranean at the canalized outlet of **Lake Bizerte**. Pop: 98 900 (1994)

Bizet (ˈbiːzeɪ; *French* bizɛ) *n* **Georges** (ʒɔrʒ) 1838–75, French composer, whose works include the opera *Carmen* (1875) and incidental music to Daudet's *L'Arlésienne* (1872)

bizzo (ˈbɪzəʊ) ▷ *n Austral inf* **1** empty and irrelevant talk or ideas; nonsense: *all that bizzo* **2** a businessman's club

bizzy (ˈbɪzɪ) *n, pl* **bizzies** *Brit sl, chiefly Liverpudlian* a policeman [c20 from BUSY]

Björneborg (bjœrnəˈbɔrj) *n* the Swedish name for **Pori**

bk *abbrev for:* **1** bank **2** book

Bk *the chemical symbol for* berkelium

bkg *abbrev for* banking

BL *abbrev for:* **1** Bachelor of Law **2** Bachelor of Letters **3** Barrister-at-Law **4** British Library

B/L, b/l, *or* **b.l.** *pl* **Bs/L, bs/l,** *or* **bs.l.** *abbrev for* bill of lading

blab (blæb) *vb* **blabs, blabbing, blabbed** **1** to divulge (secrets, etc) indiscreetly **2** (*intr*) to chatter thoughtlessly; prattle ▷ *n* **3** a less common word for **blabber** [c14 of Gmc origin]

blabber (ˈblæbə) *n* **1** a person who blabs **2** idle chatter ▷ *vb* **3** (*intr*) to talk without thinking; chatter [c15 *blabberen*, prob. imit.]

black (blæk) *adj* **1** of the colour of jet or carbon black, having no hue due to the absorption of all or nearly all incident light **2** without light; completely dark **3** without hope of alleviation; gloomy: *the future looked black* **4** very dirty or soiled **5** angry or resentful: *black looks* **6** (of a play or other work) dealing with the unpleasant realities of life, esp in a cynical or macabre manner: *black comedy* **7** (of coffee or tea) without milk or cream **8a** wicked or harmful: *a black lie* **8b** (*in combination*): *black-hearted* **9** *Brit* (of goods, jobs, works, etc) being subject to boycott by trade unionists ▷ *n* **10** a black colour **11** a dye or pigment of or producing this colour **12** black clothing, worn esp as a sign of mourning **13** *chess, draughts* a black or dark-coloured piece or square **14** complete darkness: *the black of the night* **15** **in the black** in credit or without debt ▷ *vb* **16** another word for **blacken** **17** (*tr*) to polish (shoes, etc) with blacking **18** (*tr*) *Brit, Austral, & NZ* (of trade unionists) to organize a boycott of (specified goods, jobs, work, etc) ▷ See also **blackout** [OE *blæc*] > **ˈblackness** *n*

Black[1] (blæk) *n* **1** *sometimes derog* a member of a dark-skinned race, esp someone of Negroid or Australoid origin ▷ *adj* **2** of or relating to a Black person or Black people

Black[2] (blæk) *n* **1** Sir **James** (**Whyte**) born 1924, British biochemist. He discovered beta-blockers and drugs for peptic ulcers: Nobel prize for physiology or medicine 1988 **2** **Joseph** 1728–99, Scottish physician and chemist, noted for his pioneering work on carbon dioxide and heat

blackamoor (ˈblækəˌmʊə, -ˌmɔː) *n arch* a Black person or other person with dark skin [c16 see BLACK[1], MOOR]

black-and-blue *adj* **1** (of the skin) discoloured, as from a bruise **2** feeling pain or soreness, as from a beating

Black and Tans *pl n* **the** a specially recruited armed force sent to Ireland in 1921 by the British Government to combat Sinn Féin [named after the colour of their uniforms]

black-and-white *n* **1a** a photograph, picture, sketch, etc, in black, white, and shades of grey rather than in colour **1b** (*as modifier*): *black-and-white film* **2** **in black and white** **2a** in print or writing **2b** in extremes: *he always saw things in black and white*

black art *n* **the** another name for **black magic**

black-backed gull *n* either of two common black-and-white European coastal gulls, **lesser black-backed gull** and **great black-backed gull**

blackball (ˈblækˌbɔːl) *n* **1** a negative vote or veto **2** a black wooden ball used to indicate disapproval or to veto in a vote ▷ *vb* (*tr*) **3** to vote against **4** to exclude (someone) from a group, profession, etc; ostracize [c18 from *black ball* used to veto]

black bean *n* an Australian leguminous tree: used in furniture manufacture. Also called: **Moreton Bay chestnut**

black bear *n* **1** **American black bear** a bear inhabiting forests of North America. It is smaller and less ferocious than the brown bear **2** **Asiatic black bear** a bear of central and E Asia, black with a pale V-shaped mark on the chest

Bb

black belt *n judo, karate, etc* **a** a black belt worn by an instructor or expert **b** a person entitled to wear this

blackberry (ˈblækbərɪ) *n, pl* **blackberries** **1** Also called: **bramble** any of several woody rosaceous plants that have thorny stems and black or purple edible berry-like fruits **2** the fruit of any of these plants ▷ *vb* **blackberries, blackberrying, blackberried** **3** (*intr*) to gather blackberries

blackbird (ˈblækˌbɜːd) *n* **1** a common European thrush in which the male has black plumage and a yellow bill **2** any of various American orioles having dark plumage **3** (formerly) a person, esp a South Sea Islander, who was kidnapped and sold as a slave, esp in Australia ▷ *vb* **4** (*tr*) (formerly) to kidnap and sell into slavery

blackboard (ˈblækˌbɔːd) *n* a hard or rigid surface made of a smooth usually dark substance, used for writing or drawing on with chalk, esp in teaching

black body *n physics* a hypothetical body capable of absorbing all the electromagnetic radiation falling on it. Also called: **full radiator**

black book *n* **1** a book containing the names of people to be punished, blacklisted, etc **2** **in someone's black books** *inf* out of favour with someone

black box *n* **1** a self-contained unit in an electronic or computer system whose circuitry need not be known to understand its function **2** an informal name for **flight recorder**

blackboy (ˈblækˌbɔɪ) *n* another name for **grass tree** (sense 1)

black bream *n* **1** another name for **luderick** **2** a dark-coloured food and game fish, *Acanthopagrus australis*, of E Australian seas

blackbuck (ˈblækˌbʌk) *n* an Indian antelope, the male of which has a dark back

Blackburn (ˈblækbɜːn) *n* **1** a city in NW England, in

Blackburn with Darwen unitary authority, Lancashire: formerly important for textiles, now has mixed industries. Pop: 105 994 (1991) **2 Mount** a mountain in SE Alaska, the highest peak in the Wrangell Mountains. Height: 5037 m (16 523 ft)

Blackburn with Darwen ('dɑːwɛn) *n* a unitary authority in NW England, in Lancashire. Pop: 137 471 (2001). Area: 137 sq km (53 sq miles)

blackbutt ('blæk,bʌt) *n* any of various Australian eucalyptus trees having rough fibrous bark and hard wood used as timber

blackcap ('blæk,kæp) *n* a brownish-grey Old World warbler, the male of which has a black crown

Black Caps *pl n* **the** the international cricket team of New Zealand [c20 so named because of the players' black caps]

blackcock ('blæk,kɒk) *n* the male of the black grouse

black coral *n* a dark coral with concentric rings, found deep in the sea, and, once polished, prized in the Caribbean as a semiprecious gem

Black Country *n* **the** the formerly heavily industrialized region of central England, northwest of Birmingham

blackcurrant (,blæk'kʌrənt) *n* **1** a N temperate shrub having red or white flowers and small edible black berries **2** its fruit

blackdamp ('blæk,dæmp) *n* air that is low in oxygen content and high in carbon dioxide as a result of an explosion in a mine. Also called: **chokedamp**

Black Death *n* **the** a form of bubonic plague pandemic in Europe and Asia during the 14th century. See **bubonic plague**

black disc *n* a conventional black vinyl gramophone record as opposed to a compact disc

black earth *n* another name for **chernozem**

black economy *n* that portion of the income of a nation that remains illegally undeclared

blacken ('blækən) *vb* **1** to make or become black or dirty **2** *(tr)* to defame; slander (esp in **blacken someone's name**)

Blackett ('blækɪt) *n* **Patrick Maynard Stuart**, Baron. 1897–1974, English physicist, noted for his work on cosmic radiation and his discovery of the positron. Nobel prize for physics 1948

black eye *n* bruising round the eye

black-eyed Susan ('suːzᵊn) *n* any of several North American plants having flower heads of orange-yellow rays and brown-black centres

blackface ('blæk,feɪs) *n* **1** a variety of sheep with a black face **2** the make-up used by a White performer imitating a Black person

blackfish ('blæk,fɪʃ) *n, pl* **blackfish** *or* **blackfishes** **1** any of various dark fishes, esp a common edible Australian estuary fish **2** a female salmon that has recently spawned ▹ Cf **redfish** (sense 1)

black flag *n* another name for the **Jolly Roger**

blackfly ('blæk,flaɪ) *n, pl* **blackflies** a black aphid that infests beans, sugar beet, and other plants. Also called: **bean aphid**

Black Forest *n* **the** a hilly wooded region of SW Germany, in Baden-Württemberg: a popular resort area. German name: **Schwarzwald**

Black Friar *n* a Dominican friar

black grouse *n* **1** a large N European grouse, the male of which has a bluish-black plumage **2** a related and similar species of W Asia

blackguard ('blægɑːd, -gəd) *n* **1** an unprincipled contemptible person; scoundrel ▹ *vb* **2** *(tr)* to ridicule or denounce with abusive language **3** *(intr)* to behave like a blackguard [c16 see BLACK, GUARD] > '**blackguardism** *n* > '**blackguardly** *adj*

blackhead ('blæk,hɛd) *n* **1** a black-tipped plug of fatty matter clogging a pore of the skin **2** any of various birds with black plumage on the head

Blackheath ('blækhiːθ) *n* a residential district in SE London, mainly in the boroughs of Lewisham and Greenwich: a large heath formerly notorious for highwaymen

Black Hills *pl n* a group of mountains in W South Dakota and NE Wyoming: famous for the gigantic sculptures of US presidents on the side of Mount Rushmore Highest peak: Harney Peak, 2207 m (7242 ft)

black hole *n* **1a** *astron* a hypothetical region of space resulting from the gravitational collapse of a star and surrounded by a gravitational field so high that neither matter nor radiation could escape from it **1b** a similar but much more massive region of space at the centre of a galaxy **2** any place regarded as resembling a black hole in that items or information entering it cannot be retrieved

black ice *n* a thin transparent layer of new ice on a road or similar surface

blacking ('blækɪŋ) *n* any preparation for giving a black finish to shoes, metals, etc

Black Isle *n* **the** a peninsula in NE Scotland, in Highland council area, between the Cromarty and Moray Firths [so called because until the late 18th century much of it was uncultivated black moor]

blackjack[1] ('blæk,dʒæk) *chiefly US & Canad* ▹ *n* **1** a truncheon of leather-covered lead with a flexible shaft ▹ *vb (tr)* **2** to hit as with a blackjack **3** to compel (a person) by threats [c19 from BLACK + JACK (implement)]

blackjack[2] ('blæk,dʒæk) *n* pontoon or any similar card game [c20 from BLACK + JACK (the knave)]

black knight *n commerce* a person or firm that makes an unwelcome takeover bid for a company ▹ Cf **grey knight, white knight**

black lead (lɛd) *n* another name for **graphite**

blackleg ('blæklɛg) *n* **1** Also called **scab** *Brit* a person who acts against the interests of a trade union, as by continuing to work during a strike or taking over a striker's job ▹ *vb* **blacklegs, blacklegging, blacklegged** **2** *(intr) Brit* to act against the interests of a trade union, esp by refusing to join a strike

black light *n* the invisible electromagnetic radiation in the ultraviolet and infrared regions of the spectrum

blacklist ('blæk,lɪst) *n* **1** a list of persons or organizations under suspicion, or considered untrustworthy, disloyal, etc ▹ *vb* **2** *(tr)* to put on a blacklist

black magic *n* magic used for evil purposes

blackmail ('blæk,meɪl) *n* **1** the act of attempting to obtain money by intimidation, as by threats to disclose discreditable information **2** the exertion of pressure, esp unfairly, in an attempt to influence someone ▹ *vb (tr)* **3** to exact or attempt to exact (money or anything of value) from (a person) by threats or intimidation; extort **4** to attempt to influence (a person), esp by unfair pressure [c16 from BLACK + OE *māl* terms] > '**black,mailer** *n*

Black Maria (mə'raɪə) *n* a police van for transporting prisoners

black mark *n* an indication of disapproval, failure, etc

black market *n* **1** any system in which goods or currencies are sold and bought illegally, esp in violation of controls or rationing **2** the place where such a system operates ▹ *vb* **black-market** **3** to sell (goods) on the black market > **black marketeer** *n*

black mass *n (sometimes caps)* a blasphemous travesty of the Christian Mass, performed by practitioners of black magic

black money *n* **1** that part of a nation's income that relates to its black economy **2** any money that a person or organization acquires illegally, as by a means that involves tax evasion **3** *US* money to fund a government project that is concealed in the cost of some other project

Blackmore ('blæk,mɔː) *n* **R(ichard) D(oddridge)**

1825–1900, English novelist; author of *Lorna Doone* (1869)

Black Mountain *n* **the** a mountain range in S Wales, in E Carmarthenshire and W Powys. Highest peak: Carmarthen Van, 802 m (2632 ft)

Black Mountains *pl n* a mountain range running from N Monmouthshire and SE Powys (Wales) to SW Herefordshire (England). Highest peak: Waun Fach, 811 m (2660 ft)

Black Muslim *n* (esp in the US) a member of an Islamic political movement of Black people who seek to establish a new Black nation

black nightshade *n* a common poisonous weed in cultivated land, having white flowers and black berry-like fruits

blackout ('blækaʊt) *n* **1** the extinguishing or hiding of all artificial light, esp in a city visible to an air attack **2** a momentary loss of consciousness, vision, or memory **3** a temporary electrical power failure or cut **4** the suspension of broadcasting, as by a strike or for political reasons ▷ *vb* **black out** (*adv*) **5** (*tr*) to obliterate or extinguish (lights) **6** (*tr*) to create a blackout in (a city, etc) **7** (*intr*) to lose vision, consciousness, or memory temporarily **8** (*tr*) to stop (news, a television programme, etc) from being broadcast

black pepper *n* a pungent condiment made by grinding the dried unripe berries and husks of the pepper plant

Blackpool ('blæk,puːl) *n* **1** a town and resort in NW England, in Blackpool unitary authority, Lancashire on the Irish Sea: famous for its tower, 158 m (518 ft) high, and its illuminations. Pop: 146 262 (1991) **2** a unitary authority in NW England, in Lancashire. Pop: 142 284 (2001). Area: 35 sq km (13 sq miles)

Black Power *n* a social, economic, and political movement of Black people, esp in the US, to obtain equality with Whites

Black Prince *n* **the** See **Edward** (Prince of Wales)

black pudding *n* a kind of black sausage made from minced pork fat, pig's blood, and other ingredients. Also called: **blood pudding**

Black Rod *n* (in Britain) an officer of the House of Lords and of the Order of the Garter, whose main duty is summoning the Commons at the opening and proroguing of Parliament

Black Sea *n* an inland sea between SE Europe and Asia: connected to the Aegean Sea by the Bosporus, the Sea of Marmara, and the Dardanelles, and to the Sea of Azov by the Kerch Strait. Area: about 415 000 sq km (160 000 sq miles). Also called: **Euxine Sea**. Ancient name: **Pontus Euxinus**

black section *n* (in Britain) an unofficial group within the Labour Party in any constituency which represents the interests of local Black people

black sheep *n* a person who is regarded as a disgrace or failure by his or her family or peer group

Blackshirt ('blæk,ʃɜːt) *n* (in Europe) a member of a fascist organization, esp the Italian Fascist party before and during World War II

blacksmith ('blæk,smɪθ) *n* an artisan who works iron with a furnace, anvil, hammer, etc [c14 see BLACK, SMITH]

black snake *n* **1** any of several Old World black venomous snakes, esp the **Australian black snake** **2** any of various dark nonvenomous snakes

black spot *n* **1** a place on a road where accidents frequently occur **2** any dangerous or difficult place **3** a fungal disease of roses that results in black blotches on the leaves

black stump *n* **the** *Austral* an imaginary marker of the extent of civilization (esp in **beyond the black stump**)

black tea *n* tea made from fermented tea leaves

blackthorn ('blæk,θɔːn) *n* a thorny Eurasian shrub with black twigs, white flowers, and small sour plumlike fruits. Also called: **sloe**

black tie *n* **1** a black bow tie worn with a dinner jacket **2** (*modifier*) denoting an occasion when a dinner jacket should be worn

blacktop ('blæk,tɒp) *n chiefly US & Canad* a bituminous mixture used for paving

Black tracker *n Austral* an Aboriginal tracker working for the police

black velvet *n* a mixture of stout and champagne in equal proportions

Black Volta *n* a river in W Africa, rising in SW Burkina-Faso and flowing northeast, then south into Lake Volta: forms part of the border of Ghana with Burkina-Faso and with the Ivory Coast. Length: about 800 km (500 miles)

Black Watch *n* **the** the Royal Highland Regiment in the British Army

blackwater fever ('blæk,wɔːtə) *n* a rare and serious complication of malaria, characterized by massive destruction of red blood cells, producing dark red or blackish urine

blackwater rafting *n NZ* the sport of riding through underground caves on a large rubber tube. Also called: **cave tubing**

black wattle *n* **1** a small Australian acacia tree, *A. mearnsii*, with yellow flowers **2** a tall Australian shrub, *Callicoma serratifolia*

black widow *n* an American spider, the female of which is highly venomous, and commonly eats its mate

Blackwood[1] ('blæk,wʊd) *n bridge* a conventional bidding sequence of four and five no-trumps, which are requests to the partner to show aces and kings respectively [c20 after E. F. *Blackwood*, its US inventor]

Blackwood[2] ('blæk,wʊd) *n* **Algernon** (**Henry**) 1869–1951, British novelist and short- story writer; noted for his supernatural tales

bladder ('blædə) *n* **1** *anat* a distensible membranous sac, usually containing liquid or gas, esp the urinary bladder **2** an inflatable part of something **3** a hollow saclike part or organ in certain plants, such as the bladderwort or bladderwrack [OE *blǣdre*] > '**bladdery** *adj*

bladderwort ('blædə,wɜːt) *n* an aquatic plant some of whose leaves are modified as small bladders to trap minute aquatic animals

bladderwrack ('blædə,ræk) *n* any of several seaweeds that grow in the intertidal regions of rocky shores and have branched brown fronds with air bladders

blade (bleɪd) *n* **1** the part of a sharp weapon, tool, etc, that forms the cutting edge **2** the thin flattish part of various tools, implements, etc, as of a propeller, turbine, etc **3** the flattened expanded part of a leaf, sepal, or petal **4** the long narrow leaf of a grass or related plant **5** the striking surface of a bat, club, stick, or oar **6** the metal runner on an ice skate **7** the upper part of the tongue lying directly behind the tip **8** *arch* a dashing or swaggering young man **9** short for **shoulder blade** **10** a poetic word for a **sword** or **swordsman** [OE *blæd*] > '**bladed** *adj*

blaeberry ('bleɪbərɪ) *n, pl* **blaeberries** *Brit* another name for **bilberry** (senses 1, 2) [c15 from dialect *blae* bluish + BERRY]

Blaenau Gwent ('blaɪ,naʊ 'gwɛnt) *n* a county borough of SE Wales, created in 1996 from NW Gwent. Administrative centre: Ebbw Vale. Pop: 76 058 (2001). Area: 109 sq km (42 sq miles)

blag (blæg) *sl* ▷ *n* **1** a robbery, esp with violence ▷ *vb* **blags, blagging, blagged** (*tr*) **2** to obtain by wheedling or cadging: *she blagged free tickets for the show from her mate* **3** to snatch (wages, someone's handbag, etc); steal **4** to rob (esp a bank or post office) [c19 from ?] > '**blagger** *n*

Blagoveshchensk (*Russian* bləga'vjeʃtʃɪnsk) *n* a city and port in E Russia, in Siberia on the Amur River. Pop: 220 900 (1999 est)

blah *or* **blah blah** (blɑː) *n sl* worthless or silly talk [C20 imit.]

blain (bleɪn) *n* a blister, blotch, or sore on the skin [OE *blegen*]

Blair (blɛə) *n* **Tony**, full name *Anthony Charles Lynton Blair*. born 1953, British politician; leader of the Labour Party from 1994; prime minister from 1997

Blairite (ˈblɛəraɪt) *adj* **1** of or relating to the modernizing policies of Tony Blair ▷ *n* **2** a supporter of the modernizing policies of Tony Blair

Blake (bleɪk) *n* **1 Sir Peter** born 1932, British painter, a leading exponent of pop art in the 1960s: co-founder of the Brotherhood of Ruralists (1969) **2 Quentin (Saxby)** born 1932, British artist, illustrator, and children's writer; noted esp for his illustrations to books by Roald Dahl **3 Robert** 1599–1657, English admiral, who commanded Cromwell's fleet against the Royalists, the Dutch, and the Spanish **4 William** 1757–1827, English poet, painter, engraver, and mystic. His literary works include *Songs of Innocence* (1789) and *Songs of Experience* (1794), *The Marriage of Heaven and Hell* (1793), and *Jerusalem* (1820). His chief works in the visual arts include engravings of a visionary nature, such as the illustrations for *The Book of Job* (1826), for Dante's poems, and for his own *Prophetic Books* (1783–1804)

blame (bleɪm) *n* **1** responsibility for something that is wrong; culpability **2** an expression of condemnation ▷ *vb* **blames, blaming, blamed** (*tr*) **3** (usually foll by *for*) to attribute responsibility to: *I blame him for the failure* **4** (usually foll by *on*) to ascribe responsibility for (something) to: *I blame the failure on him* **5** to find fault with **6 be to blame** to be at fault [C12 from OF *blasmer*, ult. from LL *blasphēmāre* to blaspheme] > ˈ**blamable** *or* ˈ**blameable** *adj* > ˈ**blamably** *or* ˈ**blameably** *adv*

blame culture *n* the tendency to look for one person or organization that can be held responsible for a bad state of affairs, an accident, etc

blameful (ˈbleɪmfʊl) *adj* deserving blame; guilty > ˈ**blamefully** *adv* > ˈ**blamefulness** *n*

blameless (ˈbleɪmlɪs) *adj* free from blame; innocent > ˈ**blamelessness** *n*

blameworthy (ˈbleɪmˌwɜːðɪ) *adj* deserving censure > ˈ**blameˌworthiness** *n*

Blanc[1] (*French* blɑ̃) *n* **1 Mont** See **Mont Blanc 2 Cape** a headland in N Tunisia: the northernmost point of Africa **3 Cape** Also called: **Cape Blanco** (ˈblæŋkəʊ) a peninsula in Mauritania, on the Atlantic coast

Blanc[2] (*French* blɑ̃) *n* **(Jean Joseph Charles) Louis** (lwi) 1811–82, French socialist and historian: author of *L'Organisation du travail* (1840), in which he advocated the establishment of cooperative workshops subsidized by the state

blanch (blɑːntʃ) *vb* (*mainly tr*) **1** to remove colour from; whiten **2** (*usually intr*) to become or cause to become pale, as with sickness or fear **3** to prepare (meat, green vegetables, nuts, etc) by plunging them in boiling water **4** to cause (celery, chicory, etc) to grow free of chlorophyll by the exclusion of sunlight [C14 from OF *blanchir*, from *blanc* white; see BLANK]

Blanchett (ˈblɑːntʃət) *n* **Cate** (keɪt), full name *Catherine Elise Blanchett*. born 1969, Australian actress; her films include *Elizabeth* (1998) and the *Lord of the Rings* trilogy (2001–03)

blancmange (bləˈmɒnʒ) *n* a jelly-like dessert of milk, stiffened usually with cornflour [C14 from OF *blanc manger*, lit.: white food]

Blanco (*French* blanko) *n* **Serge** (sɛrʒ) born 1958, French Rugby Union footballer

bland (blænd) *adj* **1** devoid of distinctive or stimulating characteristics; uninteresting **2** gentle and agreeable; suave **3** mild and soothing [C15 from L *blandus* flattering] > ˈ**blandly** *adv* > ˈ**blandness** *n*

blandish (ˈblændɪʃ) *vb* (*tr*) to seek to persuade or influence by mild flattery; coax [C14 from OF *blandir*, from L *blandīrī*]

blandishments (ˈblændɪʃmənts) *pl n* (*rarely sing*) flattery intended to coax or cajole

blank (blæŋk) *adj* **1** (of a writing surface) bearing no marks; not written on **2** (of a form, etc) with spaces left for details to be filled in **3** without ornament or break **4** not filled in; empty **5** exhibiting no interest or expression: *a blank look* **6** lacking understanding; confused: *he looked blank* **7** absolute; complete: *blank rejection* **8** devoid of ideas or inspiration: *his mind went blank* ▷ *n* **9** an emptiness; void; blank space **10** an empty space for writing in **11** a printed form containing such empty spaces **12** something characterized by incomprehension or confusion: *my mind went a complete blank* **13** a mark, often a dash, in place of a word, esp a taboo word **14** short for **blank cartridge 15** a piece of material prepared for stamping, punching, forging, or some other operation **16 draw a blank** to get no results from something ▷ *vb* (*tr*) **17** (usually foll by *out*) to cross out, blot, or obscure [C15 from OF *blanc* white, of Gmc origin] > ˈ**blankness** *n*

blank cartridge *n* a cartridge containing powder but no bullet

blank cheque *n* **1** a cheque that has been signed but on which the amount payable has not been specified **2** complete freedom of action

blanket (ˈblæŋkɪt) *n* **1** a large piece of thick cloth for use as a bed covering, animal covering, etc **2** a concealing cover, as of smoke, leaves, or snow **3** (*modifier*) applying to or covering a wide group or variety of people, conditions, situations, etc: *blanket insurance against loss, injury, and theft* **4 (born) on the wrong side of the blanket** *inf* illegitimate **5 on the blanket** *Irish* (of an imprisoned terrorist) wearing only a blanket instead of prison uniform, as a protest against not being recognized as a political prisoner ▷ *vb* (*tr*) **6** to cover as with a blanket; overlie **7** to cover a wide area; give blanket coverage **8** (usually foll by *out*) to obscure or suppress [C13 from OF *blancquete*, from *blanc*; see BLANK]

blanket bath *n* an all-over wash given to a person confined to bed

blanket bog *n* a very acid peat bog, low in nutrients, extending widely over a flat terrain, found in cold wet climates

blanket stitch *n* a strong reinforcing stitch for the edges of blankets and other thick material

blankety (ˈblæŋkɪtɪ) *adj, adv* a euphemism for any taboo word [C20 from BLANK]

blank verse *n prosody* unrhymed verse, esp in iambic pentameters

Blantyre-Limbe (blænˈtaɪəˈlɪmbeɪ) *n* a city in S Malawi: largest city in the country; formed in 1956 from the adjoining towns of Blantyre and Limbe. Pop: 478 155 (1998 est)

blare (blɛə) *vb* **blares, blaring, blared 1** to sound loudly and harshly **2** to proclaim loudly and sensationally ▷ *n* **3** a loud harsh noise [C14 from MDu. *bleren*; imit.]

blarney (ˈblɑːnɪ) *n* flattering talk [C19 after the *Blarney* Stone in SW Ireland, said to endow whoever kisses it with skill in flattery]

blasé (ˈblɑːzeɪ) *adj* **1** indifferent to something because of familiarity **2** lacking enthusiasm; bored [C19 from F, p.p. of *blaser* to cloy]

blaspheme (blæsˈfiːm) *vb* **blasphemes, blaspheming, blasphemed 1** (*tr*) to show contempt or disrespect for (God or sacred things), esp in speech **2** (*intr*) to utter profanities or curses [C14 from LL, from Gk, from *blasphēmos* BLASPHEMOUS] > **blasˈphemer** *n*

blasphemous (ˈblæsfɪməs) *adj* involving impiousness or gross irreverence towards God or something sacred [C15 via LL, from Gk *blasphēmos* evil-speaking, from *blapsis* evil + *phēmē* speech]

blasphemy ('blæsfɪmɪ) *n, pl* **blasphemies** **1** blasphemous behaviour or language **2** Also called: **blasphemous libel** *law* the crime committed if a person insults, offends, or vilifies the deity, Christ, or the Christian religion

blast (blɑːst) *n* **1** an explosion, as of dynamite **2** the rapid movement of air away from the centre of an explosion; shock wave **3** the charge used in a single explosion **4** a sudden strong gust of wind or air **5** a sudden loud sound, as of a trumpet **6** a violent verbal outburst, as of criticism **7** a forcible jet of air, esp one used to intensify the heating effect of a furnace **8** any of several diseases of plants and animals **9** *US sl* a very enjoyable or thrilling experience: *the party was a blast* **10** (at) **full blast** at maximum speed, volume, etc ▷ *interj* **11** *sl* an exclamation of annoyance ▷ *vb* **12** (*tr*) to destroy or blow up with explosives, shells, etc **13** to make or cause to make a loud harsh noise **14** to wither or cause to wither; blight or be blighted **15** (*tr*) to criticize severely [OE *blǣst*] > **'blaster** *n*

-blast *n combining form* (in biology) indicating an embryonic cell or formative layer: *mesoblast* [from Gk *blastos* bud]

blasted ('blɑːstɪd) *adj* **1** blighted or withered ▷ *adj (prenominal), adv* **2** *sl* (intensifier): *a blasted idiot*

blast furnace *n* a vertical cylindrical furnace for smelting into which a blast of preheated air is forced

blasto- *combining form* indicating an embryo or bud [see BLAST]

blastoff ('blɑːst,ɒf) *n* **1** the launching of a rocket under its own power **2** the time at which this occurs ▷ *vb* **blast off** **3** (*adv; when tr, usually passive*) to be launched

blastula ('blæstjʊlə) *n, pl* **blastulas** *or* **blastulae** (-liː) an early form of an animal embryo that develops a sphere of cells with a central cavity. Also called: **blastosphere** [C19 NL from Gk, from dim. of *blastos* bud] > **'blastular** *adj*

blat (blæt) *n sl* a newspaper [C20 from G *Blatt* leaf, sheet of paper]

blatant ('bleɪtᵊnt) *adj* **1** glaringly conspicuous or obvious: *a blatant lie* **2** offensively noticeable; obtrusive **3** offensively noisy [C16 coined by Edmund Spenser; prob. infl. by L *blatīre* to babble] > **'blatancy** *n*

blather ('blæðə) *vb, n* a variant of **blether**

blatherskite ('blæðə,skaɪt) *n* **1** a talkative silly person **2** foolish talk; nonsense [C17 from BLATHER + Scot. & N English dialect *skate* fellow]

Blavatsky (blə'vætskɪ) *n* **Elena Petrovna** (jɪ'ljɛnə pɪ'trɔvnə), called *Madame Blavatsky*. 1831–91, Russian theosophist; author of *Isis Unveiled* (1877)

Blaxland ('blækslənd) *n* **Gregory** 1788–1855, Australian explorer and pioneer, born in Britain; with William Lawson and William Wentworth he led the first European passage through the Blue Mountains, thus opening up the Australian interior for settlement

blaxploitation (,blæksplɔɪ'teɪʃən) *n* exploitative use of stereotypical images of Black people in films, books, etc [C20 from BLACK[1] + EXPLOITATION]

▷ www.blaxploitation.com

▷ www.blackvoices.com/feature/blk_history_98

Blaydon ('bleɪdᵊn) *n* an industrial town in NE England, in Gateshead unitary authority, Tyne and Wear. Pop: 15 510 (1991)

blaze[1] (bleɪz) *n* **1** a strong fire or flame **2** a very bright light or glare **3** an outburst (of passion, acclaim, patriotism, etc) **4** brilliance; brightness ▷ *vb* **blazes, blazing, blazed** (*intr*) **5** to burn fiercely **6** to shine brightly **7** (often foll by *up*) to become stirred, as with anger or excitement **8** (usually foll by *away*) to shoot continuously ▷ See also **blazes** [OE *blæse*]

blaze[2] (bleɪz) *n* **1** a mark, usually indicating a path, made on a tree **2** a light-coloured marking on the face of a domestic animal ▷ *vb* **blazes, blazing, blazed** (*tr*) **3** to mark (a tree, path, etc) with a blaze **4** **blaze a trail** to explore new territories, areas of knowledge, etc, so that others can follow [C17 prob. from MLow G *bles* white marking]

blaze[3] (bleɪz) *vb* **blazes, blazing, blazed** (*tr;* often foll by *abroad*) to make widely known; proclaim [C14 from MDu. *blāsen*, from OHG *blāsan*]

blazer ('bleɪzə) *n* a fairly lightweight jacket, often in the colours of a sports club, school, etc

blazes ('bleɪzɪz) *pl n* **1** *sl* a euphemistic word for **hell** **2** *inf* (intensifier): *to run like blazes*

blazon ('bleɪzᵊn) *vb* (*tr*) **1** (often foll by *abroad*) to proclaim publicly **2** *heraldry* to describe (heraldic arms) in proper terms **3** to draw and colour (heraldic arms) conventionally ▷ *n* **4** *heraldry* a conventional description or depiction of heraldic arms [C13 from OF *blason* coat of arms] > **'blazoner** *n*

blazonry ('bleɪzənrɪ) *n, pl* **blazonries** **1** the art or process of describing heraldic arms in proper form **2** heraldic arms collectively **3** colourful or ostentatious display

bldg *abbrev for* building

bleach (bliːtʃ) *vb* **1** to make or become white or colourless, as by exposure to sunlight, by the action of chemical agents, etc ▷ *n* **2** a bleaching agent **3** the act of bleaching [OE *blǣcan*] > **'bleacher** *n*

bleaching powder *n* a white powder consisting of chlorinated calcium hydroxide. Also called: **chloride of lime, chlorinated lime**

bleak[1] (bliːk) *adj* **1** exposed and barren **2** cold and raw **3** offering little hope; dismal: *a bleak future* [OE *blāc* bright, pale] > **'bleakness** *n*

bleak[2] (bliːk) *n* any of various European cyprinid fishes occurring in slow-flowing rivers [C15 prob. from ON *bleikja* white colour]

blear (blɪə) *arch* ▷ *vb* **1** (*tr*) to make (eyes or sight) dim as with tears; blur ▷ *adj* **2** a less common word for **bleary** [C13 *blere* to make dim]

bleary ('blɪərɪ) *adj* **blearier, bleariest** **1** (of eyes or vision) dimmed or blurred, as by tears or tiredness **2** indistinct or unclear > **'bleariness** *n*

Bb

bleary-eyed *or* **blear-eyed** *adj* with eyes blurred, as with old age or after waking

Bleasdale ('bliːzdeɪl) *n* **Alan** born 1946, British playwright, best known for his television series *The Boys From the Blackstuff* (1983) and *GBH* (1991)

bleat (bliːt) *vb* **1** (*intr*) (of a sheep, goat, or calf) to utter its characteristic plaintive cry **2** (*intr*) to speak with any similar sound **3** to whine; whimper ▷ *n* **4** the characteristic cry of sheep, goats, and calves **5** any sound similar to this **6** a weak complaint or whine [OE *blǣtan*] > **'bleater** *n* > **'bleating** *n, adj*

bleb (blɛb) *n* **1** a fluid-filled blister on the skin **2** a small air bubble [C17 var. of BLOB]

bleed (bliːd) *vb* **bleeds, bleeding, bled** (blɛd) **1** (*intr*) to lose or emit blood **2** (*tr*) to remove or draw blood from (a person or animal) **3** (*intr*) to be injured or die, as for a cause **4** (of plants) to exude (sap or resin), esp from a cut **5** (*tr*) *inf* to obtain money, etc, from, esp by extortion **6** (*tr*) to draw liquid or gas from (a container or enclosed system): *to bleed the hydraulic brakes* **7** (*intr*) (of dye or paint) to run or become mixed, as when wet **8** to print or be printed so that text, illustrations, etc, run off the trimmed page **9** **one's heart bleeds** used to express sympathetic grief, often ironically [OE *blēdan*]

bleeder ('bliːdə) *n* **1** *sl* **1a** *derog* a despicable person **1b** any person **2** *pathol* a nontechnical name for a **haemophiliac**

bleeding ('bliːdɪŋ) *adj, adv Brit sl* (intensifier): *a bleeding fool*

bleeding heart *n* **1** any of several plants, esp a widely cultivated Japanese species which has heart-shaped nodding pink flowers **2** *inf* **2a** an excessively softhearted person **2b** (*as modifier*): *bleeding-heart liberals*

bleep (bliːp) *n* **1** a single short high-pitched signal made by an electronic apparatus; beep **2** another word for **bleeper** ▷ *vb* **3** (*intr*) to make such a noise **4** (*tr*) to call (somebody) by means of a bleeper [c20 imit.]

bleeper ('bliːpə) *n* a small portable radio receiver, carried esp by doctors, that sounds a coded bleeping signal to call the carrier. Also called: **bleep**

blemish ('blɛmɪʃ) *n* **1** a defect; flaw; stain ▷ *vb* **2** (*tr*) to flaw the perfection of; spoil; tarnish [c14 from OF *blemir* to make pale]

blench (blɛntʃ) *vb* (*intr*) to shy away, as in fear; quail [OE *blencan* to deceive]

blend (blɛnd) *vb* **1** to mix or mingle (components) together thoroughly **2** (*tr*) to mix (different grades or varieties of tea, whisky, etc) **3** (*intr*) to look good together; harmonize **4** (*intr*) (esp of colours) to shade imperceptibly into each other ▷ *n* **5** a mixture or type produced by blending **6** the act of blending **7** Also called: **portmanteau word** a word formed by joining together the beginning and the end of two other words: *"brunch" is a blend of "breakfast" and "lunch."* [OE *blandan*]

blende (blɛnd) *n* **1** another name for **sphalerite** **2** any of several sulphide ores [c17 G, from *blenden* to deceive, BLIND; so called because it is easily mistaken for galena]

blended learning *n education* the use of both classroom teaching and on-line learning in education

blender ('blɛndə) *n* **1** a person or thing that blends **2** Also called: **liquidizer** a kitchen appliance with blades used for puréeing vegetables, blending liquids, etc

Blenheim[1] ('blɛnɪm) *n* a village in SW Germany, site of a victory of Anglo-Austrian forces under the Duke of Marlborough and Prince Eugène of Savoy that saved Vienna from the French and Bavarians (1704) during the War of the Spanish Succession. Modern name: **Blindheim**

blenny ('blɛnɪ) *n, pl* **blennies** any of various small fishes of coastal waters having a tapering scaleless body, a long dorsal fin, and long raylike pelvic fins [c18 from L, from Gk *blennos* slime]

blent (blɛnt) *vb arch or literary* a past participle of **blend**

blepharitis (ˌblɛfəˈraɪtɪs) *n* inflammation of the eyelids [c19 from Gk *blephar(on)* eyelid + -ITIS]

Blériot (*French* blerjo) *n* **Louis** (lwi) 1872–1936, French aviator and aeronautical engineer: made the first flight across the English Channel (1909)

blesbok *or* **blesbuck** ('blɛsˌbʌk) *n, pl* **blesboks, blesbok** *or* **blesbucks, blesbuck** an antelope of southern Africa. The coat is reddish brown with a white blaze between the eyes; the horns are lyre-shaped [c19 Afrik., from Du. *bles* BLAZE[2] + *bok* BUCK[1]]

bless (blɛs) *vb* **blesses, blessing, blessed** *or* **blest** (*tr*) **1** to consecrate or render holy by means of a religious rite **2** to give honour or glory to (a person or thing) as holy **3** to call upon God to protect; give a benediction to **4** to worship or adore (God) **5** (*often passive*) to grant happiness, health, or prosperity to **6** (*usually passive*) to endow with a talent, beauty, etc **7** *rare* to protect against evil or harm **8** **bless you!** (*interj*) **8a** a traditional phrase said to a person who has just sneezed **8b** an exclamation of well-wishing or surprise **9** **bless me!** *or* (**God**) **bless my soul!** (*interj*) an exclamation of surprise [OE *blǣdsian* to sprinkle with sacrificial blood]

blessed ('blɛsɪd, blɛst) *adj* **1** made holy; consecrated **2** worthy of deep reverence or respect **3** *RC Church* (of a person) beatified by the pope **4** characterized by happiness or good fortune **5** bringing great happiness or good fortune **6** a euphemistic word for **damned,** used in mild oaths: *I'm blessed if I know* > **'blessedly** *adv* > **'blessedness** *n*

Blessed Sacrament *n chiefly RC Church* the consecrated elements of the Eucharist

Blessed Virgin *n chiefly RC Church* another name for **Mary** (sense 1a)

blessing ('blɛsɪŋ) *n* **1** the act of invoking divine protection or aid **2** the words or ceremony used for this **3** a short prayer before or after a meal; grace **4** approval; good wishes **5** the bestowal of a divine gift or favour **6** a happy event

blest (blɛst) *vb* a past tense and past participle of **bless**

blether ('blɛðə) *Scot* ▷ *vb* **1** (*intr*) to speak foolishly ▷ *n* **2** foolish talk; nonsense [c16 from ON *blathr* nonsense]

blethered ('blɛðəd) *adj Northern English dialect* weary

blew (bluː) *vb* the past tense of **blow**[1] and **blow**[3]

Blida ('bliːdə) *n* a city in N Algeria, on the edge of the Mitidja Plain. Pop (urban area): 226 512 (1998)

Bligh (blaɪ) *n* **William** 1754–1817, British admiral; Governor of New South Wales (1806–9), deposed by the New South Wales Corps: as a captain, commander of *H.M.S. Bounty* when the crew mutinied in 1789

blight (blaɪt) *n* **1** any plant disease characterized by withering and shrivelling without rotting. See also **potato blight** **2** any factor that causes the symptoms of blight in plants **3** a person or thing that mars or prevents growth **4** an ugly urban district ▷ *vb* **5** to cause or suffer a blight **6** (*tr*) to frustrate or disappoint **7** (*tr*) to spoil; destroy [c17 ? rel. to OE *blǣce* rash]

blighter ('blaɪtə) *n Brit inf* **1** a fellow **2** a despicable or irritating person or thing

Blighty ('blaɪtɪ) *n* (*sometimes not cap*) *Brit sl* (used esp by troops serving abroad) **1** England; home **2** (*pl* **Blighties**) Also called: **a blighty one** (esp in World War I) a wound that causes the recipient to be sent home to England [c20 from Hindi *bilāyatī* foreign land, England, from Ar. *wilāyat* country]

blimey ('blaɪmɪ) *interj Brit sl* an exclamation of surprise or annoyance [c19 short for *gorblimey* God blind me]

blimp[1] (blɪmp) *n* **1** a small nonrigid airship **2** *films* a soundproof cover fixed over a camera during shooting [c20 prob. from (*type*) *B-limp*]

blimp[2] (blɪmp) *n* (*often cap*) *chiefly Brit* a person, esp a military officer, who is stupidly complacent and reactionary. Also called: **Colonel Blimp** [c20 from a character created by David Low] > **'blimpish** *adj*

blimp out *vb* (*intr, adv*) *sl* to become greatly overweight

blind (blaɪnd) *adj* **1a** unable to see; sightless **1b** (*as collective n; preceded by the*): *the blind* **2** (usually foll by *to*) unable or unwilling to understand or discern **3** not determined by reason: *blind hatred* **4** acting or performed without control or preparation **5** done without being able to see, relying on instruments for information **6** hidden from sight: *a blind corner* **7** closed at one end: *a blind alley* **8** completely lacking awareness or consciousness: *a blind stupor* **9** *inf* very drunk **10** having no openings or outlets: *a blind wall* **11** (intensifier): *not a blind bit of notice* ▷ *adv* **12** without being able to see ahead or using only instruments: *to drive blind; flying blind* **13** without adequate knowledge or information; carelessly: *to buy a house blind* **14** **bake blind** to bake (an empty pastry case) by half filling with dried peas, crusts, etc, to keep it in shape ▷ *vb* (*mainly tr*) **15** to deprive of sight permanently or temporarily **16** to deprive of good sense, reason, or judgment **17** to darken; conceal **18** (foll by *with*) to overwhelm by showing detailed knowledge: *to blind somebody with science* ▷ *n* **19** (*modifier*) for or intended to help the blind: *a blind school* **20** a shade for a window, usually on a roller **21** any obstruction or hindrance to sight, light, or air **22** a person, action, or thing that serves to deceive or conceal the truth **23** Also: **blinder** *Brit sl* a drunken binge [OE *blind*] > **'blindly** *adv* > **'blindness** *n*

USAGE See at **disabled**

▷ www.eyecarefoundation.org

blind alley *n* **1** an alley open at one end only; cul-de-sac **2** *inf* a situation in which no further progress can be made

blind date *n inf* a prearranged social meeting between a man and a woman who have not met before

blinder ('blaɪndə) *n* **1** an outstanding performance in sport **2** *Brit sl* another name for **blind** (sense 23)

blinders ('blaɪndəz) *pl n* the usual US & Canad word for **blinkers**

blindfold ('blaɪnd,fəʊld) *vb (tr)* **1** to prevent (a person or animal) from seeing by covering (the eyes) ▷ *n* **2** a piece of cloth, bandage, etc, used to cover the eyes ▷ *adj, adv* **3** having the eyes covered with a cloth or bandage **4** rash; inconsiderate [changed (c16) through association with FOLD[1] from OE *blindfellian* to strike blind; see BLIND, FELL[2]]

blinding ('blaɪndɪŋ) *n* **1** sand or grit spread over a road surface to fill up cracks **2** the process of laying blinding ▷ *adj* **3** making one blind or as if blind **4** most noticeable; brilliant or dazzling > **blindingly** *adv*

blind man's buff *n* a game in which a blindfolded person tries to catch and identify the other players [c16 *buff*, ?from OF *buffe* a blow; see BUFFET[2]]

blind register *n* (in Britain) a list of those who are blind and are therefore entitled to financial and other benefits

blind side *n* **1** *rugby* the side of the field between the scrum or ruck and the nearer touchline **2** the side on which a person's vision is obscured

blindsight ('blaɪnd,saɪt) *n* the ability to respond to visual stimuli without having any conscious visual experience; it can occur after some forms of brain damage

blind spot *n* **1** a small oval-shaped area of the retina, where the optic nerve enters, in which vision is not experienced **2** a place or area where vision is obscured **3** a subject about which a person is ignorant or prejudiced

blind trust *n* a trust fund that manages the financial affairs of a person without informing him or her of any investments made, usually so that the beneficiary cannot be accused of using public office for private gain

blindworm ('blaɪnd,wɜːm) *n* another name for **slowworm**

bling-bling ('blɪŋ,blɪŋ) *or* **bling** *sl* ▷ *adj* **1** flashy; ostentatious; glitzy ▷ *n* **2** ostentatious jewellery [c20 imitative of jewellery clashing together or of light reflecting off jewellery]

blink (blɪŋk) *vb* **1** to close and immediately reopen (the eyes or an eye), usually involuntarily **2** *(intr)* to look with the eyes partially closed **3** to shine intermittently or unsteadily **4** *(tr; foll by away, from, etc)* to clear the eyes of (dust, tears, etc) **5** (when *tr*, usually foll by *at*) to be surprised or amazed **6** (when *intr*, foll by *at*) to pretend not to know or see (a fault, injustice, etc) ▷ *n* **7** the act or an instance of blinking **8** a glance; glimpse **9** short for **iceblink** (sense 1) **10 on the blink** *sl* not working properly [c14 var. of BLENCH]

blinker[1] ('blɪŋkə) *n* **1** a flashing light for sending messages, as a warning device, etc, such as a direction indicator on a road vehicle **2** *(often pl)* a slang word for **eye**[1] (sense 1)

blinker[2] ('blɪŋkə) *vb (tr)* **1** to provide (a horse) with blinkers **2** to obscure or be obscured with or as with blinkers > '**blinkered** *adj*

blinkers ('blɪŋkəz) *pl n (sometimes sing) chiefly Brit* leather sidepieces attached to a horse's bridle to prevent sideways vision

blinking ('blɪŋkɪŋ) *adj, adv inf* (intensifier): *a blinking fool; a blinking good film*

blip (blɪp) *n* **1** a repetitive sound, such as that produced by an electronic device **2** Also called: **pip** the spot of light on a radar screen indicating the position of an object **3** a temporary irregularity recorded in the performance of something ▷ *vb* **blips, blipping, blipped** **4** *(intr)* to produce a blip [c20 imit.]

blipvert ('blɪp,vɜːt) *n* a very short television advertisement [c20 from BLIP + (AD)VERT]

bliss (blɪs) *n* **1** perfect happiness; serene joy **2** the ecstatic joy of heaven [OE *blīths*; rel. to *blīthe* BLITHE]

Bliss (blɪs) *n* Sir **Arthur** 1891–1975, British composer; Master of the Queen's Musick (1953–75). His works include the *Colour Symphony* (1922), film and ballet music, and a cello concerto (1970)

blissful ('blɪsfʊl) *adj* **1** serenely joyful or glad **2 blissful ignorance** unawareness or inexperience of something unpleasant > '**blissfully** *adv* > '**blissfulness** *n*

B list *n* **a** a category considered to be slightly below the most socially desirable **b** *(as modifier)*: *B-list celebrities* ▷ Cf **A list**

blister ('blɪstə) *n* **1** a small bubble-like elevation of the skin filled with serum, produced as a reaction to a burn, mechanical irritation, etc **2** a swelling containing air or liquid, as on a painted surface **3** *NZ sl* **3a** a rebuke **3b** a summons to court ▷ *vb* **4** to have or cause to have blisters **5** *(tr)* to attack verbally with great scorn or sarcasm [c13 from OF *blestre*] > '**blistered** *adj*

blister pack *n* a type of pack for small goods, consisting of a transparent dome on a firm backing. Also called: **bubble pack**

BLit *abbrev for* Bachelor of Literature

blithe (blaɪð) *adj* **1** very happy or cheerful; gay **2** heedless; casual and indifferent [OE *blīthe*] > '**blithely** *adv* > '**blitheness** *n*

blithering ('blɪðərɪŋ) *adj* **1** talking foolishly; jabbering **2** *inf* stupid; foolish: *you blithering idiot* [c19 var. of BLETHER + -ING[2]]

blithesome ('blaɪðsəm) *adj literary* cheery; merry

BLitt *abbrev for* Bachelor of Letters [L *Baccalaureus Litterarum*]

blitz (blɪts) *n* **1** a violent and sustained attack, esp with intensive aerial bombardment **2** any sudden intensive attack or concerted effort **3** *American football* a defensive charge on the quarterback ▷ *vb* **4** *(tr)* to attack suddenly and intensively [c20 shortened from G *Blitzkrieg* lightning war]

Blitz (blɪts) *n* **the** the systematic bombing of Britain in 1940–41 by the German Luftwaffe

blitzkrieg ('blɪts,kriːg) *n* a swift intensive military attack designed to defeat the opposition quickly [c20 from G: lightning war]

Blixen ('blɪksən) *n* **Karen** See (Isak) **Dinesen**

blizzard ('blɪzəd) *n* a strong cold wind accompanied by widespread heavy snowfall [c19 from ?]

bloat (bləʊt) *vb* **1** to swell or cause to swell, as with a liquid or air **2** to become or cause to be puffed up, as with conceit **3** *(tr)* to cure (fish, esp herring) by half drying in smoke [c17 prob. rel. to ON *blautr* soaked] > '**bloated** *adj*

bloater ('bləʊtə) *n* a herring that has been salted in brine, smoked, and cured

blob (blɒb) *n* **1** a soft mass or drop **2** a spot, dab, or blotch of colour, ink, etc **3** an indistinct or shapeless form or object [c15 ? imit.]

bloc (blɒk) *n* a group of people or countries combined by a common interest [from F: BLOCK]

Bloch (blɒk) *n* **1 Ernest** 1880–1959, US composer, born in Switzerland, who found inspiration in Jewish liturgical and folk music: his works include the symphonies *Israel* (1916) and *America* (1926) **2 Felix** 1905–83, US physicist, born in Switzerland: Nobel prize for physics (1952) for his work on the magnetic moments of atomic particles **3 Konrad Emil** 1912–2000, US biochemist, born in Germany: shared the Nobel prize for physiology or medicine in 1964 for his work on fatty-acid metabolism **4** (*French* blɔk) **Marc** 1886–1944, French historian and Resistance fighter; author of *Feudal Society* (1935) and *Strange Defeat* (1940), an essay on the fall of France: killed by the Nazis

block (blɒk) *n* **1** a large solid piece of wood, stone, or other material usually having at least one face fairly flat **2** such a piece on which particular tasks may be done, as chopping, cutting, or beheading **3** Also called:

building block one of a set of wooden or plastic cubes as a child's toy **4** a form on which things are shaped: *a wig block* **5** *sl* a person's head **6 do one's block** *Austral & NZ sl* to become angry **7** a dull, unemotional, or hardhearted person **8** a large building of offices, flats, etc **9a** a group of buildings in a city bounded by intersecting streets on each side **9b** the area or distance between such intersecting streets **10** *Austral & NZ* an area of land for a house, farm, etc **11** *NZ* an area of bush reserved by licence for a trapper or hunter **12** a piece of wood, metal, or other material having a design in relief, used for printing **13** *Austral & NZ* a log, usually of willow, fastened to a timber base and used in a wood-chopping competition **14** a casing housing one or more freely rotating pulleys. See also **block and tackle** **15** an obstruction or hindrance **16** *pathol* **16a** interference in the normal physiological functioning of an organ or part **16b** See **heart block** **16c** See **nerve block** **17** *psychol* a short interruption of perceptual or thought processes **18** obstruction of an opponent in a sport **19a** a quantity handled or considered as a single unit **19b** (*as modifier*): *a block booking* **20** *athletics* short for **starting block** ▷ *vb* (*mainly tr*) **21** (often foll by *up*) to obstruct (a passage, channel, etc) or prevent or impede the motion or flow of (something or someone) by introducing an obstacle: *to block the traffic; to block up a pipe* **22** to impede, retard, or prevent (an action, procedure, etc) **23** to stamp (a title, design, etc) on (a book cover, etc) esp using gold leaf **24** to shape by use of a block: *to block a hat* **25** (*also intr*) *Sport.* to obstruct or impede movement by (an opponent) **26** to interrupt a physiological function, as by use of an anaesthetic **27** (*also intr*) *Cricket.* to play (a ball) defensively ▷ See also **block in, block out** [C14 from OF *bloc*, from Du. *blok*] > **'blocker** *n*

blockade (blɒ'keɪd) *n* **1** *mil* the interdiction of a nation's sea lines of communications, esp of an individual port by the use of sea power **2** something that prevents access or progress **3** *med* the inhibition of the effect of a hormone or a drug, or the action of a nerve by a drug ▷ *vb* **blockades, blockading, blockaded** (*tr*) **4** to impose a blockade on **5** to obstruct the way to [C17 from BLOCK + *-ade*, as in AMBUSCADE] > **block'ader** *n*

blockage ('blɒkɪdʒ) *n* **1** the act of blocking or state of being blocked **2** an object causing an obstruction

block and tackle *n* a hoisting device in which a rope or chain is passed around a pair of blocks containing one or more pulleys

blockboard ('blɒkˌbɔːd) *n* a bonded board in which strips of soft wood are sandwiched between two layers of veneer

blockbuster ('blɒkˌbʌstə) *n inf* **1** a large bomb used to demolish extensive areas **2** a very successful, effective, or forceful person, thing, etc **3** a lavish film, show, novel, etc, that proves to be an outstanding popular success

block diagram *n* **1** a diagram showing the interconnections between the parts of an industrial process **2** *computing* a diagram showing the interconnections between electronic components or parts of a program

blockhead ('blɒkˌhɛd) *n derog* a stupid person > **'blockˌheaded** *adj*

blockhouse ('blɒkˌhaʊs) *n* **1** (formerly) a wooden fortification with ports for defensive fire, observation, etc **2** a concrete structure strengthened to give protection against enemy fire, with apertures to allow defensive gunfire **3** a building constructed of logs or squared timber

block in *vb* (*tr, adv*) to sketch or outline with little detail

blockish ('blɒkɪʃ) *adj* lacking vivacity or imagination; stupid > **'blockishly** *adv*

block letter *n* **1** *printing* a less common name for **sans serif** **2** Also called: **block capital** a plain capital letter

block out *vb* (*tr, adv*) **1** to plan or describe (something) in a general fashion **2** to prevent the entry or consideration of (something)

block release *n Brit* the release of industrial trainees from work for study at a college for several weeks

block vote *n Brit* (at a trade-union conference) the system whereby each delegate's vote has a value in proportion to the number of people he represents

Bloemfontein ('bluːmfɒnˌteɪn) *n* a city in central South Africa: capital of Free State province and judicial capital of the country. Pop (urban area): 333 769 (1996)

blog (blɒg) *n* a journal written on-line and accessible to users of the Internet > **'blogger** *n*

Blois (*French* blwa) *n* a city in N central France, on the Loire: 13th-century castle. Pop: 51 550 (1990)

bloke (bləʊk) *n Brit & Austral* an informal word for **man** [C19 from Shelta]

blokeish *or* **blokish** ('bləʊkɪʃ) *adj Brit inf, sometimes derog* denoting or exhibiting the characteristics believed typical of an ordinary man. Also: **blokey** ('bləʊkɪ) > **'blokeishness** *or* **'blokishness** *n*

blonde *or* (*masc*) **blond** (blɒnd) *adj* **1** (of hair) of a light colour; fair **2** (of people or a race) having fair hair, a light complexion, and, typically, blue or grey eyes ▷ *n* **3** a person having light-coloured hair and skin [C15 from OF *blond* (fem *blonde*), prob. of Gmc origin] > **'blondeness** *or* **'blondness** *n*

Blondin (*French* blɔ̃dɛ̃) *n* **Charles**, real name *Jean-François Gravelet*. 1824–97, French acrobat and tightrope walker; best known for walking a tightrope across Niagara Falls (1859)

blood (blʌd) *n* **1** a reddish fluid in vertebrates that is pumped by the heart through the arteries and veins **2** a similar fluid in invertebrates **3** bloodshed, esp when resulting in murder **4** life itself; lifeblood **5** relationship through being of the same family, race, or kind; kinship **6 flesh and blood** **6a** near kindred or kinship, esp that between a parent and child **6b** human nature (esp in **it's more than flesh and blood can stand**) **7 in one's blood** as a natural or inherited characteristic or talent **8 the blood** royal or noble descent: *a prince of the blood* **9** temperament; disposition; temper **10a** good or pure breeding; pedigree **10b** (*as modifier*): *blood horses* **11** people viewed as members of a group, esp as an invigorating force (**new blood, young blood**) **12** *chiefly Brit, rare* a dashing young man **13 in cold blood** showing no passion; deliberately; ruthlessly **14 make one's blood boil** to cause to be angry or indignant **15 make one's blood run cold** to fill with horror ▷ *vb* (*tr*) **16** *hunting* to cause (young hounds) to taste the blood of a freshly killed quarry **17** to initiate (a person) to war or hunting [OE *blōd*]

blood-and-thunder *adj* denoting or relating to a melodramatic adventure story

blood bank *n* a place where whole blood, blood plasma, or other blood products are stored until required in transfusion

blood bath *n* indiscriminate slaughter; a massacre

blood brother *n* **1** a brother by birth **2** a man or boy who has sworn to treat another as his brother, often in a ceremony in which their blood is mingled

blood count *n* the number of red and white blood corpuscles and platelets in a specific sample of blood

bloodcurdling ('blʌdˌkɜːdlɪŋ) *adj* terrifying; horrifying > **'bloodˌcurdlingly** *adv*

blood donor *n* a person who gives his or her blood to be used for transfusion

blood doping *n* the illegal practice of removing a quantity of blood from an athlete long before a race and reinjecting it shortly before a race, so boosting oxygenation of the blood

blooded ('blʌdɪd) *adj* **1** (of horses, cattle, etc) of good breeding **2** (*in combination*) having blood or temperament as specified: *hot-blooded, cold-blooded, warm-blooded, red-blooded*

blood group *n* any one of the various groups into which human blood is classified on the basis of its specific agglutinating properties. Also called: **blood type**

blood heat *n* the normal temperature of the human body, 98.4°F or 37°C

bloodhound ('blʌd,haʊnd) *n* a large breed of hound, formerly used in tracking and police work

bloodless ('blʌdlɪs) *adj* **1** without blood **2** conducted without violence (esp in **bloodless revolution**) **3** anaemic-looking; pale **4** lacking vitality; lifeless **5** lacking in emotion; unfeeling > '**bloodlessly** *adv* > '**bloodlessness** *n*

blood-letting ('blʌd,lɛtɪŋ) *n* **1** the therapeutic removal of blood. See also **phlebotomy** **2** bloodshed, esp in a feud

bloodline ('blʌd,laɪn) *n* all the members of a family group over generations, esp regarding characteristics common to that group; pedigree

blood money *n* **1** compensation paid to the relatives of a murdered person **2** money paid to a hired murderer **3** a reward for information about a criminal, esp a murderer

blood orange *n* a variety of orange all or part of the pulp of which is dark red when ripe

blood poisoning *n* a nontechnical term for **septicaemia**

blood pressure *n* the pressure exerted by the blood on the inner walls of the arteries, being relative to the elasticity and diameter of the vessels and the force of the heartbeat

blood pudding *n* another name for **black pudding**

blood relation *or* **relative** *n* a person related to another by birth, as distinct from one related by marriage

bloodshed ('blʌd,ʃɛd) *n* slaughter; killing

bloodshot ('blʌd,ʃɒt) *adj* (of an eye) inflamed

blood sport *n* any sport involving the killing of an animal, esp hunting

bloodstain ('blʌd,steɪn) *n* a dark discoloration caused by blood, esp dried blood > '**blood,stained** *adj*

bloodstock ('blʌd,stɒk) *n* thoroughbred horses

bloodstone ('blʌd,stəʊn) *n* a dark green variety of chalcedony with red spots: used as a gemstone. Also called: **heliotrope**

bloodstream ('blʌd,stri:m) *n* the flow of blood through the vessels of a living body

blood substitute *n* a substance such as plasma, albumin, or dextran-, used to replace lost blood or increase the blood volume

bloodsucker ('blʌd,sʌkə) *n* **1** an animal that sucks blood, esp a leech or mosquito **2** *inf* a person or thing that preys upon another person, esp by extorting money > '**blood,sucking** *adj*

blood sugar *n med* the glucose concentration in the blood: the normal fasting value is between 3·9 and 5·6 millimoles per litre

bloodthirsty ('blʌd,θɜ:stɪ) *adj* **bloodthirstier, bloodthirstiest** **1** murderous; cruel **2** taking pleasure in bloodshed or violence **3** describing or depicting killing and violence; gruesome > '**blood,thirstily** *adv* > '**blood,thirstiness** *n*

blood type *n* another name for **blood group**

blood vessel *n* an artery, capillary, or vein

bloodwood ('blʌd,wʊd) *n* any of several species of Australian eucalyptus with red sap

bloody ('blʌdɪ) *adj* **bloodier, bloodiest** **1** covered or stained with blood **2** resembling or composed of blood **3** marked by much killing and bloodshed: *a bloody war* **4** cruel or murderous: *a bloody tyrant* ▷ *adv, adj* **5** *sl* (intensifier): *a bloody fool* ▷ *vb* **bloodies, bloodying, bloodied** **6** (*tr*) to stain with blood > '**bloodily** *adv* > '**bloodiness** *n*

Bloody Mary *n* **1** nickname of **Mary I** **2** a drink consisting of tomato juice and vodka

bloody-minded *adj Brit inf* deliberately obstructive and unhelpful

bloom[1] (blu:m) *n* **1** a blossom on a flowering plant; a flower **2** the state, time, or period when flowers open **3** open flowers collectively **4** a healthy, vigorous, or flourishing condition; prime **5** youthful or healthy rosiness in the cheeks or face; glow **6** a fine whitish coating on the surface of fruits, leaves, etc **7** Also called: **chill** a dull area on the surface of old gloss paint, lacquer, or varnish **8** *ecology* a visible increase in the algal constituent of plankton, which may be due to excessive organic pollution ▷ *vb* (*intr*) **9** (of flowers) to open; come into flower **10** to bear flowers; blossom **11** to flourish or grow **12** to be in a healthy, glowing, or flourishing condition [C13 of Gmc origin; cf. ON *blōm* flower]

bloom[2] (blu:m) *n* a rectangular mass of metal obtained by rolling or forging a cast ingot [OE *blōma* lump of metal]

bloomer[1] ('blu:mə) *n* a plant that flowers, esp in a specified way: *a night bloomer*

bloomer[2] ('blu:mə) *n Brit inf* a stupid mistake; blunder [C20 from BLOOMING]

bloomer[3] ('blu:mə) *n Brit* a medium-sized loaf, glazed and notched on top [C20 from?]

bloomers ('blu:məz) *pl n* **1** *inf* women's baggy knickers **2** (formerly) loose trousers gathered at the knee worn by women for cycling, etc **3** *history* loose trousers gathered at the ankle and worn under a shorter skirt [after Amelia *Bloomer* (1818–94), US social reformer]

Bloomfield ('blu:m,fi:ld) *n* **Leonard** 1887–1949, US linguist, influential for his strictly scientific and descriptive approach to comparative linguistics; author of *Language* (1933)

blooming ('blu:mɪŋ) *adv, adj Brit inf* (intensifier): *a blooming genius; blooming painful* [C19 euphemistic for BLOODY]

Bloomington ('blu:mɪŋtən) *n* a city in central Indiana: seat of the University of Indiana (1820). Pop: 60 633 (1990)

Bb

Bloomsbury ('blu:mzbərɪ, -brɪ) *n* **1** a district of central London in the borough of Camden: contains the British Museum, part of the University of London, and many publishers' offices ▷ *adj* **2** relating to or characteristic of the Bloomsbury Group

Bloomsbury Group *n* a group of writers, artists, and intellectuals living and working in and around Bloomsbury from about 1907 to 1930. They included Leonard and Virginia Woolf, Roger Fry, E. M. Forster, Lytton Strachey, and John Maynard Keynes

blossom ('blɒsəm) *n* **1** the flower or flowers of a plant, esp producing edible fruit **2** the time or period of flowering ▷ *vb* (*intr*) **3** (of plants) to come into flower **4** to develop or come to a promising stage [OE *blōstm*] > '**blossomy** *adj*

blot (blɒt) *n* **1** a stain or spot of ink, paint, dirt, etc **2** something that spoils **3** a blemish or stain on one's character or reputation **4** *Austral sl* the anus ▷ *vb* **blots, blotting, blotted** **5** (of ink, dye, etc) to form spots or blobs on (a material) or (of a person) to cause such spots or blobs to form on (a material) **6** (*intr*) to stain or become stained or spotted **7** (*tr*) to cause a blemish in or on; disgrace **8** to soak up (excess ink, etc) by using blotting paper **9** (of blotting paper) to absorb (excess ink, etc) **10** (*tr*; often foll by *out*) **10a** to darken or hide completely; obscure; obliterate **10b** to destroy; annihilate [C14 prob. of Gmc origin]

blotch (blɒtʃ) *n* **1** an irregular spot or discoloration, esp a dark and relatively large one ▷ *vb* **2** to become or cause to become marked by such discoloration [C17 prob. from BOTCH, infl. by BLOT] > '**blotchy** *adj*

blotter ('blɒtə) *n* something used to absorb excess ink, esp a sheet of blotting paper

blotting paper *n* a soft absorbent unsized paper, used esp for soaking up surplus ink

blotto ('blɒtəʊ) *adj sl* unconscious, esp through drunkenness [C20 from BLOT (vb)]

blouse (blaʊz) *n* **1** a woman's shirtlike garment **2** a waist-length belted jacket worn by soldiers ▷ *vb* **blouses, blousing, bloused 3** to hang or make so as to hang in full loose folds [C19 from F, from ?]

blouson ('blu:zɒn) *n* a tight-waisted jacket or top that blouses out [C20 from F]

blow[1] (bləʊ) *vb* **blows, blowing, blew, blown 1** (of a current of air, the wind, etc) to be or cause to be in motion **2** (*intr*) to move or be carried by or as if by wind **3** to expel (air, cigarette smoke, etc) through the mouth or nose **4** to force or cause (air, dust, etc) to move (into, in, over, etc) by using an instrument or by expelling breath **5** (*intr*) to breathe hard; pant **6** (sometimes foll by *up*) to inflate with air or the breath **7** (*intr*) (of wind, a storm, etc) to make a roaring sound **8** to cause (a whistle, siren, etc) to sound by forcing air into it or (of a whistle, etc) to sound thus **9** (*tr*) to force air from the lungs through (the nose) to clear out mucus **10** (often foll by *up, down, in,* etc) to explode, break, or disintegrate completely **11** *electronics* to burn out (a fuse, valve, etc) because of excessive current or (of a fuse, valve, etc) to burn out **12** (*tr*) to wind (a horse) by making it run excessively **13** to cause (a wind instrument) to sound by forcing one's breath into the mouthpiece or (of such an instrument) to sound in this way **14** (*intr*) (of flies) to lay eggs (in) **15** to shape (glass, ornaments, etc) by forcing air or gas through the material when molten **16** (*tr*) *sl* to spend (money) freely **17** (*tr*) *sl* to use (an opportunity) ineffectively **18** *sl* to go suddenly away (from) **19** (*tr*) *sl* to expose or betray (a secret) **20** (p.p. **blowed**) *inf* another word for **damn 21 blow hot and cold** *inf* to vacillate **22 blow one's top** *inf* to lose one's temper ▷ *n* **23** the act or an instance of blowing **24** the sound produced by blowing **25** a blast of air or wind **26a** *Brit* a slang name for **cannabis** (sense 2) **26b** *US* a slang name for **cocaine 27** *Austral sl* a brief rest; a breather ▷ See also **blow away, blow in,** etc [OE *blāwan*]

blow[2] (bləʊ) *n* **1** a powerful or heavy stroke with the fist, a weapon, etc **2 at one** *or* **a blow** by or with only one action **3** a sudden setback **4 come to blows 4a** to fight **4b** to result in a fight **5** an attacking action: *a blow for freedom* **6** *Austral & NZ* a stroke of the shears in sheep-shearing [C15 prob. of Gmc origin]

blow[3] (bləʊ) *archaic vb* **blows, blowing, blew, blown 1** (*intr*) (of a plant or flower) to blossom or open out ▷ *n* **2** a mass of blossoms **3** the state or period of blossoming [OE *blōwan*]

blow away *vb* (*tr, adv*) *sl, chiefly US* **1** to kill (someone) by shooting **2** to defeat decisively

blow-by-blow *adj* (*prenominal*) explained in great detail: *a blow-by-blow account*

blow-dry *vb* **blow-dries, blow-drying, blow-dried 1** (*tr*) to style (the hair) while drying it with a hand-held hair dryer ▷ *n* **2** this method of styling hair

blower ('bləʊə) *n* **1** a mechanical device, such as a fan, that blows **2** a low-pressure compressor, esp in a furnace or internal-combustion engine **3** an informal name for **telephone**

blowfish ('bləʊ,fɪʃ) *n, pl* **blowfish** *or* **blowfishes** a popular name for **puffer** (sense 2)

blowfly ('bləʊ,flaɪ) *n, pl* **blowflies** any of various flies that lay their eggs in rotting meat, dung, carrion, and open wounds. Also called: **bluebottle**

blowgun ('bləʊ,gʌn) *n* the US word for **blowpipe** (sense 1)

blowhard ('bləʊ,hɑ:d) *inf* ▷ *n* **1** a boastful person ▷ *adj* **2** blustering or boastful

blowhole ('bləʊ,həʊl) *n* **1** the nostril of whales, situated far back on the skull **2** a hole in ice through which whales, seals, etc, breathe **3** *geol* a hole in a cliff top leading to a sea cave through which air is forced by the action of the sea **4a** a vent for air or gas **4b** *NZ* a hole emitting gas or steam in a volcanic region

blow in *inf* ▷ *vb* **1** (*intr, adv*) to arrive or enter suddenly ▷ *n* **blow-in 2** *Austral* a newcomer

blow job *taboo* a slang term for **fellatio**

blowlamp ('bləʊ,læmp) *n* another name for **blowtorch**

blown (bləʊn) *vb* the past participle of **blow**[1] and **blow**[3]

blow out *vb* (*adv*) **1** to extinguish (a flame, candle, etc) or (of a flame, etc) to become extinguished **2** (*intr*) (of a tyre) to puncture suddenly, esp at high speed **3** (*intr*) (of a fuse) to melt suddenly **4** (*tr; often reflexive*) to diminish or use up the energy of: *the storm blew itself out* **5** (*intr*) (of an oil or gas well) to lose oil or gas in an uncontrolled manner ▷ *n* **blowout 6** the sudden melting of an electrical fuse **7** a sudden burst in a tyre **8** the uncontrolled escape of oil or gas from an oil or gas well **9** *sl* a large filling meal or lavish entertainment

blow over *vb* (*intr, adv*) **1** to cease or be finished: *the storm blew over* **2** to be forgotten

blowpipe ('bləʊ,paɪp) *n* **1** a long tube from which pellets, poisoned darts, etc, are shot by blowing **2** Also called: **blow tube** a tube for blowing air or oxygen into a flame to intensify its heat **3** a long narrow iron pipe used to gather molten glass and blow it into shape

blowsy *or* **blowzy** ('blaʊzɪ) *adj* **blowsier, blowsiest** *or* **blowzier, blowziest 1** (esp of a woman) untidy in appearance; slovenly or sluttish **2** (of a woman) ruddy in complexion [C18 from dialect *blowze* beggar girl, from ?]

blow through *vb* (*intr, adv*) *Austral inf* to leave; make off

blowtorch ('bləʊ,tɔ:tʃ) *n* a small burner that produces a very hot flame, used to remove paint, melt soft metal, etc

blow up *vb* (*adv*) **1** to explode or cause to explode **2** (*tr*) to increase the importance of (something): *they blew the whole affair up* **3** (*intr*) to arise: *we lived very quietly before this affair blew up* **4** (*intr*) to come into existence with sudden force: *a storm had blown up* **5** (*intr*) *inf* to lose one's temper (with a person) **6** (*tr*) *inf* to reprimand **7** (*tr*) *inf* to enlarge the size of (a photograph) ▷ *n* **blow-up 8** an explosion **9** *inf* an enlarged photograph or part of a photograph **10** *inf* a fit of temper

blowy ('bləʊɪ) *adj* **blowier, blowiest** another word for **windy** (sense 1)

blub (blʌb) *vb* **blubs, blubbing, blubbed** *Brit* a slang word for **blubber** (senses 1–3)

blubber ('blʌbə) *vb* **1** to sob without restraint **2** to utter while sobbing **3** (*tr*) to make (the face) wet and swollen by crying ▷ *n* **4** the fatty tissue of aquatic mammals such as the whale **5** *inf* flabby body fat **6** the act or an instance of weeping without restraint ▷ *adj* **7** (*often in combination*) swollen or fleshy: *blubber-faced* [C12 ?from Low G *blubbern* to BUBBLE, imit.] > '**blubberer** *n* > '**blubbery** *adj*

Blücher (*German* 'blyçər) *n* **Gebhard Leberecht von** ('gɛphart 'le:bərɛçt fɔn) 1742–1819, Prussian field marshal, who commanded the Prussian army against Napoleon at Waterloo (1815)

bludge (blʌdʒ) *Austral & NZ inf* ▷ *vb* **bludges, bludging, bludged 1** (often foll by *on* or *off*) to scrounge from (someone) **2** (*intr*) to skive ▷ *n* **3** a very easy task [C19 back formation from *bludger* pimp, from BLUDGEON]

bludgeon ('blʌdʒən) *n* **1** a stout heavy club, typically thicker at one end **2** a person, line of argument, etc, that is effective but unsubtle ▷ *vb* (*tr*) **3** to hit as with a bludgeon **4** (often foll by *into*) to force; bully; coerce [C18 from ?]

bludger ('blʌdʒə) *n Austral & NZ inf* **1** a person who scrounges **2** a person who avoids work **3** a person in authority regarded as ineffectual by those working under him or her

blue (blu:) *n* **1** any of a group of colours, such as that of a clear unclouded sky or the deep sea **2** a dye or pigment of any of these colours **3** blue cloth or clothing: *dressed in* blue 4 a sportsman who represents or has represented Oxford or Cambridge University and has the right to wear the university colour 5 *Brit* an informal name for **Tory** 6 any of numerous small blue-winged butterflies 7 a blue substance used in laundering 8 *Austral & NZ sl* an argument or fight: *he had a blue with a taxi driver* 9 Also: **bluey** *Austral & NZ sl* a court summons 10 *Austral & NZ inf* a mistake; error 11 **out of the blue** apparently from nowhere; unexpectedly ▷ *adj* **bluer, bluest** 12 of the colour blue 13 (of the flesh) having a purple tinge, as from cold or contusion 14 depressed, moody, or unhappy 15 indecent, titillating, or pornographic: *blue films* ▷ *vb* **blues, blueing** *or* **bluing, blued** 16 to make, dye, or become blue 17 (*tr*) to treat (laundry) with blue 18 (*tr*) *sl* to spend extravagantly or wastefully; squander ▷ See also **blues** [c13 from OF *bleu*, of Gmc origin] > **'blueness** *n*

Blue (bluː) *or* **Bluey** ('bluːɪ) *n Austral inf* a person with red hair

blue baby *n* a baby born with a bluish tinge to the skin because of lack of oxygen in the blood

Bluebeard ('bluːˌbɪəd) *n* 1 a villain in European folk tales who marries several wives and murders them in turn 2 a man who has had several wives

bluebell ('bluːˌbɛl) *n* 1 Also called: **wild** or **wood hyacinth** a European woodland plant having a one-sided cluster of blue bell-shaped flowers 2 Also called: **Spanish bluebell** a similar and related plant widely grown in gardens and becoming naturalized 3 a Scottish name for **harebell** 4 any of various other plants with blue bell-shaped flowers

blueberry ('bluːbərɪ, -brɪ) *n, pl* **blueberries** 1 Also called: **huckleberry** any of several North American ericaceous shrubs that have blue-black edible berries with tiny seeds. See also **bilberry** 2 the fruit of any of these plants

bluebird ('bluːˌbɜːd) *n* 1 a North American songbird of the thrush family having a blue or partly blue plumage 2 any of various other birds having a blue plumage

blue blood *n* royal or aristocratic descent [c19 translation of Sp. *sangre azul*] > **ˌblue-'blooded** *adj*

blue book *n* 1 (in Britain) a government publication bound in a stiff blue paper cover: usually the report of a royal commission or a committee 2 (in Canada) an annual statement of government accounts

bluebottle ('bluːˌbɒtᵊl) *n* 1 another name for the **blowfly** 2 any of various blue-flowered plants, esp the cornflower 3 *Brit* an informal word for a **policeman** 4 *Austral & NZ* an informal name for **Portuguese man-of-war**

blue box *n Canad* a blue plastic container for domestic refuse that is to be collected and recycled

bluebush ('bluːˌbʊʃ) *n* any of various blue-grey herbaceous Australian shrubs of the genus *Maireana*

blue button *n* a trainee market maker on the London stock exchange [c20 from the *blue button* badge worn in the lapel]

blue cattle dog *n* an Australian breed of dog with a bluish coat, developed for herding cattle. Also called: **Australian cattle dog, blue heeler**

blue cheese *n* cheese containing a blue mould, esp Stilton, Roquefort, or Danish Blue

blue chip *n* 1 a gambling chip with the highest value 2 *finance* a stock considered reliable with respect to both dividend income and capital value 3 (*modifier*) denoting something considered to be a valuable asset

blue-collar *adj* of or designating manual industrial workers ▷ Cf **white-collar**

blue-eyed boy *n inf, chiefly Brit* the favourite or darling of a person or group

bluefish ('bluːˌfɪʃ) *n, pl* **bluefish** *or* **bluefishes** 1 Also called: **snapper** a bluish marine food and game fish, related to the horse mackerel 2 any of various other bluish fishes

Blue Flag *n* an award given to a seaside resort that meets EU standards of cleanliness and safety of beaches and purity of water in bathing areas

blue fox *n* 1 a variety of the arctic fox that has a pale grey winter coat 2 the fur of this animal

blue funk *n sl* a state of great terror

bluegrass ('bluːˌgrɑːs) *n* 1 any of several North American bluish-green grasses, esp **Kentucky bluegrass,** grown for forage 2 a type of folk music originating in Kentucky

blue-green algae *pl n* the former name for **cyanobacteria**

blue ground *n mineralogy* another name for **kimberlite**

blue gum *n* a tall fast-growing widely cultivated Australian eucalyptus, having bluish aromatic leaves containing a medicinal oil, bark that peels off in shreds, and hard timber

blue heeler *n Austral* a type of dog with dark speckled markings: used for herding cattle

bluejacket ('bluːˌdʒækɪt) *n* a sailor in the Navy

blue jay *n* a common North American jay having bright blue plumage

blue moon *n* **once in a blue moon** *inf* very rarely; almost never

blue mould *n* any fungus that forms a bluish mass on decaying food, leather, etc. Also called: **green mould**

Blue Mountains *pl n* 1 a mountain range in the US, in NE Oregon and SE Washington. Highest peak: Rock Creek Butte, 2773 m (9097 ft) 2 a mountain range in the Caribbean, in E Jamaica: Blue Mountain coffee is grown on its slopes. Highest peak: Blue Mountain Peak, 2256 m (7402 ft) 3 a plateau in SE Australia, in E New South Wales: part of the Great Dividing Range. Highest part: about 1134 m (3871 ft)

Blue Nile *n* a river in E Africa, rising in central Ethiopia as the Abbai and flowing southeast, then northwest to join the White Nile. Length: about 1530 km (950 miles)

blue-on-blue *adj military* of or relating to friendly fire: *blue-on-blue contacts* [c20 from the colour used to mark a country's own troops and allies on a military map]

blue pencil *n* 1 deletion, alteration, or censorship of the contents of a book or other work ▷ *vb* **blue-pencil, blue-pencils, blue-pencilling, blue-pencilled** *or US* **blue-pencils, blue-penciling, blue-penciled** 2 (*tr*) to alter or delete parts of (a book, film, etc), esp to censor

blue peter *n* a signal flag of blue with a white square at the centre, displayed by a vessel about to leave port [c19 from the name *Peter*]

blue pointer *n* a large shark of Australian coastal waters, having a blue back and pointed snout

blueprint ('bluːˌprɪnt) *n* 1 Also called: **cyanotype** a photographic print of plans, technical drawings, etc, consisting of white lines on a blue background 2 an original plan or prototype ▷ *vb* 3 (*tr*) to make a blueprint of (a plan, etc)

blue ribbon *n* 1 (in Britain) a badge of blue silk worn by members of the Order of the Garter 2 a badge awarded as the first prize in a competition

Blue Ridge Mountains *pl n* a mountain range in the eastern US, extending from West Virginia into Georgia: part of the Appalachian mountains. Highest peak: Mount Mitchell, 2038 m (6684 ft)

blue-ringed octopus *n* a highly venomous octopus of E Australia, which exhibits blue bands on its tentacles when disturbed

blues (bluːz) *pl n* (*sometimes functioning as sing*) **the** 1 a feeling of depression or deep unhappiness 2 a type of folk song devised by Black Americans, usually employing a basic 12-bar chorus and frequent minor intervals

▷ http://members.lycos.nl/bluesmanharry
▷ www.allmusic.com
▷ www.jazzinamerica.org

blue screen *n* a special effects film technique involving filming actors against a blue screen on which effects

Bb

such as computerized graphics can be added later and integrated into a single sequence

blue-singlet *adj Austral* working-class

blue-sky *n* (*modifier*) of or denoting theoretical research without regard to any future application of its result: *a blue-sky project*

blue-sky thinking *n* creative ideas that are not limited by current thinking or beliefs

bluestocking (ˈbluːˌstɒkɪŋ) *n usually disparaging* a scholarly or intellectual woman [from the blue worsted stockings worn by members of an 18th-cent. literary society]

bluestone (ˈbluːˌstəʊn) *n* 1 a blue-grey sandstone containing much clay, used for building and paving 2 the blue crystalline form of copper sulphate

blue swimmer *n* 1 an edible bluish Australian swimming crab, *Portunus pelagicus* 2 *Austral inf* an Australian ten-dollar note

bluetit (ˈbluːˌtɪt) *n* a common European tit having a blue crown, wings, and tail, yellow underparts, and a black-and-grey head

blue whale *n* the largest mammal: a widely distributed bluish-grey whalebone whale, closely related and similar to the rorquals

bluey (ˈbluːɪ) *n Austral inf* 1 a blanket 2 a swagman's bundle 3 **hump (one's) bluey** to carry one's bundle; tramp 4 a variant of **blue** (sense 9) 5 a cattle dog [(for senses 1, 2, 4) C19 from BLUE (on account of their colour) + -Y²]

Bluey (ˈbluːɪ) *n* a variant of **Blue**

bluff¹ (blʌf) *vb* 1 to pretend to be confident about an uncertain issue in order to influence (someone) ▷ *n* 2 deliberate deception intended to create the impression of a stronger position than one actually has 3 **call someone's bluff** to challenge someone to give proof of his or her claims [C19 orig. US poker-playing term, from Du. *bluffen* to boast] > ˈ**bluffer** *n*

bluff² (blʌf) *n* 1 a steep promontory, bank, or cliff 2 *Canad* a clump of trees on the prairie; copse ▷ *adj* 3 good-naturedly frank and hearty 4 (of a bank, cliff, etc) presenting a steep broad face [C17 (in the sense: nearly perpendicular): ?from MDu. *blaf* broad] > ˈ**bluffly** *adv* > ˈ**bluffness** *n*

bluish *or* **blueish** (ˈbluːɪʃ) *adj* somewhat blue

Blum (bluːm) *n* **Léon** (leɔ̃) 1872–1950, French socialist statesman; premier of France (1936–37; 1938; 1946–47)

Blunden (ˈblʌndən) *n* **Edmund (Charles)** 1896–1974, British poet and scholar, noted esp for *Undertones of War*(1928), a memoir of World War I in verse and prose

blunder (ˈblʌndə) *n* 1 a stupid or clumsy mistake 2 a foolish tactless remark ▷ *vb* (*mainly intr*) 3 to make stupid or clumsy mistakes 4 to make foolish tactless remarks 5 (often foll by *about, into,* etc) to act clumsily; stumble 6 (*tr*) to mismanage; botch [C14 of Scand. origin; cf. ON *blunda* to close one's eyes] > ˈ**blunderer** *n* > ˈ**blundering** *n, adj*

blunderbuss (ˈblʌndəˌbʌs) *n* an obsolete short musket with large bore and flared muzzle [C17 changed (infl. by BLUNDER) from Du. *donderbus;* from *donder* THUNDER + obs. *bus* gun]

blunge (blʌndʒ) *vb* **blunges, blunging, blunged** (*tr*) to mix (clay or a similar substance) with water in order to form a suspension for use in ceramics [C19 prob. from BLEND + PLUNGE] > ˈ**blunger** *n*

Blunkett (ˈblʌnkɪt) *n* **David** born 1947, British Labour politician; secretary of state for education and employment (1997–2001); home secretary (2001–)

blunt (blʌnt) *adj* 1 (esp of a knife or blade) lacking sharpness or keenness; dull 2 not having a sharp edge or point: *a blunt instrument* 3 (of people, manner of speaking, etc) straightforward and uncomplicated ▷ *vb* (*tr*) 4 to make less sharp 5 to diminish the sensitivity or perception of; make dull [C12 prob. of Scand. origin] > ˈ**bluntly** *adv* > ˈ**bluntness** *n*

Blunt (blʌnt) *n* 1 **Anthony** 1907–83, British art historian and Soviet spy 2 **Wilfred Scawen** 1840–1922, British poet, traveller, and anti- imperialist

blur (blɜː) *vb* **blurs, blurring, blurred** 1 to make or become vague or less distinct 2 to smear or smudge 3 (*tr*) to make (the judgment, memory, or perception) less clear; dim ▷ *n* 4 something vague, hazy, or indistinct 5 a smear or smudge [C16 ? var. of BLEAR] > **blurred** *adj* > ˈ**blurry** *adj*

blurb (blɜːb) *n* a promotional description, as on the jackets of books [C20 coined by G. Burgess (1866–1951), US humorist & illustrator]

blurt (blɜːt) *vb* (*tr;* often foll by *out*) to utter suddenly and involuntarily [C16 prob. imit.]

blush (blʌʃ) *vb* 1 (*intr*) to become suddenly red in the face from embarrassment, shame, modesty, or guilt; redden 2 to make or become reddish or rosy ▷ *n* 3 a sudden reddening of the face from embarrassment, shame, modesty, or guilt 4 a rosy glow 5 a cloudy area on the surface of freshly applied gloss paint 6 another word for **rosé** 7 **at first blush** when first seen; as a first impression [OE *blӯscan*]

blusher (ˈblʌʃə) *n* a cosmetic applied to the cheeks to give a rosy colour

bluster (ˈblʌstə) *vb* 1 to speak or say loudly or boastfully 2 to act in a bullying way 3 (*tr;* foll by *into*) to force or attempt to force (a person) into doing something by behaving thus 4 (*intr*) (of the wind) to be noisy or gusty ▷ *n* 5 boisterous talk or action; swagger 6 empty threats or protests 7 a strong wind; gale [C15 prob. from MLow G *blüsteren* to storm, blow violently] > ˈ**blusterer** *n* > ˈ**blustery** *adj*

Blu-tack (ˈbluːtæk) *n* 1 *trademark* a type of blue, malleable, sticky material used to attach paper, card, etc to walls and other surfaces ▷ *vb* 2 to attach (paper, card, etc) to a wall or other surface by means of this material

Blvd *abbrev for* Boulevard

Blyth (blaɪð) *n* a port in N England, in SE Northumberland, on the North Sea. Pop: 35 327 (1991)

Blyton (ˈblaɪtᵊn) *n* **Enid (Mary)** 1897–1968, British writer of children's books; creator of Noddy and the *Famous Five* series of adventure stories

BM *abbrev for:* 1 Bachelor of Medicine 2 *surveying* benchmark 3 British Museum

BMA *abbrev for* British Medical Association ▷ www.bma.org.uk

BMC *abbrev for* British Medical Council

B-movie *n* a film originally made (esp in the 1940s and 50s) as a supporting film, now often considered as a genre in its own right

BMus *abbrev for* Bachelor of Music

BMX 1 *abbrev. for* bicycle motocross: stunt riding over an obstacle course on a bicycle ▷ *n* 2 a bicycle designed for bicycle motocross

Bn *abbrev for:* 1 Baron 2 Battalion

B4N *text messaging abbrev for* bye for now

BNFL *abbrev for* British Nuclear Fuels Limited

BNP *abbrev for* British National Party

bo *or* **boh** (bəʊ) *interj* an exclamation to startle or surprise someone, esp a child in a game

BO *abbrev for:* 1 *inf* body odour 2 box office

b.o. *abbrev for:* 1 back order 2 branch office 3 broker's order 4 buyer's option

boa (ˈbəʊə) *n* 1 any of various large nonvenomous snakes of Central and South America and the Caribbean. They kill their prey by constriction 2 a woman's long thin scarf, usually of feathers or fur [C19 from NL, from L]

boa constrictor *n* a very large snake of tropical America and the Caribbean that kills its prey by constriction

Boadicea (ˌbəʊədɪˈsiːə) *n* another name for **Boudicca**

boar (bɔː) *n* **1** an uncastrated male pig **2** ▷ See **wild boar** [OE *bār*]

board (bɔːd) *n* **1** a long wide flat piece of sawn timber **2a** a smaller flat piece of rigid material for a specific purpose: *ironing board* **2b** (*in combination*): *breadboard* **3** a person's meals, provided regularly for money **4** *arch* a table, esp when laden with food **5a** (*sometimes functioning as pl*) a group of people who officially administer a company, trust, etc **5b** (*as modifier*): *a board meeting* **6** any other committee or council: *a board of interviewers* **7** stiff cardboard or similar material, used for the outside covers of a book **8** a flat thin rectangular sheet of composite material, such as plasterboard or chipboard **9** *chiefly US* **9a** a list of stock-exchange prices **9b** *inf* the stock exchange itself **10** *naut* the side of a ship **11** *Austral & NZ* the part of the floor of a sheep-shearing shed where the shearers work **12** any of various portable surfaces specially designed for indoor games such as chess, backgammon, etc **13 go by the board** *inf* to be in disuse, neglected, or lost: *in these days courtesy goes by the board* **14 on board** on or in a ship, boat, aeroplane, or other vehicle **15 the boards** the stage ▷ *vb* **16** to go aboard (a vessel, train, aircraft, or other vehicle) **17** to attack (a ship) by forcing one's way aboard **18** (*tr; often foll by up, in*, etc) to cover or shut with boards **19** (*intr*) to receive meals or meals and lodging in return for money **20** (sometimes foll by *out*) to arrange for (someone, esp a child) to receive food and lodging away from home **21** (in ice hockey and box lacrosse) to bodycheck an opponent against the boards ▷ See also **boards** [OE *bord*]

boarder ('bɔːdə) *n* **1** a pupil who lives at school during term time **2** another word for **lodger** **3** a person who boards a ship, esp in an attack

▷ boardgames.about.com

boarding ('bɔːdɪŋ) *n* **1** a structure of boards **2** timber boards collectively **3a** the act of embarking on an aircraft, train, ship, etc **3b** (*as modifier*): *a boarding pass* **4** (in ice hockey and box lacrosse) an act of bodychecking an opponent against the boards

boarding house *n* a private house in which accommodation and meals are provided for paying guests

boarding school *n* a school providing living accommodation for some or all of its pupils

Board of Trade *n* (in Britain) a part of the Department of Trade and Industry responsible for the supervision of commerce and the promotion of export trade

boardroom ('bɔːdˌruːm, -ˌrʊm) *n* a room where the board of directors of a company meets

boards (bɔːdz) *pl n* a wooden wall about one metre high forming the enclosure in which ice hockey or box lacrosse is played

board school *n* (formerly) a school managed by a board of local ratepayers

board shorts *pl n* shorts with longer legs, originally meant to protect a surfer's legs against the surfboard

boardwalk ('bɔːdˌwɔːk) *n US & Canad* a promenade, esp along a beach, usually made of planks

boast (bəʊst) *vb* **1** (*intr; sometimes foll by of or about*) to speak in excessively proud terms of one's possessions, skills, or superior qualities; brag **2** (*tr*) to possess (something to be proud of): *the city boasts a fine cathedral* ▷ *n* **3** a bragging statement **4** a possession, attribute, etc, that is or may be bragged about [C13 from ?] > **'boaster** *n* > **'boasting** *n, adj*

boastful ('bəʊstfʊl) *adj* tending to boast; characterized by boasting > **'boastfully** *adv* > **'boastfulness** *n*

boat (bəʊt) *n* **1** a small vessel propelled by oars, paddle, sails, or motor **2** (not in technical use) another word for **ship** **3** a container for gravy, sauce, etc **4 burn one's boats** ▷ See **burn**[1] (sense 13) **5 in the same boat** sharing the same problems **6 miss the boat** to lose an opportunity **7 rock the boat** *inf* to cause a disturbance in the existing situation ▷ *vb* **8** (*intr*) to travel or go in a boat, esp as a form of recreation **9** (*tr*) to transport or carry in a boat [OE *bāt*]

boater ('bəʊtə) *n* a stiff straw hat with a straight brim and flat crown

boathook ('bəʊtˌhʊk) *n* a pole with a hook at one end, used aboard a vessel for fending off other vessels or for catching a mooring buoy

boathouse ('bəʊtˌhaʊs) *n* a shelter by the edge of a river, lake, etc, for housing boats

boatie ('bəʊtɪ) *n Austral & NZ inf* a boating enthusiast

boating ('bəʊtɪŋ) *n* rowing, sailing, or cruising in boats as a form of recreation

boatload ('bəʊtˌləʊd) *n* the amount of cargo or number of people held by a boat or ship

boatman ('bəʊtmən) *n, pl* **boatmen** a man who works on, hires out, or repairs a boat or boats

boatswain, bosun, *or* **bo's'n** ('bəʊsᵊn) *n* a petty officer or a warrant officer who is responsible for the maintenance of a ship and its equipment [OE *bātswegen*; see BOAT, SWAIN]

boat train *n* a train scheduled to take passengers to or from a particular ship

Boa Vista (*Portuguese* 'boːə 'viʃtə) *n* a town in N Brazil, capital of the federal territory of Roraima, on the Rio Branco. Pop: 196 942 (2000)

Boaz ('bəʊæz) *n Old Testament* a kinsman of Naomi, who married her daughter-in-law Ruth (Ruth 2–4); one of David's ancestors

bob[1] (bɒb) *vb* **bobs, bobbing, bobbed** **1** to move or cause to move up and down repeatedly, as while floating in water **2** to move or cause to move with a short abrupt movement, as of the head **3** (*intr; usually foll by up*) to appear or emerge suddenly **4** (*intr; usually foll by for*) to attempt to get hold (of a floating or hanging object, esp an apple) in the teeth as a game ▷ *n* **5** a short abrupt movement, as of the head [C14 from ?]

bob[2] (bɒb) *n* **1** a hairstyle for women and children in which the hair is cut short evenly all round the head **2** a dangling or hanging object, such as the weight on a pendulum or on a plumb line **3** short for **bobsleigh** **4** a docked tail, esp of a horse ▷ *vb* **bobs, bobbing, bobbed** **5** (*tr*) to cut (the hair) in a bob **6** (*tr*) to cut short (something, esp the tail of an animal); dock or crop **7** (*intr*) to ride on a bobsleigh [C14 *bobbe* bunch of flowers]

Bb

bob[3] (bɒb) *n, pl* **bob** *Brit* (formerly) an informal word for a **shilling** [C19 from ?]

bobbejaan ('bɒbəˌjɑːn) *n S African* **1** a baboon **2** a large black spider **3** a monkey wrench [from Afrik., from MDu. *babiaen*]

bobbin ('bɒbɪn) *n* a spool or reel on which thread or yarn is wound [C16 from OF *bobine*, from ?]

bobble ('bɒbᵊl) *n* **1** a short jerky motion, as of a cork floating on disturbed water; bobbing movement **2** a tufted ball, usually for ornament, as on a knitted hat ▷ *vb* **3** (*intr*) *sport* (of a ball) to bounce with a rapid, erratic motion due to an uneven playing surface [C19 from BOB[1] (vb)]

bobby ('bɒbɪ) *n, pl* **bobbies** *inf* a British policeman [C19 from *Bobby*, after *Robert* PEEL, who set up the Metropolitan Police Force in 1828]

bobby calf *n* an unweaned calf culled for slaughter

bobby-dazzler *n dialect* anything outstanding, striking, or showy [C19 expanded from *dazzler* something striking or attractive]

bobby pin *n US, Canad, & Austral* a metal hairpin bent in order to hold the hair in place

bobby socks *pl n* ankle-length socks worn by teenage girls, esp in the US in the 1940s

bobcat ('bɒbˌkæt) *n* a North American feline mammal, closely related to but smaller than the lynx, having reddish-brown fur with dark spots or stripes, tufted ears, and a short tail. [C19 from BOB[2] + CAT[1]]

Bobo-Dioulasso (ˈbəʊbəʊdjuːˈlæsəʊ) *n* a city in W Burkina-Faso. Pop: 300 000 (1993 est)

bobolink (ˈbɒbəˌlɪŋk) *n* an American songbird, the male of which has a white back and black underparts [c18 imit.]

bobotie (bʊˈbʊtɪ) *n* a South African dish consisting of curried mincemeat with a topping of beaten egg baked to a crust [c19 from Afrik., prob. from Malay]

Bobruisk *or* **Bobruysk** (bɔˈbruːɪsk) *n* a port in Belarus, on the River Berezina: engineering, timber, tyre manufacturing. Pop: 227 000 (1998 est)

bobsleigh (ˈbɒbˌsleɪ) *n* **1** a racing sledge for two or more people, with a steering mechanism enabling the driver to direct it down a steeply banked ice-covered run ▷ *vb* **2** (*intr*) to ride on a bobsleigh. Also called (esp US and Canad): **bobsled** (ˈbɒbˌslɛd) [c19 BOB[2] + SLEIGH]

bobstay (ˈbɒbˌsteɪ) *n* a strong stay between a bowsprit and the stem of a vessel for holding down the bowsprit [c18 ?from BOB[1] + STAY[3]]

bobsy-die (ˈbɒbzɪˌdaɪ) *n NZ inf* fuss; confusion (esp in **kick up bobsy-die**) [from c19 *Bob's a-dying*]

bobtail (ˈbɒbˌteɪl) *n* **1** a docked or diminutive tail **2** an animal with such a tail ▷ *adj also* **bobtailed 3** having the tail cut short ▷ *vb* (*tr*) **4** to dock the tail of **5** to cut short; curtail

Boccaccio (*Italian* bokˈkattʃo) *n* **Giovanni** (dʒoˈvani) 1313–75, Italian poet and writer, noted particularly for his *Decameron*(1353), a collection of 100 short stories. His other works include *Filostrato*(?1338) and *Teseida* (1341)

Boccherini (*Italian* bokkeˈrini) *n* **Luigi** (luˈidʒi) 1743–1805, Italian composer and cellist

Boche (bɒʃ) *n derog sl* (esp in World Wars I and II) **1** a German, esp a German soldier **2 the** (*usually functioning as pl*) Germans collectively, esp German soldiers regarded as the enemy [c20 from F, prob. shortened from *alboche* German, from *allemand* German + *caboche* pate]

Bochum (*German* ˈboːxum) *n* an industrial city in NW Germany, in W North Rhine-Westphalia: university (1965). Pop: 392 900 (1999 est)

bockedy (ˈbɒkədɪ) *adj Irish* (of a structure, piece of furniture, etc) unsteady [from Irish Gaelic *bacaideach* limping]

bod (bɒd) *n inf* **1** a fellow; chap: *he's a queer bod* **2** another word for **body** (sense 1) [c18 short for BODY]

BOD *abbrev for:* biochemical oxygen demand

bodacious (bəʊˈdeɪʃəs) *adj sl, chiefly US* impressive or remarkable; excellent [c19 from E dialect; blend of BOLD and AUDACIOUS]

bode[1] (bəʊd) *vb* **bodes, boding, boded 1** to be an omen of (good or ill, esp of ill); portend; presage **2** (*tr*) *arch* to predict; foretell [OE *bodian*] > ˈ**bodement** *n*

bode[2] (bəʊd) *vb* a past tense of **bide**

bodega (bəʊˈdiːgə) *n* a shop selling wine and sometimes groceries, esp in a Spanish-speaking country [c19 from Sp., ult. from Gk *apothēkē* storehouse]

Bodensee (ˈboːdənzeː) *n* the German name for (Lake) **Constance**

bodge (bɒdʒ) *vb* **bodges, bodging, bodged 1** *inf* to make a mess of; botch **2** *Austral inf* to make or adjust in a false or clumsy way: *they bodged the figures* [c16 changed from BOTCH]

bodgie (ˈbɒdʒɪ) *Austral & NZ sl* ▷ *n* **1** an unruly or uncouth young man, esp in the 1950s; teddy boy ▷ *adj* **2** inferior; worthless [c20 from BODGE]

Bodh Gaya (ˈbɒd gəˈjɑː) *n* a variant spelling of **Buddh Gaya**

Bodhidharma (ˌbəʊdɪˈdɑːmə, ˌbɒd-) *n* 6th century AD, Indian Buddhist monk, who taught in China (from 520): considered to be the founder of Zen Buddhism

Bodhisattva (ˌbəʊdɪˈsætvə, -wə, ˌbɒd-) *n* (in Buddhism) a divine being worthy of nirvana who remains on the human plane to help men to salvation [Sansk., from *bodhi* enlightenment + *sattva* essence]

bodice (ˈbɒdɪs) *n* **1** the upper part of a woman's dress, from the shoulder to the waist **2** a tight-fitting corset worn laced over a blouse, or (formerly) as a woman's undergarment [c16 orig. Scot. *bodies*, pl. of BODY]

bodice ripper *n inf* a romantic novel, usually on a historical theme, that involves some sex and violence

-bodied *adj* (*in combination*) having a body or bodies as specified: *able-bodied; long-bodied*

bodiless (ˈbɒdɪlɪs) *adj* having no body or substance; incorporeal or insubstantial

bodily (ˈbɒdɪlɪ) *adj* **1** relating to or being a part of the human body ▷ *adv* **2** by taking hold of the body: *he threw him bodily from the platform* **3** in person; in the flesh

bodkin (ˈbɒdkɪn) *n* **1** a blunt large-eyed needle **2** *arch* a dagger **3** *arch* a long ornamental hairpin [c14 prob. of Celtic origin]

Bodmin (ˈbɒdmɪn) *n* a market town in SW England, in Cornwall, near **Bodmin Moor**, a granite upland rising to 420 m (1375 ft) Pop: 12 553 (1991)

body (ˈbɒdɪ) *n, pl* **bodies 1a** the entire physical structure of an animal or human being. Related adj: **corporeal 1b** (*as modifier*): *body odour* **2** the trunk or torso **3** a dead human or animal; corpse **4** the flesh as opposed to the spirit **5** the largest or main part of anything: *the body of a vehicle; the body of a plant* **6** a separate or distinct mass of water or land **7** a number of individuals regarded as a single entity; group **8** fullness in the appearance of the hair **9** the characteristic full quality of certain wines **10** firmness, esp of cloth **11a** the pigment contained in or added to paint, dye, etc **11b** the opacity of a paint **11c** (*as modifier*): *body colour* **12** an informal or dialect word for a **person 13** another word for **bodysuit** (sense 1) **14 keep body and soul together** to manage to keep alive; survive ▷ *vb* **bodies, bodying, bodied** (*tr*) **15** (usually foll by *forth*) to give a body or shape to [OE *bodig*]

body blow *n* **1** *boxing* a blow to an opponent's body **2** a severe disappointment or setback

bodyboard (ˈbɒdɪˌbɔːd) *n* a surfboard that is shorter and blunter than the standard board and on which the surfer lies rather than stands > ˈ**bodyˌboarder** *n* > ˈ**bodyˌboarding** *n*

body building *n* the practice of exercises to make the muscles of the body conspicuous

bodycheck (ˈbɒdɪˌtʃɛk) *ice hockey, etc* ▷ *n* **1** obstruction of another player ▷ *vb* **2** (*tr*) to deliver a bodycheck to (an opponent)

body double *n films* a person who substitutes for a star for the filming of a scene that involves shots of the body rather than the face

bodyguard (ˈbɒdɪˌgɑːd) *n* a person or group of people who escort and protect someone

body horror *n* a genre of horror film in which the main feature is the graphically depicted destruction or degeneration of a human body or bodies

body language *n* the nonverbal imparting of information by means of conscious or subconscious bodily gestures, posture, etc

body-line *adj cricket* denoting or relating to fast bowling aimed at the batsman's body

body mass index *n* an index used to indicate whether a person is over- or underweight. It is obtained by dividing a person's weight in kilograms by the square of their height in metres. An index of 20–25 is normal. Abbrev: **BMI**

body-packer *n* a person who smuggles illicit drugs in balloons, condoms, or similar plastic bags which have either been swallowed or inserted in the rectum or vagina

body politic *n* **the** the people of a nation or the nation itself considered as a political entity

body search *n* **1** a form of search by police, customs officials, etc, that involves examination of a prisoner's or suspect's bodily orifices ▷ *vb* **body-search 2** (*tr*) to

search (a prisoner or suspect) in this manner
bodyshell ('bɒdɪˌʃɛl) *n* the external shell of a motor vehicle
body shop *n* a repair yard for vehicle bodywork
body snatcher *n* (formerly) a person who robbed graves and sold the corpses for dissection
body stocking *n* a one-piece undergarment for women, usually of nylon, covering the torso
bodysuit ('bɒdɪˌsuːt, -ˌsjuːt) *n* **1** a woman's close-fitting one-piece garment for the torso. Sometimes shortened to **body 2** a one-piece undergarment for a baby
body swerve *n* **1** *sport* (esp in football games) the act or an instance of swerving past an opponent **2** *Scot* the act or an instance of avoiding (a situation considered unpleasant): *I think I'll give the meeting a body swerve* ▷ *vb* **body-swerve, body-swerves, body-swerving, body-swerved 3** *sport* (esp in football games) to pass (an opponent) using a body swerve **4** *Scot* to avoid (a situation or person considered unpleasant)
body warmer *n* a sleeveless type of jerkin, usually quilted, worn as an outer garment
bodywork ('bɒdɪˌwɜːk) *n* the external shell of a motor vehicle
Boeotia (bɪ'əʊʃɪə) *n* **1** a region of ancient Greece, northwest of Athens. It consisted of ten city-states, which formed the Boeotian League, led by Thebes: at its height in the 4th century BC **2** transliteration of the Modern Greek name for **Voiotia**
Boeotian (bɪ'əʊʃɪən) *adj* **1** of Boeotia **2** dull or stupid ▷ *n* **3** a person from Boeotia **4** a dull or stupid person
Boer (bʊə) *n* **a** a descendant of any of the Dutch or Huguenot colonists who settled in South Africa **b** (*as modifier*): *a Boer farmer* [c19 from Du. *Boer*; see BOOR]
▷ www.wikipedia.org/wiki/Boer_War
▷ www.nationmaster.com/encyclopedia/Boer-War
boerbul ('bʊəbəl) *n S African* a crossbred mastiff used esp as a watchdog [from Afrik. *boerboel*, from *boel* large dog]
boeremusiek ('bʊərəˌmœsɪk) *n S African* light music associated with the culture of the Afrikaners [from Afrik. *boere* country, folk + *musiek* music]
▷ www.accordions.com/index/his/his_afr.shtml
boet (bʊt) *or* **boetie** *n S African inf* a friend [from Afrik.: brother]
Boethius (bəʊ'iːθɪəs) *n* **Anicius Manlius Severinus** (ə'nɪsɪəs 'mænlɪəs ˌsɛvə'raɪnəs) ?480–?524 AD, Roman philosopher and statesman, noted particularly for his work *De Consolatione Philosophiae*. He was accused of treason and executed by Theodoric
boffin ('bɒfɪn) *n Brit inf* **1** a scientist, esp one carrying out military research **2** a person who has extensive skill or knowledge in a particular field: *a Treasury boffin* [c20 from ?]
boffo ('bɒfəʊ) *adj sl* very good; highly successful [c20 from ?]
Bofors gun ('bəʊfəz) *n* an automatic 40 mm anti-aircraft gun, one or more of which are controlled by a radar-operated computer system mounted on a lightweight vehicle [c20 after the Swedish armament firm that developed it]
bog (bɒg) *n* **1** wet spongy ground consisting of decomposing vegetation **2** an area of such ground **3** a slang word for **lavatory** [c13 from Gaelic *bogach* swamp, from *bog* soft] > '**boggy** *adj* > '**bogginess** *n*
bogan[1] ('bəʊgən) *n Canad* (esp in the Maritime Provinces) a sluggish side stream. Also called: **logan, pokelogan** [of Algonquian origin]
bogan[2] ('bəʊgən) ▷ *n Austral inf* **1** a fool **2** a hooligan [c20 of unknown origin]
bogan[2] ('bəʊgən) *n Austral & NZ inf* a young person who behaves rebelliously [c20 from ?]
Bogarde ('bəʊgɑːd) *n* Sir **Dirk**, real name *Derek Jules Gaspard Ulric Niven van den Bogaerde*. 1920–99, British film actor and writer: his films include *The Servant* (1963) and *Death in Venice* (1970). His writings include the autobiographical *A Postillion Struck by Lightning* (1977) and the novel *A Period of Adjustment* (1994)
Bogart ('bəʊgɑːt) *n* **Humphrey** (**DeForest**) nicknamed *Bogie*. 1899–1957, US film actor: his films include *High Sierra* (1941), *Casablanca* (1942), *The Big Sleep* (1946), *The African Queen* (1951), and *The Caine Mutiny* (1954)
Boğazköy (*Turkish* bɔː'ɑzkœi) *n* a village in central Asia Minor: site of the ancient Hittite capital
bogbean ('bɒgˌbiːn) *n* another name for **buckbean**
bog down *vb* **bogs, bogging, bogged** (*adv; when tr, often passive*) to impede or be impeded physically or mentally
bogey *or* **bogy** ('bəʊgɪ) *n* **1** an evil or mischievous spirit **2** something that worries or annoys **3** *golf* **3a** a score of one stroke over par on a hole ▷ Cf **par** (sense 5) **3b** *obs* a standard score for a hole or course, regarded as one that a good player should make **4** *sl* a piece of dried mucus discharged from the nose [c19 prob. rel. to obs. *bug* an evil spirit and BOGLE]
bogeyman ('bəʊgɪˌmæn) *n, pl* **bogeymen** a person, real or imaginary, used as a threat, esp to children
bogger (bɒgə) *n Austral sl* a lavatory
boggle ('bɒgᵊl) *vb* **boggles, boggling, boggled** (*intr; often foll by at*) **1** to be surprised, confused, or alarmed (esp in **the mind boggles**) **2** to hesitate or be evasive when confronted with a problem [c16 prob. var. of BOGLE]
bogie *or* **bogy** ('bəʊgɪ) *n* **1** an assembly of four or six wheels forming a pivoted support at either end of a railway coach **2** *chiefly Brit* a small railway truck of short wheelbase, used for conveying coal, ores, etc [c19 from ?]
bogle ('bəʊgᵊl, 'bɒg-) *n* a dialect or archaic word for **bogey** (sense 1) [c16 from Scot. *bogill*]
bog myrtle *n* another name for **sweet gale**
Bognor Regis ('bɒgnə 'riːdʒɪs) *n* a resort in S England, in West Sussex on the English Channel: electronics industries. *Regis* was added to the name after King George V's convalescence there in 1929. Pop: 56 744 (1991)
bog oak *n* oak found preserved in peat bogs
bog off *Brit sl* ▷ *interj* **1** go away! ▷ *vb* **bogs, bogging, bogged 2** (*intr, adv*) to go away
bogong ('bəʊˌgɒŋ) *or* **bugong** ('buːˌgɒŋ) *n* an edible dark-coloured Australian noctuid moth
Bogor ('bəʊgɔː) *n* a city in Indonesia, in W Java: botanical gardens and research institutions. Pop: 285 114 (1995 est). Former name: **Buitenzorg**
Bogotá (ˌbəʊgə'tɑː; *Spanish* boɣo'ta) *n* the capital of Colombia, on a central plateau of the E Andes: originally the centre of Chibcha civilization; founded as a city in 1538 by the Spaniards. Pop: 6 260 862 (1999 est)
▷ www.bogota-dc.com
bog-standard *adj Brit & Irish sl* completely ordinary; run-of-the-mill
bogtrotter ('bɒgˌtrɒtə) *n* a derogatory term for an Irishman, esp an Irish peasant
bogus ('bəʊgəs) *adj* spurious or counterfeit; not genuine [c19 from *bogus* apparatus for making counterfeit money] > '**bogusly** *adv* > '**bogusness** *n*
bogy ('bəʊgɪ) *n, pl* **bogies** a variant spelling of **bogey** or **bogie**
Bohai ('bɔː'haɪ) *or* **Pohai** *n* a large inlet of the Yellow Sea on the coast of NE China. Also called: (Gulf of) **Chihli**
bohea (bəʊ'hiː) *n* a black Chinese tea, once regarded as the choicest, but now as an inferior grade [c18 from Chinese *Wu-i Shan*, range of hills on which this tea was grown]
Bohemia (bəʊ'hiːmɪə) *n* **1** a former kingdom of central Europe, surrounded by mountains: independent from the 9th to the 13th century; belonged to the Hapsburgs from 1526 until 1918 **2** an area of the W Czech Republic, formerly a province of Czechoslovakia (1918–1949). From 1939 until 1945 it formed part of the German protectorate of **Bohemia-Moravia**. Czech name: **Čechy**.

Bb

German name: **Böhmen** (ˈbøːmən) **3** a district frequented by unconventional people, esp artists or writers

Bohemian (bəʊˈhiːmɪən) *n* **1** a native or inhabitant of Bohemia; a Czech **2** *(often not cap)* a person, esp an artist or writer, who lives an unconventional life **3** the Czech language ▷ *adj* **4** of, relating to, or characteristic of Bohemia, its people, or their language **5** *(often not cap)* unconventional in appearance, behaviour, etc

Bohemian Forest *n* a mountain range between the SW Czech Republic and SE Germany. Highest peak: Arber, 1457 m (4780 ft). Czech name: **Český Les** (ˈtʃɛski: ˈlɛs) German name: **Böhmerwald** (ˈbøːmər,valt)

Bohemianism (bəʊˈhiːmɪə,nɪzəm) *n* unconventional behaviour or appearance, esp of an artist

Böhm (*German* bøːm) *n* **Karl** (karl) 1894–1981, Austrian orchestral conductor

boho (ˈbəʊhəʊ) *n, pl* **bohos,** *adj* short for **Bohemian** (senses 2, 5)

Bohol (bəʊˈhɔːl) *n* an island of the central Philippines. Chief town: Tagbilaran. Pop: 948 000 (1990). Area: about 3900 sq km (1500 sq miles)

Bohr (bɔː; *Danish* boːr) *n* **1 Aage Niels** (ˈɔgə neːls) born 1922, Danish physicist, noted for his work on nuclear structure. He shared the Nobel prize for physics 1975 **2** his father, **Niels** (**Henrik David**) 1885–1962, Danish physicist, who applied the quantum theory to Rutherford's model of the atom to explain spectral lines: Nobel prize for physics 1922

bohrium (ˈbɔːrɪəm) *n* a transuranic element artificially produced in minute quantities by bombarding ^{204}Bi atoms with ^{54}Cr nuclei. Symbol: Bh; atomic no.: 107. Former names: **element 107, unnilheptium** [c20 after N. BOHR]

boil¹ (bɔɪl) *vb* **1** to change or cause to change from a liquid to a vapour so rapidly that bubbles of vapour are formed in the liquid **2** to reach or cause to reach boiling point **3** to cook or be cooked by the process of boiling **4** *(intr)* to bubble and be agitated like something boiling; seethe: *the ocean was boiling* **5** *(intr)* to be extremely angry or indignant ▷ *n* **6** the state or action of boiling ▷ See also **boil away, boil down, boil over** [c13 from OF, from L, from *bulla* a bubble]

boil² (bɔɪl) *n* a red painful swelling with a hard pus-filled core caused by bacterial infection of the skin. Technical name: **furuncle** [OE *bȳle*]

boil away *vb (adv)* to cause (liquid) to evaporate completely by boiling or (of liquid) to evaporate completely

boil down *vb (adv)* **1** to reduce or be reduced in quantity by boiling **2 boil down to 2a** *(intr)* to be the essential element in something **2b** *(tr)* to summarize; reduce to essentials

Boileau (*French* bwalo) *n* **Nicolas** (nikɔla) full name *Nicolas Boileau-Despréaux.* 1636–1711, French poet and critic; author of satires, epistles, and *L'Art poétique* (1674), in which he laid down the basic principles of French classical literature

boiled shirt *n inf* a dress shirt with a stiff front

boiler (ˈbɔɪlə) *n* **1** a closed vessel in which water is heated to supply steam or provide heat **2** a domestic device to provide hot water, esp for central heating **3** a large tub for boiling laundry

boilermaker (ˈbɔɪlə,meɪkə) *n* a person who works with metal in heavy industry; plater or welder

boilerplate (ˈbɔɪlə,pleɪt) *n* **1** a form of mild-steel plate used in the production of boiler shells **2** a copy made with the intention of making other copies from it **3** a set of instructions incorporated in several places in a computer program or a standard form of words used repeatedly in drafting contracts, guarantees, etc **4** a draft contract that can be modified to cover various types of transaction

boiler room *n* **1** any room in a building (often in the basement) that contains a boiler for central heating, etc **2** the part of a steam ship that houses the boilers and furnaces **3** the room or department in which the work of an organization goes on unseen **4** *chiefly US* an office used by a team of telephone salespeople, esp of stocks and shares, operating under high pressure

boiler suit *n Brit* a one-piece overall work garment

boiling point *n* **1** the temperature at which a liquid boils at sea level **2** *inf* the condition of being angered or highly excited

boiling-water reactor *n* a nuclear reactor using water as coolant and moderator, steam being produced in the reactor itself. Abbrev: **BWR**

boil over *vb (adv)* **1** to overflow or cause to overflow while boiling **2** *(intr)* to burst out in anger or excitement

boilover (ˈbɔɪl,əʊvə) *n Austral* **1** a surprising result in a sporting event, esp in a horse race **2** a sudden conflict

Bois de Boulogne (*French* bwa də bulɔŋ) *n* a large park in W Paris, formerly a forest: includes the racecourses of Auteuil and Longchamp

Boise *or* **Boise City** (ˈbɔɪzɪ, -sɪ) *n* a city in SW Idaho: the state capital. Pop: 185 787 (2000)

Bois-le-Duc (bwa lə dyk) *n* the French name for **'s Hertogenbosch**

boisterous (ˈbɔɪstərəs, -strəs) *adj* **1** noisy and lively; unruly **2** (of the wind, sea, etc) stormy [c13 *boistuous,* from ?] > ˈ**boisterously** *adv* > ˈ**boisterousness** *n*

Boito (*Italian* ˈbɔːito) *n* **Arrigo** (arˈrigo) 1842–1918, Italian operatic composer and librettist, whose works include the opera *Mefistofele* (1868) and the librettos for Verdi's *Otello* and *Falstaff*

Bokassa I (bəˈkæsə) *n* original name *Jean Bedel Bokassa.* 1921–96, president of the Central African Republic (1972–76); emperor of the renamed Central African Empire from 1976 until overthrown in 1979

bok choy (ˈbɒk ˈtʃɔɪ) *n* a Chinese plant that is related to the cabbage and has edible stalks and leaves. Also called: **Chinese cabbage, Chinese leaf** [from Chinese dialect, lit.: white vegetable]

Bokhara (bʊˈxɑːrə) *n* a variant spelling of **Bukhara**

Bol. *abbrev for* Bolivia(n)

bola (ˈbəʊlə) *or* **bolas** (ˈbəʊləs) *n, pl* **bolas** *or* **bolases** a missile used by gauchos and Indians of South America, consisting of heavy balls on a cord. It is hurled at a running quarry, so as to entangle its legs [Sp.: ball, from L *bulla* knob]

Boland (ˈbʊəlant) *n* an area of high altitude in S South Africa

Bolan Pass (bəʊˈlɑːn) *n* a mountain pass in W central Pakistan through the Brahui Range, between Sibi and Quetta, rising to 1800 m (5900 ft)

bold (bəʊld) *adj* **1** courageous, confident, and fearless; ready to take risks **2** showing or requiring courage: *a bold plan* **3** immodest or impudent: *she gave him a bold look* **4** standing out distinctly; conspicuous: *a figure carved in bold relief* **5** very steep: *the bold face of the cliff* **6** imaginative in thought or expression [OE *beald*] > ˈ**boldly** *adv* > ˈ**boldness** *n*

bold face *printing* ▷ *n* **1** a weight of type characterized by thick heavy lines, as the entry words in this dictionary ▷ *adj* **boldface 2** (of type) having this weight

Boldrewood (ˈbəʊldə,wʊd) *n* **Rolf,** real name *Thomas Alexander Browne.* 1826–1915, Australian writer, born in the UK, noted for his novels of the Australian outback, esp *Robbery Under Arms* (1882–3)

bole (bəʊl) *n* the trunk of a tree [c14 from ON *bolr*]

bolero (bəˈlɛərəʊ) *n, pl* **boleros 1** a Spanish dance, usually in triple time **2** a piece of music for or in the rhythm of this dance **3** *(also* ˈbɒlərəʊ) a short open bodice-like jacket not reaching the waist [c18 from Sp.]

Boleyn (bʊˈlɪn, ˈbʊlɪn) *n* **Anne** 1507–36, second wife of Henry VIII of England; mother of Elizabeth I. She was executed on a charge of adultery

Bolingbroke ('bɒlɪŋˌbrʊk) *n* 1 the surname of **Henry IV** of England 2 **Henry St John**, 1st Viscount Bolingbroke. 1678–1751, English politician; fled to France in 1714 and acted as secretary of state to the Old Pretender; returned to England in 1723. His writings include *A Dissertation on Parties* (1733–34) and *Idea of a Patriot King* (1738)

bolívar[1] ('bɒlɪˌvɑː; *Spanish*. bo'liβar) *n* the standard monetary unit of Venezuela, equal to 100 céntimos

Bolivar ('bɒlɪˌvɑː; *Spanish* bo'liβar) *n* **Simon** (si'mon) 1783–1830, South American soldier and liberator. He drove the Spaniards from Venezuela, Colombia, Ecuador, and Peru and hoped to set up a republican confederation, but was prevented by separatist movements in Venezuela and Colombia (1829–30). Upper Peru became a separate state and was called Bolivia in his honour

Bolivia (bə'lɪvɪə) *n* an inland republic in central S America: original Aymará Indian population conquered by the Incas in the 13th century; colonized by Spain from 1538; became a republic in 1825; consists of low plains in the east, with ranges of the Andes rising to over 6400 m (21 000 ft) and the Altiplano, a plateau averaging 3900 m (13 000 ft) in the west; contains some of the world's highest inhabited regions; important producer of tin and other minerals. Official languages: Spanish, Quechua, and Aymara. Religion: Roman Catholic. Currency: boliviano. Capital: La Paz (administrative); Sucre (judicial). Pop: 8 516 000 (2001 est). Area: 1 098 580 sq km (424 260 sq miles) > **Bo'livian** *adj, n*

▷ www.bolivia.gov.bo

▷ www.bolivia-tourism.com

boliviano (bəˌlɪvɪ'ɑːnəʊ; *Spanish* boli'βjano) **bolivianos** (-nəʊz; *Spanish* -nos) (until 1963 and from 1987) the standard monetary unit of Bolivia, equal to 100 centavos

boll (bəʊl) *n* the fruit of such plants as flax and cotton, consisting of a rounded capsule containing the seeds [c13 from Du. *bolle*; rel. to OE *bolla* BOWL[1]]

bollard ('bɒlɑːd, 'bɒləd) *n* 1 a strong wooden or metal post on a wharf, quay, etc, used for securing mooring lines 2 *Brit* a small post placed on a kerb or traffic island to make it conspicuous to motorists [c14 ?from BOLE + -ARD]

bollocking ('bɒləkɪŋ) *n sl* a severe telling-off [from *bollock* (vb) in the sense "to reprimand"]

bollocks ('bɒləks) *or* **ballocks** *Taboo sl* ▷ *pl n* 1 another word for **testicles** 2 nonsense; rubbish ▷ *interj* 3 an exclamation of annoyance, disbelief, etc [OE *beallucas*; see BALL[1]]

boll weevil *n* a greyish weevil of the southern US and Mexico, whose larvae live in and destroy cotton bolls

Bollywood ('bɒlɪˌwʊd) *n inf* **a** the Indian film industry **b** (*as modifier*): *a Bollywood star* [c20 from BO(MBAY) + (HO)LLYWOOD]

▷ www.bollywoodworld.com

▷ www.planetbollywood.com

Bologna[1] (bə'ləʊnjə; *Italian* bo'loɲɲa) *n* a city in N Italy, at the foot of the Apennines: became a free city in the Middle Ages; university (1088). Pop: 381 161 (2000 est). Ancient name: **Bononia** (bə'nəʊnɪə) > **Bolognese** (ˌbɒlə'niːz, -'neɪz) *adj, n*

Bologna[2] (bə'ləʊnjə; *Italian* bo'loɲɲa) *n* **Giovanni da** ▷ See **Giambologna**

bologna sausage (bə'ləʊnjə) *n chiefly US & Canad* a large smoked sausage made of seasoned mixed meats. Also called: **baloney, boloney,** (esp Brit) **polony**

bolometer (bəʊ'lɒmɪtə) *n* a sensitive instrument for measuring radiant energy [c19 from Gk *bolē* ray of light, from *ballein* to throw + -METER] > **bolometric** (ˌbəʊlə'mɛtrɪk) *adj*

boloney (bə'ləʊnɪ) *n* 1 a variant of **baloney** 2 another name for **bologna sausage**

Bolshevik ('bɒlʃɪvɪk) *n, pl* **Bolsheviks** *or* **Bolsheviki** (ˌbɒlʃɪ'viːkɪ) 1 (formerly) a Russian Communist ▷ Cf **Menshevik** 2 any Communist 3 (*often not cap*) *inf & derog*. any political radical, esp a revolutionary [c20 from Russian *Bol'shevik* majority, from *bol'shoi* great] > **'Bolsheˌvism** *n* > **'Bolshevist** *adj, n*

▷ www.imternationalist.org/stalinism &Bolshevism.html

▷ www.1upinfo.com/encyclopedia/B/Bolshevism.html

bolshie *or* **bolshy** ('bɒlʃɪ) (*sometimes cap*) *Brit inf* ▷ *adj* 1 difficult to manage; rebellious 2 politically radical or left-wing ▷ *n, pl* **bolshies** 3 *derog* any political radical [c20 shortened from BOLSHEVIK]

bolster ('bəʊlstə) *vb* (*tr*) 1 (often foll by *up*) to support or reinforce; strengthen: *to bolster morale* 2 to prop up with a pillow or cushion ▷ *n* 3 a long narrow pillow or cushion 4 any pad or padded support 5 a cold chisel used for cutting stone slabs, etc [OE *bolster*]

bolt[1] (bəʊlt) *n* 1 a bar that can be slid into a socket to lock a door, gate, etc 2 a bar or rod that forms part of a locking mechanism and is moved by a key or a knob 3 a metal rod or pin that has a head and a screw thread to take a nut 4 a sliding bar in a breech-loading firearm that ejects the empty cartridge, replaces it with a new one, and closes the breech 5 a flash of lightning 6 a sudden start or movement, esp in order to escape 7 a roll of something, such as cloth, wallpaper, etc 8 an arrow, esp for a crossbow 9 **a bolt from the blue** a sudden, unexpected, and usually unwelcome event 10 **shoot one's bolt** to exhaust one's efforts ▷ *vb* 11 (*tr*) to secure or lock with or as with a bolt 12 (*tr*) to eat hurriedly 13 (*intr*; usually foll by *from* or *out*) to move or jump suddenly: *he bolted from the chair* 14 (*intr*) (esp of a horse) to start hurriedly and run away without warning 15 (*tr*) to roll (cloth, wallpaper, etc) into bolts 16 (*intr*) (of cultivated plants) to produce flowers and seeds prematurely ▷ *adv* 17 stiffly, firmly, or rigidly (archaic except in **bolt upright**) [OE *bolt* arrow] > **'bolter** *n*

Bb

bolt[2] *or* **boult** (bəʊlt) *vb* (*tr*) 1 to pass (a powder, etc) through a sieve 2 to examine and separate [c13 from OF *bulter*, prob. of Gmc origin] > **'bolter** *or* **'boulter** *n*

Bolt (bəʊlt) *n* **Robert** (**Oxton**) 1924–95, British playwright. His plays include *A Man for All Seasons* (1960) and he also wrote a number of screenplays

bolt hole *n* a place of escape from danger

Bolton ('bəʊltən) *n* 1 a town in NW England, in Bolton unitary authority, Greater Manchester: centre of the woollen trade since the 14th century; later important for cotton. Pop: 139 020 (1991) 2 a unitary authority in NW England, in Greater Manchester. Pop: 261 035 (2001). Area: 140 sq km (54 sq miles)

boltrope ('bəʊltˌrəʊp) *n naut* a rope sewn to the foot or luff of a sail to strengthen it

Boltzmann (*German* 'bɔltsman) *n* **Ludwig** ('luːtvɪç) 1844–1906, Austrian physicist. He established the principle of the equipartition of energy and developed the kinetic theory of gases with J. C. Maxwell

bolus ('bəʊləs) *n, pl* **boluses** 1 a small round soft mass, esp of chewed food 2 a large pill or tablet used in veterinary and clinical medicine [c17 from NL, from Gk *bōlos* clod, lump]

Bolzano (*Italian* bol'tsano) *n* a city in NE Italy, in Trentino-Alto Adige: belonged to Austria until 1919. Pop: 100 380 (1990). German name: **Bozen**

Boma ('bəʊmə) *n* a port in the Democratic Republic of Congo (formerly Zaïre), on the Congo River, capital of the Belgian Congo until 1926: forest products. Pop: 135 284 (1994 est)

bomb (bɒm) *n* 1a a hollow projectile containing explosive, incendiary, or other destructive substance 1b (*as modifier*): *bomb disposal; a bomb bay* 1c (*in combination*): *bombproof* 2 an object in which an explosive device has been planted: *a car bomb; a letter bomb* 3 a round mass of

volcanic rock, solidified from molten lava that has been thrown into the air **4** *med* a container for radioactive material, applied therapeutically to any part of the body: *a cobalt bomb* **5** *Brit sl* a large sum of money **6** *US & Canad sl* a disastrous failure: *the new play was a total bomb* **7** *Austral & NZ sl* an old or dilapidated motorcar **8** *American football* a very long high pass **9** (in rugby union) another name for **up-and-under** **10** like a bomb. *Brit & NZ inf* with great speed or success; very well **11** **the bomb** a hydrogen or an atomic bomb considered as the ultimate destructive weapon ▷ *vb* **12** to attack with or as if with a bomb or bombs; drop bombs (on) **13** (*intr; often foll by off, along,* etc) *inf* to move or drive very quickly **14** (*intr*) *US sl* to fail disastrously [C17 from F, from It., from L, from Gk *bombos,* imit.]
▷ www.fas.org/man/dod-101/sys/dumb

bombard (bɒmˈbɑːd) *vb* (*tr*) **1** to attack with concentrated artillery fire or bombs **2** to attack with vigour and persistence **3** to attack verbally, esp with questions **4** *physics* to direct high-energy particles or photons against (atoms, nuclei, etc) ▷ *n* (ˈbɒmbɑːd) **5** an ancient type of cannon that threw stone balls [C15 from OF, from *bombarde* stone-throwing cannon, prob. from L *bombus* booming sound; see BOMB] > **bomˈbardment** *n*

bombardier (ˌbɒmbəˈdɪə) *n* **1** the member of a bomber aircrew responsible for aiming and releasing the bombs **2** *Brit* a noncommissioned rank, below the rank of sergeant, in the Royal Artillery [C16 from OF; see BOMBARD]

Bombardier (ˌbɒmbəˈdɪə) *n Canad trademark* a snow tractor, usually having caterpillar tracks at the rear and skis at the front [C20 after J. A. *Bombardier*, Canadian inventor and manufacturer]

bombast (ˈbɒmbæst) *n* pompous and grandiloquent language [C16 from OF, from Med. L *bombāx* cotton] > **bomˈbastic** *adj* > **bomˈbastically** *adv*

Bombay (bɒmˈbeɪ) *n* **1** a port in W India, capital of Maharashtra state, on the Arabian Sea: ceded by Portugal to England in 1661 and of major importance in British India; commercial and industrial centre, esp for cotton. Pop: 9 925 891 (1991). Official and Hindi name: **Mumbai** **2** a breed of black short-haired medium-sized cat

Bombay duck *n* a fish that is eaten dried with curry dishes as a savoury. Also called: **bummalo** [C19 changed from *bombil* through association with Bombay, from which it was exported]

bombazine *or* **bombasine** (ˌbɒmbəˈziːn, ˈbɒmbəˌziːn) *n* a twilled fabric, esp one of silk and worsted, formerly worn dyed black for mourning [C16 from OF, from L, from *bombyx* silk]

bomber (ˈbɒmə) *n* **1** a military aircraft designed to carry out bombing missions **2** a person who plants bombs
▷ www.aeroimage.com/Bomber.htm

bomber jacket *n* a short jacket finishing at the waist with an elasticated band, usually having a zip front

bomblet (ˈbɒmlɪt) *n* one of a number of small bombs contained in a larger bomb

bombora (bɒmˈbɔːrə) *n Austral* **1** a submerged reef **2** a turbulent area of sea over such a reef [from Abor.]

bombshell (ˈbɒmˌʃɛl) *n* **1** (esp formerly) a bomb or artillery shell **2** a shocking or unwelcome surprise

bombsight (ˈbɒmˌsaɪt) *n* a mechanical or electronic device in an aircraft for aiming bombs

Bomu (ˈbəʊmuː) *or* **Mbomu** (ᵊmˈbəʊmuː) *n* a river in central Africa, rising in the SE Central African Republic and flowing west into the Uele River, forming the Ubangi River. Length: about 800 km (500 miles)

Bon[2] (bɒn) *n* **Cape** a peninsula of NE Tunisia

Bona (ˈbəʊnə) *n* **Mount** a mountain in S Alaska, in the Wrangell Mountains. Height: 5005 m (16 420 ft)

bona fide (ˈbəʊnə ˈfaɪdɪ) *adj* **1** real or genuine: *a bona fide Medieval manuscript* **2** undertaken in good faith: *we had a bona fide agreement* [C16 from L]

bona fides (ˈbəʊnə ˈfaɪdiːz) *n law* good faith; honest intention [L]

Bonaire (bɒnˈɛə) *n* an island in the S Caribbean, in the E Netherlands Antilles: one of the Leeward Islands. Chief town: Kralendijk. Pop: 12 533 (1994 est). Area: about 288 sq km (111 sq miles)

bonanza (bəˈnænzə) *n* **1** a source, usually sudden and unexpected, of luck or wealth **2** *US & Canad* a mine or vein rich in ore [C19 from Sp., lit.: calm sea, hence, good luck, from Med. L, from L *bonus* good + *malacia* calm, from Gk *malakia* softness]

Bonaparte (ˈbəʊnəˌpɑːt; *French* bɔnapart) *n* **1** See **Napoleon I** **2** **Jérôme** (ʒerom), brother of Napoleon I. 1784–1860, king of Westphalia (1807–13) **3** **Joseph** (ʒozɛf), brother of Napoleon I. 1768–1844, king of Naples (1806–08) and of Spain (1808–13) **4** **Louis** (lwi), brother of Napoleon I. 1778–1846, king of Holland (1806–10) **5** **Lucien** (lysjɛ̃), brother of Napoleon I. 1775–1840, prince of Canino

Bonaventura (ˌbɒnəvɛnˈtjʊərə) *or* **Bonaventure** (ˈbɒnəˌvɛntʃə) *n* **Saint**, called *the Seraphic Doctor*. 1221–74, Italian Franciscan monk, mystic, theologian, and philosopher; author of a *Life of St Francis* and *Journey of the Soul to God* Feast day: July 14

bonbon (ˈbɒnbɒn) *n* a sweet [C19 from F, orig. a children's word from *bon* good]

bonce (bɒns) *n Brit sl* the head [C19 (orig.: a large playing marble): from ?]

bond (bɒnd) *n* **1** something that binds, fastens, or holds together **2** (*often pl*) something that brings or holds people together; tie: *a bond of friendship* **3** (*pl*) something that restrains or imprisons; captivity or imprisonment **4** a written or spoken agreement, esp a promise **5** *finance* a certificate of debt issued in order to raise funds. It is repayable with or without security at a specified future date **6** *law* a written acknowledgment of an obligation to pay a sum or to perform a contract **7** *S African* a mortgage **8** any of various arrangements of bricks or stones in a wall in which they overlap so as to provide strength **9** **chemical bond** a mutual attraction between two atoms resulting from a redistribution of their outer electrons, determining chemical properties; shown in some formulae by a dot (.) or score (—) **10** See **bond paper** **11** **in bond** *commerce* deposited in a bonded warehouse ▷ *vb* (*mainly tr*) **12** (*also intr*) to hold or be held together, as by a rope or an adhesive; bind; connect **13** (*intr*) to become emotionally attached **14** to put or hold (goods) in bond **15** *law* to place under bond **16** *finance* to issue bonds on; mortgage [C13 from ON *band;* see BAND[2]]

Bond (bɒnd) *n* **Edward** born 1934, British dramatist: his plays, including *Saved* (1965), *Lear* (1971), *Restoration* (1981), and *In the Company of Men* (1990), are noted for their violent imagery and socialist commitment

bondage (ˈbɒndɪdʒ) *n* **1** slavery or serfdom; servitude **2** subjection to some influence or duty **3** a sexual practice in which one participant is physically bound

bonded (ˈbɒndɪd) *adj* **1** *finance* consisting of, secured by, or operating under a bond or bonds **2** *commerce* deposited in a bonded warehouse

bonded warehouse *n* a warehouse in which goods are deposited until duty is paid

bondholder (ˈbɒndˌhəʊldə) *n* an owner of bonds issued by a company or other institution

Bondi (ˈbɒndɪ) *n* Sir **Hermann** born 1919, British mathematician and cosmologist, born in Austria; joint originator (with Sir Fred Hoyle and Thomas Gold) of the steady-state theory of the universe

Bondi Beach (ˈbɒndaɪ) *n* a beach in Sydney, Australia, popular with surfers

bonding (ˈbɒndɪŋ) *n* the process by which individuals become emotionally attached to one another

bondmaid ('bɒnd,meɪd) *n* an unmarried female serf or slave

bond paper *n* a superior quality of strong white paper, used esp for writing and typing

bondservant ('bɒnd,sɜːvənt) *n* a serf or slave

bondsman ('bɒndzmən) *n, pl* **bondsmen** 1 *law* a person bound by bond to act as surety for another 2 another word for **bondservant**

bond washing *n* a series of illegal deals in bonds made with the intention of avoiding taxation

bone (bəʊn) *n* 1 any of the various structures that make up the skeleton in most vertebrates 2 the porous rigid tissue of which these parts are made 3 something consisting of bone or a bonelike substance 4 (*pl*) the human skeleton or body 5 a thin strip of whalebone, plastic, etc, used to stiffen corsets and brassieres 6 (*pl*) the essentials (esp in **the bare bones**) 7 (*pl*) dice 8 **close** *or* **near to the bone** 8a risqué or indecent 8b in poverty; destitute 9 **feel in one's bones** to have an intuition of 10 **have a bone to pick** to have grounds for a quarrel 11 **make no bones about** 11a to be direct and candid about 11b to have no scruples about 12 **point the bone** (often foll by *at*) *Austral* 12a to wish bad luck (on) 12b to cast a spell (on) in order to kill ▷ *vb* **bones, boning, boned** (*mainly tr*) 13 to remove the bones from (meat for cooking, etc) 14 to stiffen (a corset, etc) by inserting bones 15 *Brit* a slang word for **steal** ▷ See also **bone up** [OE *bān*] > '**boneless** *adj*

Bône (*French* bon) *n* a former name of **Annaba**

bone ash *n* ash obtained when bones are burnt in air, consisting mainly of calcium phosphate

bone china *n* porcelain containing bone ash

bone-dry *adj inf* **a** completely dry: *a bone-dry well* **b** (*postpositive*): *the well was bone dry*

bonehead ('bəʊn,hɛd) *n sl* a stupid or obstinate person > '**bone,headed** *adj*

bone idle *adj* very idle; extremely lazy

bone marrow *n* See **marrow** (sense 1)

bone meal *n* dried and ground animal bones, used as a fertilizer or in stock feeds

boner ('bəʊnə) *n sl* a blunder

bonesetter ('bəʊn,sɛtə) *n* a person who sets broken or dislocated bones, esp one who has no formal medical qualifications

boneshaker ('bəʊn,ʃeɪkə) *n* 1 an early type of bicycle having solid tyres and no springs 2 *sl* any decrepit or rickety vehicle

bone up *vb* (*adv; when intr, usually foll by on*) *inf* to study intensively

bonfire ('bɒn,faɪə) *n* a large outdoor fire [C15 alteration (infl. by F *bon* good) of *bone-fire*; from the use of bones as fuel]

bong (bɒŋ) *n* 1 a deep reverberating sound, as of a large bell ▷ *vb* 2 to make a deep reverberating sound [C20 imit.]

bongo[1] ('bɒŋgəʊ) *n, pl* **bongo** *or* **bongos** a rare spiral-horned antelope inhabiting forests of central Africa. The coat is bright red-brown with narrow vertical stripes [of African origin]

bongo[2] ('bɒŋgəʊ) *n, pl* **bongos** *or* **bongoes** a small bucket-shaped drum, usually one of a pair, played by beating with the fingers [American Sp., prob. imit.]

Bonhoeffer (*German* 'boːnhœfər) *n* **Dietrich** ('diːtrɪç) 1906–45, German Lutheran theologian: executed by the Nazis

bonhomie ('bɒnəmiː) *n* exuberant friendliness [C18 from F, from *bon* good + *homme* man]

Boniface ('bɒnɪ,feɪs) *n* **Saint** original name *Wynfrith*. ?680–?755 AD. Anglo-Saxon missionary: archbishop of Mainz (746–755). Feast day: June 5

Boniface VIII *n* original name *Benedict Caetano*. ?1234–1303, pope (1294–1303)

Bonington ('bɒnɪŋtən) *n* 1 Sir **Chris(tian John Storey)** born 1934, British mountaineer and writer; led 1970 Annapurna I and 1975 Everest expeditions; reached Everest summit in 1985 2 **Richard Parkes** 1801–28, British painter of landscapes and historical scenes

Bonin Islands ('bəʊnɪn) *pl n* a group of 27 volcanic islands in the W Pacific: occupied by the US after World War II; returned to Japan in 1968. Largest island: Chichijima. Area: 103 sq km (40 sq miles). Japanese name: **Ogasawara Gunto**

bonito (bə'niːtəʊ) *n, pl* **bonitos** any of various small tunny-like marine food fishes of warm Atlantic and Pacific waters [C16 from Sp., from L *bonus* good]

bonk (bɒŋk) *vb inf* 1 (*tr*) to hit 2 to have sexual intercourse (with) [C20 prob. imit.] > '**bonking** *n*

bonkbuster ('bɒŋk,bʌstə) *n inf* a novel characterized by graphic descriptions of the heroine's frequent sexual encounters [C20 from BONK (sense 2) + (BLOCK)BUSTER]

bonkers ('bɒŋkəz) *adj sl, chiefly Brit* mad; crazy [C20 from ?]

bon mot (*French* bɔ̃ mo) *n, pl* **bons mots** (bɔ̃ mo) a clever and fitting remark [F, lit.: good word]

Bonn (bɒn; *German* bɔn) *n* a city in W Germany, in North Rhine-Westphalia on the Rhine: the former capital (1949–90) of West Germany; university (1786). Pop: 304 100 (1999 est)

Bonnard (*French* bɔnar) *n* **Pierre** (pjɛr) 1867–1947, French painter and lithographer, noted for the effects of light and colour in his landscapes and sunlit interiors

bonnet ('bɒnɪt) *n* 1 any of various hats worn, esp formerly, by women and girls, and tied with ribbons under the chin 2 (in Scotland) Also: **bunnet** 2a a soft cloth cap 2b (formerly) a flat brimless cap worn by men 3 the hinged metal part of a motor vehicle body that provides access to the engine. US name: **hood** 4 a cowl on a chimney 5 *naut* a piece of sail laced to the foot of a foresail to give it greater area in light winds 6 (in the US and Canada) a headdress of feathers worn by some tribes of American Indians [C14 from OF *bonet*, from ?]

Bb

Bonnie Prince Charlie ('bɒnɪ) *n* See (Charles Edward) **Stuart**

bonny ('bɒnɪ) *adj* **bonnier, bonniest** 1 *Scot & N English dialect* beautiful or handsome: *a bonny lass* 2 good or fine 3 (esp of babies) plump [C15 from OF *bon* good, from L *bonus*]

Bonny ('bɒnɪ) *n* **Bight of** a wide bay at the E end of the Gulf of Guinea off the coasts of Nigeria and Cameroon. Former name (until 1975): **Bight of Biafra**

bonsai ('bɒnsaɪ) *n, pl* **bonsai** 1 the art of growing dwarfed ornamental varieties of trees or shrubs in small shallow pots or trays by selective pruning, etc 2 a tree or shrub grown by this method [C20 from Japanese, from *bon* bowl + *sai* to plant]

▷ www.bonsai4me.com
▷ www.bonsaiweb.com
▷ http://geocities.com/bonsai_enthusiasts/index.html
▷ www.saba.org.za

bonsela (bɒn'sɛlə) *n S African inf* a present or gratuity [from Zulu *Ibanselo* a gift]

bontebok ('bɒntɪ,bʌk) *n, pl* **bonteboks** *or* **bontebok** an antelope of southern Africa, having a deep reddish-brown coat with a white blaze, tail, and rump patch [C18 Afrik. from *bont* pied + *bok* BUCK[1]]

bonus ('bəʊnəs) *n* 1 something given, paid, or received above what is due or expected 2 *chiefly Brit* an extra dividend allotted to shareholders out of profits 3 *insurance, Brit* a dividend, esp a percentage of net profits, distributed to policyholders [C18 from L *bonus* (adj) good]

bonus issue *n Brit* a free issue of shares distributed among shareholders pro rata with their holdings

bon vivant *French* (bɔ̃ vivɑ̃) *n, pl* ***bons vivants*** (bɔ̃ vivɑ̃) a person who enjoys luxuries, esp good food and drink: *the Hollywood bons vivants*. Also called (but not in French): **bon**

viveur (ˌbɒn viːˈvɜː) [lit.: good-living (man)]

bon voyage (*French* bɔ̃ vwajaʒ) *sentence substitute* a phrase used to wish a traveller a pleasant journey [F, lit.: good journey]

bony (ˈbəʊnɪ) *adj* **bonier, boniest 1** resembling or consisting of bone **2** having many bones **3** having prominent bones **4** thin or emaciated

bony fish *n* any of a class of fishes, including most of the extant species, having a skeleton of bone rather than cartilage

Bonynge (ˈbɒnɪŋ) *n* **Richard** born 1930, Australian conductor, esp of opera; married to the soprano Joan Sutherland

bonze (bɒnz) *n* a Chinese or Japanese Buddhist priest or monk [c16 from F, from Port. *bonzo*, from Japanese *bonsō*, from Sanskrit *bon* + *sō* priest or monk]

bonzer (ˈbɒnzə) *adj Austral & NZ sl, arch* very good; excellent [c20 ?from BONANZA]

boo (buː) *interj* **1** an exclamation uttered to startle or surprise someone, esp a child **2** a shout uttered to express disgust, dissatisfaction, or contempt ▷ *vb* **boos, booing, booed 3** to shout "boo" at (someone or something), esp as an expression of disapproval

boob (buːb) *sl* ▷ *n* **1** an ignorant or foolish person **2** *Brit* an embarrassing mistake; blunder **3** a female breast ▷ *vb* **4** (*intr*) *Brit* to make a blunder [c20 back formation from BOOBY]

boobialla (ˌbuːbɪˈælə) *n Austral* **1** another name for **golden wattle** (sense 2) **2** any of various trees or shrubs of the genus *Myoporum*

boo-boo *n, pl* **boo-boos** an embarrassing mistake; blunder [c20 ?from nursery talk]

boob tube *n sl* **1** a close-fitting strapless top, worn by women **2** *chiefly US & Canad* a television receiver

booby (ˈbuːbɪ) *n, pl* **boobies 1** an ignorant or foolish person **2** *Brit* the losing player in a game **3** any of several tropical marine birds related to the gannet. They have a straight stout bill and the plumage is white with darker markings [c17 from Sp. *bobo*, from L *balbus* stammering]

booby prize *n* a mock prize given to the person having the lowest score

booby trap *n* **1** a hidden explosive device primed in such a way as to be set off by an unsuspecting victim **2** a trap for an unsuspecting person, esp one intended as a practical joke ▷ *vb* **booby-trap, booby-traps, booby-trapping, booby-trapped 3** (*tr*) to set a booby trap in or on (a building or object) or for (a person)

boodle (ˈbuːdᵊl) *n sl* money or valuables, esp when stolen, counterfeit, or used as a bribe [c19 from Du. *boedel* possessions]

boogie (ˈbuːgɪ) *vb* **boogies, boogieing, boogied** (*intr*) *sl* **1** to dance to pop music **2** to make love [c20 orig. African-American slang, ?from Bantu *mbugi* devilishly good]

boogie-woogie (ˈbʊgɪˈwʊgɪ, ˈbuːgɪˈwuːgɪ) *n* a style of piano jazz using a dotted bass pattern, usually with eight notes in a bar and the harmonies of the 12-bar blues [c20 ? imit.]

▷ www.jazzinamerica.org

boohai (buːˈhaɪ) *n* **up the boohai** *NZ inf* thoroughly lost [from the remote township of *Puhoi*]

boohoo (ˌbuːˈhuː) *vb* **boohoos, boohooing, boohooed** (*intr*) **1** to sob or pretend to sob noisily ▷ *n, pl* **boohoos 2** (*sometimes pl*) distressed or pretended sobbing [c20 nursery talk]

book (bʊk) *n* **1** a number of printed or written pages bound together along one edge and usually protected by covers **2a** a written work or composition, such as a novel, technical manual, or dictionary **2b** (*as modifier*): *book reviews* **2c** (*in combination*): *bookseller; bookshop; bookshelf* **3** a number of blank or ruled sheets of paper bound together, used to record lessons, keep accounts, etc **4** (*pl*) a record of the transactions of a business or society **5** the libretto of an opera, musical, etc **6** a major division of a written composition, as of a long novel or of the Bible **7** a number of tickets, stamps, etc, fastened together along one edge **8** a record of betting transactions **9** (in card games) the number of tricks that must be taken by a side or player before any trick has a scoring value **10** strict or rigid rules or standards (esp in **by the book**) **11** a source of knowledge or authority: *the book of life* **12 a closed book** a person or subject that is unknown or beyond comprehension: *chemistry is a closed book to him* **13 an open book** a person or subject that is thoroughly understood **14 bring to book** to reprimand or require (someone) to give an explanation of his or her conduct **15 close the books** *book-keeping* to balance accounts in order to prepare a statement or report **16 in someone's good** (*or* **bad**) **books** regarded by someone with favour (*or* disfavour) **17 keep the books** to keep written records of the finances of a business **18 on the books 18a** enrolled as a member **18b** recorded **19 the book** (*sometimes cap*) the Bible **20 throw the book at 20a** to charge with every relevant offence **20b** to inflict the most severe punishment on ▷ *vb* **21** to reserve (a place, passage, etc) or engage the services of (a performer, driver, etc) in advance **22** (*tr*) to take the name and address of (a person guilty of a minor offence) with a view to bringing a prosecution **23** (*tr*) (of a football referee) to take the name of (a player) who grossly infringes the rules **24** (*tr*) *arch* to record in a book ▷ See also **book in** [OE *bōc*; see BEECH (its bark was used as a writing surface)]

bookbinder (ˈbʊkˌbaɪndə) *n* a person whose business is binding books > ˈ**bookˌbinding** *n*

▷ www.cbbag.ca/Bookbinding.html

bookbindery (ˈbʊkˌbaɪndərɪ) *n, pl* **bookbinderies** a place in which books are bound. Often shortened to **bindery**

bookcase (ˈbʊkˌkeɪs) *n* a piece of furniture containing shelves for books

book club *n* a club that sells books at low prices to members, usually by mail order

book end *n* one of a pair of usually ornamental supports for holding a row of books upright

Booker Prize (ˈbʊkə) *n* an annual prize for a work of British, Commonwealth, or Irish fiction of £20,000, awarded since 1969 by the Booker McConnell engineering company

▷ www.bookerprize.co.uk

bookie (ˈbʊkɪ) *n inf* short for **bookmaker**

book in *vb* (*adv*) **1** to reserve a room at a hotel **2** *chiefly Brit* to register, esp one's arrival at a hotel

booking (ˈbʊkɪŋ) *n* **1** *chiefly Brit* a reservation, as of a table, room, or seat **2** *theatre* an engagement of an actor or company

bookish (ˈbʊkɪʃ) *adj* **1** fond of reading; studious **2** consisting of or forming opinions through reading rather than experience; academic **3** of or relating to books > ˈ**bookishness** *n*

book-keeping *n* the skill or occupation of systematically recording business transactions > ˈ**book-ˌkeeper** *n*

book-learning *n* knowledge gained from books rather than from experience

booklet (ˈbʊklɪt) *n* a thin book, esp one having paper covers; pamphlet

bookmaker (ˈbʊkˌmeɪkə) *n* a person who as an occupation accepts bets, esp on horseraces, and pays out to winning betters > ˈ**bookˌmaking** *n*

bookmark (ˈbʊkˌmɑːk) *n* **1** Also called: **bookmarker** a strip of some material put between the pages of a book to mark a place **2** *computing* an identifier put on a website that enables the user to return to it quickly and easily ▷ *vb* **3** (*tr*) *computing* to identify and store (a website) so that one can return to it quickly and easily

Book of Common Prayer *n* the official book of church

services of the Church of England until 1980, when the Alternative Service Book was sanctioned
▷ http://just sqanglican.org/resources/bcp/everyman_history/
▷ www.britannia.com/history/articles/prayerbk.html

bookplate ('bʊk,pleɪt) *n* a label bearing the owner's name and a design, pasted into a book

bookstall ('bʊk,stɔːl) *n* a stall or stand where periodicals, newspapers, or books are sold

book token *n Brit* a gift token to be exchanged for books

book value *n* 1 the value of an asset of a business according to its books 2 the net capital value of an enterprise as shown by the excess of book assets over book liabilities

bookworm ('bʊk,wɜːm) *n* 1 a person devoted to reading 2 any of various small insects that feed on the binding paste of books

Boole (buːl) *n* **George** 1815–64, English mathematician. In *Mathematical Analysis of Logic* (1847) and *An Investigation of the Laws of Thought* (1854), he applied mathematical formulae to logic, creating Boolean algebra

boom¹ (buːm) *vb* 1 to make a deep prolonged resonant sound 2 to prosper or cause to prosper vigorously and rapidly: *business boomed* ▷ *n* 3 a deep prolonged resonant sound 4 a period of high economic growth 5 any similar period of high activity 6 the activity itself: *a baby boom* [c15 ?from Du. *bommen*, imit.]

boom² (buːm) *n* 1 *naut* a spar to which a sail is fastened to control its position relative to the wind 2 a pole carrying an overhead microphone and projected over a film or television set 3 a barrier across a waterway, usually consisting of a chain of logs, to confine free-floating logs, protect a harbour from attack, etc [c16 from Du. *boom* tree, BEAM]

boomer ('buːmə) *n* 1 *Austral* a large male kangaroo 2 *Austral & NZ inf* anything exceptionally large

boomerang ('buːmə,ræŋ) *n* 1 a curved flat wooden missile of native Australians, which can be made to return to the thrower 2 an action or statement that recoils on its originator ▷ *vb* 3 (*intr*) (of a plan, etc) to recoil or return unexpectedly, causing harm to its originator [c19 from Abor.]

boomerang generation *n* young adults who, after having lived on their own for a time, return to live in their parental home, usually due to financial problems caused by unemployment or the high cost of living independently

boomslang ('buːm,slæŋ) *n* a large greenish venomous arboreal snake of southern Africa [c18 from Afrik., from *boom* tree + *slang* snake]

boon¹ (buːn) *n* 1 something extremely useful, helpful, or beneficial; a blessing or benefit 2 *arch* a favour; request [c12 from ON *bōn* request]

boon² (buːn) *adj* 1 close, special, or intimate (in **boon companion**) 2 *arch* jolly or convivial [c14 from OF *bon*, from L *bonus* good]

boondocks ('buːn,dɒks) *pl n* **the** *US & Canad sl* 1 wild, desolate, or uninhabitable country 2 a remote rural or provincial area [c20 from Tagalog *bundok* mountain]

boong (bʊŋ) *n Austral offens* a Black person [c20 from Abor.]

boongary (buːn'gɛərɪ) *n, pl* **-ries** a tree kangaroo of NE Queensland [from Abor.]

boor (bʊə) *n* an ill-mannered, clumsy, or insensitive person [OE *gebūr* dweller, farmer; see NEIGHBOUR] > '**boorish** *adj* > '**boorishly** *adv* > '**boorishness** *n*

boost (buːst) *n* 1 encouragement, improvement, or help: *a boost to morale* 2 an upward thrust or push 3 an increase or rise 4 the amount by which the induction pressure of a supercharged internal-combustion engine is increased ▷ *vb* (*tr*) 5 to encourage, assist, or improve: *to boost morale* 6 to lift by giving a push from below or behind 7 to increase or raise: *to boost the voltage in an electrical circuit* 8 to cause to rise; increase: *to boost sales* 9 to advertise on a big scale 10 to increase the induction pressure of (an internal-combustion engine); supercharge [c19 from ?]

booster ('buːstə) *n* 1 a person or thing that supports, assists, or increases power 2 Also called: **launch vehicle** the first stage of a multistage rocket 3 a radio-frequency amplifier to strengthen signals 4 another name for **supercharger** 5 short for **booster dose**

booster dose *n inf* a supplementary injection of a vaccine given to maintain the immunization provided by an earlier dose

boot¹ (buːt) *n* 1 a strong outer covering for the foot; shoe that extends above the ankle, often to the knee 2 *Brit* an enclosed compartment of a car for holding luggage, etc, usually at the rear. US and Canad name: **trunk** 3 an instrument of torture used to crush the foot and lower leg 4 *inf* a kick: *he gave the door a boot* 5 **boots and all** *Austral & NZ inf* making every effort 6 **die with one's boots on** to die while still active 7 **lick the boots of** to be servile towards 8 **put the boot in** *sl* 8a to kick a person, esp when he or she is already down 8b to harass someone 8c to finish off (something) with unnecessary brutality 9 **the boot** *sl* dismissal from employment; the sack 10 **the boot is on the other foot** *or* **leg** the situation is or has now reversed ▷ *vb* (*tr*) 11 to kick 12 to equip with boots 13 *inf* 13a (often foll by *out*) to eject forcibly 13b to dismiss from employment 14 to bootstrap (a computer system) [c14 *bote*, from OF, from ?]

boot² (buːt) *vb* (*usually impersonal*) 1 *arch* to be of advantage or use to (a person): *what boots it to complain?* ▷ *n* 2 *obs* an advantage 3 **to boot** as well; in addition [OE *bōt* compensation]

bootblack ('buːt,blæk) *n* (esp formerly) a person who shines boots and shoes

boot camp *n* 1 *US sl* a basic training camp for new recruits to the US Navy or Marine Corps 2 a centre for juvenile offenders with a strict disciplinary regime, hard physical exercise, and community labour programmes

boot-cut *adj* (of trousers) slightly flared at the bottom of the legs

bootee ('buːtiː, buː'tiː) *n* 1 a soft shoe for a baby, esp a knitted one 2 a boot for women and children, esp an ankle-length one

Boötes (bəʊ'əʊtiːz) *n, Latin genitive* **Boötis** (bəʊ'əʊtɪs) a constellation in the N hemisphere containing the star Arcturus [c17 via L from Gk: ploughman]

booth (buːð, buːθ) *n, pl* **booths** (buːðz) 1 a stall, esp a temporary one at a fair or market 2 a small partially enclosed cubicle, such as one for telephoning (**telephone booth**) or for voting (**polling booth**) 3 two high-backed benches with a table between, used esp in bars and restaurants 4 (formerly) a temporary structure for shelter, dwelling, storage, etc [c12 of Scand. origin]

Booth (buːð) *n* 1 **Edwin Thomas**, son of Junius Brutus Booth. 1833–93, US actor 2 **John Wilkes**, son of Junius Brutus Booth. 1838–65, US actor; assassin of Abraham Lincoln 3 **Junius Brutus** ('dʒuːnɪəs 'bruːtəs) 1796–1852, US actor, born in England 4 **William** 1829–1912, British religious leader; founder and first general of the Salvation Army (1878)

Boothia Peninsula ('buːθɪə) *n* a peninsula of N Canada: the northernmost part of the mainland of North America, lying west of the **Gulf of Boothia**, an arm of the Arctic Ocean

bootjack ('buːt,dʒæk) *n* a device that grips the heel of a boot to enable the foot to be withdrawn easily

Bootle ('buːtᵊl) *n* a port in NW England, in Sefton unitary authority, Merseyside; on the River Mersey adjoining Liverpool. Pop: 65 454 (1991)

bootleg ('bu:t,lɛg) *vb* **bootlegs, bootlegging, bootlegged** **1** to make, carry, or sell (illicit goods, esp alcohol) ▷ *n* **2** something made or sold illicitly, such as alcohol **3** an illegally made copy of a CD, tape, etc ▷ *adj* **4** produced, distributed, or sold illicitly [C17 see BOOT[1], LEG; from smugglers carrying bottles of liquor concealed in their boots] > **'boot,legger** *n*

bootless ('bu:tlɪs) *adj* of little or no use; vain; fruitless [OE *bōtlēas*, from *bōt* compensation]

bootlicker ('bu:t,lɪkə) *n inf* one who seeks favour by servile or ingratiating behaviour towards (someone, esp in authority); toady

bootstrap ('bu:t,stræp) *n* **1** a loop on a boot for pulling it on **2 by one's (own) bootstraps** by one's own efforts; unaided **3a** a technique for loading the first few program instructions into a computer main store to enable the rest of the program to be introduced from an input device **3b** (*as modifier*): *a bootstrap loader* **4** *commerce* an offer to purchase a controlling interest in a company, esp with the intention of purchasing the remainder of the equity at a lower price ▷ *vb* **bootstraps, bootstrapping, bootstrapped** (*tr*) **5** to initiate (a computer system) by executing a bootstrap; boot

booty[1] ('bu:tɪ) *n, pl* **booties** any valuable article or articles, esp when obtained as plunder [C15 from OF, from MLow G *buite* exchange]

booty[2] ('bu:tɪ) *n slang* the buttocks [C20 from BUTT[1] buttocks]

booze (bu:z) *inf* ▷ *n* **1** alcoholic drink **2** a drinking bout ▷ *vb* **boozes, boozing, boozed** **3** (*usually intr*) to drink (alcohol), esp in excess [C13 from MDu. *būsen*]

booze cruise *n Brit inf* a day trip to a foreign country, esp from England across the English Channel to France, for the purposes of buying cheap alcohol, cigarettes, etc

boozer ('bu:zə) *n inf* **1** a person who is fond of drinking **2** *Brit, Austral, & NZ* a bar or pub

booze-up *n Brit, Austral, & NZ sl* a drinking spree

boozy ('bu:zɪ) *adj* **boozier, booziest** *inf* inclined to or involving excessive drinking of alcohol; drunken: *a boozy lecturer; a boozy party*

bop (bɒp) *n* **1** a form of jazz originating in the 1940s, characterized by rhythmic and harmonic complexity and instrumental virtuosity. Originally called: **bebop** ▷ *vb* **bops, bopping, bopped** **2** (*intr*) *inf* to dance to pop music [C20 shortened from BEBOP] > **'bopper** *n*

bo-peep (,bəʊ'pi:p) *n* a game for very young children, in which one hides (esp hiding one's face in one's hands) and reappears suddenly

Bophuthatswana (,bəʊpu:tɑ:t'swɑ:nə) *n* (formerly) a Bantu homeland in N South Africa: consists of six separate areas; granted independence by South Africa in 1977 although this was not internationally recognized; abolished in 1993. Capital: Mmabatho

bora[1] ('bɔ:rə) *n* (*sometimes cap*) a violent cold north wind blowing from the Adriatic [C19 from It. dialect, from L *boreās* the north wind]

bora[2] ('bɔ:rə) *n* an initiation ceremony of native Australians, introducing youths to manhood [from Abor.]

Bora Bora ('bɔ:rə 'bɔ:rə) *n* an island in the S Pacific, in French Polynesia, in the Society Islands: one of the Leeward Islands. Area: 39 sq km (15 sq miles)

boracic (bə'ræsɪk) *adj* another word for **boric**

borage ('bɒrɪdʒ, 'bʌrɪdʒ) *n* a European plant with star-shaped blue flowers. The young leaves are sometimes used in salads [C13 from OF, ?from Ar. *abū 'āraq*, lit.: father of sweat]

Borås (*Swedish* bu'ro:s) *n* a city in SW Sweden, chiefly producing textiles. Pop: 96 123 (1994)

borate *n* ('bɔ:reɪt, -ɪt) **1** a salt or ester of boric acid ▷ *vb* ('bɔ:reɪt), **borates, borating, borated** **2** (*tr*) to treat with borax, boric acid, or borate

borax ('bɔ:ræks) *n, pl* **boraxes** *or* **boraces** (-rə,si:z) a soluble readily fusible white mineral in monoclinic crystalline form, occurring in alkaline soils and salt deposits. Formula: $Na_2B_4O_7.10H_2O$ [C14 from OF, from Med. L, from Ar., from Persian *būrah*]

borazon ('bɔ:rə,zɒn) *n* an extremely hard form of boron nitride [C20 from BOR(ON) + AZO + -ON]

borborygmus (,bɔ:bə'rɪgməs) *n, pl* **borborygmi** (-maɪ) rumbling of the stomach [C18 from Gk]

Bordeaux (bɔ:'dəʊ; *French* bɔrdo) *n* **1** a port in SW France, on the River Garonne: a major centre of the wine trade. Pop: 215 118 (1999) **2** any of several red, white, or rosé wines produced around Bordeaux. Related adjective: **Bordelais**

Bordeaux mixture *n horticulture* a fungicide consisting of a solution of equal quantities of copper sulphate and quicklime

bordello (bɔ:'dɛləʊ) *n pl* **-los** a brothel. Also called (archaic): **bordel** ('bɔ:dᵊl) [C16 from Italian, from Old French *borde* hut, cabin]

border ('bɔ:də) *n* **1** a band or margin around or along the edge of something **2** the dividing line or frontier between political or geographic regions **3** a region straddling such a boundary **4** a design around the edge of something **5** a long narrow strip of ground planted with flowers, shrubs, etc: *a herbaceous border* ▷ *vb* **6** (*tr*) to provide with a border **7** (when *intr*, foll by *on* or *upon*) **7a** to be adjacent (to); lie along the boundary (of) **7b** to be nearly the same (as); verge (on): *his stupidity borders on madness* [C14 from OF, from *bort* side of a ship, of Gmc origin]

Border[1] ('bɔ:də) *n* **the 1** (*often plural*) the area straddling the border between England and Scotland **2** the area straddling the border between Northern Ireland and the Republic of Ireland **3** the region in S South Africa around East London

Border[2] ('bɔ:də) *n* **Allan (Robert)** born 1955, Australian cricketer; captain of Australia (1985–94)

borderer ('bɔ:dərə) *n* a person who lives in a border area

borderland ('bɔ:də,lænd) *n* **1** land located on or near a frontier or boundary **2** an indeterminate state or condition

borderline ('bɔ:də,laɪn) *n* **1** a border; dividing line **2** an indeterminate position between two conditions: *the borderline between friendship and love* ▷ *adj* **3** on the edge of one category and verging on another: *a borderline failure in the exam*

Borderline Personality Disorder *n* a personality disorder involving emotional instability, an unstable self-image, and a lack of self-control

Borders Region *n* a former local government region in S Scotland, formed in 1975 from Berwick, Peebles, Roxburgh, Selkirk, and part of Midlothian; replaced in 1996 by Scottish Borders council area

bore[1] (bɔ:) *vb* **bores, boring, bored** **1** to produce (a hole) in (a material) by use of a drill, auger, or rotary cutting tool **2** to increase the diameter of (a hole), as by turning **3** (*tr*) to produce (a hole in the ground, tunnel, mine shaft, etc) by digging, drilling, etc **4** (*intr*) *inf* (of a horse or athlete in a race) to push other competitors out of the way ▷ *n* **5** a hole or tunnel in the ground, esp one drilled in search of minerals, oil, etc **6** *Austral* an artesian well **7a** the hollow part of a tube or cylinder, esp of a gun barrel **7b** the diameter of such a hollow part; calibre [OE *borian*]

bore[2] (bɔ:) *vb* **bores, boring, bored** **1** (*tr*) to tire or make weary by being dull, repetitious, or uninteresting ▷ *n* **2** a dull or repetitious person, activity, or state [C18 from ?] > **bored** *adj* > **'boring** *adj*

bore[3] (bɔ:) *n* a high steep-fronted wave moving up a narrow estuary, caused by the tide [C17 from ON *bāra* wave, billow]

bore[4] (bɔ:) *vb* the past tense of **bear**[1]

boreal ('bɔ:rɪəl) *adj* of or relating to the north or the north wind [c15 from L *boreās* the north wind]

Boreal ('bɔːrɪəl) *adj* of or denoting the coniferous forests in the north of the N hemisphere

Boreas ('bɔːrɪəs) *n Greek myth* the god personifying the north wind [c14 via L from Gk]

boredom ('bɔːdəm) *n* the state of being bored

boree ('bɔːriː) *n Austral* another name for **myall** [from Abor.]

borer ('bɔːrə) *n* **1** a tool for boring holes **2** any of various insects, insect larvae, molluscs, or crustaceans, that bore into plant material, esp wood

Borg (bɔːg; *Swedish* bɔrj) *n* **Björn** (bjœrn) born 1956, Swedish tennis player: Wimbledon champion 1976–80

Borgerhout (*Flemish* bɔrxər'hɔut) *n* a city in N Belgium, near Antwerp. Pop: 44 000 (latest est)

Borges (*Spanish* 'borxes) *n* **Jorge Luis** ('xorxe lwis) 1899–1986, Argentinian poet, short-story writer, and literary scholar. The short stories collected in *Ficciones* (1944) he described as "games with infinity"

Borgia (*Italian* 'bordʒa) *n* **1** **Cesare** ('tʃezare), son of Rodrigo Borgia (Pope Alexander VI). 1475–1507, Italian cardinal, politician, and military leader; model for Machiavelli's *The Prince* **2** his sister, **Lucrezia** (lu'krɛttsja), daughter of Rodrigo Borgia. 1480–1519, Italian noblewoman. After her third marriage (1501), to the Duke of Ferrara, she became a patron of the arts and science **3** **Rodrigo** (rod'rigo). See **Alexander VI**

boric ('bɔːrɪk) *adj* of or containing boron. Also: **boracic**

boric acid *n* a white soluble weakly acid crystalline solid used in the manufacture of heat-resistant glass and porcelain enamels, as a fireproofing material, and as a mild antiseptic. Formula: H_3BO_3. Also called: **orthoboric acid.** Systematic name: **trioxoboric(III) acid**

borlotti bean (bɔː'lɒtɪ) *n* a variety of kidney bean with a pinkish-brown speckled skin that turns brown when cooked [from It., plural of *borlotto* kidney bean]

Bormann (*German* 'bɔrman) *n* **Martin** 1900–45, German Nazi politician; Hitler's adviser and private secretary (1942–45): committed suicide

born (bɔːn) *vb* **1** the past participle (in most passive uses) of **bear**[1] (sense 4) **2** **not born yesterday** not gullible or foolish ▷ *adj* **3** possessing certain qualities from birth: *a born musician* **4a** being at birth in a particular social status or other condition as specified: *ignobly born* **4b** (*in combination*): *lowborn* **5** **in all one's born days** *inf* so far in one's life.

> **USAGE** Care should be taken not to use *born* when *borne* is intended: *he had borne* (not *born*) *his ordeal with great courage*; *the following points should be borne in mind*

Born (bɔːn) *n* **Max** 1882–1970, British nuclear physicist, born in Germany, noted for his fundamental contribution to quantum mechanics: Nobel prize for physics 1954

born-again ('bɔːnəˌgɛn) *adj* **1** having experienced conversion, esp to evangelical Christianity **2** showing the enthusiasm of one newly converted to any cause: *a born-again monetarist* ▷ *n* **3** a person who shows fervent enthusiasm for a new-found cause, belief, etc

borne (bɔːn) *vb* **1** the past participle of **bear**[1] (for all active uses of the verb; also for all passive uses except sense 4 unless foll by *by*) **2** **be borne in on** *or* **upon** (of a fact, etc) to be realized by (someone).

> **USAGE** See at **born**

Borneo ('bɔːnɪˌəʊ) *n* an island in the W Pacific, between the Sulu and Java Seas, part of the Malay Archipelago: divided into Kalimantan (**Indonesian Borneo**), the Malaysian states of Sarawak and Sabah, and the British-protected sultanate of Brunei; mountainous and densely forested. Area: about 750 000 sq km (290 000 sq miles) > '**Bornean** *adj, n*

Bornholm (*Danish* bɔrn'hɔlm) *n* an island in the Baltic Sea, south of Sweden: administratively part of Denmark. Chief town: Rønne. Pop: 44 126 (2001). Area: 588 sq km (227 sq miles)

Borno ('bɔːnəʊ) *n* a state of NE Nigeria, on Lake Chad: the second largest state, formed in 1976 from part of North-Eastern State. Capital: Maiduguri. Pop: 2 903 238 (1995 est). Area: 70 898 sq km (27 374 sq miles)

Borodin ('bɒrədɪn; *Russian* bəra'din) *n* **Aleksandr Porfirevich** (alɪk'sandr pərfi'rjevitʃ) 1834–87, Russian composer, whose works include the unfinished opera *Prince Igor*, symphonies, songs, and chamber music

Borodino (ˌbɒrə'diːnəʊ; *Russian* bərədi'nɔ) *n* a village in E central Russia, about 110 km (70 miles) west of Moscow: scene of a battle (1812) in which Napoleon defeated the Russians but irreparably weakened his army

boron ('bɔːrɒn) *n* a very hard almost colourless crystalline metalloid element that in impure form exists as a brown amorphous powder. It occurs principally in borax and is used in hardening steel. Symbol: B; atomic no.: 5; atomic wt.: 10.81 [c19 from BOR(AX) + (CARB)ON]

boron carbide *n* a black extremely hard inert substance used as an abrasive and in control rods in nuclear reactors. Formula: B_4C

boronia (bə'rəʊnɪə) *n* any aromatic shrub of the Australian genus *Boronia*

boron nitride *n* a white inert crystalline solid, used as a refractory, high-temperature lubricant and insulator, and heat shield

borosilicate glass (ˌbɔːrəʊ'sɪlɪkɪt, -ˌkeɪt) *n* any of a range of heat- and chemical-resistant glasses, such as Pyrex, prepared by fusing together oxides of boron and silicon and, usually, a metal oxide

borough ('bʌrə) *n* **1** a town, esp (in Britain) one that forms the constituency of an MP or that was originally incorporated by royal charter. See also **burgh** **2** any of the 32 constituent divisions of Greater London **3** any of the five constituent divisions of New York City **4** (in the US) a self-governing incorporated municipality [OE *burg*]

Borromini (*Italian* borro'miːni) *n* **Francesco**, original name *Francesco Castelli*. 1599–1667, Italian baroque architect, working in Rome: his buildings include the churches of San Carlo (1641) and Sant'Ivo (1660)

borrow ('bɒrəʊ) *vb* **1** to obtain or receive (something, such as money) on loan for temporary use, intending to give it, or something equivalent, back to the lender **2** to adopt (ideas, words, etc) from another source; appropriate **3** *not standard* to lend **4** (*intr*) *golf* to putt the ball uphill of the direct path to the hole: *make sure you borrow enough* [OE *borgian*] > '**borrower** *n*

> **USAGE** See at **off**

Borrow ('bɒrəʊ) *n* **George** (**Henry**) 1803–81, English traveller and writer. His best-known works are the semiautobiographical novels of Gypsy life and language, *Lavengro* (1851) and its sequel *The Romany Rye* (1857)

Bors (bɔːs) *n* **Sir** (in Arthurian legend) **1** one the knights of the Round Table, nephew of Lancelot **2** an illegitimate son of King Arthur

borscht (bɔːʃt), **borsch** (bɔːʃ), *or* **borshch** (bɔːʃtʃ) *n* a Russian and Polish soup based on beetroot [from Russian *borshch*]

borscht belt *n inf, chiefly US* a resort area of the Catskill Mountains in New York State, popular with Jewish holiday-makers; its hotels and nightclubs (the **borscht circuit**) are regarded as a training ground for entertainers

borstal ('bɔːstəl) *n* **1** (formerly, in Britain) an informal name for an establishment in which offenders aged 15 to 21 could be detained for corrective training. Since 1982 they have been replaced by **young offender institutions** **2** (formerly) a similar establishment in Australia and New Zealand [c20 after *Borstal*, village in Kent where the

Bb

first institution was founded]

bort, boart (bɔːt), *or* **bortz** (bɔːts) *n* an inferior grade of diamond used for cutting and drilling or, in powdered form, as an industrial abrasive [OE *gebrot* fragment]

borzoi (ˈbɔːzɔɪ) *n, pl* **borzois** a tall fast-moving breed of dog with a long coat. Also called: **Russian wolfhound** [c19 Russian, lit.: swift]

boscage *or* **boskage** (ˈbɒskɪdʒ) *n literary* a mass of trees and shrubs; thicket [c14 from OF *bosc*, prob. of Gmc origin; see BUSH¹, -AGE]

Bosch (bɒʃ) *n* **1** **Carl** 1874–1940, German chemist, who adapted the Haber process to produce ammonia for industrial use. He shared the Nobel prize for chemistry 1931 **2** **Hieronymus** (hɪˈrɒnɪməs), original name probably *Jerome van Aken* (or *Aeken*). ?1450–1516, Dutch painter, noted for his macabre allegorical representations of biblical subjects in brilliant transparent colours, esp the triptych *The Garden of Earthly Delights*

Bose (bəʊs) *n* **1** Sir **Jagadis Chandra** (dʒəgəˈdiːs ˈtʃʌndrə) 1858–1937, Indian physicist and plant physiologist **2** **Satyendra Nath** (səˈtjɛndrə ˈnɑːθ) 1894–1974, Indian physicist, who collaborated with Einstein in devising Bose-Einstein statistics **3** **Subhas Chandra** (sʊbˈhɑːʃ ˈtʃʌndrə), known as *Netaji*. 1897–1945, Indian nationalist leader; president of the Indian National Congress (1938–39); organized the Indian National Army, with Japanese support, in Singapore to free India from British Rule

bosh (bɒʃ) *n inf* empty or meaningless talk or opinions; nonsense [c19 from Turkish *boş* empty]

bosk (bɒsk) *n literary* a small wood of bushes and small trees [c13 var. of *busk* BUSH¹]

bosky (ˈbɒskɪ) *adj* **boskier, boskiest** *literary* containing or consisting of bushes or thickets

bo's'n (ˈbəʊsᵊn) *n naut* a variant spelling of **boatswain**

Bosnia (ˈbɒznɪə) *n* a region of central Bosnia-Herzegovina: belonged to Turkey (1463–1878), to Austria-Hungary (1879–1918), then to Yugoslavia (1918–91) > ˈ**Bosnian** *adj*
▹ www.fbihvlada.gov.ba
▹ www.bhtourism.ba

Bosnia-Herzegovina, Bosnia-Hercegovina, *or esp US* **Bosnia and Herzegovina** *n* a country in SW Europe; a constituent republic of Yugoslavia until 1991; in a state of civil war also involving Serbian and Croatian forces (1992–95): mostly barren and mountainous, with forests in the east. Language: Serbo-Croat. Religion: Muslim, Serbian Orthodox, and Roman Catholic. Currency: dinar. Capital: Sarajevo. Pop: 3 838 000 (1999 est). Area: 51 129 sq km (19 737 sq miles)

bosom (ˈbʊzəm) *n* **1** the chest or breast of a person, esp the female breasts **2** the part of a woman's dress, coat, etc, that covers the chest **3** a protective centre or part: *the bosom of the family* **4** the breast considered as the seat of emotions **5** (*modifier*) very dear; intimate: *a bosom friend* ▹ *vb (tr)* **6** to embrace **7** to conceal or carry in the bosom [OE *bōsm*]

bosomy (ˈbʊzəmɪ) *adj* (of a woman) having large breasts

boson (ˈbəʊzɒn) *n* any of a group of elementary particles, such as a photon or pion, that has zero or integral spin and does not obey the Pauli exclusion principle ▹ Cf **fermion** [c20 after S. N. BOSE; see -ON]

Bosporus (ˈbɒspərəs) *or* **Bosphorus** (ˈbɒsfərəs) *n* **the** a strait between European and Asian Turkey, linking the Black Sea and the Sea of Marmara

boss¹ (bɒs) *inf* ▹ *n* **1** a person in charge of or employing others **2** *chiefly US* a professional politician who controls a political organization, often using devious or illegal methods ▹ *vb (tr)* **3** to employ, supervise, or be in charge of **4** (usually foll by *around* or *about*) to be domineering or overbearing towards (others) ▹ *adj* **5** *sl* excellent; fine: *a boss hand at carpentry; that's boss!* [c19 from Du. *baas* master]

boss² (bɒs) *n* **1** a knob, stud, or other circular rounded protuberance, esp an ornamental one on a vault, a ceiling, or a shield **2** an area of increased thickness, usually cylindrical, that strengthens or provides room for a locating device on a shaft, hub of a wheel, etc **3** an exposed rounded mass of igneous or metamorphic rock ▹ *vb (tr)* **4** to ornament with bosses; emboss [c13 from OF *boce*; rel. to It. *bozza* metal knob, swelling]

bossa nova (ˈbɒsə ˈnəʊvə) *n* **1** a dance similar to the samba, originating in Brazil **2** a piece of music composed for or in the rhythm of this dance [c20 from Port., lit.: new voice]

bosset (ˈbɒsɪt) *n* either of the rudimentary antlers found in young deer [c19 from F *bossette* a small protuberance, from *bosse* BOSS²]

boss screen *n* a screen image within a computer game that can be activated instantly, designed to hide the evidence of game-playing, esp at work

bossy (ˈbɒsɪ) *adj* **bossier, bossiest** *inf* domineering, overbearing, or authoritarian > ˈ**bossily** *adv* > ˈ**bossiness** *n*

Boston (ˈbɒstən) *n* **1** a port in E Massachusetts, the state capital. Pop: 589 141 (2000) **2** a port in E England, in SE Lincolnshire. Pop: 34 606 (1991)

Boston bluefish *n Canad* another name for **pollack**

bosun (ˈbəʊsᵊn) *n naut* a variant spelling of **boatswain**

Boswell (ˈbɒzwəl) *n* **James** 1740–95, Scottish author and lawyer, noted particularly for his *Life of Samuel Johnson* (1791)

Bosworth Field (ˈbɒzwɜːθ, -wəθ) *n English history* the site, two miles south of Market Bosworth in Leicestershire, of the battle that ended the Wars of the Roses (August, 1485). Richard III was killed and Henry Tudor was crowned king as Henry VII

bot¹ *or* **bott** (bɒt) *n* **1** the larva of a botfly, which typically develops inside the body of a horse, sheep, or man **2** any similar larva [c15 prob. from Low G; rel. to Du. *bot*, from ?]

bot² (bɒt) *Austral inf* ▹ *vb* **bots, botting, botted** **1** to scrounge or borrow ▹ *n* **2** a scrounger **3** **on the bot (for)** wanting to scrounge [c20 ?from BOTFLY, alluding to its bite; see BITE (sense 9)]

bot³ (bɒt) *n computing* an autonomous computer program that performs time-consuming tasks, esp on the Internet [c20 from (RO)BOT]

bot. *abbrev for:* **1** botanical **2** botany

botanical (bəˈtænɪkᵊl) *or* **botanic** *adj* **1** of or relating to botany or plants ▹ *n* **2** any drug or pesticide that is made from parts of a plant [c17 from Med. L, from Gk *botanē* plant, pasture] > boˈ**tanically** *adv*
▹ www.rbgkew.org.uk
▹ www.anbg.gov.au/anbg
▹ www.botanicalsociety.org.za
▹ www.mooseyscountrygarden.com
▹ www.nbi.ac.za/frames/gardensfram.htm

botanize *or* **botanise** (ˈbɒtəˌnaɪz) *vb* **botanizes, botanizing, botanized** *or* **botanises, botanising, botanised** **1** (*intr*) to collect or study plants **2** (*tr*) to explore and study the plants in (an area or region)

botany (ˈbɒtənɪ) *n, pl* **botanies** **1** the study of plants, including their classification, structure, physiology, ecology, and economic importance **2** the plant life of a particular region or time **3** the biological characteristics of a particular group of plants [c17 from BOTANICAL; cf. ASTRONOMY, ASTRONOMICAL] > ˈ**botanist** *n*
▹ www.ou.edu/cas/botany-micro/www-vl
▹ www.botany.net/IDB
▹ www.academicinfo.net/bot.html

Botany Bay *n* **1** an inlet of the Tasman Sea, on the SE coast of Australia: surrounded by the suburbs of Sydney **2** (in the 19th century) a British penal settlement that was in fact at Port Jackson, New South Wales

Botany wool *n* a fine wool from the merino sheep [c19

from Botany Bay, where the wool came from originally]

botch (bɒtʃ) *vb* (*tr*; *often foll by up*) 1 to spoil through clumsiness or ineptitude 2 to repair badly or clumsily ▷ *n* 3 a badly done piece of work or repair (esp in **make a botch of**) [c14 from ?] > '**botcher** *n* > '**botchy** *adj*

botfly ('bɒt,flaɪ) *n*, *pl* **botflies** any of various stout-bodied hairy dipterous flies, the larvae of which are parasites of man, sheep, and horses

both (bəʊθ) *determiner* 1a the two; two considered together: *both dogs were dirty* 1b (*as pron*): *both are to blame* ▷ *conj* 2 (*coordinating*) used preceding words, phrases, or clauses joined by *and*: *both Ellen and Keith enjoyed the play; both new and exciting* [c12 from ON *bāthir*]

Botha ('bəʊtə) *n* 1 **Louis** 1862–1919, South African statesman and general; first prime minister of the Union of South Africa (1910–19) 2 **P(ieter) W(illem)** born 1916, South African politician; defence minister (1965–78); prime minister (1978–84); state president (1984–89)

Botham ('bəʊθəm) *n* **Ian (Terence)** born 1955, English cricketer: played for Somerset (1973–86), Worcestershire (1987–91), and Durham (1991–93); captained England (1980–81)

bother ('bɒðə) *vb* 1 (*tr*) to give annoyance, pain, or trouble to 2 (*tr*) to trouble (a person) by repeatedly disturbing; pester 3 (*intr*) to take the time or trouble; concern oneself: *don't bother to come with me* 4 (*tr*) to make (a person) alarmed or confused ▷ *n* 5 a state of worry, trouble, or confusion 6 a person or thing that causes fuss, trouble, or annoyance 7 *inf* a disturbance or fight; trouble (esp in **a spot of bother**) ▷ *interj* 8 *chiefly Brit* an exclamation of slight annoyance [c18 ?from Irish Gaelic *bodhar* deaf, vexed]

botheration (,bɒðə'reɪʃən) *n*, *interj* *inf* another word for **bother** (senses 5, 8)

bothersome ('bɒðəsəm) *adj* causing bother; troublesome

Bothnia ('bɒθnɪə) *n* **Gulf of** an arm of the Baltic Sea, extending north between Sweden and Finland

Bothwell ('bɒθwəl, 'bɒð-) *n* **Earl of**, title of *James Hepburn*. 1535–78, Scottish nobleman; third husband of Mary Queen of Scots. He is generally considered to have instigated the murder of Darnley (1567)

bothy ('bɒθɪ) *n*, *pl* **bothies** *chiefly Scot* 1 a cottage or hut 2 a farmworker's summer quarters [c18 ? rel. to booth]

Botox ('bəʊtɒks) *n* *trademark* a preparation of botulinum toxin used to treat muscle spasm and for the cosmetic removal of wrinkles

bo tree (bəʊ) *n* another name for the **peepul** [c19 from Sinhalese, from Pali *bodhitaru* tree of wisdom]

Botswana (bʊ'tʃwɑːnə, bʊt'swɑːnə, bɒt-) *n* a republic in southern Africa: established as the British protectorate of Bechuanaland in 1885 as a defence against the Boers; became an independent state within the Commonwealth in 1966; consists mostly of a plateau averaging 1000 m (3300 ft), with the extensive Okavango swamps in the northwest and the Kalahari Desert in the southwest. Languages: English and Tswana. Religion: animist majority. Currency: pula. Capital: Gaborone. Pop: 1 586 000 (2001 est). Area: about 570 000 sq km (220 000 sq miles)

▷ www.gov.bw

▷ www.gov.bw/tourism

bott (bɒt) *n* a variant spelling of **bot**[1]

Botticelli (*Italian* botti'tʃelli) *n* **Sandro** ('sandro), original name *Alessandro di Mariano Filipepi*. 1444–1510, Italian (Florentine) painter, illustrator, and engraver, noted for the graceful outlines and delicate details of his mythological and religious paintings

bottle ('bɒtᵊl) *n* 1a a vessel, often of glass and typically cylindrical with a narrow neck, for containing liquids 1b (*as modifier*): *a bottle rack* 2 Also called: **bottleful** the amount such a vessel will hold 3 *Brit sl* courage; nerve; initiative 4 **the bottle** *inf* drinking of alcohol, esp to excess ▷ *vb* **bottles, bottling, bottled** (*tr*) 5 to put or place in a bottle or bottles 6 to store (gas) in a portable container under pressure ▷ See also **bottle out, bottle up** [c14 from OF *botaille*, from Med. L *butticula*, from LL *buttis* cask]

bottle bank *n* a large container into which the public may throw glass bottles for recycling

bottlebrush ('bɒtᵊl,brʌʃ) *n* 1 a cylindrical brush on a thin shaft, used for cleaning bottles 2 Also called: **callistemon** any of various Australian shrubs or trees having dense spikes of large red flowers with protruding brushlike stamens

bottled (*or* **bottle**) **gas** *n* butane or propane liquefied under pressure in portable metal containers for use in camping stoves, blowtorches, etc

bottle-feed *vb* **bottle-feeds, bottle-feeding, bottle-fed** to feed (a baby) with milk from a bottle

bottle glass *n* glass used for making bottles, consisting of a silicate of sodium, calcium, and aluminium

bottle green *n*, *adj* (of) a dark green colour

bottle-jack *n* *NZ*, *old-fashioned* a large jack used for heavy lifts

bottleneck ('bɒtᵊl,nɛk) *n* 1a a narrow stretch of road or a junction at which traffic is or may be held up 1b the hold-up 2 something that holds up progress

bottlenose dolphin ('bɒtᵊl,nəʊz) *n* a type of dolphin with a bottle-shaped snout

bottle out *vb* (*intr*, *adv*) *Brit sl* to lose one's nerve

bottle party *n* a party to which guests bring drink

bottler ('bɒtᵊlə) *n* *Austral & NZ inf* an exceptional or outstanding person or thing

bottle shop *n* *Austral & NZ* a shop selling alcohol in unopened containers for consumption elsewhere. Also called (Austral): **bottle store**

bottle tree *n* 1 any of several Australian trees that have a bottle-shaped swollen trunk 2 another name for **baobab**

bottle up *vb* (*tr*, *adv*) 1 to restrain (powerful emotion) 2 to keep (an army or other force) contained or trapped

bottom ('bɒtəm) *n* 1 the lowest, deepest, or farthest removed part of a thing: *the bottom of a hill* 2 the least important or successful position: *the bottom of a class* 3 the ground underneath a sea, lake, or river 4 the inner depths of a person's true feelings (esp in **from the bottom of one's heart**) 5 the underneath part of a thing 6 *naut* the parts of a vessel's hull that are under water 7 (in literary or commercial contexts) a boat or ship 8 (*often pl*) *US & Canad* the low land bordering a river 9 (esp of horses) staying power; stamina 10 *inf* the buttocks 11 importance, seriousness, or influence: *his views have weight and bottom* 12 **at bottom** in reality; basically 13 **be at the bottom of** to be the ultimate cause of 14 **get to the bottom of** to discover the real truth about ▷ *adj* (*prenominal*) 15 lowest or last 16 **bet** (*or* **put**) **one's bottom dollar on** to be absolutely sure of 17 of, relating to, or situated at the bottom 18 fundamental; basic ▷ *vb* 19 (*tr*) to provide (a chair, etc) with a bottom or seat 20 (*tr*) to discover the full facts or truth of; fathom 21 (usually foll by *on* or *upon*) to base or be founded (on an idea, etc) [OE *botm*]

bottom drawer *n* *Brit* a young woman's collection of linen, cutlery, etc, made in anticipation of marriage. US, Canad, and NZ equivalent: **hope chest**

bottom feeder *n* 1 a fish that feeds on material at the bottom of a river, lake, sea, etc 2 an objectionable and unimpressive person or thing

bottoming ('bɒtəmɪŋ) *n* the lowest level of foundation material for a road or other structure

bottomless ('bɒtəmlɪs) *adj* 1 having no bottom 2 unlimited; inexhaustible 3 very deep

bottom line *n* 1 the last line of a financial statement

Bb

that shows the net profit or loss of a company or organization **2** the conclusion or main point of a process, discussion, etc

bottom out *vb (intr, adv)* to reach the lowest point and level out

bottomry ('bɒtəmrɪ) *n, pl* **bottomries** *maritime law* a contract whereby the owner of a ship borrows money to enable the vessel to complete the voyage and pledges the ship as security for the loan [c16 from Du. *bodemerij*, from *bodem* BOTTOM (hull of a ship) + *-erij* -RY]

bottom-up *adj* from the lowest level of a hierarchy or process to the top: *a bottom-up approach to corporate decision-making*

bottom-up processing *n* a processing technique, either in the brain or in a computer, in which incoming information is analysed in successive steps and later-stage processing does not affect processing in earlier stages

Bottrop (*German* 'bɔtrɔp) *n* an industrial city in W Germany, in North Rhine-Westphalia in the Ruhr. Pop: 121 500 (1999 est)

botulism ('bɒtjʊˌlɪzəm) *n* severe, often fatal, poisoning resulting from the potent bacterial toxin, **botulin,** produced in imperfectly preserved food, etc [c19 from G *Botulismus*, lit.: sausage poisoning, from L *botulus* sausage]

Bouaké (*French* bwake) *n* a market town in S central Côte d'Ivoire. Pop: 330 000 (1995 est)

Boucher (*French* buʃe) *n* **François** (frɑ̃swa) 1703–70, French rococo artist, noted for his delicate ornamental paintings of pastoral scenes and mythological subjects

Bouches-du-Rhône (*French* buʃdyron) *n* a department of S central France, in Provence-Alpes-Côte d'Azur region. Capital: Marseille. Pop: 1 835 719 (1999 est). Area: 5284 sq km (2047 sq miles)

bouclé ('buːkleɪ) *n* **1** a curled or looped yarn or fabric giving a thick knobbly effect ▷ *adj* **2** of or designating such a yarn or fabric [c19 from F *bouclé* curly, from *boucle* a curl]

Boudicca (bəʊ'dɪkə) *n* died 62 AD, a queen of the Iceni, who led a revolt against Roman rule in Britain; after being defeated she poisoned herself. Also called: **Boadicea**

Boudin (*French* budɛ̃) *n* **Eugène** (øʒɛn) 1824–98, French painter: one of the first French landscape painters to paint in the open air; a forerunner of impressionism

boudoir ('buːdwɑː, -dwɔː) *n* a woman's bedroom or private sitting room [c18 from F, lit.: room for sulking in, from *bouder* to sulk]

bouffant ('buːfɔːŋ) *adj* **1** (of a hairstyle) having extra height and width through backcombing; puffed out **2** (of sleeves, skirts, etc) puffed out [c20 from F, from *bouffer* to puff up]

Bougainville[1] ('buːgənˌvɪl) *n* an island in the W Pacific, in Papua New Guinea: the largest of the Solomon Islands: unilaterally declared independence in 1990; occupied by government troops in 1992, and granted autonomy in 2001. Chief town: Kieta. Area: 10 049 sq km (3880 sq miles)

Bougainville[2] (*French* bugɛ̃vil) *n* **Louis Antoine de** (lwi ɑ̃twan də) 1729–1811, French navigator

bougainvillea (ˌbuːgən'vɪlɪə) *n* a tropical woody climbing plant having inconspicuous flowers surrounded by showy red or purple bracts [c19 NL, after L. A. de BOUGAINVILLE]

bough (baʊ) *n* any of the main branches of a tree [OE *bōg* arm, twig]

bought (bɔːt) *vb* the past tense and past participle of **buy**

bougie ('buːʒiː, buː'ʒiː) *n med* a slender semiflexible instrument for inserting into body passages such as the rectum or urethra to introduce medication, etc [c18 from F, orig. a wax candle from *Bougie* (Bujiya), Algeria]

bouillabaisse (ˌbuːjə'bɛs) *n* a rich stew or soup of fish and vegetables [c19 from F, from Provençal *bouiabaisso*, lit.: boil down]

bouillon ('buːjɒn) *n* a plain unclarified broth or stock [c18 from F, from *bouillir* to BOIL[1]]

Boulanger (*French* bulɑ̃ʒe) *n* **1 Georges** (ʒɔrʒ) 1837–91, French general and minister of war (1886–87). Accused of attempting a coup d'état, he fled to Belgium, where he committed suicide **2 Nadia (Juliette)** (nadja) 1887–1979, French teacher of musical composition: her pupils included Elliott Carter, Aaron Copland, Darius Milhaud, and Virgil Thomson. She is noted also for her work in reviving the works of Monteverdi

boulder ('bəʊldə) *n* a smooth rounded mass of rock that has a diameter greater than 25 cm and has been shaped by erosion [c13 prob. from ON; cf. OSwedish *bulder* rumbling + *sten* STONE]

boulder clay *n* an unstratified glacial deposit consisting of fine clay, boulders, and pebbles

Boulder Dam *n* the former name (1933–47) of **Hoover Dam**

boule ('buːliː) *n* **1** the senate of an ancient Greek city-state **2** the parliament in modern Greece [c19 from Gk *boulē* senate]

boules *French* (bul) *n (functioning as sing)* a game, popular in France, in which metal bowls are thrown to land as near as possible to a target ball [pl. of *boule* BALL[1]: see BOWL[2]]
▷ http://boules.dsnsports.com/accueil_fib

boulevard ('buːlvɑː, -vɑːd) *n* a wide usually tree-lined road in a city [c18 from F, from MDu. *bolwerc* BULWARK; so called because orig. often built on the ruins of an old rampart]

Boulez ('buːlɛz; *French* bulɛ) *n* **Pierre** (pjɛr) born 1925, French composer and conductor, whose works employ total serialism

boulle, boule, *or* **buhl** (buːl) *adj* **1** denoting or relating to a type of marquetry of patterned inlays of brass and tortoiseshell, etc ▷ *n* **2** something ornamented with such marquetry [c18 after A. C. *Boulle* (1642–1732), F cabinet-maker]

Boulogne (bʊ'lɔɪn; *French* bulɔŋ) *n* a port in N France, on the English Channel. Pop: 44 244 (1990). Official name: **Boulogne-sur-Mer** (*French* bulɔŋsyrmɛr)

Boulogne-Billancourt (*French* bulɔŋbijɑ̃kur) *n* an industrial suburb of SW Paris. Pop: 106 367 (1999). Also called: **Boulogne-sur-Seine** (*French* bulɔŋsyrsɛn)

boult (bəʊlt) *vb* a variant spelling of **bolt**[2]

Boult (bəʊlt) *n* Sir **Adrian (Cedric)** 1889–1983, English conductor

Boulton ('bəʊltən) *n* **Matthew** 1728–1809, British engineer and manufacturer, who financed Watt's steam engine and applied it to various industrial purposes

Boumédienne (buːˌmeɪdɪ'ɛn) *n* **Houari** ('haʊərɪ) 1927–78, Algerian statesman and soldier: president of Algeria (1965–78) after overthrowing Ben Bella in a coup

bounce (baʊns) *vb* **bounces, bouncing, bounced 1** *(intr)* (of a ball, etc) to rebound from an impact **2** *(tr)* to cause (a ball, etc) to hit a solid surface and spring back **3** to move or cause to move suddenly, excitedly, or violently; spring **4** *sl* (of a bank) to send (a cheque) back or (of a cheque) to be sent back by a bank to a payee unredeemed because of lack of funds in the drawer's account **5** *(tr) sl* to force (a person) to leave a place or job; throw out; eject ▷ *n* **6** the action of rebounding from an impact **7** a leap; jump; bound **8** the quality of being able to rebound; springiness **9** *inf* vitality; vigour; resilience **10** *Brit* swagger or impudence [c13 prob. imit.; cf. Low G *bunsen* to beat, Du. *bonken* to thump]

bounce back *vb (intr, adv)* to recover one's health, good spirits, confidence, etc, easily

bouncer ('baʊnsə) *n sl* a man employed at a club, disco, etc, to eject drunks or troublemakers

bouncing ('baʊnsɪŋ) *adj* (when *postpositive*, foll by *with*) vigorous and robust (esp in **a bouncing baby**)

bouncy ('baʊnsɪ) *adj* **bouncier, bounciest 1** lively, exuberant, or self-confident **2** having the capability or quality of bouncing: *a bouncy ball* **3** responsive to bouncing; springy: *a bouncy bed*

Bouncy Castle *n trademark* a large inflatable model, usually of a castle, on which children may bounce at fairs, etc

bound¹ (baʊnd) *vb* **1** the past tense and past participle of **bind** ▷ *adj* **2** in bonds or chains; tied as with a rope **3** (*in combination*) restricted; confined: *housebound* **4** (*postpositive; foll by an infinitive*) destined; sure; certain: *it's bound to happen* **5** (*postpositive; often foll by by*) compelled or obliged **6** *rare* constipated **7** (of a book) secured within a cover or binding **8** *logic* (of a variable) occurring within the scope of a quantifier ▷ Cf **free** (sense 18) **9 bound up with** closely or inextricably linked with

bound² (baʊnd) *vb* **1** to move forwards by leaps or jumps **2** to bounce; spring away from an impact ▷ *n* **3** a jump upwards or forwards **4** a bounce, as of a ball [c16 from OF *bond* a leap]

bound³ (baʊnd) *vb* **1** (*tr*) to place restrictions on; limit **2** (when *intr*, foll by *on*) to form a boundary of ▷ *n* **3** See **bounds** [c13 from OF *bonde*, from Med. L *bodina*]

bound⁴ (baʊnd) *adj* **a** (*postpositive; often foll by for*) going or intending to go towards: *bound for Jamaica; homeward bound* **b** (*in combination*): *northbound traffic* [c13 from ON *buinn*, p.p. of *būa* to prepare]

boundary ('baʊndərɪ, -drɪ) *n, pl* **boundaries 1** something that indicates the farthest limit, as of an area; border **2** *cricket* **2a** the marked limit of the playing area **2b** a stroke that hits the ball beyond this limit **2c** the four or six runs scored with such a stroke

boundary rider *n Austral* an employee on a sheep or cattle station whose job is to maintain fences

bounden ('baʊndən) *adj* morally obligatory (arch. except in **bounden duty**) [arch. p.p. of BIND]

bounder ('baʊndə) *n old-fashioned Brit sl* a morally reprehensible person; cad

boundless ('baʊndlɪs) *adj* unlimited; vast: *boundless energy* > '**boundlessly** *adv*

bounds (baʊndz) *pl n* **1** (*sometimes sing*) a limit; boundary (esp in **know no bounds**) **2** something that restrains or confines, esp the standards of a society: *within the bounds of modesty* ▷ See also **out of bounds**

bounteous ('baʊntɪəs) *adj literary* **1** giving freely; generous **2** plentiful; abundant > '**bounteously** *adv* > '**bounteousness** *n*

bountiful ('baʊntɪfʊl) *adj* **1** plentiful; ample (esp in **a bountiful supply**) **2** giving freely; generous > '**bountifully** *adv*

bounty ('baʊntɪ) *n, pl* **bounties 1** generosity; liberality **2** a generous gift **3** a payment made by a government, as, formerly, to a sailor on enlisting or to a soldier after a campaign **4** any reward or premium [c13 (in the sense: goodness): from OF, from L, from *bonus* good]

bouquet (bu:'keɪ) *n* **1** a bunch of flowers, esp a large carefully arranged one **2** the characteristic aroma or fragrance of a wine or liqueur **3** a compliment or expression of praise [c18 from F: thicket, from OF *bosc* forest]

bouquet garni ('bu:keɪ gɑ:'ni:) *n, pl* **bouquets garnis** ('bu:keɪz gɑ:'ni:) a bunch of herbs tied together and used for flavouring soups, stews, etc [c19 from F, lit.: garnished bouquet]

bourbon ('bɜ:bᵊn) *n* a whiskey distilled, chiefly in the US, from maize, esp one containing at least 51 per cent maize [c19 after *Bourbon* county, Kentucky, where it was first made]

Bourbon ('bʊəbᵊn; *French* burbɔ̃) *n* **a** a member of the European royal line that ruled in France from 1589 to 1793 (when Louis XVI was executed by the revolutionaries) and was restored in 1815, continuing to rule in its Orleans branch from 1830 until 1848. Bourbon dynasties also ruled in Spain (1700–1808; 1813–1931) and Naples and Sicily (1734–1806; 1815–1860) **b** (*as modifier*): *the Bourbon kings*

bourdon ('bʊədᵊn, 'bɔ:dᵊn) *n* **1** a bass organ stop **2** the drone of a bagpipe [c14 from OF: drone (of a musical instrument), imit.]

bourgeois ('bʊəʒwɑ:) *often disparaging* ▷ *n, pl* **bourgeois 1** a member of the middle class, esp one regarded as being conservative and materialistic or capitalistic **2** a mediocre, unimaginative, or materialistic person ▷ *adj* **3** characteristic of, relating to, or comprising the middle class **4** conservative or materialistic in outlook **5** (in Marxist thought) dominated by capitalists or capitalist interests [c16 from OF *borjois, burgeis* burgher, citizen; see BURGESS] > **bourgeoise** ('bʊəʒwɑ:z, bʊə'ʒwɑ:z) *fem n*

bourgeoisie (ˌbʊəʒwɑ:'zi:) *n* **the 1** the middle classes **2** (in Marxist thought) the capitalist ruling class. The bourgeoisie owns the means of production, through which it exploits the working class

bourgeon ('bɜ:dʒən) *n, vb* a variant spelling of **burgeon**

Bourges (*French* burʒ) *n* a city in central France. Pop: 75 609 (1990)

Bourgogne (burgɔɲ) *n* the French name for **Burgundy**

Bourguiba (bʊə'gi:bə) *n* **Habib ben Ali** (hæ'bɪb bɛn 'ɑ:lɪ) 1903–2000, Tunisian statesman: president of Tunisia (1957–87); a moderate and an advocate of gradual social change. He was deposed in a coup and kept under house arrest for the rest of his life

bourn¹ *or* **bourne** (bɔ:n) *n arch* **1** a destination; goal **2** a boundary [c16 from OF *borne*; see BOUND³]

bourn² (bɔ:n) *n chiefly southern Brit* a stream [c16 from OF *bodne* limit; see BOUND³]

Bournemouth ('bɔ:nməθ) *n* **1** a resort in S England, in Bournemouth unitary authority, Dorset, on the English Channel. Pop: 155 488 (1991) **2** a unitary authority in SE Dorset. Pop: 163 441 (2001). Area: 46 sq km (17 sq miles)

bourrée ('bʊəreɪ) *n* **1** a traditional French dance in fast duple time **2** a piece of music in the rhythm of this dance [c18 from F]

Bourse (bʊəs) *n* a stock exchange of continental Europe, esp Paris [c19 from F, lit.: purse, from Med. L *bursa*, ult. from Gk: leather]

boustrophedon (ˌbaʊstrə'fi:dᵊn) *adj* having alternate lines written from right to left and from left to right [c17 from Gk, lit.: turning as in ploughing with oxen, from *bous* ox + *strephein* to turn]

bout (baʊt) *n* **1a** a period of time spent doing something, such as drinking **1b** a period of illness **2** a contest or fight, esp a boxing or wrestling match [c16 var. of obs. *bought* turn]

boutique (bu:'ti:k) *n* **1** a shop, esp a small one selling fashionable clothes and other items **2** (*modifier*) of or denoting a small specialized producer or business: *a boutique operation* [c18 from F, ult. from Gk *apothēkē* storehouse]

boutonniere (ˌbʊtɒnɪ'ɛə) *n* the US name for **buttonhole** (sense 2) [c19 from F: buttonhole]

bouzouki (bu:'zu:kɪ) *n* a Greek long-necked stringed musical instrument related to the mandolin [c20 from Mod. Gk, ?from Turkish *büjük* large]

bovine ('bəʊvaɪn) *adj* **1** of or relating to cattle **2** (of people) dull; sluggish; stolid [c19 from LL *bovīnus*, from L *bōs* ox, cow] > '**bovinely** *adv*

bovine somatotrophin *n* the full name for **BST** (sense 1)

bovine spongiform encephalopathy *n* the full name for **BSE**

Bovril ('bɒvrɪl) *n trademark* a concentrated beef extract, used for flavouring, as a stock, etc

bovver ('bɒvə) *n Brit sl* **a** rowdiness, esp caused by gangs

Bb

of teenage youths **b** (*as modifier*): *a bovver boy* [c20 sl. pronunciation of BOTHER]

bow[1] (baʊ) *vb* **1** to lower (one's head) or bend (one's knee or body) as a sign of respect, greeting, assent, or shame **2** to bend or cause to bend **3** (*intr; usually foll by to or before*) to comply or accept: *bow to the inevitable* **4** (*tr; foll by in, out, to*, etc) to usher (someone) in or out with bows and deference **5** (*tr; usually foll by down*) to bring (a person, nation, etc) to a state of submission **6 bow and scrape** to behave in an excessively deferential or obsequious way ▹ *n* **7** a lowering or inclination of the head or body as a mark of respect, greeting, or assent **8 take a bow** to acknowledge or receive applause or praise ▹ See also **bow out** [OE *būgan*]

bow[2] (bəʊ) *n* **1** a weapon for shooting arrows, consisting of an arch of flexible wood, plastic, etc, bent by a string fastened at each end **2a** a long stick across which are stretched strands of horsehair, used for playing the strings of a violin, viola, cello, etc **2b** a stroke with such a stick **3a** a decorative interlacing of ribbon or other fabrics, usually having two loops and two loose ends **3b** the knot forming such an interlacing **4** something that is curved, bent, or arched ▹ *vb* **5** to form or cause to form a curve or curves **6** to make strokes of a bow across (violin strings) [OE *boga* arch, bow]

bow[3] (baʊ) *n* **1** *chiefly naut* **1a** (*often pl*) the forward end or part of a vessel **1b** (*as modifier*): *the bow mooring line* **2** *rowing* the oarsman at the bow [c15 prob. from Low G *boog*]

bow compass (bəʊ) *n geom* a compass in which the legs are joined by a flexible metal bow-shaped spring rather than a hinge

bowdlerize *or* **bowdlerise** (ˈbaʊdləˌraɪz) *vb* **bowdlerizes, bowdlerizing, bowdlerized** *or* **bowdlerises, bowdlerising, bowdlerised** (*tr*) to remove passages or words regarded as indecent from (a play, novel, etc); expurgate [c19 after Thomas *Bowdler* (1754–1825), E editor who expurgated Shakespeare] > ˌ**bowdleriˈzation** *or* ˌ**bowdleriˈsation** *n* > ˈ**bowdlerism** *n*

bowel (ˈbaʊəl) *n* **1** an intestine, esp the large intestine in man **2** (*pl*) innards; entrails **3** (*pl*) the deep or innermost part (esp in **the bowels of the earth**) [c13 from OF *bouel*, from L *botellus* a little sausage]

bowel movement *n* **1** the discharge of faeces; defecation **2** the waste matter discharged; faeces

Bowen (ˈbəʊən) *n* **Elizabeth** (**Dorothea Cole**) 1899–1973, British novelist and short-story writer, born in Ireland. Her novels include *The Death of the Heart* (1938) and *The Heat of the Day* (1949)

bower[1] (ˈbaʊə) *n* **1** a shady leafy shelter or recess, as in a wood or garden; arbour **2** *literary* a lady's bedroom or apartments; boudoir [OE *būr* dwelling]

bower[2] (ˈbaʊə) *n naut* a vessel's bow anchor [c18 from BOW[3] + -ER[1]]

bowerbird (ˈbaʊəˌbɜːd) *n* **1** any of various songbirds of Australia and New Guinea. The males build bower-like display grounds to attract the females **2** *inf, chiefly Austral* a collector of unconsidered trifles

Bowery (ˈbaʊərɪ) *n* **the** a street in New York City noted for its cheap hotels and bars, frequented by vagrants and drunks [c17 from Dutch *bouwerij*, from *bouwen* to farm + *erij* -ERY; see BOOR, BOER]

bowfin (ˈbəʊˌfɪn) *n* a primitive North American freshwater bony fish with an elongated body and a very long dorsal fin

bowhead (ˈbəʊˌhɛd) *n* a large-mouthed arctic right whale. Also called: **Greenland whale**

Bowie *n* **1** (ˈbaʊɪ, ˈbəʊɪ) **David**, real name *David Jones*. born 1947, British rock singer, songwriter, and film actor. His recordings include "Space Oddity" (1969), *The Rise and Fall of Ziggy Stardust and the Spiders from Mars* (1972), *Heroes* (1977), *Let's Dance* (1983), and *Heathen* (2002) **2** (ˈbəʊɪ) **James**, known as *Jim Bowie*. 1796–1836, US frontiersman. A hero of the Texas Revolution against Mexico (1835–36), he died at the Battle of the Alamo

bowie knife (ˈbəʊɪ) *n* a stout hunting knife with a short hilt and a guard for the hand [c19 named after Jim BOWIE, who popularized it]

bowl[1] (bəʊl) *n* **1** a round container open at the top, used for holding liquid, serving food, etc **2** Also: **bowlful** the amount a bowl will hold **3** the rounded or hollow part of an object, esp of a spoon or tobacco pipe **4** any container shaped like a bowl, such as a sink or lavatory **5** a bowl-shaped building or other structure, such as an amphitheatre **6** *chiefly US* a bowl-shaped depression of the land surface **7** *literary* a drinking cup [OE *bolla*]

bowl[2] (bəʊl) *n* **1** a wooden ball used in the game of bowls, having one flattened side in order to make it run on a curved course **2** a large heavy ball with holes for gripping, used in tenpin bowling ▹ *vb* **3** to roll smoothly or cause to roll smoothly along the ground **4** (*intr; usually foll by along*) to move easily and rapidly, as in a car **5** *cricket* **5a** to send (a ball) from one's hand towards the batsman **5b** Also: **bowl out** to dismiss (the person batting) by delivering a ball that breaks the wicket **6** (*intr*) to play bowls or tenpin bowling ▹ See also **bowl over, bowls** [c15 from F *boule*, ult. from L *bulla* bubble]

bow legs (bəʊ) *pl n* a condition in which the legs curve outwards like a bow between the ankle and the thigh. Also called: **bandy legs** > **bow-legged** (bəʊˈlɛgɪd, bəʊˈlɛgd) *adj*

bowler[1] (ˈbəʊlə) *n* **1** one who bowls in cricket **2** a player at the game of bowls

bowler[2] (ˈbəʊlə) *n* a stiff felt hat with a rounded crown and narrow curved brim. US and Canad name: **derby** [c19 after John *Bowler*, 19th-cent. London hatter]

Bowles (bəʊlz) *n* **Paul** 1910–99, US novelist, short-story writer, and composer, living in Tangiers. His novels include *The Sheltering Sky* (1949) and *The Spider's House* (1955)

bowline (ˈbəʊlɪn) *n naut* **1** a line for controlling the weather leech of a square sail when a vessel is close-hauled **2** a knot used for securing a loop that will not slip at the end of a piece of rope [c14 prob. from MLow G *bōlīne*, equivalent to BOW[3] + LINE[1]]

bowling (ˈbəʊlɪŋ) *n* **1** any of various games in which a heavy ball is rolled down a special alley at a group of wooden pins **2** the game of bowls **3** *cricket* the act of delivering the ball to the batsman

bowling alley *n* **1a** a long narrow wooden lane down which the ball is rolled in tenpin bowling **1b** a similar lane or alley for playing skittles **2** a building having lanes for tenpin bowling

bowling crease *n cricket* a line marked at the wicket, over which a bowler must not advance fully before delivering the ball

bowling green *n* an area of closely mown turf on which the game of bowls is played

bowl over *vb* (*tr, adv*) **1** *inf* to surprise (a person) greatly, esp in a pleasant way; astound; amaze **2** to knock down

bowls (bəʊlz) *n* (*functioning as sing*) **1** a game played on a bowling green in which a small bowl (the jack) is pitched from a mark and two opponents take turns to roll biased wooden bowls as near the jack as possible **2** skittles or tenpin bowling

▹ www.wbc.org.uk

▹ www.lawnbowls.com

bowman (ˈbəʊmən) *n, pl* **bowmen** *arch* an archer

bow out (baʊ) *vb* (*adv; usually tr; often foll by of*) to retire or withdraw gracefully

bowser (ˈbaʊzə) *n* **1** a tanker containing fuel for aircraft, military vehicles, etc **2** *Austral & NZ obs* a petrol pump at a filling station [orig. a US proprietary name]

bowshot (ˈbəʊˌʃɒt) *n* the distance an arrow travels from the bow

bowsprit (ˈbəʊsprɪt) *n naut* a spar projecting from the bow of a vessel, esp a sailing vessel [c13 from MLow G *bōchsprēt*, from *bōch* BOW[3] + *sprēt* pole]

bowstring ('bəʊˌstrɪŋ) *n* the string of an archer's bow

bow tie (bəʊ) *n* a man's tie tied in a bow, now chiefly in plain black for formal evening wear

bow window (bəʊ) *n* a bay window in the shape of a curve

bow-wow ('baʊˌwaʊ, -'waʊ) *n* **1** a child's word for **dog** **2** an imitation of the bark of a dog ▷ *vb* **3** (*intr*) to bark or imitate a dog's bark

bowyangs ('bəʊjæŋz) *pl n Austral & NZ sl* a pair of strings or straps worn around the trouser leg below the knee, orig. esp by agricultural workers [c19 from E dialect *bowy-yanks* leggings]

box¹ (bɒks) *n* **1** a receptacle or container made of wood, cardboard, etc, usually rectangular and having a removable or hinged lid **2** Also called: **boxful** the contents of such a receptacle **3** (*often in combination*) any of various small cubicles, kiosks, or shelters: *a telephone box; a signal box* **4** a separate compartment in a public place for a small group of people, as in a theatre **5** an enclosure within a courtroom: *witness box* **6** a compartment for a horse in a stable or a vehicle **7** *Brit* a small country house occupied by sportsmen when following a field sport, esp shooting **8a** a protective housing for machinery or mechanical parts **8b** (*in combination*): *a gearbox* **9** a shaped device of light tough material worn by sportsmen to protect the genitals, esp in cricket **10** a section of printed matter on a page, enclosed by lines, a border, etc **11** a central agency to which mail is addressed and from which it is collected or redistributed: *a post-office box; a box number in a newspaper advertisement* **12** short for **penalty box** **13** the raised seat on which the driver sits in a horse-drawn coach **14** *Austral & NZ* an accidental mixing of herds or flocks **15** *Brit* (esp formerly) a present, esp of money, given at Christmas to tradesmen, etc **16** *Austral taboo sl* the female genitals **17** **out of the box** *Austral inf* outstanding or excellent **18** **the box** *Brit inf* television ▷ *vb* **19** (*tr*) to put into a box **20** (*tr*; usually foll by *in* or *up*) to prevent from moving freely; confine **21** (*tr*; foll by *in*) *printing* to enclose (text) within a ruled frame **22** *Austral & NZ* to mix (flocks or herds) or (of flocks) to become mixed accidentally **23** **box the compass** *naut* to name the compass points in order [OE *box*, from L *buxus*, from Gk *puxos* BOX³] > '**box,like** *adj*

box² (bɒks) *vb* **1** (*tr*) to fight (an opponent) in a boxing match **2** (*intr*) to engage in boxing **3** (*tr*) to hit (a person) with the fist ▷ *n* **4** a punch with the fist, esp on the ear [c14 from ?]

box³ (bɒks) *n* **1** a slow-growing evergreen tree or shrub with small shiny leaves: used for hedges **2** the wood of this tree **3** any of several trees the timber or foliage of which resembles this tree, esp various eucalyptus trees with rough bark [OE, from L *buxus*, from Gk *puxus*]

box camera *n* a simple box-shaped camera having an elementary lens, shutter, and viewfinder

box chronometer *n naut* a ship's chronometer, supported on gimbals in a wooden box

boxer ('bɒksə) *n* **1** a person who boxes; pugilist **2** a medium-sized smooth-haired breed of dog with a short nose and a docked tail

Boxer ('bɒksə) *n* a member of a nationalistic Chinese secret society that led an unsuccessful rebellion in 1900 against foreign interests in China [c18 rough translation of Chinese *I Ho Ch'üan*, lit.: virtuous harmonious fist]

boxer shorts *pl n* men's underpants shaped like shorts but having a front opening. Also called: **boxers**

box girder *n* a girder that is hollow and square or rectangular in shape

Boxgrove man ('bɒksˌgrəʊv) *n* a type of primitive man, probably dating from the Middle Palaeolithic period some 500 000 years ago; remains were found at Boxgrove in West Sussex in 1993 and 1995

boxing ('bɒksɪŋ) *n* **a** the act, art, or profession of fighting with the fists **b** (*as modifier*): *a boxing enthusiast*
▷ www.ibf-usba-boxing.com
▷ www.wbaonline.com
▷ www.wbcboxing.com
▷ www.ibuboxing.com
▷ www.aiba.net
▷ www.wibf.org

Boxing Day *n Brit & Canad* the first day (traditionally and strictly, the first weekday) after Christmas, observed as a holiday [c19 from the custom of giving Christmas boxes to tradesmen and staff on this day]

boxing glove *n* one of a pair of thickly padded mittens worn for boxing

box junction *n* (in Britain) a road junction having yellow cross-hatching painted on the road surface. Vehicles may only enter the hatched area when their exit is clear

box kite *n* a kite with a boxlike frame open at both ends

box lacrosse *n Canad* lacrosse played indoors. Also called: **boxla**

box number *n* **1** the number of an individual pigeonhole at a newspaper to which replies to an advertisement may be addressed **2** the number of an individual pigeonhole at a post office from which mail may be collected

box office *n* **1** an office at a theatre, cinema, etc, where tickets are sold **2a** the public appeal of an actor or production **2b** (*as modifier*): *a box-office success*

box pleat *n* a flat double pleat made by folding under the fabric on either side of it

boxroom ('bɒksˌruːm, -ˌrʊm) *n* a small room or large cupboard in which boxes, cases, etc, may be stored

box seat *n* **1** a seat in a theatre box **2** **in the box seat** *Brit, Austral, & NZ* in the best position

box spanner *n* a spanner consisting of a steel cylinder with a hexagonal end that fits over a nut

box spring *n* a coiled spring contained in a boxlike frame, used for mattresses, chairs, etc

boxwood ('bɒksˌwʊd) *n* **1** the hard close-grained yellow wood of the box tree, used to make tool handles, etc **2** the box tree

boxy ('bɒksɪ) *adj* squarish or chunky in style or appearance: *a boxy square-cut jacket*

boy (bɔɪ) *n* **1** a male child; lad; youth **2** a man regarded as immature or inexperienced: *he's just a boy when it comes to dealing with women* **3** See **old boy** **4** *inf* a group of men, esp a group of friends **5** *usually derog* (esp in former colonial territories) a Black or native male servant of any age **6** *Austral* a jockey or apprentice **7** short for **boyfriend** **8** **boys will be boys** youthful indiscretion or exuberance must be expected and tolerated **9** **jobs for the boys** *inf* appointment of one's supporters to posts, without reference to their qualifications or ability **10** **the boy** *Irish inf* the right tool for a particular task: *that's the boy to cut it* ▷ *interj* **11** an exclamation of surprise, pleasure, contempt, etc [c13 (in the sense: male servant; c14 young male): of uncertain origin; perhaps from Anglo-French *abuié* fettered (unattested), from Latin *boia* fetter]

Boyce (bɔɪs) *n* **William** ?1710–79, English composer, noted esp for his church music and symphonies

boycott ('bɔɪkɒt) *vb* **1** (*tr*) to refuse to have dealings with (a person, organization, etc) or refuse to buy (a product) as a protest or means of coercion ▷ *n* **2** an instance or the use of boycotting [c19 after Captain C. C. *Boycott* (1832–97), Irish land agent, a victim of such practices for refusing to reduce rents]

Boycott ('bɔɪkɒt) *n* **Geoff(rey)** born 1940, English cricketer: captained Yorkshire (1970–78); played for England (1964–74, 1977–82)

Boyd (bɔɪd) *n* **1** **Arthur** 1920–99, Australian painter and

Bb

sculptor, noted for his large ceramic sculptures and his series of engravings **2 Martin (A'Beckett)** 1893–1972, Australian novelist, author of *Lucinda Brayford* (1946) and of the Langton tetralogy *The Cardboard Crown* (1952), *A Difficult Young Man* (1955), *Outbreak of Love* (1957), and *When Blackbirds Sing* (1962) **3 Michael** born 1955, British theatre director; artistic director of the Royal Shakespeare Company from 2003

Boyer (*French* bwaje) *n* **Charles** (ʃarl), known as *the Great Lover*. 1899–1978, French film actor

boyfriend ('bɔɪˌfrɛnd) *n* a male friend with whom a person is romantically or sexually involved; sweetheart or lover

boyhood ('bɔɪhʊd) *n* the state or time of being a boy

Boyle (bɔɪl) *n* **Robert** 1627–91, Irish scientist who helped to dissociate chemistry from alchemy. He established that air has weight and studied the behaviour of gases; author of *The Sceptical Chymist* (1661)

Boyle's law *n* the principle that the pressure of a gas varies inversely with its volume at constant temperature [c18 after Robert BOYLE]

Boyne (bɔɪn) *n* a river in the E Republic of Ireland, rising in the Bog of Allen and flowing northeast to the Irish Sea: William III of England defeated the deposed James II in a battle (**Battle of the Boyne**) on its banks in 1690, completing the overthrow of the Stuart cause in Ireland. Length: about 112 km (70 miles)

boyo ('bɔɪəʊ) *n Brit inf* a boy or young man: often used in direct address [from Irish and Welsh]

Boyoma Falls (bɔɪ'əʊmə) *pl n* a series of seven cataracts in the NE Democratic Republic of Congo (formerly Zaïre), on the upper River Congo: forms an unnavigable stretch of 90 km (56 miles), which falls 60 m (200 ft). Former name: **Stanley Falls**

boy racer *n inf* **a** a young man who drives his car aggressively and at inappropriately high speeds **b** (*as modifier*): *the boy-racer market*

Boys' Brigade *n* (in Britain) an organization for boys, founded in 1883, with the aim of promoting discipline and self-respect
▷ www.boys-brigade.org.uk/international

boy scout *n* See **Scout**

boysenberry ('bɔɪzᵊnbərɪ) *n, pl* **boysenberries 1** a type of bramble: a hybrid of the loganberry and various blackberries and raspberries **2** the large red edible fruit of this plant [c20 after Rudolph *Boysen*, American botanist]

Boz (bɒz) *n* pen name of (Charles) **Dickens**

Bozcaada (ˌbɔzdʒaa'da) *n* the Turkish name for **Tenedos**

Bozen ('boːtsən) *n* the German name for **Bolzano**

bp *abbrev for:* **1** (of alcoholic density) below proof **2** boiling point **3** bishop

BP *abbrev for:* **1** blood pressure **2** British Pharmacopoeia

BPC *abbrev for* British Pharmaceutical Codex

B.P.E. (in the US and Canada) *abbrev for* Bachelor of Physical Education

BPhil *abbrev for* Bachelor of Philosophy

bpi *abbrev for* bits per inch (used of a computer tape)

BPR *abbrev for* business process re-engineering

b.pt. *abbrev for* boiling point

Bq *physics symbol for* becquerel

br *abbrev for* brother

Br 1 *abbrev. for* (in a religious order) Brother ▷ **2** *the chemical symbol for* bromine

BR *abbrev for* British Rail (British Railways)

Br. *abbrev for:* **1** Britain **2** British

bra (brɑː) *n* a woman's undergarment for covering and supporting the breasts [c20 from BRASSIERE]

braai (braɪ) *n* short for **braaivleis**

braaivleis ('braɪˌfleɪs) *n S African* a barbecue [from Afrik. *braai* grill + *vleis* meat]

Brabant (brə'bænt) *n* **1** a former duchy of W Europe: divided when Belgium became independent (1830), the south forming the Belgian provinces of Antwerp and Brabant and the north forming the province of North Brabant in the Netherlands **2** a former province of central Belgium; replaced in 1995 by the provinces of **Flemish Brabant** and **Walloon Brabant**

Brabham ('bræbəm) *n* Sir **John Arthur**, known as *Jack*. born 1926, Australian motor-racing driver: world champion 1959, 1960, and 1966

brace (breɪs) *n* **1** a hand tool for drilling holes, with a socket to hold the drill at one end and a cranked handle by which the tool can be turned. See also **brace and bit** **2** something that steadies, binds, or holds up another thing **3** a structural member, such as a beam or prop, used to stiffen a framework **4** a pair, esp of game birds **5** either of a pair of characters, { }, used for connecting lines of printing or writing **6** Also called: **accolade** a line or bracket connecting two or more staves of music **7** (*often pl*) an appliance of metal bands and wires for correcting uneven alignment of teeth **8** *med* any of various appliances for supporting the trunk, a limb, or teeth **9** See **braces** ▷ *vb* **braces, bracing, braced** (*mainly tr*) **10** to provide, strengthen, or fit with a brace **11** to steady or prepare (oneself or something) as before an impact **12** (*also intr*) to stimulate; freshen; invigorate: *sea air is bracing* [c14 from OF, from L *bracchia* arms]

brace and bit *n* a hand tool for boring holes, consisting of a cranked handle into which a drilling bit is inserted

bracelet ('breɪslɪt) *n* an ornamental chain worn around the arm or wrist [c15 from OF, from L *bracchium* arm]

bracelets ('breɪslɪts) *pl n* a slang name for **handcuffs**

bracer ('breɪsə) *n* **1** a person or thing that braces **2** *inf* a tonic, esp an alcoholic drink taken as a tonic

braces ('breɪsɪz) *pl n Brit* a pair of straps worn over the shoulders by men for holding up the trousers. US and Canad word: **suspenders**

brachial ('breɪkɪəl, 'bræk-) *adj* of or relating to the arm or to an armlike part or structure

brachiate *adj* ('breɪkɪɪt, -ˌeɪt, 'bræk-) **1** *bot* having widely divergent paired branches ▷ *vb* ('breɪkɪˌeɪt, 'bræk-), **brachiates, brachiating, brachiated 2** (*intr*) (of some arboreal apes and monkeys) to swing by the arms from one hold to the next [c19 from L *bracchiātus* with armlike branches] > ˌ**brachi'ation** *n*

brachio- *or before a vowel* **brachi-** *combining form* indicating a brachium: *brachiopod*

brachiopod ('breɪkɪəˌpɒd, 'bræk-) *n* any marine invertebrate animal having a ciliated feeding organ and a shell consisting of dorsal and ventral valves [c19 from NL *Brachiopoda*; see BRACHIUM, -POD]

brachiosaurus (ˌbreɪkɪə'sɔːrəs, ˌbræk-) *n* a dinosaur up to 30 metres long: the largest land animal ever known

brachium ('breɪkɪəm, 'bræk-) *n, pl* **brachia** (-kɪə) **1** *anat* the arm, esp the upper part **2** a corresponding part in an animal **3** *biol* a branching or armlike part [c18 NL, from L *bracchium* arm]

brachy- *combining form* indicating something short: *brachycephalic* [from Gk *brakhus* short]

brachycephalic (ˌbrækɪsɪ'fælɪk) *adj* having a head nearly as broad from side to side as from front to back. Also: **brachycephalous** (ˌbrækɪ'sɛfələs) > ˌ**brachy'cephaly** *n*

bracing ('breɪsɪŋ) *adj* **1** refreshing; stimulating; invigorating ▷ *n* **2** a system of braces used to strengthen or support

bracken ('brækən) *n* **1** Also called: **brake** any of various large coarse ferns having large fronds with spore cases along the undersides **2** a clump of any of these ferns [c14 from ON]

bracket ('brækɪt) *n* **1** an L-shaped or other support fixed to a wall to hold a shelf, etc **2** one or more wall shelves carried on brackets **3** *archit* a support projecting from the side of a wall or other structure **4** Also called: **square bracket** either of a pair of characters, [ ], used to enclose a section of writing or printing **5** a general name for **parenthesis** (sense 2), **square bracket,** and **brace** (sense 5) **6** a group or category falling within certain defined limits: *the lower income bracket* **7** the distance between two preliminary shots of artillery fire in range-finding ▷ *vb* **brackets, bracketing, bracketed** (*tr*) **8** to fix or support by means of brackets **9** to put (written or printed matter) in brackets **10** to couple or join (two lines of text, etc) with a brace **11** (often foll by *with*) to group or class together **12** to adjust (artillery fire) until the target is hit [C16 from OF *braguette* codpiece, from OProvençal *braga*, from L *brāca* breeches]

brackish (ˈbrækɪʃ) *adj* (of water) slightly briny or salty [C16 from MDu. *brac* salty; see -ISH] > ˈ**brackishness** *n*

Bracknell (ˈbræknəl) *n* a town in SE England, in Bracknell Forest unitary authority, Berkshire, designated a new town in 1949. Pop: 60 895 (1991)

Bracknell Forest *n* a unitary authority in SE England, in E Berkshire. Pop: 109 606 (2001). Area: 109 sq km (42 sq miles)

bract (brækt) *n* a specialized leaf with a single flower or inflorescence growing in its axil [C18 from L *bractea* thin metal plate, gold leaf, from ?] > ˈ**bracteal** *adj* > **bracteate** (ˈbræktɪɪt) *adj*

bracteole (ˈbræktɪˌəʊl) *n* a secondary or small bract. Also called: **bractlet** [C19 from NL *bracteola*; see BRACT]

brad (bræd) *n* a small tapered nail with a small head [OE *brord* point, prick]

bradawl (ˈbrædˌɔːl) *n* an awl used to pierce wood, leather, etc

Bradbury (ˈbrædbrɪ) *n* **1** Sir **Malcolm** (**Stanley**) 1932–2000, British novelist and critic. His novels include *The History Man* (1975), *Rates of Exchange* (1983), *Cuts* (1988), and *Doctor Criminale* (1992) **2 Ray** born 1920, US science-fiction writer. His novels include *Fahrenheit 451* (1953), *Death is a Lonely Business* (1986), and *A Graveyard for Lunatics* (1990)

Bradford (ˈbrædfəd) *n* **1** an industrial city in N England, in Bradford unitary authority, West Yorkshire: a centre of the woollen industry from the 14th century and of the worsted trade from the 18th century; university (1966). Pop: 289 376 (1991) **2** a unitary authority in West Yorkshire. Pop: 467 668 (2001). Area: 370 sq km (143 sq miles)

Bradley (ˈbrædlɪ) *n* **1 A(ndrew) C(ecil)** 1851–1935, English critic; author of *Shakespearian Tragedy* (1904) **2 F(rancis) H(erbert)** 1846–1924, English idealist philosopher and metaphysical thinker; author of *Ethical Studies* (1876), *Principles of Logic* (1883), and *Appearance and Reality* (1893) **3 Henry** 1845–1923, English lexicographer; one of the editors of the *Oxford English Dictionary* **4 James** 1693–1762, English astronomer, who discovered the aberration of light and the nutation of the earth's axis

Bradman (ˈbrædmən) *n* Sir **Don(ald George)** 1908–2001, Australian cricketer: an outstanding batsman

Bradshaw (ˈbrædˌʃɔː) *n* a British railway timetable, published annually from 1839 to 1961 [C19 after its original publisher, George *Bradshaw* (1801–53)]

bradycardia (ˌbrædɪˈkɑːdɪə) *n pathol* an abnormally slow heartbeat [C19 from Gk *bradus* slow + *kardia* heart]

brae (breɪ) *n Scot* **1** a hill or hillside **2** (*pl*) an upland area [C14 *bra*; rel to ON *brā* eyelash]

Braeburn (ˈbreɪˌbɜːn) *n* a variety of eating apple from New Zealand having sweet flesh and green and red skin

Braemar (ˌbreɪˈmɑː) *n* a village in NE Scotland, in Aberdeenshire; Balmoral Castle is nearby: site of the Royal Braemar Gathering, an annual Highland Games meeting

brag (bræg) *vb* **brags, bragging, bragged 1** to speak arrogantly and boastfully ▷ *n* **2** boastful talk or behaviour **3** something boasted of **4** a braggart; boaster **5** a card game: an old form of poker [C13 from ?] > ˈ**bragger** *n*

Braga (*Portuguese* ˈbrɑːgə) *n* a city in N Portugal: capital of the Roman province of Lusitania; 12th-century cathedral, seat of the Primate of Portugal. Pop: 105 000 (2001). Ancient name: **Bracara Augusta**

Bragg *n* **1 Billy** born 1957, British rock singer and songwriter, noted for his political protest songs; recordings include *Between the Wars* (1985), *Workers' Playtime* (1988), *Mermaid Avenue* (1998), and *England, Half English* (2002) **2 Melvyn**, Baron. born 1939, British novelist, broadcaster, and television executive; presenter of *The South Bank Show* since 1978 **3** Sir **William Henry**, 1862–1942, and his son, Sir (**William**) **Lawrence**, 1890–1971, British physicists, who shared a Nobel prize for physics (1915) for their study of crystal structures by means of X-rays

braggadocio (ˌbrægəˈdəʊtʃɪˌəʊ) *n, pl* **braggadocios 1** vain empty boasting **2** a person who boasts; braggart [C16 from *Braggadocchio*, a boastful character in Spenser's *Faerie Queene*; prob. from BRAGGART + It. *-occhio* (augmentative suffix)]

braggart (ˈbrægət) *n* **1** a person who boasts loudly or exaggeratedly; bragger ▷ *adj* **2** boastful [C16 see BRAG]

Bragi (ˈbrɑːgɪ) *or* **Brage** (ˈbrɑːgə) *n Norse myth* the god of poetry and music, son of Odin

Brahe (brɑː, ˈbrɑːhɪ; *Danish* ˈbrɑːə) *n* **Tycho** (ˈtyːço) 1546–1601, Danish astronomer, who designed and constructed instruments that he used to plot accurately the positions of the planets, sun, moon, and stars

Brahma (ˈbrɑːmə) *n* a Hindu god, the Creator [from Sansk., from *brahman* praise]

Brahman (ˈbrɑːmən) *n, pl* **Brahmans 1** (*sometimes not cap*) Also (esp formerly): **Brahmin** a member of the highest or priestly caste in the Hindu caste system **2** another name for **Brahma** [C14 from Sansk. *brahman* prayer] > **Brahmanic** (brɑːˈmænɪk) *or* **Brahˈmanical** *adj*

Brahmanism (ˈbrɑːməˌnɪzəm) *or* **Brahminism** *n* (*sometimes not cap*) the religious and social system of orthodox Hinduism > ˈ**Brahmanist** *or* ˈ**Brahminist** *n*

Bb

Brahmaputra (ˌbrɑːməˈpuːtrə) *n* a river in S Asia, rising in SW Tibet as the Tsangpo and flowing through the Himalayas and NE India to join the Ganges at its delta in Bangladesh. Length: about 2900 km (1800 miles)

Brahmin (ˈbrɑːmɪn) *n, pl* **Brahmin** *or* **Brahmins 1** the older spelling of **Brahman** (a Hindu priest) **2** *US* a highly intelligent or socially exclusive person

Brahms (brɑːmz) *n* **Johannes** (joˈhanəs) 1833–97, German composer, whose music, though classical in form, exhibits a strong lyrical romanticism. His works include four symphonies, four concertos, chamber music, and *A German Requiem* (1868)

braid (breɪd) *vb* (*tr*) **1** to interweave (hair, thread, etc); plait **2** to decorate with an ornamental trim or border ▷ *n* **3** a length of hair, fabric, etc, that has been braided; plait **4** narrow ornamental tape of woven silk, wool, etc [OE *bregdan* to move suddenly, weave together] > ˈ**braider** *n* > ˈ**braiding** *n*

Brăila (*Romanian* brəˈila) *n* a port in E Romania: belonged to Turkey (1544–1828). Pop: 234 648 (1997 est)

Braille[1] (breɪl) *n* **1** a system of writing for the blind consisting of raised dots interpreted by touch **2** any writing produced by this method ▷ *vb* **Brailles, Brailling, Brailled 3** (*tr*) to print or write using this method ▷ www.braille.org

Braille[2] (*French* braj) *n* **Louis** (lwi) 1809–52, French inventor, musician, and teacher of the blind, who himself was blind from the age of three and who devised the Braille system of raised writing

brain (breɪn) *n* **1** the soft convoluted mass of nervous tissue within the skull of vertebrates that is the controlling and coordinating centre of the nervous system and the seat of thought, memory, and emotion. Related adj: **cerebral 2** (*often pl*) *inf* intellectual ability: *he's got brains* **3** *inf* shrewdness or cunning **4** *inf* an intellectual or intelligent person **5** (*usually pl; functioning as sing*) *inf* a person who plans and organizes **6** an electronic device, such as a computer, that performs similar functions to those of the human brain **7 on the brain** *inf* constantly in mind: *I had that song on the brain* ▷ *vb* (*tr*) **8** to smash the skull of **9** *sl* to hit hard on the head [OE *brægen*]

brain candy *n inf* something that is entertaining or enjoyable but lacks depth or significance

brainchild (ˈbreɪnˌtʃaɪld) *n, pl* **brainchildren** *inf* an idea or plan produced by creative thought

braindead (ˈbreɪnˌdɛd) *adj* **1** having suffered brain death **2** *inf* not using or showing intelligence; stupid

brain death *n* irreversible cessation of respiration due to irreparable brain damage: widely considered as the criterion of death

brain drain *n inf* the emigration of scientists, technologists, academics, etc

Braine (breɪn) *n* **John** (**Gerard**) 1922–86, English novelist, whose works include *Room at the Top* (1957) and *Life at the Top* (1962)

brain fever *n* inflammation of the brain

brain gain *n inf* the immigration into a country of scientists, technologists, academics, etc, attracted by better pay, equipment, or conditions

brainiac (ˈbreɪnɪˌæk) *n inf* a highly intelligent person [c20 from a super-intelligent character in an American comic strip]

brainless (ˈbreɪnlɪs) *adj* stupid or foolish

brainpan (ˈbreɪnˌpæn) *n inf* the skull

brainstem (ˈbreɪnˌstɛm) *n* the part of the brain that controls such reflex actions as breathing and is continuous with the spinal cord

brainstorm (ˈbreɪnˌstɔːm) *n* **1** a severe outburst of excitement, often as the result of a transitory disturbance of cerebral activity **2** *Brit inf* a sudden mental aberration **3** *US & Canad inf* another word for **brainwave**

brainstorming (ˈbreɪnˌstɔːmɪŋ) *n* intensive discussion to solve problems or generate ideas

brains trust *n* a group of knowledgeable people who discuss topics in public or on radio or television

brain-teaser *or* **brain-twister** *n inf* a difficult problem

brain up *vb* (*tr, adv*) to make intellectually demanding or sophisticated: *we need to brain up the curriculum*

brainwash (ˈbreɪnˌwɒʃ) *vb* (*tr*) to effect a radical change in the ideas and beliefs of (a person), esp by methods based on isolation, sleeplessness, etc > ˈ**brainˌwashing** *n*

brainwave (ˈbreɪnˌweɪv) *n inf* a sudden idea or inspiration

brain wave *n* any of the fluctuations of electrical potential in the brain

brainy (ˈbreɪnɪ) *adj* **brainier, brainiest** *inf* clever; intelligent > ˈ**braininess** *n*

braise (breɪz) *vb* **braises, braising, braised** to cook (meat, vegetables, etc) by lightly browning in fat and then cooking slowly in a closed pan with a small amount of liquid [c18 from F *braiser*, from OF *brese* live coals]

brak[1] (brak) *n S African* a crossbred dog; mongrel [from Du. *brak* setter]

brak[2] (brak) *adj S African* (of water) brackish or salty [c19 Afrik.]

brake[1] (breɪk) *n* **1** (*often pl*) a device for slowing or stopping a vehicle, wheel, shaft, etc, or for keeping it stationary, esp by means of friction **2** a machine or tool for crushing or breaking flax or hemp to separate the fibres **3** Also called: **brake harrow** a heavy harrow for breaking up clods **4** short for **shooting brake** ▷ *vb* **brakes, braking, braked 5** to slow down or cause to slow down, by or as if by using a brake **6** (*tr*) to crush or break up using a brake [c18 from MDu. *braeke*; rel. to *breken* to BREAK] > ˈ**brakeless** *adj*

brake[2] (breɪk) *n* an area of dense undergrowth, shrubs, brushwood, etc; thicket [OE *bracu*]

brake[3] (breɪk) *n* another name for **bracken** (sense 1)

brake[4] (breɪk) *vb arch, chiefly biblical* a past tense of **break**

brake-fade *n* a decrease in the efficiency of the braking system of a motor vehicle as a result of overheating of the brakes

brake horsepower *n* the rate at which an engine does work, expressed in horsepower. It is measured by the resistance of an applied brake. Abbrev: **bhp**

brake light *n* a red light or lights at the rear of a motor vehicle that light up when the brakes are applied

brake lining *n* a renewable strip of asbestos riveted to a brake shoe

brake pad *n* the flat metal casting, together with the attached friction material, in a disc brake

brake shoe *n* **1** the curved metal casting to which the brake lining is riveted in a drum brake **2** the curved metal casting together with the attached brake lining ▷ Sometimes shortened (for both senses) to **shoe**

brakesman (ˈbreɪksmən) *n, pl* **brakesmen 1** a pithead winch operator **2** a brake operator on railway rolling stock

brake van *n railways, Brit* the coach or vehicle from which the guard applies the brakes; guard's van

Brakpan (ˈbrækˌpæn) *n* a city in E South Africa: gold-mining centre. Pop: 46 416 (latest est)

Bramante (*Italian* braˈmante) *n* **Donato** (doˈnato) ?1444–1514, Italian architect and artist of the High Renaissance. He modelled his designs for domed centrally planned churches on classical Roman architecture

bramble (ˈbræmbᵊl) *n* **1** any of various prickly rosaceous plants or shrubs, esp the blackberry **2** any of several similar and related shrubs, such as the dog rose **3** *Scot & N English* a blackberry [OE *brǣmbel*] > ˈ**brambly** *adj*

brambling (ˈbræmblɪŋ) *n* a Eurasian finch with a speckled head and back and, in the male, a reddish-brown breast

bran (bræn) *n* **1** husks of cereal grain separated from the flour **2** food prepared from these husks [c13 from OF, prob. of Gaulish origin]

branch (brɑːntʃ) *n* **1** a secondary woody stem arising from the trunk or bough of a tree or the main stem of a shrub **2** an offshoot or secondary part: *a branch of a deer's antlers* **3a** a subdivision or subsidiary section of something larger or more complex: *branches of learning; branch of the family* **3b** (*as modifier*): *a branch office* **4** *US* any small stream ▷ *vb* **5** (*intr*) (of a tree or other plant) to produce or possess branches **6** (*intr*; usually foll by *from*) (of stems, roots, etc) to grow and diverge (from another part) **7** to divide or be divided into subsidiaries or offshoots **8** (*intr*; often foll by *off*) to diverge from the main way, road, topic, etc [c13 from OF *branche*, from LL *branca* paw, foot] > ˈ**branchˌlike** *adj*

branchia (ˈbræŋkɪə) *n, pl* **branchiae** (-kɪˌiː) a gill in aquatic animals > ˈ**branchial** *or* ˈ**branchiate** *adj*

branch out *vb* (*intr, adv*; often foll by *into*) to expand or extend one's interests

branch plant *or* **factory** *n Canad* a plant or factory in Canada belonging to a company whose headquarters are in another country

Brancusi (bræŋˈkuːzɪ; *Romanian* briŋˈkuʃj) *n* **Constantin** (konstanˈtin) 1876–1957, Romanian sculptor, noted for his streamlined abstractions of animal forms

brand (brænd) *n* **1** a particular product or a characteristic that identifies a particular producer **2** a particular kind or variety **3** an identifying mark made, usually by burning, on the skin of animals or (formerly) slaves or criminals, esp as a proof of ownership **4** an iron heated and used for branding animals, etc **5** a mark of disgrace or infamy; stigma **6** a burning or burnt piece of wood, as in a fire **7** *arch or poetic* **7a** a flaming torch **7b** a sword **8** a fungal disease of garden plants characterized by brown spots on the leaves ▷ *vb (tr)* **9** to label, burn, or mark with or as with a brand **10** to place indelibly in the memory: *the scene was branded in their minds* **11** to denounce; stigmatize: *they branded him a traitor* [OE *brand-*; see BURN[1]] > ˈ**brander** *n* > ˈ**branding** *n*

brand awareness *n marketing* the extent to which consumers are aware of a particular product or service

Brandenburg (ˈbrændənˌbɜːg; *German* ˈbrandənbʊrk) *n* **1** a state in NE Germany, part of East Germany until 1990. A former electorate, it expanded under the Hohenzollerns to become the kingdom of Prussia (1701). The district east of the Oder River became Polish in 1945. Capital: Potsdam. Pop: 2 601 200 (2000 est). Area: 29 481 sq km (11 219 sq miles) **2** a city in NE Germany: former capital of the Prussian province of Brandenburg. Pop: 93 660 (latest est)

brandish (ˈbrændɪʃ) *vb* **1** *(tr)* to wave or flourish (a weapon, etc) in a triumphant, threatening, or ostentatious way ▷ *n* **2** a threatening or defiant flourish [C14 from OF *brandir*, of Gmc origin] > ˈ**brandisher** *n*

brand leader *n* the most widely sold brand of a particular product

brandling (ˈbrændlɪŋ) *n* a small red earthworm, found in manure and used as bait by anglers [C17 from BRAND (n) + -LING[1]]

brand name *n* the name used for a particular make of a commodity

brand-new *adj* absolutely new [C16 from BRAND (n) + NEW, likened to newly forged iron]

Brando (ˈbrændəʊ) *n* **Marlon** 1924–2004, US actor; his films include *On the Waterfront* (1954) and *The Godfather* (1972), for both of which he won Oscars, *Last Tango in Paris* (1972), *Apocalypse Now* (1979), *A Dry White Season* (1989), and *Don Juan de Marco* (1995)

Brandt (brænt) *n* **1 Bill**, full name *William Brandt*. 1905–83, British photographer. His photographic books include *The English at Home* (1936) and *Perspectives of Nudes* (1961) **2 Georg** (ˈgeɪɔːg) 1694–1768, Swedish chemist, who isolated cobalt (1742) and exposed fraudulent alchemists **3** (*German* brant) **Willy** (ˈvɪli) 1913–92, German statesman; socialist chancellor of West Germany (1969–74); chairman of the Social Democratic party (1964–87). His policy of détente and reconciliation with E Europe brought him international acclaim. Nobel peace prize 1971

brandy (ˈbrændɪ) *n, pl* **brandies** **1** an alcoholic spirit distilled from grape wine **2** a distillation of wines made from other fruits: *plum brandy* [C17 from earlier *brandewine*, from Du. *brandewijn* burnt (or distilled) wine]

brandy butter *n* butter and sugar creamed together with brandy and served with Christmas pudding, etc Also called: **hard sauce**

brandy snap *n* a crisp sweet biscuit, rolled into a cylinder and filled with whipped cream

Branson (ˈbrænsən) *n* Sir **Richard** born 1950, British entrepreneur. In 1969 he founded the Virgin record company, adding other interests later, including Virgin Atlantic Airways (1984), Virgin Radio (1993), and the Virgin Rail Group (1996): made the fastest crossing of the Atlantic by boat (1986) and the first of the Pacific by hot-air balloon (1991)

brant (brænt) *n, pl* **brants** *or* **brant** another name (esp US and Canad) for **brent** (the goose)

Brantford (ˈbræntfəd) *n* a city in central Canada, in SW Ontario. Pop: 84 764 (1996)

bran tub *n Brit* a tub containing bran in which small wrapped gifts are hidden

Braque (*French* brak) *n* **Georges** (ʒɔrʒ) 1882–1963, French painter who developed cubism (1908–14) with Picasso

brash[1] (bræʃ) *adj* **1** tastelessly or offensively loud, showy, or bold **2** hasty; rash **3** impudent [C19 ? infl. by RASH[1]] > ˈ**brashly** *adv* > ˈ**brashness** *n*

brash[2] (bræʃ) *n* loose rubbish, such as broken rock, hedge clippings, etc [C18 from ?] > ˈ**brashy** *adj*

brasier (ˈbreɪzɪə) *n* a less common spelling of **brazier**

Brasil (brəˈziːl) *n* the Portuguese spelling of **Brazil**

Brasília (brəˈzɪljə; *Portuguese* brəziˈliːa) *n* the capital of Brazil (since 1960), on the central plateau: the former capital was Rio de Janeiro. Pop: 1 954 442 (2000)
▷ www.infobrasilia.com.br

Braşov (*Romanian* braˈʃov) *n* an industrial city in central Romania: formerly a centre for expatriate Germans; ceded by Hungary to Romania in 1920. Pop: 317 772 (1997 est). Former name (1950–61): **Stalin** German name: **Kronstadt** Hungarian name: **Brassó**

brass (brɑːs) *n* **1** an alloy of copper and zinc containing more than 50 per cent of copper ▷ Cf **bronze** (sense 1) **2** an object, ornament, or utensil made of brass **3a** the large family of wind instruments including the trumpet, trombone, French horn, etc, made of brass **3b** (*sometimes functioning as pl*) instruments of this family forming a section in an orchestra **4** (*functioning as pl*) *inf* important or high-ranking officials, esp military officers: *the top brass*. See also **brass hat** **5** *N English dialect* money **6** *Brit* an engraved brass memorial tablet or plaque in a church **7** *inf* bold self-confidence; cheek; nerve **8** (*modifier*) of, consisting of, or relating to brass or brass instruments: *a brass ornament; a brass band* [OE *bræs*]

brassard (ˈbræsɑːd) *or* **brassart** (ˈbræsət) *n* an identifying armband or badge [C19 from F, from *bras* arm]

brass band *n* See **band**[1] (sense 2)
▷ www.bandsman.co.uk
▷ www.ibew.co.uk

brasserie (ˈbræsərɪ) *n* **1** a bar in which drinks and often food are served **2** a small and usually cheap restaurant [C19 from F, from *brasser* to stir]

brass hat *n Brit inf* a top-ranking official, esp a military officer [C20 from the gold decoration on the caps of officers of high rank]

brassica (ˈbræsɪkə) *n* any plant of the genus *Brassica*, such as cabbage, rape, turnip, and mustard [C19 from L: cabbage]

brassie *or* **brassy** (ˈbræsɪ, ˈbrɑː-) *n, pl* **brassies** *golf* a former name for a club, a No. 2 wood, originally having a brass-plated sole

brassiere (ˈbræsɪə, ˈbræz-) *n* the full name for **bra** [C20 from 17th-cent. F: bodice, from OF *braciere* a protector for the arm]

Brassó (ˈbrɔʃʃoː) *n* the Hungarian name for **Braşov**

brass rubbing *n* **1** the taking of an impression of an engraved brass tablet or plaque by rubbing a paper placed over it with heelball, chalk, etc **2** an impression made in this way

brass tacks *pl n inf* basic realities; hard facts (esp in **get down to brass tacks**)

brassy (ˈbrɑːsɪ) *adj* **brassier, brassiest** **1** insolent; brazen **2** flashy; showy **3** (of sound) harsh and strident **4** like brass, esp in colour **5** decorated with or made of brass > ˈ**brassily** *adv* > ˈ**brassiness** *n*

brat (bræt) *n* a child, esp one who is ill-mannered or unruly [C16 ?from earlier *brat* rag, from OE *bratt* cloak] > ˈ**bratty** *adj*

Bratislava (ˌbrætɪˈslɑːvə) *n* the capital of Slovakia since 1918, a port on the River Danube; capital of Hungary (1541–1784) and seat of the Hungarian parliament until 1848. Pop: 448 292 (2000 est). German name: **Pressburg** Hungarian name: **Pozsony**
▷ www.bratislava.sk
▷ http://slovakia.eunet.sk

bratpack (ˈbrætˌpæk) *n* **1** a group of precocious and successful young actors, writers, etc **2** a group of ill-mannered young people > ˈ**bratˌpacker** *n*

Brattain (ˈbrætᵊn) *n* **Walter Houser** 1902–87, US physicist, who shared the Nobel prize for physics (1956) with W. B. Shockley and John Bardeen for their invention of the transistor

brattice ('brætɪs) *n* **1** a partition of wood or treated cloth used to control ventilation in a mine **2** *Medieval fortifications* a fixed wooden tower or parapet [C13 from OF *bretesche* wooden tower]

Braun (*German* braun) *n* **1 Eva** ('e:fa) 1910–45, Adolf Hitler's mistress, whom he married shortly before their suicides in 1945 **2 Karl Ferdinand** 1850–1918, German physicist, who invented crystal diodes (leading to the development of crystal radio) and the oscilloscope. He shared the Nobel prize for physics (1909) with Marconi **3** See (Wernher) **von Braun**

Braunschweig ('braunʃvaik) *n* the German name for **Brunswick**

bravado (brə'vɑːdəʊ) *n, pl* **bravadoes** *or* **bravados** vaunted display of courage or self-confidence; swagger [C16 from Sp. *bravada*; see BRAVE]

brave (breɪv) *adj* **1a** having or displaying courage, resolution, or daring; not cowardly or timid **1b** (*as collective n; preceded by the*): *the brave* **2** fine; splendid: *a brave sight* ▷ *n* **3** a warrior of a North American Indian tribe ▷ *vb* **braves, braving, braved** (*tr*) **4** to dare or defy: *to brave the odds* **5** to confront with resolution or courage: *to brave the storm* [C15 from F, from It. *bravo* courageous, wild, ? ult. from L *barbarus* BARBAROUS] > **'bravely** *adv* > **'braveness** *n* > **'bravery** *n*

bravo *interj* **1** (brɑː'vəʊ) well done! ▷ *n* **2** (brɑː'vəʊ) *pl* **bravos** a cry of "bravo" **3** ('brɑːvəʊ) *pl* **bravoes** *or* **bravos** a hired killer or assassin [C18 from It.: splendid! see BRAVE]

bravura (brə'vjʊərə, -'vʊərə) *n* **1** a display of boldness or daring **2** *music* brilliance of execution [C18 from It.: spirit, courage; see BRAVE]

braw (brɔː, brɑː) *adj chiefly Scot* fine or excellent, esp in appearance or dress [C16 Scot. var. of BRAVE]

brawl (brɔːl) *n* **1** a loud disagreement or fight **2** *US sl* an uproarious party ▷ *vb* (*intr*) **3** to quarrel or fight noisily; squabble **4** (esp of water) to flow noisily [C14 prob. rel. to Du. *brallen* to boast, behave aggressively] > **'brawler** *n*

brawn (brɔːn) *n* **1** strong well-developed muscles **2** physical strength, esp as opposed to intelligence **3** *Brit* a seasoned jellied loaf made from the head of a pig or calf [C14 from OF *braon* slice of meat, of Gmc origin]

brawny ('brɔːnɪ) *adj* **brawnier, brawniest** muscular and strong > **'brawniness** *n*

bray (breɪ) *vb* **1** (*intr*) (of a donkey) to utter its characteristic loud harsh sound; heehaw **2** (*intr*) to make a similar sound, as in laughing **3** (*tr*) to utter with a loud harsh sound ▷ *n* **4** the loud harsh sound uttered by a donkey **5** a similar loud cry or uproar [C13 from OF *braire*, prob. of Celtic origin]

Braz. *abbrev for* Brazil(ian)

braze[1] (breɪz) *vb* **brazes, brazing, brazed** (*tr*) **1** to decorate with or make of brass **2** to make like brass, as in hardness [OE *bræsen*, from *bræs* BRASS]

braze[2] (breɪz) *vb* **brazes, brazing, brazed** (*tr*) to make a joint between (two metal surfaces) by fusing a layer of brass or high-melting solder between them [C16 from OF: to burn, of Gmc origin; see BRAISE] > **'brazer** *n*

brazen ('breɪzᵊn) *adj* **1** shameless and bold **2** made of or resembling brass **3** having a ringing metallic sound ▷ *vb* (*tr*) **4** (usually foll by *out* or *through*) to face and overcome boldly or shamelessly [OE *bræsen*, from *bræs* BRASS] > **'brazenly** *adv* > **'brazenness** *n*

brazier[1] *or* **brasier** ('breɪzɪə) *n* a person engaged in brass-working or brass-founding [C14 from OE *bræsian* to work in brass + -ER[1]] > **'braziery** *n*

brazier[2] *or* **brasier** ('breɪzɪə) *n* a portable metal receptacle for burning charcoal or coal [C17 from F *brasier*, from *braise* live coals; see BRAISE]

brazil (brə'zɪl) *n* **1** Also called: **brazil wood** the red wood obtained from various tropical leguminous trees of America: used for cabinetwork **2** the red or purple dye extracted from these woods **3** short for **brazil nut** [C14 from OSp., from *brasa* glowing coals, of Gmc origin; referring to the redness of the wood]

Brazil (brə'zɪl) *n* a republic in South America, comprising about half the area and half the population of South America: colonized by the Portuguese from 1500 onwards; became independent in 1822 and a republic in 1889; consists chiefly of the tropical Amazon basin in the north, semiarid scrub in the northeast, and a vast central tableland; an important producer of coffee and minerals, esp iron ore. Official language: Portuguese. Religion: Roman Catholic majority. Currency: real. Capital: Brasília. Pop: 172 118 000 (2001 est). Area: 8 511 957 sq km (3 286 470 sq miles) > **Bra'zilian** *adj, n*

▷ www.brazil.gov.br

brazil nut *n* **1** a tropical South American tree producing large globular capsules, each containing several closely packed triangular nuts **2** the nut, having an edible oily kernel and a woody shell ▷ Often shortened to **brazil**

Brazzaville (*French* brazavil) *n* the capital of Congo-Brazzaville, in the south on the River Congo. Pop: 937 579 (1995 est) [C19 named after Pierre de *Brazza* (1852–1905), French explorer]

▷ www.brazzaville.i-p.cm

BRB *text messaging abbrev for* be right back

BRCS *abbrev for* British Red Cross Society

breach (briːtʃ) *n* **1** a crack, break, or rupture **2** a breaking, infringement, or violation of a promise, obligation, etc **3** any severance or separation ▷ *vb* (*tr*) **4** to break through or make an opening, hole, or incursion in **5** to break a promise, law, etc [OE *bræc*]

USAGE See at **breech**

breach of promise *n law* (formerly) failure to carry out one's promise to marry

breach of the peace *n law* an offence against public order causing an unnecessary disturbance of the peace

bread (brɛd) *n* **1** a food made from a dough of flour or meal mixed with water or milk, usually raised with yeast or baking powder and then baked **2** necessary food; nourishment **3** *sl* money **4 cast one's bread upon the waters** to do good without expectation of advantage or return **5 know which side one's bread is buttered** to know what to do in order to keep one's advantages **6 take the bread out of (someone's) mouth** to deprive of a livelihood ▷ *vb* **7** (*tr*) to cover with bread-crumbs before cooking [OE *brēad*]

▷ www.howstuffworks.com/bread.htm
▷ www.breadrecipe.com
▷ www.breadnet.net

bread and butter *inf* ▷ *n* **1** a means of support or subsistence; livelihood ▷ *modifier.* **bread-and-butter** **2a** providing a basic means of subsistence **2b** expressing gratitude, as for hospitality (esp in **bread-and-butter letter**)

breadbasket ('brɛd,bɑːskɪt) *n* **1** a basket for carrying bread or rolls **2** *sl* stomach

breadboard ('brɛd,bɔːd) *n* **1** a wooden board on which bread is sliced **2** an experimental arrangement of electronic circuits

breadfruit ('brɛd,fruːt) *n, pl* **breadfruits** *or* **breadfruit** **1** a tree of the Pacific Islands, having large round edible starchy, usually seedless, fruit **2** the fruit, which is eaten baked or roasted and has a texture like bread

breadline ('brɛd,laɪn) *n* **1** a queue of people waiting for free food **2 on the breadline** impoverished; living at subsistence level

breadth (brɛdθ, brɛtθ) *n* **1** the linear extent or measurement of something from side to side; width **2** a piece of fabric, etc, having a standard or definite width **3** distance, extent, size, or dimension **4** openness and lack of restriction, esp of viewpoint or interest; liberality: *breadth of vision* [C16 from obs. *brēde* (from OE

brǣdu, from *brād* BROAD) + -TH[1]]
breadthways (ˈbrɛdθˌweɪz, ˈbrɛtθ-) *or esp US* **breadthwise** (ˈbrɛdθˌwaɪz, ˈbrɛtθ-) *adv* from side to side
breadwinner (ˈbrɛdˌwɪnə) *n* a person supporting a family with his or her earnings
break (breɪk) *vb* **breaks, breaking, broke, broken** **1** to separate or become separated into two or more pieces **2** to damage or become damaged so as to be inoperative: *my radio is broken* **3** to crack or become cracked without separating **4** to burst or cut the surface of (skin, etc) **5** to discontinue or become discontinued: *to break a journey* **6** to disperse or become dispersed: *the clouds broke* **7** (*tr*) to fail to observe (an agreement, promise, law, etc): *to break one's word* **8** (foll by *with*) to discontinue an association (with) **9** to disclose or be disclosed: *he broke the news gently* **10** (*tr*) to fracture (a bone) in (a limb, etc) **11** (*tr*) to divide (something complete or perfect): *to break a set of books* **12** to bring or come to an end: *the summer weather broke at last* **13** (*tr*) to bring to an end as by force: *to break a strike* **14** (when *intr*, often foll by *out*) to escape (from): *he broke out of jail* **15** to weaken or overwhelm or be weakened or overwhelmed, as in spirit **16** (*tr*) to cut through or penetrate: *a cry broke the silence* **17** (*tr*) to improve on or surpass: *to break a record* **18** (*tr*; often foll by *in*) to accustom (a horse) to the bridle and saddle, to being ridden, etc **19** (*tr*; often foll by *of*) to cause (a person) to give up (a habit): *this cure will break you of smoking* **20** (*tr*) to weaken the impact or force of: *this net will break his fall* **21** (*tr*) to decipher: *to break a code* **22** (*tr*) to lose the order of: *to break ranks* **23** (*tr*) to reduce to poverty or the state of bankruptcy **24** (when *intr*, foll by *into*) to obtain, give, or receive smaller units in exchange for; change: *to break a pound note* **25** (*tr*) *chiefly mil* to demote to a lower rank **26** (*intr*; often foll by *from* or *out of*) to proceed suddenly **27** (*intr*) to come into being: *light broke over the mountains* **28** (*intr*; foll by *into* or *out into*) **28a** to burst into song, laughter, etc **28b** to change to a faster pace **29** (*tr*) to open with explosives: *to break a safe* **30** (*intr*) (of waves) **30a** (often foll by *against*) to strike violently **30b** to collapse into foam or surf **31** (*intr*) (of prices, esp stock exchange quotations) to fall sharply **32** (*intr*) to make a sudden effort, as in running, horse racing, etc **33** (*intr*) *cricket* (of a ball) to change direction on bouncing **34** (*intr*) *snooker* to scatter the balls at the start of a game **35** (*intr*) *boxing, wrestling* (of two fighters) to separate from a clinch **36** (*intr*) (of the male voice) to undergo a change in register, quality, and range at puberty **37** (*tr*) to open the breech of (certain firearms) by snapping the barrel away from the butt on its hinge **38** (*tr*) to interrupt the flow of current in (an electrical circuit) **39** *inf, chiefly US* to become successful **40** **break camp** to pack up and leave a camp **41** **break service** *tennis* to win a game in which an opponent is serving **42** **break the bank** to ruin financially or deplete the resources of a bank (as in gambling) **43** **break the mould** to make a change that breaks an established habit, pattern, etc ▷ *n* **44** the act or result of breaking; fracture **45** a crack formed as the result of breaking **46** a brief respite **47** a sudden rush, esp to escape: *to make a break for freedom* **48** a breach in a relationship **49** any sudden interruption in a continuous action **50** *Brit* a short period between classes at school **51** *inf* a fortunate opportunity, esp to prove oneself **52** *inf* a piece of good or bad luck **53** (esp in a stock exchange) a sudden and substantial decline in prices **54** *billiards, snooker* a series of successful shots during one turn **55** *billiards, snooker* the opening shot that scatters the placed balls **56** Also called: **service break, break of serve** *tennis* the act or an instance of breaking an opponent's service **57a** *jazz* a short usually improvised solo passage **57b** an instrumental passage in a pop song **58** a discontinuity in an electrical circuit **59** access to a radio channel by a citizens' band radio operator **60** **break of day** the dawn ▷ *interj* **61** *boxing, wrestling* a command by a referee for two opponents to separate ▷ See also **breakaway, break down,** etc [OE *brecan*]
breakable (ˈbreɪkəbᵊl) *adj* **1** capable of being broken ▷ *n* **2** (*usually pl*) a fragile easily broken article
breakage (ˈbreɪkɪdʒ) *n* **1** the act or result of breaking **2** the quantity or amount broken **3** compensation or allowance for goods damaged while in use, transit, etc
breakaway (ˈbreɪkəˌweɪ) *n* **1a** loss or withdrawal of a group of members from an association, club, etc **1b** (*as modifier*): *a breakaway faction* **2** *Austral* a stampede of animals, esp at the smell of water ▷ *vb* **break away** (*intr, adv*) **3** (often foll by *from*) to leave hastily or escape **4** to withdraw or secede
break dance *n* **1** an acrobatic dance style originating in the 1980s ▷ *vb* **break-dance, break-dances, break-dancing, break-danced** (*intr*) **2** to perform a break dance > **break dancer** *n* > **break dancing** *n*
break down *vb* (*adv*) **1** (*intr*) to cease to function; become ineffective **2** to yield or cause to yield, esp to strong emotion or tears **3** (*tr*) to crush or destroy **4** (*intr*) to have a nervous breakdown **5** to analyse or be subjected to analysis **6** to separate or cause to separate into simpler chemical elements; decompose **7** **break it down** *Austral & NZ inf* **7a** stop it **7b** don't expect me to believe that; come off it ▷ *n* **breakdown** **8** an act or instance of breaking down; collapse **9** short for **nervous breakdown** **10** an analysis or classification of something into its component parts: *he prepared a breakdown of the report* **11** a lively American country dance
breaker (ˈbreɪkə) *n* **1** a person or thing that breaks something, such as a person or firm that breaks up old cars, etc **2** a large wave with a white crest on the open sea or one that breaks into foam on the shore **3** a citizens' band radio operator
break even *vb* **1** (*intr, adv*) to attain a level of activity, as in commerce, or a point of operation, as in gambling, at which there is neither profit nor loss ▷ *n* **breakeven** **2** *accounting* the level of commercial activity at which the total cost and total revenue of a business enterprise are equal
breakfast (ˈbrɛkfəst) *n* **1** the first meal of the day **2** the food at this meal ▷ *vb* **3** to eat or supply with breakfast [C15 from BREAK + FAST[2]] > ˈ**breakfaster** *n*
break in *vb* (*adv*) **1** (sometimes foll by *on*) to interrupt **2** (*intr*) to enter a house, etc, illegally, esp by force **3** (*tr*) to accustom (a person or animal) to normal duties or practice **4** (*tr*) to use or wear (shoes, new equipment, etc) until comfortable or running smoothly **5** *Austral* to bring new land under cultivation ▷ *n* **break-in** **6** the illegal entering of a building, esp by thieves
breaking and entering *n* (formerly) the gaining of unauthorized access to a building with intent to commit a crime
breaking point *n* the point at which something or someone gives way under strain
breakneck (ˈbreɪkˌnɛk) *adj* (*prenominal*) (of speed, pace, etc) excessive and dangerous
break off *vb* **1** to sever or detach or be severed or detached **2** (*adv*) to end (a relationship, association, etc) or (of a relationship, etc) to be ended **3** (*intr, adv*) to stop abruptly: *he broke off in the middle of his speech*
break out *vb* (*intr, adv*) **1** to begin or arise suddenly **2** to make an escape, esp from prison **3** (foll by *in*) (of the skin) to erupt (in a rash, pimples, etc) ▷ *n* **break-out** **4** an escape, esp from prison or confinement
break-out group *n* a group of people who detach themselves from a larger group or meeting in order to hold separate discussions
break through *vb* **1** (*intr*) to penetrate **2** (*intr, adv*) to achieve success, make a discovery, etc, esp after lengthy efforts ▷ *n* **breakthrough** **3** a significant development or discovery, esp in science **4** the penetration of an enemy's defensive position

Bb

breakthrough bleeding ('breɪk,θruː) *n* vaginal bleeding that occurs other than at a menstrual period while a woman is using a low-dose oral contraceptive

break up *vb (adv)* **1** to separate or cause to separate **2** to put an end to (a relationship) or (of a relationship) to come to an end **3** to dissolve or cause to dissolve; disrupt or be disrupted: *the meeting broke up at noon* **4** *(intr) Brit* (of a school) to close for the holidays **5** *(intr)* (of a person making a telephone call) to be inaudible at times, owing to variations in the signal: *you're breaking up* **6** *inf* to lose or cause to lose control of the emotions **7** *sl* to be or cause to be overcome with laughter ▷ *n* **break-up 8** a separation or disintegration **9a** in the Canadian north, the breaking up of the ice on a body of water that marks the beginning of spring **9b** this season

break-up value *n commerce* **1** the value of an organization assuming that it will not continue to trade **2** the value of a share in a company based only on the value of its assets

breakwater ('breɪk,wɔːtə) *n* **1** Also called: **mole** a massive wall built out into the sea to protect a shore or harbour from the force of waves **2** another name for **groyne**

bream[1] (briːm; *Austral* brɪm) *or Austral* **brim** (brɪm) *n, pl* **bream** *or* **brim 1** any of several Eurasian freshwater cyprinid fishes having a deep compressed body covered with silvery scales **2** short for **sea bream 3** *Austral* any of various marine fishes [C14 from OF *bresme*, of Gmc origin]

bream[2] (briːm) *vb naut* (formerly) to clean debris from (the bottom of a vessel) by heating to soften the pitch [C15 prob. from MDu. *bremme* broom; from burning broom as a source of heat]

Bream (briːm) *n* **Julian** (**Alexander**) born 1933, English guitarist and lutenist

breast (brɛst) *n* **1** the front part of the body from the neck to the abdomen; chest **2** either of the two soft fleshy milk-secreting glands on the chest in sexually mature human females **3** a similar organ in certain other mammals **4** anything that resembles a breast in shape or position: *the breast of the hill* **5** a source of nourishment **6** the source of human emotions **7** the part of a garment that covers the breast **8** a projection from the side of a wall, esp that formed by a chimney **9 beat one's breast** to display guilt and remorse publicly or ostentatiously **10 make a clean breast of** to make a confession of ▷ *vb (tr)* **11** to confront boldly; face: *breast the storm* **12** to oppose with the breast or meet at breast level: *breasting the waves* **13** to reach the summit of: *breasting the mountain top* [OE *brēost*]

breastbone ('brɛst,bəʊn) *n* the nontechnical name for **sternum**

breast-feed *vb* **breast-feeds, breast-feeding, breast-fed** to feed (a baby) with milk from the breast; suckle

breastpin ('brɛst,pɪn) *n* a brooch worn on the breast, esp to close a garment

breastplate ('brɛst,pleɪt) *n* a piece of armour covering the chest

breaststroke ('brɛst,strəʊk) *n* a swimming stroke in which the arms are extended in front of the head and swept back on either side while the legs are drawn up beneath the body and thrust back together

breastwork ('brɛst,wɜːk) *n fortifications* a temporary defensive work, usually breast-high

breath (brɛθ) *n* **1** the intake and expulsion of air during respiration **2** the air inhaled or exhaled during respiration **3** a single respiration or inhalation of air, etc **4** the vapour, heat, or odour of exhaled air **5** a slight gust of air **6** a short pause or rest **7** a brief time **8** a suggestion or slight evidence; suspicion: *a breath of scandal* **9** a whisper or soft sound **10** life, energy, or vitality: *the breath of new industry* **11** *phonetics* the exhalation of air without vibration of the vocal cords, as in pronouncing fricatives such as (f) or (h) or stops such as (p) or (k) **12 catch one's breath 12a** to rest until breathing is normal, esp after exertion **12b** to stop breathing momentarily from excitement, fear, etc **13 in the same breath** done or said at the same time **14 out of breath** gasping for air after exertion **15 save one's breath** to refrain from useless talk **16 take one's breath away** to overwhelm with surprise, etc **17 under** *or* **below one's breath** in a quiet voice or whisper [OE *brǣth*]

breathable ('briːðəbᵊl) *adj* **1** (of air) fit to be breathed **2** (of a material) allowing air to pass through so that perspiration can evaporate

Breathalyser *or* **Breathalyzer** ('brɛθə,laɪzə) *n trademark* a device for estimating the amount of alcohol in the breath: used in testing people suspected of driving under the influence of alcohol [C20 BREATH + (AN)ALYSER] > **'breatha,lyse** *or* **'breatha,lyze** *vb*

breathe (briːð) *vb* **breathes, breathing, breathed 1** to take in oxygen and give out carbon dioxide; respire **2** *(intr)* to exist; be alive **3** *(intr)* to rest to regain breath, composure, etc **4** *(intr)* (esp of air) to blow lightly **5** *(intr) machinery* to take in air, esp for combustion **6** *(tr) phonetics* to articulate (a speech sound) without vibration of the vocal cords **7** to exhale or emit: *the dragon breathed fire* **8** *(tr)* to impart; instil: *to breathe confidence into the actors* **9** *(tr)* to speak softly; whisper **10** *(tr)* to permit to rest: *to breathe a horse* **11** *(intr)* (of a material) to allow air to pass through so that perspiration can evaporate **12 breathe again, freely,** *or* **easily** to feel relief **13 breathe one's last** to die or be finished or defeated [C13 from BREATH]

breather ('briːðə) *n* **1** *inf* a short pause for rest **2** a person who breathes in a specified way: *a deep breather* **3** a vent in a container to equalize internal and external pressure

breathing ('briːðɪŋ) *n* **1** the passage of air into and out of the lungs to supply the body with oxygen **2** a single breath: *a breathing between words* **3** *phonetics* **3a** expulsion of breath (**rough breathing**) or absence of such expulsion (**smooth breathing**) preceding the pronunciation of an initial vowel or rho in ancient Greek **3b** either of two symbols indicating this

breathless ('brɛθlɪs) *adj* **1** out of breath; gasping, etc **2** holding one's breath or having it taken away by excitement, etc **3** (esp of the atmosphere) motionless and stifling **4** *rare* lifeless; dead > **'breathlessly** *adv* > **'breathlessness** *n*

breathtaking ('brɛθ,teɪkɪŋ) *adj* causing awe or excitement > **'breath,takingly** *adv*

breath test *n Brit* a chemical test of a driver's breath to determine the amount of alcohol he has consumed

breathy ('brɛθɪ) *adj* **breathier, breathiest 1** (of the speaking voice) accompanied by an audible emission of breath **2** (of the singing voice) lacking resonance > **'breathily** *adv* > **'breathiness** *n*

breccia ('brɛtʃɪə) *n* a rock consisting of angular fragments embedded in a finer matrix [C18 from Italian, from Old High German *brecha* a fragment] > **'brecci,ated** *adj*

Brecht (*German* brɛçt) *n* **Bertolt** ('bɛrtɔlt) 1898–1956, German dramatist, theatrical producer, and poet, who developed a new style of "epic" theatre and a new theory of theatrical alienation, notable also for his wit and compassion. His early works include *The Threepenny Opera* (1928) and *Rise and Fall of the City of Mahagonny* (1930) (both with music by Kurt Weill). His later plays are concerned with moral and political dilemmas and include *Mother Courage and her Children* (1941), *The Good Woman of Setzuan* (1943), and *The Caucasian Chalk Circle* (1955)

Brecon ('brɛkən) *or* **Brecknock** ('brɛknɒk) *n* **1** a town in SE Wales, in Powys: textile and leather industries. Pop: 7523 (1991) **2** short for **Breconshire**

Breconshire ('brɛkən,ʃɪə, -ʃə) *or* **Brecknockshire** ('brɛknɒk,ʃɪə, -ʃə) *n* (until 1974) a county of SE Wales, now mainly in Powys: over half its area forms the

Brecon Beacons National Park

bred (brɛd) *vb* the past tense and past participle of **breed**

Breda ('bri:də; *Dutch* bre'da:) *n* a city in the S Netherlands, in North Brabant province: residence of Charles II of England during his exile. Pop: 159 042 (1999 est)

bredie ('bri:dɪ) *n S African* a meat and vegetable stew [C19 from Port. *bredo* ragout]

breech *n* (bri:tʃ) **1** the buttocks; rump **2** the lower part or bottom of something **3** the part of a firearm behind the barrel or bore ▹ *vb* (bri:tʃ, brɪtʃ) (*tr*) **4** to fit (a gun) with a breech **5** *arch* to clothe in breeches or any other clothing [OE *brēc*, pl. of *brōc* leg covering]

USAGE *Breech* is sometimes wrongly used as a verb where *breach* is meant: *he admitted he breached* (not *breeched*) *the rules*

breechblock ('bri:tʃ,blɒk) *n* a metal block in breech-loading firearms that is withdrawn to insert the cartridge and replaced before firing

breech delivery *n* birth of a baby with the feet or buttocks appearing first

breeches ('brɪtʃɪz, 'bri:-) *pl n* **1** trousers extending to the knee or just below, worn for riding, etc **2** *inf or dialect* any trousers or pants, esp extending to the knee

breeches buoy *n* a ring-shaped life buoy with a support in the form of a pair of short breeches, in which a person is suspended for safe transfer from a ship

breeching ('brɪtʃɪŋ, 'bri:-) *n* the strap of a harness that passes behind a horse's haunches

breech-loader ('bri:tʃ,ləʊdə) *n* a firearm that is loaded at the breech > **'breech-,loading** *adj*

breed (bri:d) *vb* **breeds, breeding, bred 1** to bear (offspring) **2** (*tr*) to bring up; raise **3** to produce or cause to produce by mating; propagate **4** to produce new or improved strains of (domestic animals and plants) **5** to produce or be produced; generate: *to breed trouble* ▹ *n* **6** a group of organisms within a species, esp domestic animals, having clearly defined characteristics **7** a lineage or race **8** a kind, sort, or group [OE *brēdan*, of Gmc origin; rel. to BROOD]

▹ www.ansi.okstate.edu/library
▹ www.fanciers.com
▹ www.the-kennel-club.org.uk

breeder ('bri:də) *n* **1** a person who breeds plants or animals **2** something that reproduces **3** an animal kept for breeding purposes **4** a source or cause: *a breeder of discontent* **5** short for **breeder reactor**

breeder reactor *n* a type of nuclear reactor that produces more fissionable material than it consumes

breeding ('bri:dɪŋ) *n* **1** the process of bearing offspring; reproduction **2** the process of producing plants or animals by sexual reproduction **3** the result of good training, esp the knowledge of correct social behaviour; refinement

Breed's Hill (bri:dz) *n* a hill in E Massachusetts, adjoining Bunker Hill: site of the Battle of Bunker Hill (1775)

breeze[1] (bri:z) *n* **1** a gentle or light wind **2** *meteorol* a wind of force two to six (4–31 mph) inclusive on the Beaufort scale **3** *US & Canad inf* an easy task or state of ease **4** *inf, chiefly Brit* a disturbance, esp a lively quarrel ▹ *vb* **breezes, breezing, breezed** (*intr*) **5** to move quickly or casually: *he breezed into the room* [C16 prob. from OSp. *briza* northeast wind]

breeze[2] (bri:z) *n* ashes of coal, coke, or charcoal used to make breeze blocks [C18 from F *braise* live coals; see BRAISE]

breeze block *n* a light building brick made from the ashes of coal, coke, etc, bonded together by cement

breezeway ('bri:z,weɪ) *n* a roofed passageway connecting two buildings

breezy ('bri:zɪ) *adj* **breezier, breeziest 1** fresh; windy: *a breezy afternoon* **2** casual or carefree; lively; light-hearted: *breezy nature* > **'breezily** *adv* > **'breeziness** *n*

Bregenz (*German* bre:'gɛnts) *n* a resort in W Austria, the capital of Vorarlberg province. Pop: 26 730 (latest est)

Bremen ('breɪmən) *n* **1** a state of NW Germany, centred on the city of Bremen and its outport Bremerhaven; formerly in West Germany. Pop: 663 100 (2000 est). Area: 404 sq km (156 sq miles) **2** an industrial city and port in NW Germany, on the Weser estuary. Pop: 542 300 (1999 est)

Bremerhaven (*German* bre:mər'ha:fən) *n* a port in NW Germany: an outport for Bremen. Pop: 123 800 (1999 est). Former name (until 1947): **Wesermünde**

bremsstrahlung ('brɛmz,ʃtrɑ:lʊŋ) *n* the x-radiation produced when an electrically charged particle, such as an electron, is slowed down by the electric field of an atomic nucleus [G: braking radiation]

Brendel (*German* 'brɛndəl) *n* **Alfred** born 1931, Austrian pianist and poet

Bren gun (brɛn) *n* an air-cooled gas-operated light machine gun: used by the British in World War II [C20 after *Br(no)*, now in the Czech Republic, where it was first made and *En(field)*, England, where manufacture was continued]

Brennan ('brɛnən) *n* **Christopher John** 1870–1932, Australian poet and classical scholar, disciple of Mallarmé and exponent of French symbolism in Australian verse

Brenner Pass ('brɛnə) *n* a pass over the E Alps, between Austria and Italy. Highest point: 1372 m (4501 ft)

Brent (brɛnt) *n* a borough of NW Greater London. Pop: 263 463 (2001). Area: 44 sq km (17 sq miles)

brent goose (brɛnt) *n* a small goose that has a dark grey plumage and short neck and occurs in most northern coastal regions. Also called: **brent,** (esp US and Canad) **brant** [C16 ? of Scand. origin]

Brenton ('brɛntᵊn) *n* **Howard** born 1942, British dramatist, author of such controversial plays as *The Churchill Play* (1974), *The Romans in Britain* (1980), (with David Hare) *Pravda* (1985), and several topical satires with Tariq Ali

Bb

Brentwood ('brɛnt,wʊd) *n* a residential town in SE England, in SW Essex near London. Pop: 49 463 (1991)

Brescia (*Italian* 'breʃʃa) *n* a city in N Italy, in Lombardy: at its height in the 16th century. Pop: 191 317 (2000 est). Ancient name: **Brixia** ('brɪksɪə)

Breslau ('brɛzlau) *n* the German name for **Wrocław**

Brest (brɛst) *n* **1** a port in NW France, in Brittany: chief naval station of the country, planned by Richelieu in 1631 and fortified by Vauban. Pop: 149 634 (1999) **2** a city in SW Belarus: Polish until 1795 and from 1921 to 1945. Pop: 297 000 (1998 est). Former name (until 1921): **Brest Litovsk** (brɛst li'tɔfsk). Polish name: **Brześć nad Bugiem**

Bretagne (brətaɲ) *n* the French name for **Brittany**

brethren ('brɛðrɪn) *pl n arch except when referring to fellow members of a religion, society, etc* a plural of **brother**

Breton[1] ('brɛtᵊn) *adj* **1** of, relating to, or characteristic of Brittany, its people, or their language ▹ *n* **2** a native or inhabitant of Brittany **3** the Celtic language of Brittany

Breton[2] (*French* brətɔ̃) *n* **André** (ɑ̃dre) 1896–1966, French poet and art critic: founder and chief theorist of surrealism, publishing the first surrealist manifesto in 1924

Breuer ('brɔɪə) *n* **1 Josef** ('jo:zɛf) 1842–1925, Austrian physician: treated the mentally ill by hypnosis **2 Marcel Lajos** (mɑ:'sɛl 'lɔjoʃ) 1902–81, US architect and furniture designer, born in Hungary. He developed bent plywood and tubular metal furniture and designed the UNESCO building in Paris (1953–58)

Breughel ('brɔɪgᵊl) *n* a variant spelling of **Brueghel**

breve (bri:v) *n* **1** an accent, ˘, placed over a vowel to indicate that it is short or is pronounced in a specified way **2** *music* a note, now rarely used, equivalent to two semibreves **3** *RC Church* a less common word for **brief**

(papal letter) [c13 from Med. L, from L *brevis* short]

brevet (ˈbrɛvɪt) *n* **1** a document entitling a commissioned officer to hold temporarily a higher military rank without the appropriate pay and allowances ▷ *vb* **brevets, brevetting, brevetted** *or* **brevets, breveting, breveted 2** *(tr)* to promote by brevet [c14 from OF, from *brief* letter; see BRIEF] > **ˈbrevetcy** *n*

breviary (ˈbriːvjərɪ) *n, pl* **breviaries** *RC Church* a book of psalms, hymns, prayers, etc, to be recited daily by clerics and certain members of religious orders as part of the divine office [c16 from L *breviārium* an abridged version, from *brevis* short]

brevity (ˈbrɛvɪtɪ) *n, pl* **brevities 1** conciseness of expression; lack of verbosity **2** a short duration; brief time [c16 from L, from *brevis* BRIEF]

brew (bruː) *vb* **1** to make (beer, ale, etc) from malt and other ingredients by steeping, boiling, and fermentation **2** to prepare (a drink, such as tea) by boiling or infusing **3** *(tr)* to devise or plan: *to brew a plot* **4** *(intr)* to be in the process of being brewed **5** *(intr)* to be impending or forming: *there's a storm brewing* ▷ *n* **6** a beverage produced by brewing, esp tea or beer **7** an instance or time of brewing: *last year's brew* **8** a mixture [OE *brēowan*] > **ˈbrewer** *n*

brewery (ˈbrʊərɪ) *n, pl* **breweries** a place where beer, ale, etc, is brewed

brewing (ˈbruːɪŋ) *n* a quantity of a beverage brewed at one time
▷ www.beerinfo.com/vlib/index.html

Brezhnev (ˈbrɛʒnɛf; *Russian* ˈbrjɛʒnɪf) *n* **Leonid Ilyich** (lɪaˈnit ˈiljitʃ) 1906–82, Soviet statesman; president of the Soviet Union (1977–82); general secretary of the Soviet Communist Party (1964–82)

Brian (ˈbraɪən) *n* **Havergal** (ˈhævəgəl) 1876–1972, English composer, who wrote 32 symphonies, including the large-scale *Gothic Symphony* (1919–27)

Brian Boru (bəˈruː) *n* ?941–1014, king of Ireland (1002–14): killed during the defeat of the Danes at the battle of Clontarf

Briand (*French* briɑ̃) *n* **Aristide** (aristid) 1862–1932, French socialist statesman: prime minister of France 11 times. He was responsible for the separation of Church and State (1905) and he advocated a United States of Europe. Nobel peace prize 1926

briar[1] *or* **brier** (ˈbraɪə) *n* **1** Also called: **tree heath** a shrub of S Europe, having a hard woody root (briarroot) **2** a tobacco pipe made from the root of this plant [c19 from F *bruyère* heath] > **ˈbriary** *or* **ˈbriery** *adj*

briar[2] (ˈbraɪə) *n* a variant spelling of **brier**[1]

Briareus (braɪˈɛərɪəs) *n Greek myth* a giant with a hundred arms and fifty heads who aided Zeus and the Olympians against the Titans > **Briˈarean** *adj*

briarroot *or* **brierroot** (ˈbraɪəˌruːt) *n* the hard woody root of the briar, used for making tobacco pipes. Also called: **briarwood, brierwood**

bribe (braɪb) *vb* **bribes, bribing, bribed 1** to promise, offer, or give something, often illegally, to (a person) to procure services or gain influence ▷ *n* **2** a reward, such as money or favour, given or offered for this purpose **3** any persuasion or lure [c14 from OF *briber* to beg, from ?] > **ˈbribery** *n*

bric-a-brac (ˈbrɪkəˌbræk) *n* miscellaneous small objects, esp furniture and curios, kept because they are ornamental or rare [c19 from F]

brick (brɪk) *n* **1a** a rectangular block of clay mixed with sand and fired in a kiln or baked by the sun, used in building construction **1b** *(as modifier): a brick house* **2** the material used to make such blocks **3** any rectangular block: *a brick of ice* **4** bricks collectively **5** *inf* a reliable, trustworthy, or helpful person **6** *Brit* a child's building block **7 drop a brick** *Brit inf* to make a tactless or indiscreet remark **8 like a ton of bricks** *inf* with great force; severely ▷ *vb* **9** *(tr; usually foll by in, up, or over)* to construct, line, pave, fill, or wall up with bricks: *to brick up a window* [c15 from OF *brique*, from MDu. *bricke*] > **ˈbricky** *adj*

brickbat (ˈbrɪkˌbæt) *n* **1** a piece of brick or similar material, esp one used as a weapon **2** blunt criticism [c16 BRICK + BAT[1]]

brickie (ˈbrɪkɪ) *n inf* a bricklayer

bricklayer (ˈbrɪkˌleɪə) *n* a person trained or skilled in laying bricks > **ˈbrickˌlaying** *n*

brick red *n, adj* (of) a reddish-brown colour

bricks and clicks *n* **a** a combination of traditional business carried out on physical premises and Internet trading **b** *(as modifier): bricks-and-clicks companies* [c20 from BRICKS AND MORTAR and *click*, meaning an act of pressing and releasing a computer mouse button]

bricks and mortar *n* **1a** a building or buildings: *he invested in bricks and mortar rather than stocks and shares* **1b** *(as modifier): standard bricks-and-mortar construction* **2a** a physical business premises rather than an Internet presence **2b** *(as modifier): bricks-and-mortar firms*

brickwork (ˈbrɪkˌwɜːk) *n* **1** a structure built of bricks **2** construction using bricks

brickyard (ˈbrɪkˌjɑːd) *n* a place in which bricks are made, stored, or sold

bricolage (ˈbrɪkəˌlɑːʒ; *French* brikəlaʒ) *n archit* a jumbled effect produced by the close proximity of buildings from different periods or in different styles [F: odd jobs, do-it-yourself]

bridal (ˈbraɪdᵊl) *adj* of or relating to a bride or a wedding; nuptial [OE *brȳdealu*, lit.: "bride ale", that is, wedding feast]

bride (braɪd) *n* a woman who has just been or is about to be married [OE *brȳd*]

Bride (braɪd) *n* See (Saint) **Bridget**

bridegroom (ˈbraɪdˌgruːm, -ˌgrʊm) *n* a man who has just been or is about to be married [c14 changed (through infl. of GROOM) from OE *brȳdguma*, from *brȳd* BRIDE + *guma* man]

bride price *or* **wealth** *n* (in some societies) money, property, or services given by a bridegroom to the kinsmen of his bride

bridesmaid (ˈbraɪdzˌmeɪd) *n* a girl or young unmarried woman who attends a bride at her wedding

bridge[1] (brɪdʒ) *n* **1** a structure that spans and provides a passage over a road, railway, river, or some other obstacle **2** something that resembles this in shape or function **3** the hard ridge at the upper part of the nose, formed by the underlying nasal bones **4** the part of a pair of glasses that rests on the nose **5** Also called: **bridgework** a dental plate containing one or more artificial teeth that is secured to the surrounding natural teeth **6** a platform from which a ship is piloted and navigated **7** a piece of wood, usually fixed, supporting the strings of a violin, guitar, etc, and transmitting their vibrations to the sounding board **8** Also called: **bridge passage** a passage in a musical, literary, or dramatic work linking two or more important sections **9** Also called: **bridge circuit** *electronics* any of several networks across which a device is connected for measuring resistance, capacitance, etc **10** *computing* a device that connects networks and sends packets between them **11** *billiards, snooker* a support for a cue **12 cross a bridge when (one) comes to it** to deal with a problem only when it arises ▷ *vb* **bridges, bridging, bridged** *(tr)* **13** to build or provide a bridge over something; span: *to bridge a river* **14** to connect or reduce the distance between: *let us bridge our differences* [OE *brycg*] > **ˈbridgeable** *adj*

bridge[2] (brɪdʒ) *n* a card game for four players, based on whist, in which one hand (the dummy) is exposed and the trump suit decided by bidding between the players. See also **contract bridge, auction bridge** [c19 from ?]
▷ www.worldbridge.org

Bridge (ˈbrɪdʒ) *n* **Frank** 1879–1941, English composer, esp of chamber music. He taught Benjamin Britten

bridgehead (ˈbrɪdʒˌhɛd) *n* **1** *mil* an area of ground secured or to be taken on the enemy's side of an obstacle **2** *mil* a fortified or defensive position at the end of a bridge nearest to the enemy **3** an advantageous position gained for future expansion

Bridgend (ˌbrɪdʒˈɛnd) *n* a county borough in S Wales, created in 1996 from S Mid Glamorgan. Administrative centre: Bridgend. Pop: 128 650 (2001). Area: 264 sq km (102 sq miles)

Bridge of Sighs *n* a covered 16th-century bridge in Venice, between the Doges' Palace and the prisons, through which prisoners were formerly led to trial or execution

Bridgeport (ˈbrɪdʒˌpɔːt) *n* a port in SW Connecticut, on Long Island Sound. Pop: 139 529 (2000)

bridge roll *n* a soft bread roll in a long thin shape [C20 from BRIDGE[2] or ? BRIDGE[1]]

Bridges (ˈbrɪdʒɪz) *n* **Robert (Seymour)** 1844–1930, English poet: poet laureate (1913–30)

Bridget (ˈbrɪdʒɪt) *n* **Saint 1** Also called: **Bride, Brigid** 453–523 AD, Irish abbess; a patron saint of Ireland. Feast day: Feb 1 **2** Also called: **Birgitta** ?1303-73, Swedish nun and visionary; patron saint of Sweden. Feast day: July 23

Bridgetown (ˈbrɪdʒˌtaʊn) *n* the capital of Barbados, a port on the SW coast. Pop: 6070 (1990)
▹ www.barbados.org/btown.htm

bridgework (ˈbrɪdʒˌwɜːk) *n* a partial denture attached to the surrounding teeth

bridging loan *n* a loan made to cover the period between two transactions, such as the buying of another house before the sale of the first is completed

Bridgwater (ˈbrɪdʒˌwɔːtə) *n* a town in SW England, in central Somerset. Pop: 34 610 (1991)

Bridie (ˈbraɪdɪ) *n* **James**, real name *Osborne Henry Mavor.* 1888–1951, Scottish physician and dramatist, who founded the Glasgow Citizens' Theatre. His plays include *The Anatomist* (1930)

bridle (ˈbraɪdᵊl) *n* **1** a headgear for a horse, etc, consisting of a series of buckled straps and a metal mouthpiece (bit) by which the animal is controlled through the reins **2** something that curbs or restrains; check **3** a Y-shaped cable, rope, or chain, used for holding, towing, etc ▹ *vb* **bridles, bridling, bridled 4** (*tr*) to put a bridle on (a horse, mule, etc) **5** (*tr*) to restrain; curb: *he bridled his rage* **6** (*intr*; often foll by *at*) to show anger, scorn, or indignation [OE *brigdels*]

bridle path *n* a path suitable for riding or leading horses

Brie (briː) *n* **1** a soft creamy white cheese **2** a mainly agricultural area in N France, between the Rivers Marne and Seine: noted esp for its cheese

brief (briːf) *adj* **1** short in duration **2** short in length or extent; scanty: *a brief bikini* **3** abrupt in manner; brusque: *the professor was brief with me* **4** terse or concise ▹ *n* **5** a condensed statement or written synopsis; abstract **6** *law* a document containing all the facts and points of law of a case by which a solicitor instructs a barrister to represent a client **7** *RC Church* a letter issuing from the Roman court written in modern characters, as contrasted with a papal bull; papal brief **8** Also called: **briefing** instructions **9 hold a brief for** to argue for; champion **10 in brief** in short; to sum up ▹ *vb* (*tr*) **11** to prepare or instruct by giving a summary of relevant facts **12** to make a summary or synopsis of **13** *English law* **13a** to instruct (a barrister) by brief **13b** to retain (a barrister) as counsel [C14 from OF *bref*, from L *brevis*] > ˈ**briefly** *adv* > ˈ**briefness** *n*

briefcase (ˈbriːfˌkeɪs) *n* a flat portable case, often of leather, for carrying papers, books, etc

briefing (ˈbriːfɪŋ) *n* **1** a meeting at which information and instructions are given **2** the facts presented at such a meeting

briefless (ˈbriːflɪs) *adj Brit* (said of a barrister) without clients

briefs (briːfs) *pl n* men's underpants or women's pants without legs

brier[1] *or* **briar** (ˈbraɪə) *n* any of various thorny shrubs or other plants, such as the sweetbrier [OE *brēr, brǣr*, from ?] > ˈ**briery** *or* ˈ**briary** *adj*

brier[2] (ˈbraɪə) *n* a variant spelling of **briar[1]**

brierroot (ˈbraɪəˌruːt) *n* a variant spelling of **briarroot.** Also called: **brierwood**

brig[1] (brɪg) *n* **1** *naut* a two-masted square-rigger **2** *chiefly US* a prison, esp in a navy ship [C18 shortened from BRIGANTINE]

brig[2] (brɪg) *n* a Scot. and N English word for **bridge[1]**

Brig. *abbrev for* Brigadier

brigade (brɪˈgeɪd) *n* **1** a military formation smaller than a division and usually commanded by a brigadier **2** a group of people organized for a certain task: *a rescue brigade* ▹ *vb* **brigades, brigading, brigaded** (*tr*) **3** to organize into a brigade [C17 from OF, from OIt., from *brigare* to fight; see BRIGAND]

brigadier (ˌbrɪgəˈdɪə) *n* **1** an officer of the British Army or Royal Marines junior to a major general but senior to a colonel, usually commanding a brigade **2** an equivalent rank in other armed forces [C17 from F, from BRIGADE]

brigalow (ˈbrɪgələʊ) *n Austral* **a** any of various acacia trees, forming dense scrub **b** (*as modifier*): *brigalow country* [C19 from Abor.]

brigand (ˈbrɪgənd) *n* a bandit, esp a member of a gang operating in mountainous areas [C14 from OF, from OIt. *brigante* fighter, from *briga* strife] > ˈ**brigandage** *or* ˈ**brigandry** *n*

brigantine (ˈbrɪgənˌtiːn, -ˌtaɪn) *n* a two-masted sailing ship, rigged square on the foremast and fore-and-aft on the mainmast [C16 from OIt. *brigantino* pirate ship, from *brigante* BRIGAND]

Briggs (brɪgz) *n* **Henry** 1561–1631, English mathematician: introduced common logarithms

Brighouse[1] (ˈbrɪgˌhaʊs) *n* a town in N England, in Calderdale unitary authority, West Yorkshire: machine tools, textiles, engineering. Pop: 32 198 (1991)

Brighouse[2] (ˈbrɪgˌhaʊs) *n* **Harold** 1882–1958, British novelist and dramatist, best known for his play *Hobson's Choice* (1915)

bright (braɪt) *adj* **1** emitting or reflecting much light; shining **2** (of colours) intense or vivid **3** full of promise: *a bright future* **4** full of animation; cheerful: *a bright face* **5** *inf* quick-witted or clever: *a bright child* **6** magnificent; glorious **7** polished; glistening **8** (of a liquid) translucent and clear **9 bright and early** very early in the morning ▹ *adv* **10** brightly: *the fire was burning bright* [OE *beorht*] > ˈ**brightly** *adv* > ˈ**brightness** *n*

Bright (braɪt) *n* **John** 1811–89, British liberal statesman, economist, and advocate of free trade: with Richard Cobden he led the Anti-Corn-Law League (1838–46)

brighten (ˈbraɪtᵊn) *vb* **1** to make or become bright or brighter **2** to make or become cheerful

brightening agent *n* a compound applied to a textile to increase its brightness by the conversion of ultraviolet radiation to visible (blue) light, used in detergents

Brighton (ˈbraɪtᵊn) *n* a coastal resort in S England, in Brighton and Hove unitary authority, East Sussex: patronized by the Prince Regent, who had the Royal Pavilion built (1782); seat of the University of Sussex (1966) and the University of Brighton (1992). Pop: 124 851 (1991)

Brighton and Hove (həʊv) *n* a city and unitary authority in S England, in East Sussex. Pop: 247 820 (2001). Area: 72 sq km (28 sq miles)

Bright's disease (braɪts) *n* chronic inflammation of the kidneys; chronic nephritis [C19 after Richard *Bright* (1789–1858), E physician]

brightwork ('braɪt,wɜːk) *n* shiny metal trimmings or fittings on ships, cars, etc

Brigid ('brɪdʒɪd) *n* See (Saint) **Bridget**

brill[1] (brɪl) *n, pl* **brill** *or* **brills** a European flatfish similar to the turbot [c15 prob. from Cornish *brȳthel* mackerel, from OCornish *brȳth* speckled]

brill[2] (brɪl) *adj Brit sl* excellent or wonderful [c20 shortened form of BRILLIANT]

brilliance ('brɪljəns) *or* **brilliancy** *n* **1** great brightness; radiance **2** excellence or distinction in physical or mental ability; exceptional talent **3** splendour; magnificence

brilliant ('brɪljənt) *adj* **1** shining with light; sparkling **2** (of a colour) reflecting a considerable amount of light; vivid **3** outstanding; exceptional: *a brilliant success* **4** splendid; magnificent: *a brilliant show* **5** of outstanding intelligence or intellect: *a brilliant mind* ▷ *n* **6** Also called: **brilliant cut 6a** a cut for diamonds and other gemstones in the form of two many-faceted pyramids joined at their bases **6b** a diamond of this cut [c17 from F *brillant* shining, from It. *brillo* BERYL] > '**brilliantly** *adv*

brilliantine ('brɪljən,tiːn) *n* a perfumed oil used to make the hair smooth and shiny [c19 from F, from *brillant* shining]

brim (brɪm) *n* **1** the upper rim of a vessel: *the brim of a cup* **2** a projecting rim or edge: *the brim of a hat* **3** the brink or edge of something ▷ *vb* **brims, brimming, brimmed 4** to fill or be full to the brim: *eyes brimming with tears* [c13 from MHG *brem*] > '**brimless** *adj*

brimful *or* **brimfull** (,brɪm'fʊl) *adj (postpositive;* foll by *of)* filled up to the brim (with)

brimstone ('brɪm,stəʊn) *n* **1** an obsolete name for **sulphur 2** a common yellow butterfly of N temperate regions of the Old World [OE *brynstān;* see BURN[1], STONE]

Brindisi (*Italian* 'brindizi) *n* a port in SE Italy, in SE Apulia: important naval base in Roman times and a centre of the Crusades in the Middle Ages. Pop: 93 290 (1991). Ancient name: **Brundisium**

brindle ('brɪndᵊl) *n* **1** a brindled animal **2** a brindled colouring [c17 back formation from BRINDLED]

brindled ('brɪndᵊld) *adj* brown or grey streaked or patched with a darker colour: *a brindled dog* [c17 changed from c15 *brended,* lit.: branded]

Brindley ('brɪndlɪ) *n* **James** 1716–72, British canal builder, who constructed (1759–61) the Bridgewater Canal, the first in England

brine (braɪn) *n* **1** a strong solution of salt and water, used for salting and pickling meats, etc **2** the sea or its water ▷ *vb* **brines, brining, brined 3** *(tr)* to soak in or treat with brine [OE *brīne*] > '**brinish** *adj*

bring (brɪŋ) *vb* **brings, bringing, brought** *(tr)* **1** to carry, convey, or take (something or someone) to a designated place or person: *bring that book to me* **2** to cause to happen or occur to (oneself or another): *to bring disrespect on oneself* **3** to cause to happen as a consequence: *responsibility brings maturity* **4** to cause to come to mind: *it brought back memories* **5** to cause to be in a certain state, position, etc: *the punch brought him to his knees* **6** to force, persuade, or make (oneself): *I couldn't bring myself to do it* **7** to sell for; fetch: *the painting brought 20 pounds* **8** *law* **8a** to institute (proceedings, charges, etc) **8b** to put (evidence, etc) before a tribunal **9 bring forth** to give birth to ▷ See also **bring about, bring down,** etc [OE *bringan*] > '**bringer** *n*

bring about *vb (tr, adv)* **1** to cause to happen **2** to turn (a ship) around

bring-and-buy sale *n Brit & NZ* an informal sale, often for charity, to which people bring items for sale and buy those that others have brought. Often shortened to **bring-and-buy**

bring down *vb (tr, adv)* to cause to fall

bring forward *vb (tr, adv)* **1** to present or introduce (a subject) for discussion **2** *book-keeping* to transfer (a sum) to the top of the next page or column **3** to move to an earlier time or date: *the kickoff has been brought forward to 2 p.m.*

bring in *vb (tr, adv)* **1** to yield (income, profit, or cash) **2** to produce or return (a verdict) **3** to introduce (a legislative bill, etc)

bring off *vb (tr, adv)* to succeed in achieving (something), esp with difficulty

bring out *vb (tr, adv)* **1** to produce or publish or have published **2** to expose, reveal, or cause to be seen: *she brought out the best in me* **3** (foll by *in*) to cause (a person) to become covered (with spots, a rash, etc) **4** *Brit* to introduce (a girl) formally into society as a debutante

bring over *vb (tr, adv)* to cause (a person) to change allegiances

bring round *or* **around** *vb (tr, adv)* **1** to restore (a person) to consciousness, esp after a faint **2** to convince (another person) of an opinion or point of view

bring to *vb (tr, adv)* **1** to restore (a person) to consciousness **2** to cause (a ship) to turn into the wind and reduce her headway

bring up *vb (tr, adv)* **1** to care for and train (a child); rear **2** to raise (a subject) for discussion **3** to vomit (food)

brinjal ('brɪndʒəl) *n* (in India and Africa) another name for the **aubergine** [c17 from Port. *berinjela,* from Ar.]

brink (brɪŋk) *n* **1** the edge, border, or verge of a steep place **2** the land at the edge of a body of water **3** the verge of an event or state: *the brink of disaster* [c13 from MDu. *brinc,* of Gmc origin]

brinkmanship ('brɪŋkmən,ʃɪp) *n* the art or practice of pressing a dangerous situation, esp in international affairs, to the limit of safety and peace in order to win an advantage

briny ('braɪnɪ) *adj* **brinier, briniest 1** of or resembling brine; salty ▷ *n* **2** (preceded by *the*) *inf* the sea > '**brininess** *n*

brio ('briːəʊ) *n* liveliness or vigour; spirit. See also **con brio** [c19 from It., of Celtic origin]

brioche ('briːəʊʃ, -ɒʃ) *n* a soft roll made from a very light yeast dough [c19 from Norman dialect, from *brier* to knead, of Gmc origin]

briquette *or* **briquet** (brɪ'kɛt) *n* a small brick made of compressed coal dust, sawdust, charcoal, etc, used for fuel [c19 from F: a little brick, from *brique* BRICK]

Brisbane ('brɪzbən) *n* a port in E Australia, the capital of Queensland: founded in 1824 as a penal settlement; vast agricultural hinterland. Pop: 848 741 (1998 est)

brisk (brɪsk) *adj* **1** lively and quick; vigorous: *a brisk walk* **2** invigorating or sharp: *brisk weather* ▷ *vb* **3** (often foll by *up*) to enliven; make or become brisk [c16 prob. var. of BRUSQUE] > '**briskly** *adv* > '**briskness** *n*

brisket ('brɪskɪt) *n* **1** the breast of a four-legged animal **2** the meat from this part, esp of beef [c14 prob. from ON]

brisling ('brɪslɪŋ) *n* another name for a **sprat** [c20 from Norwegian; rel. to obs. Danish *bretling*]

bristle ('brɪsᵊl) *n* **1** any short stiff hair of an animal or plant **2** something resembling these hairs: *toothbrush bristle* ▷ *vb* **bristles, bristling, bristled 3** (when *intr,* often foll by *up*) to stand up or cause to stand up like bristles **4** (*intr;* sometimes foll by *up*) to show anger, indignation, etc: *she bristled at the suggestion* **5** *(intr)* to be thickly covered or set: *the target bristled with arrows* [c13 *bristil, brustel,* from earlier *brust,* from OE *byrst*] > '**bristly** *adj*

Bristol ('brɪstᵊl) *n* **1 City of** a port and industrial city in SW England, mainly in Bristol unitary authority, on the River Avon seven miles from its mouth on the Bristol Channel: a major port, trading with America, in the 17th and 18th centuries; the modern port consists chiefly of docks at Avonmouth and Portishead; noted for the **Clifton Suspension Bridge** (designed by I. K. Brunel, 1834) over the Avon gorge; Bristol university (1909) and University of the West of England (1992). Pop: 407 992 (1991) **2 City of** a unitary authority in SW

England, created in 1996 from part of Avon county. Pop: 380 615 (2001). Area: 110 sq km (42 sq miles)

Bristol board *n* a heavy smooth cardboard of fine quality, used for drawing

Bristol Channel *n* an inlet of the Atlantic, between S Wales and SW England, merging into the Severn estuary. Length: about 137 km (85 miles)

Bristol fashion *adv, adj (postpositive)* in good order; efficiently arranged

bristols ('brɪstᵊlz) *pl n Brit sl* a woman's breasts [c20 short for *Bristol Cities*, rhyming slang for *titties*]

Brit (brɪt) *n inf* a British person

Brit. *abbrev for:* **1** Britain **2** British

Britain ('brɪtᵊn) *n* another name for **Great Britain** or the **United Kingdom**

Britannia (brɪ'tænɪə) *n* **1** a female warrior carrying a trident and wearing a helmet, personifying Great Britain or the British Empire **2** (in the ancient Roman Empire) the S part of Great Britain **3** short for **Britannia coin**

Britannia coin *n* any of four British gold coins introduced in 1987 for investment purposes; their denominations are £100, £50, £25, and £10

Britannia metal *n* an alloy of tin with antimony and copper: used for decorative purposes and for bearings

Britannic (brɪ'tænɪk) *adj* of Britain; British (esp in **His** *or* **Her Britannic Majesty**)

Britart ('brɪt,ɑːt) *n* a movement in modern British art beginning in the late 1980s, often conceptual or using controversial materials, including such artists as Damien Hirst and Rachel Whiteread [c20 *Brit* short for *British*]

britches ('brɪtʃɪz) *pl n* a variant spelling of **breeches**

Briticism ('brɪtɪ,sɪzəm) *n* a custom, linguistic usage, or other feature peculiar to Britain or its people. Also: **Britishism**

British ('brɪtɪʃ) *adj* **1** of or denoting Britain **2** relating to, denoting, or characteristic of the inhabitants of Britain **3** relating to or denoting the English language as spoken and written in Britain **4** of or relating to the Commonwealth: *British subjects* ▷ *n* **5 the British** *(functioning as pl)* the natives or inhabitants of Britain > '**Britishness** *n*

British Antarctic Territory *n* a UK Overseas Territory in the S Atlantic: created in 1962 and consisting of the South Shetland Islands, the South Orkney Islands, and Graham Land; formerly part of the Falkland Islands Dependencies

British Cameroons *pl n* a former British trust territory of West Africa. See **Cameroon**

British Columbia *n* a province of W Canada, on the Pacific coast: largely mountainous with extensive forests, rich mineral resources, and important fisheries. Capital: Victoria. Pop: 4 095 900 (2001 est). Area: 930 532 sq km (359 279 sq miles). Abbreviation: **BC** > **British Columbian** *n, adj*

▷ www.gov.bc.ca

▷ www.bc-tourism.com

British Council *n* an organization founded (1934) to extend the influence of British culture and education throughout the world

▷ www.britishcouncil.org

British East Africa *n* the former British possessions of Uganda, Kenya, Tanganyika, and Zanzibar, before their independence in the 1960s

British Empire *n* (formerly) the United Kingdom and the territories under its control, which reached its greatest extent at the end of World War I when it embraced over a quarter of the world's population and more than a quarter of the world's land surface

▷ www.britishempire.co.uk

▷ www.empiremuseum.co.uk

Britisher ('brɪtɪʃə) *n* (not used by the British) **1** a native or inhabitant of Great Britain **2** any British subject

British Guiana *n* the former name (until 1966) of **Guyana**

British Honduras *n* the former name of **Belize**

British India *n* the 17 provinces of India formerly governed by the British under the British sovereign: ceased to exist in 1947 when the independent states of India and Pakistan were created

British Indian Ocean Territory *n* a UK Overseas Territory in the Indian Ocean: consists of the Chagos Archipelago (formerly a dependency of Mauritius) and formerly included (until 1976) Aldabra, Farquhar, and Des Roches, now administratively part of the Seychelles. Diego Garcia is an important US naval base

British Isles *pl n* a group of islands in W Europe, consisting of Great Britain, Ireland, the Isle of Man, Orkney, the Shetland Islands, the Channel Islands belonging to Great Britain, and the islands adjacent to these

Britishism ('brɪtɪ,ʃɪzəm) *n* a variant of **Briticism**

British Legion *n Brit* an organization founded in 1921 to provide services and assistance for former members of the armed forces

▷ www.britishlegion.org.uk

British North America *n* (formerly) Canada or its constituent regions or provinces that formed part of the British Empire

British Somaliland *n* a former British protectorate (1884–1960) in E Africa, on the Gulf of Aden: united with Italian Somaliland in 1960 to form the Somali Republic

British thermal unit *n* a unit of heat in the fps system equal to the quantity of heat required to raise the temperature of 1 pound of water by 1°F. 1 British thermal unit is equivalent to 1055.06 joules. Abbrev: **btu, BThU**

British Virgin Islands *pl n* a UK Overseas Territory in the Caribbean, consisting of 36 islands in the E Virgin Islands: formerly part of the Federation of the Leeward Islands (1871–1956). Capital: Road Town, on Tortola. Pop: 19 000 (1997 est). Area: 153 sq km (59 sq miles)

British West Africa *n* the former British possessions of Nigeria, The Gambia, Sierra Leone, and the Gold Coast, and the former trust territories of Togoland and Cameroons

British West Indies *pl n* the states in the Caribbean that are members of the Commonwealth: the Bahamas, Barbados, Jamaica, Trinidad and Tobago, Antigua and Barbuda, Saint Kitts-Nevis, Dominica, Grenada, Saint Lucia, and Saint Vincent and the Grenadines

Briton ('brɪtᵊn) *n* **1** a native or inhabitant of Britain **2** *history* any of the early Celtic inhabitants of S Britain [c13 from OF *Breton*, of Celtic origin]

Britpack ('brɪt,pæk) *n* **a** a group of young and successful British actors, directors, artists, etc **b** *(as modifier)*: *Britpack talent* [c20 a play on BRATPACK]

Britpop ('brɪt,pɒp) *n* the characteristic pop music performed by some British bands of the mid 1990s

▷ www.wikipedia.org/wiki/Britpop

Brittany[1] ('brɪtənɪ) *n* a region of NW France, the peninsula between the English Channel and the Bay of Biscay: settled by Celtic refugees from Wales and Cornwall during the Anglo-Saxon invasions; disputed between England and France until 1364. Breton name: **Breiz** (braɪz) French name: **Bretagne** Related adjective: **Breton**

Britten ('brɪtᵊn) *n* (**Edward**) **Benjamin**, Baron Britten. 1913–76, English composer, pianist, and conductor. His works include the operas *Peter Grimes* (1945) and *Billy Budd* (1951), the choral works *Hymn to St Cecilia* (1942) and *A War Requiem* (1962), and numerous orchestral pieces

brittle ('brɪtᵊl) *adj* **1** easily cracked, snapped, or broken; fragile **2** curt or irritable **3** hard or sharp in quality ▷ *n* **4** a crunchy sweet made with treacle and nuts: *peanut brittle* [c14 ult. from OE *brēotan* to break] > '**brittleness** *n*

Bb

brittle-star *n* an echinoderm occurring on the sea bottom and having long slender arms radiating from a small central disc

Brno ('bɜːnəʊ; *Czech* 'brnɔ) *n* a city in the Czech Republic; formerly the capital of Moravia: the country's second largest city. Pop: 383 569 (2000 est). German name: **Brünn**

bro. *abbrev for* brother

bro (bruː) *n S African inf* a friend, often used in direct address [C20 from Afrik. *broer* brother]

broach (brəʊtʃ) *vb* (*tr*) **1** to initiate (a topic) for discussion **2** to tap or pierce (a container) to draw off (a liquid): *to broach a cask* **3** to open in order to begin to use ▷ *n* **4** a long tapered toothed cutting tool for enlarging holes **5** a spit for roasting meat, etc [C14 from OF *broche*, from L *brochus* projecting]

> **USAGE** *Broach* is occasionally wrongly used as the spelling for the item of jewellery (*brooch*). The mistake does not seem to occur the other way round

broad (brɔːd) *adj* **1** having relatively great breadth or width **2** of vast extent; spacious: *a broad plain* **3** (*postpositive*) from one side to the other: *four miles broad* **4** of great scope or potential: *that invention had broad applications* **5** not detailed; general: *broad plans* **6** clear and open; full (esp in **broad daylight**) **7** obvious or plain: *broad hints* **8** liberal; tolerant: *a broad political stance* **9** widely spread; extensive: *broad support* **10** vulgar; coarse; indecent: *a broad joke* **11** (of a dialect or pronunciation) consisting of a large number of speech sounds characteristic of a particular geographic area: *a broad Yorkshire accent* **12** *finance* denoting an assessment of liquidity as including notes and coin in circulation with the public, banks' till money and balances, most private-sector bank deposits, and sterling bank-deposit certificates: *broad money* ▷ Cf **narrow** (sense 7) **13** *phonetics* the long vowel in English words such as *father*, *half*, as represented in Received Pronunciation ▷ *n* **14** the broad part of something **15** *sl, chiefly US & Canad* **15a** a girl or woman **15b** a prostitute **16** See **Broads** [OE *brād*] > **'broadly** *adv*

B-road *n* a secondary road in Britain

broad bean *n* **1** an erect annual Eurasian bean plant cultivated for its large edible flattened seeds **2** the seed of this plant

broadcast ('brɔːdˌkɑːst) *vb* **broadcasts, broadcasting, broadcast** *or* **broadcasted 1** to transmit (announcements or programmes) on radio or television **2** (*intr*) to take part in a radio or television programme **3** (*tr*) to make widely known throughout an area: *to broadcast news* **4** (*tr*) to scatter (seed, etc) over an area, esp by hand ▷ *n* **5a** a transmission or programme on radio or television **5b** (*as modifier*): *a broadcast signal* **6** the act of scattering seeds ▷ *adj* **7** dispersed over a wide area ▷ *adv* **8** far and wide > **'broadˌcaster** *n* > **'broadˌcasting** *n*

Broad Church *n* **1** a party within the Church of England which favours a broad and liberal interpretation of Anglican doctrine **2** (*usually not caps.*) a group which embraces a wide and varied number of views and opinions ▷ *adj* **Broad-Church 3** of or relating to this party in the Church of England

broadcloth ('brɔːdˌklɒθ) *n* **1** fabric woven on a wide loom **2** a closely woven fabric of wool, worsted, cotton, or rayon with lustrous finish, used for clothing

broaden ('brɔːdᵊn) *vb* to make or become broad or broader; widen

broad gauge *n* **1** a railway track with a greater distance between the lines than the standard gauge of 56½ inches (about 1·44 metres) ▷ *adj* **broad-gauge 2** of or denoting a railway having this track

broad-leaved *adj* denoting trees other than conifers; having broad rather than needle-shaped leaves

broadloom ('brɔːdˌluːm) *n* (*modifier*) of or designating carpets or carpeting woven on a wide loom

broad-minded *adj* **1** tolerant of opposing viewpoints; not prejudiced; liberal **2** not easily shocked by permissive sexual habits, pornography, etc > **ˌbroad-'mindedly** *adv* > **ˌbroad-'mindedness** *n*

Broads (brɔːdz) *pl n* **the 1** a group of shallow navigable lakes, connected by a network of rivers, in E England, in Norfolk and Suffolk **2** the region around these lakes: a tourist centre; several bird sanctuaries

broadsheet ('brɔːdˌʃiːt) *n* **1** a newspaper having a large format, approximately 15 by 24 inches (38 by 61 centimetres) **2** another word for **broadside** (sense 4)

broadside ('brɔːdˌsaɪd) *n* **1** *naut* the entire side of a vessel **2** *naval* **2a** all the armament fired from one side of a warship **2b** the simultaneous discharge of such armament **3** a strong or abusive verbal or written attack **4** Also called: **broadside ballad** a ballad or popular song printed on one side of a sheet of paper, esp in 16th-century England ▷ *adv* **5** with a broader side facing an object; sideways

broad-spectrum *n* (*modifier*) effective against a wide variety of diseases or microorganisms: *a broad-spectrum antibiotic*

broadsword ('brɔːdˌsɔːd) *n* a broad-bladed sword used for cutting rather than stabbing

broadtail ('brɔːdˌteɪl) *n* **1** the highly valued black wavy fur obtained from the skins of newly born karakul lambs; caracul **2** another name for **karakul**

Broadway ('brɔːdˌweɪ) *n* **1** a thoroughfare in New York City, famous for its theatres: the centre of the commercial theatre in the US *adj* **2** of or relating to or suitable for the commercial theatre, esp on Broadway

brocade (brəʊ'keɪd) *n* **1** a rich fabric woven with a raised design, often using gold or silver threads ▷ *vb* **brocades, brocading, brocaded 2** (*tr*) to weave with such a design [C17 from Sp. *brocado*, from It. *broccato* embossed fabric, from L *brochus* projecting]

broccoli ('brɒkəlɪ) *n* **1** a cultivated variety of cabbage having branched greenish flower heads **2** the flower head, eaten as a vegetable before the buds have opened [C17 from It., pl of *broccolo* a little sprout, from *brocco* sprout]

broch (brɒk, brɒx) *n* (in Scotland) a prehistoric circular dry-stone tower large enough to serve as a fortified home [C17 from ON *borg*; rel. to OE *burh* settlement, burgh]

brochette (brɒ'ʃɛt) *n* a skewer or small spit, used for holding pieces of meat, etc, while roasting or grilling [C19 from OF *brochete* small pointed tool; see BROACH]

brochure ('brəʊʃjʊə, -ʃə) *n* a pamphlet or booklet, esp one containing summarized or introductory information or advertising [C18 from F, from *brocher* to stitch (a book)]

brock (brɒk) *n* a Brit name for **badger** (sense 1) [OE *broc*, of Celtic origin]

Brocken (*German* 'brɔkən) *n* a mountain in central Germany, formerly in East Germany: the highest peak of the Harz Mountains; important in German folklore. Height: 1142 m (3747 ft). The **Brocken Bow** or **Brocken Spectre** is an atmospheric phenomenon in which an observer, when the sun is low, may see his enlarged shadow against the clouds, often surrounded by coloured lights

brocket ('brɒkɪt) *n* a small deer of tropical America, having small unbranched antlers [C15 from Anglo-F *broquet*, from *broque* horn]

broderie anglaise ('brəʊdəriː ɑːŋ'glɛz) *n* open embroidery on white cotton, fine linen, etc [C19 from F: English embroidery]

Broederbond ('brʊdəˌbɔːnt, 'bruːdəˌbɒnt) *n* (in South Africa) a secret society of Afrikaner Nationalists [Afrik.: band of brothers]

broekies ('brʊkiːz) *pl n S African inf* underpants [C19 Afrik.]

Broglie (brɔj) *n* **1** Prince **Louis Victor de** (lwi viktɔr də) 1892–1987, French physicist, noted for his research in quantum mechanics and his development of wave mechanics: Nobel prize for physics 1929 **2** his brother, **Maurice** (mɔris), Duc de Broglie. 1875–1960, French physicist, noted for his research into X-ray spectra

brogue[1] (brəʊg) *n* a broad gentle-sounding dialectal accent, esp that used by the Irish in speaking English [c18 from ?]

brogue[2] (brəʊg) *n* **1** a sturdy walking shoe, often with ornamental perforations **2** an untanned shoe worn formerly in Ireland and Scotland [c16 from Irish Gaelic *bróg* shoe]

broil[1] (brɔɪl) *vb* **1** the usual US and Canad word for **grill** (sense 1) **2** to become or cause to become extremely hot **3** (*intr*) to be furious [c14 from OF *bruillir* to burn]

broil[2] (brɔɪl) *arch* ▷ *n* **1** a loud quarrel or disturbance; brawl ▷ *vb* **2** (*intr*) to brawl; quarrel [c16 from OF *brouiller* to mix]

broiler (ˈbrɔɪlə) *n* **1** a young tender chicken suitable for roasting **2** a pan, grate, etc, for broiling food **3** a very hot day

broke (brəʊk) *vb* **1** the past tense of **break** ▷ *adj* **2** *inf* having no money; bankrupt **3 go for broke** *sl* to risk everything in a gambling or other venture

broken (ˈbrəʊkən) *vb* **1** the past participle of **break** ▷ *adj* **2** fractured, smashed, or splintered: *a broken vase* **3** interrupted; disturbed; disconnected: *broken sleep* **4** intermittent or discontinuous: *broken sunshine* **5** not functioning **6** spoilt or ruined by divorce (esp in **broken home, broken marriage**) **7** (of a trust, promise, contract, etc) violated; infringed **8** (of the speech of a foreigner) imperfect in grammar, vocabulary, and pronunciation: *broken English* **9** Also: **broken-in** made tame or disciplined by training **10** exhausted or weakened, as through ill-health or misfortune **11** irregular or rough; uneven: *broken ground* **12** bankrupt **13** (of colour) having a multicoloured decorative effect, as by stippling paint onto a surface > ˈ**brokenly** *adv*

broken chord *n* another term for **arpeggio**

broken-down *adj* **1** worn out, as by age or long use; dilapidated **2** not in working order

brokenhearted (ˌbrəʊkənˈhɑːtɪd) *adj* overwhelmed by grief or disappointment > ˌ**brokenˈheartedly** *adv*

Broken Hill *n* a city in SE Australia, in W New South Wales: mining centre for lead, silver, and zinc. Pop: 24 500 (latest est)

broken wind (wɪnd) *n vet science* another name for **heaves** > ˌ**brokenˈwinded** *adj*

broker (ˈbrəʊkə) *n* **1** an agent who, acting on behalf of a principal, buys or sells goods, securities, etc: *insurance broker* **2** short for **stockbroker** **3** a person who deals in second-hand goods [c14 from Anglo-F *brocour* broacher (of casks, hence, one who sells, agent), from OF *broquier* to tap a cask]

brokerage (ˈbrəʊkərɪdʒ) *n* **1** commission charged by a broker **2** a broker's business or office

broker-dealer *n* another name for **stockbroker**

brolga (ˈbrɒlgə) *n* a large grey Australian crane having a red-and-green head and a trumpeting call. Also called: **native companion** [c19 from Abor.]

brolly (ˈbrɒlɪ) *n, pl* **brollies** an informal Brit name for **umbrella** (sense 1)

Bromberg (ˈbrɔmbɛrk) *n* the German name for **Bydgoszcz**

bromeliad (brəʊˈmiːlɪˌæd) *n* any of a family of tropical American plants, typically epiphytes with a rosette of fleshy leaves, such as the pineapple and Spanish moss [c19 from NL, after Olaf *Bromelius* (1639–1705), Swedish botanist]

bromide (ˈbrəʊmaɪd) *n* **1** any salt of hydrobromic acid **2** any compound containing a bromine atom **3** a dose of sodium or potassium bromide given as a sedative **4a** a platitude **4b** a dull or boring person

bromide paper *n* a type of photographic paper coated with an emulsion of silver bromide

bromine (ˈbrəʊmiːn, -mɪn) *n* a pungent dark red volatile liquid element that occurs in brine and is used in the production of chemicals. Symbol: Br; atomic no.: 35; atomic wt.: 79.91 [c19 from F *brome* bromine, from Gk *brōmos* bad smell, from ?]

Bromley (ˈbrɒmlɪ) *n* a borough of SE Greater London. Pop: 295 530 (2001). Area: 153 sq km (59 sq miles)

Bromsgrove (ˈbrɒmzˌgrəʊv) *n* a town in W central England, in N Worcestershire. Pop: 26 366 (1991)

bronchi (ˈbrɒŋkaɪ) *n* the plural of **bronchus**

bronchial (ˈbrɒŋkɪəl) *adj* of or relating to the bronchi or the bronchial tubes > ˈ**bronchially** *adv*

bronchial tubes *pl n* the bronchi or their smaller divisions

bronchiectasis (ˌbrɒŋkɪˈɛktəsɪs) *n* chronic dilation and usually infection of the bronchi [c19 from BRONCHO- + Gk *ektasis* a stretching]

bronchiole (ˈbrɒŋkɪˌəʊl) *n* any of the smallest bronchial tubes [c19 from NL; see BRONCHUS] > ˌ**bronchiˈolar** *adj*

bronchitis (brɒŋˈkaɪtɪs) *n* inflammation of the bronchial tubes, characterized by coughing, difficulty in breathing, etc > **bronchitic** (brɒŋˈkɪtɪk) *adj, n*

broncho- *or before a vowel* **bronch-** *combining form* indicating or relating to the bronchi: *bronchitis* [from Gk: BRONCHUS]

bronchodilator (ˌbrɒŋkəʊdaɪˈleɪtə, -dɪ-) *n* any drug or other agent that causes dilatation of the bronchial tubes by relaxing bronchial muscle: used, esp in the form of aerosol sprays, for the relief of asthma

bronchopneumonia (ˌbrɒŋkəʊnjuːˈməʊnɪə) *n* inflammation of the lungs, starting in the bronchioles

bronchoscope (ˈbrɒŋkəˌskəʊp) *n* an instrument for examining and providing access to the interior of the bronchial tubes

Bb

bronchus (ˈbrɒŋkəs) *n, pl* **bronchi** either of the two main branches of the trachea [c18 from NL, from Gk *bronkhos* windpipe]

bronco *or* **broncho** (ˈbrɒŋkəʊ) *n, pl* **broncos** *or* **bronchos** (in the US and Canada) a wild or partially tamed pony or mustang of the western plains [c19 from Mexican Sp., from Sp.: rough, wild]

Brontë (ˈbrɒntɪ) *n* **1 Anne**, pen name *Acton Bell*. 1820–49, English novelist; author of *The Tenant of Wildfell Hall* (1847) **2** her sister, **Charlotte**, pen name *Currer Bell*. 1816–55, English novelist, author of *Jane Eyre* (1847), *Villette* (1853), and *The Professor* (1857) **3** her sister, **Emily (Jane)**, pen name *Ellis Bell*. 1818–48, English novelist and poet; author of *Wuthering Heights* (1847)

brontosaurus (ˌbrɒntəˈsɔːrəs) *or* **brontosaur** (ˈbrɒntəˌsɔː) *n* a very large herbivorous quadrupedal dinosaur, common in N America during late Jurassic times, having a long neck and long tail [c19 from NL, from Gk *brontē* thunder + *sauros* lizard]

Bronx (brɒŋks) *n* **the** a borough of New York City, on the mainland, separated from Manhattan by the Harlem River. Pop: 1 203 789 (1990)

Bronx cheer *n chiefly US* a loud spluttering noise made with the lips and tongue and expressing derision or contempt; raspberry

bronze (brɒnz) *n* **1** any hard water-resistant alloy consisting of copper and smaller proportions of tin and sometimes zinc and lead **2** a yellowish-brown colour or pigment **3** a statue, medal, or other object made of bronze ▷ Cf **bronze** (sense 1) ▷ *adj* **4** made of or resembling bronze **5** of a yellowish-brown colour ▷ *vb* **bronzes, bronzing, bronzed** **6** (esp of the skin) to make or become brown; tan **7** (*tr*) to give the appearance of bronze to [c18 from F, from It. *bronzo*] > ˈ**bronzy** *adj*

Bronze Age *n* **a** a technological stage between the Stone and Iron Ages, beginning in the Middle East about 4500 BC and lasting in Britain from about 2000 to 500 BC, during which weapons and tools were made of bronze **b** (*as modifier*): *a Bronze-Age tool*

bronze medal *n* a medal awarded to a competitor who comes third in a contest or race

bronze whaler *n* a shark of southern Australian waters, having a bronze-coloured back

bronzing ('brɒnzɪŋ) *n* **1** blue pigment producing a metallic lustre when ground into paint media at fairly high concentrations **2** the application of a mixture of powdered metal or pigments of a metallic lustre to a surface

Bronzino (bron'dzi:no) *n* **Il**, real name *Agnolo di Cosimo*. 1503–72, Florentine mannerist painter

brooch (brəʊtʃ) *n* an ornament with a hinged pin and catch, worn fastened to clothing [c13 from OF *broche*; see BROACH]

USAGE See at **broach**

brood (bru:d) *n* **1** a number of young animals, esp birds, produced at one hatching **2** all the offspring in one family: often used jokingly or contemptuously **3** a group of a particular kind; breed **4** (*modifier*) kept for breeding: *a brood mare* ▷ *vb* **5** (of a bird) **5a** to sit on or hatch (eggs) **5b** (*tr*) to cover (young birds) protectively with the wings **6** (when *intr*, often foll by *on*, *over*, or *upon*) to ponder morbidly or persistently [OE *brōd*] > '**brooding** *n, adj*

brooder ('bru:də) *n* **1** a structure, usually heated, used for rearing young chickens or other fowl **2** a person or thing that broods

broody ('bru:dɪ) *adj* **broodier, broodiest 1** moody; introspective **2** (of poultry) wishing to sit on or hatch eggs **3** *inf* (of a woman) wishing to have a baby > '**broodiness** *n*

brook[1] (brʊk) *n* a natural freshwater stream smaller than a river [OE *brōc*]

brook[2] (brʊk) *vb* (*tr*) (*usually used with a negative*) to bear; tolerate [OE *brūcan*]

Brooke (brʊk) *n* **1 Alan Francis** See (1st Viscount) **Alanbrooke 2** Sir **James** 1803–68, British soldier; first rajah of Sarawak (1841–63) **3 Rupert (Chawner)** 1887–1915, British lyric poet, noted for his idealistic war poetry, which made him a national hero

brooklet ('brʊklɪt) *n* a small brook

brooklime ('brʊk,laɪm) *n* either of two blue-flowered trailing plants, *Veronica americana* of North America or *V. beccabunga* of Europe and Asia, growing in moist places. See also **speedwell** [c16 from BROOK[1] + *-lemk*, from OE *hleomoce*]

Brooklyn ('brʊklɪn) *n* a borough of New York City, on the SW end of Long Island. Pop: 2 291 664 (1990)

Brooks (brʊks) *n* **1 Mel**, real name *Melvyn Kaminsky*. born 1926, US comedy writer, actor, and film director. His films include *The Producers* (1968), *Blazing Saddles* (1974), *High Anxiety* (1977), and *Dracula: Dead and Loving It* (1996) **2 (Troyal) Garth** born 1962, US country singer and songwriter; his bestselling records include *Ropin' the Wind* (1991) and *Scarecrow* (2001)

Brooks Range (brʊks) *n* a mountain range in N Alaska. Highest peak: Mount Isto, 2761 m (9058 ft)

brook trout *n* a North American trout, valued as a food and game fish

broom (bru:m, brʊm) *n* **1** an implement for sweeping consisting of a long handle to which is attached either a brush of straw or twigs, bound together, or a solid head into which are set tufts of bristles or fibres **2** any of various yellow-flowered Eurasian leguminous shrubs **3 new broom** a newly appointed official, etc, eager to make changes ▷ *vb* **4** (*tr*) to sweep with a broom [OE *brōm*]

broomrape ('bru:m,reɪp, 'brʊm-) *n* any of a genus of leafless fleshy parasitic plants growing on the roots of other plants, esp on legumes [c16 adaptation & partial translation of Med. L *rāpum genistae* tuber (hence: root nodule) of Genista (a type of broom plant)]

broomstick ('bru:m,stɪk, 'brʊm-) *n* the long handle of a broom

bros. or **Bros.** *abbrev for* brothers

brose (brəʊz) *n Scot* a porridge made by adding a boiling liquid to meal, esp oatmeal [c13 *broys*, from OF *broez*, from *breu* broth, of Gmc origin]

bro talk *n NZ* **1** Maori English **2** English spoken with a Maori accent [c20 BRO[1] (sense 1) + TALK]

broth (brɒθ) *n* **1** a soup made by boiling meat, fish, vegetables, etc, in water **2** another name for **stock** (sense 19) [OE *broth*]

brothel ('brɒθəl) *n* **1** a house where men pay to have sexual intercourse with prostitutes **2** *Austral inf* any untidy place [c16 short for *brothel-house*, from c14 *brothel* useless person, from OE *brēothan* to deteriorate]

brother ('brʌðə) *n* **1** a male person having the same parents as another person **2a** a male person belonging to the same group, profession, nationality, trade union, etc, as another or others; fellow member **2b** (*as modifier*): *brother workers* **3** comrade; friend: used as a form of address **4** *Christianity* a member of a male religious order ▷ Related adj: **fraternal** [OE *brōthor*]

brotherhood ('brʌðə,hʊd) *n* **1** the state of being related as a brother or brothers **2** an association or fellowship, such as a trade union **3** all persons engaged in a particular profession, trade, etc **4** the belief, feeling, or hope that all men should treat one another as brothers

brother-in-law *n, pl* **brothers-in-law 1** the brother of one's wife or husband **2** the husband of one's sister **3** the husband of the sister of one's husband or wife

brotherly ('brʌðəlɪ) *adj* of, resembling, or suitable to a brother, esp in showing loyalty and affection; fraternal > '**brotherliness** *n*

brougham ('bru:əm, bru:m) *n* **1** a four-wheeled horse-drawn closed carriage having a raised open driver's seat in front **2** *obs* a large car with an open compartment at the front for the driver **3** *obs* an early electric car [c19 after Lord *Brougham* (1778–1868)]

brought (brɔ:t) *vb* the past tense and past participle of **bring**

brouhaha ('bru:hɑ:hɑ:) *n* a loud confused noise; commotion; uproar [F, imit.]

brow (braʊ) *n* **1** the part of the face from the eyes to the hairline; forehead **2** short for **eyebrow 3** the expression of the face; countenance: *a troubled brow* **4** the jutting top of a hill, etc [OE *brū*]

browbeat ('braʊ,bi:t) *vb* **browbeats, browbeating, browbeat, browbeaten** (*tr*) to discourage or frighten with threats or a domineering manner; intimidate

brown (braʊn) *n* **1** any of various dark colours, such as those of wood or earth **2** a dye or pigment producing these colours ▷ *adj* **3** of the colour brown **4** (of bread) made from a flour that has not been bleached or bolted, such as wheatmeal or wholemeal flour **5** deeply tanned or sunburnt **6 in a brown study.** See **study** (sense 15) ▷ *vb* **7** to make (esp food as a result of cooking) brown or (esp of food) to become brown [OE *brūn*] > '**brownish** *or* '**browny** *adj* > '**brownness** *n*

Brown (braʊn) *n* **1** Sir **Arthur Whitten** ('wɪtᵊn) 1886–1948, British aviator who with J. W. Alcock made the first flight across the Atlantic (1919) **2 Ford Madox** 1821–93, British painter, associated with the Pre-Raphaelite Brotherhood. His paintings include *The Last of England* (1865) and *Work* (1865) **3 George (Alfred)**, Lord George-Brown. 1914–85, British Labour politician; vice-chairman and deputy leader of the Labour party (1960–70); foreign secretary 1966–68 **4 George Mackay** 1921–96, Scottish poet, novelist, and short-story writer. His works, which include the novels *Greenvoe* (1972) and *Magnus* (1973), reflect the history and culture of Orkney

5 (James) **Gordon** born 1951, British Labour politician; Chancellor of the Exchequer from 1997 6 **Herbert Charles** born 1912, US chemist, who worked on the compounds of boron. Nobel prize for chemistry 1979 7 **James** born 1928, US soul singer and songwriter, noted for his dynamic stage performances and for pioneering the funk style in the late 1960s 8 **John** 1800–59, US abolitionist leader, hanged after leading an unsuccessful rebellion of slaves at Harper's Ferry, Virginia 9 **Lancelot**, called *Capability Brown*. 1716–83, British landscape gardener 10 **Michael** (**Stuart**) born 1941, US physician: shared the Nobel prize for physiology or medicine (1985) for work on cholesterol 11 **Robert** 1773–1858, Scottish botanist who was the first to observe the Brownian movement in fluids

brown bear *n* a large ferocious brownish bear inhabiting temperate forests of North America, Europe, and Asia

brown coal *n* a low quality coal intermediate between peat and **lignite**

brown dwarf *n* a type of celestial body midway in size between a large planet and a small star, thought to be one possible explanation of dark matter in the universe

Browne (braʊn) *n* 1 **Coral** (**Edith**) 1913–91, Australian actress: married to Vincent Price 2 **Hablot Knight** See **Phiz** 3 Sir **Thomas** 1605–82, English physician and author, noted for his magniloquent prose style. His works include *Religio Medici* (1642) and *Hydriotaphia or Urn Burial* (1658)

browned-off *adj inf* thoroughly discouraged or disheartened; fed up

brown fat *n* a dark form of adipose tissue that is readily converted into energy

brownfield (ˈbraʊn,fiːld) *n* (*modifier*) denoting or located in an urban area that has previously been built on: *Hampshire has many brownfield developments*

Brownian movement (ˈbraʊnɪən) *n* random movement of microscopic particles suspended in a fluid, caused by bombardment of the particles by molecules of the fluid [c19 after Robert BROWN]

brownie (ˈbraʊnɪ) *n* 1 (in folklore) an elf said to do helpful work at night, esp household chores 2 a small square nutty chocolate cake [c16 dim. of BROWN (that is, a small brown man)]

Brownie Guide *or* **Brownie** (ˈbraʊnɪ) *n* a member of the junior branch of the Guides
▷ www.girlguiding.org.uk/members/brownies

Brownie point *n* a notional mark to one's credit for being seen to do the right thing [c20 ?from the mistaken notion that Brownie Guides earn points for good deeds]

browning (ˈbraʊnɪŋ) *n Brit* a substance used to darken soups, gravies, etc

Browning[1] (ˈbraʊnɪŋ) *n* 1 **Elizabeth Barrett** 1806–61, English poet and critic; author of the *Sonnets from the Portuguese* (1850) 2 her husband, **Robert** 1812–89, English poet, noted for his dramatic monologues and *The Ring and the Book* (1868–69)

brown paper *n* a kind of coarse unbleached paper used for wrapping

brown rice *n* unpolished rice, in which the grains retain the outer yellowish-brown layer (bran)

Brown Shirt *n* 1 (in Nazi Germany) a storm trooper 2 a member of any fascist party or group

brownstone (ˈbraʊn,stəʊn) *n US* a reddish-brown iron-rich sandstone used for building

brown sugar *n* sugar that is unrefined or only partially refined

brown toast *n Canad* toasted wholemeal bread

brown trout *n* a common brownish variety of the trout that occurs in the rivers of N Europe

browse (braʊz) *vb* **browses, browsing, browsed** 1 to look through (a book, articles for sale in a shop, etc) in a casual leisurely manner 2 *computing* to read hypertext, esp on the World Wide Web 3 (of deer, goats, etc) to feed upon (vegetation) by continual nibbling ▷ *n* 4 the act or an instance of browsing 5 the young twigs, shoots, leaves, etc, on which certain animals feed [c15 from F *broust, brost* bud, of Gmc origin]

browser (ˈbraʊzə) *n* 1 a person or animal that browses 2 *computing* a software package that enables a user to read hypertext, esp on the World Wide Web

browser skin *n computing* a changeable decorative background for a browser

Broz (*Serbo-Croat* brɔːz) *n* **Josip** (ˈjɔsip) original name of (Marshal) **Tito**

Brubeck (ˈbruːbɛk) *n* **Dave** born 1920, US modern jazz pianist and composer; formed his own quartet in 1951

Bruce[1] (bruːs) *n* 1 **James** 1730–94, British explorer, who discovered the source of the Blue Nile (1770) 2 **Lenny** 1925–66, US comedian, whose satirical sketches, esp of the sexual attitudes of his contemporaries, brought him prosecutions for obscenity, but are now regarded as full of insight as well as wit 3 **Robert the** See **Robert I** 4 **Stanley Melbourne**, 1st Viscount Bruce of Melbourne. 1883–1967, Australian statesman; prime minister, in coalition with Sir Earle Page's Country Party, of Australia (1923–29)

Bruce[2] (bruːs) *n Brit* a jocular name for an Australian man

brucellosis (,bruːsɪˈləʊsɪs) *n* an infectious disease of cattle, goats, and pigs, caused by bacteria and transmittable to man. Also called: **undulant fever** [c20 from NL *Brucella*, after Sir David *Bruce* (1855–1931), Australian bacteriologist & physician]

Bruch (*German* brʊx) *n* **Max** (maks) 1838–1920, German composer, noted chiefly for his three violin concertos

Bruckner (*German* ˈbrʊknər) *n* **Anton** (ˈantoːn) 1824–96, Austrian composer and organist in the Romantic tradition. His works include nine symphonies, four masses, and a Te Deum

Bb

Brudenell (ˈbruːdənɛl) *n* **James Thomas** See (7th Earl of) **Cardigan**[2]

Brueghel, Bruegel, *or* **Breughel** (ˈbrɔɪgᵊl; *Flemish* ˈbrøːxəl) *n* 1 **Jan** (jɑn) 1568–1625, Flemish painter, noted for his detailed still lifes and landscapes 2 his father, **Pieter** (ˈpiːtər), called *the Elder*. ?1525–69, Flemish painter, noted for his landscapes, his satirical paintings of peasant life, and his allegorical biblical scenes 3 his son, **Pieter**, called *the Younger*. ?1564–1637, Flemish painter, noted for his gruesome pictures of hell

Bruges (bruːʒ; *French* bryʒ) *n* a city in NW Belgium, capital of West Flanders province: centre of the medieval European wool and cloth trade. Pop: 116 246 (2000 est). Flemish name: **Brugge** (ˈbryxə)

bruin (ˈbruːɪn) *n* a name for a bear, used in children's tales, etc [c17 from Du. *bruin* brown]

bruise (bruːz) *vb* **bruises, bruising, bruised** (*mainly tr*) 1 (*also intr*) to injure (tissues) without breaking the skin, usually with discoloration, or (of tissues) to be injured in this way 2 to offend or injure (someone's feelings) 3 to damage the surface of (something) 4 to crush (food, etc) by pounding ▷ *n* 5 a bodily injury without a break in the skin, usually with discoloration; contusion [OE *brȳsan*]

bruiser (ˈbruːzə) *n inf* a strong tough person, esp a boxer or a bully

bruit (bruːt) *vb* 1 (*tr; often passive;* usually foll by *about*) to report; rumour ▷ *n* 2 *arch* 2a a rumour 2b a loud outcry; clamour [c15 via F from Med. L *brūgītus*, prob. from L *rugīre* to roar]

brumby (ˈbrʌmbɪ) *n, pl* **brumbies** *Austral* 1 a wild horse, esp one descended from runaway stock 2 *inf* a wild or unruly person [c19 from ?]

brume (bruːm) *n poetic* heavy mist or fog [c19 from F: mist, winter, from L *brūma*, contracted from *brevissima diēs* the shortest day] > **'brumous** *adj*

Brummagem ('brʌmədʒəm) *n* **1** an informal name for **Birmingham.** Often shortened to: **Brum 2** (*sometimes not cap*) something that is cheap and flashy, esp imitation jewellery ▷ *adj* **3** (*sometimes not cap*) cheap and gaudy; tawdry [c17 from earlier *Bromecham*, local variant of BIRMINGHAM]

Brummell ('brʌməl) *n* **George Bryan**, called *Beau Brummell*. 1778–1840, English dandy: leader of fashion in the Regency period

brunch (brʌntʃ) *n* a meal eaten late in the morning, combining breakfast with lunch [c20 from BR(EAKFAST) + (L)UNCH]

Brundisium (brʌn'dɪzɪəm) *n* the ancient name for **Brindisi**

Brunei (bru:'naɪ, 'bru:naɪ) *n* **1** a sultanate in NW Borneo, consisting of two separate areas on the South China Sea, otherwise bounded by Sarawak: controlled all of Borneo and parts of the Philippines and the Sulu Islands in the 16th century; under British protection since 1888; internally self-governing since 1971; became independent in 1984 as a member of the Commonwealth. The economy depends chiefly on oil and natural gas. Official language: Malay; English is also widely spoken. Religion: Muslim. Currency: Brunei dollar. Capital: Bandar Seri Begawan. Pop: 344 000 (2001 est). Area: 5765 sq km (2226 sq miles) **2** the former name of **Bandar Seri Begawan**
▷ www.brunei.gov.bn

Brunel (bru:'nɛl) *n* **1** **Isambard Kingdom** ('ɪzəm,bɑ:d) 1806–59, English engineer: designer of the Clifton Suspension Bridge (1828), many railway lines, tunnels, bridges, etc, and the steamships *Great Western* (1838), *Great Britain* (1845), and *Great Eastern* (1858) **2** his father, Sir **Marc Isambard** 1769–1849, French engineer in England

Brunelleschi (*Italian* brunel'leski) *n* **Filippo** (fi'lippo) 1377–1446, Italian architect, whose works in Florence include the dome of the cathedral, the Pazzi chapel of Santa Croce, and the church of San Lorenzo

brunette (bru:'nɛt) *n* **1** a girl or woman with dark brown hair ▷ *adj* **2** dark brown: *brunette hair* [c17 from F, fem of *brunet* dark, brownish, from *brun* brown]

Brunhild ('brʊnhɪld, -hɪlt) *or* **Brünnhilde** (*German* bryn'hɪldə) *n* (in the *Nibelungenlied*) a legendary queen won for King Gunther by the magic of Siegfried: corresponds to Brynhild in Norse mythology

Brünn (bryn) *n* the German name for **Brno**

Brunswick ('brʌnzwɪk) *n* **1** a former duchy (1635–1918) and state (1918–46) of central Germany, now part of the state of Lower Saxony; formerly (1949–90) part of West Germany **2** a city in central Germany: formerly capital of the duchy and state of Brunswick. Pop: 246 800 (1999 est). German name: **Braunschweig**

brunt (brʌnt) *n* the main force or shock of a blow, attack, etc (esp in **bear the brunt of**) [c14 from ?]

Brusa (*Turkish* 'bru:sa:) *n* the former name of **Bursa**

brush[1] (brʌʃ) *n* **1** a device made of bristles, hairs, wires, etc, set into a firm back or handle: used to apply paint, clean or polish surfaces, groom the hair, etc **2** the act or an instance of brushing **3** a light stroke made in passing; graze **4** a brief encounter or contact, esp an unfriendly one; skirmish **5** the bushy tail of a fox **6** an electric conductor, esp one made of carbon, that conveys current between stationary and rotating parts of a generator, motor, etc ▷ *vb* **7** (*tr*) to clean, polish, scrub, paint, etc, with a brush **8** (*tr*) to apply or remove with a brush or brushing movement **9** (*tr*) to touch lightly and briefly **10** (*intr*) to move so as to graze or touch something lightly ▷ See also **brush aside, brush off, brush up** [c14 from OF *broisse*, ?from *broce* BRUSH[2]]
> **'brusher** *n*

brush[2] (brʌʃ) *n* **1** a thick growth of shrubs and small trees; scrub **2** land covered with scrub **3** broken or cut branches or twigs; brushwood **4** wooded sparsely populated country; backwoods [c16 (dense undergrowth), c14 (cuttings of trees): from OF *broce*, from Vulgar L *bruscia* (unattested) brushwood] > **'brushy** *adj*

brush aside *or* **away** *vb* (*tr, adv*) to dismiss without consideration; disregard

brush discharge *n* a slightly luminous brushlike electrical discharge

brushed (brʌʃt) *adj textiles* treated with a brushing process to raise the nap and give a softer and warmer finish: *brushed nylon*

brushmark ('brʌʃ,mɑ:k) *n* the indented lines sometimes left by the bristles of a brush on a painted surface

brush off *sl* ▷ *vb* (*tr, adv*) **1** to dismiss and ignore (a person), esp curtly ▷ *n* **brushoff 2** an abrupt dismissal or rejection

brush-tailed possum *or* **brush-tail possum** *n* any of several widely-distributed Australian possums

brush turkey *n* any of several gallinaceous flightless birds of New Guinea and Australia, having a black plumage

brush up *vb* (*adv*) **1** (*tr; often foll by on*) to refresh one's knowledge, skill, or memory of (a subject) **2** to make (a person or oneself) clean or neat as after a journey ▷ *n* **brush-up 3** *Brit* the act or an instance of tidying one's appearance (esp in **wash and brush-up**)

brushwood ('brʌʃ,wʊd) *n* **1** cut or broken-off tree branches, twigs, etc **2** another word for **brush**[2] (sense 1)

brushwork ('brʌʃ,wɜ:k) *n* **1** a characteristic manner of applying paint with a brush: *Rembrandt's brushwork* **2** work done with a brush

brusque (bru:sk, brʊsk) *adj* blunt or curt in manner or speech [c17 from F, from It. *brusco* sour, rough, from Med. L *bruscus* butcher's broom] > **'brusquely** *adv* > **'brusqueness** *n*

Brussels ('brʌsᵊlz) *n* the capital of Belgium, in the central part: became capital of Belgium in 1830; seat of the European Commission. Pop (urban area): 1 121 000 (2000 est). Flemish name: **Brussel** ('brysəl) French name: **Bruxelles**
▷ www.brussels.org
▷ www.bruxelles.irisnet.be/En/Homeen.htm

Brussels carpet *n* a worsted carpet with a heavy pile formed by uncut loops of wool on a linen warp

Brussels lace *n* a fine lace with a raised or appliqué design

Brussels sprout *n* **1** a variety of cabbage, having a stout stem studded with budlike heads resembling tiny cabbages **2** the head of this plant, eaten as a vegetable

brut (bru:t) *adj* (of champagne or sparkling wine) very dry [F, lit.: dry]

brutal ('bru:tᵊl) *adj* **1** cruel; vicious; savage **2** extremely honest or coarse in speech or manner **3** harsh; severe; extreme: *brutal cold* > **bru'tality** *n* > **'brutally** *adv*

brutalism ('bru:tə,lɪzəm) *n* an austere style of architecture characterized by emphasis on such structural materials as undressed concrete and unconcealed service pipes. Also called: **new brutalism** > **'brutalist** *n, adj*
▷ http://students.open.ac.uk/open2net/modernity/4_15.htm
▷ www.skyscrapers.com/re/en/ab/ds/pd/bu/ca/sy/mo/br

brutalize *or* **brutalise** ('bru:tə,laɪz) *vb* **brutalizes, brutalizing, brutalized** *or* **brutalises, brutalising, brutalised 1** to make or become brutal **2** (*tr*) to treat brutally > **,brutali'zation** *or* **,brutali'sation** *n*

brute (bru:t) *n* **1a** any animal except man; beast; lower animal **1b** (*as modifier*): *brute nature* **2** a brutal person ▷ *adj* (*prenominal*) **3** wholly instinctive or physical (esp in **brute strength, brute force**) **4** without reason or intelligence **5** coarse and grossly sensual [c15 from L *brūtus* heavy, irrational]

brutish ('bru:tɪʃ) *adj* **1** of, relating to, or resembling a brute; animal **2** coarse; cruel; stupid > '**brutishly** *adv* > '**brutishness** *n*

Bruton ('bru:tᵊn) *n* **John Gerard** born 1947, Irish politician: leader of the Fine Gael party (1990–2001); prime minister of the Republic of Ireland (1994–97)

Brutus ('bru:təs) *n* **1 Lucius Junius** ('lu:ʃəs 'dʒu:nɪəs) late 6th century BC, Roman statesman who ousted the tyrant Tarquin (509) and helped found the Roman republic **2 Marcus Junius** ('mɑ:kəs 'dʒu:nɪəs) ?85–42 BC, Roman statesman who, with Cassius, led the conspiracy to assassinate Caesar (44): committed suicide after being defeated by Antony and Octavian (Augustus) at Philippi (42)

Bruxelles (brysɛl) *n* the French name for **Brussels**

Bryansk (brɪ'ænsk; *Russian* brjansk) *n* a city in W Russia. Pop: 461 100 (1999 est)

Brynhild ('brɪnhɪld) *n Norse myth* a Valkyrie won as the wife of Gunnar by Sigurd who wakes her from an enchanted sleep: corresponds to Brunhild in the *Nibelungenlied*

bryology (braɪ'ɒlədʒɪ) *n* the branch of botany concerned with the study of bryophytes > **bryological** (ˌbraɪə'lɒdʒɪkᵊl) *adj* > **bry'ologist** *n*

bryony *or* **briony** ('braɪənɪ) *n, pl* **bryonies** *or* **brionies** any of several herbaceous climbing plants of Europe and N Africa [OE *bryōnia*, from L, from Gk *bruōnia*]

bryophyte ('braɪəˌfaɪt) *n* any plant of the phyla *Bryophyta* (mosses), *Hepatophyta* (liverworts), or *Anthocerophyta* (hornworts) [c19 from Gk *bruon* moss + -PHYTE] > **bryophytic** (ˌbraɪə'fɪtɪk) *adj*

bryozoan (ˌbraɪə'zəʊən) *n* any aquatic invertebrate animal forming colonies of polyps each having a ciliated feeding organ. Popular name: **sea mat** [c19 from Gk *bruon* moss + *zōion* animal]

Brythonic (brɪ'θɒnɪk) *n* **1** the S group of Celtic languages, consisting of Welsh, Cornish, and Breton ▷ *adj* **2** of or relating to this group of languages [c19 from Welsh; see BRITON]

Brześć nad Bugiem (bʒɛʃtʃ nad 'bugjɛm) *n* the Polish name for **Brest** (sense 2)

BS *abbrev for* British Standard(s)

B.S. (in the US and Canada) *abbrev for* Bachelor of Science

BSc *abbrev for* Bachelor of Science

BSC (in Britain) *abbrev for* Broadcasting Standards Commission

BSE *abbrev for* bovine spongiform encephalopathy: a fatal prion disease of cattle, affecting the nervous system. Informal name: **mad cow disease**

BSI *abbrev for* British Standards Institution

B-side *n* the less important side of a gramophone record

BSL *abbrev for* British Sign Language

BST *abbrev for*: **1** bovine somatotrophin: a growth hormone that can be used to increase milk production in dairy cattle **2** British Summer Time

Bt *abbrev for* Baronet

BT *abbrev for* British Telecom [c20 shortened from TELECOMMUNICATIONS]

BTEC ('bi:ˌtɛk) *n* (in Britain) *acronym for* **1** Business and Technology Council **2** a certificate or diploma in a vocational subject awarded by this body

btu *or* **BThU** *abbrev for* British thermal unit. US abbrev: **BTU**

bubble ('bʌbᵊl) *n* **1** a thin film of liquid forming a hollow globule around air or a gas: *a soap bubble* **2** a small globule of air or a gas in a liquid or a solid **3** the sound made by a bubbling liquid **4** something lacking substance, stability, or seriousness **5** an unreliable scheme or enterprise **6** a dome, esp a transparent glass or plastic one ▷ *vb* **bubbles, bubbling, bubbled 7** to form or cause to form bubbles **8** (*intr*) to move or flow with a gurgling sound **9** (*intr*; often foll by *over*) to overflow (with excitement, anger, etc) [c14 prob. from ON; imit.]

bubble and squeak *n Brit & Austral* a dish of leftover boiled cabbage and potatoes fried together

bubble bath *n* **1** a powder, liquid, or crystals used to scent, soften, and foam in bath water **2** a bath to which such a substance has been added

bubble car *n Brit* (formerly) a small car with a transparent bubble-shaped top

bubble chamber *n* a device that enables the tracks of ionizing particles to be photographed as a row of bubbles in a superheated liquid

bubble gum *n* a type of chewing gum that can be blown into large bubbles

bubble-jet printer *n computing* an ink-jet printer that heats the ink before printing

bubble memory *n computing* a method of storing high volumes of data by using minute pockets of magnetism (bubbles) in a semiconducting material

bubble point *n chem* the temperature at which bubbles just start to appear in a heated liquid mixture

bubble wrap *n* a type of polythene wrapping containing many small air pockets, used as a protective covering when transporting breakable goods

bubbly ('bʌblɪ) *adj* **bubblier, bubbliest 1** full of or resembling bubbles **2** lively; animated; excited ▷ *n* **3** *inf* champagne

Buber ('bu:bə) *n* **Martin** 1878–1965, Jewish theologian, existentialist philosopher, and scholar of Hasidism, born in Austria, whose works include *I and Thou* (1923), *Between Man and Man* (1946), and *Eclipse of God* (1952)

bubo ('bju:bəʊ) *n, pl* **buboes** *pathol* inflammation and swelling of a lymph node, esp in the armpit or groin [c14 from Med. L *bubō*, from Gk *boubōn* groin] > **bubonic** (bju:'bɒnɪk) *adj*

bubonic plague *n* an acute infectious febrile disease characterized by chills, prostration, delirium, and formation of buboes: caused by the bite of an infected rat flea

Bb

Bucaramanga (*Spanish* bukara'manga) *n* a city in N central Colombia, in the Cordillera Oriental: centre of a district growing coffee, tobacco, and cotton. Pop: 515 555 (1999 est)

buccal ('bʌkᵊl) *adj* **1** of or relating to the cheek **2** of or relating to the mouth; oral [c19 from L *bucca* cheek]

buccaneer (ˌbʌkə'nɪə) *n* **1** a pirate, esp one who preyed on Spanish shipping in the Caribbean in the 17th and 18th centuries ▷ *vb* (*intr*) **2** to be or act like a buccaneer [c17 from *boucan*, dried meat taken on long voyages, from F *boucaner* to smoke meat]

buccinator ('bʌksɪˌneɪtə) *n* either of two flat cheek muscles used in chewing [c17 from L, from *buccina* a trumpet]

Buchan ('bʌkən) *n* **John**, 1st Baron Tweedsmuir. 1875–1940, Scottish statesman, historian, and writer of adventure stories, esp *The Thirty-Nine Steps* (1915) and *Greenmantle* (1916); governor general of Canada (1935–40)

Buchanan (bju:'kænən) *n* **1 George** 1506–82, Scottish historian, who was tutor to Mary, Queen of Scots and James VI; author of *History of Scotland* (1582) **2 James** 1791–1868, 15th president of the US (1857–61)

Bucharest (ˌbu:kə'rɛst, ˌbju:-) *n* the capital of Romania, in the southeast. Pop: 2 027 512 (1997 est). Romanian name: **Bucureşti**

▷ www.romaniatourism.com/main.html

▷ www.explore-bucharest.com

Buchenwald (*German* 'bu:xənvalt) *n* a village in E central Germany, near Weimar; site of a Nazi concentration camp (1937–45)

Büchner (*German* 'by:çnər) *n* **Georg** ('ge:ɔrk) 1813–37, German dramatist; regarded as a forerunner of the Expressionists: author of *Danton's Death* (1835) and *Woyzeck* (1837)

buck[1] (bʌk) *n* **1a** the male of various animals including the goat, hare, kangaroo, rabbit, and reindeer **1b** (*as modifier*): *a buck antelope* **2** *S African* an antelope or deer of either sex **3** *arch* a robust spirited young man **4** the act of bucking ▷ *vb* **5** (*intr*) (of a horse or other animal) to jump vertically, with legs stiff and back arched **6** (*tr*) (of a horse, etc) to throw (its rider) by bucking **7** (when *intr*, often foll by *against* or *at*) *chiefly US, Canad, & Austral inf* to resist or oppose obstinately **8** (*tr; usually passive*) *inf* to cheer or encourage: *I was very bucked at passing the exam* ▷ See also **buck up** [OE *bucca* he-goat] > **'bucker** *n*

buck[2] (bʌk) *n inf* **1** *US, Canad, Austral & S African* a dollar **2** *S African* a rand [c19 from ?]

buck[3] (bʌk) *n* **1** *poker* a marker in the jackpot to remind the winner of some obligation when his turn comes to deal **2** **pass the buck** *inf* to shift blame or responsibility onto another [c19 prob. from *buckhorn knife*, placed before a player in poker to indicate that he was the next dealer]

Buck (bʌk) *n* **Pearl S(ydenstricker)** 1892–1973, US novelist, noted particularly for her novel of Chinese life *The Good Earth* (1931): Nobel prize for literature 1938

buckbean ('bʌk,bi:n) *n* a marsh plant with white or pink flowers. Also called: **bogbean**

buckboard ('bʌk,bɔ:d) *n US & Canad* an open four-wheeled horse-drawn carriage with the seat attached to a flexible board between the front and rear axles

bucket ('bʌkɪt) *n* **1** an open-topped roughly cylindrical container; pail **2** Also called: **bucketful** the amount a bucket will hold **3** any of various bucket-like parts of a machine, such as the scoop on a mechanical shovel **4** *chiefly US* a turbine rotor blade **5** *Austral* a small container for ice cream **6** **kick the bucket** *sl* to die ▷ *vb* **buckets, bucketing, bucketed** **7** (*tr*) to carry in or put into a bucket **8** (*intr*; often foll by *down*) (of rain) to fall very heavily **9** (*intr*; often foll by *along*) *chiefly Brit* to travel or drive fast **10** (*tr*) *Austral sl* to criticize severely [c13 from Anglo-F *buket*, from OE *būc*]

bucket seat *n* a seat in a car, etc, having curved sides

bucket shop *n* **1** an unregistered firm of stockbrokers that engages in fraudulent speculation **2** *chiefly Brit* a firm specializing in cheap airline tickets

buckeye ('bʌk,aɪ) *n* any of several North American trees of the horse chestnut family having erect clusters of white or red flowers and prickly fruits

buckhorn ('bʌk,hɔ:n) *n* **a** horn from a buck, used for knife handles, etc **b** (*as modifier*): *a buckhorn knife*

Buckingham[1] ('bʌkɪŋəm) *n* a town in S central England, in Buckinghamshire; university (1975). Pop: 2786 (1991)

Buckingham[2] ('bʌkɪŋəm) *n* **1** **George Villiers, 1st Duke of** 1592–1628, English courtier and statesman; favourite of James I and Charles I: his arrogance, military incompetence, and greed increased the tensions between the King and Parliament that eventually led to the Civil War **2** his son, **George Villiers, 2nd Duke of** 1628–87, English courtier and writer; chief minister of Charles II and member of the Cabal (1667–73)

Buckingham Palace *n* the London residence of the British sovereign: built in 1703, rebuilt by John Nash in 1821–36 and partially redesigned in the early 20th century

Buckinghamshire ('bʌkɪŋəm,ʃɪə, -ʃə) *n* a county in SE central England, containing the Vale of Aylesbury and parts of the Chiltern Hills: the geographic and ceremonial county includes Milton Keynes, which became an independent unitary authority in 1997. Administrative centre: Aylesbury. Pop (excluding Milton Keynes): 479 028 (2001). Area (excluding Milton Keynes): 1568 sq km (605 sq miles). Abbreviation: **Bucks**

buckjumper ('bʌk,dʒʌmpə) *n Austral* an untamed horse

Buckland ('bʌklənd) *n* **William** 1784–1856, English geologist; he became a proponent of the idea of catastrophic ice ages

buckle ('bʌkᵊl) *n* **1** a clasp for fastening together two loose ends, esp of a belt or strap, usually consisting of a frame with an attached movable prong **2** an ornamental representation of a buckle, as on a shoe **3** a kink, bulge, or other distortion ▷ *vb* **buckles, buckling, buckled** **4** to fasten or be fastened with a buckle **5** to bend or cause to bend out of shape [c14 from OF, from L *buccula* a little cheek, hence, cheek strap of a helmet]

buckle down *vb* (*intr, adv*) *inf* to apply oneself with determination

buckler ('bʌklə) *n* **1** a small round shield worn on the forearm **2** a means of protection; defence [c13 from OF *bocler*, from *bocle* shield boss]

Buckley's chance ('bʌklɪz) *n Austral & NZ sl* no chance at all. Often shortened to **Buckley's** [c19 from ?]

buckminsterfullerene (,bʌkmɪnstə'fʊlə,ri:n) *n* a form of carbon that contains molecules with 60 carbon atoms arranged in a structure resembling a geodesic dome. Often shortened to: **fullerene** [c20 after Buckminster FULLER]

bucko ('bʌkəʊ) *n, pl* **buckoes** *Irish* a lively young fellow: often a term of address

buckram ('bʌkrəm) *n* **a** cotton or linen cloth stiffened with size, etc, used in lining clothes, bookbinding, etc **b** (*as modifier*): *a buckram cover* [c14 from OF *boquerant*, ult. from BUKHARA, once important for textiles]

Bucks (bʌks) *abbrev for* Buckinghamshire

buckshee (,bʌk'ʃi:) *adj Brit sl* without charge; free [c20 from BAKSHEESH]

buckshot ('bʌk,ʃɒt) *n* lead shot of large size used in shotgun shells, esp for hunting game

buckskin ('bʌk,skɪn) *n* **1** the skin of a male deer **2a** a strong greyish-yellow suede leather, originally made from deerskin but now usually made from sheepskin **2b** (*as modifier*): *buckskin boots* **3** a stiffly starched cotton cloth **4** a strong and heavy satin-woven woollen fabric

buckthorn ('bʌk,θɔ:n) *n* any of several thorny small-flowered shrubs whose berries were formerly used as a purgative [c16 from BUCK[1] (from the spiny branches resembling antlers) + THORN]

bucktooth ('bʌk,tu:θ) *n, pl* **buckteeth** *derog* a projecting upper front tooth [c18 from BUCK[1] (deer) + TOOTH]

buck up *vb* (*adv*) *inf* **1** to make or cause to make haste **2** to make or become more cheerful, confident, etc

buckwheat ('bʌk,wi:t) *n* **1** a cereal plant with fragrant white flowers, cultivated, esp in the US, for its seeds **2** the edible seeds of this plant, ground into flour or used as animal fodder **3** the flour obtained from these seeds [c16 from MDu. *boecweite*, from *boeke* BEECH + *weite* WHEAT, from the resemblance of the seeds to beechnuts]

buckyball ('bʌkɪ,bɔ:l) *n inf* a ball-like polyhedral carbon molecule, of the type found in buckminsterfullerene and other fullerenes

buckytube ('bʌkɪ,tju:b) *n* a tube of carbon atoms structurally similar to buckminsterfullerene

bucolic (bju:'kɒlɪk) *adj also* **bucolical** **1** of the countryside or country life; rustic **2** of or relating to shepherds; pastoral ▷ *n* **3** (*sometimes pl*) a pastoral poem [c16 from L, from Gk, from *boukolos* cowherd, from *bous* ox] > **bu'colically** *adv*

Bucovina (,bu:kə'vi:nə) *n* a variant spelling of **Bukovina**

Bucureşti (buku'reʃtj) *n* the Romanian name for **Bucharest**

bud (bʌd) *n* **1** a swelling on a plant stem consisting of overlapping immature leaves or petals **2a** a partially opened flower **2b** (*in combination*): *rosebud* **3** any small budlike outgrowth: *taste buds* **4** something small or immature **5** an asexually produced outgrowth in simple organisms such as yeasts that develops into a new individual **6** **nip in the bud** to put an end to (an idea, movement, etc) in its initial stages ▷ *vb* **buds, budding, budded** **7** (*intr*) (of plants and some animals) to produce buds **8** (*intr*) to begin to develop or grow **9** (*tr*) *horticulture* to graft (a bud) from one plant onto another [c14 *budde*, of Gmc origin]

Budapest (ˌbjuːdəˈpɛst; *Hungarian* ˈbudɔpɛʃt) *n* the capital of Hungary, on the River Danube: formed in 1873 from the towns of Buda and Pest. Traditionally Buda, the old Magyar capital, was the administrative and Pest the trade centre: suffered severely in the Russian siege of 1945 and in the unsuccessful revolt against the Communist regime (1956). Pop: 1 811 552 (2000 est)
▷ www.budapest.hu

Buddha (ˈbʊdə) *n* **the** ?563–483 BC, a title applied to Gautama Siddhartha, a religious teacher of N India regarded by his followers as the most recent rediscoverer of the path to enlightenment: the founder of Buddhism

Buddh Gaya (ˈbʊd gəˈjɑː), **Buddha Gaya**, *or* **Bodh Gaya** *n* a village in NE India, in Bihar: site of the sacred bo tree under which Gautama Siddhartha attained enlightenment and became the Buddha; pilgrimage centre. Pop: 21 686 (1991 est)

Buddhism (ˈbʊdɪzəm) *n* a religious teaching propagated by the Buddha and his followers, which declares that by destroying greed, hatred, and delusion, which are the causes of all suffering, man can attain perfect enlightenment > ˈ**Buddhist** *n, adj*
▷ www.buddhanet.net/

buddleia (ˈbʌdlɪə) *n* an ornamental shrub which has long spikes of mauve flowers. Also called: **butterfly bush** [c19 after A. *Buddle* (died 1715), Brit botanist]

buddy (ˈbʌdɪ) *n, pl* **buddies 1** Also (as a term of address): **bud** *chiefly US & Canad* an informal word for **friend 2** a volunteer who visits and gives help and support to a person suffering from AIDS ▷ *vb* **buddies, buddying, buddied 3** (*intr*) to act as a buddy to a person suffering from AIDS [c19 prob. baby-talk var. (US) of BROTHER]

buddy-buddy *adj inf, chiefly US* on very friendly or intimate terms

buddy movie *or* **film** *n* a genre of film dealing with the relationship and adventures of two friends

budge (bʌdʒ) *vb* **budges, budging, budged** (*usually used with a negative*) **1** to move, however slightly **2** to change or cause to change opinions, etc [c16 from OF *bouger*, from L *bullīre* to boil]

budgerigar (ˈbʌdʒərɪˌgɑː) *n* a small green Australian parrot: a popular cagebird bred in many different-coloured varieties [c19 from Abor., from *budgeri* good + *gar* cockatoo]

budget (ˈbʌdʒɪt) *n* **1** an itemized summary of expected income and expenditure over a specified period **2** (*modifier*) economical; inexpensive: *budget meals for a family* **3** the total amount of money allocated for a specific purpose during a specified period ▷ *vb* **budgets, budgeting, budgeted 4** (*tr*) to enter or provide for in a budget **5** to plan the expenditure of (money, time, etc) **6** (*intr*) to make a budget [c15 (meaning: leather pouch, wallet): from OF *bougette*, dim. of *bouge*, from L *bulga*] > ˈ**budgetary** *adj*

Budget (ˈbʌdʒɪt) *n* **the** an estimate of British government expenditures and revenues and the financial plans for the ensuing fiscal year presented annually to the House of Commons by the Chancellor of the Exchequer

budget account *n* **1** an account with a department store, etc, enabling a customer to make monthly payments to cover his past and future purchases **2** a bank account that allows the holder credit to pay certain bills in return for regular deposits

budget deficit *n* the amount by which government expenditure exceeds income from taxation, customs duties, etc, in any one fiscal year

budgie (ˈbʌdʒɪ) *n inf* short for **budgerigar**

Buenaventura (*Spanish* bwenaβenˈtura) *n* a major port in W Colombia, on the Pacific coast. Pop: 224 336 (1999 est)

Buena Vista (*Spanish* ˈbwena ˈvista) *n* a village in NE Mexico, near Saltillo: site of the defeat of the Mexicans by US forces (1847)

Buenos Aires (ˈbweɪnɒs ˈaɪrɪz; *Spanish* ˈbwenos ˈaires) *n* the capital of Argentina, a major port and industrial city on the Río de la Plata estuary: became capital in 1880; university (1821). Pop (urban area): 2 904 192 (1999 est)
▷ www.buenosaires.gov.ar

buff[1] (bʌf) *n* **1a** a soft thick flexible undyed leather made chiefly from the skins of buffalo, oxen, and elk **1b** (*as modifier*): *a buff coat* **2a** a dull yellow or yellowish-brown colour **2b** (*as adj*): *a buff envelope* **3** Also called: **buffer 3a** a cloth or pad of material used for polishing an object **3b** a disc or wheel impregnated with a fine abrasive for polishing metals, etc **4** *inf* one's bare skin (esp in **in the buff**) ▷ *vb* **5** to clean or polish (a metal, floor, shoes, etc) with a buff **6** to remove the grain surface of (a leather) [c16 from OF, from OIt. *bufalo*, from LL *būfalus* BUFFALO]

buff[2] (bʌf) *n arch* a blow or buffet (now only in **blind man's buff**) [c15 back formation from BUFFET[2]]

buff[3] (bʌf) *n inf* an expert on or devotee of a given subject [c20 orig. US: an enthusiastic fire-watcher, from the buff-coloured uniforms worn by volunteer firemen in New York City]

buffalo (ˈbʌfəˌləʊ) *n, pl* **buffaloes** *or* **buffalo 1** a type of cattle, mostly found in game reserves in southern and eastern Africa and having upward-curving horns **2** short for **water buffalo 3** a US & Canad name for **bison** (sense 1) [c16 from It. *bufalo*, ult. from Gk *bous* ox]

Buffalo (ˈbʌfəˌləʊ) *n* a port in W New York State, at the E end of Lake Erie. Pop: 292 648 (2000)

Buffalo Bill *n* nickname of *William Frederick Cody*. 1846–1917, US showman who toured Europe and the US with his famous *Wild West Show*

buffalo grass *n* **1** a short grass growing on the dry plains of the central US **2** *Austral* a grass, *Stenotaphrum americanum*, introduced from North America

buffel grass (ˈbʌfəl) *n Austral* a pasture grass native to Africa and India, introduced in N Australia

buffer[1] (ˈbʌfə) *n* **1** one of a pair of spring-loaded steel pads attached at both ends of railway vehicles and at the end of a railway track to reduce shock due to contact **2** a person or thing that lessens shock or protects from damaging impact, circumstances, etc **3** *chem* **3a** an ionic compound added to a solution to resist changes in its acidity or alkalinity and thus stabilize its pH **3b** Also called: **buffer solution** a solution containing such a compound **4** *computing* a memory device for temporarily storing data ▷ *vb* (*tr*) **5** *chem* to add a buffer to (a solution) **6** to insulate against or protect from shock [c19 from BUFF[2]]

buffer[2] (ˈbʌfə) *n* **1** any device used to shine, polish, etc; buff **2** a person who uses such a device

buffer[3] (ˈbʌfə) *n Brit inf* a stupid or bumbling man (esp in **old buffer**) [c18 ?from ME *buffer* stammerer]

buffer state *n* a small and usually neutral state between two rival powers

buffer stock *n commerce* a stock of a commodity built up by a government or trade organization with the object of using it to stabilize prices

buffet[1] *n* **1** (ˈbʊfeɪ) a counter where light refreshments are served **2** (ˈbʊfeɪ) **2a** a meal at which guests help themselves from a number of dishes **2b** (*as modifier*): *a buffet lunch* **3** (ˈbʌfɪt, ˈbʊfeɪ) (formerly) a piece of furniture used for displaying plate, etc, and typically comprising cupboards and open shelves [c18 from F]

buffet[2] (ˈbʌfɪt) *vb* **buffets, buffeting, buffeted 1** (*tr*) to knock against or about; batter **2** (*tr*) to hit, esp with the fist; cuff **3** to force (one's way), as through a crowd **4** (*intr*) to struggle; battle ▷ *n* **5** a blow, esp with a fist or

Bb

hand **6** aerodynamic oscillation of an aircraft structure by separated flows [C13 from OF *buffet* a light blow]

Buffet (*French* byfɛ) *n* **Bernard** (bɛrnar) 1928–99, French painter and engraver. His works are characterized by sombre tones and thin angular forms

buffet car ('bʊfeɪ) *n Brit* a railway coach where light refreshments are served

buffeting ('bʌfɪtɪŋ) *n* response of an aircraft structure to buffet, esp an irregular oscillation of the tail

bufflehead ('bʌfᵊl,hɛd) *n* a small North American diving duck: the male has black-and-white plumage and a fluffy head [C17 *buffle*, from obs. *buffle* wild ox, referring to the duck's head]

buffo ('bʊfəʊ) *n, pl* **buffi** (-fɪ) *or* **buffos 1** (in Italian opera of the 18th century) a comic part, esp one for a bass **2** Also called: **buffo bass, basso buffo** a bass singer who performs such a part [C18 from It. (adj): comic, from *buffo* (n) BUFFOON]

buffoon (bə'fu:n) *n* **1** a person who amuses others by ridiculous or odd behaviour, jokes, etc **2** a foolish person [C16 from F *bouffon*, from It. *buffone*, from Med. L *būfō*, from L: toad] > **buf'foonery** *n*

bufotalin (,bu:fəʊ'tælɪn) *n* the principal poisonous substance in the skin and saliva of the common European toad

bug (bʌg) *n* **1** an insect having piercing and sucking mouthparts specialized as a beak **2** *chiefly US & Canad* any insect **3** *inf* **3a** a microorganism, esp a bacterium, that produces disease **3b** a disease, esp a stomach infection, caused by a microorganism **4** *inf* an obsessive idea, hobby, etc; craze **5** *inf* a person having such a craze **6** (*often pl*) *inf* a fault, as in a machine **7** *inf* a concealed microphone used for recording conversations, as in spying ▷ *vb* **bugs, bugging, bugged** *inf* **8** (*tr*) to irritate; bother **9** (*tr*) to conceal a microphone in (a room, etc) **10** (*intr*) *US* (of eyes) to protrude [C16 from ?]

Bug (*Russian* buk) *n* **1** Also called: **Southern Bug** a river in E Europe, rising in the W Ukraine and flowing southeast to the Dnieper estuary and the Black Sea. Length: 853 km (530 miles) **2** Also called: **Western Bug** a river in E Europe, rising in the SW Ukraine and flowing northwest to the River Vistula in Poland, forming part of the border between Poland and the Ukraine. Length: 724 km (450 miles)

bugaboo ('bʌgə,bu:) *n, pl* **bugaboos** an imaginary source of fear; bugbear; bogey [C18 prob. of Celtic origin; cf. Cornish *buccaboo* the devil]

Buganda (bʊ'gændə) *n* a region of Uganda: a powerful Bantu kingdom from the 17th century

Bugatti (*Italian* bʊ'gattɪ) *n* **Ettore** (**Arco Isidoro**) ('ɛttore) 1881–1947, Italian car manufacturer; founder of the Bugatti car factory at Molsheim (1909)

bugbear ('bʌg,bɛə) *n* **1** a thing that causes obsessive anxiety **2** (in English folklore) a goblin in the form of a bear [C16 from obs. *bug* an evil spirit+ BEAR²]

bug-eyed *adj* having protruding eyes

bugger ('bʌgə) *n* **1** a person who practises buggery **2** *taboo sl* a person or thing considered to be contemptible, unpleasant, or difficult **3** *sl* a humorous or affectionate term for a man or child: *a friendly little bugger* **4** **bugger all** *sl* nothing ▷ *vb* **5** to practise buggery (with) **6** (*tr*) *sl, chiefly Brit* to ruin, complicate, or frustrate **7** (*tr*) *sl* to tire; weary ▷ *interj* **8** *taboo sl* an exclamation of annoyance or disappointment [C16 from OF *bougre*, from Med. L *Bulgarus* Bulgarian; from the condemnation of the Eastern Orthodox Bulgarians as heretics]

bugger about *or* **around** *vb* (*adv*) *sl* **1** (*intr*) to fool about and waste time **2** (*tr*) to create difficulties or complications for (a person)

bugger off *vb* (*intr, adv*) *taboo sl* to go away; depart

buggery ('bʌgərɪ) *n* anal intercourse between a man and another man, a woman, or an animal

buggy¹ ('bʌgɪ) *n, pl* **buggies 1** a light horse-drawn carriage having either four wheels (esp in the US and Canada) or two wheels (esp in Britain and India) **2** any small light cart or vehicle, such as a baby buggy [C18 from ?]

buggy² ('bʌgɪ) *adj* **buggier, buggiest** infested with bugs

bugle¹ ('bju:gᵊl) *n* **1** *music* a brass instrument similar to the cornet but usually without valves: used for military fanfares, signal calls, etc ▷ *vb* **bugles, bugling, bugled** **2** (*intr*) to play or sound (on) a bugle [C14 short for *bugle horn* ox horn, from OF *bugle*, from L *būculus* young bullock, from *bōs* ox] > **'bugler** *n*

bugle² ('bju:gᵊl) *n* any of several Eurasian plants having small blue or white flowers [C13 from LL *bugula*, from ?]

bugle³ ('bju:gᵊl) *n* a tubular glass or plastic bead sewn onto clothes for decoration [C16 from ?]

bugloss ('bju:glɒs) *n* any of various hairy Eurasian plants having clusters of blue flowers [C15 from L, from Gk *bouglōssos* ox-tongued]

bugong ('bu:gɒŋ) *n* another name for **bogong**

buhl (bu:l) *adj, n* a variant spelling of **boulle**

build (bɪld) *vb* **builds, building, built 1** to make, construct, or form by joining parts or materials: *to build a house* **2** (*tr*) to order the building of: *the government builds most of our hospitals* **3** (foll by *on* or *upon*) to base; found: *his theory was not built on facts* **4** (*tr*) to establish and develop: *it took ten years to build a business* **5** (*tr*) to make in a particular way or for a particular purpose: *the car was not built for speed* **6** (*intr*; often foll by *up*) to increase in intensity ▷ *n* **7** physical form, figure, or proportions: *a man with an athletic build* [OE *byldan*]

builder ('bɪldə) *n* a person who builds, esp one who contracts for and supervises the construction or repair of buildings

building ('bɪldɪŋ) *n* **1** something built with a roof and walls **2** the act, business, occupation, or art of building houses, boats, etc

▷ http://web.singnet.com.sg/ icyh1955/civil.html

building society *n* a cooperative banking enterprise financed by deposits on which interest is paid and from which mortgage loans are advanced on homes and real property; many now offer a range of banking services

build up *vb* (*adv*) **1** (*tr*) to construct gradually, systematically, and in stages **2** to increase, accumulate, or strengthen, esp by degrees: *the murmur built up to a roar* **3** (*tr*) to improve the health or physique of (a person) **4** (*intr*) to prepare for or gradually approach a climax ▷ *n* **build-up 5** progressive increase in number, size, etc: *the build-up of industry* **6** a gradual approach to a climax **7** extravagant publicity or praise, esp in the form of a campaign **8** *mil* the process of attaining the required strength of forces and equipment

built (bɪlt) *vb* the past tense and past participle of **build**

built-in *adj* **1** made or incorporated as an integral part: *a built-in cupboard* **2** essential; inherent ▷ *n* **3** *Austral* a built-in cupboard

built-in obsolescence *n* See **planned obsolescence**

built-up *adj* **1** having many buildings (esp in **built-up area**) **2** increased by the addition of parts: *built-up heels*

Buitenzorg (*Dutch* 'bœitənzɔrx) *n* the former name of **Bogor**

Bujumbura (,bu:dʒəm'bʊərə) *n* the capital of Burundi, a port at the NE end of Lake Tanganyika. Pop: 300 000 (1994 est). Former name: **Usumbura**

Bukavu (bu:'kɑ:vu:) *n* a port in E Democratic Republic of Congo (formerly Zaïre), on Lake Kivu: commercial and industrial centre. Pop: 201 569 (1994 est). Former name (until 1966): **Costermansville**

Bukhara *or* **Bokhara** (bʊ'xɑ:rə) *n* **1** a city in S Uzbekistan. Pop: 220 000 (1998 est) **2** a former emirate of central Asia: a powerful kingdom and centre of Islam; became a territory of the Soviet Union (1920) and was divided between the former Uzbek, Tajik, and Turkmen Soviet Socialist Republics

Bukovina *or* **Bucovina** (ˌbuːkəˈviːnə) *n* a region of E central Europe, part of the NE Carpathians: the north was seized by the Soviet Union (1940) and later became part of the Ukraine; the south remained Romanian

Bulawayo (ˌbʊləˈweɪəʊ) *n* a city in SW Zimbabwe founded (1893) on the site of the kraal of Lobengula, the last Matabele king; the country's main industrial centre. Pop: 790 000 (1998 est)

bulb (bʌlb) *n* **1** a rounded organ of vegetative reproduction in plants such as the tulip and onion: a flattened stem bearing a central shoot surrounded by fleshy nutritive inner leaves and thin brown outer leaves **2** a plant, such as a hyacinth or daffodil, that grows from a bulb **3** See **light bulb** **4** any bulb-shaped thing [C16 from L *bulbus*, from Gk *bolbos* onion] > **ˈbulbous** *adj*

bulbil (ˈbʌlbɪl) *n* **1** a small bulb produced from a parent bulb **2** a bulblike reproductive organ in a leaf axil of certain plants **3** any small bulblike structure in an animal [C19 from NL *bulbillus* BULB]

bulbul (ˈbʊlbʊl) *n* a songbird of tropical Africa and Asia having brown plumage and, in many species, a distinct crest [C18 via Persian from Ar.]

Bulg. *abbrev for* Bulgaria(n)

Bulgakov (*Russian* bʊlˈgakəf) *n* **Mikhail Afanaseyev** (ʌfʌˈnasjef) 1891–1940, Soviet novelist, dramatist, and short-story writer; his novels include *The Master and Margerita* (1966–67)

Bulganin (*Russian* bulˈganin) *n* **Nikolai Aleksandrovich** (nikaˈlaj alɪkˈsandrəvitʃ) 1895–1975, Soviet statesman and military leader; chairman of the council of ministers (1955–58)

Bulgaria (bʌlˈgɛərɪə, bʊl-) *n* a republic in SE Europe, on the Balkan Peninsula on the Black Sea: under Turkish rule from 1395 until 1878; became an independent kingdom in 1908 and a republic in 1946; consists chiefly of the Danube valley in the north, the Balkan Mountains in the central part, separated from the Rhodope Mountains of the south by the valley of the Maritsa River. Language: Bulgarian. Religion: Christian (Bulgarian Orthodox) majority. Currency: lev. Capital: Sofia. Pop: 7 953 000 (2001 est). Area: 110 911 sq km (42 823 sq miles) > **Bulˈgarian** *adj, n*

▷ www.government.bg/English

▷ www.tourism-bulgaria.com

bulge (bʌldʒ) *n* **1** a swelling or an outward curve **2** a sudden increase in number, esp of population ▷ *vb* **bulges, bulging, bulged** **3** to swell outwards [C13 from OF *bouge*, from L *bulga* bag, prob. of Gaulish origin] > **ˈbulging** *adj* > **ˈbulgy** *adj*

bulgur (ˈbʌlgə) *n* cracked wheat that has been hulled, steamed, and roasted so that it requires little or no cooking. Also called: **burghul** [C20 from Ar. *burghul*]

bulimia (bjuːˈlɪmɪə) *n* **1** pathologically insatiable hunger **2** Also called: **bulimia nervosa** a disorder characterized by compulsive overeating followed by vomiting [C17 from NL, from Gk *bous* ox + *limos* hunger]

bulk (bʌlk) *n* **1** volume, size, or magnitude, esp when great **2** the main part: *the bulk of the work is repetitious* **3** a large body, esp of a person **4** the part of food which passes unabsorbed through the digestive system **5** **in bulk** **5a** in large quantities **5b** (of a cargo, etc) unpackaged ▷ *vb* **6** to cohere or cause to cohere in a mass **7** **bulk large** to be or seem important or prominent [C15 from ON *bulki* cargo]

> USAGE The use of a plural noun after *bulk* should be avoided, though it is occasionally encountered; most commonly, according to the Bank of English, when referring to *funds* and *profits*: *the bulk of our profits stem from the sale of beer*

bulk buying *n* the purchase of goods in large amounts, often at reduced prices

bulkhead (ˈbʌlkˌhɛd) *n* any upright wall-like partition in a ship, aircraft, etc [C15 prob. from *bulk* projecting framework from ON *bálkr* + HEAD]

bulk modulus *n* a coefficient of elasticity of a substance equal to the ratio of the applied stress to the resulting fractional change in volume

bulky (ˈbʌlkɪ) *adj* **bulkier, bulkiest** very large and massive, esp so as to be unwieldy > **ˈbulkily** *adv* > **ˈbulkiness** *n*

bull¹ (bʊl) *n* **1** any male bovine animal, esp one that is sexually mature. Related adj: **taurine** **2** the male of various other animals including the elephant and whale **3** a very large, strong, or aggressive person **4** *stock exchange* **4a** a speculator who buys in anticipation of rising prices in order to make a profit on resale **4b** (*as modifier*): *a bull market* ▷ Cf **bear²** (sense 5) **5** *chiefly Brit* short for **bull's-eye** (senses 1, 2) **6** *sl* short for **bullshit** **7** **a bull in a china shop** a clumsy person **8** **take the bull by the horns** to face and tackle a difficulty without shirking ▷ *adj* **9** male; masculine: *a bull elephant* **10** large; strong [OE *bula*]

bull² (bʊl) *n* a ludicrously self-contradictory or inconsistent statement [C17 from ?]

bull³ (bʊl) *n* a formal document issued by the pope [C13 from Med. L *bulla* seal attached to a bull, from L: round object]

Bull¹ (bʊl) *n* **the** the constellation Taurus, the second sign of the zodiac

Bull² (bʊl) *n* **1** **John** 1563–1628, English composer and organist **2** See **John Bull**

Bullamakanka (ˌbuːləməˈkæŋkə) *n Austral* an imaginary very remote place

bull ant *n* any of a number of large Australian ants having a powerful stinging bite. Also called: **bulldog ant**

bull bars *pl n* a large protective metal grille on the front of some vehicles, esp four-wheel-drive vehicles

bulldog (ˈbʊlˌdɒg) *n* a sturdy thickset breed of dog with an undershot jaw, short nose, broad head, and a muscular body

bulldog clip *n* a clip for holding papers together, consisting of two T-shaped metal clamps held in place by a cylindrical spring

bulldoze (ˈbʊlˌdəʊz) *vb* **bulldozes, bulldozing, bulldozed** (*tr*) **1** to move, demolish, flatten, etc, with a bulldozer **2** *inf* to force; push **3** *inf* to intimidate or coerce [C19 prob. from BULL¹ + DOSE]

bulldozer (ˈbʊlˌdəʊzə) *n* **1** a powerful tractor fitted with caterpillar tracks and a blade at the front, used for moving earth, rocks, etc **2** *inf* a person who bulldozes

bull dust *n Austral* **1** fine dust, as on roads in outback Australia **2** *sl* nonsense

bullet (ˈbʊlɪt) *n* **1a** a small metallic missile enclosed in a cartridge, used as the projectile of a gun, rifle, etc **1b** the entire cartridge **2** something resembling a bullet, esp in shape or effect **3** *stock exchange* a fixed interest security with a single maturity date **4** *commerce* a security that offers a fixed interest and matures on a fixed date **5** *commerce* **5a** the final repayment of a loan that repays the whole of the sum borrowed, as interim payments have been for interest only **5b** (*as modifier*): *a bullet loan* [C16 from F *boulette*, dim. of *boule* ball; see BOWL²]

bulletin (ˈbʊlɪtɪn) *n* **1** an official statement on a matter of public interest **2** a broadcast summary of the news **3** a periodical publication of an association, etc ▷ *vb* **4** (*tr*) to make known by bulletin [C17 from F, from It., from *bulletta*, dim. of *bulla* papal edict, BULL³]

bulletin board *n* **1** the US and Canad name for **notice board** **2** *computing* a facility on a computer network allowing any user to leave messages that can be read by any other user, and to download software and information to the user's own computer

bullet point *n* any of a number of items printed in a list, each after a centred dot, usually the most important

Bb

points in a longer piece of text

bulletproof ('bʊlɪt,pruːf) *adj* 1 not penetrable by bullets ▷ *vb* 2 (*tr*) to make bulletproof

bulletwood ('bʊlɪt,wʊd) *n* the tough durable wood of a tropical American tree, widely used for construction

bullfight ('bʊl,faɪt) *n* a traditional Spanish, Portuguese, and Latin American spectacle in which a matador baits and usually kills a bull in an arena > **'bull,fighter** *n* > **'bull,fighting** *n*

bullfinch ('bʊl,fɪntʃ) *n* 1 a common European finch: the male has a bright red throat and breast 2 any of various similar finches [C14 see BULL[1], FINCH]

bullfrog ('bʊl,frɒg) *n* any of various large frogs having a loud deep croak, esp the **American bullfrog**

bullhead ('bʊl,hɛd) *n* any of various small northern mainly marine fishes that have a large head covered with bony plates and spines

bull-headed *adj* blindly obstinate; stupid > **,bull-'headedly** *adv* > **,bull-'headedness** *n*

bullhorn ('bʊl,hɔːn) *n* the US and Canad name for **loud-hailer**

bullion ('bʊljən) *n* 1 gold or silver in mass 2 gold or silver in the form of bars and ingots, suitable for further processing [C14 from Anglo-F: mint, prob. from OF *bouillir* to boil, from L *bullīre*]

bullish ('bʊlɪʃ) *adj* 1 like a bull 2 *stock exchange* causing, expecting, or characterized by a rise in prices 3 *inf* cheerful and optimistic > **'bullishness** *n*

bull-necked *adj* having a short thick neck

bullock ('bʊlək) *n* 1 a gelded bull; steer ▷ *vb* 2 (*intr*) *Austral & NZ inf* to work hard and long [OE *bulluc*; see BULL[1], -OCK]

bullocky ('bʊləkɪ) *n, pl* **bullockies** *Austral & NZ* a bullock driver; teamster

bullring ('bʊl,rɪŋ) *n* an arena for bullfighting

bullroarer ('bʊl,rɔːrə) *n* a wooden slat attached to a thong that makes a roaring sound when the thong is whirled: used esp by native Australians in religious rites

bull's-eye *n* 1 the small central disc of a target, usually the highest valued area 2 a shot hitting this 3 *inf* something that exactly achieves its aim 4 a small circular or oval window or opening 5 a thick disc of glass set into a ship's deck, etc, to admit light 6 the glass boss at the centre of a sheet of blown glass 7a a small thick plano-convex lens used as a condenser 7b a lamp containing such a lens 8 a peppermint-flavoured boiled sweet

bullshit ('bʊl,ʃɪt) *taboo sl* ▷ *n* 1 exaggerated or foolish talk; nonsense 2 deceitful or pretentious talk 3 (in the British Army) exaggerated zeal, esp for ceremonial drill, cleaning, etc Usually shortened to **bull** ▷ *vb* **bullshits, bullshitting, bullshitted** *or* **bullshit** 4 (*intr*) to talk in an exaggerated or foolish manner 5 (*tr*) to talk bullshit to

bullswool ('bʊlz,wʊl) *n Austral & NZ inf* a euphemism for **bullshit** (sense 1)

bull terrier *n* a breed of terrier having a muscular body and thick neck, with a short smooth coat. See also **pit bull terrier, Staffordshire bull terrier**

bully ('bʊlɪ) *n, pl* **bullies** 1 a person who hurts, persecutes, or intimidates weaker people 2 a small New Zealand freshwater fish ▷ *vb* **bullies, bullying, bullied** 3 (when *tr*, often foll by *into*) to hurt, intimidate, or persecute (a weaker or smaller person), esp to make him do something ▷ *adj* 4 dashing; jolly: *my bully boy* 5 *inf* very good; fine ▷ *interj* 6 Also: **bully for you, him,** etc *inf* well done! bravo! [C16 (in the sense: sweetheart, hence fine fellow, hence swaggering coward): prob. from MDu. *boele* lover, from MHG *buole*]

bully beef *n* canned corned beef. Often shortened to **bully** [C19 *bully*, anglicized version of F *bouilli*, from *boeuf bouilli* boiled beef]

bully-off *hockey* ▷ *n* 1 the method by which a game is restarted after a stoppage. Two opposing players stand with the ball between them and alternately strike their sticks together and against the ground three times before trying to hit the ball ▷ *vb* **bully off** 2 (*intr, adv*) to restart play with a bully-off ▷ Often shortened to **bully** [C19 from ?]

bullyrag ('bʊlɪ,ræg) *vb* **bullyrags, bullyragging, bullyragged** (*tr*) to bully, esp by means of cruel practical jokes. Also: **ballyrag** [C18 from ?]

Bülow (*German* 'byːlo) *n* Prince **Bernhard von** ('bɛrnhart fɔn) 1849–1929, chancellor of Germany (1900–09)

bulrush ('bʊl,rʌʃ) *n* 1 a popular name for **reed mace** 2 a grasslike marsh plant used for making mats, chair seats, etc 3 a biblical word for **papyrus** (the plant) [C15 *bulrish*, *bul-* ?from BULL[1] + *rish* RUSH[2]]

bulwark ('bʊlwək) *n* 1 a wall or similar structure used as a fortification; rampart 2 a person or thing acting as a defence 3 (*often pl*) *naut* a solid vertical fencelike structure along the outward sides of a deck 4 a breakwater or mole ▷ *vb* 5 (*tr*) to defend or fortify with or as if with a bulwark [C15 via Du. from MHG *bolwerk*, from *bol* plank, BOLE + *werk* WORK]

Bulwer-Lytton ('bʊlwə'lɪtən) *n* See (1st Baron) **Lytton**

bum[1] (bʌm) *n Brit sl* the buttocks or anus [C14 from ?]

bum[2] (bʌm) *inf* ▷ *n* 1 a disreputable loafer or idler 2 a tramp; hobo ▷ *vb* **bums, bumming, bummed** 3 (*tr*) to get by begging; cadge: *to bum a lift* 4 (*intr*; often foll by *around*) to live by begging or as a vagrant or loafer 5 (*intr*; usually foll by *around*) to spend time to no good purpose; loaf; idle 6 **bum (someone) off** *US & Canad sl* to disappoint, annoy, or upset (someone) ▷ *adj* 7 (*prenominal*) of poor quality; useless [C19 prob. shortened from earlier *bummer* a loafer, prob. from G *bummeln* to loaf]

bum bag *n* a small bag worn on a belt, round the waist

bumbailiff (,bʌm'beɪlɪf) *n Brit derog* (formerly) an officer employed to collect debts and arrest debtors [C17 from BUM[1] + *bailiff*, so called because he follows hard behind debtors]

bumble ('bʌmbəl) *vb* **bumbles, bumbling, bumbled** 1 to speak or do in a clumsy, muddled, or inefficient way 2 (*intr*) to proceed unsteadily [C16 ? a blend of BUNGLE + STUMBLE] > **'bumbler** *n* > **'bumbling** *adj, n*

bumblebee ('bʌmbəl,biː) *or* **humblebee** *n* any large hairy social bee of temperate regions [C16 from *bumble* to buzz + BEE[1]]

bumf *or* **bumph** (bʌmf) *n Brit* 1 *inf, derog* official documents, forms, etc 2 *sl* toilet paper [C19 short for earlier *bumfodder*; see BUM[1]]

bummer ('bʌmə) *n sl* a disappointing or unpleasant experience

bump (bʌmp) *vb* 1 (when *intr*, usually foll by *against* or *into*) to knock or strike with a jolt 2 (*intr*; often foll by *along*) to travel or proceed in jerks and jolts 3 (*tr*) to hurt by knocking 4 *cricket* to bowl (a ball) so that it bounces high on pitching or (of a ball) to bounce high when bowled 5 (*tr*) *inf* to exclude (a ticket-holding passenger) from a flight as a result of overbooking ▷ *n* 6 an impact; knock; jolt; collision 7 a dull thud or other noise from an impact or collision 8 the shock of a blow or collision 9 a lump on the body caused by a blow 10 a protuberance, as on a road surface 11 any of the natural protuberances of the human skull, said by phrenologists to indicate underlying faculties and character ▷ See also **bump into, bump off, bump up** [C16 prob. imit.]

bumper[1] ('bʌmpə) *n* 1 a horizontal usually metal bar attached to the front or rear end of a car, lorry, etc, to protect against damage from impact 2 *cricket* a ball bowled so that it bounces high on pitching; bouncer

bumper[2] ('bʌmpə) *n* 1 a glass, tankard, etc, filled to the brim, esp as a toast 2 an unusually large or fine example of something ▷ *adj* 3 unusually large, fine, or abundant: *a bumper crop* [C17 (in the sense: a brimming glass): prob. from *bump* (obs. vb) to bulge; see BUMP]

bumph (bʌmf) *n* a variant spelling of **bumf**

bump into *vb (intr, prep) inf* to meet by chance; encounter unexpectedly

bumpkin ('bʌmpkɪn) *n* an awkward simple rustic person (esp in **country bumpkin**) [C16 ?from Du. *boomken* small tree, or from MDu. *boomekijn* small barrel]

bump off *vb (tr, adv) sl* to murder; kill

bumptious ('bʌmpʃəs) *adj* offensively self-assertive or conceited [C19 ?from BUMP + FRACTIOUS] > '**bumptiously** *adv* > '**bumptiousness** *n*

bump up *vb (tr, adv) inf* to raise or increase

bumpy ('bʌmpɪ) *adj* **bumpier, bumpiest 1** having an uneven surface **2** full of jolts; rough > '**bumpily** *adv* > '**bumpiness** *n*

bun (bʌn) *n* **1** a small roll, similar to bread but usually containing sweetening, currants, etc **2** any of various small round cakes **3** a hairstyle in which long hair is gathered into a bun shape at the back of the head [C14 from ?]

bunch (bʌntʃ) *n* **1** a number of things growing, fastened, or grouped together: *a bunch of grapes; a bunch of keys* **2** a collection; group: *a bunch of queries* **3** *inf* a group or company: *a bunch of boys* ▷ *vb* **4** (sometimes foll by *up*) to group or be grouped into a bunch [C14 from ?]

bunchberry ('bʌntʃ,bɛrɪ) *n pl* **bunchberries** a dwarf variety of dogwood native to North America, having red berries

bunchy ('bʌntʃɪ) *adj* **bunchier, bunchiest 1** composed of or resembling bunches **2** bulging

buncombe ('bʌŋkəm) *n* a variant spelling (esp US) of **bunkum**

Bundaberg ('bʊndə,bɜ:g) *n* a city in E Australia, near the E coast of Queensland: centre of a sugar-growing area, with a nearby deep-water port. Pop: 52 267 (1993)

Bundelkhand (,bʌndᵊl'kʌnd, -'xʌnd) *n* a region of central India: formerly native states, now mainly part of Madhya Pradesh

bundle ('bʌndᵊl) *n* **1** a number of things or a quantity of material gathered or loosely bound together: *a bundle of sticks*. Related adj: **fascicular 2** something wrapped or tied for carrying; package **3** *sl* a large sum of money **4 go a bundle on** *sl* to be extremely fond of **5** *biol* a collection of strands of specialized tissue such as nerve fibres **6** *bot* short for **vascular bundle 7 drop one's bundle** *sl* **7a** *Austral & NZ* to panic or give up hope **7b** NZ to give birth ▷ *vb* **bundles, bundling, bundled 8** (*tr*; often foll by *up*) to make into a bundle **9** (foll by *out, off, into,* etc) to go or cause to go, esp roughly or unceremoniously **10** (*tr*; usually foll by *into*) to push or throw, esp quickly and untidily **11** (*tr*) to give away (a relatively cheap product) when selling an expensive one to attract business: *software is often bundled with computing* **12** (*intr*) to sleep or lie in one's clothes on the same bed as one's betrothed: formerly a custom in New England, Wales, and elsewhere [C14 prob. from MDu. *bundel*; rel. to OE *bindele* bandage; see BIND, BOND] > '**bundler** *n*

bundle up *vb (adv)* **1** to dress (somebody) warmly and snugly **2** (*tr*) to make (something) into a bundle or bundles, esp by tying

bun fight *n Brit sl* **1** a tea party **2** *ironic* an official function

bung¹ (bʌŋ) *n* **1** a stopper, esp of cork or rubber, for a cask, etc **2** short for **bunghole** ▷ *vb (tr)* **3** (often foll by *up*) *inf* to close or seal with or as with a bung **4** *Brit sl* to throw; sling **5 bung it on** *Austral sl* to behave in a pretentious manner [C15 from MDu. *bonghe*]

bung² (bʌŋ) *adj Austral & NZ inf* **1** useless **2 go bung 2a** to fail or collapse **2b** to die [C19 from Abor.]

bungalow ('bʌŋgə,ləʊ) *n* a one-storey house, sometimes with an attic [C17 from Hindi *banglā* (house) of the Bengal type]

bungee jumping *or* **bungy jumping** ('bʌndʒɪ) *n* a sport in which a participant jumps from a high bridge, building, etc, secured only by a rubber cord attached to the ankles [C20 from *bungie*, slang for India rubber, of unknown origin]

bunghole ('bʌŋ,həʊl) *n* a hole in a cask, barrel, etc, through which liquid can be drained

bungle ('bʌŋgᵊl) *vb* **bungles, bungling, bungled 1** (*tr*) to spoil (an operation) through clumsiness, incompetence, etc ▷ *n* **2** a clumsy or unsuccessful performance [C16 ? of Scand. origin] > '**bungler** *n* > '**bungling** *adj, n*

bunion ('bʌnjən) *n* an inflamed swelling of the first joint of the big toe [C18 ?from obs. *bunny* a swelling, from ?]

bunk¹ (bʌŋk) *n* **1** a narrow shelflike bed fixed along a wall **2** short for **bunk bed 3** *inf* any place where one sleeps ▷ *vb* **4** (*intr*; often foll by *down*) to prepare to sleep: *he bunked down on the floor* **5** (*intr*) to occupy a bunk or bed [C19 prob. short for BUNKER]

bunk² (bʌŋk) *n inf* short for **bunkum** (sense 1)

bunk³ (bʌŋk) *n* **1** *Brit sl* a hurried departure, usually under suspicious circumstances (esp in **do a bunk**) ▷ *vb* **2** (usually foll by *off*) *Brit & NZ sl* to play truant from (school, work, etc) [C19 ?from BUNK¹ (in the sense: to occupy a bunk, hence a hurried departure)]

bunk bed *n* one of a pair of beds constructed one above the other to save space

bunker ('bʌŋkə) *n* **1** a large storage container or tank, as for coal **2** Also called (esp US and Canad): **sand trap** an obstacle on a golf course, usually a sand-filled hollow bordered by a ridge **3** an underground shelter with a bank and embrasures for guns above ground ▷ *vb* **4** (*tr*) *golf* **4a** to drive (the ball) into a bunker **4b** (*passive*) to have one's ball trapped in a bunker [C16 (in the sense: chest, box): from Scot. *bonkar*, from ?]

bunkhouse ('bʌŋk,haʊs) *n* (in the US and Canada) a building containing the sleeping quarters of workers on a ranch

bunkum *or* **buncombe** ('bʌŋkəm) *n* **1** empty talk; nonsense **2** *chiefly US* empty or insincere speechmaking by a politician [C19 after *Buncombe*, a county in North Carolina, alluded to in an inane speech by its Congressional representative Felix Walker (about 1820)]

Bb

bunny ('bʌnɪ) *n, pl* **bunnies 1** Also called: **bunny rabbit** a child's word for **rabbit** (sense 1) **2** Also called: **bunny girl** a night-club hostess whose costume includes rabbit-like tail and ears **3** *Austral sl* a mug; dupe [C17 from Scot. Gaelic *bun* scut of a rabbit]

Bunsen ('bʌnsᵊn; *German* 'bʊnzən) *n* **Robert Wilhelm** ('ro:bɛrt 'vɪlhɛlm) 1811–99, German chemist who with Kirchhoff developed spectrum analysis and discovered the elements caesium and rubidium. He invented the Bunsen burner and the ice calorimeter

Bunsen burner *n* a gas burner consisting of a metal tube with an adjustable air valve at the base [C19 after R. W. BUNSEN]

bunting¹ ('bʌntɪŋ) *n* **1** a coarse, loosely woven cotton fabric used for flags, etc **2** decorative flags, pennants, and streamers [C18 from ?]

bunting² ('bʌntɪŋ) *n* any of numerous seed-eating songbirds of the Old World and North America having short stout bills [C13 from ?]

buntline ('bʌntlɪn, -,laɪn) *n naut* one of several lines fastened to the foot of a square sail for hauling it up to the yard when furling [C17 from *bunt* centre of a sail + LINE¹ (sense 11)]

Buñuel (*Spanish* bu'ɲwel) *n* **Luis** (lwis) 1900–83, Spanish film director. He collaborated with Salvador Dali on the first surrealist films, *Un Chien andalou* (1929) and *L'Age d'or* (1930). His later films include *Viridiana* (1961), *Belle de jour* (1966), and *The Discreet Charm of the Bourgeoisie* (1972)

bunya ('bʌnjə) *n* a tall dome-shaped Australian coniferous tree having edible cones (**bunya nuts**) and thickish flattened needles. Also called: **bunya-bunya** [c19 from Abor.]

Bunyan ('bʌnjən) *n* **John** 1628–88, English preacher and writer, noted particularly for his allegory *The Pilgrim's Progress* (1678)

bunyip ('bʌnjɪp) *n Austral* a legendary monster said to inhabit swamps and lagoons [c19 from Abor.]

Buonaparte (bwona'parte) *n* the Italian spelling of **Bonaparte**

Buonarroti (*Italian* bwonar'roti) *n* See **Michelangelo**

buoy (bɔɪ; *US* 'buːɪ) *n* **1** a distinctively shaped and coloured float, anchored to the bottom, for designating moorings, navigable channels, or obstructions in a body of water. See also **life buoy** ▷ *vb* **2** (*tr; usually foll by up*) to prevent from sinking: *the life belt buoyed him up* **3** (*tr; usually foll by up*) to raise the spirits of; hearten **4** (*tr*) *naut* to mark (a channel or obstruction) with a buoy or buoys **5** (*intr*) to rise to the surface; float [c13 prob. of Gmc origin]

buoyancy ('bɔɪənsɪ) *n* **1** the ability to float in a liquid or to rise in liquid, air, or other gas **2** the tendency of a fluid to keep a body afloat **3** the ability to recover quickly after setbacks; resilience **4** cheerfulness

buoyant ('bɔɪənt) *adj* **1** able to float in or rise to the surface of a liquid **2** (of a liquid or gas) able to keep a body afloat **3** cheerful or resilient [c16 prob. from Sp. *boyante*, from *boyar* to float]

BUPA ('buːpə) *n acronym for* The British United Provident Association Limited: a company which provides private medical insurance

bupivacaine (bjuː'pɪvəˌkeɪn) *n* a local anaesthetic of long duration, used for nerve blocks [c20 ?from BU(TYL) + *pi(pecoloxylidide)* + *-vacaine*, from (NO)VOCAINE]

bur (bɜː) *n* **1** a seed vessel or flower head having hooks or prickles **2** any plant that produces burs **3** a person or thing that clings like a bur **4** a small surgical or dental drill ▷ *vb* **burs, burring, burred** **5** (*tr*) to remove burs from. Also: **burr** [c14 prob. from ON]

Buraydah *or* **Buraida** (bʊ'raɪdə) *n* a town and oasis in central Saudi Arabia. Pop: 69 940 (latest est)

Burbage ('bɜːbɪdʒ) *n* **1 James** ?1530–97, English actor and theatre manager, who built (1576) the first theatre in England **2** his son, **Richard** ?1567–1619, English actor, associated with Shakespeare

burble ('bɜːbᵊl) *vb* **burbles, burbling, burbled** **1** to make or utter with a bubbling sound; gurgle **2** (*intr; often foll by away or on*) to talk quickly and excitedly ▷ *n* **3** a bubbling or gurgling sound **4** a flow of excited speech [c14 prob. imit.] > **'burbler** *n*

burbot ('bɜːbət) *n, pl* **burbots** *or* **burbot** a freshwater gadoid food fish that has barbels around its mouth and occurs in Europe, Asia, and North America [c14 from OF *bourbotte*, from *bourbeter* to wallow in mud, from *bourbe* mud]

Burckhardt (*German* 'bʊrkhart) *n* **Jacob Christoph** 1818–97, Swiss art and cultural historian; author of *The Civilisation of the Renaissance in Italy* (1860)

burden[1] ('bɜːdᵊn) *n* **1** something that is carried; load **2** something that is exacting, oppressive, or difficult to bear. Related adj: **onerous** **3** *naut* **3a** the cargo capacity of a ship **3b** the weight of a ship's cargo ▷ *vb* (*tr*) **4** (*sometimes foll by up*) to put or impose a burden on; load **5** to weigh down; oppress [OE *byrthen*]

burden[2] ('bɜːdᵊn) *n* **1** a line of words recurring at the end of each verse of a song; chorus or refrain **2** the theme of a speech, book, etc **3** another word for **bourdon** [c16 from OF *bourdon* bass horn, droning sound, imit.]

burden of proof *n law* the obligation to provide evidence that will convince the court or jury of the truth of one's contention

burdensome ('bɜːdᵊnsəm) *adj* hard to bear

burdock ('bɜːˌdɒk) *n* a coarse weedy Eurasian plant having large heart-shaped leaves, tiny purple flowers surrounded by hooked bristles, and burlike fruits [c16 from BUR + DOCK[4]]

bureau ('bjʊərəʊ) *n, pl* **bureaus** *or* **bureaux** **1** *chiefly Brit* a writing desk with pigeonholes, drawers, etc, against which the writing surface can be closed when not in use **2** *US* a chest of drawers **3** an office or agency, esp one providing services for the public **4** a government department [c17 from F, orig.: type of cloth used for covering desks, from OF *burel*]

bureaucracy (bjʊə'rɒkrəsɪ) *n, pl* **bureaucracies** **1** a system of administration based upon organization into bureaus, division of labour, a hierarchy of authority, etc **2** government by such a system **3** government or other officials collectively **4** any administration in which action is impeded by unnecessary official procedures

bureaucrat ('bjʊərəˌkræt) *n* **1** an official in a bureaucracy **2** an official who adheres to bureaucracy, esp rigidly > **ˌbureau'cratic** *adj* > **ˌbureau'cratically** *adv*

bureaucratize *or* **bureaucratise** (bjʊə'rɒkrəˌtaɪz) *vb* **bureaucratizes, bureaucratizing, bureaucratized** *or* **bureaucratises, bureaucratising, bureaucratised** (*tr*) to administer by or transform into a bureaucracy > **buˌreaucrati'zation** *or* **buˌreaucrati'sation** *n*

bureaux ('bjʊərəʊz) *n* a plural of **bureau**

burette *or US* **buret** (bjʊ'rɛt) *n* a graduated glass tube with a stopcock on one end for dispensing and transferring known volumes of fluids, esp liquids [c15 from F, from OF *buire* ewer]

burg (bɜːg) *n* **1** *history* a fortified town **2** *US inf* a town or city [c18 (in the sense: fortress): from OHG *burg*]

burgage ('bɜːgɪdʒ) *n history* **1** (in England) tenure of land or tenement in a town or city, which originally involved a fixed money rent **2** (in Scotland) the tenure of land direct from the crown in Scottish royal burghs in return for watching and warding [c14 from Med. L *burgāgium*, from OE *burg*]

Burgas (*Bulgarian* bur'gas) *n* a port in SE Bulgaria on an inlet of the Black Sea. Pop: 195 255 (1999 est)

Burgenland (*German* 'bʊrgənˌlant) *n* a state of E Austria. Capital: Eisenstadt. Pop: 278 600 (2001). Area: 3965 sq km (1531 sq miles)

burgeon *or* **bourgeon** ('bɜːdʒən) *vb* **1** (*often foll by forth or out*) (of a plant) to sprout (buds) **2** (*intr; often foll by forth or out*) to develop or grow rapidly; flourish [c13 from OF *burjon*]

burger ('bɜːgə) *n inf* **a** short for **hamburger** **b** (*in combination*): *a cheeseburger*

burgess ('bɜːdʒɪs) *n* **1** (in England) a citizen, freeman, or inhabitant of a borough **2** *English history* a Member of Parliament from a borough, corporate town, or university [c13 from OF *burgeis*; see BOROUGH]

Burgess ('bɜːdʒɪs) *n* **1 Anthony**, real name *John Burgess Wilson*. 1917–93, English novelist and critic: his novels include *A Clockwork Orange* (1962), *Tremor of Intent* (1966), *Earthly Powers* (1980), and *Any Old Iron* (1989) **2 Guy** 1911–63, British spy, who fled to the Soviet Union (with Donald Maclean) in 1951

Burgess Shale *n* a bed of Cambrian sedimentary rock in the Rocky Mountains in British Columbia containing many unique invertebrate fossils [named after the *Burgess* Pass, where the bed is exposed]

burgh ('bʌrə) *n* **1** (in Scotland until 1975) a town, esp one incorporated by charter, that enjoyed a degree of self-government **2** an archaic form of **borough** [c14 Scot. form of BOROUGH] > **burghal** ('bɜːgᵊl) *adj*

burgher ('bɜːgə) *n* **1** a member of the trading or mercantile class of a medieval city **2** a respectable citizen; bourgeois **3** *arch* a citizen or inhabitant of a corporate town, esp on the Continent **4** *S African history* a citizen of the Cape Colony or of one of the Transvaal and Free State republics [c16 from G *Bürger* or Du. *burger* freeman of a BOROUGH]

Burghley *or* **Burleigh** ('bɜːlɪ) *n* **William Cecil**, 1st Baron

Burghley. 1520–98, English statesman: chief adviser to Elizabeth I; secretary of state (1558–72) and Lord High Treasurer (1572–98)

burghul (bɜːˈguːl) *n* another name for **bulgur**

burglar (ˈbɜːglə) *n* a person who commits burglary; housebreaker [C15 from Anglo-F, from Med. L *burglātor*, prob. from *burgāre* to thieve]

burglary (ˈbɜːglərɪ) *n, pl* **burglaries** the crime of entering a building as a trespasser to commit theft or another offence > **burglarious** (bɜːˈglɛərɪəs) *adj*

burgle (ˈbɜːgᵊl) *vb* **burgles, burgling, burgled** to commit burglary upon (a house, etc)

burgomaster (ˈbɜːgəˌmɑːstə) *n* the chief magistrate of a town in Austria, Belgium, Germany, or the Netherlands; mayor [C16 partial translation of Du. *burgemeester*; see BOROUGH, MASTER]

Burgos (ˈbɜːgɒs) *n* a city in N Spain, in Old Castile: cathedral. Pop: 161 984 (1998 est)

Burgoyne (bɜːˈgɔɪn) *n* **John** 1722–92, British general in the War of American Independence who was forced to surrender at Saratoga (1777)

Burgundy (ˈbɜːgəndɪ) *n pl* **-dies** 1 a region of E France famous for its wines, lying west of the Saône: formerly a semi-independent duchy; annexed to France in 1482. French name: **Bourgogne** 2 **Free County of** another name for **Franche-Comté** 3 a monarchy (1384–1477) of medieval Europe, at its height including the Low Countries, the duchy of Burgundy, and Franche-Comté 4 **Kingdom of** a kingdom in E France, established in the early 6th century AD, eventually including the later duchy of Burgundy, Franche-Comté, and the Kingdom of Provence: known as the Kingdom of Arles from the 13th century 5a any red or white wine produced in the region of Burgundy, around Dijon 5b any heavy red table wine 6 (*often not capital*) a blackish-purple to purplish-red colour > **Burgundian** (bɜːˈgʌndɪən) *adj, n*

burial (ˈbɛrɪəl) *n* the act of burying, esp the interment of a dead body [OE *byrgels* burial place, tomb; see BURY, -AL²]

burial ground *n* a graveyard or cemetery

burin (ˈbjʊərɪn) *n* 1 a chisel of tempered steel used for engraving metal, wood, or marble 2 *archaeol* a prehistoric flint tool [C17 from F, ?from It. *burino*, of Gmc origin]

burk (bɜːk) *n* a variant spelling of **berk**

burka (ˈbɜːkə) *n* a variant spelling of **burqa** [C19 from Arabic]

Burke (bɜːk) *n* 1 **Edmund** 1729–97, British Whig statesman, conservative political theorist, and orator, born in Ireland: defended parliamentary government and campaigned for a more liberal treatment of the American colonies; denounced the French Revolution 2 **Robert O'Hara** 1820–61, Irish explorer, who led the first expedition (1860–61) across Australia from south to north. He was accompanied by W. J. Wills, George Grey, and John King; King alone survived the return journey 3 **William** 1792–1829, Irish murderer and body snatcher; associate of William Hare

Burkina-Faso (bɜːˈkiːnəˈfæsəʊ) *n* an inland republic in W Africa: dominated by Mossi kingdoms (10th–19th centuries); French protectorate established in 1896; became an independent republic in 1960; consists mainly of a flat savanna plateau. Official language: French; Mossi and other African languages also widely spoken. Religion: mostly animist, with a large Muslim minority. Currency: franc. Capital: Ouagadougou. Pop: 12 272 000 (2001 est). Area: 273 200 sq km (105 900 sq miles). Former name (until 1984): **Upper Volta**
▹ www.primature.gov.bf

burl¹ (bɜːl) *n* 1 a small knot or lump in wool 2 a roundish warty outgrowth from certain trees ▹ *vb* 3 (*tr*) to remove the burls from (cloth) [C15 from OF *burle* tuft of wool, prob. ult. from LL *burra* shaggy cloth]

burl² *or* **birl** (bɜːl) *n inf* 1 *Scot, Austral, & NZ* an attempt; try (esp in **give it a burl**) 2 *Austral, & NZ* a ride in a car [C20 ?from BIRL in Scots sense: to spin or turn]

burlap (ˈbɜːlæp) *n* a coarse fabric woven from jute, hemp, or the like [C17 from *borel* coarse cloth, from OF *burel* (see BUREAU) + LAP¹]

Burleigh (ˈbɜːlɪ) *n* a variant spelling of **Burghley**

burlesque (bɜːˈlɛsk) *n* 1 an artistic work, esp literary or dramatic, satirizing a subject by caricaturing it 2 a ludicrous imitation or caricature 3 Also: **burlesk** *US & Canad theatre* a bawdy comedy show of the late 19th and early 20th centuries: the striptease eventually became one of its chief elements ▹ *adj* 4 of, relating to, or characteristic of a burlesque ▹ *vb* **burlesques, burlesquing, burlesqued** 5 to represent or imitate (a person or thing) in a ludicrous way; caricature [C17 from F, from It., from *burla* a jest, piece of nonsense] > **burˈlesquer** *n*

burley (ˈbɜːlɪ) *n* a variant spelling of **berley**

Burlington (ˈbɜːlɪŋtən) *n* 1 a city in S Canada on Lake Ontario, northeast of Hamilton. Pop: 136 976 (1996) 2 a city in NW Vermont on Lake Champlain: largest city in the state; University of Vermont (1791). Pop: 39 127 (1990)

burly (ˈbɜːlɪ) *adj* **burlier, burliest** large and thick of build; sturdy [C13 of Gmc origin] > **ˈburliness** *n*

Burma (ˈbɜːmə) *n* the former name (until 1989) of **Myanmar**

Burma Road *n* the route extending from Lashio in Burma (now Myanmar) to Chongqing in China, which was used by the Allies during World War II to supply military equipment to Chiang Kai-shek's forces in China

Burmese (bɜːˈmiːz) *adj also* **Burman** 1 of or denoting Burma (Myanmar), or its inhabitants, their customs, etc ▹ *n* 2 (*pl* **Burmese**) a native or inhabitant of Burma (Myanmar) 3 the language of the Burmese

burn¹ (bɜːn) *vb* **burns, burning, burnt** *or* **burned** 1 to undergo or cause to undergo combustion 2 to destroy or be destroyed by fire 3 to die or put to death by fire: *to burn at the stake* 4 (*tr*) to damage, injure, or mark by heat: *he burnt his hand; she was burnt by the sun* 5 to die or put to death by fire 6 (*intr*) to be or feel hot: *my forehead burns* 7 to smart or cause to smart: *brandy burns one's throat* 8 (*intr*) to feel strong emotion, esp anger or passion 9 (*tr*) to use for the purposes of light, heat, or power: *to burn coal* 10 (*tr*) to form by or as if by fire: *to burn a hole* 11 to char or become charred: *the potatoes are burning* 12 (*tr*) to brand or cauterize 13 to produce by or subject to heat as part of a process: *to burn charcoal* 14 **burn one's bridges** *or* **boats** to commit oneself to a particular course of action with no possibility of turning back 15 **burn one's fingers** to suffer from having meddled or interfered ▹ *n* 16 an injury caused by exposure to heat, electrical, chemical, or radioactive agents 17 a mark, e.g. on wood, caused by burning 18 a controlled use of rocket propellant, esp for a course correction 19 a hot painful sensation in a muscle, experienced during vigorous exercise 20 *sl* tobacco or a cigarette ▹ See also **burn out** [OE *beornan* (intr), *bærnan* (tr)]

Bb

burn² (bɜːn) *n Scot & N English* a small stream; brook [OE *burna*; rel. to ON *brunnr* spring]

Burne-Jones (bɜːndʒəʊnz) *n* Sir **Edward** 1833–98, English Pre-Raphaelite painter and designer of stained-glass windows and tapestries

burner (ˈbɜːnə) *n* 1 the part of a stove, lamp, etc, that produces flame or heat 2 an apparatus for burning something, as fuel or refuse

burnet (ˈbɜːnɪt) *n* 1 a plant of the rose family which has purple-tinged green flowers and leaves 2 **burnet rose** a very prickly Eurasian rose with white flowers and purplish-black fruits 3 a moth with red-spotted dark green wings and antennae with enlarged tips [C14 from OF *burnete*, var. of *brunete* BRUNETTE]

Burnet (bəˈnɛt, ˈbɜːnɪt) *n* 1 **Gilbert** 1643–1715, Scottish bishop and historian, who played a prominent role in the Glorious Revolution (1688–89); author of *The History of My Own Times* (2 vols: 1724 and 1734) **2** Sir (**Frank**) **Macfarlane** (mək'fɑːlən) 1899–1985, Australian physician and virologist, who shared a Nobel prize for physiology or medicine in 1960 with P. B. Medawar for their work in immunology **3** **Thomas** 1635–1715, English theologian who tried to reconcile science and religion in his *Sacred Theory of the Earth* (1680–89)

Burnett (bɜː'nɛt) *n* **Frances Hodgson** ('hɒdʒsən) 1849–1924, US novelist, born in England; author of *Little Lord Fauntleroy* (1886) and *The Secret Garden* (1911)

Burney ('bɜːnɪ) *n* **1** **Charles** 1726–1814, English composer and music historian, whose books include *A General History of Music* (1776–89) **2** his daughter, **Frances** known as *Fanny*; married name *Madame D'Arblay*. 1752–1840, English novelist and diarist: author of *Evelina* (1778) Her *Diaries and Letters* (1768–1840) are of historical interest

burning ('bɜːnɪŋ) *adj* **1** intense; passionate **2** urgent; crucial: *a burning problem*

burning bush *n* **1** a shrub of S Europe and Asia, whose glands release a volatile inflammable oil than can burn without harming the plant: identified as the bush from which God spoke to Moses (Exodus 3:2–4) **2** any of several shrubs or trees that have bright red fruits or seeds **3** any of several plants with a bright red autumn foliage

burning glass *n* a convex lens for concentrating the sun's rays to produce fire

burnish ('bɜːnɪʃ) *vb* **1** to make or become shiny or smooth by friction; polish ▷ *n* **2** a shiny finish; lustre [C14 *burnischen*, from OF *brunir* to make brown, from *brun* BROWN] > '**burnisher** *n*

Burnley ('bɜːnlɪ) *n* an industrial town in NW England, in E Lancashire. Pop: 74 661 (1991)

burnoose, burnous, *or* **burnouse** (bɜː'nuːs, -'nuːz) *n* a long circular cloak with a hood attached, worn esp by Arabs [C20 via F *burnous* from Ar. *burnus*, from Gk *birros* cloak]

burn out *vb* (*adv*) **1** to become or cause to become inoperative as a result of heat or friction: *the clutch burnt out* **2** (*intr*) (of a rocket, jet engine, etc) to cease functioning as a result of exhaustion of the fuel supply **3** (*tr; usually passive*) to destroy by fire **4** to become or cause to become exhausted through overwork or dissipation

Burns (bɜːnz) *n* **Robert** 1759–96, Scottish lyric poet. His verse, written mostly in dialect, includes love songs, nature poetry, and satires. *Auld Lang Syne* and *Tam o' Shanter* are among his best known poems

burnt (bɜːnt) *vb* **1** a past tense and past participle of **burn**[1] ▷ *adj* **2** affected by or as if by burning; charred

burnt offering *n* a sacrificial offering burnt, usually on an altar, to honour, propitiate, or supplicate a deity

burnt sienna *n* **1** a reddish-brown pigment obtained by roasting raw sienna ▷ *n, adj* **2** (of) a reddish-brown colour

burnt umber *n* **1** a brown pigment obtained by heating umber ▷ *n, adj* **2** (of) a dark brown colour

burp (bɜːp) *n* **1** *inf* a belch ▷ *vb* **2** (*intr*) *inf* to belch **3** (*tr*) to cause (a baby) to burp [C20 imit.]

burqa *or* **burka** ('bɜːkə) *n* a long enveloping garment worn by Muslim women in public [C19 from Arabic]

burr[1] (bɜː) *n* **1** a small power-driven hand-operated rotary file, esp for removing burrs or for machining recesses **2** a rough edge left on a workpiece after cutting, drilling, etc **3** a rough or irregular protuberance, such as a burl on a tree **4** a variant spelling of **bur** [C14 var. of BUR]

burr[2] (bɜː) *n* **1** an articulation of (r) characteristic of certain English dialects, esp the uvular fricative trill of Northumberland or the retroflex *r* of the West of England **2** a whirring sound ▷ *vb* **3** to pronounce (words) with a burr **4** (*intr*) to make a whirring sound [C18 either special use of BUR (in the sense: rough sound) or imit.]

Burrell ('bʌrəl) *n* **Paul** born 1958, British butler and confidant to Diana, Princess of Wales. After her death he was charged with but (2003) acquitted of stealing from her estate. His book, *A Royal Duty* (2003), revealed intimate details of her life

Burren ('bʌrən) *n* **the** a limestone area on the North Clare coast in the Irish Republic, famous for its wild flowers, caves, and dolmens

burrito (bə'riːtəʊ) *n, pl* **burritos** *Mexican cookery* a tortilla folded over a filling of minced beef, chicken, cheese, or beans [C20 from Mexican Sp., from Sp.: literally, a young donkey]

burro ('bʊrəʊ) *n, pl* **burros** a donkey, esp one used as a pack animal [C19 Sp., from Port., from *burrico*]

Burroughs ('bʌrəʊz) *n* **1** **Edgar Rice** 1875–1950, US novelist, author of the *Tarzan* stories **2** **William S(eward)** 1914–97, US novelist, noted for his experimental works exploring themes of drug addiction, violence, and homosexuality. His novels include *Junkie* (1953), *The Naked Lunch* (1959), and *Interzone* (1989)

burrow ('bʌrəʊ) *n* **1** a hole dug in the ground by a rabbit or other small animal **2** a small snug place affording shelter or retreat ▷ *vb* **3** to dig (a burrow) in, through, or under (ground) **4** (*intr; often foll by through*) to move through by or as by digging **5** (*intr*) to hide or live in a burrow **6** (*intr*) to delve deeply: *he burrowed into his pockets* **7** to hide (oneself) [C13 prob. var. of BOROUGH] > '**burrower** *n*

burry ('bɜːrɪ) *adj* **burrier, burriest** **1** full of or covered in burs **2** resembling burs; prickly

bursa ('bɜːsə) *n, pl* **bursae** (-siː) *or* **bursas** **1** *anat* a small fluid-filled sac that reduces friction, esp at joints **2** *zool* any saclike cavity or structure [C19 from Med. L: bag, pouch, from Gk: skin, hide; see PURSE] > '**bursal** *adj*

Bursa ('bɜːsə) *n* a city in NW Turkey: founded in the 2nd century BC; seat of Bithynian kings. Pop: 1 066 559 (1997). Former name: **Brusa**

bursar ('bɜːsə) *n* **1** a treasurer of a school, college, or university **2** *chiefly Scot & NZ* a student holding a bursary [C13 from Med. L *bursārius* keeper of the purse, from *bursa* purse]

bursary ('bɜːsərɪ) *n, pl* **bursaries** **1** Also called: '**bursar,ship** a scholarship awarded esp in Scottish and New Zealand schools and universities **2** *Brit* the treasury of a college, etc > **bursarial** (bɜː'sɛərɪəl) *adj*

bursitis (bɜː'saɪtɪs) *n* inflammation of a bursa

burst (bɜːst) *vb* **bursts, bursting, burst** **1** to break or cause to break open or apart suddenly and noisily; explode **2** (*intr*) to come, go, etc, suddenly and forcibly: *he burst into the room* **3** (*intr*) to be full to the point of breaking open **4** (*intr*) to give vent (to) suddenly or loudly: *to burst into song* **5** (*tr*) to cause or suffer the rupture of: *to burst a blood vessel* ▷ *n* **6** a sudden breaking open; explosion **7** a break; breach; rupture **8** a sudden display or increase of effort; spurt: *a burst of speed* **9** a sudden and violent emission, occurrence, or outbreak: *a burst of applause* **10** a volley of fire from a weapon [OE *berstan*]

burthen ('bɜːðən) *n, vb* an archaic word for **burden**[1] > '**burthensome** *adj*

burton ('bɜːtᵊn) *n* **go for a burton** *Brit sl* **a** to be broken, useless, or lost **b** to die [C20 from ?]

Burton ('bɜːtᵊn) *n* **1** Sir **Richard Francis** 1821–90, English explorer, Orientalist, and writer who discovered Lake Tanganyika with John Speke (1858); produced the first unabridged translation of *The Thousand Nights and a Night* (1885–88) **2** **Richard**, real name *Richard Jenkins*. 1925–84, Welsh stage and film actor: films include *Becket* (1964), *Who's Afraid of Virginia Woolf?* (1966), and *Equus* (1977) **3** **Robert**, pen name *Democritus Junior*. 1577–1640, English clergyman, scholar, and writer, noted for his *Anatomy of Melancholy* (1621) **4 Tim** born 1958, US film director whose work includes *Beetlejuice* (1988), *Batman* (1989), *Ed Wood* (1994), and *Planet of the Apes* (2001)

Burton-upon-Trent *n* a town in W central England, in E Staffordshire: famous for brewing. Pop: 60 525 (1991)

Burundi (bəˈrʊndɪ) *n* a republic in E central Africa: inhabited chiefly by the Hutu, Tutsi, and Twa (Pygmy); made part of German East Africa in 1899; part of the Belgian territory of Ruanda-Urundi from 1923 until it became independent in 1962; ethnic violence has continued since independence; consists mainly of high plateaus along the main Nile-Congo dividing range, dropping rapidly to the Great Rift Valley in the west. Official languages: Kirundi and French. Religion: Christian majority. Currency: Burundi franc. Capital: Bujumbura. Pop: 6 224 000 (2001 est). Area: 27 731 sq km (10 707 sq miles). Former name (until 1962): **Urundi** > **Buˈrundian** *adj, n*

▹ http://burundi.gov.bi

bury (ˈbɛrɪ) *vb* **buries, burying, buried** (*tr*) **1** to place (a corpse) in a grave; inter **2** to place in the earth and cover with soil **3** to cover from sight; hide **4** to embed; sink: *to bury a nail in plaster* **5** to occupy (oneself) with deep concentration; engross: *to be buried in a book* **6** to dismiss from the mind; abandon: *to bury old hatreds* [OE *byrgan*]

Bury (ˈbɛrɪ) *n* **1** a town in NW England, in Bury unitary authority, Greater Manchester: an early textile centre. Pop: 62 633 (1991) **2** a unitary authority in NW England, in Greater Manchester. Pop: 180 612 (2001). Area: 99 sq km (38 sq miles)

Buryat Republic *or* **Buryatia** (bʊəˈjɑːtɪə; *Russian* buˈrjaːtija) *n* a constituent republic of SE central Russia, on Lake Baikal: mountainous, with forests covering over half the total area. Capital: Ulan-Ude. Pop: 1 035 000 (2000 est). Area: 351 300 sq km (135 608 sq miles)

Bury St Edmunds (ˈbɛrɪ sənt ˈɛdməndz) *n* a market town in E England, in Suffolk. Pop: 31 237 (1991)

bus (bʌs) *n, pl* **buses** *or* **busses** **1** a large motor vehicle designed to carry passengers between stopping places along a regular route. More formal name: **omnibus** **2** (*modifier*) of or relating to a bus or buses: *a bus driver; a bus station* **3** *inf* a car or aircraft, esp one that is old and shaky **4** *electronics, computers* short for **busbar** **5** *astronautics* a platform in a space vehicle used for various experiments and processes **6** **miss the bus** to miss an opportunity ▹ *vb* **buses, busing, bused** *or* **busses, bussing, bussed** **7** to travel or transport by bus **8** *chiefly US* to transport (children) by bus from one area to another in order to create racially integrated schools [c19 short for OMNIBUS]

▹ http://routesinternational.com/buslines.htm

▹ www.busesintl.com

busbar (ˈbʌzˌbɑː) *n* **1** an electrical conductor usually used to make a common connection between several circuits **2** a group of such electrical conductors maintained at a low voltage, used for carrying data in binary form between the various parts of a computer or its peripherals

busby (ˈbʌzbɪ) *n, pl* **busbies** **1** a tall fur helmet worn by hussars **2** (not in official usage) another name for **bearskin** (the hat) [c18 ?from a proper name]

Busby (ˈbʌzbɪ) *n* Sir **Matthew**, known as *Matt*. 1909–94, British footballer. He managed Manchester United (1946–69)

bush[1] (bʊʃ) *n* **1** a dense woody plant, smaller than a tree, with many branches arising from the lower part of the stem; shrub **2** a dense cluster of such shrubs; thicket **3** something resembling a bush, esp in density: *a bush of hair* **4** (often preceded by *the*) an uncultivated or sparsely settled area, covered with trees or shrubs, which can vary from open, shrubby country to dense rainforest **5** a forested area; woodland **6** *Canad* Also called: **bush lot, woodlot** an area on a farm on which timber is grown and cut **7** (often preceded by *the*) *inf* the countryside, as opposed to the city: *out in the bush* **8** *obs* a bunch of ivy hung as a vintner's sign in front of a tavern **9** **beat about the bush** to avoid the point at issue; prevaricate ▹ *adj* **10** *Austral & NZ inf* rough-and-ready **11** *US & Canad inf* unprofessional, unpolished, or second-rate **12** **go bush** *inf* **12a** *Austral & NZ* to abandon city amenities and live rough **12b** *Austral* to go into hiding ▹ *vb* **13** (*intr*) to grow thick and bushy **14** (*tr*) to cover, decorate, support, etc, with bushes **15** **bush it** *Austral* to camp out in the bush [c13 of Gmc origin]

bush[2] (bʊʃ) *n* **1** a thin metal sleeve or tubular lining serving as a bearing ▹ *vb* **2** to fit a bush to (a bearing, etc) [c15 from MDu. *busse* box, bush; rel. to LL *buxis* BOX[1]]

Bush (bʊʃ) *n* **1 George** born 1924, US Republican politician; vice president of the US (1981–89): 41st president of the US (1989–93) **2** his son, **George W(alker)** born 1946, US Republican statesman: 43rd president of the US (from 2001)

bushbaby (ˈbʊʃˌbeɪbɪ) *n, pl* **bushbabies** an agile nocturnal arboreal primate occurring in Africa south of the Sahara. It has large eyes and ears and a long tail. Also called: **galago**

bush-bash *vb Austral sl* (*intr*) **1** to clear scrubland **2** to drive through thick scrubland. Also called: **scrub-bash**

bushbuck (ˈbʊʃˌbʌk) *or* **boschbok** (ˈbɒʃˌbʌk) *n, pl* **bushbucks, bushbuck** *or* **boschboks, boschbok** a small nocturnal spiral-horned antelope of the bush and tropical forest of Africa

bush carpenter *n Austral & NZ sl* a rough-and-ready unskilled workman

bushed (bʊʃt) *adj inf* **1** (*postpositive*) extremely tired; exhausted **2** *Canad* mentally disturbed from living in isolation **3** *Austral & NZ* lost or bewildered, as in the bush

bushel (ˈbʊʃəl) *n* **1** a British unit of dry or liquid measure equal to 8 Imperial gallons. 1 Imperial bushel is equivalent to 0.036 37 cubic metres **2** a US unit of dry measure equal to 64 US pints. 1 US bushel is equivalent to 0.035 24 cubic metres **3** a container with a capacity equal to either of these quantities **4** *US inf* a large amount **5** **hide one's light under a bushel** to conceal one's abilities or good qualities [c14 from OF *boissel*]

bushfire (ˈbʊʃˌfaɪə) *n* an uncontrolled fire in the bush; a scrub or forest fire

bushfly (ˈbʊʃˌflaɪ) *n pl* **bushflies** any of various small black dipterous flies of Australia that breed in faeces and dung

bush house *n chiefly Austral* a shed or hut in the bush or a garden

Bushido (ˌbuːʃɪˈdəʊ) *n* (*sometimes not cap*) the feudal code of the Japanese samurai [c19 from Japanese *bushi* warrior + *dō* way]

▹ http://mcel.pacificu.edu/as/students/bushido/bindex.html

▹ http://www.bushido-online.com/

bushie (ˈbʊʃɪ) *n* a variant spelling of **bushy**[2]

bushing (ˈbʊʃɪŋ) *n* **1** another word for **bush**[2] **2** an adaptor used to connect pipes of different sizes **3** a layer of electrical insulation enabling a live conductor to pass through an earthed wall, etc

Bushire (bjuːˈʃaɪə) *n* a port in SW Iran, on the Persian Gulf. Pop: 143 641 (1996). Persian name: **Bushehr** (buˈʃehr)

bush jacket *or* **shirt** *n* a casual jacket or shirt having four patch pockets and a belt

bushland (ˈbʊʃˌlænd) *n* uncultivated land (esp in Australia) that is covered with trees, shrubs, or other natural vegetation

bush lawyer *n Austral & NZ* **1** any of several trailing plants with sharp hooks **2** *inf* a person who gives legal

Bb

opinions but is not qualified to do so
bush line *n* an airline operating in the bush country of Canada's northern regions
bush lot *n Canad* another name for **bush**[1] (sense 6)
bushman ('bʊʃmən) *n, pl* **bushmen** *Austral & NZ* a person who lives or travels in the bush, esp one versed in bush lore
Bushman ('bʊʃmən) *n, pl* **Bushmen** a member of a hunting and gathering people of southern Africa [C18 from Afrik. *boschjesman*]
bushmaster ('bʊʃ,mɑːstə) *n* a large greyish-brown highly venomous snake of tropical America
bushmeat ('bʊʃ,miːt) *n* meat taken from any animal native to African forests, including species that may be endangered or not usually eaten outside Africa
bush pilot *n Canad* a pilot who operates in the bush country
bushranger ('bʊʃ,reɪndʒə) *n* **1** *Austral* (formerly) an outlaw living in the bush **2** *US* a person who lives away from civilization
bush singlet *n NZ* a black woollen singlet often worn by farm labourers
bush tea *n* **1** a leguminous shrub of southern Africa **2** a beverage prepared from the dried leaves of such a plant
bush telegraph *n* a means of spreading rumour, gossip, etc
Bushveld ('bʊʃ,fɛlt, -,vɛlt) *n* **the** an area of low altitude in NE South Africa, having scrub vegetation. Also called: **Lowveld**
bushwhack ('bʊʃ,wæk) *vb* **1** *(tr) US, Canad, & Austral* to ambush **2** *(intr) US, Canad, & Austral* to cut or beat one's way through thick woods **3** *(intr) US, Canad, & Austral* to range or move around in woods or the bush **4** *(intr) NZ* to work in the bush **5** *(intr) US & Canad* to fight as a guerrilla in wild regions
bushwhacker ('bʊʃ,wækə) *n* **1** *US, Canad, & Austral* a person who travels around or lives in thinly populated woodlands **2** *Austral sl* an unsophisticated person **3** *NZ* a person who works in the bush **4** a Confederate guerrilla in the American Civil War **5** *US* any guerrilla
bushy[1] ('bʊʃɪ) *adj* **bushier, bushiest** **1** covered or overgrown with bushes **2** thick and shaggy > '**bushily** *adv* > '**bushiness** *n*
bushy[2] *or* **bushie** ('bʊʃɪ) *n, pl* **bushies** *Austral inf* **1** a person who lives in the bush **2** an unsophisticated uncouth person
business ('bɪznɪs) *n* **1** a trade or profession **2** the purchase and sale of goods and services **3** a commercial or industrial establishment **4** commercial activity; dealings (esp in **do business**) **5** volume of commercial activity: *business is poor today* **6** commercial policy: *overcharging is bad business* **7** proper or rightful concern or responsibility (often in **mind one's own business**) **8** a special task; assignment **9** an affair; matter **10** serious work or activity: *get down to business* **11** a difficult or complicated matter **12** *theatre* an incidental action performed by an actor for dramatic effect **13** **do the business** *inf* to achieve what is required: *it tastes vile, but it does the business* **14** **mean business** to be in earnest [OE *bisignis* solicitude, from *bisig* BUSY + *-nis* -NESS]
business casual *n inf* a style of casual clothing worn by businesspeople at work instead of more formal attire
business college *n* a college providing courses in secretarial studies, business management, accounting, commerce, etc
businesslike ('bɪznɪs,laɪk) *adj* efficient and methodical
businessman ('bɪznɪs,mæn, -mən) *or (fem)* **businesswoman** *n, pl* **businessmen** *or* **businesswomen** a person engaged in commercial or industrial business, esp as an owner or executive
business park *n* an area specially designated and landscaped to accommodate offices, warehouses, etc
businessperson ('bɪznɪs,pɜrsən) *n, pl* **businesspeople** *or* **businesspersons** a person engaged in commercial or industrial business, esp as an owner or executive
business plan *n* a detailed plan setting out the objectives of a business, the strategy and tactics planned to achieve them, and the expected profits
business process re-engineering *n* restructuring an organization by means of a reassessment of its core processes and predominant competencies. Abbrev: **BPR**
business school *n* an institution that offers courses in aspects of business, such as marketing, finance, and law, designed to train managers in industry and commerce to do their jobs effectively
businesswoman ('bɪznɪs,wʊmən) *n, pl* **businesswomen** a woman engaged in commercial or industrial business, esp as an owner or executive
busk (bʌsk) *vb (intr) Brit* to make money singing, playing an instrument, performing, or dancing in public places [C20 ?from Sp. *buscar* to look for] > '**busker** *n*
buskin ('bʌskɪn) *n* **1** (formerly) a sandal-like covering for the foot and leg, reaching the calf **2** a thick-soled laced half-boot worn esp by actors of ancient Greece **3** (usually preceded by *the*) *chiefly literary.* tragic drama [C16 ?from Sp. *borzeguí;* rel. to OF *bouzequin*]
busman's holiday ('bʌsmənz) *n inf* a holiday spent doing the same as one does at work [C20 from a bus driver having a driving holiday]
Busra *or* **Busrah** ('bʌsrə) *n* variant spellings of **Basra**
buss (bʌs) *n, vb* an archaic or dialect word for **kiss** [C16 prob. imit.]
Buss (bʌs) *n* **Frances Mary** 1827–94, British educationalist; a pioneer of secondary education for girls, who campaigned for women's admission to university
Bussell ('bʌsəl) *n* **Darcey** (**Andrea**) born 1969, British ballet dancer, principal ballerina with the Royal Ballet from 1989
bust[1] (bʌst) *n* **1** the chest of a human being, esp a woman's bosom **2** a sculpture of the head, shoulders, and upper chest of a person [C17 from F, from It. *busto* a sculpture, from ?]
bust[2] (bʌst) *inf* ▷ *vb* **busts, busting, busted** *or* **bust** **1** to burst or break **2** to make or become bankrupt **3** *(tr)* (of the police) to raid, search, or arrest **4** *(tr) US & Canad* to demote, esp in military rank ▷ *n* **5** a raid, search, or arrest by the police **6** *chiefly US* a punch **7** *US & Canad* a failure, esp bankruptcy **8** a drunken party ▷ *adj* **9** broken **10** bankrupt **11** **go bust** to become bankrupt [C19 from a dialect pronunciation of BURST]
bustard ('bʌstəd) *n* a large terrestrial bird inhabiting open regions of the Old World. It has long strong legs, a heavy body, a long neck, and speckled plumage [C15 from OF *bistarde,* from L *avis tarda* slow bird]
bustier ('buːstɪeɪ) *n* a type of close-fitting usually strapless top worn by women
bustle[1] ('bʌsᵊl) *vb* **bustles, bustling, bustled** **1** (when *intr,* often foll by *about*) to hurry or cause to hurry with a great show of energy or activity ▷ *n* **2** energetic and noisy activity [C16 prob. from obs. *buskle* to make energetic preparation] > '**bustling** *adj*
bustle[2] ('bʌsᵊl) *n* a cushion or framework worn by women in the late 19th century at the back in order to expand the skirt [C18 from ?]
bust-up *inf* ▷ *n* **1** a quarrel, esp a serious one ending a friendship, etc **2** *Brit* a disturbance or brawl ▷ *vb* **bust up** *(adv)* **3** *(intr)* to quarrel and part **4** *(tr)* to disrupt (a meeting), esp violently
busy ('bɪzɪ) *adj* **busier, busiest** **1** actively or fully engaged; occupied **2** crowded with or characterized by activity **3** *chiefly US & Canad* (of a room, telephone line, etc) in use; engaged **4** overcrowded with detail: *a busy painting* **5** meddlesome; inquisitive ▷ *vb* **busies, busying, busied** **6** *(tr)* to make or keep (someone, esp oneself) busy [OE *bisig*] > '**busily** *adv* > '**busyness** *n*

busybody ('bɪzɪˌbɒdɪ) *n, pl* **busybodies** a meddlesome, prying, or officious person
busy Lizzie ('lɪzɪ) *n* a flowering plant that has pink, red, or white flowers and is often grown as a pot plant
but[1] (bʌt; *unstressed* bət) *conj (coordinating)* **1** contrary to expectation: *he cut his knee but didn't cry* **2** in contrast; on the contrary: *I like opera but my husband doesn't* **3** *(usually used after a negative)* other than: *we can't do anything but wait* ▷ *conj (subordinating)* **4** *(usually used after a negative)* without it happening: *we never go out but it rains* **5** (foll by *that*) except that: *nothing is impossible but that we live forever* **6** *arch* if not; unless ▷ *prep* **7** except; save: *they saved all but one* **8 but for** were it not for: *but for you, we couldn't have managed* ▷ *adv* **9** just; merely: *he was but a child* **10** *dialect & Austral* though; however: *it's a rainy day; warm, but* ▷ *n* **11** an objection (esp in **ifs and buts**) [OE *būtan* without, outside, except, from *be* BY + *ūtan* OUT]
but[2] (bʌt) *n Scot* the outer room of a two-roomed cottage ▷ Cf **ben**[1] [C18 from *but* (adv) outside; see BUT[1]]
butadiene (ˌbju:tə'daɪi:n) *n* a colourless flammable gas used mainly in the manufacture of synthetic rubbers. Formula: CH_2:CHCH:CH_2. Systematic name: **buta-1,3-diene** [C20 from BUTA(NE) + DI-[1] + -ENE]
butane ('bju:teɪn, bju:'teɪn) *n* a colourless flammable gaseous alkane used mainly in the manufacture of rubber and fuels. Formula: C_4H_{10} [C20 from BUT(YL) + -ANE]
butanoic acid (ˌbju:tə'nəʊɪk) *n* a carboxylic acid that produces the smell in rancid butter. Formula: $CH_3(CH_2)_2COOH$. Also called: **butyric acid** [C20 from BUTAN(E) + -OIC]
butanol ('bju:təˌnɒl) *n* a colourless substance existing in four isomeric forms. The three liquid isomers are used as solvents and in the manufacture of organic compounds. Formula: C_4H_9OH. Also called: **butyl alcohol**
butanone ('bju:təˌnəʊn) *n* a colourless flammable liquid used as a resin solvent, and paint remover, and in lacquers, adhesives, etc Formula: $CH_3COC_2H_5$
butch (bʊtʃ) *sl* ▷ *adj* **1** (of a woman or man) markedly or aggressively masculine ▷ *n* **2** a lesbian who is noticeably masculine **3** a strong rugged man [C18 back formation from BUTCHER]
butcher ('bʊtʃə) *n* **1** a retailer of meat **2** a person who slaughters or dresses meat **3** an indiscriminate or brutal murderer ▷ *vb (tr)* **4** to slaughter or dress (animals) for meat **5** to kill indiscriminately or brutally **6** to make a mess of; botch [C13 from OF *bouchier*, from *bouc* he-goat]
butcherbird ('bʊtʃəˌbɜ:d) *n* **1** a shrike, esp of the genus *Lanius* **2** any of several Australian magpies that impale their prey on thorns
butcher's-broom *n* an evergreen shrub with stiff prickle-tipped flattened green stems, formerly used for making brooms
butchery ('bʊtʃərɪ) *n, pl* **butcheries** **1** the business of a butcher **2** wanton and indiscriminate slaughter **3** a slaughterhouse
Bute[1] [1](bju:t) *n* an island off the coast of SW Scotland, in Argyll and Bute council area: situated in the Firth of Clyde, separated from the Cowal peninsula by the **Kyles of Bute** Chief town: Rothesay. Pop: 8000 (latest est) Area: 121 sq km (47 sq miles)
Bute[2] (bju:t) *n* **John Stuart**, 3rd Earl of Bute. 1713–92, British Tory statesman; prime minister (1762–63)
Butenandt (*German* 'butənant) *n* **Adolf Frederick Johann** 1903–95, German organic chemist. He shared the Nobel prize for chemistry (1939) for his pioneering work on sex hormones
Buteshire ('bju:tˌʃɪə, -ʃə) *n* (until 1975) a county of SW Scotland, consisting of islands in the Firth of Clyde and Kilbrannan Sound: formerly part of Strathclyde region (1975–96), now part of Argyll and Bute council area
Buteyko method (ˌbu:'teɪkəʊ) *n* a breath control technique used to prevent hyperventilation and treat asthma without drugs [C20 named after Konstantin P. *Buteyko* (born 1923), Russian physician]
Buthelezi (ˌbʊtə'leɪzɪ) *n* **Mangosouthu Gatsha** (ˌmæŋgəʊ'su:tu: 'gætʃə), known as *Chief Buthelezi*. born 1928, Zulu leader, chief minister of the KwaZulu territory of South Africa from 1970 until its abolition in 1994; founder of the Inkatha movement and advocate of Zulu autonomy; minister of home affairs from 1994
butler ('bʌtlə) *n* the male servant of a household in charge of the wines, table, etc: usually the head servant [C13 from OF, from *bouteille* BOTTLE]
Butler ('bʌtlə) *n* **1 Joseph** 1692–1752, English bishop and theologian, author of *Analogy of Religion* (1736) **2 Josephine (Elizabeth)** 1828–1906, British social reformer, noted esp for her campaigns against state regulation of prostitution **3 Reg**, full name *Reginald Cotterell Butler*. 1913–81, British metal sculptor; his works include *The Unknown Political Prisoner* (1953) **4 R(ichard) A(usten)**, Baron Butler of Saffron Walden, known as *Rab Butler*. 1902–82, British Conservative politician: Chancellor of the Exchequer (1951–55); Home Secretary (1957–62); Foreign Secretary (1963–64) **5 Samuel** 1612–80, English poet and satirist; author of *Hudibras* (1663–78) **6 Samuel** 1835–1902, British novelist, noted for his satirical work *Erewhon* (1872) and his autobiographical novel *The Way of All Flesh* (1903)
butlery ('bʌtlərɪ) *n, pl* **butleries** **1** a butler's room **2** another name for **buttery**[2]
butt[1] (bʌt) *n* **1** the thicker or blunt end of something, such as the end of the stock of a rifle **2** the unused end of something, esp of a cigarette; stub **3** *inf, chiefly US & Canad* the buttocks **4** *US* a slang word for **cigarette** **5** *building* short for **butt joint** [C15 (in the sense: thick end of something, buttock): rel. to OE *buttuc* end, ridge]
butt[2] (bʌt) *n* **1** a person or thing that is the target of ridicule, wit, etc **2** *shooting, archery* **2a** a mound of earth behind the target that stops bullets or wide shots **2b** the target itself **2c** *(pl)* the target range **3** a low barrier behind which sportsmen shoot game birds, esp grouse ▷ *vb* **4** (usually foll by *on* or *against*) to lie or be placed end on to; abut [C14 (in the sense: mark for archery practice): from OF *but*]
butt[3] (bʌt) *vb* **1** to strike or push (something) with the head or horns **2** *(intr)* to project; jut **3** *(intr;* foll by *in* or *into)* to intrude, esp into a conversation; interfere ▷ *n* **4** a blow with the head or horns [C12 from OF *boter*, of Gmc origin]
butt[4] (bʌt) *n* a large cask for storing wine or beer [C14 from OF *botte*, from LL *buttis* cask]
butte (bju:t) *n US & Canad* an isolated steep flat-topped hill [C19 F, from OF *bute* mound behind a target; see BUTT[2]]
butter ('bʌtə) *n* **1** an edible fatty whitish-yellow solid made from cream by churning **2** any substance with a butter-like consistency, such as peanut butter **3 look as if butter wouldn't melt in one's mouth** to look innocent, although probably not so ▷ *vb (tr)* **4** to put butter on or in **5** to flatter ▷ See also **butter up** [OE *butere*, from L, from Gk *bouturon*, from *bous* cow + *turos* cheese]
▷ www.butterisbest.com
▷ www.foodsci.uoguelph.ca/dairyedu/butter.html
▷ www.cooking.com
butter bean *n* a variety of lima bean that has large pale flat edible seeds
butterbur ('bʌtəˌbɜ:) *n* a plant of the composite family with fragrant whitish or purple flowers, and large leaves formerly used to wrap butter
buttercup ('bʌtəˌkʌp) *n* any of various yellow-flowered plants of the genus *Ranunculus* of Europe, Asia, and North America
butterfat ('bʌtəˌfæt) *n* the fatty substance of milk from

Bb

which butter is made, consisting of a mixture of glycerides

Butterfield (ˈbʌtəˌfiːld) *n* **William** 1814–1900, British architect of the Gothic Revival; his buildings include Keble College, Oxford (1870) and All Saints, Margaret Street, London (1849–59)

butterfingers (ˈbʌtəˌfɪŋgəz) *n (functioning as sing) inf* a person who drops things inadvertently or fails to catch things > ˈ**butterˌfingered** *adj*

butterfish (ˈbʌtəˌfɪʃ) *n, pl* **butterfish** *or* **butterfishes** any of several species of fishes having a slippery skin

butterflies (ˈbʌtəˌflaɪz) *pl n inf* tremors in the stomach region due to nervousness

butterfly (ˈbʌtəˌflaɪ) *n, pl* **butterflies** **1** any diurnal insect that has a slender body with clubbed antennae and typically rests with the wings (often brightly coloured) closed over the back **2** a person who never settles with one interest or occupation for long **3** a swimming stroke in which the arms are plunged forward together in large circular movements **4** *commerce* the simultaneous purchase and sale of traded call options, at different exercise prices or with different expiry dates, on a stock exchange or commodity market [OE *buttorflēoge*]

butterfly collar *n* the Irish name for **wing collar**

butterfly effect *n* the idea, used in chaos theory, that a very small difference in the initial state of a physical system can make a significant difference to the state at some later time [C20 from the theory that a butterfly flapping its wings in one part of the world might ultimately cause a hurricane in another part of the world]

butterfly nut *n* another name for **wing nut**

Buttermere (ˈbʌtəˌmɪə) *n* a lake in NW England, in Cumbria, in the Lake District, southwest of Keswick. Length: 2 km (1.25 miles)

buttermilk (ˈbʌtəˌmɪlk) *n* the sourish liquid remaining after the butter has been separated from milk

butter muslin *n* a fine loosely woven cotton material originally used for wrapping butter

butternut (ˈbʌtəˌnʌt) *n* **1** *Austral & NZ* a type of small edible pumpkin **2a** a walnut tree of North America **2b** its oily edible nut

butterscotch (ˈbʌtəˌskɒtʃ) *n* **1** a kind of hard brittle toffee made with butter, brown sugar, etc **2** a flavouring made from these ingredients [C19 ? first made in Scotland]

butter tart *n Canad* a kind of tart made with butter, brown sugar, and raisins

butter up *vb (tr, adv)* to flatter

butterwort (ˈbʌtəˌwɜːt) *n* a plant that grows in wet places and has violet-blue spurred flowers and fleshy greasy glandular leaves on which insects are trapped and digested

Butterworth (ˈbʌtəwəθ) *n* **George** 1885–1916, British composer, noted for his interest in folk song and his settings of Housman's poems **2** **Nick** born 1946, English writer and illustrator of children's books, many of which feature Percy, the animal-loving park keeper

buttery[1] (ˈbʌtərɪ) *adj* containing, like, or coated with butter > ˈ**butteriness** *n*

buttery[2] (ˈbʌtərɪ) *n, pl* **butteries** **1** a room for storing foods or wines **2** *Brit* (in some universities) a room in which food and drink are supplied or sold to students [C14 from Anglo-F *boterie*, prob. from L *butta* cask, BUTT[4]]

butt joint *n* a joint between two plates, planks, etc, fastened end to end without overlapping or interlocking. Sometimes shortened to **butt**

buttock (ˈbʌtək) *n* **1** either of the two large fleshy masses of thick muscular tissue that form the human rump. See also **gluteus**. Related adj: **gluteal** **2** the analogous part in some mammals [C13 ?from OE *buttuc* round slope]

button (ˈbʌtᵊn) *n* **1** a disc or knob of plastic, wood, etc, attached to a garment, etc, usually for fastening two surfaces together by passing it through a buttonhole or loop **2** a small round object, such as any of various sweets, decorations, or badges **3** a small disc that completes an electric circuit when pushed, as one that operates a machine **4** *biol* any rounded knoblike part or organ, such as an unripe mushroom **5** *fencing* the protective knob fixed to the point of a foil **6** *Brit* an object of no value (esp in **not worth a button**) ▷ *vb* **7** to fasten with a button or buttons **8** *(tr)* to provide with buttons [C14 from OF *boton*, from *boter* to thrust, butt; see BUTT[3]] > ˈ**buttoner** *n* > ˈ**buttonless** *adj*

buttonhole (ˈbʌtᵊnˌhəʊl) *n* **1** a slit in a garment, etc, through which a button is passed to fasten two surfaces together **2** a flower or small bunch of flowers worn pinned to the lapel or in the buttonhole, esp at weddings. US name: **boutonniere** ▷ *vb* **buttonholes, buttonholing, buttonholed** *(tr)* **3** to detain (a person) in conversation **4** to make buttonholes in

buttonhook (ˈbʌtᵊnˌhʊk) *n* a thin tapering hooked instrument formerly used for pulling buttons through the buttonholes of shoes

button up *vb (tr, adv)* **1** to fasten (a garment) with a button or buttons **2** *inf* to conclude (business) satisfactorily **3** **button up one's lip** *or* **mouth** *sl* to be silent

buttress (ˈbʌtrɪs) *n* **1** Also called: **pier** a construction, usually of brick or stone, built to support a wall **2** any support or prop **3** something shaped like a buttress, such as a projection from a mountainside ▷ *vb (tr)* **4** to support (a wall) with a buttress **5** to support or sustain [C13 from OF *bouterez*, from *bouter* to thrust, BUTT[3]]

butty[1] (ˈbʌtɪ) *n, pl* **butties** *chiefly N English dialect* a sandwich: *a jam butty* [C19 from *buttered* (bread)]

butty[2] (ˈbʌtɪ) *n, pl* **butties** *English dialect* (esp in mining parlance) a friend or workmate [C19 ?from obs. *booty* sharing, from BOOT[2]]

Butung (ˈbuːtʊŋ) *n* an island of Indonesia, southeast of Sulawesi: hilly and forested. Chief town: Baubau. Pop: 317 124 (latest est). Area: 4555 sq km (1759 sq miles)

butyl (ˈbjuːˌtaɪl, -tɪl) *n (modifier)* of or containing any of four isomeric forms of the group C_4H_9–: *butyl rubber* [C19 from BUT(YRIC ACID) + -YL]

butyl alcohol *n* another name for **butanol**

butyl rubber *n* a copolymer of isobutene and isoprene, used in tyres and as a waterproofing material

butyric acid (bjuːˈtɪrɪk) *n* another name for **butanoic acid** [C19 *butyric*, from L *būtyrum* BUTTER]

buxom (ˈbʌksəm) *adj* **1** (esp of a woman) healthily plump, attractive, and vigorous **2** (of a woman) full-bosomed [C12 *buhsum* compliant, pliant, from OE *būgan* to bend, BOW[1]] > ˈ**buxomness** *n*

Buxtehude (*German* bʊkstəˈhuːdə) *n* **Dietrich** (ˈdiːtrɪç) 1637–1707, Danish composer and organist, resident in Germany from 1668, who influenced Bach and Handel

Buxton (ˈbʌkstən) *n* a town in N England, in NW Derbyshire in the Peak District: thermal springs. Pop: 19 854 (1991)

buy (baɪ) *vb* **buys, buying, bought** *(mainly tr)* **1** to acquire by paying or promising to pay a sum of money; purchase **2** to be capable of purchasing: *money can't buy love* **3** to acquire by any exchange or sacrifice: *to buy time by equivocation* **4** to bribe or corrupt; hire by or as by bribery **5** *sl* to accept as true, practical, etc **6** *(intr; foll by into)* to purchase shares of (a company) ▷ *n* **7** a purchase (often in **good** or **bad buy**) ▷ See also **buy in, buy into,** etc [OE *bycgan*]

USAGE See at **off**

buy-back *n commerce* the repurchase by a company of some or all of its shares from an investor, who acquired them by putting venture capital into the company when it was formed

buyer (ˈbaɪə) *n* **1** a person who buys; customer **2** a person employed to buy merchandise, materials, etc, as for a shop or factory

buy in *vb (adv)* **1** *(tr)* to buy back for the owner (an item in an auction) at or below the reserve price **2** *(intr)* to purchase shares in a company **3** *(tr)* Also: **buy into** *US inf* to pay money to secure a position or place for (someone, esp oneself) in some organization, esp a business or club **4** to purchase (goods, etc) in large quantities ▷ *n* **buy-in** **5** the purchase of a company by a manager or group who does not work for that company

buy into *vb (intr, prep)* **1** to agree with or accept as valid (an argument, theory, etc) **2** *Austral & NZ inf* to get involved in (an argument, fight, etc)

buy off *vb (tr, adv)* to pay (a person or group) to drop a charge, end opposition, etc

buy out *vb (tr, adv)* **1** to purchase the ownership, controlling interest, shares, etc, of (a company, etc) **2** to gain the release of (a person) from the armed forces by payment **3** to pay (a person) to give up ownership of (property, etc) ▷ *n* **buy-out** **4** the purchase of a company, esp by its former management or staff ▷ See also **leveraged buyout, management buyout**

buy-to-let *n (modifier)* of or relating to the practice of buying a property to let to tenants rather than to live in oneself: *the buy-to-let boom*

buy up *vb (tr, adv)* **1** to purchase all, or all that is available, of (something) **2** to purchase a controlling interest in (a company, etc)

buzz (bʌz) *n* **1** a rapidly vibrating humming sound, as of a bee **2** a low sound, as of many voices in conversation **3** a rumour; report; gossip **4** *inf* a telephone call **5** *inf* **5a** a pleasant sensation **5b** a sense of excitement; kick **6** *(modifier)* fashionable, trendy ▷ *vb* **7** *(intr)* to make a vibrating sound like that of a prolonged *z* **8** *(intr)* to talk or gossip with an air of excitement: *the town buzzed with the news* **9** *(tr)* to utter or spread (a rumour) **10** *(intr; often foll by about)* to move around quickly and busily **11** *(tr)* to signal or summon with a buzzer **12** *(tr) inf* to call by telephone **13** *(tr) inf* to fly an aircraft very low over (an object) **14** *(tr)* (esp of insects) to make a buzzing sound with (wings, etc) [C16 imit.] > ˈ**buzzy** *adj*

buzzard (ˈbʌzəd) *n* a diurnal bird of prey of the hawk family, typically having broad wings and tail and a soaring flight [C13 from OF *buisard*, from L *būteō* hawk]

buzzer (ˈbʌzə) *n* **1** a device that produces a buzzing sound, esp one similar to an electric bell **2** NZ a wood-planing machine

buzz off *vb (intr, adv; often imperative) inf, chiefly Brit* to go away; leave; depart

buzz word *n inf* a word, originally from a particular jargon, which becomes a popular vogue word [C20 from ?]

BVM *abbrev for* Beata Virgo Maria [L: Blessed Virgin Mary]

bwana (ˈbwɑːnə) *n* (in E Africa) a master, often used as a form of address corresponding to *sir* [Swahili, from Ar. *abūna* our father]

by (baɪ) *prep* **1** used to indicate the agent after a passive verb: *seeds eaten by the birds* **2** used to indicate the person responsible for a creative work: *this song is by Schubert* **3** via; through: *enter by the back door* **4** foll by a gerund to indicate a means used: *he frightened her by hiding behind the door* **5** beside; next to; near: *a tree by the house* **6** passing the position of; past: *he drove by the old cottage* **7** not later than; before: *return the books by Tuesday* **8** used to indicate extent, after a comparative: *it is hotter by five degrees* **9** (esp in oaths) invoking the name of: *I swear by all the gods* **10** multiplied by: *four by three equals twelve* **11** during the passing of (esp in **by day, by night**) **12** placed between measurements of the various dimensions of something: *a pane four inches by seven* ▷ *adv* **13** near: *the house is close by* **14** away; aside: *he put some money by each week* **15** passing a point near something; past: *he drove by* ▷ *n, pl* **byes** **16** a variant spelling of **bye**[1] [OE *bī*]

by- *or* **bye-** *prefix* **1** near: *bystander* **2** secondary or incidental: *by-election; by-product* [from BY]

by and by *adv* presently or eventually

by and large *adv* in general; on the whole [C17 orig. nautical: to the wind and off it]

Byatt (ˈbaɪət) *n* **Dame A(ntonia) S(usan)** born 1936, British novelist; her books include *The Virgin in the Garden* (1978), *Possession* (1990), and *A Whistling Woman* (2002)

by-catch *n* unwanted fish and other sea animals caught in a fishing net along with the desired kind of fish

Bydgoszcz (*Polish* ˈbidgɔʃtʃ) *n* an industrial city and port in N Poland: under Prussian rule from 1772 to 1919. Pop: 386 855 (1999 est). German name: **Bromberg**

bye[1] (baɪ) *n* **1** *sport* the situation in which a player or team wins a preliminary round by virtue of having no opponent **2** *golf* one or more holes that are left unplayed after the match has been decided **3** *cricket* a run scored off a ball not struck by the batsman **4** something incidental or secondary **5** **by the bye** incidentally; by the way [C16 var. of BY]

bye[2] *or* **bye-bye** *sentence substitute Brit inf* goodbye

bye-byes *n (functioning as sing)* an informal word for **sleep,** used esp to children (as in **go to bye-byes**)

by-election *or* **bye-election** *n* (in Great Britain and other countries of the Commonwealth) an election held during the life of a parliament to fill a vacant seat

Byelgorod-Dnestrovski *n* a variant spelling of **Belgorod-Dnestrovski**

Byelorussia *n* a variant spelling of **Belarus** > **Byelorussian** (ˌbjɛləʊˈrʌʃən) *adj, n*

Byelostok (bjɪlaˈstɔk) *n* a Russian name for **Białystok**

Byelovo *or* **Belovo** (*Russian* ˈbjɛləvə) *n* a city in W central Russia. Pop: 118 000 (latest est)

bygone (ˈbaɪˌgɒn) *adj* **1** *(usually prenominal)* past; former ▷ *n* **2** *(often pl)* a past occurrence **3** an artefact, implement, etc, of former domestic or industrial use **4** **let bygones be bygones** to agree to forget past quarrels

bylaw *or* **bye-law** (ˈbaɪˌlɔː) *n* **1** a rule made by a local authority **2** a regulation of a company, society, etc [C13 prob. of Scand. orig.; cf. ON *býr* dwelling, town]

by-line *n* **1** a line under the title of a newspaper or magazine article giving the author's name **2** another word for **touchline**

Byng (bɪŋ) *n* **1** **George**, Viscount Torrington. 1663–1733, British admiral: defeated fleet of James Edward Stuart, the Old Pretender, off Scotland (1708); defeated Spanish fleet off Messina (1717) **2** his son **John** 1704–57, English admiral: executed after failing to relieve Minorca **3** **Julian Hedworth George**, 1st Viscount Byng of Vimy. 1862–1935, British general in World War I; governor general of Canada (1921–26)

BYO(G) *n Austral & NZ* an unlicensed restaurant at which diners may drink their own wine, etc [C20 from *bring your own (grog)*]

bypass (ˈbaɪˌpɑːs) *n* **1** a main road built to avoid a city or other congested area **2** a means of redirecting the flow of a substance around an appliance through which it would otherwise pass **3** *surgery* **3a** the redirection of blood flow, either to avoid a diseased blood vessel or in order to perform heart surgery. See **coronary bypass** **3b** *(as modifier)*: *bypass surgery* **4** *electronics* an electrical circuit connected in parallel around one or more components, providing an alternative path for certain frequencies ▷ *vb (tr)* **5** to go around or avoid (a city, obstruction, problem, etc) **6** to cause (traffic, fluid, etc) to go through a bypass **7** to proceed without reference to (regulations, a superior, etc); get round; avoid

bypass engine *n* a gas turbine in which part of the compressor delivery bypasses the combustion zone, flowing directly into or around the exhaust to provide additional thrust

bypath (ˈbaɪˌpɑːθ) *n* a little-used path or track
by-play *n* secondary action or talking carried on apart while the main action proceeds, esp in a play
by-product *n* **1** a secondary or incidental product of a manufacturing process **2** a side effect
Byrd (bɜːd) *n* **1 Richard Evelyn** 1888–1957, US rear admiral, aviator, and polar explorer **2 William** 1543–1623, English composer and organist, noted for his madrigals, masses, and music for virginals
Byrd Land *n* a part of Antarctica, east of the Ross Ice Shelf and the Ross Sea: claimed for the US by Richard E. Byrd in 1929. Former name: **Marie Byrd Land**
byre (ˈbaɪə) *n Brit* a shelter for cows [OE *bȳre;* rel. to *būr* hut, cottage]
byroad (ˈbaɪˌrəʊd) *n* a secondary or side road
Byron (ˈbaɪərən) *n* **George Gordon**, 6th Baron. 1788–1824, British Romantic poet, noted also for his passionate and disastrous love affairs. His major works include *Childe Harold's Pilgrimage* (1812–18), and *Don Juan* (1819–24). He spent much of his life abroad and died while fighting for Greek independence
byssinosis (ˌbɪsɪˈnəʊsɪs) *n* a lung disease caused by prolonged inhalation of fibre dust [c19 from NL, from Gk *bussinos* of linen + -OSIS]
bystander (ˈbaɪˌstændə) *n* a person present but not involved; onlooker; spectator
byte (baɪt) *n computing* **1** a group of bits processed as one unit of data **2** the storage space allocated to such a group of bits **3** a subdivision of a word [c20 prob. a blend of BIT[4] + BITE]
Bytom (*Polish* ˈbitɔm) *n* an industrial city in SW Poland, in Upper Silesia: under Prussian and German rule from 1742 to 1945. Pop: 205 560 (1999 est). German name: **Beuthen**
byway (ˈbaɪˌweɪ) *n* **1** a secondary road, esp in the country **2** an area, field of study, etc, that is very obscure or of secondary importance: *the byways of canine history*
byword (ˈbaɪˌwɜːd) *n* **1** a person or thing regarded as a perfect or proverbial example of something: *their name is a byword for good service* **2** an object of scorn or derision **3** a common saying; proverb [OE *bīwyrde;* see BY, WORD]
Byzantine (bɪˈzænˌtaɪn, -ˌtiːn, baɪ-; ˈbɪzənˌtiːn, -ˌtaɪn) *adj* **1** of, characteristic of, or relating to Byzantium or the Byzantine Empire **2** of, relating to, or characterizing the Orthodox Church or its rites and liturgy **3** of or relating to the highly coloured stylized form of religious art developed in the Byzantine Empire **4** of or relating to the style of architecture developed in the Byzantine Empire, characterized by massive domes with square bases, rounded arches, spires and minarets, and the extensive use of mosaics **5** denoting the Medieval Greek spoken in the Byzantine Empire **6** (of attitudes, etc) inflexible or complicated ▷ *n* **7** an inhabitant of Byzantium > **Byzantinism** (bɪˈzæntaɪˌnɪzəm, -tiː, baɪ-; ˈbɪzəntiːˌnɪzəm, -taɪ-) *n*
▷ www.archaeolink.com/byzantine_civilization.htm
▷ www.metmuseum.org/explore/Byzantium/art.html
▷ http://historymedren.about.com/cs/byzantinestudies
Byzantine Empire *n* the continuation of the Roman Empire in the East, esp after the deposition of the last emperor in Rome (476 AD). It was finally extinguished by the fall of Constantinople, its capital, in 1453
▷ http://chaos1.hypermart.net/byz/tbe.html
▷ www.gogreece.com/learn/history/Byzantine_empire.html
Byzantium (bɪˈzæntɪəm, baɪ-) *n* an ancient Greek city on the Bosphorus: founded about 660 BC; rebuilt by Constantine I in 330 AD and called Constantinople; present-day Istanbul
Bz *or* **bz.** *abbrev for* benzene.

c *or* **C** (siː) *n, pl* **c's, C's,** *or* **Cs 1** the third letter of the English alphabet **2** a speech sound represented by this letter, usually either as in *cigar* or as in *case* **3** the third in a series, esp the third highest grade in an examination **4** something shaped like a C

c *symbol for:* **1** centi- **2** *maths* constant **3** cubic **4** cycle **5** specific heat capacity **6** the speed of light and other types of electromagnetic radiation in free space

C *symbol for:* **1** *music* **1a** the first degree of a major scale containing no sharps or flats (**C major**) **1b** the major or minor key having this note as its tonic **1c** a time signature denoting four crotchet beats to the bar. See also **alla breve** (sense 2), **common time 2** *chem* carbon **3** *biochem* cytosine **4** capacitance **5** heat capacity **6** cold (water) **7** *physics* compliance **8** Celsius **9** centigrade **10** century: C20 **11** coulomb **12** *the Roman numeral for* 100 ▷ *n* **13** a type of high-level computer programming language

c. *abbrev for:* **1** carat **2** *cricket* caught **3** cent(s) **4** century *or* centuries **5** (used esp preceding a date) circa: *c. 1800* [L: about] **6** coulomb

C. *abbrev for:* **1** (on maps as part of name) Cape **2** Catholic **3** Celtic **4** Conservative **5** Corps

c/- (in Australia) *abbrev for* care of

C1 (ˈsiːˈwʌn) *n* **a** a person whose job is supervisory or clerical, or who works in junior management **b** (*as adj*): *a C1 worker* ▷ See also **occupation groupings**

C2 (ˈsiːˈtuː) *n* **a** a skilled manual worker, or a manual worker with responsibility for other people **b** (*as adj*): *a C2 worker* ▷ See also **occupation groupings**

Ca *the chemical symbol for* calcium

CA *abbrev for:* **1** California **2** Central America **3** chartered accountant **4** Civil Aviation **5** (in Britain) Consumers' Association

ca. *abbrev for* circa [L: about]

CAA (in Britain) *abbrev for* Civil Aviation Authority

Caaba (ˈkɑːbə) *n* a variant spelling of **Kaaba**

cab (kæb) *n* **1a** a taxi **1b** (*as modifier*): *a cab rank* **2** the enclosed compartment of a lorry, crane, etc, from which it is driven **3** (formerly) a horse-drawn vehicle used for public hire [C19 from CABRIOLET]

CAB (in Britain) *abbrev for* Citizens Advice Bureau

cabal (kəˈbæl) *n* **1** a small group of intriguers, esp one formed for political purposes **2** a secret plot; conspiracy **3** a clique ▷ *vb* **cabals, caballing, caballed 4** (*intr*) to form a cabal; plot [C17 from F *cabale*, from Med. L *cabala*]

cabala (kəˈbɑːlə) *n* a variant spelling of **cabbala**

Caballé (*Spanish* kaβaˈʎe) *n* **Montserrat** (monserˈrat) born 1933, Spanish operatic soprano

caballero (ˌkæbəˈljɛərəʊ) *n, pl* **caballeros** (-rəʊz) a Spanish gentleman [C19 from Sp.: gentleman, from LL *caballārius* rider, from *caballus* horse]

cabana (kəˈbɑːnə) *n chiefly US* a tent used as a dressing room by the sea [from Sp. *cabaña:* CABIN]

cabaret (ˈkæbəˌreɪ) *n* **1** a floor show of dancing, singing, etc, at a nightclub or restaurant **2** *chiefly US* a nightclub or restaurant providing such entertainment [C17 from Norman F: tavern, prob. from LL *camera* an arched roof]

cabbage (ˈkæbɪdʒ) *n* **1** Also called: **cole** any of various cultivated varieties of a plant of the genus *Brassica* having a short thick stalk and a large head of green or reddish edible leaves. See also **brassica 2a** the head of a cabbage **2b** the edible leaf bud of the cabbage palm **3** *inf* a dull or unimaginative person **4** *inf* a person who has no mental faculties and is dependent on others [C14 from Norman F *caboche* head]

cabbage palm *n* **1** a West Indian palm whose leaf buds are eaten like cabbage **2** a similar Brazilian palm

cabbage rose *n* a rose with a round compact full-petalled head

cabbage tree *n* **1** a tall palmlike ornamental New Zealand tree **2** any of several other similar trees
cabbage white *n* a large white butterfly, the larvae of which feed on the leaves of cabbages and related vegetables
cabbala, cabala, kabbala, *or* **kabala** (kəˈbɑːlə) *n* **1** an ancient Jewish mystical tradition **2** any secret or occult doctrine [c16 from Med. L, from Heb. *qabbālāh* tradition, from *qābal* to receive] > **cabbalism, cabalism, kabballism,** *or* **kabalism** (ˈkæbəˌlɪzəm) *n* > **ˈcabbalist, ˈcabalist, ˈkabbalist,** *or* **ˈkabalist** *n* > **ˌcabbaˈlistic, ˌcabaˈlistic, ˌkabbaˈlistic,** *or* **ˌkabaˈlistic** *adj*
cabbie *or* **cabby** (ˈkæbɪ) *n, pl* **cabbies** *inf* a cab driver
CABE (in Britain) *abbrev for* Commission for Architecture and the Built Environment
caber (ˈkeɪbə) *n Scot* a heavy section of trimmed tree trunk thrown in competition at Highland games (**tossing the caber**) [c16 from Gaelic *cabar* pole]
Cabernet Sauvignon (ˈkæbəneɪ ˈsəʊvɪnjɒn; *French* kabɛrnɛ sovinɔ̃) *n* (*sometimes not caps*) **1** a black grape grown in the Bordeaux area of France and now throughout the wine-producing world **2** any of various red wines made from this grape [F]
cabin (ˈkæbɪn) *n* **1** a small simple dwelling; hut **2** a simple house providing accommodation for travellers or holiday-makers **3** a room used as an office or living quarters in a ship **4** a covered compartment used for shelter in a small boat **5** *Brit* another name for **signal box** **6a** the enclosed part of a light aircraft in which the pilot and passengers sit **6b** the part of an aircraft for passengers or cargo ▹ *vb* **7** (*tr*) to confine in a small space [c14 from OF *cabane*, from OProvençal *cabana*, from LL *capanna* hut]
cabin boy *n* a boy who waits on the officers and passengers of a ship
cabin cruiser *n* a power boat fitted with a cabin for pleasure cruising or racing
Cabinda (kəˈbiːndə) *n* an exclave of Angola, separated from the rest of the country by part of the Democratic Republic of Congo (formerly Zaïre). Pop: 174 000 (1993 est). Area: 7270 sq km (2807 sq miles)
cabinet (ˈkæbɪnɪt) *n* **1** a piece of furniture containing shelves, cupboards, or drawers for storage or display **2** the outer case of a television, radio, etc **3a** (*often cap*) the executive and policy-making body of a country, consisting of senior government ministers **3b** (*sometimes cap*) an advisory council to a president, governor, etc **3c** (*as modifier*): *a cabinet reshuffle* **4a** a standard size of paper, 6 × 4 inches (15 × 10 cm), for mounted photographs **4b** (*as modifier*): *a cabinet photograph* **5** *arch* a private room [c16 from OF, dim. of *cabine*, from ?]
cabinet-maker *n* a craftsman specializing in making fine furniture > **ˈcabinet-ˌmaking** *n*
cabinetwork (ˈkæbɪnɪtˌwɜːk) *n* **1** the making of furniture, esp of fine quality **2** an article made by a cabinet-maker
cabin fever *n* acute depression resulting from being isolated or sharing cramped quarters in the wilderness
cable (ˈkeɪbᵊl) *n* **1** a strong thick rope, usually of twisted hemp or steel wire **2** *naut* an anchor chain or rope **3a** a unit of distance in navigation, equal to one tenth of a sea mile (about 600 ft) **3b** Also called: **cable length, cable's length** a unit of length in nautical use that has various values, including 100 fathoms (600 ft) **4** a wire or bundle of wires that conducts electricity: *a submarine cable* **5** Also called: **cablegram** a telegram sent abroad by submarine cable, telephone line, etc **6** Also called: **cable stitch** a knitting pattern resembling a twisted rope ▹ *vb* **cables, cabling, cabled** **7** to send (a message) to (someone) by cable **8** (*tr*) to fasten or provide with a cable or cables **9** (*tr*) to supply (a place) with cable television [c13 from OF, from LL *capulum* halter]
cable car *n* **1** a cabin suspended from and moved by an overhead cable in a mountain area **2** the passenger car on a **cable railway**, drawn along by a strong cable operated by a motor
cable television *n* a television service in which the subscriber's television is connected to the supplier by cable, enabling a much greater choice of channels to be provided
cabochon (ˈkæbəˌʃɒn) *n* a smooth domed gem, polished but unfaceted [c16 from OF, from *caboche* head]
caboodle (kəˈbuːdᵊl) *n inf* a lot, bunch, or group (esp in **the whole caboodle**) [c19 prob. contraction of KIT[1] & BOODLE]
caboose (kəˈbuːs) *n* **1** *US inf* short for **calaboose** **2** *railways US & Canad* a guard's van **3** *naut* **3a** a deckhouse for a galley aboard ship **3b** *chiefly Brit* the galley itself **4** *Canad* **4a** a mobile bunkhouse used by lumbermen, etc **4b** an insulated cabin on runners, equipped with a stove [c18 from Du. *cabūse*, from ?]
Cabot (ˈkæbət) *n* **1** **John** Italian name *Giovanni Caboto*. 1450–98, Italian explorer, who landed in North America in 1497, under patent from Henry VII of England, and explored the coast from Nova Scotia to Newfoundland **2** his son, **Sebastian** ?1476–1557, Italian navigator and cartographer, who served the English and Spanish crowns: explored the La Plata region of Brazil (1526–30)
cabotage (ˈkæbəˌtɑːʒ) *n* **1** *naut* coastal navigation or shipping **2** reservation to a country's carriers of its internal traffic, esp air traffic [c19 from F, from *caboter* to sail near the coast, apparently from Sp. *cabo* CAPE[2]]
Cabral (*Portuguese* kəˈbral) *n* **Pedro Álvarez** (ˈpɛːdru ˈalvərəʃ) ?1460–?1526, Portuguese navigator: discovered and took possession of Brazil for Portugal in 1500
cabriole (ˈkæbrɪˌəʊl) *n* a type of curved furniture leg, popular in the first half of the 18th century. Also called: **cabriole leg** [c18 from F, from *cabrioler* to caper; from its being based on the leg of a capering animal]
cabriolet (ˌkæbrɪəʊˈleɪ) *n* **1** a small two-wheeled horse-drawn carriage with two seats and a folding hood **2** a type of motorcar with a folding top [c18 from F, lit.: a little skip, from L, from *caper* goat; referring to the lightness of movement]
cacao (kəˈkɑːəʊ, -ˈkeɪəʊ) *n* **1** a small tropical American evergreen tree having reddish-brown seed pods from which cocoa and chocolate are prepared **2** **cacao bean** the seed pod; cocoa bean **3** **cacao butter** another name for **cocoa butter** [c16 from Sp., from Nahuatl *cacauatl* cacao beans]
cachalot (ˈkæʃəˌlɒt) *n* another name for **sperm whale** [c18 from F, from Port. *cachalote*, from ?]
cache (kæʃ) *n* **1** a hidden store of provisions, weapons, treasure, etc **2** the place where such a store is hidden **3** *computing* a small high-speed memory that improves computer performance ▹ *vb* **caches, caching, cached** **4** (*tr*) to store in a cache [c19 from F, from *cacher* to hide]
cachepot (ˈkæʃˌpɒt, kæʃˈpəʊ) *n* an ornamental container for a flowerpot [F: pot-hider]
cachet (ˈkæʃeɪ) *n* **1** an official seal on a document, letter, etc **2** a distinguishing mark **3** prestige; distinction **4** *philately* a mark stamped by hand on mail for commemorative purposes **5** a hollow wafer, formerly used for enclosing an unpleasant-tasting medicine [c17 from OF, from *cacher* to hide]
cachexia (kəˈkɛksɪə) *or* **cachexy** *n* a weakened condition of body or mind resulting from any debilitating disease [c16 from LL, from Gk, from *kakos* bad + *hexis* condition]
cachinnate (ˈkækɪˌneɪt) *vb* **cachinnates, cachinnating, cachinnated** (*intr*) to laugh loudly [c19 from L *cacchināre*, prob. imit.] > **ˌcachinˈnation** *n* > **ˌcachinˈnatory** *adj*
cachou (ˈkæʃuː, kæˈʃuː) *n* **1** a lozenge eaten to sweeten the breath **2** another name for **catechu** [c18 via F from Port., from Malay *kāchu*]
cacique (kəˈsiːk) *or* **cazique** (kəˈziːk) *n* **1** an American

Indian chief in a Spanish-speaking region **2** (esp in Spanish America) a local political boss [c16 from Sp., of Amerind origin]

cack-handed (ˌkækˈhændɪd) *adj inf* **1** left-handed **2** clumsy [from dialect *cack* excrement]

cackle (ˈkækəl) *vb* **cackles, cackling, cackled 1** (*intr*) (esp of a hen) to squawk with shrill broken notes **2** (*intr*) to laugh or chatter raucously **3** (*tr*) to utter in a cackling manner ▷ *n* **4** the noise or act of cackling **5** noisy chatter **6 cut the cackle** *inf* to be quiet [c13 prob. from MLow G *kākelen*, imit.]

caco- *combining form* bad, unpleasant, or incorrect: *cacophony* [from Gk *kakos* bad]

cacodyl (ˈkækəˌdaɪl) *n* an oily poisonous liquid with a strong garlic smell; tetramethyldiarsine [c19 from Gk, from *kakos* CACO- + *ozein* to smell + -YL]

cacoethes (ˌkækəʊˈiːθiːz) *n* an uncontrollable urge or desire: *a cacoethes for smoking* [c16 from L *cacoēthes* malignant disease, from Gk, from *kakos* CACO- + *ēthos* character]

cacography (kæˈkɒɡrəfɪ) *n* **1** bad handwriting **2** incorrect spelling > **cacographic** (ˌkækəˈɡræfɪk) *adj*

cacophony (kəˈkɒfənɪ) *n, pl* **cacophonies** harsh discordant sound > **caˈcophonous** *adj*

cactoblastis (ˌkæktəʊˈblɑːstɪs) *n* a moth, *Cactoblastis cactorum*, that was introduced into Australia to act as a biological control on the prickly pear

cactus (ˈkæktəs) *n, pl* **cactuses** *or* **cacti** (-taɪ) **1** any of a family of spiny succulent plants of the arid regions of America with swollen tough stems and leaves reduced to spines **2 cactus dahlia** a double-flowered variety of dahlia [c17 from L: prickly plant, from Gk *kaktos* cardoon] > **cactaceous** (kækˈteɪʃəs) *adj*

> USAGE The plural *cacti* is the preferred form in all contexts, according to the Bank of English. It is about ten times commoner than the alternative plural, *cactuses*

cacuminal (kæˈkjuːmɪnəl) *phonetics* ▷ *adj* **1** denoting a consonant articulated with the tip of the tongue turned back towards the hard palate ▷ *n* **2** a consonant articulated in this manner [c19 from L *cacūmen* point]

cad (kæd) *n Brit inf old-fashioned* a man who does not behave in a gentlemanly manner towards others [c18 from CADDIE] > **ˈcaddish** *adj*

CAD (kæd) *n acronym for* computer-aided design

cadaver (kəˈdeɪvə, -ˈdɑːv-) *n med* a corpse [c16 from L, from *cadere* to fall] > **cadaveric** (kəˈdævərɪk) *adj*

cadaverous (kəˈdævərəs) *adj* **1** of or like a corpse, esp in being deathly pale **2** thin and haggard > **caˈdaverousness** *n*

Cadbury (ˈkædbərɪ) *n* **George** 1839–1922, British Quaker industrialist and philanthropist. He established, with his brother **Richard Cadbury** (1835–99), the chocolate-making company Cadbury Brothers and the garden village Bournville, near Birmingham, for their workers

CADCAM (ˈkædˌkæm) *n acronym for* computer-aided design and manufacture

caddie *or* **caddy** (ˈkædɪ) *Golf* ▷ *n, pl* **caddies 1** an attendant who carries clubs, etc, for a player ▷ *vb* **caddies, caddying, caddied 2** (*intr*) to act as a caddie [c17 (c18 (Scot.): an errand-boy): from F CADET]

caddis fly *n* a small mothlike insect having two pairs of hairy wings and aquatic larvae (caddis worms) [c17 from ?]

caddis worm *or* **caddis** (ˈkædɪs) *n* the aquatic larva of a caddis fly, which constructs a protective case around itself made of silk, sand, stones, etc. Also called: **caseworm, strawworm**

caddy[1] (ˈkædɪ) *n, pl* **caddies** *chiefly Brit* a small container, esp for tea [c18 from Malay *kati*]

caddy[2] (ˈkædɪ) *n, pl* **caddies**, *vb* **caddies, caddying, caddied** a variant spelling of **caddie**

Cade (keɪd) *n* **Jack** died 1450, English leader of the Kentish rebellion against the misgovernment of Henry VI (1450)

cadence (ˈkeɪdəns) *or* **cadency** *n, pl* **cadences** *or* **cadencies 1** the beat or measure of something rhythmic **2** a fall in the pitch of the voice, as at the end of a sentence **3** intonation **4** rhythm in verse or prose **5** the close of a musical phrase [c14 from OF, from OIt. *cadenza*, lit.: a falling, from L *cadere* to fall]

cadenza (kəˈdɛnzə) *n* **1** a virtuoso solo passage occurring near the end of a piece of music, formerly improvised by the soloist **2** *S African inf* a fit or convulsion [c19 from It.; see CADENCE]

cadet (kəˈdɛt) *n* **1** a young person undergoing preliminary training, usually before full entry to the uniformed services, police, etc **2** (in England and in France before 1789) a gentleman who entered the army to prepare for a commission **3** a younger son **4 cadet branch** the family of a younger son **5** (in New Zealand, formerly) a person learning sheep farming on a sheep station [c17 from F, from dialect *capdet* captain, ult. from L *caput* head] > **caˈdetship** *n*

cadge (kædʒ) *vb* **cadges, cadging, cadged 1** to get (food, money, etc) by sponging or begging ▷ *n* **2** *Brit* a person who cadges [c17 from ?] > **ˈcadger** *n*

cadi *or* **kadi** (ˈkɑːdɪ, ˈkeɪdɪ) *n, pl* **cadis** *or* **kadis** a judge in a Muslim community [c16 from Ar. *qādī* judge]

Cádiz (kəˈdɪz; *Spanish* ˈkaðiθ) *n* a port in SW Spain, on a narrow peninsula that forms the **Bay of Cádiz** at the E end of the **Gulf of Cádiz**: founded about 1100 BC as a Phoenician trading colony; centre of trade with America from the 16th to 18th centuries. Pop: 143 121 (1998 est)

Cadmean victory (ˈkædmɪən) *n* another name for **Pyrrhic victory**

cadmium (ˈkædmɪəm) *n* a malleable bluish-white metallic element that occurs in association with zinc ores. It is used in electroplating and alloys. Symbol: Cd; atomic no.: 48; atomic wt.: 112.4 [c19 from NL, from L *cadmīa* zinc ore, CALAMINE: both calamine and cadmium are found in the ore]

cadmium yellow *n* an orange or yellow insoluble solid (cadmium sulphide) used as a pigment in paints, etc

Cadmus (ˈkædməs) *n Greek myth* a Phoenician prince who killed a dragon and planted its teeth, from which sprang a multitude of warriors who fought among themselves until only five remained, who joined Cadmus to found Thebes > **ˈCadmean** *adj*

cadre (ˈkɑːdə) *n* **1** the nucleus of trained professional servicemen forming the basis for military expansion **2** a group of activists, esp in the Communist Party **3** a basic unit or structure; nucleus **4** a member of a cadre [c19 from F, from It. *quadro*, from L *quadrum* square]

caduceus (kəˈdjuːsɪəs) *n, pl* **caducei** (-sɪˌaɪ) **1** *classical myth* a winged staff entwined with two serpents carried by Hermes (Mercury) as messenger of the gods **2** an insignia resembling this staff used as an emblem of the medical profession [c16 from L, from Doric Gk *karukeion*, from *karux* herald]

caducous (kəˈdjuːkəs) *adj biol* (of parts of a plant or animal) shed during the life of the organism [c17 from L, from *cadere* to fall]

Cadwalader (kædˈwɒlədə) *n* 7th century AD, legendary king of the Britons, probably a confusion of several historical figures

caecilian (siːˈsɪlɪən) *n* a tropical limbless cylindrical amphibian resembling the earthworm and inhabiting moist soil [c19 from L, from *caecus* blind]

caecum *or US* **cecum** (ˈsiːkəm) *n, pl* **caeca** *or US* **ceca** (-kə) *anat* any structure that ends in a blind sac or pouch, esp that at the beginning of the large intestine [c18 short for L *intestinum caecum* blind intestine, translation of Gk *tuphlon enteron*] > **ˈcaecal** *or US* **ˈcecal** *adj*

Cc

Cædmon ('kædmən) *n* 7th century AD, Anglo-Saxon poet and monk, the earliest English poet whose name survives

Caelian ('si:lɪən) *n* the southeasternmost of the Seven Hills of Rome

Caen (kɒŋ; *French* kɑ̃) *n* an industrial city in NW France. Pop: 113 987 (1999)

Caenozoic (ˌsi:nə'zəʊɪk) *adj* a variant spelling of **Cenozoic**

Caernarfon, Caernarvon, *or* **Carnarvon** (kɑ:'nɑ:vᵊn) *n* a port and resort in NW Wales, in Gwynedd on the Menai Strait: 13th-century castle. Pop: 9695 (1991)

Caernarvonshire (kɑ:'nɑ:vᵊnʃɪə, -ʃə) *n* (until 1974) a county of NW Wales, now part of Gwynedd

Caerphilly (kɛə'fɪlɪ) *n* **1** a market town in SE Wales, in Caerphilly county borough: site of the largest castle in Wales (13th–14th centuries). Pop: 28 481 (1991) **2** a county borough in SE Wales, created in 1996 from parts of Mid Glamorgan and Gwent. Pop: 169 521 (2001). Area: 275 sq km (106 sq miles) **3** a creamy white mild-flavoured cheese

Caesar ('si:zə) *n* **1 Gaius Julius** ('gaɪəs 'dʒu:lɪəs) 100–44 BC, Roman general, statesman, and historian. He formed the first triumvirate with Pompey and Crassus (60), conquered Gaul (58–50), invaded Britain (55–54), mastered Italy (49), and defeated Pompey (46). As dictator of the Roman Empire (49–44) he destroyed the power of the corrupt Roman nobility. He also introduced the Julian calendar and planned further reforms, but fear of his sovereign power led to his assassination (44) by conspirators led by Marcus Brutus and Cassius Longinus **2** any Roman emperor **3** (*sometimes not cap*) any emperor, autocrat, dictator, or other powerful ruler **4** a title of the Roman emperors from Augustus to Hadrian **5** (in the Roman Empire) **5a** a title borne by the imperial heir from the reign of Hadrian **5b** the heir, deputy, and subordinate ruler to either of the two emperors under Diocletian's system of government

Caesaraugusta (ˌsi:zərɔ:'gʌstə) *n* the Latin name for **Zaragoza**

Caesarea (ˌsi:zə'rɪə) *n* an ancient port in NW Israel, capital of Roman Palestine: founded by Herod the Great

Caesarean, Caesarian, *or US* **Cesarean, Cesarian** (sɪ'zɛərɪən) *adj* **1** of or relating to any of the Caesars, esp Julius Caesar ▷ *n* **2** (*sometimes not cap*) *surgery* **2a** a Caesarean section **2b** (*as modifier*): *Caesarean operation*

Caesarean section *n* surgical incision through the abdominal and uterine walls in order to deliver a baby [C17 from the belief that Julius Caesar was so delivered, the name allegedly being derived from *caedere* to cut]

caesious *or US* **cesious** ('si:zɪəs) *adj bot* having a waxy bluish-grey coating [C19 from L *caesius* bluish grey]

caesium *or US* **cesium** ('si:zɪəm) *n* a ductile silvery-white element of the alkali metal group. It is used in photocells and in an atomic clock (**caesium clock**) that uses the frequency of radiation from changing the spin of electrons. The radioisotope **caesium-137,** with a half-life of 30.2 years, is used in radiotherapy. Symbol: Cs; atomic no.: 55; atomic wt.: 132.905

caesura (sɪ'zjʊərə) *n, pl* **caesuras** *or* **caesurae** (-ri:) **1** (in modern prosody) a pause, esp for sense, usually near the middle of a verse line **2** (in classical prosody) a break between words within a metrical foot [C16 from L, lit.: a cutting, from *caedere* to cut] > **cae'sural** *adj*

Caetano (kaɪ'tɑ:nəʊ; *Portuguese* kɑi'tɐnu) *n* **Marcello** (mar'selu) 1906–80, prime minister of Portugal from 1968 until he was replaced by an army coup in 1974

café ('kæfeɪ, 'kæfɪ) *n* **1** a small or inexpensive restaurant serving light or easily prepared meals and refreshments **2** *S African* a corner shop or grocer [C19 from F: COFFEE]

café au lait *French* (kafe o lɛ) *n* **1** coffee with milk **2a** a light brown colour **2b** (*as adj*): *café au lait brocade*

café noir *French* (kafe nwar) *n* black coffee

cafeteria (ˌkæfɪ'tɪərɪə) *n* a self-service restaurant [C20 from American Sp.: coffee shop]

caff (kæf) *n* a slang word for **café** (sense 1)

caffeinated ('kæfɪˌneɪtəd) *adj* **1a** with no natural caffeine removed **1b** with added caffeine **2** highly stimulated by caffeine

caffeine *or* **caffein** ('kæfi:n) *n* a white crystalline bitter alkaloid responsible for the stimulant action of tea, coffee, and cocoa [C19 from G *Kaffein*, from *Kaffee* COFFEE]

caftan ('kæfˌtæn, -ˌtɑ:n) *n* a variant spelling of **kaftan**

cage (keɪdʒ) *n* **1a** an enclosure, usually made with bars or wire, for keeping birds, monkeys, etc **1b** (*in combination*): *cagebird* **2** a thing or place that confines **3** something resembling a cage in function or structure: *the rib cage* **4** the enclosed platform of a lift, esp as used in a mine ▷ *vb* **cages, caging, caged 5** (*tr*) to confine in or as in a cage [C13 from OF, from L *cavea* enclosure, from *cavus* hollow]

Cage (keɪdʒ) *n* **John** 1912–92, US composer of experimental music for a variety of conventional, modified, or invented instruments. He evolved a type of music apparently undetermined by the composer, such as in *Imaginary Landscape* (1951) for 12 radio sets. Other works include *Reunion* (1968), *Apartment Building 1776* (1976), and *Europeras 3 and 4* (1990)

cagey *or* **cagy** ('keɪdʒɪ) *adj* **cagier, cagiest** *inf* not frank; wary [C20 from ?] > **'caginess** *n*

Cagliari (kæl'jɑ:rɪ; *Italian* kaʎ'ʎari) *n* a port in Italy, the capital of Sardinia, on the S coast. Pop: 165 926 (2000 est)

Cagney ('kægnɪ) *n* **James** 1899–1986, US film actor, esp in gangster roles; his films include *The Public Enemy* (1931), *Angels with Dirty Faces* (1938), *The Roaring Twenties* (1939), and *Yankee Doodle Dandy* (1942) for which he won an Oscar

cagoule (kə'gu:l) *n* a lightweight usually knee-length type of anorak [C20 from F]

Cahokia Mounds (kə'həʊkɪə) *pl n* the largest group of prehistoric Indian earthworks in the US, located northeast of East St Louis

cahoots (kə'hu:ts) *pl n* (*sometimes sing*) *inf* **1** *US* partnership; league **2 in cahoots** in collusion [C19 from ?]

Caiaphas ('kaɪəˌfæs) *n New Testament* the high priest at the beginning of John the Baptist's preaching and during the trial of Jesus (Luke 3:2; Matthew 26)

Caicos Islands ('keɪkəs) *pl n* a group of islands in the Caribbean: part of the British dependency of the **Turks and Caicos Islands**

caiman ('keɪmən) *n, pl* **caimans** a variant spelling of **cayman**

Cain (keɪn) *n* **1** The first son of Adam and Eve, who killed his brother Abel (Genesis 4:1–16) **2 raise Cain 2a** to cause a commotion **2b** to react or protest heatedly

Caine (keɪn) *n* Sir **Michael**, real name *Maurice Micklewhite*. born 1933, British film actor. His films include *The Ipcress File* (1965), *Get Carter* (1971), *Educating Rita* (1983), *Hannah and Her Sisters* (1986), *The Cider House Rules* (1999), and *The Quiet American* (2002)

Cainozoic (ˌkaɪnəʊ'zəʊɪk, ˌkeɪ-) *adj* a variant spelling of **Cenozoic**

caïque (kaɪ'i:k) *n* **1** a long rowing skiff used on the Bosporus **2** a sailing vessel of the E Mediterranean with a square topsail [C17 from F, from It. *caicco*, from Turkish *kayik*]

Caird Coast (kɛəd) *n* a region of Antarctica: a part of Coats Land on the SE coast of the Weddell Sea; now included in the British Antarctic Territory

Cairene ('kaɪri:n) *adj* **1** of or relating to Cairo or its inhabitants ▷ *n* **2** a native or inhabitant of Cairo

cairn (kɛən) *n* **1** a mound of stones erected as a memorial or marker, esp on a hilltop **2** Also called: **cairn terrier** a small rough-haired breed of terrier originally from

Scotland [c15 from Gaelic *carn*]

cairngorm (ˌkɛənˈgɔːm) *n* a smoky yellow or brown variety of quartz, used as a gemstone. Also called: **smoky quartz** [c18 from *Cairn Gorm* (lit.: blue cairn), mountain in Scotland]

Cairngorm Mountains *pl n* a mountain range of NE Scotland, part of the Grampians; designated a national park in 2003. Highest peak: Ben Macdhui, 1309 m (4296 ft). Also called: **the Cairngorms**

Cairns (kænz, kɛənz) *n* a port in NE Australia, in Queensland. Pop: 100 900 (1995 est)

Cairo (ˈkaɪrəʊ) *n* the capital of Egypt, on the Nile: the largest city in Africa and in the Middle East; industrial centre; site of the university and mosque of Al Azhar (founded in 972). Pop: 6 789 479 (1996). Arabic name: **El Qahira** (ɛl ˈkahiːrɔ)

▷ www.cairotourist.com

caisson (kəˈsuːn, ˈkeɪsᵊn) *n* **1** a watertight chamber open at the bottom and containing air under pressure, used to carry out construction work under water **2** a watertight float filled with air, used to raise sunken ships **3** a watertight structure placed across the entrance of a dry dock, etc, to exclude water **4a** a box containing explosives formerly used as a mine **4b** an ammunition chest [c18 from F, assimilated to *caisse* CASE²]

caisson disease *n* another name for **decompression sickness**

Caithness (keɪθˈnɛs, ˈkeɪθnɛs) *n* (until 1975) a county of NE Scotland, now part of Highland

caitiff (ˈkeɪtɪf) *arch or poetic* ▷ *n* **1** a cowardly or base person ▷ *adj* **2** cowardly [c13 from OF, from L *captīvus* CAPTIVE]

Caius (ˈkaɪəs) *n* a variant of **Gaius**

cajole (kəˈdʒəʊl) *vb* **cajoles, cajoling, cajoled** to persuade (someone) by flattery to do what one wants; wheedle; coax [c17 from F *cajoler* to coax, from ?] > **caˈjolement** *n* > **caˈjoler** *n* > **caˈjolery** *n*

cake (keɪk) *n* **1** a baked food, usually in loaf or layer form, made from a mixture of flour, sugar, and eggs **2** a flat thin mass of bread, esp unleavened bread **3** a shaped mass of dough or other food: *a fish cake* **4** a mass, slab, or crust of a solidified substance, as of soap **5 go** *or* **sell like hot cakes** *inf* to be sold very quickly **6 have one's cake and eat it** to enjoy both of two desirable but incompatible alternatives **7 piece of cake** *inf* something that is easily achieved or obtained **8 take the cake** *inf* to surpass all others, esp in stupidity, folly, etc **9** *inf* the whole of something that is to be shared or divided: *a larger slice of the cake* ▷ *vb* **cakes, caking, caked 10** (*tr*) to encrust: *the hull was caked with salt* **11** to form or be formed into a hardened mass [c13 from ON *kaka*]

▷ www.cakerecipe.com
▷ www.nicecupofteaandasitdown.com
▷ www.cake-links.com
▷ www.pastrywiz.com/cakes

cakewalk (ˈkeɪkˌwɔːk) *n* **1** a dance based on a march with intricate steps, orig. performed by African-Americans for the prize of a cake **2** a piece of music for this dance **3** *inf* an easy task

CAL (kæl) *n acronym for* computer-aided (*or* -assisted) learning

cal. *abbrev for:* **1** calendar **2** calibre **3** calorie (small)

Cal. *abbrev for* Calorie (large)

Calabar (ˈkæləˌbɑː) *n* a port in SE Nigeria, capital of Cross River state. Pop: 174 400 (1996 est)

calabash (ˈkæləˌbæʃ) *n* **1** Also called: **calabash tree** a tropical American evergreen tree that produces large round gourds **2** the gourd **3** the dried hollow shell of a gourd used as the bowl of a tobacco pipe, a bottle, etc **4 calabash nutmeg** a tropical African shrub whose seeds can be used as nutmegs [c17 from obs. F *calabasse*, from Sp., ?from Ar., from *qar'ah* gourd + *yābisah* dry]

calabogus (ˌkæləˈbəʊgəs) *n Canad* a mixed drink containing rum, spruce beer, and molasses [c18 from ?]

calaboose (ˈkæləˌbuːs) *n US inf* a prison [c18 from Creole F, from Sp. *calabozo* dungeon, from ?]

calabrese (ˌkæləˈbreɪzɪ) *n* a variety of green sprouting broccoli [c20 from It.: Calabrian]

Calabria (kəˈlæbrɪə) *n* **1** a region of SW Italy: mostly mountainous and subject to earthquakes. Chief town: Reggio di Calabria. Pop: 2 050 478 (2000 est). Area: 15 080 sq km (5822 sq miles) **2** an ancient region of extreme SE Italy (3rd century BC to about 668 AD); now part of Apulia

Calabrian (kəˈlæbrɪən) *adj* **1** of or relating to Calabria or its inhabitants ▷ *n* **2** a native or inhabitant of Calabria

Calais (ˈkæleɪ, ˈkælɪ; *French* kalɛ) *n* a port in N France, on the Strait of Dover: the nearest French port to England; belonged to England 1347–1558. Pop: 75 309 (1990)

calamander (ˈkæləˌmændə) *n* the hard black-and-brown striped wood of several trees of India and Sri Lanka, used in making furniture. See also **ebony** (sense 2) [c19 metathetic var. of *coromandel* in COROMANDEL COAST]

calamari (ˌkæləˈmɑːrɪ) *n* squid cooked for eating, esp cut into rings and fried in batter [c20 from Italian, pl of *calamaro* squid, from Latin *calamarium* pen-case, referring to the squid's internal shell, from Greek *kalamos* reed]

calamine (ˈkæləˌmaɪn) *n* a pink powder consisting of zinc oxide and iron(III) oxide, used medicinally in the form of soothing lotions or ointments [c17 from OF, from Med. L *calamīna*, from L *cadmīa*; see CADMIUM]

calamint (ˈkæləmɪnt) *n* an aromatic Eurasian plant having clusters of purple or pink flowers [c14 from OF *calament*, from Med. L *calamentum*, from Gk *kalaminthē*]

calamitous (kəˈlæmɪtəs) *adj* causing, involving, or resulting in a calamity; disastrous

calamity (kəˈlæmɪtɪ) *n, pl* **calamities 1** a disaster or misfortune, esp one causing distress or misery **2** a state or feeling of deep distress or misery [c15 from F *calamité*, from L *calamitās*]

Calamity Jane *n* real name **Martha Canary** ?1852–1903, US frontierswoman, noted for her skill at shooting and riding

calamus (ˈkæləməs) *n, pl* **calami** (-ˌmaɪ) **1** any of a genus of tropical Asian palms, some of which are a source of rattan and canes **2** another name for **sweet flag** **3** *ornithol* a quill [c14 from L, from Gk *kalamos* reed, stem]

calandria (kəˈlændrɪə) *n* a cylindrical vessel through which vertical tubes pass, esp one forming part of a heat exchanger or nuclear reactor [c20 arbitrarily named, from Sp., lit.: lark]

calash (kəˈlæʃ) *or* **calèche** *n* **1** a horse-drawn carriage with low wheels and a folding top **2** a woman's folding hooped hood worn in the 18th century [c17 from F, from G, from Czech *kolesa* wheels]

calcaneus (kælˈkeɪnɪəs) *or* **calcaneum** *n, pl* **calcanei** (-nɪˌaɪ) the largest tarsal bone, forming the heel in man. Nontechnical name: **heel bone** [c19 from LL: heel, from L *calx* heel]

calcareous (kælˈkɛərɪəs) *adj* of, containing, or resembling calcium carbonate; chalky [c17 from L *calcārius*, from *calx* lime]

calceolaria (ˌkælsɪəˈlɛərɪə) *n* a tropical American plant cultivated for its speckled slipper-shaped flowers. Also called: **slipperwort** [c18 from L *calceolus* small shoe, from *calceus*]

calces (ˈkælsiːz) *n* a plural of **calx**

calci- *or before a vowel* **calc-** *combining form* indicating lime or calcium: *calcify* [from L *calx*, *calc-* limestone]

calciferol (kælˈsɪfərɒl) *n* a fat-soluble steroid, found esp in fish-liver oils and used in the treatment of rickets. Also called: **vitamin D_2** [c20 from CALCIF(EROUS) + (ERGOST)EROL]

calciferous (kælˈsɪfərəs) *adj* producing salts of calcium, esp calcium carbonate

Cc

calcify (ˈkælsɪˌfaɪ) *vb* **calcifies, calcifying, calcified 1** to convert or be converted into lime **2** to harden or become hardened by impregnation with calcium salts > ˌ**calcifiˈcation** *n*

calcine (ˈkælsaɪn, -sɪn) *vb* **calcines, calcining, calcined 1** (*tr*) to heat (a substance) so that it is oxidized, is reduced, or loses water **2** (*intr*) to oxidize as a result of heating [c14 from Med. L *calcināre* to heat, from L *calx* lime] > **calcination** (ˌkælsɪˈneɪʃən) *n*

calcite (ˈkælsaɪt) *n* a colourless or white mineral consisting of crystalline calcium carbonate: the transparent variety is Iceland spar. Formula: $CaCO_3$

calcium (ˈkælsɪəm) *n* a malleable silvery-white metallic element of the alkaline earth group, occurring esp as forms of calcium carbonate. It is an essential constituent of bones and teeth. Symbol: Ca; atomic no.: 20; atomic wt.: 40.08 [c19 from NL, from L *calx* lime]

calcium antagonist *or* **blocker** *n* any drug that prevents the influx of calcium ions into cardiac and smooth muscle: used to treat high blood pressure and angina

calcium carbide *n* a grey salt of calcium used in the production of acetylene. Formula: CaC_2. Sometimes shortened to **carbide**

calcium carbonate *n* a white crystalline salt occurring in limestone, chalk, and pearl: used in the production of lime. Formula: $CaCO_3$

calcium chloride *n* a white deliquescent salt occurring naturally in seawater and used in the de-icing of roads. Formula: $CaCl_2$

calcium hydroxide *n* a white crystalline slightly soluble alkali with many uses, esp in cement, water softening, and the neutralization of acid soils. Formula: $Ca(OH)_2$. Also called: **lime, slaked lime, caustic lime**

calcium oxide *n* a white crystalline base used in the production of calcium hydroxide and in the manufacture of glass and steel. Formula: CaO. Also called: **lime, quicklime, calx**

calcium phosphate *n* an insoluble nonacid calcium salt that occurs in bones and is the main constituent of bone ash. Formula: $Ca_3(PO_4)_2$

calcspar (ˈkælkˌspɑː) *n* another name for **calcite** [c19 from Swedish *kalkspat*, from *kalk* lime (ult. from L *calx*) + *spat* SPAR[3]]

calculable (ˈkælkjʊləbᵊl) *adj* **1** that may be computed or estimated **2** predictable > ˌ**calculaˈbility** *n* > ˈ**calculably** *adv*

calculate (ˈkælkjʊˌleɪt) *vb* **calculates, calculating, calculated 1** to solve (one or more problems) by a mathematical procedure **2** (*tr; may take a clause as object*) to determine beforehand by judgment, etc; estimate **3** (*tr; usually passive*) to aim: *the car was calculated to appeal to women* **4** (*intr;* foll by *on* or *upon*) to rely **5** (*tr; may take a clause as object*) *US dialect* to suppose [c16 from LL *calculāre*, from *calculus* pebble used as a counter] > **calculative** (ˈkælkjʊlətɪv) *adj*

calculated (ˈkælkjʊˌleɪtɪd) *adj* (*usually prenominal*) **1** undertaken after considering the likelihood of success or failure: *the project was a calculated risk* **2** premeditated: *a calculated insult*

calculating (ˈkælkjʊˌleɪtɪŋ) *adj* **1** selfishly scheming **2** shrewd > ˈ**calcuˌlatingly** *adv*

calculation (ˌkælkjʊˈleɪʃən) *n* **1** the act, process, or result of calculating **2** a forecast **3** careful planning, esp for selfish motives

calculator (ˈkælkjʊˌleɪtə) *n* **1** a device for performing mathematical calculations, esp an electronic device that can be held in the hand **2** a person or thing that calculates **3** a set of tables used as an aid to calculations

calculous (ˈkælkjʊləs) *adj pathol* of or suffering from a calculus

calculus (ˈkælkjʊləs) *n, pl* **calculuses 1** a branch of mathematics, developed independently by Newton and Leibnitz. Both **differential calculus** and **integral calculus** are concerned with the effect on a function of an infinitesimal change in the independent variable **2** any mathematical system of calculation involving the use of symbols **3** (*pl* **calculi** (-ˌlaɪ)) *pathol* a stonelike concretion of minerals found in organs of the body [c17 from L: pebble, from *calx* small stone, counter]

Calcutta (kælˈkʌtə) *n* a port in E India, capital of West Bengal state, on the Hooghly River: former capital of the country (1833–1912); major commercial and industrial centre; three universities. Pop: 4 399 819 (1991). Official name: **Kolkata**

Calder (ˈkɔːldə) *n* **Alexander** 1898–1976, US sculptor, who originated mobiles and stabiles (moving or static abstract sculptures, generally suspended from wire)

caldera (kælˈdɛərə) *n* a large basin-shaped crater at the top of a volcano, formed by the collapse of the cone [c19 from Sp. *caldera*, lit.: CAULDRON]

Calderdale (ˈkɔːldəˌdeɪl) *n* a unitary authority in N England, in West Yorkshire. Pop: 192 396 (2001). Area: 364 sq km (140 sq miles)

caldron (ˈkɔːldrən) *n* a variant spelling of **cauldron**

Caldwell (ˈkɔːldwɛl, -wəl) *n* **Erskine** (ˈɜːskɪn) 1903–87, US novelist whose works include *Tobacco Road* (1933)

calèche (*French* kalɛʃ) *n* a variant of **calash**

Caledonia (ˌkælɪˈdəʊnɪə) *n* the Roman name for **Scotland**: used poetically in later times

Caledonian (ˌkælɪˈdəʊnɪən) *adj* **1** relating to Scotland **2** of a period of mountain building in NW Europe in the Palaeozoic era ▷ *n* **3** *literary* a native or inhabitant of Scotland

Caledonian Canal *n* a canal in N Scotland, linking the Atlantic with the North Sea through the Great Glen: built 1803–47; now little used

calefacient (ˌkælɪˈfeɪʃənt) *adj* **1** causing warmth ▷ *n* **2** *med* an agent that warms, such as a mustard plaster [c17 from L, from *calefacere* to heat]

calendar (ˈkælɪndə) *n* **1** a system for determining the beginning, length, and order of years and their divisions **2** a table showing any such arrangement, esp as applied to one or more successive years **3** a list or schedule of pending court cases, appointments, etc ▷ *vb* **calendars, calendaring, calendared 4** (*tr*) to enter in a calendar; schedule [c13 via Norman F from Med. L *kalendārium* account book, from *Kalendae* the CALENDS] > **calendrical** (kæˈlɛndrɪkᵊl) *or* **caˈlendric** *adj*

calendar month *n* See **month** (sense 1)

calendar year *n* See **year** (sense 1)

calender (ˈkælɪndə) *n* **1** a machine in which paper or cloth is smoothed by passing between rollers ▷ *vb* **2** (*tr*) to subject (material) to such a process [c17 from F *calandre*, from ?]

calends *or* **kalends** (ˈkælɪndz) *pl n* the first day of each month in the ancient Roman calendar [c14 from L *kalendae*]

calendula (kæˈlɛndjʊlə) *n* any of a genus of Eurasian plants, esp the pot marigold, having orange-and-yellow rayed flowers [c19 from Med. L, from L *kalendae* CALENDS]

calf[1] (kɑːf) *n, pl* **calves 1** the young of cattle, esp domestic cattle **2** the young of certain other mammals, such as the buffalo and whale **3** a large piece of floating ice detached from an iceberg, etc **4 kill the fatted calf** to celebrate lavishly, esp as a welcome [OE *cealf*]

calf[2] (kɑːf) *n, pl* **calves** the thick fleshy part of the back of the leg between the ankle and the knee [c14 from ON *kalfi*]

calf love *n* temporary infatuation of an adolescent for a member of the opposite sex

calf's-foot jelly *n* a jelly made from the stock of boiled calves' feet and flavourings

calfskin (ˈkɑːfˌskɪn) *n* **1** the skin or hide of a calf **2** Also called: **calf 2a** fine leather made from this skin **2b** (*as modifier*): *calfskin boots*

Calgary (ˈkælgərɪ) *n* a city in Canada, in S Alberta: centre of a large agricultural region; oilfields. Pop: 768 082 (1996)

Calgon (ˈkælgɒn) *n trademark* a chemical compound, sodium hexametaphosphate, with water-softening properties, used in detergents

calibrate (ˈkælɪˌbreɪt) *vb* **calibrates, calibrating, calibrated** (*tr*) **1** to measure the calibre of (a gun, etc) **2** to mark (the scale of a measuring instrument) so that readings can be made in appropriate units **3** to determine the accuracy of (a measuring instrument, etc) > ˌ**caliˈbration** *n* > ˈ**caliˌbrator** *n*

calibre *or US* **caliber** (ˈkælɪbə) *n* **1** the diameter of a cylindrical body, esp the internal diameter of a tube or the bore of a firearm **2** the diameter of a shell or bullet **3** ability; distinction **4** personal character: *a man of high calibre* [c16 from OF, from It. *calibro*, from Ar. *qālib* shoemaker's last] > ˈ**calibred** *or US* ˈ**calibered** *adj*

calices (ˈkælɪˌsiːz) *n* the plural of **calix**

calico (ˈkælɪˌkəʊ) *n, pl* **calicoes** *or* **calicos** **1** a white or unbleached cotton fabric **2** *chiefly US* a coarse printed cotton fabric [c16 based on *Calicut*, town in India]

calif (ˈkeɪlɪf, ˈkæl-) *n* a variant spelling of **caliph**

Calif. *abbrev for* California

California (ˌkælɪˈfɔːnɪə) *n* **1** a state on the W coast of the US: the third largest state in area and the largest in population; consists of a narrow, warm coastal plain rising to the Coast Range, deserts in the south, the fertile central valleys of the Sacramento and San Joaquin Rivers, and the mountains of the Sierra Nevada in the east; major industries include the growing of citrus fruits and grapes, fishing, oil production, electronics, information technology, and films. Capital: Sacramento. Pop: 33 871 648 (2000 est). Area: 411 015 sq km (158 693 sq miles). Abbreviations: **Cal., Calif.** or (with zip code) **CA** **2** **Gulf of** an arm of the Pacific Ocean, between Sonora and Lower California

Californian (ˌkælɪˈfɔːnɪən) *adj* **1** of or relating to California or its inhabitants ▷ *n* **2** a native or inhabitant of California

California poppy *n* a plant of the poppy family, native to the Pacific coast of North America, having yellow or orange flowers and finely dissected bluish-green leaves. Also called: **eschscholzia** *or* **eschscholtzia**

californium (ˌkælɪˈfɔːnɪəm) *n* a transuranic element artificially produced from curium. Symbol: Cf; atomic no.: 98; half-life of most stable isotope, ^{251}Cf: 800 years (approx.) [c20 NL; discovered at the University of *California*]

Caligula (kəˈlɪgjʊlə) *n* original name *Gaius Caesar*, son of Germanicus. 12–41 AD, Roman emperor (37–41), noted for his cruelty and tyranny; assassinated

calipash *or* **callipash** (ˈkælɪˌpæʃ) *n* the greenish glutinous edible part of the turtle found next to the upper shell [c17 ? changed from Sp. *carapacho* CARAPACE]

calipee (ˈkælɪˌpiː) *n* the yellow glutinous edible part of the turtle found next to the lower shell [c17 ? a var. of CALIPASH]

caliper (ˈkælɪpə) *n* the usual US spelling of **calliper**

caliph, calif, *or* **khalif** (ˈkeɪlɪf, ˈkæl-) *n Islam* the title of the successors of Mohammed as rulers of the Islamic world [c14 from OF, from Ar. *khalīfa* successor]

caliphate, califate *or* **khalifate** (ˈkeɪlɪˌfeɪt) *n* the office, jurisdiction, or reign of a caliph

calisthenics (ˌkælɪsˈθɛnɪks) *n* a variant spelling (esp US) of **callisthenics**

calix (ˈkeɪlɪks, ˈkæ-) *n, pl* **calices** a cup; chalice [c18 from L: CHALICE]

calk[1] (kɔːk) *vb* a variant spelling of **caulk**

calk[2] (kɔːk) *or* **calkin** (ˈkɔːkɪn, ˈkæl-) *n* **1** a metal projection on a horse's shoe to prevent slipping ▷ *vb* (*tr*) **2** to provide with calks [c17 from L *calx* heel]

call (kɔːl) *vb* **1** (often foll by *out*) to speak or utter (words, sounds, etc) loudly so as to attract attention: *he called out her name* **2** (*tr*) to ask or order to come: *to call a policeman* **3** (*intr*; sometimes foll by *on*) to make a visit (to): *she called on him* **4** (often foll by *up*) to telephone (a person) **5** (*tr*) to summon to a specific office, profession, etc **6** (of animals or birds) to utter (a characteristic sound or cry) **7** (*tr*) to summon (a bird or animal), as by imitating its cry **8** (*tr*) to name or style: *they called the dog Rover* **9** (*tr*) to designate: *they called him a coward* **10** (*tr*) to regard in a specific way: *I call it a foolish waste of time* **11** (*tr*) to attract (attention) **12** (*tr*) to read (a list, etc) aloud to check for omissions or absentees **13** (when *tr*, usually foll by *for*) to give an order (for): *to call a strike* **14** (*intr*) to try to predict the result of tossing a coin **15** (*tr*) to awaken: *I was called early this morning* **16** (*tr*) to cause to assemble **17** (*tr*) *sport* (of an umpire, etc) to pass judgment upon (a shot, etc) with a call **18** (*tr*) *Austral inf* to broadcast a commentary on (a horse race, etc) **19** (*tr*) to demand repayment of (a loan, security, etc) **20** (*tr*) *Brit* to award (a student at an Inn of Court) the degree of barrister (esp in **call to the bar**) **21** (*tr*) *poker* to demand that (a player) expose his or her hand, after equalling his or her bet **22** (*intr*) *bridge* to make a bid **23** (in square-dancing) to call out (instructions) to the dancers **24** (*intr*; foll by *for*) **24a** to require: *this problem calls for study* **24b** to come or go (for) in order to fetch **25** (*intr*; foll by *on* or *upon*) to make an appeal or request (to): *they called upon him to reply* **26** (*tr*) to predict the outcome of an event: *we don't know yet if the plan has succeeded because it's too soon to call* **27** **call into being** to create **28** **call someone's bluff** see **bluff**[1] **29** **call to mind** to remember or cause to be remembered ▷ *n* **30** a cry or shout **31** the characteristic cry of a bird or animal **32** a device, such as a whistle, intended to imitate the cry of a bird or animal **33** a summons or invitation **34** a summons or signal sounded on a horn, bugle, etc **35** a short visit: *the doctor made six calls this morning* **36** an inner urge to some task or profession; vocation **37** allure or fascination, esp of a place: *the call of the forest* **38** need, demand, or occasion: *there is no call to shout* **39** demand or claim (esp in **the call of duty**) **40** *theatre* a notice to actors informing them of times of rehearsals **41** a conversation or a request for a connection by telephone **42** *commerce* **42a** a demand for repayment of a loan **42b** (*as modifier*): *call money* **43** *finance* a demand for redeemable bonds or shares to be presented for repayment **44** *poker* a demand for a hand or hands to be exposed **45** *bridge* a bid or a player's turn to bid **46** *sport* a decision of an umpire or referee regarding a shot, pitch, etc **47** *Austral* a broadcast commentary on a horse race, etc **48** Also called: **call option** *stock exchange* an option to buy a stated amount of securities at a specified price during a specified period **49** **on call** **49a** (of a loan, etc) repayable on demand **49b** available to be called for work outside normal working hours **50** **within call** accessible ▷ See also **call down, call forth,** etc [OE *ceallian*]

calla (ˈkælə) *n* **1** Also called: **calla lily, arum lily** a southern African plant which has a white funnel-shaped spathe enclosing a yellow spadix **2** a plant that grows in wet places and has a white spathe and red berries [c19 from NL, prob. from Gk *kalleia* wattles on a cock, prob. from *kallos* beauty]

Callaghan (ˈkæləˌhæn) *n* (**Leonard**) **James,** Baron Callaghan of Cardiff. born 1912, British Labour statesman; prime minister (1976–79)

Callanetics (ˌkæləˈnɛtɪks) *n* (*functioning as sing*) *trademark* a system of exercise involving frequent repetition of small muscular movements and squeezes, designed to improve muscle tone [c20 after *Callan* Pinckney (born 1939), its US inventor]

Callas (ˈkæləs) *n* **Maria,** real name *Maria Anna Cecilia Kalageropoulos*. 1923–77, Greek operatic soprano, born in the US

Cc

call bird *n marketing* a cheap article displayed in a shop to attract custom, in the hope of selling expensive items

call box *n* a soundproof enclosure for a public telephone. Also called: **telephone kiosk**

callboy ('kɔːlˌbɔɪ) *n* a person who notifies actors when it is time to go on stage

call centre *n* an office where staff carry out an organization's telephone transactions

call down *vb (tr, adv)* to request or invoke: *to call down God's anger*

caller ('kɔːlə) *n* **1** a person or thing that calls, esp a person who makes a brief visit **2** *Austral* a racing commentator

call forth *vb (tr, adv)* to cause (something) to come into action or existence

call girl *n* a prostitute with whom appointments are made by telephone

Callicrates (kəˈlɪkrəˌtiːz) *n* 5th century BC, Greek architect: with Ictinus, designed the Parthenon

calligraphy (kəˈlɪɡrəfɪ) *n* handwriting, esp beautiful handwriting > **calˈligrapher** *or* **calˈligraphist** *n* > **calligraphic** (ˌkælɪˈɡræfɪk) *adj*

▷ www.chinapage.com/callig1.htm
▷ www.sakkal.com/ArtArabicCalligraphy.htm
▷ www.islamicart.com/main/calligraphy

Callimachus (kəˈlɪməkəs) *n* **1** late 5th century BC, Greek sculptor, reputed to have invented the Corinthian capital **2** ?305–?240 BC, Greek poet of the Alexandrian School; author of hymns and epigrams

call in *vb (adv)* **1** *(intr; often foll by on)* to pay a visit, esp a brief one: *call in if you are in the neighbourhood* **2** *(tr)* to demand payment of: *to call in a loan* **3** *(tr)* to take (something) out of circulation, because it is defective **4** to summon to one's assistance: *to call in a specialist*

calling ('kɔːlɪŋ) *n* **1** a strong inner urge to follow an occupation, etc; vocation **2** an occupation, profession, or trade

calling card *n* the usual US and Canad term for **visiting card**

calliope (kəˈlaɪəpɪ) *n US & Canad* a steam organ [after CALLIOPE (lit.: beautiful-voiced)]

Calliope (kəˈlaɪəpɪ) *n Greek myth* the Muse of epic poetry

calliper *or US* **caliper** ('kælɪpə) *n* **1** *(often pl)* Also called: **calliper compasses** an instrument for measuring internal or external dimensions, consisting of two steel legs hinged together **2** Also called: **calliper splint** *med* a metal splint for supporting the leg ▷ *vb* **3** *(tr)* to measure with callipers [c16 var. of CALIBRE]

calliper rule *n* a measuring instrument having two parallel jaws, one fixed and the other sliding

callistemon (kəˈlɪstəmən) *n* another name for **bottlebrush** (sense 1)

callisthenics *or* **calisthenics** (ˌkælɪsˈθɛnɪks) *n* **1** *(functioning as pl)* light exercises designed to promote general fitness **2** *(functioning as sing)* the practice of callisthenic exercises [c19 from Gk *kalli-* beautiful + *sthenos* strength] > ˌ**callisˈthenic** *or* ˌ**calisˈthenic** *adj*

Callisto (kəˈlɪstəʊ) *n Greek myth* a nymph who attracted the love of Zeus and was changed into a bear by Hera. Zeus then set her in the sky as the constellation Ursa Major

call loan *n* a loan that is repayable on demand. Also called: **demand loan**

call off *vb (tr, adv)* **1** to cancel or abandon: *the game was called off* **2** to order (an animal or person) to desist: *the man called off his dog* **3** to stop (something)

callose ('kæləʊz, -ləʊs) *n* a carbohydrate, a polymer of glucose, found in plants

callosity (kəˈlɒsɪtɪ) *n, pl* **callosities** **1** hard-heartedness **2** a callus

callous ('kæləs) *adj* **1** unfeeling; insensitive: *a callous disregard for others* **2** (of skin) hardened and thickened ▷ *vb* **3** *pathol* to make or become callous [c16 from L *callōsus*; see CALLUS] > ˈ**callously** *adv* > ˈ**callousness** *n*

call out *vb (adv)* **1** to utter aloud, esp loudly **2** *(tr)* to summon: *call out the troops* **3** *(tr)* to order (workers) to strike **4** *(tr)* to challenge to a duel

callow ('kæləʊ) *adj* lacking experience of life; immature [OE *calu*] > ˈ**callowness** *n*

call sign *n* a group of letters and numbers identifying a radio transmitting station

call up *vb (tr, adv)* **1** to summon to report for active military service, as in time of war **2** to recall (something); evoke **3** to bring or summon (people, etc) into action **4** to telephone ▷ *n* **call-up** **5a** a general order to report for military service **5b** the number of men so summoned

callus ('kæləs) *n, pl* **calluses** **1** Also called: **callosity** an area of skin that is hard or thick, esp on the sole of the foot **2** an area of bony tissue formed during the healing of a fractured bone **3** *bot* a mass of hard protective tissue produced in woody plants at the site of an injury **4** a mass of undifferentiated cells produced as the first stage in tissue culture [c16 from L, var. of *callum* hardened skin]

calm (kɑːm) *adj* **1** still: *a calm sea* **2** *meteorol* without wind, or with wind of less than 1 mph **3** not disturbed, agitated, or excited **4** tranquil; serene: *a calm voice* ▷ *n* **5** an absence of disturbance or rough motion **6** absence of wind **7** tranquillity ▷ *vb* **8** (often foll by *down*) to make or become calm [c14 from OF *calme*, from OIt., from LL *cauma* heat, hence a rest during the heat of the day, from Gk, from *kaiein* to burn] > ˈ**calmly** *adv* > ˈ**calmness** *n*

calmative ('kælmətɪv, 'kɑːmə-) *adj* (of a remedy or agent) sedative

caló (kəˈləʊ; *Spanish* kaˈlo) *n* a form of Mexican Spanish incorporating many slang terms and English words: spoken esp by Mexican Americans in the SW US

calomel ('kæləˌmɛl, -məl) *n* a colourless tasteless powder consisting chiefly of mercurous chloride, used medicinally, esp as a cathartic [c17 ?from NL *calomelas* (unattested), lit.: beautiful black, from Gk *kalos* beautiful + *melas* black]

Calor Gas ('kælə) *n trademark* butane gas liquefied under pressure in portable containers for domestic use

caloric (kəˈlɒrɪk) *adj* **1** of or concerned with heat or calories ▷ *n* **2** *obs* a hypothetical elastic fluid, the embodiment of heat

calorie *or* **calory** ('kælərɪ) *n, pl* **calories** a unit of heat, equal to 4.1868 joules (**International Table calorie**): formerly defined as the quantity of heat required to raise the temperature of 1 gram of water by 1°C. Abbrev: **cal.** Also called: **small calorie** [c19 from F, from L *calor* heat]

Calorie ('kælərɪ) *n* **1** Also called: **kilogram calorie, large calorie** a unit of heat, equal to one thousand calories. Abbrev: **Cal** **2** the amount of a specific food capable of producing one thousand calories of energy

calorific (ˌkæləˈrɪfɪk) *adj* of, concerning, or generating heat > ˌ**caloˈrifically** *adv*

calorific value *n* the quantity of heat produced by the complete combustion of a given mass of a fuel

calorimeter (ˌkæləˈrɪmɪtə) *n* an apparatus for measuring amounts of heat, esp to find calorific values, etc > **calorimetric** (ˌkælərɪˈmɛtrɪk) *adj* > ˌ**caloˈrimetry** *n*

calorize *or* **calorise** ('kæləˌraɪz) *vb* **calorizes, calorizing, calorized** *or* **calorises, calorising, calorised** *(tr)* to coat (a ferrous metal) by spraying with aluminium powder and then heating

Calpe ('kælpɪ) *n* the ancient name for (the Rock of) **Gibraltar**

calque (kælk) *n* another word for **loan translation** [c20 from F: a tracing, from L *calcāre* to tread]

calumet ('kæljʊˌmɛt) *n* a less common name for **peace pipe** [c18 from Canad F, from F: straw, from LL *calamellus*

a little reed, from L: CALAMUS]
calumniate (kəˈlʌmnɪˌeɪt) *vb* **calumniates, calumniating, calumniated** (*tr*) to slander > **caˌlumniˈation** *n* > **caˈlumniˌator** *n*
calumny (ˈkæləmnɪ) *n, pl* **calumnies** **1** the malicious utterance of false charges or misrepresentation **2** such a false charge or misrepresentation [c15 from L *calumnia* deception, slander] > **calumnious** (kəˈlʌmnɪəs) *or* **caˈlumniatory** *adj*
Calvados (ˈkælvəˌdɒs) *n* **1** a department of N France in the Basse-Normandie region. Capital: Caen. Pop: 648 385 (1999). Area: 5693 sq km (2198 sq miles) **2** an apple brandy distilled from cider in this region
Calvary (ˈkælvərɪ) *n* the place just outside the walls of Jerusalem where Jesus was crucified. Also called: **Golgotha** [from LL *Calvāria*, translation of Gk *kranion* skull, translation of Aramaic *gulgulta* Golgotha]
calve (kɑːv) *vb* **calves, calving, calved** **1** to give birth to (a calf) **2** (of a glacier or iceberg) to release (masses of ice) in breaking up
Calvert (ˈkælvət) *n* **1** Sir **George,** 1st Baron Baltimore. ?1580–1632, English statesman; founder of the colony of Maryland **2** his son, **Leonard** 1606–47, English statesman; first colonial governor of Maryland (1634–47)
calves (kɑːvz) *n* the plural of **calf**[1] and **calf**[2]
Calvin (ˈkælvɪn) *n* **1 John,** original name *Jean Cauvin, Caulvin*, or *Chauvin*. 1509–64, French theologian: a leader of the Protestant Reformation in France and Switzerland, establishing the first presbyterian government in Geneva. His theological system is described in his *Institutes of the Christian Religion* (1536) **2 Melvin** 1911–97, US chemist, noted particularly for his research on photosynthesis: Nobel prize for chemistry 1961
Calvin cycle *n bot* a series of reactions, occurring during photosynthesis, in which glucose is synthesized from carbon dioxide and water [c20 named after M. CALVIN, who elucidated it]
Calvinism (ˈkælvɪˌnɪzəm) *n* the theological system of John Calvin and his followers, characterized by emphasis on predestination and justification by faith > **ˈCalvinist** *n, adj* > **ˌCalvinˈistic** *or* **ˌCalvinˈistical** *adj*
Calvino (kælˈviːnəʊ) *n* **Italo** 1923–85, Italian novelist and short-story writer. His works include *Our Ancestors* (1960) and *Invisible Cities* (1972)
calx (kælks) *n, pl* **calxes** *or* **calces** **1** the powdery metallic oxide formed when an ore or mineral is roasted **2** calcium oxide **3** *anat* the heel [c15 from L: lime, from Gk *khalix* pebble]
calypso (kəˈlɪpsəʊ) *n, pl* **calypsos** a popular type of satirical West Indian ballad, esp from Trinidad, usually extemporized to a syncopated accompaniment [c20 prob. from CALYPSO]
Calypso (kəˈlɪpsəʊ) *n Greek myth* (in Homer's *Odyssey*) a sea nymph who detained Odysseus on the island of Ogygia for seven years
calypsonian (ˌkælɪpˈsəʊnɪən) *n* a performer or writer of calypsos
calyx (ˈkeɪlɪks, ˈkælɪks) *n, pl* **calyxes** *or* **calyces** (ˈkælɪˌsiːz, ˈkeɪlɪ-) **1** the sepals of a flower collectively that protect the developing flower bud **2** any cup-shaped cavity or structure [c17 from L, from Gk *kalux* shell, from *kaluptein* to cover]
calzone (kælˈtsəʊnɪ) *n* a dish of Italian origin consisting of pizza dough folded over a filling of cheese and tomatoes, herbs, ham, etc [c20 It., lit.: trouser leg, from *calzoni* trousers]
cam (kæm) *n* a slider or roller attached to a moving shaft to give a particular type of motion to a part in contact with it [c16 from Du. *kam* comb]
Cam (kæm) *n* a river in E England, in Cambridgeshire, flowing through Cambridge to the River Ouse. Length: about 64 km (40 miles)
CAM (kæm) *n acronym for* computer-aided manufacture
-cam *n combining form* a camera: *webcam*
cama (ˈkɑːmə) *n* the hybrid offspring of a camel and a llama
Camagüey (ˈkæməˌgweɪ; *Spanish* kamaˈɣwej) *n* a city in E central Cuba. Pop: 293 961 (1994 est)
camaraderie (ˌkæməˈrɑːdərɪ) *n* a spirit of familiarity and trust existing between friends [c19 from F, from *camarade* COMRADE]
Camargue (kæˈmɑːg) *n* **la** (la) a delta region in S France, between the channels of the Grand and Petit Rhône: cattle, esp bulls for the Spanish bullrings, and horses are reared
camarilla (ˌkæməˈrɪlə) *n* a group of confidential advisers, esp formerly, to the Spanish kings [c19 from Sp., lit.: a little room]
Cambay (kæmˈbeɪ) *n* **Gulf of** an inlet of the Arabian Sea on the W coast of India, southeast of the Kathiawar Peninsula
camber (ˈkæmbə) *n* **1** a slight upward curve to the centre of the surface of a road, ship's deck, etc **2** another name for **bank**[2] (sense 8) **3** an outward inclination of the front wheels of a road vehicle so that they are slightly closer together at the bottom **4** aerofoil curvature expressed by the ratio of the maximum height of the aerofoil mean line to its chord ▷ *vb* **5** to form or be formed with a surface that curves upwards to its centre [c17 from OF *cambre* curved, from L *camurus*]
Camberwell carrot *n inf* a large, almost conical, marijuana cigarette
cambium (ˈkæmbɪəm) *n, pl* **cambiums** *or* **cambia** (-bɪə) *bot* a layer of cells that increases the girth of stems and roots [c17 from Med. L: exchange, from LL *cambiāre* to exchange] > **ˈcambial** *adj*
Cambodia (kæmˈbəʊdɪə) *n* a country in SE Asia: became part of French Indochina in 1887; achieved self-government in 1949 and independence in 1953; civil war (1970–74) ended in victory for the Khmer Rouge, who renamed the country Kampuchea (1975); Vietnamese forces ousted the Khmer Rouge in 1979 and set up a pro-Vietnamese government who reverted (1981) to the name Cambodia; in 1982 exiled factions formed the Coalition Government of Democratic Kampuchea (CGDK); after the Vietnamese withdrawal in 1989 CGDK guerrillas continued to engage government forces; a peace settlement was followed in 1993 by elections and the adoption of a democratic monarchist constitution restoring Sihanouk to the throne: contains the central plains of the Mekong River and the Cardamom Mountains in the SW. Official language: Khmer; French is also widely spoken. Currency: riel. Capital: Phnom Penh. Pop: 12 720 000 (2001 est). Area: 181 000 sq km (69 895 sq miles)
▷ www.camnet.com.kh/ocm
Cambodian (kæmˈbəʊdɪən) *adj* **1** of or relating to Cambodia or its inhabitants ▷ *n* **2** a native or inhabitant of Cambodia
Cambrai (*French* kɑ̃brɛ) *n* a town in NE France: textile industry: scene of a battle in which massed tanks were first used and broke through the German line (November, 1917). Pop: 34 210 (1990)
Cambria (ˈkæmbrɪə) *n* the Medieval Latin name for **Wales**
Cambrian (ˈkæmbrɪən) *adj* **1** of or formed in the first 65 million years of the Palaeozoic era **2** of or relating to Wales ▷ *n* **3 the** the Cambrian period or rock system **4** a Welshman
Cambrian Mountains *pl n* a mountain range in Wales, extending from Carmarthenshire in the S to Denbighshire in the N. Highest peak: Aran Fawddwy, 891 m (2970 ft)
cambric (ˈkeɪmbrɪk) *n* a fine white linen fabric [c16 from Flemish *Kamerijk* CAMBRAI]

Cambridge ('keɪmbrɪdʒ) *n* **1** a city in E England, administrative centre of Cambridgeshire, on the River Cam: centred around the university, founded in the 12th century: electronics, biotechnology. Pop: 113 800 (1994 est). Medieval Latin name: **Cantabrigia** **2** short for **Cambridgeshire** **3** a city in the US, in E Massachusetts: educational centre, with Harvard University (1636) and the Massachusetts Institute of Technology. Pop: 101 355 (2000). Related adj: **Cantabrigian**

Cambridgeshire ('keɪmbrɪdʒʃɪə, -ʃə) *n* a county of E England, in East Anglia: includes the former counties of the Isle of Ely and Huntingdon and lies largely in the Fens: Peterborough became an independent unitary authority in 1998. Administrative centre: Cambridge. Pop (excluding Peterborough): 552 655 (2001). Area (excluding Peterborough): 3068 sq km (184 sq miles)

Cambs *abbrev for* Cambridgeshire

Cambyses (kæm'baɪsiːz) *n* died ?522 BC, king of Persia (529–522 BC), who conquered Egypt (525); son of Cyrus the Great

camcorder ('kæm,kɔːdə) *n* a video camera and recorder combined in a portable unit

Camden[1] ('kæmdən) *n* a borough of N Greater London. Pop: 198 027 (2001 est). Area: 21 sq km (8 sq miles)

Camden[2] ('kæmdən) *n* **William** 1551–1623, English antiquary and historian; author of *Britannia* (1586)

came (keɪm) *vb* the past tense of **come**

camel ('kæməl) *n* **1** either of two cud-chewing, humped mammals (see **Arabian camel, Bactrian camel**) that are adapted for surviving long periods without food or water in desert regions **2** a float attached to a vessel to increase its buoyancy **3a** a fawn colour **3b** (*as adj*): *a camel coat* [OE, from L, from Gk *kamēlos*, of Semitic origin]

cameleer (,kæmɪ'lɪə) *n* a camel driver

camel hair *or* **camel's hair** *n* **1** the hair of the camel, used in rugs, etc **2a** soft cloth made of or containing this hair or a substitute, usually tan in colour **2b** (*as modifier*): *a camelhair coat* **3a** the hair of the squirrel's tail, used for paintbrushes **3b** (*as modifier*): *a camelhair brush*

camellia (kə'miːlɪə) *n* any of a genus of ornamental shrubs having glossy evergreen leaves and showy white, pink, or red flowers. Also called: **japonica** [C18 NL, after Georg Josef *Kamel* (1661–1706), Moravian Jesuit missionary]

camelopard ('kæmɪlə,pɑːd, kə'mɛl-) *n* an obsolete word for **giraffe** [C14 from Med. L, from Gk, from *kamēlos* CAMEL + *pardalis* LEOPARD, because the giraffe was thought to have a head like a camel's and spots like a leopard's]

Camelot ('kæmɪ,lɒt) *n* (in Arthurian legend) the English town where King Arthur's palace and court were situated

Camembert ('kæməm,bɛə) *n* a soft creamy cheese [F, from *Camembert*, a village in Normandy]

cameo ('kæmɪ,əʊ) *n, pl* **cameos** **1** a medallion, as on a brooch or ring, with a profile head carved in relief **2** an engraving upon a gem or other stone so that the background is of a different colour from the raised design **3** a stone with such an engraving **4a** a brief dramatic scene played by a well-known actor or actress in a film or television play **4b** (*as modifier*): *a cameo performance* **5** a short literary work [C15 from It. *cammeo*, from ?]

camera ('kæmərə) *n* **1** an optical device consisting of a lens system set in a light-proof construction inside which a light-sensitive film or plate can be positioned **2** *television* the equipment used to convert the optical image of a scene into the corresponding electrical signals **3** (*pl* **camerae** (-ə,riː)). a judge's private room **4** **in camera** **4a** *law* relating to a hearing from which members of the public are excluded **4b** in private [C18 from L: vault, from Gk *kamara*]

cameraman ('kæmərə,mæn) *n, pl* **cameramen** a person who operates a film or television camera

camera obscura (ɒb'skjʊərə) *n* a darkened chamber with an aperture, in which images of outside objects are projected onto a flat surface [NL: dark chamber]

Cameron ('kæmərən) *n* **1** (**Mark**) **James** (**Walter**) 1911–85, British journalist, author, and broadcaster. His books include *Witness in Vietnam* (1966) and *Point of Departure* (1967) **2** **James** born 1954, Canadian film director and screenwriter; his films include *The Terminator* (1984), *Aliens* (1986) and *Titanic* (1997) **3** **Julia Margaret** 1815–79, British photographer, born in India, renowned for her portrait photographs

Cameroon (,kæmə'ruːn, 'kæmə,ruːn) *n* **1** a republic in West Africa, on the Gulf of Guinea: became a German colony in 1884; divided in 1919 into the **Cameroons** (administered by Britain) and **Cameroun** (administered by France); Cameroun and the S part of the Cameroons formed a republic in 1961 (the N part joined Nigeria); became a member of the Commonwealth in 1995. Official languages: French and English. Religions: Christian, Muslim, and animist. Currency: franc. Capital: Yaoundé. Pop: 15 803 000 (2001 est). Area: 475 500 sq km (183 591 sq miles). French name: **Cameroun** German name: **Kamerun** **2** an active volcano in W Cameroon: the highest peak on the West African coast. Height: 4070 m (13 352 ft)
▷ www.spm.gov.cm
▷ www.camnet.cm/mintour/tourisme

Cameroun (kamrun) *n* the French name for **Cameroon**

camiknickers ('kæmɪ,nɪkəz) *pl n* women's knickers attached to a camisole top

camisole ('kæmɪ,səʊl) *n* **1** a woman's underbodice with shoulder straps, originally designed as a cover for a corset **2** a woman's short negligee [C19 from F, from Provençal *camisola*, from *camisa* shirt, from LL *camīsia*]

camomile *or* **chamomile** ('kæmə,maɪl) *n* **1** any of a genus of aromatic plants whose finely dissected leaves and daisy-like flowers are used medicinally **2** any plant of a related genus known as **German** or **wild camomile** **3** **camomile tea** a herbal beverage made from the fragrant leaves and flowers of any of these plants [C14 from OF, from Med. L, from Gk *khamaimēlon* lit., earth-apple (referring to the scent of the flowers)]

camouflage ('kæmə,flɑːʒ) *n* **1** the exploitation of natural surroundings or artificial aids to conceal or disguise the presence of military units, etc **2** (*modifier*) (of fabric or clothing) having a design of irregular patches, in dull colours (such as browns and greens), as used in military camouflage **3** the means by which animals escape the notice of predators **4** a device or expedient designed to conceal or deceive
▷ *vb* **camouflages, camouflaging, camouflaged** **5** (*tr*) to conceal by camouflage [C20 from F, from *camoufler*, from It. *camuffare* to disguise, from ?]

camp[1] (kæmp) *n* **1** a place where tents, cabins, etc, are erected for the use of military troops, etc **2** tents, cabins, etc, used as temporary lodgings by holiday-makers, Scouts, Gypsies, etc **3** the group of people living in such lodgings **4** a group supporting a given doctrine: *the socialist camp* **5** (*modifier*) suitable for use in temporary quarters, on holiday, etc: *a camp bed; a camp chair* **6** *S African* a field or pasture **7** *Austral* a place where sheep or cattle gather to rest ▷ *vb* (*intr*) **8** (often foll by *down*) to establish or set up a camp **9** (often foll by *out*) to live temporarily in or as if in a tent [C16 from OF, ult. from L *campus* field] > '**camping** *n*

camp[2] (kæmp) *inf* ▷ *adj* **1** effeminate; affected **2** homosexual **3** consciously artificial, vulgar, or mannered ▷ *vb* **4** (*tr*) to perform or invest with a camp quality **5** **camp it up** **5a** to overact **5b** to flaunt one's homosexuality [C20 from ?] > '**campness** *n* > '**campy** *adj*

Campagna (kæm'pɑːnjə) *n* a low-lying plain surrounding Rome, Italy: once fertile, it deteriorated to malarial marshes; recently reclaimed. Area: about 2000 sq km (800 sq miles). Also called: **Campagna di Roma** (dɪ 'rəʊmə)

campaign (kæm'peɪn) *n* **1** a series of coordinated activities, such as public speaking, designed to achieve a social, political, or commercial goal: *a presidential campaign* **2** *mil* a number of operations aimed at achieving a single objective ▷ *vb* **3** (*intr; often foll by for*) to conduct, serve in, or go on a campaign [c17 from F *campagne* open country, from It., from LL, from L *campus* field] > **cam'paigner** *n*

Campanella (*Italian* kampa'nɛlla) *n* **Tommaso** 1568–1639, Italian philosopher and Dominican friar. During his imprisonment by the Spaniards (1599–1626) he wrote his celebrated utopian fantasy, *La città del sole*

Campania (kæm'peɪnɪə; *Italian* kam'paɲɲa) *n* a region of SW Italy: includes the islands of Capri and Ischia. Chief town: Naples. Pop: 5 780 958 (2000 est). Area: 13 595 sq km (5248 sq miles)

campanile (ˌkæmpə'niːlɪ) *n* (esp in Italy) a bell tower, not usually attached to another building [c17 from It., from *campana* bell]

campanology (ˌkæmpə'nɒlədʒɪ) *n* the art or skill of ringing bells [c19 from NL, from LL *campāna* bell] > **campanological** (ˌkæmpənə'lɒdʒɪkᵊl) *adj* > **ˌcampa'nologist** *or* **ˌcampa'nologer** *n*

campanula (kæm'pænjʊlə) *n* any of a genus of N temperate plants having blue or white bell-shaped flowers. Also called: **bellflower** [c17 from NL: a little bell, from LL *campāna* bell]

Campbell ('kæmbᵊl) *n* **1** Sir **Colin,** Baron Clyde. 1792–1863, British field marshal who relieved Lucknow for the second time (1857) and commanded in Oudh, suppressing the Indian Mutiny **2** **Donald** 1921–67, English water speed record-holder **3** Sir **Malcolm,** father of Donald Campbell. 1885–1948, English racing driver and land speed record-holder **4** Mrs **Patrick,** original name *Beatrice Stella Tanner.* 1865–1940, English actress **5** **Roy** 1901–57, South African poet. His poetry is often satirical and includes *The Flaming Terrapin* (1924) **6** **Thomas** 1777–1844, Scottish poet and critic, noted particularly for his war poems *Hohenlinden* and *Ye Mariners of England*

Campbell-Bannerman ('kæmbᵊl'bænəmən) *n* Sir **Henry** 1836–1908, British statesman and leader of the Liberal Party (1899–1908); prime minister (1905–08), who granted self-government to the Transvaal and the Orange River Colony

Camp David ('deɪvɪd) *n* the US president's retreat in the Appalachian Mountains, Maryland: scene of the **Camp David Agreement** (Sept, 1978) between Anwar Sadat of Egypt and Menachem Begin of Israel, mediated by Jimmy Carter, which outlined a framework for establishing peace in the Middle East. This agreement was the basis of the peace treaty between Israel and Egypt signed in Washington (March, 1979)

camp drafting *n Austral* a competitive test of horsemen's skill in drafting cattle

Campeche (*Spanish* kam'petʃe) *n* **1** a state of SE Mexico, on the SW of the Yucatán peninsula: forestry and fishing. Capital: Campeche. Pop: 689 656 (2000 est). Area: 56 114 sq km (21 666 sq miles) **2** a port in SE Mexico, capital of Campeche state. Pop: 195 000 (2000 est) **3** **Bay of** the SW part of the Gulf of Mexico. Also called: **Gulf of Campeche**

camper ('kæmpə) *n* **1** a person who lives or temporarily stays in a tent, cabin, etc **2** *US & Canad* a vehicle equipped for camping out

Campese (kæm'peɪzɪ) *n* **David** born 1962, Australian rugby union player

camp follower *n* **1** any civilian, esp a prostitute, who unofficially provides services to military personnel **2** a nonmember who is sympathetic to a particular group, theory, etc

camphor ('kæmfə) *n* a whitish crystalline aromatic ketone obtained from the wood of an Asian or Australian laurel (**camphor tree**): used in medicine as a liniment [c15 from OF *camphre*, from Med. L *camphora*, from Ar. *kāfūr*, from Malay *kāpūr* chalk] > **camphoric** (kæm'fɒrɪk) *adj*

camphorate ('kæmfəˌreɪt) *vb* **camphorates, camphorating, camphorated** (*tr*) to apply, treat with, or impregnate with camphor

camphor ball *n* another name for **mothball** (sense 1)

camphor ice *n* an ointment consisting of camphor, white wax, spermaceti, and castor oil, used to treat skin ailments, esp chapped skin

camphor laurel *n* an Australian name for the camphor tree, now occurring in the wild in parts of Australia

camphor wood *n Austral* a popular name for any of several trees with pungent-smelling wood

Campin ('kæmpɪn) *n* **Robert** 1379–1444, Flemish painter, noted esp for his altarpieces: usually identified with the so-called Master of Flémalle

campion ('kæmpɪən) *n* any of various plants related to the pink, having red, pink, or white flowers [c16 prob. from *campion*, obs. var. of CHAMPION]

Campion ('kæmpɪən) *n* **1** Saint **Edmund** 1540–81, English Jesuit martyr. He joined the Jesuits in 1573 and returned to England (1580) as a missionary. He was charged with treason and hanged **2** **Jane** born 1954, New Zealand film director and screenwriter: her films include *An Angel at My Table* (1990), *The Piano* (1993), *Holy Smoke* (1999), and *In The Cut* (2003) **3** **Thomas** 1567–1620, English poet and musician, noted particularly for his songs for the lute

Campobello (ˌkæmpə'bɛləʊ) *n* an island in the Bay of Fundy, off the coast of SE Canada: part of New Brunswick province. Area: about 52 sq km (20 sq miles). Pop: 1317 (1991)

Campo Formio (*Italian* 'kampo 'fɔrmjo) *n* a village in NE Italy, in Friuli-Venezia Giulia: scene of the signing of a treaty in 1797 that ended the war between revolutionary France and Austria. Modern name: **Campoformido** (kampo'fɔrmido)

Cc

Campo Grande (*Portuguese* 'kə:mpu 'grə:ndə) *n* a city in SW Brazil, capital of Mato Grosso do Sul state on the São Paulo–Corumbá railway: market centre. Pop: 654 832 (2000)

camp oven *n Austral & NZ* a heavy metal pot or box with a lid, used for baking over an open fire

camp pie *n Austral* tinned meat

camp site *n* an area on which holiday-makers may pitch a tent, etc. Also called: **camping site**

campus ('kæmpəs) *n, pl* **campuses** **1** the grounds and buildings of a university **2** *chiefly US* the outside area of a college, etc [c18 from L: field]

campylobacter ('kæmpɪləʊˌbæktə) *n* a rod-shaped bacterium that causes infections in animals and man; a common cause of gastroenteritis [from Gk *kampulos* bent + BACTER(IUM)]

Cam Ranh ('kæm 'ræn) *n* a port in SE Vietnam: large natural harbour, in recent years used as a naval base by French, Japanese, US, and Russian forces successively. Pop: 114 041 (1992 est)

camshaft ('kæmˌʃɑːft) *n* a shaft having one or more cams attached to it

Camus (*French* kamy) *n* **Albert** (albɛr) 1913–60, French novelist, dramatist, and essayist, noted for his pessimistic portrayal of man's condition of isolation in an absurd world: author of the novels *L'Étranger* (1942) and *La Peste* (1947), the plays *Le Malentendu* (1945) and *Caligula* (1946), and the essays *Le Mythe de Sisyphe* (1942) and *L'Homme révolté* (1951): Nobel prize for literature 1957

can[1] (kæn; *unstressed* kən) *vb, past* **could** (takes an infinitive without *to* or an implied infinitive) used as an auxiliary: **1** to indicate ability, skill, or fitness to perform a task: *I can run* **2** to indicate permission or the right to something: *can I have a drink?* **3** to indicate knowledge of how to do something **4** to indicate the possibility, opportunity, or likelihood [OE *cunnan*]

can² (kæn) *n* **1** a container, esp for liquids, usually of thin metal: *a petrol can* **2** a tin (metal container): *a beer can* **3** Also: **canful** the contents of a can or the amount a can will hold **4** a slang word for **prison** **5** *US & Canad* a slang word for **toilet** **6** a shallow cylindrical metal container used for storing and handling film **7** **can of worms** *inf* a complicated problem **8** **in the can** **8a** (of a film, piece of music, etc) having been recorded, edited, etc **8b** *inf* agreed: *the contract is in the can* ▹ *vb* **cans, canning, canned** **9** to put (food, etc) into a can or cans [OE *canne*] > **'canner** *n*

Can. *abbrev for:* **1** Canada **2** Canadian

Cana ('keɪnə) *n New Testament* the town in Galilee, north of Nazareth, where Jesus performed his first miracle by changing water into wine (John 2:1, 11)

Canaan ('keɪnən) *n* an ancient region between the River Jordan and the Mediterranean: the Promised Land of the Israelites

Canaanite ('keɪnəˌnaɪt) *n* a member of an ancient Semitic people who occupied the land of Canaan before the Israelite conquest

Canada ('kænədə) *n* a country in North America: the second largest country in the world; first permanent settlements made by the French from 1605; ceded to Britain in 1763 after a series of colonial wars; established as the Dominion of Canada in 1867; a member of the Commonwealth. It consists generally of sparsely inhabited tundra regions, rich in natural resources, in the north, the Rocky Mountains in the west, the Canadian Shield in the east, and vast central prairies; the bulk of the population is concentrated along the US border and the Great Lakes in the south. Languages: English and French. Religion: Christian majority. Currency: Canadian dollar. Capital: Ottawa. Pop: 31 081 900 (2001 est). Area: 9 976 185 sq km (3 851 809 sq miles)
▹ http://canada.gc.ca
▹ www.travelcanada.org

Canada balsam *n* **1** a yellow transparent resin obtained from the balsam fir. Because its refractive index is similar to that of glass, it is used as a mounting medium for microscope specimens **2** another name for **balsam fir**

Canada Day *n* (in Canada) July 1, the anniversary of the day in 1867 when Canada received dominion status: a public holiday

Canada goose *n* a large common greyish-brown North American goose with a black neck and head and a white throat patch

Canada jay *n* a grey crestless jay, notorious in northern parts of N America for its stealing. Also called: **camp robber, whisky-jack**

Canadarm ('kænədˌɑːm) *n* a type of robotic arm, developed in Canada, used on space vehicles

Canadian (kə'neɪdɪən) *adj* **1** of or relating to Canada or its people ▹ *n* **2** a native, citizen, or inhabitant of Canada

Canadiana (kəˌneɪdɪ'ɑːnə; *Canad* -'ænə) *pl n* objects, such as books, furniture, and antiques, relating to Canadian history and culture

Canadian Alliance *n* a Canadian right-wing federal political party, founded in 2000

Canadian bacon *n* the US name for **back bacon**

Canadian English *n* the English language as spoken in Canada

Canadian football *n* a game like American football played on a grass pitch between teams of 12 players
▹ www.cfl.ca

Canadian Forces *pl n* the official name for the military forces of Canada

Canadianism (kə'neɪdɪəˌnɪzəm) *n* **1** the Canadian national character or spirit **2** a linguistic usage, custom, or other feature peculiar to Canada, its people, or their culture

Canadianize *or* **Canadianise** (kə'neɪdɪəˌnaɪz) *vb* **Canadianizes, Canadianizing, Canadianized** *or* **Canadianises, Canadianising, Canadianised** to make or become Canadian by changing customs, ownership, character, content, etc > **Caˌnadiani'zation** *or* **Caˌnadiani'sation** *n*

Canadian River *n* a river in the southern US, rising in NE New Mexico and flowing east to the Arkansas River in E Oklahoma. Length: 1458 km (906 miles)

Canadian Shield *n* the wide area of Precambrian rock extending over most of E and central Canada: rich in minerals. Also called: **Laurentian Shield**

Canadien (*French* kanadjɛ̃; *English* kəˌnædɪ'ɛn) *or* (*fem*) **Canadienne** (*French* kanadjɛn; *English* kəˌnædɪ'ɛn) *n* a French Canadian

canaille *French* (kanɑj) *n* the masses; mob; rabble [c17 from F, from It. *canaglia* pack of dogs]

canakin ('kænɪkɪn) *n* a variant spelling of **cannikin**

canal (kə'næl) *n* **1** an artificial waterway constructed for navigation, irrigation, etc **2** any of various passages or ducts: *the alimentary canal* **3** any of various intercellular spaces in plants **4** *astron* any of the indistinct surface features of Mars orig. thought to be a network of channels ▹ *vb* **canals, canalling, canalled** *or US* **canals, canaling, canaled** (*tr*) **5** to dig a canal through **6** to provide with a canal or canals [c15 (in the sense: pipe, tube): from L *canālis* channel, from *canna* reed]

canal boat *n* a long narrow boat used on canals, esp for carrying freight

Canaletto (*Italian* kana'lɛtto) *n* original name *Giovanni Antonio Canale*. 1697–1768, Italian painter and etcher, noted particularly for his highly detailed paintings of cities, esp Venice, which are marked by strong contrasts of light and shade

canaliculus (ˌkænə'lɪkjʊləs) *n, pl* **canaliculi** (-ˌlaɪ) a small channel or groove, as in some bones [c16 from L: a little channel, from *canālis* CANAL] > **ˌcana'licular** *or* **ˌcana'liculate** *adj*

canalize *or* **canalise** ('kænəˌlaɪz) *vb* **canalizes, canalizing, canalized** *or* **canalises, canalising, canalised** (*tr*) **1** to provide with or convert into a canal or canals **2** to give a particular direction to or provide an outlet for > **ˌcanali'zation** *or* **ˌcanali'sation** *n*

canal ray *n physics* a stream of positive ions produced in a discharge tube by allowing them to pass through holes in the cathode

Canal Zone *n* a former administrative region of the US, on the Isthmus of Panama around the Panama Canal: bordered on each side by the Republic of Panama, into which it was incorporated in 1979. Also called: **Panama Canal Zone**

canapé ('kænəpɪ, -ˌpeɪ) *n* a small piece of bread, toast, etc, spread with a savoury topping, often served at parties [c19 from F: sofa]

Canara (kə'nɑːrə) *n* a variant spelling of **Kanara**

canard (kæ'nɑːd) *n* **1** a false report; rumour or hoax **2** an aircraft in which the tailplane is mounted in front of the wing [c19 from F: a duck, from OF *caner* to quack, imit.]

canary (kə'nɛərɪ) *n, pl* **canaries** **1** a small finch of the Canary Islands and Azores: a popular cagebird noted for its singing **2** **canary yellow** **2a** a light yellow **2b** (*as adj*): *a canary-yellow car* **3** *arch* a sweet wine from the Canary Islands similar to Madeira [c16 from OSp. *canario* of or from the Canary Islands]

Canary Islands *or* **Canaries** *pl n* a group of mountainous islands in the Atlantic off the NW coast of Africa, forming an Autonomous Community of Spain. Pop: 1 716 276 (2000 est)

canasta (kəˈnæstə) *n* **1** a card game for two to six players who seek to amass points by declaring sets of cards **2** Also called: **meld** a declared set in this game, containing seven or more like cards [c20 from Sp.: basket (because two packs of cards are required), from L *canistrum*; see CANISTER]

canaster (ˈkænəstə) *n* coarsely broken dried tobacco leaves [c19 (meaning: basket in which tobacco was packed): from Sp.; see CANISTER]

Canaveral (kəˈnævərəl) *n* **Cape** a cape on the E coast of Florida: site of the US Air Force Missile Test Centre, from which the majority of US space missions have been launched. Former name (1963–73): Cape **Kennedy**
▷ www.ksc.nasa.gov

Canberra (ˈkænbərə, -brə) *n* the capital of Australia, in Australian Capital Territory: founded in 1913 as a planned capital. Pop: 306 600 (1998 est)
▷ www.act.gov.au
▷ www.nationalcapital.gov.au

cancan (ˈkænˌkæn) *n* a high-kicking dance performed by a female chorus, originating in the music halls of 19th-century Paris [c19 from F, from ?]

cancel (ˈkænsᵊl) *vb* **cancels, cancelling, cancelled** *or US* **cancels, canceling, canceled** (*mainly tr*) **1** to order (something already arranged, such as a meeting or event) to be postponed indefinitely; call off **2** to revoke or annul: *the order was cancelled* **3** to delete (writing, numbers, etc); cross out **4** to mark (a cheque, stamp, etc) with an official stamp to prevent further use **5** (*also intr*; usually foll by *out*) to counterbalance: *his generosity cancelled out his past unkindness* **6** *maths* to eliminate (numbers or terms) as common factors from both the numerator and denominator of a fraction or as equal terms from opposite sides of an equation ▷ *n* **7** a new leaf or section of a book replacing one containing errors, or one that has been omitted **8** a cancellation **9** *music* a US word for **natural** (sense 16) [c14 from OF *canceller*, from Med. L, from LL: to make like a lattice, from L *cancellī* lattice] > ˈ**canceller** *or US* ˈ**canceler** *n*

cancellate (ˈkænsɪˌleɪt) *or* **cancellated** *adj* **1** *anat* having a spongy or porous internal structure: *cancellate bones* **2** *bot* forming a network [c17 from L *cancellāre* to make like a lattice]

cancellation (ˌkænsɪˈleɪʃən) *n* **1** the fact or an instance of cancelling **2** something that has been cancelled, such as a theatre ticket: *we have a cancellation in the stalls* **3** the marks made by cancelling

cancer (ˈkænsə) *n* **1** any type of malignant growth or tumour, caused by abnormal and uncontrolled cell division **2** the condition resulting from this **3** an evil influence that spreads dangerously [c14 from L: crab, a creeping tumour] > ˈ**cancerous** *adj*
▷ www.jasperweb.com/texascanceronline
▷ www.cancercare.org

Cancer (ˈkænsə) *n*, *Latin genitive* **Cancri** (ˈkæŋkriː) **1** *astron* Also called: the **Crab** a small N constellation **2** *astrol* the fourth sign of the zodiac. The sun is in this sign between about June 21 and July 22 **3** **tropic of Cancer** See **tropic** (sense 1)

cancerophobia (ˌkænsərəʊˈfəʊbɪə) *n* a morbid dread of being afflicted by cancer

cancroid (ˈkæŋkrɔɪd) *adj* **1** resembling a cancerous growth **2** resembling a crab ▷ *n* **3** a skin cancer

Cancún (kaːnˈkuːn) *n* a coastal resort in SE Mexico, on the Yucatán Peninsula. Pop (urban area): 457 000 (2004 est)

candela (kænˈdiːlə, -ˈdeɪlə) *n* the basic SI unit of luminous intensity; the intensity, in a perpendicular direction, of a surface of 1/600 000 square metre of a black body at the temperature of freezing platinum under a pressure of 101 325 newtons per square metre. Symbol: cd [c20 from L: CANDLE]

Candela (kænˈdiːlə) *n* **Felix** born 1910, Mexican architect, noted for his naturalistic modern style and thin prestressed concrete roofs

candelabrum (ˌkændɪˈlɑːbrəm) *or* **candelabra** *n, pl* **candelabra** (-brə), **candelabrums,** *or* **candelabras** a large branched candleholder or holder for overhead lights [c19 from L, from *candēla* CANDLE]

candescent (kænˈdɛsᵊnt) *adj rare* glowing or starting to glow with heat [c19 from L, from *candēre* to be white, shine] > canˈ**descence** *n*

c & f *abbrev for* cost and freight

C & G *abbrev for* City and Guilds

Candia (ˈkandja) *n* the Italian name for **Iráklion**

candid (ˈkændɪd) *adj* **1** frank and outspoken **2** without partiality; unbiased **3** unposed or informal: *a candid photograph* [c17 from L, from *candēre* to be white] > ˈ**candidly** *adv* > ˈ**candidness** *n*

candida (ˈkændɪdə) *n* any of a genus of yeastlike parasitic fungi, esp one that causes thrush (**candidiasis**)

candidate (ˈkændɪˌdeɪt) *n* **1** a person seeking or nominated for election to a position of authority or selection for a job, etc **2** a person taking an examination or test **3** a person or thing regarded as suitable or likely for a particular fate or position [c17 from L *candidātus* clothed in white (because the candidate wore a white toga), from *candidus* white] > **candidacy** (ˈkændɪdəsɪ) *or* **candidature** (ˈkændɪdətʃə) *n*

candid camera *n* a small camera that may be used to take informal photographs of people

candied (ˈkændɪd) *adj* impregnated or encrusted with or as if with sugar: *candied peel*

Candiot (ˈkændɪˌɒt) *or* **Candiote** (ˈkændɪˌəʊt) *adj* **1** of or relating to Candia (Iráklion) or Crete; Cretan ▷ *n* **2** a native or inhabitant of Crete; a Cretan

candle (ˈkændᵊl) *n* **1** a cylindrical piece of wax, tallow, or other fatty substance surrounding a wick, which is burned to produce light **2** *physics* another name for **candela** **3** **burn the candle at both ends** to exhaust oneself by doing too much, esp by being up late and getting up early to work **4** **not hold a candle to** *inf* to be inferior or contemptible in comparison with **5** **not worth the candle** *inf* not worth the price or trouble entailed ▷ *vb* **candles, candling, candled** **6** (*tr*) to examine (eggs) for freshness or the likelihood of being hatched by viewing them against a bright light [OE *candel*, from L *candēla*, from *candēre* to glitter] > ˈ**candler** *n*

Cc

candleberry (ˈkændᵊlbərɪ) *n, pl* **candleberries** another name for **wax myrtle**

candlelight (ˈkændᵊlˌlaɪt) *n* **1a** the light from a candle or candles **1b** (*as modifier*): *a candlelight dinner* **2** dusk; evening

Candlemas (ˈkændᵊlməs) *n Christianity* Feb. 2, the Feast of the Purification of the Virgin Mary and the presentation of Christ in the Temple

candlenut (ˈkændᵊlˌnʌt) *n* **1** a tree of tropical Asia and Polynesia **2** the nut of this tree, which yields an oil used in paints. In their native regions the nuts are burned as candles

candlepower (ˈkændᵊlˌpaʊə) *n* the luminous intensity of a source of light in a given direction: now expressed in candelas

candlestick (ˈkændᵊlˌstɪk) *or* **candleholder** (ˈkændᵊlˌhəʊldə) *n* a holder, usually ornamental, with a spike or socket for a candle

candlewick (ˈkændᵊlˌwɪk) *n* **1** unbleached cotton or muslin into which loops of yarn are hooked and then cut to give a tufted pattern **2** (*modifier*) being or made of candlewick fabric

C & M *abbrev for* care and maintenance

can-do *adj* confident and resourceful in the face of challenges: *a can-do attitude*

Candolle (*French* kɑ̃dɔl) *n* **Augustin Pyrame de** 1778–1841, Swiss botanist; his *Théorie élémentaire de la botanique* (1813) introduced a new system of plant classification

candour *or US* **candor** (ˈkændə) *n* **1** the quality of being open and honest; frankness **2** fairness; impartiality [C17 from L *candor*, from *candēre* to be white]

C & W *abbrev for* country and western

candy ('kændɪ) *n, pl* **candies 1** *chiefly US & Canad* sweets, chocolate, etc ▷ *vb* **candies, candying, candied 2** to cause (sugar, etc) to become crystalline or (of sugar) to become crystalline **3** (*tr*) to preserve (fruit peel, ginger, etc) by boiling in sugar **4** (*tr*) to cover with any crystalline substance, such as ice or sugar [C18 from OF *sucre candi* candied sugar, from Ar. *qandi* candied, from *qand* cane sugar]

candyfloss ('kændɪˌflɒs) *n Brit* a very light fluffy confection made from coloured spun sugar, usually held on a stick. US and Canad name: **cotton candy** Austral name: **fairyfloss**

candy-striped *adj* (esp of clothing fabric) having narrow coloured stripes on a white background > **candy stripe** *n*

candytuft ('kændɪˌtʌft) *n* either of two species of *Iberis* having clusters of white, red, or purplish flowers [C17 *Candy*, obs. var. of CANDIA + TUFT]

cane (keɪn) *n* **1a** the long jointed pithy or hollow flexible stem of the bamboo, rattan, or any similar plant **1b** any plant having such a stem **2a** strips of such stems, woven or interlaced to make wickerwork, etc **2b** (*as modifier*): *a cane chair* **3** the woody stem of a reed, blackberry, or loganberry **4** a flexible rod with which to administer a beating **5** a slender rod used as a walking stick **6** See **sugar cane** ▷ *vb* **canes, caning, caned** (*tr*) **7** to whip or beat with or as if with a cane **8** to make or repair with cane **9** *inf* to defeat: *we got well caned in the match* [C14 from OF, from L *canna*, from Gk *kanna*, of Semitic origin] > **'caner** *n*

Canea (kæ'nɪə) *n* another name for **Chania**

canebrake ('keɪnˌbreɪk) *n US* a thicket of canes

cane sugar *n* **1** the sucrose obtained from sugar cane **2** another name for **sucrose**

Canetti (kə'nɛtɪ) *n* **Elias** 1905–94, British novelist and writer, born in Bulgaria, who usually wrote in German. His works include the novel *Auto da Fé* (1935) Nobel prize for literature 1981

canikin ('kænɪkɪn) *n* a variant spelling of **cannikin**

canine ('keɪnaɪn, 'kæn-) *adj* **1** of or resembling a dog **2** of or belonging to the Canidae, a family of mammals, including dogs, wolves, and foxes, typically having a bushy tail, erect ears, and a long muzzle **3** of or relating to any of the four teeth, two in each jaw, situated between the incisors and the premolars ▷ *n* **4** any animal of the family Canidae **5** a canine tooth [C17 from L *canīnus*, from *canis* dog]

caning ('keɪnɪŋ) *n inf* a severe defeat or punishment

Canis Major ('keɪnɪs) *n, Latin genitive* **Canis Majoris** (mə'dʒɔːrɪs) a S constellation containing Sirius, the brightest star in the sky. Also called: the **Great Dog** [L: the greater dog]

Canis Minor *n, Latin genitive* **Canis Minoris** (maɪ'nɔːrɪs) a small N constellation. Also called: the **Little Dog** [L: the lesser dog]

canister ('kænɪstə) *n* **1** a container, usually made of metal, in which dry food, such as tea or coffee, is stored **2** (formerly) **2a** a type of shrapnel shell for firing from a cannon **2b** Also called: **canister shot** the shot or shrapnel packed inside this [C17 from L *canistrum* basket woven from reeds, from Gk, from *kanna* reed]

canker ('kæŋkə) *n* **1** an ulceration, esp of the lips **2** *vet science* **2a** a disease of horses in which the horn of the hoofs becomes spongy **2b** inflammation of the lining of the external ear, esp in dogs and cats **2c** ulceration or abscess of the mouth, eyelids, ears, or cloaca of birds **3** an open wound in the stem of a tree or shrub **4** something evil that spreads and corrupts ▷ *vb* **5** to infect or become infected with or as if with canker [OE *cancer*, from L *cancer* cancerous sore] > **'cankerous** *adj*

cankerworm ('kæŋkəˌwɜːm) *n* the larva of either of two moths, which feed on and destroy fruit and shade trees in North America

CanLit (ˌkæn'lɪt) *n acronym for* Canadian Literature

canna ('kænə) *n* any of a genus of tropical plants having broad leaves and red or yellow showy flowers [C17 from NL CANE]

cannabinoid ('kænəbɪˌnɔɪd) *n* any of the narcotic chemical substances found in cannabis

cannabis ('kænəbɪs) *n* **1** another name for **hemp** (the plant), esp Indian hemp **2** the drug obtained from the dried leaves and flowers of the hemp plant, which is smoked or chewed for its psychoactive properties. See also **hashish, marijuana 3 cannabis resin** a poisonous resin obtained from the hemp plant [C18 from L, from Gk *kannabis*]

Cannae ('kæniː) *n* an ancient city in SE Italy: scene of a victory by Hannibal over the Romans (216 BC)

canned (kænd) *adj* **1** preserved and stored in airtight cans or tins **2** *inf* prepared or recorded in advance: *canned music* **3** *sl* drunk

cannel coal *or* **cannel** ('kænəl) *n* a dull coal burning with a smoky luminous flame [C16 from N English dialect *cannel* candle]

cannellini bean (ˌkænɪ'liːnɪ) *n* a cream-coloured, kidney-shaped bean with a mild flavour [It.: small tubes]

cannelloni *or* **canneloni** (ˌkænɪ'ləʊnɪ) *pl n* tubular pieces of pasta filled with meat or cheese [It., pl of *cannellone*, from *cannello* stalk]

cannery ('kænərɪ) *n, pl* **canneries** a place where foods are canned

Cannes (kæn, kænz; *French* kan) *n* a port and resort in SE France: developed in the 19th century from a fishing village; annual film festival. Pop: 335 647 (1990)

cannibal ('kænɪbəl) *n* **1** a person who eats the flesh of other human beings **2** an animal that feeds on the flesh of others of its kind [C16 from Sp. *Canibales*, the name used by Columbus to designate the Caribs of Cuba and Haiti] > **'cannibaˌlism** *n*

cannibalize *or* **cannibalise** ('kænɪbəˌlaɪz) *vb* **cannibalizes, cannibalizing, cannibalized** *or* **cannibalises, cannibalising, cannibalised** (*tr*) to use (serviceable parts from one machine or vehicle) to repair another > **ˌcannibali'zation** *or* **ˌcannibali'sation** *n*

cannikin, canakin, *or* **canikin** ('kænɪkɪn) *n* a small can, esp one used as a drinking vessel [C16 from MDu. *kanneken*; see CAN², -KIN]

canning ('kænɪŋ) *n* the process or business of sealing food in cans or tins to preserve it

Canning ('kænɪŋ) *n* **1 Charles John,** 1st Earl Canning. 1812–62, British statesman; governor general of India (1856–58) and first viceroy (1858–62) **2** his father, **George** 1770–1827, British Tory statesman; foreign secretary (1822–27) and prime minister (1827)

Cannock ('kænək) *n* a town in W central England, in S Staffordshire: **Cannock Chase** (an area of heathland) is just to the east. Pop: 60 106 (1991)

cannon ('kænən) *n, pl* **cannons** *or* **cannon 1** an automatic aircraft gun **2** *history* a heavy artillery piece consisting of a metal tube mounted on a carriage **3** a heavy tube or drum, esp one that can rotate freely **4** See **cannon bone 5** *billiards* a shot in which the cue ball is caused to contact one object ball after another. Usual US and Canad word: **carom** ▷ *vb* **6** (*intr*) to rebound; collide (*with* into) **7** (*intr*) *billiards* to make a cannon [C16 from OF *canon*, from It. *cannone* cannon, from *canna* tube]

cannonade (ˌkænə'neɪd) *n* **1** an intense and continuous artillery bombardment ▷ *vb* **cannonades, cannonading, cannonaded 2** to attack (a target) with cannon

cannonball ('kænənˌbɔːl) *n* **1** a projectile fired from a cannon: usually a solid round metal shot ▷ *vb* (*intr*) **2** (often foll by *along*, etc) to rush along ▷ *adj* **3** very fast or powerful

cannon bone *n* a bone in the legs of horses and other hoofed animals consisting of greatly elongated fused metatarsals or metacarpals

cannoneer (ˌkænəˈnɪə) *n* (formerly) a soldier who served and fired a cannon; artilleryman

cannon fodder *n* men regarded as expendable in war because they are part of a huge army

cannot (ˈkænɒt, kæˈnɒt) an auxiliary verb expressing incapacity, inability, withholding permission, etc; can not

cannula *or* **canula** (ˈkænjʊlə) *n, pl* **cannulas, cannulae** (-ˌliː), *or* **canulas, canulae** (-ˌliː) *surgery* a narrow tube for draining fluid from or introducing medication into the body [c17 from L: a small reed, from *canna* a reed]

canny (ˈkænɪ) *adj* **cannier, canniest 1** shrewd, esp in business **2** *Scot & NE English dialect* good or nice: used as a general term of approval **3** *Scot* lucky or fortunate [c16 from CAN[1] (in the sense: to know how) + -Y[1]] > **ˈcannily** *adv* > **ˈcanniness** *n*

canoe (kəˈnuː) *n* **1** a light narrow open boat, propelled by one or more paddles ▷ *vb* **canoes, canoeing, canoed 2** to go in or transport by canoe [c16 from Sp. *canoa*, of Carib origin] > **caˈnoeist** *n*

canola (kəˈnəʊlə) *n* a cooking oil extracted from a variety of rapeseed developed in Canada [c20 from CAN(ADA) + *-ola*, from OLEUM]

canon[1] (ˈkænən) *n* **1** *Christianity* a Church decree enacted to regulate morals or religious practices **2** (*often pl*) a general rule or standard, as of judgment, morals, etc **3** (*often pl*) a principle or criterion applied in a branch of learning or art **4** *RC Church* the list of the canonized saints **5** *RC Church* Also called: **Eucharistic Prayer** the prayer in the Mass in which the Host is consecrated **6** a list of writings, esp sacred writings, recognized as genuine **7** a piece of music in which an extended melody in one part is imitated successively in one or more other parts **8** a list of the works of an author that are accepted as authentic [OE, from L, from Gk *kanōn* rule, rod for measuring]

canon[2] (ˈkænən) *n* **1** one of several priests on the permanent staff of a cathedral, who are responsible for organizing services, maintaining the fabric, etc **2** *RC Church* Also called: **canon regular** a member of either of two religious orders living communally as monks but performing clerical duties. [c13 from Anglo-F, from LL *canonicus* one living under a rule, from CANON[1]]

canonical (kəˈnɒnɪkᵊl) *or* **canonic** *adj* **1** included in a canon of sacred or other officially recognized writings **2** in conformity with canon law **3** accepted; authoritative **4** *music* in the form of a canon **5** of or relating to a cathedral chapter **6** of a canon (clergyman) > **caˈnonically** *adv*

canonical hour *n* **1** *RC Church* one of the seven prayer times appointed for each day by canon law **2** *Church of England* any time at which marriages may lawfully be celebrated

canonicals (kəˈnɒnɪkᵊlz) *pl n* the vestments worn by clergy when officiating

canonicity (ˌkænəˈnɪsɪtɪ) *n* the fact or quality of being canonical

canonist (ˈkænənɪst) *n* a specialist in canon law

canonize *or* **canonise** (ˈkænəˌnaɪz) *vb* **canonizes, canonizing, canonized** *or* **canonises, canonising, canonised** (*tr*) **1** *RC Church* to declare (a person) to be a saint **2** to regard as a saint **3** to sanction by canon law > **ˌcanoniˈzation** *or* **ˌcanoniˈsation** *n*

canon law *n* the codified body of laws enacted by the supreme authorities of a Christian Church

canonry (ˈkænənrɪ) *n, pl* **canonries 1** the office, benefice, or status of a canon **2** canons collectively [c15 from CANON[2] + -RY]

canoodle (kəˈnuːdᵊl) *vb* **canoodles, canoodling, canoodled** (*intr; often foll by with*) *sl* to kiss and cuddle; fondle; pet [c19 from ?] > **caˈnoodler** *n*

Canopic jar, urn, *or* **vase** (kəˈnəʊpɪk) *n* (in ancient Egypt) one of four containers for holding the entrails of a mummy

Canopus (kəˈnəʊpəs) *n* a port in ancient Egypt east of Alexandria where granite monuments have been found inscribed with the name of Rameses II and written in languages similar to those of the Rosetta stone > **Caˈnopic** *adj*

canopy (ˈkænəpɪ) *n, pl* **canopies 1** an ornamental awning above a throne, bed, person, etc **2** a rooflike covering over an altar, niche, etc **3** a roofed structure serving as a sheltered passageway **4** a large or wide covering: *the sky was a grey canopy* **5** the hemisphere that forms the supporting surface of a parachute **6** the transparent cover of an aircraft cockpit **7** the highest level of foliage in a forest, formed by the crowns of the trees ▷ *vb* **canopies, canopying, canopied 8** (*tr*) to cover with or as with a canopy [c14 from Med. L *canōpeum* mosquito net, from L, from Gk *kōnōpeion* bed with protective net]

canst (kænst) *vb arch* the form of **can[1]** used with the pronoun *thou* or its relative form

cant[1] (kænt) *n* **1** insincere talk, esp concerning religion or morals **2** phrases that have become meaningless through repetition **3** specialized vocabulary of a particular group, such as thieves, journalists, or lawyers ▷ *vb* **4** (*intr*) to speak in or use cant [c16 prob. via Norman F *canter* to sing, from L *cantāre*; used disparagingly, from the 12th cent., of chanting in religious services] > **ˈcantingly** *adv*

cant[2] (kænt) *n* **1** inclination from a vertical or horizontal plane **2** a sudden movement that tilts or turns something **3** the angle or tilt thus caused **4** a corner or outer angle **5** an oblique or slanting surface, edge, or line ▷ *vb* (*tr*) **6** to tip, tilt, or overturn **7** to set in an oblique position **8** another word for **bevel** (sense 1) ▷ *adj* **9** oblique; slanting **10** having flat surfaces [c14 (in the sense: edge): ?from L *canthus* iron hoop round a wheel, from ?]

Cant. *abbrev for:* **1** Canterbury **2** *Bible* Canticles

can't (kɑːnt) *contraction of* cannot

Cantab. (kænˈtæb) *abbrev for* Cantabrigiensis [L: of Cambridge]

cantabile (kænˈtɑːbɪlɪ) *music* ▷ *adj, adv* **1** (to be performed) flowingly and melodiously ▷ *n* **2** a piece or passage performed in this way [It., from LL, from L *cantāre* to sing]

Cantabrian Mountains (kænˈteɪbrɪən) *pl n* a mountain chain along the N coast of Spain, consisting of a series of high ridges that rise over 2400 m (8000 ft): rich in minerals (esp coal and iron)

Cantabrigian (ˌkæntəˈbrɪdʒɪən) *adj* **1** of, relating to, or characteristic of Cambridge or Cambridge University, or of Cambridge, Massachusetts, or Harvard University ▷ *n* **2** a member or graduate of Cambridge University or Harvard University **3** an inhabitant or native of Cambridge [c17 from Medieval Latin *Cantabrigia*]

Cantal (*French* kɑ̃tal) *n* **1** a department of S central France, in the Auvergne region. Capital: Aurillac. Pop: 150 778 (1999). Area: 5779 sq km (2254 sq miles) **2** a hard strong cheese made in this area

cantaloupe *or* **cantaloup** (ˈkæntəˌluːp) *n* **1** a cultivated variety of muskmelon with ribbed warty rind and orange flesh **2** any of several other muskmelons [c18 from F, from *Cantaluppi*, near Rome, where first cultivated in Europe]

cantankerous (kænˈtæŋkərəs) *adj* quarrelsome; irascible [c18 ?from c14 (obs.) *conteckour* a contentious person, from Anglo-F *contek* strife, from ?] > **canˈtankerously** *adv* > **canˈtankerousness** *n*

cantata (kænˈtɑːtə) *n* a musical setting of a text, esp a religious text, consisting of arias, duets, and choruses

Cc

[c18 from It., from *cantare* to sing, from L]

canteen (kæn'tiːn) *n* **1** a restaurant attached to a factory, school, etc, providing meals for large numbers **2a** a small shop that provides a limited range of items to a military unit **2b** a recreation centre for military personnel **3** a temporary or mobile stand at which food is provided **4a** a box in which a set of cutlery is laid out **4b** the cutlery itself **5** a flask for carrying water or other liquids [c18 from F, from It. *cantina* wine cellar, from *canto* corner, from L *canthus* iron hoop encircling chariot wheel]

Canteloube ('kæntəˌluːb; *French* kɑ̃tlub) *n* **(Marie) Joseph** (*French* ʒozɛf) 1879–1957, French composer, best known for his *Chants d'Auvergne* (1923–30)

canter ('kæntə) *n* **1** a gait of horses, etc, between a trot and a gallop in speed **2** **at a canter** easily; without effort ▷ *vb* **3** to move or cause to move at a canter [c18 short for *Canterbury trot*, the supposed pace at which pilgrims rode to Canterbury]

Canterbury ('kæntəbərɪ, -brɪ) *n* **1** a city in SE England, in E Kent: starting point for St Augustine's mission to England (597 AD); cathedral where St Thomas à Becket was martyred (1170); seat of the archbishop and primate of England; seat of the University of Kent (1965). Pop: 36 464 (1991). Latin name: **Durovernum** (ˌduːrəʊ'vɜːnəm, ˌdjʊə-) **2** a regional council area of New Zealand, on E central South Island on **Canterbury Bight**: mountainous with coastal lowlands; agricultural. Chief town: Christchurch. Pop: 491 565 (2001) Area: 43 371 sq km (16 742 sq miles)
▷ www.ecan.govt.nz
▷ www.canterbury.net.nz

Canterbury bell *n* a biennial European plant related to the campanula and widely cultivated for its blue, violet, or white flowers

cantharides (kæn'θærɪˌdiːz) *pl n, sing* **cantharis** ('kænθərɪs) a diuretic and urogenital stimulant prepared from the dried bodies of Spanish fly. Also called: **Spanish fly** [c15 from L, pl of *cantharis*, from Gk *kantharis* Spanish fly]

cant hook *or* **dog** *n forestry* a wooden pole with a blunt steel tip and an adjustable hook at one end, used for handling logs

canthus ('kænθəs) *n, pl* **canthi** (-ˌθaɪ) the inner or outer corner of the eye, formed by the natural junction of the eyelids [c17 from NL, from L: iron tyre]

canticle ('kæntɪkᵊl) *n* a nonmetrical hymn, derived from the Bible and used in the liturgy of certain Christian churches [c13 from L *canticulum*, dim. of *canticus* a song, from *canere* to sing]

cantilena (ˌkæntɪ'leɪnə) *n* a smooth flowing style in the writing of vocal music [c18 It.]

cantilever ('kæntɪˌliːvə) *n* **1** a beam, girder, or structural framework that is fixed at one end only **2** a part of a beam or a structure projecting outwards beyond its support [c17 ?from CANT[2] + LEVER]

cantilever bridge *n* a bridge having spans that are constructed as cantilevers

cantillate ('kæntɪˌleɪt) *vb* **cantillates, cantillating, cantillated** **1** to chant (passages of the Hebrew Scriptures) according to the traditional Jewish melody **2** to intone or chant [c19 from LL *cantillāre* to sing softly, from L *cantāre* to sing] > ˌ**cantil'lation** *n*

cantle ('kæntᵊl) *n* **1** the back part of a saddle that slopes upwards **2** a broken-off piece [c14 from OF *cantel*, from *cant* corner]

canto ('kæntəʊ) *n, pl* **cantos** a main division of a long poem [c16 from It.: song, from L, from *canere* to sing]

canto fermo ('kæntəʊ 'fɜːməʊ) *or* **cantus firmus** ('kæntəs 'fɜːməs) *n* **1** a melody that is the basis to which other parts are added in polyphonic music **2** the traditional Church plainchant as prescribed by use and regulation [It., from Med L: fixed song]

canton *n* **1** ('kæntɒn, kæn'tɒn) a political division of Switzerland **2** ('kæntən) *heraldry* a small square charge on a shield, usually in the top left corner ▷ *vb* **3** (kæn'tɒn) (*tr*) to divide into cantons **4** (kən'tuːn) (esp formerly) to allocate accommodation to (military personnel, etc) [c16 from OF: corner, from It., from *canto* corner, from L *canthus* iron rim] > '**cantonal** *adj*

Canton *n* **1** (kæn'tɒn) a port in SE China, capital of Guangdong province, on the Zhu Jiang (Pearl River): the first Chinese port open to European trade. Pop: 3 306 277 (1999 est). Chinese names: **Guangzhou, Kwangchow** **2** ('kæntən) a city in the US, in NE Ohio. Pop: 80 806 (2000)

Cantonese (ˌkæntə'niːz) *n* **1** the Chinese language spoken in the city of Canton, Guangdong and Guanxi provinces, Hong Kong, and elsewhere inside and outside China **2** (*pl* **Cantonese**) a native or inhabitant of Canton city or Guangdong province ▷ *adj* **3** of or relating to Canton or Guangdong or the Chinese language spoken there

cantonment (kən'tuːnmənt) *n mil* (esp formerly) **1** a large training camp **2** the winter quarters of a campaigning army **3** *history* a permanent military camp in British India

Canton River (kæn'tɒn) *n* another name for the **Zhu Jiang**

cantor ('kæntɔː) *n* **1** *Judaism* a man employed to lead synagogue services **2** *Christianity* the leader of the singing in a church choir [c16 from L: singer, from *canere* to sing]

cantorial (kæn'tɔːrɪəl) *adj* **1** of a precentor **2** (of part of a choir) on the same side of a cathedral, etc, as the precentor

cantoris (kæn'tɔːrɪs) *adj* (in antiphonal music) to be sung by the cantorial side of a choir ▷ Cf **decani** [L: genitive of *cantor* precentor]

Cantuar. ('kæntjʊˌɑː) *abbrev for* Cantuariensis [L: (Archbishop) of Canterbury]

Canuck (kə'nʌk) *n, adj US & Canad inf* Canadian [c19 from ?]

Canute, Cnut, *or* **Knut** (kə'njuːt) *n* died 1035, Danish king of England (1016–35), Denmark (1018–35), and Norway (1028–35). He defeated Edmund II of England (1016), but divided the kingdom with him until Edmund's death. An able ruler, he invaded Scotland (1027) and drove Olaf II from Norway (1028)

canvas ('kænvəs) *n* **1a** a heavy cloth made of cotton, hemp, or jute, used for sails, tents, etc **1b** (*as modifier*): *a canvas bag* **2a** a piece of canvas, etc, on which a painting is done, usually in oils **2b** an oil painting **3** a tent or tents collectively **4** *naut* the sails of a vessel collectively **5** any coarse loosely woven cloth on which tapestry, etc, is done **6** (preceded by *the*) the floor of a boxing or wrestling ring **7** *rowing* the covered part at either end of a racing boat: *to win by a canvas* **8** **under canvas** **8a** in tents **8b** *naut* with sails unfurled [c14 from Norman F *canevas*, ult. from L *cannabis* hemp]

canvasback ('kænvəsˌbæk) *n, pl* **canvasbacks** *or* **canvasback** a North American diving duck, the male of which has a reddish-brown head

canvass ('kænvəs) *vb* **1** to solicit votes, orders, etc, (from) **2** to determine the opinions of (voters before an election, etc), esp by conducting a survey **3** to investigate (something) thoroughly, esp by discussion **4** *chiefly US* to inspect (votes) to determine their validity ▷ *n* **5** a solicitation of opinions, votes, etc [c16 prob. from obs. sense of CANVAS (to toss someone in a canvas sheet, hence, to criticize)] > '**canvasser** *n*

canyon *or* **cañon** ('kænjən) *n* a gorge or ravine, esp in North America, usually formed by a river [c19 from Sp., from *caña* tube, from L *canna* cane]

canzonetta (ˌkænzə'nɛtə) *or* **canzonet** (ˌkænzə'nɛt) *n* a short, lively song, typically of the 16th to 18th centuries [c16 It.: dim. of *canzone*, from L *canere* to sing]

caoutchouc ('kaʊtʃʊk) *n* another name for **rubber**[1] (sense 1) [C18 from F, from obs. Sp., from Quechua]

cap (kæp) *n* **1** a covering for the head, esp a small close-fitting one **2** such a covering serving to identify the wearer's rank, occupation, etc: *a nurse's cap* **3** something that protects or covers: *lens cap* **4** an uppermost surface or part: *the cap of a wave* **5a** See **percussion cap** **5b** a small amount of explosive enclosed in paper and used in a toy gun **6** *sport, chiefly Brit* **6a** an emblematic hat or beret given to someone chosen for a representative team **6b** a player chosen for such a team **7** any part like a cap in shape **8** *bot* the pileus of a mushroom or toadstool **9** *hunting* money contributed to the funds of a hunt by a follower who is neither a subscriber nor a farmer, in return for a day's hunting **10** *anat* **10a** the natural enamel covering a tooth **10b** an artificial protective covering for a tooth **11** Also: **Dutch cap, diaphragm** a contraceptive membrane placed over the mouth of the cervix **12** an upper financial limit **13** a mortarboard worn at an academic ceremony (esp in **cap and gown**) **14** *meteorol* **14a** the cloud covering the peak of a mountain **14b** the transient top of detached clouds above an increasing cumulus **15 set one's cap at** (of a woman) to be determined to win as a husband or lover **16 cap in hand** humbly, as when asking a favour ▷ *vb* **caps, capping, capped** (*tr*) **17** to cover, as with a cap: *snow capped the mountain tops* **18** *inf* to outdo; excel **19 cap it all** to provide the finishing touch **20** *sport, Brit* to select (a player) for a representative team **21** to seal off (an oil or gas well) **22** to impose an upper limit on the level of increase of (a tax): *charge-cap* **23** *chiefly Scot & NZ* to award a degree to [OE *cæppe*, from LL *cappa* hood, ?from L *caput* head]

CAP *abbrev for:* Common Agricultural Policy: (in the EU) the system for supporting farm incomes by maintaining agricultural prices at agreed levels

cap. *abbrev for:* **1** capital **2** capitalize **3** capital letter

Capa ('kæpə) *n* **Robert,** real name *André Friedmann.* 1913–54, Hungarian photographer, who established his reputation as a photojournalist during the Spanish Civil War

capability (ˌkeɪpə'bɪlɪtɪ) *n, pl* **capabilities** **1** the quality of being capable; ability **2** the quality of being susceptible to the use or treatment indicated: *the capability of a metal to be fused* **3** (*usually pl*) potential aptitude

Capablanca (*Spanish* kapa'βlaŋka) *n* **José Raúl** (xo'se ra'ul), called *Capa* or *the Chess Machine* 1888–1942, Cuban chess player; world champion 1921–27

capable ('keɪpəb°l) *adj* **1** having ability; competent **2** (*postpositive; foll by of*) able or having the skill (to do something): *she is capable of hard work* **3** (*postpositive; foll by of*) having the temperament or inclination (to do something): *he seemed capable of murder* [C16 from F, from LL *capābilis* able to take in, from L *capere* to take] > '**capableness** *n* > '**capably** *adv*

capacious (kə'peɪʃəs) *adj* capable of holding much; roomy [C17 from L, from *capere* to take] > ca'**paciously** *adv* > ca'**paciousness** *n*

capacitance (kə'pæsɪtəns) *n* **1** the property of a system that enables it to store electric charge **2** a measure of this, equal to the charge that must be added to such a system to raise its electrical potential by one unit. Former name: **capacity** [C20 from CAPACIT(Y) + -ANCE] > ca'**pacitive** *adj*

capacitor (kə'pæsɪtə) *n* a device for accumulating electric charge, usually consisting of two conducting surfaces separated by a dielectric. Former name: **condenser**

capacity (kə'pæsɪtɪ) *n, pl* **capacities** **1** the ability or power to contain, absorb, or hold **2** the amount that can be contained: *a capacity of six gallons* **3a** the maximum amount something can contain or absorb (esp in **filled to capacity**) **3b** (*as modifier*): *a capacity crowd* **4** the ability to understand or learn: *he has a great capacity for Greek* **5** the ability to do or produce: *the factory's output was not at capacity* **6** a specified position or function **7** a measure of the electrical output of a piece of apparatus such as a generator or accumulator **8** *electronics* a former name for **capacitance** **9** *computing* **9a** the number of words or characters that can be stored in a storage device **9b** the range of numbers that can be processed in a register **10** legal competence: *the capacity to make a will* [C15 from OF *capacite*, from L, from *capāx* spacious, from *capere* to take]

cap and bells *n* the traditional garb of a court jester, including a cap with bells

cap-a-pie (ˌkæpə'piː) *adv* (dressed, armed, etc) from head to foot [C16 from OF]

caparison (kə'pærɪs°n) *n* **1** a decorated covering for a horse **2** rich or elaborate clothing and ornaments ▷ *vb* **3** (*tr*) to put a caparison on [C16 via obs. F from OSp. *caparazón* saddlecloth, prob. from *capa* CAPE[1]]

cape[1] (keɪp) *n* a sleeveless garment like a cloak but usually shorter [C16 from F, from Provençal *capa*, from LL *cappa*; see CAP]

cape[2] (keɪp) *n* a headland or promontory [C14 from OF *cap*, from OProvençal, from L *caput* head]

Cape (keɪp) *n* **the 1** the SW region of South Africa, in Western Cape province **2** See **Cape of Good Hope**

Cape Barren goose *n* a greyish Australian goose, *Cereopsis novaehollandiae*, having a black bill with a greenish cere [C19 named after *Cape Barren* Island in the Bass Strait]

Cape Breton Island *n* an island off SE Canada, in NE Nova Scotia, separated from the mainland by the Strait of Canso: its easternmost point is **Cape Breton.** Pop: 120 098 (1991) Area: 10 280 sq km (3970 sq miles)

Cape Cod *n* **1** a long sandy peninsula in SE Massachusetts, between **Cape Cod Bay** and the Atlantic **2** Also called: **Cape Cod cottage** a one-storey cottage of timber construction with a simple gable roof and a large central chimney: originated on Cape Cod in the 18th century

Cc

Cape Colony *n* the name from 1652 until 1910 of the former **Cape Province** of South Africa

Cape Coloured *n* (in South Africa) another name for a **Coloured** (sense 2)

Cape doctor *n S African inf* a strong fresh SE wind blowing in the vicinity of Cape Town, esp in the summer

Cape Dutch *n* **1** (in South Africa) a distinctive style in furniture or buildings **2** an obsolete name for **Afrikaans**
▷ www.artnet.com/library/01/0138/T013814.ASP

Cape Flats *pl n* the strip of low-lying land in South Africa joining the Cape Peninsula proper to the African mainland

Cape gooseberry *n* another name for **strawberry tomato**

Cape Horn *n* a rocky headland on an island at the extreme S tip of South America, belonging to Chile. It is notorious for gales and heavy seas; until the building of the Panama Canal it lay on the only sea route between the Atlantic and the Pacific. Also called: **the Horn**

Čapek (*Czech* 'tʃapɛk) *n* **Karel** ('karɛl) 1890–1938, Czech dramatist and novelist; author of R.U.R. (1921), which introduced the word "robot", and (with his brother **Josef**) *The Insect Play* (1921)

capelin ('kæpəlɪn) *or* **caplin** ('kæplɪn) *n* a small marine food fish of northern and Arctic seas [C17 from F *capelan*, from OProvençal, lit.: chaplain]

capellmeister *or* **kapellmeister** (kæ'pɛlˌmaɪstə) *n* a person in charge of an orchestra, esp in an 18th-century princely household [from G, from *Kapelle* chapel + *Meister* MASTER]

Cape of Good Hope *n* a cape in SW South Africa south of Cape Town

Cape Peninsula *n* (in South Africa) the peninsula and the part of the mainland on which Cape Town and most of its suburbs are located
Cape pigeon *n* a kind of petrel common in S Africa
Cape Province *n* a former province of S South Africa; replaced in 1994 by the new provinces of Northern Cape, Western Cape, Eastern Cape and part of North-West. Capital: Cape Town. Official name: **Cape of Good Hope Province.** Former name (1652–1910): **Cape Colony**
caper[1] ('keɪpə) *n* **1** a playful skip or leap **2** a high-spirited escapade **3 cut a caper** *or* **capers** to skip, leap, or frolic **4** *US & Canad sl* a crime ▷ *vb* **5** (*intr*) to leap or dance about in a light-hearted manner [c16 prob. from CAPRIOLE]
caper[2] ('keɪpə) *n* **1** a spiny trailing Mediterranean shrub with edible flower buds **2** its pickled flower buds, used in sauces [c15 from earlier *capers, capres* (assumed to be pl), from L, from Gk *kapparis*]
capercaillie *or* **capercailzie** (ˌkæpəˈkeɪljɪ) *n* a large European woodland grouse having a black plumage [c16 from Scot. Gaelic *capull coille* horse of the woods]
Capernaum (kəˈpɜːnɪəm) *n* a ruined town in N Israel, on the NW shore of the Sea of Galilee: closely associated with Jesus Christ during his ministry
Cape smoke *n S African inf* South African brandy
Cape sparrow *n* a sparrow very common in southern Africa. Also called (esp S African): **mossie**
Capet (ˈkæpɪt, kæˈpɛt; *French* kapɛ) *n* **Hugh** or **Hugues** (yg) ?938–996 AD, king of France (987–96); founder of the Capetian dynasty
Cape Town *n* the legislative capital of South Africa and capital of Western Cape province, situated in the southwest on Table Bay: founded in 1652, the first White settlement in southern Africa; important port. Pop (urban area): 2 415 408 (1996)
▷ www.ctcc.gov.za
▷ www.capetown.co.za
▷ www.sa-venues.com/wcattractions_peninsula.htm
Cape Verde (vɜːd) *n* a republic in the Atlantic off the coast of West Africa, consisting of a group of ten islands and five islets: an overseas territory of Portugal until 1975, when the islands became independent. Official language: Portuguese. Religion: Christian (Roman Catholic) majority; animist minority. Currency: Cape Verdean escudo. Capital: Praia. Pop: 446 000 (2001 est). Area: 4033 sq km (1557 sq miles)
▷ www.governo.cv
Cape Verdean (ˈvɜːdɪən) *adj* **1** of or relating to Cape Verde or its inhabitants ▷ *n* **2** a native or inhabitant of Cape Verde
Cape York *n* the northernmost point of the Australian mainland, in N Queensland on the Torres Strait at the tip of **Cape York Peninsula** (a peninsula between the Coral Sea and the Gulf of Carpentaria)
Cap-Haitien (*French* kapaisjɛ̃, -tjɛ̃) *n* a port in N Haiti: capital during the French colonial period. Pop: 107 026 (1997 est). Also called: **le Cap** (lə kap)
capias (ˈkeɪpɪˌæs, ˈkæp-) *n law* a writ directing a sheriff or other officer to arrest a named person [c15 from L, lit.: you must take, from *capere*]
capillarity (ˌkæpɪˈlærɪtɪ) *n* a phenomenon caused by surface tension and resulting in the elevation or depression of the surface of a liquid in contact with a solid. Also called: **capillary action**
capillary (kəˈpɪlərɪ) *adj* **1** resembling a hair; slender **2** (of tubes) having a fine bore **3** *anat* of the delicate thin-walled blood vessels that interconnect between the arterioles and the venules **4** *physics* of or relating to capillarity ▷ *n, pl* **capillaries 5** *anat* any of the capillary blood vessels [c17 from L *capillāris*, from *capillus* hair]
capital[1] (ˈkæpɪtᵊl) *n* **1a** the seat of government of a country **1b** (*as modifier*): *a capital city* **2** material wealth owned by an individual or business enterprise **3** wealth available for or capable of use in the production of further wealth, as by industrial investment **4 make capital (out) of** to get advantage from **5** (*sometimes cap*) the capitalist class or their interests: *capital versus labour* **6** *accounting* **6a** the ownership interests of a business as represented by the excess of assets over liabilities **6b** the nominal value of the issued shares **7** any assets or resources **8a** a capital letter. Abbrev: **cap. 8b** (*as modifier*): *capital B* ▷ *adj* **9** (*prenominal*) *law* involving or punishable by death: *a capital offence* **10** very serious: *a capital error* **11** primary, chief, or principal: *our capital concern* **12** of, relating to, or designating the large letter used chiefly as the initial letter in personal names and place names and often for abbreviations and acronyms. See also **upper case 13** *chiefly Brit* excellent; first-rate: *a capital idea* [c13 from L *capitālis* (adj) concerning the head, from *caput* head]
capital[2] (ˈkæpɪtᵊl) *n* the upper part of a column or pier that supports the entablature [c14 from OF, from LL *capitellum*, dim. of *caput* head]
capital account *n* **1** *econ* that part of a balance of payments composed of movements of capital **2** *accounting* a financial statement showing the net value of a company at a specified date
capital expenditure *n* expenditure to increase fixed assets
capital gain *n* the amount by which the selling price of a financial asset exceeds its cost
capital gains tax *n* a tax on the profit made from sale of an asset
capital goods *pl n econ* goods that are themselves utilized in the production of other goods
capitalism (ˈkæpɪtəˌlɪzəm) *n* an economic system based on the private ownership of the means of production, distribution, and exchange. Also called: **free enterprise, private enterprise** ▷ Cf **socialism** (sense 1)
capitalist (ˈkæpɪtəlɪst) *n* **1** a person who owns capital, esp capital invested in a business **2** *politics* a supporter of capitalism ▷ *adj* **3** relating to capital, capitalists, or capitalism > ˌ**capitalˈistic** *adj*
capitalization *or* **capitalisation** (ˌkæpɪtəlaɪˈzeɪʃən) *n* **1a** the act of capitalizing **1b** the sum so derived **2** *accounting* the par value of the total share capital issued by a company **3** the act of estimating the present value of future payments, etc
capitalize *or* **capitalise** (ˈkæpɪtəˌlaɪz) *vb* **capitalizes, capitalizing, capitalized** *or* **capitalises, capitalising, capitalised.** (*mainly tr*) **1** (*intr*; foll by *on*) to take advantage (of) **2** to write or print (text) in capital letters **3** to convert (debt or earnings) into capital stock **4** to authorize (a business enterprise) to issue a specified amount of capital stock **5** to provide with capital **6** *accounting* to treat (expenditures) as assets **7a** to estimate the present value of (a periodical income) **7b** to compute the present value of (a business) from actual or potential earnings
capitally (ˈkæpɪtəlɪ) *adv chiefly Brit* in an excellent manner; admirably
capital punishment *n* the punishment of death for a crime; death penalty
capital ship *n* one of the largest and most heavily armed ships in a naval fleet
capital stock *n* **1** the par value of the total share capital that a company is authorized to issue **2** the total physical capital existing in an economy at any moment of time
capitation (ˌkæpɪˈteɪʃən) *n* **1** a tax levied on the basis of a fixed amount per head **2 capitation grant** a grant of money given to every person who qualifies under certain conditions [c17 from LL, from L *caput* head]
Capitol (ˈkæpɪtᵊl) *n* **1a** another name for the **Capitoline 1b** the temple on the Capitoline **2 the** the main building of the US Congress **3** (*sometimes not cap*) Also

called: **statehouse** (in the US) the building housing any state legislature [c14 from Latin *Capitōlium*, from *caput* head]

Capitoline ('kæpɪtᵊ,laɪn, kə'pɪtəʊ-) *n* **1 the** the most important of the Seven Hills of Rome. The temple of Jupiter was on the southern summit and the ancient citadel on the northern summit ▷ *adj* **2** of or relating to the Capitoline or the temple of Jupiter

capitulate (kə'pɪtjʊ,leɪt) *vb* **capitulates, capitulating, capitulated** (*intr*) to surrender, esp under agreed conditions [c16 (meaning: to draw up in order): from Med. L *capitulare* to draw up under heads, from *capitulum* CHAPTER] > **ca'pitu,lator** *n*

capitulation (kə,pɪtjʊ'leɪʃən) *n* **1** the act of capitulating **2** a document containing terms of surrender **3** a statement summarizing the main divisions of a subject > **ca'pitulatory** *adj*

capitulum (kə'pɪtjʊləm) *n, pl* **capitula** (-lə) an inflorescence in the form of a disc, the youngest flowers at the centre. It occurs in the daisy and related plants [c18 from L, lit.: a little head, from *caput* head]

capo ('kæpəʊ) *n, pl* **capos** a device fitted across all the strings of a guitar, lute, etc, so as to raise the pitch of each string simultaneously. Also called: **capo tasto** ('tæstəʊ) [from It. *capo tasto* head stop]

capoeira (,kæpʊ'eɪrə) *n* a movement discipline combining martial art and dance, which originated among African slaves in 19th-century Brazil [c20 from Portuguese]

capon ('keɪpən) *n* a castrated cock fowl fattened for eating [OE *capun*, from L *cāpō* capon] > **'capon,ize** *or* **'capon,ise** *vb*

Capone (kə'pəʊn) *n* **Alphonse,** called *Al*. 1899–1947, US gangster in Chicago during Prohibition

Caporetto (kapo'retto) *n* the Italian name for **Kobarid**

capote (kə'pəʊt) *n* a long cloak or soldier's coat, usually with a hood [c19 from F: cloak, from *cape*]

Capote (kə'pəʊtɪ) *n* **Truman** 1924–84, US writer; his novels include *Other Voices, Other Rooms* (1948) and *In Cold Blood* (1964), based on an actual multiple murder

Capp (kæp) *n* **Al,** full name *Alfred Caplin*. 1909–79, US cartoonist, famous for his comic strip *Li'l Abner*

Cappadocia (,kæpə'dəʊsɪə) *n* an ancient region of E Asia Minor famous for its horses

Cappadocian (,kæpə'dəʊsɪən) *adj* **1** of or relating to Cappadocia or its inhabitants ▷ *n* **2** a native or inhabitant of Cappadocia

capping ('kæpɪŋ) *n* *Scot & NZ* **a** the act of conferring an academic degree **b** (*as modifier*): *Capping Day*

cappuccino (,kæpʊ'tʃi:nəʊ) *n, pl* **cappuccinos** coffee with steamed milk, usually sprinkled with powdered chocolate [It.: CAPUCHIN]

Capra ('kæprə) *n* **Frank** 1896–1992, US film director born in Italy. His films include *It Happened One Night* (1934), *It's a Wonderful Life* (1946), and several propaganda films during World War II

Capri (kə'pri:; *Italian* 'kapri) *n* an island off W Italy, in the Bay of Naples: resort since Roman times. Pop: 8000 (latest est). Area: about 13 sq km (5 sq miles)

capriccio (kə'prɪtʃɪ,əʊ) *or* **caprice** *n, pl* **capriccios, capricci** (-'pri:tʃɪ), *or* **caprices** *music* a lively piece of irregular musical form [c17 from It.: CAPRICE]

capriccioso (kə,prɪtʃɪ'əʊzəʊ) *adv* *music* to be played in a free and lively style [It.: from *capriccio* CAPRICE]

caprice (kə'pri:s) *n* **1** a sudden change of attitude, behaviour, etc **2** a tendency to such changes **3** another word for **capriccio** [c17 from F, from It. *capriccio* a shiver, caprice, from *capo* head + *riccio* lit.: hedgehog]

capricious (kə'prɪʃəs) *adj* characterized by or liable to sudden unpredictable changes in attitude or behaviour > **ca'priciously** *adv*

Capricorn ('kæprɪ,kɔ:n) *n* **1** *astrol* Also called: the **Goat, Capricornus** the tenth sign of the zodiac. The sun is in this sign between about Dec 22 and Jan 19 **2** *astron* a S constellation **3 tropic of Capricorn** See **tropic** (sense 1) [c14 from L *Capricornus*, from *caper* goat + *cornū* horn]

Capricornia (,kæprɪ'kɔ:nɪə) *n* the regions of Australia in the tropic of Capricorn

caprine ('kæpraɪn) *adj* of or resembling a goat [c17 from L *caprīnus*, from *caper* goat]

capriole ('kæprɪ,əʊl) *n* **1** *dressage* a high upward but not forward leap made by a horse with all four feet off the ground ▷ *vb* **caprioles, caprioling, caprioled 2** (*intr*) to perform a capriole [c16 from F, from OIt., from *capriolo* roebuck, from L *capreolus*, *caper* goat]

caps. *abbrev for* capital letters

capsicum ('kæpsɪkəm) *n* **1** any of a genus of tropical American plants related to the potato, having mild or pungent seeds enclosed in a bell-shaped fruit **2** the fruit of any of these plants, used as a vegetable or ground to produce a condiment ▷ See also **pepper** (sense 4) [c18 from NL, from L *capsa* box]

capsid[1] ('kæpsɪd) *n* a bug related to the water bug that feeds on plant tissues, causing damage to crops [c19 from NL *Capsus* (genus)]

capsid[2] ('kæpsɪd) *n* the outer protein coat of a mature virus [c20 from F *capside*, from L *capsa* box]

capsize (kæp'saɪz) *vb* **capsizes, capsizing, capsized** to overturn accidentally; upset [c18 from ?] > **cap'sizal** *n*

capstan ('kæpstən) *n* **1** a machine with a drum equipped with a ratchet, used for hauling in heavy ropes, etc **2** the rotating shaft in a tape recorder that pulls the tape past the head [c14 from OProvençal *cabestan*, from L *capistrum* a halter, from *capere* to seize]

capstan lathe *n* a lathe for repetitive work, having a rotatable turret to hold tools for successive operations. Also called: **turret lathe**

capstone ('kæp,stəʊn) *n* another word for **copestone** (sense 2)

capsule ('kæpsju:l) *n* **1** a soluble case of gelatine enclosing a dose of medicine **2** a thin metal cap, seal, or cover **3** *bot* **3a** a dry fruit that liberates its seeds by splitting, as in the violet, or through pores, as in the poppy **3b** the spore-producing organ of mosses and liverworts **4** *anat* a membranous envelope surrounding any of certain organs or parts **5** See **space capsule 6** an aeroplane cockpit that can be ejected in a flight emergency, complete with crew, instruments, etc **7** (*modifier*) in a highly concise form: *a capsule summary* [c17 from F, from L *capsula*, dim. of *capsa* box] > **'capsu,late** *adj*

capsulize *or* **capsulise** ('kæpsjʊ,laɪz) *vb* **capsulizes, capsulizing, capsulized** *or* **capsulises, capsulising, capsulised** (*tr*) **1** to state (information, etc) in a highly condensed form **2** to enclose in a capsule

Capt. *abbrev for* Captain

captain ('kæptɪn) *n* **1** the person in charge of a vessel **2** an officer of the navy who holds a rank junior to a rear admiral **3** an officer of the army, certain air forces, and the marines who holds a rank junior to a major **4** the officer in command of a civil aircraft **5** the leader of a team in games **6** a person in command over a group, organization, etc: *a captain of industry* **7** *US* a policeman in charge of a precinct ▷ *vb* **8** (*tr*) to be captain of [c14 from OF, from LL *capitāneus* chief, from L *caput* head] > **'captaincy** *or* **'captainship** *n*

Captain Cooker ('kʊkə) *n* *NZ* a wild pig [from Captain James COOK, who first released pigs in the New Zealand bush]

caption ('kæpʃən) *n* **1** a title, brief explanation, or comment accompanying an illustration **2** a heading or title of a chapter, article, etc **3** graphic material used in television presentation **4** another name for **subtitle** (sense 2) **5** the formal heading of a legal document ▷ *vb* **6** to provide with a caption or captions [c14 (meaning: seizure): from L *captiō* a seizing, from *capere* to take]

captious ('kæpʃəs) *adj* apt to make trivial criticisms [c14

Cc

(meaning: catching in error): from L *captiōsus*, from *captiō* a seizing] > **'captiously** *adv* > **'captiousness** *n*

captivate ('kæptɪ,veɪt) *vb* **captivates, captivating, captivated** (*tr*) to hold the attention of by fascinating; enchant [C16 from LL *captivāre*, from *captīvus* CAPTIVE] > **'capti,vating** *adj* > **,capti'vation** *n*

captive ('kæptɪv) *n* **1** a person or animal that is confined or restrained **2** a person whose behaviour is dominated by some emotion: *a captive of love* ▷ *adj* **3** held as prisoner **4** held under restriction or control; confined **5** captivated **6** unable to avoid speeches, advertisements, etc: *a captive audience* [C14 from L *captīvus*, from *capere* to take]

captivity (kæp'tɪvɪtɪ) *n, pl* **captivities 1** imprisonment **2** the period of imprisonment

captor ('kæptə) *n* a person or animal that holds another captive [C17 from L, from *capere* to take]

capture ('kæptʃə) *vb* **captures, capturing, captured** (*tr*) **1** to take prisoner or gain control over: *to capture a town* **2** (in a game) to win possession of: *to capture a pawn in chess* **3** to succeed in representing (something elusive): *the artist captured her likeness* **4** *physics* (of an atom, etc) to acquire (an additional particle) **5** to insert or transfer (data) into a computer ▷ *n* **6** the act of taking by force **7** the person or thing captured **8** *physics* a process by which an atom, etc, acquires an additional particle **9** *geog* the process by which the headwaters of one river are diverted into another **10** *computing* the collection of data for processing [C16 from L *captūra* a catching, that which is caught, from *capere* to take] > **'capturer** *n*

Capua ('kæpjʊə; *Italian* 'kapua) *n* a town in S Italy, in NW Campania: strategically important in ancient times, situated on the Appian Way. Pop: 19 520 (1990)

Capuana (*Italian* ka'pwa:na) *n* **Luigi** 1839–1915, Italian realist novelist, dramatist, and critic. His works include the novel *Giacinta* (1879) and the play *Malia* (1895)

capuchin ('kæpjʊtʃɪn, -jʊʃɪn) *n* **1** an agile intelligent S American monkey having a cowl of thick hair on the top of the head **2** a woman's hooded cloak **3** (*sometimes cap*) a variety of domestic fancy pigeon [C16 from F, from It., from *cappuccio* hood]

Capuchin ('kæpjʊtʃɪn, -jʊʃɪn) *n* **1** a friar belonging to a branch of the Franciscan Order founded in 1525 ▷ *adj* **2** of or relating to this order [C16 from F, from It. *cappuccio* hood]

capybara (,kæpɪ'bɑ:rə) *n* the largest rodent, resembling a guinea pig and native to Central and South America [C18 from Port. *capibara*, from Tupi]

Caquetá (*Spanish* kake'ta) *n* the Japurá River from its source in Colombia to the border with Brazil

car (kɑ:) *n* **1a** Also called: **motorcar, automobile** a self-propelled road vehicle designed to carry passengers, that is powered by an internal-combustion engine **1b** (*as modifier*): *car coat* **2** a conveyance for passengers, freight, etc, such as a cable car or the carrier of an airship or balloon **3** *Brit* a railway vehicle for passengers only **4** *chiefly US & Canad* a railway carriage or van **5** a poetic word for **chariot** [C14 from Anglo-F *carre*, ult. rel. to L *carra*, *carrum* two-wheeled wagon, prob. of Celtic origin]
▷ www.planet-cars.net
▷ www.britishcarlinks.com

CAR *abbrev for* compound annual return

carabineer *or* **carabinier** (,kærəbɪ'nɪə) *n* variants of **carbineer**

carabiner (,kærə'bi:nə) *n* a variant of **karabiner**

caracal ('kærə,kæl) *n* **1** a lynxlike feline mammal inhabiting deserts of N Africa and S Asia, having a smooth coat of reddish fur **2** this fur [C18 from F, from Turkish *kara kūlāk*, lit.: black ear]

Caracalla (,kærə'kælə) *n* real name *Marcus Aurelius Antoninus*, original name *Bassianus*. 188–217 AD, Roman emperor (211–17): ruled with cruelty and extravagance; assassinated

caracara (,kɑ:rə'kɑ:rə) *n* a large carrion-eating bird of prey of Central and South America, having long legs [C19 from Sp. or Port., from Tupi; imit.]

Caracas (kə'rækəs, -'rɑ:-; *Spanish* ka'rakas) *n* the capital of Venezuela, in the north: founded in 1567; major industrial and commercial centre, notably for oil companies. Pop: 1 975 787 (2000 est)
▷ www.discovervenezuela.com/caracas.cfm

caracole ('kærə,kəʊl) *or* **caracol** ('kærə,kɒl) *dressage* ▷ *n* **1** a half turn to the right or left ▷ *vb* **caracoles, caracoling, caracoled** *or* **caracols, caracoling, caracoled** (*intr*) **2** to execute a half turn [C17 from F, from Sp. *caracol* snail, spiral staircase]

Caractacus (kə'ræktəkəs) *n* a variant of **Caratacus**

caracul ('kærə,kʌl) *n* **1** Also called: **Persian lamb** the black loosely curled fur obtained from the skins of newly born lambs of the karakul sheep **2** a variant spelling of **karakul**

carafe (kə'ræf, -'rɑ:f) *n* an open-topped glass container for serving water or wine at table [C18 from F, from It., from Sp., from Ar. *gharrāfah* vessel]

carageen ('kærə,gi:n) *n* a variant spelling of **carrageen**

carambola (,kærəm'bəʊlə) *n* the yellow edible star-shaped fruit of a Brazilian tree, cultivated in the tropics, esp SE Asia. Also called: **star fruit** [Sp., from Port.]

caramel ('kærəməl) *n* **1** burnt sugar, used for colouring and flavouring food **2** a chewy sweet made from sugar, milk, etc [C18 from F, from Sp. *caramelo*, from ?]

caramelize *or* **caramelise** ('kærəmə,laɪz) *vb* **caramelizes, caramelizing, caramelized** *or* **caramelises, caramelising, caramelised** to convert or be converted into caramel

carapace ('kærə,peɪs) *n* the thick hard shield that covers part of the body of crabs, tortoises, etc [C19 from F, from Sp. *carapacho*, from ?]

carat ('kærət) *n* **1** a measure of the weight of precious stones, esp diamonds, now standardized as 0.20 grams **2** Usual US and Canad spelling: **karat** a measure of the gold in an alloy, expressed as the number of parts of gold in 24 parts of the alloy [C16 from OF, from Med. L, from Ar. *qīrāt* weight of four grains, from Gk, from *keras* horn]

Caratacus (kə'rætəkəs), **Caractacus**, *or* **Caradoc** (kə'rædək) *n* died ?54 AD, British chieftain: led an unsuccessful resistance against the Romans (43–50)

Caravaggio (*Italian* kara'vaddʒo) *n* **Michelangelo Merisi da** (mike'landʒelo me'ri:zi da) 1571–1610, Italian painter, noted for his realistic depiction of religious subjects and for his dramatic use of chiaroscuro

caravan ('kærə,væn) *n* **1a** a large enclosed vehicle capable of being pulled by a car and equipped to be lived in. US and Canad name: **trailer 1b** (*as modifier*): *a caravan site* **2** (esp in some parts of Asia and Africa) a company of traders or other travellers journeying together **3** a large covered vehicle, esp a gaily coloured one used by Gypsies, circuses, etc ▷ *vb* **caravans, caravanning, caravanned 4** (*intr*) *Brit* to travel or have a holiday in a caravan [C16 from It. *caravana*, from Persian *kārwān*]

caravanserai (,kærə'vænsə,raɪ) *or* **caravansary** (,kærə'vænsərɪ) *n, pl* **caravanserais** *or* **caravansaries** (in some Eastern countries) a large inn enclosing a courtyard, providing accommodation for caravans [C16 from Persian *kārwānsarāī* caravan inn]

caravel ('kærə,vɛl) *or* **carvel** *n* a two- or three-masted sailing ship used by the Spanish and Portuguese in the 15th and 16th centuries [C16 from Port. *caravela*, dim. of *caravo* ship, ult. from Gk *karabos* crab]

caraway ('kærə,weɪ) *n* **1** an umbelliferous Eurasian plant having finely divided leaves and clusters of small whitish flowers **2 caraway seed** the pungent aromatic fruit of this plant, used in cooking [C14 prob. from Med. L *carvi*, from Ar. *karawyā*, from Gk *karon*]

carb (kɑːb) *n inf* **1** short for **carburettor** **2** short for **carbohydrate**
carbaryl (ˈkɑːbərɪl) *n* an organic compound of the carbamate group: used as an insecticide, esp to treat head lice
carbide (ˈkɑːbaɪd) *n* **1** a binary compound of carbon with a metal **2** See **calcium carbide**
carbine (ˈkɑːbaɪn) *n* **1** a light automatic or semiautomatic rifle **2** a light short-barrelled rifle formerly used by cavalry [C17 from F *carabine*, from OF *carabin* carabineer]
carbineer (ˌkɑːbɪˈnɪə), **carabineer,** *or* **carabinier** (ˌkærəbɪˈnɪə) *n* (formerly) a soldier equipped with a carbine
carbo- *or before a vowel* **carb-** *combining form* carbon: *carbohydrate; carbonate*
carbocyclic (ˌkɑːbəʊˈsaɪklɪk) *adj* (of a chemical compound) containing a closed ring of carbon atoms
carbohydrate (ˌkɑːbəʊˈhaɪdreɪt) *n* any of a large group of organic compounds, including sugars and starch, that contain carbon, hydrogen, and oxygen, with the general formula $C_m(H_2O)_n$: a source of food and energy for animals
carbolic acid (kɑːˈbɒlɪk) *n* another name for **phenol**, esp when used as a disinfectant [C19 from CARBO- + -OL[1] + -IC]
carbon (ˈkɑːbᵊn) *n* **1a** a nonmetallic element existing in three crystalline forms: graphite, diamond, and buckminsterfullerene: occurring in all organic compounds. The isotope **carbon-12** is the standard for atomic weight; **carbon-14** is used in radiocarbon dating and as a tracer. Symbol: C; atomic no.: 6; atomic wt.: 12.011 15 **1b** (*as modifier*): *a carbon compound* **2** short for **carbon paper** or **carbon copy** **3** a carbon electrode used in a carbon-arc light **4** a rod or plate, made of carbon, used in some types of battery [C18 from F, from L *carbō* charcoal]
carbon-14 dating *n* another name for **carbon dating**
carbonaceous (ˌkɑːbəˈneɪʃəs) *adj* of, resembling, or containing carbon
carbonade (ˌkɑːbəˈneɪd, -ˈnɑːd) *n* beef and onions stewed in beer [C20 F]
carbonado (ˌkɑːbəˈneɪdəʊ) *n, pl* **carbonados** *or* **carbonadoes** an inferior variety of diamond used in industry. Also called: **black diamond** [Port., lit.: carbonated]
carbon arc *n* an electric arc between two carbon electrodes or between a carbon electrode and materials to be welded
carbonate *n* (ˈkɑːbəˌneɪt, -nɪt) **1** a salt or ester of carbonic acid ▷ *vb* (ˈkɑːbəˌneɪt), **carbonates, carbonating, carbonated** **2** to turn into a carbonate **3** (*tr*) to treat with carbon dioxide, as in the manufacture of soft drinks [C18 from F, from *carbone* CARBON]
carbon black *n* a finely divided form of carbon produced by incomplete combustion of natural gas or petroleum: used in pigments and ink
carbon brush *n* a small spring-loaded block of carbon used to convey current between the stationary and moving parts of an electric generator, motor, etc
carbon copy *n* **1** a duplicate copy of writing, typewriting, or drawing obtained by using carbon paper **2** *inf* a person or thing that is identical to another: *a carbon copy of his first wife*
carbon dating *n* a technique for determining the age of organic materials, such as wood, based on their content of the radioisotope ^{14}C acquired from the atmosphere when they formed part of a living plant
carbon dioxide *n* a colourless odourless incombustible gas present in the atmosphere and formed during respiration, etc: used in fire extinguishers, and as dry ice for refrigeration. Formula: CO_2. Also called: **carbonic-acid gas**
carbonette (ˌkɑːbəˈnɛt) *n* NZ a ball of compressed coal dust used as fuel
carbon fibre *n* a thread of pure carbon used because of its lightness and strength at high temperatures for reinforcing resins, ceramics, and metals, and for fishing rods
carbonic (kɑːˈbɒnɪk) *adj* (of a compound) containing carbon, esp tetravalent carbon
carbonic acid *n* a weak acid formed when carbon dioxide combines with water. Formula: H_2CO_3
carboniferous (ˌkɑːbəˈnɪfərəs) *adj* yielding coal or carbon
Carboniferous (ˌkɑːbəˈnɪfərəs) *adj* **1** of, denoting, or formed in the fifth period of the Palaeozoic era, lasting for 64 million years, during which coal measures were formed ▷ *n* **2 the** the Carboniferous period or rock system divided into the **Upper Carboniferous** period and the **Lower Carboniferous** period
carbonize *or* **carbonise** (ˈkɑːbəˌnaɪz) *vb* **carbonizes, carbonizing, carbonized** *or* **carbonises, carbonising, carbonised** **1** to turn or be turned into carbon as a result of heating, fossilization, chemical treatment, etc **2** (*tr*) to coat (a substance) with carbon > **ˌcarboniˈzation** *or* **ˌcarboniˈsation** *n*
carbon monoxide *n* a colourless odourless poisonous gas formed when carbon compounds burn in insufficient air. Formula: CO
carbon paper *n* a thin sheet of paper coated on one side with a dark waxy pigment, often containing carbon, that is transferred by pressure onto the copying surface below
carbon sink *n* areas of vegetation, especially forests, and the phytoplankton-rich seas that absorb the carbon dioxide produced by the burning of fossil fuels
carbon tax *n* a tax on the emissions caused by the burning of coal, gas, and oil, aimed at reducing the production of greenhouse gases
carbon tetrachloride *n* a colourless volatile nonflammable liquid made from chlorine and used as a solvent, cleaning fluid, and insecticide. Formula: CCl_4. Systematic name: **tetrachloromethane**
car-boot sale *n* a sale of goods from car boots in a site hired for the occasion
Carborundum (ˌkɑːbəˈrʌndəm) *n trademark* any of various abrasive materials, esp one consisting of silicon carbide
carboxyl group *or* **radical** (kɑːˈbɒksaɪl) *n* the monovalent group -COOH: the functional group in organic acids [C19 *carboxyl*, from CARBO- + OXY-[2] + -YL]
carboxylic acid (ˌkɑːbɒkˈsɪlɪk) *n* any of a class of organic acids containing the carboxyl group. See also **fatty acid**
carboy (ˈkɑːˌbɔɪ) *n* a large bottle, usually protected by a basket or box, used for containing corrosive liquids [C18 from Persian *qarāba*]
carbuncle (ˈkɑːˌbʌŋkᵊl) *n* **1** an extensive skin eruption, similar to a boil, with several openings **2** a rounded gemstone, esp a garnet cut without facets [C13 from L *carbunculus*, dim. of *carbō* coal] > **carbuncular** (kɑːˈbʌŋkjʊlə) *adj*
carburation (ˌkɑːbjʊˈreɪʃən) *n* the process of mixing a hydrocarbon fuel with air to make an explosive mixture for an internal-combustion engine
carburet (ˈkɑːbjʊˌrɛt, ˌkɑːbjʊˈrɛt) *vb* **carburets, carburetting, carburetted** *or US* **carburets, carbureting, carbureted** (*tr*) to combine or mix (a gas, etc) with carbon or carbon compounds [C18 from CARB(ON) + -URET]
carburettor, carburetter (ˌkɑːbəˈrɛtə, ˈkɑːbəˌrɛtə), *or US & Canad* **carburetor** (ˈkɑːbəˌreɪtə) *n* a device used in some petrol engines for mixing atomized petrol with air, and regulating the intake of the mixture into the engine
carcajou (ˈkɑːkəˌdʒuː, -kəˌʒuː) *n* a North American name

Cc

for **wolverine** [c18 from Canad F, from Algonquian *karkajou*]

carcass *or* **carcase** ('kɑːkəs) *n* **1** the dead body of an animal, esp one that has been slaughtered for food **2** *inf, usually facetious or derog* a person's body **3** the skeleton or framework of a structure **4** the remains of anything when its life or vitality is gone [c14 from OF *carcasse*]

Carcassonne (*French* karkasɔn) *n* a city in SW France: extensive remains of medieval fortifications. Pop: 44 990 (1990)

carcinogen (kɑː'sɪnədʒən) *n pathol* any substance that produces cancer [c20 from Gk *karkinos* CANCER + -GEN] > ˌ**carcino'genic** *adj*

carcinogenesis (ˌkɑːsɪnəʊ'dʒɛnɪsɪs) *n pathol* the development of cancerous cells from normal ones

carcinoma (ˌkɑːsɪ'nəʊmə) *n, pl* **carcinomas** *or* **carcinomata** (-mətə) *pathol* any malignant tumour derived from epithelial tissue [c18 from L, from Gk, from *karkinos* CANCER]

card[1] (kɑːd) *n* **1** a piece of stiff paper or thin cardboard, usually rectangular, with varied uses, as for bearing a written notice for display, etc **2** such a card used for identification, reference, proof of membership, etc: *identity card* **3** such a card used for sending greetings, messages, or invitations: *birthday card* **4a** one of a set of small pieces of cardboard, marked with figures, symbols, etc, used for playing games or for fortune-telling. See also **playing card** **4b** (*as modifier*): *a card game* **5** short for **cheque card** or **credit card** **6** *inf* a witty or eccentric person **7** See **compass card** **8** Also called: **racecard** *horse racing* a daily programme of all the races at a meeting **9** **a card up one's sleeve** a thing or action used in order to gain an advantage, esp one kept in reserve until needed ▹ See also **cards** [c15 from OF *carte*, from L *charta* leaf of papyrus, from Gk *khartēs*, prob. of Egyptian origin]

card[2] (kɑːd) *vb* **1** (*tr*) to comb out and clean (fibres of wool or cotton) before spinning ▹ *n* **2** (formerly) a machine or comblike tool for carding fabrics or for raising the nap on cloth [c15 from OF *carde* card, teasel, from L *carduus* thistle] > '**carder** *n* > '**carding** *n*

cardamom ('kɑːdəməm) *or* **cardamon** ('kɑːdəmən) *n* **1** a tropical Asian plant that has large hairy leaves **2** the seeds of this plant, used esp as a spice or condiment [c15 from L, from Gk, from *kardamon* cress + *amōmon* an Indian spice]

cardboard ('kɑːdˌbɔːd) *n* **1a** a thin stiff board made from paper pulp **1b** (*as modifier*): *cardboard boxes* ▹ *adj* **2** (*prenominal*) without substance

cardboard city *n inf* an area of a city in which homeless people sleep rough, often in cardboard boxes

card-carrying *adj* being an official member of an organization: *a card-carrying Communist*

Cardenal (*Spanish* karðɛ'nal) *n* **Ernesto** ('ɜːnɛstəʊ) born 1925, Nicaraguan poet, revolutionary, and Roman Catholic priest; an influential figure in the Sandinista movement

cardiac ('kɑːdɪˌæk) *adj* **1** of or relating to the heart **2** of or relating to the portion of the stomach connected to the oesophagus ▹ *n* **3** a person with a heart disorder [c17 from L *cardiacus*, from Gk, from *kardia* heart]

cardiac arrest *n* failure of the pumping action of the heart, resulting in loss of consciousness and absence of pulse and breathing: a medical emergency requiring immediate resuscitative treatment

cardie *or* **cardy** ('kɑːdɪ) *n, pl* **cardies** *inf* short for **cardigan**

Cardiff ('kɑːdɪf) *n* **1** the capital of Wales, situated in the southeast, in Cardiff county borough: formerly an important port; seat of the Welsh assembly (1999); university (1883). Pop: 272 129 (1991) **2** a county borough in SE Wales, created in 1996 from part of South Glamorgan. Pop: 305 340 (2001). Area: 139 sq km (54 sq miles)

cardigan ('kɑːdɪgən) *n* a knitted jacket or sweater with buttons up the front [c19 after 7th Earl of CARDIGAN]

Cardigan ('kɑːdɪgən) *n* **7th Earl of**, title of *James Thomas Brudenell*. 1797–1868, British cavalry officer. He led the charge of the Light Brigade at Balaklava (1854) during the Crimean War

Cardigan Bay *n* an inlet of St George's Channel, on the W coast of Wales

Cardiganshire ('kɑːdɪgənˌʃɪə, -ʃə) *n* a former county of W Wales: became part of Dyfed in 1974; reinstated as **Ceredigion** in 1996

cardinal ('kɑːdɪnᵊl) *n* **1** RC *Church* any of the members of the Sacred College who elect the pope and act as his chief counsellors **2** Also called: **cardinal red** a deep red colour **3** See **cardinal number** **4** Also called (US): **redbird** a crested North American bunting, the male of which has a bright red plumage **5** a woman's hooded shoulder cape worn in the 17th and 18th centuries ▹ *adj* **6** (*usually prenominal*) fundamentally important; principal **7** of a deep red [c13 from L *cardinālis*, lit.: relating to a hinge, from *cardō* hinge] > '**cardinally** *adv*

cardinalate ('kɑːdɪnᵊˌleɪt) *or* **cardinalship** *n* **1** the rank, office, or term of office of a cardinal **2** the cardinals collectively

cardinal flower *n* a lobelia of E North America that has brilliant scarlet flowers

cardinal number *or* **numeral** *n* a number denoting quantity but not order in a group. Sometimes shortened to **cardinal** ▹ Cf **ordinal number**

cardinal points *pl n* the four main points of the compass: north, south, east, and west

cardinal virtues *pl n* the most important moral qualities, traditionally justice, prudence, temperance, and fortitude

cardinal vowels *pl n* a set of theoretical vowel sounds, based on the shape of the mouth needed to articulate them, that can be used to classify the vowel sounds of any speaker in any language

card index *or* **file** *n* **1** an index in which each item is separately listed on systematically arranged cards ▹ *vb* **card-index** *or* **card-file, card-indexes, card-indexing, card-indexed** *or* **card-files, card-filing, card-filed** (*tr*) **2** to make such an index of (a book, etc)

cardio- *or before a vowel* **cardi-** *combining form* heart: *cardiogram* [from Gk *kardia* heart]

cardiocentesis (ˌkɑːdɪəʊsɛn'tiːsɪs) *n med* surgical puncture of the heart

cardiogram ('kɑːdɪəʊˌgræm) *n* short for **electrocardiogram**. See **electrocardiograph**

cardiograph ('kɑːdɪəʊˌgrɑːf) *n* **1** an instrument for recording heart movements **2** short for **electrocardiograph** > **cardiographer** (ˌkɑːdɪ'ɒgrəfə) *n* > ˌ**cardi'ography** *n*

cardiology (ˌkɑːdɪ'ɒlədʒɪ) *n* the branch of medical science concerned with the heart and its diseases > ˌ**cardi'ologist** *n*

cardioplegia (ˌkɑːdɪəʊ'pliːdʒə) *n med* deliberate arrest of the action of the heart, as by hypothermia or the injection of chemicals, to enable complex heart surgery to be carried out

cardiopulmonary resuscitation (ˌkɑːdɪəʊ'pʌlmənərɪ, -'pʊl-) *n* an emergency measure to revive a patient whose heart has stopped beating, in which compressions applied with the hands to the patient's chest are alternated with mouth-to-mouth respiration. Abbrev: **CPR**

cardiovascular (ˌkɑːdɪəʊ'væskjʊlə) *adj* of or relating to the heart and the blood vessels

cardoon (kɑː'duːn) *n* a thistle-like relative of the artichoke with an edible leafstalk [c17 from F, from L *carduus* thistle, artichoke]

Cardoso (*Portuguese* kɑ'dozo) *n* **Fernando Henrique** born 1931, Brazilian statesman; president (1995–2002)

cardphone ('kɑːdfəʊn) *n* a public telephone operated by the insertion of a phonecard instead of coins

card punch *n* a device, no longer widely used, controlled by a computer, for transferring information from the central processing unit onto punched cards which can then be read by a **card reader**

card reader *n* a device, no longer widely used, for reading information on a punched card and transferring it to a computer or storage device

cards (kɑːdz) *n* **1** (*usually functioning as sing*) **1a** any game played with cards, esp playing cards **1b** the playing of such a game **2** an employee's tax and national insurance documents or information held by the employer **3 ask for** *or* **get one's cards** to ask *or* be told to terminate one's employment **4 on the cards** possible **5 play one's cards (right)** to manoeuvre (cleverly) **6 put** *or* **lay one's cards on the table** to declare one's intentions, etc

▹ http://thehouseofhttp://thehouseofcards.com

cardsharp ('kɑːdʃɑːp) *or* **cardsharper** *n* a professional card player who cheats

Cardus ('kɑːdəs) *n* Sir **Neville** 1889–1975, British music critic and cricket writer

card vote *n Brit* a vote by delegates, esp at a trade-union conference, in which each delegate's vote counts as a vote by all his constituents

care (kɛə) *vb* **cares, caring, cared 1** (when *tr, may take a clause as object*) to be troubled or concerned: *he is dying, and she doesn't care* **2** (*intr;* foll by *for* or *about*) to have regard or consideration (for): *he cares more for his hobby than his job* **3** (*intr;* foll by *for*) to have a desire or taste (for): *would you care for tea?* **4** (*intr;* foll by *for*) to provide physical needs, help, or comfort (for) **5** (*tr*) to agree or like (to do something): *would you care to sit down?* **6 for all I care** *or* **I couldn't care less** I am completely indifferent ▹ *n* **7** careful or serious attention: *he does his work with care* **8** protective or supervisory control: *in the care of a doctor* **9** (*often pl*) trouble; worry **10** an object of or cause for concern **11** caution: *handle with care* **12 care of** at the address of: written on envelopes. Usual abbrev: **c/o** **13 in** (*or* **into**) **care** *Brit* made the legal responsibility of a local authority by order of a court [OE *cearu* (n), *cearian* (vb), of Gmc origin] > **'carer** *n*

CARE (kɛə) *n acronym for:* **1** Cooperative for American Relief Everywhere **2** communicated authenticity, regard, empathy: the three qualities believed to be essential in the therapist practising client-centred therapy

care and maintenance *n commerce* the state of a building, ship, machinery, etc, that is not in current use although it is kept in good condition to enable it to be brought into service quickly if there is a demand for it. Abbrev: **C&M**

careen (kə'riːn) *vb* **1** to sway or cause to sway over to one side **2** (*tr*) *naut* to cause (a vessel) to keel over to one side, esp in order to clean its bottom **3** (*intr*) *naut* (of a vessel) to keel over to one side [c17 from F, from It., from L *carīna* keel] > **ca'reenage** *n*

career (kə'rɪə) *n* **1** a path through life or history **2a** a profession or occupation chosen as one's life's work **2b** (*as modifier*): *a career diplomat* **3** a course or path, esp a headlong one ▹ *vb* **4** (*intr*) to rush in an uncontrolled way [c16 from F, from LL *carrāria* carriage road, from L *carrus* two-wheeled wagon]

career girl *or* **woman** *n* a woman, often unmarried, who follows a profession

careerist (kə'rɪərɪst) *n* a person who seeks to advance his or her career by any possible means

carefree ('kɛəˌfriː) *adj* without worry or responsibility > **'care,freeness** *n*

careful ('kɛəfʊl) *adj* **1** cautious in attitude or action **2** painstaking in one's work; exact and thorough **3** (*usually postpositive;* foll by *of, in,* or *about*) solicitous; protective **4** *Brit* mean or miserly > **'carefully** *adv* > **'carefulness** *n*

careless ('kɛəlɪs) *adj* **1** done with or acting with insufficient attention **2** (often foll by *in, of,* or *about*) unconcerned in attitude or action **3** (*usually prenominal*) carefree **4** (*usually prenominal*) unstudied: *careless elegance* > **'carelessly** *adv* > **'carelessness** *n*

Carême (karɛm) *n* **Marie Antonin** 1784–1833, French chef, regarded as the founder of *haute cuisine*

care plan *n* a plan for the medical care of a particular patient or the welfare of a child in care

caress (kə'rɛs) *n* **1** a gentle touch or embrace, esp one given to show affection ▹ *vb* **2** (*tr*) to touch or stroke gently with or as with affection [c17 from F, from It., from L *cārus* dear]

caret ('kærɪt) *n* a symbol used to indicate the place in written or printed matter at which something is to be inserted [c17 from L, lit.: there is missing, from *carēre* to lack]

caretaker ('kɛəˌteɪkə) *n* **1** a person who looks after a place or thing, esp in the owner's absence **2** (*modifier*) interim: *a caretaker government*

Carew (kə'ruː) *n* **Thomas** ?1595–?1639, English Cavalier poet

careworn ('kɛəˌwɔːn) *adj* showing signs of care, stress, worry, etc: *a careworn face*

Carey ('kɛərɪ) *n* **1 Peter** born 1943, Australian novelist and writer; his novels include *Illywhacker* (1985), *Oscar and Lucinda* (1988), and *The True History of the Kelly Gang* (2001) **2 William** 1761–1834, British orientalist and pioneer Baptist missionary in India

Carey Street ('kɛərɪ) *n* **1** (formerly) the street in which the London bankruptcy court was situated **2** the state of bankruptcy

cargo ('kɑːgəʊ) *n, pl* **cargoes** *or esp US* **cargos 1a** goods carried by a ship, aircraft, or other vehicle; freight **1b** (*as modifier*): *a cargo vessel* **2** any load: *a cargo of new arrivals* [c17 from Sp.: from *cargar* to load, from LL, from L *carrus* CAR]

Cc

cargo pants *or* **trousers** *pl n* loose trousers with a large external pocket on the side of each leg

Carib ('kærɪb) *n* **1** (*pl* **Caribs** *or* **Carib**) a member of a group of American Indian peoples of NE South America and the Lesser Antilles **2** the family of languages spoken by these peoples [c16 from Sp. *Caribe*, from Amerind]

Caribbean (ˌkærɪ'biːən; *US* kə'rɪbɪən) *adj* **1** of or relating to the Caribbean Sea and its islands **2** of or relating to the Carib or any of their languages ▹ *n* **3 the** short for the **Caribbean Sea** **4 the** the states and islands of the Caribbean, esp when considered as a geopolitical region **5** a member of any of the peoples inhabiting the islands of the Caribbean Sea, such as a West Indian or a Carib.

> **USAGE** This word is stressed on the third syllable in the UK, and on the second in the US and in the Caribbean itself

Caribbean Sea *n* an almost landlocked sea, part of the Atlantic Ocean, bounded by the Caribbean islands, Central America, and the N coast of South America. Area: 2 718 200 sq km (1 049 500 sq miles)

Caribbees ('kærɪˌbiːz) *pl n* **the** another name for the **Lesser Antilles**

Cariboo ('kærɪˌbuː) *n* **the** *Canad* a region in the W foothills of the Cariboo Mountains, scene of a gold rush beginning in 1860

Cariboo Mountains *pl n* a mountain range in SW Canada, in SE British Columbia. Highest peak: Mount Sir Wilfrid Laurier, 3582 m (11 750 ft)

caribou ('kærɪˌbuː) *n, pl* **caribou** *or* **caribous** a large North American reindeer [c18 from Canad F, of Algonquian origin]

caricature ('kærɪkəˌtjʊə) *n* **1** a pictorial, written, or acted representation of a person, which exaggerates his characteristic traits for comic effect **2** an inadequate or inaccurate imitation ▷ *vb* **caricatures, caricaturing, caricatured** 3 (*tr*) to represent in caricature or produce a caricature of [c18 from It. *caricatura* a distortion, from *caricare* to load, exaggerate] > **'carica,turist** *n*

CARICOM ('kærɪ,kɒm) *n acronym for* Caribbean Community and Common Market
▷ www.caricom.org

caries ('kɛəriːz) *n, pl* **caries** progressive decay of a bone or a tooth [c17 from L: decay]

carillon (kə'rɪljən) *n music* 1 a set of bells usually hung in a tower 2 a tune played on such bells 3 a mixture stop on an organ giving the effect of a bell [c18 from F: set of bells, from OF *quarregnon*, ult. from L *quattuor* four]

carina (kə'riːnə, -'raɪ-) *n, pl* **carinae** (-niː) *or* **carinas** a keel-like part or ridge, as in the breastbone of birds or the fused lower petals of a leguminous flower [c18 from L: keel]

carinate ('kærɪ,neɪt) *or* **carinated** *adj biol* having a keel or ridge [c17 from L *carīnāre*, from *carīna* keel]

caring ('kɛərɪŋ) *adj* 1 showing care and compassion: *a caring attitude* 2 of or relating to professional social or medical care: *nursing is a caring job* ▷ *n* 3 the practice of providing care

Carinthia (kə'rɪnθɪə) *n* a state of S Austria: an independent duchy from 976 to 1276; mainly mountainous, with many lakes and resorts. Capital: Klagenfurt. Pop: 561 114 (2001). Area: 9533 sq km (3681 sq miles). German name: **Kärnten**

carioca (,kærɪ'əʊkə) *n* 1 a Brazilian dance similar to the samba 2 a piece of music for this dance [c19 from Brazilian Port.]

cariogenic (,kɛərɪəʊ'dʒɛnɪk) *adj* (of a substance) producing caries of the teeth

cariole *or* **carriole** ('kærɪ,əʊl) *n* 1 a small open two-wheeled horse-drawn vehicle 2 a covered cart [c19 from F, ult. from L *carrus*; see CAR]

carious ('kɛərɪəs) *or* **cariose** ('kɛərɪ,əʊz) *adj* (of teeth or bone) affected with caries; decayed

carjack ('kɑː,dʒæk) *vb* (*tr*) to attack (a driver in a car) in order to rob the driver or to steal the car for another crime [c20 CAR + (HI)JACK]

cark (kɑːk) *vb* (*intr*) *Austral & NZ sl* to die (esp in **cark it**) [?from the cry of a crow, as a carrion-feeding bird]

carl *or* **carle** (kɑːl) *n arch or Scot* another word for **churl** [OE, from ON *karl*]

Carling ('kɑːlɪŋ) *n* **Will(iam)** born 1965, British rugby union footballer; captain of England (1988–96)

Carlisle (kɑː'laɪl, 'kɑːlaɪl) *n* a city in NW England, administrative centre of Cumbria: railway and industrial centre. Pop: 72 439 (1991). Latin name: **Luguvallum** (,luːguː'væləm)

Carlos ('kɑːlɒs) *n* **Don** full name *Carlos María Isidro de Borbón*. 1788–1855, second son of Charles IV: pretender to the Spanish throne and leader of the Carlists

Carlota (*Spanish* kar'lota) *n* original name *Marie Charlotte Amélie Augustine Victoire Clémentine Léopoldine*. 1840–1927, wife of Maximilian; empress of Mexico (1864–67)

Carlovingian (,kɑːləʊ'vɪndʒɪən) *adj, n hist* a variant of **Carolingian**

Carlow ('kɑːləʊ) *n* 1 a county of SE Republic of Ireland, in Leinster: mostly flat, with barren mountains in the southeast. County town: Carlow. Pop: 41 616 (1996). Area: 896 sq km (346 sq miles) 2 a town in SE Republic of Ireland, county town of Co. Carlow. Pop: 11 275 (1991)

Carlyle (kɑː'laɪl) *n* 1 **Robert** born 1961, Scottish actor; his work includes the television series *Cracker* and *Hamish Macbeth* and the films *Trainspotting* (1996), *The Full Monty* (1997), and *The Beach* (2000) 2 **Thomas** 1795–1881, Scottish essayist and historian. His works include *Sartor Resartus* (1833–34), a spiritual autobiography, *The French Revolution* (1837), lectures *On Heroes, Hero-Worship, and the Heroic in History* (1841), and the *History of Frederick the Great* (1858–65)

carmagnole (,kɑːmən'jəʊl) *n* 1 a dance and song popular during the French Revolution 2 the costume worn by many French Revolutionaries [c18 from F, prob. after *Carmagnola*, Italy]

Carmarthen (kɑː'mɑːðən) *n* a market town in S Wales, the administrative centre of Carmarthenshire: Norman castle. Pop: 13 524 (1991)

Carmarthenshire (kɑː'mɑːðən,ʃɪə, -ʃə) *n* a county of S Wales, formerly part of Dyfed (1974–96): on Carmarthen Bay, with the Cambrian Mountains in the N: generally agricultural (esp dairying). Administrative centre: Carmarthen. Pop: 173 635 (2001). Area: 2398 sq km (926 sq miles)

Carmel ('kɑːməl) *n* **Mount** a mountain ridge in NW Israel, extending from the Samarian Hills to the Mediterranean. Highest point: about 540 m (1800 ft)

Carmelite ('kɑːmə,laɪt) *n RC Church* 1 a member of an order of mendicant friars founded about 1154 2 a member of a corresponding order of nuns founded in 1452, noted for its austere rule ▷ *adj* 3 of or relating to either of these orders [c14 from F, after Mount CARMEL, where the order was founded]

Carmichael (kɑː'maɪkᵊl) *n* **Hoaglund Howard** ('həʊglənd), known as *Hoagy*. 1899–1981, US pianist, singer, and composer of such standards as "Star Dust" (1929)

carminative ('kɑːmɪnətɪv) *adj* 1 able to relieve flatulence ▷ *n* 2 a carminative drug [c15 from F, from L *carmināre* to card wool]

carmine ('kɑːmaɪn) *n* 1a a vivid red colour 1b (*as adj*): *carmine paint* 2 a pigment of this colour obtained from cochineal [c18 from Med. L *carmīnus*, from Ar. *qirmiz* KERMES]

Carnac ('kɑːnæk) *n* a village in NW France: noted for its many megalithic monuments, including alignments of stone menhirs

carnage ('kɑːnɪdʒ) *n* extensive slaughter [c16 from F, from It., from Med. L, from L *carō* flesh]

carnal ('kɑːnᵊl) *adj* relating to the appetites and passions of the body [c15 from LL, from L *carō* flesh] > **car'nality** *n* > **'carnally** *adv*

carnal knowledge *n chiefly law* sexual intercourse

Carnap ('kɑːnæp) *n* **Rudolf** 1891–1970, US logical positivist philosopher, born in Germany: attempted to construct a formal language for the empirical sciences that would eliminate ambiguity

Carnarvon (kɑː'nɑːvᵊn) *n* a variant spelling of **Caernarfon**

carnation (kɑː'neɪʃən) *n* 1 Also called: **clove pink** a Eurasian plant cultivated in many varieties for its white, pink, or red flowers, which have a fragrant scent of cloves 2 the flower of this plant 3a a pink or reddish-pink colour 3b (*as adj*): *a carnation dress* [c16 from F: flesh colour, from LL, from L *carō* flesh]

carnauba (kɑː'naʊbə) *n* 1 Also called: **wax palm** a Brazilian fan palm 2 Also called: **carnauba wax** the wax obtained from the young leaves of this tree [from Brazilian Port., prob. of Tupi origin]

Carné ('kɑːneɪ; *French* karne) *n* **Marcel** (marsɛl) 1906–96, French film director. His films include *Le Jour se lève* (1939), *Les Portes de la nuit* (1946), and *La Bible* (1976)

Carnegie ('kɑːnəgɪ, kɑː'neɪ-) *n* **Andrew** 1835–1919, US steel manufacturer and philanthropist, born in Scotland: endowed public libraries, education, and research trusts

Carnegie Hall ('kɑːnəgɪ) *n* a famous concert hall in New York (opened 1891); endowed by Andrew Carnegie (1835–1919)S
▷ www.carnegiehall.org/intro.jsp

carnelian (kɑː'niːljən) *n* a reddish-yellow translucent variety of chalcedony, used as a gemstone [c17 var. of *cornelian*, from OF, from ?]

carnet ('kɑːneɪ) *n* 1 a customs licence authorizing the temporary importation of a motor vehicle 2 an official document permitting motorists to cross certain frontiers [F: notebook, from OF, ult. from L *quaternī* four at a time]

Carniola (ˌkɑːnɪˈəʊlə) *n* a region of N Slovenia: a former duchy of Austria (1335–1919); divided between Yugoslavia and Italy in 1919; part of Yugoslavia (1947–92). German name: **Krain** (krain) Slovene name: **Kranj**

carnival (ˈkɑːnɪvəl) *n* **1a** a festive period marked by merrymaking, etc: esp in some Roman Catholic countries, the period just before Lent **1b** (*as modifier*): *a carnival atmosphere* **2** a travelling fair having sideshows, rides, etc **3** a show or display arranged as an amusement **4** *Austral* a sports meeting [c16 from It., from OIt. *carnelevare* a removing of meat (referring to the Lenten fast)]

carnivore (ˈkɑːnɪˌvɔː) *n* **1** any of an order of mammals having large pointed canine teeth specialized for eating flesh. The order includes cats, dogs, bears, and weasels **2** any other animal or any plant that feeds on animals **3** *inf* an aggressively ambitious person [c19 prob. back formation from CARNIVOROUS]

carnivorous (kɑːˈnɪvərəs) *adj* **1** (esp of animals) feeding on flesh **2** (of plants such as the pitcher plant and sundew) able to trap and digest insects **3** of or relating to the carnivores **4** *inf* aggressively ambitious or reactionary [c17 from L, from *carō* flesh + *vorāre* to consume] > **carˈnivorousness** *n*

Carnot (ˈkɑːnəʊ; *French* karno) *n* **1** **Lazare** (**Nicolas Marguerite**) (lazar), known as *the Organizer of Victory*. 1753–1823, French military engineer and administrator: organized the French Revolutionary army (1793–95) **2** **Nicolas Léonard Sadi** (nikɔla leɔnar sadi) 1796–1832, French physicist, whose work formed the basis for the second law of thermodynamics, enunciated in 1850; author of *Réflexions sur la puissance motrice du feu* (1824)

Caro *n* **1** (ˈkærəʊ) Sir **Antony** born 1924, British sculptor, best known for his abstract steel sculptures **2** (ˈkɑːrəʊ) **Joseph** (**ben Ephraim**) 1488–1575, Jewish legal scholar and mystic, born in Spain; compiler of the *Shulhan Arukh* (1564–65), the most authoritative Jewish legal code

carob (ˈkærəb) *n* **1** an evergreen Mediterranean tree with compound leaves and edible pods **2** the long blackish sugary pod of this tree, used for animal fodder and sometimes for human food [c16 from OF, from Med. L *carrūbium*, from Ar. *al kharrūbah*]

carol (ˈkærəl) *n* **1** a joyful hymn or religious song, esp one (a **Christmas carol**) celebrating the birth of Christ ▷ *vb* **carols, carolling, carolled** *or US* **carols, caroling, caroled** **2** (*intr*) to sing carols at Christmas **3** to sing (something) in a joyful manner [c13 from OF, from ?]

Carol II (ˈkærəl) *n* 1893–1953, king of Romania (1930–40), who was deposed by the Iron Guard

Carolina (ˌkærəˈlaɪnə) *n* a former English colony on the E coast of North America, first established in 1663: divided in 1729 into North and South Carolina, which are often referred to as **the Carolinas**

Caroline (ˈkærəˌlaɪn) *or* **Carolean** (ˌkærəˈliːən) *adj* characteristic of or relating to Charles I or Charles II (kings of England, Scotland, and Ireland), the society over which they ruled, or their government. Also called: **Carolinian**

Caroline Islands *pl n* an archipelago of over 500 islands and islets in the W Pacific Ocean east of the Philippines, all are now part of the Federated States of Micronesia, except for the Belau group: formerly part of the US Trust Territory of the Pacific Islands; centre of a typhoon zone. Area: (land) 1183 sq km (457 sq miles)

Carolingian (ˌkærəˈlɪndʒɪən) *adj* **1** of or relating to the Frankish dynasty founded by Pepin the Short which ruled in France from 751–987 AD and in Germany until 911 AD ▷ *n* **2** a member of the dynasty of the Carolingian Franks ▷ Also: **Carlovingian, Carolinian**

Carolinian[1] (ˌkærəˈlɪnɪən) *adj, n* a variant of **Caroline** or **Carolingian**

Carolinian[2] (ˌkærəˈlɪnɪən) *adj* **1** of or relating to North or South Carolina ▷ *n* **2** a native or inhabitant of North or South Carolina

carom (ˈkærəm) *n billiards* another word (esp US & Canad) for **cannon** (sense 5) [c18 from earlier *carambole* (taken as *carom ball*), from Sp. *carambola* a CARAMBOLA]

carotene (ˈkærəˌtiːn) *or* **carotin** (ˈkærətɪn) *n* any of four orange-red isomers of a hydrocarbon present in many plants and converted to vitamin A in the liver [c19 *carotin*, from L *carōta* CARROT]

carotenoid *or* **carotinoid** (kəˈrɒtɪˌnɔɪd) *n* any of a group of red or yellow pigments, including carotenes, found in plants and certain animal tissues

carotid (kəˈrɒtɪd) *n* **1** either of the two principal arteries that supply blood to the head and neck ▷ *adj* **2** of either of these arteries [c17 from F, from Gk, from *karoun* to stupefy; so named because pressure on them produced unconsciousness]

carousal (kəˈraʊzəl) *n* a merry drinking party

carouse (kəˈraʊz) *vb* **carouses, carousing, caroused** **1** (*intr*) to have a merry drinking spree ▷ *n* **2** another word for **carousal** [c16 via F *carrousser* from G (*trinken*) *gar aus* (to drink) right out] > **caˈrouser** *n*

carousel (ˌkærəˈsɛl, -ˈzɛl) *n* **1** a circular tray in which slides for a projector are held in slots from which they can be released in turn **2** a revolving luggage conveyor, as at an airport **3** *US & Canad* a merry-go-round **4** *history* a tournament in which horsemen took part in races [c17 from F, from It. *carosello*, from ?]

carp[1] (kɑːp) *n, pl* **carp** *or* **carps** **1** a freshwater food fish having one long dorsal fin, and two barbels on each side of the mouth **2** a cyprinid [c14 from OF *carpe*, of Gmc origin]

carp[2] (kɑːp) *vb* (*intr*; often foll by *at*) to complain or find fault [c13 from ON *karpa* to boast] > **ˈcarper** *n* > **ˈcarping** *adj, n*

Cc

-carp *n combining form* (in botany) fruit or a reproductive structure that develops into a particular part of the fruit: *epicarp* [from NL *-carpium*, from Gk *-karpion*, from *karpos* fruit]

carpaccio (ˌkɑːˈpætʃɪəʊ; *Italian* karˈpattʃo) *n pl* **-os** an Italian dish of thin slices of raw meat or fish [possibly after CARPACCIO]

Carpaccio (ˌkɑːˈpætʃɪəʊ, -tʃəʊ; *Italian* karˈpattʃo) *n* **Vittore** (vitˈtoːre) ?1460–?1525, Italian painter of the Venetian school

carpal (ˈkɑːpəl) *n* **a** any bone of the wrist **b** (*as modifier*): *carpal bones* [c18 from NL *carpālis*, from Gk *karpos* wrist]

car park *n* an area or building reserved for parking cars. Usual US and Canad term: **parking lot**

Carpathian Mountains (kɑːˈpeɪθɪən) *or* **Carpathians** *pl n* a mountain system of central and E Europe, extending from Slovakia to central Romania: mainly forested, with rich iron ore resources. Highest peak: Gerlachovka, 2663 m (8788 ft)

Carpatho-Ukraine (kɑːˈpeɪθəʊjuːˈkreɪn) *n* another name for **Ruthenia**

carpe diem *Latin* (ˈkɑːpɪ ˈdiːɛm) *sentence substitute* enjoy the pleasures of the moment, without concern for the future [lit.: seize the day!]

carpel (ˈkɑːpəl) *n* the female reproductive organ of flowering plants, consisting of an ovary, style, and stigma [c19 from NL *carpellum*, from Gk *karpos* fruit] > **ˈcarpellary** *adj*

Carpentaria (ˌkɑːpənˈtɛərɪə) *n* **Gulf of** a shallow inlet of the Arafura Sea, in N Australia between Arnhem Land and Cape York Peninsula

carpenter (ˈkɑːpɪntə) *n* **1** a person skilled in woodwork, esp in buildings, ships, etc ▷ *vb* **2** (*intr*) to do the work of a carpenter **3** (*tr*) to make by or as if by carpentry [c14 from Anglo-F, from L, from *carpentum* wagon]

Carpenter ('kɑːpɪntə) *n* **John Alden** 1876–1951, US composer, who used jazz rhythms in orchestral music: his works include the ballet *Skyscrapers* (1926) and the orchestral suite *Adventures in a Perambulator* (1915)
Carpentier (*French* karpɑ̃tje) *n* **Georges** (ʒɔrʒ), known as *Gorgeous Georges*. 1894–1975, French boxer: world light-heavyweight champion (1920–22)
carpentry ('kɑːpɪntrɪ) *n* **1** the art or technique of working wood **2** the work produced by a carpenter; woodwork
carpet ('kɑːpɪt) *n* **1** a heavy fabric for covering floors **2** a covering like a carpet: *a carpet of leaves* **3** **on the carpet** *inf* **3a** before authority to be reproved **3b** under consideration ▷ *vb* **carpets, carpeting, carpeted** (*tr*) **4** to cover with or as if with a carpet **5** *inf* to reprimand [c14 from OF, from OIt., from LL *carpeta*, from L *carpere* to pluck, card]
carpetbag ('kɑːpɪtˌbæg) *n* a travelling bag originally made of carpeting
carpetbagger ('kɑːpɪtˌbægə) *n* **1** a politician who seeks public office in a locality where he or she has no real connections **2** *Brit* a person who makes a short-term investment in a mutual savings or life-assurance organization in order to benefit from free shares issued following the organization's conversion to a public limited company
carpet beetle *or US* **carpet bug** *n* any of various beetles, the larvae of which feed on carpets, furnishing fabrics, etc
carpet bombing *n* systematic intensive bombing of an area
carpeting ('kɑːpɪtɪŋ) *n* carpet material or carpets in general
carpet slipper *n* one of a pair of slippers, originally one made with woollen uppers resembling carpeting
carpet snake *or* **python** *n* a large nonvenomous Australian snake having a carpet-like pattern on its back
carpet-sweeper *n* a household device with a revolving brush for sweeping carpets
car phone *n* a telephone that operates by cellular radio for use in a car
carpo- *combining form* (in botany) indicating fruit or a seed [from Gk *karpos* fruit]
carport ('kɑːˌpɔːt) *n* a shelter for a car usually consisting of a roof built out from the side of a building and supported by posts
-carpous *or* **-carpic** *adj combining form* (in botany) indicating a certain kind or number of fruit: *apocarpous* [from NL, from Gk *karpos* fruit]
carpus ('kɑːpəs) *n, pl* **carpi** ('kɑːpaɪ) **1** the technical name for **wrist** **2** the eight small bones of the human wrist [c17 NL, from Gk *karpos*]
Carracci (kə'rɑːtʃɪ; *Italian* kar'rattʃi) *n* a family of Italian painters, born in Bologna: **Agostino** (agos'tiːno) (1557–1602); his brother, **Annibale** (an'niːbale) (1560–1609), noted for his frescoes, esp in the Palazzo Farnese, Rome; and their cousin, **Ludovico** (ludo'viːko) (1555–1619). They were influential in reviving the classical tradition of the Renaissance and founded a teaching academy (1582) in Bologna
carrack ('kærək) *n* a galleon sailed in the Mediterranean as a merchantman in the 15th and 16th centuries [c14 from OF *caraque*, from OSp. *carraca*, from Ar. *qarāqīr* merchant ships]
carrageen, carragheen, *or* **carageen** ('kærəˌgiːn) *n* an edible red seaweed of North America and N Europe. Also called: **Irish moss** [c19 from *Carragheen*, near Waterford, Ireland]
carrageenan, carragheenan, *or* **carageenan** (ˌkærə'giːnən) *n* a carbohydrate extracted from carrageen, used to make a beverage, medicine, and jelly, and as an emulsifying and gelling agent (**E407**) in various processed desserts and drinks
Carrara (kə'rɑːrə; *Italian* kar'raːra) *n* a town in NW Italy, in NW Tuscany: famous for its marble. Pop: 68 480 (1990)
carrel *or* **carrell** ('kærəl) *n* a small individual study room or private desk, often in a library [c20 from obs. *carrel* study area, var. of CAROL]
Carrel (kə'rɛl, 'kærəl; *French* karɛl) *n* **Alexis** (ə'lɛksɪs; *French* alɛksi) 1873–1944, French surgeon and biologist, active in the US (1905–39): developed a method of suturing blood vessels, making the transplantation of arteries and organs possible: Nobel prize for physiology or medicine 1912
Carreras (kə'rɛərəs) *n* **José** (həʊs'zeɪ) born 1947, Spanish tenor
Carrey ('kærɪ) *n* **Jim** born 1962, Canadian-born Hollywood actor noted for his comedy roles; films include *Ace Ventura, Pet Detective* (1994), *Liar Liar* (1997), *The Truman Show* (1998), *The Majestic* (2001), and *Eternal Sunshine of the Spotless Mind* (2004)
carriage ('kærɪdʒ) *n* **1** *Brit* a railway coach for passengers **2** the manner in which a person holds and moves his or her head and body **3** a four-wheeled horse-drawn vehicle for persons **4** the moving part of a machine that bears another part: *a typewriter carriage* **5** ('kærɪdʒ, 'kærɪɪdʒ) **5a** the act of conveying **5b** the charge made for conveying (esp in **carriage forward,** when the charge is to be paid by the receiver, and **carriage paid**) [c14 from OF *cariage*, from *carier* to CARRY]
carriage clock *n* a portable clock, usually in a rectangular case, originally used by travellers
carriage trade *n* trade from the wealthy part of society
carriageway ('kærɪdʒˌweɪ) *n* *Brit* the part of a road along which traffic passes in a single line moving in one direction only: *a dual carriageway*
Carrickfergus (ˌkærɪk'fɜːgəs) *n* **1** a town in E Northern Ireland, in Carrickfergus district, Co. Antrim; historic settlement of Scottish Protestants on Belfast Lough; Norman castle. Pop: 22 885 (1991) **2** a district of E Northern Ireland, in Co. Antrim. Pop: 37 659 (2001). Area: 83 sq km (32 sq miles)
carrier ('kærɪə) *n* **1** a person, thing, or organization employed to carry goods, etc **2** a mechanism by which something is carried or moved, such as a device for transmitting rotation from the faceplate of a lathe to the workpiece **3** *pathol* another name for **vector** (sense 3) **4** *pathol* a person or animal that, without having any symptoms of a disease, is capable of transmitting it to others **5** Also called: **charge carrier** *physics* an electron or hole that carries the charge in a conductor or semiconductor **6** short for **carrier wave** **7** *chem* **7a** an inert substance used to absorb a dyestuff, transport a sample through a gas chromatography column, contain a radioisotope for radioactive tracing, etc **7b** a substance used to support a catalyst **8** See **aircraft carrier**
Carrier ('kærɪə) *n* a member of an Athapaskan Native North American people of British Columbia
carrier bag *n* *Brit* a large paper or plastic bag for carrying shopping, etc
carrier pigeon *n* any homing pigeon, esp one used for carrying messages
carrier wave *n* *radio* a wave modulated in amplitude, frequency, or phase in order to carry a signal in radio transmission, etc
Carrington ('kærɪŋtən) *n* **Dora,** known as *Carrington*. 1893–1932, British painter, engraver, and letter writer; a member of the Bloomsbury Group
carriole ('kærɪˌəʊl) *n* a variant spelling of **cariole**
carrion ('kærɪən) *n* **1** dead and rotting flesh **2** (*modifier*) eating carrion **3** something rotten [c13 from Anglo-F *caroine*, ult. from L *carō* flesh]
carrion crow *n* a common predatory and scavenging

European crow similar to the rook but having a pure black bill

Carroll ('kærəl) *n* **Lewis** real name *the Reverend Charles Lutwidge Dodgson*. 1832–98, English writer; an Oxford mathematics don who wrote *Alice's Adventures in Wonderland* (1865) and *Through the Looking-Glass* (1872) and the nonsense poem *The Hunting of the Snark* (1876)

carrot ('kærət) *n* **1** an umbelliferous plant with finely divided leaves **2** the long tapering orange root of this plant, eaten as a vegetable **3a** something offered as a lure or incentive **3b** **carrot and stick** reward and punishment as methods of persuasion [C16 from OF *carotte*, from LL *carōta*, from Gk *karōton*]

carroty ('kærətɪ) *adj* **1** of a reddish or yellowish-orange colour **2** having red hair

carrousel (ˌkærə'sɛl, -'zɛl) *n* a variant spelling of **carousel**

carry ('kærɪ) *vb* **carries, carrying, carried** (*mainly tr*) **1** (*also intr*) to take or bear (something) from one place to another **2** to transfer for consideration: *he carried his complaints to her superior* **3** to have on one's person: *he carries a watch* **4** (*also intr*) to be transmitted or serve as a medium for transmitting: *sound carries over water* **5** to bear or be able to bear the weight, pressure, or responsibility of: *her efforts carry the whole production* **6** to have as an attribute or result: *this crime carries a heavy penalty* **7** to bring or communicate: *to carry news* **8** (*also intr*) to be pregnant with (young) **9** to bear (the head, body, etc) in a specified manner: *she carried her head high* **10** to conduct or bear (oneself) in a specified manner: *she carried herself well* **11** to continue or extend: *the war was carried into enemy territory* **12** to cause to move or go: *desire for riches carried him to the city* **13** to influence, esp by emotional appeal: *his words carried the crowd* **14** to secure the passage of (a bill, motion, etc) **15** to win (an election) **16** to obtain victory for (a candidate) **17** *chiefly US* to win a majority of votes in (a district, etc): *the candidate carried 40 states* **18** to capture: *our troops carried the town* **19** (of communications media) to include as the content: *this newspaper carries no book reviews* **20** Also (esp US): **carry over** *book-keeping* to transfer (an item) to another account, esp to transfer to the following year's account: *to carry a loss* **21** *maths* to transfer (a number) from one column of figures to the next **22** (of a shop, trader, etc) to keep in stock: *to carry confectionery* **23** to support (a musical part or melody) against the other parts **24** (*intr*) (of a ball, projectile, etc) to travel through the air or reach a specified point: *his first drive carried to the green* **25** *inf* to imbibe (alcoholic drink) without showing ill effects **26** (*intr*) *sl* to have drugs on one's person **27** **carry all before** (**one**) to win unanimous support or approval for (oneself) **28** **carry the can** (**for**) *inf* to take responsibility for some misdemeanour, etc (on behalf of) **29** **carry the day** to be successful ▷ *n, pl* **carries** **30** the act of carrying **31** *US & Canad* a portion of land over which a boat must be portaged **32** the range of a firearm or its projectile **33** *golf* the distance from where the ball is struck to where it first touches the ground ▷ See also **carry away, carry forward,** etc [C14 *carien*, from OF *carier* to move by vehicle, from *car*, from L *carrum* transport wagon]

carryall ('kærɪˌɔːl) *n* the usual US and Canad name for a **holdall**

carry away *vb* (*tr, adv*) **1** to remove forcefully **2** (*usually passive*) to cause (a person) to lose self-control **3** (*usually passive*) to delight: *he was carried away by your gift*

carrycot ('kærɪˌkɒt) *n* a light cot with handles, similar to but smaller than the body of a pram

carry forward *vb* (*tr, adv*) **1** *book-keeping* to transfer (a balance) to the next column, etc **2** *tax accounting* to apply (a legally permitted credit, esp an operating loss) to the taxable income of following years ▷ Also: **carry over**

carrying-on *n, pl* **carryings-on** *inf* **1** unconventional behaviour **2** excited or flirtatious behaviour

carry off *vb* (*tr, adv*) **1** to remove forcefully **2** to win **3** to handle (a situation) successfully: *he carried off the introductions well* **4** to cause to die: *he was carried off by pneumonia*

carry on *vb* (*adv*) **1** (*intr*) to continue or persevere **2** (*tr*) to conduct: *to carry on a business* **3** (*intr; often foll by with*) *inf* to have an affair **4** (*intr*) *inf* to cause a fuss or commotion ▷ *n* **carry-on** **5** *inf, chiefly Brit* a fuss

carry out *vb* (*tr, adv*) **1** to perform or cause to be implemented: *I wish he could afford to carry out his plan* **2** to accomplish ▷ *n* **carry-out** *chiefly Scot* **3** alcohol bought at an off-licence, etc, for consumption elsewhere **4a** a shop which sells hot cooked food for consumption away from the premises **4b** (*as modifier*): *a carry-out shop*

carry over *vb* (*tr, adv*) **1** to postpone or defer **2** *book-keeping, tax accounting* another term for **carry forward** ▷ *n* **carry-over** **3** something left over for future use, esp goods to be sold **4** *book-keeping* a sum or balance carried forward

carry through *vb* (*tr, adv*) **1** to bring to completion **2** to enable to endure (hardship, trouble, etc); support

carse (kɑːs) *n* *Scot* a riverside area of flat fertile alluvium [C14 from ?]

carsick ('kɑːˌsɪk) *adj* nauseated from riding in a car or other vehicle > **'carˌsickness** *n*

Carson ('kɑːsᵊn) *n* **1** **Christopher,** known as *Kit Carson*. 1809–68, US frontiersman, trapper, scout, and Indian agent **2** **Edward Henry,** Baron. 1854–1935, Anglo-Irish politician and lawyer; led northern Irish resistance to the British government's plan for home rule for Ireland **3** **Rachel** (**Louise**) 1907–64, US marine biologist and science writer; author of *Silent Spring* (1962) **4** **Willie,** full name *William Hunter Fisher Carson*. born 1942, Scottish jockey; retired in 1997

Carson City ('kɑːsᵊn) *n* a city in W Nevada, capital of the state. Pop: 46 770 (1995 est)

Carstensz ('kɑːstənz) *n* **Mount** a former name of (Mount) **Jaya**

Cc

cart (kɑːt) *n* **1** a heavy open vehicle, usually having two wheels and drawn by horses **2** a light open horse-drawn vehicle for business or pleasure **3** any small vehicle drawn or pushed by hand, such as a trolley **4** **in the cart** **4a** in an awkward situation **4b** in the lurch **5** **put the cart before the horse** to reverse the usual order of things ▷ *vb* **6** (*usually tr*) to use or draw a cart to convey (goods, etc) **7** (*tr*) to carry with effort: *to cart wood home* [C13 from ON *kartr*] > **'carter** *n*

cartage ('kɑːtɪdʒ) *n* the process or cost of carting

Cartagena (ˌkɑːtə'dʒiːnə; *Spanish* karta'xena) *n* **1** a port in NW Colombia, on the Caribbean: centre for the Inquisition and the slave trade in the 16th century; chief oil port of Colombia. Pop: 805 757 (1999 est) **2** a port in SE Spain, on the Mediterranean: important since Carthaginian and Roman times for its minerals. Pop: 175 628 (1998 est)

carte blanche ('kɑːt 'blɑːntʃ) *n, pl* **cartes blanches** ('kɑːts 'blɑːntʃ) complete discretion or authority: *the government gave their negotiator carte blanche* [C18 from F: blank paper]

cartel (kɑː'tɛl) *n* **1** Also called: **trust** a collusive association of independent enterprises formed to monopolize production and distribution of a product or service **2** *politics* an alliance of parties to further common aims [C20 from G *Kartell*, from F, from It. *cartello* public notice, dim. of *carta* CARD[1]]

Carter ('kɑːtə) *n* **1** **Angela** 1940–92, British novelist and writer; her novels include *The Magic Toyshop* (1967) and *Nights at the Circus* (1984) **2** **Elliot** (**Cook**) born 1908, US composer. His works include the *Piano Sonata* (1945–46), four string quartets, and other orchestral pieces: Pulitzer Prize 1960, 1973 **3** **Howard** 1873–1939, English Egyptologist: excavated the tomb of the Pharaoh Tutankhamen **4** **James Earl,** known as *Jimmy*. born 1924, US Democratic statesman; 39th president of the US

(1977–81): Nobel peace prize 2002

Carteret (ˈkɑːtərɪt) *n* **John,** 1st Earl Granville. 1690–1763, British statesman, diplomat, and orator who led the opposition to Walpole (1730–42), after whose fall he became a leading minister as secretary of state (1742–44)

Cartesian (kɑːˈtiːzɪən) *adj* **1** of or relating to the works of Descartes **2** of or used in Descartes' mathematical system > **Carˈtesian,ism** *n*

Cartesian coordinates *pl n* a system of coordinates that defines the location of a point in space in terms of its perpendicular distance from each of a set of mutually perpendicular axes

Carthage (ˈkɑːθɪdʒ) *n* an ancient city state, on the N African coast near present-day Tunis. Founded about 800 BC by Phoenician traders, it grew into an empire dominating N Africa and the Mediterranean. Destroyed and then rebuilt by Rome, it was finally razed by the Arabs in 697 AD. See also **Punic Wars**

Carthaginian (ˌkɑːθəˈdʒɪnɪən) *adj* **1** of or relating to Carthage or its inhabitants ▷ *n* **2** a native or inhabitant of Carthage

carthorse (ˈkɑːtˌhɔːs) *n* a large heavily built horse kept for pulling carts or carriages

Carthusian (kɑːˈθjuːzɪən) *RC Church* ▷ *n* **1** a member of a monastic order founded by Saint Bruno in 1084 near Grenoble, France ▷ *adj* **2** of or relating to this order: *a Carthusian monastery* [c14 from Med. L, from L *Carthusia* Chartreuse, near Grenoble]

Cartier (*French* kartje) *n* **Jacques** (ʒɑk) 1491–1557, French navigator and explorer in Canada, who discovered the St Lawrence River (1535)

Cartier-Bresson (*French* kartjebrɛsɔ̃) *n* **Henri** (ɑ̃ri) born 1908, French photographer

cartilage (ˈkɑːtɪlɪdʒ) *n* a tough elastic tissue composing most of the embryonic skeleton of vertebrates. In the adults of higher vertebrates it is mostly converted into bone. Nontechnical name: **gristle** [c16 from L *cartilāgō*] > **cartilaginous** (ˌkɑːtɪˈlædʒɪnəs) *adj*

cartilaginous fish *n* any of a class of fish including the sharks and rays, having a skeleton composed entirely of cartilage

Cartland (ˈkɑːtlənd) *n* Dame **Barbara** (**Hamilton**) 1901–2000, British novelist, noted for her prolific output of popular romantic fiction

cartload (ˈkɑːtˌləʊd) *n* the amount a cart can hold

cart off, away, *or* **out** *vb (tr, adv) inf* to carry or remove brusquely or by force

cartogram (ˈkɑːtəˌɡræm) *n* a map showing statistical information in diagrammatic form [c20 from F *cartogramme*, from *carte* map, CHART]

cartography (kɑːˈtɒɡrəfɪ) *n* the art, technique, or practice of compiling or drawing maps or charts [c19 from F *cartographie*, from *carte* map, CHART] > **carˈtographer** *n* > **cartographic** (ˌkɑːtəˈɡræfɪk) *or* **ˌcartoˈgraphical** *adj*

carton (ˈkɑːtᵊn) *n* **1** a cardboard box for containing goods **2** a container of waxed paper in which liquids, such as milk, are sold [c19 from F, from It. *cartone* pasteboard, from *carta* CARD[1]]

cartoon (kɑːˈtuːn) *n* **1** a humorous or satirical drawing, esp one in a newspaper or magazine **2** Also called: **comic strip** a sequence of drawings in a newspaper, magazine, etc **3** See **animated cartoon** **4** a full-size preparatory sketch for a fresco, tapestry, mosaic, etc [c17 from It. *cartone* pasteboard] > **carˈtoonist** *n*

cartouche *or* **cartouch** (kɑːˈtuːʃ) *n* **1** a carved or cast ornamental tablet or panel in the form of a scroll **2** an oblong figure enclosing characters expressing royal or divine names in Egyptian hieroglyphics [c17 from F: scroll, cartridge, from It., from *carta* paper]

cartridge (ˈkɑːtrɪdʒ) *n* **1** a metal casing containing an explosive charge and often a bullet, for a rifle or other small arms **2** a stylus unit of a record player, either containing a piezoelectric crystal (**crystal cartridge**) or an induction coil that moves in the field of a permanent magnet (**magnetic cartridge**) **3** an enclosed container of magnetic tape, photographic film, ink, etc, for insertion into a tape deck, camera, pen, etc **4** *computing* a removable unit in a computer, such as an integrated circuit, containing software [c16 from earlier *cartage*, var. of CARTOUCHE (cartridge)]

cartridge belt *n* a belt with pockets for cartridge clips or loops for cartridges

cartridge clip *n* a metallic container holding cartridges for an automatic firearm

cartridge paper *n* **1** an uncoated type of drawing or printing paper **2** a heavy paper used in making cartridges or as drawing or printing paper

cartwheel (ˈkɑːtˌwiːl) *n* **1** the wheel of a cart, usually having wooden spokes **2** an acrobatic movement in which the body makes a revolution supported on the hands with legs outstretched

Cartwright (ˈkɑːtˌraɪt) *n* **1 Edmund** 1743–1823, British clergyman, who invented the power loom **2** Dame **Silvia** (née *Poulter*) born 1943, New Zealand lawyer. She became a High Court judge in 1993 and governor general of New Zealand in 2001

caruncle (ˈkærəŋkᵊl, kəˈrʌŋ-) *n* **1** a fleshy outgrowth on the heads of certain birds, such as a cock's comb **2** an outgrowth near the hilum on the seeds of some plants [c17 from obs. F *caruncule*, from L *caruncula* a small piece of flesh, from *carō* flesh] > **caruncular** (kəˈrʌŋkjʊlə) *or* **caˈrunculous** *adj*

Caruso (*Italian* kaˈruːso) *n* **Enrico** (enˈriːko) 1873–1921, an outstanding Italian operatic tenor; one of the first to make gramophone records

carve (kɑːv) *vb* **carves, carving, carved** **1** (*tr*) to cut or chip in order to form something: *to carve wood* **2** to form (something) by cutting or chipping: *to carve statues* **3** to slice (meat) into pieces ▷ See also **carve out, carve up** [OE *ceorfan*]

carvel (ˈkɑːvᵊl) *n* another word for **caravel**

carvel-built *adj* (of a vessel) having a hull with planks made flush at the seams ▷ Cf **clinker-built**

carven (ˈkɑːvᵊn) *vb* an archaic or literary past participle of **carve**

carve out *vb (tr, adv) inf* to make or create (a career): *he carved out his own future*

carver (ˈkɑːvə) *n* **1** a carving knife **2** (*pl*) a large matched knife and fork for carving meat **3** *Brit* a chair having arms that forms part of a set of dining chairs

carvery (ˈkɑːvərɪ) *n, pl* **carveries** an eating establishment at which customers pay a set price for unrestricted helpings from a variety of meats, salads, etc

carve up *vb (tr, adv)* **1** to cut (something) into pieces **2** to divide (land, etc) ▷ *n* **carve-up** **3** *inf* an act or instance of dishonestly prearranging the result of a competition **4** *sl* the distribution of something

carving (ˈkɑːvɪŋ) *n* a figure or design produced by carving stone, wood, etc

carving knife *n* a long-bladed knife for carving cooked meat for serving

Cary (ˈkɛərɪ, ˈkærɪ) *n* (**Arthur**) **Joyce** (**Lunel**) 1888–1957, British novelist; author of *Mister Johnson* (1939), *A House of Children* (1941), and *The Horse's Mouth* (1944)

caryatid (ˌkærɪˈætɪd) *n, pl* **caryatids** *or* **caryatides** (-ɪˌdiːz) a column, used to support an entablature, in the form of a draped female figure [c16 from L, from Gk *Karuatides* priestesses of Artemis at *Karuai* (Caryae), in Laconia]

CAS (in Canada) *abbrev for* Children's Aid Society

Casablanca (ˌkæsəˈblæŋkə) *n* a port in NW Morocco, on the Atlantic: largest city in the country; industrial centre. Pop: 523 279 (1994)

Casals (*Spanish* kaˈsals) *n* **Pablo** (ˈpaβlo) 1876–1973, Spanish cellist and composer, noted for his interpretation of J. S. Bach's cello suites

Casanova (ˌkæsəˈnəʊvə) *n* **1 Giovanni Jacopo** (dʒoˈvanni ˈjaːkopo) 1725–98, Italian adventurer noted for his *Mémoires*, a vivid account of his sexual adventures and of contemporary society **2** any man noted for his amorous adventures; a rake

casbah (ˈkæzbɑː) *n* (*sometimes cap*) a variant spelling of **kasbah**

cascade (kæsˈkeɪd) *n* **1** a waterfall or series of waterfalls over rocks **2** something resembling this, such as folds of lace **3** a consecutive sequence of chemical or physical processes **4** a series of stages or devices in which each operates the next in turn ▷ *vb* **cascades, cascading, cascaded 5** (*intr*) to flow or fall in or like a cascade [C17 from F, from It., ult. from L *cadere* to fall]

Cascade Range *n* a chain of mountains in the US and Canada: a continuation of the Sierra Nevada range from N California through Oregon and Washington to British Columbia. Highest peak: Mount Rainier, 4392 m (14 408 ft)

cascading style sheet *n computing* a file recording style details, such as fonts, colours, etc, that is read by browsers so that style is consistent over multiple web pages. Abbrev: **CSS**

cascara (kæsˈkɑːrə) *n* **1** Also called: **cascara sagrada** the dried bark of the cascara buckthorn, used as a laxative and stimulant **2** Also called: **cascara buckthorn** a shrub or small tree of NW North America [C19 from Sp.: bark]

case[1] (keɪs) *n* **1** a single instance or example of something **2** an instance of disease, injury, etc **3** a question or matter for discussion **4** a specific condition or state of affairs; situation **5** a set of arguments supporting a particular action, cause, etc **6a** a person attended or served by a doctor, social worker, solicitor, etc **6b** (*as modifier*): *a case study* **7a** an action or suit at law: *he has a good case* **7b** the evidence offered in court to support a claim **8** *grammar* **8a** a set of grammatical categories of nouns, pronouns, and adjectives indicating the relation of the noun, adjective, or pronoun to other words in the sentence **8b** any one of these categories: *the dative case* **9** *inf* an eccentric **10 in any case** (*adv*) no matter what **11 in case** (*adv*) **11a** in order to allow for eventualities **11b** (*conj*) in order to allow for the possibility that: *take your coat in case it rains* **12 in case of** (*prep*) in the event of **13 in no case** (*adv*) under no circumstances [OE *casus* (grammatical) case, associated also with OF *cas* a happening; both from L *cāsus*, a befalling, from *cadere* to fall]

case[2] (keɪs) *n* **1a** a container, such as a box or chest **1b** (*in combination*): *suitcase* **2** an outer cover, esp for a watch **3** a receptacle and its contents: *a case of ammunition* **4** *archit* another word for **casing** (sense 3) **5** a cover ready to be fastened to a book to form its binding **6** *printing* a tray in which a compositor keeps individual metal types of a particular size and style. Cases were originally used in pairs, one (the **upper case**) for capitals, the other (the **lower case**) for small letters ▷ *vb* **cases, casing, cased** (*tr*) **7** to put into or cover with a case **8** *sl* to inspect carefully (esp a place to be robbed) [C13 from OF *casse*, from L, from *capere* to take, hold]

casebook (ˈkeɪsˌbʊk) *n* a book in which records of legal or medical cases are kept

case-harden *vb* (*tr*) **1** *metallurgy* to form a hard surface layer of high carbon content on (a steel component) **2** to make callous: *experience case-hardened the judge*

case history *n* a record of a person's background, medical history, etc

casein (ˈkeɪsiːɪn, -siːn) *n* a protein, precipitated from milk by the action of rennin, forming the basis of cheese [C19 from L *cāseus* cheese + -IN]

case law *n* law established by following judicial decisions given in earlier cases ▷ Cf **statute law**

caseload (ˈkeɪsˌləʊd) *n* the number of cases constituting the work of a doctor, solicitor, social worker, etc, over a specified period: *constantly increasing caseload*

casemate (ˈkeɪsˌmeɪt) *n* an armoured compartment in a ship or fortification in which guns are mounted [C16 from F, from It. *casamatta*, ?from Gk *khasmata* apertures]

casement (ˈkeɪsmənt) *n* **1** a window frame that is hinged on one side **2** a window containing frames hinged at the side **3** a poetic word for **window** [C15 prob. from OF *encassement* frame, from *encasser* to encase, from *casse* framework]

Casement (ˈkeɪsmənt) *n* Sir **Roger** (**David**) 1864–1916, British diplomat and Irish nationalist: hanged by the British for treason in attempting to gain German support for Irish independence

caseous (ˈkeɪsɪəs) *adj* of or like cheese [C17 from L *cāseus* CHEESE]

casern *or* **caserne** (kəˈzɜːn) *n* (formerly) a billet or accommodation for soldiers in a town [C17 from F *caserne*, from OProvençal *cazerna* group of four men, ult. from L *quattuor* four]

Caserta (*Italian* kaˈzɛrta) *n* a town in S Italy, in Campania: centre of Garibaldi's campaigns for the unification of Italy (1860); Allied headquarters in World War II. Pop: 69 350 (1990)

case-sensitive *adj* distinguishing between upper-case and lower-case letters: *users can now perform case-sensitive searches*

casework (ˈkeɪsˌwɜːk) *n* social work based on close study of the personal histories and circumstances of individuals and families > ˈ**caseˌworker** *n*

cash[1] (kæʃ) *n* **1** banknotes and coins, esp when readily available **2** immediate payment for goods or services (esp in **cash down**) **3** (*modifier*) of, for, or paid by cash: *a cash transaction* ▷ *vb* **4** (*tr*) to obtain or pay ready money for ▷ See also **cash in, cash up** [C16 from OIt. *cassa* money box, from L *capsa* CASE[2]] > ˈ**cashable** *adj*

cash[2] (kæʃ) *n, pl* **cash** any of various Chinese or Indian coins of low value [C16 from Port. *caixa*, from Tamil *kāsu*, from Sansk. *karsa* weight of gold]

Cash (kæʃ) *n* **Johnny** 1932–2003, US country-and-western singer, guitarist, and songwriter. His hits include "I Walk the Line" (1956), "Ring of Fire" (1963), and "A Boy named Sue" (1969)

cash-and-carry *adj, adv* **1** sold or operated on a basis of cash payment for merchandise that is not delivered but removed by the purchaser ▷ *n, pl* **cash-and-carries 2** a wholesale store, esp for groceries, that operates on this basis **3** an operation on a commodities futures market in which spot goods are purchased for cash and sold at a profit on a futures contract, after paying interest and storage charges

cashback (ˈkæʃˌbæk) *n* **1a** a discount offered in return for immediate payment **1b** (*as modifier*): *cashback price £519.99 – save £30!* **2a** a service provided by some supermarkets in which customers paying by debit card can draw cash **2b** the cash so drawn

cash-book *n book-keeping* a journal in which all receipts and disbursements are recorded

cash card *n* an embossed plastic card bearing the name and account details of a bank or building-society customer, used with a personal identification number to obtain money from a cash dispenser: may also function as a cheque card or debit card or both. Also called: **cash-point card**

cash cow *n* a product, acquisition, etc, that produces a steady flow of cash, esp one with a well-known brand name commanding a high market share

cash crop *n* a crop grown for sale rather than for subsistence

cash desk *n* a counter or till in a shop where purchases are paid for

cash discount *n* a discount granted to a purchaser who pays before a stipulated date

cash dispenser *n* a computerized device that supplies

Cc

cash when the user inserts his or her cash card and keys in his or her identification number. Also called: **automated teller machine**

cashew ('kæʃuː, kæ'ʃuː) *n* **1** a tropical American evergreen tree, bearing kidney-shaped nuts **2** Also called: **cashew nut** the edible nut of this tree [c18 from Port. *cajú*, from Tupi *acajú*]

cash flow *n* **1** the movement of money into and out of a business **2** a document that records or predicts this movement

cashier[1] (kæ'ʃɪə) *n* **1** a person responsible for receiving payments for goods, services, etc, as in a shop **2** an employee of a bank responsible for receiving deposits, cashing cheques, etc: bank clerk **3** any person responsible for handling cash in a business [c16 from Du. or F, from *casse* money chest]

cashier[2] (kæ'ʃɪə) *vb* (*tr*) to dismiss with dishonour, esp from the armed forces [c16 from MDu., from OF, from L *quassāre* to QUASH]

cash in *vb* (*adv*) **1** (*tr*) to give (something) in exchange **2** (*intr*; *often foll by* *on*) *Inf* **2a** to profit (from) **2b** to take advantage (of)

cashmere *or* **kashmir** ('kæʃmɪə) *n* **1** a fine soft wool from goats of the Kashmir area **2a** cloth or knitted material made from this or similar wool **2b** (*as modifier*): *a cashmere sweater*

Cashmere (kæʃ'mɪə) *n* a variant spelling of **Kashmir**

cash on delivery *n* a service entailing cash payment to the carrier on delivery of merchandise. Abbrev: **COD**

cashpoint ('kæʃ,pɔɪnt) *n* a cash dispenser

cash register *n* a till with a keyboard that operates a mechanism for displaying and adding the amounts of cash received in individual sales

cash-strapped *adj* short of money; impoverished: *cash-strapped local authorities*

cash up *vb* (*intr, adv*) *Brit* (of cashiers, shopkeepers, etc) to add up the money taken, esp at the end of a working day

casing ('keɪsɪŋ) *n* **1** a protective case or cover **2** material for a case or cover **3** Also called: **case** a frame containing a door or window

casino (kə'siːnəʊ) *n, pl* **casinos** **1** a public building or room in which gaming takes place **2** a variant spelling of **cassino** [c18 from It., dim. of *casa* house, from L]

cask (kɑːsk) *n* **1** a strong wooden barrel used mainly to hold alcoholic drink: *a wine cask* **2** any barrel **3** the quantity contained in a cask **4** *Austral* a lightweight cardboard container used to hold and serve wine [c15 from Sp. *casco* helmet]

casket ('kɑːskɪt) *n* **1** a small box or chest for valuables, esp jewels **2** *chiefly US* another word for **coffin** (sense 1) [c15 prob. from OF *cassette* little box]

Caspar ('kæspə, 'kæspɑː) *or* **Gaspar** *n* (in Christian tradition) one of the Magi, the other two being Melchior and Balthazar

Caspian Sea ('kæspɪən) *n* a salt lake between SE Europe and Asia: the largest inland sea in the world; fed mainly by the River Volga. Area: 394 299 sq km (152 239 sq miles)

casque (kæsk) *n* *zool* a helmet or a helmet-like structure, as on the bill of most hornbills [c17 from F, from Sp. *casco*] > **casqued** *adj*

Cassatt (kə'sæt) *n* **Mary** 1845–1926, US impressionist painter, who lived in France

cassava (kə'sɑːvə) *n* **1** Also called: **manioc** any of various tropical plants, esp the widely cultivated American species (**bitter cassava, sweet cassava**) **2** a starch derived from the root of this plant: a source of tapioca [c16 from Sp. *cazabe* cassava bread, from Taino *caçábi*]

casserole ('kæsə,rəʊl) *n* **1** a covered dish of earthenware, glass, etc, in which food is cooked and served **2** any food cooked and served in such a dish: *chicken casserole* ▷ *vb* **casseroles, casseroling, casseroled** **3** to cook or be cooked in a casserole [c18 from F, from OF *casse* ladle, from OProvençal, from LL *cattia* dipper, from Gk *kuathion*, dim. of *kuathos* cup]

cassette (kæ'sɛt) *n* **1a** a plastic container for magnetic tape, inserted into a tape deck to be played or used **1b** (*as modifier*): *a cassette recorder* **2** *photog* another term for **cartridge** (sense 3) **3** the injection of genes from one species into the fertilized egg of another species [c18 from F: little box]

cassia ('kæsɪə) *n* **1** any of a genus of tropical plants whose pods yield **cassia pulp**, a mild laxative. See also **senna** **2** a lauraceous tree of tropical Asia **3** **cassia bark** the cinnamon-like bark of this tree, used as a spice [OE, from L *casia*, from Gk *kasia*, of Semitic origin]

Cassini (kæ'siːnɪ) *n* **Giovanni Domenico** 1625–1712, French astronomer, born in Italy. He discovered (1675) **Cassini's division** and four of Saturn's moons

Cassini's division *n* the gap that divides Saturn's rings into two parts, discovered by Cassini

cassino *or* **casino** (kə'siːnəʊ) *n* a card game for two to four players in which players pair cards with those exposed on the table

Cassiodorus (,kæsɪəʊ'dɔːrəs) *n* **Flavius Magnus Aurelius** ('fleɪvɪəs 'mægnəs ɔː'riːlɪəs) ?490–?585 AD, Roman statesman, writer, and monk; author of *Variae*, a collection of official documents written for the Ostrogoths

Cassiopeia[1] (,kæsɪə'piːə) *n* *Greek myth* the wife of Cepheus and mother of Andromeda

Cassiopeia[2] (,kæsɪə'piːə) *n, Latin genitive* **Cassiopeiae** (,kæsɪə'piːiː) a very conspicuous W-shaped constellation near the Pole Star

Cassirer (*German* ka'siːrər) *n* **Ernst** (ɛrnst) 1874–1945, German neo-Kantian philosopher. *The Philosophy of Symbolic Forms* (1923–29) analyses the symbols that underlie all manifestations, including myths and language, of human culture

cassis (kɑː'siːs) *n* a blackcurrant cordial [c19 from F]

cassiterite (kə'sɪtə,raɪt) *n* a hard heavy brownish-black mineral, the chief ore of tin. Formula: SnO_2. Also called: **tinstone** [c19 from Gk *kassiteros* tin]

Cassius Longinus ('kæsɪəs lɒn'dʒaɪnəs) *n* **Gaius** ('gaɪəs) died 42 BC, Roman general: led the conspiracy against Julius Caesar (44); defeated at Philippi by Antony (42)

Cassivelaunus (,kæsɪvə'lɔːnəs) *n* 1st century BC, British chieftain, king of the Catuvellauni tribe, who organized resistance to Caesar's invasion of Britain (54 BC)

cassock ('kæsək) *n* an ankle-length garment, usually black, worn by Christian priests [c16 from OF, from It. *casacca* a long coat, from ?]

Casson ('kæsᵊn) *n* **Sir Hugh (Maxwell)** 1910–99, British architect; president of the Royal Academy of Arts (1976–84)

cassowary ('kæsə,wɛərɪ) *n, pl* **cassowaries** a large flightless bird inhabiting forests in NE Australia, New Guinea, and adjacent islands, having a horny head crest, black plumage, and brightly coloured neck [c17 from Malay *kĕsuari*]

cast (kɑːst) *vb* **casts, casting, cast** (*mainly tr*) **1** to throw or expel with force **2** to throw off or away: *she cast her clothes to the ground* **3** to reject: *he cast the idea from his mind* **4** to shed or drop: *the horse cast a shoe* **5** to cause to appear: *to cast a shadow* **6** to express (doubts, etc) or cause (them) to be felt **7** to direct (a glance, etc): *cast your eye over this* **8** to place, esp violently: *he was cast into prison* **9** (*also intr*) *Angling.* to throw (a line) into the water **10** to draw or choose (lots) **11** to give or deposit (a vote) **12** to select (actors) to play parts in (a play, etc) **13a** to shape (molten metal, glass, etc) by pouring into a mould **13b** to make (an object) by such a process **14** (*also intr*; *often foll by* *up*) to compute (figures or a total) **15** *astrol* to draw on (a horoscope) details concerning the positions of the planets in the signs of the zodiac at a particular time for interpretation **16** to contrive (esp in **cast a spell**) **17** to formulate: *he cast his work in the form of a chart* **18** (*also intr*) to twist or cause to twist **19** (*intr*) (of birds of prey) to eject from the crop and bill a pellet consisting of the indigestible parts of birds or animals previously eaten **20** *printing* to stereotype or electrotype **21** **be cast** NZ (of sheep) to have fallen and been unable to rise ▷ *n* **22** the act of casting or throwing **23a** Also called: **casting** something that is shed, dropped, or egested, such as the coil of earth left by an earthworm **23b** another name for **pellet** (sense 4) **24** the distance an object is or may be thrown **25a** a throw at dice **25b** the resulting number shown **26** *angling* the act or an instance of casting a line **27** the wide sweep made by a sheepdog to get behind a flock of sheep or by a hunting dog in search of a scent **28a** the actors in a play collectively **28b** (*as modifier*): *a cast list* **29a** an object made of metal, glass, etc, that has been shaped in a molten state by being poured or pressed into a mould **29b** the mould used to shape such an object **30** form or appearance **31** a sort, kind, or style **32** a fixed twist or defect, esp in the eye **33** a distortion of shape **34** *surgery* a rigid encircling casing, often made of plaster of Paris (**plaster cast**), for immobilizing broken bones while they heal **35** a slight tinge or trace, as of colour **36** fortune or stroke of fate ▷ See also **cast about, castaway,** etc [C13 from ON *kasta*]

cast about *or* **around** *vb* (*intr, adv*) to make a mental or visual search: *to cast about for a plot*

Castalia (kæˈsteɪlɪə) *n* a spring on Mount Parnassus: in ancient Greece sacred to Apollo and the Muses and believed to be a source of inspiration

castanets (ˌkæstəˈnɛts) *pl n* curved pieces of hollow wood, usually held between the fingers and thumb and made to click together: used esp by Spanish dancers [C17 *castanet*, from Sp. *castañeta*, dim. of *castaña* CHESTNUT]

castaway (ˈkɑːstəˌweɪ) *n* **1** a person who has been shipwrecked ▷ *adj* (*prenominal*) **2** shipwrecked **3** thrown away or rejected ▷ *vb* **cast away** **4** (*tr, adv; often passive*) to cause (a ship, person, etc) to be shipwrecked

cast back *vb* (*adv*) to turn (the mind) to the past

cast down *vb* (*tr, adv*) to make (a person) discouraged

caste (kɑːst) *n* **1a** any of the four major hereditary classes, namely the **Brahman, Kshatriya, Vaisya,** and **Sudra,** into which Hindu society is divided **1b** Also called: **caste system** the system or basis of such classes **2** any social class or system based on such distinctions as heredity, rank, wealth, etc **3** the position conferred by such a system **4** **lose caste** *inf* to lose one's social position **5** *entomol* any of various types of individual, such as the worker, in social insects [C16 from Port. *casta* race, from *casto* pure, chaste, from L *castus*]

Castellammare di Stabia (*Italian* kastɛllamˈmaːre di ˈstabja) *n* a port and resort in SW Italy, in Campania on the Bay of Naples: site of the Roman resort of Stabiae, which was destroyed by the eruption of Vesuvius in 79 AD Pop: 67 974 (1993 est)

castellan (ˈkæstɪlən) *n rare* a keeper or governor of a castle. Also called: **chatelain** [C14 from L *castellānus*, from *castellum* CASTLE]

castellated (ˈkæstɪˌleɪtɪd) *adj* **1** having turrets and battlements, like a castle **2** having indentations similar to battlements: *a castellated nut* [C17 from Med. L *castellātus*, from *castellāre* to fortify as a CASTLE] > ˌ**castelˈlation** *n*

caster (ˈkɑːstə) *n* **1** a person or thing that casts **2** a bottle with a perforated top for sprinkling sugar, etc **3** a small swivelled wheel fixed to a piece of furniture to enable it to be moved easily in any direction ▷ Also (for senses 2, 3): **castor**

caster sugar (ˈkɑːstə) *n* finely ground white sugar

castigate (ˈkæstɪˌgeɪt) *vb* **castigates, castigating, castigated** (*tr*) to rebuke or criticize in a severe manner [C17 from L *castīgāre* to correct, from *castum* pure + *agere* to compel (to be)] > ˌ**castiˈgation** *n* > ˈ**castiˌgator** *n*

Castiglione (ˌkæstɪlˈjəʊnɪ; *Italian* kastiˈʎoːne) *n* Count **Baldassare** (baldasˈsaːre) 1478–1529, Italian diplomat and writer, noted particularly for his dialogue on ideal courtly life, *Il Libro del Cortegiano* (The Courtier) (1528)

Castile (kæˈstiːl) *or* **Castilla** (*Spanish* kasˈtiʎa) *n* a former kingdom comprising most of modern Spain: originally part of León, it became an independent kingdom in the 10th century and united with Aragon (1469), the first step in the formation of the Spanish state

Castile soap *n* a hard soap made from olive oil and sodium hydroxide

Castilian (kæˈstɪljən) *n* **1** the Spanish dialect of Castile; the standard form of European Spanish **2** a native or inhabitant of Castile ▷ *adj* **3** denoting or of Castile, its inhabitants, or the standard form of European Spanish

Castilla la Vieja (kasˈtiʎa la ˈbjexa) *n* the Spanish name for **Old Castile**

casting (ˈkɑːstɪŋ) *n* **1** an object that has been cast, esp in metal from a mould **2** the process of transferring molten steel to a mould **3** the choosing of actors for a production **4** *zool* another word for **cast** (sense 23) or **pellet** (sense 4)

casting couch *n inf* a couch on which a casting director is said to seduce girls seeking a part in a film or play

casting vote *n* the deciding vote used by the presiding officer of an assembly when votes cast on both sides are equal in number

cast iron *n* **1** iron containing so much carbon that it cannot be wrought and must be cast into shape ▷ *adj* **cast-iron** **2** made of cast iron **3** rigid or unyielding: *a cast-iron decision*

castle (ˈkɑːsᵊl) *n* **1** a fortified building or set of buildings as in medieval Europe **2** any fortified place or structure **3** a large magnificent house, esp when the present or former home of a nobleman or prince **4** *chess* another name for **rook**[2] ▷ *vb* **castles, castling, castled** **5** *chess* to move (the king) two squares laterally on the first rank and place the nearest rook on the square passed over by the king [C11 from L *castellum*, dim. of *castrum* fort]

Castlebar (ˌkɑːsᵊlˈbɑː) *n* the county town of Co. Mayo, Republic of Ireland; site of the battle (1798) between the French and British known as Castlebar Races. Pop: 6070 (1991)

castle in the air *or* **in Spain** *n* a hope or desire unlikely to be realized; daydream

Castlereagh[1] (ˈkɑːsᵊlˌreɪ) *n* a district of E Northern Ireland, in Co. Down. Pop: 66 488 (2001). Area.: 85 sq km (33 sq miles)

Castlereagh[2] (ˈkɑːsᵊlˌreɪ) *n* **Viscount** title of *Robert Stewart*, Marquis of Londonderry. 1769–1822, British statesman: as foreign secretary (1812–22) led the Grand Alliance against Napoleon and attended the Congress of Vienna (1815)

Castner (ˈkæstnə) *n* **Hamilton Young** 1858–98, US chemist, who devised the **Castner process** for extracting sodium from sodium hydroxide

cast-off *adj* **1** (*prenominal*) abandoned: *cast-off shoes* ▷ *n* **castoff** **2** a person or thing that has been discarded or abandoned **3** *printing* an estimate of the amount of space that a piece of copy will occupy ▷ *vb* **cast off** (*adv*) **4** to remove (mooring lines) that hold (a vessel) to a dock **5** to knot (a row of stitches, esp the final row) in finishing off knitted or woven material **6** *printing* to estimate the amount of space that will be taken up by (a book, piece of copy, etc)

cast on *vb* (*adv*) to form (the first row of stitches) in knitting and weaving

castor[1] (ˈkɑːstə) *n* **1** the aromatic secretion of a beaver, used in perfumery and medicine **2** the fur of the beaver **3** a hat made of beaver or similar fur [C14 from L, from Gk *kastōr* beaver]

castor[2] (ˈkɑːstə) *n* a variant spelling of **caster** (senses 2, 3)

Cc

Castor and Pollux *n classical myth* the twin sons of Leda: Pollux was fathered by Zeus, Castor by the mortal Tyndareus. After Castor's death, Pollux spent half his days with his half-brother in Hades and half with the gods in Olympus

castor oil *n* an oil obtained from the seeds of the castor-oil plant and used as a lubricant and cathartic

castor-oil plant *n* a tall Indian plant cultivated for its poisonous seeds, from which castor oil is extracted

castrate (kæ'streɪt) *vb* **castrates, castrating, castrated** (*tr*) **1** to remove the testicles of **2** to deprive of vigour, masculinity, etc **3** to remove the ovaries of; spay [C17 from L *castrāre* to emasculate, geld] > **cas'tration** *n*

castrato (kæ'strɑːtəʊ) *n, pl* **castrati** (-tɪ) *or* **castratos** (in 17th- and 18th-century opera, etc) a male singer whose testicles were removed before puberty, allowing the retention of a soprano or alto voice [C18 from It., from L *castrātus* castrated]

Castries (kæs'triːs) *n* the capital and chief port of St Lucia. Pop: 13 615 (1992 est)
▷ http://stlucia.rezrez.com/whattoseedo/attractions/castries/index.htm

Castro ('kæstrəʊ; *Spanish* 'kastro) *n* **Fidel** (fɪ'dɛl; *Spanish* fi'ðɛl) full name *Fidel Castro Ruz*. born 1927, Cuban statesman: prime minister from 1959, when he led the Communist overthrow of Batista, and president from 1976

cast steel *n* steel containing varying amounts of carbon, manganese, etc, that is cast into shape rather than wrought

cast stone *n building trades* a building component, such as a block or lintel, made from cast concrete with a facing that resembles natural stone

casual ('kæʒjʊəl) *adj* **1** happening by accident or chance **2** offhand: *a casual remark* **3** shallow or superficial: *a casual affair* **4** being or seeming unconcerned or apathetic: *he assumed a casual attitude* **5** (esp of dress) for informal wear: *a casual coat* **6** occasional or irregular: *a casual labourer* ▷ *n* **7** (*usually pl*) an informal article of clothing or footwear **8** an occasional worker **9** (*usually pl*) a young man dressed in expensive casual clothes who goes to football matches in order to start fights [C14 from LL *cāsuālis* happening by chance, from L *cāsus* event, from *cadere* to fall] > **'casually** *adv* > **'casualness** *n*

casualization *or* **casualisation** (ˌkæʒjʊəlaɪ'zeɪʃən) *n* the altering of working practices so that regular workers are re-employed on a casual or short-term basis

casualty ('kæʒjʊəltɪ) *n, pl* **casualties** **1** a serviceman who is killed, wounded, captured, or missing as a result of enemy action **2** a person who is injured or killed in an accident **3** the hospital department treating victims of accidents **4** anything that is lost, damaged, or destroyed as the result of an accident, etc

casuarina (ˌkæzjʊə'riːnə) *n* any of a genus of trees of Australia and the East Indies, having jointed leafless branchlets [C19 from NL, from Malay *kĕsuari* CASSOWARY, referring to the resemblance of the branches to the feathers of the cassowary]

casuist ('kæzjʊɪst) *n* **1** a person, esp a theologian, who attempts to resolve moral dilemmas by the application of general rules and the careful distinction of special cases **2** a sophist [C17 from F, from Sp. *casuista*, from L *cāsus* CASE[1]] > ˌ**casu'istic** *or* ˌ**casu'istical** *adj*

casuistry ('kæzjʊɪstrɪ) *n, pl* **casuistries** **1** *philosophy* the resolution of particular moral dilemmas, esp those arising from conflicting general moral rules, by the careful distinction of the cases to which these rules apply **2** reasoning that is specious or oversubtle

cat[1] (kæt) *n* **1** Also called: **domestic cat** a small domesticated feline mammal having thick soft fur and occurring in many breeds in which the colour of the fur varies greatly: kept as a pet or to catch rats and mice **2** Also called: **big cat** any of the larger felines, such as a lion or tiger **3** any wild feline mammal such as the lynx or serval, resembling the domestic cat **4** *inf* a woman who gossips maliciously **5** *sl* a man **6** *naut* a heavy tackle for hoisting an anchor to the cathead **7** *Austral sl* a coward **8** short for **catboat** **9** *inf* short for **caterpillar** (the vehicle) **10** short for **cat-o'-nine-tails** **11 a bag of cats** *Irish inf* a bad-tempered person: *she's a real bag of cats this morning* **12 fight like Kilkenny cats** to fight until both parties are destroyed **13 let the cat out of the bag** to disclose a secret, often by mistake **14 like a cat on a hot tin roof** *or* **on hot bricks** in an uneasy or agitated state **15 put, set,** etc, **the cat among the pigeons** to introduce some violently disturbing new element **16 rain cats and dogs** to rain very heavily ▷ *vb* **cats, catting, catted** **17** (*tr*) *naut* to hoist (an anchor) to the cathead **18** (*intr*) *sl* to vomit [OE *catte*, from L *cattus*; rel. to OF *chat*] > **'catˌlike** *adj* > **'cattish** *adj*

cat[2] (kæt) *adj* short for **catalytic**: *a cat cracker*

CAT *abbrev for* computer-assisted trading

cat. *abbrev for*: **1** catalogue **2** catamaran

cata-, kata-, *before an aspirate* **cath-,** *or before a vowel* **cat-** *prefix* **1** down; downwards; lower in position: *catadromous* **2** indicating reversal, opposition, degeneration, etc: *catatonia* [from Gk *kata-*, from *kata*. In compound words borrowed from Gk *kata-* means: down, away, off, against, according to, and thoroughly]

catabolism *or* **katabolism** (kə'tæbəˌlɪzəm) *n* a metabolic process in which complex molecules are broken down into simple ones with the release of energy; destructive metabolism [C19 from Gk *katabolē* a throwing down, from *kata-* down + *ballein* to throw] > **catabolic** *or* **katabolic** (ˌkætə'bɒlɪk) *adj*

catachresis (ˌkætə'kriːsɪs) *n* the incorrect use of words, as *luxuriant* for *luxurious* [C16 from L, from Gk *katakhrēsis* a misusing, from *khrēsthai* to use] > **catachrestic** (ˌkætə'krɛstɪk) *adj*

cataclysm ('kætəˌklɪzəm) *n* **1** a violent upheaval, esp of a political, military, or social nature **2** a disastrous flood [C17 via F from L, from Gk, from *katakluzein* to flood, from *kluzein* to wash] > ˌ**cata'clysmic** *or* ˌ**cata'clysmal** *adj* > ˌ**cata'clysmically** *adv*

catacomb ('kætəˌkəʊm) *n* **1** (*usually pl*) an underground burial place, esp in Rome, consisting of tunnels with niches leading off them for tombs **2** a series of interconnected underground tunnels or caves [OE *catacumbe*, from LL *catacumbas* (sing), name of the cemetery under the Basilica of St Sebastian, near Rome; from ?]

catadioptric (ˌkætədaɪ'ɒptrɪk) *adj* involving a combination of reflecting and refracting components: *a catadioptric telescope* [C18 from CATA- + DIOPTRIC(S)]

catadromous (kə'tædrəməs) *adj* (of fishes such as the eel) migrating down rivers to the sea in order to breed ▷ Cf **anadromous** [C19 from Gk, from *kata-* down + *dromos*, from *dremein* to run]

catafalque ('kætəˌfælk) *n* a temporary raised platform on which a body lies in state before or during a funeral [C17 from F, from It. *catafalco*, from ?]

Catalan ('kætəˌlæn) *n* **1** a language of Catalonia, closely related to Spanish and Provençal **2** a native or inhabitant of Catalonia ▷ *adj* **3** denoting or characteristic of Catalonia, its inhabitants, or their language

catalepsy ('kætəˌlɛpsɪ) *n* a state of prolonged rigid posture, occurring for example in schizophrenia [C16 from LL *catalēpsis*, from Gk *katalēpsis*, lit.: a seizing, from *kata-* down + *lambanein* to grasp] > ˌ**cata'leptic** *adj*

catalogue *or US* **catalog** ('kætəˌlɒg) *n* **1** a complete, usually alphabetical, list of items **2** a book, usually illustrated, containing details of items for sale **3** a list of all the books of a library **4** *US & Canad* a publication issued by a university, college, etc, listing courses offered, regulations, services, etc ▷ *vb* **catalogues,**

cataloguing, catalogued *or US* **catalogs, cataloging, cataloged** 5 to compile a catalogue of (a library, etc) 6 to add (books, items, etc) to an existing catalogue [C15 from LL *catalogus*, from Gk, from *katalegein* to list, from *kata-* completely + *legein* to collect] > **ˈcataˌloguer** *n*

Catalonia (ˌkætəˈləʊnɪə) *n* a region of NE Spain, with a strong separatist tradition: became an autonomous region with its own parliament in 1979; an important agricultural and industrial region, with many resorts. Pop: 6 261 999 (2000 est). Area: 31 929 sq km (12 328 sq miles). Catalan name: **Catalunya** (ˌkatəˈluːnɪə) Spanish name: **Cataluña** (kataˈluɲa)

catalpa (kəˈtælpə) *n* any of a genus of trees of North America and Asia, having large leaves, bell-shaped whitish flowers, and long slender pods [C18 NL, from Carolina Creek *kutuhlpa*, lit.: winged head]

catalyse *or US* **catalyze** (ˈkætəˌlaɪz) *vb* **catalyses, catalysing, catalysed** *or US* **catalyzes, catalyzing, catalyzed** (*tr*) to influence (a chemical reaction) by catalysis

catalysis (kəˈtælɪsɪs) *n, pl* **catalyses** (-ˌsiːz) acceleration of a chemical reaction by the action of a catalyst [C17 from NL, from Gk, from *kataluein* to dissolve] > **catalytic** (ˌkætəˈlɪtɪk) *adj*

catalyst (ˈkætəlɪst) *n* 1 a substance that increases the rate of a chemical reaction without itself suffering any permanent chemical change 2 a person or thing that causes a change

catalytic converter *n* a device using three-way catalysts to reduce the poisonous products of combustion (mainly oxides of nitrogen, carbon monoxide, and unburnt hydrocarbons) from the exhaust of motor vehicles

catalytic cracker *n* a unit in an oil refinery in which mineral oils with high boiling points are converted to fuels with lower boiling points by a catalytic process

catamaran (ˌkætəməˈræn) *n* 1 a vessel, usually a sailing vessel, with twin hulls held parallel by a rigid framework 2 a primitive raft made of logs lashed together 3 *inf* a quarrelsome woman [C17 from Tamil *kattumaram* tied timber]

catamite (ˈkætəˌmaɪt) *n* a boy kept for homosexual purposes [C16 from L *Catamītus*, var. of *Ganymēdēs* GANYMEDE]

catamount (ˈkætəˌmaʊnt) *or* **catamountain** *n* any of various felines, such as the puma or lynx [C17 short for *cat of the mountain*]

catananche (kætənˈæŋkɪ) *n* any herb of the genus *Catananche*, having blue or yellow flowers [C18 NL, from L, from Gk *kata* down + *anagkē* compulsion (from its use by ancient Greeks as a philtre)]

Catania (*Italian* kaˈtaːnja) *n* a port in E Sicily, near Mount Etna. Pop: 337 862 (2000 est)

cataplexy (ˈkætəˌplɛksɪ) *n* 1 sudden temporary paralysis, brought on by severe shock 2 a state assumed by animals while shamming death [C19 from Gk *kataplēxis* amazement, from *kataplēssein*, from *kata-* down + *plēssein* to strike] > ˌ**cataˈplectic** *adj*

catapult (ˈkætəˌpʌlt) *n* 1 a Y-shaped implement with a loop of elastic fastened to the ends of the prongs, used mainly by children for shooting stones, etc US and Canad name: **slingshot** 2 a war engine used formerly for hurling stones, etc 3 a device installed in warships to launch aircraft ▷ *vb* 4 (*tr*) to shoot forth from or as if from a catapult 5 (foll by *over, into*, etc) to move precipitately [C16 from L, from Gk *katapeltēs*, from *kata-* down + *pallein* to hurl]

cataract (ˈkætəˌrækt) *n* 1 a large waterfall or rapids 2 a downpour 3 *pathol* 3a partial or total opacity of the lens of the eye 3b the opaque area [C15 from L, from Gk, from *katarassein* to dash down, from *arassein* to strike]

catarrh (kəˈtɑː) *n* 1 inflammation of a mucous membrane with increased production of mucus, esp affecting the nose and throat 2 the mucus so formed [C16 via F from LL, from Gk, from *katarrhein* to flow down, from *kata-* down + *rhein* to flow] > **caˈtarrhal** *adj*

catarrhine (ˈkætəˌraɪn) *adj* 1 (of apes and Old World monkeys) having the nostrils set close together and opening to the front of the face ▷ *n* 2 an animal with this characteristic [C19 ult. from Gk *katarrhin* having a hooked nose, from *kata-* down + *rhis* nose]

catastrophe (kəˈtæstrəfɪ) *n* 1 a sudden, extensive disaster or misfortune 2 the denouement of a play 3 a final decisive event, usually causing a disastrous end [C16 from Gk, from *katastrephein* to overturn, from *strephein* to turn] > **catastrophic** (ˌkætəˈstrɒfɪk) *adj* > ˌ**cataˈstrophically** *adv*

catastrophism (kəˈtæstrəˌfɪzəm) *n* 1 a former doctrine that the earth was formed by sudden divine acts rather than by evolutionary processes 2 a modern doctrine that the evolutionary processes shaping the earth have in the past been supplemented by the effects of huge natural catastrophes

catatonia (ˌkætəˈtəʊnɪə) *n* a form of schizophrenia characterized by stupor, with outbreaks of excitement [C20 NL, from G *Katatonie*, from CATA- + Gk *tonos* tension] > **catatonic** (ˌkætəˈtɒnɪk) *adj, n*

catbird (ˈkætˌbɜːd) *n* 1 any of several North American songbirds whose call resembles the mewing of a cat 2 any of several Australian bowerbirds having a catlike call

catboat (ˈkætˌbəʊt) *n* a sailing vessel with a single mast, set well forward, and a large sail. Shortened form: **cat**

cat burglar *n* a burglar who enters buildings by climbing through upper windows, etc

catcall (ˈkætˌkɔːl) *n* 1 a shrill whistle or cry expressing disapproval, as at a public meeting, etc ▷ *vb* 2 to utter such a call (at)

catch (kætʃ) *vb* **catches, catching, caught** 1 (*tr*) to take hold of so as to retain or restrain 2 (*tr*) to take or capture, esp after pursuit 3 (*tr*) to ensnare or deceive 4 (*tr*) to surprise or detect in an act: *he caught the dog rifling the larder* 5 (*tr*) to reach with a blow: *the stone caught him on the side of the head* 6 (*tr*) to overtake or reach in time to board 7 (*tr*) to see or hear; attend 8 (*tr*) to be infected with: *to catch a cold* 9 to hook or entangle or become hooked or entangled 10 to fasten or be fastened with or as if with a latch or other device 11 (*tr*) to attract: *she tried to catch his eye* 12 (*tr*) to comprehend: *I didn't catch his meaning* 13 (*tr*) to hear accurately: *I didn't catch what you said* 14 (*tr*) to captivate or charm 15 (*tr*) to reproduce accurately: *the painter managed to catch his model's beauty* 16 (*tr*) to hold back or restrain: *he caught his breath in surprise* 17 (*intr*) to become alight: *the fire won't catch* 18 (*tr*) *cricket* to dismiss (the person batting) by intercepting and holding a ball struck by him or her before it touches the ground 19 (*intr; often foll by at*) 19a to grasp or attempt to grasp 19b to take advantage (of): *he caught at the chance* 20 **catch it** *inf* to be scolded or reprimanded ▷ *n* 21 the act of catching or grasping 22 a device that catches and fastens, such as a latch 23 anything that is caught 24 the amount or number caught 25 *inf* an eligible matrimonial prospect 26 a check or break in the voice 27 *inf* 27a a concealed, unexpected, or unforeseen drawback 27b (*as modifier*): *a catch question* 28 *cricket* the catching of a ball struck by a batsman before it touches the ground, resulting in him being out 29 *music* a type of round having a humorous text that is often indecent or bawdy and hard to articulate ▷ See also **catch on, catch out, catch up** [C13 *cacchen* to pursue, from OF *cachier*, from L *captāre* to snatch, from *capere* to seize] > **ˈcatchable** *adj*

catch-22 *n* a situation in which a person is frustrated by a set of circumstances that preclude any attempt to escape from them [C20 from the title of a novel (1961) by J. Heller]

catch-as-catch-can *n* a style of wrestling in which

Cc

trips, holds below the waist, etc, are allowed

catchcry ('kætʃ,kraɪ) *n pl* **-cries** *Austral* a well-known, frequently used phrase, esp one associated with a particular group, etc

catchfly ('kætʃ,flaɪ) *n, pl* **catchflies** any of various plants that have sticky calyxes and stems on which insects are sometimes trapped

catching ('kætʃɪŋ) *adj* **1** infectious **2** attractive; captivating

catching pen *n Austral & NZ* a pen adjacent to a shearer's stand containing the sheep ready for shearing

catchment ('kætʃmənt) *n* **1** the act of catching or collecting water **2** a structure in which water is collected **3** the water so collected **4** *Brit* the intake of a school from one catchment area

catchment area *n* **1** the area of land bounded by watersheds draining into a river, basin, or reservoir **2** the area from which people are allocated to a particular school, hospital, etc

catch on *vb (intr, adv) Inf* **1** to become popular or fashionable **2** to understand

catch out *vb (tr, adv) inf, chiefly Brit* to trap (a person), esp in an error

catchpenny ('kætʃ,pɛnɪ) *adj (prenominal)* designed to have instant appeal, esp in order to sell quickly: *catchpenny ornaments*

catch phrase *n* a well-known frequently used phrase, esp one associated with a particular group, etc

catch up *vb (adv)* **1** *(tr)* to seize and take up (something) quickly **2** (when *intr*, often foll by *with*) to reach or pass (someone or something): *he caught him up* **3** *(intr;* usually foll by *on* or *with)* to make up for lost ground or deal with a backlog **4** *(tr; often passive)* to absorb or involve: *she was caught up in her reading* **5** *(tr)* to raise by or as if by fastening

catchweight ('kætʃ,weɪt) *adj wrestling* of or relating to a contest in which normal weight categories have been waived by agreement

catchword ('kætʃ,wɜːd) *n* **1** a word or phrase made temporarily popular; slogan **2** a word printed as a running head in a book **3** *theatre* an actor's cue to speak or enter **4** the first word of a page repeated at the bottom of the page preceding

catchy ('kætʃɪ) *adj* **catchier, catchiest** **1** (of a tune, etc) pleasant and easily remembered **2** deceptive: *a catchy question* **3** irregular: *a catchy breeze*

cat cracker *n* an informal name for **catalytic cracker**

catechetical (,kætɪ'kɛtɪkᵊl) *or* **catechetic** *adj* of or relating to teaching by question and answer > ,**cate'chetically** *adv*

catechism ('kætɪ,kɪzəm) *n* instruction by a series of questions and answers, esp a book containing such instruction on the religious doctrine of a Christian Church [c16 from LL, ult. from Gk *katēkhizein* to CATECHIZE] > ,**cate'chismal** *adj*

catechize *or* **catechise** ('kætɪ,kaɪz) *vb* **catechizes, catechizing, catechized** *or* **catechises, catechising, catechised** *(tr)* **1** to teach or examine by means of questions and answers **2** to give oral instruction in Christianity, esp by using a catechism **3** to put questions to (someone) [c15 from LL, from Gk *katēkhizein*, from *katēkhein* to instruct orally, from *kata-* down + *ēkhein* to sound] > '**catechist**, '**cate,chizer** *or* '**cate,chiser** *n*

catechu ('kætɪ,tʃuː) *or* **cachou** *n* an astringent resinous substance obtained from certain tropical plants, and used in medicine, tanning, and dyeing [c17 prob. from Malay *kachu*]

catechumen (,kætɪ'kjuːmɛn) *n Christianity* a person, esp in the early Church, undergoing instruction prior to baptism [c15 via OF, from LL, from Gk *katēkhoumenos* one being instructed verbally]

categorial (,kætɪ'gɔːrɪəl) *adj* **1** of or relating to a category **2** *logic* (of a statement) consisting of a subject, S, and a predicate, P, each of which denote a class, as in: *all S are P*

categorical (,kætɪ'gɒrɪkᵊl) *or* **categoric** *adj* **1** unqualified; unconditional: *a categorical statement* **2** relating to or included in a category **3** another word for **categorial** (sense 2) > ,**cate'gorically** *adv*

categorize *or* **categorise** ('kætɪgə,raɪz) *vb* **categorizes, categorizing, categorized** *or* **categorises, categorising, categorised** *(tr)* to place in a category > ,**categori'zation** *or* ,**categori'sation** *n*

category ('kætɪgərɪ) *n, pl* **categories** **1** a class or group of things, people, etc, possessing some quality or qualities in common **2** *metaphysics* one of the most basic classes into which objects and concepts can be analysed **3a** (in the philosophy of Aristotle) any one of ten most fundamental modes of being, such as quantity, quality, and substance **3b** (in the philosophy of Kant) one of twelve concepts required by human beings to interpret the empirical world [c15 from LL, from Gk *katēgoria*, from *kategorein* to accuse, assert]

category killer *n* a person, product, or business that dominates a particular market

catena (kə'tiːnə) *n, pl* **catenae** (-niː) a connected series, esp of patristic comments on the Bible [c17 from L: chain]

catenaccio (*Italian* kate'nattʃo) *n soccer* an extremely defensive style of play [c20 from L *catena* chain]

catenary (kə'tiːnərɪ) *n, pl* **catenaries** **1** the curve formed by a heavy uniform flexible cord hanging freely from two points **2** the hanging cable between pylons along a railway track, from which the trolley wire is suspended ▷ *adj* **3** of, resembling, relating to, or constructed using a catenary or suspended chain [c18 from L *catēnārius* relating to a chain]

catenate ('kætɪ,neɪt) *vb* **catenates, catenating, catenated** *biol* to arrange or be arranged in a series of chains or rings [c17 from L *catēnāre* to bind with chains] > ,**cate'nation** *n*

cater ('keɪtə) *vb* **1** *(intr;* foll by *for* or *to)* to provide what is required or desired (for) **2** (when *intr*, foll by *for*) to provide food, services, etc (for): *we cater for parties* [c16 from earlier *catour* purchaser, var. of *acatour*, from Anglo-Norman *acater* to buy] > '**catering** *n*

cater-cornered ('kætə,kɔːnəd) *adj, adv US & Canad inf* diagonal. Also: **catty-cornered, kitty-cornered** [c16 from dialect *cater* (adv) diagonally, from obs. *cater* (n) four-spot of dice, from OF *quatre* four, from L *quattuor*]

caterer ('keɪtərə) *n* one who as a profession provides food for large social events, etc

caterpillar ('kætə,pɪlə) *n* **1** the wormlike larva of butterflies and moths, having numerous pairs of legs and powerful biting jaws **2** *trademark* an endless track, driven by sprockets or wheels, used to propel a heavy vehicle **3** *trademark* a vehicle, such as a tractor, tank, etc, driven by such tracks [c15 *catyrpel*, prob. from OF *catepelose*, lit.: hairy cat]

caterwaul ('kætə,wɔːl) *vb (intr)* **1** to make a yowling noise, as a cat on heat ▷ *n* **2** a yell made by or sounding like a cat on heat [c14 imit.]

Catesby ('keɪtzbɪ) *n* **Robert** 1573–1605, English conspirator, leader of the Gunpowder Plot (1605): killed while resisting arrest

catfight ('kæt,faɪt) *n inf* a fight between two women

catfish ('kæt,fɪʃ) *n, pl* **catfish** *or* **catfishes** **1** any of numerous mainly freshwater fishes having whisker-like barbels around the mouth **2** another name for **wolffish**

cat flap *or* **door** *n* a small flap or door in a larger door through which a cat can pass

catgut ('kæt,gʌt) *n* a strong cord made from the dried intestines of sheep and other animals that is used for stringing certain musical instruments and sports rackets

cath- *prefix* a variant of **cata-** before an aspirate: *cathode*

Cathar ('kæθə) *or* **Catharist** ('kæθərɪst) *n, pl* **Cathars,**

Cathari (-ərɪ) *or* **Catharists** a member of a Christian sect in Provence in the 12th and 13th centuries who believed the material world was evil and only the spiritual was good [from Med. L, from Gk *katharoi* the pure] > **'Cathar,ism** *n*

catharsis (kə'θɑːsɪs) *n, pl* **catharses** (-siːz) **1** the purging or purification of the emotions through the evocation of pity and fear, as in tragedy **2** *psychoanal* the bringing of repressed ideas or experiences into consciousness, thus relieving tensions **3** purgation, esp of the bowels [c19 NL, from Gk *katharsis*, from *kathairein* to purge, purify]

cathartic (kə'θɑːtɪk) *adj* **1** purgative **2** effecting catharsis ▹ *n* **3** a purgative drug or agent > **ca'thartically** *adv*

Cathay (kæ'θeɪ) *n* a literary or archaic name for **China** [c14 from Medieval Latin *Cataya*, of Turkic origin]

cathead ('kæt,hɛd) *n* a fitting at the bow of a vessel for securing the anchor when raised

cathedral (kə'θiːdrəl) *n* **a** the principal church of a diocese, containing the bishop's official throne **b** (*as modifier*): *a cathedral city* [c13 from LL (*ecclesia*) *cathedrālis* cathedral (church), from Gk *kathedra* seat]

Cather ('kæðə) *n* **Willa (Sibert)** 1873–1947, US novelist, whose works include *O Pioneers!* (1913) and *My Ántonia* (1918)

Catherine ('kæθrɪn) *n* **Saint** died 307 AD, legendary Christian martyr of Alexandria, who was tortured on a spiked wheel and beheaded

Catherine I *n* ?1684–1727, second wife of Peter the Great, whom she succeeded as empress of Russia (1725–27)

Catherine II *n* known as *Catherine the Great*. 1729–96, empress of Russia (1762–96), during whose reign Russia extended her boundaries at the expense of Turkey, Sweden, and Poland: she was a patron of literature and the arts

Catherine de' Medici *or* **de Médicis** *n* 1519–89, queen of Henry II of France; mother of Francis II, Charles IX, and Henry III of France; regent of France (1560–74). She was largely responsible for the massacre of Protestants on Saint Bartholomew's Day (1572)

Catherine of Aragon *n* 1485–1536, first wife of Henry VIII of England and mother of Mary I. The annulment of Henry's marriage to her (1533) against papal authority marked an initial stage in the English Reformation

Catherine of Braganza *n* 1638–1705, wife of Charles II of England, daughter of John IV of Portugal

Catherine of Siena *n* **Saint** 1347–80, Italian mystic and ascetic; patron saint of the Dominican order. Feast day: April 29

Catherine wheel *n* **1** a firework which rotates, producing coloured flame **2** a circular window having ribs radiating from the centre [c16 after St CATHERINE of Alexandria]

catheter ('kæθɪtə) *n med* a long slender flexible tube for inserting into a bodily cavity for introducing or withdrawing fluid [c17 from LL, from Gk *kathetēr*, from *kathienai* to insert]

catheterize *or* **catheterise** ('kæθɪtə,raɪz) *vb* **catheterizes, catheterizing, catheterized** *or* **catheterises, catheterising, catheterised** (*tr*) to insert a catheter into

cathexis (kə'θɛksɪs) *n, pl* **cathexes** (-'θɛksiːz) *Psychoanal.* concentration of psychic energy on a single goal [c20 from NL, from Gk *kathexis*, from *katekhein* to hold fast]

cathode ('kæθəʊd) *n* **1** the negative electrode in an electrolytic cell **2** the negatively charged electron source in an electronic valve **3** the positive terminal of a primary cell ▹ Cf **anode** [c19 from Gk *kathodos* a descent, from *kata-* down + *hodos* way] > **cathodal** (kæ'θəʊdᵊl) *or* **cathodic** (kæ'θɒdɪk, -'θəʊ-) *adj*

cathode rays *pl n* a stream of electrons emitted from the surface of a cathode in a vacuum tube

cathode-ray tube *n* a vacuum tube in which a beam of electrons is focused onto a fluorescent screen to give a visible spot of light. The device is used in television receivers, visual display units, etc

catholic ('kæθəlɪk, 'kæθlɪk) *adj* **1** universal; relating to all men **2** broad-minded; liberal [c14 from L, from Gk *katholikos* universal, from *kata-* according to + *holos* whole] > **catholically** *or* **catholicly** (kə'θɒlɪklɪ) *adv*

Catholic ('kæθəlɪk, 'kæθlɪk) *Christianity* ▹ *adj* **1** denoting or relating to the entire body of Christians, esp to the Church before separation into the Eastern and Western Churches **2** denoting or relating to the Latin or Western Church after this separation **3** denoting or relating to the Roman Catholic Church ▹ *n* **4** a member of the Roman Catholic Church

Catholicism (kə'θɒlɪ,sɪzəm) *n* **1** short for **Roman Catholicism** **2** the beliefs, practices, etc, of any Catholic Church

catholicity (,kæθə'lɪsɪtɪ) *n* **1** a wide range of interests, tastes, etc **2** comprehensiveness

catholicize *or* **catholicise** (kə'θɒlɪ,saɪz) *vb* **catholicizes, catholicizing, catholicized** *or* **catholicises, catholicising, catholicised** **1** to make or become catholic **2** (*often cap*) to convert to or become converted to Catholicism

Catiline ('kætɪ,laɪn) *n* Latin name *Lucius Sergius Catilina*. ?108–62 BC, Roman politician: organized an unsuccessful conspiracy against Cicero (63–62)

cation ('kætaɪən) *n* a positively charged ion; an ion that is attracted to the cathode during electrolysis ▹ Cf **anion** [c19 from CATA- + ION] > **cationic** (,kætaɪ'ɒnɪk) *adj*

catkin ('kætkɪn) *n* an inflorescence consisting of a spike, usually hanging, of much reduced flowers of either sex: occurs in birch, hazel, etc [c16 from obs. Du. *katteken* kitten]

cat litter *n* absorbent material used to line a receptacle in which a domestic cat can urinate and defecate

catmint ('kæt,mɪnt) *n* a Eurasian plant having spikes of purple-spotted white flowers and scented leaves of which cats are fond. Also called: **catnip**

catnap ('kæt,næp) *n* **1** a short sleep or doze ▹ *vb* **catnaps, catnapping, catnapped** **2** (*intr*) to sleep or doze for a short time or intermittently

Cato ('keɪtəʊ) *n* **1** **Marcus Porcius** ('mɑːkəs 'pɔːʃɪəs), known as *Cato the Elder* or *the Censor*. 234–149 BC, Roman statesman and writer, noted for his relentless opposition to Carthage **2** his great-grandson, **Marcus Porcius**, known as *Cato the Younger* or *Uticensis*. 95–46 BC, Roman statesman, general, and Stoic philosopher; opponent of Catiline and Caesar

cat-o'-nine-tails *n, pl* **cat-o'-nine-tails** a rope whip consisting of nine knotted thongs, used formerly to flog prisoners. Often shortened to **cat**

CATS (kæts) *n acronym for* credit accumulation transfer scheme: a scheme enabling school-leavers and others to acquire transferable certificates for relevant work experience and study towards a recognized qualification

CAT scanner (kæt) *n* former name for **CT scanner** [c20 from Computerized Axial Tomography]

cat's cradle *n* a game played by making patterns with a loop of string between the fingers

cat's-eye *n* any of a group of gemstones that reflect a streak of light when cut in a rounded unfaceted shape

Catseye ('kætsaɪ) *n trademark, Brit* a glass reflector set into a small fixture, placed at intervals along roads to indicate traffic lanes at night

Catskill Mountains ('kætskɪl) *pl n* a mountain range in SE New York State: resort. Highest peak: Slide Mountain, 1261 m (4204 ft). Also called: **Catskills**

cat's-paw *n* **1** a person used by another as a tool; dupe **2** a pattern of ripples on the surface of water caused by a light wind [(sense 1) c18 so called from the tale of the monkey who used a cat's paw to draw chestnuts out of a fire]

catsup ('kætsəp) *n* a variant spelling (esp US) of **ketchup**

cat's whisker *n* a pointed wire formerly used to make contact with the crystal in a crystal radio receiver

cat's whiskers *or* **cat's pyjamas** *n* **the** *sl* a person or thing that is excellent or superior

Cattegat ('kætɪ,gæt) *n* a variant spelling of **Kattegat**

cattery ('kætərɪ) *n, pl* **catteries** a place where cats are bred or looked after

cattle ('kætᵊl) *n* (*functioning as pl*) **1** bovid mammals of the tribe *Bovini* (bovines) **2** Also called: **domestic cattle** any domesticated bovine mammals [c13 from OF *chatel* CHATTEL]

cattle-cake *n* concentrated food for cattle in the form of cakes

cattle dog *n Austral inf* a catalogue [supposedly imitative of CATALOGUE]

cattle-grid *n* a grid of metal bars covering a hole dug in a roadway intended to prevent the passage of livestock while allowing vehicles, etc, to pass unhindered

cattleman ('kætᵊlmən) *n, pl* **cattlemen** **1** a person who breeds, rears, or tends cattle **2** *chiefly US & Canad* a person who rears cattle on a large scale

cattle market *n* **1** a place in which cattle are bought and sold **2** *Brit sl* a situation or place in which women are on display and judged solely by their appearance

cattle-stop *n* the New Zealand name for a **cattle-grid**

catty ('kætɪ) *or* **cattish** *adj* **cattier, cattiest** **1** *inf* spiteful: *a catty remark* **2** of or resembling a cat > **'cattily** *or* **'cattishly** *adv* > **'cattiness** *or* **'cattishness** *n*

Catullus (kə'tʌləs) *n* **Gaius Valerius** ('gaɪəs və'lɪərɪəs) ?84–?54 BC, Roman lyric poet, noted particularly for his love poems

CATV *abbrev for* community antenna television

catwalk ('kæt,wɔ:k) *n* **1** a narrow ramp extending from the stage into the audience in a theatre etc, esp as used by models in a fashion show **2** a narrow pathway over the stage of a theatre, along a bridge, etc

Cauca (*Spanish* 'kauka) *n* a river in W Colombia, rising in the northwest and flowing north to the Magdalena River. Length: about 1350 km (840 miles)

Caucasia (kɔ:'keɪzɪə, -ʒə) *n* a region in SW Russia, Georgia, Armenia, and Azerbaijan, between the Caspian Sea and the Black Sea: contains the Caucasus Mountains, dividing it into Ciscaucasia in the north and Transcaucasia in the south; one of the most complex ethnic areas in the world, with over 50 different peoples. Also called: **the Caucasus**

Caucasian (kɔ:'keɪzɪən) *adj* **1** another word for **Caucasoid** **2** of or relating to Caucasia or the Caucasus ▷ *n* **3** a member of the Caucasoid race; a White person **4** a native or inhabitant of Caucasia or the Caucasus

Caucasoid ('kɔ:kə,zɔɪd) *adj* **1** denoting or belonging to the light-complexioned racial group of mankind, which includes the peoples indigenous to Europe, N Africa, SW Asia, and the Indian subcontinent ▷ *n* **2** a member of this racial group

Caucasus ('kɔ:kəsəs) *n* **the** **1** a mountain range in SW Russia, running along the N borders of Georgia and Azerbaijan, between the Black Sea and the Caspian Sea: mostly over 2700 m (9000 ft). Highest peak: Mount Elbrus, 5642 m (18 510 ft). Also called: **Caucasus Mountains** **2** another name for **Caucasia**

Cauchy ('kaʊʃɪ; *French* koʃi) *n* **Augustin Louis** (ogystɛ̃ lwi), Baron Cauchy. 1789–1857, French mathematician, noted for his work on the theory of functions and the wave theory of light

caucus ('kɔ:kəs) *n, pl* **caucuses** **1** *chiefly US & Canad* a closed meeting of the members of one party in a legislative chamber, etc, to coordinate policy, choose candidates, etc **2** *chiefly US* a local meeting of party members **3** *Brit* a group or faction within a larger group, esp a political party, who discuss tactics, choose candidates, etc **4** *NZ* a formal meeting of all MPs of one party **5** *Austral* a group of MPs from one party who meet to discuss tactics, etc ▷ *vb* **6** (*intr*) to hold a caucus [c18 prob. of Algonquian origin]

caudal ('kɔ:dᵊl) *adj* **1** *anat* of the posterior part of the body **2** *zool* resembling or in the position of the tail [c17 from NL, from L *cauda* tail] > **'caudally** *adv*

caudal fin *n* the tail fin of fishes and some other aquatic vertebrates, used for propulsion

caudate ('kɔ:deɪt) *or* **caudated** *adj* having a tail or a tail-like appendage [c17 from NL *caudātus*, from L *cauda* tail] > **cau'dation** *n*

caudillo (kɔ:'di:ljəʊ) *n, pl* **caudillos** (-ljəʊz) (in Spanish-speaking countries) a military or political leader [Sp., from LL *capitellum*, dim. of L *caput* head]

caudle ('kɔ:dᵊl) *n* a hot spiced wine drink made with gruel, formerly used medicinally [c13 from OF *caudel*, from Med. L, from L *calidus* warm]

caught (kɔ:t) *vb* the past tense and past participle of **catch**

caul (kɔ:l) *n anat* a portion of the amniotic sac sometimes covering a child's head at birth [c13 from OF *cale*, back formation from *calotte* close-fitting cap, of Gmc origin]

cauldron *or* **caldron** ('kɔ:ldrən) *n* a large pot used for boiling, esp one with handles [c13 from Anglo-F, from L *caldārium* hot bath, from *calidus* warm]

Caulfield ('kɔ:lfi:ld) *n* **Patrick (Joseph)** born 1936, British painter and printmaker

cauliflower ('kɒlɪ,flaʊə) *n* **1** a variety of cabbage having a large edible head of crowded white flowers on a very short thick stem **2** the flower head of this plant, used as a vegetable [c16 from It. *caoli fiori*, lit.: cabbage flowers]

cauliflower ear *n* permanent swelling and distortion of the external ear as the result of ruptures of the blood vessels: usually caused by blows received in boxing

caulk *or* **calk** (kɔ:k) *vb* **1** to stop up (cracks, crevices, etc) with a filler **2** *naut* to pack (the seams) between the planks of the bottom of (a vessel) with waterproof material to prevent leakage [c15 from OF *cauquer* to press down, from L *calcāre* to trample, from *calx* heel]

causal ('kɔ:zᵊl) *adj* **1** acting as or being a cause **2** stating, involving, or implying a cause: *the causal part of the argument* > **'causally** *adv*

causality (kɔ:'zælɪtɪ) *n, pl* **causalities** **1a** the relationship of cause and effect **1b** the principle that nothing can happen without being caused **2** causal agency or quality

causation (kɔ:'zeɪʃən) *n* **1** the production of an effect by a cause **2** the relationship of cause and effect > **cau'sational** *adj*

causative ('kɔ:zətɪv) *adj* **1** *grammar* relating to a form or class of verbs, such as *persuade*, that express causation **2** (*often postpositive* and foll by *of*) producing an effect ▷ *n* **3** the causative form or class of verbs > **'causatively** *adv*

cause (kɔ:z) *n* **1** a person, thing, event, state, or action that produces an effect **2** grounds for action; justification: *she had good cause to shout like that* **3** the ideals, etc, of a group or movement: *the Palestinian cause* **4** the welfare or interests of a person or group in a dispute: *they fought for the miners' cause* **5a** a ground for legal action; matter giving rise to a lawsuit **5b** the lawsuit itself **6** *arch* a subject of debate or discussion **7** **make common cause with** to join with (a person, group, etc) for a common objective ▷ *vb* **causes, causing, caused** **8** (*tr*) to be the cause of; bring about [c13 from L *causa* cause, reason, motive] > **'causeless** *adj*

cause célèbre ('kɔ:z sə'lɛbrə) *n, pl* **causes célèbres** ('kɔ:z sə'lɛbrəz) a famous lawsuit, trial, or controversy [c19 from F: famous case]

causerie ('kəʊzərɪ) *n* an informal talk or conversational piece of writing [c19 from F, from *causer* to chat]

causeway ('kɔ:z,weɪ) *n* **1** a raised path or road crossing water, marshland, sand, etc **2** a paved footpath [c15 *cauciwey* (from *cauci* + WAY); *cauci* paved road, from Med. L, (via) *calciātus*, from L *calx* limestone]

caustic ('kɔːstɪk) *adj* **1** capable of burning or corroding by chemical action: *caustic soda* **2** sarcastic; cutting: *a caustic reply* ▷ *n* **3** Also called: **caustic surface** a surface that envelops the light rays reflected or refracted by a curved surface **4** Also called: **caustic curve** a curve formed by the intersection of a caustic surface with a plane **5** *chem* a caustic substance, esp an alkali [C14 from L, from Gk *kaustikos*, from *kaiein* to burn] > **'caustically** *adv* > **causticity** (kɔː'stɪsɪtɪ) *n*

caustic potash *n* another name for **potassium hydroxide**

caustic soda *n* another name for **sodium hydroxide**

cauterize *or* **cauterise** ('kɔːtəˌraɪz) *vb* **cauterizes, cauterizing, cauterized** *or* **cauterises, cauterising, cauterised** (*tr*) (esp in the treatment of a wound) to burn or sear (body tissue) with a hot iron or caustic agent [C14 from OF, from LL, from *cautērium* branding iron, from Gk *kautērion*, from *kaiein* to burn] > **ˌcauteri'zation** *or* **ˌcauteri'sation** *n*

cautery ('kɔːtərɪ) *n, pl* **cauteries** **1** the coagulation of blood or destruction of body tissue by cauterizing **2** an instrument or agent for cauterizing [C14 from OF *cautère*, from L *cautērium*]

caution ('kɔːʃən) *n* **1** care, forethought, or prudence, esp in the face of danger **2** something intended or serving as a warning **3** *law, chiefly Brit* a formal warning given to a person suspected of an offence that his words will be taken down and may be used in evidence **4** *inf* an amusing or surprising person or thing ▷ *vb* **5** (*tr*) to warn (a person) to be careful **6** (*tr*) *law, chiefly Brit* to give a caution to (a person) **7** (*intr*) to warn, urge, or advise: *he cautioned against optimism* [C13 from OF, from L *cautiō*, from *cavēre* to beware]

cautionary ('kɔːʃənərɪ) *adj* serving as a warning; intended to warn: *a cautionary tale*

cautious ('kɔːʃəs) *adj* showing or having caution > **'cautiously** *adv* > **'cautiousness** *n*

cava ('kɑːvə) *n* a Spanish sparkling wine produced by a method similar to that used for champagne [from Spanish]

Cavafy (kə'vɑːfɪ) *n* **Constantine** Greek name *Kavafis*.1863–1933, Greek poet of Alexandria in Egypt

cavalcade (ˌkævəl'keɪd) *n* **1** a procession of people on horseback, in cars, etc **2** any procession [C16 from F, from It., from *cavalcare* to ride on horseback, from LL, from *caballus* horse]

Cavalcanti (*Italian* kaval'kanti) *n* **Guido** ('gwiːdo) ?1255–1300, Italian poet, noted for his love poems

cavalier (ˌkævə'lɪə) *adj* **1** supercilious; offhand ▷ *n* **2** a courtly gentleman, esp one acting as a lady's escort **3** *arch* a horseman, esp one who is armed [C16 from It., from OProvençal, from LL *caballārius* rider, from *caballus* horse, from ?] > **ˌcava'lierly** *adv*

Cavalier (ˌkævə'lɪə) *n* a supporter of Charles I during the English Civil War

Cavallini (*Italian* kaval'liːni) *n* **Pietro** ('pjɛːtro) ?1250–?1330, Italian fresco painter and mosaicist. His works include the mosaics of the *Life of the Virgin* in Santa Maria, Trastevere, Rome

cavalry ('kævəlrɪ) *n, pl* **cavalries** **1** (esp formerly) the part of an army composed of mounted troops **2** the armoured element of a modern army **3** (*as modifier*): *a cavalry unit* [C16 from F *cavallerie*, from It., from *cavaliere* horseman] > **'cavalryman** *n*

Cavan ('kævᵊn) *n* **1** a county of N Republic of Ireland: hilly, with many small lakes and bogs. County town: Cavan. Pop: 52 944 (1996). Area: 1890 sq km (730 sq miles) **2** a market town in N Republic of Ireland, county town of Co. Cavan. Pop: 4500 (latest est)

cavatina (ˌkævə'tiːnə) *n, pl* **cavatine** (-nɪ) **1** a simple solo song **2** an instrumental composition reminiscent of this [C19 from It.]

cave¹ (keɪv) *n* **1** an underground hollow with access from the ground surface or from the sea **2** *Brit history* a secession or a group seceding from a political party on some issue **3** (*modifier*) living in caves ▷ *vb* **caves, caving, caved** **4** (*tr*) to hollow out [C13 from OF, from L *cava*, pl. of *cavum* cavity, from *cavus* hollow]

cave² ('keɪvɪ) *Brit school sl* ▷ *n* **1** lookout: *keep cave* ▷ *sentence substitute* **2** watch out! [from L *cavē* beware!]

caveat ('keɪvɪˌæt, 'kæv-) *n* **1** *law* a formal notice requesting the court not to take a certain action without warning the person lodging the caveat **2** a caution [C16 from L, lit.: let him beware]

caveat emptor ('ɛmptɔː) *n* the principle that the buyer must bear the risk for the quality of goods purchased [L: let the buyer beware]

cave in *vb* (*intr, adv*) **1** to collapse; subside **2** *inf* to yield completely, esp under pressure ▷ *n* **cave-in** **3** the sudden collapse of a roof, piece of ground, etc **4** the site of such a collapse, as at a mine or tunnel

cavel ('keɪvᵊl) *n* NZ a drawing of lots among miners for an easy and profitable place at the coalface [C19 from E dialect *cavel* to cast lots, apportion]

Cavell ('kævᵊl) *n* **Edith Louisa** 1865–1915, English nurse: executed by the Germans in World War I for helping Allied prisoners to escape

caveman ('keɪvˌmæn) *n, pl* **cavemen** **1** a man of the Palaeolithic age; cave dweller **2** *inf* a man who is primitive or brutal in behaviour, etc

cavendish ('kævəndɪʃ) *n* tobacco that has been sweetened and pressed into moulds to form bars [C19 ?from the name of the first maker]

Cavendish ('kævəndɪʃ) *n* **Henry** 1731–1810, British physicist and chemist: recognized hydrogen, determined the composition of water, and calculated the density of the earth by an experiment named after him

cavern ('kævᵊn) *n* **1** a cave, esp when large ▷ *vb* (*tr*) **2** to shut in or as if in a cavern **3** to hollow out [C14 from OF *caverne*, from L *caverna*, from *cavus* hollow]

cavernous ('kævənəs) *adj* **1** suggestive of a cavern in vastness, etc: *cavernous eyes* **2** filled with small cavities **3** (of rocks) containing caverns

caviar *or* **caviare** ('kævɪˌɑː, ˌkævɪ'ɑː) *n* the salted roe of sturgeon, usually served as an hors d'oeuvre [C16 from earlier *cavery*, from OIt. *caviari*, pl. of *caviaro* caviar, from Turkish *havyār*]

▷ www.foodsubs.com/Caviar.html

▷ whatscookingamerica.net/caviar.htm

cavil ('kævɪl) *vb* **cavils, cavilling, cavilled** *or* *US* **cavils, caviling, caviled** **1** (*intr; foll by at or about*) to raise annoying petty objections ▷ *n* **2** a trifling objection [C16 from OF, from L *cavillārī* to jeer, from *cavilla* raillery] > **'caviller** *n*

caving ('keɪvɪŋ) *n* the sport of climbing in and exploring caves > **'caver** *n*

cavity ('kævɪtɪ) *n, pl* **cavities** **1** a hollow space **2** *dentistry* a decayed area on a tooth **3** any empty or hollow space within the body [C16 from F, from LL *cavitās*, from L *cavus* hollow]

cavity wall *n* a wall that consists of two separate walls with an airspace between them

cavort (kə'vɔːt) *vb* (*intr*) to prance; caper [C19 ?from CURVET] > **ca'vorter** *n*

Cavour (*Italian* ka'vur) *n* Conte **Camillo Benso di** (ka'millo 'bɛnzo di) 1810–61, Italian statesman and premier of Piedmont-Sardinia (1852–59; 1860–61): a leader of the movement for the unification of Italy

cavy ('keɪvɪ) *n, pl* **cavies** a small South American rodent having a thickset body and very small tail. See also **guinea pig** [C18 from NL *Cavia*, from Carib *cabiai*]

caw (kɔː) *n* **1** the cry of a crow, rook, or raven ▷ *vb* **2** (*intr*) to make this cry [C16 imit.]

CAW *abbrev for* Canadian Auto Workers (trade union)

Cc

Cawley (ˈkɔːlɪ) *n* **Evonne** (née *Goolagong*) born 1951, Australian tennis player: Wimbledon champion 1971 and 1980; Australian champion 1974–76

Cawnpore (ˌkɔːnˈpɔː) *or* **Cawnpur** (ˌkɔːnˈpʊə) *n* the former name of **Kanpur**

Caxton (ˈkækstən) *n* **William** ?1422–91, English printer and translator: published, in Bruges, the first book printed in English (1475) and established the first printing press in England (1477)

cay (keɪ, kiː) *n* a small low island or bank composed of sand and coral fragments [c18 from Sp. *cayo*, prob. from OF *quai* QUAY]

Cayenne (keɪˈɛn) *n* the capital of French Guiana, on an island at the mouth of the Cayenne River: French penal settlement from 1854 to 1938. Pop: 50 594 (1999)

cayenne pepper (keɪˈɛn) *n* a very hot red condiment made from the dried seeds of various capsicums. Often shortened to **cayenne.** Also called: **red pepper** [c18 ult. from Tupi *quiynha*]

Cayes (keɪ; *French* kaj) *n* short for **Les Cayes**

Cayley (ˈkeɪlɪ) *n* **1 Arthur** 1821–93, British mathematician, who invented matrices **2** Sir **George** 1773–1857, British engineer and pioneer of aerial navigation. He constructed the first man-carrying glider (1853) and invented the caterpillar tractor

cayman *or* **caiman** (ˈkeɪmən) *n, pl* **caymans** *or* **caimans** a tropical American crocodilian similar to alligators but with a more heavily armoured belly [c16 from Sp. *caimán*, from Carib *cayman*]

Cayman Islands (ˈkeɪmən) *pl n* three coral islands in the Caribbean Sea northwest of Jamaica: a dependency of Jamaica until 1962, now a UK Overseas Territory. Capital: Georgetown. Pop: 38 000 (1998 est). Area: about 260 sq km (100 sq miles)

CB *abbrev for:* **1** Citizens' Band **2** Companion of the (Order of the) Bath (a Brit title) **3** County Borough

CBC *abbrev for* Canadian Broadcasting Corporation ▷ www.cbc.ca

CBE *abbrev for* Commander of the (Order of the) British Empire

CBI *abbrev for:* **1** *US* Central Bureau of Investigation **2** Confederation of British Industry ▷ www.cbi.org.uk

CBT *abbrev for:* **1** computer-based training **2** cognitive behavioural therapy

cc *or* **c.c.** *abbrev for:* **1** carbon copy *or* copies **2** cubic centimetre(s)

CC *abbrev for:* **1** City Council **2** (in Britain) Competition Commission **3** County Council **4** Cricket Club

cc. *abbrev for* chapters

c.c.c. *abbrev for* cwmni cyfyngedig cyhoeddus; a public limited company in Wales

C clef *n music* a symbol (𝄡), placed at the beginning of the staff, establishing the position of middle C: see **alto clef, soprano clef, tenor clef**

CCTA (in Britain) *abbrev for* Central Computer and Telecommunications Agency

CCTV *abbrev for* closed-circuit television

cd *symbol for* candela

Cd *the chemical symbol for* cadmium

CD *abbrev for:* **1** compact disc **2** Civil Defence (Corps) **3** Corps Diplomatique (Diplomatic Corps) **4** Conference on Disarmament: a United Nations standing conference, held in Geneva, to negotiate a global ban on chemical weapons

CDC *abbrev for* **1** (in the US) Center for Disease Control **2** Commonwealth Development Corporation

CDE *abbrev for:* compact disc erasable: a compact disc that can be used to record and rerecord ▷ Cf **CDR**

CDI *abbrev for* compact disc interactive

Cdn *abbrev for* Canadian

cDNA *abbrev for* complementary DNA

CD player *n* a device for playing compact discs

Cdr *mil abbrev for* Commander

CDR *abbrev for* compact disc recordable: a compact disc that can be used to record only once ▷ Cf **CDE**

CD-ROM (ˌsiːdiːˈrɒm) *abbrev for* compact disc read only memory; a compact disc used for storing written information to be displayed on a visual-display unit

CDT *abbrev for:* **1** *US & Canad* Central Daylight Time **2** Craft, Design, and Technology: a subject on the GCSE syllabus, related to the National Curriculum

CDV *abbrev for* compact disc video

CD-video *n* a compact-disc player that, when connected to a television and hi-fi, produces high-quality stereo sound and synchronized pictures from a disc resembling a compact audio disc. In full **compact-disc video**

CD writer *n computing* a device on a computer for writing CDs

Ce *the chemical symbol for* cerium

CE *abbrev for:* **1** Church of England **2** civil engineer **3** Common Era

Ceará (*Portuguese* siaˈra) *n* **1** a state of NE Brazil: sandy coastal plain, rising to a high plateau. Capital: Fortaleza. Pop: 7 417 402 (2000). Area: 150 630 sq km (58 746 sq miles) **2** another name for **Fortaleza**

cease (siːs) *vb* **ceases, ceasing, ceased 1** (when *tr*, may take a gerund or an infinitive as object) to bring or come to an end ▷ *n* **2 without cease** without stopping; incessantly [c14 from OF, from L *cessāre*, frequentative of *cēdere* to yield]

ceasefire (ˈsiːsˌfaɪə) *chiefly mil* ▷ *n* **1** a period of truce, esp one that is temporary ▷ *sentence substitute, n* **2** the order to stop firing

ceaseless (ˈsiːslɪs) *adj* without stop or pause; incessant > ˈ**ceaselessly** *adv*

Ceauşescu (tʃaʊˈʃɛskuː) *n* **Nicolae** (ˌnɪkɒˈlaɪ) 1918–89, Romanian statesman; chairman of the state council (1967–89) and president of Romania (1974–89): deposed and executed

Cebú (sɪˈbuː) *n* **1** an island in the central Philippines. Pop: 2 091 602 (latest est). Area: 4422 sq km (1707 sq miles) **2** a port in the Philippines, on E Cebú island. Pop: 718 821 (2000)

Čechy (ˈtʃɛxi) *n* the Czech name for **Bohemia**

Cecil (ˈsɛsəl, ˈsɪs-) *n* **1** Lord **David** 1902–86, English literary critic and biographer **2 Robert** See (3rd Marquess of) **Salisbury 3 William** See (William Cecil) **Burghley**

Cecilia (sɪˈsiːljə) *n* **Saint** died ?230 AD, Roman martyr; patron saint of music. Feast day: Nov 22

cecum (ˈsiːkəm) *n, pl* **ceca** (-kə) *US*. a variant spelling of **caecum** > ˈ**cecal** *adj*

cedar (ˈsiːdə) *n* **1** any of a genus of Old World coniferous trees having needle-like evergreen leaves, and erect barrel-shaped cones. See also **cedar of Lebanon, deodar 2** any of various other conifers, such as the red cedars and white cedars **3** the wood of any of these trees ▷ *adj* **4** made of the wood of a cedar tree [c13 from OF, from L *cedrus*, from Gk *kedros*]

cedar of Lebanon (ˈlɛbənən) *n* a cedar of SW Asia with level spreading branches and fragrant wood

cede (siːd) *vb* **cedes, ceding, ceded 1** (when *intr*, often foll by *to*) to transfer, make over, or surrender (something, esp territory or legal rights) **2** (*tr*) to allow or concede (a point in an argument, etc) [c17 from L *cēdere* to yield] > ˈ**ceder** *n*

cedilla (sɪˈdɪlə) *n* a character (̧) placed underneath a *c* before *a, o*, or *u*, esp in French, Portuguese, or Catalan, denoting that it is to be pronounced (s), not (k) [c16 from Sp.: little *z*, from *ceda* zed, from LL *zeta*]

Ceefax (ˈsiːfæks) *n trademark* the BBC Teletext service. See **Teletext**

CEGB (in Britain) *abbrev for* (the former) Central Electricity Generating Board

ceil (siːl) *vb* (*tr*) **1** to line (a ceiling) with plaster, etc **2** to provide with a ceiling [C15 *celen*, ? back formation from CEILING]

ceilidh ('keɪlɪ) *n* (esp in Scotland and Ireland) an informal social gathering with singing, dancing, and storytelling [C19 from Gaelic]

ceiling ('si:lɪŋ) *n* **1** the inner upper surface of a room **2** an upper limit, such as one set by regulation on prices or wages **3** the upper altitude to which an aircraft can climb measured under specified conditions **4** *meteorol* the highest level in the atmosphere from which the earth's surface is visible at a particular time, usually the base of a cloud layer [C14 from ?]

Cela (*Spanish* 'θela) *n* **Camilo José** (ka'milo xo'se) 1916–2002, Spanish novelist and essayist. His works include *The Family of Pascual Duarte* (1942), *La Colmena* (1951), and *La Cruz de San Andres* (1994). Nobel prize for literature 1989

celadon ('sɛlə,dɒn) *n* **1** a type of porcelain having a greyish-green glaze: mainly Chinese **2a** a pale greyish-green colour **2b** (*as adj*): *a celadon jar* [C18 from F, from the name of the shepherd hero of *L'Astrée* (1610), a romance by Honoré d'Urfé]

Celan ('sɛlæn) *n* **Paul**, real name *Paul Antschel*. 1920–70, Romanian Jewish poet, writing in German, whose work reflects the experience of Nazi persecution

celandine ('sɛlən,daɪn) *n* either of two unrelated plants, **greater celandine** or **lesser celandine**, with yellow flowers [C13 earlier *celydon*, from L, from Gk *khelidōn* swallow; the plant's season was believed to parallel the migration of swallows]

-cele *n combining form* tumour or hernia: *hydrocele* [from Gk *kēlē* tumour]

celeb (sɪ'lɛb) *n inf* a celebrity

Celebes ('sɛlɪbi:z, sɛ'li:bɪz) *n* the English name for **Sulawesi**

Celebes Sea *n* the part of the Pacific Ocean between Sulawesi, Borneo, and Mindanao

celebrant ('sɛlɪbrənt) *n* a person participating in a religious ceremony, esp at the Eucharist

celebrate ('sɛlɪ,breɪt) *vb* **celebrates, celebrating, celebrated** **1** to rejoice in or have special festivities to mark (a happy day, event, etc) **2** (*tr*) to observe (a birthday, anniversary, etc) **3** (*tr*) to perform (a solemn or religious ceremony), esp to officiate at (Mass) **4** (*tr*) to praise publicly; proclaim [C15 from L, from *celeber* numerous, renowned] > ,**cele'bration** *n* > '**cele,brator** *n* > '**cele,bratory** *adj*

celebrated ('sɛlɪ,breɪtɪd) *adj* (*usually prenominal*) famous: *a celebrated pianist*

celebrity (sɪ'lɛbrɪtɪ) *n, pl* **celebrities** **1** a famous person **2** fame or notoriety

celeriac (sɪ'lɛrɪ,æk) *n* a variety of celery with a large turnip-like root, used as a vegetable [C18 from CELERY + *-ac*, from ?]

celerity (sɪ'lɛrɪtɪ) *n* rapidity; swiftness; speed [C15 from OF *celerite*, from L *celeritās*, from *celer* swift]

celery ('sɛlərɪ) *n* **1** an umbelliferous Eurasian plant whose blanched leafstalks are used in salads or cooked as a vegetable **2** **wild celery** a related and similar plant [C17 from F *céleri*, from It. (Lombardy) dialect *selleri* (pl), from Gk *selinon* parsley]

celesta (sɪ'lɛstə) *or* **celeste** (sɪ'lɛst) *n music* a keyboard percussion instrument consisting of a set of steel plates of graduated length that are struck with key-operated hammers [C19 from F, Latinized var. of *céleste* heavenly]

celestial (sɪ'lɛstɪəl) *adj* **1** heavenly; divine: *celestial peace* **2** of or relating to the sky: *celestial bodies* **3** of or connected with the celestial sphere: *celestial pole* [C14 from Med. L, from L *caelestis*, from *caelum* heaven] > **ce'lestially** *adv*

Celestial Empire *n* an archaic or literary name for the **Chinese Empire**

celestial equator *n* the great circle lying on the celestial sphere the plane of which is perpendicular to the line joining the north and south celestial poles. Also called: **equinoctial, equinoctial circle**

celestial mechanics *n* the study of the motion of celestial bodies under the influence of gravitational fields

celestial sphere *n* an imaginary sphere of infinitely large radius enclosing the universe so that all celestial bodies appear to be projected onto its surface

celiac ('si:lɪ,æk) *adj anat* the usual US spelling of **coeliac**

celibate ('sɛlɪbɪt) *n* **1** a person who is unmarried, esp one who has taken a religious vow of chastity ▷ *adj* **2** abstaining from sexual intercourse **3** unmarried [C17 from L, from *caelebs* unmarried, from ?] > '**celibacy** *n*

Céline (seɪ'li:n) *n* **Louis-Ferdinand** (lwifɛrdinɑ̃), real name *Louis-Ferdinand Destouches*. 1894–1961, French novelist and physician; became famous with his controversial first novel *Journey to the End of the Night* (1932)

cell (sɛl) *n* **1** a small simple room, as in a prison, convent, etc **2** any small compartment: *the cells of a honeycomb* **3** *biol* the basic structural and functional unit of living organisms. It consists of a nucleus, containing the genetic material, surrounded by the cytoplasm **4** *biol* any small cavity, such as the cavity containing pollen in an anther **5** a device for converting chemical energy into electrical energy, usually consisting of a container with two electrodes immersed in an electrolyte. See also **dry cell, fuel cell** **6** In full: **electrolytic cell** a device in which electrolysis occurs **7** a small religious house dependent upon a larger one **8** a small group of persons operating as a nucleus of a larger organization: *Communist cell* **9** the geographical area served by an individual transmitter in a cellular-radio network [C12 from Med. L *cella* monk's cell, from L: room, storeroom]

cellar ('sɛlə) *n* **1** an underground room, or storey of a building, usually used for storage **2** a place where wine is stored **3** a stock of bottled wines ▷ *vb* **4** (*tr*) to store in a cellar [C13 from Anglo-F, from L *cellārium* foodstore, from *cella* cell]

Cc

cellarage ('sɛlərɪdʒ) *n* **1** an area of a cellar **2** a charge for storing goods in a cellar, etc

cellar dwellers *pl n Austral sl* the team at the bottom of a sports league

cellarer ('sɛlərə) *n* a monastic official responsible for food, drink, etc

cellaret (,sɛlə'rɛt) *n* a cabinet or sideboard with compartments for holding wine bottles

Cellini (tʃɪ'li:nɪ; *Italian* tʃɛl'li:ni) *n* **Benvenuto** (benve'nu:to) 1500–71, Italian sculptor, goldsmith, and engraver, noted also for his autobiography

cell line *n biol* a clone of animal or plant cells that can be grown in a suitable nutrient culture medium in the laboratory

Cellnet ('sɛl,nɛt) *n trademark* a British Telecom mobile phone

cello ('tʃɛləʊ) *n, pl* **cellos** *music* a bowed stringed instrument of the violin family. It has four strings, is held between the knees, and has a metal spike at the lower end, which acts as a support. Full name: **violoncello** > '**cellist** *n*

Cellophane ('sɛlə,feɪn) *n trademark* a flexible thin transparent sheeting made from wood pulp and used as a moisture-proof wrapping [C20 from CELLULOSE + -PHANE]

cellphone ('sɛl,fəʊn) *n* a portable telephone operated by cellular radio. In full: **cellular telephone**

cellular ('sɛljʊlə) *adj* **1** of, relating to, or composed of a cell or cells **2** having cells or small cavities; porous **3** divided into a network of cells **4** *textiles* woven with an open texture: *a cellular blanket* **5** designed for or involving cellular radio

cellular radio *n* radio communication based on a network of transmitters each serving a small area known as a cell: used esp in car phones in which the receiver switches frequencies automatically as it passes from one cell to another

cellule ('sɛlju:l) *n* a very small cell [c17 from L *cellula*, dim. of *cella* CELL]

cellulite ('sɛljʊˌlaɪt) *n* subcutaneous fat alleged to resist dieting

cellulitis (ˌsɛljʊ'laɪtɪs) *n* inflammation of body tissue, with fever, pain, and swelling [c19 from L *cellula* CELLULE + -ITIS]

celluloid ('sɛljʊˌlɔɪd) *n* **1** a flammable material consisting of cellulose nitrate and camphor: used in sheets, rods, etc **2a** a cellulose derivative used for coating film **2b** cinema film

cellulose ('sɛljʊˌləʊz, -ˌləʊs) *n* a substance which is the main constituent of plant cell walls and used in making paper, rayon, and film [c18 from F *cellule* cell (see CELLULE) + -OSE[2]]

cellulose acetate *n* nonflammable material used in the manufacture of film, dopes, lacquers, and artificial fibres

cellulose nitrate *n* cellulose treated with nitric and sulphuric acids, used in plastics, lacquers, and explosives. See also **guncotton**

Celsius ('sɛlsɪəs) *adj* denoting a measurement on the Celsius scale. Symbol: C [c18 after Anders *Celsius* (1701–44), Swedish astronomer who invented it]

Celsius scale *n* a scale of temperature in which 0° represents the melting point of ice and 100° represents the boiling point of water. See also **centigrade** ▷ Cf **Fahrenheit scale**

celt (sɛlt) *n archaeol* a stone or metal axelike instrument [c18 from LL *celtes* chisel, from ?]

Celt (kɛlt, sɛlt) *or* **Kelt** *n* **1** a person who speaks a Celtic language **2** a member of an Indo-European people who in pre-Roman times inhabited Britain, Gaul, and Spain
▷ www.ibiblio.org/gaelic/celts.html
▷ http://celt.net/Celtic/celtopedia/indices/encyintro.html

Celtic ('kɛltɪk, 'sɛl-) *or* **Keltic** *n* **1** a branch of the Indo-European family of languages that includes Gaelic, Welsh, and Breton. Modern Celtic is divided into the Brythonic (southern) and Goidelic (northern) groups ▷ *adj* **2** of, relating to, or characteristic of the Celts or the Celtic languages > **Celticism** ('kɛltɪˌsɪzəm, 'sɛl-) *or* '**Keltiˌcism** *n*

Celtic cross *n* a Latin cross with a broad ring surrounding the point of intersection

Celtic Sea *n* the relatively shallow part of the Atlantic Ocean lying between S Ireland, SW Wales, Cornwall, and W Brittany

cembalo ('tʃɛmbələʊ) *n, pl* **cembali** (-lɪ) *or* **cembalos** another word for **harpsichord** [c19 from It. *clavicembalo* from Med. L *clāvis* key + *cymbalum* CYMBAL]

cement (sɪ'mɛnt) *n* **1** a fine grey powder made of a mixture of limestone and clay, used with water and sand to make mortar, or with water, sand, and aggregate, to make concrete **2** a binder, glue, or adhesive **3** something that unites or joins **4** *dentistry* any of various materials used in filling teeth **5** another word for **cementum** ▷ *vb (tr)* **6** to join, bind, or glue together with or as if with cement **7** to coat or cover with cement [c13 from OF, from L *caementum* stone from the quarry, from *caedere* to hew]

cementum (sɪ'mɛntəm) *n* a thin bonelike tissue that covers the dentine in the root of a tooth [c19 NL, from L: CEMENT]

cemetery ('sɛmɪtrɪ) *n, pl* **cemeteries** a place where the dead are buried, esp one not attached to a church [c14 from LL, from Gk *koimētērion*, from *koiman* to put to sleep]

-cene *n and adj combining form* denoting a recent geological period [from Gk *kainos* new]

Cenis (*French* səni) *n* **Mont** a pass over the Graian Alps in SE France, between Lanslebourg (France) and Susa (Italy): nearby tunnel, opened in 1871. Highest point: 2082 m (6831 ft). Italian name: **Monte Cenisio** ('monte tʃe'ni:zjo)

cenobite ('si:nəʊˌbaɪt) *n* a variant spelling of **coenobite**

cenotaph ('sɛnəˌtɑ:f) *n* a monument honouring a dead person or persons buried elsewhere [c17 from L, from Gk, from *kenos* empty + *taphos* tomb]

Cenotaph ('sɛnəˌtɑ:f) *n* **the** the monument in Whitehall, London, honouring the dead of both World Wars: designed by Sir Edwin Lutyens: erected in 1920

Cenozoic, Caenozoic (ˌsi:nəʊ'zəʊɪk), *or* **Cainozoic** *adj* **1** of, denoting, or relating to the most recent geological era, which began 65 million years ago: characterized by the development and increase of the mammals ▷ *n* **2** **the** the Cenozoic era [c19 from Gk *kainos* recent + *zōikos*, from *zōion* animal]

censer ('sɛnsə) *n* a container for burning incense. Also called: **thurible**

censor ('sɛnsə) *n* **1** a person authorized to examine publications, films, letters, etc, in order to suppress in whole or part those considered obscene, politically unacceptable, etc **2** any person who controls or suppresses the behaviour of others, usually on moral grounds **3** (in republican Rome) either of two senior magistrates elected to keep the list of citizens up to date, and supervise public morals **4** *psychoanal* the postulated factor responsible for regulating the translation of ideas and desires from the unconscious to the conscious mind ▷ *vb (tr)* **5** to ban or cut portions of (a film, letter, etc) **6** to act as a censor of (behaviour, etc) [c16 from L, from *cēnsēre* to consider] > **censorial** (sɛn'sɔ:rɪəl) *adj*

censorious (sɛn'sɔ:rɪəs) *adj* harshly critical; fault-finding > **cen'soriously** *adv*

censorship ('sɛnsəʃɪp) *n* **1** a policy or programme of censoring **2** the act or system of censoring

censure ('sɛnʃə) *n* **1** severe disapproval ▷ *vb* **censures, censuring, censured** **2** to criticize (someone or something) severely [c14 from L *censūra*, from *cēnsērē*: see CENSOR] > '**censurable** *adj*

census ('sɛnsəs) *n, pl* **censuses** **1** an official periodic count of a population including such information as sex, age, occupation, etc **2** any official count: *a traffic census* **3** (in ancient Rome) a registration of the population and a property evaluation for taxation [c17 from L, from *cēnsēre* to assess]
▷ www.census.gov/ipc/www/idbnew.html

cent (sɛnt) *n* a monetary unit of American Samoa, Andorra, Antigua and Barbuda, Aruba, Australia, Austria, the Bahamas, Barbados, Belgium, Belize, Bermuda, Bosnia and Herzegovina, Brunei, Canada, the Cayman Islands, Cyprus, Dominica, East Timor, Ecuador, El Salvador, Ethiopia, Fiji, Finland, France, French Guiana, Germany, Greece, Grenada, Guadeloupe, Guam, Guyana, Hong Kong, Ireland, Jamaica, Kenya, Kiribati, Kosovo, Liberia, Luxembourg, Malaysia, Malta, the Marshall Islands, Martinique, Mauritius, Mayotte, Micronesia, Monaco, Montenegro, Namibia, Nauru, the Netherlands, the Netherlands Antilles, New Zealand, the Northern Mariana Islands, Palau, Portugal, Puerto Rico, Réunion, Saint Kitts and Nevis, Saint Lucia, Saint Vincent and the Grenadines, San Marino, the Seychelles, Sierra Leone, Singapore, the Solomon Islands, Somalia, South Africa, Spain, Sri Lanka, Surinam, Swaziland, Taiwan, Tanzania, Trinidad and Tobago, Tuvalu, Uganda, the United States, the Vatican City, the Virgin Islands, and Zimbabwe. It is worth one hundredth of their respective standard units [c16 from L *centēsimus* hundredth, from *centum* hundred]

centaur ('sɛntɔ:) *n Greek myth* one of a race of creatures with the head, arms, and torso of a man, and the lower body and legs of a horse [c14 from L, from Gk *kentauros*]

centaurea (sɛntɔːˈrɪə, sɛnˈtɔːrɪə) *n* any plant of the genus *Centaurea* which includes the cornflower and knapweed [c19 ult. from Gk *Kentauros* the Centaur; see CENTAURY]

centaury (ˈsɛntɔːrɪ) *n, pl* **centauries** any of a genus of Eurasian plants having purplish-pink flowers and formerly believed to have medicinal properties [c14 ult. from Gk *Kentauros* the Centaur; from the legend that Chiron the Centaur divulged its healing properties]

centavo (sɛnˈtɑːvəʊ) *n, pl* **centavos** 1 a monetary unit of Argentina, Bolivia, Brazil, Cape Verde, Chile, Colombia, Cuba, the Dominican Republic, Guatemala, Guinea-Bissau, Honduras, Mexico, Mozambique, Nicaragua, and the Philippines. It is worth one hundredth of their respective standard units 2 a former monetary unit of Ecuador, El Salvador, and Portugal, worth one hundredth of their former standard units [Sp.: one hundredth part]

centenarian (ˌsɛntɪˈnɛərɪən) *n* 1 a person who is at least 100 years old ▷ *adj* 2 being at least 100 years old 3 of or relating to a centenarian

centenary (sɛnˈtiːnərɪ) *adj* 1 of or relating to a period of 100 years 2 occurring once every 100 years ▷ *n, pl* **centenaries** 3 a 100th anniversary or its celebration [c17 from L, from *centēnī* a hundred each, from *centum* hundred]

centennial (sɛnˈtɛnɪəl) *adj* 1 relating to or completing a period of 100 years 2 occurring every 100 years ▷ *n* 3 *US & Canad* another name for **centenary** [c18 from L *centum* hundred, on the model of BIENNIAL]

center (ˈsɛntə) *n, vb* the US spelling of **centre**

centesimal (sɛnˈtɛsɪməl) *n* 1 hundredth ▷ *adj* 2 relating to division into hundredths [c17 from L, from *centum* hundred] > **cenˈtesimally** *adv*

centesimo (sɛnˈtɛsɪˌməʊ) *n* a former monetary unit of Italy, San Marino, and the Vatican City worth one hundredth of a lira [c19 from It., from L *centēsimus* hundredth, from *centum* hundred]

centésimo (sɛnˈtɛsɪˌməʊ) *n, pl* **centésimos** *or* **centésimi** a monetary unit of Panama and Uruguay. It is worth one hundredth of their respective standard units [c19 from Sp. & It., from L, from *centum* hundred]

centi- *or before a vowel* **cent-** *prefix* 1 denoting one hundredth: *centimetre; centilitre* Symbol: c 2 *rare* denoting a hundred: *centipede* [from F, from L *centum* hundred]

centiare (ˈsɛntɪˌɛə) *or* **centare** (ˈsɛntɛə) *n* a unit of area equal to one square metre [F, from CENTI- + *are* from L *ārea*]

centigrade (ˈsɛntɪˌgreɪd) *adj* 1 a former name for **Celsius** ▷ *n* 2 a unit of angle equal to one hundredth of a grade

centigram *or* **centigramme** (ˈsɛntɪˌgræm) *n* one hundredth of a gram

centilitre *or US* **centiliter** (ˈsɛntɪˌliːtə) *n* one hundredth of a litre

centime (ˈsɒnˌtiːm; *French* sɑ̃tim) *n* 1 a monetary unit of Algeria, Benin, Burkina-Faso, Burundi, Cameroon, the Central African Republic, Chad, Comoros, Democratic Republic of Congo, Congo-Brazzaville, Côte d'Ivoire, Djibouti, Equatorial Guinea, French Polynesia, Gabon, Guinea, Guinea-Bissau, Haiti, Liechtenstein, Madagascar, Mali, Mayotte, Morocco, New Caledonia, Niger, Rwanda, Senegal, Switzerland, and Togo. It is worth one hundredth of their respective standard units 2 a former monetary unit of Andorra, Belgium, France, French Guiana, Guadeloupe, Luxembourg, Martinique, Monaco, and Réunion, worth one hundredth of a franc [c18 from F, from OF, from L, from *centum* hundred]

centimetre *or US* **centimeter** (ˈsɛntɪˌmiːtə) *n* one hundredth of a metre

centimetre-gram-second *n* See **cgs units**

céntimo (ˈsɛntɪˌməʊ) *n, pl* **céntimos** 1 a monetary unit of Costa Rica, Paraguay, Peru, and Venezuela. It is worth one hundredth of their respective standard currency units 2 a former monetary unit of Andorra and Spain, worth one hundredth of a peseta [from Sp.; see CENTIME]

cêntimo (ˈsɛntɪˌməʊ) *n* a monetary unit of São Tomé e Principe, worth one hundredth of a dobra

centipede (ˈsɛntɪˌpiːd) *n* a carnivorous arthropod having a body of between 15 and 190 segments, each bearing one pair of legs

cento (ˈsɛntəʊ) *n, pl* **centos** a piece of writing, esp a poem, composed of quotations from other authors [c17 from L, lit.: patchwork garment]

CENTO (ˈsɛntəʊ) *n acronym for* Central Treaty Organization; an organization for military and economic cooperation formed in 1959 by the UK, Iran, Pakistan, and Turkey: disbanded 1979

central (ˈsɛntrəl) *adj* 1 in, at, of, from, containing, or forming the centre of something: *the central street in a city* 2 main, principal, or chief: *the central cause of a problem* > **centrality** (sɛnˈtrælɪtɪ) *n* > **ˈcentrally** *adv*

Central African Federation *n* another name for the **Federation of Rhodesia and Nyasaland**

Central African Republic *n* a landlocked country of central Africa: joined with Chad as a territory of French Equatorial Africa in 1910; became an independent republic in 1960; a parliamentary monarchy (1976–79); consists of a huge plateau, mostly savanna, with dense forests in the south; drained chiefly by the Shari and Ubangi Rivers. Official language: French; Sango is the national language. Religion: Christian and animist. Currency: franc. Capital: Bangui. Pop: 3 577 000 (2001 est). Area: 622 577 sq km (240 376 sq miles). Former names: **Ubangi-Shari** (until 1958), **Central African Empire** (1976–79) French name: **République Centrafricaine** (repyblik sɑ̃trafrikɛn)
▷ http://segegob.cl

Central America *n* an isthmus joining the continents of North and South America, extending from the S border of Mexico to the NW border of Colombia and consisting of Belize, Guatemala, Honduras, El Salvador, Nicaragua, Costa Rica, and Panama. Area: about 518 000 sq km (200 000 sq miles)

Central American *adj* 1 of or relating to Central America or its inhabitants ▷ *n* 2 a native or inhabitant of Central America

central bank *n* a national bank that does business mainly with a government and with other banks: it regulates the volume of credit
▷ www.bankofengland.co.uk
▷ www.rba.gov.au
▷ www.rbnz.govt.nz
▷ www.resbank.co.za
▷ www.bankofcanada.ca/en/

central heating *n* a system for heating the rooms of a building by means of radiators or air vents connected to a central source of heat

Central India Agency *n* a former group of 89 states in India, under the supervision of a British political agent until 1947: most important were Indore, Bhopal, and Rewa

centralism (ˈsɛntrəˌlɪzəm) *n* the principle or act of bringing something under central control > **ˈcentralist** *n, adj*

centralize *or* **centralise** (ˈsɛntrəˌlaɪz) *vb* **centralizes, centralizing, centralized** *or* **centralises, centralising, centralised** 1 to draw or move (something) to or towards a centre 2 to bring or come under central, esp governmental, control > **ˌcentraliˈzation** *or* **ˌcentraliˈsation** *n*

Central Karoo (kəˈruː) *n* an arid plateau of S central South Africa, in Cape Province, separated from the Little Karoo to the southwest by the Swartberg range. Average height: 750 m (2500 ft.)

central limit theorem *n statistics* the fundamental

Cc

result that the sum of independent identically distributed random variables with finite variance approaches a normally distributed random variable as their number increases

central locking *n* a system by which all the doors of a motor vehicle can be locked simultaneously

central nervous system *n* the mass of nerve tissue that controls and coordinates the activities of an animal. In vertebrates it consists of the brain and spinal cord

central processing unit *n* the part of a computer that performs logical and arithmetical operations on the data. Abbrev: **CPU**

Central Provinces *pl n* **the** the Canadian provinces of Ontario and Quebec

Central Region *n* a former local government region in central Scotland, formed in 1975 from Clackmannanshire, most of Stirlingshire, and parts of Perthshire, West Lothian, Fife, and Kinross-shire; in 1996 it was replaced by the council areas of Stirling, Clackmannanshire, and Falkirk

central reserve *or* **reservation** *n Brit & Austral* the strip, often covered with grass, that separates the two sides of a motorway or dual carriageway

central tendency *n statistics* the tendency of the values of a random variable to cluster around the mean, median, and mode

centre *or US* **center** ('sɛntə) *n* **1** *geom* **1a** the midpoint of any line or figure, esp the point within a circle or sphere that is equidistant from any point on the circumference or surface **1b** the point within a body through which a specified force may be considered to act, such as the centre of gravity **2** the point, axis, or pivot about which a body rotates **3** a point, area, or part that is approximately in the middle of a larger area or volume **4** a place at which some specified activity is concentrated: *a shopping centre* **5** a person or thing that is a focus of interest **6** a place of activity or influence: *a centre of power* **7** a person, group, or thing in the middle **8** (*usually cap*) *politics* a political party or group favouring moderation **9** a bar with a conical point upon which a workpiece or part may be turned or ground **10** *football, hockey, etc* **10a** a player who plays in the middle of the forward line **10b** an instance of passing the ball from a wing to the middle of the field, etc ▷ *vb* **centres, centring, centred** *or US* **centers, centering, centered** **11** to move towards, mark, put, or be at a centre **12** (*tr*) to focus or bring together: *to centre one's thoughts* **13** (*intr*; often foll by *on*) to have as a main theme: *the novel centred on crime* **14** (*intr*; foll by *on* or *round*) to have as a centre **15** (*tr*) *football, hockey, etc* to pass (the ball) into the middle of the field or court [C14 from L *centrum* the stationary point of a compass, from Gk *kentron* needle, from *kentein* to prick]

Centre *n* **1** ('sɛntə) **the** the sparsely inhabited central region of Australia **2** (*French* sɑ̃trə) a region of central France: generally low-lying; drained chiefly by the Rivers Loire, Loir, and Cher

centre bit *n* a drilling bit with a central point and two side cutters

centreboard ('sɛntəˌbɔːd) *n* a supplementary keel for a sailing vessel

centrefold *or US* **centerfold** ('sɛntəˌfəʊld) *n* **1** a large coloured illustration folded so that it forms the central spread of a magazine **2a** a photograph of a nude or nearly nude woman (or man) in a magazine on such a spread **2b** the subject of such a photograph

centre forward *n soccer, hockey, etc* the central forward in the attack

centre half *or* **centre back** *n soccer* a defender who plays in the middle of the defence

centre of gravity *n* the point through which the resultant of the gravitational forces on a body always acts

centre pass *n hockey* a push or hit made in any direction to start the game or restart the game after a goal has been scored

centrepiece ('sɛntəˌpiːs) *n* an object used as the centre of something, esp for decoration

centre spread *n* **1** the pair of two facing pages in the middle of a magazine, newspaper, etc **2a** a photograph of a nude or nearly nude woman (or man) in a magazine on such pages **2b** the subject of such a photograph

centri- *combining form* a variant of **centro-**

centric ('sɛntrɪk) *or* **centrical** *adj* **1** being central or having a centre **2** relating to a nerve centre > **centricity** (sɛn'trɪsɪtɪ) *n*

-centric *suffix forming adjectives* having a centre as specified: *heliocentric* [abstracted from ECCENTRIC, CONCENTRIC, etc]

centrifugal (sɛn'trɪfjʊgᵊl, 'sɛntrɪˌfjuːgᵊl) *adj* **1** acting, moving, or tending to move away from a centre. Cf **centripetal** **2** of, concerned with, or operated by centrifugal force: *centrifugal pump* [C18 from NL, from CENTRI- + L *fugere* to flee] > **cen'trifugally** *adv*

centrifugal force *n* a fictitious force that can be thought of as acting outwards on any body that rotates or moves along a curved path

centrifuge ('sɛntrɪˌfjuːdʒ) *n* **1** any of various rotating machines that separate liquids from solids or other liquids by the action of centrifugal force **2** any of various rotating devices for subjecting human beings or animals to varying accelerations ▷ *vb* **centrifuges, centrifuging, centrifuged** **3** (*tr*) to subject to the action of a centrifuge > **centrifugation** (ˌsɛntrɪfjʊ'geɪʃən) *n*

centring ('sɛntrɪŋ) *or US* **centering** ('sɛntərɪŋ) *n* a temporary structure, esp one made of timber, used to support an arch during construction

centripetal (sɛn'trɪpɪtᵊl, 'sɛntrɪˌpiːtᵊl) *adj* **1** acting, moving, or tending to move towards a centre. Cf **centrifugal** **2** of, concerned with, or operated by centripetal force [C17 from NL *centripetus* seeking the centre] > **cen'tripetally** *adv*

centripetal force *n* a force that acts inwards on any body that rotates or moves along a curved path

centrist ('sɛntrɪst) *n* a person holding moderate political views > **'centrism** *n*

centro-, centri-, *or before a vowel* **centr-** *combining form* denoting a centre: *centrosome; centrist* [from Gk *kentron* CENTRE]

centuplicate *vb* (sɛn'tjuːplɪˌkeɪt), **centuplicates, centuplicating, centuplicated** **1** (*tr*) to increase 100 times ▷ *adj* (sɛn'tjuːplɪkɪt) **2** increased a hundredfold ▷ *n* (sɛn'tjuːplɪkɪt) **3** one hundredfold. Also **centuple** ('sɛntjʊpᵊl) [C17 from LL, from *centuplex* hundredfold, from L *centum* hundred + *-plex* -fold]

centurion (sɛn'tjʊərɪən) *n* the officer commanding a Roman century [C14 from L *centuriō*, from *centuria* CENTURY]

century ('sɛntʃərɪ) *n, pl* **centuries** **1** a period of 100 years **2** one of the successive periods of 100 years dated before or after an epoch or event, esp the birth of Christ **3** a score or grouping of 100: *to score a century in cricket* **4** (in ancient Rome) a unit of foot soldiers, originally consisting of 100 men **5** (in ancient Rome) a division of the people for purposes of voting [C16 from L *centuria*, from *centum* hundred]

cep (sɛp) *n* an edible woodland fungus with a brown shining cap and a rich nutty flavour [C19 from F, from Gascon dialect *cep*, from L *cippus* stake]

cephalic (sɪ'fælɪk) *adj* **1** of or relating to the head **2** situated in, on, or near the head

-cephalic *or* **-cephalous** *adj combining form* indicating skull or head; -headed: *brachycephalic* [from Gk *-kephalos*] > **-cephaly** *or* **-cephalism** *n combining form*

cephalic index *n* the ratio of the greatest width of the human head to its greatest length, multiplied by 100.

cephalic version *n* another name for **version** (sense 5)
cephalo- *or before a vowel* **cephal-** *combining form* indicating the head: *cephalopod* [via L from Gk, from *kephalē* head]
Cephalonia (ˌsɛfəˈləʊnɪə) *n* a mountainous island in the Ionian Sea, the largest of the Ionian Islands, off the W coast of Greece. Pop: 32 474 (1991). Area: 935 sq km (365 sq miles). Modern Greek name: **Kephallinía**
cephalopod (ˈsɛfələˌpɒd) *n* any of various marine molluscs, characterized by well-developed head and eyes and a ring of sucker-bearing tentacles, including the octopuses, squids, and cuttlefish > ˌ**cephaˈlopodan** *adj, n*
cephalothorax (ˌsɛfələʊˈθɔːræks) *n, pl* **cephalothoraxes** *or* **cephalothoraces** (-rəˌsiːz) the anterior part of many crustaceans and some other arthropods consisting of a united head and thorax
-cephalus *n combining form* denoting a cephalic abnormality: *hydrocephalus* [NL *-cephalus;* see -CEPHALIC]
Cepheid variable (ˈsiːfɪɪd) *n astron* any of a class of variable stars with regular cycles of variations in luminosity, which are used for measuring distances
Cepheus (ˈsiːfjuːs) *n Greek myth* a king of Ethiopia, father of Andromeda and husband of Cassiopeia
Ceram (sɪˈræm) *n* a variant spelling of **Seram**
ceramic (sɪˈræmɪk) *n* **1** a hard brittle material made by firing clay and similar substances **2** an object made from such a material ▷ *adj* **3** of or made from a ceramic **4** of or relating to ceramics: *ceramic arts* [c19 from Gk, from *keramos* potter's clay]
ceramic hob *n* (on an electric cooker) a flat ceramic cooking surface having heating elements fitted on the underside
ceramic oxide *n* a compound of oxygen with nonorganic material: recently discovered to act as a high-temperature superconductor
ceramics (sɪˈræmɪks) *n (functioning as sing)* the art and techniques of producing articles of clay, porcelain, etc > **ceramist** (ˈsɛrəmɪst) *n*

▷ www.acers.org
▷ www.ceramicsmonthly.org
▷ www.ceramicstoday.com

ceramide (ˈsɛrəˌmaɪd) *n* any of a class of biologically important compounds used as moisturizers in skin-care preparations
Cerberus (ˈsɜːbərəs) *n* **1** *Greek myth* a dog, usually represented as having three heads, that guarded the entrance to Hades **2** **a sop to Cerberus** a bribe or something given to propitiate a potential source of danger or problems > **Cerberean** (səˈbɪərɪən) *adj*
cere (sɪə) *n* a soft waxy swelling, containing the nostrils, at the base of the upper beak, as in the parrot [c15 from OF *cire* wax, from L *cēra*]
cereal (ˈsɪərɪəl) *n* **1** any grass that produces an edible grain, such as oat, wheat, rice, maize, and millet **2** the grain produced by such a plant **3** any food made from this grain, esp breakfast food **4** *(modifier)* of or relating to any of these plants or their products [c19 from L *cereālis* concerning agriculture]
cerebellum (ˌsɛrɪˈbɛləm) *n, pl* **cerebellums** *or* **cerebella** (-lə) one of the major divisions of the vertebrate brain whose function is coordination of voluntary movements [c16 from L, dim. of CEREBRUM] > ˌ**cereˈbellar** *adj*
cerebral (ˈsɛrɪbrəl; *US also* səˈriːbrəl) *adj* **1** of or relating to the cerebrum or to the entire brain **2** involving intelligence rather than emotions or instinct **3** *phonetics* another word for **cacuminal** > ˈ**cerebrally** *adv*
cerebral haemorrhage *n* bleeding from an artery in the brain, which in severe cases causes a stroke
cerebral palsy *n* a nonprogressive impairment of muscular function and weakness of the limbs, caused by lack of oxygen to the brain immediately after birth, brain injury during birth, or viral infection
cerebrate (ˈsɛrɪˌbreɪt) *vb* **cerebrates, cerebrating, cerebrated** *(intr) usually facetious* to use the mind; think; ponder; consider > ˌ**cereˈbration** *n*
cerebro- *or before a vowel* **cerebr-** *combining form* indicating the brain: *cerebrospinal* [from CEREBRUM]
cerebrospinal (ˌsɛrɪbrəʊˈspaɪnᵊl) *adj* of or relating to the brain and spinal cord: *cerebrospinal fluid*
cerebrovascular (ˌsɛrɪbrəʊˈvæskjʊlə) *adj* of or relating to the blood vessels and the blood supply of the brain
cerebrum (ˈsɛrɪbrəm) *n, pl* **cerebrums** *or* **cerebra** (-brə) **1** the anterior portion of the brain of vertebrates, consisting of two lateral hemispheres: the dominant part of the brain in man, associated with intellectual function, emotion, and personality **2** the brain considered as a whole [c17 from L: the brain] > ˈ**cerebric** *adj*
cerecloth (ˈsɪəˌklɒθ) *n* waxed waterproof cloth of a kind formerly used as a shroud [c15 from earlier *cered cloth,* from L *cērāre* to wax]
Ceredigion (ˌkɛrəˈdɪgjᵊn) *n* a county of W Wales, on Cardigan Bay: created in 1996 from part of Dyfed; corresponds to the former Cardiganshire (abolished 1974): mainly agricultural, with the Cambrian Mountains in the E and N. Administrative centre: Aberaeron. Pop: 75 384 (2001). Area: 1793 sq km (692 sq miles)
cerement (ˈsɪəmənt) *n* **1** cerecloth **2** any burial clothes [c17 from F, from *cirer* to wax]
ceremonial (ˌsɛrɪˈməʊnɪəl) *adj* **1** involving or relating to ceremony or ritual ▷ *n* **2** the observance of formality, esp in etiquette **3** a plan for formal observances; ritual **4** *Christianity* **4a** the prescribed order of rites and ceremonies **4b** a book containing this > ˌ**cereˈmonialism** *n* > ˌ**cereˈmonialist** *n* > ˌ**cereˈmonially** *adv*
ceremonious (ˌsɛrɪˈməʊnɪəs) *adj* **1** especially or excessively polite or formal **2** involving formalities > ˌ**cereˈmoniously** *adv*
ceremony (ˈsɛrɪmənɪ) *n, pl* **ceremonies** **1** a formal act or ritual, often set by custom or tradition, performed in observation of an event or anniversary **2** a religious rite or series of rites **3** a courteous gesture or act: *the ceremony of toasting the Queen* **4** ceremonial observances or gestures collectively **5** **stand on ceremony** to insist on or act with excessive formality [c14 from Med. L, from L *caerimōnia* what is sacred]
Cerenkov (*Russian* tʃɪˈrjɛnkəf) *n* See (Pavel Alekseyevich) **Cherenkov**
Ceres (ˈsɪəriːz) *n* the Roman goddess of agriculture. Greek counterpart: **Demeter**
cerise (səˈriːz, -ˈriːs) *n, adj* (of) a moderate to dark red colour [c19 from F: CHERRY]
cerium (ˈsɪərɪəm) *n* a malleable ductile steel-grey element of the lanthanide series of metals, used in lighter flints. Symbol: Ce; atomic no.: 58; atomic wt.: 140.12 [c19 NL, from *Ceres* (the asteroid) + -IUM]
CERN (sɜːn) *n acronym for* Conseil Européen pour la Recherche Nucléaire; an organization of European states with a centre in Geneva, for research in high-energy particle physics, now called the European Laboratory for Particle Physics

▷ http://public.web.cern.ch/public

Cernăuţi (tʃernəˈutsj) *n* the Romanian name for **Chernovtsy**
Cernuda (*Spanish* θɛrˈnuða) *n* **Luis** (lwiʃ) 1902–63, Spanish poet. His major work is the autobiographical *Reality and Desire* (1936–64)
Ceroc (səˈrɒk) *n trademark* a form of dance combining elements of jive and salsa
cerography (sɪəˈrɒgrəfɪ) *n* the art of engraving on a waxed plate on which a printing surface is created by electrotyping

Cc

ceroplastic (ˌsɪərəʊˈplæstɪk) *adj* **1** relating to wax modelling **2** modelled in wax

Cerro de Pasco (*Spanish* ˈθɛrrɔ ðe ˈpasko) *n* a town in central Peru, in the Andes: one of the highest towns in the world, 4400 m (14 436 ft) above sea level; mining centre. Pop: 62 749 (1993)

cert (sɜːt) *n inf* something that is a certainty, esp a horse that is certain to win a race

certain (ˈsɜːtᵊn) *adj* **1** (*postpositive*) positive and confident about the truth of something; convinced: *I am certain that he wrote a book* **2** (*usually postpositive*) definitely known: *it is certain that they were on the bus* **3** (*usually postpositive*) sure; bound: *he was certain to fail* **4** fixed: *the date is already certain for the invasion* **5** reliable: *his judgment is certain* **6** moderate or minimum: *to a certain extent* **7** **for certain** without a doubt ▷ *determiner* **8a** known but not specified or named: *certain people* **8b** (*as pron; functioning as pl*): *certain of the members have not paid* **9** named but not known: *he had written to a certain Mrs Smith* [c13 from OF, from L *certus* sure, from *cernere* to decide]

certainly (ˈsɜːtᵊnlɪ) *adv* **1** without doubt: *he certainly rides very well* ▷ *sentence substitute* **2** by all means; definitely

certainty (ˈsɜːtᵊntɪ) *n, pl* **certainties** **1** the condition of being certain **2** something established as inevitable **3** **for a certainty** without doubt

CertEd (in Britain) *abbrev for* Certificate in Education

certes (ˈsɜːtɪz) *adv arch* with certainty; truly [c13 from OF, ult. from L *certus* CERTAIN]

certificate *n* (səˈtɪfɪkɪt) **1** an official document attesting the truth of the facts stated, as of birth, death, completion of an academic course, ownership of shares, etc ▷ *vb* (səˈtɪfɪˌkeɪt), **certificates, certificating, certificated** **2** (*tr*) to authorize by or present with an official document [c15 from OF, from *certifier* to CERTIFY] > **cerˈtificatory** *adj*

Certificate of Secondary Education *n* the full name for **CSE**

certification (ˌsɜːtɪfɪˈkeɪʃən) *n* **1** the act of certifying or state of being certified **2** *law* a document attesting the truth of a fact or statement

certified (ˈsɜːtɪˌfaɪd) *adj* **1** holding or guaranteed by a certificate **2** endorsed or guaranteed: *a certified cheque* **3** (of a person) declared legally insane

certified accountant *n* (in Britain) a member of the Chartered Association of Certified Accountants, who is authorized to audit company accounts ▷ Cf **chartered accountant**

certify (ˈsɜːtɪˌfaɪ) *vb* **certifies, certifying, certified** **1** to confirm or attest (to), usually in writing **2** (*tr*) to endorse or guarantee that certain required standards have been met **3** to give reliable information or assurances: *he certified that it was Walter's handwriting* **4** (*tr*) to declare legally insane [c14 from OF, from Med. L, from L *certus* CERTAIN + *facere* to make] > **ˈcertiˌfiable** *adj*

certiorari (ˌsɜːtɪɔːˈrɛəraɪ) *n law* an order of a superior court directing that a record of proceedings in a lower court be sent up for review [c15 from legal L: to be informed]

certitude (ˈsɜːtɪˌtjuːd) *n* confidence; certainty [c15 from Church L *certitūdō*, from L *certus* CERTAIN]

cerulean (sɪˈruːlɪən) *n, adj* (of) a deep blue colour [c17 from L *caeruleus*, prob. from *caelum* sky]

cerumen (sɪˈruːmɛn) *n* the soft brownish-yellow wax secreted by glands in the external ear. Nontechnical name: **earwax** [c18 from NL, from L *cēra* wax + ALBUMEN] > **ceˈruminous** *adj*

Cervantes (səˈvæntiːz; *Spanish* θɛrˈβantes) *n* **Miguel de** (miˈɣɛl ðe), full surname *Cervantes Saavedra*. 1547–1616, Spanish dramatist, poet, and prose writer, most famous for *Don Quixote* (1605), which satirizes the chivalric romances and greatly influenced the development of the novel

cervelat (ˈsɜːvəˌlæt, -ˌlɑː) *n* a smoked sausage made from pork and beef [c17 via obs. F from It. *cervellata*]

cervena (ˌsɜːˈvɛnə) *n trademark NZ* farm-produced venison

cervical (səˈvaɪkᵊl, ˈsɜːvɪkᵊl) *adj* of or relating to the neck or cervix [c17 from NL, from L *cervīx* neck]

cervical smear *n med* a smear taken from the neck (cervix) of the uterus for detection of cancer. See also **Pap test** *or* **smear**

Cervin (sɛrvɛ̃) *n* **Mont** the French name for the **Matterhorn**

cervine (ˈsɜːvaɪn) *adj* resembling or relating to a deer [c19 from L *cervīnus*, from *cervus* a deer]

cervix (ˈsɜːvɪks) *n, pl* **cervixes** *or* **cervices** (səˈvaɪsiːz) **1** the technical name for **neck** **2** any necklike part, esp the lower part of the uterus that extends into the vagina [c18 from L]

cesium (ˈsiːzɪəm) *n* the usual US spelling of **caesium**

Československo (ˈtʃɛskɔslɔvɛnskɔ) *n* the Czech name for **Czechoslovakia**

cess[1] (sɛs) *n Brit* any of several special taxes, such as a land tax in Scotland [c16 short for ASSESSMENT]

cess[2] (sɛs) *n* an Irish slang word for **luck** (esp in **bad cess to you!**) [c19 prob. from CESS[1]]

cessation (sɛˈseɪʃən) *n* a ceasing or stopping; pause: *temporary cessation of hostilities* [c14 from L, from *cessāre* to be idle, from *cēdere* to yield]

cession (ˈsɛʃən) *n* **1** the act of ceding **2** something that is ceded, esp land or territory [c14 from L *cessiō*, from *cēdere* to yield]

cessionary (ˈsɛʃənərɪ) *n, pl* **cessionaries** *law* a person to whom something is transferred

cesspool (ˈsɛsˌpuːl) *or* **cesspit** (ˈsɛsˌpɪt) *n* **1** Also called: **sink, sump** a covered cistern, etc, for collecting and storing sewage or waste water **2** a filthy or corrupt place: *a cesspool of iniquity* [c17 ? changed from earlier *cesperalle*, from OF *souspirail* vent, air, from *soupirer* to sigh]

cestoid (ˈsɛstɔɪd) *adj* (esp of tapeworms and similar animals) ribbon-like in form

cesura (sɪˈzjʊərə) *n, pl* **cesuras** *or* **cesurae** (-riː) *prosody* a variant spelling of **caesura**

cetacean (sɪˈteɪʃən) *adj* **1** *also* **cetaceous** of or belonging to an order of aquatic placental mammals having no hind limbs and a blowhole for breathing: includes toothed whales (dolphins, porpoises, etc) and whalebone whales (rorquals, etc) ▷ *n* **2** a whale [c19 from NL, ult. from L *cētus* whale, from Gk *kētos*]

cetane (ˈsiːteɪn) *n* a colourless insoluble liquid hydrocarbon used in the determination of the cetane number of diesel fuel. Also called: **hexadecane** [c19 from L *cētus* whale + -ANE]

cetane number *n* a measure of the quality of a diesel fuel expressed as the percentage of cetane. Also called: **cetane rating** ▷ Cf **octane number**

Cetatea Albă (tʃeˈtatea ˈalbə) *n* the Romanian name for **Byelgorod-Dnestrovski**

Cetinje (*Serbo-Croat* ˈtsɛtinjɛ) *n* a city in Serbia and Montenegro, in SW Montenegro: former capital of Montenegro (until 1945); palace and fortified monastery, residences of Montenegrin prince-bishops. Pop: 15 924 (1991)

cetrimide (ˈsɛtrɪˌmaɪd) *n* an ammonium compound used as a detergent and, having powerful antiseptic properties, for sterilizing surgical instruments, cleaning wounds, etc

Cetshwayo *or* **Cetewayo** (*Zulu* kɛˈtʃwɑːjɒ) *n* ?1826–84, king of the Zulus (1873–79): defeated the British at Isandhlwana (1879) but was overwhelmed by them at Ulundi (1879); captured, he stated his case in London, and was reinstated as ruler of part of Zululand (1883)

Ceuta (*Spanish* ˈθeuta) *n* an enclave in Morocco on the Strait of Gibraltar, consisting of a port and military station: held by Spain since 1580. Pop: 75 241 (2000 est)

Cévennes (*French* sevɛn) *n* a mountain range in S central

France, on the SE edge of the Massif Central. Highest peak: 1754 m (5755 ft)

Ceylon (sɪˈlɒn) *n* **1** the former name (until 1972) of **Sri Lanka** **2** an island in the Indian Ocean, off the SE coast of India: consists politically of the republic of Sri Lanka. Area: 64 644 sq km (24 959 sq miles)

Ceylonese (ˌsɛləˈniːz, ˌsiːlə-) *adj* of or relating to Ceylon or its inhabitants

Cézanne (*French* sezan) *n* **Paul** (pɔl) 1839–1906, French postimpressionist painter, who was a major influence on modern art, esp cubism, in stressing the structural elements latent in nature, such as the sphere and the cone

Cf *the chemical symbol for* californium

CF *abbrev for* Canadian Forces

cf. *abbrev for:* **1** (in bookbinding, etc) calfskin **2** compare [L: *confer*]

CFB *abbrev for* Canadian Forces Base

CFC *abbrev for* chlorofluorocarbon

CFL *abbrev for* Canadian Football League

CFS *abbrev for* chronic fatigue syndrome

cg *abbrev for* centigram

CGBR *abbrev for* Central Government Borrowing Requirement

cgs units *pl n* a metric system of units based on the centimetre, gram, and second. For scientific and technical purposes these units have been replaced by SI units

CGT *abbrev for* Capital Gains Tax

CH **1** *abbrev. for* Companion of Honour (a Brit title) **2** *international car registration for* Switzerland [from F *Confédération Helvétique*]

ch. *abbrev for:* **1** chain (unit of measure) **2** chapter **3** *chess* check **4** chief **5** church

Chablis (ˈʃæblɪ) *n* (*sometimes not cap*) a dry white wine made around Chablis, France

Chabrier (ˈʃæbrɪeɪ; *French* ʃabrie) *n* (**Alexis**) **Emmanuel** (emanɥɛl) 1841–94, French composer; noted esp for the orchestral rhapsody *España* (1883)

Chabrol (*French* ʃabrɔl) *n* **Claude** (klod) born 1930, French film director, whose films, such as *Le Beau Serge* (1958), *Les Biches* (1968), *Le Boucher* (1969), and *La Fleur du mal* (2003) explore themes of jealousy, guilt, and murder

cha-cha-cha (ˌtʃɑːtʃɑːˈtʃɑː) *or* **cha-cha** *n* **1** a modern ballroom dance from Latin America with small steps and swaying hip movements **2** a piece of music composed for this dance ▷ *vb* (*intr*) **3** to perform this dance [c20 from American (Cuban) Sp.]

Chaco (*Spanish* ˈtʃako) *n* See **Gran Chaco**

chaconne (ʃəˈkɒn) *n* **1** a musical form consisting of a set of continuous variations upon a ground bass **2** *arch* a dance in slow triple time probably originating in Spain [c17 from F, from Sp. *chacona*]

Chad (tʃæd) *n* **1** a republic in N central Africa: made a territory of French Equatorial Africa in 1910; became independent in 1960; contains much desert and the Tibesti Mountains, with Lake Chad in the west; produces chiefly cotton and livestock; has suffered intermittent civil war from 1963 and prolonged drought. Official languages: Arabic; French. Religion: Muslim majority, also Christian and animist. Currency: franc. Capital: Ndjamena. Pop: 8 707 000 (2001 est). Area: 1 284 000 sq km (495 750 sq miles). French name: **Tchad** **2** **Lake** a lake in N central Africa: fed chiefly by the Shari River, it has no apparent outlet. Area: 10 000 to 26 000 sq km (4000 to 10 000 sq miles), varying seasonally

chadri (ˈtʃædriː) *n* a shroudlike garment which covers the body from heat to foot, usually worn by females in Islamic countries

Chadwick (ˈtʃædwɪk) *n* **1** Sir **Edwin** 1800–90, British social reformer, known for his *Report on the Sanitary Condition of the Labouring Population of Great Britain* (1842) **2** Sir **James** 1891–1974, British physicist: discovered the neutron (1932): Nobel prize for physics 1935 **3** **Lynn** (**Russell**) born 1914, British sculptor in metal

chafe (tʃeɪf) *vb* **chafes, chafing, chafed** **1** to make or become sore or worn by rubbing **2** (*tr*) to warm (the hands, etc) by rubbing **3** to irritate or be irritated or impatient **4** (*intr; often foll by on, against, etc*) to rub ▷ *n* **5** a soreness or irritation caused by friction [c14 from OF *chaufer* to warm, ult. from L, from *calēre* to be warm + *facere* to make]

chafer (ˈtʃeɪfə) *n* any of various beetles, such as the cockchafer [OE *ceafor*]

chaff[1] (tʃɑːf) *n* **1** the mass of husks, etc, separated from the seeds during threshing **2** finely cut straw and hay used to feed cattle **3** something of little worth; rubbish: *to separate the wheat from the chaff* **4** thin strips of metallic foil released into the earth's atmosphere to deflect radar signals and prevent detection [OE *ceaf*] > ˈ**chaffy** *adj*

chaff[2] (tʃɑːf) *n* **1** light-hearted teasing or joking; banter ▷ *vb* **2** to tease good-naturedly [c19 prob. slang var. of CHAFE] > ˈ**chaffer** *n*

chaffer (ˈtʃæfə) *vb* **1** (*intr*) to haggle or bargain **2** to chatter, talk, or say idly ▷ *n* **3** haggling or bargaining [c13 *chaffare*, from *chep* bargain + *fare* journey] > ˈ**chafferer** *n*

chaffinch (ˈtʃæfɪntʃ) *n* a European finch with black-and-white wings and, in the male, a reddish body and blue-grey head [OE *ceaffinc*, from *ceaf* CHAFF[1] + *finc* FINCH]

chafing dish *n* a vessel with a heating apparatus beneath it, for cooking or keeping food warm at the table

Chagall (*French* ʃagal) *n* **Marc** (mark) 1887–1985, French painter and illustrator, born in Russia, noted for his richly coloured pictures of men, animals, and objects in fantastic combinations and often suspended in space: his work includes 12 stained glass windows for a synagogue in Jerusalem (1961) and the decorations for the ceiling of the Paris Opera House (1964)

Cc

chagrin (ˈʃægrɪn) *n* **1** a feeling of annoyance or mortification ▷ *vb* **2** to embarrass and annoy [c17 from F *chagrin, chagriner*, from ?]

chain (tʃeɪn) *n* **1** a flexible length of metal links, used for confining, connecting, etc, or in jewellery **2** (*usually pl*) anything that confines or restrains: *the chains of poverty* **3** (*usually pl*) a set of metal links that fit over the tyre of a motor vehicle to reduce skidding on an icy surface **4** a series of related or connected facts, events, etc **5a** a number of establishments such as hotels, shops, etc, having the same owner or management **5b** (*as modifier*): *a chain store* **6** a series of deals in which each depends on a purchaser selling before being able to buy **7** Also called: **Gunter's chain** a unit of length equal to 22 yards **8** Also called: **engineer's chain** a unit of length equal to 100 feet **9** Also called: **nautical chain** a unit of length equal to 15 feet **10** *chem* two or more atoms or groups bonded together so that the resulting molecule, ion, or radical resembles a chain **11** *geog* a series of natural features, esp mountain ranges **12** **jerk** *or* **yank** (someone's) **chain** *inf* to tease, mislead, or harass (someone) ▷ *vb* (*tr; often foll by up*) to confine, tie, or make fast with or as if with a chain [c13 from OF, ult. from L; see CATENA]

Chain (tʃeɪn) *n* Sir **Ernst Boris** 1906–79, British biochemist, born in Germany: purified and adapted penicillin for clinical use; with Fleming and Florey shared the Nobel prize for physiology or medicine 1945

chain gang *n* *US* a group of convicted prisoners chained together

chain letter *n* a letter, often with a request for and promise of money, that is sent to many people who add to or recopy it and send it on

chain mail *n* **a** another term for **mail**[2] (sense 1) **b** (*as*

modifier): *a chain-mail hood; a chain-mail tunic*
chain printer *n* a line printer in which the type is on a continuous chain
chain reaction *n* **1** a process in which a neutron colliding with an atomic nucleus causes fission and the ejection of one or more other neutrons **2** a chemical reaction in which the product of one step is a reactant in the following step **3** a series of events, each of which precipitates the next > ,**chain-re'act** *vb* (*intr*)
chain saw *n* a motor-driven saw in which the cutting teeth form links in a continuous chain
chain-smoke *vb* **chain-smokes, chain-smoking, chain-smoked** to smoke (cigarettes, etc) continually, esp lighting one from the preceding one > **chain smoker** *n*
chain stitch *n* **1** a looped embroidery stitch resembling the links of a chain ▷ *vb* **chain-stitch 2** to sew (something) with this stitch
chainwheel ('tʃeɪn,wiːl) *n* (esp on a bicycle) a toothed wheel that transmits drive via the chain
chair (tʃɛə) *n* **1** a seat with a back on which one person sits, typically having four legs and often having arms **2** an official position of authority **3** the chairman of a debate or meeting: *the speaker addressed the chair* **4** a professorship **5** *railways* an iron or steel cradle bolted to a sleeper in which the rail is locked **6** short for **sedan chair 7 take the chair** to preside as chairman for a meeting, etc **8 the chair** *inf* the electric chair ▷ *vb* (*tr*) **9** to preside over (a meeting) **10** *Brit* to carry aloft in a sitting position after a triumph **11** to provide with a chair of office **12** to install in a chair [C13 from OF, from L *cathedra*, from Gk *kathedra*, from *kata-* down + *hedra* seat]
chairlift ('tʃɛə,lɪft) *n* a series of chairs suspended from a power-driven cable for conveying people, esp skiers, up a mountain
chairman ('tʃɛəmən) *n, pl* **chairmen** a person who presides over a company's board of directors, a committee, a debate, etc. Also: **chair, chairperson,** *or* (*fem*) **chairwoman**

> USAGE The general trend of nonsexist language is to find a term which can apply to both sexes equally, as in the use of *actor* to refer to both men and women. Since *chairman* can seem inappropriate when applied to a woman, while *chairwoman* specifies gender, the terms *chair* and *chairperson* are generally preferred

chaise (ʃeɪz) *n* **1** a light open horse-drawn carriage, esp one with two wheels **2** short for **post chaise** and **chaise longue** [C18 from F, var. of OF *chaiere* CHAIR]
chaise longue ('ʃeɪz 'lɒŋ) *n, pl* **chaise longues** *or* **chaises longues** ('ʃeɪz 'lɒŋ) a long low chair with a back and single armrest [C19 from F: long chair]
Chaka ('ʃaka) *n* a variant spelling of **Shaka**
chakalaka (ˌʃaka'laka) *n S African* a relish made from tomatoes, onions, and spices [from ?]
chakra ('tʃækrə, 'tʃʌkrə) *n* (in yoga) any of the seven major energy centres in the human body [C19 from Sansk. *cakra* wheel, circle]
chalaza (kə'leɪzə) *n, pl* **chalazas** *or* **chalazae** (-ziː) one of a pair of spiral threads holding the yolk of a bird's egg in position [C18 NL, from Gk: hailstone]
chalcedony (kæl'sɛdənɪ) *n, pl* **chalcedonies** a form of quartz with crystals arranged in parallel fibres: a gemstone [C15 from LL, from Gk *khalkēdōn* a precious stone, ? after *Khalkēdōn* Chalcedon, town in Asia Minor] > **chalcedonic** (ˌkælsɪ'dɒnɪk) *adj*
Chalcidice (kæl'sɪdɪsɪ) *n* a peninsula of N central Greece, in Macedonia Central, ending in the three promontories of Kassandra, Sithonia, and Akti. Area: 2945 sq km (1149 sq miles). Modern Greek name: **Khalkidíki**
Chalcis ('kælsɪs) *n* a city in SE Greece, at the narrowest point of the Euripus strait: important since the 7th century BC, founding many colonies in ancient times. Pop: 47 600 (1995 est). Modern Greek name: **Khalkís.** Medieval English name: **Negropont**
chalcogen ('kælkəˌdʒɛn) *n* any of the elements oxygen, sulphur, selenium, tellurium, or polonium, of group 6A of the periodic table [C20 from CHALCO(PYRITE) + -GEN]
chalcolithic (ˌkælkə'lɪθɪk) *adj archaeol* of or relating to the period in which both stone and bronze tools were used [C19 from Gk *khalkos* copper + *lithos* stone]
chalcopyrite (ˌkælkə'paɪraɪt) *n* a common ore of copper, a crystalline sulphide of copper and iron. Formula: $CuFeS_2$. Also called: **copper pyrites**
Chaldea *or* **Chaldaea** (kæl'diːə) *n* **1** an ancient region of Babylonia; the land lying between the Euphrates delta, the Persian Gulf, and the Arabian desert **2** another name for **Babylonia**
chaldron ('tʃɔːldrən) *n* a unit of capacity equal to 36 bushels [C17 from OF *chauderon* CAULDRON]
chalet ('ʃæleɪ) *n* **1** a type of wooden house of Swiss origin, with wide projecting eaves **2** a similar house used as a ski lodge, etc [C19 from F (Swiss dialect)]
Chaliapin (*Russian* ʃa'ljapin) *n* **Fyodor Ivanovich** ('fjɔdər i'vanəvitʃ) 1873–1938, Russian operatic bass singer
chalice ('tʃælɪs) *n* **1** *poetic* a drinking cup; goblet **2** *Christianity* a gold or silver cup containing the wine at Mass **3** the calyx of a flower, esp a a cup-shaped calyx [C13 from OF, from L *calix* cup]
chalk (tʃɔːk) *n* **1** a soft fine-grained white sedimentary rock consisting of nearly pure calcium carbonate, containing minute fossil fragments of marine organisms **2** a piece of chalk, or substance like chalk, often coloured, used for writing and drawing on blackboards **3 as alike** (*or* **different**) **as chalk and cheese** *inf* totally different in essentials **4 by a long chalk** *Brit inf* by far **5 not by a long chalk** *Brit inf* by no means **6** (*modifier*) made of chalk ▷ *vb* **7** to draw or mark (something) with chalk **8** (*tr*) to mark, rub, or whiten with or as with chalk [OE *cealc*, from L *calx* limestone, from Gk *khalix* pebble] > **'chalk,like** *adj* > **'chalky** *adj* > **'chalkiness** *n*
chalk out *vb* (*tr, adv*) to outline (a plan, scheme, etc); sketch
chalkpit ('tʃɔːk,pɪt) *n* a quarry for chalk
chalk up *vb* (*tr, adv*) *Inf* **1** to score or register (something) **2** to credit (money) to an account, etc (esp in **chalk it up**)
challenge ('tʃælɪndʒ) *vb* **challenges, challenging, challenged** (*mainly tr*) **1** to invite or summon (someone to do something, esp to take part in a contest) **2** (*also intr*) to call (something) into question **3** to make demands on; stimulate: *the job challenges his ingenuity* **4** to order (a person) to halt and be identified **5** *law* to make formal objection to (a juror or jury) **6** to lay claim to (attention, etc) **7** to inject (an experimental animal immunized with a test substance) with disease microorganisms to test for immunity to the disease ▷ *n* **8** a call to engage in a fight, argument, or contest **9** a questioning of a statement or fact **10** a demanding or stimulating situation, career, etc **11** a demand by a sentry, etc, for identification or a password **12** *law* a formal objection to a person selected to serve on a jury or to the whole body of jurors [C13 from OF *chalenge*, from L *calumnia* CALUMNY] > **'challengeable** *adj* > **'challenger** *n* > **'challenging** *adj*
challenged ('tʃælɪndʒd) *adj* disabled in a manner specified: *physically challenged; mentally challenged*
challis ('ʃælɪ, -lɪs) *or* **challie** ('ʃælɪ) *n* a lightweight fabric of wool, cotton, etc, usually with a printed design [C19 prob. from a surname]
Châlons-sur-Marne (*French* ʃalɔ̃syrmarn) *n* a city in NE France, on the River Marne: scene of Attila's defeat by the Romans (451 AD). Pop: 51 530 (1990). Shortened form: **Châlons**
Chalon-sur-Saône (*French* ʃalɔ̃syrson) *n* an industrial city in E central France, on the Saône River. Pop: 54 575

(1990). Shortened form: **Chalon**

chalybeate (kəˈlɪbɪɪt) *adj* containing or impregnated with iron salts [c17 from NL *chalybēātus*, ult. from Gk *khalups* iron]

chamber (ˈtʃeɪmbə) *n* **1** a meeting hall, esp one used for a legislative or judicial assembly **2** a reception room in an official residence, palace, etc **3** *arch or poetic* a room in a private house, esp a bedroom **4a** a legislative, judicial, or administrative assembly **4b** any of the houses of a legislature **5** an enclosed space; compartment; cavity **6** an enclosure for a cartridge in the cylinder of a revolver or for a shell in the breech of a cannon **7** short for **chamber pot** **8** (*modifier*) of, relating to, or suitable for chamber music: *a chamber concert* **9** (*modifier*) on a small, quasi-domestic scale ▷ See also **chambers** [c13 from OF, from LL *camera* room, L: vault, from Gk *kamara*]

chamberlain (ˈtʃeɪmbəlɪn) *n* **1** an officer who manages the household of a king **2** the steward of a nobleman or landowner **3** the treasurer of a municipal corporation [c13 from OF *chamberlayn*, of Frankish origin]

Chamberlain (ˈtʃeɪmbəlɪn) *n* **1** Sir (**Joseph**) **Austen** 1863–1937, British Conservative statesman; foreign secretary (1924–29); awarded a Nobel peace prize for his negotiation of the Locarno Pact (1925) **2** his father, **Joseph** 1836–1914, British statesman; originally a Liberal, he resigned in 1886 over Home Rule for Ireland and became leader of the Liberal Unionists; a leading advocate of preferential trading agreements with members of the British Empire **3** his son, (**Arthur**) **Neville** 1869–1940, British Conservative statesman; prime minister (1937–40): pursued a policy of appeasement towards Germany; following the German invasion of Poland, he declared war on Germany on Sept. 3, 1939 **4** **Owen** born 1920, US physicist, who discovered the antiproton. Nobel prize for physics jointly with Emilio Segré 1959

chambermaid (ˈtʃeɪmbəˌmeɪd) *n* a woman employed to clean bedrooms, esp in hotels

chamber music *n* music for performance by a small group of instrumentalists

chamber of commerce *n* (*sometimes cap*) an organization composed mainly of local businessmen to promote, regulate, and protect their interests
▷ www.iccwbo.org
▷ www.chamberonline.co.uk
▷ www.acci.asn.au
▷ www.cec-cce.ca
▷ www.bsa.org.za
▷ www.businessnz.org.nz

chamber orchestra *n* a small orchestra of about 25 players, used for the authentic performance of baroque and early classical music as well as modern music

chamber pot *n* a vessel for urine, used in bedrooms

chambers (ˈtʃeɪmbəz) *pl n* **1** a judge's room for hearing private cases not taken in open court **2** (in England) the set of rooms occupied by barristers where clients are interviewed

Chambéry (*French* ʃɑ̃beri) *n* a city in SE France, in the Alps: skiing centre; former capital of the duchy of Savoy. Pop: 54 120 (1990)

chambray (ˈʃæmbreɪ) *n* a smooth light fabric of cotton, linen, etc, with white weft and a coloured warp. [c19 after CAMBRAI]

chameleon (kəˈmiːlɪən) *n* **1** a lizard of Africa and Madagascar, having long slender legs, a prehensile tail and tongue, and the ability to change colour **2** a changeable or fickle person [c14 from L, from Gk *khamaileōn*, from *khamai* on the ground + *leōn* LION]
> **chameleonic** (kəˌmiːlɪˈɒnɪk) *adj*

chamfer (ˈtʃæmfə) *n* **1** a narrow flat surface at the corner of a beam, post, etc, esp one at an angle of 45° ▷ *vb* (*tr*) **2** to cut such a surface on (a beam, etc) [c16 back formation from *chamfering*, from OF, from *chant* edge (see CANT²) + *fraindre* to break, from L *frangere*]

chamois (ˈʃæmɪ; *for senses 1 and 4* ˈʃæmwɑː) *n, pl* **chamois** **1** a sure-footed goat antelope of Europe and SW Asia, having vertical horns with backward-pointing tips **2** a soft suede leather formerly made from this animal, now obtained from the skins of sheep and goats **3** Also called: **chamois leather, shammy** (**leather**), **chammy** (**leather**) a piece of such leather or similar material used for polishing, etc **4a** a greyish-yellow colour **4b** (*as adj*): *a chamois stamp* ▷ *vb* (*tr*) **5** to dress (leather or skin) like chamois **6** to polish with a chamois [c16 from OF, from LL *camox*, from ?]

chamomile (ˈkæməˌmaɪl) *n* a variant spelling of **camomile**

Chamonix (ˈʃæmənɪ; *French* ʃamɔni) *n* a town in SE France, in the Alps at the foot of Mont Blanc: skiing and tourist centre. Pop: 9255 (latest est)

champ¹ (tʃæmp) *vb* **1** to munch (food) noisily like a horse **2** (when *intr*, often foll by *on, at*, etc) to bite (something) nervously or impatiently **3** **champ** (*or* **chafe**) **at the bit** *inf* to be impatient to start work, a journey, etc ▷ *n* **4** the act or noise of champing [c16 prob. imit.]

champ² (tʃæmp) *n inf* short for **champion**

champagne (ʃæmˈpeɪn) *n* **1** (*sometimes cap*) a white sparkling wine produced around Reims and Épernay, France **2** (loosely) any effervescent white wine **3a** a pale tawny colour **3b** (*as adj*): *champagne tights* **4** (*modifier*) denoting a luxurious lifestyle: *a champagne capitalist* [from *Champagne*, a region of NE France]
▷ www.champagne.com

Champagne-Ardenne (ʃæmˈpeɪnɑːˈdɛn; *French* ʃɑ̃paɲardɛn) *n* a region of NE France: a countship and commercial centre in medieval times; it consists of a great plain, with sheep and dairy farms and many vineyards

champagne socialist *n* a professed socialist who enjoys an extravagant lifestyle

Champaigne (ʃæmˈpeɪn; *French* ʃɑ̃pɛɲ) *n* **Philippe de** (filip də) 1602–74, French painter, born in Brussels: noted particularly for his portraits and historical and religious scenes

champers (ˈʃæmpəz) *n* (*functioning as sing*) *sl* champagne

champerty (ˈtʃæmpətɪ) *n, pl* **champerties** *law* (formerly) an illegal bargain between a party to litigation and an outsider whereby the latter agrees to pay for the action and thereby share in any proceeds recovered [c14 from Anglo-F *champartie*, from OF *champart* share of produce, from *champ* field + *part* share]

Champigny-sur-Marne (*French* ʃɑ̃piɲisyrmarn) *n* a suburb of Paris, on the River Marne. Pop: 80 290 (latest est)

champion (ˈtʃæmpɪən) *n* **1a** a person, plant, or animal that has defeated all others in a competition: *a chess champion* **1b** (*as modifier*): *a champion team; a champion marrow* **2** a person who defends a person or cause: *champion of the underprivileged* **3** (formerly) a knight who did battle for another, esp a king or queen ▷ *adj* **4** *N English dialect* excellent ▷ *adv* **5** *N English dialect* very well ▷ *vb* (*tr*) **6** to support: *we champion the cause of liberty* [c13 from OF, from LL *campiō*, from L *campus* field]

championship (ˈtʃæmpɪənˌʃɪp) *n* **1** (*sometimes pl*) any of various contests held to determine a champion **2** the title of being a champion **3** support for a cause, person, etc

Champlain¹ (ʃæmˈpleɪn) *n* **Lake** a lake in the northeastern US, between the Green Mountains and the Adirondack Mountains: linked by the **Champlain Canal** to the Hudson River and by the Richelieu River to the St Lawrence; a major communications route in colonial times

Champlain² (ʃæmˈpleɪn; *French* ʃɑ̃plɛ̃) *n* **Samuel de** (samyɛl də) ?1567–1635, French explorer; founder of

Cc

Quebec (1608) and governor of New France (1633–35)
champlevé *French* (ʃɑ̃lve) *adj* **1** of a process of enamelling by which grooves are cut into a metal base and filled with enamel colours ▷ *n* **2** an object enamelled by this process [c19 from *champ* field (level surface) + *levé* raised]
Champollion (*French* ʃɑ̃pɔljɔ̃) *n* **Jean François** (ʒɑ̃ frɑ̃swa) 1790–1832, French Egyptologist, who deciphered the hieroglyphics on the Rosetta stone
Champs Elysées (ʃɒnz eɪ'liːzeɪ; *French* ʃɑ̃z elize) *n* a major boulevard in Paris, leading from the Arc de Triomphe: site of the Elysées Palace and government offices
chance (tʃɑːns) *n* **1a** the unknown and unpredictable element that causes an event to result in a certain way rather than another, spoken of as a real force **1b** (*as modifier*): *a chance meeting*. Related adj: **fortuitous** **2** fortune; luck; fate **3** an opportunity or occasion **4** a risk; gamble **5** the extent to which an event is likely to occur; probability **6** an unpredicted event, esp a fortunate one **7** **by chance** accidentally: *he slipped by chance* **8** **on the** (**off**) **chance** acting on the (remote) possibility ▷ *vb* **chances, chancing, chanced** **9** (*tr*) to risk; hazard **10** (*intr*) to happen by chance: *I chanced to catch sight of her* **11** **chance on** (*or* **upon**) to come upon by accident **12** **chance one's arm** to attempt to do something although the chance of success may be slight [c13 from OF, from *cheoir* to occur, from L *cadere*] > **'chanceful** *adj*
chancel ('tʃɑːnsəl) *n* the part of a church containing the altar, sanctuary, and choir [c14 from OF, from L *cancellī* (pl) lattice]
chancellery *or* **chancellory** ('tʃɑːnsələrɪ) *n, pl* **chancelleries** *or* **chancellories** **1** the building or room occupied by a chancellor's office **2** the position or office of a chancellor **3** *US* the office of an embassy or legation [c14 from Anglo-F *chancellerie*, from OF *chancelier* CHANCELLOR]
chancellor ('tʃɑːnsələ) *n* **1** the head of the government in several European countries **2** *US* the president of a university **3** *Brit & Canad* the honorary head of a university. Cf **vice chancellor** **4** *Christianity* a clergyman acting as the law officer of a bishop [c11 from Anglo-F *chanceler*, from LL *cancellārius* porter, from L *cancellī* lattice] > **'chancellor,ship** *n*
Chancellor of the Exchequer *n Brit* the cabinet minister responsible for finance
chance-medley *n law* a sudden quarrel in which one party kills another [c15 from Anglo-F *chance medlee* mixed chance]
chancer ('tʃɑːnsə) *n sl* an unscrupulous or dishonest opportunist [c19 from CHANCE + -ER[1]]
chancery ('tʃɑːnsərɪ) *n, pl* **chanceries** (*usually cap*) **1** Also called: **Chancery Division** (in England) the Lord Chancellor's court, now a division of the High Court of Justice **2** Also called: **court of chancery** (in the US) a court of equity **3** *Brit* the political section or offices of an embassy or legation **4** another name for **chancellery** **5** a court of public records **6** *Christianity* a diocesan office under the supervision of a bishop's chancellor **7** **in chancery** **7a** *law* (of a suit) pending in a court of equity **7b** in an awkward situation [c14 shortened from CHANCELLERY]
chancre ('ʃæŋkə) *n pathol* a small hard growth, which is the first sign of syphilis [c16 from F, from L: CANCER] > **'chancrous** *adj*
chancroid ('ʃæŋkrɔɪd) *n* **1** a soft venereal ulcer, esp of the male genitals ▷ *adj* **2** relating to or resembling a chancroid or chancre
chancy *or* **chancey** ('tʃɑːnsɪ) *adj* **chancier, chanciest** *inf* uncertain; risky
chandelier (ʃændɪ'lɪə) *n* an ornamental hanging light with branches and holders for several candles or bulbs [c17 from F: candleholder, from L CANDELABRUM]
Chandernagore (ˌtʃʌndənə'gɔː) *n* a port in E India, in S West Bengal on the Hooghly River: a former French settlement (1686–1950). Pop: 120 378 (1991)
Chandigarh (ˌtʃʌndɪ'gɑː) *n* a city and Union Territory of N India, joint capital of the Punjab and Haryana: modern city planned in the 1950s by Le Corbusier. Pop: 504 094 (1991), of city; 900 414 (2001), of union territory. Area (of union territory): 114 sq km (44 sq miles)
chandler ('tʃɑːndlə) *n* **1** a dealer in a specified trade or merchandise: *ship's chandler* **2** a person who makes or sells candles [c14 from OF *chandelier* one who makes or deals in candles, from *chandelle* CANDLE] > **'chandlery** *n*
Chandler ('tʃɑːndlə) *n* **Raymond** (**Thornton**) 1888–1959, US thriller writer: created Philip Marlowe, one of the first detective heroes in fiction
Chandragupta (ˌtʃʌndrə'gʊptə) *n* Greek name *Sandracottos*. died ?297 BC, ruler of N India, who founded the Maurya dynasty (325) and defeated Seleucus (?305)
Chandrasekhar (ˌtʃændrə'siːkə) *n* **Subrahmanyan** (ˌsʊbrə'mænjən) 1910–95, US astronomer born in Lahore, India (now Pakistan). His work on stellar evolution led to an understanding of white dwarfs: shared the Nobel prize for physics 1983
Chandrasekhar limit *n astron* the upper limit to the mass of a white dwarf, equal to 1.44 solar masses. A star with greater mass will continue to collapse to form a neutron star. [c20 named after S. CHANDRASEKHAR]
Chanel (*French* ʃanɛl) *n* **Gabrielle** (gabriɛl), known as *Coco Chanel*. 1883–1971, French couturière and perfumer, who created "the little black dress" and the perfume Chanel No. 5
Chqng (tʃæŋ) *n* another name for the **Yangtze**
Changan ('tʃæŋ'ɑːn) *n* a former name of **Xi An**
Changchiakow *or* **Changchiak'ou** ('tʃæŋ'tʃjɑː'kəʊ) *n* a variant transliteration of the Chinese name for **Zhangjiakou**
Changchow *or* **Ch'ang-chou** ('tʃæŋ'tʃaʊ) *n* a variant transliteration of the Chinese name for **Zhangzhou**
Changchun *or* **Ch'ang Ch'un** ('tʃæŋ'tʃʊn) *n* a city in NE China, capital of Jilin province: as **Hsinking**, capital of the Japanese state of Manchukuo (1932–45) Pop: 2 072 324 (1999 est)
Changde ('tʃæŋ'deɪ), **Changteh**, *or* **Ch'ang-te** *n* a port in SE central China, in N Hunan province, near the mouth of the Yuan River: severely damaged by the Japanese in World War II. Pop: 384 433 (1999 est)
change (tʃeɪndʒ) *vb* **changes, changing, changed** **1** to make or become different; alter **2** (*tr*) to replace with or exchange for another: *to change one's name* **3** (sometimes foll by *to* or *into*) to transform or convert or be transformed or converted **4** to give and receive (something) in return: *to change places* **5** (*tr*) to give or receive (money) in exchange for the equivalent sum in a smaller denomination or different currency **6** (*tr*) to remove or replace the coverings of: *to change a baby* **7** (when *intr*, may be foll by *into* or *out of*) to put on other clothes **8** to operate (the gear lever of a motor vehicle): *to change gear* **9** to alight from (one bus, train, etc) and board another ▷ *n* **10** the act or fact of changing or being changed **11** a variation or modification **12** the substitution of one thing for another **13** anything that is or may be substituted for something else **14** variety or novelty (esp in **for a change**) **15** a different set, esp of clothes **16** money given or received in return for its equivalent in a larger denomination or in a different currency **17** the balance of money when the amount tendered is larger than the amount due **18** coins of a small denomination **19** (*often cap*) *arch* a place where merchants meet to transact business **20** the act of passing from one state or phase to another **21** the transition from one phase of the moon to the next **22** the order in which a peal of bells may be rung **23** **get no change out of** (**someone**) *sl* not to be successful in attempts to exploit (someone) **24** **ring the changes** to

vary the manner or performance of an action that is often repeated ▷ See also **change down, changeover, change up** [C13 from OF, from L *cambīre* to exchange, barter] > **'changeful** *adj* > **'changeless** *adj* > **'changer** *n*

changeable ('tʃeɪndʒəbᵊl) *adj* **1** able to change or be changed: *changeable weather* **2** varying in colour as when viewed from different angles > **,changea'bility** *n* > **'changeably** *adv*

change down *vb* (*intr, adv*) to select a lower gear when driving

changeling ('tʃeɪndʒlɪŋ) *n* a child believed to have been exchanged by fairies for the parents' true child

change of life *n* a nontechnical name for **menopause**

changeover ('tʃeɪndʒ,əʊvə) *n* **1** an alteration or complete reversal from one method, system, or product to another **2** a reversal of a situation, attitude, etc **3** *sport* the act of transferring to or being relieved by a team-mate in a relay race, as by handing over a baton, etc ▷ *vb* **change over** (*adv*) **4** to adopt (a different position or attitude): *the driver and navigator changed over*

change-ringing *n* the art of bell-ringing in which a set of bells is rung in an established order which is then changed

change up *vb* (*intr, adv*) to select a higher gear when driving

Changsha *or* **Ch'ang-sha** ('tʃæŋ'ʃɑː) *n* a port in SE China, capital of Hunan province, on the Xiang River. Pop: 1 334 036 (1999 est)

Changteh *or* **Ch'ang-te** ('tʃæŋ'teɪ) *n* a variant transliteration of the Chinese name for **Changde**

Chania *or* **Hania** ('hɑːnɪə) *n* the chief port of Crete, on the NW coast. Pop: 50 000 (latest est). Greek name: **Khaniá**

channel ('tʃænᵊl) *n* **1** a broad strait connecting two areas of sea **2** the bed or course of a river, stream, or canal **3** a navigable course through a body of water **4** (*often pl*) a means or agency of access, communication, etc: *through official channels* **5** a course into which something can be directed or moved **6** *electronics* **6a** a band of radio frequencies assigned for a particular purpose, esp the broadcasting of a television signal **6b** a path for an electrical signal: *a stereo set has two channels* **7** a tubular passage for fluids **8** a groove, as in the shaft of a column **9** *computing* **9a** a path along which data can be transmitted **9b** one of the lines along the length of a paper tape on which information can be stored in the form of punched holes ▷ *vb* **channels, channelling, channelled** *or US* **channels, channeling, channeled** **10** to make or cut channels in (something) **11** (*tr*) to guide into or convey through a channel or channels: *information was channelled through to them* **12** to serve as a medium through whom the spirit of (a person of a former age) allegedly communicates with the living **13** (*tr*) to form a groove or flute in (a column, etc) [C13 from OF, from L *canālis* pipe, groove, conduit]

Channel ('tʃænᵊl) *n* **the** short for **English Channel**

Channel Country *n* **the** an area of E central Australia, in SW Queensland: crossed by intermittent rivers and subject to both flooding and long periods of drought

channel-hop *vb* **channel-hops, channel-hopping, channel-hopped** (*intr*) to change television channels repeatedly using a remote control device

Channel Islands *pl n* a group of islands in the English Channel, off the NW coast of France, consisting of Jersey, Guernsey, Alderney, Brechou, Great Sark, Little Sark, Herm, Jethou, and Lihou (British crown dependencies), and the Roches Douvres and the Îles Chausey (which belong to France): the only part of the duchy of Normandy remaining to Britain. Pop: 153 700 (2001 est). Area: 194 sq km (75 sq miles)

Channel Tunnel *n* the Anglo-French railway tunnel that runs beneath the English Channel, between Folkestone and Coquelles, near Calais, opened in 1994. Also called: **Chunnel, Eurotunnel**

chanson de geste *French* (ʃɑ̃sɔ̃ də ʒɛst) *n* one of a genre of Old French epic poems, the most famous of which is the *Chanson de Roland* [lit.: song of exploits]

chant (tʃɑːnt) *n* **1** a simple song **2** a short simple melody in which several words or syllables are assigned to one note **3** a psalm or canticle performed by using such a melody **4** a rhythmic or repetitious slogan, usually spoken or sung, as by sports supporters, etc ▷ *vb* **5** to sing or recite (a psalm, etc) as a chant **6** to intone (a slogan) [C14 from OF *chanter* to sing, from L *cantāre*, frequentative of *canere* to sing] > **'chanting** *n, adj*

chanter ('tʃɑːntə) *n* the pipe on a set of bagpipes on which the melody is played

chanterelle (,tʃæntə'rɛl) *n* any of a genus of fungi having an edible yellow funnel-shaped mushroom [C18 from F, from L *cantharus* drinking vessel, from Gk *kantharos*]

chanteuse (*French* ʃɑ̃tøz) *n* a female singer, esp in a nightclub or cabaret [F: singer]

chanticleer (,tʃæntɪ'klɪə) *n* a name for a cock, used esp in fables [C13 from OF, from *chanter cler* to sing clearly]

Chantilly (ʃæn'tɪlɪ; *French* ʃɑ̃tiji) *n* **1** a town in N France, near the **Forest of Chantilly** formerly famous for lace and porcelain. Pop: 11 341 (1990) **2** Also called: **Tiffany** a breed of medium-sized cat with silky semi-long hair. *adj* **3** (of cream) lightly sweetened and whipped

chantry ('tʃɑːntrɪ) *n, pl* **chantries** *Christianity* **1** an endowment for the singing of Masses for the soul of the founder **2** a chapel or altar so endowed [C14 from OF, from *chanter* to sing; see CHANT]

chanty ('ʃæntɪ, 'tʃæn-) *n, pl* **chanties** a variant of **shanty**²

Chanukah *or* **Hanukkah** ('hɑːnəkə, -nʊ,kɑː) *n* the eight-day Jewish festival of lights commemorating the rededication of the temple by Judas Maccabaeus in 165 BC. Also called: **Feast of Dedication, Feast of Lights** [from Heb., lit.: a dedication]

Chaoan ('tʃaʊ'ɑːn) *n* a city in SE China, in E Guangdong province, on the Han River: river port. Pop: 313 469 (1990). Also called: **Chaochow** Cc

Chaochow ('tʃaʊ'tʃəʊ) *n* another name for **Chaoan**

chaology (keɪ'ɒlədʒɪ) *n* the study of chaos theory > **cha'ologist** *n*

chaos ('keɪɒs) *n* **1** (*usually cap*) the disordered formless matter supposed to have existed before the ordered universe **2** complete disorder; utter confusion [C15 from L, from Gk *khaos*] > **chaotic** (keɪ'ɒtɪk) *adj* > **cha'otically** *adv*

chaos theory *n* a theory, applied in various branches of science, that apparently random phenomena have underlying order

chap¹ (tʃæp) *vb* **chaps, chapping, chapped** **1** (of the skin) to make or become raw and cracked, esp by exposure to cold ▷ *n* **2** (*usually pl*) a cracked patch on the skin [C14 prob. of Gmc origin]

chap² (tʃæp) *n inf* a man or boy; fellow [C16 (in the sense: buyer): shortened from CHAPMAN]

chap³ (tʃɒp, tʃæp) *n* a less common word for **chop**³

chaparejos *or* **chaparajos** (ʃæpə'reɪəʊs) *pl n* another name for **chaps** [from Mexican Sp.]

chaparral (,tʃæpə'ræl, ʃæp-) *n* (in the southwestern US) a dense growth of shrubs and trees [C19 from Sp., from *chaparra* evergreen oak]

chapati *or* **chapatti** (tʃə'pætɪ, -'pɑːtɪ) *n, pl* **chapati, chapatis, chapaties** *or* **chapatti, chapattis, chapatties** (in Indian cookery) a flat unleavened bread resembling a pancake [from Hindi]

chapel ('tʃæpᵊl) *n* **1** a place of Christian worship, esp with a separate altar, in a church or cathedral **2** a similar place of worship in a large house or institution, such as a college **3** a church subordinate to a parish church **4** (in Britain) **4a** a Nonconformist place of worship **4b** Nonconformist religious practices or doctrine **5a** the members of a trade union in a newspaper office, printing house, etc **5b** a meeting of these members [c13 from OF, from LL *cappella*, dim. of *cappa* cloak (see CAP); orig. the sanctuary where the cloak of St Martin was kept]

chaperon *or* **chaperone** ('ʃæpəˌrəʊn) *n* **1** (esp formerly) an older or married woman who accompanies or supervises a young unmarried woman on social occasions ▷ *vb* **chaperons, chaperoning, chaperoned** *or* **chaperones, chaperoning, chaperoned** **2** to act as a chaperon to [c14 from OF, from *chape* hood; see CAP] > **'chaperˌonage** *n*

chapfallen ('tʃæpˌfɔːlən) *or* **chopfallen** *adj* dejected; downhearted [c16 from CHOPS + FALLEN]

chaplain ('tʃæplɪn) *n* a Christian clergyman attached to a chapel of an institution or ministering to a military body, etc [c12 from OF, from LL, from *cappella* CHAPEL] > **'chaplaincy** *n*

chaplet ('tʃæplɪt) *n* **1** an ornamental wreath of flowers worn on the head **2** a string of beads **3** *RC Church* **3a** a string of prayer beads constituting one third of the rosary **3b** the prayers counted on this string **4** a narrow moulding in the form of a string of beads; astragal [c14 from OF, from *chapel* hat] > **'chapleted** *adj*

Chaplin ('tʃæplɪn) *n* Sir **Charles Spencer,** known as *Charlie Chaplin*. 1889–1977, English comedian, film actor, and director. He is renowned for his portrayal of a downtrodden little man with baggy trousers, bowler hat, and cane. His films, most of which were made in Hollywood, include *The Gold Rush* (1924), *Modern Times* (1936), and *The Great Dictator* (1940)

chapman ('tʃæpmən) *n, pl* **chapmen** *arch* a trader, esp an itinerant pedlar [OE *cēapman*, from *cēap* buying and selling]

Chapman ('tʃæpmən) *n* **George** 1559–1634, English dramatist and poet, noted for his translation of Homer

Chappell ('tʃæpᵊl) *n* **Greg(ory Stephen)** born 1948, Australian cricketer: first Australian to score over 7000 test runs

chappie ('tʃæpɪ) *n inf* another word for **chap²**

chaps (tʃæps, ʃæps) *pl n* leather overleggings without a seat, worn by cowboys. Also called: **chaparajos, chaparejos** [c19 shortened from CHAPAREJOS]

chapter ('tʃæptə) *n* **1** a division of a written work **2** a sequence of events: *a chapter of disasters* **3** a period in a life, history, etc **4** a numbered reference to that part of a Parliamentary session which relates to a specified Act of Parliament **5** a branch of some societies, clubs, etc **6** the collective body or a meeting of the canons of a cathedral or of the members of a monastic or knightly order **7** **chapter and verse** exact authority for an action or statement ▷ *vb* **8** (*tr*) to divide into chapters [c13 from OF *chapitre*, from L *capitulum*, lit.: little head, hence, section of writing, from *caput* head]

chapterhouse ('tʃæptəˌhaʊs) *n* **1** the building in which a chapter meets. See **chapter** (sense 6) **2** *US* the meeting place of a college fraternity or sorority

char¹ (tʃɑː) *vb* **chars, charring, charred** **1** to burn or be burned partially; scorch **2** (*tr*) to reduce (wood) to charcoal by partial combustion [c17 short for CHARCOAL]

char² *or* **charr** (tʃɑː) *n, pl* **char, chars** *or* **charr, charrs** any of various troutlike fishes occurring in cold lakes and northern seas [c17 from ?]

char³ (tʃɑː) *n* **1** *inf* short for **charwoman** ▷ *vb* **chars, charring, charred** **2** (*intr*) *Brit inf* to do cleaning as a job [c18 from OE *cęrran*]

char⁴ (tʃɑː) *n Brit* a slang word for **tea** [from Chinese *ch'a*]

charabanc ('ʃærəˌbæŋ) *n Brit* a coach, esp for sightseeing [c19 from F: wagon with seats]

character ('kærɪktə) *n* **1** the combination of traits and qualities distinguishing the individual nature of a person or thing **2** one such distinguishing quality; characteristic **3** moral force: *a man of character* **4a** reputation, esp a good reputation **4b** (*as modifier*): *character assassination* **5** a person represented in a play, film, story, etc; role **6** an outstanding person: *one of the great characters of the century* **7** *inf* an odd, eccentric, or unusual person: *he's quite a character* **8** an informal word for **person**: *a shady character* **9** a symbol used in a writing system, such as a letter of the alphabet **10** Also called: **sort** *printing* any single letter, numeral, etc, cast as a type **11** *computing* any letter, numeral, etc, which can be represented uniquely by a binary pattern **12** a style of writing or printing **13** *genetics* any structure, function, attribute, etc, in an organism, which may or may not be determined by a gene or group of genes **14** a short prose sketch of a distinctive type of person **15** **in** (*or* **out of**) **character** typical (*or* not typical) of the apparent character of a person [c14 from L: distinguishing mark, from Gk *kharaktēr* engraver's tool] > **'characterful** *adj* > **'characterless** *adj*

character actor *n* an actor who specializes in playing odd or eccentric characters

character assassination *n* the act of deliberately attempting to destroy a person's reputation by defamatory remarks

characteristic (ˌkærɪktə'rɪstɪk) *n* **1** a distinguishing quality, attribute, or trait **2** *maths* **2a** the integral part of a common logarithm: *the characteristic of 2.4771 is 2* **2b** another name for **exponent** (sense 4) ▷ *adj* **3** indicative of a distinctive quality, etc; typical > ˌ**character'istically** *adv*

characterize *or* **characterise** ('kærɪktəˌraɪz) *vb* **characterizes, characterizing, characterized** *or* **characterises, characterising, characterised** (*tr*) **1** to be a characteristic of **2** to distinguish or mark as a characteristic **3** to describe or portray the character of > ˌ**characteri'zation** *or* ˌ**characteri'sation** *n*

charade (ʃə'rɑːd) *n* **1** an act in the game of charades **2** *chiefly Brit* an absurd act; travesty

charades (ʃə'rɑːdz) *n* (*functioning as sing*) a parlour game in which one team acts out each syllable of a word, the other team having to guess the word [c18 from F, from Provençal *charrado* chat, from *charra* chatter]

charcoal ('tʃɑːˌkəʊl) *n* **1** a black amorphous form of carbon made by heating wood or other organic matter in the absence of air **2** a stick of this for drawing **3** a drawing done in charcoal **4** Also: **charcoal grey** **4a** a dark grey colour **4b** (*as adj*): *a charcoal suit* ▷ *vb* **5** (*tr*) to write, draw, or blacken with charcoal [c14 from *char* (from ?) + COAL]

Charcot (*French* ʃarko) *n* **Jean Martin** (ʒɑ̃ martɛ̃) 1825–93, French neurologist, noted for his attempt using hypnotism to find an organic cause for hysteria, which influenced Freud

charcuterie (ʃɑː'kuːtəriː) *n* **1** cooked cold meats **2** a shop selling cooked cold meats [F]

chard (tʃɑːd) *n* a variety of beet with large succulent leaves and thick stalks, used as a vegetable. Also called: **Swiss chard** [c17 prob. from F *carde*, ult. from L *carduus* thistle]

Chardin (*French* ʃardɛ̃) *n* **Jean-Baptiste Siméon** (ʒɑ̃batist simeɔ̃) 1699–1779, French still-life and genre painter, noted for his subtle use of scumbled colour

Chardonnay ('ʃɑːdəˌneɪ) *n* (*sometimes not cap*) **1** a white grape grown in the Burgundy region of France and now throughout the wine-producing world **2** any of various white wines made from this grape [F]

Chardonnet (*French* ʃardɔnɛ) *n* **(Louis Marie) Hilaire Bernigaud** (ilɛr bɛrnigo), Comte de. 1839–1924, French chemist and industrialist who produced rayon, the first artificial fibre

Charente (*French* ʃarɑ̃t) *n* **1** a department of W central France, in Poitou-Charentes region. Capital: Angoulême. Pop: 339 628 (1999). Area: 5972 sq km (2329 sq miles) **2** a river in W France, flowing west to the Bay of

Biscay. Length: 362 km (225 miles)

Charente-Maritime (*French* ʃarɑ̃tmaritim) *n* a department of W France, in Poitou-Charentes region. Capital: La Rochelle. Pop: 557 024 (1999). Area: 7232 sq km (2820 sq miles)

charge (tʃɑːdʒ) *vb* **charges, charging, charged 1** to set or demand (a price) **2** (*tr*) to enter a debit against a person or his account **3** (*tr*) to accuse or impute a fault to (a person, etc), as formally in a court of law **4** (*tr*) to command; place a burden upon or assign responsibility to: *I was charged to take the message to headquarters* **5** to make a rush at or sudden attack upon (a person or thing) **6** (*tr*) to fill (a receptacle) with the proper quantity **7** (often foll by *up*) to cause (an accumulator, capacitor, etc) to take or store electricity or (of an accumulator) to have electricity fed into it **8** to fill or be filled with matter by dispersion, solution, or absorption: *to charge water with carbon dioxide* **9** (*tr*) to fill or suffuse with feeling, emotion, etc: *the atmosphere was charged with excitement* **10** (*tr*) *law* (of a judge) to address (a jury) authoritatively **11** (*tr*) to load (a firearm) **12** (*tr*) *heraldry* to paint (a shield, banner, etc) with a charge ▷ *n* **13** a price charged for some article or service; cost **14** a financial liability, such as a tax **15** a debt or a book entry recording it **16** an accusation or allegation, such as a formal accusation of a crime in law **17a** an onrush, attack, or assault **17b** the call to such an attack in battle **18** custody or guardianship **19** a person or thing committed to someone's care **20a** a cartridge or shell **20b** the explosive required to discharge a firearm **20c** an amount of explosive to be detonated at any one time **21** the quantity of anything that a receptacle is intended to hold **22** *physics* **22a** the attribute of matter responsible for all electrical phenomena, existing in two forms: *negative charge; positive charge* **22b** an excess or deficiency of electrons in a system **22c** a quantity of electricity determined by the product of an electric current and the time for which it flows, measured in coulombs **22d** the total amount of electricity stored in a capacitor or an accumulator **23** a load or burden **24** a duty or responsibility; control **25** a command, injunction, or order **26** *heraldry* a design depicted on heraldic arms **27** **in charge** in command **28** **in charge of** **28a** having responsibility for **28b** US under the care of [C13 from OF *chargier* to load, from LL *carricāre*; see CARRY]

chargeable (ˈtʃɑːdʒəbᵊl) *adj* **1** liable to be charged **2** liable to result in a legal charge

chargeable asset *n* any asset that can give rise to assessment for capital gains tax on its disposal. Exempt assets include principal private residences, cars, investments held in a personal equity plan, and government securities

charge account *n* another term for **credit account**

charge card *n* a card issued by a chain store, shop, or organization, that enables customers to obtain goods and services for which they pay at a later date

charge carrier *n* an electron, hole, or ion that transports the electric charge in an electric current

chargé d'affaires (ˈʃɑːʒeɪ dæˈfɛə) *n, pl* **chargés d'affaires** (ˈʃɑːʒeɪ, -ʒeɪz) **1** the temporary head of a diplomatic mission in the absence of the ambassador or minister **2** the head of a diplomatic mission of the lowest level [C18 from F: (one) charged with affairs]

charge hand *n Brit* a workman whose grade of responsibility is just below that of a foreman

charge nurse *n Brit* a nurse in charge of a ward in a hospital. Male equivalent of **sister**

charger[1] (ˈtʃɑːdʒə) *n* **1** a person or thing that charges **2** a horse formerly ridden into battle **3** a device for charging an accumulator

charger[2] (ˈtʃɑːdʒə) *n antiques* a large dish [C14 *chargeour*, from *chargen* to CHARGE]

charge sheet *n Brit* a document on which a police officer enters details of the charge against a prisoner and the court in which he will appear

char-grilled *adj* (of food) grilled over charcoal

Chari (ˈtʃɑːrɪ) *or* **Shari** *n* a river in N central Africa, rising in the N Central African Republic and flowing north to Lake Chad. Length: about 2250 km (1400 miles)

charily (ˈtʃɛərɪlɪ) *adv* **1** cautiously; carefully **2** sparingly

chariness (ˈtʃɛərɪnɪs) *n* the state of being chary

Charing Cross (ˈtʃærɪŋ) *n* a district of London, in the city of Westminster: the modern cross (1863) in front of Charing Cross railway station replaces the one erected by Edward I (1290), the last of twelve marking the route of the funeral procession of his queen, Eleanor

chariot (ˈtʃærɪət) *n* **1** a two-wheeled horse-drawn vehicle used in ancient wars, races, etc **2** a light four-wheeled horse-drawn ceremonial carriage **3** *poetic* any stately vehicle [C14 from OF, augmentative of *char* CAR]

charioteer (ˌtʃærɪəˈtɪə) *n* the driver of a chariot

charisma (kəˈrɪzmə) *or* **charism** (ˈkærɪzəm) *n* **1** a special personal quality or power making an individual capable of influencing or inspiring people **2** a quality inherent in a thing, such as a particular type of car, which inspires great enthusiasm and devotion **3** *Christianity* a divinely bestowed power or talent [C17 from Church L, from Gk *kharisma*, from *kharis* grace, favour] > **charismatic** (ˌkærɪzˈmætɪk) *adj*

charismatic movement *n Christianity* any of various groups, within existing denominations, emphasizing the charismatic gifts of speaking in tongues, healing, etc

charitable (ˈtʃærɪtəbᵊl) *adj* **1** generous in giving to the needy **2** kind or lenient in one's attitude towards others **3** of or for charity > ˈ**charitableness** *n* > ˈ**charitably** *adv*

charitable trust *n* a trust set up for the benefit of a charity that complies with the regulations of the Charity Commissioners to enable it to be exempt from paying income tax

charity (ˈtʃærɪtɪ) *n, pl* **charities 1a** the giving of help, money, food, etc, to those in need **1b** (*as modifier*): *a charity show* **2** an institution or organization set up to provide help, money, etc, to those in need **3** the help, money, etc, given to the needy; alms **4** a kindly attitude towards people **5** love of one's fellow men [C13 from OF, from L *cāritās* affection, from *cārus* dear]

charivari (ˌʃɑːrɪˈvɑːrɪ), **shivaree,** *or esp US.* **chivaree** *n* **1** a discordant mock serenade to newlyweds, made with pans, kettles, etc **2** a confused noise; din [C17 from F, from LL, from Gk *karēbaria*, from *karē* head + *barus* heavy]

charlady (ˈtʃɑːˌleɪdɪ) *n, pl* **charladies** another name for **charwoman**

charlatan (ˈʃɑːlətᵊn) *n* someone who professes expertise, esp in medicine, that he does not have; quack [C17 from F, from It., from *ciarlare* to chatter] > ˈ**charlatanˌism** *or* ˈ**charlatanry** *n*

Charlemagne (ˈʃɑːləˌmeɪn) *n* ?742–814 AD, king of the Franks (768–814) and, as Charles I, Holy Roman Emperor (800–814). He conquered the Lombards (774), the Saxons (772–804), and the Avars (791–799). He instituted many judicial and ecclesiastical reforms, and promoted commerce and agriculture throughout his empire, which extended from the Ebro to the Elbe. Under Alcuin his court at Aachen became the centre of a revival of learning

Charles (tʃɑːlz) *n* **1** *Prince of Wales.* born 1948, son of Elizabeth II; heir apparent to the throne of Great Britain and Northern Ireland. He married (1981) Lady Diana Spencer; they separated in 1992 and were divorced in 1996; their son, Prince William of Wales, was born in 1982 and their second son, Prince Henry, in 1984 **2** **Ray** real name *Ray Charles Robinson.* 1930–2004, US singer, pianist, and songwriter, whose work spans jazz, blues, gospel, pop, and country music

Cc

Charles I *n* **1** title as Holy Roman Emperor of **Charlemagne** **2** title as king of France of **Charles II** (Holy Roman Emperor) **3** title as king of Spain of **Charles V** (Holy Roman Emperor) **4** title of **Charles Stuart** 1600–49, king of England, Scotland, and Ireland (1625–49); son of James I. He ruled for 11 years (1629–40) without parliament, advised by his minister Strafford, until rebellion broke out in Scotland. Conflict with the Long Parliament led to the Civil War and after his defeat at Naseby (1645) he sought refuge with the Scots (1646). He was handed over to the English army under Cromwell (1647) and executed **5** 1887–1922, emperor of Austria, and, as Charles IV, king of Hungary (1916–18) The last ruler of the Austro-Hungarian monarchy, he was forced to abdicate at the end of World War I

Charles II *n* **1** known as *Charles the Bald*. 823–877 AD, Holy Roman Emperor (875–877) and, as Charles I, king of France (843–877) **2** the title as king of France of **Charles III** (Holy Roman Emperor) **3** 1630–85, king of England, Scotland, and Ireland (1660–85) following the Restoration (1660); son of Charles I. He did much to promote commerce, science, and the Navy, but his Roman Catholic sympathies caused widespread distrust **4** 1661–1700, the last Hapsburg king of Spain: his reign saw the end of Spanish power in Europe

Charles III *n* **1** known as *Charles the Fat*. 839–888 AD, Holy Roman Emperor (881–887) and, as Charles II, king of France (884–887). He briefly reunited the empire of Charlemagne **2** 1716–88, king of Spain (1759–88), who curbed the power of the Church and tried to modernize his country

Charles IV *n* **1** known as *Charles the Fair*. 1294–1328, king of France (1322–28): brother of Isabella of France, with whom he intrigued against her husband, Edward II of England **2** 1316–78, king of Bohemia (1346–78) and Holy Roman Emperor (1355–78) **3** 1748–1819, king of Spain (1788–1808), whose reign saw the domination of Spain by Napoleonic France: abdicated **4** title as king of Hungary of **Charles I** (sense 5)

Charles V *n* **1** known as *Charles the Wise*. 1337–80, king of France (1364–80) during the Hundred Years' War **2** 1500–58, Holy Roman Emperor (1519–56), king of Burgundy and the Netherlands (1506–55), and, as Charles I, king of Spain (1516–56): his reign saw the empire threatened by Francis I of France, the Turks, and the spread of Protestantism; abdicated

Charles VI *n* **1** known as *Charles the Mad* or *Charles the Well-Beloved*. 1368–1422, king of France (1380–1422): defeated by Henry V of England at Agincourt (1415), he was forced by the Treaty of Troyes (1420) to recognize Henry as his successor **2** 1685–1740, Holy Roman Emperor (1711–40) His claim to the Spanish throne (1700) led to the War of the Spanish Succession

Charles VII *n* **1** 1403–61, king of France (1422–61), son of Charles VI. He was excluded from the French throne by the Treaty of Troyes, but following Joan of Arc's victory over the English at Orléans (1429), was crowned **2** 1697–1745, Holy Roman Emperor (1742–45) during the War of the Austrian Succession

Charles IX *n* 1550–74, king of France (1560–74), son of Catherine de' Medici and Henry II: his reign was marked by war between Huguenots and Catholics

Charles X *n* **1** title of *Charles Gustavus*. 1622–60, king of Sweden, who warred with Poland and Denmark in an attempt to create a unified Baltic state **2** 1757–1836, king of France (1824–30): his attempt to restore absolutism led to his enforced exile

Charles XIV *n* the title as king of Sweden and Norway of (Jean Baptiste Jules) **Bernadotte**

Charles Edward Stuart *n* See (Charles Edward) **Stuart**

Charles Martel (mɑːˈtɛl) *n* grandfather of Charlemagne. ?688–741 AD, Frankish ruler of Austrasia (715–41), who checked the Muslim invasion of Europe by defeating the Moors at Poitiers (732)

Charles's Wain (weɪn) *n* another name for the **Plough** [OE *Carles wægn*, from *Carl* CHARLEMAGNE + *wægn* WAIN]

Charles the Great *n* another name for **Charlemagne**

charleston (ˈtʃɑːlstən) *n* a fast rhythmic dance of the 1920s, characterized by kicking and by twisting of the legs from the knee down [named after *Charleston*, South Carolina]

Charleston (ˈtʃɑːlstən) *n* **1** a city in central West Virginia: the state capital. Pop: 59 371 (1985 est) **2** a port in SE South Carolina, on the Atlantic: scene of the first action in the Civil War. Pop: 96 650 (2000)

Charleville-Mézières (*French* ʃarləvilmezjɛr) *n* twin towns on opposite sides of the River Meuse in NE France. Pop: 59 440 (1990). See **Mézières**

charley horse (ˈtʃɑːlɪ) *n* *US & Canad inf* cramp following strenuous athletic exercise [c19 from ?]

charlie (ˈtʃɑːlɪ) *n* *Brit inf* a silly person; fool

charlock (ˈtʃɑːlɒk) *n* a weedy Eurasian plant with hairy stems and foliage and yellow flowers. Also called: **wild mustard** [OE *cerlic*, from ?]

charlotte (ˈʃɑːlət) *n* **1** a dessert made with fruit and layers or a casing of bread or cake crumbs, sponge cake, etc: *apple charlotte* **2** short for **charlotte russe** [c19 from F, from the name *Charlotte*]

Charlotte (ˈʃɑːlət) *n* a city in S North Carolina: the largest city in the state. Pop: 540 828 (2000)

Charlotte Amalie (ˈʃɑːlət əˈmɑːlɪə) *n* the capital of the Virgin Islands of the United States, a port on St Thomas Island. Pop: 12 331 (1990). Former name (1921–37): **Saint Thomas**

Charlottenburg (*German* ʃarˈlɔtənbʊrk) *n* a district of Berlin (of West Berlin until 1990), formerly an independent city. Pop: 145 564 (latest est)

charlotte russe (ruːs) *n* a cold dessert made with sponge fingers enclosing a mixture of cream, custard, etc [F.: Russian charlotte]

Charlottetown (ˈʃɑːlətˌtaʊn) *n* a port in SE Canada, capital of the province of Prince Edward Island. Pop: 15 396 (1991)

Charlton (ˈtʃɑːltᵊn) *n* **1** **Bobby**, full name *Sir Robert Charlton*. born 1937, English footballer; played for England over 100 times **2** his brother, **Jack**, full name *John Charlton*. born 1935, English footballer; played for Leeds United (1952–73) and England; manager of the Republic of Ireland soccer team (1986–95)

charm (tʃɑːm) *n* **1** the quality of pleasing, fascinating, or attracting people **2** a pleasing or attractive feature **3** a small object worn for supposed magical powers; amulet **4** a trinket worn on a bracelet **5** a magic spell **6** a formula used in casting such a spell **7** *physics* a property of certain elementary particles, used to explain some scattering experiments **8** **like a charm** perfectly; successfully ▷ *vb* **9** to attract or fascinate; delight greatly **10** to cast a magic spell on **11** to protect, influence, or heal, supposedly by magic **12** (*tr*) to influence or obtain by personal charm [c13 from OF, from L *carmen* song] > **ˈcharmer** *n*

charming (ˈtʃɑːmɪŋ) *adj* delightful; pleasant; attractive > **ˈcharmingly** *adv*

charm offensive *n* a concentrated attempt to gain favour or respectability by conspicuously cooperative and obliging behaviour

charnel (ˈtʃɑːnᵊl) *n* **1** short for **charnel house** ▷ *adj* **2** ghastly; sepulchral; deathly [c14 from OF: burial place, from L *carnālis* fleshly, CARNAL]

charnel house *n* (esp formerly) a building or vault where corpses or bones are deposited

Charnley (ˈtʃɑːnlɪ) *n* Sir **John** 1911–82, British surgeon noted for his invention of an artificial hip joint and his development of hip-replacement surgery

Charon (ˈkɛərən) *n* *Greek myth* the ferryman who brought the dead across the rivers Styx or Acheron to Hades

Charpentier (*French* ʃarpɑ̃tje) *n* **1 Gustave** (gystav) 1860–1956, French composer, whose best-known work is the opera *Louise* (1900) **2 Marc-Antoine** ?1645–1704, French composer, best known for his sacred music, particularly the *Te Deum*

chart (tʃɑːt) *n* **1** a map designed to aid navigation by sea or air **2** an outline map, esp one on which weather information is plotted **3** a sheet giving graphical, tabular, or diagrammatical information **4 the charts** *inf* the lists produced weekly of the bestselling pop singles and albums or the most popular videos ▷ *vb* **5** (*tr*) to make a chart of **6** (*tr*) to plot or outline the course of **7** (*intr*) (of a record) to appear in the charts [C16 from L, from Gk *khartēs* papyrus] > **ˈchartless** *adj*

charter (ˈtʃɑːtə) *n* **1** a formal document from the sovereign or state incorporating a city, bank, college, etc, and specifying its purposes and rights **2** (*sometimes cap*) a formal document granting or demanding certain rights or liberties **3** a document issued by a society or an organization authorizing the establishment of a local branch or chapter **4** a special privilege or exemption **5** (*often cap*) the fundamental principles of an organization; constitution **6a** the hire or lease of transportation **6b** (*as modifier*): *a charter flight* ▷ *vb* (*tr*) **7** a law, policy, or decision containing a loophole that allows a specified group to engage more easily in an activity considered undesirable: *a beggars' charter* **8** to lease or hire by charter **9** to hire (a vehicle, etc) **10** to grant a charter to (a group or person) [C13 from OF, from L *chartula*, dim. of *charta* leaf of papyrus; see CHART] > **ˈcharterer** *n*

chartered accountant *n* (in Britain) an accountant who has passed the examinations of the Institute of Chartered Accountants

chartered bank *n Canad* a privately owned bank that has been incorporated by Parliament to operate in the commercial banking system

chartered librarian *n* (in Britain) a librarian who has obtained a qualification from the Library Association in addition to a degree or diploma in librarianship

chartered surveyor *n* (in Britain) a member of the Royal Institution of Chartered Surveyors

Charteris (ˈtʃɑːtərɪs) *n* **Leslie,** original name *Leslie Charles Bowyer Yin*. 1907–93, British novelist, born in Singapore: created the character Simon Templar, known as The Saint, the central character in many adventure novels

Chartism (ˈtʃɑːtɪzəm) *n English history* a movement (1838–48) to achieve certain political reforms, demand for which was embodied in charters presented to Parliament > **ˈChartist** *n, adj*

Chartres (ˈʃɑːtrə, ʃɑːt; *French* ʃartrə) *n* a city in NW France: Gothic cathedral; market town. Pop: 41 850 (1990)

chartreuse (ʃɑːˈtrɜːz; *French* ʃartrøz) *n* **1** either of two liqueurs, green or yellow, made from herbs **2a** a yellowish-green colour **2b** (*as adj*): *a chartreuse dress* [C19 from F, after *La Grande Chartreuse*, monastery near Grenoble, where the liqueur is produced]

charwoman (ˈtʃɑːˌwʊmən) *n, pl* **charwomen** *Brit* a woman who is hired to clean a house

chary (ˈtʃɛərɪ) *adj* **charier, chariest 1** wary; careful **2** choosy; finicky **3** shy **4** sparing; mean [OE *cearig*; rel. to *caru* CARE]

Charybdis (kəˈrɪbdɪs) *n* a ship-devouring monster in classical mythology, identified with a whirlpool off the coast of Sicily ▷ Cf **Scylla**

chase[1] (tʃeɪs) *vb* **chases, chasing, chased 1** to follow or run after (a person, animal, or goal) persistently or quickly **2** (*tr; often foll by out, away,* or *off*) to force to run (away); drive (out) **3** (*tr*) *inf* to court (a member of the opposite sex) in an unsubtle manner **4** (*tr; often foll by up*) *inf* to pursue persistently and energetically in order to obtain results, information, etc **5** (*intr*) *inf* to hurry; rush ▷ *n* **6** the act of chasing; pursuit **7** any quarry that is pursued **8** *Brit* an unenclosed area of land where wild animals are preserved to be hunted **9** *Brit* the right to hunt a particular quarry over the land of others **10 the chase** the act or sport of hunting **11** short for **steeplechase 12 give chase** to pursue (a person, animal, or thing) actively [C13 from OF *chacier*, from Vulgar L *captiāre* (unattested), from L, from *capere* to take; see CATCH]

chase[2] (tʃeɪs) *n* **1** *letterpress printing* a rectangular steel frame into which metal type and blocks are locked for printing **2** the part of a gun barrel from the trunnions to the muzzle **3** a groove or channel, esp to take a pipe, cable, etc ▷ *vb* **chases, chasing, chased** (*tr*) **4** Also: **chamfer** to cut a groove, furrow, or flute in (a surface, column, etc) [C17 prob. from F *châsse* frame, from OF *chas* enclosure, from LL *capsus* pen for animals; both from L *capsa* CASE[2]]

chase[3] (tʃeɪs) *vb* **chases, chasing, chased** (*tr*) to ornament (metal) by engraving or embossing. Also: **enchase** [C14 from OF *enchasser* ENCHASE]

chaser (ˈtʃeɪsə) *n* **1** a person or thing that chases **2** a drink drunk after another of a different kind, as beer after spirits

chasm (ˈkæzəm) *n* **1** a deep cleft in the ground; abyss **2** a break in continuity; gap **3** a wide difference in interests, feelings, etc [C17 from L, from Gk *khasma*; rel. to *khainein* to gape] > **chasmal** (ˈkæzməl) *or* **ˈchasmic** *adj*

chasseur (ʃæˈsɜː) *n* **1** *French army* a member of a unit specially trained for swift deployment **2** a uniformed attendant ▷ *adj* **3** (*often postpositive*) designating or cooked in a sauce consisting of white wine and mushrooms [C18 from F: huntsman]

Chassid *or* **Hassid** (ˈhæsɪd) *n pl* **Chassidim** *or* **Hassidim** (ˈhæsɪˌdiːm, -dɪm) **1** a sect of Jewish mystics founded in Poland about 1750, characterized by religious zeal and a spirit of prayer, joy, and charity **2** a Jewish sect of the 2nd century BC, formed to combat Hellenistic influences > **Chassidic** *or* **Hassidic** (həˈsɪdɪk) *adj*

Cc

chassis (ˈʃæsɪ) *n, pl* **chassis** (-sɪz) **1** the steel frame, wheels, and mechanical parts of a motor vehicle **2** *electronics* a mounting for the circuit components of an electrical or electronic device, such as a radio or television **3** the landing gear of an aircraft **4** the frame on which a cannon carriage moves [C17 (meaning: window frame): from F *châssis*, from Vulgar L *capsicum* (unattested), ult. from L *capsa* CASE[2]]

chaste (tʃeɪst) *adj* **1** not having experienced sexual intercourse; virginal **2** abstaining from unlawful sexual intercourse **3** abstaining from all sexual intercourse **4** (of conduct, speech, etc) pure; decent; modest **5** (of style) simple; restrained [C13 from OF, from L *castus* pure] > **ˈchastely** *adv* > **ˈchasteness** *n*

chasten (ˈtʃeɪsᵊn) *vb* (*tr*) **1** to bring to submission; subdue **2** to discipline or correct by punishment **3** to moderate; restrain [C16 from OF, from L *castigāre*; see CASTIGATE] > **ˈchastener** *n*

chastise (tʃæsˈtaɪz) *vb* **chastises, chastising, chastised** (*tr*) **1** to punish, esp by beating **2** to scold severely [C14 *chastisen*, irregularly from *chastien* to CHASTEN] > **chastisement** (ˈtʃæstɪzmənt, tʃæsˈtaɪz-) *n* > **chasˈtiser** *n*

chastity (ˈtʃæstɪtɪ) *n* **1** the state of being chaste; purity **2** abstention from sexual intercourse; virginity or celibacy [C13 from OF, from L, from *castus* CHASTE]

chasuble (ˈtʃæzjʊbᵊl) *n Christianity* a long sleeveless outer vestment worn by a priest when celebrating Mass [C13 from F, from LL *casubla* garment with a hood]

chat (tʃæt) *n* **1** informal conversation or talk in an easy familiar manner **2** the exchange of messages in an Internet or other network chatroom **3** an Old World songbird of the thrush family, having a harsh chattering cry **4** any of various North American warblers **5** any of various Australian wrens ▷ *vb* **chats, chatting, chatted 6** (*intr*) to talk in an easy familiar way

7 (*intr*) to exchange messages in a chatroom ▷ See also **chat up** [C16 short for CHATTER]

chatbot ('tʃæt,bɒt) *n* a computer program in the form of a virtual e-mail correspondent that can reply to messages from computer users [C20 from CHAT[1] + (RO)BOT]

chateau *or* **château** ('ʃætəʊ) *n, pl* **chateaux** (-təʊ, -təʊz), **chateaus** *or* **châteaux, châteaus** 1 a country house or castle, esp in France 2 (in the name of a wine) estate or vineyard [C18 from F, from OF, from L *castellum* CASTLE]

Chateaubriand (*French* ʃɑtobrijɑ̃) *n* 1 **François René** (frɑ̃swa rəne), Vicomte de Chateaubriand. 1768–1848, French writer and statesman: a precursor of the romantic movement in France; his works include *Le Génie du Christianisme* (1802) and *Mémoires d'outre-tombe* (1849–50) 2 a thick steak cut from the fillet of beef

chateau cardboard *n NZ inf* wine sold in a winebox

Châteauroux (*French* ʃɑtoru) *n* a city in central France: tenth-century castle (**Château-Raoul**). Pop: 52 950 (1990)

Château-Thierry ('ʃætəʊ'tɪərɪ; *French* ʃɑtotjɛri) *n* a town in N central France, on the River Marne: scene of the second battle of the Marne (1918) during World War I. Pop: 15 830 (1990)

chatelaine ('ʃætə,leɪn) *n* 1 (esp formerly) the mistress of a castle or large household 2 a chain or clasp worn at the waist by women in the 16th to the 19th centuries, with handkerchief, keys, etc, attached [from F, from OF, ult. from L *castellum* CASTLE]

Chatham[1] ('tʃætəm) *n* 1 a town in SE England, in N Kent on the River Medway: formerly royal naval dockyard. Pop: 71 691 (1991) 2 a city in SE Canada, in SE Ontario on the Thames River. Pop: 43 557 (1991)

Chatham[2] ('tʃætəm) *n* 1 **1st Earl of** title of the elder (William) **Pitt**

Chatham Island *n* another name for **San Cristóbal** (sense 1)

Chatham Islands *pl n* a group of islands in the S Pacific Ocean, forming a county of South Island, New Zealand: consists of the main islands of Chatham, Pitt, and several rocky islets. Chief settlement: Waitangi. Pop: 769 (1991). Area: 963 sq km (372 sq miles)

chatline ('tʃæt,laɪn) *n* a telephone service enabling callers to join in general conversation with each other

chatroom ('tʃæt,ru:m) *n* a site on the Internet, or another computer network, where users have group discussions in real time, typically about one subject

chat show *n Brit* a television or radio show in which guests, esp celebrities, are interviewed informally. US name: **talk show**

Chattanooga (,tʃætᵊ'nu:gə) *n* a city in SE Tennessee, on the Tennessee River: scene of two battles during the Civil War, in which the North defeated the Confederates, cleared Tennessee, and opened the way to Georgia (1863). Pop: 155 554 (2000)

chattel ('tʃætᵊl) *n* 1 (*often pl*) *Property law* 1a **chattel personal** an item of movable personal property, such as furniture, etc 1b **chattel real** an interest in land less than a freehold 2 **goods and chattels** personal property [C13 from OF *chatel* personal property, from Med. L *capitāle* wealth]

chatter ('tʃætə) *vb* 1 to speak (about unimportant matters) rapidly and incessantly 2 (*intr*) (of birds, monkeys, etc) to make rapid repetitive high-pitched noises 3 (*intr*) (of the teeth) to click together rapidly through cold or fear 4 (*intr*) to make rapid intermittent contact with a component, as in machining ▷ *n* 5 idle or foolish talk; gossip 6 the high-pitched repetitive noise made by a bird, monkey, etc 7 the rattling of objects, such as parts of a machine [C13 imit.] > '**chatterer** *n*

chatterati (,tʃætə'rɑti:) *n inf* another word for **chattering classes** [C20 from CHATTER + *-ati* as in LITERATI]

chatterbox ('tʃætə,bɒks) *n inf* a person who talks constantly, esp about trivial matters

chattering classes *n inf, often derog* (usually preceded by *the*) those members of the educated sections of society who enjoy talking about politics, society, culture, etc

Chatterton ('tʃætətən) *n* **Thomas** 1752–70, British poet; author of spurious medieval verse and prose: he committed suicide at the age of 17

chatty ('tʃætɪ) *adj* **chattier, chattiest** 1 full of trivial conversation; talkative 2 informal and friendly; gossipy > '**chattily** *adv* > '**chattiness** *n*

chat up *vb (tr, adv) Brit inf* 1 to talk flirtatiously to (someone) with a view to starting a romantic or sexual relationship 2 to talk persuasively to (a person), esp with an ulterior motive

Chaucer ('tʃɔ:sə) *n* **Geoffrey** ?1340–1400, English poet, noted for his narrative skill, humour, and insight, particularly in his most famous work, *The Canterbury Tales*. He was influenced by the continental tradition of rhyming verse. His other works include *Troilus and Criseyde, The Legende of Good Women*, and *The Parlement of Foules*

chauffeur ('ʃəʊfə, ʃəʊ'fɜ:) *n* 1 a person employed to drive a car ▷ *vb* 2 to act as driver for (a person, etc): *he chauffeured me to the stadium* [C20 from F, lit.: stoker, from *chauffer* to heat] > **chauffeuse** (ʃəʊ'fɜ:z) *fem n*

chaunt (tʃɔ:nt) *n* a less common variant of **chant**

chauvinism ('ʃəʊvɪ,nɪzəm) *n* 1 aggressive or fanatical patriotism; jingoism 2 enthusiastic devotion to a cause 3 smug irrational belief in the superiority of one's own race, party, sex, etc: *male chauvinism* [C19 from F, after Nicolas *Chauvin*, F soldier under Napoleon, noted for his unthinking patriotism] > '**chauvinist** *n, adj* > ,**chauvin'istic** *adj* > ,**chauvin'istically** *adv*

cheap (tʃi:p) *adj* 1 costing relatively little; inexpensive; of good value 2 charging low prices: *a cheap hairdresser* 3 of poor quality; shoddy: *cheap furniture* 4 worth relatively little: *promises are cheap* 5 not worthy of respect; vulgar 6 ashamed; embarrassed: *to feel cheap* 7 stingy; miserly 8 *inf* mean; despicable: *a cheap liar* ▷ *n* 9 **on the cheap** *Brit inf* at a low cost ▷ *adv* 10 at very little cost [OE *ceap* barter, bargain, price, property] > '**cheaply** *adv* > '**cheapness** *n*

cheapen ('tʃi:pᵊn) *vb* 1 to make or become lower in reputation, quality, etc 2 to make or become cheap or cheaper > '**cheapener** *n*

cheap-jack *inf* ▷ *n* 1 a person who sells cheap and shoddy goods ▷ *adj* 2 shoddy or inferior [C19 from CHEAP + JACK]

cheapo ('tʃi:pəʊ) *adj inf* very cheap and possibly shoddy

cheapskate ('tʃi:p,skeɪt) *n inf* a miserly person

cheat (tʃi:t) *vb* 1 to deceive or practise deceit, esp for one's own gain; trick or swindle (someone) 2 (*intr*) to obtain unfair advantage by trickery, as in a game of cards 3 (*tr*) to escape or avoid (something unpleasant) by luck or cunning: *to cheat death* 4 (when *intr*, usually foll by *on*) *inf* to be sexually unfaithful to (one's wife, husband, or lover) ▷ *n* 5 a person who cheats 6 a deliberately dishonest transaction, esp for gain; fraud 7 *inf* sham 8 *law* the obtaining of another's property by fraudulent means [C14 short for ESCHEAT] > '**cheater** *n*

Cheb (*Czech* xɛp) *n* a town in the W Czech Republic, in W Bohemia on the Ohře River: 12th-century castle where Wallenstein was murdered (1634); a centre of the Sudeten-German movement after World War I. Pop: 31 847 (1991). German name: **Eger**

Cheboksary (*Russian* tʃɪbak'sari) *n* a port in W central Russia on the River Volga: capital of the Chuvash Republic. Pop: 458 000 (1999 est)

check (tʃɛk) *vb* 1 to pause or cause to pause, esp abruptly 2 (*tr*) to restrain or control: *to check one's tears* 3 (*tr*) to slow the growth or progress of; retard 4 (*tr*) to rebuke or rebuff 5 (when *intr*, often foll by *on* or *up on*) to examine, investigate, or make an inquiry into (facts, a product, etc) for accuracy, quality, or progress **6** (*tr*) *chiefly US & Canad* to mark off so as to indicate approval, correctness, or preference **7** (*intr; often foll by with*) *chiefly US & Canad* to correspond or agree: *this report checks with the other* **8** (*tr*) *chiefly US, Canad, & NZ* to leave in or accept (property) for temporary custody **9** *chess* to place (an opponent's king) in check **10** (*tr*) to mark with a pattern of squares or crossed lines **11** to crack or cause to crack **12** (*tr*) *ice hockey* to impede (an opponent) **13** (*intr*) *hunting* (of hounds) to pause while relocating a lost scent ▹ *n* **14** a break in progress; stoppage **15** a restraint or rebuff **16** a person or thing that restrains, halts, etc **17** a control, esp a rapid or informal one, to ensure accuracy, progress, etc **18** a means or standard to ensure against fraud or error **19** the US word for **tick**[1] (senses 3, 6) **20** the US spelling of **cheque** **21** *US & Canad* the bill in a restaurant **22** *chiefly US & Canad* a tag used to identify property deposited for custody **23** a pattern of squares or crossed lines **24** a single square in such a pattern **25** fabric with a pattern of squares or crossed lines **26** *chess* the state or position of a king under direct attack **27** a small crack, as one that occurs in timber during drying **28** a chip or counter used in some card and gambling games **29** *hunting* a pause by the hounds owing to loss of the scent **30** *ice hockey* the act of impeding an opponent with one's body or stick **31** **in check** under control or restraint ▹ *sentence substitute* **32** *chess* a call made to an opponent indicating that his or her king is in check **33** *chiefly US & Canad* an expression of agreement ▹ See also **check in, check out, checkup** [C14 from OF *eschec* a check at chess, via Ar. from Persian *shāh* the king] > **'checkable** *adj*

checked (tʃɛkt) *adj* having a pattern of squares

checker[1] ('tʃɛkə) *n, vb* **1** the usual US spelling of **chequer** ▹ *n* **2** *textiles* the US spelling of **chequer** (sense 2) **3** the US and Canad name for **draughtsman** (sense 3)

checker[2] ('tʃɛkə) *n chiefly US* **1** a cashier, esp in a supermarket **2** an attendant in a cloakroom, left-luggage office, etc

checkerboard ('tʃɛkə,bɔ:d) *n* the US and Canad name for a **draughtboard**

checkers ('tʃɛkəz) *n* (*functioning as sing*) the US and Canad name for **draughts**

check in *vb* (*adv*) **1** (*intr*) to record one's arrival, as at a hotel or for work; sign in or report **2** (*tr*) to register the arrival of (passengers, etc) ▹ *n* **check-in** **3** the formal registration of arrival, as at an airport or a hotel **4** the place where one registers arrival at an airport, etc

check list *n* a list of items, names, etc, to be referred to for identification or verification

checkmate ('tʃɛk,meɪt) *n* **1** *chess* **1a** the winning position in which an opponent's king is under attack and unable to escape **1b** the move by which this position is achieved **2** utter defeat ▹ *vb* **checkmates, checkmating, checkmated** (*tr*) **3** *chess* to place (an opponent's king) in checkmate **4** to thwart or render powerless ▹ *sentence substitute* **5** *chess* a call made when placing an opponent's king in checkmate [C14 from OF, from Ar. *shāh māt* the king is dead; see CHECK]

check out *vb* (*adv*) **1** (*intr*) to pay the bill and depart, esp from a hotel **2** (*intr*) to depart from a place; record one's departure from work **3** (*tr*) to investigate or prove to be in order after investigation: *the police checked out all the statements* **4** (*tr*) *inf* to have a look at; inspect ▹ *n* **checkout** **5** the latest time for vacating a room in a hotel, etc **6** a counter, esp in a supermarket, where customers pay

checkpoint ('tʃɛk,pɔɪnt) *n* a place, as at a frontier, where vehicles or travellers are stopped for official identification, inspection, etc

checkup ('tʃɛk,ʌp) *n* **1** an examination to see if something is in order **2** *med* a medical examination, esp one taken at regular intervals ▹ *vb* **check up** **3** (*intr, adv; sometimes foll by on*) to investigate or make an inquiry into (a person's character, evidence, etc)

Cheddar ('tʃɛdə) *n* **1** (*sometimes not cap*) any of several types of smooth hard yellow or whitish cheese **2** a village in SW England, in N Somerset: situated near **Cheddar Gorge**, a pass through the Mendip Hills renowned for its stalactitic caverns and rare limestone flora. Pop: 4484 (1991)

cheek (tʃi:k) *n* **1** either side of the face, esp that part below the eye **2** *inf* impudence; effrontery **3** (*often pl*) *inf* either side of the buttocks **4** (*often pl*) a side of a door jamb **5** one of the jaws of a vice **6** **cheek by jowl** close together; intimately linked **7** **turn the other cheek** to be submissive and refuse to retaliate ▹ *vb* **8** (*tr*) *inf* to speak or behave disrespectfully to [OE *ceace*]

cheekbone ('tʃi:k,bəʊn) *n* the nontechnical name for **zygomatic bone**

cheeky ('tʃi:kɪ) *adj* **cheekier, cheekiest** disrespectful in speech or behaviour; impudent > **'cheekily** *adv* > **'cheekiness** *n*

cheep (tʃi:p) *n* **1** the short weak high-pitched cry of a young bird; chirp ▹ *vb* **2** (*intr*) (of young birds) to utter such sounds > **'cheeper** *n*

cheer (tʃɪə) *vb* **1** (usually foll by *up*) to make or become happy or hopeful; comfort or be comforted **2** to applaud with shouts **3** (when *tr*, sometimes foll by *on*) to encourage (a team, etc) with shouts ▹ *n* **4** a shout or cry of approval, encouragement, etc, often using **hurrah!** **5** **three cheers** three shouts of hurrah given in unison to honour someone or celebrate something **6** happiness; good spirits **7** state of mind; spirits (archaic, except in **be of good cheer, with good cheer**) **8** *arch* provisions for a feast; fare [C13 (in the sense: face, welcoming aspect): from OF *chere*, from LL *cara* face, from Gk *kara* head]

cheerful ('tʃɪəfʊl) *adj* **1** having a happy disposition; in good spirits **2** pleasantly bright: *a cheerful room* **3** ungrudging: *cheerful help* > **'cheerfully** *adv* > **'cheerfulness** *n*

Cc

cheerio (,tʃɪərɪ'əʊ) *inf* ▹ *sentence substitute* *chiefly Brit* **1** a farewell greeting **2** a drinking toast ▹ *n, pl* **cheerios** **3** *NZ* a type of small sausage

cheerleader ('tʃɪə,li:də) *n US & Canad* a person who leads a crowd in cheers, esp at sports events

cheerless ('tʃɪəlɪs) *adj* dreary or gloomy > **'cheerlessly** *adv* > **'cheerlessness** *n*

cheers (tʃɪəz) *sentence substitute inf, chiefly Brit* **1** a drinking toast **2** goodbye! cheerio! **3** thanks!

cheery ('tʃɪərɪ) *adj* **cheerier, cheeriest** showing or inspiring cheerfulness > **'cheerily** *adv* > **'cheeriness** *n*

cheese (tʃi:z) *n* **1** the curd of milk separated from the whey and variously prepared as a food **2** a mass or cake of this substance **3** any of various substances of similar consistency, etc: *lemon cheese* **4** *sl* an important person (esp in **big cheese**) [OE *cēse*, from L *cāseus* cheese]

▹ www.cheeseboard.co.uk
▹ www.cheese.com
▹ www.cheesesociety.org

cheeseburger ('tʃi:z,bɜ:gə) *n* a hamburger cooked with a slice of cheese on top of it

cheesecake ('tʃi:z,keɪk) *n* **1** a rich tart filled with cheese, esp cream cheese, cream, sugar, etc **2** *sl* women displayed for their sex appeal, as in photographs in magazines or films

cheesecloth ('tʃi:z,klɒθ) *n* a loosely woven cotton cloth formerly used for wrapping cheese

cheesed off *adj* (*usually postpositive*) *Brit sl* bored, disgusted, or angry [C20 from ?]

cheeseparing ('tʃi:z,pɛərɪŋ) *adj* **1** penny-pinching ▹ *n* **2a** a paring of cheese rind **2b** anything similarly worthless **3** stinginess

cheesy ('tʃi:zɪ) *adj* **cheesier, cheesiest** **1** like cheese in flavour, smell, or consistency **2** *inf* (of a smile) broad but possibly insincere: *a big cheesy grin* **3** *inf* banal or trite; in poor taste > **'cheesiness** *n*

cheetah *or* **chetah** ('tʃi:tə) *n* a large feline of Africa and SW Asia: the swiftest mammal, having very long legs, and a black-spotted coat [c18 from Hindi *cītā*, from Sansk. *citra* speckled]

Cheever ('tʃi:və) *n* **John** 1912–82, US novelist and short-story writer. His novels include *The Wapshot Chronicle* (1957) and *Bullet Park* (1969)

chef (ʃɛf) *n* a cook, esp the principal cook in a restaurant [c19 from F, from OF *chief* head, CHIEF]
▷ http://chef2chef.net

chef-d'œuvre *French* (ʃɛdœvrə) *n, pl* ***chefs-d'œuvre*** (ʃɛdœvrə). a masterpiece

Chefoo ('tʃi:'fu:) *n* another name for **Yantai**

Che Guevara (tʃeɪ gə'vɑ:rə; *Spanish* tʃe ge'βara) *n* See **Guevara**

Cheiron ('kaɪrɒn, -rən) *n* a variant spelling of **Chiron**

Cheju ('tʃɛ'dʒu:) *n* a volcanic island in the N East China Sea, southwest of Korea: constitutes a province (Cheju-do) of South Korea. Capital: Cheju. Pop: 513 000 (2000). Area: 1792 sq km (692 sq miles). Also called: **Quelpart**

Chekhov *or* **Chekov** ('tʃɛkɒf; *Russian* 'tʃɛxəf) *n* **Anton Pavlovich** (an'tɔn 'pavləvitʃ) 1860–1904, Russian dramatist and short-story writer. His plays include *The Seagull* (1896), *Uncle Vanya* (1900), *The Three Sisters* (1901), and *The Cherry Orchard* (1904)

Chekiang ('tʃɛ'kjæŋ, -kaɪ'æŋ) *n* a variant transliteration of the Chinese name for **Zhejiang**

chela[1] ('ki:lə) *n, pl* **chelae** (-li:) a large pincer-like claw of such arthropods as the crab and scorpion [c17 NL, from Gk *khēlē* claw]

chela[2] ('tʃeɪlə) *n Hinduism* a disciple of a religious teacher [c19 from Hindi *celā*, from Sansk. *ceta* servant, slave]

chelate ('ki:leɪt) *n* **1** *chem* a chemical compound whose molecules contain a closed ring of atoms of which one is a metal atom ▷ *adj* **2** *zool* of or possessing chelae **3** *chem* of a chelate ▷ *vb* **chelates, chelating, chelated 4** (*intr*) *chem* to form a chelate [c20 from CHELA[1]] > **che'lation** *n*

chelicera (kɪ'lɪsərə) *n, pl* **chelicerae** (-ə,ri:) one of a pair of appendages on the head of spiders and other arachnids: often modified as food-catching claws [c19 from NL, from Gk *khēle* claw + *keras* horn]

Chelmsford ('tʃɛlmzfəd) *n* a city in SE England, administrative centre of Essex: electronics, retail; university (1992). Pop: 197 451 (1991)

cheloid ('ki:lɔɪd) *n pathol* a variant spelling of **keloid** > **che'loidal** *adj*

chelonian (kɪ'ləʊnɪən) *n* **1** any reptile of the order *Chelonia*, including the tortoises and turtles, in which most of the body is enclosed in a bony capsule ▷ *adj* **2** of or belonging to the *Chelonia* [c19 from NL, from Gk *khelōnē* tortoise]

Chelsea ('tʃɛlsɪ) *n* a residential district of SW London, in the Royal Borough of Kensington and Chelsea: site of the Chelsea Royal Hospital for old and invalid soldiers (**Chelsea Pensioners**)

Cheltenham ('tʃɛlt[ə]nəm) *n* **1** a town in W England, in central Gloucestershire: famous for its schools, racecourse, and saline springs (discovered in 1716). Pop: 91 301 (1991) **2** a style of type

Chelyabinsk (*Russian* tʃɪ'ljabinsk) *n* an industrial city in SW Russia. Pop: 1 086 300 (1999 est)

Chelyuskin (*Russian* tʃɪ'ljuskin) *n* **Cape** a cape in N central Russia, in N Siberia at the end of the Taimyr Peninsula: the northernmost point of Asia

chem. *abbrev for:* **1** chemical **2** chemist **3** chemistry

chem- *combining form* a variant of **chemo-** before a vowel

chemical ('kɛmɪk[ə]l) *n* **1** any substance used in or resulting from a reaction involving changes to atoms or molecules **2** a compound that has been produced artificially ▷ *adj* **3** of or used in chemistry **4** of, made from, or using chemicals: *chemical fertilizer* > '**chemically** *adv*

chemical engineering *n* the branch of engineering concerned with the design and manufacture of the plant used in industrial chemical processes > **chemical engineer** *n*
▷ www.che.ufl.edu/www-che

chemical warfare *n* warfare using asphyxiating or nerve gases, poisons, defoliants, etc
▷ www.howstuffworks.com/biochem_war.htm

chemiluminescence (,kɛmɪ,lu:mɪ'nɛsəns) *n* the phenomenon in which a chemical reaction leads to the emission of light without incandescence > ,**chemi,lumi'nescent** *adj*

chemin de fer (ʃə'mæn də 'fɛə) *n* a gambling game, a variation of baccarat [F: railway, referring to the fast tempo of the game]

chemise (ʃə'mi:z) *n* **1** an unwaisted loose-fitting dress hanging straight from the shoulders **2** a loose shirtlike undergarment ▷ Also called: **shift** [c14 from OF: shirt, from LL *camisa*]

chemist ('kɛmɪst) *n* **1** *Brit* a shop selling medicines, cosmetics, etc **2** *Brit* a qualified dispenser of prescribed medicines **3** a person studying, trained in, or engaged in chemistry [c16 from earlier *chimist*, from NL, shortened from Med. L *alchimista* ALCHEMIST]

chemistry ('kɛmɪstrɪ) *n, pl* **chemistries 1** the branch of physical science concerned with the composition, properties, and reactions of substances **2** the composition, properties, and reactions of a particular substance **3** the nature and effects of any complex phenomenon: *the chemistry of humour* [c17 from earlier *chimistrie*, from *chimist* CHEMIST]
▷ www.chemweb.com
▷ www.psigate.ac.uk/newsite
▷ http://people.ouc.bc.ca/woodcock/nomenclature/index-2.htm
▷ www.psigate.ac.uk/newsite/reference/periodic-table.html

Chemnitz (*German* 'kɛmnɪts) *n* a city in E Germany, in Saxony, at the foot of the Erzgebirge: textiles, engineering. Pop: 266 000 (1999 est). Also called (1953–90): **Karl-Marx-Stadt**

chemo ('ki:məʊ) *n inf* short for **chemotherapy**

chemo-, chemi-, *or before a vowel* **chem-** *combining form* indicating that chemicals or chemical reactions are involved: *chemotherapy* [NL, from LGk *khēmeia*; see ALCHEMY]

chemoreceptor (,ki:məʊrɪ'sɛptə) *or* **chemoceptor** *n* a sensory receptor in a biological cell membrane to which an external molecule binds to generate a smell or taste sensation

chemosynthesis (,ki:məʊ'sɪnθɪsɪs) *n* the formation of organic material by some bacteria using energy from simple chemical reactions

chemotherapy (,ki:məʊ'θɛrəpɪ) *n* treatment of disease, esp cancer, by means of chemical agents. Cf **radiotherapy** > ,**chemo'therapist** *n*

Chemulpo (,tʃɛmʊl'pəʊ) *n* a former name of **Inchon**

chemurgy ('kɛmɜ:dʒɪ) *n* the branch of chemistry concerned with the industrial use of organic raw materials, esp of agricultural origin > **chem'urgic** *or* **chem'urgical** *adj*

Chenab (tʃɪ'næb) *n* a river rising in the Himalayas and flowing southwest to the Sutlej River in Pakistan. Length: 1087 km (675 miles)

Cheney ('tʃeɪnɪ) *n* **Richard B**(**ruce**), known as *Dick*. born 1941, U.S. Republican politician; vice-president from 2001

Cheng-chiang ('tʃɛŋ'tʃæŋ) *n* a variant transliteration of the Chinese name for **Jinjiang**

Chengchow *or* **Cheng-chou** ('tʃɛŋ'tʃaʊ) *n* a variant transliteration of the Chinese name for **Zhengzhou**

Chengde, Chengteh, *or* **Ch'eng-te** ('tʃɛŋ'teɪ) *n* a city in NE China, in Hebei on the Luan River: summer residence of the Manchu emperors. Pop: 298 895 (1999 est)

Chengdu, Chengtu, *or* **Ch'eng-tu** ('tʃɛŋ'tu:) *n* a city in S central China, capital of Sichuan province. Pop: 2 146 126 (1999 est)

Chénier (*French* ʃenje) *n* **1 André (Marie de)** (ɑ̃dre) 1762–94, French poet; his work was influenced by the ancient Greek elegiac poets. He was guillotined during the French Revolution **2** his brother, **Marie-Joseph (Blaise de)** 1764–1811, French dramatist and politician. He wrote patriotic songs and historical plays, such as *Charles IX* (1789)

chenille (ʃə'ni:l) *n* **1** a thick soft tufty silk or worsted velvet cord or yarn used in embroidery and for trimmings, etc **2** a fabric of such yarn **3** a carpet of such fabric [c18 from F, lit.: hairy caterpillar, from L *canicula*, dim. of *canis* dog]

Chennai (tʃɪ'naɪ) *n* the official name for **Madras**

cheongsam ('tʃɒŋ'sæm) *n* a straight dress with a stand-up collar and a slit in one side of the skirt, worn by Chinese women [from Chinese *ch'ang shan* long jacket]

Cheops ('ki:ɒps) *n* original name *Khufu*. Egyptian king of the fourth dynasty (?2613–?2494 BC), who built the largest pyramid at El Gîza

Chepstow ('tʃɛpstəʊ) *n* a town in S Wales, in Monmouthshire on the River Wye: tourism, light industry. Pop: 9461 (1991)

cheque *or US* **check** (tʃɛk) *n* **1** a bill of exchange drawn on a bank by the holder of a current account **2** *Austral & NZ* the total sum of money received for contract work or a crop **3** *Austral & NZ* wages [c18 from CHECK, in the sense: means of verification]

cheque account *n* an account at a bank or a building society upon which cheques can be drawn

chequebook *or US* **checkbook** ('tʃɛk,bʊk) *n* a book of detachable blank cheques issued by a bank or building society to holders of cheque accounts

chequebook journalism *n* the practice of securing exclusive rights to material for newspaper stories by paying a high price, regardless of any moral implications

cheque card *n* a card issued by a bank or building society, guaranteeing payment of a customer's cheques up to a stated value: may also function as a cash card or debit card or both

chequer *or US* **checker** ('tʃɛkə) *n* **1** any of the marbles, pegs, or other pieces used in the game of Chinese chequers **2a** a pattern of squares **2b** one of the squares in such a pattern ▷ *vb (tr)* **3** to make irregular in colour or character; variegate **4** to mark off with alternating squares of colour ▷ See also **chequers** [c13 chessboard, from Anglo-F *escheker*, from *eschec* CHECK]

chequered *or esp US* **checkered** ('tʃɛkəd) *adj* marked by fluctuations of fortune (esp in **a chequered career**)

chequers ('tʃɛkəz) *n (functioning as sing)* another name for **draughts**

Chequers ('tʃɛkəz) *n* an estate and country house in S England, in central Buckinghamshire: the official country residence of the British prime minister

Cher (*French* ʃɛr) *n* **1** a department of central France, in E Centre region. Capital: Bourges. Pop: 314 428 (1999 est). Area: 7304 sq km (2849 sq miles) **2** a river in central France, rising in the Massif Central and flowing northwest to the Loire. Length: 354 km (220 miles)

Cherbourg ('ʃɛəbʊəg; *French* ʃɛrbur) *n* a port in NW France, on the English Channel. Pop: 28 773 (1990)

Cherenkov *or* **Cerenkov** (tʃɪ'rɛŋkɒf; *Russian* tʃɪ'rjenkəf) *n* **Pavel Alekseyevich** ('pavɪl alɪk'sjejɪvɪtʃ) 1904–90, Soviet physicist: noted for work on the effects produced by high-energy particles: shared Nobel prize for physics 1958

cherish ('tʃɛrɪʃ) *vb (tr)* **1** to feel or show great tenderness or care for **2** to cling fondly to (a hope, idea, etc); nurse: *to cherish ambitions* [c14 from OF, from *cher* dear, from L *cārus*]

Chernenko (tʃɜ:'ŋɛŋkəʊ) *n* **Konstantin (Ustinovich)** (kənstan'tin) 1911–85, Soviet statesman; general secretary of the Soviet Communist Party (1984–85)

Chernobyl (tʃɜ:'nəʊbᵊl, -'nɒbᵊl) *n* a town in the N Ukraine; site of a nuclear power station accident in 1986

Chernovtsy (*Russian* tʃɪrnaf'tsi) *n* a city in the Ukraine on the Prut River: formerly under Polish, Austro-Hungarian, and Romanian rule; part of the Soviet Union (1947–91). Pop: 259 000 (1998 est). German name: **Czernowitz**. Romanian name: **Cernăuţi**

chernozem ('tʃɜ:nəʊ,zɛm) *n* a rich black soil found in temperate semiarid regions, such as the grasslands of Russia [from Russian *chernaya zemlya* black earth]

Cherokee ('tʃɛrə,ki:) *n* **1** (*pl* **Cherokees** *or* **Cherokee**) a member of a North American Indian people formerly living in the Appalachian Mountains **2** the Iroquois language of this people

cheroot (ʃə'ru:t) *n* a cigar with both ends cut off squarely [c17 from Tamil *curuttu* curl, roll]

cherry ('tʃɛrɪ) *n, pl* **cherries** **1** any of several trees of the genus *Prunus*, having a small fleshy rounded fruit containing a hard stone **2** the fruit or wood of any of these trees **3** any of various unrelated plants, such as the ground cherry and Jerusalem cherry **4a** a bright red colour; cerise **4b** *(as adj)*: *a cherry coat* **5** *sl* virginity or the hymen as its symbol [c14 back formation from OE *ciris* (mistakenly thought to be pl), ult. from LL *ceresia*, ?from L *cerasus* cherry tree, from Gk *kerasios*]

cherry tomato *n* a miniature tomato not much bigger than a cherry

chert (tʃɜ:t) *n* an impure black or grey microcrystalline variety of quartz that resembles flint [c17 from ?] > **'cherty** *adj*

Chertsey ('tʃɜ:tsɪ) *n* a town in S England, in N Surrey on the River Thames. Pop: 11 786 (1991)

cherub ('tʃɛrəb) *n, pl* **cherubs** *or (for sense 1)* **cherubim** ('tʃɛrəbɪm, -ʊbɪm) **1** a member of the second order of angels, often represented as a winged child **2** an innocent or sweet child [OE, from Heb. *kĕrūbh*] > **cherubic** (tʃə'ru:bɪk) *or* **che'rubical** *adj* > **che'rubically** *adv*

Cherubini (,kɛrʊ'bi:nɪ) *n* **(Maria) Luigi (Carlo Zenobio Salvatore)** (lu'i:dʒi) 1760–1842, Italian composer, noted particularly for his church music and his operas

chervil ('tʃɜ:vɪl) *n* an aromatic umbelliferous Eurasian plant with small white flowers and aniseed-flavoured leaves used as herbs in soups and salads [OE *cerfelle*, from L, from Gk, from *khairein* to enjoy + *phullon* leaf]

Cherwell ('tʃɑ:wəl) *n* **1 1st Viscount** title of *Frederick Alexander Lindemann* ('lɪndəmən). 1886–1957, British physicist, born in Germany, noted for his research on heat capacity, aeronautics, and atomic physics. He was scientific adviser to Winston Churchill during World War II

Ches. *abbrev for* Cheshire

Chesapeake Bay ('tʃɛsə,pi:k) *n* the largest inlet of the Atlantic in the coast of the US: bordered by Maryland and Virginia

Cheshire[1] ('tʃɛʃə, 'tʃɛʃɪə) *n* a county of NW England: low-lying and undulating, bordering on the Pennines in the east; mainly agricultural: the geographic and ceremonial county includes Warrington and Halton, which became independent unitary authorities in 1998. Administrative centre: Chester. Pop (excluding unitary authorities): 673 777 (2001). Area (excluding unitary authorites): 2077 sq km (802 sq miles). Abbrev: **Ches.**

Cheshire[2] ('tʃɛʃə) *n* Group Captain **(Geoffrey) Leonard** 1917–92, British philanthropist: awarded the Victoria Cross in World War II; founded the Leonard Cheshire Foundation Homes for the Disabled: married Sue, Baroness Ryder

Cc

Cheshire cheese *n* a mild-flavoured cheese with a crumbly texture, originally made in Cheshire

chess (tʃɛs) *n* a game of skill for two players using a chessboard on which chessmen are moved. The object is to checkmate the opponent's king [C13 from OF *esches*, pl. of *eschec* CHECK]
▷ www.fide.com

chessboard ('tʃɛs,bɔːd) *n* a square board divided into 64 squares of two alternating colours, used for playing chess or draughts

chessman ('tʃɛs,mæn, -mən) *n, pl* **chessmen** any of the pieces and pawns used in a game of chess [C17 from *chessmen*, from ME *chessemeyne* chess company]

chest (tʃɛst) *n* **1a** the front part of the trunk from the neck to the belly. Related adj: **pectoral** **1b** (*as modifier*): *a chest cold* **2** **get (something) off one's chest** *inf* to unburden oneself of troubles, worries, etc, by talking about them **3** a box used for storage or shipping: *a tea chest* [OE *cest*, from L, from Gk *kistē* box] > '**chested** *adj*

Chester ('tʃɛstə) *n* a city in NW England, administrative centre of Cheshire, on the River Dee: intact surrounding walls; 16th- and 17th-century double-tier shops. Pop: 80 110 (1991). Latin name: **Deva**

chesterfield ('tʃɛstə,fiːld) *n* **1** a man's overcoat, usually with a velvet collar **2** a large tightly stuffed sofa, with straight upholstered arms of the same height as the back [C19 after a 19th-cent. Earl of *Chesterfield*]

Chesterfield[1] ('tʃɛstə,fiːld) *n* an industrial town in N central England, in Derbyshire: famous 14th-century church with twisted spire. Pop: 71 945 (1991)

Chesterfield[2] ('tʃɛstə,fiːld) *n* **Philip Dormer Stanhope,** 4th Earl of Chesterfield. 1694–1773, English statesman and writer, noted for his elegance, suavity, and wit; author of *Letters to His Son* (1774)

Chesterton ('tʃɛstətᵊn) *n* **G(ilbert) K(eith)** 1874–1936, English essayist, novelist, poet, and critic

chestnut ('tʃɛs,nʌt) *n* **1** a N temperate tree such as the **sweet** or **Spanish chestnut**, which produces flowers in long catkins and nuts in a prickly bur. Cf **horse chestnut** **2** the edible nut of any of these trees **3** the hard wood of any of these trees, used in making furniture, etc **4a** a reddish-brown colour **4b** (*as adj*): *chestnut hair* **5** a horse of a golden-brown colour **6** *inf* an old or stale joke [C16 from earlier *chesten nut: chesten*, from OF, from L, from Gk *kastanea*]

chest of drawers *n* a piece of furniture consisting of a set of drawers in a frame

chesty ('tʃɛstɪ) *adj* **chestier, chestiest** *inf* **1** *Brit* suffering from or symptomatic of chest disease: *a chesty cough* **2** having a large well-developed chest or bosom > '**chestiness** *n*

cheval glass (ʃə'væl) *n* a full-length mirror mounted so as to swivel within a frame [C19 from F *cheval* support (lit.: horse)]

chevalier (ʃɛvə'lɪə) *n* **1** a member of certain orders of merit, such as the French Legion of Honour **2** the lowest title of rank in the old French nobility **3** an archaic word for **knight** **4** a chivalrous man; gallant [C14 from OF, from Med. L *caballārius* horseman, CAVALIER]

Chevalier *n* **1** (ʃɛvə'lɪə) **Albert** 1861–1923, British music hall entertainer, remembered for his cockney songs **2** (ʃɛ'vælɪə; *French* ʃəvalje) **Maurice** (mɔris) 1888–1972, French singer and film actor

Cheviot ('tʃiːvɪət, 'tʃɛv-) *n* **1** a large British breed of sheep reared for its wool **2** (*often not cap*) a rough twill-weave woollen suiting fabric

Cheviot Hills *pl n* a range of hills on the border between England and Scotland, mainly in Northumberland

chèvre ('ʃɛvrə) *n* any cheese made from goats' milk [C20 from F, lit.: goat]

chevron ('ʃɛvrən) *n* **1** *mil* a badge or insignia consisting of one or more V-shaped stripes to indicate a noncommissioned rank or length of service **2** *heraldry* an inverted V-shaped charge on a shield **3** (*usually pl*) a pattern of horizontal black and white V-shapes on a road sign indicating a sharp bend **4** any V-shaped pattern or device [C14 from OF, ult. from L *caper* goat; cf. L *capreoli* pair of rafters (lit.: little goats)]

chevrotain ('ʃɛvrə,teɪn, -tɪn) *n* a small timid ruminant mammal of S and SE Asia. Also called: **mouse deer** [C18 from F, from OF *chevrot* kid, from *chèvre* goat, ult. from L *caper* goat]

chevy ('tʃɛvɪ) *n, vb* a variant spelling of **chivy**

chew (tʃuː) *vb* **1** to work the jaws and teeth in order to grind (food); masticate **2** to bite repeatedly: *she chewed her nails anxiously* **3** (*intr*) to use chewing tobacco **4** **chew the fat** *or* **rag** *sl* **4a** to argue over a point **4b** to talk idly; gossip ▷ *n* **5** the act of chewing **6** something that is chewed [OE *ceowan*] > '**chewable** *adj* > '**chewer** *n*

chewing gum *n* a preparation for chewing, usually made of flavoured and sweetened chicle or such substitutes as polyvinyl acetate

chew over *vb* (*tr, adv*) to consider carefully

chewy ('tʃuːɪ) *adj* **chewier, chewiest** of a consistency requiring chewing

Cheyenne (ʃaɪ'æn, -'ɛn) *n* a city in SE Wyoming, capital of the state. Pop: 50 008 (1990)

chez *French* (ʃe) *prep* **1** at the home of **2** with, among, or in the manner of

Chhattisgarh (,tʃʌtɪs'gɑː) *n* a state of E central India, created from the SE part of Madhya Pradesh, consists of a hilly plateau, with extensive forests; agricultural. Capital: Raipur. Pop.: 20 795 956 (2001). Area 135 194 sq km (52 199 sq miles).

chi[1] (kaɪ) *n* the 22nd letter of the Greek alphabet (Χ, χ)

chi[2] *or* **ch'i** *or* **qi** (tʃiː) *n* (*sometimes cap*) (in Oriental medicine, martial arts, etc) vital energy believed to circulate round the body in currents [Chinese, lit.: energy]

chiack *or* **chyack** ('tʃaɪæk) *Austral inf* ▷ *vb* (*tr*) **1** to tease or banter ▷ *n* **2** good-humoured banter [C19 from *chi-hike*, a shout of greeting]

Chian ('kaɪən) *adj* **1** of or relating to Chios ▷ *n* **2** a native or inhabitant of Chios

Chiang Ch'ing ('tʃæŋ 'tʃɪŋ) *n* a variant transliteration of the Chinese name for **Jiang Qing**

Chiang Ching-kuo ('tʃæŋ tʃɪŋ'kwəʊ) *or* **Jiang Jing Guo** *n* 1910–88, Chinese statesman; the son of Chiang Kai-shek. He was prime minister of Taiwan (1971–78); president (1978–88)

Chiang Kai-shek ('tʃæŋ kaɪ'ʃɛk) *or* **Jiang Jie Shi** *n* original name *Chiang Chung-cheng*, 1887–1975, Chinese general: president of China (1928–31; 1943–49) and of the Republic of China (Taiwan) (1950–75). As chairman of the Kuomintang, he allied with the Communists against the Japanese (1937–45), but in the Civil War that followed was forced to withdraw to Taiwan after his defeat by the Communists (1949)

chianti (kɪ'æntɪ) *n* (*sometimes cap*) a dry red wine produced in Tuscany, Italy

Chiapas (*Spanish* 'tʃjapas) *n* a state of S Mexico: mountainous and forested; Maya ruins in the northeast; rich mineral resources. Capital: Tuxtla Gutiérrez. Pop: 3 920 515 (2000). Area: 73 887 sq km (28 816 sq miles)

chiaroscuro (kɪ,ɑːrə'skʊərəʊ) *n, pl* **chiaroscuros** **1** the artistic distribution of light and dark masses in a picture **2** monochrome painting using light and dark only [C17 from It., from *chiaro* CLEAR + *oscuro* OBSCURE]

chiasma (kaɪ'æzmə) *n, pl* **chiasmas, chiasmata** (-mətə) **1** *cytology* the cross-shaped connection produced by the crossing over of pairing chromosomes during meiosis **2** *anat* the crossing over of two parts or structures [C19 from Gk *khiasma*, from *khi* CHI[1]]

chiasmus (kaɪ'æzməs) *n, pl* **chiasmi** (-maɪ) *rhetoric* reversal of word order in the second of two parallel

phrases: *he came in triumph and in defeat departs* [NL from Gk: see CHIASMA] > **chiastic** (kaɪˈæstɪk) *adj*
Chiba (ˈtʃiːba) *n* an industrial city in central Japan, in SE Honshu on Tokyo Bay. Pop: 856 882 (1995)
chic (ʃiːk, ʃɪk) *adj* **1** (esp of fashionable clothes, women, etc) stylish or elegant ▷ *n* **2** stylishness, esp in dress; modishness; fashionable good taste [c19 from F, from ?] > ˈ**chicly** *adv*
Chicago (ʃɪˈkɑːgəʊ) *n* a port in NE Illinois, on Lake Michigan: the third largest city in the US; it is a major railway and air traffic centre. Pop: 2 896 016 (1996 est)
chicane (ʃɪˈkeɪn) *n* **1** a bridge or whist hand without trumps **2** *motor racing* a short section of sharp narrow bends formed by barriers placed on a motor-racing circuit **3** a less common word for **chicanery** ▷ *vb* **chicanes, chicaning, chicaned 4** (*tr*) to deceive or trick by chicanery **5** (*intr*) to use tricks or chicanery [c17 from F *chicaner* to quibble, from ?] > **chiˈcaner** *n*
chicanery (ʃɪˈkeɪnərɪ) *n, pl* **chicaneries 1** verbal deception or trickery, dishonest or sharp practice **2** a trick, deception, or quibble
chicano (tʃɪˈkɑːnəʊ) *n, pl* **chicanos** *US* an American citizen of Mexican origin [c20 from Sp. *mejicano* Mexican]
Chichagof Island (ˈtʃɪtʃəˌgɔːf) *n* an island of Alaska, in the Alexander Archipelago. Area: 5439 sq km (2100 sq miles)
Chichen Itzá (*Spanish* tʃiˈtʃen itˈsa) *n* a village in Yucatán state in Mexico: site of important Mayan ruins
Chichester[1] (ˈtʃɪtʃɪstə) *n* a city in S England, administrative centre of West Sussex: Roman ruins; 11th-century cathedral; Festival Theatre. Pop: 26 572 (1991)
Chichester[2] (ˈtʃɪtʃɪstə) *n* Sir **Francis** 1901–72, British yachtsman, who sailed alone round the world in *Gipsy Moth IV* (1966–67)
chichi (ˈʃiːʃiː) *adj* **1** affectedly pretty or stylish ▷ *n* **2** the quality of being affectedly pretty or stylish [c20 from F]
Chichihaerh *or* **Ch'i-ch'i-haerh** (ˈtʃiːˌtʃiːˈhɑː) *n* a variant transliteration of the Chinese name for **Qiqihar**
chick (tʃɪk) *n* **1** the young of a bird, esp of a domestic fowl **2** *sl* a girl or young woman, esp an attractive one **3** a young child: used as a term of endearment [c14 short for CHICKEN]
chickadee (ˈtʃɪkəˌdiː) *n* any of various small North American songbirds, typically having grey-and-black plumage [c19 imit.]
chicken (ˈtʃɪkɪn) *n* **1** a domestic fowl bred for its flesh or eggs **2** the flesh of such a bird used for food **3** any of various similar birds, such as a prairie chicken **4** *sl* a cowardly person **5** *sl* a young inexperienced person **6** *inf* any of various, often dangerous, games or challenges in which the object is to make one's opponent lose his nerve **7 count one's chickens before they are hatched** to be over-optimistic in acting on expectations which are not yet fulfilled ▷ *adj* **8** *sl* easily scared; cowardly; timid [OE *ciecen*]
chicken feed *n sl* a trifling amount of money
chicken fillet *n* **1** a fillet cut from a chicken **2** a gel-filled pad inserted under clothing to enlarge the appearance of a woman's breast
chicken-hearted *or* **chicken-livered** *adj* easily frightened; cowardly
chicken out *vb* (*intr, adv*) *inf* to fail to do something through fear or lack of conviction
chickenpox (ˈtʃɪkɪnˌpɒks) *n* a highly communicable viral disease most commonly affecting children, characterized by slight fever and the eruption of a rash
chicken wire *n* wire netting with a hexagonal mesh
chickpea (ˈtʃɪkˌpiː) *n* **1** a bushy leguminous plant, cultivated for its edible pealike seeds **2** the seed of this plant [c16 *ciche peasen*, from *ciche* (from F, from L *cicer* chickpea) + *peasen*; see PEA]
chickweed (ˈtʃɪkˌwiːd) *n* any of various plants of the pink family, esp a common garden weed with small white flowers
Chiclayo (*Spanish* tʃiˈklajo) *n* a city in NW Peru. Pop: 469 200 (1998 est)
chicle (ˈtʃɪkᵊl) *n* a gumlike substance obtained from the sapodilla; the main ingredient of chewing gum [from Sp., from Nahuatl *chictli*]
chicory (ˈtʃɪkərɪ) *n, pl* **chicories 1** a blue-flowered plant, cultivated for its leaves, which are used in salads, and for its roots **2** the root of this plant, roasted, dried, and used as a coffee substitute ▷ Cf **endive** [c15 from OF, from L *cichorium*, from Gk *kikhōrion*]
chide (tʃaɪd) *vb* **chides, chiding, chided** *or* **chid** (tʃɪd); **chided, chid** *or* **chidden** (ˈtʃɪdᵊn) **1** to rebuke or scold **2** (*tr*) to goad into action [OE *cīdan*] > ˈ**chider** *n* > ˈ**chidingly** *adv*
chief (tʃiːf) *n* **1** the head or leader of a group or body of people **2** *heraldry* the upper third of a shield **3 in chief** primarily; especially ▷ *adj* **4** (*prenominal*) **4a** most important; principal **4b** highest in rank or authority ▷ *adv* **5** *arch* principally [c13 from OF, from L *caput* head]
chief executive *n* the person with overall responsibility for the efficient running of a company, organization, etc
chief justice *n* **1** (in any of several Commonwealth countries) the judge presiding over a supreme court **2** (in the US) the presiding judge of a court composed of a number of members ▷ See also **Lord Chief Justice**
chiefly (ˈtʃiːflɪ) *adv* **1** especially or essentially; above all **2** in general; mainly; mostly ▷ *adj* **3** of or relating to a chief or chieftain
Chief of Staff *n* **1** the senior staff officer under the commander of a major military formation or organization **2** the senior officer of each service of the armed forces
chief petty officer *n* the senior naval rank for personnel without commissioned or warrant rank
chieftain (ˈtʃiːftən, -tɪn) *n* the head or leader of a tribe or clan [c14 from OF, from LL *capitāneus* commander; see CAPTAIN] > ˈ**chieftaincy** *or* ˈ**chieftainˌship** *n*
chief technician *n* a noncommissioned officer in the Royal Air Force, junior to a flight sergeant
chiffchaff (ˈtʃɪfˌtʃæf) *n* a common European warbler with a yellowish-brown plumage [c18 imit.]
chiffon (ʃɪˈfɒn, ˈʃɪfɒn) *n* **1** a fine almost transparent fabric of silk, nylon, etc **2** (*often pl*) *now rare* feminine finery ▷ *adj* **3** made of chiffon **4** (of soufflés, pies, cakes, etc) having a very light fluffy texture [c18 from F, from *chiffe* rag]
chiffonier *or* **chiffonnier** (ʃɪfəˈnɪə) *n* **1** a tall, elegant chest of drawers **2** a wide low open-fronted cabinet [c19 from F, from *chiffon* rag]
Chifley (ˈtʃɪflɪ) *n* **Joseph Benedict** 1885–1951, Australian statesman; prime minister of Australia (1945–49)
chigetai (ˌtʃɪgɪˈtaɪ) *n* a variety of the Asiatic wild ass of Mongolia. Also spelled: **dziggetai** [from Mongolian *tchikhitei* long-eared, from *tchikhi* ear]
chigger (ˈtʃɪgə) *n* **1** *US & Canad* the parasitic larva of a mite, which causes intense itching **2** another name for **chigoe**
chignon (ˈʃiːnjɒn) *n* an arrangement of long hair in a roll or knot at the back of the head [c18 from F, from OF *chaignon* link, from *chaine* CHAIN; infl. also by OF *tignon* coil of hair]
chigoe (ˈtʃɪgəʊ) *n* **1** a tropical flea, the female of which burrows into the skin of its host, which includes man **2** another name for **chigger** [c17 from Carib *chigo*]
Chigwell (ˈtʃɪgwəl) *n* a town in S England, in W Essex. Pop: 10 332 (1991)
Chihli (ˈtʃiːliː) *n* **Gulf of** another name for the **Bohai**
Chihuahua (tʃɪˈwɑːwɑː, -wə) *n* **1** a state of N Mexico: mostly high plateau; important mineral resources, with many silver mines. Capital: Chihuahua. Pop:

3 047 867 (2000). Area: 247 087 sq km (153 194 sq miles) **2** a city in N Mexico, capital of Chihuahua state. Pop: 650 000 (2000 est) **3** a breed of tiny dog originally from Mexico, having short smooth hair, large erect ears, and protruding eyes

chilblain ('tʃɪlˌbleɪn) *n (usually pl)* an inflammation of the fingers or toes, caused by exposure to cold [c16 from CHILL (n) + BLAIN] > **'chilˌblained** *adj*

child (tʃaɪld) *n, pl* **children 1a** a boy or girl between birth and puberty **1b** *(as modifier): child labour* **2** a baby or infant **3** an unborn baby **4 with child** an old-fashioned term for **pregnant 5** a human offspring; a son or daughter. Related adj: **filial 6** a childish or immature person **7** a member of a family or tribe; descendant: *a child of Israel* **8** a person or thing regarded as the product of an influence or environment: *a child of nature* [OE *cild*] > **'childless** *adj* > **'childlessness** *n*

child abuse *n* physical, sexual, or emotional ill-treatment of a child by its parents or other adults responsible for its welfare

child-bearing *n* **a** the act or process of carrying and giving birth to a child **b** *(as modifier): of child-bearing age*

childbed ('tʃaɪldˌbɛd) *n* (often preceded by *in*) the condition of giving birth to a child

child benefit *n* (in Britain and New Zealand) a regular government payment to parents of children up to a certain age

childbirth ('tʃaɪldˌbɜːθ) *n* the act of giving birth to a child

childcare ('tʃaɪldˌkɛə) *n Brit* **1** care provided for children without homes (or with a seriously disturbed home life) by a local authority **2** care and supervision of children whose parents are working, provided by a childminder or local authority

child endowment *n* (in Australia) a social security payment for dependent children

Childers ('tʃɪldəz) *n* (**Robert**) **Erskine** 1870–1922, Irish politician, executed by the Irish Free State for his IRA activities: author of the spy story *The Riddle of the Sands* (1903)

childhood ('tʃaɪldhʊd) *n* the condition of being a child; the period of life before puberty

childish ('tʃaɪldɪʃ) *adj* **1** in the manner of or suitable to a child **2** foolish or petty: *childish fears* > **'childishly** *adv* > **'childishness** *n*

childlike ('tʃaɪldˌlaɪk) *adj* like or befitting a child, as in being innocent, trustful, etc

childminder ('tʃaɪldˌmaɪndə) *n* a person who looks after children, esp those whose parents are working

children ('tʃɪldrən) *n* the plural of **child**

Children of Israel *pl n* the Jewish people or nation

child-resistant *adj* (of packaging etc, esp of drugs) designed to be difficult for children to open or tamper with. Also: **child-proof**

child's play *n inf* something easy to do

chile ('tʃɪlɪ) *n* a variant spelling of **chilli**

Chile ('tʃɪlɪ) *n* a republic in South America, on the Pacific, with a total length of about 4090 km (2650 miles) and an average width of only 177 km (110 miles): gained independence from Spain in 1818; the government of President Allende (elected 1970) attempted the implementation of Marxist policies within a democratic system until overthrown by a military coup (1973); democracy restored 1988. Chile consists chiefly of the Andes in the east, the Atacama Desert in the north, a central fertile region, and a huge S region of almost uninhabitable mountains, glaciers, fjords, and islands; an important producer of copper, iron ore, nitrates, etc Language: Spanish. Religion: Roman Catholic majority. Currency: peso. Capital: Santiago. Pop: 15 402 000 (2001 est). Area: 756 945 sq km (292 256 sq miles)
▷ www.gov.cl
▷ www.sernatur.cl

Chilean ('tʃɪlɪən) *adj* **1** of or relating to Chile or its inhabitants ▷ *n* **2** a native or inhabitant of Chile

Chile pine *n* another name for the **monkey puzzle**

Chile saltpetre *or* **nitre** *n* a naturally occurring form of sodium nitrate

chiliad ('kɪlɪˌæd) *n* **1** a group of one thousand **2** one thousand years [c16 from Gk, from *khilioi* a thousand]

chill (tʃɪl) *n* **1** a moderate coldness **2** a sensation of coldness resulting from a cold or damp environment, or from a sudden emotional reaction **3** a feverish cold **4** a check on enthusiasm or joy. ▷ *adj* **5** another word for **chilly** ▷ *vb* **6** to make or become cold **7** *(tr)* to cool or freeze (food, drinks, etc) **8** *(tr)* **8a** to depress (enthusiasm, etc) **8b** to discourage **9** *(intr) sl, chiefly US* to relax; calm oneself ▷ See also **chill out** [OE *ciele*] > **'chilling** *adj* > **'chillingly** *adv* > **'chillness** *n*

chilled (tʃɪld) *adj* **1** (of a person) feeling cold **2** (of food or drink) kept cool **3** *inf* Also: **chilled-out** relaxed or easy-going in character or behaviour

chiller ('tʃɪlə) *n* **1** short for **spine-chiller 2** *NZ* a refrigerated storage area for meat

chilli *or* **chili** ('tʃɪlɪ) *n, pl* **chillies** *or* **chilies** the small red hot-tasting pod of a type of capsicum used for flavouring sauces, etc [c17 from Sp., from Nahuatl *chilli*]
▷ www.iisr.org/spices/chilli.htm
▷ www.spicesvalley.com/spices/chilli.asp

chilli con carne ('tʃɪlɪ kɒn 'kɑːnɪ) *n* a highly seasoned Mexican dish of meat, onions, beans, and chilli powder [from Sp.: chilli with meat]

chilli dog *n US* a frankfurter garnished with chilli con carne, served in a roll

chilli powder *n* ground chilli blended with other spices, used in cooking

chilli sauce *n* a highly seasoned sauce made of tomatoes cooked with chilli and other spices

chill out *inf* ▷ *vb* **1** *(intr, adv)* to relax, esp after energetic dancing at a rave ▷ *adj* **chill-out 2** suitable for relaxation after energetic dancing: *a chill-out area; chill-out music*

chilly ('tʃɪlɪ) *adj* **chillier, chilliest 1** causing or feeling cool or moderately cold **2** without warmth; unfriendly **3** (of people) sensitive to cold > **'chilliness** *n*

chilly bin *n NZ inf* a portable insulated container with provision for packing food and drink in ice

Chiloé Island (ˌtʃɪləʊ'eɪ) *n* an island administered by Chile, off the W coast of South America in the Pacific Ocean: timber. Pop: 116 000 (latest est). Area: 8394 sq km (3240 sq miles)

Chilpancingo (*Spanish* tʃilpan'θiŋgo) *n* a town in S Mexico, capital of Guerrero state, in the Sierra Madre del Sur. Pop: 140 000 (2000 est)

Chiltern Hills ('tʃɪltən) *pl n* a range of low chalk hills in SE England extending northwards from the Thames valley. Highest point: 260 m (852 ft)

Chiltern Hundreds ('tʃɪltən) *pl n* (in Britain) short for **Stewardship of the Chiltern Hundreds;** a nominal office that an MP applies for in order to resign his seat

Chilung *or* **Chi-lung** ('tʃiː'lʊŋ) *n* a port in N Taiwan: fishing and industrial centre. Pop: 385 201 (2000 est). Also called: **Keelung, Kilung**

Chimborazo (ˌtʃɪmbə'rɑːzəʊ, -'reɪ-; *Spanish* tʃimbo'raθo) *n* an extinct volcano in central Ecuador, in the Andes: the highest peak in Ecuador. Height: 6267 m (20 561 ft)

Chimbote (*Spanish* tʃim'bote) *n* a port in N central Peru: contains Peru's first steelworks (1958), using hydroelectric power from the Santa River. Pop: 298 800 (1998 est)

chime¹ (tʃaɪm) *n* **1** an individual bell or the sound it makes when struck **2** *(often pl)* the machinery employed to sound a bell in this way **3** Also called: **bell** a percussion instrument consisting of a set of vertical metal tubes of graduated length, suspended in a frame and struck with a hammer **4** agreement; concord ▷ *vb* **chimes, chiming, chimed 5a** to sound (a bell) or (of a bell) to be sounded by a clapper or hammer **5b** to produce (music or sounds) by chiming **6** *(tr)* to indicate or show (time or the hours) by chiming **7** *(intr; foll by with)* to agree or harmonize [c13 prob. shortened from earlier *chymbe bell*, ult. from L *cymbalum* CYMBAL] > **'chimer** *n*

chime², **chimb** (tʃaɪm), *or* **chine** *n* the projecting rim of a cask or barrel [OE *cimb-*]

chime in *vb (intr, adv) inf* **1** to join in or interrupt (a conversation), esp repeatedly and unwelcomely **2** to voice agreement

chimera *or* **chimaera** (kaɪ'mɪərə, kɪ-) *n* **1** a wild and unrealistic dream or notion **2** *(often cap) Greek myth* a fire-breathing monster with the head of a lion, body of a goat, and tail of a serpent **3** a fabulous beast made up of parts taken from various animals **4** *biol* an organism consisting of at least two genetically different kinds of tissue as a result of mutation, grafting, etc [c16 from L, from Gk *khimaira* she-goat]

chimerical (kaɪ'mɛrɪkᵊl, kɪ-) *or* **chimeric** *adj* **1** wildly fanciful; imaginary **2** given to or indulging in fantasies > **chi'merically** *adv*

Chimkent (tʃɪm'kɛnt) *n* a city in S Kazakhstan; a major railway junction. Pop: 360 100 (1999 est)

chimney ('tʃɪmnɪ) *n* **1** a vertical structure of brick, masonry, or steel that carries smoke or steam away from a fire, engine, etc **2** another name for **flue** (sense 1) **3** short for **chimney stack** **4** an open-ended glass tube fitting around the flame of an oil or gas lamp in order to exclude draughts **5** *Brit* a fireplace, esp an old and large one **6** the vent of a volcano **7** *mountaineering* a vertical fissure large enough for a person's body to enter [c14 from OF *cheminée*, from LL *camīnāta*, from L *camīnus* furnace, from Gk *kaminos* oven]

chimney breast *n* the wall or walls that surround the base of a chimney or fireplace

chimneypot ('tʃɪmnɪˌpɒt) *n* a short pipe on the top of a chimney

chimney stack *n* the part of a chimney that rises above the roof of a building

chimney sweep *or* **sweeper** *n* a person who cleans soot from chimneys

chimp (tʃɪmp) *n inf* short for **chimpanzee**

chimpanzee (ˌtʃɪmpæn'ziː) *n* a gregarious and intelligent anthropoid ape, inhabiting forests in central W Africa [c18 from Central African dialect]

chin (tʃɪn) *n* **1** the protruding part of the lower jaw **2** the front part of the face below the lips **3** **keep one's chin up** *inf* to keep cheerful under difficult circumstances **4** **take it on the chin** *inf* to face squarely up to a defeat, adversity, etc ▷ *vb* **chins, chinning, chinned** **5** *gymnastics* to raise one's chin to (a horizontal bar, etc) when hanging by the arms [OE *cinn*]

Chin. *abbrev for:* **1** China **2** Chinese

china¹ ('tʃaɪnə) *n* **1** ceramic ware of a type originally from China **2** any porcelain or similar ware **3** cups, saucers, etc, collectively **4** *(modifier)* made of china [c16 *chiny*, from Persian *chīnī*]
▷ http://entertainment.howstuffworks.com/lenox.htm
▷ www.pbs.org/wgbh/pages/roadshow/speak/china.html
▷ www.netcentral.co.uk/steveb/types/bonechina.htm

china² ('tʃaɪnə) *n Brit & S African inf* a friend or companion [c19 orig. Cockney rhyming sl: *china plate, mate*]

China ('tʃaɪnə) *n* **1** **People's Republic of** Also called: **Communist China, Red China** a republic in E Asia: the third largest and the most populous country in the world; the oldest continuing civilization (beginning over 2000 years BC); republic established in 1911 after the overthrow of the Manchu dynasty by Sun Yat-sen; People's Republic formed in 1949; the 1980s and 1990s saw economic liberalization but a rejection of political reform; contains vast deserts, steppes, great mountain ranges (Himalayas, Kunlun, Tian Shan, and Nan Shan), a central rugged plateau, and intensively cultivated E plains. Language: Chinese in various dialects, the chief of which is Mandarin. Religion: nonreligious majority; Buddhist and Taoist minorities. Currency: yuan. Capital: Beijing. Pop: 1 274 915 000 (2001 est). Area: 9 560 990 sq km (3 691 502 sq miles) **2** **Republic of** Also called: **Nationalist China, Taiwan** a republic (recognized as independent by less than 40 nations) in E Asia occupying the island of Taiwan, 13 nearby islands, and 64 islands of the Penghu (Pescadores) group: established in 1949 by the Nationalist government of China under Chiang Kai-shek after its expulsion by the Communists from the mainland; under US protection 1954–79; lost its seat at the U.N. to the People's Republic of China in 1971; state of war with the People's Republic of China formally ended in 1991. Language: Mandarin Chinese. Religion: nonreligious majority, Buddhist and Taoist minorities. Currency: New Taiwan dollar. Capital: Taipei. Pop: 22 340 000 (2001). Area: 35 981 sq km (13 892 sq miles). Former name: **Formosa** ▷ Related adj: **Sinitic**
▷ www.china.org.cn/english
▷ www.cnto.org.au

CHINESE ANIMAL YEARS

CHINESE	ENGLISH	YEARS
Shu	Rat	1960, 1972, 1984, 1996, 2008
Niu	Ox	1961, 1973, 1985, 1997, 2009
Hu	Tiger	1962, 1974, 1986, 1998, 2010
Tu	Hare	1963, 1975, 1987, 1999, 2011
Long	Dragon	1964, 1976, 1988, 2000, 2012
She	Serpent	1965, 1977, 1989, 2001, 2013
Ma	Horse	1966, 1978, 1990, 2002, 2014
Yang	Sheep	1967, 1979, 1991, 2003, 2015
Hou	Monkey	1968, 1980, 1992, 2004, 2016
Ji	Cock	1969, 1981, 1993, 2005, 2017
Gou	Dog	1970, 1982, 1994, 2006, 2018
Zhu	Boar	1971, 1983, 1995, 2007, 2019

china clay *n* another name for **kaolin**

Chinagraph ('tʃaɪnəˌgrɑːf) *n trademark* a coloured pencil used for writing on china, glass, etc

Chinaman ('tʃaɪnəmən) *n, pl* **Chinamen** **1** *arch or derog* a native or inhabitant of China **2** *(often not cap) Cricket.* a ball bowled by a left-handed bowler to a right-handed batsman that spins from off to leg

Chinan *or* **Chi-nan** ('tʃiː'næn) *n* a variant transliteration of the Chinese name for **Jinan**

China Sea *n* part of the Pacific Ocean off the coast of China: divided by Taiwan into the East China Sea in the north and the South China Sea in the south

china stone *n* **1** a type of kaolinized granitic rock containing unaltered plagioclase **2** any of certain limestones having a very fine grain and smooth texture

Chinatown ('tʃaɪnəˌtaʊn) *n* a quarter of any city or town outside China with a predominantly Chinese population

chinaware ('tʃaɪnəˌwɛə) *n* articles made of china, esp those made for domestic use

chincherinchee (ˌtʃɪntʃərɪn'tʃiː, -'rɪntʃɪ) *n* a bulbous South African liliaceous plant having long spikes of white or yellow long-lasting flowers [from ?]

chinchilla (tʃɪn'tʃɪlə) *n* **1** a small gregarious rodent inhabiting mountainous regions of South America. It is bred in captivity for its soft silvery grey fur **2** the highly valued fur of this animal **3** a thick napped woollen

cloth used for coats [c17 from Sp., ?from Aymara]
chin-chin *sentence substitute inf* a greeting or toast [c18 from Chinese (Peking) *ch'ing-ch'ing*, please-please]
Chin-Chou *or* **Chin-chow** ('tʃɪn'tʃaʊ) *n* a variant transliteration of the Chinese name for **Jinzhou**
Chindit ('tʃɪndɪt) *n* a member of the Allied forces fighting behind the Japanese lines in Burma (1943–45) [c20 from Burmese *chinthé* a fabulous lion]
Chindwin ('tʃɪn'dwɪn) *n* a river in N Myanmar, rising in the Kumôn Range and flowing northwest then south to the Irrawaddy, of which it is the main tributary. Length: about 966 km (600 miles)
chine[1] (tʃaɪn) *n* **1** the backbone **2** the backbone of an animal with adjoining meat, cut for cooking **3** a ridge or crest of land ▷ *vb* **chines, chining, chined** **4** (*tr*) to cut (meat) along or across the backbone [c14 from OF *eschine*, of Gmc origin; see SHIN]
chine[2] (tʃaɪn) *n S English dialect* a deep fissure in the wall of a cliff [OE *cīnan* to crack]
Chinese (tʃaɪ'ni:z) *adj* **1** of, relating to, or characteristic of China, its people, or their languages ▷ *n* **2** (*pl* **Chinese**) a native or inhabitant of China or a descendant of one **3** any of the languages of China
Chinese cabbage *n* **1** a Chinese plant that is related to the cabbage and has crisp edible leaves growing in a loose cylindrical head **2** another name for **bok choy**
Chinese chequers *n* (*functioning as sing*) a board game played with marbles or pegs
Chinese Empire *n* China as ruled by the emperors until the establishment of the republic in 1911–12
▷ www.wsu.edu/~dee/CHEMPIRE/CHEMPIRE.HTM
▷ http://ancienthistory.about.com/library/bl/bl_maps_chineseempire_index.htm
Chinese gooseberry *n* another name for **kiwi fruit**
Chinese lantern *n* **1** a collapsible lantern made of thin coloured paper **2** an Asian plant, cultivated for its attractive orange-red inflated calyx
Chinese leaf *n* another name for **bok choy**
Chinese puzzle *n* **1** an intricate puzzle, esp one consisting of boxes within boxes **2** a complicated problem
Chinese Turkestan *n* the E part of the central Asian region of Turkestan: corresponds generally to the present-day Xinjiang Uygur Autonomous Region of China
Chinese wall *n* (esp in financial institutions) a notional barrier between departments in the same company in order to avoid conflicts of interest between them
Chinghai *or* **Ch'ing-hai** ('tʃɪŋ'haɪ) *n* a variant transliteration of the Chinese name for **Qinghai**
Chingtao *or* **Ch'ing-tao** ('tʃɪŋ'taʊ) *n* a variant transliteration of the Chinese name for **Qingdao**
Ch'ing-yüan ('tʃɪŋ'ju:ɑ:n) *n* a former name of **Baoding**
Chin-Hsien ('tʃɪn'ʃjɛn) *n* the former name (1913–47) of **Jinzhou**
chink[1] (tʃɪŋk) *n* **1** a small narrow opening, such as a fissure or crack **2** **chink in one's armour** a small but fatal weakness [c16 ? var. of earlier *chine*, from OE *cine* crack; rel. to MDu. *kene*]
chink[2] (tʃɪŋk) *vb* **1** to make or cause to make a light ringing sound, as by the striking of glasses or coins ▷ *n* **2** such a sound [c16 imit.]
Chinkiang ('tʃɪn'kjæŋ, -kaɪ'æŋ) *n* a variant transliteration of the Chinese name for **Jinjiang**
chinless wonder ('tʃɪnlɪs) *n Brit inf* a person, esp upper-class, lacking strength of character
chinoiserie (ʃi:n,wɑ:zə'ri:, -'wɑ:zərɪ) *n* **1** a style of decorative or fine art based on imitations of Chinese motifs **2** an object or objects in this style [F, from *chinois* CHINESE; see -ERY]
chinook (tʃɪ'nu:k, -'nʊk) *n* **1** a warm dry southwesterly wind blowing down the eastern slopes of the Rocky Mountains **2** a warm moist wind blowing onto the Washington and Oregon coasts from the sea [c19 from Amerind]
Chinook (tʃɪ'nu:k, -'nʊk) *n* **1** (*pl* **Chinook** *or* **Chinooks**) a North American Indian people of the Pacific coast near the Columbia River **2** the language of this people
Chinook Jargon *n* a pidgin language containing elements of North American Indian languages, English, and French: formerly used among fur traders and Indians on the NW coast of North America
Chinook salmon *n* a Pacific salmon valued as a food fish
chinos ('tʃi:nəʊz) *pl n* trousers made of a durable cotton twill cloth [c20 from *chino*, the cloth, from ?]
chintz (tʃɪnts) *n* a printed, patterned cotton fabric, with glazed finish [c17 from Hindi *chīnt*, from Sansk. *citra* gaily-coloured]
chintzy ('tʃɪntsɪ) *adj* **chintzier, chintziest** **1** of, resembling, or covered with chintz **2** *Brit inf* typical of the décor associated with the use of chintz soft furnishings
chinwag ('tʃɪn,wæg) *n Brit inf* a chat
Chios ('kaɪɒs, -əʊs, 'ki:-) *n* **1** an island in the Aegean Sea, off the coast of Turkey: belongs to Greece. Capital: Chios. Pop: 52 184 (1991). Area: 904 sq km (353 sq miles) **2** a port on the island of Chios: in ancient times, one of the 12 Ionian city-states. Pop: 54 000 (1995 est). Modern Greek name: **Khíos**
chip (tʃɪp) *n* **1** a small piece removed by chopping, cutting, or breaking **2** a mark left after a small piece has been broken off something **3** (in some games) a counter used to represent money **4** a thin strip of potato fried in deep fat **5** the US, Canad, Austral, and NZ name for **crisp** (sense 10) **6** *sport* a shot, kick, etc, lofted into the air, and travelling only a short distance **7** *electronics* Also called: **microchip** a tiny wafer of semiconductor material, such as silicon, processed to form a type of integrated circuit or component such as a transistor **8** a thin strip of wood or straw used for making woven hats, baskets, etc **9** NZ a container for soft fruit, made of thin sheets of wood; punnet **10** **chip off the old block** *inf* a person who resembles one of his or her parents in behaviour **11** **have a chip on one's shoulder** *inf* to be aggressive or bear a grudge **12** **have had one's chips** *Brit inf* to be defeated, condemned to die, killed, etc **13** **when the chips are down** *inf* at a time of crisis ▷ *vb* **chips, chipping, chipped** **14** to break small pieces from or become broken off in small pieces: *will the paint chip?* **15** (*tr*) to break or cut into small pieces: *to chip ice* **16** (*tr*) to shape by chipping **17** *Austral* to dig or weed (a crop) with a hoe **18** *sport* to strike or kick (a ball) in a high arc [OE *cipp* (n), *cippian* (vb), from ?]
chip-based *adj* using or incorporating microchips in electronic equipment
chipboard ('tʃɪp,bɔ:d) *n* a thin rigid sheet made of compressed wood chips
chip heater *n Austral & NZ* a domestic water heater that burns chips of wood
chip in *vb* (*adv*) *inf* **1** to contribute (money, time, etc) to a cause or fund **2** (*intr*) to interpose a remark or interrupt with a remark
chipmunk ('tʃɪp,mʌŋk) *n* a burrowing rodent of North America and Asia, typically having black-striped yellowish fur and cheek pouches for storing food [c19 of Algonquian origin]
chipolata (,tʃɪpə'lɑ:tə) *n chiefly Brit* a small sausage [via F from It., from *cipolla* onion]
Chippendale ('tʃɪpᵊn,deɪl) *n* **1** **Thomas** ?1718–79, English cabinet-maker and furniture designer ▷ *adj* **2** (of furniture) designed by, made by, or in the style of Thomas Chippendale, characterized by the use of Chinese and Gothic motifs, cabriole legs, and massive carving
▷ www.britainexpress.com/History/bio
chipper ('tʃɪpə) *adj inf* **1** cheerful **2** smartly dressed

chippy[1] ('tʃɪpɪ) *n, pl* **chippies** 1 *Brit inf* a fish-and-chip shop 2 *Brit and NZ* a slang word for **carpenter** 3 Also: **chippie** *NZ* a potato crisp

chippy[2] ('tʃɪpɪ) *adj* **chippier, chippiest** *inf* resentful or oversensitive about being perceived as inferior: *a chippy miner's son* [c20 from CHIP (sense 11)] > '**chippiness** *n*

chipset ('tʃɪpsɛt) *n* 1 a highly integrated circuit on the motherboard of a computer that controls many of its data transfer functions 2 *computing* the main processing circuitry on many video cards

chip shot *n golf* a short approach shot to the green, esp one that is lofted

chip wagon *n Canad* a small van in which chips are cooked and sold

Chirac (*French* ʃirak) *n* **Jacques (René)** (ʒɑk) born 1932, French Gaullist politician: president of France from 1995; prime minister (1974–76 and 1986–88); mayor of Paris (1977–95)

chiral ('kaɪrəl) *adj* relating to chirality [c20 from CHIRO- + -AL[1]]

chirality (kaɪ'rælɪtɪ) *n* right- or left-handedness in an asymmetric molecule

Chirico (*Italian* 'ki:riko) *n* **Giorgio de** ('dʒordʒo de) 1888–1978, Italian artist born in Greece: profoundly influenced the surrealist movement

chiro- *or* **cheiro-** *combining form* of or by means of the hand: *chiromancy; chiropractic* [via L from Gk *kheir* hand]

chirography (kaɪ'rɒgrəfɪ) *n* another name for **calligraphy** > **chi'rographer** *n* > **chirographic** (,kaɪrə'græfɪk) *or* ,**chiro'graphical** *adj*

chiromancy ('kaɪrə,mænsɪ) *n* another word for **palmistry** > '**chiro,mancer** *n*

Chiron *or* **Cheiron** ('kaɪrɒn, -rən) *n* 1 *Greek myth* a wise and kind centaur who taught many great heroes in their youth, including Achilles, Actaeon, and Jason 2 a minor planet, discovered by Charles Kowal in 1977, revolving round the sun between the orbits of Saturn and Uranus

chiropody (kɪ'rɒpədɪ) *n* the treatment of the feet, esp corns, verrucas, etc > **chi'ropodist** *n*

chiropractic (,kaɪrə'præktɪk) *n* a system of treating bodily disorders by manipulation of the spine and other parts [c20 from CHIRO- + Gk *praktikos* PRACTICAL] > '**chiro,practor** *n*

chirp (tʃɜ:p) *vb (intr)* 1 (esp of some birds and insects) to make a short high-pitched sound 2 to speak in a lively fashion ▷ *n* 3 a chirping sound [c15 (as *chirpinge*, gerund): imit.] > '**chirper** *n*

chirpy ('tʃɜ:pɪ) *adj* **chirpier, chirpiest** *inf* cheerful; lively > '**chirpily** *adv* > '**chirpiness** *n*

chirr *or* **churr** (tʃɜ:) *vb* 1 *(intr)* (esp of certain insects, such as crickets) to make a shrill trilled sound ▷ *n* 2 such a sound [c17 imit.]

chirrup ('tʃɪrəp) *vb (intr)* 1 (esp of some birds) to chirp repeatedly 2 to make clucking sounds with the lips ▷ *n* 3 such a sound [c16 var. of CHIRP] > '**chirruper** *n* > '**chirrupy** *adj*

chisel ('tʃɪzᵊl) *n* 1a a hand tool for working wood, consisting of a flat steel blade with a handle 1b a similar tool without a handle for working stone or metal ▷ *vb* **chisels, chiselling, chiselled** *or US* **chisels, chiseling, chiseled** 2 to carve (wood, stone, metal, etc) or form (an engraving, statue, etc) with or as with a chisel 3 *sl* to cheat or obtain by cheating [c14 via OF, from Vulgar L *cīsellus* (unattested), from L *caesus* cut]

chiseller ('tʃɪzᵊlə) *n* 1 a person who uses a chisel 2 *inf* a cheat 3 *Dublin sl* a child

Chishima (,tʃi:ʃi:'ma) *n* the Japanese name for the **Kuril Islands**

Chisimaio (,ki:zɪ'mɑ:jəʊ) *n* a port in S Somalia, on the Indian Ocean. Pop: 200 000 (latest est). Also called: **Kismayu**

Chişinău (kiʃi'nəu) *n* the Romanian name for **Kishinev**

chi-square distribution *n statistics* a continuous single-parameter distribution used esp to measure goodness of fit and to test hypotheses

chi-square test *n statistics* a test derived from the chi-square distribution to compare the goodness of fit of theoretical and observed frequency distributions

chit[1] (tʃɪt) *n* 1 a voucher for a sum of money owed, esp for food or drink 2 Also called: **chitty** *chiefly Brit* 2a a note or memorandum 2b a requisition or receipt [c18 from earlier *chitty*, from Hindi *cittha* note, from Sansk. *citra* marked]

chit[2] (tʃɪt) *n facetious or derog* a pert, impudent, or self-confident girl or child [c14 (in the sense: young of an animal, kitten): from ?]

Chita (*Russian* tʃi'ta) *n* an industrial city in SE Russia, on the Trans-Siberian railway. Pop: 314 300 (1995 est)

chital ('tʃi:tᵊl) *n* another name for **axis**[2] (the deer) [from Hindi]

chitchat ('tʃɪt,tʃæt) *n* 1 gossip ▷ *vb* **chitchats, chitchatting, chitchatted** 2 *(intr)* to gossip

chitin ('kaɪtɪn) *n* a polysaccharide that is the principal component of the exoskeletons of arthropods and of the bodies of fungi [c19 from F, from Gk *khitōn* CHITON + -IN] > '**chitinous** *adj*

chiton ('kaɪtᵊn, -tɒn) *n* 1 (in ancient Greece) a loose woollen tunic worn by men and women 2 any small primitive marine mollusc having an elongated body covered with eight overlapping shell plates [c19 from Gk *khitōn* coat of mail]

Chittagong ('tʃɪtə,gɒŋ) *n* a port in E Bangladesh, on the Bay of Bengal: industrial centre. Pop: 1 599 000 (1991)

chitterlings ('tʃɪtəlɪŋz) *or* **chitlings** ('tʃɪtlɪŋz) *pl n* *(sometimes sing)* the intestines of a pig or other animal prepared as a dish [c13 from ?]

chiv (tʃɪv, ʃɪv) *or* **shiv** (ʃɪv) *Sl* ▷ *n* 1 a knife ▷ *vb* **chivs, chivving, chivved** *or* **shivs, shivving, shivved** 2 to stab (someone) [c17 ?from Romany *chiv* blade]

chivalrous ('ʃɪvəlrəs) *adj* 1 gallant; courteous 2 involving chivalry [c14 from OF, from CHEVALIER] > '**chivalrously** *adv* > '**chivalrousness** *n*

chivalry ('ʃɪvəlrɪ) *n, pl* **chivalries** 1 the combination of qualities expected of an ideal knight, esp courage, honour, justice, and a readiness to help the weak 2 courteous behaviour, esp towards women 3 the medieval system and principles of knighthood 4 knights, noblemen, etc, collectively [c13 from OF *chevalerie*, from CHEVALIER] > '**chivalric** *adj*

chive (tʃaɪv) *n* a small Eurasian purple-flowered alliaceous plant, whose long slender hollow leaves are used in cooking. Also called: **chives** [c14 from OF *cive*, ult. from L *caepa* onion]

chivy, chivvy ('tʃɪvɪ), *or* **chevy** *Brit* ▷ *vb* **chivies, chivying, chivied, chivvies, chivvying, chivvied,** *or* **chevies, chevying, chevied** 1 *(tr)* to harass or nag 2 *(tr)* to hunt 3 *(intr)* to run about ▷ *n, pl* **chivies, chivvies,** *or* **chevies** 4 a hunt 5 *obs* a hunting cry [c19 var. of *chevy*, prob. from *Chevy Chase*, title of a Scottish border ballad]

Chkalov (*Russian* 'tʃkaləf) *n* the former name (1938–57) of **Orenburg**

chlamydia (klə'mɪdɪə) *n* any of a genus of parasitic Gram-negative bacteria responsible for such diseases as trachoma, psittacosis, and some sexually transmitted diseases [c20 NL, from Gk *khlamus* mantle + -IA]

chloral ('klɔ:rəl) *n* 1 a colourless oily liquid with a pungent odour, made from chlorine and acetaldehyde and used in preparing chloral hydrate and DDT. Formula: CCl_3CHO 2 short for **chloral hydrate**

chloral hydrate *n* a colourless crystalline soluble solid produced by the reaction of chloral with water and used as a sedative and hypnotic. Formula: $CCl_3C(OH)_3$

chloramphenicol (,klɔ:ræm'fɛnɪ,kɒl) *n* a broad-spectrum antibiotic used esp in treating typhoid fever and rickettsial infections [c20 from CHLORO- +

Cc

AM(IDE)- + PHE(NO)- + NI(TRO)- + (GLY)COL]
chlorate ('klɔːreɪt, -rɪt) *n* any salt of chloric acid, containing the monovalent ion ClO_3^-
chlordane ('klɔːdeɪn) *or* **chlordan** *n* a white insoluble toxic solid used as an insecticide [c20 from CHLORO- + (IN)D(OLE + -ENE) + -ANE]
chlorhexidine (klɔː'hɛksɪdiːn) *n* an antiseptic compound used in skin cleansers, mouthwashes, etc [c20 from CHLOR(O)- + HEX(ANE) + -I(DE) + (AM)INE]
chloric ('klɔːrɪk) *adj* of or containing chlorine in the pentavalent state
chloric acid *n* a strong acid with a pungent smell, known only in solution and in the form of chlorate salts. Formula: $HClO_3$
chloride ('klɔːraɪd) *n* **1** any salt of hydrochloric acid, containing the chloride ion Cl^- **2** any compound containing a chlorine atom, such as methyl chloride (chloromethane), CH_3Cl
chloride of lime *or* **chlorinated lime** *n* another name for **bleaching powder**
chlorinate ('klɔːrɪˌneɪt) *vb* **chlorinates, chlorinating, chlorinated** (*tr*) **1** to combine or treat (a substance) with chlorine **2** to disinfect (water) with chlorine > ˌ**chlorin'ation** *n* > '**chlorinˌator** *n*
chlorine ('klɔːriːn) *or* **chlorin** ('klɔːrɪn) *n* a toxic pungent greenish-yellow gas of the halogen group; occurring only in the combined state, mainly in common salt: used in the manufacture of many organic chemicals, in water purification, and as a disinfectant and bleaching agent. Symbol: Cl; atomic no.: 17; atomic wt.: 35.453 [c19 (coined by Sir Humphrey Davy): from CHLORO- + -INE[2], referring to its colour]
chlorite[1] ('klɔːraɪt) *n* any of a group of green soft secondary minerals consisting of the hydrated silicates of aluminium, iron, and magnesium [c18 from L, from Gk, from *khlōros* greenish yellow] > **chloritic** (klɔː'rɪtɪk) *adj*
chlorite[2] ('klɔːraɪt) *n* any salt of chlorous acid
chloro- *or before a vowel* **chlor-** *combining form* **1** indicating the colour green: *chlorophyll* **2** chlorine: *chloroform*
chlorofluorocarbon (ˌklɔːrəˌflʊərəʊ'kɑːbən) *n chem* any of various gaseous compounds of carbon, hydrogen, chlorine, and fluorine, used as refrigerants, aerosol propellants, solvents, and in foam: some cause a breakdown of ozone in the earth's atmosphere
chloroform ('klɔːrəˌfɔːm) *n* a heavy volatile liquid with a sweet taste and odour, used as a solvent and cleansing agent and in refrigerants: formerly used as an inhalation anaesthetic. Formula: $CHCl_3$. Systematic name: **trichloromethane** [c19 from CHLORO- + *formyl* from FORMIC]
Chloromycetin (ˌklɔːrəʊmaɪ'siːtɪn) *n trademark* a brand of **chloramphenicol**
chlorophyll *or US* **chlorophyl** ('klɔːrəfɪl) *n* the green pigment of plants and photosynthetic algae and bacteria that traps the energy of sunlight for photosynthesis: used as a colouring agent (**E140**) in medicines and food > '**chloroˌphylloid** *adj* > ˌ**chloro'phyllous** *adj*
chloroplast ('klɔːrəʊˌplæst) *n* a plastid containing chlorophyll and other pigments, occurring in plants and algae that carry out photosynthesis
chlorosis (klɔː'rəʊsɪs) *n* **1** Also called: **greensickness** *pathol* a once-common iron-deficiency disease of adolescent girls, characterized by greenish-yellow skin colour, weakness, and palpitation **2** *bot* a deficiency of chlorophyll in green plants caused by mineral deficiency, lack of light, disease, etc, the leaves appearing uncharacteristically pale [c17 from CHLORO- + -OSIS] > **chlorotic** (klɔː'rɒtɪk) *adj*
chlorous ('klɔːrəs) *adj* **1** of or containing chlorine in the trivalent state **2** of or containing chlorous acid
chlorous acid *n* an unstable acid that is a strong oxidizing agent. Formula: $HClO_2$
chlorpromazine (klɔː'prɒməˌziːn) *n* a drug used as a tranquillizer and sedative [c20 from CHLORO- + PRO(PYL + A)M(INE) + AZINE]
chlortetracycline (klɔːˌtɛtrə'saɪkliːn) *n* an antibiotic used in treating many bacterial and rickettsial infections and some viral infections
chock (tʃɒk) *n* **1** a block or wedge of wood used to prevent the sliding or rolling of a heavy object **2** *naut* **2a** a ringlike device with an opening at the top through which a rope is placed **2b** a cradle-like support for a boat, barrel, etc ▷ *vb* (*tr*) **3** (usually foll by *up*) *Brit* to cram full **4** to fit with or secure by a chock **5** to support (a boat, barrel, etc) on chocks ▷ *adv* **6** as closely or tightly as possible: *chock against the wall* [c17 from ?; ? rel. to OF *çoche* log]
chock-a-block *adj, adv* **1** filled to capacity; in a crammed state **2** *naut* with the blocks brought close together, as when a tackle is pulled as tight as possible
chocker ('tʃɒkə) *adj* **1** *inf* full up; packed **2** *Brit sl* irritated; fed up [c20 from CHOCK-A-BLOCK]
chock-full *or* **choke-full** *adj* (*postpositive*) completely full [c17 *choke-full*; see CHOKE, FULL[1]]
choco *or* **chocko** ('tʃɒkəʊ) *n, pl* **chocos** *or* **chockos** *Austral sl* a conscript or militiaman [from *chocolate soldier*]
chocolate ('tʃɒkəlɪt, 'tʃɒklɪt, -lət) *n* **1** a food preparation made from roasted ground cacao seeds, usually sweetened and flavoured **2** a drink or sweetmeat made from this **3a** a deep brown colour **3b** (*as adj*): *a chocolate carpet* [c17 from Sp., from Aztec *xocolatl*, from *xococ* sour + *atl* water] > '**chocolaty** *adj*
chocolate-box *n* (*modifier*) *inf* sentimentally pretty or appealing
Choctaw ('tʃɒktɔː) *n* **1** (*pl* **-taws** *or* **-taw**) a member of a N American people originally of Alabama **2** their language [c18 from Choctaw *Chahta*]
choice (tʃɔɪs) *n* **1** the act or an instance of choosing or selecting **2** the opportunity or power of choosing **3** a person or thing chosen or that may be chosen: *he was a possible choice* **4** an alternative action or possibility: *what choice did I have?* **5** a supply from which to select ▷ *adj* **6** of superior quality; excellent: *choice wine* **7** carefully chosen, appropriate: *a few choice words will do the trick* **8** vulgar or rude: *choice language* **9** **of choice** preferred; favourite [c13 from OF, from *choisir* to CHOOSE] > '**choicely** *adv* > '**choiceness** *n*
choir ('kwaɪə) *n* **1** an organized group of singers, esp for singing in church services **2** the part of a cathedral, abbey, or church in front of the altar and used by the choir and clergy **3** a number of instruments of the same family playing together: *a brass choir* **4** Also called: **choir organ** one of the manuals on an organ controlling a set of soft sweet-toned pipes [c13 *quer*, from OF *cuer*, from L CHORUS]
choirboy ('kwaɪəˌbɔɪ) *n* a young boy who sings the treble part in a church choir
choir school *n* (in Britain) a school attached to a cathedral, college, etc, offering general education to boys whose singing ability is good
Choiseul (*French* ʃwazœl) *n* an island in the SW Pacific Ocean, in the Solomon Islands: hilly and densely forested. Area: 3885 sq km (1500 sq miles)
choke (tʃəʊk) *vb* **chokes, choking, choked** **1** (*tr*) to hinder or stop the breathing of (a person or animal), esp by constricting the windpipe or by asphyxiation **2** (*intr*) to have trouble or fail in breathing, swallowing, or speaking **3** (*tr*) to block or clog up (a passage, pipe, street, etc) **4** (*tr*) to retard the growth or action of: *the weeds are choking my plants* **5** (*tr*) to enrich the petrol-air mixture by reducing the air supply to (a carburettor, petrol engine, etc) ▷ *n* **6** the act or sound of choking **7** a device in the carburettor of a petrol engine that enriches the petrol-air mixture by reducing the air

supply **8** any mechanism for reducing the flow of a fluid in a pipe, tube, etc **9** Also called: **choke coil** *electronics* an inductor having a relatively high impedance, used to prevent the passage of high frequencies or to smooth the output of a rectifier [OE *ācēocian*] > **'choky** *or* **'chokey** *adj*

choke back *or* **down** *vb (tr, adv)* to suppress (anger, tears, etc)

choke chain *n* a collar and lead for a dog so designed that if the dog drags on the lead the collar tightens round its neck

choked (tʃəʊkt) *adj Brit inf* annoyed or disappointed

choker ('tʃəʊkə) *n* **1** a woman's high collar **2** any neckband or necklace worn tightly around the throat **3** a high clerical collar; stock **4** a person who chokes **5** something that causes a person to choke

choke up *vb (tr, adv)* **1** to block (a drain, pipe, etc) completely **2** *inf (usually passive)* to overcome (a person) with emotion

chokey *or* **choky** ('tʃəʊkɪ) *n Brit sl* prison [c17 from Anglo-Indian, from Hindi *caukī* a lockup]

choko ('tʃəʊkəʊ) *n, pl* **chokos** *Austral & NZ* the cucumber-like fruit of a tropical American vine: eaten as a vegetable in the Caribbean, Australia, and New Zealand [c18 from Brazilian Indian]

cholangiography (kəˌlændʒɪ'ɒgrəfɪ) *n* radiographic examination of the bile ducts after the introduction into them of a contrast medium

chole- *or before a vowel* **chol-** *combining form* bile or gall: *cholesterol* [from Gk *kholē*]

choler ('kɒlə) *n* **1** anger or ill humour **2** *arch* one of the four bodily humours; yellow bile [c14 from OF, from Med. L, from L: jaundice, CHOLERA]

cholera ('kɒlərə) *n* an acute intestinal infection characterized by severe diarrhoea, cramp, etc: caused by ingestion of water or food contaminated with the bacterium *Vibrio comma* [c14 from L, from Gk *kholera* jaundice, from *kholē* bile] > **choleraic** (ˌkɒlə'reɪɪk) *adj*

choleric ('kɒlərɪk) *adj* **1** bad-tempered **2** *obs* bilious or causing biliousness > **'cholerically** *adv*

cholesterol (kə'lɛstəˌrɒl) *or* **cholesterin** (kə'lɛstərɪn) *n* a sterol found in all animal tissues, blood, bile, and animal fats. A high level of cholesterol is implicated in some cases of atherosclerosis [c19 from CHOLE- + Gk *stereos* solid]

choline ('kəʊliːn, -ɪn, 'kɒl-) *n* a colourless viscous soluble alkaline substance present in animal tissues, esp as a constituent of lecithin [c19 from CHOLE- + -INE[2]]

Cholula (*Spanish* tʃo'lula) *n* a town in S Mexico, in Puebla state: ancient ruins, notably a pyramid, 53 m (177 ft) high. Pop: 37 791 (1990)

choma ('tʃɒmə) *n S African inf* a friend, used esp by Black males [probably from Afrik. *tjommie*, from CHUM[1]]

chomp (tʃɒmp) *or* **chump** *vb* **1** to chew (food) noisily; champ ▷ *n* **2** the act or sound of chewing in this manner [var. of CHAMP[1]]

Chomsky ('tʃɒmskɪ) *n* **(Avram) Noam** ('nəʊəm) born 1928, US linguist and political critic. His theory of language structure, transformational generative grammar, superseded the structuralist and behaviourist view of Bloomfield

Chondokyo (ˌtʃɒndəʊ'kjəʊ) *n* an indigenous religion of Korea, incorporating elements of Buddhism, Confucianism, Christianity, and shamanism. Former name: **Tongchak** [c20 from Korean: Religion of the Heavenly Way]

chondrite ('kɒndraɪt) *n* a stony meteorite consisting mainly of silicate minerals in small spherical masses

Chongqing ('tʃʊŋ'tʃɪŋ), **Chungking**, *or* **Ch'ung-ch'ing** *n* a port in SW China, in Sichuan province at the confluence of the Yangtze and Jialing rivers: site of a city since the 3rd millennium BC; wartime capital of China (1938–45); major trade centre for W China. Pop: 3 193 889 (1999 est). Also called: **Pahsien**

choof off (tʃʊf) *vb (intr, adv) Austral sl* to go away; make off

chook (tʃʊk) *n inf, chiefly Austral & NZ* a hen or chicken. Also called: **chookie**

choose (tʃuːz) *vb* **chooses, choosing, chose, chosen** **1** to select (a person, thing, course of action, etc) from a number of alternatives **2** *(tr; takes a clause as object or an infinitive)* to consider it desirable or proper: *I don't choose to read that book* **3** *(intr)* to like; please: *you may stand if you choose* [OE *ceosan*] > **'chooser** *n*

choosy ('tʃuːzɪ) *adj* **choosier, choosiest** *inf* particular in making a choice; difficult to please

chop[1] (tʃɒp) *vb* **chops, chopping, chopped** **1** (often foll by *down* or *off*) to cut (something) with a blow from an axe or other sharp tool **2** *(tr; often foll by up)* to cut into pieces **3** *(tr) Brit inf* to dispense with or reduce **4** *(intr)* to move quickly or violently **5** *tennis, cricket, etc* to hit (a ball) sharply downwards **6** *boxing, karate, etc* to punch or strike (an opponent) with a short sharp blow ▷ *n* **7** a cutting blow **8** the act or an instance of chopping **9** a piece chopped off **10** a slice of mutton, lamb, or pork, generally including a rib **11** *Austral & NZ sl* a share (esp in **get** *or* **hop in for one's chop**) **12** *Austral & NZ* a competition of skill and speed in chopping logs **13** *sport* a sharp downward blow or stroke **14** **not much chop** *Austral & NZ inf* not much good; poor **15** **the chop** *Brit & Austral sl* dismissal from employment [c16 var. of CHAP[1]]

chop[2] (tʃɒp) *vb* **chops, chopping, chopped** **1** *(intr)* to change direction suddenly; vacillate (esp in **chop and change**) **2** **chop logic** use excessively subtle or involved argument [OE *ceapian* to barter]

chop[3] (tʃɒp) *n* a design stamped on goods as a trademark, esp in the Far East [c17 from Hindi *chhāp*]

chop chop *adv* pidgin English for **quickly** [c19 from Chinese dialect]

chophouse ('tʃɒpˌhaʊs) *n* a restaurant specializing in steaks, grills, chops, etc

Chopin ('ʃɒpæn; *French* ʃɔpɛ̃) *n* **Frédéric (François)** (frederik) 1810–49, Polish composer and pianist active in France, who wrote chiefly for the piano: noted for his harmonic imagination and his lyrical and melancholy qualities

chopper ('tʃɒpə) *n* **1** *chiefly Brit* a small hand axe **2** a butcher's cleaver **3** a person or thing that cuts or chops **4** an informal name for a **helicopter** **5** a device for periodically interrupting an electric current or beam of radiation to produce a pulsed current or beam **6** a type of bicycle or motorcycle with very high handlebars **7** *sl, chiefly US* a sub-machine-gun

choppy ('tʃɒpɪ) *adj* **choppier, choppiest** (of the sea, weather, etc) fairly rough > **'choppily** *adv* > **'choppiness** *n*

chops (tʃɒps) *pl n* **1** the jaws or cheeks; jowls **2** the mouth **3** **lick one's chops** *inf* to anticipate with pleasure [c16 from ?]

chopsticks ('tʃɒpstɪks) *pl n* a pair of thin sticks, of ivory, wood, etc, used for eating Chinese or other East Asian food [c17 from pidgin E, from *chop* quick, from Chinese dialect + STICK[1]]

chop suey ('suːɪ) *n* a Chinese-style dish originating in the US, consisting of meat, bean sprouts, etc, served with rice [c19 from Chinese *tsap sui* odds and ends]

choral ('kɔːrəl) *adj* relating to, sung by, or designed for a chorus or choir > **'chorally** *adv*

chorale *or* **choral** (kɒ'rɑːl) *n* **1** a slow stately hymn tune **2** *chiefly US* a choir or chorus [c19 from G *Choralgesang*, translation of L *cantus chorālis* choral song]

chord[1] (kɔːd) *n* **1** *maths* a straight line connecting two points on a curve or curved surface **2** *engineering* one of the principal members of a truss, esp one that lies along the top or the bottom **3** *anat* a variant spelling of **cord** **4** an emotional response, esp one of sympathy: *the story struck the right chord* [c16 from L, from Gk *khordē* gut, string; see CORD]

Cc

chord² (kɔːd) *n* **1** the simultaneous sounding of a group of musical notes, usually three or more in number ▷ *vb* **2** (*tr*) to provide (a melodic line) with chords [c15 short for ACCORD; spelling infl. by CHORD¹] > '**chordal** *adj*

chordate ('kɔːdeɪt) *n* **1** an animal with a backbone or notochord ▷ *adj* **2** of or relating to the chordates [c19 from Med. L *chordata*: see CHORD¹ & -ATE¹]

chore (tʃɔː) *n* **1** a routine task, esp a domestic one **2** a boring task [c19 from ME *chare*, from OE *cierr* a job]

-chore *n combining form* (in botany) indicating a plant that is distributed by a certain means: *anemochore* [from Gk *khōrein* to move] > **-chorous** *or* **-choric** *adj combining form*

chorea (kɒ'rɪə) *n* a disorder of the central nervous system characterized by uncontrollable irregular jerky movements. See **Huntington's disease**, **Sydenham's chorea** [c19 from NL, from L: dance, from Gk *khoreia*; see CHORUS]

choreograph ('kɒrɪəˌgrɑːf) *vb* (*tr*) to compose the steps and dances for (a ballet, etc)

choreography (ˌkɒrɪ'ɒgrəfɪ) *or* **choregraphy** (kɒ'rɛgrəfɪ) *n* **1** the composition of dance steps and sequences for ballet and stage and film dancing **2** the steps and sequences of a ballet or dance **3** the notation representing such steps **4** the art of dancing [c18 from Gk *khoreia* dance + -GRAPHY] > ˌ**chore'ographer** *or* **cho'regrapher** *n* > **choreographic** (ˌkɒrɪə'græfɪk) *or* **choregraphic** (ˌkɒrə'græfɪk) *adj* > ˌ**choreo'graphically** *or* ˌ**chore'graphically** *adv*

▷ www.instchordance.com

▷ www.culturekiosque.com/dance

choric ('kɒrɪk) *adj* of, like, or for a chorus, esp of singing, dancing, or the speaking of verse

chorion ('kɔːrɪən) *n* the outer membrane surrounding an embryo [c16 from Gk *khorion* afterbirth] > **chorionic** (ˌkɔːrɪ'ɒnɪk) *adj*

chorionic gonadotrophin *n* a hormone, secreted by the placenta in mammals, that promotes the secretion of progesterone. See **HCG**

chorionic villus sampling *n* a method of diagnosing genetic disorders early in pregnancy by the removal by catheter through the cervix of a tiny sample of tissue from the chorionic villi. Abbrev: **CVS**

chorister ('kɒrɪstə) *n* a singer in a choir, esp a choirboy [c14 from Med. L *chorista*]

Chorley ('tʃɔːlɪ) *n* a town in NW England, in S Lancashire: cotton textiles. Pop: 33 536 (1991)

choroid ('kɔːrɔɪd) *or* **chorioid** ('kɔːrɪˌɔɪd) *adj* **1** resembling the chorion, esp in being vascular ▷ *n* **2** the vascular membrane of the eyeball between the sclera and the retina [c18 from Gk *khoroeidēs*, erroneously for *khorioeidēs*, from CHORION]

choropleth ('kɔrəˌplɛθ) *n* **a** a symbol or marked and bounded area on a map denoting the distribution of some property **b** (*as modifier*): *a choropleth map* [c20 from Gk *khōra* place + *plēthos* multitude]

chorrie ('tʃɒrɪ) *n S African inf* a dilapidated old car [c20 from Afrik. *tjor* a crock]

chortle ('tʃɔːtᵊl) *vb* **chortles, chortling, chortled** **1** (*intr*) to chuckle gleefully ▷ *n* **2** a gleeful chuckle [c19 coined (1871) by Lewis Carroll; prob. a blend of CHUCKLE + SNORT] > '**chortler** *n*

chorus ('kɔːrəs) *n, pl* **choruses** **1** a large choir of singers or a piece of music composed for such a choir **2** a body of singers or dancers who perform together **3** a section of a song in which a soloist is joined by a group of singers, esp in a recurring refrain **4** an intermediate section of a pop song, blues, etc, as distinct from the verse **5** *jazz* any of a series of variations on a theme **6** (in ancient Greece) **6a** a lyric poem sung by a group of dancers, originally as a religious rite **6b** an ode or series of odes sung by a group of actors **6c** the actors who sang the chorus and commented on the action of the play **7a** (esp in Elizabethan drama) the actor who spoke the prologue, etc **7b** the part spoken by this actor **8** a group of people or animals producing words or sounds simultaneously **9** any speech, song, or utterance produced by a group of people or animals simultaneously: *the dawn chorus* **10** **in chorus** in unison ▷ *vb* **11** to speak, sing, or utter (words, sounds, etc) in unison [c16 from L, from Gk *khoros*]

chorus girl *n* a girl who dances or sings in the chorus of a musical comedy, revue, etc

Chorzów (*Polish* 'xɔʒuf) *n* an industrial city in SW Poland: under German administration from 1794 to 1921. Pop: 121 708 (1999 est). German name: **Königshütte**

chose (tʃəʊz) *vb* the past tense of **choose**

chosen ('tʃəʊzᵊn) *vb* **1** the past participle of **choose** ▷ *adj* **2** selected, esp for some special quality

Chosen ('tʃəʊ'sɛn) *n* the official name for **Korea** as a Japanese province (1910–45)

Chosŏn ('tʃəʊ'sɒn) *n* the Korean name for **North Korea**

Chota Nagpur ('tʃəʊtə 'nɑːgpʊə) *n* a plateau in E India, mainly in Jharkand state since 2000: forested, with rich mineral resources and much heavy industry; produces chiefly lac (world's leading supplier), coal (half India's total output), and mica

Chou En-lai (tʃəʊ ɛn'laɪ) *or* **Zhou En Lai** *n* 1898–1976, Chinese Communist statesman; foreign minister of the People's Republic of China (1949–58) and premier (1949–76)

chough (tʃʌf) *n* a large black passerine bird of parts of Europe, Asia, and Africa, with a long downward-curving red bill: family Corvidae (crows) [c14 from ?]

choux pastry (ʃuː) *n* a very light pastry made with eggs, used for éclairs, etc [partial translation of F *pâte choux* cabbage dough]

chow (tʃaʊ) *n* **1** *inf* food **2** short for **chow-chow** (sense 1)

chow-chow *n* **1** a thick-coated breed of dog with a curled tail and a characteristic blue-black tongue, originally from China. Often shortened to **chow** **2** a Chinese preserve of ginger, orange peel, etc, in syrup **3** a mixed vegetable pickle [c19 from pidgin E, prob. based on Chinese *cha* miscellaneous]

chowder ('tʃaʊdə) *n chiefly US & Canad* a thick soup or stew containing clams or fish [c18 from F *chaudière* kettle, from LL *caldāria*; see CAULDRON]

chow mein (meɪn) *n* a Chinese-American dish, consisting of mushrooms, meat, shrimps, etc, served with fried noodles [from Chinese *ch'ao mien* fried noodles]

Chrétien (*French* kretjɛ̃) *n* (**Joseph Jacques**) **Jean** born 1934, Canadian Liberal politician; prime minister of Canada (1993–2003)

Chrétien de Troyes (*French* kretjɛ̃ də trwa) *n* 12th century, French poet, who wrote the five Arthurian romances *Erec*; *Cligès*; *Lancelot, le chevalier de la charette*; *Yvain, le chevalier au lion*; and *Perceval, le conte del Graal* (?1155–?1190), the first courtly romances

chrism *or* **chrisom** ('krɪzəm) *n* a mixture of olive oil and balsam used for sacramental anointing in the Greek Orthodox and Roman Catholic Churches [OE, from Med. L, from Gk, from *khriein* to anoint] > **chrismal** ('krɪzməl) *adj*

Christ (kraɪst) *n* **1** Jesus of Nazareth (Jesus Christ), regarded by Christians as fulfilling Old Testament prophecies of the Messiah **2** the Messiah or anointed one of God as the subject of Old Testament prophecies **3** an image or picture of Christ ▷ *interj* **4** *taboo sl* an oath expressing anger, etc ▷ See also **Jesus** [OE *Crīst*, from L *Chrīstus*, from Gk *khristos* anointed one (from *khriein* to anoint), translating Heb. *māshīah* MESSIAH] > '**Christly** *adj*

Christadelphian (ˌkrɪstə'dɛlfɪən) *n* **1** a member of a Christian millenarian sect founded in the US about 1848, holding that only the just will enter eternal life, and that the ignorant and unconverted will not be raised from the dead ▷ *adj* **2** of or relating to this body or its beliefs and practices [c19 from LGk *khristadelphos*, *khristos* CHRIST + *adelpos* brother]

Christchurch (ˈkraɪstˌtʃɜːtʃ) *n* **1** a city in New Zealand, on E South Island: manufacturing centre of a rich agricultural region. Pop (urban area): 324 300 (1999 est) **2** a town and resort in S England, in SE Dorset. Pop: 36 379 (1991)

christen (ˈkrɪsᵊn) *vb* (*tr*) **1** to give a Christian name to in baptism as a sign of incorporation into a Christian Church **2** another word for **baptize** **3** to give a name to anything, esp with some ceremony **4** *inf* to use for the first time [OE *cristnian*, from *Crīst* CHRIST] > ˈ**christening** *n*

Christendom (ˈkrɪsᵊndəm) *n* the collective body of Christians throughout the world

Christian¹ (ˈkrɪstʃən) *n* **1a** a person who believes in and follows Jesus Christ **1b** a member of a Christian Church or denomination **2** *inf* a person who possesses Christian virtues ▷ *adj* **3** of, relating to, or derived from Jesus Christ, his teachings, example, or followers **4** (*sometimes not cap*) exhibiting kindness or goodness > ˈ**Christianly** *adj, adv*

Christian² (ˈkrɪstʃən) *n* **Charlie** 1919–42, US jazz guitarist

Christian IV (ˈkrɪstʃən; *Danish* ˈkresdjan) *n* 1577–1648, king of Denmark and Norway (1588–1648): defeated in the Thirty Years' War (1629) and by Sweden (1645)

Christian X *n* 1890–1947, king of Denmark (1912–47) and Iceland (1918–44)

Christian Democrat *n* a member or supporter of any of various right-of-centre political parties in Europe and Latin America that combine moderate conservatism with historical links to the Christian Church > **Christian Democracy** *n* > **Christian Democratic** *adj*

Christian Era *n* the period beginning with the year of Christ's birth

Christiania (ˌkrɪstɪˈɑːnɪə) *n* a former name (1624–1877) of **Oslo**

Christianity (ˌkrɪstɪˈænɪtɪ) *n* **1** the Christian religion **2** Christian beliefs or practices **3** a less common word for **Christendom**

Christianize *or* **Christianise** (ˈkrɪstʃəˌnaɪz) *vb* **Christianizes, Christianizing, Christianized** *or* **Christianises, Christianising, Christianised** (*tr*) **1** to make Christian or convert to Christianity **2** to imbue with Christian principles, spirit, or outlook > ˌ**Christianiˈzation** *or* ˌ**Christianiˈsation** *n*

Christian name *n* a personal name formally given to Christians at christening: loosely used to mean any person's first name.

> **USAGE** There are more multicultural alternatives for this term, such as *first name* and *forename*. In US usage, *given name* is also often used

Christiansand (ˈkrɪstʃənˌsænd; *Norwegian* kristianˈsan) *n* a variant spelling of **Kristiansand**

Christian Science *n* the religious system of the Church of Christ, Scientist, founded by Mary Baker Eddy (1879), emphasizing spiritual regeneration and healing through prayer alone > **Christian Scientist** *n*
▷ www.tfccs.com

Christie (ˈkrɪstɪ) *n* **1** Dame **Agatha** (**Mary Clarissa**) 1890–1976, British author of detective stories, many featuring Hercule Poirot, and several plays, including *The Mousetrap* (1952) **2** **John** (**Reginald Halliday**) 1898–1953, British murderer. His trial influenced legislation regarding the death penalty after he was found guilty of a murder for which Timothy Evans had been hanged **3** **William** (**Lincoln**) born 1944, French harpsichord player, organist, and conductor, born in the US; founder (1979) and director of the early-music group Les Arts Florissants

Christina (krɪˈstiːnə) *n* 1626–89, queen of Sweden (1632–54), daughter of Gustavus Adolphus, noted particularly for her patronage of literature

Christine de Pisan (*French* kristin də pizɑ̃) *n* ?1364–?1430, French poet and prose writer, born in Venice. Her works include ballads, rondeaux, lays, and a biography of Charles V of France

Christingle (ˌkrɪsˈtɪŋgl) *n* (in Britain) a Christian service for children held shortly before Christmas, in which each child is given a decorated fruit with a lighted candle in it [c20 from CHRIST(MAS) + INGLE]

Christlike (ˈkraɪstˌlaɪk) *adj* resembling the spirit of Jesus Christ > ˈ**Christˌlikeness** *n*

Christmas (ˈkrɪsməs) *n* **1a** the annual commemoration by Christians of the birth of Jesus Christ, on Dec 25 **1b** Also called: **Christmas Day** Dec 25, observed as a day of secular celebrations when gifts and greetings are exchanged **1c** (*as modifier*): *Christmas celebrations* **2** Also called: **Christmastide** the season of Christmas extending from Dec 24 (Christmas Eve) to Jan 6 (the festival of the Epiphany or Twelfth Night) [OE *Crīstes mæsse* MASS of CHRIST] > ˈ**Christmassy** *adj*

Christmas box *n* a tip or present given at Christmas, esp to postmen, tradesmen, etc

Christmas Eve *n* the evening or the whole day before Christmas Day

Christmas Island *n* **1** the former name (until 1981) of **Kiritimati** **2** an island in the Indian Ocean, south of Java: administered by Singapore (1900–58), now by Australia; phosphate mining. Pop: 2500 (1994 est). Area: 135 sq km (52 sq miles)

Christmas pudding *n* *Brit* a rich steamed pudding containing suet, dried fruit, spices, etc. Also called: **plum pudding**

Christmas rose *n* an evergreen plant of S Europe and W Asia with white or pinkish winter-blooming flowers. Also called: **hellebore, winter rose**

Christmastide (ˈkrɪsməsˌtaɪd) *n* another name for **Christmas** (sense 2)

Christmas tree *n* **1** an evergreen tree or an imitation of one, decorated as part of Christmas celebrations **2** Also called: **Christmas bush** *Austral* any of various trees or shrubs flowering at Christmas and used for decoration **3** *NZ* another name for the **pohutukawa**

Christo (ˈkrɪstəʊ) *n* full name **Christo Jaracheff** born 1935, U.S. artist, born in Bulgaria; best known for works in which he wraps buildings, monuments, or natural features in canvas or plastic

Christoff (ˈkrɪstɒf) *n* **Boris** 1919–93, Bulgarian bass-baritone, noted esp for his performance in the title role of Mussorgsky's *Boris Godunov*

Christopher (ˈkrɪstəfə) *n* **Saint** 3rd century AD, Christian martyr; patron saint of travellers

Christy *or* **Christie** (ˈkrɪstɪ) *n, pl* **Christies** (*sometimes not cap*) *skiing* a turn in which the body is swung sharply round with the skis parallel: used for stopping or changing direction quickly [c20 from CHRISTIANIA]

chroma (ˈkrəʊmə) *n* the attribute of a colour that enables an observer to judge how much chromatic colour it contains. See also **saturation** (sense 4) [c19 from Gk *khrōma* colour]

chromate (ˈkrəʊmeɪt) *n* any salt or ester of chromic acid

chromatic (krəˈmætɪk) *adj* **1** of, relating to, or characterized by a colour or colours **2** *music* **2a** involving the sharpening or flattening of notes or the use of such notes in chords and harmonic progressions **2b** of or relating to the chromatic scale or an instrument capable of producing it [c17 from Gk, from *khrōma* colour] > **chroˈmatically** *adv* > **chroˈmaticism** *n* > **chromaticity** (ˌkrəʊməˈtɪsɪtɪ) *n*

chromatic aberration *n* a defect in a lens system in which different wavelengths of light are focused at different distances because they are refracted through different angles. It produces a blurred image with coloured fringes

Cc

chromatics (krəʊˈmætɪks) *n (functioning as sing)* the science of colour

chromatic scale *n* a twelve-note scale including all the semitones of the octave

chromatin (ˈkrəʊmətɪn) *n* the part of the nucleus that consists of DNA, and proteins, forms the chromosomes, and stains with basic dyes

chromato- *or before a vowel* **chromat-** *combining form* **1** indicating colour or coloured: *chromatophore* **2** indicating chromatin: *chromatolysis* [from Gk *khrōma, khrōmat-* colour]

chromatography (ˌkrəʊməˈtɒɡrəfɪ) *n* the technique of separating and analysing the components of a mixture of liquids or gases by selective adsorption > ˌ**chromaˈtographer** *n*

chrome (krəʊm) *n* **1a** another word for **chromium**, esp when present in a pigment or dye **1b** *(as modifier)*: *a chrome dye* **2** anything plated with chromium **3** a pigment or dye that contains chromium ▷ *vb* **chromes, chroming, chromed 4** to plate or be plated with chromium **5** to treat or be treated with a chromium compound, as in dyeing or tanning [C19 via F from Gk *khrōma* colour]

-chrome *n and adj combining form* colour, coloured, or pigment: *monochrome* [from Gk *khrōma* colour]

chrome dioxide *n* another name for **chromium dioxide**

chromel (ˈkrəʊmɛl) *n* a nickel-based alloy containing about 10 per cent chromium, used in heating elements [C20 from CHRO(MIUM) + ME(TA)L]

chrome steel *n* any of various hard rust-resistant steels containing chromium

chrome yellow *n* any yellow pigment consisting of lead chromate

chromic (ˈkrəʊmɪk) *adj* **1** of or containing chromium in the trivalent state **2** of or derived from chromic acid

chromic acid *n* an unstable dibasic oxidizing acid known only in solution and as chromate salts. Formula: H_2CrO_4

chromite (ˈkrəʊmaɪt) *n* a brownish-black mineral consisting of a ferrous chromic oxide in crystalline form: the only commercial source of chromium. Formula: $FeCr_2O_4$

chromium (ˈkrəʊmɪəm) *n* a hard grey metallic element, used in steel alloys and electroplating to increase hardness and corrosion-resistance. Symbol: Cr; atomic no.: 24; atomic wt.: 51.996 [C19 from NL, from F: CHROME]

chromium dioxide *n* a chemical compound used as a magnetic coating on cassette tapes; chromium(IV) oxide. Formula: CrO_2. Also called *(not in technical usage)*: **chrome dioxide**

chromium steel *n* another name for **chrome steel**

chromo (ˈkrəʊməʊ) *n, pl* **chromos** short for **chromolithograph**

chromo- *or before a vowel* **chrom-** *combining form* **1** indicating colour, coloured, or pigment: *chromogen* **2** indicating chromium: *chromyl* [from Gk *khrōma* colour]

chromolithograph (ˌkrəʊməʊˈlɪθəˌɡrɑːf) *n* a picture produced by chromolithography

chromolithography (ˌkrəʊməʊlɪˈθɒɡrəfɪ) *n* the process of making coloured prints by lithography > ˌ**chromoliˈthographer** *n* > **chromolithographic** (ˌkrəʊməʊlɪθəˈɡræfɪk) *adj*

chromosome (ˈkrəʊməˌsəʊm) *n* any of the microscopic rod-shaped structures that appear in a cell nucleus during cell division, consisting of nucleoprotein arranged into units (genes) that are responsible for the transmission of hereditary characteristics > ˌ**chromoˈsomal** *adj*

chromosome map *n* a graphic representation of the positions of genes on chromosomes, obtained by observation of stained chromosomes or by determining the degree of linkage between genes. See also **genetic map** > **chromosome mapping** *n*

chromosphere (ˈkrəʊməˌsfɪə) *n* a gaseous layer of the sun's atmosphere extending from the photosphere to the corona > **chromospheric** (ˌkrəʊməˈsfɛrɪk) *adj*

chromous (ˈkrəʊməs) *adj* of or containing chromium in the divalent state

Chron. *Bible abbrev for* Chronicles

chronic (ˈkrɒnɪk) *adj* **1** continuing for a long time; constantly recurring **2** (of a disease) developing slowly, or of long duration ▷ Cf **acute** (sense 7) **3** inveterate; habitual: *a chronic smoker* **4** *inf* **4a** very bad: *the play was chronic* **4b** very serious: *he left her in a chronic condition* [C15 from L, from Gk, from *khronos* time] > ˈ**chronically** *adv* > **chronicity** (krɒˈnɪsɪtɪ) *n*

chronic fatigue syndrome *n* another name for **myalgic encephalopathy.** Abbrev: **CFS**

chronicle (ˈkrɒnɪkᵊl) *n* **1** a record or register of events in chronological order ▷ *vb* **chronicles, chronicling, chronicled 2** *(tr)* to record in or as if in a chronicle [C14 from Anglo-F, via L *chronica* (pl), from Gk *khronika* annals; see CHRONIC] > ˈ**chronicler** *n*

chrono- *or before a vowel* **chron-** *combining form* time: *chronology* [from Gk *khronos* time]

chronograph (ˈkrɒnəˌɡrɑːf, ˈkrəʊnə-) *n* **1** an accurate instrument for recording small intervals of time **2** any timepiece, esp a wristwatch designed for maximum accuracy > **chronographic** (ˌkrɒnəˈɡræfɪk) *adj*

chronological (ˌkrɒnəˈlɒdʒɪkᵊl, ˌkrəʊ-) *or* **chronologic** *adj* **1** (esp of a sequence of events) arranged in order of occurrence **2** relating to or in accordance with chronology > ˌ**chronoˈlogically** *adv*

chronology (krəˈnɒlədʒɪ) *n, pl* **chronologies 1** the determination of the proper sequence of past events **2** the arrangement of dates, events, etc, in order of occurrence **3** a table of events arranged in order of occurrence > **chroˈnologist** *n*

chronometer (krəˈnɒmɪtə) *n* a timepiece designed to be accurate in all conditions of temperature, pressure, etc, used esp at sea > **chronometric** (ˌkrɒnəˈmɛtrɪk) *or* ˌ**chronoˈmetrical** *adj* > ˌ**chronoˈmetrically** *adv*

chronometry (krəˈnɒmɪtrɪ) *n* the science of measuring time with extreme accuracy

chronon (ˈkrəʊnɒn) *n* a unit of time equal to the time that a photon would take to traverse the diameter of an electron: about 10^{-24} seconds

chrysalid (ˈkrɪsəlɪd) *n* **1** another name for **chrysalis** ▷ *adj* **2** of or relating to a chrysalis

chrysalis (ˈkrɪsəlɪs) *n, pl* **chrysalises** *or* **chrysalides** (krɪˈsælɪˌdiːz) **1** the pupa of a moth or butterfly, in a case or cocoon **2** anything in the process of developing [C17 from L, from Gk *khrusallis*, from *khrusos* gold]

chrysanthemum (krɪˈsænθəməm) *n* **1** any of various widely cultivated plants of the family Asteraceae, having brightly coloured showy flower heads in autumn **2** any other plant of the genus *Chrysanthemum*, such as the oxeye daisy [C16 from L: marigold, from Gk, from *khrusos* gold + *anthemon* flower]

chryselephantine (ˌkrɪsɛlɪˈfæntɪn) *adj* (of ancient Greek statues, etc) made of or overlaid with gold and ivory [C19 from Gk, from *khrusos* gold + *elephas* ivory]

chrysoberyl (ˈkrɪsəˌbɛrɪl) *n* a rare very hard greenish-yellow mineral consisting of beryllium aluminate: used as a gemstone. Formula: $BeAl_2O_4$ [C17 from L, from Gk, from *khrusos* gold + *bērullos* beryl]

chrysolite (ˈkrɪsəˌlaɪt) *n* another name for **olivine** [C14 *crisolite*, from OF, from L, from Gk, from *khrusos* gold + *lithos* stone]

chrysoprase (ˈkrɪsəˌpreɪz) *n* an apple-green variety of chalcedony: used as a gemstone [C13 *crisopace*, from OF, from L, from Gk, from *khrusos* gold + *prason* leek]

Chrysostom (ˈkrɪsəstəm) *n* Saint **John** ?345–407 AD, Greek patriarch; archbishop of Constantinople (398–404) Feast day: Sept 13 or Nov 13

chthonian (ˈθəʊnɪən) *or* **chthonic** (ˈθɒnɪk) *adj* of or relating to the underworld [c19 from Gk *khthonios* in or under the earth, from *khthōn* earth]

chub (tʃʌb) *n, pl* **chub** *or* **chubs** 1 a common European freshwater cyprinid game fish, having a cylindrical dark greenish body 2 any of various North American fishes, esp certain whitefishes and minnows [c15 from ?]

chubby (ˈtʃʌbɪ) *adj* **chubbier, chubbiest** (esp of the human form) plump [c17 ?from CHUB] > ˈ**chubbiness** *n*

Chu Chiang (ˈtʃuː ˈtʃæŋ, tʃaɪˈœŋ) *n* a variant transliteration of the Chinese name for the **Zhu Jiang**

chuck[1] (tʃʌk) *vb (mainly tr)* 1 *inf* to throw 2 to pat affectionately, esp under the chin 3 *inf* (sometimes foll by *in* or *up*) to give up; reject: *he chucked up his job* 4 *US, Austral & NZ sl* to vomit ▷ *n* 5 a throw or toss 6 a pat under the chin 7 **the chuck** *inf* dismissal ▷ See also **chuck in, chuck off, chuck out** [c16 from ?]

chuck[2] (tʃʌk) *n* 1 Also called: **chuck steak** a cut of beef from the neck to the shoulder blade 2 a device that holds a workpiece in a lathe or tool in a drill [c17 var. of CHOCK]

chuck[3] (tʃʌk) *n W Canad* 1 a large body of water 2 In full: **saltchuck** the sea [c19 from Chinook Jargon, of Amerind origin, from *chauk*]

chuck in *vb (adv)* 1 *(tr) Brit inf* to abandon or give up: *to chuck in a hopeless attempt* 2 *(intr) Austral inf* to contribute to the cost of something

chuckle (ˈtʃʌkᵊl) *vb* **chuckles, chuckling, chuckled** *(intr)* 1 to laugh softly or to oneself 2 (of animals, esp hens) to make a clucking sound ▷ *n* 3 a partly suppressed laugh [c16 prob. from *chuck* cluck + *le*]

chucklehead (ˈtʃʌkᵊlˌhɛd) *n inf* a stupid person; dolt

chuck off *vb (intr, adv; often foll by at) Austral & NZ inf* to abuse or make fun of

chuck out *vb (tr, adv; often foll by of) inf* to eject forcibly (from); throw out (of)

chuddies (ˈtʃʌdɪz) *pl n Indian inf* underpants [c20 possibly from Hindi *chuddar* large shawl or veil]

chuddy (ˈtʃʌdɪ) *n Austral & NZ* an informal name for **chewing gum**

Chudskoye Ozero (*Russian* ˈtʃutskəjɪ ˈɔzɪrə) *n* the Russian name for Lake **Peipus**

chuff[1] (tʃʌf) *n* 1 a puffing sound as of a steam engine ▷ *vb* 2 *(intr)* to move while emitting such sounds [c20 imit.]

chuff[2] (tʃʌf) *vb (tr; usually passive) Brit sl* to please or delight: *he was chuffed by his pay rise* [prob. from *chuff* (adj) pleased, happy]

chug (tʃʌg) *n* 1 a short dull sound, such as that made by an engine ▷ *vb* **chugs, chugging, chugged** 2 *(intr)* (of an engine, etc) to operate while making such sounds [c19 imit.]

chukar (tʃʌˈkɑː) *n* a common Indian partridge having a red bill and black-barred sandy plumage [from Hindi *cakor*, from Sansk. *cakora*, prob. imit.]

Chu Kiang (ˈtʃuː ˈkjæŋ, kaɪˈæŋ) *n* a variant transliteration of the Chinese name for the **Zhu Jiang**

chukka *or US* **chukker** (ˈtʃʌkə) *n polo* a period of continuous play, generally lasting 7½ minutes [c20 from Hindi *cakkar*, from Sansk. *cakra* wheel]

chukka boot (ˈtʃʌkə) *or* **chukka** *n* an ankle-high boot worn for playing polo [c19 from CHUKKA]

chum (tʃʌm) *n* 1 *inf* a close friend ▷ *vb* **chums, chumming, chummed** 2 *(intr; usually foll by up with)* to be or become an intimate friend (of) [c17 (meaning: a person sharing rooms with another): prob. shortened from *chamber fellow*]

chummy (ˈtʃʌmɪ) *adj* **chummier, chummiest** *inf* friendly > ˈ**chummily** *adv* > ˈ**chumminess** *n*

chump (tʃʌmp) *n* 1 *inf* a stupid person 2 a thick heavy block of wood 3 the thick blunt end of anything, esp of a piece of meat 4 *Brit sl* the head (esp in **off one's chump**) [c18 ? a blend of CHUNK + LUMP[1]]

chunder (ˈtʃʌndə) *sl, chiefly Austral* ▷ *vb (intr)* 1 to vomit ▷ *n* 2 vomit [c20 from ?]

Chungking (ˈtʃʊŋˈkɪŋ, ˈtʃʌŋ-) *or* **Ch'ung-ch'ing** (ˈtʃʊŋˈtʃɪŋ, ˈtʃʌŋ-) *n* a variant transliteration of the Chinese name for **Chongqing**

chunk (tʃʌŋk) *n* 1 a thick solid piece, as of meat, wood, etc 2 a considerable amount [c17 var. of CHUCK[2]]

chunky (ˈtʃʌŋkɪ) *adj* **chunkier, chunkiest** 1 thick and short 2 containing thick pieces 3 *chiefly Brit* (of clothes, esp knitwear) made of thick bulky material > ˈ**chunkiness** *n*

Chunnel (ˈtʃʌnᵊl) *n* an informal name for **Channel Tunnel** [c20 from CH(ANNEL) + T(UNNEL)]

chunter (ˈtʃʌntə) *vb (intr; often foll by on) Brit inf* to mutter or grumble incessantly in a meaningless fashion [c16 prob. imit.]

Chuquisaca (*Spanish* tʃukiˈsaka) *n* the former name (until 1839) of **Sucre**[1]

Chur (*German* kuːr) *n* a city in E Switzerland, capital of Grisons canton. Pop: 30 236 (1990). Ancient name: **Curia Rhaetorum** (ˈkuːrɪə riːˈtəʊrəm, ˈkjuː-) French name: **Coire**

church (tʃɜːtʃ) *n* 1 a building for public worship, esp Christian worship 2 an occasion of public worship 3 the clergy as distinguished from the laity 4 *(usually cap)* institutionalized forms of religion as a political or social force: *conflict between Church and State* 5 *(usually cap)* the collective body of all Christians 6 *(often cap)* a particular Christian denomination or group 7 *(often cap)* the Christian religion ▷ Related adj: **ecclesiastical** ▷ *vb (tr)* 8 *Church of England* to bring (someone, esp a woman after childbirth) to church for special ceremonies [OE *cirice*, from LGk, from Gk *kuriakon* (*dōma*) the Lord's (house), from *kurios* master, from *kuros* power]

Church (tʃɜːtʃ) *n* **Charlotte** born 1986, Welsh soprano, who made her name with the album *Voice of an Angel* (1998) when she was 12

Church Army *n* a voluntary Anglican organization founded to assist the parish clergy

Church Commissioners *pl n Brit* a group of representatives of Church and State that administers the property of the Church of England

churchgoer (ˈtʃɜːtʃˌgəʊə) *n* a person who attends church regularly > ˈ**church,going** *adj, n*

Churchill[1] (ˈtʃɜːtʃɪl) *n* 1 a river in E Canada, rising in SE Labrador and flowing north and southeast over Churchill Falls, then east to the Atlantic. Length: about 1000 km (600 miles). Former name: **Hamilton River** 2 a river in central Canada, rising in NW Saskatchewan and flowing east through several lakes to Hudson Bay. Length: about 1600 km (1000 miles)

Churchill[2] (ˈtʃɜːtʃɪl) *n* 1 **Caryl** born 1938, British playwright; her plays include *Cloud Nine* (1978), *Top Girls* (1982), *Serious Money* (1987), and *Far Away* (2000) 2 **Charles** 1731–64, British poet, noted for his polemical satires. His works include *The Rosciad* (1761) and *The Prophecy of Famine* (1763) 3 **John** See (1st Duke of) **Marlborough** 4 Lord **Randolph** 1849–95, British Conservative politician: secretary of state for India (1885–86) and chancellor of the Exchequer and leader of the House of Commons (1886) 5 his son, Sir **Winston** (**Leonard Spencer**) 1874–1965, British Conservative statesman, orator, and writer, noted for his leadership during World War II. He held various posts under both Conservative and Liberal governments, including 1st Lord of the Admiralty (1911–15), before becoming prime minister (1940–45; 1951–55). His writings include *The World Crisis* (1923–29), *Marlborough* (1933–38), *The Second World War* (1948–54), and *History of the English-Speaking Peoples* (1956–58): Nobel prize for literature 1953

Churchill Falls *pl n* a waterfall in E Canada, in SW Labrador on the Churchill River: site of one of the largest hydroelectric power projects in the world.

Height: 75 m (245 ft). Former name: **Grand Falls**

churchly (ˈtʃɜːtʃlɪ) *adj* appropriate to or associated with the church > ˈ**churchliness** *n*

churchman (ˈtʃɜːtʃmən) *n, pl* **churchmen** 1 a clergyman 2 a male member of a church

Church of Christ, Scientist *n* See **Christian Science**

Church of England *n* the reformed established state Church in England, with the Sovereign as its temporal head

Church of Jesus Christ of Latter-Day Saints *n* See **Mormon** (sense 1)

churchwarden (ˌtʃɜːtʃˈwɔːdᵊn) *n* 1 *Church of England, Episcopal Church* one of two assistants of a parish priest who administer the secular affairs of the church 2 a long-stemmed tobacco pipe made of clay

churchwoman (ˈtʃɜːtʃˌwʊmən) *n, pl* **churchwomen** a female member of a church

churchyard (ˈtʃɜːtʃˌjɑːd) *n* the grounds round a church, used as a graveyard

churinga (tʃəˈrɪŋgə) *n, pl* **churinga** *or* **churingas** a sacred amulet of the native Australians [from Abor.]

churl (tʃɜːl) *n* 1 a surly ill-bred person 2 *arch* a farm labourer 3 *arch* a miserly person [OE *ceorl*]

churlish (ˈtʃɜːlɪʃ) *adj* 1 rude or surly 2 of or relating to peasants 3 miserly > ˈ**churlishly** *adv* > ˈ**churlishness** *n*

churn (tʃɜːn) *n* 1 *Brit* a large container for milk 2 a vessel or machine in which cream or whole milk is vigorously agitated to produce butter 3 the number of customers who switch from one supplier to another ▷ *vb* 4a to agitate (milk or cream) to make butter 4b to make (butter) by this process 5 (sometimes foll by *up*) to move or cause to move with agitation 6 (of a bank, broker, etc) to encourage an investor or policyholder to change investments, endowment policies, etc, to increase commissions at the client's expense 7 (of a government) to pay benefits to a wide category of people and claw it back by taxation from the well off 8 to promote the turnover of existing subscribers leasing, and new subscribers joining, a cable television system or mobile phone company [OE *ciern*] > ˈ**churner** *n*

churn out *vb (tr, adv) inf* 1 to produce (something) at a rapid rate: *to churn out ideas* 2 to perform (something) mechanically: *to churn out a song*

churr (tʃɜː) *vb, n* a variant spelling of **chirr**

chute[1] (ʃuːt) *n* 1 an inclined channel or vertical passage down which water, parcels, coal, etc, may be dropped 2 a steep slope, used as a slide as for toboggans 3 a slide into a swimming pool 4 a rapid or waterfall [C19 from OF *cheoite*, fem. p.p. of *cheoir* to fall, from L *cadere*; in some senses, var. spelling of SHOOT]

chute[2] (ʃuːt) *n, vb* **chutes, chuting, chuted** *inf* short for **parachute** > ˈ**chutist** *n*

Chu Teh (ˈtʃuː ˈteɪ) *or* **Zhu De** *n* 1886–1976, Chinese military leader and politician; he became commander in chief of the Red Army (1931) and was chairman of the Standing Committee of the National People's Congress of the People's Republic of China (1959–76)

chutney (ˈtʃʌtnɪ) *n* a pickle of Indian origin, made from fruit, vinegar, spices, sugar, etc: *mango chutney* [C19 from Hindi *catni*, from ?]

chutzpah (ˈxʊtspə) *n US & Canad inf* shameless audacity; impudence [C20 from Yiddish]

Chuvash Republic (ˈtʃuːvaːʃ) *n* a constituent republic of W central Russia, in the middle Volga valley: generally low-lying with undulating plains and large areas of forest. Capital: Cheboksary. Pop: 1 357 000 (2000 est). Area: 18 300 sq km (7064 sq miles). Also called: **Chuvashia** (tʃuːˈvɑːʃɪə)

chyack (ˈtʃaɪæk) *vb, n* a variant spelling of **chiack**

chyle (kaɪl) *n* a milky fluid composed of lymph and emulsified fat globules, formed in the small intestine during digestion [C17 from LL, from Gk *khulos* juice] > **chylaceous** (kaɪˈleɪʃəs) *or* ˈ**chylous** *adj*

chyme (kaɪm) *n* the thick fluid mass of partially digested food that leaves the stomach [C17 from LL, from Gk *khumos* juice] > ˈ**chymous** *adj*

chypre *French* (ʃiprə) *n* a perfume made from sandalwood [lit.: Cyprus, ? where it originated]

Ci *symbol for* curie

CI *abbrev for* Channel Islands

CIA *abbrev for* Central Intelligence Agency; a federal US bureau created in 1947 to coordinate and conduct espionage and intelligence activities

ciabatta (tʃəˈbætə) *n* a type of open-textured bread made with olive oil [C20 from It., lit.: slipper]

Ciano (ˈtʃɑːnəʊ) *n* **Galeazzo,** full name *Conte Galeazzo Ciano di Cortellazzo.* 1903–44, Italian fascist politician; minister of foreign affairs (1936–43) and son-in-law of Mussolini, whose supporters shot him

CIB *abbrev for* Criminal Investigation Branch (of the New Zealand and Australian police)
▷ www.police.govt.nz/service/cib

Cibber (ˈsɪbə) *n* **Colley** (ˈkɒlɪ) 1671–1757, English actor and dramatist; poet laureate (1730–57)

ciborium (sɪˈbɔːrɪəm) *n, pl* **ciboria** (-rɪə) *Christianity* 1 a goblet-shaped lidded vessel used to hold consecrated wafers in Holy Communion 2 a canopy fixed over an altar [C17 from Med. L, from L, from Gk *kibōrion* cup-shaped seed vessel of the Egyptian lotus]

CICA (in Britain) *abbrev for* Criminal Injuries Compensation Authority

cicada (sɪˈkɑːdə) *or* **cicala** *n, pl* **cicadas, cicadae** (-diː) *or* **cicale** (-leɪ) any large broad insect, most common in warm regions, having membranous wings: the males produce a high-pitched drone by vibration of a pair of drumlike abdominal organs [C19 from L]

cicatrix (ˈsɪkətrɪks) *n, pl* **cicatrices** (ˌsɪkəˈtraɪsiːz) 1 the tissue that forms in a wound during healing; scar 2 a scar on a plant indicating the former point of attachment of a part, esp a leaf [C17 from L: scar, from ?] > **cicatricial** (ˌsɪkəˈtrɪʃəl) *adj*

cicatrize *or* **cicatrise** (ˈsɪkəˌtraɪz) *vb* **cicatrizes, cicatrizing, cicatrized** *or* **cicatrises, cicatrising, cicatrised** (of a wound or defect in tissue) to be closed by scar formation; heal > ˌ**cicatriˈzation** *or* ˌ**cicatriˈsation** *n*

cicely (ˈsɪsəlɪ) *n, pl* **cicelies** short for **sweet cicely** [C16 from L *seselis*, from Gk, from ?]

Cicero (ˈsɪsəˌrəʊ) *n* **Marcus Tullius** (ˈmɑːkəs ˈtʌlɪəs) 106–43 BC, Roman consul, orator, and writer. He foiled Catiline's conspiracy (63) and was killed by Mark Antony's agents after he denounced Antony in the *Philippics*. His writings are regarded as a model of Latin prose. Formerly known in English as: **Tully**

cicerone (ˌsɪsəˈrəʊnɪ, ˌtʃɪtʃ-) *n, pl* **cicerones** *or* **ciceroni** (-nɪ) a person who conducts and informs sightseers [C18 from It.: antiquarian scholar, guide, after CICERO]

ciclosporin (ˌsaɪkləʊˈspɔːrɪn-) *or* **cyclosporin** *n* a drug extracted from a fungus and used to suppress the body's immune mechanisms, and so prevent rejection of an organ

Cid (sɪd; *Spanish* θið) *n* **El** *or* **the** original name *Rodrigo Diaz de Vivar.* ?1043–99, Spanish soldier and hero of the wars against the Moors

CID (in Britain) *abbrev for* Criminal Investigation Department; the detective division of a police force

-cide *n combining form* 1 indicating a person or thing that kills: *insecticide* 2 indicating a killing; murder: *homicide* [from L *-cīda* (agent), *-cīdium* (act), from *caedere* to kill] > **-cidal** *adj combining form*

cider *or* **cyder** (ˈsaɪdə) *n* 1 an alcoholic drink made from the fermented juice of apples 2 Also called: **sweet cider** *US & Canad* an unfermented drink made from apple juice [C14 from OF, via Med. L, from LGk *sikera* strong drink, from Heb. *shēkhār*]

c.i.f. *or* **CIF** *abbrev for* cost, insurance, and freight (included in the price quoted)

c.i.f.c.i. *abbrev for* cost, insurance, freight, commission, and interest (included in the price quoted)
cig (sɪg) *or* **ciggy** ('sɪgɪ) *n, pl* **cigs** *or* **ciggies** *inf* a cigarette
cigar (sɪ'gɑː) *n* a cylindrical roll of cured tobacco leaves, for smoking [c18 from Sp. *cigarro*]
cigarette *or US (sometimes)* **cigaret** (ˌsɪgə'rɛt) *n* a short tightly rolled cylinder of tobacco, wrapped in thin paper for smoking [c19 from F, lit.: a little CIGAR]
cigarette card *n* a small picture card, formerly given away with cigarettes, now collected as a hobby
cigarillo (ˌsɪgə'rɪləʊ) *n, pl* **cigarillos** a small cigar, often only slightly larger than a cigarette
cilantro (sɪ'læntrəʊ) *n* the US and Canad name for **coriander** [c20 Sp.]
ciliary ('sɪlɪərɪ) *adj* of or relating to cilia
ciliary body *n* the part of the eye that joins the choroid to the iris
Cilician (sɪ'lɪʃɪən) *adj* **1** of or relating to Cilicia (an ancient region of SE Asia Minor) or its inhabitants ▷ *n* **2** a native or inhabitant of Cilicia
Cilician Gates *pl n* a pass in S Turkey, over the Taurus Mountains. Turkish name: **Gülek Bogaz**
cilium ('sɪlɪəm) *n, pl* **cilia** ('sɪlɪə) **1** any of the short threadlike projections on the surface of a cell, organism, etc, whose rhythmic beating causes movement **2** the technical name for **eyelash** [c18 NL, from L: (lower) eyelid, eyelash] > **ciliate** ('sɪlɪɪt, -eɪt) *or* **'cili,ated** *adj*
Cimarosa (ˌtʃiːmə'rəʊzə) *n* **Domenico** 1749–1801, Italian composer, chiefly remembered for his opera buffa *The Secret Marriage* (1792)
C in C *or* **C.-in-C.** *mil abbrev for* Commander in Chief
cinch (sɪntʃ) *n* **1** *sl* an easy task **2** *sl* a certainty **3** a US and Canad name for **girth** (sense 2) **4** *US inf* a firm grip ▷ *vb* **5** (often foll by *up*) *US & Canad* to fasten a girth around (a horse) **6** (*tr*) *inf* to make sure of **7** (*tr*) *inf, chiefly US* to get a firm grip on [c19 from Sp., from L, from *cingere* to encircle]
cinchona (sɪŋ'kəʊnə) *n* **1** any tree or shrub of the South American genus *Cinchona*, having medicinal bark **2** the dried bark of any of these trees, which yields quinine **3** any of the drugs derived from cinchona bark [c18 NL, after the Countess of *Chinchón* (1576–1639), vicereine of Peru] > **cinchonic** (sɪŋ'kɒnɪk) *adj*
Cincinnati (ˌsɪnsɪ'nætɪ) *n* a city in SW Ohio, on the Ohio River. Pop: 331 285 (2000)
Cincinnatus (ˌsɪnsɪ'nɑːtəs) *n* **Lucius Quinctius** ('luːsɪəs 'kwɪŋktɪəs) ?519–438 BC, Roman general and statesman, regarded as a model of simple virtue; dictator of Rome during two crises (458; 439), retiring to his farm after each one
cincture ('sɪŋktʃə) *n* something that encircles, esp a belt or girdle [c16 from L, from *cingere* to gird]
cinder ('sɪndə) *n* **1** a piece of incombustible material left after the combustion of coal, coke, etc; clinker **2** a piece of charred material that burns without flames; ember **3** any solid waste from smelting or refining **4** (*pl*) fragments of volcanic lava; scoriae [OE *sinder*] > **'cindery** *adj*
Cinderella (ˌsɪndə'rɛlə) *n* **1** a girl who achieves fame after being obscure **2** a poor, neglected, or unsuccessful person or thing [c19 after *Cinderella*, the heroine of a fairy tale]
cine- *combining form* indicating motion picture or cinema: *cine camera; cinephotography*
cineaste ('sɪnɪˌæst) *n* an enthusiast for films [c20 F]
cinema ('sɪnɪmə) *n* **1** *chiefly Brit* a place designed for the exhibition of films **2** **the cinema** **2a** the art or business of making films **2b** films collectively [c19 (earlier spelling: *kinema*): shortened from CINEMATOGRAPH] > **cinematic** (ˌsɪnɪ'mætɪk) *adj* > ˌ**cine'matically** *adv*
▷ www.cinema.com
▷ www.sensesofcinema.com
▷ www.learner.org/exhibits/cinema
▷ www.scoot.co.uk/cinemafinder/default.asp
cinematograph (ˌsɪnɪ'mætəˌgrɑːf) *chiefly Brit* ▷ *n* **1** a combined camera, printer, and projector ▷ *vb* **2** to take (pictures) with a film camera [c19 (earlier spelling: *kinematograph*): from Gk *kinēma* motion + -GRAPH]
cinematography (ˌsɪnɪmə'tɒgrəfɪ) *n* the art or science of photographing films > **cinematographer** (ˌsɪnɪmə'tɒgrəfə) *n* > **cinematographic** (ˌsɪnɪˌmætə'græfɪk) *adj* > ˌ**cine**ˌ**mato'graphically** *adv*
▷ www.cinematographersday.com
▷ www.zerocut.com/tech/film_terms.html
▷ www.cinematographer.com
cinéma vérité (*French* sinema verite) *n* films characterized by subjects, actions, etc, that have the appearance of real life [F, lit.: truth cinema]
▷ www.brightlightsfilm.com/31/cinemaverite.html
▷ www.scottschirmer.com/gender-essays-Cinema-Verite.html
cinephile ('sɪnɪˌfaɪl) *n* a person who loves films and cinema
cineraria (ˌsɪnə'rɛərɪə) *n* a plant of the Canary Islands, widely cultivated for its blue, purple, red, or variegated daisy-like flowers [c16 from NL, from L, from *cinis* ashes; from its downy leaves]
cinerarium (ˌsɪnə'rɛərɪəm) *n, pl* **cineraria** (-'rɛərɪə) a place for keeping the ashes of the dead after cremation [c19 from L, from *cinerārius* relating to ashes] > **cinerary** ('sɪnərərɪ) *adj*
cinerator ('sɪnəˌreɪtə) *n chiefly US* a furnace for cremating corpses > ˌ**cine'ration** *n*
cinnabar ('sɪnəˌbɑː) *n* **1** a heavy red mineral consisting of mercury(II) sulphide: the chief ore of mercury. Formula: HgS **2** the red form of mercury(II) sulphide, esp when used as a pigment **3a** a bright red; vermilion **3b** (*as adj*): *a cinnabar tint* **4** a large red-and-black European moth [c15 from OF, from L, from Gk *kinnabari*, of Oriental origin]
cinnamon ('sɪnəmən) *n* **1** a tropical Asian tree, having aromatic yellowish-brown bark **2** the spice obtained from the bark of this tree, used for flavouring food and drink **3a** a light yellowish brown **3b** (*as adj*): *a cinnamon coat* [c15 from OF, via L & Gk, from Heb. *qinnamown*]
cinque (sɪŋk) *n* the number five in cards, dice, etc [c14 from OF *cinq* five]
cinquecento (ˌtʃɪŋkwɪ'tʃɛntəʊ) *n* the 16th century, esp in reference to Italian art, architecture, or literature [c18 It., shortened from *milcinquecento* 1500]
cinquefoil ('sɪŋkˌfɔɪl) *n* **1** any plant of the N temperate rosaceous genus *Potentilla*, typically having five-lobed compound leaves **2** an ornamental carving in the form of five arcs arranged in a circle and separated by cusps [c13 *sink foil*, from OF, from L *quinquefolium* plant with five leaves]
Cinque Ports (sɪŋk) *pl n* an association of ports on the SE coast of England, which from late Anglo-Saxon times until 1685 provided ships for the king's service in return for the profits of justice in their courts
Cintra ('sɪntrə) *n* the former name for **Sintra**
cipher *or* **cypher** ('saɪfə) *n* **1** a method of secret writing using substitution of letters according to a key **2** a secret message **3** the key to a secret message **4** an obsolete name for **zero** (sense 1) **5** any of the Arabic numerals or the Arabic system of numbering **6** a person or thing of no importance; nonentity **7** a design consisting of interwoven letters; monogram ▷ *vb* **8** to put (a message) into secret writing **9** *rare* to perform (a calculation) arithmetically [c14 from OF *cifre* zero, from Med. L, from Ar. *sifr* zero]
circa ('sɜːkə) *prep* (used with a date) at the approximate time of: *circa 1182 BC*. Abbrev: **c, ca** [L: about]
circadian (sɜː'keɪdɪən) *adj* of or relating to biological processes that occur regularly at 24-hour intervals. See

Cc

also **biological clock** [c20 from L *circa* about + *diēs* day]

Circassia (sɜːˈkæsɪə) *n* a region of S Russia, on the Black Sea north of the Caucasus Mountains

Circassian (sɜːˈkæsɪən) *n* **1** a native of Circassia **2** a language or languages spoken in Circassia, belonging to the North-West Caucasian family. See also **Adygei, Kabardian** ▷ *adj also* **Circassic 3** relating to Circassia, its people, or language

Circe (ˈsɜːsɪ) *n Greek myth* an enchantress who detained Odysseus on her island and turned his men into swine > **Circean** (sɜːˈsɪən) *adj*

circle (ˈsɜːkᵊl) *n* **1** a closed plane curve every point of which is equidistant from a given fixed point, the centre **2** the figure enclosed by such a curve **3** *theatre* the section of seats above the main level of the auditorium, usually comprising the dress circle and the upper circle **4** something formed or arranged in the shape of a circle **5** a group of people sharing an interest, activity, upbringing, etc; set: *golf circles; a family circle* **6** a domain or area of activity, interest, or influence **7** a circuit **8** a process or chain of events or parts that forms a connected whole; cycle **9** a parallel of latitude. See also **great circle, small circle 10** one of a number of Neolithic or Bronze Age rings of standing stones, such as Stonehenge **11 come full circle** to arrive back at one's starting point. See also **vicious circle** ▷ *vb* **circles, circling, circled 12** to move in a circle (around) **13** (*tr*) to enclose in a circle; encircle [c14 from L *circulus*, from *circus* ring, circle] > ˈ**circler** *n*

circlet (ˈsɜːklɪt) *n* a small circle or ring, esp a circular ornament worn on the head [c15 from OF *cerclet* a little CIRCLE]

circuit (ˈsɜːkɪt) *n* **1a** a complete route or course, esp one that is curved or circular or that lies around an object **1b** the area enclosed within such a route **2** the act of following such a route: *we made three circuits of the course* **3a** a complete path through which an electric current can flow **3b** (*as modifier*): *a circuit diagram* **4a** a periodical journey around an area, as made by judges, salesmen, etc **4b** the places visited on such a journey **4c** the persons making such a journey **5** an administrative division of the Methodist Church comprising a number of neighbouring churches **6** a number of theatres, cinemas, etc, under one management **7** *sport* **7a** a series of tournaments in which the same players regularly take part: *the international tennis circuit* **7b** (usually preceded by *the*) the contestants who take part in such a series **8** *chiefly Brit* a motor-racing track, usually of irregular shape ▷ *vb* **9** to make or travel in a circuit around (something) [c14 from L *circuitus*, from *circum* around + *īre* to go] > ˈ**circuital** *adj*

circuit breaker *n* a device that under abnormal conditions, such as a short circuit, stops the flow of current in an electrical circuit

circuitous (səˈkjuːɪtəs) *adj* indirect and lengthy; roundabout: *a circuitous route* > **cirˈcuitously** *adv* > **cirˈcuitousness** *n*

circuitry (ˈsɜːkɪtrɪ) *n* **1** the design of an electrical circuit **2** the system of circuits used in an electronic device

circuity (səˈkjuːɪtɪ) *n, pl* **circuities** (of speech, reasoning, etc) a roundabout or devious quality

circular (ˈsɜːkjʊlə) *adj* **1** of, involving, resembling, or shaped like a circle **2** circuitous **3** (of arguments) futile because the truth of the premises cannot be established independently of the conclusion **4** travelling or occurring in a cycle **5** (of letters, announcements, etc) intended for general distribution ▷ *n* **6** a printed advertisement or notice for mass distribution > **circularity** (ˌsɜːkjʊˈlærɪtɪ) *n* > ˈ**circularly** *adv*

circular breathing *n* a technique for sustaining a phrase on a wind instrument, using the cheeks to force air out of the mouth while breathing in through the nose

circularize *or* **circularise** (ˈsɜːkjʊləˌraɪz) *vb* **circularizes, circularizing, circularized** *or* **circularises, circularising, circularised** (*tr*) **1** to distribute circulars to **2** to canvass or petition (people), as for support, votes, etc, by distributing letters, etc **3** to make circular > ˌ**circulariˈzation** *or* ˌ**circulariˈsation** *n*

circular saw *n* a power-driven saw in which a circular disc with a toothed edge is rotated at high speed

circulate (ˈsɜːkjʊˌleɪt) *vb* **circulates, circulating, circulated 1** to send, go, or pass from place to place or person to person: *don't circulate the news* **2** to distribute or be distributed over a wide area **3** to move or cause to move through a circuit, system, etc, returning to the starting point: *blood circulates through the body* **4** to move in a circle [c15 from L *circulārī*, from *circulus* CIRCLE] > ˈ**circulative** *adj* > ˈ**circuˌlator** *n* > ˈ**circulatory** *adj*

circulating library *n* **1** another word (esp US) for **lending library 2** a small library circulated in turn to a group of institutions

circulation (ˌsɜːkjʊˈleɪʃən) *n* **1** the transport of oxygenated blood through the arteries, and the return of oxygen-depleted blood through the veins to the heart, where the cycle is renewed **2** the flow of sap through a plant **3** any movement through a closed circuit **4** the spreading or transmission of something to a wider group of people or area **5** (of air and water) free movement within an area or volume **6a** the distribution of newspapers, magazines, etc **6b** the number of copies of an issue that are distributed **7 in circulation 7a** (of currency) serving as a medium of exchange **7b** (of people) active in a social or business context

circulatory system *n anat, zool* the system concerned with the transport of blood and lymph, consisting of the heart, blood vessels, lymph vessels, etc

circum- *prefix* around; surrounding; on all sides: *circumlocution; circumpolar* [from L *circum* around, from *circus* circle]

circumambient (ˌsɜːkəmˈæmbɪənt) *adj* surrounding [c17 from LL, from L CIRCUM- + *ambīre* to go round] > ˌ**circumˈambience** *or* ˌ**circumˈambiency** *n*

circumambulate (ˌsɜːkəmˈæmbjʊˌleɪt) *vb* **circumambulates, circumambulating, circumambulated 1** to walk around (something) **2** (*intr*) to avoid the point [c17 from LL, from L CIRCUM- + *ambulāre* to walk] > ˌ**circumˌambuˈlation** *n*

circumcise (ˈsɜːkəmˌsaɪz) *vb* **circumcises, circumcising, circumcised** (*tr*) **1** to remove the foreskin of (a male) **2** to incise surgically the skin over the clitoris of (a female) **3** to remove the clitoris of (a female) **4** to perform such an operation as a religious rite on (someone) [c13 from L from CIRCUM- + *caedere* to cut] > **circumcision** (ˌsɜːkəmˈsɪʒən) *n*

circumference (səˈkʌmfərəns) *n* **1** the boundary of a specific area or figure, esp of a circle **2** the length of a closed geometric curve, esp of a circle [c14 from OF, from L from CIRCUM- + *ferre* to bear] > **circumferential** (səˌkʌmfəˈrɛnʃəl) *adj* > **cirˌcumferˈentially** *adv*

circumflex (ˈsɜːkəmˌflɛks) *n* **1** a mark (^) placed over a vowel to show that it is pronounced with rising and falling pitch, as in ancient Greek, or as a long vowel, as in French ▷ *adj* **2** (of nerves, arteries, etc) bending or curving around [c16 from L, from CIRCUM- + *flectere* to bend] > ˌ**circumˈflexion** *n*

circumfuse (ˌsɜːkəmˈfjuːz) *vb* **circumfuses, circumfusing, circumfused** (*tr*) **1** to pour or spread (a liquid, powder, etc) around **2** to surround with a substance, such as a liquid [c16 from L *circumfūsus*, from CIRCUM- + *fundere* to pour] > **circumfusion** (ˌsɜːkəmˈfjuːʒən) *n*

circumlocution (ˌsɜːkəmləˈkjuːʃən) *n* **1** an indirect way of expressing something **2** an indirect expression > **circumlocutory** (ˌsɜːkəmˈlɒkjətərɪ, -trɪ) *adj*

circumnavigate (ˌsɜːkəmˈnævɪˌgeɪt) *vb* **circumnavigates, circumnavigating, circumnavigated** (*tr*) to sail or fly completely around > ˌ**circumˌnaviˈgation** *n* > ˌ**circumˈnaviˌgator** *n*
circumscribe (ˌsɜːkəmˈskraɪb, ˈsɜːkəmˌskraɪb) *vb* **circumscribes, circumscribing, circumscribed** (*tr*) **1** to restrict within limits **2** to mark or set the bounds of **3** to draw a geometric construction around (another construction) so that the two are in contact but do not intersect **4** to draw a line round [c15 from L from CIRCUM- + *scrībere* to write] > ˌ**circumˈscribable** *adj* > ˌ**circumˈscriber** *n* > **circumscription** (ˌsɜːkəmˈskrɪpʃən) *n*
circumspect (ˈsɜːkəmˌspɛkt) *adj* cautious, prudent, or discreet [c15 from L, from CIRCUM- + *specere* to look] > ˌ**circumˈspection** *n* > ˈ**circumˌspectly** *adv*
circumstance (ˈsɜːkəmstəns) *n* **1** (*usually pl*) a condition of time, place, etc, that accompanies or influences an event or condition **2** an incident or occurrence, esp a chance one **3** accessory information or detail **4** formal display or ceremony (archaic except in **pomp and circumstance**) **5 under** *or* **in no circumstances** in no case; never **6 under the circumstances** because of conditions; this being the case ▷ *vb* **circumstances, circumstancing, circumstanced** (*tr*) **7** to place in a particular condition or situation [c13 from OF, from L *circumstantia*, from CIRCUM- + *stāre* to stand]
circumstantial (ˌsɜːkəmˈstænʃəl) *adj* **1** of or dependent on circumstances **2** fully detailed **3** incidental > ˌ**circumˌstantiˈality** *n* > ˌ**circumˈstantially** *adv*
circumstantial evidence *n* indirect evidence that tends to establish a conclusion by inference
circumstantiate (ˌsɜːkəmˈstænʃɪˌeɪt) *vb* **circumstantiates, circumstantiating, circumstantiated** (*tr*) to support by giving particulars > ˌ**circumˌstantiˈation** *n*
circumvallate (ˌsɜːkəmˈvæleɪt) *vb* **circumvallates, circumvallating, circumvallated** (*tr*) to surround with a defensive fortification [c19 from L, from CIRCUM- + *vallum* rampart] > ˌ**circumvalˈlation** *n*
circumvent (ˌsɜːkəmˈvɛnt) *vb* (*tr*) **1** to evade or go around **2** to outwit **3** to encircle (an enemy) so as to intercept or capture [c15 from L, from CIRCUM- + *venīre* to come] > ˌ**circumˈvention** *n*
circus (ˈsɜːkəs) *n, pl* **circuses 1** a travelling company of entertainers such as acrobats, clowns, trapeze artists, and trained animals **2** a public performance given by such a company **3** an arena, usually tented, in which such a performance is held **4** a travelling group of professional sportsmen: *a cricket circus* **5** (in ancient Rome) **5a** an open-air stadium, usually oval or oblong, for chariot races or public games **5b** the games themselves **6** *Brit* **6a** an open place, usually circular, where several streets converge **6b** (*cap. when part of a name*): *Piccadilly Circus* **7** *inf* noisy or rowdy behaviour **8** *inf* a group of people travelling together and putting on a display [c16 from L, from Gk *kirkos* ring]
▷ www.circusweb.com
ciré (ˈsɪəreɪ) *adj* **1** (of fabric) treated with a heat or wax process to make it smooth ▷ *n* **2** such a surface on a fabric **3** a fabric having such a surface [c20 F, from L *cēra* wax]
Cirencester (ˈsaɪrənˌsɛstə) *n* a market town in S England, in Gloucestershire: Roman amphitheatre. Pop: 15 221 (1991). Latin name: **Corinium**
cirque (sɜːk) *n* a steep-sided semicircular or crescent-shaped depression formed in mountainous regions by the erosive action of a glacier [c17 from F, from L *circus* ring]
cirrhosis (sɪˈrəʊsɪs) *n* any of various chronic progressive diseases of the liver, characterized by death of liver cells, irreversible fibrosis, etc [c19 NL, from Gk *kirrhos* orange-coloured + -OSIS; referring to the appearance of the diseased liver] > **cirrhotic** (sɪˈrɒtɪk) *adj*
cirripede (ˈsɪrɪˌpiːd) *or* **cirriped** (ˈsɪrɪˌpɛd) *n* **1** any marine crustacean of the subclass *Cirripedia*, including the barnacles ▷ *adj* **2** of, relating to, or belonging to the *Cirripedia*
cirrocumulus (ˌsɪrəʊˈkjuːmjʊləs) *n, pl* **cirrocumuli** (-ˌlaɪ) a high cloud of ice crystals grouped into small separate globular masses
cirrostratus (ˌsɪrəʊˈstrɑːtəs) *n, pl* **cirrostrati** (-taɪ) a uniform layer of cloud above about 6000 metres
cirrus (ˈsɪrəs) *n, pl* **cirri** (-raɪ) **1** a thin wispy fibrous cloud at high altitudes, composed of ice particles **2** a plant tendril or similar part **3a** a slender tentacle or filament in barnacles and other marine invertebrates **3b** any of various hairlike structures in other animals [c18 from L: curl]
CIS *abbrev for* Commonwealth of Independent States
cis- *prefix* on this side of, as in **cismontane** on this side of the mountains. Often retains the original Latin sense of 'side nearest Rome', as in **cispadane** on this (the southern) side of the Po [from L]
cisalpine (sɪsˈælpaɪn) *adj* on this (the southern) side of the Alps, as viewed from Rome
Cisalpine Gaul *n* (in the ancient world) that part of Gaul between the Alps and the Apennines
Ciscaucasia (ˌsɪskɔːˈkeɪzɪə, -ʒə) *n* the part of Caucasia north of the Caucasus Mountains
cisco (ˈsɪskəʊ) *n, pl* **ciscoes** *or* **ciscos** any of various whitefish, esp the lake herring of cold deep lakes of North America [c19 short for Canad F *ciscoette*, of Algonquian origin]
Ciskei (ˈsɪskaɪ) *n* (formerly) a Bantustan in SE South Africa; granted independence in 1981 but this was not recognized outside South Africa; abolished in 1993. Capital: Bisho
cislunar (sɪsˈluːnə) *adj* of or relating to the space between the earth and the moon
cisplatin (sɪsˈplætɪn) *n* a cytotoxic drug that acts by preventing DNA replication and hence cell divisions, used in the treatment of tumours of the ovary and testis [c20 from CIS- + PLATIN(UM)]
cissing (ˈsɪsɪŋ) *n building trades* the appearance of pinholes, craters, etc, in paintwork due to poor adhesion of the paint to the surface
cissy (ˈsɪsɪ) *n, pl* **-sies** a variant spelling of **sissy**
cist[1] (sɪst) *n* a wooden box for holding ritual objects used in ancient Rome and Greece [c19 from L *cista* box, from Gk *kistē*]
cist[2] (sɪst) *or* **kist** *n* a box-shaped burial chamber made from stone slabs or a hollowed tree trunk [c19 from Welsh: chest, from L; see CIST[1]]
Cistercian (sɪˈstɜːʃən) *n* **1** Also called: **White Monk** a member of a Christian order of monks and nuns founded in 1098, which follows an especially strict form of the Benedictine rule ▷ *adj* **2** of or relating to this order [c17 from F, from Med. L, from *Cistercium* (modern *Cîteaux*), original home of the order]
cistern (ˈsɪstən) *n* **1** a tank for the storage of water, esp on or within the roof of a house or connected to a WC **2** an underground reservoir for the storage of a liquid, esp rainwater **3** Also called: **cisterna** *anat* a sac or partially enclosed space containing body fluid [c13 from OF, from L *cisterna* underground tank, from *cista* box]
cistus (ˈsɪstəs) *n* any plant of the genus *Cistus*. See **rockrose** [c16 NL, from Gk *kistos*]
citadel (ˈsɪtədᵊl, -ˌdɛl) *n* **1** a stronghold within or close to a city **2** any strongly fortified building or place of safety; refuge [c16 from OF, from OIt. *cittadella* a little city, from L *cīvitās*]
citation (saɪˈteɪʃən) *n* **1** the quoting of a book or author **2** a passage or source cited **3a** an official commendation or award, esp for bravery or outstanding service **3b** a formal public statement of this **4** *law* **4a** an official

Cc

summons to appear in court **4b** the document containing such a summons > **citatory** ('saɪtətərɪ) *adj*

cite (saɪt) *vb* **cites, citing, cited** (*tr*) **1** to quote or refer to (a passage, book, or author) **2** to mention or commend (a soldier, etc) for outstanding bravery or meritorious action **3** to summon to appear before a court of law **4** to enumerate: *he cited the king's virtues* [C15 from OF *citer* to summon, ult. from L *ciēre* to excite] > **'citable** *or* **'citeable** *adj*

cithara ('sɪθərə) *or* **kithara** ('kɪθərə) *n* a stringed musical instrument of ancient Greece, similar to the lyre [C18 from Gk *kithara*]

cither ('sɪθə) *or* **cithern** ('sɪθən) *n* a variant spelling of **cittern** [C17 from L, from Gk *kithara*]

citified *or* **cityfied** ('sɪtɪˌfaɪd) *adj often derog* having the customs, manners, or dress of city people

citizen ('sɪtɪzᵊn) *n* **1** a native registered or naturalized member of a state, nation, or other political community **2** an inhabitant of a city or town **3** a civilian, as opposed to a soldier, public official, etc [C14 from Anglo-F *citesein*, from OF *citeien*, from *cité* CITY]

citizenry ('sɪtɪzənrɪ) *n, pl* **citizenries** citizens collectively

citizen's arrest *n* an arrest carried out by an ordinary member of the public rather than an officer of the law

Citizens' Band *n* a range of radio frequencies assigned officially for use by the public for private communication. Abbrev: **CB**
▹ www.bcbc.cwc.net

citizenship ('sɪtɪzənʃɪp) *n* **1** the condition or status of a citizen, with its rights and duties **2** a person's conduct as a citizen

Citlaltépetl (ˌsiːtlɑːl'teɪpɛtᵊl) *n* a volcano in SE Mexico, in central Veracruz state: the highest peak in the country. Height: 5699 m (18 698 ft). Spanish name: **Pico de Orizaba** (piko de ori'saba)

citrate ('sɪtreɪt, -rɪt; 'saɪtreɪt) *n* any salt or ester of citric acid [C18 from CITR(US) + -ATE[1]]

citric ('sɪtrɪk) *adj* of or derived from citrus fruits or citric acid

citric acid *n* a water-soluble weak tribasic acid found in many fruits, esp citrus fruits, and used in pharmaceuticals and as a flavouring (**E330**). Formula: $CH_2(COOH)C(OH)(COOH)CH_2COOH$

citrine ('sɪtrɪn) *n* **1** a brownish-yellow variety of quartz: a gemstone; false topaz **2a** the yellow colour of a lemon **2b** (*as adj*): *citrine hair*

citron ('sɪtrən) *n* **1** a small Asian tree, having lemon-like fruit with a thick aromatic rind **2** the fruit of this tree **3** the rind of this fruit candied and used for decoration and flavouring of foods [C16 from OF, from L *citrus* citrus tree]

citronella (ˌsɪtrə'nɛlə) *n* **1** a tropical Asian grass with bluish-green lemon-scented leaves **2** Also called: **citronella oil** the yellow aromatic oil obtained from this grass, used in insect repellents, soaps, perfumes, etc [C19 NL, from F, from *citron* lemon]

citrus ('sɪtrəs) *n, pl* **citruses 1** any tree or shrub of the tropical and subtropical genus *Citrus*, which includes the orange, lemon, and lime ▹ *adj* **2** *also* **citrous** of or relating to the genus *Citrus* or to the fruits of plants of this genus [C19 from L: citrus tree]

Città del Vaticano (tʃit'ta del vati'kaːno) *n* the Italian name for **Vatican City**

cittern ('sɪtɜːn), **cither,** *or* **cithern** *n* a medieval stringed instrument resembling a lute but having wire strings and a flat back [C16 ? a blend of CITHER + GITTERN]

city ('sɪtɪ) *n, pl* **cities 1** any large town or populous place **2** (in Britain) a town that has received this title from the Crown: usually the seat of a bishop **3** (in the US) an incorporated urban centre with its own government and administration established by state charter **4** (in Canada) a similar urban municipality incorporated by the provincial government **5** the people of a city collectively **6** (*modifier*) in or characteristic of a city: *city habits* ▹ Related adjs.: **civic, urban, municipal** [C13 from OF *cité*, from L *cīvitās* state, from *cīvis* citizen]

City ('sɪtɪ) *n* **the 1** short for **City of London**: the original settlement of London on the N bank of the Thames; a municipality governed by the Lord Mayor and Corporation. Resident pop.: 7186 (2001) **2** the area in central London in which the United Kingdom's major financial business is transacted **3** the various financial institutions located in this area

City and Guilds Institute *n* (in Britain) an examining body for technical and craft skills

city chambers *n* (*functioning as sing*) (in Scotland) the municipal buildings of a city; town hall

City Code *n* (in Britain) short for **City Code on Takeovers and Mergers**: a code laid down in 1968 (later modified) to control takeovers and mergers

city desk *n* the editorial section of a newspaper dealing in Britain with financial news, in the US and Canada with local news

city editor *n* (on a newspaper) **1** *Brit* the editor in charge of financial and commercial news **2** *US & Canad* the editor in charge of local news

city father *n* a person who is active or prominent in the public affairs of a city

cityscape ('sɪtɪˌskeɪp) *n* an urban landscape; view of a city

city-state *n ancient history* a state consisting of a sovereign city and its dependencies

city technology college *n* (in Britain) a type of senior secondary school specializing in technological subjects, set up in inner-city areas with funding from industry as well as the government

Ciudad Bolívar (*Spanish* θiu'ðað bo'liβar) *n* a port in E Venezuela, on the Orinoco River: accessible to ocean-going vessels. Pop: 312 691 (2000 est). Former name (1764–1846): **Angostura**

Ciudad Guayana (*Spanish* θiu'ðað gwa'jana) *n* an industrial conurbation in E Venezuela, on the River Orinoco: iron and steel processing, gold mining. Pop (urban area): 704 168 (2000 est). Former name: **Santo Tomé de Guayana**

Ciudad Juárez (*Spanish* θiu'ðað 'xwarɛθ) *n* a city in N Mexico, in Chihuahua state on the Río Grande, opposite El Paso, Texas. Pop (urban area): 1 190 000 (2000 est). Former name (until 1888): **El Paso del Norte** (ɛl 'paso del 'nɔrte)

Ciudad Trujillo (*Spanish* θiu'ðað tru'xiʎo) *n* the former name (1936–61) of **Santo Domingo**

Ciudad Victoria (*Spanish* θiu'ðað bik'torja) *n* a city in E central Mexico, capital of Tamaulipas state. Pop: 248 000 (2000 est)

civet ('sɪvɪt) *n* **1** a catlike mammal of Africa and S Asia, typically having spotted fur and secreting a powerfully smelling fluid from anal glands **2** the yellowish fatty secretion of such an animal, used as a fixative in the manufacture of perfumes **3** the fur of such an animal [C16 from OF, from It., from Ar. *zabād* civet perfume]

civic ('sɪvɪk) *adj* of or relating to a city, citizens, or citizenship [C16 from L, from *cīvis* citizen] > **'civically** *adv*

civic centre *n Brit* the public buildings of a town, including recreational facilities and offices of local administration

civics ('sɪvɪks) *n* (*functioning as sing*) the study of the rights and responsibilities of citizenship

civies ('sɪvɪz) *pl n inf* a variant spelling of **civvies** See **civvy** (sense 2)

civil ('sɪvᵊl) *adj* **1** of the ordinary life of citizens as distinguished from military, legal, or ecclesiastical affairs **2** of or relating to the citizen as an individual: *civil rights* **3** of or occurring within the state or between citizens: *civil strife* **4** polite or courteous: *a civil manner* **5** of or in accordance with Roman law [C14 from OF, from L *cīvīlis*, from *cīvis* citizen] > ˈ**civilly** *adv*

civil defence *n* the organizing of civilians to deal with enemy attacks

civil disobedience *n* a refusal to obey laws, pay taxes, etc: a nonviolent means of protesting

civil engineer *n* a person qualified to design and construct public works, such as roads, bridges, harbours, etc > **civil engineering** *n*

▷ www.ce.gatech.edu/WWW-CE/

civilian (sɪˈvɪljən) *n* **a** a person whose occupation is civil or nonmilitary **b** (*as modifier*): *civilian life* [c14 (orig.: a practitioner of civil law): from *civile* (from L *jūs cīvīle* civil law) + -IAN]

civility (sɪˈvɪlɪtɪ) *n, pl* **civilities** **1** politeness or courtesy **2** (*often pl*) an act of politeness

civilization *or* **civilisation** (ˌsɪvɪlaɪˈzeɪʃən) *n* **1** a human society that has a complex cultural, political, and legal organization; an advanced state in social development **2** the peoples or nations collectively who have achieved such a state **3** the total culture and way of life of a particular people, nation, region, or period **4** the process of bringing or achieving civilization **5** intellectual, cultural, and moral refinement **6** cities or populated areas, as contrasted with sparsely inhabited areas, deserts, etc

civilize *or* **civilise** (ˈsɪvɪˌlaɪz) *vb* **civilizes, civilizing, civilized** *or* **civilises, civilising, civilised** (*tr*) **1** to bring out of savagery or barbarism into a state characteristic of civilization **2** to refine, educate, or enlighten

civilized *or* **civilised** (ˈsɪvɪˌlaɪzd) *adj* **1** having a high state of culture and social development **2** cultured; polite: *everything had been done in a civilized manner*

civil law *n* **1** the law of a state relating to private and civilian affairs **2** the body of law in ancient Rome, esp as applicable to private citizens **3** law based on the Roman system as distinguished from common law and canon law

civil liberty *n* the right of an individual to certain freedoms of speech and action

civil list *n* (in Britain) the annuities voted by Parliament for the support of the royal household and the royal family

civil marriage *n law* a marriage performed by an official other than a clergyman

civil rights *pl n* **1** the personal rights of the individual citizen **2** (*modifier*) of, relating to, or promoting equality in social, economic, and political rights

civil servant *n* a member of the civil service

civil service *n* **1** the service responsible for the public administration of the government of a country. It excludes the legislative, judicial, and military branches **2** the members of the civil service collectively

civil society *n* the elements such as freedom of speech, an independent judiciary, etc, that make up a democratic society

civil war *n* war between parties or factions within the same nation

Civil War *n* **1** *English history* the conflict between Charles I and the Parliamentarians resulting from disputes over their respective prerogatives. Parliament gained decisive victories at Marston Moor in 1644 and Naseby in 1645, and Charles was executed in 1649 **2** *US history* the war fought from 1861 to 1865 between the North and the South, sparked off by Lincoln's election as president but with deep-rooted political and economic causes, exacerbated by the slavery issue. The advantages of the North in terms of population, finance, and communications brought about the South's eventual surrender at Appomattox

▷ http://americancivilwar.com
▷ www.civilwar.com
▷ www.open2.net/civilwar
▷ http://easyweb.easynet.co.uk/~crossby/ECW

civvy (ˈsɪvɪ) *n, pl* **civvies** *sl* **1** a civilian **2** (*pl*) Also: **civies** civilian dress as opposed to uniform **3** **civvy street** civilian life

CJ *abbrev for* Chief Justice

CJA (in Britain) *abbrev for* Criminal Justice Act

CJD *abbrev for* Creutzfeldt-Jakob disease

Cl *the chemical symbol for* chlorine

clachan (*Gaelic* ˈklaxən; *English* ˈklæ-) *n Scot & Irish dialect* a small village; hamlet [c15 from Scot. Gaelic: prob. from *clach* stone]

clack (klæk) *vb* **1** to make or cause to make a sound like that of two pieces of wood hitting each other **2** (*intr*) to jabber ▷ *n* **3** a short sharp sound **4** chatter **5** Also called: **clack valve** a simple nonreturn valve using a hinged flap or a ball [c13 prob. from ON *klaka* to twitter, imit.] > ˈ**clacker** *n*

Clackmannanshire (klækˈmænənʃɪə, -ʃə) *n* a council area and historical county of central Scotland; became part of the Central region in 1975 but reinstated as an independent unitary authority in 1996; mainly agricultural. Administrative centre: Alloa. Pop: 48 077 (2001). Area: 142 sq km (55 sq miles)

Clacton *or* **Clacton-on-Sea** (ˈklæktən) *n* a town and resort in SE England, in E Essex. Pop: 45 065 (1991)

clad[1] (klæd) *vb* a past tense and past participle of **clothe** [OE *clāthode* clothed, from *clāthian* to CLOTHE]

clad[2] (klæd) *vb* **clads, cladding, clad** (*tr*) to bond a metal to (another metal), esp to form a protective coating [c14 special use of CLAD[1]]

cladding (ˈklædɪŋ) *n* **1** the process of protecting one metal by bonding a second metal to its surface **2** the protective coating so bonded to metal **3** the material used for the outside facing of a building, etc

clade (kleɪd) *n biol* a group of organisms considered as having evolved from a common ancestor [c20 from Gk *klados* branch, shoot]

cladistics (kləˈdɪstɪks) *n* (*functioning as sing*) a method of grouping animals that makes use of lines of descent rather than structural similarities [c20 NL from Gk *klados* branch, shoot] > **cladism** (ˈklædɪzəm) *n* > **cladist** (ˈklædɪst) *n*

Cc

claim (kleɪm) *vb* (*mainly tr*) **1** to demand as being due or as one's property; assert one's title or right to: *he claimed the record* **2** (*takes a clause as object or an infinitive*) to assert as a fact; maintain against denial: *he claimed to be telling the truth* **3** to call for or need; deserve: *this problem claims our attention* **4** to take: *the accident claimed four lives* ▷ *n* **5** an assertion of a right; a demand for something as due **6** an assertion of something as true, real, or factual **7** a right or just title to something; basis for demand: *a claim to fame* **8** anything that is claimed, such as a piece of land staked out by a miner **9a** a demand for payment in connection with an insurance policy, etc **9b** the sum of money demanded [c13 from OF *claimer* to call, from L *clāmāre* to shout] > ˈ**claimable** *adj* > ˈ**claimant** *or* ˈ**claimer** *n*

Clair (*French* klɛr) *n* **René** (rəne), real name *René Chomette*. 1898–1981, French film director; noted for his comedies including *An Italian Straw Hat* (1928) and pioneering sound films such as *Sous les toits de Paris* (1930); later films include *Les Belles de nuit* (1952)

clairvoyance (klɛəˈvɔɪəns) *n* **1** the alleged power of perceiving things beyond the natural range of the senses **2** keen intuitive understanding [c19 from F: clear-seeing, from *clair* clear + *voyance*, from *voir* to see]

clairvoyant (klɛəˈvɔɪənt) *adj* **1** of or possessing clairvoyance **2** having great insight ▷ *n* **3** a person claiming to have the power to foretell future events > **clairˈvoyantly** *adv*

clam (klæm) *n* **1** any of various burrowing bivalve molluscs **2** the edible flesh of such a mollusc **3** *inf* a reticent person ▷ *vb* **clams, clamming, clammed** **4** (*intr*) *chiefly US* to gather clams ▷ See also **clam up** [c16 from earlier *clamshell*, that is, shell that clamps]

clamant ('kleɪmənt) *adj* **1** noisy **2** calling urgently [c17 from L, from *clāmāre* to shout]
clambake ('klæm,beɪk) *n US & Canad* a picnic, often by the sea, at which clams, etc, are baked
clamber ('klæmbə) *vb* **1** (usually foll by *up, over,* etc) to climb (something) awkwardly, esp by using both hands and feet ▷ *n* **2** a climb performed in this manner [c15 prob. var. of CLIMB] > '**clamberer** *n*
clam-diggers *pl n* calf-length trousers
clammy ('klæmɪ) *adj* **clammier, clammiest** **1** unpleasantly sticky; moist **2** (of the weather) close; humid [c14 from OE *clǣman* to smear] > '**clammily** *adv* > '**clamminess** *n*
clamour *or US* **clamor** ('klæmə) *n* **1** a loud persistent outcry **2** a vehement expression of collective feeling or outrage: *a clamour against higher prices* **3** a loud and persistent noise: *the clamour of traffic* ▷ *vb* **4** (*intr;* often foll by *for* or *against*) to make a loud noise or outcry; make a public demand **5** (*tr*) to move or force by outcry [c14 from OF, from L, from *clāmāre* to cry out] > '**clamorous** *adj* > '**clamorously** *adv* > '**clamorousness** *n*
clamp[1] (klæmp) *n* **1** a mechanical device with movable jaws with which an object can be secured to a bench or with which two objects may be secured together **2** See **wheel clamp** ▷ *vb* (*tr*) **3** to fix or fasten with or as if with a clamp **4** to immobilize (a car) by means of a wheel clamp **5** to inflict or impose forcefully: *they clamped a curfew on the town* [c14 from Du. or Low G *klamp*]
clamp[2] (klæmp) *n* **1** a mound of a harvested root crop, covered with straw and earth to protect it from winter weather ▷ *vb* **2** (*tr*) to enclose (a harvested root crop) in a mound [c16 from MDu. *klamp* heap]
clamp down *vb* (*intr, adv;* often foll by *on*) **1** to behave repressively; attempt to suppress something regarded as undesirable ▷ *n* **clampdown** **2** a sudden restrictive measure
clam up *vb* (*intr, adv*) *inf* to keep or become silent or withhold information
clan (klæn) *n* **1** a group of people interrelated by ancestry or marriage **2** a group of families with a common surname and a common ancestor, esp among the Scots and the Irish **3** a group of people united by common characteristics, aims, or interests [c14 from Scot. Gaelic *clann* family, descendants, from L *planta* sprout]
Clancy ('klænsɪ) *n* **Tom** born 1947, U.S. novelist; his thrillers, many of which have been filmed, include *The Hunt for Red October* (1984), *Clear and Present Danger* (1989), *Debt of Honour* (1994) and *Red Rabbit* (2002)
clandestine (klæn'dɛstɪn) *adj* secret and concealed, often for illicit reasons; furtive [c16 from L, from *clam* secretly] > **clan'destinely** *adv*
clang (klæŋ) *vb* **1** to make or cause to make a loud resounding noise, as metal when struck **2** (*intr*) to move or operate making such a sound ▷ *n* **3** a resounding metallic noise **4** the harsh cry of certain birds [c16 from L *clangere*]
clanger ('klæŋə) *n* **1** *inf* a conspicuous mistake (esp in **drop a clanger**) **2** something that clangs or causes a clang [c20 from CLANG]
clangour *or US* **clangor** ('klæŋgə, 'klæŋə) *n* **1** a loud resonant often-repeated noise **2** an uproar ▷ *vb* **3** (*intr*) to make or produce a loud resonant noise > '**clangorous** *adj* > '**clangorously** *adv*
clank (klæŋk) *n* **1** an abrupt harsh metallic sound ▷ *vb* **2** to make or cause to make such a sound **3** (*intr*) to move or operate making such a sound [c17 imit.] > '**clankingly** *adv*
clannish ('klænɪʃ) *adj* **1** of or characteristic of a clan **2** tending to associate closely within a group to the exclusion of outsiders; cliquish > '**clannishly** *adv* > '**clannishness** *n*
clansman ('klænzmən) *or* (*fem*) **clanswoman** *n, pl* **clansmen** *or* **clanswomen** a person belonging to a clan
clap[1] (klæp) *vb* **claps, clapping, clapped** **1** to make or cause to make a sound abrupt sound, as of two nonmetallic objects struck together **2** to applaud (someone or something) by striking the palms of the hands together sharply **3** (*tr*) to strike (a person) lightly with an open hand, in greeting, etc **4** (*tr*) to place or put quickly or forcibly: *they clapped him into jail* **5** (of certain birds) to flap (the wings) noisily **6** (*intr;* foll by *up* or *together*) to contrive or put together hastily **7** **clap eyes on** *inf* to catch sight of **8** **clap hold of** *inf* to grasp suddenly or forcibly ▷ *n* **9** the sharp abrupt sound produced by striking the hands together **10** the act of clapping, esp in applause **11** a sudden sharp sound, esp of thunder **12** a light blow **13** *arch* a sudden action or mishap [OE *clæppan;* imit.]
clap[2] (klæp) *n* (usually preceded by *the*) a slang word for **gonorrhoea** [c16 from OF *clapoir* venereal sore, from *clapier* brothel, from ?]
clapboard ('klæp,bɔːd, 'klæbəd) *n* **1** a long thin timber board, used esp in the US and Canada in wood-frame construction by lapping each board over the one below ▷ *vb* **2** (*tr*) to cover with such boards [c16 partial translation of Low G *klappholt,* from *klappen* to crack + *holt* wood]
clapped out *adj* (**clapped-out** *when prenominal*) *inf* **1** *Brit, Austral & NZ* worn out; dilapidated **2** *Austral & NZ* extremely tired; exhausted
clapper ('klæpə) *n* **1** a person or thing that claps **2** Also called: **tongue** a small piece of metal suspended within a bell that causes it to sound when made to strike against its side **3** **go (run, move) like the clappers** *Brit inf* to move extremely fast
clapperboard ('klæpə,bɔːd) *n* a pair of hinged boards clapped together during film shooting to aid in synchronizing sound and picture prints
Clapton ('klæptən) *n* **Eric** born 1945, British rock guitarist, noted for his virtuoso style, his work with the Yardbirds (1963–65), Cream (1966–68), and, with Derek and the Dominos, the album *Layla* (1970); later solo work includes *Unplugged* (1992)
claptrap ('klæp,træp) *n inf* **1** contrived but foolish talk **2** insincere and pretentious talk: *politicians' claptrap* [c18 from CLAP[1] + TRAP[1]]
claque (klæk) *n* **1** a group of people hired to applaud **2** a group of fawning admirers [c19 from F, from *claquer* to clap, imit.]
Clare[1] (klɛə) *n* a county of W Republic of Ireland, in Munster between Galway Bay and the Shannon estuary. County town: Ennis. Pop: 94 006 (1996). Area: 3188 sq km (1231 sq miles)
Clare[2] (klɛə) *n* **1** **Anthony** (**Ward**) born 1942, Irish psychiatrist and broadcaster; presenter of the radio series *In the Psychiatrist's Chair* from 1982 **2** **John** 1793–1864, English poet, noted for his descriptions of country life, particularly in *The Shepherd's Calendar* (1827) and *The Rural Muse* (1835). He was confined in a lunatic asylum from 1837
Clarendon[1] ('klærəndən) *n* a village near Salisbury in S England: site of a council held by Henry II in 1164 that produced a code of laws (the **Constitutions of Clarendon**) defining relations between church and state
Clarendon[2] ('klærəndən) *n* **1st Earl of,** title of *Edward Hyde.* 1609–74, English statesman and historian; chief adviser to Charles II (1660–67); author of *History of the Rebellion and Civil Wars in England* (1704–07)
Clare of Assisi *n* **Saint** 1194–1253, Italian nun; founder of the Franciscan Order of Poor Clares. Feast day: Aug. 11
claret ('klærət) *n* **1** a red wine, esp one from the Bordeaux district of France **2a** a purplish-red colour **2b** (*as adj*): *a claret football strip* [c14 from OF (*vin*) *claret* clear (wine), from Med. L *clārātum,* from L *clārus* clear]
clarify ('klærɪ,faɪ) *vb* **clarifies, clarifying, clarified** **1** to make or become clear or easy to understand **2** to make

or become free of impurities **3** to make (fat, butter, etc) clear by heating, etc, or (of fat, etc) to become clear as a result of such a process [c14 from OF, from LL, from L *clārus* clear + *facere* to make] > ˌ**clarifiˈcation** *n* > ˈ**clariˌfier** *n*

clarinet (ˌklærɪˈnɛt) *n music* **1** a keyed woodwind instrument with a cylindrical bore and a single reed **2** an orchestral musician who plays the clarinet [c18 from F, prob. from It., from *clarino* trumpet] > ˌ**clariˈnettist** *or US sometimes* ˌ**clariˈnetist** *n*

clarion (ˈklærɪən) *n* **1** a stop of trumpet quality on an organ **2** an obsolete, high-pitched, small-bore trumpet **3** the sound of such an instrument or any similar sound ▷ *adj* **4** (*prenominal*) clear and ringing; inspiring: *a clarion call to action* ▷ *vb* **5** to proclaim loudly [c14 from Med. L *clāriō* trumpet, from L *clārus* clear]

clarity (ˈklærɪtɪ) *n* **1** clearness, as of expression **2** clearness, as of water [c16 from L *clāritās*, from *clārus* clear]

Clark (klɑːk) *n* **1 Helen** born 1950, New Zealand politician; Labour prime minister from 1999 **2 James,** known as *Jim*. 1936–68, Scottish racing driver; World Champion (1963, 1965) **3 Kenneth,** Baron Clark of Saltwood. 1903–83, English art historian: his books include *Civilization* (1969), which he first presented as a television series **4 William** 1770–1838, US explorer and frontiersman: best known for his expedition to the Pacific Northwest (1804–06) with Meriwether Lewis

Clarke (klɑːk) *n* **1** Sir **Arthur C(harles)** born 1917, British science-fiction writer, who helped to develop the first communications satellites. He scripted the film *2001, A Space Odyssey* (1968) **2 Austin** 1896–1974, Irish poet and verse dramatist. His volumes include *The Vengeance of Fionn* (1917), *Night and Morning* (1938), and *Ancient Lights* (1955) **3 Jeremiah** ?1673-1707, English composer and organist, best known for his *Trumpet Voluntary*, formerly attributed to Purcell **4 Marcus** (**Andrew Hislop**) 1846–81, Australian novelist born in England, noted for his novel *For the Term of His Natural Life*, published in serial form (1870–72); other works include *Twixt Shadow and Shine* (1875)

clarkia (ˈklɑːkɪə) *n* any North American plant of the genus *Clarkia*: cultivated for their red, purple, or pink flowers [c19 NL, after William CLARK]

Clarkson (ˈklɑːksən) *n* **Thomas** 1760–1846, British campaigner for the abolition of slavery

clary (ˈklɛərɪ) *n, pl* **claries** any of several European plants having aromatic leaves and blue flowers [c14 from earlier *sclarreye*, from Med. L *sclareia*, from ?]

-clase *n combining form* (in mineralogy) indicating a particular type of cleavage: *plagioclase* [via F from Gk *klasis* a breaking]

clash (klæʃ) *vb* **1** to make or cause to make a loud harsh sound, esp by striking together **2** (*intr*) to be incompatible **3** (*intr*) to engage together in conflict **4** (*intr*) (of dates or events) to coincide **5** (*intr*) (of colours) to look inharmonious together ▷ *n* **6** a loud harsh noise **7** a collision or conflict [c16 imit.] > ˈ**clasher** *n*

clasp (klɑːsp) *n* **1** a fastening, such as a catch or hook, for holding things together **2** a firm grasp or embrace **3** *mil* a bar on a medal ribbon, to indicate either a second award or the battle, campaign, or reason for its award ▷ *vb* (*tr*) **4** to hold in a firm grasp **5** to grasp firmly with the hand **6** to fasten together with or as if with a clasp [c14 from ?] > ˈ**clasper** *n*

claspers (ˈklɑːspəz) *pl n zool* **1** a paired organ of male insects, used to clasp the female during copulation **2** a paired organ of male sharks and related fish, used to assist the transfer of spermatozoa into the body of the female during copulation

clasp knife *n* a large knife with one or more blades or other devices folding into the handle

class (klɑːs) *n* **1** a collection or division of people or things sharing a common characteristic **2** a group of persons sharing a similar social and economic position **3a** the pattern of divisions that exist within a society on the basis of rank, economic status, etc **3b** (*as modifier*): *the class struggle; class distinctions* **4a** a group of pupils or students who are taught together **4b** a meeting of a group of students for tuition **5** *US* a group of students who graduated in a specified year: *the class of '53* **6** (*in combination and as modifier*) *Brit* a grade of attainment in a university honours degree: *second-class honours* **7** one of several standards of accommodation in public transport **8** *inf* excellence or elegance, esp in dress, design, or behaviour **9** *biol* any of the taxonomic groups into which a phylum is divided and which contains one or more orders **10** *maths* another name for **set²** (sense 3) **11 in a class of its own** *or* **in a class by oneself** unequalled; unparalleled ▷ *vb* **12** to have or assign a place within a group, grade, or class [c17 from L *classis* class, rank, fleet]

class A drug *n law* (in Britain) any of the most dangerous group of controlled drugs, including heroin, cocaine, and MDMA ▷ Cf **class B drug, class C drug**

class B drug *n law* (in Britain) any of the second most dangerous group of controlled drugs, including amphetamine ▷ Cf **class A drug, class C drug**

class C drug *n law* (in Britain) any of the least dangerous group of controlled drugs, including cannabis and temazepam ▷ Cf **class A drug, class B drug**

class-conscious *adj* aware of belonging to a particular social rank > ˌ**class-ˈconsciousness** *n*

classic (ˈklæsɪk) *adj* **1** of the highest class, esp in art or literature **2** serving as a standard or model of its kind **3** adhering to an established set of principles in the arts or sciences: *a classic proof* **4** characterized by simplicity, balance, regularity, and purity of form; classical **5** of lasting interest or significance **6** continuously in fashion because of its simple style: *a classic dress* ▷ *n* **7** an author, artist, or work of art of the highest excellence **8** a creation or work considered as definitive **9** *horse racing* any of the five principal races for three-year-old horses in Britain, namely the One Thousand Guineas, Two Thousand Guineas, Derby, Oaks, and Saint Leger [c17 from L *classicus* of the first rank, from *classis* division, rank, class]

classical (ˈklæsɪkᵊl) *adj* **1** of, relating to, or characteristic of the ancient Greeks and Romans or their civilization **2** designating, following, or influenced by the art or culture of ancient Greece or Rome: *classical architecture* **3** *music* **3a** of, relating to, or denoting any music or its period of composition marked by stability of form, intellectualism, and restraint. Cf **romantic** (sense 5) **3b** accepted as a standard: *the classical suite* **3c** denoting serious art music in general. Cf **pop²** **4** denoting or relating to a style in any of the arts characterized by emotional restraint and conservatism: *a classical style of painting* **5** (of an education) based on the humanities and the study of Latin and Greek **6** *physics* not involving the quantum theory or the theory of relativity: *classical mechanics* > ˌ**classiˈcality** *or* ˈ**classicalness** *n* > ˈ**classically** *adv*

▷ www.wilhelm-aerospace.org/Architecture/classical
▷ www.le.ac.uk/ur/urarch5.html
▷ www.classicalmus.hispeed.com/classical.html

Classical school *n* economic theory based on the works of Adam Smith and David Ricardo, which explains the creation of wealth and advocates free trade

▷ www.frbsf.org/publications/education/unfrmd.great/greatschls.html
▷ www.ku.edu/~jsic/econ-524/forclass.html
▷ www.eh.net/HE/he_resources/classical.php

classic car *n chiefly Brit* a car that is more than twenty five years old ▷ Cf **veteran car, vintage car**

classicism (ˈklæsɪˌsɪzəm) *or* **classicalism** (ˈklæsɪkəˌlɪzəm) *n* **1** a style based on the study of Greek

Cc

and Roman models, characterized by emotional restraint and regularity of form; the antithesis of romanticism **2** knowledge of the culture of ancient Greece and Rome **3a** a Greek or Latin expression **3b** an expression in a modern language that is modelled on a Greek or Latin form > **'classicist** *n*

classicize *or* **classicise** ('klæsɪˌsaɪz) *vb* **classicizes, classicizing, classicized** *or* **classicises, classicising, classicised 1** (*tr*) to make classic **2** (*intr*) to imitate classical style

classics ('klæsɪks) *n* **1 the** a body of literature regarded as great or lasting, esp that of ancient Greece or Rome **2 the** the ancient Greek and Latin languages **3** (*functioning as sing*) ancient Greek and Roman culture as a subject for academic study

classification (ˌklæsɪfɪ'keɪʃən) *n* **1** systematic placement in categories **2** one of the divisions in a system of classifying **3** *biol* **3a** the placing of animals and plants in a series of increasingly specialized groups because of similarities in structure, origin, etc, that indicate a common relationship **3b** the study of the principles and practice of this process; taxonomy [C18 from F; see CLASS, -IFY, -ATION] > **'classificatory** *adj*

classified ('klæsɪˌfaɪd) *adj* **1** arranged according to some system of classification **2** *government* (of information) not available to people outside a restricted group, esp for reasons of national security **3** *US & Canad inf* (of information) closely concealed or secret **4** (of advertisements in newspapers, etc) arranged according to type **5** *Brit* (of newspapers) containing sports results **6** (of British roads) having a number in the national road system

classify ('klæsɪˌfaɪ) *vb* **classifies, classifying, classified** (*tr*) **1** to arrange or order by classes; categorize **2** *government* to declare (information, documents, etc) of possible aid to an enemy and therefore not available to people outside a restricted group [C18 back formation from CLASSIFICATION] > **'classiˌfiable** *adj* > **'classiˌfier** *n*

class interval *n statistics* one of the intervals into which the range of a variable of a distribution is divided, esp one of the divisions of the base line of a bar chart or histogram

classless ('klɑːslɪs) *adj* **1** not belonging to a class **2** characterized by the absence of economic and social distinctions > **'classlessness** *n*

class list *n* (in Britain) a list categorizing students according to the class of honours they have obtained in their degree examination

classmate ('klɑːsˌmeɪt) *n* a friend or contemporary of the same class in a school

classroom ('klɑːsˌruːm, -ˌrʊm) *n* a room in which classes are conducted, esp in a school

classroom assistant *n* a person whose job is to help a schoolteacher in the classroom

class struggle *n* **the** *Marxism* the continual conflict between the capitalist and working classes for economic and political power

classy ('klɑːsɪ) *adj* **classier, classiest** *sl* elegant; stylish > **'classiness** *n*

clatter ('klætə) *vb* **1** to make or cause to make a rattling noise, esp as a result of movement **2** (*intr*) to chatter ▹ *n* **3** a rattling sound or noise **4** a noisy commotion, such as loud chatter [OE *clatrung* clattering (gerund)] > **'clatterer** *n* > **'clatteringly** *adv*

Claude Lorrain (*French* klod lɔrɛ̃) *n* real name *Claude Gelée*. 1600–82, French painter, esp of idealized landscapes, noted for his subtle depiction of light

Claudius ('klɔːdɪəs) *n* full name *Tiberius Claudius Drusus Nero Germanicus*. 10 BC–54 AD, Roman emperor (41–54); invaded Britain (43); poisoned by his fourth wife, Agrippina

Claudius II *n* full name *Marcus Aurelius Claudius*, called *Gothicus*. 214–270 AD, Roman emperor (268–270)

clause (klɔːz) *n* **1** *grammar* a group of words, consisting of a subject and a predicate including a finite verb, that does not necessarily constitute a sentence ▹ Cf **phrase** See also **main clause, subordinate clause 2** a section of a legal document such as a contract, will, or draft statute [C13 from OF, from Med. L *clausa* a closing (of a rhetorical period), from L, from *claudere* to close] > **'clausal** *adj*

Clausewitz (*German* 'klauzəvɪts) *n* **Karl von** (karl fɔn) 1780–1831, Prussian general, noted for his works on military strategy, esp *Vom Kriege* (1833)

Clausius (*German* 'klauziʊs) *n* **Rudolf Julius** ('ruːdɔlf 'juːliʊs) 1822–88, German physicist and mathematician. He enunciated the second law of thermodynamics (1850) and developed the kinetic theory of gases

claustrophobia (ˌklɔːstrə'fəʊbɪə, ˌklɒs-) *n* an abnormal fear of being in a confined space [C19 NL from L *claustrum* CLOISTER + -PHOBIA] > **'claustroˌphobe** *n* > **ˌclaustro'phobic** *adj*

clavate ('kleɪveɪt, -vɪt) *or* **claviform** ('klævɪˌfɔːm) *adj biol* shaped like a club [C19 from L *clāva* club] > **'clavately** *adv*

clave[1] (kleɪv, klɑːv) *n music* one of a pair of hardwood sticks struck together to make a hollow sound, esp to mark the beat in Latin-American dance music [C20 from American Sp., from L *clavis* key]

clave[2] (kleɪv) *vb arch* a past tense of **cleave**

clavichord ('klævɪˌkɔːd) *n* a keyboard instrument consisting of a number of thin wire strings struck from below by brass tangents [C15 from Med. L, from L *clāvis* key + *chorda* CHORD[1]]

clavicle ('klævɪkᵊl) *n* **1** either of the two bones connecting the shoulder blades with the upper part of the breastbone. Nontechnical name: **collarbone 2** the corresponding structure in other vertebrates [C17 from Med. L *clāvicula*, from L *clāvis* key] > **clavicular** (klə'vɪkjʊlə) *adj*

clavier (klə'vɪə, 'klævɪə) *n* **a** any keyboard instrument **b** the keyboard itself [C18 from F: keyboard, from L *clāvis* key]

claw (klɔː) *n* **1** a curved pointed horny process on the end of each digit in birds, some reptiles, and certain mammals **2** a corresponding structure in some invertebrates, such as the pincer of a crab **3** a part or member like a claw in function or appearance ▹ *vb* **4** to scrape, tear, or dig (something or someone) with claws, etc **5** (*tr*) to create by scratching as with claws: *to claw an opening* [OE *clawu*] > **'clawer** *n*

claw back *vb* (*tr, adv*) **1** to get back (something) with difficulty **2** to recover (a sum of money), esp by taxation or a penalty ▹ *n* **clawback 3** the recovery of a sum of money, esp by taxation or a penalty **4** the sum so recovered

claw hammer *n* a hammer with a cleft at one end of the head for extracting nails

clay (kleɪ) *n* **1** a very fine-grained material that occurs as sedimentary rocks, soils, and other deposits. It becomes plastic when moist but hardens on heating and is used in the manufacture of bricks, ceramics, etc **2** earth or mud **3** *poetic* the material of the human body [OE *clǣg*] > **'clayey, 'clayish,** *or* **'clayˌlike** *adj*

Clay (kleɪ) *n* **1 Cassius** See **Muhammad Ali 2 Henry** 1777–1852, US statesman and orator; secretary of state (1825–29)

claymation (ˌkleɪ'meɪʃən) *n* the techniques of animation applied to clay models [C20 from CLAY + (ANI)MATION]

claymore ('kleɪˌmɔː) *n* a large two-edged broadsword used formerly by Scottish Highlanders [C18 from Gaelic *claidheamh mōr* great sword]

clay pigeon *n* a disc of baked clay hurled into the air from a machine as a target to be shot at

CLC *abbrev for* Canadian Labour Congress

-cle *suffix forming nouns* indicating smallness: *cubicle; particle* [via OF from L *-culus*. See -CULE]

clean (kliːn) *adj* 1 without dirt or other impurities; unsoiled 2 without anything in it or on it: *a clean page* 3 recently washed; fresh 4 without extraneous or foreign materials 5 without defect, difficulties, or problems 6 (of a nuclear weapon) producing little or no radioactive fallout or contamination 7 (of a wound, etc) having no pus or other sign of infection 8 pure; morally sound 9 without objectionable language or obscenity 10 thorough or complete: *a clean break* 11 dexterous or adroit: *a clean throw* 12 *sport* played fairly and without fouls 13 simple in design: *a ship's clean lines* 14 *aeronautics* causing little turbulence; streamlined 15 honourable or respectable 16 habitually neat 17 (esp of a driving licence) showing or having no record of offences 18 *sl* 18a innocent; not guilty 18b not carrying illegal drugs, weapons, etc ▷ *vb* 19 to make or become free of dirt, filth, etc: *the stove cleans easily* 20 (*tr*) to remove in making clean: *to clean marks off the wall* 21 (*tr*) to prepare (fish, poultry, etc) for cooking: *to clean a chicken* ▷ *adv* 22 in a clean way; cleanly 23 *not standard* (intensifier): *clean forgotten* 24 **come clean** *inf* to make a revelation or confession ▷ *n* 25 the act or an instance of cleaning: *he gave his shoes a clean* 26 **clean sweep** See **sweep** (sense 28) ▷ See also **clean out, clean up** [OE *clǣne*] > **'cleanable** *adj* > **'cleanness** *n*

clean-cut *adj* 1 clearly outlined; neat: *clean-cut lines of a ship* 2 definite

cleaner ('kliːnə) *n* 1 a person, device, chemical agent, etc, that removes dirt, as from clothes or carpets 2 (*usually pl*) a shop, etc, that provides a dry-cleaning service 3 **take (a person) to the cleaners** *inf* to rob or defraud (a person)

cleanly ('kliːnlɪ) *adv* 1 in a fair manner 2 easily or smoothly ▷ *adj* ('klɛnlɪ), **cleanlier, cleanliest** 3 habitually clean or neat > **cleanlily** ('klɛnlɪlɪ) *adv* > **cleanliness** ('klɛnlɪnɪs) *n*

clean out *vb* (*tr, adv*) 1 (foll by *of* or *from*) to remove (something) (from or away from) 2 *sl* to leave (someone) with no money 3 *inf* to exhaust (stocks, goods, etc) completely

cleanse (klɛnz) *vb* **cleanses, cleansing, cleansed** (*tr*) 1 to remove dirt, filth, etc, from 2 to remove guilt from 3 to remove a group of people from (an area) by means of ethnic cleansing 4 *arch* to cure [OE *clǣnsian*; see CLEAN]

cleanser ('klɛnzə) *n* a cleansing agent

clean-shaven *adj* (of men) having the facial hair shaved off

clean sheet *n* *sport* an instance of conceding no goals or points in a match or competition (esp in **keep a clean sheet**)

clean up *vb* (*adv*) 1 to rid (something) of dirt, filth, or other impurities 2 to make (someone or something) orderly or presentable 3 (*tr*) to rid (a place) of undesirable people or conditions 4 *inf, chiefly US & Canad* to make (a great profit) ▷ *n* **cleanup** 5 the process of cleaning up 6 *inf, chiefly US* a great profit

clear (klɪə) *adj* 1 free from darkness or obscurity; bright 2 (of weather) free from dullness or clouds 3 transparent 4 even and pure in tone or colour 5 without blemish: *a clear skin* 6 easy to see or hear; distinct 7 free from doubt or confusion 8 (*postpositive*) certain in the mind; sure: *are you clear?* 9 (*in combination*) perceptive, alert: *clear-headed* 10 evident or obvious: *it is clear that he won't come now* 11 (of sounds or the voice) not harsh or hoarse 12 serene; calm 13 without qualification; complete: *a clear victory* 14 free of suspicion, guilt, or blame: *a clear conscience* 15 free of obstruction; open: *a clear passage* 16 free from debt or obligation 17 (of money, profits, etc) without deduction; net 18 emptied of freight or cargo 19 *showjumping* (of a round) ridden without any points being lost ▷ *adv* 20 in a clear or distinct manner 21 completely or utterly 22 (*postpositive; often foll by of*) not in contact (with); free: *stand clear of the gates* ▷ *n* 23 a clear space 24 **in the clear** 24a free of suspicion, guilt, or blame 24b *sport* able to receive a pass without being tackled ▷ *vb* 25 to make or become free from darkness, obscurity, etc 26 (*intr*) 26a (of the weather) to become free from dullness, fog, rain, etc 26b (of mist, fog, etc) to disappear 27 (*tr*) to free from impurity or blemish 28 (*tr*) to free from doubt or confusion 29 (*tr*) to rid of objects, obstructions, etc 30 (*tr*) to make or form (a path, way, etc) by removing obstructions 31 (*tr*) to free or remove (a person or thing) from something, as of suspicion, blame, or guilt 32 (*tr*) to move or pass by or over without contact: *he cleared the wall easily* 33 (*tr*) to rid (the throat) of phlegm 34 (*tr*) to make or gain (money) as profit 35 (*tr; often foll by off*) to discharge or settle (a debt) 36 (*tr*) to free (a debtor) from obligation 37 (*intr*) (of a cheque) to pass through one's bank and be charged against one's account 38 *banking* to settle accounts by exchanging (commercial documents) in a clearing house 39 to permit (ships, aircraft, cargo, passengers, etc) to unload, disembark, depart, etc, or (of ships, etc) to be permitted to unload, etc 40 to obtain or give (clearance) 41 (*tr*) to obtain clearance from 42 (*tr*) to permit (a person, company, etc) to see or handle classified information 43 (*tr*) *mil, etc* to decode (a message, etc) 44 (*tr*) *computing* to remove data from a storage device and revert to zero 45 **clear the air** to dispel tension, confusion, etc, by settling misunderstandings, etc ▷ See also **clear away, clear off,** etc [C13 *clere*, from OF *cler*, from L *clārus* clear] > **'clearer** *n* > **'clearness** *n*

clearance ('klɪərəns) *n* 1a the process or an instance of clearing: *slum clearance* 1b (*as modifier*): *a clearance order* 2 space between two parts in motion or in relative motion 3 permission for an aircraft, ship, passengers, etc, to proceed 4 official permission to have access to secret information, projects, areas, etc 5 *banking* the exchange of commercial documents drawn on the members of a clearing house 6a the disposal of merchandise at reduced prices 6b (*as modifier*): *a clearance sale* 7 the act of clearing an area of land by mass eviction: *the Highland Clearances*

clear away *vb* (*adv*) to remove (objects) from (the table) after a meal

clear-cut *adj* (**clear cut** *when postpositive*) 1 definite; not vague: *a clear-cut proposal* 2 clearly outlined

clearing ('klɪərɪŋ) *n* an area with few or no trees or shrubs in wooded or overgrown land

clearing bank *n* (in Britain) any bank that makes use of the central clearing house in London

clearing house *n* 1 *banking* an institution where cheques and other commercial papers drawn on member banks are cancelled against each other so that only net balances are payable 2 a central agency for the collection and distribution of information or materials

clearly ('klɪəlɪ) *adv* 1 in a clear, distinct, or obvious manner: *I could see everything quite clearly* 2 (*sentence modifier*) it is obvious that; evidently: *clearly the social services must be flexible*

clear off *vb* (*intr, adv*) *inf* to go away: often used imperatively

clear out *vb* (*adv*) 1 (*intr*) *inf* to go away: often used imperatively 2 (*tr*) to remove and sort the contents of (a room, etc) 3 (*tr*) *sl* to leave (someone) with no money 4 (*tr*) *sl* to exhaust (stocks, goods, etc) completely

clearstory ('klɪəˌstɔːrɪ) *n* a variant of **clerestory**

clear up *vb* (*adv*) 1 (*tr*) to explain or solve (a mystery, misunderstanding, etc) 2 to put (a place or thing that is disordered) in order 3 (*intr*) (of the weather) to become brighter

clearway ('klɪəˌweɪ) *n* 1 *Brit* a stretch of road on which motorists may stop only in an emergency: *urban clearway* 2 an area at the end of a runway over which an aircraft

Cc

taking off makes its initial climb

cleat (kliːt) *n* **1** a wedge-shaped block attached to a structure to act as a support **2** a device consisting of two hornlike prongs projecting horizontally in opposite directions from a central base, used for securing lines on vessels, wharves, etc ▷ *vb (tr)* **3** to supply or support with a cleat or cleats **4** to secure (a line) on a cleat [C14 of Gmc origin]

cleavage (ˈkliːvɪdʒ) *n* **1** *inf* the separation between a woman's breasts, esp as revealed by a low-cut dress **2** a division or split **3** (of crystals) the act of splitting or the tendency to split along definite planes so as to yield smooth surfaces **4** Also called: **segmentation** (in animals) the repeated division of a fertilized ovum into a solid ball of cells **5** the breaking of a chemical bond in a molecule to give smaller molecules or radicals **6** *geol* the natural splitting of certain rocks, such as slates, into thin plates

cleave[1] (kliːv) *vb* **cleaves, cleaving; cleft, cleaved,** *or* **clove; cleft, cleaved,** *or* **cloven 1** to split or cause to split, esp along a natural weakness **2** *(tr)* to make by or as if by cutting: *to cleave a path* **3** (when *intr*, foll by *through*) to penetrate or traverse [OE *clēofan*] > ˈ**cleavable** *adj*

cleave[2] (kliːv) *vb* **cleaves, cleaving, cleaved** *(intr;* foll by *to)* to cling or adhere [OE *cleofian*]

cleaver (ˈkliːvə) *n* a heavy knife or long-bladed hatchet, esp one used by butchers

cleavers (ˈkliːvəz) *n (functioning as sing)* a Eurasian plant, having small white flowers and prickly stems and fruits. Also called: **goosegrass, hairif** [OE *clīfe*; see CLEAVE[2]]

Cleethorpes (ˈkliːθɔːps) *n* a resort in E England, in North East Lincolnshire unitary authority, Lincolnshire. Pop: 32 719 (1991)

clef (klɛf) *n* one of several symbols placed on the left-hand side beginning of each stave indicating the pitch of the music written after it [C16 from F: key, clef, from L *clāvis*]

cleft (klɛft) *vb* **1** a past tense and past participle of **cleave**[1] ▷ *n* **2** a fissure or crevice **3** an indentation or split in something, such as the chin, palate, etc ▷ *adj* **4** split; divided [OE *geclyft* (n); see CLEAVE[1]]

cleft palate *n* a congenital crack or fissure in the midline of the hard palate, often associated with a harelip

cleg (klɛg) *n* another name for a **horsefly** [C15 from ON *kleggi*]

Cleland (ˈklɛlənd) *n* **John** 1709–89, British writer, best known for his bawdy novel *Fanny Hill* (1748–49)

clematis (ˈklɛmətɪs, kləˈmeɪtɪs) *n* any N temperate climbing plant of the genus *Clematis*. Many species are cultivated for their large colourful flowers [C16 from L, from Gk, from *klēma* vine twig]

Clemenceau (*French* klemɑ̃so) *n* **Georges Eugène Benjamin** (ʒɔrʒ œʒɛn bɛ̃ʒamɛ̃) 1841–1929, French statesman; prime minister of France (1906–09; 1917–20); negotiated the Treaty of Versailles (1919)

clemency (ˈklɛmənsɪ) *n, pl* **clemencies 1** mercy or leniency **2** mildness, esp of the weather [C15 from L, from *clēmēns* gentle]

Clemens (ˈklɛmənz) *n* **Samuel Langhorne** (ˈlæŋˌhɔːn) See (Mark) **Twain**

clement (ˈklɛmənt) *adj* **1** merciful **2** (of the weather) mild [C15 from L *clēmēns* mild]

Clement I (ˈklɛmənt) *n* **Saint,** called *Clement of Rome*. pope (?88–?97 AD). Feast day: Nov 23

Clement V *n* original name *Bertrand de Got*. ?1264–1314, pope (1305–14): removed the papal seat from Rome to Avignon in France (1309)

Clement VII *n* original name *Giulio de' Medici*. 1478–1534, pope (1523–34): refused to authorize the annulment of the marriage of Henry VIII of England to Catherine of Aragon (1533)

clementine (ˈklɛmənˌtiːn, -ˌtaɪn) *n* a citrus fruit thought to be either a variety of tangerine or a hybrid between a tangerine and sweet orange [C20 from F *clémentine*]

Clement of Alexandria *n* **Saint** original name *Titus Flavius Clemens*. ?150–?215 AD, Greek Christian theologian: head of the catechetical school at Alexandria; teacher of Origen. Feast day: Dec 5

clench (klɛntʃ) *vb (tr)* **1** to close or squeeze together (the teeth, a fist, etc) tightly **2** to grasp or grip firmly ▷ *n* **3** a firm grasp or grip **4** a device that grasps or grips ▷ *n, vb* **5** another word for **clinch** [OE *beclencan*]

Cleon (ˈkliːɒn) *n* died 422 BC, Athenian demagogue and military leader

Cleopatra (ˌkliːəˈpætrə, -ˈpɑː-) *n* ?69–30 BC, queen of Egypt (51–30), renowned for her beauty: the mistress of Julius Caesar and later of Mark Antony. She killed herself with an asp to avoid capture by Octavian (Augustus)

Cleopatra's Needle *n* either of two Egyptian obelisks, originally set up at Heliopolis about 1500 BC: one was moved to the Thames Embankment, London, in 1878, the other to Central Park, New York, in 1880

clepsydra (ˈklɛpsɪdrə) *n, pl* **clepsydras** *or* **clepsydrae** (-ˌdriː) an ancient device for measuring time by the flow of water or mercury through a small aperture. Also called: **water clock** [C17 from L, from Gk, from *kleptein* to steal + *hudōr* water]

cleptomania (ˌklɛptəʊˈmeɪnɪə) *n* a variant spelling of **kleptomania**

clerestory *or* **clearstory** (ˈklɪəˌstɔːrɪ) *n, pl* **clerestories** *or* **clearstories 1** a row of windows in the upper part of the wall of a church that divides the nave from the aisle **2** the part of the wall in which these windows are set [C15 from CLEAR + STOREY] > ˈ**cereˌstoried** *or* ˈ**clearˌstoried** *adj*

clergy (ˈklɜːdʒɪ) *n, pl* **clergies** the collective body of men and women ordained as religious ministers, esp of the Christian Church [C13 from OF; see CLERK]

clergyman (ˈklɜːdʒɪmən) *n, pl* **clergymen** a member of the clergy

cleric (ˈklɛrɪk) *n* a member of the clergy [C17 from Church L *clēricus* priest, CLERK]

clerical (ˈklɛrɪkᵊl) *adj* **1** relating to or associated with the clergy: *clerical dress* **2** of or relating to office clerks or their work: *a clerical error* **3** supporting or advocating clericalism > ˈ**clerically** *adv*

clerical collar *n* a stiff white collar with no opening at the front that buttons at the back of the neck; the distinctive mark of the clergy in certain Churches. Informal name: **dog collar**

clericalism (ˈklɛrɪkᵊˌlɪzəm) *n* **1** a policy of upholding the power of the clergy **2** the power of the clergy > ˈ**clericalist** *n*

clericals (ˈklɛrɪkᵊlz) *pl n* the distinctive dress of a clergyman

clerihew (ˈklɛrɪˌhjuː) *n* a form of comic or satiric verse, consisting of two couplets of metrically irregular lines, containing the name of a well-known person [C20 after E. *Clerihew* BENTLEY, its inventor]

clerk (klɑːk; *US & Canad* klɜːrk) *n* **1** a worker, esp in an office, who keeps records, files, etc **2** an employee of a court, legislature, board, corporation, etc, who keeps records and accounts, etc: *a town clerk* **3** Also called: **clerk in holy orders** a cleric **4** *US & Canad* short for **salesclerk** **5** Also called: **desk clerk** *US & Canad* a hotel receptionist **6** *arch* a scholar ▷ *vb* **7** *(intr)* to serve as a clerk [OE *clerc*, from Church L *clēricus*, from Gk *klērikos* cleric, from *klēros* heritage] > ˈ**clerkess** *fem n (chiefly Scot)* > ˈ**clerkish** *adj* > ˈ**clerkship** *n*

clerk of works *n* an employee who supervises building work in progress

Clermont-Ferrand (*French* klɛrmɔ̃fɛrɑ̃) *n* a city in S central France: capital of Puy-de-Dôme department; industrial centre. Pop: 137 140 (1999)

Cleveland[1] (ˈkliːvlənd) *n* **1** a former county of NE England formed in 1974 from parts of E Durham and N

Yorkshire; replaced in 1996 by the unitary authorities of Hartlepool (Durham), Stockton-on-Tees (Durham), Middlesbrough (North Yorkshire) and Redcar and Cleveland (North Yorkshire) **2** a port in NE Ohio, on Lake Erie: major heavy industries. Pop: 478 403 (2000) **3** a hilly region of NE England, extending from the **Cleveland Hills** to the River Tees

Cleveland² ('kli:vlənd) *n* **Stephen Grover** 1837–1908, US Democratic politician; the 22nd and 24th president of the US (1885–89; 1893–97)

clever ('klɛvə) *adj* **1** displaying sharp intelligence or mental alertness **2** adroit or dexterous, esp with the hands **3** smart in a superficial way **4** *Brit inf* sly; cunning [C13 *cliver* (in the sense: quick to seize, adroit), from ?] > **'cleverly** *adv* > **'cleverness** *n*

clevis ('klɛvɪs) *n* the U-shaped component of a shackle [C16 rel. to CLEAVE¹]

clew (klu:) *n* **1** a ball of thread, yarn, or twine **2** *naut* either of the lower corners of a square sail or the after lower corner of a fore-and-aft sail ▷ *vb* **3** (*tr*) to coil into a ball [OE *cliewen* (vb)]

clianthus (klɪ'ænθəs) *n* a leguminous plant of Australia and New Zealand with ornamental clusters of slender flowers. See also **desert pea** [C19 NL, prob. from Gk *klei-, kleos* glory + *anthos* flower]

cliché ('kli:ʃeɪ) *n* **1** a word or expression that has lost much of its force through overexposure **2** an idea, action, or habit that has become trite from overuse **3** *printing, chiefly Brit* a stereotype or electrotype plate [C19 from F, from *clicher* to stereotype; imit.] > **'clichéd** *or* **'cliché'd** *adj*

click (klɪk) *n* **1** a short light often metallic sound **2** the locking member of a ratchet mechanism, such as a pawl or detent **3** *phonetics* any of various stop consonants that are produced by the suction of air into the mouth ▷ *vb* **4** to make or cause to make a clicking sound: *to click one's heels* **5** (usually foll by *on*) *computing* to press and release (a button on a mouse) or to select (a particular function) by pressing and releasing a button on a mouse **6** (*intr*) *sl* to be a great success: *that idea really clicked* **7** (*intr*) *inf* to become suddenly clear: *it finally clicked* **8** (*intr*) *sl* to get on well ▷ See also **click through** [C17 imit.] > **'clicker** *n*

clicks and mortar *adj* making use of traditional trading methods in conjunction with Internet trading. Abbreviation: **C & M** [C20 pun on *bricks and mortar*, with CLICK referring to the computing sense]

click through *vb* (*tr, adverb*) **1** to navigate around (a website) using the links provided to move onto different pages ▷ *adj* **click-through 2** (of a website) able to be navigated by means of links between different pages

client ('klaɪənt) *n* **1** a person, company, etc, that seeks the advice of a professional man or woman **2** a customer **3** a person for whom a social worker, etc, is responsible **4** *computing* a program or work station that requests data or information from a server [C14 from L *cliēns* retainer, dependent] > **cliental** (klaɪ'ɛntᵊl) *adj*

clientele (ˌkli:ɒn'tɛl) *or* **clientage** ('klaɪəntɪdʒ) *n* customers or clients collectively [C16 from L, from *cliēns* CLIENT]

cliff (klɪf) *n* a steep high rock face, esp one that runs along the seashore [OE *clif*] > **'cliffy** *adj*

cliffhanger ('klɪfˌhæŋə) *n* **1a** a situation of imminent disaster usually occurring at the end of each episode of a serialized film **1b** the serialized film itself **2** a situation that is dramatic or uncertain > **'cliffˌhanging** *adj*

climacteric (klaɪ'mæktərɪk, ˌklaɪmæk'tɛrɪk) *n* **1** a critical event or period **2** another name for **menopause** **3** the period in the life of a man corresponding to the menopause, chiefly characterized by diminished sexual activity ▷ *adj* **4** *also* **climacterical** (ˌklaɪmæk'tɛrɪkᵊl) involving a crucial event or period [C16 from L, from Gk, from *klimaktēr* rung of a ladder from *klimax* ladder]

climactic (klaɪ'mæktɪk) *or* **climactical** *adj* consisting of, involving, or causing a climax > **cli'mactically** *adv*

USAGE See at **climate**

climate ('klaɪmɪt) *n* **1** the long-term prevalent weather conditions of an area, determined by latitude, altitude, etc **2** an area having a particular kind of climate **3** a prevailing trend: *the political climate* [C14 from LL, from Gk *klima* inclination, region] > **climatic** (klaɪ'mætɪk), **cli'matical,** *or* **'climatal** *adj* > **cli'matically** *adv*

USAGE *Climatic* is sometimes wrongly used where *climactic* is meant. *Climatic* should be used to talk about things relating to climate; *climactic* is used to describe something which forms a climax: *...the climactic moment of the Revolution*

climatic zone *n* any of the eight principal zones, roughly demarcated by lines of latitude, into which the earth can be divided on the basis of climate

climatology (ˌklaɪmə'tɒlədʒɪ) *n* the study of climate > **climatologic** (ˌklaɪmətə'lɒdʒɪk) *or* **ˌclimato'logical** *adj* > **ˌclima'tologist** *n*

climax ('klaɪmæks) *n* **1** the most intense or highest point of an experience or of a series of events: *the party was the climax of the week* **2** a decisive moment in a dramatic or other work **3** a rhetorical device by which a series of sentences, clauses, or phrases are arranged in order of increasing intensity **4** *ecology* the stage in the development of a community during which it remains stable under the prevailing environmental conditions **5** another word for **orgasm** ▷ *vb* **6** to reach or bring to a climax [C16 from LL, from Gk *klimax* ladder]

climb (klaɪm) *vb* (*mainly intr*) **1** (*also tr;* often foll by *up*) to go up or ascend (stairs, a mountain, etc) **2** (often foll by *along*) to progress with difficulty: *to climb along a ledge* **3** to rise to a higher point or intensity: *the temperature climbed* **4** to incline or slope upwards: *the road began to climb* **5** to ascend in social position **6** (of plants) to grow upwards by twining, using tendrils or suckers, etc **7** *inf* (foll by *into*) to put (on) or get (into) **8** to be a climber or mountaineer ▷ *n* **9** the act or an instance of climbing **10** a place or thing to be climbed, esp a route in mountaineering [OE *climban*] > **'climbable** *adj*

climb down *vb* (*intr, adv*) **1** to descend **2** (often foll by *from*) to retreat (from an opinion, position, etc) ▷ *n* **climb-down 3** a retreat from an opinion, etc

climber ('klaɪmə) *n* **1** a person or thing that climbs, esp a mountaineer **2** a plant that grows upwards by twining or clinging with tendrils and suckers **3** *chiefly Brit* short for **social climber**

clime (klaɪm) *n* *poetic* a region or its climate [C16 from LL *clima;* see CLIMATE]

clinch (klɪntʃ) *vb* **1** (*tr*) to secure (a driven nail), by bending the protruding point over **2** (*tr*) to hold together in such a manner **3** (*tr*) to settle (something, such as an argument, bargain, etc) in a definite way **4** (*tr*) *naut* to fasten by means of a clinch **5** (*intr*) to engage in a clinch, as in boxing or wrestling ▷ *n* **6** the act of clinching **7a** a nail with its point bent over **7b** the part of such a nail, etc, that has been bent over **8** *boxing, wrestling, etc* an act or an instance in which one or both competitors hold on to the other to avoid punches, regain wind, etc **9** *sl* a lovers' embrace **10** *naut* a loop or eye formed in a line ▷ Also (for senses 1, 2, 4, 7, 8, 10): **clench** [C16 var. of CLENCH]

clincher ('klɪntʃə) *n* **1** *inf* something decisive, such as fact, score, etc **2** a person or thing that clinches

cline (klaɪn) *n* the range of variation of form within a species [C20 from Gk *klinein* to lean] > **'clinal** *adj*

-cline *n combining form* indicating a slope: *anticline* [back formation from INCLINE] > **-clinal** *adj combining form*

Cline (klaɪn) *n* **Patsy,** original name *Virginia Patterson Hensley.* 1932–63, US country singer; her bestselling records include "Walking After Midnight", "I Fall to

Cc

Pieces", and "Leavin' On Your Mind"

cling (klɪŋ) *vb* **clings, clinging, clung** (*intr*) **1** (often foll by *to*) to hold fast or adhere closely (to something), as by gripping or sticking **2** (foll by *together*) to remain in contact (with each other) **3** to be or remain physically or emotionally close ▷ *n* **4** short for **clingstone** [OE *clingan*] > **'clinging** *adj* > **'clingingly** *adv* > **'clingy** *adj* > **'clinginess** *or* **'clingingness** *n*

clingfilm ('klɪŋˌfɪlm) *n* a thin polythene material having the power to adhere closely: used for wrapping food

clingstone ('klɪŋˌstəʊn) *n* **a** a fruit, such as certain peaches, in which the flesh adheres to the stone **b** (*as modifier*): *a clingstone peach*

clinic ('klɪnɪk) *n* **1** a place in which outpatients are given medical treatment or advice **2** a similar place staffed by specialist physicians or surgeons: *eye clinic* **3** *Brit* a private hospital or nursing home **4** *obsolete* the teaching of medicine to students at the bedside **5** *chiefly US & Canad* a group or centre that offers advice or instruction [c17 from L *clīnicus* one on a sickbed, from Gk, from *klinē* bed]

clinical ('klɪnɪkᵊl) *adj* **1** of or relating to a clinic **2** of or relating to the observation and treatment of patients directly: *clinical medicine* **3** scientifically detached; strictly objective: *a clinical attitude to life* **4** plain, simple, and usually unattractive > **'clinically** *adv*

clinical governance *n* a systematic approach to raising standards of health care and tackling poor performance in hospitals

clinically dead *adj* having no respiration, no heartbeat, and with no contraction of the pupils when exposed to a strong light

clinically obese *adj* in the state at which being overweight causes medical complications

clinical psychology *n* the branch of psychology that studies and treats mental illness and mental retardation

clinical thermometer *n* a thermometer for determining the temperature of the body

clinician (klɪ'nɪʃən) *n* a physician, psychiatrist, etc, who specializes in clinical work as opposed to one engaged in experimental studies

clink¹ (klɪŋk) *vb* **1** to make or cause to make a light and sharply ringing sound ▷ *n* **2** such a sound [c14 ?from MDu. *klinken*]

clink² (klɪŋk) *n* a slang word for **prison** [c16 after *Clink*, a prison in Southwark, London]

clinker ('klɪŋkə) *n* **1** the ash and partially fused residues from a coal-fired furnace or fire **2** a partially vitrified brick or mass of brick **3** *sl, chiefly US* something of poor quality, such as a film ▷ *vb* **4** (*intr*) to form clinker [c17 from Du. *klinker* a type of brick, from *klinken* to CLINK¹]

clinker-built *or* **clincher-built** *adj* (of a boat or ship) having a hull constructed with each plank overlapping that below [c18 *clinker* a nailing together, prob. from CLINCH]

clinometer (klaɪ'nɒmɪtə) *n* an instrument used in surveying for measuring an angle of inclination > **clinometric** (ˌklaɪnə'mɛtrɪk) *or* **ˌclino'metrical** *adj* > **cli'nometry** *n*

Clinton ('klɪntən) *n* **1 Hillary (Rodham)** born 1947, US Democrat politician, wife of Bill Clinton; senator for New York from 2000 **2 William Jefferson**, known as *Bill*. born 1946, US Democrat politician; 42nd president of the US (1993–2001)

Clio ('klaɪəʊ) *n Greek myth* the Muse of history [c19 from L, from Gk *Kleiō*, from *kleein* to celebrate]

clip¹ (klɪp) *vb* **clips, clipping, clipped** (*mainly tr*) **1** (*also intr*) to cut or trim with scissors or shears, esp in order to shorten or remove a part **2** *Brit* to punch (a hole) in something, esp a ticket **3** to curtail **4** to move a short section from (a film, etc) **5** to shorten (a word) **6** *inf* to strike with a sharp, often slanting, blow **7** *sl* to obtain (money) by deception or cheating ▷ *n* **8** the act or process of clipping **9** something clipped off **10** a short extract from a film, etc **11** *inf* a sharp, often slanting, blow **12** *inf* speed: *a rapid clip* **13** *Austral & NZ* the total quantity of wool shorn, as in one season, etc **14** another word for **clipped form** [c12 from ON *klippa* to cut]

clip² (klɪp) *n* **1** any of various small implements used to hold loose articles together or to attach one article to another **2** an article of jewellery that can be clipped onto a dress, hat, etc **3** short for **paperclip** or **cartridge clip** ▷ *vb* **clips, clipping, clipped** (*tr*) **4** to hold together tightly, as with a clip [OE *clyppan* to embrace]

clipboard ('klɪpˌbɔːd) *n* **1** a portable writing board with a clip at the top for holding paper **2** *computing* a temporary storage area in desktop publishing and other programs where text or graphics are held when cut or copied

clip joint *n sl* a place, such as a nightclub or restaurant, in which customers are overcharged

clipped (klɪpt) *adj* (of speech or tone of voice) abrupt, terse, and distinct

clipped form *n* a shortened form of a word

clipper ('klɪpə) *n* **1** any fast sailing ship **2** a person or thing that cuts or clips

clippers ('klɪpəz) *or* **clips** *pl n* **1** a hand tool for clipping fingernails, veneers, etc **2** a hairdresser's tool for cutting short hair

clipping ('klɪpɪŋ) *n* **1** something cut out, esp an article from a newspaper; cutting **2** the distortion of an audio or visual signal in which the tops of peaks with a high amplitude are cut off, caused by, for example, overloading of amplifier circuits

clique (kliːk, klɪk) *n* a small exclusive group of friends or associates [c18 from F, ?from OF: latch, from *cliquer* to click] > **'cliquey** *or* **'cliquy** *adj* > **'cliquish** *adj* > **'cliquishly** *adv* > **'cliquishness** *n*

clitoridectomy (ˌklɪtərɪ'dɛktəmɪ) *n* surgical removal of the clitoris: a form of female circumcision, esp practised as a religious or ethnic rite

clitoris ('klɪtərɪs, 'klaɪ-) *n* a part of the female genitalia consisting of a small elongated highly sensitive erectile organ at the front of the vulva [c17 from NL, from Gk *kleitoris*] > **'clitoral** *adj*

Clive (klaɪv) *n* **Robert,** Baron Clive of Plassey. 1725–74, British general and statesman, whose victory at Plassey (1757) strengthened British control in India

Cllr *abbrev for* Councillor

cloaca (kləʊ'eɪkə) *n, pl* **cloacae** (-kiː) **1** a cavity in most vertebrates, except higher mammals, and certain invertebrates, into which the alimentary canal and the genital and urinary ducts open **2** a sewer [c18 from L: sewer] > **clo'acal** *adj*

cloak (kləʊk) *n* **1** a wraplike outer garment fastened at the throat and falling straight from the shoulders **2** something that covers or conceals ▷ *vb* (*tr*) **3** to cover with or as if with a cloak **4** to hide or disguise [c13 from OF *cloque*, from Med. L *clocca* cloak, bell]

cloak-and-dagger *n* (*modifier*) characteristic of or concerned with intrigue and espionage

cloakroom ('kləʊkˌruːm, -rʊm) *n* **1** a room in which hats, coats, etc, may be temporarily deposited **2** *Brit* a euphemistic word for **toilet**

clobber¹ ('klɒbə) *vb* (*tr*) *sl* **1** to batter **2** to defeat utterly **3** to criticize severely [c20 from ?]

clobber² ('klɒbə) *n Brit sl* personal belongings, such as clothes [c19 from ?]

clobbering machine *n NZ inf* pressure to conform with accepted standards

cloche (klɒʃ) *n* **1** a bell-shaped cover used to protect young plants **2** a woman's close-fitting hat [c19 from F: bell, from Med. L *clocca*]

clock¹ (klɒk) *n* **1** a timepiece having mechanically or electrically driven pointers that move constantly over a dial showing the numbers of the hours ▷ Cf **watch** (sense 7) **2** any clocklike device for recording or measuring, such as a taximeter or pressure gauge **3** the downy head of a dandelion that has gone to seed **4** short for **time clock** **5** (usually preceded by *the*) an informal word for **speedometer** or **mileometer** **6** *Brit* a slang word for **face** **7** **around** *or* **round the clock** all day and all night ▷ *vb (tr)* **8** *Brit, Austral, & NZ sl* to strike, esp on the face or head **9** to record time as with a stopwatch, esp in the calculation of speed **10** *inf* to turn back the mileometer on (a car) illegally so that its mileage appears less [C14 from MDu. *clocke* clock, from Med. L *clocca* bell, ult. of Celtic origin]

clock² (klɒk) *n* an ornamental design on the side of a stocking [C16 see CLOCK¹]

clock off *or* **out** *vb (intr, adv)* to depart from work, esp when it involves registering the time of departure on a card

clock on *or* **in** *vb (intr, adv)* to arrive at work, esp when it involves registering the time of arrival on a card

clock up *vb (tr, adv)* to record or register: *this car has clocked up 80 000 miles*

clock-watcher *n* an employee who frequently checks the time in anticipation of a break or of the end of the working day

clockwise (ˈklɒkˌwaɪz) *adv, adj* in the direction that the hands of a clock rotate; from top to bottom towards the right when seen from the front

clockwork (ˈklɒkˌwɜːk) *n* **1** the mechanism of a clock **2** any similar mechanism, as in a wind-up toy **3** **like clockwork** with complete regularity and precision; smoothly

clod (klɒd) *n* **1** a lump of earth or clay **2** earth, esp when heavy or in hard lumps **3** Also called: **clod poll, clodpate** a dull or stupid person [OE *clod-* (occurring in compound words) lump] > ˈ**cloddy** *adj* > ˈ**cloddish** *adj* > ˈ**cloddishly** *adv* > ˈ**cloddishness** *n*

clodhopper (ˈklɒdˌhɒpə) *n inf* **1** a clumsy person; lout **2** (*usually pl*) a large heavy shoe

clog (klɒg) *vb* **clogs, clogging, clogged** **1** to obstruct or become obstructed with thick or sticky matter **2** *(tr)* to encumber; hinder **3** *(intr)* to adhere or stick in a mass ▷ *n* **4a** any of various wooden or wooden-soled shoes **4b** (*as modifier*): *clog dance* **5** a heavy block, esp of wood, fastened to the leg of a person or animal to impede motion **6** something that impedes motion or action; hindrance [C14 (in the sense: block of wood): from ?]

cloisonné (klwɑːˈzɒneɪ) *n* **1a** a design made by filling in with coloured enamel an outline of flattened wire **1b** the method of doing this ▷ *adj* **2** of or made by cloisonné [C19 from F, from *cloisonner* to divide into compartments, ult. from L *claudere* to close]

cloister (ˈklɔɪstə) *n* **1** a covered walk, usually around a quadrangle in a religious institution, having an open colonnade on the inside **2** (*sometimes pl*) a place of religious seclusion, such as a monastery **3** life in a monastery or convent ▷ *vb* **4** *(tr)* to confine or seclude in or as if in a monastery [C13 from OF *cloistre*, from Med. L *claustrum* monastic cell, from L *claudere* to close] > ˈ**cloistered** *adj* > ˈ**cloistral** *adj*

clomb (kləʊm) *vb arch* a past tense and past participle of **climb**

clomp (klɒmp) *n, vb* a less common word for **clump** (senses 2, 7)

clone (kləʊn) *n* **1** a group of organisms or cells of the same genetic constitution that are descended from a common ancestor by asexual reproduction, as by cuttings, grafting, etc, or by transplantation of parent nuclei into donor egg cells whose nuclei have been removed **2** Also called: **gene clone** a segment of DNA that has been isolated and replicated by laboratory manipulation **3** *inf* a person or thing that closely resembles another **4** *sl* **4a** a mobile phone that has been given the electronic identity of an existing mobile phone, so that calls made on either phone are charged to the same account **4b** any similar object, such as a credit card, that has been given the electronic identity of another device, usually in order to commit theft **5** a microcomputer designed to simulate the operating characteristics of another type of microcomputer ▷ *vb* **clones, cloning, cloned** **6** to produce or cause to produce a clone **7** *inf* to produce near copies of (a person or thing) **8** *(tr)* to give (a phone or other device) the same electronic identity as an existing device [C20 from Gk *klōn* twig, shoot] > ˈ**cloning** *n*

clonk (klɒŋk) *vb* **1** *(intr)* to make a loud dull thud **2** *(tr) inf* to hit ▷ *n* **3** a loud thud [C20 imit.]

Clonmel (klɒnˈmɛl) *n* the county town of Co. Tipperary, Republic of Ireland; birthplace of Laurence Sterne; meat processing and enamelware. Pop: 14 500 (1991)

clonus (ˈkləʊnəs) *n* a type of convulsion characterized by rapid contraction and relaxation of a muscle [C19 from NL, from Gk *klonos* turmoil] > **clonic** (ˈklɒnɪk) *adj* > **clonicity** (klɒˈnɪsɪtɪ) *n*

Clooney (ˈkluːnɪ) *n* **George** born 1961, U.S. film actor; he starred in the television series ER (1994–99) and the films *The Perfect Storm* (2000), and *Ocean's Eleven* (2001), and *Confessions of a Dangerous Mind*, (2002, also directed)

clop (klɒp) *vb* **clops, clopping, clopped** **1** *(intr)* to make or move along with a sound as of a horse's hooves striking the ground ▷ *n* **2** a sound of this nature [C20 imit.]

close¹ (kləʊs) *adj* **1** near in space or time; in proximity **2** having the parts near together; dense: *a close formation* **3** near to the surface; short: *a close haircut* **4** near in relationship: *a close relative* **5** intimate: *a close friend* **6** almost equal: *a close contest* **7** not deviating or varying greatly from a model or standard: *a close resemblance; a close translation* **8** careful, strict, or searching: *a close study* **9** confined or enclosed **10** shut or shut tight **11** oppressive, heavy, or airless: *a close atmosphere* **12** strictly guarded: *a close prisoner* **13** neat or tight in fit **14** secretive or reticent **15** miserly; not generous, esp with money **16** (of money or credit) hard to obtain **17** restricted as to public admission or membership **18** hidden or secluded **19** Also: **closed** restricted or prohibited as to the type of game or fish able to be taken ▷ *adv* **20** closely; tightly **21** near or in proximity **22** **close to the wind** *naut* sailing as nearly as possible towards the direction from which the wind is blowing. See also **wind¹** (sense 23) [C13 from OF *clos*, from L *clausus*, from *claudere* to close] > ˈ**closely** *adv* > ˈ**closeness** *n*

close² (kləʊz) *vb* **closes, closing, closed** **1** to put or be put in such a position as to cover an opening; shut: *the door closed behind him* **2** *(tr)* to bar, obstruct, or fill up (an entrance, a hole, etc): *to close a road* **3** to bring the parts or edges of (a wound, etc) together or (of a wound, etc) to be brought together **4** (*intr; foll by on, over,* etc) to take hold: *his hand closed over the money* **5** to bring or be brought to an end; terminate **6** (of agreements, deals, etc) to complete or be completed successfully **7** to cease or cause to cease to render service: *the shop closed at six* **8** *(intr) stock exchange* to have a value at the end of a day's trading, as specified: *steels closed two points down* **9** *(tr) arch* to enclose or shut in ▷ *n* **10** the act of closing **11** the end or conclusion: *the close of the day* **12** (kləʊs) *Brit* a courtyard or quadrangle enclosed by buildings or an entry leading to such a courtyard **13** (kləʊs) *Brit* (*cap when part of a street name*) a small quiet residential road: *Hillside Close* **14** (kləʊs) the precincts of a cathedral or similar building **15** (kləʊs) *Scot* the entry from the street to a tenement building ▷ See also **close down, close in,** etc [C13 from OF *clos*, from L *clausus*, from *claudere* to close] > ˈ**closer** *n*

close company *n* a company that is controlled by its directors or by five or fewer participants

close corporation *n S African* a small private limited company

closed (kləʊzd) *adj* **1** blocked against entry; shut **2** restricted; exclusive **3** not open to question or debate **4** (of a hunting season, etc) close **5** *maths* **5a** (of a curve or surface) completely enclosing an area or volume

Cc

5b (of a set) having members that can be produced by a specific operation on other members of the same set **6** *phonetics* denoting a syllable that ends in a consonant **7** not open to public entry or membership: *a closed society*

closed chain *n chem* another name for **ring**[1] (sense 17)

closed circuit *n* a complete electrical circuit through which current can flow

closed-circuit television *n* a television system in which signals are transmitted from the television camera to the receivers by cables or telephone links

close corporation (kləʊs) *n S African* a small private limited company. Abbrev: **c.c.**

close down (kləʊz) *vb* (*adv*) **1** to cease or cause to cease operations **2** (*tr*) *soccer* to deny (an opposing player) space to run with the ball or to make or receive a pass ▷ *n* **close-down 3** a closure or stoppage, esp in a factory **4** *Brit radio, television* the end of a period of broadcasting, esp late at night

closed shop *n* (formerly) an industrial establishment in which there exists a contract between a trade union and the employer permitting the employment of the union's members only

close-fisted (ˌkləʊsˈfɪstɪd) *adj* very careful with money; mean > ˌ**close-ˈfistedness** *n*

close harmony (kləʊs) *n* a type of singing in which all the parts except the bass lie close together

close-hauled (ˌkləʊsˈhɔːld) *adj naut* with the sails flat, so as to sail as close to the wind as possible

close in (kləʊz) *vb* (*intr, adv*) **1** (of days) to become shorter with the approach of winter **2** (foll by *on* or *upon*) to advance (on) so as to encircle or surround

close out (kləʊz) *vb* (*adv*) to terminate (a client's or other account) usually by sale of securities to realize cash

close punctuation (kləʊs) *n* punctuation in which many commas, full stops, etc, are used ▷ Cf **open punctuation**

close quarters (kləʊs) *pl n* **1** a narrow cramped space or position **2 at close quarters 2a** engaged in hand-to-hand combat **2b** in close proximity; very near together

close season (kləʊs) *or* **closed season** *n* **1** the period of the year when it is prohibited to kill certain game or fish **2** *sport* the period of the year when there is no domestic competition

close shave (kləʊs) *n inf* a narrow escape

closet (ˈklɒzɪt) *n* **1** a small cupboard or recess **2** a small private room **3** short for **water closet 4** (*modifier*) private or secret ▷ *vb* **closets, closeting, closeted 5** (*tr*) to shut up or confine in a small private room, esp for conference or meditation [C14 from OF, from *clos* enclosure; see CLOSE[1]]

close-up (ˈkləʊsˌʌp) *n* **1** a photograph or film or television shot taken at close range **2** a detailed or intimate view or examination ▷ *vb* **close up** (kləʊz) (*adv*) **3** to shut entirely **4** (*intr*) to draw together: *the ranks closed up* **5** (*intr*) (of wounds) to heal completely

close with (kləʊz) *vb* (*intr, prep*) to engage in battle with (an enemy)

closure (ˈkləʊʒə) *n* **1** the act of closing or the state of being closed **2** an end or conclusion **3** something that closes or shuts, such as a cap or seal for a container **4** Also called: **gag** (in a deliberative body) a procedure by which debate may be halted and an immediate vote taken **5** *chiefly US* **5a** the resolution of a significant event or relationship in a person's life **5b** a sense of contentment experienced after such a resolution ▷ *vb* **closures, closuring, closured 6** (*tr*) (in a deliberative body) to end (debate) by closure [C14 from OF, from LL, from L *claudere* to close]

clot (klɒt) *n* **1** a soft thick lump or mass **2** *Brit inf* a stupid person; fool ▷ *vb* **clots, clotting, clotted 3** to form or cause to form into a soft thick lump or lumps [OE *clott*, of Gmc origin]

cloth (klɒθ) *n, pl* **cloths** (klɒθs, klɒðz) **1a** a fabric formed by weaving, felting or knitting wool, cotton, etc **1b** (*as modifier*): *a cloth bag* **2** a piece of such fabric used for a particular purpose, as for a dishcloth **3** (usually preceded by *the*) the clergy [OE *clāth*]

clothe (kləʊð) *vb* **clothes, clothing, clothed** *or* **clad** (*tr*) **1** to dress or attire (a person) **2** to provide with clothing **3** to conceal or disguise **4** to endow or invest [OE *clāthian*, from *clāth* cloth]

clothes (kləʊðz) *pl n* **1** articles of dress **2** *chiefly Brit* short for **bedclothes** [OE *clāthas*, pl. of *clāth* cloth]

clotheshorse (ˈkləʊðzˌhɔːs) *n* **1** a frame on which to hang laundry for drying or airing **2** *inf* an excessively fashionable person

clothesline (ˈkləʊðzˌlaɪn) *n* a piece of rope or wire on which clean washing is hung to dry

clothes peg *n* a small wooden or plastic clip for attaching washing to a clothesline

clothes pole *n* a post to which a clothesline is attached. Also called: **clothes post**

clothes-press *n* a piece of furniture for storing clothes, usually containing wide drawers

clothes prop *n* a long wooden pole with a forked end used to raise a line of washing to enable it to catch the breeze

clothier (ˈkləʊðɪə) *n* a person who makes, sells, or deals in clothes or cloth

clothing (ˈkləʊðɪŋ) *n* **1** garments collectively **2** something that covers or clothes

Clotho (ˈkləʊθəʊ) *n Greek myth* one of the three Fates, spinner of the thread of life [L, from Gk *Klōtho*, one who spins, from *klōthein* to spin]

cloth of gold *n* cloth woven from silk threads interspersed with gold

clotted cream *n Brit* a thick cream made from scalded milk, esp in SW England

clotting factor *n* any one of a group of substances, including factor VIII, the presence of which in the blood is essential for blood clotting to occur. Also called: **coagulation factor**

cloture (ˈkləʊtʃə) *n* **1** closure in the US Senate ▷ *vb* **clotures, cloturing, clotured 2** (*tr*) to end (debate) by cloture [C19 from F *clôture*, from OF CLOSURE]

cloud (klaʊd) *n* **1** a mass of water or ice particles visible in the sky **2** any collection of particles visible in the air, esp of smoke or dust **3** a large number of insects or other small animals in flight **4** something that darkens, threatens, or carries gloom **5** *jewellery* a cloudlike blemish in a transparent stone **6 in the clouds** not in contact with reality **7 on cloud nine** *inf* elated; very happy **8 under a cloud 8a** under reproach or suspicion **8b** in a state of gloom or bad temper ▷ *vb* **9** (when *intr*, often foll by *over* or *up*) to make or become cloudy, overcast, or indistinct **10** (*tr*) to make obscure; darken **11** to make or become gloomy or depressed **12** (*tr*) to place under or render liable to suspicion or disgrace **13** to render (liquids) milky or dull or (of liquids) to become milky or dull [C13 (in the sense: a mass of vapour): from OE *clūd* rock, hill] > ˈ**cloudless** *adj* > ˈ**cloudlessly** *adv* > ˈ**cloudlessness** *n*

cloudberry (ˈklaʊdbərɪ, brɪ) *n, pl* **cloudberries** a creeping Eurasian herbaceous rosaceous plant with white flowers and orange berry-like fruits

cloudburst (ˈklaʊdˌbɜːst) *n* a heavy downpour

cloud chamber *n physics* an apparatus for detecting high-energy particles by observing their tracks through a chamber containing a supersaturated vapour

cloud-cuckoo-land *n* a realm of fantasy, dreams, or impractical notions

cloudy (ˈklaʊdɪ) *adj* **cloudier, cloudiest 1** covered with cloud or clouds **2** of or like clouds **3** streaked or mottled like a cloud **4** opaque or muddy **5** obscure or unclear **6** troubled or gloomy > ˈ**cloudily** *adv* > ˈ**cloudiness** *n*

clough (klʌf) *n dialect* a ravine [OE *clōh*]
Clough (klʌf) *n* **Arthur Hugh** 1819–61, British poet, author of *Amours de Voyage* (1858) and *Dipsychus* (1865)
clout (klaʊt) *n* **1** *inf* a blow with the hand or a hard object **2** power or influence, esp political **3** Also called: **clout nail** a short, flat-headed nail **4** *dialect* **4a** a piece of cloth: *a dish clout* **4b** a garment ▹ *vb* (*tr*) **5** *inf* to give a hard blow to, esp with the hand [OE *clūt* piece of metal or cloth, *clūtian* to patch (c14 to strike with the hand)]
clove[1] (kləʊv) *n* **1** a tropical evergreen tree of the myrtle family **2** the dried unopened flower buds of this tree, used as a pungent fragrant spice [c14 from OF, lit.: nail of clove, *clou* from L *clāvus* nail + *girofle* clove tree]
clove[2] (kləʊv) *n* any of the segments of a compound bulb that arise from the axils of the scales of a large bulb [OE *clufu* bulb; see CLEAVE[1]]
clove[3] (kləʊv) *vb* a past tense of **cleave[1]**
clove hitch *n* a knot or hitch used for securing a rope to a spar, post, or larger rope
Clovelly (klə'vɛlɪ) *n* a village in SW England, in Devon on the Bristol Channel: famous for its steep cobbled streets: tourism, fishing. Pop: 500 (latest est)
cloven ('kləʊvən) *vb* **1** a past participle of **cleave[1]** ▹ *adj* **2** split; cleft; divided
cloven hoof *or* **foot** *n* **1** the divided hoof of a pig, goat, cow, deer, or related animal **2** the mark or symbol of Satan > ˌ**cloven-'hoofed** *or* ˌ**cloven-'footed** *adj*
clove oil *n* a volatile pale-yellow aromatic oil obtained from clove flowers, formerly much used in confectionery, dentistry, and microscopy. Also called: **oil of cloves**
clover ('kləʊvə) *n* **1** a leguminous fodder plant having trifoliate leaves and dense flower heads **2** any of various similar or related plants **3** **in clover** *inf* in a state of ease or luxury [OE *clāfre*]
cloverleaf ('kləʊvəˌliːf) *n, pl* **cloverleaves** **1** an arrangement of connecting roads, resembling a four-leaf clover in form, that joins two intersecting main roads **2** (*modifier*) in the shape or pattern of a leaf of clover
Clovis I ('kləʊvɪs) *n* German name *Chlodwig*. ?466–511 AD, king of the Franks (481–511), who extended the Merovingian kingdom to include most of Gaul and SW Germany
clown (klaʊn) *n* **1** a comic entertainer, usually grotesquely costumed and made up, appearing in the circus **2** a person who acts in a comic or buffoon-like manner **3** a clumsy rude person; boor **4** *arch* a countryman or rustic ▹ *vb* (*intr*) **5** to perform as a clown **6** to play jokes or tricks **7** to act foolishly [c16 ?from Low G] > '**clownery** *n* > '**clownish** *adj* > '**clownishly** *adv* > '**clownishness** *n*
cloy (klɔɪ) *vb* to make weary or cause weariness through an excess of something initially pleasurable or sweet [c14 (orig.: to nail, hence, to obstruct): from earlier *acloyen*, from OF, from Med. L *inclavāre*, from L, from *clāvus* a nail]
cloying ('klɔɪɪŋ) *adj* initially pleasurable or sweet but wearying in excess > '**cloyingly** *adv*
cloze test (kləʊz) *n* a test of the ability to comprehend text in which the reader has to supply the missing words that have been removed from the text [c20 altered from *close* to complete a pattern (in Gestalt theory)]
club (klʌb) *n* **1** a stout stick, usually with one end thicker than the other, esp one used as a weapon **2** a stick or bat used to strike the ball in various sports, esp golf. See **golf club** **3** short for **Indian club** **4** a group or association of people with common aims or interests **5** the room, building, or facilities used by such a group **6** a building in which elected, fee-paying members go to meet, dine, read, etc **7** a commercial establishment in which people can drink and dance; disco. See also **nightclub** **8** *chiefly Brit* an organization, esp in a shop, set up as a means of saving **9** *Brit* an informal word for **friendly society** **10a** the black trefoil symbol on a playing card **10b** a card with one or more of these symbols or (*when pl*) the suit of cards so marked **11** **in the club** *Brit sl* pregnant ▹ *vb* **clubs, clubbing, clubbed** **12** (*tr*) to beat with or as if with a club **13** (often foll by *together*) to gather or become gathered into a group **14** (often foll by *together*) to unite or combine (resources, efforts, etc) for a common purpose [c13 from ON *klubba*, rel. to CLUMP]
clubbed (klʌbd) *adj* having a thickened end, like a club
clubber ('klʌbə) *n* a person who regularly frequents nightclubs and similar establishments
clubbing ('klʌbɪŋ) *n* the activity of frequenting nightclubs
club class *n* **1** a class of air travel that is less luxurious than first class but more luxurious than economy class ▹ *adj* **club-class** **2** of or relating to this class of travel
club foot *n* **1** a congenital deformity of the foot, esp one in which the foot is twisted so that most of the weight rests on the heel. Technical name: **talipes** **2** a foot so deformed > ˌ**club-'footed** *adj*
clubhouse ('klʌbˌhaʊs) *n* the premises of a sports or other club, esp a golf club
clubman ('klʌbmən) *or* (*fem*) **clubwoman** *n, pl* **clubmen** *or* **clubwomen** a person who is an enthusiastic member of a club or clubs
club root *n* a fungal disease of cabbages and related plants, in which the roots become thickened and distorted
cluck (klʌk) *n* **1** the low clicking sound made by a hen or any similar sound ▹ *vb* **2** (*intr*) (of a hen) to make a clicking sound **3** (*tr*) to call or express (a feeling) by making a similar sound [c17 imit.]
clucky ('klʌkɪ) *adj Austral inf* **1** wanting to have a baby **2** excessively protective towards children
clue (kluː) *n* **1** something that helps to solve a problem or unravel a mystery **2** **not have a clue** **2a** to be completely baffled **2b** to be ignorant or incompetent ▹ *vb* **clues, cluing, clued** **3** (*tr*; usually foll by *in* or *up*) to provide with helpful information [c15 var. of CLEW]
clued-up *adj inf* shrewd; well-informed
clueless ('kluːlɪs) *adj sl* helpless; stupid
Cluj (klʊʃ, kluːʒ) *n* an industrial city in NW Romania, on the Someşul-Mic River: former capital of Transylvania. Pop: 332 792 (1997 est). German name: **Klausenburg** Hungarian name: **Kolozsvár**
clump (klʌmp) *n* **1** a cluster, as of trees or plants **2** a dull heavy tread or any similar sound **3** an irregular mass **4** an inactive mass of microorganisms, esp a mass of bacteria produced as a result of agglutination **5** an extra sole on a shoe **6** *sl* a blow ▹ *vb* **7** (*intr*) to walk or tread heavily **8** to gather or be gathered into clumps, clusters, clots, etc **9** to collect together or (of bacteria) cause to to collect together **10** (*tr*) *sl* to punch (someone) [OE *clympe*] > '**clumpy** *adj*
clumsy ('klʌmzɪ) *adj* **clumsier, clumsiest** **1** lacking in skill or physical coordination **2** awkwardly constructed or contrived [c16 (in obs. sense: benumbed with cold; hence, awkward): ?from c13 dialect *clumse* to benumb, prob. of Scand. origin] > '**clumsily** *adv* > '**clumsiness** *n*
clung (klʌŋ) *vb* the past tense and past participle of **cling**
Cluniac ('kluːnɪˌæk) *adj* of or relating to a reformed Benedictine order founded at the French town of Cluny in 910
clunk (klʌŋk) *n* **1** a blow or the sound of a blow **2** a dull metallic sound ▹ *vb* **3** to make or cause to make such a sound [c19 imit.]
clunker ('klʌŋkə) *n inf* **1** *chiefly US* a dilapidated old car or other machine **2** something that fails: *the novel's last line is a clunker*
clunky ('klʌŋkɪ) *adj* **clunkier, clunkiest** **1** making a clunking noise **2** clumsy or inelegant: *clunky ankle-strap*

Cc

shoes **3** awkward or unsophisticated: *then you guffaw at clunky dialogue*

Cluny ('klu:nɪ; *French* klyni) *n* a town in E central France: reformed Benedictine order founded here in 910; important religious and cultural centre in the Middle Ages. Pop: 4724 (1990)

cluster ('klʌstə) *n* **1** a number of things growing, fastened, or occurring close together **2** a number of persons or things grouped together ▹ *vb* **3** to gather or be gathered in clusters [OE *clyster*] > **'clustered** *adj* > **'clustery** *adj*

clutch[1] (klʌtʃ) *vb* **1** (*tr*) to seize with or as if with hands or claws **2** (*tr*) to grasp or hold firmly **3** (*intr*; usually foll by *at*) to attempt to get hold or possession (of) ▹ *n* **4** a device that enables two revolving shafts to be joined or disconnected, esp one that transmits the drive from the engine to the gearbox in a vehicle **5** a device for holding fast **6** a firm grasp **7** a hand, claw, or talon in the act of clutching: *in the clutches of a bear* **8** (*often pl*) power or control: *in the clutches of the Mafia* [OE *clyccan*]

clutch[2] (klʌtʃ) *n* **1** a hatch of eggs laid by a particular bird or laid in a single nest **2** a brood of chickens **3** *inf* a group or cluster ▹ *vb* **4** (*tr*) to hatch (chickens) [C17 (N English dialect) *cletch*, from ON *klekja* to hatch]

Clutha ('klu:θə) *n* a river in New Zealand, the longest river in South Island; rising in the Southern Alps it flows southeast to the Pacific. Length: 338 km (210 miles)

clutter ('klʌtə) *vb* **1** (*usually tr*; often foll by *up*) to strew or amass (objects) in a disorderly manner **2** (*intr*) to move about in a bustling manner ▹ *n* **3** a disordered heap or mass of objects **4** a state of disorder **5** unwanted echoes that confuse the observation of signals on a radar screen [C15 *clotter*, from *clotteren* to CLOT]

Clwyd ('klu:ɪd) *n* a former county in NE Wales, formed in 1974 from Flintshire, most of Denbighshire, and part of Merionethshire; replaced in 1996 by Flintshire, Denbighshire, Wrexham county borough, and part of Conwy county borough

Clyde (klaɪd) *n* **1 Firth of** an inlet of the Atlantic in SW Scotland. Length: 103 km (64 miles) **2** a river in S Scotland, rising in South Lanarkshire and flowing northwest to the Firth of Clyde: formerly extensive shipyards. Length: 170 km (106 miles)

Clydebank (,klaɪd'bæŋk, 'klaɪd,bæŋk) *n* a town in W Scotland, in West Dunbartonshire on the north bank of the River Clyde. Pop: 29 171 (1991)

Clydesdale ('klaɪdz,deɪl) *n* a heavy powerful breed of carthorse, originally from Scotland

clypeus ('klɪpɪəs) *n, pl* **clypei** ('klɪpɪ,aɪ) a cuticular plate on the head of some insects [C19 from NL, from L *clipeus* round shield] > **'clypeal** *adj* > **clypeate** ('klɪpɪ,eɪt) *adj*

Clytemnestra *or* **Clytaemnestra** (,klaɪtɪm'nɛstrə) *n Greek myth* the wife of Agamemnon, whom she killed on his return from the Trojan War

cm *symbol for* centimetre

Cm *the chemical symbol for* curium

CM *abbrev for* Member of the Order of Canada

Cmdr *mil abbrev for* Commander

CMEA *abbrev for* Council for Mutual Economic Assistance. See **Comecon**

CMG *abbrev for* Companion of St Michael and St George (a Brit title)

CMOS ('si:mɒs) *adj computing acronym for* complementary metal oxide silicon: *CMOS memory*

CMV *abbrev for* cytomegalovirus

CNAA *abbrev for* Council for National Academic Awards

CNAR *abbrev for* compound net annual rate

CND *chiefly Brit abbrev for* Campaign for Nuclear Disarmament

CNG *abbrev for* compressed natural gas

CNN *abbrev for* Cable Network News

Cnossus ('nɒsəs, 'knɒs-) *n* a variant spelling of **Knossos**

CNR *abbrev for* Canadian National Railways

Cnut (kə'nju:t) *n* a variant spelling of **Canute**

Co *the chemical symbol for* cobalt

CO *abbrev for:* **1** Commanding Officer **2** conscientious objector

Co. *or* **co.** *abbrev for:* **1** (esp in names of business organizations) Company **2 and co** (kəʊ) *inf* and the rest of them: *Harold and co*

Co. *abbrev for* County

co- *prefix* **1** together; joint or jointly; mutual or mutually: *coproduction* **2** indicating partnership or equality: *cofounder; copilot* **3** to the same or a similar degree: *coextend* **4** (in mathematics and astronomy) of the complement of an angle: *cosecant* [from L, reduced form of COM-]

c/o *abbrev for:* **1** care of **2** *book-keeping* carried over

coach (kəʊtʃ) *n* **1** a large vehicle for several passengers, used for transport over long distances, sightseeing, etc **2** a large four-wheeled enclosed carriage, usually horse-drawn **3** a railway carriage **4** a trainer or instructor: *a drama coach* **5** a tutor who prepares students for examinations ▹ *vb* **6** to give tuition or instruction to (a pupil) **7** (*tr*) to transport in a bus or coach [C16 from F *coche*, from Hungarian *kocsi szekér* wagon of Kocs, village in Hungary where coaches were first made] > **'coacher** *n*

coach-built *adj* (of a vehicle) having specially built bodywork > **'coach-,builder** *n*

coach class *n* the US and Canad term for **economy class**

coachman ('kəʊtʃmən) *n, pl* **coachmen** the driver of a coach or carriage

coachwork ('kəʊtʃ,wɜ:k) *n* **1** the design and manufacture of car bodies **2** the body of a car

coadjutor (kəʊ'ædʒʊtə) *n* **1** a bishop appointed as assistant to a diocesan bishop **2** *rare* an assistant [C15 via OF from L *co-* together + *adjūtor* helper, from *adjūtāre* to assist]

coagulate *vb* (kəʊ'ægjʊ,leɪt), **coagulates, coagulating, coagulated** **1** to cause (a fluid, such as blood) to change into a soft semisolid mass or (of such a fluid) to change into such a mass; clot; curdle ▹ *n* (kəʊ'ægjʊlɪt, -,leɪt) **2** the solid or semisolid substance produced by coagulation [C16 from L *coāgulāre*, from *coāgulum* rennet, from *cōgere* to drive together] > **co'agulant** *or* **co'agu,lator** *n* > **co,agu'lation** *n* > **coagulative** (kəʊ'ægjʊlətɪv) *adj*

coagulation factor *n med* another name for **clotting factor**

Coahuila (*Spanish* koa'wila) *n* a state of N Mexico: mainly plateau, crossed by several mountain ranges that contain rich mineral resources. Capital: Saltillo. Pop: 2 295 808 (2000). Area: 151 571 sq km (59 112 sq miles)

coal (kəʊl) *n* **1a** a combustible compact black or dark brown carbonaceous rock formed from compaction of layers of partially decomposed vegetation: a fuel and a source of coke, coal gas, and coal tar **1b** (*as modifier*): *coal cellar; coal mine; coal dust* **2** one or more lumps of coal **3** short for **charcoal** **4 coals to Newcastle** something supplied where it is already plentiful ▹ *vb* **5** to take in, provide with, or turn into coal [OE *col*] > **'coaly** *adj*

coaler ('kəʊlə) *n* a ship, train, etc, used to carry or supply coal

coalesce (,kəʊə'lɛs) *vb* **coalesces, coalescing, coalesced** (*intr*) to unite or come together in one body or mass; merge; fuse; blend [C16 from L *co-* + *alēscere* to increase, from *alere* to nourish] > **,coa'lescence** *n* > **,coa'lescent** *adj*

coalface ('kəʊl,feɪs) *n* the exposed seam of coal in a mine

coalfield ('kəʊl,fi:ld) *n* an area rich in deposits of coal

coalfish ('kəʊl,fɪʃ) *n, pl* **coalfish** *or* **coalfishes** a dark-coloured gadoid food fish occurring in northern seas. Also called (Brit): **saithe, coley**

coal gas *n* a mixture of gases produced by the distillation of bituminous coal and used for heating and lighting

coalition (,kəʊə'lɪʃən) *n* **1a** an alliance between groups or parties, esp for some temporary and specific reason **1b** (*as modifier*): *a coalition government* **2** a fusion or merging into one body or mass [C17 from Med. L *coalitiō*, from L *coalēscere* to COALESCE] > ˌ**coa'litionist** *n*

Coal Measures *pl n* **the** a series of coal-bearing rocks formed in the upper Carboniferous period

coal miner's lung *n* an informal name for **anthracosis**

coal scuttle *n* a container to supply coal to a domestic fire

coal tar *n* a black tar, produced by the distillation of bituminous coal, that can be further distilled to yield benzene, toluene, etc

coal tit *n* a small European songbird having a black head with a white patch on the nape

coaming ('kəʊmɪŋ) *n* a raised frame round a ship's hatchway for keeping out water [C17 from ?]

coarse (kɔːs) *adj* **1** rough in texture, structure, etc; not fine: *coarse sand* **2** lacking refinement or taste; indelicate; vulgar: *coarse jokes* **3** of inferior quality **4** (of a metal) not refined [C14 from ?] > '**coarsely** *adv* > '**coarseness** *n*

coarse fish *n* a freshwater fish that is not of the salmon family > **coarse fishing** *n*

coarsen ('kɔːsᵊn) *vb* to make or become coarse

coast (kəʊst) *n* **1** the line or zone where the land meets the sea. Related adj: **littoral** **2** *Brit* the seaside **3** *US* **3a** a slope down which a sledge may slide **3b** the act or an instance of sliding down a slope **4** **the coast is clear** *inf* the obstacles or dangers are gone ▷ *vb* **5** to move or cause to move by momentum or force of gravity **6** (*intr*) to proceed without great effort: *to coast to victory* **7** to sail along (a coast) [C13 from OF *coste*, from L *costa* side, rib] > '**coastal** *adj*

coaster ('kəʊstə) *n* **1** *Brit* a vessel engaged in coastal commerce **2** a small tray for holding a decanter, wine bottle, etc **3** a person or thing that coasts **4** a protective mat for glasses **5** *US* short for **roller coaster**

Coaster ('kəʊstə) *n* *NZ* a person from the West Coast of the South Island, New Zealand

coastguard ('kəʊstˌgɑːd) *n* **1** a maritime force which aids shipping, saves lives at sea, prevents smuggling, etc **2** Also called: **coastguardsman** a member of such a force

coastline ('kəʊstˌlaɪn) *n* the outline of a coast

Coast Mountains *pl n* a mountain range in Canada, on the Pacific coast of British Columbia. Highest peak: Mount Waddington, 4043 m (13 266 ft)

coat (kəʊt) *n* **1** an outdoor garment with sleeves, covering the body from the shoulders to waist, knees, or feet **2** any similar garment, esp one forming the top to a suit **3** a layer that covers or conceals a surface: *a coat of dust* **4** the hair, wool, or fur of an animal ▷ *vb* (*tr*) **5** (often foll by *with*) to cover (with) a layer or covering **6** to provide with a coat [C16 from OF *cote*, of Gmc origin]

Coates (kəʊts) *n* **Joseph Gordon** 1878–1943, New Zealand statesman; prime minister of New Zealand (1925–28)

coat hanger *n* a curved piece of wood, wire, etc, with a hook, used to hang up clothes

coati (kəʊ'ɑːtɪ), **coati-mondi,** *or* **coati-mundi** (kəʊˌɑːtɪ'mʌndɪ) *n, pl* **coatis, coati-mondis,** *or* **coati-mundis** an omnivorous mammal of Central and South America, related to but larger than the raccoons, having a long flexible snout and a brindled coat [C17 from Port., from Tupi, lit.: belt-nosed, from *cua* belt + *tim* nose]

coating ('kəʊtɪŋ) *n* **1** a layer or film spread over a surface **2** fabric suitable for coats

coat of arms *n* the heraldic bearings of a person, family, or corporation

coat of mail *n* a protective garment made of linked metal rings or overlapping metal plates

coat-tail *n* the long tapering tails at the back of a man's tailed coat

coauthor (kəʊ'ɔːθə) *n* **1** a person who shares the writing of a book, etc, with another ▷ *vb* **2** (*tr*) to be the joint author of (a book, etc)

coax (kəʊks) *vb* **1** to seek to manipulate or persuade (someone) by tenderness, flattery, pleading, etc **2** (*tr*) to obtain by persistent coaxing **3** (*tr*) to work on (something) carefully and patiently so as to make it function as desired: *he coaxed the engine into starting* [C16 verb formed from obs. noun *cokes* fool, from ?] > '**coaxer** *n* > '**coaxingly** *adv*

coaxial (kəʊ'æksɪəl) *or* **coaxal** (kəʊ'æksᵊl) *adj* **1** having or mounted on a common axis **2** *geom* (of a set of circles) having the same radical axis **3** *electronics* formed from, using, or connected to a coaxial cable

coaxial cable *n* a cable consisting of an inner insulated core of stranded or solid wire surrounded by an outer insulated flexible wire braid, used esp as a transmission line for radio-frequency signals. Often shortened to **coax** ('kəʊæks)

cob (kɒb) *n* **1** a male swan **2** a thickset short-legged type of riding and draught horse **3** short for **corncob** or **cobnut** **4** *Brit* another name for **hazel** (sense 1) **5** a small rounded lump or heap of coal, ore, etc **6** *Brit & NZ* a building material consisting of a mixture of clay and chopped straw **7** *Brit* a round loaf of bread [C15 from ?]

cobalt ('kəʊbɔːlt) *n* a brittle hard silvery-white element that is a ferromagnetic metal: used in alloys. The radioisotope **cobalt-60** is used in radiotherapy and as a tracer. Symbol: Co; atomic no.: 27; atomic wt.: 58.933 [C17 G *Kobalt*, from MHG *kobolt* goblin; from the miners' belief that goblins placed it in the silver ore]

cobalt blue *n* **1** any greenish-blue pigment containing cobalt aluminate **2a** a deep blue colour **2b** (*as adj*): *a cobalt-blue car*

cobalt bomb *n* **1** a cobalt-60 device used in radiotherapy **2** a nuclear weapon consisting of a hydrogen bomb encased in cobalt, which releases large quantities of radioactive cobalt-60 into the atmosphere

cobber ('kɒbə) *n* *Austral arch & NZ* a friend; mate: used as a term of address to males [C19 from E dialect *cob* to take a liking to someone]

Cobbett ('kɒbɪt) *n* **William** 1763–1835, English journalist and social reformer; founded *The Political Register* (1802); author of *Rural Rides* (1830)

cobble[1] ('kɒbᵊl) *n* **1** short for **cobblestone** ▷ *vb* **cobbles, cobbling, cobbled** **2** (*tr*) to pave (a road, etc) with cobblestones [C15 (in *cobblestone*): from COB]

cobble[2] ('kɒbᵊl) *vb* **cobbles, cobbling, cobbled** (*tr*) **1** to make or mend (shoes) **2** to put together clumsily [C15 back formation from COBBLER[1]]

cobbler[1] ('kɒblə) *n* a person who makes or mends shoes [C13 (as surname): from ?]

cobbler[2] ('kɒblə) *n* **1** a sweetened iced drink, usually made from fruit and wine **2** *chiefly US* a hot dessert made of fruit covered with a rich cakelike crust [C19 (for sense 1) ? shortened from *cobbler's punch*]

cobblers ('kɒbləz) *pl n* *Brit sl* **1** another word for **testicles** **2** (**a load of old**) **cobblers** rubbish; nonsense [C20 from rhyming sl *cobblers' awls* balls]

cobblestone ('kɒbᵊlˌstəʊn) *n* a rounded stone used for paving. Sometimes shortened to **cobble**

Cobden ('kɒbdən) *n* **Richard** 1804–65, British economist and statesman: with John Bright a leader of the successful campaign to abolish the Corn Laws (1846)

cobelligerent (ˌkəʊbɪ'lɪdʒərənt) *n* a country fighting in a war on the side of another country

Cobham ('kɒbəm) *n* **Lord,** title of (Sir John) **Oldcastle**

Coblenz (*German* 'koːblɛnts) *n* a variant spelling of **Koblenz**

cobnut ('kɒbˌnʌt) *or* **cob** *n* other names for a **hazelnut** [C16 from earlier *cobylle nut*]

COBOL *or* **Cobol** ('kəʊˌbɒl) *n* a high-level computer

Cc

programming language designed for general commercial use [c20 *co(mmon) b(usiness) o(riented) l(anguage)*]

cobra ('kəʊbrə) *n* any of several highly venomous snakes of tropical Africa and Asia. When alarmed they spread the skin of the neck region into a hood [c19 from Port. *cobra (de capello)* snake (with a hood), from L *colubra* snake]

Coburg ('kəʊbɜːg; *German* 'koːbʊrk) *n* a city in E Germany, in N Bavaria. Pop: 44 690 (1991)

cobweb ('kɒbˌwɛb) *n* **1** a web spun by certain spiders **2** a single thread of such a web **3** something like a cobweb, as in its flimsiness or ability to trap [c14 *cob*, from OE *(ātor)coppe* spider] > **'cobˌwebbed** *adj* > **'cobˌwebby** *adj*

cobwebs ('kɒbˌwɛbz) *pl n* **1** mustiness, confusion, or obscurity **2** *inf* stickiness of the eyelids experienced upon first awakening

coca ('kəʊkə) *n* either of two shrubs, native to the Andes, the dried leaves of which contain cocaine and are chewed for their stimulating effects [c17 from Sp., from Quechuan *kúka*]

Coca-Cola (ˌkəʊkə'kəʊlə) *n* **1** *trademark* a carbonated soft drink flavoured with coca leaves, cola nuts, caramel, etc **2** (*modifier*) denoting the spread of American culture and values to other parts of the world: *Coca-Cola generation*

cocaine *or* **cocain** (kə'keɪn) *n* an addictive narcotic drug derived from coca leaves or synthesized, used medicinally as a topical anaesthetic [c19 from COCA + -INE[1]]

coccus ('kɒkəs) *n, pl* **cocci** (-kaɪ, -kiː) any spherical or nearly spherical bacterium, such as a staphylococcus [c18 from NL, from Gk *kokkos* berry, grain] > **'coccoid** *or* **'coccal** *adj*

coccyx ('kɒksɪks) *n, pl* **coccyges** (kɒk'saɪdʒiːz) a small triangular bone at the end of the spinal column in man and some apes [c17 from NL, from Gk *kokkux* cuckoo, imit.; from its likeness to a cuckoo's beak] > **coccygeal** (kɒk'sɪdʒɪəl) *adj*

Cochin ('kəʊtʃɪn, 'kɒtʃ-) *n* **1** a region and former state of SW India: part of Kerala state since 1956 **2** a port in SW India, on the Malabar Coast: the first European settlement in India, founded by Vasco da Gama in 1502: shipbuilding, engineering. Pop: 564 589 (1991) **3** a large breed of domestic fowl, with dense plumage and feathered legs, that originated in Cochin China

Cochin China *n* a former French colony of Indochina (1862–1948): now the part of Vietnam that lies south of Phan Thiet

cochineal (ˌkɒtʃɪ'niːl, 'kɒtʃɪˌniːl) *n* **1** a Mexican insect that feeds on cacti **2** a crimson substance obtained from the crushed bodies of these insects, used for colouring food and for dyeing **3** the colour of this dye [c16 from OSp. *cochinilla*, from L *coccineus* scarlet-coloured, from Gk *kokkos* kermes berry]

cochlea ('kɒklɪə) *n, pl* **cochleae** (-lɪˌiː) the spiral tube that forms part of the internal ear, converting sound vibrations into nerve impulses [c16 from L: snail, spiral, from Gk *kokhlias*] > **'cochlear** *adj*

cochlear implant ('kɒklɪə) *n* a device that stimulates the acoustic nerve in the inner ear in order to produce some form of hearing in people who are deaf from inner ear disease

cochleate ('kɒklɪˌeɪt, -lɪɪt) *or* **cochleated** *adj biol* shaped like a snail's shell

cock[1] (kɒk) *n* **1** the male of the domestic fowl **2a** any other male bird **2b** the male of certain other animals, such as the lobster **2c** (*as modifier*): *a cock sparrow* **3** short for **stopcock** or **weathercock** **4** a taboo slang word for **penis** **5a** the hammer of a firearm **5b** its position when the firearm is ready to be discharged **6** *Brit inf* a friend, mate, or fellow **7** a jaunty or significant tilting upwards: *a cock of the head* ▹ *vb* **8** (*tr*) to set the firing pin, hammer, or breech block of (a firearm) so that a pull on the trigger will release it and thus fire the weapon **9** (*tr*; sometimes foll by *up*) to raise in an alert or jaunty manner **10** (*intr*) to stick or stand up conspicuously ▹ See also **cockup** [OE *cocc*, ult. imit.]

cock[2] (kɒk) *n* **1** a small, cone-shaped heap of hay, straw, etc ▹ *vb* **2** (*tr*) to stack (hay, etc) in such heaps [c14 ? of Scand. origin]

cockabully (ˌkɒkə'bʊlɪ) *n, pl* **cockabullies** any of several small freshwater fish of New Zealand [Maori *kokopu*]

cockade (kɒ'keɪd) *n* a feather or ribbon worn on military headwear [c18 changed from earlier *cockard*, from F, from *coq* COCK[1]] > **cock'aded** *adj*

cock-a-doodle-doo (ˌkɒkəˌduːdᵊl'duː) *interj* an imitation or representation of a cock crowing

cock-a-hoop *adj* (*usually postpositive*) **1** in very high spirits **2** boastful **3** askew; confused [c16 ?from *set the cock a hoop*: to put a cock on a *hoop*, a full measure of grain]

cockalorum (ˌkɒkə'lɔːrəm) *n* **1** a self-important little man **2** bragging talk [c18 from COCK[1] + *-alorum*, var. of L genitive pl ending; ? intended to suggest: the cock of all cocks]

cockamamie (ˌkɒkə'meɪmɪ) *adj sl, chiefly US* ridiculous or nonsensical: *a cockamamie story* [c20 in an earlier sense: a paper transfer, prob. from DECALCOMANIA]

cock-and-bull story *n inf* an obviously improbable story, esp one used as an excuse

cockatoo (ˌkɒkə'tuː, 'kɒkəˌtuː) *n, pl* **cockatoos** **1** any of a genus of parrots having an erectile crest and light-coloured plumage **2** *Austral & NZ obs* a small farmer or settler **3** *Austral inf* a lookout during some illegal activity [c17 from Du., from Malay *kakatua*]

cockatrice ('kɒkətrɪs, -ˌtraɪs) *n* **1** a legendary monster, part snake and part cock, that could kill with a glance **2** another name for **basilisk** (sense 1) [c14 from OF, ult. from L *calcāre* to tread, from *calx* heel]

cockboat ('kɒkˌbəʊt) *or* **cockleboat** *n* a ship's small boat [c15 *cokbote*, ? ult. from LL *caudica* dugout canoe, from L *caudex* tree trunk]

cockchafer ('kɒkˌtʃeɪfə) *n* any of various Old World beetles, whose larvae feed on crops and grasses. Also called: **May beetle, May bug** [c18 from COCK[1] + CHAFER]

Cockcroft ('kɒkˌkrɒft) *n* Sir **John Douglas** 1897–1967, English nuclear physicist. With E. T. S. Walton, he produced the first artificial transmutation of an atomic nucleus (1932) and shared the Nobel prize for physics 1951

cockcrow ('kɒkˌkrəʊ) *n* daybreak

cocked hat *n* **1** a hat with brims turned up and caught together in order to give two points (bicorn) or three points (tricorn) **2** **knock into a cocked hat** *sl* to outdo or defeat

Cocker ('kɒkə) *n* **1** **Edward** 1631–75, English arithmetician **2** **according to cocker** reliable or reliably; correct or correctly

cockerel ('kɒkərəl, 'kɒkrəl) *n* a young domestic cock, less than a year old [c15 dim. of COCK[1]]

Cockerell ('kɒkərəl) *n* Sir **Christopher Sydney** 1910–99, British engineer, who invented the hovercraft

cocker spaniel ('kɒkə) *n* a small compact breed of spaniel [c19 from *cocking* hunting woodcocks]

cockeyed ('kɒkˌaɪd) *adj inf* **1** afflicted with strabismus or squint **2** physically or logically abnormal, absurd, etc; crooked; askew: *cockeyed ideas* **3** drunk

cockfight ('kɒkˌfaɪt) *n* a fight between two gamecocks fitted with sharp metal spurs > **'cockˌfighting** *n*

cockhorse (ˌkɒk'hɔːs) *n* another name for **rocking horse** or **hobbyhorse**

cockieleekie, cockyleeky, *or* **cock-a-leekie** ('kɒkə'liːkɪ) *n Scot* a soup made from a fowl boiled with leeks

cockle[1] ('kɒkᵊl) *n* **1** any edible sand-burrowing bivalve mollusc of Europe, typically having a rounded shell with radiating ribs **2** any of certain similar or related molluscs **3** short for **cockleshell** (sense 1) **4** a wrinkle or puckering **5** one's deepest feelings (esp in **warm the cockles of one's heart**) ▷ *vb* **cockles, cockling, cockled** **6** to contract or cause to contract into wrinkles [C14 from OF *coquille* shell, from L *conchȳlium* shellfish, from Gk *konkhule* mussel; see CONCH]

cockle[2] ('kɒkᵊl) *n* any of several plants, esp the corn cockle, that grow as weeds in cornfields

cockleshell ('kɒkᵊlˌʃɛl) *n* **1** the shell of the cockle **2** any of the shells of certain other molluscs **3** any small light boat

cockney ('kɒknɪ) *(often cap)* ▷ *n* **1** a native of London, esp of the East End, speaking a characteristic dialect of English. Traditionally defined as someone born within the sound of the bells of St Mary-le-Bow church **2** the urban dialect of London or its East End ▷ *adj* **3** characteristic of cockneys or their dialect of English [C14 from *cokeney*, lit.: cock's egg, later applied contemptuously to townsmen, from *cokene*, genitive pl of *cok* COCK[1] + *ey* EGG[1]] > **'cockneyish** *adj* > **'cockneyˌism** *n*

cock of the walk *n inf* a person who asserts himself in a strutting pompous way

cockpit ('kɒkˌpɪt) *n* **1** the compartment in a small aircraft in which the pilot, crew, and sometimes the passengers sit ▷ Cf **flight deck** (sense 1) **2** the driver's compartment in a racing car **3** *naut* an enclosed or recessed area towards the stern of a small vessel from which it is steered **4** the site of numerous battles or campaigns **5** an enclosure used for cockfights

cockroach ('kɒkˌrəʊtʃ) *n* an insect having an oval flattened body with long antennae and biting mouthparts: a household pest [C17 from Sp. *cucaracha*, from ?]

cockscomb *or* **coxcomb** ('kɒksˌkəʊm) *n* **1** the comb of a domestic cock **2** a garden plant with yellow, crimson, or purple feathery plumelike flowers in a broad spike resembling the comb of a cock **3** *inf* a conceited dandy

cockshy ('kɒkˌʃaɪ) *n, pl* **cockshies** *Brit* **1** a target aimed at in throwing games **2** the throw itself ▷ Often shortened to **shy** [C18 from shying at a cock, the prize for the person who hit it]

cocksure (ˌkɒk'ʃʊə, -'ʃɔː) *adj* overconfident; arrogant [C16 from ?] > ˌ**cock'sureness** *n*

cocktail ('kɒkˌteɪl) *n* **1a** any mixed drink with a spirit base **1b** *(as modifier): the cocktail hour* **2** an appetizer of seafood, mixed fruits, etc **3** any combination of diverse elements, esp one considered potent **4** *(modifier)* appropriate for formal occasions: *a cocktail dress* [C19 from ?]

▷ www.cocktail.com
▷ www.cocktail.uk.com

cockup ('kɒkˌʌp) *n* **1** *Brit sl* something done badly ▷ *vb* **cock up** *(tr, adv)* **2** (of an animal) to raise (its ears etc), esp in an alert manner **3** *Brit sl* to botch

cocky[1] ('kɒkɪ) *adj* **cockier, cockiest** excessively proud of oneself > **'cockily** *adv* > **'cockiness** *n*

cocky[2] ('kɒkɪ) *n, pl* **cockies** *Austral & NZ inf* short for **cockatoo** (sense 2)

coco ('kəʊkəʊ) *n, pl* **cocos** short for **coconut** or **coconut palm** [C16 from Port. *coco* grimace; from the likeness of the three holes of the nut to a face]

cocoa ('kəʊkəʊ) *or* **cacao** *n* **1** a powder made from cocoa beans after they have been roasted and ground **2** a hot or cold drink made from cocoa and milk or water **3a** a light to moderate brown colour **3b** *(as adj): cocoa paint* [C18 altered from CACAO]

cocoa bean *n* the seed of the cacao

cocoa butter *n* a yellowish-white waxy solid that is obtained from cocoa beans and used for confectionery, soap, etc

coconut *or* **cocoanut** ('kəʊkəˌnʌt) *n* **1** the fruit of the coconut palm, consisting of a thick fibrous oval husk inside which is a thin hard shell enclosing edible white meat. The hollow centre is filled with a milky fluid (**coconut milk**) **2** the meat of the coconut, often shredded and used in cakes, curries, etc [C18 see COCO]

coconut matting *n* a form of coarse matting made from the fibrous husk of the coconut

coconut oil *n* the oil obtained from the meat of the coconut and used for making soap, etc

coconut palm *n* a tall palm tree, widely planted throughout the tropics, having coconuts as fruits. Also called: **coco palm, coconut tree**

cocoon (kə'kuːn) *n* **1** a silky protective envelope secreted by silkworms and certain other insect larvae, in which the pupae develop **2** a protective spray covering used as a seal on machinery **3** a cosy warm covering ▷ *vb* **4** *(tr)* to wrap in a cocoon [C17 from F, from Provençal *coucoun* eggshell, from *coco* shell]

cocopan ('kəʊkəʊˌpæn) *n* (in South Africa) a small wagon running on narrow-gauge railway lines used in mines. Also called: **hopper** [C20 from Zulu *'ngkumbana* short truck]

Cocos Islands ('kəʊkɒs, 'kəʊkəs) *pl n* a group of 27 coral islands in the Indian Ocean, southwest of Java: a Territory of Australia since 1955. Pop: 593 (1993). Area: 13 sq km (5 sq miles). Also called: **Keeling Islands**

cocotte (kəʊ'kɒt, kə-) *n* **1** a small fireproof dish in which individual portions of food are cooked and served **2** a prostitute or promiscuous woman [C19 from F, from fem of *coq* COCK[1]]

Cocteau *(French* kɔkto) *n* **Jean** (ʒɑ̃) 1889–1963, French dramatist, novelist, poet, critic, designer, and film director. His works include the novel *Les Enfants terribles* (1929) and the play *La Machine infernale* (1934)

cod[1] (kɒd) *n, pl* **cod** *or* **cods** **1** any of the gadoid food fishes which occur in the North Atlantic and have a long body with three rounded dorsal fins **2** any of various Australian fishes of fresh or salt water, such as the Murray cod or the red cod [C13 prob. of Gmc origin]

cod[2] (kɒd) *n* **1** *Brit & US dialect* a pod or husk **2** an obsolete word for **scrotum** [OE *codd* husk, bag]

cod[3] (kɒd) *Brit sl* ▷ *vb* **cods, codding, codded** *(tr)* **1** to make fun of; tease **2** to play a trick on; befool ▷ *n* **3** a hoax or trick [C19 ?from earlier *cod* a fool]

Cod *n* **Cape** See **Cape Cod**

COD *abbrev for:* **1** cash on delivery **2** (in the US) collect on delivery

coda ('kəʊdə) *n* **1** *music* the final passage of a musical structure **2** a concluding part of a literary work that rounds off the main work but is independent of it [C18 from It.: tail, from L *cauda*]

cod-act *vb (intr) Irish inf* to play tricks; fool [from COD[3] + ACT]

coddle ('kɒdᵊl) *vb* **coddles, coddling, coddled** *(tr)* **1** to treat with indulgence **2** to cook (something, esp eggs) in water just below the boiling point [C16 from ?; ? rel. to CAUDLE] > **'coddler** *n*

code (kəʊd) *n* **1** a system of letters or symbols, by which information can be communicated secretly, briefly, etc: *binary code; Morse code*. See also **genetic code** **2** a message in code **3** a symbol used in a code **4** a conventionalized set of principles or rules: *a code of behaviour* **5** a system of letters or digits used for identification purposes ▷ *vb* **codes, coding, coded** *(tr)* **6** to translate or arrange into a code [C14 from F, from L *cōdex* book, CODEX] > **'coder** *n*

codeine ('kəʊdiːn) *n* a white crystalline alkaloid prepared mainly from morphine. It is used as an analgesic, an antidiarrhoeal, and to relieve coughing [C19 from Gk *kōdeia* head of a poppy, from *kōos* hollow place + -INE[2]]

co-dependency (ˌkəʊdɪ'pɛndənsɪ) *n psychol* a state of mutual dependence between two people, esp when one partner relies emotionally on supporting and caring for the other partner > ˌ**co-de'pendent** *adj, n*

Co. Derry *abbrev for* County Londonderry

Cc

codex ('kəʊdɛks) *n, pl* **codices** ('kəʊdɪˌsiːz, 'kɒdɪ-) **1** a volume of manuscripts of an ancient text **2** *obs* a legal code [c16 from L: tree trunk, wooden block, book]
codfish ('kɒdˌfɪʃ) *n, pl* **codfish** *or* **codfishes** a cod
codger ('kɒdʒə) *n inf* a man, esp an old or eccentric one: often in **old codger** [c18 prob. var. of CADGER]
codicil ('kɒdɪsɪl) *n* **1** *law* a supplement modifying a will or revoking some provision of it **2** an additional provision; appendix [c15 from LL dim. of CODEX] > ˌ**codi'cillary** *adj*
codify ('kəʊdɪˌfaɪ, 'kɒ-) *vb* **codifies, codifying, codified** *(tr)* to organize or collect together (laws, rules, procedures, etc) into a system or code > '**codiˌfier** *n* > ˌ**codifi'cation** *n*
codling[1] ('kɒdlɪŋ) *or* **codlin** ('kɒdlɪn) *n* **1** any of several varieties of long tapering apples **2** any unripe apple [c15 *querdlyng*, from ?]
codling[2] ('kɒdlɪŋ) *n* a codfish, esp a young one
cod-liver oil *n* an oil extracted from the livers of cod and related fish, rich in vitamins A and D
codology (kɒd'ɒlədʒɪ) *n Irish inf* the art or practice of bluffing or deception
codpiece ('kɒdˌpiːs) *n* a bag covering the male genitals, attached to breeches: worn in the 15th and 16th centuries [c15 from COD[2] + PIECE]
codswallop ('kɒdzˌwɒləp) *n Brit sl* nonsense [c20 from ?]
Co. Durham *abbrev for* County Durham
Cody ('kəʊdɪ) *n* **William Frederick** the real name of **Buffalo Bill**
Coe (kəʊ) *n* **Sebastian** Baron. born 1956, English middle-distance runner and Conservative politician: winner of the 1500 metres in the 1980 and 1984 Olympic Games; holds 1000m record; held records at 800m, 1500m, and a mile: member of parliament (1992–97)
co-ed (ˌkəʊ'ɛd) *adj* **1** coeducational ▷ *n* **2** *US* a female student in a coeducational college or university **3** *Brit* a school or college providing coeducation
coeducation (ˌkəʊɛdjʊ'keɪʃən) *n* instruction in schools, colleges, etc, attended by both sexes > ˌ**coedu'cational** *adj* > ˌ**coedu'cationally** *adv*
coefficient (ˌkəʊɪ'fɪʃənt) *n* **1** *maths* a numerical or constant factor in an algebraic term: *the coefficient of the term 3xyz is 3* **2** *physics* a number that is the value of a given substance under specified conditions [c17 from NL, from L *co-* together + *efficere* to EFFECT]
coefficient of variation *n statistics* a measure of the relative variation of distributions independent of the units of measurement; the standard deviation divided by the mean, sometimes expressed as a percentage
coel- *prefix* indicating a cavity within a body or a hollow organ or part: *coelacanth; coelenterate* [NL, from Gk *koilos* hollow]
coelacanth ('siːləˌkænθ) *n* a primitive marine bony fish, having fleshy limblike pectoral fins: thought to be extinct until a living specimen was discovered in 1938 [c19 from NL, from COEL- + Gk *akanthos* spine]
coelenterate (sɪ'lɛntəˌreɪt, -rɪt) *n* any of various invertebrates having a saclike body with a single opening (mouth), such as jellyfishes, sea anemones, and corals [c19 from NL *Coelenterata*, hollow-intestined (creatures)]
coeliac *or US* **celiac** ('siːlɪˌæk) *adj* of the abdomen [c17 from L, from Gk, from *koilia* belly]
coeliac disease *n* an illness, esp of children, in which the lining of the small intestine is sensitive to gluten in the diet, causing an impairment of food absorption
coelom *or esp US* **celom** ('siːləʊm, -ləm) *n* the body cavity of many multicellular animals, containing the digestive tract and other visceral organs [c19 from Gk, from *koilos* hollow] > **coelomic** *or esp US* **celomic** (sɪ'lɒmɪk) *adj*
coeno- *or before a vowel* **coen-** *combining form* common: *coenobite* [NL, from Gk *koinos*]
coenobite *or* **cenobite** ('siːnəʊˌbaɪt) *n* a member of a religious order following a communal rule of life [c17 from OF or ecclesiastical L, from Gk *koinobion* convent, from *koinos* common + *bios* life] > **coenobitic** (ˌsiːnəʊ'bɪtɪk), ˌ**coeno'bitical** *or* ˌ**ceno'bitic,** ˌ**ceno'bitical** *adj*
coenzyme (kəʊ'ɛnzaɪm) *n biochem* a nonprotein organic molecule that forms a complex with certain enzymes and is essential for their activity
coequal (kəʊ'iːkwəl) *adj* **1** of the same size, rank, etc ▷ *n* **2** a person or thing equal with another > **coequality** (ˌkəʊɪ'kwɒlɪtɪ) *n*
coerce (kəʊ'ɜːs) *vb* **coerces, coercing, coerced** *(tr)* to compel or restrain by force or authority without regard to individual wishes or desires [c17 from L, from *co-* together + *arcēre* to enclose] > **co'ercer** *n* > **co'ercible** *adj*
coercion (kəʊ'ɜːʃən) *n* **1** the act or power of coercing **2** government by force > **coercive** (kəʊ'ɜːsɪv) *adj* > **co'ercively** *adv*
Coetzee ('kɜːtzɪ) *n* **J(ohn) M(ichael)** born 1940, South African novelist: his works include *Life and Times of Michael K* (1983), *Age of Iron* (1990), *Disgrace* (1999), and *Youth* (2002); Nobel prize for literature 2003
Coeur (kɜː; *French* kœr) *n* **Jacques** ?1395–1456, French merchant; councillor and court banker to Charles VII of France
coeval (kəʊ'iːvᵊl) *adj* **1** of or belonging to the same age or generation ▷ *n* **2** a contemporary [c17 from LL, from L *co-* + *aevum* age] > **coevality** (ˌkəʊɪ'vælɪtɪ) *n* > **co'evally** *adv*
coexecutor (ˌkəʊɪg'zɛkjʊtə) *n law* a person acting jointly with another or others as executor
coexist (ˌkəʊɪg'zɪst) *vb (intr)* **1** to exist together at the same time or in the same place **2** to exist together in peace > ˌ**coex'istence** *n* > ˌ**coex'istent** *adj*
coextend (ˌkəʊɪk'stɛnd) *vb* to extend or cause to extend equally in space or time > ˌ**coex'tension** *n*
coextensive (ˌkəʊɪk'stɛnsɪv) *adj* of the same limits or extent > ˌ**coex'tensively** *adv*
C of E *abbrev for* Church of England
coffee ('kɒfɪ) *n* **1a** a drink consisting of an infusion of the roasted and ground seeds of the coffee tree **1b** *(as modifier): coffee grounds* **2** Also called: **coffee beans** the beanlike seeds of the coffee tree, used to make this beverage **3** the tree yielding these seeds **4a** a light brown colour **4b** *(as adj): a coffee carpet* [c16 from It. *caffè*, from Turkish *kahve*, from Ar. *qahwah* coffee, wine]
▷ www.coffeeresearch.org
▷ www.ico.org
▷ www.nationalgeographic.com/coffee
▷ www.coffeescience.org/css.html
▷ www.ineedcoffee.com
▷ www.ncausa.org
coffee bar *n* a café; snack bar
coffee cup *n* a small cup for serving coffee
coffee house *n* a place where coffee is served, esp one that was a fashionable meeting place in 18th-century London
coffee mill *n* a machine for grinding roasted coffee beans
coffeepot ('kɒfɪˌpɒt) *n* a pot in which coffee is brewed or served
coffee shop *n* a shop where coffee is sold or drunk
coffee table *n* a low table on which coffee may be served
coffee-table book *n* a book, usually glossily illustrated, designed chiefly to be looked at, rather than read
coffer ('kɒfə) *n* **1** a chest, esp for storing valuables **2** *(usually pl)* a store of money **3** an ornamental sunken panel in a ceiling, dome, etc **4** a watertight box or chamber **5** short for **cofferdam** ▷ *vb (tr)* **6** to store, as in a coffer **7** to decorate (a ceiling, dome, etc) with coffers [c13 from OF *coffre*, from L, from Gk *kophinos* basket]
cofferdam ('kɒfəˌdæm) *n* **1** a watertight structure that encloses an area under water, pumped dry to enable construction work to be carried out **2** (on a ship) a

compartment separating two bulkheads, as for insulation or to serve as a barrier against the escape of gas, etc ▷ Often shortened to **coffer**

coffin ('kɒfɪn) *n* **1** a box in which a corpse is buried or cremated **2** the bony part of a horse's foot ▷ *vb* **3** (*tr*) to place in or as in a coffin [C14 from OF *cofin*, from L *cophinus* basket]

coffin nail *n* a slang term for **cigarette**

coffle ('kɒfᵊl) *n* a line of slaves, beasts, etc, fastened together [C18 from Ar. *qāfilah* caravan]

C of S *abbrev for* Church of Scotland

cog[1] (kɒg) *n* **1** any of the teeth or projections on the rim of a gearwheel **2** a gearwheel, esp a small one **3** a person or thing playing a small part in a large organization or process [C13 of Scand. origin]

cog[2] (kɒg) *n* **1** a tenon that projects from the end of a timber beam for fitting into a mortise ▷ *vb* **cogs, cogging, cogged 2** (*tr*) to join (pieces of wood) with cogs [C19 from ?]

cogent ('kəʊdʒənt) *adj* compelling belief or assent; forcefully convincing [C17 from L *cōgent-, cōgēns*, from *co-* together + *agere* to drive] > **'cogency** *n* > **'cogently** *adv*

cogitate ('kɒdʒɪˌteɪt) *vb* **cogitates, cogitating, cogitated** to think deeply about (a problem, possibility, etc); ponder [C16 from L, from *co-* (intensive) + *agitāre* to turn over] > **ˌcogi'tation** *n* > **'cogitative** *adj* > **'cogiˌtator** *n*

Cognac ('kɒnjæk; *French* kɔɲak) *n* **1** a town in SW France: centre of the district famed for its brandy. Pop: 21 000 (latest est) **2** (*sometimes not capital*) a high-quality grape brandy

cognate ('kɒgneɪt) *adj* **1** akin; related: *cognate languages* **2** related by blood or descended from a common maternal ancestor ▷ *n* **3** something that is cognate with something else [C17 from L, from *co-* same + *gnātus* born, var. of *nātus*, p.p. of *nāscī* to be born] > **'cognately** *adv* > **'cognateness** *n* > **cog'nation** *n*

cognition (kɒg'nɪʃən) *n* **1** the mental act or process by which knowledge is acquired, including perception, intuition, and reasoning **2** the knowledge that results from such an act or process [C15 from L, from *co-* (intensive) + *nōscere* to learn] > **cog'nitional** *adj* > **'cognitive** *adj*

cognitive behavioural therapy *n* a form of therapy in which, having learnt to understand their anxiety, patients attempt to overcome their usual behavioural responses to it

cognitive therapy *n psychol* a form of psychotherapy in which the patient is encouraged to change the way he sees the world and himself: used particularly to treat depression

cognizable *or* **cognisable** ('kɒgnɪzəbᵊl, 'kɒnɪ-) *adj* **1** perceptible **2** *law* susceptible to the jurisdiction of a court

cognizance *or* **cognisance** ('kɒgnɪzəns, 'kɒnɪ-) *n* **1** knowledge; acknowledgment **2 take cognizance of** to take notice of; acknowledge, esp officially **3** the range or scope of knowledge or perception **4** *law* the right of a court to hear and determine a cause or matter **5** *heraldry* a distinguishing badge or bearing [C14 from OF, from L *cognōscere* to learn; see COGNITION]

cognizant *or* **cognisant** ('kɒgnɪzənt, 'kɒnɪ-) *adj* (usually foll by *of*) aware; having knowledge

cognomen (kɒg'nəʊmɛn) *n, pl* **cognomens** *or* **cognomina** (-'nɒmɪnə, -'nəʊ-) (originally) an ancient Roman's third name or nickname, which later became his family name [C19 from L: additional name, from *co-* together + *nōmen* name] > **cognominal** (kɒg'nɒmɪnᵊl, -'nəʊ-) *adj*

cognoscenti (ˌkɒnjəʊ'ʃɛntɪ, ˌkɒgnəʊ-) *or* **conoscenti** (ˌkɒnəʊ'ʃɛntɪ) *pl n, sing* **cognoscente** *or* **conoscente** (-tiː) (*sometimes sing*) people with informed appreciation of a particular field, esp in the fine arts; connoisseurs [C18 from obs. It., from L *cognōscere* to learn]

cogwheel ('kɒgˌwiːl) *n* another name for **gearwheel**

cohab ('kəʊˌhæb) *n* a sexual partner with whom one lives but to whom one is not married [C20 a shortened form of *cohabitee*; see COHABIT]

cohabit (kəʊ'hæbɪt) *vb* (*intr*) to live together as husband and wife, esp without being married [C16 from L *co-* together + *habitāre* to live] > **ˌcohabi'tee, co'habitant,** *or* **co'habiter** *n*

cohabitation (kəʊˌhæbɪ'teɪʃən) *n* **1** the state or condition of living together as husband and wife without being married **2** (of political parties) the state or condition of cooperating for specific purposes without forming a coalition

coheir (kəʊ'ɛə) *n* a person who inherits jointly with others > **co'heiress** *fem n*

Cohen *n* **Leonard** born 1934, Canadian singer, songwriter, and poet; recordings include *Songs of Leonard Cohen* (1968), *Songs of Love and Hate* (1971), *I'm Your Man* (1988), and *Ten New Songs* (2001)

cohere (kəʊ'hɪə) *vb* **coheres, cohering, cohered** (*intr*) **1** to hold or stick firmly together **2** to be connected logically; be consistent **3** *physics* to be held together by the action of molecular forces [C16 from L *co-* together + *haerēre* to cling]

coherence (kəʊ'hɪərəns) *or* **coherency** *n* **1** logical or natural connection or consistency **2** another word for **cohesion** (sense 1)

coherent (kəʊ'hɪərənt) *adj* **1** capable of intelligible speech **2** logical; consistent and orderly **3** cohering or sticking together **4** *physics* (of two or more waves) having the same phase or a fixed phase difference: *coherent light* > **co'herently** *adv*

cohesion (kəʊ'hiːʒən) *n* **1** the act or state of cohering; tendency to unite **2** *physics* the force that holds together the atoms or molecules in a solid or liquid, as distinguished from adhesion **3** *bot* the fusion in some plants of flower parts, such as petals, that are usually separate [C17 from L *cohaesus*, p.p. of *cohaerēre* to COHERE] > **co'hesive** *adj*

Cc

coho ('kəʊhəʊ) *n, pl* **coho** *or* **cohos** a Pacific salmon. Also called: **silver salmon** [from ?]

cohort ('kəʊhɔːt) *n* **1** one of the ten units of an ancient Roman Legion **2** any band of warriors or associates: *the cohorts of Satan* **3** *chiefly US* an associate or follower [C15 from L *cohors* yard, company of soldiers]

COI (in Britain) *abbrev for* Central Office of Information

coif (kɔɪf) *n* **1** a close-fitting cap worn under a veil in the Middle Ages **2** a leather cap worn under a chain-mail hood **3** (kwɑːf) a less common word for **coiffure** (sense 1) ▷ *vb* **coifs, coiffing, coiffed** (*tr*) **4** to cover with or as if with a coif **5** (kwɑːf) to arrange (the hair) [C14 from OF *coiffe*, from LL *cofea* helmet, cap, from ?]

coiffeur (kwɑː'fɜː) *n* a hairdresser > **coiffeuse** (kwɑː'fɜːz) *fem n*

coiffure (kwɑː'fjʊə) *n* **1** a hairstyle **2** an obsolete word for **headdress** ▷ *vb* **coiffures, coiffuring, coiffured 3** (*tr*) to dress or arrange (the hair)

coign of vantage (kɔɪn) *n* an advantageous position for observation or action

coil[1] (kɔɪl) *vb* **1** to wind or gather (ropes, hair, etc) into loops or (of ropes, hair, etc) to be formed in such loops **2** (*intr*) to move in a winding course ▷ *n* **3** something wound in a connected series of loops **4** a single loop of such a series **5** an arrangement of pipes in a spiral or loop, as in a condenser **6** an electrical conductor wound into the form of a spiral, to provide inductance or a magnetic field **7** an intrauterine contraceptive device in the shape of a coil **8** the transformer in a petrol engine that supplies the high voltage to the sparking plugs [C16 from OF *coillir* to collect together; see CULL]

coil[2] (kɔɪl) *n* the troubles of the world (in Shakespeare's phrase **this mortal coil**) [C16 from ?]

Coimbra (*Portuguese* 'kuimbrə) *n* a city in central Portugal: capital of Portugal from 1190 to 1260; seat of the country's oldest university. Pop: 103 000 (2001)

coin (kɔɪn) *n* **1** a metal disc or piece used as money **2** metal currency, as opposed to paper currency, etc **3** *archit* a variant spelling of **quoin** **4** **pay (a person) back in (his** *or* **her) own coin** to treat (a person) in the way that he or she has treated others ▷ *vb (tr)* **5** to make or stamp (coins) **6** to make into a coin **7** to fabricate or invent (words, etc) **8** *inf* to make (money) rapidly (esp in **coin it in**) [C14 from OF: stamping die, from L *cuneus* wedge]

coinage ('kɔɪnɪdʒ) *n* **1** coins collectively **2** the act of striking coins **3** the currency of a country **4** the act of inventing something, esp a word or phrase **5** a newly invented word, phrase, usage, etc

coincide (ˌkəʊɪn'saɪd) *vb* **coincides, coinciding, coincided** *(intr)* **1** to occur or exist simultaneously **2** to be identical in nature, character, etc **3** to agree [C18 from Med. L, from L *co-* together + *incidere* to occur, befall, from *cadere* to fall]

coincidence (kəʊ'ɪnsɪdəns) *n* **1** a chance occurrence of events remarkable either for being simultaneous or for apparently being connected **2** the fact, condition, or state of coinciding **3** *(modifier) electronics* of or relating to a circuit that produces an output pulse only when both its input terminals receive pulses within a specified interval: *coincidence gate*

coincident (kəʊ'ɪnsɪdənt) *adj* **1** having the same position in space or time **2** (usually *postpositive* and foll by *with*) in exact agreement

coincidental (kəʊˌɪnsɪ'dɛntᵊl) *adj* of or happening by a coincidence; fortuitous > **coˌinci'dentally** *adv*

coin-op ('kɔɪnˌɒp) *n* a launderette or other installation in which the machines are operated by the insertion of coins > **'coin-ˌoperˌated** *adj*

Cointreau ('kwɑːntrəʊ) *n trademark* a colourless liqueur with orange flavouring

coir ('kɔɪə) *n* the fibre from the husk of the coconut, used in making rope and matting [C16 from Malayalam *kāyar* rope, from *kāyaru* to be twisted]

Coire (kwar) *n* the French name for **Chur**

coitus ('kəʊɪtəs) *or* **coition** (kəʊ'ɪʃən) *n* a technical term for **sexual intercourse** [C18 from L, from *coīre* to meet, from *īre* to go] > **'coital** *adj*

coke¹ (kəʊk) *n* **1** a solid-fuel product produced by distillation of coal to drive off its volatile constituents: used as a fuel **2** the layer formed in the cylinders of a car engine by incomplete combustion of the fuel ▷ *vb* **cokes, coking, coked** **3** to become or convert into coke [C17 prob. var. of C14 N English dialect *colk* core, from ?]

coke² (kəʊk) *n sl* short for **cocaine** (kəʊk) *n trademark* short for **Coca-Cola**

Coke¹ (kəʊk) *n trademark* short for **Coca-Cola**

Coke² (kʊk, kəʊk) *n* **1** Sir **Edward** 1552–1634, English jurist, noted for his defence of the common law against encroachment from the Crown: the Petition of Right (1628) was largely his work **2** (kʊk) **Thomas William,** 1st Earl of Leicester, known as *Coke of Holkham*. 1752–1842, English agriculturist: pioneered agricultural improvement and considerably improved productivity at his Holkham estate in Norfolk

coked-up ('kəʊkdʌp) *adj sl* showing the effects of having taken cocaine

col (kɒl) *n* **1** Also called: **saddle** the lowest point of a ridge connecting two mountain peaks **2** *meteorol* a low-pressure region between two anticyclones [C19 from F: neck, col, from L *collum* neck]

Col. *abbrev for:* **1** Colombia(n) **2** Colonel **3** *Bible* Colossians

col- *prefix* a variant of **com-** before *l: collateral*

cola *or* **kola** ('kəʊlə) *n* **1** either of two trees widely cultivated in tropical regions for their seeds (see **cola nut**) **2** a sweet carbonated drink flavoured with cola nuts [C18 from *kola*, prob. var. of W African *kolo* nut]

colander ('kɒləndə, 'kʌl-) *or* **cullender** *n* a pan with a perforated bottom for straining or rinsing foods [C14 *colyndore*, prob. from OProvençal *colador*, from LL, from L *cōlum* sieve]

cola nut *n* any of the seeds of the cola tree, which contain caffeine and theobromine and are used medicinally and in soft drinks

Colbert (*French* kɔlbɛr) *n* **1** **Claudette**, real name *Claudette Lily Chauchoin*. 1905–96, French-born Hollywood actress, noted for her sophisticated comedy roles; her films include *It Happened One Night* (1934) and *The Palm Beach Story* (1942) **2** **Jean Baptiste** (ʒɑ̃ batist) 1619–83, French statesman; chief minister to Louis XIV: reformed the taille and pursued a mercantilist policy, creating a powerful navy and merchant fleet and building roads and canals

Colby ('kɒlbɪ) *n* a type of mild-tasting hard cheese from *Colby*, a town in Wisconsin

Colchester ('kəʊltʃɪstə) *n* a town in E England, in NE Essex; university (1964). Pop: 96 063 (1991). Latin name: **Camulodunum** (ˌkæmjʊləʊ'djuːnəm, ˌkæmʊləʊ'duːnəm)

colchicine ('kɒltʃɪˌsiːn, -sɪn, 'kɒlkɪ-) *n* a pale yellow crystalline alkaloid extracted from seeds or corms of the autumn crocus and used in the treatment of gout [C19 from COLCHICUM + -INE²]

colchicum ('kɒltʃɪkəm, 'kɒlkɪ-) *n* **1** any Eurasian plant of the lily family, such as the autumn crocus **2** the dried seeds or corms of the autumn crocus [C16 from L, from Gk, from *kolkhikos* of COLCHIS]

Colchis ('kɒlkɪs) *n* an ancient country on the Black Sea south of the Caucasus; the land of Medea and the Golden Fleece in Greek mythology

cold (kəʊld) *adj* **1** having relatively little warmth; of a rather low temperature: *cold weather; cold hands* **2** without proper warmth: *this meal is cold* **3** lacking in affection or enthusiasm: *a cold manner* **4** not affected by emotion: *cold logic* **5** dead **6** sexually unresponsive or frigid **7** lacking in freshness: *a cold scent; cold news* **8** chilling to the spirit; depressing **9** (of a colour) having violet, blue, or green predominating; giving no sensation of warmth **10** *sl* unconscious **11** *inf* (of a seeker) far from the object of a search **12** denoting the contacting of potential customers, voters, etc, without previously approaching them in order to establish their interest: *cold mailing* **13** **cold comfort** little or no comfort **14** **leave (someone) cold** *inf* to fail to excite: *the performance left me cold* **15** **throw cold water on** *inf* to be unenthusiastic about or discourage ▷ *n* **16** the absence of heat regarded as a positive force: *the cold took away our breath* **17** the sensation caused by loss or lack of heat **18** **(out) in the cold** *inf* neglected; ignored **19** an acute viral infection of the upper respiratory passages characterized by discharge of watery mucus from the nose, sneezing, etc **20** **catch a cold** *inf* to make a financial loss ▷ *adv* **21** *inf* without preparation: *he played his part cold* [OE *ceald*] > **'coldish** *adj* > **'coldly** *adv* > **'coldness** *n*

cold-blooded *adj* **1** having or showing a lack of feeling or pity **2** *inf* particularly sensitive to cold **3** (of all animals except birds and mammals) having a body temperature that varies with that of the surroundings. Technical name: **poikilothermic** > **ˌcold-'bloodedly** *adv* > **ˌcold-'bloodedness** *n*

cold cathode *n electronics* a cathode from which electrons are emitted at an ambient temperature

cold chisel *n* a toughened steel chisel

cold cream *n* an emulsion of water and fat used for softening and cleansing the skin

cold cuts *pl n* cooked meats sliced and served cold

cold feet *n inf* loss or lack of confidence

cold frame *n* an unheated wooden frame with a glass top, used to protect young plants

cold front *n meteorol* the boundary line between a warm air mass and the cold air pushing it from beneath and behind as it moves

cold-hearted *adj* lacking in feeling or warmth; unkind > ˌ**cold-'heartedly** *adv* > ˌ**cold-'heartedness** *n*
Colditz ('kəʊldɪts) *n* a town in E Germany, on the River Mulde: during World War II its castle was used as a top-security camp for Allied prisoners of war; many daring escape attempts, some successful, were made
cold-rolled *adj* (of metal sheets, etc) having been rolled without heating, producing a smooth surface finish
cold shoulder *inf* ▷ *n* **1** (often preceded by *the*) a show of indifference; a slight ▷ *vb* **cold-shoulder** (*tr*) **2** to treat with indifference
cold sore *n* a cluster of blisters at the margin of the lips: a form of herpes simplex
cold start *n computing* the reloading of a program or operating system
cold storage *n* **1** the storage of things in an artificially cooled place for preservation **2** *inf* a state of temporary suspension: *to put an idea into cold storage*
Coldstream ('kəʊldˌstriːm) *n* a town in SE Scotland, in Scottish Borders on the English border: the Coldstream Guards were formed here (1660). Pop: 1746 (1991)
cold sweat *n inf* a bodily reaction to fear or nervousness, characterized by chill and moist skin
cold turkey *n sl* **1** a method of curing drug addiction by abrupt withdrawal of all doses **2** the withdrawal symptoms, esp nausea and shivering, brought on by this method
cold war *n* a state of political hostility and military tension between two countries or power blocs, involving propaganda, threats, etc, esp that between the American and Soviet blocs after World War II (the **Cold War**)
▷ www.coldwar.org
▷ www.fas.harvard.edu/hpcws
cold wave *n* **1** *meteorol* a sudden spell of low temperatures over a wide area **2** *hairdressing* a permanent wave made by chemical agents applied at normal temperatures
cole (kəʊl) *n* any of various plants such as the cabbage and rape. Also called: **colewort** [OE *cāl*, from L *caulis* cabbage]
Cole (kəʊl) *n* **Nat 'King'**, real name *Nathaniel Adams Cole*. 1917–65, US popular singer and jazz pianist
Coleman ('kəʊlmən) *n* **Ornette** (ɔː'nɛt) born 1930, US avant-garde jazz alto saxophonist and multi-instrumentalist
coleopter (ˌkɒlɪ'ɒptə) *n aeronautics* an aircraft that has an annular wing with the fuselage and engine on the centre line
coleopteran (ˌkɒlɪ'ɒptərən) *n also* **coleopteron** **1** any of the order of insects in which the forewings are modified to form shell-like protective elytra. It includes the beetles and weevils ▷ *adj* **2** *also* **coleopterous** of, relating to, or belonging to this order [c18 from NL, from Gk, from *koleon* sheath + *pteron* wing]
Coleraine ('kəʊl'reɪn) *n* **1** a town in N Northern Ireland, in Coleraine district, Co. Antrim, on the River Bann; light industries; university (1965). Pop: 20 721 (1991) **2** a district in N Northern Ireland, in Co. Antrim and Co. Londonderry. Pop: 56 315 (2001). Area: 485 sq km (187 sq miles)
Coleridge ('kəʊlərɪdʒ) *n* **Samuel Taylor** 1772–1834, English Romantic poet and critic, noted for poems such as *The Rime of the Ancient Mariner* (1798), *Kubla Khan* (1816), and *Christabel* (1816), and for his critical work *Biographia Literaria* (1817)
Coleridge-Taylor (ˌkəʊlərɪdʒ'teɪlə) *n* **Samuel** 1875–1912, British composer, best known for his trilogy of oratorios *Song of Hiawatha* (1898–1900)
coleslaw ('kəʊlˌslɔː) *n* a salad of shredded cabbage, mayonnaise, carrots, onions, etc [c19 from Du. *koolsla*, from *koolsalade*, lit.: cabbage salad]
colestipol (kə'lɛstɪˌpɒl) *n* a drug that reduces the concentration of cholesterol in the blood: used to prevent atherosclerosis
Colet ('kɒlɪt) *n* **John** ?1467–1519, English humanist and theologian; founder of St. Paul's School, London (1509)
coletit ('kəʊltɪt) *n* another name for **coal tit**
Colette (kɒ'lɛt) *n* full name *Sidonie Gabrielle Claudine Colette*. 1873–1954, French novelist; her works include *Chéri* (1920), *Gigi* (1944), and the series of *Claudine* books
coleus ('kəʊlɪəs) *n, pl* **coleuses** any plant of the Old World genus *Coleus*: cultivated for their variegated leaves [c19 from NL, from Gk, var. of *koleon* sheath]
coley ('kəʊlɪ, 'kɒlɪ) *n Brit* any of various edible fishes, esp the coalfish
colic ('kɒlɪk) *n* a condition characterized by acute spasmodic abdominal pain, esp that caused by inflammation, distention, etc, of the gastrointestinal tract [c15 from OF, from LL, from Gk *kōlon*, var. of *kolon* COLON[2]] > '**colicky** *adj*
coliform bacteria ('kɒlɪfɔːm) *pl n* a large group of bacteria, inhabiting the intestinal tract of humans and animals, that may cause disease and whose presence in water is an indicator of faecal pollution
Coligny *or* **Coligni** (*French* kɔliɲi) *n* **Gaspard de** (gaspar də), Seigneur de Châtillon. 1519–72, French Huguenot leader
Colima (*Spanish* ko'lima) *n* **1** a state of SW Mexico, on the Pacific coast: mainly a coastal plain, rising to the foothills of the Sierra Madre, with important mineral resources. Capital: Colima. Pop: 540 679 (2000). Area: 5455 sq km (2106 sq miles) **2** a city in SW Mexico, capital of Colima state, on the Colima River. Pop: 106 967 (1990) **3** **Nevado de** a volcano in SW Mexico, in Jalisco state. Height: 4339 m (14 235 ft)
coliseum (ˌkɒlɪ'sɪəm) *or* **colosseum** (ˌkɒlə'sɪəm) *n* a large building, such as a stadium, used for entertainments, sports, etc [c18 from Med. L, var. of COLOSSEUM]
colitis (kɒ'laɪtɪs) *n* inflammation of the colon
collaborate (kə'læbəˌreɪt) *vb* **collaborates, collaborating, collaborated** (*intr*) **1** (often foll by *on*, *with*, etc) to work with another or others on a joint project **2** to cooperate as a traitor, esp with an enemy occupying one's own country [c19 from LL, from L *com-* together + *labōrāre* to work] > **colˌlabo'ration** *n* > **col'laborative** *adj* > **col'laboˌrator** *n*
collage (kə'lɑːʒ, kɒ-) *n* **1** an art form in which compositions are made out of pieces of paper, cloth, photographs, etc, pasted on a dry ground **2** a composition made in this way **3** any work, such as a piece of music, created by combining unrelated styles [c20 F, from *colle* glue, from Gk *kolla*] > **col'lagist** *n*
collagen ('kɒlədʒən) *n* a fibrous protein of connective tissue and bones that yields gelatine on boiling [c19 from Gk *kolla* glue + -GEN]
collapsar (kɒ'læpsɑː) *n astron* another name for **black hole**
collapse (kə'læps) *vb* **collapses, collapsing, collapsed** **1** (*intr*) to fall down or cave in suddenly: *the whole building collapsed* **2** (*intr*) to fail completely **3** (*intr*) to break down or fall down from lack of strength **4** to fold (furniture, etc) compactly or (of furniture, etc) to be designed to fold compactly ▷ *n* **5** the act or instance of suddenly falling down, caving in, or crumbling **6** a sudden failure or breakdown [c18 from L, from *collābī* to fall in ruins, from *lābī* to fall] > **col'lapsible** *or* **col'lapsable** *adj* > **colˌlapsi'bility** *n*
collar ('kɒlə) *n* **1** the part of a garment around the neck and shoulders, often detachable or folded over **2** any band, necklace, garland, etc, encircling the neck **3** a band or chain of leather, rope, or metal placed around an animal's neck **4** *biol* a marking resembling a collar, such as that found around the necks of some birds **5** a section of a shaft or rod having a locally increased

Cc

diameter to provide a bearing seat or a locating ring **6** a cut of meat, esp bacon, taken from around the neck of an animal ▷ *vb* (*tr*) **7** to put a collar on; furnish with a collar **8** to seize by the collar **9** *inf* to seize; arrest; detain [C13 from L *collāre* neckband, from *collum* neck]

collarbone ('kɒləˌbəʊn) *n* the nontechnical name for **clavicle**

collard ('kɒləd) *n* a variety of the cabbage, having a crown of edible leaves. See also **kale** [C18 var. of *colewort*, from COLE + WORT]

collate (kɒ'leɪt, kə-) *vb* **collates, collating, collated** (*tr*) **1** to examine and compare (texts, statements, etc) in order to note points of agreement and disagreement **2** to check the number and order of (the pages of a book) **3** *bookbinding* **3a** to check the sequence of (the sections of a book) after gathering **3b** a nontechnical word for **gather** (sense 8) **4** (often foll by *to*) *Christianity* to appoint (an incumbent) to a benefice [C16 from L, from *com-* together + *lātus*, p.p. of *ferre* to bring] > **col'lator** *n*

collateral (kɒ'lætərəl, kə-) *n* **1a** security pledged for the repayment of a loan **1b** (*as modifier*): *a collateral loan* **2** a person, animal, or plant descended from the same ancestor as another but through a different line ▷ *adj* **3** situated or running side by side **4** descended from a common ancestor but through different lines **5** serving to support or corroborate [C14 from Med. L, from L *com-* together + *laterālis* of the side, from *latus* side] > **col'laterally** *adv*

collateral damage *n mil* unintentional damage to civil property and civilian casualties, caused by military operations

collation (kɒ'leɪʃən, kə-) *n* **1** the act or process of collating **2** a description of the technical features of a book **3** *RC Church* a light meal permitted on fast days **4** any light informal meal

colleague ('kɒliːg) *n* a fellow worker or member of a staff, department, profession, etc [C16 from F, from L *collēga*, from *com-* together + *lēgāre* to choose]

collect[1] (kə'lɛkt) *vb* **1** to gather together or be gathered together **2** to accumulate (stamps, books, etc) as a hobby or for study **3** (*tr*) to call for or receive payment of (taxes, dues, etc) **4** (*tr*) to regain control of (oneself, one's emotions, etc) as after a shock or surprise: *he collected his wits* **5** (*tr*) to fetch: *collect your own post* **6** (*intr*; sometimes foll by *on*) *sl* to receive large sums of money **7** (*tr*) *Austral & NZ inf* to collide with; be hit by ▷ *adv, adj* **8** *US* (of telephone calls, etc) on a reverse-charge basis [C16 from L, from *com-* together + *legere* to gather]

collect[2] ('kɒlɛkt) *n Christianity* a short Church prayer in Communion and other services [C13 from Med. L *collecta* (from *ōrātiō ad collēctam* prayer at the assembly), from L *colligere* to COLLECT[1]]

collectable *or* **collectible** (kə'lɛktəbᵊl) *adj* **1** (of antiques) of interest to a collector ▷ *n* **2** (*often pl*) any object regarded as being of interest to a collector

collected (kə'lɛktɪd) *adj* **1** in full control of one's faculties; composed **2** assembled in totality or brought together into one volume or a set of volumes: *the collected works of Dickens* > **col'lectedly** *adv* > **col'lectedness** *n*

collection (kə'lɛkʃən) *n* **1** the act or process of collecting **2** a number of things collected or assembled together **3** something gathered into a mass or pile; accumulation: *a collection of rubbish* **4** a sum of money collected or solicited, as in church **5** removal, esp regular removal of letters from a postbox **6** (*often pl*) (at Oxford University) a college examination or an oral report by a tutor

collective (kə'lɛktɪv) *adj* **1** formed or assembled by collection **2** forming a whole or aggregate **3** of, done by, or characteristic of individuals acting in cooperation ▷ *n* **4a** a cooperative enterprise or unit, such as a collective farm **4b** the members of such a cooperative **5** short for **collective noun** > **col'lectively** *adv* > **col'lectiveness** *n* > **ˌcollec'tivity** *n*

collective bargaining *n* negotiation between a trade union and an employer or an employers' organization on the incomes and working conditions of the employees

collective noun *n* a noun that is singular in form but that refers to a group of people or things.

> USAGE Collective nouns are often used with singular verbs: *the family is on holiday*; *General Motors is mounting a big sales campaign*. In British usage, however, plural verbs are often employed in this context, especially where reference is being made to a collection of individual objects or people rather than to the group as a unit: *the family are all on holiday*. Care should be taken that the same collective noun is not treated as both singular and plural in the same sentence: *the family is well and sends its best wishes* or *the family are all well and send their best wishes*, but not *the family is well and send their best wishes*

collective ownership *n* ownership by a group for the benefit of members of that group

collective unconscious *n* (in Jungian psychological theory) a part of the unconscious mind incorporating patterns of memories, instincts, and experiences common to all mankind

collectivism (kə'lɛktɪˌvɪzəm) *n* the principle of ownership of the means of production by the state or the people > **col'lectivist** *n* > **colˌlectiv'istic** *adj*

collectivize *or* **collectivise** (kə'lɛktɪˌvaɪz) *vb* **collectivizes, collectivizing, collectivized** *or* **collectivises, collectivising, collectivised** (*tr*) to organize according to the principles of collectivism > **colˌlectivi'zation** *or* **colˌlectivi'sation** *n*

collector (kə'lɛktə) *n* **1** a person or thing that collects **2** a person employed to collect debts, rents, etc **3** a person who collects objects as a hobby **4** (in India, formerly) the head of a district administration **5** *electronics* the region in a transistor into which charge carriers flow from the base

colleen ('kɒliːn, kɒ'liːn) *n* an Irish word for **girl** [C19 from Irish Gaelic *cailīn*]

college ('kɒlɪdʒ) *n* **1** an institution of higher education; part of a university **2** a school or an institution providing specialized courses: *a college of music* **3** the buildings in which a college is housed **4** the staff and students of a college **5** an organized body of persons with specific rights and duties: *an electoral college* **6** a body organized within a particular profession, concerned with regulating standards **7** *Brit* a name given to some secondary schools [C14 from L, from *collēga*; see COLLEAGUE]

College of Cardinals *n RC Church* the collective body of cardinals having the function of electing and advising the pope

college of education *n Brit* a professional training college for teachers

collegian (kə'liːdʒɪən) *n* a member of a college

collegiate (kə'liːdʒɪɪt) *adj* **1** Also: **col'legial** of or relating to a college or college students **2** (of a university) composed of various colleges of equal standing

collegiate church *n* **1** *RC Church, Church of England* a church that has an endowed chapter of canons and prebendaries attached to it but that is not a cathedral **2** *US Protestantism* one of a group of churches presided over by a body of pastors **3** *Scot Protestantism* a church served by two or more ministers

collegiate institute *n Canad* (in certain provinces) a large secondary school meeting set requirements in terms of courses, facilities, and specialist staff

col legno ('kɒl 'lɛgnəʊ, 'leɪnjəʊ) *adv music* to be played (on a stringed instrument) with the back of the bow [It.: with the wood]

Colles' fracture ('kɒlɪs) *n* a fracture of the radius just above the wrist with backward and outward displacement of the hand [c19 after Abraham *Colles* (d. 1843), Irish surgeon]

collet ('kɒlɪt) *n* **1** (in a jewellery setting) a band or coronet-shaped claw that holds an individual stone **2** *mechanical engineering* an externally tapered sleeve made in two or more segments and used to grip a shaft passed through its centre **3** *horology* a small metal collar that supports the inner end of the hairspring [c16 from OF: a little collar, from *col*, from L *collum* neck]

collide (kə'laɪd) *vb* **collides, colliding, collided** (*intr*) **1** to crash together with a violent impact **2** to conflict; clash; disagree [c17 from L, from *com-* together + *laedere* to strike]

collider (kə'laɪdə) *n physics* a particle accelerator in which beams of particles are made to collide

collie ('kɒlɪ) *n* any of several silky-coated breeds of dog developed for herding sheep and cattle [c17 Scot., prob. from earlier *colie* black from *cole* coal]

collier ('kɒlɪə) *n chiefly Brit* **1** a coal miner **2a** a ship designed to transport coal **2b** a member of its crew [c14 from COAL + -IER]

colliery ('kɒljərɪ) *n, pl* **collieries** *chiefly Brit* a coal mine

collimate ('kɒlɪˌmeɪt) *vb* **collimates, collimating, collimated** (*tr*) **1** to adjust the line of sight of (an optical instrument) **2** to use a collimator on (a beam of radiation) **3** to make parallel or bring into line [c17 from NL *collimāre*, erroneously for L *collīneāre* to aim, from *com-* (intensive) + *līneāre*, from *līnea* line] > ˌ**colli'mation** *n*

collimator ('kɒlɪˌmeɪtə) *n* **1** a small telescope attached to a larger optical instrument as an aid in fixing its line of sight **2** an optical system of lenses and slits producing a nondivergent beam of light **3** any device for limiting the size and angle of spread of a beam of radiation or particles

collinear (kɒ'lɪnɪə) *adj* lying on the same straight line > **collinearity** (ˌkɒlɪnɪ'ærɪtɪ) *n*

collins ('kɒlɪnz) *n* (*functioning as sing*) an iced drink made with gin, vodka, rum, etc, mixed with fruit juice, soda water, and sugar [c20 prob. from the name *Collins*]

Collins ('kɒlɪnz) *n* **1 Michael** 1890–1922, Irish republican revolutionary: a leader of Sinn Féin; member of the Irish delegation that negotiated the treaty with Great Britain (1921) that established the Irish Free State **2** (**William**) **Wilkie** 1824–89, British author, noted particularly for his suspense novel *The Moonstone* (1868) **3 William** 1721–59, British poet, noted for his odes; regarded as a precursor of romanticism

collision (kə'lɪʒən) *n* **1** a violent impact of moving objects; crash **2** the conflict of opposed ideas, wishes, attitudes, etc [c15 from LL, from L *collīdere* to COLLIDE]

collocate ('kɒləˌkeɪt) *vb* **collocates, collocating, collocated** (*tr*) to group or place together in some system or order [c16 from L, from *com-* together + *locāre* to place] > ˌ**collo'cation** *n*

collocutor ('kɒləˌkjuːtə) *n* a person who talks or engages in conversation with another

collodion (kə'ləʊdɪən) *or* **collodium** (kə'ləʊdɪəm) *n* a syrupy liquid that consists of a solution of pyroxylin in ether and alcohol: used in medicine and in the manufacture of photographic plates, lacquers, etc [c19 from NL, from Gk *kollōdēs* glutinous, from *kolla* glue]

collogue (kɒ'ləʊg) *vb* **collogues, colloguing, collogued** (*intr*; usually foll by *with*) to confer confidentially; conspire [c16 ?from obs. *colleague* (vb) to conspire, infl. by L *colloquī* to talk with]

colloid ('kɒlɔɪd) *n* **1** a mixture having particles of one component suspended in a continuous phase of another component. The mixture has properties between those of a solution and a fine suspension **2** *physiol* a gelatinous substance of the thyroid follicles that holds the hormonal secretions of the thyroid gland [c19 from Gk *kolla* glue + -OID] > **col'loidal** *adj*

collop ('kɒləp) *n dialect* **1** a slice of meat **2** a small piece of anything [c14 of Scand. origin]

colloq. *abbrev for* colloquial(ly)

colloquial (kə'ləʊkwɪəl) *adj* **1** of or relating to conversation **2** denoting or characterized by informal or conversational idiom or vocabulary > **col'loquially** *adv* > **col'loquialness** *n*

colloquialism (kə'ləʊkwɪəˌlɪzəm) *n* **1** a word or phrase appropriate to conversation and other informal situations **2** the use of colloquial words and phrases

colloquium (kə'ləʊkwɪəm) *n, pl* **colloquiums** *or* **colloquia** (-kwɪə) **1** a gathering for discussion **2** an academic seminar [c17 from L: COLLOQUY]

colloquy ('kɒləkwɪ) *n, pl* **colloquies** **1** a formal conversation or conference **2** an informal conference on religious or theological matters [c16 from L *colloquium*, from *com-* together + *loquī* to speak] > **'colloquist** *n*

collotype ('kɒləʊˌtaɪp) *n* **1** a method of lithographic printing (usually of high-quality reproductions) from a plate of hardened gelatine **2** a print so made

collude (kə'luːd) *vb* **colludes, colluding, colluded** (*intr*) to conspire together, esp in planning a fraud [c16 from L, from *com-* together + *lūdere* to play] > **col'luder** *n*

collusion (kə'luːʒən) *n* **1** secret agreement for a fraudulent purpose; conspiracy **2** a secret agreement between opponents at law for some improper purpose [c14 from L, from *collūdere* to COLLUDE] > **col'lusive** *adj*

collywobbles ('kɒlɪˌwɒbᵊlz) *pl n* (usually preceded by *the*) *Sl* **1** an upset stomach **2** an intense feeling of nervousness [c19 prob. from NL *cholera morbus*, infl. through folk etymology by COLIC and WOBBLE]

Colmar (*French* kɔlmar) *n* a city in NE France: annexed to Germany 1871–1919 and 1940–45; textile industry. Pop: 63 498 (1990). German name: **Kolmar**

Colo. *abbrev for* Colorado

colobus ('kɒləbəs) *n* any leaf-eating arboreal Old World monkey of W and central Africa, having long silky fur and reduced or absent thumbs [c19 NL, from Gk *kolobos* cut short; referring to its thumb]

cologarithm (kəʊ'lɒgəˌrɪðəm) *n* the logarithm of the reciprocal of a number; the negative value of the logarithm: *the cologarithm of 4 is log ¼*. Abbrev: **colog**

cologne (kə'ləʊn) *n* a perfumed liquid or solid made of fragrant essential oils and alcohol. Also called: **Cologne water, eau de cologne** [c18 *Cologne water* from COLOGNE, where it was first manufactured (1709)]

Cologne (kə'ləʊn) *n* an industrial city and river port in W Germany, in North Rhine-Westphalia on the Rhine: important commercially since ancient times; university (1388). Pop: 963 200 (1999 est). German name: **Köln**

Colomb-Béchar (*French* kɔlɔ̃beʃar) *n* the former name of **Béchar**

Colombes (*French* kɔlɔ̃b) *n* an industrial and residential suburb of NW Paris. Pop: 79 060 (1990)

Colombia (kə'lɒmbɪə) *n* a republic in NW South America: inhabited by Chibchas and other Indians before Spanish colonization in the 16th century; independence won by Bolívar in 1819; became the Republic of Colombia in 1886; violence and unrest have been endemic since the 1970s. It consists chiefly of a hot swampy coastal plain, separated by ranges of the Andes from the pampas and the equatorial forests of the Amazon basin in the east. Language: Spanish. Religion: Roman Catholic majority. Currency: peso. Capital: Bogotá. Pop: 43 071 000 (2001 est). Area: 1 138 908 sq km (439 735 sq miles)

▷ www.gobiernoenlinea.gov.co

▷ www.turismocolombia.com/home-E.htm

Colombian (kə'lɒmbɪən) *adj* **1** of or relating to Colombia

Cc

or its inhabitants ▷ *n* **2** a native or inhabitant of Colombia

Colombo (kəˈlʌmbəʊ) *n* the capital and chief port of Sri Lanka, on the W coast, with one of the largest artificial harbours in the world. Pop: 800 982 (1997 est)
▷ www.atsrilanka.com/cityofcolombo.htm
▷ www.explorelanka.com/places/colombo.htm

colon[1] (ˈkəʊlən) *n, pl* **colons** **1** the punctuation mark :, usually preceding an explanation or an example, a list, or an extended quotation **2** this mark used for certain other purposes, such as when a ratio is given in figures, as in 5:3 [C16 from L, from Gk *kōlon* limb, clause]

colon[2] (ˈkəʊlən) *n, pl* **colons** *or* **cola** (-lə) the part of the large intestine between the caecum and the rectum [C16 from L: large intestine, from Gk *kolon*] > **colonic** (kəˈlɒnɪk) *adj*

colón (kəʊˈləʊn; *Spanish* koˈlon) *n, pl* **colons** *or* **colones** (*Spanish* -ˈlones) **1** the standard monetary unit of Costa Rica, divided into 100 céntimos **2** the former standard monetary unit of El Salvador, divided into 100 centavos; replaced by the U.S. dollar in 2001 [C19 American Sp., from Sp., after Cristóbal *Colón* Christopher Columbus]

Colón (kɒˈlɒn; *Spanish* koˈlɔn) *n* **1** a port in Panama, at the Caribbean entrance to the Panama Canal. Chief Caribbean port. Pop: 137 825 (1992 est). Former name: **Aspinwall** **2** **Archipiélago de** (ˌartʃiˈpjelaɣo ðe) the official name of the **Galápagos Islands**

colonel (ˈkɜːnəl) *n* an officer of land or air forces junior to a brigadier but senior to a lieutenant colonel [C16 via OF, from OIt. *colonnello* column of soldiers, from *colonna* COLUMN] > **ˈcolonelcy** *or* **ˈcolonelship** *n*

colonial (kəˈləʊnɪəl) *adj* **1** of, characteristic of, relating to, possessing, or inhabiting a colony or colonies **2** (*often cap*) characteristic of or relating to the 13 British colonies that became the United States of America (1776) **3** (*often cap*) of or relating to the colonies of the British Empire **4** denoting or having the style of Neoclassical architecture used in the British colonies in America in the 17th and 18th centuries **5** of or relating to the period of Australian history before federation (1901) **6** (of animals and plants) having become established in a community in a new environment ▷ *n* **7** a native of a colony > **coˈlonially** *adv*

colonial goose *n* NZ an old-fashioned name for stuffed roast mutton

colonialism (kəˈləʊnɪəˌlɪzəm) *n* the policy and practice of a power in extending control over weaker peoples or areas. Also called: **imperialism** > **coˈlonialist** *n, adj*

Colonies (ˈkɒlənɪz) *pl n* **the** **1** *Brit* the subject territories formerly in the British Empire **2** *US history* the 13 states forming the original United States of America when they declared their independence (1776)

colonist (ˈkɒlənɪst) *n* **1** a person who settles or colonizes an area **2** an inhabitant of a colony

colonize *or* **colonise** (ˈkɒləˌnaɪz) *vb* **colonizes, colonizing, colonized** *or* **colonises, colonising, colonised** **1** to send colonists to or establish a colony in (an area) **2** to settle in (an area) as colonists **3** (*tr*) to transform (a community, etc) into a colony **4** (of plants and animals) to become established in (a new environment) > **ˌcoloniˈzation** *or* **ˌcoloniˈsation** *n* > **ˈcoloˌnizer** *or* **ˈcoloˌniser** *n*

colonnade (ˌkɒləˈneɪd) *n* **1** a set of evenly spaced columns **2** a row of regularly spaced trees [C18 from F, from *colonne* COLUMN; on the model of It. *colonnato*] > **ˌcolonˈnaded** *adj*

Colonsay (ˈkɒlənseɪ, -zeɪ) *n* an island in W Scotland, in the Inner Hebrides. Area: about 41 sq km (16 sq miles)

colony (ˈkɒlənɪ) *n, pl* **colonies** **1** a body of people who settle in a country distant from their homeland but maintain ties with it **2** the community formed by such settlers **3** a subject territory occupied by a settlement from the ruling state **4a** a community of people who form a national, racial, or cultural minority concentrated in a particular place: *an artists' colony* **4b** the area itself **5** *zool* a group of the same type of animal or plant living or growing together esp in large numbers **6** *bacteriol* a group of bacteria, fungi, etc, derived from one or a few spores, esp when grown on a culture medium [C16 from L, from *colere* to cultivate, inhabit]

colony-stimulating factor *n immunol* any of a number of substances, secreted by the bone marrow, that stimulate the formation of blood cells. Synthetic forms are being tested for their ability to reduce the toxic effects of chemotherapy. Abbrev: **CSF**

colophon (ˈkɒləˌfɒn, -fən) *n* **1** a publisher's emblem on a book **2** (formerly) an inscription at the end of a book showing the title, printer, date, etc [C17 via LL, from Gk *kolophōn* a finishing stroke]

colophony (kɒˈlɒfənɪ) *n* another name for **rosin** (sense 1) [C14 from L: resin from Colophon, town in Lydia]

color (ˈkʌlə) *n, vb* the US spelling of **colour**

Colorado (ˌkɒləˈrɑːdəʊ) *n* **1** a state of the central US: consists of the Great Plains in the east and the Rockies in the west; drained chiefly by the Colorado, Arkansas, South Platte, and Rio Grande Rivers. Capital: Denver. Pop: 4 301 261 (2000). Area: 269 998 sq km (104 247 sq miles). Abbreviations: **Colo** or (with zip code) **CO** **2** a river in SW North America, rising in the Rocky Mountains and flowing southwest to the Gulf of California: famous for the 1600 km (1000 miles) of canyons along its course. Length: about 2320 km (1440 miles) **3** a river in central Texas, flowing southeast to the Gulf of Mexico. Length: about 1450 km (900 miles) **4** a river in central Argentina, flowing southeast to the Atlantic. Length: about 850 km (530 miles) [Spanish, literally: red, from Latin *colōrātus* coloured, tinted red; see COLOUR]

Colorado beetle *n* a black-and-yellow beetle that is a serious pest of potatoes, feeding on the leaves

Colorado Desert *n* an arid region of SE California and NW Mexico, West of the Colorado River. Area: over 5000 sq km (2000 sq miles)

Colorado Springs *n* a city and resort in central Colorado. Pop: 360 890 (2000)

colorant (ˈkʌlərənt) *n* any substance that imparts colour, such as a pigment, dye, or ink

coloration *or* **colouration** (ˌkʌləˈreɪʃən) *n* **1** arrangement of colour; colouring **2** the colouring or markings of insects, birds, etc

coloratura (ˌkɒlərəˈtʊərə) *n music* **1** (in 18th- and 19th-century arias) a florid virtuoso passage **2** Also called: **coloratura soprano** a soprano who specializes in such music [C19 from obs. It., lit.: colouring.]

colorific (ˌkʌləˈrɪfɪk) *adj* producing, imparting, or relating to colour

colorimeter (ˌkʌləˈrɪmɪtə) *n* apparatus for measuring the quality of a colour by comparison with standard colours or combinations of colours > **colorimetric** (ˌkʌlərɪˈmɛtrɪk) *adj* > **ˌcolorˈimetry** *n*

colossal (kəˈlɒsəl) *adj* **1** of immense size; huge; gigantic **2** (in figure sculpture) approximately twice life-size **3** *archit* of the order of columns that extend more than one storey in a façade > **coˈlossally** *adv*

Colosseum (ˌkɒləˈsɪəm) *n* an amphitheatre in Rome built about 75–80 AD

colossus (kəˈlɒsəs) *n, pl* **colossi** (-saɪ) *or* **colossuses** something very large, esp a statue [C14 from L, from Gk *kolossos*]

Colossus of Rhodes *n* a giant bronze statue of Apollo built on Rhodes in about 292–280 BC; destroyed by an earthquake in 225 BC; one of the Seven Wonders of the World

colostomy (kəˈlɒstəmɪ) *n, pl* **colostomies** the surgical formation of an opening from the colon onto the surface of the body, which functions as an anus

colostrum (kəˈlɒstrəm) *n* the thin milky secretion from the nipples that precedes and follows true lactation [C16 from L, from ?]

colotomy (kəˈlɒtəmɪ) *n, pl* **colotomies** a colonic incision [C19 COLON² + -TOMY]

colour *or US* **color** (ˈkʌlə) *n* **1a** an attribute of things that results from the light they reflect or emit in so far as this causes a visual sensation that depends on its wavelengths **1b** the aspect of visual perception by which an observer recognizes this attribute **1c** the quality of the light producing this visual perception **2** Also called: **chromatic colour 2a** a colour, such as red or green, that possesses hue, as opposed to achromatic colours such as white or black **2b** (*as modifier*): *colour television* **3** a substance, such as a dye or paint, that imparts colour **4a** the skin complexion of a person, esp as determined by race **4b** (*as modifier*): *colour prejudice* **5** the use of all the hues in painting as distinct from composition, form, and light and shade **6** the quantity and quality of ink used in a printing process **7** the distinctive tone of a musical sound **8** vividness or authenticity: *period colour* **9** semblance or pretext: *under colour of* **10** *physics* one of three characteristics of quarks, designated red, blue, or green, but having only a remote formal relationship with the physical sensation ▷ *vb* **11** (*tr*) to apply colour to (something) **12** (*tr*) to give a convincing appearance to: *to colour an alibi* **13** (*tr*) to influence or distort: *anger coloured her judgment* **14** (*intr*; often foll by *up*) to become red in the face, esp when embarrassed or annoyed ▷ See also **colours** [C13 from OF *colour* from L *color* tint, hue]

colourable (ˈkʌlərəbᵊl) *adj* **1** capable of being coloured **2** appearing to be true; plausible **3** pretended; feigned

colour bar *n* discrimination against people of a different race, esp as practised by Whites against Blacks

colour-blind *adj* of or relating to any defect in the normal ability to distinguish certain colours > **colour blindness** *n*

colour code *n* a system of easily distinguishable colours, as for the identification of electrical wires or resistors

colour commentator *n* a sports celebrity who works as part of a commentary team

coloured (ˈkʌləd) *adj* **1** possessing colour **2** having a strong element of fiction or fantasy; distorted (esp in **highly coloured**)

Coloured (ˈkʌləd) *n* **1** an individual who is not a White person, esp a Black person **2** Also called: **Cape Coloured** (in South Africa) a person of racially mixed parentage or descent ▷ *adj* **3a** (in South Africa) designating or relating to a person or people of racially mixed descent **3b** designating or relating to a person or people who are not White.

> **USAGE** The use of *Coloured* to refer to people is now generally considered to be offensive

colourfast (ˈkʌləˌfɑːst) *adj* (of a fabric) having a colour that does not run or change when washed or worn > ˈ**colourˌfastness** *n*

colourful (ˈkʌləfʊl) *adj* **1** having intense colour or richly varied colours **2** vivid, rich, or distinctive in character > ˈ**colourfully** *adv*

colour guard *n* a military guard in a parade, ceremony, etc, that carries and escorts the flag

colouring (ˈkʌlərɪŋ) *n* **1** the process or art of applying colour **2** anything used to give colour, such as paint **3** appearance with regard to shade and colour **4** arrangements of colours, as in the markings of birds **5** the colour of a person's complexion **6** a false or misleading appearance

colourist (ˈkʌlərɪst) *n* a person who uses colour, esp an artist

colourize, colourise, *or US* **colorize** (ˈkʌləˌraɪz) *vb* **colourizes, colourizing, colourized** *or* **colourises, colourising, colourised** *or US* **colorizes, colorizing, colorized** (*tr*) to add colour electronically to (an old black-and-white film) > ˌ**colouriˈzation**, ˌ**colouriˈsation** *or US* ˌ**coloriˈzation** *n*

colourless (ˈkʌləlɪs) *adj* **1** without colour **2** lacking in interest: *a colourless individual* **3** grey or pallid in tone or hue **4** without prejudice; neutral > ˈ**colourlessly** *adv*

colours (ˈkʌləz) *pl n* **1a** the flag that indicates nationality **1b** *mil* the ceremony of hoisting or lowering the colours **2** a pair of silk flags borne by a military unit and showing its crest and battle honours **3** true nature or character (esp in **show one's colours**) **4** a distinguishing badge or flag **5** *sport, Brit* a badge or other symbol denoting membership of a team, esp at a school or college **6 nail one's colours to the mast 6a** to commit oneself publicly and irrevocably to some party, course of action, etc **6b** to refuse to admit defeat

colour sergeant *n* a sergeant who carries the regimental, battalion, or national colours

colour supplement *n Brit* an illustrated magazine accompanying a newspaper

colourway (ˈkʌləˌweɪ) *n* one of several different combinations of colours in which a given pattern is printed on fabrics or wallpapers, etc

colposcope (ˈkɒlpəˌskəʊp) *n* an instrument for examining the uterine cervix [C20 from Gk *kolpos* womb + -SCOPE] > **colposcopy** (kɒlˈpɒskəpɪ) *n*

colt (kəʊlt) *n* **1** a male horse or pony under the age of four **2** *sport* **2a** a young and inexperienced player **2b** a member of a junior team [OE *colt* young ass]

colter (ˈkəʊltə) *n* a variant spelling (esp US) of **coulter**

coltish (ˈkəʊltɪʃ) *adj* **1** inexperienced; unruly **2** playful and lively > ˈ**coltishness** *n*

Coltrane (kɒlˈtreɪn) *n* **John (William)** 1926–67, US jazz tenor and soprano saxophonist and composer

coltsfoot (ˈkəʊltsˌfʊt) *n, pl* **coltsfoots** a European plant with yellow daisy-like flowers and heart-shaped leaves: a common weed

colubrine (ˈkɒljʊˌbraɪn) *adj* **1** of or resembling a snake **2** of or belonging to the Colubrinae, a subfamily of harmless snakes [C16 from L *colubrīnus*, from *coluber* snake]

Colum (ˈkɒləm) *n* **Padraic** (ˈpɑːdrɪk) 1881–1972, Irish lyric poet, resident in the US (1914–72)

Columba (kəˈlʌmbə) *n* **Saint** ?521–597 AD, Irish missionary: founded the monastery at Iona (563) from which the Picts were converted to Christianity. Feast day: June 9

Columbia (kəˈlʌmbɪə) *n* **1** a river in NW North America, rising in the Rocky Mountains and flowing through British Columbia, then west to the Pacific. Length: about 1930 km (1200 miles) **2** a city in central South Carolina, on the Congaree River: the state capital. Pop: 116 278 (2000)

Columbian (kəˈlʌmbɪən) *adj* **1** of or relating to the United States **2** relating to Christopher **Columbus** ▷ *n* **3** a size of printer's type, approximately equal to 16 point; two-line Brevier

columbine (ˈkɒləmˌbaɪn) *n* any plant of the genus *Aquilegia*, having flowers with five spurred petals. Also called: **aquilegia** [C13 from Med. L *columbīna herba* dovelike plant]

Columbine (ˈkɒləmˌbaɪn) *n* the sweetheart of Harlequin in English pantomime

Columbus¹ (kəˈlʌmbəs) *n* **1** a city in central Ohio: the state capital. Pop: 711 470 (2000) **2** a city in W Georgia, on the Chattahoochee River. Pop: 185 781 (2000)

Columbus² (kəˈlʌmbəs) *n* **Christopher** Spanish name *Cristóbal Colón*, Italian name *Cristoforo Colombo*. 1451–1506, Italian navigator and explorer in the service of Spain, who discovered the New World (1492)

column (ˈkɒləm) *n* **1** an upright pillar usually having a cylindrical shaft, a base, and a capital **2a** a form or

Cc

structure in the shape of a column: *a column of air* **2b** a monument **3** a line, as of people in a queue **4** *mil* a narrow formation in which individuals or units follow one behind the other **5** *journalism* **5a** any of two or more vertical sections of type on a printed page, esp on a newspaper page **5b** a regular feature in a paper: *the fashion column* **6** a vertical array of numbers [C15 from L *columna*, from *columen* top, peak] > **columnar** (kəˈlʌmnə) *adj* > ˈ**columned** *adj*

column inch *n* a unit of measurement for advertising space, one inch deep and one column wide

columnist (ˈkɒləmnɪst, -əmɪst) *n* a journalist who writes a regular feature in a newspaper

colure (kəˈlʊə, ˈkəʊlʊə) *n* either of two great circles on the celestial sphere, one passing through the poles and the equinoxes, the other through the poles and the solstices [C16 from LL, from Gk *kolourai*, dock-tailed, from *kolos* docked + *oura* tail (because the lower portion is not visible)]

Colwyn Bay (ˈkɒlwɪn) *n* a town and resort in N Wales, in Conwy county borough. Pop: 29 883 (1991)

colza (ˈkɒlzə) *n* another name for **rape**[2] [C18 via F (Walloon) from Du., from *kool* cabbage, COLE + *zaad* SEED]

com *an Internet domain name for* a commercial company

COM (kɒm) *n* direct conversion of computer output to microfiche or film [C20 C(*omputer*) O(*utput on*) M(*icrofilm*)]

Com. *abbrev for:* **1** Commander **2** Committee **3** Commodore

com- *or* **con-** *prefix* together; with; jointly: *commingle* [from L *com-*; rel. to *cum* with. In compound words of L origin, *com-* becomes *col-* and *cor-* before *l* and *r*, *co-* before *gn*, *h*, and most vowels, and *con-* before consonants other than *b*, *p*, and *m*]

coma[1] (ˈkəʊmə) *n, pl* **comas** a state of unconsciousness from which a person cannot be aroused, caused by injury, narcotics, poisons, etc [C17 from medical L, from Gk *kōma* heavy sleep]

coma[2] (ˈkəʊmə) *n, pl* **comae** (-miː) **1** *astron* the luminous cloud surrounding the nucleus in the head of a comet **2** *bot* **2a** a tuft of hairs attached to the seed coat of some seeds **2b** the terminal crown of leaves of palms and moss stems [C17 from L: hair of the head, from Gk *komē*]

comanche (kəˈmæntʃɪ) *n* **1** (*pl* **comanches** *or* **comanche**) a member of a North American Indian people formerly inhabiting the W plains of the US **2** the language of this people

comatose (ˈkəʊməˌtəʊs) *adj* **1** in a state of coma **2** torpid; lethargic

comb (kəʊm) *n* **1** a toothed device for disentangling or arranging hair **2** a tool or machine that cleans and straightens wool, cotton, etc **3** *Austral & NZ* the fixed cutter on a sheep-shearing machine **4** anything resembling a comb in form or function **5** the fleshy serrated outgrowth on the heads of certain birds, esp the domestic fowl **6** a honeycomb ▷ *vb* **7** (*tr*) to use a comb on **8** (when *tr*, often foll by *through*) to search with great care: *the police combed the woods* ▷ See also **comb out** [OE *camb*]

combat *n* (ˈkɒmbæt, -bət, ˈkʌm-) **1** a fight, conflict, or struggle **2a** an action fought between two military forces **2b** (*as modifier*): *a combat jacket* **3 single combat** a duel ▷ *vb* (kəmˈbæt; ˈkɒmbæt, ˈkʌm-) **-bats, -bating, -bated 4** (*tr*) to fight **5** (*intr*; often foll by *with* or *against*) to struggle or strive (against): *to combat against disease* [C16 from F, from OF *combattre*, from Vulgar L *combattere* (unattested), from L *com-* with + *battuere* to beat]

combatant (ˈkɒmbətᵊnt, ˈkʌm-) *n* **1** a person or group engaged in or prepared for a fight ▷ *adj* **2** engaged in or ready for combat

combat boot *n* a heavy army boot

combat fatigue *n* another term for **battle fatigue**

combative (ˈkɒmbətɪv, ˈkʌm-) *adj* eager or ready to fight, argue, etc > ˈ**combativeness** *n*

combat trousers *or* **combats** (ˈkɒmbæts, -bəts, ˈkʌm-) *pl n* loose casual trousers with large pockets on the legs

combe *or* **comb** (kuːm) *n* variant spellings of **coomb**

comber (ˈkəʊmə) *n* **1** a person, tool, or machine that combs wool, flax, etc **2** a long curling wave; roller

combination (ˌkɒmbɪˈneɪʃən) *n* **1** the act of combining or state of being combined **2** a union of separate parts, qualities, etc **3** an alliance of people or parties **4** the set of numbers that opens a combination lock **5** *Brit* a motorcycle with a sidecar attached **6** *maths* an arrangement of the numbers, terms, etc, of a set into specified groups without regard to order in the group **7** the chemical reaction of two or more compounds, usually to form one other compound **8** *chess* a tactical manoeuvre involving a sequence of moves and more than one piece > ˌ**combiˈnational** *adj*

combination lock *n* a type of lock that can only be opened when a set of dials is turned to show a specific sequence of numbers

combinations (ˌkɒmbɪˈneɪʃənz) *pl n Brit* a one-piece undergarment with long sleeves and legs. Often shortened to **combs** or **coms**

combine *vb* (kəmˈbaɪn), **combines, combining, combined 1** to join together **2** to unite or cause to unite to form a chemical compound ▷ *n* (ˈkɒmbaɪn) **3** short for **combine harvester 4** an association of enterprises, esp in order to gain a monopoly of a market **5** an association of related bodies, such as business corporations or sports clubs, for a common purpose [C15 from LL *combīnāre*, from L *com-* together + *bīnī* two by two] > **comˈbinable** *adj* > **comˌbinaˈbility** *n* > **combinative** (ˈkɒmbɪˌneɪtɪv) *or* **combinatory** (ˈkɒmbɪˌneɪtərɪ) *adj*

combine harvester (ˈkɒmbaɪn) *n* a machine that simultaneously cuts, threshes, and cleans a standing crop of grain

combings (ˈkəʊmɪŋz) *pl n* **1** the loose hair removed by combing **2** the unwanted fibres removed in combing cotton, etc

combining form *n* a linguistic element that occurs only as part of a compound word, such as *anthropo-* in *anthropology* and *anthropomorph*

combo (ˈkɒmbəʊ) *n, pl* **combos 1** a small group of jazz musicians **2** *inf* any combination

comb out *vb* (*tr, adv*) **1** to remove (tangles) from (the hair) with a comb **2** to remove for a purpose **3** to examine systematically

combustible (kəmˈbʌstɪbᵊl) *adj* **1** capable of igniting and burning **2** easily annoyed; excitable ▷ *n* **3** a combustible substance > **comˌbustiˈbility** *or* **comˈbustibleness** *n*

combustion (kəmˈbʌstʃən) *n* **1** the process of burning **2** any process in which a substance reacts to produce a significant rise in temperature and the emission of light **3** a process in which a compound reacts slowly with oxygen to produce little heat and no light [C15 from OF, from L *combūrere* to burn up] > **comˈbustive** *n, adj*

combustion chamber *n* an enclosed space in which combustion takes place, such as the space above the piston in the cylinder head of an internal-combustion engine

combustor (kəmˈbʌstə) *n* the combustion system of a jet engine or ramjet

Comdr *mil abbrev for* Commander

Comdt *mil abbrev for* Commandant

come (kʌm) *vb* **comes, coming, came, come** (*mainly intr*) **1** to move towards a specified person or place **2** to arrive by movement or by making progress **3** to become perceptible: *light came into the sky* **4** to occur: *Christmas comes but once a year* **5** to happen as a result: *no good will come of this* **6** to be derived: *good may come of evil* **7** to occur to the mind: *the truth suddenly came to me* **8** to reach: *she comes up to my shoulder* **9** to be produced: *that dress comes in red* **10** to arrive at or be brought into a particular state:

you will soon come to grief **11** (foll by *from*) to be or have been a resident or native (of): *I come from London* **12** to become: *your wishes will come true* **13** (*tr; takes an infinitive*) to be given awareness: *I came to realize its value* **14** *sl* to have an orgasm **15** (*tr*) *Brit inf* to play the part of: *don't come the fine gentleman with me* **16** (*tr*) *Brit inf* to cause or produce: *don't come that nonsense* **17** (*subjunctive use*): *come next August, he will be fifty years old:* when next August arrives **18** **as … as they come** the most characteristic example of a type **19** **come again?** *inf* what did you say? **20** **come good** to recover and perform well after a setback or poor start **21** **come to light** to be revealed **22** **come to light with** *Austral & NZ inf* to find or produce ▷ *interj* **23** an exclamation expressing annoyance, etc: *come now!* ▷ See also **come about, come across,** etc [OE *cuman*]

come about *vb* (*intr, adv*) **1** to take place; happen **2** *naut* to change tacks

come across *vb* (*intr*) **1** (*prep*) to meet or find by accident **2** (*adv*) to communicate the intended meaning or impression **3** (often foll by *with*) to provide what is expected

come at *vb* (*intr, prep*) **1** to discover (facts, the truth, etc) **2** to attack: *he came at me with an axe* **3** (*usually used with a negative*) *Austral sl* to agree to do (something)

comeback ('kʌm,bæk) *n inf* **1** a return to a former position, status, etc **2** a response, esp recriminatory **3** a quick retort ▷ *vb* **come back** (*intr, adv*) **4** to return, esp to the memory **5** to become fashionable again **6** **come back to (someone)** (of something forgotten) to return to (someone's) memory

come between *vb* (*intr, prep*) to cause the estrangement or separation of (two people)

come by *vb* (*intr, prep*) to find or obtain, esp accidentally: *do you ever come by any old books?*

Comecon ('kɒmɪ,kɒn) *n* (formerly) an association of Soviet-oriented Communist nations, founded in 1949 to coordinate economic development, etc: disbanded in 1991 [c20 *Co*(*uncil for*) *M*(*utual*) *Econ*(*omic Aid*)]

comedian (kə'miːdɪən) *n* **1** an entertainer who specializes in jokes, comic skits, etc **2** an actor in comedy **3** an amusing person: sometimes used ironically

comedienne (kə,miːdɪ'ɛn) *n* a female comedian

comedo ('kɒmɪ,dəʊ) *n, pl* **comedos** *or* **comedones** (ˌkɒmɪ'dəʊniːz) *pathol* the technical name for **blackhead** [c19 from NL, from L: glutton]

comedown ('kʌm,daʊn) *n* **1** a decline in status or prosperity **2** *inf* a disappointment ▷ *vb* **come down** (*intr, adv*) **3** to come to a place regarded as lower **4** to lose status, etc (esp in **come down in the world**) **5** (of prices) to become lower **6** to reach a decision: *the report came down in favour of a pay increase* **7** (often foll by *to*) to be handed down by tradition or inheritance **8** *Brit* to leave university **9** (foll by *with*) to succumb (to illness) **10** (foll by *on*) to rebuke harshly **11** (foll by *to*) to amount in essence (to): *it comes down to two choices*

comedy ('kɒmɪdɪ) *n, pl* **comedies** **1** a dramatic or other work of light and amusing character **2** the genre of drama represented by works of this type **3** (in classical literature) a play in which the main characters triumph over adversity **4** the humorous aspect of life or of events **5** an amusing event or sequence of events **6** humour: *the comedy of Chaplin* [c14 from OF, from L, from Gk *kōmōidia*, from *kōmos* village festival + *aeidein* to sing] > **comedic** (kə'miːdɪk) *adj*

▷ www.comedy-zone.net
▷ www.comedy.com
▷ www.bbc.co.uk/comedy

comedy of manners *n* a comedy dealing with the way of life and foibles of a social group

come forward *vb* (*intr, adv*) **1** to offer one's services; volunteer **2** to present oneself

come-hither *adj* (*usually prenominal*) *inf* alluring; seductive: *she gave me a come-hither look*

come in *vb* (*intr, mainly adv*) **1** to enter **2** to prove to be: *it came in useful* **3** to become fashionable or seasonable **4** *cricket* to begin an innings **5** to finish a race (in a certain position) **6** to be received: *news is coming in of a big fire in Glasgow* **7** (of money) to be received as income **8** to play a role: *where do I come in?* **9** (foll by *for*) to be the object of: *the Chancellor came in for a lot of criticism*

come into *vb* (*intr, prep*) **1** to enter **2** to inherit

comely ('kʌmlɪ) *adj* **comelier, comeliest** **1** good-looking; attractive **2** *arch* suitable; fitting [OE *cȳmlīc* beautiful] > '**comeliness** *n*

come of *vb* (*intr, prep*) **1** to be descended from **2** to result from: *nothing came of it*

come off *vb* (*intr, mainly adv*) **1** (*also prep*) to fall (from) **2** to become detached **3** (*prep*) to be removed from (a price, tax, etc): *will anything come off income tax in the budget?* **4** (*copula*) to emerge from or as if from a contest: *he came off the winner* **5** *inf* to happen **6** *inf* to have the intended effect: *his jokes did not come off* **7** *taboo sl* to have an orgasm

come on *vb* (*intr, mainly adv*) **1** (of power, water, etc) to start running or functioning **2** to progress: *my plants are coming on nicely* **3** to advance, esp in battle **4** to begin: *she felt a cold coming on* **5** to make an entrance on stage **6** **come on!** **6a** hurry up! **6b** cheer up! pull yourself together! **6c** make an effort! **6d** don't exaggerate! stick to the facts! **7** to attempt to give a specified impression: *he came on like a hard man* **8** **come on strong** to make a forceful or exaggerated impression **9** **come on to** *inf* to make sexual advances to ▷ *n* **come-on** **10** anything that serves as a lure or enticement

come out *vb* (*intr, adv*) **1** to be made public or revealed: *the news of her death came out last week* **2** to make a debut in society **3** Also: **come out of the closet** **3a** to declare openly that one is a homosexual **3b** to reveal or declare any practice or habit formerly concealed **4** *chiefly Brit* to go on strike **5** to declare oneself: *the government came out in favour of scrapping the project* **6** to be shown clearly: *you came out very well in the photos* **7** to yield a satisfactory solution: *these sums just won't come out* **8** to be published: *the paper comes out on Fridays* **9** (foll by *in*) to become covered (with) **10** (foll by *with*) to declare openly: *you can rely on him to come out with the facts*

come over *vb* (*intr, adv*) **1** to communicate the intended meaning or impression: *he came over very well* **2** to change allegiances **3** *inf* to feel a particular sensation: *I came over funny*

comer ('kʌmə) *n* **1** (*in combination*) a person who comes: *all-comers; newcomers* **2** *inf* a potential success

come round *vb* (*intr, adv*) **1** to be restored to consciousness **2** to modify one's opinion

comestible (kə'mɛstɪbᵊl) *n* (*usually pl*) food [c15 from LL *comestibilis*, from *comedere* to eat up]

comet ('kɒmɪt) *n* a celestial body that travels around the sun, usually in a highly elliptical orbit: thought to consist of a frozen nucleus, part of which vaporizes on approaching the sun to form a long luminous tail [c13 from OF, from L, from Gk *komētēs* long-haired] > '**cometary** *or* **cometic** (kɒ'mɛtɪk) *adj*

come through *vb* (*intr*) **1** (*adv*) to emerge successfully **2** (*prep*) to survive (an illness, etc)

come to *vb* (*intr*) **1** (*adv or prep and reflexive*) to regain consciousness **2** (*adv*) *naut* to slow a vessel or bring her to a stop **3** (*prep*) to amount to (a sum of money) **4** (*prep*) to arrive at: *what is the world coming to?*

come up *vb* (*intr, adv*) **1** to come to a place regarded as higher **2** (of the sun) to rise **3** to present itself: *that question will come up again* **4** *Brit* to begin a term at a university **5** to appear from out of the ground: *my beans have come up early* **6** *inf* to win: *have your premium bonds ever come up?* **7** **come up against** to come into conflict with **8** **come up to** to meet a standard **9** **come up with** to produce

come upon *vb (intr, prep)* to meet or encounter unexpectedly

comeuppance (ˌkʌmˈʌpəns) *n inf* just retribution [c19 from *come up* (in the sense): to appear before a court]

comfit (ˈkʌmfɪt, ˈkɒm-) *n* a sugar-coated sweet containing a nut or seed [c15 from OF, from L *confectum* something prepared]

comfort (ˈkʌmfət) *n* **1** a state of ease or well-being **2** relief from affliction, grief, etc **3** a person, thing, or event that brings solace or ease **4** *(usually pl)* something that affords physical ease and relaxation ▷ *vb (tr)* **5** to soothe; cheer **6** to bring physical ease to [c13 from OF *confort*, from LL *confortāre* to strengthen, from L *con-* (intensive) + *fortis* strong] > **ˈcomforting** *adj* > **ˈcomfortless** *adj*

comfortable (ˈkʌmftəbᵊl) *adj* **1** giving comfort **2** at ease **3** free from affliction or pain **4** (of a person or situation) relaxing **5** *inf* having adequate income **6** *inf* (of income, etc) adequate to provide comfort > **ˈcomfortably** *adv*

comforter (ˈkʌmfətə) *n* **1** a person or thing that comforts **2** *chiefly Brit* a woollen scarf **3** a baby's dummy **4** *US* a quilted bed covering

Comforter (ˈkʌmfətə) *n Christianity* an epithet of the Holy Spirit [c14 translation of L *consolātor*, representing Gk *paraklētos* advocate]

comfort food *n* food that is enjoyable to eat and makes the eater feel better emotionally

comfrey (ˈkʌmfrɪ) *n* a hairy Eurasian plant having blue, purplish-pink, or white flowers [c15 from OF *cunfirie*, from L *conferva* water plant]

comfy (ˈkʌmfɪ) *adj* **comfier, comfiest** *inf* short for **comfortable**

comic (ˈkɒmɪk) *adj* **1** of, characterized by, or characteristic of comedy **2** *(prenominal)* acting in or composing comedy: *a comic writer* **3** humorous; funny ▷ *n* **4** a person who is comic; comedian **5** a book or magazine containing comic strips [c16 from L *cōmicus*, from Gk *kōmikos*]

comical (ˈkɒmɪkᵊl) *adj* **1** causing laughter **2** ludicrous; laughable > **ˈcomically** *adv*

comic opera *n* a play largely set to music, employing comic effects or situations

comic strip *n* a sequence of drawings in a newspaper, magazine, etc, relating a humorous story or an adventure

coming (ˈkʌmɪŋ) *adj* **1** *(prenominal)* (of time, events, etc) approaching or next **2** promising (esp in **up and coming**) **3** of future importance: *this is the coming thing* **4** **have it coming to one** *inf* to deserve what one is about to suffer ▷ *n* **5** arrival or approach

Comintern *or* **Komintern** (ˈkɒmɪnˌtɜːn) *n* short for **Communist International**; an international Communist organization founded by Lenin in 1919 and dissolved in 1943; it degenerated under Stalin into an instrument of Soviet politics. Also called: **Third International**

comity (ˈkɒmɪtɪ) *n, pl* **comities** **1** mutual civility; courtesy **2** short for **comity of nations** [c16 from L *cōmitās*, from *cōmis* affable]

comity of nations *n* the friendly recognition accorded by one nation to the laws and usages of another

comma (ˈkɒmə) *n* **1** the punctuation mark , indicating a slight pause and used where there is a listing of items or to separate a nonrestrictive clause from a main clause **2** *music* a minute difference in pitch [c16 from L, from Gk *komma* clause, from *koptein* to cut]

comma bacillus *n* a comma-shaped bacterium that causes cholera in man

command (kəˈmɑːnd) *vb* **1** (when *tr*, may take a clause as object or an infinitive) to order or compel **2** to have or be in control or authority over **3** *(tr)* to receive as due: *his nature commands respect* **4** to dominate (a view, etc) as from a height ▷ *n* **5** an order **6** the act of commanding **7** the right to command **8** the exercise of the power to command **9** knowledge; control: *a command of French* **10** *chiefly mil* the jurisdiction of a commander **11** a military unit or units commanding a specific function, as in the RAF **12** *Brit* **12a** an invitation from the monarch **12b** *(as modifier)*: *a command performance* **13** *computing* a word or phrase that can be selected from a menu or typed after a prompt in order to carry out an action [c13 from OF *commander*, from L *com-* (intensive) + *mandāre* to enjoin]

Command (kəˈmɑːnd) *n* any of the three main branches of the Canadian military forces

commandant (ˈkɒmənˌdænt, -ˌdɑːnt) *n* an officer commanding a group or establishment

command economy *n* an economy in which business activities and the allocation of resources are determined by government order rather than market forces. Also called: **planned economy**

commandeer (ˌkɒmənˈdɪə) *vb (tr)* **1** to seize for public or military use **2** to seize arbitrarily [c19 from Afrik. *kommandeer*, from F *commander* to COMMAND]

commander (kəˈmɑːndə) *n* **1** an officer in command of a military formation or operation **2** a naval commissioned rank junior to captain but senior to lieutenant commander **3** the second in command of larger British warships **4** someone who holds authority **5** a high-ranking member of some knightly orders **6** an officer responsible for a district of the Metropolitan Police in London > **comˈmanderˌship** *n*

commander in chief *n, pl* **commanders in chief** the officer holding supreme command of the forces in an area or operation

commanding (kəˈmɑːndɪŋ) *adj (usually prenominal)* **1** being in command **2** having the air of authority: *a commanding voice* **3** (of a situation) exerting control **4** (of a viewpoint, etc) overlooking; advantageous > **comˈmandingly** *adv*

commanding officer *n* an officer in command of a military unit

command language *n computing* the language used to access a computer system

commandment (kəˈmɑːndmənt) *n* **1** a divine command, esp one of the Ten Commandments of the Old Testament **2** *literary* any command

command module *n* the module used as the living quarters in an Apollo spacecraft and functioning as the splashdown vehicle

commando (kəˈmɑːndəʊ) *n, pl* **commandos** *or* **commandoes** **1a** an amphibious military unit trained for raiding **1b** a member of such a unit **2** the basic unit of the Royal Marine Corps **3** (originally) an armed force raised by Boers during the Boer War **4** *(modifier)* denoting or relating to commandos: *a commando unit* [c19 from Afrik. *kommando*, from Du. *commando* command]

command paper *n* (in Britain) a government document that is presented to Parliament, in theory by royal command

command post *n mil* the position from which a commander exercises command

commedia dell'arte (*Italian* komˈmeːdia delˈlarte) *n* a form of popular improvised comedy in Italy during the 16th to 18th centuries, with stock characters such as Punchinello, Harlequin, and Columbine [It., lit.: comedy of art]

comme il faut *French* (kɔm il fo) correct or correctly

commemorate (kəˈmɛməˌreɪt) *vb* **commemorates, commemorating, commemorated** *(tr)* to honour or keep alive the memory of [c16 from L *commemorāre*, from *com-* (intensive) + *memorāre* to remind] > **comˌmemoˈration** *n* > **comˈmemorative** *adj* > **comˈmemoˌrator** *n*

commence (kəˈmɛns) *vb* **commences, commencing, commenced** to start or begin; come or cause to come into being, operation, etc: *let battle commence* [c14 from OF *comencer*, from Vulgar L *cominitiāre* (unattested), from L *com-* (intensive) + *initiāre* to begin]

commencement (kəˈmɛnsmənt) *n* 1 the beginning; start 2 *US* a ceremony for the conferment of academic degrees 3 *US & Canad* a ceremony for the presentation of awards at secondary schools

commend (kəˈmɛnd) *vb* (*tr*) 1 to represent as being worthy of regard, confidence, etc; recommend 2 to give in charge; entrust 3 to praise 4 to give the regards of: *commend me to your aunt* [C14 from L *commendāre*, from *com-* (intensive) + *mandāre* to entrust] > **comˈmendable** *adj* > **comˈmendably** *adv* > **comˈmendatory** *adj*

commendation (ˌkɒmɛnˈdeɪʃən) *n* 1 the act of commending; praise 2 *US* an award

commensal (kəˈmɛnsəl) *adj* 1 (of two different species of plant or animal) living in close association such that one species benefits without harming the other. See also **inquiline** (sense 1) 2 *rare* of or relating to eating together, esp at the same table ▷ *n* 3 a commensal plant or animal 4 *rare* a companion at table [C14 from Med. L *commensālis*, from L *com-* together + *mensa* table] > **comˈmensalism** *n* > **commensality** (ˌkɒmɛnˈsælɪtɪ) *n*

commensurable (kəˈmɛnsərəbəl, -ʃə-) *adj* 1 *maths* 1a having a common factor 1b having units of the same dimensions and being related by whole numbers 2 proportionate > **comˌmensuraˈbility** *n* > **comˈmensurably** *adv*

commensurate (kəˈmɛnsərɪt, -ʃə-) *adj* 1 having the same extent or duration 2 corresponding in degree, amount, or size; proportionate 3 commensurable [C17 from LL *commēnsūrātus*, from L *com-* same + *mēnsurāre* to MEASURE] > **comˈmensurately** *adv*

comment (ˈkɒmɛnt) *n* 1 a remark, criticism, or observation 2 talk or gossip 3 a note explaining or criticizing a passage in a text 4 explanatory or critical matter added to a text ▷ *vb* 5 (when *intr*, often foll by *on*; when *tr*, takes a clause as object) to remark or express an opinion 6 (*intr*) to write notes explaining or criticizing a text [C15 from L *commentum* invention, from *comminiscī* to contrive] > **ˈcommenter** *n*

commentariat (ˌkɒmənˈtɛərɪæt) *n inf* the journalists and broadcasters who analyse and comment on current affairs [C20 from COMMEN(TATOR) + (PROLE)TARIAT]

commentary (ˈkɒməntərɪ) *n, pl* **commentaries** 1 an explanatory series of notes 2 a spoken accompaniment to a broadcast, film, etc 3 an explanatory treatise on a text 4 (*usually pl*) a personal record of events: *the commentaries of Caesar*

commentate (ˈkɒmənˌteɪt) *vb* **commentates, commentating, commentated** 1 (*intr*) to serve as a commentator 2 (*tr*) *US* to make a commentary on

commentator (ˈkɒmənˌteɪtə) *n* 1 a person who provides a spoken commentary for a broadcast, film, etc, esp of a sporting event 2 a person who writes notes on a text, etc

commerce (ˈkɒmɜːs) *n* 1 the activity embracing all forms of the purchase and sale of goods and services 2 social relations 3 *arch* sexual intercourse [C16 from L *commercium*, from *commercārī*, from *mercārī* to trade, from *merx* merchandise]

commercial (kəˈmɜːʃəl) *adj* 1 of or engaged in commerce 2 sponsored or paid for by an advertiser: *commercial television* 3 having profit as the main aim: *commercial music* 4 (of chemicals, etc) unrefined and produced in bulk for use in industry ▷ *n* 5 a commercially sponsored advertisement on radio or television > **commerciality** (kəˌmɜːʃɪˈælɪtɪ) *n* > **comˈmercially** *adv*

commercial art *n* graphic art for commercial uses such as advertising, packaging, etc

commercial bank *n* a bank primarily engaged in making short-term loans from funds deposited in current accounts

commercial break *n* an interruption in a radio or television programme for the broadcasting of advertisements

commercialism (kəˈmɜːʃəˌlɪzəm) *n* 1 the spirit, principles, or procedure of commerce 2 exclusive or inappropriate emphasis on profit

commercialize *or* **commercialise** (kəˈmɜːʃəˌlaɪz) *vb* **commercializes, commercializing, commercialized** *or* **commercialises, commercialising, commercialised** (*tr*) 1 to make commercial 2 to exploit for profit, esp at the expense of quality > **comˌmercialiˈzation** *or* **comˌmercialiˈsation** *n*

commercial paper *n* a short-term negotiable document, such as a bill of exchange, calling for the transference of a specified sum of money at a designated date

commercial traveller *n* another name for a **travelling salesman**

commercial vehicle *n* a vehicle for carrying goods or (less commonly) passengers

commie *or* **commy** (ˈkɒmɪ) *n, pl* **commies**, *adj inf & derog* short for **communist**

commination (ˌkɒmɪˈneɪʃən) *n* 1 the act of threatening punishment or vengeance 2 *Church of England* a recital of prayers, including a list of God's judgments against sinners, in the office for Ash Wednesday [C15 from L *comminātiō*, from *com-* (intensive) + *minārī* to threaten] > **comminatory** (ˈkɒmɪnətərɪ) *adj*

commingle (kɒˈmɪŋgəl) *vb* **commingles, commingling, commingled** to mix or be mixed

comminute (ˈkɒmɪˌnjuːt) *vb* **comminutes, comminuting, comminuted** 1 to break (a bone) into small fragments 2 to divide (property) into small lots [C17 from L *comminuere*, from *com-* (intensive) + *minuere* to reduce] > **ˌcommiˈnution** *n*

commis (ˈkɒmɪs, ˈkɒmɪ) *n, pl* **commis** 1 an agent or deputy ▷ *adj* 2 (of a waiter or chef) apprentice [C16 (meaning: deputy): from F, from *commettre* to employ]

commiserate (kəˈmɪzəˌreɪt) *vb* **commiserates, commiserating, commiserated** (when *intr*, usually foll by *with*) to feel or express sympathy or compassion (for) [C17 from L *commiserārī*, from *com-* together + *miserārī* to bewail] > **comˌmiserˈation** *n* > **comˈmiserˌator** *n*

commissar (ˈkɒmɪˌsɑː, ˌkɒmɪˈsɑː) *n* (in the former Soviet Union) 1 an official of the Communist Party responsible for political education 2 (before 1946) the head of a government department [C20 from Russian *kommissar*]

commissariat (ˌkɒmɪˈsɛərɪət) *n* 1 (in the former Soviet Union) a government department before 1946 2 a military department in charge of food supplies, etc [C17 from NL *commissāriātus*, from Med. L *commissārius* COMMISSARY]

commissary (ˈkɒmɪsərɪ) *n, pl* **commissaries** 1 *US* a shop supplying food or equipment, as in a military camp 2 *US army* an officer responsible for supplies 3 *US* a restaurant in a film studio 4 a representative or deputy, esp of a bishop [C14 from Med. L *commissārius* official in charge, from L *committere* to COMMIT] > **commissarial** (ˌkɒmɪˈsɛərɪəl) *adj*

commission (kəˈmɪʃən) *n* 1 a duty committed to a person or group to perform 2 authority to perform certain duties 3 a document granting such authority 4 *mil* 4a a document conferring a rank on an officer 4b the rank granted 5 a group charged with certain duties: *a commission of inquiry* 6 a government board empowered to exercise administrative, judicial, or legislative authority. See also **Royal Commission** 7a the authority given to a person or organization to act as an agent to a principal in commercial transactions 7b the fee allotted to an agent for services rendered 8 the state of being charged with specific responsibilities 9 the act of committing a sin, crime, etc 10 good working condition or (esp of a ship) active service (esp in **in commission, out of commission**) ▷ *vb* (*mainly tr*) 11 to grant authority to 12 *mil* to confer a rank on 13 to equip

Cc

and test (a ship) for active service **14** to place an order for (something): *to commission a portrait* **15** to make or become operative or operable: *the plant is due to commission next year* [C14 from OF, from L *commissiō* a bringing together, from *committere* to COMMIT]
commissionaire (kəˌmɪʃəˈnɛə) *n chiefly Brit* a uniformed doorman at a hotel, theatre, etc [C18 from F, from COMMISSION]
commissioned officer *n* a military officer holding a commission, such as Second Lieutenant in the British Army, Acting Sub-Lieutenant in the Royal Navy, Pilot Officer in the Royal Air Force, and officers of all ranks senior to these
commissioner (kəˈmɪʃənə) *n* **1** a person endowed with certain powers **2** any of several types of civil servant **3** a member of a commission > **comˈmissionerˌship** *n*
commissioner for oaths *n* a solicitor authorized to authenticate oaths on sworn statements
commit (kəˈmɪt) *vb* **commits, committing, committed** (*tr*) **1** to hand over, as for safekeeping; entrust **2 commit to memory** to memorize **3** to take into custody: *to commit someone to prison* **4** (*usually passive*) to pledge or align (oneself), as to a particular cause: *a committed radical* **5** to order (forces) into action **6** to perform (a crime, error, etc) **7** to surrender, esp for destruction: *she committed the letter to the fire* **8** to refer (a bill, etc) to a committee [C14 from L *committere* to join, from *com-* together + *mittere* to send] > **comˈmittable** *adj* > **comˈmitter** *n*
commitment (kəˈmɪtmənt) *n* **1** the act of committing or pledging **2** the state of being committed or pledged **3** an obligation, promise, etc, that restricts freedom of action **4** Also called (esp formerly): **mittimus** *law* a written order of a court directing that a person be imprisoned **5** a future financial obligation or contingent liability ▷ Also called (esp for sense 4): **committal** (kəˈmɪtᵊl)
committee *n* **1** (kəˈmɪtɪ) a group of people appointed to perform a specified service or function **2** (ˌkɒmɪˈtiː) (formerly) a person to whom the care of a mentally incompetent person or his or her property was entrusted by a court [C15 from *committen* to entrust + -EE]
committeeman (kəˈmɪtɪmən, -ˌmæn) *n, pl* **committeemen** *chiefly US* a member of one or more committees > **comˈmitteeˌwoman** *fem n*
Committee of the Whole House *n* (in Britain) an informal sitting of the House of Commons to discuss and amend a bill
commode (kəˈməʊd) *n* **1** a piece of furniture, usually highly ornamented, containing drawers or shelves **2** a bedside table with a cabinet for a chamber pot or washbasin **3** a chair with a hinged flap concealing a chamber pot [C17 from F, from L *commodus* COMMODIOUS]
commodious (kəˈməʊdɪəs) *adj* **1** roomy; spacious **2** *arch* convenient [C15 from Med. L, from L *commodus* convenient, from *com-* with + *modus* measure] > **comˈmodiousness** *n*
commodity (kəˈmɒdɪtɪ) *n, pl* **commodities 1** an article of commerce **2** something of use or profit **3** *econ* an exchangeable unit of economic wealth, such as a primary product [C14 from OF *commodité*, from L *commoditās* suitability; see COMMODIOUS]
commodo (kəˈməʊdəʊ) *adv* a variant spelling of **comodo**
commodore (ˈkɒməˌdɔː) *n* **1** *Brit* a naval rank junior to rear admiral and senior to captain **2** the captain of a shipping line **3** the officer in command of a merchant convoy **4** the titular head of a yacht club [C17 prob. from Du. *commandeur*, from F, from OF *commander* to COMMAND]
Commodus (kəˈməʊdəs, ˈkɒmədəs) *n* **Lucius Aelius Aurelius** (ˈluːsɪəs ˈiːlɪəs ɔːˈriːlɪəs), son of Marcus Aurelius. 161–192 AD, Roman emperor (180–192), noted for his tyrannical reign
common (ˈkɒmən) *adj* **1** belonging to two or more people: *common property* **2** belonging to members of one or more communities; public: *a common culture* **3** of ordinary standard; average **4** prevailing; widespread: *common opinion* **5** frequently encountered; ordinary: *a common brand of soap* **6** notorious: *a common nuisance* **7** *derog* considered by the speaker to be low-class, vulgar, or coarse **8** (*prenominal*) having no special distinction: *the common man* **9** *maths* having a specified relationship with a group of numbers or quantities: *common denominator* **10** *prosody* (of a syllable) able to be long or short **11** *grammar* (in certain languages) denoting or belonging to a gender of nouns that includes both masculine and feminine referents **12 common or garden** *inf* ordinary; unexceptional ▷ *n* **13** a tract of open public land **14** *law* the right to go onto someone else's property and remove natural products, as by pasturing cattle (esp in **right of common**) **15** *Christianity* **15a** a form of the proper of the Mass used on festivals that have no special proper of their own **15b** the ordinary of the Mass **16 in common** mutually held or used ▷ See also **commons** [C13 from OF *commun*, from L *commūnis* general] > **ˈcommonly** *adv* > **ˈcommonness** *n*
commonage (ˈkɒmənɪdʒ) *n* **1** *chiefly law* **1a** the use of something, esp a pasture, in common with others **1b** the right to such use **2** the state of being held in common **3** another word for **commonalty** (sense 1)
Common Agricultural Policy *n* the full name for **CAP**
commonality (ˌkɒməˈnælɪtɪ) *n, pl* **commonalities 1** the fact of being common **2** another word for **commonalty** (sense 1)
commonalty (ˈkɒmənəltɪ) *n, pl* **commonalties 1** the ordinary people as distinct from those with rank or title **2** the members of an incorporated society [C13 from OF *comunalte*, from *comunal* communal]
common carrier *n* a person or firm engaged in the business of transporting goods or passengers
common chord *n music* a chord consisting of the keynote, a major or minor third, and a perfect fifth
common cold *n* a mild viral infection of the upper respiratory tract, characterized by sneezing, coughing, etc
commoner (ˈkɒmənə) *n* **1** a person who does not belong to the nobility **2** a person who has a right in or over common land **3** *Brit* a student at a university who is not on a scholarship
common fraction *n* another name for **simple fraction**
common knowledge *n* something widely or generally known
common law *n* **1** the body of law based on judicial decisions and custom, as distinct from statute law **2** (*modifier*) of or denoting a marriage that is deemed to exist after a man and a woman have cohabited for a number of years: *common-law marriage*; *common-law wife*; *common-law husband*
Common Market *n* **the** an informal name for the **European Economic Community** (now the European Union, part of the wider European Community) and its politics of greater economic cooperation between member states
common noun *n grammar* a noun that refers to each member of a whole class sharing the features connoted by the noun, as for example *orange* and *drum* ▷ Cf **proper noun**
commonplace (ˈkɒmənˌpleɪs) *adj* **1** ordinary; everyday **2** dull; trite: *commonplace prose* ▷ *n* **3** a platitude; truism **4** a passage in a book marked for inclusion in a commonplace book, etc **5** an ordinary thing [C16 translation of L *locus commūnis* argument of wide application] > **ˈcommonˌplaceness** *n*
commonplace book *n* a notebook in which quotations, poems, etc, that catch the owner's attention are entered
common room *n chiefly Brit* a sitting room in schools, colleges, etc
commons (ˈkɒmənz) *n* **1** (*functioning as pl*) the lower

classes as contrasted with the ruling or noble classes of society **2** *(functioning as sing) Brit* a hall for dining, recreation, etc, usually attached to a college, etc **3** *(usually functioning as pl) Brit* food or rations (esp in **short commons**)

Commons ('kɒmənz) *n* **the** See **House of Commons**

common sense *n* **1** sound practical sense ▹ *adj* **common-sense;** *also* **common-sensical 2** inspired by or displaying this

common time *n music* a time signature indicating four crotchet beats to the bar; four-four time. Symbol: **C**

commonweal ('kɒmən,wi:l) *n arch* **1** the public good **2** another name for **commonwealth**

commonwealth ('kɒmən,wɛlθ) *n* **1** the people of a state or nation viewed politically; body politic **2** a state in which the people possess sovereignty; republic **3** a group of persons united by some common interest

Commonwealth ('kɒmən,wɛlθ) *n* **the 1** Official name: **the Commonwealth of Nations** an association of sovereign states, most of which are or at some time were ruled by Britain **2** the republic that existed in Britain from 1649 to 1660 **3** the official designation of Australia, four states of the US (Kentucky, Massachusetts, Pennsylvania, and Virginia), and Puerto Rico
▹ www.thecommonwealth.org

Commonwealth Day *n* the anniversary of Queen Victoria's birth, May 24, celebrated (now on the second Monday in March) in many parts of the Commonwealth. Former name: **Empire Day**

Commonwealth of Independent States *n* a loose organization of former Soviet republics, excluding the Baltic States, formed in 1991. Abbrev: **CIS**
▹ www.cisstat.com

commotion (kə'məʊʃən) *n* **1** violent disturbance; upheaval **2** political insurrection **3** a confused noise; din [C15 from L *commōtiō*, from *commovēre*, from *com-* (intensive) + *movēre* to MOVE]

communal ('kɒmjʊnᵊl) *adj* **1** belonging to a community as a whole **2** of a commune or a religious community > **communality** (,kɒmjʊ'nælɪtɪ) *n* > **'communally** *adv*

communalism ('kɒmjʊnə,lɪzəm) *n* **1** a system or theory of government in which the state is seen as a loose federation of self-governing communities **2** the practice or advocacy of communal living or ownership > **'communalist** *n* > **,communal'istic** *adj*

communalize *or* **communalise** ('kɒmjʊnə,laɪz) *vb* **communalizes, communalizing, communalized** *or* **communalises, communalising, communalised** (*tr*) to render (something) the property of a commune or community > **,communali'zation** *or* **,communali'sation** *n*

communautaire *French* (kɔmynotɛr) *adj* supporting the principles of the European Union [lit.: community (as modifier)]

commune¹ *vb* (kə'mju:n), **communes, communing, communed** (*intr;* usually foll by *with*) **1** to talk intimately **2** to experience strong emotion (for): *to commune with nature* ▹ *n* ('kɒmju:n) **3** intimate conversation; communion [C13 from OF *comuner* to hold in common, from *comun* COMMON]

commune² ('kɒmju:n) *n* **1** a group of families or individuals living together and sharing possessions and responsibilities **2** any small group of people having common interests or responsibilities **3** the smallest administrative unit in Belgium, France, Italy, and Switzerland **4** a medieval town enjoying a large degree of autonomy [C18 from F, from Med. L *commūnia*, from L: things held in common]

Commune ('kɒmju:n) *n French history* **1** See **Paris Commune 2** a committee that governed Paris during the French Revolution: suppressed 1794

communicable (kə'mju:nɪkəbᵊl) *adj* **1** capable of being communicated **2** (of a disease) capable of being passed on readily > **com,munica'bility** *n* > **com'municably** *adv*

communicant (kə'mju:nɪkənt) *n* **1** *Christianity* a person who receives Communion **2** a person who communicates or informs

communicate (kə'mju:nɪ,keɪt) *vb* **communicates, communicating, communicated 1** to impart (knowledge) or exchange (thoughts) by speech, writing, gestures, etc **2** (*tr;* usually foll by *to*) to transmit (to): *the dog communicated his fear to the other animals* **3** (*intr*) to have a sympathetic mutual understanding **4** (*intr;* usually foll by *with*) to make or have a connecting passage: *the kitchen communicates with the dining room* **5** (*tr*) to transmit (a disease) **6** (*intr*) *Christianity* to receive Communion [C16 from L *commūnicāre* to share, from *commūnis* COMMON] > **com'muni,cator** *n* > **com'municatory** *adj*

communication (kə,mju:nɪ'keɪʃən) *n* **1** the imparting or exchange of information, ideas, or feelings **2** something communicated, such as a message **3** *(usually pl; sometimes functioning as sing)* the study of ways in which human beings communicate **4** a connecting route or link **5** (*pl*) *mil* the system of routes by which forces, supplies, etc, are moved within an area of operations

communication cord *n Brit* a cord or chain in a train which may be pulled by a passenger to stop the train in an emergency

communications satellite *n* an artificial satellite used to relay radio, television, and telephone signals around the earth's surface, usually in geostationary orbit

communicative (kə'mju:nɪkətɪv) *adj* **1** inclined or able to communicate readily; talkative **2** of or relating to communication

communion (kə'mju:njən) *n* **1** an exchange of thoughts, emotions, etc **2** sharing in common; participation **3** (foll by *with*) strong feelings (for): *communion with nature* **4** a religious group or denomination having common beliefs and practices **5** spiritual union [C14 from L *commūniō*, from *commūnis* COMMON]

Communion (kə'mju:njən) *n Christianity* **1** the act of participating in the Eucharist **2** the celebration of the Eucharist **3** the consecrated elements of the Eucharist ▹ Also called: **Holy Communion**

communiqué (kə'mju:nɪ,keɪ) *n* an official communication or announcement, esp to the press or public [C19 from F]

communism ('kɒmjʊ,nɪzəm) *n* **1** advocacy of a classless society in which private ownership has been abolished and the means of production belong to the community **2** any movement or doctrine aimed at achieving such a society **3** *(usually cap)* a political movement based upon the writings of Marx that considers history in terms of class conflict and revolutionary struggle **4** *(usually cap)* a system of government established by a ruling Communist Party, esp in the former Soviet Union **5** communal living [C19 from F *communisme*, from *commun* COMMON]

communist ('kɒmjʊnɪst) *n* **1** a supporter of communism **2** *(often cap)* a supporter of a Communist movement or state **3** *(often cap)* a member of a Communist party **4** *(often cap) chiefly US* any person holding left-wing views, esp when considered subversive **5** a person who practises communal living ▹ *adj* **6** of, favouring, or relating to communism > **,commu'nistic** *adj*

Communist China *n* another name for (the People's Republic of) **China**

community (kə'mju:nɪtɪ) *n, pl* **communities 1a** the people living in one locality **1b** the locality in which they live **1c** *(as modifier)*: *community spirit* **2** a group of people having cultural, religious, or other characteristics in common: *the Protestant community* **3** a group of nations having certain interests in common

Cc

4 the public; society 5 common ownership 6 similarity or agreement: *community of interests* 7 (in Wales and Scotland) the smallest unit of local government 8 *ecology* a group of interdependent plants and animals inhabiting the same region [C14 from L *commūnitās*, from *commūnis* COMMON]

community centre *n* a building used by a community for social gatherings, etc

community charge *n* (formerly in Britain) a flat-rate charge paid by each adult in a community to their local authority in place of rates. Also called (informal): **poll tax**

community chest *n US* a fund raised by voluntary contribution for local welfare activities

community council *n* (in Scotland and Wales) an independent voluntary local body set up to attend to local interests and organize community activities

community education *n* the provision of a wide range of educational and special-interest courses and activities by a local authority

community home *n* (in Britain) 1 a home provided by a local authority for children who cannot remain with their parents 2 a boarding school for young offenders

community medicine *n* the branch of medicine concerned with evaluating and providing for the health needs of populations, esp through monitoring and preventive measures

community policing *n* the assigning of the same one or two policemen to a particular area so that they become familiar with the residents and they with them, as a way of reducing crime

community service *n* work undertaken for the community by an offender without pay, by the order of a court

communize *or* **communise** (ˈkɒmjʊˌnaɪz) *vb* **communizes, communizing, communized** *or* **communises, communising, communised** (*tr*) (*sometimes cap*) 1 to make (property) public; nationalize 2 to make (a person or country) communist > **ˌcommuniˈzation** *or* **ˌcommuniˈsation** *n*

commutate (ˈkɒmjʊˌteɪt) *vb* **commutates, commutating, commutated** (*tr*) 1 to reverse the direction of (an electric current) 2 to convert (an alternating current) into a direct current

commutation (ˌkɒmjʊˈteɪʃən) *n* 1 a substitution or exchange 2 the replacement of one method of payment by another 3 the reduction in severity of a penalty imposed by law 4 the process of commutating an electric current

commutative (kəˈmjuːtətɪv, ˈkɒmjʊˌteɪtɪv) *adj* 1 relating to or involving substitution 2 *maths, logic* 2a giving the same result irrespective of the order of the arguments; thus addition is commutative but subtraction is not 2b relating to this property: *the commutative law of addition*

commutator (ˈkɒmjʊˌteɪtə) *n* 1 a device used to reverse the direction of flow of an electric current 2 the segmented metal cylinder or disc of an electric motor, generator, etc, used to make electrical contact with the rotating coils

commute (kəˈmjuːt) *vb* **commutes, commuting, commuted** 1 (*intr*) to travel some distance regularly between one's home and one's place of work 2 (*tr*) to substitute 3 (*tr*) *law* to reduce (a sentence) to one less severe 4 to pay (an annuity, etc) at one time, instead of in instalments 5 to change: *to commute base metal into gold* [C17 from L *commūtāre*, from *com-* mutually + *mūtāre* to change] > **comˈmutable** *adj* > **comˌmutaˈbility** *n*

commuter (kəˈmjuːtə) *n* a person who travels to work over an appreciable distance, usually from the suburbs to the centre of a city

Como (ˈkəʊməʊ; *Italian* ˈkɔːmo) *n* a city in N Italy, in Lombardy at the SW end of **Lake Como**: tourist centre. Pop: 96 900 (1995 est) Latin name: **Comum** (ˈkəʊmʊm)

comodo *or* **commodo** (kəˈməʊdəʊ) *adv music* in a convenient tempo [It.: comfortable, from L *commodus* convenient: see COMMODIOUS]

Comoros (ˈkɒməˌrəʊz, kəˈmɔːrəʊz) *pl n* a republic consisting of three volcanic islands in the Indian Ocean, off the NW coast of Madagascar; a French territory from 1947; became independent in 1976 except for Mayotte, the fourth island in the group, which chose to remain French. Official languages: Comorian, French, and Arabic; Swahili is used commercially. Religion: Muslim. Currency: franc. Capital: Moroni. Pop: 566 000 (2001 est). Area: 1862 sq km (719 sq miles). Official name: **Federal Islamic Republic of the Comoros**
▷ www.presidence-uniondescomores.com/v3/us/

comose (ˈkəʊməʊs, kəʊˈməʊs) *adj bot* having tufts of hair; hairy. Also: **comate** [C18 from L *comōsus* hairy]

Comox (ˈkəʊmɒks) *n* a member of a Salishan Native Canadian people living on Vancouver Island

comp (kɒmp) *inf* ▷ *n* 1 a compositor 2 an accompaniment 3 a competition ▷ *vb* 4 (*intr*) to work as a compositor in the printing industry 5 to play an accompaniment (to)

compact[1] *adj* (kəmˈpækt, ˈkɒmpækt) 1 closely packed together 2 neatly fitted into a restricted space 3 concise; brief 4 well constructed; solid; firm 5 (foll by *of*) composed (of) ▷ *vb* (kəmˈpækt) (*tr*) 6 to pack closely together; compress 7 (foll by *of*) to form by pressing together: *sediment compacted of three types of clay* 8 *metallurgy* to compress (a metal powder) to form a stable product suitable for sintering ▷ *n* (ˈkɒmpækt) 9 a small flat case containing a mirror, face powder, and powder puff, designed to be carried in a woman's handbag 10 *US & Canad* a small and economical car [C16 from L *compactus*, from *compingere*, from *com-* together + *pangere* to fasten] > **comˈpactly** *adv* > **comˈpactness** *n*

compact[2] (ˈkɒmpækt) *n* an official contract or agreement [C16 from L *compactum*, from *compaciscī*, from *com-* together + *paciscī* to contract]

compact disc (ˈkɒmpækt) *n* a small digital audio disc on which sound is recorded as a series of metallic pits enclosed in PVC and read by an optical laser system. Also called: **compact audio disc**. Abbrev: **CD, CAD**

compact disc erasable *n* see **CDE**

compact disc recordable *n* see **CDR**

compact video disc *n* a compact laser disc that plays both pictures and sound

compages (kəmˈpeɪdʒiːz) *n* (*functioning as sing*) a structure or framework [C17 from L: from *com-* together + *pangēre* to fasten]

companion[1] (kəmˈpænjən) *n* 1 a person who is an associate of another or others; comrade 2 (esp formerly) an employee, usually a woman, who provides company for an employer 3a one of a pair 3b (*as modifier*): *a companion volume* 4 a guidebook or handbook 5 a member of the lowest rank of certain orders of knighthood 6 *astron* the fainter of the two components of a double star ▷ *vb* 7 (*tr*) to accompany [C13 from LL *compāniō*, lit.: one who eats bread with another, from L *com-* with + *pānis* bread] > **comˈpanionˌship** *n*

companion[2] (kəmˈpænjən) *n naut* a raised frame on an upper deck with windows to give light to the deck below [C18 from Du. *kompanje* quarterdeck, from OF *compagne*, from OIt. *compagna* pantry, ? ult. from L *pānis* bread]

companionable (kəmˈpænjənəbᵊl) *adj* sociable > **comˈpanionableness** *n* > **comˈpanionably** *adv*

companion animal *n* an animal kept as a pet

companionate (kəmˈpænjənɪt) *adj* 1 resembling, appropriate to, or acting as a companion 2 harmoniously suited

companionway (kəmˈpænjənˌweɪ) *n* a ladder from one deck to another in a ship

company (ˈkʌmpənɪ) *n, pl* **companies** 1 a number of

people gathered together; assembly **2** the fact of being with someone; companionship: *I enjoy her company* **3** a guest or guests **4** a business enterprise **5** the members of an enterprise not specifically mentioned in the enterprise's title. Abbrev: **Co., co. 6** a group of actors **7** a small unit of troops **8** the officers and crew of a ship **9** a unit of Guides **10** *English history* a medieval guild **11 keep company 11a** to accompany (someone) **11b** (esp of lovers) to spend time together ▷ *vb* **companies, companying, companied 12** *arch* to associate (with someone) [C13 from OF *compaignie*, from LL *compāniō*; see COMPANION[1]]

company doctor *n* **1** a businessman or accountant who specializes in turning ailing companies into profitable enterprises **2** a physician employed by a company to look after its staff and to advise on health matters

company sergeant major *n mil* the senior noncommissioned officer in a company

company town *n US & Canad* a town built by a company for its employees

comparable ('kɒmpərəbᵊl) *adj* **1** worthy of comparison **2** able to be compared (with) > ˌ**compara'bility** *or* '**comparableness** *n*

comparative (kəm'pærətɪv) *adj* **1** denoting or involving comparison: *comparative literature* **2** relative: *a comparative loss of prestige* **3** *grammar* denoting the form of an adjective that indicates that the quality denoted is possessed to a greater extent. In English the comparative is marked by the suffix *-er* or the word *more* ▷ *n* **4** the comparative form of an adjective > **com'paratively** *adv* > **com'parativeness** *n*

comparative advertising *n* the usual US term for **knocking copy**

compare (kəm'pɛə) *vb* **compares, comparing, compared 1** (*tr; foll by to*) to regard as similar; liken: *the general has been compared to Napoleon* **2** (*tr*) to examine in order to observe resemblances or differences: *to compare rum and gin* **3** (*intr; usually foll by with*) to be the same or similar: *gin compares with rum in alcoholic content* **4** (*intr*) to bear a specified relation when examined: *this car compares badly with the other* **5** (*tr*) *grammar* to give the positive, comparative, and superlative forms of (an adjective) **6 compare notes** to exchange opinions ▷ *n* **7** comparison (esp in **beyond compare**) [C15 from OF, from L *comparāre*, from *compar*, from *com-* together + *par* equal]

comparison (kəm'pærɪsᵊn) *n* **1** the act of comparing **2** the state of being compared **3** likeness: *there was no comparison between them* **4** a rhetorical device involving comparison, such as a simile **5** Also called: **degrees of comparison** *grammar* the listing of the positive, comparative, and superlative forms of an adjective or adverb **6 bear** *or* **stand comparison (with)** to be sufficiently similar to be compared with (something else), esp favourably

compartment (kəm'pɑːtmənt) *n* **1** one of the sections into which an area, esp an enclosed space, is partitioned **2** any separate section: *a compartment of the mind* **3** a small storage space [C16 from F *compartiment*, ult. from LL *compartīrī* to share] > **compartmental** (ˌkɒmpɑːt'mɛntᵊl) *adj* > ˌ**compart'mentally** *adv*

compartmentalize *or* **compartmentalise** (ˌkɒmpɑːt'mɛntᵊˌlaɪz) *vb* **compartmentalizes, compartmentalizing, compartmentalized** *or* **compartmentalises, compartmentalising, compartmentalised** (*usually tr*) to put into categories, etc, esp to an excessive degree > ˌ**compartˌmentali'zation** *or* ˌ**compartˌmentali'sation** *n*

compass ('kʌmpəs) *n* **1** Also called: **magnetic compass** an instrument for finding direction, having a magnetized needle which points to magnetic north **2** (*often pl*) Also called: **pair of compasses** an instrument used for drawing circles, measuring distances, etc, that consists of two arms, joined at one end **3** limits or range: *within the compass of education* **4** *music* the interval between the lowest and highest note attainable ▷ *vb* (*tr*) **5** to surround; hem in **6** to grasp mentally **7** to achieve; accomplish **8** *obs* to plot [C13 from OF *compas*, from Vulgar L *compassāre* (unattested) to pace out, ult. from L *passus* step] > '**compassable** *adj*

compass card *n* a compass in the form of a card that rotates so that "0°" or "North" points to magnetic north

compassion (kəm'pæʃən) *n* a feeling of distress and pity for the suffering or misfortune of another [C14 from OF, from LL *compassiō*, from L *com-* with + *patī* to suffer]

compassionate (kəm'pæʃənɪt) *adj* showing or having compassion > **com'passionately** *adv*

compassionate leave *n* leave granted on the grounds of bereavement, family illness, etc

compassion fatigue *n* the inability to react sympathetically to a crisis, disaster, etc, because of overexposure to previous crises, disasters, etc

compass rose *n* a circle or decorative device printed on a map or chart showing the points of the compass

compass saw *n* a hand saw with a narrow tapered blade for making a curved cut

compatible (kəm'pætɪbᵊl) *adj* **1** (usually foll by *with*) able to exist together harmoniously **2** (usually foll by *with*) consistent: *her deeds were not compatible with her ideology* **3** (of pieces of machinery, etc) capable of being used together without modification or adaptation [C15 from Med. L *compatibilis*, from LL *compatī*; see COMPASSION] > **comˌpati'bility** *n* > **com'patibly** *adv*

compatriot (kəm'pætrɪət) *n* a fellow countryman [C17 from F *compatriote*, from LL; see PATRIOT] > **comˌpatri'otic** *adj*

compeer ('kɒmpɪə) *n* **1** a person of equal rank, status, or ability **2** a comrade [C13 from OF *comper*, from Med. L *compater* godfather]

compel (kəm'pɛl) *vb* **compels, compelling, compelled** (*tr*) **1** to cause (someone) by force (to be or do something) **2** to obtain by force; exact: *to compel obedience* [C14 from L *compellere*, from *com-* together + *pellere* to drive] > **com'pellable** *adj*

compelling (kəm'pɛlɪŋ) *adj* **1** arousing or denoting strong interest, esp admiring interest **2** (of an argument, evidence, etc) convincing

compendious (kəm'pɛndɪəs) *adj* stating the essentials of a subject in a concise form > **com'pendiously** *adv* > **com'pendiousness** *n*

compendium (kəm'pɛndɪəm) *n, pl* **compendiums** *or* **compendia** (-dɪə) **1** *Brit* a book containing a collection of useful hints **2** *Brit* a selection, esp of different games in one container **3** a summary [C16 from L: a saving, lit.: something weighed]

compensate ('kɒmpɛnˌseɪt) *vb* **compensates, compensating, compensated 1** to make amends to (someone), esp for loss or injury **2** (*tr*) to serve as compensation or damages for (injury, loss, etc) **3** to counterbalance the effects of (a force, weight, etc) so as to produce equilibrium **4** (*intr*) to attempt to conceal one's shortcomings by the exaggerated exhibition of qualities regarded as desirable [C17 from L *compēnsāre*, from *pendere* to weigh] > **compensatory** ('kɒmpɛnˌseɪtərɪ, kəm'pɛnsətərɪ) *or* **compensative** ('kɒmpɛnˌseɪtɪv, kəm'pɛnsə-) *adj*

compensation (ˌkɒmpɛn'seɪʃən) *n* **1** the act of making amends for something **2** something given as reparation for loss, injury, etc **3** the attempt to conceal one's shortcomings by the exaggerated exhibition of qualities regarded as desirable > ˌ**compen'sational** *adj*

compensation culture *n* a culture in which people are very ready to go to law over even relatively minor incidents in the hope of gaining compensation

comper ('kɒmpə) *n inf* a person who regularly enters competitions in newspapers, magazines, etc, esp

Cc

competitions offering consumer goods as prizes [C20 COMP(ETITION) + -ER[1]] > 'comping *n*

compere ('kɒmpɛə) *Brit* ▷ *n* **1** a master of ceremonies who introduces cabaret, television acts, etc ▷ *vb* **comperes, compering, compered** **2** to act as a compere (for) [C20 from F, lit.: godfather]

compete (kəm'pi:t) *vb* **competes, competing, competed** (*intr; often foll by with*) to contend (against) for profit, an award, etc [C17 from LL *competere*, from L, from *com-* together + *petere* to seek]

competence ('kɒmpɪtəns) *or* **competency** *n* **1** the condition of being capable; ability **2** a sufficient income to live on **3** the state of being legally competent or qualified

competent ('kɒmpɪtənt) *adj* **1** having sufficient skill, knowledge, etc; capable **2** suitable or sufficient for the purpose: *a competent answer* **3** *law* (of a witness, etc) qualified to testify, etc [C14 from L *competēns*, from *competere*; see COMPETE] > '**competently** *adv*

competition (ˌkɒmpɪ'tɪʃən) *n* **1** the act of competing **2** a contest in which a winner is selected from among two or more entrants **3** a series of games, sports events, etc **4** the opposition offered by competitors **5** competitors offering opposition

competitive (kəm'pɛtɪtɪv) *adj* **1** involving rivalry: *competitive sports* **2** sufficiently low in price or high in quality to be successful against commercial rivals **3** characterized by an urge to compete: *a competitive personality* > **com'petitiveness** *n*

competitor (kəm'pɛtɪtə) *n* a person, group, team, firm, etc, that vies or competes; rival

Compiègne (*French* kɔ̃pjɛɲ) *n* a city in N France, on the Oise River: scene of the armistice at the end of World War I (1918) and of the Franco-German armistice of 1940. Pop: 44 703 (1990)

compile (kəm'paɪl) *vb* **compiles, compiling, compiled** (*tr*) **1** to make or compose from other sources: *to compile a list of names* **2** to collect for a book, hobby, etc **3** *computing* to create (a set of machine instructions) from a high-level programming language, using a compiler [C14 from L *compīlāre*, from *com-* together + *pīlāre* to thrust down, pack] > **compilation** (ˌkɒmpɪ'leɪʃən) *n*

compiler (kəm'paɪlə) *n* **1** a person who compiles something **2** a computer program by which a high-level programming language is converted into machine language that can be acted upon by a computer ▷ Cf **assembler**

complacency (kəm'pleɪsənsɪ) *or* **complacence** *n* extreme self-satisfaction; smugness

complacent (kəm'pleɪsᵊnt) *adj* extremely self-satisfied [C17 from L *complacēns* very pleasing, from *complacēre*, from *com-* (intensive) + *placēre* to please] > **com'placently** *adv*

complain (kəm'pleɪn) *vb* (*intr*) **1** to express resentment, displeasure, etc; grumble **2** (foll by *of*) to state the presence of pain, illness, etc: *she complained of a headache* [C14 from OF *complaindre*, from Vulgar L *complangere* (unattested), from L *com-* (intensive) + *plangere* to bewail] > **com'plainer** *n* > **com'plainingly** *adv*

complainant (kəm'pleɪnənt) *n* *law* a plaintiff

complaint (kəm'pleɪnt) *n* **1** the act of complaining **2** a cause for complaining; grievance **3** a mild ailment

complaisant (kəm'pleɪzᵊnt) *adj* showing a desire to comply or oblige; polite [C17 from F *complaire*, from L *complacēre* to please greatly; cf. COMPLACENT] > **com'plaisance** *n*

complement *n* ('kɒmplɪmənt) **1** a person or thing that completes something **2** a complete amount, number, etc (often in **full complement**) **3** the officers and crew needed to man a ship **4** *grammar* a word, phrase, or clause that completes the meaning of the predicate, as *an idiot* in *He is an idiot* or *that he would be early* in *I hoped that he would be early* **5** *maths* the angle that when added to a specified angle produces a right angle **6** *logic* the class of all the things that are not members of a given class **7** *immunol* a group of proteins in the blood serum that, when activated by antibodies, destroys alien cells, such as bacteria ▷ *vb* ('kɒmplɪˌmɛnt) **8** (*tr*) to complete or form a complement to [C14 from L *complēmentum*, from *complēre*, from *com-* (intensive) + *plēre* to fill] > ˌ**complemen'tation** *n*

> **USAGE** This is sometimes confused with **compliment**

complementary (ˌkɒmplɪ'mɛntərɪ) *adj* **1** forming a complement **2** forming a satisfactory or balanced whole **3** involving or using the treatments and techniques of alternative (complementary) medicine > ˌ**comple'mentarily** *adv* > ˌ**comple'mentariness** *n*

complementary angle *n* either of two angles whose sum is 90° ▷ Cf **supplementary angle**

complementary colour *n* one of any pair of colours, such as yellow and blue, that give white or grey when mixed in the correct proportions

complementary DNA *n* a form of DNA artificially synthesized from a messenger RNA template and used in genetic engineering to produce gene clones. Abbrev: **cDNA**

complementary medicine *n* another name for **alternative medicine**

complete (kəm'pli:t) *adj* **1** having every necessary part; entire **2** finished **3** (*prenominal*) thorough: *he is a complete rogue* **4** perfect in quality or kind: *he is a complete scholar* **5** (of a logical system) constituted such that a contradiction or inconsistency arises on the addition of an axiom that cannot be deduced from the axioms of the system **6** *arch* skilled; accomplished ▷ *vb* **completes, completing, completed** (*tr*) **7** to make perfect **8** to finish **9** (in land law) to pay any outstanding balance on a contract for the conveyance of land in exchange for the title deeds, so that the ownership of the land changes hands **10** *American football* (of a quarterback) to make a forward pass successfully [C14 from L *complētus*, p.p. of *complēre* to fill up; see COMPLEMENT] > **com'pletely** *adv* > **com'pleteness** *n* > **com'pletion** *n*

completist (kəm'pli:tɪst) *n* a person who collects objects or memorabilia obsessively

complex ('kɒmplɛks) *adj* **1** made up of interconnected parts **2** (of thoughts, writing, etc) intricate **3** *maths* **3a** of or involving complex numbers **3b** consisting of a real and an imaginary part, either of which can be zero ▷ *n* **4** a whole made up of related parts: *a building complex* **5** *psychoanal* a group of emotional impulses that have been banished from the conscious mind but continue to influence a person's behaviour **6** *inf* an obsession: *he's got a complex about cats* **7** any chemical compound in which one molecule is linked to another by a coordinate bond [C17 from L *complexus*, from *complectī*, from *com-* together + *plectere* to braid] > '**complexness** *n*

> **USAGE** *Complex* is sometimes used where *complicated* is meant. *Complex* should be used to say only that something consists of several parts rather than that it is difficult to understand, analyse, or deal with, which is what *complicated* inherently means. In the following real example a clear distinction is made between the two words: *the British benefits system is phenomenally complex and is administered by a complicated range of agencies*

complex fraction *n* *maths* a fraction in which the numerator or denominator or both contain fractions. Also called: **compound fraction**

complexion (kəm'plɛkʃən) *n* **1** the colour and general appearance of a person's skin, esp of the face **2** aspect or nature: *the general complexion of a nation's finances* **3** *obs* temperament [C14 from L *complexiō* a combination, from *complectī* to embrace; see COMPLEX] > **com'plexional** *adj*

complexioned (kəm'plɛkʃənd) *adj* of a specified complexion: *light-complexioned*

complexity (kəm'plɛksɪtɪ) *n, pl* **complexities** 1 the state or quality of being intricate or complex 2 something intricate or complex; complication

complex number *n* any number of the form *a* + *b*i, where *a* and *b* are real numbers and i = √–1

complex sentence *n grammar* a sentence containing at least one main clause and one subordinate clause

compliance (kəm'plaɪəns) *or* **compliancy** *n* 1 acquiescence 2 a disposition to yield to others 3 a measure of the ability of a mechanical system to respond to an applied vibrating force

compliance officer *or* **lawyer** *n* a specialist, usually a lawyer, employed by a financial group operating in a variety of fields and for multiple clients to ensure that no conflict of interest arises and that all obligations and regulations are complied with

compliant (kəm'plaɪənt) *adj* complying, obliging, or yielding > **com'pliantly** *adv*

complicate *vb* ('kɒmplɪˌkeɪt), **complicates, complicating, complicated** 1 to make or become complex, etc ▷ *adj* ('kɒmplɪkɪt) 2 *biol* folded on itself: *a complicate leaf* [c17 from L *complicāre* to fold together]

complicated ('kɒmplɪˌkeɪtɪd) *adj* made up of intricate parts or aspects that are difficult to understand or analyse > **'compliˌcatedly** *adv*

USAGE See at **complex**

complication (ˌkɒmplɪ'keɪʃən) *n* 1 a condition, event, etc, that is complex or confused 2 the act of complicating 3 an event or condition that complicates or frustrates: *her coming was a serious complication* 4 a disease arising as a consequence of another

complicity (kəm'plɪsɪtɪ) *n, pl* **complicities** 1 the fact of being an accomplice, esp in a criminal act 2 a less common word for **complexity**

compliment *n* ('kɒmplɪmənt) 1 a remark or act expressing respect, admiration, etc 2 (*usually pl*) a greeting of respect or regard ▷ *vb* ('kɒmplɪˌmɛnt) (*tr*) 3 to express admiration for; congratulate 4 to express or show regard for, esp by a gift [c17 from F, from It. *complimento*, from Sp. *cumplimiento*, from *cumplir* to complete]

USAGE This is sometimes confused with **complement**

complimentary (ˌkɒmplɪ'mɛntərɪ) *adj* 1 conveying a compliment 2 flattering 3 given free, esp as a courtesy or for publicity purposes > ˌ**compli'mentarily** *adv*

compline ('kɒmplɪn, -plaɪn) *or* **complin** ('kɒmplɪn) *n RC Church* the last of the seven canonical hours of the divine office [c13 from OF *complie*, from Med. L *hōra complēta*, lit.: the completed hour]

comply (kəm'plaɪ) *vb* **complies, complying, complied** (*intr*) (usually foll by *with*) to act in accordance with rules, wishes, etc; be obedient (to) [c17 from It. *complire*, from Sp. *cumplir* to complete]

compo ('kɒmpəʊ) *n, pl* **compos** 1 a mixture of materials, such as mortar, plaster, etc 2 *Austral & NZ inf* compensation, esp for injury or loss of work ▷ *adj* 3 *mil* intended to last for several days: *a compo pack* [short for *composition, compensation, composite*]

component (kəm'pəʊnənt) *n* 1 a constituent part or aspect of something more complex 2 any electrical device that has distinct electrical characteristics and may be connected to other devices to form a circuit 3 *maths* one of a set of two or more vectors whose resultant is a given vector 4 See **phase rule** ▷ *adj* 5 forming or functioning as a part or aspect; constituent [c17 from L *compōnere* to put together] > **componential** (ˌkɒmpə'nɛnʃəl) *adj*

comport (kəm'pɔːt) *vb* 1 (*tr*) to conduct or bear (oneself) in a specified way 2 (*intr; foll by with*) to agree (with); correspond (to) [c16 from L *comportāre* collect, from *com-* together + *portāre* to carry] > **com'portment** *n*

compose (kəm'pəʊz) *vb* **composes, composing, composed** (*mainly tr*) 1 to put together or make up 2 to be the component elements of 3 to create (a musical or literary work) 4 (*intr*) to write music 5 to calm (someone, esp oneself); make quiet 6 to adjust or settle (a quarrel, etc) 7 to order the elements of (a painting, sculpture, etc); design 8 *printing* to set up (type) [c15 from OF *composer*, from L *compōnere* to put in place]

composed (kəm'pəʊzd) *adj* (of people) calm; tranquil > **composedly** (kəm'pəʊzɪdlɪ) *adv*

composer (kəm'pəʊzə) *n* 1 a person who composes music 2 a person or machine that composes anything, esp type for printing

composite *adj* ('kɒmpəzɪt) 1 composed of separate parts; compound 2 of or belonging to the plant family Asteraceae 3 *maths* capable of being factorized: *a composite function* 4 (*sometimes cap*) denoting one of the five classical orders of architecture: characterized by a combination of the Ionic and Corinthian styles ▷ *n* ('kɒmpəzɪt) 5 something composed of separate parts; compound 6 any plant of the family Asteraceae (formerly Compositae), having flower heads composed of many small flowers (e.g. dandelion, daisy) 7 a material, such as reinforced concrete, made of two or more distinct materials 8 a proposal that has been composited ▷ *vb* ('kɒmpəˌzaɪt), **composites, compositing, composited** (*tr*) 9 to merge related motions from local branches (of a political party, trade union, etc) so as to produce a manageable number of proposals for discussion at national level [c16 from L *compositus* well arranged, from *compōnere* to arrange] > **'compositely** *adv* > **'compositeness** *n*

composite school *n E Canad* a secondary school offering both academic and nonacademic courses

composition (ˌkɒmpə'zɪʃən) *n* 1 the act of putting together or making up by combining parts 2 something formed in this manner; a mixture 3 the parts of which something is composed; constitution 4 a work of music, art, or literature 5 the harmonious arrangement of the parts of a work of art in relation to each other 6 a piece of writing undertaken as an academic exercise; an essay 7 *printing* the act or technique of setting up type 8 a settlement by mutual consent, esp a legal agreement whereby the creditors agree to accept partial payment of a debt in full settlement [c14 from OF, from L *compositus*; see COMPOSITE, -ION]

compositor (kəm'pɒzɪtə) *n printing* a person who sets and corrects type

compos mentis *Latin* ('kɒmpəs 'mɛntɪs) *adj* (*postpositive*) of sound mind; sane

compost ('kɒmpɒst) *n* 1 a mixture of organic residues such as decomposed vegetation, manure, etc, used as a fertilizer 2 a mixture, normally of plant remains, peat, charcoal, etc, in which plants are grown, esp in pots 3 *rare* a mixture ▷ *vb* (*tr*) 4 to make (vegetable matter) into compost 5 to fertilize with compost [c14 from OF *compost*, from L *compositus* put together]

Compostela (*Spanish* kɔmpɔs'tela) *n* See **Santiago de Compostela**

composure (kəm'pəʊʒə) *n* calmness, esp of the mind; tranquillity; serenity

compote ('kɒmpəʊt) *n* a dish of fruit stewed with sugar or in a syrup [c17 from F *composte*, from L *compositus* put in place]

compound[1] *n* ('kɒmpaʊnd) 1 a substance that contains atoms of two or more chemical elements held together by chemical bonds 2 any combination of two or more parts, aspects, etc 3 a word formed from two existing words or combining forms ▷ *vb* (kəm'paʊnd) (*mainly tr*) 4 to combine so as to create a compound 5 to make by combining parts, aspects, etc: *to compound a new plastic*

Cc

6 to intensify by an added element: *his anxiety was compounded by her crying* 7 (*also intr*) to come to an agreement in (a dispute, etc) or to settle (a debt, etc) for less than what is owed; compromise 8 *law* to agree not to prosecute in return for a consideration: *to compound a crime* ▷ *adj* ('kɒmpaʊnd) 9 composed of two or more parts, elements, etc 10 (of a word) consisting of elements that are also words or combining forms 11 *grammar* (of tense, mood, etc) formed by using an auxiliary verb in addition to the main verb 12 *music* 12a denoting a time in which the number of beats per bar is a multiple of three: *six-four is an example of compound time* 12b (of an interval) greater than an octave 13 (of a steam engine, etc) having multiple stages in which the steam or working fluid from one stage is used in a subsequent stage 14 (of a piston engine) having a supercharger powered by a turbine in the exhaust stream [C14 from earlier *compounen*, from OF *compondre* to set in order, from L *compōnere*] > **com'poundable** *adj*

compound² ('kɒmpaʊnd) *n* 1 (esp formerly in South Africa) an enclosure, esp on the mines, containing the living quarters for Black workers 2 any similar enclosure, such as a camp for prisoners of war [C17 from Malay *kampong* village]

compound eye *n* the convex eye of insects and some crustaceans, consisting of numerous separate light-sensitive units (ommatidia)

compound fraction *n* another name for **complex fraction**

compound fracture *n* a fracture in which the broken bone pierces the skin

compound interest *n* interest calculated on both the principal and its accrued interest

compound leaf *n* a leaf consisting of two or more leaflets borne on the same leafstalk

compound number *n* a quantity expressed in two or more different but related units: *3 hours 10 seconds is a compound number*

compound sentence *n* a sentence containing at least two coordinate clauses

compound time *n* See **compound¹** (sense 12)

comprehend (ˌkɒmprɪ'hɛnd) *vb* 1 to understand 2 (*tr*) to comprise; include [C14 from L *comprehendere*, from *prehendere* to seize]

comprehensible (ˌkɒmprɪ'hɛnsəbᵊl) *adj* capable of being comprehended > **ˌcompreˌhensi'bility** *n* > **ˌcompre'hensibly** *adv*

comprehension (ˌkɒmprɪ'hɛnʃən) *n* 1 the act or capacity of understanding 2 the state of including; comprehensiveness

comprehensive (ˌkɒmprɪ'hɛnsɪv) *adj* 1 of broad scope or content 2 (of a car insurance policy) providing protection against most risks, including third-party liability, fire, theft, and damage 3 of or being a comprehensive school ▷ *n* 4 short for **comprehensive school** > **ˌcompre'hensively** *adv* > **ˌcompre'hensiveness** *n*

comprehensive school *n chiefly Brit* a secondary school for children of all abilities from the same district

compress *vb* (*tr*) (kəm'prɛs) 1 to squeeze together; condense 2 to apply a compression program to (electronic data) so that it takes up less space ▷ *n* ('kɒmprɛs) 3 a cloth or gauze pad applied firmly to some part of the body to relieve discomfort, reduce fever, etc [C14 from LL *compressāre*, from L *comprimere*, from *premere* to press] > **com'pressible** *adj* > **com'pressive** *adj*

compressed air *n* air at a higher pressure than atmospheric pressure: used esp as a source of power for machines

compressibility (kəmˌprɛsɪ'bɪlɪtɪ) *n* 1 the ability to be compressed 2 *physics* the reciprocal of the bulk modulus; the ratio of volume strain to stress at constant temperature. Symbol: *k*

compression (kəm'prɛʃən) *n* 1 the act of compressing or the condition of being compressed 2 an increase in pressure of the charge in an engine or compressor obtained by reducing its volume

compressor (kəm'prɛsə) *n* 1 any device that compresses a gas 2 the part of a gas turbine that compresses the air before it enters the combustion chambers 3 any muscle that causes compression 4 an electronic device for reducing the variation in signal amplitude in a transmission system

comprise (kəm'praɪz) *vb* **comprises, comprising, comprised** (*tr*) 1 to be made up of 2 to constitute the whole of; consist of: *her singing comprised the entertainment* [C15 from F *compris* included, from *comprendre* to COMPREHEND] > **com'prisable** *adj*

> **USAGE** The use of *of* after *comprise* should be avoided: *the library comprises* (not *comprises of*) *500,000 books and manuscripts*

compromise ('kɒmprəˌmaɪz) *n* 1 settlement of a dispute by concessions on both or all sides 2 the terms of such a settlement 3 something midway between different things ▷ *vb* **compromises, compromising, compromised** 4 to settle (a dispute) by making concessions 5 (*tr*) to expose (oneself or another) to disrepute [C15 from OF *compromis*, from L, from *comprōmittere*, from *prōmittere* to promise] > **'comproˌmiser** *n* > **'comproˌmisingly** *adv*

compte rendu *French* (kɔ̃t rɑ̃dy) *n, pl* ***comptes rendus*** (kɔ̃t rɑ̃dy) 1 a review or notice 2 an account [lit.: account rendered]

Compton *n* 1 ('kɒmptən) **Arthur Holly** 1892–1962, US physicist, noted for his research on X-rays, gamma rays, and nuclear energy: Nobel prize for physics 1927 2 ('kʌmptən) **Denis** 1918–97, English cricketer, who played for Middlesex and England (1937–57); broke two records in 1947 scoring 3816 runs and 18 centuries in one season

Compton-Burnett ('kɒmptənbɜː'nɛt, -'bɜːnɪt) *n* Dame **Ivy** 1884–1969, English novelist. Her novels include *Men and Wives* (1931) and *Mother and Son* (1955)

comptroller (kən'trəʊlə) *n* a variant spelling of **controller** (sense 2), esp as a title of any of various financial executives

compulsion (kəm'pʌlʃən) *n* 1 the act of compelling or the state of being compelled 2 something that compels 3 *psychiatry* an inner drive that causes a person to perform actions, often repetitive, against his or her will. See also **obsession** [C15 from OF, from L *compellere* to COMPEL]

compulsive (kəm'pʌlsɪv) *adj* relating to or involving compulsion > **com'pulsively** *adv*

compulsory (kəm'pʌlsərɪ) *adj* 1 required by regulations or laws; obligatory 2 involving or employing compulsion; compelling; essential > **com'pulsorily** *adv* > **com'pulsoriness** *n*

compulsory purchase *n* purchase of a property by a local authority or government department for public use or development, regardless of whether or not the owner wishes to sell

compunction (kəm'pʌŋkʃən) *n* a feeling of remorse, guilt, or regret [C14 from Church L *compunctiō*, from L *compungere* to sting] > **com'punctious** *adj* > **com'punctiously** *adv*

computation (ˌkɒmpjʊ'teɪʃən) *n* a calculation involving numbers or quantities > **ˌcompu'tational** *adj*

compute (kəm'pjuːt) *vb* **computes, computing, computed** to calculate (an answer, result, etc), often with the aid of a computer [C17 from L *computāre*, from *putāre* to think] > **com'putable** *adj* > **comˌputa'bility** *n*

computed tomography *n med* another name (esp US) for **computerized tomography**

computer (kəm'pjuːtə) *n* 1a a device, usually electronic, that processes data according to a set of instructions. The **digital computer** stores data in discrete units and performs operations at very high speed. The **analog**

computer has no memory and is slower than the digital computer but has a continuous rather than a discrete input **1b** (*as modifier*): *computer technology* **2** a person who computes or calculates

computer-aided design *n* the use of computer techniques in designing products, esp involving the use of computer graphics. Abbrev: **CAD**

computer-aided engineering *n* the use of computers to automate manufacturing processes. Abbrev: **CAE**

computer architecture *n* the structure, behaviour, and design of computing

computerate (kəm'pjuːtərɪt) *adj* able to use computing [C20 COMPUTER + -ATE[1], by analogy with *literate*]

computer dating *n* the use of computers by dating agencies to match their clients

computer game *n* any of various games for use in a home computer, that are played by manipulating a mouse, joystick or the keys on the keyboard in response to the graphics on the screen

computer graphics *n* (*functioning as sing*) the use of a computer to produce and manipulate pictorial images on a video screen, as in animation techniques or the production of audiovisual aids

computerize *or* **computerise** (kəm'pjuːtəˌraɪz) *vb* **computerizes, computerizing, computerized** *or* **computerises, computerising, computerised** **1** (*tr*) to cause (certain operations) to be performed by a computer, esp as a replacement for human labour **2** (*intr*) to install a computer **3** (*tr*) to control or perform (operations) by means of a computer **4** (*tr*) to process or store (information) by or in a computer > **comˌputeri'zation** *or* **comˌputeri'sation** *n*

computerized tomography *n med* a radiological technique that produces images of cross sections through a patient's body. Also called (esp US): **computed tomography**. Abbrev: **CT** See also **CT scanner**

computer language *n* another term for **programming language**

computer science *n* the study of computers and their application

▷ http://foldoc.doc.ic.ac.uk/foldoc/index.html
▷ http://carbon.cudenver.edu/~hgreenbe/glossary/index.php
▷ www.eevl.ac.uk/computing/index.htm
▷ www.vlib.org/Computing.html

comrade ('kɒmreɪd, -rɪd) *n* **1** a companion **2** a fellow member of a political party, esp a fellow Communist [C16 from F *camarade*, from Sp. *camarada* group of soldiers sharing a billet, from *cámara* room, from L] > **'comradely** *adj* > **'comradeˌship** *n*

Comsat ('kɒmsæt) *n trademark* short for **communications satellite**

Comte (*French* kɔ̃t) *n* (**Isidore**) **Auguste** (**Marie François**) (ogyst) 1798–1857, French mathematician and philosopher; the founder of positivism

Comus ('kəʊməs) *n* (in late Roman mythology) a god of revelry [C17 from L, from Gk *kōmos* a revel]

con[1] (kɒn) *inf* ▷ *n* **1a** short for **confidence trick** **1b** (*as modifier*): *con man* ▷ *vb* **cons, conning, conned** **2** (*tr*) to swindle or defraud [C19 from CONFIDENCE]

con[2] (kɒn) *n* (*usually pl*) an argument or vote against a proposal, motion, etc. See also **pros and cons** [from L *contrā* against]

con[3] *or esp US* **conn** (kɒn) *vb* **cons** *or esp US* **conns, conning, conned** (*tr*) *naut* to direct the steering of (a vessel) [C17 *cun*, from earlier *condien* to guide, from OF *conduire*, from L *condūcere*; see CONDUCT]

con[4] (kɒn) *vb* **cons, conning, conned** (*tr*) *arch* to study attentively or learn [C15 var. of CAN[1] in the sense: to come to know]

con[5] (kɒn) *prep music* with [It.]

con- *prefix* a variant of **com-**

Conakry *or* **Konakri** (*French* kɔnakri) *n* the capital of Guinea, a port on the island of Tombo. Pop: 1 764 000 (1999 est)

▷ www.gn.refer.org

con amore (kɒn æ'mɔːrɪ) *adj, adv music* (to be performed) lovingly [C19 from It.: with love]

Conan Doyle ('kəʊnən 'dɔɪl, 'kɒnən) *n* Sir **Arthur** 1859–1930, British author of detective stories and historical romances and the creator of *Sherlock Holmes*

con brio (kɒn 'briːəʊ) *adj, adv music* (to be performed) with liveliness or spirit [It.: with energy]

concatenate (kɒn'kætɪˌneɪt) *vb* **concatenates, concatenating, concatenated** (*tr*) to link or join together, esp in a chain or series [C16 from LL *concatēnāre*, from L *com-* together + *catēna* CHAIN] > **ˌconcate'nation** *n*

concave ('kɒnkeɪv, kɒn'keɪv) *adj* **1** curving inwards; having the shape of a section of the interior of a sphere, paraboloid, etc: *a concave lens* ▷ *vb* **2** (*tr*) to make concave [C15 from L *concavus* arched, from *cavus* hollow] > **'concavely** *adv* > **'concaveness** *n*

concavity (kɒn'kævɪtɪ) *n, pl* **concavities** **1** the state of being concave **2** a concave surface or thing

concavo-concave (kɒnˌkeɪvəʊkɒn'keɪv) *adj* (esp of a lens) having both sides concave

concavo-convex *adj* **1** having one side concave and the other side convex **2** (of a lens) having a concave face with greater curvature than the convex face

conceal (kən'siːl) *vb* (*tr*) **1** to keep from discovery; hide **2** to keep secret [C14 from OF *conceler*, from L *concēlāre*, from *com-* (intensive) + *cēlāre* to hide] > **con'cealer** *n* > **con'cealment** *n*

concede (kən'siːd) *vb* **concedes, conceding, conceded** **1** (when *tr*, *may take a clause as object*) to admit or acknowledge (something) as true or correct **2** to yield or allow (something, such as a right) **3** (*tr*) to admit as certain in outcome: *to concede an election* [C17 from L *concēdere*, from *cēdere* to give way] > **con'ceder** *n*

conceit (kən'siːt) *n* **1** a high, often exaggerated, opinion of oneself or one's accomplishments **2** *literary* an elaborate image or far-fetched comparison **3** *arch* **3a** a witty expression **3b** fancy; imagination **3c** an idea ▷ *vb* (*tr*) **4** *obs* to think [C14 from CONCEIVE]

Cc

conceited (kən'siːtɪd) *adj* having an exaggerated opinion of oneself or one's accomplishments > **con'ceitedly** *adv* > **con'ceitedness** *n*

conceivable (kən'siːvəbᵊl) *adj* capable of being understood, believed, or imagined; possible > **conˌceiva'bility** *n* > **con'ceivably** *adv*

conceive (kən'siːv) *vb* **conceives, conceiving, conceived** **1** (when *intr*, foll by *of*; when *tr*, *often takes a clause as object*) to have an idea (of); imagine; think **2** (*tr; takes a clause as object or an infinitive*) to believe **3** (*tr*) to develop: *she conceived a passion for music* **4** to become pregnant with (a child) **5** (*tr*) *rare* to express in words [C13 from OF *conceivre*, from L *concipere* to take in, from *capere* to take]

concelebrate (kən'sɛlɪˌbreɪt) *vb* **concelebrates, concelebrating, concelebrated** *Christianity* to celebrate (the Eucharist or Mass) jointly with one or more other priests [C16 from L *concelebrāre*] > **conˌcele'bration** *n*

concentrate ('kɒnsənˌtreɪt) *vb* **concentrates, concentrating, concentrated** **1** to come or cause to come to a single purpose or aim: *to concentrate one's hopes on winning* **2** to make or become denser or purer by the removal of certain elements **3** (*intr;* often foll by *on*) to think intensely (about) ▷ *n* **4** a concentrated material or solution [C17 back formation from CONCENTRATION, ult. from L *com-* same + *centrum* CENTRE] > **'concenˌtrative** *adj* > **'concenˌtrator** *n*

concentration (ˌkɒnsən'treɪʃən) *n* **1** intense mental application **2** the act of concentrating; complete attention **3** something that is concentrated **4** the strength of a solution, esp the amount of dissolved substance in a given volume of solvent **5** *mil* **5a** the act of bringing together military forces **5b** the application

of fire from a number of weapons against a target
concentration camp *n* a guarded prison camp for nonmilitary prisoners, esp one in Nazi Germany
concentre *or US* **concenter** (kən'sɛntə) *vb* **concentres, concentring, concentred** *or US* **concenters, concentering, concentered** to converge or cause to converge on a common centre; concentrate [C16 from F *concentrer*]
concentric (kən'sɛntrɪk) *adj* having a common centre: *concentric circles* [C14 from Med. L *concentricus*, from L *com-* same + *centrum* CENTRE] > **con'centrically** *adv*
Concepción (*Spanish* konθep'θjon) *n* an industrial city in S central Chile. Pop: 362 589 (1999 est)
concept ('kɒnsɛpt) *n* **1** an idea, esp an abstract idea: *the concepts of biology* **2** *philosophy* a general idea that corresponds to some class of entities and consists of the essential features of the class **3** a new idea; invention **4** (*modifier*) (of a product, esp a car) created to demonstrate the technical skills and imagination of the designers, and not for mass production or sale [C16 from L *conceptum*, from *concipere* to CONCEIVE]
conception (kən'sɛpʃən) *n* **1** something conceived; notion, idea, or plan **2** the description under which someone considers something: *a strange conception of freedom* **3** the fertilization of an ovum by a sperm in the Fallopian tube followed by implantation in the womb **4** origin or beginning [C13 from L *conceptiō*, from *concipere* to CONCEIVE] > **con'ceptional** *or* **con'ceptive** *adj*
conceptual (kən'sɛptjʊəl) *adj* of or characterized by concepts > **con'ceptually** *adv*
conceptualize *or* **conceptualise** (kən'sɛptjʊə,laɪz) *vb* **conceptualizes, conceptualizing, conceptualized** *or* **conceptualises, conceptualising, conceptualised** to form (a concept or concepts) out of observations, experience, data, etc > **con,ceptuali'zation** *or* **con,ceptuali'sation** *n*
concern (kən'sɜːn) *vb* (*tr*) **1** to relate to; affect **2** (usually foll by *with* or *in*) to involve or interest (oneself): *he concerns himself with other people's affairs* ▷ *n* **3** something that affects a person; affair; business **4** regard or interest: *he felt a strong concern for her* **5** anxiety or solicitude **6** important relation: *his news has great concern for us* **7** a commercial company **8** *inf* a material thing, esp one of which one has a low opinion [C15 from LL *concernere*, from L *com-* together + *cernere* to sift]
concerned (kən'sɜːnd) *adj* **1** (*postpositive*) interested, guilty, or involved: *I shall find the boy concerned and punish him* **2** worried or solicitous > **concernedly** (kən'sɜːnɪdlɪ) *adv*
concerning (kən'sɜːnɪŋ) *prep* **1** about; regarding ▷ *adj* **2** worrying or troublesome
concernment (kən'sɜːnmənt) *n rare* affair or business; concern
concert *n* ('kɒnsɜːt) **1a** a performance of music by players or singers that does not involve theatrical staging **1b** (*as modifier*): *a concert version of an opera* **2** agreement in design, plan, or action **3 in concert 3a** acting with a common purpose **3b** (of musicians, etc) performing live ▷ *vb* (kən'sɜːt) **4** to arrange or contrive (a plan) by mutual agreement [C16 from F *concerter* to bring into agreement, from It., from LL *concertāre* to work together, from L *certāre* to contend]
concertante (,kɒntʃə'tæntɪ) *adj music* characterized by contrasting alternating tutti and solo passages [It.: from *concertare* to perform a CONCERT]
concerted (kən'sɜːtɪd) *adj* **1** mutually contrived, planned, or arranged; combined: *a concerted effort* **2** *music* arranged in parts for a group of singers or players
Concertgebouw (*Dutch* kɔn'sɛrtxəbɔu) *n* a concert hall in Amsterdam, inaugurated in 1888: the **Concertgebouw Orchestra** established in 1888, has been independent of the hall since World War II
concert grand *n* a grand piano of the largest size
concertina (,kɒnsə'tiːnə) *n* **1** a hexagonal musical instrument similar to the accordion, in which metallic reeds are vibrated by air from a set of bellows operated by the player's hands ▷ *vb* **concertinas, concertinaing, concertinaed 2** (*intr*) to collapse or fold up like the bellows of a concertina [C19 CONCERT + *-ina*] > **,concer'tinist** *n*
concertino (,kɒntʃə'tiːnəʊ) *n, pl* **concertini** (-nɪ) *music* **1** the solo group in a concerto grosso **2** a short concerto [It.: a little CONCERTO]
concertmaster ('kɒnsət,mɑːstə) *n* a US and Canad word for **leader** (of an orchestra)
concerto (kən'tʃɛətəʊ) *n, pl* **concertos** *or* **concerti** (-tɪ) a composition for an orchestra and one or more soloists [C18 from It.: CONCERT]
concerto grosso ('grɒsəʊ) *n, pl* **concerti grossi** ('grɒsɪ) *or* **concerto grossos** a composition for an orchestra and a group of soloists [It., lit.: big concerto]
concert party *n* **1** a musical entertainment popular in the early 20th century, esp one at a British seaside resort **2** *stock exchange inf* a group of individuals or companies who secretly agree together to purchase shares separately in a particular company which they plan to amalgamate later into a single holding: a malpractice which is illegal in some countries
concert pitch *n* **1** the frequency of 440 hertz assigned to the A above middle C **2** *inf* a state of extreme readiness
concession (kən'sɛʃən) *n* **1** the act of yielding or conceding **2** something conceded **3** *Brit* a reduction in the usual price of a ticket granted to a special group of customers: *a student concession* **4** any grant of rights, land, or property by a government, local authority, corporation, or individual **5** the right, esp an exclusive right, to market a particular product in a given area **6** *Canad* **6a** a land subdivision in a township survey **6b** another name for a **concession road** [C16 from L *concēssiō*, from *concēdere* to CONCEDE] > **con'cessible** *adj* > **con'cessive** *adj*
concessionaire (kən,sɛʃə'nɛə), **concessioner** (kən'sɛʃənə), *or* **concessionary** *n* someone who holds or operates a concession
concessionary (kən'sɛʃənərɪ) *adj* **1** of, granted, or obtained by a concession ▷ *n, pl* **concessionaries 2** another word for **concessionaire**
concession road *n Canad* one of a series of roads separating concessions in a township
conch (kɒŋk, kɒntʃ) *n, pl* **conchs** (kɒŋks) *or* **conches** ('kɒntʃɪz) **1** any of various tropical marine gastropod molluscs characterized by a large brightly coloured spiral shell **2** the shell of such a mollusc, used as a trumpet [C16 from L *concha*, from Gk *konkhē* shellfish]
conchie *or* **conchy** ('kɒntʃɪ) *n, pl* **conchies** *inf* short for **conscientious objector**
Conchobar ('kɒŋkəʊwə, 'kɒnʊə) *n* (in Irish legend) a king of Ulster at about the beginning of the Christian era. See also **Deirdre**
conchology (kɒŋ'kɒlədʒɪ) *n* the study of mollusc shells > **con'chologist** *n*
concierge (,kɒnsɪ'ɛəʒ) *n* (esp in France) a caretaker of a block of flats, hotel, etc, esp one who lives on the premises [C17 from F, ult. from L *conservus*, from *servus* slave]
conciliar (kən'sɪlɪə) *adj* of, from, or by means of a council, esp an ecclesiastical one
conciliate (kən'sɪlɪ,eɪt) *vb* **conciliates, conciliating, conciliated** (*tr*) **1** to overcome the hostility of; win over **2** to gain (favour, regard, etc), esp by making friendly overtures [C16 from L *conciliāre* to bring together, from *concilium* COUNCIL] > **con'ciliable** *adj* > **con'cili,ator** *n*
conciliation (kən,sɪlɪ'eɪʃən) *n* **1** the act or process of conciliating **2** a method of helping the parties in a dispute to reach agreement, esp divorcing or separating couples to part amicably

conciliatory (kənˈsɪljətərɪ) *or* **conciliative** (kənˈsɪljətɪv) *adj* intended to placate or reconcile > **conˈciliatorily** *adv*

concise (kənˈsaɪs) *adj* brief and to the point [c16 from L *concīsus* cut short, from *concīdere*, from *caedere* to cut, strike down] > **conˈcisely** *adv* > **conˈciseness** *or* **concision** (kənˈsɪʒən) *n*

conclave (ˈkɒnkleɪv) *n* **1** a secret meeting **2** *RC Church* **2a** the closed apartments where the college of cardinals elects a new pope **2b** a meeting of the college of cardinals for this purpose [c14 from Med. L *conclāve*, from L: place that may be locked, from *clāvis* key]

conclude (kənˈklu:d) *vb* **concludes, concluding, concluded** (*mainly tr*) **1** (*also intr*) to come or cause to come to an end **2** (*takes a clause as object*) to decide by reasoning; deduce: *the judge concluded that the witness had told the truth* **3** to settle: *to conclude a treaty* **4** *obs* to confine [c14 from L *conclūdere*, from *claudere* to close]

conclusion (kənˈklu:ʒən) *n* **1** end or termination **2** the last main division of a speech, essay, etc **3** outcome or result (esp in **a foregone conclusion**) **4** a final decision or judgment (esp in **come to a conclusion**) **5** *logic* **5a** a statement that purports to follow from another or others (the **premises**) by means of an argument **5b** a statement that does validly follow from given premises **6** *law* **6a** an admission or statement binding on the party making it; estoppel **6b** the close of a pleading or of a conveyance **7 in conclusion** lastly; to sum up **8 jump to conclusions** to come to a conclusion prematurely, without sufficient thought or on incomplete evidence [c14 via OF from L; see CONCLUDE, -ION]

conclusive (kənˈklu:sɪv) *adj* **1** putting an end to doubt; decisive; final **2** approaching or involving an end > **conˈclusively** *adv*

concoct (kənˈkɒkt) *vb* (*tr*) **1** to make by combining different ingredients **2** to invent; make up; contrive [c16 from L *concoctus* cooked together, from *coquere* to cook] > **conˈcocter** *or* **conˈcoctor** *n* > **conˈcoction** *n*

concomitance (kənˈkɒmɪtəns) *n* **1** existence together **2** *Christianity.* the doctrine that the body and blood of Christ are present in the Eucharist

concomitant (kənˈkɒmɪtənt) *adj* **1** existing or occurring together ▷ *n* **2** a concomitant act, person, etc [c17 from LL *concomitārī* to accompany, from *com-* with + *comes* companion]

concord (ˈkɒnkɔ:d) *n* **1** agreement or harmony **2** a treaty establishing peaceful relations between nations **3** *music* a combination of musical notes, esp one containing a series of consonant intervals **4** *grammar* another word for **agreement** (sense 6) [c13 from OF *concorde*, from L *concordia*, from *com-* same + *cor* heart]

Concord (ˈkɒŋkəd) *n* **1** a town in NE Massachusetts: scene of one of the opening military actions (1775) of the War of American Independence. Pop: 17 080 (1990) **2** a city in New Hampshire, the state capital: printing, publishing. Pop: 36 364 (1992)

concordance (kənˈkɔ:dᵊns) *n* **1** a state of harmony **2** a book that indexes the principal words in a literary work, often with the immediate context and an account of the meaning **3** an index produced by computer or machine

concordant (kənˈkɔ:dᵊnt) *adj* being in agreement; harmonious > **conˈcordantly** *adv*

concordat (kɒnˈkɔ:dæt) *n* a pact or treaty, esp one between the Vatican and another state concerning the interests of religion in that state [c17 via F, from Med. L *concordātum*, from L: something agreed; see CONCORD]

concourse (ˈkɒnkɔ:s) *n* **1** a crowd; throng **2** a coming together; confluence **3** a large open space for the gathering of people in a public place [c14 from OF *concours*, ult. from L *concurrere* to run together]

concrete (ˈkɒnkri:t) *n* **1** a construction material made of cement, sand, stone and water that hardens to a stonelike mass ▷ *adj* **2** relating to a particular instance; specific as opposed to general **3** relating to things capable of being perceived by the senses, as opposed to abstractions **4** formed by the coalescence of particles; condensed; solid ▷ *vb* **concretes, concreting, concreted** **5** (*tr*) to construct in or cover with concrete **6** (kənˈkri:t) to become or cause to become solid; coalesce [c14 from L *concrētus*, from *concrēscere* to grow together] > **ˈconcretely** *adv* > **ˈconcreteness** *n*

concrete music *n* music consisting of an electronically modified montage of tape-recorded sounds
▷ www.intuitivemusic.com/tguideconcrete.html

concrete noun *n* a noun that refers to a material object

concrete poetry *n* poetry in which the visual form of the poem is used to convey meaning

concretion (kənˈkri:ʃən) *n* **1** the act of growing together; coalescence **2** a solidified mass **3** something made real, tangible, or specific **4** a rounded or irregular mineral mass different in composition from the sedimentary rock that surrounds it **5** *pathol* another word for **calculus** > **conˈcretionary** *adj*

concretize *or* **concretise** (ˈkɒnkrɪˌtaɪz) *vb* **concretizes, concretizing, concretized** *or* **concretises, concretising, concretised** (*tr*) to render concrete; make real or specific

concubine (ˈkɒŋkjʊˌbaɪn, ˈkɒn-) *n* **1** (in polygamous societies) a secondary wife **2** a woman who cohabits with a man, esp (formerly) the mistress of a king, nobleman, etc [c13 from OF, from L *concubīna*, from *concumbere* to lie together] > **concubinage** (kɒnˈkju:bɪnɪdʒ) *n* > **conˈcubinary** *adj*

concupiscence (kənˈkju:pɪsəns) *n* strong desire, esp sexual desire [c14 from Church L *concupiscentia*, from L *concupiscere* to covet] > **conˈcupiscent** *adj*

concur (kənˈkɜ:) *vb* **concurs, concurring, concurred** (*intr*) **1** to agree; be in accord **2** to combine or cooperate **3** to occur simultaneously; coincide [c15 from L *concurrere* to run together]

concurrence (kənˈkʌrəns) *n* **1** the act of concurring **2** agreement; accord **3** cooperation or combination **4** simultaneous occurrence

concurrent (kənˈkʌrənt) *adj* **1** taking place at the same time or in the same location **2** cooperating **3** meeting at, approaching, or having a common point: *concurrent lines* **4** in agreement; harmonious > **conˈcurrently** *adv*

concurrent engineering *n* a method of designing and marketing new products in which development stages are run in parallel rather than in series, to reduce lead times and costs. Also called: **interactive engineering**

concurrent versions system *n computing* a system that allows more than one person to work on the same file at the same time, merging their changes but keeping records of the different versions

concuss (kənˈkʌs) *vb* (*tr*) **1** to injure (the brain) by a violent blow, fall, etc **2** to shake violently [c16 from L *concussus*, from *concutere* to disturb greatly, from *quatere* to shake]

concussion (kənˈkʌʃən) *n* **1** a jarring of the brain, caused by a blow or a fall, usually resulting in loss of consciousness **2** any violent shaking

Condé (*French* kɔ̃de) *n* **Prince de** (prɛ̃s də), title of *Louis II de Bourbon, Duc d'Enghien*, called *the Great Condé*. 1621–86, French general, who led Louis XIV's armies against the Fronde (1649) but joined the Fronde in a new revolt (1650–52). He later fought for both France and Spain

condemn (kənˈdɛm) *vb* (*tr*) **1** to express strong disapproval of **2** to pronounce judicial sentence on **3** to demonstrate the guilt of: *his secretive behaviour condemned him* **4** to judge or pronounce unfit for use **5** to force into a particular state: *his disposition condemned him to boredom* [c13 from OF *condempner*, from L *condemnāre*, from *damnāre* to condemn] > **condemnable** (kənˈdɛmnəbᵊl) *adj* > **ˌcondemˈnation** *n* > **condemnatory** (kənˈdɛmnətərɪ) *adj*

condensate (kənˈdɛnseɪt) *n* a substance formed by

Cc

condensation, such as a liquid from a vapour
condensation (ˌkɒndɛnˈseɪʃən) *n* **1** the act or process of condensing, or the state of being condensed **2** anything that has condensed from a vapour, esp on a window **3** *chem* a type of reaction in which two organic molecules combine to form a larger molecule as well as a simple molecule such as water, etc **4** an abridged version of a book > ˌ**condenˈsational** *adj*
condensation trail *n* another name for **vapour trail**
condense (kənˈdɛns) *vb* **condenses, condensing, condensed 1** (*tr*) to increase the density of; compress **2** to reduce or be reduced in volume or size **3** to change or cause to change from a gaseous to a liquid or solid state **4** *chem* to undergo or cause to undergo condensation [C15 from L *condēnsāre*, from *dēnsāre* to make thick, from *dēnsus* DENSE] > **conˈdensable** *or* **conˈdensible** *adj*
condensed matter *n physics* **a** crystalline and amorphous solids and liquids, including liquid crystals, glasses, polymers, and gels **b** (*as modifier*): *condensed-matter physics*
condensed milk *n* milk reduced by evaporation to a thick concentration, with sugar added
condenser (kənˈdɛnsə) *n* **1a** an apparatus for reducing gases to their liquid or solid form by the abstraction of heat **1b** a device for abstracting heat, as in a refrigeration unit **2** a lens that concentrates light **3** another name for **capacitor 4** a person or device that condenses
condescend (ˌkɒndɪˈsɛnd) *vb* (*intr*) **1** to act graciously towards another or others regarded as being on a lower level; behave patronizingly **2** to do something that one regards as below one's dignity [C14 from Church L *condēscendere*, from L *dēscendere* to DESCEND] > ˌ**condeˈscending** *adj* > ˌ**condeˈscendingly** *adv* > ˌ**condeˈscension** *n*
condign (kənˈdaɪn) *adj* (esp of a punishment) fitting; deserved [C15 from OF *condigne*, from L *condignus*, from *dignus* worthy] > **conˈdignly** *adv*
condiment (ˈkɒndɪmənt) *n* any spice or sauce such as salt, pepper, mustard, etc [C15 from L *condīmentum* seasoning, from *condīre* to pickle]
condition (kənˈdɪʃən) *n* **1** a particular state of being or existence: *the human condition* **2** something that limits or restricts; a qualification **3** (*pl*) circumstances: *conditions were right for a takeover* **4** state of physical fitness, esp good health: *out of condition* **5** an ailment: *a heart condition* **6** something indispensable: *your happiness is a condition of mine* **7** something required as part of an agreement; term: *the conditions of the lease are set out* **8** *law* **8a** a provision in a will, contract, etc, that makes some right or liability contingent upon the happening of some event **8b** the event itself **9** *logic* a statement whose truth is either required for the truth of a given statement (a **necessary condition**) or sufficient to guarantee the truth of the given statement (a **sufficient condition**) **10** rank, status, or position **11 on condition that** (*conj*) provided that ▷ *vb* (*mainly tr*) **12** *psychol* **12a** to alter the response of (a person or animal) to a particular stimulus or situation **12b** to establish a conditioned response in **13** to put into a fit condition **14** to improve the condition of (one's hair) by use of special cosmetics **15** to accustom or inure **16** to subject to a condition [C14 from L *conditiō*, from *condīcere* to discuss, from *con-* together + *dīcere* to say] > **conˈditioner** *n* > **conˈditioning** *n, adj*
conditional (kənˈdɪʃənᵊl) *adj* **1** depending on other factors **2** *grammar* expressing a condition on which something else is contingent: *"If he comes" is a conditional clause in the sentence "If he comes I shall go"* **3** *logic* Also called: **hypothetical** (of a proposition) consisting of two component propositions associated by the words *if...then* so that the proposition is false only when the antecedent is true and the consequent false ▷ *n* **4** a conditional verb form, clause, sentence, etc > **conˌditionˈality** *n* > **conˈditionally** *adv*
conditional access *n* the distortion of television programme transmissions so that only authorized subscribers with suitable decoding apparatus may have access to them
conditioned response *n psychol* a response that is transferred from the second to the first of a pair of stimuli. A well-known Pavlovian example is salivation by a dog when it hears a bell ring, because food has always been presented when the bell has been rung previously. Also called (esp formerly): **conditioned reflex**
condo (ˈkɒndəʊ) *n, pl* **condos** *US & Canad inf* a condominium building or apartment
condole (kənˈdəʊl) *vb* **condoles, condoling, condoled** (*intr;* foll by *with*) to express sympathy with someone in grief, pain, etc [C16 from Church L *condolēre*, from L *com-* together + *dolēre* to grieve]
condolence (kənˈdəʊləns) *or* **condolement** *n* (*often plural*) an expression of sympathy with someone in grief, etc
condom (ˈkɒndɒm, ˈkɒndəm) *n* a rubber sheath worn on the penis or in the vagina during sexual intercourse to prevent conception or infection [C18 from ?]
condominium (ˌkɒndəˈmɪnɪəm) *n, pl* **condominiums 1** joint rule or sovereignty **2** a country ruled by two or more foreign powers **3** *US & Canad* **3a** an apartment building in which each apartment is individually owned and the common areas are jointly owned **3b** an apartment in such a building. Sometimes shortened to **condo** [C18 from NL, from L *com-* together + *dominium* ownership]
condone (kənˈdəʊn) *vb* **condones, condoning, condoned** (*tr*) **1** to overlook or forgive (an offence, etc) **2** *law* (esp of a spouse) to pardon or overlook (an offence, usually adultery) [C19 from L *condōnāre*, from *com-* (intensive) + *dōnāre* to donate] > **condonation** (ˌkɒndəʊˈneɪʃən) *n* > **conˈdoner** *n*
condor (ˈkɒndɔː) *n* either of two very large rare New World vultures, the **Andean condor**, which has black plumage with white around the neck, and the **California condor**, which is nearly extinct [C17 from Sp. *cóndor*, from Quechuan *kuntur*]
condottiere (ˌkɒndɒˈtjɛərɪ) *n, pl* **condottieri** (-riː) a commander or soldier in a professional mercenary company in Europe from the 13th to the 16th centuries [C18 from It., from *condotto* leadership, from *condurre* to lead, from L *condūcere*]
conduce (kənˈdjuːs) *vb* **conduces, conducing, conduced** (*intr;* foll by *to*) to lead or contribute (to a result) [C15 from L *condūcere*, from *com-* together + *dūcere* to lead]
conducive (kənˈdjuːsɪv) *adj* (when *postpositive*, foll by *to*) contributing, leading, or tending
conduct *n* (ˈkɒndʌkt) **1** behaviour **2** the way of managing a business, affair, etc; handling **3** *rare* the act of leading ▷ *vb* (kənˈdʌkt) **4** (*tr*) to accompany and guide (people, a party, etc) (esp in **conducted tour**) **5** (*tr*) to direct (affairs, business, etc); control **6** (*tr*) to carry out; organize: *conduct a survey* **7** (*tr*) to behave (oneself) **8** to control (an orchestra, etc) by the movements of the hands or a baton **9** to transmit (heat, electricity, etc) [C15 from Med. L *conductus* escorted, from L, from *condūcere* to CONDUCE] > **conˈductible** *adj* > **conˌductiˈbility** *n*
conductance (kənˈdʌktəns) *n* the ability of a system to conduct electricity, measured by the ratio of the current flowing through the system to the potential difference across it. Symbol: G
conducting tissue *n bot* another name for **vascular tissue**
conduction (kənˈdʌkʃən) *n* **1** the transfer of energy by a medium without bulk movement of the medium itself

▷ Cf **convection** (sense 1) **2** the transmission of an impulse along a nerve fibre **3** the act of conveying or conducting, as through a pipe **4** *physics* another name for **conductivity** (sense 1) > **con'ductional** *adj*

conductive (kən'dʌktɪv) *adj* of, denoting, or having the property of conduction

conductive education *n* an educational system, developed in Hungary, in which teachers (**conductors**) teach children and adults with motor disorders to function independently, by guiding them to attain their own goals in their own way

▷ www.conductive-education.org.uk

conductivity (ˌkɒndʌk'tɪvɪtɪ) *n, pl* **conductivities 1** the property of transmitting heat, electricity, or sound **2** a measure of the ability of a substance to conduct electricity. Symbol: κ

conductivity water *n* water that has a conductivity of less than 0.043×10^{-6} S cm^{-1}

conductor (kən'dʌktə) *n* **1** an official on a bus who collects fares **2** a person who conducts an orchestra, choir, etc **3** a person who leads or guides **4** *US & Canad* a railway official in charge of a train **5** a substance, body, or system that conducts electricity, heat, etc **6** See **lightning conductor** > **con'ductorship** *n* > **conductress** (kən'dʌktrɪs) *fem n*

conduit ('kɒndɪt, -djʊɪt) *n* **1** a pipe or channel for carrying a fluid **2** a rigid tube for carrying electrical cables **3** an agency or means of access, communication, etc [C14 from OF, from Med. L *conductus* channel, from L *condūcere* to lead]

condyle ('kɒndɪl) *n* the rounded projection on the articulating end of a bone [C17 from L *condylus*, from Gk *kondulos*] > **'condylar** *adj*

cone (kəʊn) *n* **1** a geometric solid consisting of a plane base bounded by a closed curve, usually a circle or an ellipse, every point of which is joined to a fixed point lying outside the plane of the base **2** anything that tapers from a circular section to a point, such as a wafer shell used to contain ice cream **3a** the reproductive body of conifers and related plants, made up of overlapping scales **3b** a similar structure in horsetails, club mosses, etc **4** a small cone used as a temporary traffic marker on roads **5** any one of the cone-shaped cells in the retina of the eye, sensitive to colour and bright light ▷ *vb* **cones, coning, coned 6** (*tr*) to shape like a cone [C16 from L *cōnus*, from Gk *kōnus* pine cone, geometrical cone]

cone off *vb* (*tr, adv*) *Brit* to close (one carriageway of a motorway) by placing warning cones across it

coney ('kəʊnɪ) *n* a variant spelling of **cony**

Coney Island ('kəʊnɪ) *n* an island off the S shore of Long Island, New York: site of a large amusement park

confab ('kɒnfæb) *inf* ▷ *n* **1** a conversation ▷ *vb* **confabs, confabbing, confabbed 2** (*intr*) to converse

confabulate (kən'fæbjʊˌleɪt) *vb* **confabulates, confabulating, confabulated** (*intr*) **1** to talk together; chat **2** *psychiatry* to replace the gaps left by a disorder of the memory with imaginary remembered experiences consistently believed to be true [C17 from L *confābulārī*, from *fābulārī* to talk, from *fābula* a story] > **conˌfabu'lation** *n*

confect (kən'fɛkt) *vb* (*tr*) **1** to prepare by combining ingredients **2** to make; construct [C16 from L *confectus* prepared, from *conficere*, from *com-* (intensive) + *facere* to make]

confection (kən'fɛkʃən) *n* **1** the act of compounding or mixing **2** any sweet preparation, such as a preserve or a sweet **3** *old-fashioned* an elaborate article of clothing, esp for women [C14 from OF, from L *confectiō* a preparing, from *conficere*; see CONFECT]

confectioner (kən'fɛkʃənə) *n* a person who makes or sells sweets or confections

confectionery (kən'fɛkʃənərɪ) *n, pl* **confectioneries 1** sweets and other confections collectively **2** the art or business of a confectioner

confederacy (kən'fɛdərəsɪ) *n, pl* **confederacies 1** a union of states, etc; alliance; league **2** a combination of groups or individuals for unlawful purposes [C14 from OF *confederacie*, from LL *confoederātiō* agreement] > **con'federal** *adj*

Confederacy (kən'fɛdərəsɪ, -'fɛdrəsɪ) *n* **the** another name for the **Confederate States of America**

confederate *n* (kən'fɛdərɪt) **1** a nation, state, or individual that is part of a confederacy **2** someone who is part of a conspiracy ▷ *adj* (kən'fɛdərɪt) **3** united; allied ▷ *vb* (kən'fɛdəˌreɪt), **confederates, confederating, confederated 4** to form into or become part of a confederacy [C14 from LL *confoederātus*, from *confoederāre* to unite by a league]

Confederate (kən'fɛdərɪt) *adj* **1** of or supporting the Confederate States of America ▷ *n* **2** a supporter of the Confederate States

Confederate States of America *pl n US History*. the 11 Southern states (Alabama, Arkansas, Florida, Georgia, North Carolina, South Carolina, Texas, Virginia, Tennessee, Louisiana, and Mississippi) that seceded from the Union in 1861, precipitating a civil war with the North. The Confederacy was defeated in 1865 and the South reincorporated into the US

confederation (kənˌfɛdə'reɪʃən) *n* **1** the act of confederating or the state of being confederated **2** a loose alliance of political units **3** (esp in Canada) another name for a **federation** > **conˌfeder'ationist** *n*

Confederation (kənˌfɛdə'reɪʃən) *n* **1 the** *US history* the original 13 states of the United States of America constituted under the Articles of Confederation and superseded by the more formal union established in 1789 **2** the federation of Canada, formed with four original provinces in 1867 and since joined by eight more

confer (kən'fɜː) *vb* **confers, conferring, conferred 1** (*tr*; foll by *on* or *upon*) to grant or bestow (an honour, gift, etc) **2** (*intr*) to consult together [C16 from L *conferre*, from *com-* together + *ferre* to bring] > **con'ferment** *or* **con'ferral** *n* > **con'ferrable** *adj*

conferee *or* **conferree** (ˌkɒnfɜː'riː) *n* **1** a person who takes part in a conference **2** a person on whom an honour or gift is conferred

conference ('kɒnfərəns) *n* **1** a meeting for consultation or discussion, esp one with a formal agenda **2** an assembly of the clergy or of clergy and laity of any of certain Protestant Churches acting as representatives of their denomination **3** *sport, US & Canad* a league or division of clubs or teams [C16 from Med. L *conferentia*, from L *conferre* to bring together] > **conferential** (ˌkɒnfə'rɛnʃəl) *adj*

conference call *n* a special telephone facility by which three or more people using conventional or cellular phones can be linked up to speak to one another

conferencing ('kɒnfərənsɪŋ) *n* the practice of holding a conference, esp by means of a telephone service. See **conference call**

confess (kən'fɛs) *vb* (when *tr*, *may take a clause as object*) **1** (when *intr*, often foll by *to*) to make an admission (of faults, crimes, etc) **2** (*tr*) to admit to be true; concede **3** *Christianity* to declare (one's sins) to God or to a priest as his representative, so as to obtain pardon and absolution [C14 from OF *confesser*, from LL, from L *confessus* confessed, from *confitērī* to admit]

confessedly (kən'fɛsɪdlɪ) *adv* (*sentence modifier*) by admission or confession; avowedly

confession (kən'fɛʃən) *n* **1** the act of confessing **2** something confessed **3** an acknowledgment, esp of one's faults or crimes **4** *Christianity* the act of a penitent accusing himself of his sins **5** **confession of faith** a formal public avowal of religious beliefs **6** a religious

Cc

sect united by common beliefs > **con'fessionary** *adj*
confessional (kən'fɛʃənᵊl) *adj* **1** of or suited to a confession ▷ *n* **2** *Christianity* a small stall where a priest hears confessions
confessor (kən'fɛsə) *n* **1** *Christianity* a priest who hears confessions and sometimes acts as a spiritual counsellor **2** *history* a person who bears witness to the Christian religious faith by the holiness of his or her life, but does not suffer martyrdom **3** a person who makes a confession
confetti (kən'fɛtɪ) *n* small pieces of coloured paper thrown on festive occasions, esp at weddings [C19 from It., pl of *confetto*, orig., a bonbon]
confidant *or (fem)* **confidante** (ˌkɒnfɪ'dænt, 'kɒnfɪˌdænt) *n* a person to whom private matters are confided [C17 from F *confident*, from It. *confidente*, n. use of adj: trustworthy]
confide (kən'faɪd) *vb* **confides, confiding, confided** **1** (usually foll by *in*; when *tr*, *may take a clause as object*) to disclose (secret or personal matters) in confidence (to) **2** (*intr*; foll by *in*) to have complete trust **3** (*tr*) to entrust into another's keeping [C15 from L *confīdere*, from *fīdere* to trust] > **con'fider** *n*
confidence ('kɒnfɪdəns) *n* **1** trust in a person or thing **2** belief in one's own abilities; self-assurance **3** trust or a trustful relationship: *take me into your confidence* **4** something confided; secret **5 in confidence** as a secret
confidence trick *or US & Canad* **confidence game** *n* a swindle involving money in which the victim's trust is won by the swindler
confident ('kɒnfɪdənt) *adj* **1** (*postpositive*; foll by *of*) having or showing certainty; sure: *confident of success* **2** sure of oneself **3** presumptuous [C16 from L *confīdens*, from *confīdere* to have complete trust in] > **'confidently** *adv*
confidential (ˌkɒnfɪ'dɛnʃəl) *adj* **1** spoken or given in confidence; private **2** entrusted with another's secret affairs: *a confidential secretary* **3** suggestive of intimacy: *a confidential approach* > **ˌconfiˌdenti'ality** *n* > **ˌconfi'dentially** *adv*
confiding (kən'faɪdɪŋ) *adj* unsuspicious; trustful > **con'fidingly** *adv* > **con'fidingness** *n*
configuration (kənˌfɪgjʊ'reɪʃən) *n* **1** the arrangement of the parts of something **2** the external form or outline achieved by such an arrangement **3** *psychol* the unit or pattern in perception studied by Gestalt psychologists [C16 from LL *configūrātiō*, from *configūrāre* to model on something, from *figūrāre* to shape, fashion] > **conˌfigu'rational** *or* **con'figurative** *adj*
configure (ˌkən'fɪgə) *vb (tr)* **1** to arrange or organize **2** *computing* to set up (a piece of hardware or software) as required
confine *vb* (kən'faɪn), **confines, confining, confined** (*tr*) **1** to keep within bounds; limit; restrict **2** to restrict the free movement of: *arthritis confined him to bed* ▷ *n* ('kɒnfaɪn) **3** (*often pl*) a limit; boundary [C16 from Med. L *confīnāre*, from L *confīnis* adjacent, from *fīnis* boundary] > **con'finer** *n*
confined (kən'faɪnd) *adj* **1** enclosed; limited **2** in childbed; undergoing childbirth
confinement (kən'faɪnmənt) *n* **1** the act of confining or the state of being confined **2** the period of the birth of a child
confirm (kən'fɜːm) *vb (tr)* **1** (*may take a clause as object*) to prove to be true or valid; corroborate **2** (*may take a clause as object*) to assert for a further time, so as to make more definite: *he confirmed that he would appear in court* **3** to strengthen: *his story confirmed my doubts* **4** to make valid by a formal act; ratify **5** to administer the rite of confirmation to [C13 from OF *confermer*, from L *confirmāre*, from *firmus* FIRM[1]] > **con'firmatory** *or* **con'firmative** *adj*
confirmation (ˌkɒnfə'meɪʃən) *n* **1** the act of confirming **2** something that confirms **3** a rite in several Christian churches that confirms a baptized person in his faith and admits him to full participation in the church
confirmed (kən'fɜːmd) *adj* **1** (*prenominal*) long-established in a habit, way of life, etc **2** having received the rite of confirmation
confiscate ('kɒnfɪˌskeɪt) *vb* **confiscates, confiscating, confiscated** (*tr*) **1** to seize (property), esp for public use and esp by way of a penalty ▷ *adj* **2** confiscated; forfeit [C16 from L *confiscāre* to seize for the public treasury, from *fiscus* treasury] > **ˌconfis'cation** *n* > **'confisˌcator** *n* > **confiscatory** (kən'fɪskətərɪ) *adj*
Confiteor (kən'fɪtɪˌɔː) *n* *RC Church* a prayer consisting of a general confession of sinfulness and an entreaty for forgiveness [C13 from L: I confess]
conflagration (ˌkɒnflə'greɪʃən) *n* a large destructive fire [C16 from L *conflagrātiō*, from *conflagrāre*, from *com-* (intensive) + *flagrāre* to burn]
conflate (kən'fleɪt) *vb* **conflates, conflating, conflated** (*tr*) to combine or blend (two things, esp two versions of a text) so as to form a whole [C16 from L *conflāre* to blow together, from *flāre* to blow] > **con'flation** *n*
conflict *n* ('kɒnflɪkt) **1** a struggle between opposing forces; battle **2** opposition between ideas, interests, etc; controversy **3** *psychol* opposition between two simultaneous but incompatible wishes or drives, sometimes leading to emotional tension ▷ *vb* (kən'flɪkt) (*intr*) **4** to come into opposition; clash **5** to fight [C15 from L *conflictus*, from *confligere* to combat, from *flīgere* to strike] > **con'flicting** *adj* > **con'flictingly** *adv* > **con'fliction** *n*
confluence ('kɒnflʊəns) *or* **conflux** ('kɒnflʌks) *n* **1** a flowing together, esp of rivers **2** a gathering > **'confluent** *adj*
conform (kən'fɔːm) *vb* **1** (*intr*; usually foll by *to*) to comply in actions, behaviour, etc, with accepted standards **2** (*intr*; usually foll by *with*) to be in accordance: *he conforms with my idea of a teacher* **3** to make or become similar **4** (*intr*) to comply with the practices of an established church, esp the Church of England [C14 from OF *conformer*, from L *confirmāre* to strengthen, from *firmāre* to make firm] > **con'former** *n* > **con'formist** *n, adj*
conformable (kən'fɔːməbᵊl) *adj* **1** corresponding in character; similar **2** obedient; submissive **3** (foll by *to*) consistent (with) **4** (of rock strata) lying in a parallel arrangement so that their original relative positions have remained undisturbed > **conˌforma'bility** *n* > **con'formably** *adv*
conformal (kən'fɔːməl) *adj* (of a map projection) maintaining true shape over a small area and scale in every direction [C17 from LL *conformālis*, from L *com-* same + *forma* shape]
conformation (ˌkɒnfɔː'meɪʃən) *n* **1** the general shape of an object; configuration **2** the arrangement of the parts of an object **3** *chem* the three-dimensional arrangement of the atoms in a molecule
conformity (kən'fɔːmɪtɪ) *or* **conformance** *n, pl* **conformities** *or* **conformances** **1** compliance in actions, behaviour, etc, with certain accepted standards **2** likeness; congruity; agreement **3** compliance with the practices of an established church
confound (kən'faʊnd) *vb (tr)* **1** to astound; bewilder **2** to confuse **3** to treat mistakenly as similar to or identical with **4** (kɒn'faʊnd) to curse (usually in **confound it!**) **5** to contradict or refute (an argument, etc) **6** to rout or defeat (an enemy) [C13 from OF *confondre*, from L *confundere* to mingle, pour together] > **con'founder** *n*
confounded (kən'faʊndɪd) *adj* **1** bewildered; confused **2** (*prenominal*) *inf* execrable; damned > **con'foundedly** *adv*
confraternity (ˌkɒnfrə'tɜːnɪtɪ) *n, pl* **confraternities** a group of men united for some particular purpose, esp Christian laymen organized for religious or charitable service; brotherhood [C15 from Med. L *confrāternitās*, ult. from L *frāter* brother]
confrère ('kɒnfrɛə) *n* a fellow member of a profession,

etc [c15 from OF, from Med. L *confrāter*]

confront (kən'frʌnt) *vb* (*tr*) **1** (usually foll by *with*) to present (with something), esp in order to accuse or criticize **2** to face boldly; oppose in hostility **3** to be face to face with [c16 from Med. L *confrontārī*, from *frons* forehead] > **confrontation** (ˌkɒnfrʌn'teɪʃən) *n* > ˌ**confron'tational** *adj*

Confucian (kən'fjuːʃən) *adj* **1** of or relating to the doctrines of Confucius: *Confucian philosophy* ▷ *n* **2** a follower of Confucius

Confucianism (kən'fjuːʃəˌnɪzəm) *n* the ethical system of Confucius, emphasizing moral order, the virtue of China's ancient rules, and gentlemanly education > **Con'fucianist** *n*

Confucius (kən'fjuːʃəs) *n* Chinese name *Kong Zi* or *K'ung Fu-tse*. 551–479 BC, Chinese philosopher and teacher of ethics (see **Confucianism**). His doctrines were compiled after his death under the title *The Analects of Confucius*

confuse (kən'fjuːz) *vb* **confuses, confusing, confused** (*tr*) **1** to bewilder; perplex **2** to mix up (things, ideas, etc) **3** to make unclear: *he confused his talk with irrelevant details* **4** to mistake (one thing) for another **5** to disconcert; embarrass **6** to cause to become disordered: *the enemy ranks were confused by gas* [c18 back formation from *confused*, from L *confūsus*, from *confundere* to pour together] > **con'fusable** *adj* > **confusedly** (kən'fjuːzɪdlɪ, -'fjuːzd-) *adv* > **con'fusing** *adj* > **con'fusingly** *adv*

confusion (kən'fjuːʒən) *n* **1** the act of confusing or the state of being confused **2** disorder **3** bewilderment; perplexity **4** lack of clarity **5** embarrassment; abashment

confute (kən'fjuːt) *vb* **confutes, confuting, confuted** (*tr*) to prove (a person or thing) wrong, invalid, or mistaken; disprove [c16 from L *confūtāre* to check, silence] > **con'futable** *adj* > **confutation** (ˌkɒnfjʊ'teɪʃən) *n*

conga ('kɒŋgə) *n* **1** a Latin American dance of three steps and a kick to each bar, performed by a number of people in single file **2** Also called: **conga drum** a large tubular bass drum played with the hands ▷ *vb* **congas, congaing, congaed 3** (*intr*) to perform this dance [c20 from American Sp., fem of *congo* belonging to the *Congo*]

congé ('kɒnʒeɪ) *n* **1** permission to depart or dismissal, esp when formal **2** a farewell [c16 from OF *congié*, from L *commeātus* leave of absence, from *meāre* to go]

congeal (kən'dʒiːl) *vb* **1** to change or cause to change from a soft or fluid state to a firm state **2** to form or cause to form into a coagulated mass; jell [c14 from OF *congeler*, from L *congelāre*, from *com-* together + *gelāre* to freeze] > **con'gealable** *adj* > **con'gealment** *n*

congelation (ˌkɒndʒɪ'leɪʃən) *n* **1** the process of congealing **2** something formed by this process

congener (kən'dʒiːnə, 'kɒndʒɪnə) *n* a member of a class, group, or other category, esp any animal of a specified genus [c18 from L, from *com-* same + *genus* kind]

congenial (kən'dʒiːnjəl) *adj* **1** friendly, pleasant, or agreeable: *a congenial atmosphere to work in* **2** having a similar disposition, tastes, etc; compatible [c17 from CON- (same) + GENIAL[1]] > **congeniality** (kənˌdʒiːnɪ'ælɪtɪ) *n*

congenital (kən'dʒɛnɪtᵊl) *adj* **1** denoting any nonhereditary condition, esp an abnormal condition, existing at birth: *congenital blindness* **2** *inf* complete, as if from birth: *a congenital idiot* [c18 from L *congenitus*, from *genitus* born, from *gignere* to bear] > **con'genitally** *adv*

conger ('kɒŋgə) *n* a large marine eel occurring in temperate and tropical coastal waters [c14 from OF *congre*, from L *conger*, from Gk *gongros*]

congeries (kɒn'dʒɪəriːz) *n* (*functioning as sing or pl*) a collection; mass; heap [c17 from L, from *congerere* to pile up, from *gerere* to carry]

congest (kən'dʒɛst) *vb* **1** to crowd or become crowded to excess; overfill **2** to clog (an organ) with blood or (of an organ) to become clogged with blood **3** (*tr; usually passive*) to block (the nose) with mucus [c16 from L *congestus*, from *congerere*; see CONGERIES]

congestion (kən'dʒɛstʃən) *n* **1** the state of being overcrowded, esp with traffic or people **2** the state of being overloaded or clogged with blood **3** the state of being blocked with mucus

congestion charging *n* the practice of charging motorists for the right to drive on busy roads, esp at busy times > **congestion charge** *n*

conglomerate *n* (kən'glɒmərɪt) **1** a thing composed of heterogeneous elements **2** any coarse-grained sedimentary rock consisting of rounded fragments of rock embedded in a finer matrix **3** a large corporation consisting of a group of companies dealing in widely diversified goods, services, etc ▷ *vb* (kən'glɒməˌreɪt), **conglomerates, conglomerating, conglomerated 4** to form into a mass ▷ *adj* (kən'glɒmərɪt) **5** made up of heterogeneous elements **6** (of sedimentary rocks) consisting of rounded fragments within a finer matrix [c16 from L *conglomerāre* to roll up, from *glomerāre* to wind into a ball, from *glomus* ball of thread] > **conˌglomer'ation** *n*

Congo ('kɒŋgəʊ) *n* **1 Democratic Republic of** a republic in S central Africa, with a narrow strip of land along the Congo estuary leading to the Atlantic in the west: Congo Free State established in 1885, with Leopold II of Belgium as absolute monarch; became the Belgian Congo colony in 1908; gained independence in 1960, followed by civil war and the secession of Katanga (until 1963); President Mobutu Sese Seko seized power in 1965; declared a one-party state in 1978, and was overthrown by rebels in 1997. The country consists chiefly of the Congo basin, with large areas of dense tropical forest and marshes, and the Mitumba highlands reaching over 5000 m (16 000 ft) in the east. Official language: French. Religion: Christian majority, animist minority. Currency: Congolese franc. Capital: Kinshasa. Pop: 53 625 000 (2001 est). Area: 2 344 116 sq km (905 063 sq miles). Former names: **Congo Free State** (1885–1908), **Belgian Congo** (1908–60), **Congo-Kinshasa** (1960–71), **Zaïre** (1971–97) **2 Republic of** a former name (1960–99) of Congo-Brazzaville **3** the second longest river in Africa, rising as the Lualaba on the Katanga plateau in the Democratic Republic of Congo and flowing in a wide northerly curve to the Atlantic: forms the border between Congo-Brazzaville and the Democratic Republic of Congo Length: about 4800 km (3000 miles). Area of basin: about 3 000 000 sq km (1 425 000 sq miles). Former Zaïrese name (1971–97): **Zaïre 4** a variant spelling of **Kongo** (the people and language)

▷ www.rdcongo.org

Congo-Brazzaville *n* a republic in W Central Africa: formerly the French colony of Middle Congo, part of French Equatorial Africa, it became independent in 1960; consists mostly of equatorial forest, with savanna and extensive swamps; drained chiefly by the Rivers Congo and Ubangi. Official language: French. Religion: Christian majority. Currency: franc. Capital: Brazzaville. Pop: 2 894 000 (2001 est). Area: 342 000 sq km (132 018 sq miles). Former names: **Middle Congo** (until 1958), **Republic of Congo** (1960–99)

▷ www.congo-site.cg

Congo Free State *n* a former name (1885–1908) of (**Democratic Republic of**) **Congo** (sense 2)

Congolese (ˌkɒŋgə'liːz) *adj* **1** of or relating to the People's Republic of the Congo or the Democratic Republic of the Congo or their inhabitants ▷ *n* **2** a native or inhabitant of the People's Republic of the Congo or the Democratic Republic of the Congo

congrats (kən'græts) *pl n, sentence substitute* informal shortened form of **congratulations**

congratulate (kən'grætjʊˌleɪt) *vb* **congratulates, congratulating, congratulated** (*tr*) **1** (usually foll by *on*)

Cc

to communicate pleasure, approval, or praise to; compliment **2** (often foll by *on*) to consider (oneself) clever or fortunate (as a result of): *she congratulated herself on her tact* **3** *obs* to greet; salute [C16 from L *congrātulārī*, from *grātulārī* to rejoice, from *grātus* pleasing] > **con,gratu'lation** *n* > **con'gratulatory** *or* **con'gratulative** *adj*

congratulations (kən,grætjʊ'leɪʃənz) *pl n, sentence substitute* expressions of pleasure or joy on another's success, good fortune, etc

congregate ('kɒŋgrɪ,geɪt) *vb* **congregates, congregating, congregated** to collect together in a body or crowd; assemble [C15 from L *congregāre* to collect into a flock, from *grex* flock]

congregation (,kɒŋgrɪ'geɪʃən) *n* **1** a group of persons gathered for worship, prayer, etc, esp in a church **2** the act of congregating together **3** a group collected together; assemblage **4** the group of persons habitually attending a given church, chapel, etc **5** *RC Church* **5a** a society of persons who follow a common rule of life but who are bound only by simple vows **5b** an administrative subdivision of the papal curia **6** *chiefly Brit* an assembly of senior members of a university

congregational (,kɒŋgrɪ'geɪʃənᵊl) *adj* **1** of or relating to a congregation **2** (*usually cap*) of or denoting Congregationalism

Congregationalism (,kɒŋgrɪ'geɪʃənə,lɪzəm) *n* a system of Christian doctrines and ecclesiastical government in which each congregation is self-governing > **,Congre'gationalist** *adj, n*
▷ http://wikipedia.org/wiki/Congregationalism

congress ('kɒŋgrɛs) *n* **1** a meeting or conference, esp of representatives of sovereign states **2** a national legislative assembly **3** a society or association [C16 from L *congressus*, from *congredī*, from *com-* together + *gradī* to walk]

Congress ('kɒŋgrɛs) *n* **1** the bicameral federal legislature of the US, consisting of the House of Representatives and the Senate **2** Also called: **Congress Party** (in India) a major political party > **Con'gressional** *adj*

congressional (kən'grɛʃənᵊl) *adj* of or relating to a congress > **con'gressionalist** *n*

Congressman ('kɒŋgrɛsmən) *or* (*fem*) **Congresswoman** *n, pl* **Congressmen** *or* **Congresswomen** (in the US) a member of Congress, esp of the House of Representatives

Congreve ('kɒŋgriːv) *n* **William** 1670–1729, English dramatist, a major exponent of Restoration comedy; author of *Love for Love* (1695) and *The Way of the World* (1700)

congruence ('kɒŋgrʊəns) *or* **congruency** *n* **1** the quality or state of corresponding, agreeing, or being congruent **2** *maths* the relationship between two integers, *x* and *y*, such that their difference, with respect to another integer called the modulus, *n*, is a multiple of the modulus

congruent ('kɒŋgrʊənt) *adj* **1** agreeing; corresponding **2** having identical shapes so that all parts correspond: *congruent triangles* **3** of or concerning two integers related by a congruence [C15 from L *congruere* to agree]

congruous ('kɒŋgrʊəs) *adj* **1** corresponding or agreeing **2** appropriate [C16 from L *congruus*; see CONGRUENT] > **congruity** (kən'gruːɪtɪ) *n*

conic ('kɒnɪk) *adj also* **conical 1a** having the shape of a cone **1b** of a cone ▷ *n* **2** another name for **conic section** > **'conically** *adv*

conics ('kɒnɪks) *n* (*functioning as sing*) the geometry of the parabola, ellipse, and hyperbola

conic section *n* one of a group of curves formed by the intersection of a plane and a right circular cone. It is either a circle, ellipse, parabola, or hyperbola

conidium (kəʊ'nɪdɪəm) *n, pl* **conidia** (-'nɪdɪə) an asexual spore formed at the tip of a specialized hypha in fungi such as *Penicillium* [C19 from NL, from Gk *konis* dust + -IUM]

conifer ('kəʊnɪfə, 'kɒn-) *n* any tree or shrub of the phylum *Coniferophyta*, typically bearing cones and evergreen leaves. The group includes the pines, spruces, firs, larches, etc [C19 from L, from *cōnus* CONE + *ferre* to bear] > **co'niferous** *adj*

Coniston Water ('kɒnɪstən) *n* a lake in NW England, in Cumbria: scene of the establishment of world water speed records by Sir Malcolm Campbell (1939) and his son Donald Campbell (1959). Length: 8 km (5 miles)

conj. *abbrev for* conjugation

conjectural (kən'dʒɛktʃərəl) *adj* involving or inclined to conjecture > **con'jecturally** *adv*

conjecture (kən'dʒɛktʃə) *n* **1** the formation of conclusions from incomplete evidence; guess **2** the conclusion so formed ▷ *vb* **conjectures, conjecturing, conjectured 3** to infer or arrive at (an opinion, conclusion, etc) from incomplete evidence [C14 from L *conjectūra*, from *conjicere* to throw together, from *jacere* to throw] > **con'jecturable** *adj*

conjoin (kən'dʒɔɪn) *vb* to join or become joined [C14 from OF *conjoindre*, from L *conjungere*, from *jungere* to JOIN] > **con'joiner** *n*

conjoined twins *pl n* twin babies joined together at some point, such as the hips. Also called (not in technical usage): **Siamese twins**

conjoint (kən'dʒɔɪnt) *adj* united, joint, or associated > **con'jointly** *adv*

conjugal ('kɒndʒʊgᵊl) *adj* of or relating to marriage or the relationship between husband and wife: *conjugal rights* [C16 from L *conjugālis*, from *conjunx* wife or husband] > **conjugality** (,kɒndʒʊ'gælɪtɪ) *n* > **'conjugally** *adv*

conjugate *vb* ('kɒndʒʊ,geɪt), **conjugates, conjugating, conjugated 1** (*tr*) *grammar* to state or set out the conjugation of (a verb) **2** (*intr*) (of a verb) to undergo inflection according to a specific set of rules **3** (*intr*) *biol* to undergo conjugation **4** (*tr*) *obs* to join together, esp in marriage ▷ *adj* ('kɒndʒʊgɪt, -,geɪt) **5** joined together in pairs **6** *maths* **6a** (of two angles) having a sum of 360° **6b** (of two complex numbers) differing only in the sign of the imaginary part as $4 + 3i$ and $4 - 3i$ **7** *chem* of the state of equilibrium in which two liquids can exist as separate phases that are both solutions **8** *chem* (of acids and bases) related by loss or gain of a proton **9** (of a compound leaf) having one pair of leaflets **10** (of words) cognate; related in origin ▷ *n* ('kɒndʒʊgɪt) **11** one of a pair or set of conjugate substances, values, quantities, words, etc [C15 from L *conjugāre*, from *com-* together + *jugāre* to connect, from *jugum* a yoke] > **'conju,gative** *adj* > **'conju,gator** *n*

conjugation (,kɒndʒʊ'geɪʃən) *n* **1** *grammar* **1a** inflection of a verb for person, number, tense, voice, mood, etc **1b** the complete set of the inflections of a given verb **2** a joining **3** a type of sexual reproduction in ciliate protozoans involving the temporary union of two individuals and the subsequent migration and fusion of the gametic nuclei **4** (in bacteria) the direct transfer of DNA between two cells that are temporarily joined **5** the union of gametes, as in some fungi **6** the pairing of chromosomes in the early phase of a meiotic division **7** *chem* the existence of alternating double or triple bonds in a chemical compound, with consequent electron delocalization over part of the molecule > **,conju'gational** *adj*

conjunct ('kɒndʒʌŋkt, kən'dʒʌŋkt) *n logic* one of the propositions or formulas in a conjunction

conjunction (kən'dʒʌŋkʃən) *n* **1** the act of joining together; union **2** simultaneous occurrence of events; coincidence **3** any word or group of words, other than a relative pronoun, that connects words, phrases, or clauses; for example *and* and *while* **4** *astron* **4a** the position of a planet when it is in line with the sun as seen from the earth **4b** the apparent proximity or coincidence of two celestial bodies on the celestial sphere **5** *logic* **5a** the operator that forms a compound sentence from two given sentences, and corresponds to the English *and* **5b** a sentence so formed: it is true only when both the component sentences are true **5c** the relation between such sentences > **con'junctional** *adj*

conjunctiva (ˌkɒndʒʌŋk'taɪvə) *n, pl* **conjunctivas** *or* **conjunctivae** (-viː) the delicate mucous membrane that covers the eyeball and the under surface of the eyelid [C16 from NL *membrāna conjunctīva* the conjunctive membrane] > ˌ**conjunc'tival** *adj*

conjunctive (kən'dʒʌŋktɪv) *adj* **1** joining; connective **2** joined **3** of or relating to conjunctions ▷ *n* **4** a less common word for **conjunction** (sense 3) [C15 from LL *conjunctīvus*, from L *conjungere* to CONJOIN]

conjunctivitis (kənˌdʒʌŋktɪ'vaɪtɪs) *n* inflammation of the conjunctiva

conjuncture (kən'dʒʌŋktʃə) *n* a combination of events, esp a critical one

conjuration (ˌkɒndʒʊ'reɪʃən) *n* **1** a magic spell; incantation **2** a less common word for **conjuring 3** *arch* supplication; entreaty

conjure ('kʌndʒə) *vb* **conjures, conjuring, conjured 1** (*intr*) to practise conjuring **2** (*intr*) to call upon supposed supernatural forces by spells and incantations **3** (kən'dʒʊə) (*tr*) to appeal earnestly to: *I conjure you to help me* **4 a name to conjure with 4a** a person thought to have great power or influence **4b** any name that excites the imagination [C13 from OF *conjurer* to plot, from L *conjūrāre* to swear together]

conjure up *vb* (*tr, adv*) **1** to present to the mind; evoke or imagine: *he conjured up a picture of his childhood* **2** to call up or command (a spirit or devil) by an incantation

conjuring ('kʌndʒərɪŋ) *n* **1** the performance of tricks that appear to defy natural laws ▷ *adj* **2** denoting or of such tricks or entertainment

conjuror *or* **conjurer** ('kʌndʒərə) *n* **1** a person who practises conjuring, esp for people's entertainment **2** a sorcerer

conk (kɒŋk) *sl* ▷ *vb* **1** to strike (someone) a blow, esp on the head or nose ▷ *n* **2** a punch or blow, esp on the head or nose **3** the head or nose [C19 prob. changed from CONCH]

conker ('kɒŋkə) *n* an informal name for the **horse chestnut** (sense 2)

conkers ('kɒŋkəz) *n* (*functioning as sing*) *Brit* a game in which a player swings a horse chestnut (conker), threaded onto a string, against that of another player to try to break it [C19 from dialect *conker* snail shell, orig. used in the game]

conk out *vb* (*intr, adv*) *Inf* **1** (of machines, cars, etc) to fail suddenly **2** to tire suddenly or collapse [C20 from ?]

con man *n inf* a person who swindles another by means of a confidence trick. More formal term: **confidence man**

con moto (kɒn 'məʊtəʊ) *adj, adv music* (to be performed) in a brisk or lively manner [It., lit.: with movement]

conn (kɒn) *vb, n* a variant spelling (esp US) of **con³**

Conn (kɒn) *n* 2nd century AD, king of Leinster and high king of Ireland

Conn. *abbrev for* Connecticut

Connacht ('kɒnət) *n* a province and ancient kingdom of NW Republic of Ireland: consists of the counties of Galway, Leitrim, Mayo, Roscommon, and Sligo. Pop: 433 231 (1996). Area: 17 122 sq km (6611 sq miles). Former name: **Connaught**

connate ('kɒneɪt) *adj* **1** existing from birth; congenital or innate **2** allied in nature or origin **3** *biol* (of similar parts or organs) closely joined or united by growth **4** *geol* (of fluids) produced at the same time as the rocks surrounding them; *connate water* [C17 from LL *connātus* born at the same time]

connect (kə'nɛkt) *vb* **1** to link or be linked **2** (*tr*) to associate: *I connect him with my childhood* **3** (*tr*) to establish telephone communications with or between **4** (*intr*) to be meaningful or meaningfully related **5** (*intr*) (of two public vehicles, such as trains or buses) to have the arrival of one timed to occur just before the departure of the other, for the convenient transfer of passengers **6** (*intr*) *inf* to hit, punch, kick, etc, solidly [C17 from L *connectere* to bind together, from *nectere* to tie] > **con'nectible** *or* **con'nectable** *adj* > **con'nector** *or* **con'necter** *n*

Connecticut (kə'nɛtɪkət) *n* **1** a state of the northeastern US, in New England. Capital: Hartford Pop: 3 405 565 (1997 est). Area: 12 973 sq km (5009 sq miles). Abbreviations: **Conn.** or (with zip code) **CT 2** a river in the northeastern US, rising in N New Hampshire and flowing south to Long Island Sound. Length: 651 km (407 miles)

connecting rod *n* **1** a rod or bar for transmitting motion, esp one that connects a rotating part to a reciprocating part **2** such a rod that connects the piston to the crankshaft in an internal-combustion engine or reciprocating pump

connection *or* **connexion** (kə'nɛkʃən) *n* **1** the act of connecting; union **2** something that connects or relates; link or bond **3** a relationship or association **4** logical sequence in thought or expression; coherence **5** the relation of a word or phrase to its context: *in this connection the word has no political significance* **6** (*often pl*) an acquaintance, esp one who is influential **7** a relative, esp if distant and related by marriage **8a** an opportunity to transfer from one train, bus, etc, to another **8b** the vehicle scheduled to provide such an opportunity **9** a link, usually a wire or metallic strip, between two components in an electric circuit **10** a communications link, esp by telephone **11** *sl* a supplier of illegal drugs, such as heroin **12** *rare* sexual intercourse > **con'nectional** *or* **con'nexional** *adj*

Cc

connective (kə'nɛktɪv) *adj* **1** connecting ▷ *n* **2** a thing that connects **3** *grammar, logic* **3a** any word that connects phrases, clauses, or individual words **3b** a symbol used in a formal language in the construction of compound sentences, corresponding to terms such as *or*, *and*, etc, in ordinary speech **4** *bot* the tissue of a stamen that connects the two lobes of the anther

connective tissue *n* an animal tissue that supports organs, fills the spaces between them, and forms tendons and ligaments

connectivity (ˌkɒnɛk'tɪvɪtɪ) *n* **1** the state of being or being able to be connected **2** *computing* the state of being connected to the Internet **3** *computing* the capacity of a machine or appliance to be connected to other machines, appliances, or facilities

Connell ('kɒnəl) *n* **Desmond** born 1926, Irish cardinal; Archbishop of Dublin and primate of Ireland from 1988

Connemara (ˌkɒnɪ'mɑːrə) *n* a barren coastal region of W Republic of Ireland, in Co. Galway: consists of quartzite mountains, peat bogs, and many lakes; noted for its breed of pony originating from the hilly regions

Connery ('kɒnərɪ) *n* Sir **Sean,** real name *Thomas Connery*. born 1929, Scottish film actor, who played James Bond in such films as *Goldfinger* (1964). His later films include *The Name of the Rose* (1986), *Indiana Jones and the Last Crusade* (1989), and *Finding Forrester* (2000)

conning tower ('kɒnɪŋ) *n* **1** a superstructure of a submarine, used as the bridge when the vessel is on the surface **2** the armoured pilot house of a warship [C19 see CON³]

connivance (kə'naɪvəns) *n* **1** the act or fact of conniving **2** *law* the tacit encouragement of or assent to another's wrongdoing

connive (kə'naɪv) *vb* **connives, conniving, connived** (*intr*) **1** to plot together; conspire **2** (foll by *at*) *law* to give assent or encouragement (to the commission of a wrong) [c17 from F *conniver*, from L *connīvēre* to blink, hence, leave uncensured] > **con'niver** *n*

connoisseur (ˌkɒnɪˈsɜː) *n* a person with special knowledge or appreciation of a field, esp in the arts [c18 from F, from OF *conoiseor*, from *connoistre* to know, from L *cognōscere*] > **ˌconnois'seurship** *n*

Connolly (ˈkɒnəlɪ) *n* **1 Billy** born 1942, Scottish comedian **2 Cyril (Vernon)** 1903–74, British critic and writer, founder and editor of *Horizon* (1939–50): his books include *Enemies of Promise* (1938) **3 James** 1868–1916, Irish labour leader: executed by the British for his part in the Easter Rising (1916)

connotation (ˌkɒnəˈteɪʃən) *n* **1** an association or idea suggested by a word or phrase **2** the act of connoting **3** *logic* the characteristic or set of characteristics that determines to which object the common name properly applies. In traditional logic synonymous with **intension** > **connotative** (ˈkɒnəˌteɪtɪv, kəˈnəʊtə-) *or* **con'notive** *adj*

connote (kɒˈnəʊt) *vb* **connotes, connoting, connoted** (*tr; often takes a clause as object*) **1** (of a word, phrase, etc) to imply or suggest (associations or ideas) other than the literal meaning: *the word "maiden" connotes modesty* **2** to involve as a consequence or condition [c17 from Med. L *connotāre*, from L *notāre* to mark, note, from *nota* sign, note]

connubial (kəˈnjuːbɪəl) *adj* of or relating to marriage: *connubial bliss* [c17 from L *cōnūbiālis*, from *cōnūbium* marriage] > **conˌnubi'ality** *n*

conoid (ˈkəʊnɔɪd) *n* **1** a cone-shaped object ▷ *adj also* **conoidal** (kəʊˈnɔɪdᵊl) **2** cone-shaped [c17 from Gk *kōnoeidēs*, from *kōnos* CONE] > **co'noidally** *adv*

conquer (ˈkɒŋkə) *vb* **1** to overcome (an enemy, army, etc); defeat **2** to overcome (an obstacle, desire, etc); surmount **3** (*tr*) to gain possession or control of as by force or war; win [c13 from OF *conquerre*, from Vulgar L *conquērere* (unattested) to obtain, from L *conquīrere* to search for, from *quaerere* to seek] > **'conquerable** *adj* > **'conquering** *adj* > **'conqueror** *n*

Conqueror (ˈkɒŋkərə) *n* **William the** See **William I**

conquest (ˈkɒnkwɛst) *n* **1** the act of conquering or the state of having been conquered; victory **2** a person, thing, etc, that has been conquered **3** a person, whose compliance, love, etc, has been won [c13 from OF *conqueste*, from Vulgar L *conquēsta* (unattested), from L *conquīsīta*, fem. p.p. of *conquīrere*; see CONQUER]

Conquest (ˈkɒnkwɛst) *n* **the** See **Norman Conquest**

conquistador (kɒnˈkwɪstəˌdɔː) *n, pl* **conquistadors** *or* **conquistadores** (kɒnˌkwɪstəˈdɔːrɛs) an adventurer or conqueror, esp one of the Spanish conquerors of the New World in the 16th century [c19 from Sp., from *conquistar* to conquer]

▷ www.bbc.co.uk/history/discovery/exploration/conquistadors

▷ www.incaconquest.com

Conrad (ˈkɒnræd) *n* **Joseph** real name *Teodor Josef Konrad Korzeniowski*. 1857–1924, British novelist born in Poland, noted for sea stories such as *The Nigger of the Narcissus* (1897) and *Lord Jim* (1900) and novels of politics and revolution such as *Nostromo* (1904) and *Under Western Eyes* (1911)

Cons. *abbrev for* Conservative

consanguinity (ˌkɒnsæŋˈgwɪnɪtɪ) *n* **1** relationship by blood; kinship **2** close affinity or connection [c14 see CON-, SANGUINE] > **ˌconsan'guineous** *or* **con'sanguine** *adj*

conscience (ˈkɒnʃəns) *n* **1** the sense of right and wrong that governs a person's thoughts and actions **2** conscientiousness; diligence **3** a feeling of guilt or anxiety: *he has a conscience about his unkind action* **4 in (all) conscience 4a** with regard to truth and justice **4b** certainly **5 on one's conscience** causing feelings of guilt or remorse [c13 from OF, from L *conscientia* knowledge, from *conscīre* to know; see CONSCIOUS]

conscience clause *n* a clause in a law or contract exempting persons with moral scruples

conscience money *n* money paid voluntarily to compensate for dishonesty, esp for taxes formerly evaded

conscience-stricken *adj* feeling anxious or guilty. Also: **conscience-smitten**

conscientious (ˌkɒnʃɪˈɛnʃəs) *adj* **1** involving or taking great care; painstaking **2** governed by or done according to conscience > **ˌconsci'entiously** *adv* > **ˌconsci'entiousness** *n*

conscientious objector *n* a person who refuses to serve in the armed forces on the grounds of conscience

conscious (ˈkɒnʃəs) *adj* **1** alert and awake **2** aware of one's surroundings, one's own motivations and thoughts, etc **3a** aware (of) and giving value and emphasis (to a particular fact): *I am conscious of your great kindness to me* **3b** (*in combination*): *clothes-conscious* **4** deliberate or intended: *a conscious effort; conscious rudeness* **5a** denoting a part of the human mind that is aware of a person's self, environment, and mental activity and that to a certain extent determines his choices of action **5b** (*as n*): *the conscious is only a small part of the mind* [c17 from L *conscius* sharing knowledge, from *com-* with + *scīre* to know] > **'consciously** *adv* > **'consciousness** *n*

consciousness raising *n* **a** the process of developing awareness in a person or group of a situation regarded as wrong or unjust, with the aim of producing active participation in changing it **b** (*as modifier*): *a consciousness-raising group*

conscript *n* (ˈkɒnskrɪpt) **1a** a person who is enrolled for compulsory military service **1b** (*as modifier*): *a conscript army* ▷ *vb* (kənˈskrɪpt) **2** (*tr*) to enrol (youths, civilians, etc) for compulsory military service [c15 from L *conscrīptus*, p.p. of *conscrībere* to enrol, from *scrībere* to write]

conscription (kənˈskrɪpʃən) *n* compulsory military service

consecrate (ˈkɒnsɪˌkreɪt) *vb* **consecrates, consecrating, consecrated** (*tr*) **1** to make or declare sacred or holy **2** to dedicate (one's life, time, etc) to a specific purpose **3** *Christianity* to sanctify (bread and wine) for the Eucharist to be received as the body and blood of Christ **4** to cause to be respected or revered: *time has consecrated this custom* [c15 from L *consecrāre*, from *com-* (intensive) + *sacrāre* to devote, from *sacer* sacred] > **ˌconse'cration** *n* > **'conseˌcrator** *n* > **'conseˌcratory** *adj*

Consecration (ˌkɒnsɪˈkreɪʃən) *n* *RC Church* the part of the Mass after the sermon during which the bread and wine are believed to change into the Body and Blood of Christ

consecutive (kənˈsɛkjʊtɪv) *adj* **1** (of a narrative, account, etc) following chronological sequence **2** following one another without interruption; successive **3** characterized by logical sequence **4** *grammar* expressing consequence or result: *consecutive clauses* **5** *music* another word for **parallel** (sense 3) [c17 from F *consécutif*, from L *consecūtus*, from *consequī* to pursue] > **con'secutively** *adv* > **con'secutiveness** *n*

consensual (kənˈsɛnsjʊəl) *adj* **1** *law* (of a contract, etc) existing by consent **2** (of reflex actions of the body) responding to stimulation of another part > **con'sensually** *adv*

consensus (kənˈsɛnsəs) *n* general or widespread agreement (esp in **consensus of opinion**) [c19 from L, from *consentīre*; see CONSENT]

> USAGE Given the word's original meaning, namely referring to a collective opinion, some purists would argue that the phrase *consensus of opinion* is tautological and should therefore be avoided. Nevertheless, it is an extremely common use of the word, and is unlikely to jar with the majority of speakers

consent (kən'sɛnt) *vb* **1** to give assent or permission; agree ▷ *n* **2** acquiescence to or acceptance of something done or planned by another **3** harmony in opinion; agreement (esp in **with one consent**) [C13 from OF *consentir*, from L *consentīre* to agree, from *sentīre* to feel] > **con'senting** *adj*

consequence ('kɒnsɪkwəns) *n* **1** a result or effect **2** an unpleasant result (esp in **take the consequences**) **3** an inference reached by reasoning; conclusion **4** significance or importance: *it's of no consequence; a man of consequence* **5** **in consequence** as a result

consequent ('kɒnsɪkwənt) *adj* **1** following as an effect **2** following as a logical conclusion **3** (of a river) flowing in the direction of the original slope of the land ▷ *n* **4** something that follows something else, esp as a result **5** *logic* the resultant clause in a conditional sentence [C15 from L *consequēns* following closely, from *consequī* to pursue]

consequential (ˌkɒnsɪ'kwɛnʃəl) *adj* **1** important or significant **2** self-important **3** following as a consequence, esp indirectly: *consequential loss* > ˌ**conseˌquenti'ality** *n* > ˌ**conse'quentially** *adv*

consequently ('kɒnsɪkwəntlɪ) *adv, sentence connector.* as a result or effect; therefore; hence

conservancy (kən'sɜːvənsɪ) *n, pl* **conservancies** **1** (in Britain) a court or commission with jurisdiction over a river, port, area of countryside, etc **2** another word for **conservation** (sense 2)

conservation (ˌkɒnsə'veɪʃən) *n* **1** the act of conserving or keeping from change, loss, injury, etc **2a** protection, preservation, and careful management of natural resources **2b** (*as modifier*): *a conservation area* **3** *physics, etc* the preservation of a specified aspect or value of a system, as in **conservation of charge, conservation of momentum, conservation of parity** > ˌ**conser'vational** *adj* > ˌ**conser'vationist** *n*

conservation grade *adj* relating to food produced using traditional methods where possible, and following strict specifications regarding animal feeds and welfare, the use of chemical fertilizers, wildlife conservation, and land management

conservation of energy *n* the principle that the total energy of any isolated system is constant and independent of any changes occurring within the system

conservation of mass *n* the principle that the total mass of any isolated system is constant and is independent of any chemical and physical changes taking place within the system

conservatism (kən'sɜːvəˌtɪzəm) *n* **1** opposition to change and innovation **2** a political philosophy advocating the preservation of the best of the established order in society

conservative (kən'sɜːvətɪv) *adj* **1** favouring the preservation of established customs, values, etc, and opposing innovation **2** of conservatism **3** moderate or cautious: *a conservative estimate* **4** conventional in style: *a conservative suit* **5** *med* (of treatment) designed to alleviate symptoms. Cf **radical** (sense 4) ▷ *n* **6** a person who is reluctant to change or consider new ideas; conformist **7** a supporter of conservatism > **con'servatively** *adv* > **con'servativeness** *n*

Conservative (kən'sɜːvətɪv) ▷ *adj* **1** (in Britain and elsewhere) of, supporting, or relating to a Conservative Party **2** (in Canada) of, supporting, or relating to the Progressive Conservative Party **3** of, relating to, or characterizing Conservative Judaism ▷ *n* **4** a supporter or member of a Conservative Party, or, (in Canada) of the Progressive Conservative Party

Conservative Judaism *n* a movement rejecting extreme change and advocating moderate relaxations of traditional Jewish law

Conservative Party *n* **1** (in Britain) the major right-wing party, which developed from the Tories in the 1830s. It encourages property owning and free enterprise **2** (in Canada) short for Progressive Conservative Party **3** (in other countries) any of various political parties generally opposing change

conservatoire (kən'sɜːvəˌtwɑː) *n* an institution or school for instruction in music. Also called: **conservatory** [C18 from F: CONSERVATORY]

conservator ('kɒnsəˌveɪtə, kən'sɜːvə-) *n* a custodian, guardian, or protector

conservatorium (kənˌsɜːvə'tɔːrɪəm) *n Austral* the usual term for **conservatoire**

conservatory (kən'sɜːvətrɪ) *n, pl* **conservatories** **1** a greenhouse, esp one attached to a house **2** another word for **conservatoire**

conserve *vb* (kən'sɜːv), **conserves, conserving, conserved** (*tr*) **1** to keep or protect from harm, decay, loss, etc **2** to preserve (a foodstuff, esp fruit) with sugar ▷ *n* ('kɒnsɜːv, kən'sɜːv) **3** a preparation similar to jam but usually containing whole pieces of fruit [(vb) C14 from L *conservāre* to keep safe, from *servāre* to save; (n) C14 from Med. L *conserva*, from L *conservāre*]

consider (kən'sɪdə) *vb* (*mainly tr*) **1** (*also intr*) to think carefully about (a problem, decision, etc) **2** (*may take a clause as object*) to judge; deem: *I consider him a fool* **3** to have regard for: *consider your mother's feelings* **4** to look at: *he considered her face* **5** (*may take a clause as object*) to bear in mind: *when buying a car consider this make* **6** to describe or discuss [C14 from L *consīderāre* to inspect closely]

considerable (kən'sɪdərəbᵊl) *adj* **1** large enough to reckon with: *a considerable quantity* **2** a lot of; much: *he had considerable courage* **3** worthy of respect: *a considerable man in the scientific world* > **con'siderably** *adv*

considerate (kən'sɪdərɪt) *adj* **1** thoughtful towards other people; kind **2** *rare* carefully thought out; considered > **con'siderately** *adv*

consideration (kənˌsɪdə'reɪʃən) *n* **1** deliberation; contemplation **2** **take into consideration** to bear in mind; consider **3** **under consideration** being currently discussed **4** a fact to be taken into account when making a judgment or decision **5** thoughtfulness for other people; kindness **6** payment for a service **7** thought resulting from deliberation; opinion **8** *law* the promise, object, etc, given by one party to persuade another to enter into a contract **9** esteem **10** **in consideration of** **10a** because of **10b** in return for

considered (kən'sɪdəd) *adj* **1** presented or thought out with care: *a considered opinion* **2** (*qualified by a preceding adverb*) esteemed: *highly considered*

considering (kən'sɪdərɪŋ) *prep* **1** in view of ▷ *adv* **2** *inf* all in all; taking into account the circumstances: *it's not bad considering* ▷ *conj* **3** (*subordinating*) in view of the fact that

consign (kən'saɪn) *vb* (*mainly tr*) **1** to give into the care or charge of; entrust **2** to commit irrevocably: *he consigned the papers to the flames* **3** to commit: *to consign someone to jail* **4** to address or deliver (goods): *it was consigned to his London address* [C15 from OF *consigner*, from L *consignāre* to put one's seal to, sign, from *signum* mark] > **con'signable** *adj* > ˌ**consign'ee** *n* > **con'signor** *or* **con'signer** *n*

consignment (kən'saɪnmənt) *n* **1** the act of consigning; commitment **2** a shipment of goods consigned **3** **on consignment** for payment by the consignee after sale

consist (kən'sɪst) *vb* (*intr*) **1** (foll by *of* or *in*) to be composed (of) **2** (foll by *in* or *of*) to have its existence (in): *his religion consists only in going to church* **3** to be consistent; accord [C16 from L *consistere* to stand firm, from *sistere* to stand]

consistency (kən'sɪstənsɪ) *or* **consistence** *n, pl* **consistencies** *or* **consistences** **1** agreement or accordance **2** degree of viscosity or firmness **3** the state or quality of holding or sticking together and retaining shape **4** conformity with previous attitudes, behaviour, practice, etc

Cc

consistent (kənˈsɪstənt) *adj* **1** (usually foll by *with*) showing consistency or harmony **2** steady; even: *consistent growth* **3** *logic* (of a logical system) constituted so that the propositions deduced from different axioms of the system do not contradict each other > **conˈsistently** *adv*

consistory (kənˈsɪstərɪ) *n, pl* **consistories 1** *Church of England* the court of a diocese (other than Canterbury) administering ecclesiastical law **2** *RC Church* an assembly of the cardinals and the pope **3** (in certain Reformed Churches) the governing body of a local congregation **4** *arch* a council [c14 from OF, from Med. L *consistōrium* ecclesiastical tribunal, ult. from L *consistere* to stand still] > **consistorial** (ˌkɒnsɪˈstɔːrɪəl) *adj*

consolation (ˌkɒnsəˈleɪʃən) *n* **1** the act of consoling or state of being consoled **2** a person or thing that is a comfort in a time of grief, disappointment, etc > **consolatory** (kənˈsɒlətərɪ) *adj*

consolation prize *n* a prize given to console a loser of a game

console[1] (kənˈsəʊl) *vb* **consoles, consoling, consoled** to serve as a comfort to (someone) in disappointment, sadness, etc [c17 from L *consōlārī*, from *sōlārī* to comfort] > **conˈsolable** *adj* > **conˈsoler** *n* > **conˈsolingly** *adv*

console[2] (ˈkɒnsəʊl) *n* **1** an ornamental bracket used to support a wall fixture, etc **2** the part of an organ comprising the manuals, pedals, stops, etc **3** a unit on which the controls of an electronic system are mounted **4** a cabinet for a television, etc, designed to stand on the floor **5** See **console table** [c18 from F, from OF *consolateur* one that provides support; see CONSOLE[1]]

console table *n* a table with one or more curved legs of bracket-like construction, designed to stand against a wall

consolidate (kənˈsɒlɪˌdeɪt) *vb* **consolidates, consolidating, consolidated 1** to form or cause to form into a whole **2** to make or become stronger or more stable **3** *mil* to strengthen one's control over (a situation, area, etc) [c16 from L *consolidāre* to make firm, from *solidus* strong] > **conˌsoliˈdation** *n* > **conˈsoliˌdator** *n*

consolidated fund *n Brit* a fund maintained from tax revenue to meet standing charges, esp national debt interest

consols (ˈkɒnsɒlz, kənˈsɒlz) *pl n* irredeemable British government securities carrying annual interest [short for *consolidated stock*]

consommé (kənˈsɒmeɪ) *n* a clear soup made from meat stock [c19 from F, from *consommer* to use up]

consonance (ˈkɒnsənəns) *n* **1** agreement, harmony, or accord **2** *prosody* similarity between consonants, but not between vowels, as between the *s* and *t* sounds in *sweet silent thought* **3** *music* a combination of notes which can sound together without harshness

consonant (ˈkɒnsənənt) *n* **1** a speech sound or letter of the alphabet other than a vowel ▷ *adj* **2** (*postpositive*; foll by *with* or *to*) consistent; in agreement **3** harmonious **4** *music* characterized by the presence of a consonance [c14 from L *consonāns*, from *consonāre* to sound at the same time, from *sonāre* to sound] > **ˈconsonantly** *adv*

consonantal (ˌkɒnsəˈnæntᵊl) *adj* relating to, functioning as, or characterized by consonants

consort *vb* (kənˈsɔːt). (*intr*) **1** (usually foll by *with*) to keep company (with undesirable people); associate **2** to harmonize ▷ *n* (ˈkɒnsɔːt) **3** (esp formerly) a small group of instruments, either of the same type (**a whole consort**) or of different types (**a broken consort**) **4** the husband or wife of a reigning monarch **5** a husband or wife **6** a ship that escorts another [c15 from OF, from L *consors* partner, from *sors* lot, portion]

consortium (kənˈsɔːtɪəm) *n, pl* **consortia** (kənˈsɔːtɪə) **1** an association of financiers, companies, etc, esp for a particular purpose **2** *law* the right of husband or wife to the company and affection of the other [c19 from L: community of goods, partnership; see CONSORT]

conspectus (kənˈspɛktəs) *n* **1** an overall view; survey **2** a summary; résumé [c19 from L: a viewing, from *conspicere*, from *specere* to look]

conspicuous (kənˈspɪkjʊəs) *adj* **1** clearly visible **2** attracting attention because of a striking feature: *conspicuous stupidity* [c16 from L *conspicuus*, from *conspicere* to perceive; see CONSPECTUS] > **conˈspicuously** *adv* > **conˈspicuousness** *n*

conspiracy (kənˈspɪrəsɪ) *n, pl* **conspiracies 1** a secret plan to carry out an illegal or harmful act, esp with political motivation; plot **2** the act of making such plans in secret > **conˈspirator** *n* > **conˌspiraˈtorial** *adj*

conspiracy theory *n* the belief that the government or a covert organization is responsible for an unusual or unexplained event

conspire (kənˈspaɪə) *vb* **conspires, conspiring, conspired** (when *intr*, sometimes foll by *against*) **1** to plan (a crime) together in secret **2** (*intr*) to act together as if by design: *the elements conspired to spoil our picnic* [c14 from OF, from L *conspīrāre* to plot together, lit.: to breathe together, from *spīrāre* to breathe]

con spirito (kɒn ˈspɪrɪtəʊ) *adj, adv music* (to be performed) in a spirited or lively manner [It.: with spirit]

constable (ˈkʌnstəbᵊl, ˈkɒn-) *n* **1** (in Britain, Australia, New Zealand, Canada, etc) a police officer of the lowest rank **2** any of various officers of the peace, esp one who arrests offenders, serves writs, etc **3** the keeper of a royal castle **4** (in medieval Europe) the chief military officer and functionary of a royal household **5** an officer of a hundred in medieval England [c13 from OF, from LL *comes stabulī* officer in charge of the stable] > **ˈconstableˌship** *n*

Constable (ˈkʌnstəbᵊl) *n* **John** 1776–1837, English landscape painter, noted particularly for his skill in rendering atmospheric effects of changing light

constabulary (kənˈstæbjʊlərɪ) *chiefly Brit* ▷ *n, pl* **constabularies 1** the police force of a town or district ▷ *adj* **2** of or relating to constables

Constance (ˈkɒnstəns) *n* **1** a city in S Germany, in Baden-Württemberg on Lake Constance: tourist centre. Pop: 72 860 (latest est). German name: **Konstanz 2 Lake** a lake in W Europe, bounded by S Germany, W Austria, and N Switzerland, through which the Rhine flows. Area: 536 sq km. (207 sq miles). German name: **Bodensee**

constant (ˈkɒnstənt) *adj* **1** unchanging **2** incessant: *constant interruptions* **3** resolute; loyal ▷ *n* **4** something that is unchanging **5** a specific quantity that is invariable: *the velocity of light is a constant* **6a** *maths* a symbol representing an unspecified number that remains invariable throughout a particular series of operations **6b** *physics* a quantity or property that is considered invariable throughout a particular series of experiments [c14 from OF, from L *constāns*, from *constāre* to be steadfast, from *stāre* to stand] > **ˈconstancy** *n* > **ˈconstantly** *adv*

▷ http://physics.nist.gov/cuu/Constants/index.html

Constanța (*Romanian* konˈstantsa) *n* a port and resort in SE Romania, on the Black Sea: founded by the Greeks in the 6th century BC and rebuilt by Constantine the Great (4th century); exports petroleum. Pop: 344 876 (1997 est)

Constantia (kɒnˈstænʃə) *n* **1** a region of the Cape Peninsula of South Africa **2** any of several red or white wines produced around Constantia

Constantine (ˈkɒnstənˌtaɪn; *French* kɔ̃stɑ̃tin) *n* a walled city in NE Algeria: built on an isolated rock; military and trading centre. Pop: 462 187 (1998)

Constantine I (ˈkɒnstənˌtaɪn, -ˌtiːn) *n* **1** known as *Constantine the Great*. Latin name *Flavius Valerius Aurelius Constantinus*. ?280–337 AD, first Christian Roman emperor (306–337): moved his capital to Byzantium, which he renamed Constantinople (330) **2** 1868–1923, king of Greece (1913–17; 1920–22): deposed (1917), recalled by a plebiscite (1920), but forced to abdicate again (1922) after defeat by the Turks

Constantine VII *n* known as *Porphyrogenitus*. 905–59 AD, Byzantine emperor (913–59) and scholar: his writings are an important source for Byzantine history

Constantine XI *n* 1404–53, last Byzantine emperor (1448–53): killed when Constantinople was captured by the Turks

Constantinople (ˌkɒnstæntɪˈnəʊpᵊl) *n* the former name (330–1926) of **Istanbul**

constellate (ˈkɒnstɪˌleɪt) *vb* **constellates, constellating, constellated** to form into clusters in or as if in constellations

constellation (ˌkɒnstɪˈleɪʃən) *n* **1** any of the 88 groups of stars as seen from the earth, many of which were named by the ancient Greeks after animals, objects, or mythological persons **2** a gathering of brilliant people or things **3** *psychoanal* a group of ideas felt to be related [C14 from LL *constellātiō*, from L *com-* together + *stella* star] > **constellatory** (kənˈstɛlətərɪ) *adj*

consternate (ˈkɒnstəˌneɪt) *vb* **consternates, consternating, consternated** (*tr; usually passive*) to fill with anxiety, dismay, dread, or confusion [C17 from L *consternāre*, from *sternere* to lay low]

consternation (ˌkɒnstəˈneɪʃən) *n* a feeling of anxiety, dismay, dread, or confusion

constipate (ˈkɒnstɪˌpeɪt) *vb* **constipates, constipating, constipated** (*tr*) to cause constipation in [C16 from L *constīpāre* to press closely together]

constipated (ˈkɒnstɪˌpeɪtɪd) *adj* **1** suffering from constipation **2** subject to restriction or blockage in a flow of productive activity or creativity

constipation (ˌkɒnstɪˈpeɪʃən) *n* infrequent or difficult evacuation of the bowels

constituency (kənˈstɪtjʊənsɪ) *n, pl* **constituencies** **1** the whole body of voters who elect one representative to a legislature or all the residents represented by one deputy **2** a district that sends one representative to a legislature

constituent (kənˈstɪtjʊənt) *adj* (*prenominal*) **1** forming part of a whole; component **2** having the power to frame a constitution or to constitute a government: *constituent assembly* ▷ *n* **3** a component part; ingredient **4** a resident of a constituency, esp one entitled to vote **5** *chiefly law* a person who appoints another to act on his or her behalf [C17 from L *constituēns*, from *constituere* to establish, CONSTITUTE] > **conˈstituently** *adv*

constitute (ˈkɒnstɪˌtjuːt) *vb* **constitutes, constituting, constituted** (*tr*) **1** to form; compose: *the people who constitute a jury* **2** to appoint to an office: *a legally constituted officer* **3** to set up (an institution) formally; found **4** *law* to give legal form to (a court, assembly, etc) [C15 from L *constituere*, from *com-* (intensive) + *statuere* to place] > **ˈconstiˌtutor** *n*

constitution (ˌkɒnstɪˈtjuːʃən) *n* **1** the act of constituting or state of being constituted **2** physical make-up; structure **3** the fundamental principles on which a state is governed, esp when considered as embodying the rights of the subjects **4** (*often cap*) (in certain countries, esp the US and Australia) a statute embodying such principles **5** a person's state of health **6** a person's temperament

▷ www.psa.ac.uk/www/constitutions.htm

constitutional (ˌkɒnstɪˈtjuːʃənᵊl) *adj* **1** of a constitution **2** authorized by or subject to a constitution: *constitutional monarchy* **3** inherent in the nature of a person or thing: *a constitutional weakness* **4** beneficial to one's physical wellbeing ▷ *n* **5** a regular walk taken for the benefit of one's health > **ˌconstiˌtutionˈality** *n* > **ˌconstiˈtutionally** *adv*

constitutionalism (ˌkɒnstɪˈtjuːʃənəˌlɪzəm) *n* **1** the principles or system of government in accord with a constitution **2** adherence to or advocacy of such a system > **ˌconstiˈtutionalist** *n*

constitutive (ˈkɒnstɪˌtjuːtɪv) *adj* **1** having power to enact or establish **2** another word for **constituent** (sense 1) > **ˈconstiˌtutively** *adv*

constrain (kənˈstreɪn) *vb* (*tr*) **1** to compel, esp by circumstances, etc **2** to restrain as by force [C14 from OF, from L *constringere* to bind together] > **conˈstrainer** *n*

constrained (kənˈstreɪnd) *adj* embarrassed, unnatural, or forced: *a constrained smile*

constraint (kənˈstreɪnt) *n* **1** compulsion or restraint **2** repression of natural feelings **3** a forced unnatural manner **4** something that serves to constrain; restrictive condition

constrict (kənˈstrɪkt) *vb* (*tr*) **1** to make smaller or narrower, esp by contracting at one place **2** to hold in or inhibit; limit [C18 from L *constrictus*, from *constringere* to tie up together]

constriction (kənˈstrɪkʃən) *n* **1** a feeling of tightness in some part of the body, such as the chest **2** the act of constricting or condition of being constricted **3** something that is constricted > **conˈstrictive** *adj*

constrictor (kənˈstrɪktə) *n* **1** any of various nonvenomous snakes, such as the boas, that coil around and squeeze their prey to kill it **2** any muscle that constricts; sphincter

construct *vb* (kənˈstrʌkt). (*tr*) **1** to put together substances or parts systematically; build; assemble **2** to frame mentally (an argument, sentence, etc) **3** *geom* to draw (a line, angle, or figure) so that certain requirements are satisfied ▷ *n* (ˈkɒnstrʌkt) **4** something formulated or built systematically **5** a complex idea resulting from a synthesis of simpler ideas [C17 from L *constructus*, from *construere* to build, from *struere* to arrange, erect] > **conˈstructor** *or* **conˈstructer** *n*

construction (kənˈstrʌkʃən) *n* **1** the act of constructing or manner in which a thing is constructed **2** a structure **3a** the business or work of building dwellings, offices, etc **3b** (*as modifier*): *a construction site* **4** an interpretation: *they put a sympathetic construction on her behaviour* **5** *grammar* a group of words that make up one of the constituents into which a sentence may be analysed; a phrase or clause **6** an abstract work of art in three dimensions > **conˈstructional** *adj* > **conˈstructionally** *adv*

Cc

constructive (kənˈstrʌktɪv) *adj* **1** serving to improve; positive: *constructive criticism* **2** *law* deduced by inference; not expressed **3** another word for **structural** > **conˈstructively** *adv*

constructivism (kənˈstrʌktɪˌvɪzəm) *n* a movement in abstract art evolved after World War I, which explored the use of movement and machine-age materials in sculpture > **conˈstructivist** *adj, n*

▷ www.kmtspace.com/constructivism.htm

construe (kənˈstruː) *vb* **construes, construing, construed** (*mainly tr*) **1** to interpret the meaning of (something): *you can construe that in different ways* **2** (*may take a clause as object*) to infer; deduce **3** to analyse the grammatical structure of; parse (esp a Latin or Greek text as a preliminary to translation) **4** to combine words syntactically **5** (*also intr*) *Old-fashioned.* to translate literally, esp aloud [C14 from L *construere*; see CONSTRUCT] > **conˈstruable** *adj*

consubstantial (ˌkɒnsəbˈstænʃəl) *adj* *Christian theol* (esp of the three persons of the Trinity) regarded as identical in essence though different in aspect [C15 from Church L, from L *com-* COM- + *substantia* SUBSTANCE] > **ˌconsubˌstantiˈality** *n*

consubstantiation (ˌkɒnsəbˌstænʃɪˈeɪʃən) *n* *Christian theol* (in the Lutheran branch of Protestantism) the doctrine that after the consecration of the Eucharist the substance of the body and blood of Christ coexists within the substance of the consecrated bread and wine ▷ Cf **transubstantiation**

consuetude ('kɒnswɪˌtjuːd) *n* an established custom or usage, esp one having legal force [c14 from L *consuētūdō*, from *consuēscere*, from CON- + *suēscere* to be wont]

consul ('kɒnsᵊl) *n* **1** an official appointed by a sovereign state to protect its commercial interests and aid its citizens in a foreign city **2** (in ancient Rome) either of two annually elected magistrates who jointly exercised the highest authority in the republic **3** (in France from 1799 to 1804) any of the three chief magistrates of the First Republic [c14 from L, from *consulere* to CONSULT] > **consular** ('kɒnsjʊlə) *adj* > **'consulˌship** *n*

consulate ('kɒnsjʊlɪt) *n* **1** the premises of a consul **2** government by consuls **3** the office or period of office of a consul **4** (*often cap*) **4a** the government of France by the three consuls from 1799 to 1804 **4b** this period **5** (*often cap*) the consular government of the Roman republic

consul general *n, pl* **consuls general** a consul of the highest grade, usually stationed in a city of considerable commercial importance

consult (kən'sʌlt) *vb* **1** (when *intr*, often foll by *with*) to ask advice from (someone) **2** (*tr*) to refer to for information: *to consult a map* **3** (*tr*) to have regard for (a person's feelings, interests, etc); consider [c17 from F, from L *consultāre*, from *consulere* to consult]

consultant (kən'sʌltᵊnt) *n* **1a** a specialist physician who is asked to confirm a diagnosis or treatment or to provide an opinion **1b** a physician or surgeon holding the highest appointment in a particular branch of medicine or surgery in a hospital **2** a specialist who gives expert advice or information **3** a person who asks advice in a consultation > **con'sultancy** *n*

consultant nurse *n* (in Britain) an experienced senior nurse responsible for running clinics and managing nursing teams

consultation (ˌkɒnsᵊl'teɪʃən) *n* **1** the act of consulting **2** a conference for discussion or the seeking of advice > **consultative** (kən'sʌltətɪv) *adj*

consulting (kən'sʌltɪŋ) *adj* (*prenominal*) acting in an advisory capacity on professional matters: *a consulting engineer*

consulting room *n* a room in which a doctor sees patients

consume (kən'sjuːm) *vb* **consumes, consuming, consumed** **1** (*tr*) to eat or drink **2** (*tr; often passive*) to obsess **3** (*tr*) to use up; expend **4** to destroy or be destroyed by: *fire consumed the forest* **5** (*tr*) to waste **6** (*passive*) to waste away [c14 from L *consūmere*, from *com-* (intensive) + *sūmere* to take up] > **con'sumable** *adj* > **con'suming** *adj*

consumedly (kən'sjuːmɪdlɪ) *adv Old-fashioned.* (intensifier): *consumedly fascinating*

consumer (kən'sjuːmə) *n* **1** a person who purchases goods and services for his own personal needs. Cf **producer** (sense 6) **2** a person or thing that consumes

consumer durable *n* a manufactured product that has a relatively long useful life, such as a car or a television

consumer goods *pl n* goods that satisfy personal needs rather than those required for the production of other goods or services

consumerism (kən'sjuːməˌrɪzəm) *n* **1** protection of the interests of consumers **2** advocacy of a high rate of consumption as a basis for a sound economy > **con'sumerist** *n, adj*

consumer terrorism *n* the practice of introducing dangerous substances to foodstuffs or other consumer products, esp to extort money from the manufacturers

consummate *vb* ('kɒnsəˌmeɪt), **consummates, consummating, consummated** (*tr*) **1** to bring to completion; fulfil **2** to complete (a marriage) legally by sexual intercourse ▷ *adj* (kən'sʌmɪt, 'kɒnsəmɪt) **3** supremely skilled: *a consummate artist* **4** (*prenominal*) (intensifier): *a consummate fool* [c15 from L *consummāre* to complete, from *summus* utmost] > **con'summately** *adv* > **ˌconsum'mation** *n*

consumption (kən'sʌmpʃən) *n* **1** the act of consuming or the state of being consumed, esp by eating, burning, etc **2** *econ* expenditure on goods and services for final personal use **3** the quantity consumed **4** a wasting away of the tissues of the body, esp in tuberculosis of the lungs [c14 from L *consumptiō*, from *consūmere* to CONSUME]

consumptive (kən'sʌmptɪv) *adj* **1** causing consumption; wasteful; destructive **2** relating to or affected with tuberculosis of the lungs ▷ *n* **3** *pathol* a person who suffers from consumption > **con'sumptively** *adv* > **con'sumptiveness** *n*

contact *n* ('kɒntækt) **1** the act or state of touching **2** the state or fact of communication (esp in **in contact, make contact**) **3a** a junction of electrical conductors **3b** the part of the conductors that makes the junction **3c** the part of an electrical device to which such connections are made **4** an acquaintance, esp one who might be useful in business, etc **5** any person who has been exposed to a contagious disease **6** (*modifier*) caused by touching the causative agent: *contact dermatitis* **7** (*modifier*) denoting a herbicide or insecticide that kills on contact **8** (*modifier*) of or maintaining contact **9** (*modifier*) requiring or involving (physical) contact: *a contact sport* ▷ *vb* ('kɒntækt, kən'tækt) **10** (when *intr*, often foll by *with*) to put, come, or be in association, touch, or communication [c17 from L *contactus*, from *contingere* to touch on all sides, from *tangere* to touch] > **contactual** (kɒn'tæktjʊəl) *adj*

contact centre *n* another name for **call centre**

contact lens *n* a thin convex lens, usually of plastic, which floats on the layer of tears in front of the cornea to correct defects of vision

contact print *n* a photographic print made by exposing the printing paper through a negative placed directly on to it

contagion (kən'teɪdʒən) *n* **1** the transmission of disease from one person to another by contact **2** a contagious disease **3** a corrupting influence that tends to spread **4** the spreading of an emotional or mental state among a number of people: *the contagion of mirth* [c14 from L *contāgiō* infection, from *contingere*; see CONTACT]

contagious (kən'teɪdʒəs) *adj* **1** (of a disease) capable of being passed on by direct contact with a diseased individual or by handling his clothing, etc **2** (of an organism) harbouring the causative agent of a transmissible disease **3** causing or likely to cause the same reaction in several people: *her laughter was contagious*

contain (kən'teɪn) *vb* (*tr*) **1** to hold or be capable of holding: *this contains five pints* **2** to restrain (feelings, behaviour, etc) **3** to consist of: *the book contains three sections* **4** *mil* to prevent (enemy forces) from operating beyond a certain area **5** to be a multiple of, leaving no remainder: *6 contains 2 and 3* [c13 from OF, from L *continēre*, from *com-* together + *tenēre* to hold] > **con'tainable** *adj*

container (kən'teɪnə) *n* **1** an object used for or capable of holding, esp for transport or storage **2a** a large cargo-carrying standard-sized container that can be loaded from one mode of transport to another **2b** (*as modifier*): *a container ship*

containerize *or* **containerise** (kən'teɪnəˌraɪz) *vb* **containerizes, containerizing, containerized** *or* **containerises, containerising, containerised** (*tr*) **1** to convey (cargo) in standard-sized containers **2** to adapt (a port or transportation system) to the use of standard-sized containers > **conˌtaineri'zation** *or* **conˌtaineri'sation** *n*

containment (kən'teɪnmənt) *n* the act of containing,

esp of restraining the power of a hostile country or the operations of a hostile military force

contaminate (kən'tæmɪˌneɪt) *vb* **contaminates, contaminating, contaminated** (*tr*) **1** to make impure; pollute **2** to make radioactive by the addition of radioactive material [c15 from L *contamināre* to defile] > **con'taminable** *adj* > **con'taminant** *n* > **conˌtami'nation** *n* > **con'tamiˌnator** *n*

contango (kən'tæŋgəʊ) *n, pl* **contangos 1** (formerly, on the London Stock Exchange) postponement of payment for and delivery of stock from one account day to the next **2** the fee paid for such a postponement. Also called: **carry-over, continuation** ▷ Cf **backwardation** [c19 apparently an arbitrary coinage]

conte *French* (kɔ̃t) *n* a tale or short story

contemn (kən'tɛm) *vb* (*tr*) *formal* to regard with contempt; scorn [c15 from L *contemnere*, from *temnere* to slight] > **contemner** (kən'tɛmnə, -'tɛmə) *n*

contemplate ('kɒntɛmˌpleɪt) *vb* **contemplates, contemplating, contemplated** (*mainly tr*) **1** to think about intently and at length **2** (*intr*) to think intently and at length, esp for spiritual reasons; meditate **3** to look at thoughtfully **4** to have in mind as a possibility [c16 from L *contemplāre*, from *templum* TEMPLE[1]] > ˌ**contem'plation** *n* > '**contemˌplator** *n*

contemplative ('kɒntɛmˌpleɪtɪv, -təm-; kən'tɛmplə-) *adj* **1** denoting, concerned with, or inclined to contemplation; meditative ▷ *n* **2** a person dedicated to religious contemplation

contemporaneous (kənˌtɛmpə'reɪnɪəs) *adj* existing, beginning, or occurring in the same period of time > **contemporaneity** (kənˌtɛmpərə'niːɪtɪ) *or* **conˌtempo'raneousness** *n*

contemporary (kən'tɛmprərɪ) *adj* **1** living or occurring in the same period **2** existing or occurring at the present time **3** conforming to modern ideas in style, fashion, etc **4** having approximately the same age as one another ▷ *n, pl* **contemporaries 5** a person living at the same time or of approximately the same age as another **6** something that is contemporary [c17 from Med. L *contemporārius*, from L *com-* together + *temporārius* relating to time, from *tempus* time] > **con'temporarily** *adv* > **con'temporariness** *n*

> USAGE Since *contemporary* can mean either of the same period or of the present period, it is best to avoid it where ambiguity might arise, as in *...a production of* Othello *in contemporary dress*. Specifying either *modern dress* or *Elizabethan dress*, according to whichever was intended, would avoid any possible confusion in this particular example

contemporize *or* **contemporise** (kən'tɛmpəˌraɪz) *vb* **contemporizes, contemporizing, contemporized** *or* **contemporises, contemporising, contemporised** to be or make contemporary

contempt (kən'tɛmpt) *n* **1** the feeling of a person towards a person or thing that he considers despicable; scorn **2** the state of being scorned; disgrace (esp in **hold in contempt**) **3** wilful disregard of the authority of a court of law or legislative body: *contempt of court* [c14 from L *contemptus*, from *contemnere* to CONTEMN]

contemptible (kən'tɛmptɪbᵊl) *adj* deserving or worthy of contempt > **conˌtempti'bility** *or* **con'temptibleness** *n* > **con'temptibly** *adv*

contemptuous (kən'tɛmptjʊəs) *adj* (when *predicative*, often foll by *of*) showing or feeling contempt; disdainful > **con'temptuously** *adv*

contend (kən'tɛnd) *vb* **1** (*intr*; often foll by *with*) to struggle in rivalry, battle, etc; vie **2** to argue earnestly **3** (*tr*; *may take a clause as object*) to assert [c15 from L *contendere* to strive, from *com-* with + *tendere* to stretch] > **con'tender** *n*

content[1] ('kɒntɛnt) *n* **1** (*often pl*) everything inside a container **2** (*usually pl*) **2a** the chapters or divisions of a book **2b** a list of these printed at the front of a book **3** the meaning or significance of a work of art, as distinguished from its style or form **4** all that is contained or dealt with in a piece of writing, etc; substance **5** the capacity or size of a thing **6** the proportion of a substance contained in an alloy, mixture, etc: *the lead content of petrol* [c15 from L *contentus* contained, from *continēre* to CONTAIN]

content[2] (kən'tɛnt) *adj* (*postpositive*) **1** satisfied with things as they are **2** assenting to or willing to accept circumstances, a proposed course of action, etc ▷ *vb* **3** (*tr*) to make (oneself or another person) satisfied ▷ *n* **4** peace of mind [c14 from OF, from L *contentus* contented, having restrained desires, from *continēre* to restrain] > **con'tentment** *n*

contented (kən'tɛntɪd) *adj* accepting one's situation or life with equanimity and satisfaction > **con'tentedly** *adv* > **con'tentedness** *n*

contention (kən'tɛnʃən) *n* **1** a struggling between opponents; competition **2** a point of dispute (esp in **bone of contention**) **3** a point asserted in argument [c14 from L *contentiō*, from *contendere* to CONTEND]

contentious (kən'tɛnʃəs) *adj* **1** tending to quarrel **2** causing or characterized by dispute; controversial > **con'tentiousness** *n*

conterminous (kən'tɜːmɪnəs) *or* **coterminous** (kəʊ'tɜːmɪnəs) *adj* **1** enclosed within a common boundary **2** without a break or interruption [c17 from L *conterminus*, from CON- + *terminus* boundary]

contest *n* ('kɒntɛst) **1** a formal game or match in which people, teams, etc, compete **2** a struggle for victory between opposing forces ▷ *vb* (kən'tɛst) **3** (*tr*) to try to disprove; call in question **4** (when *intr*, foll by *with* or *against*) to dispute or contend (with): *to contest an election* [c16 from L *contestārī* to introduce a lawsuit, from *testis* witness] > **con'testable** *adj* > **con'tester** *n*

contestant (kən'tɛstənt) *n* a person who takes part in a contest; competitor

context ('kɒntɛkst) *n* **1** the parts of a piece of writing, speech, etc, that precede and follow a word or passage and contribute to its full meaning: *it is unfair to quote out of context* **2** the circumstances that are relevant to an event, fact, etc [c15 from L *contextus* a putting together, from *contexere*, from *com-* together + *texere* to weave] > **con'textual** *adj*

contiguous (kən'tɪgjʊəs) *adj* **1** touching along the side or boundary; in contact **2** neighbouring **3** preceding or following in time [c17 from L *contiguus*, from *contingere* to touch; see CONTACT] > **con'tiguously** *adv*

continent[1] ('kɒntɪnənt) *n* **1** one of the earth's large land masses (Asia, Australia, Africa, Europe, North and South America, and Antarctica) **2** *obs* **2a** mainland **2b** a continuous extent of land [c16 from the L phrase *terra continens* continuous land] > **continental** (ˌkɒntɪ'nɛntᵊl) *adj* > ˌ**conti'nentally** *adv*

continent[2] ('kɒntɪnənt) *adj* **1** able to control urination and defecation **2** exercising self-restraint, esp from sexual activity; chaste [c14 from L *continēre*; see CONTAIN] > '**continence** *n*

Continent ('kɒntɪnənt) *n* **the** *Brit* the mainland of Europe as distinguished from the British Isles

Continental (ˌkɒntɪ'nɛntᵊl) *adj* **1** of or characteristic of Europe, excluding the British Isles **2** of or relating to the 13 original British North American colonies during the War of American Independence ▷ *n* **3** (*sometimes not cap*) an inhabitant of Europe, excluding the British Isles **4** a regular soldier of the rebel army during the War of American Independence

continental breakfast *n* a light breakfast of coffee and rolls

continental climate *n* a climate characterized by hot

Cc

summers, cold winters, and little rainfall, typical of the interior of a continent

continental drift *n geol* the theory that the earth's continents move gradually over the surface of the planet on a substratum of magma

continental quilt *n Brit* a quilt, stuffed with down or a synthetic material, used as a bed cover in place of the top sheet and blankets. Also called: **duvet**, (Austral) **doona**

continental shelf *n* the sea bed surrounding a continent at depths of up to about 200 metres (100 fathoms), at the edge of which the **continental slope** drops steeply

contingency (kən'tɪndʒənsɪ) *or* **contingence** (kən'tɪndʒəns) *n, pl* **contingencies** *or* **contingences** **1a** a possible but not very likely future event or condition **1b** (*as modifier*): *a contingency plan* **2** something dependent on a possible future event **3** a fact, event, etc, incidental to something else **4** *logic* the state of being contingent **5** uncertainty **6** *statistics* **6a** the degree of association between theoretical and observed common frequencies of two graded or classified variables **6b** (*as modifier*): *a contingency table*

contingent (kən'tɪndʒənt) *adj* **1** (when *postpositive*, often foll by *on* or *upon*) dependent on events, conditions, etc, not yet known; conditional **2** *logic* (of a proposition) true under certain conditions, false under others; not logically necessary **3** happening by chance; accidental **4** uncertain ▷ *n* **5** a part of a military force, parade, etc **6** a group distinguished by common interests, etc, that is part of a larger group **7** a chance occurrence [C14 from L *contingere* to touch, befall]

continual (kən'tɪnjʊəl) *adj* **1** recurring frequently, esp at regular intervals **2** occurring without interruption; continuous in time [C14 from OF *continuel*, from L *continuus* uninterrupted, from *continēre* to CONTAIN] > **con'tinually** *adv*

continuance (kən'tɪnjʊəns) *n* **1** the act of continuing **2** the duration of an action, etc **3** *US* the adjournment of a legal proceeding

continuant (kən'tɪnjʊənt) *phonetics* ▷ *n* **1** a speech sound, such as (l), (r), (f), or (s), in which the closure of the vocal tract is incomplete, allowing the continuous passage of the breath ▷ *adj* **2** relating to or denoting a continuant

continuation (kən,tɪnjʊ'eɪʃən) *n* **1** a part or thing added, esp to a book or play; sequel **2** a renewal of an interrupted action, process, etc; resumption **3** the act of continuing; prolongation **4** another word for **contango**

continue (kən'tɪnju:) *vb* **continues, continuing, continued** **1** (when *tr*, may take an infinitive) to remain or cause to remain in a particular condition or place **2** (when *tr*, may take an infinitive) to carry on uninterruptedly (a course of action): *he continued running* **3** (when *tr*, may take an infinitive) to resume after an interruption: *we'll continue after lunch* **4** to prolong or be prolonged: *continue the chord until it meets the tangent* **5** (*tr*) *law, chiefly Scots* to adjourn (legal proceedings) [C14 from OF *continuer*, from L *continuāre* to join together]

continuity (,kɒntɪ'nju:ɪtɪ) *n, pl* **continuities** **1** logical sequence **2** a continuous or connected whole **3** the comprehensive script or scenario of detail in a film or broadcast **4** the continuous projection of a film

continuity girl *or* **man** *n* a woman or man whose job is to ensure continuity and consistency in successive shots of a film

continuo (kən'tɪnjʊəʊ) *n, pl* **continuos** **1** *music* **1a** a shortened form of **basso continuo** (see **thorough bass**) **1b** (*as modifier*): *a continuo accompaniment* **2** the thorough-bass part as played on a keyboard instrument [It., lit.: continuous]

continuous (kən'tɪnjʊəs) *adj* **1** unceasing: *a continuous noise* **2** in an unbroken series or pattern **3** *statistics* (of a variable) having a continuum of possible values so that its distribution requires integration rather than summation to determine its cumulative probability **4** *grammar* another word for **progressive** (sense 7) [C17 from L *continuus*, from *continēre* to CONTAIN] > **con'tinuously** *adv*

continuous assessment *n* the assessment of a pupil's progress throughout a course of study rather than exclusively by examination at the end of it

continuous creation *n* the theory that matter is created continuously in the universe. See **steady-state theory**

continuum (kən'tɪnjʊəm) *n, pl* **continua** (-'tɪnjʊə) *or* **continuums** a continuous series or whole, no part of which is perceptibly different from the adjacent parts [C17 from L, neuter of *continuus* CONTINUOUS]

contort (kən'tɔ:t) *vb* to twist or bend out of place or shape [C15 from L *contortus* intricate, from *contorquēre* to whirl around, from *torquēre* to twist] > **con'tortion** *n* > **con'tortive** *adj*

contortionist (kən'tɔ:ʃənɪst) *n* **1** a performer who contorts his or her body for the entertainment of others **2** a person who twists or warps meaning

contour ('kɒntʊə) *n* **1** the outline of a mass of land, figure, or body; a defining line **2a** See **contour line** **2b** (*as modifier*): *a contour map* **3** (*often pl*) the shape of a curving form: *the contours of her body were full and round* ▷ *vb* (*tr*) **4** to shape so as to form the contour of something **5** to mark contour lines on **6** to construct (a road, railway, etc) to follow the outline of the land [C17 from F, from It. *contorno*, from *contornare* to sketch, from *tornare* to TURN]

contour line *n* a line on a map or chart joining points of equal height or depth

contour ploughing *n* ploughing along the contours of the land to minimize erosion

Contra ('kɒntrə) *n* a member of a US-backed guerrilla army, founded in 1979, whose aim was to overthrow the Sandinista government in Nicaragua

contra- *prefix* **1** against; contrary; opposing; contrasting: *contraceptive* **2** (in music) pitched below: *contrabass* [from L, from *contrā* against]

contraband ('kɒntrə,bænd) *n* **1a** goods that are prohibited by law from being exported or imported **1b** illegally imported or exported goods **2** illegal traffic in such goods; smuggling **3** Also called: **contraband of war** goods that a neutral country may not supply to a belligerent ▷ *adj* **4** (of goods) **4a** forbidden by law from being imported or exported **4b** illegally imported or exported [C16 from Sp. *contrabanda*, from It., from Med. L, from CONTRA- + *bannum* ban] > **'contra,bandist** *n*

contrabass (,kɒntrə'beɪs) *n* **1** another name for **double bass** ▷ *adj* **2** denoting the instrument of a family that is lower than the bass

contrabassoon (,kɒntrəbə'su:n) *n* the largest instrument in the oboe family, pitched an octave below the bassoon; double bassoon

contraception (,kɒntrə'sɛpʃən) *n* the intentional prevention of conception by artificial or natural means [C19 from CONTRA- + CONCEPTION] > **,contra'ceptive** *adj, n*

contract *vb* (kən'trækt) **1** to make or become smaller, narrower, shorter, etc **2** ('kɒntrækt) (when *intr*, sometimes foll by *for*; when *tr*, may take an infinitive) to enter into an agreement with (a person, company, etc) to deliver (goods or services) or to do (something) on mutually agreed terms **3** to draw or be drawn together **4** (*tr*) to incur or become affected by (a disease, debt, etc) **5** (*tr*) to shorten (a word or phrase) by the omission of letters or syllables, usually indicated in writing by an apostrophe **6** (*tr*) to wrinkle (the brow or a muscle) **7** (*tr*) to arrange (a marriage) for; betroth ▷ *n* ('kɒntrækt) **8** a formal agreement between two or more parties **9** a document that states the terms of such an agreement **10** the branch of law treating of contracts **11** marriage considered as a formal agreement **12** See **contract bridge** **13** *bridge* **13a** the highest bid, which determines trumps and the number of tricks one side must make **13b** the number and suit of these tricks **14** *sl* **14a** a criminal agreement to kill a particular person in return for an agreed sum of money **14b** (*as modifier*): *a contract killing* [C16 from L *contractus* agreement, from *contrahere* to draw together, from *trahere* to draw] > **con'tractible** *adj*

contract bridge ('kɒntrækt) *n* the most common variety of bridge, in which the declarer receives points counting towards game and rubber only for tricks he bids as well as makes ▷ Cf **auction bridge**

contractile (kən'træktaɪl) *adj* having the power to contract or to cause contraction

contraction (kən'trækʃən) *n* **1** an instance of contracting or the state of being contracted **2** a shortening of a word or group of words, often marked by an apostrophe: *I've come* for *I have come* > **con'tractive** *adj*

contractor (kən'træktə) *n* **1** a person or firm that contracts to supply materials or labour, esp for building **2** something that contracts

contract out ('kɒntrækt) *vb* (*intr, adv*) *Brit* to agree not to participate in something, esp the state pension scheme

contractual (kən'træktjʊəl) *adj* of the nature of or assured by a contract

contradict (ˌkɒntrə'dɪkt) *vb* **1** (*tr*) to affirm the opposite of (a statement, etc) **2** (*tr*) to declare (a statement, etc) to be false or incorrect; deny **3** (*tr*) to be inconsistent with: *the facts contradicted his theory* **4** (*intr*) to be at variance; be in contradiction [C16 from L *contrādīcere*, from CONTRA- + *dīcere* to speak] > ˌ**contra'dictable** *adj* > ˌ**contra'dictor** *n*

contradiction (ˌkɒntrə'dɪkʃən) *n* **1** opposition; denial **2** a declaration of the opposite **3** a statement that is at variance with itself (often in **a contradiction in terms**) **4** conflict or inconsistency, as between events, qualities, etc **5** a person or thing containing conflicting qualities **6** *logic* a statement that is false under all circumstances; necessary falsehood

contradictory (ˌkɒntrə'dɪktərɪ) *adj* **1** inconsistent; incompatible **2** given to argument and contention: *a contradictory person* **3** *logic* (of a pair of statements) unable both to be true or both to be false under the same circumstances > ˌ**contra'dictorily** *adv* > ˌ**contra'dictoriness** *n*

contradistinction (ˌkɒntrədɪ'stɪŋkʃən) *n* a distinction made by contrasting different qualities > ˌ**contradis'tinctive** *adj*

contraflow ('kɒntrəˌfləʊ) *n* *Brit* two-way traffic on one carriageway of a motorway

contrail ('kɒntreɪl) *n* another name for **vapour trail** [C20 from CON(DENSATION) + TRAIL]

contralto (kən'træltəʊ) *n, pl* **contraltos** *or* **contralti** (-tɪ) **1** the lowest female voice: in the context of a choir often shortened to **alto** **2** a singer with such a voice ▷ *adj* **3** of or denoting a contralto: *the contralto part* [C18 from It.; see CONTRA-, ALTO]

contraposition (ˌkɒntrəpə'zɪʃən) *n* **1** the act of placing opposite or against **2** *logic* the conclusion drawn from a subject-predicate proposition by negating its terms and changing their order

contraption (kən'træpʃən) *n* *inf, often facetious or derog* a device or contrivance, esp one considered strange, unnecessarily intricate, or improvised [C19 ?from CON(TRIVANCE) + TRAP[1] + (INVEN)TION]

contrapuntal (ˌkɒntrə'pʌntᵊl) *adj* *music* characterized by counterpoint [C19 from It. *contrappunto*] > ˌ**contra'puntally** *adv* > ˌ**contra'puntist** *or* ˌ**contra'puntalist** *n*

contrariety (ˌkɒntrə'raɪətɪ) *n, pl* **contrarieties** **1** opposition between one thing and another; disagreement **2** an instance of such opposition; inconsistency; discrepancy

contrariwise ('kɒntrərɪˌwaɪz) *adv* **1** from a contrasting point of view **2** in the reverse way **3** (kən'trɛərɪˌwaɪz) in a contrary manner

contrary ('kɒntrərɪ) *adj* **1** opposed in nature, position, etc: *contrary ideas* **2** (kən'trɛərɪ) perverse; obstinate **3** (esp of wind) adverse; unfavourable **4** (of plant parts) situated at right angles to each other **5** *logic* (of a pair of propositions) related so they cannot both be true, although they may both be false ▷ *n, pl* **contraries** **6** the exact opposite (esp in **to the contrary**) **7** **on the contrary** quite the reverse **8** either of two exactly opposite objects, facts, or qualities ▷ *adv* (usually foll by *to*) **9** in an opposite or unexpected way: *contrary to usual belief* **10** in conflict (with): *contrary to nature* [C14 from L *contrārius* opposite, from *contrā* against] > **con'trarily** *adv* > **con'trariness** *n*

contrast *vb* (kən'trɑːst) **1** (often foll by *with*) to distinguish or be distinguished by comparison of unlike or opposite qualities ▷ *n* ('kɒntrɑːst) **2** distinction by comparison of opposite or dissimilar things, qualities, etc (esp in **by contrast, in contrast to** *or* **with**) **3** a person or thing showing differences when compared with another **4** the effect of the juxtaposition of different colours, tones, etc **5** the extent to which adjacent areas of an optical image, esp on a television screen or in a photograph, differ in brightness [C16 (n): via F from It., from *contrastare* (vb), from L *contra-* against + *stare* to stand] > **con'trasting** *adj* > **con'trastive** *adj*

contrast medium *n* *med* a radiopaque substance, such as barium sulphate, used to increase the contrast of an image in radiography

contravene (ˌkɒntrə'viːn) *vb* **contravenes, contravening, contravened** (*tr*) **1** to come into conflict with or infringe (rules, laws, etc) **2** to dispute or contradict (a statement, proposition, etc) [C16 from LL *contrāvenīre*, from L CONTRA- + *venīre* to come] > ˌ**contra'vener** *n* > **contravention** (ˌkɒntrə'vɛnʃən) *n*

contretemps ('kɒntrəˌtɑːn) *n, pl* **contretemps** **1** an awkward or difficult situation or mishap **2** a small disagreement that is rather embarrassing [C17 from F, from *contre* against + *temps* time]

Cc

contribute (kən'trɪbjuːt) *vb* **contributes, contributing, contributed** (often foll by *to*) **1** to give (support, money, etc) for a common purpose or fund **2** to supply (ideas, opinions, etc) **3** (*intr*) to be partly responsible (for): *drink contributed to the accident* **4** to write (articles, etc) for a publication [C16 from L *contribuere* to collect, from *tribuere* to grant] > **con'tributable** *adj* > **con'tributive** *adj* > **con'tributor** *n*

contribution (ˌkɒntrɪ'bjuːʃən) *n* **1** the act of contributing **2** something contributed, such as money **3** an article, etc, contributed to a newspaper or other publication **4** *arch* a levy

contributory (kən'trɪbjʊtərɪ, -trɪ) *adj* **1** (often foll by *to*) being partly responsible: *a contributory factor* **2** giving to a common purpose or fund **3** of or designating an insurance or pension scheme in which the premiums are paid partly by the employer and partly by the employees who benefit from it ▷ *n, pl* **contributories** **4** a person or thing that contributes **5** *company law* a member or former member of a company liable to contribute to the assets on the winding-up of the company

contrite (kən'traɪt, 'kɒntraɪt) *adj* **1** full of guilt or regret; remorseful **2** arising from a sense of shame or guilt: *contrite promises* [C14 from L *contrītus* worn out, from *conterere* to bruise, from *terere* to grind] > **con'tritely** *adv* > **con'triteness** *or* **contrition** (kən'trɪʃən) *n*

contrivance (kən'traɪvəns) *n* **1** something contrived, esp an ingenious device; contraption **2** inventive skill or ability **3** an artificial rather than natural arrangement of details, parts, etc **4** an elaborate or deceitful plan; stratagem

contrive (kən'traɪv) *vb* **contrives, contriving, contrived**

1 *(tr)* to manage (something or to do something), esp by a trick: *he contrived to make them meet* 2 *(tr)* to think up or adapt ingeniously: *he contrived a new mast for the boat* 3 to plot or scheme [C14 from OF *controver*, from LL *contropāre* to represent by figures of speech, compare] > **con'triver** *n*

contrived (kən'traɪvd) *adj* obviously planned; artificial; forced; unnatural

control (kən'trəʊl) *vb* **controls, controlling, controlled** *(tr)* 1 to command, direct, or rule 2 to check, limit, or restrain: *to control one's emotions* 3 to regulate or operate (a machine) 4 to verify (a scientific experiment) by conducting a parallel experiment in which the variable being investigated is held constant or is compared with a standard **5a** to regulate (financial affairs) **5b** to examine (financial accounts) 6 to restrict or regulate the authorized supply of (certain substances, such as drugs) ▷ *n* 7 power to direct: *under control* 8 a curb; check: *a frontier control* 9 *(often pl)* a mechanism for operating a car, aircraft, etc **10a** a standard of comparison used in a statistical analysis, etc **10b** *(as modifier)*: *a control group* **11a** a device that regulates the operation of a machine **11b** *(as modifier)*: *control room* [C15 from OF *conteroller* to regulate, from *contrerolle* duplicate register, from *contre-* COUNTER- + *rolle* ROLL] > **con'trollable** *adj* > **con,trolla'bility** *n* > **con'trollably** *adv*

control experiment *n* an experiment designed to check or correct the results of another experiment by removing the variable or variables operating in that other experiment

control freak *n inf* a person who is obsessed with gaining and exercising control

controlled explosion *n* the deliberate detonation of an explosive device under strictly controlled circumstances

controller (kən'trəʊlə) *n* 1 a person who directs 2 Also called: **comptroller** a business executive or government officer responsible for financial planning, control, etc 3 the equipment concerned with controlling the operation of an electrical device > **con'troller,ship** *n*

controlling interest *n* a quantity of shares in a business that is sufficient to ensure control over its direction

control tower *n* a tower at an airport from which air traffic is controlled

controversy ('kɒntrə,vɜːsɪ, kən'trɒvəsɪ) *n, pl* **controversies** dispute, argument, or debate, esp one concerning a matter about which there is strong disagreement and esp one carried on in public or in the press [C14 from L *contrōversia*, from *contrōversus*, from CONTRA- + *vertere* to turn] > **controversial** (,kɒntrə'vɜːʃəl) *adj* > **,contro'versial,ism** *n* > **,contro'versialist** *n*

controvert ('kɒntrə,vɜːt, ,kɒntrə'vɜːt) *vb (tr)* 1 to deny, refute, or oppose (argument or opinion) 2 to argue about [C17 from L *contrōversus*; see CONTROVERSY] > **,contro'vertible** *adj*

contumacious (,kɒntjʊ'meɪʃəs) *adj* stubbornly resistant to authority > **,contu'maciously** *adv*

contumacy ('kɒntjʊməsɪ) *n, pl* **contumacies** obstinate and wilful resistance to authority, esp refusal to comply with a court order [C14 from L *contumācia*, from *contumāx* obstinate]

contumely ('kɒntjʊmɪlɪ) *n, pl* **contumelies** 1 scornful or insulting language or behaviour 2 a humiliating insult [C14 from L *contumēlia*, from *tumēre* to swell, as with wrath] > **contumelious** (,kɒntjʊ'miːlɪəs) *adj* > **,contu'meliously** *adv*

contuse (kən'tjuːz) *vb* **contuses, contusing, contused** *(tr)* to injure (the body) without breaking the skin; bruise [C15 from L *contūsus* bruised, from *contundere* to grind, from *tundere* to beat]

contusion (kən'tjuːʒən) *n* an injury in which the skin is not broken; bruise > **con'tusioned** *adj*

conundrum (kə'nʌndrəm) *n* 1 a riddle, esp one whose answer makes a play on words 2 a puzzling question or problem [C16 from ?]

conurbation (,kɒnɜː'beɪʃən) *n* a large densely populated urban sprawl formed by the growth and coalescence of individual towns or cities [C20 from CON- + *-urbation*, from L *urbs* city]

convalesce (,kɒnvə'lɛs) *vb* **convalesces, convalescing, convalesced** *(intr)* to recover from illness, injury, or the aftereffects of a surgical operation [C15 from L *convalēscere*, from *com-* (intensive) + *valēscere* to grow strong]

convalescence (,kɒnvə'lɛsəns) *n* 1 gradual return to health after illness, injury, or an operation 2 the period during which such recovery occurs > **,conva'lescent** *n, adj*

convection (kən'vɛkʃən) *n* 1 a process of heat transfer through a gas or liquid by bulk motion of hotter material into a cooler region. Cf **conduction** (sense 1) 2 *meteorol* the process by which masses of relatively warm air are raised into the atmosphere, often cooling and forming clouds, with compensatory downward movements of cooler air [C19 from LL *convectiō*, from L *convehere* to bring together, from *vehere* to carry] > **con'vectional** *adj* > **con'vective** *adj*

convector (kən'vɛktə) *n* a space-heating device from which heat is transferred to the surrounding air by convection

convene (kən'viːn) *vb* **convenes, convening, convened** 1 to gather, call together or summon, esp for a formal meeting 2 *(tr)* to order to appear before a court of law, judge, tribunal, etc [C15 from L *convenīre* to assemble, from *venīre* to come] > **con'venable** *adj*

convener *or* **convenor** (kən'viːnə) *n* 1 a person who convenes or chairs a meeting, committee, etc, esp one who is specifically elected to do so: *a convener of shop stewards* 2 the chairman and civic head of certain Scottish councils. Cf **provost** (sense 2) > **con'venership** *or* **con'venorship** *n*

convenience (kən'viːnɪəns) *n* 1 the quality of being suitable or opportune 2 a convenient time or situation 3 **at your convenience** at a time suitable to you 4 usefulness, comfort, or facility 5 an object that is useful, esp a labour-saving device 6 *euphemistic, chiefly Brit* a lavatory, esp a public one 7 **make a convenience of** to take advantage of; impose upon

convenience food *n* food that needs little preparation, especially food that has been pre-prepared and preserved for long-term storage

convenience store *n* a shop that has long opening hours, caters to local tastes, and is conveniently situated

convenient (kən'viːnɪənt) *adj* 1 suitable; opportune 2 easy to use 3 close by; handy [C14 from L *conveniēns*, from *convenīre* to be in accord with, from *venīre* to come] > **con'veniently** *adv*

convent ('kɒnvənt) *n* 1 a building inhabited by a religious community, usually of nuns 2 the religious community inhabiting such a building 3 Also called: **convent school** a school in which the teachers are nuns [C13 from OF, from L *conventus* meeting, from *convenīre*; see CONVENE]

conventicle (kən'vɛntɪkᵊl) *n* 1 a secret or unauthorized assembly for worship 2 a small meeting house or chapel, esp of Dissenters [C14 from L *conventiculum*, from *conventus*; see CONVENT]

convention (kən'vɛnʃən) *n* 1 a large formal assembly of a group with common interests, such as a trade union 2 *US politics* an assembly of delegates of one party to select candidates for office 3 an international agreement second only to a treaty in formality 4 any agreement or contract 5 the established view of what is thought to be proper behaviour, good taste, etc 6 an accepted rule, usage, etc: *a convention used by printers* 7 *bridge* a bid or play not to be taken at its face value, which one's partner can interpret according to a prearranged bidding system [c15 from L *conventiō* an assembling]

conventional (kən'vɛnʃənᵊl) *adj* 1 following the accepted customs and proprieties, esp in a way that lacks originality 2 established by accepted usage or general agreement 3 of a convention or assembly 4 *visual arts* conventionalized 5 (of weapons, warfare, etc) not nuclear > **con'ventionalism** *n* > **con'ventionally** *adv*

conventionality (kən,vɛnʃə'nælɪtɪ) *n, pl* **conventionalities** 1 the quality of being conventional 2 (*often pl*) something conventional

conventionalize *or* **conventionalise** (kən'vɛnʃənə,laɪz) *vb* **conventionalizes, conventionalizing, conventionalized** *or* **conventionalises, conventionalising, conventionalised** (*tr*) 1 to make conventional 2 to simplify or stylize (a design, decorative device, etc) > **con,ventionali'zation** *or* **con,ventionali'sation** *n*

conventual (kən'vɛntjʊəl) *adj* 1 of, belonging to, or characteristic of a convent ▹ *n* 2 a member of a convent > **con'ventually** *adv*

converge (kən'vɜːdʒ) *vb* **converges, converging, converged** 1 to move or cause to move towards the same point 2 to meet or join 3 (*intr*) (of opinions, effects, etc) to tend towards a common conclusion or result 4 (*intr*) *maths* (of an infinite series) to approach a finite limit as the number of terms increases 5 (*intr*) (of animals and plants) to undergo convergence [c17 from LL *convergere*, from L *com-* together + *vergere* to incline] > **con'vergent** *adj*

convergence (kən'vɜːdʒəns) *n* 1 Also: **convergency** the act, degree, or a point of converging 2 Also called: **convergent evolution** the evolutionary development of a superficial resemblance between unrelated animals that occupy a similar environment, as in the evolution of wings in birds and bats

convergent thinking *n psychol* analytical, usually deductive, thinking in which ideas are examined for their logical validity or in which a set of rules is followed, for example in arithmetic

conversable (kən'vɜːsəbᵊl) *adj* 1 easy or pleasant to talk to 2 able or inclined to talk

conversant (kən'vɜːsᵊnt) *adj* (*usually postpositive* and foll by *with*) experienced (in), familiar (with), or acquainted (with) > **con'versance** *or* **con'versancy** *n* > **con'versantly** *adv*

conversation (,kɒnvə'seɪʃən) *n* the interchange through speech of information, ideas, etc; spoken communication

conversational (,kɒnvə'seɪʃənᵊl) *adj* 1 of, using, or in the manner of conversation 2 inclined to conversation; conversable > **,conver'sationalist** *n* > **,conver'sationally** *adv*

conversation piece *n* 1 something, esp an unusual object, that provokes conversation 2 (esp in 18th-century Britain) a group portrait in a landscape or domestic setting

converse¹ *vb* (kən'vɜːs), **converses, conversing, conversed** (*intr*; often foll by *with*) 1 to engage in conversation (with) 2 to commune spiritually (with) ▹ *n* ('kɒnvɜːs) 3 conversation (often in **hold converse with**) [c16 from OF *converser*, from L *conversārī* to keep company with, from *conversāre* to turn constantly, from *vertere* to turn] > **con'verser** *n*

converse² ('kɒnvɜːs) *adj* 1 (*prenominal*) reversed; opposite; contrary ▹ *n* 2 something that is opposite or contrary 3 *logic* a categorial proposition obtained from another by the transposition of the subject and predicate, as *no bad man is bald* from *no bald man is bad* [c16 from L *conversus* turned around; see CONVERSE¹] > **con'versely** *adv*

conversion (kən'vɜːʃən) *n* 1a a change or adaptation in form, character, or function 1b something changed in one of these respects 2 a change to another belief, as in a change of religion 3 alteration to the structure or fittings of a building undergoing a change in function or legal status 4 *maths* a change in the units or form of a number or expression: *the conversion of miles to kilometres* 5 *rugby* a score made after a try by kicking the ball over the crossbar from a place kick 6 *physics* a change of fertile material to fissile material in a reactor 7 an alteration to a car engine to improve its performance [c14 from L *conversiō* a turning around; see CONVERT]

conversion disorder *n* a psychological disorder in which severe physical symptoms like blindness or paralysis appear with no apparent physical cause

convert *vb* (kən'vɜːt). (*mainly tr*) 1 to change or adapt the form, character, or function of 2 to cause (someone) to change in opinion, belief, etc 3 (*intr*) to admit of being changed (into): *the table converts into a tray* 4 (*also intr*) to change or be changed into another state: *to convert water into ice* 5 *law* to assume unlawful proprietary rights over (personal property) 6 (*also intr*) *rugby* to make a conversion after (a try) 7 *logic* to transpose the subject and predicate of (a proposition) 8 to change (a value or measurement) from one system of units to another 9 to exchange (a security or bond) for something of equivalent value ▹ *n* ('kɒnvɜːt) 10 a person who has been converted to another belief, religion, etc [c13 from OF, from L *convertere* to turn around, alter, from *vertere* to turn]

converter *or* **convertor** (kən'vɜːtə) *n* 1 a person or thing that converts 2 *physics* 2a a device for converting alternating current to direct current or vice versa 2b a device for converting a signal from one frequency to another 3 a vessel in which molten metal is refined, using a blast of air or oxygen 4 *computing* a device for converting one form of coded information to another, such as an analogue-to-digital converter

converter reactor *n* a nuclear reactor for converting one fuel into another, esp fertile material into fissionable material

convertible (kən'vɜːtɪbᵊl) *adj* 1 capable of being converted 2 (of a car) having a folding or removable roof 3 *finance* 3a (of a currency) freely exchangeable into other currencies 3b (of a paper currency) exchangeable on demand for precious metal to an equivalent value 3c (of a bond, debenture, etc) able to be exchanged for a share on a specified date at a specified price ▹ *n* 4 a car with a folding or removable roof 5 any convertible document or currency > **con,verti'bility** *n* > **con'vertibly** *adv*

convex ('kɒnvɛks, kɒn'vɛks) *adj* 1 curving outwards 2 having one or two surfaces curved or ground in the shape of a section of the exterior of a sphere, ellipsoid, etc: *a convex lens* [c16 from L *convexus* vaulted, rounded] > **con'vexity** *n* > **'convexly** *adv*

convexo-concave (kən,vɛksəʊkɒn'keɪv) *adj* 1 having one side convex and the other side concave 2 (of a lens) having a convex face with greater curvature than the concave face

convexo-convex *adj* (esp of a lens) having both sides convex; biconvex

convey (kən'veɪ) *vb* (*tr*) 1 to take, carry, or transport from one place to another 2 to communicate (a message, information, etc) 3 (of a channel, path, etc) to conduct or transfer 4 *law* to transfer (the title to property) [c13 from OF *conveier*, from Med. L *conviāre* to escort, from L *com-* with + *via* way] > **con'veyable** *adj*

conveyance (kən'veɪəns) *n* 1 the act of conveying 2 a means of transport 3 *law* 3a a transfer of the legal title to property 3b the document effecting such a transfer > **con'veyancer** *n* > **con'veyancing** *n*

conveyor *or* **conveyer** (kən'veɪə) *n* 1 a person or thing that conveys 2 short for **conveyor belt**

conveyor belt *n* a flexible endless strip of fabric or

Cc

linked plates driven by rollers and used to transport objects, esp in a factory

convict *vb* (kən'vɪkt). (*tr*) **1** to pronounce (someone) guilty of an offence ▷ *n* ('kɒnvɪkt) **2** a person found guilty of an offence against the law **3** a person serving a prison sentence [C14 from L *convictus* convicted, from *convincere* to prove guilty, CONVINCE]

conviction (kən'vɪkʃən) *n* **1** the state of being convinced **2** a firmly held belief, opinion, etc **3** the act of convincing **4** the act of convicting or the state of being convicted **5 carry conviction** to be convincing > **con'victional** *adj* > **con'victive** *adj*

convince (kən'vɪns) *vb* **convinces, convincing, convinced** (*tr*) (*may take a clause as object*) to make (someone) agree, understand, or realize the truth or validity of something; persuade [C16 from L *convincere* to demonstrate incontrovertibly, from *com-* (intensive) + *vincere* to overcome] > **con'vincer** *n* > **con'vincible** *adj* > **con'vincing** *adj* > **con'vincingly** *adv*

> **USAGE** The use of *convince* to talk about persuading someone to do something is considered by many British speakers to be wrong or unacceptable

convivial (kən'vɪvɪəl) *adj* sociable; jovial or festive: *a convivial atmosphere* [C17 from LL *convīviālis*, from L *convīvium*, a living together, banquet, from *vīvere* to live] > **con,vivi'ality** *n*

convocation (,kɒnvə'keɪʃən) *n* **1** a large formal assembly **2** the act of convoking or state of being convoked **3** *Church of England* either of the synods of the provinces of Canterbury or York **4** *Episcopal Church* an assembly of the clergy and part of the laity of a diocese **5** (*sometimes cap*) (in some British universities) a legislative assembly **6** (in Australia and New Zealand) the graduate membership of a university > **,convo'cational** *adj*

convoke (kən'vəʊk) *vb* **convokes, convoking, convoked** (*tr*) to call (a meeting, assembly, etc) together; summon [C16 from L *convocāre*, from *vocāre* to call] > **con'voker** *n*

convolute ('kɒnvə,lu:t) *vb* **convolutes, convoluting, convoluted** (*tr*) **1** to form into a twisted, coiled, or rolled shape ▷ *adj* **2** *bot* rolled longitudinally upon itself: *a convolute petal* [C18 from L *convolūtus*, from *convolvere* to roll together, from *volvere* to turn]

convoluted ('kɒnvə,lu:tɪd) *adj* **1** (esp of meaning, style, etc) difficult to comprehend; involved **2** coiled > **'convo,lutedly** *adv*

convolution (,kɒnvə'lu:ʃən) *n* **1** a turn, twist, or coil **2** an intricate or confused matter or condition **3** any of the numerous convex folds of the surface of the brain > **,convo'lutional** *or* **,convo'lutionary** *adj*

convolve (kən'vɒlv) *vb* **convolves, convolving, convolved** to wind or roll together; coil; twist [C16 from L *convolvere*; see CONVOLUTE]

convolvulus (kən'vɒlvjʊləs) *n, pl* **convolvuluses** *or* **convolvuli** (-,laɪ) a twining herbaceous plant having funnel-shaped flowers and triangular leaves [C16 from L: bindweed; see CONVOLUTE]

convoy ('kɒnvɔɪ) *n* **1** a group of merchant ships with an escort of warships **2** a group of land vehicles assembled to travel together **3** the act of travelling or escorting by convoy (esp in **in convoy**) ▷ *vb* **4** (*tr*) to escort while in transit [C14 from OF *convoier* to CONVEY]

convulse (kən'vʌls) *vb* **convulses, convulsing, convulsed** **1** (*tr*) to shake or agitate violently **2** (*tr*) to cause (muscles) to undergo violent spasms or contractions **3** (*intr; often foll by with*) *inf* to shake or be overcome (with violent emotion, esp laughter) **4** (*tr*) to disrupt the normal running of (a country, etc): *student riots have convulsed India* [C17 from L *convulsus*, from *convellere*, from *vellere* to pluck, pull] > **con'vulsive** *adj* > **con'vulsively** *adv*

convulsion (kən'vʌlʃən) *n* **1** a violent involuntary muscular contraction **2** a violent upheaval, esp a social one **3** (*usually pl*) *inf* uncontrollable laughter: *I was in convulsions*

Conwy ('kɒnwɪ) *n* **1** a market town and resort in N Wales, in Conwy county borough on the estuary of the River Conwy: medieval town walls, 13th-century castle. Pop: 13 627 (1991). Former name: **Conway** **2** a county borough in N Wales, created in 1996 from parts of Gwynedd and Clwyd. Pop: 109 597 (2001 est). Area: 1130 sq km (436 sq miles)

cony *or* **coney** ('kəʊnɪ) *n, pl* **conies** *or* **coneys** **1** a rabbit or fur made from the skin of a rabbit **2** (in the Bible) another name for the **hyrax** [C13 back formation from *conies*, from OF *conis*, pl. of *conil*, from L *cunīculus* rabbit]

Conybeare ('kɒnɪ,bɪə, 'kʌn-) *n* **William Daniel** 1787–1857, British geologist. He summarized all that was known about rocks at the time in *Outlines of the Geology of England and Wales* (1822)

coo (ku:) *vb* **coos, cooing, cooed** **1** (*intr*) (of doves, pigeons, etc) to make a characteristic soft throaty call **2** (*tr*) to speak in a soft murmur **3** (*intr*) to murmur lovingly (esp in **bill and coo**) ▷ *n* **4** the sound of cooing ▷ *interj* **5** *Brit sl* an exclamation of surprise, awe, etc > **'cooing** *adj, n* > **'cooingly** *adv*

COO *abbrev for* chief operating officer

Cooch Behar *or* **Kuch Bihar** (ku:tʃ bɪ'hɑ:) *n* **1** a former state of NE India: part of West Bengal since 1950 **2** a city in India, in NE West Bengal: capital of the former state of Cooch Behar. Pop: 62 500 (latest est)

cooee *or* **cooey** ('ku:i:) *interj* **1** a call used to attract attention, esp a long loud high-pitched call on two notes ▷ *vb* **cooees, cooeeing, cooeed** *or* **cooeys, cooeying, cooeyed** **2** (*intr*) to utter this call ▷ *n* **3** *Austral & NZ inf* calling distance (esp in **within (a) cooee (of)**) [C19 from Abor.]

cook (kʊk) *vb* **1** to prepare (food) by the action of heat, or (of food) to become ready for eating through such a process. Related adj: **culinary** **2** to subject or be subjected to intense heat: *the town cooked in the sun* **3** (*tr*) *sl* to alter or falsify (figures, accounts, etc): *to cook the books* **4** (*tr*) *sl* to spoil (something) **5** (*intr*) *sl* to happen (esp in **what's cooking?**) ▷ *n* **6** a person who prepares food for eating ▷ See also **cook up** [OE *cōc* (n), from L *coquus* a cook, from *coquere* to cook] > **'cookable** *adj*

Cook[1] (kʊk) *n* **Mount** **1** Official name: **Aorangi-Mount Cook** a mountain in New Zealand, in the South Island, in the Southern Alps: the highest peak in New Zealand. Height: 3764 m (12 349 ft) **2** a mountain in SE Alaska, in the St. Elias Mountains. Height: 4194 m (13 760 ft)

Cook[2] (kʊk) *n* **1** Captain **James** 1728–79, British navigator and explorer: claimed the E coast of Australia for Britain, circumnavigated New Zealand, and discovered several Pacific and Atlantic islands (1768–79) **2** Sir **Joseph** 1860–1947, Australian statesman, born in England: prime minister of Australia (1913–14) **3 Thomas** 1808–92, British travel agent; innovator of conducted excursions and founder of the travel agents Thomas Cook and Son

cook-chill *n* a method of food preparation used by caterers, in which cooked dishes are chilled rapidly and reheated as required

Cooke *n* **Norman**, real name *Quentin Cooke*, also known as *Fatboy Slim*. born 1963, British disc jockey, pop musician, and record producer; hit records include *You've Come a Long Way, Baby* (1998) and "Praise You" (2001)

cooker ('kʊkə) *n* **1** an apparatus heated by gas, electricity, oil, or solid fuel, for cooking food **2** *Brit* another name for **cooking apple**

cookery ('kʊkərɪ) *n* **1** the art, study, or practice of cooking **2** *US* a place for cooking

▷ www.uk250.co.uk/Cookery
▷ www.cooksrecipes.com
▷ www.cookeryonline.com
▷ www.foodreference.com

cookery book *or* **cookbook** ('kʊk,bʊk) *n* a book containing recipes

cook-general *n, pl* **cooks-general** *Brit* (formerly, esp in the 1920s and 30s) a domestic servant who did cooking and housework

cookie *or* **cooky** ('kʊkɪ) *n, pl* **cookies** 1 the US and Canad word for **biscuit** 2 *inf* a person: *smart cookie* 3 *computing* a small file placed on a user's computer by a website, containing information about the user's preferences for future use in visits to the site 4 **that's the way the cookie crumbles** *inf* matters are inevitably so [c18 from Du. *koekje*, dim. of *koek* cake]

cookie-cutter *n* 1 a shape with a sharp edge for cutting individual biscuits from a sheet of dough ▷ *adj* 2 resembling many others of the same kind: *a row of cookie-cutter houses*

cooking apple *n* any large sour apple used in cooking

Cook Islands *pl n* a group of islands in the SW Pacific, an overseas territory of New Zealand: consists of the **Lower Cooks** and the **Northern Cooks.** Capital: Avarua, on Rarotonga. Pop: 18 500 (1994). Area: 234 sq km (90 sq miles)

cookout ('kʊk,aʊt) *n US & Canad* a party where a meal is cooked and eaten out of doors

cook shop *n* 1 *Brit* a shop that sells cookery equipment 2 *US* a restaurant

Cookson ('kʊksən) *n* Dame **Catherine** 1906-98, British novelist, known for her popular novels set in northeast England

Cook's tour (kʊks) *n inf* a rapid but extensive tour or survey of anything [c19 after Thomas COOK]

Cookstown ('kʊkstaʊn) *n* a district of central Northern Ireland, in Co. Tyrone. Pop: 32 581 (2001). Area: 622 sq km (240 sq miles)

Cook Strait *n* the strait between North and South Islands, New Zealand. Width: 26 km (16 miles)

Cooktown orchid ('kʊktaʊn) *n* a purple Australian orchid, *Dendrobium bigibbum*, found in Queensland, of which it is the floral emblem [named after *Cooktown*, a coastal town in NE Queensland]

cook up *vb (tr, adv)* 1 *inf* to concoct or invent (a story, alibi, etc) 2 to prepare (a meal), esp quickly 3 *sl* to prepare (a drug) by heating, as by melting heroin

cool (kuːl) *adj* 1 moderately cold: *a cool day* 2 comfortably free of heat: *a cool room* 3 calm: *a cool head* 4 lacking in enthusiasm, cordiality, etc: *a cool welcome* 5 calmly impudent 6 *inf* (of sums of money, etc) without exaggeration; actual: *a cool ten thousand* 7 (of a colour) having violet, blue, or green predominating; cold 8 (of jazz) economical and rhythmically relaxed 9 *inf* sophisticated or elegant; unruffled 10 *inf* marvellous ▷ *n* 11 coolness: *the cool of the evening* 12 *sl* calmness; composure (esp in **keep** *or* **lose one's cool**) 13 *sl* unruffled elegance or sophistication ▷ *vb* 14 (usually foll by *down* or *off*) to make or become cooler 15 (usually foll by *down* or *off*) to lessen the intensity of (anger or excitement) or (of anger or excitement) to become less intense; calm down 16 **cool it** *(usually imperative) sl* to calm down [OE *cōl*] > '**coolly** *adv* > '**coolness** *n*

coolant ('kuːlənt) *n* 1 a fluid used to cool a system or to transfer heat from one part of it to another 2 a liquid used to lubricate and cool the workpiece and cutting tool during machining

cool bag *or* **box** *n* an insulated container for keeping food cool

cool-down *n* another name for **warm-down**

cool drink *n S African* a soft drink

cooler ('kuːlə) *n* 1 a container, vessel, or apparatus for cooling, such as a heat exchanger 2 a slang word for **prison** 3 a drink consisting of wine, fruit juice, and carbonated water

cool hunter *n inf* a person who is employed to identify future trends, esp in fashion or the media

coolibah *or* **coolabah** ('kuːlə,bɑː) *n* an Australian eucalyptus that grows along rivers and has smooth bark and long narrow leaves [from Abor.]

Coolidge ('kuːlɪdʒ) *n* (**John**) **Calvin** 1872–1933, 30th president of the US (1923–29)

coolie *or* **cooly** ('kuːlɪ) *n, pl* **coolies** an unskilled Oriental labourer [c17 from Hindi *kulī*]

cooling-off period *n* 1 a period during which the contending sides to a dispute reconsider their options before taking further action 2 *Brit* a period, often 14 days, that begins when a sale contract or life-assurance policy is received by a member of the public, during which the contract or policy can be cancelled without loss

cooling tower *n* a tall, hollow structure, designed to permit free passage of air, inside which hot water trickles down, becoming cool as it does so: the water is normally reused as part of an industrial process

cool school *n NZ* a school where the students resolve conflict without the involvement of teachers

Coomaraswamy (kuː,mɑːrə'swɑːmɪ) *n* **Ananda** (**Kentish**) 1877–1947, Ceylonese art historian and interpreter of Indian culture to the West

coomb, combe, coombe, *or* **comb** (kuːm) *n* 1 *chiefly southern English* a short valley or deep hollow 2 *chiefly northern English* another name for a **cirque** [OE *cumb* (in place names), probably of Celtic origin; compare Old French *combe* small valley and Welsh *cwm* valley]

coon (kuːn) *n* 1 *inf* short for **raccoon** 2 *offens sl* a Black or a native Australian 3 *S African offens* a person of mixed race

coonskin ('kuːn,skɪn) *n* 1 the pelt of a raccoon 2 a raccoon cap with the tail hanging at the back 3 *US* an overcoat made of raccoon

coop[1] (kuːp) *n* 1 a cage or small enclosure for poultry or small animals 2 a small narrow place of confinement, esp a prison cell 3 a wicker basket for catching fish 4 **fly the coop** *US & Canad inf* to leave suddenly ▷ *vb* 5 *(tr; often foll by up or in)* to confine in a restricted area [c15 prob. from MLow G *kūpe* basket]

Cc

coop[2] *or* **co-op** ('kəʊ,ɒp) *n* a cooperative society or a shop run by a cooperative society

cooper ('kuːpə) *n* 1 a person skilled in making and repairing barrels, casks, etc ▷ *vb* 2 *(tr)* to make or mend (barrels, casks, etc) [c13 from MDu. *cūper* or MLow G *kūper*; see COOP[1]]

Cooper ('kuːpə) *n* 1 **Anthony Ashley** See (Earl of) **Shaftesbury** 2 **Cary** (**Lynn**) born 1940, British psychologist, noted for his studies of behaviour at work and the causes and treatment of stress 3 **Gary,** real name *Frank James Cooper*. 1901–61, US film actor; his many films include *Sergeant York* (1941) and *High Noon* (1952), for both of which he won Oscars 4 **James Fenimore** 1789–1851, US novelist, noted for his stories of American Indians, esp *The Last of the Mohicans* (1826) 5 **Leon Neil** born 1930, US physicist, noted for his work on the theory of superconductivity. He shared the Nobel prize for physics 1972 6 **Samuel** 1609–72, English miniaturist

cooperage ('kuːpərɪdʒ) *n* 1 Also called: **coopery** the craft, place of work, or products of a cooper 2 the labour fee charged by a cooper

cooperate *or* **co-operate** (kəʊ'ɒpə,reɪt) *vb* **cooperates, cooperating, cooperated** *or* **co-operates, co-operating, co-operated** *(intr)* 1 to work or act together 2 to be of assistance or be willing to assist 3 *econ* to engage in economic cooperation [c17 from LL *cooperārī* to combine, from L *operārī* to work] > **co'oper,ator** *or* **co-'oper,ator** *n*

cooperation *or* **co-operation** (kəʊ,ɒpə'reɪʃən) *n* 1 joint operation or action 2 assistance or willingness to assist 3 *econ* the combination of consumers, workers, etc, in activities usually embracing production, distribution, or trade > **co,oper'ationist** *or* **co-,oper'ationist** *n*

cooperative *or* **co-operative** (kəʊ'ɒpərətɪv, -'ɒprə-) *adj* 1 willing to cooperate; helpful 2 acting in conjunction with others; cooperating **3a** (of an enterprise, farm, etc) owned collectively and managed for joint economic benefit **3b** (of an economy) based on collective ownership and cooperative use of the means of production and distribution ▷ *n* **4** a cooperative organization, such as a farm

cooperative society *n* a commercial enterprise owned and managed by and for the benefit of customers or workers

Cooper Creek (ˈkuːpə) *n* an intermittent river in E central Australia, in the Channel Country: rises in central Queensland and flows generally southwest, reaching Lake Eyre only during wet-year floods; scene of the death of the explorers Burke and Wills in 1861; the surrounding basin provides cattle pastures after the floods subside. Total length: 1420 km (880 miles)

coopt *or* **co-opt** (kəʊˈɒpt) *vb* (*tr*) to add (someone) to a committee, board, etc, by the agreement of the existing members [c17 from L *cooptāre*, from *optāre* to choose] > **coˈoption, co-ˈoption** *or* **ˌcoopˈtation, ˌco-opˈtation** *n*

coordinate *or* **co-ordinate** (kəʊˈɔːdɪˌneɪt) *vb*, **coordinates, coordinating, coordinated** *or* **co-ordinates, co-ordinating, co-ordinated** **1** (*tr*) to integrate (diverse elements) in a harmonious operation **2** to place (things) in the same class, or (of things) to be placed in the same class, etc **3** (*intr*) to work together harmoniously **4** (*intr*) to take or be in the form of a harmonious order ▷ *n* (kəʊˈɔːdɪnɪt) **5** *maths* any of a set of numbers that defines the location of a point with reference to a system of axes **6** a person or thing equal in rank, type, etc ▷ *adj* (kəʊˈɔːdɪnɪt) **7** of or involving coordination **8** of the same rank, type, etc **9** of or involving the use of coordinates: *coordinate geometry* **10** *chem* denoting a type of covalent bond in which both the shared electrons are provided by one of the atoms > **coˈordiˌnator** *or* **co-ˈordiˌnator** *n*

coordinate clause *n* one of two or more clauses in a sentence having the same status and introduced by coordinating conjunctions

coordinates (kəʊˈɔːdɪnɪts) *pl n* clothes of matching or harmonious colours and design, for wearing together

coordinating conjunction *n* a conjunction that introduces coordinate clauses, such as *and*, *but*, and *or*

coordination *or* **co-ordination** (kəʊˌɔːdɪˈneɪʃən) *n* balanced and effective interaction of movement, actions, etc [c17 from LL *coordinātiō*, from L *ordinātiō* an arranging]

coot (kuːt) *n* **1** an aquatic bird of Europe and Asia, having dark plumage, and a white bill with a frontal shield: family Rallidae (rails, etc) **2** a foolish person, esp an old man [c14 prob. from Low G]

cootie (ˈkuːtɪ) *n* *US & NZ* a slang name for the body louse [c20 from Maori & ? (for US) Malay *kutu* louse]

cop¹ (kɒp) *sl* ▷ *n* **1** another name for **policeman** **2** *Brit* an arrest (esp in **a fair cop**) ▷ *vb* **cops, copping, copped** (*tr*) **3** to catch **4** to steal **5** to suffer (a punishment): *you'll cop a clout if you do that!* **6 cop it sweet** *Austral sl* **6a** to accept a punishment without complaint **6b** to have good fortune **7 cop this!** just look at this! ▷ See also **cop out** [c18 (vb) ?from obs. *cap* to arrest, from OF *caper* to seize]

cop² (kɒp) *n* **1** a conical roll of thread wound on a spindle **2** *now chiefly dialect* the top or crest, as of a hill [OE *cop*, *copp* top, summit]

cop³ (kɒp) *n* *Brit sl* (*usually used with a negative*) value: *not much cop* [c19 n use of COP¹]

copal (ˈkəʊpᵊl, -pæl) *n* a hard aromatic resin obtained from various tropical trees and used in making varnishes and lacquers [c16 from Sp., from Nahuatl *copalli*]

copartner (kəʊˈpɑːtnə) *n* a partner or associate, esp an equal partner in business > **coˈpartnership** *n*

cope¹ (kəʊp) *vb* **copes, coping, coped** (*intr*) **1** (foll by *with*) to contend (against) **2** to deal successfully (with); manage: *she coped well with the problem* [c14 from OF *coper* to strike, cut, from *coup* blow]

cope² (kəʊp) *n* **1** a large ceremonial cloak worn at liturgical functions by priests of certain Christian sects **2** any covering shaped like a cope ▷ *vb* **copes, coping, coped** **3** (*tr*) to dress (someone) in a cope [OE *cāp*, from Med. L *cāpa*, from LL *cappa* hooded cloak]

cope³ (kəʊp) *vb* **copes, coping, coped** (*tr*) **1** to provide (a wall, etc) with a coping ▷ *n* **2** another name for **coping** [c17 prob. from F *couper* to cut]

copeck (ˈkəʊpɛk) *n* a variant spelling of **kopeck**

Copenhagen (ˌkəʊpənˈheɪgən, -ˈhɑː-, ˈkəʊpənˌheɪ-, -ˌhɑː-) *n* the capital of Denmark, a port on Zealand and Amager Islands on a site inhabited for some 6000 years: exports chiefly agricultural products; iron and steel works; university (1479). Pop: 485 699 (2000 est). Danish name: **København**
▷ www.copenhagen.com

Copenhagen interpretation *n* an interpretation of quantum mechanics developed by Niels Bohr (1885–1962) and his colleagues at the University of Copenhagen, based on the concept of wave–particle duality and the idea that the observation influences the result of an experiment

copepod (ˈkəʊpɪˌpɒd) *n* a minute marine or freshwater crustacean, an important constituent of plankton [c19 from NL *copepoda*, from Gk *kōpē* oar + *pous* foot]

coper (ˈkəʊpə) *n* a horse dealer [c17 (a dealer): from dialect *cope* to buy, barter, from Low G]

Copernican system *n* the theory published in 1543 by Copernicus which stated that the earth and the planets rotated round the sun

Copernicus (kəˈpɜːnɪkəs) *n* **Nicolaus** (ˌnɪkəˈleɪəs) Polish name *Mikolaj Kopernik*. 1473–1543, Polish astronomer, whose theory of the solar system (the **Copernican system**) was published in 1543

copestone (ˈkəʊpˌstəʊn) *n* **1** Also called: **coping stone** a stone used to form a coping **2** the stone at the top of a building, wall, etc

copier (ˈkɒpɪə) *n* a person or device that copies

copilot (ˈkəʊˌpaɪlət) *n* a second or relief pilot of an aircraft

coping (ˈkəʊpɪŋ) *n* the sloping top course of a wall, usually made of masonry or brick

coping saw *n* a handsaw with a U-shaped frame used for cutting curves in a material too thick for a fret saw

copious (ˈkəʊpɪəs) *adj* **1** abundant; extensive **2** having an abundant supply **3** full of words, ideas, etc; profuse [c14 from L *cōpiōsus*, from *cōpia* abundance] > **ˈcopiously** *adv* > **ˈcopiousness** *n*

coplanar (kəʊˈpleɪnə) *adj* lying in the same plane: *coplanar lines* > **ˌcoplaˈnarity** *n*

Copland (ˈkəʊplənd) *n* **Aaron** 1900–90, US composer of orchestral and chamber music, ballets, and film music

cop off *vb* (*intr, adv*) **cop off with** *Brit inf* to establish an amorous or sexual relationship with

copolymer (kəʊˈpɒlɪmə) *n* a chemical compound of high molecular weight formed by uniting the molecules of two or more different compounds (monomers)

cop out *sl* ▷ *vb* **1** (*intr, adv*) to fail to assume responsibility or fail to perform ▷ *n* **cop-out** **2** a way or an instance of avoiding responsibility or commitment [c20 prob. from COP¹]

copper¹ (ˈkɒpə) *n* **1** a malleable reddish metallic element occurring as the free metal, copper glance, and copper pyrites: used in such alloys as brass and bronze. Symbol: Cu; atomic no.: 29; atomic wt.: 63.54. Related adjs.: **cupric, cuprous** **2a** the reddish-brown colour of copper **2b** (*as adj*): *copper hair* **3** *inf* any copper or bronze coin **4** *chiefly Brit* a large vessel, formerly of copper, used for boiling or washing **5** any of various small widely distributed butterflies having reddish-brown wings

▷ *vb* **6** (*tr*) to coat or cover with copper [OE *coper*, from L *Cyprium aes* Cyprian metal, from Gk *Kupris* Cyprus]

copper[2] ('kɒpə) *n* a slang word for **policeman** Often shortened to **cop** [c19 from COP[1] (vb)]

copperas ('kɒpərəs) *n* a less common name for **ferrous sulphate** [c14 *coperose*, via OF from Med. L *cuperosa*, ? orig. in *aqua cuprosa* copper water]

copper beech *n* a cultivated variety of European beech that has dark purple leaves

Copper Belt *n* a region of Central Africa, along the border between Zambia and the Democratic Republic of Congo: rich deposits of copper

copper-bottomed *adj* reliable, esp financially reliable [from the practice of coating bottom of ships with copper to prevent the timbers rotting]

copper-fasten *vb* (*tr*) *Irish* to make (a bargain or agreement) binding

copperhead ('kɒpə,hɛd) *n* **1** a venomous pit viper of the US, with a reddish-brown head **2** a venomous marsh snake of Australia, with a reddish band behind the head

copperplate ('kɒpə,pleɪt) *n* **1** a polished copper plate on which a design has been etched or engraved **2** a print taken from such a plate **3** a fine handwriting based upon that used on copperplate engravings

copper pyrites ('paɪraɪts) *n* (*functioning as sing*) another name for **chalcopyrite**

coppersmith ('kɒpə,smɪθ) *n* a person who works in copper

copper sulphate *n* a copper salt found naturally and made by the action of sulphuric acid on copper oxide: used as a mordant, in electroplating, and in plant sprays. Formula: $CuSO_4$

coppice ('kɒpɪs) *n* **1** a dense growth of small trees or bushes, esp one regularly trimmed back so that a continual supply of small poles and firewood is obtained ▷ *vb* **coppices, coppicing, coppiced 2** (*tr*) to trim back (trees or bushes) to form a coppice [c14 from OF *copeiz*] > **'coppiced** *adj*

Coppola ('kɒpələ) *n* **Francis Ford** born 1939, US film director. His films include *The Godfather* (1972), *Apocalypse Now* (1979), *Tucker* (1988), and *The Rainmaker* (1999)

copra ('kɒprə) *n* the dried, oil-yielding kernel of the coconut [c16 from Port., from Malayalam *koppara* coconut]

copro- *or before a vowel* **copr-** *combining form* indicating dung or obscenity, as in **cop'rology** *n* preoccupation with excrement, **cop'rophagous** *adj* feeding on dung [from Gk *kopros* dung]

copse (kɒps) *n* another word for **coppice** (sense 1) [c16 from COPPICE]

Copt (kɒpt) *n* **1** a member of the Coptic Church **2** an Egyptian descended from the ancient Egyptians [c17 from Ar., from Coptic *kyptios* Egyptian, from Gk *Aiguptios*, from *Aiguptos* Egypt]

Coptic ('kɒptɪk) *n* **1** an Afro-Asiatic language, written in the Greek alphabet but descended from ancient Egyptian. Extinct as a spoken language, it survives in the Coptic Church ▷ *adj* **2** of this language **3** of the Copts

Coptic Church *n* the ancient Christian Church of Egypt

copula ('kɒpjʊlə) *n, pl* **copulas** *or* **copulae** (-,liː) **1** a verb, such as *be, seem*, or *taste*, that is used to identify or link the subject with the complement of a sentence, as in *he became king, sugar tastes sweet* **2** anything that serves as a link [c17 from L: bond, from *co-* together + *apere* to fasten] > **'copular** *adj*

copulate ('kɒpjʊ,leɪt) *vb* **copulates, copulating, copulated** (*intr*) to perform sexual intercourse [c17 from L *copulāre* to join together; see COPULA] > **,copu'lation** *n* > **'copulatory** *adj*

copulative ('kɒpjʊlətɪv) *adj* **1** serving to join or unite **2** of copulation **3** *grammar* (of a verb) having the nature of a copula

copy ('kɒpɪ) *n, pl* **copies 1** an imitation or reproduction of an original **2** a single specimen of something that occurs in a multiple edition, such as a book **3a** matter to be reproduced in print **3b** written matter or text as distinct from graphic material in books, etc **4** the words used to present a promotional message in an advertisement **5** *journalism, inf* suitable material for an article: *disasters are always good copy* **6** *arch* a model to be copied, esp an example of penmanship ▷ *vb* **copies, copying, copied 7** (when *tr*, often foll by *out*) to make a copy (of) **8** (*tr*) to imitate as a model **9** to imitate unfairly [c14 from Med. L *cōpia* an imitation, from L: abundance]

copybook ('kɒpɪ,bʊk) *n* **1** a book of specimens, esp of penmanship, for imitation **2** *chiefly US* a book for or containing documents **3 blot one's copybook** *inf* to spoil one's reputation by a mistake or indiscretion **4** (*modifier*) trite or unoriginal

copycat ('kɒpɪ,kæt) *n inf* **a** a person, esp a child, who imitates or copies another **b** (*as modifier*): *copycat murders*

copyhold ('kɒpɪ,həʊld) *n law* (formerly) a tenure less than freehold of land in England evidenced by a copy of the Court roll

copyist ('kɒpɪɪst) *n* **1** a person who makes written copies **2** a person who imitates

copyreader ('kɒpɪ,riːdə) *n US* a person who edits and prepares newspaper copy for publication; subeditor

copyright ('kɒpɪ,raɪt) *n* **1** the exclusive right to produce copies and to control an original literary, musical, or artistic work, granted by law for a specified number of years ▷ *adj* **2** (of a work, etc) subject to copyright ▷ *vb* **3** (*tr*) to take out a copyright on

copy typist *n* a typist whose job is to type from written or typed drafts rather than dictation

copywriter ('kɒpɪ,raɪtə) *n* a person employed to write advertising copy > **'copy,writing** *n*

coquet (kəʊ'kɛt, kɒ-) *vb* **coquets, coquetting, coquetted** (*intr*) **1** to behave flirtatiously **2** to dally or trifle [c17 from F: a gallant, lit.: a little cock, from *coq* cock] > **'coquetry** *n*

coquette (kəʊ'kɛt, kɒ-) *n* **1** a woman who flirts **2** any hummingbird of the genus *Lophornis* [c17 from F, fem of COQUET] > **co'quettish** *adj* > **co'quettishness** *n*

Cor. *Bible abbrev for* Corinthians

coracle ('kɒrək[ə]l) *n* a small roundish boat made of waterproofed hides stretched over a wicker frame [c16 from Welsh *corwgl*]

coracoid ('kɒrə,kɔɪd) *n* a paired ventral bone of the pectoral girdle in vertebrates. In mammals it is reduced to a peg (the **coracoid process**) on the scapula [c18 from NL *coracoīdēs*, from Gk *korakoeidēs* like a raven, from *korax* raven]

coral ('kɒrəl) *n* **1** any of a class of marine colonial coelenterates having a calcareous, horny, or soft skeleton **2a** the calcareous or horny material forming the skeleton of certain of these animals **2b** (*as modifier*): *a coral reef* **3** a rocklike aggregation of certain of these animals or their skeletons, forming an island or reef **4a** something made of coral **4b** (*as modifier*): *a coral necklace* **5a** a yellowish-pink colour **5b** (*as adj*): *coral lipstick* **6** the roe of a lobster or crab, which becomes pink when cooked [c14 from OF, from L *corāllium*, from Gk *korallion*, prob. of Semitic origin]

coral reef *n* a marine reef consisting of coral consolidated into limestone

coralroot ('kɒrəl,ruːt) *n* a N temperate leafless orchid with branched roots resembling coral

Coral Sea *n* the SW arm of the Pacific, between Australia, New Guinea, and Vanuatu

coral snake *n* **1** a venomous snake of tropical and subtropical America, marked with red, black, yellow, and white transverse bands **2** any of various other brightly coloured snakes of Africa and SE Asia

coral trout *n* an Australian fish, *Plectropomus maculatus*, of the Great Barrier Reef which is an important food fish

cor anglais ('kɔːr 'ɑːŋgleɪ) *n, pl* **cors anglais** ('kɔːz 'ɑːŋgleɪ) *music* a woodwind instrument, the alto of the oboe family. Also called: **English horn** [c19 from F: English horn]

corbel ('kɔːbᵊl) *archit* ▷ *n* **1** a bracket, usually of stone or brick ▷ *vb* **corbels, corbelling, corbelled** *or US* **corbels, corbeling, corbeled** **2** (*tr*) to lay (a stone) so that it forms a corbel [c15 from OF, lit.: a little raven, from Med. L *corvellus*, from L *corvus* raven]

corbie ('kɔːbɪ) *n* a Scot. name for **raven**[1] (sense 1) or **crow**[1] (sense 1) [c15 from OF *corbin*, from L *corvīnus* CORVINE]

corbie-step *or* **corbel step** *n archit* any of a set of steps on the top of a gable. Also called: **crow step**

Corbusier (*French* kɔrbyzje) *n* **Le** See **Le Corbusier**

Corcovado *n* **1** (*Spanish* korko'βaðo) a volcano in S Chile, in the Andes. Height: 2300 m (7546 ft) **2** (*Portuguese* korku'vɑːdu) a mountain in SE Brazil, in SW Rio de Janeiro city. Height: 704 m (2310 ft)

Corcyra (kɔː'saɪərə) *n* the ancient name for **Corfu**

cord (kɔːd) *n* **1** string or thin rope made of twisted strands **2** a length of woven or twisted strands of silk, etc, used as a belt, etc **3** a ribbed fabric, esp corduroy **4** the US and Canad name for **flex** (sense 1) **5** *anat* any part resembling a rope: *the spinal cord* **6** a unit for measuring cut wood, equal to 128 cubic feet ▷ *vb* (*tr*) **7** to bind or furnish with a cord or cords ▷ See also **cords** [c13 from OF *corde*, from L *chorda*, from Gk *khordē*] > **'cord,like** *adj*

cordage ('kɔːdɪdʒ) *n* **1** *naut* the lines and rigging of a vessel **2** an amount of wood measured in cords

cordate ('kɔːdeɪt) *adj* heart-shaped

Corday (*French* kɔrdɛ) *n* **Charlotte** (ʃarlɔt), full name *Marie Anne Charlotte Corday d'Armont*. 1768–93, French Girondist revolutionary, who assassinated Marat

corded ('kɔːdɪd) *adj* **1** bound or fastened with cord **2** (of a fabric) ribbed **3** (of muscles) standing out like cords

cordial ('kɔːdɪəl) *adj* **1** warm and friendly: *a cordial greeting* **2** stimulating ▷ *n* **3** a drink with a fruit base: *lime cordial* **4** another word for **liqueur** [c14 from Med. L *cordiālis*, from L *cor* heart] > **'cordially** *adv*

cordiality (ˌkɔːdɪ'ælɪtɪ) *n, pl* **cordialities** warmth of feeling

cordillera (ˌkɔːdɪl'jɛərə) *n* a series of parallel ranges of mountains, esp in the northwestern US [c18 from Sp., from *cordilla*, lit.: a little cord]

Cordilleras (ˌkɔːdɪl'jɛərəz; *Spanish* korði'ʎeras) *pl n* **the** the complex of mountain ranges on the W side of the Americas, extending from Alaska to Cape Horn and including the Andes and the Rocky Mountains

cordite ('kɔːdaɪt) *n* any of various explosive materials containing cellulose nitrate, sometimes mixed with nitroglycerine [c19 from CORD + -ITE[1], from its stringy appearance]

cordless ('kɔːdlɪs) *adj* (of an electrical device) operated by an internal battery so that no connection to mains supply is needed

cordless telephone *n* a portable battery-powered telephone with a short-range radio link to a fixed base unit

Córdoba[1] (*Spanish* 'korðoβa) *n* **1** a city in central Argentina: university (1613). Pop: 1 208 713 (1991) **2** a city in S Spain, on the Guadalquivir River: centre of Moorish Spain (711–1236). Pop: 309 961 (1998 est). English name: **Cordova**

Córdoba[2] *or* **Córdova** (*Spanish* 'korðoβa) *n* **Francisco Fernández de** (fran'θisko fɛr'nandɛθ de) died 1518, Spanish soldier and explorer, who discovered Yucatán

cordon ('kɔːdᵊn) *n* **1** a chain of police, soldiers, ships, etc, stationed around an area **2** a ribbon worn as insignia of honour **3** a cord or ribbon worn as an ornament **4** *archit* another name for **string course** **5** *horticulture* a fruit tree consisting of a single stem bearing fruiting spurs, produced by cutting back all lateral branches ▷ *vb* **6** (*tr*; often foll by *off*) to put or form a cordon (around); close (off) [c16 from OF, lit.: a little cord, from *corde* CORD]

cordon bleu (*French* kɔrdɔ̃ blø) *n* **1** *French history* the sky-blue ribbon worn by members of the highest order of knighthood under the Bourbon monarchy **2** any very high distinction ▷ *adj* **3** of or denoting food prepared to a very high standard [F, lit.: blue ribbon]

cordon sanitaire *French* (kɔrdɔ̃ sanitɛr) *n* **1** a guarded line isolating an infected area **2** a line of buffer states shielding a country [c19 lit.: sanitary line]

Cordova ('kɔːdəvə) *n* the English name for **Córdoba** (sense 2)

cordovan ('kɔːdəvᵊn) *n* a fine leather now made mainly from horsehide [c16 from Sp. *cordobán* of CÓRDOBA[1]]

Cordovan ('kɔːdəvᵊn) *n* **1** a native or inhabitant of Córdoba, Spain ▷ *adj* **2** of or relating to Córdoba, Spain

cords (kɔːdz) *pl n* trousers made of corduroy

corduroy ('kɔːdəˌrɔɪ, ˌkɔːdə'rɔɪ) *n* a heavy cotton pile fabric with lengthways ribs [c18 ?from the proper name *Corderoy*]

corduroys (ˌkɔːdə'rɔɪz, 'kɔːdəˌrɔɪz) *pl n* trousers or breeches of corduroy

cordwainer ('kɔːdˌweɪnə) *n arch* a shoemaker or worker in leather [c12 *cordwaner*, from OF, from OSp. *cordován* CORDOVAN]

cordwood ('kɔːdˌwʊd) *n* wood that has been cut into lengths of four feet so that it can be stacked in cords

core (kɔː) *n* **1** the central part of certain fleshy fruits, such as the apple, consisting of the seeds **2** the central or essential part of something: *the core of the argument* **3** a piece of magnetic material, such as soft iron, inside an electromagnet or transformer **4** *geol* the central part of the earth **5** a cylindrical sample of rock, soil, etc, obtained by the use of a hollow drill **6** *physics* the region of a nuclear reactor in which the reaction takes place **7** *computing* **7a** a ferrite ring formerly used in a computer memory to store one bit of information **7b** (*as modifier*): *core memory* **8** *archaeol* a stone or flint from which flakes have been removed **9** *physics* the nucleus together with all complete electron shells of an atom ▷ *vb* **cores, coring, cored** **10** (*tr*) to remove the core from (fruit) [c14 from ?]

coreligionist (ˌkəʊrɪ'lɪdʒənɪst) *n* an adherent of the same religion as another

Corelli (kɒ'rɛlɪ) *n* ▷ **1** (*Italian* ko'rɛlli) *n* **Arcangelo** (ar'kandʒelo) 1653–1713, Italian violinist and composer of sonatas and concerti grossi **2** **Marie** , real name *Mary Mackay*. 1854–1924, British novelist. Her melodramatic works include *The Sorrows of Satan* (1895) and *The Murder of Delicia* (1896)

coreopsis (ˌkɒrɪ'ɒpsɪs) *n* a plant of America and Africa, with yellow, brown, or yellow-and-red daisy-like flowers [c18 from NL, from Gk *koris* bedbug + -OPSIS; so called from the appearance of the seed]

co-respondent (ˌkəʊrɪ'spɒndənt) *n law* a person cited in divorce proceedings, alleged to have committed adultery with the respondent

core subjects *pl n Brit education* three foundation subjects (English, mathematics, and science) that are compulsory throughout each key stage in the National Curriculum

core time *n* See **flexitime**

corf (kɔːf) *n, pl* **corves** *Brit* a wagon or basket used formerly in mines [c14 from MDu. *corf* or MLow G *korf*, prob. from L *corbis* basket]

Corfu (kɔː'fuː) *n* **1** an island in the Ionian Sea, in the Ionian Islands: forms, with neighbouring islands, a department of Greece. Pop: 107 592 (1991). Area: 641 sq km (247 sq miles) **2** a port on E Corfu island. Pop: 105 000 (1995 est). Modern Greek name: **Kérkyra** Ancient name: **Corcyra**

corgi (ˈkɔːɡɪ) *n* either of two short-legged sturdy breeds of dog, the Cardigan and the Pembroke [c20 from Welsh, from *cor* dwarf + *ci* dog]

coriander (ˌkɒrɪˈændə) *n* a European umbelliferous plant, cultivated for its aromatic seeds and leaves, used in flavouring foods. US and Canad name: **cilantro** [c14 from OF *coriandre*, from L *coriandrum*, from Gk *koriannon*, from ?]

Corinth (ˈkɒrɪnθ) *n* **1** a port in S Greece, in the NE Peloponnese: the modern town is near the site of the ancient city, the largest and richest of the city-states after Athens. Pop: 29 600 (1995 est). Modern Greek name: **Kórinthos** **2** a region of ancient Greece, occupying most of the Isthmus of Corinth and part of the NE Peloponnese **3** **Gulf of** Also called: Gulf of **Lepanto** an inlet of the Ionian Sea between the Peloponnese and central Greece **4** **Isthmus of** a narrow strip of land between the Gulf of Corinth and the Saronic Gulf: crossed by the **Corinth Canal** making navigation possible between the gulfs

Corinthian (kəˈrɪnθɪən) *adj* **1** of Corinth **2** denoting one of the five classical orders of architecture: characterized by a bell-shaped capital having carved ornaments based on acanthus leaves **3** *obs* given to luxury; dissolute ▷ *n* **4** a native or inhabitant of Corinth

▷ http://harpy.uccs.edu/greek/corinthian.htm

Coriolanus (ˌkɒrɪəˈleɪnəs) *n* **Gaius Marcius** (ˈɡaɪəs ˈmɑːsɪəs) 5th century BC, a legendary Roman general, who allegedly led an army against Rome but was dissuaded from conquering it by his mother and wife

Coriolis force (ˌkɒrɪˈəʊlɪs) *n* a hypothetical force postulated to explain a deflection in the path of a body moving relative to the earth: it is due to the earth's rotation and is to the left in the S hemisphere and to the right in the N hemisphere [c19 after Gaspard G. *Coriolis* (1792–1843), F civil engineer]

corium (ˈkɔːrɪəm) *n, pl* **coria** (-rɪə) the deep inner layer of the skin, beneath the epidermis, containing connective tissue, blood vessels, and fat. Also called: **derma, dermis** [c19 from L: rind, skin]

cork (kɔːk) *n* **1** the thick light porous outer bark of the cork oak **2** a piece of cork used as a stopper **3** an angling float **4** Also called: **phellem** *bot* a protective layer of dead impermeable cells on the outside of the stems and roots of woody plants ▷ *adj* **5** made of cork. Related adj: **suberose** ▷ *vb (tr)* **6** to stop up (a bottle, etc) with or as with a cork **7** (often foll by *up*) to restrain **8** to black (the face, hands, etc) with burnt cork [c14 prob. from Ar. *qurq*, from L *cortex* bark] > ˈ**cork**ˌ**like** *adj*

Cork (kɔːk) *n* **1** a county of SW Republic of Ireland, in Munster province: crossed by ridges of low mountains; scenic coastline. County town: Cork. Pop: 420 510 (1996). Area: 7459 sq km (2880 sq miles) **2** a city and port in S Republic of Ireland, county town of Co. Cork, at the mouth of the River Lee: seat of the University College of Cork (1849). Pop: 127 092 (1996). Gaelic name: **Corcaigh**

corkage (ˈkɔːkɪdʒ) *n* a charge made at a restaurant for serving wine, etc, bought off the premises

corked (kɔːkt) *adj* tainted through having a cork containing excess tannin

corker (ˈkɔːkə) *n old-fashioned sl* **1** something or somebody striking or outstanding **2** an irrefutable remark that puts an end to discussion

cork oak *n* an evergreen Mediterranean oak whose porous bark yields cork

corkscrew (ˈkɔːkˌskruː) *n* **1** a device for drawing corks from bottles, typically consisting of a pointed metal spiral attached to a handle or screw mechanism **2** (*modifier*) resembling a corkscrew in shape ▷ *vb* **3** to move or cause to move in a spiral or zigzag course

corm (kɔːm) *n* an organ of vegetative reproduction in plants such as the crocus, consisting of a globular stem base swollen with food and surrounded by papery scale leaves [c19 from NL *cormus*, from Gk *kormos* tree trunk from which the branches have been lopped]

cormorant (ˈkɔːmərənt) *n* an aquatic bird having a dark plumage, a long neck and body, and a slender hooked beak [c13 from OF *cormareng*, from *corp* raven + *-mareng* of the sea]

corn[1] (kɔːn) *n* **1** *Brit* **1a** any of various cereal plants, esp the predominant crop of a region, such as wheat in England and oats in Scotland **1b** the seeds of such plants, esp after harvesting **1c** a single seed of such plants; a grain **2** the usual US, Canad, Austral, and NZ name for **maize** **3** *sl* an idea, song, etc, regarded as banal or sentimental ▷ *vb (tr)* **4a** to preserve in brine **4b** to salt [OE *corn*]

corn[2] (kɔːn) *n* **1** a hardening of the skin, esp of the toes, caused by pressure **2** **tread on (someone's) corns** *Brit inf* to offend or hurt (someone) by touching on a sensitive subject [c15 from OF *corne* horn, from L *cornū*]

corn borer *n* the larva of a moth native to Europe: in E North America a serious pest of maize

corn bread *n chiefly US* bread made from maize meal. Also called: **Indian bread**

corn bunting *n* a heavily built European songbird with a streaked brown plumage

corncob (ˈkɔːnˌkɒb) *n* the core of an ear of maize, to which kernels are attached

corncob pipe *n* a pipe with a bowl made from a dried corncob

corncockle (ˈkɔːnˌkɒkᵊl) *n* a European plant that has reddish-purple flowers and grows in cornfields and by roadsides

corncrake (ˈkɔːnˌkreɪk) *n* a common Eurasian rail with a buff speckled plumage and reddish wings

corn dolly *n* a decorative figure made by plaiting straw

cornea (ˈkɔːnɪə) *n, pl* **corneas** *or* **corneae** (-nɪˌiː) the convex transparent membrane that forms the anterior covering of the eyeball [c14 from Med. L *cornea tēla* horny web, from L *cornū* HORN] > ˈ**corneal** *adj*

corned (kɔːnd) *adj* (esp of beef) cooked and then preserved or pickled in salt or brine

Corneille (*French* kɔrnɛj) *n* **Pierre** (pjɛr) 1606–84, French tragic dramatist often regarded as the founder of French classical drama. His plays include *Médée* (1635), *Le Cid* (1636), *Horace* (1640), and *Polyeucte* (1642)

cornel (ˈkɔːnᵊl) *n* any shrub of the genus *Cornus*, such as the dogwood [c16 prob. from MLow G *kornelle*, ult. from L *cornus*]

cornelian (kɔːˈniːlɪən) *n* a variant spelling of **carnelian**

corner (ˈkɔːnə) *n* **1** the place or angle formed by the meeting of two converging lines or surfaces **2** a projecting angle of a solid object **3** the place where two streets meet **4** any small, secluded, or private place **5** a dangerous position from which escape is difficult: *a tight corner* **6** any region, esp a remote place **7** something used to protect or mark a corner, as of the hard cover of a book **8** *commerce* a monopoly over the supply of a commodity so that its market price can be controlled **9** *soccer, hockey, etc* a free kick or shot from the corner of the field, taken against a defending team when the ball goes out of play over their goal line after last touching one of their players **10** either of two opposite angles of a boxing ring in which the opponents take their rests **11** **cut corners** to take the shortest or easiest way, esp at the expense of high standards **12** **turn the corner** to pass the critical point (in an illness, etc) **13** (*modifier*) on a corner: *a corner shop* ▷ *vb* **14** (*tr*) to manoeuvre (a person or animal) into a position from which escape is difficult or impossible **15** (*tr*) **15a** to acquire enough of (a commodity) to attain control of the market **15b** Also: **engross** to attain control of (a market) in such a manner **16** (*intr*) (of vehicles, etc) to turn a corner **17** (*intr*) (in soccer, etc) to take a corner [c13 from OF *corniere*, from L *cornū* point, HORN]

Corner *n* **the** *inf* an area in central Australia, at the junction of the borders of Queensland and South Australia

cornerback ('kɔːnəˌbæk) *n American football* a defensive back

cornerstone ('kɔːnəˌstəʊn) *n* **1** a stone at the corner of a wall, uniting two intersecting walls **2** a stone placed at the corner of a building during a ceremony to mark the start of construction **3** a person or thing of prime importance: *the cornerstone of the whole argument*

cornerwise ('kɔːnəˌwaɪz) *or* **cornerways** ('kɔːnəˌweɪz) *adv, adj* with a corner in front; diagonally

cornet ('kɔːnɪt) *n* **1** a three-valved brass instrument of the trumpet family **2** a person who plays the cornet **3** a cone-shaped paper container for sweets, etc **4** *Brit* a cone-shaped wafer container for ice cream **5** (formerly) the lowest rank of commissioned cavalry officer in the British Army **6** the large white headdress of some nuns [C14 from OF, from L *cornū* HORN] > **cor'netist** *or* **cor'nettist** *n*

corn exchange *n* a building where corn is bought and sold

cornfield ('kɔːnˌfiːld) *n* a field planted with cereal crops

cornflakes ('kɔːnˌfleɪks) *pl n* a breakfast cereal made from toasted maize

cornflour ('kɔːnˌflaʊə) *n* a fine maize flour, used for thickening sauces. US and Canad name: **cornstarch**

cornflower ('kɔːnˌflaʊə) *n* a herbaceous plant, with blue, purple, pink, or white flowers, formerly a common weed in cornfields

Cornforth ('kɔːnˌfɔːθ) *n* Sir **John Warcup** born 1917, Australian chemist, who shared the 1975 Nobel prize for chemistry with Vladimir Prelog for their work on stereochemistry

cornice ('kɔːnɪs) *n* **1** *archit* **1a** the top projecting mouldings of an entablature **1b** a continuous horizontal projecting course or moulding at the top of a wall, building, etc **2** an overhanging ledge of snow [C16 from OF, from It., ?from L *cornix* crow, but infl. also by L *corōnis* decorative flourish]

corniche ('kɔːnɪʃ) *n* a coastal road, esp one built into the face of a cliff [C19 from *corniche road;* see CORNICE]

Cornish ('kɔːnɪʃ) *adj* **1** of Cornwall or its inhabitants ▷ *n* **2** a former language of Cornwall: extinct by 1800 **3** **the** *(functioning as pl)* the natives or inhabitants of Cornwall > **'Cornishman** *or fem* **'Cornishwoman** *n*

Cornish pasty ('pæstɪ) *n cookery* a pastry case with a filling of meat and vegetables

corn meal *n* meal made from maize. Also called: **Indian meal**

Corno (*Italian* 'kɔrno) *n* **Monte** ('monte) a mountain in central Italy: the highest peak in the Apennines. Height: 2912 m (9554 ft)

corn salad *n* a plant which often grows in cornfields and whose leaves are sometimes used in salads. Also called: **lamb's lettuce**

cornstarch ('kɔːnˌstɑːtʃ) *n* the US and Canad name for **cornflour**

cornucopia (ˌkɔːnjʊ'kəʊpɪə) *n* **1** a representation of a horn in painting, sculpture, etc, overflowing with fruit, vegetables, etc; horn of plenty **2** a great abundance **3** a horn-shaped container [C16 from LL, from L *cornū cōpiae* horn of plenty] > ˌ**cornu'copian** *adj*

Cornwall ('kɔːnˌwɔːl, -wəl) *n* a county of SW England: hilly, with a deeply indented coastline. Administrative centre: Truro. Pop: 499 114 (2001). Area: 3564 sq km (1376 sq miles)

Cornwallis (kɔːn'wɒlɪs) *n* **Charles,** 1st Marquis Cornwallis. 1738–1805, British general in the War of American Independence: commanded forces defeated at Yorktown (1781): defeated Tipu Sahib (1791): governor general of Bengal (1786–93, 1805): negotiated the Treaty of Amiens (1801)

Cornwell ('kɔːnˌwɛl) *n* **Patricia D(aniels)** born 1956, US crime novelist; her novels, many of which feature the pathologist Dr Kay Scarpetta, include *Postmortem* (1990), *The Last Precinct* (2000), and *Isle of Dogs* (2002)

corn whisky *n* whisky made from maize

corny ('kɔːnɪ) *adj* **cornier, corniest** *sl* **1** trite or banal **2** sentimental or mawkish **3** abounding in corn [C16 (C20 in the sense banal): from CORN[1] + -Y[1]]

corolla (kə'rɒlə) *n* the petals of a flower collectively, forming an inner floral envelope [C17 dim. of L *corōna* crown]

corollary (kə'rɒlərɪ) *n, pl* **corollaries** **1** a proposition that follows directly from the proof of another proposition **2** an obvious deduction **3** a natural consequence [C14 from L *corollārium* money paid for a garland, from L *corolla* garland]

Coromandel Coast (ˌkɒrə'mændᵊl) *n* the SE coast of India, along the Bay of Bengal, extending from Point Calimere to the mouth of the Krishna River

corona (kə'rəʊnə) *n, pl* **coronas** *or* **coronae** (-niː) **1** a circle of light around a luminous body, usually the moon **2** Also called: **aureole** the outermost region of the sun's atmosphere, visible as a faint halo during a solar eclipse **3** *archit* the flat vertical face of a cornice **4** a circular chandelier **5** *bot* **5a** the trumpet-shaped part of the corolla of daffodils and similar plants **5b** a crown of leafy outgrowths from inside the petals of some flowers **6** *anat* a crownlike structure **7** a long cigar with blunt ends **8** *physics* an electrical discharge appearing around the surface of a charged conductor [C16 from L: crown]

coronach ('kɒrənəx) *n Scot & Irish* a dirge or lamentation for the dead [C16 from Scot. Gaelic *corranach*]

coronary ('kɒrənərɪ) *adj* **1** *anat* designating blood vessels, nerves, ligaments, etc, that encircle a part or structure ▷ *n, pl* **coronaries** **2** short for **coronary thrombosis** [C17 from L *corōnārius* belonging to a wreath or crown]

coronary artery *n* either of the two arteries branching from the aorta and supplying blood to the heart

coronary bypass *n* the surgical bypass of a narrowed or blocked coronary artery by grafting a section of a healthy blood vessel taken from another part of the patient's body

coronary heart disease *n* any heart disorder caused by disease of the coronary arteries

coronary thrombosis *n* a condition of interrupted blood flow to the heart due to a blood clot in a coronary artery

coronation (ˌkɒrə'neɪʃən) *n* the act or ceremony of crowning a monarch [C14 from OF, from *coroner* to crown, from L *corōnāre*]

coronation chicken *n* a dish of cold cooked chicken in a mild creamy curry sauce [C20 so-called because it was served at the coronation lunch of Elizabeth II (born 1926), queen of Great Britain and Northern Ireland from 1952]

coronavirus (kə'rəʊnəˌvaɪrəs) *n* a type of airborne virus accounting for 10-30% of all colds af [C20 so-called because of their corona-like appearance in electron micrographs]

coroner ('kɒrənə) *n* a public official responsible for the investigation of violent, sudden, or suspicious deaths [C14 from Anglo-F *corouner*, from OF *corone* CROWN] > **'coronerˌship** *n*

coronet ('kɒrənɪt) *n* **1** any small crown, esp one worn by princes or peers **2** a woman's jewelled circlet for the head **3** the margin between the skin of a horse's pastern and the horn of the hoof **4** the knob at the base of a deer's antler [C15 from OF *coronete*]

Corot (*French* kɔro) *n* **Jean Baptiste Camille** (ʒɑ̃ batist kamij) 1796–1875, French landscape and portrait painter

coroutine ('kəʊruːˌtiːn) *n computing* a section of a computer program similar to but differing from a subroutine in that it can be left and re-entered at any point

corp. *abbrev for:* **1** corporation **2** corporal

corporal[1] (ˈkɔːpərəl, ˈkɔːprəl) *adj* of or relating to the body [C14 from L *corporālis*, from *corpus* body] > ˌ**corpoˈrality** *n* > ˈ**corporally** *adv*

corporal[2] (ˈkɔːpərəl) *n* **1** a noncommissioned officer junior to a sergeant in the army, air force, or marines **2** (in the Royal Navy) a petty officer who assists the master-at-arms [C16 from OF, via It., from L *caput* head; ? also infl. in OF by *corps* body (of men)]

corporal[3] (ˈkɔːpərəl) *or* **corporale** (ˌkɔːpəˈreɪlɪ) *n* a white linen cloth on which the bread and wine are placed during the Eucharist [C14 from Med. L *corporāle pallium* eucharistic altar cloth, from L *corporālis*, from *corpus* body (of Christ)]

Corporal of Horse *n* a noncommissioned rank in the British Army, above that of sergeant and below that of staff sergeant

corporal punishment *n* punishment of a physical nature, such as caning

corporate (ˈkɔːpərɪt) *adj* **1** forming a corporation; incorporated **2** of a corporation or corporations: *corporate finance* **3** of or belonging to a united group; joint [C15 from L *corporātus*, from *corpus* body] > ˈ**corporatism** *n*

corporate advertising *n* advertising designed to publicize or create a favourable image of a company rather than a particular product

corporate anorexia *n* a malaise of a business organization resulting from making too many creative people redundant in a cost-cutting exercise

corporate culture *n* the distinctive ethos of an organization that influences the level of formality, loyalty, and general behaviour of its employees

corporate identity *or* **image** *n* the way an organization is presented to or perceived by its members and the public

corporate raider *n finance* a person or organization that acquires a substantial holding of the shares of a company in order to take it over or to force its management to act in a desired way

corporate venturing *n finance* the provision of venture capital by one company for another in order to obtain information about the company requiring capital or as a step towards acquiring it

corporation (ˌkɔːpəˈreɪʃən) *n* **1** a group of people authorized by law to act as an individual and having its own powers, duties, and liabilities **2** Also called: **municipal corporation** the municipal authorities of a city or town **3** a group of people acting as one body **4** See **public corporation** **5** *inf* a large paunch > ˈ**corporative** *adj*

corporation tax *n* a British tax on the profits of a company or other incorporated body

corporatize *or* **corporatise** (ˈkɔːpərətaɪz, -prə-) *vb* **1** to convert (a government-controlled industry or enterprise) into an independent company **2** to be influenced by or take on the features of a large commercial business, esp in being bureaucratic and uncaring

corporeal (kɔːˈpɔːrɪəl) *adj* **1** of the nature of the physical body; not spiritual **2** of a material nature; physical [C17 from L *corporeus*, from *corpus* body] > **corˌporeˈality** *or* **corporeity** (ˌkɒːpəˈriːɪtɪ) *n* > **corˈporeally** *adv*

corps (kɔː) *n, pl* **corps** (kɔːz) **1** a military formation that comprises two or more divisions **2** a military body with a specific function: *medical corps* **3** a body of people associated together: *the diplomatic corps* [C18 from F, from L *corpus* body]

corps de ballet (ˈkɔː də ˈbæleɪ) *n* the members of a ballet company who dance together in a group

corps diplomatique (ˌdɪpləʊmæˈtiːk) *n* another name for **diplomatic corps**

corpse (kɔːps) *n* a dead body, esp of a human being [C14 from OF *corps*, from L *corpus*]

corpulent (ˈkɔːpjʊlənt) *adj* physically bulky; fat [C14 from L *corpulentus*] > ˈ**corpulence** *n*

cor pulmonale (ˌkɔː ˌpʌlməˈnɑːlɪ) *n* pulmonary heart disease: a serious heart condition in which there is enlargement and failure of the right ventricle resulting from lung disease [NL]

corpus (ˈkɔːpəs) *n, pl* **corpora** (-pərə) **1** a body of writings, esp by a single author or on a specific topic: *the corpus of Dickens' works* **2** the main body or substance of something **3** *anat* **3a** any distinct mass or body **3b** the main part of an organ or structure **4** *obs* a corpse [C14 from L: body] (ˈkrɪstɪ) *n chiefly RC Church* a festival in honour of the Eucharist, observed on the Thursday after Trinity Sunday [C14 from L: body of Christ]

Corpus Christi[1] (ˈkrɪstɪ) *n chiefly RC Church* a festival in honour of the Eucharist, observed on the Thursday after Trinity Sunday [C14 from L: body of Christ]

Corpus Christi[2] (ˈkrɪstɪ) *n* a port in S Texas, on **Corpus Christi Bay**, an inlet of the Gulf of Mexico. Pop: 277 454 (2000)

corpuscle (ˈkɔːpʌsᵊl) *n* **1** any cell or similar minute body that is suspended in a fluid, esp any of the **red blood corpuscles** (see **erythrocyte**) or **white blood corpuscles** (see **leucocyte**) **2** Also: **corpuscule** (kɔːˈpʌskjuːl) any minute particle [C17 from L *corpusculum* a little body, from *corpus* body] > **corpuscular** (kɔːˈpʌskjʊlə) *adj*

corpuscular theory *n* the theory, originally proposed by Newton, that light consists of a stream of particles. Cf **wave theory**

corpus delicti (dɪˈlɪktaɪ) *n law* the body of facts that constitute an offence [NL, lit.: the body of the crime]

corpus juris (ˈdʒʊərɪs) *n* a body of law, esp of a nation or state [from LL, lit.: a body of law]

corpus luteum (ˈluːtɪəm) *n, pl* **corpora lutea** (ˈluːtɪə) a mass of tissue that forms in a Graafian follicle following release of an ovum [NL, lit.: yellow body]

Cc

corral (kɒˈrɑːl) *n* **1** *chiefly US & Canad* an enclosure for cattle or horses **2** *chiefly US* (formerly) a defensive enclosure formed by a ring of covered wagons ▷ *vb* **corrals, corralling, corralled** (*tr*) *US & Canad* **3** to drive into a corral **4** *inf* to capture [C16 from Sp., ult. from L *currere* to run]

corrasion (kəˈreɪʒən) *n* erosion of a rock surface by rock fragments transported over it by water, wind, or ice [C17 from L *corrādere* to scrape together]

correa (ˈkɒrɪə, kəˈriːə) *n* an Australian evergreen shrub with large showy tubular flowers [C19 after Jose Francesco *Correa* da Serra (1750-1823), Portuguese botanist]

correct (kəˈrɛkt) *vb* (*tr*) **1** to make free from errors **2** to indicate the errors in **3** to rebuke or punish in order to improve: *to stand corrected* **4** to rectify (a malfunction, ailment, etc) **5** to adjust or make conform, esp to a standard ▷ *adj* **6** true; accurate: *the correct version* **7** in conformity with accepted standards: *correct behaviour* [C14 from L *corrigere* to make straight, from *com-* (intensive) + *regere* to rule] > **corˈrectly** *adv* > **corˈrectness** *n*

correction (kəˈrɛkʃən) *n* **1** the act of correcting **2** something substituted for an error; an improvement **3** a reproof **4** a quantity added to or subtracted from a scientific calculation or observation to increase its accuracy > **corˈrectional** *adj*

corrective (kəˈrɛktɪv) *adj* **1** tending or intended to correct ▷ *n* **2** something that tends or is intended to correct

Correggio (*Italian* korˈreddʒo) *n* **Antonio Allegri da** (anˈtɔːnjo alˈleːgri da) 1494–1534, Italian painter, noted for his striking use of perspective and foreshortening

Corregidor (kəˈrɛgɪˌdɔː) *n* an island at the entrance to Manila Bay, in the Philippines: site of the defeat of American forces by the Japanese (1942) in World War II

correlate (ˈkɒrɪˌleɪt) *vb* **correlates, correlating, correlated 1** to place or be placed in a complementary or reciprocal relationship **2** *(tr)* to establish or show a correlation between ▷ *n* **3** either of two things mutually related

correlation (ˌkɒrɪˈleɪʃən) *n* **1** a mutual relationship between two or more things **2** the act of correlating or the state of being correlated **3** *statistics* the extent of correspondence between the ordering of two variables [C16 from Med. L *correlātiō*, from *com-* together + *relātiō* RELATION] > ˌ**correˈlational** *adj*

correlation coefficient *n statistics* a statistic measuring the degree of correlation between two variables

correlative (kɒˈrɛlətɪv) *adj* **1** in complementary or reciprocal relationship; corresponding **2** denoting words, usually conjunctions, occurring together though not adjacently in certain grammatical constructions, as *neither* and *nor* ▷ *n* **3** either of two things that are correlative **4** a correlative word > **corˈrelatively** *adv* > **corˌrelaˈtivity** *n*

correspond (ˌkɒrɪˈspɒnd) *vb (intr)* **1** (usually foll by *with* or *to*) to be consistent or compatible (with); tally (with) **2** (usually foll by *to*) to be similar in character or function **3** (usually foll by *with*) to communicate by letter [C16 from Med. L *correspondēre*, from L *rēspondēre* to RESPOND] > ˌ**correˈsponding** *adj* > ˌ**correˈspondingly** *adv*

correspondence (ˌkɒrɪˈspɒndəns) *n* **1** the condition of agreeing or corresponding **2** similarity **3** agreement or conformity **4a** communication by letters **4b** the letters so exchanged

correspondence school *n* an educational institution that offers tuition (**correspondence courses**) by post

correspondent (ˌkɒrɪˈspɒndənt) *n* **1** a person who communicates by letter **2** a person employed by a newspaper, etc, to report on a special subject or from a foreign country **3** a person or firm that has regular business relations with another, esp one abroad ▷ *adj* **4** similar or analogous

corrida (koˈrriða) *n* the Spanish word for **bullfight** [Sp., from *corrida de toros*, lit.: a running of bulls]

corridor (ˈkɒrɪˌdɔː) *n* **1** a passage connecting parts of a building **2** a strip of land or airspace that affords access, either from a landlocked country to the sea or from a state to an exclave **3** a passageway connecting the compartments of a railway coach **4** a flight path that affords safe access for intruding aircraft **5** the path that a spacecraft must follow when re-entering the atmosphere, above which lift is insufficient and below which heating effects are excessive **6 corridors of power** the higher echelons of government, the Civil Service, etc, considered as the location of power and influence [C16 from OF, from OIt. *corridore*, lit.: place for running]

corrie (ˈkɒrɪ) *n* **1** (in Scotland) another name for cirque (sense 1) **2** *geol* another name for **cirque** [C18 from Gaelic *coire* cauldron]

corrigendum (ˌkɒrɪˈdʒɛndəm) *n, pl* **corrigenda** (-də) **1** an error to be corrected **2** *(sometimes pl)* Also called: **erratum** a slip of paper inserted into a book after printing, listing corrections [C19 from L: that which is to be corrected]

corrigible (ˈkɒrɪdʒɪbᵊl) *adj* **1** capable of being corrected **2** submissive [C15 from OF, from Med. L *corrigibilis*, from L *corrigere* to CORRECT]

corroborate (kəˈrɒbəˌreɪt) *vb* **corroborates, corroborating, corroborated** *(tr)* to confirm or support (facts, opinions, etc), esp by providing fresh evidence [C16 from L *corrōborāre*, from *rōborāre* to make strong, from *rōbur* strength] > **corˌroboˈration** *n* > **corroborative** (kəˈrɒbərətɪv) *or* **corˈroboratory** *adj* > **corˈroboˌrator** *n*

corroboree (kəˈrɒbərɪ) *n Austral* **1** a native assembly of sacred, festive, or warlike character **2** *inf* any noisy gathering [C19 from Abor.]

corrode (kəˈrəʊd) *vb* **corrodes, corroding, corroded 1** to eat away or be eaten away, esp as in the oxidation or rusting of a metal **2** *(tr)* to destroy gradually: *his jealousy corroded his happiness* [C14 from L *corrōdere* to gnaw to pieces, from *rōdere* to gnaw] > **corˈrodible** *adj*

corrosion (kəˈrəʊʒən) *n* **1** a process in which a solid, esp a metal, is eaten away and changed by a chemical action, as in the oxidation of iron **2** slow deterioration by being eaten or worn away **3** the product of corrosion

corrosive (kəˈrəʊsɪv) *adj* **1** tending to eat away or consume ▷ *n* **2** a corrosive substance, such as a strong acid > **corˈrosively** *adv* > **corˈrosiveness** *n*

corrosive sublimate *n* another name for **mercuric chloride**

corrugate (ˈkɒrʊˌgeɪt) *vb* **corrugates, corrugating, corrugated** *(usually tr)* to fold or be folded into alternate furrows and ridges [C18 from L *corrūgāre*, from *rūga* a wrinkle] > **ˈcorruˌgated** *adj* > ˌ**corruˈgation** *n*

corrugated iron *n* a thin sheet of iron or steel, formed with alternating ridges and troughs

corrupt (kəˈrʌpt) *adj* **1** open to or involving bribery or other dishonest practices: *a corrupt official; corrupt practices* **2** morally depraved **3** putrid or rotten **4** (of a text or manuscript) made meaningless or different in meaning by scribal errors or alterations **5** (of computer programs or data) containing errors ▷ *vb* **6** to become or cause to become dishonest or disloyal **7** *(tr)* to deprave **8** *(tr)* to infect or contaminate **9** *(tr)* to cause to become rotten **10** *(tr)* to alter (a text, etc) from the original **11** *(tr) computing* to introduce errors into (data or a program) [C14 from L *corruptus* spoiled, from *corrumpere* to ruin, from *rumpere* to break] > **corˈrupter** *or* **corˈruptor** *n* > **corˈruptly** *adv* > **corˈruptness** *n*

corruptible (kəˈrʌptɪbᵊl) *adj* capable of being corrupted > **corˈruptibly** *adv*

corruption (kəˈrʌpʃən) *n* **1** the act of corrupting or state of being corrupt **2** depravity **3** dishonesty, esp bribery **4** decay **5** alteration, as of a manuscript **6** an altered form of a word

corsage (kɔːˈsɑːʒ) *n* **1** a small bunch of flowers worn pinned to the lapel, bosom, etc **2** the bodice of a dress [C15 from OF, from *cors* body, from L *corpus*]

corsair (ˈkɔːsɛə) *n* **1** a pirate **2** a privateer, esp of the Barbary Coast [C15 from OF *corsaire*, from Med. L *cursārius*, from L *cursus* a running]

corse (kɔːs) *n* an archaic word for **corpse**

corselet (ˈkɔːslɪt) *n* **1** Also spelt: **corslet** a piece of armour for the top part of the body **2** a one-piece foundation garment [C15 from OF, from *cors* bodice, from L *corpus* body]

corset (ˈkɔːsɪt) *n* **1a** a stiffened, elasticated, or laced foundation garment, worn esp by women **1b** a similar garment worn because of injury, weakness, etc, by either sex **2** *inf* a restriction or limitation, esp government control of bank lending ▷ *vb* **3** *(tr)* to dress or enclose in, or as in, a corset [C14 from OF, lit.: a little bodice] > **corsetière** (ˌkɔːsɛtɪˈɛə) *n* > **ˈcorsetry** *n*

Corsica (ˈkɔːsɪkə) *n* an island in the Mediterranean, west of N Italy: forms, with 43 islets, a region of France; mountainous; settled by Greeks in about 560 BC; sold by Genoa to France in 1768. Capital: Ajaccio. Pop: 260 196 (1999). Area: 8682 sq km (3367 sq miles). French name: **Corse**

Corsican (ˈkɔːsɪkən) *adj* **1** of or relating to Corsica or its inhabitants ▷ *n* **2** a native or inhabitant of Corsica

cortege *or* **cortège** (kɔːˈteɪʒ) *n* **1** a formal procession, esp a funeral procession **2** a train of attendants; retinue [C17 from F, from It. *corteggio*, from *corteggiare* to attend]

Cortés (ˈkɔːtɛz; *Spanish* korˈtes) *or* **Cortez** (kɔːˈtɛz) *n* **Hernando** (ɛrˈnando) or **Hernán** (ɛrˈnan) 1485–1547, Spanish conquistador: defeated the Aztecs and conquered Mexico (1523)

cortex (ˈkɔːtɛks) *n, pl* **cortices** (-tɪˌsiːz) **1** *anat* the outer layer of any organ or part, such as the grey matter in the brain that covers the cerebrum (**cerebral cortex**) **2** *bot* **2a** the tissue in plant stems and roots between the vascular bundles and the epidermis **2b** the outer layer of a part such as the bark of a stem [c17 from L: bark, outer layer] > **cortical** ('kɔːtɪkᵊl) *adj*

corticate ('kɔːtɪkɪt, -ˌkeɪt) *or* **corticated** *adj* (of plants, seeds, etc) having a bark, husk, or rind [c19 from L *corticātus*]

cortisone ('kɔːtɪˌzəʊn) *n* a steroid hormone, the synthetic form of which has been used in treating rheumatoid arthritis, allergic and skin diseases, leukaemia, etc [c20 from *corticosterone*, a hormone]

Cortona (kɔː'təʊnə; *Italian* kɔr'tona) *n* a town in central Italy, in Tuscany: Roman and Etruscan remains, 15th-century cathedral. Pop: 22 700 (latest est)

Cortot (*French* kɔrto) *n* **Alfred** (alfrɛd) 1877–1962, French pianist, born in Switzerland

corundum (kə'rʌndəm) *n* a hard mineral consisting of aluminium oxide: used as an abrasive. Precious varieties include ruby and white sapphire. Formula: Al_2O_3 [c18 from Tamil *kuruntam*; rel. to Sansk. *kuruvinda* ruby]

Corunna (kə'rʌnə) *n* the English name for **La Coruña**

coruscate ('kɒrəˌskeɪt) *vb* **coruscates, coruscating, coruscated** (*intr*) to emit flashes of light; sparkle [c18 from L *coruscāre* to flash] > ˌ**corus'cation** *n*

corvée ('kɔːveɪ) *n* **1** *European history* a day's unpaid labour owed by a feudal vassal to his lord **2** the practice or an instance of forced labour [c14 from OF, from LL *corrogāta* contribution, from L *corrogāre* to collect, from *rogāre* to ask]

corvette (kɔː'vɛt) *n* a lightly armed escort warship [c17 from OF, ?from MDu. *corf*]

corvine ('kɔːvaɪn) *adj* **1** of or resembling a crow **2** of the passerine bird family Corvidae, which includes the crows, ravens, rooks, jackdaws, magpies, and jays [c17 from L *corvīnus*, from *corvus* a raven]

Corvo ('kɔːvəʊ) *n* **Baron** See (Frederick William) **Rolfe**

Corybant ('kɒrɪˌbænt) *n, pl* **Corybants** *or* **Corybantes** (ˌkɒrɪ'bæntiːz) *Classical myth.* a wild attendant of the goddess Cybele [c14 from L *Corybās*, from Gk *Korubas*] > ˌ**Cory'bantic** *adj*

corymb ('kɒrɪmb, -rɪm) *n* an inflorescence in the form of a flat-topped flower cluster with the oldest flowers at the periphery [c18 from L *corymbus*, from Gk *korumbos* cluster]

coryza (kə'raɪzə) *n* acute inflammation of the mucous membrane of the nose, with discharge of mucus; a head cold [c17 from LL: catarrh, from Gk *koruza*]

cos[1] *or* **cos lettuce** (kɒs) *n* a variety of lettuce with a long slender head and crisp leaves. Usual US and Canad name: **romaine** [c17 after *Kos*, the Aegean island of its origin]

cos[2] (kɒz) *abbrev for* cosine

Cos (kɒs) *n* a variant spelling of **Kos**

Cosa Nostra ('kəʊzə 'nɒstrə) *n* the branch of the Mafia that operates in the US [It.: our thing]

COSATU (ˌkəʊ'zaːtuː) *n acronym for* Congress of South African Trade Unions

cosec ('kəʊsɛk) *abbrev for* cosecant

cosecant (kəʊ'siːkənt) *n* (of an angle) a trigonometric function that in a right-angled triangle is the ratio of the length of the hypotenuse to that of the opposite side

coset ('kəʊˌsɛt) *n maths* a set that produces a specified larger set when added to another set

Cosgrave ('kɒzgreɪv) *n* **1** **Liam** ('liːəm) born 1920, Irish statesman; prime minister of the Republic of Ireland (1973–77) **2** his father, **W**(**illiam**) **T**(**homas**) 1880–1965, Irish statesman; first prime minister (president of the executive council) of the Irish Free State (1922–32)

cosh[1] (kɒʃ) *Brit* ▷ *n* **1** a blunt weapon, often made of hard rubber; bludgeon **2** an attack with such a weapon ▷ *vb* **3** to hit with such a weapon, esp on the head: *young people were coshed and kicked* [c19 from Romany *kosh*]

cosh[2] (kɒʃ, kɒs'eɪtʃ) *n* hyperbolic cosine [c19 from COS(INE) + H(YPERBOLIC)]

cosignatory (kəʊ'sɪgnətərɪ, -trɪ) *n, pl* **cosignatories** **1** a person, country, etc, that signs a document jointly with others ▷ *adj* **2** signing jointly

Cosimo I (*Italian* 'kɔːzimo) *n* See (Cosimo I) **Medici**

cosine ('kəʊˌsaɪn) *n* (of an angle) a trigonometric function that in a right-angled triangle is the ratio of the length of the adjacent side to that of the hypotenuse [c17 from NL *cosinus*; see CO-, SINE[1]]

cosmetic (kɒz'mɛtɪk) *n* **1** any preparation applied to the body, esp the face, with the intention of beautifying it ▷ *adj* **2** serving or designed to beautify the body, esp the face **3** having no other function than to beautify: *cosmetic illustrations in a book* [c17 from Gk *kosmētikos*, from *kosmein* to arrange, from *kosmos* order] > **cos'metically** *adv*

cosmetology (ˌkɒzmɛ'tɒlədʒɪ) *n* the work of beauty therapists, including hairdressing, facials, manicures, etc

cosmic ('kɒzmɪk) *adj* **1** of or relating to the whole universe: *cosmic laws* **2** occurring or originating in outer space, esp as opposed to the vicinity of the earth: *cosmic rays* **3** immeasurably extended; vast > '**cosmically** *adv*

cosmic dust *n* fine particles of solid matter occurring throughout interstellar space and often collecting into clouds of extremely low density

cosmic rays *pl n* radiation consisting of atomic nuclei, esp protons, of very high energy, that reach the earth from outer space. Also called: **cosmic radiation**

cosmic string *n* any of a number of linear defects in space-time postulated in certain theories of cosmology to exist in the universe as a consequence of the big bang

cosmo- *or before a vowel* **cosm-** *combining form* indicating the world or universe: *cosmology; cosmonaut* [from Gk: COSMOS]

cosmogony (kɒz'mɒgənɪ) *n, pl* **cosmogonies** the study of the origin and development of the universe or of a particular system in the universe, such as the solar system [c17 from Gk *kosmogonia*, from COSMO- + *gonos* creation] > **cosmogonic** (ˌkɒzmə'gɒnɪk) *or* ˌ**cosmo'gonical** *adj* > **cos'mogonist** *n*

Cc

cosmography (kɒz'mɒgrəfɪ) *n* **1** a representation of the world or the universe **2** the science dealing with the whole order of nature > **cos'mographer** *n* > **cosmographic** (ˌkɒzmə'græfɪk) *or* ˌ**cosmo'graphical** *adj*

cosmological principle *n astron* the theory that the universe is uniform, homogenous, and isotropic, and therefore appears the same from any position

cosmology (kɒz'mɒlədʒɪ) *n* **1** the study of the origin and nature of the universe **2** a particular account of the origin or structure of the universe > **cosmological** (ˌkɒzmə'lɒdʒɪkᵊl) *or* ˌ**cosmo'logic** *adj* > **cos'mologist** *n*

▷ www.damtp.cam.ac.uk/user/gr/public/cos_home.html

▷ http://map.gsfc.nasa.gov/m_uni.html

cosmonaut ('kɒzməˌnɔːt) *n* an astronaut, esp in the former Soviet Union [c20 from Russian *kosmonavt*, from COSMO- + Gk *nautēs* sailor]

cosmopolitan (ˌkɒzmə'pɒlɪtᵊn) *n* **1** a person who has lived and travelled in many countries, esp one who is free of national prejudices ▷ *adj* **2** familiar with many parts of the world **3** sophisticated or urbane **4** composed of people or elements from all parts of the world or from many different spheres [c17 from F, ult. from Gk *kosmopolitēs*, from *kosmo-* COSMO- + *politēs* citizen] > ˌ**cosmo'politanism** *n*

cosmopolite (kɒz'mɒpəˌlaɪt) *n* **1** a less common word for **cosmopolitan** (sense 1) **2** an animal or plant that occurs in most parts of the world > **cos'mopolitˌism** *n*

cosmos ('kɒzmɒs) *n* **1** the universe considered as an ordered system **2** any ordered system **3** (*pl* **cosmos** *or* **cosmoses**) any tropical American plant of the genus

Cosmos cultivated as garden plants for their brightly coloured flowers [c17 from Gk *kosmos* order]

Cosmos ('kɒzmɒs) *n astronautics* any of various types of Soviet satellite, including Cosmos 1 (launched 1962) and nearly 2000 subsequent satellites

Cossack ('kɒsæk) *n* **1** (formerly) any of the free warrior-peasants of chiefly East Slavonic descent who served as cavalry under the tsars ▷ *adj* **2** of, relating to, or characteristic of the Cossacks: *a Cossack dance* [c16 from Russian *kazak* vagabond, of Turkic origin]

cosset ('kɒsɪt) *vb* **cossets, cosseting, cosseted 1** (*tr*) to pamper; pet ▷ *n* **2** any pet animal, esp a lamb [c16 from ?]

cost (kɒst) *n* **1** the price paid or required for acquiring, producing, or maintaining something, measured in money, time, or energy; outlay **2** suffering or sacrifice: *I know to my cost* **3a** the amount paid for a commodity by its seller: *to sell at cost* **3b** (*as modifier*): *the cost price* **4** (*pl*) *law* the expenses of judicial proceedings **5 at all costs** regardless of sacrifice involved **6 at the cost of** at the expense of losing ▷ *vb* **costs, costing, cost 7** (*tr*) to be obtained or obtainable in exchange for: *the ride cost one pound* **8** to cause or require the loss or sacrifice (of): *the accident cost him dearly* **9** (*p.t. & p.p.* **costed**) to estimate the cost of (a product, process, etc) for the purposes of pricing, budgeting, control, etc [c13 from OF (n), from *coster* to cost, from L *constāre* to stand at, cost, from *stāre* to stand]

costa ('kɒstə) *n, pl* **costae** (-ti:) **1** the technical name for **rib**[1] (sense 1) **2** a riblike part [c19 from L: rib, side] > **'costal** *adj*

Costa Brava ('kɒstə 'brɑ:və) *n* a coastal region of NE Spain along the Mediterranean, extending from Barcelona to the French border: many resorts

cost accounting *n* the recording and controlling of all the expenditures of an enterprise in order to facilitate control of separate activities. Also called: **management accounting** > **cost accountant** *n*

Costa Rica ('kɒstə 'ri:kə) *n* a republic in Central America: gained independence from Spain in 1821; mostly mountainous and volcanic, with extensive forests. Official language: Spanish. Official religion: Roman Catholic. Currency: colón. Capital: San José. Pop: 3 936 000 (2001 est). Area: 50 900 sq km (19 652 sq miles)

▷ www.casapres.go.cr
▷ http://costarica.tourism.co.cr

Costa Rican ('kɒstə 'ri:kən) *adj* **1** of or relating to Costa Rica or its inhabitants ▷ *n* **2** a native or inhabitant of Costa Rica

cost-benefit *adj* denoting or relating to a method of assessing a project that takes into account its costs and its benefits to society as well as the revenue it generates: *a cost-benefit analysis; the project was assessed on a cost-benefit basis*

cost-effective *adj* providing adequate financial return in relation to outlay > ˌ**cost-ef'fectiveness** *n*

costermonger ('kɒstəˌmʌŋgə) *or* **coster** *n Brit, rare* a person who sells fruit, vegetables, etc, from a barrow [c16 from *costard* a kind of apple + MONGER]

costive ('kɒstɪv) *adj* **1** constipated **2** niggardly [c14 from OF *costivé*, from L *constipātus*; see CONSTIPATE] > **'costiveness** *n*

costly ('kɒstlɪ) *adj* **costlier, costliest 1** expensive **2** entailing great loss or sacrifice: *a costly victory* **3** splendid; lavish > **'costliness** *n*

cost of living *n* **a** the basic cost of the food, clothing, shelter, and fuel necessary to maintain life, esp at a standard of living regarded as basic **b** (*as modifier*): *the cost-of-living index*

cost-plus *n* a method of establishing a selling price in which an agreed percentage is added to the cost price to cover profit

costume ('kɒstju:m) *n* **1** a style of dressing, including all the clothes, accessories, etc, worn at one time, as in a particular country or period **2** *old-fashioned* a woman's suit **3** a set of clothes, esp unusual or period clothes: *a jester's costume* **4** short for **swimming costume** ▷ *vb* **costumes, costuming, costumed** (*tr*) **5** to furnish the costumes for (a show, film, etc) **6** to dress (someone) in a costume [c18 from F, from It.: dress, habit, CUSTOM]

▷ www.costumes.org
▷ www.costumesocietyamerica.com/csaorg.html
▷ www.costumesociety.org.uk
▷ www.metmuseum.org/collections

costumier (kɒ'stju:mɪə) *or* **costumer** *n* a person or firm that makes or supplies theatrical or fancy costumes

cosy *or US* **cozy** ('kəʊzɪ) *adj* **cosier, cosiest** *or US* **cozier, coziest 1** warm and snug **2** intimate; friendly ▷ *n, pl* **cosies** *or US* **cozies 3** a cover for keeping things warm: *egg cosy* [c18 from Scot., from ?] > **'cosily** *or US* **'cozily** *adv* > **'cosiness** *or US* **'coziness** *n*

cot[1] (kɒt) *n* **1** a child's boxlike bed, usually incorporating vertical bars **2** a portable bed **3** a light bedstead **4** *naut* a hammock-like bed [c17 from Hindi *khāt* bedstead]

cot[2] (kɒt) *n* **1** *literary or arch* a small cottage **2** Also called: **cote 2a** a small shelter, esp one for pigeons, sheep, etc **2b** (*in combination*): *dovecot* [OE *cot*]

cot[3] (kɒt) *abbrev for* cotangent

cotangent (kəʊ'tændʒənt) *n* (of an angle) a trigonometric function that in a right-angled triangle is the ratio of the length of the adjacent side to that of the opposite side

COTC *abbrev for* Canadian Officers Training Corps

cot death *n* the unexplained sudden death of an infant during sleep. Technical name: **sudden infant death syndrome**

cote (kəʊt) *or* **cot** *n* **1** a small shelter for pigeons, sheep, etc **2** (*in combination*): *dovecote* [OE *cote*]

Côte d'Azur (*French* kot dazyr) *n* the Mediterranean coast of France, including the French Riviera: forms an administrative region with Provence

Côte d'Ivoire (*French* kot divwar) *n* a republic in West Africa, on the Gulf of Guinea: Portuguese trading for ivory and slaves began in the 16th century; made a French protectorate in 1842 and became independent in 1960; major producer of coffee and cocoa. Official language: French. Religion: Muslim majority, with animist, atheist, and Roman Catholic minorities. Currency: franc. Capital: Yamoussoukro (administrative); Abidjan (legislative). Pop: 16 393 000 (2001 est). Area: 319 820 sq km (123 483 sq miles). Former name (until 1986): **the Ivory Coast**

▷ www.presidence.gov.ci
▷ www.encodivoire.com/En/tourisme.php

Côte-d'Or (*French* kotdɔr) *n* a department of E central France, in NE Burgundy. Capital: Dijon. Pop: 506 755 (1999). Area: 8787 sq km (3427 sq miles)

coterie ('kəʊtərɪ) *n* a small exclusive group of people with common interests; clique [c18 from F, from OF: association of tenants, from *cotier* (unattested) cottager]

coterminous (kəʊ'tɜ:mɪnəs) *or* **conterminous** *adj* **1** having a common boundary **2** coextensive or coincident in range, time, etc

Côtes-d'Armor (*French* kotdarmɔr) *n* a department of W France, on the N coast of Brittany. Capital: St Brieuc. Pop: 542 373 (1999). Area: 6878 sq km (2656 sq miles). Former name: **Côtes-du-Nord**

coth (kɒθ, 'kɒt'eɪtʃ) *n* hyperbolic cotangent [c20 from COT(ANGENT) + H(YPERBOLIC)]

cotillion *or* **cotillon** (kə'tɪljən, kəʊ-) *n* **1** a French formation dance of the 18th century **2** *US* a quadrille **3** *US* a formal ball [c18 from F *cotillon* dance, from OF: petticoat]

cotinga (kə'tɪŋgə) *n* a tropical American passerine bird having a broad slightly hooked bill

cotoneaster (kəˌtəʊnɪˈæstə) *n* any Old World shrub of the rosaceous genus *Cotoneaster:* cultivated for their ornamental flowers and red or black berries [c18 from NL, from L *cotōneum* QUINCE]

Cotonou (ˌkəʊtəˈnuː) *n* the chief port and official capital of Benin, on the Bight of Benin. Pop: 750 000 (1994 est)

Cotopaxi (*Spanish* kotoˈpaksi) *n* a volcano in central Ecuador, in the Andes: the world's highest active volcano. Height: 5896 m (19 344 ft)

Cotswolds (ˈkɒtsˌwəʊldz, -wəldz) *pl n* a range of low hills in SW England, mainly in Gloucestershire: formerly a centre of the wool industry

cotta (ˈkɒtə) *n RC Church* a short form of surplice [c19 from It.: tunic]

cottage (ˈkɒtɪdʒ) *n* a small simple house, esp in a rural area [c14 from COT[2]]

cottage cheese *n* a mild loose soft white cheese made from skimmed milk curds

cottage country *n Canad* any lakeside region where many country cottages are located

cottage hospital *n Brit* a small rural hospital

cottage industry *n* an industry in which employees work in their own homes, often using their own equipment

cottage pie *n Brit* another term for **shepherd's pie**

cottager (ˈkɒtɪdʒə) *n* **1** a person who lives in a cottage **2** a rural labourer

cottaging (ˈkɒtɪdʒɪŋ) *n Brit sl* homosexual activity between men in a public lavatory

cotter[1] (ˈkɒtə) *n machinery* **1** any part, such as a pin, wedge, key, etc, that is used to secure two other parts so that relative motion between them is prevented **2** short for **cotter pin** [c14 shortened from *cotterel*, from ?]

cotter[2] (ˈkɒtə) *n* **1** *English history* a villein in late Anglo-Saxon and early Norman times occupying a cottage and land in return for labour **2** Also called: **cottar** a peasant occupying a cottage and land in the Scottish Highlands [c14 from Med. L *cotārius*, from ME *cote* COT[2]]

cotter pin *n machinery* a split pin secured, after passing through holes in the parts to be attached, by spreading the ends

Cottian Alps (ˈkɒtɪən) *pl n* a mountain range in SW Europe, between NW Italy and SE France: part of the Alps. Highest peak: Monte Viso, 3841 m (12 600 ft)

cotton (ˈkɒtᵊn) *n* **1** any of various herbaceous plants and shrubs cultivated in warm climates for the fibre surrounding the seeds and the oil within the seeds **2** the soft white downy fibre of these plants, used to manufacture textiles **3** cotton plants collectively, as a cultivated crop **4** a cloth or thread made from cotton fibres [c14 from OF *coton*, from Ar. *qutn*] > ˈ**cottony** *adj*

Cotton (ˈkɒtᵊn) *n* **Henry** 1907–87, British golfer: three times winner of the British Open

cotton bud *n* a small stick with a cotton-wool tip used for cleaning the ears, applying make-up, etc

cotton grass *n* any of various N temperate and arctic grasslike bog plants whose clusters of long silky hairs resemble cotton tufts

cotton on *vb (intr, adv; often foll by to) inf* to perceive the meaning (of)

cotton-picking *adj US & Canad sl* (intensifier qualifying something undesirable): *you cotton-picking layabout!*

cottonseed (ˈkɒtᵊnˌsiːd) *n, pl* **cottonseeds** *or* **cottonseed** the seed of the cotton plant: a source of oil and fodder

cotton wool *n* **1** *chiefly Brit* bleached and sterilized cotton from which the impurities, such as the seeds, have been removed. Usual US term: **absorbent cotton** **2** cotton in the natural state **3** *Brit inf* a state of pampered comfort and protection

cotyledon (ˌkɒtɪˈliːdᵊn) *n* a simple embryonic leaf in seed-bearing plants, which, in some species, forms the first green leaf after germination [c16 from L: a plant, navelwort, from Gk *kotulēdōn*, from *kotulē* cup, hollow] > ˌ**cotyˈledonous** *adj* > ˌ**cotyˈledonal** *adj*

coucal (ˈkuːkæl) *n* any ground-living bird of the genus *Centropus* of Africa, S Asia, and Australia [c19 from F, ?from *couc(ou)* cuckoo + *al(ouette)* lark]

couch (kaʊtʃ) *n* **1** a piece of upholstered furniture, usually having a back and armrests, for seating more than one person **2** a bed, esp one used in the daytime by the patients of a doctor or a psychoanalyst ▷ *vb* **3** *(tr)* to express in a particular style of language: *couched in an archaic style* **4** (when *tr, usually reflexive or passive*) to lie down or cause to lie down for or as for sleep **5** *(intr) arch* to crouch **6** *(intr) arch* to lie in ambush; lurk **7** *(tr) surgery* to remove (a cataract) by downward displacement of the lens of the eye **8** *(tr) arch* to lower (a lance) into a horizontal position [c14 from OF *couche* a bed, lair, from *coucher* to lay down, from L *collocāre* to arrange, from *locāre* to place]

couchant (ˈkaʊtʃənt) *adj (usually postpositive) heraldry* in a lying position: *a lion couchant* [c15 from F: lying]

couchette (kuːˈʃɛt) *n* a bed or berth in a railway carriage, esp one converted from seats [c20 from F, dim. of *couche* bed]

couch grass (kaʊtʃ, kuːtʃ) *n* a grass with a yellowish-white creeping underground stem by which it spreads quickly: a troublesome weed. Also called: **twitch grass, quitch grass**

couch potato *n sl* a lazy person whose recreation consists chiefly of watching television

Coué (*French* kue) *n* **Émile** (emil) 1857–1926, French psychologist and pharmacist: advocated psychotherapy by autosuggestion

cougar (ˈkuːgə) *n* another name for **puma** [c18 from F *couguar*, from Port., from Tupi]

cough (kɒf) *vb* **1** *(intr)* to expel air or solid matter from the lungs abruptly and explosively through the partially closed vocal chords **2** *(intr)* to make a sound similar to this **3** *(tr)* to utter or express with a cough or coughs ▷ *n* **4** an act or sound of coughing **5** a condition of the lungs or throat which causes frequent coughing [OE *cohhetten*] > ˈ**cougher** *n*

cough drop *n* a lozenge to relieve a cough

cough mixture *n* any medicine that relieves coughing

cough up *vb (adv)* **1** *inf* to surrender (money, information, etc), esp reluctantly **2** *(tr)* to bring into the mouth or eject (phlegm, food, etc) by coughing

could (kʊd) *vb* (takes an infinitive without *to* or an implied infinitive) used as an auxiliary: **1** to make the past tense of **can[1]** **2** to make the subjunctive mood of **can[1]**, esp used in polite requests or in conditional sentences: *could I see you tonight?* **3** to indicate suggestion of a course of action: *you could take the car if it's raining* **4** (often foll by *well*) to indicate a possibility: *he could well be a spy* [OE *cūthe*]

couldn't (ˈkʊdᵊnt) *contraction of* could not

couldst (kʊdst) *vb arch* the form of **could** used with the pronoun *thou* or its relative form

coulee (ˈkuːleɪ, -lɪ) *n* **1a** a flow of molten lava **1b** such lava when solidified **2** *western US & Canad* a long steep-sided ravine [c19 from Canad F *coulée* a flow, from F, from *couler* to flow, from L *cōlāre* to sift]

coulis (ˈkuːliː) *n* a thin purée of vegetables, fruit, etc, usually served as a sauce [c20 F, lit.: purée]

coulomb (ˈkuːlɒm) *n* the derived SI unit of electric charge; the quantity of electricity transported in one second by a current of 1 ampere. Symbol: C [c19 after C.A. de COULOMB]

Coulomb (ˈkuːlɒm; *French* kulɔ̃) *n* **Charles Augustin de** (ʃarl ogystɛ̃ də) 1736–1806, French physicist: made many discoveries in the field of electricity and magnetism

coulter (ˈkəʊltə) *n* a blade or sharp-edged disc attached to a plough so that it cuts through the soil vertically in

Cc

advance of the ploughshare. Also (esp US): **colter** [OE *culter*, from L: ploughshare, knife]

coumarin *or* **cumarin** ('ku:mərɪn) *n* a white vanilla-scented crystalline ester, used in perfumes and flavouring [c19 from F, from *coumarou* tonka-bean tree, from Sp., from Tupi]

council ('kaʊnsəl) *n* **1** an assembly of people meeting for discussion, consultation, etc **2a** a body of people elected or appointed to serve in an administrative, legislative, or advisory capacity: *a student council* **2b** short for **legislative council** **3** (*sometimes cap; often preceded by the*) *Brit* the local governing authority of a town, county, etc **4** *Austral* an administrative or legislative assembly, esp the upper house of a state parliament in Australia **5** a meeting of a council **6** (*modifier*) of, provided for, or used by a local council: *a council chamber; council offices* **7** (*modifier*) *Brit* provided by a local council, esp (of housing) at a subsidized rent: *a council house; a council estate; a council school* **8** *Christianity* an assembly of bishops, etc, convened for regulating matters of doctrine or discipline [c12 from OF *concile*, from L *concilium* assembly, from *com-* together + *calāre* to call]

USAGE This word is sometimes confused with **counsel**

council area *n* any of the 32 unitary authorities into which Scotland was divided for administrative purposes in 1996

councillor *or US* **councilor** ('kaʊnsələ) *n* a member of a council.

USAGE This word is sometimes confused with **counsellor**

councilman ('kaʊnsəlmən) *n, pl* **councilmen** *chiefly US* a councillor

council tax *n* (in Britain) a tax based on the relative value of property levied to fund local council services

counsel ('kaʊnsəl) *n* **1** advice or guidance on conduct, behaviour, etc **2** discussion; consultation: *to take counsel with a friend* **3** a person whose advice is sought **4** a barrister or group of barristers engaged in conducting cases in court and advising on legal matters **5** *Christianity* any of the **counsels of perfection,** namely poverty, chastity, and obedience **6** **counsel of perfection** excellent but unrealizable advice **7** private opinions (esp in **keep one's own counsel**) **8** *arch* wisdom; prudence ▷ *vb* **counsels, counselling, counselled** *or US* **counsels, counseling, counseled** **9** (*tr*) to give advice or guidance to **10** (*tr; often takes a clause as object*) to recommend; urge **11** (*intr*) *arch* to take counsel; consult [c13 from OF *counseil*, from L *consilium* deliberating body; rel. to CONSULT]

USAGE This word is sometimes confused with **council**

counselling *or US* **counseling** ('kaʊnsəlɪŋ) *n* systematic guidance offered by social workers, doctors, etc, in which a person's problems are discussed and advice is given

counsellor *or US* **counselor** ('kaʊnsələ) *n* **1** a person who gives counsel; adviser **2** Also called: **counselor-at-law** *US* a lawyer, esp one who conducts cases in court **3** a senior diplomatic officer.

USAGE This word is sometimes confused with **councillor**

count[1] (kaʊnt) *vb* **1** to add up or check (each unit in a collection) in order to ascertain the sum: *count your change* **2** (*tr*) to recite numbers in ascending order up to and including **3** (*tr; often foll by in*) to take into account or include: *we must count him in* **4** **not counting** excluding **5** (*tr*) to consider; deem: *count yourself lucky* **6** (*intr*) to have importance: *this picture counts as a rarity* **7** (*intr*) *music* to keep time by counting beats ▷ *n* **8** the act of counting **9** the number reached by counting; sum: *a blood count* **10** *law* a paragraph in an indictment containing a separate charge **11** **keep** *or* **lose count** to keep or fail to keep an accurate record of items, events, etc **12** *boxing, wrestling* the act of telling off a number of seconds by the referee, as when a boxer has been knocked down by his opponent **13** **out for the count** *boxing* knocked out and unable to continue after a count of ten by the referee ▷ See also **count against, countdown,** etc [c14 from Anglo-F *counter*, from OF *conter*, from L *computāre* to calculate] > '**countable** *adj*

count[2] (kaʊnt) *n* **1** a nobleman in any of various European countries having a rank corresponding to that of a British earl **2** any of various officials in the late Roman Empire and in the early Middle Ages [c16 from OF *conte*, from L *comes* associate, from COM- with + *īre* to go]

count against *vb* (*intr, prep*) to have influence to the disadvantage of

countdown ('kaʊnt,daʊn) *n* **1** the act of counting backwards to time a critical operation exactly, such as the launching of a rocket ▷ *vb* **count down** (*intr, adv*) **2** to count thus

countenance ('kaʊntɪnəns) *n* **1** the face, esp when considered as expressing a person's character or mood **2** support or encouragement; sanction **3** composure; self-control (esp in **keep** *or* **lose one's countenance**) ▷ *vb* **countenances, countenancing, countenanced** (*tr*) **4** to support or encourage; sanction **5** to tolerate; endure [c13 from OF *contenance* mien, behaviour, from L *continentia* restraint, control; see CONTAIN] >'**countenancer** *n*

counter[1] ('kaʊntə) *n* **1** a horizontal surface, as in a shop or bank, over which business is transacted **2** (in some cafeterias) a long table on which food is served **3a** a small flat disc of wood, metal, or plastic, used in various board games **3b** a similar disc or token used as an imitation coin **4** a person or thing that may be used or manipulated **5** **under the counter** (**under-the-counter** *when prenominal*) (of the sale of goods) clandestine or illegal **6** **over the counter** (**over-the-counter** *when prenominal*) (of security transactions) through a broker rather than on a stock exchange [c14 from OF *comptouer*, ult. from L *computāre* to COMPUTE]

counter[2] ('kaʊntə) *n* **1** a person who counts **2** an apparatus that records the number of occurrences of events [c14 from OF *conteor*, from L *computātor*; see COUNT[1]]

counter[3] ('kaʊntə) *adv* **1** in a contrary direction or manner **2** in a wrong or reverse direction **3** **run counter to** to have a contrary effect or action to ▷ *adj* **4** opposing; opposite; contrary ▷ *n* **5** something that is contrary or opposite to some other thing **6** an act, effect, or force that opposes another **7** a return attack, such as a blow in boxing **8** *fencing* a parry in which the foils move in a circular fashion **9** the portion of the stern of a boat or ship that overhangs the water aft of the rudder **10** a piece of leather forming the back of a shoe ▷ *vb* **11** to say or do (something) in retaliation or response **12** (*tr*) to move, act, or perform in a manner or direction opposite to (a person or thing) **13** to return the attack of (an opponent) [c15 from OF *contre*, from L *contrā* against]

counter- *prefix* **1** against; opposite; contrary: *counterattack* **2** complementary; corresponding: *counterfoil* **3** duplicate or substitute: *counterfeit* [via OF from L *contrā* against, opposite; see CONTRA-]

counteract (,kaʊntər'ækt) *vb* (*tr*) to oppose or neutralize by contrary action; check > ,**counter'action** *n* > ,**counter'active** *adj*

counterattack ('kaʊntərə,tæk) *n* **1** an attack in response to an attack ▷ *vb* **2** to make a counterattack (against)

counterbalance *n* ('kaʊntə,bæləns) **1** a weight or force that balances or offsets another ▷ *vb* (,kaʊntə'bæləns), **counterbalances, counterbalancing, counterbalanced** (*tr*) **2** Also: **counterweigh** to act as a counterbalance to ▷ Also: **counterpoise**

counterblast ('kaʊntəˌblɑːst) *n* an aggressive response to a verbal attack
countercheck *n* ('kaʊntəˌtʃɛk) **1** a check or restraint, esp one that acts in opposition to another **2** a double check, as for accuracy ▷ *vb* (ˌkaʊntə'tʃɛk) (*tr*) **3** to oppose by counteraction **4** to double-check
counterclaim ('kaʊntəˌkleɪm) *chiefly law* ▷ *n* **1** a claim set up in opposition to another ▷ *vb* **2** to set up (a claim) in opposition to another claim > ˌ**counter'claimant** *n*
counterclockwise (ˌkaʊntə'klɒkˌwaɪz) *adv, adj* the US and Canad equivalent of **anticlockwise**
counterculture ('kaʊntəˌkʌltʃə) *n* an alternative culture, deliberately at variance with the social norm
counterespionage (ˌkaʊntər'ɛspɪəˌnɑːʒ) *n* activities to counteract enemy espionage
counterfeit ('kaʊntəfɪt) *adj* **1** made in imitation of something genuine with the intent to deceive or defraud; forged **2** simulated; sham: *counterfeit affection* ▷ *n* **3** an imitation designed to deceive or defraud ▷ *vb* **4** (*tr*) to make a fraudulent imitation of **5** (*intr*) to make counterfeits **6** to feign; simulate [C13 from OF *contrefait*, from *contrefaire* to copy, from *contre-* COUNTER- + *faire* to make] > '**counterfeiter** *n*
counterfoil ('kaʊntəˌfɔɪl) *n* *Brit* the part of a cheque, receipt, etc, retained as a record. Also called (esp in the US and Canada): **stub**
counterforce ('kaʊntəˌfɔːs) *n* (*modifier*) denoting military strategy based on retaliation against attacking forces
counterinsurgency (ˌkaʊntərɪn'sɜːdʒənsɪ) *n* action taken by a government against rebels, guerrillas, etc
counterintelligence (ˌkaʊntərɪn'tɛlɪdʒəns) *n* activities designed to frustrate enemy espionage
counterintuitive *adj* *chiefly US* (of an idea, proposal, etc) seemingly contrary to common sense
counterirritant (ˌkaʊntər'ɪrɪtᵊnt) *n* **1** an agent that causes a superficial irritation of the skin and thereby relieves inflammation of deep structures ▷ *adj* **2** producing a counterirritation > ˌ**counterˌirri'tation** *n*
countermand *vb* (ˌkaʊntə'mɑːnd) (*tr*) **1** to revoke or cancel (a command, order, etc) **2** to order (forces, etc) to retreat; recall ▷ *n* ('kaʊntəˌmɑːnd) **3** a command revoking another [C15 from OF *contremander*, from *contre-* COUNTER- + *mander* to command, from L *mandāre*]
countermarch ('kaʊntəˌmɑːtʃ) *chiefly mil* ▷ *vb* **1** to march or cause to march back or in the opposite direction ▷ *n* **2** the act or an instance of countermarching
countermeasure ('kaʊntəˌmɛʒə) *n* action taken to oppose, neutralize, or retaliate against some other action
countermove ('kaʊntəˌmuːv) *n* **1** an opposing move ▷ *vb* **countermoves, countermoving, countermoved** **2** to make or do (something) as an opposing move > '**counterˌmovement** *n*
counteroffensive ('kaʊntərəˌfɛnsɪv) *n* a series of attacks by a defending force against an attacking enemy
counteroffer ('kaʊntərˌɒfə) *n* a response to a bid in which a seller amends his or her original offer, making it more favourable to the buyer
counterpane ('kaʊntəˌpeɪn) *n* another word for **bedspread** [C17 from obs. *counterpoint* (infl. by *pane* coverlet), changed from OF *coutepointe* quilt, from Med. L *culcita puncta* quilted mattress]
counterpart ('kaʊntəˌpɑːt) *n* **1** a person or thing identical to or closely resembling another **2** one of two parts that complement or correspond to each other **3** a duplicate, esp of a legal document; copy
counterparty ('kaʊntəˌpɑːtɪ) *n* a person who is a party to a contract
counterplot ('kaʊntəˌplɒt) *n* **1** a plot designed to frustrate another plot ▷ *vb* **counterplots, counterplotting, counterplotted** **2** (*tr*) to oppose with a counterplot
counterpoint ('kaʊntəˌpɔɪnt) *n* **1** the technique involving the simultaneous sounding of two or more parts or melodies **2** a melody or part combined with another melody or part **3** the musical texture resulting from the simultaneous sounding of two or more melodies or parts ▷ *vb* **4** (*tr*) to set in contrast ▷ Related adj: **contrapuntal** [C15 from OF *contrepoint*, from *contre-* COUNTER- + *point* dot, note in musical notation, i.e. an accompaniment set against the notes of a melody]
counterpoise ('kaʊntəˌpɔɪz) *n* **1** a force, influence, etc, that counterbalances another **2** a state of balance; equilibrium **3** a weight that balances another ▷ *vb* **counterpoises, counterpoising, counterpoised** (*tr*) **4** to oppose with something of equal effect, weight, or force; offset **5** to bring into equilibrium
counterproductive (ˌkaʊntəprə'dʌktɪv) *adj* tending to hinder the achievement of an aim; having effects contrary to those intended
counterproposal ('kaʊntəprəˌpəʊzᵊl) *n* a proposal offered as an alternative to a previous proposal
Counter-Reformation (ˌkaʊntəˌrɛfə'meɪʃən) *n* the reform movement of the Roman Catholic Church in the 16th and early 17th centuries considered as a reaction to the Reformation
▷ http://www.lepg.org/religion.htm
counter-revolution (ˌkaʊntəˌrɛvə'luːʃən) *n* a revolution opposed to a previous revolution > ˌ**counter-ˌrevo'lutionist** *n* > **counter-ˌrevo'lutionary** *n, adj*
countershaft ('kaʊntəˌʃɑːft) *n* an intermediate shaft driven by a main shaft, esp in a gear train
countersign *vb* ('kaʊntəˌsaɪn, ˌkaʊntə'saɪn) **1** (*tr*) to sign (a document already signed by another) ▷ *n* ('kaʊntəˌsaɪn) **2** Also called: **countersignature** the signature so written **3** a secret sign given in response to another sign **4** *chiefly mil* a password
countersink ('kaʊntəˌsɪŋk) *vb* **countersinks, countersinking, countersank, countersunk** (*tr*) **1** to enlarge the upper part of (a hole) in timber, metal, etc, so that the head of a bolt or screw can be sunk below the surface **2** to drive (a screw) or sink (a bolt) into such a hole ▷ *n* **3** Also called: **countersink bit** a tool for countersinking **4** a countersunk hole
countertenor (ˌkaʊntə'tɛnə) *n* **1** an adult male voice with an alto range **2** a singer with such a voice
counterterrorism (ˌkəʊntə'tɛrəˌrɪzəm) *n* activities that are intended to prevent terrorist acts or to eradicate terrorist groups > ˌ**counter'terrorist** *adj*
countervail (ˌkaʊntə'veɪl, 'kaʊntəˌveɪl) *vb* **1** (when *intr*, usually foll by *against*) to act or act against with equal power or force **2** (*tr*) to make up for; compensate; offset [C14 from OF *contrevaloir*, from L *contrā valēre*, from *contrā* against + *valēre* to be strong]
countervailing duty *n* an extra import duty imposed by a country on certain imports, esp to prevent dumping or to counteract subsidies in the exporting country
counterweigh (ˌkaʊntə'weɪ) *vb* another word for **counterbalance** (sense 2)
counterweight ('kaʊntəˌweɪt) *n* a counterbalancing weight, influence, or force
countess ('kaʊntɪs) *n* **1** the wife or widow of a count or earl **2** a woman of the rank of count or earl
counting house *n* *rare, chiefly Brit* a room or building used by the accountants of a business
countless ('kaʊntlɪs) *adj* innumerable; myriad
count noun *n* a noun that can be qualified by the indefinite article and may be used in the plural, as *telephone* and *thing* but not *airs and graces* or *bravery*. Cf **mass noun**
count on *vb* (*intr, prep*) to rely or depend on
count out *vb* (*tr, adv*) **1** *inf* to leave out; exclude **2** (of a boxing referee) to judge (a floored boxer) to have failed to recover within the specified time

count palatine *n, pl* **counts palatine** *history* **1** (in the Holy Roman Empire) a count who exercised royal authority in his own domain **2** (in England and Ireland) the lord of a county palatine

countrified *or* **countryfied** ('kʌntrɪˌfaɪd) *adj* in the style, manners, etc, of the country; rural

country ('kʌntrɪ) *n, pl* **countries 1** a territory distinguished by its people, culture, geography, etc **2** an area of land distinguished by its political autonomy; state **3** the people of a territory or state **4a** the part of the land that is away from cities or industrial areas; rural districts **4b** *(as modifier): country cottage*. Related adjs.: **pastoral, rural 5** short for **country music 6 across country** not keeping to roads, etc **7 go** *or* **appeal to the country** *chiefly Brit* to dissolve Parliament and hold an election **8 up country** away from the coast or the capital **9** one's native land or nation of citizenship [C13 from OF *contrée*, from Med. L *contrāta*, lit.: that which lies opposite, from L *contrā* opposite]

country and western *n* another name for **country music**

country club *n* a club in the country, having sporting and social facilities

country dance *n* a type of folk dance in which couples face one another in a line
▷ www.cdss.org
▷ www.cam.ac.uk/societies/round/dances/elements.htm

country house *n* a large house in the country, esp belonging to a wealthy family

countryman ('kʌntrɪmən) *n, pl* **countrymen 1** a person who lives in the country **2** a person from a particular country or from one's own country > **'country,woman** *fem n*

country music *n* a type of 20th-century popular music based on White folk music of the southeastern US
▷ www.cmt.com

country park *n Brit* an area of countryside set aside for public recreation

country seat *n* a large estate or property in the country

countryside ('kʌntrɪˌsaɪd) *n* a rural area or its population

county ('kaʊntɪ) *n, pl* **counties 1a** any of various administrative, political, judicial, or geographic subdivisions of certain English-speaking countries or states **1b** *(as modifier): county cricket* ▷ *adj* **2** *Brit inf* upper class; of or like the landed gentry [C14 from OF *conté* land belonging to a count, from LL *comes* COUNT²]

county borough *n* **1** (in England from 1888 to 1974 and in Wales from 1888 to 1974 and from 1996) a borough administered independently of any higher tier of local government **2** (in the Republic of Ireland) a borough governed by an elected council that constitutes an all-purpose authority

county palatine *n, pl* **counties palatine 1** the lands of a count palatine **2** (in England and Ireland) a county in which the earl (or other lord) exercised many royal powers, esp judicial authority

county town *n* the town in which a county's affairs are or were administered

coup (kuː) *n* **1** a brilliant and successful stroke or action **2** short for **coup d'état** [C18 from F: blow, from L *colaphus* blow with the fist, from Gk *kolaphos*]

coup de grâce *French* (ku də grɑs) *n, pl* ***coups de grâce*** (ku də grɑs) **1** a mortal or finishing blow, esp one delivered as an act of mercy to a sufferer **2** a final or decisive stroke [lit.: blow of mercy]

coup d'état ('kuː deɪ'tɑː) *n, pl* **coups d'état** ('kuːz deɪ'tɑː) a sudden violent or illegal seizure of government [F, lit.: stroke of state]

coupe (kuːp) *n* **1** a dessert of fruit and ice cream **2** a dish or stemmed glass bowl designed for this dessert [C19 from F: goblet, CUP]

coupé ('kuːpeɪ) *n* **1** a four-seater car with a sloping back, and usually two doors **2** a four-wheeled horse-drawn carriage with two seats inside and one outside for the driver [C19 from F *carrosse coupé*, lit.: cut-off carriage]

Couperin (*French* kuprɛ̃) *n* **François** (frɑ̃swa) 1668–1733, French composer, noted for his harpsichord suites and organ music

Coupland ('kəʊplənd) *n* **Douglas** born 1961, Canadian novelist and journalist; novels include *Generation X* (1991), *Girlfriend in a Coma* (1998), and *City of Glass* (2000)

couple ('kʌpᵊl) *n* **1** two people who regularly associate with each other or live together: *an engaged couple* **2** *(functioning as sing or pl)* two people considered as a pair, for or as if for dancing, games, etc **3** a pair of equal and opposite parallel forces that have a tendency to produce rotation **4** a connector or link between two members, such as a tie connecting a pair of rafters in a roof **5 a couple of** *(functioning as sing or pl)* **5a** a combination of two; a pair of: *a couple of men* **5b** *inf* a small number of; a few: *a couple of days* ▷ *pron* **6** (usually preceded by *a; functioning as sing or pl*) two; a pair: *give him a couple* ▷ *vb* **couples, coupling, coupled 7** *(tr)* to connect (two things) together or to connect (one thing) to (another): *to couple railway carriages* **8** to form or be formed into a pair or pairs **9** to associate, put, or connect together **10** *(intr)* to have sexual intercourse [C13 from OF: a pair, from L *cōpula* a bond; see COPULA]

coupledom ('kʌpᵊldəm) *n* the state of living as a couple

coupler ('kʌplə) *n music* a device on an organ or harpsichord connecting two keys, two manuals, etc, so that both may be played at once

couplet ('kʌplɪt) *n* two successive lines of verse, usually rhymed and of the same metre [C16 from F, lit.: a little pair; see COUPLE]

coupling ('kʌplɪŋ) *n* **1** a mechanical device that connects two things **2** a device for connecting railway cars or trucks together

coupon ('kuːpɒn) *n* **1a** a detachable part of a ticket or advertisement entitling the holder to a discount, free gift, etc **1b** a detachable slip usable as a commercial order form **1c** a voucher given away with certain goods, a certain number of which are exchangeable for goods offered by the manufacturers **2** one of a number of detachable certificates attached to a bond, the surrender of which entitles the bearer to receive interest payments **3** *Brit* a detachable entry form for any of certain competitions, esp football pools [C19 from F, from OF *colpon* piece cut off, from *colper* to cut, var. of *couper*]

courage ('kʌrɪdʒ) *n* **1** the power or quality of dealing with or facing danger, fear, pain, etc **2 the courage of one's convictions** the confidence to act in accordance with one's beliefs [C13 from OF *corage*, from *cuer* heart, from L *cor*]

courageous (kə'reɪdʒəs) *adj* possessing or expressing courage > **cou'rageously** *adv* > **cou'rageousness** *n*

courante (kʊ'rɑːnt) *n music* **1** an old dance in quick triple time **2** a movement of a (mostly) 16th- to 18th-century suite based on this [C16 from F, lit.: running, from *courir* to run, from L *currere*]

Courantyne ('kɜːrənˌtaɪn) *n* a river in N South America, rising in S Guyana and flowing north to the Atlantic, forming the boundary between Guyana and Surinam. Length: 765 km (475 miles). Dutch name: **Corantijn**

courbaril ('kʊəbərɪl) *n* a tropical American leguminous tree: its wood is a useful timber and its gum is a source of copal. Also called: **West Indian locust** [C18 from Amerind]

Courbet (*French* kurbɛ) *n* **Gustave** (gystav) 1819–77, French painter, a leader of the realist movement; noted for his depiction of contemporary life

coureur de bois (*French* kurœr də bwa) *n, pl* **coureurs de bois** (kurœr də bwa) *Canad history* a French Canadian woodsman or Métis who traded with Indians for furs [Canad F: trapper (lit.: wood-runner)]

courgette (kʊəˈʒɛt) *n* a small variety of vegetable marrow. US, Canad, and Austral name: **zucchini** [from F, dim. of *courge* marrow, gourd]

courier (ˈkʊərɪə) *n* **1** a special messenger, esp one carrying diplomatic correspondence **2** a person employed to collect and deliver parcels, packages, etc **3** a person who makes arrangements for or accompanies a group of travellers on a journey or tour ▷ *vb* **4** (*tr*) to send (a parcel, letter, etc) by courier [c16 from OF *courrier*, from OIt. *correre* to run, from L *currere*]

Cournand (ˈkʊənənd, -nænd; *French* kurnɑ̃) *n* **André (Frederic)** 1895–1988, US physician, born in France: shared the 1956 Nobel prize for physiology or medicine for his work on heart catheterization

Courrèges (*French* kurɛʒ) *n* **André** (ɑ̃dre) born 1923, French couturier: helped to launch unisex fashion in the mid-1960s

course (kɔːs) *n* **1** a continuous progression in time or space; onward movement **2** a route or direction followed **3** the path or channel along which something moves: *the course of a river* **4** an area or stretch of land or water on which a sport is played or a race is run: *a golf course* **5** a period of time; duration: *in the course of the next hour* **6** the usual order of and time required for a sequence of events; regular procedure: *the illness ran its course* **7** a mode of conduct or action: *if you follow that course, you will fail* **8** a connected series of events, actions, etc **9a** a prescribed number of lessons, lectures, etc, in an educational curriculum **9b** the material covered in such a curriculum **10** a regimen prescribed for a specific period of time: *a course of treatment* **11** a part of a meal served at one time **12** a continuous, usually horizontal, layer of building material, such as a row of bricks, tiles, etc **13 as a matter of course** as a natural or normal consequence, mode of action, or event **14 in course of** in the process of **15 in due course** at some future time, esp the natural or appropriate time **16 of course 16a** (*adv*) as expected; naturally **16b** (*sentence substitute*) certainly; definitely **17 the course of nature** the ordinary course of events ▷ *vb* **courses, coursing, coursed 18** (*intr*) to run, race, or flow **19** to cause (hounds) to hunt by sight rather than scent or (of hounds) to hunt (a quarry) thus [c13 from OF *cours*, from L *cursus* a running, from *currere* to run]

courser[1] (ˈkɔːsə) *n* **1** a person who courses hounds or dogs, esp greyhounds **2** a hound or dog trained for coursing

courser[2] (ˈkɔːsə) *n literary* a swift horse; steed [c13 from OF *coursier*, from *cours* COURSE]

coursework (ˈkɔːsˌwɜːk) *n* written or oral work completed by a student within a given period, which is assessed as part of an educational course

coursing (ˈkɔːsɪŋ) *n* **1** hunting with hounds or dogs that follow their quarry by sight **2** a sport in which hounds are matched against one another in pairs for the hunting of hares by sight

court (kɔːt) *n* **1** an area of ground wholly or partly surrounded by walls or buildings **2** *Brit* **2a** a block of flats **2b** a mansion or country house **2c** a short street, sometimes closed at one end **3a** the residence, retinues, or household of a sovereign or nobleman **3b** (*as modifier*): *a court ball* **4** a sovereign or prince and his retinue, advisers, etc **5** any formal assembly held by a sovereign or nobleman **6** homage, flattering attention, or amorous approaches (esp in **pay court to someone**) **7** *law* **7a** a tribunal having power to adjudicate in civil, criminal, military, or ecclesiastical matters **7b** the regular sitting of such a judicial tribunal **7c** the room or building in which such a tribunal sits **8a** a marked outdoor or enclosed area used for any of various ball games, such as tennis, squash, etc **8b** a marked section of such an area **9 go to court** to take legal action **10 hold court** to preside over admirers, attendants, etc **11 out of court** without a trial or legal case **12 the ball is in your court** you are obliged to make the next move ▷ *vb* **13** to attempt to gain the love of; woo **14** (*tr*) to pay attention to (someone) in order to gain favour **15** (*tr*) to try to obtain (fame, honour, etc) **16** (*tr*) to invite, usually foolishly, as by taking risks [c12 from OF, from L *cohors* COHORT]

Court (kɔːt) *n* **Margaret** (née *Smith*) born 1942, Australian tennis player: Australian champion 1960–66, 1969–71, and 1973; US champion 1962, 1965, 1969–70, and 1973; Wimbledon champion 1963, 1965, and 1970

court-bouillon (ˈkʊətˈbuːjɒn) *n* a stock made from root vegetables, water, and wine or vinegar, used primarily for poaching fish [from F, from *court* short, + *bouillon* broth, from *bouillir* to BOIL[1]]

court card *n* (in a pack of playing cards) a king, queen, or jack of any suit [c17 altered from earlier *coat-card*, from the decorative coats worn by the figures depicted]

court circular *n* a daily report of the activities, engagements, etc, of the sovereign, published in a national newspaper

Courtelle (kɔːˈtɛl) *n trademark* a synthetic acrylic fibre resembling wool

Courtenay (ˈkɔːtnɪ) *n* **Bryce** (braɪs) born 1933, Australian author and businessman, born in South Africa. His bestselling novels include *The Power of One* (1989), *Tandia* (1991), and *The Potato Factory* (1995), and *Thommo and Hawk* (1998)

courteous (ˈkɜːtɪəs) *adj* polite and considerate in manner [c13 *corteis*, lit.: with courtly manners, from OF; see COURT] > ˈ**courteously** *adv* > ˈ**courteousness** *n*

courtesan *or* **courtezan** (ˌkɔːtɪˈzæn) *n* (esp formerly) a prostitute, or the mistress of a man of rank [c16 from OF *courtisane*, from It. *cortigiana* female courtier, from *corte* COURT]

courtesy (ˈkɜːtɪsɪ) *n, pl* **courtesies 1** politeness; good manners **2** a courteous gesture or remark **3** favour or consent (esp in (**by**) **courtesy of**) **4** common consent as opposed to right (esp in **by courtesy**) [c13 *curteisie*, from OF, from *corteis* COURTEOUS]

Cc

courtesy light *n* the interior light in a motor vehicle

courtesy title *n* any of several titles having no legal significance, such as those borne by the children of peers

courthouse (ˈkɔːtˌhaʊs) *n* a public building in which courts of law are held

courtier (ˈkɔːtɪə) *n* **1** an attendant at a court **2** a person who seeks favour in an ingratiating manner [c13 from Anglo-F *courteour* (unattested), from OF *corteier* to attend at court]

courtly (ˈkɔːtlɪ) *adj* **courtlier, courtliest 1** of or suitable for a royal court **2** refined in manner **3** ingratiating > ˈ**courtliness** *n*

court martial *n, pl* **court martials** *or* **courts martial 1** a military court that tries persons subject to military law ▷ *vb* **court-martial, court-martials, court-martialling, court-martialled** *or US* **court-martials, court-martialing, court-martialed 2** (*tr*) to try by court martial

Court of Appeal *n* a court that hears appeals from the High Court in both criminal and civil matters and from the county and crown courts

Court of St James's *n* the official name of the royal court of Britain

court plaster *n* a plaster, composed of isinglass on silk, formerly used to cover superficial wounds [c18 so called because formerly used by court ladies for beauty spots]

courtroom (ˈkɔːtˌruːm, -ˌrʊm) *n* a room in which the sittings of a law court are held

courtship (ˈkɔːtʃɪp) *n* **1** the act, period, or art of seeking the love of someone with intent to marry **2** the seeking or soliciting of favours

court shoe *n* a low-cut shoe for women, without any laces or straps

courtyard ('kɔːtˌjɑːd) *n* an open area of ground surrounded by walls or buildings; court

couscous ('kuːskuːs) *n* **1** a type of semolina originating in North Africa, consisting of granules of crushed durum wheat **2** a spicy North African dish consisting of steamed semolina with meat, vegetables, or fruit [C17 via F from Ar. *kouskous*, from *kaskasa* to pound until fine]

cousin ('kʌzᵊn) *n* **1** Also called: **first cousin, cousin-german, full cousin** the child of one's aunt or uncle **2** a relative descended from one of one's common ancestors **3** a title used by a sovereign when addressing another sovereign or a nobleman [C13 from OF *cosin*, from L *consōbrīnus*, from *sōbrīnus* cousin on the mother's side] > **'cousinˌhood** *or* **'cousinˌship** *n* > **'cousinly** *adj, adv*

Cousin (*French* kuzɛ̃) *n* **Victor** (viktɔr) 1792–1867, French philosopher and educational reformer

Cousteau (*French* kusto) *n* **Jacques Yves** (ʒɑk iv) 1910–97, French underwater explorer

couture (kuː'tʊə) *n* **a** high-fashion designing and dressmaking **b** (*as modifier*): *couture clothes* [from F: sewing, from OF *cousture* seam, from L *consuere* to stitch together]

couturier (kuː'tʊərɪˌeɪ) *n* a person who designs, makes, and sells fashion clothes for women [from F: dressmaker; see COUTURE] > **couturière** (kuːˌtuːrɪ'ɛə) *fem n*

▷ www.fashion.net/sites/fashiondesigners

▷ www.fashionshowroom.com

couvade (kuː'vɑːd) *n anthropol* the custom in certain cultures of treating the husband of a woman giving birth as if he were bearing the child [C19 from F, from *couver* to hatch, from L *cubāre* to lie down]

covalency (kəʊ'veɪlənsɪ) *or US* **covalence** *n* **1** the formation and nature of covalent bonds, that is, chemical bonds involving the sharing of electrons between atoms in a molecule **2** the number of covalent bonds that a particular atom can make with other atoms in forming a molecule > **co'valent** *adj* > **co'valently** *adv*

cove[1] (kəʊv) *n* **1** a small bay or inlet **2** a narrow cavern in the side of a cliff, mountain, etc **3** Also called: **coving** *archit* a concave curved surface between the wall and ceiling of a room [OE *cofa*]

cove[2] (kəʊv) *n sl, Brit old-fashioned & Austral* a fellow; chap [C16 prob. from Romany *kova* thing, person]

coven ('kʌvᵊn) *n* a meeting of witches [C16 prob. from OF *covin* group, ult. from L *convenīre* to come together]

covenant ('kʌvənənt) *n* **1** a binding agreement; contract **2** *law* an agreement in writing under seal, as to pay a stated annual sum to a charity **3** *Bible* God's promise to the Israelites and their commitment to worship him alone ▷ *vb* **4** to agree to a covenant (concerning) [C13 from OF, from *covenir* to agree, from L *convenīre* to come together, make an agreement; see CONVENE] > **covenantal** (ˌkʌvə'næntᵊl) *adj* > **'covenantor** *or* **'covenanter** *n*

Covenanter ('kʌvənəntə, ˌkʌvə'næntə) *n Scot history* a person upholding either of two 17th-century covenants to establish and defend Presbyterianism

▷ www.tartans.com/articles/covmain.html

▷ www.sorbie.net/covenanters.htm

Covent Garden ('kʌvənt, 'kɒv-) *n* **1** a district of central London: famous for its former fruit, vegetable, and flower market, now a shopping precinct **2** the Royal Opera House (built 1858) in Covent Garden

▷ www.royalopera.org

Coventry ('kɒvəntrɪ) *n* **1** a city in central England, in Coventry unitary authority, West Midlands: devastated in World War II; modern cathedral (1954–62); industrial centre, esp for motor vehicles; two universities (1965, 1992). Pop: 299 316 (1991) **2** a unitary authority in central England, in West Midlands. Pop: 300 844 (2001). Area: 97 sq km (37 sq miles) **3** **send to Coventry** to ostracize or ignore

cover ('kʌvə) *vb* (*mainly tr*) **1** to place or spread something over so as to protect or conceal **2** to provide with a covering; clothe **3** to put a garment, esp a hat, on (the body or head) **4** to extend over or lie thickly on the surface of: *snow covered the fields* **5** to bring upon (oneself); invest (oneself) as if with a covering: *covered with shame* **6** (sometimes foll by *up*) to act as a screen or concealment for; hide from view **7** *mil* to protect (an individual, formation, or place) by taking up a position from which fire may be returned if those being protected are fired upon **8** (*also intr*, sometimes foll by *for*) to assume responsibility for (a person or thing) **9** (*intr*; foll by *for* or *up for*) to provide an alibi (for) **10** to have as one's territory: *this salesman covers your area* **11** to travel over **12** to have or place in the aim and within the range of (a firearm) **13** to include or deal with **14** (of an asset or income) to be sufficient to meet (a liability or expense) **15a** to insure against loss, risk, etc **15b** to provide for (loss, risk, etc) by insurance **16** to deposit (an equivalent stake) in a bet **17** to act as reporter or photographer on (a news event, etc) for a newspaper or magazine: *to cover sports events* **18** *music* to record a cover version of **19** *sport* to guard or protect (an opponent, team-mate, or area) **20** (of a male animal, esp a horse) to copulate with (a female animal) ▷ *n* **21** anything that covers, spreads over, protects, or conceals **22a** a blanket used on a bed for warmth **22b** another word for **bedspread** **23** a pretext, disguise, or false identity: *the thief sold brushes as a cover* **24** an envelope or package for sending through the post: *under plain cover* **25a** an individual table setting, esp in a restaurant **25b** (*as modifier*): *a cover charge* **26** Also called: **cover version** a version by a different artist of a previously recorded musical item **27** *cricket* **27a** (*often pl*) the area more or less at right angles to the pitch on the off side and usually about halfway to the boundary **27b** (*as modifier*): *a cover drive* **28** *philately* an entire envelope that has been postmarked **29** **break cover** to come out from a shelter or hiding place **30** **take cover** to make for a place of safety or shelter **31** **under cover** protected, concealed, or in secret ▷ See also **cover-up** [C13 from OF *covrir*, from L *cooperīre* to cover completely, from *operīre* to cover over]

coverage ('kʌvərɪdʒ) *n* **1** the amount or extent to which something is covered **2** *journalism* the amount and quality of reporting or analysis given to a particular subject or event **3** the extent of the protection provided by insurance

cover crop *n* a crop planted between main crops to prevent leaching or soil erosion or to provide green manure

Coverdale ('kʌvəˌdeɪl) *n* **Miles** 1488–1568, the first translator of the complete Bible into English (1535)

covered wagon *n US & Canad* a large horse-drawn wagon with an arched canvas top, used formerly for prairie travel

cover girl *n* a glamorous woman whose picture appears on the cover of a magazine

covering letter *n* an accompanying letter sent as an explanation, introduction, or record

coverlet ('kʌvəlɪt) *n* another word for **bedspread**

cover note *n Brit* a certificate issued by an insurance company stating that a policy is operative: used as a temporary measure between the commencement of cover and the issue of the policy

cover point *n cricket* **a** a fielding position in the covers **b** a fielder in this position

cover slip *n* a very thin piece of glass placed over a specimen on a glass slide that is to be examined under a microscope

covert ('kʌvət) *adj* **1** concealed or secret ▷ *n* **2** a shelter or disguise **3** a thicket or woodland providing shelter for game **4** short for **covert cloth** **5** *ornithol* Also called: **tectrix** any of the small feathers on the wings and tail of a bird that surround the bases of the larger feathers [C14 from OF: covered, from *covrir* to COVER] > **'covertly** *adv*

covert cloth *n* a twill-weave cotton or worsted suiting fabric

coverture ('kʌvətʃə) *n rare* shelter, concealment, or disguise [C13 from OF, from *covert* covered; see COVERT]

cover-up *n* **1** concealment or attempted concealment of a mistake, crime, etc ▷ *vb* **cover up** (*adv*) **2** (*tr*) to cover completely **3** (when *intr*, often foll by *for*) to attempt to conceal (a mistake or crime)

cover version *n* another name for **cover** (sense 26)

covet ('kʌvɪt) *vb* **covets, coveting, coveted** (*tr*) to wish, long, or crave for (something, esp the property of another person) [C13 from OF *coveitier*, from *coveitié* eager desire, ult. from L *cupiditās* CUPIDITY] > **'covetable** *adj*

covetous ('kʌvɪtəs) *adj* (*usually postpositive* and foll by *of*) jealously eager for the possession of something (esp the property of another person) > **'covetously** *adv* > **'covetousness** *n*

covey ('kʌvɪ) *n* **1** a small flock of grouse or partridge **2** a small group, as of people [C14 from OF *covee*, from *cover* to sit on, hatch]

cow[1] (kaʊ) *n* **1** the mature female of any species of cattle, esp domesticated cattle **2** the mature female of various other mammals, such as the elephant, whale, and seal **3** (not in technical use) any domestic species of cattle **4** *inf* a disagreeable woman **5** *Austral & NZ sl* something objectionable (esp in **a fair cow**) [OE *cū*]

cow[2] (kaʊ) *vb* (*tr*) to frighten or overawe, as with threats [C17 from ON *kūga* to oppress]

coward ('kaʊəd) *n* a person who shrinks from or avoids danger, pain, or difficulty [C13 from OF *cuard*, from *coue* tail, from L *cauda*; ? suggestive of a frightened animal with its tail between its legs]

Coward ('kaʊəd) *n* Sir **Noël** (**Pierce**) 1899–1973, English dramatist, actor, and composer, noted for his sophisticated comedies, which include *Private Lives* (1930) and *Blithe Spirit* (1941)

cowardice ('kaʊədɪs) *n* lack of courage in facing danger, pain, or difficulty

cowardly ('kaʊədlɪ) *adj* of or characteristic of a coward; lacking courage > **'cowardliness** *n*

cowbell ('kaʊˌbɛl) *n* a bell hung around a cow's neck so that the cow can be easily located

cowberry ('kaʊbərɪ, -brɪ) *n, pl* **cowberries** **1** a creeping evergreen shrub of N temperate and arctic regions, with pink or red flowers and edible slightly acid berries **2** the berry of this plant

cowbird ('kaʊˌbɜːd) *n* any of various American orioles, having dark plumage and a short bill

cowboy ('kaʊˌbɔɪ) *n* **1** Also called: **cowhand** a hired man who herds and tends cattle, usually on horseback, esp in the western US **2** a conventional character of Wild West folklore, films, etc, esp one involved in fighting Indians **3** *inf* an irresponsible or unscrupulous operator in business, etc > **'cowˌgirl** *fem n*

cowcatcher ('kaʊˌkætʃə) *n* a metal frame on the front of a locomotive to clear the track of animals or other obstructions

cow-cocky *n, pl* **cow-cockies** *Austral & NZ* a one-man dairy farmer

Cowdrey ('kaʊdrɪ) *n* (**Michael**) **Colin**, Baron. 1932–2000, English cricketer. He played for Kent and in 114 Test matches (captaining England 27 times)

Cowell ('kaʊəl) *n* **Simon** born 1959, British manager of pop groups and TV personality, best known as an outspoken judge on the TV talent contest *Pop Idol*

cower ('kaʊə) *vb* (*intr*) to crouch or cringe, as in fear [C13 from MLow G *kūren* to lie in wait; rel. to Swedish *kura*]

Cowes (kaʊz) *n* a town in S England, on the Isle of Wight: famous for its annual regatta. Pop: 16 335 (1991)

cowherd ('kaʊˌhɜːd) *n* a person employed to tend cattle

cowhide ('kaʊˌhaɪd) *n* **1** the hide of a cow **2** the leather made from such a hide

cowl (kaʊl) *n* **1** a hood, esp a loose one **2** the hooded habit of a monk **3** a cover fitted to a chimney to increase ventilation and prevent draughts **4** the part of a car body that supports the windscreen and the bonnet ▷ *vb* (*tr*) **5** to cover or provide with a cowl [OE *cugele*, from LL *cuculla* cowl, from L *cucullus* hood]

cowlick ('kaʊˌlɪk) *n* a tuft of hair over the forehead

cowling ('kaʊlɪŋ) *n* a streamlined metal covering, esp around an aircraft engine

cowman ('kaʊmən) *n, pl* **cowmen** **1** *Brit* another name for **cowherd** **2** *US & Canad* a man who owns cattle; rancher

co-worker *n* a fellow worker; associate

cow parsley *n* a common Eurasian umbelliferous hedgerow plant having umbrella-shaped clusters of white flowers

cowpat ('kaʊˌpæt) *n* a single dropping of cow dung

cowpea ('kaʊˌpiː) *n* **1** a leguminous tropical climbing plant producing pods containing edible pealike seeds **2** the seed of this plant

Cowper ('kuːpə, 'kaʊ-) *n* **William** 1731–1800, English poet, noted for his nature poetry, such as in *The Task* (1785), and his hymns

cowpox ('kaʊˌpɒks) *n* a contagious viral disease of cows characterized by vesicles, esp on the teats and udder. Inoculation of humans with this virus provides temporary immunity to smallpox

cowpuncher ('kaʊˌpʌntʃə) *or* **cowpoke** ('kaʊˌpəʊk) *n US & Canad* an informal word for **cowboy**

cowrie *or* **cowry** ('kaʊrɪ) *n, pl* **cowries** **1** any marine gastropod mollusc of a mostly tropical family having a glossy brightly marked shell **2** the shell of any of these molluscs, esp the money cowrie, used as money in parts of Africa and S Asia [C17 from Hindi *kaurī*, from Sansk. *kaparda*]

Cc

cowslip ('kaʊˌslɪp) *n* **1** a primrose native to temperate regions of the Old World, having yellow flowers **2** *US & Canad* another name for **marsh marigold** [OE *cūslyppe*; see COW[1], SLIP[3]]

cox (kɒks) *n* **1** a coxswain ▷ *vb* **2** to act as coxswain of (a boat) > **'coxless** *adj*

coxa ('kɒksə) *n, pl* **coxae** ('kɒksiː) **1** a technical name for the hipbone or hip joint **2** the basal segment of the leg of an insect [C18 from L: hip] > **'coxal** *adj*

coxalgia (kɒk'sældʒɪə) *n* **1** pain in the hip joint **2** disease of the hip joint causing pain [C19 from COXA + -ALGIA] > **cox'algic** *adj*

coxcomb ('kɒksˌkəʊm) *n* **1** a variant spelling of **cockscomb** **2** *obs* the cap, resembling a cock's comb, worn by a jester > **'coxˌcombry** *n*

coxswain ('kɒksən, -ˌsweɪn) *n* **1** (usually shortened to **cox** in competitive rowing) the helmsman of a lifeboat, racing shell, etc **2** the senior petty officer on a small naval craft ▷ Also called: **cockswain** [C15 from *cock* a ship's boat + SWAIN]

coy (kɔɪ) *adj* **1** affectedly demure, esp in a playful or provocative manner **2** shy; modest **3** evasive, esp in an annoying way [C14 from OF *coi* reserved, from L *quiētus* QUIET] > **'coyly** *adv* > **'coyness** *n*

Coy. *mil abbrev for* company

coyote ('kɔɪəʊt, kɔɪ'əʊtɪ; *esp US.* 'kaɪəʊt, kaɪ'əʊtɪ) *n, pl* **coyotes** *or* **coyote** a predatory canine mammal of the deserts and prairies of North America. Also called: **prairie wolf** [C19 from Mexican Sp., from Nahuatl *coyotl*]

coypu ('kɔɪpuː) *n, pl* **coypus** *or* **coypu** **1** an aquatic South American rodent, naturalized in Europe. It resembles a small beaver and is bred for its fur **2** the fur of this animal ▷ Also called: **nutria** [C18 from American Sp. *coipú*, from Amerind *kóypu*]

coz (kʌz) *n* an archaic word for **cousin**

cozen ('kʌzən) *vb* to cheat or trick (someone) [C16 cant term ? rel. to COUSIN] > '**cozenage** *n*

cozy ('kəʊzɪ) *adj, n* the usual US spelling of **cosy**

CP *abbrev for:* **1** Canadian Pacific **2** Common Prayer **3** Communist Party

cp. *abbrev for* compare

CPAG *abbrev for* Child Poverty Action Group

cpd *abbrev for* compound

cpi *abbrev for* characters per inch

Cpl *abbrev for* Corporal

CPO *abbrev for* Chief Petty Officer

CPR *abbrev for* cardiopulmonary resuscitation

cps *abbrev for:* **1** *physics* cycles per second **2** *computing* characters per second

CPS (in England and Wales) *abbrev for* Crown Prosecution Service
▷ www.cps.gov.uk

CPSA *abbrev for* Civil and Public Services Association

CPVE (in Britain) *abbrev for* Certificate of Pre-vocational Education: a certificate awarded for completion of a broad-based course of study offered as a less advanced alternative to traditional school-leaving qualifications

CQ a symbol transmitted by an amateur radio operator requesting communication with any other amateur radio operator

Cr **1** *abbrev for* Councillor **2** *the chemical symbol for* chromium

cr. *abbrev for:* **1** credit **2** creditor

crab[1] (kræb) *n* **1** any chiefly marine decapod crustacean having a broad flattened carapace covering the cephalothorax, beneath which is folded the abdomen. The first pair of limbs are pincers **2** any of various similar or related arthropods **3** short for **crab louse** **4** a mechanical lifting device, esp the travelling hoist of a gantry crane **5** **catch a crab** *rowing* to make a stroke in which the oar either misses the water or digs too deeply, causing the rower to fall backwards ▷ *vb* **crabs, crabbing, crabbed** **6** (*intr*) to hunt or catch crabs [OE *crabba*]

crab[2] (kræb) *inf* ▷ *vb* **crabs, crabbing, crabbed** **1** (*intr*) to find fault; grumble ▷ *n* **2** an irritable person [C16 prob. back formation from CRABBED]

crab[3] (kræb) *n* short for **crab apple** [C15 ? of Scand. origin; cf. Swedish *skrabbe* crab apple]

Crab (kræb) *n* **the** the constellation Cancer, the fourth sign of the zodiac

crab apple *n* **1** any of several rosaceous trees that have white, pink, or red flowers and small sour apple-like fruits **2** the fruit of any of these trees, used to make jam

Crabbe (kræb) *n* **George** 1754–1832, English narrative poet, noted for his depiction of impoverished rural life in *The Village* (1783) and *The Borough* (1810)

crabbed ('kræbɪd) *adj* **1** surly; irritable; perverse **2** (esp of handwriting) cramped and hard to decipher **3** *rare* abstruse [C13 prob. from CRAB[1] (from its wayward gait), infl. by CRAB (APPLE) (from its tartness)] > '**crabbedly** *adv* > '**crabbedness** *n*

crabby ('kræbɪ) *adj* **crabbier, crabbiest** bad-tempered

crab louse *n* a parasitic louse that infests the pubic region in man

crabwise ('kræbˌwaɪz) *adj, adv* (of motion) sideways; like a crab

crack (kræk) *vb* **1** to break or cause to break without complete separation of the parts **2** to break or cause to break with a sudden sharp sound; snap **3** to make or cause to make a sudden sharp sound: *to crack a whip* **4** to cause (the voice) to change tone or become harsh or (of the voice) to change tone, esp to a higher register; break **5** *inf* to fail or cause to fail **6** to yield or cause to yield **7** (*tr*) to hit with a forceful or resounding blow **8** (*tr*) to break into or force open: *to crack a safe* **9** (*tr*) to solve or decipher (a code, problem, etc) **10** (*tr*) *inf* to tell (a joke, etc) **11** (*tr*) to break (a molecule) into smaller molecules or radicals by the action of heat, as in the distillation of petroleum **12** (*tr*) to open (a bottle) for drinking **13** (*intr*) *Scot & N English dialect* to chat; gossip **14** (*tr*) *inf* to achieve (esp in **crack it**) **15** **crack a smile** *inf* to break into a smile **16** **crack hardy** *or* **hearty** *Austral & NZ inf* to disguise one's discomfort, etc; put on a bold front ▷ *n* **17** a sudden sharp noise **18** a break or fracture without complete separation of the two parts **19** a narrow opening or fissure **20** *inf* a resounding blow **21** a physical or mental defect; flaw **22** a moment or specific instant: *the crack of day* **23** a broken or cracked tone of voice, as a boy's during puberty **24** (often foll by *at*) *inf* an attempt; opportunity to try **25** *sl* a gibe; wisecrack; joke **26** *sl* a person that excels **27** *Scot & N English dialect* a talk; chat **28** *sl* a concentrated highly addictive form of cocaine made into pellets or powder and smoked **29** Also: **craic** *inf, chiefly Irish* fun; informal entertainment: *the crack was great in here last night* **30** **a fair crack of the whip** *inf* a fair chance or opportunity **31** **crack of doom** doomsday; the end of the world; the Day of Judgment ▷ *adj* **32** (*prenominal*) *sl* first-class; excellent: *a crack shot* ▷ See also **crack down, crack up** [OE *cracian*]

crackbrained ('krækˌbreɪnd) *adj* insane, idiotic, or crazy

crack down *vb* (*intr, adv;* often foll by *on*) **1** to take severe measures (against); become stricter (with) ▷ *n* **crackdown** **2** severe or repressive measures

cracked (krækt) *adj* **1** damaged by cracking **2** *inf* crazy

cracked wheat *n* whole wheat cracked between rollers so that it will cook more quickly

cracker ('krækə) *n* **1** a decorated cardboard tube that emits a bang when pulled apart, releasing a toy, a joke, or a paper hat **2** short for **firecracker** **3** a thin crisp biscuit, usually unsweetened **4** a person or thing that cracks **5** *Brit, Austral, & NZ sl* a thing or person of notable qualities or abilities **6** See **catalytic cracker**

crackerjack ('krækəˌdʒæk) *inf* ▷ *adj* **1** excellent ▷ *n* **2** a person or thing of exceptional quality or ability [C20 changed from CRACK (first-class) + JACK (man)]

crackers ('krækəz) *adj* (*postpositive*) *Brit* a slang word for **insane**

crackhead ('krækˌhɛd) *n sl* a person addicted to the drug crack

cracking ('krækɪŋ) *adj* **1** (*prenominal*) *inf* fast; vigorous (esp in **a cracking pace**) **2** **get cracking** *inf* to start doing something quickly or with increased speed ▷ *adv, adj* **3** *Brit inf* first-class; excellent ▷ *n* **4** the process in which molecules are cracked, esp the oil-refining process in which heavy oils are broken down into hydrocarbons of lower molecular weight by heat or catalysis

crackjaw ('krækˌdʒɔː) *inf* ▷ *adj* **1** difficult to pronounce ▷ *n* **2** a word or phrase that is difficult to pronounce

crackle ('krækəl) *vb* **crackles, crackling, crackled** **1** to make or cause to make a series of slight sharp noises, as of paper being crushed **2** (*tr*) to decorate (porcelain or pottery) by causing fine cracks to appear in the glaze **3** (*intr*) to abound in vivacity or energy ▷ *n* **4** the act or sound of crackling **5** intentional crazing in the glaze of porcelain or pottery **6** Also called: **crackleware** porcelain or pottery so decorated > '**crackly** *adj*

crackling ('kræklɪŋ) *n* the crisp browned skin of roast pork

crack on *vb* (*intr;* often foll by *with*) *inf* to continue to do something as quickly as possible

crackpot ('krækˌpɒt) *inf* ▷ *n* **1** an eccentric person; crank ▷ *adj* **2** eccentric; crazy

crack up *vb* (*adv*) **1** (*intr*) to break into pieces **2** (*intr*) *inf* to undergo a physical or mental breakdown **3** (*tr*) *inf* to present or report, esp in glowing terms: *it's not all it's cracked up to be* **4** *inf, chiefly US & Canad* to laugh or cause to laugh uncontrollably ▷ *n* **crackup** **5** *inf* a physical or mental breakdown

Cracow ('krækaʊ, -əʊ, -ɒf) *n* an industrial city in S Poland, on the River Vistula: former capital of the country (1320–1609); university (1364). Pop: 740 000 (1999 est). Polish name: **Kraków** German name: **Krakau**

-cracy *n combining form* indicating a type of government or rule: *plutocracy; mobocracy*. See also **-crat** [from Gk *-kratia*, from *kratos* power]

cradle ('kreɪdᵊl) *n* **1** a baby's bed, often with rockers **2** a place where something originates **3** a frame, rest, or trolley made to support a piece of equipment, aircraft, ship, etc **4** a platform or trolley in which workmen are suspended on the side of a building or ship **5** *agriculture* **5a** a framework of several wooden fingers attached to a scythe to gather the grain into bunches as it is cut **5b** a scythe with such a cradle **6** Also called: **rocker** a boxlike apparatus for washing rocks, sand, etc, containing gold or gemstones **7** **rob the cradle** *inf* to take for a lover, husband, or wife a person much younger than oneself ▷ *vb* **cradles, cradling, cradled** (*tr*) **8** to rock or place in or as if in a cradle; hold tenderly **9** to nurture in or bring up from infancy **10** to wash (soil bearing gold, etc) in a cradle [OE *cradol*]

cradle snatcher *n inf* another name for **baby snatcher** (sense 2)

cradlesong ('kreɪdᵊlˌsɒŋ) *n* a lullaby

craft (krɑːft) *n* **1** skill or ability **2** skill in deception and trickery **3** an occupation or trade requiring special skill, esp manual dexterity **4a** the members of such a trade, regarded collectively **4b** (*as modifier*): *a craft union* **5** a single vessel, aircraft, or spacecraft **6** (*functioning as pl*) ships, boats, aircraft, or spacecraft collectively ▷ *vb* **7** (*tr*) to make or fashion with skill, esp by hand [OE *cræft* skill, strength]

▷ www.craftsitedirectory.com

▷ www.artpromote.com/craft.shtml

craftsman ('krɑːftsmən) *n, pl* **craftsmen** **1** a member of a skilled trade; someone who practises a craft; artisan **2** an artist skilled in an art or craft > **'craftsmanˌship** *n*

crafty ('krɑːftɪ) *adj* **craftier, craftiest** **1** skilled in deception; shrewd; cunning **2** *arch* skilful > **'craftily** *adv* > **'craftiness** *n*

crag (kræg) *n* a steep rugged rock or peak [c13 of Celtic origin]

craggy ('krægɪ) *or US* **cragged** ('krægɪd) *adj* **craggier, craggiest** **1** having many crags **2** (of the face) rugged; rocklike > **'cragginess** *n*

craic (kræk) *n* an Irish spelling of **crack** (sense 29)

Craig (kreɪg) *n* **Edward Gordon** 1872–1966, English theatrical designer, actor, and director. His nonrealistic scenic design greatly influenced theatre in Europe and the US

Craigavon (ˌkreɪg'ævᵊn) *n* a district in central Northern Ireland, in Co. Armagh. Pop: 80 671 (2001). Area: 279 sq km (108 sq miles)

Craigie ('kreɪgɪ) *n* Sir **William A(lexander)** 1867–1957, Scottish lexicographer; joint editor of the *Oxford English Dictionary* (1901–33), and of *A Dictionary of American English on Historical Principles* (1938–44)

crake (kreɪk) *n zool* any of several rails of the Old World, such as the corncrake [c14 from ON *krāka* crow or *krākr* raven, imit.]

cram (kræm) *vb* **crams, cramming, crammed** **1** (*tr*) to force more (people, material, etc) into (a room, container, etc) than it can hold; stuff **2** to eat or cause to eat more than necessary **3** *inf* to study or cause to study (facts, etc), esp for an examination, by hastily memorizing ▷ *n* **4** the act or condition of cramming **5** a crush [OE *crammian*]

crambo ('kræmbəʊ) *n* a word game in which one team says a rhyme or rhyming line for a word or line given by the other team [c17 from earlier *crambe*, prob. from L *crambē repetīta* cabbage repeated, hence an old story]

crammer ('kræmə) *n* a person or school that prepares pupils for an examination

cramp¹ (kræmp) *n* **1** a painful involuntary contraction of a muscle, typically caused by overexertion, heat, or chill **2** temporary partial paralysis of a muscle group: *writer's cramp* **3** (*usually pl in the US and Canada*) severe abdominal pain ▷ *vb* **4** (*tr*) to affect with or as if with a cramp [c14 from OF *crampe*, of Gmc origin]

cramp² (kræmp) *n* **1** Also called: **cramp iron** a strip of metal with its ends bent at right angles, used to bind masonry **2** a device for holding pieces of wood while they are glued; clamp **3** something that confines or restricts ▷ *vb* (*tr*) **4** to hold with a cramp **5** to confine or restrict **6** **cramp (someone's) style** *inf* to prevent (a person) from using his or her abilities or from acting freely and confidently [c15 from MDu. *crampe* cramp, hook, of Gmc origin]

cramped (kræmpt) *adj* **1** closed in; restricted **2** (esp of handwriting) small and irregular

crampon ('kræmpən) *or* **crampoon** (kræm'puːn) *n* **1** one of a pair of pivoted steel levers used to lift heavy objects; grappling iron **2** (*often pl*) one of a pair of frames each with 10 or 12 metal spikes, strapped to boots for climbing or walking on ice or snow [c15 from F, from MDu. *crampe* hook; see CRAMP²]

cran (kræn) *n* a unit of capacity used for fresh herring, equal to 37.5 gallons [c18 from ?]

Cranach (*German* 'kraːnax) *n* **Lucas** ('luːkas), known as *the Elder*, real name *Lucas Müller*. 1472–1553, German painter, etcher, and designer of woodcuts

cranberry ('krænbərɪ, -brɪ) *n, pl* **cranberries** **1** any of several trailing shrubs that bear sour edible red berries **2** the berry of this plant [c17 from Low G *kraanbere*, from *kraan* CRANE + *bere* BERRY]

crane (kreɪn) *n* **1** a large long-necked long-legged wading bird inhabiting marshes and plains in most parts of the world **2** (not in ornithological use) any similar bird, such as a heron **3** a device for lifting and moving heavy objects, typically consisting of a pivoted boom rotating about a vertical axis with lifting gear suspended from the end of the boom ▷ *vb* **cranes, craning, craned** **4** (*tr*) to lift or move (an object) by or as if by a crane **5** to stretch out (esp the neck), as to see over other people's heads [OE *cran*]

Crane (kreɪn) *n* **1** **(Harold) Hart** 1899–1932, US poet; author of *The Bridge* (1930) **2** **Stephen** 1871–1900, US novelist and short-story writer, noted particularly for his novel *The Red Badge of Courage* (1895) **3** **Walter** 1845–1915, British painter, illustrator of children's books, and designer of textiles and wallpaper

crane fly *n* a dipterous fly having long legs, slender wings, and a narrow body. Also called (Brit): **daddy-longlegs**

cranesbill ('kreɪnzˌbɪl) *n* any of various plants of the genus *Geranium*, having pink or purple flowers and long slender beaked fruits

cranial ('kreɪnɪəl) *adj* of or relating to the skull > **'cranially** *adv*

cranial index *n* the ratio of the greatest length to the greatest width of the cranium, multiplied by 100

cranial nerve *n* any of the 12 paired nerves that have their origin in the brain

craniate ('kreɪnɪɪt, -ˌeɪt) *adj* **1** having a skull or cranium ▷ *adj, n* **2** another word for **vertebrate**

cranio- *or before a vowel* **crani-** *combining form* indicating the cranium or cranial

craniology (ˌkreɪnɪ'ɒlədʒɪ) *n* the branch of science concerned with the shape and size of the human skull > **craniological** (ˌkreɪnɪə'lɒdʒɪkᵊl) *adj* > **ˌcranio'logically** *adv* > **ˌcrani'ologist** *n*

craniometry (ˌkreɪnɪ'ɒmɪtrɪ) *n* the study and measurement of skulls > **craniometric** (ˌkreɪnɪə'mɛtrɪk) *or* **ˌcranio'metrical** *adj* > **ˌcranio'metrically** *adv* > **ˌcrani'ometrist** *n*

craniotomy (ˌkreɪnɪ'ɒtəmɪ) *n, pl* **craniotomies** **1** a surgical incision into the skull **2** surgical crushing of a

Cc

fetal skull to extract a dead fetus

cranium ('kreɪnɪəm) *n, pl* **craniums** *or* **crania** (-nɪə) **1** the skull of a vertebrate **2** the part of the skull that encloses the brain [C16 from Med. L *crānium* skull, from Gk *kranion*]

crank (kræŋk) *n* **1** a device for communicating or converting motion, consisting of an arm projecting from a shaft, often with a second member attached to it parallel to the shaft **2** Also called: **crank handle, starting handle** a handle incorporating a crank, used to start an engine or motor **3** *inf* **3a** an eccentric or odd person **3b** *US, Canad, Austral, & Irish* a bad-tempered person ▷ *vb (tr)* **4** to rotate (a shaft) by means of a crank **5** to start (an engine, motor, etc) by means of a crank handle [OE *cranc*]

crankcase ('kræŋk,keɪs) *n* the metal housing that encloses the crankshaft, connecting rods, etc, in an internal-combustion engine

Cranko ('kræŋkəʊ) *n* **John** 1927–73, British choreographer, born in South Africa: director of the Stuttgart Ballet (1961–73)

crankpin ('kræŋk,pɪn) *n* a short cylindrical surface fitted between two arms of a crank parallel to the main shaft of the crankshaft

crankshaft ('kræŋk,ʃɑːft) *n* a shaft having one or more cranks, to which the connecting rods are attached

crank up *vb (adv) Sl* **1** *(tr)* to increase (loudness, output, etc): *he cranked up his pace* **2** *(tr)* to set in motion or invigorate: *news editors have to crank up tired reporters* **3** *(intr)* to inject a narcotic drug

cranky ('kræŋkɪ) *adj* **crankier, crankiest 1** *inf* eccentric **2** *inf* fussy and bad-tempered **3** shaky; out of order > **'crankily** *adv* > **'crankiness** *n*

Cranmer ('krænmə) *n* **Thomas** 1489–1556, the first Protestant archbishop of Canterbury (1533–56) and principal author of the Book of Common Prayer. He was burnt as a heretic by Mary I

crannog ('krænəg) *n* an ancient Celtic lake or bog dwelling [C19 from Irish Gaelic *crannóg*, from OIrish *crann* tree]

cranny ('krænɪ) *n, pl* **crannies** a narrow opening, as in a wall or rock face; chink; crevice (esp in **every nook and cranny**) [C15 from OF *cran* notch, fissure; cf. CRENEL] > **'crannied** *adj*

Cranwell ('krænwəl) *n* a village in E England, in Lincolnshire: Royal Air Force College (1920)

crap[1] (kræp) *n* **1** a losing throw in the game of craps **2** another name for **craps** [C20 back formation from CRAPS]

crap[2] (kræp) *sl* ▷ *n* **1** nonsense **2** rubbish **3** another word for **faeces** ▷ *vb* **craps, crapping, crapped 4** *(intr)* another word for **defecate** [C15 *crappe* chaff, from MDu., prob. from *crappen* to break off]

crape (kreɪp) *n* **1** a variant spelling of **crepe 2** crepe, esp when used for mourning clothes **3** a band of black crepe worn in mourning

crap out *vb (intr, adv) sl* **1** *US* to make a losing throw in craps **2** *US* to fail; withdraw **3** to fail to attempt something through fear

craps (kræps) *n (usually functioning as sing)* **1** a gambling game using two dice **2 shoot craps** to play this game [C19 prob. from *crabs* lowest throw at dice, pl of CRAB[1]] > **'crap,shooter** *n*

crapulent ('kræpjʊlənt) *or* **crapulous** ('kræpjʊləs) *adj* **1** given to or resulting from intemperance **2** suffering from intemperance; drunken [C18 from LL *crāpulentus* drunk, from L *crāpula*, from Gk *kraipalē* drunkenness, headache resulting therefrom] > **'crapulence** *n*

crash[1] (kræʃ) *vb* **1** to make or cause to make a loud noise as of solid objects smashing or clattering **2** to fall or cause to fall with force, breaking in pieces with a loud noise **3** *(intr)* to break or smash in pieces with a loud noise **4** *(intr)* to collapse or fail suddenly **5** to cause (an aircraft) to land violently resulting in severe damage or (of an aircraft) to land in this way **6** to cause (a car, etc) to collide with another car or other object or (of two or more cars) to be involved in a collision **7** to move or cause to move violently or noisily **8** *(intr)* (of a computer system or program) to fail suddenly because of a malfunction **9** *Brit inf* short for **gate-crash** ▷ *n* **10** an act or instance of breaking and falling to pieces **11** a sudden loud noise **12** a collision, as between vehicles **13** a sudden descent of an aircraft as a result of which it hits land or water **14** the sudden collapse of a business, stock exchange, etc **15** *(modifier)* requiring or using intensive effort and all possible resources in order to accomplish something quickly: *a crash course* [C14 prob. from *crasen* to smash, shatter + *dasshen* to strike violently, DASH[1]; see CRAZE]

crash[2] (kræʃ) *n* a coarse cotton or linen cloth [C19 from Russian *krashenina* coloured linen]

Crashaw ('kreɪʃɔː) *n* **Richard** 1613–49, English religious poet, noted esp for the *Steps to the Temple* (1646)

crash barrier *n* a barrier erected along the centre of a motorway, around a racetrack, etc, for safety purposes

crash dive *n* **1** a sudden steep dive from the surface by a submarine ▷ *vb* **crash-dive, crash-dives, crash-diving, crash-dived 2** *(intr)* (usually of an aircraft) to descend steeply and rapidly, before hitting the ground **3** to perform or cause to perform a crash dive

crash helmet *n* a padded helmet worn for motorcycling, flying, etc, to protect the head

crashing ('kræʃɪŋ) *adj (prenominal) inf* (intensifier) (esp in **a crashing bore**)

crash-land *vb* to land (an aircraft) causing some damage to it or (of an aircraft) to land in this way > **'crash-,landing** *n*

crash team *n* a medical team with special equipment able to be mobilized quickly to treat cardiac arrest

crass (kræs) *adj* **1** stupid; gross **2** *rare* thick or coarse [C16 from L *crassus* thick, dense, gross] > **'crassly** *adv* > **'crassness** *or* **'crassi,tude** *n*

Crassus ('kræsəs) *n* **Marcus Licinius** ('mɑːkəs lɪ'sɪnɪəs) ?115–53 BC, Roman general; member of the first triumvirate with Caesar and Pompey

-crat *n combining form* indicating a person who takes part in or is a member of a form of government or class [from Gk *-kratēs*, from *-kratia* -CRACY] > **-cratic** *or* **-cratical** *adj combining form*

crate (kreɪt) *n* **1** a fairly large container, usually made of wooden slats or wickerwork, used for packing, storing, or transporting goods **2** *sl* an old car, aeroplane, etc ▷ *vb* **crates, crating, crated 3** *(tr)* to pack or place in a crate [C16 from L *crātis* wickerwork, hurdle] > **'crater** *n* > **'crateful** *n*

crater ('kreɪtə) *n* **1** the bowl-shaped opening in a volcano or a geyser **2** a similar depression formed by the impact of a meteorite or exploding bomb **3** any of the roughly circular or polygonal walled formations on the moon and some planets **4** a large open bowl with two handles, used for mixing wines, esp in ancient Greece ▷ *vb* **5** to make or form craters in (a surface, such as the ground) [C17 from L: mixing bowl, crater, from Gk *kratēr*, from *kerannunai* to mix] > **'crater-,like** *adj* > **'craterous** *adj*

cravat (krə'væt) *n* a scarf worn round the neck instead of a tie, esp by men [C17 from F *cravate*, from Serbo-Croat *Hrvat* Croat; so called because worn by Croats in the French army during the Thirty Years' War]

crave (kreɪv) *vb* **craves, craving, craved 1** (when *intr*, foll by *for* or *after*) to desire intensely; long (for) **2** *(tr)* to need greatly or urgently **3** *(tr)* to beg or plead for [OE *crafian*] > **'craver** *n* > **'craving** *n*

craven ('kreɪvᵊn) *adj* **1** cowardly ▷ *n* **2** a coward [C13 *cravant*, prob. from OF *crevant* bursting, from *crever* to burst, die, from L *crepāre* to burst, crack] > **'cravenly** *adv* > **'cravenness** *n*

craw (krɔː) *n* **1** a less common word for **crop** (sense 6)

2 the stomach of an animal 3 **stick in one's craw** *inf* to be difficult, or against one's conscience, for one to accept, utter, etc [c14 rel. to MHG *krage*, MDu. *crāghe* neck, Icelandic *kragi* collar]

crawfish ('krɔːˌfɪʃ) *n, pl* **crawfish** *or* **crawfishes** a variant of **crayfish** (esp sense 2)

Crawford ('krɔːfəd) *n* 1 **Joan**, real name *Lucille le Sueur*. 1908–77, US film actress, who portrayed ambitious women in such films as *Mildred Pierce* (1945) 2 **Michael**, real name *Michael Dumbell Smith*. born 1942, British actor

crawl[1] (krɔːl) *vb* (*intr*) 1 to move slowly, either by dragging the body along the ground or on the hands and knees 2 to proceed very slowly or laboriously 3 to act in a servile manner; fawn 4 to be or feel as if overrun by something unpleasant, esp crawling creatures: *the pile of refuse crawled with insects* 5 (of insects, worms, snakes, etc) to move with the body close to the ground 6 to swim the crawl ▷ *n* 7 a slow creeping pace or motion 8 *swimming* a stroke in which the feet are kicked like paddles while each arm in turn reaches forward and pulls back through the water [c14 prob. from ON *krafla* to creep] > '**crawlingly** *adv*

crawl[2] (krɔːl) *n* an enclosure in shallow, coastal water for fish, lobsters, etc [c17 from Du. KRAAL]

crawler ('krɔːlə) *n* 1 *sl* a servile flatterer 2 a person or animal that crawls 3 *US* an informal name for **earthworm** 4 (*pl*) a baby's overalls; rompers 5 a computer program that is capable of performing recursive searches on the World Wide Web. Also called: **spider**

crawler lane *n* a lane on an uphill section of a motorway reserved for slow vehicles

Crawley ('krɔːlɪ) *n* a town in S England, in NE West Sussex: designated a new town in 1956. Pop: 88 203 (1991)

crawling ('krɔːlɪŋ) *n* a defect in freshly applied paint or varnish characterized by bare patches and ridging

crawly ('krɔːlɪ) *adj* **crawlier, crawliest** *inf* feeling or causing a sensation like creatures crawling on one's skin

crayfish ('kreɪˌfɪʃ) *or esp US* **crawfish** *n, pl* **crayfish** *or* **crayfishes** 1 a freshwater decapod crustacean resembling a small lobster 2 any of various similar crustaceans, esp the spiny lobster [c14 *cray*, by folk etymology, from OF *crevice* crab, from OHG *krebiz* + fish]

crayon ('kreɪən, -ɒn) *n* 1 a small stick or pencil of charcoal, wax, clay, or chalk mixed with coloured pigment 2 a drawing made with crayons ▷ *vb* 3 to draw or colour with crayons [c17 from F, from *craie*, from L *crēta* chalk] > '**crayonist** *n*

craze (kreɪz) *n* 1 a short-lived fashion 2 a wild or exaggerated enthusiasm ▷ *vb* **crazes, crazing, crazed** 3 to make or become mad 4 *ceramics, metallurgy* to develop or cause to develop fine cracks [c14 (in the sense: to break, shatter): prob. from ON]

crazy ('kreɪzɪ) *adj* **crazier, craziest** 1 *inf* insane 2 fantastic; strange; ridiculous 3 (*postpositive*; foll by *about* or *over*) *inf* extremely fond (of) > '**crazily** *adv* > '**craziness** *n*

Crazy Horse *n* Indian name *Ta-Sunko-Witko*. ?1849–77, Sioux Indian chief, remembered for his attempts to resist White settlement in Sioux territory

crazy paving *n Brit* a form of paving, as for a path, made of irregular slabs of stone

creak (kriːk) *vb* 1 to make or cause to make a harsh squeaking sound 2 (*intr*) to make such sounds while moving: *the old car creaked along* ▷ *n* 3 a harsh squeaking sound [c14 var. of CROAK, imit.] > '**creaky** *adj* > '**creakily** *adv* > '**creakiness** *n* > '**creakingly** *adv*

cream (kriːm) *n* 1a the fatty part of milk, which rises to the top 1b (*as modifier*): *cream buns* 2 anything resembling cream in consistency 3 the best one or most essential part of something; pick 4 a soup containing cream or milk: *cream of chicken soup* 5 any of various foods resembling or containing cream 6a a yellowish-white colour 6b (*as adj*): *cream wallpaper* ▷ *vb* (*tr*) 7 to skim or otherwise separate the cream from (milk) 8 to beat (foodstuffs) to a light creamy consistency 9 to add or apply cream or any creamlike substance to 10 (sometimes foll by *off*) to take away the best part of 11 to prepare or cook (vegetables, chicken, etc) with cream or milk [c14 from OF *cresme*, from LL *crāmum* cream, of Celtic origin; infl. by Church L *chrisma* unction, CHRISM] > '**cream,like** *adj*

cream cheese *n* a smooth soft white cheese made from soured cream or milk

cream cracker *n Brit* a crisp unsweetened biscuit, often eaten with cheese

creamer ('kriːmə) *n* 1 a vessel or device for separating cream from milk 2 a powdered substitute for cream, used in coffee 3 *now chiefly US & Canad* a small jug or pitcher for serving cream

creamery ('kriːmərɪ) *n, pl* **creameries** 1 an establishment where milk and cream are made into butter and cheese 2 a place where dairy products are sold

cream of tartar *n* potassium hydrogen tartrate, esp when used in baking powders

cream puff *n* a shell of light pastry with a custard or cream filling

cream soda *n* a soft drink flavoured with vanilla

cream tea *n* afternoon tea including bread or scones served with clotted cream and jam

creamy ('kriːmɪ) *adj* **creamier, creamiest** 1 resembling cream in colour, taste, or consistency 2 containing cream > '**creaminess** *n*

crease (kriːs) *n* 1 a line or mark produced by folding, pressing, or wrinkling 2 a wrinkle or furrow, esp on the face 3 *cricket* any of four lines near each wicket marking positions for the bowler or batsman. See also **bowling crease, popping crease, return crease** ▷ *vb* **creases, creasing, creased** 4 to make or become wrinkled or furrowed 5 (*tr*) to graze with a bullet [c15 from earlier *crēst*; prob. rel. to OF *cresté* wrinkled] > '**creaser** *n* > '**creasy** *adj*

Cc

create (kriːˈeɪt) *vb* **creates, creating, created** 1 (*tr*) to cause to come into existence 2 (*tr*) to invest with a new honour, office, or title; appoint 3 (*tr*) to be the cause of 4 (*tr*) to act (a role) in the first production of a play 5 (*intr*) *Brit sl* to make a fuss or uproar [c14 *creat* created, from L *creātus*, from *creāre* to produce, make]

creatine ('kriːəˌtiːn, -tɪn) *n* an important compound involved in many biochemical reactions and present in many types of living cells [c19 from Gk *kreas* flesh + -INE[2]]

creation (kriːˈeɪʃən) *n* 1 the act or process of creating 2 the fact of being created or produced 3 something brought into existence or created 4 the whole universe

Creation (kriːˈeɪʃən) *n Christianity* 1 (often preceded by *the*) God's act of bringing the universe into being 2 the universe as thus brought into being by God

creative (kriːˈeɪtɪv) *adj* 1 having the ability to create 2 characterized by originality of thought; having or showing imagination 3 designed to or tending to stimulate the imagination 4 characterized by sophisticated bending of the rules or conventions: *creative accounting* ▷ *n* 5 a creative person, esp one who devises advertising campaigns > **cre'atively** *adv* > **cre'ativeness** *n* > **,crea'tivity** *n*

creator (kriːˈeɪtə) *n* a person or thing that creates; originator > **cre'atorship** *n*

Creator (kriːˈeɪtə) *n* (usually preceded by *the*) an epithet of God

creature ('kriːtʃə) *n* 1 a living being, esp an animal 2 something that has been created, whether animate or inanimate 3 a human being; person: used as a term of scorn, pity, or endearment 4 a person who is dependent upon another; tool [c13 from Church L *creātūra*, from L

crēare to create] > **'creatural** *or* **'creaturely** *adj*
creature feature *n* a horror film featuring a monster
CREB *abbrev for* cyclic amp-response element binding protein: a protein involved in the long-term memory process
crèche (krɛʃ, kreɪʃ) *n* **1** *chiefly Brit* **1a** a day nursery for very young children **1b** a supervised play area provided for young children for short periods **2** a tableau of Christ's Nativity [C19 from OF: manger, crib, ult. of Gmc origin]
Crécy ('krɛsɪ; *French* kresi) *n* a village in N France: scene of the first decisive battle of the Hundred Years' War when the English defeated the French (1346). Official name: **Crécy-en-Ponthieu** (-ɑ̃pɔ̃tjø) English name: **Cressy**
cred (krɛd) *n sl* short for **credibility** (esp in **street cred**)
credence ('kriːdᵊns) *n* **1** acceptance or belief, esp with regard to the evidence of others **2** something supporting a claim to belief; credential (esp in **letters of credence**) **3** short for **credence table** [C14 from Med. L *crēdentia* trust, credit, from L *crēdere* to believe]
credence table *n Christianity* a small table on which the Eucharistic bread and wine are placed
credential (krɪ'dɛnʃəl) *n* **1** something that entitles a person to confidence, authority, etc **2** (*pl*) a letter or certificate giving evidence of the bearer's identity or competence [C16 from Med. L *crēdentia* credit, trust; see CREDENCE]
credenza (krɪ'dɛnzə) *n* another name for **credence table** [It.: see CREDENCE]
credibility gap *n* a disparity between claims or statements made and the evident facts of the situation or circumstances to which they relate
credible ('krɛdɪbᵊl) *adj* **1** capable of being believed **2** trustworthy or reliable: *the latest claim is the only one to involve a credible witness* [C14 from L *crēdibilis*, from L *crēdere* to believe] > **'credibleness** *or* **,credi'bility** *n* > **'credibly** *adv*
credit ('krɛdɪt) *n* **1** commendation or approval, as for an act or quality **2** a person or thing serving as a source of good influence, repute, etc **3** influence or reputation coming from the good opinion of others **4** belief in the truth, reliability, quality, etc, of someone or something **5** a sum of money or equivalent purchasing power, available for a person's use **6a** the positive balance in a person's bank account **6b** the sum of money that a bank makes available to a client in excess of any deposit **7a** the practice of permitting a buyer to receive goods or services before payment **7b** the time permitted for paying for such goods or services **8** reputation for solvency and probity, inducing confidence among creditors **9** *accounting* **9a** acknowledgment of an income, liability, or capital item by entry on the right-hand side of an account **9b** the right-hand side of an account **9c** an entry on this side **9d** the total of such entries **9e** (*as modifier*): *credit entries* **10** short for **tax credit** **11** *education* **11a** a distinction awarded to an examination candidate obtaining good marks **11b** a section of an examination syllabus satisfactorily completed **12** **on credit** with payment to be made at a future date ▷ *vb* **credits, crediting, credited** (*tr*) **13** (foll by *with*) to ascribe (to); give credit (for) **14** to accept as true; believe **15** to do credit to **16** *accounting* **16a** to enter (an item) as a credit in an account **16b** to acknowledge (a payer) by making such an entry ▷ See also **credits** [C16 from OF *crédit*, from It. *credito*, from L *crēditum* loan, from *crēdere* to believe]
creditable ('krɛdɪtəbᵊl) *adj* deserving credit, honour, etc; praiseworthy > **,credita'bility** *n* > **'creditably** *adv*
credit account *n Brit* a credit system by means of which customers may obtain goods and services before payment
credit card *n* a card issued by banks, businesses, etc, enabling the holder to obtain goods and services on credit
creditor ('krɛdɪtə) *n* a person or commercial enterprise to whom money is owed
credit rating *n* an evaluation of the creditworthiness of an individual or business
credits ('krɛdɪts) *pl n* a list of those responsible for the production of a film or a television programme
credit transfer *n* a method of settling a debt by transferring money through a bank or post office, esp for those who do not have cheque accounts
creditworthy ('krɛdɪt,wɜːðɪ) *adj* (of an individual or business) adjudged as meriting credit on the basis of earning power, previous record of debt repayment, etc > **'credit,worthiness** *n*
credo ('kriːdəʊ, 'kreɪ-) *n, pl* **credos** any formal statement of beliefs, principles, or opinions: *the American credo of individual freedom*
Credo ('kriːdəʊ, 'kreɪ-) *n, pl* **Credos** **1** the Apostles' or Nicene Creed **2** a musical setting of the Creed [C12 from L, lit.: I believe; first word of the Apostles' and Nicene Creeds]
credulity (krɪ'djuːlɪtɪ) *n* disposition to believe something on little evidence; gullibility
credulous ('krɛdjʊləs) *adj* **1** tending to believe something on little evidence **2** arising from or characterized by credulity: *credulous beliefs* [C16 from L *crēdulus*, from *crēdere* to believe] > **'credulously** *adv* > **'credulousness** *n*
Cree (kriː) *n* **1** (*pl* **Cree** *or* **Crees**) a member of a N American Indian people living in Ontario, Saskatchewan, and Manitoba **2** the language of this people
creed (kriːd) *n* **1** a concise, formal statement of the essential articles of Christian belief, such as the Apostles' Creed or the Nicene Creed **2** any statement or system of beliefs or principles [OE *crēda*, from L *crēdo* I believe] > **'creedal** *or* **'credal** *adj*
creek (kriːk) *n* **1** *chiefly Brit* a narrow inlet or bay, esp of the sea **2** *US, Canad, Austral, & NZ* a small stream or tributary **3** **up the creek** *sl* in trouble; in a difficult position [C13 from ON *kriki* nook; rel. to MDu. *krēke* creek, inlet]
Creek (kriːk) *n* **1** (*pl* **Creek** *or* **Creeks**) a member of a confederacy of N American Indian tribes formerly living in Georgia and Alabama **2** any of their languages
creel (kriːl) *n* **1** a wickerwork basket, esp one used to hold fish **2** a wickerwork trap for catching lobsters, etc [C15 from Scot., from ?]
creep (kriːp) *vb* **creeps, creeping, crept** (*intr*) **1** to crawl with the body near to or touching the ground **2** to move slowly, quietly, or cautiously **3** to act in a servile way; fawn; cringe **4** to move or slip out of place, as from pressure or wear **5** (of plants) to grow along the ground or over rocks **6** to develop gradually: *creeping unrest* **7** to have the sensation of something crawling over the skin ▷ *n* **8** the act of creeping or a creeping movement **9** *sl* a person considered to be obnoxious or servile **10** *geol* the gradual downward movement of loose rock material, soil, etc, on a slope [OE *crēopan*]
creeper ('kriːpə) *n* **1** a person or animal that creeps **2** a plant, such as the ivy, that grows by creeping **3** the US and Canad name for the **tree creeper** **4** a hooked instrument for dragging deep water **5** *inf* a shoe with a soft sole
creeps (kriːps) *pl n* (preceded by *the*) *inf* a feeling of fear, repulsion, disgust, etc
creepy ('kriːpɪ) *adj* **creepier, creepiest** **1** *inf* having or causing a sensation of repulsion or fear, as of creatures crawling on the skin **2** creeping; slow-moving > **'creepily** *adv* > **'creepiness** *n*
creepy-crawly *Brit inf* ▷ *n, pl* **creepy-crawlies** **1** a small crawling creature ▷ *adj* **2** feeling or causing a sensation as of creatures crawling on one's skin
cremate (krɪ'meɪt) *vb* **cremates, cremating, cremated**

(*tr*) to burn up (something, esp a corpse) and reduce to ash [c19 from L *cremāre*] > **cre'mation** *n* > **cre'mator** *n* > **crematory** ('krɛmətərɪ, -trɪ) *adj*

crematorium (,krɛmə'tɔ:rɪəm) *n, pl* **crematoriums** *or* **crematoria** (-rɪə) a building in which corpses are cremated. Also called (esp US): **crematory**

crème (krɛm, kri:m, kreɪm; *French* krɛm) *n* **1** cream **2** any of various sweet liqueurs: *crème de moka* ▷ *adj* **3** (of a liqueur) rich and sweet

crème de la crème *French* (krɛm də la krɛm) *n* the very best [lit.: cream of the cream]

crème de menthe ('krɛm də 'mɛnθ, 'mɪnt; 'kri:m, 'kreɪm) *n* a liqueur flavoured with peppermint [F, lit.: cream of mint]

crème fraîche ('krɛm 'frɛʃ) *n* thickened and slightly fermented cream [F, lit.: fresh cream]

Cremona (*Italian* kre'mo:na) *n* a city in N Italy, in Lombardy on the River Po: noted for the manufacture of fine violins in the 16th–18th centuries. Pop: 75 160 (1990)

crenate ('kri:neɪt) *or* **crenated** *adj* having a scalloped margin, as certain leaves [c18 from NL *crēnātus*, from Med. L, prob. from LL *crēna* a notch] > **'crenately** *adv* > **crenation** (krɪ'neɪʃən) *n*

crenel ('krɛn[ə]l) *or* **crenelle** (krɪ'nɛl) *n* any of a set of openings formed in the top of a wall or parapet and having slanting sides, as in a battlement [c15 from OF, lit.: a little notch, from *cren* notch, from LL *crēna*]

crenellate *or US* **crenelate** ('krɛnɪ,leɪt) *vb* **crenellates, crenellating, crenellated** *or US* **crenelates, crenelating, crenelated** (*tr*) to supply with battlements [c19 from OF *creneler*, from CRENEL] > **,crenel'lation** *or US* **,crenel'ation** *n*

crenellated *or US* **crenelated** ('krɛnɪ,leɪtɪd) *adj* **1** having battlements **2** (of a moulding, etc) having square indentations

creole ('kri:əʊl) *n* **1** a language that has its origin in extended contact between two language communities, one of which is European ▷ *adj* **2** of or relating to creole **3** (of a sauce or dish) containing or cooked with tomatoes, green peppers, onions, etc [c17 via F & Sp., prob. from Port. *crioulo* slave born in one's household, prob. from *criar* to bring up, from L *creāre* to CREATE]

Creole ('kri:əʊl) *n* **1** (*sometimes not cap*) (in the Caribbean and Latin America) **1a** a native-born person of European ancestry **1b** a native-born person of mixed European and African ancestry who speaks a creole **2** (in Louisiana and other Gulf States of the US) a native-born person of French ancestry **3** the French Creole spoken in Louisiana ▷ *adj* **4** of or relating to any of these peoples

Creon ('kri:ɒn) *n* *Greek myth* the successor to Oedipus as king of Thebes; the brother of Jocasta. See also **Antigone**

creosol ('kri:ə,sɒl) *n* a colourless or pale yellow insoluble oily liquid with a smoky odour and a burning taste [c19 from CREOS(OTE) + -OL[1]]

creosote ('krɪə,səʊt) *n* **1** a colourless or pale yellow liquid with a burning taste and penetrating odour distilled from wood tar. It is used as an antiseptic **2** a thick dark liquid mixture prepared from coal tar: used as a preservative for wood ▷ *vb* **creosotes, creosoting, creosoted 3** to treat (wood) with creosote [c19 from Gk *kreas* flesh + *sōtēr* preserver, from *sōzein* to keep safe] > **creosotic** (,krɪə'sɒtɪk) *adj*

crepe *or* **crape** (kreɪp) *n* **1a** a light cotton, silk, or other fabric with a fine ridged or crinkled surface **1b** (*as modifier*): *a crepe dress* **2** a black armband originally made of this, worn as a sign of mourning **3** a very thin pancake, often folded around a filling **4** short for **crepe paper** or **crepe rubber** [c19 from F *crêpe*, from L *crispus* curled, uneven, wrinkled]

crepe de Chine (kreɪp də ʃi:n) *n* a very thin crepe of silk or a similar light fabric [c19 from F: Chinese crepe]

crepe paper *n* thin crinkled coloured paper, resembling crepe and used for decorations

creperie ('krɛpərɪ, 'kreɪp-) *n* an eating establishment that specializes in pancakes

crepe rubber *n* a type of rubber in the form of colourless or pale yellow crinkled sheets: used for the soles of shoes

crêpe suzette (kreɪp su:'zɛt) *n, pl* **crêpes suzettes** (*sometimes pl*) an orange-flavoured pancake flambéed in a liqueur or brandy

crepitate ('krɛpɪ,teɪt) *vb* **crepitates, crepitating, crepitated** (*intr*) to make a rattling or crackling sound [c17 from L *crepitāre*] > **'crepitant** *adj* > **,crepi'tation** *n*

crepitus ('krɛpɪtəs) *n* **1** a crackling chest sound heard in pneumonia, etc **2** the grating sound of two ends of a broken bone rubbing together ▷ Also called: **crepitation** [c19 from L, from *crepāre* to crack, creak]

crept (krɛpt) *vb* the past tense and past participle of **creep**

crepuscular (krɪ'pʌskjʊlə) *adj* **1** of or like twilight; dim **2** (of certain creatures) active at twilight or just before dawn [c17 from L *crepusculum* dusk, from *creper* dark]

crepy *or* **crepey** ('kreɪpɪ) *adj* **crepier, crepiest** (esp of the skin) having a dry wrinkled appearance

Cres. *abbrev for* Crescent

crescendo (krɪ'ʃɛndəʊ) *n, pl* **crescendos** *or* **crescendi** (-dɪ) **1** *music* **1a** a gradual increase in loudness or the musical direction or symbol indicating this. Abbrev: **cresc** Symbol: < **1b** (*as modifier*): *a crescendo passage* **2** any similar gradual increase in loudness **3** a peak of noise or intensity: *the cheers reached a crescendo* ▷ *vb* **crescendos, crescendoing, crescendoed 4** (*intr*) to increase in loudness or force ▷ *adv* **5** with a crescendo [c18 from It., lit.: increasing, from *crescere* to grow, from L]

crescent ('krɛs[ə]nt, -z[ə]nt) *n* **1** the curved shape of the moon in its first or last quarter **2** any shape or object resembling this **3** *chiefly Brit* a crescent-shaped street **4** (*often cap* and preceded by *the*) **4a** the emblem of Islam or Turkey **4b** Islamic or Turkish power ▷ *adj* **5** *arch or poetic* increasing or growing [c14 from L *crescēns* increasing, from *crescere* to grow]

Cc

cresol ('kri:sɒl) *n* an aromatic compound found in coal tar and creosote and used in making synthetic resins and as an antiseptic and disinfectant. Formula: $C_6H_4(CH_3)OH$. Systematic name: **methylphenol**

cress (krɛs) *n* any of various plants having pungent-tasting leaves often used in salads and as a garnish [OE *cressa*]

cresset ('krɛsɪt) *n* *history* a metal basket mounted on a pole in which oil or pitch was burned for illumination [c14 from OF *craisset*, from *craisse* GREASE]

Cressida ('krɛsɪdə), **Criseyde,** *or* **Cressid** *n* (in medieval adaptations of the story of Troy) a lady who deserts her Trojan lover Troilus for the Greek Diomedes

Cressy ('krɛsɪ) *n* *rare* the English name for **Crécy**

crest (krɛst) *n* **1** a tuft or growth of feathers, fur, or skin along the top of the heads of some birds, reptiles, and other animals **2** something resembling or suggesting this **3** the top, highest point, or highest stage of something **4** an ornamental piece, such as a plume, on top of a helmet **5** *heraldry* a symbol of a family or office, borne in addition to a coat of arms and used in medieval times to decorate the helmet ▷ *vb* **6** (*intr*) to come or rise to a high point **7** (*tr*) to lie at the top of; cap **8** (*tr*) to reach the top of (a hill, wave, etc) [c14 from OF *creste*, from L *crista*] > **'crested** *adj* > **'crestless** *adj*

crestfallen ('krɛst,fɔ:lən) *adj* dejected or disheartened > **'crest,fallenly** *adv*

cretaceous (krɪ'teɪʃəs) *adj* consisting of or resembling chalk [c17 from L *crētāceus*, from *crēta*, lit.: Cretan earth, that is, chalk]

Cretaceous (krɪ'teɪʃəs) *adj* **1** of, denoting, or formed in the last period of the Mesozoic era, lasting 80 million years, during which chalk deposits were formed ▷ *n* **2 the** the Cretaceous period or rock system

Cretan ('kri:tən) *adj* **1** of or relating to Crete or its

inhabitants ▷ *n* **2** a native or inhabitant of Crete
Crete (kri:t) *n* a mountainous island in the E Mediterranean, the largest island of Greece: of archaeological importance for the ruins of Minoan civilization. Pop: 601 159 (2001). Area: 8331 sq km (3216 sq miles). Modern Greek name: **Kríti**
cretin ('krɛtɪn) *n* **1** a person afflicted with cretinism **2** a person considered to be extremely stupid [c18 from F *crétin*, from Swiss F *crestin*, from L *Chrīstiānus* Christian, alluding to the humanity of such people, despite their handicaps] > **'cretinous** *adj*
cretinism ('krɛtɪˌnɪzəm) *n* a condition arising from a deficiency of thyroid hormone, present from birth, characterized by dwarfism and mental retardation. See also **myxoedema**
cretonne (krɛ'tɒn, 'krɛtɒn) *n* a heavy cotton or linen fabric with a printed design, used for furnishing [c19 from F, from *Creton* Norman village where it originated]
Creutzfeldt-Jakob disease ('krɔɪtsfɛlt 'jɑ:kɒp) *n* a fatal slow-developing disease that affects the central nervous system, characterized by mental deterioration and loss of coordination of the limbs. It is thought to be caused by an abnormal prion protein in the brain. Abbrev: **CJD** [c20 after Hans G. *Creutzfeldt* (1885–1964) and Alfons *Jakob* (1884–1931), German physicians]
crevasse (krɪ'væs) *n* **1** a deep crack or fissure, esp in the ice of a glacier **2** *US* a break in a river embankment ▷ *vb* **crevasses, crevassing, crevassed 3** (*tr*) *US* to make a break or fissure in (a wall, etc) [c19 from F: CREVICE]
crevice ('krɛvɪs) *n* a narrow fissure or crack; split; cleft [c14 from OF *crevace*, from *crever* to burst, from L *crepāre* to crack]
crew[1] (kru:) *n* (*sometimes functioning as pl*) **1** the people who man a ship, boat, aircraft, etc **2** *naut* a group of people assigned to a particular job or type of work **3** *inf* a gang, company, or crowd ▷ *vb* **4** to serve on (a ship) as a member of the crew [c15 *crue* (military) reinforcement, from OF *creue* augmentation, from OF *creistre* to increase, from L *crescere*]
crew[2] (kru:) *vb arch* a past tense of **crow**[2]
crew cut *n* a closely cropped haircut for men [c20 from the style of haircut worn by the boat crews at Harvard and Yale Universities]
Crewe (kru:) *n* a town in NW England, in Cheshire: major railway junction. Pop: 63 351 (1991)
crewel ('kru:ɪl) *n* a loosely twisted worsted yarn, used in fancy work and embroidery [c15 from ?] > **'crewelist** *n* > **'crewelˌwork** *n*
crew neck *n* a plain round neckline in sweaters > **'crew-ˌneck** *or* **'crew-ˌnecked** *adj*
crib (krɪb) *n* **1** a child's bed with slatted wooden sides; cot **2** a cattle stall or pen **3** a fodder rack or manger **4** a small crude cottage or room **5** *NZ* a weekend cottage: term is South Island usage only **6** any small confined space **7** a representation of the manger in which the infant Jesus was laid at birth **8** *inf* a theft, esp of another's writing or thoughts **9** *inf, chiefly Brit* a translation of a foreign text or a list of answers used by students, often illicitly, as an aid in lessons, examinations, etc **10** short for **cribbage 11** *cribbage* the discard pile **12** Also called: **cribwork** a framework of heavy timbers used in the construction of foundations, mines, etc ▷ *vb* **cribs, cribbing, cribbed 13** (*tr*) to put or enclose in or as if in a crib; furnish with a crib **14** (*tr*) *inf* to steal (another's writings or thoughts) **15** (*intr*) *inf* to copy either from a crib or from someone else during a lesson or examination **16** (*intr*) *inf* to grumble [OE *cribb*] > **'cribber** *n*
cribbage ('krɪbɪdʒ) *n* a game of cards for two to four, in which players try to win a set number of points before their opponents [c17 from ?]
cribbage board *n* a board, with pegs and holes, used for scoring at cribbage
crib-biting *n* a harmful habit of horses in which the animal leans on the manger or seizes it with the teeth and swallows a gulp of air
crib-wall *n NZ* a supporting wall constructed by laying cribs at right angles to each other, as in cribwork
Crichton ('kraɪtᵊn) *n* **James** 1560–82, Scottish scholar and writer, called *the Admirable Crichton* because of his talents **2** **(John) Michael** born 1942, US novelist, screenwriter, and film director; his thrillers, many of which have been filmed, include *The Andromeda Strain* (1969), *Jurassic Park* (1990), *Disclosure* (1994), and *Prey* (2002)
crick (krɪk) *inf* ▷ *n* **1** a painful muscle spasm or cramp, esp in the neck or back ▷ *vb* **2** (*tr*) to cause a crick in [c15 from ?]
Crick (krɪk) *n* **Francis Harry Compton** born 1916, English molecular biologist: helped to discover the helical structure of DNA; Nobel prize for physiology or medicine shared with James Watson and Maurice Wilkins 1962
cricket[1] ('krɪkɪt) *n* an insect having long antennae and, in the males, the ability to produce a chirping sound by rubbing together the leathery forewings [c14 from OF *criquet*, from *criquer* to creak, imit.]
cricket[2] ('krɪkɪt) *n* **1a** a game played by two teams of eleven players on a field with a wicket at either end of a 22-yard pitch, the object being for one side to score runs by hitting a hard leather-covered ball with a bat while the other side tries to dismiss them by bowling, catching, running them out, etc **1b** (*as modifier*): *a cricket bat* **2** **not cricket** *inf* not fair play ▷ *vb* (*intr*) **3** to play cricket [c16 from OF *criquet* goalpost, wicket, from ?] > **'cricketer** *n*
▷ www.cricket.org
cricoid ('kraɪkɔɪd) *adj* **1** of or relating to the ring-shaped lowermost cartilage of the larynx ▷ *n* **2** this cartilage [c18 from NL *cricoīdes*, from Gk *krikoeidēs* ring-shaped, from *krikos* ring]
cri de coeur (kri: də kɜ:) *n, pl* **cris de coeur** (kri: də kɜ:) a heartfelt or impassioned appeal [c20 altered from F *cri du coeur*]
crier ('kraɪə) *n* **1** a person or animal that cries **2** (formerly) an official who made public announcements, esp in a town or court
crikey ('kraɪkɪ) *interj sl* an expression of surprise [c19 euphemistic for *Christ!*]
crime (kraɪm) *n* **1** an act or omission prohibited and punished by law **2** unlawful acts in general **3** an evil act **4** *inf* something to be regretted [c14 from OF, from L *crīmen* verdict, accusation, crime]
▷ www.unodc.org/unodc/crime_cicp_sitemap.html
Crimea (kraɪ'mɪə) *n* a peninsula and autonomous region in the Ukraine between the Black Sea and the Sea of Azov: a former autonomous republic of the Soviet Union (1921–45), part of the Ukrainian SSR from 1945 until 1991. Russian name: **Krym**
Crimean (kraɪ'mɪən) *adj* **1** of or relating to the Crimea or its inhabitants ▷ *n* **2** a native or inhabitant of the Crimea
crimen injuria ('krɪmɛn ɪn'dʒu:rɪə) *n S African law* the crime of injuring the dignity of a person by using racist or foul language, obscene gestures, etc [L, lit.: crime of insult]
crimewave ('kraɪmˌweɪv) *n* a period of increased criminal activity
criminal ('krɪmɪnᵊl) *n* **1** a person charged with and convicted of crime **2** a person who commits crimes for a living ▷ *adj* **3** of, involving, or guilty of crime **4** (*prenominal*) of or relating to crime or its punishment: *the criminal justice system* **5** *inf* senseless or deplorable [c15 from LL *crīminālis*; see CRIME, -AL[1]] > **'criminally** *adv* > **ˌcrimi'nality** *n*
criminal conversation *n* another term for **adultery**
criminalize *or* **criminalise** ('krɪmɪnəˌlaɪz)

vb **criminalizes, criminalizing, criminalized** *or* **criminalises, criminalising, criminalised** (*tr*) **1** to make (an action or activity) criminal **2** to treat (a person) as a criminal > ˌ**criminaliˈzation** *or* ˌ**criminaliˈsation** *n*

criminal law *n* the body of law dealing with offences and offenders

Criminal Records Bureau *n* (in England and Wales) a service offering employers and voluntary organizations access to police, health, and education records

criminology (ˌkrɪmɪˈnɒlədʒɪ) *n* the scientific study of crime [c19 from L *crimin-* CRIME, + -LOGY] > **criminological** (ˌkrɪmɪnəˈlɒdʒɪkᵊl) *or* ˌ**criminoˈlogic** *adj* > ˌ**criminoˈlogically** *adv* > ˌ**crimiˈnologist** *n*

crimp (krɪmp) *vb* (*tr*) **1** to fold or press into ridges **2** to fold and pinch together (something, such as two pieces of metal) **3** to curl or wave (the hair) tightly, esp with curling tongs **4** *inf, chiefly US* to hinder ▷ *n* **5** the act or result of folding or pressing together or into ridges **6** a tight wave or curl in the hair [OE *crympan*; rel. to *crump* bent; see CRAMP] > ˈ**crimper** *n* > ˈ**crimpy** *adj*

Crimplene (ˈkrɪmpliːn) *n trademark* a synthetic material similar to Terylene, characterized by its crease-resistance

crimson (ˈkrɪmzən) *n* **1a** a deep or vivid red colour **1b** (*as adj*): *a crimson rose* ▷ *vb* **2** to make or become crimson **3** (*intr*) to blush [c14 from OSp. *cremesin*, from Ar. *qirmizi* red of the kermes, from *qirmiz* KERMES] > ˈ**crimsonness** *n*

cringe (krɪndʒ) *vb* **cringes, cringing, cringed** (*intr*) **1** to shrink or flinch, esp in fear or servility **2** to behave in a servile or timid way **3** *inf* to experience a sudden feeling of embarrassment or distaste ▷ *n* **4** the act of cringing **5 the cultural cringe** *Austral* subservience to overseas cultural standards [OE *cringan* to yield in battle] > ˈ**cringer** *n*

cringle (ˈkrɪŋgᵊl) *n* an eyelet at the edge of a sail [c17 from Low G *Kringel* small ring]

crinkle (ˈkrɪŋkᵊl) *vb* **crinkles, crinkling, crinkled 1** to form or cause to form wrinkles, twists, or folds **2** to make or cause to make a rustling noise ▷ *n* **3** a wrinkle, twist, or fold **4** a rustling noise [OE *crincan* to bend, give way]

crinkly (ˈkrɪŋklɪ) *adj* **1** wrinkled; crinkled ▷ *n, pl* **crinklies 2** *sl* an old person

crinoid (ˈkraɪnɔɪd, ˈkrɪn-) *n* **1** a primitive echinoderm having delicate feathery arms radiating from a central disc ▷ *adj* **2** of, relating to, or belonging to the *Crinoidea* **3** shaped like a lily [c19 from Gk *krinoeidēs* lily-like] > **criˈnoidal** *adj*

crinoline (ˈkrɪnᵊlɪn) *n* **1** a stiff fabric, originally of horsehair and linen used in lining garments **2** a petticoat stiffened with this, worn to distend skirts, esp in the mid-19th century **3** a framework of steel hoops worn for the same purpose [c19 from F, from It. *crinolino*, from *crino* horsehair, from L *crīnis* hair + *lino* flax, from L *līnum*]

Crippen (ˈkrɪpᵊn) *n* **Hawley Harvey,** known as *Doctor Crippen*. 1862–1910, US doctor living in England: executed for poisoning his wife; the first criminal to be apprehended by the use of radiotelegraphy

cripple (ˈkrɪpᵊl) *n* **1** *offens* a person who is lame **2** *offens* a person who is or seems disabled or deficient in some way: *a mental cripple* ▷ *vb* **cripples, crippling, crippled 3** (*tr*) to make a cripple of; disable [OE *crypel*; rel. to *crēopan* to creep] > ˈ**crippler** *n*

Cripple Creek *n* a village in central Colorado: gold-mining centre since 1891, once the richest in the world

Cripps (krɪps) *n* Sir (**Richard**) **Stafford** 1889–1952, British Labour statesman; Chancellor of the Exchequer (1947–50)

Criseyde (krɪˈseɪdə) *n* a variant of **Cressida**

crisis (ˈkraɪsɪs) *n, pl* **crises** (-siːz) **1** a crucial stage or turning point, esp in a sequence of events or a disease **2** an unstable period, esp one of extreme trouble or danger **3** *pathol* a sudden change in the course of a disease [c15 from L: decision, from Gk *krisis*, from *krinein* to decide]

crisp (krɪsp) *adj* **1** dry and brittle **2** fresh and firm **3** invigorating or bracing: *a crisp breeze* **4** clear; sharp: *crisp reasoning* **5** lively or stimulating **6** clean and orderly **7** concise and pithy **8** wrinkled or curly: *crisp hair* ▷ *vb* **9** to make or become crisp ▷ *n* **10** *Brit* a very thin slice of potato fried and eaten cold as a snack **11** something that is crisp [OE, from L *crispus* curled, uneven, wrinkled] > ˈ**crisply** *adv* > ˈ**crispness** *n*

crispbread (ˈkrɪspˌbrɛd) *n* a thin dry biscuit made of wheat or rye

crisper (ˈkrɪspə) *n* a compartment in a refrigerator for storing salads, vegetables, etc, in order to keep them fresh

Crispin (ˈkrɪspɪn) *n* **Saint,** 3rd century AD, legendary Roman Christian martyr, with his brother **Crispinian** (krɪˈspɪnɪən): they are the patron saints of shoemakers. Feast day: Oct. 25

crispy (ˈkrɪspɪ) *adj* **crispier, crispiest 1** crisp **2** having waves or curls > ˈ**crispiness** *n*

crisscross (ˈkrɪsˌkrɒs) *vb* **1** to move or cause to move in a crosswise pattern **2** to mark with or consist of a pattern of crossing lines ▷ *adj* **3** (esp of lines) crossing one another in different directions ▷ *n* **4** a pattern made of crossing lines ▷ *adv* **5** in a crosswise manner or pattern

crit. *abbrev for:* **1** *med* critical **2** criticism

criterion (kraɪˈtɪərɪən) *n, pl* **criteria** (-rɪə) *or* **criterions** a standard by which something can be judged or decided [c17 from Gk *kritērion*, from *kritēs* judge, from *krinein* to decide]

> USAGE *Criteria*, the plural of *criterion*, is occasionally mistakenly used as a singular noun: *this criterion is not valid*; *these criteria are not valid*

critic (ˈkrɪtɪk) *n* **1** a person who judges something **2** a professional judge of art, music, literature, etc **3** a person who often finds fault and criticizes [c16 from L *criticus*, from Gk *kritikos* capable of judging, from *kritēs* judge; see CRITERION]

critical (ˈkrɪtɪkᵊl) *adj* **1** containing or making severe or negative judgments **2** containing analytical evaluations **3** of a critic or criticism **4** of or forming a crisis; crucial **5** urgently needed **6** *inf* so seriously injured or ill as to be in danger of dying **7** *physics* of, denoting, or concerned with a state in which the properties of a system undergo an abrupt change **8 go critical** (of a nuclear power station or reactor) to reach a state in which a nuclear-fission chain reaction becomes self-sustaining > ˌ**critiˈcality** *n* > ˈ**critically** *adv* > ˈ**criticalness** *n*

critical mass *n* the minimum mass of fissionable material that can sustain a nuclear chain reaction

critical path analysis *n* a technique for planning projects with reference to the critical path, which is the sequence of stages requiring the longest time

critical temperature *n* the temperature of a substance in its critical state. A gas can only be liquefied at temperatures below this

criticism (ˈkrɪtɪˌsɪzəm) *n* **1** the act or an instance of making an unfavourable or severe judgment, comment, etc **2** the analysis or evaluation of a work of art, literature, etc **3** the occupation of a critic **4** a work that sets out to evaluate or analyse

criticize *or* **criticise** (ˈkrɪtɪˌsaɪz) *vb* **criticizes, criticizing, criticized** *or* **criticises, criticising, criticised 1** to judge (something) with disapproval; censure **2** to evaluate or analyse (something) > ˈ**critiˌcizable** *or* ˈ**critiˌcisable** *adj* > ˈ**critiˌcizer** *or* ˈ**critiˌciser** *n*

critique (krɪˈtiːk) *n* **1** a critical essay or commentary, esp of an artistic work **2** the act or art of criticizing [c17

Cc

from F, from Gk *kritikē*, from *kritikos* able to discern]

croak (krəʊk) *vb* **1** *(intr)* (of frogs, crows, etc) to make a low, hoarse cry **2** to utter (something) in this manner **3** *(intr)* to grumble or be pessimistic **4** *sl* **4a** *(intr)* to die **4b** *(tr)* to kill ▷ *n* **5** a low hoarse utterance or sound [OE *crācettan*] > **'croaky** *adj* > **'croakiness** *n*

croaker ('krəʊkə) *n* **1** an animal, bird, etc, that croaks **2** a grumbling person

Croat ('krəʊæt) *n* **1a** a native or inhabitant of Croatia **1b** a speaker of Croatian ▷ *n, adj* **2** another word for **Croatian**

Croatia (krəʊ'eɪʃə) *n* a republic in SE Europe: settled by Croats in the 7th century; belonged successively to Hungary, Turkey, and Austria; formed part of Yugoslavia (1918–91); became independent in 1991 but was invaded by Serbia and fighting continued until 1995; involved in the civil war in Bosnia-Herzegovina (1991–95). Language: Croatian. Religion: Roman Catholic majority. Currency: kuna. Capital: Zagreb. Pop: 4 393 000 (2001 est). Area: 55 322 sq km (21 359 sq miles). Croatian name: **Hrvatska**

▷ www.vlada.hr
▷ www.croatia.hr/home/Default.aspx
▷ www.hr/index.en.shtml

Croatian (krəʊ'eɪʃən) *adj* **1** of or relating to Croatia, its people, or their language ▷ *n* **2** the official language of Croatia, a dialect of Serbo-Croat **3a** a native or inhabitant of Croatia **3b** a speaker of Croatian

Croatian (krəʊ'eɪʃən) *adj* **1** of, relating to, or characteristic of Croatia, its people, or their language ▷ *n* **2** the language that is spoken in Croatia, a dialect of Serbo-Croat (Croato-Serb) **3a** a native or inhabitant of Croatia **3b** a speaker of Croatian

croc (krɒk) *n* short for **crocodile** (senses 1 and 2)

Croce (*Italian* 'kro:tʃe) *n* **Benedetto** (bene'detto) 1866–1952, Italian philosopher, critic, and statesman: an opponent of Fascism, he helped re-establish liberalism in postwar Italy

crochet ('krəʊʃeɪ, -ʃɪ) *vb* **crochets, crocheting** (-ʃeɪɪŋ, -ʃɪɪŋ), **crocheted** (-ʃeɪd, -ʃɪd) **1** to make (a piece of needlework, a garment, etc) by looping and intertwining thread with a hooked needle (**crochet hook**) ▷ *n* **2** work made by crocheting [c19 from F *crochet*, dim. of *croc* hook, prob. of Scand. origin] > **'crocheter** *n*

▷ www.crochet.org

crock¹ (krɒk) *n* **1** an earthen pot, jar, etc **2** a piece of broken earthenware [OE *crocc* pot]

crock² (krɒk) *sl, chiefly Brit* ▷ *n* **1** a person or thing that is old or decrepit (esp in **old crock**) ▷ *vb* **2** to become or cause to become weak or disabled [c15 orig. Scot.; rel. to Norwegian *krake* unhealthy animal, Du. *kraak* decrepit person or animal]

crockery ('krɒkərɪ) *n* china dishes, earthen vessels, etc, collectively

crocket ('krɒkɪt) *n* a carved ornament in the form of a curled leaf or cusp, used in Gothic architecture [c17 from Anglo-F *croket* a little hook, from *croc* hook, of Scand. origin]

Crockett ('krɒkɪt) *n* **David,** known as *Davy Crockett.* 1786–1836, US frontiersman, politician, and soldier

crocodile ('krɒkəˌdaɪl) *n* **1** a large tropical reptile having a broad head, tapering snout, massive jaws, and a thick outer covering of bony plates **2a** leather made from the skin of any of these animals **2b** *(as modifier): crocodile shoes* **3** *Brit inf* a line of people, esp schoolchildren, walking two by two [c13 via OF, from L *crocodīlus*, from Gk *krokodeilos* lizard, ult. from *krokē* pebble + *drilos* worm; referring to its basking on shingle]

crocodile clip *n* a clasp with serrated interlocking edges used for making electrical connections, etc

Crocodile River *n* **1** a river in N South Africa, rising north of Johannesburg and flowing north-westerly into the Marico River on the Botswanan border; a tributary of the Limpopo **2** a river that rises in NE South Africa, in the Kruger National Park and flows south-easterly into Mozambique

crocodile tears *pl n* an insincere show of grief; false tears [from the belief that crocodiles wept over their prey to allure further victims]

crocodilian (ˌkrɒkə'dɪlɪən) *n* **1** any large predatory reptile of the order *Crocodilia*, which includes the crocodiles, alligators, and caymans ▷ *adj* **2** of, relating to, or belonging to the *Crocodilia* **3** of, relating to, or resembling a crocodile

crocus ('krəʊkəs) *n, pl* **crocuses** any plant of the iridaceous genus *Crocus*, having white, yellow, or purple flowers [c17 from NL, from L *crocus*, from Gk *krokos* saffron]

Croesus ('kri:səs) *n* **1** died ?546 BC, the last king of Lydia (560–546), noted for his great wealth **2** any very rich man

croft (krɒft) *n Brit* a small enclosed plot of land, adjoining a house, worked by the occupier and his family, esp in Scotland [OE *croft*] > **'crofter** *n* > **'crofting** *adj, n*

Crohn's disease (krəʊnz) *n* inflammation, thickening, and ulceration of any of various parts of the intestine, esp the ileum. Also called: **regional enteritis.** See also **Johne's disease** [c20 named after B. B. *Crohn* (1884–1983), US physician]

croissant ('krwʌsɒŋ) *n* a flaky crescent-shaped bread roll [F, lit.: crescent]

Croix de Guerre *French* (krwa də gɛr) *n* a French military decoration awarded for gallantry in battle: established 1915 [lit.: cross of war]

Cro-Magnon man ('krəʊ'mænjɒn, -'mægnɒn) *n* an early type of modern man, *Homo sapiens*, who lived in Europe during late Palaeolithic times [c19 after the cave (Cro-Magnon), Dordogne, France, where the remains were first found]

Cromer ('krəʊmə) *n* **1 1st Earl of,** title of (Evelyn) **Baring**

cromlech ('krɒmlɛk) *n* **1** a circle of prehistoric standing stones **2** (no longer in technical usage) a megalithic chamber tomb or dolmen [c17 from Welsh, from *crom*, fem. of *crwm* bent, arched + *llech* flat stone]

Crompton ('krɒmptən) *n* **1 Richmal,** full name *Richmal Crompton Lamburn.* 1890–1969, British children's author, best known for her *Just William* stories **2 Samuel** 1753–1827, British inventor of the spinning mule (1779)

Cromwell ('krɒmwəl, -wɛl) *n* **1 Oliver** 1599–1658, English general and statesman. A convinced Puritan, he was an effective leader of the parliamentary army in the Civil War. After the execution of Charles I he quelled the Royalists in Scotland and Ireland, and became Lord Protector of the Commonwealth (1653–58) **2** his son, **Richard** 1626–1712, Lord Protector of the Commonwealth (1658–59) **3 Thomas,** Earl of Essex. ?1485–1540, English statesman. He was secretary to Cardinal Wolsey (1514), after whose fall he became chief adviser to Henry VIII. He drafted most of the Reformation legislation, securing its passage through parliament, the power of which he thereby greatly enhanced. He was executed after losing Henry's favour

crone (krəʊn) *n* a witchlike old woman [c14 from OF *carogne* carrion, ult. from L *caro* flesh]

Cronin ('krəʊnɪn) *n* **1 A**(**rchibald**) **J**(**oseph**) 1896–1981, British novelist and physician. His works include *Hatter's Castle* (1931), *The Judas Tree* (1961), and *Dr Finlay's Casebook*, a TV series based on his medical experiences **2 James Watson** born 1931, US physicist; shared the Nobel prize for physics (1980) for his work on parity conservation in weak interactions

cronk (krɒŋk) *adj Austral sl* **1** unfit; unsound **2** dishonest [c19 ?from G *krank* ill]

Cronus ('krəʊnəs), **Cronos,** *or* **Kronos** ('krəʊnɒs) *n Greek myth* a Titan, son of Uranus (sky) and Gaea (earth), who ruled the world until his son Zeus dethroned him. Roman counterpart: **Saturn**

crony ('krəʊnɪ) *n, pl* **cronies** a friend or companion [c17 student sl (Cambridge), from Gk *khronios* of long duration, from *khronos* time]

cronyism ('krəʊnɪˌɪzəm) *n* the practice of appointing friends to high-level posts, esp political posts, regardless of their suitability

crook (krʊk) *n* **1** a curved or hooked thing **2** a staff with a hooked end, such as a bishop's crosier or shepherd's staff **3** a turn or curve; bend **4** *inf* a dishonest person, esp a swindler or thief ▷ *vb* **5** to bend or curve or cause to bend or curve ▷ *adj* **6** *Austral & NZ sl* **6a** ill **6b** of poor quality **6c** unpleasant; bad **7 go (off) crook** *Austral & NZ sl* to lose one's temper **8 go crook at** *or* **on** *Austral & NZ sl* to rebuke or upbraid [c12 from ON *krokr* hook]

crooked ('krʊkɪd) *adj* **1** bent, angled or winding **2** set at an angle; not straight **3** deformed or contorted **4** *inf* dishonest or illegal **5 crooked on** (*also* krʊkt) *Austral inf* hostile or averse to > **'crookedly** *adv* > **'crookedness** *n*

Crookes (krʊks) *n* Sir **William** 1832–1919, English chemist and physicist: he investigated the properties of cathode rays and invented a type of radiometer and the lens named after him

crool (kru:l) *vb Austral slang* **1** to spoil: *don't crool your chances* **2 crool someone's pitch** to spoil an opportunity for someone

croon (kru:n) *vb* **1** to sing or speak in a soft low tone ▷ *n* **2** a soft low singing or humming [c14 via MDu. *crōnen* to groan] > **'crooner** *n*

crop (krɒp) *n* **1** the produce of cultivated plants, esp cereals, vegetables, and fruit **2a** the amount of such produce in any particular season **2b** the yield of some other farm produce: *the lamb crop* **3** a group of products, thoughts, people, etc, appearing at one time or in one season **4** the stock of a thonged whip **5** short for **riding crop** **6** a pouchlike part of the oesophagus of birds, in which food is stored or partially digested before passing on to the gizzard **7** a short cropped hairstyle **8** a notch in or a piece cut out of the ear of an animal **9** the act of cropping ▷ *vb* **crops, cropping, cropped** (*mainly tr*) **10** to cut (hair, grass, etc) very short **11** to cut and collect (mature produce) from the land or plant on which it has been grown **12** to clip part of (the ear or ears) of (an animal), esp as a means of identification **13** (of herbivorous animals) to graze on (grass or similar vegetation) ▷ See also **crop out, crop up** [OE *cropp*]

crop-dusting *n* the spreading of fungicide, etc, on crops in the form of dust, often from an aircraft

crop-eared *adj* having the ears or hair cut short

crop out *vb (intr, adv)* (of a formation of rock strata) to appear or be exposed at the surface

cropper ('krɒpə) *n* **1** a person who cultivates or harvests a crop **2 come a cropper** *inf* **2a** to fall heavily **2b** to fail completely

crop rotation *n* the system of growing a sequence of different crops on the same ground so as to maintain or increase its fertility

crop top *n* a short T-shirt or vest that reveals the wearer's midriff

crop up *vb (intr, adv) inf* to occur or appear, esp unexpectedly

croquet ('krəʊkeɪ, -kɪ) *n* a game for two to four players who hit a wooden ball through iron hoops with mallets in order to hit a peg [c19 ?from F dialect, var. of CROCHET (little hook)]

▷ www.croquet.org.uk

▷ www.croquetamerica.com

croquette (krəʊ'kɛt, krɒ-) *n* a savoury cake of minced meat, fish, etc, fried in breadcrumbs [c18 from F, from *croquer* to crunch, imit.]

Crosby ('krɒzbɪ) *n* **Bing**, real name *Harry Lillis Crosby*. 1904–77, US singer and film actor; famous for his style of crooning: best known for the song "White Christmas" from the film *Holiday Inn* (1942)

crosier *or* **crozier** ('krəʊʒə) *n* a staff surmounted by a crook or cross, carried by bishops as a symbol of pastoral office [c14 from OF *crossier* staff bearer, from *crosse* pastoral staff]

cross (krɒs) *n* **1** a structure or symbol consisting of two intersecting lines or pieces at right angles to one another **2** a wooden structure used as a means of execution, consisting of an upright post with a transverse piece to which people were nailed or tied **3** a representation of the Cross used as an emblem of Christianity or as a reminder of Christ's death **4** any mark or shape consisting of two intersecting lines, esp such a symbol (×) used as a signature, error mark, etc **5** a sign representing the Cross made either by tracing a figure in the air or by touching the forehead, breast, and either shoulder in turn **6** any variation of the Christian symbol, such as a Maltese or Greek cross **7** a cruciform emblem awarded to indicate membership of an order or as a decoration for distinguished service **8** (*sometimes cap*) Christianity or Christendom, esp as contrasted with non-Christian religions **9** the place in a town or village where a cross has been set up **10** *biol* **10a** the process of crossing; hybridization **10b** an individual produced as a result of this process **11** a mixture of two qualities or types **12** an opposition, hindrance, or misfortune; affliction (esp in **bear one's cross**) **13** *boxing* a straight punch delivered from the side, esp with the right hand **14** *football* the act or an instance of passing the ball from a wing to the middle of the field ▷ *vb* **15** (sometimes foll by *over*) to move or go across (something); traverse or intersect **16a** to meet and pass **16b** (of each of two letters in the post) to be dispatched before receipt of the other **17** (*tr*; usually foll by *out, off,* or *through*) to cancel with a cross or with lines; delete **18** (*tr*) to place or put in a form resembling a cross: *to cross one's legs* **19** (*tr*) to mark with a cross or crosses **20** (*tr*) *Brit* to draw two parallel lines across the face of (a cheque) and so make it payable only into a bank account **21** (*tr*) **21a** to trace the form of the Cross upon (someone or something) in token of blessing **21b** to make the sign of the Cross upon (oneself) **22** (*intr*) (of telephone lines) to interfere with each other so that several callers are connected together at one time **23** to cause fertilization between (plants or animals of different breeds, races, varieties, etc) **24** (*tr*) to oppose the wishes or plans of; thwart **25** *football* to pass (the ball) from a wing to the middle of the field **26 cross one's fingers** to fold one finger across another in the hope of bringing good luck **27 cross one's heart** to promise or pledge, esp by making the sign of a cross over one's heart **28 cross one's mind** to occur to one briefly or suddenly **29 cross the path** (**of**) to meet or thwart (someone) **30 cross swords** to argue or fight ▷ *adj* **31** angry; ill-humoured; vexed **32** lying or placed across; transverse: *a cross timber* **33** involving interchange; reciprocal **34** contrary or unfavourable **35** another word for **crossbred** [OE *cros*, from OIrish *cross* (unattested), from L *crux*; see CRUX] > **'crossly** *adv* > **'crossness** *n*

Cross[1] (krɒs) *n* **the 1** the cross on which Jesus Christ was crucified **2** the Crucifixion of Jesus

Cross[2] (krɒs) *n* **Richard Assheton**, 1st Viscount. 1823–1914, British Conservative statesman, home secretary (1874–80); noted for reforms affecting housing, public health, and the employment of women and children in factories

cross- *combining form* **1** indicating action from one individual, group, etc, to another: *cross-cultural; cross-fertilize; cross-refer* **2** indicating movement, position, etc, across something: *crosscurrent; crosstalk* **3** indicating a crosslike figure or intersection: *crossbones* [from CROSS (in various senses)]

Cc

crossbar ('krɒs,bɑː) *n* 1 a horizontal bar, line, stripe, etc 2 a horizontal beam across a pair of goalposts 3 the horizontal bar on a man's bicycle

crossbeam ('krɒs,biːm) *n* a beam that spans from one support to another

cross-bench *n* (*usually pl*) *Brit* a seat in Parliament occupied by a neutral or independent member > **'cross-,bencher** *n*

crossbill ('krɒs,bɪl) *n* any of various widely distributed finches that occur in coniferous woods and have a bill with crossed tips

crossbones ('krɒs,bəʊnz) *pl n* See **skull and crossbones**

crossbow ('krɒs,bəʊ) *n* a type of medieval bow fixed transversely on a stock grooved to direct a square-headed arrow > **'cross,bowman** *n*

crossbred ('krɒs,brɛd) *adj* 1 (of plants or animals) produced as a result of crossbreeding ▷ *n* 2 a crossbred plant or animal

crossbreed ('krɒs,briːd) *vb* **crossbreeds, crossbreeding, crossbred** 1 Also: **interbreed** to breed (animals or plants) using parents of different races, varieties, breeds, etc ▷ *n* 2 the offspring produced by such a breeding

crosscheck (,krɒs'tʃɛk) *vb* 1 to verify (a fact, report, etc) by considering conflicting opinions or consulting other sources ▷ *n* 2 the act or an instance of crosschecking

cross-country *adj, adv* 1 by way of fields, etc, as opposed to roads 2 across a country ▷ *n* 3 a long race held over open ground

crosscurrent ('krɒs,kʌrənt) *n* 1 a current flowing across another current 2 a conflicting tendency moving counter to the usual trend

cross-curricular *adj Brit education* denoting or relating to an approach to a topic that includes contributions from several different disciplines and viewpoints

crosscut ('krɒs,kʌt) *adj* 1 cut at right angles or obliquely to the major axis ▷ *n* 2 a transverse cut or course 3 *mining* a tunnel through a vein of ore or from the shaft to a vein ▷ *vb* **crosscuts, crosscutting, crosscut** 4 to cut across

crosscut saw *n* a saw for cutting timber across the grain

crosse (krɒs) *n* a light staff with a triangular frame to which a network is attached, used in playing lacrosse [F, from OF *croce* CROSIER]

cross-examine *vb* **cross-examines, cross-examining, cross-examined** (*tr*) 1 *law* to examine (a witness for the opposing side), as in attempting to discredit his testimony 2 to examine closely or relentlessly > **'cross-ex,ami'nation** *n* > **,cross-ex'aminer** *n*

cross-eye *n* a turning inwards towards the nose of one or both eyes, caused by abnormal alignment > **'cross-,eyed** *adj*

cross-fertilize *vb* **cross-fertilizes, cross-fertilizing, cross-fertilized** 1 to fertilize by fusion of male and female gametes from different individuals of the same species 2 a non-technical term for **cross-pollinate** > **'cross-,fertili'zation** *n*

crossfire ('krɒs,faɪə) *n* 1 *mil, etc* converging fire from one or more positions 2 a lively exchange of ideas, opinions, etc

cross-grained *adj* 1 (of timber) having the fibres arranged irregularly or across the axis of the piece 2 perverse, cantankerous, or stubborn

cross hairs *pl n* two fine mutually perpendicular lines or wires that cross in the focal plane of a theodolite, gunsight, or other optical instrument and are used to define the line of sight. Also called: **cross wires**

crosshatch ('krɒs,hætʃ) *vb drawing* to shade or hatch with two or more sets of parallel lines that cross one another

crossing ('krɒsɪŋ) *n* 1 the place where one thing crosses another 2 a place, often shown by lights or markings, where a street, railway, etc, may be crossed 3 the act or an instance of travelling across something, esp the sea 4 the act or process of crossbreeding

crossing over *n genetics* the interchange of sections between pairing chromosomes during meiosis that produces variations in inherited characteristics by rearranging genes

cross-legged ('krɒs'lɛgɪd, -'lɛgd) *adj* standing or sitting with one leg crossed over the other

Crossman ('krɒsmən) *n* **Richard** (**Howard Stafford**) 1907–74, British Labour politician. His diaries, published posthumously as the *Crossman Papers* (1975), revealed details of cabinet discussions

cross-match *vb immunol* to test the compatibility of (a donor's and recipient's blood) by checking that the red cells of each do not agglutinate in the other's serum

crossover ('krɒs,əʊvə) *n* 1 a place at which a crossing is made 2 *railways* a point of transfer between two main lines 3 short for **crossover network** 4 *genetics* another term for **crossing over** 5 a recording, book, or other product that becomes popular in a genre other than its own ▷ *adj* 6 (of music, fashion, art, etc) combining two distinct styles 7 (of a performer, writer, recording, book, etc) having become popular in more than one genre

crossover network *n electronics* an arrangement in a loudspeaker system that separates the signal into two or more frequency bands for feeding into different speakers

crosspatch ('krɒs,pætʃ) *n inf* a bad-tempered person [C18 from CROSS + obs. *patch* fool]

crosspiece ('krɒs,piːs) *n* a transverse beam, joist, etc

cross-ply *adj* (of a motor tyre) having the fabric cords in the outer casing running diagonally to stiffen the sidewalls

cross-pollinate *vb* **cross-pollinates, cross-pollinating, cross-pollinated** to transfer pollen from the anthers of one flower to the stigma of another > **,cross-polli'nation** *n*

cross-purpose *n* 1 a contrary aim or purpose 2 **at cross-purposes** conflicting; opposed; disagreeing

cross-question *vb* 1 to cross-examine ▷ *n* 2 a question asked in cross-examination

cross-refer *vb* to refer from one part of something, esp a book, to another

cross-reference *n* 1 a reference within a text to another part of the text ▷ *vb* **cross-references, cross-referencing, cross-referenced** 2 to cross-refer

crossroad ('krɒs,rəʊd) *n US & Canad* 1 a road that crosses another road 2 Also called: **crossway** a road that crosses from one main road to another

crossroads ('krɒs,rəʊdz) *n* (*functioning as sing*) 1 the point at which two or more roads cross each other 2 the point at which an important choice has to be made (esp in **at the crossroads**)

crossruff ('krɒs,rʌf) *bridge, whist* ▷ *n* 1 the alternate trumping of each other's leads by two partners, or by declarer and dummy ▷ *vb* 2 (*intr*) to trump alternately in this way

cross section *n* 1 *maths* a plane surface formed by cutting across a solid, esp perpendicular to its longest axis 2 a section cut off in this way 3 the act of cutting anything in this way 4 a random sample, esp one regarded as representative > **,cross-'sectional** *adj*

cross-stitch *n* 1 an embroidery stitch made by two stitches forming a cross 2 embroidery worked with this stitch ▷ *vb* 3 to embroider (a piece of needlework) with cross-stitch

crosstalk ('krɒs,tɔːk) *n* 1 unwanted signals in one channel of a communications system as a result of a transfer of energy from other channels 2 *Brit* rapid or witty talk

cross training *n* training in two or more sports to improve performance, esp in one's main sport

crosstree ('krɒs,triː) *n naut* either of a pair of wooden or metal braces on the head of a mast to support the topmast, etc

crosswise ('krɒs,waɪz) *or* **crossways** ('krɒs,weɪz) *adj, adv* **1** across; transversely **2** in the shape of a cross

crossword puzzle ('krɒs,wɜːd) *n* a puzzle in which the solver guesses words suggested by numbered clues and writes them into a grid to form a vertical and horizontal pattern
▷ www.crossword-puzzles.co.uk

crotch (krɒtʃ) *n* **1** Also called (Brit): **crutch 1a** the angle formed by the legs where they join the human trunk **1b** the human genital area **1c** the corresponding part of a pair of trousers, pants, etc **2** a forked region formed by the junction of two members **3** a forked pole or stick [C16 prob. var. of CRUTCH] > **crotched** *adj*

crotchet ('krɒtʃɪt) *n* **1** *music* Also called (US and Canad): **quarter note** a note having the time value of a quarter of a semibreve **2** a perverse notion [C14 from OF *crochet*, lit.: little hook, from *croche* hook; see CROCKET]

crotchety ('krɒtʃɪtɪ) *adj* **1** *inf* irritable; contrary **2** full of crotchets > '**crotchetiness** *n*

croton ('krəʊtᵊn) *n* **1** any shrub or tree of the chiefly tropical genus *Croton*, esp *C. tiglium*, the seeds of which yield croton oil, formerly used as a purgative **2** any of various tropical plants of the related genus *Codiaeum* [C18 from NL, from Gk *krotōn* tick, castor-oil plant (whose berries resemble ticks)]

crouch (kraʊtʃ) *vb* (*intr*) **1** to bend low with the limbs pulled up close together, esp (of an animal) in readiness to pounce **2** to cringe, as in humility or fear ▷ *n* **3** the act of stooping or bending [C14 ?from OF *crochir* to become bent like a hook, from *croche* hook]

croup¹ (kruːp) *n* a throat condition, occurring usually in children, characterized by a hoarse cough and laboured breathing, resulting from inflammation of the larynx [C16 *croup* to cry hoarsely, prob. imit.] > '**croupous** *or* '**croupy** *adj*

croup² (kruːp) *n* the hindquarters, esp of a horse [C13 from OF *croupe*; rel. to G *Kruppe*]

croupier ('kruːpɪə) *n* a person who deals cards, collects bets, etc, at a gaming table [C18 lit.: one who rides behind another, from F *croupe* CROUP²]

crouton ('kruːtɒn) *n* a small piece of fried or toasted bread, usually served in soup [F: dim. of *croûte* CRUST]

crow¹ (krəʊ) *n* **1** any large gregarious songbird of the genus *Corvus* of Europe and Asia, such as the raven, rook, and jackdaw. All have a heavy bill, glossy black plumage, and rounded wings **2** any of various similar birds **3** *sl* an old or ugly woman **4 as the crow flies** as directly as possible **5 eat crow** *US & Canad inf* to be forced to do something humiliating **6 stone the crows** (*interj*) *Brit & Austral sl* an expression of surprise, dismay, etc [OE *crāwa*]

crow² (krəʊ) *vb* (*intr*) **1** (p.t. **crowed** *or* **crew**) to utter a shrill squawking sound, as a cock **2** (often foll by *over*) to boast one's superiority **3** (esp of babies) to utter cries of pleasure ▷ *n* **4** an act or instance of crowing [OE *crāwan*; rel. to OHG *krāen*, Du. *kraaien*] > '**crowingly** *adv*

crowbar ('krəʊ,bɑː) *n* a heavy iron lever with one end forged into a wedge shape

crowd (kraʊd) *n* **1** a large number of things or people gathered or considered together **2** a particular group of people, esp considered as a set: *the crowd from the office* **3** (preceded by *the*) the common people; the masses ▷ *vb* **4** (*intr*) to gather together in large numbers; throng **5** (*tr*) to press together into a confined space **6** (*tr*) to fill to excess; fill by pushing into **7** (*tr*) *inf* to urge or harass by urging [OE *crūdan*] > '**crowded** *adj* > '**crowdedness** *n*

Crowe (krəʊ) *n* **Russell** born 1964, Australian film actor, born in New Zealand. His films include *LA Confidential* (1997), *Gladiator* (2000), for which he won an Oscar, *A Beautiful Mind* (2001), and *Master and Commander* (2003)

crowfoot ('krəʊ,fʊt) *n, pl* **crowfoots** any of several plants that have yellow or white flowers and divided leaves resembling the foot of a crow

crown (kraʊn) *n* **1** an ornamental headdress denoting sovereignty, usually made of gold embedded with precious stones **2** a wreath or garland for the head, awarded as a sign of victory, success, honour, etc **3** (*sometimes cap*) monarchy or kingship **4** an award, distinction, or title, given as an honour to reward merit, victory, etc **5** anything resembling or symbolizing a crown **6a** a coin worth five shillings (25 pence) **6b** a coin worth £5 **6c** any of several continental coins, such as the krona or krone, with a name meaning *crown* **7** the top or summit of something: *crown of a hill* **8** the centre part of a road, esp when it is cambered **9** the outstanding quality, achievement, state, etc: *the crown of his achievements* **10a** the enamel-covered part of a tooth above the gum **10b artificial crown** a substitute crown, usually of gold, porcelain, or acrylic resin, fitted over a decayed or broken tooth **11** the part of an anchor where the arms are joined to the shank ▷ *vb* (*tr*) **12** to put a crown on the head of, symbolically vesting with royal title, powers, etc **13** to place a crown, wreath, garland, etc, on the head of **14** to place something on or over the head or top of **15** to confer a title, dignity, or reward upon **16** to form the summit or topmost part of **17** to cap or put the finishing touch to (a series of events): *to crown it all it rained, too* **18** *draughts* to promote (a draught) to a king by placing another draught on top of it **19** to attach a crown to (a tooth) **20** *sl* to hit over the head [C12 from OF *corone*, from L *corōna* wreath, crown, from Gk *korōnē* crown, something curved]

Crown (kraʊn) *n* (*sometimes not cap*; usually preceded by *the*) **1** the sovereignty or realm of a monarch **2a** the government of a monarchy **2b** (*as modifier*): *Crown property*

crown colony *n* a British colony whose administration is controlled by the Crown

crown court *n English law* a court of criminal jurisdiction holding sessions in towns throughout England and Wales

Crown Derby *n* **1** a type of porcelain manufactured at Derby from 1784–1848 **2** *trademark* shortened form of Royal Crown Derby

crown glass *n* **1** another name for **optical crown 2** an old form of window glass made by blowing a globe and spinning it until it forms a flat disc

crown green *n* a type of bowling green in which the sides are lower than the middle

crowning ('kraʊnɪŋ) *n obstetrics* the stage of labour at which the infant's head is passing through the vaginal opening

crown jewels *pl n* the jewellery, including the regalia, used by a sovereign on a state occasion
▷ www.royal.gov.uk/output/Page450.asp

Crown Office *n* (in Britain) an administrative office of the Queen's Bench Division of the High Court, where actions are entered for trial

crown prince *n* the male heir to a sovereign throne

crown princess *n* **1** the wife of a crown prince **2** the female heir to a sovereign throne

Crown Prosecution Service *n* (in England and Wales) an independent prosecuting body, established in 1986, that decides whether cases brought by the police should go to the courts: headed by the Director of Public Prosecutions ▷ Cf **procurator fiscal** Abbrev: **CPS**

crown wheel *n* **1** *horology* a wheel that has one set of teeth at right angles to another **2** the larger of two wheels in a bevel gear

crow's-foot *n, pl* **crow's-feet** (*often pl*) a wrinkle at the outer corner of the eye

crow's-nest *n* a lookout platform high up on a ship's mast

crow step *n* another term for **corbie-step**

Croydon ('krɔɪdᵊn) *n* a borough in S Greater London

(since 1965): formerly important for its airport (1915–59). Pop: 330 688 (2001). Area: 87 sq km (33 sq miles)

crozier ('krəʊʒə) *n* a variant spelling of **crosier**

CRP *abbrev for* C-reactive protein; a chemical in the blood that can be measured to indicate inflammation in the body and a person's risk of suffering a heart attack

CRT *abbrev for:* **1** cathode-ray tube **2** (in Britain) composite rate tax: a system of paying interest to savers by which a rate of tax for a period is determined in advance and interest is paid net of tax which is deducted at source

crucial ('kru:ʃəl) *adj* **1** involving a final or supremely important decision or event; decisive; critical **2** *inf* very important **3** *sl* very good [c18 from F, from L *crux* CROSS] > **'crucially** *adv*

crucible ('kru:sɪbᵊl) *n* **1** a vessel in which substances are heated to high temperatures **2** the hearth at the bottom of a metallurgical furnace in which the metal collects **3** a severe trial or test [c15 *corusible*, from Med. L *crūcibulum* night lamp, crucible, from ?]

crucifix ('kru:sɪfɪks) *n* a cross or image of a cross with a figure of Christ upon it [c13 from Church L *crucifixus* the crucified Christ, from *crucifigere* to CRUCIFY]

crucifixion (ˌkru:sɪ'fɪkʃən) *n* a method of putting to death by nailing or binding to a cross, normally by the hands and feet

Crucifixion (ˌkru:sɪ'fɪkʃən) *n* **1** (usually preceded by *the*) the crucifying of Christ **2** a picture or representation of this

cruciform ('kru:sɪˌfɔ:m) *adj* shaped like a cross [c17 from L *crux* cross + -FORM] > **'cruciˌformly** *adv*

crucify ('kru:sɪˌfaɪ) *vb* **crucifies, crucifying, crucified** (*tr*) **1** to put to death by crucifixion **2** *sl* to defeat, ridicule, etc, totally **3** to treat very cruelly; torment [c13 from OF *crucifier*, from LL *crucifigere* to crucify, to fasten to a cross, from L *crux* cross + *figere* to fasten] > **'cruciˌfier** *n*

crud (krʌd) *n* **1** *sl* a sticky substance, esp when dirty and encrusted **2** *sl* something or someone that is worthless, disgusting, or contemptible **3** an undesirable residue, esp one inside a nuclear reactor [c14 earlier form of CURD] > **'cruddy** *adj*

crude (kru:d) *adj* **1** lacking taste, tact, or refinement; vulgar: *a crude joke* **2** in a natural or unrefined state **3** lacking care, knowledge, or skill: *a crude sketch* **4** (*prenominal*) stark; blunt ▷ *n* **5** short for **crude oil** [c14 from L *crūdus* bloody, raw; rel. to L *cruor* blood] > **'crudely** *adv* > **'crudity** *or* **'crudeness** *n*

Cruden ('kru:dᵊn) *n* **Alexander** 1701–70, Scottish bookseller and compiler of a well- known biblical concordance (1737)

crude oil *n* unrefined petroleum

crudités (ˌkru:dɪ'teɪ) *pl n* a selection of raw vegetables, served as an hors d'oeuvre [c20 from F, pl of *crudité*, lit.: rawness]

cruel ('kru:əl) *adj* **1** causing or inflicting pain without pity **2** causing pain or suffering ▷ *vb* **cruels, cruelling, cruelled** *or US* **cruels, crueling, crueled** (*tr*) **3 cruel someone's pitch** *Austral sl* to ruin someone's chances [c13 from OF, from L *crūdēlis*, from *crūdus* raw, bloody] > **'cruelly** *adv* > **'cruelness** *n*

cruelty ('kru:əltɪ) *n, pl* **cruelties 1** deliberate infliction of pain or suffering **2** the quality or characteristic of being cruel **3** a cruel action **4** *law* conduct that causes danger to life or limb or a threat to bodily or mental health

cruelty-free *adj* (of a cosmetic or other product) developed without being tested on animals

cruet ('kru:ɪt) *n* **1** a small container for holding pepper, salt, vinegar, oil, etc, at table **2** a set of such containers, esp on a stand [c13 from Anglo-F, dim. of OF *crue* flask, of Gmc origin]

Cruft (krʌft) *n* **Charles** 1852–1938, British dog breeder, who organized the first (1886) of the annual dog shows known as Cruft's

Cruikshank ('krʊkˌʃæŋk) *n* **George** 1792–1878, English illustrator and caricaturist

cruise (kru:z) *vb* **cruises, cruising, cruised 1** (*intr*) to make a trip by sea for pleasure, usually calling at a number of ports **2** to sail or travel over (a body of water) for pleasure **3** (*intr*) to search for enemy vessels in a warship **4** (*intr*) (of a vehicle, aircraft, or vessel) to travel at a moderate and efficient speed ▷ *n* **5** an act or instance of cruising, esp a trip by sea [c17 from Du. *kruisen* to cross, from *cruis* CROSS]

cruise control *n* a system in a road vehicle that automatically maintains a selected speed until cancelled

cruise missile *n* a low-flying subsonic missile that is guided throughout its flight

cruiser ('kru:zə) *n* **1** a high-speed, long-range warship armed with medium-calibre weapons **2** Also called: **cabin cruiser** a pleasure boat, esp one that is power-driven and has a cabin **3** any person or thing that cruises

cruiserweight ('kru:zəˌweɪt) *n boxing* another term (esp Brit) for **light heavyweight**

crumb (krʌm) *n* **1** a small fragment of bread, cake, or other baked foods **2** a small piece or bit **3** the soft inner part of bread **4** *sl* a contemptible person ▷ *vb* **5** (*tr*) to prepare or cover (food) with breadcrumbs **6** to break into small fragments [OE *cruma*]

crumble ('krʌmbᵊl) *vb* **crumbles, crumbling, crumbled 1** to break or be broken into crumbs or fragments **2** (*intr*) to fall apart or away ▷ *n* **3** *Brit, Austral, & NZ* a baked pudding consisting of a crumbly mixture of flour, fat, and sugar over stewed fruit: *apple crumble* [c16 var. of *crimble*, of Gmc origin]

crumbly ('krʌmblɪ) *adj* **crumblier, crumbliest 1** easily crumbled or crumbling ▷ *n, pl* **crumblies 2** *Brit sl* an older person > **'crumbliness** *n*

crumby ('krʌmɪ) *adj* **crumbier, crumbiest 1** full of or littered with crumbs **2** soft, like the inside of bread **3** a variant spelling of **crummy**

crummy ('krʌmɪ) *adj* **crummier, crummiest** *sl* **1** of little value; contemptible **2** unwell or depressed: *to feel crummy* [c19 var. spelling of CRUMBY]

crumpet ('krʌmpɪt) *n chiefly Brit* **1** a light soft yeast cake, eaten toasted and buttered **2** *sl* women collectively [c17 from ?]

crumple ('krʌmpᵊl) *vb* **crumples, crumpling, crumpled 1** (when *intr*, often foll by *up*) to collapse or cause to collapse **2** (when *tr*, often foll by *up*) to crush or cause to be crushed so as to form wrinkles or creases ▷ *n* **3** a loose crease or wrinkle [c16 from obs. *crump* to bend]

crumple zones *pl n* parts of a motor vehicle, at the front and the rear, that are designed to crumple in a collision, thereby absorbing part of the energy of the impact

crunch (krʌntʃ) *vb* **1** to bite or chew with a crushing or crackling sound **2** to make or cause to make a crisp or brittle sound ▷ *n* **3** the sound or act of crunching **4 the crunch** *inf* the critical moment or situation ▷ *adj* **5** *inf* critical; decisive: *crunch time* [c19 changed (through infl. of MUNCH) from earlier *craunch*, imit.] > **'crunchy** *adj* > **'crunchily** *adv* > **'crunchiness** *n*

crupper ('krʌpə) *n* **1** a strap from the back of a saddle that passes under a horse's tail **2** the horse's rump [c13 from OF *crupiere*, from *crupe* CROUP²]

crusade (kru:'seɪd) *n* **1** (*often cap*) any of the military expeditions undertaken in the 11th, 12th, and 13th centuries by the Christian powers of Europe to recapture the Holy Land from the Muslims **2** (formerly) any holy war **3** a vigorous and dedicated action or movement in favour of a cause ▷ *vb* **crusades, crusading, crusaded** (*intr*) **4** to campaign vigorously for something **5** to go on a crusade [c16 from earlier *croisade*, from OF *crois* cross, from L *crux*; infl. also by Sp. *cruzada*, from *cruzar* to take up the cross] > **cru'sader** *n*

▷ www.medievalcrusades.com
▷ www.fordham.edu/halsall/sbook.1k.html

cruse (kruːz) *n* a small earthenware container used, esp formerly, for liquids [OE *crūse*]

crush (krʌʃ) *vb (mainly tr)* **1** to press, mash, or squeeze so as to injure, break, crease, etc **2** to break or grind into small particles **3** to put down or subdue, esp by force **4** to extract (juice, water, etc) by pressing **5** to oppress harshly **6** to hug or clasp tightly **7** to defeat or humiliate utterly, as in argument or by a cruel remark **8** *(intr)* to crowd; throng **9** *(intr)* to become injured, broken, or distorted by pressure ▷ *n* **10** a dense crowd, esp at a social occasion **11** the act of crushing; pressure **12** a drink or pulp prepared by or as if by crushing fruit: *orange crush* **13** *inf* **13a** an infatuation: *she had a crush on him* **13b** the person with whom one is infatuated [C14 from OF *croissir*, of Gmc origin] > **'crushable** *adj* > **'crusher** *n*

crush barrier *n* a barrier erected to separate sections of large crowds

crust (krʌst) *n* **1a** the hard outer part of bread **1b** a piece of bread consisting mainly of this **2** the baked shell of a pie, tart, etc **3** any hard or stiff outer covering or surface: *a crust of ice* **4** the solid outer shell of the earth **5** the dry covering of a skin sore or lesion; scab **6** *sl* impertinence **7** *Brit, Austral, & NZ sl* a living (esp in **earn a crust**) ▷ *vb* **8** to cover with or acquire a crust **9** to form or be formed into a crust [C14 from L *crūsta* hard surface, rind, shell]

crustacean (krʌ'steɪʃən) *n* **1** any arthropod of the mainly aquatic class *Crustacea*, typically having a carapace and including the lobsters, crabs, woodlice, and water fleas ▷ *adj* **2** *also* **crustaceous** of, relating to, or belonging to the *Crustacea* [C19 from NL *crūstāceus* hard-shelled, from L *crūsta* shell]

crustal ('krʌstᵊl) *adj* of or relating to the earth's crust

crusty ('krʌstɪ) *adj* **crustier, crustiest** **1** having or characterized by a crust **2** having a rude or harsh character or exterior > **'crustily** *adv* > **'crustiness** *n*

crutch (krʌtʃ) *n* **1** a long staff having a rest for the armpit, for supporting the weight of the body **2** something that supports, helps, or sustains **3** *Brit* another word for **crotch** (sense 1) ▷ *vb* **4** *(tr)* to support or sustain (a person or thing) as with a crutch **5** *Austral & NZ* to clip (wool) from the hindquarters of a sheep [OE *crycc*]

crutchings ('krʌtʃɪŋz) *pl n Austral & NZ* wool clipped from a sheep's hindquarters

crux (krʌks) *n, pl* **cruxes** *or* **cruces** ('kruːsiːz) **1** a vital or decisive stage, point, etc (often in **the crux of the matter**) **2** a baffling problem or difficulty [C18 from L: cross]

cruzado (kruː'zeɪdəʊ) *n, pl* **cruzadoes** *or* **cruzados** (-dəʊz) a former standard monetary unit of Brazil [C16 lit., marked with a cross, from *cruzar* to bear a cross; see CRUSADE]

cruzeiro (kruː'zɛərəʊ) *n, pl* **cruzeiros** (-rəʊz) a former standard monetary unit of Brazil [Port.: from *cruz* CROSS]

cry (kraɪ) *vb* **cries, crying, cried** **1** *(intr)* to utter inarticulate sounds, esp when weeping; sob **2** *(intr)* to shed tears; weep **3** *(intr; usually foll by out)* to scream or shout in pain, terror, etc **4** *(tr; often foll by out)* to utter or shout (words of appeal, exclamation, fear, etc) **5** *(intr; often foll by out)* (of animals, birds, etc) to utter loud characteristic sounds **6** *(tr)* to hawk or sell by public announcement: *to cry newspapers* **7** to announce (something) publicly or in the streets **8** *(intr; foll by for)* to clamour or beg **9** **cry for the moon** to desire the unattainable **10** **cry one's eyes** *or* **heart out** to weep bitterly ▷ *n, pl* **cries** **11** the act or sound of crying; a shout, scream, or wail **12** the characteristic utterance of an animal or bird **13** a fit of weeping **14** *hunting* the baying of a pack of hounds hunting their quarry by scent **15** **a far cry** **15a** a long way **15b** something very different **16** **in full cry** (esp of a pack of hounds) in hot pursuit of a quarry ▷ See also **cry down, cry off**, etc [C13 from OF *crier*, from L *quirītāre* to call for help]

crybaby ('kraɪˌbeɪbɪ) *n, pl* **crybabies** a person, esp a child, given to frequent crying or complaint

cry down *vb (tr, adv)* to belittle; disparage

crying ('kraɪɪŋ) *adj (prenominal)* notorious; lamentable (esp in **crying shame**)

cryo- *combining form* cold or freezing: *cryogenics* [from Gk *kruos* icy cold, frost]

cryobiology (ˌkraɪəʊbaɪ'ɒlədʒɪ) *n* the biology of the effects of very low temperatures on organisms > **ˌcryobi'ologist** *n*

cry off *vb (intr) inf* to withdraw from or cancel (an agreement or arrangement)

cryogen ('kraɪədʒən) *n* a substance used to produce low temperatures; a freezing mixture

cryogenics (ˌkraɪə'dʒɛnɪks) *n (functioning as sing)* the branch of physics concerned with very low temperatures and the phenomena occurring at these temperatures > **ˌcryo'genic** *adj*

cryolite ('kraɪəˌlaɪt) *n* a white or colourless fluoride of sodium and aluminium: used in the production of aluminium, glass, and enamel. Formula: Na_3AlF_6

cryonics (kraɪ'ɒnɪks) *n (functioning as sing)* the practice of freezing a human corpse in the hope of restoring it to life later

cryoprecipitate (ˌkraɪəʊprɪ'sɪpɪtɪt) *n* a precipitate obtained by controlled thawing of a previously frozen substance. Factor VIII, for treating haemophilia, is often obtained as a cryoprecipitate from frozen blood

cryostat ('kraɪəˌstæt) *n* an apparatus for maintaining a constant low temperature

cryosurgery (ˌkraɪəʊ'sɜːdʒərɪ) *n* surgery involving quick freezing for therapeutic benefit

cry out *vb (intr, adv)* **1** to scream or shout aloud, esp in pain, terror, etc **2** (often foll by *for*) *inf* to demand in an obvious manner

crypt (krɪpt) *n* a vault or underground chamber, esp beneath a church, often used as a chapel, burial place, etc [C18 from L *crypta*, from Gk *kruptē* vault, secret place, ult. from *kruptein* to hide]

cryptanalysis (ˌkrɪptə'nælɪsɪs) *n* the study of codes and ciphers; cryptography [C20 from CRYPTO- + ANALYSIS] > **cryptanalytic** (ˌkrɪptænə'lɪtɪk) *adj* > **crypt'analyst** *n*

cryptic ('krɪptɪk) *adj* **1** hidden; secret **2** esoteric or obscure in meaning **3** (of coloration) effecting camouflage or concealment [C17 from LL *crypticus*, from Gk *kruptikos*, from *kruptos* concealed; see CRYPT] > **'cryptically** *adv*

crypto- *or before a vowel* **crypt-** *combining form* secret, hidden, or concealed [NL, from Gk *kruptos* hidden, from *kruptein* to hide]

cryptocrystalline (ˌkrɪptəʊ'krɪstəlaɪn) *adj* (of rocks) composed of crystals visible only under a polarizing microscope

cryptogam ('krɪptəʊˌgæm) *n* (in former plant classification schemes) any organism that does not produce seeds, including algae, fungi, mosses, and ferns [C19 from NL *Cryptogamia*, from CRYPTO- + Gk *gamos* marriage] > **ˌcrypto'gamic** *or* **cryptogamous** (krɪp'tɒgəməs) *adj*

cryptograph ('krɪptəʊˌgrɑːf) *n* **1** something written in code or cipher **2** a code using secret symbols (**cryptograms**)

cryptography (krɪp'tɒgrəfɪ) *n* the science or study of analysing and deciphering codes, ciphers, etc. Also called: **cryptanalysis** > **cryp'tographer** *or* **cryp'tographist** *n* > **cryptographic** (ˌkrɪptə'græfɪk) *or* **ˌcrypto'graphical** *adj* > **ˌcrypto'graphically** *adv*

crystal ('krɪstᵊl) *n* **1** a solid, such as quartz, with a regular shape in which plane faces intersect at definite angles **2** a single grain of a crystalline substance

Cc

3 anything resembling a crystal, such as a piece of cut glass **4a** a highly transparent and brilliant type of glass **4b** (*as modifier*): *a crystal chandelier* **5** something made of or resembling crystal **6** crystal glass articles collectively **7** *electronics* **7a** a crystalline element used in certain electronic devices as a detector, oscillator, etc **7b** (*as modifier*): *crystal pick-up* **8** a transparent cover for the face of a watch **9** (*modifier*) of or relating to a crystal or the regular atomic arrangement of crystals: *crystal structure* ▷ *adj* **10** resembling crystal; transparent: *crystal water* [OE *cristalla*, from L *crystallum*, from Gk *krustallos* ice, crystal, from *krustainein* to freeze]

crystal ball *n* the glass globe used in crystal gazing

crystal class *n crystallog* any of 32 possible types of crystals, classified according to their rotational symmetry about axes through a point. Also called: **point group**

crystal detector *n electronics* a demodulator, used esp in early radio receivers, incorporating a semiconductor crystal

crystal gazing *n* **1** the act of staring into a crystal ball supposedly in order to arouse visual perceptions of the future, etc **2** the act of trying to foresee or predict > **crystal gazer** *n*

crystal healing *n* (in alternative therapy) the use of the supposed power of crystals to affect the human energy field

crystal lattice *n* the regular array of points about which the atoms, ions, or molecules composing a crystal are centred

crystalline (ˈkrɪstəˌlaɪn) *adj* **1** having the characteristics or structure of crystals **2** consisting of or containing crystals **3** made of or like crystal; transparent; clear

crystalline lens *n* a biconvex transparent elastic lens in the eye

crystallize *or* **crystallise** (ˈkrɪstəˌlaɪz) *vb* **crystallizes, crystallizing, crystallized** *or* **crystallises, crystallising, crystallised** **1** to form or cause to form crystals; assume or cause to assume a crystalline form or structure **2** to coat or become coated with sugar **3** to give a definite form or expression to (an idea, argument, etc) or (of an idea, argument, etc) to assume a definite form > **ˈcrystalˌlizable** *or* **ˈcrystalˌlisable** *adj* > **ˌcrystalliˈzation** *or* **ˌcrystalliˈsation** *n*

crystallo- *or before a vowel* **crystall-** *combining form* crystal: *crystallography*

crystallography (ˌkrɪstəˈlɒgrəfɪ) *n* the science of crystal structure > **ˌcrystalˈlographer** *n* > **crystallographic** (ˌkrɪstələʊˈgræfɪk) *adj*

crystalloid (ˈkrɪstəˌlɔɪd) *adj* **1** resembling or having the properties of a crystal ▷ *n* **2** a substance that in solution can pass through a semipermeable membrane

Crystal Palace *n* a building of glass and iron designed by Joseph Paxton to house the Great Exhibition of 1851. Erected in Hyde Park, London, it was moved to Sydenham (1852–53): destroyed by fire in 1936

crystal set *n* an early form of radio receiver having a crystal detector

cry up *vb* (*tr, adv*) to praise highly; extol

Cs *the chemical symbol for* caesium

CS *abbrev for:* **1** Also: **cs** capital stock **2** chartered surveyor **3** Christian Science **4** Civil Service **5** Also: **cs** Court of Session

CSA (in Britain) *abbrev for* Child Support Agency

csc *abbrev for* cosecant

CSC *abbrev for* Civil Service Commission

CSE (in Britain, formerly) *abbrev for* Certificate of Secondary Education

CSF *abbrev for:* **1** cerebrospinal fluid **2** *immunol* colony-stimulating factor

CS gas *n* a gas causing tears, salivation, and painful breathing, used for crowd control and dispersal in civil disturbances [c20 from the surname initials of its US inventors, Ben Carson and Roger Staughton]

CSIRO (in Australia) *abbrev for* Commonwealth Scientific and Industrial Research Organization
▷ www.csiro.au

CSM (in Britain) *abbrev for* Company Sergeant-Major

C-spanner *n* a sickle-shaped spanner having a projection at the end of the curve, used for turning large narrow nuts that have an indentation into which the projection on the spanner fits

CSS *computing abbrev for* cascading style sheet

CST (in the US and Canada) *abbrev for* Central Standard Time

ct *abbrev for:* **1** carat **2** cent **3** court

CTC (in Britain) *abbrev for* city technology college

ctenophore (ˈtɛnəˌfɔː, ˈtiːnə-) *n* any marine invertebrate of the phylum *Ctenophora*, whose body bears eight rows of fused cilia, for locomotion [c19 from NL *ctenophorus*, from Gk *kteno-*, *kteis* comb + -PHORE]

ctn *abbrev for* cotangent

CT scanner *n* computerized tomography scanner: an X-ray machine that can produce multiple cross-sectional images of the soft tissues (**CT scans**). Former name: **CAT scanner**

CTU (in New Zealand) *abbrev for* Conference of Trade Unions

CTV *abbrev for* Canadian Television (Network Limited)
▷ www.ctv.ca

Cu *the chemical symbol for* copper [from LL *cuprum*]

CU *text messaging abbrev for* see you

cu. *abbrev for* cubic

cub (kʌb) *n* **1** the young of certain animals, such as the lion, bear, etc **2** a young or inexperienced person ▷ *vb* **cubs, cubbing, cubbed** **3** to give birth to (cubs) [c16 ?from ON *kubbi* young seal] > **ˈcubbish** *adj*

Cub (kʌb) *n* short for **Cub Scout**

Cuba (ˈkjuːbə) *n* a republic and the largest island in the Caribbean, at the entrance to the Gulf of Mexico: became a Spanish colony after its discovery by Columbus in 1492; gained independence after the Spanish-American War of 1898 but remained subject to US influence until declared a people's republic under Castro in 1960; subject of an international crisis in 1962, when the US blockaded the island in order to compel the Soviet Union to dismantle its nuclear missile base. Sugar comprises about 80 per cent of total exports; the economy has been devastated by loss of trade following the collapse of the Soviet Union and by the continuing US trade embargo. Language: Spanish. Religion: nonreligious majority. Currency: peso. Capital: Havana. Pop: 11 190 000 (2001 est). Area: 110 922 sq km (42 827 sq miles)
▷ www.cubagob.cu/ingles
▷ www.cubatravel.cu

Cuban (ˈkjuːbən) *adj* **1** of or relating to Cuba or its inhabitants ▷ *n* **2** a native or inhabitant of Cuba

cubby (ˈkʌbɪ) *n, pl* **cubbies** *Austral* a small room or enclosed area, esp one used as a child's play area

cubbyhole (ˈkʌbɪˌhəʊl) *n* a small enclosed space or room [c19 from dialect *cub* cattle pen]

cube (kjuːb) *n* **1** a solid having six plane square faces in which the angle between two adjacent sides is a right angle **2** the product of three equal factors **3** something in the form of a cube ▷ *vb* **cubes, cubing, cubed** **4** to raise (a number or quantity) to the third power **5** (*tr*) to make, shape, or cut (something) into cubes [c16 from L *cubus* die, cube, from Gk *kubos*] > **ˈcuber** *n*

cubeb (ˈkjuːbɛb) *n* **1** a SE Asian treelike climbing plant **2** its spicy fruit, dried and used as a stimulant and diuretic and sometimes smoked in cigarettes [c14 from OF *cubebe*, from Med. L *cubēba*, from Ar. *kubābah*]

cube root *n* the number or quantity whose cube is a given number or quantity: 2 is the cube root of 8 (usually written $\sqrt[3]{8}$ or $8^{1/3}$)

cubic ('kju:bɪk) *adj* **1** having the shape of a cube **2a** having three dimensions **2b** denoting or relating to a linear measure that is raised to the third power: *a cubic metre* **3** *maths* of, relating to, or containing a variable to the third power or a term in which the sum of the exponents of the variables is three > '**cubical** *adj*

cubicle ('kju:bɪkᵊl) *n* an enclosed compartment, screened for privacy, as in a dormitory, shower, etc [C15 from L *cubiculum*, from *cubāre* to lie down]

cubic measure *n* a system of units for the measurement of volumes

cubiform ('kju:bɪˌfɔ:m) *adj* having the shape of a cube

cubism ('kju:bɪzəm) *n* (*often cap*) a French school of art, initiated in 1907 by Picasso and Braque, which amalgamated viewpoints of natural forms into a multifaceted surface of geometrical planes > '**cubist** *adj, n* > **cu'bistic** *adj*

▹ www.artlex.com/ArtLex/c/cubism.html
▹ http://wwar.com/categories/Artists/Masters/Cubism
▹ http://abstractart.20m.com/cubism.htm

cubit ('kju:bɪt) *n* an ancient measure of length based on the length of the forearm [C14 from L *cubitum* elbow, cubit]

cuboid ('kju:bɔɪd) *adj also* **cuboidal** (kju:'bɔɪdᵊl) **1** shaped like a cube; cubic **2** of or denoting the cuboid bone ▹ *n* **3** the cubelike bone of the foot **4** *maths* a geometric solid whose six faces are rectangles

Cub Scout *or* **Cub** *n* a member of the junior branch of the Scout Association

▹ www.scoutbase.org.uk

Cuchulain, Cuchulainn, *or* **Cuchullain** (ku:'kʌlɪn, kʊ'xʊlɪn) *n Celtic myth* a legendary hero of Ulster

cucking stool ('kʌkɪŋ) *n history* a stool to which suspected witches, scolds, etc, were tied and pelted or ducked into water [C13 *cucking stol*, lit.: defecating chair, from *cukken* to defecate]

cuckold ('kʌkəld) *n* **1** a man whose wife has committed adultery ▹ *vb* **2** (*tr*) to make a cuckold of [C13 *cukeweld*, from OF *cucuault*, from *cucu* CUCKOO; ? an allusion to cuckoos that lay eggs in the nests of other birds] > '**cuckoldry** *n*

cuckoo ('kʊku:) *n, pl* **cuckoos** **1** any bird of the family Cuculidae, having pointed wings and a long tail. Many species, including the **European cuckoo,** lay their eggs in the nests of other birds and have a two-note call **2** *inf* an insane or foolish person ▹ *adj* **3** *inf* insane or foolish ▹ *interj* **4** an imitation or representation of the call of a cuckoo ▹ *vb* **cuckoos, cuckooing, cuckooed** **5** (*intr*) to make the sound imitated by the word *cuckoo* [C13 from OF *cucu*, imit.]

cuckoo clock *n* a clock in which a mechanical cuckoo pops out with a sound like a cuckoo's call when the clock strikes

cuckoopint ('kʊku:ˌpaɪnt, -ˌpɪnt) *n* a European plant with arrow-shaped leaves, a spathe marked with purple, a pale purple spadix, and scarlet berries. Also called: **lords-and-ladies**

cuckoo spit *n* a white frothy mass on the stems and leaves of many plants, produced by froghopper larvae

cucumber ('kju:ˌkʌmbə) *n* **1** a creeping plant cultivated in many forms for its edible fruit **2** the cylindrical fruit of this plant, which has hard thin green rind and white crisp flesh [C14 from L *cucumis*, from ?]

cucurbit (kju:'kɜ:bɪt) *n* any of a family of creeping flowering plants that includes the pumpkin, cucumber, and gourds [C14 from OF, from L *cucurbita* gourd, cup] > **cuˌcurbi'taceous** *adj*

cud (kʌd) *n* **1** partially digested food regurgitated from the first stomach of ruminants to the mouth for a second chewing **2** **chew the cud** to reflect or think over something [OE *cudu*, from *cwidu* what has been chewed]

cuddle ('kʌdᵊl) *vb* **cuddles, cuddling, cuddled** **1** to hold close or (of two people, etc) to hold each other close, as for affection or warmth; hug **2** (*intr*; foll by *up*) to curl or snuggle up into a comfortable or warm position ▹ *n* **3** a close embrace, esp when prolonged [C18 from ?] > '**cuddlesome** *adj* > '**cuddly** *adj*

cuddy ('kʌdɪ) *n, pl* **cuddies** a small cabin in a boat [C17 ?from Du. *kajute*]

cudgel ('kʌdʒəl) *n* **1** a short stout stick used as a weapon **2** **take up the cudgels** (often foll by *for* or *on behalf of*) to join in a dispute, esp to defend oneself or another ▹ *vb* **cudgels, cudgelling, cudgelled** *or US* **cudgels, cudgeling, cudgeled** **3** (*tr*) to strike with a cudgel **4** **cudgel one's brains** to think hard [OE *cycgel*]

cudgerie ('kʌdʒərɪ) *n Austral* any of various large rainforest trees, such as the pink poplar or blush cudgerie, with pink wood [from Abor.]

Cudlipp ('kʌdlɪp) *n* **Hugh,** Baron. 1913–98, British newspaper editor, a pioneer of tabloid journalism: editorial director of the *Daily Mirror* (1952–63)

cudweed ('kʌdˌwi:d) *n* any of various temperate woolly plants having clusters of whitish or yellow button-like flowers

cue[1] (kju:) *n* **1a** (in the theatre, films, music, etc) anything that serves as a signal to an actor, musician, etc, to follow with specific lines or action **1b** **on cue** at the right moment **2** a signal or reminder to do something ▹ *vb* **cues, cueing, cued** **3** (*tr*) to give a cue or cues to (an actor) **4** (usually foll by *in* or *into*) to signal (to something or somebody) at a specific moment in a musical or dramatic performance [C16 prob. from name of the letter *q*, used in an actor's script to represent L *quando* when]

cue[2] (kju:) *n* **1** *billiards, etc* a long tapered shaft used to drive the balls **2** hair caught at the back forming a tail or braid ▹ *vb* **cues, cueing, cued** **3** to drive (a ball) with a cue [C18 var. of QUEUE]

cue ball *n billiards, etc* the ball struck by the cue, as distinguished from the object balls

Cuernavaca (*Spanish* kwɛrna'βaka) *n* a city in S central Mexico, capital of Morelos state: resort with nearby Cacahuamilpa Caverns. Pop: 330 000 (2000 est)

cuesta ('kwɛstə) *n* a long low ridge with a steep scarp slope and a gentle back slope [Sp.: shoulder, from L *costa* side, rib]

cuff[1] (kʌf) *n* **1** the end of a sleeve, sometimes turned back **2** the part of a glove that extends past the wrist **3** the US, Canad, and Austral name for **turn-up** (sense 4) **4** **off the cuff** *inf* improvised; extemporary [C14 *cuffe* glove, from ?]

cuff[2] (kʌf) *vb* **1** (*tr*) to strike with an open hand ▹ *n* **2** a blow of this kind [C16 from ?]

cuff link *n* one of a pair of linked buttons, used to join the buttonholes on the cuffs of a shirt

Cuiabá (*Portuguese* kuia'ba) *n* **1** a port in W Brazil, capital of Mato Grosso state, on the Cuibá River. Pop (urban area): 475 632 (2000) **2** a river in SW Brazil, rising on the Mato Grosso plateau and flowing southwest into the São Lourenço River. Length: 483 km (300 miles)

cui bono *Latin* (kwi: 'bəʊnəʊ) for whose benefit? for what purpose?

cuirass (kwɪ'ræs) *n* **1** a piece of armour covering the chest and back ▹ *vb* **2** (*tr*) to equip with a cuirass [C15 from F *cuirasse*, from LL *coriacea*, from *coriaceus* made of leather]

cuirassier (ˌkwɪərə'sɪə) *n* a mounted soldier, esp of the 16th century, who wore a cuirass

Cuisenaire rod (ˌkwɪzə'nɛə) *n trademark* one of a set of rods of various colours and lengths representing different numbers, used to teach arithmetic to young children [C20 after Emil-Georges *Cuisenaire* (?1891–1976), Belgian educationalist]

cuisine (kwɪ'zi:n) *n* **1** a style or manner of cooking: *French cuisine* **2** the food prepared by a restaurant, household,

Cc

etc [c18 from F, lit.: kitchen, from LL *coquīna*, from L *coquere* to cook]
▷ http://directory.google.com/Top/Home/Cooking/World_Cuisines
▷ www.globalgourmet.com/destinations/
▷ www.foodreference.com/
▷ www.cooking2000.com
▷ www.italiancookingandliving.com
▷ www.ruscuisine.com
▷ www.thaitable.com
▷ www.cajuncookery.esmartweb.com/recipes.html
▷ http://virtual.finland.fi/finfo/english/gasteng.html
▷ www.koshercooking.com
▷ www.dezi.com
▷ www.rainbownation.com/recipes

cuisse (kwɪs) *or* **cuish** (kwɪʃ) *n* a piece of armour for the thigh [c15 back formation from *cuisses* (pl), from OF *cuisseaux*, from *cuisse* thigh]

Culbertson ('kʌlbətsᵊn) *n* **Ely** ('iːlaɪ) 1891–1955, US authority on contract bridge

cul-de-sac ('kʌldəˌsæk, 'kʊl-) *n, pl* **culs-de-sac** *or* **cul-de-sacs** **1** a road with one end blocked off; dead end **2** an inescapable position [c18 from F, lit.: bottom of the bag]

-cule *suffix forming nouns* indicating smallness [from L *-culus*, dim. suffix]

Culebra Cut (kuː'lɛbrə) *n* the former name of the **Gaillard Cut**

culex ('kjuːlɛks) *n, pl* **culices** (-lɪˌsiːz) any mosquito of the genus *Culex*, such as *C. pipiens*, the common mosquito [c15 from L: midge, gnat]

Culham ('kʌləm) *n* a village in S central England, in Oxfordshire: site of the UK centre for thermonuclear reactor research and of the Joint European Torus (JET) programme

Culiacán (*Spanish* kulja'kan) *n* a city in NW Mexico, capital of Sinaloa state. Pop: 536 942 (2000 est)

culinary ('kʌlɪnərɪ) *adj* of, relating to, or used in the kitchen or in cookery [c17 from L *culīnārius*, from *culīna* kitchen] > '**culinarily** *adv*

cull (kʌl) *vb* (*tr*) **1** to choose or gather the best or required examples of **2** to take out (an animal, esp an inferior one) from a herd or group **3** to reduce the size of (a herd, etc) by killing a proportion of its members **4** to gather (flowers, fruit, etc) ▷ *n* **5** the act or product of culling **6** an inferior animal taken from a herd or group [c15 from OF *coillir* to pick, from L *colligere*; see COLLECT[1]]

Cullen ('kʌlən) *n* **William Douglas**, Baron. born 1935, Scottish judge who conducted public inquiries into the Piper Alpha disaster (1990), the Dunblane school shootings (1996), and the Ladbroke Grove rail disaster (1999)

Culloden (kə'lɒdᵊn) *n* a moor near Inverness in N Scotland: site of a battle in 1746 in which government troops under the Duke of Cumberland defeated the Jacobites under Prince Charles Edward Stuart

culm¹ (kʌlm) *n mining* **1** coal-mine waste **2** inferior anthracite [c14 prob. rel. to COAL]

culm² (kʌlm) *n* the hollow jointed stem of a grass or sedge [c17 from L *culmus* stalk; see HAULM]

culminate ('kʌlmɪˌneɪt) *vb* **culminates, culminating, culminated** **1** (when *intr*, usually foll by *in*) to reach or bring to a final or climactic stage **2** (*intr*) (of a celestial body) to cross the meridian [c17 from LL *culmināre* to reach the highest point, from L *culmen* top] > '**culminant** *adj*

culmination (ˌkʌlmɪ'neɪʃən) *n* **1** the final or highest point **2** the act of culminating **3** *astron* the highest or lowest altitude attained by a heavenly body as it crosses the meridian

culottes (kjuː'lɒts) *pl n* women's flared trousers cut to look like a skirt [c20 from F, lit.: breeches, from *cul* bottom]

culpable ('kʌlpəbᵊl) *adj* deserving censure; blameworthy [c14 from OF *coupable*, from L *culpābilis*, from *culpāre* to blame, from *culpa* fault] > ˌ**culpa'bility** *n* > '**culpably** *adv*

culpable homicide *n Scots law* manslaughter

Culpeper ('kʌlpɛpə) *n* **Nicholas** 1616–54, English herbalist and astrologer; his unauthorized translation (1649) of the College of Physicians' *Pharmacopoeia* and his *Herbal* (1653) popularized herbalism

culprit ('kʌlprɪt) *n* **1** *law* a person awaiting trial **2** the person responsible for a particular offence, misdeed, etc [c17 from Anglo-F *cul-*, short for *culpable* guilty + *prit* ready, indicating that the prosecution was ready to prove the guilt of the one charged]

CUL8R *text messaging abbrev for* see you later

cult (kʌlt) *n* **1** a specific system of religious worship **2** a sect devoted to such a system **3** a quasi-religious organization using devious psychological techniques to gain and control adherents **4** intense interest in and devotion to a person, idea, or activity **5** the person, idea, etc, arousing such devotion **6** something regarded as fashionable or significant by a particular group; craze **7** (*modifier*) of, relating to, or characteristic of a cult or cults: *a cult figure; a cult show* [c17 from L *cultus* cultivation, refinement, from *colere* to till] > '**cultism** *n* > '**cultist** *n*

cultic ('kʌltɪk) *adj* of or relating to a religious cult

cultish ('kʌltɪʃ) *or* **culty** ('kʌltɪ) *adj* intended to appeal to a small group of fashionable people

cultivable ('kʌltɪvəbᵊl) *or* **cultivatable** ('kʌltɪˌveɪtəbᵊl) *adj* (of land) capable of being cultivated [c17 from F, from OF *cultiver* to CULTIVATE] > ˌ**cultiva'bility** *n*

cultivar ('kʌltɪˌvɑː) *n* a variety of a plant produced from a natural species and maintained by cultivation [c20 from CULTI(VATED) + VAR(IETY)]

cultivate ('kʌltɪˌveɪt) *vb* **cultivates, cultivating, cultivated** (*tr*) **1** to prepare (land or soil) for the growth of crops **2** to plant, tend, harvest, or improve (plants) **3** to break up (land or soil) with a cultivator or hoe **4** to improve (the mind, body, etc) as by study, education, or labour **5** to give special attention to: *to cultivate a friendship* [c17 from Med. L *cultivāre* to till, from *cultīvus* cultivable, from L *cultus* cultivated, from *colere* to till, toil over] > '**cultiˌvated** *adj*

cultivation (ˌkʌltɪ'veɪʃən) *n* **1** *agriculture* **1a** the cultivating of crops or plants **1b** the preparation of ground to promote their growth **2** development, esp through education, training, etc **3** culture or sophistication

cultivator ('kʌltɪˌveɪtə) *n* **1** a farm implement used to break up soil and remove weeds **2** a person or thing that cultivates

cultural ('kʌltʃərəl) *adj* **1** of or relating to artistic or social pursuits or events considered valuable or enlightened **2** of or relating to a culture **3** obtained by specialized breeding

culture ('kʌltʃə) *n* **1** the total of the inherited ideas, beliefs, values, and knowledge, which constitute the shared bases of social action **2** the total range of activities and ideas of a people **3** a particular civilization at a particular period **4** the artistic and social pursuits, expression, and tastes valued by a society or class **5** the enlightenment or refinement resulting from these pursuits **6** the attitudes and general behaviour of a particular social group, profession, etc **7** the cultivation of plants to improve stock or to produce new ones **8** the rearing and breeding of animals, esp with a view to improving the strain **9** the act or practice of tilling or cultivating the soil **10** *biol* **10a** the experimental growth of microorganisms in a nutrient substance **10b** a group of microorganisms grown in this way ▷ *vb* **cultures, culturing, cultured** (*tr*) **11** to cultivate (plants or animals) **12** to grow (microorganisms) in a culture medium [c15 from OF, from L *cultūra* a cultivating, from *colere* to till; see CULT] > '**culturist** *n*

cultured ('kʌltʃəd) *adj* **1** showing or having good taste, manners, and education **2** artificially grown or synthesized: *cultured pearls* **3** treated by a culture of microorganisms

cultured pearl *n* a pearl induced to grow in the shell of an oyster or clam, by the insertion of a small object

culture jamming *n* a form of political and social activism which, by means of fake adverts, hoax news stories, pastiches of company logos and product labels, computer hacking, etc, draws attention to and at the same time subverts the power of the media, governments, and large corporations to control and distort the information that they give to the public in order to promote consumerism, militarism, etc

culture shock *n sociol* the feelings of isolation, rejection, etc, experienced when one culture is brought into sudden contact with another

culture vulture *n inf* a person considered to be excessively, and often pretentiously, interested in the arts

cultus ('kʌltəs) *n, pl* **cultuses** *or* **culti** (-taɪ) another word for **cult** (sense 1) [C17 from L: a toiling over something, refinement, CULT]

culverin ('kʌlvərɪn) *n* **1** a medium-to-heavy cannon used during the 15th, 16th, and 17th centuries **2** a medieval musket [C15 from OF *coulevrine*, from *couleuvre*, from L *coluber* serpent]

culvert ('kʌlvət) *n* **1** a drain or covered channel that crosses under a road, railway, etc **2** a channel for an electric cable [C18 from ?]

cum (kʌm) *prep* used between nouns to designate a combined nature: *a kitchen-cum-dining room* [L: with, together with]

Cumae ('kju:mi:) *n* the oldest Greek colony in Italy, founded about 750 BC near Naples > **Cu'maean** *adj*

cumber ('kʌmbə) *vb (tr)* **1** to obstruct or hinder **2** *obs* to inconvenience [C13 prob. from OF *combrer* to impede, prevent, from *combre* barrier; see ENCUMBER]

Cumberland[1] ('kʌmbələnd) *n* (until 1974) a county of NW England, now part of Cumbria

Cumberland[2] ('kʌmbələnd) *n* **1 Richard** 1631–1718, English theologian and moral philosopher; bishop of Peterborough (1691–1718) **2 William Augustus,** Duke of Cumberland, known as *Butcher Cumberland.* 1721–65, English soldier, younger son of George II, noted for his defeat of Charles Edward Stuart at Culloden (1746) and his subsequent ruthless destruction of Jacobite rebels

cumbersome ('kʌmbəsəm) *or* **cumbrous** ('kʌmbrəs) *adj* **1** awkward because of size, weight, or shape **2** difficult because of extent or complexity: *cumbersome accounts* [C14 *cumber*, short for ENCUMBER + -SOME[1]] > '**cumbersomeness** *or* '**cumbrousness** *n*

Cumbria ('kʌmbrɪə) *n* (since 1974) a county of NW England comprising the former counties of Westmorland and Cumberland together with N Lancashire: includes the Lake District mountain area and surrounding coastal lowlands with the Pennine uplands in the extreme east. Administrative centre: Carlisle. Pop: 487 607 (2001). Area: 6810 sq km (2629 sq miles)

Cumbrian ('kʌmbrɪən) *adj* **1** of or relating to Cumbria or its inhabitants ▷ *n* **2** a native or inhabitant of Cumbria

Cumbrian Mountains ('kʌmbrɪən) *pl n* a mountain range in NW England, in Cumbria. Highest peak: Scafell Pike, 978 m (3210 ft)

cumin *or* **cummin** ('kʌmɪn) *n* **1** an umbelliferous Mediterranean plant with small white or pink flowers **2** the aromatic seeds (collectively) of this plant, used as a condiment and a flavouring [C12 from OF, from L *cumīnum*, from Gk *kuminon*, of Semitic origin]

cummerbund ('kʌmə,bʌnd) *n* a wide sash worn round the waist, esp with a dinner jacket [C17 from Hindi *kamarband*, from Persian, from *kamar* loins, waist + *band* band]

Cummings ('kʌmɪŋz) *n* **Edward Estlin** ('ɛstlɪn), (preferred typographical representation of name **e e cummings**) 1894–1962, US poet

cum new *adv, adj* (of shares, etc) with the right to take up any scrip issue or rights issue ▷ Cf **ex new**

cumquat ('kʌmkwɒt) *n* a variant spelling of **kumquat**

cumulate *vb* ('kju:mjʊ,leɪt), **cumulates, cumulating, cumulated 1** to accumulate **2** *(tr)* to combine (two or more sequences) into one ▷ *adj* ('kju:mjʊlɪt) **3** heaped up [C16 from L *cumulāre* from *cumulus* heap] > ,**cumu'lation** *n*

cumulative ('kju:mjʊlətɪv) *adj* **1** growing in quantity, strength, or effect by successive additions **2** (of dividends or interest) intended to be accumulated **3** *statistics* **3a** (of a frequency) including all values of a variable either below or above a specified value **3b** (of error) tending to increase as the sample size is increased > '**cumulatively** *adv* > '**cumulativeness** *n*

cumulonimbus (,kju:mjʊləʊ'nɪmbəs) *n, pl* **cumulonimbi** (-baɪ) *or* **cumulonimbuses** *meteorol* a cumulus cloud of great vertical extent, the bottom being dark-coloured, indicating rain or hail

cumulus ('kju:mjʊləs) *n, pl* **cumuli** (-,laɪ) a bulbous or billowing white or dark grey cloud [C17 from L: mass] > '**cumulous** *adj*

Cunaxa (kju:'næksə) *n* the site near the lower Euphrates where Artaxerxes II defeated Cyrus the Younger in 401 BC

cuneate ('kju:nɪɪt, -,eɪt) *adj* wedge-shaped [C19 from L *cuneāre* to make wedge-shaped, from *cuneus* a wedge] > '**cuneately** *adv* > '**cuneal** *adj*

cuneiform ('kju:nɪ,fɔ:m) *adj* **1** Also: **cuneal** wedge-shaped **2** of, relating to, or denoting the wedge-shaped characters in several ancient languages of Mesopotamia and Persia **3** of or relating to a tablet in which this script is employed ▷ *n* **4** cuneiform characters [C17 prob. from OF *cunéiforme*, from L *cuneus* wedge]

Cc

cunjevoi ('kʌndʒɪ,vɔɪ) *n Austral* **1** an arum of tropical Asia and Australia, cultivated for its edible rhizome **2** a sea squirt. Often shortened to **cunjie, cunjy** [C19 from Abor.]

cunnilingus (,kʌnɪ'lɪŋgəs) *or* **cunnilinctus** (,kʌnɪ'lɪŋktəs) *n* a sexual activity in which the female genitalia are stimulated by the partner's lips and tongue ▷ Cf **fellatio** [C19 from NL, from L *cunnus* vulva + *lingere* to lick]

cunning ('kʌnɪŋ) *adj* **1** crafty and shrewd, esp in deception **2** made with or showing skill; ingenious ▷ *n* **3** craftiness, esp in deceiving **4** skill or ingenuity [OE *cunnende*; rel. to *cunnan* to know (see CAN[1])] > '**cunningly** *adv* > '**cunningness** *n*

Cunningham ('kʌnɪŋəm) *n* **Merce** (mɜ:s) born 1919, US dancer and choreographer. His experimental ballets include *Suit for Five* (1956) and *Travelogue* (1977)

Cunninghame Graham ('kʌnɪŋəm 'greɪəm) *n* **R(obert) B(ontine)** 1852–1936, Scottish traveller, writer, and politician, noted for his essays and short stories: first president (1928) of the Scottish Nationalist Party

Cunobelinus (kju:,nɒbə'laɪnəs) *n* also called *Cymbeline.* died ?42 AD, British ruler of the Catuvellauni tribe (?10–?42); founder of Colchester (?10)

cunt (kʌnt) *n taboo* **1** the female genitals **2** *offens sl* a woman considered sexually **3** *offens sl* a mean or obnoxious person [C13 of Gmc origin; rel. to ON *kunta*, MLow G *kunte*]

cup (kʌp) *n* **1** a small open container, usually having one handle, used for drinking from **2** the contents of such a container **3** Also called: **teacup, cupful** a unit of capacity used in cooking **4** something resembling a cup **5** either of two cup-shaped parts of a brassiere **6** a cup-shaped trophy awarded as a prize **7** *Brit* **7a** a sporting contest in which a cup is awarded to the winner **7b** (*as modifier*): *a cup competition* **8** a mixed drink with one ingredient as a base: *claret cup* **9** *golf* the hole or metal container in the hole on a green **10** the chalice or the consecrated wine used in the Eucharist **11** one's lot in life **12** **in one's cups** drunk **13** **one's cup of tea** *inf* one's chosen or preferred thing, task, company, etc ▷ *vb* **cups, cupping, cupped** (*tr*) **14** to form (something, such as the hands) into the shape of a cup **15** to put into or as if into a cup **16** *arch* to draw blood to the surface of the body of (a person) by cupping [OE *cuppe*, from LL *cuppa* cup, alteration of L *cūpa* cask]

cupbearer ('kʌpˌbɛərə) *n* an attendant who fills and serves wine cups, as in a royal household

cupboard ('kʌbəd) *n* a piece of furniture or a recessed area of a room, with a door concealing storage space

cupboard love *n* a show of love inspired only by some selfish or greedy motive

cupcake ('kʌpˌkeɪk) *n* a small cake baked in a cup-shaped foil or paper case

CUPE ('kju:pɪ) *n abbrev. or acronym for* Canadian Union of Public Employees

cupel ('kju:pᵊl, kjʊ'pɛl) *n* **1** a refractory pot in which gold or silver is refined **2** a small bowl in which gold and silver are recovered during assaying ▷ *vb* **cupels, cupelling, cupelled** *or US* **cupels, cupeling, cupeled** **3** (*tr*) to refine (gold or silver) using a cupel [c17 from F *coupelle*, dim. of *coupe* CUP] > ˌ**cupel'lation** *n*

Cup Final *n* **1** (often preceded by *the*) the annual final of the FA or Scottish Cup soccer competition **2** (*often not cap*) the final of any cup competition

Cupid ('kju:pɪd) *n* **1** the Roman god of love, represented as a winged boy with a bow and arrow. Greek counterpart: **Eros** **2** (*not cap*) any similar figure [c14 from L *Cupīdō*, from *cupīdō* desire, from *cupidus* desirous; see CUPIDITY]

cupidity (kju:'pɪdɪtɪ) *n* strong desire, esp for wealth; greed [c15 from L *cupiditās*, from *cupidus* eagerly desiring, from *cupere* to long for]

cupola ('kju:pələ) *n* **1** a roof or ceiling in the form of a dome **2** a small structure, usually domed, on the top of a roof or dome **3** a protective dome for a gun on a warship **4** a furnace in which iron is remelted [c16 from It., from LL *cūpula* a small cask, from L *cūpa* tub] > '**cupoˌlated** *adj*

cuppa *or* **cupper** ('kʌpə) *n Brit inf* a cup of tea

cupping ('kʌpɪŋ) *n med* formerly, the use of an evacuated glass cup to draw blood to the surface of the skin for blood-letting

cupreous ('kju:prɪəs) *adj* **1** of, containing, or resembling copper **2** of the colour of copper [c17 from LL *cupreus*, from *cuprum* COPPER[1]]

cupressus (kə'prɛsəs) *n* any evergreen tree of the genus *Cupressus*

cupric ('kju:prɪk) *adj* of or containing copper in the divalent state [c18 from LL *cuprum* copper]

cupriferous (kju:'prɪfərəs) *adj* (of a substance such as an ore) containing or yielding copper

cupro-, cupri-, *or before a vowel* **cupr-** *combining form* indicating copper [from L *cuprum*]

cupronickel (ˌkju:prəʊ'nɪkᵊl) *n* any copper alloy containing up to 40 per cent nickel: used in coins, condenser tubes, etc

cuprous ('kju:prəs) *adj* of or containing copper in the monovalent state

cup tie *n sport* an eliminating match or round between two teams in a cup competition

cupule ('kju:pju:l) *n biol* a cup-shaped part or structure [c19 from LL *cūpula*; see CUPOLA]

cur (kɜ:) *n* **1** any vicious dog, esp a mongrel **2** a despicable or cowardly person [c13 from *kurdogge*; prob. rel. to ON *kurra* to growl]

curable ('kjʊərəbᵊl) *adj* capable of being cured > ˌ**cura'bility** *or* '**curableness** *n*

Curaçao (ˌkjʊərə'səʊ) *n* **1** an island in the Caribbean, the largest in the Netherlands Antilles. Capital: Willemstad. Pop: 143 387 (2000 est). Area: 444 sq km (171 sq miles) **2** an orange-flavoured liqueur originally made there

curacy ('kjʊərəsɪ) *n, pl* **curacies** the office or position of a curate

curare *or* **curari** (kjʊ'rɑ:rɪ) *n* **1** black resin obtained from certain tropical South American trees, which causes muscular paralysis by acting on the motor nerves: used medicinally as a muscle relaxant and by South American Indians as an arrow poison **2** any of various trees from which this resin is obtained [c18 from Port. & Sp., from Carib *kurari*]

curassow ('kjʊərəˌsəʊ) *n* any of various ground-nesting birds of S North, Central, and South America, having long legs and tail and a crest of curled feathers [c17 anglicized from CURAÇAO (island)]

curate ('kjʊərɪt) *n* **1** a clergyman appointed to assist a parish priest **2** *Irish* an assistant barman [c14 from Med. L *cūrātus*, from *cūra* spiritual oversight, CURE]

curate's egg *n* something that has good and bad parts [c20 derived from a cartoon in *Punch* (Nov, 1895) in which a timid curate, who has been served a bad egg while breakfasting with his bishop, says that parts of the egg are excellent]

curative ('kjʊərətɪv) *adj* **1** able or tending to cure ▷ *n* **2** anything able to heal or cure > '**curatively** *adv* > '**curativeness** *n*

curator (kjʊə'reɪtə) *n* the administrative head of a museum, art gallery, etc [c14 from L: one who cares, from *cūrāre* to care for, from *cūra* care] > **curatorial** (ˌkjʊərə'tɔ:rɪəl) *adj* > **cu'ratorˌship** *n*

curb (kɜ:b) *n* **1** something that restrains or holds back **2** any enclosing framework, such as a wall around the top of a well **3** Also called: **curb bit** a horse's bit with an attached chain or strap, which checks the horse ▷ *vb* (*tr*) **4** to control with or as if with a curb; restrain ▷ See also **kerb** [c15 from OF *courbe* curved piece of wood or metal, from L *curvus* curved]

curcuma ('kɜ:kjʊmə) *n* any tropical Asian tuberous plant of the genus *Curcuma*, such as *C. longa*, which is the source of turmeric [c17 from NL, from Ar. *kurkum* turmeric]

curd (kɜ:d) *n* **1** (*often pl*) a substance formed from the coagulation of milk, used in making cheese or eaten as a food **2** something similar in consistency ▷ *vb* **3** to turn into or become curd [c15 from earlier *crud*, from ?] > '**curdy** *adj*

curdle ('kɜ:dᵊl) *vb* **curdles, curdling, curdled** **1** to turn or cause to turn into curd **2** **curdle someone's blood** to fill someone with fear [c16 (*crudled*, p.p.): from CURD]

cure (kjʊə) *vb* **cures, curing, cured** **1** (*tr*) to get rid of (an ailment or problem); heal **2** (*tr*) to restore to health or good condition **3** (*intr*) to bring about a cure **4** (*tr*) to preserve (meat, fish, etc) by salting, smoking, etc **5** (*tr*) **5a** to treat or finish (a substance) by chemical or physical means **5b** to vulcanize (rubber) **6** (*tr*) to assist the hardening of (concrete, mortar, etc) by keeping it moist ▷ *n* **7** a return to health **8** any course of medical therapy, esp one proved effective **9** a means of restoring health or improving a situation, etc **10** the spiritual and pastoral charge of a parish **11** a process or method of preserving meat, fish, etc [(n) c13 from OF, from L *cūra* care; in ecclesiastical sense, from Med. L *cūra* spiritual charge; (vb) c14 from OF *curer*, from L *cūrāre* to attend to, heal, from *cūra* care] > '**cureless** *adj* > '**curer** *n*

curé ('kjʊəreɪ) *n* a parish priest in France [F, from Med. L *cūrātus*; see CURATE]

cure-all *n* something reputed to cure all ailments

curettage (ˌkjʊərɪ'tɑ:ʒ, kjʊə'rɛtɪdʒ) *or* **curettement**

(kjʊəˈrɛtmənt) *n* the process of using a curette. See also **D and C**

curette *or* **curet** (kjʊəˈrɛt) *n* **1** a surgical instrument for removing dead tissue, growths, etc, from the walls of body cavities ▷ *vb* **curettes** *or* **curets, curetting, curetted** **2** (*tr*) to scrape or clean with such an instrument [c18 from F *curette*, from *curer* to heal, make clean; see CURE]

curfew (ˈkɜːfjuː) *n* **1** an official regulation setting restrictions on movement, esp after a specific time at night **2** the time set as a deadline by such a regulation **3** (in medieval Europe) **3a** the ringing of a bell to prompt people to extinguish fires and lights **3b** the time at which the curfew bell was rung **3c** the bell itself [c13 from OF *cuevrefeu*, lit.: cover the fire]

curia (ˈkjʊərɪə) *n, pl* **curiae** (-rɪˌiː) **1** (*sometimes cap*) the papal court and government of the Roman Catholic Church **2** (in the Middle Ages) a court held in the king's name [c16 from L, from OL *coviria* (unattested), from *co-* + *vir* man] > **ˈcurial** *adj*

curie (ˈkjʊərɪ, -riː) *n* a unit of radioactivity equal to 3.7×10^{10} disintegrations per second [c20 after Pierre CURIE]

Curie (ˈkjʊərɪ, -riː; *French* kyri) *n* **1** **Marie** (mari) 1867–1934, French physicist and chemist, born in Poland: discovered with her husband Pierre the radioactivity of thorium, and discovered and isolated radium and polonium. She shared a Nobel prize for physics (1903) with her husband and Henri Becquerel, and was awarded a Nobel prize for chemistry (1911) **2** her husband, **Pierre** (pjɛr) 1859–1906, French physicist and chemist

curio (ˈkjʊərɪˌəʊ) *n, pl* **curios** a small article valued as a collector's item, esp something unusual [c19 shortened from CURIOSITY]

curiosity (ˌkjʊərɪˈɒsɪtɪ) *n, pl* **curiosities** **1** an eager desire to know; inquisitiveness **2** the quality of being curious; strangeness **3** something strange or fascinating

curious (ˈkjʊərɪəs) *adj* **1** eager to learn; inquisitive **2** overinquisitive; prying **3** interesting because of oddness or novelty [c14 from L *cūriōsus* taking pains over something, from *cūra* care] > **ˈcuriously** *adv* > **ˈcuriousness** *n*

Curitiba (ˌkʊərɪˈtiːbə) *n* a city in SE Brazil, capital of Paraná state: seat of the University of Paraná (1946). Pop (urban area): 1 586 898 (2000)

curium (ˈkjʊərɪəm) *n* a silvery-white metallic transuranic element artificially produced from plutonium. Symbol: Cm; at. no.: 96; half-life of most stable isotope, ^{247}Cm: 1.6×10^7 years [c20 NL, after Pierre and Marie CURIE]

curl (kɜːl) *vb* **1** (*intr*) (esp of hair) to grow into curves or ringlets **2** (*tr*; sometimes foll by *up*) to twist or roll (esp hair) into coils or ringlets **3** (often foll by *up*) to become or cause to become spiral-shaped or curved **4** (*intr*) to move in a curving or twisting manner **5** (*intr*) to play the game of curling **6** **curl one's lip** to show contempt, as by raising a corner of the lip ▷ *n* **7** a curve or coil of hair **8** a curved or spiral shape or mark **9** the act of curling or state of being curled ▷ See also **curl up** [c14 prob. from MDu. *crullen* to curl]

curler (ˈkɜːlə) *n* **1** any of various pins, clasps, or rollers used to curl or wave hair **2** a person or thing that curls **3** a person who plays curling

curlew (ˈkɜːljuː) *n* any of certain large shore birds of Europe and Asia. They have a long downward-curving bill and occur in northern and arctic regions [c14 from OF *corlieu*, ? imit.]

curlicue (ˈkɜːlɪˌkjuː) *n* an intricate ornamental curl or twist [c19 from CURLY + CUE[2]]

curling (ˈkɜːlɪŋ) *n* a game played on ice, esp in Scotland, in which heavy stones with handles (**curling stones**) are slid towards a target (**tee**)

▷ http://icing.org

curling tongs *pl n* a metal scissor-like device that is heated, so that strands of hair may be twined around it in order to form curls. Also called: **curling iron, curling irons, curling pins**

curl up *vb* (*adv*) **1** (*intr*) to adopt a reclining position with the legs close to the body and the back rounded **2** to become or cause to become spiral-shaped or curved **3** (*intr*) to retire to a quiet cosy setting: *to curl up with a good novel* **4** *Brit inf* to be or cause to be embarrassed or disgusted (esp in **curl up and die**)

curly (ˈkɜːlɪ) *adj* **curlier, curliest** **1** tending to curl; curling **2** having curls **3** (of timber) having waves in the grain > **ˈcurliness** *n*

curmudgeon (kɜːˈmʌdʒən) *n* a surly or miserly person [c16 from ?] > **curˈmudgeonly** *adj*

Curnow (kɜːnaʊ) *n* (**Thomas**) **Allen** (**Monro**) 1911–2001, New Zealand poet and anthologist

currach *or* **curragh** *Gaelic* (ˈkʌrəx, ˈkʌrə) *n* a Scottish or Irish name for **coracle** [c15 from Irish Gaelic *currach*; Cf CORACLE]

currajong (ˈkʌrəˌdʒɒŋ) *n* a variant spelling of **kurrajong**

currant (ˈkʌrənt) *n* **1** a small dried seedless grape of the Mediterranean region **2** any of several mainly N temperate shrubs, esp redcurrant and blackcurrant **3** the small acid fruit of any of these plants [c16 shortened from *rayson of Corannte* raisin of Corinth]

currawong (ˈkʌrəˌwɒŋ) *n* any Australian crowlike songbird of the genus *Strepera*, having black, grey, and white plumage. Also called: **bell-magpie** [from Abor.]

currency (ˈkʌrənsɪ) *n, pl* **currencies** **1** a metal or paper medium of exchange in current use in a particular country **2** general acceptance or circulation; prevalence **3** the period of time during which something is valid, accepted, or in force ▷ *adj* **4** *Austral inf* native-born as distinct from immigrant: *a currency lad* [c17 from Med. L *currentia*, lit.: a flowing, from L *currere* to run, flow]

Currencies

COUNTRY	CODE	CURRENCY
Afghanistan	AFA	afghani
Albania	ALL	lek
Algeria	DZD	dinar
American Samoa	USD	US dollar $
Andorra	EUR	euro €
Angola	KWA	kwanza
Anguilla	XCD	East Caribbean dollar
Antarctica	NOK	Norwegian krone
Antigua and Barbuda	XCD	East Caribbean dollar
Argentina	ARS	Argentine peso
Armenia	AMD	dram
Aruba	AWG	Arubian guilder
Australia	AUD	Australian dollar
Austria	EUR	euro €
Azerbaijan	AZM	manat
Bahamas	BSD	Bahamanian dollar
Bahrain	BHD	Bahraini dinar
Bangladesh	BDT	taka
Barbados	BBD	Barbados dollar
Belarus	BYR	Belarussian rouble
Belgium	EUR	euro €
Belize	BZD	Belize dollar
Benin	XOF	CFA franc BCEAO
Bermuda	BMD	Bermudian dollar
Bhutan	BTN	ngultrum
Bolivia	BOB	boliviano
Bosnia-Herzegovina	BAM	convertible marka

Country	Code	Currency
Botswana	BWP	pula
Brazil	BRL	real
British Virgin Islands	USD	US dollar $
Brunei	BND	Bruneian dollar
Bulgaria	BGN	lev
Burkina Faso	XOF	CFA franc BCEAO
Burundi	BIF	Burundi franc
Cambodia	KHR	riel
Cameroon	XAF	CFA franc BEAC
Canada	CAD	Canadian dollar
Cape Verde	CVE	Cape Verde escudo
Cayman Islands	KYD	Cayman Islands dollar
Central African Republic	XAF	CFA franc BEAC
Chad	XAF	CFA franc BEAC
Chile	CLP	Chilean peso
China	CNY	yuan renminbi
Christmas Island	AUD	Australian dollar
Cocos (Keeling) Islands	AUD	Australian dollar
Colombia	COP	Colombian peso
Comoros	KMF	Comoro franc
Congo	XAF	CFA franc BEAC
Congo, Democratic Republic of	CDF	Congolese franc
Cook Islands	NZD	New Zealand dollar
Costa Rica	CRC	Costa Rican colon
Côte d'Ivoire	XOF	CFA franc BCEAO
Croatia	HRK	kuna
Cuba	CUP	Cuban peso
Cyprus	CYP	Cyprus pound
Czech Republic	CZK	Czech koruna
Denmark	DKK	Danish krone
Djibouti	DJF	Djibouti franc
Dominica	XCD	East Caribbean dollar
Dominican Republic	DOP	Dominican peso
East Timor	TPE	Timor escudo
Ecuador	USD	US dollar $
Egypt	EGP	Egyptian pound
El Salvador	SVC	El Salvador colon
Equatorial Guinea	XAF	CFA franc BEAC
Eritrea	ERN	nakfa
Estonia	EEK	kroon
Ethiopia	ETB	Ethiopian birr
Falkland Islands	FKP	Falkland Islands pound
Faroe Islands	DKK	Danish krone
Fiji	FJD	Fiji dollar
Finland	EUR	euro €
France	EUR	euro €
French Guiana	EUR	euro €
French Polynesia	XPF	CFP franc
French Southern and Antarctic Territories	EUR	euro €
Gabon	XAF	CFA franc BEAC
Gambia	GMD	dalasi
Georgia	GEL	lari
Germany	EUR	euro €
Ghana	GHC	cedi
Gibraltar	GIP	Gibraltar pound
Greece	EUR	euro €
Greenland	DKK	Danish krone
Grenada	XCD	East Caribbean dollar
Guadeloupe	EUR	euro €
Guam	USD	US dollar $
Guatemala	GTQ	Quetzal
Guinea	GNF	Guinea franc
Guinea-Bissau	GWP	Guinea-Bissau peso
Guyana	GYD	Guyana dollar
Haiti	HTG	gourde
Heard and McDonald Islands	AUD	Australian dollar
Honduras	HNL	lempira
Hong Kong	HKD	Hong Kong dollar
Hungary	FOR	forint
Iceland	ISK	Iceland krona
India	INR	Indian rupee
Indonesia	IDR	rupiah
Iran	IRR	Iranian rial
Iraq	IQD	Iraqi dinar
Ireland	EUR	euro €
Israel	ILS	Israeli sheqel
Italy	EUR	euro €
Jamaica	JMD	Jamaican dollar
Japan	JPY	yen
Jordan	JOD	Jordanian dinar
Kazakhstan	KZT	tenge
Kenya	KES	Kenyan shilling
Kiribati	AUD	Australian dollar
Korea (North)	KPW	North Korean won
Korea (South)	KRW	won
Kuwait	KWD	Kuwaiti dinar
Kyrgyzstan	KGS	som
Lao People's Democratic Republic	LAK	kip
Latvia	LVL	lats
Lebanon	LBP	Lebanese pound
Lesotho	LSL	loti
Liberia	LRD	Liberian dollar
Libya	LYD	Libyan dinar
Liechtenstein	CHF	Swiss franc
Lithuania	LTL	litus
Luxembourg	EUR	euro €
Macau	MOP	pataca
Macedonia, FYR of	MKD	denar
Madagascar	MGF	Malagasy franc
Malawi	MWK	kwacha
Malaysia	MYR	Malaysian ringgit
Maldives	MVR	rufiyaa
Mali	XOF	CFA franc BCEAO
Malta	MTL	Maltese lira
Marshall Islands	USD	US dollar $
Martinique	EUR	euro €
Mauritania	MRO	ouguiya
Mauritius	MUR	Mauritius rupee
Mayotte	EUR	euro €
Mexico	MXN	Mexican peso
Micronesia (Federated States of)	USD	US dollar $
Moldova	MDL	Moldovan leu
Monaco	EUR	euro €
Mongolia	MNT	tugrik
Montserrat	XCD	East Caribbean dollar
Morocco	MAD	Moroccan dirham
Mozambique	MZM	metical
Myanmar	MMK	kyat
Namibia	ZAR	rand
Nauru	AUD	Australian dollar
Nepal	NPR	Nepalese rupee
Netherlands	EUR	euro €
Netherlands Antilles	ANG	Netherlands Antillian guilder
New Caledonia	XPF	CFP franc
New Zealand	NZD	New Zealand dollar
Nicaragua	NIO	cordoba oro
Niger	XOF	CFA franc BCEAO
Nigeria	NGN	naira
Niue	NZD	New Zealand dollar
Norfolk Island	AUD	Australian dollar

Country	Code	Currency
Northern Mariana Islands	USD	US dollar $
Norway	NOK	Norwegian krone
Oman	OMR	rial Omani
Pakistan	PKR	Pakistan rupee
Palau	USD	US dollar $
Panama	PAB	balboa
Papua New Guinea	PGK	kina
Paraguay	PYG	guarani
Peru	PEN	new sol
Philippines	PHP	Philippine peso
Pitcairn Island	NZD	New Zealand dollar
Poland	PLN	zloty
Portugal	EUR	euro €
Puerto Rico	USD	US dollar $
Qatar	QAR	Qatari rial
Réunion	EUR	euro €
Romania	ROL	leu
Russian Federation	RUR	Russian ruble
Rwanda	RWF	Rwanda franc
Saint Helena	SHP	Saint Helena pound
Saint Kitts and Nevis	XCD	East Caribbean dollar
Saint Lucia	XCD	East Caribbean dollar
Saint Pierre and Miquelon	EUR	euro €
Saint Vincent and the Grenadines	XCD	East Caribbean dollar
Samoa	WST	tala
San Marino	EUR	euro €
São Tomé and Príncipe	STD	dobra
Saudi Arabia	SAR	Saudi riyal
Senegal	XOF	Senegal franc BCEAO
Serbia and Montenegro	EUR	euro €
Seychelles	SCR	Seychelles rupee
Sierra Leone	SLL	leone
Singapore	SGD	Singapore dollar
Slovakia	SKK	Slovak koruna
Slovenia	SIT	tolar
Soloman Islands	SBD	Soloman Islands dollar
Somalia	SOS	Somali shilling
South Africa	ZAR	rand
Spain	EUR	euro €
Sri Lanka	LKR	Sri Lanka rupee
Sudan	SDD	Sudanese dinar
Suriname	SRG	Suriname guilder
Svalbard and Jan Mayen	NOK	Norwegian krone
Swaziland	SZL	lilangeni
Sweden	SEK	Swedish krona
Switzerland	CHF	Swiss franc
Syria	SYP	Syrian pound
Taiwan	TWD	New Taiwan dollar
Tajikistan	TJS	somoni
Tanzania	TZS	Tanzanian shilling
Thailand	THB	baht
Togo	XOF	CFA franc BCEAO
Tokelau	NZD	New Zealand dollar
Tonga	TOP	pa'anga
Trinidad and Tobago	TTD	Trinidad and Tobago dollar
Tunisia	TND	Tunisian dinar
Turkey	TRL	Turkish lira
Turkmenistan	TMM	manat
Turks and Caicos Islands	USD	US dollar $
Tuvalu	AUD	Australian dollar
Uganda	UGX	Ugandan shilling
Ukraine	UAH	hryvnia
United Arab Emirates	AED	UAE dirham
United Kingdom	GBP	pound sterling £
United States	USD	US dollar $
Uruuguay	UYU	Uruguayan peso
Uzbekistan	UZS	Uzbekistan sum
Vanuatu	VUV	vatu
Vatican City	EUR	euro €
Venezuela	VEB	bolivar
Vietnam	VND	dong
Virgin Islands (UK)	USD	US dollar $
Virgin Islands (US)	USD	US dollar $
Wallis and Futuna	XPF	CFP franc
Western Sahara	MAD	Moroccan dirham
Yemen	YER	Yemeni rial
Zambia	ZMK	kwacha
Zimbabwe	ZWD	Zimbabwe dollar

▷ www.exchangerate.com/indication_rates.html
▷ www.xe.com/ucc
▷ www.uta.fi/~ktmatu/rate-symbols.html

current ('kʌrənt) *adj* **1** of the immediate present; in progress **2** most recent; up-to-date **3** commonly known, practised, or accepted **4** circulating and valid at present: *current coins* ▷ *n* **5** (esp of water or air) a steady, usually natural, flow **6** a mass of air, body of water, etc, that has a steady flow in a particular direction **7** the rate of flow of such a mass **8** *physics* **8a** a flow of electric charge through a conductor **8b** the rate of flow of this charge **9** a general trend or drift: *currents of opinion* [c13 from OF *corant*, lit.: running, from *corre* to run, from L *currere*] > '**currently** *adv* > '**currentness** *n*

current account *n* an account at a bank or building society against which cheques may be drawn at any time

current-cost accounting *n* a method of accounting that values assets at their current replacement cost rather than their original cost. It is often used in times of high inflation ▷ Cf **historical-cost accounting**

curricle ('kʌrɪk^{ə}l) *n* a two-wheeled open carriage drawn by two horses side by side [c18 from L *curriculum* from *currus* chariot, from *currere* to run]

curriculum (kə'rɪkjʊləm) *n, pl* **curricula** (-lə) *or* **curriculums** **1** a course of study in one subject at a school or college **2** a list of all the courses of study offered by a school or college **3** a plan of activities [c19 from L: course, from *currere* to run] > **cur'ricular** *adj*

curriculum vitae (kə'rɪkjʊləm 'viːtaɪ, 'vaɪtiː) *n, pl* **curricula vitae** (kə'rɪkjʊlə) an outline of a person's educational and professional history, usually prepared for job applications [L, lit.: the course of one's life]

currish ('kɜːrɪʃ) *adj* of or like a cur; rude or bad-tempered > '**currishly** *adv* > '**currishness** *n*

curry[1] ('kʌrɪ) *n, pl* **curries** **1** a spicy dish of oriental, esp Indian, origin that usually consists of meat or fish prepared in a hot piquant sauce **2** curry seasoning or sauce **3 give someone curry** *Austral sl* to assault (a person) verbally or physically ▷ *vb* **curries, currying, curried** **4** (*tr*) to prepare (food) with curry powder or sauce [c16 from Tamil *kari* sauce, relish]
▷ www.recipesource.com
▷ www.indiatastes.com
▷ www.wikipedia.org/wiki/Curry

curry[2] ('kʌrɪ) *vb* **curries, currying, curried** **1** to beat vigorously, as in order to clean **2** to dress and finish (leather) after it has been tanned **3** to groom (a horse) **4 curry favour** to ingratiate oneself, esp with superiors [c13 from OF *correer* to make ready]

currycomb ('kʌrɪˌkəʊm) *n* a square comb used for grooming horses

curry powder *n* a mixture of finely ground pungent

spices, such as turmeric, cumin, coriander, ginger, etc, used in making curries

curse (kɜːs) *n* **1** a profane or obscene expression of anger, disgust, surprise, etc; oath **2** an appeal to a supernatural power for harm to come to a specific person, group, etc **3** harm resulting from an appeal to a supernatural power **4** something that brings or causes great trouble or harm **5** (preceded by *the*) *inf* menstruation or a menstrual period ▷ *vb* **curses, cursing, cursed** *or* (*arch*) **curst 6** (*intr*) to utter obscenities or oaths **7** (*tr*) to abuse (someone) with obscenities or oaths **8** (*tr*) to invoke supernatural powers to bring harm to (someone or something) **9** (*tr*) to bring harm upon [OE *cursian* to curse, from *curs* a curse] > **'curser** *n*

cursed ('kɜːsɪd, kɜːst) *or* **curst** *adj* **1** under a curse **2** deserving to be cursed; detestable; hateful > **'cursedly** *adv* > **'cursedness** *n*

cursive ('kɜːsɪv) *adj* **1** of or relating to handwriting in which letters are joined in a flowing style **2** *printing* of or relating to typefaces that resemble handwriting ▷ *n* **3** a cursive letter or printing type [c18 from Med. L *cursīvus* running, ult. from L *currere* to run] > **'cursively** *adv*

cursor ('kɜːsə) *n* **1** the sliding part of a measuring instrument, esp on a slide rule **2** any of various means, typically a flashing bar or underline, of identifying a particular position on a computer screen

cursorial (kɜː'sɔːrɪəl) *adj zool* adapted for running: *a cursorial skeleton; cursorial birds*

cursory ('kɜːsərɪ) *adj* hasty and usually superficial; quick [c17 from LL *cursōrius* of running, from L *cursus* a course, from *currere* to run] > **'cursorily** *adv* > **'cursoriness** *n*

curst (kɜːst) *vb* **1** *arch* a past tense and past participle of **curse** ▷ *adj* **2** a variant of **cursed**

curt (kɜːt) *adj* **1** rudely blunt and brief **2** short or concise [c17 from L *curtus* cut short, mutilated] > **'curtly** *adv* > **'curtness** *n*

curtail (kɜː'teɪl) *vb* (*tr*) to cut short; abridge [c16 changed (through infl. of TAIL[1]) from obs. *curtal* to dock] > **cur'tailer** *n* > **cur'tailment** *n*

curtain ('kɜːtᵊn) *n* **1** a piece of material that can be drawn across an opening or window, to shut out light or to provide privacy **2** a barrier to vision, access, or communication **3** a hanging cloth or similar barrier for concealing all or part of a theatre stage from the audience **4** (often preceded by *the*) the end of a scene of a play, opera, etc, marked by the fall or closing of the curtain **5** the rise or opening of the curtain at the start of a performance ▷ *vb* **6** (*tr*; sometimes foll by *off*) to shut off or conceal as with a curtain **7** (*tr*) to provide (a window, etc) with curtains [c13 from OF *courtine*, from LL *cortīna* enclosed place, curtain, prob. from L *cohors* courtyard]

curtain call *n* the appearance of performers at the end of a theatrical performance to acknowledge applause

curtain lecture *n* a scolding or rebuke given in private, esp by a wife to her husband [alluding to the curtained beds where such rebukes were once given]

curtain-raiser *n* **1** *theatre* a short dramatic piece presented before the main play **2** any preliminary event

curtains ('kɜːtᵊnz) *pl n inf* death or ruin: the end

curtain wall *n* a non-load-bearing external wall attached to a framed structure

Curtin ('kɜːtɪn) *n* **John Joseph** 1885–1945, Australian statesman; prime minister of Australia (1941–45)

curtsy *or* **curtsey** ('kɜːtsɪ) *n, pl* **curtsies** *or* **curtseys 1** a formal gesture of greeting and respect made by women, in which the knees are bent and the head slightly bowed ▷ *vb* **curtsies, curtsying, curtsied** *or* **curtseys, curtseying, curtseyed 2** (*intr*) to make a curtsy [c16 var. of COURTESY]

curvaceous (kɜː'veɪʃəs) *adj inf* (of a woman) having a well-rounded body

curvature ('kɜːvətʃə) *n* **1** something curved or a curved part of a thing **2** any curving of a bodily part **3** the act of curving or the state or degree of being curved or bent

curve (kɜːv) *n* **1** a continuously bending line that has no straight parts **2** something that curves or is curved **3** the act or extent of curving; curvature **4** *maths* a system of points whose coordinates satisfy a given equation **5** a line representing data on a graph **6 ahead of** *or* **behind the curve** ahead of *or* behind the times ▷ *vb* **curves, curving, curved 7** to take or cause to take the shape or path of a curve; bend [c15 from L *curvāre* to bend, from *curvus* crooked] > **'curvedness** *n* > **'curvy** *adj*

curvet (kɜː'vɛt) *n* **1** *dressage* a low leap with all four feet off the ground ▷ *vb* **curvets, curvetting, curvetted** *or* **curvets, curveting, curveted 2** *dressage* to make or cause to make such a leap **3** (*intr*) to prance or frisk about [c16 from OIt. *corvetta*, from OF *courbette*, from *courber* to bend, from L *curvāre*]

curvilinear (ˌkɜːvɪ'lɪnɪə) *or* **curvilineal** *adj* consisting of, bounded by, or characterized by a curved line

Curzon ('kɜːzᵊn) *n* **1** Sir **Clifford** 1907–82, English pianist **2 George Nathaniel**, 1st Marquis Curzon of Kedleston. 1859–1925, British Conservative statesman; viceroy of India (1898–1905)

Cusack ('kjuːsæk) *n* **Cyril** (**James**) 1910–93, Irish actor

Cusanus (kjuː'seɪnəs) *n* **Nicholas** See **Nicholas of Cusa**

Cusco (*Spanish* 'kusko) *n* a variant of **Cuzco**

cuscus ('kʌskʌs) *n, pl* **cuscuses** any of several large nocturnal phalangers of N Australia, New Guinea, and adjacent islands, having dense fur, prehensile tails, large eyes, and a yellow nose [c17 NL, prob. from a native name in New Guinea]

cusec ('kjuːsɛk) *n* a unit of flow equal to 1 cubic foot per second [c20 from *cu*(*bic foot per*) *sec*(*ond*)]

Cush *or* **Kush** (kʌʃ, kʊʃ) *n Old Testament* **1** the son of Ham and brother of Canaan (Genesis 10:6) **2** the country of the supposed descendants of Cush (ancient Ethiopia), comprising approximately Nubia and the modern Sudan, and the territory of southern (or Upper) Egypt

cushat ('kʌʃət) *n* another name for **wood pigeon** [OE *cūscote*; ? rel. to *sceōtan* to shoot]

Cushing ('kʊʃɪŋ) *n* **Harvey Williams** 1869–1939, US neurosurgeon: identified a pituitary tumour as a cause of the disease named after him

cushion ('kʊʃən) *n* **1** a bag filled with a yielding substance, used for sitting on, leaning against, etc **2** something resembling a cushion in function or appearance, esp one to support or pad or to absorb shock **3** the resilient felt-covered rim of a billiard table ▷ *vb* (*tr*) **4** to place on or as on a cushion **5** to provide with cushions **6** to protect **7** to lessen or suppress the effects of **8** to provide with a means of absorbing shock [c14 from OF *coussin*, from L *culcita* mattress] > **'cushiony** *adj*

cushion plant *n* a type of low-growing plant having many closely spaced short upright shoots, typical of alpine and arctic habitats

Cushitic (kʊ'ʃɪtɪk) *n* **1** a group of languages of Somalia, Ethiopia, and adjacent regions ▷ *adj* **2** of or relating to this group of languages

cushy ('kʊʃɪ) *adj* **cushier, cushiest** *inf* easy; comfortable [c20 from Hindi *khush* pleasant, from Persian *khōsh*]

cusp (kʌsp) *n* **1** any of the small elevations on the grinding or chewing surface of a tooth **2** any of the triangular flaps of a heart valve **3** a point or pointed end **4** *geom* a point at which two arcs of a curve intersect and at which the two tangents are coincident **5** *archit* a carving at the meeting place of two arcs **6** *astron* either of the points of a crescent moon **7** *astrol* any division between houses or signs of the zodiac [c16 from L *cuspis* point, pointed end] > **'cuspate** *adj*

cuspid ('kʌspɪd) *n* a tooth having one point; canine tooth

cuspidate ('kʌspɪˌdeɪt), **cuspidated,** *or* **cuspidal** ('kʌspɪdᵊl) *adj* **1** having a cusp or cusps **2** (esp of leaves) narrowing to a point [c17 from L *cuspidāre* to make pointed, from *cuspis* a point]

cuspidor ('kʌspɪˌdɔː) *n* another name (esp US) for **spittoon** [c18 from Port., from *cuspir* to spit, from L *conspuere*, from *spuere* to spit]

cuss (kʌs) *inf* ▷ *n* **1** a curse; an oath **2** a person or animal, esp an annoying one ▷ *vb* **3** another word for **curse** (senses 6, 7)

cussed ('kʌsɪd) *adj inf* **1** another word for **cursed** **2** obstinate **3** annoying: *a cussed nuisance* > **'cussedly** *adv* > **'cussedness** *n*

custard ('kʌstəd) *n* **1** a baked sweetened mixture of eggs and milk **2** a sauce made of milk and sugar and thickened with cornflour [c15 alteration of ME *crustade* kind of pie]

custard apple *n* **1** a West Indian tree **2** its large heart-shaped fruit, which has a fleshy edible pulp

custard pie *n* **a** a flat, open pie filled with real or artificial custard, as thrown in slapstick comedy **b** (*as modifier*): *custard-pie humour*

Custer ('kʌstə) *n* **George Armstrong** 1839–76, US cavalry general: Civil War hero, killed fighting the Sioux Indians at Little Bighorn, Montana

custodian (kʌ'stəʊdɪən) *n* **1** a person who has custody, as of a prisoner, ward, etc **2** a keeper of an art collection, etc > **cus'todianˌship** *n*

custody ('kʌstədɪ) *n, pl* **custodies** **1** the act of keeping safe or guarding **2** the state of being held by the police; arrest [c15 from L *custōdia*, from *custōs* guard, defender] > **custodial** (kʌ'stəʊdɪəl) *adj*

custom ('kʌstəm) *n* **1** a usual or habitual practice; typical mode of behaviour **2** the long-established habits or traditions of a society collectively; convention **3a** a practice which by long-established usage has come to have the force of law **3b** such practices collectively (esp in **custom and practice**) **4** habitual patronage, esp of a shop or business **5** the customers of a shop or business collectively ▷ *adj* **6** made to the specifications of an individual customer ▷ See also **customs** [c12 from OF *costume*, from L *consuētūdō*, from *consuēscere* to grow accustomed to]

customary ('kʌstəmərɪ, -təmrɪ) *adj* **1** in accordance with custom or habitual practice; usual **2** *law* **2a** founded upon long-continued practices and usage **2b** (of land) held by custom ▷ *n, pl* **customaries** **3** a statement in writing of customary laws and practices > **'customarily** *adv* > **'customariness** *n*

custom-built *adj* (of cars, houses, etc) made according to the specifications of an individual buyer

customer ('kʌstəmə) *n* **1** a person who buys **2** *inf* a person with whom one has dealings

customer-facing *adj* interacting or communicating directly with customers: *good customer-facing skills*

custom house *n* a government office, esp at a port, where customs are collected and ships cleared for entry

customize *or* **customise** ('kʌstəˌmaɪz) *vb* **customizes, customizing, customized** *or* **customises, customising, customised** (*tr*) to make (something) according to a customer's individual requirements

custom-made *adj* (of suits, dresses, etc) made according to the specifications of an individual buyer

customs ('kʌstəmz) *n* (*functioning as sing or pl*) **1** duty on imports or exports **2** the government department responsible for the collection of these duties **3** the part of a port, airport, etc, where baggage and freight are examined for dutiable goods and contraband

cut (kʌt) *vb* **cuts, cutting, cut** **1** to open up or incise (a person or thing) with a sharp edge or instrument **2** (of a sharp instrument) to penetrate or incise (a person or thing) **3** to divide or be divided with or as if with a sharp instrument **4** (*intr*) to use an instrument that cuts **5** (*tr*) to trim or prune by or as if by clipping **6** (*tr*) to reap or mow (a crop, grass, etc) **7** (*tr; sometimes foll by out*) to make, form, or shape by cutting **8** (*tr*) to hollow or dig out; excavate **9** to strike (an object) sharply **10** *cricket* to hit (the ball) to the off side with a roughly horizontal bat **11** to hurt the feelings of (a person) **12** (*tr*) *inf* to refuse to recognize; snub **13** (*tr*) *inf* to absent oneself from, esp without permission or in haste: *to cut a class* **14** (*tr*) to abridge or shorten **15** (*tr; often foll by down*) to lower, reduce, or curtail **16** (*tr*) to dilute or weaken: *to cut whisky with water* **17** (*tr*) to dissolve or break up: *to cut fat* **18** (when *intr*, foll by *across* or *through*) to cross or traverse **19** (*intr*) to make a sharp or sudden change in direction; veer **20** to grow (teeth) through the gums or (of teeth) to appear through the gums **21** (*intr*) *films* **21a** to call a halt to a shooting sequence **21b** (foll by *to*) to move quickly to another scene **22** *films* to edit (film) **23** to switch off (a light, car engine, etc) **24** (*tr*) to make (a record or tape of a song, performance, etc) **25** *cards* **25a** to divide (the pack) at random into two parts after shuffling **25b** (*intr*) to pick cards from a spread pack to decide dealer, partners, etc **26** (*tr*) (of a tool) to bite into (an object) **27** **cut a dash** to make a stylish impression **28** **cut (a person) dead** *inf* to ignore (a person) completely **29** **cut a (good, poor, etc) figure** to appear or behave in a specified manner **30** **cut and run** *inf* to make a rapid escape **31** **cut both ways** **31a** to have both good and bad effects **31b** to affect both sides, as two parties in an argument, etc **32** **cut it** *sl* to be successful in doing something **33** **cut it fine** *inf* to allow little margin of time, space etc **34** **cut loose** to free or become freed from restraint, custody, anchorage, etc **35** **cut no ice** *inf* to fail to make an impression **36** **cut one's teeth on** *inf* **36a** to use at an early age or stage **36b** to practise on ▷ *adj* **37** detached, divided, or separated by cutting **38** made, shaped, or fashioned by cutting **39** reduced or diminished as by cutting: *cut prices* **40** weakened or diluted **41** *Brit* a slang word for **drunk**: *half cut* **42** **cut and dried** *inf* settled or arranged in advance ▷ *n* **43** the act of cutting **44** a stroke or incision made by cutting; gash **45** a piece or part cut off: *a cut of meat* **46** the edge of anything cut or sliced **47** a passage, channel, path, etc, cut or hollowed out **48** an omission or deletion, esp in a text, film, or play **49** a reduction in price, salary, etc **50** a decrease in government finance in a particular department or area **51** *inf* a portion or share **52** *inf* a straw, slip of paper, etc, used in drawing lots **53** the manner or style in which a thing, esp a garment, is cut **54a** *Irish inf* a person's general appearance: *I didn't like the cut of him* **54b** *Irish derog* a dirty or untidy condition: *look at the cut of your shoes* **55** a direct route; short cut **56** the US name for **block** (sense 13) **57** *cricket* a stroke made to the off side with the bat in a roughly horizontal position **58** *films* an immediate transition from one shot to the next **59** words or an action that hurt another person's feelings **60** a refusal to recognize an acquaintance; snub **61** *Brit* a stretch of water, esp a canal **62** **a cut above** *inf* superior to; better than ▷ See also **cut across, cutback,** etc [c13 prob. from ON]

cut across *vb* (*intr, prep*) **1** to be contrary to ordinary procedure or limitations **2** to cross or traverse, making a shorter route

cut and paste *n* a technique used in word processing by which a section of text can be moved within a document

cutaneous (kjuː'teɪnɪəs) *adj* of or relating to the skin [c16 from NL *cutāneus*, from L *cutis* skin]

cutaway ('kʌtəˌweɪ) *n* **1** a man's coat cut diagonally from the front waist to the back of the knees **2a** a drawing or model of a machine, engine, etc, in which part of the casing is omitted to reveal the workings **2b** (*as modifier*): *a cutaway model* **3** *films, television* a shot separate from the main action of a scene

cutback ('kʌtˌbæk) *n* **1** a decrease or reduction ▷ *vb* **cut back** (*adv*) **2** (*tr*) to shorten by cutting off the end

3 (when *intr*, foll by *on*) to reduce or make a reduction (in)
cut down *vb (adv)* 1 (*tr*) to fell 2 (when *intr*, often foll by *on*) to reduce or make a reduction (in) 3 (*tr*) to remake (an old garment) in order to make a smaller one 4 (*tr*) to kill 5 **cut (a person) down to size** to reduce in importance or decrease the conceit of (a person)
cute (kju:t) *adj* 1 appealing or attractive, esp in a pretty way 2 *inf* affecting cleverness or prettiness 3 clever; shrewd [C18 (in the sense: clever): shortened from ACUTE] > **'cutely** *adv* > **'cuteness** *n*
cut glass *n* 1a glass, esp bowls, vases, etc, decorated by facet-cutting or grinding 1b (*as modifier*): *a cut-glass vase* 2 (*modifier*) (of an accent) upper-class; refined
Cuthbert ('kʌθbət) *n* **Saint** ?635–87AD, English monk; bishop of Lindisfarne. Feast day: March 20
cuticle ('kju:tɪkᵊl) *n* 1 dead skin, esp round the base of a fingernail or toenail 2 another name for **epidermis** 3 the protective layer that covers the epidermis of higher plants 4 the protective layer covering the epidermis of many invertebrates [C17 from L *cutīcula* dim. of *cutis* skin] > **cuticular** (kju:'tɪkjʊlə) *adj*
cut in *vb (adv)* 1 (*intr*; often foll by *on*) Also: **cut into** to break in or interrupt 2 (*intr*) to interrupt a dancing couple to dance with one of them 3 (*intr*) (of a driver, motor vehicle, etc) to draw in front of another vehicle leaving too little space 4 (*tr*) *inf* to allow to have a share 5 (*intr*) to take the place of a person in a card game
cutis ('kju:tɪs) *n, pl* **cutes** (-ti:z) *or* **cutises** *anat* a technical name for the **skin** [C17 from L: skin]
cutlass ('kʌtləs) *n* a curved, one-edged sword formerly used by sailors [C16 from F *coutelas*, from *coutel* knife, ult. from L *culter* knife]
cutler ('kʌtlə) *n* a person who makes or sells cutlery [C14 from F *coutelier*, ult. from L *culter* knife]
cutlery ('kʌtlərɪ) *n* 1 implements used for eating, such as knives, forks, and spoons 2 instruments used for cutting 3 the art or business of a cutler
cutlet ('kʌtlɪt) *n* 1 a piece of meat taken esp from the best end of neck of lamb, pork, etc 2 a flat croquette of minced chicken, lobster, etc [C18 from OF *costelette*, lit.: a little rib, from *coste* rib, from L *costa*]
cut off *vb (tr, adv)* 1 to remove by cutting 2 to intercept or interrupt something, esp a telephone conversation 3 to discontinue the supply of 4 to bring to an end 5 to deprive of rights; disinherit: *cut off without a penny* 6 to sever or separate 7 to occupy a position so as to prevent or obstruct (a retreat or escape) ▷ *n* **cutoff** 8a the act of cutting off; limit or termination 8b (*as modifier*): *the cutoff point* 9 *chiefly US* a short cut 10 a device to terminate the flow of a fluid in a pipe or duct
cut-offs ('kʌtɒfs) *pl n* trousers that have been shortened to calf length or to make shorts
cut out *vb (adv)* 1 (*tr*) to delete or remove 2 (*tr*) to shape or form by cutting 3 (*tr*; *usually passive*) to suit or equip for: *you're not cut out for this job* 4 (*intr*) (of an engine, etc) to cease to operate suddenly 5 (*intr*) (of an electrical device) to switch off, usually automatically 6 (*tr*) *inf* to oust and supplant (a rival) 7 (*intr*) (of a person) to be excluded from a card game 8 (*tr*) *inf* to cease doing something, esp something undesirable (esp in **cut it out**) 9 (*tr*) *soccer* to intercept (a pass) 10 (*tr*) to separate (cattle) from a herd 11 (*intr*) *Austral* to end or finish: *the road cuts out at the creek* 12 **have one's work cut out** to have as much work as one can manage ▷ *n* **cutout** 13 something that has been or is intended to be cut out from something else 14 a device that switches off or interrupts an electric circuit, esp as a safety device 15 *Austral sl* the end of shearing
cut-price *or esp US* **cut-rate** *adj* 1 available at prices or rates below the standard price or rate 2 (*prenominal*) offering goods or services at prices below the standard price
cutpurse ('kʌt,pɜ:s) *n* an archaic word for **pickpocket**
cutter ('kʌtə) *n* 1 a person or thing that cuts, esp a person who cuts cloth for clothing 2 a sailing boat with its mast stepped further aft than that of a sloop 3 a ship's boat, powered by oars or sail, for carrying passengers or light cargo 4 a small lightly armed boat, as used in the enforcement of customs regulations
cut-throat ('kʌt,θrəʊt) *n* 1 a person who cuts throats; murderer 2 Also called: **cut-throat razor, straight razor** *Brit* a razor with a long blade that usually folds into the handle ▷ *adj* 3 bloodthirsty or murderous; cruel 4 fierce or relentless in competition: *cut-throat prices* 5 (of some games) played by three people: *cut-throat poker*
cutting ('kʌtɪŋ) *n* 1 a piece cut off from something 2 *horticulture* 2a a method of propagation in which a part of a plant is induced to form its own roots 2b a part separated for this purpose 3 Also called (esp US and Canad): **clipping** an article, photograph, etc, cut from a publication 4 the editing process of a film 5 an excavation in a piece of high land for a road, railway, etc 6 *Irish inf* sharp-wittedness: *there is no cutting in him* ▷ *adj* 7 designed for or adapted to cutting; sharp 8 keen; piercing 9 tending to hurt the feelings: *a cutting remark* > **'cuttingly** *adv*
cutting compound *n engineering* a mixture, such as oil, water, and soap, used for cooling drills and other cutting tools
cutting edge *n* 1 the leading position in any field; forefront: *on the cutting edge of space technology* ▷ *adj* **cutting-edge** 2 at the forefront of people or things in a field of activity; leading: *cutting-edge technology*
cuttlebone ('kʌtᵊl,bəʊn) *n* the internal calcareous shell of the cuttlefish, used as a mineral supplement to the diet of cagebirds and as a polishing agent [C16 OE *cudele* + BONE]
cuttlefish ('kʌtᵊl,fɪʃ) *n, pl* **cuttlefish** *or* **cuttlefishes** a cephalopod mollusc which occurs near the bottom of inshore waters and has a broad flattened body. Sometimes shortened to **cuttle**
cut up *vb (tr, adv)* 1 to cut into pieces 2 to inflict injuries on 3 (*usually passive*) *inf* to affect the feelings of deeply 4 *inf* to subject to severe criticism 5 *inf* (of a driver) to overtake or pull in front of (another driver) in a dangerous manner 6 **cut up rough** *Brit inf* to become angry or bad-tempered ▷ *n* **cut-up** 7 *inf, chiefly US* a joker or prankster
cutwater ('kʌt,wɔ:tə) *n* the forward part of the stem of a vessel, which cuts through the water
cutworm ('kʌt,wɜ:m) *n* the caterpillar of various noctuid moths, which is a pest of young crop plants in North America
cuvée (ku:'veɪ) *n* an individual batch or blend of wine [C19 from F, lit.: put in a cask, from *cuve* cask]
Cuxhaven ('kʊks,hɑ:vᵊn; *German* kʊks'ha:fən) *n* a port in NW Germany, at the mouth of the River Elbe. Pop: 55 250 (latest est)
Cuyp *or* **Kuyp** (kaɪp; *Dutch* kœip) *n* **Aelbert** ('a:lbert) 1620–91, Dutch painter of landscapes and animals
cuz (kʌz) *n inf* 1 Also: **cuzzie** NZ a term used by a Maori to refer to or address a family member 2 *Austral* a term used by an Aboriginal person to refer to or address a family member [shorted from COUSIN]
Cuzco (*Spanish* 'kuθko) *or* **Cusco** *n* a city in S central Peru: former capital of the Inca Empire, with extensive Inca remains; university (1692). Pop: 278 590 (1998 est)
CV *abbrev for* curriculum vitae
CVS *abbrev for* 1 chorionic villus sampling 2 *computing* concurrent versions system
Cwlth *abbrev for* Commonwealth
cwm (ku:m) *n* 1 (in Wales) a valley 2 *geol* another name for **cirque**
c.w.o. *or* **CWO** *abbrev for* cash with order
CWS *abbrev for* Cooperative Wholesale Society
cwt *abbrev for* hundredweight [c, from the L numeral C one hundred (*centum*)]

CWU (in Britain) *abbrev for* Communication Workers Union
-cy *suffix* **1** indicating state, quality, or condition: *plutocracy; lunacy* **2** rank or office: *captaincy* [via OF from L *-cia, -tia*, Gk *-kia, -tia*, abstract noun suffixes]
CYA *text messaging abbrev for* see you: as a farewell [c20]
cyan ('saɪæn, 'saɪən) *n* **1** a green-blue colour ▷ *adj* **2** of this colour [c19 from Gk *kuanos* dark blue]
cyanate ('saɪəˌneɪt) *n* any salt or ester of cyanic acid
cyanic (saɪ'ænɪk) *adj* **1** of or containing cyanogen **2** blue
cyanic acid *n* a colourless poisonous volatile liquid acid. Formula: HOCN
cyanide ('saɪəˌnaɪd) *or* **cyanid** ('saɪənɪd) *n* any salt of hydrocyanic acid. Cyanides are extremely poisonous > ˌ**cyani'dation** *n*
cyanite ('saɪəˌnaɪt) *n* a variant spelling of **kyanite** > **cyanitic** (ˌsaɪə'nɪtɪk) *adj*
cyano- *or before a vowel* **cyan-** *combining form* **1** blue or dark blue **2** indicating cyanogen **3** indicating cyanide [from Gk *kuanos* (adj) dark blue, (n) dark blue enamel, lapis lazuli]
cyanobacteria (ˌsaɪənəʊbæk'tɪərɪə) *pl n*, *sing* **cyanobacterium** (-rɪəm) a group of photosynthetic bacteria (phylum *Cyanobacteria*) containing a blue photosynthetic pigment. Former name: **blue-green algae**
cyanocobalamin (ˌsaɪənəʊkəʊ'bæləmɪn) *n* vitamin B_{12}, a complex crystalline compound of cobalt and cyanide, lack of which leads to pernicious anaemia [c20 from CYANO- + COBAL(T) + (VIT)AMIN]
cyanogen (saɪ'ænədʒɪn) *n* an extremely poisonous colourless flammable gas. Formula: $(CN)_2$ [c19 from F *cyanogène*; see CYANO-, -GEN; so named because it is one of the constituents of Prussian blue]
cyanosis (ˌsaɪə'nəʊsɪs) *n pathol* a bluish-purple discoloration of skin and mucous membranes usually resulting from a deficiency of oxygen in the blood > **cyanotic** (ˌsaɪə'nɒtɪk) *adj*
Cybele ('sɪbɪlɪ) *n classical myth* the Phrygian goddess of nature, mother of all living things and consort of Attis; identified with the Greek Rhea or Demeter
cyber- *combining form* indicating computers: *cyberphobia* [c20 back formation from CYBERNETICS]
cybercafé ('saɪbəˌkæfɪ, -ˌkæfeɪ) *n* a café with computer equipment that gives public access to the Internet
cybercrime ('saɪbəˌkraɪm) *n* **1** the illegal use of computers and the Internet **2** crime committed by means of computers or the Internet > ˌ**cyber'criminal** *n*
cybernate ('saɪbəˌneɪt) *vb* **cybernates, cybernating, cybernated** to control with a servomechanism or to be controlled by a servomechanism [c20 from CYBER(NETICS) + -ATE[1]] > ˌ**cyber'nation** *n*
cybernetics (ˌsaɪbə'nɛtɪks) *n (functioning as sing)* the branch of science concerned with control systems and comparisons between man-made and biological systems [c20 from Gk *kubernētēs* steersman, from *kubernan* to steer] > ˌ**cyber'netic** *adj* > ˌ**cyber'neticist** *n*
cyberpet ('saɪbəˌpɛt) *n* an electronic toy that simulates the activities of a pet, requiring the owner to feed, discipline, and entertain it
cyberphobia (ˌsaɪbə'fəʊbɪə) *n* an irrational fear of computing > ˌ**cyber'phobic** *adj*
cyberpunk ('saɪbəˌpʌŋk) *n* **1** a genre of science fiction that features rebellious computer hackers and is set in a society integrated by computer networks **2** a writer of cyberpunk
cybersecurity (ˌsaɪbəsɪ'kjʊərɪtɪ) *n computing* the state of being safe from electronic crime and the measures taken to achieve this
cybersex ('saɪbəˌsɛks) *n* **1** the exchanging of sexual messages or information via the Internet **2** sexual activity performed in hyperspace by means of virtual reality equipment
cyberspace ('saɪbəˌspeɪs) *n* all of the data stored in a large computer or network represented as a three-dimensional model through which a virtual-reality user can move
cybersquatting ('saɪbəˌskwɒtɪŋ) *n* the practice of registering an Internet domain name that is likely to be wanted by another person, business, or organization in the hope that it can be sold to them for a profit > '**cyber,squatter** *n*
cyberterrorism ('saɪbəˌtɛrərɪzəm) *n* the illegal use of computers and the Internet to achieve some political goal > '**cyber,terrorist** *n*
cycad ('saɪkæd) *n* a tropical or subtropical plant, having an unbranched stem with fernlike leaves crowded at the top [c19 from NL *Cycas* name of genus, from Gk *kukas*, scribe's error for *koïkas*, from *koïx* a kind of palm] > ˌ**cyca'daceous** *adj*
Cyclades ('sɪkləˌdiːz) *pl n* a group of over 200 islands in the S Aegean Sea, forming a department of Greece. Capital: Hermoupolis (Siros). Pop: 94 005 (1991). Area: 2572 sq km (993 sq miles). Modern Greek name: **Kikládhes**
Cycladic (sɪ'klædɪk) *adj* of or relating to the Cyclades or their inhabitants
cyclamate ('saɪkləˌmeɪt, 'sɪkləmeɪt) *n* any of certain compounds formerly used as food additives and sugar substitutes [c20 *cycl(ohexyl-sulph)amate*]
cyclamen ('sɪkləmən, -ˌmɛn) *n* **1** any Old World plant of the genus *Cyclamen*, having white, pink, or red flowers, with reflexed petals ▷ *adj* **2** of a dark reddish-purple colour [c16 from Med. L, from L *cyclamīnos*, from Gk *kuklaminos*, prob. from *kuklos* circle, referring to the bulblike roots]
cycle ('saɪk^{ə}l) *n* **1** a recurring period of time in which certain events or phenomena occur and reach completion **2** a completed series of events that follows or is followed by another series of similar events occurring in the same sequence **3** the time taken or needed for one such series **4** a vast period of time; age; aeon **5** a group of poems or prose narratives about a central figure or event: *the Arthurian cycle* **6** short for **bicycle, motorcycle,** etc **7** a recurrent series of events or processes in plants and animals: *a life cycle* **8** one of a series of repeated changes in the magnitude of a periodically varying quantity, such as current or voltage ▷ *vb* **cycles, cycling, cycled 9** *(tr)* to process through a cycle or system **10** *(intr)* to move in or pass through cycles **11** to travel by or ride a bicycle or tricycle [c14 from LL *cyclus*, from Gk *kuklos* cycle, circle, ring, wheel]
▷ www.uci.ch
▷ www.usacycling.org
cyclic ('saɪklɪk, 'sɪklɪk) *or* **cyclical** *adj* **1** recurring or revolving in cycles **2** (of an organic compound) containing a closed saturated or unsaturated ring of atoms **3** *bot* **3a** arranged in whorls: *cyclic petals* **3b** having parts arranged in this way: *cyclic flowers* > '**cyclically** *adv*
cycling shorts *pl n* tight-fitting shorts reaching partway to the knee for cycling, sport, etc
cyclist ('saɪklɪst) *or US* **cycler** *n* a person who rides or travels by bicycle, motorcycle, etc
cyclo- *or before a vowel* **cycl-** *combining form* **1** indicating a circle or ring: *cyclotron* **2** denoting a cyclic compound: *cyclopropane* [from Gk *kuklos* CYCLE]
cyclogiro ('saɪkləʊˌdʒaɪrəʊ) *n, pl* **cyclogiros** *aeronautics* an aircraft lifted and propelled by pivoted blades rotating parallel to roughly horizontal transverse axes
cyclohexanone (ˌsaɪkləʊ'hɛksəˌnəʊn) *n* a colourless liquid used as a solvent for cellulose lacquers. Formula: $C_6H_{10}O$
cycloid ('saɪklɔɪd) *adj* **1** resembling a circle ▷ *n* **2** *geom* the curve described by a point on the circumference of a circle as the circle rolls along a straight line

Cc

cyclometer (saɪˈklɒmɪtə) *n* a device that records the number of revolutions made by a wheel and hence the distance travelled

cyclone (ˈsaɪkləʊn) *n* **1** *meteorol* another name for **depression** (sense 6) **2** a violent tropical storm; hurricane ▷ *adj* **3** *Austral & NZ trademark* (of fencing) made of interlaced wire and metal [c19 from Gk *kuklōn* a turning around, from *kuklos* wheel] > **cyclonic** (saɪˈklɒnɪk) *adj* > **cyˈclonically** *adv*

Cyclopean (ˌsaɪkləʊˈpiːən, saɪˈkləʊpɪən) *adj* **1** of, relating to, or resembling the Cyclops **2** denoting or having the kind of masonry used in preclassical Greek architecture, characterized by large undressed blocks of stone

cyclopedia *or* **cyclopaedia** (ˌsaɪkləʊˈpiːdɪə) *n* a less common word for **encyclopedia**

cyclopentadiene (ˌsaɪkləʊˌpɛntəˈdaɪiːn) *n* a colourless liquid unsaturated cyclic hydrocarbon obtained in the cracking of petroleum hydrocarbons and the distillation of coal tar: used in the manufacture of plastics and insecticides. Formula: C_5H_6

cyclophosphamide (ˌsaɪkləʊˈfɒsfəˌmaɪd) *n* a cytotoxic drug used in the treatment of leukaemia and lymphoma [c20 from CYCLO- + PHOSPH(ORUS) + AMIDE]

cyclopropane (ˌsaɪkləʊˈprəʊpeɪn) *n* a colourless gaseous hydrocarbon, used in medicine as an anaesthetic. Formula: C_3H_6

Cyclops (ˈsaɪklɒps) *n, pl* **Cyclopes** (saɪˈkləʊpiːz) *or* **Cyclopses** *classical myth* one of a race of giants having a single eye in the middle of the forehead [c15 from L *Cyclōps*, from Gk *Kuklōps*, lit.: round eye, from *kuklos* circle + *ōps* eye]

cyclorama (ˌsaɪkləʊˈrɑːmə) *n* **1** a large picture on the interior wall of a cylindrical room, designed to appear in natural perspective to a spectator **2** *theatre* a curtain or wall curving along the back of a stage, usually painted to represent the sky [c19 CYCLO- + Gk *horama* view, sight, on the model of *panorama*] > **cycloramic** (ˌsaɪkləʊˈræmɪk) *adj*

cyclostome (ˈsaɪkləˌstəʊm, ˈsɪk-) *n* any primitive aquatic jawless vertebrate, such as the lamprey, having a round sucking mouth > **cyclostomate** (saɪˈklɒstəmɪt, -ˌmeɪt) *or* **cyclostomatous** (ˌsaɪkləʊˈstɒmətəs, -ˈstəʊmə-, ˌsɪk-) *adj*

cyclostyle (ˈsaɪkləˌstaɪl) *n* **1** a kind of pen with a small toothed wheel, used for cutting holes in a specially prepared stencil **2** an office duplicator using such a stencil ▷ *vb* **cyclostyles, cyclostyling, cyclostyled** **3** (*tr*) to print using such a stencil > **ˈcycloˌstyled** *adj*

cyclothymia (ˌsaɪkləʊˈθaɪmɪə) *n* *psychiatry* a condition characterized by alternating periods of excitement and depression [from CYCLO- + Gk *thumos*, cast of mind + -IA] > **ˌcycloˈthymic** *adj*

cyclotron (ˈsaɪkləˌtrɒn) *n* a type of particle accelerator in which the particles spiral under the effect of a strong vertical magnetic field

cyder (ˈsaɪdə) *n* a variant spelling of **cider**

cygnet (ˈsɪɡnɪt) *n* a young swan [c15 *sygnett*, from OF *cygne* swan, from L *cygnus*, from Gk *kuknos*]

cylinder (ˈsɪlɪndə) *n* **1** a solid consisting of two parallel planes bounded by identical closed curves, usually circles, that are interconnected at every point by a set of parallel lines, usually perpendicular to the planes **2** a surface formed by a line moving round a closed plane curve at a fixed angle to it **3** any object shaped like a cylinder **4** the chamber in a reciprocating internal-combustion engine, pump, or compressor within which the piston moves. The cylinders are housed in the metal **cylinder block**, which is topped by the **cylinder head** **5** the rotating mechanism of a revolver, containing cartridge chambers **6** *printing* any of the rotating drums on a printing press **7** Also called: **cylinder seal** an ancient cylindrical seal found in the Middle East and Balkans [c16 from L *cylindrus*, from Gk *kulindros* a roller, from *kulindein* to roll] > **ˈcylinder-ˌlike** *adj*

cylindrical (sɪˈlɪndrɪkᵊl) *or* **cylindric** *adj* of, shaped like, or characteristic of a cylinder > **cyˌlindriˈcality** *n* > **cyˈlindrically** *adv*

cymbal (ˈsɪmbᵊl) *n* a percussion instrument consisting of a thin circular piece of brass, which vibrates when clashed together with another cymbal or struck with a stick [OE *cymbala*, from L *cymbalum*, from Gk *kumbalon*, from *kumbē* something hollow] > **ˈcymbalist** *n*

Cymbeline (ˈsɪmbəliːn) *n* See **Cunobelinus**

cyme (saɪm) *n* an inflorescence in which the first flower is the terminal bud of the main stem and subsequent flowers develop as terminal buds of lateral stems [c18 from L *cȳma* cabbage sprout, from Gk *kuma* anything swollen] > **cymiferous** (saɪˈmɪfərəs) *adj* > **cymose** (ˈsaɪməʊs, -məʊz, saɪˈməʊs) *adj*

Cymric *or* **Kymric** (ˈkɪmrɪk) *n* **1** the Welsh language **2** the Brythonic group of Celtic languages ▷ *adj* **3** of or relating to the Cymry, any of their languages, Wales, or the Welsh

Cymru (*Welsh* kumˈri) *n* the Welsh name for **Wales**

Cymry *or* **Kymry** (ˈkɪmrɪ) *n* **the** (*functioning as pl*) **1** the Brythonic Celts, comprising the present-day Welsh, Cornish, and Bretons **2** the Welsh people [Welsh: the Welsh]

Cynewulf, Kynewulf (ˈkɪnɪˌwʊlf), *or* **Cynwulf** (ˈkɪnˌwʊlf) *n* ?8th century AD, Anglo-Saxon poet; author of *Juliana, The Ascension, Elene*, and *The Fates of the Apostles*

cynic (ˈsɪnɪk) *n* **1** a person who believes the worst about people or the outcome of events ▷ *adj* **2** a less common word for **cynical** [c16 via L from Gk *Kunikos*, from *kuōn* dog]

Cynic (ˈsɪnɪk) *n* a member of an ancient Greek sect that scorned worldly things

cynical (ˈsɪnɪkᵊl) *adj* **1** believing the worst of others, esp that all acts are selfish **2** sarcastic; mocking **3** showing contempt for accepted standards, esp of honesty or morality > **ˈcynically** *adv* > **ˈcynicalness** *n*

cynicism (ˈsɪnɪˌsɪzəm) *n* **1** the attitude or beliefs of a cynic **2** a cynical action, idea, etc

Cynicism (ˈsɪnɪˌsɪzəm) *n* the doctrines of the Cynics

cynosure (ˈsɪnəˌzjʊə, -ʃʊə) *n* **1** a person or thing that attracts notice **2** something that serves as a guide [c16 from L *Cynosūra* the constellation of Ursa Minor, from Gk *Kunosoura*, from *kuōn* dog + *oura* tail]

Cynthia (ˈsɪnθɪə) *n* another name for **Artemis** (Diana)

cypher (ˈsaɪfə) *n, vb* a variant spelling of **cipher**

cypress (ˈsaɪprəs) *n* **1** any coniferous tree of a N temperate genus having dark green scalelike leaves and rounded cones **2** any of several similar and related trees **3** the wood of any of these trees **4** cypress branches used as a symbol of mourning [OE *cypresse*, from L *cyparissus*, from Gk *kuparissos*; rel. to L *cupressus*]

cypress pine *n* any coniferous tree of an Australian genus yielding valuable timber

Cyprian[1] (ˈsɪprɪən) *adj* **1** of or relating to Cyprus **2** of or resembling the ancient orgiastic worship of Aphrodite on Cyprus ▷ *n* **3** (*often not cap*) *obs* a licentious person, esp a prostitute or dancer ▷ *n, adj* **4** another word for **Cypriot**

Cyprian[2] (ˈsɪprɪən) *n* **Saint** ?200–258 AD, bishop of Carthage and martyr. Feast day: Sept 26 or 16

cyprinid (sɪˈpraɪnɪd, ˈsɪprɪnɪd) *n* **1** any teleost fish of the mainly freshwater family Cyprinidae, typically having toothless jaws and including the carp, tench, and dace ▷ *adj* **2** of, relating to, or belonging to the Cyprinidae **3** resembling a carp; cyprinoid [c19 from NL *Cyprīnidae*, from L *cyprīnus* carp, from Gk *kuprinos*]

cyprinoid (ˈsɪprɪˌnɔɪd, sɪˈpraɪnɔɪd) *adj* **1** of or relating to the Cyprinoidea, a large suborder of teleost fishes including the cyprinids, electric eels, and loaches **2** of, relating to, or resembling the carp ▷ *n* **3** any fish belonging to the Cyprinoidea [c19 from L *cyprīnus* carp]

Cypriot (ˈsɪprɪət) *or* **Cypriote** (ˈsɪprɪˌəʊt) *n* **1** a native or inhabitant of Cyprus **2** the dialect of Greek spoken in Cyprus ▷ *adj* **3** denoting or relating to Cyprus, its inhabitants, or dialects

cypripedium (ˌsɪprɪˈpiːdɪəm) *n* any orchid of a genus having large flowers with an inflated pouchlike lip. See also **lady's-slipper** [c18 from NL, from L *Cypria* the Cyprian, that is, Venus + *pēs* foot (that is, Venus' slipper)]

Cyprus (ˈsaɪprəs) *n* an island in the E Mediterranean: ceded to Britain by Turkey in 1878 and made a colony in 1925; became an independent republic in 1960 as a member of the Commonwealth; invaded by Turkey in 1974 following a Greek-supported military coup, leading to the virtual partition of the island. In 1983 the Turkish-controlled northern sector declared itself to be an independent state as the Turkish Republic of Northern Cyprus but failed to receive international recognition. Attempts by the U.N. to broker a reunification agreement have failed. Cyprus joined the EU in 2004. Languages: Greek and Turkish. Religions: Greek Orthodox and Muslim. Currency: pound and Turkish lira. Capital: Nicosia. Pop (Greek): 675 000 (2001 est); (Turkish): 198 000 (2001 est). Area: 9251 sq km (3571 sq miles)
▷ www.pio.gov.cy
▷ www.cyprustourism.org

Cyrano de Bergerac (*French* sirano də bɛrʒərak) *n* **Savinien** (savinjɛ̃) 1619–55, French writer and soldier, famous as a duellist and for his large nose. He became widely known through the verse drama *Cyrano de Bergerac* (1897) by Edmond Rostand

Cyrenaic (ˌsaɪrəˈneɪɪk, ˌsɪrə-) *adj* **1** of or relating to the ancient Greek city of Cyrene **2** of or relating to the philosophical school founded by Aristippus in Cyrene that held pleasure to be the highest good ▷ *n* **3** a follower of the Cyrenaica school of philosophy

Cyrene (saɪˈriːnɪ) *n* an ancient Greek city of N Africa, near the coast of Cyrenaica: famous for its medical school

Cyril (ˈsɪrəl) *n* **Saint** ?827–869 AD, Greek Christian theologian, missionary to the Moravians and inventor of the Cyrillic alphabet; he and his brother Saint Methodius were called *the Apostles of the Slavs*. Feast day: Feb 14 or May 11

Cyrillic (sɪˈrɪlɪk) *adj* **1** denoting or relating to the alphabet said to have been devised by Saint Cyril, for Slavonic languages: now used primarily for Russian and Bulgarian ▷ *n* **2** this alphabet

Cyril of Alexandria *n* **Saint** ?375–444 AD, Christian theologian and patriarch of Alexandria. Feast day: June 27 or June 9

Cyrus (ˈsaɪrəs) *n* **1** known as *Cyrus the Great* or *Cyrus the Elder*. died ?529 BC, king of Persia and founder of the Persian empire **2** called *the Younger*. died 401 BC, Persian satrap of Lydia: revolted against his brother Artaxerxes II, but was killed at the battle of Cunaxa. See also **anabasis, katabasis**

cyst (sɪst) *n* **1** *pathol* any abnormal membranous sac or blister-like pouch containing fluid or semisolid material **2** *anat* any normal sac in the body **3** a protective membrane enclosing a cell, larva, or organism [c18 from NL *cystis*, from Gk *kustis* pouch, bag, bladder]

-cyst *n combining form* indicating a bladder or sac: *otocyst* [from Gk *kustis* bladder]

cystectomy (sɪˈstɛktəmɪ) *n, pl* **cystectomies** **1** surgical removal of the gall bladder or part of the urinary bladder **2** surgical removal of a cyst

cystic (ˈsɪstɪk) *adj* **1** of, relating to, or resembling a cyst **2** having or enclosed within a cyst; encysted **3** relating to the gall bladder or urinary bladder

cysticercus (ˌsɪstɪˈsɜːkəs) *n, pl* **cysticerci** (-saɪ) an encysted larval form of many tapeworms, consisting of a head inverted in a fluid-filled bladder [c19 from NL, from Gk *kustis* pouch, bladder + *kerkos* tail]

cystic fibrosis *n* an inheritable disease of the exocrine glands, controlled by a recessive gene: affected children inherit defective alleles from both parents. It is characterized by chronic infection of the respiratory tract and by pancreatic insufficiency

cystitis (sɪˈstaɪtɪs) *n* inflammation of the urinary bladder

cysto- *or before a vowel* **cyst-** *combining form* indicating a cyst or bladder: *cystoscope*

cystoid (ˈsɪstɔɪd) *adj* **1** resembling a cyst or bladder ▷ *n* **2** a tissue mass that resembles a cyst but lacks an outer membrane

cystoscope (ˈsɪstəˌskəʊp) *n* a slender tubular medical instrument for examining the interior of the urethra and urinary bladder > **cystoscopic** (ˌsɪstəˈskɒpɪk) *adj* > **cystoscopy** (sɪsˈtɒskəpɪ) *n*

-cyte *n combining form* indicating a cell [from NL *-cyta*, from Gk *kutos* vessel]

Cythera (sɪˈθɪərə) *n* **1** a Greek island off the SE coast of the Peloponnese: in ancient times a centre of the worship of Aphrodite. Pop: 3500 (latest est). Area: about 285 sq km (110 sq miles) **2** the chief town of this island, on the S coast. Pop: 300 (latest est) ▷ Modern Greek name **Kíthira**

Cytherea (ˌsɪθəˈriːə) *n* another name for **Aphrodite** (Venus) > ˌ**Cytherˈean** *adj*

cyto- *combining form* indicating a cell: *cytoplasm* [from Gk *kutos* vessel]

cytogenetics (ˌsaɪtəʊdʒɪˈnɛtɪks) *n* (*functioning as sing*) the branch of genetics that correlates the structure, number, and behaviour of chromosomes with heredity and variation > ˌ**cytogeˈnetic** *adj*

cytokine (ˈsaɪtəʊˌkaɪn) *n* any of various proteins, secreted by cells, that carry signals to neighbouring cells. Cytokines include interferon

cytokinin (ˌsaɪtəʊˈkaɪnɪn) *n* any of a group of plant hormones that promote cell division and retard ageing. Also called: **kinin**

cytology (saɪˈtɒlədʒɪ) *n* **1** the study of plant and animal cells **2** the detailed structure of a tissue as revealed by microscopic examination > **cytological** (ˌsaɪtəˈlɒdʒɪkəl) *adj* > ˌ**cytoˈlogically** *adv* > **cyˈtologist** *n*

cytomegalovirus (ˌsaɪtəʊˌmɛɡələʊˈvaɪrəs) *n* a virus of the herpes virus that may cause serious disease in patients whose immune systems are compromised. Abbrev: **CMV**

cytoplasm (ˈsaɪtəʊˌplæzəm) *n* the protoplasm of a cell excluding the nucleus > ˌ**cytoˈplasmic** *adj*

cytosine (ˈsaɪtəsɪn) *n* a white crystalline base occurring in nucleic acids [c19 from CYTO- + -OSE[2] + -INE[2]]

cytotoxic (ˌsaɪtəʊˈtɒksɪk) *adj* destructive to cells, esp to cancer cells: *cytotoxic drugs* > **cytotoxicity** (ˌsaɪtəʊtɒkˈsɪsɪtɪ) *n*

cytotoxin (ˌsaɪtəʊˈtɒksɪn) *n* any substance that is poisonous to living cells

Cyzicus (ˈsɪzɪkəs) *n* an ancient Greek colony in NW Asia Minor on the S shore of the Sea of Marmara: site of Alcibiades' naval victory over the Peloponnesians (410 BC)

czar (zɑː) *n* a variant spelling (esp US) of **tsar** > ˈ**czardom** *n* > ˈ**Czarevitch, czaˈrevna, czaˈrina, ˈczarism, ˈczarist**: see **ts-** spellings

czardas (ˈtʃɑːdæʃ) *n* **1** a Hungarian national dance of alternating slow and fast sections **2** music for this dance [from Hungarian *csárdás*]

Czech (tʃɛk) *adj* **1a** of, relating to, or characteristic of the Czech Republic, its people, or their language **1b** of, relating to, or characteristic of Bohemia and Moravia, their people, or their language **1c** (loosely) of, relating to, or characteristic of the former Czechoslovakia or its

Cc

people ▷ *n* **2** the official languages of the Czech Republic, belonging to the West Slavonic branch of the Indo-European family. Czech is closely related to Slovak; they are mutually intelligible **3a** a native or inhabitant of the Czech Republic **3b** a native or inhabitant of Bohemia or Moravia **3c** (loosely) a native, inhabitant, or citizen of the former Czechoslovakia [C19 from Polish, from Czech *Čech*]

Czechoslovak (ˌtʃɛkəʊˈsləʊvæk) *or* **Czechoslovakian** (ˌtʃɛkəʊsləʊˈvækɪən) *adj* **1** of or relating to the former Czechoslovakia, its peoples, or languages ▷ *n* **2** (loosely) either of the two languages of the former Czechoslovakia: Czech or Slovak

Czechoslovakia (ˌtʃɛkəʊsləʊˈvækɪə) *n* a former republic in central Europe: formed after the defeat of Austria-Hungary (1918) as a nation of Czechs in Bohemia and Moravia and Slovaks in Slovakia; occupied by Germany from 1939 until its liberation by the Soviet Union in 1945; became a people's republic under the Communists in 1948; invaded by Warsaw Pact troops in 1968, ending Dubček's attempt to liberalize communism; in 1989 popular unrest led to the resignation of the politburo and the formation of a non-Communist government. It consisted of two federal republics, the **Czech Republic** and the **Slovak Republic**, which became independent in 1993. Czech name: **Československo**

Czechoslovakian (ˌtʃɛkəʊsləʊˈvækɪən) *adj* **1** of, relating to, or characteristic of the former republic of Czechoslovakia, its peoples, or their languages ▷ *n* **2** a native or inhabitant of the former republic of Czechoslovakia

Czech Republic *n* a country in central Europe; formed part of Czechoslovakia until 1993; mostly wooded, with lowlands surrounding the River Morava, rising to the Bohemian plateau in the W and to highlands in the N; joined the EU in 2004. Language: Czech. Religion: Christian majority. Currency: koruna. Capital Prague. Pop: 10 269 000 (2001 est). Area: 78 864 sq km (30 450 sq miles)

▷ http://wtd.vlada.cz/eng/aktuality.htm
▷ www.czech.cz
▷ www.visitczech.cz

Czernowitz (ˈtʃɛrnovɪts) *n* the German name for **Chernovtsy**

Czerny (*German* ˈtʃɛrni) *n* **Karl** (karl) 1791–1857, Austrian pianist, composer, and teacher, noted for his studies

Częstochowa (*Polish* tʃɛ̃stɔˈxɔva) *n* an industrial city in S Poland, on the River Warta: pilgrimage centre. Pop: 259 800 (1995 est).

d *or* **D** (diː) *n, pl* **d's, D's,** *or* **Ds** 1 the fourth letter of the modern English alphabet 2 a speech sound represented by this letter

d *symbol for physics* density

D *symbol for:* 1 *music* 1a the second note of the scale of C major 1b the major or minor key having this note as its tonic 2 *chem* deuterium 3a a semiskilled or unskilled manual worker, or a trainee or apprentice to a skilled worker 3b (*as modifier*): *D worker* ▷ See also **occupation groupings** ▷ 4 *the Roman numeral for* 500

2,4-D *n* a synthetic auxin widely used as a weedkiller; 2,4-dichlorophenoxyacetic acid

d. *abbrev for:* 1 daughter 2 *Brit currency before decimalization* penny *or* pennies [L *denarius* or *denarii*] 3 diameter 4 died 5 dose

D. *abbrev for:* 1 US Democrat(ic) 2 Department 3 Dutch

'd *contraction for* would *or* had: *I'd; you'd*

DA *abbrev for:* 1 (in the US) District Attorney 2 Diploma of Art 3 duck's arse (hairstyle) 4 drug addict

dab[1] (dæb) *vb* **dabs, dabbing, dabbed** 1 to touch or pat lightly and quickly 2 (*tr*) to daub with short tapping strokes: *to dab the wall with paint* 3 (*tr*) to apply (paint, cream, etc) with short tapping strokes ▷ *n* 4 a small amount, esp of something soft or moist 5 a light stroke or tap, as with the hand 6 (*often pl*) *chiefly Brit* a slang word for **fingerprint** [c14 imit.] > **'dabber** *n*

dab[2] (dæb) *n* 1 a small common European flatfish covered with rough toothed scales 2 any of various other small flatfish [c15 from Anglo-F *dabbe*, from ?]

DAB *abbrev for* digital audio broadcasting
▷ www.worlddab.org

dabble ('dæbᵊl) *vb* **dabbles, dabbling, dabbled** 1 to dip, move, or splash (the fingers, feet, etc) in a liquid 2 (*intr; usually foll by in, with, or at*) to deal (with) or work (at) frivolously or superficially 3 (*tr*) to splash or smear [c16 prob. from Du. *dabbelen*] > **'dabbler** *n*

dabchick ('dæbˌtʃɪk) *n* any of several small grebes [c16 prob. from OE *dop* to dive + CHICK]

dab hand *n Brit inf* a person who is particularly skilled at something: *a dab hand at chess* [?from DAB[1]]

da capo (dɑː 'kɑːpəʊ) *adj, adv music* to be repeated from the beginning [c18 from It., lit.: from the head]

Dacca ('dækə) *n* the former name (until 1982) of **Dhaka**

dace (deɪs) *n, pl* **dace** *or* **daces** 1 a European freshwater fish of the carp family 2 any of various similar fishes [c15 from OF *dars* DART]

dacha *or* **datcha** ('dætʃə) *n* a country house or cottage in Russia [from Russian: a giving, gift]

Dachau (*German* 'daxau) *n* a town in S Germany, in Bavaria: site of a Nazi concentration camp. Pop: 33 200 (latest est)

dachshund ('dæksˌhʊnd, 'dæʃənd) *n* a long-bodied short-legged breed of dog [c19 from G, from *Dachs* badger + *Hund* dog]

Dacia ('deɪsɪə) *n* an ancient region bounded by the Carpathians, the Tisza, and the Danube, roughly corresponding to modern Romania. United under kings from about 60 BC, it later contained the Roman province of the same name (about 105 to 270 AD) > **'Dacian** *adj, n*

dacks (dæks) *pl n Austral* another word for **daks**

dacoit (də'kɔɪt) *n* (in India and Myanmar) a member of a gang of armed robbers [c19 from Hindi *dakait*, from *dākā* robbery]

Dacron ('deɪkrɒn, 'dæk-) *n* the US name (trademark) for **Terylene**

dactyl ('dæktɪl) *n prosody* a metrical foot of three syllables, one long followed by two short (–⏑⏑) [c14 via L from Gk *daktulos* finger, comparing the finger's three joints to the three syllables]

dactylic (dæk'tɪlɪk) *adj* 1 of, relating to, or having a dactyl: *dactylic verse* ▷ *n* **2** a variant of **dactyl** > **dac'tylically** *adv*

dad (dæd) *n* an informal word for **father** [C16 childish word]

Dada ('dɑ:dɑ:) *or* **Dadaism** ('dɑ:dɑ:ˌɪzəm) *n* a nihilistic artistic movement of the early 20th century, founded on principles of irrationality, incongruity, and irreverence towards accepted aesthetic criteria [C20 from F, from children's word for hobbyhorse] > **'Dadaist** *n, adj* > **ˌDada'istic** *adj*

▷ www.peak.org/~dadaist/English/Graphics

daddy ('dædɪ) *n, pl* **daddies 1** an informal word for **father 2 the daddy** *sl, chiefly US, Canad, & Austral* the supreme or finest example

daddy-longlegs *n* **1** *Brit, Austral, & NZ* an informal name for **crane fly 2** *US, Canad, Austral, & NZ* an informal name for **harvestman** (sense 2)

dado ('deɪdəʊ) *n, pl* **dadoes** *or* **dados 1** the lower part of an interior wall that is decorated differently from the upper part **2** *archit* the part of a pedestal between the base and the cornice ▷ *vb* **3** (*tr*) to provide with a dado [C17 from It.: die, die-shaped pedestal]

Dadra and Nagar Haveli (də'drɑ: 'nʌgə ə'vɛlɪ) *n* a union territory of W India, on the Gulf of Cambay: until 1961 administratively part of Portuguese Damão. Capital: Silvassa. Pop: 220 451 (2001). Area: 489 sq km (191 sq miles)

Daedalus ('di:dələs) *n Greek myth* an Athenian architect and inventor who built the labyrinth for Minos on Crete and fashioned wings for himself and his son Icarus to flee their imprisonment on the island > **Daedalian, Daedalean** (dɪ'deɪlɪən), *or* **Daedalic** (dɪ'dælɪk) *adj*

daemon ('di:mən) *or* **daimon** *n* **1** a demigod **2** the guardian spirit of a place or person **3** a variant spelling of **demon** (sense 3) > **daemonic** (di:'mɒnɪk) *adj*

daff (dæf) *n inf* short for **daffodil**

daffodil ('dæfədɪl) *n* **1** Also called: **Lent lily** a widely cultivated Eurasian plant, *Narcissus pseudonarcissus*, having spring-blooming yellow nodding flowers **2** any other plant of the genus *Narcissus* **3a** a brilliant yellow colour **3b** (*as adj*): *daffodil paint* **4** a daffodil as a national emblem of Wales [C14 from Med. L *affodillus*, var. of L *asphodelus* ASPHODEL]

daffy ('dæfɪ) *adj* **daffier, daffiest** *inf* another word for **daft** (senses 1, 2) [C19 from obs. *daff* fool]

daft (dɑ:ft) *adj chiefly Brit* **1** *inf* foolish, simple, or stupid **2** a slang word for **insane 3** (*postpositive; foll by about*) *inf* extremely fond (of) **4** *sl* frivolous; giddy [OE *gedæfte* gentle, foolish] > **'daftness** *n*

daftie ('dɑ:ftɪ) *n inf* a daft person

Dafydd ap Gruffudd (*Welsh* 'dævɪθ æp 'grɪfɪθ) *n* died 1283, Welsh leader. Claiming the title Prince of Wales (1282), he led an unsuccessful revolt against Edward I: executed

Dafydd ap Gwilym (*Welsh* 'dævɪθ æp 'gwɪlɪm) *n* ?1320–?1380, Welsh poet

dag¹ (dæg) *n* **1** short for **daglock** ▷ *vb* **dags, dagging, dagged 2** to cut the daglock away from (a sheep) [C18 from ?] > **'dagger** *n*

dag² (dæg) *n Austral & NZ inf* **1** a character; eccentric **2** a person who is untidily dressed **3** a person with a good sense of humour **4 rattle one's dags** to hurry up [back formation from DAGGY]

Da Gama (də 'gɑ:mə) *n* See (Vasco da) **Gama**

Dagan ('dɑ:gən) *n* an earth god of the Babylonians and Assyrians

Dagenham ('dægənəm) *n* part of the Greater London borough of Barking and Dagenham: engineering and chemicals

Dagestan Republic (ˌdɑ:gɪ'stɑ:n) *n* a constituent republic of S Russia, on the Caspian Sea: annexed from Persia in 1813; rich mineral resources. Capital: Makhachkala. Pop: 2 149 000 (2000 est). Area: 50 278 sq km (19 416 sq miles). Also called: **Dagestan** *or* **Daghestan**

dagga ('daxə, 'dɑ:gə) *n S African inf* a local name for marijuana [C19 from Afrik., from Khoikhoi *dagab*]

dagger ('dægə) *n* **1** a short stabbing weapon with a pointed blade **2** Also called: **obelisk** a character (†) used in printing to indicate a cross reference **3 at daggers drawn** in a state of open hostility **4 look daggers** to glare with hostility; scowl [C14 from ?]

daggy ('dægɪ) *adj* **daggier, daggiest** *Austral and NZ inf* **1** untidy; dishevelled **2** eccentric [from DAG¹]

daglock ('dæg,lɒk) *n* a dung-caked lock of wool around the hindquarters of a sheep [C17 see DAG¹, LOCK²]

dago ('deɪgəʊ) *n, pl* **dagos** *or* **dagoes** *derog* a foreigner, esp a Spaniard or Portuguese [C19 from *Diego*, a common Sp. name]

Dagon ('deɪgɒn) *n Bible* a god worshipped by the Philistines, represented as half man and half fish [C14 via L and Gk from Heb. *Dāgōn*, lit.: little fish]

Daguerre (*French* dagɛr) *n* **Louis Jacques Mandé** (lwi ʒɑk mɑ̃de) 1789–1851, French inventor, who devised one of the first practical photographic processes (1838)

daguerreotype (də'gɛrəʊ,taɪp) *n* **1** one of the earliest photographic processes, in which the image was produced on iodine-sensitized silver and developed in mercury vapour **2** a photograph formed by this process > **da'guerreo,typy** *n*

Dahl (dɑ:l) *n* **Roald** ('rəʊəld) 1916–90, British writer with Norwegian parents, noted for his short stories and such children's books as *Charlie and the Chocolate Factory* (1964)

dahlia ('deɪljə) *n* **1** any herbaceous perennial plant of the Mexican genus *Dahlia*, having showy flowers and tuberous roots **2** the flower or root of any of these plants [C19 after Anders *Dahl*, 18th-cent. Swedish botanist]

Dahna ('dɑ:xnɑ:) *n* another name for **Rub' al Khali**

Dahomey (də'həʊmɪ) *n* the former name (until 1975) of **Benin**

Dáil Éireann ('dɑ:l 'e:rɪn) *or* **Dáil** *n* (in the Republic of Ireland) the lower chamber of parliament [from Irish *dáil* assembly + *Éireann* of Eire]

daily ('deɪlɪ) *adj* **1** of or occurring every day or every weekday ▷ *n, pl* **dailies 2** a daily newspaper **3** *Brit* a charwoman ▷ *adv* **4** every day **5** constantly; often [OE *dæglīc*]

Daimler ('deɪmlə) *n* **Gottlieb (Wilhelm)** (*German* 'gɔtli:p 'vɪlhɛlm) 1834–1900, German engineer and car manufacturer, who collaborated with Nikolaus Otto in inventing the first internal-combustion engine (1876)

daimon ('daɪmɒn) *n* a variant spelling of **daemon** or **demon** (sense 3) > **dai'monic** *adj*

daimyo bond ('daɪmjəʊ) *n* a bearer bond issued in Japan and the eurobond market by the World Bank [from Japanese, from Ancient Chinese]

dainty ('deɪntɪ) *adj* **daintier, daintiest 1** delicate or elegant **2** choice; delicious: *a dainty morsel* **3** excessively genteel; fastidious ▷ *n, pl* **dainties 4** a choice piece of food; delicacy [C13 from OF *deintié*, from L *dignitās* DIGNITY] > **'daintily** *adv*

daiquiri ('daɪkɪrɪ, 'dæk-) *n, pl* **daiquiris** an iced drink containing rum, lime juice, and sugar [C20 after *Daiquiri*, town in Cuba]

dairy ('dɛərɪ) *n, pl* **dairies 1** a company that supplies milk and milk products **2** a room or building where milk and cream are stored or made into butter and cheese **3a** (*modifier*) of, relating to, or containing milk and milk products **3b** (*in combination*): *a dairymaid* **4a** a general shop, selling provisions, esp milk and milk products **4b** *NZ* a shop selling milk and groceries that remains open outside normal trading hours [C13 *daierie*, from OE *dǣge* servant girl, one who kneads bread]

dairying ('dɛərɪɪŋ) *n* the business of producing, processing, and selling dairy products

dairyman ('dɛərɪmən) *n, pl* **dairymen** a man who works in a dairy

dais (ˈdeɪɪs, deɪs) *n* a raised platform, usually at one end of a hall, used by speakers, etc [c13 from OF *deis*, from L *discus* DISCUS]

daisy (ˈdeɪzɪ) *n, pl* **daisies** **1** a small low-growing European plant having flower heads with a yellow centre and pinkish-white outer rays **2** any of various other composite plants having conspicuous ray flowers **3** *sl* an excellent person or thing **4** **pushing up the daisies** dead and buried [OE *dægesēge* day's eye] > ˈ**daisied** *adj*

daisy chain *n* a garland made, esp by children, by threading daisies together

daisycutter (ˈdeɪzɪˌkʌtə) *n cricket* a ball bowled, hit, or kicked so that it rolls along the ground

daisywheel (ˈdeɪzɪˌwiːl) *n computing* a component of a computer printer shaped like a wheel with many spokes that prints using a disk with characters around the circumference. Also called: **printwheel**

Dak. *abbrev for* Dakota

Dakar (ˈdækə) *n* the capital and chief port of Senegal, on the SE side of Cape Verde peninsula. Pop: 1 999 000 (1998 est)

Dakota (dəˈkəʊtə) *n* a former territory of the US: divided into the states of North Dakota and South Dakota in 1889

Dakotan (dəˈkəʊtən) *adj* **1** of or relating to Dakota or its inhabitants ▷ *n* **2** a native or inhabitant of Dakota

daks *or* **dacks** (dæks) *pl n Austral* an informal name for **trousers** [from a brand name]

dal (dɑːl) *n* **1** split grain, a common foodstuff in India; pulse **2** a variant spelling of **dhal**

Daladier (*French* daladje) *n* **Édouard** (edwar) 1884–1970, French radical socialist statesman; premier of France (1933; 1934; 1938–40) and signatory of the Munich Pact (1938)

Dalai Lama (ˈdælaɪ ˈlɑːmə) *n* **1** (until 1959) the chief lama and ruler of Tibet **2** born 1935, the 14th holder of this office (1940), who fled to India (1959): Nobel peace prize 1989 [from Mongolian *dalai* ocean; see LAMA]

dale (deɪl) *n* an open valley [OE *dæl*]

Dale (deɪl) *n* Sir **Henry Hallet** 1875–1968, English physiologist: shared a Nobel prize for physiology or medicine in 1936 with Otto Loewi for their work on the chemical transmission of nerve impulses

Dalek (ˈdɑːlɛk) *n* a fictional robot-like creation that is aggressive, mobile, and produces rasping staccato speech [c20 from a children's television series, *Dr Who*]

d'Alembert (*French* dalɑ̃bɛr) *n* See (Jean le Rond d') **Alembert**

Dales (deɪlz) *pl n* (*sometimes not capital*) **the** the short for the **Yorkshire Dales**

dalesman (ˈdeɪlzmən) *n, pl* **dalesmen** a person living in a dale, esp in the Yorkshire Dales

Dalglish (dælˈgliːʃ, dəl-) *n* **Kenny** born 1951, Scottish footballer and manager: Scotland's most-capped footballer

Dalhousie (dælˈhaʊzɪ) *n* **1** **9th Earl of**, title of *George Ramsay*. 1770–1838, British general; governor of the British colonies in Canada (1819–28) **2** his son, **1st Marquis and 10th Earl of**, title of *James Andrew Broun Ramsay*. 1812–60, British statesman: governor general of India (1848–56)

Dali (ˈdɑːlɪ; *Spanish* daˈliː) *n* **Salvador** (ˈsælvədɔː) 1904–89, Spanish surrealist painter

Dalian (dɑːlˈjɛn) *or* **Talien** (tɑːlˈjɛn) *n* a city in NE China, at the end of the Liaodong Peninsula: with the adjoining city of Lü-shun comprises the port complex of Lüda. Pop: 2 000 944 (1999 est). Former name: **Dairen**

Dallapiccola (*Italian* dallaˈpikkola) *n* **Luigi** (luˈiːdʒi) 1904–75, Italian composer of twelve-tone music. His works include the opera *Il Prigioniero* (1944–48) and the ballet *Marsia* (1948)

Dallas (ˈdæləs) *n* a city in NE Texas, on the Trinity River: scene of the assassination of President John F. Kennedy (1963). Pop: 1 188 580 (2000)

dalles (ˈdæləs, dælz) *pl n Canad* a stretch of river between high rock walls, with rapids and dangerous currents [from Canad F.: sink; see DALE]

dalliance (ˈdælɪəns) *n* waste of time in frivolous action or in dawdling

dally (ˈdælɪ) *vb* **dallies, dallying, dallied** (*intr*) **1** to waste time idly; dawdle **2** (usually foll by *with*) to deal frivolously; trifle: *to dally with someone's affections* [c14 from Anglo-F *dalier* to gossip, from ?]

Dalmatia (dælˈmeɪʃə) *n* a region of W Croatia along the Adriatic: mountainous, with many offshore islands

Dalmatian (dælˈmeɪʃən) *n* **1** a large breed of dog having a short smooth white coat with black or brown spots **2** a native or inhabitant of Dalmatia ▷ *adj* **3** of Dalmatia or its inhabitants

dalmatic (dælˈmætɪk) *n* a wide-sleeved tunic-like vestment open at the sides, worn by deacons and bishops, and by a king at his coronation [c15 from LL *dalmatica* (*vestis*) Dalmatian (robe) (orig. made of Dalmatian wool)]

dal segno (ˈdæl ˈsɛnjəʊ) *adj, adv music* to be repeated from the point marked with a sign to the word *fine* [It., lit.: from the sign]

dalton (ˈdɔːltən) *n* another name for **atomic mass unit** [c20 after J. DALTON]

Dalton (ˈdɔːltən) *n* **John** 1766–1844, English chemist and physicist, who formulated the modern form of the atomic theory and the law of partial pressures for gases. He also gave the first accurate description of colour blindness, from which he suffered

daltonism (ˈdɔːltəˌnɪzəm) *n* colour blindness, esp the confusion of red and green [c19 from F *daltonisme*, after J. DALTON]

Dalton's atomic theory *n chem* the theory that matter consists of indivisible particles called atoms and that atoms of a given element are all identical and can neither be created nor destroyed [c19 after J. DALTON]

Dd

dam¹ (dæm) *n* **1** a barrier of concrete, earth, etc, built across a river to create a body of water **2** a reservoir of water created by such a barrier **3** something that resembles or functions as a dam ▷ *vb* **dams, damming, dammed** **4** (*tr*; often foll by *up*) to restrict by a dam [c12 prob. from MLow G]

dam² (dæm) *n* the female parent of an animal, esp of domestic livestock [c13 var. of DAME]

damage (ˈdæmɪdʒ) *n* **1** injury or harm impairing the function or condition of a person or thing **2** loss of something desirable **3** *inf* cost; expense ▷ *vb* **damages, damaging, damaged** **4** (*tr*) to cause damage to **5** (*intr*) to suffer damage [c14 from OF, from L *damnum* injury, loss] > ˈ**damaging** *adj*

damages (ˈdæmɪdʒɪz) *pl n law* money to be paid as compensation for injury, loss, etc

Daman (dɑːˈmɑːn) *n* a coastal town in W India, the chief town of Daman and Diu. Pop: 26 895 (1991 est). Portuguese name: **Damão**

Daman and Diu (dɑːˈmɑːn ˈdiːuː) *n* a union territory in W India: formerly a district of Portuguese India (1559–1961) then part of the union territory of Goa, Daman, and Diu (1961–87). Area: 112 sq km (43 sq miles). Pop: 158 059 (2001)

damascene (ˈdæməˌsiːn) *vb* **damascenes, damascening, damascened** **1** (*tr*) to ornament (metal, esp steel) by etching or by inlaying other metals, usually gold or silver ▷ *n* **2** a design or article produced by this process ▷ *adj* **3** of or relating to this process [c14 from L *damascēnus* of Damascus]

Damascene (ˈdæməˌsiːn) *adj* **1** of Damascus ▷ *n* **2** a native or inhabitant of Damascus

Damascus (dəˈmɑːskəs, -ˈmæs-) *n* the capital of Syria, in the southwest: reputedly the oldest city in the world,

having been inhabited continuously since before 2000 BC. Pop: 1 394 322 (1994). Arabic names: **Dimashq, Esh Sham** (ɛʃ ʃæm)
▷ www.syriatourism.org/new/index.html
▷ www.made-in-syria.com/damascus.htm

Damascus steel *or* **damask steel** *n history* a hard flexible steel with wavy markings, used for sword blades

damask ('dæməsk) *n* **1a** a reversible fabric, usually silk or linen, with a pattern woven into it. It is used for table linen, curtains, etc **1b** table linen made from this **1c** *(as modifier): a damask tablecloth* **2** short for **Damascus steel** **3** the wavy markings on such steel **4a** the greyish-pink colour of the damask rose **4b** *(as adj): damask wallpaper* ▷ *vb* **5** *(tr)* another word for **damascene** [C14 from Med. L *damascus*, from Damascus, where fabric orig. made]

damask rose *n* a rose with fragrant flowers, which are used to make the perfume attar [C16 from Med. L *rosa damascēna* rose of Damascus]

dame (deɪm) *n* **1** (formerly) a woman of rank or dignity; lady **2** *arch, chiefly Brit* an elderly woman **3** *sl, chiefly US & Canad* a woman **4** *Brit* the role of a comic old woman in a pantomime, usually played by a man [C13 from OF, from L *domina* lady, mistress of household]

Dame (deɪm) *n* (in Britain) **1** the title of a woman who has been awarded the Order of the British Empire or any of certain other orders of chivalry **2** the title of the wife of a knight or baronet

dame school *n* (formerly) a small school, offering basic education, usually run by an elderly woman in her own home

Damien (*French* damjɛ̃) *n* **Joseph** (ʒozɛf), known as *Father Damien*. 1840–89, Belgian Roman Catholic missionary to the leper colony at Molokai, Hawaii

damn (dæm) *interj* **1** *sl* an exclamation of annoyance **2** *inf* an exclamation of surprise or pleasure ▷ *adj* **3** *(prenominal) sl* deserving damnation ▷ *adv, adj (prenominal)* **4** *sl* (intensifier): *a damn good pianist* ▷ *adv* **5** **damn all** *sl* absolutely nothing ▷ *vb (mainly tr)* **6** to condemn as bad, worthless, etc **7** to curse **8** to condemn to eternal damnation **9** *(often passive)* to doom to ruin **10** *(also intr)* to prove (someone) guilty: *damning evidence* **11** **damn with faint praise** to praise so unenthusiastically that the effect is condemnation ▷ *n* **12** *sl* something of negligible value(esp in **not worth a damn**) **13** **not give a damn** *inf* not care [C13 from OF *dampner*, from L *damnāre*, from *damnum* loss, injury]

damnable ('dæmnəbᵊl) *adj* **1** execrable; detestable **2** liable to or deserving damnation > '**damnableness** *or* ˌ**damna'bility** *n*

damnably ('dæmnəblɪ) *adv* **1** in a detestable manner **2** (intensifier): *it was damnably unfair*

damnation (dæm'neɪʃən) *n* **1** the act of damning or state of being damned ▷ *interj* **2** an exclamation of anger, disappointment, etc

damnatory ('dæmnətərɪ) *adj* threatening or occasioning condemnation

damned (dæmd) *adj* **1a** condemned to hell **1b** *(as collective n; preceded by the): the damned* ▷ *adv, adj sl* **2** (intensifier): *a damned good try* **3** used to indicate amazement, disavowal, or refusal (as in **damned if I care**)

damnedest ('dæmdɪst) *n inf* utmost; best(esp in the phrases **do** or **try one's damnedest**)

damnify ('dæmnɪˌfaɪ) *vb* **damnifies, damnifying, damnified** *(tr) law* to cause loss or damage to (a person); injure [C16 from OF *damnifier*, ult. from L *damnum* harm, + *facere* to make] > ˌ**damnifi'cation** *n*

Damocles ('dæməˌkli:z) *n classical legend* a sycophant forced by Dionysius, tyrant of Syracuse, to sit under a sword suspended by a hair to demonstrate that being a king was not the happy state Damocles had said it was. See also **Sword of Damocles** > ˌ**Damo'clean** *adj*

Damodar ('dæməˌdɑ:) *n* a river in NE India, rising in Jharkand and flowing east through West Bengal to the Hooghly River: the **Damodar Valley** is an important centre of heavy industry

damoiselle, damosel, *or* **damozel** (ˌdæmə'zɛl) *n* archaic variants of **damsel**

damp (dæmp) *adj* **1** slightly wet ▷ *n* **2** slight wetness; moisture **3** rank air or poisonous gas, esp in a mine **4** a discouragement; damper ▷ *vb (tr)* **5** to make slightly wet **6** (often foll by *down*) to stifle or deaden: *to damp one's ardour* **7** (often foll by *down*) to reduce the flow of air to (a fire) to make it burn more slowly **8** *physics* to reduce the amplitude of (an oscillation or wave) **9** *music* to muffle (the sound of an instrument) [C14 from MLow G *damp* steam] > '**dampness** *n*

dampcourse ('dæmpˌkɔ:s) *n* a layer of impervious material in a wall, to stop moisture rising. Also called: **damp-proof course**

dampen ('dæmpən) *vb* **1** to make or become damp **2** *(tr)* to stifle; deaden > '**dampener** *n*

damper ('dæmpə) *n* **1** a person, event, or circumstance that depresses or discourages **2** **put a damper on** to produce a depressing or stultifying effect on **3** a movable plate to regulate the draught in a stove or furnace flue **4** a device to reduce electronic, mechanical, acoustic, or aerodynamic oscillations in a system **5** the pad in a piano or harpsichord that deadens the vibration of each string as its key is released **6** *chiefly Austral & NZ* any of various unleavened loaves and scones, typically cooked on an open fire

damping off *n* any of various diseases of plants caused by fungi in conditions of excessive moisture

damp-proof *building trades* ▷ *vb* **1** to protect against the incursion of damp by adding a dampcourse or by coating with a moisture-resistant preparation ▷ *adj* **2** protected against damp or causing protection against damp: *a damp-proof course*

damsel ('dæmzᵊl) *n arch or poetic* a young unmarried woman; maiden [C13 from OF *damoisele*, from Vulgar L *domnicella* (unattested) young lady, from L *domina* mistress]

damselfly ('dæmzᵊlˌflaɪ) *n, pl* **damselflies** any of various insects similar to dragonflies but usually resting with the wings closed over the back

damson ('dæmzən) *n* **1** a small tree cultivated for its blue-black edible plumlike fruit **2** the fruit of this tree [C14 from L *prūnum damascēnum* Damascus plum]

dan (dæn) *n judo, karate, etc* **1** any one of the 10 black-belt grades of proficiency **2** a competitor entitled to dan grading [Japanese]

Dan (dæn) *n Old Testament* **1a** the fourth son of Jacob (Genesis 30:1–6) **1b** the tribe descended from him **2** a city in the northern territory of Canaan

Dan. *abbrev for:* **1** *Bible* Daniel **2** Danish

Dana ('deɪnə) *n* **James Dwight** (dwaɪt) 1813–95, American geologist; noted for his work *The System of Mineralogy* (1837)

Danaë ('dæneɪˌi:) *n Greek myth* the mother of Perseus by Zeus, who came to her in prison as a shower of gold

Danaides (də'neɪɪˌdi:z) *pl n, sing* **Danaid** *Greek myth* the fifty daughters of Danaüs. All but Hypermnestra murdered their bridegrooms and were punished in Hades by having to pour water perpetually into a jar with a hole in the bottom > **Danaidean** (ˌdænɪ'ɪdɪən, ˌdænɪə'di:ən) *adj*

Da Nang ('dɑ: 'næŋ) *n* a port in central Vietnam, on the South China Sea. Pop: 382 674 (1992 est). Former name: **Tourane**

Danaüs ('dænɪəs) *n Greek myth* a king of Argos who told his fifty daughters, the Danaides, to kill their bridegrooms on their wedding night

dance (dɑ:ns) *vb* **dances, dancing, danced** **1** *(intr)* to move the feet and body rhythmically, esp in time to music **2** (*tr*) to perform (a particular dance) **3** (*intr*) to skip or leap **4** to move or cause to move in a rhythmic way **5 dance attendance on (someone)** to attend (someone) solicitously or obsequiously ▷ *n* **6** a series of rhythmic steps and movements, usually in time to music **7** an act of dancing **8a** a social meeting arranged for dancing **8b** (*as modifier*): *a dance hall* **9** a piece of music in the rhythm of a particular dance form **10** dancelike movements **11 lead (someone) a dance** *Brit inf* to cause (someone) continued worry and exasperation [C13 from OF *dancier*] > **'danceable** *adj* > **'dancer** *n* > **'dancing** *n, adj*

▷ www.culturekiosque.com/dance
▷ www.streetswing.com/histmain/z3modrn1.htm
▷ www.sapphireswan.com/dance/links/modern.htm
▷ www.artindia.net/modern.html
▷ www.britisharts.co.uk/moddance.htm

dance floor *n* **a** an area of floor in a disco, etc, where patrons may dance **b** (*as modifier*): *dancefloor music*

dancehall ('dɑːns,hɔːl) *n* **1** a style of dance-oriented reggae, originating in the late 1980s **2** a style of dancing associated with this music, involving close body contact with one's partner or partners

dance of death *n* a medieval representation of a dance in which people are led off to their graves, by a personification of death. Also called (French): **danse macabre**

D and C *n med* dilation (of the cervix) and curettage (of the uterus)

dandelion ('dændɪ,laɪən) *n* **1** a plant native to Europe and Asia and naturalized as a weed in North America, having yellow rayed flowers and deeply notched leaves **2** any of several similar plants [C15 from OF *dent de lion*, lit.: tooth of a lion, referring to its leaves]

dander ('dændə) *n* **1** small particles of hair or feathers **2 get one's** (*or* **someone's**) **dander up** *inf* to become (*or* cause to become) annoyed or angry [C19 from DANDRUFF]

dandify ('dændɪ,faɪ) *vb* **dandifies, dandifying, dandified** (*tr*) to dress like or cause to resemble a dandy

dandle ('dændᵊl) *vb* **dandles, dandling, dandled** (*tr*) **1** to move (a young child) up and down (on the knee or in the arms) **2** to pet; fondle [C16 from ?] > **'dandler** *n*

dandruff ('dændrəf) *n* loose scales of dry dead skin shed from the scalp [C16 *dand-* from ? + *-ruff*, prob. from ME *roufe* scab, from ON *hrūfa*]

dandy ('dændɪ) *n, pl* **dandies 1** a man greatly concerned with smartness of dress ▷ *adj* **dandier, dandiest 2** *inf* good or fine [C18 ? short for *jack-a-dandy*] > **'dandyish** *adj*

dandy-brush *n* a stiff brush used for grooming a horse

dandy roll *or* **roller** *n* a roller used in the manufacture of paper to produce watermarks

Dane (deɪn) *n* **1** a native, citizen, or inhabitant of Denmark **2** any of the Vikings who invaded England from the late 8th to the 11th century AD

Danegeld ('deɪn,gɛld) *or* **Danegelt** ('deɪn,gɛlt) *n* the tax levied in Anglo-Saxon England to provide protection money for or to finance forces to oppose Viking invaders [C11 from *Dan* Dane + *geld* tribute; see YIELD]

Danelaw ('deɪn,lɔː) *n* the parts of Anglo-Saxon England in which Danish law and custom were observed [OE *Dena lagu* Danes' law]

danger ('deɪndʒə) *n* **1** the state of being vulnerable to injury, loss, or evil; risk **2** a person or thing that may cause injury, pain, etc **3 in danger of** liable to **4 on the danger list** critically ill in hospital [C13 *daunger* power, hence power to inflict injury, from OF *dongier* from L *dominium* ownership] > **'dangerless** *adj*

danger money *n* extra money paid to compensate for the risks involved in certain dangerous jobs

dangerous ('deɪndʒərəs) *adj* causing danger; perilous > **'dangerously** *adv*

dangle ('dæŋgᵊl) *vb* **dangles, dangling, dangled 1** to hang or cause to hang freely: *his legs dangled over the wall* **2** (*tr*) to display as an enticement [C16 ?from Danish *dangle*, prob. imit.] > **'dangler** *n*

Daniel[1] ('dænjəl) *n* **1** *Old Testament* **1a** a youth who was taken into the household of Nebuchadnezzar, received guidance and apocalyptic visions from God, and was given divine protection when thrown into the lions' den **1b** the book that recounts these experiences and visions (in full **The Book of the Prophet Daniel**) **2** (often preceded by *a*) a wise upright person [sense 2: referring to Daniel in the Apocryphal *Book of Susanna*]

Daniel[2] *n* **Paul** (**Wilson**) born 1958, British conductor; musical director of the English National Opera 1997–2003

Danish ('deɪnɪʃ) *adj* **1** of Denmark, its people, or their language ▷ *n* **2** the official language of Denmark

Danish blue *n* a strong-tasting white cheese with blue veins

Danish pastry *n* a rich puff pastry filled with apple, almond paste, icing, etc

Danish West Indies *pl n* the former possession of Denmark in the W Lesser Antilles, sold to the US in 1917 and since then named the **Virgin Islands of the United States**

dank (dæŋk) *adj* (esp of cellars, caves, etc) unpleasantly damp and chilly [C14 prob. from ON] > **'dankly** *adv* > **'dankness** *n*

Danmark ('danmarg) *n* the Danish name for **Denmark**

D'Annunzio (*Italian* dan'nuntsjo) *n* **Gabriele** (ga'brjɛːle) 1863–1938, Italian poet, dramatist, novelist, national hero, and Fascist. His works include the poems in *Alcione* (1904) and the drama *La Figlia di Iorio* (1904)

danseur *French* (dɑ̃sœr) *or* (*fem*) ***danseuse*** (dɑ̃søz) *n* a ballet dancer

Dante ('dæntɪ, 'dɑːnteɪ; *Italian* 'dante) *n* full name **Dante Alighieri** (*Italian* ali'gjɛːri) 1265–1321, Italian poet famous for *La Divina Commedia* (?1309–?1320), an allegorical account of his journey through Hell, Purgatory, and Paradise, guided by Virgil and his idealized love Beatrice. His other works include *La Vita Nuova* (?1292), in which he celebrates his love for Beatrice > **Dantean** ('dæntɪən, dæn'tiːən), *or* **Dantesque** (dæn'tɛsk) *adj*

Danton ('dæntən; *French* dɑ̃tɔ̃) *n* **Georges Jacques** (ʒɔrʒ ʒɑk) 1759–94, French revolutionary leader: a founder member of the Committee of Public Safety (1793) and minister of justice (1792–94). He was overthrown by Robespierre and guillotined

Danube ('dænjuːb) *n* a river in central and SE Europe, rising in the Black Forest in Germany and flowing to the Black Sea. Length: 2859 km (1776 miles). German name: **Donau** Czech name: **Dunaj** Hungarian name: **Duna** Serbo-Croat name: **Dunav** ('dunaf) Romanian name: **Dunărea**

Danubian (dæn'juːbɪən) *adj* of or relating to the river Danube

Danzig ('dænsɪg; *German* 'dantsɪç) *n* **1** the German name for **Gdańsk** **2** a rare variety of domestic fancy pigeon originating in this area

dap (dæp) *vb* **daps, dapping, dapped 1** *angling* to fly-fish so that the fly bobs on and off the water **2** (*intr*) to dip lightly into water **3** to bounce or cause to bounce [C17 imit.]

daphne ('dæfnɪ) *n* any of various Eurasian ornamental shrubs with shiny evergreen leaves and clusters of small bell-shaped flowers [via L from Gk: laurel]

Daphne ('dæfnɪ) *n Greek myth* a nymph who was saved from the amorous attentions of Apollo by being changed into a laurel tree

daphnia ('dæfnɪə) *n* any of several waterfleas having a rounded body enclosed in a transparent shell [C19 prob. from DAPHNE]

Daphnis ('dæfnɪs) *n Greek myth* a Sicilian shepherd, the son of Hermes and a nymph, who was regarded as the inventor of pastoral poetry

Da Ponte (*Italian* da 'pɔnte) *n* **Lorenzo** (lo'rɛntso), real name *Emmanuele Conegliano*. 1749–1838, Italian writer; Mozart's librettist for *The Marriage of Figaro* (1786), *Don Giovanni* (1787), and *Così fan tutte* (1790)

dapper ('dæpə) *adj* **1** neat in dress and bearing **2** small and nimble [C15 from MDu.: active, nimble] > **'dapperly** *adv* > **'dapperness** *n*

dapple ('dæpᵊl) *vb* **dapples, dappling, dappled** **1** to mark or become marked with spots of a different colour; mottle ▷ *n* **2** mottled or spotted markings **3** a dappled horse, etc ▷ *adj* **4** marked with dapples or spots [C14 from ?]

dapple-grey *n* a horse with a grey coat having spots of darker colour

Dapsang (dʌp'sʌŋ) *n* another name for **K2**

darbies ('dɑːbɪz) *pl n Brit* a slang term for **handcuffs** [C16 ?from *Father Derby's* (or *Darby's*) *bonds*, a rigid agreement between a usurer and his client]

Darby and Joan ('dɑːbɪ) *n* **1** an ideal elderly married couple living in domestic harmony **2** **Darby and Joan Club** a club for elderly people [C18 couple in 18th-cent. English ballad]

Darcy ('dɑːsɪ) *n* **(James) Les(lie)** 1895–1917, Australian boxer and folk hero, who lost only five professional fights and was never knocked out, considered a martyr after his death from septicaemia during a tour of the United States

Dardanelles (ˌdɑːdə'nɛlz) *n* the strait between the Aegean and the Sea of Marmara, separating European from Asian Turkey. Ancient name: **Hellespont**

dare (dɛə) *vb* **dares, daring, dared** **1** (*tr*) to challenge (a person to do something) as proof of courage **2** (can take an infinitive with or without *to*) to be courageous enough to try (to do something) **3** (*tr*) *rare* to oppose without fear; defy **4** **I dare say** **4a** (it is) quite possible (that) **4b** probably ▷ *n* **5** a challenge to do something as proof of courage **6** something done in response to such a challenge [OE *durran*] > **'darer** *n*

daredevil ('dɛəˌdɛvᵊl) *n* **1** a recklessly bold person ▷ *adj* **2** reckless; daring; bold > **'dareˌdevilry** *or* **'dareˌdeviltry** *n*

Dar es Salaam ('dɑːr ɛs sə'lɑːm) *n* the chief port of Tanzania, on the Indian Ocean: capital of German East Africa (1891–1916); capital of Tanzania until 1983 when it was replaced by Dodoma; university (1963). Pop: 1 360 850 (latest est)

Darfur (dɑː'fʊə) *n* a region of the W Sudan; an independent kingdom until conquered by Egypt in 1874

Darien ('dɛərɪən, 'dæ-) *n* **1** the E part of the Isthmus of Panama, between the **Gulf of Darien** on the Caribbean coast and the Gulf of San Miguel on the Pacific coast; chiefly within the republic of Panama but extending also into Colombia: site of a disastrous attempt to establish a Scottish colony in 1698 **2** **Isthmus of** the former name of the Isthmus of **Panama** ▷ Spanish name **Darién** (da'rjen)

daring ('dɛərɪŋ) *adj* **1** bold or adventurous ▷ *n* **2** courage in taking risks; boldness

Dario (*Spanish* da'rio) *n* **Rubén** (ru'βen), real name *Félix Rubén García Sarmiento*. 1867–1916, Nicaraguan poet whose poetry includes *Prosas Profanas* (1896)

Darius I (də'raɪəs) *n* known as *Darius the Great*, surname *Hystaspis*. ?550–486 BC, king of Persia (521–486), who extended the Persian empire and crushed the revolt of the Ionian city states (500). He led two expeditions against Greece but was defeated at Marathon (490)

Darjeeling (dɑː'dʒiːlɪŋ) *n* **1** a town in NE India, in West Bengal in the Himalayas, at an altitude of about 2250 m (7500 ft). Pop: 73 090 (1991) **2** a high-quality black tea grown in the mountains around Darjeeling

dark (dɑːk) *adj* **1** having little or no light **2** (of a colour) reflecting or transmitting little light: *dark brown* **3** (of complexion, hair colour, etc) not fair; swarthy; brunette **4** gloomy or dismal **5** sinister; evil: *a dark purpose* **6** sullen or angry **7** ignorant or unenlightened: *a dark period in our history* **8** secret or mysterious ▷ *n* **9** absence of light; darkness **10** night or nightfall **11** a dark place **12** a state of ignorance (esp in **in the dark**) [OE *deorc*] > **'darkish** *adj* > **'darkly** *adv* > **'darkness** *n*

Dark Ages *pl n European history*. the period from about the late 5th century AD to about 1000 AD, once considered an unenlightened period

▷ http://cfcc.net/dutch/DarkAges.htm

▷ www.fernweb.pwp.blueyonder.co.uk/mf

Dark Continent *n* **the** a term for Africa when it was relatively unexplored

darken ('dɑːkən) *vb* **1** to make or become dark or darker **2** to make or become gloomy, angry, or sad **3** **darken (someone's) door** (*usually used with a negative*) to visit someone: *never darken my door again!* > **'darkener** *n*

dark horse *n* **1** a competitor in a race or contest about whom little is known **2** a person who reveals little about himself or herself, esp one who has unexpected talents **3** *US politics* a candidate who is unexpectedly nominated or elected

dark lantern *n* a lantern having a sliding shutter or panel to dim or hide the light

darkling ('dɑːklɪŋ) *adv, adj Poetic*. in the dark or night [C15 from DARK + -LING[2]]

dark matter *n astron* matter known to make up a substantial part of the mass of the universe, but not detectable by its absorption or emission of electromagnetic radiation

darkroom ('dɑːkˌruːm, -ˌrʊm) *n* a room in which photographs are processed in darkness or safe light

darksome ('dɑːksəm) *adj literary* dark or darkish

dark star *n* an invisible star known to exist only from observation of its radio, infrared, or other spectrum or of its gravitational effect

Darlan (*French* darlɑ̃) *n* **Jean Louis Xavier François** (ʒɑ̃ lwi gzavje frɑ̃swa) 1881–1942, French admiral and member of the Vichy government. He cooperated with the Allies after their invasion of North Africa; assassinated

darling ('dɑːlɪŋ) *n* **1** a person very much loved **2** a favourite ▷ *adj* (*prenominal*) **3** beloved **4** much admired; pleasing: *a darling hat* [OE *dēorling*; see DEAR, -LING[1]]

Darling ('dɑːlɪŋ) *n* **Grace** 1815–42, English national heroine, famous for her rescue (1838) of some shipwrecked sailors with her father, a lighthouse keeper

Darling Downs *pl n* a plateau in NE Australia, in SE Queensland: a vast agricultural and stock-raising area

Darling Range *n* a ridge in SW Western Australia, parallel to the coast. Highest point: about 582 m (1669 ft)

Darling River *n* a river in SE Australia, rising in the Eastern Highlands and flowing southwest to the Murray River. Length: 2740 km (1702 miles)

Darlington ('dɑːlɪŋtən) *n* **1** an industrial town in NE England in Darlington unitary authority, S Durham: developed mainly with the opening of the Stockton-Darlington railway (1825). Pop: 86 767 (1991) **2** a unitary authority in NE England, in Durham. Pop: 97 822 (2001). Area: 198 sq km (77 sq miles)

Darmstadt ('dɑːmstæt; *German* 'darmʃtat) *n* an industrial city in central Germany, in Hesse: former capital of the grand duchy of Hesse-Darmstadt (1567–1945). Pop: 137 600 (1999 est)

darmstadtium ('dɑːmstætɪəm) *n* a transuranic element artificially produced by bombardment of lead with nickel nuclei. Symbol: Ds; atomic no.: 110; half-life of most stable isotope, ^{269}Ds: 1.7×10^{-4} s [C20 after DARMSTADT, where it was discovered]

darn[1] (dɑːn) *vb* **1** to mend (a hole or a garment) with a series of crossing or interwoven stitches ▷ *n* **2** a patch of darned work on a garment [C16 prob. from F (dialect) *darner*] > **'darner** *n*

darn[2] (dɑːn) *interj, adj, adv, n* a euphemistic word for **damn** (senses 1–5, 12, 13)

darnel ('dɑːnᵊl) *n* any of several grasses that grow as weeds in grain fields in Europe and Asia [C14 prob. rel. to F (dialect) *darnelle*, from ?]

darning ('dɑːnɪŋ) *n* **1** the act of mending a hole using interwoven stitches **2** garments needing to be darned

darning needle *n* a long needle with a large eye used for darning

Darnley ('dɑːnlɪ) *n* **Lord** title of *Henry Stuart* (or *Stewart*). 1545–67, Scottish nobleman; second husband of Mary, Queen of Scots and father of James I of England. After murdering his wife's secretary, Rizzio (1566), he was himself assassinated (1567)

dart (dɑːt) *n* **1** a small narrow pointed missile that is thrown or shot, as in the game of darts **2** a sudden quick movement **3** *zool* a slender pointed structure, as in snails for aiding copulation **4** a tapered tuck made in dressmaking ▷ *vb* **5** to move or throw swiftly and suddenly; shoot [C14 from OF, of Gmc origin] > **'darting** *adj*

dartboard ('dɑːtˌbɔːd) *n* a circular piece of wood, cork, etc, used as the target in the game of darts

darter ('dɑːtə) *n* **1** Also called: **anhinga, snakebird** any of various aquatic birds of tropical and subtropical inland waters, having a long slender neck and bill **2** any of various small brightly coloured North American freshwater fish

Dartford ('dɑːtfəd) *n* a town in SE England, in NW Kent. Pop: 59 411 (1991)

Dartmoor ('dɑːtˌmʊə) *n* **1** a moorland plateau in SW England, in SW Devon: a national park since 1951. Area: 945 sq km (365 sq miles) **2** a prison in SW England, on Dartmoor: England's main prison for long-term convicts **3** a small strong breed of pony, originally from Dartmoor **4** a hardy coarse-woolled breed of sheep originally from Dartmoor

Dartmouth ('dɑːtməθ) *n* **1** a port in SW England, in S Devon: Royal Naval College (1905). Pop: 5676 (1991) **2** a city in SE Canada, in S Nova Scotia, on Halifax Harbour: oil refineries and shipyards. Pop: 67 798 (1991)

darts (dɑːts) *n* (*functioning as sing*) any of various competitive games in which darts are thrown at a dartboard

▷ www.dartswdf.com

Darwin[1] ('dɑːwɪn) *n* a port in N Australia, capital of the Northern Territory: destroyed by a cyclone in 1974 but rebuilt on the same site. Pop: 78 100 (1994). Former name (1869–1911): **Palmerston**

Darwin[2] ('dɑːwɪn) *n* **1** **Charles** (**Robert**) 1809–82, English naturalist who formulated the theory of evolution by natural selection, expounded in *On the Origin of Species* (1859) and applied to man in *The Descent of Man* (1871) **2** his grandfather, **Erasmus** 1731–1802, English physician and poet; author of *Zoonomia, or the Laws of Organic Life* (1794–96), anticipating Lamarck's views on evolution **3** Sir **George Howard**, son of Charles Darwin. 1845–1912, English astronomer and mathematician noted for his work on tidal friction

Darwinian (dɑːˈwɪnɪən) *adj* **1** of or relating to Charles Darwin or his theory of evolution ▷ *n* **2** a person who accepts, supports, or uses this theory

Darwinism ('dɑːwɪˌnɪzəm) *or* **Darwinian theory** *n* the theory of the origin of animal and plant species by evolution through a process of natural selection > **'Darwinist** *n, adj*

dash[1] (dæʃ) *vb* (*mainly tr*) **1** to hurl; crash: *he dashed the cup to the floor* **2** to mix: *white paint dashed with blue* **3** (*intr*) to move hastily or recklessly; rush **4** (usually foll by *off* or *down*) to write (down) or finish (off) hastily **5** to frustrate: *his hopes were dashed* **6** to daunt (someone); discourage ▷ *n* **7** a sudden quick movement **8** a small admixture: *coffee with a dash of cream* **9** a violent stroke or blow **10** the sound of splashing or smashing **11** panache; style: *he rides with dash* **12** Also called: **rule** the punctuation mark—, used to indicate a sudden change of subject or to enclose a parenthetical remark **13** the symbol (–) used, in combination with the symbol *dot* (•), in the written representation of Morse and other telegraphic codes **14** *athletics* another word (*esp US & Canad*) for **sprint** [ME *daschen, dassen*, ?from ON]

dash[2] (dæʃ) *interj inf* a euphemistic word for **damn** (senses 1, 2)

dashboard ('dæʃˌbɔːd) *n* **1** Also called (*Brit*): **fascia** the instrument panel in a car, boat, or aircraft **2** *obs* a board at the side of a carriage or boat to protect against splashing

dasher ('dæʃə) *n* **1** one that dashes **2** *Canad* the ledge along the top of the boards of an ice hockey rink

dashiki (dɑːˈʃiːkɪ) *n* a large loose-fitting upper garment worn esp by Blacks in the US, Africa, and the Caribbean [C20 of W African origin]

dashing ('dæʃɪŋ) *adj* **1** spirited; lively: *a dashing young man* **2** stylish; showy

dashlight ('dæʃˌlaɪt) *n* a light that illuminates the dashboard of a car, esp at night

Dasht-i-Kavir *or* **Dasht-e-Kavir** (ˌdæʃtiːkæˈvɪə) *n* a salt waste on the central plateau of Iran: a treacherous marsh beneath a salt crust. Also called: **Kavir Desert**

Dasht-i-Lut *or* **Dasht-e-Lut** (ˌdæʃtiːˈlʊt) *n* a desert plateau in central and E central Iran

Dassehra ('dæsεəræ) *n* an annual Hindu festival celebrated on the 10th lunar day of Navaratri; images of the goddess Durga are immersed in water

dassie ('dæsɪ) *n* another name for a **hyrax,** esp the rock hyrax [C19 from Afrik.]

dastardly ('dæstədlɪ) *adj* mean and cowardly [C15 *dastard* (in the sense: dullard): prob. from ON *dæstr* exhausted, out of breath] > **'dastardliness** *n*

dasyure ('dæsɪˌjʊə) *n* **1** any of several small carnivorous marsupials of Australia, New Guinea, and adjacent islands **2** the ursine dasyure ▷ See **Tasmanian devil** [C19 from NL, from Gk *dasus* shaggy + *oura* tail]

DAT *abbrev for* digital audio tape

dat. *abbrev for* dative

data ('deɪtə, 'dɑːtə) *pl n* **1** a series of observations, measurements, or facts; information **2** Also called: **information** *computing* the information operated on by a computer program [C17 from L, lit.: (things) given, from *dare* to give]

USAGE From a historical point of view only, the word *data* is a plural. In fact, in many cases it is not clear from context if it is being used as a singular or plural, so there is no issue: *when next needed the data can be accessed very quickly*. When it is necessary to specify, the preferred usage nowadays in general language is to treat it as singular, as in: *this data is useful to the government in the planning of housing services*. There are rather more examples in the Bank of English of *these data* than *this data*, with a marked preference for the plural in academic and scientific writing. As regards *data is* versus *data are*, the preference for the plural form overall is even more marked in that kind of writing. When speaking, however, it is best to opt for treating the word as singular, except in precise scientific contexts. The singular form *datum* is comparatively rare in the sense of a single item of data

database ('deɪtəˌbeɪs) *n* **1** Also called: **data bank** a store of a large amount of information, esp in a form that can be handled by a computer **2** *inf* any large store of information: *a database of knowledge*

data capture *n* any process for converting information into a form that can be handled by a computer

data mining *n* the gathering of information from pre-existing data stored in a database, such as one held

Dd

by a supermarket with details of customers' shopping habits

data pen *n* a device for reading or scanning magnetically coded data on labels, packets, etc

data processing *n* **a** a sequence of operations performed on data, esp by a computer, in order to extract information, reorder files, etc **b** *(as modifier): a data-processing centre*

data protection *n* (in Britain) safeguards for individuals relating to personal data stored on a computer

data set *n computing* another name for **file**[1] (sense 6)

date[1] (deɪt) *n* **1** a specified day of the month **2** the particular day or year of an event **3** an inscription on a coin, letter, etc, stating when it was made or written **4a** an appointment for a particular time, esp with a person to whom one is sexually or romantically attached **4b** the person with whom the appointment is made **5** the present moment; now(esp in **to date, up to date**) ▷ *vb* **dates, dating, dated 6** *(tr)* to mark (a letter, coin, etc) with the day, month, or year **7** *(tr)* to assign a date of occurrence or creation to **8** *(intr; foll by from or back to)* to have originated (at a specified time) **9** *(tr)* to reveal the age of: *that dress dates her* **10** to make or become old-fashioned: *some good films hardly date at all* **11** *inf, chiefly US & Canad* **11a** to be a boyfriend or girlfriend of **11b** to accompany (someone to whom one is sexually or romantically attached) on a date [c14 from OF, from L *dare* to give, as in *epistula data Romae* letter handed over at Rome] > '**datable** *or* '**dateable** *adj*

USAGE See at **year**

date[2] (deɪt) *n* **1** the fruit of the date palm, having sweet edible flesh and a single large woody seed **2** short for **date palm** [c13 from OF, from L, from Gk *daktulos* finger]

dated ('deɪtɪd) *adj* **1** unfashionable; outmoded **2** (of a security) having a fixed date for redemption

dateless ('deɪtlɪs) *adj* likely to remain fashionable, good, or interesting regardless of age

dateline ('deɪtˌlaɪn) *n journalism* the date and location of a story, placed at the top of an article

date line *n (often caps.)* short for **International Date Line**

date palm *n* a tall feather palm grown in warm to temperate and subtropical regions for its sweet edible fruit (dates)

date rape *n* **1** the act or an instance of a man raping a woman while they are on a date together **2** an act of sexual intercourse regarded as tantamount to rape, esp if the woman was encouraged to drink excessively or was subjected to undue pressure

date stamp *n* **1** an adjustable rubber stamp for recording the date **2** an inked impression made by this

dating ('deɪtɪŋ) *n* any of several techniques, such as radioactive dating, dendrochronology, or varve dating, for establishing the age of rocks, palaeontological or archaeological specimens, etc

dating agency *n* an agency that provides introductions to people seeking a companion with similar interests

dative ('deɪtɪv) *grammar* ▷ *adj* **1** denoting a case of nouns, pronouns, and adjectives used to express the indirect object, to identify the recipients, and for other purposes ▷ *n* **2a** the dative case **2b** a word or speech element in this case [c15 from L *datīvus*, from *dare* to give] > **datival** (deɪ'taɪvᵊl) *adj* > '**datively** *adv*

datum ('deɪtəm, 'dɑːtəm) *n, pl* **data 1** a single piece of information; fact **2** a proposition taken as unquestionable, often in order to construct some theoretical framework upon it. ▷ See also **sense datum** [c17 from L: something given; see DATA]

USAGE See at **data**

datura (də'tjʊərə) *n* any of various chiefly Indian plants and shrubs with large trumpet-shaped flowers [c16 from NL, from Hindi]

daub (dɔːb) *vb* **1** *(tr)* to smear or spread (paint, mud, etc), esp carelessly **2** *(tr)* to cover or coat (with paint, plaster, etc) carelessly **3** to paint (a picture) clumsily or badly ▷ *n* **4** an unskilful or crude painting **5** something daubed on, esp as a wall covering **6** a smear (of paint, mud, etc) [c14 from OF *dauber* to paint, whitewash, from L *dealbāre*, from *albāre* to whiten] > '**dauber** *n*

Daubigny (*French* dobiɲi) *n* **Charles François** (ʃarl frɑ̃swa) 1817–78, French landscape painter associated with the Barbizon School

Daudet (*French* dodɛ) *n* **Alphonse** (alfɔ̃s) 1840–97, French novelist, short-story writer, and dramatist: noted particularly for his humorous sketches of Provençal life, as in *Lettres de mon moulin* (1866)

Daugava ('daʊgaˌva) *n* the Latvian name for the Western **Dvina**

Daugavpils (*Latvian* 'daʊgafˌpils) *n* a city in SE Latvia on the Western Dvina River: founded in 1274 by Teutonic Knights; ruled by Poland (1559–1772) and Russia (1772–1915); retaken by the Russians in 1940. Pop: 114 510 (2000 est). German name (until 1893): **Dünaburg** Former Russian name (1893–1920): **Dvinsk**

daughter ('dɔːtə) *n* **1** a female offspring; a girl or woman in relation to her parents **2** a female descendant **3** a female from a certain country, etc, or one closely connected with a certain environment, etc: *a daughter of the church* ▷ *(modifier)* **4** *biol* denoting a cell or unicellular organism produced by the division of one of its own kind **5** *physics* (of a nuclide) formed from another nuclide by radioactive decay [OE *dohtor*] > '**daughterhood** *n* > '**daughterless** *adj* > '**daughterly** *adj*

daughter-in-law *n, pl* **daughters-in-law** the wife of one's son

Daumier (*French* domje) *n* **Honoré** (ɔnɔre) 1808–79, French painter and lithographer, noted particularly for his political and social caricatures

daunt (dɔːnt) *vb (tr; often passive)* **1** to intimidate **2** to dishearten [c13 from OF *danter*, changed from *donter* to conquer, from L *domitāre* to tame]

daunting ('dɔːntɪŋ) *adj* causing fear or discouragement; intimidating > '**dauntingly** *adv*

dauntless ('dɔːntlɪs) *adj* bold; fearless; intrepid > '**dauntlessly** *adv* > '**dauntlessness** *n*

dauphin ('dɔːfɪn; *French* dofɛ̃) *n* (1349–1830) the title of the eldest son of the king of France [c15 from OF: orig. a family name]

dauphine ('dɔːfiːn; *French* dofin) *or* **dauphiness** ('dɔːfɪnɪs) *n French history* the wife of a dauphin

davenport ('dævənˌpɔːt) *n* **1** *chiefly Brit* a tall narrow writing desk with drawers **2** *US & Canad* a large sofa, esp one convertible into a bed [c19 sense 1 supposedly after Captain *Davenport*, who commissioned the first ones]

Daventry ('dævəntrɪ) *n* a town in central England, in Northamptonshire: light industries, site of an important international radio transmitter. Pop: 18 099 (1991)

David ('deɪvɪd) *n* **1** the second king of the Hebrews (about 1000–962 BC), who united Israel as a kingdom with Jerusalem as its capital **2 Elizabeth** 1914–92, British cookery writer. Her books include *Mediterranean Food* (1950) and *An Omelette and a Glass of Wine* (1984) **3** (*French* david) **Jacques Louis** (ʒɑk lwi) 1748–1825, French neoclassical painter of such works as the *Oath of the Horatii* (1784), *Death of Socrates* (1787), and *The Intervention of the Sabine Women* (1799). He actively supported the French Revolution and became court painter to Napoleon Bonaparte in 1804; banished at the Bourbon restoration **4 Saint** 6th century AD, Welsh bishop; patron saint of Wales. Feast day: March 1

David I *n* 1084–1153, king of Scotland (1124–53) who supported his niece Matilda's claim to the English throne and unsuccessfully invaded England on her behalf

David II *n* 1324–71, king of Scotland (1329–71): he was forced into exile in France (1334–41) by Edward de Baliol; captured following the battle of Neville's Cross (1346), and imprisoned by the English (1346–57)

Davies ('deɪvɪs) *n* **1** Sir **John** 1569–1626, English poet, author of *Orchestra or a Poem of Dancing* (1596) and the philosophical poem *Nosce Teipsum* (1599) **2** Sir **Peter Maxwell** born 1934, British composer whose works include the operas *Taverner* (1967), *The Martyrdom of St Magnus* (1977), and *Resurrection* (1988), six symphonies and the ten Strathclyde Concertos (1987–95); Master of the Queen's Music from 2004 **3** (**William**) **Robertson** 1913–95, Canadian novelist and dramatist. His novels include *Leaven of Malice* (1954), *The Rebel Angels* (1981), *What's Bred in the Bone* (1985), and *Murther and Walking Spirits* (1991) **4** **W**(**illiam**) **H**(**enry**) 1871–1940, Welsh poet, noted also for his *Autobiography of a Super-tramp* (1908)

da Vinci (də 'vɪntʃɪ) *n* See **Leonardo da Vinci**

Davis ('deɪvɪs) *n* **1** Sir **Andrew** (**Frank**) born 1944, British conductor; chief conductor of the BBC Symphony Orchestra (1989–2000) and of the Chicago Lyric Opera from 2000 **2** **Bette** ('bɛtɪ), real name *Ruth Elizabeth Davis.* 1908–89, US film actress, whose films include *Of Human Bondage* (1934), *Jezebel* (1938) for which she won an Oscar, *All About Eve* (1950), *Whatever Happened to Baby Jane?* (1962), *The Nanny* (1965), and *The Whales of August* (1987) **3** Sir **Colin** (**Rex**) born 1927, English conductor, noted esp for his performances of Mozart and Berlioz **4** **Jefferson** 1808–89, president of the Confederate States of America during the Civil War (1861–65) **5** **Joe** 1901–78, English billiards and snooker player: world champion from 1927 to 1946 **6** **John** Also called: **John Davys** ?1550–1605, English navigator: discovered the Falkland Islands (1592); searched for a Northwest Passage **7** **Miles** (**Dewey**) 1926–91, US jazz trumpeter and composer: his recordings include *Kind of Blue* (1960) **8** **Steve** born 1957, English snooker player: world champion 1981, 1983–84, 1987–89

Davisson ('deɪvɪsən) *n* **Clinton Joseph** 1881–1958, US physicist, noted for his discovery of electron diffraction; shared the Nobel prize for physics in 1937

Davis Strait ('deɪvɪs) *n* a strait between Baffin Island, in Canada, and Greenland [named after John *Davis* (??1550–1605), English navigator]

davit ('dævɪt, 'deɪ-) *n* a cranelike device, usually one of a pair, fitted with a tackle for suspending or lowering equipment, esp a lifeboat [c14 from Anglo-F *daviot*, dim. of *Davi* David]

Davos ('dævɒs) *n* a mountain resort in Switzerland: winter sports, site of the Parsenn ski run. Pop: 10 500 (1990). Height: about 1560 m (5118 ft). Romansh name: **Tarau**

Davy ('deɪvɪ) *n* Sir **Humphry** 1778–1829, English chemist who isolated sodium, magnesium, chlorine, and other elements and suggested the electrical nature of chemical combination. He invented the **Davy lamp**

Davy Jones *n* **1** Also called: **Davy Jones's locker** the ocean's bottom, esp when regarded as the grave of those lost or buried at sea **2** the spirit of the sea [c18 from ?]

Davy lamp *n* See **safety lamp** [c19 after Sir H. Davy, who invented it]

daw (dɔː) *n* an archaic, dialect, or poetic name for a **jackdaw** [c15 rel. to OHG *taha*]

dawdle ('dɔːdᵊl) *vb* **dawdles, dawdling, dawdled** **1** (*intr*) to be slow or lag behind **2** (when *tr*, often foll by *away*) to waste (time); trifle [c17 from ?] > '**dawdler** *n*

Dawes (dɔːz) *n* **Charles Gates** 1865–1951, US financier, diplomat, and statesman, who devised the Dawes Plan for German reparations payments after World War I; vice president of the US (1925–29); Nobel peace prize 1925

Dawkins ('dɔːkɪnz) *n* **Richard** born 1941, British zoologist, noted for such works as *The Selfish Gene* (1976), *The Blind Watchmaker* (1986), and *River Out of Eden* (1995)

dawn (dɔːn) *n* **1** daybreak. Related adj: **auroral** **2** the sky when light first appears in the morning **3** the beginning of something ▹ *vb* (*intr*) **4** to begin to grow light after the night **5** to begin to develop or appear **6** (usually foll by *on* or *upon*) to begin to become apparent (to) [OE *dagian* to dawn] > '**dawn,like** *adj*

dawn chorus *n* the singing of large numbers of birds at dawn

dawn raid *n stock exchange* an unexpected attempt to acquire a substantial proportion of a company's shares at the start of a day's trading as a preliminary to a takeover bid

Dawson Creek *n* a town in W Canada, in NE British Columbia: SE terminus of the Alaska Highway. Pop: 10 981 (1991)

day (deɪ) *n* **1** Also called: **civil day** the period of time, the **calendar day**, of 24 hours' duration reckoned from one midnight to the next **2a** the period of light between sunrise and sunset **2b** (*as modifier*): *the day shift* **3** the part of a day occupied with regular activity, esp work **4** (*sometimes pl*) a period or point in time: *in days gone by; any day now* **5** the period of time, the **sidereal day**, during which the earth makes one complete revolution on its axis relative to a particular star **6** the period of time, the **solar day**, during which the earth makes one complete revolution on its axis relative to the sun **7** the period of time taken by a specified planet to make one complete rotation on its axis: *the Martian day* **8** (*often cap*) a day designated for a special observance: *Christmas Day* **9** a time of success, recognition, etc: *his day will come* **10** a struggle or issue at hand: *the day is lost* **11** **all in a day's work** part of one's normal activity **12** **at the end of the day** in the final reckoning **13** **call it a day** to stop work or other activity **14** **day after day** without respite; relentlessly **15** **day by day** gradually or progressively **16** **day in, day out** every day and all day long **17** **day of rest** the Sabbath; Sunday **18** **every dog has his day** one's luck will come **19** **in this day and age** nowadays **20** **that will be the day** **20a** that is most unlikely to happen **20b** I look forward to that ▹ Related adj: **diurnal** ▹ See also **days** [OE *dæg*]

Dayak ('daɪæk) *n, pl* **Dayaks** *or* **Dayak** a variant spelling of **Dyak**

Dayan (daɪ'jaːn) *n* **Moshe** ('mɒʃɛ) 1915–81, Israeli soldier and statesman; minister of defence (1967; 1969–74) and foreign minister (1977–79)

day bed *n* a narrow bed intended for use as a seat and as a bed

daybook ('deɪˌbʊk) *n book-keeping* a book in which the transactions of each day are recorded as they occur

dayboy ('deɪˌbɔɪ) *n Brit* a boy who attends a boarding school daily, but returns home each evening > '**daygirl** *fem n*

daybreak ('deɪˌbreɪk) *n* the time in the morning when light first appears; dawn; sunrise

daycare ('deɪˌkɛə) *n Brit social welfare* **1** occupation, treatment, or supervision during the working day for people who might be at risk if left on their own **2** welfare services provided by a local authority, health service, etc, during the day

daycentre ('deɪˌsɛntə) *or* **day centre** *n Brit social welfare* **1** a building used for daycare or other welfare services **2** the enterprise itself, including staff, users, and organization

daydream ('deɪˌdriːm) *n* **1** a pleasant dreamlike fantasy indulged in while awake **2** a pleasant scheme or wish that is unlikely to be fulfilled ▹ *vb* **3** (*intr*) to indulge in idle fantasy > '**day,dreamer** *n* > '**day,dreamy** *adj*

Day-Glo *n trademark* **a** a brand of fluorescent colouring materials, as of paint **b** (*as modifier*): *Day-Glo colours*

day labourer *n* an unskilled worker hired and paid by the day

Day-Lewis ('deɪ'luːɪs) *or* **Day Lewis** *n* **C**(**ecil**) 1904–72, British poet, critic, and (under the pen name *Nicholas Blake*) author of detective stories; poet laureate (1968–72)

daylight ('deɪˌlaɪt) *n* **1** light from the sun **2** daytime

Dd

3 daybreak **4 see daylight 4a** to understand something previously obscure **4b** to realize that the end of a difficult task is approaching

daylight robbery *n inf* blatant overcharging

daylights ('deɪ,laɪts) *pl n* consciousness or wits(esp in **scare, knock,** or **beat the (living) daylights out of someone**)

daylight-saving time *n* time set usually one hour ahead of the local standard time, widely adopted in the summer to provide extra daylight in the evening

daylong ('deɪ,lɒŋ) *adj, adv* lasting the entire day; all day

day release *n Brit* a system whereby workers are released for part-time education without loss of pay

day return *n* a reduced fare for a journey (by train, etc) travelling both ways in one day

day room *n* a communal living room in a residential institution such as a hospital

days (deɪz) *adv inf* during the day, esp regularly: *he works days*

day school *n* **1** a private school taking day students only **2** a school giving instruction during the daytime

daytime ('deɪ,taɪm) *n* the time between dawn and dusk

day-to-day *adj* routine; everyday

day trading *n* the practice of buying shares and selling them later the same day, often via the Internet, in order to make a quick profit > **day trader** *n*

day trip *n* a journey made to and from a place within one day > **'day-,tripper** *n*

Da Yunhe ('dæ 'ju:nhə) *n* the Pinyin transliteration of the Chinese name for the **Grand Canal** (sense 1)

daze (deɪz) *vb* **dazes, dazing, dazed** (*tr*) **1** to stun, esp by a blow or shock **2** to bewilder or amaze ▷ *n* **3** a state of stunned confusion or shock(esp in **in a daze**) [C14 from ON *dasa-*, as in *dasast* to grow weary]

dazzle ('dæzᵊl) *vb* **dazzles, dazzling, dazzled 1** (*usually tr*) to blind or be blinded partially and temporarily by sudden excessive light **2** (*tr*) to amaze, as with brilliance ▷ *n* **3** bright light that dazzles **4** bewilderment caused by glamour, brilliance, etc: *the dazzle of fame* [C15 from DAZE] > **'dazzler** *n* > **'dazzling** *adj* > **'dazzlingly** *adv*

dazzle gun *n* a weapon consisting of a laser gun used to dazzle enemy pilots

dB *or* **db** *symbol for* decibel *or* decibels

DBE *abbrev for* Dame (Commander of the Order) of the British Empire (a Brit title)

DBMS *abbrev for* database management system

DBS *abbrev for* direct broadcasting by satellite
▷ www.dbsforums.com

dbx *or* **DBX** *n trademark, electronics* a noise-reduction system that works across the full frequency spectrum

DC *abbrev for:* **1** *music* da capo **2** direct current ▷ Cf **AC** **3** Also: **D.C.** District of Columbia

DCB *abbrev for* Dame Commander of the Order of the Bath (a Brit title)

DCC *abbrev for* digital compact cassette

DCM *Brit mil abbrev for* Distinguished Conduct Medal

DCMS (in Britain) *abbrev for* Department for Culture, Media, and Sport

DD *abbrev for:* **1** Doctor of Divinity **2** Also: **dd** direct debit

D-day *n* the day selected for the start of some operation, esp of the Allied invasion of Europe on June 6, 1944 [C20 from *D(ay)-day*]
▷ www.dday.co.uk
▷ www.ddaymuseum.org

DDR *abbrev for* Deutsche Demokratische Republik (the former East Germany; GDR)

DDS *or* **DDSc** *abbrev for* Doctor of Dental Surgery *or* Science

DDT *n* dichlorodiphenyltrichloroethane; a colourless odourless substance used as an insecticide. It is now banned in the UK

de- *prefix forming verbs and verbal derivatives* **1** removal of or from something: *deforest; dethrone* **2** reversal of something: *decode; desegregate* **3** departure from: *decamp* [from L, from *dē* (prep) from, away from, out of, etc In compound words of Latin origin, *de-* also means away, away from (*decease*); down (*degrade*); reversal (*detect*); removal (*defoliate*); and is used intensively (*devote*) and pejoratively (*detest*)]

deacon ('di:kən) *n Christianity* **1** (in the Roman Catholic and other episcopal churches) an ordained minister ranking immediately below a priest **2** (in some other churches) a lay official who assists the minister, esp in secular affairs [OE, ult. from Gk *diakonos* servant] > **'deaconate** *n* > **'deacon,ship** *n*

deaconess ('di:kənɪs) *n Christianity* (in the early church and in some modern Churches) a female member of the laity with duties similar to those of a deacon

deactivate (di:'æktɪ,veɪt) *vb* **deactivates, deactivating, deactivated 1** (*tr*) to make (a bomb, etc) harmless or inoperative **2** (*intr*) to become less radioactive > **de'acti,vator** *n*

dead (dɛd) *adj* **1a** no longer alive **1b** (*as collective n; preceded by the*): *the dead* **2** not endowed with life; inanimate **3** no longer in use, effective, or relevant: *a dead issue; a dead language* **4** unresponsive or unaware **5** lacking in freshness or vitality **6** lacking activity or excitement: *this place is dead at night* **7** devoid of physical sensation; numb **8** resembling death: *a dead sleep* **9** no longer burning or hot: *dead coals* **10** (of flowers or foliage) withered; faded **11** (*prenominal*) (intensifier): *a dead stop* **12** *inf* very tired **13** *electronics* **13a** drained of electric charge **13b** not connected to a source of potential difference or electric charge **14** lacking acoustic reverberation: *a dead sound* **15** *sport* (of a ball, etc) out of play **16** accurate; precise(esp in **a dead shot**) **17** lacking resilience or bounce: *a dead ball* **18** not yielding a return: *dead capital* **19** (of colours) not glossy or bright **20** stagnant: *dead air* **21** *mil* shielded from view, as by a geographic feature **22 dead from the neck up** *inf* stupid **23 dead to the world** *inf* unaware of one's surroundings, esp asleep or drunk ▷ *n* **24** a period during which coldness, darkness, etc is at its most intense: *the dead of winter* ▷ *adv* **25** (intensifier): *dead easy; stop dead* **26 dead on** exactly right [OE *dēad*] > **'deadness** *n*

dead-and-alive *adj Brit* (of a place, activity, or person) dull; uninteresting

dead-ball line *n rugby* a line behind the goal line beyond which the ball is out of play

deadbeat ('dɛd,bi:t) *n* **1** *inf* a lazy or socially undesirable person **2** *chiefly US* **2a** a person who makes a habit of evading his or her responsibilities or debts **2b** (*as modifier*): *a deadbeat dad* **3** a high grade escapement used in pendulum clocks **4** (*modifier*) without recoil

dead beat *adj inf* very tired; exhausted

dead-cat bounce *n stock exchange inf* a temporary recovery in prices following a substantial fall as a result of speculators buying stocks they have already sold rather than as a result of a genuine reversal of the downward trend

dead centre *n* **1** the exact top or bottom of the piston stroke in a reciprocating engine or pump **2** a rod mounted in the tailstock of a lathe to support a workpiece ▷ Also called: **dead point**

dead data *n computing* data that is no longer relevant

dead duck *n sl* a person or thing doomed to death, failure, etc, esp because of a mistake

deaden ('dɛdᵊn) *vb* **1** to make or become less sensitive, intense, lively, etc **2** (*tr*) to make acoustically less resonant > **'deadening** *adj*

dead end *n* **1** a cul-de-sac **2** a situation in which further progress is impossible

deadeye ('dɛd,aɪ) *n* **1** *naut* either of a pair of disclike wooden blocks, supported by straps in grooves around them, between which a line is rove so as to draw them together to tighten a shroud **2** *inf, chiefly US* an expert marksman

deadfall ('dɛd,fɔːl) *n* a trap in which a heavy weight falls to crush the prey

deadhead ('dɛd,hɛd) *n* **1** a person who uses a free ticket, as for the theatre, etc **2** a train, etc, travelling empty **3** *US & Canad* a dull person **4** *US & Canad* a totally or partially submerged log floating in a lake, etc ▷ *vb* **5** (*intr*) *US & Canad* to drive an empty bus, train, etc **6** (*tr*) to remove dead flower heads

Dead Heart *n* (usually preceded by *the*) *Austral* the remote interior of Australia [c20 from the title *The Dead Heart of Australia* (1906) by J. W. Gregory (1864–1932), British geologist]

dead heat *n* **a** a race or contest in which two or more participants tie for first place **b** a tie between two or more contestants in any position

dead leg *n inf* temporary loss of sensation in the leg, caused by a blow to a muscle

dead letter *n* **1** a law or ordinance that is no longer enforced **2** a letter that cannot be delivered or returned because it lacks adequate directions

deadlight ('dɛd,laɪt) *n* **1** *naut* **1a** a bull's-eye to admit light to a cabin **1b** a shutter for sealing off a porthole or cabin window **2** a skylight designed not to be opened

deadline ('dɛd,laɪn) *n* a time limit for any activity

deadlock ('dɛd,lɒk) *n* **1** a state of affairs in which further action between two opposing forces is impossible **2** a tie between opponents **3** a lock having a bolt that can be opened only with a key ▷ *vb* **4** to bring or come to a deadlock

dead loss *n* **1** a complete loss for which no compensation is paid **2** *inf* a useless person or thing

deadly ('dɛdlɪ) *adj* **deadlier, deadliest 1** likely to cause death **2** *inf* extremely boring ▷ *adv, adj* **3** like death in appearance or certainty

deadly nightshade *n* a poisonous Eurasian plant having purple bell-shaped flowers and black berries. Also called: **belladonna, dwale**

deadly sins *pl n* the sins of pride, covetousness, lust, envy, gluttony, anger, and sloth

dead man's handle *or* **pedal** *n* a safety switch on a piece of machinery that allows operation only while depressed by the operator

dead march *n* a piece of solemn funeral music played to accompany a procession

dead-nettle *n* any of several Eurasian plants having leaves resembling nettles but lacking stinging hairs

deadpan ('dɛd,pæn) *adj, adv* with a deliberately emotionless face or manner

dead reckoning *n* a method of establishing one's position using the distance and direction travelled rather than astronomical observations

Dead Sea *n* a lake between Israel and Jordan, 397 m (1302 ft) below sea level: the lowest lake in the world, with no outlet and very high salinity. Area: 1020 sq km (394 sq miles)

dead set *adv* **1** absolutely: *he is dead set against going to Spain* ▷ *n* **2** the motionless position of a dog when pointing towards game ▷ *adj* **3** (of a hunting dog) in this position

dead soldier *or* **marine** *n inf* an empty beer bottle

dead time *n electronics* the time immediately following a stimulus, during which an electrical device, component, etc is insensitive to a further stimulus

dead weight *n* **1** a heavy weight or load **2** an oppressive burden **3** the difference between the loaded and the unloaded weights of a ship **4** the intrinsic invariable weight of a structure, such as a bridge

deadwood ('dɛd,wʊd) *n* **1** dead trees or branches **2** *inf* a useless person; encumbrance

deaf (dɛf) *adj* **1a** partially or totally unable to hear **1b** (*as collective n*; preceded by *the*): *the deaf* **2** refusing to heed [OE *dēaf*] > '**deafness** *n*

USAGE See at **disabled**

▷ www.drf.org

deaf aid *n* another name for **hearing aid**

deaf-and-dumb *offens* ▷ *adj* **1** unable to hear or speak ▷ *n* **2** a deaf-mute person

deafblind ('dɛf,blaɪnd) *adj* **a** unable to hear or see **b** (*as collective n*; preceded by *the*): *the deafblind.*

USAGE See at **disabled**

deafen ('dɛfᵊn) *vb* (*tr*) to make deaf, esp momentarily, as by a loud noise

deafening ('dɛfᵊnɪŋ) *adj* **1** excessively loud: *deafening music* **2** complete; absolute: *the government's deafening silence* > '**deafeningly** *adv*

deaf-mute *n* **1** a person who is unable to hear or speak. See also **mute** (sense 7) ▷ *adj* **2** unable to hear or speak [c19 translation of F *sourd-muet*]

USAGE Nowadays this word would be considered offensive, and should be replaced by *profoundly deaf*

Deakin ('diːkɪn) *n* **Alfred** 1856–1919, Australian statesman. He was a leader of the movement for Australian federation; prime minister of Australia (1903–04; 1905–08; 1909–10)

deal[1] (diːl) *vb* **deals, dealing, dealt 1** (*intr*; foll by *in*) to engage in commercially: *to deal in upholstery* **2** (often foll by *out*) to apportion or distribute **3** (*tr*) to give (a blow, etc) to (someone); inflict **4** (*intr*) *sl* to sell any illegal drug ▷ *n* **5** *inf* a bargain, transaction, or agreement **6** a particular type of treatment received, esp as the result of an agreement: *a fair deal* **7** an indefinite amount(esp in **good** *or* **great deal**) **8** *cards* **8a** the process of distributing the cards **8b** a player's turn to do this **8c** a single round in a card game **9 big deal** *sl* an important person, event, or matter: often used sarcastically **10 cut a deal** *inf, chiefly US* to come to an arrangement; make a deal ▷ See also **deal with** [OE *dǣlan*, from *dǣl* a part; cf. OHG *teil* a part, ON *deild* a share]

deal[2] (diːl) *n* **1** a plank of softwood timber, such as fir or pine, or such planks collectively **2** the sawn wood of various coniferous trees ▷ *adj* **3** of fir or pine [c14 from MLow G *dele* plank]

Dd

Deal (diːl) *n* a town in SE England, in Kent, on the English Channel: two 16th-century castles: tourism, light industries. Pop: 28 504 (1991)

dealer ('diːlə) *n* **1** a person or firm engaged in commercial purchase and sale; trader: *a car dealer* **2** *cards* the person who distributes the cards **3** *sl* a person who sells illegal drugs

dealings ('diːlɪŋz) *pl n* (*sometimes sing*) transactions or business relations

dealt (dɛlt) *vb* the past tense and past participle of **deal**[1]

deal with *vb* (*tr, adv*) **1** to take action on: *to deal with each problem in turn* **2** to punish: *the headmaster will deal with the culprit* **3** to treat or be concerned with: *the book deals with architecture* **4** to conduct onself (towards others), esp with regard to fairness **5** to do business with: *we deal with many suppliers*

dean (diːn) *n* **1** the chief administrative official of a college or university faculty **2** (at Oxford and Cambridge universities) a college fellow with responsibility for undergraduate discipline **3** *chiefly Church of England* the head of a chapter of canons and administrator of a cathedral or collegiate church **4** *RC Church* the cardinal bishop senior by consecration and head of the college of cardinals. Related adj: **decanal**. ▷ See also **rural dean** [c14 from OF *deien*, from LL *decānus* one set over ten persons, from L *decem* ten]

Dean[1] (diːn) *n* **Forest of** a forest in W England, in Gloucestershire, between the Rivers Severn and Wye: formerly a royal hunting ground

Dean[2] (diːn) *n* **1 Christopher** See **Torvill and Dean** **2 James** (**Byron**) 1931–55, US film actor, who became a cult figure; his films include *East of Eden* and *Rebel Without a Cause* (both 1955). He died in a car crash

Deane (diːn) *n* Sir **William Patrick** born 1931, Australian lawyer. He became a High Court judge in 1982 and governor-general of Australia (1995–2001)

deanery ('diːnərɪ) *n, pl* **deaneries** 1 the office or residence of a dean 2 the group of parishes presided over by a rural dean

dear (dɪə) *adj* 1 beloved; precious 2 used in conventional forms of address, as in *Dear Sir* 3 (*postpositive; foll by to*) important; close 4a highly priced 4b charging high prices 5 appealing 6 **for dear life** with extreme vigour or desperation ▷ *interj* 7 used in exclamations of surprise or dismay, such as *Oh dear!* ▷ *n* 8 Also: **dearest** (*often used in direct address*) someone regarded with affection and tenderness ▷ *adv* 9 dearly [OE *dēore*] > **'dearness** *n*

dearly ('dɪəlɪ) *adv* 1 very much 2 affectionately 3 at a great cost

dearth (dɜːθ) *n* an inadequate amount, esp of food; scarcity [C13 *derthe*, from *dēr* DEAR]

deary *or* **dearie** ('dɪərɪ) *n* 1 (*pl* **dearies**) *inf* a term of affection: now often sarcastic or facetious ▷ *interj* 2 **deary** *or* **dearie me!** an exclamation of surprise or dismay

death (dɛθ) *n* 1 the permanent end of all functions of life in an organism 2 an instance of this: *his death ended an era* 3 a murder or killing 4 termination or destruction 5 a state of affairs or an experience considered as terrible as death 6 a cause or source of death 7 (*usually cap*) a personification of death, usually a skeleton or an old man holding a scythe 8 **at death's door** likely to die soon 9 **catch one's death (of cold)** *inf* to contract a severe cold 10 **do to death** 10a to kill 10b to overuse 11 **in at the death** 11a present when a hunted animal is killed 11b present at the finish or climax 12 **like death warmed up** *inf* very ill 13 **like grim death** as if afraid of one's life 14 **put to death** to kill deliberately or execute 15 **to death** 15a until dead 15b very much ▷ Related adjs.: **fatal, lethal, mortal** [OE *dēath*]

death adder *n* a venomous thick-bodied Australian snake

deathbed ('dɛθˌbɛd) *n* the bed in which a person is about to die

deathblow ('dɛθˌbləʊ) *n* a thing or event that destroys life or hope, esp suddenly

death camp *n* a concentration camp in which the conditions are so brutal that few prisoners survive, or one to which prisoners are sent for execution

death cap *or* **angel** *n* a poisonous woodland fungus with white gills and a cuplike structure at the base of the stalk

death certificate *n* a legal document issued by a qualified medical practitioner certifying the death of a person and stating the cause if known

death duty *n* a tax on property inheritances, in Britain replaced by capital transfer tax in 1975 and since 1986 by inheritance tax. Also called: **estate duty**

death futures *pl n* life insurance policies of terminally ill people that are bought speculatively for a lump sum by a company, enabling it to collect the proceeds of the policies when the ill people die

death knell *or* **bell** *n* 1 something that heralds death or destruction 2 a bell rung to announce a death

deathless ('dɛθlɪs) *adj* immortal, esp because of greatness; everlasting > **'deathlessness** *n*

deathly ('dɛθlɪ) *adj* 1 deadly 2 resembling death: *a deathly quiet*

death mask *n* a cast of a dead person's face

death rate *n* the ratio of deaths in a specified area, group, etc, to the population of that area, group, etc. Also called: **mortality rate**

death rattle *n* a low-pitched gurgling sound sometimes made by a dying person

death's-head *n* a human skull or a representation of one

death's-head moth *n* a European hawk moth having markings resembling a human skull on its upper thorax

death star *n* a weapon consisting of a flat star-shaped piece of metal with sharpened points that is thrown at an opponent. Also called: **throwing star**

death tourist *n inf* a seriously ill person who seeks to terminate his or her own life by travelling to a country where medically assisted suicide is legal

death trap *n* a building, vehicle, etc, that is considered very unsafe

Death Valley *n* a desert valley in E California and W Nevada: the lowest, hottest, and driest area of the US. Lowest point: 86 m (282 ft) below sea level. Area: about 3885 sq km (1500 sq miles)

death warrant *n* 1 the official authorization for carrying out a sentence of death 2 **sign one's (own) death warrant** to cause one's own destruction

deathwatch ('dɛθˌwɒtʃ) *n* 1 a vigil held beside a dying or dead person 2 **deathwatch beetle** a beetle whose woodboring larvae are a serious pest. The adult produces a tapping sound that was once supposed to presage death

death wish *n* (in Freudian psychology) the desire for self-annihilation

Deauville ('dəʊviːl; *French* dovil) *n* a town and resort in NW France: casino. Pop: 4770 (latest est)

deb (dɛb) *n inf* short for **debutante**

debacle (deɪ'bɑːkᵊl, dɪ-) *n* 1 a sudden disastrous collapse or defeat; rout 2 the breaking up of ice in a river, often causing flooding 3 a violent rush of water carrying along debris [C19 from F, from OF *desbacler* to unbolt]

debag (diː'bæg) *vb* **debags, debagging, debagged** (*tr*) *Brit sl* to remove the trousers from (someone) by force

debar (dɪ'bɑː) *vb* **debars, debarring, debarred** (*tr; usually foll by from*) to exclude from a place, a right, etc; bar > **de'barment** *n*

USAGE See at **disbar**

debark[1] (dɪ'bɑːk) *vb* another word for **disembark** [C17 from F *débarquer*, from *dé-* DIS-[1] + *barque* BARQUE] > **debarkation** (ˌdiːbɑː'keɪʃən) *n*

debark[2] (diː'bɑːk) *vb* (*tr*) to remove the bark from (a tree) [C18 from DE- + BARK[2]]

debase (dɪ'beɪs) *vb* **debases, debasing, debased** (*tr*) to lower in quality, character, or value; adulterate [C16 see DE-, BASE[2]] > **de'basement** *n* > **de'baser** *n*

debate (dɪ'beɪt) *n* 1 a formal discussion, as in a legislative body, in which opposing arguments are put forward 2 discussion or dispute 3 the formal presentation and opposition of a specific motion, followed by a vote ▷ *vb* **debates, debating, debated** 4 to discuss (a motion, etc), esp in a formal assembly 5 to deliberate upon (something) [C13 from OF *debatre* to discuss, argue, from L *battuere*] > **de'batable** *adj* > **de'bater** *n*

debauch (dɪ'bɔːtʃ) *vb* 1 (*when tr, usually passive*) to lead into a life of depraved self-indulgence 2 (*tr*) to seduce (a woman) ▷ *n* 3 an instance or period of extreme dissipation [C16 from OF *desbaucher* to corrupt, lit.: to shape (timber) roughly, from *bauch* beam, of Gmc origin] > **de'baucher** *n* > **de'bauchery** *n*

debauchee (ˌdɛbɔː'tʃiː) *n* a man who leads a life of promiscuity and self-indulgence

debenture (dɪ'bɛntʃə) *n* 1 a long-term bond, bearing fixed interest and usually unsecured, issued by a company or governmental agency 2 a certificate acknowledging a debt 3 a customs certificate providing for a refund of excise or import duty [C15 from L *dēbentur mihi* there are owed to me, from *dēbēre*] > **de'bentured** *adj*

debenture stock *n* shares issued by a company, which guarantee a fixed return at regular intervals

debilitate (dɪ'bɪlɪˌteɪt) *vb* **debilitates, debilitating, debilitated** (*tr*) to make feeble; weaken [C16 from L, from *dēbilis* weak] > **deˌbili'tation** *n* > **de'bilitative** *adj*

debility (dɪ'bɪlɪtɪ) *n, pl* **debilities** weakness or infirmity

debit ('dɛbɪt) *n* **1a** acknowledgment of a sum owing by entry on the left side of an account **1b** the left side of an account **1c** an entry on this side **1d** the total of such entries **1e** (*as modifier*): *a debit balance* ▷ *vb* **debits, debiting, debited 2** (*tr*) **2a** to record (an item) as a debit in an account **2b** to charge (a person or his or her account) with a debt [C15 from L *dēbitum* DEBT]

debit card *n* an embossed plastic card issued by a bank or building society to enable its customers to pay for goods or services by inserting it into a computer-controlled device at the place of sale, which is connected through the telephone network to the bank or building society. It may also function as a cash card, a cheque card, or both

debonair *or* **debonnaire** (ˌdɛbə'nɛə) *adj* **1** suave and refined **2** carefree; light-hearted **3** courteous and cheerful [C13 from OF, from *de bon aire* having a good disposition] > ˌ**debo'nairly** *adv* > ˌ**debo'nairness** *n*

Deborah ('dɛbərə, -brə) *n Old Testament* **1** a prophetess and judge of Israel who fought the Canaanites (Judges 4, 5) **2** Rebecca's nurse (Genesis 35:8)

debouch (dɪ'baʊtʃ) *vb* (*intr*) **1** (esp of troops) to move into a more open space **2** (of a river, glacier, etc) to flow into a larger area or body [C18 from F *déboucher*, from *dé-* DIS-[1] + *bouche* mouth] > **de'bouchment** *n*

Debrett (də'brɛt) *n* a list, considered exclusive, of the British aristocracy. In full: **Debrett's Peerage** [C19 after J. Debrett (c 1750–1822), London publisher who first issued it]

debrief (diː'briːf) *vb* (*tr*) to elicit a report from (a soldier, diplomat, etc) after a mission or event > **de'briefing** *n*

debris *or* **débris** ('deɪbrɪ, 'dɛbrɪ) *n* **1** fragments of something destroyed or broken; rubble **2** a collection of loose material derived from rocks, or an accumulation of animal or vegetable matter [C18 from F, from obs. *debrisier* to break into pieces, of Celtic origin]

de Broglie (*French* də brɔj) *n* See (Louis Victor de) **Broglie**

debt (dɛt) *n* **1** something owed, such as money, goods, or services **2 bad debt** a debt that has little prospect of being paid **3** an obligation to pay or perform something **4** the state of owing something, or of being under an obligation(esp in **in debt, in** (**someone's**) **debt**) [C13 from OF *dette*, from L *dēbitum*, from *dēbēre* to owe, from DE- + *habēre* to have]

debt collector *n* a person employed to collect debts for creditors

debt of honour *n* a debt that is morally but not legally binding

debtor ('dɛtə) *n* a person or commercial enterprise that owes a financial obligation

debt swap *n* See **swap** (sense 4)

debud (diː'bʌd) *vb* **debuds, debudding, debudded** another word for **disbud**

debug (diː'bʌg) *vb* **debugs, debugging, debugged** (*tr*) *inf* **1** to locate and remove concealed microphones from (a room, etc) **2** to locate and remove defects in (a device, system, plan, etc) **3** to remove insects from [C20 from DE- + BUG]

debunk (diː'bʌŋk) *vb* (*tr*) *inf* to expose the pretensions or falseness of, esp by ridicule [C20 from DE- + BUNK[2]] > **de'bunker** *n*

debus (diː'bʌs) *vb* **debuses, debusing, debused** *or* **debusses, debussing, debussed** to unload (goods, etc) or(esp of troops) to alight from a bus

Debussy (də'bjuːsɪ, 'deɪbjuːsɪ; *French* dəbysi) *n* (**Achille**) **Claude** (klod) 1862–1918, French composer and critic, the creator of impressionism in music and a profound influence on contemporary composition. His works include *Prélude à l'après- midi d'un faune* (1894) and *La Mer* (1905) for orchestra, the opera *Pelléas et Mélisande* (1902), and many piano pieces and song settings

debut ('deɪbjuː, 'dɛbjuː) *n* **1a** the first public appearance of an actor, musician, etc **1b** (*as modifier*): *debut album* **2** the presentation of a debutante [C18 from F, from OF *desbuter* to play first, from *des-* DE- + *but* goal, target]

debutant ('dɛbjʊˌtɑːnt, -ˌtænt) *n* a person who is making a first appearance in a particular capacity, such as a sportsperson playing in a first game for a team

debutante ('dɛbjʊˌtɑːnt, -ˌtænt) *n* **1** a young upper-class woman who is formally presented to society **2** a young woman regarded as being upper-class, wealthy, and frivolous [C19 from F, from *débuter* to lead off in a game, make one's first appearance; see DEBUT]

Debye (*Dutch* de'bɛiə) *n* **Peter Joseph Wilhelm** 1884–1966, Dutch chemist and physicist, working in the US: Nobel prize for chemistry (1936) for his work on dipole moments

dec. *abbrev for:* **1** deceased **2** decimal **3** decimetre **4** *music* decrescendo

Dec. *abbrev for* December

deca-, deka- *or before a vowel* **dec-, dek-** *prefix* denoting ten: *decagon*. In conjunction with scientific units the symbol **da** is used [from Gk *deka*]

decade ('dɛkeɪd, dɪ'keɪd) *n* **1** a period of ten years **2** a group of ten [C15 from OF, from LL, from Gk, from *deka* ten] > **de'cadal** *adj*

> USAGE Though this word may be pronounced with the stress on the first or the second syllable, stressing the first syllable is preferable

decadence ('dɛkədəns) *or* **decadency** *n* **1** deterioration, esp of morality or culture **2** the state reached through such a process **3** (*often cap*) the period or style associated with the 19th-century decadents [C16 from F, from Med. L *dēcadentia*, lit.: a falling away; see DECAY]

decadent ('dɛkədənt) *adj* **1** characterized by decline, as in being self-indulgent or morally corrupt **2** belonging to a period of decline in artistic standards ▷ *n* **3** a decadent person **4** (*often cap*) one of a group of French and English writers of the late 19th century whose works were characterized by refinement of style and a tendency toward the artificial and abnormal

Dd

decaf ('diːkæf) *inf* ▷ *n* **1** decaffeinated coffee ▷ *adj* **2** decaffeinated

decaffeinate (dɪ'kæfɪˌneɪt) *vb* **decaffeinates, decaffeinating, decaffeinated** (*tr*) to remove all or part of the caffeine from (coffee, tea, etc)

decagon ('dɛkəˌgɒn) *n* a polygon having ten sides > **decagonal** (dɪ'kægənᵊl) *adj*

decahedron (ˌdɛkə'hiːdrən) *n* a solid figure having ten plane faces > ˌ**deca'hedral** *adj*

decal (dɪ'kæl, 'diːkæl) *n* **1** short for **decalcomania** ▷ *vb* **decals, decalling, decalled** *or US* **decals, decaling, decaled 2** to transfer (a design, etc) by decalcomania

decalcify (diː'kælsɪˌfaɪ) *vb* **decalcifies, decalcifying, decalcified** (*tr*) to remove calcium or lime from (bones, etc) > **de'calciˌfier** *n*

decalcomania (dɪˌkælkə'meɪnɪə) *n* **1** the process of transferring a design from prepared paper onto another surface, such as glass or paper **2** a design so transferred [C19 from F, from *décalquer*, from *de-* DE- + *calquer* to trace + *-manie* -MANIA]

decalitre *or US* **decaliter** ('dɛkəˌliːtə) *n* a metric measure of volume equivalent to 10 litres

Decalogue ('dɛkəˌlɒg) *n* another name for the **Ten Commandments** [C14 from Church L *decalogus*, from Gk, from *deka* ten + *logos* word]

decametre *or US* **decameter** ('dɛkəˌmiːtə) *n* a metric measure of length equivalent to 10 metres

decamp (dɪ'kæmp) *vb* (*intr*) **1** to leave a camp; break camp **2** to depart secretly or suddenly; abscond > **de'campment** *n*

decanal (dɪ'keɪnᵊl) *adj* **1** of a dean or deanery **2** on the same side of a cathedral, etc, as the dean; on the S side of the choir [C18 from Med. L *decānālis*, *decānus* DEAN]

decani (dɪ'keɪnaɪ) *adj, adv music* to be sung by the decanal side of a choir. ▷ Cf **cantoris** [L: genitive of *decānus*]

decant (dɪˈkænt) *vb* **1** to pour (a liquid, such as wine) from one container to another, esp without disturbing any sediment **2** (*tr*) to rehouse (people) while their homes are being rebuilt or refurbished [C17 from Med. L *dēcanthāre*, from *canthus* spout, rim]

decanter (dɪˈkæntə) *n* a stoppered bottle, into which a drink is poured for serving

decapitate (dɪˈkæpɪˌteɪt) *vb* **decapitates, decapitating, decapitated** (*tr*) to behead [C17 from LL *dēcapitāre*, from L DE- + *caput* head] > **deˌcapiˈtation** *n* > **deˈcapiˌtator** *n*

decapod (ˈdɛkəˌpɒd) *n* **1** any crustacean having five pairs of walking limbs, as a crab, lobster, shrimp, etc **2** any cephalopod mollusc having eight short tentacles and two longer ones, as a squid or cuttlefish > **decapodal** (dɪˈkæpədᵊl), **deˈcapodan,** *or* **deˈcapodous** *adj*

decarbonate (diːˈkɑːbəˌneɪt) *vb* **decarbonates, decarbonating, decarbonated** (*tr*) to remove carbon dioxide from > **deˌcarbonˈation** *n* > **deˈcarbonˌator** *n*

decarbonize *or* **decarbonise** (diːˈkɑːbəˌnaɪz) *vb* **decarbonizes, decarbonizing, decarbonized** *or* **decarbonises, decarbonising, decarbonised** (*tr*) to remove carbon from (an internal-combustion engine, etc). Also: **decoke, decarburize** > **deˌcarboniˈzation** *or* **deˌcarboniˈsation** *n* > **deˈcarbonˌizer** *or* **deˈcarbonˌiser** *n*

decarboxylase (ˌdiːkɑːˈbɒksɪˌleɪz) *n* an enzyme that catalyses the removal of carbon dioxide from a compound

decastyle (ˈdɛkəˌstaɪl) *n* *archit* a portico consisting of ten columns

decasyllable (ˈdɛkəˌsɪləbᵊl) *n* a word or line of verse consisting of ten syllables > **decasyllabic** (ˌdɛkəsɪˈlæbɪk) *adj*

decathlon (dɪˈkæθlɒn) *n* an athletic contest in which each athlete competes in ten different events [C20 from DECA- + Gk *athlon* contest, prize; see ATHLETE] > **deˈcathlete** *n*

decay (dɪˈkeɪ) *vb* **1** to decline or cause to decline gradually in health, prosperity, excellence, etc; deteriorate **2** to rot or cause to rot; decompose **3** (*intr*) Also: **disintegrate** *physics* **3a** (of an atomic nucleus) to undergo radioactive disintegration **3b** (of an elementary particle) to transform into two or more different elementary particles **4** (*intr*) *physics* (of a stored charge, magnetic flux, etc) to decrease gradually when the source of energy has been removed ▷ *n* **5** the process of decline, as in health, mentality, etc **6** the state brought about by this process **7** decomposition **8** rotten or decayed matter **9** *physics* **9a** See **radioactive decay** **9b** a spontaneous transformation of an elementary particle into two or more different particles **10** *physics* a gradual decrease of a stored charge, current, etc, when the source of energy has been removed [C15 from OF *decaïr*, from LL *dēcadere*, lit.: to fall away, from L *cadere* to fall] > **deˈcayable** *adj*

Deccan (ˈdɛkən) *n* **the 1** a plateau in S India, between the Eastern Ghats, the Western Ghats, and the Narmada River **2** the whole Indian peninsula south of the Narmada River

decease (dɪˈsiːs) *n* **1** a more formal word for **death** ▷ *vb* **deceases, deceasing, deceased 2** (*intr*) a more formal word for **die**[1] [C14 (n): from OF, from L *dēcēdere* to depart]

deceased (dɪˈsiːst) *adj* **a** a more formal word for **dead** (sense 1) **b** (*as n; preceded by the*): *the deceased*

deceit (dɪˈsiːt) *n* **1** the act or practice of deceiving **2** a statement, act, or device intended to mislead; fraud; trick **3** a tendency to deceive [C13 from OF, from *deceivre* to DECEIVE]

deceitful (dɪˈsiːtfʊl) *adj* full of deceit

deceive (dɪˈsiːv) *vb* **deceives, deceiving, deceived** (*tr*) **1** to mislead by deliberate misrepresentation or lies **2** to delude (oneself) **3** to be unfaithful to (one's sexual partner) **4** *arch* to disappoint [C13 from OF *deceivre*, from L *dēcipere* to ensnare, cheat, from *capere* to take] > **deˈceivable** *adj* > **deˈceiver** *n*

decelerate (diːˈsɛləˌreɪt) *vb* **decelerates, decelerating, decelerated** to slow down or cause to slow down [C19 from DE- + (AC)CELERATE] > **deˌcelerˈation** *n* > **deˈcelerˌator** *n*

December (dɪˈsɛmbə) *n* the twelfth month of the year, consisting of 31 days [C13 from OF, from L: the tenth month (the Roman year orig. began with March), from *decem* ten]

decencies (ˈdiːsᵊnsɪz) *pl n* **1 the** those things that are considered necessary for a decent life **2** another word for **proprieties**, see **propriety** (sense 3)

decency (ˈdiːsᵊnsɪ) *n, pl* **decencies 1** conformity to the prevailing standards of propriety, morality, modesty, etc **2** the quality of being decent

decennial (dɪˈsɛnɪəl) *adj* **1** lasting for ten years **2** occurring every ten years ▷ *n* **3** a tenth anniversary > **deˈcennially** *adv*

decent (ˈdiːsᵊnt) *adj* **1** polite or respectable **2** proper and suitable; fitting **3** conforming to conventions of sexual behaviour; not indecent **4** free of oaths, blasphemy, etc **5** good or adequate: *a decent wage* **6** *inf* kind; generous **7** *inf* sufficiently clothed to be seen by other people: *are you decent?* [C16 from L *decēns* suitable, from *decēre* to be fitting] > **ˈdecently** *adv*

decentralize *or* **decentralise** (diːˈsɛntrəˌlaɪz) *vb* **decentralizes, decentralizing, decentralized** *or* **decentralises, decentralising, decentralised 1** to reorganize into smaller more autonomous units **2** to disperse (a concentration, as of industry or population) > **deˈcentralist** *n, adj* > **deˌcentraliˈzation** *or* **deˌcentraliˈsation** *n*

deception (dɪˈsɛpʃən) *n* **1** the act of deceiving or the state of being deceived **2** something that deceives; trick

deceptive (dɪˈsɛptɪv) *adj* likely or designed to deceive; misleading > **deˈceptively** *adv* > **deˈceptiveness** *n*

decertify (diːˈsɜːtɪˌfaɪ) *vb* **decertifies, decertifying, decertified** (*tr*) to withdraw or remove a certificate or certification from (a person, organization, or country) > **deˌcertifiˈcation** *n*

de Chastelain (də ˈʃæstəlɪn) *n* **(Alfred) John (Gardyne Drummond)** born 1937, Canadian general and diplomat; chairman of the international body on arms decommissioning in Northern Ireland from 1997

deci- *prefix* denoting one tenth: *decimetre*. Symbol: d [from F *déci-*, from L *decimus* tenth]

decibel (ˈdɛsɪˌbɛl) *n* **1** a unit for comparing two currents, voltages, or power levels, equal to one tenth of a bel **2** a similar unit for measuring the intensity of a sound. Abbrev: **dB**

decide (dɪˈsaɪd) *vb* **decides, deciding, decided 1** (*may take a clause or an infinitive as object;* when *intr*, sometimes foll by *on* or *about*) to reach a decision: *decide what you want; he decided to go* **2** (*tr*) to cause to reach a decision **3** (*tr*) to determine or settle (a contest or question) **4** (*tr*) to influence decisively the outcome of (a contest or question) **5** (*intr;* foll by *for* or *against*) to pronounce a formal verdict [C14 from OF, from L *dēcīdere*, lit.: to cut off, from *caedere* to cut] > **deˈcidable** *adj*

decided (dɪˈsaɪdɪd) *adj* (*prenominal*) **1** unmistakable **2** determined; resolute: *a girl of decided character* > **deˈcidedly** *adv*

decider (dɪˈsaɪdə) *n* the point, goal, game, etc, that determines who wins a match or championship

deciduous (dɪˈsɪdjʊəs) *adj* **1** (of trees and shrubs) shedding all leaves annually at the end of the growing season and then having a dormant period without leaves. ▷ Cf **evergreen 2** (of antlers, teeth, etc) being shed at the end of a period of growth [C17 from L: falling off, from *dēcidere* to fall down, from *cadere* to fall] > **deˈciduousness** *n*

decilitre *or US* **deciliter** (ˈdɛsɪˌliːtə) *n* a metric measure of volume equivalent to one tenth of a litre

decillion (dɪˈsɪljən) *n* **1** (in Britain, France, and Germany) the number represented as one followed by 60 zeros (10^{60}) **2** (in the US and Canada) the number represented as one followed by 33 zeros (10^{33}) [c19 from L *decem* ten + *-illion* as in *million*] > **deˈcillionth** *adj*

decimal (ˈdɛsɪməl) *n* **1** Also called: **decimal fraction** a fraction that has an unwritten denominator of a power of ten. It is indicated by a decimal point to the left of the numerator: *.2=2/10* **2** any number used in the decimal system ▷ *adj* **3a** relating to or using powers of ten **3b** of the base ten **4** (*prenominal*) expressed as a decimal [c17 from Med. L *decimālis* of tithes, from L *decima* a tenth] > **ˈdecimally** *adv*

decimal classification *n* another term for **Dewey Decimal System**

decimal currency *n* a system of currency in which the monetary units are parts or powers of ten

decimalize *or* **decimalise** (ˈdɛsɪməˌlaɪz) *vb* **decimalizes, decimalizing, decimalized** *or* **decimalises, decimalising, decimalised** to change (a system, number, etc) to the decimal system > **ˌdecimaliˈzation** *or* **ˌdecimaliˈsation** *n*

decimal place *n* **1** the position of a digit after the decimal point **2** the number of digits to the right of the decimal point

decimal point *n* a full stop or a raised full stop placed between the integral and fractional parts of a number in the decimal system.

> **USAGE** Conventions relating to the use of the decimal point are confused. The IX General Conference on Weights and Measures resolved in 1948 that the decimal point should be a point on the line or a comma, but not a centre dot. It also resolved that figures could be grouped in threes about the decimal point, but that no point or comma should be used for this purpose. These conventions are adopted in this dictionary. However, the Decimal Currency Board recommended that for sums of money the centre dot should be used as the decimal point and that the comma should be used as the thousand marker. Moreover, in some countries the position is reversed, the comma being used as the decimal point and the dot as the thousand marker

decimal system *n* **1** the number system in general use, having a base of ten, in which numbers are expressed by combinations of the ten digits 0 to 9 **2** a system of measurement in which the multiple and submultiple units are related to a basic unit by powers of ten

decimate (ˈdɛsɪˌmeɪt) *vb* **decimates, decimating, decimated** (*tr*) **1** to destroy or kill a large proportion of **2** (esp in the ancient Roman army) to kill every tenth man of (a mutinous section) [c17 from L *decimāre*, from *decem* ten] > **ˌdeciˈmation** *n* > **ˈdeciˌmator** *n*

> **USAGE** The antiquarian view that this word is only properly used to refer to slaughtering one in ten of a population, because of what it meant in Latin, now seems wilfully obscurantist. Nowadays the word is used not only to describe the destruction of people and animals, but also of institutions: *overseas visitors will stay away in droves, decimating the tourist industry*. When using this word it is advisable to refer to its effects on the whole of something, not on a part: *disease decimated the population*, not *disease decimated most of the population*

decimetre *or US* **decimeter** (ˈdɛsɪˌmiːtə) *n* one tenth of a metre. Symbol: **dm**

decipher (dɪˈsaɪfə) *vb* (*tr*) **1** to determine the meaning of (something obscure or illegible) **2** to convert from code into plain text; decode > **deˈcipherable** *adj* > **deˈcipherment** *n*

decision (dɪˈsɪʒən) *n* **1** a judgment, conclusion, or resolution reached or given; verdict **2** the act of making up one's mind **3** firmness of purpose or character; determination [c15 from OF, from L *dēcīsiō*, lit.: a cutting off; see DECIDE]

decision tree *n* a treelike diagram illustrating the choices available to a decision maker, each possible decision and its estimated outcome being shown as a separate branch of the tree

decisive (dɪˈsaɪsɪv) *adj* **1** influential; conclusive **2** characterized by the ability to make decisions, esp quickly; resolute > **deˈcisively** *adv* > **deˈcisiveness** *n*

deck (dɛk) *n* **1** *naut* any of various platforms built into a vessel **2** a similar platform, as in a bus **3a** the horizontal platform that supports the turntable and pick-up of a record player **3b** See **tape deck** **4** *chiefly US* a pack of playing cards **5** *computing* a collection of punched cards relevant to a particular program **6** **clear the decks** *inf* to prepare for action, as by removing obstacles **7** **hit the deck** *inf* **7a** to fall to the ground, esp to avoid injury **7b** to prepare for action **7c** to get out of bed ▷ *vb* (*tr*) **8** (often foll by *out*) to dress or decorate **9** to build a deck on (a vessel) **10** *sl* to knock (someone) to the floor or ground [c15 from MDu. *dec* a covering]

deck-access *adj* (of a block of flats) having a continuous balcony at each level onto which the front door of each flat opens

deck chair *n* a folding chair consisting of a wooden frame suspending a length of canvas

-decker *adj* (*in combination*) having a certain specified number of levels or layers: *a double-decker bus*

Decker (ˈdɛkə) *n* a variant spelling of (Thomas) **Dekker**

deck hand *n* **1** a seaman assigned duties on the deck of a ship **2** (in Britain) a seaman who has seen sea duty for at least one year **3** a helper aboard a yacht

Dd

decking (ˈdɛkɪŋ) *n* a form of floor covering, used in gardens, made from varnished or stained wooden boards or tiles

deckle *or* **deckel** (ˈdɛkᵊl) *n* **1** a frame used to contain pulp on the mould in the making of handmade paper **2** a strap on a paper-making machine that fixes the width of the paper [c19 from G *Deckel* lid, from *decken* to cover]

deckle edge *n* **1** the rough edge of paper made using a deckle, often left as ornamentation **2** an imitation of this > **ˈdeckle-ˈedged** *adj*

declaim (dɪˈkleɪm) *vb* **1** to make (a speech, etc) loudly and in a rhetorical manner **2** to speak lines from (a play, poem, etc) with studied eloquence **3** (*intr*; foll by *against*) to protest (against) loudly and publicly [c14 from L *dēclāmāre*, from *clāmāre* to call out] > **deˈclaimer** *n* > **declamatory** (dɪˈklæmətərɪ) *adj*

declamation (ˌdɛkləˈmeɪʃən) *n* **1** a rhetorical or emotional speech, made esp in order to protest; tirade **2** a speech, verse, etc, that is or can be spoken **3** the act or art of declaiming

declaration (ˌdɛkləˈreɪʃən) *n* **1** an explicit or emphatic statement **2** a formal statement or announcement **3** the act of declaring **4** the ruling of a judge or court on a question of law **5** *law* an unsworn statement of a witness admissible in evidence under certain conditions **6** *cricket* the voluntary closure of an innings before all ten wickets have fallen **7** *contract bridge* the final contract **8** a statement or inventory of goods, etc, submitted for tax assessment

declarative (dɪˈklærətɪv) *or* **declaratory** (dɪˈklærətərɪ, -trɪ) *adj* making or having the nature of a declaration > **deˈclaratively** *or* **deˈclaratorily** *adv*

declare (dɪˈklɛə) *vb* **declares, declaring, declared** (*mainly* tr) 1 (*may take a clause as object*) to make clearly known or announce officially: *war was declared* 2 to state officially that (a person, fact, etc) is as specified: *he declared him fit* 3 (*may take a clause as object*) to state emphatically; assert 4 to show, reveal, or manifest 5 (*intr; often foll by for or against*) to make known one's choice or opinion 6 to make a statement of (dutiable goods, etc) 7 (*also intr*) *Cards* 7a to display (cards) on the table so as to add to one's score 7b to decide (the trump suit) by making the final bid 8 (*intr*) *cricket* to close an innings voluntarily before all ten wickets have fallen 9 to authorize payment of (a dividend) [c14 from L *dēclārāre* to make clear, from *clārus* clear] > **de'clarable** *adj* > **de'clarer** *n*

declassify (di:'klæsɪ,faɪ) *vb* **declassifies, declassifying, declassified** (*tr*) to release (a document or information) from the security list > **de,classifi'cation** *n*

declension (dɪ'klɛnʃən) *n* 1 *grammar* 1a inflection of nouns, pronouns, or adjectives for case, number, and gender 1b the complete set of the inflections of such a word 2 a decline or deviation 3 a downward slope [c15 from L *dēclīnātiō*, lit.: a bending aside, hence variation; see DECLINE] > **de'clensional** *adj*

declination (,dɛklɪ'neɪʃən) *n* 1 *astron* the angular distance of a star, planet, etc, north or south from the celestial equator. Symbol: δ 2 the angle made by a compass needle with the direction of the geographical north pole 3 a refusal, esp a courteous or formal one > **,decli'national** *adj*

decline (dɪ'klaɪn) *vb* **declines, declining, declined** 1 to refuse to do or accept (something), esp politely 2 (*intr*) to grow smaller; diminish 3 to slope or cause to slope downwards 4 (*intr*) to deteriorate gradually 5 *grammar* to list the inflections of (a noun, adjective, or pronoun), or (of a noun, adjective, or pronoun) to be inflected for number, case, or gender ▷ *n* 6 gradual deterioration or loss 7 a movement downward; diminution 8 a downward slope 9 *arch* any slowly progressive disease, such as tuberculosis [c14 from OF *decliner*, from L *dēclīnāre* to bend away, inflect grammatically] > **de'clinable** *adj* > **de'cliner** *n*

declivity (dɪ'klɪvɪtɪ) *n, pl* **declivities** a downward slope, esp of the ground [c17 from L *dēclīvitās*, from DE- + *clīvus* a slope, hill] > **de'clivitous** *adj*

declutch (dɪ'klʌtʃ) *vb* (*intr*) to disengage the clutch of a motor vehicle

declutter (di:'klʌtə) *vb* to simplify or get rid of mess, disorder, complications, etc: *declutter your life*

decoct (dɪ'kɒkt) *vb* to extract the essence or active principle from (a medicinal or similar substance) by boiling [c15 see DECOCTION]

decoction (dɪ'kɒkʃən) *n* 1 *pharmacol* the extraction of the water-soluble substances of a drug or medicinal plants by boiling 2 the liquor resulting from this [c14 from OF, from LL, from *dēcoquere* to boil down, from *coquere* to cook]

decode (di:'kəʊd) *vb* **decodes, decoding, decoded** to convert from code into ordinary language > **de'coder** *n*

decoke (di:'kəʊk) *vb* **decokes, decoking, decoked** (*tr*) another word for **decarbonize**

décolletage (,deɪkɒl'tɑ:ʒ) *n* a low-cut dress or neckline [c19 from F; see DÉCOLLETÉ]

décolleté (deɪ'kɒlteɪ) *adj* 1 (of a woman's garment) low-cut 2 wearing a low-cut garment ▷ *n* 3 a low-cut neckline [c19 from F *décolleter* to cut out the neck (of a dress), from *collet* collar]

decolonize *or* **decolonise** (di:'kɒlə,naɪz) *vb* **decolonizes, decolonizing, decolonized** *or* **decolonises, decolonising, decolonised** (*tr*) to grant independence to (a colony) > **de,coloni'zation** *or* **de,coloni'sation** *n*

decolour (di:'kʌlə), **decolorize,** *or* **decolorise** *vb* **decolorizes, decolorizing, decolorized** *or* **decolorises, decolorising, decolorised** (*tr*) to deprive of colour > **de,colori'zation** *or* **de,colori'sation** *n*

decommission (,di:kə'mɪʃən) *vb* (*tr*) to dismantle or remove from service (a nuclear reactor, weapon, ship, etc which is no longer required)

decompose (,di:kəm'pəʊz) *vb* **decomposes, decomposing, decomposed** 1 to break down or be broken down physically and chemically by bacterial or fungal action; rot 2 *chem* to break down or cause to break down into simpler chemical compounds 3 to break up or separate into constituent parts > **decomposition** (,di:kɒmpə'zɪʃən) *n*

decomposer (,di:kəm'pəʊzə) *n* a person or thing that causes decomposition, esp any of the organisms, such as bacteria or fungi, that break down dead tissue enabling the constituents to be recycled to the environment

decompress (,di:kəm'prɛs) *vb* 1 to relieve or be relieved of pressure 2 to return (a diver, etc) to a condition of normal atmospheric pressure or to be returned to such a condition > **,decom'pression** *n*

decompression chamber *n* a chamber in which the pressure of air can be varied slowly for returning people safely from abnormal pressures to atmospheric pressure

decompression sickness *or* **illness** *n* a disorder characterized by severe pain, cramp, and difficulty in breathing, caused by a sudden and sustained decrease in atmospheric pressure

decongestant (,di:kən'dʒɛstənt) *adj* 1 relieving congestion, esp nasal congestion ▷ *n* 2 a decongestant drug

deconsecrate (di:'kɒnsɪ,kreɪt) *vb* **deconsecrates, deconsecrating, deconsecrated** (*tr*) to transfer (a church, etc) to secular use > **de,conse'cration** *n*

deconstruct (,di:kən'strʌkt) *vb* (*tr*) 1 to apply the theories of deconstruction to (a text, film, etc) 2 to expose or dismantle the existing structure in (a system, organization, etc)

deconstruction (,di:kən'strʌkʃən) *n* a technique of literary analysis that regards meaning as resulting from the differences between words rather than their reference to the things they stand for

decontaminate (,di:kən'tæmɪ,neɪt) *vb* **decontaminates, decontaminating, decontaminated** (*tr*) to render harmless by the removal or neutralization of poisons, radioactivity, etc > **,decon,tami'nation** *n*

decontrol (,di:kən'trəʊl) *vb* **decontrols, decontrolling, decontrolled** (*tr*) to free of restraints or controls, esp government controls: *to decontrol prices*

décor *or* **decor** ('deɪkɔ:) *n* 1 a style or scheme of interior decoration, furnishings, etc, as in a room or house 2 stage decoration; scenery [c19 from F, from *décorer* to DECORATE]

decorate ('dɛkə,reɪt) *vb* **decorates, decorating, decorated** 1 (*tr*) to ornament; adorn 2 to paint or wallpaper 3 (*tr*) to confer a mark of distinction, esp a medal, upon [c16 from L *decorāre*, from *decus* adornment] > **'decorative** *adj*

Decorated style *n* a 14th-century style of English architecture characterized by geometrical tracery and floral decoration
▷ www.britainexpress.com/architecture/decorated.htm

decoration (,dɛkə'reɪʃən) *n* 1 an addition that renders something more attractive or ornate 2 the act or art of decorating 3 a medal, etc, conferred as a mark of honour

decorator ('dɛkə,reɪtə) *n* 1 *Brit* a person whose profession is the painting and wallpapering of buildings or their interiors 2 a person who decorates

decorous ('dɛkərəs) *adj* characterized by propriety in manners, conduct, etc [c17 from L, from *decor* elegance] > **'decorously** *adv* > **'decorousness** *n*

decorum (dɪ'kɔ:rəm) *n* 1 propriety, esp in behaviour or conduct 2 a requirement of correct behaviour in polite society [c16 from L: propriety]

decoupage (ˌdeɪkuːˈpɑːʒ) *n* the decoration of a surface with cutout shapes or illustrations [c20 from F, from *découper*, from DE- + *couper* to cut]
▷ www.decoupage.org

decoy *n* (ˈdiːkɔɪ, dɪˈkɔɪ) **1** a person or thing used to lure someone into danger **2** *mil* something designed to deceive an enemy **3** a bird or animal, or an image of one, used to lure game into a trap or within shooting range **4** a place into which game can be lured for capture **5** *Canad* another word for **deke** (sense 2) ▷ *vb* (dɪˈkɔɪ) **6** to lure or be lured by or as if by means of a decoy **7** (*tr*) *Canad* another word for **deke** (sense 1) [c17 prob. from Du. *de kooi*, lit.: the cage, from L *cavea* CAGE]

decrease *vb* (dɪˈkriːs). **decreases, decreasing, decreased** **1** to diminish or cause to diminish in size, strength, etc ▷ *n* (ˈdiːkriːs, dɪˈkriːs) **2** a diminution; reduction **3** the amount by which something has been diminished [c14 from OF, from L *dēcrescere* to grow less, from DE- + *crescere* to grow] > **deˈcreasing** *adj* > **deˈcreasingly** *adv*

decree (dɪˈkriː) *n* **1** an edict, law, etc, made by someone in authority **2** an order or judgment of a court ▷ *vb* **decrees, decreeing, decreed** **3** to order, adjudge, or ordain by decree [c14 from OF, from L *dēcrētum* ordinance, from *dēcrētus* decided, p.p. of *dēcernere*]

decree absolute *n* the final decree in divorce proceedings, which leaves the parties free to remarry

decree nisi (ˈnaɪsaɪ) *n* a provisional decree, esp in divorce proceedings, which will later be made absolute unless cause is shown why it should not

decrement (ˈdɛkrɪmənt) *n* **1** the act of decreasing; diminution **2** *maths* a negative increment **3** *physics* a measure of the damping of an oscillator or oscillation, expressed by the ratio of amplitudes in successive cycles [c17 from L *dēcrēmentum*, from *dēcrescere* to DECREASE]

decrepit (dɪˈkrɛpɪt) *adj* **1** enfeebled by old age; infirm **2** broken down or worn out by hard or long use; dilapidated [c15 from L *dēcrepitus*, from *crepāre* to creak] > **deˈcrepiˌtude** *n*

decrescendo (ˌdiːkrɪˈʃɛndəʊ) *n, adj* another word for **diminuendo** [It., from *decrescere* to DECREASE]

decrescent (dɪˈkrɛsənt) *adj* (esp of the moon) decreasing; waning [c17 from L *dēcrescēns* growing less; see DECREASE] > **deˈcrescence** *n*

decretal (dɪˈkriːtᵊl) *n* **1** *RC Church* a papal decree; edict on doctrine or church law ▷ *adj* **2** of or relating to a decree [c15 from OF, from LL *dēcrētālis*; see DECREE]

decriminalize *or* **decriminalise** (diːˈkrɪmɪnᵊˌlaɪz) *vb* **decriminalizes, decriminalizing, decriminalized** *or* **decriminalises, decriminalising, decriminalised** (*tr*) to remove (an action) from the legal category of criminal offence: *to decriminalize the possession of marijuana*

decry (dɪˈkraɪ) *vb* **decries, decrying, decried** (*tr*) **1** to express open disapproval of; disparage **2** to depreciate by proclamation: *to decry obsolete coinage* [c17 from OF *descrier*, from *des-* DIS-¹ + *crier* to CRY]

decumbent (dɪˈkʌmbənt) *adj* **1** lying down **2** *bot* (of stems) lying flat with the tip growing upwards [c17 from L, present participle of *dēcumbere* to lie down] > **deˈcumbency** *n*

Dedéagach, Dedeagatch, *or* **Dedeağaç** (ˈdɛdeɪɑːˈgɑːtʃ) *n* a former name (until the end of World War I) of **Alexandroúpolis**

Dedekind (*German* ˈdedəˌkɪnt) *n* (**Julius Wilhelm**) **Richard** (ˈjuːlɪʊs ˈvɪlhɛlm ˈrɪxɑːt) 1831–1916, German mathematician, who devised a way (the **Dedekind cut**) of according irrational and rational numbers the same status

dedicate (ˈdɛdɪˌkeɪt) *vb* **dedicates, dedicating, dedicated** (*tr*) **1** (often foll by *to*) to devote (oneself, one's time, etc) wholly to a special purpose or cause **2** (foll by *to*) to address a book, performance, etc, to a person, cause, etc, as a token of affection or respect **3** (foll by *to*) to request or play (a record) on radio for another person as a greeting **4** to assign or allocate to a particular project, function, etc **5** to set apart for a deity or for sacred uses [c15 from L *dēdicāre* to announce, from *dicāre* to make known] > **ˈdediˌcator** *n* > **dedicatory** (ˈdɛdɪˌkeɪtərɪ, ˈdɛdɪkətərɪ) *or* **ˈdediˌcative** *adj*

dedicated (ˈdɛdɪˌkeɪtɪd) *adj* **1** devoted to a particular purpose or cause **2** assigned or allocated to a particular project, function, etc: *a dedicated transmission line* **3** *computing* designed to fulfil one function

dedication (ˌdɛdɪˈkeɪʃən) *n* **1** the act of dedicating or being dedicated **2** an inscription prefixed to a book, etc, dedicating it to a person or thing **3** wholehearted devotion, esp to a career, ideal, etc > **ˌdediˈcational** *adj*

deduce (dɪˈdjuːs) *vb* **deduces, deducing, deduced** (*tr*) **1** (*may take a clause as object*) to reach (a conclusion) by reasoning; conclude (that); infer **2** *arch* to trace the origin or derivation of [c15 from L *dēdūcere* to lead away, derive, from DE- + *dūcere* to lead] > **deˈducible** *adj*

deduct (dɪˈdʌkt) *vb* (*tr*) to take away or subtract (a number, quantity, part, etc) [c15 from L *dēductus*, p.p. of *dēdūcere* to DEDUCE]

deductible (dɪˈdʌktɪbᵊl) *adj* **1** capable of being deducted **2** *US* short for **tax-deductible** ▷ *n* **3** *insurance* the US name for **excess** (sense 5)

deduction (dɪˈdʌkʃən) *n* **1** the act or process of deducting or subtracting **2** something that is or may be deducted **3** *logic* **3a** a process of reasoning by which a specific conclusion necessarily follows from a set of general premises **3b** a logical conclusion reached by this process > **deˈductive** *adj*

Dee (diː) *n* **1** a river in N Wales and NW England, rising in S Gwynedd and flowing east and north to the Irish Sea. Length: about 112 km (70 miles) **2** a river in NE Scotland, rising in the Cairngorms and flowing east to the North Sea. Length: about 140 km (87 miles) **3** a river in S Scotland, flowing south to the Solway Firth. Length: about 80 km (50 miles)

Dd

deed (diːd) *n* **1** something that is done or performed; act **2** a notable achievement **3** action as opposed to words **4** *law* a legal document signed, witnessed, and delivered to effect a conveyance or transfer of property or to create a legal contract ▷ *vb* **5** (*tr*) *US* to convey or transfer (property) by deed [OE *dēd*]

deed box *n* a strong box in which deeds and other documents are kept

deed poll *n law* a deed made by one party only, esp one by which a person changes his name

deejay (ˈdiːˌdʒeɪ) *n* an informal name for **disc jockey** [c20 from the initials DJ (disc jockey)]

deem (diːm) *vb* (*tr*) to judge or consider [OE *dēman*]

de-emphasize *or* **de-emphasise** (diːˈɛmfəˌsaɪz) *vb* **de-emphasizes, de-emphasizing, de-emphasized** *or* **de-emphasises, de-emphasising, de-emphasised** (*tr*) to remove emphasis from

deemster (ˈdiːmstə) *n* the title of one of the two justices in the Isle of Man. Also called: **dempster**

de-energize *or* **de-energise** (diːˈɛnədʒaɪz) *vb* **de-energizes, de-energizing, de-energized** *or* **de-energises, de-energising, de-energised** (*tr*) *electrical engineering* to disconnect (an electrical circuit) from its source > **de-ˌenergiˈzation** *or* **de-ˌenergiˈsation** *n*

deep (diːp) *adj* **1** extending or situated far down from a surface: *a deep pool* **2** extending or situated far inwards, backwards, or sideways **3** *cricket* far from the pitch: *the deep field* **4** (*postpositive*) of a specified dimension downwards, inwards, or backwards: *six feet deep* **5** coming from or penetrating to a great depth **6** difficult to understand; abstruse **7** intellectually demanding: *a deep discussion* **8** of great intensity: *deep trouble* **9** (*postpositive*; foll by *in*) absorbed (by); immersed (in): *deep in study* **10** very cunning; devious **11** mysterious: *a deep secret* **12** (of a colour) having an intense or dark hue **13** low in pitch: *a deep voice* **14** **go off**

the deep end *inf* **14a** to lose one's temper; react angrily **14b** *chiefly US* to act rashly **15 in deep water** *inf* in a tricky position or in trouble ▹ *n* **16** any deep place on land or under water **17 the deep 17a** a poetic term for the **ocean 17b** *cricket* the area of the field relatively far from the pitch **18** the most profound, intense, or central part: *the deep of winter* **19** a vast extent, as of space or time ▹ *adv* **20** far on in time; late: *they worked deep into the night* **21** profoundly or intensely **22 deep down** *inf* in reality, esp as opposed to appearance [OE *dēop*] > **'deeply** *adv* > **'deepness** *n*

deep-discount bond *n* a fixed-interest security that pays little or no interest but is issued at a substantial discount to its redemption value, thus largely substituting capital gain for income

deepen ('diːpᵊn) *vb* to make or become deep, deeper, or more intense > **'deepener** *n*

deepfreeze (ˌdiːp'friːz) *n* **1** another name for **freezer 2** storage in a freezer **3** *inf* a state of suspended activity ▹ *vb* **deep-freeze, deep-freezes, deep-freezing, deep-froze, deep-frozen 4** *(tr)* to freeze (food) or keep (food) in a freezer

deep-fry *vb* **deep-fries, deep-frying, deep-fried** to cook (fish, etc) in sufficient hot fat to cover the food

deep-laid *adj* (of a plot or plan) carefully worked out and kept secret

deep-rooted *or* **deep-seated** *adj* (of ideas, beliefs, etc) firmly fixed or held; ingrained

deep-sea *n (modifier)* of, found in, or characteristic of the deep parts of the sea

deep-set *adj* (esp of eyes) deeply set

Deep South *n* the SE part of the US, esp South Carolina, Georgia, Alabama, Mississippi, and Louisiana

deep space *n* any region of outer space beyond the system of the earth and moon

deep structure *n generative grammar* a representation of a sentence at a level where logical or grammatical relations are made explicit ▹ Cf **surface structure**

deep-vein thrombosis *n, pl* **thromboses** (-siːz) a blood clot in one of the major veins, usually in the legs or pelvis; can be caused by prolonged sitting in the same position, as on long-haul air flights. Abbrev: **DVT**

deer (dɪə) *n, pl* **deer** *or* **deers** any of a family of hoofed, ruminant mammals including reindeer, elk, and roe deer, typically having antlers in the male. Related adj: **cervine** [OE *dēor* beast]

deer lick *n* a naturally or artificially salty area of ground where deer come to lick the salt

deerskin ('dɪəˌskɪn) *n* **a** the hide of a deer **b** *(as modifier)*: *a deerskin jacket*

deerstalker ('dɪəˌstɔːkə) *n* **1** a person who stalks deer, esp in order to shoot them **2** a hat, peaked in front and behind, with earflaps usually tied together on the top > **'deerˌstalking** *adj, n*

de-escalate (diː'ɛskəˌleɪt) *vb* **de-escalates, de-escalating, de-escalated** to reduce the level or intensity of (a crisis, etc) or (of a crisis, etc) to decrease in level or intensity > **de-ˌesca'lation** *n*

def (dɛf) *adj sl* very good [c20 ?from *definitive*]

def. *abbrev for* definition

DEFA ('diːfə) (in Britain) *n acronym for* Department of the Environment, Fisheries, and Agriculture

deface (dɪ'feɪs) *vb* **defaces, defacing, defaced** *(tr)* to spoil or mar the surface or appearance of; disfigure > **de'faceable** *adj* > **de'facement** *n* > **de'facer** *n*

de facto (deɪ 'fæktəʊ) *adv* **1** in fact ▹ *adj* **2** existing in fact, whether legally recognized or not: *a de facto regime* ▹ Cf **de jure** ▹ *n, pl* **de factos 3** *Austral & NZ* a de facto wife or husband [c17 L]

defalcate ('diːfælˌkeɪt) *vb* **defalcates, defalcating, defalcated** *(intr) law* to misuse or misappropriate property or funds entrusted to one [c15 from Med. L *dēfalcāre* to cut off, from L DE- + *falx* sickle] > **'defalˌcator** *n*

defame (dɪ'feɪm) *vb* **defames, defaming, defamed** *(tr)* to attack the good name or reputation of; slander; libel [c14 from OF, from L, from *diffāmāre* to spread by unfavourable report, from *fāma* FAME] > **defamation** (ˌdɛfə'meɪʃən) *n* > **defamatory** (dɪ'fæmətərɪ) *adj*

default (dɪ'fɔːlt) *n* **1** a failure to act, esp a failure to meet a financial obligation or to appear in a court of law at a time specified **2** absence or lack **3 by default** in the absence of opposition or a better alternative: *he became prime minister by default* **4 in default of** through or in the lack or absence of **5 judgment by** *or* **in default** *law* a judgment in the plaintiff's favour when the defendant fails to plead or to appear **6** *(also* 'diːfɔːlt) *Computing* **6a** the preset selection of an option offered by a system, which will always be followed except when explicitly altered **6b** *(as modifier)*: *default setting* ▹ *vb* **7** *(intr; often foll by on or in)* to fail to make payment when due **8** *(intr)* to fail to fulfil an obligation **9** *law* to lose (a case) by failure to appear in court [c13 from OF *defaute*, from *defaillir* to fail, from Vulgar L *dēfallīre* (unattested) to be lacking]

defaulter (dɪ'fɔːltə) *n* **1** a person who defaults **2** *chiefly Brit* a person, esp a soldier, who has broken the disciplinary code of his service

defeat (dɪ'fiːt) *vb (tr)* **1** to overcome; win a victory over **2** to thwart or frustrate **3** *law* to render null and void ▹ *n* **4** a defeating or being defeated [c14 from OF, from *desfaire* to undo, ruin, from *des-* DIS-[1] + *faire* to do, from L *facere*]

defeatism (dɪ'fiːtɪzəm) *n* a ready acceptance or expectation of defeat > **de'featist** *n, adj*

defecate ('dɛfɪˌkeɪt) *vb* **defecates, defecating, defecated 1** *(intr)* to discharge waste from the body through the anus **2** *(tr)* to remove impurities from [c16 from L *dēfaecāre* to cleanse from dregs, from DE- + *faex* dregs] > **ˌdefe'cation** *n* > **'defeˌcator** *n*

defect *n* ('diːfɛkt) **1** a lack of something necessary for completeness; deficiency **2** an imperfection or blemish ▹ *vb* (dɪ'fɛkt) **3** *(intr)* to desert one's country, cause, etc, esp in order to join the opposing forces [c15 from L, from *dēficere* to forsake, fail] > **de'fector** *n*

defection (dɪ'fɛkʃən) *n* **1** abandonment of duty, allegiance, principles, etc **2** a shortcoming

defective (dɪ'fɛktɪv) *adj* **1** having a defect or flaw; imperfect **2** (of a person) below the usual standard or level, esp in intelligence **3** *grammar* lacking the full range of inflections characteristic of its form class > **de'fectiveness** *n*

defence *or US* **defense** (dɪ'fɛns) *n* **1** resistance against danger or attack **2** a person or thing that provides such resistance **3** a plea, essay, etc, in support of something **4** a country's military measures or resources **5** *law* a defendant's denial of the truth of the allegations or charge against him or her **6** *law* the defendant and his or her legal advisers collectively **7** *sport* **7a** the action of protecting oneself or part of the playing area against an opponent's attacks **7b** (usually preceded by *the*) the players in a team whose function is to do this **8** *American football* (usually preceded by *the*) **8a** the team that does not have possession of the ball **8b** the members of a team that play in such circumstances **9** *(pl)* fortifications [c13 from OF, from LL *dēfensum*, p.p. of *dēfendere* to DEFEND] > **de'fenceless** *or US* **de'fenseless** *adj*

defence mechanism *n* **1** *psychoanal* an unconscious mental process designed to reduce anxiety or shame **2** *physiol* the protective response of the body against disease

defend (dɪ'fɛnd) *vb* **1** *(tr)* to protect from harm or danger **2** *(tr)* to support in the face of criticism, esp by argument **3** to represent (a defendant) in court **4** *sport* to guard (one's goal, etc) against attack **5** *(tr)* to protect (a title, etc) against a challenge [c13 from OF, from L *dēfendere* to ward off, from DE- + *-fendere* to strike] > **de'fender** *n*

defendant (dɪ'fɛndənt) *n* **1** a person against whom an action or claim is brought in a court of law ▷ Cf **plaintiff** ▷ *adj* **2** defending

defenestration (diːˌfɛnɪˈstreɪʃən) *n* the act of throwing someone out of a window [C17 from NL *dēfenestrātiō*, from L DE- + *fenestra* window]

defensible (dɪˈfɛnsɪbᵊl) *adj* capable of being defended, as in war, an argument, etc > **deˌfensiˈbility** *or* **deˈfensibleness** *n*

defensive (dɪˈfɛnsɪv) *adj* **1** intended for defence **2** rejecting criticisms of oneself ▷ *n* **3** a position of defence **4 on the defensive** in a position of defence, as in being ready to reject criticism > **deˈfensively** *adv*

defer[1] (dɪˈfɜː) *vb* **defers, deferring, deferred** (*tr*) to delay until a future time; postpone [C14 from OF *differer* to be different, postpone; see DIFFER] > **deˈferment** *or* **deˈferral** *n* > **deˈferrer** *n*

defer[2] (dɪˈfɜː) *vb* **defers, deferring, deferred** (*intr*; foll by *to*) to yield to or comply with the wishes or judgments (of) [C15 from L *dēferre*, lit.: to bear down, from DE- + *ferre* to bear]

deference (ˈdɛfərəns) *n* **1** compliance with the wishes of another **2** courteous regard; respect [C17 from F *déférence*; see DEFER[2]]

deferent[1] (ˈdɛfərənt) *adj* another word for **deferential**

deferent[2] (ˈdɛfərənt) *adj* (esp of a nerve or duct) conveying an impulse, fluid, etc, down or away; efferent [C17 from L *dēferre*; see DEFER[2]]

deferential (ˌdɛfəˈrɛnʃəl) *adj* showing deference; respectful > **ˌdeferˈentially** *adv*

defiance (dɪˈfaɪəns) *n* **1** open or bold resistance to authority, opposition, or power **2** a challenge > **deˈfiant** *adj*

defibrillation (dɪˌfaɪbrɪˈleɪʃən) *n med* the application of an electric current to the heart to restore normal contractions after the onset of atrial or ventricular fibrillation

defibrillator (dɪˈfaɪbrɪˌleɪtə) *n med* an apparatus for stopping fibrillation of the heart by application of an electric current

deficiency (dɪˈfɪʃənsɪ) *n, pl* **deficiencies 1** the state or quality of being deficient **2** a lack or insufficiency; shortage **3** a deficit **4** *biol* the absence of a gene or a region of a chromosome normally present

deficiency disease *n* **1** *med* any condition, such as pellagra, beriberi, or scurvy, produced by a lack of vitamins or other essential substances **2** *bot* any disease caused by lack of essential minerals

deficient (dɪˈfɪʃənt) *adj* **1** lacking some essential; incomplete; defective **2** inadequate in quantity or supply; insufficient [C16 from L *dēficiēns* lacking, from *dēficere* to fall short] > **deˈficiently** *adv*

deficit (ˈdɛfɪsɪt, dɪˈfɪsɪt) *n* **1** the amount by which an actual sum is lower than that expected or required **2a** an excess of liabilities over assets **2b** an excess of expenditures over revenues [C18 from L, lit.: there is lacking, from *dēficere*]

deficit financing *n* government spending in excess of revenues so that a budget deficit is incurred, which is financed by borrowing

defile[1] (dɪˈfaɪl) *vb* **defiles, defiling, defiled** (*tr*) **1** to make foul or dirty; pollute **2** to taint; corrupt **3** to damage or sully (someone's reputation, etc) **4** to make unfit for ceremonial use **5** to violate the chastity of [C14 from earlier *defoilen*, from OF *defouler* to trample underfoot, abuse, from DE- + *fouler* to tread upon; see FULL[2]] > **deˈfilement** *n*

defile[2] (ˈdiːfaɪl, dɪˈfaɪl) *n* **1** a narrow pass or gorge **2** a single file of soldiers, etc ▷ *vb* **defiles, defiling, defiled 3** (*intr*) to march in single file [C17 from F, from *défiler* to file off, from *filer* to march in a column, from OF, from L *fīlum* thread]

define (dɪˈfaɪn) *vb* **defines, defining, defined** (*tr*) **1** to state precisely the meaning of (words, terms, etc) **2** to describe the nature, properties, or essential qualities of **3** to determine the boundary or extent of **4** (*often passive*) to delineate the form or outline of: *the shape of the tree was clearly defined by the light behind it* **5** to fix with precision; specify [C14 from OF: to determine, from L *dēfinīre* to set bounds to, from *fīnīre* to FINISH] > **deˈfinable** *adj* > **deˈfiner** *n*

defined-benefit *adj* denoting an occupational pension scheme that guarantees a specified payout, usually based on an employee's final salary and years of service. Abbreviation: **DB** Also called: **final-salary**

definite (ˈdɛfɪnɪt) *adj* **1** clearly defined; exact **2** having precise limits or boundaries **3** known for certain [C15 from L *dēfīnītus* limited, distinct; see DEFINE] > **ˈdefiniteness** *n*

> USAGE *Definite* and *definitive* should be carefully distinguished. *Definite* indicates precision and firmness, as in *a definite decision*. *Definitive* includes these senses but also indicates conclusiveness. *A definite answer* indicates a clear and firm answer to a particular question; *a definitive answer* implies an authoritative resolution of a complex question

definite article *n grammar* a determiner that expresses specificity of reference, such as *the* in English ▷ Cf **indefinite article**

definite integral *n* See **integral**

definitely (ˈdɛfɪnɪtlɪ) *adv* **1** in a definite manner **2** (*sentence modifier*) certainly: *he said he was coming, definitely* ▷ *sentence substitute* **3** unquestionably

definition (ˌdɛfɪˈnɪʃən) *n* **1** a formal and concise statement of the meaning of a word, phrase, etc **2** the act of defining **3** specification of the essential properties of something **4** the act of making clear or definite **5** the state of being clearly defined **6** a measure of the clarity of an optical, photographic, or television image as characterized by its sharpness and contrast

Dd

definitive (dɪˈfɪnɪtɪv) *adj* **1** serving to decide or settle finally **2** most reliable or authoritative **3** serving to define or outline **4** *zool* fully developed **5** (of postage stamps) permanently on sale ▷ *n* **6** *grammar* a word indicating specificity of reference > **deˈfinitively** *adv*

deflate (diːˈfleɪt) *vb* **deflates, deflating, deflated 1** to collapse through the release of gas **2** (*tr*) to take away the self-esteem or conceit from **3** (*tr*) to take away the enthusiasm or excitement from **4** *econ* to cause deflation of (an economy, the money supply, etc) [C19 from DE- + (IN)FLATE] > **deˈflator** *n*

deflation (diːˈfleɪʃən) *n* **1** the act of deflating or the state of being deflated **2** *econ* a reduction in spending and economic activity resulting in lower levels of output, employment, investment, trade, profits, and prices **3** the removal of loose rock material, etc, by wind > **deˈflationary** *adj* > **deˈflationist** *n, adj*

deflect (dɪˈflɛkt) *vb* to turn or cause to turn aside from a course [C17 from L *dēflectere*, from *flectere* to bend] > **deˈflector** *n*

deflection *or* **deflexion** (dɪˈflɛkʃən) *n* **1** a deflecting or being deflected **2** the amount of deviation **3** the change in direction of a light beam as it crosses a boundary between two media with different refractive indexes **4** a deviation of the indicator of a measuring instrument from its zero position > **deˈflective** *adj*

deflocculate (diːˈflɒkjʊˌleɪt) *vb* **deflocculates, deflocculating, deflocculated** (*tr*) to cause (an aggregate) to separate into particles > **deˌfloccuˈlation** *n* > **deˈflocculant** *n*

deflower (diːˈflaʊə) *vb* (*tr*) **1** to deprive(esp a woman) of virginity **2** to despoil of beauty, innocence, etc **3** to rob or despoil of flowers > **ˌdefloˈration** *n*

Defoe (dɪˈfəʊ) *n* **Daniel** ?1660–1731, English novelist, journalist, spymaster, and pamphleteer, noted particularly for his novel *Robinson Crusoe* (1719) His other novels include *Moll Flanders* (1722) and *A Journal of the Plague Year* (1722)

defoliant (diːˈfəʊlɪənt) *n* a chemical sprayed or dusted onto trees to cause their leaves to fall, esp to remove cover from an enemy in warfare

defoliate (diːˈfəʊlɪˌeɪt) *vb* **defoliates, defoliating, defoliated** to deprive (a plant) of its leaves [C18 from Med. L *dēfoliāre*, from L DE- + *folium* leaf] > **deˌfoliˈation** *n*

deforest (diːˈfɒrɪst) *vb* (*tr*) to clear of trees. Also: **disforest** > **deˌforesˈtation** *n*

De Forest (də ˈfɒrɪst) *n* **Lee** 1873–1961, US inventor of telegraphic, telephonic, and radio equipment: patented the first triode valve (1907)

deform (dɪˈfɔːm) *vb* **1** to make or become misshapen or distorted **2** (*tr*) to mar the beauty of; disfigure **3** (*tr*) to subject or be subjected to a stress that causes a change of dimensions [C15 from L *dēformāre*, from DE- + *forma* shape, beauty] > **deˈformable** *adj* > **ˌdeforˈmation** *n*

deformed (dɪˈfɔːmd) *adj* **1** disfigured or misshapen **2** morally perverted; warped

deformity (dɪˈfɔːmɪtɪ) *n, pl* **deformities 1** a deformed condition **2** *pathol* a distortion of an organ or part **3** a deformed person or thing **4** a defect, esp of the mind or morals; depravity

Defra (ˈdɛfrə) (in Britain) *n acronym for* Department for Environment, Food and Rural Affairs

defraud (dɪˈfrɔːd) *vb* (*tr*) to take away or withhold money, rights, property, etc, from (a person) by fraud; swindle > **deˈfrauder** *n*

defray (dɪˈfreɪ) *vb* (*tr*) to provide money for (costs, expenses, etc); pay [C16 from OF *deffroier* to pay expenses, from *de-* DIS-[1] + *frai* expenditure] > **deˈfrayable** *adj* > **deˈfrayal** *or* **deˈfrayment** *n*

defrock (diːˈfrɒk) *vb* (*tr*) to deprive (a person in holy orders) of ecclesiastical status; unfrock

defrost (diːˈfrɒst) *vb* **1** to make or become free of frost or ice **2** to thaw, esp through removal from a deepfreeze

defroster (diːˈfrɒstə) *n* a device by which a de-icing process, as of a refrigerator, is accelerated

deft (dɛft) *adj* quick and neat in movement; nimble; dexterous [C13 (in the sense: gentle): see DAFT] > **ˈdeftly** *adv* > **ˈdeftness** *n*

defunct (dɪˈfʌŋkt) *adj* **1** no longer living; dead or extinct **2** no longer operative or valid [C16 from L *dēfungī* to discharge (one's obligations), die; see DE-, FUNCTION] > **deˈfunctness** *n*

defuse *or US (sometimes)* **defuze** (diːˈfjuːz) *vb* **defuses, defusing, defused** *or US (sometimes)* **defuzes, defuzing, defuzed** (*tr*) **1** to remove the triggering device of (a bomb, etc) **2** to remove the cause of tension from (a crisis, etc).

USAGE See at **diffuse**

defy (dɪˈfaɪ) *vb* **defies, defying, defied** (*tr*) **1** to resist openly and boldly **2** to elude, esp in a baffling way **3** *formal* to challenge (someone to do something); dare **4** *arch* to invite to do battle or combat [C14 from OF *desfier*, from *des-* DE- + *fier* to trust, from L *fidere*] > **deˈfier** *n*

deg. *abbrev for* degree

Degas (ˈdeɪgɑː; *French* dəgɑ) *n* **Hilaire Germain Edgar** (ilɛr ʒɛrmɛ̃ ɛdgar) 1834–1917, French impressionist painter and sculptor, noted for his brilliant draughtsmanship and ability to convey movement, esp in his studies of horse racing and ballet dancers

De Gasperi (*Italian* de ˈgasperi) *n* **Alcide** (alˈtʃiːde) 1881–1954, Italian statesman; prime minister (1945–53). An antifascist, he led the Christian Democratic party during World War II from the Vatican City

de Gaulle (*French* də gol) *n* **Charles** (**André Joseph Marie**) (ʃarl) 1890–1970, French general and statesman. During World War II, he refused to accept Pétain's armistice with Germany and founded the Free French movement in England (1940). He was head of the provisional governments (1944–46) and, as first president of the Fifth Republic (1959–69), he restored political and economic stability to France

degauss (diːˈgaʊs) *vb* (*tr*) to neutralize by producing an opposing magnetic field > **deˈgausser** *n*

degeneracy (dɪˈdʒɛnərəsɪ) *n, pl* **degeneracies 1** the act or state of being degenerate **2** the process of becoming degenerate

degenerate *vb* (dɪˈdʒɛnəˌreɪt). **degenerates, degenerating, degenerated** (*intr*) **1** to become degenerate **2** *biol* (of organisms or their parts) to become less specialized or functionally useless ▷ *adj* (dɪˈdʒɛnərɪt) **3** having declined or deteriorated to a lower mental, moral, or physical level; degraded; corrupt ▷ *n* (dɪˈdʒɛnərɪt) **4** a degenerate person [C15 from L, from *dēgener* departing from its kind, ignoble, from DE- + *genus* race] > **deˈgenerately** *adv* > **deˈgenerateness** *n* > **deˈgenerative** *adj*

degenerate matter *n astrophysics* the highly compressed state of a star's matter when its atoms virtually touch in the final stage of its evolution into a white dwarf

degeneration (dɪˌdʒɛnəˈreɪʃən) *n* **1** the process of degenerating **2** the state of being degenerate **3** *biol* the loss of specialization, function, or structure by organisms and their parts **4** impairment or loss of the function and structure of cells or tissues, as by disease or injury **5** *electronics* negative feedback of a signal

deglaze (diːˈgleɪz) *vb* to dilute meat sediments in (a pan) in order to make a sauce or gravy

degradable (dɪˈgreɪdəbᵊl) *adj* **1** capable of being decomposed chemically or biologically **2** capable of being degraded

degradation (ˌdɛgrəˈdeɪʃən) *n* **1** a degrading or being degraded **2** a state of degeneration or squalor **3** some act, constraint, etc, that is degrading **4** the wearing down of the surface of rocks, cliffs, etc, by erosion **5** *chem* a breakdown of a molecule into atoms or smaller molecules **6** *physics* an irreversible process in which the energy available to do work is decreased **7** *RC Church* the permanent unfrocking of a priest

degrade (dɪˈgreɪd) *vb* **degrades, degrading, degraded 1** (*tr*) to reduce in worth, character, etc; disgrace **2** (diːˈgreɪd) (*tr*) to reduce in rank or status; demote **3** (*tr*) to reduce in strength, quality, etc **4** to reduce or be reduced by erosion or down-cutting, as a land surface or bed of a river **5** *chem* to decompose into atoms or smaller molecules [C14 from LL *dēgradāre*, from L DE- + *gradus* rank, degree] > **deˈgrader** *n*

degrading (dɪˈgreɪdɪŋ) *adj* causing humiliation; debasing > **deˈgradingly** *adv*

degree (dɪˈgriː) *n* **1** a stage in a scale of relative amount or intensity: *a high degree of competence* **2** an academic award conferred by a university or college on successful completion of a course or as an honorary distinction (**honorary degree**) **3** any of three categories of seriousness of a burn **4** (in the US) any of the categories into which a crime is divided according to its seriousness **5** *genealogy* a step in a line of descent **6** *grammar* any of the forms of an adjective used to indicate relative amount or intensity: in English they are *positive, comparative,* and *superlative* **7** *music* any note of a diatonic scale relative to the other notes in that scale **8** a unit of temperature on a specified scale. Symbol: °. See also **Celsius scale, Fahrenheit scale 9** a measure of angle equal to one three-hundred-and-sixtieth of the angle traced by one complete revolution of a line about one of its ends. Symbol: ° **10** a unit of latitude or longitude used to define points on the earth's surface. Symbol: ° **11** a unit on any of several scales of measurement, as for specific gravity. Symbol: ° **12** *maths* **12a** the highest power or the sum of the powers of any term in a polynomial or by itself: $x^4 + x + 3$ *and* xyz^2 *are of the* *fourth degree* **12b** the greatest power of the highest order derivative in a differential equation **13** *obs* a step; rung **14** *arch* a stage in social status or rank **15** **by degrees** little by little; gradually **16** **one degree under** *inf* off colour; ill **17** **to a degree** somewhat; rather [C13 from OF *degre*, from L DE- + *gradus* step]

degree of freedom *n* **1** *chem* the least number of independently variable properties needed to determine the state of a system. See also **phase rule** **2** one of the independent components of motion (translation, vibration, and rotation) of an atom or molecule

de Havilland (də 'hævɪlənd) *n* Sir **Geoffrey** 1882–1965, British aircraft designer. He produced many military aircraft and the first jet airliners

dehisce (dɪ'hɪs) *vb* **dehisces, dehiscing, dehisced** (*intr*) (of fruits, anthers, etc) to burst open spontaneously, releasing seeds, pollen, etc [C17 from L *dēhiscere* to split open, from DE- + *hiscere* to yawn, gape] > **de'hiscent** *adj*

dehorn (diː'hɔːn) *vb* (*tr*) to remove the horns of (cattle, sheep, or goats)

dehumanize *or* **dehumanise** (diː'hjuːməˌnaɪz) *vb* **dehumanizes, dehumanizing, dehumanized** *or* **dehumanises, dehumanising, dehumanised** (*tr*) **1** to deprive of human qualities **2** to render mechanical, artificial, or routine > **deˌhumani'zation** *or* **deˌhumani'sation** *n*

dehumidifier (ˌdiːhjuː'mɪdɪˌfaɪə) *n* a device for reducing the moisture content of the atmosphere

dehumidify (ˌdiːhjuː'mɪdɪˌfaɪ) *vb* **dehumidifies, dehumidifying, dehumidified** (*tr*) to remove water from (the air, etc) > **ˌdehuˌmidifi'cation** *n*

dehydrate (diː'haɪdreɪt, ˌdiːhaɪ'dreɪt) *vb* **dehydrates, dehydrating, dehydrated** **1** to lose or cause to lose water **2** to lose or deprive of water, as the body or tissues > **ˌdehy'dration** *n* > **de'hydrator** *n*

dehydroepiandrosterone (diːˌhaɪdrəʊˌɛpɪæn'drɒstəˌrəʊn) *n* the most abundant steroid in the human body, that is involved in the manufacture of testosterone, oestrogen, progesterone, and corticosteroine

dehydrogenate (diː'haɪdrədʒəˌneɪt), **dehydrogenize,** *or* **dehydrogenise** (diː'haɪdrədʒəˌnaɪz) *vb* **dehydrogenates, dehydrogenating, dehydrogenated, dehydrogenizes, dehydrogenizing, dehydrogenized** *or* **dehydrogenises, dehydrogenising, dehydrogenised** (*tr*) to remove hydrogen from > **deˌhydroge'nation, deˌhydrogeni'zation,** *or* **deˌhydrogeni'sation** *n*

de-ice (diː'aɪs) *vb* **de-ices, de-icing, de-iced** to free or be freed of ice

de-icer (diː'aɪsə) *n* **1** a mechanical or thermal device designed to melt or stop the formation of ice on an aircraft **2** a substance used for this purpose, esp an aerosol that can be sprayed on car windscreens to remove ice or frost

deictic ('daɪktɪk) *adj* **1** *logic* proving by direct argument ▷ Cf **elenctic** (see **elenchus**) ▷ *n* **2** another word for **indexical** (sense 2) [C17 from Gk *deiktikos* concerning proof, from *deiknunai* to show]

deify ('diːɪˌfaɪ, 'deɪɪ-) *vb* **deifies, deifying, deified** (*tr*) **1** to exalt to the position of a god or personify as a god **2** to accord divine honour or worship to [C14 from OF, from LL *deificāre*, from L *deus* god + *facere* to make] > **ˌdeifi'cation** *n* > **'deiˌfier** *n*

Deighton ('deɪtᵊn) *n* **Len** born 1929, British thriller writer. His books include *The Ipcress File* (1962), *Bomber* (1970), and the trilogy *Berlin Game*, *Mexico Set*, and *London Match* (1983–85)

deign (deɪn) *vb* **1** (*intr*) to think it fit or worthy of oneself (to do something); condescend **2** (*tr*) *arch* to vouchsafe [C13 from OF, from L *dignārī* to consider worthy, from *dignus*]

deindividuation (diːˌɪndɪˌvɪdjʊ'eɪʃən) *n* *psychol* the loss of a person's sense of individuality and responsibility

de-industrialization *or* **de-industrialisation** (diːɪndʌstrɪəlaɪ'zeɪʃən) *n* a decline in importance of a country's manufacturing industry

de-ionize *or* **de-ionise** (diː'aɪəˌnaɪz) *vb* **de-ionizes, de-ionizing, de-ionized** *or* **de-ionises, de-ionising, de-ionised** (*tr*) to remove ions from (water, etc), esp by ion exchange > **deˌioni'zation** *or* **deˌioni'sation** *n*

Deirdre ('dɪədrɪ) *n* *Irish myth* a beautiful girl who was raised by Conchobar to be his wife but eloped with Naoise. When Conchobar treacherously killed Naoise she took her own life: often used to symbolize Ireland. See also **Naoise**

deism ('diːɪzəm, 'deɪ-) *n* belief in the existence of God based on natural reason, without revelation ▷ Cf **theism** [C17 from F *déisme*, from L *deus* god] > **'deist** *n, adj* > **de'istic** *or* **de'istical** *adj* > **de'istically** *adv*

deity ('deɪɪtɪ, 'diːɪ-) *n, pl* **deities** **1** a god or goddess **2** the state of being divine; godhead **3** the rank of a god **4** the nature or character of God [C14 from OF, from LL *deitās*, from L *deus* god]

Deity ('deɪɪtɪ, 'diːɪ-) *n* **the** God

déjà vu ('deɪʒæ 'vuː) *n* the experience of perceiving a new situation as if it had occurred before [from F, lit.: already seen]

deject (dɪ'dʒɛkt) *vb* (*tr*) to have a depressing effect on; dispirit; dishearten [C15 from L *dēicere* to cast down, from DE- + *iacere* to throw]

dejected (dɪ'dʒɛktɪd) *adj* miserable; despondent; downhearted > **de'jectedly** *adv*

dejection (dɪ'dʒɛkʃən) *n* **1** lowness of spirits; depression **2a** faecal matter **2b** defecation

de jure (deɪ 'dʒʊəreɪ) *adv* according to law; by right; legally ▷ Cf **de facto** [L]

deka- *or* **dek-** *combining form.* variants of **deca-**

deke (diːk) *Canad sl* ▷ *vb* **dekes, deking, deked** **1** (*tr*) (in ice hockey or box lacrosse) to draw a defending player out of position by faking a shot or movement ▷ *n* **2** such a shot or movement. Also: **decoy** [C20 from DECOY]

Dekker *or* **Decker** ('dɛkə) *n* **Thomas** ?1572–?1632, English dramatist and pamphleteer, noted particularly for his comedy *The Shoemaker's Holiday* (1600) and his satirical pamphlet *The Gull's Hornbook* (1609)

dekko ('dɛkəʊ) *n, pl* **dekkos** *Brit sl* a look; glance [C19 from Hindi *dekho!* look! from *dekhnā* to see]

de Klerk (də 'klɜːk) *n* **F(rederik) W(illem)** born 1936, South African statesman; president (1989–94), second executive deputy president (1994–97). In 1990 he legalized the ANC and released Nelson Mandela from prison, and initiated the abolition of apartheid: Nobel peace prize 1993 jointly with Mandela

de Kooning (də 'kuːnɪŋ) *n* **Willem** See (Willem de) **Kooning**

del (dɛl) *n* *maths* the differential operator $\mathbf{i}(\partial/\partial x) + \mathbf{j}(\partial/\partial y) + \mathbf{k}(\partial/\partial z)$, where $\mathbf{i}$, $\mathbf{j}$, and $\mathbf{k}$ are unit vectors in the x, y, and z directions. Symbol: ∇ Also called: **nabla**

del. *abbrev for* delegate

Del. *abbrev for* Delaware

Delacroix (*French* dəlakrwa) *n* **(Ferdinand Victor) Eugène** (øʒɛn) 1798–1863, French romantic painter whose use of colour and free composition influenced impressionism. His paintings of historical and contemporary scenes include *The Massacre at Chios* (1824)

Delagoa Bay (ˌdɛlə'gəʊə) *n* an inlet of the Indian Ocean, in S Mozambique. Official name: **Baía de Lourenço Marques**

de la Mare (də lɑː mɛə) *n* **Walter (John)** 1873–1956, English poet and novelist, noted esp for his evocative verse for children. His works include the volumes of poetry *The Listeners and Other Poems* (1912) and *Peacock Pie* (1913) and the novel *Memoirs of a Midget* (1921)

Delaroche (*French* dəlarɔʃ) *n* **(Hippolyte) Paul** 1797–1859,

Dd

French painter of portraits and sentimental historical scenes, such as *The Children of Edward IV in the Tower* (1830)

Delaunay (*French* dəlonɛ) *n* **Robert** (rɔbɛr) 1885–1941, French painter, whose abstract use of colour characterized Orphism, an attempt to introduce more colour into austere forms of Cubism

Delaware[1] (ˈdɛləˌwɛə) *n* **1** (*pl* **Delawares** *or* **Delaware**) a member of a North American Indian people formerly livingnear the Delaware River **2** the language of this people

Delaware[2] (ˈdɛləˌwɛə) *n* **1** a state of the northeastern US, on the Delmarva Peninsula: mostly flat and low-lying, with hills in the extreme north and cypress swamps in the extreme south. Capital: Dover. Pop: 783 600 (2000). Area: 5004 sq km (1932 sq miles). Abbreviations: **Del.** or (with zip code) **DE** **2** a river in the northeastern US, rising in the Catskill Mountains and flowing south into **Delaware Bay**, an inlet of the Atlantic. Length 660 km (410 miles)

Delawarean (ˌdɛləˈwɛərɪən) *adj* **1** of or relating to the state of Delaware or its inhabitants **2** of or relating to the Delaware river

De La Warr (ˈdɛləˌwɛə) *n* **Baron,** title of *Thomas West*, known as *Lord Delaware*. 1577–1618, English administrator in America; first governor of Virginia (1610)

delay (dɪˈleɪ) *vb* **1** (*tr*) to put off to a later time; defer **2** (*tr*) to slow up or cause to be late **3** (*intr*) to be irresolute or put off doing something **4** (*intr*) to linger; dawdle ▷ *n* **5** a delaying or being delayed **6** the interval between one event and another [c13 from OF, from *des-* off + *laier* to leave, from L *laxāre* to loosen] > **deˈlayer** *n*

delayed action *or* **delay action** *n* a device for operating a mechanism, such as a camera shutter, a short time after setting

delayed drop *n aeronautics* a parachute descent in which the opening of the parachute is delayed for a predetermined time

delayering (diːˈleɪərɪŋ) *n* the process of pruning the administrative structure of a large organization by reducing the number of tiers in its hierarchy

dele (ˈdiːlɪ) *n, pl* **deles** **1** a sign (δ) indicating that typeset matter is to be deleted ▷ *vb* **deles, deleing, deled** **2** (*tr*) to mark (matter to be deleted) with a dele [c18 from L: delete (imperative), from *dēlēre* to destroy, obliterate]

delectable (dɪˈlɛktəbᵊl) *adj* highly enjoyable, esp pleasing to the taste; delightful [c14 from L *dēlectābilis*, from *dēlectāre* to DELIGHT] > **deˈlectableness** *or* **deˌlectaˈbility** *n*

delectation (ˌdiːlɛkˈteɪʃən) *n* pleasure; enjoyment

delegate *n* (ˈdɛlɪˌgeɪt, -gɪt) **1** a person chosen to act for another or others, esp at a conference or meeting ▷ *vb* (ˈdɛlɪˌgeɪt), **delegates, delegating, delegated** **2** to give (duties, powers, etc) to another as representative; depute **3** (*tr*) to authorize (a person) as representative [c14 from L *dēlēgāre* to send on a mission, from *lēgāre* to send, depute] > **ˈdelegable** *adj*

delegation (ˌdɛlɪˈgeɪʃən) *n* **1** a person or group chosen to represent another or others **2** a delegating or being delegated

de Lesseps (*French* də lɛsɛps) *n* **Vicomte** title of (Ferdinand Marie) **Lesseps**

delete (dɪˈliːt) *vb* **deletes, deleting, deleted** (*tr*) to remove (something printed or written); erase; strike out [c17 from L *dēlēre* to destroy, obliterate] > **deˈletion** *n*

deleterious (ˌdɛlɪˈtɪərɪəs) *adj* harmful; injurious; hurtful [c17 from NL, from Gk *dēlētērios*, from *dēleisthai* to hurt] > ˌ**deleˈteriousness** *n*

Delft (dɛlft) *n* **1** a town in the SW Netherlands, in South Holland province. Pop: 91 941 (1994) **2** Also called: **delftware** tin-glazed earthenware made in Delft since the 17th century, typically having blue decoration on a white ground **3** a similar earthenware made in England

Delhi (ˈdɛlɪ) *n* **1** the capital of India, in the N central part, on the Jumna river: consists of **Old Delhi** (a walled city reconstructed in 1639 on the site of former cities of Delhi, which date from the 15th century BC) and **New Delhi** to the south, chosen as the capital in 1912, replacing Calcutta; university (1922). Pop: (total) 9 882 000 (1995) **2** an administrative division (National Capital Territory) of N India, formerly a Union Territory. Capital: Delhi. Area: 1483 sq km (572 sq miles). Pop: 13 782 976 (2001)
▷ http://delhigovt.nic.in

deli (ˈdɛlɪ) *n, pl* **delis** an informal word for **delicatessen**

Delian (ˈdiːlɪən) *n* **1** a native or inhabitant of Delos ▷ *adj* **2** of or relating to Delos **3** of or relating to Delius

deliberate *adj* (dɪˈlɪbərɪt) **1** carefully thought out in advance; intentional **2** careful or unhurried: *a deliberate pace* ▷ *vb* (dɪˈlɪbəˌreɪt) **deliberates, deliberating, deliberated** **3** to consider (something) deeply; think over [c15 from L *dēlīberāre*, from *lībrāre* to weigh, from *lībra* scales] > **deˈliberately** *adv* > **deˈliberateness** *n* > **deˈliberˌator** *n*

deliberation (dɪˌlɪbəˈreɪʃən) *n* **1** careful consideration **2** (*often pl*) formal discussion, as of a committee **3** care or absence of hurry

deliberative (dɪˈlɪbərətɪv) *adj* **1** of or for deliberating: *a deliberative assembly* **2** characterized by deliberation > **deˈliberatively** *adv* > **deˈliberativeness** *n*

Delibes (*French* dəlib) *n* (**Clément Philibert**) **Léo** (leo) 1836–91, French composer, noted particularly for his ballets *Coppélia* (1870) and *Sylvia* (1876), and the opera *Lakmé* (1883)

delicacy (ˈdɛlɪkəsɪ) *n, pl* **delicacies** **1** fine or subtle quality, character, construction, etc **2** fragile or graceful beauty **3** something that is considered choice to eat, such as caviar **4** fragile construction or constitution **5** refinement of feeling, manner, or appreciation **6** fussy or squeamish refinement, esp in matters of taste, propriety, etc **7** need for tactful or sensitive handling **8** sensitivity of response, as of an instrument

delicate (ˈdɛlɪkɪt) *adj* **1** fine or subtle in quality, character, construction, etc **2** having a soft or fragile beauty **3** (of colour, tone, taste, etc) pleasantly subtle **4** easily damaged or injured; fragile **5** precise or sensitive in action: *a delicate mechanism* **6** requiring tact **7** showing regard for the feelings of others **8** excessively refined; squeamish [c14 from L *dēlicātus* affording pleasure, from *dēliciae* (pl) delight, pleasure] > **ˈdelicately** *adv* > **ˈdelicateness** *n*

delicatessen (ˌdɛlɪkəˈtɛsᵊn) *n* **1** a shop selling various foods, esp unusual or imported foods, already cooked or prepared **2** such foods [c19 from G *Delikatessen*, lit.: delicacies, from F *délicatesse*]

delicious (dɪˈlɪʃəs) *adj* **1** very appealing, esp to taste or smell **2** extremely enjoyable [c13 from OF, from LL *dēliciōsus*, from L *dēliciae* delights, from *dēlicere* to entice; see DELIGHT] > **deˈliciously** *adv* > **deˈliciousness** *n*

delight (dɪˈlaɪt) *vb* **1** (*tr*) to please greatly **2** (*intr; foll by in*) to take great pleasure (in) ▷ *n* **3** extreme pleasure **4** something that causes this [c13 from OF, from *deleitier* to please, from L *dēlectāre*, from *dēlicere* to allure, from DE- + *lacere* to entice]

delighted (dɪˈlaɪtɪd) *adj* **1** (often foll by an infinitive) extremely pleased (to do something): *I'm delighted to hear it!* ▷ *sentence substitute* **2** I should be delighted to! > **deˈlightedly** *adv*

delightful (dɪˈlaɪtfʊl) *adj* giving great delight; very pleasing, beautiful, charming, etc > **deˈlightfully** *adv* > **deˈlightfulness** *n*

Delilah (dɪˈlaɪlə) *n* **1** Samson's Philistine mistress, who betrayed him (Judges 16) **2** a voluptuous and treacherous woman; temptress

delimit (diːˈlɪmɪt) *or* **delimitate** *vb* **delimits, delimiting,**

delimited *or* **delimitates, delimitating, delimitated** (*tr*) to mark or prescribe the limits or boundaries of
> **deˌlimiˈtation** *n* > **deˈlimitative** *adj*

delineate (dɪˈlɪnɪˌeɪt) *vb* **delineates, delineating, delineated** (*tr*) **1** to trace the outline of **2** to represent pictorially; depict **3** to portray in words; describe [C16 from L *dēlīneāre* to sketch out, from *līnea* LINE[1]]
> **deˌlineˈation** *n* > **deˈlineative** *adj*

delinquency (dɪˈlɪŋkwənsɪ) *n, pl* **delinquencies 1** an offence or misdeed, esp one committed by a young person. See **juvenile delinquency 2** failure or negligence in duty or obligation **3** a delinquent nature or delinquent behaviour [C17 from LL *dēlinquentia* fault, offence, from L *dēlinquere* to transgress, from DE- + *linquere* to forsake]

delinquent (dɪˈlɪŋkwənt) *n* **1** someone, esp a young person, guilty of delinquency ▷ *adj* **2** guilty of an offence or misdeed **3** failing in or neglectful of duty or obligation [C17 from L *dēlinquēns* offending; see DELINQUENCY]

deliquesce (ˌdɛlɪˈkwɛs) *vb* **deliquesces, deliquescing, deliquesced** (*intr*)(esp of certain salts) to dissolve gradually in water absorbed from the air [C18 from L *dēliquēscere*, from DE- + *liquēscere* to melt, from *liquēre* to be liquid] > ˌ**deliˈquescence** *n* > ˌ**deliˈquescent** *adj*

delirious (dɪˈlɪrɪəs) *adj* **1** affected with delirium **2** wildly excited, esp with joy or enthusiasm > **deˈliriously** *adv*

delirium (dɪˈlɪrɪəm) *n, pl* **deliriums** *or* **deliria** (-ˈlɪrɪə) **1** a state of excitement and mental confusion, often accompanied by hallucinations, caused by high fever, poisoning, brain injury, etc **2** violent excitement or emotion; frenzy [C16 from L: madness, from *dēlīrāre*, lit.: to swerve from a furrow, hence be crazy, from DE- + *līra* furrow]

delirium tremens (ˈtrɛmɛnz, ˈtriː-) *n* a severe psychotic condition occurring in some persons with chronic alcoholism, characterized by delirium, tremor, anxiety, and vivid hallucinations. Abbrevs.: **DT's** (informal), **dt** [C19 NL, lit.: trembling delirium]

delist (diːˈlɪst) *vb* (*tr*) **1** to remove from a list **2** *stock exchange* to remove (a security) from the register of those that may be traded on the recognized market

Delius (ˈdiːlɪəs) *n* **Frederick** 1862–1934, English composer, who drew inspiration from folk tunes and the sounds of nature. His works include the opera *A Village Romeo and Juliet* (1901), *A Mass of Life* (1905), and the orchestral variations *Brigg Fair* (1907)

deliver (dɪˈlɪvə) *vb* (*mainly tr*) **1** to carry to a destination, esp to distribute (goods, mail, etc) to several places **2** (often foll by *over* or *up*) to hand over or transfer **3** (often foll by *from*) to release or rescue (from captivity, harm, etc) **4** (*also intr*) **4a** to aid in the birth of (offspring) **4b** to give birth to (offspring) **4c** (usually foll by *of*) to aid (a female) in the birth (of offspring) **4d** (*passive*; foll by *of*) to give birth (to offspring) **5** to present (a speech, idea, etc) **6** to utter: *to deliver a cry of exultation* **7** to discharge or release (something, such as a blow or shot) suddenly **8** (*intr*) *inf* Also: **deliver the goods** to produce something promised or expected **9** *chiefly US* to cause (voters, etc) to support a given candidate, cause, etc **10 deliver oneself of** to speak with deliberation or at length [C13 from OF, from LL *dēlīberāre* to set free, from L DE- + *līberāre* to free] > **deˈliverable** *adj* > **deˈliverer** *n*

deliverance (dɪˈlɪvərəns) *n* **1** a formal expression of opinion **2** rescue from moral corruption or evil; salvation

delivery (dɪˈlɪvərɪ) *n, pl* **deliveries 1a** the act of delivering or distributing goods, mail, etc **1b** something that is delivered **2** the act of giving birth to a child **3** manner or style of utterance, esp in public speaking: *the chairman had a clear delivery* **4** the act of giving or transferring or the state of being given or transferred **5** a rescuing or being rescued; liberation **6** *sport* the act or manner of bowling or throwing a ball **7** the handing over of property, a deed, etc **8** *S African* the supply of basic services to communities deprived under apartheid

dell (dɛl) *n* a small, esp wooded hollow [OE]

della Robbia (*Italian* ˈdɛlla ˈrobbja) *n* See (Luca della) **Robbia**

Deller (ˈdɛlə) *n* **Alfred** (**George**) 1912–79, British countertenor

Del Mar (dɛl ˈmɑː) *n* **Norman** 1919–94, British conductor, associated esp with 20th-century British music

Delmarva Peninsula (dɛlˈmɑːvə) *n* a peninsula of the northeast US, between Chesapeake Bay and the Atlantic

Delors (dəlɔː) *n* **Jacques** (**Lucien Jean**) born 1925, French politician and economist, President of the European Commission (1985–94): originator of the **Delors plan** for closer European union

Delos (ˈdiːlɒs) *n* a Greek island in the SW Aegean Sea, in the Cyclades: a commercial centre in ancient times; the legendary birthplace of Apollo and Artemis. Area: about 5 sq km (2 sq miles). Modern Greek name: **Dhílos**

de los Angeles (*Spanish* de los ˈaŋxeles) *n* **Victoria** (bikˈtorja) born 1923, Spanish soprano

delouse (diːˈlaʊs, -ˈlaʊz) *vb* **delouses, delousing, deloused** (*tr*) to rid (a person or animal) of lice as a sanitary measure

Delphi (ˈdɛlfɪ) *n* an ancient Greek city on the S slopes of Mount Parnassus: site of the most famous oracle of Apollo

Delphic (ˈdɛlfɪk) *or* **Delphian** *adj* **1** of or relating to the ancient Greek city of Delphi or its oracle or temple **2** obscure or ambiguous

Delphic oracle *n* the oracle of Apollo at Delphi that gave answers held by the ancient Greeks to be of great authority but also noted for their ambiguity

delphinium (dɛlˈfɪnɪəm) *n, pl* **delphiniums** *or* **delphinia** (-ɪə) a plant with spikes of blue, pink, or white spurred flowers. See also **larkspur** [C17 NL, from Gk *delphinion* larkspur, from *delphis* dolphin, referring to the shape of the nectary]

Dd

del Sarto (*Italian* dɛl ˈsarto) *n* See (Andrea del) **Sarto**

delta (ˈdɛltə) *n* **1** the fourth letter in the Greek alphabet (Δ or δ) **2** (*cap. when part of name*) the flat alluvial area at the mouth of some rivers where the mainstream splits up into several distributaries **3** *maths* a finite increment in a variable [C16 via L from Gk, of Semitic origin]
> **deltaic** (dɛlˈteɪɪk) *or* ˈ**deltic** *adj*

delta connection *n* a connection used in a three-phase electrical system in which three elements in series form a triangle, the supply being input and output at the three junctions

Delta Force *n* (in the US) an élite army unit involved in counterterrorist operations abroad

delta particle *n Physics* a very short-lived type of hyperon

delta ray *n* a particle, esp an electron, ejected from matter by ionizing radiation

delta rhythm *or* **wave** *n physiol* the normal electrical activity of the cerebral cortex during deep sleep. See also **brain wave**

delta stock *n* any of the fourth rank of active securities on the London stock exchange. Market makers need not display prices of these securities continuously

delta wing *n* a triangular swept-back aircraft wing

deltiology (ˌdɛltɪˈɒlədʒɪ) *n* the collection and study of postcards [C20 from Gk *deltion*, dim. of *deltos* a writing tablet + -LOGY] > ˌ**deltiˈologist** *n*

deltoid (ˈdɛltɔɪd) *n* a thick muscle of the shoulder that acts to raise the arm [C18 from Gk *deltoeidēs* triangular, from DELTA]

delude (dɪˈluːd) *vb* **deludes, deluding, deluded** (*tr*) to deceive; mislead; beguile [C15 from L *dēlūdere* to mock, play false, from DE- + *lūdere* to play] > **deˈludable** *adj*
> **deˈluder** *n*

deluge (ˈdɛljuːdʒ) *n* **1** a great flood of water **2** torrential rain **3** an overwhelming rush or number ▷ *vb* **deluges, deluging, deluged** (*tr*) **4** to flood **5** to overwhelm; inundate [C14 from OF, from L *dīluvium*, from *dīluere* to wash away, drench, from *di-* DIS-[1] + *-luere*, from *lavere* to wash]

Deluge ('dɛlju:dʒ) *n* **the** another name for the **Flood**

delusion (dɪ'lu:ʒən) *n* **1** a mistaken idea, belief, etc **2** *psychiatry* a belief held in the face of evidence to the contrary, that is resistant to all reason **3** a deluding or being deluded > **de'lusional** *adj* > **de'lusive** *adj* > **delusory** (dɪ'lu:sərɪ) *adj*

de luxe (də 'lʌks, 'lʊks) *adj* **1** rich or sumptuous; superior in quality: *the de luxe model of a car* ▷ *adv* **2** *chiefly US* in a luxurious manner [C19 from F, lit.: of luxury]

delve (dɛlv) *vb* **delves, delving, delved** (*mainly intr;* often foll by *in* or *into*) **1** to research deeply or intensively (for information, etc) **2** to search or rummage **3** to dig or burrow deeply **4** (*also tr*) *arch or Brit dialect* to dig [OE *delfan*] > **'delver** *n*

Dem. (in the US) *abbrev for* Democrat(ic)

demagnetize *or* **demagnetise** (di:'mægnə,taɪz) *vb* **demagnetizes, demagnetizing, demagnetized** *or* **demagnetises, demagnetising, demagnetised** to remove or lose magnetic properties. Also: **degauss** > **de,magneti'zation** *or* **de,magneti'sation** *n* > **de'magnet,izer** *or* **de'magnet,iser** *n*

demagogue *or US* (*sometimes*) **demagog** ('dɛmə,gɒg) *n* **1** a political agitator who appeals with crude oratory to the prejudice and passions of the mob **2** (esp in the ancient world) any popular political leader or orator [C17 from Gk *dēmagōgos* people's leader, from *dēmos* people + *agein* to lead] > **,dema'gogic** *adj* > **,dema'goguery** *n*

demagogy ('dɛmə,gɒgɪ) *n, pl* **demagogies** **1** demagoguery **2** rule by a demagogue or by demagogues **3** a group of demagogues

demand (dɪ'mɑ:nd) *vb* (*tr; may take a clause as object or an infinitive*) **1** to request peremptorily or urgently **2** to require as just, urgent, etc: *the situation demands attention* **3** to claim as a right; exact **4** *law* to make a formal legal claim to (property) ▷ *n* **5** an urgent or peremptory requirement or request **6** something that requires special effort or sacrifice **7** the act of demanding something or the thing demanded **8** an insistent question **9** *econ* **9a** willingness and ability to purchase goods and services **9b** the amount of a commodity that consumers are willing and able to purchase at a specified price ▷ Cf **supply**[1] (sense 9) **10** *law* a formal legal claim, esp to real property **11 in demand** sought after **12 on demand** as soon as requested [C13 from Anglo-F, from Med. L *dēmandāre*, from L: to commit to, from DE- + *mandāre* to command, entrust] > **de'mandable** *adj* > **de'mander** *n*

demand feeding *n* the practice of feeding a baby whenever it is hungry, rather than at set intervals

demanding (dɪ'mɑ:ndɪŋ) *adj* requiring great patience, skill, etc: *a demanding job*

demarcate ('di:mɑ:,keɪt) *vb* **demarcates, demarcating, demarcated** (*tr*) **1** to mark the boundaries, limits, etc, of **2** to separate; distinguish > **'demar,cator** *n*

demarcation *or* **demarkation** (,di:mɑ:'keɪʃən) *n* **1** the act of establishing limits or boundaries **2** a limit or boundary **3a** a strict separation of the kinds of work performed by members of different trade unions **3b** (*as modifier*): *demarcation dispute* **4** separation or distinction (as in **line of demarcation**) [C18 from Sp. *demarcar* to appoint the boundaries of, from *marcar* to mark, from It., of Gmc origin]

démarche *French* (demarʃ) *n* a move, step, or manoeuvre, esp in diplomatic affairs [C17 lit.: walk, gait, from OF *demarcher* to tread, trample]

dematerialize *or* **dematerialise** (di:mə'tɪərɪə,laɪz) *vb* **dematerializes, dematerializing, dematerialized** *or* **dematerialises, dematerialising, dematerialised** (*intr*) **1** to cease to have material existence, as in science fiction or spiritualism **2** to vanish > **dema,teriali'zation** *or* **dema,teriali'sation** *n*

deme (di:m) *n* **1** (in ancient Attica) a geographical unit of local government **2** *biol* a group of individuals within a species that possess particular characteristics of cytology, genetics, etc [C19 from Gk *dēmos* district in local government, the populace]

demean[1] (dɪ'mi:n) *vb* (*tr*) to lower (oneself) in dignity, status, or character; humble; debase [C17 see DE-, MEAN[2]]

demean[2] (dɪ'mi:n) *vb* (*tr*) *rare* to behave or conduct (oneself) [C13 from OF, from DE- + *mener* to lead, from L *mināre* to drive (animals), from *minārī* to use threats]

demeanour *or US* **demeanor** (dɪ'mi:nə) *n* **1** the way a person behaves towards others **2** bearing or mien [C15 see DEMEAN[2]]

dement (dɪ'mɛnt) *vb* **1** (*intr*) to deteriorate mentally, esp because of old age **2** (*tr*) *rare* to drive mad; make insane [C16 from LL *dēmentāre* to drive mad, from L DE- + *mēns* mind]

demented (dɪ'mɛntɪd) *adj* mad; insane > **de'mentedly** *adv* > **de'mentedness** *n*

dementia (dɪ'mɛnʃə, -ʃɪə) *n* a state of serious mental deterioration, of organic or functional origin [C19 from L: madness; see DEMENT]

dementia praecox ('pri:kɒks) *n* a former name for **schizophrenia** [C19 NL, lit.: premature dementia]

demerara (,dɛmə'rɛərə, -'rɑ:rə) *n* brown crystallized cane sugar from the Caribbean [C19 after *Demerara*, a region of Guyana]

Demerara (,dɛmə'rɛərə, -'rɑ:rə) *n* **the** a river in Guyana, rising in the central forest area and flowing north to the Atlantic at Georgetown. Length: 346 km (215 miles)

demerit (di:'mɛrɪt) *n* **1** something that deserves censure **2** *US & Canad* a mark given against a student, etc, for failure or misconduct **3** a fault [C14 (orig.: worth, desert, ult.: something worthy of blame): from L *dēmerērī* to deserve] > **de,meri'torious** *adj*

demersal (dɪ'mɜ:s^əl) *adj* living or occurring in deep water or on the bottom of a sea or lake [C19 from L *dēmersus* submerged (from *mergere* to dip) + -AL[1]]

demesne (dɪ'meɪn, -'mi:n) *n* **1** land surrounding a house or manor **2** *property law* the possession and use of one's own property or land **3** realm; domain **4** a region or district [C14 from OF *demeine;* see DOMAIN]

Demeter (dɪ'mi:tə) *n* *Greek myth* the goddess of agricultural fertility and protector of marriage and women. Roman counterpart: **Ceres**

demi- *prefix* **1** half: *demirelief* **2** of less than full size, status, or rank: *demigod* [via F from Med. L, from L *dīmīdius* half, from *dis-* apart + *medius* middle]

demigod ('dɛmɪ,gɒd) *n* **1a** a being who is part mortal, part god **1b** a lesser deity **2** a person with godlike attributes [C16 translation of L *sēmideus*] > **'demi,goddess** *fem n*

demijohn ('dɛmɪ,dʒɒn) *n* a large bottle with a short narrow neck, often encased in wickerwork [C18 prob. from F *dame-jeanne*, from *dame* lady + *Jeanne* Jane]

demilitarize *or* **demilitarise** (di:'mɪlɪtə,raɪz) *vb* **demilitarizes, demilitarizing, demilitarized** *or* **demilitarises, demilitarising, demilitarised** (*tr*) **1** to remove and prohibit any military presence or function in (an area): *demilitarized zone* **2** to free of military character, purpose, etc > **de,militari'zation** *or* **de,militari'sation** *n*

De Mille (də 'mɪl) *n* **Cecil B(lount)** 1881–1959, US film producer and director

demimondaine (,dɛmɪ'mɒndeɪn) *n* a woman of the demimonde [C19 from F]

demimonde (,dɛmɪ'mɒnd) *n* **1** (esp in the 19th century) those women considered to be outside respectable society, esp on account of sexual promiscuity **2** any group considered to be not wholly respectable: *the*

gambling demimonde [c19 from F, lit.: half-world]
de-mining *n* the process of removing landmines
demise (dɪˈmaɪz) *n* **1** failure or termination **2** a euphemistic or formal word for **death** **3** *property law* a transfer of an estate by lease or on the death of the owner **4** the transfer of sovereignty to a successor upon the death, abdication, etc, of a ruler(esp in **demise of the crown**) ▷ *vb* **demises, demising, demised** **5** to transfer or be transferred by inheritance, will, or succession **6** (*tr*) *property law* to transfer for a limited period; lease **7** (*tr*) to transfer (sovereignty, a title, etc) [c16 from OF, fem of *demis* dismissed, from *demettre* to send away, from L *dīmittere*] > **deˈmisable** *adj*
demi-sec (ˌdɛmɪˈsɛk) *adj* (of wine) medium-dry [c20 from F, from *demi* half + *sec* dry]
demisemiquaver (ˈdɛmɪˌsɛmɪˌkweɪvə) *n* *music* a note having the time value of one thirty-second of a semibreve. Usual US and Canad name: **thirty-second note**
demist (diːˈmɪst) *vb* to free or become free of condensation > **deˈmister** *n*
demitasse (ˈdɛmɪˌtæs) *n* **1** a small cup used to serve coffee, esp after a meal **2** the coffee itself [c19 F, lit.: half-cup]
demiurge (ˈdɛmɪˌɜːdʒ) *n* **1** (in the philosophy of Plato) the creator of the universe **2** (in Gnostic philosophy) the creator of the universe, supernatural but subordinate to the Supreme Being [c17 from Church L, from Gk *dēmiourgos* skilled workman, lit.: one who works for the people, from *dēmos* people + *ergon* work] > ˌ**demiˈurgic** *or* ˌ**demiˈurgical** *adj*
demiveg (ˈdɛmɪˌvɛdʒ) *inf* ▷ *n* **1** a person who eats poultry and fish, but no red meat ▷ *adj* **2** denoting a person who eats poultry and fish, but no red meat [c20 from DEMI- + VEG(ETARIAN)]
demo (ˈdɛməʊ) *n, pl* **demos** *inf* **1** short for **demonstration** (sense 4) **2** a demonstration record or tape
demo- *or before a vowel* **dem-** *combining form*. indicating people or population: *demography* [from Gk *dēmos*]
demob *Brit inf* ▷ *vb* (diːˈmɒb), **demobs, demobbing, demobbed** **1** to demobilize ▷ *n* (ˈdiːmɒb) **2** demobilization
demobilize *or* **demobilise** (diːˈməʊbɪˌlaɪz) *vb* **demobilizes, demobilizing, demobilized** *or* **demobilises, demobilising, demobilised** to disband, as troops, etc > **deˌmobiliˈzation** *or* **deˌmobiliˈsation** *n*
Demochristian (ˌdɛməʊˈkrɪstʃən) *n* an informal name for a **Christian Democrat**
democracy (dɪˈmɒkrəsɪ) *n, pl* **democracies** **1** government by the people or their elected representatives **2** a political or social unit governed ultimately by all its members **3** the practice or spirit of social equality **4** a social condition of classlessness and equality [c16 from F, from LL, from Gk *dēmokratia* government by the people]
democrat (ˈdɛməˌkræt) *n* **1** an advocate of democracy **2** a member or supporter of a democratic party or movement
Democrat (ˈdɛməˌkræt) *n* (in the US) a member or supporter of the Democratic Party > ˌ**Demoˈcratic** *adj*
democratic (ˌdɛməˈkrætɪk) *adj* **1** of or relating to the principles of democracy **2** upholding democracy or the interests of the common people **3** popular with or for the benefit of all > ˌ**demoˈcratically** *adv*
democratic centralism *n* the Leninist principle that policy should be decided centrally by officials, who are nominally democratically elected
Democratic Republic of Congo *n* **the** See **Congo** (sense 2)
democratize *or* **democratise** (dɪˈmɒkrəˌtaɪz) *vb* **democratizes, democratizing, democratized** *or* **democratises, democratising, democratised** (*tr*) to make democratic > **deˌmocratiˈzation** *or* **deˌmocratiˈsation** *n*
Democritus (dɪˈmɒkrɪtəs) *n* ?460–?370 BC, Greek philosopher who developed the atomist theory of matter of his teacher, Leucippus. See also **atomism**
démodé *French* (demɔde) *adj* outmoded [F, from *dé-* out of + *mode* fashion]
demodulate (diːˈmɒdjʊˌleɪt) *vb* **demodulates, demodulating, demodulated** to carry out demodulation on > **deˈmoduˌlator** *n*
demodulation (ˌdiːmɒdjʊˈleɪʃən) *n* *electronics* the act or process by which an output wave or signal is obtained having the characteristics of the original modulating wave or signal; the reverse of modulation
demographic (ˌdɛməˈɡræfɪk, ˌdiːmə-) *adj* **1** Also: **demographical** of or relating to demography ▷ *n* **2** a section of the population sharing common characteristics, such as age, sex, class, ethnic background, etc: *this programme appeals to a young demographic*
demographic timebomb *n* *chiefly Brit* a predicted shortage of school-leavers and consequently of available workers, caused by an earlier drop in the birth rate
demography (dɪˈmɒɡrəfɪ) *n* the scientific study of human populations, esp of their size, distribution, etc [c19 from F, from Gk *dēmos* the populace; see -GRAPHY] > **deˈmographer** *n*
▷ www.un.org/popin/data.html
▷ http://unstats.un.org/unsd/demographic/social/default.htm
demoiselle (dəmwɑːˈzɛl) *n* **1** a small crane of central Asia, N Africa, and SE Europe, having a grey plumage with black breast feathers and white ear tufts **2** a less common name for a **damselfly** **3** a literary word for **damsel** [c16 from F: young woman; see DAMSEL]
demolish (dɪˈmɒlɪʃ) *vb* (*tr*) **1** to tear down or break up (buildings, etc) **2** to put an end to (an argument, etc) **3** *facetious* to eat up [c16 from F, from L *dēmōlīrī* to throw down, from DE- + *mōlīrī* to construct, from *mōles* mass] > **deˈmolisher** *n*
demolition (ˌdɛməˈlɪʃən, ˌdiː-) *n* **1** a demolishing or being demolished **2** *chiefly mil* destruction by explosives > ˌ**demoˈlitionist** *n, adj*
demon (ˈdiːmən) *n* **1** an evil spirit or devil **2** a person, obsession, etc, thought of as evil or cruel **3** Also called: **daemon, daimon** an attendant or ministering spirit; genius: *the demon of inspiration* **4a** a person extremely skilful in or devoted to a given activity, esp a sport: *a demon at cycling* **4b** (*as modifier*): *a demon cyclist* **5** a variant spelling of **daemon** (senses 1, 2) **6** *Austral & NZ sl* a detective or policeman, esp one in plain clothes **7** a part of a computer program such as a help facility, that can run in the background behind the current task or application, and which will only begin to work when certain conditions are met or when it is specifically invoked [c15 from L *daemōn* (evil) spirit, from Gk *daimōn* spirit, deity, fate] > **demonic** (dɪˈmɒnɪk) *adj*
demonetize *or* **demonetise** (diːˈmʌnɪˌtaɪz) *vb* **demonetizes, demonetizing, demonetized** *or* **demonetises, demonetising, demonetised** (*tr*) **1** to deprive (a metal) of its capacity as a monetary standard **2** to withdraw from use as currency > **deˌmonetiˈzation** *or* **deˌmonetiˈsation** *n*
demoniac (dɪˈməʊnɪˌæk) *adj* also **demoniacal** (ˌdiːməˈnaɪəkᵊl) **1** of or like a demon **2** suggesting inner possession or inspiration **3** frantic; frenzied ▷ *n* **4** a person possessed by a demon > ˌ**demoˈniacally** *adv*
demonism (ˈdiːməˌnɪzəm) *n* **1** belief in the existence and power of demons **2** another name for **demonology** (sense 1) > ˈ**demonist** *n*
demonize *or* **demonise** (ˌdiːməˌnaɪz) *vb* (*tr*) **1** to make into or like a demon **2** to subject to demonic influence **3** to mark out or describe as evil or culpable: *they demonized the enemy in the run-up to war*

Dd

demonolatry (ˌdiːməˈnɒlətrɪ) *n* the worship of demons [C17 see DEMON, -LATRY]

demonology (ˌdiːməˈnɒlədʒɪ) *n* **1** Also called: **demonism** the study of demons or demonic beliefs **2** a set of people or things that are disliked or feared: *Adolf Hitler's place in contemporary demonology* > ˌ**demonˈologist** *n*

demonstrable (ˈdɛmənstrəbᵊl, dɪˈmɒn-) *adj* able to be demonstrated or proved > ˌ**demonstraˈbility** *n* > ˈ**demonstrably** *adv*

demonstrate (ˈdɛmənˌstreɪt) *vb* **demonstrates, demonstrating, demonstrated 1** (*tr*) to show or prove, esp by reasoning, evidence, etc **2** (*tr*) to evince; reveal the existence of **3** (*tr*) to explain by experiment, example, etc **4** (*tr*) to display and explain the workings of (a machine, product, etc) **5** (*intr*) to manifest support, protest, etc, by public parades or rallies **6** (*intr*) to be employed as a demonstrator of machinery, etc **7** (*intr*) *mil* to make a show of force [C16 from L *dēmonstrāre* to point out, from *monstrāre* to show]

demonstration (ˌdɛmənˈstreɪʃən) *n* **1** the act of demonstrating **2** proof or evidence leading to proof **3** an explanation, illustration, or experiment showing how something works **4** Also: **demo** a manifestation of support or protest by public rallies, parades, etc **5** a manifestation of emotion **6** a show of military force > ˌ**demonˈstrational** *adj* > ˌ**demonˈstrationist** *n*

demonstration model *n* a nearly new product, such as a car, that has been used to demonstrate its performance by a dealer and is offered at a discount

demonstrative (dɪˈmɒnstrətɪv) *adj* **1** tending to express one's feelings easily or unreservedly **2** (*postpositive; foll by of*) serving as proof; indicative **3** involving or characterized by demonstration **4** conclusive **5** *grammar* denoting or belonging to a class of determiners used to point out the individual referent or referents intended, such as *this* and *those* ▷ Cf **interrogative, relative** ▷ *n* **6** *grammar* a demonstrative word > **deˈmonstratively** *adv* > **deˈmonstrativeness** *n*

demonstrator (ˈdɛmənˌstreɪtə) *n* **1** a person who demonstrates equipment, machines, products, etc **2** a person who takes part in a public demonstration

demoralize *or* **demoralise** (dɪˈmɒrəˌlaɪz) *vb* **demoralizes, demoralizing, demoralized** *or* **demoralises, demoralising, demoralised** (*tr*) **1** to undermine the morale of; dishearten **2** to corrupt **3** to throw into confusion > **deˌmoraliˈzation** *or* **deˌmoraliˈsation** *n*

Demosthenes (dɪˈmɒsθəˌniːz) *n* 384–322 BC, Athenian statesman, orator, and lifelong opponent of the power of Macedonia over Greece

demote (dɪˈməʊt) *vb* **demotes, demoting, demoted** (*tr*) to lower in rank or position; relegate [C19 from DE- + (PRO)MOTE] > **deˈmotion** *n*

demotic (dɪˈmɒtɪk) *adj* **1** of or relating to the common people; popular **2** of or relating to a simplified form of hieroglyphics used in ancient Egypt. Cf **hieratic** ▷ *n* **3** the demotic script of ancient Egypt [C19 from Gk *dēmotikos* of the people, from *dēmotēs* a man of the people, commoner] > **deˈmotist** *n*

Dempsey (ˈdɛmpsɪ) *n* **Jack** real name *William Harrison Dempsey*. 1895–1983, US boxer; world heavyweight champion (1919–26)

dempster (ˈdɛmpstə) *n* a variant spelling of **deemster**

demulcent (dɪˈmʌlsᵊnt) *adj* **1** soothing ▷ *n* **2** a drug or agent that soothes irritation [C18 from L *dēmulcēre*, from DE- + *mulcēre* to stroke]

demur (dɪˈmɜː) *vb* **demurs, demurring, demurred** (*intr*) **1** to show reluctance **2** *law* to raise an objection by entering a demurrer ▷ *n* also **demurral** (dɪˈmʌrəl) **3** the act of demurring **4** an objection raised [C13 from OF, from L *dēmorārī*, from *morārī* to delay] > **deˈmurrable** *adj*

demure (dɪˈmjʊə) *adj* **1** sedate; decorous; reserved **2** affectedly modest or prim; coy [C14 ?from OF *demorer* to delay, linger; ? infl. by *meur* ripe, MATURE] > **deˈmurely** *adv* > **deˈmureness** *n*

demurrage (dɪˈmʌrɪdʒ) *n* **1** the delaying of a ship, etc, caused by the charterer's failure to load, unload, etc, before the time of scheduled departure **2** the extra charge required for such delay [C14 from OF *demorage, demourage;* see DEMUR]

demurrer (dɪˈmʌrə) *n* **1** *law* a pleading that admits an opponent's point but denies that it is relevant or valid **2** any objection raised

demutualize *or* **demutualise** (diːˈmjuːtjʊəˌlaɪz) *vb* **demutualizes, demutualizing, demutualized** *or* **demutualises, demutualising, demutualised** (*intr*) (of a mutual savings or life-assurance organization) to convert to a public limited company > ˌ**demutualiˈzation** *or* ˌ**demutualiˈsation** *n*

demy (dɪˈmaɪ) *n, pl* **demies 1** a size of printing paper, 17½ by 22½ inches (444.5 × 571.5 mm) **2** a size of writing paper, 15½ by 20 inches (Brit) (393.7 × 508 mm) or 16 by 21 inches (US) (406.4 × 533.4 mm) [C16 see DEMI-]

demystify (diːˈmɪstɪˌfaɪ) *vb* **demystifies, demystifying, demystified** (*tr*) to remove the mystery from > **deˌmystifiˈcation** *n*

demythologize *or* **demythologise** (ˌdiːmɪˈθɒləˌdʒaɪz) *vb* **demythologizes, demythologizing, demythologized** *or* **demythologises, demythologising, demythologised** (*tr*) **1** to eliminate mythical elements from (a piece of writing, esp the Bible) **2** to restate (a religious message) in rational terms

den (dɛn) *n* **1** the habitat or retreat of a wild animal; lair **2** a small or secluded room in a home, often used for carrying on a hobby **3** a squalid room or retreat **4** a site or haunt: *a den of vice* **5** *Scot* a small wooded valley ▷ *vb* **dens, denning, denned 6** (*intr*) to live in or as if in a den [OE *denn*]

Den. *abbrev for* Denmark

denar (dɪˈnɑː) *n* the standard monetary unit of (the Former Yugoslav Republic of) Macedonia, divided into 100 deni

denarius (dɪˈnɛərɪəs) *n, pl* **denarii** (-ˈnɛərɪˌaɪ) **1** a silver coin of ancient Rome, often called a penny in translation **2** a gold coin worth 25 silver denarii [C16 from L: coin orig. equal to ten asses, from *dēnārius* (adj) containing ten, from *decem* ten]

denary (ˈdiːnərɪ) *adj* **1** calculated by tens; decimal **2** containing ten parts; tenfold [C16 from L *dēnārius;* see DENARIUS]

denationalize *or* **denationalise** (diːˈnæʃənᵊˌlaɪz) *vb* **denationalizes, denationalizing, denationalized** *or* **denationalises, denationalising, denationalised 1** to transfer (an industry, etc) from public to private ownership **2** to deprive of national character or nationality > **deˌnationaliˈzation** *or* **deˌnationaliˈsation** *n*

denaturalize *or* **denaturalise** (diːˈnætʃrəˌlaɪz) *vb* **denaturalizes, denaturalizing, denaturalized** *or* **denaturalises, denaturalising, denaturalised** (*tr*) **1** to deprive of nationality **2** to make unnatural > **deˌnaturaliˈzation** *or* **deˌnaturaliˈsation** *n*

denature (diːˈneɪtʃə) *or* **denaturize, denaturise** (diːˈneɪtʃəˌraɪz) *vb* **denatures, denaturing, denatured** *or* **denaturizes, denaturizing, denaturized; denaturises, denaturising, denaturised** (*tr*) **1** to change the nature of **2** to change the properties of (a protein), as by the action of acid or heat **3** to render (something, such as alcohol) unfit for consumption by adding nauseous substances **4** to render (fissile material) unfit for use in nuclear weapons by addition of an isotope > **deˈnaturant** *n* > **deˌnaturˈation** *n*

Denbighshire (ˈdɛnbɪʃɪə, -ʃə) *n* a county of N Wales: split between Clwyd and Gwynedd in 1974; reinstated with different boundaries in 1996: borders the Irish Sea, with the Cambrian Mountains in the south: chiefly agricultural. Administrative centre: Ruthin. Pop: 93 092

(2001). Area: 844 sq km (327 sq miles)

Den Bosch (dən bɔs) *n* another name for **'s Hertogenbosch**

Dench (dɛntʃ) *n* Dame **Judi (Olivia)** born 1934, British actress and theatre director

dendrite ('dɛndraɪt) *n* **1** Also called: **dendron** any of the branched extensions of a nerve cell, which conduct impulses towards the cell body **2** a branching mosslike crystalline structure in some rocks and minerals **3** a crystal that has branched during growth [c18 from Gk *dendritēs* relating to a tree] > **dendritic** (dɛn'drɪtɪk) *adj*

dendro-, dendri-, *or before a vowel* **dendr-** *combining form.* tree: *dendrochronology* [NL, from Gk, from *dendron* tree]

dendrochronology (ˌdɛndrəʊkrə'nɒlədʒɪ) *n* the study of the annual rings of trees, used esp to date past events

dendrology (dɛn'drɒlədʒɪ) *n* the branch of botany that is concerned with the natural history of trees > **dendrological** (ˌdɛndrə'lɒdʒɪkᵊl) *or* ˌ**dendro'logic** *adj* > **den'drologist** *n*

dene[1] *or* **dean** (diːn) *n Brit* a narrow wooded valley [OE *denu* valley]

dene[2] *or* **dean** (diːn) *n dialect, chiefly southern English* a sandy stretch of land or dune near the sea [c13 prob. rel. to OE *dūn* hill]

denervate ('dɛnəˌveɪt) *vb* **denervates, denervating, denervated** (*tr*) to deprive (a tissue or organ) of its nerve supply > ˌ**dener'vation** *n*

Deneuve (*French* dənøv) *n* **Catherine**, original name *Catherine Dorléac.* born 1943, French film actress: her films include *Les Parapluies de Cherbourg* (1964), *Belle de Jour* (1967), *Indochine* (1992), and *Dancer in the Dark* (2000)

dengue ('dɛŋgɪ) *or* **dandy** ('dændɪ) *n* an acute viral disease transmitted by mosquitoes, characterized by headache, fever, pains in the joints, and skin rash [c19 from Sp., prob. of African origin]

Deng Xiaoping ('dʌŋ 'sjaʊpɪŋ) *or* **Teng Hsiao-ping** *n* 1904–97, Chinese Communist statesman; deputy prime minister (1973–76; 1977–80) and the dominant figure in the Chinese government from 1977 until his death. He was twice removed from office (1967–73, 1976–77) and rehabilitated. He introduced economic liberalization, but suppressed demands for political reform, most notably in 1989 when over 2500 demonstrators were killed by the military in Tiananmen Square in Beijing

Den Haag (dɛn 'haːx) *n* the Dutch name for (The) **Hague**

deni (dɪ'nɪ) *n* a monetary unit of (the former Yugoslav Republic of) Macedonia, worth one hundredth of a denar

deniable (dɪ'naɪəbᵊl) *adj* able to be denied; questionable > **de'niably** *adv*

denial (dɪ'naɪəl) *n* **1** a refusal to agree or comply with a statement **2** the rejection of the truth of a proposition, doctrine, etc **3** a rejection of a request **4** a refusal to acknowledge; disavowal **5** a psychological process by which painful truths are not admitted into an individual's consciousness **6** abstinence; self-denial

denier[1] *n* **1** ('dɛnɪˌeɪ, 'dɛnjə) a unit of weight used to measure the fineness of silk and man-made fibres, esp when woven into women's tights, etc **2** (də'njeɪ, -'nɪə) any of several former European coins of various denominations [c15 from OF: coin, from L *dēnārius* DENARIUS]

denier[2] (dɪ'naɪə) *n* a person who denies

denigrate ('dɛnɪˌgreɪt) *vb* **denigrates, denigrating, denigrated** (*tr*) to belittle or disparage the character of; defame [c16 from L *dēnigrāre* to make very black, from *nigrāre*, from *niger* black] > ˌ**deni'gration** *n* > '**deniˌgrator** *n*

denim ('dɛnɪm) *n* **1** a hard-wearing twill-weave cotton fabric used for trousers, work clothes, etc **2** a similar lighter fabric used in upholstery [c17 from F (*serge*) *de Nîmes* (serge) of Nîmes, in S France]

denims ('dɛnɪmz) *pl n* jeans or overalls made of denim

De Niro (də 'nɪərəʊ) *n* **Robert** born 1943, US film actor. His films include *Taxi Driver* (1976), *Raging Bull* (1980), *GoodFellas* (1990), *Casino* (1995), and *Analyze This* (1999)

Denis ('dɛnɪs; *French* dəni) *n* **1 Maurice** (mɔris) 1870–1943, French painter and writer on art. One of the leading Nabis, he defined a picture as "essentially a flat surface covered with colours assembled in a certain order" **2 Saint** Also: **Denys** 3rd century AD, first bishop of Paris; patron saint of France. Feast day: Oct 9

denizen ('dɛnɪzən) *n* **1** an inhabitant; resident **2** *Brit* an individual permanently resident in a foreign country where he or she enjoys certain rights of citizenship **3** a plant or animal established in a place to which it is not native **4** a naturalized foreign word [c15 from Anglo-F *denisein*, from OF *denzein*, from *denz* within, from L *de intus* from within]

Denmark ('dɛnmɑːk) *n* a kingdom in N Europe, between the Baltic and the North Sea: consists of the mainland of Jutland and about 100 inhabited islands (chiefly Zealand, Lolland, Funen, Falster, Langeland, and Bornholm); extended its territory throughout the Middle Ages, ruling Sweden until 1523 and Norway until 1814, and incorporating Greenland as a province from 1953 to 1979; joined the Common Market (now the EU) in 1973; an important exporter of dairy produce. Language: Danish. Religion: Christian, Lutheran majority. Currency: krone. Capital: Copenhagen. Pop: 5 358 000 (2001 est). Area: 43 031 sq km (16 614 sq miles). Danish name: **Danmark** Related adj: **Danish**

▹ www.denmark.dk
▹ www.visitdenmark.com

Denmark Strait *n* a channel between SE Greenland and Iceland, linking the Arctic Ocean with the Atlantic

Dennis ('dɛnɪs) *n* **C(larence) J(ames)** 1876–1938, the poet of the Australian larrikin, esp in *The Songs of a Sentimental Bloke* (1915) and *The Moods of Ginger Mick* (1916)

denominate *vb* (dɪ'nɒmɪˌneɪt). **denominates, denominating, denominated** **1** (*tr*) to give a specific name to; designate ▹ *adj* (dɪ'nɒmɪnɪt, -ˌneɪt) **2** *maths* (of a number) representing a multiple of a unit of measurement: *4 is the denominate number in 4 miles* [c16 from L *dēnōmināre* from DE- (intensive) + *nōmināre* to name]

denomination (dɪˌnɒmɪ'neɪʃən) *n* **1** a group having a distinctive interpretation of a religious faith and usually its own organization **2** a grade or unit in a series of designations of value, weight, measure, etc **3** a name given to a class or group; classification **4** the act of giving a name **5** a name; designation > **deˌnomi'national** *adj*

denominative (dɪ'nɒmɪnətɪv) *adj* **1** giving or constituting a name **2** *grammar* **2a** formed from or having the same form as a noun **2b** (*as n*): *the verb "to mushroom" is a denominative*

denominator (dɪ'nɒmɪˌneɪtə) *n* the divisor of a fraction, as 8 in ⅞ ▹ Cf **numerator**

denotation (ˌdiːnəʊ'teɪʃən) *n* **1** a denoting; indication **2** a particular meaning given by a sign or symbol **3** specific meaning as distinguished from suggestive meaning and associations **4** *logic* another word for **extension** (sense 10)

denote (dɪ'nəʊt) *vb* **denotes, denoting, denoted** (*tr; may take a clause as object*) **1** to be a sign of; designate **2** (of words, phrases, etc) to have as a literal or obvious meaning [c16 from L *dēnotāre* to mark, from *notāre* to mark, NOTE] > **de'notative** *adj*

denouement (deɪ'nuːmɒn) *or* **dénouement** (*French* denumɑ̃) *n* **1** the clarification or resolution of a plot in a play or other work **2** final outcome; solution [c18 from F, lit.: an untying, from OF *desnoer*, from *des-* DE- + *noer* to tie, from L *nōdus* a knot]

denounce (dɪ'naʊns) *vb* **denounces, denouncing, denounced** (*tr*) **1** to condemn openly or vehemently **2** to give information against; accuse **3** to announce

Dd

formally the termination of (a treaty, etc) [c13 from OF *denoncier*, from L *dēnuntiāre* to make an official proclamation, threaten, from DE- + *nuntiāre* to announce] > **de'nouncement** *n* > **de'nouncer** *n*

de novo *Latin* (di: 'nəʊvəʊ) *adv* from the beginning; anew

dense (dɛns) *adj* **1** thickly crowded or closely set **2** thick; impenetrable **3** *physics* having a high density **4** stupid; dull **5** (of a photographic negative) having many dark or exposed areas [c15 from L *densus* thick] > **'densely** *adv* > **'denseness** *n*

densimeter (dɛn'sɪmɪtə) *n physics* any instrument for measuring density > **densimetric** (ˌdɛnsɪ'mɛtrɪk) *adj* > **den'simetry** *n*

density ('dɛnsɪtɪ) *n, pl* **densities** **1** the degree to which something is filled or occupied: *high density of building in towns* **2** stupidity **3** a measure of the compactness of a substance, expressed as its mass per unit volume. Symbol: ρ. See also **relative density** **4** a measure of a physical quantity per unit of length, area, or volume **5** *physics, photog* a measure of the extent to which a substance or surface transmits or reflects light

dent (dɛnt) *n* **1** a hollow in a surface, as one made by pressure or a blow **2** an appreciable effect, esp of lessening: *a dent in our resources* ▷ *vb (tr)* **3** to make a dent in [c13 (in the sense: a stroke, blow): var. of DINT]

dental ('dɛntᵊl) *adj* **1** of or relating to the teeth or dentistry **2** *phonetics* pronounced with the tip of the tongue touching the backs of the upper teeth, as for *t* in French *tout* ▷ *n* **3** *phonetics* a dental consonant [c16 from Med. L *dentālis*, from L *dens* tooth]

dental floss *n* a waxed thread used to remove food particles from between the teeth

dental plaque *n* a filmy deposit on the surface of a tooth consisting of a mixture of mucus, bacteria, food, etc

dental surgeon *n* another name for **dentist**

dentate ('dɛnteɪt) *adj* **1** having teeth or toothlike processes **2** (of leaves) having a toothed margin [c19 from L *dentātus*] > **'dentately** *adv*

denti- *or before a vowel* **dent-** *combining form.* indicating a tooth: *dentine* [from L *dens, dent-*]

denticulate (dɛn'tɪkjʊlɪt, -ˌleɪt) *adj* **1** *biol* very finely toothed: *denticulate leaves* **2** *arch* having dentils [c17 from L *denticulātus* having small teeth]

dentifrice ('dɛntɪfrɪs) *n* any substance, esp paste or powder, for use in cleaning the teeth [c16 from L *dentifricium*, from *dent-, dens* tooth + *fricāre* to rub]

dentil ('dɛntɪl) *n* one of a set of small square or rectangular blocks evenly spaced to form an ornamental row [c17 from F, from obs. *dentille* a little tooth, from *dent* tooth]

dentine ('dɛnti:n) *or* **dentin** ('dɛntɪn) *n* the calcified tissue comprising the bulk of a tooth [c19 from DENTI- + -IN] > **'dentinal** *adj*

dentist ('dɛntɪst) *n* a person qualified to practise dentistry [c18 from F *dentiste*, from *dent* tooth]

dentistry ('dɛntɪstrɪ) *n* the branch of medical science concerned with the diagnosis and treatment of disorders of the teeth and gums

▷ www.dental-health.com

▷ http://dir.yahoo.com/Health/Medicine/Dentistry

dentition (dɛn'tɪʃən) *n* **1** the arrangement, type, and number of the teeth in a particular species **2** the time or process of teething [c17 from L *dentītiō* a teething]

Denton ('dɜntən) *n* **Andrew** born 1960, Australian chat-show host and television producer

D'Entrecasteaux Islands (*French* dɑ̃trəkasto) *pl n* a group of volcanic islands in the Pacific, off the SE coast of New Guinea: part of Papua New Guinea. Pop: 49 167 (1990 est). Area: 3141 sq km (1213 sq miles)

denture ('dɛntʃə) *n (usually pl)* **1** a partial or full set of artificial teeth **2** *rare* a set of natural teeth [c19 from F, from *dent* tooth + -URE]

denuclearize *or* **denuclearise** (dɪ'nju:klɪəˌraɪz) *vb* **denuclearizes, denuclearizing, denuclearized** *or* **denuclearises, denuclearising, denuclearised** *(tr)* to deprive (a state, etc) of nuclear weapons > **deˌnucleari'zation** *or* **deˌnucleari'sation** *n*

denudate ('dɛnjʊˌdeɪt, dɪ'nju:deɪt) *vb* **denudates, denudating, denudated** **1** a less common word for **denude** ▷ *adj* **2** denuded

denude (dɪ'nju:d) *vb* **denudes, denuding, denuded** *(tr)* **1** to make bare; strip **2** to expose (rock) by the erosion of the layers above > **denudation** (ˌdɛnjʊ'deɪʃən) *n*

denumerable (dɪ'nju:mərəbᵊl) *adj maths* capable of being put into a one-to-one correspondence with the positive integers; countable > **de'numerably** *adv*

denunciate (dɪ'nʌnsɪˌeɪt) *vb* **denunciates, denunciating, denunciated** *(tr)* to condemn; denounce [c16 from L *dēnuntiāre*; see DENOUNCE] > **de'nunciˌator** *n* > **de'nunciatory** *adj*

denunciation (dɪˌnʌnsɪ'eɪʃən) *n* **1** open condemnation; denouncing **2** *law, obsolete* a charge or accusation of crime made before a public prosecutor or tribunal **3** a formal announcement of the termination of a treaty

Denver ('dɛnvə) *n* a city in central Colorado: the state capital. Pop: 554 636 (2000)

Denver boot *n* a slang name for **wheel clamp** [c20 from DENVER, where the device was first used]

deny (dɪ'naɪ) *vb* **denies, denying, denied** *(tr)* **1** to declare (a statement, etc) to be untrue **2** to reject as false **3** to withhold **4** to refuse to fulfil the expectations of: *it is hard to deny a child* **5** to refuse to acknowledge; disown **6** to refuse (oneself) things desired [c13 from OF *denier*, from L *dēnegāre*, from *negāre*]

Denys ('dɛnɪs; *French* dəni) *n* **Saint** a variant spelling of (Saint) **Denis**

deodar ('di:əʊˌdɑ:) *n* **1** a Himalayan cedar with drooping branches **2** the durable fragrant highly valued wood of this tree [c19 from Hindi, from Sansk. *devadāru*, lit.: wood of the gods]

deodorant (di:'əʊdərənt) *n* **1** a substance applied to the body to suppress or mask the odour of perspiration **2** any substance for destroying or masking odours

deodorize *or* **deodorise** (di:'əʊdəˌraɪz) *vb* **deodorizes, deodorizing, deodorized** *or* **deodorises, deodorising, deodorised** *(tr)* to remove, disguise, or absorb the odour of, esp when unpleasant > **deˌodori'zation** *or* **deˌodori'sation** *n* > **de'odorˌizer** *or* **de'odorˌiser** *n*

deontic (di:'ɒntɪk) *adj logic* **a** of such ethical concepts as obligation and permissibility **b** designating the branch of logic that deals with the formalization of these concepts [c19 from Gk *deon* duty, from impersonal *dei* it behoves, it is binding] > **ˌdeon'tology** *n*

deoxidize *or* **deoxidise** (di:'ɒksɪˌdaɪz) *vb* **deoxidizes, deoxidizing, deoxidized** *or* **deoxidises, deoxidising, deoxidised** **1** *(tr)* to remove oxygen atoms from (a compound, molecule, etc) **2** another word for **reduce** (sense 12) > **deˌoxidi'zation** *or* **deˌoxidi'sation** *n* > **de'oxiˌdizer** *or* **de'oxiˌdiser** *n*

deoxygenate (di:'ɒksɪdʒɪˌneɪt) *or* **deoxygenize, deoxygenise** (di:'ɒksɪdʒɪˌnaɪz) *vb* **deoxygenates, deoxygenating, deoxygenated** *or* **deoxygenizes, deoxygenizing, deoxygenized; deoxygenises, deoxygenising, deoxygenised** *(tr)* to remove oxygen from > **deˌoxygen'ation** *n*

deoxyribonuclease (di:'ɒksɪˌraɪbəʊ'nju:klɪeɪz) *n* the full name for **DNAase**

deoxyribonucleic acid (di:ˌɒksɪˌraɪbəʊnju:'kleɪɪk) *or* **desoxyribonucleic acid** *n* the full name for **DNA**

dep. *abbrev for:* **1** department **2** departure **3** deposit **4** depot **5** deputy

dépanneur (ˌdɛpə'nɜ:) *n Canad* (in Quebec) a convenience store [CF]

Depardieu (*French* dəpɑdjø) *n* **Gérard** born 1948, French film actor. His films include *Jean de Florette* (1986), *Trop Belle pour Toi* (1989), *Cyrano de Bergerac* (1990), *The Man in the*

Iron Mask (1997), and *Tais-toi* (2003)

depart (dɪˈpɑːt) *vb* (*mainly intr*) **1** to leave **2** to set forth **3** (usually foll by *from*) to differ; vary: *to depart from normal procedure* **4** (*tr*) to quit (arch, except in **depart this life**) [C13 from OF *departir*, from DE- + *partir* to go away, divide, from L *partīrī* to divide, distribute, from *pars* a part]

departed (dɪˈpɑːtɪd) *adj euphemistic* **a** dead **b** (*as sing or collective n*; preceded by *the*): *the departed*

department (dɪˈpɑːtmənt) *n* **1** a specialized division of a large concern, such as a business, store, or university **2** a major subdivision of the administration of a government **3** a branch of learning **4** an administrative division in several countries, such as France **5** *inf* a specialized sphere of skill or activity: *wine-making is my wife's department* [C18 from F *département*, from *départir* to divide; see DEPART] > **departmental** (ˌdiːpɑːtˈmɛntᵊl) *adj*

departmentalize *or* **departmentalise** (ˌdiːpɑːtˈmɛntᵊˌlaɪz) *vb* **departmentalizes, departmentalizing, departmentalized** *or* **departmentalises, departmentalising, departmentalised** (*tr*) to organize into departments, esp excessively > **ˌdepartˌmentaliˈzation** *or* **ˌdepartˌmentaliˈsation** *n*

department store *n* a large shop divided into departments selling a great many kinds of goods

departure (dɪˈpɑːtʃə) *n* **1** the act or an instance of departing **2** a variation from previous custom **3** a course of action, venture, etc: *selling is a new departure for him* **4** *naut* the net distance travelled due east or west by a vessel **5** a euphemistic word for **death**

depend (dɪˈpɛnd) *vb* (*intr*) **1** (foll by *on* or *upon*) to put trust (in); rely (on) **2** (usually foll by *on* or *upon*) to be influenced or determined (by): *it all depends on you* **3** (foll by *on* or *upon*) to rely (on) for income, support, etc **4** (foll by *from*) *Rare*. to hang down **5** to be undecided [C15 from OF, from L *dēpendēre* to hang from, from DE- + *pendēre*]

dependable (dɪˈpɛndəbᵊl) *adj* able to be depended on; reliable > **deˌpendaˈbility** *or* **deˈpendableness** *n* > **deˈpendably** *adv*

dependant (dɪˈpɛndənt) *n* a person who depends on another person, organization, etc, for support, aid, or sustenance, esp financial support.

> USAGE *Dependant* is the generally accepted correct spelling in British usage for the noun: *if you are single and have no dependants,...* The adjective should be spelt *dependent: ... tax allowance for dependent* (not *dependant*) *children...* American usage spells both adjective and noun with an *e* in the last syllable

dependence *or US* (*sometimes*) **dependance** (dɪˈpɛndəns) *n* **1** the state or fact of being dependent, esp for support or help **2** reliance; trust; confidence

dependency *or US* (*sometimes*) **dependancy** (dɪˈpɛndənsɪ) *n, pl* **dependencies** *or US* (*sometimes*) **dependancies** **1** a territory subject to a state on which it does not border **2** a dependent or subordinate person or thing **3** *psychol* overreliance on another person or on a drug, etc **4** another word for **dependence**

dependent *or US* (*sometimes*) **dependant** (dɪˈpɛndənt) *adj* **1** depending on a person or thing for aid, support, etc **2** (*postpositive*; foll by *on* or *upon*) influenced or conditioned (by); contingent (on) **3** subordinate; subject **4** *obs* hanging down ▷ *n* **5** a variant spelling (esp US) of **dependant** > **deˈpendently** *adv*

> USAGE See at **dependant**

dependent clause *n grammar* another term for **subordinate clause**

dependent variable *n* a variable in a mathematical equation or statement whose value depends on that taken on by the independent variable

depersonalize *or* **depersonalise** (dɪˈpɜːsnᵊˌlaɪz) *vb* **depersonalizes, depersonalizing, depersonalized** *or* **depersonalises, depersonalising, depersonalised** (*tr*) **1** to deprive (a person, organization, etc) of individual or personal qualities **2** to cause (someone) to lose his or her sense of identity > **deˌpersonaliˈzation** *or* **deˌpersonaliˈsation** *n*

depict (dɪˈpɪkt) *vb* (*tr*) **1** to represent by drawing, sculpture, painting, etc; delineate; portray **2** to represent in words; describe [C17 from L *dēpingere*, from *pingere* to paint] > **deˈpicter** *or* **deˈpictor** *n* > **deˈpiction** *n* > **deˈpictive** *adj*

depilate (ˈdɛpɪˌleɪt) *vb* **depilates, depilating, depilated** (*tr*) to remove the hair from [C16 from L *dēpilāre*, from *pilāre* to make bald, from *pilus* hair] > **ˌdepiˈlation** *n* > **ˈdepiˌlator** *n*

depilatory (dɪˈpɪlətərɪ, -trɪ) *adj* **1** able or serving to remove hair ▷ *n, pl* **depilatories** **2** a chemical used to remove hair from the body

deplane (diːˈpleɪn) *vb* **deplanes, deplaning, deplaned** (*intr*) *chiefly US & Canad* to disembark from an aeroplane [C20 from DE- + PLANE[1]]

deplete (dɪˈpliːt) *vb* **depletes, depleting, depleted** (*tr*) **1** to use up (supplies, money, etc); exhaust **2** to empty entirely or partially [C19 from L *dēplēre* to empty out, from DE- + *plēre* to fill] > **deˈpletion** *n*

depleted uranium *n* uranium from which most of the radioactive uranium-235 isotope has been removed, used in armour-piercing shells. Abbrev: **DU**

depletion layer *n* a region at the interface between dissimilar zones of conductivity in a semiconductor, in which there are few charge carriers

deplorable (dɪˈplɔːrəbᵊl) *adj* **1** lamentable **2** worthy of censure or reproach; very bad > **deˈplorably** *adv*

deplore (dɪˈplɔː) *vb* **deplores, deploring, deplored** (*tr*) **1** to express or feel sorrow about **2** to express or feel strong disapproval of; censure [C16 from OF, from L *dēplōrāre* to weep bitterly, from *plōrāre* to weep] > **deˈploringly** *adv*

Dd

deploy (dɪˈplɔɪ) *vb chiefly mil* **1** to adopt or cause to adopt a battle formation **2** (*tr*) to redistribute (forces) to or within a given area [C18 from F, from L *displicāre* to unfold; see DISPLAY] > **deˈployment** *n*

depolarize *or* **depolarise** (diːˈpəʊləˌraɪz) *vb* **depolarizes, depolarizing, depolarized** *or* **depolarises, depolarising, depolarised** to undergo or cause to undergo a loss of polarity or polarization > **deˌpolariˈzation** *or* **deˌpolariˈsation** *n*

deponent (dɪˈpəʊnənt) *adj* **1** *grammar* (of a verb, esp in Latin) having the inflectional endings of a passive verb but the meaning of an active verb ▷ *n* **2** *grammar* a deponent verb **3** *law* a person who makes an affidavit or a deposition [C16 from L *dēpōnēns* putting aside, putting down, from *dēpōnere*]

depopulate (dɪˈpɒpjʊˌleɪt) *vb* **depopulates, depopulating, depopulated** to be or cause to be reduced in population > **deˌpopuˈlation** *n*

deport (dɪˈpɔːt) *vb* (*tr*) **1** to remove forcibly from a country; expel **2** to conduct, hold, or behave (oneself) in a specified manner [C15 from F, from L *dēportāre* to carry away, banish, from DE- + *portāre* to carry] > **deˈportable** *adj*

deportation (ˌdiːpɔːˈteɪʃən) *n* the act of expelling someone from a country

deportee (ˌdiːpɔːˈtiː) *n* a person deported or awaiting deportation

deportment (dɪˈpɔːtmənt) *n* the manner in which a person behaves, esp in physical bearing: *military deportment* [C17 from F, from OF *deporter* to conduct (oneself); see DEPORT]

depose (dɪˈpəʊz) *vb* **deposes, deposing, deposed** **1** (*tr*) to remove from an office or position of power **2** *law* to testify or give (evidence, etc) on oath [C13 from OF: to put away, put down, from LL *dēpōnere* to depose from office, from L: to put aside]

deposit (dɪˈpɒzɪt) *vb (tr)* **1** to put or set down, esp carefully; place **2** to entrust for safekeeping **3** to place (money) in a bank or similar institution to earn interest or for safekeeping **4** to give (money) in part payment or as security **5** to lay down naturally: *the river deposits silt* ▷ *n* **6a** an instance of entrusting money or valuables to a bank or similar institution **6b** the money or valuables so entrusted **7** money given in part payment or as security **8** an accumulation of sediments, minerals, coal, etc **9** any deposited material, such as a sediment **10** a depository or storehouse **11 on deposit** payable as the first instalment, as when buying on hire-purchase [C17 from Med. L *dēpositāre*, from L *dēpositus* put down]

deposit account *n Brit* a bank account that earns interest and usually requires notice of withdrawal

depositary (dɪˈpɒzɪtərɪ, -trɪ) *n, pl* **depositaries** **1** a person or group to whom something is entrusted for safety **2** a variant spelling of **depository**

deposition (ˌdɛpəˈzɪʃən) *n* **1** *law* **1a** the giving of testimony on oath **1b** the testimony given **1c** the sworn statement of a witness used in court in his or her absence **2** the act or an instance of deposing **3** the act or an instance of depositing **4** something deposited [C14 from LL *dēpositiō* a laying down, disposal, burying, testimony]

depositor (dɪˈpɒzɪtə) *n* a person who places or has money on deposit, esp in a bank

depository (dɪˈpɒzɪtərɪ, -trɪ) *n, pl* **depositories** **1** a store for furniture, valuables, etc; repository **2** a variant spelling of **depositary** [C17 (in the sense: place of a deposit): from Med. L *dēpositōrium*; C18 (in the sense: depositary): see DEPOSIT, -ORY[1]]

depot (ˈdɛpəʊ; *US & Canad* ˈdiːpəʊ) *n* **1** a storehouse or warehouse **2** *mil* **2a** a store for supplies **2b** a training and holding centre for recruits and replacements **3** *chiefly Brit* a building used for the storage and servicing of buses or railway engines **4** *US & Canad* a bus or railway station [C18 from F *dépôt*, from L *dēpositum* a deposit, trust]

deprave (dɪˈpreɪv) *vb* **depraves, depraving, depraved** *(tr)* to make morally bad; corrupt [C14 from L *dēprāvāre* to distort, corrupt, from DE- + *prāvus* crooked] > **depravation** (ˌdɛprəˈveɪʃən) *n*

depraved (dɪˈpreɪvd) *adj* morally bad or debased; corrupt; perverted

depravity (dɪˈprævɪtɪ) *n, pl* **depravities** the state or an instance of moral corruption

deprecate (ˈdɛprɪˌkeɪt) *vb* **deprecates, deprecating, deprecated** *(tr)* **1** to express disapproval of; protest against **2** to depreciate; belittle [C17 from L *dēprecārī* to avert, ward off by entreaty, from DE- + *precārī* to PRAY] > **ˈdepreˌcating** *adj* > **ˈdepreˌcatingly** *adv* > **ˌdepreˈcation** *n* > **ˈdeprecative** *adj* > **ˈdepreˌcator** *n*

USAGE See at **depreciate**

deprecatory (ˈdɛprɪkətərɪ) *adj* **1** expressing disapproval; protesting **2** expressing apology; apologetic > **ˈdeprecatorily** *adv*

depreciate (dɪˈpriːʃɪˌeɪt) *vb* **depreciates, depreciating, depreciated** **1** to reduce or decline in value or price **2** *(tr)* to lessen the value of by derision, criticism, etc [C15 from LL *dēpretiāre* to lower the price of, from L DE- + *pretium* PRICE] > **deˈpreciˌatingly** *adv* > **depreciatory** (dɪˈpriːʃɪətərɪ) *or* **deˈpreciative** *adj*

USAGE The form *self-depreciating*, which used to be considered incorrect, is now in quite common use, and is generally agreed to be an acceptable alternative to *self-deprecating*

depreciation (dɪˌpriːʃɪˈeɪʃən) *n* **1** *accounting* **1a** the reduction in value of a fixed asset due to use, obsolescence, etc **1b** the amount deducted from gross profit to allow for this **2** the act or an instance of depreciating or belittling **3** a decrease in the exchange value of a currency brought about by excess supply of that currency under conditions of fluctuating exchange rates

depredation (ˌdɛprɪˈdeɪʃən) *n* the act or an instance of plundering; pillage [C15 from LL *dēpraedārī* to ravage]

depress (dɪˈprɛs) *vb (tr)* **1** to lower in spirits; make gloomy **2** to weaken the force, or energy of **3** to lower prices of **4** to press or push down [C14 from OF *depresser*, from L *dēprimere* from DE- + *premere* to PRESS[1]] > **deˈpressing** *adj* > **deˈpressingly** *adv*

depressant (dɪˈprɛsᵊnt) *adj* **1** *med* able to reduce nervous or functional activity **2** causing gloom; depressing ▷ *n* **3** a depressant drug

depressed (dɪˈprɛst) *adj* **1** low in spirits; downcast **2** lower than the surrounding surface **3** pressed down or flattened **4** Also: **distressed** characterized by economic hardship, such as unemployment: *a depressed area* **5** lowered in force, intensity, or amount **6** *bot, zool* flattened

depression (dɪˈprɛʃən) *n* **1** a depressing or being depressed **2** a sunken place **3** a mental disorder characterized by feelings of gloom and inadequacy **4** *pathol* an abnormal lowering of the rate of any physiological activity or function **5** an economic condition characterized by unemployment, low investment, etc; slump **6** Also called: **cyclone, low** *meteorol* a large body of rotating and rising air below normal atmospheric pressure, which often brings rain **7** (esp in surveying and astronomy) the angular distance of an object below the horizontal plane

Depression (dɪˈprɛʃən) *n* (usually preceded by *the*) the worldwide economic depression of the early 1930s, when there was mass unemployment

depressive (dɪˈprɛsɪv) *adj* **1** tending to depress **2** *psychol* tending to be subject to periods of depression > **deˈpressively** *adv*

depressor (dɪˈprɛsə) *n* **1** a person or thing that depresses **2** any muscle that draws down a part **3** *med* an instrument used to press down or aside an organ or part

depressurize *or* **depressurise** (dɪˈprɛʃəˌraɪz) *vb* **depressurizes, depressurizing, depressurized** *or* **depressurises, depressurising, depressurised** *(tr)* to reduce the pressure of a gas inside (an enclosed space), as in an aircraft cabin > **deˌpressuriˈzation** *or* **deˌpressuriˈsation** *n*

deprive (dɪˈpraɪv) *vb* **deprives, depriving, deprived** *(tr)* **1** (foll by *of*) to prevent from possessing or enjoying; dispossess (of) **2** *arch* to depose; demote [C14 from OF, from Med. L *dēprīvāre*, from L DE- + *prīvāre* to deprive of] > **deˈprival** *n* > **deprivation** (ˌdɛprɪˈveɪʃən) *n*

deprived (dɪˈpraɪvd) *adj* lacking adequate food, shelter, education, etc: *deprived inner-city areas*

deprogramme *or esp US* **deprogram** (diːˈprəʊgræm) *vb* **deprogrammes, deprogramming, deprogrammed** *or esp US* **deprograms, deprogramming, deprogrammed** to attempt to reverse the brainwashing of (a person)

dept *abbrev for* department

depth (dɛpθ) *n* **1** the distance downwards, backwards, or inwards **2** the quality of being deep; deepness **3** intensity of emotion **4** profundity of moral character; sagacity; integrity **5** complexity or abstruseness, as of thought **6** intensity, as of silence, colour, etc **7** lowness of pitch **8** (*often pl*) a deep, inner, or remote part, such as an inaccessible region of a country **9** (*often pl*) the most intense or severe part: *the depths of winter* **10** (*usually pl*) a low moral state **11** (*often pl*) a vast space or abyss **12 beyond** *or* **out of one's depth** **12a** in water deeper than one is tall **12b** beyond the range of one's competence or understanding [C14 from *dep* DEEP + -TH[1]]

depth charge *or* **bomb** *n* a bomb used to attack submarines that explodes at a preset depth of water

depth gauge *n* a device attached to a drill bit to prevent the hole from exceeding a predetermined depth

depth of field *n* the range of distance in front of and behind an object focused by an optical instrument, such as a camera or microscope, within which other objects will also appear sharply defined in the resulting image

depth psychology *n psychol* the study of unconscious motives and attitudes

depuration (ˌdɛpjʊˈreɪʃən) *n* the act or process of eliminating impurities; self-purification [c17 from F or Med. L, ult. from L *pūrus* pure]

deputation (ˌdɛpjʊˈteɪʃən) *n* **1** the act of appointing a person or body of people to represent others **2** a person or body of people so appointed; delegation

depute *vb* (dɪˈpjuːt), **deputes, deputing, deputed** (*tr*) **1** to appoint as an agent **2** to assign (authority, duties, etc) to a deputy ▷ *n* (ˈdɛpjuːt) **3** *Scot* **3a** a deputy **3b** (*as modifier, usually postpositive*): *a sheriff-depute* [c15 from OF, from LL *dēputāre* to assign, allot, from L DE- + *putāre* to think, consider]

deputize *or* **deputise** (ˈdɛpjʊˌtaɪz) *vb* **deputizes, deputizing, deputized** *or* **deputises, deputising, deputised** to appoint or act as deputy

deputy (ˈdɛpjʊtɪ) *n, pl* **deputies 1a** a person appointed to act on behalf of or represent another **1b** (*as modifier*): *the deputy chairman* **2** a member of a legislative assembly in various countries, such as France [c16 from OF, from *deputer* to appoint; see DEPUTE]

De Quincey (də ˈkwɪnsɪ) *n* **Thomas** 1785–1859, English critic and essayist, noted particularly for his *Confessions of an English Opium Eater* (1821)

der. *abbrev for*: **1** derivation **2** derivative

deracinate (dɪˈræsɪˌneɪt) *vb* **deracinates, deracinating, deracinated** (*tr*) to pull up by or as if by the roots; uproot [c16 from OF *desraciner*, from *des-* DIS-[1] + *racine* root, from LL, from L *rādīx* a root] > **deˌraciˈnation** *n*

derail (dɪˈreɪl) *vb* to go or cause to go off the rails, as a train, tram, etc > **deˈrailment** *n*

Derain (*French* dərɛ̃) *n* **André** (ɑ̃dre) 1880–1954, French painter, noted for his Fauvist pictures (1905–08)

derange (dɪˈreɪndʒ) *vb* **deranges, deranging, deranged** (*tr*) **1** to throw into disorder; disarrange **2** to disturb the action of **3** to make insane [c18 from OF *desrengier*, from des- DIS-[1] + *reng* row, order] > **deˈrangement** *n*

derby (ˈdɜːrbɪ) *n, pl* **derbies** the US and Canad name for **bowler**[2]

Derby[1] (ˈdɑːbɪ; US ˈdɜːrbɪ) *n, pl* **Derbies 1 the** an annual horse race run at Epsom Downs, Surrey, since 1780 **2** (*usually not cap*) any of various other horse races **3 local derby** a football match between two teams from the same area [c18 after the twelfth Earl of *Derby* (died 1834), who founded the race in 1780]

Derby[2] (ˈdɑːbɪ) *n* **1** a city in central England, in Derby unitary authority, Derbyshire: engineering industries(esp aircraft engines and railway rolling stock); university (1991). Pop: 223 836 (1991) **2** a unitary authority in central England, in Derbyshire. Pop: 221 716 (2001 est). Area: 78 sq km (30 sq miles) **3** a firm-textured pale-coloured type of cheese **4 sage Derby** a green-and-white Derby cheese flavoured with sage

Derby[3] (ˈdɑːbɪ) *n* **Earl of** title of *Edward George Geoffrey Smith Stanley*. 1799–1869, British statesman; Conservative prime minister (1852; 1858–59; 1866–68)

Derbyshire (ˈdɑːbɪˌʃɪə, -ʃə) *n* a county of N central England: contains the Peak District and several resorts with mineral springs: the geographical and ceremonial county includes the city of Derby, which became an independent unitary authority in 1997. Administrative centre: Matlock. Pop (excluding Derby city): 734 581 (2001). Area (excluding Derby city): 2551 sq km (985 sq miles)

derecognize *or* **derecognise** (diːˈrɛkəgˌnaɪz) *vb* **derecognizes, derecognizing, derecognized** *or* **derecognises, derecognising, derecognised** (*tr*) to cease to recognize (a trade union) as having special negotiating rights within a company or industry > ˌ**derecogˈnition** *n*

deregulate (diːˈrɛgjʊˌleɪt) *vb* **deregulates, deregulating, deregulated** (*tr*) to remove regulations from > **deˌreguˈlation** *n*

derelict (ˈdɛrɪlɪkt) *adj* **1** deserted or abandoned, as by an owner, occupant, etc **2** falling into ruins **3** neglectful of duty; remiss ▷ *n* **4** a social outcast or vagrant **5** property deserted or abandoned by an owner, occupant, etc **6** a vessel abandoned at sea **7** a person who is neglectful of duty [c17 from L, from *dērelinquere* to abandon, from DE- + *relinquere* to leave]

dereliction (ˌdɛrɪˈlɪkʃən) *n* **1** conscious or wilful neglect(esp in **dereliction of duty**) **2** an abandoning or being abandoned **3** *law* accretion of dry land gained by the gradual receding of the sea

derestrict (ˌdiːrɪˈstrɪkt) *vb* (*tr*) to render or leave free from restriction, esp a road from speed limits > ˌ**dereˈstriction** *n*

deride (dɪˈraɪd) *vb* **derides, deriding, derided** (*tr*) to speak of or treat with contempt or ridicule; scoff at [c16 from L *dērīdēre* to laugh to scorn, from DE- + *rīdēre* to laugh, smile] > **deˈrider** *n* > **deˈridingly** *adv*

de rigueur *French* (də rigœr) *adj* required by etiquette or fashion [lit.: of strictness]

derision (dɪˈrɪʒən) *n* the act of deriding; mockery; scorn [c15 from LL *dērīsiō*, from L *dērīsus*; see DERIDE] > **deˈrisible** *adj*

derisive (dɪˈraɪsɪv) *adj* characterized by derision; mocking; scornful > **deˈrisively** *adv* > **deˈrisiveness** *n*

derisory (dɪˈraɪsərɪ) *adj* **1** subject to or worthy of derision **2** another word for **derisive**

derivation (ˌdɛrɪˈveɪʃən) *n* **1** a deriving or being derived **2** the origin or descent of something, such as a word **3** something derived; a derivative **4a** the process of deducing a mathematical theorem, formula, etc, as a necessary consequence of a set of accepted statements **4b** this sequence of statements > ˌ**deriˈvational** *adj*

Dd

derivative (dɪˈrɪvətɪv) *adj* **1** derived **2** based on other sources; not original ▷ *n* **3** a term, idea, etc, that is based on or derived from another in the same class **4** a word derived from another word **5** *chem* a compound that is formed from, or can be regarded as formed from, a structurally related compound **6** *maths* **6a** Also called: **differential coefficient, first derivative** the change of a function, f(*x*), with respect to an infinitesimally small change in the independent variable, *x* **6b** the rate of change of one quantity with respect to another **7** *finance* a financial instrument, such as a futures contract or option, the price of which is largely determined by the commodity, currency, share price, interest rate, etc, to which it is linked > **deˈrivatively** *adv*

derive (dɪˈraɪv) *vb* **derives, deriving, derived 1** (usually foll by *from*) to draw or be drawn (from) in source or origin **2** (*tr*) to obtain by reasoning; deduce; infer **3** (*tr*) to trace the source or development of **4** (usually foll by *from*) to produce or be produced (from) by a chemical reaction [c14 from OF: to spring from, from L *dērīvāre* to draw off, from DE- + *rīvus* a stream] > **deˈrivable** *adj* > **deˈriver** *n*

derived unit *n* a unit of measurement obtained by multiplication or division of the base units of a system without the introduction of numerical factors

-derm *n combining form* indicating skin: *endoderm* [via F from Gk *derma* skin]

derma (ˈdɜːmə) *n* another name for **corium.** Also: **derm** [c18 NL, from Gk: skin]

dermal (ˈdɛːməl) *adj* of or relating to the skin

dermatitis (ˌdɜːməˈtaɪtɪs) *n* inflammation of the skin

dermato-, derma- *or before a vowel* **dermat-, derm-** *combining form.* indicating skin: *dermatitis* [from Gk *derma* skin]

dermatology (ˌdɜːməˈtɒlədʒɪ) *n* the branch of medicine

concerned with the skin and its diseases
> **dermatological** (ˌdɜːmətəˈlɒdʒɪkᵊl) *adj*
> ˌ**dermaˈtologist** *n*
▹ www.aad.org

dermis (ˈdɜːmɪs) *n* another name for **corium** [C19 NL, from EPIDERMIS] > ˈ**dermic** *adj*

dernier cri *French* (dɛrnje kri) *n* **le** (lə) the latest fashion; the last word [lit.: last cry]

derogate (ˈdɛrəˌɡeɪt) *vb* **derogates, derogating, derogated** 1 (*intr*; foll by *from*) to cause to seem inferior; detract 2 (*intr*; foll by *from*) to deviate in standard or quality 3 (*tr*) to cause to seem inferior, etc; disparage 4 (*tr*) to curtail the application of (a law or regulation) [C15 from L *dērogāre* to repeal some part of a law, modify it, from DE- + *rogāre* to ask, propose a law] > ˌ**deroˈgation** *n* > **derogative** (dɪˈrɒɡətɪv) *adj*

derogatory (dɪˈrɒɡətərɪ) *adj* tending or intended to detract, disparage, or belittle; intentionally offensive > **deˈrogatorily** *adv*

derrick (ˈdɛrɪk) *n* 1 a simple crane having lifting tackle slung from a boom 2 the framework erected over an oil well to enable drill tubes to be raised and lowered [C17 (in the sense: gallows): from *Derrick*, celebrated hangman at Tyburn, London]

Derrida (*French* dɛrɪda) *n* **Jacques** born 1930, French philosopher and literary critic, regarded as the founder of deconstruction: author of *L'Ecriture et la différence* (1967)

derrière (ˌdɛrɪˈɛə) *n* a euphemistic word for **buttocks** [C18 lit.: behind (prep), from OF *deriere*, from L *dē retrō* from the back]

derring-do (ˈdɛrɪŋˈduː) *n arch or literary* boldness or bold action [C16 from ME *durring don* daring to do, from *durren* to dare + *don* to do]

derringer *or* **deringer** (ˈdɛrɪndʒə) *n* a short-barrelled pocket pistol of large calibre [C19 after Henry *Deringer*, US gunsmith, who invented it]

derris (ˈdɛrɪs) *n* 1 an East Indian woody climbing plant 2 an insecticide made from its powdered roots [C19 NL, from Gk: covering, leather, from *deros* skin, hide, from *derein* to skin]

derro (ˈdɛrəʊ) *n, pl* **derros** *Austral sl* a vagrant [from DERELICT]

Derry (ˈdɛrɪ) *n* 1 a district in NW Northern Ireland, in Co. Londonderry. Pop: 106 066 (2001). Area: 387 sq km (149 sq miles) 2 another name for **Londonderry**

derv (dɜːv) *n* a Brit name for **diesel oil** when used for road transport [C20 from *d(iesel) e(ngine) r(oad) v(ehicle)*]

dervish (ˈdɜːvɪʃ) *n* a member of any of various Muslim orders of ascetics, some of which (**whirling dervishes**) are noted for a frenzied, ecstatic, whirling dance [C16 from Turkish, from Persian *darvīsh* mendicant monk]

Derwent (ˈdɜːwənt) *n* 1 a river in S Australia, in S Tasmania, flowing southeast to the Tasman Sea. Length: 172 km (107 miles) 2 a river in N central England, in N Derbyshire, flowing southeast to the River Trent. Length: 96 km (60 miles) 3 a river in N England, in Yorkshire, rising on the North York Moors and flowing south to the River Ouse. Length: 92 km (57 miles) 4 a river in NW England, in Cumbria, rising on the Borrowdale Fells and flowing north and west to the Irish Sea. Length: 54 km (34 miles)

Derwentwater (ˈdɜːwəntˌwɔːtə) *n* a lake in NW England, in Cumbria in the Lake District. Area: about 8 sq km (3 sq miles)

DES (in Britain) *abbrev for* (the former) Department of Education and Science

Desai (dɛˈsaɪ) *n* **Morarji (Ranchhodji)** (məˈrɑːdʒɪ) 1896–1995, Indian statesman, noted for his asceticism. He founded the Janata party in opposition to Indira Gandhi, whom he defeated in the 1977 election; prime minister of India (1977–79)

desalination (diːˌsælɪˈneɪʃən) *or* **desalinization, desalinisation** *n* **a** the process of removing salt, esp from sea water **b** (*as modifier*): **desalination techniques**

descale (ˌdiːˈskeɪl) *vb* **descales, descaling, descaled** (*tr*) to remove the hard deposit formed by chemicals in water from (a kettle, pipe, etc)

descant (ˈdɛskænt) *n* 1 Also called: **discant** a decorative counterpoint added above a basic melody 2 a comment or discourse ▹ *adj* 3 Also: **discant** of the highest member in common use in a family of musical instruments: *a descant recorder* ▹ *vb* (*intr*) 4 Also: **discant** (often foll by *on* or *upon*) to perform a descant 5 (often foll by *on* or *upon*) to discourse or make comments 6 *arch* to sing sweetly [C14 from OF, from Med. L *discanthus*, from L DIS-[1] + *cantus* song] > **desˈcanter** *n*

Descartes (ˈdeɪˌkɑːt; *French* dekart) *n* **René** (rəne) 1596–1650, French philosopher and mathematician. He provided a mechanistic basis for the philosophical theory of dualism and is regarded as the founder of modern philosophy. He also founded analytical geometry and contributed greatly to the science of optics. His works include *Discours de la méthode* (1637), *Meditationes de Prima Philosophia* (1641), and *Principia Philosophiae* (1644). Related adj: **Cartesian**

descend (dɪˈsɛnd) *vb* (*mainly intr*) 1 (*also tr*) to move down (a slope, staircase, etc) 2 to lead or extend down; slope 3 to move to a lower level, pitch, etc; fall 4 (often foll by *from*) to be connected by a blood relationship (to a dead or extinct individual, species, etc) 5 to be inherited 6 to sink or come down in morals or behaviour 7 (often foll by *on* or *upon*) to arrive or attack in a sudden or overwhelming way 8 (of the sun, moon, etc) to move towards the horizon [C13 from OF, from L *dēscendere*, from DE- + *scandere* to climb] > **desˈcendable** *or* **desˈcendible** *adj*

descendant (dɪˈsɛndənt) *n* 1 a person, animal, or plant when described as descended from an individual, race, species, etc 2 something that derives from an earlier form ▹ *adj* 3 a variant spelling of **descendent**

descendent (dɪˈsɛndənt) *adj* descending

descender (dɪˈsɛndə) *n* 1 *printing* the part of certain lower-case letters, such as j, p, or y, that extends below the body of the letter 2 a person or thing that descends

descent (dɪˈsɛnt) *n* 1 the act of descending 2 a downward slope 3 a path or way leading downwards 4 derivation from an ancestor; lineage 5 a generation in a particular lineage 6 a decline or degeneration 7 a movement or passage in degree or state from higher to lower 8 (often foll by *on*) a sudden and overwhelming arrival or attack 9 *property law* (formerly) the transmission of real property to the heir

deschool (ˌdiːˈskuːl) *vb* (*tr*) to separate education from the institution of school and operate through the pupil's life experience as opposed to a set curriculum

describe (dɪˈskraɪb) *vb* **describes, describing, described** (*tr*) 1 to give an account or representation of in words 2 to pronounce or label 3 to draw a line or figure, such as a circle [C15 from L *dēscrībere* to copy off, write out, from DE- + *scrībere* to write] > **deˈscribable** *adj* > **deˈscriber** *n*

description (dɪˈskrɪpʃən) *n* 1 a statement or account that describes 2 the act, process, or technique of describing 3 sort or variety: *reptiles of every description*

descriptive (dɪˈskrɪptɪv) *adj* 1 characterized by or containing description 2 *grammar* (of an adjective) serving to describe the referent of the noun modified, as for example the adjective *brown* as contrasted with *my* 3 relating to description or classification rather than explanation or prescription > **deˈscriptively** *adv* > **deˈscriptiveness** *n*

descry (dɪˈskraɪ) *vb* **descries, descrying, descried** (*tr*) 1 to catch sight of 2 to discover by looking carefully [C14 from OF *descrier* to proclaim, DECRY]

desecrate (ˈdɛsɪˌkreɪt) *vb* **desecrates, desecrating, desecrated** (*tr*) 1 to violate the sacred character of (an object or place) by destructive, blasphemous, or sacrilegious action **2** to deconsecrate [C17 from DE- + CONSECRATE] > **'dese,crator** or **'dese,crater** *n* > **,dese'cration** *n*

desegregate (diː'sɛgrɪ,geɪt) *vb* **desegregates, desegregating, desegregated** to end racial segregation in (a school or other public institution) > **,desegre'gation** *n*

deselect (,diːsɪ'lɛkt) *vb* (*tr*) **1** *Brit politics* (of a constituency organization) to refuse to select (an existing MP) for re-election **2** *computing* to cancel (a highlighted selection of data) on a computer screen **3** *computing* to remove (the check mark) at an option in a dialogue box > **,dese'lection** *n*

desensitize *or* **desensitise** (diː'sɛnsɪ,taɪz) *vb* **desensitizes, desensitizing, desensitized** *or* **desensitises, desensitising, desensitised** (*tr*) to render less sensitive or insensitive: *the patient was desensitized to the allergen* > **de,sensiti'zation** *or* **de,sensiti'sation** *n* > **de'sensi,tizer** *or* **de'sensi,tiser** *n*

desert[1] ('dɛzət) *n* **1** a region that is devoid or almost devoid of vegetation, esp because of low rainfall **2** an uncultivated uninhabited region **3** a place which lacks some desirable feature or quality: *a cultural desert* **4** (*modifier*) of, relating to, or like a desert [C13 from OF, from Church L *dēsertum*, from L *dēserere* to abandon, lit.: to sever one's links with, from DE- + *serere* to bind together]

desert[2] (dɪ'zɜːt) *vb* **1** (*tr*) to abandon (a person, place, etc) without intending to return, esp in violation of a promise or obligation **2** *mil* to abscond from (a post or duty) with no intention of returning **3** (*tr*) to fail (someone) in time of need [C15 from F *déserter*, from LL *dēsertāre*, from L *dēserere* to forsake; see DESERT[1]] > **de'serted** *adj* > **de'serter** *n*

desert[3] (dɪ'zɜːt) *n* **1** (*often pl*) just reward or punishment **2** the state of deserving a reward or punishment [C13 from OF *deserte*, from *deservir* to DESERVE]

desert boots *pl n* ankle-high boots, often of suede, with laces and soft soles

desertification (dɪ,zɛːtɪfɪ'keɪʃən) *n* the transformation of fertile land into an arid or semiarid region as a result of intensive farming, soil erosion, etc

desertion (dɪ'zɜːʃən) *n* **1** a deserting or being deserted **2** *law* wilful abandonment, esp of one's spouse or children

desert island *n* a small remote tropical island

desert pea *n* an Australian trailing leguminous plant with scarlet flowers

desert rat *n* **1** a jerboa inhabiting the deserts of N Africa **2** *Brit inf* a soldier who served in North Africa with the British 7th Armoured Division in 1941–42

deserve (dɪ'zɜːv) *vb* **deserves, deserving, deserved 1** (*tr*) to be entitled to or worthy of; merit **2** (*intr*; foll by *of*) *Obs.* to be worthy [C13 from OF *deservir*, from L *dēservīre* to serve devotedly, from DE- + *servīre* to SERVE]

deserved (dɪ'zɜːvd) *adj* rightfully earned; justified; warranted > **deservedly** (dɪ'zɜːvɪdlɪ) *adv* > **deservedness** (dɪ'zɜːvɪdnɪs) *n*

deserving (dɪ'zɜːvɪŋ) *adj* (often *postpositive* and foll by *of*) worthy, esp of praise or reward > **de'servingly** *adv* > **de'servingness** *n*

deshabille (,deɪzæ'biːl) *or* **dishabille** *n* the state of being partly or carelessly dressed [C17 from F *déshabillé*, from *dés* DIS-[1] + *habiller* to dress]

de Sica (*Italian* de 'siːka) *n* **Vittorio** (vit'tɔːrjo) 1902–74, Italian film actor and director. His films, in the neorealist tradition, include *Shoeshine* (1946) and *Bicycle Thieves* (1948)

desiccant ('dɛsɪkənt) *adj* **1** drying ▷ *n* **2** a substance that absorbs water and is used to remove moisture [C17 from L *dēsiccāns* drying up; see DESICCATE]

desiccate ('dɛsɪ,keɪt) *vb* **desiccates, desiccating, desiccated 1** (*tr*) to remove most of the water from; dehydrate **2** (*tr*) to preserve (food) by removing moisture; dry **3** (*intr*) to become dried up [C16 from L *dēsiccāre* to dry up, from DE- + *siccāre*, from *siccus* dry] > **,desic'cation** *n*

desiccated ('dɛsɪ,keɪtɪd) *adj* **1** dehydrated and powdered: *desiccated coconut* **2** lacking in spirit or animation

desiderate (dɪ'zɪdə,reɪt) *vb* **desiderates, desiderating, desiderated** (*tr*) to feel the lack of or need for; miss [C17 from L *dēsīderāre*, from DE- + *sīdus* star; see DESIRE] > **de,sider'ation** *n*

desideratum (dɪ,zɪdə'rɑːtəm) *n, pl* **desiderata** (-tə) something lacked and wanted [C17 from L; see DESIDERATE]

design (dɪ'zaɪn) *vb* **1** to work out the structure or form of (something), as by making a sketch or plans **2** to plan and make (something) artistically or skilfully **3** (*tr*) to invent **4** (*tr*) to intend, as for a specific purpose; plan ▷ *n* **5** a plan or preliminary drawing **6** the arrangement, elements, or features of an artistic or decorative work: *the design of the desk is Chippendale* **7** a finished artistic or decorative creation **8** the art of designing **9** a plan or project **10** an intention; purpose **11** (*often pl*; often foll by *on* or *against*) a plot, often to gain possession of (something) by illegitimate means [C16 from L *dēsignāre* to mark out, describe, from DE- + *signāre*, from *signum* a mark] > **de'signable** *adj*

designate *vb* ('dɛzɪg,neɪt) **designates, designating, designated** (*tr*) **1** to indicate or specify **2** to give a name to; style; entitle **3** to select or name for an office or duty; appoint ▷ *adj* ('dɛzɪgnɪt, -,neɪt) **4** (*immediately postpositive*) appointed, but not yet in office: *a minister designate* [C15 from L *dēsignātus* marked out, defined; see DESIGN] > **'desig,nator** *n*

designation (,dɛzɪg'neɪʃən) *n* **1** something that designates, such as a name **2** the act of designating or the fact of being designated

designedly (dɪ'zaɪnɪdlɪ) *adv* by intention or design; on purpose

designer (dɪ'zaɪnə) *n* **1** a person who devises and executes designs, as for clothes, machines, etc **2** (*modifier*) designed by and bearing the label of a well-known fashion designer: *designer jeans* **3** (*modifier*) (of things, ideas, etc) fashionably trendy: *designer stubble* **4** (*modifier*) (of cells, chemicals, etc) designed or produced to perform a specific function or combat a specific problem: *designer insecticide* **5** a person who devises plots; intriguer

▷ www.fashion.net/sites/fashiondesigners

designer baby *n inf* a baby that is the product of genetic engineering

designer drug *n* **1** *med* a synthetic drug that has the same properties as an illegal narcotic or hallucinogen but can be manufactured legally **2** a drug designed to act on a specific molecular target

designing (dɪ'zaɪnɪŋ) *adj* artful and scheming

desirable (dɪ'zaɪərəbᵊl) *adj* **1** worthy of desire: *a desirable residence* **2** arousing desire, esp sexual desire; attractive > **de,sira'bility** *or* **de'sirableness** *n* > **de'sirably** *adv*

desire (dɪ'zaɪə) *vb* **desires, desiring, desired** (*tr*) **1** to wish or long for; crave **2** to request; ask for ▷ *n* **3** a wish or longing **4** an expressed wish; request **5** sexual appetite **6** a person or thing that is desired [C13 from OF, from L *dēsīderāre* to desire earnestly; see DESIDERATE] > **de'sirer** *n*

desirous (dɪ'zaɪərəs) *adj* (usually *postpositive* and foll by *of*) having or expressing desire (for)

desist (dɪ'zɪst) *vb* (*intr*; often foll by *from*) to cease, as from an action; stop or abstain [C15 from OF, from L *dēsistere* to leave off, stand apart, from DE- + *sistere* to stand, halt]

desk (dɛsk) *n* **1** a piece of furniture with a writing surface and usually drawers or other compartments **2** a service counter or table in a public building, such as a hotel **3** a support for the book from which services are read in a church **4** the editorial section of a newspaper, etc, responsible for a particular subject: *the news desk* **5** a music stand shared by two orchestral players [c14 from Med. L *desca* table, from L *discus* disc, dish]

desk-bound *adj* obliged by one's occupation to work sitting at a desk

desk editor *n* (in a publishing house) an editor responsible for the preparation and checking of manuscripts for printing

deskfast ('dɛskfəst) *n* breakfast eaten at one's desk at work [c20 from DESK + (BREAK)FAST]

deskill (diːˈskɪl) *vb (tr)* **1** to mechanize or computerize (a job) so that little skill is required to do it **2** to deprive (employees) of the opportunity for skilled work

desktop ('dɛsk,tɒp) *n (modifier)* denoting a computer system, esp for word processing, that is small enough to use at a desk

desktop publishing *n* a means of publishing reports, advertising material, etc, to near-typeset quality using a desktop computer and a laser printer. Abbrev: **DTP**
▷ www.desktoppublishing.com

desman ('dɛsmən) *n, pl* **desmans** either of two molelike amphibious mammals, the Russian desman or the Pyrenean desman, with dense fur and webbed feet [c18 from Swedish *desmansråtta*, from *desman* musk + *råtta* rat]

Des Moines (də 'mɔɪn, 'mɔɪnz) *n* **1** a city in S central Iowa: state capital. Pop: 198 682 (2000) **2** a river in the N central US, rising in SW Minnesota and flowing southeast to join the Mississippi. Length: 861 km (535 miles)

Desmond Tutu (,dɛzmənd 'tuːtuː) *n Brit inf* a university degree graded 2:2 (second class lower bracket). Often shortened to: **Desmond** [c20 rhyming slang, after Desmond *Tutu* (born 1931), South African clergyman and anti-apartheid campaigner]

Desmoulins (*French* dɛmulɛ̃) *n* **(Lucie Simplice) Camille (Benoît)** (kamij) 1760–94, French revolutionary leader, pamphleteer, and orator

desolate *adj* ('dɛsəlɪt) **1** uninhabited; deserted **2** made uninhabitable; laid waste; devastated **3** without friends, hope, or encouragement **4** dismal; depressing ▷ *vb* ('dɛsə,leɪt), **desolates, desolating, desolated** *(tr)* **5** to deprive of inhabitants; depopulate **6** to lay waste; devastate **7** to make wretched or forlorn **8** to forsake or abandon [c14 from L *dēsōlāre* to leave alone, from DE- + *sōlāre* to make lonely, lay waste, from *sōlus* alone] > **'deso,later** *or* **'deso,lator** *n* > **'desolately** *adv* > **'desolateness** *n*

desolation (,dɛsə'leɪʃən) *n* **1** a desolating or being desolated; ruin or devastation **2** solitary misery; wretchedness **3** a desolate region

De Soto (də 'səʊtəʊ; *Spanish* de 'soto) *n* **Hernando** (ɛr'nando) ?1500–42, Spanish explorer, who discovered the Mississippi River (1541). Also called: **Fernando De Soto** (fɛr'nando)

despair (dɪ'spɛə) *vb* **1** *(intr; often foll by of)* to lose or give up hope: *I despair of his coming* ▷ *n* **2** total loss of hope **3** a person or thing that causes hopelessness or for which there is no hope [c14 from OF *despoir* hopelessness, from *desperer* to despair, from L *dēspērāre*, from DE- + *spērāre* to hope]

despairing (dɪ'spɛərɪŋ) *adj* hopeless, despondent; feeling or showing despair > **de'spairingly** *adv*

despatch (dɪ'spætʃ) *vb (tr), n* a less common spelling of **dispatch** > **des'patcher** *n*

Despenser (dɪs'pɛnsə) *n* **Hugh le,** Earl of Winchester. 1262–1326, English statesman, a favourite of Edward II. Together with his son **Hugh,** *the Younger* (?1290–1326), he was executed by the king's enemies

desperado (,dɛspə'rɑːdəʊ) *n, pl* **desperadoes** *or* **desperados** a reckless or desperate person, esp one ready to commit any violent illegal act [c17 prob. pseudo-Spanish var. of obs. *desperate* (n)]

desperate ('dɛspərɪt, -prɪt) *adj* **1** careless of danger, as from despair **2** (of an act) reckless; risky **3** used or undertaken as a last resort **4** critical; very grave: *in desperate need* **5** *(often postpositive and foll by for)* in distress and having a great need or desire **6** moved by or showing despair [c15 from L *dēspērāre* to have no hope; see DESPAIR] > **'desperately** *adv* > **'desperateness** *n*

desperation (,dɛspə'reɪʃən) *n* **1** desperate recklessness **2** the state of being desperate

despicable (dɪ'spɪkəbᵊl, 'dɛspɪk-) *adj* worthy of being despised; contemptible; mean [c16 from LL *dēspicābilis*, from *dēspicārī* to disdain; cf. DESPISE] > **de'spicably** *adv*

despise (dɪ'spaɪz) *vb* **despises, despising, despised** *(tr)* to look down on with contempt; scorn: *he despises flattery* [c13 from OF *despire*, from L *dēspicere* to look down, from DE- + *specere* to look] > **de'spiser** *n*

despite (dɪ'spaɪt) *prep* **1** in spite of; undeterred by ▷ *n* **2** *arch* contempt; insult **3** **in despite of** *(prep) Rare.* in spite of [c13 from OF *despit*, from L *dēspectus* contempt; see DESPISE]

despoil (dɪ'spɔɪl) *vb (tr)* to deprive by force; plunder; loot [c13 from OF, from L *dēspoliāre*, from DE- + *spoliāre* to rob(esp of clothing)] > **de'spoiler** *n* > **de'spoilment** *n*

despoliation (dɪ,spəʊlɪ'eɪʃən) *n* **1** plunder or pillage **2** the state of being despoiled

despond (dɪ'spɒnd) *vb (intr)* **1** to become disheartened; despair ▷ *n* **2** *arch* despondency [c17 from L *dēspondēre* to promise, make over to, yield, lose heart, from DE- + *spondēre* to promise] > **de'spondingly** *adv*

despondent (dɪ'spɒndənt) *adj* downcast or disheartened; dejected > **de'spondence** *or* **de'spondency** *n* > **de'spondently** *adv*

despot ('dɛspɒt) *n* **1** an absolute or tyrannical ruler **2** any person in power who acts tyrannically [c16 from Med. L *despota*, from Gk *despotēs* lord, master] > **despotic** (dɛs'pɒtɪk) *or* **des'potical** *adj* > **des'potically** *adv*

despotism ('dɛspə,tɪzəm) *n* **1** the rule of a despot; absolute or tyrannical government **2** arbitrary or tyrannical authority or behaviour

des Prés *or* **Desprez** (*French* de pre) *n* **Josquin** (ʒɔskɛ̃) ?1450–1521, Flemish Renaissance composer of masses, motets, and chansons

des res ('dɛz 'rɛz) *n* (in estate agents' jargon) a desirable residence

Dessau (*German* 'dɛsau) *n* an industrial city in E Germany, in Saxony-Anhalt: capital of Anhalt state from 1340 to 1918. Pop: 95 100 (1991)

dessert (dɪ'zɜːt) *n* **1** the sweet, usually last course of a meal **2** *chiefly Brit (esp formerly) fruit, dates, nuts, etc, served at the end of a meal* [c17 from F, from *desservir* to clear a table, from *des-* DIS-¹ + *servir* to SERVE]
▷ www.cooksrecipes.com/category/dessert.html
▷ http://dessert.allrecipes.com

dessertspoon (dɪ'zɜːt,spuːn) *n* a spoon intermediate in size between a tablespoon and a teaspoon

destination (,dɛstɪ'neɪʃən) *n* **1** the predetermined end of a journey **2** the end or purpose for which something is created or a person is destined

destine ('dɛstɪn) *vb* **destines, destining, destined** *(tr)* to set apart (for a certain purpose or person); intend; design [c14 from OF, from L *dēstināre* to appoint, from DE- + *-stināre*, from *stāre* to stand]

destined ('dɛstɪnd) *adj (postpositive)* **1** foreordained; meant **2** (usually foll by *for*) heading (towards a specific destination)

destiny ('dɛstɪnɪ) *n, pl* **destinies** **1** the future destined for a person or thing **2** the predetermined or inevitable course of events **3** the power that predetermines the course of events [c14 from OF, from *destiner* to DESTINE]

destitute ('dɛstɪ,tjuːt) *adj* **1** lacking the means of subsistence; totally impoverished **2** *(postpositive; foll by of)* completely lacking: *destitute of words* [c14 from L, from *dēstituere* to leave alone, from *statuere* to place]

destitution (,dɛstɪ'tjuːʃən) *n* the state of being destitute

de-stress *vb* to become or cause to become less stressed or anxious

destrier ('dɛstrɪə) *n arch* a warhorse [c13 from OF, from *destre* right hand, from L *dextra;* from the fact that a squire led a knight's horse with his right hand]

destroy (dɪ'strɔɪ) *vb* (*mainly tr*) **1** to ruin; spoil **2** to tear down or demolish **3** to put an end to **4** to kill or annihilate **5** to crush or defeat **6** (*intr*) to be destructive or cause destruction [c13 from OF, from L *dēstruere* to pull down, from DE- + *struere* to pile up, build]

destroyer (dɪ'strɔɪə) *n* **1** a small fast lightly armoured but heavily armed warship **2** a person or thing that destroys

destruct (dɪ'strʌkt) *vb* **1** to destroy (one's own missile, etc) for safety **2** (*intr*) (of a missile, etc) to be destroyed, for safety, by those controlling it ▷ *n* **3** the act of destructing ▷ *adj* **4** designed to be capable of destroying itself or the object containing it: *to disarm the destruct device*

destructible (dɪ'strʌktɪbᵊl) *adj* capable of being or liable to be destroyed

destruction (dɪ'strʌkʃən) *n* **1** the act of destroying or state of being destroyed; demolition **2** a cause of ruin or means of destroying [c14 from L *dēstructiō* a pulling down; see DESTROY]

destructive (dɪ'strʌktɪv) *adj* **1** (often *postpositive* and foll by *of* or *to*) causing or tending to cause the destruction (of) **2** intended to discredit, esp without positive suggestions or help; negative: *destructive criticism* > **de'structively** *adv* > **de'structiveness** *n*

destructive distillation *n* the decomposition of a complex substance, such as wood or coal, by heating it in the absence of air and collecting the volatile products

destructor (dɪ'strʌktə) *n* **1** a furnace or incinerator for the disposal of refuse **2** a device used to blow up a defective missile

desuetude (dɪ'sju:ɪ,tju:d, 'dɛswɪ,tju:d) *n formal* the condition of not being in use or practice; disuse [c15 from L, from *dēsuescere* to lay aside a habit, from DE- + *suescere* to grow accustomed]

desulphurize *or* **desulphurise** (di:'sʌlfjʊ,raɪz) *vb* **desulphurizes, desulphurizing, desulphurized** *or* **desulphurises, desulphurising, desulphurised** to free or become free from sulphur

desultory ('dɛsəltərɪ, -trɪ) *adj* **1** passing from one thing to another, esp in a fitful way; unmethodical; disconnected **2** random or incidental: *a desultory thought* [c16 from L: relating to one who vaults or jumps, hence superficial, from *dēsilīre* to jump down, from DE- + *salīre*] > **'desultorily** *adv* > **'desultoriness** *n*

Det. *abbrev for* Detective

detach (dɪ'tætʃ) *vb* (*tr*) **1** to disengage and separate or remove; unfasten; disconnect **2** *mil* to separate (a small unit) from a larger, esp for a special assignment [c17 from OF *destachier*, from *des-* DIS-¹ + *atachier* to ATTACH] > **de'tachable** *adj* > **de,tacha'bility** *n*

detached (dɪ'tætʃt) *adj* **1** disconnected or standing apart; not attached: *a detached house* **2** showing no bias or emotional involvement **3** *ophthalmol* (of the retina) separated from the choroid layer of the eyeball to which it is normally attached, resulting in loss of vision in the affected part

detachment (dɪ'tætʃmənt) *n* **1** indifference; aloofness **2** freedom from self-interest or bias; disinterest **3** the act of detaching something **4** the condition of being detached; disconnection **5** *mil* **5a** the separation of a small unit from its main body **5b** the unit so detached **6** *Canad* a branch office of a police force

detail ('di:teɪl) *n* **1** an item that is considered separately; particular **2** an item that is unimportant: *passengers' comfort was regarded as a detail* **3** treatment of particulars: *this essay includes too much detail* **4** items collectively; particulars **5** a small section or element in a painting, building, statue, etc, esp when considered in isolation **6** *mil* **6a** the act of assigning personnel for a specific duty **6b** the personnel selected **6c** the duty **7 in detail** including all or most particulars or items thoroughly ▷ *vb* (*tr*) **8** to list or relate fully **9** *mil* to select (personnel) for a specific duty [c17 from F, from OF *detailler* to cut in pieces, from *de-* DIS-¹ + *tailler* to cut]

detailed ('di:teɪld) *adj* having many details or giving careful attention to details

detain (dɪ'teɪn) *vb* (*tr*) **1** to delay; hold back **2** to confine or hold in custody [c15 from OF, from L *dētinēre* to hold off, keep back, from DE- + *tenēre* to hold] > **de'tainable** *adj* > **detainee** (,di:teɪ'ni:) *n* > **de'tainment** *n*

detect (dɪ'tɛkt) *vb* (*tr*) **1** to perceive or notice **2** to discover the existence or presence of(esp something likely to elude observation) **3** *obs* to discover, or reveal (a crime, criminal, etc) **4** to extract information from (an electromagnetic wave) [c15 from L *dētectus*, from *dētegere* to uncover, from DE- + *tegere* to cover] > **de'tectable** *or* **de'tectible** *adj*

detection (dɪ'tɛkʃən) *n* **1** the act of discovering or the fact of being discovered **2** the act or process of extracting information, esp at audio or video frequencies, from an electromagnetic wave; demodulation

detective (dɪ'tɛktɪv) *n* **1a** a police officer who investigates crimes **1b** See **private detective** **1c** (*as modifier*): *a detective story* ▷ *adj* **2** of or for detection

detector (dɪ'tɛktə) *n* **1** a person or thing that detects **2** any mechanical sensing device **3** *electronics* a device used in the detection of radio signals

detent (dɪ'tɛnt) *n* the locking piece of a mechanism, often spring-loaded to check the movement of a wheel in only one direction [c17 from OF *destente* a loosening, trigger; see DÉTENTE]

détente (deɪ'tɑ:nt; *French* detɑ̃t) *n* the relaxing or easing of tension, esp between nations [F, lit.: a loosening, from OF *destendre* to release, from *tendre* to stretch]

Dd

detention (dɪ'tɛnʃən) *n* **1** a detaining or being detained **2a** custody or confinement, esp of a suspect awaiting trial **2b** (*as modifier*): *a detention order* **3** a form of punishment in which a pupil is detained after school [c16 from L *dētentiō* a keeping back; see DETAIN]

detention centre *n* (formerly) a place in which young persons could be detained for short periods by order of a court

deter (dɪ'tɜ:) *vb* **deters, deterring, deterred** (*tr*) to discourage (from acting) or prevent (from occurring), usually by instilling fear, doubt, or anxiety [c16 from L *dēterrēre*, from DE- + *terrēre* to frighten] > **de'terment** *n*

deterge (dɪ'tɜ:dʒ) *vb* **deterges, deterging, deterged** (*tr*) to cleanse: *to deterge a wound* [c17 from L *dētergēre* to wipe away, from DE- + *tergēre* to wipe]

detergent (dɪ'tɜ:dʒənt) *n* **1** a cleansing agent, esp a chemical such as an alkyl sulphonate, widely used in industry, laundering, etc ▷ *adj* **2** having cleansing power [c17 from L *dētergēns* wiping off; see DETERGE]

deteriorate (dɪ'tɪərɪə,reɪt) *vb* **deteriorates, deteriorating, deteriorated** **1** to make or become worse; depreciate **2** (*intr*) to wear away or disintegrate [c16 from LL *dēteriōrāre*, from L *dēterior* worse] > **de,terio'ration** *n* > **de'teriorative** *adj*

determinacy (dɪ'tɜ:mɪnəsɪ) *n* **1** the quality of being defined or fixed **2** the condition of being predicted or deduced

determinant (dɪ'tɜ:mɪnənt) *adj* **1** serving to determine ▷ *n* **2** a factor that influences or determines **3** *maths* a square array of elements that represents the sum of certain products of these elements, used to solve simultaneous equations, in vector studies, etc

determinate (dɪ'tɜ:mɪnɪt) *adj* **1** definitely limited, defined, or fixed **2** determined **3** able to be predicted or deduced **4** *bot* having the main and branch stems ending in flowers and unable to grow further > **de'terminateness** *n*

determination (dɪˌtɜːmɪ'neɪʃən) *n* **1** the act of making a decision **2** the condition of being determined; resoluteness **3** an ending of an argument by the decision of an authority **4** the act of fixing the quality, limit, position, etc, of something **5** a decision or opinion reached **6** a resolute movement towards some object or end **7** *law* the termination of an estate or interest **8** *law* the decision reached by a court of justice on a disputed matter

determinative (dɪ'tɜːmɪnətɪv) *adj* **1** serving to settle or determine; deciding ▷ *n* **2** a factor, circumstance, etc, that settles or determines > **de'terminatively** *adv* > **de'terminativeness** *n*

determine (dɪ'tɜːmɪn) *vb* **determines, determining, determined 1** to settle or decide (an argument, question, etc) conclusively **2** (*tr*) to conclude, esp after observation or consideration **3** (*tr*) to influence; give direction to **4** (*tr*) to fix in scope, variety, etc: *the river determined the edge of the property* **5** to make or cause to make a decision **6** (*tr*) *logic* to define or limit (a notion) by adding or requiring certain features or characteristics **7** (*tr*) *geom* to fix or specify the position or form of **8** *chiefly law* to come or bring to an end, as an estate [C14 from OF, from L *dētermināre* to set boundaries to, from DE- + *termināre* to limit] > **de'terminable** *adj*

determined (dɪ'tɜːmɪnd) *adj* of unwavering mind; resolute; firm > **de'terminedly** *adv*

determiner (dɪ'tɜːmɪnə) *n* **1** a word, such as a number, article, or personal pronoun, that determines (limits) the meaning of a noun phrase, e.g. *their* in 'their black cat' **2** a person or thing that determines

determinism (dɪ'tɜːmɪˌnɪzəm) *n* the philosophical doctrine that all events, including human actions, are fully determined by preceding events, and so freedom of choice is illusory. Also called: **necessitarianism** ▷ Cf **free will** > **de'terminist** *n, adj* > **deˌtermin'istic** *adj*

deterrent (dɪ'tɛrənt) *n* **1** something that deters **2** a weapon, esp nuclear, held by one state, etc, to deter attack by another ▷ *adj* **3** tending or used to deter [C19 from L *dēterrēns* hindering; see DETER] > **de'terrence** *n*

detest (dɪ'tɛst) *vb* (*tr*) to dislike intensely; loathe [C16 from L *dētestārī* to curse (while invoking a god as witness), from DE- + *testārī*, from *testis* a witness] > **de'tester** *n*

detestable (dɪ'tɛstəbᵊl) *adj* being or deserving to be abhorred or detested > **deˌtesta'bility** *or* **de'testableness** *n* > **de'testably** *adv*

detestation (ˌdiːtɛs'teɪʃən) *n* **1** intense hatred; abhorrence **2** a person or thing that is detested

dethrone (dɪ'θrəʊn) *vb* **dethrones, dethroning, dethroned** (*tr*) to remove from a throne or deprive of any high position or title > **de'thronement** *n* > **de'throner** *n*

detonate ('dɛtəˌneɪt) *vb* **detonates, detonating, detonated** to cause (a bomb, mine, etc) to explode or (of a bomb, mine, etc) to explode [C18 from L *dētonāre* to thunder down, from DE- + *tonāre* to THUNDER] > **ˌdeto'nation** *n*

detonator ('dɛtəˌneɪtə) *n* **1** a small amount of explosive, as in a percussion cap, used to initiate a larger explosion **2** a device, such as an electrical generator, used to set off an explosion from a distance **3** an explosive

detour ('diːtʊə) *n* **1** a deviation from a direct route or course of action ▷ *vb* **2** to deviate or cause to deviate from a direct route or course of action [C18 from F, from OF *destorner* to divert, turn away, from *des-* DE- + *torner* to TURN]

detox ('diːˌtɒks) *inf* ▷ *n* **1** treatment designed to rid the body of poisonous substances, esp alcohol and drugs ▷ *vb* (*intr*) **2** to undergo treatment to rid the body of poisonous substances, esp alcohol and drugs

detoxification centre *n* a place that specializes in the treatment of alcoholism or drug addiction

detoxify (diː'tɒksɪˌfaɪ) *vb* **detoxifies, detoxifying, detoxified** (*tr*) **1** to remove poison from **2** to treat (a person) for alcoholism or drug dependency > **deˌtoxifi'cation** *n*

DETR (in Britain) *abbrev for* Department of the Environment, Transport, and the Regions

detract (dɪ'trækt) *vb* **1** (when *intr*, usually foll by *from*) to take away a part (of); diminish: *her anger detracts from her beauty* **2** (*tr*) to distract or divert **3** (*tr*) *obs* to belittle or disparage [C15 from L *dētractus*, from *dētrahere* to pull away, disparage, from DE- + *trahere* to drag] > **de'tractive** *adj* > **de'tractor** *n* > **de'traction** *n*

USAGE *Detract* is sometimes wrongly used where *distract* is meant: *a noise distracted* (not *detracted*) *my attention*

detrain (diː'treɪn) *vb* to leave or cause to leave a railway train > **de'trainment** *n*

detriment ('dɛtrɪmənt) *n* **1** disadvantage or damage **2** a cause of disadvantage or damage [C15 from L *dētrīmentum*, a rubbing off, hence damage, from *dēterere*, from DE- + *terere* to rub]

detrimental (ˌdɛtrɪ'mɛntᵊl) *adj* (when *postpositive*, foll by *to*) harmful; injurious

detritus (dɪ'traɪtəs) *n* **1** a loose mass of stones, silt, etc, worn away from rocks **2** the organic debris formed from the decay of organisms [C18 from F, from L: a rubbing away; see DETRIMENT] > **de'trital** *adj*

Detroit (dɪ'trɔɪt) *n* **1** a city in SE Michigan, on the Detroit River: a major Great Lakes port; largest car-manufacturing centre in the world. Pop: 951 270 (2000) **2** a river in central North America, flowing along the US-Canadian border from Lake St Clair to Lake Erie

de trop *French* (də tro) *adj* (*postpositive*) not wanted; in the way [lit.: of too much]

detumescence (ˌdiːtjʊ'mɛsəns) *n* the subsidence of a swelling [C17 from L *dētumescere* to cease swelling, from DE- + *tumescere*, from *tumēre* to swell]

deuce[1] (djuːs) *n* **1a** a playing card or dice with two spots **1b** a throw of two in dice **2** *tennis, etc* a tied score that requires one player to gain two successive points to win the game [C15 from OF *deus* two, from L *duos*, from *duo* two]

deuce[2] (djuːs) *inf* ▷ *interj* **1** an expression of annoyance or frustration ▷ *n* **2** **the deuce** (intensifier) used in such phrases as **what the deuce, where the deuce,** etc [C17 prob. special use of DEUCE[1] (in the sense: lowest throw at dice)]

deuced ('djuːsɪd, djuːst) *Brit inf* ▷ *adj* **1** (intensifier) confounded: *he's a deuced idiot* ▷ *adv* **2** (intensifier): *deuced good luck*

Deus *Latin* ('deɪʊs) *n* God [rel. to Gk *Zeus*]

deus ex machina *Latin* ('deɪʊs ɛks 'mækɪnə) *n* **1** (in ancient Greek and Roman drama) a god introduced into a play to resolve the plot **2** any unlikely device serving this purpose [lit.: god out of a machine]

Deut. *Bible. abbrev for* Deuteronomy

deuteride ('djuːtəˌraɪd) *n* a compound of deuterium and another element

deuterium (djuː'tɪərɪəm) *n* a stable isotope of hydrogen, occurring in natural hydrogen and in heavy water. Symbol: D or ^{2}H; atomic no.: 1; atomic wt.: 2.014 [C20 NL; see DEUTERO-, -IUM; from the fact that it is the second heaviest hydrogen isotope]

deuterium oxide *n* the compound D_2O; water in which the normal hydrogen atoms are replaced by deuterium atoms. See also **heavy water**

deutero-, deuto- *or before a vowel* **deuter-, deut-** *combining form.* second or secondary: *deuterium* [from Gk *deuteros* second]

deuteron ('djuːtəˌrɒn) *n* the nucleus of a deuterium atom

Deutsch (dɔɪtʃ; *German* dɔytʃ) *n* **Otto Erich** ('ɔto 'e:rɪç) 1883–1967, Austrian music historian and art critic, noted for his catalogue of Schubert's works (1951)

Deutschland ('dɔytʃlant) *n* the German name for Germany

Deutschmark ('dɔɪtʃˌmɑ:k) *or* **Deutsche Mark** ('dɔɪtʃə) *n* the former standard monetary unit of Germany divided into 100 pfennigs; replaced by the euro in 2002; until 1990 the standard monetary unit of West Germany

deutzia ('dju:tsɪə,'dɔɪtsɪə) *n* any of various shrubs with white, pink, or purplish flowers in early summer [C19 NL, after J. *Deutz*, 18th-cent. Du. patron of botany]

Deux-Sèvres (*French* døsɛvrə) *n* a department of W France, in Poitou-Charentes region. Capital: Niort. Pop: 344 392 (1999). Area: 6054 sq km (2337 sq miles)

de Valera (də vəˈlɛərə, -ˈlɪə-) *n* **Eamon** ('eɪmən) 1882–1975, Irish statesman; president of Sinn Fé in (1917–26) and of the Dáil (1918–22); formed the Fianna Fáil party (1927); prime minister (1937–48; 1951–54; 1957–59) and president (1959–73) of the Irish Republic

de Valois (də 'vælwɑ:) *n* See (Ninette de) **Valois**[3]

devalue (di:'vælju:) *or* **devaluate** (di:'vælju:ˌeɪt) *vb* **devalues, devaluing, devalued** *or* **devaluates, devaluating, devaluated** **1** to reduce (a currency) or (of a currency) be reduced in exchange value **2** (*tr*) to reduce the value of > **deˌvaluˈation** *n*

Devanagari (ˌdeɪvəˈnɑ:gərɪ) *n* a syllabic script in which Sanskrit, Hindi, and other modern languages of India are written [C18 from Sansk.: alphabet of the gods]

devastate ('dɛvəˌsteɪt) *vb* **devastates, devastating, devastated** (*tr*) **1** to lay waste or make desolate; ravage; destroy **2** to confound or overwhelm [C17 from L *dēvastāre*, from DE- + *vastāre* to ravage; rel. to *vastus* waste, empty] > ˌ**devasˈtation** *n* > '**devasˌtator** *n*

develop (dɪ'vɛləp) *vb* **1** to come or bring to a later or more advanced or expanded stage; grow or cause to grow gradually **2** (*tr*) to work out in detail **3** to disclose or unfold (thoughts, a plot, etc) gradually or (of thoughts, etc) to be gradually disclosed or unfolded **4** to come or bring into existence: *he developed a new faith in God* **5** (*intr*) to follow as a result of something; ensue: *a row developed after her remarks* **6** (*tr*) to contract (a disease or illness) **7** (*tr*) to improve the value or change the use of (land) **8** to exploit or make available the natural resources of (a country or region) **9** (*tr*) *photog* to treat (exposed film, plate, or paper) with chemical solutions in order to produce a visible image **10** *biol* to progress or cause to progress from simple to complex stages in the growth of an individual or the evolution of a species **11** (*tr*) to elaborate upon (a musical theme) by varying the melody, key, etc **12** (*tr*) *maths* to expand (a function or expression) in the form of a series **13** (*tr*) *geom* to project or roll out (a surface) onto a plane without stretching or shrinking any element **14** *chess* to bring (a piece) into play from its initial position on the back rank [C19 from OF *desveloper* to unwrap, from *des-* DIS-[1] + *veloper* to wrap; see ENVELOP] > **deˈvelopable** *adj*

developer (dɪ'vɛləpə) *n* **1** a person or thing that develops something, esp a person who develops property **2** Also called: **developing agent** *photog* a chemical used to convert the latent image recorded in the emulsion of a film or paper into a visible image

developing country *n* a poor or non-industrial country that is seeking to develop its resources by industrialization

development (dɪ'vɛləpmənt) *n* **1** the act or process of growing or developing **2** the product of developing **3** a fact or event, esp one that changes a situation **4** an area of land that has been developed **5** the section of a movement, usually in sonata form, in which the basic musical themes are developed **6** *chess* the process of developing pieces > **deˌvelopˈmental** *adj*

developmental disorder *n psychiatry* any condition, such as autism or dyslexia, that appears in childhood and is characterized by delay in the development of one or more psychological functions, such as language skill

development area *n* (in Britain) an area which has experienced economic depression because of the decline of its main industry or industries, and which is given government assistance to establish new industry

Devereux ('dɛvərə) *n* **Robert** See (2nd Earl of) **Essex**

Devi ('deɪvi:) *n* a Hindu goddess and embodiment of the female energy of Siva [Sansk.: goddess]

deviance ('di:vɪəns) *n* **1** Also called: **deviancy** the act or state of being deviant **2** *statistics* a measure of the degree of fit of a statistical model compared to that of a more complete model

deviant ('di:vɪənt) *adj* **1** deviating, as from what is considered acceptable behaviour ▷ *n* **2** a person whose behaviour, esp sexual behaviour, deviates from what is considered to be acceptable

deviate *vb* ('di:vɪˌeɪt), **deviates, deviating, deviated** **1** (*usually intr*) to differ or cause to differ, as in belief or thought **2** (*usually intr*) to turn aside or cause to turn aside **3** (*intr*) *psychol* to depart from an accepted standard ▷ *n, adj* ('di:vɪɪt) **4** another word for **deviant** [C17 from LL *dēviāre* to turn aside from the direct road, from DE- + *via* road] > '**deviˌator** *n* > '**deviatory** *adj*

deviation (ˌdi:vɪ'eɪʃən) *n* **1** an act or result of deviating **2** *statistics* the difference between an observed value in a series of such values and their arithmetic mean **3** the error of a compass due to local magnetic disturbances

device (dɪ'vaɪs) *n* **1** a machine or tool used for a specific task **2** *euphemistic* a bomb **3** a plan, esp a clever or evil one; trick **4** any ornamental pattern or picture, as in embroidery **5** computer hardware designed for a specific function **6** a design or figure, used as a heraldic sign, emblem, etc **7** a particular pattern of words, figures of speech, etc, used in literature to produce an effect on the reader **8** **leave (someone) to his** (*or* **her**) **own devices** to leave (someone) alone to do as he or she wishes [C13 from OF *devis* purpose, contrivance & *devise* difference, intention, from *deviser* to divide, control; see DEVISE] Dd

devil ('dɛvᵊl) *n* **1** (*often cap*) *Theol.* the chief spirit of evil and enemy of God, often depicted as a human figure with horns, cloven hoofs, and tail **2** any subordinate evil spirit **3** a person or animal regarded as wicked or ill-natured **4** a person or animal regarded as unfortunate or wretched **5** a person or animal regarded as daring, mischievous, or energetic **6** *inf* something difficult or annoying **7** *Christian Science* an error, lie, or false belief **8** (in Malaysia) a ghost **9** a portable furnace or brazier **10** any of various mechanical devices, such as a machine for making wooden screws or a rag-tearing machine **11** See **printer's devil** **12** *law* (in England) a junior barrister who does work for another in order to gain experience, usually for a half fee **13** *meteorol* a small whirlwind in arid areas that raises dust or sand in a column **14** **between the devil and the deep blue sea** between equally undesirable alternatives **15** **devil of** **15a** *inf* (intensifier): *a devil of a fine horse* **16** **give the devil his due** to acknowledge the talent or success of an unpleasant person **17** **go to the devil** **17a** to fail or become dissipated **17b** (*interj*) used to express annoyance with the person causing it **18** (**let**) **the devil take the hindmost** look after oneself and leave others to their fate **19** **talk** (*or* **speak**) **of the devil!** used when an absent person who has been the subject of conversation appears **20** **the devil!** (intensifier): **20a** used in **what the devil, where the devil**, etc **20b** an exclamation of anger, surprise, disgust, etc **21** **the devil to pay** trouble to be faced as a consequence of an action ▷ *vb* **devils, devilling, devilled** *or US* **devils, deviling, deviled** **22** (*tr*) to prepare (food) by coating with a highly flavoured spiced paste or mixture of condiments before cooking **23** (*tr*) to tear (rags) with a devil **24** (*intr*) to serve as a printer's devil **25** (*intr*) *chiefly Brit* to do hackwork, esp for a lawyer or author **26** (*tr*) *US inf* to harass, vex, etc [OE *dēofol*, from L *diabolus*, from Gk *diabolos* enemy, accuser, slanderer]

devilfish ('dɛvᵊlˌfɪʃ) *n, pl* **devilfish** *or* **devilfishes** **1** Also called: **devil ray** another name for **manta** (the fish) **2** another name for **octopus**

devilish ('dɛvəlɪʃ) *adj* **1** of, resembling, or befitting a devil; diabolic; fiendish ▷ *adv, adj* **2** *inf* (intensifier): *devilish good food* > '**devilishly** *adv* > '**devilishness** *n*

devil-may-care *adj* careless or reckless; happy-go-lucky: *a devil-may-care attitude*

devilment ('dɛvᵊlmənt) *n* devilish or mischievous conduct

devilry ('dɛvᵊlrɪ) *or* **deviltry** *n, pl* **devilries** *or* **deviltries** **1** reckless or malicious fun or mischief **2** wickedness **3** black magic or other forms of diabolism [C18 from F *diablerie*, from *diable* DEVIL]

devil's advocate *n* **1** a person who advocates an opposing or unpopular view, often for the sake of argument **2** *RC Church* the official appointed to put the case against the beatification or canonization of a candidate [translation of NL *advocātus diabolī*]

devil's coach-horse *n* a large black beetle with large jaws and ferocious habits

devil's food cake *n chiefly US & Canad* a rich chocolate cake

Devil's Island *n* one of the three Safety Islands, off the coast of French Guiana: formerly a leper colony, then a French penal colony from 1895 until 1938. Area: less than 2 sq km (1 sq mile). French name: **Île du Diable**

Devine (də'viːn) *n* **George** (**Alexander Cassady**) 1910–65, British stage director and actor: founded (1956) the English Stage Company in London's Royal Court Theatre

devious ('diːvɪəs) *adj* **1** not sincere or candid; deceitful **2** (of a route or course of action) rambling; indirect **3** going astray; erring [C16 from L *dēvius* lying to one side of the road, from DE- + *via* road] > '**deviously** *adv* > '**deviousness** *n*

devise (dɪ'vaɪz) *vb* **devises, devising, devised** **1** to work out or plan (something) in one's mind **2** (*tr*) *law* to dispose of (real property) by will ▷ *n law* **3** a disposition of property by will **4** a will or clause in a will disposing of real property [C15 from OF *deviser* to divide, apportion, intend, from L *dīvidere* to DIVIDE] > **de'viser** *n*

devitalize *or* **devitalise** (diː'vaɪtəˌlaɪz) *vb* **devitalizes, devitalizing, devitalized** *or* **devitalises, devitalising, devitalised** (*tr*) to lower or destroy the vitality of; make weak or lifeless > **deˌvitali'zation** *or* **deˌvitali'sation** *n*

Devizes (də'vaɪzəz) *n* a market town in S England, in Wiltshire: agricultural and dairy products. Pop: 13 205 (1991)

devoid (dɪ'vɔɪd) *adj* (*postpositive*; foll by *of*) destitute or void (of); free (from) [C15 orig. p.p. of *devoid* (*vb*) to remove, from OF *devoider* from DE- + *voider* to void]

devoirs (də'vwɑː) *pl n* (*sometimes sing*) compliments or respects [C13 from OF: duty, from *devoir* to be obliged to, owe, from L *dēbēre*]

devolution (ˌdiːvə'luːʃən) *n* **1** a devolving **2** a passing onwards or downwards from one stage to another **3** a transfer of authority from a central government to regional governments [C16 from Med. L *dēvolūtiō* a rolling down, from L *dēvolvere*; see DEVOLVE] > ˌ**devo'lutionary** *adj* > ˌ**devo'lutionist** *n, adj*

devolve (dɪ'vɒlv) *vb* **devolves, devolving, devolved** **1** (foll by *on, upon, to*, etc) to pass or cause to pass to a successor or substitute, as duties, power, etc **2** (*intr*; foll by *on* or *upon*) *law* (of an estate, etc) to pass to another by operation of law [C15 from L *dēvolvere* to roll down, fall into, from DE- + *volvere* to roll] > **de'volvement** *n*

Devon ('dɛvᵊn) *n* **1** Also called: **Devonshire** a county of SW England, between the Bristol Channel and the English Channel, including the island of Lundy: the geographic and ceremonial county includes Plymouth and Torbay, which became independent unitary authorities in 1998; hilly, rising to the uplands of Exmoor and Dartmoor, with wooded river valleys and a rugged coastline. Administrative centre: Exeter. Pop (excluding unitary authorities): 704 499 (2001). Area (excluding unitary authorities): 6569 sq km (2536 sq miles) **2** a breed of large red beef cattle originally from Devon

Devonian (də'vəʊnɪən) *adj* **1** of, denoting, or formed in the fourth period of the Palaeozoic era, between the Silurian and Carboniferous periods, lasting for 60–70 million years during which amphibians first appeared **2** of or relating to Devon ▷ *n* **3** **the** the Devonian period or rock system

Devonshire ('dɛvᵊnʃɪə, -ʃə) *n* **8th Duke of**, title of *Spencer Compton Cavendish*. 1833–1908, British politician, also known (1858–91) as Lord Hartington. He led the Liberal Party (1874–80) and left it to found the Liberal Unionist Party (1886)

Devonshire split *n* a kind of yeast bun split open and served with cream or jam

devoré (də'vɔreɪ) *n* a velvet fabric with a raised pattern created by disintegrating some of the pile with chemicals [from F, p.p. of *dévorer* to devour]

devote (dɪ'vəʊt) *vb* **devotes, devoting, devoted** (*tr*) to apply or dedicate (oneself, money, etc) to some pursuit, cause, etc [C16 from L *dēvōtus* devoted, solemnly promised, from *dēvovēre* to vow; see DE-, VOW]

devoted (dɪ'vəʊtɪd) *adj* **1** feeling or demonstrating loyalty or devotion; devout **2** (*postpositive*; foll by *to*) dedicated or consecrated > **de'votedly** *adv* > **de'votedness** *n*

devotee (ˌdɛvə'tiː) *n* **1** a person ardently enthusiastic about something, such as a sport or pastime **2** a zealous follower of a religion

devotion (dɪ'vəʊʃən) *n* **1** (often foll by *to*) strong attachment (to) or affection (for a cause, person, etc) marked by dedicated loyalty **2** religious zeal; piety **3** (*often pl*) religious observance or prayers > **de'votional** *adj*

devour (dɪ'vaʊə) *vb* (*tr*) **1** to eat up greedily or voraciously **2** to waste or destroy; consume **3** to consume greedily or avidly with the senses or mind **4** to engulf or absorb [C14 from OF, from L *dēvorāre* to gulp down, from DE- + *vorāre*; see VORACIOUS] > **de'vourer** *n* > **de'vouring** *adj*

devout (dɪ'vaʊt) *adj* **1** deeply religious; reverent **2** sincere; earnest; heartfelt [C13 from OF *devot*, from LL *dēvōtus*, from L: faithful; see DEVOTE] > **de'voutly** *adv* > **de'voutness** *n*

De Vries (*Dutch* də 'vriːs) *n* **Hugo** ('hyːxoː) 1848–1935, Dutch botanist, who rediscovered Mendel's laws and developed the mutation theory of evolution

dew (djuː) *n* **1** drops of water condensed on a cool surface, esp at night, from vapour in the air **2** something like this, esp in freshness: *the dew of youth* **3** small drops of moisture, such as tears ▷ *vb* **4** (*tr*) to moisten with or as with dew [OE *dēaw*]

Dewar ('djuːə) *n* Sir **James** 1842–1923, Scottish chemist and physicist. He worked on the liquefaction of gases and the properties of matter at low temperature, invented the vacuum flask, and (with Sir Frederick Abel) was the first to prepare cordite

dewberry ('djuːbərɪ, -brɪ) *n, pl* **dewberries** **1** any trailing bramble having blue-black fruits **2** the fruit of any such plant

dewclaw ('djuːˌklɔː) *n* **1** a nonfunctional claw in dogs **2** an analogous rudimentary hoof in deer, goats, etc > '**dewˌclawed** *adj*

dewdrop ('djuːˌdrɒp) *n* a drop of dew

de Wet (də 'vɛt) *n* **Christian Rudolf** 1854–1922, Afrikaner military commander and politician, who led the

Orange Free State army in the second Boer War (1899–1902) He was imprisoned for treason (1914) after organizing an Afrikaner nationalist rebellion

Dewey ('dju:ɪ) *n* **John** 1859–1952, US pragmatist philosopher and educator: an exponent of progressivism in education, he formulated an instrumentalist theory of learning through experience. His works include *The School and Society* (1899), *Democracy and Education* (1916), and *Logic: the Theory of Inquiry* (1938)

Dewey Decimal System ('dju:ɪ) *n* a system of library book classification with ten main subject classes. Also called: **decimal classification** [c19 after Melvil *Dewey* (1851–1931), US educator]
▷ www.oclc.org/dewey

dewlap ('dju:ˌlæp) *n* **1** a loose fold of skin hanging from beneath the throat in cattle, dogs, etc **2** loose skin on an elderly person's throat [c14 *dewlappe*, from DEW (prob. from an earlier form of different meaning) + LAP[1] (from OE *læppa* hanging flap), ?from ON]

DEW line (dju:) *n acronym for* distant early warning line, a network of radar stations situated mainly in Arctic regions of North America

dew point *n* the temperature at which water vapour in the air becomes saturated and water droplets begin to form

dew pond *n* a shallow pond, usually man-made, that is kept full by dew and mist

dewy ('dju:ɪ) *adj* **dewier, dewiest 1** moist with or as with dew **2** of or resembling dew **3** *poetic* suggesting, falling, or refreshing like dew: *dewy sleep* > '**dewily** *adv* > '**dewiness** *n*

dexter ('dɛkstə) *adj* **1** *arch* of or located on the right side **2** *(usually postpositive) heraldry* of, on, or starting from the right side of a shield from the bearer's point of view and therefore on the spectator's left ▷ Cf **sinister** [c16 from L; cf. Gk *dexios* on the right hand]

dexterity (dɛk'stɛrɪtɪ) *n* **1** physical, esp manual, skill or nimbleness **2** mental skill or adroitness [c16 from L *dexteritās* aptness, readiness; see DEXTER]

dexterous ('dɛkstrəs) *adj* possessing or done with dexterity > '**dexterously** *adv* > '**dexterousness** *n*

dextral ('dɛkstrəl) *adj* **1** of or located on the right side, esp of the body **2** of a person who prefers to use his or her right foot, hand, or eye; right-handed **3** (of shells) coiling in an anticlockwise direction from the apex > **dextrality** (dɛk'strælɪtɪ) *n* > '**dextrally** *adv*

dextran ('dɛkstrən) *n biochem* a chainlike polymer of glucose produced by the action of bacteria on sucrose: used as a substitute for plasma in blood transfusions [c19 from DEXTRO- + -AN]

dextrin ('dɛkstrɪn) *or* **dextrine** ('dɛkstrɪn, -tri:n) *n* any of a group of sticky substances obtained from starch: used as thickening agents in foods and as gums [c19 from F *dextrine*; see DEXTRO-, -IN]

dextro- *or before a vowel* **dextr-** *combining form.* on or towards the right: *dextrorotation* [from L, from *dexter* on the right side]

dextrorotation (ˌdɛkstrəʊrəʊ'teɪʃən) *n* a rotation to the right; clockwise rotation, esp of the plane of polarization of plane-polarized light ▷ Cf **laevorotation** > **dextrorotatory** (ˌdɛkstrəʊ'rəʊtətərɪ, -trɪ) *or* ˌ**dextro'rotary** *adj*

dextrorse ('dɛkstrɔ:s) *or* **dextrorsal** (dɛk'strɔ:s[ə]l) *adj* (of some climbing plants) growing upwards in a helix from left to right or anticlockwise [c19 from L *dextrorsum* towards the right, from DEXTRO- + *vorsus*, var. of *versus*, from *vertere* to turn] > '**dextrorsely** *adv*

dextrose ('dɛkstrəʊz, -trəʊs) *n* a glucose occurring widely in fruit, honey, and in the blood and tissue of animals. Formula: $C_6H_{12}O_6$. Also called: **grape sugar, dextroglucose**

dextrous ('dɛkstrəs) *adj* a variant spelling of **dexterous** > '**dextrously** *adv* > '**dextrousness** *n*

Dezhnev (*Russian* dɪʒ'njɔf) *n* **Cape** a cape in NE Russia at the E end of Chukotski Peninsula: the northeasternmost point of Asia. Former name: **East Cape**

DF *abbrev for* Defender of the Faith

D/F *or* **DF** *Telecomm* ▷ *abbrev for:* **1** direction finder **2** direction finding

DFC *abbrev for* Distinguished Flying Cross

DfEE (in Britain) *abbrev for* Department for Education and Employment

DFID (in Britain) *abbrev for* Department for International Development

DFM *abbrev for* Distinguished Flying Medal

dg *symbol for* decigram

Dhahran (dɑ:'rɑ:n) *n* a town in E Saudi Arabia: site of the original discovery of oil in the country (1938)

Dhaka *or* **Dacca** ('dækə) *n* the capital of Bangladesh, in the E central part: capital of Bengal (1608–39; 1660–1704) and of East Pakistan (1949–71); jute and cotton mills; university (1921). Pop: 3 839 000 (1991)
▷ www.dhaka-bangladesh.com

dhal, dal, *or* **dholl** (dɑ:l) *n* **1** a tropical African and Asian shrub cultivated for its nutritious pealike seeds **2** the seed of this shrub **3** a curry made from lentils or other pulses [c17 from Hindi, from Sansk. *dal* to split]

dharma ('dɑ:mə) *n* **1** *Hinduism* social custom regarded as a religious and moral duty **2** *Hinduism* **2a** the essential principle of the cosmos; natural law **2b** conduct that conforms with this **3** *Buddhism* ideal truth [Sansk.: habit, usage, law]

DHB (in New Zealand) *abbrev for* District Health Board

DHEA *abbrev for* dehydroepiandrosterone

Dhílos ('ðilɔs) *n* transliteration of the Modern Greek name for **Delos**

dhobi ('dəʊbɪ) *n, pl* **dhobis** (in India, E Africa, etc) a washerman [c19 from Hindi, from *dhōb* washing]

Dhodhekánisos (ðɔðɛ'kanisɔs) *n* a transliteration of the modern Greek name for the **Dodecanese**

dhoti ('dəʊtɪ), **dhooti, dhootie,** *or* **dhuti** ('du:tɪ) *n, pl* **dhotis** a long loincloth worn by men in India [c17 from Hindi]

dhow (daʊ) *n* a lateen-rigged coastal Arab sailing vessel [c19 from Ar.]

DHS (in Canada) *abbrev for* district high school

DHSS (formerly, in Britain) *abbrev for* Department of Health and Social Security

DI *abbrev for* donor insemination

di-[1] *prefix* **1** twice; two; double: *dicotyledon* **2a** containing two specified atoms or groups of atoms: *carbon dioxide* **2b** a nontechnical equivalent of **bi-** (sense 5) [via L from Gk, from *dis* twice, double, rel. to *duo* two. Cf BI-]

di-[2] *combining form.* a variant of **dia-** before a vowel: *dioptre*

dia- *or* **di-** *prefix* **1** through or during: *diachronic* **2** across: *diactinic* **3** apart: *diacritic.* [from Gk *dia* through, between, across, by]

diabetes (ˌdaɪə'bi:tɪs, -ti:z) *n* any of various disorders, esp diabetes mellitus, characterized by excessive thirst and excretion of an abnormally large amount of urine [c16 from L: siphon, from Gk, lit.: a passing through]
▷ www.insulinchoice.org
▷ www.diabetes.org.uk

diabetes mellitus (mə'laɪtəs) *n* a form of diabetes, caused by a deficiency of insulin, in which the body is unable to metabolize sugars [c18 NL, lit.: honey-sweet diabetes]

diabetic (ˌdaɪə'bɛtɪk) *adj* **1** of, relating to, or having diabetes **2** for the use of diabetics ▷ *n* **3** a person who has diabetes

diablerie (dɪ'ɑ:blərɪ) *n* **1** magic or witchcraft connected with devils **2** esoteric knowledge of devils **3** devilry; mischief [c18 from OF, from *diable* devil, from L *diabolus*; see DEVIL]

diabolic (ˌdaɪə'bɒlɪk) *adj* **1** of the devil; satanic

Dd

2 extremely cruel or wicked; fiendish 3 very difficult or unpleasant [c14 from LL, from Gk *diabolikos*, from *diabolos* DEVIL] > ˌ**dia'bolically** *adv* > ˌ**dia'bolicalness** *n*

diabolical (ˌdaɪə'bɒlɪkᵊl) *adj inf* 1 excruciatingly bad 2 (intensifier): *a diabolical liberty* > ˌ**dia'bolically** *adv* > ˌ**dia'bolicalness** *n*

diabolism (daɪ'æbəˌlɪzəm) *n* 1a witchcraft or sorcery 1b worship of devils or beliefs concerning them 2 character or conduct that is devilish > **di'abolist** *n*

diabolo (dɪ'æbəˌləʊ) *n, pl* **diabolos** 1 a game in which one throws and catches a top on a cord fastened to two sticks 2 the top used in this [c20 from It., lit.: devil]

diachronic (ˌdaɪə'krɒnɪk) *adj* of, relating to, or studying the development of a phenomenon through time; historical ▷ Cf **synchronic** [c19 from DIA- + Gk *khronos* time]

diacidic (ˌdaɪə'sɪdɪk) *adj* (of a base) capable of neutralizing two protons with one of its molecules. Also: **diacid**

diaconal (daɪ'ækənᵊl) *adj* of or associated with a deacon or the diaconate [c17 from LL *diāconālis*, from *diāconus* DEACON]

diaconate (daɪ'ækənɪt, -ˌneɪt) *n* the office, sacramental status, or period of office of a deacon [c17 from LL *diāconātus*; see DEACON]

diacritic (ˌdaɪə'krɪtɪk) *n* 1 a sign placed above or below a character or letter to indicate that it has a different phonetic value, is stressed, or for some other reason ▷ *adj* 2 another word for **diacritical** [c17 from Gk *diakritikos* serving to distinguish, from *diakrinein*, from DIA- + *krinein* to separate]

diacritical (ˌdaɪə'krɪtɪkᵊl) *adj* 1 of or relating to a diacritic 2 showing up a distinction

diadem ('daɪəˌdɛm) *n* 1 a royal crown, esp a light jewelled circlet 2 royal dignity or power [c13 from L, from Gk: fillet, royal headdress, from *diadein*, from DIA- + *dein* to bind]

diaeresis *or* **dieresis** (daɪ'ɛrɪsɪs) *n, pl* **diaereses** *or* **diereses** (-ˌsiːz) 1 the mark ¨ placed over the second of two adjacent vowels to indicate that it is to be pronounced separately, as in some spellings of *coöperate*, *naïve*, etc 2 this mark used for any other purpose, such as to indicate a special pronunciation for a particular vowel 3 a pause in a line of verse when the end of a foot coincides with the end of a word [c17 from L, from Gk: a division, from *diairein*, from DIA- + *hairein* to take; cf. HERESY] > **diaeretic** *or* **dieretic** (ˌdaɪə'rɛtɪk) *adj*

diag. *abbrev for* diagram

Diaghilev (*Russian* 'djagɪlif) *n* **Sergei Pavlovich** (sɪr'gjej 'pavləvitʃ) 1872–1929, Russian ballet impresario. He founded (1909) and directed (1909–29) the *Ballet Russe* in Paris, introducing Russian ballet to the West

diagnose ('daɪəgˌnəʊz) *vb* **diagnoses, diagnosing, diagnosed** 1 to determine by diagnosis 2 (*tr*) to examine (a person or thing), as for a disease > ˌ**diag'nosable** *adj*

diagnosis (ˌdaɪəg'nəʊsɪs) *n, pl* **diagnoses** (-siːz) 1a the identification of diseases by the examination of symptoms and signs and by other investigations 1b an opinion so reached 2a thorough analysis of facts or problems in order to gain understanding 2b an opinion reached through such analysis [c17 NL, from Gk: a distinguishing, from *diagignōskein*, from *gignōskein* to perceive, KNOW] > **diagnostic** (ˌdaɪəg'nɒstɪk) *adj*

diagonal (daɪ'ægənᵊl) *adj* 1 *maths* connecting any two vertices that in a polygon are not adjacent and in a polyhedron are not in the same face 2 slanting; oblique 3 marked with slanting lines or patterns ▷ *n* 4 a diagonal line, plane, or pattern 5 something put, set, or drawn obliquely [c16 from L, from Gk *diagōnios*, from DIA- + *gōnia* angle] > **di'agonally** *adv*

diagram ('daɪəˌgræm) *n* 1 a sketch or plan demonstrating the form or workings of something 2 *maths* a pictorial representation of a quantity or of a relationship ▷ *vb* **diagrams, diagramming, diagrammed** *or US* **diagrams, diagraming, diagramed** 3 to show in or as if in a diagram [c17 from L, from Gk, from *diagraphein*, from *graphein* to write] > **diagrammatic** (ˌdaɪəgrə'mætɪk) *adj*

dial ('daɪəl) *n* 1 the face of a watch, clock, etc, marked with divisions representing units of time 2 the graduated disc of various measuring instruments 3a the control on a radio or television set used to change the station or channel 3b the panel on a radio on which the frequency, wavelength, or station is indicated 4 a numbered disc on a telephone that is rotated a set distance for each digit of a number being called 5 *Brit* a slang word for **face** ▷ *vb* **dials, dialling, dialled** *or US* **dials, dialing, dialed** 6 to try to establish a telephone connection with (a subscriber) by operating the dial or buttons on a telephone 7 (*tr*) to indicate, measure, or operate with a dial [c14 from Med. L *diālis* daily, from L *diēs* day] > **'dialler** *or US* **'dialer** *n*

dial. *abbrev for* dialect(al)

dialect ('daɪəˌlɛkt) *n* a a form of a language spoken in a particular geographical area or by members of a particular social class or occupational group, distinguished by its vocabulary, grammar, and pronunciation b a form of a language that is considered inferior [c16 from L, from Gk *dialektos* speech, dialect, discourse, from *dialegesthai* to converse, from *legein* to talk, speak] > ˌ**dia'lectal** *adj*

dialectic (ˌdaɪə'lɛktɪk) *n* 1 disputation or debate, esp when intended to resolve differences between two views 2 logical argumentation 3 a variant of **dialectics** (sense 1) 4 *philosophy* an interpretive method used by Hegel in which contradictions are resolved at a higher level of truth (synthesis) ▷ *adj* 5 of or relating to logical disputation [c17 from L, from Gk *dialektikē* (*tekhnē*) (the art) of argument; see DIALECT] > ˌ**dialec'tician** *n*

dialectical (ˌdaɪə'lɛktɪkᵊl) *adj* of or relating to dialectic or dialectics > ˌ**dia'lectically** *adv*

dialectical materialism *n* the economic, political, and philosophical system of Marx and Engels that combines traditional materialism and Hegelian dialectic

dialectics (ˌdaɪə'lɛktɪks) *n* (*functioning as pl or (sometimes) sing*) 1 the study of reasoning 2 a particular methodology or system 3 the application of the Hegelian dialectic or the rationale of dialectical materialism

dialling code *n* a sequence of numbers which is dialled for connection with another exchange before an individual subscriber's telephone number is dialled

dialling tone *or US & Canad* **dial tone** *n* a continuous sound, either purring or high-pitched, heard over a telephone indicating that a number can be dialled

dialogue *or US (often)* **dialog** ('daɪəˌlɒg) *n* 1 conversation between two or more people 2 an exchange of opinions; discussion 3 the lines spoken by characters in drama or fiction 4 a passage of conversation in a literary or dramatic work 5 a literary composition in the form of a dialogue 6 a political discussion between representatives of two nations or groups [c13 from OF, from L, from Gk, from *dialegesthai*; see DIALECT]

dialogue *or* **dialog box** *n computing* a window that may appear on a VDU display to prompt the user to enter further information or select an option

dialyse *or US* **dialyze** ('daɪəˌlaɪz) *vb* **dialyses, dialysing, dialysed** *or US* **dialyzes, dialyzing, dialyzed** (*tr*) to separate by dialysis > ˌ**dialy'sation** *or US* ˌ**dialy'zation** *n*

dialyser *or US* **dialyzer** ('daɪəˌlaɪzə) *n* a machine that performs dialysis, esp one that removes impurities from the blood of patients with malfunctioning kidneys; kidney machine

dialysis (daɪ'ælɪsɪs) *n, pl* **dialyses** (-ˌsiːz) 1 the separation of small molecules from large molecules and colloids in a solution by the selective diffusion of the small molecules through a semipermeable membrane **2** *med* the filtering of blood through a semipermeable membrane to remove waste products [C16 from LL: a separation, from Gk *dialusis*, from *dialuein* to tear apart, dissolve, from *luein* to loosen] > **dialytic** (ˌdaɪəˈlɪtɪk) *adj*

diam. *abbrev for* diameter

diamagnetic (ˌdaɪəmæɡˈnɛtɪk) *adj* of, exhibiting, or concerned with diamagnetism

diamagnetism (ˌdaɪəˈmæɡnɪˌtɪzəm) *n* the phenomenon exhibited by substances that have a relative permeability less than unity and a negative susceptibility; caused by the orbital motion of electrons in the atoms of the material

diamanté (ˌdaɪəˈmæntɪ) *adj* **1** decorated with glittering ornaments, such as sequins ▷ *n* **2** a fabric so covered [C20 from F, from *diamanter* to adorn with diamonds]

diameter (daɪˈæmɪtə) *n* **1a** a straight line connecting the centre of a circle, sphere, etc with two points on the perimeter or surface **1b** the length of such a line **2** the thickness of something, esp with circular cross section [C14 from Med. L, from Gk: diameter, diagonal, from DIA- + *metron* measure]

diametric (ˌdaɪəˈmɛtrɪk) *or* **diametrical** *adj* **1** Also: **diametral** of, related to, or along a diameter **2** completely opposed

diametrically (ˌdaɪəˈmɛtrɪkəlɪ) *adv* completely; utterly(esp in **diametrically opposed**)

diamond (ˈdaɪəmənd) *n* **1a** a usually colourless exceptionally hard form of carbon in cubic crystalline form. It is used as a precious stone and for industrial cutting or abrading **1b** (*as modifier*): *a diamond ring* **2** *geom* a figure having four sides of equal length forming two acute angles and two obtuse angles; rhombus **3a** a red lozenge-shaped symbol on a playing card **3b** a card with one or more of these symbols or (*when pl*) the suit of cards so marked **4** *baseball* **4a** the whole playing field **4b** the square formed by the four bases ▷ *vb* **5** (*tr*) to decorate with or as with diamonds [C13 from OF *diamant*, from Med. L *diamas*, from L *adamas* the hardest iron or steel, diamond; see ADAMANT] > **diamantine** (ˌdaɪəˈmæntaɪn) *adj*

▷ www.adiamondisforever.com

▷ www.amnh.org/exhibitions/diamonds

diamond anniversary *n* a 60th, or occasionally 75th, anniversary

diamondback (ˈdaɪəmənd,bæk) *n* **1** Also called: **diamondback terrapin** *or* **turtle** any edible North American terrapin having diamond-shaped markings on the shell **2** a large North American rattlesnake having diamond-shaped markings

diamond wedding *n* the 60th, or occasionally the 75th, anniversary of a marriage

diamorphine (ˌdaɪəˈmɔːfiːn) *n* a technical name for **heroin**

Diana (daɪˈænə) *n* **1** the virginal Roman goddess of the hunt and the moon. Greek counterpart: **Artemis** **2** title *Diana, Princess of Wales*, original name *Lady Diana Frances Spencer*. 1961–97, she married Charles, Prince of Wales, in 1981; they were divorced in 1996

dianthus (daɪˈænθəs) *n, pl* **dianthuses** any Eurasian plant of the widely cultivated genus *Dianthus*, such as the carnation, pink, and sweet william [C19 NL, from Gk DI-[1] + *anthos* flower]

diapason (ˌdaɪəˈpeɪzᵊn) *n* *music* **1** either of two stops (**open** and **stopped diapason**) found throughout the compass of a pipe organ that give it its characteristic tone colour **2** the compass of an instrument or voice **3a** a standard pitch used for tuning **3b** a tuning fork or pitch pipe **4** (in classical Greece) an octave [C14 from L: the whole octave, from Gk: (*hē*) *dia pasōn* (*khordōn sumphōnia*) (concord) through all (the notes)]

diapause (ˈdaɪə,pɔːz) *n* a period of suspended development and growth accompanied by decreased metabolism in insects and some other animals [C19 from Gk *diapausis* pause, from *diapauein* to pause, bring to an end, from DIA- + *pauein* to stop]

diaper (ˈdaɪəpə) *n* **1** the US and Canad word for **nappy**[1] **2a** a fabric having a pattern of a small repeating design, esp diamonds **2b** such a pattern, used as decoration ▷ *vb* **3** (*tr*) to decorate with such a pattern [C14 from OF *diaspre*, from Med. L *diasprus* made of diaper, from Med. Gk *diaspros* pure white, from DIA- + *aspros* white, shining]

diaphanous (daɪˈæfənəs) *adj* (usually of fabrics) fine and translucent [C17 from Med. L, from Gk *diaphanēs* transparent, from DIA- + *phainein* to show] > **diˈaphanously** *adv*

diaphoresis (ˌdaɪəfəˈriːsɪs) *n* sweating, esp when perceptible and excessive [C17 via LL from Gk, from *diaphorein* to disperse by perspiration, from DIA- + *phorein* to carry]

diaphoretic (ˌdaɪəfəˈrɛtɪk) *adj* **1** relating to or causing sweating ▷ *n* **2** a diaphoretic drug

diaphragm (ˈdaɪə,fræm) *n* **1** *anat* any separating membrane, esp the muscular partition that separates the abdominal and thoracic cavities in mammals **2** another name for **cap** (sense 11) **3** any thin dividing membrane **4** Also called: **stop** a device to control the amount of light entering an optical instrument, such as a camera **5** a thin vibrating disc used to convert sound signals to electrical signals or vice versa in telephones, etc [C17 from LL, from Gk, from DIA- + *phragma* fence] > **diaphragmatic** (ˌdaɪəfræɡˈmætɪk) *adj*

diapositive (ˌdaɪəˈpɒzɪtɪv) *n* a positive transparency; slide

diarist (ˈdaɪərɪst) *n* a person who writes a diary, esp one that is subsequently published

diarrhoea *or esp US* **diarrhea** (ˌdaɪəˈrɪə) *n* frequent and copious discharge of abnormally liquid faeces [C16 from LL, from Gk, from *diarrhein*, from DIA- + *rhein* to flow] > **ˌdiarˈrhoeal**, **ˌdiarˈrhoeic** *or esp US* **ˌdiarˈrheal**, **ˌdiarˈrheic** *adj*

Dd

diary (ˈdaɪərɪ) *n, pl* **diaries** **1** a personal record of daily events, appointments, observations, etc **2** a book for this [C16 from L *diārium* daily allocation of food or money, journal, from *diēs* day]

Dias *or* **Diaz** (ˈdiːəs; *Portuguese* ˈdiəʃ) *n* **Bartholomeu** (ˌbərtuluˈmeu) ?1450–1500, Portuguese navigator who discovered the sea route from Europe to the East via the Cape of Good Hope (1488)

Diaspora (daɪˈæspərə) *n* **1a** the dispersion of the Jews after the Babylonian and Roman conquests of Palestine **1b** the Jewish people and communities outside Israel **2** (*often not cap*) a dispersion, as of people originally belonging to one nation **3** *Caribbean* the descendants of Sub-Saharan African peoples living anywhere in the Western hemisphere [C19 from Gk: a scattering, from *diaspeirein*, from DIA- + *speirein* to scatter, sow] > **Diasporic** *or* **diasporic** (ˌdaɪəˈspɒrɪk) *adj*

diastalsis (ˌdaɪəˈstælsɪs) *n, pl* **diastalses** (-siːz) *Physiol.* a downward wave of contraction occurring in the intestine during digestion [C20 NL, from DIA- + (PERI)STALSIS] > **ˌdiaˈstaltic** *adj*

diastase (ˈdaɪə,steɪs, -,steɪz) *n* any of a group of enzymes that hydrolyse starch to maltose. They are present in germinated barley and in the pancreas [C19 from F, from Gk *diastasis* a separation] > **ˌdiaˈstasic** *adj*

diastole (daɪˈæstəlɪ) *n* the dilatation of the chambers of the heart that follows each contraction, during which they refill with blood ▷ Cf **systole** [C16 via LL from Gk, from *diastellein* to expand, from DIA- + *stellein* to place, bring together, make ready] > **diastolic** (ˌdaɪəˈstɒlɪk) *adj*

diastrophism (daɪˈæstrə,fɪzəm) *n* the process of movement of the earth's crust that gives rise to mountains, continents, and other large-scale features [C19 from Gk *diastrophē* a twisting; see DIA-, STROPHE] > **diastrophic** (ˌdaɪəˈstrɒfɪk) *adj*

diathermancy (ˌdaɪəˈθɜːmənsɪ) *n, pl* **diathermancies** the property of transmitting infrared radiation [C19 from F, from DIA- + Gk *thermansis* heating, from *thermos* hot] > ˌ**diaˈthermanous** *adj*

diathermy (ˈdaɪəˌθɜːmɪ) *or* **diathermia** (ˌdaɪəˈθɜːmɪə) *n* local heating of the body tissues with an electric current for medical purposes [C20 from NL, from DIA- + Gk *thermē* heat]

diatom (ˈdaɪətəm) *n* a microscopic unicellular alga having a cell wall impregnated with silica [C19 from NL, from Gk *diatomos* cut in two, from DIA- + *temnein* to cut]

diatomaceous (ˌdaɪətəˈmeɪʃəs) *adj* of or containing diatoms or their fossil remains

diatomic (ˌdaɪəˈtɒmɪk) *adj* (of a compound or molecule) containing two atoms

diatomite (daɪˈætəˌmaɪt) *n* a soft whitish rock consisting of the siliceous remains of diatoms

diatonic (ˌdaɪəˈtɒnɪk) *adj* **1** of, relating to, or based upon any scale of five tones and two semitones produced by playing the white keys of a keyboard instrument **2** not involving the sharpening or flattening of the notes of the major or minor scale nor the use of such notes as modified by accidentals [C16 from LL, from Gk, from *diatonos* extending, from DIA- + *teinein* to stretch]

diatonic scale *n music* the major and minor scales, made up of both tones and semitones

diatribe (ˈdaɪəˌtraɪb) *n* a bitter or violent criticism or attack [C16 from L *diatriba* learned debate, from Gk *diatribē* discourse, pastime, from *diatribein* to while away, from DIA- + *tribein* to rub]

Diaz (ˈdɪæz) *n* **Cameron** born 1972, U.S. film actress; films include *The Mask* (1994), *There's Something About Mary* (1998), and *The Gangs of New York* (2003)

Díaz de Vivar (*Spanish* ˈdiaθ dɛ biˈβar) *n* **Rodrigo** (rɔˈðriɣo) the original name of (El) **Cid**

diazepam (daɪˈæzəˌpæm) *n* a chemical compound used as a minor tranquillizer and muscle relaxant and to treat acute epilepsy [C20 from DI-¹ + *azo-* + *ep(oxide)* + *-am*]

diazo (daɪˈeɪzəʊ) *adj* **1** of, consisting of, or containing the divalent group, =N:N, or the divalent group, -N:N- **2** of the reproduction of documents using the bleaching action of ultraviolet radiation on diazonium salts ▷ *n, pl* **diazos** *or* **diazoes** **3** a document produced by this method

diazonium (ˌdaɪəˈzəʊnɪəm) *n* (*modifier*) of, consisting of, or containing the group ArN:N–, where Ar is an aryl group: *a diazonium salt*

dibasic (daɪˈbeɪsɪk) *adj* **1** (of an acid) containing two acidic hydrogen atoms **2** (of a salt) derived by replacing two acidic hydrogen atoms > **dibasicity** (ˌdaɪbeɪˈsɪsɪtɪ) *n*

dibble (ˈdɪbᵊl) *n* **1** Also: **dibber** a small hand tool used to make holes in the ground for bulbs, seeds, or roots ▷ *vb* **dibbles, dibbling, dibbled** **2** to make a hole in (the ground) with a dibble **3** to plant (seeds, etc) with a dibble [C15 from ?]

dibs (dɪbz) *pl n* **1** another word for **jacks** **2** *sl* money **3** (foll by *on*) *inf* rights (to) or claims (on): used mainly by children [C18 from *dibstones* game played with knucklebones or pebbles, prob. from *dib* to tap]

DiCaprio (dɪˈkæprɪəʊ) *n* **Leonardo** born 1974, U.S. film actor; his films include *Romeo and Juliet* (1996), *Titanic* (1997), and *The Gangs of New York* (2003)

dice (daɪs) *pl n* **1** cubes of wood, plastic, etc, each of whose sides has a different number of spots (1 to 6), used in games of chance **2** (*functioning as sing*) Also called: **die** one of these cubes **3** small cubes as of vegetables, meat, etc **4** **no dice** *sl, chiefly US & Canad* an expression of refusal ▷ *vb* **dices, dicing, diced** **5** to cut (food, etc) into small cubes **6** (*intr*) to gamble or play with dice **7** (*intr*) to take a chance or risk (esp in **dice with death**) **8** (*tr*) *Austral inf* to abandon or reject [C14 pl of DIE²] > ˈ**dicer** *n*

dicey (ˈdaɪsɪ) *adj* **dicier, diciest** *inf, chiefly Brit* difficult or dangerous; risky; tricky

dichloride (daɪˈklɔːraɪd) *n* a compound in which two atoms of chlorine are combined with another atom or group. Also called: **bichloride**

dichlorodiphenyltrichloroethane (daɪˌklɔːrəʊdaɪˌfiːnaɪltraɪˌklɔːrəʊˈiːθeɪn) *n* the full name for **DDT**

dichloromethane (daɪˌklɔːrəʊˈmiːθeɪn) *n* a noxious colourless liquid widely used as a solvent, e.g. in paint strippers. Formula: CH_2Cl_2. Traditional name: **methylene dichloride**

dichotomy (daɪˈkɒtəmɪ) *n, pl* **dichotomies** **1** division into two parts or classifications, esp when they are sharply distinguished or opposed **2** *bot* a simple method of branching by repeated division into two equal parts > **diˈchotomous** *adj*

> **USAGE** *Dichotomy* should always refer to a division of some kind into two groups. It is sometimes used to refer to a puzzling situation which seems to involve a contradiction, but this use is thought by many to be incorrect, and *dilemma* is often more appropriate

dichroism (ˈdaɪkrəʊˌɪzəm) *n* a property of a uniaxial crystal of showing a difference in colour when viewed along two different axes (in transmitted white light). Also called: **dichromaticism**. See also **pleochroism** > **diˈchroic** *adj*

dichromate (daɪˈkrəʊmeɪt) *n* any salt or ester of dichromic acid. Also called: **bichromate**

dichromatic (ˌdaɪkrəʊˈmætɪk) *adj* **1** Also: **dichroic** having two colours **2** (of animal species) having two different colour varieties **3** able to perceive only two colours (and mixes of them) > **dichromatism** (daɪˈkrəʊməˌtɪzəm) *n*

dichromic (daɪˈkrəʊmɪk) *adj* of or involving only two colours; dichromatic

dick (dɪk) *n sl* **1** *Brit* a fellow or person **2** **clever dick** *Brit* an opinionated person; know-all **3** a slang word for **penis** [C16 (meaning: fellow): from *Dick*, familiar form of *Richard*, applied to any fellow, lad, etc; hence, C19 penis]

dickens (ˈdɪkɪnz) *n inf* a euphemistic word for **devil** (used as intensifier in **what the dickens**) [C16 from the name *Dickens*]

Dickens (ˈdɪkɪnz) *n* **Charles** (**John Huffam**), pen name *Boz*. 1812–70, English novelist, famous for the humour and sympathy of his characterization and his criticism of social injustice. His major works include *The Pickwick Papers* (1837), *Oliver Twist* (1839), *Nicholas Nickleby* (1839), *Old Curiosity Shop* (1840–41), *Martin Chuzzlewit* (1844), *David Copperfield* (1850), *Bleak House* (1853), *Little Dorrit* (1857), and *Great Expectations* (1861)

Dickensian (dɪˈkɛnzɪən) *adj* **1** of Charles Dickens or his novels **2a** denoting poverty, distress, and exploitation as depicted in the novels of Dickens **2b** grotesquely comic, as some of the characters of Dickens

dicker (ˈdɪkə) *vb* **1** to trade (goods) by bargaining; barter ▷ *n* **2** a petty bargain or barter [C12 ult. from L *decuria* company of ten, from *decem* ten]

dickhead (ˈdɪkˌhɛd) *n sl* a stupid or despicable man or boy [C20 from DICK (in the sense: penis) + HEAD]

Dickinson (ˈdɪkɪnsᵊn) *n* **Emily** 1830–86, US poet, noted for her short mostly unrhymed mystical lyrics

dicky¹ *or* **dickey** (ˈdɪkɪ) *n, pl* **dickies** *or* **dickeys** **1** a false blouse or shirt front **2** Also called: **dicky bow** *Brit* a bow tie **3** Also called: **dicky-bird, dickeybird** a child's word for a bird **4** a folding outside seat at the rear of some early cars [C18 (in the sense: shirt front): from *Dickey*, dim. of *Dick* (name)]

dicky² *or* **dickey** (ˈdɪkɪ) *adj* **dickier, dickiest** *Brit inf* shaky, unsteady, or unreliable: *I feel a bit dicky today* [C18 ?from *as queer as Dick's hatband* feeling ill]

diclinous (ˈdaɪklɪnəs) *adj* **1** (of flowering plants) bearing unisexual flowers **2** (of flowers) unisexual ▷ Cf

monoclinous > ˈ**diclinism** *n* > ˈ**dicling** *n*
dicotyledon (ˌdaɪkɒtɪˈliːdᵊn) *n* a flowering plant having two embryonic seed leaves and leaves with netlike veins > ˌ**dicotyˈledonous** *adj*
dicta (ˈdɪktə) *n* a plural of **dictum**
Dictaphone (ˈdɪktəˌfəʊn) *n trademark* a tape recorder designed for recording dictation for subsequent typing
dictate *vb* (dɪkˈteɪt), **dictates, dictating, dictated** 1 to say (letters, speeches, etc) aloud for mechanical recording or verbatim transcription by another person 2 (*tr*) to prescribe (commands, etc) authoritatively 3 (*intr*) to seek to impose one's will on others ▷ *n* (ˈdɪkteɪt) 4 an authoritative command 5 a guiding principle: *the dictates of reason* [c17 from L *dictāre* to say repeatedly, order, from *dīcere* to say]
dictation (dɪkˈteɪʃən) *n* 1 the act of dictating material to be recorded or taken down in writing 2 the material dictated 3 authoritative commands or the act of giving them
dictator (dɪkˈteɪtə) *n* 1a a ruler who is not effectively restricted by a constitution, laws, etc 1b an absolute, esp tyrannical, ruler 2 (in ancient Rome) a person appointed during a crisis to exercise supreme authority 3 a person who makes pronouncements, which are regarded as authoritative 4 a person who behaves in an authoritarian or tyrannical manner
dictatorial (ˌdɪktəˈtɔːrɪəl) *adj* 1 of or characteristic of a dictator 2 tending to dictate; tyrannical; overbearing > ˌ**dictaˈtorially** *adv*
dictatorship (dɪkˈteɪtəˌʃɪp) *n* 1 the rank, office, or period of rule of a dictator 2 government by a dictator 3 a country ruled by a dictator 4 absolute power or authority
diction (ˈdɪkʃən) *n* 1 the choice of words in writing or speech 2 the manner of enunciating words and sounds [c15 from L *dictiō* a saying, mode of expression, from *dīcere* to speak, say]
dictionary (ˈdɪkʃənərɪ) *n, pl* **dictionaries** 1a a book that consists of an alphabetical list of words with their meanings, parts of speech, pronunciations, etymologies, etc 1b a similar book giving equivalent words in two or more languages 2 a reference book listing words or terms and giving information about a particular subject or activity 3 a collection of information or examples with the entries alphabetically arranged: *a dictionary of quotations* [c16 from Med. L *dictiōnārium* collection of words, from LL *dictiō* word; see DICTION]
▷ www.fireandwater.co.uk
▷ http://titania.cobuild.collins.co.uk
▷ www.cogsci.princeton.edu/~wn/
dictum (ˈdɪktəm) *n, pl* **dictums** *or* **dicta** 1 a formal or authoritative statement; pronouncement 2 a popular saying or maxim 3 *law* See **obiter dictum** [c16 from L, from *dīcere* to say]
did (dɪd) *vb* the past tense of **do**[1]
didactic (dɪˈdæktɪk) *adj* 1 intended to instruct, esp excessively 2 morally instructive 3 (of works of art or literature) containing a political or moral message to which aesthetic considerations are subordinated [c17 from Gk *didaktikos* skilled in teaching, from *didaskein*] > **diˈdactically** *adv* > **diˈdacticism** *n*
didactics (dɪˈdæktɪks) *n* (*functioning as sing*) the art or science of teaching
diddle (ˈdɪdᵊl) *vb* **diddles, diddling, diddled** (*tr*) *inf* to cheat or swindle [c19 back formation from Jeremy *Diddler*, a scrounger in J. Kenney's farce *Raising the Wind* (1803)] > ˈ**diddler** *n*
Diderot (ˈdiːdərəʊ; *French* didro) *n* **Denis** (dəni) 1713–84, French philosopher, noted particularly for his direction (1745–72) of the great French *Encyclopédie*
didgeridoo (ˌdɪdʒərɪˈduː) *n music* a native deep-toned Australian wind instrument [c20 imit.]
didn't (ˈdɪdᵊnt) *contraction of* did not
dido (ˈdaɪdəʊ) *n, pl* **didos** *or* **didoes** (*usually pl*) *inf* an antic; prank; trick [c19 from ?]
Dido (ˈdaɪdəʊ) *n classical myth* a princess of Tyre who founded Carthage and became its queen. Virgil tells of her suicide when abandoned by her lover Aeneas
didst (dɪdst) *vb arch* (used with *thou*) a form of the past tense of **do**[1]
didymium (daɪˈdɪmɪəm) *n* a mixture of the metallic rare earths neodymium and praseodymium, once thought to be an element [c19 from NL, from Gk *didumos* twin + -IUM]
die[1] (daɪ) *vb* **dies, dying, died** (*mainly intr*) 1 (of an organism, organs, etc) to cease all biological activity permanently 2 (of something inanimate) to cease to exist 3 (often foll by *away, down,* or *out*) to lose strength, power, or energy, esp by degrees 4 (often foll by *away* or *down*) to become calm; subside 5 to stop functioning: *the engine died* 6 to languish, as with love, longing, etc 7 (usually foll by *of*) *inf* to be nearly overcome (with laughter, boredom, etc) 8 *Christianity* to lack spiritual life within the soul 9 (*tr*) to suffer (a death of a specified kind): *he died a saintly death* 10 **be dying** (foll by *for* or an infinitive) to be eager or desperate (for something or to do something) 11 **die hard** to cease to exist after a struggle: *old habits die hard* 12 **die in harness** to die while still working or active 13 **never say die** *inf* never give up ▷ See also **die down, die out** [OE *dīegan*, prob. of Scand. origin]
die[2] (daɪ) *n* 1a a shaped block used to cut or form metal in a drop forge, press, etc 1b a tool with a conical hole through which wires, etc are drawn to reduce their diameter 2 an internally-threaded tool for cutting external threads 3 a casting mould 4 *archit* the dado of a pedestal, usually cubic 5 another name for **dice** (sense 2) 6 **the die is cast** the irrevocable decision has been taken [c13 *dee*, from OF *de*, ?from Vulgar L *datum* (unattested) a piece in games, from L *dare* to give, play]
die-cast *vb* **die-casts, die-casting, die-cast** (*tr*) to shape or form (an object) by introducing molten metal or plastic into a reusable mould, esp under pressure > ˈ**die-ˌcasting** *n*
die down *vb* (*intr, adv*) 1 (of plants) to wither above ground, leaving only the root alive during the winter 2 to lose strength or power, esp by degrees 3 to become calm
Diefenbaker (ˈdiːfᵊnˌbeɪkə) *n* **John George** 1895–1979, Canadian Conservative statesman; prime minister of Canada (1957–63)
die-hard *n* 1 a person who resists change or who holds onto an untenable position 2 (*modifier*) obstinately resistant to change
dieldrin (ˈdiːldrɪn) *n* a crystalline substance, consisting of a chlorinated derivative of naphthalene: a contact insecticide the use of which is now restricted [c20 from *Diel(s-Al)d(e)r (reaction)* + -IN; Diels & Alder were G chemists]
dielectric (ˌdaɪɪˈlɛktrɪk) *n* 1 a substance that can sustain an electric field 2 a substance of very low electrical conductivity; insulator ▷ *adj* 3 concerned with or having the properties of a dielectric [from DIA- + ELECTRIC] > ˌ**dieˈlectrically** *adv*
Dien Bien Phu (ˌdjɛn bjɛn ˈfuː) *n* a village in NW Vietnam: French military post during the Indochina War; scene of a major defeat of French forces by the Vietminh (1954)
diene (ˈdaɪiːn) *n chem* a hydrocarbon that contains two carbon-to-carbon double bonds in its molecules [from DI-[1] + -ENE]
die out *or* **off** *vb* (*intr, adv*) 1 to die one after another until few or none are left 2 to become extinct, esp after a period of gradual decline
Dieppe (dɪˈɛp; *French* djɛp) *n* a port and resort in N

France, on the English Channel. Pop: 36 600 (1990)
dieresis (daɪˈɛrɪsɪs) *n, pl* **diereses** (-ˌsiːz) a variant spelling of **diaeresis**
diesel (ˈdiːzᵊl) *n* 1 See **diesel engine** 2 a ship, locomotive, lorry, etc, driven by a diesel engine 3 *inf* short for **diesel oil** (*or* **fuel**)
Diesel (ˈdiːzᵊl) *n* **Rudolf** (ˈruːdɔlf) 1858–1913, German engineer, who invented the diesel engine (1892)
diesel-electric *n* 1 a locomotive fitted with a diesel engine driving an electric generator that feeds electric traction motors ▷ *adj* 2 of or relating to such a locomotive or system
diesel engine *or* **motor** *n* a type of internal-combustion engine in which atomized fuel oil is ignited by compression alone
diesel oil *or* **fuel** *n* a fuel obtained from petroleum distillation that is used in diesel engines. Also called (Brit): **derv**
Dies Irae *Latin* (ˈdiːeɪz ˈɪəraɪ) *n* 1 a Latin hymn of the 13th century, describing the Last Judgment. It is used in the Mass for the dead 2 a musical setting of this [lit.: day of wrath]
diesis (ˈdaɪɪsɪs) *n, pl* **dieses** (-ˌsiːz) *printing* another name for **double dagger** [c16 via L from Gk: a quarter tone, lit.: a sending through, from *diienai*; the double dagger was orig. used in musical notation]
diestock (ˈdaɪˌstɒk) *n* the device holding the dies used to cut an external screw thread
diet[1] (ˈdaɪət) *n* 1 a specific allowance or selection of food, esp prescribed to control weight or for health reasons: *a salt-free diet* 2 the food and drink that a person or animal regularly consumes 3 regular activities or occupations ▷ *vb* 4 (*usually intr*) to follow or cause to follow a dietary regimen [c13 from OF *diete*, from L *diaeta*, from Gk *diaita* mode of living, from *diaitan* to direct one's own life] > ˈ**dieter** *n*
diet[2] (ˈdaɪət) *n* 1 (*sometimes cap*) a legislative assembly in various countries 2 (*sometimes cap*) the assembly of the estates of the Holy Roman Empire 3 *Scots law* a single session of a court [c15 from Med. L *diēta* public meeting, prob. from L *diaeta* DIET[1] but associated with L *diēs* day]
dietary (ˈdaɪətərɪ, -trɪ) *adj* 1 of or relating to a diet ▷ *n, pl* **dietaries** 2 a regulated diet 3 a system of dieting
dietary fibre *n* fibrous substances in fruits and vegetables, such as the structural polymers of cell walls, which aid digestion. Also called: **roughage**
dietetic (ˌdaɪɪˈtɛtɪk) *or* **dietetical** *adj* 1 denoting or relating to diet 2 prepared for special dietary requirements > ˌ**dieˈtetically** *adv*
dietetics (ˌdaɪɪˈtɛtɪks) *n* (*functioning as sing*) the scientific study and regulation of food intake and preparation
diethylene glycol *n* a colourless soluble liquid used as an antifreeze and solvent
dietician *or* **dietitian** (ˌdaɪɪˈtɪʃən) *n* a person who specializes in dietetics
Dietrich (*German* ˈdiːtrɪç) *n* **Marlene** (marˈleːnə), real name *Maria Magdalene von Losch*. 1901–92, US film actress and cabaret singer, born in Germany
differ (ˈdɪfə) *vb* (*intr*) 1 (often foll by *from*) to be dissimilar in quality, nature, or degree (to); vary (from) 2 (often foll by *from* or *with*) to disagree (with) 3 *dialect* to quarrel or dispute [c14 from L *differre*, to scatter, put off, be different, from *dis-* apart + *ferre* to bear]
difference (ˈdɪfərəns) *n* 1 the state or quality of being unlike 2 a specific instance of being unlike 3 a distinguishing mark or feature 4 a significant change 5 a disagreement or argument 6 a degree of distinctness, as between two people or things 7 Also called: **remainder** the result of the subtraction of one number, quantity, etc, from another 8 *maths* (of two sets) the set of members of the first that are not members of the second 9 *heraldry* an addition to the arms of a family to represent a younger branch 10 **make a difference** 10a to have an effect 10b to treat differently 11 **split the difference** 11a to compromise 11b to divide a remainder equally 12 **with a difference** with some distinguishing quality, good or bad
different (ˈdɪfərənt) *adj* 1 partly or completely unlike 2 not identical or the same; other 3 unusual > ˈ**differently** *adv* > ˈ**differentness** *n*

> USAGE The constructions *different from*, *different to*, and *different than* are all found in the works of writers of English during the past. Nowadays, however, the most widely acceptable preposition to use after *different* is *from*. *Different to* is common in British English, but is considered by some people to be incorrect, or less acceptable. *Different than* is a standard construction in American English. As, however, this structure is not regarded as totally acceptable in British usage, it is preferable either to use *different from*: *this result is only slightly different from that obtained in the US* or to rephrase the sentence: *this result differs only slightly from that in the US*. See also at **disabled**

differentia (ˌdɪfəˈrɛnʃɪə) *n, pl* **differentiae** (-ʃɪˌiː) *Logic*. a feature by which two subclasses of the same class of named objects can be distinguished [c19 from L: diversity]
differential (ˌdɪfəˈrɛnʃəl) *adj* 1 of, relating to, or using a difference 2 constituting a difference; distinguishing 3 *maths* involving one or more derivatives or differentials 4 *physics, engineering* relating to, operating on, or based on the difference between two opposing effects, motions, forces, etc ▷ *n* 5 a factor that differentiates between two comparable things 6 *maths* 6a an increment in a given function, expressed as the product of the derivative of that function and the corresponding increment in the independent variable 6b an increment in a given function of two or more variables, $f(x_1, x_2, \dots x_n)$, expressed as the sum of the products of each partial derivative and the increment in the corresponding variable 7 See **differential gear** 8 *chiefly Brit* the difference between rates of pay for different types of labour, esp when forming a pay structure within an industry 9 (in commerce) a difference in rates, esp between comparable services > ˌ**differˈentially** *adv*
differential calculus *n* the branch of calculus concerned with the study, evaluation, and use of derivatives and differentials
differential equation *n* an equation containing differentials or derivatives of a function of one independent variable
differential gear *n* the epicyclic gear mounted in the driving axle of a road vehicle that permits one driving wheel to rotate faster than the other, as when cornering
differential operator *n* the mathematical operator del, ∇, used in vector analysis
differentiate (ˌdɪfəˈrɛnʃɪˌeɪt) *vb* **differentiates, differentiating, differentiated** 1 (*tr*) to serve to distinguish between 2 (when *intr*, often foll by *between*) to perceive, show, or make a difference (in or between); discriminate 3 (*intr*) to become dissimilar or distinct 4 *maths* to perform a differentiation on (a quantity, expression, etc) 5 (*intr*) (of unspecialized cells, etc) to change during development to more specialized forms > ˌ**differˈentiˌator** *n*
differentiation (ˌdɪfəˌrɛnʃɪˈeɪʃən) *n* 1 the act, process, or result of differentiating 2 *maths* an operation used in calculus in which the derivative of a function or variable is determined
difficult (ˈdɪfɪkᵊlt) *adj* 1 not easy to do; requiring effort 2 not easy to understand or solve 3 troublesome: *a difficult child* 4 not easily convinced, pleased, or satisfied

5 full of hardships or trials [c14 back formation from DIFFICULTY] > '**difficultly** *adv*

difficulty ('dɪfɪkəltɪ) *n, pl* **difficulties** 1 the state or quality of being difficult 2 a task, problem, etc, that is hard to deal with 3 (*often pl*) a troublesome or embarrassing situation, esp a financial one 4 a disagreement 5 (*often pl*) an objection or obstacle 6 a trouble or source of trouble; worry 7 lack of ease; awkwardness [c14 from L *difficultās*, from *difficilis*, from *dis-* not + *facilis* easy]

diffident ('dɪfɪdənt) *adj* lacking self-confidence; shy [c15 from L *diffīdere*, from *dis-* not + *fīdere* to trust] > '**diffidence** *n* > '**diffidently** *adv*

diffract (dɪ'frækt) *vb* to undergo or cause to undergo diffraction > **dif'fractive** *adj* > **dif'fractively** *adv* > **dif'fractiveness** *n*

diffraction (dɪ'frækʃən) *n* 1 *physics* a deviation in the direction of a wave at the edge of an obstacle in its path 2 any phenomenon caused by diffraction, such as the formation of light and dark fringes by the passage of light through a small aperture [c17 from NL *diffractiō* a breaking to pieces, from L *diffringere* to shatter, from *dis-* apart + *frangere* to break]

diffuse *vb* (dɪ'fjuːz), **diffuses, diffusing, diffused** 1 to spread in all directions 2 to undergo or cause to undergo diffusion 3 to scatter; disperse ▷ *adj* (dɪ'fjuːs) 4 spread out over a wide area 5 lacking conciseness 6 characterized by diffusion [c15 from L *diffūsus* spread abroad, from *diffundere* to pour forth, from *dis-* away + *fundere* to pour] > **diffusely** (dɪ'fjuːslɪ) *adv* > **dif'fuseness** *n* > **diffusible** (dɪ'fjuːzɪbəl) *adj*

USAGE This word is quite commonly misused instead of *defuse*, when talking about calming down a situation

diffuser *or* **diffusor** (dɪ'fjuːzə) *n* 1 a person or thing that diffuses 2 a part of a lighting fixture, as a translucent covering, used to scatter the light and prevent glare 3 a cone, wedge, or baffle placed in front of the diaphragm of a loudspeaker to diffuse the sound waves 4 a duct, esp in a wind tunnel or jet engine, that reduces the speed and increases the pressure of the air or fluid 5 *photog* a light-scattering medium, such as a screen of fine fabric, used to reduce the sharpness of shadows and thus soften the lighting 6 a device attached to a hair dryer that diffuses the warm air as it comes out

diffusion (dɪ'fjuːʒən) *n* 1 a diffusing or being diffused; dispersion 2 verbosity 3 *physics* 3a the random thermal motion of atoms, molecules, etc, in gases, liquids, and some solids 3b the transfer of atoms or molecules by their random motion from one part of a medium to another 4 *physics* the transmission or reflection of electromagnetic radiation, esp light, in which the radiation is scattered in many directions 5 *anthropol* the transmission of social institutions, skills, and myths from one culture to another

diffusionism (dɪ'fjuːʒənˌɪzəm) *n anthropol* the theory that diffusion is responsible for the similarities between different cultures > **dif'fusionist** *n, adj*

diffusive (dɪ'fjuːsɪv) *adj* characterized by diffusion > **dif'fusively** *adv* > **dif'fusiveness** *n*

dig (dɪg) *vb* **digs, digging, dug** 1 (when *tr*, often foll by *up*) to cut into, break up, and turn over or remove (earth, etc), esp with a spade 2 to excavate (a hole, tunnel, etc) by digging, usually with an implement or (of animals) with claws, etc 3 (often foll by *through*) to make or force (one's way): *he dug his way through the crowd* 4 (*tr*; often foll by *out* or *up*) to obtain by digging 5 (*tr*; often foll by *out* or *up*) to find by effort or searching: *to dig out facts* 6 (*tr*; foll by *in* or *into*) to thrust or jab 7 (*tr*; foll by *in* or *into*) to mix (compost, etc) with soil by digging 8 (*intr*; foll by *in* or *into*) *inf* to begin vigorously to do something 9 (*tr*) *inf* to like, understand, or appreciate 10 (*intr*) *US sl* to work hard, esp for an examination ▷ *n* 11 the act of digging 12 a thrust or poke 13 a cutting remark 14 *inf* an archaeological excavation 15 *Austral & NZ inf* short for **digger** (sense 4) ▷ See also **dig in** [c13 *diggen*, from ?]

Digby chicken *or* **chick** ('dɪgbɪ) *n Canad inf* dried herring [after *Digby*, a town in Nova Scotia, Canada]

digerati (ˌdɪdʒə'rɑːtɪ) *pl n* the people who earn large amounts of money through Internet-related business

digest *vb* (dɪ'dʒɛst, daɪ-) 1 to subject (food) to a process of digestion 2 (*tr*) to assimilate mentally 3 *chem* to soften or disintegrate by the action of heat, moisture, or chemicals 4 (*tr*) to arrange in a methodical order; classify 5 (*tr*) to reduce to a summary ▷ *n* ('daɪdʒɛst) 6 a comprehensive and systematic compilation of information or material, often condensed 7 a magazine, periodical, etc, that summarizes news 8 a compilation of rules of law [c14 from LL *dīgesta* writings grouped under various heads, from L *dīgerere* to divide, from *di-* apart + *gerere* to bear]

Digest ('daɪdʒɛst) *n Roman law* the books of law compiled by order of Justinian in the sixth century AD

digestible (dɪ'dʒɛstɪbəl, daɪ-) *adj* capable of being digested > **diˌgesti'bility** *n*

digestion (dɪ'dʒɛstʃən, daɪ-) *n* 1 the act or process in living organisms of breaking down food into easily absorbed substances by the action of enzymes, etc 2 mental assimilation, esp of ideas 3 the decomposition of sewage by bacteria 4 *chem* the treatment of material with heat, solvents, etc, to cause decomposition [c14 from OF, from L *digestiō* a dissolving, digestion] > **di'gestional** *adj*

digestive (dɪ'dʒɛstɪv, daɪ-) *or* **digestant** (daɪ'dʒɛstənt) *adj* 1 relating to, aiding, or subjecting to digestion ▷ *n* 2 any substance that aids digestion > **di'gestively** *adv*

digestive biscuit *n* a round semisweet biscuit made from wholemeal flour

digger ('dɪgə) *n* 1 a person, animal, or machine that digs 2 a miner 3 a tool or machine used for excavation 4 (*sometimes cap*) *Austral inf* an Australian, esp a soldier: often used as a friendly term of address

Dd

diggings ('dɪgɪŋz) *pl n* 1 (*functioning as pl*) material that has been dug out 2 (*functioning as sing or pl*) a place where mining has taken place 3 (*functioning as pl*) *Brit inf* a less common name for **digs**

dight (daɪt) *vb* **dights, dighting, dight** *or* **dighted** (*tr*) *arch* to adorn or equip, as for battle [OE *dihtan* to compose, from L *dictāre* to DICTATE]

Digibox ('dɪdʒɪbɒks) *n trademark* a device which converts the signals from a digital television broadcast into a form which can be viewed on a standard television set [c20 from DIGI(TAL) (sense 3) + BOX[1]]

dig in *vb* (*adv*) 1 *mil* to dig foxholes, trenches, etc 2 *inf* to entrench (oneself) 3 (*intr*) *inf* to defend a position firmly, as in an argument 4 (*intr*) *inf* to begin to eat vigorously: *don't wait, just dig in* 5 **dig one's heels in** *inf* to refuse to move or be persuaded

digit ('dɪdʒɪt) *n* 1 a finger or toe 2 any of the ten Arabic numerals from 0 to 9 [c15 from L *digitus* toe, finger]

digital ('dɪdʒɪtəl) *adj* 1 of, resembling, or possessing a digit or digits 2 performed with the fingers 3 representing data as a series of numerical values 4 displaying information as numbers rather than by a pointer moving over a dial ▷ *n* 5 *music* a key on a piano, harpsichord, etc > '**digitally** *adv*

digital audio tape *n* magnetic tape on which sound is recorded digitally, giving high-fidelity reproduction. Abbrev: **DAT**

digital camera *n* a camera that produces digital images, which can be stored on a computer, displayed on a screen, and printed

digital clock *or* **watch** *n* a clock or watch in which the time is indicated by digits rather than by hands on a dial

digital compact cassette *n* a magnetic tape cassette on which sound can be recorded in digital format. Abbrev: **DCC**

digital computer *n* an electronic computer in which the input is discrete, consisting of numbers, letters, etc that are represented internally in binary notation
digital divide *n inf* the gap between those people who have Internet access and those who do not
digitalin (ˌdɪdʒɪˈteɪlɪn) *n* a poisonous mixture of glycosides extracted from digitalis and formerly used in treating heart disease [C19 from DIGITAL(IS) + -IN]
digitalis (ˌdɪdʒɪˈteɪlɪs) *n* **1** any of a genus of Eurasian plants such as the foxglove, having long spikes of bell-shaped flowers **2** a drug prepared from the dried leaves of the foxglove: used medicinally to treat heart failure and some abnormal heart rhythms [C17 from NL, from L: relating to a finger; based on G *Fingerhut* foxglove, lit.: finger-hat or thimble]
digitalize *or* **digitalise** (ˈdɪdʒɪtəˌlaɪz) *vb* **digitalizes, digitalizing, digitalized** *or* **digitalises, digitalising, digitalised** (*tr*) another word for **digitize**
digital mapping *n* a method of preparing maps in which the data is stored in a computer for ease of access and updating > **digital map** *n*
digital radio *n* **1** radio in which the audio information is transmitted in digital form and decoded at the radio receiver **2** a radio that can receive and decode digital audio information
▷ www.drm.org
digital recording *n* a sound recording process that converts audio or analogue signals into a series of pulses that correspond to the voltage level
digital signature *n computing* electronic proof of a person's identity involving the use of encryption; used to authenticate documents
digital television *n* **1** television in which the picture information is transmitted in digital form and decoded at the receiver **2** a television set that can receive and decode digital information
▷ www.digitaltelevision.gov.uk
digital versatile disk *n* a disk similar to a CD but with much greater capacity, used for storing and distributing films, multimedia, etc. Also called(esp formerly): **digital video disk** Abbrev: **DVD**
digital video *n* video output based on digital rather than analogue signals
digitate (ˈdɪdʒɪˌteɪt) *or* **digitated** *adj* **1** (of leaves) having the leaflets in the form of a spread hand **2** (of animals) having digits > **ˈdigiˌtately** *adv* > **ˌdigiˈtation** *n*
digitigrade (ˈdɪdʒɪtɪˌgreɪd) *adj* **1** (of dogs, cats, horses, etc) walking so that only the toes touch the ground ▷ *n* **2** a digitigrade animal
digitize *or* **digitise** (ˈdɪdʒɪˌtaɪz) *vb* **digitizes, digitizing, digitized** *or* **digitises, digitising, digitised** (*tr*) to transcribe (data) into a digital form for processing by a computer > **ˌdigitiˈzation** *or* **ˌdigitiˈsation** *n* > **ˈdigiˌtizer** *or* **ˈdigiˌtiser** *n*
digitized *or* **digitised** (ˈdɪdʒɪˌtaɪzd) *adj computing* recorded or stored in digital form: *export your digitized colour photos*
dignified (ˈdɪgnɪˌfaɪd) *adj* characterized by dignity of manner or appearance; stately; noble > **ˈdigniˌfiedly** *adv* > **ˈdigniˌfiedness** *n*
dignify (ˈdɪgnɪˌfaɪ) *vb* **dignifies, dignifying, dignified** (*tr*) **1** to invest with honour or dignity **2** to add distinction to **3** to add a semblance of dignity to, esp by the use of a pretentious name or title [C15 from OF *dignifier*, from LL *dignificāre*, from L *dignus* worthy + *facere* to make]
dignitary (ˈdɪgnɪtərɪ) *n, pl* **dignitaries** a person of high official position or rank
dignity (ˈdɪgnɪtɪ) *n, pl* **dignities** **1** a formal, stately, or grave bearing **2** the state or quality of being worthy of honour **3** relative importance; rank **4** sense of self-importance (often in **stand** (*or* **be**) **on one's dignity, beneath one's dignity**) **5** high rank, esp in government or the church [C13 from OF *dignite*, from L *dignitās* merit, from *dignus* worthy]
digoxin (daɪˈdʒɒksɪn) *n* a glycoside extracted from the leaves of the woolly foxglove and used in the treatment of heart failure
digraph (ˈdaɪgrɑːf) *n* a combination of two letters used to represent a single sound such as *gh* in *tough* > **digraphic** (daɪˈgræfɪk) *adj*
digress (daɪˈgrɛs) *vb* (*intr*) **1** to depart from the main subject in speech or writing **2** to wander from one's path [C16 from L *dīgressus* turned aside, from *dīgredī*, from *dis-* apart + *gradī* to go] > **diˈgresser** *n* > **diˈgression** *n*
digressive (daɪˈgrɛsɪv) *adj* characterized by digression or tending to digress > **diˈgressively** *adv* > **diˈgressiveness** *n*
digs (dɪgz) *pl n Brit inf* lodgings [C19 from DIGGINGS, ? referring to where one *digs* or works, but see also DIG IN]
dihedral (daɪˈhiːdrəl) *adj* **1** having or formed by two intersecting planes ▷ *n* **2** Also called: **dihedron, dihedral angle** the figure formed by two intersecting planes **3** the upward inclination of an aircraft wing in relation to the lateral axis
Dijon (*French* diʒɔ̃) *n* a city in E France: capital of the former duchy of Burgundy. Pop: 149 867 (1999)
dik-dik (ˈdɪkˌdɪk) *n* any of several small antelopes inhabiting semiarid regions of Africa [C19 E African, prob. imit.]
dike (daɪk) *n, vb* **dikes, diking, diked** a variant spelling of **dyke**[1]
diktat (ˈdɪktɑːt) *n* **1** a decree or settlement imposed, esp by a ruler or a victorious nation **2** a dogmatic statement [from G: dictation, from L *dictātum*, from *dictāre* to DICTATE]
dilapidate (dɪˈlæpɪˌdeɪt) *vb* **dilapidates, dilapidating, dilapidated** to fall or cause to fall into ruin [C16 from L *dīlapidāre* to waste, from *dis-* apart + *lapidāre* to stone, from *lapis* stone] > **diˌlapiˈdation** *n*
dilapidated (dɪˈlæpɪˌdeɪtɪd) *adj* falling to pieces or in a state of disrepair; shabby
dilate (daɪˈleɪt, dɪ-) *vb* **dilates, dilating, dilated** **1** to make or become wider or larger **2** (*intr*; *often foll by on or upon*) to speak or write at length [C14 from L *dīlātāre* to spread out, from *dis-* apart + *lātus* wide] > **diˈlatable** *adj* > **diˌlataˈbility** *n* > **diˈlation** *or* **dilatation** (ˌdaɪləˈteɪʃən) *n* > **dilative** (daɪˈleɪtɪv) *adj*
dilatory (ˈdɪlətərɪ, -trɪ) *adj* **1** tending to delay or waste time **2** intended to waste time or defer action [C15 from LL *dīlātōrius* inclined to delay, from *differre* to postpone; see DIFFER] > **ˈdilatorily** *adv* > **ˈdilatoriness** *n*
dildo *or* **dildoe** (ˈdɪldəʊ) *n, pl* **dildos** *or* **dildoes** an object used as a substitute for an erect penis [C16 from ?]
dilemma (dɪˈlɛmə, daɪ-) *n* **1** a situation necessitating a choice between two equally undesirable alternatives **2** a problem that seems incapable of a solution **3** *logic* a type of argument which forces the maintainer of a proposition to accept one of two conclusions each of which contradicts the original assertion **4** **on the horns of a dilemma** **4a** faced with the choice between two equally unpalatable alternatives **4b** in an awkward situation [C16 via L from Gk, from DI-[1] + *lēmma* proposition, from *lambanein* to grasp] > **dilemmatic** (ˌdɪlɪˈmætɪk) *adj*

> USAGE The use of *dilemma* to refer to a problem that seems incapable of a solution is considered by some people to be incorrect

dilettante (ˌdɪlɪˈtɑːntɪ) *n, pl* **dilettantes** *or* **dilettanti** (-ˈtɑːntɪ) **1** a person whose interest in a subject is superficial rather than professional **2** a person who loves the arts ▷ *adj* **3** of or characteristic of a dilettante [C18 from It., from *dilettare* to delight, from L *dēlectāre*] > **ˌdiletˈtantish** *or* **ˌdiletˈtanteish** *adj* > **ˌdiletˈtantism** *or* **ˌdiletˈtanteism** *n*
diligence[1] (ˈdɪlɪdʒəns) *n* **1** steady and careful

application **2** proper attention or care [c14 from L *dīligentia* care]

diligence[2] ('dɪlɪdʒəns) *n history* a stagecoach [c18 from F, shortened from *carosse de diligence*, lit.: coach of speed]

diligent ('dɪlɪdʒənt) *adj* **1** careful and persevering in carrying out tasks or duties **2** carried out with care and perseverance: *diligent work* [c14 from OF, from L *dīligere* to value, from *dis-* apart + *legere* to read] > **'diligently** *adv*

dill[1] (dɪl) *n* **1** an aromatic Eurasian plant with umbrella-shaped clusters of yellow flowers **2** the leaves or fruits of this plant, used for flavouring and in medicine [OE *dile*]

dill[2] (dɪl) *n Austral & NZ sl* a fool [c20 from DILLY[2]]

dill pickle *n* a pickled cucumber flavoured with dill

dilly[1] ('dɪlɪ) *n, pl* **dillies** *sl, chiefly US & Canad* a person or thing that is remarkable [c20 ?from girl's name *Dilly*]

dilly[2] ('dɪlɪ) *adj* **dillier, dilliest** *Austral sl* silly [c20 from E dialect, ?from SILLY]

dilly bag *n Austral* a small bag, esp, formerly, one made of plaited grass, etc, often used for carrying food [from Abor. *dilly* small bag or basket]

dilly-dally (ˌdɪlɪ'dælɪ) *vb* **dilly-dallies, dilly-dallying, dilly-dallied** (*intr*) *inf* to loiter or vacillate [c17 by reduplication from DALLY]

dilute (daɪ'luːt) *vb* **dilutes, diluting, diluted** **1** to make or become less concentrated, esp by adding water or a thinner **2** to make or become weaker in force, effect, etc ▷ *adj* **3** *chem* **3a** (of a solution, etc) having a low concentration **3b** (of a substance) present in solution, esp a weak solution in water: *dilute acetic acid* [c16 from L *dīluere*, from *dis-* apart + *-luere*, from *lavāre* to wash] > **di'luter** *n*

dilution (daɪ'luːʃən) *n* **1** the act of diluting or state of being diluted **2** a diluted solution

diluvial (daɪ'luːvɪəl, dɪ-) *or* **diluvian** *adj* of or connected with a deluge, esp with the great Flood described in Genesis [c17 from LL *dīluviālis*, from L *dīluere* to wash away; see DILUTE]

dim (dɪm) *adj* **dimmer, dimmest** **1** badly illuminated **2** not clearly seen; faint **3** having weak or indistinct vision **4** mentally dull **5** not clear in the mind; obscure: *a dim memory* **6** lacking in brightness or lustre **7** unfavourable, gloomy or disapproving(esp in **take a dim view**) ▷ *vb* **dims, dimming, dimmed** **8** to become or cause to become dim **9** (*tr*) to cause to seem less bright **10** the US and Canad word for **dip** (sense 5) [OE *dimm*] > **'dimly** *adv* > **'dimness** *n*

dim. *or* **dimin.** *music abbrev for* diminuendo

Dimashq (diː'mæʃk) *n* an Arabic name for **Damascus**

Dimbleby ('dɪmbᵊlbɪ) *n* **Richard** 1913–65, British broadcaster

dime (daɪm) *n* **1** a coin of the US and Canada, worth one tenth of a dollar or ten cents **2** **a dime a dozen** very cheap or common [c14 from OF *disme*, from L *decimus* tenth, from *decem* ten]

dimenhydrinate (ˌdaɪmɛn'haɪdrɪˌneɪt) *n* a crystalline substance: an antihistamine used in the prevention of nausea, esp in travel sickness [from DI-[1] + ME(THYL) + (AMI)N(E) + (*diphen*)*hydr*(*am*)*in*(*e*) + -ATE[1]]

dime novel *n US* (formerly) a cheap melodramatic novel, usually in paperback

dimension (dɪ'mɛnʃən) *n* **1** (*often pl*) a measurement of the size of something in a particular direction, such as the length, width, height, or diameter **2** (*often pl*) scope; size; extent **3** aspect: *a new dimension to politics* **4** *maths* the number of coordinates required to locate a point in space ▷ *vb* **5** (*tr*) *chiefly US* to cut to or mark with specified dimensions [c14 from OF, from L *dīmensiō* an extent, from *dīmētīrī* to measure out, from *mētīrī*] > **di'mensional** *adj* > **di'mensionless** *adj*

dimer ('daɪmə) *n chem* a compound the molecule of which is formed by the linking of two identical molecules [c20 from DI-[1] + -MER]

dimerize *or* **dimerise** ('daɪməˌraɪz) *vb* **dimerizes, dimerizing, dimerized** *or* **dimerises, dimerising, dimerised** to react or cause to react to form a dimer > **ˌdimeri'zation** *or* **ˌdimeri'sation** *n*

dimeter ('dɪmɪtə) *n prosody* a line of verse consisting of two metrical feet or a verse written in this metre

dimethylformamide (daɪˌmiːθaɪl'fɔːməˌmaɪd) *n* a colourless liquid widely used as a solvent and sometimes as a catalyst. Formula: $(CH_3)_2NCHO$. Abbrev: **DMF**

dimethylsulphoxide *or* **dimethylsulfoxide** (daɪˌmiːθaɪlsʌl'fɒksaɪd) *n* a liquid used as a solvent and in medicine to improve the penetration of drugs applied to the skin. Abbrev: **DMSO**

diminish (dɪ'mɪnɪʃ) *vb* **1** to make or become smaller, fewer, or less **2** (*tr*) *archit* to cause to taper **3** (*tr*) *music* to decrease (a minor or perfect interval) by a semitone **4** to reduce in authority, status, etc [c15 blend of *diminuen* to lessen (from L *dēminuere*, from *minuere*) + archaic *minish* to lessen] > **di'minishable** *adj*

diminished (dɪ'mɪnɪʃt) *adj* **1** reduced or lessened; made smaller **2** *music* denoting any minor or perfect interval reduced by a semitone

diminished responsibility *n law* a plea under which mental derangement is submitted as demonstrating lack of criminal responsibility

diminishing returns *pl n Econ.* progressively smaller increases in output resulting from equal increases in production

diminuendo (dɪˌmɪnjʊ'ɛndəʊ) *music* ▷ *n, pl* **diminuendos** **1a** a gradual decrease in loudness. Symbol: > **1b** a musical passage affected by a diminuendo ▷ *adj* **2** gradually decreasing in loudness **3** with a diminuendo [c18 from It., from *diminuire* to DIMINISH]

diminution (ˌdɪmɪ'njuːʃən) *n* **1** reduction; decrease **2** *music* the presentation of the subject of a fugue, etc, in which the note values are reduced in length [c14 from L *dēminūtiō*; see DIMINISH]

Dd

diminutive (dɪ'mɪnjʊtɪv) *adj* **1** very small; tiny **2** *grammar* **2a** denoting an affix added to a word to convey the meaning *small* or *unimportant* or to express affection **2b** denoting a word formed by the addition of a diminutive affix ▷ *n* **3** *grammar* a diminutive word or affix **4** a tiny person or thing > **di'minutively** *adv* > **di'minutiveness** *n*

dimissory (dɪ'mɪsərɪ) *adj* **1** granting permission to be ordained: *a bishop's dimissory letter* **2** granting permission to depart

Dimitrovo (*Bulgarian* di'mitrovo) *n* the former name (1949–62) of **Pernik**

dimity ('dɪmɪtɪ) *n, pl* **dimities** **a** a light strong cotton fabric with woven stripes or squares **b** (*as modifier*) *a dimity bonnet* [c15 from Med. L *dimitum*, from Gk *dimiton*, from DI-[1] + *mitos* thread of the warp]

dimmer ('dɪmə) *n* **1** a device for dimming an electric light **2** (*often pl*) *US* **2a** a dipped headlight on a road vehicle **2b** a parking light on a car

dimorphism (daɪ'mɔːfɪzəm) *n* **1** the occurrence within a plant of two distinct forms of any part **2** the occurrence in an animal or plant species of two distinct types of individual **3** a property of certain substances that enables them to exist in two distinct crystalline forms > **di'morphic** *or* **di'morphous** *adj*

dimple ('dɪmpᵊl) *n* **1** a small natural dent, esp on the cheeks or chin **2** any slight depression in a surface ▷ *vb* **dimples, dimpling, dimpled** **3** to make or become dimpled **4** (*intr*) to produce dimples by smiling [c13 *dympull*] > **'dimply** *adj*

dim sum (ˌdɪm 'sʌm) *n* a Chinese appetizer of steamed dumplings containing various fillings [Cantonese]

dimwit ('dɪmˌwɪt) *n inf* a stupid or silly person > **ˌdim-'witted** *adj* > **ˌdim-'wittedness** *n*

din (dɪn) *n* **1** a loud discordant confused noise ▷ *vb* **dins,**

dinning, dinned 2 (*tr; usually foll by into*) to instil by constant repetition **3** (*tr*) to subject to a din **4** (*intr*) to make a din [OE *dynn*]

DIN *n* **1** a formerly used logarithmic expression of the speed of a photographic film, plate, etc; high-speed films have high numbers **2** a system of standard plugs, sockets, etc formerly used for interconnecting domestic audio and video equipment [c20 from G *D(eutsche) I(ndustrie) N(ormen)* German Industry Standards]

dinar ('diːnɑː) *n* the standard monetary unit of Algeria, Bahrain, Iraq, Jordan, Kuwait, Libya, Serbia, Sudan, and Tunisia [c17 from Ar., from LGk *dēnarion*, from L *dēnārius* DENARIUS]

d'Indy (*French* dɛ̃di) *n* (**Paul Marie Theodore**) **Vincent** 1851–1931, French composer. His works include operas, chamber music, and the *Symphony on a French Mountaineer's Song* (1866)

dine (daɪn) *vb* **dines, dining, dined 1** (*intr*) to eat dinner **2** (*intr; often foll by on, off, or upon*) to make one's meal (of): *the guests dined upon roast beef* **3** (*tr*) *inf* to entertain to dinner (esp in **wine and dine someone**) [c13 from OF *disner*, from Vulgar L *disjējūnāre* (unattested), from *dis-* not + LL *jējūnāre* to fast]

dine out *vb* (*intr, adv*) **1** to dine away from home **2** (*foll by on*) to have dinner at the expense of someone else mainly for the sake of one's conversation about (a subject or story)

diner ('daɪnə) *n* **1** a person eating a meal, esp in a restaurant **2** *chiefly US & Canad* a small cheap restaurant **3** a fashionable bar, or a section of one, where food is served

Dinesen ('dɪnɪsᵊn) *n* **Isak** ('aɪzək), pen name of *Baroness Karen Blixen*. 1885–1962, Danish author of short stories in Danish and English, including *Seven Gothic Tales* (1934) and *Winter's Tales* (1942). Her life story was told in the film *Out of Africa* (1986)

dinette (daɪ'nɛt) *n* an alcove or small area for use as a dining room

ding (dɪŋ) *vb* **1** to ring, esp with tedious repetition **2** (*tr*) another word for **din** (sense 2) ▷ *n* **3** an imitation of the sound of a bell [c13 prob. imit., but infl. by DIN + RING²]

dingbat ('dɪŋˌbæt) *n Austral sl* a crazy or stupid person

dingbats ('dɪŋˌbæts) *pl n Austral & NZ sl* an attack of nervousness, irritation, or loathing: *he had the dingbats*

ding-dong *n* **1** the sound of a bell or bells **2** an imitation of the sound of a bell **3a** a violent exchange of blows or words **3b** (*as modifier*): *a ding-dong battle* ▷ *adj* **4** sounding or ringing repeatedly [c16 imit.; see DING]

dinges ('dɪŋəs) *n S African inf* a jocular word for something whose name is unknown or forgotten; thingumabob [from Afrik., from Du. *dinges* thing]

dinghy ('dɪŋɪ, 'dɪŋgɪ) *n, pl* **dinghies** any small boat, powered by sail, oars, or outboard motor. Also(esp formerly): **dingy, dingey** [c19 from Hindi or Bengali *dingi*]

dingle ('dɪŋgᵊl) *n* a small wooded dell [c13 from ?]

dingo ('dɪŋgəʊ) *n, pl* **dingoes** a wild dog of Australia, having a yellowish-brown coat and resembling a wolf [c18 from Abor.]

dingy ('dɪndʒɪ) *adj* **dingier, dingiest 1** lacking light or brightness; drab **2** dirty; discoloured [c18 perhaps from an earlier dialect word rel. to OE *dynge* dung] > '**dingily** *adv* > '**dinginess** *n*

dining car *n* a railway coach in which meals are served at tables. Also called: **restaurant car**

dining room *n* a room where meals are eaten

dinitrogen oxide (daɪ'naɪtrədʒən) *n* the systematic name for **nitrous oxide**

dinkie ('dɪŋkɪ) *n* **1** an affluent married childless person ▷ *adj* **2** designed for or appealing to dinkies [c20 from *d(ouble) i(ncome) n(o) k(ids)* + -IE]

dinkum ('dɪŋkəm) *adj Austral & NZ inf* **1** genuine or right: *he made us a fair dinkum offer* **2 dinkum oil** the truth [c19 from E dialect: work, from ?]

dinky ('dɪŋkɪ) *adj* **dinkier, dinkiest** *inf* **1** *Brit* small and neat; dainty **2** *US* inconsequential; insignificant [c18 from Scot. & N English dialect *dink* neat, neatly dressed]

dinky-di ('dɪŋkɪ'daɪ) *adj Austral inf* typical: *dinky-di Pom idleness* [c20 var. of DINKUM]

dinner ('dɪnə) *n* **1** a meal taken in the evening **2** a meal taken at midday, esp when it is the main meal of the day; lunch **3** a formal meal or banquet in honour of someone or something **4** (*as modifier*): *dinner table; dinner hour* [c13 from OF *disner*; see DINE]

dinner dance *n* a formal dinner followed by dancing

dinner jacket *n* a man's semiformal evening jacket without tails, usually black. US and Canad name: **tuxedo**

dinner service *n* a set of matching plates, dishes, etc, suitable for serving a meal

Dinnigan ('dɪnɪgən) *n* **Collette** born 1966, Australian fashion designer

dinosaur ('daɪnəˌsɔː) *n* **1** any of a large order of extinct reptiles many of which were of gigantic size and abundant in the Mesozoic era **2** a person or thing that is considered to be out of date [c19 from NL *dinosaurus*, from Gk *deinos* fearful + *sauros* lizard] > ˌ**dino'saurian** *adj*

dint (dɪnt) *n* **1 by dint of** by means or use of: *by dint of hard work* **2** *arch* a blow or a mark made by a blow ▷ *vb* **3** (*tr*) to mark with dints [OE *dynt*]

Dio Cassius ('daɪəʊ 'kæsɪəs) *n* ?155–?230 AD, Roman historian. His *History of Rome* covers the period of Rome's transition from Republic to Empire

diocesan (daɪ'ɒsɪsᵊn) *adj* **1** of or relating to a diocese ▷ *n* **2** the bishop of a diocese

diocese ('daɪəsɪs) *n* the district under the jurisdiction of a bishop [c14 from OF, from LL *diocēsis*, from Gk *dioikēsis* administration, from *dioikein* to manage a household, from *oikos* house]

Dio Chrysostom (*Greek* 'diːo 'krizəstəm) *n* 2nd century AD, Greek orator and philosopher

Diocletian (ˌdaɪə'kliːʃən) *n* full name *Gaius Aurelius Valerius Diocletianus*. 245–313 AD, Roman emperor (284–305), who divided the empire into four administrative units (293) and instigated the last severe persecution of the Christians (303)

diode ('daɪəʊd) *n* **1** a semiconductor device used in circuits for converting alternating current to direct current **2** the earliest type of electronic valve having two electrodes between which a current can flow only in one direction [c20 from DI-¹ + -ODE²]

dioecious (daɪ'iːʃəs) *adj* (of plants) having the male and female reproductive organs on separate plants [c18 from NL *Dioecia* name of class, from DI-¹ + Gk *oikia* house]

Diogenes (daɪ'ɒdʒɪˌniːz) *n* ?412–?323 BC, Greek Cynic philosopher, who rejected social conventions and advocated self-sufficiency and simplicity of life

Diomede Islands ('daɪəˌmiːd) *pl n* two small islands in the Bering Strait, separated by the international date line and by the boundary line between the US and Russia

Diomedes (ˌdaɪə'miːdiːz), **Diomede,** *or* **Diomed** ('daɪəˌmɛd) *n Greek myth* a king of Argos, and suitor of Helen, who fought with the Greeks at Troy

Dionysian (ˌdaɪə'nɪzɪən) *adj* **1** of or relating to Dionysus **2** (*often not cap*) wild or orgiastic

Dionysius (ˌdaɪə'nɪsɪəs) *n* called *the Elder*. ?430–367 BC, tyrant of Syracuse (405–367), noted for his successful campaigns against Carthage and S Italy

Dionysus *or* **Dionysos** (ˌdaɪə'naɪsəs) *n* the Greek god of wine, fruitfulness, and vegetation, worshipped in orgiastic rites. He was also known as the bestower of ecstasy and god of the drama, and identified with Bacchus

Diophantine equation (ˌdaɪəʊ'fæntaɪn) *n* (in number theory) an equation in more than one variable, for

which integral solutions are sought [from DIOPHANTUS]
Diophantus (ˌdaɪəʊˈfæntəs) *n* 3rd century AD, Greek mathematician, noted for his treatise on the theory of numbers, *Arithmetica*
dioptre *or US* **diopter** (daɪˈɒptə) *n* a unit for measuring the refractive power of a lens: the reciprocal of the focal length of the lens expressed in metres [c16 from L *dioptra* optical instrument, from Gk, from *dia-* through + *opsesthai* to see] > **diˈoptral** *adj*
dioptrics (daɪˈɒptrɪks) *n (functioning as sing)* the branch of geometrical optics concerned with the formation of images by lenses [c20 from DIOPTRE + -ICS]
Dior (diːˈɔː; *French* djɔr) *n* **Christian** (ˈkrɪstʃən; *French* kristjɑ̃) 1905–57, French couturier, noted for his New Look of narrow waist with a long full skirt (1947); he also created the waistless sack dress
diorama (ˌdaɪəˈrɑːmə) *n* **1** a miniature three-dimensional scene, in which models of figures are seen against a background **2** a picture made up of illuminated translucent curtains, viewed through an aperture **3** a museum display, as of an animal, of a specimen in its natural setting [c19 from F, from Gk *dia-* through + *horama* view, from *horan* to see] > **dioramic** (ˌdaɪəˈræmɪk) *adj*
dioxide (daɪˈɒksaɪd) *n* any oxide containing two oxygen atoms per molecule, both of which are bonded to an atom of another element
dioxin (daɪˈɒksɪn) *n* any of various chemical by-products of the manufacture of certain herbicides and bactericides, esp the extremely toxic tetrachlorodibenzoparadioxin (TCDD)
dip (dɪp) *vb* **dips, dipping, dipped** **1** to plunge or be plunged quickly or briefly into a liquid, esp to wet or coat **2** *(intr)* to undergo a slight decline, esp temporarily: *sales dipped in November* **3** *(intr)* to slope downwards **4** *(intr)* to sink quickly **5** *(tr)* to switch (car headlights) from the main to the lower beam. US and Canad word: **dim** **6** *(tr)* **6a** to immerse (sheep, etc) briefly in a chemical to rid them of or prevent infestation by insects, etc **6b** to immerse (grain, vegetables, or wood) in a preservative liquid **7** *(tr)* to dye by immersing in a liquid **8** *(tr)* to baptize (someone) by immersion **9** *(tr)* to plate or galvanize (a metal, etc) by immersion in an electrolyte or electrolytic cell **10** *(tr)* to scoop up a liquid or something from a liquid in the hands or in a container **11** to lower or be lowered briefly **12** *(tr)* to make (a candle) by plunging the wick into melted wax **13** *(intr)* to plunge a container, the hands, etc, into something, esp to obtain an object **14** *(intr)* (of an aircraft) to drop suddenly and then regain height ▷ *n* **15** the act of dipping or state of being dipped **16** a brief swim in water **17a** any liquid chemical in which sheep, etc are dipped **17b** any liquid preservative into which objects are dipped **18** a dye into which fabric is immersed **19** a depression, esp in a landscape **20** something taken up by dipping **21** a container used for dipping; dipper **22** a momentary sinking down **23** the angle of slope of rock strata, etc, from the horizontal plane **24** the angle between the direction of the earth's magnetic field and the plane of the horizon; the angle that a magnetic needle free to swing in a vertical plane makes with the horizontal **25** a creamy savoury mixture into which pieces of food are dipped before being eaten **26** *surveying* the angular distance of the horizon below the plane of observation **27** a candle made by plunging a wick into wax **28** a momentary loss of altitude when flying ▷ See also **dip into** [OE *dyppan*]
dip. *or* **Dip.** *abbrev for* diploma
DipAD *abbrev for* Diploma in Art and Design
DipEd (in Britain) *abbrev for* Diploma in Education
diphtheria (dɪpˈθɪərɪə) *n* an acute contagious disease caused by a bacillus, producing fever, severe prostration, and difficulty in breathing and swallowing as the result of swelling of the throat and the formation of a false membrane [c19 NL, from F *diphthérie*, from Gk *diphthera* leather; from the nature of the membrane] > **diphˈtherial, diphtheritic** (ˌdɪpθəˈrɪtɪk), *or* **diphtheric** (dɪpˈθɛrɪk) *adj*
diphthong (ˈdɪfθɒŋ) *n* **1** a vowel sound, occupying a single syllable, during the articulation of which the tongue moves continuously from one position to another, as in the pronunciation of *a* in *late* **2** a digraph or ligature representing a composite vowel such as this, as *ae* in *Caesar* [c15 from LL *diphthongus*, from Gk *diphthongos*, from DI-[1] + *phthongos* sound] > **diphˈthongal** *adj*
diphthongize *or* **diphthongise** (ˈdɪfθɒŋˌaɪz) *vb* **diphthongizes, diphthongizing, diphthongized** *or* **diphthongises, diphthongising, diphthongised** *(often passive)* to make (a simple vowel) into a diphthong > ˌ**diphthongiˈzation** *or* ˌ**diphthongiˈsation** *n*
dip into *vb (intr, prep)* **1** to draw upon: *he dipped into his savings* **2** to dabble (in); play at **3** to read passages at random from (a book, newspaper, etc)
diplodocus (ˌdɪpləʊˈdəʊkəs, dɪˈplɒdəkəs) *n, pl* **diplodocuses** a herbivorous dinosaur characterized by a very long neck and tail and a total body length of 27 metres [c19 from NL, from Gk *diplo-*, (from *diploos*, from DI-[1] + *-ploos* -fold)+ *dokos* beam]
diploid (ˈdɪplɔɪd) *adj* **1** *biol* (of cells or organisms) having pairs of homologous chromosomes so that twice the haploid number is present **2** double or twofold ▷ *n* **3** a diploid cell or organism > **dipˈloidic** *adj*
diploma (dɪˈpləʊmə) *n* **1** a document conferring a qualification, recording success in examinations or successful completion of a course of study **2** an official document that confers an honour or privilege [c17 from L: official letter or document, lit.: letter folded double, from Gk]
diplomacy (dɪˈpləʊməsɪ) *n, pl* **diplomacies** **1** the conduct of the relations of one state with another by peaceful means **2** skill in the management of international relations **3** tact, skill, or cunning in dealing with people [c18 from F *diplomatie*, from *diplomatique* DIPLOMATIC]
diplomat (ˈdɪpləˌmæt) *n* **1** an official such as an ambassador, engaged in diplomacy **2** a person who deals with people tactfully or skilfully ▷ Also called: **diplomatist** (dɪˈpləʊmətɪst)
diplomatic (ˌdɪpləˈmætɪk) *adj* **1** of or relating to diplomacy or diplomats **2** skilled in negotiating, esp between states or people **3** tactful in dealing with people [c18 from F *diplomatique* concerning the documents of diplomacy, from NL *diplōmaticus*; see DIPLOMA] > ˌ**diploˈmatically** *adv*
diplomatic bag *n* a container or bag in which official mail is sent, free from customs inspection, to and from an embassy or consulate
diplomatic corps *or* **body** *n* the entire body of diplomats accredited to a given state
diplomatic immunity *n* the immunity from local jurisdiction and exemption from taxation in the country to which they are accredited afforded to diplomats
Diplomatic Service *n* **1** (in Britain) the division of the Civil Service which provides diplomats to represent the UK abroad **2** *(not caps.)* the equivalent institution of any other country
dipole (ˈdaɪˌpəʊl) *n* **1** two equal but opposite electric charges or magnetic poles separated by a small distance **2** a molecule in which the centre of positive charge does not coincide with the centre of negative charge **3** a directional aerial consisting of two metal rods with a connecting wire fixed between them in the form of a T > **diˈpolar** *adj*
dipole moment *n chem* a measure of the polarity in a

Dd

chemical bond or molecule, equal to the product of one charge and the distance between the charges. Symbol: μ

dipper ('dɪpə) *n* **1** a ladle used for dipping **2** Also called: **water ouzel** any of a genus of aquatic songbirds that inhabit fast-flowing streams **3** a person or thing that dips **4** *arch* an Anabaptist ▷ See also **big dipper**

dippy ('dɪpɪ) *adj* **dippier, dippiest** *sl* odd, eccentric, or crazy [c20 from ?]

diprotodon (daɪ'prəʊtəʊˌdɒn) *n* a large extinct marsupial of the Australian genus *Diprotodon* [c19 from Greek from DI-[1] + PROTO- + -ODONT, from its two prominent lower incisors]

dipsomania (ˌdɪpsəʊ'meɪnɪə) *n* a compulsive desire to drink alcoholic beverages [c19 NL, from Gk *dipsa* thirst + -MANIA] > ˌ**dipso'maniac** *n, adj*

dipstick ('dɪpˌstɪk) *n* **1** a graduated rod or strip dipped into a container to indicate the fluid level **2** *Brit sl* a fool

dip switch *n* a device for dipping car headlights

dipteran ('dɪptərən) *or* **dipteron** ('dɪptəˌrɒn) *n* **1** any dipterous insect ▷ *adj* **2** another word for **dipterous** (sense 1)

dipterous ('dɪptərəs) *adj* **1** Also: **dipteran** of a large order of insects having a single pair of wings and sucking or piercing mouthparts. The group includes flies, mosquitoes, and midges **2** *bot* having two winglike parts [c18 from Gk *dipteros* two-winged]

diptych ('dɪptɪk) *n* **1** a pair of hinged wooden tablets with waxed surfaces for writing **2** a painting or carving on two hinged panels [c17 from Gk *diptukhos* folded together, from DI-[1] + *ptukhos* fold]

Dirac (dɪ'ræk) *n* **Paul Adrien Maurice** 1902–84, English physicist, noted for his work on the application of relativity to quantum mechanics and his prediction of electron spin and the positron: shared the Nobel prize for physics 1933

dire ('daɪə) *adj* (*usually prenominal*) **1** Also: **direful** disastrous; fearful **2** desperate; urgent: *a dire need* **3** foreboding disaster; ominous [c16 from L *dīrus* ominous] > '**direly** *adv* > '**direness** *n*

direct (dɪ'rɛkt, daɪ-) *vb* (*mainly tr*) **1** to conduct or control the affairs of **2** (*also intr*) to give commands or orders with authority to (a person or group) **3** to tell or show (someone) the way to a place **4** to aim, point, or cause to move towards a goal **5** to address (a letter, etc) **6** to address (remarks, etc) **7** (*also intr*) **7a** to provide guidance to (actors, cameramen, etc) in a play or film **7b** to supervise the making or staging of (a film or play) **8** (*also intr*) to conduct (a piece of music or musicians), usually while performing oneself ▷ *adj* **9** without delay or evasion; straightforward **10** without turning aside; shortest; straight: *a direct route* **11** without intervening persons or agencies: *a direct link* **12** honest; frank **13** (*usually prenominal*) precise; exact: *a direct quotation* **14** diametrical: *the direct opposite* **15** in an unbroken line of descent: *a direct descendant* **16** (of government, decisions, etc) by or from the electorate rather than through representatives **17** *logic, maths* (of a proof) progressing from the premises to the conclusion, rather than eliminating the possibility of the falsehood of the conclusion ▷ Cf **indirect proof** **18** *astron* moving from west to east ▷ Cf **retrograde** **19** of or relating to direct current **20** *music* (of an interval or chord) in root position; not inverted ▷ *adv* **21** directly; straight [c14 from L *dīrectus*, from *dīrigere* to guide, from *dis-* apart + *regere* to rule] > **di'rectness** *n*

direct access *n* a method of reading data from a computer file without reading through the file from the beginning

direct action *n* action such as strikes or civil disobedience employed to obtain demands from an employer, government, etc

direct current *n* a continuous electric current that flows in one direction only

direct debit *n* an order given to a bank or building society by a holder of an account, instructing it to pay to a specified person or organization any sum demanded by that person or organization ▷ Cf **standing order**

direct-grant school *n* (in Britain, formerly) a school financed by endowment, fees, and a state grant conditional upon admittance of a percentage of nonpaying pupils

direction (dɪ'rɛkʃən, daɪ-) *n* **1** the act of directing or the state of being directed **2** management, control, or guidance **3** the work of a stage or film director **4** the course or line along which a person or thing moves, points, or lies **5** the place towards which a person or thing is directed **6** a line of action; course **7** the name and address on a letter, parcel, etc **8** *music* the process of conducting an orchestra, choir, etc **9** *music* an instruction to indicate tempo, dynamics, mood, etc

directional (dɪ'rɛkʃənᵊl, daɪ-) *adj* **1** of or relating to a spatial direction **2** *electronics* **2a** having or relating to an increased sensitivity to radio waves, nuclear particles, etc, coming from a particular direction **2b** (of an aerial) transmitting or receiving radio waves more effectively in some directions than in others **3** *physics, electronics* concentrated in, following, or producing motion in a particular direction > **diˌrection'ality** *n*

directional drilling *n* a method of drilling for oil in which the well is not drilled vertically, as when a number of wells are to be drilled from a single platform. Also called: **deviated drilling**

direction finder *n* a device to determine the direction of incoming radio signals, used esp as a navigation aid

directions (dɪ'rɛkʃənz, daɪ-) *pl n* (*sometimes sing*) instructions for doing something or for reaching a place

directive (dɪ'rɛktɪv, daɪ-) *n* **1** an instruction; order ▷ *adj* **2** tending to direct; directing **3** indicating direction

directly (dɪ'rɛktlɪ, daɪ-) *adv* **1** in a direct manner **2** at once; without delay **3** (foll by *before* or *after*) immediately; just ▷ *conj* **4** (*subordinating*) as soon as

direct marketing *n* selling goods directly to consumers rather than through retailers, as by mail order, telephone selling, the Internet, or television home-shopping channels. Also called: **direct selling**

direct object *n grammar* a noun, pronoun, or noun phrase whose referent receives the direct action of a verb. For example, *a book* in *They bought Anne a book*

directoire (dɪ'rɛktwɑː) *adj* (of ladies' knickers) knee-length, with elastic at waist and knees [c19 after fashions of the period of the French *Directoire* Directorate (1795–99)]

director (dɪ'rɛktə, daɪ-) *n* **1** a person or thing that directs, controls, or regulates **2** a member of the governing board of a business concern **3** a person who directs the affairs of an institution, trust, etc **4** the person responsible for the artistic and technical aspects of the making of a film or television programme or the staging of a play ▷ Cf **producer** (sense 3) **5** *music* another word(esp US) for **conductor** > ˌ**direc'torial** *adj* > ˌ**di'rectorˌship** *n* > **di'rectress** *fem n*

directorate (dɪ'rɛktərɪt, daɪ-) *n* **1** a board of directors **2** Also: **directorship** the position of director

director-general *n, pl* **directors-general** the head of a large organization such as the CBI or BBC

Director of Public Prosecutions *n* (in Britain) an official who, as head of the Crown Prosecution Service, is responsible for conducting all criminal prosecutions initiated by the police. Abbrev: **DPP**

director's chair *n* a light wooden folding chair with arm rests and a canvas seat and back, as used by film directors

directory (dɪ'rɛktərɪ, -trɪ; daɪ-) *n, pl* **directories** **1** a book listing names, addresses, telephone numbers, etc, of individuals or firms **2** a book giving directions **3** a book containing the rules to be observed in the forms of worship used in churches **4** a directorate **5** *computing* an area of a disk, Winchester disk, or floppy disk that contains the names and locations of files currently held on that disk ▷ *adj* **6** directing

Directory (dɪˈrɛktərɪ, -trɪ; daɪ-) *n* **the** *history* the body of five directors in power in France from 1795 until their overthrow by Napoleon in 1799. Also called: **French Directory**

direct primary *n US government* a primary in which voters directly select the candidates who will run for office

direct selling *n* another name for **direct marketing**

direct speech *or esp US* **direct discourse** *n* the reporting of what someone has said or written by quoting his or her exact words

direct tax *n* a tax paid by the person or organization on which it is levied

dirge (dɜːdʒ) *n* **1** a chant of lamentation for the dead **2** the funeral service in its solemn or sung forms **3** any mourning song or melody [c13 from L *dīrigē* direct (imperative), opening word of antiphon used in the office of the dead] > **ˈdirgeful** *adj*

dirham (ˈdɪəræm) *n* **1** the standard monetary unit of Morocco and the United Arab Emirates **2** a monetary unit of Kuwait, Libya, Qatar, and Tunisia **3** any of various N African coins [c18 from Ar., from L: DRACHMA]

dirigible (ˈdɪrɪdʒɪbᵊl) *adj* **1** able to be steered or directed ▷ *n* **2** another name for **airship** [c16 from L *dīrigere* to DIRECT] > **ˌdirigiˈbility** *n*

dirigisme (diːriːˈʒiːzəm) *n* control by the state of economic and social matters [c20 from F] > **diriˈgiste** *adj*

dirk (dɜːk) *n* **1** a dagger, esp as formerly worn by Scottish Highlanders ▷ *vb* **2** (*tr*) to stab with a dirk [c16 from Scot. *durk*, ?from G *Dolch* dagger]

dirndl (ˈdɜːndᵊl) *n* **1** a woman's dress with a full gathered skirt and fitted bodice; originating from Tyrolean peasant wear **2** a gathered skirt of this kind [G (Bavarian and Austrian): from *Dirndlkleid*, from *Dirndl* little girl + *Kleid* dress]

dirt (dɜːt) *n* **1** any unclean substance, such as mud, etc; filth **2** loose earth; soil **3a** packed earth, gravel, cinders, etc, used to make a racetrack **3b** (*as modifier*): *a dirt track* **4** *mining* the gravel or soil from which minerals are extracted **5** a person or thing regarded as worthless **6** obscene or indecent speech or writing **7** *sl* gossip; scandalous information **8** moral corruption **9 do (someone) dirt** *sl* to do something vicious to (someone) **10 eat dirt** *sl* to accept insult without complaining [c13 from ON *drit* excrement]

dirt bike *n* a type of motorbike designed for use over rough ground

dirt-cheap *adj, adv inf* at an extremely low price

dirt road *n Austral & NZ* a road without shingle or any form of sealing

dirty (ˈdɜːtɪ) *adj* **dirtier, dirtiest 1** covered or marked with dirt; filthy **2a** obscene: *dirty books* **2b** sexually clandestine: *a dirty weekend* **3** causing one to become grimy: *a dirty job* **4** (of a colour) not clear and bright **5** unfair; dishonest **6** mean; nasty: *a dirty cheat* **7** scandalous; unkind **8** revealing dislike or anger **9** (of weather) rainy or squally; stormy **10 dirty linen** *inf* intimate secrets, esp those that might give rise to gossip **11 dirty work** unpleasant or illicit activity ▷ *n* **12 do the dirty on** *inf* to behave meanly towards ▷ *vb* **dirties, dirtying, dirtied 13** to make or become dirty; stain; soil > **ˈdirtily** *adv* > **ˈdirtiness** *n*

dirty bomb *n inf* a bomb made from nuclear waste combined with conventional explosives that is capable of spreading radioactive material over a very wide area

dis (dɪs) *vb* a variant spelling of **diss**

Dis (dɪs) *n* **1** Also called: **Orcus, Pluto** the Roman god of the underworld **2** the abode of the dead; underworld ▷ Greek equivalent: **Hades**

dis-¹ *prefix* **1** indicating reversal: *disconnect* **2** indicating negation, lack, or deprivation: *dissimilar; disgrace* **3** indicating removal or release: *disembowel* **4** expressing intensive force: *dissever* [from L *dis-* apart; in some cases, via OF *des-*. In compound words of L origin, *dis-* becomes *dif-* before *f*, and *di-* before some consonants]

dis-² *combining form* a variant of **di-¹** before *s*: *dissyllable*

disability (ˌdɪsəˈbɪlɪtɪ) *n, pl* **disabilities 1** the condition of being physically or mentally impaired **2** something that disables; handicap **3** lack of necessary intelligence, strength, etc **4** an incapacity in the eyes of the law to enter into certain transactions

▷ www.disabilityworld.org

disable (dɪsˈeɪbᵊl) *vb* **disables, disabling, disabled** (*tr*) **1** to make ineffective, unfit, or incapable, as by crippling **2** to make or pronounce legally incapable **3** to switch off (an electronic device) > **disˈablement** *n*

disabled (dɪˈseɪbᵊld) *adj* **a** lacking one or more physical powers, such as the ability to walk or to coordinate one's movements **b** (*as collective n*; preceded by *the*): *the disabled*. See usage note below.

> **USAGE** The use of *the disabled, the blind*, etc can be offensive, and should be avoided. Instead you should talk about *disabled people, blind people*, etc. An acceptable alternative to the word *disabled* is *differently abled*

disabled list *n* the US term for **injury list**

disabuse (ˌdɪsəˈbjuːz) *vb* **disabuses, disabusing, disabused** (*tr*; usually foll by *of*) to rid of a mistaken idea; set right

disadvantage (ˌdɪsədˈvɑːntɪdʒ) *n* **1** an unfavourable circumstance, thing, person, etc **2** injury, loss, or detriment **3** an unfavourable situation(esp in **at a disadvantage**) ▷ *vb* **disadvantages, disadvantaging, disadvantaged 4** (*tr*) to put at a disadvantage; handicap

disadvantaged (ˌdɪsədˈvɑːntɪdʒd) *adj* socially or economically deprived or discriminated against

disadvantageous (ˌdɪsædvɑːnˈteɪdʒəs, dɪsˌædvənˈteɪdʒəs) *adj* unfavourable; detrimental > **ˌdisadvanˈtageously** *adv* > **ˌdisadvanˈtageousness** *n*

disaffect (ˌdɪsəˈfɛkt) *vb* (*tr; often passive*) to cause to lose loyalty or affection; alienate > **ˌdisafˈfectedly** *adv*

disaffection (ˌdɪsəˈfɛkʃən) *n* a state of dissatisfaction or alienation: *the growing disaffection between players*

disaffiliate (ˌdɪsəˈfɪlɪˌeɪt) *vb* **disaffiliates, disaffiliating, disaffiliated** to sever an affiliation (with) > **ˌdisafˌfiliˈation** *n*

disafforest (ˌdɪsəˈfɒrɪst) *vb* (*tr*) *law* to reduce (land) from the status of a forest to the state of ordinary ground > **ˌdisafˌforesˈtation** *n*

disaggregate (dɪsˈægrɪˌgeɪt) *vb* **disaggregates, disaggregating, disaggregated 1** to separate from a group or mass **2** to divide into parts > **ˌdisaggreˈgation** *n*

disagree (ˌdɪsəˈgriː) *vb* **disagrees, disagreeing, disagreed** (*intr*; often foll by *with*) **1** to dissent in opinion or dispute (about an idea, fact, etc) **2** to fail to correspond; conflict **3** to be unacceptable (to) or unfavourable (for): *curry disagrees with me* **4** to be opposed (to)

disagreeable (ˌdɪsəˈgrɪəbᵊl) *adj* **1** not likable; bad-tempered, esp disobliging, etc **2** not to one's liking; unpleasant > **ˌdisaˈgreeableness** *n* > **ˌdisaˈgreeably** *adv*

disagreement (ˌdɪsəˈgriːmənt) *n* **1** refusal or failure to agree **2** a failure to correspond **3** an argument or dispute

disallow (ˌdɪsəˈlaʊ) *vb* (*tr*) **1** to reject as untrue or invalid **2** to cancel > **ˌdisalˈlowable** *adj* > **ˌdisalˈlowance** *n*

disappear (ˌdɪsəˈpɪə) *vb* **1** (*intr*) to cease to be visible; vanish **2** (*intr*) to go away or become lost, esp without explanation **3** (*intr*) to cease to exist; become extinct or lost **4** (*tr*)(esp in South and Central America) to arrest secretly and presumably imprison or kill (a member of an opposing political group) > **ˌdisapˈpearance** *n*

disapplication (ˌdɪsæplɪˈkeɪʃən) *n Brit education* a provision for exempting schools or individuals from the

Dd

requirements of the National Curriculum in special circumstances
disappoint (ˌdɪsəˈpɔɪnt) *vb* (*tr*) **1** to fail to meet the expectations, hopes, etc of; let down **2** to prevent the fulfilment of (a plan, etc); frustrate [C15 (orig. meaning: to remove from office): from OF *desapointier*; see DIS-[1], APPOINT]
disappointed (ˌdɪsəˈpɔɪntɪd) *adj* saddened by the failure of an expectation, etc > ˌ**disapˈpointedly** *adv*
disappointing (ˌdɪsəˈpɔɪntɪŋ) *adj* failing to meet one's expectations, hopes, desires, or standards > ˌ**disapˈpointingly** *adv*
disappointment (ˌdɪsəˈpɔɪntmənt) *n* **1** a disappointing or being disappointed **2** a person or thing that disappoints
disapprobation (ˌdɪsæprəʊˈbeɪʃən) *n* moral or social disapproval
disapproval (ˌdɪsəˈpruːvəl) *n* the act or a state or feeling of disapproving; censure
disapprove (ˌdɪsəˈpruːv) *vb* **disapproves, disapproving, disapproved 1** (*intr; often foll by* of) to consider wrong, bad, etc **2** (*tr*) to withhold approval from > ˌ**disapˈproving** *adj* > ˌ**disapˈprovingly** *adv*
disarm (dɪsˈɑːm) *vb* **1** (*tr*) to remove defensive or offensive capability from (a country, army, etc) **2** (*tr*) to deprive of weapons **3** (*tr*) to win the confidence or affection of **4** (*intr*) (of a nation, etc) to decrease the size and capability of one's armed forces **5** (*intr*) to lay down weapons > **disˈarmer** *n*
disarmament (dɪsˈɑːməmənt) *n* **1** the reduction of fighting capability, as by a nation **2** a disarming or being disarmed
disarming (dɪsˈɑːmɪŋ) *adj* tending to neutralize hostility, suspicion, etc > **disˈarmingly** *adv*
disarrange (ˌdɪsəˈreɪndʒ) *vb* **disarranges, disarranging, disarranged** (*tr*) to throw into disorder > ˌ**disarˈrangement** *n*
disarray (ˌdɪsəˈreɪ) *n* **1** confusion, dismay, and lack of discipline **2** (esp of clothing) disorderliness; untidiness ▷ *vb* (*tr*) **3** to throw into confusion **4** *arch* to undress
disassemble (ˌdɪsəˈsɛmbəl) *vb* **disassembles, disassembling, disassembled** (*tr*) to take apart (a piece of machinery, etc); dismantle
disassembler (ˌdɪsəˈsɛmblə) *n* *computing* a computer program that translates machine code into assembly language
disassociate (ˌdɪsəˈsəʊʃɪˌeɪt, -sɪ-) *vb* **disassociates, disassociating, disassociated** a less common word for **dissociate** > ˌ**disasˌsociˈation** *n*
disaster (dɪˈzɑːstə) *n* **1** an occurrence that causes great distress or destruction **2** a thing, project, etc, that fails or has been ruined [C16 (orig. in the sense: malevolent astral influence): from It. *disastro*, from *dis-* (pejorative) + *astro* star, ult. from Gk *astron*] > **disˈastrous** *adj*
disavow (ˌdɪsəˈvaʊ) *vb* (*tr*) to deny knowledge of, connection with, or responsibility for > ˌ**disaˈvowal** *n* > **disavowedly** (ˌdɪsəˈvaʊɪdlɪ) *adv*
disband (dɪsˈbænd) *vb* to cease to function or cause to stop functioning, as a unit, group, etc > **disˈbandment** *n*
disbar (dɪsˈbɑː) *vb* **disbars, disbarring, disbarred** (*tr*) *law* to deprive of the status of barrister; expel from the Bar > **disˈbarment** *n*

USAGE *Disbar* should only be used when talking about a barrister, and should not be confused with *debar*, in the sense of 'prevent'

disbelief (ˌdɪsbɪˈliːf) *n* refusal or reluctance to believe
disbelieve (ˌdɪsbɪˈliːv) *vb* **disbelieves, disbelieving, disbelieved 1** (*tr*) to reject as false or lying **2** (*intr; usually foll by* in) to have no faith (in) > ˌ**disbeˈliever** *n* > ˌ**disbeˈlieving** *adj*
disbud (dɪsˈbʌd) *or* **debud** (diːˈbʌd) *vb* **disbuds, disbudding, disbudded** *or* **debuds, debudding, debudded 1** to remove superfluous buds from (a plant) **2** *vet science* to remove the horn buds of (calves, lambs, and kids)
disburden (dɪsˈbɜːdən) *vb* **1** to remove a load from **2** (*tr*) to relieve (one's mind, etc) of a distressing worry
disburse (dɪsˈbɜːs) *vb* **disburses, disbursing, disbursed** (*tr*) to pay out [C16 from OF *desborser*, from *des-* DIS-[1] + *borser* to obtain money, from *borse* bag, from LL *bursa*] > **disˈbursable** *adj* > **disˈbursement** *n* > **disˈburser** *n*

USAGE *Disburse* is sometimes wrongly used where *disperse* is meant: *the police used water cannon to disperse* (not *disburse*) *the crowd*

disc (dɪsk) *n* **1** a flat circular plate **2** something resembling this **3** a gramophone record **4** *anat* any approximately circular flat structure in the body, esp an intervertebral disc **5a** the flat receptacle of composite flowers, such as the daisy **5b** (*as a modifier*) a disc floret **6a** Also called: **parking disc** a marker or device for display in a parked vehicle showing the time of arrival or the latest permitted time of departure or both **6b** (*as modifier*): *disc parking* **7** *computing* a variant spelling of **disk** [C18 from L *discus* DISCUS] > **ˈdiscal** *adj*

USAGE See at **disk**

discard *vb* (dɪsˈkɑːd) **1** (*tr*) to get rid of as useless or undesirable **2** *cards* to throw out (a card or cards) from one's hand **3** *cards* to play (a card not of the suit led nor a trump) when unable to follow suit ▷ *n* (ˈdɪskɑːd) **4** a person or thing that has been cast aside **5** *cards* a discarded card **6** the act of discarding
disc brake *n* a type of brake in which two pads rub against a flat disc attached to the wheel hub when the brake is applied
discern (dɪˈsɜːn) *vb* **1** (*tr*) to recognize or perceive clearly **2** to recognize or perceive (differences) [C14 from OF *discerner*, from L *discernere* to divide, from DIS-[1] apart + *cernere* to separate] > **disˈcernible** *adj* > **disˈcernibly** *adv*
discerning (dɪˈsɜːnɪŋ) *adj* having or showing good taste or judgment; discriminating
discernment (dɪˈsɜːnmənt) *n* keen perception or judgment
disc floret *or* **flower** *n* any of the small tubular flowers at the centre of the flower head of certain composite plants, such as the daisy
discharge *vb* (dɪsˈtʃɑːdʒ). **discharges, discharging, discharged 1** (*tr*) to release or allow to go **2** (*tr*) to dismiss from or relieve of duty, employment, etc **3** to fire or be fired, as a gun **4** to pour forth or cause to pour forth: *the boil discharges pus* **5** (*tr*) to remove (the cargo) from (a boat, etc); unload **6** (*tr*) to perform the duties of or meet the demands of (an office, obligation, etc) **7** (*tr*) to relieve (oneself) of (a responsibility, debt, etc) **8** (*intr*) *physics* **8a** to lose or remove electric charge **8b** to form an arc, spark, or corona in a gas **8c** to take or supply electrical current from a cell or battery **9** (*tr*) *law* to release (a prisoner from custody, etc) ▷ *n* (ˈdɪstʃɑːdʒ, dɪsˈtʃɑːdʒ) **10** a person or thing that is discharged **11a** dismissal or release from an office, job, institution, etc **11b** the document certifying such release **12** the fulfilment of an obligation or release from a responsibility or liability **13** the act of removing a load, as of cargo **14** a pouring forth of a fluid; emission **15a** the act of firing a projectile **15b** the volley, bullet, etc, fired **16** *law* **16a** a release, as of a person held under legal restraint **16b** an annulment, as of a court order **17** *physics* **17a** the act or process of removing or losing charge **17b** a conduction of electricity through a gas by the formation and movement of electrons and ions in an applied electric field > **disˈchargeable** *adj* > **disˈcharger** *n*
discharge tube *n* *electronics* an electrical device in which current flow is by electrons and ions in an ionized gas, as in a fluorescent light or neon tube
disc harrow *n* a harrow with sharp-edged discs used to cut clods on the surface of the soil or to cover seed after planting

disciple (dɪˈsaɪpᵊl) *n* **1** a follower of the doctrines of a teacher or a school of thought **2** one of the personal followers of Christ (including his 12 apostles) during his earthly life [OE *discipul*, from L *discipulus* pupil, from *discere* to learn] > **disˈciple,ship** *n* > **discipular** (dɪˈsɪpjʊlə) *adj*

disciplinarian (ˌdɪsɪplɪˈnɛərɪən) *n* a person who imposes or advocates strict discipline

disciplinary (ˈdɪsɪˌplɪnərɪ) *adj* **1** of, promoting, or used for discipline; corrective **2** relating to a branch of learning

discipline (ˈdɪsɪplɪn) *n* **1** training or conditions imposed for the improvement of physical powers, self-control, etc **2** systematic training in obedience **3** the state of improved behaviour, etc, resulting from such training **4** punishment or chastisement **5** a system of rules for behaviour, etc **6** a branch of learning or instruction **7** the laws governing members of a Church ▷ *vb* **disciplines, disciplining, disciplined** (*tr*) **8** to improve or attempt to improve the behaviour, orderliness, etc, of by training, conditions, or rules **9** to punish or correct [c13 from L *disciplīna* teaching, from *discipulus* DISCIPLE] > **ˈdisci,plinable** *adj* > **disciplinal** (ˌdɪsɪˈplaɪnᵊl) *adj* > **ˈdisci,pliner** *n*

disc jockey *n* a person who announces and plays recorded music, esp pop music, on a radio programme, etc

disclaim (dɪsˈkleɪm) *vb* **1** (*tr*) to deny or renounce (any claim, connection, etc) **2** (*tr*) to deny the validity or authority of **3** *law* to renounce or repudiate (a legal claim or right)

disclaimer (dɪsˈkleɪmə) *n* a repudiation or denial

disclose (dɪsˈkləʊz) *vb* **discloses, disclosing, disclosed** (*tr*) **1** to make known **2** to allow to be seen > **disˈcloser** *n*

disclosure (dɪsˈkləʊʒə) *n* **1** something that is disclosed **2** the act of disclosing; revelation

Discman (ˈdɪskmən) *n* *trademark* a small portable CD player with light headphones

disco (ˈdɪskəʊ) *n, pl* **discos** **1a** an occasion at which people dance to pop records **1b** (*as modifier*): *disco music* **2** a nightclub or other public place where such dances are held **3** mobile equipment for providing music for a disco [c20 from DISCOTHEQUE]
▷ www.discomusic.com

discobolus (dɪsˈkɒbələs) *n, pl* **discoboli** (-ˌlaɪ) a discus thrower [c18 from L, from Gk, from *diskos* DISCUS + *-bolos*, from *ballein* to throw]

discography (dɪsˈkɒgrəfɪ) *n* a classified list of gramophone records > **disˈcographer** *n*

discoid (ˈdɪskɔɪd) *adj* also **discoidal** **1** like a disc ▷ *n* **2** a disclike object

discolour *or US* **discolor** (dɪsˈkʌlə) *vb* to change in colour; fade or stain > **dis,colorˈation** *or* **dis,colourˈation** *n*

discombobulate (ˌdɪskəmˈbɒbjʊˌleɪt) *vb* **discombobulates, discombobulating, discombobulated** (*tr*) *inf, chiefly US & Canad* to throw into confusion [c20 prob. a whimsical alteration of DISCOMPOSE or DISCOMFIT]

discomfit (dɪsˈkʌmfɪt) *vb* (*tr*) **1** to make uneasy or confused **2** to frustrate the plans or purpose of **3** *arch* to defeat [c14 from OF *desconfire* to destroy, from *des-* (indicating reversal) + *confire* to make, from L *conficere* to produce] > **disˈcomfiture** *n*

discomfort (dɪsˈkʌmfət) *n* **1** an inconvenience, distress, or mild pain **2** something that disturbs or deprives of ease ▷ *vb* **3** (*tr*) to make uncomfortable or uneasy

discommode (ˌdɪskəˈməʊd) *vb* **discommodes, discommoding, discommoded** (*tr*) to cause inconvenience to; disturb > **ˌdiscomˈmodious** *adj*

discompose (ˌdɪskəmˈpəʊz) *vb* **discomposes, discomposing, discomposed** (*tr*) **1** to disturb the composure of; disconcert **2** *now rare* to disarrange > **ˌdiscomˈposure** *n*

disconcert (ˌdɪskənˈsɜːt) *vb* (*tr*) **1** to disturb the composure of **2** to frustrate or upset > **ˌdisconˈcerted** *adj* > **ˌdisconˈcertion** *n*

disconcerting (ˌdɪskənˈsɜːtɪŋ) *adj* causing a feeling of disturbance, embarrassment, or confusion; perturbing; worrying > **ˌdisconˈcertingly** *adv*

disconformity (ˌdɪskənˈfɔːmɪtɪ) *n, pl* **disconformities** **1** lack of conformity; discrepancy **2** the junction between two parallel series of stratified rocks

disconnect (ˌdɪskəˈnɛkt) *vb* (*tr*) to undo or break the connection of or between (something, as a plug and a socket) > **ˌdisconˈnection** *n*

disconnected (ˌdɪskəˈnɛktɪd) *adj* **1** not rationally connected; confused or incoherent **2** not connected or joined

disconsolate (dɪsˈkɒnsəlɪt) *adj* **1** sad beyond comfort; inconsolable **2** disappointed; dejected [c14 from Med. L *disconsōlātus*, from DIS-¹ + *consōlātus* comforted] > **disˈconsolately** *adv* > **disˈconsolateness** *or* **dis,consoˈlation** *n*

discontent (ˌdɪskənˈtɛnt) *n* **1** Also called: **discontentment** lack of contentment, as with one's condition or lot in life ▷ *vb* **2** (*tr*) to make dissatisfied > **ˌdisconˈtented** *adj* > **ˌdisconˈtentedness** *n*

discontinue (ˌdɪskənˈtɪnjuː) *vb* **discontinues, discontinuing, discontinued** **1** to come or bring to an end; interrupt or be interrupted; stop **2** (*tr*) *law* to terminate or abandon (an action, suit, etc) > **ˌdisconˈtinuance** *n* > **ˌdiscon,tinuˈation** *n*

discontinuity (ˌdɪskɒntɪˈnjuːɪtɪ, dɪsˌkɒntɪ-) *n, pl* **discontinuities** **1** lack of rational connection or cohesion **2** a break or interruption

discontinuous (ˌdɪskənˈtɪnjʊəs) *adj* characterized by interruptions or breaks; intermittent > **ˌdisconˈtinuously** *adv* > **ˌdisconˈtinuousness** *n*

discord *n* (ˈdɪskɔːd) **1** lack of agreement or harmony **2** harsh confused mingling of sounds **3** a combination of musical notes, esp one containing one or more dissonant intervals ▷ *vb* (dɪsˈkɔːd) **4** (*intr*) to disagree; clash [c13 from OF *descort*, from *descorder* to disagree, from L *discordāre*, from *discors* at variance, from DIS-¹ + *cor* heart]

discordant (dɪsˈkɔːdᵊnt) *adj* **1** at variance; disagreeing **2** harsh in sound; inharmonious > **disˈcordance** *n* > **disˈcordantly** *adv*

discotheque (ˈdɪskəˌtɛk) *n* the full term for **disco** [c20 from F *discothèque*, from Gk *diskos* disc + *-o-* + Gk *thēkē* case]

discount *vb* (dɪsˈkaʊnt, ˈdɪskaʊnt). (*mainly tr*) **1** to leave out of account as being unreliable, prejudiced, or irrelevant **2** to anticipate and make allowance for **3a** to deduct (an amount or percentage) from the price, cost, etc **3b** to reduce (the regular price, etc) by a percentage or amount **4** to sell or offer for sale at a reduced price **5** to buy or sell (a bill of exchange, etc) before maturity, with a deduction for interest **6** (*also intr*) to loan money on (a negotiable instrument) with a deduction for interest ▷ *n* (ˈdɪskaʊnt) **7** a deduction from the full amount of a price or debt. See also **cash discount, trade discount** **8** Also called: **discount rate** **8a** the amount of interest deducted in the purchase or sale of or the loan of money on unmatured negotiable instruments **8b** the rate of interest deducted **9** (in the issue of shares) a percentage deducted from the par value to give a reduced amount payable by subscribers **10** a discounting **11** **at a discount** **11a** below the regular price **11b** held in low regard **12** (*modifier*) offering or selling at reduced prices: *a discount shop* > **disˈcountable** *adj* > **ˈdiscounter** *n*

discounted cash flow *n* the cash flow of an organization taking into account the future values of benefits and assets in addition to their present values

discountenance (dɪsˈkaʊntɪnəns) *vb* **discountenances, discountenancing, discountenanced** (*tr*) **1** to make ashamed or confused **2** to disapprove of

Dd

discount house *n* **1** *chiefly Brit* a financial organization engaged in discounting bills of exchange, etc, on a large scale **2** Also called: **discount store** *chiefly US* a shop offering for sale most of its merchandise at prices below the recommended prices

discount market *n* the part of the money market consisting of banks, discount houses, and brokers on which bills are discounted

discourage (dɪsˈkʌrɪdʒ) *vb* **discourages, discouraging, discouraged** (*tr*) **1** to deprive of the will to persist in something **2** to inhibit; prevent: *this solution discourages rust* **3** to oppose by expressing disapproval > **disˈcouragement** *n* > **disˈcouragingly** *adv*

discourse *n* (ˈdɪskɔːs, dɪsˈkɔːs) **1** verbal communication; talk; conversation **2** a formal treatment of a subject in speech or writing **3** a unit of text used by linguists for the analysis of linguistic phenomena that range over more than one sentence **4** *arch* the ability to reason ▷ *vb* (dɪsˈkɔːs), **discourses, discoursing, discoursed** **5** (*intr; often foll by on or upon*) to speak or write (about) formally **6** (*intr*) to hold a discussion **7** (*tr*) *arch* to give forth (music) [C14 from Med. L *discursus* argument, from L: a running to and fro, from *discurrere*, from DIS-[1] + *currere* to run]

discourteous (dɪsˈkɜːtɪəs) *adj* showing bad manners; impolite; rude > **disˈcourteously** *adv* > **disˈcourteousness** *n*

discourtesy (dɪsˈkɜːtɪsɪ) *n, pl* **discourtesies** **1** bad manners; rudeness **2** a rude remark or act

discover (dɪˈskʌvə) *vb* (*tr; may take a clause as object*) **1** to be the first to find or find out about: *Fleming discovered penicillin* **2** to learn about for the first time; realize **3** to find after study or search **4** to reveal or make known > **disˈcoverable** *adj* > **disˈcoverer** *n*

discovery (dɪˈskʌvərɪ) *n, pl* **discoveries** **1** the act, process, or an instance of discovering **2** a person, place, or thing that has been discovered **3** *law* the compulsory disclosure by a party to an action of relevant documents in his possession

discredit (dɪsˈkrɛdɪt) *vb* (*tr*) **1** to damage the reputation of **2** to cause to be disbelieved or distrusted **3** to reject as untrue ▷ *n* **4** something that causes disgrace **5** damage to a reputation **6** lack of belief or confidence

discreditable (dɪsˈkrɛdɪtəbᵊl) *adj* tending to bring discredit; shameful or unworthy

discreet (dɪˈskriːt) *adj* **1** careful to avoid embarrassment, esp by keeping confidences secret; tactful **2** unobtrusive [C14 from OF *discret*, from Med. L *discrētus*, from L *discernere* to DISCERN] > **disˈcreetly** *adv* > **disˈcreetness** *n*

USAGE See at **discrete**

discrepancy (dɪˈskrɛpənsɪ) *n, pl* **discrepancies** a conflict or variation, as between facts, figures, or claims [C15 from L *discrepāns*, from *discrepāre* to differ in sound, from DIS-[1] + *crepāre* to be noisy] > **disˈcrepant** *adj*

discrete (dɪsˈkriːt) *adj* **1** separate or distinct **2** consisting of distinct or separate parts [C14 from L *discrētus* separated; see DISCREET] > **disˈcretely** *adv* > **disˈcreteness** *n*

USAGE This word is quite often used by mistake where *discreet* is intended: *reading is a set of discrete skills; she was discreet* (not *discrete*) *about the affair*

discretion (dɪˈskrɛʃən) *n* **1** the quality of behaving so as to avoid social embarrassment or distress **2** freedom or authority to make judgments and to act as one sees fit(esp in **at one's own discretion, at the discretion of**) **3** **age** *or* **years of discretion** the age at which a person is thought able to manage his or her own affairs

discretionary (dɪˈskrɛʃənərɪ, -ənrɪ) *or* **discretional** *adj* having or using the ability to decide at one's own discretion: *discretionary powers*

discretionary trust *n* a trust in which the beneficiaries' shares are not fixed in the trust deed but are left to the discretion of other persons, often the trustees

discriminate *vb* (dɪˈskrɪmɪˌneɪt). **discriminates, discriminating, discriminated** **1** (*intr; usually foll by in favour of or against*) to single out a particular person, group, etc, for special favour or, esp, disfavour **2** (when *intr*, foll by *between* or *among*) to recognize or understand the difference (between); distinguish **3** (*intr*) to constitute or mark a difference **4** (*intr*) to be discerning in matters of taste ▷ *adj* (dɪˈskrɪmɪnɪt) **5** showing or marked by discrimination [C17 from L *discrīmināre* to divide, from *discrīmen* a separation, from *discernere* to DISCERN] > **disˈcriminately** *adv*

discriminating (dɪˈskrɪmɪˌneɪtɪŋ) *adj* **1** able to see fine distinctions and differences **2** discerning in matters of taste **3** (of a tariff, import duty, etc) levied at differential rates

discrimination (dɪˌskrɪmɪˈneɪʃən) *n* **1** unfair treatment of a person, racial group, minority, etc; action based on prejudice **2** subtle appreciation in matters of taste **3** the ability to see fine distinctions and differences

discriminatory (dɪˈskrɪmɪnətərɪ, -trɪ) *or* **discriminative** (dɪˈskrɪmɪnətɪv) *adj* **1** based on or showing prejudice; biased **2** capable of making fine distinctions

discursive (dɪˈskɜːsɪv) *adj* **1** passing from one topic to another; digressive **2** *philosophy* of or relating to knowledge obtained by reason and argument rather than intuition [C16 from Med. L *discursīvus*, from LL *discursus* DISCOURSE] > **disˈcursively** *adv* > **disˈcursiveness** *n*

discus (ˈdɪskəs) *n, pl* **discuses** *or* **disci** (ˈdɪskaɪ) **1** (originally) a circular stone or plate used in throwing competitions by the ancient Greeks **2** *field sports* a similar disc-shaped object with a heavy middle, thrown by athletes **3** (preceded by *the*) the event or sport of throwing the discus [C17 from L, from Gk *diskos*, from *dikein* to throw]

discuss (dɪˈskʌs) *vb* (*tr*) **1** to have a conversation about; consider by talking over **2** to treat (a subject) in speech or writing [C14 from LL *discussus* examined, from *discutere*, from L: to dash to pieces, from DIS-[1] + *quatere* to shake] > **disˈcussant** *or* **disˈcusser** *n* > **disˈcussible** *or* **disˈcussable** *adj*

discussion (dɪˈskʌʃən) *n* the examination or consideration of a matter in speech or writing

disdain (dɪsˈdeɪn) *n* **1** a feeling or show of superiority and dislike; contempt; scorn ▷ *vb* **2** (*tr; may take an infinitive*) to refuse or reject with disdain [C13 *dedeyne*, from OF *desdeign*, from *desdeigner* to reject as unworthy, from L *dēdignārī*; see DIS-[1], DEIGN] > **disˈdainful** *adj*

disease (dɪˈziːz) *n* **1** any impairment of normal physiological function affecting an organism, esp a change caused by infection, stress, etc, producing characteristic symptoms; illness or sickness in general **2** a corresponding condition in plants **3** any condition likened to this [C14 from OF *desaise*; see DIS-[1], EASE] > **disˈeased** *adj*

diseconomy (ˌdɪsɪˈkɒnəmɪ) *n* *econ* disadvantage, such as lower efficiency or higher costs, resulting from the scale on which an enterprise operates

disembark (ˌdɪsɪmˈbɑːk) *vb* to land or cause to land from a ship, aircraft, etc > **disembarkation** (dɪsˌɛmbɑːˈkeɪʃən) *n*

disembarrass (ˌdɪsɪmˈbærəs) *vb* (*tr*) **1** to free from embarrassment, entanglement, etc **2** to relieve or rid of something burdensome

disembodied (ˌdɪsɪmˈbɒdɪd) *adj* **1** lacking a body or freed from the body **2** lacking in substance or any firm relation to reality

disembody (ˌdɪsɪmˈbɒdɪ) *vb* **disembodies, disembodying, disembodied** (*tr*) to free from the body or from physical form > ˌ**disemˈbodiment** *n*

disembogue (ˌdɪsɪmˈbəʊg) *vb* **disembogues,**

disemboguing, disembogued 1 (of a river, stream, etc) to discharge (water) at the mouth 2 (*intr*) to flow out [C16 from Sp. *desembocar*, from *des-* DIS-[1] + *embocar* to put into the mouth] > ˌdisemˈboguement *n*

disembowel (ˌdɪsɪmˈbaʊəl) *vb* **disembowels, disembowelling, disembowelled** *or US* **disembowels, disemboweling, disemboweled** (*tr*) to remove the entrails of > ˌ**disemˈbowelment** *n*

disempower (ˌdɪsɪmˈpaʊə) *vb* (*tr*) to deprive (a person) of power or authority > ˌ**disemˈpowerment** *n*

disenchant (ˌdɪsɪnˈtʃɑːnt) *vb* (*tr*) to free from or as if from an enchantment; disillusion > ˌ**disenˈchantingly** *adv*

disenchantment (ˌdɪsɪnˈtʃɑːntmənt) *n* a state of disappointment or dissillusionment

disencumber (ˌdɪsɪnˈkʌmbə) *vb* (*tr*) to free from encumbrances > ˌ**disenˈcumberment** *n*

disenfranchise (ˌdɪsɪnˈfræntʃaɪz) *or* **disfranchise** *vb* **disenfranchises, disenfranchising, disenfranchised** *or* **disfranchises, disfranchising, disfranchised** (*tr*) 1 to deprive (a person) of the right to vote or other rights of citizenship 2 to deprive (a place) of the right to send representatives to an elected body 3 to deprive (a person, place, etc) of any franchise or right > **disenfranchisement** (ˌdɪsɪnˈfræntʃɪzmənt) *or* **disˈfranchisement** *n*

disengage (ˌdɪsɪnˈgeɪdʒ) *vb* **disengages, disengaging, disengaged** 1 to release or become released from a connection, obligation, etc 2 *mil* to withdraw (forces) from close action 3 *fencing* to move (one's blade) from one side of an opponent's blade to another in a circular motion > ˌ**disenˈgaged** *adj* > ˌ**disenˈgagement** *n*

disentangle (ˌdɪsɪnˈtæŋgəl) *vb* **disentangles, disentangling, disentangled** 1 to release or become free from entanglement or confusion 2 (*tr*) to unravel or work out > ˌ**disenˈtanglement** *n*

disequilibrium (ˌdɪsiːkwɪˈlɪbrɪəm) *n* a loss or absence of equilibrium, esp in an economy

disestablish (ˌdɪsɪˈstæblɪʃ) *vb* (*tr*) to deprive (a church, custom, institution, etc) of established status > ˌ**disesˈtablishment** *n*

disesteem (ˌdɪsɪˈstiːm) *vb* 1 (*tr*) to think little of ▷ *n* 2 lack of esteem

disfavour *or US* **disfavor** (dɪsˈfeɪvə) *n* 1 disapproval or dislike 2 the state of being disapproved of or disliked 3 an unkind act ▷ *vb* 4 (*tr*) to treat with disapproval or dislike

disfigure (dɪsˈfɪgə) *vb* **disfigures, disfiguring, disfigured** (*tr*) 1 to spoil the appearance or shape of; deface 2 to mar the effect or quality of > **disˈfigurement** *n*

disforest (dɪsˈfɒrɪst) *vb* (*tr*) 1 another word for **deforest** 2 *English law* a less common word for **disafforest** > **disˌforesˈtation** *n*

disfranchise (dɪsˈfræntʃaɪz) *vb* another word for **disenfranchise**

disgorge (dɪsˈgɔːdʒ) *vb* **disgorges, disgorging, disgorged** 1 to throw out (food, etc) from the throat or stomach; vomit 2 to discharge or empty of (contents) 3 (*tr*) to yield up unwillingly > **disˈgorgement** *n*

disgrace (dɪsˈgreɪs) *n* 1 a condition of shame, loss of reputation, or dishonour 2 a shameful person or thing 3 exclusion from confidence or trust: *he is in disgrace with his father* ▷ *vb* **disgraces, disgracing, disgraced** (*tr*) 4 to bring shame upon 5 to treat or cause to be treated with disfavour

disgraceful (dɪsˈgreɪsfʊl) *adj* shameful; scandalous > **disˈgracefully** *adv*

disgruntle (dɪsˈgrʌntəl) *vb* **disgruntles, disgruntling, disgruntled** (*tr*) to make sulky or discontented [C17 DIS-[1] + obs. *gruntle* to complain] > **disˈgruntlement** *n*

disgruntled (dɪsˈgrntəld) *adj* feeling or expressing discontent or anger

disguise (dɪsˈgaɪz) *vb* **disguises, disguising, disguised** 1 to modify the appearance or manner in order to conceal the identity of (someone or something) 2 (*tr*) to misrepresent in order to obscure the actual nature or meaning ▷ *n* 3 a mask, costume, or manner that disguises 4 a disguising or being disguised [C14 from OF *desguisier*, from *des-* DIS-[1] + *guise* manner] > **disˈguised** *adj*

disgust (dɪsˈgʌst) *vb* (*tr*) 1 to sicken or fill with loathing 2 to offend the moral sense of ▷ *n* 3 a great loathing or distaste 4 **in disgust** as a result of disgust [C16 from OF *desgouster*, from *des-* DIS-[1] + *gouster* to taste, from L *gustus* taste] > **disˈgustedly** *adv* > **disˈgustedness** *n*

dish (dɪʃ) *n* 1 a container used for holding or serving food, esp an open shallow container 2 the food in a dish 3 a particular kind of food 4 Also called: **dishful** the amount contained in a dish 5 something resembling a dish 6 a concavity 7 short for **dish aerial**. 8 *inf* an attractive person ▷ *vb* (*tr*) 9 to put into a dish 10 to make concave 11 *Brit inf* to ruin or spoil ▷ See also **dish out, dish up** [OE *disc*, from L *discus* quoit] > **ˈdishˌlike** *adj*

dishabille (ˌdɪsæˈbiːl) *n* a variant of **deshabille**

dish aerial *n* a microwave aerial, used esp in radar, radio telescopes, and satellite broadcasting (**satellite dish aerial**), consisting of a parabolic reflector. Formal name: **parabolic aerial** ▷ Also called: **dish antenna.** Often shortened to **dish**

disharmony (dɪsˈhɑːmənɪ) *n, pl* **disharmonies** 1 lack of accord or harmony 2 a situation, circumstance, etc, that is inharmonious > **disharmonious** (ˌdɪshɑːˈməʊnɪəs) *adj*

dishcloth (ˈdɪʃˌklɒθ) *n* a cloth or rag for washing or drying dishes

dishearten (dɪsˈhɑːtən) *vb* (*tr*) to weaken or destroy the hope, courage, enthusiasm, etc, of > **disˈhearteningly** *adv* > **disˈheartenment** *n*

dished (dɪʃt) *adj* 1 shaped like a dish 2 (of wheels) closer to one another at the bottom than at the top 3 *inf* exhausted or defeated

dishevel (dɪˈʃɛvəl) *vb* **dishevels, dishevelling, dishevelled** *or US* **dishevels, disheveling, disheveled** to disarrange (the hair or clothes) of (someone) [C15 back formation from DISHEVELLED] > **diˈshevelment** *n*

dishevelled *or US* **disheveled** (dɪˈʃɛvəld) *adj* 1 (esp of hair) hanging loosely 2 unkempt; untidy [C15 *dischevelee*, from OF *deschevelé*, from *des-* DIS-[1] + *chevel* hair, from L *capillus*]

dishonest (dɪsˈɒnɪst) *adj* not honest or fair; deceiving or fraudulent > **disˈhonestly** *adv*

dishonesty (dɪsˈɒnɪstɪ) *n, pl* **dishonesties** 1 lack of honesty 2 a deceiving act or statement

dishonour *or US* **dishonor** (dɪsˈɒnə) *vb* (*tr*) 1 to treat with disrespect 2 to fail or refuse to pay (a cheque, etc) 3 to cause the disgrace of (a woman) by seduction or rape ▷ *n* 4 a lack of honour or respect 5 a state of shame or disgrace 6 a person or thing that causes a loss of honour 7 an insult; affront 8 refusal or failure to accept or pay a commercial paper

dishonourable *or US* **dishonorable** (dɪsˈɒnərəbəl) *adj* 1 characterized by or causing dishonour or discredit 2 having little or no integrity; unprincipled > **disˈhonourableness** *or US* **disˈhonorableness** *n* > **disˈhonourably** *or US* **disˈhonorably** *adv*

dish out *vb* (*tr, adv*) 1 *inf* to distribute 2 **dish it out** to inflict punishment

dishtowel (ˈdɪʃˌtaʊəl) *n* another name (*esp Scot, US, & Canad*) for a **tea towel**

dish up *vb* (*adv*) 1 to serve (a meal, food, etc) 2 (*tr*) *inf* to prepare or present, esp in an attractive manner

dishwasher (ˈdɪʃˌwɒʃə) *n* 1 a machine for washing dishes, etc 2 a person who washes dishes, etc

dishwater (ˈdɪʃˌwɔːtə) *n* 1 water in which dishes have been washed 2 something resembling this

dishy (ˈdɪʃɪ) *adj* **dishier, dishiest** *inf, chiefly Brit* good-looking or attractive

disillusion (ˌdɪsɪˈluːʒən) *vb* 1 (*tr*) to destroy the ideals,

Dd

illusions, or false ideas of ▷ *n* also **disillusionment** 2 the act of disillusioning or the state of being disillusioned
disincentive (ˌdɪsɪnˈsɛntɪv) *n* 1 something that acts as a deterrent ▷ *adj* 2 acting as a deterrent: *a disincentive effect on productivity*
disincline (ˌdɪsɪnˈklaɪn) *vb* **disinclines, disinclining, disinclined** to make or be unwilling, reluctant, or averse > **disinclination** (ˌdɪsɪnklɪˈneɪʃən) *n*
disinfect (ˌdɪsɪnˈfɛkt) *vb (tr)* to rid of microorganisms potentially harmful to man, esp by chemical means > **ˌdisinˈfection** *n*
disinfectant (ˌdɪsɪnˈfɛktənt) *n* an agent that destroys or inhibits the activity of microorganisms that cause disease
disinfest (ˌdɪsɪnˈfɛst) *vb (tr)* to rid of vermin > **ˌdisinfesˈtation** *n*
disinflation (ˌdɪsɪnˈfleɪʃən) *n econ* a reduction or stabilization of the general price level intended to improve the balance of payments without incurring reductions in output, employment, etc
disinformation (ˌdɪsɪnfəˈmeɪʃən) *n* false information intended to deceive or mislead
disingenuous (ˌdɪsɪnˈdʒɛnjʊəs) *adj* not sincere; lacking candour > **ˌdisinˈgenuously** *adv* > **ˌdisinˈgenuousness** *n*
disinherit (ˌdɪsɪnˈhɛrɪt) *vb (tr)* 1 *law* to deprive (an heir or next of kin) of inheritance or right to inherit 2 to deprive of a right or heritage > **ˌdisinˈheritance** *n*
disintegrate (dɪsˈɪntɪˌɡreɪt) *vb* **disintegrates, disintegrating, disintegrated** 1 to break or be broken into fragments or parts; shatter 2 to lose or cause to lose cohesion 3 *(intr)* to lose judgment or control 4 *physics* 4a to induce or undergo nuclear fission 4b another word for **decay** (sense 3) > **disˌinteˈgration** *n* > **disˈinteˌgrator** *n*
disinter (ˌdɪsɪnˈtɜː) *vb* **disinters, disinterring, disinterred** *(tr)* 1 to remove or dig up; exhume 2 to bring to light; expose > **ˌdisinˈterment** *n*
disinterest (dɪsˈɪntrɪst, -tərɪst) *n* 1 freedom from bias or involvement 2 lack of interest
disinterested (dɪsˈɪntrɪstɪd, -tərɪs-) *adj* 1 free from bias or partiality; objective 2 not interested > **disˈinterestedly** *adv* > **disˈinterestedness** *n*

> USAGE *Disinterested* is now so commonly used to mean 'not interested' that to avoid ambiguity it is often advisable to replace it by a synonym when the meaning intended is 'impartial, unbiased'. In the Bank of English about 10% of the examples of the word occur followed by *in*, and overall about a third of examples are of this usage

disintermediation (dɪsˌɪntəˌmiːdɪˈeɪʃən) *n finance* the elimination of such financial intermediaries as banks and brokers in transactions between principals, often as a result of deregulation and the use of computing
disinvest (dɪsɪnˈvɛst) *vb econ* 1 (usually foll by *in*) to remove investment (from) 2 *(intr)* to reduce the capital stock of an economy or enterprise, as by not replacing obsolete machinery > **ˌdisinˈvestment** *n*
disjoin (dɪsˈdʒɔɪn) *vb* to disconnect or become disconnected; separate > **disˈjoinable** *adj*
disjoint (dɪsˈdʒɔɪnt) *vb* 1 to take apart or come apart at the joints 2 *(tr)* to disunite or disjoin 3 to dislocate or become dislocated 4 *(tr; usually passive)* to end the unity, sequence, or coherence of
disjointed (dɪsˈdʒɔɪntɪd) *adj* 1 having no coherence; disconnected 2 separated at the joint 3 dislocated > **disˈjointedly** *adv*
disjunct (ˈdɪsdʒʌŋkt) *n logic* one of the propositions in a disjunction
disjunction (dɪsˈdʒʌŋkʃən) *n* 1 Also called: **disjuncture** a disconnecting or being disconnected; separation 2 *logic* 2a the operator that forms a compound sentence from two given sentences and corresponds to the English *or* 2b the relation between such sentences
disjunctive (dɪsˈdʒʌŋktɪv) *adj* 1 serving to disconnect or separate 2 *grammar* denoting a word, esp a conjunction, that serves to express opposition or contrast: *but* in *She was poor but she was honest* 3 *logic* relating to, characterized by, or containing disjunction ▷ *n* 4 *grammar* a disjunctive word, esp a conjunction 5 *logic* a disjunctive proposition > **disˈjunctively** *adv*
disk (dɪsk) *n* 1 a variant spelling (esp US and Canad) of **disc** 2 Also called: **magnetic disk, hard disk** *computing* a direct-access storage device consisting of a stack of plates coated with a magnetic layer, the whole assembly rotating rapidly as a single unit.

> USAGE *Disk* is the preferred US spelling of *disc* in all its senses, and is also the majority spelling in the computer industry

disk drive *n computing* the controller and mechanism for reading and writing data on computer disks
diskette (dɪsˈkɛt) *n* another name for **floppy disk**
disk operating system *n* an operating system used on a computer system with one or more disk drives. Often shortened to: **DOS**
dislike (dɪsˈlaɪk) *vb* **dislikes, disliking, disliked** 1 *(tr)* to consider unpleasant or disagreeable ▷ *n* 2 a feeling of aversion or antipathy > **disˈlikable** *or* **disˈlikeable** *adj*
dislocate (ˈdɪsləˌkeɪt) *vb* **dislocates, dislocating, dislocated** *(tr)* 1 to disrupt or shift out of place 2 to displace from its normal position, esp a bone from its joint
dislocation (ˌdɪsləˈkeɪʃən) *n* 1 a displacing or being displaced 2 the state or condition of being dislocated
dislodge (dɪsˈlɒdʒ) *vb* **dislodges, dislodging, dislodged** to remove from or leave a lodging place, hiding place, or previously fixed position > **disˈlodgment** *or* **disˈlodgement** *n*
disloyal (dɪsˈlɔɪəl) *adj* not loyal or faithful; deserting one's allegiance > **disˈloyally** *adv*
disloyalty (dɪsˈlɔɪəltɪ) *n, pl* **disloyalties** the condition or an instance of being unfaithful or disloyal
dismal (ˈdɪzməl) *adj* 1 causing gloom or depression 2 causing dismay or terror 3 of poor quality or a low standard; feeble [C13 from *dismal* (n) list of 24 unlucky days in the year, from Med. L *diēs malī*, from L *diēs* day + *malus* bad] > **ˈdismally** *adv* > **ˈdismalness** *n*
dismantle (dɪsˈmænt^əl) *vb* **dismantles, dismantling, dismantled** *(tr)* 1 to take apart 2 to demolish or raze 3 to strip of covering [C17 from OF *desmanteler* to remove a cloak from] > **disˈmantlement** *n*
dismast (dɪsˈmɑːst) *vb (tr)* to break off the mast or masts of (a sailing vessel)
dismay (dɪsˈmeɪ) *vb (tr)* 1 to fill with apprehension or alarm 2 to fill with depression or discouragement ▷ *n* 3 consternation or agitation [C13 from OF *desmaiier* (unattested), from *des-* DIS-[1] + *esmayer* to frighten, ult. of Gmc origin] > **disˈmaying** *adj*
dismember (dɪsˈmɛmbə) *vb (tr)* 1 to remove the limbs or members of 2 to cut to pieces 3 to divide or partition (something, such as an empire) > **disˈmemberment** *n*
dismiss (dɪsˈmɪs) *vb (tr)* 1 to remove or discharge from employment or service 2 to send away or allow to go 3 to dispel from one's mind; discard 4 to cease to consider (a subject) 5 to decline further hearing to (a claim or action) 6 *cricket* to bowl out a side for a particular number of runs [C15 from Med. L *dismissus* sent away, from *dīmittere*, from *dī-* DIS-[1] + *mittere* to send] > **disˈmissal** *n* > **disˈmissible** *adj* > **disˈmissive** *adj*
dismount (dɪsˈmaʊnt) *vb* 1 to get off a horse, bicycle, etc 2 *(tr)* to disassemble or remove from a mounting ▷ *n* 3 the act of dismounting
Disney (ˈdɪznɪ) *n* **Walt(er Elias)** 1901–66, US film producer, who pioneered animated cartoons: noted esp for his creations *Mickey Mouse* and *Donald Duck* and films such as *Fantasia* (1940)

Disneyfy (ˈdɪznɪˌfaɪ) *vb* **Disneyfies, Disneyfying, Disneyfied** (*tr*) to transform (historic places, local customs, etc) into trivial entertainment for tourists [c20 from the *Disneyland* amusement park in California] > **ˌDisneyfiˈcation** *n*

disobedience (ˌdɪsəˈbiːdɪəns) *n* lack of obedience

disobedient (ˌdɪsəˈbiːdɪənt) *adj* not obedient; neglecting or refusing to obey > **ˌdisoˈbediently** *adv*

disobey (ˌdɪsəˈbeɪ) *vb* to neglect or refuse to obey (someone, an order, etc) > **ˌdisoˈbeyer** *n*

disoblige (ˌdɪsəˈblaɪdʒ) *vb* **disobliges, disobliging, disobliged** (*tr*) **1** to disregard the desires of **2** to slight; insult **3** *inf* to cause trouble or inconvenience to > **ˌdisoˈbliging** *adj*

disorder (dɪsˈɔːdə) *n* **1** a lack of order; confusion **2** a disturbance of public order **3** an upset of health; ailment **4** a deviation from the normal system or order ▷ *vb* (*tr*) **5** to upset the order of **6** to disturb the health or mind of

disorderly (dɪsˈɔːdəlɪ) *adj* **1** untidy; irregular **2** uncontrolled; unruly **3** *law* violating public peace or order > **disˈorderliness** *n*

disorderly house *n law* an establishment in which unruly behaviour habitually occurs, esp a brothel or a gaming house

disorganize *or* **disorganise** (dɪsˈɔːgəˌnaɪz) *vb* **disorganizes, disorganizing, disorganized** *or* **disorganises, disorganising, disorganised** (*tr*) to disrupt the arrangement, system, or unity of > **disˌorganiˈzation** *or* **disˌorganiˈsation** *n*

disorientate (dɪsˈɔːrɪɛnˌteɪt) *or* **disorient** *vb* **disorientates, disorientating, disorientated** *or* **disorients, disorienting, disoriented** (*tr*) **1** to cause (someone) to lose his or her bearings **2** to perplex; confuse > **disˌorienˈtation** *n*

disown (dɪsˈəʊn) *vb* (*tr*) to deny any connection with; refuse to acknowledge > **disˈowner** *n*

disparage (dɪˈspærɪdʒ) *vb* **disparages, disparaging, disparaged** (*tr*) **1** to speak contemptuously of; belittle **2** to damage the reputation of [c14 from OF *desparagier*, from *des-* DIS-[1] + *parage* equality, from L *par* equal] > **disˈparagement** *n* > **disˈparaging** *adj*

disparate (ˈdɪspərɪt) *adj* **1** utterly different or distinct in kind ▷ *n* **2** (*pl*) unlike things or people [c16 from L *disparāre* to divide, from DIS-[1] + *parāre* to prepare; also infl. by L *dispar* unequal] > **ˈdisparately** *adv* > **ˈdisparateness** *n*

disparity (dɪˈspærɪtɪ) *n, pl* **disparities 1** inequality or difference, as in age, rank, wages, etc **2** dissimilarity

dispassionate (dɪsˈpæʃənɪt) *adj* devoid of or uninfluenced by emotion or prejudice; objective; impartial > **disˈpassionately** *adv*

dispatch *or* **despatch** (dɪˈspætʃ) *vb* (*tr*) **1** to send off promptly, as to a destination or to perform a task **2** to discharge or complete (a duty, etc) promptly **3** *inf* to eat up quickly **4** to murder or execute ▷ *n* **5** the act of sending off a letter, messenger, etc **6** prompt action or speed (often in **with dispatch**) **7** an official communication or report, sent in haste **8** a report sent to a newspaper, etc, by a correspondent **9** murder or execution [c16 from It. *dispacciare*, from Provençal *despachar*, from OF *despeechier* to set free, from *des-* DIS-[1] + *-peechier*, ult. from L *pedica* a fetter] > **disˈpatcher** *n*

dispatch box *n* a case or box used to hold valuables or documents, esp official state documents

dispatch case *n* a case used for carrying papers, documents, books, etc

dispatch rider *n* a horseman or motorcyclist who carries dispatches

dispel (dɪˈspɛl) *vb* **dispels, dispelling, dispelled** (*tr*) to disperse or drive away [c17 from L *dispellere*, from DIS-[1] + *pellere* to drive] > **disˈpeller** *n*

dispensable (dɪˈspɛnsəbᵊl) *adj* **1** not essential; expendable **2** (of a law, vow, etc) able to be relaxed > **disˌpensaˈbility** *or* **disˈpensableness** *n*

dispensary (dɪˈspɛnsərɪ) *n, pl* **dispensaries** a place where medicine, etc, is dispensed

dispensation (ˌdɪspɛnˈseɪʃən) *n* **1** the act of distributing or dispensing **2** something distributed or dispensed **3** a system or plan of administering or dispensing **4** *chiefly RC Church* permission to dispense with an obligation of church law **5** any exemption from an obligation **6a** the ordering of life and events by God **6b** a religious system or code of prescriptions for life and conduct regarded as of divine origin > **ˌdispenˈsational** *adj*

dispensatory (dɪˈspɛnsətərɪ, -trɪ) *n, pl* **dispensatories** a book listing the composition, preparation, and application of various drugs

dispense (dɪˈspɛns) *vb* **dispenses, dispensing, dispensed 1** (*tr*) to give out or distribute in portions **2** (*tr*) to prepare and distribute (medicine), esp on prescription **3** (*tr*) to administer (the law, etc) **4** (*intr*; foll by *with*) to do away (with) or manage (without) **5** to grant a dispensation to **6** to exempt or excuse from a rule or obligation [c14 from Med. L *dispensāre* to pardon, from L *dispendere* to weigh out, from DIS-[1] + *pendere*]

dispenser (dɪˈspɛnsə) *n* **1** a device that automatically dispenses a single item or a measured quantity **2** a person or thing that dispenses

dispensing optician *n* See **optician**

dispersal (dɪˈspɜːsᵊl) *n* **1** a dispersing or being dispersed **2** the spread of animals, plants, or seeds to new areas

dispersant (dɪsˈpɜːsənt) *n* a liquid or gas used to disperse small particles or droplets, as in an aerosol

disperse (dɪˈspɜːs) *vb* **disperses, dispersing, dispersed 1** to scatter; distribute over a wide area **2** to dissipate **3** to leave or cause to leave a gathering **4** to separate or be separated by dispersion **5** (*tr*) to spread (news, etc) **6** to separate (particles) throughout a solid, liquid, or gas ▷ *adj* **7** of or consisting of the particles in a colloid or suspension: *disperse phase* [c14 from L *dispērsus*, from *dispergere* to scatter widely, from DI-[2] + *spargere* to strew] > **disˈperser** *n*

USAGE See at **disburse**

dispersion (dɪˈspɜːʃən) *n* **1** another word for **dispersal** **2** *physics* **2a** the separation of electromagnetic radiation into constituents of different wavelengths **2b** a measure of the ability of a substance to separate by refraction **3** *statistics* the degree to which values of a frequency distribution are scattered around some central point, usually the arithmetic mean or median **4** *chem* a system containing particles dispersed in a solid, liquid, or gas **5** *ecology* the distribution pattern of a population of animals or plants

dispirit (dɪˈspɪrɪt) *vb* (*tr*) to lower the spirit of; make downhearted; discourage

dispirited (dɪˈspɪrɪtɪd) *adj* low in spirit or enthusiasm; downhearted or depressed; discouraged > **disˈpiritedly** *adv* > **disˈpiritedness** *n*

dispiriting (dɪˈspɪrɪtɪŋ) *adj* tending to lower the spirit or enthusiasm; depressing; discouraging > **disˈpiritingly** *adv*

displace (dɪsˈpleɪs) *vb* **displaces, displacing, displaced** (*tr*) **1** to move from the usual or correct location **2** to remove from office or employment **3** to occupy the place of; replace; supplant

displaced person *n* a person forced from his or her home or country, esp by war or revolution

displacement (dɪsˈpleɪsmənt) *n* **1** a displacing or being displaced **2** the weight or volume displaced by a body in a fluid **3** *psychoanal* the transferring of emotional feelings from their original object to one that disguises their real nature **4** *maths* the distance measured in a particular direction from a reference point. Symbol: *s*

displacement activity *n psychol* behaviour that occurs typically when there is a conflict of motives and that has no relevance to either motive: e.g. head scratching

Dd

display (dɪˈspleɪ) *vb* 1 (*tr*) to show or make visible 2 (*tr*) to put out to be seen; exhibit 3 (*tr*) to disclose; reveal 4 (*tr*) to flaunt in an ostentatious way 5 (*tr*) to spread out; unfold 6 (*tr*) to give prominence to 7 (*intr*) *zool* to engage in a display ▷ *n* 8 an exhibiting or displaying; show 9 something exhibited or displayed 10 an ostentatious exhibition 11 an arrangement of certain typefaces to give prominence to headings, etc 12 *electronics* 12a a device capable of representing information visually, as on a cathode-ray tube screen 12b the information so presented 13 *zool* a pattern of behaviour by which the animal attracts attention while it is courting the female, defending its territory, etc 14 (*modifier*) designating typefaces that give prominence to the words they are used to set [C14 from Anglo-F *despleier* to unfold, from LL *displicāre* to scatter, from DIS-¹ + *plicāre* to fold] > **disˈplayer** *n*

displease (dɪsˈpliːz) *vb* **displeases, displeasing, displeased** to annoy, offend, or cause displeasure to (someone) > **disˈpleasing** *adj* > **disˈpleasingly** *adv*

displeasure (dɪsˈplɛʒə) *n* 1 the condition of being displeased 2 *arch* 2a pain 2b an act or cause of offence

disport (dɪˈspɔːt) *vb* 1 (*tr*) to indulge (oneself) in pleasure 2 (*intr*) to frolic or gambol ▷ *n* 3 *arch* amusement [C14 from Anglo-F *desporter*, from *des-* DIS-¹ + *porter* to carry]

disposable (dɪˈspəʊzəbᵊl) *adj* 1 designed for disposal after use: *disposable cups* 2 available for use if needed: *disposable assets* ▷ *n* 3 something, such as a baby's nappy, that is designed for disposal 4 (*pl*) short for **disposable goods** > **dis͵posaˈbility** *or* **disˈposableness** *n*

disposable goods *pl n* consumer goods that are used up a short time after purchase, including perishables, newspapers, clothes, etc. Also called: **disposables**

disposable income *n* 1 the money a person has available to spend after paying taxes, pension contributions, etc 2 the total amount of money that the individuals in a community, country, etc, have available to buy consumer goods

disposal (dɪˈspəʊzᵊl) *n* 1 the act or means of getting rid of something 2 arrangement in a particular order 3 a specific method of tending to matters, as in business 4 the act or process of transferring something to or providing something for another 5 the power or opportunity to make use of someone or something(esp in **at one's disposal**)

dispose (dɪˈspəʊz) *vb* **disposes, disposing, disposed** 1 (*intr*; foll by *of*) 1a to deal with or settle 1b to give, sell, or transfer to another 1c to throw out or away 1d to consume, esp hurriedly 1e to kill 2 to arrange or settle (matters) 3 (*tr*) to make willing or receptive 4 (*tr*) to place in a certain order 5 (*tr*; often foll by *to*) to accustom or condition [C14 from OF *disposer*, from L *dispōnere* to set in different places, from DIS-¹ + *pōnere* to place] > **disˈposer** *n*

disposed (dɪˈspəʊzd) *adj* **a** having an inclination as specified (towards something) **b** (*in combination*): *well-disposed*

disposition (͵dɪspəˈzɪʃən) *n* 1 a person's usual temperament or frame of mind 2 a tendency, inclination, or habit 3 another word for **disposal** (senses 2–5) 4 *arch* manner of placing or arranging

dispossess (͵dɪspəˈzɛs) *vb* (*tr*) to take away possession of something, esp property; expel > ͵**disposˈsession** *n* > ͵**disposˈsessor** *n*

dispraise (dɪsˈpreɪz) *vb* **dispraises, dispraising, dispraised** 1 (*tr*) to express disapproval or condemnation of ▷ *n* 2 the disapproval, etc, expressed > **disˈpraiser** *n*

disproof (dɪsˈpruːf) *n* 1 facts that disprove something 2 the act of disproving

disproportion (͵dɪsprəˈpɔːʃən) *n* 1 lack of proportion or equality 2 an instance of disparity or inequality ▷ *vb* 3 (*tr*) to cause to become exaggerated or unequal > ͵**disproˈportional** *adj*

disproportionate (͵dɪsprəˈpɔːʃənɪt) *adj* out of proportion; unequal > ͵**disproˈportionately** *adv* > ͵**disproˈportionateness** *n*

disprove (dɪsˈpruːv) *vb* **disproves, disproving, disproved** (*tr*) to show (an assertion, claim, etc) to be incorrect > **disˈprovable** *adj* > **disˈproval** *n*

disputable (dɪˈspjuːtəbᵊl, ˈdɪspjʊtə-) *adj* capable of being argued; debatable > **dis͵putaˈbility** *or* **disˈputableness** *n* > **disˈputably** *adv*

disputant (dɪˈspjuːtᵊnt, ˈdɪspjʊtənt) *n* 1 a person who argues; contestant ▷ *adj* 2 engaged in argument

disputation (͵dɪspjʊˈteɪʃən) *n* 1 the act or an instance of arguing 2 a formal academic debate on a thesis 3 an obsolete word for **conversation**

disputatious (͵dɪspjʊˈteɪʃəs) *or* **disputative** (dɪˈspjuːtətɪv) *adj* inclined to argument > ͵**dispuˈtatiousness** *or* **disˈputativeness** *n*

dispute *vb* (dɪˈspjuːt) **disputes, disputing, disputed** 1 to argue, debate, or quarrel about (something) 2 (*tr; may take a clause as object*) to doubt the validity, etc, of 3 (*tr*) to seek to win; contest for 4 (*tr*) to struggle against; resist ▷ *n* (dɪˈspjuːt, ˈdɪspjuːt) 5 an argument or quarrel 6 *rare* a fight [C13 from LL *disputāre* to contend verbally, from L: to discuss, from DIS-¹ + *putāre* to think] > **disˈputer** *n*

disqualify (dɪsˈkwɒlɪ͵faɪ) *vb* **disqualifies, disqualifying, disqualified** (*tr*) 1 to make unfit or unqualified 2 to make ineligible, as for entry to an examination 3 to debar from a contest 4 to deprive of rights, powers, or privileges > **dis͵qualifiˈcation** *n*

disquiet (dɪsˈkwaɪət) *n* 1 a feeling or condition of anxiety or uneasiness ▷ *vb* 2 (*tr*) to make anxious or upset > **disˈquieting** *adj*

disquietude (dɪsˈkwaɪɪ͵tjuːd) *n* a feeling or state of anxiety or uneasiness

disquisition (͵dɪskwɪˈzɪʃən) *n* a formal examination of a subject [C17 from L *disquīsītiō*, from *disquīrere* to make an investigation, from DIS-¹ + *quaerere* to seek] > ͵**disquiˈsitional** *adj*

Disraeli (dɪzˈreɪlɪ) *n* **Benjamin,** 1st Earl of Beaconsfield. 1804–81, British Tory statesman and novelist; prime minister (1868; 1874–80) He gave coherence to the Tory principles of protectionism and imperialism, was responsible for the Reform Bill (1867) and, as prime minister, bought a controlling interest in the Suez Canal. His novels include *Coningsby* (1844) and *Sybil* (1845)

disregard (͵dɪsrɪˈgɑːd) *vb* (*tr*) 1 to give little or no attention to; ignore 2 to treat as unworthy of consideration or respect ▷ *n* 3 lack of attention or respect > ͵**disreˈgardful** *adj*

disremember (͵dɪsrɪˈmɛmbə) *vb inf, chiefly US* to fail to recall

disrepair (͵dɪsrɪˈpɛə) *n* the condition of being worn out or in poor working order; a condition requiring repairs

disreputable (dɪsˈrɛpjʊtəbᵊl) *adj* 1 having or causing a lack of repute 2 disordered in appearance > **disˈreputably** *adv*

disrepute (͵dɪsrɪˈpjuːt) *n* a loss or lack of credit or repute

disrespect (͵dɪsrɪˈspɛkt) *n* contempt; rudeness; lack of respect > ͵**disreˈspectful** *adj*

disrobe (dɪsˈrəʊb) *vb* **disrobes, disrobing, disrobed** 1 to undress 2 (*tr*) to divest of authority, etc > **disˈrobement** *n*

disrupt (dɪsˈrʌpt) *vb* 1 (*tr*) to throw into turmoil or disorder 2 (*tr*) to interrupt the progress of 3 to break or split apart [C17 from L *disruptus* burst asunder, from *dīrumpere* to dash to pieces, from DIS-¹ + *rumpere* to burst] > **disˈrupter** *or* **disˈruptor** *n* > **disˈruption** *n*

disruptive (dɪsˈrʌptɪv) *adj* involving, causing, or tending to cause disruption

diss *or* **dis** (dɪs) *vb* **disses, dissing, dissed** *sl, chiefly US* to treat (someone) with contempt [C20 orig. US Black rap slang, short for DISRESPECT]

dissatisfaction (͵dɪsætɪsˈfækʃən) *n* the state of being unsatisfied or disappointed > ͵**dissatisˈfactory** *adj*

dissatisfy (dɪsˈsætɪsˌfaɪ) *vb* **dissatisfies, dissatisfying, dissatisfied** (*tr*) to fail to satisfy; disappoint

dissect (dɪˈsɛkt, daɪ-) *vb* **1** to cut open and examine the structure of (a dead animal or plant) **2** (*tr*) to examine critically and minutely [C17 from L *dissecāre*, from DIS-[1] + *secāre* to cut] > **disˈsection** *n* > **disˈsector** *n*

dissected (dɪˈsɛktɪd, daɪ-) *adj* **1** *bot* in the form of narrow lobes or segments **2** *geol* cut by erosion into hills and valleys

disselboom (ˈdɪsᵊlˌbuːm) *n S African* the single shaft of a wagon, esp an ox wagon [from Du. *dissel* shaft + *boom* beam]

dissemble (dɪˈsɛmbᵊl) *vb* **dissembles, dissembling, dissembled 1** to conceal (one's real motives, emotions, etc) by pretence **2** (*tr*) to pretend; simulate [C15 from earlier *dissimulen*, from L *dissimulāre*; prob. infl. by obs. *semble* to resemble] > **disˈsemblance** *n* > **disˈsembler** *n*

disseminate (dɪˈsɛmɪˌneɪt) *vb* **disseminates, disseminating, disseminated** (*tr*) to distribute or scatter about; diffuse [C17 from L *dissēmināre*, from DIS-[1] + *sēmināre* to sow, from *sēmen* seed] > **disˌsemiˈnation** *n* > **disˈsemiˌnator** *n*

disseminated sclerosis *n* another name for **multiple sclerosis**

dissension (dɪˈsɛnʃən) *n* disagreement, esp when leading to a quarrel [C13 from L *dissentīre* to DISSENT]

dissent (dɪˈsɛnt) *vb* (*intr*) **1** to have a disagreement or withhold assent **2** *Christianity* to reject the doctrines, beliefs, or practices of an established church, and to adhere to a different system of beliefs ▷ *n* **3** a difference of opinion **4** *Christianity* separation from an established church; Nonconformism **5** the voicing of a minority opinion in the decision on a case at law [C16 from L *dissentīre* to disagree, from DIS-[1] + *sentīre* to feel] > **disˈsenter** *n* > **disˈsenting** *adj*

Dissenter (dɪˈsɛntə) *n Christianity, chiefly Brit* a Nonconformist or a person who refuses to conform to the established church

dissentient (dɪˈsɛnʃənt) *adj* **1** dissenting, esp from the opinion of the majority ▷ *n* **2** a dissenter > **disˈsentience** *or* **disˈsentiency** *n*

dissertation (ˌdɪsəˈteɪʃən) *n* **1** a written thesis, often based on original research, usually required for a higher degree **2** a formal discourse [C17 from L *dissertāre* to debate, from *disserere* to examine, from DIS-[1] + *serere* to arrange] > **ˌdisserˈtational** *adj*

disserve (dɪsˈsɜːv) *vb* **disserves, disserving, disserved** (*tr*) *arch* to do a disservice to

disservice (dɪsˈsɜːvɪs) *n* an ill turn; wrong; injury, esp when trying to help

dissever (dɪˈsɛvə) *vb* **1** to break off or become broken off **2** (*tr*) to divide up into parts [C13 from OF *dessevrer*, from LL DIS-[1] + *sēparāre* to SEPARATE] > **disˈseverance** *or* **disˈseverment** *n*

dissident (ˈdɪsɪdənt) *adj* **1** disagreeing; dissenting ▷ *n* **2** a person who disagrees, esp one who disagrees with the government [C16 from L *dissidēre* to be remote from, from DIS-[1] + *sedēre* to sit] > **ˈdissidence** *n* > **ˈdissidently** *adv*

dissimilar (dɪˈsɪmɪlə) *adj* not alike; not similar; different > **disˈsimilarly** *adv* > **ˌdissimiˈlarity** *n*

dissimilate (dɪˈsɪmɪˌleɪt) *vb* **dissimilates, dissimilating, dissimilated 1** to make or become dissimilar **2** (usually foll by *to*) *Phonetics.* to change or displace (a consonant) or (of a consonant) to be changed to or displaced by (another consonant) so that its manner of articulation becomes less similar to a speech sound in the same word. Thus (r) in the final syllable of French *marbre* is dissimilated to (l) in its English form *marble* [C19 from DIS-[1] + ASSIMILATE]

dissimilation (ˌdɪsɪmɪˈleɪʃən) *n* **1** the act or an instance of making dissimilar **2** *phonetics* the alteration or omission of a consonant as a result of being dissimilated

dissimilitude (ˌdɪsɪˈmɪlɪˌtjuːd) *n* **1** dissimilarity; difference **2** a point of difference

dissimulate (dɪˈsɪmjʊˌleɪt) *vb* **dissimulates, dissimulating, dissimulated** to conceal (one's real feelings) by pretence > **disˌsimuˈlation** *n* > **disˈsimuˌlator** *n*

dissipate (ˈdɪsɪˌpeɪt) *vb* **dissipates, dissipating, dissipated 1** to exhaust or be exhausted by dispersion **2** (*tr*) to scatter or break up **3** (*intr*) to indulge in the pursuit of pleasure [C15 from L *dissipāre* to disperse, from DIS-[1] + *supāre* to throw] > **ˈdissiˌpater** *or* **ˈdissiˌpator** *n* > **ˈdissiˌpative** *adj*

dissipated (ˈdɪsɪˌpeɪtɪd) *adj* **1** indulging without restraint in the pursuit of pleasure; debauched **2** wasted, scattered, or exhausted > **ˈdissiˌpatedly** *adv* > **ˈdissiˌpatedness** *n*

dissipation (ˌdɪsɪˈpeɪʃən) *n* **1** a dissipating or being dissipated **2** unrestrained indulgence in physical pleasures **3** excessive expenditure; wastefulness

dissociate (dɪˈsəʊʃɪˌeɪt, -sɪ-) *vb* **dissociates, dissociating, dissociated 1** to break or cause to break the association between (people, organizations, etc) **2** (*tr*) to regard or treat as separate or unconnected **3** to undergo or subject to dissociation > **disˈsociative** *adj*

dissociation (dɪˌsəʊsɪˈeɪʃən, -ʃɪ-) *n* **1** a dissociating or being dissociated **2** *chem* the decomposition of the molecules of a single compound into two or more other compounds, atoms, ions, or radicals **3** *psychiatry* the separation of a group of mental processes or ideas from the rest of the personality, so that they lead an independent existence, as in cases of multiple personality

dissoluble (dɪˈsɒljʊbᵊl) *adj* a less common word for **soluble** [C16 from L *dissolūbilis*, from *dissolvere* to DISSOLVE] > **disˌsoluˈbility** *n*

dissolute (ˈdɪsəˌluːt) *adj* given to dissipation; debauched [C14 from L *dissolūtus* loose, from *dissolvere* to DISSOLVE] > **ˈdissoˌlutely** *adv* > **ˈdissoˌluteness** *n*

Dd

dissolution (ˌdɪsəˈluːʃən) *n* **1** separation into component parts; disintegration **2** destruction by breaking up and dispersing **3** the termination of a meeting or assembly, such as Parliament **4** the termination of a formal or legal relationship, such as a business, marriage, etc **5** the act or process of dissolving

dissolve (dɪˈzɒlv) *vb* **dissolves, dissolving, dissolved 1** to go or cause to go into solution **2** to become or cause to become liquid; melt **3** to disintegrate or disperse **4** to come or bring to an end **5** to dismiss (a meeting, Parliament, etc) or (of a meeting, etc) to be dismissed **6** to collapse or cause to collapse emotionally: *to dissolve into tears* **7** to lose or cause to lose distinctness **8** (*tr*) to terminate legally, as a marriage, etc **9** (*intr*) *films, television* to fade out one scene and replace with another to make two scenes merge imperceptibly or slowly overlap ▷ *n* **10** *films, television* a scene filmed or televised by dissolving [C14 from L *dissolvere* to make loose, from DIS-[1] + *solvere* to release] > **disˈsolvable** *adj*

dissonance (ˈdɪsənəns) *or* **dissonancy** *n* **1** a discordant combination of sounds **2** lack of agreement or consistency **3** *music* **3a** a sensation of harshness and incompleteness associated with certain intervals and chords **3b** an interval or chord of this kind

dissonant (ˈdɪsənənt) *adj* **1** discordant **2** incongruous or discrepant **3** *music* characterized by dissonance [C15 from L *dissonāre* to be discordant, from DIS-[1] + *sonāre* to sound]

dissuade (dɪˈsweɪd) *vb* **dissuades, dissuading, dissuaded** (*tr*) **1** (often foll by *from*) to deter (someone) by persuasion from a course of action, policy, etc **2** to advise against (an action, etc) [C15 from L *dissuādēre*, from DIS-[1] + *suādēre* to persuade] > **disˈsuader** *n* > **disˈsuasion** *n* > **disˈsuasive** *adj*

dissyllable (dɪˈsɪləbᵊl) *or* **disyllable** *n* a word of two syllables > **dissyllabic** (ˌdɪsɪˈlæbɪk) *or* **disyllabic** (ˌdaɪsɪˈlæbɪk) *adj*

dissymmetry (dɪˈsɪmɪtrɪ, dɪsˈsɪm-) *n, pl* **dissymmetries** 1 lack of symmetry 2 the relationship between two objects when one is the mirror image of the other > **dissymmetric** (ˌdɪsɪˈmɛtrɪk, ˌdɪssɪ-) *or* ˌ**dissym**ˈ**metrical** *adj*

distaff (ˈdɪstɑːf) *n* 1 the rod on which flax is wound preparatory to spinning 2 *figurative* women's work [OE *distæf*, from *dis-* bunch of flax + *stæf* STAFF[1]]

distaff side *n* the female side of a family

distal (ˈdɪstᵊl) *adj anat* situated farthest from the centre or point of attachment or origin [C19 from DISTANT + -AL[1]] > ˈ**distally** *adv*

distance (ˈdɪstəns) *n* 1 the space between two points 2 the length of this gap 3 the state of being apart in space; remoteness 4 an interval between two points in time 5 the extent of progress 6 a distant place or time 7 a separation or remoteness in relationship 8 (preceded by *the*) the most distant or a faraway part of the visible scene 9 *horse racing* 9a *Brit* a point on a racecourse 240 yards from the winning post 9b *US* the part of a racecourse that a horse must reach before the winner passes the finishing line in order to qualify for later heats 10 **go the distance** 10a *boxing* to complete a bout without being knocked out 10b to be able to complete an assigned task or responsibility 11 **keep one's distance** to maintain a reserve in respect of another person 12 **middle distance** halfway between the foreground or the observer and the horizon ▷ *vb* **distances, distancing, distanced** (*tr*) 13 to hold or place at a distance 14 to separate (oneself) mentally from something 15 to outdo; outstrip

distance learning *n* a teaching system consisting of video, audio, and written material designed for a person to use in studying a subject at home

distant (ˈdɪstənt) *adj* 1 far apart in space or time 2 (*postpositive*) separated in space or time by a specified distance 3 apart in relationship: *a distant cousin* 4 coming from or going to a faraway place 5 remote in manner; aloof 6 abstracted; absent: *a distant look* [C14 from L *distāre* to be distant, from DIS-[1] + *stāre* to stand] > ˈ**distantly** *adv* > ˈ**distantness** *n*

distaste (dɪsˈteɪst) *n* (often foll by *for*) a dislike (of); aversion (to)

distasteful (dɪsˈteɪstfʊl) *adj* unpleasant or offensive > **dis**ˈ**tastefulness** *n*

Di Stéfano (*Spanish* di ˈstefano) *n* **Alfredo** (alˈfredo) born 1926, Argentinian-born football player, who played for Argentina, Colombia, Spain, and Real Madrid

distemper[1] (dɪsˈtɛmpə) *n* 1 any of various infectious diseases of animals, esp **canine distemper,** a highly contagious viral disease of dogs 2 *arch* 2a a disorder 2b disturbance 2c discontent [C14 from LL *distemperāre* to derange the health of, from L DIS-[1] + *temperāre* to mix in correct proportions]

distemper[2] (dɪsˈtɛmpə) *n* 1 a technique of painting in which the pigments are mixed with water, glue, size, etc: used for poster, mural, and scene painting 2 the paint used in this technique or any of various water-based paints ▷ *vb* 3 to paint (something) with distemper [C14 from Med. L *distemperāre* to soak, from L DIS-[1] + *temperāre* to mingle]

distend (dɪˈstɛnd) *vb* 1 to expand by or as if by pressure from within; swell; inflate 2 (*tr*) to stretch out or extend [C14 from L *distendere*, from DIS-[1] + *tendere* to stretch] > **dis**ˈ**tensible** *adj* > **dis**ˈ**tension** *or* **dis**ˈ**tention** *n*

distich (ˈdɪstɪk) *n prosody* a unit of two verse lines, usually a couplet [C16 from Gk *distikhos* having two lines, from DI-[1] + *stikhos* row, line]

distil *or US* **distill** (dɪsˈtɪl) *vb* **distils, distilling, distilled** *or US* **distills, distilling, distilled** 1 to subject to or undergo distillation 2 (sometimes foll by *out* or *off*) to purify, separate, or concentrate, or be purified, separated, or concentrated by distillation 3 to obtain or be obtained by distillation 4 to exude or give off (a substance) in drops 5 (*tr*) to extract the essence of [C14 from L *dēstillāre* to distil, from DE- + *stillāre* to drip]

distillate (ˈdɪstɪlɪt) *n* 1 the product of distillation 2 a concentrated essence

distillation (ˌdɪstɪˈleɪʃən) *n* 1 a distilling 2 the process of evaporating or boiling a liquid and condensing its vapour 3 purification or separation of mixtures by using different evaporation rates or boiling points of their components 4 the process of obtaining the essence or an extract of a substance, usually by heating it in a solvent 5 a distillate 6 a concentrated essence > **dis**ˈ**tillatory** *adj*

distiller (dɪˈstɪlə) *n* a person or organization that distils, esp a company that makes spirits

distillery (dɪˈstɪlərɪ) *n, pl* **distilleries** a place where alcoholic drinks, etc, are made by distillation

distinct (dɪˈstɪŋkt) *adj* 1 easily sensed or understood; clear 2 (when *postpositive*, foll by *from*) not the same (as); separate (from) 3 not alike; different 4 sharp; clear 5 recognizable; definite 6 explicit; unequivocal 7 *bot* (of parts of a plant) not joined together; separate [C14 from L *distinctus*, from *distinguere* to DISTINGUISH] > **dis**ˈ**tinctly** *adv* > **dis**ˈ**tinctness** *n*

distinction (dɪˈstɪŋkʃən) *n* 1 the act or an instance of distinguishing or differentiating 2 a distinguishing feature 3 the state of being different or distinguishable 4 special honour, recognition, or fame 5 excellence of character; distinctive qualities 6 distinguished appearance 7 a symbol of honour or rank

distinctive (dɪˈstɪŋktɪv) *adj* serving or tending to distinguish; characteristic > **dis**ˈ**tinctively** *adv* > **dis**ˈ**tinctiveness** *n*

distingué *French* (distɛ̃ge) *adj* distinguished or noble

distinguish (dɪˈstɪŋgwɪʃ) *vb* (*mainly tr*) 1 (when *intr*, foll by *between* or *among*) to make, show, or recognize a difference (between or among); differentiate (between) 2 to be a distinctive feature of; characterize 3 to make out; perceive 4 to mark for a special honour 5 to make (oneself) noteworthy 6 to classify [C16 from L *distinguere* to separate] > **dis**ˈ**tinguishable** *adj* > **dis**ˈ**tinguishing** *adj*

distinguished (dɪˈstɪŋgwɪʃt) *adj* 1 noble or dignified in appearance or behaviour 2 eminent; famous; celebrated

distort (dɪˈstɔːt) *vb* (*tr*) 1 (*often passive*) to twist or pull out of shape; contort; deform 2 to alter or misrepresent (facts, etc) 3 *electronics* to reproduce or amplify (a signal) inaccurately [C16 from L *distortus*, from *distorquēre* to turn different ways, from DIS-[1] + *torquēre* to twist] > **dis**ˈ**torted** *adj*

distortion (dɪˈstɔːʃən) *n* 1 a distorting or being distorted 2 something that is distorted 3 *electronics* an undesired change in the shape of an electrical wave or signal resulting in a loss of clarity in radio reception or sound reproduction > **dis**ˈ**tortional** *adj*

distract (dɪˈstrækt) *vb* (*tr*) 1 (*often passive*) to draw the attention of (a person) away from something 2 to divide or confuse the attention of (a person) 3 to amuse or entertain 4 to trouble greatly 5 to make mad [C14 from L *distractus* perplexed, from *distrahere* to pull in different directions, from DIS-[1] + *trahere* to drag]

USAGE See at **detract**

distracted (dɪˈstræktɪd) *adj* 1 bewildered; confused 2 mad > **dis**ˈ**tractedly** *adv*

distraction (dɪˈstrækʃən) *n* 1 a distracting or being distracted 2 something that serves as a diversion or entertainment 3 an interruption; obstacle to concentration 4 mental turmoil or madness

distrain (dɪˈstreɪn) *vb law* to seize (personal property) as security or indemnity for a debt [C13 from OF *destreindre*, from L *distringere* to impede, from DIS-¹ + *stringere* to draw tight] > **dis'trainment** *n* > **dis'trainor** *or* **dis'trainer** *n*

distraint (dɪ'streɪnt) *n law* the act or process of distraining; distress

distrait (dɪ'streɪ; *French* distrɛ) *adj* absent-minded; abstracted [C18 from F, from *distraire* to DISTRACT]

distraught (dɪ'strɔːt) *adj* **1** distracted or agitated **2** *rare* mad [C14 changed from obs. *distract* through influence of obs. *straught*, p.p. of STRETCH]

distress (dɪ'strɛs) *vb* (*tr*) **1** to cause mental pain to; upset badly **2** (*usually passive*) to subject to financial or other trouble **3** to treat (something, esp furniture or fabric) in order to make it appear older than it is **4** *law* a less common word for **distrain** ▷ *n* **5** mental pain; anguish **6** a distressing or being distressed **7** physical or financial trouble **8** **in distress** (of a ship, etc) in dire need of help **9** *law* **9a** the seizure of property as security for or in satisfaction of a debt, claim, etc; distraint **9b** the property thus seized **9c** (*as modifier*) *US: distress merchandise* [C13 from OF *destresse*, via Vulgar L, from L *districtus* divided in mind] > **dis'tressful** *adj* > **dis'tressing** *adj* > **dis'tressingly** *adv*

distressed (dɪ'strɛst) *adj* **1** much troubled; upset; afflicted **2** in financial straits; poor **3** (of furniture, fabric, etc) having signs of ageing artificially applied **4** *econ* another word for **depressed**

distress signal *n* a signal by radio, Very light, etc, from a ship in need of immediate assistance

distribute (dɪ'strɪbjuːt) *vb* **distributes, distributing, distributed** (*tr*) **1** to give out in shares; dispense **2** to hand out or deliver **3** (*often passive*) to spread throughout an area **4** (*often passive*) to divide into classes or categories **5** *printing* to return (used type) to the correct positions in the typecase **6** *logic* to incorporate in a distributed term of a categorical proposition **7** *maths* to expand an expression containing two operators so as to change the order, as in expressing $a(b + c)$ as $ab + ac$ [C15 from L *distribuere*, from DIS-¹ + *tribuere* to give] > **dis'tributable** *adj*

distributed logic *n* a computer system in which remote terminals and electronic devices supplement the main computer by doing some of the computing or decision making

distributed term *n logic* a term applying equally to every member of the class it designates, as *men* in *all men are mortal*

distribution (ˌdɪstrɪ'bjuːʃən) *n* **1** the act of distributing or the state or manner of being distributed **2** a thing or portion distributed **3** arrangement or location **4** the process of physically satisfying the demand for goods and services **5** *econ* the division of the total income of a community among its members **6** *statistics* the set of possible values of a random variable, considered in terms of theoretical or observed frequency **7** *law* the apportioning of the estate of a deceased intestate **8** *law* the lawful division of the assets of a bankrupt among his or her creditors **9** *finance* **9a** the division of part of a company's profit as a dividend to its shareholders **9b** the amount paid by dividend in a particular distribution **10** *engineering* the way in which the fuel-air mixture is supplied to each cylinder of a multicylinder internal-combustion engine > ˌ**distri'butional** *adj*

distributive (dɪ'strɪbjʊtɪv) *adj* **1** characterized by or relating to distribution **2** *grammar* referring separately to the individual people or items in a group, as the words *each* and *every* ▷ *n* **3** *grammar* a distributive word > **dis'tributively** *adv* > **dis'tributiveness** *n*

distributive law *n maths, logic* a theorem asserting that one operator can validly be distributed over another. See **distribute** (sense 7)

distributor (dɪ'strɪbjʊtə) *n* **1** a person or thing that distributes **2** a wholesaler or middleman engaged in the distribution of a category of goods, esp to retailers in a specific area **3** the device in a petrol engine that distributes the high-tension voltage to the sparking plugs

district ('dɪstrɪkt) *n* **1a** an area of land marked off for administrative or other purposes **1b** (*as modifier*): *district nurse* **2** a locality separated by geographical attributes; region **3** any subdivision of a territory, region, etc **4** a political subdivision of a county, region, etc, that elects a council responsible for certain local services ▷ *vb* **5** (*tr*) to divide into districts [C17 from Med. L *districtus* area of jurisdiction, from L *distringere* to stretch out]

district attorney *n* (in the US) the state prosecuting officer in a specified judicial district

District Court *n* **1** (in Scotland) a court of summary jurisdiction which deals with minor criminal offences **2** (in the US) **2a** a Federal trial court in each US district **2b** in some states, a court of general jurisdiction **3** (in New Zealand) a court lower than a High Court. Formerly called: **magistrates' court**

district high school *n* (in New Zealand) a school in a rural area providing both primary and secondary education

district nurse *n* (in Britain) a nurse appointed to attend patients within a particular district, usually in the patients' homes

District of Columbia *n* a federal district of the eastern US, coextensive with the federal capital, Washington. Pop: 572 059 (2000). Area: 178 sq km (69 sq miles). Abbreviations: **D.C.** with zip code **DC**

distrust (dɪs'trʌst) *vb* **1** to regard as untrustworthy or dishonest ▷ *n* **2** suspicion; doubt > **dis'truster** *n* > **dis'trustful** *adj*

disturb (dɪ'stɜːb) *vb* (*tr*) **1** to intrude on; interrupt **2** to destroy the quietness or peace of **3** to disarrange; muddle **4** (*often passive*) to upset; trouble **5** to inconvenience; put out [C13 from L *disturbāre*, from DIS-¹ + *turbāre* to confuse] > **dis'turber** *n* > **dis'turbing** *adj* > **dis'turbingly** *adv*

Dd

disturbance (dɪ'stɜːbəns) *n* **1** a disturbing or being disturbed **2** an interruption or intrusion **3** an unruly outburst or tumult **4** *law* an interference with another's rights **5** *geol* a minor movement of the earth causing a small earthquake **6** *meteorol* a small depression **7** *psychiatry* a mental or emotional disorder

disturbed (dɪ'stɜːbd) *adj psychiatry* emotionally upset, troubled, or maladjusted

disulphide (daɪ'sʌlfaɪd) *n* any chemical compound containing two sulphur atoms per molecule

disunite (ˌdɪsjʊ'naɪt) *vb* **disunites, disuniting, disunited** **1** to separate; disrupt **2** (*tr*) to set at variance; estrange > **dis'union** *n*

disunity (dɪs'juːnɪtɪ) *n, pl* **disunities** dissension or disagreement

disuse (dɪs'juːs) *n* the condition of being unused; neglect (often in **in** *or* **into disuse**)

disutility (ˌdɪsjuː'tɪlɪtɪ) *n, pl* **disutilities** *econ* the shortcomings of a commodity or activity in satisfying human wants ▷ Cf **utility** (sense 4)

disyllable ('daɪˌsɪləbᵊl) *n* a variant of **dissyllable**

ditch (dɪtʃ) *n* **1** a narrow channel dug in the earth, usually used for drainage, irrigation, or as a boundary marker ▷ *vb* **2** to make a ditch in **3** (*intr*) to edge with a ditch **4** *sl* to crash, esp deliberately, as to avoid more unpleasant circumstances: *he had to ditch the car* **5** (*tr*) *sl* to abandon **6** *sl* to land (an aircraft) on water in an emergency **7** (*tr*) *US sl* to evade [OE *dīc*] > **'ditcher** *n*

ditchwater ('dɪtʃˌwɔːtə) *n* **1** stagnant water, esp found in ditches **2** **as dull as ditchwater** very dull; very uninteresting

dither ('dɪðə) *vb* (*intr*) **1** *chiefly Brit* to be uncertain or indecisive **2** *chiefly US* to be in an agitated state **3** to tremble, as with cold ▷ *n* **4** *chiefly Brit* a state of indecision **5** a state of agitation [C17 var. of C14 (N

English dialect) *didder*, from ?] > **'ditherer** *n* > **'dithery** *adj*

dithyramb ('dɪθɪˌræm, -ˌræmb) *n* **1** (in ancient Greece) a passionate choral hymn in honour of Dionysus **2** any utterance or a piece of writing that resembles this [c17 from L *dīthyrambus*, from Gk *dithurambos*] > **ˌdithy'rambic** *adj*

dittany ('dɪtənɪ) *n, pl* **dittanies** **1** an aromatic Cretan plant with pink flowers: formerly credited with medicinal properties **2** a North American plant with purplish flowers [c14 from OF *ditan*, from L *dictamnus*, from Gk *diktamnon*, ?from *Diktē*, mountain in Crete]

ditto ('dɪtəʊ) *n, pl* **dittos** **1** the aforementioned; the above; the same. Used in accounts, lists, etc, to avoid repetition, and symbolized by two small marks (") known as **ditto marks,** placed under the thing repeated **2** *inf* a duplicate ▷ *adv* **3** in the same way ▷ *sentence substitute* **4** *inf* used to avoid repeating or to confirm agreement with an immediately preceding sentence ▷ *vb* **dittos, dittoing, dittoed** **5** *(tr)* to copy; repeat [c17 from It. (dialect): var. of *detto* said, from *dicere* to say, from L]

ditty ('dɪtɪ) *n, pl* **ditties** a short simple song or poem [c13 from OF *ditie* poem, from *ditier* to compose, from L *dictāre* to DICTATE]

ditty bag *or* **box** *n* a sailor's bag or box for personal belongings or tools [c19 ?from obs. *dutty* calico, from Hindi *dhōtī* loincloth]

ditzy *or* **ditsy** ('dɪtzɪ, 'dɪtsɪ) *adj* **ditzier, ditziest** *or* **ditsier, ditsiest** *sl* silly and scatterbrained [c20 perhaps from DOTTY + DIZZY]

Diu ('di:u:) *n* a small island off the NW coast of India: together with a mainland area, it formed a district of Portuguese India (1535–1961); formerly part of the Indian Union Territory of Goa, Daman, and Diu (1962–87)

diuretic (ˌdaɪjʊ'rɛtɪk) *adj* **1** acting to increase the flow of urine ▷ *n* **2** a drug or agent that increases the flow of urine [ME, from LL, from Gk, from *dia-* through + *ourein* to urinate] > **diuresis** (ˌdaɪjʊ'ri:sɪs) *n*

diurnal (daɪ'ɜ:nᵊl) *adj* **1** happening during the day or daily **2** (of flowers) open during the day and closed at night **3** (of animals) active during the day ▷ Cf **nocturnal** [c15 from LL *diurnālis*, from L *diurnus*, from *diēs* day] > **di'urnally** *adv*

div (dɪv) *n sl* a shortened form of **divvy**[1]

diva ('di:və) *n, pl* **divas** *or* **dive** (-vɪ) a highly distinguished female singer; prima donna [c19 via It. from L: a goddess, from *dīvus* DIVINE]

divagate ('daɪvəˌgeɪt) *vb* **divagates, divagating, divagated** *(intr) rare* to digress or wander [c16 from L DI-[2] + *vagārī* to wander] > **ˌdiva'gation** *n*

divalent (daɪ'veɪlənt, 'daɪˌveɪ-) *adj chem* **1** having a valency of two **2** having two valencies ▷ Also: **bivalent** > **di'valency** *n*

divan (dɪ'væn) *n* **1a** a backless sofa or couch **1b** a bed resembling such a couch **2** (esp formerly) a smoking room **3a** a Muslim law court, council chamber, or counting house **3b** a Muslim council of state [c16 from Turkish *dīvān*, from Persian *dīwān*]

dive (daɪv) *vb* **dives, diving, dived** *or US* **dove** (dəʊv), **dived** *(mainly intr)* **1** to plunge headfirst into water **2** (of a submarine, etc) to submerge under water **3** *(also tr)* to fly in a steep nose-down descending path **4** to rush, go, or reach quickly, as in a headlong plunge: *he dived for the ball* **5** *(also tr; foll by in or into)* to dip or put (one's hand) quickly or forcefully (into) **6** (usually foll by *in* or *into*) to involve oneself (in something), as in eating food ▷ *n* **7** a headlong plunge into water **8** an act or instance of diving **9** a steep nose-down descent of an aircraft **10** *sl* a disreputable bar or club **11** *boxing sl* the act of a boxer pretending to be knocked down or out [OE *dӯfan*]

dive bomber *n* a military aircraft designed to release its bombs on a target during a steep dive > **'dive-bomb** *vb* *(tr)*

diver ('daɪvə) *n* **1** a person or thing that dives **2** a person who works or explores underwater **3** any of various aquatic birds of northern oceans: noted for skill in diving. US and Canad name: **loon** **4** any of various other diving birds

diverge (daɪ'vɜ:dʒ) *vb* **diverges, diverging, diverged** **1** to separate or cause to separate and go in different directions from a point **2** *(intr)* to be at variance; differ **3** *(intr)* to deviate from a prescribed course **4** *(intr) maths* (of a series) to have no limit [c17 from Med. L *dīvergere*, from L DI-[2] + *vergere* to turn]

divergence (daɪ'vɜ:dʒəns) *or* **divergency** *n* **1** the act or result of diverging or the amount by which something diverges **2** the condition of being divergent

divergent (daɪ'vɜ:dʒənt) *adj* **1** diverging or causing divergence **2** *maths* (of a series) having no limit > **di'vergently** *adv*

> USAGE The use of *divergent* to mean different as in *they hold widely divergent views* is considered by some people to be incorrect

divergent thinking *n psychol* thinking in an unusual and unstereotyped way, for instance to generate several possible solutions to a problem

divers ('daɪvəz) *determiner arch or literary* various; sundry; some [c13 from OF, from L *dīversus* turned in different directions]

diverse (daɪ'vɜ:s, 'daɪvɜ:s) *adj* **1** having variety; assorted **2** distinct in kind [c13 from L *dīversus*; see DIVERS] > **di'versely** *adv*

diversify (daɪ'vɜ:sɪˌfaɪ) *vb* **diversifies, diversifying, diversified** **1** *(tr)* to create different forms of; variegate; vary **2** (of an enterprise) to vary (products, operations, etc) in order to spread risk, expand, etc **3** to distribute (investments) among several securities in order to spread risk [c15 from OF *diversifier*, from Med. L *dīversificāre*, from L *dīversus* DIVERSE + *facere* to make] > **diˌversifi'cation** *n*

diversion (daɪ'vɜ:ʃən) *n* **1** the act of diverting from a specified course **2** *chiefly Brit* an official detour used by traffic when a main route is closed **3** something that distracts from business, etc; amusement **4** *mil* a feint attack designed to draw an enemy away from the main attack > **di'versional** *or* **di'versionary** *adj*

diversity (daɪ'vɜ:sɪtɪ) *n* **1** the state or quality of being different or varied **2** a point of difference

divert (daɪ'vɜ:t) *vb* **1** to turn aside; deflect **2** *(tr)* to entertain; amuse **3** *(tr)* to distract the attention of [c15 from F *divertir*, from L *dīvertere* to turn aside, from DI-[2] + *vertere* to turn] > **di'verting** *adj* > **di'vertingly** *adv*

diverticulitis (ˌdaɪvəˌtɪkjʊ'laɪtɪs) *n* inflammation of one or more diverticula, esp of the colon

diverticulum (ˌdaɪvə'tɪkjʊləm) *n, pl* **diverticula** (-lə) any sac or pouch formed by herniation of the wall of a tubular organ or part, esp the intestines [c16 from NL, from L *dēverticulum* by-path, from *dēvertere* to turn aside, from *vertere* to turn]

divertimento (dɪˌvɜ:tɪ'mɛntəʊ) *n, pl* **divertimenti** (-tɪ) **1** a piece of entertaining music, often scored for a mixed ensemble and having no fixed form **2** an episode in a fugue [c18 from It.]

divertissement (dɪ'vɜ:tɪsmənt) *n* a brief entertainment or diversion, usually between the acts of a play [c18 from F: entertainment]

Dives ('daɪvi:z) *n* **1** a rich man in the parable in Luke 16:19–31 **2** a very rich man

divest (daɪ'vɛst) *vb (tr; usually foll by of)* **1** to strip (of clothes) **2** to deprive or dispossess [c17 changed from earlier *devest*] > **divestiture** (daɪ'vɛstɪtʃə), **divesture** (daɪ'vɛstʃə), *or* **di'vestment** *n*

divi ('dɪvɪ) *n* an alternative spelling of **divvy**[1]

divide (dɪ'vaɪd) *vb* **divides, dividing, divided** **1** to separate into parts; split up **2** to share or be shared out in parts; distribute **3** to diverge or cause to diverge in opinion or aim **4** (*tr*) to keep apart or be a boundary between **5** (*intr*) to vote by separating into two groups **6** to categorize; classify **7** to calculate the quotient of (one number or quantity) and (another number or quantity) by division **8** (*intr*) to diverge: *the roads divide* **9** (*tr*) to mark increments of (length, angle, etc) ▷ *n* **10** *chiefly US & Canad* an area of relatively high ground separating drainage basins; watershed **11** a division; split [C14 from L *dīvidere* to force apart, from DIS-[1] + *vid-* separate, from the source of *viduus* bereaved]

divided (dɪˈvaɪdɪd) *adj* **1** *bot* another word for **dissected** (sense 1) **2** split; not united

dividend (ˈdɪvɪˌdɛnd) *n* **1a** a distribution from the net profits of a company to its shareholders **1b** a portion of this distribution received by a shareholder **2** the share of a cooperative society's surplus allocated to members **3** *insurance* a sum of money distributed from a company's net profits to the holders of certain policies **4** something extra; a bonus **5** a number or quantity to be divided by another number or quantity **6** *law* the proportion of an insolvent estate payable to the creditors [C15 from L *dīvidendum* what is to be divided]

divider (dɪˈvaɪdə) *n* **1** Also called: **room divider** a screen or piece of furniture placed so as to divide a room into separate areas **2** a person or thing that divides **3** *electronics* an electrical circuit with an output that is a well-defined fraction of a given input: *a voltage divider*

dividers (dɪˈvaɪdəz) *pl n* a type of compass with two pointed arms, used for measuring lines or dividing them

divination (ˌdɪvɪˈneɪʃən) *n* **1** the art or practice of discovering future events or unknown things, as though by supernatural powers **2** a prophecy **3** a guess > **divinatory** (dɪˈvɪnətərɪ, -trɪ) *adj*

divine (dɪˈvaɪn) *adj* **1** of God or a deity **2** godlike **3** of or associated with religion or worship **4** of supreme excellence or worth **5** *inf* splendid; perfect ▷ *n* **6** (*often cap;* preceded by *the*) another term for **God** **7** a priest, esp one learned in theology ▷ *vb* **divines, divining, divined** **8** to perceive (something) by intuition **9** to conjecture (something); guess **10** to discern (a hidden or future reality) as though by supernatural power **11** (*tr*) to search for (water, metal, etc) using a divining rod [C14 from L *dīvīnus*, from *dīvus* a god] > **diˈvinely** *adv* > **diˈviner** *n*

divine office *n* (*sometimes cap*) the canonical prayers recited daily by priests, etc. Also called: **Liturgy of the Hours**

divine right of kings *n history* the concept that the right to rule derives from God and that kings are answerable for their actions to God alone

diving bell *n* an early diving submersible having an open bottom and being supplied with compressed air

diving board *n* a platform or springboard from which swimmers may dive

diving suit *or* **dress** *n* a waterproof suit used by divers, having a heavy detachable helmet and an air supply

divining rod *n* a forked twig said to move when held over ground in which water, metal, etc, is to be found. Also called: **dowsing rod**

divinity (dɪˈvɪnɪtɪ) *n, pl* **divinities** **1** the nature of a deity or the state of being divine **2** a god **3** (*often cap;* preceded by *the*) another term for **God** **4** another word for **theology**

divisible (dɪˈvɪzɪbəl) *adj* capable of being divided, usually with no remainder > **diˌvisiˈbility** *or* **diˈvisibleness** *n* > **diˈvisibly** *adv*

division (dɪˈvɪʒən) *n* **1** a dividing or being divided **2** the act of sharing out; distribution **3** something that divides; boundary **4** one of the parts, groups, etc, into which something is divided **5** a part of a government, business, etc, that has been made into a unit for administrative or other reasons **6** a formal vote in Parliament or a similar legislative body **7** a difference of opinion **8** (in sports) a section or class organized according to age, weight, skill, etc **9** a mathematical operation in which the quotient of two numbers or quantities is calculated. Usually written: $a \div b$, a/b, $\frac{a}{b}$ **10** *army* a major formation, larger than a brigade but smaller than a corps, containing the necessary arms to sustain independent combat **11** *biol* (in traditional classification systems) a major category of the plant kingdom that contains one or more related classes. Cf **phylum** (sense 1) [C14 from L *dīvīsiō*, from *dīvidere* to DIVIDE] > **diˈvisional** *or* **diˈvisionary** *adj* > **diˈvisionally** *adv*

division sign *n* the symbol ÷, placed between the dividend and the divisor to indicate division, as in $12 \div 6 = 2$

divisive (dɪˈvaɪsɪv) *adj* tending to cause disagreement or dissension > **diˈvisively** *adv* > **diˈvisiveness** *n*

divisor (dɪˈvaɪzə) *n* **1** a number or quantity to be divided into another number or quantity (the dividend) **2** a number that is a factor of another number

divorce (dɪˈvɔːs) *n* **1** the legal dissolution of a marriage **2** a judicial decree declaring a marriage to be dissolved **3** a separation, esp one that is total or complete ▷ *vb* **divorces, divorcing, divorced** **4** to separate or be separated by divorce; give or obtain a divorce **5** (*tr*) to remove or separate, esp completely [C14 from OF, from L *dīvortium*, from *dīvertere* to separate] > **diˈvorceable** *adj*

divorcée (dɪvɔːˈsiː) *or* (*masc*) **divorcé** (dɪˈvɔːseɪ) *n* a person who has been divorced

divot (ˈdɪvət) *n* a piece of turf dug out of a grass surface, esp by a golf club or by horses' hooves [C16 from Scot., from ?]

divulge (daɪˈvʌldʒ) *vb* **divulges, divulging, divulged** (*tr; may take a clause as object*) to make known; disclose [C15 from L *dīvulgāre*, from DI-[2] + *vulgāre* to spread among people, from *vulgus* the common people] > **diˈvulgence** *or* **diˈvulgement** *n* > **diˈvulger** *n*

divvy[1] (ˈdɪvɪ) *inf* ▷ *n, pl* **divvies** **1** *Brit* short for **dividend**, esp (formerly) one paid by a cooperative society **2** *US & Canad* a share; portion ▷ *vb* **divvies, divvying, divvied** **3** (*tr;* usually foll by *up*) to divide and share

divvy[2] (ˈdɪvɪ) *n, pl* **divvies** *sl* a stupid or odd person; misfit [C20 ? from DEVIANT]

Diwali (dɪˈwɑːlɪ) *n* a major Hindu religious festival, honouring Lakshmi, the goddess of wealth. Held over the New Year according to the Vikrama calendar, it is marked by feasting, gifts, and the lighting of lamps

dixie (ˈdɪksɪ) *n* **1** *chiefly mil* a large metal pot for cooking, brewing tea, etc **2** a mess tin [C19 from Hindi *degcī*, dim. of *degcā* pot]

Dixie (ˈdɪksɪ) *n* **1** Also called: **Dixieland** the southern states of the US ▷ *adj* **2** of the southern states of the US [C19 ?from the nickname of New Orleans, from *dixie* a ten-dollar bill printed there, from F *dix* ten]

Dixieland (ˈdɪksɪˌlænd) *n* **1** a form of jazz that originated in New Orleans in the 1920s **2** a revival of this style in the 1950s **3** See **Dixie** (sense 1)

▷ www.jazzinamerica.org

▷ http://nfo.net/usa/JO.html

Dixon (ˈdɪksən) *n* **Willie**, full name *William James Dixon*. 1915–92, U.S. blues musician, songwriter, and record producer, whose songs have been recorded by many other artists

DIY *or* **d.i.y.** *Brit, Austral, Canad, & NZ abbrev for* do-it-yourself

▷ http://doityourself.com

dizzy (ˈdɪzɪ) *adj* **dizzier, dizziest** **1** affected with a whirling or reeling sensation; giddy **2** mentally confused or bewildered **3** causing or tending to cause vertigo or bewilderment **4** *inf* foolish or flighty ▷ *vb* **dizzies, dizzying, dizzied** **5** (*tr*) to make dizzy [OE *dysig* silly] > **ˈdizzily** *adv* > **ˈdizziness** *n*

DJ *or* **dj** (ˈdiːˌdʒeɪ) *n* **1** a variant of **deejay** **2** an informal term for **dinner jacket**

Dd

Djailolo *or* **Jilolo** (dʒaɪˈləʊləʊ) *n* the Dutch name for **Halmahera**
Djakarta (dʒəˈkɑːtə) *n* a variant spelling of **Jakarta**
djellaba, djellabah *or* **jellaba, jellabah** (ˈdʒɛləbə) *n* a kind of loose cloak with a hood, worn by men esp in N Africa and the Middle East [from Ar. *jallabah*]
Djibouti *or* **Jibouti** (dʒɪˈbuːtɪ) *n* **1** a republic in E Africa, on the Gulf of Aden: a French overseas territory (1946–77); became independent in 1977; mainly desert. Official languages: Arabic and French. Religion: Muslim majority. Currency: Djibouti franc. Capital: Djibouti. Pop: 461 000 (2001 est). Area: 23 200 sq km (8950 sq miles). Former name (until 1977): (Territory of the) Afars and the Issas **2** the capital of Djibouti, a port on the Gulf of Aden: an outlet for Ethiopian goods. Pop: 383 000 (1995)
▷ www.republique-djibouti.com/gouvernement.htm
djinni *or* **djinny** (dʒɪˈniː, ˈdʒɪnɪ) *n, pl* **djinn** (dʒɪn) variant spellings of **jinni**
dl *symbol for* decilitre
DLitt *or* **DLit** *abbrev for:* **1** Doctor of Letters **2** Doctor of Literature [L *Doctor Litterarum*]
dm *symbol for* decimetre
DM *abbrev for* (the former) Deutschmark
DMA *computing abbrev for* direct memory access
D-mark *or* **D-Mark** *n* short for (the former) **Deutschmark**
DMF *abbrev for* dimethylformamide
DMs *inf abbrev for* Doc Martens
DMus *abbrev for* Doctor of Music
DMV *in the US and Canada abbrev for* Department of Motor Vehicles
DNA *n* deoxyribonucleic acid, the main constituent of the chromosomes of all organisms (except some viruses) in the form of a double helix. DNA is self-replicating and is responsible for the transmission of hereditary characteristics
DNAase (ˌdiːɛnˈeɪeɪz) *or* **DNase** (ˌdiːɛnˈeɪz) *n* deoxyribonuclease; any of a number of enzymes that hydrolyse DNA
DNA fingerprinting *or* **profiling** *n* another name for **genetic fingerprinting**
Dnepropetrovsk (*Russian* dnɪprəpɪˈtrɔfsk) *n* a city in the E central Ukraine on the Dnieper River: a major centre of the metallurgical industry. Pop: 1 122 400 (1998 est). Former name (1787–1796, 1802–1926): **Yekaterinoslav**
Dnieper (ˈdniːpə) *n* a river in NE Europe, rising in Russia, in the Valdai Hills NE of Smolensk and flowing south to the Black Sea: the third longest river in Europe; a major navigable waterway. Length: 2200 km (1370 miles). Russian name: **Dnepr** (ˈdnjɛpə)
Dniester (ˈdniːstə) *n* a river in E Europe, rising in the Ukraine, in the Carpathian Mountains and flowing generally southeast to the Black Sea. Length: 1411 km (877 miles). Russian name: **Dnestr** (ˈdnjɛstə)
D-notice *n Brit* an official notice sent to newspapers prohibiting the publication of certain security information [c20 from their administrative classification letter]
do¹ (duː; *unstressed* dʊ, də) *vb* **does, doing, did, done 1** to perform or complete (a deed or action): *to do a portrait* **2** (often *intr;* foll by *for*) to serve the needs of; be suitable for; suffice **3** (*tr*) to arrange or fix **4** (*tr*) to prepare or provide; serve: *this restaurant doesn't do lunch on Sundays* **5** (*tr*) to make tidy, elegant, ready, etc: *to do one's hair* **6** (*tr*) to improve(esp in **do something to** *or* **for**) **7** (*tr*) to find an answer to (a problem or puzzle) **8** (*tr*) to translate or adapt the form or language of: *the book was done into a play* **9** (*intr*) to conduct oneself: *do as you please* **10** (*intr*) to fare or manage **11** (*tr*) to cause or produce: *complaints do nothing to help* **12** (*tr*) to give or render: *do me a favour* **13** (*tr*) to work at, esp as a course of study or a profession **14** (*tr*) to perform (a play, etc); act **15** (*tr*) to mimic or play the part of: *she does a wonderful elderly aunt* **16** (*tr*) to travel at a specified speed, esp as a maximum **17** (*tr*) to travel or traverse (a distance) **18** (takes an infinitive without *to*) used as an auxiliary **18a** before the subject of an interrogative sentence as a way of forming a question: *do you agree?* **18b** to intensify positive statements and commands: *I do like your new house; do hurry!* **18c** before a negative adverb to form negative statements or commands: *do not leave me here alone!* **18d** in inverted constructions: *little did he realize that* **19** used as an auxiliary to replace an earlier verb or verb phrase: *he likes you as much as I do* **20** (*tr*) *inf* to visit as a sightseer or tourist **21** (*tr*) to wear out; exhaust **22** (*intr*) to happen(esp in **nothing doing**) **23** (*tr*) *sl* to serve (a period of time) as a prison sentence **24** (*tr*) *inf* to cheat or swindle **25** (*tr*) *sl* to rob **26** (*tr*) *sl* **26a** to arrest **26b** to convict of a crime **27** (*tr*) *Austral sl* to spend (money) **28** (*tr*) *sl, chiefly Brit* to treat violently; assault **29** *sl* to take or use (a drug) **30** (*tr*) *taboo sl* (of a male) to have sexual intercourse with **31 do or die** to make a final or supreme effort **32 make do** to manage with whatever is available ▷ *n, pl* **dos** *or* **do's 33** *sl* an act or instance of cheating or swindling **34** *inf, chiefly Brit & NZ* a formal or festive gathering; party **35 do's and don'ts** *inf* rules ▷ See also **do away with, do by,** etc [OE *dōn*]
do² (dəʊ) *n, pl* **dos** a variant spelling of **doh**
do. *abbrev for* ditto
DOA *abbrev for* dead on arrival
doable (ˈduːəbᵊl) *adj* capable of being done
do away with *vb* (*intr, adv + prep*) **1** to kill or destroy **2** to discard or abolish
dobbin (ˈdɒbɪn) *n* a name for a horse, esp a workhorse [c16 from *Robin*, pet form of *Robert*]
Dobell (dəʊˈbɛl) *n* Sir **William** 1899–1970, Australian portrait and landscape painter. Awarded the Archibald prize (1943) for his famous painting of *Joshua Smith* which resulted in a heated clash between the conservatives and the moderns and led to a lawsuit. His other works include *The Cypriot* (1940), *The Billy Boy* (1943), and *Portrait of a strapper* (1941)
Doberman pinscher (ˈdəʊbəmən ˈpɪnʃə) *or* **Doberman** *n* a breed of large dog with a glossy black-and-tan coat. Also: **Dobermann** [c19 after L. *Dobermann* (19th-cent. G dog breeder) who bred it + *Pinscher*, ? after *Pinzgau*, district in Austria]
dob in *vb* **dobs, dobbing, dobbed** (*adv*) *Austral & NZ sl* **1** (*tr*) to inform against, esp to the police **2** to contribute to a fund
dobra (ˈdəʊbrə) *n* the standard monetary unit of São Tomé e Principe, divided into 100 cêntimos
Dobruja (*Bulgarian* ˈdɔbrudʒa) *n* a region of E Europe, between the River Danube and the Black Sea: the north passed to Romania and the south to Bulgaria after the Berlin Congress (1878). Romanian name: **Dobrogea** (doˈbrodʒea)
do by *vb* (*intr, prep*) to treat in the manner specified
doc (dɒk) *n inf* short for **doctor**
DOC *abbrev for* Denominazione di Origine Controllata: used of wines [It., lit.: name of origin controlled]
docent (ˈdəʊsᵊnt) *n* a voluntary worker acting as a guide in a museum, art gallery, etc [c19 from G *Dozent*, from L *docēns* from *docēre* to teach]
DOCG *abbrev for* Denominazione di Origine Controllata Garantita: used of wines [It., lit: name of origin guaranteed controlled]
docile (ˈdəʊsaɪl) *adj* **1** easy to manage or discipline; submissive **2** *rare* easy to teach [c15 from L *docilis* easily taught, from *docēre* to teach] > **ˈdocilely** *adv* > **docility** (dəʊˈsɪlɪtɪ) *n*
dock¹ (dɒk) *n* **1** a wharf or pier **2** a space between two wharves or piers for the mooring of ships **3** an area of water that can accommodate a ship and can be closed off to allow regulation of the water level **4** short for **dry**

dock 5 **in** *or* **into dock** *Brit inf* **5a** (of people) in hospital **5b** (of cars, etc) in a repair shop **6** *chiefly US & Canad* a platform from which lorries, goods trains, etc, are loaded and unloaded ▷ *vb* **7** to moor or be moored at a dock **8** to put (a vessel) into, or (of a vessel) to come into a dry dock **9** (of two spacecraft) to link together in space or link together (two spacecraft) in space [c14 from MDu. *docke*; ? rel. to L *ducere* to lead]

dock² (dɒk) *n* **1** the bony part of the tail of an animal **2** the part of an animal's tail left after the major part of it has been cut off ▷ *vb (tr)* **3** to remove (the tail or part of the tail) of (an animal) by cutting through the bone **4** to deduct (an amount) from (a person's wages, pension, etc) [c14 *dok* from ?]

dock³ (dɒk) *n* an enclosed space in a court of law where the accused sits or stands during his trial [c16 from Flemish *dok* sty]

dock⁴ (dɒk) *n* any of various weedy plants having greenish or reddish flowers and broad leaves [OE *docce*]

dockage (ˈdɒkɪdʒ) *n* **1** a charge levied upon a vessel for using a dock **2** facilities for docking vessels **3** the practice of docking vessels

docker (ˈdɒkə) *n Brit* a man employed in the loading or unloading of ships. US and Canad equivalent: **longshoreman** Austral and NZ equivalent: **watersider, wharfie** See also **stevedore**

docket (ˈdɒkɪt) *n* **1** *chiefly Brit* a piece of paper accompanying or referring to a package or other delivery, stating contents, delivery instructions, etc, sometimes serving as a receipt **2** *law* **2a** a summary of the proceedings in a court **2b** a register containing this **3** *Brit* **3a** a customs certificate declaring that duty has been paid **3b** a certificate giving particulars of a shipment **4** a summary of contents, as in a document **5** *US* a list of things to be done **6** *US law* a list of cases awaiting trial ▷ *vb* **dockets, docketing, docketed** *(tr)* **7** to fix a docket to (a package, etc) **8** *law* **8a** to make a summary of (a judgment, etc) **8b** to abstract and enter in a register **9** to endorse (a document, etc) with a summary [c15 from ?]

docking station *n* a device used to connect one appliance to another, esp a portable computer and a desktop computer, to make use of its external power supply, monitor, and keyboard, esp to enable the transfer of data between the machines

dockland (ˈdɒkˌlænd) *n* the area around the docks

dockside (ˈdɒkˌsaɪd) *n* an area beside a dock

dockyard (ˈdɒkˌjɑːd) *n* a naval establishment with docks, workshops, etc, for the building, fitting out, and repair of vessels

Doc Martens (dɒk ˈmɑːtənz) *pl n trademark.* a brand of lace-up boots with thick lightweight resistant soles. In full: **Doctor Martens.** Abbrev: **DMs**

doctor (ˈdɒktə) *n* **1** a person licensed to practise medicine **2** a person who has been awarded a higher academic degree in any field of knowledge **3** *chiefly US & Canad* a person licensed to practise dentistry or veterinary medicine **4** *(often cap)* Also called: **Doctor of the Church** a title given to any of several of the early Fathers of the Christian Church **5** *angling* any of various artificial flies **6** *inf* a person who mends or repairs things **7** *sl* a cook on a ship or at a camp **8** *arch* a man, esp a teacher, of learning **9** a cool sea breeze blowing in some warm countries: *the Cape doctor* **10** **go for the doctor** *Austral sl* to make a great effort or move very fast **11** **what the doctor ordered** something needed or desired ▷ *vb* **12** *(tr)* to give medical treatment to **13** *(intr) inf* to practise medicine **14** *(tr)* to repair or mend **15** *(tr)* to make different in order to deceive **16** *(tr)* to adapt **17** *(tr) inf* to castrate (a cat, dog, etc) [c14 from L: teacher, from *docēre* to teach] > **ˈdoctoral** *or* **doctorial** (dɒkˈtɔːrɪəl) *adj*

doctorate (ˈdɒktərɪt, -trɪt) *n* the highest academic degree in any field of knowledge

Doctor of Philosophy *n* a doctorate awarded for original research in any subject except law, medicine, or theology

doctrinaire (ˌdɒktrɪˈnɛə) *adj* **1** stubbornly insistent on the observation of the niceties of a theory, esp without regard to practicality, suitability, etc **2** theoretical; impractical ▷ *n* **3** a person who stubbornly attempts to apply a theory without regard to practical difficulties > ˌ**doctriˈnairism** *n* > ˌ**doctriˈnarian** *n*

doctrine (ˈdɒktrɪn) *n* **1** a creed or body of teachings of a religious, political, or philosophical group presented for acceptance or belief; dogma **2** a principle or body of principles that is taught or advocated [c14 from OF, from L *doctrīna* teaching, from *doctor*; see DOCTOR] > **doctrinal** (dɒkˈtraɪnᵊl) *adj* > **docˈtrinally** *adv*

docudrama (ˈdɒkjʊˌdrɑːmə) *n* a film or television programme based on true events, presented in a dramatized form

document *n* (ˈdɒkjʊmənt) **1** a piece of paper, booklet, etc, providing information, esp of an official nature **2** a piece of text or graphics, such as a letter or article, stored in a computer as a file for manipulation by document processing software **3** *arch* proof ▷ *vb* (ˈdɒkjʊˌmɛnt) *(tr)* **4** to record or report in detail, as in the press, on television, etc **5** to support (statements in a book) with references, etc **6** to support (a claim, etc) with evidence **7** to furnish (a vessel) with documents specifying its registration, dimensions, etc [c15 from L *documentum* a lesson, from *docēre* to teach]

documentarian (ˌdɒkjʊmənˈtɛərɪən) *n chiefly US* a person who makes documentary films

documentary (ˌdɒkjʊˈmɛntərɪ) *adj* **1** Also: **documental** consisting of or relating to documents **2** presenting factual material with few or no fictional additions ▷ *n, pl* **documentaries** **3** a factual film or television programme about an event, person, etc, presenting the facts with little or no fiction > ˌ**docuˈmentarily** *adv*

Dd

documentation (ˌdɒkjʊmɛnˈteɪʃən) *n* **1** the act of supplying with or using documents or references **2** the documents or references supplied

document reader *n computing* a device that reads and inputs into a computer marks and characters on a special form, as by optical or magnetic character recognition

docu-soap *or* **docusoap** (ˈdɒkjʊˌsəʊp) *n* a television documentary series in which the lives of the people filmed are presented as entertainment or drama [c20 from DOCU(MENTARY) + SOAP (OPERA)]

▷ www.memorabletv.com/documentary/docusoap.htm

dodder¹ (ˈdɒdə) *vb (intr)* **1** to move unsteadily; totter **2** to shake or tremble, as from age [c17 var. of earlier *dadder*] > ˈ**dodderer** *n* > ˈ**doddery** *adj*

dodder² (ˈdɒdə) *n* any of a genus of rootless parasitic plants lacking chlorophyll and having suckers for drawing nourishment from the host plant [c13 of Gmc origin]

doddle (ˈdɒdᵊl) *n Brit inf* something easily accomplished [c20 ?from *doddle* (vb) to totter]

dodeca- *combining form.* indicating twelve: *dodecaphonic* [from Gk *dōdeka* twelve]

dodecagon (dəʊˈdɛkəˌgɒn) *n* a polygon having twelve sides

dodecahedron (ˌdəʊdɛkəˈhiːdrən) *n* a solid figure having twelve plane faces > ˌ**dodecaˈhedral** *adj*

Dodecanese (ˌdəʊdɪkəˈniːz) *pl n* a group of islands in the SE Aegean Sea, forming a department of Greece: part of the Southern Sporades. Capital: Rhodes. Pop: 162 439 (1991). Area: 2663 sq km (1028 sq miles). Modern Greek name: **Dhodhekánisos**

dodecaphonic (ˌdəʊdɛkəˈfɒnɪk) *adj* of or relating to the twelve-tone system of serial music

dodge (dɒdʒ) *vb* **dodges, dodging, dodged** **1** to avoid or attempt to avoid (a blow, discovery, etc), as by moving suddenly **2** to evade by cleverness or trickery **3** (*intr*) *change-ringing* to make a bell change places with its neighbour when sounding in successive changes **4** (*tr*) *photog* to lighten or darken (selected areas on a print) ▷ *n* **5** a plan contrived to deceive **6** a sudden evasive movement **7** a clever contrivance **8** *change-ringing* the act of dodging [C16 from ?]

Dodge City *n* a city in SW Kansas, on the Arkansas River: famous as a frontier town on the Santa Fe Trail. Pop: 21 130 (1990)

Dodgem ('dɒdʒəm) *n trademark* an electrically propelled vehicle driven and bumped against similar cars in a rink at a funfair

dodger ('dɒdʒə) *n* **1** a person who evades or shirks **2** a shifty dishonest person **3** a canvas shelter on a ship's bridge, etc, to protect the helmsman from bad weather **4** *dialect & Austral* food, esp bread

dodgy ('dɒdʒɪ) *adj* **dodgier, dodgiest** *Brit, Austral & NZ inf* **1** risky, difficult, or dangerous **2** uncertain or unreliable; tricky

dodo ('dəʊdəʊ) *n, pl* **dodos** *or* **dodoes** **1** any of a now extinct family of flightless birds formerly found on Mauritius. They had a hooked bill and short stout legs **2** *inf* an intensely conservative person who is unaware of changing fashions, ideas, etc **3** (**as**) **dead as a dodo** irretrievably defunct or out of date [C17 from Port. *doudo*, from *duodo* stupid]

Dodoma ('dəʊdəmə) *n* a city in central Tanzania, the legislative capital of the country. Pop: 203 833 (latest est) ▷ www.itanzania.info/Dodoma_Region.htm

Dodona (dəʊ'dəʊnə) *n* an ancient Greek town in Epirus: seat of an ancient sanctuary and oracle of Zeus and later the religious centre of Pyrrhus' kingdom > **Dodonaean** *or* **Dodonean** (ˌdəʊdəʊ'niːən) *adj*

do down *vb* (*tr, adv*) **1** to belittle or humiliate **2** to deceive or cheat

doe (dəʊ) *n, pl* **does** *or* **doe** the female of the deer, hare, rabbit, and certain other animals [OE *dā*]

Doe (dəʊ) *n* **John** *law* **1** (formerly) the plaintiff in a fictitious action, Doe versus Roe, to test a point of law. See also **Roe** **2** Also: **Jane Doe** US an unknown or unidentified person

DOE (in Britain) *abbrev for* (the former) Department of the Environment

doek (dʊk) *n S African inf* a square of cloth worn mainly by African women to cover the head [C18 from Afrik.: cloth]

Doenitz (*German* 'døːnɪts) *n* a variant spelling of (Karl) **Dönitz**

doer ('duːə) *n* **1** a person or thing that does something **2** an active or energetic person **3** a thriving animal, esp a horse

does[1] (dʌz) *vb* (used with a singular noun or the pronouns *he, she,* or *it*) a form of the present tense (indicative mood) of **do**[1]

does[2] (dʊəs) *n S African taboo sl* a foolish or despicable person [Afrik.]

doeskin ('dəʊˌskɪn) *n* **1** the skin of a deer, lamb, or sheep **2** a very supple leather made from this **3** a heavy smooth cloth

doff (dɒf) *vb* (*tr*) **1** to take off or lift (one's hat) in salutation **2** to remove (clothing) [OE *dōn of*; see DO[1], OFF; cf. DON[1]] > '**doffer** *n*

do for *vb* (*prep*) *Inf* **1** (*tr*) to convict of a crime or offence **2** (*intr*) to cause the ruin, death, or defeat of **3** (*intr*) to do housework for **4** **do well for oneself** to thrive or succeed

dog (dɒg) *n* **1** a domesticated canine mammal occurring in many breeds that show a great variety in size and form **2** any other carnivore of the dog family, such as the dingo and coyote **3** the male of animals of the dog family **4** (*modifier*) spurious, inferior, or useless **5** a mechanical device for gripping or holding **6** *inf* a fellow; chap **7** *inf* a man or boy regarded as unpleasant or wretched **8** *sl* an unattractive girl or woman **9** *US & Canad inf* something unsatisfactory or inferior **10** short for **firedog** **11** **a dog's chance** no chance at all **12** **a dog's dinner** *or* **breakfast** *inf* something messy or bungled **13** **a dog's life** a wretched existence **14** **dog eat dog** ruthless competition **15** **like a dog's dinner** dressed smartly or ostentatiously **16** **put on the dog** *US & Canad inf* to behave or dress in an ostentatious manner ▷ *vb* **dogs, dogging, dogged** (*tr*) **17** to pursue or follow after with determination **18** to trouble; plague **19** to chase with a dog **20** to grip or secure by a mechanical device ▷ *adv* **21** (*usually in combination*) thoroughly; utterly: *dog-tired* ▷ See also **dogs** [OE *docga*, from ?]

dog and bone *n Brit sl* a telephone [rhyming sl for *phone*]

dog biscuit *n* a hard biscuit for dogs

dog box *n NZ inf* disgrace; disfavour: *in the dog box*

dogcart ('dɒgˌkɑːt) *n* a light horse-drawn two-wheeled vehicle

dog-catcher *n now chiefly US & Canad* a local official whose job is to impound and dispose of stray dogs

dog collar *n* **1** a collar for a dog **2** *inf* a clerical collar **3** *inf* a tight-fitting necklace

dog days *pl n* the hot period of the summer reckoned in ancient times from the heliacal rising of Sirius (the Dog Star) [C16 translation of LL *diēs caniculārēs*, translation of Gk *hēmerai kunades*]

doge (dəʊdʒ) *n* (formerly) the chief magistrate in the republics of Venice and Genoa [C16 via F from It. (Venetian dialect), from L *dux* leader]

dog-ear *vb* **1** (*tr*) to fold down the corner of (a page) ▷ *n* also **dog's-ear** **2** a folded-down corner of a page

dog-eared *adj* **1** having dog-ears **2** shabby or worn

dog-end *n inf* a cigarette end

dogfight ('dɒgˌfaɪt) *n* **1** close-quarters combat between fighter aircraft **2** any rough fight

dogfish ('dɒgˌfɪʃ) *n, pl* **dogfish** *or* **dogfishes** **1** any of several small sharks **2** a less common name for the **bowfin**

dog fouling *n* the offence of being in charge of a dog and failing to remove the faeces after it defecates in a public place

dogged ('dɒgɪd) *adj* obstinately determined; wilful or tenacious > '**doggedly** *adv* > '**doggedness** *n*

Dogger Bank ('dɒgə) *n* an extensive submerged sandbank in the North Sea between N England and Denmark: fishing ground

doggerel ('dɒgərəl) *or* **dogrel** ('dɒgrəl) *n* **1a** comic verse, usually irregular in measure **1b** (*as modifier*): *a doggerel rhythm* **2** nonsense [C14 *dogerel* worthless, ?from *dogge* DOG]

doggish ('dɒgɪʃ) *adj* **1** of or like a dog **2** surly; snappish

doggo ('dɒgəʊ) *adv Brit inf* in hiding and keeping quiet(esp in **lie doggo**) [C19 prob. from DOG]

doggone ('dɒgɒn) *US & Canad* ▷ *interj* **1** an exclamation of annoyance, etc ▷ *adj* (*prenominal*), *adv* **2** Also: **doggoned** another word for **damn** [C19 euphemism for *God damn*]

doggy *or* **doggie** ('dɒgɪ) *n, pl* **doggies** **1** a child's word for a dog ▷ *adj* **doggier, doggiest** **2** of, like, or relating to a dog **3** fond of dogs

doggy bag *n* a bag in which leftovers from a meal may be taken away, supposedly for the diner's dog

doggy paddle *or* **doggie paddle** *n, vb* another word for **dog paddle**

doghouse ('dɒgˌhaʊs) *n* **1** the US and Canad name for **kennel** **2** *inf* disfavour (in **in the doghouse**)

dogie, dogy, *or* **dogey** ('dəʊgɪ) *n, pl* **dogies** *or* **dogeys** *US & Canad* a motherless calf [C19 from *dough-guts*, because they were fed on flour-and-water paste]

dog in the manger *n* a person who prevents others from using something he or she has no use for

dog Latin *n* spurious or incorrect Latin

dogleg ('dɒgˌlɛg) *n* **1** a sharp bend or angle ▷ *vb* **doglegs, doglegging, doglegged** **2** (*intr*) to go off at an angle ▷ *adj*

3 of or with the shape of a dogleg > **doglegged** (ˌdɒg'lɛgɪd, 'dɒgˌlɛgd) *adj*

dogma ('dɒgmə) *n, pl* **dogmas** *or* **dogmata** (-mətə) **1** a religious doctrine or system of doctrines proclaimed by ecclesiastical authority as true **2** a belief, principle, or doctrine or a code of beliefs, principles, or doctrines [C17 via L from Gk: opinion, from *dokein* to seem good]

dogman ('dɒgmən) *n, pl* **dogmen** *Austral* a person who directs the operation of a crane whilst riding on an object being lifted by it

dogmatic (dɒg'mætɪk) *or* **dogmatical** *adj* **1a** (of a statement, opinion, etc) forcibly asserted as if authoritative and unchallengeable **1b** (of a person) prone to making such statements **2** of or constituting dogma **3** based on assumption rather than observation > **dog'matically** *adv*

dogmatics (dɒg'mætɪks) *n (functioning as sing)* the study of religious dogmas and doctrines. Also called: **dogmatic** (*or* **doctrinal**) **theology**

dogmatize *or* **dogmatise** ('dɒgməˌtaɪz) *vb* **dogmatizes, dogmatizing, dogmatized** *or* **dogmatises, dogmatising, dogmatised** to say or state (something) in a dogmatic manner > **'dogmatism** *n* > **'dogmatist** *n*

do-gooder *n inf* a well-intentioned person, esp a naive or impractical one > **ˌdo-'gooding** *n, adj*

dog paddle *n* **1** a swimming stroke in which the swimmer paddles his or her hands in imitation of a swimming dog ▷ *vb* **dog-paddle, dog-paddles, dog-paddling, dog-paddled 2** *(intr)* to swim using the dog paddle. Also: **doggy paddle** *or* **doggie paddle**

Dogrib ('dɒgˌrɪb) *n* **1** a member of a Dene Native Canadian people of northern Canada **2** the Athapascan language of this people [from Dogrib *Thlingchadinne*, dog's flank, referring to the people's belief that they are descended from a dog]

dog-roll *n NZ* a large sausage-shaped roll of processed meat used for dog food

dog rose *n* a prickly wild European rose that has pink or white scentless flowers [from belief that its root was effective against the bite of a mad dog]

dogs (dɒgz) *pl n* **1** *sl* the feet **2** *marketing, inf* goods with a low market share, which are unlikely to yield substantial profits **3 go to the dogs** *inf* to go to ruin physically or morally **4 let sleeping dogs lie** to leave things undisturbed **5 the dogs** *Brit inf* greyhound racing

Dogs (dɒgz) *n* **Isle of** a district in the East End of London, bounded on three sides by the River Thames

dogsbody ('dɒgzˌbɒdɪ) *inf* ▷ *n, pl* **dogsbodies 1** a person who carries out menial tasks for others ▷ *vb* **dogsbodies, dogsbodying, dogsbodied** *(intr)* **2** to act as a dogsbody

dog's disease *n Austral inf* influenza

dogsled ('dɒgˌslɛd) *n chiefly US & Canad* a sleigh drawn by dogs. Also called *(Brit)*: **dog sledge**

Dog Star *n* **the** another name for **Sirius**

dog-tired *adj (usually postpositive) inf* exhausted

dogtooth ('dɒgˌtuːθ) *n, pl* **dogteeth** *archit* a carved ornament in the form of a series of four-cornered pyramids set diagonally and often decorated with leaf shapes along each edge, used in England in the 13th century

dogtooth violet *n* any of a genus of plants, esp a European plant with purple flowers

dogtrot ('dɒgˌtrɒt) *n* a gently paced trot

dog violet *n* any of three wild violets found in Britain and northern Europe

dogwatch ('dɒgˌwɒtʃ) *n* either of two two-hour watches aboard ship, from four to six p.m. or from six to eight pm

dogwood ('dɒgˌwʊd) *n* any of various trees or shrubs, esp a European shrub with small white flowers and black berries

dogy ('dəʊgɪ) *n, pl* **dogies** a variant of **dogie**

doh (dəʊ) *n music* (in tonic sol-fa) the first degree of any major scale [C18 from It., replacing *ut*; see GAMUT]

DOH (in Britain) *abbrev for* Department of Health

Doha ('dəʊhɑː, 'dəʊə) *n* the capital and chief port of Qatar, on the E coast of the peninsula. Pop: 264 009 (1997). Former name: **Bida, El Beda**
▷ www.qatartourism.org

Dohnányi (dɒk'nɑːnjɪ, dɒx-; *Hungarian* 'dohnaːnji) *n* **Ernö** ('ɛrnøː) or **Ernst von** (ɛrnst fɔn) 1877–1960, Hungarian pianist and composer whose works include *Variations on a Nursery Theme* (1913) for piano and orchestra

doily *or* **doyley** ('dɔɪlɪ) *n, pl* **doilies** *or* **doileys** a decorative mat of lace or lacelike paper, etc, laid on plates [C18 after *Doily*, a London draper]

do in *vb (tr, adv) Sl* **1** to kill **2** to exhaust

doing ('duːɪŋ) *n* **1** an action or the performance of an action: *whose doing is this?* **2** *inf* a beating or castigation

doings ('duːɪŋz) *n* **1** *(functioning as pl)* deeds, actions, or events **2** *(functioning as sing) inf* anything of which the name is not known, or euphemistically left unsaid, etc

do-it-yourself *n* **a** the hobby or process of constructing and repairing things oneself **b** *(as modifier)*: *a do-it-yourself kit*

dol. *abbrev for*: **1** *music* dolce **2** *(pl* **dols.**) dollar

Dolby ('dɒlbɪ) *n trademark* any of various specialized electronic circuits, esp those used in tape recorders for noise reduction in high-frequency signals [after R. *Dolby* (born 1933), US inventor]

dolce ('dɒltʃɪ) *adj, adv music* (to be performed) gently and sweetly [It.]

Dolcelatte (ˌdɒltʃiː'lɑːtɪ) *n* a soft creamy blue-veined Italian cheese [It., lit: sweet milk]

dolce vita ('dɒltʃɪ 'viːtə) *n* a life of luxury [It., lit.: sweet life]

doldrums ('dɒldrəmz) *n* **the 1** a depressed or bored state of mind **2** a state of inactivity or stagnation **3** a belt of light winds or calms along the equator [C19 prob. from OE *dol* DULL, infl. by TANTRUM]

Dd

dole[1] (dəʊl) *n* **1** (usually preceded by *the*) *Brit & Austral inf* money received from the state while out of work **2 on the dole** *Brit & Austral inf* receiving such money **3** a small portion of money or food given to a poor person **4** the act of distributing such portions **5** *arch* fate ▷ *vb* **doles, doling, doled 6** *(tr; usually foll by out)* to distribute, esp in small portions [OE *dāl* share]

dole[2] (dəʊl) *n arch* grief or mourning [C13 from OF, from LL *dolus*, from L *dolēre* to lament]

dole-bludger *n Austral & NZ sl* a person who draws unemployment benefit without making any attempt to get work

doleful ('dəʊlfʊl) *adj* dreary; mournful > **'dolefully** *adv* > **'dolefulness** *n*

dolerite ('dɒləˌraɪt) *n* **1** a dark basic intrusive igneous rock; a coarse-grained basalt **2** any dark igneous rock whose composition cannot be determined with the naked eye [C19 from F *dolérite*, from Gk *doleros* deceitful; from the difficulty in determining its composition]

Dolgellau (dɒl'gɛθlaɪ; *Welsh* dɒl'gɛhlaɪ) *n* a market town and tourist centre in NW Wales, in Gwynedd. Pop: 2396 (1991)

dolichocephalic (ˌdɒlɪkəʊsɪ'fælɪk) *or* **dolichocephalous** (ˌdɒlɪkəʊ'sɛfələs) *adj* having a head much longer than it is broad [C19 from Gk *dolichos* long + -CEPHALIC]

Dolin ('dəʊlɪn) *n* Sir **Anton**, real name *Sydney Healey-Kay*. 1904–83, British ballet dancer and choreographer: with Alicia Markova he founded (1949) the London Festival Ballet

doll (dɒl) *n* **1** a small model or dummy of a human being, used as a toy **2** *sl* a pretty girl or woman of little intelligence [C16 prob. from *Doll*, pet name for *Dorothy*]

dollar ('dɒlə) *n* **1** the standard monetary unit of the US, divided into 100 cents **2** the standard monetary unit, comprising 100 cents, of the following countries or territories: Antigua and Barbuda, Australia, the

Bahamas, Barbados, Belize, Bermuda, the British Virgin Islands, Brunei, Canada, the Cayman Islands, Dominica, East Timor, Ecuador, El Salvador, Fiji, Grenada, Guatemale, Guyana, Hong Kong, Jamaica, Kiribati, Liberia, Malaysia, the Marshall Islands, Micronesia, Namibia, Nauru, New Zealand, Saint Kitts and Nevis, Saint Lucia, Saint Vincent and the Grenadines, Singapore, Solomon Islands, Taiwan, Trinidad and Tobago, Tuvulu, and Zimbabwe [c16 from Low G *daler*, from G *Taler*, *Thaler*, short for *Joachimsthaler*, coin made from metal mined in *Joachimsthal* Jachymov, town in the Czech Republic]

dollarbird ('dɒlə,bɜːd) *n* a bird of S and SE Asia and Australia with a round white spot on each wing

dollar diplomacy *n chiefly US* **1** a foreign policy that encourages and protects commercial and financial involvement abroad **2** use of financial power as a diplomatic weapon

Dollfuss (*German* 'dɔlfuːs) *n* **Engelbert** ('ɛŋəlbɛrt) 1892–1934, Austrian statesman, chancellor (1932–34), who was assassinated by Austrian Nazis

dollop ('dɒləp) *inf* ▷ *n* **1** a semisolid lump **2** a measure or serving ▷ *vb* **3** (*tr; foll by out*) to serve out (food) [c16 from ?]

doll up *vb* (*tr, adv*) *sl* to dress in a stylish or showy manner

dolly ('dɒlɪ) *n, pl* **dollies** **1** a child's word for a **doll** **2** *films, etc* a wheeled support on which a camera may be mounted **3** a cup-shaped anvil used to hold a rivet **4** *cricket* **4a** a simple catch **4b** a full toss bowled in a slow high arc **5** Also called: **dolly bird** *sl, chiefly Brit* an attractive and fashionable girl ▷ *vb* **dollies, dollying, dollied** **6** *films, etc* to wheel (a camera) backwards or forwards on a dolly

dolly mixture *n* **1** a mixture of tiny coloured sweets **2** one such sweet

dolma ('dɒlmə) *n, pl* **dolmas** *or* **dolmades** (dɒl'mɑːdiːz) a vine leaf stuffed with a filling of meat and rice [c19 Turkish *dolma* lit. something filled]

dolman sleeve ('dɒlmən) *n* a sleeve that is very wide at the armhole and tapers to a tight wrist [c19 from *dolman*, a type of Turkish robe, ult. from Turkish *dolamak* to wind]

dolmen ('dɒlmɛn) *n* a Neolithic stone formation, consisting of a horizontal stone supported by several vertical stones, and thought to be a tomb [c19 from F, prob. from OBreton *tol* table, from L *tabula* board + Breton *mēn* stone, of Celtic origin]

Dolmetsch ('dɒlmɛtʃ) *n* **Arnold** 1858–1940, British musician, born in France. He contributed greatly to the revival of interest in early music and instruments

dolomite ('dɒlə,maɪt) *n* **1** a mineral consisting of calcium magnesium carbonate **2** a rock resembling limestone but consisting principally of the mineral dolomite [c18 after Déodat de *Dolomieu* (1750–1801), F mineralogist] > **dolomitic** (,dɒlə'mɪtɪk) *adj*

Dolomites ('dɒlə,maɪts) *pl n* a mountain range in NE Italy: part of the Alps; formed of dolomitic limestone. Highest peak: Marmolada, 3342 m (10 965 ft)

doloroso (,dɒlə'rəʊsəʊ) *adj, adv music* (to be performed) in a sorrowful manner [It.]

dolorous ('dɒlərəs) *adj* causing or involving pain or sorrow > '**dolorously** *adv*

dolos ('dɒlɒs) *n, pl* **dolosse** *S African* a knucklebone of a sheep, buck, etc, used esp by diviners [from ?]

dolour *or US* **dolor** ('dɒlə) *n poetic* grief or sorrow [c14 from L, from *dolēre* to grieve]

dolphin ('dɒlfɪn) *n* **1** any of various marine mammals that are typically smaller than whales and larger than porpoises and have a beaklike snout **2** **river dolphin** any of various freshwater mammals inhabiting rivers of North and South America and S Asia **3** Also called: **dorado** either of two large marine fishes that have an iridescent coloration **4** *naut* a post or buoy for mooring a vessel [c13 from OF *dauphin*, via L, from Gk *delphin-*, *delphis*]

dolphinarium (,dɒlfɪ'nɛərɪəm) *n, pl* **dolphinariums** *or* **dolphinaria** (-ɪə) a pool or aquarium for dolphins, esp one in which they give public displays

dolt (dəʊlt) *n* a slow-witted or stupid person [c16 prob. rel. to OE *dol* stupid] > '**doltish** *adj* > '**doltishness** *n*

-dom *suffix forming nouns* **1** state or condition: *freedom* **2** rank, office, or domain of: *earldom* **3** a collection of persons: *officialdom* [OE *-dōm*]

Domagk (*German* 'doːmak) *n* **Gerhard** ('geːrhart) 1895–1964, German biochemist: Nobel prize for medicine (1939) for isolating sulphanilamide for treating bacterial infections

domain (də'meɪn) *n* **1** land governed by a ruler or government **2** land owned by one person or family **3** a field or scope of knowledge or activity **4** a region having specific characteristics **5** *Austral & NZ* a park or recreation reserve maintained by a public authority, often the government **6** *law* the absolute ownership and right to dispose of land **7** *maths* the set of values of the independent variable of a function for which the functional value exists **8** *logic* another term for **universe of discourse** **9** *philosophy* range of significance **10** *physics* one of the regions in a ferromagnetic solid in which all the atoms have their magnetic moments aligned in the same direction **11** *computing* a group of computers that have the same suffix (**domain name**) in their names on the Internet, specifying the country, type of institution, etc where they are located **12** Also called **superkingdom** *biol* the highest level of classification of living organisms [c17 from F *domaine*, from L *dominium* property, from *dominus* lord]

domain name *n computing* the suffix in a computer's Internet name, specifying the country, type of institution, etc, where it is located

dome (dəʊm) *n* **1** a hemispherical roof or vault **2** something shaped like this **3** a slang word for the **head** ▷ *vb* **domes, doming, domed** (*tr*) **4** to cover with or as if with a dome **5** to shape like a dome [c16 from F, from It. *duomo* cathedral, from L *domus* house] > '**dome,like** *adj* > **domical** ('dəʊmɪkᵊl, 'dɒm-) *adj*

Dome of the Rock *n* the mosque in Jerusalem, Israel, built in 691 AD by caliph 'Abd al-Malik: the third most holy place of Islam; stands on the Temple Mount alongside the **al-Aqsa** mosque. Also called (not in Muslim usage): **Mosque of Omar**

Domesday Book *or* **Doomsday Book** ('duːmz,deɪ) *n history* the record of a survey of the land of England carried out by the commissioners of William I in 1086
▷ www.domesdaybook.co.uk
▷ www.pro.gov.uk/virtualmuseum/millennium/domesday/book

domestic (də'mɛstɪk) *adj* **1** of the home or family **2** enjoying or accustomed to home or family life **3** (of an animal) bred or kept by man as a pet or for purposes such as the supply of food **4** of one's own country or a specific country: *domestic and foreign affairs* ▷ *n* **5** a household servant [c16 from OF *domestique*, from L *domesticus* belonging to the house, from *domus* house] > **do'mestically** *adv*

domesticate (də'mɛstɪ,keɪt) *or US* (*sometimes*) **domesticize** (də'mɛstɪ,saɪz) *vb* **domesticates, domesticating, domesticated** *or US* **domesticizes, domesticizing, domesticized** (*tr*) **1** to bring or keep (wild animals or plants) under control or cultivation **2** to accustom to home life **3** to adapt to an environment > **do'mesticable** *adj* > **do,mesti'cation** *n*

domesticity (,dəʊmɛ'stɪsɪtɪ) *n, pl* **domesticities** **1** home life **2** devotion to or familiarity with home life **3** (*usually pl*) a domestic duty or matter

domestic science *n* the study of cooking, needlework, and other subjects concerned with household skills

domicile ('dɒmɪ,saɪl) *or* **domicil** ('dɒmɪsɪl) *Formal* ▷ *n* **1** a dwelling place **2** a permanent legal residence **3** *commerce, Brit* the place where a bill of exchange is to be paid ▷ *vb also* **domiciliate** (ˌdɒmɪˈsɪlɪˌeɪt), **domiciles, domiciling, domiciled** *or* **domiciliates, domiciliating, domiciliated** **4** to establish or be established in a dwelling place [c15 from L *domicilium*, from *domus* house] > **domiciliary** (ˌdɒmɪˈsɪlɪərɪ) *adj*

dominance (ˈdɒmɪnəns) *n* control; ascendancy

dominant (ˈdɒmɪnənt) *adj* **1** having primary authority or influence; governing; ruling **2** predominant or primary: *the dominant topic of the day* **3** occupying a commanding position **4** *genetics* (of an allele) producing the same phenotype in the organism irrespective of whether the allele of the same gene is identical or dissimilar ▷ Cf **recessive** **5** *music* of or relating to the fifth degree of a scale **6** *ecology* (of a plant or animal species) more prevalent than any other species and determining the appearance and composition of the community ▷ *n* **7** *genetics* a dominant gene **8** *music* **8a** the fifth degree of a scale **8b** a key or chord based on this **9** *ecology* a dominant plant or animal in a community > ˈ**dominantly** *adv*

dominant seventh chord *n music* a chord consisting of the dominant and the major third, perfect fifth, and minor seventh above it

dominate (ˈdɒmɪˌneɪt) *vb* **dominates, dominating, dominated** **1** to control, rule, or govern **2** to tower above (surroundings, etc) **3** (*tr; usually passive*) to predominate in [c17 from L *dominārī* to be lord over, from *dominus* lord] > ˈ**domiˌnating** *adj* > ˌ**domiˈnation** *n*

dominatrix (ˌdɒmɪˈneɪtrɪks) *n, pl* **dominatrices** (ˌdɒmɪnəˈtraɪsiːz) **1** a woman who is the dominant sexual partner in a sadomasochistic relationship **2** a dominant woman [c16 from L, fem of *dominātor*, from *dominārī* to be lord over]

dominee (ˈduːmɪnɪ, ˈdʊə-) *n* (in South Africa) a minister in any of the Afrikaner Churches [from Afrik., from Du.; cf. DOMINIE]

domineer (ˌdɒmɪˈnɪə) *vb* (*intr; often foll by* *over*) to act with arrogance or tyranny; behave imperiously [c16 from Du. *domineren*, from F *dominer* to DOMINATE]

domineering (ˌdɒmɪˈnɪərɪŋ) *adj* acting with or showing arrogance or tyranny; imperious > ˌ**domiˈneeringly** *adv*

Domingo (*Spanish* doˈmiŋgo) *n* **Placido** (ˈplaθiðo) born 1941, Spanish operatic tenor

Dominic (ˈdɒmɪnɪk) *n* **Saint** original name *Domingo de Guzman*. ?1170–1221, Spanish priest; founder of the Dominican order. Feast day: Aug. 7

Dominica (ˌdɒmɪˈniːkə, dəˈmɪnɪkə) *n* a republic in the E Caribbean, comprising a volcanic island in the Windward Islands group; a former British colony; became independent as a member of the Commonwealth in 1978. Official language: English. Religion: Roman Catholic majority. Currency: East Caribbean dollar. Capital: Roseau. Pop: 71 700 (2001 est). Area: 751 sq km (290 sq miles). Official name: **Commonwealth of Dominica**

▷ www.ndcdominica.dm

dominical (dəˈmɪnɪkᵊl) *adj* **1** of Jesus Christ as Lord **2** of Sunday as the Lord's Day [c15 from LL *dominicālis*, from L *dominus* lord]

Dominican¹ (dəˈmɪnɪkən) *n* **1a** a member of an order of preaching friars founded by Saint Dominic in 1215; a Blackfriar **1b** a nun of one of the orders founded under his patronage ▷ *adj* **2** of Saint Dominic or the Dominican order

Dominican² (dəˈmɪnɪkən) *adj* **1** of or relating to the Dominican Republic or Dominica ▷ *n* **2** a native or inhabitant of the Dominican Republic or Dominica

Dominican Republic *n* a republic in the Caribbean, occupying the eastern half of the island of Hispaniola: colonized by the Spanish after its discovery by Columbus in 1492; gained independence from Spain in 1821. It is generally mountainous, dominated by the Cordillera Central, which rises over 3000 m (10 000 ft), with fertile lowlands. Language: Spanish. Religion: Roman Catholic majority. Currency: peso. Capital: Santo Domingo. Pop: 8 693 000 (2001 est). Area: 48 441 sq km (18 703 sq miles). Former name (until 1844): **Santo Domingo**

▷ www.presidencia.gov.do/Ingles/welcome.htm
▷ www.dominicanrepublic.com
▷ www.dominicanrepublic.com/Tourism

dominie (ˈdɒmɪnɪ) *n* **1** a Scots word for **schoolmaster** **2** a minister or clergyman [c17 from L *dominē*, vocative case of *dominus* lord]

dominion (dəˈmɪnjən) *n* **1** rule; authority **2** the land governed by one ruler or government **3** sphere of influence; area of control **4** a name formerly applied to self-governing divisions of the British Empire **5** **the Dominion** New Zealand [c15 from OF, from L *dominium* ownership, from *dominus* master]

Dominion Day *n* the former name for **Canada Day**

domino¹ (ˈdɒmɪˌnəʊ) *n, pl* **dominoes** a small rectangular block marked with dots, used in dominoes [c19 from F, from It., ?from *domino!* master!, said by the winner]

domino² (ˈdɒmɪˌnəʊ) *n, pl* **dominoes** *or* **dominos** **1** a large hooded cloak worn with an eye mask at a masquerade **2** the eye mask worn with such a cloak [c18 from F or It., prob. from L *dominus* lord, master]

Domino (ˈdɒmɪnəʊ) *n* **Fats** real name *Antoine Domino*. born 1928, US rhythm-and-blues and rock-and-roll pianist, singer, and songwriter. His singles include "Ain't that a Shame" (1955) and "Blueberry Hill" (1956)

domino effect *n* a series of similar or related events occurring as a direct and inevitable result of one initial event [c20 alluding to a row of dominoes, each standing on end, all of which fall when one is pushed]

dominoes (ˈdɒmɪˌnəʊz) *n* (*functioning as sing*) any of several games in which dominoes with matching halves are laid together

▷ www.idf.statecraft.net/idf.htm

Dominus *Latin* (ˈdɒmɪnʊs) *n* God or Christ

Domitian (dəˈmɪʃən) *n* full name *Titus Flavius Domitianus*. 51–96 AD, Roman emperor (81–96): instigated a reign of terror (93); assassinated

Domrémy-la-Pucelle (*French* dɔ̃remilapysɛl) *or* **Domrémy** *n* a village in NE France, in the Vosges: birthplace of Joan of Arc

don¹ (dɒn) *vb* **dons, donning, donned** (*tr*) to put on (clothing) [c14 from DO¹ + ON; cf. DOFF]

don² (dɒn) *n* **1** *Brit* a member of the teaching staff at a university or college, esp at Oxford or Cambridge **2** the head of a student dormitory at certain Canadian universities and colleges **3** a Spanish gentleman or nobleman **4** (in the Mafia) the head of the family **5** *arch* a person of rank [c17 ult. from L *dominus* lord]

Don¹ (dɒn) *n* a Spanish title equivalent to *Mr* [c16 via Sp., from L *dominus* lord]

Don² (dɒn) *n* **1** a river rising in W Russia, southeast of Tula and flowing generally south, to the Sea of Azov: linked by canal to the River Volga. Length: 1870 km (1162 miles) **2** a river in NE Scotland, rising in the Cairngorm Mountains and flowing east to the North Sea. Length: 100 km (62 miles) **3** a river in N central England, rising in S Yorkshire and flowing northeast to the Humber. Length: about 96 km (60 miles)

Doña (ˈdɒnjə) *n* a Spanish title of address equivalent to *Mrs* or *Madam* [c17 via Sp., from L *domina*]

Donar (ˈdəʊnɑː; *German* ˈdoːnar) *n* the Germanic god of thunder, corresponding to Thor in Norse mythology

donate (dəʊˈneɪt) *vb* **donates, donating, donated** to give (money, time, etc), esp to a charity > **doˈnator** *n*

Donatello (*Italian* donaˈtɛllo) *n* real name *Donato di Betto Bardi*. 1386–1466, Florentine sculptor, regarded as the greatest sculptor of the quattrocento, who was greatly

Dd

influenced by classical sculpture and contemporary humanist theories. His marble relief of *St George Killing the Dragon* (1416–17) shows his innovative use of perspective. Other outstanding works are the classic bronze *David*, and the bronze equestrian monument to Gattamelatta, which became the model of subsequent equestrian sculpture

donation (dəʊ'neɪʃən) *n* **1** the act of donating **2** a contribution [C15 from L *dōnātiō* a presenting, from *dōnāre* to give, from *dōnum* gift]

donative ('dəʊnətɪv) *n* **1** a gift or donation **2** a benefice capable of being conferred as a gift ▷ *adj* **3** of or like a donation **4** being or relating to a benefice [C15 from L *dōnātīvum* a donation made to soldiers by a Roman emperor, from *dōnāre* to present]

Donatus (dəʊ'nɑːtəs) *n* **1** **Aelius** ('iːlɪəs) 4th century AD, Latin grammarian, who taught Saint Jerome; his textbook *Ars Grammatica* was used throughout the Middle Ages **2** 4th century AD, bishop of Carthage; leader of the Donatists, a heretical Christian sect originating in N Africa in 311 AD

Donau ('doːnau) *n* the German name for the **Danube**

Donbass *or* **Donbas** (dɒn'bɑːs) *n* an industrial region in the E Ukraine in the plain of the Rivers Donets and lower Dnieper: the site of a major coalfield. Also called: **Donets Basin**

Doncaster ('dɒŋkəstə) *n* **1** an industrial town in N England, in Doncaster unitary authority, South Yorkshire, on the River Don. Pop: 71 595 (1991) **2** a unitary authority in N England, in South Yorkshire. Pop: 286 865 (2001). Area: 582 sq km (225 sq miles)

donder ('dɒndə) *S African sl* ▷ *vb* **1** (*tr*) to beat (someone) up ▷ *n* **2** a wretch; swine [from Afrik., from Du. *donderen* to swear, bully]

done (dʌn) *vb* **1** the past participle of **do**[1] **2** **be** *or* **have done with** to end relations with **3** **have done** to be completely finished: *have you done?* ▷ *interj* **4** an expression of agreement, as on the settlement of a bargain ▷ *adj* **5** completed **6** cooked enough **7** used up **8** socially acceptable **9** *inf* cheated; tricked **10** **done for** *inf* **10a** dead or almost dead **10b** in serious difficulty **11** **done in** *or* **up** *inf* exhausted

donee (dəʊ'niː) *n* a person who receives a gift [C16 from DON(OR) + -EE]

Donegal ('dɒnɪˌɡɔːl, ˌdɒnɪ'ɡɔːl) *n* a county in NW Republic of Ireland, on the Atlantic: mountainous, with a rugged coastline and many offshore islands. County town: Lifford. Pop: 129 994 (1996). Area: 4830 sq km (1865 sq miles)

doner kebab ('dɒnə) *n* a fast-food dish comprising grilled meat and salad served in pitta bread with chilli sauce [from Turkish *döner* rotating + KEBAB]

Donets (*Russian* da'njɛts) *n* a river rising in SW Russia, in the Kursk steppe and flowing southeast, through the Ukraine, to the Don River. Length: about 1078 km (670 miles)

Donets Basin (də'nɛts) *n* another name for the **Donbass**

Donetsk (*Russian* da'njɛtsk) *n* a city in the E Ukraine: the chief industrial centre of the Donbass; first ironworks founded by a Welshman, John Hughes (1872), after whom the town was named **Yuzovka** (Hughesovka) Pop: 1 065 400 (1998 est). Former names (from 1924 until 1961): **Stalin** *or* **Stalino**

dong (dɒŋ) *n* **1** an imitation of the sound of a bell **2** *Austral & NZ inf* a heavy blow ▷ *vb* **3** (*intr*) to make such a sound **4** *Austral & NZ inf* to strike or punch [C19 imit.]

donga ('dɒŋɡə) *n S African & Austral* a steep-sided gully created by soil erosion [C19 from Afrik., from Zulu]

Dongola ('dɒŋɡələ) *n* a small town in the N Sudan, on the Nile: built on the site of Old Dongola, the capital of the Christian Kingdom of Nubia (6th to 14th centuries). Pop: 5937 (latest est)

Dongting ('dʊŋ'tɪŋ), **Tungting**, *or* **Tung-t'ing** *n* a lake in S China, in NE Hunan province: main outlet flows to the Yangtze; rice-growing in winter. Area: (in winter) 3900 sq km (1500 sq miles)

Dönitz *or* **Doenitz** (*German* 'døːnɪts) *n* **Karl** (karl) 1891–1980, German admiral; commander in chief of the German navy (1943–45); as head of state after Hitler's death he surrendered to the Allies (May 7, 1945)

Donizetti (ˌdɒnɪ'zɛtɪ; *Italian* donid'dzetti) *n* **Gaetano** (gae'taːno) 1797–1848, Italian operatic composer: his works include *Lucia di Lammermoor* (1835), *La Fille du régiment* (1840), and *Don Pasquale* (1843)

donjon ('dʌndʒən, 'dɒn-) *n* the heavily fortified central tower or keep of a medieval castle. Also: **dungeon** [C14 arch var. of *dungeon*]

Don Juan ('dɒn 'dʒuːən) *n* **1** a legendary Spanish nobleman and philanderer: hero of many poems, plays, and operas **2** a successful seducer of women

donkey ('dɒŋkɪ) *n* **1** a long-eared member of the horse family **2** a stupid or stubborn person **3** **talk the hind leg(s) off a donkey** to talk endlessly [C18 ?from *dun* dark + *-key*, as in *monkey*]

donkey jacket *n* a thick hip-length jacket, usually navy blue, with a waterproof panel across the shoulders

donkey's years *pl n inf* a long time

donkey vote *n Austral* a vote in which the voter's order of preference follows the order in which the candidates are listed

donkey-work *n* **1** groundwork **2** drudgery

Donna ('dɒnə) *n* an Italian title of address equivalent to *Madam* [C17 from It., from L *domina* lady]

Donne (dʌn) *n* **John** 1573–1631, English metaphysical poet and preacher. He wrote love and religious poems, sermons, epigrams, and elegies

Donnelly ('donəlɪ) *n* **Declan** ('dɛklᵊn) born 1975, British television presenter, who appears with Antony McPartlin as Ant and Dec

donnish ('dɒnɪʃ) *adj* of or resembling a university don, esp denoting pedantry or fussiness > '**donnishness** *n*

donnybrook ('dɒnɪˌbrʊk) *n* a rowdy brawl [C19 after *Donnybrook Fair*, an annual event until 1855 near Dublin]

donor ('dəʊnə) *n* **1** a person who makes a donation **2** *med* any person who gives blood, organs, etc, for use in the treatment of another person **3** the atom supplying both electrons in a coordinate bond [C15 from OF *doneur*, from L *dōnātor*, from *dōnāre* to give]

donor card *n* a card carried to show that the bodily organs specified on it may be used for transplants after the carrier's death

Don Quixote ('dɒn kiː'həʊtiː, 'kwɪksət) *n* an impractical idealist [after the hero of Cervantes' *Don Quixote de la Mancha* (1605)]

don't (dəʊnt) *contraction of* do not

don't know *n* a person who has no definite opinion, esp as a response to a questionnaire

doodah ('duːdɑː) *or US & Canad* **doodad** ('duːdæd) *n inf* an unnamed thing, esp an object the name of which is unknown or forgotten [C20 from ?]

doodle ('duːdᵊl) *inf* ▷ *vb* **doodles, doodling, doodled** **1** to scribble or draw aimlessly **2** to play or improvise idly **3** (*intr*; often foll by *away*) *US* to dawdle or waste time ▷ *n* **4** a shape, picture, etc, drawn aimlessly [C20 ?from C17 a foolish person, but infl. in meaning by DAWDLE] > '**doodler** *n*

doodlebug ('duːdᵊlˌbʌg) *n* **1** another name for the **V-1** **2** a diviner's rod **3** a US name for an **antlion** (the larva) [C20 prob. from DOODLE + BUG]

doo-doo ('duːˌduː) *n US & Canad inf* a child's word for **excrement**

Doohan ('duːən) *n* **Michael K** (**Mick**) born 1965, Australian racing motorcyclist; 500 cc world champion 1994–98

doohickey ('duːˌhɪkɪ) *n US & Canad inf* another name for **doodah**

Doolittle ('du:lɪtᵊl) *n* **Hilda** known as *H.D.* 1886–1961, US imagist poet and novelist, living in Europe
doom (du:m) *n* **1** death or a terrible fate **2** a judgment **3** (*sometimes cap*) another term for the **Last Judgment** ▷ *vb* **4** (*tr*) to destine or condemn to death or a terrible fate [OE *dōm*]
doomsday *or* **domesday** ('du:mz,deɪ) *n* **1** (*sometimes cap*) the day on which the Last Judgment will occur **2** any day of reckoning **3** (*modifier*) characterized by predictions of disaster: *doomsday scenario* [OE *dōmes dæg* Judgment Day]
doona ('du:nə) *n* the Austral name for **continental quilt** [from a trademark]
door (dɔ:) *n* **1** a hinged or sliding panel for closing the entrance to a room, cupboard, etc **2** a doorway or entrance **3** a means of access or escape: *a door to success* **4** **lay at someone's door** to lay (the blame or responsibility) on someone **5** **out of doors** in or into the open air **6** **show someone the door** to order someone to leave [OE *duru*]
do-or-die *adj* (*prenominal*) of a determined and sometimes reckless effort to succeed
door furniture *n* locks, handles, etc, designed for use on doors
doorjamb ('dɔ:,dʒæm) *n* one of the two vertical members forming the sides of a doorframe. Also called: **doorpost**
doorkeeper ('dɔ:,ki:pə) *n* a person attending or guarding a door or gateway
doorman ('dɔ:,mæn, -mən) *n, pl* **doormen** a man employed to attend the doors of certain buildings
doormat ('dɔ:,mæt) *n* **1** a mat, placed at an entrance, for wiping dirt from shoes **2** *inf* a person who offers little resistance to ill-treatment
Doorn (*Dutch* do:rn) *n* a town in the central Netherlands, in Utrecht province: residence of Kaiser William II of Germany from his abdication (1919) until his death (1941)
doornail ('dɔ:,neɪl) *n* (**as**) **dead as a doornail** dead beyond any doubt
Doornik ('do:rnɪk) *n* the Flemish name for **Tournai**
doorsill ('dɔ:,sɪl) *n* a horizontal member of wood, stone, etc, forming the bottom of a doorframe
doorstep ('dɔ:,stɛp) *n* **1** a step in front of a door **2** *inf* a thick slice of bread ▷ *vb* **doorsteps, doorstepping, doorstepped** (*tr*) **3** to canvass (a district or member of the public) by or in the course of door-to-door visiting **4** (of journalists) to wait outside the house of (someone) in order to obtain an interview or photograph when he or she emerges
doorstop ('dɔ:,stɒp) *n* **1** any device which prevents an open door from moving **2** a piece of rubber, etc, fixed to the floor to stop a door striking a wall
door to door *adj* (**door-to-door** *when prenominal*), *adv* **1** (of selling, etc) from one house to the next **2** (of journeys, etc) direct
doorway ('dɔ:,weɪ) *n* **1** an opening into a building, room, etc, esp one that has a door **2** a means of access or escape: *a doorway to freedom*
do over *vb* (*tr, adv*) **1** *inf* to redecorate **2** *Brit, Austral & NZ sl* to beat up; thrash
doo-wop ('du:,wɒp) *n* vocalizing based on rhythm-and-blues harmony [c20 imit.]
dop (dɒp) *n* *S African sl* **1** Cape brandy **2** a tot of this [from Afrik., from ?]
dope (dəʊp) *n* **1** any of a number of preparations applied to fabric in order to improve strength, tautness, etc **2** an additive, such as an antiknock compound added to petrol **3** a thick liquid, such as a lubricant, applied to a surface **4** a combustible absorbent material used to hold the nitroglycerine in dynamite **5** *sl* an illegal drug, usually cannabis **6** a drug administered to a racehorse or greyhound to affect its performance **7** *inf* a stupid or slow-witted person **8** *inf* news or facts, esp confidential information ▷ *vb* **dopes, doping, doped** (*tr*) **9** *electronics* to add impurities to (a semiconductor) in order to produce or modify its properties **10** to apply or add dope to **11** to administer a drug to (oneself or another) [c19 from Du. *doop* sauce, from *doopen* to dip] > '**doper** *n*
dopey *or* **dopy** ('dəʊpɪ) *adj* **dopier, dopiest** **1** *sl* silly **2** *inf* half-asleep or semiconscious, as when under the influence of a drug
doppelgänger ('dɒpᵊl,gɛŋə) *n* *legend* a ghostly duplicate of a living person [from G *Doppelgänger*, lit.: double-goer]
Doppler effect ('dɒplə) *n* a change in the apparent frequency of a sound or light wave, etc, as a result of relative motion between the observer and the source. Also called: **Doppler shift** [c19 after C. J. *Doppler* (1803–53), Austrian physicist]
Doráti (də'rɑ:tɪ) *n* **Antal** ('æntæl) 1906–88, US conductor and composer
Dorcas ('dɔ:kəs) *n* a charitable woman of Joppa (Acts 9:36–42)
Dorchester ('dɔ:tʃɪstə) *n* a town in S England, administrative centre of Dorset: associated with Thomas Hardy, esp as the Casterbridge of his novels. Pop: 15 037 (1991). Latin name: **Durnovaria** (,djʊrnəʊ'veɪrɪə)
Dordogne (*French* dɔrdɔɲ) *n* **1** a river in SW France, rising in the Auvergne Mountains and flowing southwest and west to join the Garonne river and form the Gironde estuary. Length: 472 km (293 miles) **2** a department of SW France, in Aquitaine region. Capital: Périgueux. Pop: 388 293 (1999). Area: 9224 sq km (3597 sq miles)
Dordrecht (*Dutch* 'dɔrdrɛxt) *n* a port in the SW Netherlands, in South Holland province: chief port of the Netherlands until the 17th century. Pop: 119 462 (1999 est). Also called: **Dort**
doré ('dɔreɪ, -ri:) *n* another name for **walleye** (the fish) [c18 from F, gilded; see DORY]
Doré (*French* dɔre) *n* (**Paul**) **Gustave** (gystav) 1832–83, French illustrator, whose style tended towards the grotesque. He illustrated the Bible, Dante's *Inferno*, Cervantes' *Don Quixote*, and works by Rabelais
Doric ('dɒrɪk) *adj* **1** of the inhabitants of Doris in ancient Greece or their dialect **2** of or denoting one of the five classical orders of architecture: characterized by a heavy fluted column and a simple capital **3** (*sometimes not cap*) rustic ▷ *n* **4** one of four chief dialects of Ancient Greek **5** any rural dialect of English, esp that spoken in the northeast of Scotland
▷ www.hellenism.net/eng/doric.htm
Doris[1] ('dɒrɪs) *n* (in ancient Greece) **1** a small landlocked area north of the Gulf of Corinth. Traditionally regarded as the home of the Dorians, it was perhaps settled by some of them during their southward migration **2** the coastal area of Caria in SW Asia Minor, settled by Dorians
▷ www.helios.gr/rhodes/dorians.htm
Doris[2] ('dɒrɪs) *n* *Greek myth* a sea nymph
dork (dɔ:k) *n* *sl* a stupid or incompetent person [c20 from ?]
dorm (dɔ:m) *n* *inf* short for **dormitory**
dormant ('dɔ:mənt) *adj* **1** quiet and inactive, as during sleep **2** latent or inoperative **3** (of a volcano) neither extinct nor erupting **4** *biol* alive but in a resting condition with reduced metabolism **5** (*usually postpositive*) *Heraldry*. (of a beast) in a sleeping position [c14 from OF *dormant*, from *dormir* to sleep, from L *dormīre*] > '**dormancy** *n*
dormer ('dɔ:mə) *n* a construction with a gable roof and a window that projects from a sloping roof. Also called: **dormer window** [c16 from OF *dormoir*, from L *dormītōrium* DORMITORY]
dormie *or* **dormy** ('dɔ:mɪ) *adj* *golf* as many holes ahead

Dd

of an opponent as there are still to play: *dormie three* [c19 from ?]

dormitory (ˈdɔːmɪtərɪ, -trɪ) *n, pl* **dormitories** 1 a large room, esp at a school, containing several beds 2 *US* a building, esp at a college or camp, providing living and sleeping accommodation 3 *(modifier) Brit* denoting or relating to an area from which most of the residents commute to work(esp in **dormitory suburb**) [c15 from L *dormītōrium*, from *dormīre* to sleep]

Dormobile (ˈdɔːməʊˌbiːl) *n trademark* a vanlike vehicle specially equipped for living in while travelling

dormouse (ˈdɔːˌmaʊs) *n, pl* **dormice** a small Eurasian rodent resembling a mouse with a furry tail [c15 *dor-*, ?from OF *dormir* to sleep, (from L *dormīre)* + MOUSE]

dorp (dɔːp) *n S African* a small town or village [c16 from Du.]

Dorpat (ˈdɔrpat) *n* the German name for **Tartu**

dorsal (ˈdɔːsᵊl) *adj anat, zool.* relating to the back or spinal part of the body [c15 from Med. L *dorsālis*, from L *dorsum* back] > ˈ**dorsally** *adv*

dorsal fin *n* an unpaired fin on the back of a fish that maintains balance during locomotion

Dorset (ˈdɔːsɪt) *n* a county in SW England, on the English Channel: mainly hilly but low-lying in the east: the geographical and ceremonial county includes Bournemouth and Poole, which became independent unitary authorities in 1997. Administrative centre: Dorchester. Pop (excluding unitary authorities): 390 986 (2001 est). Area (excluding unitary authorities): 2544 sq km (982 sq miles)

Dort (*Dutch* dɔrt) *n* another name for **Dordrecht**

Dortmund (ˈdɔːtmənd; *German* ˈdɔrtmʊnt) *n* an industrial city in W Germany, in North Rhine-Westphalia at the head of the **Dortmund-Ems Canal**: university (1966) Pop: 590 300 (1999 est)

dory[1] (ˈdɔːrɪ) *n, pl* **dories** any of various spiny-finned food fishes, esp the John Dory [c14 from F *dorée* gilded, from LL *deaurāre* to gild, ult. from L *aurum* gold]

dory[2] (ˈdɔːrɪ) *n, pl* **dories** *US & Canad* a flat-bottomed rowing boat with a high bow, stern, and sides [c18 from Amerind *dóri* dugout]

DOS (dɒs) *n computers trademark acronym for* disk-operating system, often prefixed, as in MS-DOS and PC-DOS; a computer operating system

dosage (ˈdəʊsɪdʒ) *n* 1 the administration of a drug or agent in prescribed amounts and at prescribed intervals 2 the optimum therapeutic dose and interval between doses 3 another name for **dose** (senses 3, 4)

dose (dəʊs) *n* 1 *med* a specific quantity of a therapeutic drug or agent taken at any one time or at specified intervals 2 *inf* something unpleasant to experience: *a dose of influenza* 3 Also called: **dosage** the total energy of ionizing radiation absorbed by unit mass of material, esp of living tissue; usually measured in grays (SI unit) or rads 4 Also called: **dosage** a small amount of syrup added to wine during bottling 5 *sl* a sexually transmitted infection ▷ *vb* **doses, dosing, dosed** *(tr)* 6 to administer a dose to (someone) 7 *med* to give (a drug) in appropriate quantities 8 to add syrup to (wine) during bottling [c15 from F, from LL *dosis*, from Gk: a giving, from *didonai* to give]

dosh (dɒʃ) *n Brit* a slang word for **money** [c20 of unknown origin]

dosimeter (dəʊˈsɪmɪtə) *n* an instrument for measuring the dose of radiation absorbed by matter or the intensity of a source of radiation > **dosimetric** (ˌdəʊsɪˈmɛtrɪk) *adj*

dosing strip *n* (in New Zealand) an area set aside for treating dogs suspected of having hydatid disease

Dos Passos (ˈdɒs ˈpæsɒs) *n* **John (Roderigo)** 1896–1970, US novelist of the Lost Generation; author of *Three Soldiers* (1921), *Manhattan Transfer* (1925), and the trilogy *USA.* (1930–36)

doss (dɒs) *Brit sl* ▷ *vb* 1 *(intr; often foll by down)* to sleep, esp in a dosshouse 2 *(intr; often foll by around)* to pass time aimlessly ▷ *n* 3 a bed, esp in a dosshouse 4 another word for **sleep** 5 short for **dosshouse** 6 a task or pastime requiring little effort: *making a film is a bit of a doss* [c18 from ?]

dosser (ˈdɒsə) *n* 1 *Brit sl* a person who sleeps in dosshouses 2 *Brit sl* another word for **dosshouse** 3 *sl* a lazy person

dosshouse (ˈdɒsˌhaʊs) *n Brit sl* a cheap lodging house, esp one used by tramps. US name: **flophouse**

dossier (ˈdɒsɪˌeɪ) *n* a collection of papers about a subject or person [c19 from F: a file with a label on the back, from *dos* back, from L *dorsum*]

dost (dʌst) *vb arch or dialect* (used with *thou*) a singular form of the present tense (indicative mood) of **do**[1]

Dostoevsky, Dostoyevsky, Dostoevski, *or* **Dostoyevski** (ˌdɒstɔɪˈɛfskɪ; *Russian* dəstaˈjɛfskij) *n* **Fyodor Mikhailovich** (ˈfjɔdər miˈxajləvitʃ) 1821–81, Russian novelist, the psychological perception of whose works has greatly influenced the subsequent development of the novel. His best-known works are *Crime and Punishment* (1866), *The Idiot* (1868), *The Possessed* (1871), and *The Brothers Karamazov* (1879–80)

dot[1] (dɒt) *n* 1 a small round mark; spot; point 2 anything resembling a dot; a small amount 3 the mark (·) above the letters *i, j* 4 *music* 4a the symbol (•) placed after a note or rest to increase its time value by half 4b this symbol written above or below a note indicating staccato 5 *maths, logic* 5a the symbol (.) indicating multiplication or logical conjunction 5b a decimal point 6 the symbol (•) used, in combination with the symbol for *dash* (—), in Morse and other codes 7 **on the dot** at exactly the arranged time ▷ *vb* **dots, dotting, dotted** 8 *(tr)* to mark or form with a dot 9 *(tr)* to scatter or intersperse (as with dots): *bushes dotting the plain* 10 *(intr)* to make a dot or dots 11 **dot one's i's and cross one's t's** *inf* to pay meticulous attention to detail [OE *dott* head of a boil] > ˈ**dotter** *n*

dot[2] (dɒt) *n* a woman's dowry [c19 from F from L *dōs*; rel. to *dōtāre* to endow, *dāre* to give]

dotage (ˈdəʊtɪdʒ) *n* 1 feebleness of mind, esp as a result of old age 2 foolish infatuation [c14 from DOTE + -AGE]

dotard (ˈdəʊtəd) *n* a person who is weak-minded, esp through senility [c14 from DOTE + -ARD] > ˈ**dotardly** *adj*

dotcom *or* **dot.com** *n* a a company that conducts most of its business on the Internet b *(as modifier)*: *dotcom stocks* [c20 from *.com*, the domain-name suffix of businesses trading on the Internet]

dotcommer (dɒtˈkɒmə) *n* a person who carries out business on the Internet

dote (dəʊt) *vb* **dotes, doting, doted** *(intr)* 1 (foll by *on* or *upon*) to love to an excessive or foolish degree 2 to be foolish or weak-minded, esp as a result of old age [c13 rel. to MDu. *doten* to be silly] > ˈ**doter** *n*

doth (dʌθ) *vb arch or dialect* (used with *he, she,* or *it*) a singular form of the present tense of **do**[1]

dot-matrix printer *n computing* a printer in which each character is produced by a subset of an array of needles

dotterel *or* **dottrel** (ˈdɒtrəl) *n* 1 a rare Eurasian plover with white bands around the head and neck 2 *dialect* a person who is foolish or easily duped [c15 *dotrelle*; see DOTE]

dottle (ˈdɒtᵊl) *n* the plug of tobacco left in a pipe after smoking [c15 dim. of *dot* lump]

dotty (ˈdɒtɪ) *adj* **dottier, dottiest** 1 *sl, chiefly Brit* feeble-minded; slightly crazy 2 *Brit sl* (foll by *about*) extremely fond (of) 3 marked with dots [c19 from DOT[1]] > ˈ**dottily** *adv* > ˈ**dottiness** *n*

Douai (ˈduːeɪ; *French* dwɛ) *n* an industrial city in N France: the political and religious centre of exiled English Roman Catholics in the 16th and 17th centuries. Pop: 199 562 (1990)

Douala *or* **Duala** (dʊˈɑːlə) *n* the chief port and largest city in W Cameroon, on the Bight of Bonny: capital of the German colony of Kamerun (1901–16). Pop: 1 200 000 (1992 est)

Douay Bible *or* **Version** (ˈduːeɪ) *n* an English translation of the Bible from the Vulgate by Catholic scholars at Douai in 1610

double (ˈdʌbᵊl) *adj (usually prenominal)* **1** as much again in size, strength, number, etc: *a double portion* **2** composed of two equal or similar parts **3** designed for two users: *a double room* **4** folded in two; composed of two layers **5** stooping; bent over **6** having two aspects; ambiguous: *a double meaning* **7** false, deceitful, or hypocritical: *a double life* **8** (of flowers) having more than the normal number of petals **9** *music* **9a** (of an instrument) sounding an octave lower: *a double bass* **9b** (of time) duple ▷ *adv* **10** twice over; twofold **11** two together; two at a time(esp in **see double**) ▷ *n* **12** twice the number, amount, size, etc **13** a double measure of spirits **14** a duplicate or counterpart, esp a person who closely resembles another; understudy **15** a ghostly apparition of a living person; doppelgänger **16** a sharp turn, esp a return on one's own tracks **17** *bridge* a call that increases certain scoring points if the last preceding bid becomes the contract **18** *billiards, etc* a strike in which the object ball is struck so as to make it rebound against the cushion to an opposite pocket **19** a bet on two horses in different races in which any winnings from the first race are placed on the horse in the later race **20a** the narrow outermost ring on a dartboard **20b** a hit on this ring **21 at** *or* **on the double 21a** at twice normal marching speed **21b** quickly or immediately ▷ *vb* **doubles, doubling, doubled 22** to make or become twice as much **23** to bend or fold (material, etc) **24** (*tr; sometimes foll by up*) to clench (a fist) **25** (*tr; often foll by together or up*) to join or couple **26** (*tr*) to repeat exactly; copy **27** (*intr*) to play two parts or serve two roles **28** (*intr*) to turn sharply; follow a winding course **29** *naut* to sail around (a headland or other point) **30** *music* **30a** to duplicate (a part) either in unison or at the octave above or below it **30b** (*intr; usually foll by on*) to be capable of performing (upon an additional instrument) **31** *bridge* to make a call that will double certain scoring points if the preceding bid becomes the contract **32** *billiards, etc* to cause (a ball) to rebound or (of a ball) to rebound from a cushion **33** (*intr; foll by for*) to act as substitute **34** (*intr*) to go or march at twice the normal speed ▷ See also **double back, doubles, double up** [c13 from OF, from L *duplus* twofold, from *duo* two + *-plus* -FOLD] > ˈ**doubler** *n*

double agent *n* a spy employed by two mutually antagonistic countries, companies, etc

double back *vb* (*intr, adv*) to go back in the opposite direction(esp in **double back on one's tracks**)

double-bank *vb Austral & NZ inf* to carry (a second person) on (a horse, bicycle, etc). Also: **dub**

double bar *n music* a symbol, consisting of two ordinary bar lines or a single heavy one, that marks the end of a composition or section

double-barrelled *or US* **double-barreled** *adj* **1** (of a gun) having two barrels **2** extremely forceful **3** *Brit* (of a surname) having hyphenated parts **4** serving two purposes; ambiguous: *a double-barrelled remark*

double bass (beɪs) *n* **1** Also called (US): **bass viol** a stringed instrument, the largest and lowest member of the violin family with a range of almost three octaves. Inf. name: **bass fiddle** ▷ *adj* **double-bass 2** of an instrument whose pitch lies below the bass; contrabass

double bassoon *n music* the lowest and largest instrument in the oboe class; contrabassoon

double-blind *adj* of or denoting an experimental study of a new drug in which neither the experimenters nor the patients know which are the test subjects and which are the controls: *double-blind trials*

double boiler *n* the US and Canad name for **double saucepan**

double-breasted *adj* (of a garment) having overlapping fronts

double-check *vb* **1** to check again; verify ▷ *n* **double check 2** a second examination or verification **3** *chess* a simultaneous check from two pieces

double chin *n* a fold of fat under the chin > ˌ**double-ˈchinned** *adj*

double concerto *n* a concerto for two solo instruments and orchestra

double cream *n Brit* thick cream with a high fat content

double-cross *vb* **1** (*tr*) to cheat or betray ▷ *n* **2** the act or an instance of double-crossing; betrayal > ˌ**double-ˈcrosser** *n*

double dagger *n* a character (‡) used in printing to indicate a cross-reference. Also called: **diesis, double obelisk**

double-dealing *n* **a** action characterized by treachery or deceit **b** (*as modifier*): *double-dealing treachery* > ˌ**double-ˈdealer** *n*

double-decker *n* **1** *chiefly Brit* a bus with two passenger decks **2** *inf* **2a** a thing or structure having two decks, layers, etc **2b** (*as modifier*): *a double-decker sandwich*

double-declutch *vb* (*intr*) *Brit, Austral, & NZ* to change to a lower gear in a motor vehicle by first placing the gear lever into neutral before engaging the desired gear. US term: **double-clutch**

double dip *n econ* **a** a recession in which a brief recovery in output is followed by another fall, because demand remains low **b** (*as modifier*): *a double-dip recession*

double Dutch *n Brit inf* incomprehensible talk; gibberish

double-edged *adj* **1** acting in two ways **2** (of a remark, etc) having two possible interpretations, esp applicable both for and against, or being malicious though apparently innocuous **3** (of a knife, etc) having a cutting edge on either side of the blade

double entendre (ɑːnˈtɑːndrə) *n* **1** a word, phrase, etc, that can be interpreted in two ways, esp one having one meaning that is indelicate **2** the type of humour that depends upon this [c17 from obs. F: double meaning]

double entry *n* **a** a book-keeping system in which any commercial transaction is entered as a debit in one account and as a credit in another **b** (*as modifier*): *double-entry book-keeping*

double exposure *n* **1** the act or process of recording two superimposed images on a photographic medium **2** the photograph resulting from such an act

double-faced *adj* **1** (of textiles) having a finished nap on each side; reversible **2** insincere or deceitful

double feature *n films* a programme showing two full-length films. Inf. name (US): **twin bill**

double first *n Brit* a first-class honours degree in two subjects

double glazing *n* **1** two panes of glass in a window, fitted to reduce heat loss, etc **2** the fitting of glass in such a manner

double-header *n* **1** a train drawn by two locomotives coupled together **2** Also called: **twin bill** *sport, US & Canad* two games played consecutively **3** *Austral & NZ inf* a coin with the impression of a head on each side **4** *Austral inf* a double ice-cream cone

double helix *n* the form of the molecular structure of DNA, consisting of two helical chains coiled around the same axis

double-jointed *adj* having unusually flexible joints permitting an abnormal degree of motion

double knitting *n* a widely used medium thickness of knitting wool

double negative *n* a construction, often considered ungrammatical, in which two negatives are used where

Dd

one is needed, as in *I wouldn't never have believed it.*

> USAGE There are two contexts where double negatives are found. An adjective with negative force is often used with a negative in order to express a nuance of meaning somewhere between the positive and the negative: *he was a not infrequent visitor; it is not an uncommon sight.* Two negatives are also found together where they reinforce each other rather than conflict: *he never went back, not even to collect his belongings.* These two uses of what is technically a double negative are acceptable. A third case, illustrated by *I shouldn't wonder if it didn't rain today*, has the force of a weak positive statement (*I expect it to rain today*) and is common in informal English

double-park *vb* to park (a vehicle) alongside or opposite another already parked by the roadside, thereby causing an obstruction

double pneumonia *n* pneumonia affecting both lungs

double-quick *adj* **1** very quick; rapid ▷ *adv* **2** in a very quick or rapid manner

double-reed *adj* relating to or denoting a wind instrument having two reeds that vibrate against each other

double refraction *n* the splitting of a ray of unpolarized light into two unequally refracted rays polarized in mutually perpendicular planes. Also called: **birefringence**

doubles ('dʌbᵊlz) *n (functioning as sing or pl)* **a** a game between two pairs of players **b** *(as modifier): a doubles match*

double saucepan *n Brit* a cooking utensil consisting of two saucepans: the lower pan is used to boil water to heat food in the upper pan. US and Canad name: **double boiler**

double-space *vb* **double-spaces, double-spacing, double-spaced** to type (copy) with a full space between lines

doublespeak ('dʌbᵊlˌspiːk) *n* the practice of using ambiguous language regarding political, military, or corporate matters in a deliberate attempt to disguise the truth

double spread *n printing* two facing pages of a publication treated as a single unit

double standard *n* a set of principles that allows greater freedom to one person or group than to another

double-stop *vb* **double-stops, double-stopping, double-stopped** to play (two notes or parts) simultaneously on a violin or related instrument

doublet ('dʌblɪt) *n* **1** (formerly) a man's close-fitting jacket, with or without sleeves(esp in **doublet and hose**) **2a** a pair of similar things, esp two words deriving ultimately from the same source **2b** one of such a pair **3** *jewellery* a false gem made by welding or fusing stones together **4** *physics* a closely spaced pair of related spectral lines **5** *(pl)* two dice each showing the same number of spots on one throw [C14 from OF, from DOUBLE]

double take *n* (esp in comedy) a delayed reaction by a person to a remark, situation, etc

double talk *n* **1** rapid speech with a mixture of nonsense syllables and real words; gibberish **2** empty, deceptive, or ambiguous talk

doublethink ('dʌbᵊlˌθɪŋk) *n* deliberate, perverse, or unconscious acceptance or promulgation of conflicting facts, principles, etc

double time *n* **1** a doubled wage rate, paid for working on public holidays, etc **2** *music* two beats per bar **3** a slow running pace, keeping in step **4** *US army* a fast march

double up *vb (adv)* **1** to bend or cause to bend in two **2** *(intr)* to share a room or bed designed for one person, family, etc **3** *(intr) Brit* to use the winnings from one bet as the stake for another. US and Canad term: **parlay**

double whammy *n inf, chiefly US* a devastating setback made up of two elements

doubloon (dʌ'bluːn) *n* **1** a former Spanish gold coin **2** *(pl) sl* money [C17 from Sp. *doblón*, from *dobla*, from L *dupla*, fem. of *duplus* twofold]

doubly ('dʌblɪ) *adv* **1** to or in a double degree, quantity, or measure **2** in two ways

Doubs (*French* du) *n* **1** a department of E France, in Franche-Comté region. Capital: Besançon. Pop: 499 062 (1999). Area: 5258 sq km (2030 sq miles) **2** a river in E France, rising in the Jura Mountains, becoming part of the border between France and Switzerland and flowing generally southwest to the Saône River. Length: 430 km (267 miles)

doubt (daʊt) *n* **1** uncertainty about the truth, fact, or existence of something(esp in **in doubt, without doubt,** etc) **2** *(often pl)* lack of belief in or conviction about something **3** an unresolved difficulty, point, etc **4** *obs* fear **5 give (someone) the benefit of the doubt** to presume (someone suspected of guilt) innocent **6 no doubt** almost certainly ▷ *vb* **7** *(tr; may take a clause as object)* to be inclined to disbelieve **8** *(tr)* to distrust or be suspicious of **9** *(intr)* to feel uncertainty or be undecided **10** *(tr) arch* to fear [C13 from OF *douter*, from L *dubitāre*] > **'doubtable** *adj* > **'doubter** *n* > **'doubtingly** *adv*

> USAGE When a clause follows *doubt* in an affirmative sentence it was formerly considered correct only to use *whether*: (*I doubt whether he will come*), but nowadays *if* and *that* are also common and acceptable. In negative statements, *doubt* is invariably followed by *that*: *I do not doubt that he is telling the truth.* In such sentences, *but* (*I do not doubt but that he is telling the truth*) is rather rare, and will tend to sound either formal or pompous

doubtful ('daʊtfʊl) *adj* **1** unlikely; improbable **2** uncertain: *a doubtful answer* **3** unsettled; unresolved **4** of questionable reputation or morality **5** having reservations or misgivings > **'doubtfully** *adv* > **'doubtfulness** *n*

> USAGE It was formerly considered correct to use *whether* after *doubtful* (*it is doubtful whether he will come*), but now *if* and *that* are also acceptable

doubting Thomas *n* a person who insists on proof before he or she will believe anything [after THOMAS (the apostle), who did not believe that Jesus had been resurrected]

doubtless ('daʊtlɪs) *adv* also **doubtlessly** *(sentence modifier), sentence substitute* **1** certainly **2** probably ▷ *adj* **3** certain; assured > **'doubtlessness** *n*

douche (duːʃ) *n* **1** a stream of water directed onto or into the body for cleansing or medical purposes **2** the application of such a stream of water **3** an instrument for applying a douche ▷ *vb* **douches, douching, douched** **4** to cleanse or treat or be cleansed or treated by means of a douche [C18 from F, from It. *doccia* pipe]

dough (dəʊ) *n* **1** a thick mixture of flour or meal and water or milk, used for making bread, pastry, etc **2** any similar pasty mass **3** a slang word for **money** [OE *dāg*]

doughboy ('dəʊˌbɔɪ) *n* **1** *US inf* an infantryman, esp in World War I **2** dough that is boiled or steamed as a dumpling

doughnut ('dəʊnʌt) *n* **1** a small cake of sweetened dough, often ring-shaped, cooked in hot fat **2** anything shaped like a ring, such as the reaction vessel of a thermonuclear reactor ▷ *vb* **doughnuts, doughnutting, doughnutted** **3** *(tr) inf* (of Members of Parliament) to surround (a speaker) during the televising of Parliament to give the impression that the chamber is crowded or the speaker is well supported

doughty ('daʊtɪ) *adj* **doughtier, doughtiest** hardy; resolute [OE *dohtig*] > **'doughtily** *adv* > **'doughtiness** *n*

doughy ('dəʊɪ) *adj* **doughier, doughiest** resembling dough; soft, pallid, or flabby

Douglas[1] ('dʌgləs) *n* a town and resort on the Isle of Man, capital of the island, on the E coast. Pop: 23 487 (1996)

Douglas[2] ('dʌgləs) *n* **1 C(lifford) H(ugh)** 1879–1952, British economist, who originated the theory of social credit **2 Gavin** ?1474–1522, Scottish poet, the first British translator of the *Aeneid* **3 Keith (Castellain)** 1920–44, British poet, noted for his poems of World War II: killed in action **4 Michael K(irk)** born 1944, US film actor; his films include *Romancing the Stone* (1984), *Wall Street* (1987), *Basic Instinct* (1992), and *Wonder Boys* (2000) **5 (George) Norman** 1868–1952, British writer, esp of books on southern Italy such as *South Wind* (1917)

Douglas fir, spruce, *or* **hemlock** *n* a North American pyramidal coniferous tree, widely planted for ornament and for timber [c19 after David *Douglas* (1798–1834), Scot. botanist]

Douglas-Home ('dʌgləs'hjuːm) *n* Sir **Alexander** See (Baron Alexander) **Home of the Hirsel**

Douglas Hurd (ˌdʌgləs 'hɜːd) *n Brit inf* a third-class university degree. Often shortened to: **Douglas** [c20 rhyming slang, after Douglas *Hurd* (born 1930), British Conservative politician]

Doukhobor *or* **Dukhobor** ('duːkəʊˌbɔː) *n* a member of a Russian sect of Christians that originated in the 18th century. In the late 19th century a large number emigrated to W Canada, where most Doukhobors now live [c19 from Russian *dukhoborets* spirit wrestlers]

doula ('duːlə) *n* a woman who is trained to provide support to women and their families during pregnancy, childbirth, and the period of time following the birth [c20 from Greek *doule* female slave]

Dounreay (duːn'reɪ) *n* the site in N Scotland of a nuclear power station, which contained the world's first fast-breeder reactor (1962–77). A prototype fast-breeder operated from 1974 until 1994: a nuclear fuel re-processing plant has also operated at the site

do up *vb* (*adv; mainly tr*) **1** to wrap and make into a bundle: *to do up a parcel* **2** to beautify or adorn **3** (*also intr*) to fasten or be fastened **4** *inf* to renovate or redecorate **5** *sl* to assault **6** *inf* to cause the downfall of (a person)

dour (dʊə, 'daʊə) *adj* **1** sullen **2** hard or obstinate [c14 prob. from L *dūrus* hard] > **'dourly** *adv* > **'dourness** *n*

douroucouli (ˌduːruː'kuːlɪ) *n* a nocturnal New World monkey of Central and South America with thick fur and large eyes [from Amerind]

douse *or* **dowse** (daʊs) *vb* **douses, dousing, doused** *or* **dowses, dowsing, dowsed 1** to plunge or be plunged into liquid; duck **2** (*tr*) to drench with water **3** (*tr*) to put out (a light, candle, etc) ▷ *n* **4** an immersion [c16 ? rel. to obs. *douse* to strike, from ?]

dove (dʌv) *n* **1** any of a family of birds having a heavy body, small head, short legs, and long pointed wings **2** *politics* a person opposed to war **3** a gentle or innocent person: used as a term of endearment **4a** a greyish-brown colour **4b** (*as adj*): *dove walls* [OE *dūfe* (unattested except as a fem proper name)] > **'doveˌlike** *adj*

Dove (dʌv) *n* **the** *Christianity* a manifestation of the Holy Spirit (John 1:32)

dovecote ('dʌvˌkəʊt) *or* **dovecot** ('dʌvˌkɒt) *n* a structure for housing pigeons

Dover ('dəʊvə) *n* **1** a port in SE England, in E Kent on the Strait of Dover: the only one of the Cinque Ports that is still important; a stronghold since ancient times and Caesar's first point of attack in the invasion of Britain (55 BC). Pop: 34 179 (1991) **2 Strait of** a strait between SE England and N France, linking the English Channel with the North Sea. Width: about 32 km (20 miles). French name: **Pas de Calais 3** a city in the US, the capital of Delaware, founded in 1683: 18th-century buildings. Pop: 27 630 (1990)

dovetail ('dʌvˌteɪl) *n* **1** a wedge-shaped tenon **2** Also called: **dovetail joint** a joint containing such tenons ▷ *vb* **3** (*tr*) to join by means of dovetails **4** to fit or cause to fit together closely or neatly

dowager ('daʊədʒə) *n* **1a** a widow possessing property or a title obtained from her husband **1b** (*as modifier*): *the dowager duchess* **2** a wealthy or dignified elderly woman [c16 from OF *douagiere*, from *douage* DOWER]

Dowding ('daʊdɪŋ) *n* Baron **Hugh Caswall Tremenheere,** nicknamed *Stuffy*. 1882–1970, British air chief marshal. As commander in chief of Fighter Command (1936–40), he contributed greatly to the British victory in the Battle of Britain (1940)

dowdy ('daʊdɪ) *adj* **dowdier, dowdiest 1** (esp of a woman or a woman's dress) shabby or old-fashioned ▷ *n, pl* **dowdies 2** a dowdy woman [c14 *dowd* slut, from ?] > **'dowdily** *adv* > **'dowdiness** *n* > **'dowdyish** *adj*

dowel ('daʊəl) *n* a wooden or metal peg that fits into two corresponding holes to join two adjacent parts [c14 from MLow G *dövel* plug, from OHG *tubili*]

dower ('daʊə) *n* **1** the life interest in a part of her husband's estate allotted to a widow by law **2** an archaic word for **dowry** (sense 1) **3** a natural gift ▷ *vb* **4** (*tr*) to endow [c14 from OF *douaire*, from Med. L *dōtārium*, from L *dōs* gift]

dower house *n* a house for the use of a widow, often on her deceased husband's estate

do with *vb* **1 could** *or* **can do with** to find useful; benefit from **2 have to do with** to be involved in or connected with **3 to do with** concerning; related to **4 what...do with 4a** to put or place: *what did you do with my coat?* **4b** to handle or treat **4c** to fill one's time usefully: *she didn't know what to do with herself when the project was finished*

do without *vb* (*intr*) **1** to forgo; manage without **2** (*prep*) not to require (uncalled-for comments): *we can do without your criticisms*

Dd

Dow-Jones average (daʊ'dʒəʊnz) *n US* a daily index of average stock-exchange prices [c20 after Charles H. *Dow* (died 1902) & Edward D. *Jones* (died 1920), American financial statisticians]

Dowland ('daʊlənd) *n* **John** ?1563–1626, English lutenist and composer of songs and lute music

down[1] (daʊn) *prep* **1** used to indicate movement from a higher to a lower position **2** at a lower or further level or position on, in, or along: *he ran down the street* ▷ *adv* **3** downwards; at or to a lower level or position **4** (*particle*) used with many verbs when the result of the verb's action is to lower or destroy its object: *knock down* **5** (*particle*) used with several verbs to indicate intensity or completion: *calm down* **6** immediately: *cash down* **7** on paper: *write this down* **8** arranged; scheduled **9** in a helpless position **10a** away from a more important place **10b** away from a more northerly place **10c** (of a member of some British universities) away from the university **10d** in a particular part of a country: *down south* **11** *naut* (of a helm) having the rudder to windward **12** reduced to a state of lack or want: *down to the last pound* **13** lacking a specified amount **14** lower in price **15** including all intermediate grades **16** from an earlier to a later time **17** to a finer or more concentrated state: *to grind down* **18** *sport* being a specified number of points, goals, etc, behind another competitor, team, etc **19** (of a person) being inactive, owing to illness: *down with flu* **20** (*functioning as imperative*) (to dogs): *down, Rover!* **21** (*functioning as imperative*) **down with** wanting the end of somebody or something: *down with the king!* **22 get down on something** *Austral & NZ* to procure something, esp in advance of needs or in anticipation of someone else ▷ *adj* **23** (*postpositive*) depressed **24** (*prenominal*) of or relating to a train or trains from a more important place or one regarded as higher: *the down line* **25** (*postpositive*) (of a device, machine, etc, esp a computer) temporarily out of action **26** made in cash: *a down payment* **27 down to** the responsibility or fault of: *this defeat was down to me* ▷ *vb* (*tr*) **28** to knock, push, or pull down **29** to cause to go or come down **30** *inf* to drink, esp quickly **31** to bring (someone) down, esp by tackling ▷ *n* **32** a descent; downward movement **33** a lowering or a poor period (esp in **ups and downs**) **34** (in American football) any of a series of four attempts to advance the ball ten yards **35 have a down on** *inf* to bear ill will towards [OE *dūne*, short for *adūne*, var. of *of dūne*, lit.: from the hill]

down² (daʊn) *n* **1** soft fine feathers **2** another name for **eiderdown** (sense 1) **3** *bot* a fine coating of soft hairs, as on certain leaves, fruits, and seeds **4** any growth or coating of soft fine hair [c14 from ON]

down³ (daʊn) *n arch* a hill, esp a sand dune. See also **downs** [OE *dūn*]

Down (daʊn) *n* **1** a district of SE Northern Ireland, in Co. Down. Pop: 63 828 (2001). Area: 649 sq km (250 sq miles) **2** a historical county of SE Northern Ireland, on the Irish Sea: generally hilly, rising to the Mountains of Mourne: in 1973 it was replaced for administrative purposes by the districts of Ards, Banbridge, Castlereagh, Down, Newry and Mourne, North Down, and part of Lisburn. Area: 2466 sq km (952 sq miles)

down and dirty *adj* (**down-and-dirty** *when prenominal*) *inf, chiefly US* **1** ruthlessly competitive or underhand: *if Bush gets down and dirty the Governor will give as good as he gets* **2** uninhibited; frank

down-and-out *adj* **1** without any means of livelihood; poor and, often, socially outcast ▷ *n* **2** a person who is destitute and, often, homeless

downbeat (ˈdaʊnˌbiːt) *n* **1** *music* the first beat of a bar or the downward gesture of a conductor's baton indicating this ▷ *adj inf* **2** depressed; gloomy **3** relaxed

downcast (ˈdaʊnˌkɑːst) *adj* **1** dejected **2** (esp of the eyes) directed downwards ▷ *n* **3** *mining* a ventilation shaft

downer (ˈdaʊnə) *n sl* **1** a barbiturate, tranquillizer, or narcotic **2** a depressing experience **3** a state of depression

downfall (ˈdaʊnˌfɔːl) *n* **1** a sudden loss of position, health, or reputation **2** a fall of rain, snow, etc, esp a sudden heavy one

downgrade (ˈdaʊnˌgreɪd) *vb* **downgrades, downgrading, downgraded** (*tr*) **1** to reduce in importance or value, esp to demote (a person) to a poorer job **2** to speak of disparagingly ▷ *n* **3** *chiefly US & Canad* a downward slope **4 on the downgrade** waning in importance, health, etc

downhearted (ˌdaʊnˈhɑːtɪd) *adj* discouraged; dejected > ˌ**downˈheartedly** *adv*

downhill (ˈdaʊnˈhɪl) *adj* **1** going or sloping down ▷ *adv* **2** towards the bottom of a hill; downwards **3 go downhill** *inf* to decline; deteriorate ▷ *n* **4** the downward slope of a hill; a descent **5** a skiing race downhill

downhole (ˈdaʊnˌhəʊl) *adj* (in the oil industry) denoting any piece of equipment used in the well itself

downhome (ˌdaʊnˈhəʊm) *adj sl, chiefly US* of, relating to, or reminiscent of rural life, esp in the southern US; unsophisticated; homely

Downing Street (ˈdaʊnɪŋ) *n* **1** a street in W central London, in Westminster: official residences of the British prime minister and the chancellor of the exchequer **2** *inf* the prime minister or the British Government [named after Sir George *Downing* (1623–84), English statesman]

download (ˈdaʊnˌləʊd) *vb* **1** (*tr*) to copy or transfer (data or a program) from one computer's memory to that of another, esp in a network of computing. *n* **2** a file transferred onto a computer from another computer or the Internet ▷ Cf **upload** > ˌ**downˈloadable** *adj*

down-market *adj* relating to commercial products, services, etc, that are cheap, unfashionable, or poor quality

Downpatrick (ˌdaʊnˈpætrɪk) *n* a market town in Northern Ireland: reputedly the burial place of Saint Patrick. Pop: 10 257 (1991)

down payment *n* the deposit paid on an item purchased on hire-purchase, mortgage, etc

downpipe (ˈdaʊnˌpaɪp) *n Brit and NZ* a pipe for carrying rainwater from a roof gutter to ground level. Usual US & Canad name: **downspout**

downpour (ˈdaʊnˌpɔː) *n* a heavy continuous fall of rain

downrange (ˈdaʊnˈreɪndʒ) *adj, adv* in the direction of the intended flight path of a rocket or missile

downright (ˈdaʊnˌraɪt) *adj* **1** frank or straightforward; blunt ▷ *adv, adj* (*prenominal*) **2** (intensifier): *downright rude* > ˈ**downˌrightly** *adv* > ˈ**downˌrightness** *n*

downs (daʊnz) *pl n* **1** rolling upland, esp in the chalk areas of S Britain, characterized by lack of trees and used mainly as pasture **2** *Austral & NZ* a flat grassy area, not necessarily of uplands

Downs (daʊnz) *pl, n* **the 1** any of various ranges of low chalk hills in S England, esp the **South Downs** in Sussex **2** a roadstead off the SE coast of Kent, protected by the Goodwin Sands

downshifting (ˈdaʊnˌʃɪftɪŋ) *n* the practice of simplifying one's lifestyle and becoming less materialistic > ˈ**downˌshifter** *n*

downside (ˈdaʊnˌsaɪd) *n* the disadvantageous aspect of a situation: *the downside of twentieth-century living*

downsize (ˈdaʊnˌsaɪz) *vb* **downsizes, downsizing, downsized** (*tr*) **1** to reduce the number of people employed by (a company) **2** to upgrade (a computer system) by replacing a mainframe or minicomputer with a network of microcomputing ▷ Cf **rightsize**

Down's syndrome (daʊnz) *n* **a** *pathol* a chromosomal abnormality resulting in a flat face and nose, a vertical fold of skin at the inner edge of the eye, and mental retardation. Former name: **mongolism b** (*as modifier*): *a Down's syndrome baby* [c19 after John *Langdon-Down* (1828–96), Brit physician]

downstage (ˈdaʊnˈsteɪdʒ) *theatre* ▷ *adv* **1** at or towards the front of the stage ▷ *adj* **2** of or relating to the front of the stage

downstairs (ˈdaʊnˈstɛəz) *adv* **1** down the stairs; to or on a lower floor ▷ *n* **2a** a lower or ground floor **2b** (*as modifier*): *a downstairs room* **3** *Brit inf, old-fashioned* the servants of a household collectively

downstream (ˈdaʊnˈstriːm) *adv, adj* in or towards the lower part of a stream; with the current ▷ Cf **upstream** (sense 1)

downswing (ˈdaʊnˌswɪŋ) *n* a statistical downward trend in business activity, the death rate, etc

downtime (ˈdaʊnˌtaɪm) *n commerce* time during which a computer or machine is not working, as when under repair

down-to-earth *adj* sensible; practical; realistic

downtown (ˈdaʊnˈtaʊn) *chiefly US, Canad, & NZ* ▷ *n* **1** the central or lower part of a city, esp the main commercial area ▷ *adv* **2** towards, to, or into this area ▷ *adj* **3** of, relating to, or situated in the downtown area: *a downtown cinema*

downtrodden (ˈdaʊnˌtrɒdᵊn) *adj* **1** subjugated; oppressed **2** trodden down

downturn (ˈdaʊnˌtɜːn) *n* a drop or reduction in the success of a business or economy

down under *inf* ▷ *n* **1** Australia or New Zealand ▷ *adv* **2** in or to Australia or New Zealand

downward (ˈdaʊnwəd) *adj* **1** descending from a higher to a lower level, condition, position, etc **2** descending from a beginning ▷ *adv* **3** a variant of **downwards** > ˈ**downwardly** *adv*

downwards (ˈdaʊnwədz) *or* **downward** *adv* **1** from a higher to a lower place, level, etc **2** from an earlier time

or source to a later: *from the Tudors downwards*
downwind ('daʊn'wɪnd) *adv, adj* in the same direction towards which the wind is blowing; with the wind from behind
downy ('daʊnɪ) *adj* **downier, downiest** 1 covered with soft fine hair or feathers 2 light, soft, and fluffy 3 made from or filled with down 4 *Brit sl* sharp-witted > '**downiness** *n*
dowry ('daʊərɪ) *n, pl* **dowries** 1 the property brought by a woman to her husband at marriage 2 a natural talent or gift [C14 from Anglo-F *douarie*, from Med. L *dōtārium*; see DOWER]
dowse (daʊz) *vb* **dowses, dowsing, dowsed** (*intr*) to search for underground water, minerals, etc, using a divining rod; divine [C17 from ?] > '**dowser** *n*
Dowson ('daʊsᵊn) *n* **Ernest (Christopher)** 1867–1900, English Decadent poet noted for his lyric *Cynara*
doxology (dɒk'sɒlədʒɪ) *n, pl* **doxologies** a hymn, verse, or form of words in Christian liturgy glorifying God [C17 from Med. L *doxologia*, from Gk, from *doxologos* uttering praise, from *doxa* praise; see -LOGY] > **doxological** (ˌdɒksə'lɒdʒɪkᵊl) *adj*
doxy ('dɒksɪ) *n, pl* **doxies** *arch sl* a prostitute or mistress [C16 prob. from MFlemish *docke* doll]
doyen ('dɔɪən) *n* the senior member of a group, profession, or society [C17 from F, from LL *decānus* leader of a group of ten] > **doyenne** (dɔɪ'ɛn) *fem n*
doyley ('dɔɪlɪ) *n* a variant spelling of **doily**
D'Oyly Carte ('dɔɪlɪ kɑːt) *n* **Richard** 1844–1901, British impresario noted for his productions of the operettas of Gilbert and Sullivan
doz. *abbrev for* dozen
doze (dəʊz) *vb* **dozes, dozing, dozed** (*intr*) 1 to sleep lightly or intermittently 2 (often foll by *off*) to fall into a light sleep ▷ *n* 3 a short sleep [C17 prob. from ON *dūs* lull] > '**dozer** *n*
dozen ('dʌzᵊn) *determiner* 1 (preceded by *a* or a numeral) twelve or a group of twelve ▷ *n, pl* **dozens** *or* **dozen** 2 **by the dozen** in large quantities 3 **daily dozen** *Brit* regular physical exercises 4 **talk nineteen to the dozen** to talk without stopping [C13 from OF *douzaine*, from *douze* twelve, from L *duodecim*, from *duo* two + *decem* ten] > '**dozenth** *adj*
dozy ('dəʊzɪ) *adj* **dozier, doziest** 1 drowsy 2 *Brit inf* stupid > '**dozily** *adv* > '**doziness** *n*
DP *abbrev for:* 1 data processing 2 displaced person 3 (in South Africa) Democratic Party
DPB (in New Zealand) *abbrev for* domestic purposes benefit: an allowance paid to single parents
DPhil *or* **DPh** *abbrev for* Doctor of Philosophy. Also: **PhD**
dpi *abbrev for* dots per inch: a measure of the resolution of a typesetting machine, computer screen, etc
DPP (in Britain) *abbrev for* Director of Public Prosecutions
dpt *abbrev for:* 1 department 2 depot
dr *abbrev for:* 1 Also: **dr** dram 2 debtor
Dr *abbrev for:* 1 Doctor 2 Drive
DR *abbrev for* dry riser
dr. *abbrev for:* 1 debit 2 (the former) drachma
drab¹ (dræb) *adj* **drabber, drabbest** 1 dull; dingy 2 cheerless; dreary 3 of the colour drab ▷ *n* 4 a light olive-brown colour [C16 from OF *drap* cloth, from LL *drappus*, ? of Celtic origin] > '**drably** *adv* > '**drabness** *n*
drab² (dræb) *arch* ▷ *n* 1 a slatternly woman 2 a whore ▷ *vb* **drabs, drabbing, drabbed** 3 (*intr*) to consort with prostitutes [C16 of Celtic origin]
drachm (dræm) *n* 1 Also called: **fluid dram** *Brit* one eighth of a fluid ounce 2 *US* another name for **dram** (sense 2) 3 another name for **drachma** [C14 learned var. of DRAM]
drachma ('drækmə) *n, pl* **drachmas** *or* **drachmae** (-miː) 1 the former standard monetary unit of Greece, replaced by the euro in 2002 2 *US* another name for **dram** (sense 2) 3 a silver coin of ancient Greece [C16 from L, from Gk *drakhmē* a handful, from *drassesthai* to seize]
drack *or* **drac** (dræk) *adj Austral sl* (of a woman) unattractive [C20 ?from *Dracula's* daughter]
Draco ('dreɪkəʊ) *n* 7th century BC, Athenian statesman and lawmaker, whose code of laws (621) prescribed death for most offences
Draconian (dreɪ'kəʊnɪən) *or* **Draconic** (dreɪ'kɒnɪk) *adj* (*sometimes not cap*) 1 of or relating to Draco or his code of laws 2 harsh > **Dra'conianism** *n* > **Dra'conically** *adv*
Dracula ('drækjʊlə) *n* 1 a cruel or bloodthirsty person 2 a person who preys ruthlessly on others [C20 from the vampire in Bram Stoker's Gothic novel *Dracula* (1897)]
draff (dræf) *n* the residue of husks after fermentation of the grain in brewing, used as cattle fodder [C13 from ON *draf*]
draft (drɑːft) *n* 1 a plan, sketch, or drawing of something 2 a preliminary outline of a book, speech, etc 3 another word for **bill of exchange** 4 a demand or drain on something 5 *US & Austral* selection for compulsory military service 6 detachment of military personnel from one unit to another 7 *Austral & NZ* a group of livestock separated from the rest of the herd or flock ▷ *vb* (*tr*) 8 to draw up an outline or sketch for 9 to prepare a plan or design of 10 to detach (military personnel) from one unit to another 11 *US & Austral* to select for compulsory military service 12 *Austral & NZ* 12a to select (cattle or sheep) from a herd or flock 12b to select (farm stock) for sale ▷ *n, vb* 13 the usual US spelling of **draught** [C16 var. of DRAUGHT] > '**drafter** *n*
draftee (drɑːf'tiː) *n US* a conscript
drafty ('drɑːftɪ) *adj* **draftier, draftiest** the usual US spelling of **draughty**
drag (dræg) *vb* **drags, dragging, dragged** 1 to pull or be pulled with force, esp along the ground 2 (*tr*; often foll by *away* or *from*) to persuade to come away 3 to trail or cause to trail on the ground 4 (*tr*) to move with effort or difficulty 5 to linger behind 6 (often foll by *on* or *out*) to prolong or be prolonged unnecessarily or tediously: *his talk dragged on for hours* 7 (when *intr*, usually foll by *for*) to search (the bed of a river, etc) with a dragnet or hook 8 (*tr*; foll by *out* or *from*) to crush (clods) or level (a soil surface) by use of a drag 9 (of hounds) to follow (a fox or its trail) 10 (*intr*) *sl* to draw (on a cigarette, etc) 11 *computing* to move (a graphics image) from one place to another on the screen using a mouse 12 **drag anchor** (of a vessel) to move away from its mooring because the anchor has failed to hold 13 **drag one's feet** *or* **heels** *inf* to act with deliberate slowness ▷ *n* 14 the act of dragging or the state of being dragged 15 an implement, such as a dragnet, dredge, etc, used for dragging 16 a type of harrow used to crush clods, level soil, etc 17 a coach with seats inside and out, usually drawn by four horses 18 a braking device 19 a person or thing that slows up progress 20 slow progress or movement 21 *aeronautics* the resistance to the motion of a body passing through a fluid, esp through air 22 the trail of scent left by a fox, etc 23 an artificial trail of scent drawn over the ground for hounds to follow 24 See **drag hunt** 25 *inf* a person or thing that is very tedious 26 *sl* a car 27 short for **drag race** 28 *sl* 28a women's clothes worn by a man(esp in **in drag**) 28b (*as modifier*): *a drag show* 28c clothes collectively 29 *inf* a draw on a cigarette, etc 30 *US sl* influence 31 *chiefly US sl* a street(esp in **main drag**) ▷ See also **drag out of, drag up** [OE *dragan* to DRAW]
dragée (dræ'ʒeɪ) *n* 1 a sweet coated with a hard sugar icing 2 a tiny beadlike sweet used for decorating cakes, etc 3 a medicinal formulation coated with sugar [C19 from F; see DREDGE²]
draggle ('drægᵊl) *vb* **draggles, draggling, draggled** 1 to make or become wet or dirty by trailing on the ground; bedraggle 2 (*intr*) to lag; dawdle [ME, prob. frequentative of DRAG]

drag hunt *n* **1** a hunt in which hounds follow an artificial trail of scent **2** a club that organizes such hunts > **ˈdrag-ˌhunt** *vb*

dragnet (ˈdræɡˌnɛt) *n* **1** a net used to scour the bottom of a pond, river, etc, as when searching for something **2** any system of coordinated efforts to track down wanted persons

dragoman (ˈdræɡəʊmən) *n, pl* **dragomans** *or* **dragomen** (in some Middle Eastern countries, esp formerly) a professional interpreter or guide [C14 from F, from It., from Med. Gk *dragoumanos*, from Ar. *targumān*, ult. from Akkadian]

dragon (ˈdræɡən) *n* **1** a mythical monster usually represented as breathing fire and having a scaly reptilian body, wings, claws, and a long tail **2** *inf* a fierce person, esp a woman **3** any of various very large lizards, esp the Komodo dragon **4** *commerce* a newly industrialized country, esp one in SE Asia **5** **chase the dragon** *sl* to smoke opium or heroin [C13 from OF, from L *dracō*, from Gk *drakōn*]

dragonet (ˈdræɡənɪt) *n* a small fish with spiny fins, a flat head, and a slender tapering brighty coloured body [C14 (meaning: small dragon): from F; applied to fish C18]

dragonfly (ˈdræɡənˌflaɪ) *n, pl* **dragonflies** a predatory insect having a long slender body and two pairs of iridescent wings that are outspread at rest

dragon light *n* an extremely powerful light used by police to dazzle and immobilize criminal suspects

dragonnade (ˌdræɡəˈneɪd) *n* **1** *history* the persecution of French Huguenots during the reign of Louis XIV by dragoons quartered in their villages and homes **2** subjection by military force ▷ *vb* **dragonnades, dragonnading, dragonnaded** **3** (*tr*) to subject to persecution by military troops [C18 from F, from *dragon* DRAGOON]

dragoon (drəˈɡuːn) *n* **1** (originally) a mounted infantryman armed with a carbine **2** (*sometimes cap*) a domestic fancy pigeon **3a** a type of cavalryman **3b** (*pl; cap when part of a name*): *the Royal Dragoons* ▷ *vb* (*tr*) **4** to coerce; force **5** to persecute by military force [C17 from F *dragon* (special use of DRAGON), soldier armed with a carbine]

drag out of *vb* (*tr, adv + prep*) to obtain or extract (a confession, statement, etc), esp by force. Also: **drag from**

drag race *n* a type of motor race in which specially built or modified cars or motorcycles are timed over a measured course > **drag racing** *n*

dragster (ˈdræɡstə) *n* a car specially built or modified for drag racing

▷ www.eurodragster.com

▷ www.ihra.com

drag up *vb* (*tr, adv*) *Inf* **1** to rear (a child) poorly and in an undisciplined manner **2** to introduce or revive (an unpleasant fact or story)

drain (dreɪn) *n* **1** a pipe or channel that carries off water, sewage, etc **2** an instance or cause of continuous diminution in resources or energy; depletion **3** *surgery* a device, such as a tube, to drain off pus, etc **4** **down the drain** wasted ▷ *vb* **5** (*tr; often foll by off*) to draw off or remove (liquid) from **6** (*intr; often foll by away*) to flow (away) or filter (off) **7** (*intr*) to dry or be emptied as a result of liquid running off or flowing away **8** (*tr*) to drink the entire contents of (a glass, etc) **9** (*tr*) to consume or make constant demands on (resources, energy, etc); exhaust **10** (*intr*) to disappear or leave, esp gradually **11** (of a river, etc) to carry off the surface water from (an area) **12** (*intr*) (of an area) to discharge its surface water into rivers, streams, etc [OE *drēahnian*] > **ˈdrainer** *n*

drainage (ˈdreɪnɪdʒ) *n* **1** the process or a method of draining **2** a system of watercourses or drains **3** liquid, sewage, etc, that is drained away

drainage basin *or* **area** *n* another name for **catchment area**

draining board *n* a sloping grooved surface at the side of a sink, used for draining washed dishes, etc.

drainlayer (ˈdreɪnˌleɪə) *n* NZ a person trained to build or repair drains

drainpipe (ˈdreɪnˌpaɪp) *n* a pipe for carrying off rainwater, sewage, etc; downpipe

drainpipes (ˈdreɪnˌpaɪps) *pl n* trousers with very narrow legs, worn esp by teddy boys in the 1950s

drake (dreɪk) *n* the male of any duck [C13 ?from Low G]

Drake (dreɪk) *n* Sir **Francis** ?1540–96, English navigator and buccaneer, the first Englishman to sail around the world (1577–80) He commanded a fleet against the Spanish Armada (1588) and contributed greatly to its defeat

Drakensberg (ˈdrɑːkənzˌbɜːɡ) *n* a mountain range in southern Africa, extending through Lesotho, E South Africa, and Swaziland. Highest peak: Thabana Ntlenyana, 3482 m (11 425 ft). Sotho name: **Quathlamba**

Dralon (ˈdreɪlɒn) *n trademark* an acrylic fibre fabric used esp for upholstery

dram (dræm) *n* **1** one sixteenth of an ounce (avoirdupois). 1 dram is equivalent to 0.0018 kilogram **2** *US* one eighth of an apothecaries' ounce; 60 grains. 1 dram is equivalent to 0.0039 kilogram **3** a small amount of an alcoholic drink, esp a spirit; tot **4** the standard monetary unit of Armenia [C15 from OF *dragme*, from LL *dragma*, from Gk *drakhmē*; see DRACHMA]

DRAM *or* **D-RAM** (ˈdiːræm) *n acronym for* dynamic random access memory: **a** a widely used type of random access memory. See **RAM¹** **b** a chip containing such a memory

drama (ˈdrɑːmə) *n* **1** a work to be performed by actors; play **2** the genre of literature represented by works intended for the stage **3** the art of the writing and production of plays **4** a situation that is highly emotional, tragic, or turbulent [C17 from LL: a play, from Gk: something performed, from *drān* to do]

▷ http://vl-theatre.com

drama queen *n inf* a person who tends to react to every situation in an overdramatic or exaggerated manner

dramatic (drəˈmætɪk) *adj* **1** of drama **2** like a drama in suddenness, emotional impact, etc **3** striking; effective **4** acting or performed in a flamboyant way > **draˈmatically** *adv*

dramatic irony *n theatre* the irony occurring when the implications of a situation, speech, etc, are understood by the audience but not by the characters in the play

dramatics (drəˈmætɪks) *n* **1** (*functioning as sing or pl*) **1a** the art of acting or producing plays **1b** dramatic productions **2** (*usually functioning as pl*) histrionic behaviour

dramatis personae (ˈdrɑːmətɪs pəˈsəʊnaɪ) *pl n* (*often functioning as sing*) the characters in a play [C18 from NL]

dramatist (ˈdræmətɪst) *n* a playwright

dramatize *or* **dramatise** (ˈdræməˌtaɪz) *vb* **dramatizes, dramatizing, dramatized** *or* **dramatises, dramatising, dramatised** **1** (*tr*) to put into dramatic form **2** to express (something) in a dramatic or exaggerated way > **ˌdramatiˈzation** *or* **ˌdramatiˈsation** *n*

dramaturge (ˈdræməˌtɜːdʒ) *n* **1** Also called: **dramaturgist** a dramatist **2** Also called: **dramaturg** a literary adviser on the staff of a theatre, film company, etc [C19 prob. from F, from Gk *dramatourgos* playwright, from DRAMA + *ergon* work]

dramaturgy (ˈdræməˌtɜːdʒɪ) *n* the art and technique of the theatre; dramatics > **ˌdramaˈturgic** *or* **ˌdramaˈturgical** *adj*

dramedy (ˈdrɑːmɪdɪ) *n, pl* **dramedies** a television or film drama in which there are important elements of comedy [C20 from DRAM(A) + (COM)EDY]

drank (dræŋk) *vb* the past tense of **drink**

drape (dreɪp) *vb* **drapes, draping, draped** 1 (*tr*) to hang or cover with material or fabric, usually in folds 2 to hang or arrange or be hung or arranged, esp in folds 3 (*tr*) to place casually and loosely ▷ *n* 4 (*often pl*) a cloth or hanging that covers something in folds 5 the way in which fabric hangs [c15 from OF *draper*, from *drap* piece of cloth; see DRAB[1]]

draper (ˈdreɪpə) *n* 1 *Brit* a dealer in fabrics and sewing materials 2 *arch* a maker of cloth

drapery (ˈdreɪpərɪ) *n, pl* **draperies** 1 fabric or clothing arranged and draped 2 (*often pl*) curtains or hangings that drape 3 *Brit* the occupation or shop of a draper 4 fabrics and cloth collectively > ˈ**draperied** *adj*

drapes (dreɪps) *or* **draperies** (ˈdreɪpərɪz) *pl n chiefly US & Canad* curtains, esp ones of heavy fabric

drastic (ˈdræstɪk) *adj* extreme or forceful; severe [c17 from Gk *drastikos*, from *drān* to do, act] > ˈ**drastically** *adv*

drat (dræt) *interj sl* an exclamation of annoyance [c19 prob. alteration of *God rot*]

draught *or US* **draft** (drɑːft) *n* 1 a current of air, esp in an enclosed space 2a the act of pulling a load, as by a vehicle or animal 2b (*as modifier*): *a draught horse* 3 the load or quantity drawn 4 a portion of liquid to be drunk, esp a dose of medicine 5 the act or an instance of drinking; a gulp or swallow 6 the act or process of drawing air, etc, into the lungs 7 the amount of air, etc, inhaled 8a beer, wine, etc, stored in bulk, esp in a cask 8b (*as modifier*): *draught beer* 8c **on draught** drawn from a cask or keg 9 any one of the flat discs used in the game of draughts. US and Canad equivalent: **checker** 10 the depth of a loaded vessel in the water 11 **feel the draught** to be short of money [c14 prob. from ON *drahtr*, of Gmc origin]

draughtboard (ˈdrɑːftˌbɔːd) *n* a square board divided into 64 squares of alternating colours, used for playing draughts or chess

draughts (drɑːfts) *n* (*functioning as sing*) a game for two players using a draughtboard and 12 draughtsmen each. US and Canad name: **checkers** [c14 pl of DRAUGHT (in obs. sense: a chess move)]
▷ www.fmjd.nl

draughtsman *or US* **draftsman** (ˈdrɑːftsmən) *n, pl* **draughtsmen** *or US* **draftsmen** 1 a person employed to prepare detailed scale drawings of machinery, buildings, etc 2 a person skilled in drawing 3 *Brit* any of the flat discs used in the game of draughts. US and Canad equivalent: **checker** > ˈ**draughtsmanˌship** *or US* ˈ**draftsmanˌship** *n*

draughty *or US* **drafty** (ˈdrɑːftɪ) *adj* **draughtier, draughtiest** *or US* **draftier, draftiest** characterized by or exposed to draughts of air > ˈ**draughtily** *or US* ˈ**draftily** *adv* > ˈ**draughtiness** *or US* ˈ**draftiness** *n*

Dravidian (drəˈvɪdɪən) *n* 1 a family of languages spoken in S and central India and Sri Lanka, including Tamil, Malayalam, etc 2 a member of one of the aboriginal races of India, pushed south by the Indo-Europeans and now mixed with them ▷ *adj* 3 of or denoting this family of languages or these peoples

draw (drɔː) *vb* **draws, drawing, drew, drawn** 1 to cause (a person or thing) to move towards or away by pulling 2 to bring, take, or pull (something) out, as from a drawer, holster, etc 3 (*tr*) to extract or pull or take out: *to draw teeth* 4 (*tr; often foll by off*) to take (liquid) out of a cask, etc, by means of a tap 5 (*intr*) to move, esp in a specified direction: *to draw alongside* 6 (*tr*) to attract: *to draw attention* 7 (*tr*) to cause to flow: *to draw blood* 8 to depict or sketch (a figure, picture, etc) in lines, as with a pencil or pen 9 (*tr*) to make, formulate, or derive: *to draw conclusions* 10 (*tr*) to write (a legal document) in proper form 11 (*tr; sometimes foll by in*) to suck or take in (air, etc) 12 (*intr*) to induce or allow a draught to carry off air, smoke, etc 13 (*tr*) to take or receive from a source: *to draw money from the bank* 14 (*tr*) to earn: *draw interest* 15 (*tr*) to write out (a bill of exchange, etc) 16 (*tr*) to choose at random 17 (*tr*) to reduce the diameter of (a wire) by pulling it through a die 18 (*tr*) to shape (metal or glass) by rolling, by pulling through a die, or by stretching 19 *archery* to bend (a bow) by pulling the string 20 to steep (tea) or (of tea) to steep in boiling water 21 (*tr*) to disembowel 22 (*tr*) to cause (pus, etc) to discharge from an abscess or wound 23 (*intr*) (of two teams, etc) to finish a game with an equal number of points, goals, etc; tie 24 (*tr*) *bridge, whist* to keep leading a suit in order to force out (all outstanding cards) 25 **draw trumps** *bridge, whist* to play the trump suit until the opponents have none left 26 (*tr*) *billiards* to cause (the cue ball) to spin back after a direct impact with another ball 27 (*tr*) to search (a place) in order to find wild animals, etc, for hunting 28 *golf* to cause (a golf ball) to move with a controlled right-to-left trajectory or (of a golf ball) to veer gradually from right to left 29 (*tr*) *naut* (of a vessel) to require (a certain depth) in which to float 30 **draw and quarter** to disembowel and dismember (a person) after hanging 31 **draw stumps** *cricket* to close play 32 **draw the shot** *bowls* to deliver the bowl in such a way that it approaches the jack ▷ *n* 33 the act of drawing 34 *US* a sum of money advanced to finance anticipated expenses 35 *inf* an event, act, etc, that attracts a large audience 36 a raffle or lottery 37 something taken at random, as a ticket in a lottery 38 a contest or game ending in a tie 39 *US & Canad* a small natural drainage way or gully ▷ See also **drawback, draw in,** etc [OE *dragan*]

drawback (ˈdrɔːˌbæk) *n* 1 a disadvantage or hindrance 2 a refund of customs or excise paid on goods that are being exported or used in making goods for export ▷ *vb* **draw back** (*intr, adv; often foll by from*) 3 to retreat; move backwards 4 to turn aside from an undertaking

drawbridge (ˈdrɔːˌbrɪdʒ) *n* a bridge that may be raised to prevent access or to enable vessels to pass

drawee (drɔːˈiː) *n* the person or organization on which an order for payment is drawn

drawer (ˈdrɔːə) *n* 1 a person or thing that draws, esp a draughtsman 2 a person who draws a cheque. See **draw** (sense 15) 3 a person who draws up a commercial paper 4 *arch* a person who draws beer, etc, in a bar 5 (drɔː) a boxlike container in a chest, table, etc, made for sliding in and out

drawers (drɔːz) *pl n* a legged undergarment for either sex, worn below the waist

draw in *vb* (*intr, adv*) 1 (of hours of daylight) to become shorter 2 (of a train) to arrive at a station

drawing (ˈdrɔːɪŋ) *n* 1 a picture or plan made by means of lines on a surface, esp one made with a pencil or pen 2 a sketch or outline 3 the art of making drawings; draughtsmanship

drawing pin *n Brit* a short tack with a broad smooth head for fastening papers to a drawing board, etc US and Canad name: **thumbtack**

drawing room *n* 1 a room where visitors are received and entertained; living room; sitting room 2 *arch* a formal reception

drawknife (ˈdrɔːˌnaɪf) *or* **drawshave** *n, pl* **drawknives** *or* **drawshaves** a tool with two handles, used to shave wood. US name: **spokeshave**

drawl (drɔːl) *vb* 1 to speak or utter (words) slowly, esp prolonging the vowel sounds ▷ *n* 2 the way of speech of someone who drawls [c16 prob. frequentative of DRAW] > ˈ**drawling** *adj*

drawn (drɔːn) *vb* 1 the past participle of **draw** ▷ *adj* 2 haggard, tired, or tense in appearance

drawn work *n* ornamental needlework done by drawing threads out of the fabric and using the remaining threads to form lacelike patterns. Also called: **drawn-thread work**

draw off *vb* (*adv*) 1 (*tr*) to cause (a liquid) to flow from

Dd

something **2** to withdraw (troops)

draw on *vb* **1** (*intr, prep*) to use or exploit (a source, fund, etc) **2** (*intr, adv*) to come near **3** (*tr, prep*) to withdraw (money) from (an account) **4** (*tr, adv*) to put on (clothes) **5** (*tr, adv*) to lead further; entice

draw out *vb* (*adv*) **1** to extend **2** (*tr*) to cause (a person) to talk freely **3** (*tr; foll by of*) Also: **draw from** to elicit (information) (from) **4** (*tr*) to withdraw (money) as from a bank account **5** (*intr*) (of hours of daylight) to become longer **6** (*intr*) (of a train) to leave a station **7** (*tr*) to extend (troops) in line **8** (*intr*) (of troops) to proceed from camp

drawstring (ˈdrɔːˌstrɪŋ) *n* a cord, etc, run through a hem around an opening, so that when it is pulled tighter, the opening closes

draw up *vb* (*adv*) **1** to come or cause to come to a halt **2** (*tr*) **2a** to prepare a draft of (a document, etc) **2b** to formulate and write out: *to draw up a contract* **3** (*used reflexively*) to straighten oneself **4** to form or arrange (a body of soldiers, etc) in order or formation

dray[1] (dreɪ) *n* **a** a low cart used for carrying heavy loads **b** (*in combination*): *a drayman* [OE *drǣge* dragnet]

dray[2] (dreɪ) *n* a variant spelling of **drey**

Drayton (ˈdreɪtᵊn) *n* **Michael** 1563–1631, English poet. His work includes odes and pastorals, and *Poly-Olbion* (1613–22), on the topography of England

dread (drɛd) *vb* (*tr*) **1** to anticipate with apprehension or terror **2** to fear greatly **3** *arch* to be in awe of ▷ *n* **4** great fear **5** an object of terror **6** *sl* a Rastafarian **7** *arch* deep reverence [OE *ondrǣdan*]

dreadful (ˈdrɛdfʊl) *adj* **1** extremely disagreeable, shocking, or bad **2** (intensifier): *a dreadful waste of time* **3** causing dread; terrifying **4** *arch* inspiring awe

dreadfully (ˈdrɛdfʊlɪ) *adv* **1** in a shocking or disagreeable manner **2** (intensifier): *you're dreadfully kind*

dreadlocks (ˈdrɛdˌlɒks) *pl n inf* hair worn in the Rastafarian style of long tightly-curled strands

dreadnought (ˈdrɛdˌnɔːt) *n* **1** a battleship armed with heavy guns of uniform calibre **2** an overcoat made of heavy cloth

dream (driːm) *n* **1a** mental activity, usually an imagined series of events, occurring during sleep **1b** (*as modifier*): *a dream sequence* **1c** (*in combination*): *dreamland* **2a** a sequence of imaginative thoughts indulged in while awake; daydream; fantasy **2b** (*as modifier*): *a dream world* **3** a person or thing seen or occurring in a dream **4** a cherished hope; aspiration **5** a vain hope **6** a person or thing that is as pleasant or seemingly unreal as a dream **7 go like a dream** to move, develop, or work very well ▷ *vb* **dreams, dreaming, dreamed** *or* **dreamt 8** (*may take a clause as object*) to undergo or experience (a dream or dreams) **9** (*intr*) to indulge in daydreams **10** (*intr*) to suffer delusions; be unrealistic **11** (when *intr*, foll by *of* or *about*) to have an image (of) or fantasy (about) in or as if in a dream **12** (*intr; foll by of*) to consider the possibility (of) ▷ *adj* **13** too good to be true; ideal: *dream kitchen* [OE *drēam* song] > ˈ**dreamer** *n*

dreamboat (ˈdriːmˌbəʊt) *n sl* an ideal or desirable person, esp one of the opposite sex

dreamt (drɛmt) *vb* a past tense and past participle of **dream**

dream team *n inf* a group of people regarded as having the perfect combination of talents

dream ticket *n* a combination of two people, usually candidates in an election, that is considered to be ideal

Dreamtime (ˈdriːmˌtaɪm) *n* **1** Also called: **alcheringa** (in the mythology of Australian Aboriginal peoples) a mythical golden age of the past, when the first men were created **2** *Austral inf* any remote period, out of touch with the realities of the present

dream up *vb* (*tr, adv*) to invent by ingenuity and imagination: *to dream up an excuse*

dreamy (ˈdriːmɪ) *adj* **dreamier, dreamiest 1** vague or impractical **2** resembling a dream **3** relaxing; gentle **4** *inf* wonderful **5** having dreams, esp daydreams > ˈ**dreamily** *adv* > ˈ**dreaminess** *n*

dreary (ˈdrɪərɪ) *adj* **drearier, dreariest 1** sad or dull **2** wearying; boring ▷ Also (literary): **drear** [OE *drēorig* gory] > ˈ**drearily** *adv* > ˈ**dreariness** *n*

dredge[1] (drɛdʒ) *n* **1** a machine used to scoop or suck up material from a riverbed, channel, etc **2** another name for **dredger** ▷ *vb* **dredges, dredging, dredged 3** to remove (material) from a riverbed, etc, by means of a dredge **4** (*tr*) to search for (a submerged object) with or as if with a dredge; drag [C16 ? ult. from OE *dragan* to DRAW]

dredge[2] (drɛdʒ) *vb* **dredges, dredging, dredged** to sprinkle or coat (food) with flour, etc [C16 from OF *dragie*, ?from L *tragēmata* spices, from Gk] > ˈ**dredger** *n*

dredger (ˈdrɛdʒə) *n* **1** a vessel used for dredging **2** another name for **dredge**[1] (sense 1)

dredge up *vb* (*tr, adv*) **1** *inf* to bring to notice, esp with effort and from an obscure source **2** to raise, as with a dredge

dree (driː) *Scot, literary* ▷ *vb* **drees, dreeing, dreed 1** (*tr*) to endure ▷ *adj* **2** dreary [OE *drēogan*]

D region *or* **layer** *n* the lowest region of the ionosphere, extending from a height of about 60 km to about 90 km

dregs (drɛgz) *pl n* **1** solid particles that settle at the bottom of some liquids **2** residue or remains **3 the dregs** *Brit sl* a despicable person or people [C14 *dreg*, from ON *dregg*]

dreich *or* **dreigh** (driːx) *adj Scot dialect* dreary [ME *dreig*, *drih* enduring, from OE *drēog* (unattested)]

drench (drɛntʃ) *vb* (*tr*) **1** to make completely wet; soak **2** to give liquid medicine to (an animal) ▷ *n* **3** a drenching **4** a dose of liquid medicine given to an animal [OE *drencan* to cause to drink] > ˈ**drenching** *n, adj*

Drenthe (*Dutch* ˈdrɛntə) *n* a province of the NE Netherlands: a low plateau, with many raised bogs, partially reclaimed; agricultural, with oil deposits. Capital: Assen. Pop: 469 800 (2000 est). Area: 2647 sq km (1032 sq miles)

Dresden (ˈdrɛzdᵊn) *n* **1** an industrial city in SE Germany, the capital of Saxony on the River Elbe: it was severely damaged in the Seven Years' War (1760); the baroque city was almost totally destroyed in World War II by Allied bombing (1945). Pop: 477 700 (1999 est). *adj* **2** relating to, designating, or made of Dresden china

Dresden china *n* porcelain ware, esp delicate and elegantly decorative objects and figures of high quality, made at Meissen, near Dresden, since 1710
▷ www.collectics.com/education_meissen.html

dress (drɛs) *vb* **1** to put clothes on; attire **2** (*intr*) to put on more formal attire **3** (*tr*) to provide (someone) with clothing; clothe **4** (*tr*) to arrange merchandise in (a shop window) **5** (*tr*) to arrange (the hair) **6** (*tr*) to apply protective or therapeutic covering to (a wound, sore, etc) **7** (*tr*) to prepare (food, esp fowl and fish) by cleaning, gutting, etc **8** (*tr*) to put a finish on (stone, metal, etc) **9** (*tr*) to cultivate (land), esp by applying fertilizer **10** (*tr*) to trim (trees, etc) **11** (*tr*) to groom (a horse) **12** (*tr*) to convert (tanned hides) into leather **13** *angling* to tie (a fly) **14** *mil* to bring (troops) into line or (of troops) to come into line(esp in **dress ranks**) **15 dress ship** *naut* to decorate a vessel by displaying signal flags on lines ▷ *n* **16** a one-piece garment for a woman, consisting of a skirt and bodice **17** complete style of clothing; costume: *military dress* **18** (*modifier*) suitable for a formal occasion: *a dress shirt* **19** outer covering or appearance ▷ See also **dress down, dress up** [C14 from OF *drecier*, ult. from L *dīrigere* to DIRECT]

dressage (ˈdrɛsɑːʒ) *n* **a** the training of a horse to perform manoeuvres in response to the rider's body signals **b** the manoeuvres performed [F: preparation, from OF *dresser* to prepare; see DRESS]

dress circle *n* a tier of seats in a theatre or other auditorium, usually the first gallery, in which evening dress formerly had to be worn
dress code *n* a set of rules or guidelines regarding the manner of dress acceptable in an office, restaurant, etc
dress down *vb* (*adv*) **1** (*tr*) *inf* to reprimand severely or scold (a person) **2** (*intr*) to dress in casual clothes
dresser[1] ('drɛsə) *n* **1** a set of shelves, usually also with cupboards, for storing or displaying dishes, etc **2** *US* a chest of drawers for storing clothing, often having a mirror on top [C14 *dressour*, from OF *dreceore*, from *drecier* to arrange; see DRESS]
dresser[2] ('drɛsə) *n* **1** a person who dresses in a specified way: *a fashionable dresser* **2** *theatre* a person employed to assist actors with their costumes **3** a tool used for dressing stone, etc **4** *Brit* a person who assists a surgeon during operations **5** *Brit* See **window-dresser**
dressing ('drɛsɪŋ) *n* **1** a sauce for food, esp for salad **2** the US and Canad name for **stuffing** (sense 2) **3** a covering for a wound, etc **4** fertilizer spread on land **5** size used for stiffening textiles **6** the processes in the conversion of hides into leather
dressing-down *n* *inf* a severe scolding
dressing gown *n* a full robe worn before dressing or for lounging
dressing room *n* **1** *theatre* a room backstage for an actor to change clothing and to make up **2** any room used for changing clothes
dressing station *n* *mil* a first-aid post close to a combat area
dressing table *n* a piece of bedroom furniture with a mirror and a set of drawers for clothes, cosmetics, etc
dressmaker ('drɛsˌmeɪkə) *n* a person whose occupation is making clothes, esp for women > **'dressˌmaking** *n*
dress parade *n* *mil* a formal parade in dress uniform
dress rehearsal *n* **1** the last rehearsal of a play, etc, using costumes, lighting, etc, as for the first night **2** any full-scale practice
dress shirt *n* a man's evening shirt, worn as part of formal evening dress
dress suit *n* a man's evening suit, esp tails
dress uniform *n* *mil* formal ceremonial uniform
dress up *vb* (*adv*) **1** to attire (oneself or another) very smartly or elaborately **2** to put fancy dress, etc, on **3** (*tr*) to improve the appearance or impression of: *to dress up the facts*
dressy ('drɛsɪ) *adj* **dressier, dressiest 1** (of clothes) elegant **2** (of persons) dressing stylishly **3** overelegant > **'dressiness** *n*
drew (druː) *vb* the past tense of **draw**
drey *or* **dray** (dreɪ) *n* a squirrel's nest [C17 from ?]
Dreyfus ('dreɪfəs; *French* drɛfys) *n* **Alfred** (alfrɛd) 1859–1935, French army officer, a Jew whose false imprisonment for treason (1894) raised issues of anti-semitism and militarism that dominated French politics until his release (1906)
dribble ('drɪbᵊl) *vb* **dribbles, dribbling, dribbled 1** (*usually intr*) to flow or allow to flow in a thin stream or drops; trickle **2** (*intr*) to allow saliva to trickle from the mouth **3** (in soccer, basketball, hockey, etc) to propel (the ball) by repeatedly tapping it with the hand, foot, or a stick ▷ *n* **4** a small quantity of liquid falling in drops or flowing in a thin stream **5** a small quantity or supply **6** an act or instance of dribbling [C16 frequentative of *drib*, var. of DRIP] > **'dribbler** *n* > **'dribbly** *adj*
driblet *or* **dribblet** ('drɪblɪt) *n* a small amount [C17 from obs. *drib* to fall bit by bit + -LET]
dribs and drabs (drɪbz) *pl, n inf* small sporadic amounts
dried (draɪd) *vb* the past tense and past participle of **dry**
drier[1] ('draɪə) *adj* a comparative of **dry**
drier[2] ('draɪə) *n* a variant spelling of **dryer**[1]
driest ('draɪɪst) *adj* a superlative of **dry**
drift (drɪft) *vb* (*mainly intr*) **1** (*also tr*) to be carried along as by currents of air or water or (of a current) to carry (a vessel, etc) along **2** to move aimlessly from one place or activity to another **3** to wander away from a fixed course or point; stray **4** (*also tr*) (of snow, etc) to accumulate in heaps or to drive (snow, etc) into heaps ▷ *n* **5** something piled up by the wind or current, as a snowdrift **6** tendency or meaning: *the drift of the argument* **7** a state of indecision or inaction **8** the extent to which a vessel, aircraft, etc, is driven off course by winds, etc **9** a general tendency of surface ocean water to flow in the direction of the prevailing winds **10** a driving movement, force, or influence; impulse **11** a controlled four-wheel skid used to take bends at high speed **12** a deposit of sand, gravel, etc, esp one transported and deposited by a glacier **13** a horizontal passage in a mine that follows the mineral vein **14** something, esp a group of animals, driven along **15** a steel tool driven into holes to enlarge or align them **16** an uncontrolled slow change in some operating characteristic of a piece of equipment **17** *S African* a ford [C13 from ON: snowdrift]
driftage ('drɪftɪdʒ) *n* **1** the act of drifting **2** matter carried along by drifting **3** the amount by which an aircraft or vessel has drifted
drifter ('drɪftə) *n* **1** a person or thing that drifts **2** a person who moves aimlessly from place to place **3** a boat used for drift-net fishing
drift ice *n* masses of ice floating in the sea
drift net *n* a large fishing net that is allowed to drift with the tide or current
driftwood ('drɪftˌwʊd) *n* wood floating on or washed ashore by the sea or other body of water
drill[1] (drɪl) *n* **1** a machine or tool for boring holes **2** *mil* **2a** training in procedures or movements, as for parades or the use of weapons **2b** (*as modifier*): *drill hall* **3** strict and often repetitious training or exercises used in teaching **4** *inf* correct procedure **5** a marine mollusc that preys on oysters ▷ *vb* **6** to pierce, bore, or cut (a hole) in (material) with or as if with a drill **7** to instruct or be instructed in military procedures or movements **8** (*tr*) to teach by rigorous exercises or training **9** (*tr*) *inf* to riddle with bullets [C17 from MDu. *drillen*] > **'driller** *n*
drill[2] (drɪl) *n* **1** a machine for planting seeds in rows **2** a furrow in which seeds are sown **3** a row of seeds planted by means of a drill ▷ *vb* **4** to plant (seeds) by means of a drill [C18 from ?; cf. G *Rille* furrow] > **'driller** *n*
drill[3] (drɪl) *n* a hard-wearing twill-weave cotton cloth, used for uniforms, etc [C18 var. of G *Drillich*, from L *trilīx*, from TRI- + *līcium* thread]
drill[4] (drɪl) *n* an Old World monkey of W Africa, related to the mandrill [C17 from a West African word]
drill down *vb adv* to look at or examine something in depth: *to drill down through financial data*
drilling fluid *n* a fluid, usually consisting of a suspension of clay in water, pumped down when an oil well is being drilled. Also called: **mud**
drilling platform *n* a structure, either fixed to the sea bed or mobile, which supports the drilling rig, stores, etc, required for drilling an offshore oil well
drilling rig *n* **1** the complete machinery, equipment, and structures needed to drill an oil well **2** a mobile drilling platform used for exploratory offshore drilling
drillmaster ('drɪlˌmɑːstə) *n* **1** Also called: **drill sergeant** a military drill instructor **2** a person who instructs in a strict manner
drill press *n* a machine tool for boring holes
drily *or* **dryly** ('draɪlɪ) *adv* in a dry manner
drink (drɪŋk) *vb* **drinks, drinking, drank, drunk 1** to swallow (a liquid) **2** (*tr*) to soak up (liquid); absorb **3** (*tr; usually foll by in*) to pay close attention to **4** (*tr*) to bring (oneself) into a certain condition by consuming alcohol **5** (*tr; often foll by away*) to dispose of or ruin by excessive expenditure on alcohol **6** (*intr*) to consume alcohol, esp to excess **7** (when *intr*, foll by *to*) to drink (a toast) **8** **drink**

Dd

the health of to salute or celebrate with a toast 9 **drink with the flies** *Austral inf* to drink alone ▷ *n* 10 liquid suitable for drinking 11 alcohol or its habitual or excessive consumption 12 a portion of liquid for drinking; draught 13 **the drink** *inf* the sea [OE *drincan*] > **'drinkable** *adj* > **'drinker** *n*

drink-driving *n* (*modifier*) of or relating to driving a car after drinking alcohol: *drink-driving offences*

drinking fountain *n* a device for providing a flow or jet of drinking water, esp in public places

drinking-up time *n* (in Britain) a short time for finishing drinks after last orders in a public house

drinking water *n* water reserved or suitable for drinking

Drinkwater ('drɪŋk,wɔːtə) *n* **John** 1882–1937, English dramatist, poet, and critic; author of chronicle plays such as *Abraham Lincoln* (1918) and *Mary Stuart* (1921)

drip (drɪp) *vb* **drips, dripping, dripped** 1 to fall or let fall in drops ▷ *n* 2 the formation and falling of drops of liquid 3 the sound made by falling drops 4 a projection at the edge of a sill or cornice designed to throw water clear of the wall 5 *inf* an inane, insipid person 6 *med* 6a the apparatus used for the intravenous drop-by-drop administration of a solution 6b the solution so administered [OE *dryppan*, from *dropa* DROP]

drip-dry *adj* 1 designating clothing or a fabric that will dry relatively free of creases if hung up when wet ▷ *vb* **drip-dries, drip-drying, drip-dried** 2 to dry or become dry thus

drip-feed *vb* **drip-feeds, drip-feeding, drip-fed** (*tr*) 1 to feed (someone) a liquid drop by drop, esp intravenously 2 *inf* to fund (a new company) in stages rather than by injecting a large sum at its inception 3 to supply information constantly but in small amounts ▷ *n* **drip feed** 4 another term for **drip** (sense 6) 5 a constant supply of small amounts of information

dripping ('drɪpɪŋ) *n* 1 the fat exuded by roasting meat 2 (*often pl*) liquid that falls in drops ▷ *adv* 3 (intensifier): *dripping wet*

drippy ('drɪpɪ) *adj* **drippier, drippiest** 1 *inf* mawkish, insipid, or inane 2 tending to drip

drive (draɪv) *vb* **drives, driving, drove, driven** 1 to push, propel, or be pushed or propelled 2 to guide the movement of (a vehicle, animal, etc) 3 (*tr*) to compel or urge to work or act, esp excessively 4 (*tr*) to goad into a specified attitude or state: *work drove him mad* 5 (*tr*) to cause (an object) to make (a hole, crack, etc) 6 to move rapidly by striking or throwing with force 7 *sport* to hit (a ball) very hard and straight 8 *golf* to strike (the ball) with a driver 9 (*tr*) to chase (game) from cover 10 to transport or be transported in a vehicle 11 (*intr*) to rush or dash violently, esp against an obstacle 12 (*tr*) to transact with vigour(esp in **drive a hard bargain**) 13 (*tr*) to force (a component) into or out of its location by means of blows or a press 14 (*tr*) *mining* to excavate horizontally 15 **drive home** 15a to cause to penetrate to the fullest extent 15b to make clear by special emphasis ▷ *n* 16 the act of driving 17 a journey in a driven vehicle 18 a road for vehicles, esp a private road leading to a house 19 vigorous pressure, as in business 20 a united effort, esp towards a common goal 21 *Brit* a large gathering of persons to play cards, etc 22 energy, ambition, or initiative 23 *psychol* a motive or interest, such as sex or ambition 24 a sustained and powerful military offensive 25a the means by which force, motion, etc, is transmitted in a mechanism 25b (*as modifier*): *a drive shaft* 26 *sport* a hard straight shot or stroke 27 a search for and chasing of game towards waiting guns 28 *electronics* the signal applied to the input of an amplifier [OE *drīfan*] > **'drivable** *or* **'driveable** *adj*

drive at *vb* (*intr, prep*) *inf* to intend or mean: *what are you driving at?*

drive-by shooting *n* an incident in which a person, building, or vehicle is shot at by someone in a moving vehicle. Sometimes shortened to **drive-by**

drive-in *adj* 1 denoting a public facility or service designed to be used by patrons seated in their cars: *a drive-in bank* ▷ *n* 2 *chiefly US & Canad* a cinema designed to be used in such a manner

drivel ('drɪvᵊl) *vb* **drivels, drivelling, drivelled** *or US* **drivels, driveling, driveled** 1 to allow (saliva) to flow from the mouth; dribble 2 (*intr*) to speak foolishly ▷ *n* 3 foolish or senseless talk 4 saliva flowing from the mouth; slaver [OE *dreflian* to slaver] > **'driveller** *or US* **'driveler** *n*

driven ('drɪvᵊn) *vb* the past participle of **drive**

driver ('draɪvə) *n* 1 a person who drives a vehicle 2 **in the driver's seat** in a position of control 3 a person who drives animals 4 a mechanical component that exerts a force on another to produce motion 5 *golf* a club, a No. 1 wood, used for tee shots 6 *electronics* a circuit whose output provides the input of another circuit 7 *computing* a computer program that controls a device > **'driverless** *adj*

drive-thru *n* a a takeaway restaurant, bank, etc, designed so that customers can use it without leaving their cars b (*as modifier*): *a drive-thru restaurant*

drive-time *n* a the time of day when many people are driving to or from work, considered as a broadcasting slot b (*as modifier*): *the daily drive-time show*

driveway ('draɪv,weɪ) *n* a path for vehicles, often connecting a house with a public road

driving chain *n engineering* a roller chain that transmits power from one toothed wheel to another. Also called: **drive chain**

driving licence *n* an official document authorizing a person to drive a motor vehicle

drizzle ('drɪzᵊl) *n* 1 very light rain ▷ *vb* **drizzles, drizzling, drizzled** 2 (*intr*) to rain lightly [OE *drēosan* to fall] > **'drizzly** *adj*

Drogheda ('drɔɪɪdə) *n* a port in NE Republic of Ireland, in Co. Louth near the mouth of the River Boyne: captured by Cromwell in 1649 and its inhabitants massacred. Pop: 23 800 (1991)

drogue (drəʊg) *n* 1 any funnel-like device used as a sea anchor 2a a small parachute released behind an aircraft to reduce its landing speed 2b a small parachute released during the landing of a spacecraft 3 a device towed behind an aircraft as a target for firing practice 4 a device on the end of the hose of a tanker aircraft, to assist location of the probe of the receiving aircraft 5 a windsock [c18 prob. based ult. on OE *dragan* to DRAW]

droll (drəʊl) *adj* amusing in a quaint or odd manner; comical [c17 from F *drôle* scamp, from MDu.: imp] > **'drollness** *n* > **'drolly** *adv*

drollery ('drəʊlərɪ) *n, pl* **drolleries** 1 humour; comedy 2 *rare* a droll act, story, or remark

-drome *n combining form* 1 a course or race-course: *hippodrome* 2 a large place for a special purpose: *aerodrome* [via L from Gk *dromos* race, course]

Drôme (*French* drom) *n* a department of SE France, in Rhône-Alpes region. Capital: Valence. Pop: 437 778 (1999). Area: 6561 sq km (2559 sq miles)

dromedary ('drʌmədərɪ) *n, pl* **dromedaries** a type of Arabian camel bred for racing and riding, having a single hump [c14 from LL *dromedārius (camēlus)*, from Gk *dromas* running]

-dromous *adj combining form.* moving or running: *anadromous; catadromous* [via NL from Gk *-dromos*, from *dromos* a running]

drone[1] (drəʊn) *n* 1 a male honeybee whose sole function is to mate with the queen 2 a person who lives off the work of others 3 a drone aircraft [OE *drān*; see DRONE[2]]

drone[2] (drəʊn) *vb* **drones, droning, droned** 1 (*intr*) to make a monotonous low dull sound 2 (when *intr*, often foll by *on*) to utter (words) in a monotonous tone, esp to talk without stopping ▷ *n* **3** a monotonous low dull sound **4** *music* a sustained bass note or chord **5** one of the single-reed pipes in a set of bagpipes **6** a person who speaks in a low monotonous tone [c16 rel. to DRONE[1] & MDu. *drōnen*, G *dröhnen*] > **'droning** *adj*

drone aircraft *n* a pilotless radio-controlled aircraft used for reconnaissance or bombing

drongo ('drɒŋgəʊ) *n, pl* **drongos 1** any of various songbirds of the Old World tropics, having a glossy black plumage **2** *Austral & NZ sl* a slow-witted person [c19 from Malagasy]

drool (dru:l) *vb* **1** (*intr*; often foll by *over*) to show excessive enthusiasm (for) or pleasure (in); gloat (over) ▷ *vb, n* **2** another word for **drivel** (senses 1, 2, 4) [c19 prob. alteration of DRIVEL]

droop (dru:p) *vb* **1** to sag or allow to sag, as from weakness **2** (*intr*) to be overcome by weariness **3** (*intr*) to lose courage ▷ *n* **4** the act or state of drooping [c13 from ON *drūpa*] > **'drooping** *adj* > **'droopy** *adj*

drop (drɒp) *n* **1** a small quantity of liquid that forms or falls in a spherical mass **2** a very small quantity of liquid **3** a very small quantity of anything **4** something resembling a drop in shape or size **5** the act or an instance of falling; descent **6** a decrease in amount or value **7** the vertical distance that anything may fall **8** a steep incline or slope **9** short for **fruit drop 10** the act of unloading troops, etc, by parachute **11** (in cable television) a short spur from a trunk cable that feeds signals to an individual house **12** *theatre* See **drop curtain 13** another word for **trap door** or **gallows 14** *chiefly US & Canad* a slot through which an object can be dropped into a receptacle **15** *Austral cricket sl* a fall of the wicket **16** See **drop shot 17 at the drop of a hat** without hesitation or delay **18 have the drop on (someone)** *US & NZ* to have the advantage over (someone) ▷ *vb* **drops, dropping, dropped 19** (of liquids) to fall or allow to fall in globules **20** to fall or allow to fall vertically **21** (*tr*) to allow to fall by letting go of **22** to sink or fall or cause to sink to the ground, as from a blow, weariness, etc **23** (*intr*; foll by *back, behind*, etc) to move in a specified manner, direction, etc **24** (*intr*; foll by *in, by*, etc) *inf* to pay a casual visit (to) **25** to decrease in amount or value **26** to sink or cause to sink to a lower position **27** to make or become less in strength, volume, etc **28** (*intr*) to decline in health or condition **29** (*intr*; sometimes foll by *into*) to pass easily into a condition: *to drop into a habit* **30** (*intr*) to move gently as with a current of air **31** (*tr*) to mention casually: *to drop a hint* **32** (*tr*) to leave out (a word or letter) **33** (*tr*) to set down (passengers or goods) **34** (*tr*) to send or post: *drop me a line* **35** (*tr*) to discontinue: *let's drop the matter* **36** (*tr*) to cease to associate with **37** (*tr*) *sl, chiefly US* to cease to employ **38** (*tr*; sometimes foll by *in, off*, etc) *inf* to leave or deposit **39** (of animals) to give birth to (offspring) **40** *sl, chiefly US & Canad* to lose (money) **41** (*tr*) to lengthen (a hem, etc) **42** (*tr*) to unload (troops, etc) by parachute **43** (*tr*) *naut* to sail out of sight of **44** (*tr*) *sport* to omit (a player) from a team **45** (*tr*) to lose (a game, etc) **46** (*tr*) *golf, basketball, etc* to hit or throw (a ball) into a goal **47** (*tr*) to hit (a ball) with a drop shot ▷ *n, vb* **48** *rugby* short for **drop kick** or **drop-kick** ▷ See also **drop off, dropout, drops** [OE *dropian*]

drop curtain *n theatre* a curtain that can be raised and lowered onto the stage

drop-dead *adv sl* outstandingly or exceptionally: *drop-dead gorgeous*

drop-down menu *n* a menu that appears on a computer screen when its title is selected and remains on display until dismissed

drop forge *n* a device for forging metal between two dies, one of which is fixed, the other acting by gravity or by pressure > **'drop-,forge** *vb* (*tr*)

drop goal *n rugby* a goal scored with a drop kick during the run of play

drop hammer *n* another name for **drop forge**

drop-in centre *n* (in Britain) a daycentre run by the social services or a charity that clients may attend on an informal basis

drop kick *n* **1** a kick in which the ball is dropped and kicked as it bounces from the ground **2** a wrestling attack in which a wrestler leaps in the air and kicks his opponent ▷ *vb* **drop-kick 3** to kick (a ball, a wrestling opponent, etc) by the use of a drop kick

drop leaf *n* **a** a hinged flap on a table that can be raised to extend the surface **b** (*as modifier*): *a drop-leaf table*

droplet ('drɒplɪt) *n* a tiny drop

drop lock *n finance* a variable-rate bank loan that is automatically replaced by a fixed-rate long-term bond if the long-term interest rates fall to a specified level

drop off *vb* (*adv*) **1** (*intr*) to grow smaller or less **2** (*tr*) to set down **3** (*intr*) *inf* to fall asleep ▷ *n* **drop-off 4** a steep descent **5** a sharp decrease

dropout ('drɒp,aʊt) *n* **1** a student who fails to complete a course **2** a person who rejects conventional society **3 drop-out** *rugby* a drop kick taken to restart play ▷ *vb* **drop out** (*intr, adv*; often foll by *of*) **4** to abandon or withdraw from (a school, job, etc)

dropper ('drɒpə) *n* **1** a small tube having a rubber bulb at one end for dispensing drops of liquid **2** a person or thing that drops

droppings ('drɒpɪŋz) *pl n* the dung of certain animals, such as rabbits, sheep, and birds

drops (drɒps) *pl n* any liquid medication applied by means of a dropper

drop scone *n* a flat spongy cake made by dropping a spoonful of batter on a hot griddle

drop shot *n* **a** *tennis* a softly played return that drops abruptly after clearing the net **b** *squash* a shot that stops abruptly after hitting the front wall of the court

dropsy ('drɒpsɪ) *n* **1** *pathol* a condition characterized by an accumulation of watery fluid in the tissues or in a body cavity **2** *sl* a tip or bribe [c13 from *ydropesie*, from L *hydrōpisis*, from Gk *hudrōps*, from *hudōr* water] > **dropsical** ('drɒpsɪkᵊl) *adj*

droshky ('drɒʃkɪ) *or* **drosky** ('drɒskɪ) *n, pl* **droshkies** *or* **droskies** an open four-wheeled carriage, formerly used in Russia [c19 from Russian, dim. of *drogi* wagon]

drosophila (drɒ'sɒfɪlə) *n, pl* **drosophilas** *or* **drosophilae** (-,li:) any of a genus of small flies that are widely used in laboratory genetics studies. Also called: **fruit fly** [c19 NL, from Gk *drosos* dew + *-phila* -PHILE]

dross (drɒs) *n* **1** the scum formed on the surfaces of molten metals **2** worthless matter; waste [OE *drōs* dregs] > **'drossy** *adj* > **'drossiness** *n*

drought (draʊt) *n* **1** a prolonged period of scanty rainfall **2** a prolonged shortage [OE *drūgoth*] > **'droughty** *adj*

drove[1] (drəʊv) *vb* the past tense of **drive**

drove[2] (drəʊv) *n* **1** a herd of livestock being driven together **2** (*often pl*) a moving crowd of people ▷ *vb* **droves, droving, droved** (*tr*) **3** to drive (livestock), usually for a considerable distance [OE *drāf* herd]

drover ('drəʊvə) *n* a person who drives sheep or cattle, esp to and from market

drown (draʊn) *vb* **1** to die or kill by immersion in liquid **2** (*tr*) to get rid of: *he drowned his sorrows in drink* **3** (*tr*) to drench thoroughly **4** (*tr*; sometimes foll by *out*) to render (a sound) inaudible by making a loud noise [c13 prob. from OE *druncnian*]

drowse (draʊz) *vb* **drowses, drowsing, drowsed 1** to be or cause to be sleepy, dull, or sluggish ▷ *n* **2** the state of being drowsy [c16 prob. from OE *drūsian* to sink]

drowsy ('draʊzɪ) *adj* **drowsier, drowsiest 1** heavy with sleepiness; sleepy **2** inducing sleep; soporific **3** sluggish or lethargic; dull > **'drowsily** *adv* > **'drowsiness** *n*

drub (drʌb) *vb* **drubs, drubbing, drubbed** (*tr*) **1** to beat as with a stick **2** to defeat utterly, as in a contest **3** to drum

Dd

or stamp (the feet) 4 to instil with force or repetition ▷ *n* 5 a blow, as from a stick [c17 prob. from Ar. *dáraba* to beat]

drubbing ('drʌbɪŋ) *n* 1 a beating 2 a total defeat

drudge (drʌdʒ) *n* 1 a person who works hard at wearisome menial tasks ▷ *vb* **drudges, drudging, drudged** 2 (*intr*) to toil at such tasks [c16 ?from *druggen* to toil] > **'drudger** *n* > **'drudgingly** *adv*

drudgery ('drʌdʒərɪ) *n, pl* **drudgeries** hard, menial, and monotonous work

drug (drʌg) *n* 1 any substance used in the treatment, prevention, or diagnosis of disease. Related adj: **pharmaceutical** 2 a chemical substance, esp a narcotic, taken for the effects it produces 3 **drug on the market** a commodity available in excess of demand ▷ *vb* **drugs, drugging, drugged** (*tr*) 4 to mix a drug with (food, etc) 5 to administer a drug to 6 to stupefy or poison with or as if with a drug [c14 from OF *drogue*, prob. of Gmc origin]

drug addict *n* any person who is abnormally dependent on narcotic drugs

drugget ('drʌgɪt) *n* a coarse fabric used as a protective floor covering, etc [c16 from F *droguet* useless fabric, from *drogue* trash]

druggie ('drʌgɪ) *n inf* a drug addict

druggist ('drʌgɪst) *n* a US and Canad term for **pharmacist**

druglord ('drʌg,lɔ:d) *n* a criminal who controls the distribution and sale of large quantities of illegal drugs

drugstore ('drʌg,stɔ:) *n US & Canad* a shop where medical prescriptions are made up and a wide variety of goods and sometimes light meals are sold

druid ('dru:ɪd) *n* (*sometimes cap*) 1 a member of an ancient order of priests in Gaul, Britain, and Ireland in the pre-Christian era 2 a member of any of several modern movements attempting to revive druidism [c16 from L *druides*, of Gaulish origin] > **'druidess** *fem n* > **dru'idic** *or* **dru'idical** *adj* > **'druid,ism** *n*

▷ www.crystalinks.com/druids.html
▷ http://celt.net/Celtic/History/druidsintro.html
▷ http://www.adf.org/core/

drum (drʌm) *n* 1 a percussion instrument sounded by striking a membrane stretched across the opening of a hollow cylinder or hemisphere 2 the sound produced by a drum or any similar sound 3 an object that resembles a drum in shape, such as a large spool or a cylindrical container 4 *archit* a cylindrical block of stone used to construct the shaft of a column 5 short for **eardrum** 6 any of various North American fishes that utter a drumming sound 7 a type of hollow rotor for steam turbines or axial compressors 8 *arch* a drummer 9 **beat the drum for** *inf* to attempt to arouse interest in 10 **the drum** *Austral inf* the necessary information(esp in **give (someone) the drum**) ▷ *vb* **drums, drumming, drummed** 11 to play (music) on or as if on a drum 12 to tap rhythmically or regularly 13 (*tr*; sometimes foll by *up*) to summon or call by drumming 14 (*tr*) to instil by constant repetition ▷ See also **drum up** [c16 prob. from MDu. *tromme*, imit.]

drumbeat ('drʌm,bi:t) *n* the sound made by beating a drum

drum brake *n* a type of brake used on the wheels of vehicles, consisting of two shoes that rub against the brake drum when the brake is applied

drumhead ('drʌm,hɛd) *n* 1 the part of a drum that is actually struck 2 the head of a capstan 3 another name for **eardrum**

drumlin ('drʌmlɪn) *n* a streamlined mound of glacial drift [c19 from Irish Gaelic *druim* ridge + *-lin* -LING[1]]

drum machine *n* a synthesizer specially programmed to reproduce the sound of drums and other percussion instruments in variable rhythms and combinations selected by the musician; the resulting beat is produced continually until stopped or changed

drum major *n* the noncommissioned officer, usually of warrant officer's rank, who commands the corps of drums of a military band and who is in command of both the drums and the band when paraded together

drum majorette *n* a girl who marches at the head of a procession, twirling a baton

drummer ('drʌmə) *n* 1 a drum player 2 *chiefly US* a travelling salesman

drum'n'bass *or* **drum and bass** *n* **a** a type of electronic dance music using mainly bass guitar and drum sounds **b** (*as modifier*): *a drum'n'bass backing*

drumstick ('drʌm,stɪk) *n* 1 a stick used for playing a drum 2 the lower joint of the leg of a cooked fowl

drum up *vb* (*tr, adv*) to obtain (support, business, etc) by solicitation or canvassing

drunk (drʌŋk) *adj* 1 intoxicated with alcohol to the extent of losing control over normal functions 2 overwhelmed by strong influence or emotion ▷ *n* 3 a person who is drunk 4 *inf* a drinking bout [OE *druncen*, p.p. of *drincan* to drink]

drunkard ('drʌŋkəd) *n* a person who is frequently or habitually drunk

drunkathon ('drʌŋkə,θɒn) *n inf* a session in which excessive quantities of alcohol are consumed

drunken ('drʌŋkən) *adj* 1 intoxicated 2 habitually drunk 3 (*prenominal*) caused by or relating to alcoholic intoxication: *a drunken brawl* > **'drunkenly** *adv* > **'drunkenness** *n*

drupe (dru:p) *n* any fruit that has a fleshy or fibrous part around a stone that encloses a seed, as in the peach, plum, and cherry [c18 from L *druppa* wrinkled overripe olive, from Gk: olive] > **drupaceous** (dru:'peɪʃəs) *adj*

drupelet ('dru:plɪt) *or* **drupel** ('dru:pəl) *n* a small drupe, usually one of a number forming a compound fruit

Druse *or* **Druze** (dru:z) *n, pl* **Druse** *or* **Druze** **a** a member of a religious sect, mainly living in Syria, Lebanon, and Israel, having certain characteristics in common with Muslims **b** (*as modifier*): *Druse customs* [c18 from Arabic *Durūz*, after Ismail al-*Darazi*, 11th-century founder of the sect]

dry (draɪ) *adj* **drier, driest** *or* **dryer, dryest** 1 lacking moisture; not damp or wet 2 having little or no rainfall 3 not in or under water 4 having the water drained away or evaporated: *a dry river* 5 not providing milk: *a dry cow* 6 (of the eyes) free from tears 7a *inf* thirsty 7b causing thirst 8 eaten without butter, jam, etc: *dry toast* 9 *electronics* (of a soldered joint) imperfect because the solder has not adhered to the metal 10 (of wine, etc) not sweet 11 not producing a mucous or watery discharge: *a dry cough* 12 consisting of solid as opposed to liquid substances 13 without adornment; plain: *dry facts* 14 lacking interest: *a dry book* 15 lacking warmth: *a dry greeting* 16 (of humour) shrewd and keen in an impersonal, sarcastic, or laconic way 17 *inf* opposed to or prohibiting the sale of alcoholic liquor: *a dry country* ▷ *vb* **dries, drying, dried** 18 (when *intr*, often foll by *off*) to make or become dry 19 (*tr*) to preserve (fruit, etc) by removing the moisture ▷ *n, pl* **drys** *or* **dries** 20 *Brit inf* a Conservative politician who is a hardliner 21 **the dry** (*sometimes cap*) *Austral inf* the dry season ▷ See also **dry out, dry up** [OE *drȳge*] > **'dryness** *n*

dryad ('draɪəd, -æd) *n, pl* **dryads** *or* **dryades** (-ə,di:z) *Greek myth* a nymph or divinity of the woods [c14 from L *Dryas*, from Gk *Druas*, from *drus* tree]

dry battery *n* an electric battery consisting of two or more dry cells

dry cell *n* a primary cell in which the electrolyte is in the form of a paste or is treated in some way to prevent it from spilling

dry-clean *vb* (*tr*) to clean (fabrics, etc) with a solvent other than water > **,dry-'cleaner** *n* > **,dry-'cleaning** *n*

Dryden ('draɪdən) *n* **John** 1631–1700, English poet, dramatist, and critic of the Augustan period, commonly regarded as the chief exponent of heroic tragedy. His major works include the tragedy *All for Love* (1677), the verse satire *Absalom and Achitophel* (1681), and the *Essay of Dramatick Poesie* (1668)

dry dock *n* a dock that can be pumped dry for work on a ship's bottom

dry drunk *n* an alcoholic who is not currently drinking alcohol but is still following an irregular undisciplined lifestyle like that of a drunkard

dryer[1] ('draɪə) *n* **1** a person or thing that dries **2** an apparatus for removing moisture by forced draught, heating, or centrifuging **3** any of certain chemicals added to oils to accelerate their drying when used in paints, etc

dryer[2] ('draɪə) *adj* a variant spelling of **drier**[1]

dry fly *n angling* **a** an artificial fly designed to be floated on the surface of the water **b** (*as modifier*): *dry-fly fishing*

dry hole *n* (in the oil industry) a well which proves unsuccessful

dry ice *n* solid carbon dioxide used as a refrigerant, and to create billows of smoke in stage shows. Also called: **carbon dioxide snow**

drying ('draɪɪŋ) *n* the processing of timber until it has a moisture content suitable for the purposes for which it is to be used

dryly ('draɪlɪ) *adv* a variant spelling of **drily**

dry measure *n* a unit or system of units for measuring dry goods, such as fruit, grains, etc

dry out *vb* (*adv*) **1** to make or become dry **2** to undergo or cause to undergo treatment for alcoholism or drug addiction

dry point *n* **1** a technique of intaglio engraving with a hard steel needle, without acid, on a copper plate **2** the sharp steel needle used **3** the engraving or print produced

dry riser *n* a vertical pipe, not containing water, having connections on different floors of a building for a fireman's hose to be attached. A fire tender can be connected at the lowest level to make water rise under pressure within the pipe. Abbrev: **DR**

dry rot *n* **1** crumbling and drying of timber, bulbs, potatoes, or fruit, caused by certain fungi **2** any fungus causing this decay **3** moral degeneration or corruption

dry run *n* **1** *mil* practice in firing without live ammunition **2** *inf* a rehearsal

drysalter ('draɪˌsɔːltə) *n obs* a dealer in dyestuffs and gums, and in dried, tinned, or salted foods and edible oils

Drysdale[1] ('draɪzdeɪl) *n* Sir **George Russell** 1912–81, Australian painter, esp of landscapes

dry slope *n* an artificial ski slope used for tuition and practice. Also called: **dry-ski slope**

dry stock *n NZ* cattle that are raised for meat

dry-stone *adj* (of a wall) made without mortar

dry up *vb* (*adv*) **1** (*intr*) to become barren or unproductive; fail **2** to dry (dishes, cutlery, etc) with a tea towel after they have been washed **3** (*intr*) *inf* to stop talking or speaking

DS *or* **ds** *music abbrev for* dal segno

Ds *the chemical symbol for* darmstadtium

DSc *abbrev for* Doctor of Science

DSC *mil abbrev for* Distinguished Service Cross

DSM *mil abbrev for* Distinguished Service Medal

DSO *Brit mil abbrev for* Distinguished Service Order

DSS *Brit abbrev for*: **1** Department of Social Security **2** Director of Social Services

DST *abbrev for* Daylight Saving Time

DTI (in Britain) *abbrev for* Department of Trade and Industry

DTP *abbrev for* desktop publishing

DT's *inf abbrev for* delirium tremens

DTT *abbrev for* digital terrestrial television

DU *abbrev for* depleted uranium

Du. *abbrev for* Dutch

dual ('djuːəl) *adj* **1** relating to or denoting two **2** twofold; double **3** (in the grammar of some languages) denoting a form of a word indicating that exactly two referents are being referred to **4** *maths, logic* (of a pair of operators) convertible into one another by the distribution of negation over either ▷ *n* **5** *grammar* **5a** the dual number **5b** a dual form of a word [c17 from L *duālis* concerning two, from *duo* two] > '**dually** *adv* > **duality** (djuːˈælɪtɪ) *n*

dual carriageway *n Brit* a road on which traffic travelling in opposite directions is separated by a central strip of turf, etc. US and Canad name: **divided highway**

dualism ('djuːəˌlɪzəm) *n* **1** the state of being twofold or double **2** *philosophy* the doctrine that reality consists of two basic types of substance, usually taken to be mind and matter or mental and physical entities ▷ Cf **monism** (sense 1) **3a** the theory that the universe has been ruled from its origins by two conflicting powers, one good and one evil **3b** the theory that there are two personalities, one human and one divine, in Christ > '**dualist** *n* > **dual'istic** *adj*

dub[1] (dʌb) *vb* **dubs, dubbing, dubbed 1** (*tr*) to invest (a person) with knighthood by tapping on the shoulder with a sword **2** (*tr*) to invest with a title, name, or nickname **3** (*tr*) to dress (leather) by rubbing **4** *angling* to dress (a fly) [OE *dubbian*]

dub[2] (dʌb) *vb* **dubs, dubbing, dubbed 1** to alter the soundtrack of (a film, etc) **2** (*tr*) to provide (a film) with a new soundtrack, esp in a different language **3** (*tr*) to provide (a film or tape) with a soundtrack ▷ *n* **4** the new sounds added **5** *music* a style of record production associated with reggae, involving the use of echo, delay, etc [c20 shortened from DOUBLE]

dub[3] (dʌb) *vb* **dubs, dubbing, dubbed** *Austral & NZ inf* short for **double-bank**

Dubai (duːˈbaɪ) *n* a sheikhdom in the NE United Arab Emirates, consisting principally of the port of Dubai, on the Persian Gulf: oilfields. Pop: 913 000 (2001 est)

du Barry (djuː ˈbærɪ; *French* dy bari) *n* **Comtesse** (kɔ̃tɛs), original name *Marie Jeanne Bécu*. ?1743–93, mistress of Louis XV, guillotined in the French Revolution

dubbin ('dʌbɪn) *n Brit* a greasy preparation applied to leather to soften it and make it waterproof [c18 from *dub* to dress leather]

dubbing[1] ('dʌbɪŋ) *n films* **1** the replacement of a soundtrack, esp by one in another language **2** the combination of several soundtracks **3** the addition of a soundtrack to a film, etc

dubbing[2] ('dʌbɪŋ) *n* **1** *angling* fibrous material used for the body of an artificial fly **2** a variant of **dubbin**

Dubček (*Czech* 'duptʃɛk) *n* **Alexander** ('aleksandᵊr) 1921–92, Czechoslovak statesman. His reforms as first secretary of the Czechoslovak Communist Party (1968–69) prompted the Russian occupation (1968) and his enforced resignation. Following the uprising of 1989 he was elected chairman of the new Czechoslovak Federal Assembly

du Bellay (*French* dy bɛlɛ) *n* See (Joachim du) **Bellay**

dubiety (djuːˈbaɪɪtɪ) *n, pl* **dubieties 1** the state of being doubtful **2** a doubtful matter [c18 from LL *dubietās*, from L *dubius* DUBIOUS]

dub in *or* **up** *vb* (*adv*) *sl* to contribute to the cost of something: *we'll all dub in a fiver for the trip*

dubious ('djuːbɪəs) *adj* **1** marked by or causing doubt **2** uncertain; doubtful **3** of doubtful quality; untrustworthy **4** not certain in outcome [c16 from L *dubius* wavering] > '**dubiously** *adv* > '**dubiousness** *n*

Dublin ('dʌblɪn) *n* **1** the capital of the Republic of Ireland, on **Dublin Bay**: under English rule from 1171 until 1922; commercial and cultural centre; contains one of the world's largest breweries and exports whiskey, stout, and agricultural produce. Pop: 480 996 (1996) Gaelic name: **Baile Átha Cliath 2** a county in E Republic of Ireland, in Leinster on the Irish Sea: mountainous in

the south but low-lying in the north and centre. County seat: Dublin. Pop: 1 058 264 (1996). Area: 922 sq km (356 sq miles)
▷ www.visitdublin.com

Dublin Bay prawn ('dʌblɪn) *n* a large prawn usually used in a dish of scampi

dubnium ('dʌbnɪəm) *n* a synthetic transactinide element produced in minute quantities by bombarding plutonium with high-energy neon ions. Symbol: Du; atomic no. 105 [c20 from *Dubna*, city in Russia where it was first reported]

Dubrovnik (dʊ'brɒvnɪk) *n* a port in W Croatia, on the Dalmatian coast: an important commercial centre in the Middle Ages; damaged in 1991 when it was shelled by Serbian artillery. Pop: 49 730 (1991). Former Italian name (until 1918): **Ragusa**

Dubuffet (*French* dybyfɛ) *n* **Jean** (ʒɑ̃) 1901–85, French painter, inspired by graffiti and the untrained art of children and psychotics

ducal ('dju:kᵊl) *adj* of a duke or duchy [c16 from F, from LL *ducālis* of a leader, from L *dux* leader]

ducat ('dʌkət) *n* **1** any of various former European gold or silver coins **2** (*often pl*) money [c14 from OF, from OIt. *ducato* coin stamped with the doge's image]

Duccio di Buoninsegna (*Italian* 'duttʃo di buonin'seɲɲa) *n* ?1255–?1318, Italian painter; founder of the Sienese school

duce ('du:tʃɪ) *n* leader [c20 from It., from L *dux*]

Duce (*Italian* 'du:tʃe) *n* **Il** (il) the title assumed by Mussolini as leader of Fascist Italy (1922–43)

Duchamp (*French* dyʃɑ̃) *n* **Marcel** (marsɛl) 1887–1968, US painter and sculptor, born in France; noted as a leading exponent of Dada. His best-known work is *Nude Descending a Staircase* (1912)

Duchenne dystrophy (dʊ'ʃɛn) *or* **Duchenne muscular dystrophy** *n* the most common form of muscular dystrophy, usually affecting only boys [after Guillaume *Duchenne* (1806–75), F neurologist]

duchess ('dʌtʃɪs) *n* **1** the wife or widow of a duke **2** a woman who holds the rank of duke in her own right ▷ *vb* **3** (*tr*) *Austral inf* to overwhelm with flattering attention [c14 from OF *duchesse*]

duchesse ('dʌtʃɪs) *n Austral & NZ* a dressing table or chest of drawers with a mirror

duchy ('dʌtʃɪ) *n, pl* **duchies** the territory of a duke or duchess; dukedom [c14 from OF *duche*, from *duc* DUKE]

duck¹ (dʌk) *n, pl* **ducks** *or* **duck** **1** any of a family of aquatic birds, esp those having short legs, webbed feet, and a broad blunt bill **2** the flesh of this bird, used as food **3** the female of such a bird, as opposed to the male (drake) **4** Also: **ducks** *Brit inf* dear or darling: used as a term of address. See also **ducky** **5** *cricket* a score of nothing by a batsman **6 like water off a duck's back** *inf* without effect [OE *dūce* duck, diver; rel. to DUCK²]

duck² (dʌk) *vb* **1** to move (the head or body) quickly downwards or away, esp to escape observation or evade a blow **2** to plunge suddenly under water **3** (when *intr*, often foll by *out*) *inf* to dodge or escape (a person, duty, etc) **4** (*intr*) *bridge* to play a low card rather than try to win a trick ▷ *n* **5** the act or an instance of ducking [c14 rel. to OHG *tūhhan* to dive, MDu. *dūken*] > '**ducker** *n*

duck³ (dʌk) *n* a heavy cotton fabric of plain weave, used for clothing, tents, etc [c17 from MDu. *doek*]

duck⁴ (dʌk) *n* an amphibious vehicle used in World War II [c20 from code name DUKW]

duck-billed platypus *n* an amphibious egg-laying mammal of E Australia having dense fur, a broad bill and tail, and webbed feet

duckboard ('dʌk,bɔ:d) *n* a board or boards laid so as to form a path over wet or muddy ground

ducking stool *n history* a chair used for punishing offenders by plunging them into water

duckling ('dʌklɪŋ) *n* a young duck

ducks and drakes *n* (*functioning as sing*) **1** a game in which a flat stone is bounced across the surface of water **2 make ducks and drakes of** *or* **play (at) ducks and drakes with** *inf* to use recklessly; squander

duck's arse *n* a hairstyle in which the hair is swept back to a point at the nape of the neck, resembling a duck's tail. Abbrev: **DA**

duck soup *n US sl* something that is easy to do

duckweed ('dʌk,wi:d) *n* any of various small stemless aquatic plants that occur floating on still water in temperate regions

ducky *or* **duckie** ('dʌkɪ) *Inf* ▷ *n, pl* **duckies** **1** *Brit* darling or dear: a term of endearment ▷ *adj* **duckier, duckiest** **2** delightful; fine

duct (dʌkt) *n* **1** a tube, pipe, or canal by means of which a substance, esp a fluid or gas, is conveyed **2** any bodily passage, esp one conveying secretions or excretions **3** a narrow tubular cavity in plants **4** a channel or pipe carrying electric wires **5** a passage through which air can flow, as in air conditioning [c17 from L *ductus* a leading (in Med. L: aqueduct), from *dūcere* to lead] > '**ductless** *adj*

ductile ('dʌktaɪl) *adj* **1** (of a metal) able to sustain large deformations without fracture and able to be hammered into sheets or drawn out into wires **2** able to be moulded **3** easily led or influenced [c14 from OF, from L *ductilis*, from *dūcere* to lead] > **ductility** (dʌk'tɪlɪtɪ) *n*

ductless gland *n anat* See **endocrine gland**

dud (dʌd) *inf* ▷ *n* **1** a person or thing that proves ineffectual **2** a shell, etc, that fails to explode **3** (*pl*) *Old-fashioned*. clothes or other belongings ▷ *adj* **4** failing in its purpose or function [c15 (in the sense: an article of clothing, a thing, used disparagingly): from ?]

dude (du:d, dju:d) *n inf* **1** *western US & Canad* a city dweller, esp one holidaying on a ranch **2** *US & Canad* a dandy **3** *US & Canad* any person: often used to any male in direct address [c19 from ?] > '**dudish** *adj* > '**dudishly** *adv*

dude ranch *n US & Canad* a ranch used as a holiday resort

dudgeon ('dʌdʒən) *n* anger or resentment (arch, except in **in high dudgeon**) [c16 from ?]

Dudley¹ ('dʌdlɪ) *n* **1** a town in W central England, in Dudley unitary authority, West Midlands: wrought-iron industry. Pop: 192 171 (1991) **2** a unitary authority in W central England, in West Midlands. Pop: 305 164 (2001). Area: 98 sq km (38 sq miles)

Dudley² ('dʌdlɪ) *n* **Robert** See (Earl of) **Leicester**

due (dju:) *adj* **1** (*postpositive*) immediately payable **2** (*postpositive*) owed as a debt **3** fitting; proper **4** (*prenominal*) adequate or sufficient **5** (*postpositive*) expected or appointed to be present or arrive **6 due to** attributable to or caused by ▷ *n* **7** something that is owed, required, or due **8 give (a person) his due** to give or allow what is deserved or right ▷ *adv* **9** directly or exactly [c13 from OF *deu*, from *devoir* to owe, from L *debēre*]

> **USAGE** In usage debates over the years, there can have been few more contentious subjects than the use of *due to* as a compound preposition. It used to be claimed that a sentence such as *the late arrival of the 10.15 from Guildford is due to snow on the lines* was correct, while *the trains are running late due to snow on the lines* was incorrect. The reasoning was that in the first case *due* is being used as an adjective synonymous with 'attributable', followed by *to* and a complement, whereas in the second case there is no explicit noun which *due* as an adjective can be said to modify. Nowadays, while the construction is quite common, it may be advisable in certain types of writing to replace it with an uncontentious alternative, such as *on account of*, *because of*, or *owing to*

duel ('dju:əl) *n* **1** a formal prearranged combat with deadly weapons between two people in the presence of seconds, usually to settle a quarrel **2** a contest or conflict between two persons or parties ▷ *vb* **duels, duelling, duelled** *or US* **duels, dueling, dueled** (*intr*) **3** to fight in a duel **4** to contest closely [c15 from Med. L *duellum*, from L, poetical var. of *bellum* war; associated with L *duo* two] > '**dueller**, '**duellist** *or US* '**dueler**, '**duelist** *n*
duenna (dju:'ɛnə) *n* (in Spain and Portugal, etc) an elderly woman retained by a family to act as governess and chaperon to girls [c17 from Sp. *dueña*, from L *domina* lady]
due process of law *n* the administration of justice in accordance with established rules and principles
dues (dju:z) *pl n* (*sometimes sing*) charges, as for membership of a club or organization; fees
duet (dju:'ɛt) *n* **1** a musical composition for two performers or voices **2** a pair of closely connected individuals; duo [c18 from It. *duetto* a little duet, from *duo* duet, from L: two] > **du'ettist** *n*
duff[1] (dʌf) *n* **1** a thick flour pudding boiled in a cloth bag **2 up the duff** *sl* pregnant [c19 N English var. of DOUGH]
duff[2] (dʌf) *vb* (*tr*) **1** *sl* to give a false appearance to (old or stolen goods); fake **2** (foll by *up*) *Brit sl* to beat (a person) severely **3** *Austral sl* to steal (cattle), altering the brand **4** *golf, inf* to bungle a shot by hitting the ground behind the ball ▷ *adj* **5** *Brit, Austral, & NZ inf* bad or useless [c19 prob. back formation from DUFFER]
duffel *or* **duffle** ('dʌfᵊl) *n* **1** a heavy woollen cloth **2** *chiefly US & Canad* equipment or supplies [c17 after *Duffel*, Belgian town]
duffel bag *n* a cylindrical drawstring canvas bag, originally used esp by sailors for carrying personal articles
duffel coat *n* a usually knee-length wool coat, usually with a hood and fastened with toggles
duffer ('dʌfə) *n* **1** *inf* a dull or incompetent person **2** *sl* something worthless **3** *Austral sl* **3a** an unproductive mine **3b** a person who steals cattle [c19 from ?]
Duffy ('dʌfɪ) *n* **Carol Ann** born 1955, British poet and writer; her collections include *Standing Female Nude* (1985) and *The World's Wife* (1999(
Dufy (*French* dyfi) *n* **Raoul** (raul) 1877–1953, French painter and designer whose style is characterized by swift calligraphic draughtsmanship and bright colouring
dug[1] (dʌg) *vb* the past tense and past participle of **dig**
dug[2] (dʌg) *n* a nipple, teat, udder, or breast [c16 of Scand. origin]
dugong ('du:gɒŋ) *n* a whalelike mammal occurring in shallow tropical waters from E Africa to Australia [c19 from Malay *duyong*]
dugout ('dʌg,aʊt) *n* **1** a canoe made by hollowing out a log **2** *mil* a covered excavation dug to provide shelter **3** (at a sports ground) the covered bench where managers, substitutes, etc, sit **4** (in the Canadian prairies) a reservoir dug on a farm in which water from rain and snow is collected for use in irrigation, watering livestock, etc
duiker *or* **duyker** ('daɪkə) *n, pl* **duikers, duiker** *or* **duykers, duyker 1** Also: **duikerbok** any of various small African antelopes **2** *S African* any of several cormorants, esp the long-tailed shag [c18 via Afrik., from Du. *duiker* diver, from *duiken* to dive]
Duisburg (*German* 'dy:sbʊrk) *n* an industrial city in NW Germany, in North Rhine-Westphalia at the confluence of the Rivers Rhine and Ruhr: one of the world's largest and busiest inland ports; university (1972). Pop: 521 300 (1999 est)
Duisenberg (*Dutch* 'dys:ʊn,berk) *n* **Willem Frederik**, known as *Wim*. born 1935, Dutch economist; president of the European Central Bank from 1998
du jour (du: 'ʒɔ:; *French* dy ʒur) *n inf* currently very fashionable or popular: *the young writer du jour* [c20 from French, literally: of the day (as used on restaurant menus of items that change daily)]
Dukas (*French* dyka) *n* **Paul** (pɔl) 1865–1935, French composer best known for the orchestral scherzo *The Sorcerer's Apprentice* (1897)
duke (dju:k) *n* **1** a nobleman of high rank: in the British Isles standing above the other grades of the nobility **2** the prince or ruler of a small principality or duchy [c12 from OF *duc*, from L *dux* leader] > '**dukedom** *n*
dukes (dju:ks) *pl n sl* the fists [c19 from *Duke of Yorks* rhyming sl for *forks* (fingers)]
dulcet ('dʌlsɪt) *adj* (of a sound) soothing or pleasant; sweet [c14 from L *dulcis* sweet]
dulcimer ('dʌlsɪmə) *n* **1** a tuned percussion instrument consisting of a set of strings stretched over a sounding board and struck with hammers **2** an instrument used in US folk music, with an elliptical body and usually three strings plucked with a goose quill [c15 from OF *doulcemer*, from OIt. *dolcimelo*, from *dolce* (from L *dulcis* sweet) + *-melo*, ?from Gk *melos* song]
dull (dʌl) *adj* **1** slow to think or understand; stupid **2** lacking in interest **3** lacking in perception; insensitive **4** lacking sharpness **5** not acute, intense, or piercing **6** (of weather) not bright or clear **7** not active, busy, or brisk **8** lacking in spirit; listless **9** (of colour) lacking brilliance; sombre **10** not loud or clear; muffled ▷ *vb* **11** to make or become dull [OE *dol*] > '**dullish** *adj* > '**dullness** *or* '**dulness** *n* > '**dully** *adv*
dullard ('dʌləd) *n* a dull or stupid person
dulse (dʌls) *n* any of several seaweeds that occur on rocks and have large red edible fronds [c17 from OIrish *duilesc* seaweed]
Dulwich ('dʌlɪtʃ) *n* a residential district in the Greater London borough of Southwark: site of an art gallery and the public school, Dulwich College
duly ('dju:lɪ) *adv* **1** in a proper manner **2** at the proper time [c14 see DUE, -LY[2]]
duma *Russian* ('du:mə) *n Russian history* **1** (*usually cap*) the elective legislative assembly established by Tsar Nicholas II in 1905: overthrown in 1917 **2** (before 1917) any official assembly or council **3** short for **State Duma**, the lower chamber of the Russian parliament [c20 from *duma* thought, of Gmc origin]
Dumas (*French* dyma) *n* **1 Alexandre** (alɛksɑ̃drə), known as *Dumas père*. 1802–70, French novelist and dramatist, noted for his historical romances *The Count of Monte Cristo* (1844) and *The Three Musketeers* (1844) **2** his son, **Alexandre,** known as *Dumas fils*. 1824–95, French novelist and dramatist, noted esp for the play he adapted from an earlier novel, *La Dame aux camélias* (1852) **3 Jean-Baptiste André** (ʒɑ̃batist ɑ̃dre) 1800–84, French chemist, noted for his research on vapour density and atomic weight
Du Maurier (dju: 'mɒrɪ,eɪ) *n* **1** Dame **Daphne** 1907–89, English novelist; author of *Rebecca* (1938) and *My Cousin Rachel* (1951) **2** her grandfather, **George Louis Palmella Busson** ('pælmɛlə 'bju:sᵊn) 1834–96, English novelist, caricaturist, and illustrator; author of *Peter Ibbetson* (1891) and *Trilby* (1894) **3** his son, Sir **Gerald** (**Hubert Edward**) 1873–1934, British actor-manager: father of Daphne Du Maurier
dumb (dʌm) *adj* **1** lacking the power to speak; mute **2** lacking the power of human speech: *dumb animals* **3** temporarily bereft of the power to speak: *struck dumb* **4** refraining from speech; uncommunicative **5** producing no sound: *a dumb piano* **6** made, done, or performed without speech **7** *inf* **7a** dim-witted **7b** foolish ▷ See also **dumb down** [OE] > '**dumbly** *adv* > '**dumbness** *n*
Dumbarton (dʌm'bɑ:tᵊn) *n* a town in W Scotland, in West Dunbartonshire near the confluence of the Rivers Leven and Clyde: centred around the **Rock of**

Dd

Dumbarton, an important stronghold since ancient times; engineering and distilling. Pop: 21 962 (1991)

Dumbarton Oaks ('dʌm,bɑːtᵊn) *n* an estate in the District of Columbia in the US: scene of conferences in 1944 concerned with creating the United Nations

dumbbell ('dʌm,bɛl) *n* **1** an exercising weight consisting of a short bar with a heavy ball or disc at either end, used for single-arm movements **2** a small wooden or rubber object of a similar shape used to train dogs in retrieval **3** *sl, chiefly US & Canad* a fool

dumb down *vb (tr)* to make less intellectually demanding or sophisticated: *the alleged dumbing down of BBC radio*

dumbfound *or* **dumfound** (dʌm'faʊnd) *vb (tr)* to strike dumb with astonishment; amaze [C17 from DUMB + (CON)FOUND]

dumbledore ('dʌmbᵊl,dɔː) *n English dialect* a bumblebee. Also (Southwest English): **drumbledrane** [Old English *dumble*, variant of *drumble* to move sluggishly + *dor* humming insect]

dumbo ('dʌmbəʊ) *n, pl* **dumbos** *sl* a slow-witted unintelligent person [C20 after the flying elephant in *Dumbo*, the Walt Disney cartoon released in 1941]

dumb show *n* **1** formerly, a part of a play acted in pantomime **2** meaningful gestures

dumbstruck ('dʌm,strʌk) *adj* temporarily deprived of speech through shock or surprise

dumbwaiter ('dʌm,weɪtə) *n* **1** *Brit* **1a** a stand placed near a dining table to hold food **1b** a revolving circular tray placed on a table to hold food. US and Canad name: **lazy Susan** **2** a lift for carrying food, rubbish, etc, between floors

dumdum ('dʌm,dʌm) *n* a soft-nosed bullet that expands on impact and inflicts extensive laceration [C19 after *Dum-Dum*, town near Calcutta where orig. made]

dumela (dʊ'mɛla) *sentence substitute S African* hello; good morning [Sotho]

Dumfries (dʌm'friːs) *n* a town in S Scotland on the River Nith, administrative centre of Dumfries and Galloway. Pop: 32 136 (1991)

Dumfries and Galloway *n* a council area in SW Scotland: created in 1975 from the counties of Dumfries, Kirkcudbright, and Wigtown; became a unitary authority in 1996; chiefly agricultural. Administrative centre: Dumfries. Pop: 147 765 (2001). Area: 6439 sq km (2486 sq miles)

Dumfriesshire (dʌm'friːsʃɪə, -ʃə) *n* (until 1975) a county in S Scotland, on the Solway Firth, now part of Dumfries and Galloway

dummelhead ('dʌməl,hɛd) *n Northern English dialect* a stupid or slow-witted person

dummy ('dʌmɪ) *n, pl* **dummies** **1** a figure representing the human form, used for displaying clothes, as a target, etc **2a** a copy of an object, often lacking some essential feature of the original **2b** *(as modifier)*: *a dummy drawer* **3** *sl* a stupid person **4** *derog, sl* a person without the power of speech **5** *inf* a person who says or does nothing **6a** a person who appears to act for himself or herself while acting on behalf of another **6b** *(as modifier)*: *a dummy buyer* **7** *mil* a weighted round without explosives **8** *bridge* **8a** the hand exposed on the table by the declarer's partner and played by the declarer **8b** the declarer's partner **9a** a prototype of a book, indicating the appearance of the finished product **9b** a designer's layout of a page **10** *sport* a feigned pass or move **11** *Brit* a rubber teat for babies to suck or bite on. US and Canad equivalent: **pacifier** **12** *(modifier)* counterfeit; sham **13** *(modifier)* (of a card game) played with one hand exposed or unplayed **14** **sell (someone) a dummy** *sport* to trick (an opponent) with a dummy pass [C16 see DUMB, -Y³]

dummy run *n* an experimental run; practice; rehearsal

Du Mont ('djuː,mɒnt) *n* **Allen Balcom** 1901–65, US inventor and electronics manufacturer. He developed the cathode-ray tube used in television sets and oscilloscopes

dump (dʌmp) *vb* **1** to drop, fall, or let fall heavily or in a mass **2** *(tr)* to empty (objects or material) out of a container **3** to unload or empty (a container), as by overturning **4** *(tr)* **4a** *inf* to dispose of without subtlety or proper care **4b** to dispose of (nuclear waste) **5** *commerce* to market (goods) in bulk and at low prices, esp abroad, in order to maintain a high price in the home market and obtain a share of the foreign markets **6** *(tr)* to store (supplies, etc) temporarily **7** *(intr) sl, chiefly US* to defecate **8** *(tr) surfing* (of a wave) to hurl a swimmer or surfer down **9** *(tr) Austral & NZ* to compact (bales of wool) by hydraulic pressure **10** *(tr) computing* to record (the contents of the memory) on a storage device at a series of points during a computer run ▷ *n* **11** a place or area where waste materials are dumped **12** a pile or accumulation of rubbish **13** the act of dumping **14** *inf* a dirty or unkempt place **15** *mil* a place where weapons, supplies, etc, are stored **16** *sl, chiefly US* an act of defecation [C14 prob. from ON]

dumper ('dʌmpə) *n* **1** a person or thing that dumps **2** *surfing* a wave that hurls a swimmer or surfer down

dumpling ('dʌmplɪŋ) *n* **1** a small ball of dough cooked and served with stew **2** a pudding consisting of a round pastry case filled with fruit: *apple dumpling* **3** *inf* a short plump person [C16 *dump-*, ? var. of LUMP¹ + -LING¹]

dumps (dʌmps) *pl n inf* a state of melancholy or depression(esp in **down in the dumps**) [C16 prob. from MDu. *domp* haze]

dump truck *or* **dumper-truck** *n* a small truck used on building sites, having a load-bearing container at the front that can be tipped up to dump the contents

dumpy ('dʌmpɪ) *adj* **dumpier, dumpiest** short and plump; squat [C18 ? rel. to DUMPLING] > **'dumpily** *adv* > **'dumpiness** *n*

dun¹ (dʌn) *vb* **duns, dunning, dunned** **1** *(tr)* to press (a debtor) for payment ▷ *n* **2** a person, esp a hired agent, who importunes another for the payment of a debt **3** a demand for payment [C17 from ?]

dun² (dʌn) *n* **1** a brownish-grey colour **2** a horse of this colour **3** *angling* **3a** an immature adult mayfly **3b** an artificial fly resembling this ▷ *adj* **dunner, dunnest** **4** of a dun colour **5** dark and gloomy [OE *dunn*]

Duna ('dunɔ) *n* the Hungarian name for the **Danube**

Dünaburg ('dyːnabʊrk) *n* the German name (until 1893) for **Daugavpils**

Dunaj ('dunaj) *n* the Czech name for the **Danube**

Dunant (*French* dynɑ̃) *n* **Jean Henri** (ʒɑ̃ ɑ̃ri) 1828–1910, Swiss humanitarian, founder of the International Red Cross (1864): shared the Nobel peace prize 1901

Dunărea ('dunərja) *n* the Romanian name for the **Danube**

Dunbar¹ (dʌn'bɑː) *n* a port and resort in SE Scotland, in East Lothian: scene of Cromwell's defeat of the Scots (1650). Pop: 6518 (1991)

Dunbar² (dʌn'bɑː) *n* **William** ?1460–?1520, Scottish poet, noted for his satirical, allegorical, and elegiac works

Dunbartonshire (dʌn'bɑːtᵊnʃɪə, -ʃə) *n* a historical county of W Scotland: became part of Strathclyde region in 1975; administered since 1996 by the council areas of East Dunbartonshire and West Dunbartonshire

Duncan ('dʌŋkən) *n* **Isadora** (,ɪzə'dɔːrə) 1878–1927, US dancer and choreographer, who influenced modern ballet by introducing greater freedom of movement

Duncan I ('dʌŋkən) *n* died 1040, king of Scotland (1034–40); killed by Macbeth

Duncan Smith ('dʌŋkən 'smɪθ) *n* **(George) Iain** born 1954, British politician; leader of the Conservative Party from 2001

dunce (dʌns) *n* a person who is stupid or slow to learn [C16 from *Dunses* or *Dunsmen*, term of ridicule applied to the followers of John *Duns Scotus* (?1265–1308), Scot. scholastic theologian, esp by 16th-cent. humanists]

dunce cap *or* **dunce's cap** *n* a conical paper hat, formerly placed on the head of a dull child at school

Dundalk (dʌn'dɔ:k) *n* a town in NE Republic of Ireland, on **Dundalk Bay**: county town of Co. Louth. Pop: 25 800 (1991)

Dundee[1] (dʌn'di:) *n* **1** a port in E Scotland, in City of Dundee council area, on the Firth of Tay: centre of the former British jute industry; university (1967). Pop: 158 981 (1991) **2 City of** a council area in E Scotland. Pop: 145 663 (1996 est). Area: 65 sq km (25 sq miles)

Dundee[2] (dʌn'di:) *n* **1 1st Viscount**, title of *John Graham of Claverhouse*. ?1649–89, Scottish Jacobite leader, who died from his wounds after winning the battle of Killiecrankie

Dundee cake (dʌn'di:) *n chiefly Brit* a fairly rich fruit cake decorated with almonds

dunderhead ('dʌndə,hɛd) *n* a slow-witted person [C17 prob. from Du. *donder* thunder + HEAD] > **'dunder,headed** *adj*

Dundonian (dʌn'dəʊnɪən) *n* **1** a native or inhabitant of Dundee ▹ *adj* **2** of or relating to Dundee or its inhabitants

dune (dju:n) *n* a mound or ridge of drifted sand [C18 via OF from MDu. *dūne*]

Dunedin (dʌn'i:dɪn) *n* a port in New Zealand, on SE South Island: founded (1848) by Scottish settlers. Pop (urban area): 119 600 (1999 est)

Dunfermline (dʌn'fɜ:mlɪn) *n* a city in E Scotland, in SW Fife: ruined palace, a former residence of Scottish kings. Pop: 55 083 (1991)

dung (dʌŋ) *n* **1** excrement, esp of animals; manure **2** something filthy ▹ *vb* **3** (*tr*) to cover with manure [OE: prison; rel. to OHG *tunc* cellar roofed with dung, ON *dyngja* manure heap]

Dungannon (dʌn'gænən) *n* a district of S Northern Ireland, in Co. Tyrone. Pop: 47 735 (2001). Area: 783 sq km (302 sq miles)

dungaree (,dʌŋgə'ri:) *n* **1** a coarse cotton fabric used chiefly for work clothes, etc **2** (*pl*) **2a** a suit of workman's overalls made of this material, consisting of trousers with a bib attached **2b** a casual garment resembling this, usually worn by women or children **3** (*pl*) *US* jeans [C17 from Hindi, after *Dungrī*, district of Bombay, where this fabric originated]

Dungeness (,dʌndʒə'nɛs) *n* a low shingle headland on the S coast of England, in Kent: two nuclear power stations: automatic lighthouse

dungeon ('dʌndʒən) *n* **1** a prison cell, often underground **2** a variant spelling of **donjon** [C14 from OF *donjon*]

dunger ('dʌŋə) *n NZ inf* **1** an old decrepit car **2** any old worn-out machine

dunghill ('dʌŋ,hɪl) *n* **1** a heap of dung **2** a foul place, condition, or person

dunk (dʌŋk) *vb* **1** to dip (bread, etc) in tea, soup, etc, before eating **2** to submerge or be submerged [C20 from Pennsylvania Du., from MHG *dunken*, from OHG *dunkōn*] > **'dunker** *n*

Dunkerque (*French* dœ̃kɛrk) *n* a port in N France, on the Strait of Dover: scene of the evacuation of British and other Allied troops after the fall of France in 1940; industrial centre with an oil refinery and naval shipbuilding yards. Pop: 190 879 (1990). English name: **Dunkirk** (dʌn'kɜ:k)

Dún Laoghaire (du:n 'lɪərɪ) *n* a port in E Republic of Ireland, on Dublin Bay. Pop: 189 999 (1996). Former names: **Dunleary** (until 1821), **Kingstown** (1821–1921)

dunlin ('dʌnlɪn) *n* a small sandpiper of northern and arctic regions, having a brown back and black breast in summer [C16 DUN[2] + -LING[1]]

Dunlop ('dʌnlɒp) *n* **John Boyd** 1840–1921, Scottish veterinary surgeon, who devised the first successful pneumatic tyre, which was manufactured by the company named after him

dunnage ('dʌnɪdʒ) *n* loose material used for packing cargo [C14 from ?]

dunnart ('dʌnɑ:t) *n* a mouselike insectivorous marsupial of the genus *Sminthopsis* of Australia and New Guinea [C20 from a native Australian language]

dunno (dʌ'nəʊ, də-) *sl contraction of* (I) do not know

dunnock ('dʌnək) *n* another name for a **hedge sparrow** [C15 from DUN[2] + -OCK]

dunny ('dʌnɪ) *n, pl* **dunnies 1** *Scot dialect* a cellar or basement **2** *Austral & NZ inf* **2a** a lavatory, esp one which is outside **2b** (*as modifier*): *a dunny roll; a dunny seat* [C20 from ?]

Dunsinane (dʌn'sɪnən) *n* a hill in central Scotland, in the Sidlaw Hills: the ruined fort at its summit is regarded as Macbeth's castle. Height: 308 m (1012 ft).

> **USAGE** The pronunciation ('dʌnsɪ,neɪn) is used in Shakespeare's *Macbeth* for the purposes of rhyme

Duns Scotus ('dʌnz 'skɒtəs) *n* **John** ?1265–1308, Scottish scholastic theologian and Franciscan priest: opposed the theology of St. Thomas Aquinas. See also **Scotism**

Dunstable ('dʌnstəbᵊl) *n* an industrial town in SE central England, in Bedfordshire. Pop: 49 666 (1991)

Dunstan ('dʌnstən) *n* **Saint** ?909–988 AD, English prelate and statesman; archbishop of Canterbury (959–988) He revived monasticism in England on Benedictine lines and promoted education. Feast day: May 19

duo ('dju:əʊ) *n, pl* **duos** *or* **dui** ('dju:i:) **1** *music* **1a** a pair of performers **1b** a duet **2** a pair of actors, etc **3** *inf* a pair of closely connected individuals [C16 via It. from L: two]

duo- *combining form.* indicating two [from L]

duodecimal (,dju:əʊ'dɛsɪməl) *adj* **1** relating to twelve or twelfths ▹ *n* **2** a twelfth **3** one of the numbers used in a duodecimal number system > **,duo'decimally** *adv*

duodecimo (,dju:əʊ'dɛsɪ,məʊ) *n, pl* **duodecimos 1** Also called: **twelvemo** a book size resulting from folding a sheet of paper into twelve leaves **2** a book of this size [C17 from L *in duodecimō* in twelfth]

duodenum (,dju:əʊ'di:nəm) *n, pl* **duodena** (-nə) *or* **duodenums** the first part of the small intestine, between the stomach and the jejunum [C14 from Med. L, from *intestinum duodenum digitorum* intestine of twelve fingers' length] > **,duo'denal** *adj*

duologue *or US (sometimes)* **duolog** ('dju:ə,lɒg) *n* **1** a part or all of a play in which the speaking roles are limited to two actors **2** a less common word for **dialogue**

duopoly (djʊ'ɒpəlɪ) *n, pl* **duopolies** a situation in which control of a commodity or service in a particular market is vested in two producers or suppliers > **du,opo'listic** *adj*

Duo-Tang ('dju:ə,tæŋ) *n Canad trademark* a type of folder with flexible metal fasteners

dupe (dju:p) *n* **1** a person who is easily deceived ▹ *vb* **dupes, duping, duped 2** (*tr*) to deceive; cheat; fool [C17 from F, from OF *duppe*, contraction of *de huppe* of (a) hoopoe; from the bird's reputation for stupidity] > **'dupable** *adj* > **'duper** *n* > **'dupery** *n*

duple ('dju:pᵊl) *adj* **1** a less common word for **double** **2** *music* (of time or music) having two beats in a bar [C16 from L *duplus* twofold, double]

duplex ('dju:plɛks) *n* **1** *US & Canad* a duplex apartment or house **2** *biochem* a double-stranded region in a nucleic acid molecule ▹ *adj* **3** having two parts **4** having pairs of components of independent but identical function **5** permitting the transmission of simultaneous signals in both directions [C19 from L: twofold, from *duo* two + *-plex* -FOLD] > **du'plexity** *n*

duplex apartment *n US & Canad* an apartment on two floors

duplex house *n US & Canad* a house divided into two separate dwellings. Also called (*US*): **semidetached**

Dd

duplicate *adj* ('dju:plɪkɪt) **1** copied exactly from an original **2** identical **3** existing as a pair or in pairs ▷ *n* ('dju:plɪkɪt) **4** an exact copy **5** something additional of the same kind **6** two exact copies(esp in **in duplicate**) ▷ *vb* ('dju:plɪˌkeɪt), **duplicates, duplicating, duplicated** (*tr*) **7** to make a replica of **8** to do or make again **9** to make in a pair; make double [c15 from L *duplicāre* to double, from *duo* two + *plicāre* to fold] > **'duplicable** *adj*

duplication (ˌdju:plɪ'keɪʃən) *n* **1** the act of duplicating or the state of being duplicated **2** a copy; duplicate **3** *genetics* a mutation in which there are two or more copies of a gene or of a segment of a chromosome

duplicator ('dju:plɪˌkeɪtə) *n* an apparatus for making replicas of an original, such as a machine using a stencil wrapped on an ink-loaded drum

duplicity (dju:'plɪsɪtɪ) *n, pl* **duplicities** deception; double-dealing [c15 from OF *duplicite*, from LL *duplicitās* a being double, from L DUPLEX]

du Pré (du: preɪ) *n* **Jacqueline** 1945–87, English cellist. Multiple sclerosis ended her performing career (1973) after which she became a cello teacher

Dupré (*French* dypre) *n* **Marcel** (marsɛl) 1886–1971, French organist and composer, noted as an improviser

Duque de Caxias (*Portuguese* 'du:ke 'də: kə'ʃiəʃ) *n* a city in SE Brazil, near Rio de Janeiro. Pop: 767 724 (2000)

Dur. *abbrev for* Durham

durable ('djʊərəbᵊl) *adj* long-lasting; enduring [c14 from OF, from L *dūrābilis*, from *dūrāre* to last] > ˌ**dura'bility** *n* > **'durably** *adv*

durable goods *pl n* goods that require infrequent replacement. Also called: **durables**

dural ('djʊərəl) *adj* relating to or affecting the dura mater

Duralumin (djʊ'ræljʊmɪn) *n trademark* a light strong aluminium alloy containing copper, silicon, magnesium, and manganese

dura mater ('djʊərə 'meɪtə) *n* the outermost and toughest of the three membranes covering the brain and spinal cord. Often shortened to **dura** [c15 from Med. L: hard mother]

duramen (djʊ'reɪmɛn) *n* another name for **heartwood** [c19 from L: hardness, from *dūrāre* to harden]

durance ('djʊərəns) *n arch or literary* **1** imprisonment **2** duration [c15 from OF, from *durer* to last, from L *dūrāre*]

Durango (djʊ'ræŋgəʊ; *Spanish* du'raŋgo) *n* **1** a state in N central Mexico: high plateau, with the Sierra Madre Occidental in the west; irrigated agriculture(esp cotton) and rich mineral resources. Capital: Durango. Pop: 1 445 922 (1995 est). Area: 119 648 sq km (46 662 sq miles) **2** a city in NW central Mexico, capital of Durango state: mining centre. Pop: 430 000 (2000 est). Official name: **Victoria de Durango**

Durante (də'ræntɪ) *n* **Jimmy**, known as *Schnozzle*. 1893–1980, US comedian

Duras (*French* dyra) *n* **Marguerite**, real name *Marguerite Donnadieu*. 1914–96, French novelist born in Giadinh, Indochina (now in Vietnam) Her works include *The Sea Wall* (1950), *Practicalities* (1990), *Écrire* (1993), and the script for the film *Hiroshima mon amour* (1960)

duration (djʊ'reɪʃən) *n* the length of time that something lasts or continues [c14 from Med. L *dūrātiō*, from L *dūrāre* to last] > **du'rational** *adj*

durative ('djʊərətɪv) *grammar* ▷ *adj* **1** denoting an aspect of verbs that includes the imperfective and the progressive ▷ *n* **2a** the durative aspect of a verb **2b** a verb in this aspect

Durban ('dɜ:bᵊn) *n* a port in E South Africa, in E KwaZulu/Natal province on the Indian Ocean: University of Natal (1909); resort and industrial centre, with oil refineries, shipbuilding yards, etc Pop (urban area): 2 117 650 (1996)

Durban poison *n S African sl* a particularly potent variety of cannabis grown in Natal

durbar ('dɜ:bɑ:, ˌdɜ:'bɑ:) *n* **a** (formerly) the court of a native ruler or a governor in India **b** a levee at such a court [c17 from Hindi *darbār*, from Persian, from *dar* door + *bār* entry, audience]

Dürer (*German* 'dy:rər) *n* **Albrecht** ('albrɛçt) 1471–1528, German painter and engraver, regarded as the greatest artist of the German Renaissance and noted particularly as a draughtsman and for his copper engravings and woodcuts

duress (djʊ'rɛs, djʊə-) *n* **1** compulsion by use of force or threat; coercion (often in **under duress**) **2** imprisonment [c14 from OF *duresse*, from L *dūritia* hardness, from *dūrus* hard]

Durga Puja (ˌdʊəgə 'pu:dʒə) *n* another name for **Navaratri** [from Sanskr. *Durga* (Hindu goddess) and *puja* worship]

Durham ('dʌrəm) *n* **1** a county of NE England, on the North Sea: rises to the N Pennines in the west: the geographical and ceremonial county includes the unitary authorities of Hartlepool and Stockton-on-Tees (both part of Cleveland until 1996) and Darlington (created in 1997). Administrative centre: Durham. Pop (excluding unitary authorities): 493 470 (1994 est). Area (excluding unitary authorities): 2434 sq km (940 sq miles). Abbreviation: **Dur.** **2** a city in NE England, administrative centre of Co. Durham, on the River Wear: Norman cathedral; 11th-century castle (founded by William the Conqueror), now occupied by the University of Durham (1832). Pop: 36 937 (1991) **3** a rare variety of shorthorn cattle. See **shorthorn**

during ('djʊərɪŋ) *prep* **1** concurrently with (some other activity) **2** within the limit of (a period of time) [c14 from *duren* to last, ult. from L *dūrare* to last]

Durkan ('dɜ:kən) *n* **(John) Mark** born 1960, Northern Irish politician; leader of the Social Democratic and Labour Party (SDLP) from 2001

Durkheim ('dɜ:khaɪm; *French* dyrkɛm) *n* **Émile** (emil) 1858–1917, French sociologist, whose pioneering works include *De la Division du travail social* (1893)

durmast *or* **durmast oak** ('dɜ:ˌmɑ:st) *n* a large Eurasian oak tree with lobed leaves and sessile acorns. Also called: **sessile oak** [c18 prob. from DUN[2] + MAST[2]]

durra ('dʌrə) *n* an Old World variety of sorghum, cultivated for grain and fodder [c18 from Ar. *dhurah* grain]

Durrell ('dʌrəl) *n* **1** **Gerald** (**Malcolm**) 1925–95, British zoologist and writer: his books include *The Bafut Beagles* (1954), *My Family and Other Animals* (1956), and *The Aye-aye and I* (1992) **2** his brother, **Lawrence** (**George**) 1912–90, British poet and novelist; author of *The Alexandria Quartet* of novels, consisting of *Justine* (1957), *Balthazar* (1958), *Mountolive* (1958), and *Clea* (1960). Later works include *The Avignon Quintet* of novels (1974–85)

Dürrenmatt ('dyrənmat) *n* **Friedrich** ('fri:drɪç) 1921–90, Swiss dramatist and writer of detective stories, noted for his grotesque and paradoxical treatment of the modern world: author of *The Visit* (1956) and *The Physicists* (1962)

durry ('dʌrɪ) *n, pl* **durries** *Austral sl* a cigarette [from *durrie* a type of Indian carpet]

durst (dɜ:st) *vb* an archaic past tense of **dare**

durum *or* **durum wheat** ('djʊərəm) *n* a variety of wheat with a high gluten content, used chiefly to make pastas [c20 from NL *trīticum dūrum*, lit.: hard wheat]

Duse (*Italian* 'du:ze) *n* **Eleonora** (ˌɛlɪə'nɔ:rə) 1858–1924, Italian actress, noted as a tragedienne

Dushanbe (du:'ʃɑ:nbɪ) *n* the capital of Tajikistan; a cultural centre. Pop: 513 000 (1998 est). Former name (1929–61): **Stalinabad**

dusk (dʌsk) *n* **1** the darker part of twilight **2** *poetic* gloom; shade ▷ *adj* **3** *poetic* shady; gloomy ▷ *vb* **4** *poetic* to make or become dark [OE *dox*]

dusky ('dʌskɪ) *adj* **duskier, duskiest** **1** dark in colour;

swarthy or dark-skinned **2** dim > **'duskily** *adv* > **'duskiness** *n*

Düsseldorf ('dʊsəl,dɔ:f; *German* 'dysəldɔrf) *n* an industrial city in W Germany, capital of North Rhine-Westphalia, on the Rhine: commercial centre of the Rhine-Ruhr industrial area. Pop: 568 500 (1999 est)

dust (dʌst) *n* **1** dry fine powdery material, such as particles of dirt, earth, or pollen **2** a cloud of such fine particles **3a** the mortal body of man **3b** the corpse of a dead person **4** the earth; ground **5** *inf* a disturbance; fuss(esp in **kick up a dust, raise a dust**) **6** something of little worth **7** short for **gold dust** **8** ashes or household refuse **9** **dust and ashes** something that is very disappointing **10** **shake the dust off** (*or* **from**) **one's feet** to depart angrily or contemptuously **11** **throw dust in the eyes of** to confuse or mislead ▷ *vb* **12** (*tr*) to sprinkle or cover (something) with (dust or some other powdery substance) **13** to remove dust (from) by wiping, sweeping, or brushing **14** *arch* to make or become dirty with dust ▷ See also **dust down, dust-up** [OE *dūst*] > **'dustless** *adj*

dustbin ('dʌst,bɪn) *n* a large, usually cylindrical container for rubbish, esp one used by a household. US and Canad names: **garbage can, trash can**

dust bowl *n* a semiarid area in which the surface soil is exposed to wind erosion

Dust Bowl *n* **the** the area of the south central US that became denuded of topsoil by wind erosion during the droughts of the mid-1930s

dustcart ('dʌst,kɑ:t) *n* a road vehicle for collecting refuse. US and Canad name: **garbage truck**

dust cover *n* **1** another name for **dustsheet** **2** another name for **dust jacket** **3** a Perspex cover for the turntable of a record player

dust devil *n* a strong miniature whirlwind that whips up dust, litter, leaves, etc, into the air

dust down *vb* (*tr, adv*) **1** to remove dust from by brushing or wiping **2** to reprimand severely > **dusting down** *n*

duster ('dʌstə) *n* **1** a cloth used for dusting. US name: **dust cloth** **2** a machine for blowing out dust **3** a person or thing that dusts

dusting-powder *n* fine powder (such as talcum powder) used to absorb moisture, etc

dust jacket *or* **cover** *n* a removable paper cover used to protect a bound book

dustman ('dʌstmən) *n, pl* **dustmen** *Brit* a man whose job is to collect domestic refuse

dustpan ('dʌst,pæn) *n* a short-handled hooded shovel into which dust is swept from floors, etc

dustsheet ('dʌst,ʃi:t) *n Brit* a large cloth used to protect furniture from dust

dust storm *n* a windstorm that whips up clouds of dust

dust-up *inf* ▷ *n* **1** a fight or argument ▷ *vb* **dust up** **2** (*tr, adv*) to attack (someone)

dusty ('dʌstɪ) *adj* **dustier, dustiest** **1** covered with or involving dust **2** like dust **3** (of a colour) tinged with grey; pale **4** **give** (*or* **get**) **a dusty answer** to give (*or* get) an unhelpful or bad-tempered reply > **'dustily** *adv* > **'dustiness** *n*

Dutch (dʌtʃ) *n* **1** the language of the Netherlands **2** **the Dutch** (*functioning as pl*) the natives, citizens, or inhabitants of the Netherlands **3** See **double Dutch** **4** **in Dutch** *sl* in trouble ▷ *adj* **5** of the Netherlands, its inhabitants, or their language ▷ *adv* **6** **go Dutch** *inf* to share expenses equally

Dutch auction *n* an auction in which the price is lowered by stages until a buyer is found

Dutch barn *n Brit* a farm building consisting of a steel frame and a curved roof

Dutch courage *n* **1** false courage gained from drinking alcohol **2** alcoholic drink

Dutch door *n* the US and Canad name for **stable door**

Dutch East Indies *n* **the** a former name (1798–1945) of **Indonesia** Also called: **Netherlands East Indies**

Dutch elm disease *n* a fungal disease of elm trees characterized by withering of the foliage and stems and eventual death of the tree

Dutch Guiana *or* **Netherlands Guiana** *n* the former name of **Surinam**

Dutchman ('dʌtʃmən) *n, pl* **Dutchmen** **1** a native, citizen, or inhabitant of the Netherlands **2** *S African derog* an Afrikaner

Dutch New Guinea *n* a former name (until 1963) of **Irian Jaya**

Dutch oven *n* **1** an iron or earthenware container with a cover, used for stews, etc **2** a metal box, open in front, for cooking in front of an open fire

Dutch treat *n inf* an entertainment, meal, etc, where each person pays for himself

Dutch uncle *n inf* a person who criticizes or reproves frankly and severely

Dutch West Indies *pl n* **the** a former name of the **Netherlands Antilles**

duteous ('dju:tɪəs) *adj formal or arch* dutiful; obedient > **'duteously** *adv*

dutiable ('dju:tɪəbᵊl) *adj* (of goods) liable to duty > **,dutia'bility** *n*

dutiful ('dju:tɪfʊl) *adj* **1** exhibiting or having a sense of duty **2** characterized by or resulting from a sense of duty: *a dutiful answer*

duty ('dju:tɪ) *n, pl* **duties** **1** a task or action that a person is bound to perform for moral or legal reasons **2** respect or obedience due to a superior, older persons, etc **3** the force that binds one morally or legally to one's obligations **4** a government tax, esp on imports **5** *Brit* **5a** the quantity of work for which a machine is designed **5b** a measure of the efficiency of a machine **6a** a job or service allocated **6b** (*as modifier*): *duty rota* **7** **do duty for** to act as a substitute for **8** **on** (*or* **off**) **duty** at (*or* not at) work [c13 from Anglo-F *dueté*, from OF *deu* DUE]

duty-bound *adj* morally obliged

duty-free *adj, adv* **1** with exemption from customs or excise duties ▷ *n* **2** goods sold in a duty-free shop

duty-free shop *n* a shop, esp one at an airport or on board a ship, that sells perfume, tobacco, etc, at duty-free prices

duumvir (dju:'ʌmvə) *n, pl* **duumvirs** *or* **duumviri** (-vɪ,ri:) **1** *Roman history* one of two coequal magistrates **2** either of two men who exercise a joint authority [c16 from L, from *duo* two + *vir* man] > **duumvirate** (dju:'ʌmvɪrɪt) *n*

Duvalier (*French* dyvalje) *n* **1** **François** (frɑ̃swa), known as *Papa Doc*. 1907–71, president of Haiti (1957–71) **2** his son, **Jean-Claude** (ʒɑ̃klod), known as *Baby Doc*. born 1951, Haitian statesman; president of Haiti 1971–86; deposed and exiled

duvet ('du:veɪ) *n* **1** another name for **continental quilt** **2** Also called: **duvet jacket** a down-filled jacket [c18 from F, from earlier *dumet*, from OF *dum* DOWN²]

dux (dʌks) *n* (esp in Scottish schools) the top pupil in a class or school [L: leader]

DV *abbrev for:* **1** Deo volente [L: God willing] **2** Douay Version (of the Bible)

DVD *abbrev for* digital versatile disk or (formerly) digital video disk

DVD writer *n computing* a device on a computer for writing DVDs

Dvina (*Russian* dvi'na) *n* **1** **Northern** a river in NW Russia, formed by the confluence of the Sukhona and Yug Rivers and flowing northwest to *Dvina Bay* in the White Sea. Length: 750 km (466 miles). Russian name: **Severnaya Dvina** **2** **Western** a river rising in W Russia, in the Valdai Hills and flowing south and southwest then northwest to the Gulf of Riga. Length: 1021 km (634 miles). Russian name: **Zapadnaya Dvina** ('zapədnəjə) Latvian name: **Daugava**

Dvina Bay *or* **Dvina Gulf** *n* an inlet of the White Sea, off the coast of NW Russia
Dvinsk (dvinsk) *n* transliteration of the former Russian name for **Daugavpils**
DVLA *abbrev for* Driver and Vehicle Licensing Agency
Dvořák (ˈdvɔːʒæk; *Czech* ˈdvɔrʒaːk) *n* **Antonín** (ˈantɔnjiːn), known as *Anton Dvořák*. 1841–1904, Czech composer, much of whose work reflects the influence of folk music. His best-known work is the *Symphony No. 9 From the New World* (1893)
DVT *abbrev for* deep-vein thrombosis
dwaal (dwɑːl) *n S African* a state of befuddlement; daze [from Afrik. *dwaal* wander]
dwale (dweɪl) *n* another name for **deadly nightshade** [c14 ?from ON]
dwarf (dwɔːf) *n, pl* **dwarfs** *or* **dwarves** (dwɔːvz) **1** an abnormally undersized person **2a** an animal or plant much below the average height for the species **2b** (*as modifier*): *a dwarf tree* **3** (in folklore) a small ugly manlike creature, often possessing magical powers **4** *astron* short for **dwarf star** ▷ *vb* **5** to become or cause to become comparatively small in size, importance, etc **6** (*tr*) to stunt the growth of [OE *dweorg*] > **ˈdwarfish** *adj*
dwarf star *n* any unevolved star, such as the sun, lying in the main sequence of the Hertzsprung-Russell diagram. Also called: **main sequence star.** See also **red dwarf, white dwarf**
dwell (dwɛl) *vb* **dwells, dwelling, dwelt** *or* **dwelled** (*intr*) **1** *formal, literary* to live as a permanent resident **2** to live (in a specified state): *to dwell in poverty* ▷ *n* **3** a regular pause in the operation of a machine [OE *dwellan* to seduce, get lost] > **ˈdweller** *n*
dwelling (ˈdwɛlɪŋ) *n formal, literary* a place of residence
dwell on *or* **upon** *vb* (*intr, prep*) to think, speak, or write at length about
dwelt (dwɛlt) *vb* a past tense and past participle of **dwell**
dwindle (ˈdwɪndᵊl) *vb* **dwindles, dwindling, dwindled** to grow or cause to grow less in size, intensity, or number [c16 from OE *dwīnan* to waste away]
DWP (in Britain) *abbrev for* Department for Work and Pensions
Dy *the chemical symbol for* dysprosium
dyad (ˈdaɪæd) *n* **1** *maths* an operator that is the unspecified product of two vectors **2** an atom or group that has a valency of two **3** a group of two; couple [c17 from LL *dyas*, from Gk *duas* two] > **dyˈadic** *adj*
Dyak *or* **Dayak** (ˈdaɪæk) *n, pl* **Dyaks, Dyak** *or* **Dayaks, Dayak** a member of a Malaysian people of Borneo [from Malay: upcountry, from *darat* land]
dybbuk (ˈdɪbək) *n, pl* **dybbuks** *or* **dybbukkim** *judaism* (in folklore) the soul of a dead sinner that has transmigrated into the body of a living person [from Yiddish: devil, from Heb.]
dye (daɪ) *n* **1** a staining or colouring substance **2** a liquid that contains a colouring material and can be used to stain fabrics, skins, etc **3** the colour produced by dyeing ▷ *vb* **dyes, dyeing, dyed 4** (*tr*) to impart a colour or stain to (fabric, hair, etc) by or as if by the application of a dye [OE *dēagian*, from *dēag* a dye] > **ˈdyable** *or* **ˈdyeable** *adj* > **ˈdyer** *n*
dyed-in-the-wool *adj* **1** uncompromising or unchanging in attitude, opinion, etc **2** (of a fabric) made of dyed yarn
dyeing (ˈdaɪɪŋ) *n* the process or industry of colouring yarns, fabric, etc
▷ www.straw.com/sig/dyehist.html
▷ www.ritdye.com
dyestuff (ˈdaɪˌstʌf) *n* a substance that can be used as a dye or which yields a dye
Dyfed (ˈdʌvɛd) *n* a former county in SW Wales: created in 1974 from Cardiganshire, Pembrokeshire, and Carmarthenshire; in 1996 it was replaced by Pembrokeshire, Carmarthenshire, and Ceredigion
dying (ˈdaɪɪŋ) *vb* **1** the present participle of **die**[1] ▷ *adj* **2** relating to or occurring at the moment of death: *a dying wish*
dyke[1] *or* **dike** (daɪk) *n* **1** an embankment constructed to prevent flooding, keep out the sea, or confine a river to a particular course **2** a ditch or watercourse **3** a bank made of earth alongside a ditch **4** *Scot* a wall, esp a dry-stone wall **5** a barrier or obstruction **6** a wall-like mass of igneous rock in older sedimentary rock **7** *Austral & NZ inf* a lavatory ▷ *vb* **dykes, dyking, dyked 8** (*tr*) to protect, enclose, or drain (land) with a dyke [c13 from OE *dic* ditch]
dyke[2] *or* **dike** (daɪk) *n sl* a lesbian [c20 from ?]
Dyke (daɪk) *n* **Greg(ory)** born 1947, British television executive; director-general of the BBC from 2000
Dylan (ˈdɪlən) *n* **Bob** real name *Robert Allen Zimmerman*. born 1941, US rock singer and songwriter, also noted for his acoustic protest songs in the early 1960s. His albums include *The Freewheelin' Bob Dylan* (1963), *Highway 61 Revisited* (1965), *Blonde on Blonde* (1966), *John Wesley Harding* (1968), *Blood on the Tracks* (1974), *Oh Mercy* (1989), *Time Out of Mind* (1997), and *Love and Theft* (2001)
dynamic (daɪˈnæmɪk) *adj* **1** of or concerned with energy or forces that produce motion, as opposed to *static* **2** of or concerned with dynamics **3** Also: **dynamical** characterized by force of personality, ambition, energy, etc **4** *computing* (of a memory) needing its contents refreshed periodically [c19 from F *dynamique*, from Gk *dunamikos* powerful, from *dunamis* power, from *dunasthai* to be able] > **dyˈnamically** *adv*
dynamic link library *n computing* a set of programs that can be activated and then discarded by other programs. Abbrev: **DLL**
dynamic range *n* the range of signal amplitudes over which an electronic communications channel can operate within acceptable limits of distortion. The range is determined by system noise at the lower end and by the onset of overload at the upper end
dynamics (daɪˈnæmɪks) *n* **1** (*functioning as sing*) the branch of mechanics concerned with the forces that change or produce the motions of bodies **2** (*functioning as sing*) the branch of mechanics that includes statics and kinetics **3** (*functioning as sing*) the branch of any science concerned with forces **4** (*functioning as pl*) those forces that produce change in any field or system **5** (*functioning as pl*) *Music* **5a** the various degrees of loudness called for in performance **5b** directions and symbols used to indicate degrees of loudness
dynamism (ˈdaɪnəˌmɪzəm) *n* **1** *philosophy* any of several theories that attempt to explain phenomena in terms of an immanent force or energy **2** the forcefulness of an energetic personality > **ˈdynamist** *n* > **ˌdynaˈmistic** *adj*
dynamite (ˈdaɪnəˌmaɪt) *n* **1** an explosive consisting of nitroglycerine mixed with an absorbent **2** *inf* a spectacular or potentially dangerous person or thing ▷ *vb* **dynamites, dynamiting, dynamited 3** (*tr*) to mine or blow up with dynamite [c19 (coined by Alfred Nobel): from DYNAMO- + -ITE[1]] > **ˈdynaˌmiter** *n*
dynamo (ˈdaɪnəˌməʊ) *n, pl* **dynamos 1** a device for converting mechanical energy into electrical energy **2** *inf* an energetic hard-working person [c19 short for *dynamoelectric machine*]
dynamo- *or sometimes before a vowel* **dynam-** *combining form* indicating power: *dynamite* [from Gk, from *dunamis* power]
dynamoelectric (ˌdaɪnəməʊɪˈlɛktrɪk) *or* **dynamoelectrical** *adj* of or concerned with the interconversion of mechanical and electrical energy
dynamometer (ˌdaɪnəˈmɒmɪtə) *n* an instrument for measuring power or force
dynamotor (ˈdaɪnəˌməʊtə) *n* an electrical machine having two independent armature windings of which one acts as a motor and the other a generator: used to

convert direct current into alternating current

dynast (ˈdɪnəst, -æst) *n* a ruler, esp a hereditary one [C17 from L *dynastēs*, from Gk, from *dunasthai* to be powerful]

dynasty (ˈdɪnəstɪ) *n, pl* **dynasties** **1** a sequence of hereditary rulers **2** any sequence of powerful leaders of the same family [C15 via LL from Gk, from *dunastēs* DYNAST] > **dynastic** (dɪˈnæstɪk) *adj*

dyne (daɪn) *n* the cgs unit of force; the force that imparts an acceleration of 1 centimetre per second per second to a mass of 1 gram. 1 dyne is equivalent to 10^{-5} newton or 7.233×10^{-5} poundal [C19 from F, from Gk *dunamis* power, force]

dys- *prefix* **1** diseased, abnormal, or faulty **2** difficult or painful **3** unfavourable or bad [via L from Gk *dus-*]

dysentery (ˈdɪsᵊntrɪ) *n* infection of the intestine marked by severe diarrhoea with the passage of mucus and blood [C14 via L from Gk, from *dusentera*, lit.: bad bowels, from DYS- + *enteron* intestine] > **dysenteric** (ˌdɪsᵊnˈtɛrɪk) *adj*

dysfunction (dɪsˈfʌŋkʃən) *n* **1** *med* any disturbance or abnormality in the function of an organ or part **2** (esp of a family) failure to show the characteristics or fulfil the purposes accepted as normal or beneficial

dysfunctional (dɪsˈfʌŋkʃənᵊl) *adj* **1** *med* (of an organ or part) not functioning normally **2** (esp of a family) characterized by a breakdown of normal or beneficial relationships between the members of a group

dysgraphia (dɪsˈgræfɪə) *n* inability to write correctly, caused by disease of part of the brain

dyslexia (dɪsˈlɛksɪə) *n* a developmental disorder which can cause learning difficulty in one or more of the areas of reading, writing, and numeracy [C19 NL, from DYS- + *-lexia*, from Gk *lexis* word] > **dyslectic** (dɪsˈlɛktɪk) *adj* > **dysˈlexic** *adj, n*

dysmenorrhoea *or esp US* **dysmenorrhea** (ˌdɪsmɛnəˈrɪə) *n* abnormally difficult or painful menstruation [C19 from DYS- + Gk *mēn* month + *rhoia* a flowing]

Dyson (ˈdaɪsən) *n* **James** born 1947, British businessman and industrial designer; inventor of the bagless vacuum cleaner (1979–93)

dyspepsia (dɪsˈpɛpsɪə) *n* indigestion or upset stomach [C18 from L, from Gk *duspepsia*, from DYS- + *pepsis* digestion]

dyspeptic (dɪsˈpɛptɪk) *adj* **1** relating to or suffering from dyspepsia **2** irritable ▷ *n* **3** a person suffering from dyspepsia

dysphasia (dɪsˈfeɪzɪə) *n* a disorder of language caused by a brain lesion > **dysˈphasic** *adj, n*

dysphoria (dɪsˈfɔːrɪə) *n* a feeling of being ill at ease [C20 NL, from Gk DYS- + *-phoria*, from *pherein* to bear]

dyspnoea *or US* **dyspnea** (dɪspˈniːə) *n* difficulty in breathing or in catching the breath [C17 via L from Gk *duspnoia*, from DYS- + *pnoē* breath, from *pnein* to breathe] > **dyspˈnoeal, dyspˈnoeic** *or US* **dyspˈneal, dyspˈneic** *adj*

dysprosium (dɪsˈprəʊsɪəm) *n* a metallic element of the lanthanide series: used in laser materials and as a neutron absorber in nuclear control rods. Symbol: Dy; atomic no.: 66; atomic wt.: 162.50 [C20 NL, from Gk *dusprositos* difficult to get near + -IUM]

dysthymia (dɪsˈθaɪmɪə) *n psychiatry* the characteristics of the neurotic and introverted, including anxiety, depression, and compulsive behaviour [C19 NL, from Gk *dusthumia*, from DYS- + *thumos* mind] > **dysˈthymic** *adj*

dysthymic disorder *n* a psychiatric disorder characterized by generalized depression that lasts for at least a year

dystrophy (ˈdɪstrəfɪ) *n* any of various bodily disorders, characterized by wasting of tissues. See also **muscular dystrophy** [C19 NL *dystrophia*, from DYS- + Gk *trophē* food] > **dystrophic** (dɪsˈtrɒfɪk) *adj*

Dzaudzhikau (dzəudʒiˈkau) *n* the former name (1944–54) of **Vladikavkaz**

dzo (zəʊ) *n, pl* **dzos** *or* **dzo** a variant spelling of **zo**

Dzungaria (dzʊŋˈgɛərɪə, zʊŋ-) *n* a variant transliteration of the Chinese name for **Junggar Pendi**

Ee

e *or* **E** (iː) *n, pl* **e's, E's,** *or* **Es** **1** the fifth letter and second vowel of the English alphabet **2** any of several speech sounds represented by this letter, as in *he, bet,* or *below*

e *symbol for:* **1** *maths* a transcendental number used as the base of natural logarithms. Approximate value: 2.718 282... **2** electron

E *symbol for:* **1** *music* **1a** the third note of the scale of C major **1b** the major or minor key having this note as its tonic **2** earth **3** East **4** English **5** Egypt(ian) **6** *physics* **6a** energy **6b** electromotive force **7** exa- **8a** a person without a regular income, or who is dependent on the state on a long-term basis because of unemployment, sickness, old age, etc **8b** (*as modifier*): *E worker* ▷ See also **occupation groupings** **9** the drug ecstasy

E. *abbrev for* Earl

e- *prefix* electronic, indicating the involvement of the Internet: *e-mail; e-money*

E- *prefix* used with numbers indicating a standardized system within the European Union, as of food additives. See also **E number**

ea. *abbrev for* each

each (iːtʃ) *determiner* **1a** every (one) of two or more considered individually: *each day; each person* **1b** (*as pron*): *each gave according to his ability* ▷ *adv* **2** for, to, or from each one; apiece: *four apples each* [OE *ǣlc*]

> **USAGE** *Each* is a singular pronoun and should be used with a singular form of a verb: *each of the candidates was* (not *were*) *interviewed separately*. See also at **either**

e-address *n* an e-mail address

Eadred (ˈɛdrɪd) *n* died 955 AD, king of England (946–55): regained Northumbria (954) from the Norwegian king Eric Bloodaxe

eager (ˈiːɡə) *adj* **1** (*postpositive; often foll by to or for*) impatiently desirous (of); anxious or avid (for) **2** characterized by or feeling expectancy or great desire: *an eager look* **3** *arch* biting; sharp [C13 from OF *egre*, from L *acer* sharp, keen] > ˈ**eagerly** *adv* > ˈ**eagerness** *n*

eager beaver *n inf* a person who displays conspicuous diligence

eagle (ˈiːɡᵊl) *n* **1** any of various birds of prey having large broad wings and strong soaring flight. Related adj: **aquiline** **2** a representation of an eagle used as an emblem, etc, esp representing power: *the Roman eagle* **3** a standard, seal, etc, bearing the figure of an eagle **4** *golf* a score of two strokes under par for a hole **5** a former US gold coin worth ten dollars ▷ *vb* **6** *golf* to score two strokes under par for a hole [C14 from OF *aigle*, from OProvençal *aigla*, from L *aquila*]

eagle-eyed *adj* having keen or piercing eyesight

eagle-hawk *n* a large brown Australian eagle. Also called: **wedge-tailed eagle**

eagle owl *n* a large Eurasian owl with brownish speckled plumage and large ear tufts

eaglet (ˈiːɡlɪt) *n* a young eagle

Eakins (ˈiːkɪnz) *n* **Thomas** 1844–1916, US painter of portraits and sporting life: a noted realist

ealdorman (ˈɔːldəmən) *n, pl* **ealdormen** an official of Anglo-Saxon England, appointed by the king, and responsible for law and order in his shire and for leading local militia [OE *ealdor* lord + MAN]

Ealing (ˈiːlɪŋ) *n* a borough of W Greater London, formed in 1965 from Acton, Ealing, and Southall. Pop: 300 947 (2001). Area: 55 sq km (21 sq miles)

-ean *suffix forming adjectives and nouns* a variant of **-an**: *Caesarean*

ear[1] (ɪə) *n* **1** the organ of hearing and balance in higher vertebrates (see **middle ear**). Related adj: **aural** **2** the outermost cartilaginous part of the ear in mammals, esp man **3** the sense of hearing **4** sensitivity to musical sounds, poetic diction, etc: *he has an ear for music* 5 attention; consideration (esp in **give ear to, lend an ear**) 6 an object resembling the external ear 7 **all ears** very attentive; listening carefully 8 **a thick ear** *inf* a blow on the ear 9 **fall on deaf ears** to be ignored or pass unnoticed 10 **in one ear and out the other** heard but unheeded 11 **keep** (*or* **have**) **one's ear to the ground** to be or try to be well informed about current trends and opinions 12 **out on one's ear** *inf* dismissed unceremoniously 13 **play by ear** 13a *inf* to act according to the demands of a situation; improvise 13b to perform a musical piece on an instrument without written music 14 **turn a deaf ear** to be deliberately unresponsive 15 **up to one's ears** *inf* deeply involved, as in work or debt [OE *ēare*] > **eared** *adj* > **'earless** *adj*

ear² (ɪə) *n* 1 the part of a cereal plant, such as wheat or barley, that contains the seeds, grains, or kernels ▷ *vb* 2 (*intr*) (of cereal plants) to develop such parts [OE *ēar*]

earache ('ɪərˌeɪk) *n* pain in the ear

earbash ('ɪəˌbæʃ) *vb* (*intr*) *Austral & NZ sl* to talk incessantly > **'earˌbashing** *n* > **'earˌbasher** *n*

earbash ('ɪəˌbæʃ) *vb* (*intr*) *Austral and NZ slang.* to talk incessantly > **'earˌbasher** *n* > **'earˌbashing** *n*

eardrum ('ɪəˌdrʌm) *n* the nontechnical name for **tympanic membrane**

earful ('ɪəfʊl) *n inf* 1 something heard or overheard 2 a rebuke or scolding

Earhart ('ɛəˌhɑːt) *n* **Amelia** 1898–1937, US aviator: the first woman to fly the Atlantic (1928). She disappeared on a Pacific flight (1937)

earl (ɜːl) *n* (in Britain) a nobleman ranking below a marquess and above a viscount. Female equivalent: **countess** [OE *eorl*] > **'earldom** *n*

Earl Grey *n* a variety of China tea flavoured with oil of bergamot

Earl Marshal *n* an officer of the English peerage who presides over the College of Heralds and organizes royal processions and other important ceremonies

early ('ɜːlɪ) *adj, adv* **earlier, earliest** 1 before the expected or usual time 2 occurring in or characteristic of the first part of a period or sequence 3 occurring in or characteristic of a period far back in time 4 occurring in the near future 5 **in the early days** during the first years of any enterprise, such as marriage [OE *ǣrlīce*, from *ǣr* ERE + *-līce* -LY²] > **'earliness** *n*

early closing *n Brit* the shutting of shops in a town one afternoon each week

Early English *n* a style of architecture used in England in the 12th and 13th centuries, characterized by lancet arches and plate tracery
▷ www.britainexpress.com/architecture/early-english.htm

early music *n* 1 music of the Middle Ages and Renaissance, sometimes also including music of the baroque and early classical periods ▷ (*modifier*) **early-music** 2 of or denoting an approach to musical performance emphasizing the use of period instruments and historically researched scores and playing techniques: *the early-music movement*
▷ www.kings-music.co.uk/emr.htm
▷ www.s-hamilton.k12.ia.us/antiqua/instrumt.html

early warning *n* advance notice of some impending event

earmark ('ɪəˌmɑːk) *vb* (*tr*) 1 to set aside or mark out for a specific purpose 2 to make an identification mark on the ear of (a domestic animal) ▷ *n* 3 such a mark of identification 4 any distinguishing mark or characteristic

earmuff ('ɪəˌmʌf) *n* one of a joined pair of pads of fur or cloth for keeping the ears warm

earn (ɜːn) *vb* 1 to gain or be paid (money or other payment) in return for work or service 2 (*tr*) to acquire or deserve through behaviour or action 3 (*tr*) (of securities, investments, etc) to gain (interest, profit, etc) [OE *earnian*]

earned income *n* income derived from paid employment

earner ('ɜːnə) *n* 1 a person who earns money 2 *sl* an activity or thing that produces income, esp illicitly: *a nice little earner*

earnest¹ ('ɜːnɪst) *adj* 1 serious in mind or intention 2 characterized by sincerity of intention 3 demanding or receiving serious attention ▷ *n* 4 **in earnest** with serious or sincere intentions [OE *eornost*] > **'earnestly** *adv* > **'earnestness** *n*

earnest² ('ɜːnɪst) *n* 1 a part of something given in advance as a guarantee of the remainder 2 Also called: **earnest money** *contract law* something given, usually a nominal sum of money, to confirm a contract 3 any token of something to follow [C13 from OF *erres* pledges, pl of *erre* earnest money, from L *arrha*, from *arrabō* pledge, from Gk *arrabon*, from Heb. *'ērābhōn* pledge]

earnings ('ɜːnɪŋz) *pl n* 1 money or other payment earned 2 the profits of an enterprise

EAROM ('ɪərɒm) *n computing acronym for* electrically alterable read only memory

earphone ('ɪəˌfəʊn) *n* a device for converting electric currents into sound waves, held close to or inserted into the ear

ear piercing *n* 1 the making of a hole in the lobe of an ear, using a sterilized needle, so that earrings may be worn fastened in the hole ▷ *adj* **ear-piercing** 2 so loud or shrill as to hurt the ears

earplug ('ɪəˌplʌg) *n* a piece of soft material placed in the ear to keep out noise or water

earring ('ɪəˌrɪŋ) *n* an ornament for the ear, usually clipped onto the lobe or fastened through a hole pierced in the lobe

earshot ('ɪəˌʃɒt) *n* the range or distance within which sound may be heard (esp in **out of earshot,** etc)

ear-splitting *adj* so loud or shrill as to hurt the ears

earth (ɜːθ) *n* 1 (*sometimes cap*) the third planet from the sun, the only planet on which life is known to exist. Related adjs.: **terrestrial, telluric** 2 the inhabitants of this planet: *the whole earth rejoiced* 3 the dry surface of this planet; land; ground 4 the loose soft material on the surface of the ground that consists of disintegrated rock particles, mould, clay, etc; soil 5 worldly or temporal matters as opposed to the concerns of the spirit 6 the hole in which some species of burrowing animals, esp foxes, live 7 *chem* See **rare earth, alkaline earth** 8 Also (US and Canad): **ground** 8a a connection between an electric circuit or device and the earth, which is at zero potential 8b a terminal to which this connection is made 9 (*modifier*) *astrol* of or relating to a group of three signs of the zodiac: Taurus, Virgo, and Capricorn 10 **come back** *or* **down to earth** to return to reality from a fantasy or daydream 11 **on earth** used as an intensifier in **what on earth, who on earth,** etc 12 **run to earth** 12a to hunt (an animal, esp a fox) to its earth and trap it there 12b to find (someone) after hunting ▷ *vb* 13 Also (US and Canad): **ground** (*tr*) to connect (a circuit, device, etc) to earth ▷ See also **earth up** [OE *eorthe*]
▷ http://earthobservatory.nasa.gov
▷ www.earth.nasa.gov
▷ www.itc.nl

earthbound ('ɜːθˌbaʊnd) *adj* 1 confined to the earth 2 heading towards the earth

earth closet *n* a type of lavatory in which earth is used to cover excreta

earthen ('ɜːθən) *adj* (*prenominal*) 1 made of baked clay: *an earthen pot* 2 made of earth

earthenware ('ɜːθənˌwɛə) *n* **a** vessels, etc, made of baked clay **b** (*as adj*): *an earthenware pot*

earth-grazer *n* an asteroid in an orbit that takes it close to the earth. Also called: **near-earth asteroid**

earthly ('ɜːθlɪ) *adj* **earthlier, earthliest 1** of or characteristic of the earth as opposed to heaven; materialistic; worldly **2** (*usually with a negative*) *inf* conceivable or possible (in **not an earthly (chance)**, etc) > **'earthliness** *n*

earthman ('ɜːθ,mæn) *n, pl* **earthmen** (esp in science fiction) an inhabitant or native of the earth. Also called: **earthling**

earthnut ('ɜːθ,nʌt) *n* **1** a perennial umbelliferous plant of Europe and Asia, having edible dark brown tubers **2** any of various plants having an edible root, tuber, or underground pod, such as the peanut or truffle

earthquake ('ɜːθ,kweɪk) *n* a series of vibrations at the earth's surface caused by movement along a fault plane, volcanic activity, etc. Related adj: **seismic**

earth science *n* any of various sciences, such as geology and geography, that are concerned with the structure, age, etc, of the earth
▷ www.geologylink.com
▷ www.psigate.ac.uk/newsite/earth-gateway.html
▷ http://personal.cmich.edu/~francım/homepage.htm
▷ www.geologynet.com/indexa.htm
▷ www.iers.org/links/geo/

earth up *vb* (*tr, adv*) to cover (part of a plant) with soil to protect from frost, light, etc

earthward ('ɜːθwəd) *adj* **1** directed towards the earth ▷ *adv* **2** a variant of **earthwards**

earthwards ('ɜːθwədz) *or* **earthward** *adv* towards the earth

earthwork ('ɜːθ,wɜːk) *n* **1** excavation of earth, as in engineering construction **2** a fortification made of earth

earthworm ('ɜːθ,wɜːm) *n* any of numerous worms which burrow in the soil and help aerate and break up the ground

earthy ('ɜːθɪ) *adj* **earthier, earthiest 1** of, composed of, or characteristic of earth **2** unrefined, coarse, or crude > **'earthily** *adv* > **'earthiness** *n*

ear trumpet *n* a trumpet-shaped instrument held to the ear: an old form of hearing aid

earwax ('ɪə,wæks) *n* the nontechnical name for **cerumen**

earwig ('ɪə,wɪg) *n* **1** any of various insects that typically have an elongated body with small leathery forewings, semicircular membranous hindwings, and curved forceps at the tip of the abdomen ▷ *vb* **earwigs, earwigging, earwigged 2** (*intr*) *inf* to eavesdrop **3** (*tr*) *arch* to attempt to influence (a person) by private insinuation [OE *ēarwicga*, from *ēare* ear + *wicga* beetle, insect; prob. from superstition that the insect crept into human ears]

earwigging ('ɪə,wɪgɪŋ) *n inf* a scolding or harangue: *I'll give him an earwigging about that*

earworm ('ɪə,wɜːm) *n inf* an irritatingly catchy tune [C20 from German *Ohrwurm* earwig]

ease (iːz) *n* **1** freedom from discomfort, worry, or anxiety **2** lack of difficulty, labour, or awkwardness **3** rest, leisure, or relaxation **4** freedom from poverty; affluence: *a life of ease* **5** lack of restraint, embarrassment, or stiffness: *ease of manner* **6 at ease 6a** *mil* (of a standing soldier, etc) in a relaxed position with the feet apart, rather than at attention **6b** a command to adopt such a position **6c** in a relaxed attitude or frame of mind ▷ *vb* **eases, easing, eased 7** to make or become less burdensome **8** (*tr*) to relieve (a person) of worry or care; comfort **9** (*tr*) to make comfortable or give rest to **10** (*tr*) to make less difficult; facilitate **11** to move or cause to move into, out of, etc, with careful manipulation **12** (when *intr*, often foll by *off* or *up*) to lessen or cause to lessen in severity, pressure, tension, or strain **13 ease oneself** *or* **ease nature** *arch, euphemistic* to urinate or defecate [C13 from OF *aise* ease, opportunity, from L *adjacēns* neighbouring (area); see ADJACENT] > **'easeful** *adj*

easel ('iːzᵊl) *n* a frame, usually an upright tripod, for supporting or displaying an artist's canvas, a blackboard, etc [C17 from Du. *ezel*; ult. from L *asinus* ass]

easement ('iːzmənt) *n* **1** *property law* the right enjoyed by a landowner of making limited use of his neighbour's land, as by crossing it to reach his own property **2** the act of easing or something that brings ease

easily ('iːzɪlɪ) *adv* **1** with ease; without difficulty or exertion **2** by far; undoubtedly: *easily the best* **3** probably; almost certainly

easiness ('iːzɪnɪs) *n* **1** the quality or condition of being easy to accomplish, do, obtain, etc **2** ease or relaxation of manner; nonchalance

east (iːst) *n* **1** the direction along a parallel towards the sunrise, at 90° to north; the direction of the earth's rotation **2 the east** (*often cap*) any area lying in or towards the east. Related adj: **oriental 3** (*usually cap*) *cards* the player or position at the table corresponding to east on the compass ▷ *adj* **4** situated in, moving towards, or facing the east **5** (esp of the wind) from the east ▷ *adv* **6** in, to, or towards the east **7 back East** *Canad* in or to E Canada, esp east of Quebec ▷ Symbol: E [OE *ēast*]

East (iːst) *n* **the 1** the continent of Asia regarded as culturally distinct from Europe and the West; the Orient **2** the countries under Communist rule and those under Communist rule until *c.* 1991, lying mainly in the E hemisphere ▷ *adj* **3** of or denoting the eastern part of a specified country, area, etc

East Africa *n* a region of Africa comprising Kenya, Uganda, and Tanzania

East African *adj* **1** of or relating to East Africa or its inhabitants ▷ *n* **2** a native or inhabitant of East Africa

East Anglia *n* **1** a region of E England south of the Wash: consists of Norfolk and Suffolk, and parts of Essex and Cambridgeshire **2** an Anglo-Saxon kingdom that consisted of Norfolk and Suffolk in the 6th century AD; became a dependency of Mercia in the 8th century

East Anglian *adj* **1** of or relating to East Anglia or its inhabitants ▷ *n* **2** a native or inhabitant of East Anglia

East Ayrshire *n* a council area of SW Scotland, comprising the E part of the historical county of Ayrshire: part of Strathclyde region from 1975 to 1996: chiefly agricultural. Administrative centre: Kilmarnock. Pop: 120 235 (2001). Area: 1252 sq km (483 sq miles)

East Bengal *n* the part of the former Indian province of Bengal assigned to Pakistan in 1947 (now Bangladesh)

East Bengali *adj* **1** of or relating to East Bengal (now Bangladesh) or its inhabitants ▷ *n* **2** a native or inhabitant of East Bengal

East Berlin *n* (formerly) the part of Berlin under East German control

eastbound ('iːst,baʊnd) *adj* going or leading towards the east

Eastbourne ('iːst,bɔːn) *n* a resort in SE England, in East Sussex on the English Channel. Pop: 83 200 (1991 est)

east by north *n* one point on the compass north of east

east by south *n* one point on the compass south of east

East Cape *n* **1** the easternmost point of New Guinea, on Milne Bay **2** the easternmost point of New Zealand, on North Island **3** the former name for Cape **Dezhnev**

East China Sea *n* part of the N Pacific, between the E coast of China and the Ryukyu Islands

East Dunbartonshire *n* a council area of central Scotland to the N of Glasgow: part of Strathclyde region from 1975 until 1996: mainly agricultural and residential. Administrative centre: Kirkintilloch. Pop: 108 243 (2001). Area: 172 sq km (66 sq miles)

East End *n* **the** a densely populated part of E London containing former industrial and dock areas

Easter ('iːstə) *n* **1** a festival of the Christian Church commemorating the Resurrection of Christ: falls on the Sunday following the first full moon after the vernal equinox **2** Also called: **Easter Sunday, Easter Day** the day on which this festival is celebrated **3** the period between Good Friday and Easter Monday ▷ Related adj: **Paschal** [OE *ēastre*]

Easter cactus *n* a Brazilian cactus, *Rhipsalidopsis gaertneri*, widely cultivated as an ornamental for its showy red flowers

Easter egg *n* **1** an egg given to children at Easter, usually a chocolate egg or a hen's egg with its shell painted **2** *computing* an unexpected entertaining effect in an applications program, initiated when certain actions are carried out, such as pressing certain key combinations

Easter Island *n* an isolated volcanic island in the Pacific, 3700 km (2300 miles) west of Chile, of which it is a dependency: discovered on Easter Sunday, 1722; annexed by Chile in 1888; noted for the remains of an aboriginal culture, which includes gigantic stone figures. Pop: 2000 (latest est). Area: 166 sq km (64 sq miles). Also called: **Rapa Nui**

easterly (ˈiːstəlɪ) *adj* **1** of or in the east ▷ *adv, adj* **2** towards the east **3** from the east: *an easterly wind* ▷ *n, pl* **easterlies 4** a wind from the east

eastern (ˈiːstən) *adj* **1** situated in or towards the east **2** facing or moving towards the east

Eastern Cape *n* a province of S South Africa; formed in 1994 from the E part of the former Cape Province: service industries, agriculture, and mining. Capital: Bisho. Pop: 6 658 670 (1999 est). Area: 169 600 sq km (65 483 sq miles). Also called: **Eastern Province**
▷ www.ecprov.gov.za
▷ www.ectourism.co.za

Eastern Church *n* **1** any of the Christian Churches of the former Byzantine Empire **2** any Church owing allegiance to the Orthodox Church **3** any Church having Eastern forms of liturgy and institutions

Easterner (ˈiːstənə) *n* (*sometimes not cap*) a native or inhabitant of the east of any specified region

Eastern Ghats *pl n* a mountain range in S India, parallel to the Bay of Bengal: united with the Western Ghats by the Nilgiri Hills; forms the E margin of the Deccan plateau

eastern hemisphere *n* (*often caps*) **1** that half of the globe containing Europe, Asia, Africa, and Australia, lying east of the Greenwich meridian **2** the lands in this, esp Asia

Eastern Orthodox Church *n* another name for the **Orthodox Church**

Eastern Townships *n* an area of central Canada, in S Quebec: consists of 11 townships south of the St Lawrence

Eastertide (ˈiːstəˌtaɪd) *n* the Easter season

East Flanders *n* a province of W Belgium: low-lying, with reclaimed land in the northeast: textile industries. Capital: Ghent. Pop: 1 361 623 (2000 est). Area: 2979 sq km (1150 sq miles)

East German *adj* **1** of or relating to the former republic of East Germany or its inhabitants ▷ *n* **2** a native or inhabitant of the former East Germany

East Germany *n* a former republic in N central Europe: established in 1949 and declared a sovereign state by the Soviet Union in 1954; Communist regime replaced by a multiparty democracy in 1989; reunited with West Germany in 1990. Official name: **German Democratic Republic** Abbreviations: **DDR, GDR.** See also **Germany**

East Indian *n* **1** Also called: **Indo-Caribbean** *Caribbean* an immigrant to the countries of the Caribbean (West Indies) who is of Indian origin; an Asian West Indian ▷ *adj* **2** *US & Canad* of, relating to, or originating in the East Indies

East Indies *pl n* **the 1** the Malay Archipelago, including or excluding the Philippines **2** SE Asia in general

easting (ˈiːstɪŋ) *n* **1** *naut* the net distance eastwards made by a vessel moving towards the east **2** *cartography* the distance eastwards of a point from a given meridian indicated by the first half of a map grid reference

East Kilbride (kɪlˈbraɪd) *n* a town in W Scotland, in South Lanarkshire near Glasgow: designated a new town in 1947. Pop: 70 422 (1991)

Eastleigh (ˈiːstˌliː) *n* a town in S England, in S Hampshire: railway engineering industry. Pop: 49 934 (1991)

East London *n* a port in S South Africa, in S Eastern Cape province. Pop: 102 325 (1991)

East Lothian *n* a council area and historical county of E central Scotland, on the Firth of Forth and the North Sea: part of Lothian region from 1975 to 1996: chiefly agricultural. Administrative centre: Haddington. Pop: 90 088 (2001). Area: 678 sq km (262 sq miles)

Eastman (ˈiːstmən) *n* **George** 1854–1932, US manufacturer of photographic equipment: noted for the introduction of roll film and developments in colour photography

east-northeast *n* **1** the point on the compass or the direction midway between northeast and east ▷ *adj, adv* **2** in, from, or towards this direction

East Pakistan *n* the former name (until 1971) of **Bangladesh**

East Pakistani *adj* **1** of or relating to East Pakistan (now Bangladesh) or its inhabitants ▷ *n* **2** a native or inhabitant of the former East Pakistan

East Prussia *n* a former province of NE Germany on the Baltic Sea: separated in 1919 from the rest of Germany by the Polish Corridor and Danzig: in 1945 Poland received the south part, the Soviet Union the north. German name: **Ostpreussen** (ostˈprɔysən)

East Prussian *adj* **1** of or relating to the former German province of East Prussia or its inhabitants ▷ *n* **2** a native or inhabitant of the former East Prussia

East Renfrewshire *n* a council area of W central Scotland, comprising part of the historical county of Renfrewshire; part of Strathclyde region from 1975 to 1996: chiefly agricultural and residential. Administrative centre: Giffnock. Pop: 89 311 (2001). Area: 173 sq km (67 sq miles)

East Riding of Yorkshire *n* a county of NE England, a historical division of Yorkshire on the North Sea and the Humber estuary: became part of Humberside in 1974; reinstated as an independent unitary authority in 1996, with a separate authority for Kingston upon Hull: chiefly agricultural and low-lying, with various industries in Hull. Administrative centre: Beverley. Pop (excluding Hull): 314 076 (2001). Area (excluding Hull): 748 sq km (675 sq miles)

east-southeast *n* **1** the point on the compass or the direction midway between east and southeast ▷ *adj, adv* **2** in, from, or towards this direction

East Sussex *n* a county of SE England comprising part of the former county of Sussex: mainly undulating agricultural land, with the South Downs and seaside resorts in the south: Brighton and Hove became an independent unitary authority in 1997 but is part of the geographical and ceremonial county. Administrative centre: Lewes. Pop (excluding Brighton and Hove): 492 324 (2001). Area (excluding Brighton and Hove): 1795 sq km (693 sq miles)

East Timor *n* a small country in SE Asia, comprising part of the island of Timor: colonized by Portugal in the 19th century; declared independence in 1975 but immediately invaded by Indonesia; under UN administration from 1999 and an independent state from 2002. It is mountainous with a monsoon climate; subsistence agriculture is the main occupation. Languages: Portuguese, Tetun (a lingua franca), and

Bahasa Indonesia. Religion: Roman Catholic majority. Currency: US dollar. Capital: Dilli. Pop: 750 000 (2002 est). Area: 14 874 sq km (5743 sq miles)
▷ www.gov.east-timor.org

East Timorese *adj* **1** of or relating to East Timor or its inhabitants ▷ *n* **2** a native or inhabitant of East Timor

eastward ('i:stwəd) *adj* **1** situated or directed towards the east ▷ *adv* **2** a variant of **eastwards** ▷ *n* **3** the eastward part, direction, etc > '**eastwardly** *adv, adj*

eastwards ('i:stwədz) *or* **eastward** *adv* towards the east

Eastwood ('i:stwʊd) *n* **Clint** born 1930, US film actor and director. His films as an actor include *The Good The Bad and The Ugly* (1966), and *Dirty Harry* (1971), and as actor and director *Play Misty for Me* (1971), *Unforgiven* (1993), and *Mystic River* (2003)

easy ('i:zɪ) *adj* **easier, easiest 1** not requiring much labour or effort; not difficult **2** free from pain, care, or anxiety **3** not restricting; lenient: *easy laws* **4** tolerant and undemanding; easy-going: *an easy disposition* **5** readily influenced; pliant: *an easy victim* **6** not constricting; loose: *an easy fit* **7** not strained or extreme; moderate: *an easy pace* **8** *inf* ready to fall in with any suggestion made; not predisposed: *he is easy about what to do* **9** *sl* sexually available ▷ *adv* **10** *inf* in an easy or relaxed manner **11 easy does it** *inf* go slowly and carefully; be careful **12 go easy** (*usually imperative;* often foll by *on*) to exercise moderation **13 stand easy** *mil* a command to soldiers standing at ease that they may relax further **14 take it easy 14a** to avoid stress or undue hurry **14b** to remain calm [C12 from OF *aisié*, p.p. of *aisier* to relieve, EASE]

easy-care *adj* (esp of a fabric or garment) hard-wearing and requiring no special treatment during washing, etc

easy chair *n* a comfortable upholstered armchair

easy-going ('i:zɪ'gəʊɪŋ) *adj* **1** relaxed in manner or attitude; excessively tolerant **2** moving at a comfortable pace: *an easy-going horse*

easy meat *n inf* **1** someone easily seduced or deceived **2** something easy

easy money *n* **1** money made with little effort, sometimes dishonestly **2** *commerce* money that can be borrowed at a low interest rate

Easy Street *n* (*sometimes not caps*) *inf* a state of financial security

eat (i:t) *vb* **eats, eating, ate, eaten 1** to take into the mouth and swallow (food, etc), esp after biting and chewing **2** (*tr;* often foll by *away* or *up*) to destroy as if by eating: *the damp had eaten away the woodwork* **3** (often foll by *into*) to use up or waste: *taxes ate into his inheritance* **4** (often foll by *into* or *through*) to make (a hole, passage, etc) by eating or gnawing: *rats ate through the floor* **5** to take or have (a meal or meals): *we eat at six* **6** (*tr*) to include as part of one's diet: *he doesn't eat fish* **7** (*tr*) *inf* to cause to worry: *what's eating you?* ▷ See also **eat out, eats, eat up** [OE *etan*] > '**eater** *n*

eatable ('i:təbᵊl) *adj* fit or suitable for eating; edible

eatables ('i:təbᵊlz) *pl n* food

eating ('i:tɪŋ) *n* **1** food, esp in relation to quality or taste: *this fruit makes excellent eating* ▷ *adj* **2** suitable for eating uncooked: *eating apples* **3** relating to or for eating: *an eating house*

eat out *vb* (*intr, adv*) to eat away from home, esp in a restaurant

eats (i:ts) *pl n inf* articles of food; provisions

eat up *vb* (*adv, mainly tr*) **1** (*also intr*) to eat or consume entirely **2** *inf* to listen to with enthusiasm or appreciation: *the audience ate up his every word* **3** (*often passive*) *inf* to affect grossly: *she was eaten up by jealousy* **4** *inf* to travel (a distance) quickly: *we just ate up the miles*

eau de Cologne (ˌəʊ də kə'ləʊn) *n* See **cologne** [F, lit.: water of Cologne]

eau de nil (ˌəʊ də 'ni:l) *n, adj* (of) a pale yellowish-green colour [F, lit.: water of (the) Nile]

eau de vie (ˌəʊ də 'vi:) *n* brandy or other spirits [F, lit.: water of life]

eaves (i:vz) *pl n* the edge of a roof that projects beyond the wall [OE *efes*]

eavesdrop ('i:vzˌdrɒp) *vb* **eavesdrops, eavesdropping, eavesdropped** (*intr*) to listen secretly to the private conversation of others [C17 back formation from *evesdropper*, from OE *yfesdrype* water dripping from the eaves] > '**eavesˌdropper** *n*

ebb (ɛb) *vb* (*intr*) **1** (of tide water) to flow back or recede. ▷ Cf **flow** (sense 8) **2** to fall away or decline ▷ *n* **3a** the flowing back of the tide from high to low water or the period in which this takes place **3b** (*as modifier*): *the ebb tide.* ▷ Cf **flood** (sense 3) **4 at a low ebb** in a state of weakness or decline [OE *ebba*]

Ebbinghaus ('ɛbɪŋhaʊs) *n* **Hermann** ('hɛrman) 1850–1909, German experimental psychologist who undertook the first systematic and large-scale studies of memory and devised tests using nonsense syllables

Ebbw Vale ('ɛbu: veɪl) *n* a town in S Wales, in Blaenau Gwent county borough: a former coal mining centre. Pop: 19 484 (1991)

EBCDIC ('ɛpsɪˌdɪk) *n acronym for* extended binary-coded decimal-interchange code: a computer code for representing alphanumeric characters

Ebert (*German* 'e:bərt) *n* **Friedrich** ('fri:drɪç) 1871–1925, German Social Democratic statesman; first president of the German Republic (1919–25)

ebon ('ɛbᵊn) *adj, n* a poetic word for **ebony** [C14 from L *hebenus;* see EBONY]

ebonite ('ɛbəˌnaɪt) *n* another name for **vulcanite**

ebonize *or* **ebonise** ('ɛbəˌnaɪz) *vb* **ebonizes, ebonizing, ebonized** *or* **ebonises, ebonising, ebonised** (*tr*) to stain or otherwise finish in imitation of ebony

ebony ('ɛbənɪ) *n, pl* **ebonies 1** any of various tropical and subtropical trees that have hard dark wood **2** the wood of such a tree **3a** a black colour **3b** (*as adj*): *an ebony skin* [C16 *hebeny*, from LL, from Gk, from *ebenos* ebony, from Egyptian]

e-book *n* a book in electronic form [C20 electronic *book*]

Ebor. ('i:bɔ:) *abbrev for* Eboracensis [L.: (Archbishop) of York]

Eboracum (i:'bɒrəkəm, ˌi:bɔ:'rɑ:kəm) *n* the Roman name for **York** (sense 1)

EBRD *abbrev for* European Bank for Reconstruction and Development
▷ www.ebrd.com

Ebro ('i:brəʊ; *Spanish* 'eβro) *n* the second largest river in Spain, rising in the Cantabrian Mountains and flowing southeast to the Mediterranean. Length: 910 km (565 miles)

ebullient (ɪ'bʌljənt, ɪ'bʊl-) *adj* **1** overflowing with enthusiasm or excitement **2** boiling [C16 from L *ēbullīre* to bubble forth, be boisterous, from *bullīre* to BOIL[1]] > **e'bullience** *or* **e'bulliency** *n*

ebulliometer (ɪˌbʌlɪ'ɒmɪtə) *n physics* a device used to determine the boiling point of a solution

ebullition (ˌɛbə'lɪʃən) *n* **1** the process of boiling **2** a sudden outburst, as of intense emotion [C16 from LL *ēbullītiō;* see EBULLIENT]

EC *abbrev for:* **1** European Community (now subsumed within the European Union) **2** (in London postal codes) East Central

ec- *combining form* out from; away from: *eccentric; ecdysis* [from Gk *ek* (before a vowel *ex*) out of, away from; see EX-[1]]

ECB *abbrev for* European Central Bank
▷ www.ecb.int

Ecbatana (ɛk'bætənə) *n* an ancient city in Iran, on the site of modern Hamadān; capital of Media and royal residence of the Persians and Parthians

eccentric (ɪk'sɛntrɪk) *adj* **1** deviating or departing from convention; irregular or odd **2** situated away from the centre or the axis **3** not having a common centre: *eccentric circles* **4** not precisely circular ▷ *n* **5** a person who deviates from normal forms of behaviour **6** a device for converting rotary motion to reciprocating motion [C16 from Med. L *eccentricus*, from Gk *ekkentros*, from *ek-* EX-[1] + *kentron* centre] > **ec'centrically** *adv*

eccentricity (ˌɛksɛn'trɪsɪtɪ) *n, pl* **eccentricities** **1** unconventional or irregular behaviour **2** the state of being eccentric **3** deviation from a circular path or orbit **4** *geom* a number that expresses the shape of a conic section **5** the degree of displacement of the geometric centre of a part from the true centre, esp of the axis of rotation of a wheel

eccl. *or* **eccles.** *abbrev for* ecclesiastic(al)

Eccles¹ ('ɛkᵊlz) *n* a town in NW England, in Salford unitary authority, Greater Manchester. Pop: 36 000 (1991)

Eccles² ('ɛkᵊlz) *n* Sir **John Carew** 1903–97, Australian physiologist: shared the Nobel prize for physiology (1963) with A. L. Hodgkin and A. F. Huxley for their work on conduction of nervous impulses

Eccles. *or* **Eccl.** *Bible. abbrev for* Ecclesiastes

ecclesiastic (ɪˌkliːzɪ'æstɪk) *n* **1** a clergyman or other person in holy orders ▷ *adj* **2** of or associated with the Christian Church or clergy

ecclesiastical (ɪˌkliːzɪ'æstɪkᵊl) *adj* of or relating to the Christian Church > **ecˌclesi'astically** *adv*

ecclesiasticism (ɪˌkliːzɪ'æstɪˌsɪzəm) *n* exaggerated attachment to the practices or principles of the Christian Church

ecclesiology (ɪˌkliːzɪ'ɒlədʒɪ) *n* **1** the study of the Christian Church **2** the study of Church architecture and decoration > **ecclesiological** (ɪˌkliːzɪə'lɒdʒɪkᵊl) *adj*

Ecclestone ('ɛkəlstən) *n* **Bernard**, known as *Bernie*. born 1930, British businessman and sports administrator; head of Formula One motor racing from 1995

eccrine ('ɛkrɪn) *adj* of or denoting glands that secrete externally, esp the sweat glands. ▷ Cf **apocrine** [from Gk *ekkrinein*, from *ek-* EC- + *krinein* to separate] > **eccrinology** (ˌɛkrɪ'nɒlədʒɪ) *n*

ecdemic (ɛk'dɛmɪk) *adj* not indigenous or endemic; foreign: *an ecdemic disease*

ecdysis ('ɛkdɪsɪs) *n, pl* **ecdyses** (-ˌsiːz) the periodic shedding of the cuticle in insects and other arthropods or the outer epidermal layer in reptiles [C19 NL, from Gk *ekdusis*, from *ekduein* to strip, from *ek-* EX-[1] + *duein* to put on]

Ecevit ('ɛʃəvɪt) *n* **Bülent** ('buːlənt) born 1925, Turkish politician and journalist: prime minister of Turkey (1974, 1977, 1978–79, 1998–2002)

ECG *abbrev for:* **1** electrocardiogram **2** electrocardiograph

echelon ('ɛʃəˌlɒn) *n* **1** a level of command, responsibility, etc (esp in **the upper echelons**) **2** *mil* **2a** a formation in which units follow one another but are offset sufficiently to allow each unit a line of fire ahead **2b** a group formed in this way ▷ *vb* **3** to assemble in echelon [C18 from F *échelon*, lit.: rung of a ladder, from OF *eschiele* ladder, from L *scāla*]

echidna (ɪ'kɪdnə) *n, pl* **echidnas** *or* **echidnae** (-niː) a spine-covered monotreme mammal of Australia and New Guinea, having a long snout and claws. Also called: **spiny anteater** [C19 from NL, from L: viper, from Gk *ekhidna*]

echinoderm (ɪ'kaɪnəʊˌdɜːm) *n* any of various marine invertebrates characterized by tube feet, a calcite body-covering, and a five-part symmetrical body. The group includes the starfish, sea urchins, and sea cucumbers

echinus (ɪ'kaɪnəs) *n, pl* **echini** (-naɪ) **1** *archit* a moulding between the shaft and the abacus of a Doric column **2** any sea urchin of the genus *Echinus*, such as the Mediterranean edible sea urchin [C14 from L, from Gk *ekhinos*]

echo ('ɛkəʊ) *n, pl* **echoes** **1a** the reflection of sound or other radiation by a reflecting medium, esp a solid object **1b** the sound so reflected **2** a repetition or imitation, esp an unoriginal reproduction of another's opinions **3** something that evokes memories **4** (*sometimes pl*) an effect that continues after the original cause has disappeared: *echoes of the French Revolution* **5** a person who copies another, esp one who obsequiously agrees with another's opinions **6a** the signal reflected by a radar target **6b** the trace produced by such a signal on a radar screen ▷ *vb* **echoes, echoing, echoed** **7** to resound or cause to resound with an echo **8** (*intr*) (of sounds) to repeat or resound by echoes; reverberate **9** (*tr*) (of persons) to repeat (words, opinions, etc) in imitation, agreement, or flattery **10** (*tr*) (of things) to resemble or imitate (another style, an earlier model, etc) [C14 via L from Gk *ēkhō*; rel. to Gk *ēkhē* sound] > **'echoing** *adj* > **'echoless** *adj* > **'echo-ˌlike** *adj*

Echo ('ɛkəʊ) *n Greek myth* a nymph who, spurned by Narcissus, pined away until only her voice remained

echocardiography (ˌɛkəʊˌkɑːdɪ'ɒgrəfɪ) *n* examination of the heart using ultrasound techniques

echo chamber *n* a room with walls that reflect sound. It is used to make acoustic measurements and as a recording studio when echo effects are required. Also called: **reverberation chamber**

echography (ɛ'kɒgrəfɪ) *n* medical examination of the internal structures of the body by means of ultrasound

echoic (ɛ'kəʊɪk) *adj* **1** characteristic of or resembling an echo **2** onomatopoeic; imitative

echolalia (ˌɛkəʊ'leɪlɪə) *n psychiatry* the tendency to repeat mechanically words just spoken by another person [C19 from NL, from ECHO + Gk *lalia* talk, chatter]

echolocation (ˌɛkəʊləʊ'keɪʃən) *n* determination of the position of an object by measuring the time taken for an echo to return from it and its direction

echo sounder *n* a navigation device that determines depth by measuring the time taken for a pulse of sound to reach the sea bed or a submerged object and for the echo to return > **echo sounding** *n*

echovirus *or* **ECHO virus** ('ɛkəʊˌvaɪrəs) *n* any of a group of viruses that can cause symptoms of mild meningitis, the common cold, or infections of the intestinal and respiratory tracts [C20 from initials of *Enteric Cytopathic Human Orphan* ("orphan" because orig. believed to be unrelated to any disease) + VIRUS]

Eck (ɛk) *n* **Johann** (jo'han), original name *Johann Mayer*. 1486–1543, German Roman Catholic theologian; opponent of Luther and the Reformation

Eckert ('ɛkət) *n* **John Presper** 1919–95, US electronics engineer: built the first electronic computer with John W. Mauchly in 1946

éclair (eɪ'klɛə, ɪ'klɛə) *n* a finger-shaped cake of choux pastry, usually filled with cream and covered with chocolate [C19 from F, lit.: lightning (prob. because it does not last long)]

eclampsia (ɪ'klæmpsɪə) *n pathol* a toxic condition that sometimes develops in the last three months of pregnancy, characterized by high blood pressure, weight gain, and convulsions [C19 from NL, from Gk *eklampsis* a shining forth]

éclat (eɪ'klɑː) *n* **1** brilliant or conspicuous success, effect, etc **2** showy display; ostentation **3** social distinction **4** approval; acclaim; applause [C17 from F, from *éclater* to burst]

eclectic (ɪ'klɛktɪk, ɛ'klɛk-) *adj* **1** selecting from various styles, ideas, methods, etc **2** composed of elements drawn from a variety of sources, styles, etc ▷ *n* **3** a person who favours an eclectic approach [C17 from Gk *eklektikos*, from *eklegein* to select, from *legein* to gather] > **e'clectically** *adv* > **e'clecticism** *n*

eclipse (ɪ'klɪps) *n* **1** the total or partial obscuring of one celestial body by another (**total eclipse** *or* **partial eclipse**).

Ee

A **solar eclipse** occurs when the moon passes between the sun and the earth; a **lunar eclipse** when the earth passes between the sun and the moon **2** the period of time during which such a phenomenon occurs **3** any dimming or obstruction of light **4** a loss of importance, power, fame, etc, esp through overshadowing by another ▷ *vb* **eclipses, eclipsing, eclipsed** (*tr*) **5** to cause an eclipse of **6** to cast a shadow upon; obscure **7** to overshadow or surpass [C13 back formation from OE *eclypsis*, from L, from Gk *ekleipsis* a forsaking, from *ekleipein* to abandon] > **e'clipser** *n*

eclipsing binary *n* a binary star whose orbital plane lies in or near the line of sight so that one component is regularly eclipsed by its companion

ecliptic (ɪ'klɪptɪk) *n* **1** *astron* **1a** the great circle on the celestial sphere representing the apparent annual path of the sun relative to the stars **1b** (*as modifier*): *the ecliptic plane* **2** an equivalent great circle on the terrestrial globe ▷ *adj* **3** of or relating to an eclipse > **e'cliptically** *adv*

eclogue ('ɛklɒg) *n* a pastoral or idyllic poem, usually in the form of a conversation [C15 from L *ecloga* short poem, collection of extracts, from Gk *eklogē* selection]

eclosion (ɪ'kləʊʒən) *n* the emergence of an insect larva from the egg or an adult from the pupal case [C19 from F, from *éclore* to hatch, ult. from L *exclūdere* to shut out]

Eco ('ɛkəʊ) *n* **Umberto** born 1932, Italian writer. His novels include *The Name of the Rose* (1981) and *The Island of the Day Before* (1995)

eco- *combining form* denoting ecology or ecological: *ecocide; ecosphere*

ecocentric (ˌiːkəʊ'sɛntrɪk) *adj* having a serious concern for environmental issues: *ecocentric management*

Ecofin ('ɛkəʊˌfɪn) *n* the council of European finance ministers

ecofriendly ('iːkəʊˌfrɛndlɪ) *adj* having a beneficial effect on the environment or at least not causing environmental damage

ecol. *abbrev for:* **1** ecological **2** ecology

E. coli (iː'kəʊlaɪ) *n* short for *Escherichia coli*, see ***Escherichia***

ecological (ˌiːkə'lɒdʒɪkᵊl) *adj* **1** of or relating to ecology **2** (of a practice, policy, product, etc) tending to benefit or cause minimal damage to the environment > ˌ**eco'logically** *adv*

ecological footprint *n* the amount of productive land appropriated on average by each person (in the world, a country, etc) for food, water, transport, housing, waste management, and other purposes

ecology (ɪ'kɒlədʒɪ) *n* **1** the study of the relationships between living organisms and their environment **2** the set of relationships of a particular organism with its environment [C19 from G *Ökologie*, from Gk *oikos* house (hence, environment)] > **e'cologist** *n*

e-commerce *or* **ecommerce** ('iː'kɒmɜːs) *n* business transactions conducted on the Internet [C20 from E- + COMMERCE]

econ. *abbrev for:* **1** economical **2** economics **3** economy

econometrics (ɪˌkɒnə'mɛtrɪks) *n* (*functioning as sing*) the application of mathematical and statistical techniques to economic theories > **eˌcono'metric** *or* **eˌcono'metrical** *adj* > **econometrician** (ɪˌkɒnəmə'trɪʃən) *or* **econometrist** (ˌiːkə'nɒmətrɪst, ˌɛkə-) *n*

▷ www.econometricsociety.org
▷ www.res.org.uk/econometrics/econometricshome.asp

economic (ˌiːkə'nɒmɪk, ˌɛkə-) *adj* **1** of or relating to an economy, economics, or finance **2** *Brit* capable of being produced, operated, etc, for profit; profitable **3** concerning or affecting material resources or welfare: *economic pests* **4** concerned with or relating to the necessities of life; utilitarian **5** a variant of **economical** **6** *inf* inexpensive; cheap

economical (ˌiːkə'nɒmɪkᵊl, ˌɛkə-) *adj* **1** using the minimum required; not wasteful **2** frugal; thrifty **3** a variant of **economic** (senses 1–4) **4** *euphemistic* deliberately withholding information (esp in **economical with the truth**) > ˌ**eco'nomically** *adv*

economic indicator *n* a statistical measure representing an economic variable: *the retail price index is an economic indicator of the actual level of prices*

economic migrant *or* **refugee** *n* a person who emigrates from a poor country to a developed one in the hope of improving his or her standard of living

economic rationalism *n Austral & NZ* an economic policy based on the efficiency of market forces, characterized by minimal government intervention, tax cuts, privatization, and deregulation of labour markets

economics (ˌiːkə'nɒmɪks, ˌɛkə-) *n* **1** (*functioning as sing*) the social science concerned with the production and consumption of goods and services and the analysis of the commercial activities of a society **2** (*functioning as pl*) financial aspects

▷ http://economics.about.com
▷ www.res.org.uk
▷ http://allserv.rug.ac.be/~gdegeest

economic sanctions *pl n* any actions taken by one nation or group of nations to harm the economy of another nation or group, often to force a political change

economist (ɪ'kɒnəmɪst) *n* a specialist in economics

economize *or* **economise** (ɪ'kɒnəˌmaɪz) *vb* **economizes, economizing, economized** *or* **economises, economising, economised** (often foll by *on*) to limit or reduce (expense, waste, etc) > **eˌconomi'zation** *or* **eˌconomi'sation** *n*

economy (ɪ'kɒnəmɪ) *n, pl* **economies** **1** careful management of resources to avoid unnecessary expenditure or waste; thrift **2** a means or instance of this; saving **3** sparing, restrained, or efficient use **4a** the complex of activities concerned with the production, distribution, and consumption of goods and services **4b** a particular type or branch of this: *a socialist economy* **5** the management of the resources, finances, income, and expenditure of a community, business enterprise, etc **6a** a class of travel in aircraft, cheaper and less luxurious than first class **6b** (*as modifier*): *economy class* **7** (*modifier*) purporting to offer a larger quantity for a lower price: *economy pack* **8** the orderly interplay between the parts of a system or structure [C16 via L from Gk *oikonomia* domestic management, from *oikos* house + *-nomia*, from *nemein* to manage]

economy class *n* **1** the cheapest class of air travel, offering the most basic service, the narrowest seats, and the most restricted legroom ▷ *adj* **2** of or relating to this class of travel.

economy-class syndrome *n* (*not in technical usage*) a deep-vein thrombosis that has developed in the legs or pelvis of a person travelling for a long period of time in cramped conditions [C20 reference to the restricted legroom of cheaper seats on passenger aircraft]

ecoregion ('iːkəʊˌriːdʒən) *n* an area defined by its environmental conditions, esp climate, landforms, and soil characteristics

ecosphere ('iːkəʊˌsfɪə, 'ɛkəʊ-) *n* the planetary ecosystem, consisting of all living organisms and their environment

écossaise (ˌeɪkɒ'seɪz) *n* **1** a lively dance in two-four time **2** the tune for such a dance [C19 F, lit.: Scottish (dance)]

ecosystem ('iːkəʊˌsɪstəm, 'ɛkəʊ-) *n ecology* a system involving the interactions between a community of living organisms in a particular area and its nonliving environment [C20 from ECO- + SYSTEM]

ecoterrorist ('iːkəʊˌtɛrərɪst) *n* a person who uses violence in order to achieve environmentalist aims

ecotourism ('iːkəʊˌtʊərɪzəm) *n* tourism which is designed to contribute to the protection of the environment or at least minimize damage to it, often involving travel to areas of natural interest in developing countries or participation in environmental projects > ˈ**eco**ˌ**tourist** *n*

eco-warrior (ˈiːkəʊˌwɒrɪə) *n inf* a person who zealously pursues environmentalist aims

▷ www.ecowas.int

ecru (ˈɛkruː, ˈeɪkruː) *n, adj* (of) a greyish-yellow to a light greyish colour [c19 from F, from *é-* (intensive) + *cru* raw, from L *crūdus*; see CRUDE]

ecstasy (ˈɛkstəsɪ) *n, pl* **ecstasies** **1** (*often pl*) a state of exalted delight, joy, etc; rapture **2** intense emotion of any kind: *an ecstasy of rage* **3** *psychol* overpowering emotion sometimes involving temporary loss of consciousness: often associated with mysticism **4** *sl* 3,4-methylenedioxymethamphetamine (MDMA): a powerful drug that acts as a stimulant and can produce hallucinations [c14 from OF via Med. L from Gk *ekstasis* displacement, trance, from *ex-* out + *histanai* to cause to stand]

ecstatic (ɛkˈstætɪk) *adj* **1** in a trancelike state of rapture or delight **2** showing or feeling great enthusiasm ▷ *n* **3** a person who has periods of intense trancelike joy > **ec**ˈ**statically** *adv*

ECT *abbrev for* electroconvulsive therapy

ecto- *combining form* indicating outer, outside [from Gk *ektos* outside, from *ek, ex* out]

ectoblast (ˈɛktəʊˌblæst) *n* another name for **ectoderm** > ˌ**ecto**ˈ**blastic** *adj*

ectoderm (ˈɛktəʊˌdɜːm) *or* **exoderm** *n* the outer germ layer of an animal embryo, which gives rise to epidermis and nervous tissue > ˌ**ecto**ˈ**dermal** *or* ˌ**ecto**ˈ**dermic** *adj*

ectomorph (ˈɛktəʊˌmɔːf) *n* a type of person having a body build characterized by thinness, weakness, and a lack of weight > ˌ**ecto**ˈ**morphic** *adj* > ˈ**ecto**ˌ**morphy** *n*

-ectomy *n combining form* indicating surgical excision of a part: *appendectomy* [from NL *-ectomia*, from Gk *ek-* out + -TOMY]

ectopic pregnancy (ɛkˈtɒpɪk) *n pathol* the abnormal development of a fertilized egg outside the uterus, usually within a Fallopian tube

ectoplasm (ˈɛktəʊˌplæzəm) *n* **1** *cytology* in some cells, the outer layer of cytoplasm **2** *spiritualism* the substance supposedly emanating from the body of a medium during trances > ˌ**ecto**ˈ**plasmic** *adj*

ECU (ˈeɪkjuː; *sometimes* ˈiːˈsiːˈjuː) *n acronym for* European Currency Unit: a former unit of currency based on the composite value of several different currencies in the European Union and functioning both as the reserve asset and accounting unit of the European Monetary System; replaced by the euro in 1999

Ecua. *abbrev for* Ecuador

Ecuador (ˈɛkwəˌdɔː) *n* a republic in South America, on the Pacific: under the Incas when Spanish colonization began in 1532; gained independence in 1822; declared a republic in 1830. It consists chiefly of a coastal plain in the west, separated from the densely forested upper Amazon basin (Oriente) by ranges and plateaus of the Andes. Official language: Spanish; Quechua is also widely spoken. Religion: Roman Catholic majority. Currency: US dollar. Capital: Quito. Pop: 12 879 000 (2001 est). Area: 283 560 sq km (109 483 sq miles)

▷ www.ec-gov.net

▷ www.vivecuador.com/html2/eng/tourism_news.htm

Ecuadorean (ˌɛkwəˈdɔːrɪən) *adj* **1** of or relating to Ecuador or its inhabitants ▷ *n* **2** a native or inhabitant of Ecuador

ecumenical, oecumenical (ˌiːkjʊˈmɛnɪkəl, ˌɛk-) *or* **ecumenic, oecumenic** *adj* **1** of or relating to the Christian Church throughout the world, esp with regard to its unity **2** tending to promote unity among Churches **3** *rare* universal; general [c16 via LL from Gk *oikoumenikos*, from *oikein* to inhabit, from *oikos* house] > ˌ**ecu**ˈ**menically** *or* ˌ**oecu**ˈ**menically** *adv*

ecumenism (ɪˈkjuːməˌnɪzəm, ˈekjʊm-), **ecumenicism** (ˌiːkjʊˈmɛnɪˌsɪzəm, ˌɛk-) *or* **ecumenicalism** (ˌiːkjʊˈmɛnɪkəˌlɪzəm, ˌɛk-) *n* the aim of unity among all Christian churches throughout the world

▷ http://ecumenism.net/

eczema (ˈɛksɪmə; ɪgˈziːmə) *n pathol* a skin inflammation with lesions that scale, crust, or ooze a serous fluid, often accompanied by intense itching [c18 from NL, from Gk *ekzema*, from *ek-* out + *zein* to boil] > **eczematous** (ɛkˈsɛmətəs) *adj*

ed. *abbrev for:* **1** edited **2** (*pl* **eds.**) edition **3** (*pl* **eds.**) editor

-ed[1] *suffix.* forming the past tense of most English verbs [OE *-de, -ede, -ode, -ade*]

-ed[2] *suffix* forming the past participle of most English verbs [OE *-ed, -od, -ad*]

-ed[3] *suffix forming adjectives from nouns* possessing or having the characteristics of: *salaried; red-blooded* [OE *-ede*]

Edam (ˈiːdæm) *n* **1** a town in the NW Netherlands, in North Holland province, on the IJsselmeer: cheese, light manufacturing. Pop: 24 572 (latest est) **2** a hard round mild-tasting Dutch cheese, yellow in colour with a red outside covering

EDC *abbrev for* European Defence Community

Edda (ˈɛdə) *n* **1** Also called: **Elder Edda, Poetic Edda** a 12th-century collection of mythological Old Norse poems **2** Also called: **Younger Edda, Prose Edda** a treatise on versification together with a collection of Scandinavian myths, legends, and poems (?1222) [c18 ON] > **Eddaic** (ɛˈdeɪɪk) *adj*

Eddington (ˈɛdɪŋtən) *n* Sir **Arthur Stanley** 1882–1944, English astronomer and physicist, noted for his research on the motion, internal constitution, and luminosity of stars and for his elucidation of the theory of relativity

eddo (ˈɛdəʊ) *n, pl* **eddoes** another name for **taro**

eddy (ˈɛdɪ) *n, pl* **eddies** **1** a movement in air, water, or other fluid in which the current doubles back on itself causing a miniature whirlwind or whirlpool **2** a deviation from or disturbance in the main trend of thought, life, etc ▷ *vb* **eddies, eddying, eddied** **3** to move or cause to move against the main current [c15 prob. from ON]

Eddy (ˈɛdɪ) *n* **Mary Baker** 1821–1910, US religious leader; founder of the Christian Science movement (1866)

eddy current *n* an electric current induced in a massive conductor by an alternating magnetic field

Eddystone Rocks (ˈɛdɪstən) *n* a dangerous group of rocks at the W end of the English Channel, southwest of Plymouth: lighthouse

Ede (ˈeɪdə) *n* a city in the central Netherlands, in Gelderland province. Pop: 101 542 (1999 est)

Edelman (ˈɛdᵊlmən) *n* **Gerald Maurice** born 1929, US biochemist: he shared the Nobel prize for physiology or medicine (1972) with Rodney Porter for determining the structure of antibodies

edelweiss (ˈeɪdᵊlˌvaɪs) *n* a small alpine flowering plant having white woolly oblong leaves and a tuft of floral leaves surrounding the flowers [c19 G, lit.: noble white]

edema (ɪˈdiːmə) *n, pl* **edemata** (-mətə) the usual US spelling of **oedema**

Eden (ˈiːdᵊn) *n* Sir (**Robert**) **Anthony,** Earl of Avon. 1897–1977, British Conservative statesman; foreign secretary (1935–38; 1940–45; 1951–55) and prime minister (1955–57). He resigned after the controversy caused by the occupation of the Suez Canal zone by British and French forces (1956)

Eden Project *n* the world's largest greenhouse, built in a disused clay pit near St Austell, Cornwall, to study plant populations in a variety of environments

edentate (iːˈdɛnteɪt) *n* **1** any mammal of the order *Edentata*, of tropical Central and South America, which have few or no teeth. The order includes anteaters, sloths, and armadillos ▷ *adj* **2** of or relating to the order *Edentata* [C19 from L *ēdentātus* lacking teeth, from *ēdentāre* to render toothless, from *e-* out + *dēns* tooth]

Edessa (ɪ'dɛsə) *n* **1** an ancient city on the N edge of the Syrian plateau, founded as a Macedonian colony by Seleucus I: a centre of early Christianity. Modern name: **Urfa** **2** a market town in Greece: ancient capital of Macedonia. Pop: 15 980 (latest est). Ancient name: **Aegae** ('iːgiː) Modern Greek name: **Édhessa**

Edgar ('ɛdgə) *n* **1** 944–975 AD, king of Mercia and Northumbria (957–975) and of England (959–975) **2** ?1074–1107, king of Scotland (1097–1107), fourth son of Malcolm III. He overthrew his uncle Donald to gain the throne **3** **David** born 1948, British dramatist, noted for political plays such as *Destiny* (1976), *Maydays* (1983), and *Albert Speer* (1999): he adapted (1980) *Nicholas Nickleby* for the RSC

Edgar Atheling ('æθɪlɪŋ) *n* ?1050–?1125, grandson of Edmund II; Anglo-Saxon pretender to the English throne in 1066

edge (ɛdʒ) *n* **1** a border, brim, or margin **2** a brink or verge **3** a line along which two faces or surfaces of a solid meet **4** the sharp cutting side of a blade **5** keenness, sharpness, or urgency **6** force, effectiveness, or incisiveness: *the performance lacked edge* **7** a ridge **8** **have the edge on** *or* **over** to have a slight advantage or superiority over **9** **on edge** **9a** nervously irritable; tense **9b** nervously excited or eager **10** **set (someone's) teeth on edge** to make (someone) acutely irritated or uncomfortable ▷ *vb* **edges, edging, edged** **11** (*tr*) to provide an edge or border for **12** (*tr*) to shape or trim the edge or border of (something) **13** to push (one's way, someone, something, etc) gradually, esp edgeways **14** (*tr*) *cricket* to hit (a bowled ball) with the edge of the bat **15** (*tr*) to sharpen (a knife, etc) [OE *ecg*] > **'edger** *n*

Edgehill (ˌɛdʒ'hɪl) *n* a ridge in S Warwickshire: site of the indecisive first battle between Charles I and the Parliamentarians (1642) in the Civil War

edgeways ('ɛdʒˌweɪz) *or esp US & Canad* **edgewise** ('ɛdʒˌwaɪz) *adv* **1** with the edge forwards or uppermost **2** on, by, with, or towards the edge **3** **get a word in edgeways** (*usually with a negative*) to interrupt a conversation in which someone else is talking incessantly

Edgeworth ('ɛdʒwɜːθ) *n* **Maria** 1767–1849, Anglo-Irish novelist: her works include *Castle Rackrent* (1800) and *The Absentee* (1812)

edging ('ɛdʒɪŋ) *n* **1** anything placed along an edge to finish it, esp as an ornament **2** the act of making an edge ▷ *adj* **3** used for making an edge: *edging shears*

edgy ('ɛdʒɪ) *adj* **edgier, edgiest** (*usually postpositive*) nervous, irritable, tense, or anxious > **'edgily** *adv* > **'edginess** *n*

edh (ɛð) *or* **eth** (ɛθ, ɛð) *n* a character of the runic alphabet (ð) used to represent the voiced dental fricative as in *then, mother, bathe*

Édhessa (*Greek* 'ɛðɛsa) *n* transliteration of the Modern Greek name for **Edessa**

edible ('ɛdɪbᵊl) *adj* fit to be eaten; eatable [C17 from LL *edibilis*, from L *edere* to eat] > ˌ**edi'bility** *n*

edibles ('ɛdɪbᵊlz) *pl n* articles fit to eat; food

edict ('iːdɪkt) *n* **1** a decree or order issued by any authority **2** any formal or authoritative command, proclamation, etc [C15 from L *ēdictum*, from *ēdīcere* to declare] > **e'dictal** *adj*

edifice ('ɛdɪfɪs) *n* **1** a building, esp a large or imposing one **2** a complex or elaborate institution or organization [C14 from OF, from L *aedificium*, from *aedificāre* to build; see EDIFY]

edify ('ɛdɪˌfaɪ) *vb* **edifies, edifying, edified** (*tr*) to improve the morality, intellect, etc, of, esp by instruction [C14 from OF, from L *aedificāre* to construct, from *aedēs* a dwelling, temple + *facere* to make] > ˌ**edifi'cation** *n* > **'edifiˌer** *n* > **'ediˌfying** *adj* > **'ediˌfyingly** *adv*

Edinburgh[1] ('ɛdɪnbərə, -brə) *n* **1** the capital of Scotland and seat of the Scottish Parliament (from 1999), in City of Edinburgh council area on the S side of the Firth of Forth: became the capital in the 15th century; castle; universities (1583, 1966); commercial and cultural centre, noted for its annual festival. Pop: 401 910 (1991) **2** **City of** a council area in central Scotland, created from part of Lothian region in 1996. Pop: 448 624 (2001). Area: 262 sq km (101 sq miles)

Edinburgh[2] ('ɛdɪnbərə, -brə) *n* **Duke of,** title of Prince *Philip Mountbatten*. born 1921, husband of Elizabeth II of Great Britain and Northern Ireland

Edirne (ɛ'dirnɛ) *n* a city in NW Turkey: a Thracian town, rebuilt and renamed by the Roman emperor Hadrian. Pop: 115 083 (1997). Former name: **Adrianople**

Edison ('ɛdɪsᵊn) *n* **Thomas Alva** 1847–1931, US inventor. He patented more than a thousand inventions, including the phonograph, the incandescent electric lamp, the microphone, and the kinetoscope

edit ('ɛdɪt) *vb* **edits, editing, edited** (*tr*) **1** to prepare (text) for publication by checking and improving its accuracy, clarity, etc **2** to be in charge of (a publication, esp a periodical) **3** to prepare (a film, tape, etc) by rearrangement or selection of material **4** (*tr*) to modify (a computer file) **5** (often foll by *out*) to remove, as from a manuscript or film [C18 back formation from EDITOR]

edit. *abbrev for:* **1** edited **2** edition **3** editor

edition (ɪ'dɪʃən) *n* **1** *printing* **1a** the entire number of copies of a book or other publication printed at one time **1b** a copy from this number: *a first edition* **2** one of a number of printings of a book or other publication, issued at separate times with alterations, amendments, etc **3a** an issue of a work identified by its format: *a leather-bound edition* **3b** an issue of a work identified by its editor or publisher: *the Oxford edition* **4** a particular instance of a television or radio programme broadcast [C16 from L *ēditiō* a bringing forth, publishing, from *ēdere* to give out; see EDITOR]

editor ('ɛdɪtə) *n* **1** a person who edits written material for publication **2** a person in overall charge of a newspaper or periodical **3** a person in charge of one section of a newspaper or periodical: *the sports editor* **4** *films* a person who makes a selection and arrangement of shots **5** a person in overall control of a television or radio programme that consists of various items [C17 from LL: producer, exhibitor, from *ēdere* to give out, publish, from *ē-* out + *dāre* to give] > **'editorˌship** *n*

editorial (ˌɛdɪ'tɔːrɪəl) *adj* **1** of or relating to editing or editors **2** of, relating to, or expressed in an editorial **3** of or relating to the content of a publication ▷ *n* **4** an article in a newspaper, etc, expressing the opinion of the editor or the publishers > ˌ**edi'torially** *adv*

editorialize *or* **editorialise** (ˌɛdɪ'tɔːrɪəˌlaɪz) *vb* **editorializes, editorializing, editorialized** *or* **editorialises, editorialising, editorialised** (*intr*) to express an opinion as in an editorial > ˌ**ediˌtoriali'zation** *or* ˌ**ediˌtoriali'sation** *n*

Edmonton ('ɛdməntən) *n* a city in W Canada, capital of Alberta: oil industry. Pop: 616 306 (1991)

Edmund ('ɛdmənd) *n* **Saint,** also called *Saint Edmund Rich.* 1175–1240, English churchman: archbishop of Canterbury (1234–40). Feast day: Nov. 16

Edmund I *n* ?922–946 AD, king of England (940–946)

Edmund II *n* called *Edmund Ironside.* ?980–1016, king of England in 1016. His succession was contested by Canute and they divided the kingdom between them

EDT (in the US and Canada) *abbrev for* Eastern Daylight Time

educate ('ɛdjʊˌkeɪt) *vb* **educates, educating, educated** (*mainly tr*) **1** (*also intr*) to impart knowledge by formal instruction to (a pupil); teach **2** to provide schooling for **3** to improve or develop (a person, taste, skills, etc) **4** to train for some particular purpose or occupation [c15 from L *ēducāre* to rear, educate, from *dūcere* to lead] > ˈ**educable** *or* ˈ**eduˌcatable** *adj* > ˌ**educaˈbility** *or* ˌ**eduˌcataˈbility** *n* > ˈ**educative** *adj*

educated (ˈɛdjʊˌkeɪtɪd) *adj* **1** having an education, esp a good one **2** displaying culture, taste, and knowledge; cultivated **3** (*prenominal*) based on experience or information (esp in **an educated guess**)

education (ˌɛdjʊˈkeɪʃən) *n* **1** the act or process of acquiring knowledge **2** the knowledge or training acquired by this process **3** the act or process of imparting knowledge, esp at a school, college, or university **4** the theory of teaching and learning **5** a particular kind of instruction or training: *a university education* > ˌ**eduˈcationalist** *or* ˌ**eduˈcationist** *n*
▷ www.dfes.gov.uk/index.htm
▷ www.sosig.ac.uk/education
▷ http://canada.gc.ca/azind/eindex_e.html
▷ www.fed.gov.au/KSP
▷ www.minedu.govt.nz
▷ http://education.pwv.gov.za/

educational (ˌɛdjʊˈkeɪʃənᵊl) *adj* **1** providing knowledge; instructive or informative: *an educational toy* **2** of or relating to education > ˌ**eduˈcationally** *adv*

educator (ˈɛdjʊˌkeɪtə) *n* **1** a person who educates; teacher **2** a specialist in education

educe (ɪˈdjuːs) *vb* **educes, educing, educed** (*tr*) *rare* **1** to evolve or develop **2** to draw out or elicit (information, solutions, etc) [c15 from L *ēdūcere*, from *ē-* out + *dūcere* to lead] > **eˈducible** *adj* > **eductive** (ɪˈdʌktɪv) *adj*

Edward[1] (ˈɛdwəd) *n* **Lake** a lake in central Africa, between Uganda and the Democratic Republic of Congo (formerly Zaïre) in the Great Rift Valley: empties through the Semliki River into Lake Albert. Area: about 2150 sq km (830 sq miles). Former official name: **Lake Amin**

Edward[2] (ˈɛdwəd) *n* known as *the Black Prince*. 1330–76, Prince of Wales, the son of Edward III of England. He won victories over the French at Crécy (1346) and Poitiers (1356) in the Hundred Years' War

Edward I *n* 1239–1307, king of England (1272–1307); son of Henry III. He conquered Wales (1284) but failed to subdue Scotland

Edward II *n* 1284–1327, king of England (1307–27); son of Edward I. He invaded Scotland but was defeated by Robert Bruce at Bannockburn (1314). He was deposed by his wife Isabella and Roger Mortimer; died in prison

Edward III *n* 1312–77, king of England (1327–77); son of Edward II. His claim to the French throne in right of his mother Isabella provoked the Hundred Years' War (1337)

Edward IV *n* 1442–83, king of England (1461–70; 1471–83); son of Richard, duke of York. He defeated Henry VI in the Wars of the Roses and became king (1461). In 1470 Henry was restored to the throne, but Edward recovered the crown by his victory at Tewkesbury

Edward V *n* 1470–?83, king of England in 1483; son of Edward IV. He was deposed by his uncle, Richard, Duke of Gloucester (Richard III), and is thought to have been murdered with his brother in the Tower of London

Edward VI *n* 1537–53, king of England (1547–53), son of Henry VIII and Jane Seymour. His uncle the Duke of Somerset was regent until 1552, when he was executed. Edward then came under the control of Dudley, Duke of Northumberland

Edward VII *n* 1841–1910, king of Great Britain and Ireland (1901–10); son of Queen Victoria

Edward VIII *n* 1894–1972, king of Great Britain and Ireland in 1936; son of George V and brother of George VI. He abdicated in order to marry an American divorcée, Mrs Wallis Simpson (1896–1986); created Duke of Windsor (1937)

Edwardian (ɛdˈwɔːdɪən) *adj* of or characteristic of the reign of Edward VII > **Edˈwardianˌism** *n*

Edwards (ˈɛdwədz) *n* **Jonathan** born 1966, British athlete: gold medallist in the Olympic triple jump (2000)

Edward the Confessor *n* **Saint** ?1002–66, king of England (1042–66); son of Ethelred II; founder of Westminster Abbey. Feast day: Oct 13

Edward the Elder *n* died 924 AD, king of England (899–924), son of Alfred the Great

Edward the Martyr *n* **Saint** ?963–978 AD, king of England (975–78), son of Edgar: murdered. Feast day: March 18

Edwin (ˈɛdwɪn) *n* ?585–633 AD, king of Northumbria (617–633) and overlord of all England except Kent

-ee *suffix forming nouns* **1** indicating a recipient of an action (as opposed, esp in legal terminology, to the agent): *assignee; lessee* **2** indicating a person in a specified state or condition: *absentee* **3** indicating a diminutive form of something: *bootee* [via OF *-é, -ée*, p.p. endings, from L *-ātus, -āta* -ATE[1]]

EEC *abbrev for* European Economic Community (now subsumed within the European Union)
▷ www.encyclopedia.com/html/E/EuropnE1C1.asp

EEG *abbrev for:* **1** electroencephalogram **2** electroencephalograph

eel (iːl) *n* **1** any teleost fish such as the European freshwater eel, having a long snakelike body, a smooth slimy skin, and reduced fins **2** any of various similar animals, such as the mud eel and the electric eel **3** an evasive or untrustworthy person [OE *ǣl*] > ˈ**eel-ˌlike** *adj* > ˈ**eely** *adj*

eelgrass (ˈiːlˌgrɑːs) *n* any of several perennial submerged marine plants having grasslike leaves

eelpout (ˈiːlˌpaʊt) *n* **1** a marine eel-like fish **2** another name for **burbot** [OE *ǣlepūte*]

eelworm (ˈiːlˌwɜːm) *n* any of various nematode worms, esp the wheatworm and the vinegar eel

e'en (iːn) *adv, n poetic or arch* contraction of **even**[2] or **evening**

e'er (ɛə) *adv poetic or arch* contraction of **ever**

-eer *or* **-ier** *suffix* **1** (*forming nouns*) indicating a person who is concerned with or who does something specified: *auctioneer; engineer; profiteer; mutineer* **2** (*forming verbs*) to be concerned with something specified: *electioneer* [from OF *-ier*, from L *-arius* -ARY]

eerie (ˈɪərɪ) *adj* **eerier, eeriest** uncannily frightening or disturbing; weird [c13 orig. Scot. & N English, prob. from OE *earg* cowardly] > ˈ**eerily** *adv* > ˈ**eeriness** *n*

EFA *abbrev for* European Fighter Aircraft

eff (ɛf) *vb* **1** euphemism for **fuck** (esp in **eff off**) **2 eff and blind** *sl* to use obscene language > ˈ**effing** *n, adj, adv*

efface (ɪˈfeɪs) *vb* **effaces, effacing, effaced** (*tr*) **1** to obliterate or make dim **2** to make (oneself) inconspicuous or humble **3** to rub out; erase [c15 from F *effacer*, lit.: to obliterate the face; see FACE] > **efˈfaceable** *adj* > **efˈfacement** *n* > **efˈfacer** *n*

effect (ɪˈfɛkt) *n* **1** something produced by a cause or agent; result **2** power to influence or produce a result **3** the condition of being operative (esp in **in** *or* **into effect**) **4 take effect** to become operative or begin to produce results **5** basic meaning or purpose (esp in **to that effect**) **6** an impression, usually contrived (esp in **for effect**) **7** a scientific phenomenon: *the Doppler effect* **8 in effect 8a** in fact; actually **8b** for all practical purposes **9** the overall impression or result ▷ *vb* **10** (*tr*) to cause to occur; accomplish [c14 from L *effectus* a performing, tendency, from *efficere* to accomplish, from *facere* to do] > **efˈfecter** *n* > **efˈfectible** *adj*

> USAGE It is quite common for *effect* to be mistakenly used where *affect* is intended, in the verb use. With initial *e* the verb is relatively uncommon and rather formal, and is a synonym of 'bring about'. Conversely, the noun is quite often

Ee

mistakenly written with an initial *a*. The following are correct: *the group is still recovering from the effects of the recession; they really are powerless to effect any change*. The next two examples are incorrect: *the full affects of the shutdown won't be felt for several more days; ...men whose lack of hair doesn't effect their self-esteem*

effective (ɪ'fɛktɪv) *adj* **1** productive of or capable of producing a result **2** in effect; operative **3** impressive: *an effective entrance* **4** (*prenominal*) actual rather than theoretical **5** (of a military force, etc) equipped and prepared for action ▷ *n* **6** a serviceman equipped and prepared for action > **ef'fectively** *adv* > **ef'fectiveness** *n*

effects (ɪ'fɛkts) *pl n* **1** Also called: **personal effects** personal belongings **2** lighting, sounds, etc, to accompany a stage, film, or broadcast production

effectual (ɪ'fɛktjʊəl) *adj* **1** capable of or successful in producing an intended result; effective **2** (of documents, etc) having legal force > **ef,fectu'ality** *or* **ef'fectualness** *n*

effectually (ɪ'fɛktjʊəlɪ) *adv* **1** with the intended effect **2** in effect

effectuate (ɪ'fɛktjʊ,eɪt) *vb* **effectuates, effectuating, effectuated** (*tr*) to cause to happen; effect; accomplish > **ef,fectu'ation** *n*

effeminate (ɪ'fɛmɪnɪt) *adj* (of a man or boy) displaying characteristics regarded as typical of a woman; not manly [C14 from L *effēmināre* to make into a woman, from *fēmina* woman] > **ef'feminacy** *or* **ef'feminateness** *n*

effendi (ɛ'fɛndɪ) *n, pl* **effendis 1** (in the Ottoman Empire) a title of respect **2** (in Turkey since 1934) the oral title of address equivalent to *Mr* [C17 from Turkish *efendi* master, from Mod. Gk *aphentēs*, from Gk *authentēs* lord, doer]

efferent ('ɛfərənt) *adj physiol* carrying or conducting outwards, esp from the brain or spinal cord. ▷ Cf **afferent** [C19 from L *efferre* to bear off, from *ferre* to bear] > **'efference** *n*

effervesce (,ɛfə'vɛs) *vb* **effervesces, effervescing, effervesced** (*intr*) **1** (of a liquid) to give off bubbles of gas **2** (of a gas) to issue in bubbles from a liquid **3** to exhibit great excitement, vivacity, etc [C18 from L *effervescere* to foam up, ults from *fervēre* to boil, ferment] > **,effer'vescingly** *adv*

effervescent (,ɛfə'vɛsᵊnt) *adj* **1** (of a liquid) giving off bubbles of gas **2** high-spirited; vivacious > **,effer'vescence** *n*

effete (ɪ'fi:t) *adj* **1** weak or decadent **2** exhausted; spent **3** (of animals or plants) no longer capable of reproduction [C17 from L *effētus* exhausted by bearing, from *fētus* having brought forth; see FETUS] > **ef'feteness** *n*

efficacious (,ɛfɪ'keɪʃəs) *adj* capable of or successful in producing an intended result; effective [C16 from L *efficāx* powerful, efficient, from *efficere* to achieve] > **efficacy** ('ɛfɪkəsɪ) *or* **,effi'caciousness** *n*

efficiency (ɪ'fɪʃənsɪ) *n, pl* **efficiencies 1** the quality or state of being efficient **2** the ratio of the useful work done by a machine, etc, to the energy input, often expressed as a percentage

efficient (ɪ'fɪʃənt) *adj* **1** functioning or producing effectively and with the least waste of effort; competent **2** *philosophy* producing a direct effect [C14 from L *efficiēns* effecting]

effigy ('ɛfɪdʒɪ) *n, pl* **effigies 1** a portrait, esp as a monument **2** a crude representation of someone, used as a focus for contempt or ridicule (often in **burn** *or* **hang in effigy**) [C18 from L *effigiēs*, from *effingere* to form, portray, from *fingere* to shape]

effleurage (,ɛflɜ:'rɑ:ʒ) *n med* a light stroking movement used in massage [C19 from F]

effloresce (,ɛflɔ:'rɛs) *vb* **effloresces, efflorescing, effloresced** (*intr*) **1** to burst forth as into flower; bloom **2** to become powdery by loss of water or crystallization **3** to become encrusted with powder or crystals as a result of chemical change or evaporation [C18 from L *efflōrēscere* to blossom, from *flōrēscere*, from *flōs* flower]

efflorescence (,ɛflɔ:'rɛsᵊns) *n* **1** a bursting forth or flowering **2** *chem, geol* **2a** the process of efflorescing **2b** the powdery substance formed as a result of this process **3** any skin rash or eruption > **,efflo'rescent** *adj*

effluence ('ɛflʊəns) *or* **efflux** ('ɛflʌks) *n* **1** the act or process of flowing out **2** something that flows out

effluent ('ɛflʊənt) *n* **1** liquid discharged as waste, as from an industrial plant or sewage works **2** radioactive waste released from a nuclear power station **3** a stream that flows out of another body of water **4** something that flows out or forth ▷ *adj* **5** flowing out or forth [C18 from L *effluere* to run forth, from *fluere* to flow]

effluvium (ɛ'flu:vɪəm) *n, pl* **effluvia** (-vɪə) *or* **effluviums** an unpleasant smell or exhalation, as of gaseous waste or decaying matter [C17 from L: a flowing out; see EFFLUENT] > **ef'fluvial** *adj*

effort ('ɛfət) *n* **1** physical or mental exertion **2** a determined attempt **3** achievement; creation [C15 from OF *esfort*, from *esforcier* to force, ult. from L *fortis* strong] > **'effortful** *adj* > **'effortless** *adj*

effrontery (ɪ'frʌntərɪ) *n, pl* **effronteries** shameless or insolent boldness [C18 from F, from OF *esfront* barefaced, shameless, from LL *effrons*, lit.: putting forth one's forehead]

effulgent (ɪ'fʌldʒənt) *adj* radiant; brilliant [C18 from L *effulgēre* to shine forth, from *fulgēre* to shine] > **ef'fulgence** *n* > **ef'fulgently** *adv*

effuse *vb* (ɪ'fju:z), **effuses, effusing, effused 1** to pour or flow out **2** to spread out; diffuse ▷ *adj* (ɪ'fju:s) **3** *bot* (esp of an inflorescence) spreading out loosely [C16 from L *effūsus* poured out, from *effundere* to shed]

effusion (ɪ'fju:ʒən) *n* **1** an unrestrained outpouring in speech or words **2** the act or process of being poured out **3** something that is poured out **4** *med* **4a** the escape of blood or other fluid into a body cavity or tissue **4b** the fluid that has escaped

effusive (ɪ'fju:sɪv) *adj* **1** extravagantly demonstrative of emotion; gushing **2** (of rock) formed by the solidification of magma > **ef'fusively** *adv* > **ef'fusiveness** *n*

E-FIT ('i:fɪt) *n trademark* **1** a technique which uses psychological principles and computer technology to generate a likeness of a face: used by the police to trace suspects from witnesses' descriptions **2** an image generated by this technique [C20 from Electronic Facial Identification Technique]

EFL *abbrev for* English as a Foreign Language

eft (ɛft) *n* a dialect or archaic name for a **newt** [OE *efeta*]

EFTA ('ɛftə) *n acronym for* European Free Trade Association; established in 1960 to eliminate trade tariffs on industrial products; the current members are Austria, Iceland, Norway, Sweden, and Switzerland ▷ www.efta.int

EFTPOS ('ɛftpɒs) *n acronym for* electronic funds transfer at point of sale

EFTS *abbrev for* electronic funds transfer system

Eg. *abbrev for:* **1** Egypt(ian) **2** Egyptology

e.g., eg, *or* **eg.** *abbrev for* exempli gratia [L: for example]

USAGE In careful writing which is not technical, it is best to avoid using this abbreviation and write *for example* instead. In the Bank of English the abbreviation occurs most commonly in magazines and miscellaneous brochures and junk mail, and relatively infrequently in books. There is occasional confusion between *e.g.* and *i.e.* as in *the item just got lost in the system (e.g. stuck at the bottom of a mailbag)*. Here *i.e.* was clearly meant. The correct form of the abbreviation is with two stops, although it is frequently encountered with none, or with one after the *g*

egad (ɪ'gæd, iː'gæd) *interj arch* a mild oath [c17 prob. var. of *Ah God!*]

egalitarian (ɪˌgælɪ'tɛərɪən) *adj* **1** of or upholding the doctrine of the equality of mankind ▷ *n* **2** an adherent of egalitarian principles [c19 alteration of *equalitarian*, through infl. of F *égal* equal] > **eˌgali'tarianˌism** *n*

Egbert ('ɛgbɜːt) *n* ?775–839 AD, king of Wessex (802–839); first overlord of all England (829–830)

Eger *n* **1** (*Hungarian* 'ɛgɛr) a city in N central Hungary. Pop: 60 000 (1995 est) **2** ('eːgər) the German name for **Cheb**

egg¹ (ɛg) *n* **1** the oval or round reproductive body laid by the females of birds, reptiles, fishes, insects, and some other animals, consisting of a developing embryo, its food store, and sometimes jelly or albumen, all surrounded by an outer shell or membrane **2** Also called: **egg cell** any female gamete; ovum **3** the egg of the domestic hen used as food **4** something resembling an egg, esp in shape **5** **good** (*or* **bad**) **egg** *old-fashioned inf* a good (or bad) person **6** **put** *or* **have all one's eggs in one basket** to stake everything on a single venture **7** **teach one's grandmother to suck eggs** *inf* to presume to teach someone something that he or she knows already **8** **with egg on one's face** *inf* made to look ridiculous [c14 from ON *egg*; rel. to OE *ǣg*]

egg² (ɛg) *vb* (*tr*; usually foll by *on*) to urge or incite, esp to daring or foolish acts [OE *eggian*]

egg-and-spoon race *n* a race in which runners carry an egg balanced in a spoon

eggbeater ('ɛgˌbiːtə) *n* **1** Also called: **eggwhisk** a utensil for beating eggs; whisk **2** *chiefly US & Canad* an informal name for **helicopter**

egger *or* **eggar** ('ɛgə) *n* any of various European moths having brown bodies and wings [c18 from EGG¹, from the egg-shaped cocoon]

egghead ('ɛgˌhɛd) *n inf* an intellectual

eggnog (ˌɛg'nɒg) *n* a drink made of eggs, milk, sugar, spice, and brandy, rum, or other spirit. Also called: **egg flip** [c19 from EGG¹ + NOG]

eggplant ('ɛgˌplɑːnt) *n* another name (esp US, Canad, & Austral) for **aubergine**

eggshell ('ɛgˌʃɛl) *n* **1** the hard porous outer layer of a bird's egg **2** (*modifier*) (of paint) having a very slight sheen

eggshell porcelain *or* **china** *n* a very thin translucent porcelain originally from China

egg tooth *n* (in embryo reptiles) a temporary tooth or (in birds) projection of the beak used for piercing the eggshell

Egham ('ɛgəm) *n* a town in S England, in N Surrey on the River Thames. Pop: 23 816 (1991)

eglantine ('ɛglənˌtaɪn) *n* another name for **sweetbrier** [c14 from OF *aiglent*, ult. from L *acus* needle, from *acer* sharp, keen]

EGM *abbrev for* extraordinary general meeting

Egmont¹ ('ɛgmɒnt) *n* an extinct volcano in New Zealand, in W central North Island in the **Egmont National Park**: an almost perfect cone. Height: 2518 m (8261 ft)

Egmont² ('ɛgmɒnt) *n* **Lamoral** (lamo'ral), Count of Egmont, Prince of Gavre. 1522–68, Flemish statesman and soldier. He attempted to secure limited reforms and religious tolerance in the Spanish government of the Netherlands, refused to join William the Silent's rebellion, but was nevertheless executed for treason by the Duke of Alva

ego ('iːgəʊ, 'ɛgəʊ) *n, pl* **egos** **1** the self of an individual person; the conscious subject **2** *psychoanal* the conscious mind, based on perception of the environment: modifies the antisocial instincts of the id and is itself modified by the conscience (superego) **3** one's image of oneself; morale **4** egotism; conceit [c19 from L: I]

egocentric (ˌiːgəʊ'sɛntrɪk, ˌɛg-) *adj* **1** regarding everything only in relation to oneself; self-centred ▷ *n* **2** a self-centred person; egotist > **ˌegocen'tricity** *n* > **ˌego'centrism** *n*

egoism ('iːgəʊˌɪzəm, 'ɛg-) *n* **1** concern for one's own interests and welfare **2** *ethics* the theory that the pursuit of one's own welfare is the highest good **3** self-centredness; egotism > **'egoist** *n* > **ˌego'istic** *or* **ˌego'istical** *adj*

Egoli (ɛ'gəʊlɪ) an informal name for **Johannesburg** [from Zulu *eGoli* place of gold]

egomania (ˌiːgəʊ'meɪnɪə, ˌɛg-) *n psychiatry* obsessive love for oneself > **ˌego'maniˌac** *n* > **egomaniacal** (ˌiːgəʊmə'naɪɪkᵊl, ˌɛg-) *adj*

egotism ('iːgəˌtɪzəm, 'ɛgə-) *n* **1** an inflated sense of self-importance or superiority; self-centredness **2** excessive reference to oneself [c18 from L *ego* I + -ISM] > **'egotist** *n* > **ˌego'tistic** *or* **ˌego'tistical** *adj*

ego trip *n inf* something undertaken to boost or draw attention to a person's own image or appraisal of himself

e-government *n* the provision of government information and services by means of the Internet and other computer resources [c20 *e*lectronic *government*]

egregious (ɪ'griːdʒəs, -dʒɪəs) *adj* **1** outstandingly bad; flagrant **2** *arch* distinguished; eminent [c16 from L *ēgregius* outstanding (lit.: standing out from the herd), from *ē-* out + *grex* flock, herd] > **e'gregiousness** *n*

egress ('iːgrɛs) *n* **1** Also: **egression** the act of going or coming out; emergence **2** a way out; exit **3** the right to go out or depart [c16 from L *ēgredī* to come forth, depart, from *gradī* to move, step]

egret ('iːgrɪt) *n* any of various wading birds similar to herons but usually having white plumage and, in the breeding season, long feathery plumes [c15 from OF *aigrette*, of Gmc origin]

Egypt ('iːdʒɪpt) *n* a republic in NE Africa, on the Mediterranean and Red Sea: its history dates back about 5000 years. Occupied by the British from 1882, it became an independent kingdom in 1922 and a republic in 1953. Over 96 per cent of the total area is desert, with the chief areas of habitation and cultivation in the Nile delta and valley. Cotton is the main export. Official language: Arabic. Official religion: Muslim; Sunni majority. Currency: pound. Capital: Cairo. Pop: 65 239 000 (2001 est). Area: 997 739 sq km (385 229 sq miles). Official name: **Arab Republic of Egypt**. Former official name (1958–71): **United Arab Republic**

▷ www.sis.gov.eg
▷ www.egypttourism.org
▷ www.ancientegypt.co.uk
▷ www.ancient-egypt.org

Egyptian (ɪ'dʒɪpʃən) *adj* **1** of or relating to Egypt, its inhabitants, or their dialect of Arabic **2** of or characteristic of the ancient Egyptians, their language, or culture ▷ *n* **3** a native or inhabitant of Egypt **4** a member of a people who established an advanced civilization in Egypt that flourished from the late fourth millennium BC **5** the extinct language of the ancient Egyptians

Egyptology (ˌiːdʒɪp'tɒlədʒɪ) *n* the study of the archaeology and language of ancient Egypt > **ˌEgyp'tologist** *n*

eh (eɪ) *interj* an exclamation used to express questioning surprise or to seek the repetition or confirmation of a statement or question

EHF *abbrev for* extremely high frequency

Ehrenburg *or* **Erenburg** ('ɛərənˌbɜːg; *Russian* erɪn'burk) *n* **Ilya Grigorievich** (ilj'ja gri'gɔrjɪvitʃ) 1891–1967, Soviet novelist and journalist. His novel *The Thaw* (1954) was the first published in the Soviet Union to deal with repression under Stalin

Ehrlich (*German* 'eːrlɪç) *n* **Paul** (paul) 1854–1915, German

Ee

bacteriologist, noted for his pioneering work in immunology and chemotherapy and for his discovery of a remedy for syphilis: Nobel prize for physiology or medicine 1908

EI *abbrev for:* **1** East Indian **2** East Indies **3** (in Canada) Employment Insurance

EIB *abbrev for* European Investment Bank

Eichler (*German* 'aiçlər) *n* **August Wilhelm** ('aʊgʊst 'vilhɛlm) 1839–87, German botanist: devised the system on which modern plant classification is based

Eichmann (*German* 'aiçman) *n* **Karl Adolf** ('a:dɔlf) 1902–62, Austrian Nazi official, who took a leading role in organizing the extermination of the European Jews. He escaped to Argentina after World War II, but was captured and executed in Israel as a war criminal

eider *or* **eider duck** ('aɪdə) *n* any of several sea ducks of the N hemisphere. See **eiderdown** [c18 from ON *æthr*]

eiderdown ('aɪdə,daʊn) *n* **1** the breast down of the female eider duck, used for stuffing pillows, quilts, etc **2** a thick, warm cover for a bed, enclosing a soft filling

eidetic (aɪ'dɛtɪk) *adj psychol* **1** (of visual, or sometimes auditory, images) very vivid and allowing detailed recall of something previously perceived: thought to be common in children **2** relating to or subject to such imagery [c20 from Gk *eidētikos*, from *eidos* shape, form] > **ei'detically** *adv*

Eid-ul-Adha ('i:dʊl,ɑ:də) *n* an annual Muslim festival marking the end of the pilgrimage to Mecca. Animals are sacrificed and their meat shared among the poor [from Ar. *id ul adha* festival of sacrifice]

Eid-ul-Fitr ('i:dʊl,fi:tə) *n* an annual Muslim festival marking the end of Ramadan, involving the exchange of gifts and a festive meal [from Ar. *id ul fitr* festival of fast-breaking]

Eifel ('aɪfəl; *German* 'aifəl) *n* a plateau region in W Germany, between the River Moselle and the Belgian frontier: quarrying

Eiffel ('aɪfᵊl; *French* ɛfɛl) *n* **Alexandre Gustave** (alɛksɑ̃drə gystav) 1832–1923, French engineer

Eiffel Tower ('aɪfᵊl) *n* a tower in Paris: designed by A. G. Eiffel; erected for the 1889 Paris Exposition. Height: 300 m (984 ft), raised in 1959 to 321 m (1052 ft)

Eigen (*German* 'aigən) *n* **Manfred** born 1927, German physical chemist: shared the Nobel prize for chemistry (1967) for developing his relaxation technique for studying fast reactions

Eiger (*German* 'aigər) *n* a mountain in central Switzerland, in the Bernese Alps. Height: 3970 m (13 025 ft)

eight (eɪt) *n* **1** the cardinal number that is the sum of one and seven and the product of two and four **2** a numeral, 8, VIII, etc, representing this number **3** the amount or quantity that is one greater than seven **4** something representing, represented by, or consisting of eight units **5** *rowing* **5a** a racing shell propelled by eight oarsmen **5b** the crew of such a shell **6** Also called: **eight o'clock** eight hours after noon or midnight **7** **have one over the eight** *sl* to be drunk ▷ *determiner* **8a** amounting to eight **8b** *(as pron): I could only find eight* [OE *eahta*]

eighteen ('eɪ'ti:n) *n* **1** the cardinal number that is the sum of ten and eight and the product of two and nine **2** a numeral, 18, XVIII, etc, representing this number **3** the amount or quantity that is eight more than ten **4** something represented by, representing, or consisting of 18 units ▷ *determiner* **5a** amounting to eighteen: *eighteen weeks* **5b** *(as pron): eighteen of them knew* [OE *eahtatēne*] > **'eigh'teenth** *adj, n*

eightfold ('eɪt,fəʊld) *adj* **1** equal to or having eight times as many or as much **2** composed of eight parts ▷ *adv* **3** by eight times as much

eighth (eɪtθ) *adj* **1** *(usually prenominal)* **1a** coming after the seventh and before the ninth in numbering, position, etc; being the ordinal number of *eight:* often written 8th **1b** *(as n): the eighth in line* ▷ *n* **2a** one of eight equal parts of something **2b** *(as modifier): an eighth part* **3** the fraction one divided by eight (⅛) **4** another word for **octave** ▷ *adv* **5** Also: **eighthly** after the seventh person, position, event, etc

eighth note *n music* the usual US and Canad name for **quaver**

eightsome reel ('eɪtsəm) *n* a Scottish dance for eight people

eighty ('eɪtɪ) *n, pl* **eighties** **1** the cardinal number that is the product of ten and eight **2** a numeral, 80, LXXX, etc, representing this number **3** *(pl)* the numbers 80–89, esp the 80th to the 89th year of a person's life or of a century **4** the amount or quantity that is eight times ten **5** something represented by, representing, or consisting of 80 units ▷ *determiner* **6a** amounting to eighty: *eighty pages of nonsense* **6b** *(as pron): eighty are expected* [OE *eahtatig*] > **'eightieth** *adj, n*

Eilat, Elat, *or* **Elath** (eɪ'lɑ:t) *n* a port in S Israel, on the Gulf of Aqaba: Israel's only outlet to the Red Sea. Pop: 26 010 (latest est)

eina ('eɪ,nɑ:) *interj S African* an exclamation of sudden pain [c19 Afrik., from Khoi]

Eindhoven (*Dutch* 'aɪnt,həʊvᵊn, 'ɛintho:və) *n* a city in the SE Netherlands, in North Brabant province: radio and electrical industry. Pop: 199 877 (1999 est)

Einstein ('aɪnstaɪn) *n* **Albert** 1879–1955, US physicist and mathematician, born in Germany. He formulated the special theory of relativity (1905) and the general theory of relativity (1916), and made major contributions to the quantum theory, for which he was awarded the Nobel prize for physics in 1921. He was noted also for his work for world peace

einsteinium (aɪn'staɪnɪəm) *n* a radioactive metallic transuranic element artificially produced from plutonium. Symbol: Es; atomic no.: 99; half-life of most stable isotope, ^{252}Es: 276 days [c20 NL, after Albert EINSTEIN]

Einthoven (*Dutch* 'ɛɪntho:və) *n* **Willem** 1860–1927, Dutch physiologist. A pioneer of electrocardiography, he was awarded the Nobel prize for physiology or medicine in 1924

Eire ('ɛərə) *n* **1** the Irish Gaelic name for **Ireland**[1]: often used to mean the **Republic of Ireland** **2** a former name for the **Republic of Ireland** (1937–49)

Eisenach (*German* 'aizənax) *n* a city in central Germany, in Thuringia: birthplace of Johann Sebastian Bach. Pop: 48 361 (latest est)

Eisenhower ('aɪzən,haʊə) *n* **Dwight David,** known as *Ike.* 1890–1969, US general and Republican statesman; Supreme Commander of the Allied Expeditionary Force (1943–45) and 34th president of the US (1953–61). He commanded Allied forces in Europe and North Africa (1942), directed the invasion of Italy (1943), and was Supreme Commander of the combined land forces of NATO (1950–52)

Eisenstadt (*German* 'aizənʃtat) *n* a town in E Austria, capital of Burgenland province: Hungarian until 1921. Pop: 10 506 (1991)

Eisenstein ('aɪzᵊn,staɪn; *Russian* ejzɪn'ʃtjejn) *n* **Sergei Mikhailovich** (sɪr'gjej mi'xajləvitʃ) 1898–1948, Soviet film director. His films include *Battleship Potemkin* (1925), *Alexander Nevsky* (1938), and *Ivan the Terrible* (1944)

Eisk *or* **Eysk** (*Russian* jejsk) *n* variant transliterations of the Russian name for **Yeisk**

eisteddfod (aɪ'stɛdfəd) *n, pl* **eisteddfods** *or* **eisteddfodau** (*Welsh* aɪ,stɛð'vɒdaɪ) any of a number of annual festivals in Wales in which competitions are held in music, poetry, drama, and the fine arts [c19 from Welsh, lit.: session, from *eistedd* to sit + *-fod*, from *bod* to be]

either ('aɪðə, 'i:ðə) *determiner* **1a** one or the other (of two) **1b** *(as pron): either is acceptable* **2** both one and the other: *at* *either end of the table* ▷ *conj* **3** (*coordinating*) used preceding two or more possibilities joined by "or" ▷ *adv* (*sentence modifier*) **4** (*with a negative*) used to indicate that the clause immediately preceding is a partial reiteration of a previous clause: *John isn't a liar, but he isn't exactly honest either* [OE *ǣgther*, short for *ǣghwæther* each of two; see WHETHER]

USAGE *Either* should be followed by a singular verb: *either is good*; *either of these books is useful*. Care should be taken to avoid ambiguity when using *either* to mean *both* or *each*, as in the following sentence: *a ship could be moored on either side of the channel*. Agreement between the verb and its subject in *either...or...* constructions follows the pattern for *neither...nor...* See at **neither**

ejaculate *vb* (ɪˈdʒækjʊˌleɪt), **ejaculates, ejaculating, ejaculated 1** to eject or discharge (semen) in orgasm **2** (*tr*) to utter abruptly; blurt out ▷ *n* (ɪˈdʒækjʊlɪt) **3** another word for **semen** [c16 from L *ējaculārī* to hurl out, from *jaculum* javelin, from *jacere* to throw] > **eˌjacuˈlation** *n* > **eˈjaculatory** *or* **eˈjaculative** *adj* > **eˈjacuˌlator** *n*

eject (ɪˈdʒɛkt) *vb* **1** (*tr*) to force out; expel or emit **2** (*tr*) to compel (a person) to leave; evict **3** (*tr*) to dismiss, as from office **4** (*intr*) to leave an aircraft rapidly, using an ejection seat or capsule [c15 from L *ejicere*, from *jacere* to throw] > **eˈjection** *n* > **eˈjective** *adj* > **eˈjector** *n*

ejection seat *or* **ejector seat** *n* a seat, esp in military aircraft, fired by a cartridge or rocket to eject the occupant in an emergency

Ekaterinburg (*Russian* jɪkətɪrinˈburk) *n* a variant transliteration of the Russian name for **Yekaterinburg**

Ekaterinodar (*Russian* jɪkətɪrinaˈdar) *n* the former name (until 1920) of **Krasnodar**

eke (iːk) *sentence connector arch* also; moreover [OE *eac*]

eke out (iːk) *vb* (*tr, adv*) **1** to make (a supply) last, esp by frugal use **2** to support (existence) with difficulty and effort **3** to add to (something insufficient), esp with effort [from obs. *eke* to enlarge]

EKG (in the US and Canada) *abbrev for* **1** electrocardiogram **2** electrocardiograph

Ekman (*Swedish* ˈɛkman) *n* **Vagn Walfrid** (vaɣᵊn waːlfriːd) 1874–1954, Swedish oceanographer: discoverer of the **Ekman Spiral** (a complex interaction on the surface of the sea between wind, rotation of the earth, and friction forces) and the **Ekman layer** (the thin top layer of the sea that flows at 90° to the wind direction)

El Aaiún (ɛl aɪˈjuːn) *n* a city in Morocco, in Western Sahara: the capital of the former Spanish Sahara; port facilities begun in 1967 at **Playa de El Aaiún** 20 km (12 miles) away, following the discovery of rich phosphate deposits. Pop (urban area): 164 000 (1998 est)

elaborate *adj* (ɪˈlæbərɪt) **1** planned with care and exactness **2** marked by complexity or detail ▷ *vb* (ɪˈlæbəˌreɪt) **elaborates, elaborating, elaborated 3** (*intr; usually foll by on or upon*) to add detail (to an account); expand (upon) **4** (*tr*) to work out in detail; develop **5** (*tr*) to produce by careful labour **6** (*tr*) *physiol* to change (food or simple substances) into more complex substances for use in the body [c16 from L *ēlabōrāre* to take pains, from *labōrāre* to toil] > **eˈlaborateness** *n* > **eˌlaboˈration** *n* > **elaborative** (ɪˈlæbərətɪv) *adj* > **eˈlaboˌrator** *n*

Elagabalus (ˌɛləˈgæbələs, ˌiːlə-) *n* a variant of **Heliogabalus**

El Alamein *or* **Alamein** (ɛl ˈæləˌmeɪn) *n* a village on the N coast of Egypt, about 112 km (70 miles) west of Alexandria: scene of a decisive Allied victory over the Axis forces (1942)

Elam (ˈiːləm) *n* an ancient kingdom east of the River Tigris: established before 4000 BC; probably inhabited by a non-Semitic people

élan (eɪˈlaːn) *n* a combination of style and vigour [c19 from F, from *élancer* to throw forth, ult. from L *lancea* LANCE]

eland (ˈiːlənd) *n* **1** a large spiral-horned antelope inhabiting bushland in eastern and southern Africa **2 giant eland** a similar but larger animal of central and W Africa [c18 via Afrik., from Du. *eland* elk]

elapse (ɪˈlæps) *vb* **elapses, elapsing, elapsed** (*intr*) (of time) to pass by [c17 from L *ēlābī* to slip away]

elasmobranch (ɪˈlæsməˌbræŋk) *n* **1** any cartilaginous fish of the subclass *Elasmobranchii*, which includes sharks, rays, and skates ▷ *adj* **2** of or relating to the *Elasmobranchii* [c19 from NL *elasmobranchii*, from Gk *elasmos* metal plate + *brankhia* gills]

elastane (ɪˈlæsteɪn) *n* a synthetic fibre characterized by its ability to revert to its original shape after being stretched

elastic (ɪˈlæstɪk) *adj* **1** (of a body or material) capable of returning to its original shape after compression, stretching, or other deformation **2** capable of adapting to change **3** quick to recover from fatigue, dejection, etc **4** springy or resilient **5** made of elastic ▷ *n* **6** tape, cord, or fabric containing flexible rubber or similar substance allowing it to stretch and return to its original shape [c17 from NL *elasticus* impulsive, from Gk *elastikos*, from *elaunein* to beat, drive] > **eˈlastically** *adv* > **elasˈticity** *n*

elasticate (ɪˈlæstɪˌkeɪt) *vb* **elasticates, elasticating, elasticated** (*tr*) to insert elastic into (a fabric or garment) > **eˌlastiˈcation** *n*

elastic band *n* another name for **rubber band**

elasticize *or* **elasticise** (ɪˈlæstɪˌsaɪz) *vb* **elasticizes, elasticizing, elasticized** *or* **elasticises, elasticising, elasticised 1** to make elastic **2** another word for **elasticate**

elastomer (ɪˈlæstəmə) *n* any material, such as rubber, able to resume its original shape when a deforming force is removed [c20 from ELASTIC + -MER] > **elastomeric** (ɪˌlæstəˈmɛrɪk) *adj*

Ee

Elastoplast (ɪˈlæstəˌplaːst) *n trademark* a gauze surgical dressing backed by adhesive tape

Elat *or* **Elath** (eɪˈlaːt) *n* variant spellings of **Eilat**

elate (ɪˈleɪt) *vb* **elates, elating, elated** (*tr*) to fill with high spirits, exhilaration, pride, or optimism [c16 from p.p. of L *efferre* to bear away, from *ferre* to carry]

elated (ɪˈleɪtɪd) *adj* full of high spirits, exhilaration, pride or optimism; very happy > **eˈlated** *adj* > **eˈlatedly** *adv*

elation (ɪˈleɪʃən) *n* joyfulness or exaltation of spirit, as from success, pleasure, or relief

E layer *n* another name for **E region**

Elba (ˈɛlbə) *n* a mountainous island off the W coast of Italy, in the Mediterranean: Napoleon Bonaparte's first place of exile (1814–15). Pop: 27 722 (1991 est). Area: 223 sq km (86 sq miles)

Elbe (ɛlb; *German* ˈɛlbə) *n* a river in central Europe, rising in the N Czech Republic and flowing generally northwest through Germany to the North Sea at Hamburg. Length: 1165 km (724 miles). Czech name: **Labe**

Elbert (ˈɛlbət) *n* **Mount** a mountain in central Colorado, in the Sawatch range. Height: 4399 m (14 431 ft)

Elbląg (*Polish* ˈɛlblɔŋk) *n* a port in N Poland: metallurgical industries. Pop: 129 782 (1999 est). German name: **Elbing** (ˈɛlbɪŋ)

elbow (ˈɛlbəʊ) *n* **1** the joint between the upper arm and the forearm **2** the corresponding joint of birds or mammals **3** the part of a garment that covers the elbow **4** something resembling an elbow, such as a sharp bend in a road **5 at one's elbow** within easy reach **6 out at elbow(s)** ragged or impoverished **7 the elbow** dismissal or rejection ▷ *vb* **8** to make (one's way) by shoving, jostling, etc **9** (*tr*) to knock or shove as with the elbow [OE *elnboga*]

elbow grease *n facetious* vigorous physical labour, esp hard rubbing

elbowroom ('ɛlbəʊˌruːm, -ˌrʊm) *n* sufficient scope to move or function

Elbrus (ɪl'bruːs) *n* a mountain in SW Russia, on the border with Georgia, in the Caucasus Mountains, with two extinct volcanic peaks: the highest mountain in Europe. Height: 5642 m (18 510 ft)

Elburz Mountains (ɛl'bʊəz) *pl n* a mountain range in N Iran, parallel to the SW and S shores of the Caspian Sea. Highest peak: Mount Demavend, 5601 m (18 376 ft)

El Capitan (ɛl ˌkæpɪ'tæn) *n* a mountain in E central California, in the Sierra Nevada: a monolith with a precipice rising over 1100 m (3600 ft) above the floor of the Yosemite Valley. Height: 2306 m (7564 ft)

Elche (*Spanish* 'ɛlke) *n* a town in S Spain, in Valencia: noted for Iberian and Roman archaeological finds and the medieval religious drama performed there annually: fruit growing, esp dates, pomegranates, figs. Pop: 191 713 (1998 est)

El Cid Campeador (*Spanish* ɛl θið kampea'ðɔr) *n* See (El) Cid

elder[1] ('ɛldə) *adj* **1** born earlier; senior. ▷ Cf **older** **2** (in certain card games) denoting or relating to the nondealer (the **elder hand**), who has certain advantages in the play **3** *arch* **3a** prior in rank or office **3b** of a previous time ▷ *n* **4** an older person; one's senior **5** *anthropol* a senior member of a tribe who has authority **6** (in certain Protestant Churches) a lay office **7** another word for **presbyter** [OE *eldra*, comp. of *eald* OLD] > '**elder,ship** *n*

elder[2] ('ɛldə) *n* any of various shrubs or small trees having clusters of small white flowers and red, purple, or black berry-like fruits. Also called: **elderberry** [OE *ellern*]

Elder ('ɛldə) *n* **Mark Philip** born 1947, British conductor; musical director of the English National Opera (1979–93) and of the Hallé Orchestra from 2000

elderberry ('ɛldəˌbɛrɪ) *n, pl* **elderberries** **1** the fruit of the elder **2** another name for **elder**[2]

elder brother *n* one of the senior members of Trinity House

elderly ('ɛldəlɪ) *adj* (of people) quite old; past middle age > '**elderliness** *n*

eldest ('ɛldɪst) *adj* being the oldest, esp the oldest surviving child of the same parents [OE *eldesta*, sup. of *eald* OLD]

El Dorado (ɛl dɒ'rɑːdəʊ) *n* **1** a fabled city in South America, rich in treasure **2** Also: **eldorado** any place of great riches or fabulous opportunity [c16 from Sp., lit.: the gilded (place)]

eldritch *or* **eldrich** ('ɛldrɪtʃ) *adj poetic, Scot* unearthly; weird [c16 ?from OE *ælf* elf + *rīce* realm]

Elea ('iːlɪə) *n* (in ancient Italy) a Greek colony on the Tyrrhenian coast of Lucana

Eleanor of Aquitaine ('ɛlɪnə, -ˌnɔː) *n* ?1122–1204, queen of France (1137–52) by her marriage to Louis VII and queen of England (1154–89) by her marriage to Henry II; mother of the English kings Richard I and John

Eleanor of Castile ('ɛlɪnə, -ˌnɔː) *n* 1246–90, Spanish wife of Edward I of England. **Eleanor Crosses** were erected at each place at which her body rested between Nottingham, where she died, and London, where she is buried

e-learning *n* an Internet-based teaching system [c20 electronic *learning*]

elect (ɪ'lɛkt) *vb* **1** (*tr*) to choose (someone) to be (a representative or official) by voting **2** to select; choose **3** (*tr*) (of God) to predestine for the grace of salvation ▷ *adj* **4** (*immediately postpositive*) voted into office but not yet installed: *president elect* **5a** chosen; elite **5b** (*as collective n*; preceded by *the*): *the elect* **6** *Christian theol* **6a** predestined by God to receive salvation **6b** (*as collective n*; preceded by *the*): *the elect* [c15 from L *ēligere* to select, from *legere* to choose] > **e'lectable** *adj*

election (ɪ'lɛkʃən) *n* **1** the selection by vote of a person or persons for a position, esp a political office **2** a public vote **3** the act or an instance of choosing **4** *Christian theol* **4a** the doctrine that God chooses individuals for salvation without reference to faith or works **4b** the doctrine that God chooses for salvation those who, by grace, persevere in faith and works
▷ www.electionworld.org/
▷ www.ifes.org/eguide/elecguide.htm

electioneer (ɪˌlɛkʃə'nɪə) *vb* (*intr*) **1** to be active in a political election or campaign ▷ *n* **2** a person who engages in this activity > **e,lection'eering** *n, adj*

elective (ɪ'lɛktɪv) *adj* **1** of or based on selection by vote **2** selected by vote **3** having the power to elect **4** open to choice; optional ▷ *n* **5** an optional course or hospital placement undertaken by a medical student > **electivity** (ˌiːlɛk'tɪvɪtɪ) *or* **e'lectiveness** *n*

elector (ɪ'lɛktə) *n* **1** someone who is eligible to vote in the election of a government **2** (*often cap*) a member of the US electoral college **3** (*often cap*) (in the Holy Roman Empire) any of the German princes entitled to take part in the election of a new emperor > **e'lector,ship** *n* > **e'lectress** *fem n*

electoral (ɪ'lɛktərəl) *adj* relating to or consisting of electors

electoral college *n* (*often cap*) **1** *US* a body of electors chosen by the voters who formally elect the president and vice president **2** any body of electors with similar functions

electorate (ɪ'lɛktərɪt) *n* **1** the body of all qualified voters **2** the rank, position, or territory of an elector of the Holy Roman Empire **3** *Austral & NZ* the area represented by a Member of Parliament **4** *Austral & NZ* the voters in a constituency

Electra (ɪ'lɛktrə) *n Greek myth* the daughter of Agamemnon and Clytemnestra. She persuaded her brother Orestes to avenge their father by killing his murderess Clytemnestra and her lover Aegisthus

electret (ɪ'lɛktrət) *n* a permanently polarized dielectric material; its field is similar to that of a permanent magnet [c20 from *electr(icity + magn)et*]

electric (ɪ'lɛktrɪk) *adj* **1** of, derived from, produced by, producing, transmitting, or powered by electricity **2** (of a musical instrument) amplified electronically **3** very tense or exciting; emotionally charged ▷ *n* **4** *inf* an electric train, car, etc **5** (*pl*) an electric circuit or electric appliances [c17 from NL *electricus* amber-like (because friction causes amber to become charged), from L *ēlectrum* amber, from Gk *ēlektron*, from ?]

electrical (ɪ'lɛktrɪkᵊl) *adj* of, relating to, or concerned with electricity > **e'lectrically** *adv*

electrical engineering *n* the branch of engineering concerned with practical applications of electricity > **electrical engineer** *n*
▷ http://webdiee.cem.itesm.mx/wwwvlee

electric blanket *n* a blanket that contains an electric heating element, used to warm a bed

electric chair *n* (in the US) **a** an electrified chair for executing criminals **b** (usually preceded by *the*) execution by this method

electric circuit *n physics* another name for **circuit** (sense 3a)

electric constant *n* the permittivity of free space, which has the value $8.854\,185 \times 10^{-12}$ farad per metre

electric discharge *n physics* another name for **discharge** (sense 17b)

electric displacement *n physics* the charge per unit area displaced across a layer of conductor in an electric field. Symbol: D Also called: **electric flux density**

electric eel *n* an eel-like freshwater fish of N South America, having electric organs in the body

electric eye *n* another name for **photocell**
electric field *n* a field of force surrounding a charged particle within which another charged particle experiences a force
electric flux *n* the amount of electricity displaced across a given area in a dielectric. Symbol: Ψ
electric flux density *n* another name for **electric displacement**
electric guitar *n* an electrically amplified guitar, used mainly in pop music
electrician (ɪlɛkˈtrɪʃən, ˌiːlɛk-) *n* a person whose occupation is the installation, maintenance, and repair of electrical devices
electricity (ɪlɛkˈtrɪsɪtɪ, ˌiːlɛk-) *n* **1** any phenomenon associated with stationary or moving electrons, ions, or other charged particles **2** the science of electricity **3** an electric current or charge **4** emotional tension or excitement
electric motor *n* a device that converts electrical energy to mechanical torque
electric organ *n* **1** *music* **1a** a pipe organ operated by electrical means **1b** another name for **electronic organ** **2** a group of cells on certain fishes, such as the electric eel, that gives an electric shock to any animal touching them
electric potential *n* **a** the work required to transfer a unit of positive electric charge from an infinite distance to a given point **b** the potential difference between the point and some other point. Sometimes shortened to **potential**
electric ray *n* any ray of tropical and temperate seas, having a flat rounded body and an organ for producing electricity in each fin
electric shock *n* the physiological reaction, characterized by pain and muscular spasm, to the passage of an electric current through the body. It can affect the respiratory system and heart rhythm. Sometimes shortened to **shock**
electric susceptibility *n* another name for **susceptibility** (sense 4a)
electrify (ɪˈlɛktrɪˌfaɪ) *vb* **electrifies, electrifying, electrified** (*tr*) **1** to adapt or equip (a system, device, etc) for operation by electrical power **2** to charge with or subject to electricity **3** to startle or excite intensely > **eˈlectriˌfiable** *adj* > **eˌlectrifiˈcation** *n* > **eˈlectriˌfier** *n*
electro (ɪˈlɛktrəʊ) *n, pl* **electros** short for **electroplate** or **electrotype**
electro- *or sometimes before a vowel* **electr-** *combining form* **1** electric or electrically: *electrodynamic* **2** electrolytic: *electrodialysis* [from NL, from L *ēlectrum* amber, from Gk *ēlektron*]
electroacoustic (ɪˌlɛktrəʊəˈkuːstɪk) *adj* (of music) combining both computer-generated and acoustic sounds
electrocardiograph (ɪˌlɛktrəʊˈkɑːdɪəʊˌɡrɑːf) *n* an instrument for making tracings (**electrocardiograms**) recording the electrical activity of the heart > **eˌlectroˌcardioˈgraphic** *or* **eˌlectroˌcardioˈgraphical** *adj* > **electrocardiography** (ɪˌlɛktrəʊˌkɑːdɪˈɒɡrəfɪ) *n*
electrochemistry (ɪˌlɛktrəʊˈkɛmɪstrɪ) *n* the branch of chemistry concerned with electric cells and electrolysis > **ˌelectroˈchemical** *adj* > **eˌlectroˈchemist** *n*
electroconvulsive therapy (ɪˌlɛktrəʊkənˈvʌlsɪv) *n med* the treatment of certain psychotic conditions by passing an electric current through the brain to induce coma or convulsions. See also **shock therapy**
electrocute (ɪˈlɛktrəˌkjuːt) *vb* **electrocutes, electrocuting, electrocuted** (*tr*) **1** to kill as a result of an electric shock **2** *US* to execute in the electric chair [c19 from ELECTRO- + (EXE)CUTE] > **eˌlectroˈcution** *n*
electrode (ɪˈlɛktrəʊd) *n* **1** a conductor through which an electric current enters or leaves an electrolyte, an electric arc, or an electronic valve or tube **2** an element in a semiconducting device that emits, collects, or controls the movement of electrons or holes
electrodeposit (ɪˌlɛktrəʊdɪˈpɒzɪt) *vb* **1** (*tr*) to deposit (a metal) by electrolysis ▷ *n* **2** the deposit so formed > **electrodeposition** (ɪˌlɛktrəʊˌdɛpəˈzɪʃən) *n*
electrodynamics (ɪˌlɛktrəʊdaɪˈnæmɪks) *n* (*functioning as sing*) the branch of physics concerned with the interactions between electrical and mechanical forces
electroencephalograph (ɪˌlɛktrəʊɛnˈsɛfələˌɡrɑːf) *n* an instrument for making tracings (**electroencephalograms**) recording the electrical activity of the brain, usually by means of electrodes placed on the scalp. See also **brain wave** > **eˌlectroenˌcephaloˈgraphic** *adj* > **electroencephalography** (ɪˌlɛktrəʊɛnˌsɛfəˈlɒɡrəfɪ) *n*
electrolyse *or US* **electrolyze** (ɪˈlɛktrəʊˌlaɪz) *vb* **electrolyses, electrolysing, electrolysed** *or US* **electrolyzes, electrolyzing, electrolyzed** (*tr*) **1** to decompose (a chemical compound) by electrolysis **2** to destroy (living tissue, such as hair roots) by electrolysis > **eˈlectroˌlyser** *or US* **eˈlectroˌlyzer** *n*
electrolysis (ɪlɛkˈtrɒlɪsɪs) *n* **1** the conduction of electricity by an electrolyte, esp the use of this process to induce chemical changes **2** the destruction of living tissue, such as hair roots, by an electric current, usually for cosmetic reasons
electrolyte (ɪˈlɛktrəʊˌlaɪt) *n* **1** a solution or molten substance that conducts electricity **2a** a chemical compound that dissociates in solution into ions **2b** any of the ions themselves
electrolytic (ɪˌlɛktrəʊˈlɪtɪk) *adj* **1** *physics* **1a** of, concerned with, or produced by electrolysis or electrodeposition **1b** of, relating to, or containing an electrolyte ▷ *n* **2** *electronics* Also called: **electrolytic capacitor** a small capacitor consisting of two electrodes separated by an electrolyte > **eˌlectroˈlytically** *adv*
electromagnet (ɪˌlɛktrəʊˈmæɡnɪt) *n* a magnet consisting of an iron or steel core wound with a coil of wire, through which a current is passed
electromagnetic (ɪˌlɛktrəʊmæɡˈnɛtɪk) *adj* **1** of, containing, or operated by an electromagnet **2** of, relating to, or consisting of electromagnetism **3** of or relating to electromagnetic radiation > **eˌlectromagˈnetically** *adv*
electromagnetic radiation *n* radiation consisting of an electric and magnetic field at right angles to each other and to the direction of propagation
electromagnetics (ɪˌlɛktrəʊmæɡˈnɛtɪks) *n* (*functioning as sing*) *physics* another name for **electromagnetism** (sense 2)
electromagnetic spectrum *n* the complete range of electromagnetic radiation from the longest radio waves to the shortest gamma radiation
electromagnetic unit *n* any unit of a system of electrical cgs units in which the magnetic constant is given the value of unity
electromagnetic wave *n* a wave of energy propagated in an electromagnetic field
electromagnetism (ɪˌlɛktrəʊˈmæɡnɪˌtɪzəm) *n* **1** magnetism produced by electric current **2** Also called: **electromagnetics** the branch of physics concerned with this magnetism and with the interaction of electric and magnetic fields
electrometer (ɪlɛkˈtrɒmɪtə, ˌiːlɛk-) *n* an instrument for detecting or measuring a potential difference or charge by the electrostatic forces between charged bodies > **electrometric** (ɪˌlɛktrəʊˈmɛtrɪk) *or* **eˌlectroˈmetrical** *adj* > **elecˈtrometry** *n*
electromotive (ɪˌlɛktrəʊˈməʊtɪv) *adj* of, concerned with, or producing an electric current
electromotive force *n physics* **a** a source of energy that can cause current to flow in an electrical circuit **b** the rate at which energy is drawn from this source when

Ee

unit current flows through the circuit, measured in volts

electromyography (ɪˌlɛktrəʊmaɪˈɒɡrəfɪ) *n med* a technique for recording the electrical activity of muscles: used in the diagnosis of nerve and muscle disorders

electron (ɪˈlɛktrɒn) *n* an elementary particle in all atoms, orbiting the nucleus in numbers equal to the atomic number of the element [C19 from ELECTRO- + -ON]

electronegative (ɪˌlɛktrəʊˈnɛɡətɪv) *adj* **1** having a negative electric charge **2** (of an atom, molecule, etc) tending to attract electrons and form negative ions or polarized bonds

electron gun *n* a heated cathode for producing and focusing a beam of electrons, used esp in cathode-ray tubes

electronic (ɪlɛkˈtrɒnɪk, ˌiːlɛk-) *adj* **1** of, concerned with, using, or operated by devices, such as transistors, in which electrons are conducted through a semiconductor, free space, or gas **2** of or concerned with electronics **3** of or concerned with electrons **4** involving or concerned with the representation, storage, or transmission of information by electronic systems: *electronic shopping* > **elecˈtronically** *adv*

electronic flash *n photog* an electronic device for producing a very bright flash of light by means of an electric discharge in a gas-filled tube

electronic footprint *n computing* data that identifies a computer that has connected to a particular website

electronic funds transfer at point of sale *n* a system for debiting a retail sale direct to the customer's bank, building-society, or credit-card account by means of a computer link using the telephone network. The customer inserts his or her debit card or credit card into the computer at the point of sale. Acronym: **EFTPOS**

electronic ignition *n* any system that uses an electronic circuit to supply the voltage to the sparking plugs of an internal-combustion engine

electronic keyboard *n* a typewriter keyboard used to operate an electronic device such as a computer

electronic mail *n* the transmission of information, messages, facsimiles, etc, from one computer terminal to another. Often shortened to **E-mail, e-mail, email**

electronic music *n* music consisting of sounds produced by electric currents either controlled from an instrument panel or keyboard or prerecorded on magnetic tape

electronic organ *n music* an instrument played by means of a keyboard, in which sounds are produced by electronic or electrical means

electronic organizer *n* a computerized personal organizer

electronic point of sale *n* a computerized system for recording sales in retail shops, using a laser scanner at the cash till to read bar codes on the packages of the items sold. The retailer's stock record is automatically adjusted and the customer receives an itemized bill. Acronym: **EPOS**

electronic publishing *n* the publication of information on magnetic tape, discs, etc, so that it can be accessed by a computer
▷ www.elpub.org

electronics (ɪlɛkˈtrɒnɪks, ˌiːlɛk-) *n* **1** (*functioning as sing*) the science and technology concerned with the development, behaviour, and applications of electronic devices and circuits **2** (*functioning as pl*) the circuits and devices of a piece of electronic equipment
▷ www.eskimo.com/~billb/amateur/elehob.html
▷ http://webdiee.cem.itesm.mx/wwwvlee
▷ www.eetuk.com

electronic signature *n computing* electronic proof of a person's identity

electronic surveillance *n* **1** the use of such electronic devices as television monitors, video cameras, etc, to prevent burglary, shop lifting, break-ins, etc **2** monitoring events, conversations, etc at a distance by electronic means, esp by such covert means as wire tapping or bugging

electronic tag *n* another name for **tag**[1] (sense 2)

electronic transfer of funds *n* the transfer of money from one bank or building-society account to another by means of a computer link using the telephone network. Abbrev: **ETF**

electron lens *n* a system, such as an arrangement of electrodes or magnets, that produces a field for focusing a beam of electrons

electron micrograph *n* a photograph or image of a specimen taken using an electron microscope

electron microscope *n* a powerful microscope that uses electrons, rather than light, and electron lenses to produce a magnified image

electron tube *n* an electrical device, such as a valve, in which a flow of electrons between electrodes takes place

electronvolt (ɪˌlɛktrɒnˈvəʊlt) *n* a unit of energy equal to the work done on an electron accelerated through a potential difference of 1 volt

electrophoresis (ɪˌlɛktrəʊfəˈriːsɪs) *n* the motion of charged particles in a colloid under the influence of an applied electric field > **electrophoretic** (ɪˌlɛktrəʊfəˈrɛtɪk) *adj*

electrophorus (ɪlɛkˈtrɒfərəs, ˌiːlɛk-) *n* an apparatus for generating static electricity by induction [C18 from ELECTRO- + *-phorus*, from Gk, from *pherein* to bear]

electroplate (ɪˈlɛktrəʊˌpleɪt) *vb* **electroplates, electroplating, electroplated 1** (*tr*) to plate (an object) by electrolysis ▷ *n* **2** electroplated articles collectively, esp when plated with silver ▷ *adj* **3** coated with metal by electrolysis > **eˈlectroˌplater** *n*

electropositive (ɪˌlɛktrəʊˈpɒzɪtɪv) *adj* **1** having a positive electric charge **2** (of an atom, molecule, etc) tending to release electrons and form positive ions or polarized bonds

electrorheology (ɪˌlɛktrəʊrɪˈɒlədʒɪ) *n* **1** the study of the flow of fluids under the influence of electric fields **2** the way in which fluid flow is influenced by an electric field > **eˌlectroˌrheoˈlogical** *adj*

electroscope (ɪˈlɛktrəʊˌskəʊp) *n* an apparatus for detecting an electric charge, typically consisting of a rod holding two gold foils that separate when a charge is applied > **electroscopic** (ɪˌlɛktrəʊˈskɒpɪk) *adj*

electroshock therapy (ɪˈlɛktrəʊˌʃɒk) *n* another name for **electroconvulsive therapy**

electrostatic (ɪˌlɛktrəʊˈstætɪk) *adj* **1** of, concerned with, producing, or caused by static electricity **2** concerned with electrostatics

electrostatics (ɪˌlɛktrəʊˈstætɪks) *n* (*functioning as sing*) the branch of physics concerned with static electricity

electrostatic unit *n* any unit of a system of electrical cgs units in which the electric constant is given the value of unity

electrotherapeutics (ɪˌlɛktrəʊˌθɛrəˈpjuːtɪks) *n* (*functioning as sing*) the branch of medical science concerned with the use of electrotherapy > **eˌlectroˌtheraˈpeutic** *or* **eˌlectroˌtheraˈpeutical** *adj*

electrotherapy (ɪˌlɛktrəʊˈθɛrəpɪ) *n* treatment in which electric currents are passed through the tissues to stimulate muscle function in paralysed patients > **eˌlectroˈtherapist** *n*

electrotype (ɪˈlɛktrəʊˌtaɪp) *n* **1** a duplicate printing plate made by electrolytically depositing a layer of copper or nickel onto a mould of the original ▷ *vb* **electrotypes, electrotyping, electrotyped 2** (*tr*) to make an electrotype of (printed matter, etc) > **eˈlectroˌtyper** *n*

electrovalent bond (ɪˌlɛktrəʊˈveɪlənt) *n* a type of

chemical bond in which one atom loses an electron to form a positive ion and the other atom gains the electron to form a negative ion. The resulting ions are held together by electrostatic attraction
> **e,lectro'valency** *n*

electroweak (ɪ,lɛktrəʊ'wi:k) *adj physics* involving both electromagnetic interaction and weak interaction

electrum (ɪ'lɛktrəm) *n* an alloy of gold and silver [C14 from L, from Gk *ēlektron* amber]

electuary (ɪ'lɛktjʊərɪ) *n, pl* **electuaries** *med archaic* a paste taken orally, containing a drug mixed with syrup or honey [C14 from LL *ēlēctuārium*, prob. from Gk *ēkleikton*, from *leikhein* to lick]

eleemosynary (,ɛlɪi:'mɒsɪnərɪ) *adj* **1** of or dependent on charity **2** given as an act of charity [C17 from Church L *eleēmosyna* ALMS]

elegance ('ɛlɪgəns) *or* **elegancy** *n, pl* **elegances** *or* **elegancies 1** dignified grace **2** good taste in design, style, arrangement, etc **3** something elegant; a refinement

elegant ('ɛlɪgənt) *adj* **1** tasteful in dress, style, or design **2** dignified and graceful **3** cleverly simple; ingenious: *an elegant solution* [C16 from L *ēlegāns* tasteful; see ELECT]

elegiac (,ɛlɪ'dʒaɪək) *adj* **1** resembling, characteristic of, relating to, or appropriate to an elegy **2** lamenting; mournful **3** denoting or written in elegiac couplets (which consist of a dactylic hexameter followed by a dactylic pentameter) or elegiac stanzas (which consist of a quatrain in iambic pentameters with alternate lines rhyming) ▷ *n* **4** (*often pl*) an elegiac couplet or stanza > ,**ele'giacally** *adv*

elegize *or* **elegise** ('ɛlɪ,dʒaɪz) *vb* **elegizes, elegizing, elegized** *or* **elegises, elegising, elegised 1** to compose an elegy (in memory of) **2** (*intr*) to write elegiacally
> **'elegist** *n*

elegy ('ɛlɪdʒɪ) *n, pl* **elegies 1** a mournful poem or song, esp a lament for the dead **2** poetry written in elegiac couplets or stanzas [C16 via F & L from Gk, from *elegos* lament sung to flute accompaniment]

element ('ɛlɪmənt) *n* **1** any of the 109 known substances that consist of atoms with the same number of protons in their nuclei **2** one of the fundamental or irreducible components making up a whole **3** a cause that contributes to a result; factor **4** any group that is part of a larger unit, such as a military formation **5** a small amount; hint **6** a distinguishable section of a social group **7** the most favourable environment for an animal or plant **8** the situation in which a person is happiest or most effective (esp in **in** *or* **out of one's element**) **9** the resistance wire that constitutes the electrical heater in a cooker, heater, etc **10** one of the four substances thought in ancient and medieval cosmology to constitute the universe (earth, air, water, or fire) **11** (*pl*) atmospheric conditions, esp wind, rain, and cold **12** (*pl*) the basic principles **13** *Christianity* the bread or wine consecrated in the Eucharist [C13 from L *elementum* a first principle, element]

elemental (,ɛlɪ'mɛntᵊl) *adj* **1** fundamental; basic **2** motivated by or symbolic of primitive powerful natural forces or passions **3** of or relating to earth, air, water, and fire considered as elements **4** of or relating to atmospheric forces, esp wind, rain, and cold **5** of or relating to a chemical element ▷ *n* **6** *rare* a spirit or force that is said to appear in physical form > ,**ele'mental,ism** *n*

elementary (,ɛlɪ'mɛntərɪ) *adj* **1** not difficult; rudimentary **2** of or concerned with the first principles of a subject; introductory or fundamental **3** *chem* another word for **elemental** (sense 5) > ,**ele'mentariness** *n*

elementary particle *n* any of several entities, such as electrons, neutrons, or protons, that are less complex than atoms

elementary school *n* **1** *Brit* a former name for **primary school 2** *US & Canad* a state school for the first six to eight years of a child's education

elenchus (ɪ'lɛŋkəs) *n, pl* **elenchi** (-kaɪ) *logic* refutation of an argument by proving the contrary of its conclusion, esp syllogistically [C17 from L, from Gk, from *elenkhein* to refute] > **e'lenctic** *adj*

elephant ('ɛlɪfənt) *n, pl* **elephants** *or* **elephant** either of two proboscidean mammals. The **African elephant** is the larger species, with large flapping ears and a less humped back than the **Indian elephant,** of S and SE Asia [C13 from L, from Gk *elephas* elephant, ivory]

elephantiasis (,ɛlɪfən'taɪəsɪs) *n pathol* a complication of chronic filariasis, in which nematode worms block the lymphatic vessels, usually in the legs or scrotum, causing extreme enlargement of the affected area [C16 via L from Gk, from *elephas* ELEPHANT + -IASIS]

elephantine (,ɛlɪ'fæntaɪn) *adj* **1** denoting, relating to, or characteristic of an elephant or elephants **2** huge, clumsy, or ponderous

elephant seal *n* either of two large earless seals, of southern oceans or of the N Atlantic, the males of which have a trunklike snout

Eleusinian mysteries *pl n* a mystical religious festival, held at Eleusis in classical times, to celebrate the gods Persephone, Demeter, and Dionysus

Eleusis (ɪ'lu:sɪs) *n* a town in Greece, in Attica about 23 km (14 miles) west of Athens, of which it is now an industrial suburb. Modern Greek name: **Elevsís**
> **'Eleusinian** (,ɛljʊ'sɪnɪən) *adj*

elevate ('ɛlɪ,veɪt) *vb* **elevates, elevating, elevated** (*tr*) **1** to move to a higher place **2** to raise in rank or status **3** to put in a cheerful mood; elate **4** to put on a higher cultural plane; uplift **5** to raise the axis of a gun **6** to raise the intensity or pitch of (the voice) [C15 from L *ēlevāre*, from *levāre* to raise, from *levis* (adj) light]
> **'ele,vatory** *adj*

elevated ('ɛlɪ,veɪtɪd) *adj* **1** raised to or being at a higher level **2** inflated or lofty; exalted **3** in a cheerful mood **4** *inf* slightly drunk

elevation (,ɛlɪ'veɪʃən) *n* **1** the act of elevating or the state of being elevated **2** the height of something above a given place, esp above sea level **3** a raised area; height **4** nobleness or grandeur **5** a drawing to scale of the external face of a building or structure **6** a ballet dancer's ability to leap high **7** *astron* another name for **altitude** (sense 3) **8** the angle formed between the muzzle of a gun and the horizontal > ,**ele'vational** *adj*

elevator ('ɛlɪ,veɪtə) *n* **1** a person or thing that elevates **2** a mechanical hoist, often consisting of a chain of scoops linked together on a conveyor belt **3** the US and Canad name for **lift** (sense 14a) **4** *chiefly US & Canad* a granary equipped with an elevator and, usually, facilities for cleaning and grading the grain **5** a control surface on the tailplane of an aircraft, for making it climb or descend **6** any muscle that raises a part of the body

eleven (ɪ'lɛvᵊn) *n* **1** the cardinal number that is the sum of ten and one **2** a numeral, 11, XI, etc, representing this number **3** something representing, represented by, or consisting of 11 units **4** (*functioning as sing or pl*) a team of 11 players in football, cricket, etc **5** Also called: **eleven o'clock** eleven hours after noon or midnight ▷ *determiner* **6a** amounting to eleven **6b** (*as pron*): *another eleven* [OE *endleofan*] > **e'leventh** *adj, n*

eleven-plus *n* (in Britain, esp formerly) an examination taken by children aged 10 or 11 that determines the type of secondary education a child will be given

elevenses (ɪ'lɛvᵊnzɪz) *pl n* (*sometimes functioning as sing*) *Brit inf* a light snack taken in mid-morning

eleventh hour *n* the latest possible time; last minute

Elevsís (,ɛlɛf'sis) *n* transliteration of the Modern Greek name for **Eleusis**

Ee

elf (ɛlf) *n, pl* **elves** **1** (in folklore) one of a kind of legendary beings, usually characterized as small, manlike, and mischievous **2** a mischievous or whimsical child [OE *ælf*] > **'elfish** *or* **'elvish** *adj*

El Faiyûm (ɛl faɪ'ju:m) *or* **Al Faiyûm** (æl faɪ'ju:m) *n* a city in N Egypt: a site of towns going back at least to the 12th dynasty. Pop: 260 964 (1996)

El Ferrol (*Spanish* ɛl fɛ'rrɔl) *n* a port in NW Spain, on the Atlantic: fortified naval base, with a deep natural harbour. Pop: 82 371 (1991). Official name (since 1939): **El Ferrol del Caudillo** (dɛl kau'ðiʎo)

elfin ('ɛlfɪn) *adj* **1** of or like an elf or elves **2** small, delicate, and charming

elflock ('ɛlf,lɒk) *n* a lock of hair, fancifully regarded as having been tangled by the elves

Elgar ('ɛlgɑ:) *n* Sir **Edward** (**William**) 1857–1934, English composer, whose works include the *Enigma Variations* (1899), the oratorio *The Dream of Gerontius* (1900), two symphonies, a cello concerto, and a violin concerto

Elgin ('ɛlgɪn) *n* a market town in NE Scotland, the administrative centre of Moray, on the River Lossie: ruined 13th-century cathedral: distilling, engineering. Pop: 19 027 (1991)

El Gîza (ɛl 'gi:zə) *n* a city in NE Egypt, on the W bank of the Nile opposite Cairo: nearby are the Great Pyramid of Cheops (Khufu) and the Sphinx. Pop: 2 221 868 (1996)

Elgon ('ɛlgɒn) *n* **Mount** an extinct volcano in E Africa, on the Kenya-Uganda border. Height: 4321m (14 178 ft)

El Greco (ɛl 'grɛkəʊ) *n* real name *Domenikos Theotocopoulos.* 1541–1614, Spanish painter, born in Crete; noted for his elongated human forms and dramatic use of colour

Eli ('i:laɪ) *n* *Old Testament* the highest priest at Shiloh and teacher of Samuel (I Samuel 1–3)

ft[1] ('i:lɪə) *n* a department of SW Greece, in the W Peloponnese: in ancient times most of the region formed the state of Elis. Pop: 179 429 (1991). Area: 2681 sq km (1035 sq miles). Modern Greek name: **Ilía**

Elia[2] ('i:lɪə) *n* the pen name of (Charles) **Lamb**

Elias (ɪ'laɪəs) *n* *Bible* the Douay spelling of **Elijah**

elicit (ɪ'lɪsɪt) *vb* (*tr*) **1** to give rise to; evoke **2** to bring to light [c17 from L *ēlicere*, from *licere* to entice] > **e'licitable** *adj* > **e,lici'tation** *n* > **e'licitor** *n*

elide (ɪ'laɪd) *vb* **elides, eliding, elided** to undergo or cause to undergo elision [c16 from L *ēlīdere* to knock, from *laedere* to hit, wound] > **e'lidible** *adj*

eligible ('ɛlɪdʒəbᵊl) *adj* **1** fit, worthy, or qualified, as for office **2** desirable, esp as a spouse [c15 from LL *ēligere* to ELECT] > **,eligi'bility** *n* > **'eligibly** *adv*

Elijah (ɪ'laɪdʒə) *n* *Old Testament* a Hebrew prophet of the 9th century BC, who was persecuted for denouncing Ahab and Jezebel (I Kings 17–21: 21; II Kings 1–2:18)

Elikón (ɛli'kɔn) *n* transliteration of the Modern Greek name for **Helicon**

eliminate (ɪ'lɪmɪ,neɪt) *vb* **eliminates, eliminating, eliminated** (*tr*) **1** to remove or take out **2** to reject; omit from consideration **3** to remove (a competitor, team, etc) from a contest, usually by defeat **4** *sl* to murder in cold blood **5** *physiol* to expel (waste) from the body **6** *maths* to remove (an unknown variable) from simultaneous equations [c16 from L *ēlīmināre* to turn out of the house, from *e-* out + *līmen* threshold] > **e'liminable** *adj* > **e,limi'nation** *n* > **e'liminative** *adj* > **e'limi,nator** *n*

Eliot ('ɛlɪət) *n* **1** **George,** real name *Mary Ann Evans.* 1819–80, English novelist, noted for her analysis of provincial Victorian society. Her best-known novels include *Adam Bede* (1859), *The Mill on the Floss* (1860), *Silas Marner* (1861), and *Middlemarch* (1872) **2** Sir **John** 1592–1632, English statesman, a leader of parliamentary opposition to Charles I **3** **T**(**homas**) **S**(**tearns**) 1888–1965, British poet, dramatist, and critic, born in the US. His poetry includes *Prufrock and Other Observations* (1917), *The Waste Land* (1922), *Ash Wednesday* (1930), and *Four Quartets* (1943). Among his verse plays are *Murder in the Cathedral* (1935), *The Family Reunion* (1939), *The Cocktail Party* (1950), and *The Confidential Clerk* (1954): Nobel prize for literature 1948

Elis ('i:lɪs) *n* an ancient city-state of SW Greece, in the NW Peloponnese: site of the ancient Olympic games

ELISA (ɪ'laɪzə) *n acronym for* enzyme-linked immunosorbent assay: an immunological technique for accurately measuring the amount of a substance, for example in a blood sample

Elisabeth (ɪ'lɪzəbəθ) *n* a variant spelling of **Elizabeth**[1] (sense 1)

Élisabethville (ɪ'lɪzəbəθ,vɪl) *n* the former name (until 1966) of **Lubumbashi**

Elisavetgrad (*Russian* jɪliza'vjɛtgrət) *n* a former name (until 1924) of **Kirovograd**

Elisavetpol (*Russian* jɪliza'vjɛtpəlj) *n* a former name (until 1920) of **Kirovabad**

Elisha (ɪ'laɪʃə) *n* *Old Testament* a Hebrew prophet of the 9th century BC: successor of Elijah (II Kings 3–9)

elision (ɪ'lɪʒən) *n* **1** omission of a syllable or vowel from a word **2** omission of parts of a book, etc [c16 from L *ēlīdere* to ELIDE]

elite *or* **élite** (ɪ'li:t, eɪ-) *n* **1** (*sometimes functioning as pl*) the most powerful, rich, or gifted members of a group, community, etc **2** a typewriter type size having 12 characters to the inch ▷ *adj* **3** of or suitable for an elite [c18 from F, from OF *eslit* chosen, from L *ēligere* to ELECT]

elitism (ɪ'li:tɪzəm, eɪ-) *n* **1a** the belief that society should be governed by an elite **1b** such government **2** pride in or awareness of being one of an elite group > **e'litist** *adj, n*

elixir (ɪ'lɪksə) *n* **1** an alchemical preparation supposed to be capable of prolonging life (**elixir of life**) or of transmuting base metals into gold **2** anything that purports to be a sovereign remedy **3** a quintessence **4** a liquid containing a medicine with syrup, glycerine, or alcohol added to mask its unpleasant taste [c14 from Med. L, from Ar., prob. from Gk *xērion* powder used for drying wounds]

Elizabeth[1] (ɪ'lɪzəbəθ) *n* **1** a city in NE New Jersey, on Newark Bay. Pop: 120 568 (2000) **2** a town in SE South Australia, near Adelaide. Pop: 34 000 (latest est)

Elizabeth[2] (ɪ'lɪzəbəθ) *n* **1** **Saint** Also: **Elisabeth** *New Testament* the wife of Zacharias, mother of John the Baptist, and kinswoman of the Virgin Mary. Feast day: Nov 5 or 8 **2** pen name *Carmen Sylva.* 1843–1916, queen of Romania (1881–1914) and author **3** Russian name *Yelizaveta Petrovna.* 1709–62, empress of Russia (1741–62); daughter of Peter the Great **4** title *the Queen Mother*; original name Lady *Elizabeth Bowes-Lyon.* 1900–2002, queen of Great Britain and Northern Ireland (1936–52) as the wife of George VI; mother of Elizabeth II

Elizabeth I *n* 1533–1603, queen of England (1558–1603); daughter of Henry VIII and Anne Boleyn. She established the Church of England (1559) and put an end to Catholic plots, notably by executing Mary Queen of Scots (1587) and defeating the Spanish Armada (1588). Her reign was notable for commercial growth, maritime expansion, and the flourishing of literature, music, and architecture

Elizabeth II *n* born 1926, queen of Great Britain and Northern Ireland from 1952; daughter of George VI

Elizabethan (ɪ,lɪzə'bi:θən) *adj* **1** of, characteristic of, or relating to the reigns of Elizabeth I or Elizabeth II **2** of, relating to, or designating a style of architecture used in England during the reign of Elizabeth I ▷ *n* **3** a person who lived in England during the reign of Elizabeth I

Elizabethan sonnet *n* another term for **Shakespearean sonnet**

Elizabeth of Hungary *n* **Saint** 1207–31, Hungarian princess who devoted herself to charity and asceticism. Feast day: Nov 17 and 19

elk (ɛlk) *n, pl* **elks** *or* **elk** **1** a large deer of N Europe and Asia: also occurs in N America, where it is called a moose **2 American elk** another name for **wapiti** [OE *eolh*]

El Khalil (ɛl xɒ'li:l) *n* transliteration of the Arabic name for **Hebron**

ell (ɛl) *n* an obsolete unit of length, approximately 45 inches [OE *eln* forearm (the measure orig. being from elbow to fingertips)]

Ellás (ɛ'las) *n* transliteration of the Modern Greek name for **Greece**

Ellesmere Island ('ɛlzmɪə) *n* a Canadian island in the Arctic Ocean: part of Nunavut; mountainous, with many glaciers. Area: 212 688 sq km (82 119 sq miles)

Ellesmere Port *n* a port in NW England, in NW Cheshire on the Mersey estuary and Manchester Ship Canal. Pop: 64 504 (1991)

Ellice Islands ('ɛlɪs) *pl n* the former name (until 1975) of **Tuvalu**

Ellington ('ɛlɪŋtən) *n* **Duke,** nickname of *Edward Kennedy Ellington*. 1899–1974, US jazz composer, pianist, and conductor, famous for such works as "Mood Indigo" and "Creole Love Call"

ellipse (ɪ'lɪps) *n* a closed conic section shaped like a flattened circle and formed by an inclined plane that does not cut the base of the cone [C18 back formation from ELLIPSIS]

ellipsis (ɪ'lɪpsɪs) *n, pl* **ellipses** (-si:z) **1** omission of parts of a word or sentence **2** *printing* a sequence of three dots (...) indicating an omission in text [C16 from L, from Gk, from *en* in + *leipein* to leave]

ellipsoid (ɪ'lɪpsɔɪd) *n* **a** a geometric surface, symmetrical about the three coordinate axes, whose plane sections are ellipses or circles **b** a solid having this shape > **ellipsoidal** (ɪlɪp'sɔɪdᵊl, ˌɛl-) *adj*

ellipsoid of revolution *n* a geometric surface produced by rotating an ellipse about one of its two axes and having circular plane sections perpendicular to the axis of revolution

elliptical (ɪ'lɪptɪkᵊl) *adj* **1** relating to or having the shape of an ellipse **2** relating to or resulting from ellipsis **3** (of speech, literary style, etc) **3a** very concise, often so as to be obscure or ambiguous **3b** circumlocutory ▷ Also (for senses 1 and 2): **elliptic** > **el'lipticalness** *n*

Ellis ('ɛlɪs) *n* **1** 1814–90, English philologist: made the first systematic survey of the phonology of British dialects **2** **(Henry) Havelock** ('hævlɒk) 1859–1939, English essayist: author of works on the psychology of sex

elm (ɛlm) *n* **1** any tree of the genus *Ulmus*, occurring in the N hemisphere, having serrated leaves and winged fruits (samaras) **2** the hard heavy wood of this tree [OE *elm*]

El Mansûra (ɛl mæn'sʊərə) *or* **Al Mansûrah** *n* a city in NE Egypt: scene of a battle (1250) in which the Crusaders were defeated by the Mamelukes and Louis IX of France was captured; cotton-manufacturing centre. Pop: 369 621 (1996)

El Minya (ɛl 'mɪnjə) *n* a river port in central Egypt on the Nile. Pop: 201 360 (1996)

El Misti (ɛl 'mi:sti:) *n* a volcano in S Peru, in the Andes. Height: 5852 m (19 199 ft)

El Niño (ɛl 'ni:njəʊ) *n* *meteorol* a warming of the eastern tropical Pacific occurring every few years, which alters the local climate and has a wider effect on the general weather pattern of the tropics [from Sp.: The Child, i.e. Christ, referring to its occurrence around Christmas time]

El Obeid (ɛl əʊ'beɪd) *n* a city in the central Sudan, in Kordofan province: scene of the defeat of a British and Egyptian army by the Mahdi (1883). Pop: 228 096 (1993)

elocution (ˌɛlə'kju:ʃən) *n* the art of public speaking [C15 from L *ēloquī*, from *loquī* to speak] > **ˌelo'cutionary** *adj* > **ˌelo'cutionist** *n*

Elohim (ɛ'ləʊhɪm, ˌɛləʊ'hi:m) *n* *Old Testament* a Hebrew word for God or gods [C17 from Heb. *'Elōhim*, pl (to indicate uniqueness) of *'Elōah* God]

Elohist (ɛ'ləʊhɪst) *n* *Bible* the supposed author or authors of the Pentateuch, identified chiefly by the use of the word *Elohim* for God

elongate ('i:lɒŋgeɪt) *vb* **elongates, elongating, elongated** **1** to make or become longer; stretch ▷ *adj* **2** long and narrow **3** lengthened or tapered [C16 from LL *ēlongāre* to keep at a distance, from *ē-* away + L *longē* (adv) far] > **ˌelon'gation** *n*

elope (ɪ'ləʊp) *vb* **elopes, eloping, eloped** (*intr*) to run away secretly with a lover, esp in order to marry [C16 from Anglo-F *aloper*, ?from MDu. *lōpen* to run; see LOPE] > **e'lopement** *n* > **e'loper** *n*

eloquence ('ɛləkwəns) *n* **1** ease in using language **2** powerful and effective language **3** the quality of being persuasive or moving

eloquent ('ɛləkwənt) *adj* **1** (of speech, writing, etc) fluent and persuasive **2** visibly or vividly expressive: *an eloquent yawn* [C14 from L *ēloquēns*, from *loquī* to speak] > **'eloquentness** *n*

El Paso (ɛl 'pæsəʊ) *n* a city in W Texas, on the Rio Grande opposite Ciudad Juárez, Mexico. Pop: 599 865 (1996 est)

El Salvador (ɛl 'sælvəˌdɔ:) *n* a republic in Central America, on the Pacific: colonized by the Spanish from 1524; declared independence in 1841, becoming a republic in 1856. It consists of coastal lowlands rising to a central plateau. Coffee constitutes over a third of the total exports. Official language: Spanish. Religion: Roman Catholic majority. Currency: US dollar. Capital: San Salvador. Pop: 6 238 000 (2001 est). Area: 21 393 sq km (8236 sq miles) > **ˌSalva'doran, ˌSalva'dorean,** *or* **ˌSalva'dorian** *adj, n*

▷ www.el-salvador.org.il

▷ www.elsalvadorturismo.gob.sv

Elsan ('ɛlsæn) *n* *trademark* a type of portable chemical lavatory [C20 from initials of *E. L.* Jackson, manufacturer + SAN(ITATION)]

Elsass ('ɛlzas) *n* the German name for **Alsace**

Elsass-Lothringen ('ɛlzas'lo:trɪŋən) *n* the German name for **Alsace-Lorraine**

else (ɛls) *determiner* (*postpositive; used after an indefinite pronoun or an interrogative*) **1** in addition; more: *there is nobody else here* **2** other; different: *where else could he be?* ▷ *adv* **3** **or else** **3a** if not, then: *go away or else I won't finish my work today* **3b** or something terrible will result: used as a threat: *sit down, or else!* [OE *elles*, genitive of *el-* strange, foreign]

elsewhere (ˌɛls'wɛə) *adv* in or to another place; somewhere else [OE *elles hwǣr*; see ELSE, WHERE]

Elsinore ('ɛlsɪˌnɔ:, ˌɛlsɪ'nɔ:) *n* the English name for **Helsingør**

ELT *abbrev for* English Language Teaching

Elton ('ɛltᵊn) *n* **1** **Ben(jamin) (Charles)** born 1959, British comedian, scriptwriter, playwright, and novelist; his work includes the *Blackadder* series for television (1987–89), the play *Gasping* (1990), and the novel *High Society* (2002) **2** **Charles Sutherland** 1900–91, British zoologist: initiated the study of animal ecology

eluate ('ɛlju:ˌeɪt) *n* a solution of adsorbed material in the eluant obtained during the process of elution

elucidate (ɪ'lu:sɪˌdeɪt) *vb* **elucidates, elucidating, elucidated** to make clear (something obscure or difficult); clarify [C16 from LL *ēlūcidāre* to enlighten; see LUCID] > **eˌluci'dation** *n* > **e'luciˌdative** *or* **e'luciˌdatory** *adj* > **e'luciˌdator** *n*

elude (ɪ'lu:d) *vb* **eludes, eluding, eluded** (*tr*) **1** to escape from or avoid, esp by cunning **2** to avoid fulfilment of (a responsibility, obligation, etc); evade **3** to escape discovery or understanding by; baffle [C16 from L *ēlūdere* to deceive, from *lūdere* to play] > **e'luder** *n* > **e'lusion** *n*

Ee

USAGE *Elude* is sometimes wrongly used where *allude* is meant: *he was alluding* (not *eluding*) *to his previous visit to the city*

eluent *or* **eluant** ('ɛljʊənt) *n* a solvent used for eluting

elusive (ɪ'lu:sɪv) *adj* **1** difficult to catch **2** preferring or living in solitude and anonymity **3** difficult to remember > **e'lusiveness** *n*

USAGE See at **illusory**

elute (i:'lu:t, ɪ'lu:t) *vb* **elutes, eluting, eluted** (*tr*) to wash out (a substance) by the action of a solvent, as in chromatography [C18 from L *ēlūtus* rinsed out, from *luere* to wash, LAVE] > **e'lution** *n*

elutriate (ɪ'lu:trɪ,eɪt) *vb* **elutriates, elutriating, elutriated** (*tr*) to purify or separate (a substance or mixture) by washing and straining or decanting [C18 from L *ēluere*, from *ē-* out + *lavere* to wash] > **e,lutri'ation** *n*

elver ('ɛlvə) *n* a young eel, esp one migrating up a river [C17 var. of *eelfare*, lit.: eel-journey; see EEL, FARE]

elves (ɛlvz) *n* the plural of **elf**

elvish ('ɛlvɪʃ) *adj* a variant of **elfish**: see **elf**

Ely ('i:lɪ) *n* **1** a cathedral city in E England, in E Cambridgeshire on the River Ouse. Pop: 10 329 (1991) **2** a former county of E England, part of Cambridgeshire since 1965

Elysée (eɪ'li:zeɪ) *n* a palace in Paris, in the Champs Elysées: official residence of the president of France

Elysium (ɪ'lɪzɪəm) *n* **1** Also called: **Elysian fields** *Greek myth* the dwelling place of the blessed after death **2** a state or place of perfect bliss [C16 from L, from Gk *Ēlusion pedion* Elysian (that is, blessed) fields]

Elytis (ɛ'laɪtɪs) *n* **Odysseus**, real name *Odysseus Alepoudelis*. 1912–96, Greek poet, author of the long poems *Axion Est* (1959) and *Maria Nefeli* (1978): Nobel prize for literature 1979

elytron ('ɛlɪ,trɒn) *or* **elytrum** ('ɛlɪtrəm) *n, pl* **elytra** (-trə) either of the horny front wings of beetles and some other insects [C18 from Gk *elutron* sheath]

em (ɛm) *n printing* **1** the square of a body of any size of type, used as a unit of measurement **2** Also called: **pica em, pica** a unit of measurement in printing, equal to twelve points or one sixth of an inch [C19 from the name of the letter *M*]

em- *prefix* a variant of **en-**[1] and **en-**[2] before *b, m*, and *p*

'em (əm) *pron* an informal variant of **them**

emaciate (ɪ'meɪsɪ,eɪt) *vb* **emaciates, emaciating, emaciated** (*usually tr*) to become or cause to become abnormally thin [C17 from L, from *macer* thin] > **e,maci'ation** *n*

emaciated (ɪ'meɪsɪ,eɪtɪd) *adj* abnormally thin

E-mail, e-mail, *or* **email** ('i:meɪl) *n* **1** short for **electronic mail** ▷ *vb* (*tr*) **2** to contact (a person) by electronic mail **3** to send (a message, document, etc) by electronic mail

emanate ('ɛmə,neɪt) *vb* **emanates, emanating, emanated** **1** (*intr*; *often foll by from*) to issue or proceed from or as from a source **2** (*tr*) to send forth; emit [C18 from L *ēmānāre* to flow out, from *mānāre* to flow] > **emanative** ('ɛmənətɪv) *adj* > **'ema,nator** *n* > **'ema,natory** *adj*

emanation (,ɛmə'neɪʃən) *n* **1** an act or instance of emanating **2** something that emanates or is produced **3** a gaseous product of radioactive decay > **,ema'national** *adj*

emancipate (ɪ'mænsɪ,peɪt) *vb* **emancipates, emancipating, emancipated** (*tr*) **1** to free from restriction or restraint, esp social or legal restraint **2** (*often passive*) to free from the inhibitions of conventional morality **3** to liberate (a slave) from bondage [C17 from L *ēmancipāre* to give independence (to a son), from *mancipāre* to transfer property; see MANCIPLE] > **e'manci,pated** *adj* > **e,manci'pation** *n* > **e'manci,pator** *n* > **emancipatory** (ɪ'mænsɪpətərɪ, -trɪ) *adj*

e-marketing *n* the practice of marketing by means of the Internet [C20 *e*lectronic *marketing*]

emasculate *vb* (ɪ'mæskjʊ,leɪt), **emasculates, emasculating, emasculated** (*tr*) **1** to remove the testicles of; castrate; geld **2** to deprive of vigour, effectiveness, etc **3** *bot* to remove the stamens from (a flower) to prevent self-pollination for the purposes of plant breeding ▷ *adj* (ɪ'mæskjʊlɪt, -,leɪt) **4** castrated; gelded **5** Also: **emasculated** deprived of strength, effectiveness, etc [C17 from L *ēmasculāre*, from *masculus* male; see MASCULINE] > **e,mascu'lation** *n* > **e'mascu,lator** *n* > **e'masculatory** *adj*

embalm (ɪm'bɑ:m) *vb* (*tr*) **1** to treat (a dead body) with preservatives to retard putrefaction **2** to preserve or cherish the memory of **3** *poetic* to give a sweet fragrance to [C13 from OF *embaumer*; see BALM] > **em'balmer** *n* > **em'balmment** *n*

embank (ɪm'bæŋk) *vb* (*tr*) to protect, enclose, or confine with an embankment

embankment (ɪm'bæŋkmənt) *n* a man-made ridge of earth or stone that carries a road or railway or confines a waterway

embargo (ɛm'bɑ:gəʊ) *n, pl* **embargoes** **1** a government order prohibiting the departure or arrival of merchant ships in its ports **2** any legal stoppage of commerce **3** a restraint or prohibition ▷ *vb* **embargoes, embargoing, embargoed** (*tr*) **4** to lay an embargo upon **5** to seize for use by the state [C16 from Sp., from *embargar*, from L IM- + *barra* BAR[1]]

embark (ɛm'bɑ:k) *vb* **1** to board (a ship or aircraft) **2** (*intr*; *usually foll by on or upon*) to commence or engage (in) a new project, venture, etc [C16 via F from OF, from EM- + *barca* boat, BARQUE] > **,embar'kation** *n*

embarrass (ɪm'bærəs) *vb* (*mainly tr*) **1** to cause to feel confusion or self-consciousness; disconcert **2** (*usually passive*) to involve in financial difficulties **3** *arch* to complicate **4** *arch* to impede or hamper [C17 (in the sense: to impede): via F & Sp. from It., from *imbarrare* to confine within bars] > **em'barrassed** *adj* > **em'barrassing** *adj* > **em'barrassment** *n*

embassy ('ɛmbəsɪ) *n, pl* **embassies** **1** the residence or place of business of an ambassador **2** an ambassador and his or her entourage collectively **3** the position, business, or mission of an ambassador **4** any important or official mission [C16 from OF *ambaisada*; see AMBASSADOR]

embattle (ɪm'bæt[ə]l) *vb* **embattles, embattling, embattled** (*tr*) **1** to deploy (troops) for battle **2** to fortify (a position, town, etc) **3** to provide with battlements [C14 from OF *embataillier*; see EN-[1] BATTLE]

embay (ɪm'beɪ) *vb* (*tr*) (*usually passive*) **1** to form into a bay **2** to enclose in or as if in a bay

embed (ɪm'bɛd) *vb* **embeds, embedding, embedded** **1** (usually foll by *in*) to fix or become fixed firmly and deeply in a surrounding solid mass **2** (*tr*) to surround closely **3** (*tr*) to fix or retain (a thought, idea, etc) in the mind **4** to assign a journalist, or be assigned as a journalist, to accompany an active military unit. Also: **imbed** > **em'bedment** *n*

embedding (ɪm'bɛdɪŋ) *n* the practice of being assigned or assigning a journalist to accompany an active military unit

embellish (ɪm'bɛlɪʃ) *vb* (*tr*) **1** to beautify; adorn **2** to make (a story, etc) more interesting by adding detail [C14 from OF *embelir*, from *bel* beautiful, from L *bellus*] > **em'bellisher** *n* > **em'bellishment** *n*

ember ('ɛmbə) *n* **1** a glowing or smouldering piece of coal or wood, as in a dying fire **2** the remains of a past emotion [OE *ǣmyrge*]

Ember days *pl n RC & Anglican Church* any of four groups in the year of three days (always Wednesday, Friday, and Saturday) of prayer and fasting [OE *ymbrendǣg*, from *ymb* around + *ryne* a course + *dǣg* day]

embezzle (ɪm'bɛzᵊl) *vb* **embezzles, embezzling, embezzled** to convert (money or property entrusted to one) fraudulently to one's own use [c15 from Anglo-F *embeseiller* to destroy, from OF *beseiller* to make away with, from ?] > **em'bezzlement** *n* > **em'bezzler** *n*

embitter (ɪm'bɪtə) *vb (tr)* **1** to make (a person) bitter **2** to aggravate (a hostile feeling, difficult situation, etc) > **em'bittered** *adj* > **em'bitterment** *n*

emblazon (ɪm'bleɪzᵊn) *vb (tr)* **1** to portray heraldic arms on (a shield, one's notepaper, etc) **2** to make bright or splendid, as with colours, flowers, etc **3** to glorify, praise, or extol > **em'blazonment** *n*

emblem ('ɛmbləm) *n* a visible object or representation that symbolizes a quality, type, group, etc [c15 from L *emblēma*, from Gk, from *emballein* to insert, from *en* in + *ballein* to throw] > ˌ**emblem'atic** *or* ˌ**emblem'atical** *adj* > ˌ**emblem'atically** *adv*

embody (ɪm'bɒdɪ) *vb* **embodies, embodying, embodied** *(tr)* **1** to give a tangible, bodily, or concrete form to (an abstract concept) **2** to be an example of or express (an idea, principle, etc) **3** (often foll by *in*) to collect or unite in a comprehensive whole **4** to invest (a spiritual entity) with bodily form > **em'bodiment** *n*

embolden (ɪm'bəʊldᵊn) *vb (tr)* to encourage; make bold

embolism ('ɛmbəˌlɪzəm) *n* the occlusion of a blood vessel by an embolus [c14 from Med. L, from LGk *embolismos*; see EMBOLUS] > **embolic** (ɛm'bɒlɪk) *adj*

embolus ('ɛmbələs) *n, pl* **emboli** (-ˌlaɪ) material, such as part of a blood clot or an air bubble, that becomes lodged within a small blood vessel and impedes the circulation [c17 via L from Gk *embolos* stopper; see EMBLEM]

embonpoint *French* (ɑ̃bɔ̃pwɛ̃) *n* **1** plumpness or stoutness ▷ *adj* **2** plump; stout [c18 from *en bon point* in good condition]

embosom (ɪm'bʊzəm) *vb (tr) arch* **1** to enclose or envelop, esp protectively **2** to clasp to the bosom; hug **3** to cherish

emboss (ɪm'bɒs) *vb* **1** to mould or carve (a decoration) on (a surface) so that it is raised above the surface in low relief **2** to cause to bulge; make protrude [c14 from OF *embocer*, from EM- + *boce* BOSS²] > **em'bossed** *adj* > **em'bosser** *n* > **em'bossment** *n*

embouchure (ˌɒmbʊ'ʃʊə) *n* **1** the mouth of a river or valley **2** *music* **2a** the correct application of the lips and tongue in playing a wind instrument **2b** the mouthpiece of a wind instrument [c18 from F, from OF, from *bouche* mouth, from L *bucca* cheek]

embower (ɪm'baʊə) *vb (tr) arch* to enclose in or as in a bower

embrace (ɪm'breɪs) *vb* **embraces, embracing, embraced** *(mainly tr)* **1** *(also intr)* (of a person) to take or clasp (another person) in the arms, or (of two people) to clasp each other, as in affection, greeting, etc; hug **2** to accept willingly or eagerly **3** to take up (a new idea, faith, etc); adopt **4** to comprise or include as an integral part **5** to encircle or enclose **6** *rare* to perceive or understand ▷ *n* **7** the act of embracing [c14 from OF, from EM- + *brace* a pair of arms, from L *bracchia* arms] > **em'braceable** *adj* > **em'bracement** *n* > **em'bracer** *n*

embrasure (ɪm'breɪʒə) *n* **1** *fortifications* an opening or indentation, as in a battlement, for shooting through **2** a door or window having splayed sides that increase the width of the opening in the interior [c18 from F, from obs. *embraser* to widen] > **em'brasured** *adj*

embrocate ('ɛmbrəʊˌkeɪt) *vb* **embrocates, embrocating, embrocated** *(tr)* to apply a liniment or lotion to (a part of the body) [c17 from Med. L *embrocha* poultice, from Gk, from *brokhē* a moistening]

embrocation (ˌɛmbrəʊ'keɪʃən) *n* a drug or agent for rubbing into the skin; liniment

embroider (ɪm'brɔɪdə) *vb* **1** to do decorative needlework (upon) **2** to add fictitious or exaggerated detail to (a story, etc) [c15 from OF *embroder*] > **em'broiderer** *n*

embroidery (ɪm'brɔɪdərɪ) *n, pl* **embroideries** **1** decorative needlework done usually on loosely woven cloth or canvas, often being a picture or pattern **2** elaboration or exaggeration, esp in writing or reporting; embellishment

▷ www.embroiderersguild.org.uk

embroil (ɪm'brɔɪl) *vb (tr)* **1** to involve (a person, oneself, etc) in trouble, conflict, or argument **2** to throw (affairs, etc) into a state of confusion or disorder; complicate; entangle [c17 from F *embrouiller*, from *brouiller* to mingle, confuse] > **em'broiler** *n* > **em'broilment** *n*

embryo ('ɛmbrɪˌəʊ) *n, pl* **embryos** **1** an animal in the early stages of development up to birth or hatching **2** the human product of conception up to approximately the end of the second month of pregnancy. ▷ Cf **fetus** **3** a plant in the early stages of development **4** an undeveloped or rudimentary state (esp in **in embryo**) **5** something in an early stage of development [c16 from LL, from Gk *embruon*, from *bruein* to swell]

embryology (ˌɛmbrɪ'ɒlədʒɪ) *n* **1** the scientific study of embryos **2** the structure and development of the embryo of a particular organism > **embryological** (ˌɛmbrɪə'lɒdʒɪkᵊl) *or* ˌ**embryo'logic** *adj* > ˌ**embry'ologist** *n*

embryonic (ˌɛmbrɪ'ɒnɪk) *or* **embryonal** ('ɛmbrɪənᵊl) *adj* **1** of or relating to an embryo **2** in an early stage; rudimentary; undeveloped > ˌ**embry'onically** *adv*

emcee (ˌɛm'siː) *inf* ▷ *n* **1** a master of ceremonies ▷ *vb* **emcees, emceeing, emceed** **2** to act as master of ceremonies (for or at) [c20 from MC]

Emden (*German* 'ɛmdən) *n* a port in NW Germany, in Lower Saxony at the mouth of the River Ems. Pop: 51 100 (1991)

-eme *suffix forming nouns linguistics* indicating a minimal distinctive unit of a specified type in a language: *morpheme; phoneme* [c20 via F, abstracted from PHONEME]

emend (ɪ'mɛnd) *vb (tr)* to make corrections or improvements in (a text) by critical editing [c15 from L, from *ē-* out + *mendum* a mistake] > **e'mendable** *adj*

emendation (ˌiːmɛn'deɪʃən) *n* **1** a correction or improvement in a text **2** the act or process of emending > **'emenˌdator** *n* > **emendatory** (ɪ'mɛndətərɪ, -trɪ) *adj*

emerald ('ɛmərəld, 'ɛmrəld) *n* **1** a green transparent variety of beryl: highly valued as a gem **2a** its clear green colour **2b** *(as adj)*: *an emerald carpet* [c13 from OF *esmeraude*, from L *smaragdus*, from Gk *smaragdos*]

Emerald Isle *n* a poetic name for **Ireland**

emerge (ɪ'mɜːdʒ) *vb* **emerges, emerging, emerged** *(intr; often foll by from)* **1** to come up to the surface of or rise from water or other liquid **2** to come into view, as from concealment or obscurity **3** (foll by *from*) to come out (of) or live (through (a difficult experience, etc)) **4** to become apparent [c17 from L *ēmergere* to rise up from, from *mergere* to dip] > **e'mergence** *n* > **e'merging** *adj*

emergency (ɪ'mɜːdʒənsɪ) *n, pl* **emergencies** **1a** an unforeseen or sudden occurrence, esp of danger demanding immediate action **1b** *(as modifier)*: *an emergency exit* **2a** a patient requiring urgent treatment **2b** *(as modifier)*: *an emergency ward* **3** NZ a player selected to stand by to replace an injured member of a team; reserve **4** **state of emergency** a condition, declared by a government, in which martial law applies, usually because of civil unrest or natural disaster

emergency medical technician *n* US a member of the emergency services who is trained to provide basic emergency medical care before a patient is taken to a hospital. Abbrev: **EMT**

emergent (ɪ'mɜːdʒənt) *adj* **1** coming into being or notice **2** (of a nation) recently independent > **e'mergently** *adv*

emeritus (ɪ'mɛrɪtəs) *adj (usually postpositive)* retired or honourably discharged from full-time work, but retaining one's title on an honorary basis: *a professor emeritus* [c19 from L, from *merēre* to deserve; see MERIT]

emersion (ɪˈmɜːʃən) *n* **1** the act or an instance of emerging **2** *astron* the reappearance of a celestial body after an eclipse or occultation [C17 from L *ēmersus*; see EMERGE]

Emerson (ˈɛməsᵊn) *n* **Ralph Waldo** (rælf ˈwɔːldəʊ) 1803–82, US poet, essayist, and transcendentalist

emery (ˈɛmərɪ) *n* **a** a hard greyish-black mineral consisting of corundum with either magnetite or haematite: used as an abrasive and polishing agent **b** (*as modifier*): *emery paper* [C15 from OF *esmeril*, ult. from Gk *smuris* powder for rubbing]

emery board *n* a strip of cardboard or wood with a rough surface of crushed emery, for filing one's nails

emetic (ɪˈmɛtɪk) *adj* **1** causing vomiting ▷ *n* **2** an emetic agent or drug [C17 from LL, from Gk *emetikos*, from *emein* to vomit]

emf *or* **EMF** *abbrev for* electromotive force

-emia *n combining form* a US variant of **-aemia**

emigrant (ˈɛmɪɡrənt) *n* **a** a person who leaves one place, esp his or her native country, to settle in another **b** (*as modifier*): *an emigrant worker*

emigrate (ˈɛmɪˌɡreɪt) *vb* **emigrates, emigrating, emigrated** (*intr*) to leave one place, esp one's native country, to settle in another [C18 from L *ēmīgrāre*, from *migrāre* to depart, MIGRATE] > ˌ**emiˈgration** *n* > ˈ**emiˌgratory** *adj*

émigré (ˈɛmɪˌɡreɪ) *n* an emigrant, esp one forced to leave his or her native country for political reasons [C18 from F, from *émigrer* to EMIGRATE]

Emilia-Romagna (ɪˈmiːlɪərəʊˈmɑːnjə; *Italian* eˈmiːlia-roˈmaɲɲa) *n* a region of N central Italy, on the Adriatic: rises from the plains of the Po valley in the north to the Apennines in the south. Capital: Bologna. Pop: 3 981 146 (2000 est). Area: 22 123 sq km (8628 sq miles)

Emin (ˈiːmɪn) *n* **Tracey** born 1963, British artist, noted for provocative multimedia works such as *Everyone I Have Ever Slept With* (1995) and *My Bed* (1999)

Eminem (ˌʒmɪˈnɜm) *n* real name *Marshall Mathers III*. born 1972, US White rap performer noted for his controversial lyrics; recordings include *The Slim Shady LP* (1999) and *The Eminem Show* (2002); he also starred in the film *8 mile* (2002)

eminence (ˈɛmɪnəns) *n* **1** a position of superiority or fame **2** a high or raised piece of ground. Also: **eminency** [C17 from F, from L *ēminentia* a standing out; see EMINENT]

Eminence (ˈɛmɪnəns) *or* **Eminency** *n, pl* **Eminences** *or* **Eminencies** (preceded by *Your* or *His*) a title used to address or refer to a cardinal

éminence grise *French* (eminɑ̃s ɡriz) *n, pl* ***éminences grises*** (eminɑ̃s ɡriz) a person who wields power and influence unofficially or behind the scenes [lit.: grey eminence, orig. applied to Père Joseph (François Le Clerc du Tremblay; died 1638), F monk, secretary of Cardinal RICHELIEU]

eminent (ˈɛmɪnənt) *adj* **1** above others in rank, merit, or reputation; distinguished **2** (*prenominal*) noteworthy or outstanding **3** projecting or protruding; prominent [C15 from L *ēminēre* to project, stand out, from *minēre* to stand]

eminent domain *n law* the right of a state to confiscate private property for public use, payment usually being made in compensation

emir (ɛˈmɪə) *n* (in the Islamic world) **1** an independent ruler or chieftain **2** a military commander or governor **3** a descendant of Mohammed [C17 via F from Sp., from Ar. ʼ*amīr* commander] > **eˈmirate** *n*

emissary (ˈɛmɪsərɪ, -ɪsrɪ) *n, pl* **emissaries 1a** an agent sent on a mission, esp one who represents a government or head of state **1b** (*as modifier*): *an emissary delegation* **2** an agent sent on a secret mission, as a spy ▷ *adj* **3** (of veins) draining blood from sinuses in the dura mater to veins outside the skull [C17 from L *ēmissārius*, from *ēmittere* to send out; see EMIT]

emission (ɪˈmɪʃən) *n* **1** the act of emitting or sending forth **2** energy, in the form of heat, light, radio waves, etc, emitted from a source **3** a substance, fluid, etc, that is emitted; discharge **4** *physiol* any bodily discharge, esp of semen [C17 from L *ēmissiō*, from *ēmittere* to send forth, EMIT] > **eˈmissive** *adj*

emission spectrum *n* the spectrum or pattern of bright lines or bands seen when the electromagnetic radiation emitted by a substance is passed into a spectrometer

emissivity (ˌiːmɪˈsɪvɪtɪ, ˌɛm-) *n* a measure of the ability of a surface to radiate energy; the ratio of the radiant flux emitted per unit area to that emitted by a black body at the same temperature

emit (ɪˈmɪt) *vb* **emits, emitting, emitted** (*tr*) **1** to give or send forth; discharge **2** to give voice to; utter **3** *physics* to give off (radiation or particles) [C17 from L *ēmittere* to send out, from *mittere* to send]

emitter (ɪˈmɪtə) *n* **1** a person or thing that emits **2** a substance that emits radiation **3** the region in a transistor in which the charge-carrying holes or electrons originate

Emmanuel (ɪˈmænjʊəl) *n* a variant spelling of **Immanuel**

Emmen (ˈɛmən; *Dutch* ˈɛmə) *n* a city in the NE Netherlands, in Drenthe province: a new town developed since World War II. Pop: 105 497 (1999 est)

Emmenthal, Emmental (ˈɛmənˌtɑːl), *or* **Emmenthaler** *n* a hard Swiss cheese with holes in it [C20 after *Emmenthal*, valley in Switzerland]

Emmet (ˈɛmɪt) *n* **Robert** 1778–1803, Irish nationalist, executed for leading an uprising for Irish independence

Emmy (ˈɛmɪ) *n, pl* **Emmys** *or* **Emmies** (in the US) one of the statuettes awarded annually for outstanding television performances and productions [C20 from *Immy*, short for *image orthicon tube*]

▷ www.emmyonline.org
▷ www.emmys.com
▷ www.howstuffworks.com/emmy.htm

emollient (ɪˈmɒljənt) *adj* **1** softening or soothing, esp to the skin **2** helping to avoid confrontation; calming ▷ *n* **3** any preparation or substance that has this effect [C17 from L *ēmollīre* to soften, from *mollis* soft] > **eˈmollience** *n*

emolument (ɪˈmɒljʊmənt) *n* the profit arising from an office or employment; fees or wages [C15 from L *ēmolumentum* benefit; orig., fee paid to a miller, from *molere* to grind]

emote (ɪˈməʊt) *vb* **emotes, emoting, emoted** (*intr*) to display exaggerated emotion, as in acting [C20 back formation from EMOTION] > **eˈmoter** *n*

emoticon (ɪˈməʊtɪˌkɒn) *n* any of several combinations of symbols used in electronic mail to indicate the state of mind of the writer, as in :-) to indicate happiness or :-o to indicate surprise [C20 from EMOT(ION) + ICON]

EMOTICONS

:-)	happy
:)	smiley without a nose
(-:	also smiling; smiling back
:))	cheerful
:)))	really happy
:>	devilish grin
:')	happy and crying
:-()	smiling with mouth open
8-)	smiling with glasses
{:-)	smiling with hair
D:-)	smiling with cap
C|:-)	smiling with top hat
(:-)	smiling with helmet

:-)= smiling with a beard
;-) twinkle
:-* kiss
:-(sad
:'-(crying
:-C unhappy
[:-(unhappy
[:-(frowning
:/ frustrated
:-|| angry
:-(o) shouting
:-@ screaming
:-< cheated
:-* bitter
'! grim
:-(*) you make me sick
:-| not talking
-!! definitely not
-!-!-! No! No! No!
:-O wow
:-9 salivating
:- surprised
:-() shocked
:-\ sceptical
%-) confused; cross-eyed
8-o Omigod
:-X not saying a word
:-& tongue-tied
|-| sleeping
|-o snoring
8-] glasses
B-) sunglasses
B:-) sunglasses on head
8:-) glasses on head
{:-) toupee
:^) broken nose
:-~) runny nose
X:-(headache
-:-) punk
:-{) with a moustache
:-{} lipstick
:-Q smoking
O :-) angel
:*) drunk
%') very drunk
#:-) bad hair day
O-====" flat on my back
:@) pig
;———-) liar; Pinocchio
@-) hypnotist
:-)))Xmas Happy Christmas
{:^=(Adolf Hitler
([(Robocop
?:^[] Jim Carrey
*<L:-) Santa Claus
%\v Pablo Picasso
(_8^(|) Homer Simpson
@@@@@:) Marge Simpson
~~~~~8) snake
(8) invisible man

▷ www.computeruser.com/resources/dictionary/emoticons.html
▷ www.pacificnet.net/jue/docs/emoticons.html
▷ www.sharpened.net/glossary/emoticons.php

emotion (ɪ'məʊʃən) *n* any strong feeling, as of joy, sorrow, or fear [C16 from F, from OF, from L *ēmovēre* to disturb, from *movēre* to MOVE]

emotional (ɪ'məʊʃənᵊl) *adj* **1** of, characteristic of, or expressive of emotion **2** readily or excessively affected by emotion **3** appealing to or arousing emotion **4** caused or determined by emotion rather than reason: *an emotional argument* > **e,motion'ality** *n*

USAGE See at **emotive**

emotional correctness *n* pressure on an individual to be seen to feel the same emotion as others

emotional intelligence *n* awareness of one's own emotions and moods and those of others, esp in managing people

emotionalism (ɪ'məʊʃənə,lɪzəm) *n* **1** emotional nature or quality **2** a tendency to yield readily to the emotions **3** an appeal to the emotions, esp as to an audience > **e'motionalist** *n* > **e,motional'istic** *adj*

emotionalize *or* **emotionalise** (ɪ'məʊʃənə,laɪz) *vb* **emotionalizes, emotionalizing, emotionalized** *or* **emotionalises, emotionalising, emotionalised** (*tr*) to make emotional; subject to emotional treatment

emotional literacy *n* the ability to deal with one's emotions and recognize their causes

emotive (ɪ'məʊtɪv) *adj* **1** tending or designed to arouse emotion **2** of or characterized by emotion > **e'motiveness** *or* **,emo'tivity** *n*

USAGE *Emotional* is the more general and neutral word for referring to anything to do with the emotions and emotional states. *Emotive* has the more restricted meaning of 'tending to arouse emotion', and is often associated with *issues, subjects, language, words*. However, since *emotional* can also mean 'arousing emotion', with certain nouns it is possible to use either word, depending on the slant one wishes to give: *...an emotive/emotional appeal on behalf of the disadvantaged young*

empanel *or* **impanel** (ɪm'pænᵊl) *vb* **empanels, empanelling, empanelled** *or US* **empanels, empaneling, empaneled** *or* **impanels, impanelling, impanelled** *or US* **impanels, impaneling, impaneled** (*tr*) *law* **1** to enter on a list (names of persons to be summoned for jury service) **2** to select (a jury) from such a list > **em'panelment** *or* **im'panelment** *n*

empathize *or* **empathise** ('ɛmpə,θaɪz) *vb* **empathizes, empathizing, empathized** *or* **empathises, empathising, empathised** (*intr*) to engage in or feel empathy

empathy ('ɛmpəθɪ) *n* **1** the power of understanding and imaginatively entering into another person's feelings **2** the attribution to an object, such as a work of art, of one's own feelings about it [C20 from Gk *empatheia* affection, passion] > **em'pathic** *or* **,empa'thetic** *adj*

Empedocles (ɛm'pɛdə,kli:z) *n* ?490–430 BC, Greek philosopher and scientist, who held that the world is composed of four elements, air, fire, earth, and water, which are governed by the opposing forces of love and discord

emperor ('ɛmpərə) *n* a monarch who rules or reigns over an empire [C13 from OF, from L *imperāre* to command, from IM- + *parāre* to make ready] > **'emperor,ship** *n*

emperor penguin *n* an Antarctic penguin with orange-yellow patches on the neck: the largest penguin, reaching a height of 1.3 m (4 ft)

emphasis ('ɛmfəsɪs) *n, pl* **emphases** (-si:z) **1** special importance or significance **2** an object, idea, etc, that is given special importance or significance **3** stress on a particular syllable, word, or phrase in speaking **4** force or intensity of expression **5** sharpness or clarity of form or outline [C16 via L from Gk: meaning, (in rhetoric) significant stress; see EMPHATIC]

emphasize *or* **emphasise** ('ɛmfə,saɪz) *vb* **emphasizes, emphasizing, emphasized** *or* **emphasises, emphasising, emphasised** (*tr*) to give emphasis or prominence to; stress

emphatic (ɪm'fætɪk) *adj* **1** expressed, spoken, or done with emphasis **2** forceful and positive; definite; direct **3** sharp or clear in form, contour, or outline
~~~~~

4 important or significant; stressed [c18 from Gk, from *emphainein* to display, from *phainein* to show]
> **em'phatically** *adv*

emphysema (ˌɛmfɪ'siːmə) *n pathol* 1 a condition in which the air sacs of the lungs are grossly enlarged, causing breathlessness and wheezing 2 the abnormal presence of air in a tissue or part [c17 from NL, from Gk *emphusēma* a swelling up, from *phusan* to blow]

empire ('ɛmpaɪə) *n* 1 an aggregate of peoples and territories under the rule of a single person, oligarchy, or sovereign state 2 any monarchy that has an emperor as head of state 3 the period during which a particular empire exists 4 supreme power; sovereignty 5 a large industrial organization with many ramifications [c13 from OF, from L, from *imperāre* to command, from *parāre* to prepare]

Empire ('ɛmpaɪə) *n* **the** 1 See **British Empire** 2 *French history* a the period of imperial rule in France from 1804 to 1815 under Napoleon Bonaparte b Also called: **Second Empire** the period from 1852 to 1870 when Napoleon III ruled as emperor ▷ *adj* 3 denoting, characteristic of, or relating to the British Empire 4 denoting, characteristic of, or relating to either French Empire, esp the first
▷ www.artlex.com/ArtLex/e/empire.html
▷ http://french.chass.utoronto.ca/fcs195

empire-builder *n inf* a person who seeks extra power, esp by increasing the number of his staff
> **'empire-ˌbuilding** *n, adj*

Empire Day *n* the former name of **Commonwealth Day**

Empire State *n* nickname of **New York** (state)

empiric (ɛm'pɪrɪk) *n* 1 a person who relies on empirical methods 2 a medical quack ▷ *adj* 3 a variant of **empirical** [c16 from L, from Gk *empeirikos* practised, from *peiran* to attempt]

empirical (ɛm'pɪrɪkᵊl) *adj* 1 derived from or relating to experiment and observation rather than theory 2 (of medical treatment) based on practical experience rather than scientific proof 3 *philosophy* (of knowledge) derived from experience rather than by logic from first principles 4 of or relating to medical quackery
> **em'piricalness** *n*

empiricism (ɛm'pɪrɪˌsɪzəm) *n* 1 *philosophy* the doctrine that all knowledge derives from experience 2 the use of empirical methods 3 medical quackery > **em'piricist** *n, adj*
▷ http://utm.edu/research/iep/e/emp-brit.htm

emplace (ɪm'pleɪs) *vb* **emplaces, emplacing, emplaced** (*tr*) to put in position

emplacement (ɪm'pleɪsmənt) *n* 1 a prepared position for a gun or other weapon 2 the act of putting or state of being put in place [c19 from F, from obs. *emplacer* to put in position, from PLACE]

emplane (ɪm'pleɪn) *vb* **emplanes, emplaning, emplaned** to board or put on board an aeroplane

employ (ɪm'plɔɪ) *vb* (*tr*) 1 to engage or make use of the services of (a person) in return for money; hire 2 to provide work or occupation for; keep busy 3 to use as a means ▷ *n* 4 the state of being employed (esp in **in someone's employ**) [c15 from OF *emploier*, from L *implicāre* to entangle, engage, from *plicāre* to fold] > **em'ployable** *adj* > **emˌploya'bility** *n*

employee *or US* **employe** (ɛm'plɔɪiː, ˌɛmplɔɪ'iː) *n* a person who is hired to work for another or for a business, firm, etc, in return for payment

employer (ɪm'plɔɪə) *n* 1 a person, firm, etc, that employs workers 2 a person who employs

employment (ɪm'plɔɪmənt) *n* 1 the act of employing or state of being employed 2 a person's work or occupation

employment office *n Brit* any government office established to collect and supply to the unemployed information about job vacancies and to employers information about availability of prospective workers. See also **Jobcentre**

employment tribunal *n* (in England, Scotland, and Wales) a tribunal that rules on disputes between employers and employees regarding unfair dismissal, redundancy, etc. See also: **industrial tribunal**

emporium (ɛm'pɔːrɪəm) *n, pl* **emporiums** *or* **emporia** (-rɪə) a large retail shop offering for sale a wide variety of merchandise [c16 from L, from Gk, from *emporos* merchant, from *poros* a journey]

empower (ɪm'paʊə) *vb* (*tr*) 1 to give power or authority to; authorize 2 to give ability to; enable or permit
> **em'powerment** *n*

empowerment (ɪm'paʊəmənt) *n* 1 the giving or delegation of power or authority; authorization 2 the giving of an ability; enablement or permission 3 (in South Africa) a policy of providing special opportunities in employment, training, etc, for Blacks and others disadvantaged under apartheid

empress ('ɛmprɪs) *n* 1 the wife or widow of an emperor 2 a woman who holds the rank of emperor in her own right [c12 from OF *empereriz*, from L *imperātrix*; see EMPEROR]

Empson ('ɛmpsᵊn) *n* Sir **William** 1906–84, English poet and critic; author of *Seven Types of Ambiguity* (1930)

empty ('ɛmptɪ) *adj* **emptier, emptiest** 1 containing nothing 2 without inhabitants; vacant or unoccupied 3 carrying no load, passengers, etc 4 without purpose, substance, or value: *an empty life* 5 insincere or trivial: *empty words* 6 not expressive or vital; vacant: *an empty look* 7 *inf* hungry 8 (*postpositive*; foll by *of*) devoid; destitute 9 *inf* drained of energy or emotion 10 *maths, logic* (of a set or class) containing no members ▷ *vb* **empties, emptying, emptied** 11 to make or become empty 12 (when *intr*, foll by *into*) to discharge (contents) 13 (*tr*; often foll by *of*) to unburden or rid (oneself) ▷ *n, pl* **empties** 14 an empty container, esp a bottle [OE *ǣmtig*]
> **'emptiable** *adj* > **'emptier** *n* > **'emptily** *adv* > **'emptiness** *n*

empty-handed *adj* 1 carrying nothing in the hands 2 having gained nothing

empty-headed *adj* lacking sense; frivolous

empty-nester (-'nɛstə) *n inf* a married person whose children have grown up and left home

empty-nest syndrome *n inf* a condition, often involving depression, loneliness, etc, experienced by parents living in a home from which the children have grown up and left

Empty Quarter *n* another name for **Rub' al Khali**

empyema (ˌɛmpaɪ'iːmə) *n, pl* **empyemata** (-'iːmətə) *or* **empyemas** a collection of pus in a body cavity, esp in the chest [c17 from Med. L, from Gk *empuēma* abscess, from *empuein* to suppurate, from *puon* pus] > **ˌempy'emic** *adj*

empyrean (ˌɛmpaɪ'riːən) *n* 1 *arch* the highest part of the heavens, thought in ancient times to contain the pure element of fire and by early Christians to be the abode of God 2 *poetic* the heavens or sky ▷ *adj also* **empyreal** 3 of or relating to the sky 4 heavenly or sublime [c17 from LL, from Gk *empurios* fiery]

empyreuma (ˌɛmpɪ'ruːmə) *n, pl* **empyreumata** (-mətə) the smell and taste associated with burning vegetable and animal matter [c17 from Gk, from *empureuein* to set on fire]

Ems (ɛmz) *n* 1 a town in W Germany, in the Rhineland-Palatinate: famous for the **Ems Telegram** (1870), Bismarck's dispatch that led to the outbreak of the Franco-Prussian War. Pop: 10 241 (latest est) 2 a river in West Germany, rising in the Teutoburger Wald and flowing generally north to the North Sea. Length: about 370 km (230 miles)

EMS *abbrev for* European Monetary System

EMT *US abbrev for* emergency medical technician

emu ('iːmjuː) *n* a large Australian flightless bird, similar

to the ostrich [c17 changed from Port. *ema* ostrich, from Ar. *Na-'amah* ostrich]
EMU *abbrev for:* 1 Economic and Monetary Union 2 European Monetary Union 3 See **e.m.u.**
e.m.u. *or* **EMU** *abbrev for* electromagnetic unit
emu-bob *Austral inf* ▷ *vb* **emu-bobs, emu-bobbing, emu-bobbed** 1 (*intr*) to bend over to collect litter or small pieces of wood ▷ *n* 2 Also called: **emu parade** a parade of soldiers or schoolchildren for litter collection > **'emu-ˌbobbing** *n*
emulate ('ɛmjʊˌleɪt) *vb* **emulates, emulating, emulated** (*tr*) 1 to attempt to equal or surpass, esp by imitation 2 to rival or compete with [c16 from L *aemulus* competing with] > **'emulative** *adj* > **ˌemu'lation** *n* > **'emuˌlator** *n*
emulous ('ɛmjʊləs) *adj* 1 desiring or aiming to equal or surpass another 2 characterized by or arising from emulation [c14 from L; see EMULATE] > **'emulousness** *n*
emulsifier (ɪ'mʌlsɪˌfaɪə) *n* an agent that forms an emulsion, esp a food additive that prevents separation of processed foods
emulsify (ɪ'mʌlsɪˌfaɪ) *vb* **emulsifies, emulsifying, emulsified** to make or form into an emulsion > **eˌmulsi'fiable** *or* **e'mulsible** *adj* > **eˌmulsifi'cation** *n*
emulsion (ɪ'mʌlʃən) *n* 1 *photog* a light-sensitive coating on a base, such as paper or film, consisting of silver bromide suspended in gelatine 2 *chem* a colloid in which both phases are liquids 3 a type of paint in which the pigment is suspended in a vehicle that is dispersed in water as an emulsion 4 *pharmacol* a mixture in which an oily medicine is dispersed in another liquid 5 any liquid resembling milk [c17 from NL *ēmulsiō*, from L, from *ēmulgēre* to milk out, from *mulgēre* to milk] > **e'mulsive** *adj*
emu oil *n* an oil obtained from the fat of the emu, traditionally used as an emollient by native Australians to relieve pain and speed healing
emu-wren *n* an Australian wren having long plumy tail feathers
en (ɛn) *n printing* a unit of measurement, half the width of an em
EN (in Britain) *abbrev for:* 1 enrolled nurse 2 English Nature
en-[1] *or* **em-** *prefix forming verbs* 1 (*from nouns*) 1a put in or on: *entomb; enthrone* 1b go on or into: *enplane* 1c surround or cover with: *enmesh* 1d furnish with: *empower* 2 (*from adjectives and nouns*) cause to be in a certain condition: *enable; enslave* [via OF from L *in-* IN-[2]]
en-[2] *or* **em-** *prefix forming nouns and adjectives* in; into; inside: *endemic* [from Gk (often via L); cf. IN-[1], IN-[2]]
-en[1] *suffix forming verbs from adjectives and nouns* cause to be; become; cause to have: *blacken; heighten* [OE *-n-*, as in *fæst-n-ian* to fasten, of Gmc origin]
-en[2] *suffix forming adjectives from nouns* of; made of; resembling: *ashen; wooden* [OE *-en*]
enable (ɪn'eɪbᵊl) *vb* **enables, enabling, enabled** (*tr*) 1 to provide (someone) with adequate power, means, opportunity, or authority (to do something) 2 to make possible > **en'ablement** *n* > **en'abler** *n*
enabling act *n* a legislative act conferring certain specified powers on a person or organization
enact (ɪn'ækt) *vb* (*tr*) 1 to make into an act or statute 2 to establish by law; decree 3 to represent or perform as in a play > **en'actable** *adj* > **en'active** *or* **en'actory** *adj* > **en'actment** *or* **en'action** *n* > **en'actor** *n*
enamel (ɪ'næməl) *n* 1 a coloured glassy substance, translucent or opaque, fused to the surface of articles made of metal, glass, etc, for ornament or protection 2 an article or articles ornamented with enamel 3 an enamel-like paint or varnish 4 any coating resembling enamel 5 the hard white substance that covers the crown of each tooth 6 (*modifier*) decorated or covered with enamel ▷ *vb* **enamels, enamelling, enamelled** *or US* **enamels, enameling, enameled** (*tr*) 7 to decorate with enamel 8 to ornament with glossy variegated colours, as if with enamel 9 to portray in enamel [c15 from OF *esmail*, of Gmc origin] > **e'nameller, e'namellist** *or US* **e'nameler, e'namelist** *n* > **e'namelˌwork** *n*
enamour *or US* **enamor** (ɪn'æmə) *vb* (*tr; usually passive* and foll by *of*) to inspire with love; captivate [c14 from OF, from *amour* love, from L *amor*]
enamoured *or US* **enamored** (ɪn'æməd) *adj* in love; captivated; charmed
en bloc *French* (ɑ̃ blɔk) *adv* in a lump or block; as a body or whole; all together
en brosse *French* (ɑ̃ brɔs) *adj, adv* (of the hair) cut very short so that the hair stands up stiffly [lit.: in the style of a brush]
enc. *abbrev for:* 1 enclosed 2 enclosure
encamp (ɪn'kæmp) *vb* to lodge or cause to lodge in a camp
encampment (ɪn'kæmpmənt) *n* 1 the act of setting up a camp 2 the place where a camp, esp a military camp, is set up
encapsulate *or* **incapsulate** (ɪn'kæpsjʊˌleɪt) *vb* **encapsulates, encapsulating, encapsulated** *or* **incapsulates, incapsulating, incapsulated** 1 to enclose or be enclosed as in a capsule 2 (*tr*) to sum up in a short or concise form > **enˌcapsu'lation** *or* **inˌcapsu'lation** *n*
encase *or* **incase** (ɪn'keɪs) *vb* **encases, encasing, encased** (*tr*) to place or enclose as in a case > **en'casement** *or* **in'casement** *n*
encash (ɪn'kæʃ) *vb* (*tr*) *Brit, formal* to exchange (a cheque) for cash > **en'cashable** *adj* > **en'cashment** *n*
encaustic (ɪn'kɒstɪk) *ceramics, etc* ▷ *adj* 1 decorated by any process involving burning in colours, esp by inlaying coloured clays and baking or by fusing wax colours to the surface ▷ *n* 2 the process of burning in colours 3 a product of such a process [c17 from L *encausticus*, from Gk, from *enkaiein* to burn in, from *kaiein* to burn] > **en'caustically** *adv*
-ence *or* **-ency** *suffix forming nouns* indicating an action, state, condition, or quality: *benevolence; residence; patience* [via OF from L *-entia*, from *-ēns*, present participial ending]
enceinte (ɒn'sænt) *adj* another word for **pregnant** [c17 from F, from L *inciēns* pregnant]
Enceladus (ɛn'sɛlədəs) *n Greek myth* a giant who was punished for his rebellion against the gods by a fatal blow from a stone cast by Athena. He was believed to be buried under Mount Etna in Sicily
encephalic (ˌɛnsɪ'fælɪk) *adj* of or relating to the brain
encephalin (ɛn'sɛfəlɪn) *n* a variant of **enkephalin**
encephalitis (ˌɛnsɛfə'laɪtɪs) *n* inflammation of the brain > **encephalitic** (ˌɛnsɛfə'lɪtɪk) *adj*
encephalitis lethargica (lɪ'θɑːdʒɪkə) *n* a technical name for **sleeping sickness** (sense 2)
encephalo- *or before a vowel* **encephal-** *combining form* indicating the brain: *encephalogram; encephalitis* [from NL, from Gk *enkephalos*, from *en-* in + *kephalē* head]
encephalogram (ɛn'sɛfələˌgræm) *n* 1 an X-ray photograph of the brain, esp one (a **pneumoencephalogram**) taken after replacing some of the cerebrospinal fluid with air or oxygen 2 short for **electroencephalogram**; see **electroencephalograph**
encephalon (ɛn'sɛfəˌlɒn) *n, pl* **encephala** (-lə) a technical name for **brain** [c18 from NL, from Gk *enkephalos* brain, from EN-[2] + *kephalē* head] > **en'cephalous** *adj*
encephalopathy (ˌɛnsɛfə'lɒpəθɪ) *n* any degenerative disease of the brain, often associated with toxic conditions. See also **BSE**
enchain (ɪn'tʃeɪn) *vb* (*tr*) 1 to bind with chains 2 to hold fast or captivate (the attention, etc) > **en'chainment** *n*
enchant (ɪn'tʃɑːnt) *vb* (*tr*) 1 to cast a spell on; bewitch 2 to delight or captivate utterly [c14 from OF, from L *incantāre*, from *cantāre* to chant] > **en'chanter** *n* > **en'chantress** *fem n*

Ee

enchanted (ɪnˈtʃɑːntɪd) *adj* **1** under a spell; bewitched; magical **2** utterly delighted or captivated; fascinated; charmed

enchanting (ɪnˈtʃɑːntɪŋ) *adj* pleasant; delightful > **enˈchantingly** *adv*

enchantment (ɪnˈtʃɑːntmənt) *n* **1** the act of enchanting or state of being enchanted **2** a magic spell **3** great charm or fascination

enchase (ɪnˈtʃeɪs) *vb* **enchases, enchasing, enchased** (*tr*) a less common word for **chase**[3] [c15 from OF *enchasser* to enclose, set, from EN-[1] + *casse* CASE[2]] > **enˈchaser** *n*

enchilada (ˌɛntʃɪˈlɑːdə) *n* a Mexican dish of a tortilla filled with meat, served with a chilli sauce [American Sp., from *enchilado*, from *enchilar* to spice with chilli]

-enchyma *n combining form* denoting cellular tissue [c20 abstracted from PARENCHYMA]

encipher (ɪnˈsaɪfə) *vb* (*tr*) to convert (a message, etc) into code or cipher > **enˈcipherer** *n* > **enˈcipherment** *n*

encircle (ɪnˈsɜːkᵊl) *vb* **encircles, encircling, encircled** (*tr*) to form a circle around; enclose within a circle; surround > **enˈcirclement** *n*

enclave (ˈɛnkleɪv) *n* a part of a country entirely surrounded by foreign territory: viewed from the position of the surrounding territories [c19 from F, from OF *enclaver* to enclose, from Vulgar L *inclāvāre* (unattested) to lock up, from L IN-[2] + *clavis* key]

enclitic (ɪnˈklɪtɪk) *adj* **1** denoting or relating to a monosyllabic word or form that is treated as a suffix of the preceding word ▷ *n* **2** an enclitic word or form [c17 from LL, from Gk, from *enklinein* to cause to lean, from EN-[2] + *klinein* to lean] > **enˈclitically** *adv*

enclose *or* **inclose** (ɪnˈkləʊz) *vb* **encloses, enclosing, enclosed** *or* **incloses, inclosing, inclosed** (*tr*) **1** to close; hem in; surround **2** to surround (land) with or as if with a fence **3** to put in an envelope or wrapper, esp together with a letter **4** to contain or hold > **enˈclosable** *or* **inˈclosable** *adj* > **enˈcloser** *or* **inˈcloser** *n*

enclosed order *n* a Christian religious order that does not permit its members to go into the outside world

enclosure *or* **inclosure** (ɪnˈkləʊʒə) *n* **1** the act of enclosing or state of being enclosed **2** an area enclosed as by a fence **3** the act of appropriating land by setting up a fence, hedge, etc, around it **4** a fence, wall, etc, that encloses **5** something enclosed within an envelope or wrapper, esp together with a letter **6** *Brit* a section of a sports ground, racecourse, etc, allotted to certain spectators

encode (ɪnˈkəʊd) *vb* **encodes, encoding, encoded** (*tr*) to convert (a message) into code > **enˈcodement** *n* > **enˈcoder** *n*

encomiast (ɛnˈkəʊmɪˌæst) *n* a person who speaks or writes an encomium [c17 from Gk, from *enkōmiazein* to utter an ENCOMIUM] > **enˌcomiˈastic** *or* **enˌcomiˈastical** *adj*

encomium (ɛnˈkəʊmɪəm) *n, pl* **encomiums** *or* **encomia** (-mɪə) a formal expression of praise; eulogy [c16 from L, from Gk, from EN-[2] + *kōmos* festivity]

encompass (ɪnˈkʌmpəs) *vb* (*tr*) **1** to enclose within a circle; surround **2** to bring about: *he encompassed the enemy's ruin* **3** to include entirely or comprehensively > **enˈcompassment** *n*

encore (ˈɒŋkɔː) *sentence substitute* **1** again: used by an audience to demand an extra or repeated performance ▷ *n* **2** an extra or repeated performance given in response to enthusiastic demand ▷ *vb* **encores, encoring, encored** **3** (*tr*) to demand an extra or repeated performance of (a work, piece of music, etc) by (a performer) [c18 from F: still, again, ?from L *in hanc hōram* until this hour]

encounter (ɪnˈkaʊntə) *vb* **1** to come upon or meet casually or unexpectedly **2** to meet (an enemy, army, etc) in battle or contest **3** (*tr*) to be faced with; contend with ▷ *n* **4** a casual or unexpected meeting **5** a hostile meeting; contest [c13 from OF, from Vulgar L *incontrāre* (unattested), from L IN-[2] + *contrā* against, opposite]

encounter group *n* a group of people who meet in order to develop self-awareness and mutual understanding by openly expressing their feelings, by confrontation, etc

encourage (ɪnˈkʌrɪdʒ) *vb* **encourages, encouraging, encouraged** (*tr*) **1** to inspire (someone) with the courage or confidence (to do something) **2** to stimulate (something or someone) by approval or help > **enˈcouragement** *n* > **enˈcourager** *n* > **enˈcouraging** *adj* > **enˈcouragingly** *adv*

encroach (ɪnˈkrəʊtʃ) *vb* (*intr*) **1** (often foll by *on* or *upon*) to intrude gradually or stealthily upon the rights, property, etc, of another **2** to advance beyond certain limits [c14 from OF *encrochier* to seize, lit.: fasten upon with hooks, of Gmc origin] > **enˈcroacher** *n* > **enˈcroachment** *n*

encrust *or* **incrust** (ɪnˈkrʌst) *vb* **1** (*tr*) to cover or overlay with or as with a crust or hard coating **2** to form or cause to form a crust or hard coating **3** (*tr*) to decorate lavishly, as with jewels > **ˌencrusˈtation** *or* **ˌincrusˈtation** *n*

encumber *or* **incumber** (ɪnˈkʌmbə) *vb* (*tr*) **1** to hinder or impede; hamper **2** to fill with superfluous or useless matter **3** to burden with debts, obligations, etc [c14 from OF, from EN-[1] + *combre* a barrier, from LL *combrus*]

encumbrance *or* **incumbrance** (ɪnˈkʌmbrəns) *n* **1** a thing that impedes or is burdensome; hindrance **2** *law* a burden or charge upon property, such as a mortgage or lien

-ency *suffix forming nouns* a variant of **-ence**: *fluency; permanency*

encyclical (ɛnˈsɪklɪkᵊl) *n* **1** a letter sent by the pope to all Roman Catholic bishops ▷ *adj also* **encyclic** **2** (of letters) intended for general circulation [c17 from LL, from Gk, from *kuklos* circle]

encyclopedia *or* **encyclopaedia** (ɛnˌsaɪkləʊˈpiːdɪə) *n* a book, often in many volumes, containing articles, often arranged in alphabetical order, dealing either with the whole range of human knowledge or with one particular subject [c16 from NL, erroneously for Gk *enkuklios paideia* general education] > **enˌcycloˈpedic** *or* **enˌcycloˈpaedic** *adj*

▷ www.kalama.com/~mariner/qserencyclo.htm

encyclopedist *or* **encyclopaedist** (ɛnˌsaɪkləʊˈpiːdɪst) *n* a person who compiles or contributes to an encyclopedia > **enˌcycloˈpedism** *or* **enˌcycloˈpaedism** *n*

encyst (ɛnˈsɪst) *vb biol* to enclose or become enclosed by a cyst, thick membrane, or shell > **enˈcystment** *or* **ˌencysˈtation** *n*

end (ɛnd) *n* **1** the extremity of the length of something, such as a road, line, etc **2** the surface at either extremity of an object **3** the extreme extent, limit, or degree of something **4** the most distant place or time that can be imagined: *the ends of the earth* **5** the time at which something is concluded **6** the last section or part **7** a share or part **8** (*often pl*) a remnant or fragment (esp in **odds and ends**) **9** a final state, esp death; destruction **10** the purpose of an action or existence **11** *sport* either of the two defended areas of a playing field, rink, etc **12** *bowls, etc* a section of play from one side of the rink to the other **13** **at an end** exhausted or completed **14** **come to an end** to become completed or exhausted **15** **have one's end away** *sl* to have sexual intercourse **16** **in the end** finally **17** **keep one's end up** **17a** to sustain one's part in a joint undertaking **17b** to hold one's own in an argument, contest, etc **18** **make (both) ends meet** to spend no more than the money one has **19** **no end (of)** *inf* (intensifier): *I had no end of work* **20** **on end** *inf* without pause or interruption **21** **the end** *sl* the worst, esp something that goes beyond the limits of endurance ▷ *vb* **22** to bring or come to a finish; conclude **23** to die or cause to die **24** (*tr*) to surpass or outdo: *a novel to end all* *novels* 25 **end it all** *inf* to commit suicide ▷ See also **end up** [OE *ende*] > **'ender** *n*

end- *combining form* a variant of **endo-** before a vowel

-end *suffix forming nouns* See **-and**

endamoeba *or US* **endameba** (ˌɛndəˈmiːbə) *n* variant spellings of **entamoeba**

endanger (ɪnˈdeɪndʒə) *vb (tr)* to put in danger or peril; imperil > **en'dangerment** *n*

endangered (ɪnˈdeɪndʒəd) *adj* in danger, esp of extinction: *an endangered species*

endear (ɪnˈdɪə) *vb (tr)* to cause to be beloved or esteemed > **en'dearing** *adj*

endearment (ɪnˈdɪəmənt) *n* something that endears, such as an affectionate utterance

endeavour *or US* **endeavor** (ɪnˈdɛvə) *vb* 1 to try (to do something) ▷ *n* 2 an effort to do or attain something [C14 *endeveren*, from EN-[1] + *-deveren* from *dever* duty, from OF *deveir*; see DEVOIRS] > **en'deavourer** *or US* **en'deavorer** *n*

endemic (ɛnˈdɛmɪk) *adj also* **endemial** (ɛnˈdɛmɪəl) *or* **endemical** 1 present within a localized area or peculiar to persons in such an area ▷ *n* 2 an endemic disease or plant [C18 from NL *endēmicus*, from Gk *endēmos* native, from EN-[2] + *dēmos* the people] > **en'demically** *adv* > **'endemism** *or* **ˌende'micity** *n*

Enderby Land (ˈɛndəbɪ) *n* part of the coastal region of Antarctica, between Kempland and Queen Maud Land: the westernmost part of the Australian Antarctic Territory; discovered in 1831

endermic (ɛnˈdɜːmɪk) *adj* (of a medicine, etc) acting by absorption through the skin [C19 from EN-[2] + Gk *derma* skin]

endgame (ˈɛndˌgeɪm) *n* the closing stage of any of certain games, esp chess, when there are only a few pieces left in play

ending (ˈɛndɪŋ) *n* 1 the act of bringing to or reaching an end 2 the last part of something 3 the final part of a word, esp a suffix

endive (ˈɛndaɪv) *n* a plant cultivated for its crisp curly leaves, which are used in salads. Cf **chicory** [C15 from OF, from Med. L, from var. of L *intubus*, *entubus*]

endless (ˈɛndlɪs) *adj* 1 having or seeming to have no end; eternal or infinite 2 continuing too long or continually recurring 3 formed with the ends joined > **'endlessness** *n*

endmost (ˈɛndˌməʊst) *adj* nearest the end; most distant

endo- *or before a vowel* **end-** *combining form* inside; within: *endocrine* [from Gk, from *endon* within]

endoblast (ˈɛndəʊˌblæst) *n* 1 *embryol* a less common name for **endoderm** 2 another name for **hypoblast** > **ˌendo'blastic** *adj*

endocarditis (ˌɛndəʊkɑːˈdaɪtɪs) *n* inflammation of the lining of the heart [C19 from NL, from ENDO- + Gk *kardia* heart + -ITIS] > **endocarditic** (ˌɛndəʊkɑːˈdɪtɪk) *adj*

endocarp (ˈɛndəˌkɑːp) *n* the inner layer of the pericarp of a fruit, such as the stone of a peach > **ˌendo'carpal** *or* **ˌendo'carpic** *adj*

endocrine (ˈɛndəʊˌkraɪn) *adj also* **ˌendo'crinal, endocrinic** (ˌɛndəʊˈkrɪnɪk) 1 of or denoting endocrine glands or their secretions ▷ *n* 2 an endocrine gland [C20 from ENDO- + *-crine*, from Gk *krinein* to separate]

endocrine gland *n* any of the glands that secrete hormones directly into the bloodstream, e.g. the pituitary, pineal, and thyroid

endocrinology (ˌɛndəʊkraɪˈnɒlədʒɪ, -krɪ-) *n* the branch of medical science concerned with the endocrine glands and their secretions > **ˌendocri'nologist** *n*

endoderm (ˈɛndəʊˌdɜːm) *or* **entoderm** *n* the inner germ layer of an animal embryo, which gives rise to the lining of the digestive and respiratory tracts > **ˌendo'dermal, ˌendo'dermic** *or* **ˌento'dermal, ˌento'dermic** *adj*

end of steel *n Canad* 1 a point up to which railway tracks have been laid 2 a town located at such a point

endogamy (ɛnˈdɒgəmɪ) *n* 1 *anthropol* marriage within one's own tribe or similar unit 2 pollination between two flowers on the same plant > **en'dogamous** *or* **endogamic** (ˌɛndəʊˈgæmɪk) *adj*

endogenous (ɛnˈdɒdʒɪnəs) *adj* 1 *biol* developing or originating within an organism or part of an organism 2 having no apparent external cause: *endogenous depression* > **en'dogeny** *n*

endometritis (ˌɛndəʊmɪˈtraɪtɪs) *n* inflammation of the endometrium, which is caused by infection, as by bacteria, foreign bodies, etc

endometrium (ˌɛndəʊˈmiːtrɪəm) *n, pl* **endometria** (-trɪə) the mucous membrane that lines the uterus [C19 NL, from ENDO- + Greek *mētra* uterus] > **ˌendo'metrial** *adj*

endomorph (ˈɛndəʊˌmɔːf) *n* 1 a type of person having a body build characterized by fatness and heaviness 2 a mineral that naturally occurs enclosed within another mineral > **ˌendo'morphic** *adj* > **'endoˌmorphy** *n*

endomorphism (ˌɛndəʊˈmɔːˌfɪzəm) *n geol* changes in a cooling body of igneous rock brought about by assimilation of fragments of, or chemical reaction with, the surrounding country rock

endophyte (ˈɛndəʊˌfaɪt) *n* any plant, parasitic fungus, or alga that lives within a plant > **endophytic** (ˌɛndəʊˈfɪtɪk) *adj*

endoplasm (ˈɛndəʊˌplæzəm) *n cytology* the inner cytoplasm of some cells > **ˌendo'plasmic** *adj*

end organ *n anat* the expanded end of a peripheral motor or sensory nerve

endorphin (ɛnˈdɔːfɪn) *n* any of a class of chemicals occurring in the brain, including enkephalin, which have a similar effect to morphine

endorsation (ˌɛndɔːˈseɪʃən) *n Canad* approval or support

endorse *or* **indorse** (ɪnˈdɔːs) *vb* **endorses, endorsing, endorsed** *or* **indorses, indorsing, indorsed** *(tr)* 1 to give approval or sanction to 2 to sign (one's name) on the back of (a cheque, etc) to specify oneself as payee 3 *commerce* 3a to sign the back of (a document) to transfer ownership of the rights to a specified payee 3b to specify (a sum) as transferable to another as payee 4 to write (a qualifying comment, etc) on the back of a document 5 to sign a document, as when confirming receipt of payment 6 *chiefly Brit* to record a conviction on (a driving licence) [C16 from OF *endosser* to put on the back, from EN-[1] + *dos* back] > **en'dorsable** *or* **in'dorsable** *adj* > **en'dorser, en'dorsor** *or* **in'dorser, in'dorsor** *n* > **enˌdor'see** *or* **inˌdor'see** *n*

endorsement *or* **indorsement** (ɪnˈdɔːsmənt) *n* 1 the act or an instance of endorsing 2 something that endorses, such as a signature 3 approval or support 4 a record of a motoring offence on a driving licence

endoscope (ˈɛndəʊˌskəʊp) *n* a medical instrument for examining the interior of hollow organs such as the stomach or bowel > **endoscopic** (ˌɛndəʊˈskɒpɪk) *adj*

endoskeleton (ˌɛndəʊˈskɛlɪtᵊn) *n* an internal skeleton, esp the bony or cartilaginous skeleton of vertebrates > **ˌendo'skeletal** *adj*

endosperm (ˈɛndəʊˌspɜːm) *n* the tissue within the seed of a flowering plant that surrounds and nourishes the embryo > **ˌendo'spermic** *adj*

endothermic (ˌɛndəʊˈθɜːmɪk) *or* **endothermal** *adj* (of a chemical reaction or compound) occurring or formed with the absorption of heat > **ˌendo'thermically** *adv* > **ˌendo'thermism** *n*

endow (ɪnˈdaʊ) *vb (tr)* 1 to provide with or bequeath a source of permanent income 2 (usually foll by *with*) to provide (with qualities, characteristics, etc) [C14 from OF, from EN-[1] + *douer*, from L *dōtāre*, from *dōs* dowry]

endowment (ɪnˈdaʊmənt) *n* 1 the income with which an institution, etc, is endowed 2 the act or process of endowing 3 (*usually pl*) natural talents or qualities

endowment assurance *or* **insurance** *n* a form of life insurance that provides for the payment of a specified

Ee

sum directly to the policyholder at a designated date or to his beneficiary should he die before this date

endpaper ('ɛnd,peɪpə) *n* either of two leaves at the front and back of a book pasted to the inside of the board covers and the first leaf of the book

end point *n* **1** *chem* the point at which a titration is complete **2** the point at which anything is complete

end product *n* the final result of a process, series, etc, esp in manufacturing

endue *or* **indue** (ɪn'dju:) *vb* **endues, enduing, endued** *or* **indues, induing, indued** (*tr*) (usually foll by *with*) to invest or provide, as with some quality or trait [c15 from OF, from L *indūcere*, from *dūcere* to lead]

end up *vb* (*adv*) **1** (*copula*) to become eventually; turn out to be **2** (*intr*) to arrive, esp by a circuitous or lengthy route or process

endurance (ɪn'djʊərəns) *n* **1** the capacity, state, or an instance of enduring **2** something endured; a hardship, strain, or privation

endure (ɪn'djʊə) *vb* **endures, enduring, endured 1** to undergo (hardship, strain, etc) without yielding; bear **2** (*tr*) to permit or tolerate **3** (*intr*) to last or continue to exist [c14 from OF, from L *indūrāre* to harden, from *dūrus* hard] > **en'durable** *adj*

enduring (ɪn'djʊərɪŋ) *adj* **1** permanent; lasting **2** having forbearance; long-suffering > **en'duringly** *adv* > **en'duringness** *n*

end user *n* **1** (in international trading) the person, organization, or nation that will be the ultimate user of goods such as arms **2** *computing* the ultimate destination of information that is being transferred within a system

endways ('ɛnd,weɪz) *or esp US & Canad* **endwise** ('ɛnd,waɪz) *adv* **1** having the end forwards or upwards ▷ *adj* **2** vertical or upright **3** lengthways **4** standing or lying end to end

Endymion (ɛn'dɪmɪən) *n Greek myth* a handsome youth who was visited every night by the moon goddess Selene, who loved him

end zone *n American football* the area behind the goals at each end of the field that the ball must cross for a touchdown to be awarded

ENE *symbol for* east-northeast

-ene *n combining form* (in chemistry) indicating an unsaturated compound containing double bonds: *benzene; ethylene* [from Gk *-ēnē*, fem. patronymic suffix]

enema ('ɛnɪmə) *n, pl* **enemas** *or* **enemata** (-mətə) *Med* **1** the introduction of liquid into the rectum to evacuate the bowels, medicate, or nourish **2** the liquid so introduced [c15 from NL, from Gk: injection, from *enienai* to send in]

enemy ('ɛnəmɪ) *n, pl* **enemies 1** a person hostile or opposed to a policy, cause, person, or group **2a** an armed adversary; opposing military force **2b** (*as modifier*): *enemy aircraft* **3a** a hostile nation or people **3b** (*as modifier*): *an enemy alien* **4** something that harms or opposes. Related adj: **inimical** [c13 from OF, from L *inimīcus* hostile, from IN-[1] + *amīcus* friend]

energetic (,ɛnə'dʒɛtɪk) *adj* having or showing energy; vigorous > ,**ener'getically** *adv*

energize *or* **energise** ('ɛnə,dʒaɪz) *vb* **energizes, energizing, energized** *or* **energises, energising, energised 1** to have or cause to have energy; invigorate **2** (*tr*) to apply electric current or electromotive force to (a circuit, etc) > **'ener,gizer** *or* **'ener,giser** *n*

energy ('ɛnədʒɪ) *n, pl* **energies 1** intensity or vitality of action or expression; forcefulness **2** capacity or tendency for intense activity; vigour **3** *physics* **3a** the capacity of a body or system to do work **3b** a measure of this capacity, measured in joules (SI units) **4** a source of power: *the energy crisis* [c16 from LL, from Gk *energeia* activity, from EN-[2] + *ergon* work]

energy band *n physics* a range of energies associated with the quantum states of electrons in a crystalline solid

energy conversion *n* the process of changing one form of energy into another, such as nuclear energy into heat or solar energy into electrical energy

energy drink *n* a soft drink containing ingredients designed to boost the drinker's energy, esp after exercise

enervate *vb* ('ɛnə,veɪt), **enervates, enervating, enervated 1** (*tr*) to deprive of strength or vitality ▷ *adj* (ɪ'nɜ:vɪt) **2** deprived of strength or vitality [c17 from L *ēnervāre* to remove the nerves from, from *nervus* nerve] > ,**ener'vation** *n*

enervating ('ɛnə,veɪtɪŋ) *adj* tending to deprive of strength or vitality; physically or mentally weakening; debilitating

Enesco (ɛ'nɛskəʊ) *n* **Georges** (ʒɔrʒ), original name *George Enescu*. 1881–1955, Romanian violinist and composer

en famille *French* (ã famij) *adv* **1** with one's family; at home **2** in a casual way; informally

enfant terrible *French* (ãfã tɛriblə) *n, pl* ***enfants terribles*** (ãfã tɛriblə) a person given to unconventional conduct or indiscreet remarks [c19 lit.: terrible child]

enfeeble (ɪn'fi:bᵊl) *vb* **enfeebles, enfeebling, enfeebled** (*tr*) to make weak > **en'feeblement** *n* > **en'feebler** *n*

en fête *French* (ã fɛt) *adv* dressed for or engaged in a festivity [c19 lit.: in festival]

Enfield ('ɛnfi:ld) *n* a borough of Greater London: a N residential suburb. Pop: 273 563 (2001 est). Area: 55 sq km (31 sq miles)

enfilade (,ɛnfɪ'leɪd) *mil* ▷ *n* **1** gunfire directed along the length of a position or formation **2** a position or formation subject to such fire ▷ *vb* **enfilades, enfilading, enfiladed** (*tr*) **3** to attack (a position or formation) with enfilade [c18 from F: suite, from *enfiler* to thread on string, from *fil* thread]

enfold *or* **infold** (ɪn'fəʊld) *vb* (*tr*) **1** to cover by enclosing **2** to embrace > **en'folder** *or* **in'folder** *n* > **en'foldment** *or* **in'foldment** *n*

enforce (ɪn'fɔ:s) *vb* **enforces, enforcing, enforced** (*tr*) **1** to ensure obedience to (a law, decision, etc) **2** to impose (obedience, etc) as by force **3** to emphasize or reinforce (an argument, etc) > **en'forceable** *adj* > **en,forcea'bility** *n* > **enforcedly** (ɪn'fɔ:sɪdlɪ) *adv* > **en'forcement** *n* > **en'forcer** *n*

enfranchise (ɪn'fræntʃaɪz) *vb* **enfranchises, enfranchising, enfranchised** (*tr*) **1** to grant the power of voting to **2** to liberate, as from servitude **3** (in England) to invest (a town, city, etc) with the right to be represented in Parliament > **en'franchisement** *n* > **en'franchiser** *n*

ENG *abbrev for* electronic news gathering: TV news obtained at the point of action by means of modern video equipment

Eng. *abbrev for:* **1** England **2** English

Engadine ('ɛŋgə,di:n) *n* the upper part of the valley of the River Inn in Switzerland, in Graubünden canton: tourist and winter sports centre

engage (ɪn'geɪdʒ) *vb* **engages, engaging, engaged** (*mainly tr*) **1** to secure the services of **2** to secure for use; reserve **3** to involve (a person or his or her attention) intensely **4** to attract (the affection) of (a person) **5** to draw (somebody) into conversation **6** (*intr*) to take part; participate **7** to promise (to do something) **8** (*also intr*) *mil* to begin an action with (an enemy) **9** to bring (a mechanism) into operation **10** (*also intr*) to undergo or cause to undergo interlocking, as of the components of a driving mechanism **11** *machinery* to locate (a locking device) in its operative position or to advance (a tool) into a workpiece to commence cutting [c15 from OF, from EN-[1] + *gage* a pledge; see GAGE[1]] > **en'gager** *n*

engagé *or* (*fem*) ***engagée*** *French* (ãgaʒe) *adj* (of an artist) committed to some ideology

engaged (ɪnˈɡeɪdʒd) *adj* 1 pledged to be married; betrothed 2 occupied or busy 3 *archit* built against or attached to a wall or similar structure 4 (of a telephone line) in use

engaged tone *n Brit* a repeated single note heard on a telephone when the number called is already in use

engagement (ɪnˈɡeɪdʒmənt) *n* 1 a pledge of marriage; betrothal 2 an appointment or arrangement, esp for business or social purposes 3 the act of engaging or condition of being engaged 4 a promise, obligation, or other condition that binds 5 a period of employment, esp a limited period 6 an action; battle

engagement ring *n* a ring given by a man to a woman as a token of their betrothal
▹ www.diamond-legend.info/people/bride.html

engaging (ɪnˈɡeɪdʒɪŋ) *adj* pleasing, charming, or winning > **enˈgagingness** *n*

en garde *French* (ɑ̃ ɡard) *sentence substitute* 1 on guard; a call to a fencer to adopt a defensive stance in readiness for an attack or bout ▹ *adj* 2 (of a fencer) in such a stance

Engels (*German* ˈɛŋəls) *n* **Friedrich** (ˈfriːdrɪç) 1820–95, German socialist leader and political philosopher, in England from 1849. He collaborated with Marx on *The Communist Manifesto* (1848) and his own works include *Condition of the Working Classes in England* (1844) and *The Origin of the Family, Private Property and the State* (1884)

engender (ɪnˈdʒɛndə) *vb* (*tr*) to bring about or give rise to; cause to be born [c14 from OF, from L *ingenerāre*, from *generāre* to beget]

engine (ˈɛndʒɪn) *n* 1 any machine designed to convert energy into mechanical work 2 a railway locomotive 3 *mil* any piece of equipment formerly used in warfare, such as a battering ram 4 *obs* any instrument or device [c13 from OF, from L *ingenium* nature, talent, ingenious contrivance, from IN-[2] + *-genium*, rel. to *gignere* to beget, produce]

engine driver *n chiefly Brit* a man who drives a railway locomotive; train driver

engineer (ˌɛndʒɪˈnɪə) *n* 1 a person trained in any branch of engineering 2 the originator or manager of a situation, system, etc 3 *US & Canad* the driver of a railway locomotive 4 an officer responsible for a ship's engines 5 a member of the armed forces trained in engineering and construction work ▹ *vb* (*tr*) 6 to originate, cause, or plan in a clever or devious manner 7 to design, plan, or construct as a professional engineer [c14 *enginer*, from OF, from *engignier* to contrive, ult. from L *ingenium* skill, talent; see ENGINE]

engineering (ˌɛndʒɪˈnɪərɪŋ) *n* the profession of applying scientific principles to the design, construction, and maintenance of engines, cars, machines, etc (**mechanical engineering**), buildings, bridges, roads, etc (**civil engineering**), electrical machines and communication systems (**electrical engineering**), chemical plant and machinery (**chemical engineering**), or aircraft (**aeronautical engineering**)
▹ www.er-online.co.uk/others.htm
▹ www.eevl.ac.uk
▹ www.e4engineering.com

England (ˈɪŋɡlənd) *n* the largest division of Great Britain, bordering on Scotland and Wales: unified in the mid-tenth century and conquered by the Normans in 1066; united with Wales in 1536 and Scotland in 1707; monarchy overthrown in 1649 but restored in 1660. Capital: London. Pop: 49 138 831 (2001). Area: 130 439 sq km (50 352 sq miles). See **United Kingdom, Great Britain**
▹ www.ukwebstart.com/listdepartments.html
▹ www.travelengland.org.uk

English (ˈɪŋɡlɪʃ) *n* 1 the official language of Britain, the US, most of the Commonwealth, and certain other countries 2 **the English** (*functioning as pl*) the natives or inhabitants of England collectively 3 (*often not cap*) the usual US & Canad term for **side** (in billiards) ▹ *adj* 4 of or relating to the English language 5 relating to or characteristic of England or the English ▹ *vb* (*tr*) 6 *arch* to translate or adapt into English > **ˈEnglishness** *n*

English Channel *n* an arm of the Atlantic Ocean between S England and N France, linked with the North Sea by the Strait of Dover. Length: about 560 km (350 miles). Width: between 32 km (20 miles) and 161 km (100 miles)

English horn *n music* another name for **cor anglais**

Englishman (ˈɪŋɡlɪʃmən) *or* (*fem*) **Englishwoman** *n, pl* **Englishmen** *or* **Englishwomen** a native or inhabitant of England

engorge (ɪnˈɡɔːdʒ) *vb* **engorges, engorging, engorged** (*tr*) 1 *pathol* to congest with blood 2 to eat (food) greedily 3 to gorge (oneself); glut > **enˈgorgement** *n*

engr *abbrev for:* 1 engineer 2 engraver

engraft *or* **ingraft** (ɪnˈɡrɑːft) *vb* (*tr*) 1 to graft (a shoot, bud, etc) onto a stock 2 to incorporate in a firm or permanent way; implant > **ˌengrafˈtation, ˌingrafˈtation** *or* **enˈgraftment, inˈgraftment** *n*

engrain (ɪnˈɡreɪn) *vb* a variant spelling of **ingrain**

engrave (ɪnˈɡreɪv) *vb* **engraves, engraving, engraved** (*tr*) 1 to inscribe (a design, writing, etc) onto (a block, plate, or other printing surface) by carving, etching, or other process 2 to print (designs or characters) from a plate so made 3 to fix deeply or permanently in the mind [c16 from EN-[1] + GRAVE[3], on the model of F *engraver*] > **enˈgraver** *n*

engraving (ɪnˈɡreɪvɪŋ) *n* 1 the art of a person who engraves 2 a printing surface that has been engraved 3 a print made from this

engross (ɪnˈɡrəʊs) *vb* (*tr*) 1 to occupy one's attention completely; absorb 2 to write or copy (manuscript) in large legible handwriting 3 *law* to write or type out formally (a document) preparatory to execution [c14 (in the sense: to buy up wholesale); c15 (in the sense: to write in large letters): from L *grossus* thick, GROSS] > **enˈgrossed** *adj* > **enˈgrossing** *adj* > **enˈgrossment** *n*

Ee

engulf *or* **ingulf** (ɪnˈɡʌlf) *vb* (*tr*) 1 to immerse, plunge, bury, or swallow up 2 (*often passive*) to overwhelm > **enˈgulfment** *n*

enhance (ɪnˈhɑːns) *vb* **enhances, enhancing, enhanced** (*tr*) to intensify or increase in quality, value, power, etc; improve; augment [c14 from OF, from EN-[1] + *haucier* to raise, from Vulgar L *altiāre* (unattested), from L *altus* high] > **enˈhancement** *n* > **enˈhancer** *n*

enharmonic (ˌɛnhɑːˈmɒnɪk) *adj music* 1 denoting or relating to a small difference in pitch between two notes, such as A flat and G sharp: not present in instruments of equal temperament, but significant in the intonation of stringed instruments 2 denoting or relating to enharmonic modulation [c17 from L, from Gk, from EN-[2] + *harmonia*; see HARMONY] > **ˌenharˈmonically** *adv*

Enid (ˈiːnɪd) *n* (in Arthurian legend) the faithful wife of Geraint

enigma (ɪˈnɪɡmə) *n* a person, thing, or situation that is mysterious, puzzling, or ambiguous [c16 from L, from Gk, from *ainissesthai* to speak in riddles, from *ainos* fable, story] > **enigmatic** (ˌɛnɪɡˈmætɪk) *or* **ˌenigˈmatical** *adj* > **ˌenigˈmatically** *adv*

Eniwetok (ˌɛnəˈwiːtɒk, əˈniːwɪˌtɔːk) *n* an atoll in the W Pacific Ocean, in the NW Marshall Islands: taken by the US from Japan in 1944; became a naval base and later a testing ground for atomic weapons. Pop: 715 (latest est)

enjambment *or* **enjambement** (ɪnˈdʒæmmənt) *n prosody* the running over of a sentence from one line of verse into the next [c19 from F, lit.: a straddling, from EN-[1] + *jambe* leg; see JAMB] > **enˈjambed** *adj*

enjoin (ɪnˈdʒɔɪn) *vb* (*tr*) 1 to order (someone) to do something 2 to impose or prescribe (a mode of behaviour, etc) 3 *law* to require (a person) to do or refrain from some act, esp by an injunction [c13 from OF *enjoindre*, from L *injungere* to fasten to, from IN-² + *jungere* to JOIN] > **en'joiner** *n* > **en'joinment** *n*

enjoy (ɪn'dʒɔɪ) *vb* (*tr*) **1** to receive pleasure from; take joy in **2** to have the benefit of; use **3** to have as a condition; experience **4** **enjoy oneself** to have a good time [c14 from OF, from EN-¹ + *joir* to find pleasure in, from L *gaudēre* to rejoice] > **en'joyable** *adj* > **en'joyableness** *n* > **en'joyably** *adv* > **en'joyer** *n*

enjoyment (ɪn'dʒɔɪmənt) *n* **1** the act or condition of receiving pleasure from something **2** the use or possession of something that is satisfying **3** something that provides joy or satisfaction

enkephalin (ɛn'kɛfəlɪn) *or* **encephalin** (ɛn'sɛfəlɪn) *n* a chemical occurring in the brain, having effects similar to those of morphine

enkindle (ɪn'kɪndᵊl) *vb* **enkindles, enkindling, enkindled** (*tr*) **1** to set on fire; kindle **2** to excite to activity or ardour; arouse

enlace (ɪn'leɪs) *vb* **enlaces, enlacing, enlaced** (*tr*) **1** to bind or encircle with or as with laces **2** to entangle; intertwine > **en'lacement** *n*

enlarge (ɪn'lɑːdʒ) *vb* **enlarges, enlarging, enlarged** **1** to make or grow larger; increase or expand **2** (*tr*) to make (a photographic print) of a larger size than the negative **3** (*intr*; foll by *on* or *upon*) to speak or write (about) in greater detail > **en'largeable** *adj* > **en'largement** *n* > **en'larger** *n*

enlighten (ɪn'laɪtᵊn) *vb* (*tr*) **1** to give information or understanding to; instruct **2** to free from prejudice, superstition, etc **3** to give spiritual or religious revelation to **4** *poetic* to shed light on > **en'lightening** *adj*

enlightened (ɪn'laɪtᵊnd) *adj* **1** well-informed, tolerant, and guided by rational thought: *an enlightened administration* **2** claiming a spiritual revelation of truth

enlightenment (ɪn'laɪtᵊnmənt) *n* the act or means of enlightening or the state of being enlightened

Enlightenment (ɪn'laɪtᵊnmənt) *n* **the** an 18th-century philosophical movement stressing the importance of reason
▷ www.wsu.edu/~dee/ENLIGHT/

enlist (ɪn'lɪst) *vb* **1** to enter or persuade to enter the armed forces **2** (*tr*) to engage or secure (a person or his or her support) for a venture, cause, etc **3** (*intr*; foll by *in*) to enter into or join an enterprise, cause, etc > **en'lister** *n* > **en'listment** *n*

enlisted man *n US* a serviceman who holds neither a commission nor a warrant

enliven (ɪn'laɪvᵊn) *vb* (*tr*) **1** to make active, vivacious, or spirited **2** to make cheerful or bright; gladden > **en'livening** *adj* > **en'livenment** *n*

en masse (*French* ɑ̃ mas) *adv* in a group or mass; as a whole; all together [c19 from F]

enmesh (ɪn'mɛʃ) *vb* (*tr*) to catch or involve in or as if in a net or snare; entangle > **en'meshment** *n*

enmity ('ɛnmɪtɪ) *n, pl* **enmities** a feeling of hostility or ill will, as between enemies [c13 from OF; see ENEMY]

Ennerdale Water ('ɛnəˌdeɪl) *n* a lake in NW England, in Cumbria in the Lake District. Length: 4 km (2.5 miles)

Ennis ('ɛnɪs) *n* a town in the W Republic of Ireland, county town of Co. Clare. Pop: 13 750 (1991)

Enniskillen (ˌɛnɪs'kɪlɪn) *or formerly* **Inniskilling** *n* a town in SW Northern Ireland, in Fermanagh, on an island in the River Erne: scene of the defeat of James II's forces in 1689. Pop: 11 436 (1991)

Ennius ('ɛnɪəs) *n* **Quintus** ('kwɪntəs) 239–169 BC, Roman epic poet and dramatist

ennoble (ɪ'nəʊbᵊl) *vb* **ennobles, ennobling, ennobled** (*tr*) **1** to make noble, honourable, or excellent; dignify; exalt **2** to raise to a noble rank > **en'noblement** *n* > **en'nobler** *n* > **en'nobling** *adj*

ennog ('ɛnɒg) *n Northern English dialect* a back alley

ennui ('ɒnwiː) *n* a feeling of listlessness and general dissatisfaction resulting from lack of activity or excitement [c18 from F: apathy, from OF *enui* annoyance, vexation; see ANNOY]

Enoch ('iːnɒk) *n Old Testament* **1** the eldest son of Cain after whom the first city was named (Genesis 4:17) **2** the father of Methuselah: said to have walked with God and to have been taken by God at the end of his earthly life (Genesis 5:24)

enology (iː'nɒlədʒɪ) *n* the usual US spelling of **oenology**

enormity (ɪ'nɔːmɪtɪ) *n, pl* **enormities** **1** the quality or character of extreme wickedness **2** an act of great wickedness; atrocity **3** *inf* vastness of size or extent [c15 from OF, from LL *ēnormitās* hugeness; see ENORMOUS]

enormous (ɪ'nɔːməs) *adj* **1** unusually large in size, extent, or degree; immense; vast **2** *arch* extremely wicked; heinous [c16 from L, from *ē-* out of, away from + *norma* rule, pattern] > **e'normously** *adv* > **e'normousness** *n*

Enos ('iːnɒs) *n Old Testament* a son of Seth (Genesis 4:26; 5:6)

enosis ('ɛnəʊsɪs) *n* the union of Greece and Cyprus: the aim of a group of Greek Cypriots [c20 Mod. Gk: from Gk *henoun* to unite, from *heis* one]

enough (ɪ'nʌf) *determiner* **1a** sufficient to answer a need, demand or supposition **1b** (*as pron*): *enough is now known* **2** **that's enough!** that will do: used to put an end to an action, speech, performance, etc ▷ *adv* **3** so as to be sufficient; as much as necessary **4** (*not used with a negative*) very or quite; rather **5** (intensifier): *oddly enough* **6** just adequately; tolerably [OE *genōh*]

en passant (ɒn pæ'sɑːnt) *adv* in passing: in chess, said of capturing a pawn that has made an initial move of two squares. The capture is made as if the captured pawn had moved one square instead of two [c17 from F]

enprint ('ɛnprɪnt) *n* a standard photographic print (5 × 3.5 in.) produced from a negative

enquire (ɪn'kwaɪə) *vb* **enquires, enquiring, enquired** a variant of **inquire** > **en'quirer** *n* > **en'quiry** *n*

enrage (ɪn'reɪdʒ) *vb* **enrages, enraging, enraged** (*tr*) to provoke to fury; put into a rage > **en'raged** *adj* > **en'ragement** *n*

en rapport *French* (ɑ̃ rapɔr) *adj* (*postpositive*), *adv* in sympathy, harmony, or accord

enrapture (ɪn'ræptʃə) *vb* **enraptures, enrapturing, enraptured** (*tr*) to fill with delight; enchant

enrich (ɪn'rɪtʃ) *vb* (*tr*) **1** to increase the wealth of **2** to endow with fine or desirable qualities **3** to make more beautiful; adorn; decorate **4** to improve in quality, colour, flavour, etc **5** to increase the food value of by adding nutrients **6** to fertilize (soil) **7** *physics* to increase the concentration or abundance of one component or isotope in (a solution or mixture) > **en'riched** *adj* > **en'richment** *n*

Enright ('ɛnraɪt) *n* **D**(**ennis**) **J**(**oseph**) 1920–2003, British poet, essayist, and editor

enrol *or US* **enroll** (ɪn'rəʊl) *vb* **enrols** *or US* **enrolls, enrolling, enrolled** (*mainly tr*) **1** to record or note in a roll or list **2** (*also intr*) to become or cause to become a member; enlist; register **3** to put on record > ˌ**enrol'lee** *n* > **en'roller** *n*

enrolment *or US* **enrollment** (ɪn'rəʊlmənt) *n* **1** the act of enrolling or state of being enrolled **2** a list of people enrolled **3** the total number of people enrolled

en route (ɒn 'ruːt) *adv* on or along the way [c18 from F]

Ens. *abbrev for* Ensign

ENSA ('ɛnsə) *n acronym for* Entertainments National Service Association

Enschede (*Dutch* 'ɛnsxədeː) *n* a city in the E Netherlands, in Overijssel province: a major centre of the Dutch cotton industry. Pop: 148 814 (1999 est)

ensconce (ɪn'skɒns) *vb* **ensconces, ensconcing, ensconced** (*tr*; *often passive*) **1** to establish or settle firmly or comfortably **2** to place in safety; hide [c16 see EN-¹, SCONCE²]

ensemble (ɒn'sɒmbᵊl) *n* **1** all the parts of something considered together **2** a person's complete costume; outfit **3** the cast of a play other than the principals **4** *music* a group of soloists singing or playing together **5** *music* the degree of precision and unity exhibited by a group of instrumentalists or singers performing together **6** the general effect of something made up of individual parts ▷ *adv* **7** all together or at once [c15 from F: together, from L, from IN-[2] + *simul* at the same time]
enshrine *or* **inshrine** (ɪn'ʃraɪn) *vb* **enshrines, enshrining, enshrined** (*tr*) **1** to place or enclose as in a shrine **2** to hold as sacred; cherish; treasure > **en'shrinement** *n*
enshroud (ɪn'ʃraʊd) *vb* (*tr*) to cover or hide as with a shroud
ensign ('ɛnsaɪn) *n* **1** (*also* 'ɛnsən) a flag flown by a ship, branch of the armed forces, etc, to indicate nationality, allegiance, etc. See also **Red Ensign, White Ensign** **2** any flag, standard, or banner **3** a standard-bearer **4** a symbol or emblem; sign **5** (in the US Navy) a commissioned officer of the lowest rank **6** (in the British infantry) a colours bearer **7** (formerly in the British infantry) a commissioned officer of the lowest rank [c14 from OF *enseigne*, from L INSIGNIA] > **'ensign,ship** *or* **'ensigncy** *n*
ensilage ('ɛnsɪlɪdʒ) *n* **1** the process of ensiling green fodder **2** a less common name for **silage**
ensile (ɛn'saɪl, 'ɛnsaɪl) *vb* **ensiles, ensiling, ensiled** (*tr*) **1** to store and preserve (green fodder) in a silo **2** to turn (green fodder) into silage by causing it to ferment in a silo [c19 from F, from Sp., from EN-[1] + *silo* SILO]
enslave (ɪn'sleɪv) *vb* **enslaves, enslaving, enslaved** (*tr*) to make a slave of; subjugate > **en'slavement** *n* > **en'slaver** *n*
ensnare *or* **insnare** (ɪn'snɛə) *vb* **ensnares, ensnaring, ensnared** *or* **insnares, insnaring, insnared** (*tr*) **1** to catch or trap as in a snare **2** to trap or gain power over (someone) by dishonest or underhand means > **en'snarement** *n* > **en'snarer** *n*
ensue (ɪn'sjuː) *vb* **ensues, ensuing, ensued** **1** (*intr*) to come next or afterwards **2** (*intr*) to occur as a consequence; result **3** (*tr*) *obs* to pursue [c14 from Anglo-F, from OF, from EN-[1] + *suivre* to follow, from L *sequī*] > **en'suing** *adj*
en suite *French* (ɑ̃ sɥit) *adv* forming a unit: *a room with bathroom en suite* [lit.: in sequence]
ensure (ɛn'ʃʊə, -'ʃɔː) *or esp US* **insure** *vb* **ensures, ensuring, ensured** *or US* **insures, insuring, insured** (*tr*) **1** (*may take a clause as object*) to make certain or sure; guarantee **2** to make safe or secure; protect > **en'surer** *n*
ENT *med abbrev for* ear, nose, and throat
-ent *suffix forming adjectives and nouns* causing or performing an action or existing in a certain condition; the agent that performs an action: *astringent; dependent* [from L *-ent-*, *-ens*, present participial ending]
entablature (ɛn'tæblətʃə) *n archit* **1** the part of a classical temple above the columns, having an architrave, a frieze, and a cornice **2** any similar construction [c17 from F, from It. *intavolatura* something put on a table, hence, something laid flat, from *tavola* table]
entablement (ɪn'teɪbᵊlmənt) *n* the platform of a pedestal, above the dado, that supports a statue [c17 from OF]
entail (ɪn'teɪl) *vb* (*tr*) **1** to bring about or impose inevitably: *this task entails careful thought* **2** *property law* to restrict (the descent of an estate) to designated heirs **3** *logic* to have as a necessary consequence ▷ *n* **4** *property law* **4a** the restriction imposed by entailing an estate **4b** an entailed estate [c14 *entaillen*, from EN-[1] + *taille* limitation, TAIL[2]] > **en'tailer** *n* > **en'tailment** *n*
entamoeba (,ɛntə'miːbə), **endamoeba** *or US* **entameba, endameba** *n, pl* **entamoebae** (-biː), **entamoebas, endamoebae, endamoebas** *or US* **entamebae, entamebas, endamebae, endamebas** any parasitic amoeba of the genus *Entamoeba* (or *Endamoeba*) which lives in the intestines of man and causes amoebic dysentery
entangle (ɪn'tæŋgᵊl) *vb* **entangles, entangling, entangled** (*tr*) **1** to catch or involve in or as if in a tangle; ensnare or enmesh **2** to make tangled or twisted; snarl **3** to make complicated; confuse **4** to involve in difficulties > **en'tanglement** *n* > **en'tangler** *n*
entasis ('ɛntəsɪs) *n, pl* **entasises** (-siːz) a slightly convex curve given to the shaft of a column, or similar structure, to correct the illusion of concavity produced by a straight shaft [c18 from Gk, from *enteinein* to stretch tight, from *teinein* to stretch]
Entebbe (ɛn'tɛbɪ) *n* a town in S Uganda, on Lake Victoria: British administrative centre of Uganda (1893–1958); international airport. Pop: 41 638 (1991)
entellus (ɛn'tɛləs) *n* an Old World monkey of S Asia [c19 NL, apparently after a character in Virgil's *Aeneid*]
entente (*French* ɑ̃tɑ̃t) *n* **1** short for **entente cordiale** **2** the parties to an entente cordiale collectively [c19 F: understanding]
entente cordiale (*French* ɑ̃tɑ̃t kɔrdjal) *n* **1** a friendly understanding between political powers **2** (*often caps*) the understanding reached by France and Britain in 1904, over colonial disputes [c19 F: cordial understanding]
enter ('ɛntə) *vb* **1** to come or go into (a place, house, etc) **2** to penetrate or pierce **3** (*tr*) to introduce or insert **4** to join (a party, organization, etc) **5** (when *intr*, foll by *into*) to become involved or take part (in) **6** (*tr*) to record (an item) in a journal, account, etc **7** (*tr*) to record (a name, etc) on a list **8** (*tr*) to present or submit: *to enter a proposal* **9** (*intr*) *theatre* to come on stage: used as a stage direction: *enter Juliet* **10** (when *intr*, often foll by *into*, *on*, or *upon*) to begin; start: *to enter upon a new career* **11** (*intr*; often foll by *upon*) to come into possession (of) **12** (*tr*) to place (evidence, etc) before a court of law [c13 from OF, from L *intrāre*, from *intrā* within] > **'enterable** *adj* > **'enterer** *n*
enteric (ɛn'tɛrɪk) *or* **enteral** ('ɛntərəl) *adj* intestinal [c19 from Gk, from *enteron* intestine]
enter into *vb* (*intr, prep*) **1** to be considered as a necessary part of (one's plans, calculations, etc) **2** to be in sympathy with
enteritis (,ɛntə'raɪtɪs) *n* inflammation of the small intestine
entero- *or before a vowel* **enter-** *combining form* indicating an intestine: *enterovirus; enteritis* [from NL, from Gk *enteron* intestine]
enterobiasis (,ɛntərəʊ'baɪəsɪs) *n* a disease, common in children, caused by infestation of the large intestine with pinworms [c20 NL, from *enterobius* (generic name of worm) + -IASIS]
enterprise ('ɛntə,praɪz) *n* **1** a project or undertaking, esp one that requires boldness or effort **2** participation in such projects **3** readiness to embark on new ventures; boldness and energy **4a** initiative in business **4b** (*as modifier*): *the enterprise culture* **5** a company or firm [c15 from OF *entreprise* (n), from *entreprendre* from *entre-* between (from L: INTER-) + *prendre* to take, from L *prehendere* to grasp] > **'enter,priser** *n*
Enterprise Allowance Scheme *n* (in Britain) a scheme to provide a weekly allowance to an unemployed person who wishes to set up a business and is willing to invest a specified amount in it during its first year
enterprise zone *n* one of several areas in the UK in which industrial development is encouraged by tax and other concessions
enterprising ('ɛntə,praɪzɪŋ) *adj* ready to embark on new ventures; full of boldness and initiative > **'enter,prisingly** *adv*
entertain (,ɛntə'teɪn) *vb* **1** to provide amusement for (a person or audience) **2** to show hospitality to (guests)

Ee

3 (*tr*) to hold in the mind [c15 from OF, from *entre-* mutually + *tenir* to hold]
entertainer (ˌɛntəˈteɪnə) *n* 1 a professional performer in public entertainments 2 any person who entertains
entertaining (ˌɛntəˈteɪnɪŋ) *adj* serving to entertain or give pleasure; diverting; amusing
entertainment (ˌɛntəˈteɪnmənt) *n* 1 the act or art of entertaining or state of being entertained 2 an act, production, etc, that entertains; diversion; amusement
enthalpy (ˈɛnθəlpɪ, ɛnˈθæl-) *n* a thermodynamic property of a system equal to the sum of its internal energy and the product of its pressure and volume. Symbol: H. Also called: **heat content, total heat** [c20 from Greek *enthalpein* to warm in, from EN-² + *thalpein* to warm]
enthral *or US* **enthrall** (ɪnˈθrɔːl) *vb* **enthrals** *or US* **enthralls, enthralling, enthralled** (*tr*) 1 to hold spellbound; enchant; captivate 2 *obs* to hold as thrall; enslave > **enˈthraller** *n* > **enˈthralling** *adj* > **enˈthralment** *or US* **enˈthrallment** *n*
enthrone (ɛnˈθrəʊn) *vb* **enthrones, enthroning, enthroned** (*tr*) 1 to place on a throne 2 to honour or exalt 3 to assign authority to > **enˈthronement** *n*
enthuse (ɪnˈθjuːz) *vb* **enthuses, enthusing, enthused** to feel or show or cause to feel or show enthusiasm
enthusiasm (ɪnˈθjuːzɪˌæzəm) *n* 1 ardent and lively interest or eagerness 2 an object of keen interest 3 *arch* extravagant religious fervour [c17 from LL, from Gk, from *enthousiazein* to be possessed by a god, from EN-² + *theos* god]
enthusiast (ɪnˈθjuːzɪˌæst) *n* 1 a person motivated by enthusiasm; fanatic 2 *arch* one whose zeal for religion is extravagant > **enˌthusiˈastic** *adj* > **enˌthusiˈastically** *adv*
enthymeme (ˈɛnθɪˌmiːm) *n logic* a syllogism in which one or more premises are unexpressed [c16 via L from Gk *enthumeisthai* to infer, from EN-² + *thumos* mind]
entice (ɪnˈtaɪs) *vb* **entices, enticing, enticed** (*tr*) to attract by exciting hope or desire; tempt; allure [c13 from OF, from Vulgar L *intitiāre* (unattested) to incite] > **enˈticement** *n* > **enˈticer** *n* > **enˈticing** *adj* > **enˈticingly** *adv*
entire (ɪnˈtaɪə) *adj* 1 (*prenominal*) whole; complete 2 (*prenominal*) without reservation or exception 3 not broken or damaged 4 undivided; continuous 5 (of leaves, petals, etc) having a smooth margin not broken up into teeth or lobes 6 not castrated: *an entire horse* 7 *obs* unmixed; pure ▷ *n* 8 an uncastrated horse [c14 from OF, from L *integer* whole, from IN-¹ + *tangere* to touch] > **enˈtireness** *n*
entirely (ɪnˈtaɪəlɪ) *adv* 1 wholly; completely 2 solely or exclusively
entirety (ɪnˈtaɪərɪtɪ) *n, pl* **entireties** 1 the state of being entire or whole; completeness 2 a thing, sum, amount, etc, that is entire; whole; total
entitle (ɪnˈtaɪtᵊl) *vb* **entitles, entitling, entitled** (*tr*) 1 to give (a person) the right to do or have something; qualify; allow 2 to give a name or title to 3 to confer a title of rank or honour upon [c14 from OF *entituler*, from LL, from L *titulus* TITLE] > **enˈtitlement** *n*
entity (ˈɛntɪtɪ) *n, pl* **entities** 1 something having real or distinct existence 2 existence or being [c16 from Med. L, from *ēns* being, from L *esse* to be] > **ˈentitative** *adj*
ento- *combining form* inside; within: *entoderm* [NL, from Gk *entos* within]
entomb (ɪnˈtuːm) *vb* (*tr*) 1 to place in or as if in a tomb; bury; inter 2 to serve as a tomb for > **enˈtombment** *n*
entomo- *combining form* indicating an insect: *entomology* [from Gk *entomon* insect]
entomol. *or* **entom.** *abbrev for* entomology
entomology (ˌɛntəˈmɒlədʒɪ) *n* the branch of science concerned with the study of insects > **ˌentomoˈlogical** *adj* > **ˌentoˈmologist** *n*
entophyte (ˈɛntəʊˌfaɪt) *n bot* a variant spelling of **endophyte** > **entophytic** (ˌɛntəʊˈfɪtɪk) *adj*
entourage (ɒntʊˈrɑːʒ) *n* 1 a group of attendants or retainers; retinue 2 surroundings [c19 from F, from *entourer* to surround, from *tour* circuit; see TOUR, TURN]
entr'acte (ɒnˈtrækt) *n* 1 an interval between two acts of a play or opera 2 (esp formerly) an entertainment during such an interval [c19 F, lit.: between-act]
entrails (ˈɛntreɪlz) *pl n* 1 the internal organs of a person or animal; intestines; guts 2 the innermost parts of anything [c13 from OF, from Med. L *intrālia*, changed from L *interānea* intestines]
entrain (ɪnˈtreɪn) *vb* to board or put aboard a train > **enˈtrainment** *n*
entrance¹ (ˈɛntrəns) *n* 1 the act or an instance of entering; entry 2 a place for entering, such as a door 3a the power, liberty, or right of entering 3b (*as modifier*): *an entrance fee* 4 the coming of an actor or other performer onto a stage [c16 from F, from *entrer* to ENTER]
entrance² (ɪnˈtrɑːns) *vb* **entrances, entrancing, entranced** (*tr*) 1 to fill with wonder and delight; enchant 2 to put into a trance; hypnotize > **enˈtrancement** *n* > **enˈtrancing** *adj*
entrant (ˈɛntrənt) *n* a person who enters [c17 from F, lit.: entering, from *entrer* to ENTER]
entrap (ɪnˈtræp) *vb* **entraps, entrapping, entrapped** (*tr*) 1 to catch or snare as in a trap 2 to trick into danger, difficulty, or embarrassment > **enˈtrapment** *n* > **enˈtrapper** *n*
entreat *or* **intreat** (ɪnˈtriːt) *vb* 1 to ask (a person) earnestly; beg or plead with; implore 2 to make an earnest request or petition for (something) 3 an archaic word for **treat** (sense 4) [c15 from OF, from EN-¹ + *traiter* to TREAT] > **enˈtreatment** *or* **inˈtreatment** *n*
entreaty (ɪnˈtriːtɪ) *n, pl* **entreaties** an earnest request or petition; supplication; plea
entrechat (*French* ɑ̃trəʃa) *n* a leap in ballet during which the dancer repeatedly crosses his or her feet or beats them together [c18 from F *entrechase*, changed by folk etymology from It. (*capriola*) *intrecciata*, lit.: entwined (caper)]
entrecôte (*French* ɑ̃trəkot) *n* a beefsteak cut from between the ribs [F, from *entre-* INTER- + *côte* rib]
entrée (ˈɒntreɪ) *n* 1 a dish served before a main course 2 *chiefly US* the main course of a meal 3 the power or right of entry [c18 from F, from *entrer* to ENTER; in cookery, so called because formerly the course was served after an intermediate course called the *relevé* (remove)]
entremets (*French* ɑ̃trəmɛ) *n, pl* **entremets** (*French* -mɛ) 1 a dessert 2 a light dish formerly served between the main course and the dessert [c18 from F, from OF, from *entre-* between + *mes* dish]
entrench *or* **intrench** (ɪnˈtrɛntʃ) *vb* 1 (*tr*) to construct a defensive position by digging trenches around it 2 (*tr*) to fix or establish firmly 3 (*intr*; foll by *on* or *upon*) to trespass or encroach > **enˈtrenched** *or* **inˈtrenched** *adj* > **enˈtrenchment** *or* **inˈtrenchment** *n*
entrepôt (*French* ɑ̃trəpo) *n* 1 a warehouse for commercial goods 2a a trading centre or port at which goods are imported and re-exported without incurring duty 2b (*as modifier*): *an entrepôt trade* [c18 F, from *entreposer*, from *entre* between + *poser* to place; formed on the model of DEPOT]
entrepreneur (ˌɒntrəprəˈnɜː) *n* 1 the owner or manager of a business enterprise who, by risk and initiative, attempts to make profits 2 a middleman or commercial intermediary [c19 from F, from *entreprendre* to undertake; see ENTERPRISE] > **ˌentrepreˈneurial** *adj* > **ˌentrepreˈneurship** *n*
entropy (ˈɛntrəpɪ) *n, pl* **entropies** 1 a thermodynamic quantity that changes in a reversible process by an amount equal to the heat absorbed or emitted divided by the thermodynamic temperature. It is measured in joules per kelvin 2 lack of pattern or organization;

disorder [C19 from EN-² + -TROPE]

entrust *or* **intrust** (ɪnˈtrʌst) *vb (tr)* **1** (usually foll by *with*) to invest or charge (with a duty, responsibility, etc) **2** (often foll by *to*) to put into the care or protection of someone > **enˈtrustment** *or* **inˈtrustment** *n*

entry (ˈɛntrɪ) *n, pl* **entries 1** the act or an instance of entering; entrance **2** a point or place for entering, such as a door, etc **3a** the right or liberty of entering **3b** (*as modifier*): *an entry permit* **4** the act of recording an item in a journal, account, etc **5** an item recorded, as in a diary, dictionary, or account **6** a person, horse, car, etc, entering a competition or contest **7** the competitors entering a contest considered collectively **8** the action of an actor in going on stage **9** *property law* the act of going upon land with the intention of asserting the right to possession **10** any point in a piece of music at which a performer commences or resumes singing or playing **11** *bridge, etc* a card that enables one to transfer the lead from one's own hand to that of one's partner or to the dummy hand **12** *dialect* a passage between the backs of two rows of houses [C13 from OF *entree*, p.p. of *entrer* to ENTER]

entryism (ˈɛntrɪɪzəm) *n* the policy or practice of joining an existing political party with the intention of changing it instead of forming a new party > **ˈentryist** *n, adj*

entry-level *adj* **1** (of a job or worker) at the most elementary level in a career structure **2** (of a product) characterized by being at the most appropriate level for use by a beginner: *an entry-level camera*

entwine *or* **intwine** (ɪnˈtwaɪn) *vb* **entwines, entwining, entwined** *or* **intwines, intwining, intwined** (of two or more things) to twine together or (of one or more things) to twine around (something else) > **enˈtwinement** *or* **inˈtwinement** *n*

Enugu (ɛˈnuːguː) *n* a city in S Nigeria, capital of Enugu state: capital of the former Eastern region and of the breakaway state of Biafra during the Civil War (1967–70): coal-mining. Pop: 316 100 (1996 est)

E number *n* any of a series of numbers with the prefix E indicating a specific food additive recognized by the European Union

enumerate (ɪˈnjuːməˌreɪt) *vb* **enumerates, enumerating, enumerated** *(tr)* **1** to name one by one; list **2** to determine the number of; count **3** *Canad* to compile or enter (a name or names) in a voting list for an area [C17 from L, from *numerāre* to count, reckon; see NUMBER] > **eˈnumerable** *adj* > **eˌnumerˈation** *n* > **eˈnumerative** *adj*

enumerator (ɪˈnjuːməˌreɪtə) *n* **1** a person or thing that enumerates **2** *Brit* a person who issues and retrieves census forms

enunciable (ɪˈnʌnsɪəbᵊl) *adj* capable of being enunciated

enunciate (ɪˈnʌnsɪˌeɪt) *vb* **enunciates, enunciating, enunciated 1** to articulate or pronounce (words), esp clearly and distinctly **2** *(tr)* to state precisely or formally [C17 from L *ēnuntiāre* to declare, from *nuntiāre* to announce] > **eˌnunciˈation** *n* > **eˈnunciative** *or* **eˈnunciatory** *adj* > **eˈnunciˌator** *n*

enuresis (ˌɛnjʊˈriːsɪs) *n* involuntary discharge of urine, esp during sleep [C19 from NL, from Gk EN-² + *ouron* urine] > **enuretic** (ˌɛnjʊˈrɛtɪk) *adj, n*

envelop (ɪnˈvɛləp) *vb* **envelops, enveloping, enveloped** *(tr)* **1** to wrap or enclose as in a covering **2** to conceal or obscure **3** to surround (an enemy force) [C14 from OF *envoluper*, from EN-¹ + *voluper, voloper*, from ?] > **enˈvelopment** *n*

envelope (ˈɛnvəˌləʊp, ˈɒn-) *n* **1** a flat covering of paper, usually rectangular and with a flap that can be sealed, used to enclose a letter, etc **2** any covering or wrapper **3** *biol* any enclosing structure, such as a membrane, shell, or skin **4** the bag enclosing gas in a balloon **5** *maths* a curve or surface that is tangential to each one of a group of curves or surfaces **6 push the envelope** *inf* to push the boundaries of what is possible [C18 from F, from *envelopper* to wrap around; see ENVELOP; sense 6 from aeronautics jargon, referring to graphs of aircraft performance]

envenom (ɪnˈvɛnəm) *vb (tr)* **1** to fill or impregnate with venom; make poisonous **2** to fill with bitterness or malice

Enver Pasha (ˈɛnvə ˈpɑːʃə) *n* 1881–1922, Turkish soldier and leader of the Young Turks: minister of war (1914–18)

enviable (ˈɛnvɪəbᵊl) *adj* exciting envy; fortunate or privileged > **ˈenviableness** *n*

envious (ˈɛnvɪəs) *adj* feeling, showing, or resulting from envy [C13 from Anglo-Norman, ult. from L *invidiōsus* full of envy, INVIDIOUS; see ENVY] > **ˈenviously** *adv* > **ˈenviousness** *n*

environ (ɪnˈvaɪrən) *vb (tr)* to encircle or surround [C14 from OF *environner* to surround, from EN-¹ + *viron* a circle, from *virer* to turn, VEER]

environment (ɪnˈvaɪrənmənt) *n* **1** external conditions or surroundings **2** *ecology* the external surroundings in which a plant or animal lives, which influence its development and behaviour **3** *computing* an operating system, program, or integrated suite of programs that provides all the facilities necessary for a particular application: *a word-processing environment* > **enˌvironˈmental** *adj*

▷ www.conservation.org

▷ www.doc.mmu.ac.uk/aric/eae/english.html

▷ http://personal.cmich.edu/francɪm/homepage.htm

environmentalist (ɪnˌvaɪrənˈmɛntəlɪst) *n* **1** a specialist in the maintenance of ecological balance and the conservation of the environment **2** a person who is concerned with issues that affect the environment, such as pollution

environs (ɪnˈvaɪrənz) *pl n* a surrounding area or region, esp the suburbs or outskirts of a city

envisage (ɪnˈvɪzɪdʒ) *vb* **envisages, envisaging, envisaged** *(tr)* **1** to form a mental image of; visualize **2** to conceive of as a possibility in the future [C19 from F, from EN-¹ + *visage* face, VISAGE] > **enˈvisagement** *n*

envision (ɪnˈvɪʒən) *vb (tr)* to conceive of as a possibility, esp in the future; foresee

envoy¹ (ˈɛnvɔɪ) *n* **1** Also called: **minister, minister plenipotentiary** a diplomat ranking between an ambassador and a minister resident **2** an accredited agent or representative [C17 from F, from *envoyer* to send, from Vulgar L *inviāre* (unattested) to send on a journey, from IN-² + *via* road] > **ˈenvoyship** *n*

envoy² *or* **envoi** (ˈɛnvɔɪ) *n* **1** a brief concluding stanza, notably in ballades **2** a postscript in other forms of verse or prose [C14 from OF, from *envoyer* to send; see ENVOY¹]

envy (ˈɛnvɪ) *n, pl* **envies 1** a feeling of grudging or somewhat admiring discontent aroused by the possessions, achievements, or qualities of another **2** the desire to have something possessed by another; covetousness **3** an object of envy ▷ *vb* **envies, envying, envied 4** to be envious of (a person or thing) [C13 via OF from L *invidia*, from *invidēre* to eye maliciously, from IN-² + *vidēre* to see] > **ˈenvier** *n* > **ˈenvyingly** *adv*

enwrap *or* **inwrap** (ɪnˈræp) *vb* **enwraps, enwrapping, enwrapped** *(tr)* **1** to wrap or cover up; envelop **2** (*usually passive*) to engross or absorb

enwreath (ɪnˈriːð) *vb (tr)* to surround or encircle with or as with a wreath or wreaths

Enzed (ˈɛnˈzɛd) *n Austral and NZ inf* **1** New Zealand **2** Also called: **Enzedder** a New Zealander

enzootic (ˌɛnzəʊˈɒtɪk) *adj* **1** (of diseases) affecting animals within a limited region ▷ *n* **2** an enzootic disease [C19 from EN-² + Gk *zōion* animal + -OTIC] > **ˌenzoˈotically** *adv*

enzyme (ˈɛnzaɪm) *n* any of a group of complex proteins produced by living cells, that act as catalysts in specific biochemical reactions [C19 from Med. Gk *enzumos*

Ee

leavened, from Gk EN-[2] + *zumē* leaven] > **enzymatic** (ˌɛnzaɪˈmætɪk, -zɪ-) *or* **enzymic** (ɛnˈzaɪmɪk, -ˈzɪm-) *adj*
enzyme-linked immunosorbent assay (ˌɪmjʊnəʊˈsɔːbənt) *n* the full name for **ELISA**
eo- *combining form* early or primeval: *Eocene; eohippus* [from Gk, from *ēōs* dawn]
EOC *abbrev for* Equal Opportunities Commission
Eocene (ˈiːəʊˌsiːn) *adj* **1** of or denoting the second epoch of the Tertiary period, during which hooved mammals appeared ▷ *n* **2 the** the Eocene epoch or rock series [C19 from EO- + -CENE]
eohippus (ˌiːəʊˈhɪpəs) *n, pl* **eohippuses** the earliest horse: an extinct Eocene dog-sized animal [C19 NL, from EO- + Gk *hippos* horse]
Eolithic (ˌiːəʊˈlɪθɪk) *adj* denoting or relating to the early part of the Stone Age, characterized by the use of crude stone tools (**eoliths**)
eon (ˈiːən, ˈiːɒn) *n* **1** the usual US spelling of **aeon** **2** *geol* the longest division of geological time, comprising two or more eras
Eos (ˈiːɒs) *n Greek myth* the winged goddess of the dawn, the daughter of Hyperion. Roman counterpart: **Aurora**
eosin (ˈiːəʊsɪn) *or* **eosine** (ˈiːəʊsɪn, -ˌsiːn) *n* **1** a red fluorescent crystalline water-insoluble compound. Its soluble salts are used as dyes **2** any of several similar dyes [C19 from Gk *ēōs* dawn + -IN; referring to colour it gives to silk]
Eötvös (ˈɜːtvɔs) *n* Baron **Roland von** 1848–1919, Hungarian physicist noted for his studies of gravity and surface tension
-eous *suffix forming adjectives* relating to or having the nature of: *gaseous* [from L *-eus*]
EP *n* an extended-play gramophone record, usually 7 inches (18 cm) in diameter: a longer recording than a single
EPA *abbrev for* eicosapentaenoic acid: a fatty acid, found in certain fish oils, that can reduce blood cholesterol
epact (ˈiːpækt) *n* **1** the difference in time, about 11 days, between the solar year and the lunar year **2** the number of days between the beginning of the calendar year and the new moon immediately preceding this [C16 via LL from Gk *epaktē*, from *epagein* to bring in, intercalate]
Epaminondas (ɛˌpæmɪˈnɒndæs) *n* ?418–362 BC, Greek Theban statesman and general: defeated the Spartans at Leuctra (371) and Mantinea (362) and restored power in Greece to Thebes
eparch (ˈɛpɑːk) *n* **1** a bishop or metropolitan in the Orthodox Church **2** a governor of a subdivision of a province of modern Greece [C17 from Gk *eparkhos*, from *epi-* over, on + -ARCH] > **ˈeparchy** *n*
epaulette *or US* **epaulet** (ˈɛpəˌlɛt, -lɪt) *n* a piece of ornamental material on the shoulder of a garment, esp a military uniform [C18 from F, from *épaule* shoulder, from L *spatula* shoulder blade]
e-payment *n* a digital payment for a transaction made on the Internet
épée (ˈɛpeɪ) *n* a sword similar to the foil but with a heavier blade [C19 from F: sword, from L *spatha*, from Gk *spathē* blade; see SPADE[1]] > **ˈépéeist** *n*
epeirogeny (ˌɛpaɪˈrɒdʒɪnɪ) *or* **epeirogenesis** (ɪˌpaɪrəʊˈdʒɛnɪsɪs) *n* the formation of continents by relatively slow displacements of the earth's crust [C19 from Gk *ēpeiros* continent + -GENY] > **epeirogenic** (ɪˌpaɪrəʊˈdʒɛnɪk) *or* **epeirogenetic** (ɪˌpaɪrəʊdʒɪˈnɛtɪk) *adj*
epergne (ɪˈpɜːn) *n* an ornamental centrepiece for a table, holding fruit, flowers, etc [C18 prob. from F *épargne* a saving, from *épargner* to economize, of Gmc origin]
epexegesis (ɛˌpɛksɪˈdʒiːsɪs) *n, pl* **epexegesises** (-ˌsiːz) *rhetoric* **1** the addition of a phrase, clause, or sentence to a text to provide further explanation **2** the phrase, clause, or sentence added for this purpose [C17 from Gk; see EPI-, EXEGESIS] > **epexegetic** (ɛˌpɛksɪˈdʒɛtɪk) *or* **epˌexeˈgetical** *adj*

Eph. *or* **Ephes.** *Bible. abbrev for* Ephesians
ephah *or* **epha** (ˈiːfə) *n* a Hebrew unit of measure equal to approximately one bushel or about 33 litres [C16 from Heb., from Egyptian]
ephedrine *or* **ephedrin** (ɪˈfɛdrɪn, ˈɛfɪˌdriːn, -drɪn) *n* a white crystalline alkaloid used for the treatment of asthma and hay fever [C19 from NL from L from Gk, from EPI- + *hedra* seat + -INE[2]]
ephemera (ɪˈfɛmərə) *n, pl* **ephemeras** *or* **ephemerae** (-əˌriː) **1** a mayfly, esp one of the genus *Ephemera* **2** something transitory or short-lived **3** (*functioning as pl*) collectable items not originally intended to be long-lasting, such as tickets, posters, etc **4** a plural of **ephemeron** [C16 see EPHEMERAL]
ephemeral (ɪˈfɛmərəl) *adj* **1** transitory; short-lived: *ephemeral pleasure* ▷ *n* **2** a short-lived organism, such as the mayfly **3** a plant that completes its life cycle in less than one year, usually less than six months [C16 from Gk *ephēmeros* lasting only a day, from *hēmera* day] > **eˌphemerˈality** *or* **eˈphemeralness** *n*
ephemerid (ɪˈfɛmərɪd) *n* any insect of the order *Ephemeroptera* (or *Ephemerida*), which comprises the mayflies. Also: **ephemeropteran** [C19 from NL, from Gk *ephēmeros* short-lived + -ID[1]]
ephemeris (ɪˈfɛmərɪs) *n, pl* **ephemerides** (ˌɛfɪˈmɛrɪˌdiːz) a table giving the future positions of a planet, comet, or satellite during a specified period [C16 from L, from Gk: diary, journal; see EPHEMERAL]
ephemeron (ɪˈfɛməˌrɒn) *n, pl* **ephemera** (-ərə) *or* **ephemerons** (*usually pl*) something transitory or short-lived [C16 see EPHEMERAL]
Ephesus (ˈɛfɪsəs) *n* (in ancient Greece) a major trading city on the W coast of Asia Minor: famous for its temple of Artemis (Diana); sacked by the Goths (262 AD)
ephod (ˈiːfɒd) *n Bible* an embroidered vestment worn by priests in ancient Israel [C14 from Heb.]
ephor (ˈɛfɔː) *n, pl* **ephors** *or* **ephori** (-əˌraɪ) (in ancient Greece) a senior magistrate, esp one of the five Spartan ephors, who wielded effective power [C16 from Gk, from *ephoran* to supervise, from EPI- + *horan* to look] > **ˈephoral** *adj* > **ˈephorate** *n*
Ephraim (ˈiːfreɪɪm) *n Old Testament* **1a** the younger son of Joseph, who received the principal blessing of his grandfather Jacob (Genesis 48:8–22) **1b** the tribe descended from him **1c** the territory of this tribe, west of the River Jordan **2** the northern kingdom of Israel after the kingdom of Solomon had been divided into two
Ephraimite (ˈiːfreɪɪˌmaɪt) *n* a member of the tribe of Ephraim
epi-, eph-, *or before a vowel* **ep-** *prefix* **1** upon; above; over: *epidermis; epicentre* **2** in addition to: *epiphenomenon* **3** after: *epilogue* **4** near; close to: *epicalyx* [from Gk, from *epi* (prep)]
epic (ˈɛpɪk) *n* **1** a long narrative poem recounting in elevated style the deeds of a legendary hero **2** the genre of epic poetry **3** any work of literature, film, etc, having qualities associated with the epic **4** an episode in the lives of men in which heroic deeds are performed ▷ *adj* **5** denoting, relating to, or characteristic of an epic or epics **6** of heroic or impressive proportions [C16 from L, from Gk *epikos*, from *epos* speech, word, song]
epicalyx (ˌɛpɪˈkeɪlɪks, -ˈkæl-) *n, pl* **epicalyxes** *or* **epicalyces** (-lɪˌsiːz) *bot* a series of small sepal-like bracts forming an outer calyx beneath the true calyx in some flowers
epicanthus (ˌɛpɪˈkænθəs) *n, pl* **epicanthi** (-θaɪ) a fold of skin extending vertically over the inner angle of the eye: characteristic of Mongolian peoples [C19 NL, from EPI- + L *canthus* corner of the eye, from Gk *kanthos*] > **ˌepiˈcanthic** *adj*
epicardium (ˌɛpɪˈkɑːdɪəm) *n, pl* **epicardia** (-dɪə) *anat* the innermost layer of the pericardium [C19 NL, from EPI- + Gk *kardia* heart] > **ˌepiˈcardiac** *or* **ˌepiˈcardial** *adj*
epicarp (ˈɛpɪˌkɑːp) *or* **exocarp** *n* the outermost layer of

the pericarp of fruits [C19 from F, from EPI- + Gk *karpos* fruit]

epicene ('ɛpɪ,si:n) *adj* **1** having the characteristics of both sexes **2** of neither sex; sexless **3** effeminate **4** *grammar* **4a** denoting a noun that may refer to a male or a female **4b** (in Latin, Greek, etc) denoting a noun that retains the same gender regardless of the sex of the referent [C15 from L *epicoenus* of both genders, from Gk *epikoinos* common to many, from *koinos* common] > ,**epi'cenism** *n*

epicentre *or US* **epicenter** ('ɛpɪ,sɛntə) *n* the point on the earth's surface immediately above the origin of an earthquake [C19 from NL, from Gk *epikentros* over the centre, from EPI- + CENTRE] > ,**epi'central** *adj*

Epictetus (,ɛpɪk'ti:təs) *n* ?50–?120 AD, Greek Stoic philosopher, who stressed self-renunciation and the brotherhood of man

epicure ('ɛpɪ,kjʊə) *n* **1** a person who cultivates a discriminating palate for good food and drink **2** a person devoted to sensual pleasures [C16 from Med. L *epicūrus*, after EPICURUS] > '**epicur,ism** *n*

epicurean (,ɛpɪkjʊ'ri:ən) *adj* **1** devoted to sensual pleasures, esp food and drink **2** suitable for an epicure ▷ *n* **3** an epicure; gourmet > ,**epicu'rean,ism** *n*

Epicurean (,ɛpɪkjʊ'ri:ən) *adj* **1** of or relating to the philosophy of Epicurus ▷ *n* **2** a follower of the philosophy of Epicurus > ,**Epicu'rean,ism** *n*

Epicurus (,ɛpɪ'kjʊərəs) *n* 341–270 BC, Greek philosopher, who held that the highest good is pleasure and that the world is a series of fortuitous combinations of atoms

epicycle ('ɛpɪ,saɪkᵊl) *n* a circle that rolls around the inside or outside of another circle [C14 from LL, from Gk; see EPI-, CYCLE] > **epicyclic** (,ɛpɪ'saɪklɪk, -'sɪklɪk) *or* ,**epi'cyclical** *adj*

epicyclic train *n* a cluster of gears consisting of a central gearwheel, a coaxial gearwheel of greater diameter, and one or more planetary gears engaging with both of them

epicycloid (,ɛpɪ'saɪklɔɪd) *n* the curve described by a point on the circumference of a circle as this circle rolls around the outside of another fixed circle > ,**epicy'cloidal** *adj*

Epidaurus (,ɛpɪ'dɔ:rəs; *Greek* ɛpi'ðaʊrɔs) *n* an ancient port in Greece, in the NE Peloponnese, in Argolis on the Saronic Gulf

epideictic (,ɛpɪ'daɪktɪk) *adj* designed to display something, esp the skill of the speaker in rhetoric. Also: **epidictic** (,ɛpɪ'dɪktɪk) [C18 from Gk, from *epideiknunai* to display, from *deiknunai* to show]

epidemic (,ɛpɪ'dɛmɪk) *adj* **1** (esp of a disease) attacking or affecting many persons simultaneously in a community or area ▷ *n* **2** a widespread occurrence of a disease **3** a rapid development, spread, or growth of something [C17 from F, via LL from Gk *epidēmia*, lit.: among the people, from EPI- + *dēmos* people] > ,**epi'demically** *adv*

epidemiology (,ɛpɪ,di:mɪ'ɒlədʒɪ) *n* the branch of medical science concerned with the occurrence, distribution, and control of diseases in populations > **epidemiological** (,ɛpɪ,di:mɪə'lɒdʒɪkᵊl) *adj* > ,**epi,demi'ologist** *n*

epidermis (,ɛpɪ'dɜ:mɪs) *n* **1** the thin protective outer layer of the skin **2** the outer layer of cells of an invertebrate **3** the outer protective layer of cells of a plant [C17 via LL from Gk, from EPI- + *derma* skin] > ,**epi'dermal**, ,**epi'dermic**, *or* ,**epi'dermoid** *adj*

epidiascope (,ɛpɪ'daɪə,skəʊp) *n* an optical device for projecting a magnified image onto a screen

epididymis (,ɛpɪ'dɪdɪmɪs) *n*, *pl* **epididymides** (-dɪ'dɪmɪ,di:z) *anat* a convoluted tube behind each testis, in which spermatozoa are stored and conveyed to the vas deferens [C17 from Gk *epididumis*, from EPI- + *didumos* twin, testicle]

epidural (,ɛpɪ'djʊərəl) *adj* **1** Also: **extradural** upon or outside the dura mater ▷ *n* **2** Also: **epidural anaesthesia, spinal anaesthesia** **2a** injection of anaesthetic into the space outside the dura mater enveloping the spinal cord **2b** anaesthesia induced by this method [C19 from EPI- + DUR(A MATER) + -AL[1]]

epigamic (,ɛpɪ'gæmɪk) *adj zool* attractive to the opposite sex: *epigamic colouration*

epigeal (,ɛpɪ'dʒi:əl), **epigean,** *or* **epigeous** *adj* **1** of or relating to seed germination in which the cotyledons appear above the ground **2** living or growing on or close to the surface of the ground [C19 from Gk *epigeios* of the earth, from EPI- + *gē* earth]

epigenetic (,ɛpɪdʒɪ'nɛtɪk) *adj* **1** of or relating to epigenesis **2** denoting processes by which heritable modifications in gene function occur without a change in the sequence of the DNA > ,**epige'netically** *adv*

epigenetics (,ɛpɪdʒɪ'nɛtɪks) *n* (*functioning as sing*) the study of heritable changes that occur without a change in the DNA sequence

epiglottis (,ɛpɪ'glɒtɪs) *n*, *pl* **epiglottises** *or* **epiglottides** (-tɪ,di:z) a thin cartilaginous flap that covers the entrance to the larynx during swallowing, preventing food from entering the trachea > ,**epi'glottal** *or* ,**epi'glottic** *adj*

Epigoni (ɪ'pɪgə,naɪ) *pl n*, *sing* **-onus** (-ənəs) *Greek myth* the descendants of the Seven against Thebes, who undertook a second expedition against the city and eventually captured and destroyed it [C20 from Gk *epigonoi* those born after]

epigram ('ɛpɪ,græm) *n* **1** a witty, often paradoxical remark, concisely expressed **2** a short poem, esp one having a witty and ingenious ending [C15 from L *epigramma*, from Gk: inscription, from *graphein* to write] > ,**epigram'matic** *adj* > ,**epigram'matically** *adv*

epigrammatize *or* **epigrammatise** (,ɛpɪ'græmə,taɪz) *vb* **epigrammatizes, epigrammatizing, epigrammatized** *or* **epigrammatises, epigrammatising, epigrammatised** to make an epigram (about) > ,**epi'grammatism** *n* > ,**epi'grammatist** *n*

epigraph ('ɛpɪ,grɑ:f) *n* **1** a quotation at the beginning of a book, chapter, etc **2** an inscription on a monument or building [C17 from Gk; see EPIGRAM] > **epigraphic** (,ɛpɪ'græfɪk) or ,**epi'graphical** *adj*

epigraphy (ɪ'pɪgrəfɪ) *n* **1** the study of ancient inscriptions **2** epigraphs collectively > **e'pigraphist** *or* **e'pigrapher** *n*

epilator ('ɛpɪ,leɪtə) *n* an electrical appliance consisting of a metal spiral head that rotates at high speed, plucking unwanted hair

epilepsy ('ɛpɪ,lɛpsɪ) *n* a disorder of the central nervous system characterized by periodic loss of consciousness with or without convulsions [C16 from LL *epilēpsia*, from Gk, from *epilambanein* to attack, seize]

▷ www.apa.org/science/efa.html

epileptic (,ɛpɪ'lɛptɪk) *adj* **1** of, relating to, or having epilepsy ▷ *n* **2** a person who has epilepsy > ,**epi'leptically** *adv*

epilogue ('ɛpɪ,lɒg) *n* **1a** a speech addressed to the audience by an actor at the end of a play **1b** the actor speaking this **2** a short postscript to any literary work [C15 from L, from Gk *epilogos*, from *logos* word, speech] > **epilogist** (ɪ'pɪlədʒɪst) *n*

epinephrine (,ɛpɪ'nɛfrɪn, -ri:n) *or* **epinephrin** *n* a US and Canad name for **adrenaline** [C19 from EPI- + *nephro-* + -INE[2]]

epiphany (ɪ'pɪfənɪ) *n*, *pl* **epiphanies** **1** the manifestation of a supernatural or divine reality **2** any moment of great or sudden revelation > **epiphanic** (,ɛpɪ'fænɪk) *adj*

Epiphany (ɪ'pɪfənɪ) *n*, *pl* **Epiphanies** a Christian festival held on Jan 6, commemorating, in the Western Church, the manifestation of Christ to the Magi [C17 via Church

Ee

L from Gk *epiphaneia* an appearing, from EPI- + *phainein* to show]

epiphenomenon (ˌɛpɪfɪˈnɒmɪnən) *n, pl* **epiphenomena** (-nə) **1** a secondary or additional phenomenon **2** *philosophy* mind or consciousness regarded as a by-product of the biological activity of the human brain **3** *pathol* an unexpected symptom or occurrence during the course of a disease > **ˌepipheˈnomenal** *adj*

epiphyte (ˈɛpɪˌfaɪt) *n* a plant that grows on another plant but is not parasitic on it [c19 via NL from Gk, from EPI- + *phusis* growth] > **epiphytic** (ˌɛpɪˈfɪtɪk), **ˌepiˈphytal,** *or* **ˌepiˈphytical** *adj*

Epirus (ɪˈpaɪərəs) *n* **1** a region of NW Greece, part of ancient Epirus ceded to Greece after independence in 1830 **2** (in ancient Greece) a region between the Pindus mountains and the Ionian Sea, straddling the modern border with Albania

Epis. *or* **Epist.** *Bible abbrev for* Epistle

episcopacy (ɪˈpɪskəpəsɪ) *n, pl* **episcopacies** **1** government of a Church by bishops **2** another word for **episcopate**

episcopal (ɪˈpɪskəpᵊl) *adj* of, denoting, governed by, or relating to a bishop or bishops [c15 from Church L, from *episcopus* BISHOP]

Episcopal (ɪˈpɪskəpᵊl) *adj* of or denoting the Episcopal Church, an autonomous church of Scotland and the US which is in full communion with the Church of England

episcopalian (ɪˌpɪskəˈpeɪlɪən) *adj also* **episcopal** **1** practising or advocating the principle of Church government by bishops ▷ *n* **2** an advocate of such Church government > **eˌpiscoˈpalianism** *n*

Episcopalian (ɪˌpɪskəˈpeɪlɪən) *adj* **1** belonging to or denoting the Episcopal Church ▷ *n* **2** a member or adherent of this Church

▷ http://wikipedia.org/wiki/Episcopalian
▷ http://holycross.net/anonline.htm
▷ http://episcopalian.org/

episcopate (ɪˈpɪskəpɪt, -ˌpeɪt) *n* **1** the office, status, or term of office of a bishop **2** bishops collectively

episiotomy (ɪˌpiːzɪˈɒtəmɪ) *n, pl* **episiotomies** surgical incision into the perineum during labour to prevent its laceration during childbirth and to make delivery easier [c20 from Gk *epision* pubic region + -TOMY]

episode (ˈɛpɪˌsəʊd) *n* **1** an event or series of events **2** any of the sections into which a serialized novel or radio or television programme is divided **3** an incident or sequence that forms part of a narrative but may be a digression from the main story **4** (in ancient Greek tragedy) a section between two choric songs **5** *music* a contrasting section between statements of the subject, as in a fugue [c17 from Gk *epeisodion* something added, from *epi-* (in addition) + *eisodios* coming in, from *eis-* in + *hodos* road]

episodic (ˌɛpɪˈsɒdɪk) *or* **episodical** *adj* **1** resembling or relating to an episode **2** divided into episodes **3** irregular or sporadic > **ˌepiˈsodically** *adv*

epistaxis (ˌɛpɪˈstæksɪs) *n* the technical name for **nosebleed** [c18 from Gk: a dropping, from *epistazein* to drop on, from *stazein* to drip]

epistemology (ɪˌpɪstɪˈmɒlədʒɪ) *n* the theory of knowledge, esp the critical study of its validity, methods, and scope [c19 from Gk *epistēmē* knowledge] > **epistemological** (ɪˌpɪstɪməˈlɒdʒɪkᵊl) *adj* > **eˌpisteˈmologist** *n*

▷ http://pespmc1.vub.ac.be/EPISTEMI.html

epistle (ɪˈpɪsᵊl) *n* **1** a letter, esp one that is long, formal, or didactic **2** a literary work in letter form, esp a verse letter [OE *epistol*, via L from Gk *epistolē*]

Epistle (ɪˈpɪsᵊl) *n* **1** *Bible* any of the letters of the apostles **2** a reading from one of the Epistles, part of the Eucharistic service in many Christian Churches

epistolary (ɪˈpɪstələrɪ) *or* (*arch*) **epistolatory** *adj* **1** relating to, denoting, conducted by, or contained in letters **2** (of a novel, etc) in the form of a series of letters

epistyle (ˈɛpɪˌstaɪl) *n* another name for **architrave** (sense 1) [c17 via L from Gk, from EPI- + *stulos* column, STYLE]

epitaph (ˈɛpɪˌtɑːf) *n* **1** a commemorative inscription on a tombstone or monument **2** a commemorative speech or written passage **3** a final judgment on a person or thing [c14 via L from Gk, from EPI- + *taphos* tomb] > **epitaphic** (ˌɛpɪˈtæfɪk) *adj* > **ˈepiˌtaphist** *n*

epitaxy (ˈɛpɪˌtæksɪ) *n* the growth of a layer of one substance on the surface of a crystal so that the layer has the same structure as the underlying crystal > **epitaxial** (ˌɛpɪˈtæksɪəl) *adj*

epithalamium (ˌɛpɪθəˈleɪmɪəm) *or* **epithalamion** *n, pl* **epithalamia** (-mɪə) a poem or song written to celebrate a marriage [c17 from L, from Gk *epithalamion* marriage song, from *thalamos* bridal chamber] > **epithalamic** (ˌɛpɪθəˈlæmɪk) *adj*

epithelium (ˌɛpɪˈθiːlɪəm) *n, pl* **epitheliums** *or* **epithelia** (-lɪə) an animal cellular tissue covering the external and internal surfaces of the body [c18 NL, from EPI- + Gk *thēlē* nipple] > **ˌepiˈthelial** *adj*

epithet (ˈɛpɪˌθɛt) *n* a descriptive word or phrase added to or substituted for a person's name [c16 from L, from Gk, from *epitithenai* to add, from *tithenai* to put] > **ˌepiˈthetic** *or* **ˌepiˈthetical** *adj*

epitome (ɪˈpɪtəmɪ) *n* **1** a typical example of a characteristic or class; embodiment; personification **2** a summary of a written work; abstract [c16 via L from Gk, from *epitemnein* to abridge, from EPI- + *temnein* to cut] > **epitomical** (ˌɛpɪˈtɒmɪkᵊl) *or* **ˌepiˈtomic** *adj*

epitomize *or* **epitomise** (ɪˈpɪtəˌmaɪz) *vb* **epitomizes, epitomizing, epitomized** *or* **epitomises, epitomising, epitomised** (*tr*) **1** to be a personification of; typify **2** to make an epitome of

epizootic (ˌɛpɪzəʊˈɒtɪk) *adj* **1** (of a disease) suddenly and temporarily affecting a large number of animals in large areas of land ▷ *n* **2** an epizootic disease

EPNS *abbrev for* electroplated nickel silver

epoch (ˈiːpɒk) *n* **1** a point in time beginning a new or distinctive period **2** a long period of time marked by some predominant characteristic; era **3** *astron* a precise date to which information relating to a celestial body is referred **4** a unit of geological time within a period during which a series of rocks is formed [c17 from NL, from Gk *epokhē* cessation] > **epochal** (ˈɛpˌɒkᵊl) *adj*

epode (ˈɛpəʊd) *n Greek prosody* **1** the part of a lyric ode that follows the strophe and the antistrophe **2** a type of lyric poem composed of couplets in which a long line is followed by a shorter one [c16 via L from Gk, from *epaidein* to sing after, from *aidein* to sing]

eponym (ˈɛpənɪm) *n* **1** a name, esp a place name, derived from the name of a real or mythical person **2** the name of the person from which such a name is derived [c19 from Gk *epōnumos* giving a significant name] > **eˈponymy** *n*

eponymous (ɪˈpɒnɪməs) *adj* **1** (of a person) being the person after whom a literary work, film, etc, is named: *the eponymous heroine in the film of Jane Eyre* **2** (of a literary work, film, etc) named after its central character or creator: *The Stooges' eponymous debut album* > **eˈponymously** *adv*

EPOS (ˈiːpɒs) *n acronym for* electronic point of sale

epoxidize *or* **epoxidise** *vb* **epoxidizes, epoxidizing, epoxidized** *or* **epoxidises, epoxidising, epoxidised** (*tr*) to convert into or treat with an epoxy resin

epoxy (ɪˈpɒksɪ) *adj chem* **1** of, consisting of, or containing an oxygen atom joined to two different groups that are themselves joined to other groups: *epoxy group* **2** of, relating to, or consisting of an epoxy resin ▷ *n, pl* **epoxies** **3** short for **epoxy resin** [c20 from EPI- + OXY-²]

epoxy *or* **epoxide resin** (ɪˈpɒksaɪd) *n* any of various tough resistant thermosetting synthetic resins containing epoxy groups: used in surface coatings, laminates, and adhesives

Epping ('ɛpɪŋ) *n* a town in E England, in Essex, on the edge of Epping Forest: a residential centre for London. Pop: 9922 (1991)

Epping Forest ('ɛpɪŋ) *n* a forest in E England, northeast of London: formerly a royal hunting ground

eps *abbrev for* earnings per share

epsilon ('ɛpsɪ,lɒn) *n* the fifth letter of the Greek alphabet (E, ε) [Gk *e psilon*, lit.: simple *e*]

Epsom ('ɛpsəm) *n* a town in SE England, in Surrey: famous for its mineral springs and for horse racing. Pop (with Ewell): 64 405 (1991)

Epsom salts *n (functioning as sing or pl)* a medicinal preparation of hydrated magnesium sulphate, used as a purgative [c18 after EPSOM, where they occur in the water]

Epstein ('ɛpstaɪn) *n* Sir **Jacob** 1880–1959, British sculptor, born in the US of Russo-Polish parents

EQ *abbrev for* **1** emotional quotient, a (notional) measure of a person's adequacy in such areas as self-awareness, empathy, and dealing sensitively with other people [late c20 by analogy with IQ] **2** equalization, the electronic balancing of sound frequencies on audio recording equipment or hi-fi to reduce distortion or achieve a specific effect

equable ('ɛkwəbᵊl) *adj* **1** even-tempered; placid **2** unvarying; uniform: *an equable climate* [c17 from L *aequābilis*, from *aequāre* to make equal] > ,**equa'bility** *or* '**equableness** *n*

equal ('i:kwəl) *adj* **1** (often foll by *to* or *with*) identical in size, quantity, degree, intensity, etc **2** having identical privileges, rights, status, etc **3** having uniform effect or application: *equal opportunities* **4** evenly balanced or proportioned **5** (usually foll by *to*) having the necessary or adequate strength, ability, means, etc (for) ▷ *n* **6** a person or thing equal to another, esp in merit, ability, etc ▷ *vb* **equals, equalling, equalled** *or US* **equals, equaling, equaled 7** *(tr)* to be equal to; match **8** *(intr; usually foll by out)* to become equal **9** *(tr)* to make or do something equal to [c14 from L *aequālis*, from *aequus* level] > '**equally** *adv*

equalitarian (ɪ,kwɒlɪ'tɛərɪən) *adj, n* a less common word for **egalitarian** > **e,quali'tarianism** *n*

equality (ɪ'kwɒlɪtɪ) *n, pl* **equalities** the state of being equal

equalization payment *or* **grant** *n Canada* a financial grant made by the federal government to a poorer province in order to facilitate a level of services equal to that of a richer province.

equalize *or* **equalise** ('i:kwə,laɪz) *vb* **equalizes, equalizing, equalized** *or* **equalises, equalising, equalised 1** *(tr)* to make equal or uniform **2** *(intr)* (in sports) to reach the same score as one's opponent or opponents > ,**equali'zation** *or* ,**equali'sation** *n*

equal opportunity *n* **a** the offering of employment, pay, or promotion without discrimination as to sex, race, etc **b** *(as modifier)*: *an equal-opportunities employer*

equal sign *or* **equals sign** *n* the symbol =, used to indicate a mathematical equality

equanimity (,i:kwə'nɪmɪtɪ, ,ɛkwə-) *n* calmness of mind or temper; composure [c17 from L, from *aequus* even, EQUAL + *animus* mind, spirit] > **equanimous** (ɪ'kwænɪməs) *adj*

equate (ɪ'kweɪt) *vb* **equates, equating, equated** *(mainly tr)* **1** to make or regard as equivalent or similar **2** *maths* to indicate the equality of; form an equation from **3** *(intr)* to be equal [c15 from L *aequāre* to make EQUAL] > **e'quatable** *adj* > **e,quata'bility** *n*

equation (ɪ'kweɪʒən, -ʃən) *n* **1** a mathematical statement that two expressions are equal **2** the act of equating **3** the state of being equal, equivalent, or equally balanced **4** a representation of a chemical reaction using symbols of the elements **5** a situation or problem in which a number of factors need to be considered > **e'quational** *adj* > **e'quationally** *adv*

equator (ɪ'kweɪtə) *n* **1** the great circle of the earth, equidistant from the poles, dividing the N and S hemispheres **2** a circle dividing a sphere into two equal parts **3** *astron* See **celestial equator** [c14 from Med. L *(circulus) aequātor (diei et noctis)* (circle) that equalizes (the day and night), from L *aequāre* to make EQUAL]

equatorial (,ɛkwə'tɔ:rɪəl) *adj* **1** of, like, or existing at or near the equator **2** *astron* of or referring to the celestial equator **3** (of a telescope) mounted on perpendicular axes, one of which is parallel to the earth's axis ▷ *n* **4** an equatorial mounting for a telescope

Equatorial Guinea *n* a republic of W Africa, consisting of Río Muni on the mainland and the island of Bioko in the Gulf of Guinea, with four smaller islands: ceded by Portugal to Spain in 1778; gained independence in 1968. Official languages: Spanish and French. Religion: Roman Catholic majority. Currency: franc. Capital: Malabo. Pop: 486 000 (2001 est). Area: 28 049 sq km (10 830 sq miles). Former name (until 1964): **Spanish Guinea**

equerry ('ɛkwərɪ; *at the British court* ɪ'kwɛrɪ) *n, pl* **equerries 1** an officer attendant upon the British sovereign **2** (formerly) an officer in a royal household responsible for the horses [c16 alteration (through infl. of L *equus* horse) of earlier *escuirie*, from OF: stable]

equestrian (ɪ'kwɛstrɪən) *adj* **1** of or relating to horses and riding **2** on horseback; mounted **3** of, relating to, or composed of knights ▷ *n* **4** a person skilled in riding and horsemanship [c17 from L *equestris*, from *equus* horse] > **e'questrian,ism** *n*

equi- *combining form* equal or equally: *equidistant; equilateral*

equiangular (,i:kwɪ'æŋgjʊlə) *adj* having all angles equal

Ee

equidistant (,i:kwɪ'dɪstənt) *adj* equally distant > ,**equi'distance** *n* > ,**equi'distantly** *adv*

equilateral (,i:kwɪ'lætərəl) *adj* **1** having all sides of equal length ▷ *n* **2** a geometric figure having all sides of equal length **3** a side that is equal in length to other sides

equilibrant (ɪ'kwɪlɪbrənt) *n* a force capable of balancing another force

equilibrate (,i:kwɪ'laɪbreɪt, ɪ'kwɪlɪ,breɪt) *vb* **equilibrates, equilibrating, equilibrated** to bring to or be in equilibrium; balance [c17 from LL, from *aequilībris* in balance; see EQUILIBRIUM] > ,**equili'bration** *n*

equilibrist (ɪ'kwɪlɪbrɪst) *n* a person who performs balancing feats, esp on a high wire > **e,quili'bristic** *adj*

equilibrium (,i:kwɪ'lɪbrɪəm) *n, pl* **equilibriums** *or* **equilibria** (-rɪə) **1** a stable condition in which forces cancel one another **2** a state or feeling of mental balance; composure **3** any unchanging state of a body, system, etc, resulting from the balance of the influences to which it is subjected **4** *physiol* a state of bodily balance, maintained primarily by receptors in the inner ear [c17 from L, from *aequi-* EQUI- + *lībra* pound, balance]

equine ('ɛkwaɪn) *adj* of, relating to, or resembling a horse [c18 from L, from *equus* horse]

equinoctial (,i:kwɪ'nɒkʃəl) *adj* **1** relating to or occurring at either or both equinoxes **2** *astron* of or relating to the celestial equator ▷ *n* **3** a storm or gale at or near an equinox **4** another name for **celestial equator** [c14 from L: see EQUINOX]

equinoctial circle *or* **line** *n* another name for **celestial equator**

equinoctial point *n* either of two points at which the celestial equator intersects the ecliptic

equinox ('i:kwɪ,nɒks; 'ɛkwɪ,nɑks) *n* **1** either of the two occasions, six months apart, when day and night are of equal length. In the N hemisphere the **vernal equinox** occurs around March 21 (Sept 23 in the S hemisphere). The **autumnal equinox** occurs around Sept 23 in the N hemisphere (March 21 in the S hemisphere) **2** another name for **equinoctial point** [C14 from Med. L *equinoxium*, changed from L *aequinoctium*, from *aequi-* EQUI- + *nox* night]

equip (ɪˈkwɪp) *vb* **equips, equipping, equipped** (*tr*) **1** to furnish (with necessary supplies, etc) **2** (*usually passive*) to provide with abilities, understanding, etc **3** to dress out; attire [C16 from OF *eschiper* to embark, fit out (a ship), of Gmc origin] > **eˈquipper** *n*

equipage (ˈɛkwɪpɪdʒ) *n* **1** a horse-drawn carriage, esp one attended by liveried footmen **2** the stores and equipment of a military unit **3** *arch* a set of useful articles

equipment (ɪˈkwɪpmənt) *n* **1** an act or instance of equipping **2** the items provided **3** a set of tools, kit, etc, assembled for a specific purpose

equipoise (ˈɛkwɪˌpɔɪz) *n* **1** even balance of weight; equilibrium **2** a counterbalance; counterpoise ▷ *vb* **equipoises, equipoising, equipoised** **3** (*tr*) to offset or balance

equipollent (ˌiːkwɪˈpɒlənt) *adj* **1** equal or equivalent in significance, power, or effect ▷ *n* **2** something that is equipollent [C15 from L *aequipollēns* of equal importance, from EQUI- + *pollēre* to be able, be strong] > ˌ**equiˈpollence** *or* ˌ**equiˈpollency** *n*

equisetum (ˌɛkwɪˈsiːtəm) *n, pl* **equisetums** *or* **equiseta** (-tə) any plant of the horsetail genus [C19 NL, from L, from *equus* horse + *saeta* bristle]

equitable (ˈɛkwɪtəbᵊl) *adj* **1** fair; just **2** *law* relating to or valid in equity, as distinct from common law or statute law [C17 from F, from *équité* EQUITY] > ˈ**equitableness** *n*

equitation (ˌɛkwɪˈteɪʃən) *n* the study and practice of riding and horsemanship [C16 from L *equitātiō*, from *equitāre* to ride, from *equus* horse]

equities (ˈɛkwɪtɪz) *pl n* another name for **ordinary shares**

equity (ˈɛkwɪtɪ) *n, pl* **equities** **1** the quality of being impartial; fairness **2** an impartial or fair act, decision, etc **3** *law* a system of jurisprudence founded on principles of natural justice and fair conduct. It supplements common law, as by providing a remedy where none exists at law **4** *law* an equitable right or claim **5** the interest of ordinary shareholders in a company **6** the value of a debtor's property in excess of debts to which it is liable [C14 from OF, from L *aequitās*, from *aequus* level, EQUAL]

Equity (ˈɛkwɪtɪ) *n* the actors' trade union

equity capital *n* the part of the share capital of a company owned by ordinary shareholders or in certain circumstances by other classes of shareholder

equity-linked policy *n* an insurance or assurance policy in which premiums are invested partially or wholly in ordinary shares for the eventual benefit of the beneficiaries of the policy

equivalence (ɪˈkwɪvələns) *or* **equivalency** *n* **1** the state of being equivalent **2** *logic, maths* another term for **biconditional**

equivalent (ɪˈkwɪvələnt) *adj* **1** equal in value, quantity, significance, etc **2** having the same or a similar effect or meaning **3** *logic, maths* (of two propositions) having a biconditional between them ▷ *n* **4** something that is equivalent **5** Also called: **equivalent weight** the weight of a substance that will combine with or displace 8 grams of oxygen or 1.007 97 grams of hydrogen [C15 from LL, from L *aequi-* EQUI- + *valēre* to be worth] > **eˈquivalently** *adv*

equivocal (ɪˈkwɪvəkᵊl) *adj* **1** capable of varying interpretations; ambiguous **2** deliberately misleading or vague **3** of doubtful character or sincerity [C17 from LL, from L EQUI- + *vōx* voice] > **eˌquivoˈcality** *or* **eˈquivocalness** *n*

equivocate (ɪˈkwɪvəˌkeɪt) *vb* **equivocates, equivocating, equivocated** (*intr*) to use equivocal language, esp to avoid speaking directly or honestly [C15 from Med. L, from LL *aequivocus* ambiguous, EQUIVOCAL] > **eˈquivoˌcatingly** *adv* > **eˌquivoˈcation** *n* > **eˈquivoˌcator** *n* > **eˈquivocatory** *adj*

er (ə, ɜː) *interj* a sound made when hesitating in speech

Er *the chemical symbol for* erbium

ER *abbrev for:* **1** (in the US) emergency room (in hospitals) **2** Elizabeth Regina [L: Queen Elizabeth] **3** Eduardus Rex [L: King Edward]

-er[1] *suffix forming nouns* **1** a person or thing that performs a specified action: *reader; lighter* **2** a person engaged in a profession, occupation, etc: *writer; baker* **3** a native or inhabitant of: *Londoner; villager* **4** a person or thing having a certain characteristic: *newcomer; fiver* [OE *-ere*]

-er[2] *suffix.* forming the comparative degree of adjectives (*deeper, freer*, etc) and adverbs (*faster, slower*, etc) [OE *-rd, -re* (adj), *-or* (adv)]

era (ˈɪərə) *n* **1** a period of time considered as being of a distinctive character; epoch **2** an extended period of time the years of which are numbered from a fixed point: *the Christian era* **3** a point in time beginning a new or distinctive period **4** a major division of geological time, divided into periods [C17 from L *aera* counters, pl of *aes* brass, pieces of brass money]

ERA (ˈɪərə) *n acronym or abbrev for* **1** (in Britain) Education Reform Act: the 1988 act which established the key elements of the National Curriculum **2** (in the US) Equal Rights Amendment: a proposed amendment to the US Constitution enshrining equality between the sexes

eradicate (ɪˈrædɪˌkeɪt) *vb* **eradicates, eradicating, eradicated** (*tr*) **1** to obliterate **2** to pull up by the roots [C16 from L *ērādīcāre* to uproot, from EX-[1] + *rādīx* root] > **eˈradicable** *adj* > **eˌradiˈcation** *n* > **eˈradicative** *adj*

erase (ɪˈreɪz) *vb* **erases, erasing, erased** **1** to obliterate or rub out (something written, typed, etc) **2** (*tr*) to destroy all traces of **3** to remove (a recording) from (magnetic tape) [C17 from L, from EX-[1] + *rādere* to scratch, scrape] > **eˈrasable** *adj*

eraser (ɪˈreɪzə) *n* an object, such as a piece of rubber, for erasing something written, typed, etc

Erasmus (ɪˈræzməs) *n* **Desiderius** (ˌdɛzɪˈdɪərɪəs), real name *Gerhard Gerhards*. ?1466–1536, Dutch humanist, the leading scholar of the Renaissance in northern Europe. He published the first Greek edition of the New Testament in 1516; his other works include the satirical *Encomium Moriae* (1509); *Colloquia* (1519), a series of dialogues; and an attack on the theology of Luther, *De Libero Arbitrio* (1524)

erasure (ɪˈreɪʒə) *n* **1** the act or an instance of erasing **2** the place or mark, as on a piece of paper, where something has been erased

Erato (ˈɛrəˌtəʊ) *n Greek myth* the Muse of love poetry

Eratosthenes (ˌɛrəˈtɒsθɪˌniːz) *n* ?276–?194 BC, Greek mathematician and astronomer, who calculated the circumference of the earth by observing the angle of the sun's rays at different places

Erbil *or* **Irbil** (ˈɜːbɪl) *n* a city in N Iraq: important in Assyrian times. Pop: 485 968 (latest est). Ancient name: **Arbela**

erbium (ˈɜːbɪəm) *n* a soft malleable silvery-white element of the lanthanide series of metals. Symbol: Er; atomic no.: 68; atomic wt.: 167.26 [C19 from NL, from (*Ytt*)*erb*(*y*), Sweden, where it was first found + -IUM]

Erciyas Dağ i (*Turkish* ˈɛrdʒijɑs dɑːˈi) *n* an extinct volcano in central Turkey. Height 3916 m (12 848 ft)

ERDF *abbrev for* European Regional Development Fund: a fund to provide money for specific projects for work on the infrastructure in countries of the European Union

ere (ɛə) *conj, prep* a poetic word for **before** [OE *ǣr*]

Erebus[1] (ˈɛrɪbəs) *n Greek myth* **1** the god of darkness, son of Chaos and brother of Night **2** the darkness below the earth, thought to be the abode of the dead or the region they pass through on their way to Hades

Erebus² (ˈɛrɪbəs) *n* **Mount** a volcano in Antarctica, on Ross Island: discovered by Sir James Ross in 1841 and named after his ship. Height: 3794 m (12 448 ft)

Erechtheum (ɪˈrɛkθɪəm, ˌɛrəkˈθiːəm) *or* **Erechtheion** (ɪˈrɛkθɪən, ˌɛrəkˈθiːən) *n* a temple on the Acropolis at Athens, which has a porch of caryatids

Erechtheus (ɛˈrɛkθjuːs, -θɪəs) *n Greek myth* a king of Athens who sacrificed one of his daughters because the oracle at Delphi said this was the only way to win the war against the Eleusinians

erect (ɪˈrɛkt) *adj* **1** upright in posture or position **2** *physiol* (of the penis, clitoris, or nipples) firm or rigid after swelling with blood, esp as a result of sexual excitement **3** (of plant parts) growing vertically or at right angles to the parts from which they arise ▷ *vb (mainly tr)* **4** to put up; build **5** to raise to an upright position **6** to found or form; set up **7** *(also intr) physiol* to become or cause to become firm or rigid by filling with blood **8** to exalt **9** to draw or construct (a line, figure, etc) on a given line or figure [c14 from L *ērigere* to set up, from *regere* to control, govern] > **eˈrectable** *adj* > **eˈrecter** *or* **eˈrector** *n* > **eˈrectness** *n*

erectile (ɪˈrɛktaɪl) *adj* **1** *physiol* (of tissues or organs, such as the penis or clitoris) capable of becoming erect **2** capable of being erected > **erectility** (ɪrɛkˈtɪlɪtɪ, ˌiːrɛk-) *n*

erection (ɪˈrɛkʃən) *n* **1** the act of erecting or the state of being erected **2** a building or construction **3** *physiol* the enlarged state of erectile tissues or organs, esp the penis, when filled with blood **4** an erect penis

E region *or* **layer** *n* a region of the ionosphere, extending from a height of 90 to about 150 kilometres. It reflects radio waves of medium wavelength

eremite (ˈɛrɪˌmaɪt) *n* a Christian hermit or recluse [c13 see HERMIT] > **eremitic** (ˌɛrɪˈmɪtɪk) or ˌ**ereˈmitical** *adj* > ˈ**eremitˌism** *n*

Erenburg (ˈɛrənbɜːg; *Russian* ɛrɪnˈburk) *n* a variant spelling of (Ilya Grigorievich) **Ehrenburg**

erepsin (ɪˈrɛpsɪn) *n* a mixture of proteolytic enzymes secreted by the small intestine [c20 *er-*, from L *ēripere* to snatch + (P)EPSIN]

erethism (ˈɛrɪˌθɪzəm) *n* **1** *physiol* an abnormal irritability or sensitivity in any part of the body **2** *psychiatry* **2a** a personality disorder resulting from mercury poisoning **2b** an abnormal tendency to become aroused quickly, esp sexually, as the result of a verbal or psychic stimulus [c18 from F, from Gk, from *erethizein* to excite, irritate]

Eretria (ɪˈrɛtrɪə) *n* an ancient city in Greece, on the S coast of Euboea: founded as an Ionian colony; destroyed by the Persians in 490 BC following which it never regained its former significance

Erevan (*Russian* jɪrɪˈvan) *n* a variant spelling of **Yerevan**

erf (ɜːf) *n, pl* **erven** (ˈɜːvən) *S African* a plot of land, usually urban [from Afrik., from Du.: inheritance]

Erf (ɜːf) *n acronym for* electrorheological fluid: a liquid that thickens when an electric current passes and returns to a liquid when the current ceases

Erfurt (*German* ˈɛrfʊrt) *n* an industrial city in central Germany, the capital of Thuringia: university (1392). Pop: 202 100 (1999 est)

erg¹ (ɜːg) *n* the cgs unit of work or energy [c19 from Gk *ergon* work]

erg² (ɜːg) *n, pl* **ergs** *or* **areg** (əˈrɛg) an area of shifting sand dunes, esp in the Sahara Desert in N Africa [c19 from Ar. *ʿirj*]

ergo (ˈɜːgəʊ) *sentence connector* therefore; hence [c14 from L: therefore]

ergonomic (ˌɜːgəˈnɒmɪk) *adj* **1** of or relating to ergonomics **2** designed to minimize physical effort and discomfort, and hence maximize efficiency

ergonomics (ˌɜːgəˈnɒmɪks) *n (functioning as sing)* the study of the relationship between workers and their environment, esp the equipment they use [c20 from Gk *ergon* work + (ECO)NOMICS] > **ergonomist** (ɜːˈgɒnəmɪst) *n*

ergosterol (ɜːˈgɒstəˌrɒl) *n* a plant sterol that is converted into vitamin D by the action of ultraviolet radiation

ergot (ˈɜːgət, -gɒt) *n* **1** a disease of cereals and other grasses caused by fungi of the genus *Claviceps* **2** any fungus causing this disease **3** the dried fungus, used as the source of certain alkaloids used in medicine [c17 from F: spur (of a cock), from ?]

ergotism (ˈɜːgəˌtɪzəm) *n* ergot poisoning, producing either burning pains and eventually gangrene or itching skin and convulsions

Erhard (*German* ˈeːrhart) *n* **Ludwig** (ˈluːtvɪç) 1897–1977, German statesman: chief architect of the *Wirtschaftswunder* ("economic miracle") of West Germany's recovery after World War II; chancellor (1963–66)

erica (ˈɛrɪkə) *n* any shrub of the ericaceous genus *Erica*, including the heaths and some heathers [c19 via L from Gk *ereikē* heath]

ericaceous (ˌɛrɪˈkeɪʃəs) *adj* of or relating to the Ericaceae, a family of trees and shrubs with typically bell-shaped flowers: includes heather, rhododendron, azalea, and arbutus

Ericson *or* **Ericsson** (ˈɛrɪksᵊn) *n* **Leif** (liːf) 10th–11th centuries AD, Norse navigator, who discovered Vinland (?1000), variously identified as the coast of New England, Labrador, or Newfoundland; son of Eric the Red

Eric the Red (ˈɛrɪk) *n* ?940–?1010 AD, Norse navigator: discovered and colonized Greenland; father of Leif Ericson

Erie (ˈɪərɪ) *n* **1 Lake** a lake between the US and Canada: the southernmost and the shallowest of the Great Lakes; empties by the Niagara River into Lake Ontario. Area: 25 718 sq km (9930 sq miles) **2** a port in NW Pennsylvania, on Lake Erie. Pop: 103 717 (2000)

Ee

Erie Canal *n* a canal in New York State between Albany and Buffalo, linking the Hudson River with Lake Erie. Length: 579 km (360 miles)

erigeron (ɪˈrɪdʒərən, -ˈrɪg-) *n* any plant of the genus *Erigeron*, whose flowers resemble asters [c17 via L from Gk, from *ēri* early + *gerōn* old man; from the white down of some species]

Eriksson (ˈɛrɪksən) *n* **Sven-Goran** (ˈsfɛnˈgɜːrən) born 1948, Swedish football manager; head coach of the England team from 2001

Erin (ˈɪərɪn, ˈɛərɪn) *n* an archaic or poetic name for **Ireland¹** [from Irish Gaelic *Éirinn*, dative of Ireland]

Erinyes (ɪˈrɪnɪˌiːz) *pl n, sing* **Erinys** (ɪˈrɪnɪs, ɪˈraɪ-) *myth* another name for the **Furies** [Gk]

Eris (ˈɛrɪs) *n Greek myth* the goddess of discord, sister of Ares

Eritrea (ˌɛrɪˈtreɪə) *n* a small country in NE Africa, on the Red Sea: became an Italian colony in 1890; federated with Ethiopia (1952–93); an independence movement was engaged in war with the Ethiopian government from 1961 until independence was gained in 1993; consists of hot and arid coastal lowlands, rising to the foothills of the Ethiopian highlands. Languages: Arabic, English, Afar, and others. Religions: Muslim and Christian. Currency: nakfa. Capital: Asmara. Pop: 4 298 000 (2001 est). Area: 117 400 sq km (45 300 sq miles)

Eritrean (ˌɛrɪˈtreɪən) *adj* **1** of or relating to Eritrea or its inhabitants ▷ *n* **2** a native or inhabitant of Eritrea

Erivan (*Russian* jɪrɪˈvan) *n* a variant spelling of **Yerevan**

erk (ɜːk) *n Brit sl* an aircraftman or naval rating [c20 ? a corruption of *AC* (aircraftman)]

Erlangen (*German* ˈɛrlaŋən) *n* a town in central Germany, in Bavaria: university (1743). Pop: 100 600 (1999 est)

Erlanger ('ɜːlæŋə) *n* **Joseph** 1874–1965, US physiologist. He shared a Nobel prize for physiology or medicine (1944) with Gasser for their work on the electrical signs of nervous activity

ERM *abbrev for* Exchange Rate Mechanism

ermine ('ɜːmɪn) *n, pl* **ermines** *or* **ermine** 1 the stoat in northern regions, where it has a white winter coat with a black-tipped tail 2 the fur of this animal 3 the dignity or office of a judge, noble, etc, whose state robes are trimmed with ermine [c12 from OF, from Med. L *Armenius (mūs)* Armenian (mouse)]

erne *or* **ern** (ɜːn) *n* a fish-eating sea eagle [OE *earn*]

Erne (ɜːn) *n* a river in N central Republic of Ireland, rising in County Cavan and flowing north across the border, through **Upper Lough Erne** and **Lower Lough Erne** and then west to Donegal Bay. Length: about 96 km (60 miles)

Ernie ('ɜːnɪ) *n* (in Britain) a machine that randomly selects winning numbers of Premium Bonds [c20 acronym of Electronic Random Number Indicator Equipment]

Ernst (*German* ɛrnst) *n* **Max** (maks) 1891–1976, German painter, resident in France and the US, a prominent exponent of Dada and surrealism: developed the technique of collage

erode (ɪ'rəʊd) *vb* **erodes, eroding, eroded** 1 to grind or wear down or away or become ground or worn down or away 2 to deteriorate or cause to deteriorate [c17 from L, from EX-[1] + *rōdere* to gnaw] > **e'rodible** *adj*

erogenous (ɪ'rɒdʒɪnəs) *or* **erogenic** (ˌɛrə'dʒɛnɪk) *adj* 1 sensitive to sexual stimulation 2 arousing sexual desire or giving sexual pleasure [c19 from Gk *erōs* love, desire + -GENOUS] > **erogeneity** (ˌɛrədʒɪ'niːɪtɪ) *n*

Eros ('ɪərɒs, 'ɛrɒs) *n Greek myth* the god of love, son of Aphrodite. Roman counterpart: **Cupid**

erosion (ɪ'rəʊʒən) *n* 1 the wearing away of rocks, soil, etc, by the action of water, ice, wind, etc 2 the act or process of eroding or the state of being eroded > **e'rosive** *or* **e'rosional** *adj*

erotic (ɪ'rɒtɪk) *adj* 1 of, concerning, or arousing sexual desire or giving sexual pleasure 2 marked by strong sexual desire or being especially sensitive to sexual stimulation. Also: **erotical** [c17 from Gk *erōtikos*, from *erōs* love] > **e'rotically** *adv*

erotica (ɪ'rɒtɪkə) *pl n* explicitly sexual literature or art [c19 from Gk: see EROTIC]

eroticism (ɪ'rɒtɪˌsɪzəm) *or* **erotism** ('ɛrəˌtɪzəm) *n* 1 erotic quality or nature 2 the use of sexually arousing or pleasing symbolism in literature or art 3 sexual excitement or desire

erotogenic (ɪˌrɒtə'dʒɛnɪk) *adj* originating from or causing sexual stimulation; erogenous

err (ɜː) *vb (intr)* 1 to make a mistake; be incorrect 2 to deviate from a moral standard 3 to act with bias, esp favourable bias: *to err on the right side* [c14 *erren* to wander, stray, from OF, from L *errāre*] > **'errancy** *n*

errand ('ɛrənd) *n* 1 a short trip undertaken to perform a task or commission (esp in **run errands**) 2 the purpose or object of such a trip [OE *ǣrende*]

errant ('ɛrənt) *adj (often postpositive)* 1 *arch or literary* wandering in search of adventure 2 erring or straying from the right course or accepted standards [c14 from OF: journeying, from Vulgar L *iterāre* (unattested), from L *iter* journey; infl. by L *errāre* to err] > **'errantly** *adv* > **'errantry** *n*

erratic (ɪ'rætɪk) *adj* 1 irregular in performance, behaviour, or attitude; unpredictable 2 having no fixed or regular course ▷ *n* 3 a piece of rock that has been transported from its place of origin, esp by glacial action [c14 from L, from *errāre* to wander, err] > **er'ratically** *adv*

erratum (ɪ'rɑːtəm) *n, pl* **errata** (-tə) 1 an error in writing or printing 2 another name for **corrigendum** [c16 from L: mistake, from *errāre* to err]

Er Rif (ɛə rɪf) *n* a mountainous region of N Morocco, near the Mediterranean coast

erroneous (ɪ'rəʊnɪəs) *adj* based on or containing error; incorrect [c14 (in the sense: deviating from what is right), from L, from *errāre* to wander] > **er'roneousness** *n*

error ('ɛrə) *n* 1 a mistake or inaccuracy 2 an incorrect belief or wrong judgment 3 the condition of deviating from accuracy or correctness 4 deviation from a moral standard; wrongdoing 5 *maths, statistics* a measure of the difference between some quantity and an approximation of it, often expressed as a percentage [c13 from L, from *errāre* to err] > **'error-ˌfree** *adj*

ersatz ('ɛəzæts, 'ɜː-) *adj* 1 made in imitation; artificial ▷ *n* 2 an ersatz substance or article [c20 G, from *ersetzen* to substitute]

Erse (ɜːs) *n* 1 another name for Irish **Gaelic** ▷ *adj* 2 of or relating to the Irish Gaelic language [c14 from Lowland Scots *Erisch* Irish]

erst (ɜːst) *adv arch* 1 long ago; formerly 2 at first [OE *ǣrest* earliest, sup. of *ǣr* early]

erstwhile ('ɜːstˌwaɪl) *adj* 1 former; one-time ▷ *adv* 2 *arch* long ago; formerly

Erté (ɛrte) *n* real name *Romain de Tirtoff*. 1892–1990, French fashion illustrator and designer, born in Russia, noted for his extravagant costumes and tableaux for the Folies-Bergère in Paris

eruct (ɪ'rʌkt) *or* **eructate** *vb* **eructs, eructing, eructed** *or* **eructates, eructating, eructated** 1 to belch 2 (of a volcano) to pour out (fumes or volcanic matter) [c17 from L, from *ructāre* to belch] > **eructation** (ɪˌrʌk'teɪʃən, ˌiːrʌk-) *n*

erudite ('ɛrʊˌdaɪt) *adj* having or showing extensive scholarship; learned [c15 from L, from *ērudīre* to polish] > **erudition** (ˌɛrʊ'dɪʃən) *or* **'eruˌditeness** *n*

erupt (ɪ'rʌpt) *vb* 1 to eject (steam, water, and volcanic material) violently or (of volcanic material, etc) to be so ejected 2 *(intr)* (of a blemish) to appear on the skin 3 *(intr)* (of a tooth) to emerge through the gum during normal tooth development 4 *(intr)* to burst forth suddenly and violently [c17 from L *ēruptus* having burst forth, from *ērumpere*, from *rumpere* to burst] > **e'ruptive** *adj* > **e'ruption** *n*

-ery *or* **-ry** *suffix forming nouns* 1 indicating a place of business or activity: *bakery; refinery* 2 indicating a class or collection of things: *cutlery* 3 indicating qualities or actions: *snobbery; trickery* 4 indicating a practice or occupation: *husbandry* 5 indicating a state or condition: *slavery* [from OF *-erie*; see -ER[1], -Y[3]]

Erymanthus (ˌɛrɪ'mænθəs) *n* **Mount** a mountain in SW Greece, in the NW Peloponnese. Height: 2224 m (7297 ft). Modern Greek name: **Erímanthos** (e'rimanθɔs)

erysipelas (ˌɛrɪ'sɪpɪləs) *n* an acute streptococcal infectious disease of the skin, characterized by fever and purplish lesions [c16 from L, from Gk, from *erusi-* red + *-pelas* skin]

erythro- *or before a vowel* **erythr-** *combining form* red: *erythrocyte* [from Gk *eruthros* red]

erythrocyte (ɪ'rɪθrəʊˌsaɪt) *n* a blood cell of vertebrates that transports oxygen and carbon dioxide, combined with haemoglobin > **erythrocytic** (ɪˌrɪθrəʊ'sɪtɪk) *adj*

erythromycin (ɪˌrɪθrəʊ'maɪsɪn) *n* an antibiotic used in treating certain bacterial infections [c20 from ERYTHRO- + Gk *mukēs* fungus + -IN]

erythropoiesis (ɪˌrɪθrəʊpɔɪ'iːsɪs) *n physiol* the formation of red blood cells [c19 from ERYTHRO- + Gk *poiēs* a making, from *poiein* to make] > **erythropoietic** (ɪˌrɪθrəʊpɔɪ'ɛtɪk) *adj*

Erzgebirge (*German* 'eːrtsgəbɪrgə) *pl n* a mountain range on the border between Germany and the Czech Republic: formerly rich in mineral resources. Highest peak: Mount Klínovec (Keilberg), 1244 m (4081 ft). Czech name: **Krušné Hory**. Also called: **Ore Mountains**

Erzurum ('ɛəzʊrʊm) *n* a city in E Turkey: a strategic centre; scene of two major battles against Russian forces (1877 and 1916); important military base and a closed city to unofficial visitors. Pop: 298 735 (1997)

Es *the chemical symbol for* einsteinium

-es *suffix* **1** a variant of **-s**[1] for nouns ending in *ch, s, sh, z,* postconsonantal *y*, for some nouns ending in a vowel, and nouns in *f* with *v* in the plural: *ashes; heroes; calves* **2** a variant of **-s**[2] for verbs ending in *ch, s, sh, z,* postconsonantal *y*, or a vowel: *preaches; steadies; echoes*

Esau (ˈiːsɔː) *n Bible* son of Isaac and Rebecca and twin brother of Jacob, to whom he sold his birthright (Genesis 25)

Esbjerg (*Danish* ˈɛsbjɛr) *n* a port in SW Denmark, in Jutland on the North Sea: Denmark's chief fishing port. Pop: 82 579 (1995 est)

escadrille (ˌɛskəˈdrɪl) *n* a French squadron of aircraft, esp in World War I [from F: flotilla, from Sp., from *escuadra* SQUADRON]

escalade (ˌɛskəˈleɪd) *n* **1** an assault using ladders, esp on a fortification ▷ *vb* **escalades, escalading, escaladed** **2** to gain access to (a place) by ladders [c16 from F, from It., from *scalare* to mount, SCALE[3]]

escalate (ˈɛskəˌleɪt) *vb* **escalates, escalating, escalated** to increase or be increased in extent, intensity, or magnitude [c20 back formation from ESCALATOR] > ˌ**escaˈlation** *n*

escalator (ˈɛskəˌleɪtə) *n* **1** a moving staircase consisting of stair treads fixed to a conveyor belt **2** short for **escalator clause** [c20 orig. a trademark]

escalator clause *n* a clause in a contract stipulating an adjustment in wages, prices, etc, in the event of specified changes in conditions, such as a large rise in the cost of living

escallop (ɛˈskɒləp, ɛˈskæl-) *n, vb* another word for **scallop**

escalope (ˈɛskəˌlɒp) *n* a thin slice of meat, usually veal [c19 from OF: shell]

escapade (ˈɛskəˌpeɪd, ˌɛskəˈpeɪd) *n* **1** an adventure, esp one that is mischievous or unlawful **2** a prank; romp [c17 from F, from OIt., from Vulgar L *excappāre* (unattested) to ESCAPE]

escape (ɪˈskeɪp) *vb* **escapes, escaping, escaped** **1** to get away or break free from (confinement, etc) **2** to manage to avoid (danger, etc) **3** (*intr; usually foll by from*) (of gases, liquids, etc) to issue gradually, as from a crack; seep; leak **4** (*tr*) to elude; be forgotten by: *the figure escapes me* **5** (*tr*) to be articulated inadvertently or involuntarily from: *a roar escaped his lips* ▷ *n* **6** the act of escaping or state of having escaped **7** avoidance of injury, harm, etc **8a** a means or way of escape **8b** (*as modifier*): *an escape route* **9** a means of distraction or relief **10** a gradual outflow; leakage; seepage **11** Also called: **escape valve, escape cock** a valve that releases air, steam, etc, above a certain pressure **12** a plant originally cultivated but now growing wild [c14 from OF, from Vulgar L *excappāre* (unattested) to escape (lit.: to slip out of one's cloak, hence free oneself), from EX-[1] + LL *cappa* cloak] > **esˈcapable** *adj* > **esˈcaper** *n*

escapee (ɪˌskeɪˈpiː) *n* a person who has escaped, esp an escaped prisoner

escapement (ɪˈskeɪpmənt) *n* **1** a mechanism consisting of a toothed wheel (**escape wheel**) and anchor, used in timepieces to provide periodic impulses to the pendulum or balance **2** any similar mechanism that regulates movement **3** in pianos, the mechanism which allows the hammer to clear the string after striking, so the string can vibrate **4** *rare* an act or means of escaping

escape road *n* a road provided on a hill for a driver to drive into if his brakes fail or on a bend if he loses control of the turn

escape velocity *n* the minimum velocity necessary for a body to escape from the gravitational field of the earth or other celestial body

escapism (ɪˈskeɪpɪzəm) *n* an inclination to retreat from unpleasant reality, as through diversion or fantasy > **esˈcapist** *n, adj*

escapologist (ˌɛskəˈpɒlədʒɪst) *n* an entertainer who specializes in freeing himself or herself from confinement > ˌ**escaˈpology** *n*

escargot *French* (ɛskargo) *n* a variety of edible snail

escarole (ˈɛskərəʊl) *n US and Canadian name* a variety of endive with broad leaves, used in salads [c20 French from Italian *scar(i)ola*, from Latin *esca* food]

escarpment (ɪˈskɑːpmənt) *n* **1** the long continuous steep face of a ridge or plateau formed by erosion or faulting; scarp **2** a steep artificial slope made immediately in front of a fortified place [c19 from F *escarpe*; see SCARP]

Escaut (ɛsko) *n* the French name for the **Scheldt**

-escent *suffix forming adjectives* beginning to be, do, show, etc: *convalescent; luminescent* [via OF from L *-ēscent-*, stem of present participial suffix of *-ēscere*, ending of inceptive verbs] > **-escence** *suffix forming nouns*

eschatology (ˌɛskəˈtɒlədʒɪ) *n* the branch of theology concerned with the end of the world [c19 from Gk *eskhatos* last] > **eschatological** (ˌɛskətəˈlɒdʒɪkᵊl) *adj* > ˌ**eschaˈtologist** *n*

escheat (ɪsˈtʃiːt) *law* ▷ *n* **1** (in England before 1926) the reversion of property to the Crown in the absence of legal heirs **2** *feudalism* the reversion of property to the feudal lord in the absence of legal heirs **3** the property so reverting ▷ *vb* **4** to take (land) by escheat or (of land) to revert by escheat [c14 from OF, from *escheoir* to fall to the lot of, from LL *excadere* (unattested), from L *cadere* to fall] > **esˈcheatable** *adj* > **esˈcheatage** *n*

Escherichia (ˌɛʃəˈrɪkɪə) *n* a genus of bacteria that are found in the intestines of humans and many animals, esp *E. coli*, which is sometimes pathogenic and is widely used in genetic research [c19 after Theodor *Escherich* (1857–1911), G paediatrician]

eschew (ɪsˈtʃuː) *vb* (*tr*) to keep clear of or abstain from (something disliked, injurious, etc); shun; avoid [c14 from OF *eschiver*, of Gmc origin; see SHY[1], SKEW] > **esˈchewal** *n* > **esˈchewer** *n*

Ee

eschscholzia *or* **eschscholtzia** (ɪsˈkɒlʃə) *n* another name for **California poppy** [c19 after J. F. von *Eschscholtz* (1793–1831), G botanist]

Escoffier (*French* ɛskɔfje) *n* (**Georges**) **Auguste** (ogyst) 1846–1935, French chef at the Savoy Hotel, London (1890–99)

Escorial (ˌɛskɒrɪˈɑːl, ɛˈskɔːrɪəl) *or* **Escurial** *n* a village in central Spain, northwest of Madrid: site of an architectural complex containing a monastery, palace, and college, built by Philip II between 1563 and 1584

escort *n* (ˈɛskɔːt) **1** one or more persons, soldiers, vehicles, etc, accompanying another or others for protection, as a mark of honour, etc **2** a man or youth who accompanies a woman or girl on a social occasion ▷ *vb* (ɪsˈkɔːt) **3** (*tr*) to accompany or attend as an escort [c16 from F, from It., from *scorgere* to guide, from L *corrigere* to straighten; see CORRECT]

escritoire (ˌɛskrɪˈtwɑː) *n* a writing desk with drawers and compartments [c18 from F, from Med. L *scrīptōrium* writing room in a monastery, from L *scrībere* to write]

escrow (ˈɛskrəʊ, ɛˈskrəʊ) *law* ▷ *n* **1** money, goods, or a written document, held by a third party pending fulfilment of some condition **2** the state or condition of being an escrow (esp in **in escrow**) ▷ *vb* (*tr*) **3** to place (money, a document, etc) in escrow [c16 from OF *escroe*, of Gmc origin; see SCREED, SHRED, SCROLL]

escudo (ɛˈskuːdəʊ) *n, pl* **escudos** **1** the standard monetary unit of Cape Verde **2** the former standard monetary unit of Portugal, divided into 100 centavos; replaced by the euro in 2002 **3** a former standard monetary unit of Chile **4** an old Spanish silver coin [c19 Sp., lit.: shield, from L *scūtum*]

esculent (ˈɛskjʊlənt) *n* **1** any edible substance ▷ *adj*

2 edible [c17 from L *ēsculentus* good to eat, from *ēsca* food, from *edere* to eat]

Escurial (ɛˌskjʊərɪˈɑːl, ɛˈskjʊərɪəl) *n* a variant of **Escorial**

escutcheon (ɪˈskʌtʃən) *n* **1** a shield, esp a heraldic one that displays a coat of arms **2** a plate or shield around a keyhole, door handle, etc **3** the place on the stern of a vessel where the name is shown **4** **blot on one's escutcheon** a stain on one's honour [c15 from OF *escuchon*, ult. from L *scūtum* shield] > **esˈcutcheoned** *adj*

Esdraelon (ˌɛsdreɪˈiːlɒn) *n* a plain in N Israel, east of Mount Carmel. Also called: (Plain of) Jezreel

ESE *symbol for* east-southeast

-ese *suffix forming adjectives and nouns* indicating place of origin, language, or style: *Cantonese; Japanese; journalese*

Eşfahān (ˌɛʃfəˈhɑːn) *n* a variant of **Isfahan**

Esher (ˈiːʃə) *n* a town in SE England, in NE Surrey near London: racecourse. Pop: 46 599 (1991)

esker (ˈɛskə) *or* **eskar** (ˈɛskɑː, -kə) *n* a long winding ridge of gravel, sand, etc, originally deposited by a meltwater stream running under a glacier [c19 from OIrish *escir* ridge]

Eskilstuna (*Swedish* ˈɛskilstuːna) *n* an industrial city in SE Sweden. Pop: 89 761 (1994)

Eskimo (ˈɛskɪˌməʊ) *n, pl* **Eskimos** *or* **Eskimo**, *adj derog* another word for **Inuit** [c18 from Algonquian Esquimawes]

> USAGE *Eskimo* is considered to be offensive, and the term *Inuit* is now preferred

Eskimo dog *n* a large powerful breed of dog with a long thick coat and curled tail, developed for hauling sledges

Eskişehir (*Turkish* ɛsˈkiʃɛˌhir) *n* an industrial city in NW Turkey: founded around hot springs in Byzantine times. Pop: 454 536 (1997)

Esky (ˈɛskɪ) *n, pl* **Eskies** (*sometimes not cap*) *Austral trademark* a portable insulated container for keeping food and drink cool [c20 from ESKIMO, alluding to the cold habitat of the Inuit]

ESN *abbrev for* educationally subnormal; formerly used to designate a person of limited intelligence who needs special schooling

esophagus (iːˈsɒfəgəs) *n* the US spelling of **oesophagus**

esoteric (ˌɛsəʊˈtɛrɪk) *adj* **1** restricted to or intended for an enlightened or initiated minority **2** difficult to understand; abstruse **3** not openly admitted; private [c17 from Gk, from *esōterō* inner] > ˌ**esoˈterically** *adv* > ˌ**esoˈteriˌcism** *n*

ESP *abbrev for:* **1** extrasensory perception **2** electronic stability programme: an electronic system that automatically stabilizes a road vehicle that is being over-steered

esp. *abbrev for* especially

espadrille (ˌɛspəˈdrɪl) *n* a light shoe with a canvas upper, esp with a braided cord sole [c19 from F, from Provençal *espardilho*, dim. of *espart* ESPARTO; from use of esparto for the soles]

espalier (ɪˈspæljə) *n* **1** an ornamental shrub or fruit tree trained to grow flat, as against a wall **2** the trellis or framework on which such plants are trained ▷ *vb* **3** (*tr*) to train (a plant) on an espalier [c17 from F: trellis, from OIt.: shoulder supports, from *spalla* shoulder]

España (esˈpaɲa) *n* the Spanish name for **Spain**

esparto *or* **esparto grass** (ɛˈspɑːtəʊ) *n, pl* **espartos** any of various grasses of S Europe and N Africa, used to make ropes, mats, etc [c18 from Sp., via L from Gk *spartos* a kind of rush]

especial (ɪˈspɛʃəl) *adj* (*prenominal*) **1** unusual; notable **2** applying to one person or thing in particular; specific; peculiar: *he had an especial dislike of relatives* [c14 from OF, from L *speciālis* individual; see SPECIAL]

especially (ɪˈspɛʃəlɪ) *adv* **1** in particular; specifically: *for everyone's sake, especially your children's* **2** very much: *especially useful for vegans*

Esperanto (ˌɛspəˈræntəʊ) *n* an international artificial language based on words common to the chief European languages [c19 lit.: the one who hopes, pseudonym of Dr L. L. Zamenhof (1859–1917), its Polish inventor] > ˌ**Espeˈrantist** *n, adj*

espial (ɪˈspaɪəl) *n arch* **1** the act or fact of being seen or discovered **2** the act of noticing **3** the act of spying upon; secret observation

espionage (ˈɛspɪəˌnɑːʒ) *n* **1** the use of spies to obtain secret information, esp by governments **2** the act of spying [c18 from F, from *espion* spy]

Espírito Santo (*Portuguese* ɪʃˈpiritu ˈsəntu) *n* a state of E Brazil, on the Atlantic: swampy coastal plain with mountains in the west; heavily forested. Capital: Vitória. Pop: 3 093 171 (2000). Area: 45 597 sq km (17 601 sq miles)

Espíritu Santo (ɛsˈpɪrɪtuː ˈsæntəʊ) *n* an island in the SW Pacific: the largest and westernmost of the Vanuatu islands. Pop: 25 581 (latest est). Area: 4856 sq km (1875 sq miles)

esplanade (ˌɛspləˈneɪd) *n* **1** a long open level stretch of ground for walking along, esp beside the seashore. ▷ Cf **promenade** (sense 1) **2** an open area in front of a fortified place [c17 from F, from OIt. *spianata*, from *spianare* to make level, from L *explānāre*; see EXPLAIN]

Espoo (*Finnish* ˈɛspoː) *n* a city in S Finland. Pop: 209 667 (2000 est)

espousal (ɪˈspaʊzᵊl) *n* **1** adoption or support: *an espousal of new beliefs* **2** (*sometimes pl*) *arch* a marriage or betrothal ceremony

espouse (ɪˈspaʊz) *vb* **espouses, espousing, espoused** (*tr*) **1** to adopt or give support to (a cause, ideal, etc): *to espouse socialism* **2** *arch* (esp of a man) to take as spouse; marry [c15 from OF *espouser*, from L *spōnsāre* to affiance, espouse] > **esˈpouser** *n*

espressivo (ˌɛsprɛˈsiːvəʊ) *adv music* in an expressive manner [It.]

espresso (ɛˈsprɛsəʊ) *n, pl* **espressos** **1** coffee made by forcing steam or boiling water through ground coffee beans **2** an apparatus for making coffee in this way [c20 It., lit.: pressed]

esprit (ɛˈspriː) *n* spirit and liveliness, esp in wit [c16 from F, from L *spīritus* a breathing, SPIRIT[1]]

esprit de corps (ɛˈspriː də ˈkɔː) *n* consciousness of and pride in belonging to a particular group; the sense of shared purpose and fellowship

espy (ɪˈspaɪ) *vb* **espies, espying, espied** (*tr*) to catch sight of or perceive; detect [c14 from OF *espier* to SPY, of Gmc origin] > **esˈpier** *n*

Esq *abbrev for* esquire

-esque *suffix forming adjectives* indicating a specified character, manner, style, or resemblance: *picturesque; Romanesque; statuesque* [via F from It. *-esco*]

Esquiline (ˈɛskwəˌlaɪn) *n* one of the seven hills on which ancient Rome was built

Esquimau (ˈɛskɪˌməʊ) *n, pl* **Esquimaus** *or* **Esquimau,** *adj* a former spelling of **Eskimo**

esquire (ɪˈskwaɪə) *n* **1** *chiefly Brit* a title of respect, usually abbreviated *Esq*, placed after a man's name **2** (in medieval times) the attendant of a knight, subsequently often knighted himself [c15 from OF *escuier*, from LL *scūtārius* shield bearer, from L *scūtum* shield]

ESRC (in Britain) *abbrev for* Economic and Social Research Council

ESRO (ˈɛzrəʊ) *n acronym for* European Space Research Organization

▷ www.esoc.esa.de/external/mso/esro.html

-ess *suffix forming nouns* indicating a female: *waitress; lioness* [via OF from LL *-issa*, from Gk]

> USAGE The suffix *-ess* in such words as *poetess, authoress* is now often regarded as disparaging; a sexually neutral term *poet, author* is preferred

Essaouira (ˌɛsəˈwɪərə) *n* a port in SW Morocco on the Atlantic. Pop: 42 000 (latest est). Former name (until 1956): **Mogador**

essay *n* (ˈɛseɪ; *senses 2, 3 also* ɛˈseɪ) **1** a short literary composition **2** an attempt; effort **3** a test or trial ▷ *vb* (ɛˈseɪ) (*tr*) **4** to attempt or try **5** to test or try out [c15 from OF *essai* an attempt, from LL *exagium* a weighing, from L *agere* to do, infl. by *exigere* to investigate]

essayist (ˈɛseɪɪst) *n* a person who writes essays

Essen (*German* ˈɛsən) *n* a city in W Germany, in North Rhine-Westphalia: the leading administrative centre of the Ruhr; university. Pop: 600 700 (1999 est)

essence (ˈɛsᵊns) *n* **1** the characteristic or intrinsic feature of a thing, which determines its identity; fundamental nature **2** a perfect or complete form of something **3** *philosophy* the unchanging and unchangeable inward nature of something **4a** the constituent of a plant, usually an oil, alkaloid, or glycoside, that determines its chemical properties **4b** an alcoholic solution of such a substance **5** a substance containing the properties of a plant or foodstuff in concentrated form: *vanilla essence* **6** a rare word for **perfume** **7** **in essence** essentially; fundamentally **8** **of the essence** indispensable; vitally important [c14 from Med. L *essentia*, from L: the being (of something), from *esse* to be]

Essene (ˈɛsiːn, ɛˈsiːn) *n Judaism* a member of an ascetic sect that flourished in Palestine from the second century BC to the second century AD > **Essenian** (ɛˈsiːnɪən) *or* **Essenic** (ɛˈsɛnɪk) *adj*

essential (ɪˈsɛnʃəl) *adj* **1** vitally important; absolutely necessary **2** basic; fundamental **3** absolute; perfect **4** derived from or relating to an extract of a plant, drug, etc: *an essential oil* **5** *biochem* (of an amino acid or a fatty acid) necessary for the normal growth of an organism but not synthesized by the organism and therefore required in the diet **6** *pathol* (of a disease) having no obvious external cause: *essential hypertension* ▷ *n* **7** something fundamental or indispensable > **essentiality** (ɪˌsɛnʃɪˈælɪtɪ) *or* **esˈsentialness** *n*

essential element *n biochem* any chemical element required by an organism for healthy growth. It may be required in large amounts (**macronutrient**) or in very small amounts (**trace element**)

essential fatty acid *n biochem* any fatty acid required by the body in manufacturing prostaglandins, found in such foods as oily fish and nuts. Abbreviation: **EFA**

essentialism (ɪˈsɛnʃəˌlɪzəm) *n philosophy* any doctrine that material objects have an essence distinguishable from their attributes and existence > **esˈsentialist** *n*

essentially (ɪˈsɛnʃəlɪ) *adv* in a fundamental or basic way; in essence

essential oil *n* any of various volatile oils in plants, having the odour or flavour of the plant from which they are extracted

Essequibo (ˌɛsɪˈkwiːbəʊ) *n* a river in Guyana, rising near the Brazilian border and flowing north to the Atlantic: drains over half of Guyana. Length: 1014 km (630 miles)

Essex¹ (ˈɛsɪks) *n* **1** a county of SE England, on the North Sea and the Thames estuary; the geographical and ceremonial county includes Thurrock and Southend-on-Sea, which became independent unitary authorities in 1998. Administrative centre: Chelmsford. Pop (excluding unitary authorities): 1 310 922 (2001). Area (excluding unitary authorities): 3446 sq km (1310 sq miles) **2** an Anglo-Saxon kingdom that in the early 7th century AD comprised the modern county of Essex and much of Hertfordshire and Surrey. By the late 8th century, Essex had become a dependency of the kingdom of Mercia

Essex² (ˈɛsɪks) *n* **2nd Earl of,** title of *Robert Devereux.* ?1566–1601, English soldier and favourite of Queen Elizabeth I; executed for treason

Essex Man *n inf, derog* a self-made man, esp of working-class origins, characterized by philistinism and bigoted right-wing views [c20 from the supposed prevalence of such people in ESSEX¹ (sense 1)]

Esslingen (ˈɛsˌlɪŋən) *n* a town in SW Germany, on the River Neckar: Gothic church, medieval buildings: wines, light industry. Pop: 91 685 (1991 est)

Essonne (*French* ɛsɔn) *n* a department of N France, south of Paris in Île-de-France region: formed in 1964. Capital: Évry. Pop: 1 134 238 (1999). Area: 1811 sq km (706 sq miles)

EST *abbrev for:* **1** (in the US, Canada, and Australia) Eastern Standard Time **2** electric-shock treatment

est. *abbrev for:* **1** established **2** estimate(d)

-est¹ *suffix* forming the superlative degree of adjectives and adverbs: *fastest* [OE *-est, -ost*]

-est² *or* **-st** *suffix* forming the archaic second person singular present and past indicative tense of verbs: *thou goest; thou hadst* [OE *-est, -ast*]

establish (ɪˈstæblɪʃ) *vb* (*tr*) **1** to make secure or permanent in a certain place, condition, job, etc **2** to create or set up (an organization, etc) as on a permanent basis **3** to prove correct; validate: *establish a fact* **4** to cause (a principle, theory, etc) to be accepted: *establish a precedent* **5** to give (a Church) the status of a national institution **6** to cause (a person) to become recognized and accepted **7** (in works of imagination) to cause (a character, place, etc) to be credible and recognized [c14 from OF, from L *stabilis* STABLE²] > **esˈtablisher** *n*

Established Church *n* a Church that is officially recognized as a national institution, esp the Church of England

establishment (ɪˈstæblɪʃmənt) *n* **1** the act of establishing or state of being established **2a** a business organization or other large institution **2b** a place of business **3** the staff and equipment of an organization **4** any large organization or system **5** a household; residence **6** a body of employees or servants **7** (*modifier*) belonging to or characteristic of the Establishment

Establishment (ɪˈstæblɪʃmənt) *n* **the** a group or class having institutional authority within a society: usually seen as conservative

estate (ɪˈsteɪt) *n* **1** a large piece of landed property, esp in the country **2** *chiefly Brit* a large area of property development, esp of new houses or (**trading estate**) of factories **3** *law* **3a** property or possessions **3b** the nature of interest that a person has in land or other property **3c** the total extent of the property of a deceased person or bankrupt **4** Also called: **estate of the realm** an order or class in a political community, regarded as a part of the body politic: the lords spiritual (**first estate**), lords temporal or peers (**second estate**), and commons (**third estate**). See also **fourth estate** **5** state, period, or position in life: *youth's estate; a poor man's estate* [c13 from OF *estat*, from L *status* condition, STATE]

estate agent *n* **1** *Brit* an agent concerned with the valuation, management, lease, and sale of property **2** the administrator of a large landed property; estate manager

estate car *n Brit* a car containing a large carrying space, reached through a rear door: usually the back seats fold forward to increase the carrying space

estate duty *n* another name for **death duty**

Este (ˈɛste) *n* a noble family of Italy founded by Alberto Azzo II (996–1097), who was invested with the town of Este in NE Italy as a fief of the Holy Roman Empire. The family governed Ferrara (13th–16th centuries), Modena, and Reggio (13th–18th centuries)

esteem (ɪˈstiːm) *vb* (*tr*) **1** to have great respect or high regard for **2** *formal* to judge or consider; deem ▷ *n* **3** high regard or respect; good opinion **4** *arch* judgment; opinion [c15 from OF *estimer*, from L *aestimāre* ESTIMATE] > **esˈteemed** *adj*

Ee

ester ('ɛstə) *n chem* any of a class of compounds produced by reaction between acids and alcohols with the elimination of water [c19 from G, prob. a contraction of *Essigäther* acetic ether, from *Essig* vinegar (ult. from L *acētum*) + *Äther* ETHER]

Esterházy ('ɛstəˌhɑːzɪ) *n* a noble Hungarian family that produced many soldiers, diplomats, and patrons of the arts. Prince **Miklós József Esterházy** (1714–90) rebuilt the family castle of Esterháza and employed Haydn as his musical director (1766–90)

Esth. *Bible abbrev for* Esther

Esther ('ɛstə) *n Old Testament* **1** a beautiful Jewish woman who became queen of Persia and saved her people from massacre **2** the book in which this episode is recounted

esthesia (iːs'θiːzɪə) *n* a US spelling of **aesthesia**

esthete ('iːsθiːt) *n* a US spelling of **aesthete**

Esthonia (ɛ'stəʊnɪə, ɛ'sθəʊ-) *n* See **Estonia**

estimable ('ɛstɪməbᵊl) *adj* worthy of respect; deserving of admiration > **'estimableness** *n* > **'estimably** *adv*

estimate *vb* ('ɛstɪˌmeɪt), **estimates, estimating, estimated 1** to form an approximate idea of (size, cost, etc); calculate roughly **2** (*tr; may take a clause as object*) to form an opinion about; judge **3** to submit (an approximate price) for (a job) to a prospective client ▷ *n* ('ɛstɪmɪt) **4** an approximate calculation **5** a statement of the likely charge for certain work **6** a judgment; appraisal [c16 from L *aestimāre* to assess the worth of, from ?] > **'estiˌmator** *n* > **'estimative** *adj*

estimation (ˌɛstɪ'meɪʃən) *n* **1** a considered opinion; judgment **2** esteem; respect **3** the act of estimating

estival (iː'staɪvᵊl, 'ɛstɪ-) *adj* the usual US spelling of **aestival**

estivate ('iːstɪˌveɪt, 'ɛs-) *vb* **estivates, estivating, estivated** (*intr*) the usual US spelling of **aestivate**

Estonia *or* **Esthonia** (ɛ'stəʊnɪə, ɛ'sθəʊ-) *n* a republic in NE Europe, on the Gulf of Finland and the Baltic: low-lying with many lakes and forests, it includes numerous islands in the Baltic Sea. It was under Scandinavian and Teutonic rule from the 13th century to 1721, when it passed to Russia: it was an independent republic from 1920 to 1940, when it was annexed by the Soviet Union; became independent in 1991 and joined the EU in 2004. Official language: Estonian. Religion: believers are mostly Christian. Currency: kroon. Capital: Tallinn. Pop: 1 363 000 (2001 est). Area: 45 227 sq km (17 462 sq miles)
▷ www.riik.ee/en/valitsus
▷ http://visitestonia.com

Estonian *or* **Esthonian** (ɛ'stəʊnɪən, ɛ'sθəʊ-) *adj* **1** of, relating to, or characteristic of Estonia, its people, or their language ▷ *n* **2** the official language of Estonia **3** a native or inhabitant of Estonia

estop (ɪ'stɒp) *vb* **estops, estopping, estopped** (*tr*) **1** *law* to preclude by estoppel **2** *arch* to stop [c15 from OF *estoper* to plug, ult. from L *stuppa* tow; see STOP] > **es'toppage** *n*

estoppel (ɪ'stɒpᵊl) *n law* a rule of evidence whereby a person is precluded from denying the truth of a statement he has previously asserted [c16 from OF *estoupail* plug; see ESTOP]

Estoril ('ɛʃtɔːˌriːl) *n* a resort in W Portugal, near Lisbon, on the Atlantic Ocean: noted esp for a famous avenue of palm trees leading to the seafront. Pop: 24 850 (1991)

estovers (ɛ'stəʊvəz) *pl n law* necessaries allowed to tenants of land, esp wood for fuel and repairs [c15 from Anglo-F., pl of *estover*, from OF *estovoir* to be necessary, from L *est opus* there is need]

estradiol (ˌɛstrə'daɪɒl, ˌiːstrə-) *n* the usual US spelling of **oestradiol**

estrange (ɪ'streɪndʒ) *vb* **estranges, estranging, estranged** (*tr*) to antagonize or lose the affection of (someone previously friendly); alienate [c15 from OF *estranger*, from LL *extrāneāre* to treat as a stranger, from L *extrāneus* foreign] > **es'trangement** *n*

estranged (ɪ'streɪndʒd) *adj* **1** separated and living apart from one's spouse **2** no longer friendly; alienated

Estremadura (*Portuguese* ɪʃtrəmə'ðurə) *n* a region of W Spain: arid and sparsely populated except in the valleys of the Tagus and Guadiana Rivers. Area: 41 593 sq km (16 059 sq miles). Spanish name: **Extremadura**

estrogen ('ɛstrədʒən, 'iːstrə-) *n* the usual US spelling of **oestrogen**

estrus ('ɛstrəs, 'iːstrəs) *n* the usual US spelling of **oestrus**

estuary ('ɛstjʊərɪ) *n, pl* **estuaries** the widening channel of a river where it nears the sea [c16 from L *aestuārium* marsh, channel, from *aestus* tide] > **estuarial** (ˌɛstjʊ'ɛərɪəl) *adj* > **'estuarine** *adj*

e.s.u. *or* **ESU** *abbrev for* electrostatic unit

E. Sussex *abbrev for* East Sussex

ET (in Britain) *abbrev for* Employment Training: a government scheme offering training in technological and business skills to unemployed people

-et *suffix of nouns* small or lesser: *islet; baronet* [from OF *-et, -ete*]

eta ('iːtə) *n* the seventh letter in the Greek alphabet (Η, η) [Gk, from Phoenician]

ETA *abbrev for* estimated time of arrival

e-tail ('iːteɪl) *or* **e-tailing** ('iːteɪlɪŋ) *n* retail conducted via the Internet [c20 E-^{2} + (RE)TAIL] > **'e-tailer** *n*

et al. *abbrev for:* **1** et alibi [L: and elsewhere] **2** et alii [L: and others]

etalon ('ɛtəˌlɒn) *n physics* a device used in spectroscopy to measure wavelengths by interference effects produced by multiple reflections between parallel half-silvered glass plates [c20 F *étalon* a standard of weights & measures]

etc. *abbrev for* et cetera

et cetera *or* **etcetera** (ɪt 'sɛtrə) *n and vb substitute* **1** and the rest; and others; and so forth **2** or the like; or something similar [from L *et* and + *cetera* the other (things)]

> USAGE It is unnecessary to use *and* before *etc* as the Latin words of which *etc* is an abbreviation already mean 'and other things'. The repetition of *etc*, as in *he brought paper, ink, notebooks, etc, etc*, should be avoided except in spoken or informal contexts

etceteras (ɪt'sɛtrəz) *pl n* miscellaneous extra things or persons

etch (ɛtʃ) *vb* **1** (*tr*) to wear away the surface of (a metal, glass, etc) by the action of an acid **2** to cut or corrode (a design, etc) on (a metal or other printing plate) by the action of acid on parts not covered by an acid-resistant coating **3** (*tr*) to cut as with a sharp implement **4** (*tr; usually passive*) to imprint vividly [c17 from Du. *etsen*, from OHG *azzen* to feed, bite] > **'etcher** *n*

etching ('ɛtʃɪŋ) *n* **1** the art, act, or process of preparing etched surfaces or of printing designs from them **2** an etched plate **3** an impression made from an etched plate

ETD *abbrev for* estimated time of departure

Eteocles (ɪ'tiːəˌkliːz, 'ɛtɪə-) *n Greek myth* a son of Oedipus and Jocasta. He and his brother, Polynices, were to share the kingdom of Thebes but Eteocles expelled Polynices from Thebes; they killed each other in single combat when Polynices returned as leader of the Seven against Thebes

eternal (ɪ'tɜːnᵊl) *adj* **1a** without beginning or end; lasting forever **1b** (*as n*): *the eternal* **2** (*often cap*) a name applied to God **3** unchanged by time; immutable: *eternal truths* **4** seemingly unceasing [c14 from LL, from L *aeternus*; rel. to L *aevum* age] > **ˌeter'nality** *or* **e'ternalness** *n* > **e'ternally** *adv*

Eternal City *n* **the** Rome

eternalize (ɪ'tɜːnəˌlaɪz) *or* **eternize** (ɪ'tɜːnaɪz),

eternalise *vb* **eternalizes, eternalizing, eternalized** *or* **eternalises, eternalising, eternalised** (*tr*) **1** to make eternal **2** to make famous forever; immortalize > **e,ternali'zation** *or* **e,terni'zation, e,ternali'sation** *n*

eternal triangle *n* an emotional relationship usually involving three people, two of whom are rival lovers of the third person

eternity (ɪ'tɜːnɪtɪ) *n, pl* **eternities 1** endless or infinite time **2** the quality, state, or condition of being eternal **3** (*usually pl*) any aspect of life and thought considered timeless **4** the timeless existence, believed by some to characterize the afterlife **5** a seemingly endless period of time

eternity ring *n* a ring given as a token of lasting affection, esp one set all around with stones to symbolize continuity

etesian (ɪ'tiːʒɪən) *adj* (of NW winds) recurring annually in the summer in the E Mediterranean [c17 from L *etēsius* yearly, from Gk *etos* year]

ETF *abbrev for* electronic transfer of funds

Eth. *abbrev for* Ethiopia(n)

-eth[1] *suffix* forming the archaic third person singular present indicative tense of verbs: *goeth; taketh* [OE *-eth, -th*]

-eth[2] *suffix forming ordinal numbers* a variant of **-th**[2]: *twentieth*

ethanal ('ɛθə,næl) *n* the systematic name for **acetaldehyde**

ethane ('iːθeɪn, 'ɛθ-) *n* a colourless odourless flammable gaseous alkane obtained from natural gas and petroleum: used as a fuel. Formula: C_2H_6 [c19 from ETH(YL)+ -ANE]

ethanediol ('iːθeɪn,daɪɒl, 'ɛθ-) *n* a colourless soluble liquid used as an antifreeze and solvent. Formula: $C_2H_4(OH)_2$ [c20 from ETHANE + DI-[1] + -OL[1]]

ethanoic acid (,ɛθə'nəʊɪk, ,iːθə-) *n* the systematic name for **acetic acid**

ethanol ('ɛθə,nɒl, 'iːθə-) *n* the systematic name for **alcohol** (sense 1)

Ethelbert ('ɛθəl,bɜːt) *or* **Æthelbert** ('æθəl,bɜːt) *n* **Saint** ?552–616 AD, king of Kent (560–616): converted to Christianity by St Augustine; issued the earliest known code of English laws. Feast day: Feb 24 or 25

Ethelred I ('ɛθəl,rɛd) *or* **Æthelred** ('æθəl,rɛd) *n* died 871, king of Wessex (866–71). He led resistance to the Danish invasion of England; died following his victory at Ashdown

Ethelred II *or* **Æthelred** *n* known as *Ethelred the Unready*. ?968–1016 AD, king of England (978–1016). He was temporarily deposed by the Danish king Sweyn (1013) but was recalled on Sweyn's death (1014)

Ethelwulf ('ɛθəl,wʊlf) *or* **Æthelwulf** ('æθəl,wʊlf) *n* died 858 AD, king of Wessex (839–858)

ethene ('ɛθiːn) *n* the systematic name for **ethylene**

ether ('iːθə) *n* **1** Also called: **diethyl ether, ethyl ether, ethoxyethane** a colourless volatile highly flammable liquid: used as a solvent and anaesthetic. Formula: $C_2H_5OC_2H_5$ **2** any of a class of organic compounds with the general formula ROR′, as in methyl ethyl ether, $CH_3OC_2H_5$ **3** the medium formerly believed to fill all space and to support the propagation of electromagnetic waves **4** *Greek myth* the upper atmosphere; clear sky or heaven ▷ Also (for senses 3 and 4): **aether** [c17 from L, from Gk *aithein* to burn] > **e'theric** *adj*

ethereal (ɪ'θɪərɪəl) *adj* **1** extremely delicate or refined **2** almost as light as air; airy **3** celestial or spiritual **4** of, containing, or dissolved in an ether, esp diethyl ether **5** of or relating to the ether [c16 from L, from Gk *aithēr* ETHER] > **e,there'ality** *or* **e'therealness** *n*

etherealize *or* **etherealise** (ɪ'θɪərɪə,laɪz) *vb* **etherealizes, etherealizing, etherealized** *or* **etherealises, etherealising, etherealised** (*tr*) **1** to make or regard as being ethereal **2** to add ether to or make into ether > **e,thereali'zation** *or* **e,thereali'sation** *n*

etherize *or* **etherise** ('iːθə,raɪz) *vb* **etherizes, etherizing, etherized** *or* **etherises, etherising, etherised** (*tr*) *obs* to subject (a person) to the anaesthetic influence of ether fumes; anaesthetize > **,etheri'zation** *or* **,etheri'sation** *n* > **'ether,izer** *or* **'ether,iser** *n*

Ethernet ('iːθə,nɛt) *n trademark, computers* a widely used type of local area network

ethic ('ɛθɪk) *n* **1** a moral principle or set of moral values held by an individual or group ▷ *adj* **2** another word for **ethical** [c15 from L, from Gk *ēthos* custom]

ethical ('ɛθɪkəl) *adj* **1** in accordance with principles of conduct that are considered correct, esp those of a given profession or group **2** of or relating to ethics **3** (of a medicinal agent) available legally only with a doctor's prescription > **'ethically** *adv* > **'ethicalness** *or* **,ethi'cality** *n*

ethical investment *n* an investment in a company whose activities or products are not considered by the investor to be unethical

ethics ('ɛθɪks) *n* **1** (*functioning as sing*) the philosophical study of the moral value of human conduct and of the rules and principles that ought to govern it **2** (*functioning as pl*) a code of behaviour considered correct, esp that of a particular group, profession, or individual **3** (*functioning as pl*) the moral fitness of a decision, course of action, etc > **ethicist** ('ɛθɪsɪst) *n*

▷ http://ethics.acusd.edu/
▷ http://www.ethics.org/

Ethiopia (,iːθɪ'əʊpɪə) *n* a state in NE Africa, on the Red Sea: consolidated as an empire under Menelik II (1889–1913); federated with Eritrea from 1952 until 1993; Emperor Haile Selassie was deposed by the military in 1974 and the monarchy was abolished in 1975; an independence movement in Eritrea was engaged in war with the government from 1961 until 1993. It lies along the Great Rift Valley and consists of deserts in the southeast and northeast and a high central plateau with many rivers (including the Blue Nile) and mountains rising over 4500 m (15 000 ft); the main export is coffee. Language: Amharic. Religion: Christian majority. Currency: birr. Capital: Addis Ababa. Pop: 65 892 000 (2001 est). Area: 1 128 215 sq km (435 614 sq miles). Former name: **Abyssinia**

▷ www.ethiopar.net/English/contents.htm
▷ www.tourismethiopia.org

Ethiopian (,iːθɪ'əʊpɪən) *adj* **1** of or relating to Ethiopia, its people, or any of their languages ▷ *n* **2** a native or inhabitant of Ethiopia **3** any of the languages of Ethiopia, esp Amharic ▷ *n, adj* **4** an archaic word for **Black**[1]

Ethiopic (,iːθɪ'ɒpɪk, -'əʊpɪk) *n* **1** the ancient Semitic language of Ethiopia: a Christian liturgical language **2** the group of languages developed from this language, including Amharic ▷ *adj* **3** denoting or relating to this language or group of languages **4** a less common word for **Ethiopian**

ethnic ('ɛθnɪk) *or* **ethnical** *adj* **1** of or relating to a human group having racial, religious, linguistic, and other traits in common **2** relating to the classification of mankind into groups, esp on the basis of racial characteristics **3** denoting or deriving from the cultural traditions of a group of people **4** characteristic of another culture, esp a peasant one ▷ *n* **5** *chiefly US* a member of an ethnic group, esp a minority one [c14 (in the senses: heathen, Gentile): from LL *ethnicus*, from Gk *ethnos* race] > **'ethnically** *adv* > **ethnicity** (ɛθ'nɪsɪtɪ) *n*

ethnic cleansing *n euphemistic* the violent removal by one ethnic group of other ethnic groups from the population of a particular area: used esp of the activities of Serbs against Croats and Muslims in the former Yugoslavia

Ee

ethno- *combining form* indicating race, people, or culture [via F from Gk *ethnos* race]

ethnocentrism (ˌɛθnəʊˈsɛnˌtrɪzəm) *n* belief in the intrinsic superiority of the nation, culture, or group to which one belongs > ˌ**ethnoˈcentric** *adj* > ˌ**ethnoˈcentrically** *adv* > ˌ**ethnocenˈtricity** *n*

ethnography (ɛθˈnɒgrəfɪ) *n* the branch of anthropology that deals with the scientific description of individual human societies > **ethˈnographer** *n* > **ethnographic** (ˌɛθnəʊˈgræfɪk) *or* ˌ**ethnoˈgraphical** *adj*

▹ www.sosig.ac.uk/roads/subject-listing/World-cat/ethnostud.html

ethnology (ɛθˈnɒlədʒɪ) *n* the branch of anthropology that deals with races and peoples, their origins, characteristics, etc > **ethnologic** (ˌɛθnəˈlɒdʒɪk) *or* ˌ**ethnoˈlogical** *adj* > **ethˈnologist** *n*

ethnomusicology (ˌɛθnəʊˌmjuːzɪˈkɒlədʒɪ) *n* the study of the origins of music, esp from non-European cultures

ethology (ɪˈθɒlədʒɪ) *n* the study of the behaviour of animals in their normal environment [C17 (in the obs. sense: mimicry): via L from Gk *ēthos* character; current sense, C19] > **ethological** (ˌɛθəˈlɒdʒɪkᵊl) *adj* > **eˈthologist** *n*

ethos (ˈiːθɒs) *n* the distinctive character, spirit, and attitudes of a people, culture, era, etc: *the revolutionary ethos* [C19 from LL: habit, from Gk]

ethyl (ˈiːθaɪl, ˈɛθɪl) *n* (*modifier*) of, consisting of, or containing the monovalent group C_2H_5– [C19 from ETH(ER) + -YL] > **ethylic** (ɪˈθɪlɪk) *adj*

ethyl acetate *n* a colourless volatile flammable liquid ester: used in perfumes and flavourings and as a solvent. Formula: $CH_3COOC_2H_5$

ethyl alcohol *n* another name for **alcohol** (sense 1)

ethylene (ˈɛθɪˌliːn) *or* **ethene** (ˈɛθiːn) *n* a colourless flammable gaseous alkene used in the manufacture of polythene and other chemicals. Formula: CH_2:CH_2 > **ethylenic** (ˌɛθɪˈliːnɪk) *adj*

ethylene glycol *n* another name for **ethanediol**

ethylene group *or* **radical** *n chem* the divalent group, –CH_2CH_2–, derived from ethylene

ethylene series *n chem* another name for **alkene series**

ethyne (ˈɛθaɪn) *n chem* the systematic name for **acetylene**

ethyne series *n chem* another name for **acetylene series**

etiolate (ˈiːtɪəʊˌleɪt) *vb* **etiolates, etiolating, etiolated** **1** *bot* to whiten (a green plant) through lack of sunlight **2** to become or cause to become pale and weak [C18 from F *étioler* to make pale, prob. from OF *estuble* straw, from L *stipula*] > ˌ**etioˈlation** *n*

etiology (ˌiːtɪˈɒlədʒɪ) *n, pl* **etiologies** a variant spelling of **aetiology**

etiquette (ˈɛtɪˌkɛt, ˌɛtɪˈkɛt) *n* **1** the customs or rules governing behaviour regarded as correct in social life **2** a conventional code of practice followed in certain professions or groups [C18 from F, from OF *estiquette* label, from *estiquier* to attach; see STICK²]

Etna (ˈɛtnə) *n* **Mount** an active volcano in E Sicily: the highest volcano in Europe and the highest peak in Italy south of the Alps. Height: 3323 m (10 902 ft)

Eton (ˈiːtᵊn) *n* **1** a town in S England, in Windsor and Maidenhead unitary authority, Berkshire, near the River Thames: site of **Eton College,** a public school for boys founded in 1440. Pop: 1974 (1991) **2** this college

Eton collar *n* (formerly) a broad stiff white collar worn outside a boy's jacket

Eton crop *n* a very short mannish hairstyle worn by women in the 1920s

Eton jacket *n* (formerly) a boy's waist-length jacket with a V-shaped back, open in front

Etruria (ɪˈtrʊərɪə) *n* **1** an ancient country of central Italy, between the Rivers Arno and Tiber, roughly corresponding to present-day Tuscany and part of Umbria **2** a factory established in Staffordshire by Josiah Wedgwood in 1769

Etruscan (ɪˈtrʌskən) *or* **Etrurian** (ɪˈtrʊərɪən) *n* **1** a member of an ancient people of Etruria whose civilization greatly influenced the Romans **2** the language of the ancient Etruscans ▹ *adj* **3** of or relating to Etruria, the Etruscans, their culture, or their language

▹ www.mysteriousetruscans.com

▹ www.crystalinks.com/etruscians.html

et seq. *abbrev for:* **1** et sequens [L: and the following] **2** Also: **et seqq.** et sequentia [L: and those that follow]

-ette *suffix of nouns* **1** small: *cigarette* **2** female: *majorette* **3** (esp in trade names) imitation: *Leatherette* [from F, fem of -ET]

étude (ˈeɪtjuːd) *n* a short musical composition for a solo instrument, esp one designed as an exercise or exploiting virtuosity [C19 from F: STUDY]

étui (ɛˈtwiː) *n, pl* **étuis** a small usually ornamented case for holding needles, cosmetics, or other small articles [C17 F, from OF *estuier* to enclose; see TWEEZERS]

etymology (ˌɛtɪˈmɒlədʒɪ) *n, pl* **etymologies** **1** the study of the sources and development of words **2** an account of the source and development of a word [C14 via L from Gk; see ETYMON, -LOGY] > **etymological** (ˌɛtɪməˈlɒdʒɪkᵊl) *adj* > ˌ**etyˈmologist** *n* > ˌ**etyˈmoloˌgize** *or* ˌ**etyˈmoloˌgise** *vb*

etymon (ˈɛtɪˌmɒn) *n, pl* **etymons** *or* **etyma** (-mə) a form of a word, usually the earliest recorded form or a reconstructed form, from which another word is derived [C16 via L from Gk *etumon* basic meaning, from *etumos* true, actual]

e-type *n inf* a person who works in or is interested in electronics [C20 electronics]

Etzel (ˈɛtsᵊl) *n German legend* a great king who, according to the *Nibelungenlied,* was the second husband of Kriemhild after the death of Siegfried: identified with Attila the Hun. ▹ Cf **Atli**

Eu *the chemical symbol for* europium

EU *abbrev for* European Union

eu- *combining form* well, pleasant, or good: *eupeptic; euphony* [via L from Gk, from *eus* good]

Euboea (juːˈbɪə) *n* an island in the W Aegean Sea: the largest island after Crete of the Greek archipelago; linked with the mainland by a bridge across the Euripus channel. Capital: Chalcis. Pop: 188 400 (latest est). Area: 3908 sq km (1509 sq miles). Modern Greek name: **Évvoia.** Former English name: **Negropont**

Euboean (juːˈbɪən) *adj* **1** of or relating to the Greek island of Euboea ▹ *n* **2** a native or inhabitant of Euboea

eucalyptus (ˌjuːkəˈlɪptəs) *or* **eucalypt** (ˈjuːkəˌlɪpt) *n, pl* **eucalyptuses, eucalypti** (-ˈlɪptaɪ), *or* **eucalypts** any tree of the mostly Australian genus *Eucalyptus,* widely cultivated for timber and gum, as ornament, and for the medicinal oil in their leaves (**eucalyptus oil**) [C19 NL, from EU- + Gk *kaluptos* covered, from *kaluptein* to cover, hide]

Eucharist (ˈjuːkərɪst) *n* **1** the Christian sacrament in which Christ's Last Supper is commemorated by the consecration of bread and wine **2** the consecrated elements of bread and wine offered in the sacrament [C14 via Church L from Gk *eukharistos* thankful, from EU- + *kharis* favour] > ˌ**Euchaˈristic** *or* ˌ**Euchaˈristical** *adj*

euchre (ˈjuːkə) *n* **1** a US and Canad card game for two, three, or four players, using a poker pack **2** an instance of euchring another player ▹ *vb* **euchres, euchring, euchred** (*tr*) **3** to prevent (a player) from making his or her contracted tricks **4** (usually foll by *out*) *US, Canad, Austral, & NZ inf* to outwit or cheat [C19 from ?]

Euclid (ˈjuːklɪd) *n* **1** 3rd century BC, Greek mathematician of Alexandria; author of *Elements,* which sets out the principles of geometry and remained a text until the 19th century at least **2** the works of Euclid, esp his system of geometry

eucryphia (juːˈkrɪfɪə) *n* any of various mostly evergreen trees and shrubs of S America and Australia, with dark

leaves [NL, from EU- + Gk *kryphios* covered]
eudiometer (ˌjuːdɪˈɒmɪtə) *n* a graduated glass tube used in the study and volumetric analysis of gas reactions [c18 from Gk *eudios*, lit.: clear-skied + -METER]
Eugène (*French* øʒɛn) *n* **Prince,** title of *François Eugène de Savoie-Carignan*. 1663–1736, Austrian general, born in France: with Marlborough defeated the French at Blenheim (1704), Oudenaarde (1708), and Malplaquet (1709)
eugenics (juːˈdʒɛnɪks) *n* (*functioning as sing*) the study of methods of improving the quality of the human race, esp by selective breeding [c19 from Gk *eugenēs* well-born, from EU- + *-genēs* born; see -GEN] > **euˈgenic** *adj* > **euˈgenically** *adv* > **euˈgenicist** *n* > **eugenist** (ˈjuːdʒənɪst) *n*
Eugénie (*French* øʒeni) *n* original name *Eugénia Maria de Montijo de Guzman, Comtesse de Téba*. 1826–1920, Empress of France (1853–71) as wife of Napoleon III
eukaryote *or* **eucaryote** (jʊˈkærɪəʊt) *n* an organism having cells each with a distinct nucleus within which the genetic material is contained. ▷ Cf **prokaryote** [from EU- + KARYO- + *-ote* as in *zygote*] > **eukaryotic** *or* **eucaryotic** (jʊˌkærɪˈɒtɪk) *adj*
Euler (*German* ˈɔɪlər) *n* **1 Leonhard** (ˈleːɔnhart) 1707–83, Swiss mathematician, noted esp for his work on the calculus of variation: considered the founder of modern mathematical analysis **2 Ulf (Svante) von** (ʊlf fɔn) 1905–83, Swedish physiologist: shared the Nobel prize (1970) for physiology or medicine with Julius Axelrod and Bernard Katz for their work on the catecholamines: son of Hans von Euler-Chelpin
Euler-Chelpin (*German* ˈɔɪlər ˈkɛlpiːn) *n* **Hans (Karl August) von** 1873–1964, Swedish biochemist, born in Germany: shared the Nobel prize for chemistry (1929) with Sir Arthur Harden for their work on enzymes: father of Ulf von Euler
eulogize *or* **eulogise** (ˈjuːləˌdʒaɪz) *vb* **eulogizes, eulogizing, eulogized** *or* **eulogises, eulogising, eulogised** to praise (a person or thing) highly in speech or writing > **ˈeulogist, ˈeuloˌgizer,** *or* **ˈeuloˌgiser** *n* > **ˌeuloˈgistic** *or* **ˌeuloˈgistical** *adj*
eulogy (ˈjuːlədʒɪ) *n, pl* **eulogies 1** a speech or piece of writing praising a person or thing, esp a person who has recently died **2** high praise or commendation. Also called (archaic): **eulogium** (juːˈləʊdʒɪəm) [c16 from LL, from Gk: praise, from EU- + -LOGY]
Eumenides (juːˈmɛnɪˌdiːz) *pl n* another name for the **Furies,** used by the Greeks as a euphemism [from Gk, lit: the benevolent ones]
eunuch (ˈjuːnək) *n* **1** a man who has been castrated, esp (formerly) for some office such as a guard in a harem **2** *inf* an ineffective man [c15 via L from Gk *eunoukhos* bedchamber attendant]
euonymus (juːˈɒnɪməs) *or* **evonymus** (ɛˈvɒnɪməs) *n* any tree or shrub of the N temperate genus *Euonymus*, such as the spindle tree [c18 from L: spindle tree, from Gk *euōnumos* fortunately named, from EU- + *onoma* NAME]
Eupen and Malmédy (*French* øpɛn; malmedi) *n* a region of Belgium in Liège province: ceded by Germany in 1919. Pop: 27 675 (latest est)
eupepsia (juːˈpɛpsɪə) *or* **eupepsy** (juːˈpɛpsɪ) *n physiol* good digestion [c18 from NL, from Gk, from EU- + *pepsis* digestion] > **eupeptic** (juːˈpɛptɪk) *adj*
euphemism (ˈjuːfɪˌmɪzəm) *n* **1** an inoffensive word or phrase substituted for one considered offensive or hurtful **2** the use of such inoffensive words or phrases [c17 from Gk, from EU- + *phēmē* speech] > **ˌeupheˈmistic** *adj* > **ˌeupheˈmistically** *adv*
euphemize *or* **euphemise** (ˈjuːfɪˌmaɪz) *vb* **euphemizes, euphemizing, euphemized** *or* **euphemises, euphemising, euphemised** to speak in euphemisms or refer to by means of a euphemism > **ˈeupheˌmizer** *or* **ˈeupheˌmiser** *n*
euphonic (juːˈfɒnɪk) *or* **euphonious** (juːˈfəʊnɪəs) *adj* **1** denoting or relating to euphony **2** (of speech sounds) altered for ease of pronunciation > **euˈphonically** *or* **euˈphoniously** *adv* > **euˈphoniousness** *n*
euphonium (juːˈfəʊnɪəm) *n* a brass musical instrument with four valves, mainly used in brass bands [c19 NL, from EUPH(ONY + HARM)ONIUM]
euphonize *or* **euphonise** (ˈjuːfəˌnaɪz) *vb* **euphonizes, euphonizing, euphonized** *or* **euphonises, euphonising, euphonised 1** to make pleasant to hear **2** to change (speech sounds) so as to facilitate pronunciation
euphony (ˈjuːfənɪ) *n, pl* **euphonies 1** the alteration of speech sounds, esp by assimilation, so as to make them easier to pronounce **2** a pleasing sound, esp in speech [c17 from LL, from Gk, from EU- + *phōnē* voice]
euphorbia (juːˈfɔːbɪə) *n* any plant of the genus *Euphorbia*, such as the spurges [c14 *euforbia*, from L *euphorbea* African plant, after *Euphorbus*, first-cent. AD Gk physician]
euphoria (juːˈfɔːrɪə) *n* a feeling of great elation, esp when exaggerated [c19 from Gk: good ability to endure, from EU- + *pherein* to bear] > **euphoric** (juːˈfɒrɪk) *adj*
euphoriant (juːˈfɔːrɪənt) *adj* **1** able to produce euphoria ▷ *n* **2** a euphoriant drug or agent
euphotic (juːˈfəʊtɪk, -ˈfɒt-) *adj* denoting or relating to the uppermost part of a sea or lake, which receives enough light for photosynthesis to take place [c20 from EU- + PHOTIC]
euphrasy (ˈjuːfrəsɪ) *n, pl* **euphrasies** another name for **eyebright** [c15 *eufrasie*, from Med. L, from Gk *euphrasia* gladness, from EU- + *phrēn* mind]
Euphrates (juːˈfreɪtiːz) *n* a river in SW Asia, rising in E Turkey and flowing south across Syria and Iraq to join the Tigris, forming the Shatt-al-Arab, which flows to the head of the Persian Gulf: important in ancient times for the extensive irrigation of its valley (in Mesopotamia). Length: 3598 km (2235 miles)
Euphrosyne (juːˈfrɒzɪˌniː) *n Greek myth* one of the three Graces [from Gk: mirth, merriment]
euphuism (ˈjuːfjuːˌɪzəm) *n* **1** an artificial prose style of the Elizabethan period, marked by extreme use of antithesis, alliteration, and extended similes and allusions **2** any stylish affectation in speech or writing [c16 after *Euphues*, prose romance by John LYLY] > **ˈeuphuist** *n* > **ˌeuphuˈistic** *or* **ˌeuphuˈistical** *adj*
eur- *combining form* (*sometimes cap*) a variant of **euro-** before a vowel
Eurasia (jʊəˈreɪʃə, -ʒə) *n* the continents of Europe and Asia considered as a whole
Eurasian (jʊəˈreɪʃən, -ʒən) *adj* **1** of or relating to Eurasia **2** of mixed European and Asian descent ▷ *n* **3** a person of mixed European and Asian descent
Euratom (jʊəˈrætəm) *n* short for **European Atomic Energy Community;** an authority established by the EEC (now the EU) to develop peaceful uses of nuclear energy
Eure (*French* œr) *n* a department of N France, in Haute-Normandie region. Capital: Évreux. Pop: 541 054 (1999). Area: 6037 sq km (2354 sq miles)
Eure-et-Loir (*French* œrelwar) *n* a department of N central France, in Centre region. Capital: Chartres. Pop: 407 665 (1999). Area: 5940 sq km (2317 sq miles)
eureka (jʊˈriːkə) *interj* an exclamation of triumph on discovering or solving something [c17 from Gk *heurēka* I have found (it), from *heuriskein* to find; traditionally the exclamation of Archimedes when he realized, during bathing, that the volume of an irregular solid could be calculated by measuring the water displaced when it was immersed]
eurhythmic (juːˈrɪðmɪk), **eurhythmical,** *or esp US* **eurythmic, eurythmical** *adj* **1** having a pleasing and harmonious rhythm, order, or structure **2** of or relating to eurhythmics [c19 from L, from Gk, from EU- + *rhuthmos* proportion, RHYTHM]

Ee

eurhythmics *or esp US* **eurythmics** (juːˈrɪðmɪks) *n (functioning as sing)* **1** a system of training through physical movement to music **2** dancing of this style [C20 from EURHYTHMIC] > **euˈrhythmy** *or* **euˈrythmy** *n*

Euripides (jʊˈrɪpɪˌdiːz) *n* ?480–406 BC, Greek tragic dramatist. His plays, 18 of which are extant, include *Alcestis, Medea, Hippolytus, Hecuba, Trojan Women, Electra, Iphigeneia in Tauris, Iphigeneia in Aulis*, and *Bacchae*

euro (ˈjʊərəʊ) *n, pl* **euros** the official currency unit, divided into 100 cents, of the member countries of the European Union who have adopted European Monetary Union

euro- (ˈjʊərəʊ) *or before a vowel* **eur-** *combining form (sometimes cap)* Europe *or* European

eurobond (ˈjʊərəʊˌbɒnd) *n (sometimes cap)* a bond issued in a eurocurrency

Eurocentric (ˌjʊərəʊˈsɛntrɪk) *adj* chiefly concerned with or concentrating on Europe and European culture: *the Eurocentric curriculum*

eurocheque (ˈjʊərəʊˌtʃɛk) *n (sometimes cap)* a cheque drawn on a European bank that can be cashed at any bank or bureau de change displaying the EU sign or that can be used to pay for goods or services at any outlet displaying this sign

Eurocommunism (ˌjʊərəʊˈkɒmjʊˌnɪzəm) *n* the policies, doctrines, and practices of Communist Parties in Western Europe in the 1970s and 1980s, esp those rejecting democratic centralism and favouring nonalignment with the Soviet Union and China > ˌ**Euroˈcommunist** *n, adj*

eurocrat (ˈjʊərəˌkræt) *n (sometimes cap)* a member of the administration of the European Union

eurocreep (ˈjʊərəˌkriːp) *n* the gradual introduction of the euro into use in Britain

eurocurrency (ˈjʊərəʊˌkʌrənsɪ) *n (sometimes cap)* the currency of any country held on deposit in Europe outside its home market: used as a source of short- or medium-term finance because of easy convertibility

eurodollar (ˈjʊərəʊˌdɒlə) *n (sometimes cap)* a US dollar as part of a European holding. See **eurocurrency**

euroland (ˈjʊərəʊˌlænd) *n (sometimes cap)* another name for **eurozone**

euromarket (ˈjʊərəʊˌmɑːkɪt) *n* **1** a market for financing international trade backed by the central banks and commercial banks of the European Union **2** the European Union treated as one large market for the sale of goods and services

Euro MP *n inf* a member of the European Parliament

euronote (ˈjʊərəʊˌnəʊt) *n* a form of euro-commercial paper consisting of short-term negotiable bearer notes

Europa (jʊˈrəʊpə) *n Greek myth* a Phoenician princess who had three children by Zeus in Crete, where he had taken her after assuming the guise of a white bull. Their offspring were Rhadamanthys, Minos, and Sarpedon

Europe (ˈjʊərəp) *n* **1** the second smallest continent, forming the W extension of Eurasia: the border with Asia runs from the Urals to the Caspian and the Black Sea. The coastline is generally extremely indented and there are several peninsulas (notably Scandinavia, Italy, and Iberia) and offshore islands (including the British Isles and Iceland). It contains a series of great mountain systems in the south (Pyrenees, Alps, Apennines, Carpathians, Caucasus), a large central plain, and a N region of lakes and mountains in Scandinavia. Pop: 729 370 000 (1996 est). Area: about 10 400 000 sq km (4 000 000 sq miles) **2** *Brit* the continent of Europe except for the British Isles: *we're going to Europe for our holiday* **3** *Brit* the European Union: *when did Britain go into Europe?*

European (ˌjʊərəˈpɪən) *adj* **1** of or relating to Europe or its inhabitants **2** native to or derived from Europe ▷ *n* **3** a native or inhabitant of Europe **4** a person of European descent **5** *S African* any White person > ˌ**Euroˈpeanˌism** *n*

European Central Bank *n* the central bank of the European Union, established in 1998 to oversee the process of European Monetary Union and subsequently to direct monetary policy within the countries using the euro. Abbreviation: **ECB**

European Commission *n* the executive body of the European Union formed in 1967, which initiates action in the EU and mediates between member governments. Former name (until 1993): **Commission of the European Communities**

▷ http://europa.eu.int/comm/index_en.htm

European Community *or* **Communities** *n* an economic and political association of European states that came into being in 1967, when the executive and legislative bodies of the European Economic Community merged with those of the European Coal and Steel Community and the European Atomic Energy Community

European Council *n* a body consisting of the heads of government of the member states of the European Union that meets three times a year to discuss major policy developments

▷ http://ue.eu.int/en/summ.htm

European Currency Unit *n* See **ECU**

European Economic Community *n* the former W European economic association created by the Treaty of Rome (1957); in 1967 its executive and legislative bodies merged with those of the European Coal and Steel Community and the European Atomic Energy Community to form the European Community. Informal name: **Common Market.** Abbrev: **EEC**

Europeanize *or* **Europeanise** (ˌjʊərəˈpɪəˌnaɪz) *vb* **Europeanizes, Europeanizing, Europeanized** *or* **Europeanises, Europeanising, Europeanised** *(tr)* **1** to make European **2** to integrate (a country, economy, etc) into the European Union > ˌ**Euroˌpeaniˈzation** *or* ˌ**Euroˌpeaniˈsation** *n*

European Monetary System *n* the system used in the European Union for stabilizing exchange rates between the currencies of member states and financing the balance-of-payments support mechanism. The original Exchange Rate Mechanism was formed in 1979 but was superseded in 1999 when the euro was adopted as official currency of 11 EU member states. A new exchange rate mechanism (ERM II) based on the euro is used to regulate the currencies of participating states that have not adopted the euro. Abbrev: **EMS**

European Monetary Union *n* the agreement between members of the European Union to establish a common currency. The current participating members are Austria, Belgium, Finland, France, Germany, Greece, Ireland, Italy, Luxembourg, the Netherlands, Portugal and Spain. Abbrev: **EMU**

European Parliament *n* the assembly of the European Union in Strasbourg

▷ www.europarl.eu.int/home/default_en.htm

European Union *n* an organization created in 1993 with the aim of achieving closer economic and political union between member states of the European Community. The current members are Austria, Belgium, Cyprus, the Czech Republic, Denmark, Estonia, Finland, France, Germany, Greece, Hungary, Ireland, Italy, Latvia, Lithuania, Luxembourg, Malta, the Netherlands, Poland, Portugal, Slovakia, Slovenia, Spain, Sweden, and the UK. Abbrev: **EU**

▷ www.europa.eu.int/index_en.htm
▷ www.eia.org.uk/websites.htm

European wasp *n Austral* a large black-and-yellow banded wasp, *Vespula germanica*, native to Europe, North Africa, and Asia, now established in Australasia and the US

Europhile ('jʊərəʊˌfaɪl) *(sometimes not cap)* ▷ *n* **1** a person who admires Europe, Europeans, or the European Union ▷ *adj* **2** marked by admiration for Europe, Europeans, or the European Union
europium (jʊ'rəʊpɪəm) *n* a silvery-white element of the lanthanide series of metals. Symbol: Eu; atomic no.: 63; atomic wt.: 151.96 [c20 after EUROPE + -IUM]
Europol ('jʊərəʊˌpɒl) *n* ▷ *acronym for* European Police Office, an international association devoted to fighting cross-border organized crime within the European Union
▷ www.europol.net
Europoort (*Dutch* 'ø:ro:po:rt) *n* a port in the Netherlands near Rotterdam: developed in the 1960s; handles chiefly oil
Eurosceptic ('jʊərəʊˌskɛptɪk) (in Britain) ▷ *n* **1** a person who is opposed to closer links with the European Union ▷ *adj* **2** opposing closer links with the European Union: *Eurosceptic MPs*
Eurotunnel ('jʊərəʊˌtʌnᵊl) *n* another name for **Channel Tunnel**
eurozone ('jʊərəʊˌzəʊn) *n* *(sometimes cap)* the geographical area containing the countries that are participating in European Monetary Union. Also called: **euroland**
Eurus ('jʊərəs) *n* *Greek myth* the east or southeast wind personified [L, from Gk *euros*]
Euryale (jʊ'raɪəlɪ) *n* *Greek myth* one of the three Gorgons
Eurydice (jʊ'rɪdɪsɪ) *n* *Greek myth* a dryad married to Orpheus, who sought her in Hades after she died. She would have been able to leave Hades with him had he not broken his pact and looked back at her
Eurystheus (jʊ'rɪsθju:s, -θɪəs) *n* *Greek myth* a grandson of Perseus, who, through the favour of Hera, inherited the kingship of Mycenae, which Zeus had intended for Hercules
eurythmics (ju:'rɪðmɪks) *n* a variant spelling (esp US) of **eurhythmics**
Eusebio (ju:'seɪbɪəʊ) *n* **Silva Ferreira da** ('sɪlvə fɛr'eɪrə də) born 1942, Portuguese footballer
Eusebius (ju:'si:bɪəs) *n* ?265–?340 AD, bishop of Caesarea: author of a history of the Christian Church to 324 AD
Eustachian tube (ju:'steɪʃən) *n* a tube that connects the middle ear with the pharynx and equalizes the pressure between the two sides of the eardrum [c18 after Bartolomeo *Eustachio*, 16th-cent. It. anatomist]
eustatic (ju:'stætɪk) *adj* denoting or relating to worldwide changes in sea level, caused by the melting of ice sheets, sedimentation, etc [c20 from Gk, from EU- + STATIC]
eutectic (ju:'tɛktɪk) *adj* **1** (of a mixture of substances) having the lowest freezing point of all possible mixtures of the substances **2** concerned with or suitable for the formation of eutectic mixtures ▷ *n* **3** a eutectic mixture **4** the temperature at which a eutectic mixture forms [c19 from Gk *eutēktos* melting readily, from EU- + *tēkein* to melt]
Euterpe (ju:'tɜ:pɪ) *n* *Greek myth* the Muse of lyric poetry and music > **Eu'terpean** *adj*
euthanasia (ˌju:θə'neɪzɪə) *n* the act of killing someone painlessly, esp to relieve suffering from an incurable illness [c17 via NL from Gk: easy death]
euthenics (ju:'θɛnɪks) *n* *(functioning as sing)* the study of the control of the environment, esp with a view to improving the health and living standards of the human race [c20 from Gk *euthēnein* to thrive] > **eu'thenist** *n*
eutrophic (ju:'trɒfɪk, -'trəʊ-) *adj* (of lakes, etc) rich in organic and mineral nutrients and supporting an abundant plant life [c18 prob. from *eutrophy*, from Gk, from *eutrophos* well-fed] > **'eutrophy** *n*
Euxine Sea ('ju:ksaɪn) *n* another name for the **Black Sea**
eV *abbrev for* electronvolt

EVA *astronautics abbrev for* extravehicular activity
evacuate (ɪ'vækjʊˌeɪt) *vb* **evacuates, evacuating, evacuated** *(mainly tr)* **1** *(also intr)* to withdraw or cause to withdraw (from a place of danger) to a place of safety **2** to make empty **3** *(also intr) physiol* **3a** to eliminate or excrete (faeces) **3b** to discharge (any waste) from (the body) **4** *(tr)* to create a vacuum in (a bulb, flask, etc) [c16 from L *ēvacuāre* to void, from *vacuus* empty] > **eˌvacu'ation** *n* > **e'vacuative** *adj* > **e'vacuˌator** *n* > **eˌvacu'ee** *n*
evade (ɪ'veɪd) *vb* **evades, evading, evaded** *(mainly tr)* **1** to get away from or avoid (imprisonment, captors, etc) **2** to get around, shirk, or dodge (the law, a duty, etc) **3** *(also intr)* to avoid answering (a question) [c16 from F, from L *ēvādere* to go forth] > **e'vadable** *adj* > **e'vader** *n*
evaginate (ɪ'vædʒɪˌneɪt) *vb* **evaginates, evaginating, evaginated** *(tr) med* to turn (an organ or part) inside out [c17 from LL *ēvāgīnare* to unsheathe, from L *vāgīna* sheath]
evaluate (ɪ'væljʊˌeɪt) *vb* **evaluates, evaluating, evaluated** *(tr)* **1** to ascertain or set the amount or value of **2** to judge or assess the worth of [c19 back formation from *evaluation*, from F, from *évaluer*; see VALUE] > **eˌvalu'ation** *n* > **e'valuative** *adj* > **e'valuˌator** *n*
evanesce (ˌɛvə'nɛs) *vb* **evanesces, evanescing, evanesced** *(intr)* (of smoke, mist, etc) to fade gradually from sight; vanish [c19 from L *ēvānēscere* to disappear; see VANISH]
evanescent (ˌɛvə'nɛsᵊnt) *adj* **1** passing out of sight; fading away; vanishing **2** ephemeral or transitory > **ˌeva'nescence** *n*
evangel (ɪ'vændʒəl) *n* **1** *arch* the gospel of Christianity **2** *(often cap)* any of the four Gospels of the New Testament **3** any body of teachings regarded as basic **4** *US* an evangelist [c14 from Church L, from Gk *evangelion* good news, from EU- + *angelos* messenger; see ANGEL]
evangelical (ˌi:væn'dʒɛlɪkᵊl) *Christianity* ▷ *adj* **1** of or following from the Gospels **2** denoting or relating to any of certain Protestant sects, which emphasize personal conversion and faith in atonement through the death of Christ as a means of salvation **3** denoting or relating to an evangelist ▷ *n* **4** a member of an evangelical sect > **ˌevan'gelicalism** *n* > **ˌevan'gelically** *adv*
▷ http://wikipedia.org/wiki/Evangelicalism
▷ http://dict.die.net/evangelical/
evangelism (ɪ'vændʒɪˌlɪzəm) *n* **1** the practice of spreading the Christian gospel **2** ardent or missionary zeal for a cause
evangelist (ɪ'vændʒɪlɪst) *n* **1** an occasional preacher, sometimes itinerant **2** a preacher of the Christian gospel > **eˌvange'listic** *adj*
Evangelist (ɪ'vændʒɪlɪst) *n* any of the writers of the New Testament Gospels: Matthew, Mark, Luke, or John
evangelize *or* **evangelise** (ɪ'vændʒɪˌlaɪz) *vb* **evangelizes, evangelizing, evangelized** *or* **evangelises, evangelising, evangelised** **1** to preach the Christian gospel (to) **2** *(intr)* to advocate a cause with the object of making converts > **eˌvangeli'zation** *or* **eˌvangeli'sation** *n* > **e'vangeˌlizer** *or* **e'vangeˌliser** *n*
Evans ('ɛvənz) *n* **1** Sir **Arthur (John)** 1851–1941, British archaeologist, whose excavations of the palace of Knossos in Crete provided evidence for the existence of the Minoan civilization **2** Dame **Edith (Mary Booth)** 1888–1976, British actress **3** Sir **Geraint (Llewellyn)** 1922–92, Welsh operatic baritone **4** **Herbert McLean** 1882–1971, US anatomist and embryologist; discoverer of vitamin E (1922) **5** **Mary Ann** real name of (George) **Eliot** **6** **Oliver** 1755–1819, US engineer: invented the continuous production line and a high-pressure steam engine **7** **Walker** 1903–75, US photographer, noted esp for his studies of rural poverty in the Great Depression
Evanston ('ɛvənstən) *n* a city in NE Illinois, on Lake Michigan north of Chicago: Northwestern University (1851). Pop: 73 233 (1990)

Ee

Evansville (ˈɛvənzˌvɪl) *n* a city in SW Indiana, on the Ohio River. Pop: 121 582 (2000)

evaporate (ɪˈvæpəˌreɪt) *vb* **evaporates, evaporating, evaporated** **1** to change or cause to change from a liquid or solid state to a vapour **2** to lose or cause to lose liquid by vaporization leaving a more concentrated residue **3** to disappear or cause to disappear [C16 from LL, from L *vapor* steam; see VAPOUR] > **eˈvaporable** *adj* > **eˌvapoˈration** *n* > **eˈvaporative** *adj* > **eˈvapoˌrator** *n*

evaporated milk *n* thick unsweetened tinned milk from which some of the water has been evaporated

evasion (ɪˈveɪʒən) *n* **1** the act of evading, esp a distasteful duty, responsibility, etc, by cunning or by illegal means: *tax evasion* **2** cunning or deception used to dodge a question, duty, etc; means of evading [C15 from LL *ēvāsio*; see EVADE]

evasive (ɪˈveɪsɪv) *adj* **1** tending or seeking to evade; not straightforward **2** avoiding or seeking to avoid trouble or difficulties **3** hard to catch or obtain; elusive > **eˈvasively** *adv* > **eˈvasiveness** *n*

eve (iːv) *n* **1** the evening or day before some special event **2** the period immediately before an event: *the eve of war* **3** an archaic word for **evening** [C13 var. of EVEN²]

Eve (iːv) *n Old Testament* the first woman; mother of the human race, fashioned by God from the rib of Adam (Genesis 2:18-25)

Evelyn (ˈiːvlɪn, ˈɛv-) *n* **John** 1620–1706, English author, noted chiefly for his diary (1640–1706)

even¹ (ˈiːvᵊn) *adj* **1** level and regular; flat **2** (*postpositive; foll by with*) on the same level or in the same plane (as) **3** without variation or fluctuation; regular; constant **4** not readily moved or excited; calm: *an even temper* **5** equally balanced between two sides: *an even game* **6** equal or identical in number, quantity, etc **7a** (of a number) divisible by two **7b** characterized or indicated by such a number: *the even pages.* ▷ Cf **odd** (sense 4) **8** relating to or denoting two or either of two alternatives, events, etc, that have an equal probability: *an even chance of missing or catching a train* **9** having no balance of debt; neither owing nor being owed **10** just and impartial; fair **11** exact in number, amount, or extent: *an even pound* **12** equal, as in score; level **13 even money 13a** a bet in which the winnings are the same as the amount staked **13b** (*as modifier*): *the even-money favourite* **14 get even (with)** *inf* to exact revenge (on); settle accounts (with) ▷ *adv* **15** (intensifier; used to suggest that the content of a statement is unexpected or paradoxical): *even an idiot can do that* **16** (intensifier; used with comparative forms): *even better* **17** notwithstanding; in spite of **18** used to introduce a more precise version of a word, phrase, or statement: *he is base, even depraved* **19** used preceding a clause of supposition or hypothesis to emphasize that whether or not the condition in it is fulfilled, the statement in the main clause remains valid: *even if she died he wouldn't care* **20** *arch* all the way; fully: *I love thee even unto death* **21 even as** (*conj*) at the very same moment or in the very same way that **22 even so** in spite of any assertion to the contrary: nevertheless ▷ See also **even out, evens, even up** [OE *efen*] > **ˈevener** *n* > **ˈevenly** *adv* > **ˈevenness** *n*

even² (ˈiːvᵊn) *n* an archaic word for **eve** or **evening** [OE *ǣfen*]

even-handed *adj* fair; impartial > **ˌeven-ˈhandedly** *adv* > **ˌeven-ˈhandedness** *n*

evening (ˈiːvnɪŋ) *n* **1** the latter part of the day, esp from late afternoon until nightfall **2** the latter or concluding period: *the evening of one's life* **3** the early part of the night spent in a specified way: *an evening at the theatre* **4** (*modifier*) of, used in, or occurring in the evening: *the evening papers* [OE *ǣfnung*]

evening dress *n* attire for a formal occasion during the evening

evening primrose *n* any plant of the genus *Oenothera*, typically having yellow flowers that open in the evening

evening primrose oil *n* an oil, obtained from the seeds of the evening primrose, that is claimed to stimulate the production of prostaglandins

evenings (ˈiːvnɪŋz) *adv inf* in the evening, esp regularly

evening star *n* a planet, usually Venus, seen just after sunset during the time that the planet is east of the sun

even out *vb* (*adv*) to make or become even, as by the removal of bumps, inequalities, etc

evens (ˈiːvənz) *adj, adv* **1** (of a bet) winning the same as the amount staked if successful **2** (of a runner) offered at such odds

evensong (ˈiːvᵊnˌsɒŋ) *n* **1** Also called: **Evening Prayer, vespers** *Church of England* the daily evening service **2** *RC Church, arch* another name for **vespers**

event (ɪˈvɛnt) *n* **1** anything that takes place, esp something important; an incident **2** the actual or final outcome (esp in **in the event, after the event**) **3** any one contest in a programme of sporting or other contests **4 in any event** *or* **at all events** regardless of circumstances; in any case **5 in the event of** in case of; if (such a thing) happens **6 in the event that** if it should happen that [C16 from L *ēvenīre* to come forth, happen]

even-tempered *adj* not easily angered or excited; calm

eventful (ɪˈvɛntfʊl) *adj* full of events > **eˈventfully** *adv* > **eˈventfulness** *n*

event horizon *n astron* the spherical boundary of a black hole: objects passing through it would disappear completely and for ever, as no information can escape across the event horizon from the interior

eventide (ˈiːvᵊnˌtaɪd) *n arch or poetic* another word for **evening**

eventide home *n euphemistic* an old people's home

eventing (ɪˈvɛntɪŋ) *n chiefly Brit* taking part in equestrian competitions (esp **three-day events**), usually involving cross-country riding, jumping, and dressage

eventize *or* **eventise** (ɪˈvɛntaɪz) *vb* (*tr*) to arrange (an occasion) so that it is seen as being a special event

event television *n* television programmes focusing on events which attract media attention and high ratings

event theatre *n* spectacular and extravagantly-mounted theatrical productions collectively

eventual (ɪˈvɛntʃʊəl) *adj* **1** (*prenominal*) happening in due course of time; ultimate **2** *arch* contingent or possible

eventuality (ɪˌvɛntʃʊˈælɪtɪ) *n, pl* **eventualities** a possible event, occurrence, or result; contingency

eventually (ɪˈvɛntʃʊəlɪ) *adv* **1** at the very end; finally **2** (*sentence modifier*) after a long time or long delay: *eventually, he arrived*

eventuate (ɪˈvɛntʃʊˌeɪt) *vb* **eventuates, eventuating, eventuated** (*intr*) **1** (often foll by *in*) to result ultimately (in) **2** to come about as a result > **eˌventuˈation** *n*

even up *vb* (*adv*) to make or become equal, esp in respect of claims or debts

ever (ˈɛvə) *adv* **1** at any time **2** by any chance; in any case: *how did you ever find out?* **3** at all times; always **4** in any possible way or manner: *come as fast as ever you can* **5** *inf, chiefly Brit* (intensifier, in **ever so, ever such,** and **ever such a**) **6 is he** *or* **she ever!** *US & Canad sl* he *or* she displays the quality concerned in abundance ▷ See also **forever** [OE *ǣfre*, from ?]

Everest (ˈɛvərɪst) *n* **1 Mount** a mountain in S Asia on the border between Nepal and Tibet, in the Himalayas: the highest mountain in the world; first climbed by a British expedition (1953). Height: 8850 m (29 035 ft) **2** any high point of ambition or achievement [C19 named after Sir G. *Everest* (1790–1866), Surveyor-General of India]

Everglades (ˈɛvəˌgleɪdz) *pl n* **the** a subtropical marshy region of Florida, south of Lake Okeechobee: contains the **Everglades National Park** established to preserve the flora and fauna of the swamps. Area: over 13 000 sq km (5000 sq miles)

evergreen ('ɛvə,gri:n) *adj* 1 (of certain trees and shrubs) bearing foliage throughout the year. ▷ Cf **deciduous** 2 remaining fresh and vital ▷ *n* 3 an evergreen tree or shrub

evergreen fund *n* a fund that provides capital for new companies and makes regular injections of capital to support their development

everlasting (,ɛvə'lɑ:stɪŋ) *adj* 1 never coming to an end; eternal 2 lasting for an indefinitely long period 3 lasting so long or occurring so often as to become tedious ▷ *n* 4 eternity 5 Also called: **everlasting flower** another name for **immortelle** > ,**ever'lastingly** *adv*

evermore (,ɛvə'mɔ:) *adv* (preceded by *for*) all time to come

evert (ɪ'vɜ:t) *vb* (*tr*) to turn (an eyelid or other bodily part) outwards or inside out [C16 from L *ēvertere* to overthrow, from *vertere* to turn] > **e'versible** *adj* > **e'version** *n*

every ('ɛvrɪ) *determiner* 1 each one (of the class specified), without exception 2 (*not used with a negative*) the greatest or best possible: *every hope* 3 each: used before a noun phrase to indicate the recurrent, intermittent, or serial nature of a thing: *every third day* 4 **every bit** (used in comparisons with *as*) quite; just; equally 5 **every other** each alternate; every second 6 **every which way** *US & Canad* 6a in all directions; everywhere 6b from all sides [C15 *everich*, from OE *ǣfre ǣlc*, from *ǣfre* EVER + *ǣlc* EACH]

everybody ('ɛvrɪ,bɒdɪ) *pron* every person; everyone.

USAGE See at **everyone**

everyday ('ɛvrɪ,deɪ) *adj* 1 happening each day 2 commonplace or usual 3 suitable for or used on ordinary days

Everyman ('ɛvrɪ,mæn) *n* 1 a medieval English morality play in which the central figure represents mankind 2 (*often not cap*) the ordinary person; common man

everyone ('ɛvrɪ,wʌn, -wən) *pron* every person; everybody.

USAGE *Everyone* and *everybody* are interchangeable, as are *no one* and *nobody*, and *someone* and *somebody*. Care should be taken to distinguish between *everyone* and *someone* as single words and *every one* and *some one* as two words, the latter form correctly being used to refer to each individual person or thing in a particular group: *every one of them is wrong*

every one *pron* each person or thing in a group, without exception

everything ('ɛvrɪ,θɪŋ) *pron* 1 the entirety of a specified or implied class 2 a great deal, esp of something very important

everywhere ('ɛvrɪ,wɛə) *adv* to or in all parts or places

Evesham ('i:vʃəm) *n* a town in W central England, in W Worcestershire, on the River Avon: scene of the Battle of Evesham in 1265 (Lord Edward's defeat of Simon de Montfort and the barons); centre of the **Vale of Evesham**, famous for market gardens and orchards. Pop: 17 823 (1991)

Evian ('ɛvian) *n trademark* a type of bottled natural mineral water [from ÉVIAN-LES-BAINS]

Évian-les-Bains (*French* eviã le bɛ̃) *n* a resort and spa town in E France, on Lake Geneva opposite Lausanne; noted for its bottled mineral waters. Pop: 6000 (latest est)

evict (ɪ'vɪkt) *vb* (*tr*) 1 to expel (a tenant) from property by process of law; turn out 2 to recover (property or the title to property) by judicial process or by virtue of a superior title [C15 from LL *ēvincere*, from L: to vanquish utterly] > **e'viction** *n* > **e'victor** *n*

evidence ('ɛvɪdəns) *n* 1 ground for belief or disbelief; data on which to base proof or to establish truth or falsehood 2 a mark or sign that makes evident 3 *law* matter produced before a court of law in an attempt to prove or disprove a point in issue 4 **in evidence** on display; apparent ▷ *vb* **evidences, evidencing, evidenced** (*tr*) 5 to make evident; show clearly 6 to give proof of or evidence for

evident ('ɛvɪdənt) *adj* easy to see or understand; apparent [C14 from L *ēvidēns*, from *vidēre* to see]

evidential (,ɛvɪ'dɛnʃəl) *adj* relating to, serving as, or based on evidence > ,**evi'dentially** *adv*

evidently ('ɛvɪdəntlɪ) *adv* 1 without question; clearly 2 to all appearances; apparently

evil ('i:vᵊl) *adj* 1 morally wrong or bad; wicked 2 causing harm or injury 3 marked or accompanied by misfortune: *an evil fate* 4 (of temper, disposition, etc) characterized by anger or spite 5 infamous: *an evil reputation* 6 offensive or unpleasant: *an evil smell* 7 *sl, chiefly US* excellent or outstanding ▷ *n* 8 the quality or an instance of being morally wrong; wickedness 9 (*sometimes cap*) a force or power that brings about wickedness or harm ▷ *adv* 10 (*now usually in combination*) in an evil manner; badly: *evil-smelling* [OE *yfel*] > '**evilly** *adv* > '**evilness** *n*

evildoer ('i:vᵊl,du:ə) *n* a person who does evil > '**evil,doing** *n*

evil eye *n* **the** 1 a look or glance superstitiously supposed to have the power of inflicting harm or injury 2 the power to inflict harm, etc, by such a look > ,**evil-'eyed** *adj*

evil-minded *adj* inclined to evil thoughts; malicious or spiteful > ,**evil-'mindedly** *adv* > ,**evil-'mindedness** *n*

evince (ɪ'vɪns) *vb* **evinces, evincing, evinced** (*tr*) to make evident; show (something) clearly [C17 from L *ēvincere* to overcome; see EVICT] > **e'vincible** *adj*

USAGE The rather bookish and highfalutin word *evince* is sometimes wrongly used where *evoke* is meant as in: *its very mention is likely to evince a smile of embarrassment* where *evoke* would have been correct

eviscerate (ɪ'vɪsə,reɪt) *vb* **eviscerates, eviscerating, eviscerated** (*tr*) 1 to remove the internal organs of; disembowel 2 to deprive of meaning or significance [C17 from L *ēviscerāre*, from *viscera* entrails] > **e,viscer'ation** *n* > **e'viscer,ator** *n*

evocation (,ɛvə'keɪʃən) *n* the act or an instance of evoking [C17 from L: see EVOKE] > **evocative** (ɪ'vɒkətɪv) *adj*

evoke (ɪ'vəʊk) *vb* **evokes, evoking, evoked** (*tr*) 1 to call or summon up (a memory, feeling, etc), esp from the past 2 to provoke; elicit 3 to cause (spirits) to appear; conjure up [C17 from L *ēvocāre* to call forth, from *vocāre* to call] > **evocable** ('ɛvəkəbᵊl) *adj* > **e'voker** *n*

USAGE See at **evince** and **invoke**

evolute ('ɛvə,lu:t) *n* 1 a geometric curve that describes the locus of the centres of curvature of another curve (the **involute**) ▷ *adj* 2 *biol* having the margins rolled outwards [C19 from L *ēvolūtus* unrolled, from *ēvolvere* to roll out, EVOLVE]

evolution (,i:və'lu:ʃən) *n* 1 *biol* a gradual change in the characteristics of a population of animals or plants over successive generations 2 a gradual development, esp to a more complex form: *the evolution of modern art* 3 the act of throwing off, as heat, gas, vapour, etc 4 a pattern formed by a series of movements or something similar 5 an algebraic operation in which the root of a number, expression, etc, is extracted 6 *mil* an exercise carried out in accordance with a set procedure or plan [C17 from L *ēvolūtiō* an unrolling, from *ēvolvere* to EVOLVE] > ,**evo'lutionary** *or* ,**evo'lutional** *adj*

evolutionary algorithm *n computing* a computer program that is designed to evolve and improve in response to input

evolutionist (,i:və'lu:ʃənɪst) *n* 1 a person who believes in a theory of evolution ▷ *adj* 2 of or relating to a theory of evolution > ,**evo'lutionism** *n* > ,**evolution'istic** *adj*

evolve (ɪ'vɒlv) *vb* **evolves, evolving, evolved** 1 to develop

Ee

or cause to develop gradually **2** (*intr*) (of animal or plant species) to undergo evolution **3** (*tr*) to yield, emit, or give off (heat, gas, vapour, etc) [C17 from L *ēvolvere* to unfold, from *volvere* to roll] > **e'volvable** *adj* > **e'volvement** *n*

Évora (*Portuguese* 'ɛvura) *n* a city in S central Portugal: ancient Roman settlement; occupied by the Moors from 712 to 1166; residence of the Portuguese court in 15th and 16th centuries. Pop: 34 100 (latest est). Ancient name: **Ebora** ('i:bərə)

Évreux (*French* evrø) *n* an industrial town in NW France: severely damaged in World War II; cathedral (12th–16th centuries). Pop: 51 450 (1990)

Évros ('ɛvrɔs) *n* transliteration of the Modern Greek name for the **Maritsa**

Évvoia ('ɛvia) *n* transliteration of the Modern Greek name for **Euboea**

evzone ('ɛvzəʊn) *n* a soldier in an elite Greek infantry regiment [C19 from Mod. Gk, from Gk *euzōnos*, lit.: well-girt, from EU- + *zōne* girdle]

e-wallet *n* computer software in which digital cash may be stored for use in paying for transactions on the Internet

ewe (ju:) *n* **a** a female sheep **b** (*as modifier*): *a ewe lamb* [OE *ēowu*]

ewer ('ju:ə) *n* a large jug or pitcher with a wide mouth [C14 from OF *evier*, from L *aquārius* water carrier, from *aqua* water]

ex[1] (ɛks) *prep* **1** *finance* excluding; without: *ex dividend* **2** *commerce* without charge to the buyer until removed from: *ex warehouse* [C19 from L: out of, from]

ex[2] (ɛks) *n inf* (a person's) former wife, husband, etc

Ex. *Bible abbrev for* Exodus

ex-[1] *prefix* **1** out of; outside of; from: *exclosure; exurbia* **2** former: *ex-wife* [from L, from *ex* (prep), identical with Gk *ex, ek*; see EC-]

ex-[2] *combining form* a variant of **exo-** before a vowel: *exergonic*

exa- *combining form* **1** denoting 10^{18}: *exametres* **2** Also: **exbi** *computing* denoting 2^{60}: *exabyte* ▷ Symbol: E.

USAGE See at **kilo-**

exacerbate (ɪg'zæsə,beɪt, ɪk'sæs-) *vb* **exacerbates, exacerbating, exacerbated** (*tr*) **1** to make (pain, disease, etc) more intense; aggravate **2** to irritate (a person) [C17 from L *exacerbāre* to irritate, from *acerbus* bitter] > **ex,acer'bation** *n*

exact (ɪg'zækt) *adj* **1** correct in every detail; strictly accurate **2** precise, as opposed to approximate **3** (*prenominal*) specific; particular **4** operating with very great precision **5** allowing no deviation from a standard; rigorous; strict **6** based on measurement and the formulation of laws, as opposed to description and classification: *an exact science* ▷ *vb* (*tr*) **7** to force or compel (payment, etc); extort: *to exact tribute* **8** to demand as a right; insist upon **9** to call for or require [C16 from L *exactus* driven out, from *exigere* to drive forth, from *agere* to drive] > **ex'actable** *adj* > **ex'actness** *n* > **ex'actor** *or* **ex'acter** *n*

exacting (ɪg'zæktɪŋ) *adj* making rigorous or excessive demands > **ex'actingness** *n*

exaction (ɪg'zækʃən) *n* **1** the act or an instance of exacting **2** an excessive or harsh demand, esp for money **3** a sum or payment exacted

exactitude (ɪg'zæktɪ,tju:d) *n* the quality of being exact; precision; accuracy

exactly (ɪg'zæktlɪ) *adv* **1** in an exact manner; accurately or precisely **2** in every respect; just ▷ *sentence substitute* **3** just so!, precisely! **4 not exactly** *ironical* not at all; by no means

exacum ('ɛksəkəm) *n* any of various Asian flowering herbs [NL, from EX-[1] + Gk *ago* to arrive]

exaggerate (ɪg'zædʒə,reɪt) *vb* **exaggerates, exaggerating, exaggerated** **1** to regard or represent as larger or greater, more important or more successful, etc, than is true **2** (*tr*) to make greater, more noticeable, etc [C16 from L *exaggerāre* to magnify, from *aggerāre* to heap, from *agger* heap] > **ex'agger,ated** *adj* > **ex,agger'ation** *n* > **ex'agger,ator** *n*

ex all *adv, adj finance* without the right to any benefits: *shares quoted ex all*

exalt (ɪg'zɔ:lt) *vb* (*tr*) **1** to elevate in rank, dignity, etc **2** to praise highly; extol **3** to stimulate; excite **4** to fill with joy or delight; elate [C15 from L *exaltāre* to raise, from *altus* high] > **ex'alted** *adj* > **ex'alter** *n*

exaltation (,ɛgzɔ:l'teɪʃən) *n* **1** the act of exalting or state of being exalted **2** exhilaration; elation; rapture

exam (ɪg'zæm) *n* short for **examination**

examination (ɪg,zæmɪ'neɪʃən) *n* **1** the act of examining or state of being examined **2** *education* **2a** written exercises, oral questions, etc, set to test a candidate's knowledge and skill **2b** (*as modifier*): *an examination paper* **3** *med* **3a** physical inspection of a patient **3b** laboratory study of secretory or excretory products, tissue samples, etc **4** *law* the formal interrogation of a person on oath > **ex,ami'national** *adj*

examine (ɪg'zæmɪn) *vb* **examines, examining, examined** (*tr*) **1** to inspect or scrutinize carefully or in detail; investigate **2** *education* to test the knowledge or skill of (a candidate) in (a subject or activity) by written or oral questions, etc **3** *law* to interrogate (a person) formally on oath **4** *med* to investigate the state of health of (a patient) [C14 from OF, from L *exāmināre* to weigh, from *exāmen* means of weighing] > **ex'aminable** *adj* > **ex,ami'nee** *n* > **ex'aminer** *n* > **ex'amining** *adj*

example (ɪg'zɑ:mpᵊl) *n* **1** a specimen or instance that is typical of its group or set; sample **2** a person, action, thing, etc, that is worthy of imitation; pattern **3** a precedent, illustration of a principle, or model **4** a punishment or the recipient of a punishment intended to serve as a warning **5 for example** as an illustration; for instance ▷ *vb* **examples, exampling, exampled** **6** (*tr; now usually passive*) to present an example of; exemplify [C14 from OF, from L *exemplum* pattern, from *eximere* to take out]

exanthema (,ɛksæn'θi:mə) *n, pl* **exanthemata** (-'θi:mətə) *or* **exanthemas** a skin rash occurring in a disease such as measles [C17 via LL from Gk, from *exanthein* to burst forth, from *anthein* to blossom]

exasperate (ɪg'zɑ:spə,reɪt) *vb* **exasperates, exasperating, exasperated** (*tr*) **1** to cause great irritation or anger to **2** to cause (something unpleasant) to worsen; aggravate [C16 from L *exasperāre* to make rough, from *asper* rough] > **ex'asper,atedly** *adv* > **ex'asper,atingly** *adv* > **ex,asper'ation** *n*

exbi- ('ɛksbɪ) *combining form computing* denoting 2^{60}: *exbibyte* [C20 from EX(A-) + BI(NARY)]

USAGE See at **kilo-**

ex cathedra (ɛks kə'θi:drə) *adj, adv* **1** with authority **2** *RC Church* (of doctrines of faith or morals) defined by the pope as infallibly true, to be accepted by all Catholics [L, lit.: from the chair]

excavate ('ɛkskə,veɪt) *vb* **excavates, excavating, excavated** **1** to remove (soil, earth, etc) by digging; dig out **2** to make (a hole or tunnel) in (solid matter) by hollowing **3** to unearth (buried objects) methodically to discover information about the past [C16 from L *cavāre* to make hollow, from *cavus* hollow] > **,exca'vation** *n* > **'exca,vator** *n*

exceed (ɪk'si:d) *vb* **1** to be superior (to); excel **2** (*tr*) to go beyond the limit or bounds of **3** (*tr*) to be greater in degree or quantity than [C14 from L *excēdere* to go beyond] > **ex'ceedable** *adj* > **ex'ceeder** *n*

exceeding (ɪk'si:dɪŋ) *adj* **1** very great; exceptional or excessive ▷ *adv* **2** *arch* to a great or unusual degree > **ex'ceedingly** *adv*

excel (ɪk'sɛl) *vb* **excels, excelling, excelled** **1** to be superior to (another or others); surpass **2** (*intr; foll by in* or *at*) to be outstandingly good or proficient [C15 from L *excellere* to rise up]

excellence ('ɛksələns) *n* **1** the state or quality of excelling or being exceptionally good; extreme merit **2** an action, feature, etc, in which a person excels

Excellency ('ɛksələnsɪ) *or* **Excellence** *n, pl* **Excellencies** *or* **Excellences** **1** (usually preceded by *Your, His,* or *Her*) a title used to address or refer to a high-ranking official, such as an ambassador **2** *RC Church* a title of bishops and archbishops in many non-English-speaking countries

excellent ('ɛksələnt) *adj* exceptionally good; extremely meritorious; superior > **'excellently** *adv*

excelsior (ɪk'sɛlsɪˌɔː) *interj, n* **1** excellent: used as a motto and as a trademark for various products **2** upward [C19 from L: higher]

except (ɪk'sɛpt) *prep* **1** Also: **except for** other than; apart from **2** **except that** (*conj*) but for the fact that; were it not true that ▷ *conj* **3** an archaic word for **unless** **4** *inf* (*not standard in the US*) except that; but for the fact that ▷ *vb* **5** (*tr*) to leave out; omit; exclude **6** (*intr;* often foll by *to*) *rare* to take exception; object [C14 from OF *excepter* to leave out, from L *excipere* to take out]

excepting (ɪk'sɛptɪŋ) *prep* **1** except; except for (esp in **not excepting**) ▷ *conj* **2** an archaic word for **unless**

> USAGE The use of *excepting* used to be considered by purists acceptable only after *not, only, always,* or *without.* Nowadays it seems to appear after these words largely in books, and is otherwise used as a more highbrow alternative to *except*

exception (ɪk'sɛpʃən) *n* **1** the act of excepting or fact of being excepted; omission **2** anything excluded from or not in conformance with a general rule, principle, class, etc **3** criticism, esp adverse; objection **4** *law* (formerly) a formal objection in legal proceedings **5** **take exception** **5a** (usually foll by *to*) to make objections (to); demur (at) **5b** (often foll by *at*) to be offended (by); be resentful (at)

exceptionable (ɪk'sɛpʃənəbᵊl) *adj* open to or subject to objection; objectionable > **ex'ceptionableness** *n* > **ex'ceptionably** *adv*

exceptional (ɪk'sɛpʃənᵊl) *adj* **1** forming an exception; not ordinary **2** having much more than average intelligence, ability, or skill

excerpt *n* ('ɛksɜːpt) **1** a part or passage taken from a book, speech, etc; extract ▷ *vb* (ɛk'sɜːpt) **2** (*tr*) to take (a part or passage) from a book, speech, etc [C17 from L *excerptum,* lit.: (something) picked out, from *excerpere* to select, from *carpere* to pluck] > **ex'cerptible** *adj* > **ex'cerption** *n* > **ex'cerptor** *n*

excess *n* (ɪk'sɛs, 'ɛksɛs) **1** the state or act of going beyond normal, sufficient, or permitted limits **2** an immoderate or abnormal amount **3** the amount, number, etc, by which one thing exceeds another **4** overindulgence or intemperance **5** *insurance, chiefly Brit* a specified contribution towards the cost of a claim, payable by the policyholder. US name: **deductible** **6** **in excess of** of more than; over **7** **to excess** to an inordinate extent; immoderately ▷ *adj* ('ɛksɛs, ɪk'sɛs) (*usually prenominal*) **8** more than normal, necessary, or permitted; surplus: *excess weight* **9** payable as a result of previous underpayment: *excess postage* [C14 from L *excēdere* to go beyond; see EXCEED]

excessive (ɪk'sɛsɪv) *adj* exceeding the normal or permitted limits; immoderate; inordinate > **ex'cessively** *adv* > **ex'cessiveness** *n*

excess luggage *or* **baggage** *n* luggage that is more in weight or number of pieces than an airline, etc, will carry free

exchange (ɪks'tʃeɪndʒ) *vb* **exchanges, exchanging, exchanged** **1** (*tr*) to give up or transfer (one thing) for an equivalent **2** (*tr*) to give and receive (information, ideas, etc); interchange **3** (*tr*) to replace (one thing) with another, esp to replace unsatisfactory goods **4** to hand over (goods) in return for the equivalent value in kind; barter; trade ▷ *n* **5** the act or process of exchanging **6a** anything given or received as an equivalent or substitute for something else **6b** (*as modifier*): *an exchange student* **7** an argument or quarrel **8** Also called: **telephone exchange** a switching centre in which telephone lines are interconnected **9** a place where securities or commodities are sold, bought, or traded, esp by brokers or merchants **10a** the system by which commercial debts are settled by commercial documents, esp bills of exchange, instead of by direct payment of money **10b** the percentage or fee charged for accepting payment in this manner **11** a transfer or interchange of sums of money of equivalent value, as between different currencies **12** **win** (*or* **lose**) **the exchange** *chess* to win (*or* lose) a rook in return for a bishop or knight ▷ See also **bill of exchange, exchange rate, labour exchange** [C14 from Anglo-French *eschaungier,* from Vulgar L *excambiāre* (unattested), from L *cambīre* to barter] > **ex'changeable** *adj* > **exˌchangea'bility** *n* > **ex'changeably** *adv* > **ex'changer** *n*

exchange rate *n* the rate at which the currency unit of one country may be exchanged for that of another

Exchange Rate Mechanism *n* the mechanism used in the European Monetary System in which participating governments commit themselves to maintain the values of their currencies in relation to the ECU. Abbrev: **ERM**

exchequer (ɪks'tʃɛkə) *n* **1** (*often cap*) *government* (in Britain and certain other countries) the accounting department of the Treasury **2** *inf* personal funds; finances [C13 (in the sense: chessboard, counting table): from OF *eschequier,* from *eschec* CHECK]

excisable (ɪk'saɪzəbᵊl) *adj* **1** liable to an excise tax **2** suitable for deletion

excise[1] *n* ('ɛksaɪz, ɛk'saɪz) **1** Also called: **excise tax** a tax on goods, such as spirits, produced for the home market **2** a tax paid for a licence to carry out various trades, sports, etc **3** *Brit* that section of the government service responsible for the collection of excise, now the Board of Customs and Excise ▷ *vb* (ɪk'saɪz), **excises, excising, excised** **4** (*tr*) *rare* to compel (a person) to pay excise [C15 prob. from MDu. *excijs,* prob. from OF *assise* a sitting, assessment, from L *assidēre* to sit beside, assist in judging] > **ex'cisable** *adj*

excise[2] (ɪk'saɪz) *vb* **excises, excising, excised** (*tr*) **1** to delete (a passage, sentence, etc) **2** to remove (an organ or part) surgically [C16 from L *excīdere* to cut down] > **excision** (ɪk'sɪʒən) *n*

exciseman ('ɛksaɪzˌmæn) *n, pl* **excisemen** *Brit* (formerly) a government agent whose function was to collect excise and prevent smuggling

excitable (ɪk'saɪtəbᵊl) *adj* **1** easily excited; volatile **2** (esp of a nerve) ready to respond to a stimulus > **exˌcita'bility** *or* **ex'citableness** *n*

excitation (ˌɛksɪ'teɪʃən) *n* **1** the act or process of exciting or state of being excited **2** a means of exciting or cause of excitement **3** the current in a field coil of a generator, motor, etc, or the magnetizing current in a transformer **4** the action of a stimulus on an animal or plant organ, inducing it to respond

excite (ɪk'saɪt) *vb* **excites, exciting, excited** (*tr*) **1** to arouse (a person), esp to pleasurable anticipation or nervous agitation **2** to arouse or elicit (an emotion, response, etc); evoke **3** to cause or bring about; stir up **4** to arouse sexually **5** *physiol* to cause a response in or increase the activity of (an organ, tissue, or part); stimulate **6** to raise (an atom, molecule, etc) from the ground state to a higher energy level **7** to supply electricity to (the coils of a generator or motor) in order to create a magnetic field [C14 from L *excīēre* to stimulate, from *cīēre* to set in motion, rouse] > **ex'citant** *n* > **ex'citative** *or* **ex'citatory** *adj* > **ex'citer** *or* **ex'citor** *n*

excited (ɪk'saɪtɪd) *adj* **1** emotionally aroused, esp to pleasure or agitation **2** characterized by excitement **3** sexually aroused **4** (of an atom, molecule, etc) having an energy level above the ground state > **ex'citedness** *n*

excitement (ɪk'saɪtmənt) *n* **1** the state of being excited **2** a person or thing that excites

exciting (ɪk'saɪtɪŋ) *adj* causing excitement; stirring; stimulating > **ex'citingly** *adv*

exclaim (ɪk'skleɪm) *vb* to cry out or speak suddenly or excitedly, as from surprise, delight, horror, etc [C16 from L *exclāmāre*, from *clāmāre* to shout] > **ex'claimer** *n*

exclamation (,ɛksklə'meɪʃən) *n* **1** an abrupt or excited cry or utterance; ejaculation **2** the act of exclaiming > **,excla'mational** *adj* > **ex'clamatory** *adj*

exclamation mark *or US* **point** *n* **1** the punctuation mark ! used after exclamations and vehement commands **2** this mark used for any other purpose, as to draw attention to an obvious mistake, in road warning signs, etc

exclave ('ɛkskleɪv) *n* a part of a country entirely surrounded by foreign territory: viewed from the position of the home country [C20 from EX-[1] + *-clave*, on the model of ENCLAVE]

exclosure (ɪk'skləʊʒə) *n* an area of land fenced round to keep out unwanted animals

exclude (ɪk'sklu:d) *vb* **excludes, excluding, excluded** (*tr*) **1** to keep out; prevent from entering **2** to bar (someone) from access to or participation in: *to exclude from school* **3** to reject or not consider; leave out **4** to expel forcibly; eject [C14 from L *exclūdere*, from *claudere* to shut] > **ex'cludable** *or* **ex'cludible** *adj* > **ex'cluder** *n*

exclusion (ɪk'sklu:ʒən) *n* the act or an instance of excluding or the state of being excluded > **ex'clusionary** *adj*

exclusion principle *n* See **Pauli exclusion principle**

exclusive (ɪk'sklu:sɪv) *adj* **1** excluding all else; rejecting other considerations, events, etc **2** belonging to a particular individual or group and to no other; not shared **3** belonging to or catering for a privileged minority, esp a fashionable clique **4** (*postpositive*; foll by *to*) limited (to); found only (in) **5** single; unique; only **6** separate and incompatible **7** (*immediately postpositive*) not including the numbers, dates, letters, etc, mentioned **8** (*postpositive*; foll by *of*) except (for); not taking account (of) **9** *logic* (of a disjunction) true if only one rather than both of its component propositions is true ▷ *n* **10** an exclusive story; a story reported in only one newspaper > **ex'clusively** *adv* > **exclusivity** (,ɛksklu:'sɪvɪtɪ) *or* **ex'clusiveness** *n*

exclusive OR circuit *or* **gate** *n electronics* a computer logic circuit having two or more input wires and one output wire and giving a high-voltage output signal if a low-voltage signal is fed to one or more, but not all, of the input wires ▷ Cf **OR circuit**

excommunicate *RC Church* ▷ *vb* (,ɛkskə'mju:nɪ,keɪt), **excommunicates, excommunicating, excommunicated** **1** (*tr*) to sentence (a member of the Church) to exclusion from the communion of believers and from the privileges and public prayers of the Church ▷ *adj* (,ɛkskə'mju:nɪkɪt, -,keɪt) **2** having incurred such a sentence ▷ *n* (,ɛkskə'mju:nɪkɪt, -,keɪt) **3** an excommunicated person [C15 from LL *excommūnicāre*, lit.: to exclude from the community, from L *commūnis* COMMON] > **,excom,muni'cation** *n* > **,excom'muni,cator** *n*

excoriate (ɪk'skɔ:rɪ,eɪt) *vb* **excoriates, excoriating, excoriated** (*tr*) **1** to strip the skin from (a person or animal) **2** to denounce vehemently [C15 from LL *excoriāre* to strip, flay, from L *corium* skin, hide] > **ex,cori'ation** *n*

excrement ('ɛkskrɪmənt) *n* waste matter discharged from the body, esp faeces; excreta [C16 from L *excernere* to sift, EXCRETE] > **excremental** (,ɛkskrɪ'mɛntᵊl) *or* **excrementitious** (,ɛkskrɪmɛn'tɪʃəs) *adj*

excrescence (ɪk'skrɛsᵊns) *n* a projection or protuberance, esp an outgrowth from an organ or part of the body > **ex'crescent** *adj* > **excrescential** (,ɛkskrɪ'sɛnʃəl) *adj*

excreta (ɪk'skri:tə) *pl n* waste matter, such as urine, faeces, or sweat, discharged from the body [C19 NL, from L: see EXCRETE] > **ex'cretal** *adj*

excrete (ɪk'skri:t) *vb* **excretes, excreting, excreted** **1** to discharge (waste matter, such as urine, sweat, or faeces) from the body **2** (of plants) to eliminate (waste matter) through the leaves, roots, etc [C17 from L *excernere* to separate, discharge, from *cernere* to sift] > **ex'creter** *n* > **ex'cretion** *n* > **ex'cretive** *or* **ex'cretory** *adj*

excruciate (ɪk'skru:ʃɪ,eɪt) *vb* **excruciates, excruciating, excruciated** (*tr*) to inflict mental suffering on; torment [C16 from L *excruciāre*, from *cruciāre* to crucify, from *crux* cross]

excruciating (ɪk'skru:ʃɪ,eɪtɪŋ) *adj* **1** unbearably painful; agonizing **2** intense; extreme **3** *inf* irritating; trying **4** *humorous* very bad: *an excruciating pun*

exculpate ('ɛkskʌl,peɪt, ɪk'skʌlpeɪt) *vb* **exculpates, exculpating, exculpated** (*tr*) to free from blame or guilt; vindicate or exonerate [C17 from Med. L, from L EX-[1] + *culpa* fault, blame] > **,excul'pation** *n* > **ex'culpatory** *adj*

excursion (ɪk'skɜ:ʃən, -ʒən) *n* **1** a short outward and return journey, esp for sightseeing, etc; outing **2** a group going on such a journey **3** (*modifier*) of or relating to reduced rates offered on certain journeys by rail: *an excursion ticket* **4** a digression or deviation; diversion **5** (formerly) a raid or attack [C16 from L *excursiō* an attack, from *excurrere* to run out, from *currere* to run] > **ex'cursionist** *n*

excursive (ɪk'skɜ:sɪv) *adj* **1** tending to digress **2** involving detours; rambling [C17 from L *excursus*, from *excurrere* to run forth] > **ex'cursively** *adv* > **ex'cursiveness** *n*

excuse *vb* (ɪk'skju:z), **excuses, excusing, excused** (*tr*) **1** to pardon or forgive **2** to seek pardon or exemption for (a person, esp oneself) **3** to make allowances for: *to excuse someone's ignorance* **4** to serve as an apology or explanation for; justify: *her age excuses her* **5** to exempt from a task, obligation, etc **6** to dismiss or allow to leave **7** to seek permission for (someone, esp oneself) to leave **8** **be excused** *euphemistic* to go to the lavatory **9** **excuse me!** an expression used to catch someone's attention or to apologize for an interruption, disagreement, etc ▷ *n* (ɪk'skju:s) **10** an explanation offered in defence of some fault or as a reason for not fulfilling an obligation, etc **11** *inf* an inferior example of something; makeshift substitute: *she is a poor excuse for a hostess* **12** the act of excusing [C13 from L, from EX-[1] + *causa* cause, accusation] > **ex'cusable** *adj* > **ex'cusableness** *n* > **ex'cusably** *adv*

excuse-me *n* a dance in which a person may take another's partner

ex-directory *adj chiefly Brit* not listed in a telephone directory, by request, and not disclosed to inquirers

ex dividend *adj, adv* without the right to the current dividend: *to quote shares ex dividend*

exeat ('ɛksɪət) *n Brit* **1** leave of absence from school or some other institution **2** a bishop's permission for a priest to leave his diocese in order to take up an appointment elsewhere [C18 L, lit.: he may go out, from *exīre*]

exec. *abbrev for:* **1** executive **2** executor

execrable ('ɛksɪkrəbᵊl) *adj* **1** deserving to be execrated; abhorrent **2** of very poor quality [C14 from L: see EXECRATE] > **'execrableness** *n* > **'execrably** *adv*

execrate ('ɛksɪ,kreɪt) *vb* **execrates, execrating, execrated** **1** (*tr*) to loathe; detest; abhor **2** (*tr*) to denounce; deplore **3** to curse (a person or thing); damn [C16 from L *exsecrārī* to curse, from EX-[1] + *-secrārī* from *sacer* SACRED] > **,exe'cration** *n* > **'exe,crative** *or* **'exe,cratory** *adj*

executable (ɛg'zɛkju:təbᵊl, ɪg-) *adj* **1** (of a computer program) able to be run ▷ *n* **2** a file containing a program that will run as soon as it is opened

execute (ˈɛksɪˌkjuːt) *vb* **executes, executing, executed** (*tr*) **1** to put (a condemned person) to death; inflict capital punishment upon **2** to carry out; complete **3** to perform; accomplish; effect **4** to make or produce: *to execute a drawing* **5** to carry into effect (a judicial sentence, the law, etc) **6** *law* to render (a deed, etc) effective, as by signing, sealing, and delivering **7** to carry out the terms of (a contract, will, etc) [C14 from OF *executer*, back formation from *executeur* EXECUTOR] > **ˈexeˌcutable** *adj* > **executant** (ɪgˈzɛkjʊtənt) *n* > **ˈexeˌcuter** *n*

execution (ˌɛksɪˈkjuːʃən) *n* **1** the act or process of executing **2** the carrying out or undergoing of a sentence of death **3** the style or manner in which something is accomplished or performed; technique **4a** the enforcement of the judgment of a court of law **4b** the writ ordering such enforcement

executioner (ˌɛksɪˈkjuːʃənə) *n* an official charged with carrying out the death sentence passed upon a condemned person

executive (ɪgˈzɛkjʊtɪv) *n* **1** a person or group responsible for the administration of a project, activity, or business **2a** the branch of government responsible for carrying out laws, decrees, etc **2b** any administration ▷ *adj* **3** having the function of carrying plans, orders, laws, etc, into effect **4** of or relating to an executive **5** *inf* very expensive or exclusive: *executive housing* > **exˈecutively** *adv*

Executive Council *n* (in Australia and New Zealand) a body of ministers of the Crown presided over by the governor or governor-general that formally approves cabinet decisions, etc

executive director *n* a member of the board of directors of a company who is also an employee (usually full-time) and who often has a specified area of responsibility, such as finance or production. ▷ Cf **nonexecutive director**

executive officer *n* the second-in-command of any of certain military units

executor (ɪgˈzɛkjʊtə) *n* **1** *law* a person appointed by a testator to carry out his will **2** a person who executes [C14 from Anglo-F *executour*, from L *execūtor*] > **exˌecuˈtorial** *adj* > **exˈecutory** *adj* > **exˈecutorˌship** *n*

executrix (ɪgˈzɛkjʊtrɪks) *n, pl* **executrices** (ɪgˌzɛkjʊˈtraɪsiːz) *or* **executrixes** *law* a female executor

exegesis (ˌɛksɪˈdʒiːsɪs) *n, pl* **exegeses** (-siːz) explanation or critical interpretation of a text, esp of the Bible [C17 from Gk, from *exēgeisthai* to interpret, from EX-[1] + *hēgeisthai* to guide] > **exegetic** (ˌɛksɪˈdʒɛtɪk) *adj*

exegete (ˈɛksɪˌdʒiːt) *or* **exegetist** (ˌɛksɪˈdʒiːtɪst, -ˈdʒɛt-) *n* a person who practises exegesis

exemplar (ɪgˈzɛmplə, -plɑː) *n* **1** a person or thing to be copied or imitated; model **2** a typical specimen or instance; example [C14 from L, from *exemplum* EXAMPLE]

exemplary (ɪgˈzɛmplərɪ) *adj* **1** fit for imitation; model **2** serving as a warning; admonitory **3** representative; typical > **exˈemplarily** *adv* > **exˈemplariness** *n*

exemplary damages *pl n law* damages awarded to a plaintiff above the value of actual loss sustained so that they serve also as a punishment to the defendant

exemplify (ɪgˈzɛmplɪˌfaɪ) *vb* **exemplifies, exemplifying, exemplified** (*tr*) **1** to show by example **2** to serve as an example of **3** *law* to make an official copy of (a document) under seal [C15 via OF from Med. L *exemplificāre*, from L *exemplum* EXAMPLE + *facere* to make] > **exˈempliˌfiable** *adj* > **exˌemplifiˈcation** *n* > **exˈemplifiˌcative** *adj* > **exˈempliˌfier** *n*

exempt (ɪgˈzɛmpt) *vb* **1** (*tr*) to release from an obligation, tax, etc; excuse ▷ *adj* **2a** freed from or not subject to an obligation, tax, etc; excused **2b** (*in combination*): *tax-exempt* ▷ *n* **3** a person who is exempt [C14 from L *exemptus* removed, from *eximere* to take out, from *emere* to buy, obtain] > **exˈemption** *n*

exequies (ˈɛksɪkwɪz) *pl n, sing* **exequy** the rites and ceremonies used at funerals [C14 from L *exequiae* (pl) funeral procession, rites, from *exequī* to follow to the end]

exercise (ˈɛksəˌsaɪz) *vb* **exercises, exercising, exercised** (*mainly tr*) **1** to put into use; employ **2** (*intr*) to take exercise or perform exercises **3** to practise using in order to develop or train **4** to perform or make use of: *to exercise one's rights* **5** to bring to bear: *to exercise one's influence* **6** (*often passive*) to occupy the attentions of, esp so as to worry or vex: *to be exercised about a decision* **7** *mil* to carry out or cause to carry out simulated combat, manoeuvres, etc ▷ *n* **8** physical exertion, esp for development, training, or keeping fit **9** mental or other activity or practice, esp to develop a skill **10** a set of movements, tasks, etc, designed to train, improve, or test one's ability: *piano exercises* **11** a performance or work of art done as practice or to demonstrate a technique **12** the performance of a function: *the exercise of one's rights* **13** (*usually pl*) *mil* a manoeuvre or simulated combat operation **14** *gymnastics* a particular event, such as the horizontal bar [C14 from OF, from L, from *exercēre* to drill, from EX-[1] + *arcēre* to ward off] > **ˈexerˌcisable** *adj* > **ˈexerˌciser** *n*

exercise bike *or* **cycle** *n* a stationary exercise machine that is pedalled like a bicycle as a method of increasing cardiovascular fitness

exercise book *n* a notebook used by pupils and students

exercise price *n stock exchange* the price at which the holder of a traded option may exercise his right to buy (or sell) a security

exert (ɪgˈzɜːt) *vb* (*tr*) **1** to use (influence, authority, etc) forcefully or effectively **2** to apply (oneself) diligently; make a strenuous effort [C17 (in the sense: push forth, emit): from L *exserere* to thrust out, from EX-[1] + *serere* to bind together, entwine] > **exˈertion** *n* > **exˈertive** *adj*

Ee

Exeter (ˈɛksɪtə) *n* a city in SW England, administrative centre of Devon; university (1955). Pop: 94 717 (1991)

exeunt (ˈɛksɪˌʌnt) *Latin* they go out: used as a stage direction

exeunt omnes (ˈɒmneɪz) *Latin* they all go out: used as a stage direction

exfoliate (ɛksˈfəʊlɪˌeɪt) *vb* **exfoliates, exfoliating, exfoliated** (of bark, skin, minerals, etc) to peel off in layers, flakes, or scales [C17 from LL *exfoliāre* to strip off leaves, from L *folium* leaf] > **exˌfoliˈation** *n* > **exˈfoliative** *adj*

ex gratia (ˈgreɪʃə) *adj* given as a favour or gratuitously where no legal obligation exists: *an ex gratia payment* [NL, lit.: out of kindness]

exhale (ɛksˈheɪl, ɪgˈzeɪl) *vb* **exhales, exhaling, exhaled** **1** to expel (breath, smoke, etc) from the lungs; breathe out **2** to give off (air, fumes, etc) or (of air, etc) to be given off [C14 from L *exhālāre*, from *hālāre* to breathe] > **exˈhalable** *adj* > **ˌexhaˈlation** *n*

exhaust (ɪgˈzɔːst) *vb* (*mainly tr*) **1** to drain the energy of; tire out **2** to deprive of resources, etc **3** to deplete totally; consume **4** to empty (a container) by drawing off or pumping out (the contents) **5** to develop or discuss thoroughly so that no further interest remains **6** to remove gas from (a vessel, etc) in order to reduce pressure or create a vacuum **7** (*intr*) (of steam or other gases) to be emitted or to escape from an engine after being expanded ▷ *n* **8** gases ejected from an engine as waste products **9** the expulsion of expanded gas or steam from an engine **10a** the parts of an engine through which exhausted gases or steam pass **10b** (*as modifier*): *exhaust pipe* [C16 from L *exhaustus* made empty, from *exhaurīre* to draw out, from *haurīre* to draw, drain] > **exˈhausted** *adj* > **exˈhaustible** *adj* > **exˈhausting** *adj*

exhaustion (ɪgˈzɔːstʃən) *n* **1** extreme tiredness; fatigue **2** the condition of being used up **3** the act of exhausting or the state of being exhausted

exhaustive (ɪg'zɔːstɪv) *adj* **1** comprehensive; thorough **2** tending to exhaust > **ex'haustively** *adv* > **ex'haustiveness** *n*

exhibit (ɪg'zɪbɪt) *vb* (*mainly tr*) **1** (*also intr*) to display (something) to the public **2** to manifest; display; show **3** *law* to produce (a document or object) in court as evidence ▷ *n* **4** an object or collection exhibited to the public **5** *law* a document or object produced in court as evidence [C15 from L *exhibēre* to hold forth, from *habēre* to have] > **ex'hibitor** *n* > **ex'hibitory** *adj*

exhibition (ˌɛksɪ'bɪʃən) *n* **1** a public display of art, skills, etc **2** the act of exhibiting or the state of being exhibited **3 make an exhibition of oneself** to behave so foolishly that one excites notice or ridicule **4** *Brit* an allowance or scholarship awarded to a student at a university or school

exhibitioner (ˌɛksɪ'bɪʃənə) *n* *Brit* a student who has been awarded an exhibition

exhibitionism (ˌɛksɪ'bɪʃəˌnɪzəm) *n* **1** a compulsive desire to attract attention to oneself, esp by exaggerated behaviour **2** a compulsive desire to expose one's genital organs publicly > ˌ**exhi'bitionist** *n* > ˌ**exhiˌbition'istic** *adj*

exhibitive (ɪg'zɪbɪtɪv) *adj* (*usually postpositive* and foll by *of*) illustrative or demonstrative

exhilarate (ɪg'zɪləˌreɪt) *vb* **exhilarates, exhilarating, exhilarated** (*tr*) to make lively and cheerful; elate [C16 from L *exhilarāre*, from *hilarāre* to cheer] > **exˌhila'ration** *n* > **ex'hilarative** *adj*

exhilarating (ɪg'zɪləˌreɪtɪŋ) *adj* causing strong feelings of excitement and happiness: *an exhilarating helicopter trip* > **ex'hilaˌratingly** *adv*

exhort (ɪg'zɔːt) *vb* to urge or persuade (someone) earnestly; advise strongly [C14 from L *exhortārī*, from *hortārī* to urge] > **ex'hortative** *or* **ex'hortatory** *adj* > ˌ**exhor'tation** *n* > **ex'horter** *n*

exhume (ɛks'hjuːm) *vb* **exhumes, exhuming, exhumed** (*tr*) **1** to dig up (something buried, esp a corpse); disinter **2** to reveal; disclose [C18 from Med. L, from L EX-[1] + *humāre* to bury, from *humus* the ground] > **exhumation** (ˌɛkshjʊ'meɪʃən) *n* > **ex'humer** *n*

ex hypothesi (ɛks haɪ'pɒθəsɪ) *adv* in accordance with the hypothesis stated [C17 NL]

exigency ('ɛksɪdʒənsɪ, ɪg'zɪdʒənsɪ) *or* **exigence** ('ɛksɪdʒəns) *n, pl* **exigencies** *or* **exigences** **1** urgency **2** (*often pl*) an urgent demand; pressing requirement **3** an emergency

exigent ('ɛksɪdʒənt) *adj* **1** urgent; pressing **2** exacting; demanding [C15 from L *exigere* to drive out, weigh out, from *agere* to drive, compel]

exiguous (ɪg'zɪgjʊəs, ɪk'sɪg-) *adj* scanty or slender; meagre [C17 from L *exiguus*, from *exigere* to weigh out; see EXIGENT] > **exiguity** (ˌɛksɪ'gjuːɪtɪ) *or* **ex'iguousness** *n*

exile ('ɛgzaɪl, 'ɛksaɪl) *n* **1** a prolonged, usually enforced absence from one's home or country **2** the official expulsion of a person from his or her native land **3** a person banished or living away from his or her home or country; expatriate ▷ *vb* **exiles, exiling, exiled** **4** (*tr*) to expel from home or country, esp by official decree; banish [C13 from L *exsilium* banishment, from *exsul* banished person] > **exilic** (ɛg'zɪlɪk, ɛk'sɪlɪk) *adj*

exist (ɪg'zɪst) *vb* (*intr*) **1** to have being or reality; be **2** to eke out a living; stay alive **3** to be living; live **4** to be present under specified conditions or in a specified place [C17 from L *exsistere* to step forth, from EX-[1] + *sistere* to stand] > **ex'istent** *adj* > **ex'isting** *adj*

USAGE See at **extant**

existence (ɪg'zɪstəns) *n* **1** the fact or state of existing; being **2** the continuance or maintenance of life; living, esp in adverse circumstances **3** something that exists; a being or entity **4** everything that exists

existential (ˌɛgzɪ'stɛnʃəl) *adj* **1** of or relating to existence, esp human existence **2** *philosophy* known by experience rather than reason **3** of a formula or proposition asserting the existence of at least one object fulfilling a given condition **4** of or relating to existentialism

existentialism (ˌɛgzɪ'stɛnʃəˌlɪzəm) *n* a modern philosophical movement stressing personal experience and responsibility and their demands on the individual, who is seen as a free agent in a deterministic and seemingly meaningless universe > ˌ**exis'tentialist** *adj, n*

▷ http://tameri.com/csw/exist/
▷ http://connect.net/ron/exist.html
▷ http://thecry.com/existentialism/

exit ('ɛgzɪt, 'ɛksɪt) *n* **1** a way out **2** the act or an instance of going out **3a** the act of leaving or right to leave a particular place **3b** (*as modifier*): *an exit visa* **4** departure from life; death **5** *theatre* the act of going offstage **6** *Brit* a point at which vehicles may leave or join a motorway ▷ *vb* **exits, exiting, exited** **7** (*intr*) to go away or out; depart **8** (*intr*) *theatre* to go offstage: used as a stage direction: *exit Hamlet* **9** *computing* to leave (a computer program or system) [C17 from L *exitus* a departure, from *exīre* to go out, from EX-[1] + *īre* to go]

exitance ('ɛksɪtəns) *n* a measure of the ability of a surface to emit radiation [C20 from EXIT + -ANCE]

exit poll *n* a poll taken by asking people how they voted in an election as they leave a polling station

exit strategy *n* a method or plan for extricating oneself from an undesirable situation

ex libris (ɛks 'liːbrɪs) *prep* **1** from the collection or library of ▷ *n* **ex-libris**, *pl* **ex-libris** **2** a bookplate bearing the owner's name, coat of arms, etc [C19 from L, lit.: from the books (of)]

Exmoor ('ɛksˌmʊə, -ˌmɔː) *n* **1** a high moorland in SW England, in W Somerset and N Devon: chiefly grazing ground for Exmoor ponies, sheep, and red deer **2** a small stocky breed of pony with a fawn-coloured nose, originally from Exmoor

Exmouth ('ɛksməθ) *n* a town in SW England, in Devon, at the mouth of the River Exe: tourism, fishing. Pop: 28 414 (1991)

ex new *adv, adj* (of shares, etc) without the right to take up any scrip issue or rights issue ▷ **cum new**

exo- *combining form* external, outside, or beyond: *exothermal* [from Gk *exō* outside]

exobiology (ˌɛksəʊbaɪ'ɒlədʒɪ) *n* another name for **astrobiology** > ˌ**exobi'ologist** *n*

exocarp ('ɛksəʊˌkɑːp) *n* another name for **epicarp**

exocrine ('ɛksəʊˌkraɪn, -krɪn) *adj* **1** of or relating to exocrine glands or their secretions ▷ *n* **2** an exocrine gland [C20 EXO- + *-crine* from Gk *krinein* to separate]

exocrine gland *n* any gland, such as a salivary or sweat gland, that secretes its products through a duct onto an epithelial surface

Exod. *Bible abbrev for* Exodus

exodus ('ɛksədəs) *n* the act or an instance of going out [C17 via L from Gk *exodos*, from EX-[1] + *hodos* way]

Exodus ('ɛksədəs) *n* **1 the** the departure of the Israelites from Egypt **2** the second book of the Old Testament, recounting the events connected with this

ex officio ('ɛks ə'fɪʃɪəʊ, ə'fɪsɪəʊ) *adv, adj* by right of position or office [L]

exogamy (ɛk'sɒgəmɪ) *n* *anthropol, sociol* marriage outside one's own tribe or similar unit > **ex'ogamous** *or* **exogamic** (ˌɛksəʊ'gæmɪk) *adj*

exogenous (ɛk'sɒdʒɪnəs) *adj* **1** having an external origin **2** *biol* **2a** originating outside an organism **2b** of or relating to external factors, such as light, that influence an organism **3** *psychiatry* (of a mental illness) caused by external factors

exon ('ɛksɒn) *n* *Brit* one of the four officers who command the Yeomen of the Guard [C17 a pronunciation spelling of F *exempt* EXEMPT]

exonerate (ɪɡˈzɒnəˌreɪt) *vb* **exonerates, exonerating, exonerated** (*tr*) **1** to absolve from blame or a criminal charge **2** to relieve from an obligation [C16 from L *exonerāre* to free from a burden, from *onus* a burden] > **exˌonerˈation** *n* > **exˈonerative** *adj* > **exˈonerˌator** *n*

exophthalmos (ˌɛksɒfˈθælmɒs), **exophthalmus** (ˌɛksɒfˈθælməs), *or* **exophthalmia** (ˌɛksɒfˈθælmɪə) *n* abnormal protrusion of the eyeball, as caused by hyperthyroidism [C19 via NL from Gk, from EX-[1] + *ophthalmos* eye] > ˌ**exophˈthalmic** *adj*

exorbitant (ɪɡˈzɔːbɪtᵊnt) *adj* (of prices, demands, etc) excessive; extravagant; immoderate [C15 from LL *exorbitāre* to deviate, from L *orbita* track] > **exˈorbitance** *n* > **exˈorbitantly** *adv*

exorcize *or* **exorcise** (ˈɛksɔːˌsaɪz) *vb* **exorcizes, exorcizing, exorcized** *or* **exorcises, exorcising, exorcised** (*tr*) to expel (evil spirits) from (a person or place), by adjurations and religious rites [C15 from LL, from Gk, from EX-[1] + *horkizein* to adjure] > ˈ**exorcism** *n* > ˈ**exorcist** *n* > ˈ**exorˌcizer** *or* ˈ**exorˌciser** *n*

exordium (ɛkˈsɔːdɪəm) *n, pl* **exordiums** *or* **exordia** (-dɪə) an introductory part or beginning, esp of an oration or discourse [C16 from L, from *exōrdīrī* to begin, from *ōrdīrī* to begin] > **exˈordial** *adj*

exoskeleton (ˌɛksəʊˈskɛlɪtᵊn) *n* the protective or supporting structure covering the outside of the body of many animals, such as the thick cuticle of arthropods > ˌ**exoˈskeletal** *adj*

exosphere (ˈɛksəʊˌsfɪə) *n* the outermost layer of the earth's atmosphere. It extends from about 400 kilometres above the earth's surface

exothermic (ˌɛksəʊˈθɜːmɪk) *or* **exothermal** *adj* (of a chemical reaction or compound) occurring or formed with the evolution of heat > ˌ**exoˈthermically** *or* ˌ**exoˈthermally** *adv*

exotic (ɪɡˈzɒtɪk) *adj* **1** originating in a foreign country, esp one in the tropics; not native: *an exotic plant* **2** having a strange or bizarre allure, beauty, or quality ▷ *n* **3** an exotic person or thing [C16 from L, from Gk *exōtikos* foreign, from *exō* outside] > **exˈotically** *adv* > **exˈotiˌcism** *n* > **exˈoticness** *n*

exotica (ɪɡˈzɒtɪkə) *pl n* exotic objects, esp when forming a collection [C19 L, neuter pl of *exōticus*; see EXOTIC]

exotic dancer *n* a striptease or belly dancer

expand (ɪkˈspænd) *vb* **1** to make or become greater in extent, volume, size, or scope **2** to spread out; unfold; stretch out **3** (*intr; often foll by on*) to enlarge or expatiate (on a story, topic, etc) **4** (*intr*) to become increasingly relaxed, friendly, or talkative **5** *maths* to express (a function or expression) as the sum or product of terms [C15 from L *expandere* to spread out] > **exˈpandable** *adj*

expanded (ɪkˈspændɪd) *adj* (of a plastic) having been foamed during manufacture by a gas to make a light packaging material or heat insulator: *expanded polystyrene*

expanded metal *n* an open mesh of metal used for reinforcing brittle or friable materials and in fencing

expander (ɪkˈspændə) *n* **1** a device for exercising and developing the muscles of the body **2** an electronic device for increasing the variations in signal amplitude in a transmission system according to a specified law

expanse (ɪkˈspæns) *n* **1** an uninterrupted surface of something that extends, esp over a wide area; stretch **2** expansion or extension [C17 from NL *expansum* the heavens, from L *expansus* spread out, from *expandere* to expand]

expansible (ɪkˈspænsəbᵊl) *adj* able to expand or be expanded > **exˌpansiˈbility** *n*

expansion (ɪkˈspænʃən) *n* **1** the act of expanding or the state of being expanded **2** something expanded **3** the degree or amount by which something expands **4** an increase or development, esp in the activities of a company **5** the increase in the dimensions of a body or substance when subjected to an increase in temperature, internal pressure, etc > **exˈpansionary** *adj*

expansionism (ɪkˈspænʃəˌnɪzəm) *n* the doctrine or practice of expanding the economy or territory of a country > **exˈpansionist** *n, adj* > **exˌpansionˈistic** *adj*

expansive (ɪkˈspænsɪv) *adj* **1** able or tending to expand or characterized by expansion **2** wide; extensive **3** friendly, open, or talkative **4** grand or extravagant > **exˈpansiveness** *n*

expansivity (ˌɛkspænˈsɪvɪtɪ) *n* the fractional increase in length or volume of a substance or body on being heated through a one degree rise in temperature; coefficient of expansion

ex parte (ɛks ˈpɑːtɪ) *adj law* (of an application in a judicial proceeding) on behalf of one side or party only: *an ex parte injunction*

expat (ˌɛksˈpæt) *n, adj inf* short for **expatriate**

expatiate (ɪkˈspeɪʃɪˌeɪt) *vb* **expatiates, expatiating, expatiated** (*intr*) **1** (foll by *on* or *upon*) to enlarge (on a theme, topic, etc); elaborate (on) **2** *rare* to wander about [C16 from L *exspatiārī* to digress, from *spatiārī* to walk about] > **exˌpatiˈation** *n* > **exˈpatiˌator** *n*

expatriate *adj* (ɛksˈpætrɪɪt, -ˌeɪt) **1** resident outside one's native country **2** exiled or banished from one's native country ▷ *n* (ɛksˈpætrɪɪt, -ˌeɪt) **3** a person living outside his native country **4** an exile; expatriate person ▷ *vb* (ɛksˈpætrɪˌeɪt), **expatriates, expatriating, expatriated** (*tr*) **5** to exile (oneself) from one's native country or cause (another) to go into exile [C18 from Med. L, from L EX-[1] + *patria* native land] > **exˌpatriˈation** *n*

expect (ɪkˈspɛkt) *vb* (*tr; may take a clause as object or an infinitive*) **1** to regard as likely; anticipate **2** to look forward to or be waiting for **3** to decide that (something) is necessary; require: *the teacher expects us to work late* ▷ See also **expecting** [C16 from L *exspectāre* to watch for, from *spectāre* to look at] > **exˈpectable** *adj*

expectancy (ɪkˈspɛktənsɪ) *or* **expectance** *n* **1** something expected, esp on the basis of a norm or average: *his life expectancy was 30 years* **2** anticipation; expectation **3** the prospect of a future interest or possession

expectant (ɪkˈspɛktənt) *adj* **1** expecting, anticipating, or hopeful **2** having expectations, esp of possession of something **3** pregnant ▷ *n* **4** a person who expects something > **exˈpectantly** *adv*

expectation (ˌɛkspɛkˈteɪʃən) *n* **1** the act or state of expecting or the state of being expected **2** (*usually pl*) something looked forward to, whether feared or hoped for **3** an attitude of expectancy or hope **4** *statistics* **4a** the numerical probability that an event will occur **4b** another term for **expected value**

expected frequency *n statistics* the number of occasions on which an event may be presumed to occur on average in a given number of trials

expected value *n statistics* the sum or integral of all possible values of a random variable, or any given function of it, multiplied by the respective probabilities of the values of the variable

expecting (ɪkˈspɛktɪŋ) *adj inf* pregnant

expectorant (ɪkˈspɛktərənt) *med* ▷ *adj* **1** promoting the secretion, liquefaction, or expulsion of sputum from the respiratory passages ▷ *n* **2** an expectorant drug or agent

expectorate (ɪkˈspɛktəˌreɪt) *vb* **expectorates, expectorating, expectorated** to cough up and spit out (sputum from the respiratory passages) [C17 from L *expectorāre*, lit.: to drive from the breast, expel, from *pectus* breast] > **exˌpectoˈration** *n* > **exˈpectoˌrator** *n*

expediency (ɪkˈspiːdɪənsɪ) *or* **expedience** *n, pl* **expediencies** *or* **expediences** **1** appropriateness; suitability **2** the use of or inclination towards methods that are advantageous rather than fair or just **3** another word for **expedient** (sense 3)

Ee

expedient (ɪk'spiːdɪənt) *adj* **1** suitable to the circumstances; appropriate **2** inclined towards methods that are advantageous rather than fair or just ▷ *n* also **expediency 3** something suitable or appropriate, esp during an urgent situation [C14 from L *expediēns* setting free; see EXPEDITE]

expedite ('ɛkspɪˌdaɪt) *vb* **expedites, expediting, expedited** (*tr*) **1** to hasten or assist the progress of **2** to do or process with speed and efficiency [C17 from L *expedīre*, lit.: to free the feet (as from a snare), hence, liberate, from EX-[1] + *pēs* foot] > **'expeˌditer** *or* **'expeˌditor** *n*

expedition (ˌɛkspɪ'dɪʃən) *n* **1** an organized journey or voyage, esp for exploration or for a scientific or military purpose **2** the people and equipment comprising an expedition **3** promptness; dispatch [C15 from L *expedīre* to prepare, EXPEDITE] > **ˌexpe'ditionary** *adj*

expeditious (ˌɛkspɪ'dɪʃəs) *adj* characterized by or done with speed and efficiency; prompt; quick > **ˌexpe'ditiously** *adv* > **ˌexpe'ditiousness** *n*

expel (ɪk'spɛl) *vb* **expels, expelling, expelled** (*tr*) **1** to eject or drive out with force **2** to deprive of participation in or membership of a school, club, etc [C14 from L *expellere* to drive out, from *pellere* to thrust, drive] > **ex'pellable** *adj* > **expellee** (ˌɛkspɛ'liː) *n* > **ex'peller** *n*

expellant *or* **expellent** (ɪk'spɛlənt) *adj* **1** forcing out or able to force out ▷ *n* **2** a medicine used to expel undesirable substances or organisms from the body

expend (ɪk'spɛnd) *vb* (*tr*) **1** to spend; disburse **2** to consume or use up [C15 from L *expendere*, from *pendere* to weigh] > **ex'pender** *n*

expendable (ɪk'spɛndəbᵊl) *adj* **1** that may be expended or used up **2** able to be sacrificed to achieve an objective, esp a military one ▷ *n* **3** something expendable > **exˌpenda'bility** *n*

expenditure (ɪk'spɛndɪtʃə) *n* **1** something expended, esp money **2** the act of expending

expense (ɪk'spɛns) *n* **1** a particular payment of money; expenditure **2** money needed for individual purchases; cost; charge **3** (*pl*) money spent in the performance of a job, etc, usually reimbursed by an employer or allowable against tax **4** something requiring money for its purchase or upkeep **5 at the expense of** to the detriment of [C14 from LL, from L *expēnsus* weighed out; see EXPEND]

expense account *n* **1** an arrangement by which an employee's expenses are refunded by his employer or deducted from his income for tax purposes **2** a record of such expenses

expensive (ɪk'spɛnsɪv) *adj* high-priced; costly; dear > **ex'pensiveness** *n*

experience (ɪk'spɪərɪəns) *n* **1** direct personal participation or observation **2** a particular incident, feeling, etc, that a person has undergone **3** accumulated knowledge, esp of practical matters ▷ *vb* **experiences, experiencing, experienced** (*tr*) **4** to participate in or undergo **5** to be moved by; feel [C14 from L *experīrī* to prove; rel. to L *perīculum* PERIL] > **ex'perienceable** *adj*

experienced (ɪk'spɪərɪənst) *adj* having become skilful or knowledgeable from extensive participation or observation

experiential (ɪkˌspɪərɪ'ɛnʃəl) *adj philosophy* relating to or derived from experience; empirical

experiment *n* (ɪk'spɛrɪmənt) **1** a test or investigation, esp one planned to provide evidence for or against a hypothesis **2** the act of conducting such an investigation or test; research **3** an attempt at something new or original ▷ *vb* (ɪk'spɛrɪˌmɛnt) **4** (*intr*) to make an experiment or experiments [C14 from L *experīmentum* proof, trial, from *experīrī* to test; see EXPERIENCE] > **ex'periˌmenter** *n*

experimental (ɪkˌspɛrɪ'mɛntᵊl) *adj* **1** relating to, based on, or having the nature of experiment **2** based on or derived from experience; empirical **3** tending to experiment **4** tentative or provisional > **exˌperi'mentalism** *n*

experimentation (ɪkˌspɛrɪmɛn'teɪʃən) *n* the act, process, or practice of experimenting

expert ('ɛkspɜːt) *n* **1** a person who has extensive skill or knowledge in a particular field ▷ *adj* **2** skilful or knowledgeable **3** of, involving, or done by an expert: *an expert job* [C14 from L *expertus* known by experience; see EXPERIENCE] > **'expertly** *adv* > **'expertness** *n*

expertise (ˌɛkspɜː'tiːz) *n* special skill, knowledge, or judgment; expertness [C19 from F: expert skill, from EXPERT]

expiate ('ɛkspɪˌeɪt) *vb* **expiates, expiating, expiated** (*tr*) to atone for (sin or wrongdoing); make amends for [C16 from L *expiāre*, from *pius* dutiful; see PIOUS] > **'expiable** *adj* > **ˌexpi'ation** *n* > **'expiˌator** *n*

expiatory ('ɛkspɪətərɪ, -trɪ) *adj* **1** capable of making expiation **2** offered in expiation

expiration (ˌɛkspɪ'reɪʃən) *n* **1** the finish of something; expiry **2** the act, process, or sound of breathing out

expire (ɪk'spaɪə) *vb* **expires, expiring, expired 1** (*intr*) to finish or run out; come to an end **2** to breathe out (air) **3** (*intr*) to die [C15 from OF, from L *exspīrāre* to breathe out, from *spīrāre* to breathe] > **ex'pirer** *n*

expiry (ɪk'spaɪərɪ) *n, pl* **expiries 1a** a coming to an end, esp of a contract period; termination **1b** (*as modifier*): *the expiry date* **2** death

explain (ɪk'spleɪn) *vb* **1** (when *tr, may take a clause as object*) to make (something) comprehensible, esp by giving a clear and detailed account of it **2** (*tr*) to justify or attempt to justify (oneself) by reasons for one's actions [C15 from L *explānāre* to flatten, from *plānus* level] > **ex'plainable** *adj* > **ex'plainer** *n*

explain away *vb* (*tr, adv*) to offer excuses or reasons for (bad conduct, mistakes, etc)

explanation (ˌɛksplə'neɪʃən) *n* **1** the act or process of explaining **2** something that explains **3** a clarification of disputed points

explanatory (ɪk'splænətərɪ, -trɪ) *or* **explanative** *adj* serving or intended to serve as an explanation > **ex'planatorily** *adv*

expletive (ɪk'spliːtɪv) *n* **1** an exclamation or swearword; an oath or sound expressing emotion rather than meaning **2** any syllable, word, or phrase conveying no independent meaning, esp one inserted in verse for the sake of metre ▷ *adj also* **expletory** (ɪk'spliːtərɪ, -trɪ) **3** without particular meaning, esp when filling out a line of verse [C17 from LL *explētīvus* for filling out, from *explēre*, from *plēre* to fill]

explicable ('ɛksplɪkəbᵊl, ɪk'splɪk-) *adj* capable of being explained

explicate ('ɛksplɪˌkeɪt) *vb* **explicates, explicating, explicated** (*tr*) *formal* **1** to make clear or explicit; explain **2** to formulate or develop (a theory, hypothesis, etc) [C16 from L *explicāre* to unfold] > **ˌexpli'cation** *n*

explicit (ɪk'splɪsɪt) *adj* **1** precisely and clearly expressed, leaving nothing to implication; fully stated **2** leaving little to the imagination; graphically detailed **3** openly expressed without reservations; unreserved [C17 from L *explicitus* unfolded] > **ex'plicitly** *adv* > **ex'plicitness** *n*

explode (ɪk'spləʊd) *vb* **explodes, exploding, exploded 1** to burst or cause to burst with great violence, esp through detonation of an explosive; blow up **2** to destroy or be destroyed in this manner **3** (of a gas) to undergo or cause (a gas) to undergo a sudden violent expansion, as a result of a fast exothermic chemical or nuclear reaction **4** (*intr*) to react suddenly or violently with emotion, etc **5** (*intr*) (esp of a population) to increase rapidly **6** (*tr*) to show (a theory, etc) to be baseless [C16 from L *explōdere* to drive off by clapping] > **ex'ploder** *n*

exploded view *n* a drawing or photograph of a mechanism that shows its parts separately, usually indicating their relative positions

exploit *n* ('ɛksplɔɪt) **1** a notable deed or feat, esp one that is heroic ▷ *vb* (ɪk'splɔɪt) *(tr)* **2** to take advantage of (a person, situation, etc) for one's own ends **3** to make the best use of [C14 from OF: accomplishment, from L *explicitum* (something) unfolded, from *explicāre* to EXPLICATE] > **ex'ploitable** *adj* > **ˌexploi'tation** *n* > **ex'ploitive** *or* **ex'ploitative** *adj*

exploration (ˌɛksplə'reɪʃən) *n* **1** the act or process of exploring **2** an organized trip into unfamiliar regions, esp for scientific purposes > **exploratory** (ɪk'splɒrətərɪ, -trɪ) *or* **ex'plorative** *adj*

explore (ɪk'splɔː) *vb* **explores, exploring, explored** **1** *(tr)* to examine or investigate, esp systematically **2** to travel into (unfamiliar regions), esp for scientific purposes **3** *(tr) med* to examine (an organ or part) for diagnostic purposes [C16 from L, from EX-[1] + *plōrāre* to cry aloud; prob. from the shouts of hunters sighting prey] > **ex'plorer** *n*

explosion (ɪk'spləʊʒən) *n* **1** the act or an instance of exploding **2** a violent release of energy resulting from a rapid chemical or nuclear reaction **3** a sudden or violent outburst of activity, noise, emotion, etc **4** a rapid increase, esp in a population [C17 from L *explōsiō*, from *explōdere* to EXPLODE]

explosive (ɪk'spləʊsɪv) *adj* **1** of, involving, or characterized by explosion **2** capable of exploding or tending to explode **3** potentially violent or hazardous: *an explosive situation* ▷ *n* **4** a substance capable of exploding or tending to explode > **ex'plosiveness** *n*

expo ('ɛkspəʊ) *n, pl* **expos** short for **exposition** (sense 3)

exponent (ɪk'spəʊnənt) *n* **1** (usually foll by *of*) a person or thing that acts as an advocate (of an idea, cause, etc) **2** a person or thing that explains or interprets **3** a performer or artist **4** Also called: **power, index** *maths* a number or variable placed as a superscript to another number or quantity to indicate the number of times the designated number or quantity should appear in a repeated multiplication, as in $x^3 = x \times x \times x$, where 3 is the exponent ▷ *adj* **5** offering a declaration, explanation, or interpretation [C16 from L *expōnere* to set out, expound]

exponential (ˌɛkspəʊ'nɛnʃəl) *adj* **1** *maths* (of a function, curve, etc) of or involving numbers or quantities raised to an exponent, esp e^x **2** *maths* raised to the power of e, the base of natural logarithms **3** of or involving an exponent or exponents **4** *inf* very rapid ▷ *n* **5** *maths* an exponential function, etc

exponential distribution *n statistics* a continuous single-parameter distribution used esp when making statements about the length of life of materials or times between random events

export *n* ('ɛkspɔːt) **1** *(often pl)* **1a** goods (**visible exports**) or services (**invisible exports**) sold to a foreign country or countries **1b** *(as modifier)*: *an export licence* ▷ *vb* (ɪk'spɔːt, 'ɛkspɔːt) **2** to sell (goods or services) or ship (goods) to a foreign country **3** *(tr)* to transmit or spread (an idea, institution, etc) abroad [C15 from L *exportāre* to carry away] > **ex'portable** *adj* > **exˌporta'bility** *n* > **ˌexpor'tation** *n* > **ex'porter** *n*

export reject *n* an article that fails to meet a standard of quality required for export and that is sold on the home market

expose (ɪk'spəʊz) *vb* **exposes, exposing, exposed** *(tr)* **1** to display for viewing; exhibit **2** to bring to public notice; disclose **3** to divulge the identity of; unmask **4** (foll by *to*) to make subject or susceptible (to attack, criticism, etc) **5** to abandon (a child, etc) in the open to die **6** (foll by *to*) to introduce (to) or acquaint (with) **7** *photog* to subject (a film or plate) to light, X-rays, etc **8** **expose oneself** to display one's sexual organs in public [C15 from OF *exposer*, from L *expōnere* to set out] > **ex'posable** *adj* > **ex'posal** *n* > **ex'poser** *n*

exposé (ɛks'pəʊzeɪ) *n* the act or an instance of bringing a scandal, crime, etc, to public notice

exposed (ɪk'spəʊzd) *adj* **1** not concealed; displayed for viewing **2** without shelter from the elements **3** susceptible to attack or criticism; vulnerable

exposition (ˌɛkspə'zɪʃən) *n* **1** a systematic, usually written statement about or explanation of a subject **2** the act of expounding or setting forth information or a viewpoint **3** a large public exhibition, esp of industrial products or arts and crafts **4** the act of exposing or the state of being exposed **5** *music* the first statement of the subjects or themes of a movement in sonata form or a fugue **6** *RC Church* the exhibiting of the consecrated Eucharistic Host or a relic for public veneration [C14 from L *expositiō* a setting forth, from *expōnere* to display] > **ˌexpo'sitional** *adj*

expositor (ɪk'spɒzɪtə) *n* a person who expounds

expository (ɪk'spɒzɪtərɪ, -trɪ) *or* **expositive** *adj* of or involving exposition; explanatory

ex post facto (ɛks pəʊst 'fæktəʊ) *adj* having retrospective effect [C17 from L *ex* from + *post* afterwards + *factus* done, from *facere* to do]

expostulate (ɪk'spɒstjʊˌleɪt) *vb* **expostulates, expostulating, expostulated** *(intr; usually foll by with)* to argue or reason (with), esp in order to dissuade [C16 from L *expostulāre* to require, from *postulāre* to demand; see POSTULATE] > **exˌpostu'lation** *n* > **ex'postuˌlator** *n*

exposure (ɪk'spəʊʒə) *n* **1** the act of exposing or the condition of being exposed **2** the position or outlook of a house, building, etc: *a southern exposure* **3** lack of shelter from the weather, esp the cold **4** a surface that is exposed **5** *photog* **5a** the act of exposing a film or plate to light, X-rays, etc **5b** an area on a film or plate that has been exposed **6** *photog* **6a** the intensity of light falling on a film or plate multiplied by the time for which it is exposed **6b** a combination of lens aperture and shutter speed used in taking a photograph **7** appearance before the public, as in a theatre, on television, etc

exposure meter *n photog* an instrument for measuring the intensity of light so that suitable camera settings can be determined. Also called: **light meter**

expound (ɪk'spaʊnd) *vb* (when *intr*, foll by *on* or *about*) to explain or set forth (an argument, theory, etc) in detail [C13 from OF, from L *expōnere* to set forth, from *pōnere* to put] > **ex'pounder** *n*

express (ɪk'sprɛs) *vb (tr)* **1** to transform (ideas) into words; utter; verbalize **2** to show or reveal **3** to communicate (emotion, etc) without words, as through music, painting, etc **4** to indicate through a symbol, formula, etc **5** to squeeze out: *to express the juice from an orange* **6** **express oneself** to communicate one's thoughts or ideas ▷ *adj (prenominal)* **7** clearly indicated; explicitly stated **8** done or planned for a definite reason; particular **9** of or designed for rapid transportation of people, mail, etc: *express delivery* ▷ *n* **10a** a system for sending mail, money, etc, rapidly **10b** mail, etc, conveyed by such a system **10c** *chiefly US & Canad* an enterprise operating such a system **11** Also: **express train** a fast train stopping at no or only a few stations between its termini ▷ *adv* **12** by means of express delivery [C14 from L *expressus*, lit.: squeezed out, hence, prominent, from *exprimere* to force out, from EX-[1] + *premere* to press] > **ex'presser** *n* > **ex'pressible** *adj*

expression (ɪk'sprɛʃən) *n* **1** the act or an instance of transforming ideas into words **2** a manifestation of an emotion, feeling, etc, without words **3** communication of emotion through music, painting, etc **4** a look on the face that indicates mood or emotion **5** the choice of words, intonation, etc, in communicating **6** a particular phrase used conventionally to express something **7** the act or process of squeezing out a liquid **8** *maths* a variable, function, or some combination of these > **ex'pressional** *adj* > **ex'pressionless** *adj*

Ee

expressionism (ɪkˈsprɛʃəˌnɪzəm) *n* (*sometimes cap*) an artistic and literary movement originating in the early 20th century, which sought to express emotions rather than to represent external reality: characterized by symbolism and distortion > **exˈpressionist** *n, adj* > **exˌpressionˈistic** *adj*
▷ www.artlex.com/ArtLex/e/Expressionism.html
▷ www.ibiblio.org/wm/paint/tl/20th/expressionism.html

expression mark *n* one of a set of musical directions, usually in Italian, indicating how a piece or passage is to be performed

expressive (ɪkˈsprɛsɪv) *adj* **1** of, involving, or full of expression **2** (*postpositive; foll by of*) indicative or suggestive (of) **3** having a particular meaning or force; significant > **exˈpressiveness** *n*

expressly (ɪkˈsprɛslɪ) *adv* **1** for an express purpose **2** plainly, exactly, or unmistakably

expresso (ɪkˈsprɛsəʊ) *n, pl* **expressos** a variant of **espresso**

expressway (ɪkˈsprɛsˌweɪ) *n* a motorway

expropriate (ɛksˈprəʊprɪˌeɪt) *vb* **expropriates, expropriating, expropriated** (*tr*) to deprive (an owner) of (property), esp by taking it for public use [c17 from Med. L *expropriāre* to deprive of possessions, from *proprius* own] > **exˌpropriˈation** *n* > **exˈpropriˌator** *n*

expulsion (ɪkˈspʌlʃən) *n* the act of expelling or the fact or condition of being expelled [c14 from L *expulsiō* a driving out, from *expellere* to EXPEL] > **exˈpulsive** *adj*

expunge (ɪkˈspʌndʒ) *vb* **expunges, expunging, expunged** (*tr*) to delete or erase; blot out; obliterate [c17 from L *expungere* to blot out, from *pungere* to prick] > **expunction** (ɪkˈspʌŋkʃən) *n* > **exˈpunger** *n*

expurgate (ˈɛkspəˌgeɪt) *vb* **expurgates, expurgating, expurgated** (*tr*) to amend (a book, text, etc) by removing (offensive sections) [c17 from L *expurgāre* to clean out, from *purgāre* to purify; see PURGE] > ˌ**expurˈgation** *n* > ˈ**expurˌgator** *n*

exquisite (ɪkˈskwɪzɪt, ˈɛkskwɪzɪt) *adj* **1** possessing qualities of unusual delicacy and craftsmanship **2** extremely beautiful **3** outstanding or excellent **4** sensitive; discriminating **5** fastidious and refined **6** intense or sharp in feeling ▷ *n* **7** *obs* a dandy [c15 from L *exquīsītus* excellent, from *exquīrere* to search out, from *quaerere* to seek] > **exˈquisitely** *adv* > **exˈquisiteness** *n*

ex-serviceman *or* (*fem*) **ex-servicewoman** *n, pl* **ex-servicemen** *or* **ex-servicewomen** a person who has served in the armed forces

extant (ɛkˈstænt, ˈɛkstənt) *adj* still in existence; surviving [c16 from L *exstāns* standing out, from *exstāre*, from *stāre* to stand]

> USAGE According to some, *extant* should properly only be used where there is a connotation of survival, often against all odds: *the oldest extant document dates from 1492*. Where the phrase *in existence* can be substituted, using *extant* would on this view be incorrect: *in existence* (not *extant*) *for nearly 15 years, they have been consistently one of the finest rock bands on the planet*. In practice, however, the distinct meanings of the two phrases often overlap: *these beasts, the largest primates on the planet and the greatest of the great apes, are man's closest living relatives and the only extant primate with which we share close physical characteristics*

extemporaneous (ɪkˌstɛmpəˈreɪnɪəs) *or* **extemporary** (ɪkˈstɛmpərərɪ) *adj* **1** spoken, performed, etc, without preparation; extempore **2** done in a temporary manner; improvised > **exˌtempoˈraneously** *or* **exˈtemporarily** *adv* > **exˌtempoˈraneousness** *or* **exˈtemporariness** *n*

extempore (ɪkˈstɛmpərɪ) *adv, adj* without planning or preparation; impromptu [c16 from L *ex tempore* instantaneously, from EX-[1] out of + *tempus* time]

extemporize *or* **extemporise** (ɪkˈstɛmpəˌraɪz) *vb* **extemporizes, extemporizing, extemporized** *or* **extemporises, extemporising, extemporised** **1** to perform, speak, or compose (an act, speech, music, etc) without preparation **2** to use a temporary solution; improvise > **exˌtemporiˈzation** *or* **exˌtemporiˈsation** *n* > **exˈtempoˌrizer** *or* **exˈtempoˌriser** *n*

extend (ɪkˈstɛnd) *vb* **1** to draw out or be drawn out; stretch **2** to last or cause to last for a certain time **3** (*intr*) to reach a certain point in time or distance **4** (*intr*) to exist or occur **5** (*tr*) to increase (a building, etc) in size; add to or enlarge **6** (*tr*) to broaden the meaning or scope of: *the law was extended* **7** (*tr*) to present or offer **8** to stretch forth (an arm, etc) **9** (*tr*) to lay out (a body) at full length **10** (*tr*) to strain or exert (a person or animal) to the maximum **11** (*tr*) to prolong (the time) for payment of (a debt or loan), completion of (a task), etc [c14 from L *extendere* to stretch out, from *tendere* to stretch] > **exˈtendible** *or* **exˈtendable** *adj* > **exˌtendiˈbility** *or* **exˌtendaˈbility** *n*

extended family *n sociol, anthropol* the nuclear family together with relatives, often spanning three or more generations

extended-play *adj* denoting an EP record

extender (ɪkˈstɛndə) *n* **1** a person or thing that extends **2** a substance added to paints to give body and decrease their rate of settlement **3** a substance added to glues and resins to dilute them or to modify their viscosity

extensible (ɪkˈstɛnsɪbᵊl) *or* **extensile** (ɪkˈstɛnsaɪl) *adj* capable of being extended > **exˌtensiˈbility** *or* **exˈtensibleness** *n*

extension (ɪkˈstɛnʃən) *n* **1** the act of extending or the condition of being extended **2** something that can be extended or that extends another object **3** the length, range, etc, over which something is extended **4** an additional telephone set connected to the same telephone line as another set **5** a room or rooms added to an existing building **6** a delay in the date originally set for payment of a debt or completion of a contract **7** the property of matter by which it occupies space **8a** the act of straightening or extending an arm or leg **8b** its position after being straightened or extended **9a** a service by which the facilities of an educational establishment, library, etc, are offered to outsiders **9b** (*as modifier*): *a university extension course* **10** *logic* the class of entities to which a given word correctly applies [c14 from LL *extensiō* a stretching out; see EXTEND] > **exˈtensional** *adj* > **exˌtensionˈality** *or* **exˈtensionalˌism** *n*

extensive (ɪkˈstɛnsɪv) *adj* **1** having a large extent, area, degree, etc **2** widespread **3** *agriculture* involving or farmed with minimum expenditure of capital or labour, esp depending on a large extent of land ▷ Cf **intensive** (sense 3) **4** of or relating to logical extension > **exˈtensiveness** *n*

extensor (ɪkˈstɛnsə, -sɔː) *n* any muscle that stretches or extends an arm, leg, or other bodily part ▷ Cf **flexor** [c18 from NL, from L *extensus* stretched out]

extent (ɪkˈstɛnt) *n* **1** the range over which something extends; scope **2** an area or volume [c14 from OF, from L *extentus* extensive, from *extendere* to EXTEND]

extenuate (ɪkˈstɛnjʊˌeɪt) *vb* **extenuates, extenuating, extenuated** (*tr*) **1** to represent (an offence, fault, etc) as being less serious than it appears, as by showing mitigating circumstances **2** to cause to be or appear less serious; mitigate **3** *arch* **3a** to emaciate or weaken **3b** to dilute or thin out [c16 from L *extenuāre* to make thin, from *tenuis* thin, frail] > **exˈtenuˌating** *adj* > **exˌtenuˈation** *n* > **exˈtenuˌator** *n*

exterior (ɪkˈstɪərɪə) *n* **1** a part, surface, or region that is on the outside **2** the outward behaviour or appearance of a person **3** a film or scene shot outside a studio ▷ *adj* **4** of, situated on, or suitable for the outside **5** coming or acting from without [c16 from L, comp. of *exterus* on the outside, from *ex* out of] > **ex'teriorly** *adv*

exterior angle *n* **1** an angle of a polygon contained between one side extended and the adjacent side **2** any of the four angles made by a transversal that are outside the region between the two intersected lines

exteriorize *or* **exteriorise** (ɪk'stɪərɪəˌraɪz) *vb* **exteriorizes, exteriorizing, exteriorized** *or* **exteriorises, exteriorising, exteriorised** (*tr*) **1** *surgery* to expose (an attached organ or part) outside the body **2** another word for **externalize** > **exˌteriori'zation** *or* **exˌteriori'sation** *n*

exterminate (ɪk'stɜːmɪˌneɪt) *vb* **exterminates, exterminating, exterminated** (*tr*) to destroy (living things, esp pests or vermin) completely; annihilate; eliminate [c16 from L *extermināre* to drive away, from *terminus* boundary] > **ex'terminable** *adj* > **exˌtermi'nation** *n* > **ex'termiˌnator** *n*

external (ɪk'stɜːnᵊl) *adj* **1** of, situated on, or suitable for the outside; outer **2** coming or acting from without **3** of or involving foreign nations **4** of, relating to, or designating a medicine that is applied to the outside of the body **5** *anat* situated on or near the outside of the body **6** (of a student) studying a university subject extramurally **7** *philosophy* (of objects, etc) taken to exist independently of a perceiving mind ▷ *n* **8** (*often pl*) an external circumstance or aspect, esp one that is superficial **9** *Austral* an extramural student [c15 from L *externus* outward, from *exterus* on the outside, from *ex* out of] > **ex'ternally** *adv* > **ˌexter'nality** *n*

External Affairs *pl n Canad* (formerly) the Canadian federal Foreign Affairs department

externalize *or* **externalise** (ɪk'stɜːnəˌlaɪz) *vb* **externalizes, externalizing, externalized** *or* **externalises, externalising, externalised** (*tr*) **1** to make external; give outward shape to **2** *psychol* to attribute (one's feelings) to one's surroundings > **exˌternali'zation** *or* **exˌternali'sation** *n*

extinct (ɪk'stɪŋkt) *adj* **1** (of an animal or plant species) having died out **2** quenched or extinguished **3** (of a volcano) no longer liable to erupt; inactive [c15 from L *exstinctus* quenched, from *exstinguere* to EXTINGUISH]

extinction (ɪk'stɪŋkʃən) *n* **1** the act of making extinct or the state of being extinct **2** the act of extinguishing or the state of being extinguished **3** complete destruction; annihilation **4** *physics* reduction of the intensity of radiation as a result of absorption or scattering by matter

extinguish (ɪk'stɪŋgwɪʃ) *vb* (*tr*) **1** to put out or quench (a light, flames, etc) **2** to remove or destroy entirely; annihilate **3** *arch* to eclipse or obscure [c16 from L *exstinguere*, from *stinguere* to quench] > **ex'tinguishable** *adj* > **ex'tinguisher** *n* > **ex'tinguishment** *n*

extirpate ('ɛkstəˌpeɪt) *vb* **extirpates, extirpating, extirpated** (*tr*) **1** to remove or destroy completely **2** to pull up or out; uproot [c16 from L *exstirpāre* to root out, from *stirps* root, stock] > **ˌextir'pation** *n* > **'extirˌpator** *n*

extol *or US* **extoll** (ɪk'stəʊl) *vb* **extols** *or US* **extolls, extolling, extolled** (*tr*) to praise lavishly; exalt [c15 from L *extollere* to elevate, from *tollere* to raise] > **ex'toller** *n* > **ex'tolment** *n*

extort (ɪk'stɔːt) *vb* (*tr*) **1** to secure (money, favours, etc) by intimidation, violence, or the misuse of authority **2** to obtain by importunate demands [c16 from L *extortus* wrenched out, from *extorquēre* to wrest away, from *torquēre* to twist, wrench] > **ex'tortion** *n* > **ex'tortioner, ex'tortionist,** *or* **ex'torter** *n* > **ex'tortive** *adj*

extortionate (ɪk'stɔːʃənɪt) *adj* **1** (of prices, etc) excessive; exorbitant **2** (of persons) using extortion > **ex'tortionately** *adv*

extra ('ɛkstrə) *adj* **1** being more than what is usual or expected; additional ▷ *n* **2** a person or thing that is additional **3** something for which an additional charge is made **4** an additional edition of a newspaper, esp to report a new development **5** *films* a person temporarily engaged, usually for crowd scenes **6** *cricket* a run not scored from the bat, such as a wide, no-ball, or bye ▷ *adv* **7** unusually; exceptionally: *an extra fast car* [c18 ? shortened from EXTRAORDINARY]

extra- *prefix* outside or beyond an area or scope: *extrasensory; extraterritorial* [from L *extrā* outside, beyond, from *extera*, from *exterus* outward]

extra cover *n cricket* a fielding position between cover and mid-off

extract *vb* (ɪk'strækt) (*tr*) **1** to pull out or uproot by force **2** to remove or separate **3** to derive (pleasure, information, etc) from some source **4** to deduce or develop (a doctrine, policy, etc) **5** *inf* to extort (money, etc) **6** to obtain (a substance) from a mixture or material by a process, such as digestion, distillation, mechanical separation, etc **7** to cut out or copy out (an article, passage, etc) from a publication **8** to determine the value of (the root of a number) ▷ *n* ('ɛkstrækt) **9** something extracted, such as a passage from a book, etc **10** a preparation containing the active principle or concentrated essence of a material [c15 from L *extractus* drawn forth, from *extrahere*, from *trahere* to drag] > **ex'tractable** *adj* > **exˌtracta'bility** *n* > **ex'tractive** *adj*

> USAGE *Extract* is occasionally wrongly used where *extricate* would be better: *he will find it difficult extricating* (not *extracting*) *himself from this situation*. The main difference between the two words is that while both can be used to refer to removing oneself from a physical situation, *extricate* has stronger overtones of difficulty, and is primarily used with *oneself*. The idea of 'entanglement' present in the Latin root is also there in *intricate*

extraction (ɪk'strækʃən) *n* **1** the act of extracting or the condition of being extracted **2** something extracted **3** the act or an instance of extracting a tooth **4** origin or ancestry

Ee

extractor (ɪk'stræktə) *n* **1** a person or thing that extracts **2** an instrument for pulling something out or removing tight-fitting components **3** short for **extractor fan**

extractor fan *or* **extraction fan** *n* a fan used in kitchens, bathrooms, workshops, etc, to remove stale air or fumes

extracurricular (ˌɛkstrəkə'rɪkjʊlə) *adj* **1** taking place outside the normal school timetable **2** beyond the regular duties, schedule, etc

extradite ('ɛkstrəˌdaɪt) *vb* **extradites, extraditing, extradited** (*tr*) **1** to surrender (an alleged offender) for trial to a foreign state **2** to procure the extradition of [c19 back formation from EXTRADITION] > **'extraˌditable** *adj*

extradition (ˌɛkstrə'dɪʃən) *n* the surrender of an alleged offender to the state where the alleged offence was committed [c19 from F, from L *trāditiō* a handing over]

extrados (ɛk'streɪdɒs) *n, pl* **extrados** (-dəʊz) *or* **extradoses** *archit* the outer curve of an arch or vault [c18 from F, from EXTRA- + *dos* back]

extradural (ˌɛkstrə'djʊərəl) *adj* another word for **epidural** (sense 1)

extragalactic (ˌɛkstrəgə'læktɪk) *adj* occurring or existing beyond the Galaxy

extramarital (ˌɛkstrə'mærɪtᵊl) *adj* (esp of sexual relations) occurring outside marriage

extramural (ˌɛkstrə'mjʊərəl) *adj* **1** connected with but outside the normal courses of a university, college, etc **2** beyond the boundaries or walls of a city, castle, etc

extraneous (ɪk'streɪnɪəs) *adj* **1** not essential **2** not pertinent; irrelevant **3** coming from without **4** not belonging [c17 from L *extrāneus* external, from *extrā* outside] > **ex'traneousness** *n*

extranet ('ɛkstrəˌnɛt) *n computing* an intranet that is modified to allow outsiders access to it, esp one belonging to a business that allows customers to access it [C20 from EXTRA- + NET[1] (sense 8), modelled on INTRANET]

extraordinary (ɪk'strɔːdᵊnrɪ) *adj* **1** very unusual or surprising **2** not in an established manner or order **3** employed for particular purposes **4** (*usually postpositive*) (of an official, etc) additional or subordinate [C15 from L *extraordinārius* beyond what is usual; see ORDINARY] > **ex'traordinarily** *adv* > **ex'traordinariness** *n*

extraordinary general meeting *n* a meeting specially called to discuss an important item of a company's business. It may be called by a group of shareholders or by the directors. Abbrev: **EGM**

extrapolate (ɪk'stræpəˌleɪt) *vb* **extrapolates, extrapolating, extrapolated 1** *maths* to estimate (a value of a function etc) beyond the known values, by the extension of a curve. ▷ Cf **interpolate** (sense 4) **2** to infer (something) by using but not strictly deducing from known facts [C19 EXTRA- + *-polate*, as in INTERPOLATE] > **exˌtrapo'lation** *n* > **ex'trapolative** *or* **ex'trapolatory** *adj* > **ex'trapoˌlator** *n*

extrasensory (ˌɛkstrə'sɛnsərɪ) *adj* of or relating to extrasensory perception

extrasensory perception *n* the supposed ability of certain individuals to obtain information about the environment without the use of normal sensory channels

extraterritorial (ˌɛkstrəˌtɛrɪ'tɔːrɪəl) *or* **exterritorial** *adj* **1** beyond the limits of a country's territory **2** of, relating to, or possessing extraterritoriality

extraterritoriality (ˌɛkstrəˌtɛrɪˌtɔːrɪ'ælɪtɪ) *n* **1** the privilege granted to some aliens, esp diplomats, of being exempt from the jurisdiction of the state in which they reside **2** the right of a state to exercise authority in certain circumstances beyond the limits of its territory

extra time *n sport* an additional period played at the end of a match, to compensate for time lost through injury or (in certain circumstances) to allow the teams to achieve a conclusive result

extravagance (ɪk'strævɪgəns) *n* **1** excessive outlay of money; wasteful spending **2** immoderate or absurd speech or behaviour

extravagant (ɪk'strævɪgənt) *adj* **1** spending money excessively or immoderately **2** going beyond usual bounds; unrestrained **3** ostentatious; showy **4** exorbitant in price; overpriced [C14 from Med. L *extravagāns*, from L EXTRA- + *vagārī* to wander]

extravaganza (ɪkˌstrævə'gænzə) *n* **1** an elaborately staged light entertainment **2** any lavish or fanciful display, literary composition, etc [C18 from It.: extravagance]

extravasate (ɪk'strævəˌseɪt) *vb* **extravasates, extravasating, extravasated** *pathol* to cause (blood or lymph) to escape or (of blood or lymph) to escape into the surrounding tissues from their proper vessels [C17 from L EXTRA- + *vās* vessel] > **exˌtrava'sation** *n*

extravehicular (ˌɛkstrəvɪ'hɪkjʊlə) *adj* occurring or used outside a spacecraft, either in space or on the surface of a planet

extraversion (ˌɛkstrə'vɜːʃən) *n* a variant spelling of **extroversion** > **'extraˌvert** *n, adj*

extra virgin *adj* (of olive oil) of the highest quality, extracted by cold pressing rather than chemical treatment

Extremadura (estrema'ðura) *n* the Spanish name for **Estremadura**

extreme (ɪk'striːm) *adj* **1** being of a high or of the highest degree or intensity **2** exceeding what is usual or reasonable; immoderate **3** very strict or severe; drastic **4** (*prenominal*) farthest or outermost ▷ *n* **5** the highest or furthest degree (often in **in the extreme, go to extremes**) **6** (*often pl*) either of the two limits or ends of a scale or range **7** *maths* the first or last term of a series or a proportion [C15 from L *extrēmus* outermost, from *exterus* on the outside; see EXTERIOR] > **ex'tremeness** *n*

USAGE See at **very**

extremely (ɪk'striːmlɪ) *adv* **1** to the extreme; exceedingly **2** (*intensifier*): *she behaved extremely badly*

extreme sport *n* a sport that is physically hazardous, such as bungee jumping or snowboarding

extreme unction *n RC Church* the former name for **anointing of the sick**

extremist (ɪk'striːmɪst) *n* **1** a person who favours immoderate or fanatical methods, esp in being politically radical ▷ *adj* **2** of or characterized by immoderate or excessive actions, opinions, etc > **ex'tremism** *n*

extremity (ɪk'strɛmɪtɪ) *n, pl* **extremities 1** the farthest or outermost point or section **2** the greatest degree **3** an extreme condition or state, as of adversity **4** a limb, such as a leg or wing, or the end of such a limb **5** (*usually pl*) *arch* a drastic or severe measure

extremophile (ɪk'strɛməˌfaɪl) *n* a microbe that lives in an environment once thought to be uninhabitable, for example in boiling or frozen water

extricate ('ɛkstrɪˌkeɪt) *vb* **extricates, extricating, extricated** (*tr*) to remove or free from complication, hindrance, or difficulty; disentangle [C17 from L *extrīcāre* to disentangle] > **'extricable** *adj* > **ˌextri'cation** *n*

USAGE See at **extract**

extrinsic (ɛk'strɪnsɪk) *adj* **1** not contained or included within; extraneous **2** originating or acting from outside [C16 from LL *extrinsecus* (adj) outward, from L (adv), ult. from *exter* outward + *secus* alongside] > **ex'trinsically** *adv*

extroversion *or* **extraversion** (ˌɛkstrə'vɜːʃən) *n psychol* the directing of one's interest outwards, esp towards social contacts [C17 from *extro-* (var. of EXTRA-, contrasting with *intro-*) + *-version*, from L *vertere* to turn] > **ˌextro'versive** *or* **ˌextra'versive** *adj*

extrovert *or* **extravert** ('ɛkstrəˌvɜːt) *psychol* ▷ *n* **1** a person concerned more with external reality than inner feelings ▷ *adj* **2** of or characterized by extroversion [C20 from *extro-* (var. of EXTRA-, contrasting with *intro-*) + *-vert*, from L *vertere* to turn] > **'extroˌverted** *or* **'extraˌverted** *adj*

extrude (ɪk'struːd) *vb* **extrudes, extruding, extruded** (*tr*) **1** to squeeze or force out **2** to produce (moulded sections of plastic, metal, etc) by ejection from a shaped nozzle or die **3** to chop up or pulverize (an item of food) and re-form it to look like a whole [C16 from L *extrūdere* to thrust out, from *trūdere* to push, thrust] > **ex'truded** *adj*

extrusion (ɪk'struːʒən) *n* **1** the act or process of extruding **2a** the movement of magma onto the surface of the earth through volcano craters and cracks in the earth's crust, forming igneous rock **2b** any igneous rock formed in this way **3** anything formed by the process of extruding > **ex'trusive** *adj*

exuberant (ɪg'zjuːbərənt) *adj* **1** abounding in vigour and high spirits **2** lavish or effusive; excessively elaborate **3** growing luxuriantly or in profusion [C15 from L *exūberāns*, from *ūberāre* to be fruitful] > **ex'uberance** *n*

exuberate (ɪg'zjuːbəˌreɪt) *vb* **exuberates, exuberating, exuberated** (*intr*) *rare* **1** to be exuberant **2** to abound [C15 from L *exūberāre* to be abundant; see EXUBERANT]

exude (ɪg'zjuːd) *vb* **exudes, exuding, exuded 1** to release or be released through pores, incisions, etc, as sweat or sap **2** (*tr*) to make apparent by mood or behaviour [C16 from L *exsūdāre*, from *sūdāre* to sweat] > **exudation** (ˌɛksjʊ'deɪʃən) *n*

exult (ɪg'zʌlt) *vb* (*intr*) **1** to be joyful or jubilant, esp because of triumph or success **2** (often foll by *over*) to triumph (over); take delight in the defeat of [C16 from L *exsultāre* to jump or leap for joy, from *saltāre* to leap]

> **exultation** (ˌɛgzʌlˈteɪʃən) *n* > **exˈultingly** *adv*
exultant (ɪgˈzʌltənt) *adj* elated or jubilant, esp because of triumph or success > **exˈultantly** *adv*
exurbia (ɛksˈɜːbɪə) *n chiefly US* the region outside the suburbs of a city, consisting of residential areas (**exurbs**) occupied predominantly by rich commuters (**exurbanites**) [C20 from EX-¹ + L *urbs* city] > **exˈurban** *adj*
exuviate (ɪgˈzjuːvɪˌeɪt) *vb* **exuviates, exuviating, exuviated** to shed (a skin or similar outer covering) [C17 from L *exuere* to strip off] > **exˌuviˈation** *n*
-ey *suffix.* a variant of **-y**¹ and **-y**²
Eyam (ˈiːjəm) *n* a village in N central England, in Derbyshire. When plague reached the village in 1665 the inhabitants isolated themselves to prevent it spreading further: as a result, most of them died
eyas (ˈaɪəs) *n* a nestling hawk or falcon, esp one reared for falconry [C15 mistaken division of earlier *a nyas*, from OF *niais* nestling, from L *nīdus* nest]
eye¹ (aɪ) *n* **1** the organ of sight of animals. Related adjs: **ocular, ophthalmic** **2** (*often pl*) the ability to see; sense of vision **3** the external part of an eye, often including the area around it **4** a look, glance, expression, or gaze **5** a sexually inviting or provocative look (esp in **give (someone) the (glad) eye, make eyes at**) **6** attention or observation (often in **catch someone's eye, keep an eye on, cast an eye over**) **7** ability to recognize, judge, or appreciate **8** (*often pl*) opinion, judgment, point of view, or authority: *in the eyes of the law* **9** a structure or marking resembling an eye, such as the bud on a potato tuber or a spot on a butterfly wing **10** a small loop or hole, as at one end of a needle **11** a small area of low pressure and calm in the centre of a storm, hurricane, or tornado **12 electric eye** another name for **photocell** **13 all eyes** *inf* acutely vigilant or observant **14 (all) my eye** *inf* rubbish; nonsense **15 an eye for an eye** retributive or vengeful justice; retaliation **16 get one's eye in** *chiefly sport* to become accustomed to the conditions, light, etc, with a consequent improvement in one's performance **17 go eyes out** *Austral & NZ* to make every possible effort **18 half an eye** a modicum of perceptiveness **19 have eyes for** to be interested in **20 in one's mind's eye** pictured within the mind; imagined or remembered vividly **21 in the public eye** exposed to public curiosity or publicity **22 keep an eye open** *or* **out (for)** to watch with special attention (for) **23 keep one's eyes peeled** (*or* **skinned**) to watch vigilantly (for) **24 lay, clap,** *or* **set eyes on** (*usually with a negative*) to see **25 look (someone) in the eye** to look openly and without shame or embarrassment at (someone) **26 make sheep's eyes (at)** *old-fashioned* to ogle amorously **27 more than meets the eye** hidden motives, meaning, or facts **28 see eye to eye (with)** to agree (with) **29 turn a blind eye to** *or* **close one's eyes to** to pretend not to notice or to ignore deliberately **30 up to one's eyes (in)** extremely busy (with) **31 with** *or* **having an eye to** (*prep*) **31a** regarding; with reference to **31b** with the intention or purpose of **32 with one's eyes open** in the full knowledge of all relevant facts **33 with one's eyes shut** **33a** with great ease, esp as a result of thorough familiarity **33b** without being aware of all the facts ▷ *vb* **eyes, eyeing** *or* **eying, eyed** (*tr*) **34** to look at carefully or warily **35** Also: **eye up** to look at in a manner indicating sexual interest; ogle [OE *ēage*] > **ˈeyeless** *adj* > **ˈeyeˌlike** *adj*
eye² (aɪ) *n* another word for **nye**
eyeball (ˈaɪˌbɔːl) *n* **1** the entire ball-shaped part of the eye **2 eyeball to eyeball** in close confrontation ▷ *vb* **3** (*tr*) *sl* to stare at
eyebank (ˈaɪˌbæŋk) *n* a place in which corneas are stored for use in corneal grafts
eyebath (ˈaɪˌbɑːθ) *n* a small vessel for applying medicated or cleansing solutions to the eye. Also called (US and Canad): **eyecup**
eyeblack (ˈaɪˌblæk) *n* another name for **mascara**
eyebright (ˈaɪˌbraɪt) *n* an annual plant having small white-and-purple flowers: formerly used in the treatment of eye disorders
eyebrow (ˈaɪˌbraʊ) *n* **1** the transverse bony ridge over each eye **2** the arch of hair that covers this ridge **3 raise an eyebrow** to give rise to doubt or disapproval
eyebrow pencil *n* a cosmetic in pencil form for applying colour and shape to the eyebrows
eye candy *n inf* **1** a person or people considered highly attractive to look at, often implying that they are lacking in intelligence or depth **2** something intended to be attractive to the eye without being demanding or contributing anything essential
eye-catching *adj* tending to attract attention; striking
eye contact *n* a direct look between two people; meeting of eyes
eyed (aɪd) *adj* **a** having an eye or eyes (as specified) **b** (*in combination*): *brown-eyed*
eye dog *n NZ* a dog trained to control sheep by staring fixedly at them. Also called: **strong-eye dog**
eyeful (ˈaɪfʊl) *n inf* **1** a view, glance, or gaze **2** a beautiful or attractive sight, esp a woman
eyeglass (ˈaɪˌglɑːs) *n* **1** a lens for aiding or correcting defective vision, esp a monocle **2** another word for **eyepiece** or **eyebath**
eyeglasses (ˈaɪˌglɑːsɪz) *pl n now chiefly US* another word for **spectacles**
eyehole (ˈaɪˌhəʊl) *n* **1** a hole through which a rope, hook, etc, is passed **2** the cavity that contains the eyeball **3** another word for **peephole**
eyelash (ˈaɪˌlæʃ) *n* **1** any one of the short curved hairs that grow from the edge of the eyelids **2** a row or fringe of these hairs
eyelet (ˈaɪlɪt) *n* **1** a small hole for a lace, cord, or hook to be passed through **2** a small metal ring or tube reinforcing an eyehole in fabric **3** a small opening, such as a peephole **4** *embroidery* a small hole with finely stitched edges **5** a small eye or eyelike marking ▷ *vb* **6** (*tr*) to supply with an eyelet or eyelets [C14 from OF *oillet*, lit.: a little eye, from *oill* eye, from L *oculus* eye]
eyelevel (ˈaɪˌlɛvᵊl) *adj* level with a person's eyes when looking straight ahead: *an eyelevel grill*
eyelid (ˈaɪˌlɪd) *n* either of the two muscular folds of skin that can be moved to cover the exposed portion of the eyeball
eyeliner (ˈaɪˌlaɪnə) *n* a cosmetic used to outline the eyes
eye-opener *n inf* **1** something startling or revealing **2** *US & Canad* an alcoholic drink taken early in the morning
eyepiece (ˈaɪˌpiːs) *n* the lens or lenses in an optical instrument nearest the eye of the observer
eye rhyme *n* a rhyme involving words that are similar in spelling but not in sound, such as *stone* and *none*
eye shadow *n* a coloured cosmetic put around the eyes
eyeshot (ˈaɪˌʃɒt) *n* range of vision; view
eyesight (ˈaɪˌsaɪt) *n* the ability to see; faculty of sight
eyesore (ˈaɪˌsɔː) *n* something very ugly
eyespot (ˈaɪˌspɒt) *n* **1** a small area of light-sensitive pigment in some simple organisms **2** an eyelike marking, as on a butterfly wing
eyestrain (ˈaɪˌstreɪn) *n* fatigue or irritation of the eyes, resulting from excessive use or uncorrected defects of vision
Eyetie (ˈaɪtaɪ) *n, adj Brit sl, offensive* Italian [C20 from jocular mispronunciation of *Italian*]
eyetooth (ˌaɪˈtuːθ) *n, pl* **eyeteeth** **1** either of the two canine teeth in the upper jaw **2 give one's eyeteeth for** to go to any lengths to achieve or obtain (something)
eyewash (ˈaɪˌwɒʃ) *n* **1** a lotion for the eyes **2** *inf* nonsense; rubbish
eyewitness (ˈaɪˌwɪtnɪs) *n* a person present at an event who can describe what happened
eyot (aɪt) *n Brit, rare* island [var. of AIT]

Ee

Eyre[1] (ɛə) *n* **Lake** a shallow salt lake in NE central South Australia, about 11 m (35 ft) below sea level. Area: 9600 sq km (3700 sq miles) [C19 named after Edward John *Eyre* (1815–1901), British explorer and colonial administrator]

Eyre[2] (ɛə) *n* **Edward John** 1815–1901, British explorer and colonial administrator. He was governor of Jamaica (1864–66) until his authorization of 400 executions to suppress an uprising led to his recall

Eyre Peninsula *n* a peninsula of South Australia, between the Great Australian Bight and Spencer Gulf

eyrie (ˈɪərɪ, ˈɛərɪ, ˈaɪərɪ) *or* **aerie** *n* **1** the nest of an eagle or other bird of prey, built in a high inaccessible place **2** any high isolated position or place [C16 from Med. L *airea*, from L *ārea* open field, hence, nest]

eyrir (ˈeɪrɪə) *n, pl* **aurar** (ˈɔɪrɑː) an Icelandic monetary unit worth one hundredth of a krona [ON: ounce (of silver), money; rel. to L *aureus* golden]

Eysenck (ˈaɪzɛŋk) *n* **Hans Jürgen** (hænz ˈjɜːgən) 1916–97, British psychologist, born in Germany, who developed a dimensional theory of personality that stressed the influence of heredity

Ez. *or* **Ezr.** *Bible abbrev for* Ezra

Ezek. *Bible abbrev for* Ezekiel

Ezekiel (ɪˈziːkɪəl) *n Old Testament* **1** a Hebrew prophet of the 6th century BC, exiled to Babylon in 597 BC **2** the book containing his oracles, which describe the downfall of Judah and Jerusalem and their subsequent restoration. Douay spelling: **Ezechiel**

e-zine (ˈiːˌziːn) *n* a magazine available only in electronic form, for example on the World Wide Web

Ezra (ˈɛzrə) *n Old Testament* **1** a Jewish priest of the 5th century BC, who was sent from Babylon by the Persian king Artaxerxes I to reconstitute observance of the Jewish law and worship in Jerusalem after the captivity **2** the book recounting his efforts to perform this task.

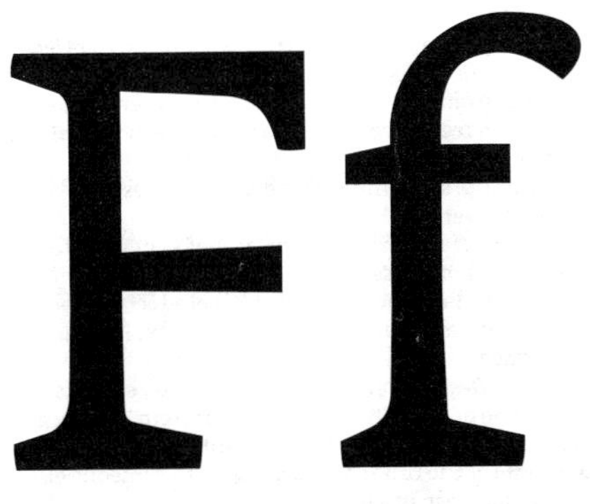

f *or* **F** (ɛf) *n, pl* **f's, F's,** *or* **Fs** **1** the sixth letter of the English alphabet **2** a speech sound represented by this letter, as in *fat*

f *symbol for:* **1** *music* forte: an instruction to play loudly **2** *physics* frequency **3** *maths* function (of) **4** *physics* femto-

f, f/, *or* **f:** *symbol for* f-number

F *symbol for:* **1** *music* **1a** the fourth note of the scale of C major **1b** the major or minor key having this note as its tonic **2** Fahrenheit **3** farad(s) **4** *chem* fluorine **5** *physics* force **6** franc(s) **7** *genetics* a generation of filial offspring, F_1 being the first generation of offspring

f. *or* **F.** *abbrev for:* **1** fathom(s) **2** female **3** *grammar* feminine **4** (*pl* **ff** *or* **FF.**) folio **5** (*pl* **ff.**) following (page)

F- (of US military aircraft) *abbrev for* fighter

fa (fɑː) *n music* the syllable used in the fixed system of solmization for the note F [C14 see GAMUT]

FA (in Britain) *abbrev for* Football Association

f.a. *or* **FA** *abbrev for* fanny adams

FAB *abbrev for* fuel air bomb

F.A.B. *interj Brit* an expression of agreement to, or acknowledgment of, a command [C20 from British television series *Thunderbirds*]

Fabergé (ˈfæbəˌʒeɪ) *n* **Peter Carl** 1846–1920, Russian goldsmith and jeweller, known for the golden Easter eggs and other ornate and fanciful objects that he created for the Russian and other royal families

Fabian (ˈfeɪbɪən) *adj* **1** of or resembling the delaying tactics of Q Fabius Maximus; cautious ▷ *n* **2** a member of or sympathizer with the Fabian Society [C19 from L *Fabiānus* of Fabius] > ˈ**Fabiaˌnism** *n*

Fabian Society *n* an association of British socialists advocating the establishment of socialism by gradual reforms

Fabius Maximus (ˈfeɪbɪəs ˈmæksɪməs) *n* full name *Quintus Fabius Maximus Verrucosus*, called *Cunctator* (the delayer). died 203 BC, Roman general and statesman. As commander of the Roman army during the Second Punic War, he withstood Hannibal by his strategy of harassing the Carthaginians while avoiding a pitched battle

fable (ˈfeɪbᵊl) *n* **1** a short moral story, esp one with animals as characters **2** a false, fictitious, or improbable account **3** a story or legend about supernatural or mythical characters or events **4** legends or myths collectively ▷ *vb* **fables, fabling, fabled** **5** to relate or tell (fables) **6** (*intr*) to tell lies **7** (*tr*) to talk about or describe in the manner of a fable [C13 from L *fābula* story, narrative, from *fārī* to speak, say] > ˈ**fabler** *n*

fabled (ˈfeɪbᵊld) *adj* **1** made famous in fable **2** fictitious

fabliau (ˈfæblɪˌəʊ) *n, pl* **fabliaux** (ˈfæblɪˌəʊz) a comic usually ribald verse tale, popular in France in the 12th and 13th centuries [C19 from F: a little tale, from *fable* tale]

Fablon (ˈfæblən, -lɒn) *n trademark* a brand of adhesive-backed plastic material used to cover and decorate shelves, worktops, etc

Fabre (*French* fabrə) *n* **Jean Henri** (ʒɑ̃ ɑ̃ri) 1823–1915, French entomologist; author of many works on insect life, remarkable for their vivid and minute observation, esp *Souvenirs Entomologiques* (1879–1907). Nobel prize for literature 1910

fabric (ˈfæbrɪk) *n* **1** any cloth made from yarn or fibres by weaving, knitting, felting, etc **2** the texture of a cloth **3** a structure or framework: *the fabric of society* **4** a style or method of construction **5** *rare* a building [C15 from L *fabrica* workshop, from *faber* craftsman]
▷ www.fabriclink.com

fabricate (ˈfæbrɪˌkeɪt) *vb* **fabricates, fabricating, fabricated** (*tr*) **1** to make, build, or construct **2** to devise or concoct (a story, etc) **3** to fake or forge [C15 from L, from *fabrica* workshop; see FABRIC] > ˌ**fabri'cation** *n* > **'fabriˌcator** *n*

Fabry (*French* fabri) *n* **Charles** (ʃarl) 1867–1945, French physicist: discovered ozone in the upper atmosphere

fabulist ('fæbjʊlɪst) *n* **1** a person who invents or recounts fables **2** a person who lies

fabulous ('fæbjʊləs) *adj* **1** almost unbelievable; astounding; legendary: *fabulous wealth* **2** *inf* extremely good: *a fabulous time at the party* **3** of, relating to, or based upon fable: *a fabulous beast* [C15 from L *fābulōsus* celebrated in fable, from *fābula* FABLE] > **'fabulously** *adv* > **'fabulousness** *n*

façade *or* **facade** (fə'sɑːd, fæ-) *n* **1** the face of a building, esp the main front **2** a front or outer appearance, esp a deceptive one [C17 from F, from It., from *faccia* FACE]

face (feɪs) *n* **1a** the front of the head from the forehead to the lower jaw **1b** (*as modifier*): *face flannel* **2a** the expression of the countenance: *a sad face* **2b** a distorted expression, esp to indicate disgust **3** *inf* make-up (esp in **put one's face on**) **4** outward appearance: *the face of the countryside is changing* **5** appearance or pretence (esp in **put a bold, good, bad,** etc, **face on**) **6** dignity (esp in **lose** *or* **save face**) **7** *inf* impudence or effrontery **8** the main side of an object, building, etc, or the front: *a cliff face* **9** the marked surface of an instrument, esp the dial of a timepiece **10** the functional or working side of an object, as of a tool or playing card **11a** the exposed area of a mine from which coal, ore, etc, may be mined **11b** (*as modifier*): *face worker* **12** the uppermost part or surface: *the face of the earth* **13** Also called: **side** any one of the plane surfaces of a crystal or other solid figure **14** Also called: **typeface** *printing* **14a** the printing surface of any type character **14b** the style or design of the character on the type **15** *NZ* the exposed slope of a hill **16** *Brit sl* a well-known or important person **17 in (the) face of** despite **18 on the face of it** to all appearances **19 set one's face against** to oppose with determination **20 show one's face** to make an appearance **21 to someone's face** in someone's presence: *I told him the truth to his face* ▷ *vb* **faces, facing, faced 22** (when *intr*, often foll by *to, towards,* or *on*) to look or be situated or placed (in a specified direction): *the house faces onto the square* **23** to be opposite: *facing page 9* **24** (*tr*) to be confronted by: *he faces many problems* **25** (*tr*) to provide with a surface of a different material **26** to dress the surface of (stone or other material) **27** (*tr*) to expose (a card) with the face uppermost **28** *mil* to order (a formation) to turn in a certain direction or (of a formation) to turn as required: *right face!* ▷ See also **face down, face up to** [C13 from OF, from Vulgar L *facia* (unattested), from L *faciēs* form]

face card *n* the usual US and Canad term for **court card**

face cloth *or* **face flannel** *n Brit* a small piece of cloth used to wash the face and hands. US equivalent: **washcloth**

face down *vb* **1** (*tr, adv*) to confront and force (someone or something) to back down ▷ *n* **facedown 2** *inf* another word for **face-off** (sense 2)

faceless ('feɪslɪs) *adj* **1** without a face **2** without identity; anonymous > **'facelessness** *n*

face-lift *n* **1** a cosmetic surgical operation for tightening sagging skin and smoothing wrinkles on the face **2** any improvement or renovation ▷ *vb* (*tr*) **3** to improve the appearance of, as by a face-lift

facemail ('feɪsˌmeɪl) *n* a computer program which uses an electronically generated face to deliver messages on screen

face-off *n* **1** *ice hockey* the method of starting a game, in which the referee drops the puck, etc between two opposing players **2** Also called **facedown** a confrontation, esp one in which each party attempts to make the other back down ▷ *vb* **face off** (*intr, adv*) **3** to start play by a face-off

face powder *n* a cosmetic powder worn to make the face look less shiny, softer, etc

faceprint ('feɪsˌprɪnt) *n* a digitally recorded representation of a person's face that can be used for security purposes because it is as individual as a fingerprint

facer ('feɪsə) *n* **1** a person or thing that faces **2** *Brit inf* a difficulty or problem

face recognition *n* the ability of a computer to scan, store, and recognize human faces for use in identifying people

face-saving *adj* maintaining dignity or prestige > **'face-ˌsaver** *n*

facet ('fæsɪt) *n* **1** any of the surfaces of a cut gemstone **2** an aspect or phase, as of a subject or personality ▷ *vb* **facets, faceting** *or* **facetting, faceted** *or* **facetted 3** (*tr*) to cut facets in (a gemstone) [C17 from F *facette* a little FACE]

facetiae (fə'siːʃɪˌiː) *pl n* **1** humorous or witty sayings **2** obscene or coarsely witty books [C17 from L: jests, pl of *facētia* witticism, from *facētus* elegant]

face time *n* the time spent dealing with someone else face to face, esp in a place of work

facetious (fə'siːʃəs) *adj* **1** characterized by love of joking **2** jocular or amusing, esp at inappropriate times: *facetious remarks* [C16 from OF *facetieux*, from *facetie* witticism; see FACETIAE] > **fa'cetiously** *adv* > **fa'cetiousness** *n*

face to face *adv, adj* (**face-to-face** *as adj*) **1** opposite one another **2** in confrontation

face up to *vb* (*intr, adv + prep*) to accept (an unpleasant fact, reality, etc)

face value *n* **1** the value written or stamped on the face of a commercial paper or coin **2** apparent worth or value

facia ('feɪʃɪə) *n* a variant spelling of **fascia**

facial ('feɪʃəl) *adj* **1** of or relating to the face ▷ *n* **2** a beauty treatment for the face involving massage and cosmetic packs > **'facially** *adv*

-facient *suffix forming adjectives and nouns* indicating a state or quality: *absorbefacient* [from L *facient-, faciēns*, present participle of *facere* to do]

facies ('feɪʃɪˌiːz) *n, pl* **facies 1** the general form and appearance of an individual or a group **2** the characteristics of a rock or rocks reflecting their appearance and conditions of formation **3** *med* the general facial expression of a patient [C17 from L: appearance, FACE]

facile ('fæsaɪl) *adj* **1** easy to perform or achieve **2** working or moving easily or smoothly **3** superficial: *a facile solution* [C15 from L *facilis* easy, from *facere* to do] > **'facilely** *adv* > **'facileness** *n*

facilitate (fə'sɪlɪˌteɪt) *vb* **facilitates, facilitating, facilitated** (*tr*) to assist the progress of > **faˌcili'tation** *n*

facility (fə'sɪlɪtɪ) *n, pl* **facilities 1** ease of action or performance **2** ready skill or ease deriving from practice or familiarity **3** (*often pl*) the means or equipment facilitating the performance of an action **4** *rare* easy-going disposition **5** (*usually pl*) a euphemistic word for **lavatory** [C15 from L *facilitās*, from *facilis* easy; see FACILE]

facing ('feɪsɪŋ) *n* **1** a piece of material used esp to conceal the seam of a garment and prevent fraying **2** (*usually pl*) the collar, cuffs, etc, of the jacket of a military uniform **3** an outer layer or coat of material applied to the surface of a wall

facsimile (fæk'sɪmɪlɪ) *n* **1** an exact copy or reproduction **2** an image produced by facsimile transmission; fax ▷ *vb* **facsimiles, facsimileing, facsimiled 3** (*tr*) to make an exact copy of [C17 from L *fac simile!* make something like it!, from *facere* to make + *similis* similar, like]

facsimile transmission *n* an international system of transmitting a written, printed, or pictorial document over the telephone system by scanning it photoelectrically and reproducing the image xerographically after transmission. Often shortened to **fax**

fact (fækt) *n* **1** an event or thing known to have happened or existed **2** a truth verifiable from experience or observation **3** a piece of information: *get me all the facts of this case* **4** (*often pl*) *law* an actual event, happening, etc, as distinguished from its legal consequences **5** **after** (*or* **before**) **the fact** *criminal law* after (or before) the commission of the offence **6** **as a matter of fact, in fact, in point of fact** in reality or actuality **7** **fact of life** an inescapable truth, esp an unpleasant one. See also **facts of life** [C16 from L *factum* something done, from *factus* made, from *facere* to do, make]

faction[1] ('fækʃən) *n* **1** a group of people forming a minority within a larger body, esp a dissentious group **2** strife or dissension within a group [C16 from L *factiō* a making, from *facere* to do, make] > **'factional** *adj*

faction[2] ('fækʃən) *n* a television programme, film, or literary work comprising a dramatized presentation of actual events [C20 a blend of FACT & FICTION]

faction fight *n* conflict between different groups within a larger body, esp in S Africa a fight between Blacks of different tribes

factious ('fækʃəs) *adj* given to, producing, or characterized by faction > **'factiously** *adv*

factitious (fæk'tɪʃəs) *adj* **1** artificial rather than natural **2** not genuine; sham: *factitious enthusiasm* [C17 from L *factīcius*, from *facere* to do, make] > **fac'titiously** *adv* > **fac'titiousness** *n*

factitive ('fæktɪtɪv) *adj grammar* denoting a verb taking a direct object as well as a noun in apposition, as for example *elect* in *They elected John president*, where *John* is the direct object and *president* is the complement [C19 from NL, from L *factitāre* to do frequently, from *facere* to do, make]

factoid ('fæktɔɪd) *n* a piece of unreliable information believed to be true because of the way it is presented or repeated in print [C20 coined by Norman MAILER, from FACT + -OID]

factor ('fæktə) *n* **1** an element or cause that contributes to a result **2** *maths* one of two or more integers or polynomials whose product is a given integer or polynomial: *2 and 3 are factors of 6* **3** (foll by identifying numeral) *med* any of several substances that participate in the clotting of blood: *factor VIII* **4** a person who acts on another's behalf, esp one who transacts business for another **5** former name for a **gene** **6** *commercial law* a person to whom goods are consigned for sale and who is paid a commission **7** (in Scotland) the manager of an estate ▷ *vb* **8** (*intr*) to engage in the business of a factor [C15 from L: one who acts, from *facere* to do, make] > **'factorable** *adj* > **'factorship** *n*

> USAGE Purists maintain that *factor* (sense 1) should only be used to refer to something that contributes to a result. It should not be used to refer to a part of something, such as a plan or arrangement; instead a word such as *component* or *element* should be used

factor VIII *n* a protein that participates in the clotting of blood. It is extracted from donated serum and used in the treatment of haemophilia

factorial (fæk'tɔːrɪəl) *maths* ▷ *n* **1** the product of all the positive integers from one up to and including a given integer: *factorial four is* $1 \times 2 \times 3 \times 4$ ▷ *adj* **2** of or involving factorials or factors > **fac'torially** *adv*

factorize *or* **factorise** ('fæktəˌraɪz) *vb* **factorizes, factorizing, factorized** *or* **factorises, factorising, factorised** (*tr*) *maths* to resolve (an integer or polynomial) into factors > **ˌfactori'zation** *or* **ˌfactori'sation** *n*

factory ('fæktərɪ) *n, pl* **factories** **a** a building or group of buildings containing a plant assembly for the manufacture of goods **b** (*as modifier*): *a factory worker* [C16 from LL *factorium*; see FACTOR] > **'factory-ˌlike** *adj*

factory farm *n* a farm in which animals are intensively reared using modern industrial methods > **factory farming** *n*

factory outlet *or* **factory shop** *n* a usually low-rent site leased by a factory to sell its end-of-line or damaged stock direct to the customer at reduced prices

factory ship *n* a vessel that processes fish supplied by a fleet

factotum (fæk'təʊtəm) *n* a person employed to do all kinds of work [C16 from Med. L, from L *fac!* do! + *tōtum*, from *tōtus* (adj) all]

facts and figures *pl n* details

factsheet ('fæktˌʃiːt) *n* a printed sheet containing information relating to items covered in a television or radio programme

facts of life *pl n* **the** the details of sexual behaviour and reproduction

factual ('fæktʃʊəl) *adj* **1** of, relating to, or characterized by facts **2** real; actual > **'factually** *adv* > **'factualness** *or* **ˌfactu'ality** *n*

facula ('fækjʊlə) *n, pl* **faculae** (-ˌliː) any of the bright areas on the sun's surface, usually appearing just before a sunspot [C18 from L: little torch, from *fax* torch] > **'facular** *adj*

facultative ('fækəltətɪv) *adj* **1** empowering but not compelling the doing of an act **2** that may or may not occur **3** *biol* able to exist under more than one set of environmental conditions **4** of or relating to a faculty > **'facultatively** *adv*

faculty ('fækəltɪ) *n, pl* **faculties** **1** one of the inherent powers of the mind or body, such as memory, sight, or hearing **2** any ability or power, whether acquired or inherent **3** a conferred power or right **4a** a department within a university or college devoted to a particular branch of knowledge **4b** the staff of such a department **4c** *chiefly US & Canad* all the teaching staff at a university, school, etc **5** all members of a learned profession [C14 (in the sense: department of learning): from L *facultās* capability; rel. to L *facilis* easy]

FA Cup *n soccer* (in England and Wales) **1** an annual knockout competition among member teams of the Football Association **2** the trophy itself

fad (fæd) *n inf* **1** an intense but short-lived fashion **2** a personal idiosyncrasy [C19 from ?] > **'faddish** *or* **'faddy** *adj*

Fadden ('fædən) *n* Sir **Arthur William** 1895–1973, Australian statesman; prime minister of Australia (1941)

fade (feɪd) *vb* **fades, fading, faded** **1** to lose or cause to lose brightness, colour, or clarity **2** (*intr*) to lose vigour or youth **3** (*intr; usually foll by* away *or* out) to vanish slowly **4a** to decrease the brightness or volume of (a television or radio programme) or (of a television programme, etc) to decrease in this way **4b** to decrease the volume of (a sound) in a recording system or (of a sound) to be so reduced in volume **5** (*intr*) (of the brakes of a vehicle) to lose power **6** to cause (a golf ball) to veer from a straight flight or (of a golf ball) to veer from a straight flight ▷ *n* **7** the act or an instance of fading [C14 from *fade* (adj) dull, from OF, from Vulgar L *fatidus* (unattested), prob. blend of L *vapidus* VAPID + L *fatuus* FATUOUS] > **'fadeless** *adj* > **'fadedness** *n* > **'fader** *n*

fade-in *n* **1** *films* an optical effect in which a shot appears gradually out of darkness ▷ *vb* **fade in** (*adv*) **2** to increase or cause to increase gradually, as vision or sound in a film or broadcast

fade-out *n* **1** *films* an optical effect in which a shot slowly disappears into darkness **2** a gradual and temporary loss of a radio or television signal **3** a slow or gradual disappearance ▷ *vb* **fade out** (*adv*) **4** to decrease or cause to decrease gradually, as vision or sound in a film or broadcast

faeces *or esp US* **feces** ('fiːsiːz) *pl n* bodily waste matter

Ff

discharged through the anus [c15 from L *faecēs*, pl. of *faex* sediment, dregs] > **faecal** *or esp US* **fecal** ('fiːkᵊl) *adj*

Faenza (*Italian* fa'ɛntsa) *n* a city in N Italy, in Emilia-Romagna: famous in the 15th and 16th centuries for its majolica earthenware, esp faïence. Pop: 54 050 (1990)

faerie *or* **faery** ('feɪərɪ, 'fɛərɪ) *n, pl* **faeries** *arch or poetic* 1 the land of fairies ▷ *adj, n* 2 a variant spelling of **fairy**

Faeroes *or* **Faroes** ('fɛərəʊz) *pl n* a group of 21 basalt islands in the North Atlantic between Iceland and the Shetland Islands: a self-governing community within the kingdom of Denmark; fishing. Capital: Thorshavn. Pop: 46 600 (2001 est). Area: 1400 sq km (540 sq miles). Also called: **Faeroe Islands** *or* **Faroe Islands**

Faeroese *or* **Faroese** (ˌfɛərəʊ'iːz) *adj* 1 of or characteristic of the Faeroes, their inhabitants, or their language ▷ *n* 2 the language of the Faeroes, closely related to Icelandic 3 (*pl* **Faeroese** *or* **Faroese**) a native or inhabitant of the Faeroes

faff (fæf) *vb* (*intr; often foll by about*) *Brit inf* to dither or fuss [c19 from ?]

Fafnir ('fæfnɪə, 'fæv-) *n Norse myth* the son of Hreidmar, whom he killed to gain the cursed treasure of Andvari. He became a dragon and was slain by Sigurd while guarding the treasure

fag[1] (fæg) *n* 1 *inf* a boring or wearisome task 2 *Brit* (esp formerly) a young public school boy who performs menial chores for an older boy or prefect ▷ *vb* **fags, fagging, fagged** 3 (when *tr*, often foll by *out*) *inf* to become or cause to become exhausted by hard work 4 (*usually intr*) *Brit* to do or cause to do menial chores in a public school [c18 from ?]

fag[2] (fæg) *n Brit sl* a cigarette [c16 (in the sense: something hanging loose, flap): from ?]

fag[3] (fæg) *n sl, chiefly US & Canad* short for **faggot**[2]

fag end *n* 1 the last and worst part 2 *Brit inf* the stub of a cigarette [c17 see FAG[2]]

faggot[1] *or esp US* **fagot** ('fægət) *n* 1 a bundle of sticks or twigs, esp when used as fuel 2 a bundle of iron bars, esp to be forged into wrought iron 3 a ball of chopped meat bound with herbs and bread and eaten fried ▷ *vb* (*tr*) 4 to collect into a bundle or bundles 5 *needlework* to do faggoting on (a garment, etc) [c14 from OF, ?from Gk *phakelos* bundle]

faggot[2] ('fægət) *n sl, chiefly US & Canad* a male homosexual [c20 special use of FAGGOT[1]]

faggoting *or esp US* **fagoting** ('fægətɪŋ) *n* 1 decorative needlework done by tying vertical threads together in bundles 2 a decorative way of joining two hems by crisscross stitches

fag hag *n sl, usually derog* a heterosexual woman who prefers the company of homosexual men

fah *n music* (in tonic sol-fa) the fourth degree of any major scale [c14 later variant of *fa*; see GAMUT]

Fahd ibn Abdul Aziz (fɑːd 'ɪbᵊn 'æbdʊl ə'ziːz) *n* born 1923, king of Saudi Arabia from 1982

Fahrenheit[1] ('færənˌhaɪt) *adj* of or measured according to the Fahrenheit scale of temperature. Symbol: F

Fahrenheit[2] (*German* 'faːrənhait) *n* **Gabriel Daniel** ('gaːbrieːl 'daːnieːl) 1686–1736, German physicist, who invented the mercury thermometer and devised the temperature scale that bears his name

Fahrenheit scale *n* a scale of temperatures in which 32° represents the melting point of ice and 212° represents the boiling point of pure water under standard atmospheric pressure. Cf **Celsius scale**

Faial *or* **Fayal** (*Portuguese* fə'ial) *n* an island in the central Azores archipelago. Chief town: Horta. Area: 171 sq km (66 sq miles)

faïence (faɪ'ɑːns, feɪ-) *n* tin-glazed earthenware, usually that of French, German, Italian, or Scandinavian origin [c18 from F, strictly: pottery from FAENZA]

fail (feɪl) *vb* 1 to be unsuccessful in an attempt (at something or to do something) 2 (*intr*) to stop operating or working properly: *the steering failed suddenly* 3 to judge or be judged as being below the officially accepted standard required in (a course, examination, etc) 4 (*tr*) to prove disappointing or useless to (someone) 5 (*tr*) to neglect or be unable (to do something) 6 (*intr*) to prove insufficient in quantity or extent 7 (*intr*) to weaken 8 (*intr*) to go bankrupt ▷ *n* 9 a failure to attain the required standard 10 **without fail** definitely [c13 from OF *faillir*, ult. from L *fallere* to disappoint]

failing ('feɪlɪŋ) *n* 1 a weak point ▷ *prep* 2 (*used to express a condition*) in default of: *failing a solution, the problem will have to wait until Monday*

fail-safe *adj* 1 designed to return to a safe condition in the event of a failure or malfunction 2 safe from failure; foolproof

failure ('feɪljə) *n* 1 the act or an instance of failing 2 a person or thing that is unsuccessful or disappointing 3 nonperformance of something required or expected: *failure to attend will be punished* 4 cessation of normal operation: *a power failure* 5 an insufficiency: *a crop failure* 6 a decline or loss, as in health 7 the fact of not reaching the required standard in an examination, test, etc 8 bankruptcy

fain (feɪn) *adv* 1 (usually with *would*) *arch* gladly: *she would fain be dead* ▷ *adj* 2 *obs* 2a willing 2b compelled [OE *fægen*; see FAWN[2]]

faint (feɪnt) *adj* 1 lacking clarity, brightness, volume, etc 2 lacking conviction or force: *faint praise* 3 feeling dizzy or weak as if about to lose consciousness 4 timid (esp in **faint-hearted**) 5 **not the faintest** (**idea** *or* **notion**) no idea whatsoever: *I haven't the faintest* ▷ *vb* (*intr*) 6 to lose consciousness, as through weakness 7 *arch or poetic* to become weak, esp in courage ▷ *n* 8 a sudden spontaneous loss of consciousness caused by an insufficient supply of blood to the brain [c13 from OF, from *faindre* to be idle] > '**faintish** *adj* > '**faintly** *adv* > '**faintness** *n*

fair[1] (fɛə) *adj* 1 free from discrimination, dishonesty, etc 2 in conformity with rules or standards: *a fair fight* 3 (of the hair or complexion) light in colour 4 beautiful to look at 5 quite good: *a fair piece of work* 6 unblemished; untainted 7 (of the tide or wind) favourable to the passage of a vessel 8 fine or cloudless 9 pleasant or courteous 10 apparently good or valuable: *fair words* 11 **fair and square** in a correct or just way ▷ *adv* 12 in a fair way: *act fair, now!* 13 absolutely or squarely; quite ▷ *vb* 14 (*intr*) *dialect* (of the weather) to become fine ▷ *n* 15 *arch* a person or thing that is beautiful or valuable [OE *fæger*] > '**fairish** *adj* > '**fairness** *n*

fair[2] (fɛə) *n* 1 a travelling entertainment with sideshows, rides, etc 2 a gathering of producers of and dealers in a given class of products to facilitate business: *a book fair* 3 a regular assembly at a specific place for the sale of goods, esp livestock [c13 from OF *feire*, from LL *fēria* holiday, from L *fēriae* days of rest]

Fairbanks[1] ('fɛəˌbæŋks) *n* a city in central Alaska, at the terminus of the Alaska Highway. Pop: 30 800 (1990)

Fairbanks[2] ('fɛəˌbæŋks) *n* 1 **Douglas** (**Elton**), real name *Julius Ullman*. 1883–1939, US film actor and producer 2 his son, **Douglas, Jnr** 1909–2000, US film actor

Fairfax ('fɛəfæks) *n* **Thomas**, 3rd Baron Fairfax. 1612–71, English general and statesman: commanded the Parliamentary army (1645–50), defeating Charles I at Naseby (1645). He was instrumental in restoring Charles II to the throne (1660)

fair game *n* a legitimate object for ridicule or attack

fairground ('fɛəˌgraʊnd) *n* an open space used for a fair or exhibition

fairing[1] ('fɛərɪŋ) *n* an external metal structure fitted around parts of an aircraft, car, etc, to reduce drag [c20 from *fair* to streamline + -ING[1]]

fairing[2] ('fɛərɪŋ) *n arch* a present, esp from a fair

Fair Isle *n* an intricate multicoloured pattern knitted with Shetland wool into various garments, such as sweaters [c19 after one of the Shetland Islands, where this type of pattern originated]

fairly ('fɛəlɪ) *adv* **1** (*not used with a negative*) moderately **2** as deserved; justly **3** (*not used with a negative*) positively: *the hall fairly rang with applause*

fair-minded *adj* just or impartial > ˌ**fair-'mindedness** *n*

fair play *n* **1** an established standard of decency, etc **2** abidance by this standard

fair sex *n* **the** women collectively

fair-spoken *adj* civil, courteous, or elegant in speech > ˌ**fair-'spokenness** *n*

fair trade *n* **a** the practice of directly benefiting producers in the developing world by buying straight from them at a guaranteed price **b** (*as modifier*): *fair-trade coffee*

fairway ('fɛəˌweɪ) *n* **1** (on a golf course) the avenue approaching a green bordered by rough **2** *naut* the navigable part of a river, harbour, etc

fair-weather *adj* **1** suitable for use in fair weather only **2** not reliable in situations of difficulty: *fair-weather friend*

fairy ('fɛərɪ) *n, pl* **fairies 1** an imaginary supernatural being, usually represented in diminutive human form and characterized as having magical powers **2** *sl* a male homosexual ▷ *adj* (*prenominal*) **3** of a fairy or fairies **4** resembling a fairy or fairies [c14 from OF *faerie* fairyland, from *feie* fairy, from L *Fāta* the Fates; see FATE, FAY] > '**fairy-ˌlike** *adj*

fairy cycle *n* a child's bicycle

fairyfloss ('fɛərɪˌflɒs) *n* the Australian word for **candyfloss**

fairy godmother *n* a benefactress, esp an unknown one

fairyland ('fɛərɪˌlænd) *n* **1** the imaginary domain of the fairies **2** a fantasy world, esp one resulting from a person's wild imaginings

fairy lights *pl n* small coloured or white electric bulbs strung together and used as decoration, esp on a Christmas tree

fairy penguin *n* a small penguin with a bluish head and back, found on the Australian coast. Also called: **little** or **blue penguin**

fairy ring *n* a ring of dark luxuriant vegetation in grassy ground corresponding to the edge of an underground fungal mycelium

fairy-tale *adj* **1** of or relating to a fairy tale **2** resembling a fairy tale, esp in being extremely happy or fortunate: *a fairy-tale ending* **3** highly improbable: *a fairy-tale account*

fairy tale *or* **story** *n* **1** a story about fairies or other mythical or magical beings **2** a highly improbable account

Faisal I *or* **Feisal I** ('faɪsᵊl) *n* 1885–1933, king of Syria (1920) and first king of Iraq (1921–33): a leader of the Arab revolt against the Turks (1916–18)

Faisal II *or* **Feisal II** *n* 1935–58, last king of Iraq (1939–58)

Faisalabad (faɪˈzɑːləˌbɑːd) *n* a city in NE Pakistan: commercial and manufacturing centre of a cotton- and wheat-growing region; university (1961). Pop: 1 977 246 (1998). Former name (until 1979): **Lyallpur**

Faisal Ibn Abdul Aziz ('ɪbᵊn æb'dʊl æ'ziːz) *n* 1905–75, king of Saudi Arabia (1964–75)

fait accompli *French* (fɛt akɔ̃pli) *n, pl* ***faits accomplis*** (fɛz akɔ̃pli) something already done and beyond alteration [lit.: accomplished fact]

faith (feɪθ) *n* **1** strong or unshakable belief in something, esp without proof **2** a specific system of religious beliefs: *the Jewish faith* **3** *Christianity* trust in God and in his actions and promises **4** a conviction of the truth of certain doctrines of religion **5** complete confidence or trust in a person, remedy, etc **6** loyalty, as to a person or cause (esp in **keep faith, break faith**) **7 bad faith** dishonesty **8 good faith** honesty **9** (*modifier*) using or relating to the supposed ability to cure bodily ailments by means of religious faith: *a faith healer* ▷ *interj* **10** *arch* indeed [c12 from Anglo-F *feid*, from L *fidēs* trust, confidence]

faithful ('feɪθfʊl) *adj* **1** remaining true or loyal **2** maintaining sexual loyalty to one's lover or spouse **3** consistently reliable: *a faithful worker* **4** reliable or truthful **5** accurate in detail: *a faithful translation* ▷ *n* **6 the faithful** (*functioning as pl*) **6a** the believers in a religious faith, esp Christianity **6b** any group of loyal and steadfast followers > '**faithfully** *adv* > '**faithfulness** *n*

faithless ('feɪθlɪs) *adj* **1** unreliable or treacherous **2** dishonest or disloyal **3** lacking religious faith > '**faithlessness** *n*

faith school *n Brit* a school that provides a general education within a framework of a specific religious belief

Faiyûm *or* **Fayum** (faɪ'juːm) *n* See **El Faiyûm**

fajitas (fə'hiːtəz) *pl n* a Mexican dish of soft tortillas wrapped round fried strips of meat, vegetables, etc [Mexican Sp.]

fake (feɪk) *vb* **fakes, faking, faked 1** (*tr*) to cause (something inferior or not genuine) to appear more valuable or real by fraud or pretence **2** to pretend to have (an illness, emotion, etc) ▷ *n* **3** an object, person, or act that is not genuine; sham ▷ *adj* **4** not genuine [c18 prob. ult. from It. *facciare* to make or do] > '**faker** *n* > '**fakery** *n*

fakir ('feɪkɪə, fə'kɪə) *n* **1** a Muslim ascetic who spurns worldly possessions **2** a Hindu ascetic mendicant [c17 from Ar. *faqīr* poor]

falafel *or* **felafel** (fə'lɑːfəl) *n* a ball or cake of ground spiced chickpeas, deep-fried and often served with pitta bread [c20 from Ar. *felāfil*]

Falange ('fælændʒ) *n* the Fascist movement founded in Spain in 1933 [Sp.: PHALANX] > **Fa'langist** *n, adj*

falcate ('fælkeɪt) *or* **falciform** ('fælsɪˌfɔːm) *adj biol* shaped like a sickle [c19 from L *falcātus*, from *falx* sickle]

falchion ('fɔːltʃən, 'fɔːlʃən) *n* **1** a short and slightly curved medieval sword **2** an archaic word for **sword** [c14 from It., from *falce*, from L *falx* sickle]

falcon ('fɔːlkən, 'fɔːkən) *n* **1** a diurnal bird of prey such as the gyrfalcon, peregrine falcon, etc, having pointed wings and a long tail **2a** any of these or related birds, trained to hunt small game **2b** the female of such a bird (cf. **tercel**) [c13 from OF, from LL *falcō* hawk, prob. of Gmc origin; ? rel. to L *falx* sickle]

falconet ('fɔːlkəˌnɛt, 'fɔːkə-) *n* **1** any of various small falcons **2** a small light cannon used from the 15th to 17th centuries

falconry ('fɔːlkənrɪ, 'fɔːkən-) *n* the art of keeping falcons and training them to return from flight to a lure or to hunt quarry > '**falconer** *n*
▷ www.falconry.com

falderal ('fældəˌræl) *or* **folderol** ('fɒldəˌrɒl) *n* **1** a showy but worthless trifle **2** foolish nonsense **3** a nonsensical refrain in old songs

Faldo ('fældəʊ) *n* **Nick** born 1957, British golfer: winner of the British Open Championship (1987, 1990, 1992) and the US Masters (1989, 1990, 1996)

faldstool ('fɔːldˌstuːl) *n* a backless seat, sometimes capable of being folded, used by bishops and certain other prelates [c11 *fyldestol*, prob. a translation of Med. L *faldistolium* folding stool, of Gmc origin; cf. OHG *faldstuol*]

Falerii (fə'lɪərɪˌaɪ) *n* an ancient city of S Italy, in Latium: important in pre-Roman times

Faliraki (ˌfælɪ'rɑːkɪ) *n* a coastal resort in SE Greece, on Rhodes. Pop: 400 (2000 est)

Falkirk ('fɔːlkɜːk) *n* **1** a town in Scotland, the administrative centre of Falkirk council area: scene of Edward I's defeat of Wallace (1298) and Prince Charles Edward's defeat of General Hawley (1746); ironworks. Pop: 35 610 (1991) **2** a council area in central Scotland, on the Firth of Forth: created in 1996 from part of Central

Region: largely agricultural, with heavy industry in Falkirk and Grangemouth. Administrative centre: Falkirk. Pop: 145 191 (2001). Area: 299 sq km (115 sq miles)

Falkland Islands ('fɔːlklənd) *pl n* a group of over 100 islands in the S Atlantic: a UK Overseas Territory; invaded by Argentina, who had long laid claim to the islands, on 2 April 1982; recaptured by a British expeditionary force on 14 June 1982. Chief town: Stanley. Pop: 2221 (1996). Area: about 12 200 sq km (4700 sq miles). Spanish name: **Islas Malvinas**

Falkland Islands Dependencies *pl n* the former name (until 1985) for South Georgia and the South Sandwich Islands

Falkner ('fɔːknə) *n* a variant spelling of (William) **Faulkner**

fall (fɔːl) *vb* **falls, falling, fell, fallen** *(mainly intr)* **1** to descend by the force of gravity from a higher to a lower place **2** to drop suddenly from an erect position **3** to collapse to the ground, esp in pieces **4** to become less or lower in number, quality, etc: *prices fell* **5** to become lower in pitch **6** to extend downwards: *her hair fell to her waist* **7** to be badly wounded or killed **8** to slope in a downward direction **9** to yield to temptation or sin **10** to diminish in status, estimation, etc **11** to yield to attack: *the city fell under the assault* **12** to lose power: *the government fell after the riots* **13** to pass into or take on a specified condition: *to fall asleep* **14** to adopt a despondent expression: *her face fell* **15** to be averted: *her gaze fell* **16** to come by chance or presumption: *suspicion fell on the butler* **17** to occur; take place: *night fell* **18** (foll by *back, behind*, etc) to move in a specified direction **19** to occur at a specified place: *the accent falls on the last syllable* **20** (foll by *to*) to be inherited (by): *the estate falls to the eldest son* **21** (often foll by *into, under*, etc) to be classified: *the subject falls into two main areas* **22** to issue forth: *a curse fell from her lips* **23** *(tr) dialect, Austral & NZ* to fell (trees) **24** *cricket* (of a batsman's wicket) to be taken by the bowling side: *the sixth wicket fell for 96* **25** **fall short 25a** to prove inadequate **25b** (often foll by *of*) to fail to reach or measure up to (a standard) ▷ *n* **26** an act or instance of falling **27** something that falls: *a fall of snow* **28** *chiefly US* autumn **29** the distance that something falls: *a hundred-foot fall* **30** a sudden drop from an upright position **31** *(often pl)* **31a** a waterfall or cataract **31b** *(cap when part of a name)*: *Niagara Falls* **32** a downward slope or decline **33** a decrease in value, number, etc **34** a decline in status or importance **35** a capture or overthrow: *the fall of the city* **36** *machinery, naut* the end of a tackle to which power is applied to hoist it **37** Also called: **pinfall** *wrestling* a scoring move, pinning both shoulders of one's opponent to the floor for a specified period **38a** the birth of an animal **38b** the animals produced at a single birth ▷ See also **fall about, fall apart**, etc [OE *feallan*: cf. FELL[2]]

Fall (fɔːl) *n* **the** *theol* Adam's sin of disobedience and the state of innate sinfulness ensuing from this for himself and all mankind

Falla (*Spanish* 'faʎa) *n* **Manuel de** (ma'nwɛl de) 1876–1946, Spanish composer and pianist, composer of the opera *La Vida Breve* (1905), the ballet *The Three-Cornered Hat* (1919), guitar and piano music, and songs

fall about *vb (intr, adv)* to laugh in an uncontrolled manner: *we fell about at the sight*

fallacious (fə'leɪʃəs) *adj* **1** containing or involving a fallacy **2** tending to mislead **3** delusive or disappointing > **fal'laciously** *adv*

fallacy ('fæləsɪ) *n, pl* **fallacies 1** an incorrect or misleading notion or opinion based on inaccurate facts or invalid reasoning **2** unsound reasoning **3** the tendency to mislead **4** *logic* an error in reasoning that renders an argument logically invalid [C15 from L, from *fallax* deceitful, from *fallere* to deceive]

fall apart *vb (intr, adv)* **1** to break owing to long use or poor construction: *the chassis is falling apart* **2** to become disorganized and ineffective: *since you resigned, the office has fallen apart*

fall away *vb (intr, adv)* **1** (of friendship, etc) to be withdrawn **2** to slope down

fall back *vb (intr, adv)* **1** to recede or retreat **2** (foll by *on* or *upon*) to have recourse (to) ▷ *n* **fall-back 3** a retreat **4** a reserve, esp money, that can be called upon in need **5a** anything to which one can have recourse as a second choice **5b** *(as modifier)*: *a fall-back position*

fall behind *vb (intr, adv)* **1** to drop back; fail to keep up **2** to be in arrears, as with a payment

fall down *vb (intr, adv)* **1** to drop suddenly or collapse **2** (often foll by *on*) *inf* to fail

fallen ('fɔːlən) *vb* **1** the past participle of **fall** ▷ *adj* **2** having sunk in reputation or honour: *a fallen woman* **3** killed in battle with glory

fallen arch *n* collapse of the arch formed by the instep of the foot, resulting in flat feet

fall for *vb (intr, prep)* **1** to become infatuated with (a person) **2** to allow oneself to be deceived by (a lie, trick, etc)

fall guy *n inf* **1** a person who is the victim of a confidence trick **2** a scapegoat

fallible ('fælɪbᵊl) *adj* **1** capable of being mistaken **2** liable to mislead [C15 from Med. L *fallibilis*, from L *fallere* to deceive] > ˌ**falli'bility** *n*

fall in *vb (intr, adv)* **1** to collapse **2** to adopt a military formation, esp as a soldier taking his place in a line **3** (of a lease) to expire **4** (often foll by *with*) **4a** to meet and join **4b** to agree with or support a person, suggestion, etc

falling sickness *or* **evil** *n* a former name (nontechnical) for **epilepsy**

falling star *n* an informal name for **meteor**

Fall Line *n* a natural junction, running parallel to the E coast of the US, between the hard rocks of the Appalachians and the softer coastal plain, along which rivers form falls and rapids

fall off *vb (intr)* **1** to drop unintentionally to the ground from (a high object, bicycle, etc), esp after losing one's balance **2** *(adv)* to diminish in size, intensity, etc ▷ *n* **fall-off 3** a decline or drop

fall on *vb (intr, prep)* **1** Also: **fall upon** to attack or snatch (an army, booty, etc) **2** **fall on one's feet** to emerge unexpectedly well from a difficult situation

Fallopian tube (fə'ləʊpɪən) *n* either of a pair of slender tubes through which ova pass from the ovaries to the uterus in female mammals [C18 after Gabriello *Fallopio* (1523–62), It. anatomist who first described the tubes]

fallout ('fɔːlˌaʊt) *n* **1** the descent of radioactive material following a nuclear explosion **2** any particles that so descend **3** secondary consequences ▷ *vb* **fall out** *(intr, adv)* **4** *inf* to disagree **5** *(intr)* to occur **6** *mil* to leave a disciplinary formation

fallow[1] ('fæləʊ) *adj* **1** (of land) left unseeded after being ploughed to regain fertility for a crop **2** (of an idea, etc) undeveloped, but potentially useful ▷ *n* **3** land treated in this way ▷ *vb* **4** *(tr)* to leave (land) unseeded after ploughing it [OE *fealga*] > '**fallowness** *n*

fallow[2] ('fæləʊ) *n, adj* (of) a light yellowish-brown colour [OE *fealu*]

fallow deer *n* either of two species of deer, one of which is native to the Mediterranean region and the other to Persia. The summer coat is reddish with white spots

fall through *vb (intr, adv)* to fail

fall to *vb (intr)* **1** *(adv)* to begin some activity, as eating, working, or fighting **2** *(prep)* to devolve on (a person): *the task fell to me*

Falmouth ('fælməθ) *n* a port and resort in SW England, in S Cornwall. Pop: 20 297 (1991)

false (fɔːls) *adj* **1** not in accordance with the truth or facts **2** irregular or invalid: *a false start* **3** untruthful or lying: *a false account* **4** artificial; fake: *false teeth* **5** being or intended to be misleading or deceptive: *a false rumour* **6** treacherous: *a false friend* **7** based on mistaken or irrelevant ideas or facts: *a false argument* **8** (*prenominal*) (esp of plants) superficially resembling the species specified: *false hellebore* **9** serving to supplement or replace, often temporarily: *a false keel* **10** *music* (of a note, interval, etc) out of tune ▷ *adv* **11** in a false or dishonest manner (esp in **play (someone) false**) [OE *fals*] > **'falsely** *adv* > **'falseness** *n*

false colour *n* colour used in a computer or photographic display to help in interpreting the image, as in the use of red to show high temperatures and blue to show low temperatures in an infrared image converter

false dawn *n* light appearing just before sunrise

false diamond *n* any of a number of semiprecious stones that resemble diamond, such as zircon and white topaz

falsehood ('fɔːls,hʊd) *n* **1** the quality of being untrue **2** an untrue statement; lie **3** the act of deceiving or lying

false imprisonment *n law* the restraint of a person's liberty without lawful authority

false pretences *pl n* a misrepresentation used to obtain anything, such as trust or affection (esp in **under false pretences**)

false ribs *pl n* any of the lower five pairs of ribs in man, not attached directly to the breastbone

false step *n* **1** an unwise action **2** a stumble; slip

falsetto (fɔːl'sɛtəʊ) *n, pl* **falsettos** a form of vocal production used by male singers to extend their range upwards by limiting the vibration of the vocal cords [C18 from It., from *falso* false]

falsies ('fɔːlsɪz) *pl n inf* pads of soft material, such as foam rubber, worn to exaggerate the size of a woman's breasts

falsify ('fɔːlsɪ,faɪ) *vb* **falsifies, falsifying, falsified** (*tr*) **1** to make (a report, evidence, etc) false or inaccurate by alteration, esp in order to deceive **2** to prove false [C15 from OF, from LL, from L *falsus* FALSE + *facere* to do, make] > **'falsi,fiable** *adj* > **falsification** (,fɔːlsɪfɪ'keɪʃən) *n*

falsity ('fɔːlsɪtɪ) *n, pl* **falsities** **1** the state of being false or untrue **2** a lie or deception

Falstaffian (fɔːl'stɑːfɪən) *adj* jovial, plump, and dissolute [C19 after Sir John *Falstaff*, a character in Shakespeare's play *Henry IV*]

Falster ('fɑːlstə) *n* an island in the Baltic Sea, part of SE Denmark. Chief town: Nykøbing. Pop: 42 846 (1990 est). Area: 513 sq km (198 sq miles)

falter ('fɔːltə) *vb* **1** (*intr*) to be hesitant, weak, or unsure **2** (*intr*) to move unsteadily or hesitantly **3** to utter haltingly or hesitantly ▷ *n* **4** hesitancy in speech or action **5** a quavering sound [C14 prob. from ON] > **'falterer** *n* > **'falteringly** *adv*

Falun (,fɑː'lʌn) *n* a city in central Sweden: iron and pyrites mines. Pop: 55 014 (1994)

Famagusta (,fæmə'gʊstə) *n* a port in E Cyprus, on **Famagusta Bay**: became one of the richest cities in Christendom in the 14th century. Pop: 67 167 (1994)

fame (feɪm) *n* **1** the state of being widely known or recognized **2** *arch* rumour or public report ▷ *vb* **fames, faming, famed** **3** (*tr; now usually passive*) to make famous: *he was famed for his ruthlessness* [C13 from L *fāma* report; rel. to *fārī* to say]

familial (fə'mɪlɪəl) *adj* **1** of or relating to the family **2** occurring in the members of a family: *a familial disease*

familiar (fə'mɪlɪə) *adj* **1** well-known: *a familiar figure* **2** frequent or customary: *a familiar excuse* **3** (*postpositive; foll by* with) acquainted **4** friendly; informal **5** close; intimate **6** more intimate than is acceptable; presumptuous ▷ *n* **7** Also called: **familiar spirit** a supernatural spirit supposed to attend and aid a witch, wizard, etc **8** a person attached to the household of the pope or a bishop, who renders service in return for support **9** a friend [C14 from L *familiāris* domestic, from *familia* FAMILY] > **fa'miliarly** *adv* > **fa'miliarness** *n*

familiarity (fə,mɪlɪ'ærɪtɪ) *n, pl* **familiarities** **1** knowledge, as of a subject or place **2** close acquaintanceship **3** undue intimacy **4** (*sometimes pl*) an instance of unwarranted intimacy

familiarize *or* **familiarise** (fə'mɪljə,raɪz) *vb* **familiarizes, familiarizing, familiarized** *or* **familiarises, familiarising, familiarised** (*tr*) **1** to make (oneself or someone else) familiar, as with a particular subject **2** to make (something) generally known > **fa,miliari'zation** *or* **fa,miliari'sation** *n*

famille *French* (famij) *n* a type of Chinese porcelain characterized either by a design on a background of yellow (***famille jaune***) or black (***famille noire***) or by a design in which the predominant colour is pink (***famille rose***) or green (***famille verte***) [C19 lit.: family]

family ('fæmɪlɪ, 'fæmlɪ) *n, pl* **families** **1a** a primary social group consisting of parents and their offspring **1b** (*as modifier*): *a family unit* **2** one's wife or husband and one's children **3** one's children, as distinguished from one's husband or wife **4** a group descended from a common ancestor **5** all the persons living together in one household **6** any group of related things or beings, esp when scientifically categorized **7** *biol* any of the taxonomic groups into which an order is divided and which contains one or more genera **8** a group of historically related languages assumed to derive from one original language **9** *maths* a group of curves or surfaces whose equations differ from a given equation only in the values assigned to one or more constants **10 in the family way** *inf* pregnant [C15 from L *familia* a household, servants of the house, from *famulus* servant]

family allowance *n* **1** (in Britain) a former name for **child benefit** **2** (*caps*) the Canadian equivalent of **child benefit**

family balancing *n US* the choosing of the sex of a future child on the basis of how many children of each sex a family already has

family Bible *n* a large Bible in which births, marriages, and deaths of the members of a family are recorded

Family Compact *n Canad* **1 the** the ruling oligarchy in Upper Canada in the early 19th century **2** (*often not cap*) any influential clique

family man *n* a man who is married and has children, esp one who is devoted to his family

family name *n* a surname, esp when regarded as representing the family honour

family planning *n* the control of the number of children in a family and of the intervals between them, esp by the use of contraceptives

▷ www.icea.org

family support *n NZ* a means-tested allowance for families in need

family therapy *n* a form of psychotherapy in which the members of a family participate, with the aim of improving communications between them and the ways in which they relate to each other

family tree *n* a chart showing the genealogical relationships and lines of descent of a family. Also called: **genealogical tree**

famine ('fæmɪn) *n* **1** a severe shortage of food, as through crop failure or overpopulation **2** acute shortage of anything **3** violent hunger [C14 from OF, via Vulgar L, from L *famēs* hunger]

famish ('fæmɪʃ) *vb* (*now usually passive*) to be or make very hungry or weak [C14 from OF, from L *famēs* FAMINE]

famous ('feɪməs) *adj* **1** known to or recognized by many people **2** *inf* excellent; splendid [C14 from L *fāmōsus*; see

FAME] > **'famously** *adv* > **'famousness** *n*

fan¹ (fæn) *n* **1** any device for creating a current of air by movement of a surface or number of surfaces, esp a rotating device consisting of a number of blades attached to a central hub **2** any of various hand-agitated devices for cooling oneself, esp a collapsible semicircular series of flat segments of paper, ivory, etc **3** something shaped like such a fan, such as the tail of certain birds **4** *agriculture* a kind of basket formerly used for winnowing grain ▷ *vb* **fans, fanning, fanned** (*mainly tr*) **5** to cause a current of air to blow upon, as by means of a fan: *to fan one's face* **6** to agitate or move (air, etc) with or as if with a fan **7** to make fiercer, more ardent, etc: *fan one's passion* **8** (*also intr; often foll by out*) to spread out or cause to spread out in the shape of a fan **9** to winnow (grain) by blowing the chaff away from it [OE *fann*, from L *vannus*] > **'fanlike** *adj* > **'fanner** *n*

fan² (fæn) *n* **1** an ardent admirer of a pop star, football team, etc **2** a devotee of a sport, hobby, etc [C17, re-formed C19 from FAN(ATIC)] > **'fandom** *n*

Fanagalo ('fænəgələʊ) *or* **Fanakalo** *n* (in South Africa) a Zulu-based pidgin with English and Afrikaans components [C20 from Fanagalo *fana ga lo*, lit.: to be like this]

fanatic (fə'nætɪk) *n* **1** a person whose enthusiasm or zeal for something is extreme or beyond normal limits **2** *inf* a person devoted to a particular hobby or pastime ▷ *adj* **3** a variant of **fanatical** [C16 from L *fānāticus* belonging to a temple, hence, inspired by a god, frenzied, from *fānum* temple]

fanatical (fə'nætɪkᵊl) *adj* surpassing what is normal or accepted in enthusiasm for or belief in something > **fa'natically** *adv*

fanaticism (fə'nætɪˌsɪzəm) *n* wildly excessive or irrational devotion, dedication, or enthusiasm

fan belt *n* the belt that drives a cooling fan in a car engine

fancied ('fænsɪd) *adj* **1** imaginary; unreal **2** thought likely to win or succeed: *a fancied runner*

fancier ('fænsɪə) *n* **1** a person with a special interest in something **2** a person who breeds special varieties of plants or animals: *a pigeon fancier*

fanciful ('fænsɪfʊl) *adj* **1** not based on fact: *fanciful notions* **2** made or designed in a curious, intricate, or imaginative way **3** indulging in or influenced by fancy > **'fancifully** *adv* > **'fancifulness** *n*

fan club *n* **1** an organized group of admirers of a particular pop singer, film star, etc **2 be a member of someone's fan club** *inf* to approve of someone strongly

fancy ('fænsɪ) *adj* **fancier, fanciest 1** ornamented or decorative: *fancy clothes* **2** requiring skill to perform: *a fancy dance routine* **3** capricious or illusory **4** (often used ironically) superior in quality **5** higher than expected: *fancy prices* **6** (of a domestic animal) bred for particular qualities ▷ *n, pl* **fancies 7** a sudden capricious idea **8** a sudden or irrational liking for a person or thing **9** the power to conceive and represent decorative and novel imagery, esp in poetry **10** an idea or thing produced by this **11** a mental image **12** *music* a composition for solo lute, keyboard, etc, current during the 16th and 17th centuries **13 the fancy** *arch* those who follow a particular sport, esp prize fighting ▷ *vb* **fancies, fancying, fancied** (*tr*) **14** to picture in the imagination **15** to imagine: *I fancy it will rain* **16** (*often used with a negative*) to like: *I don't fancy your chances!* **17** (*reflexive*) to have a high or ill-founded opinion of oneself **18** *inf* to have a wish for: *she fancied some chocolate* **19** *Brit inf* to be physically attracted to (another person) **20** to breed (animals) for particular characteristics ▷ *interj* **21** Also: **fancy that!** an exclamation of surprise [C15 *fantsy*, shortened from *fantasie*; see FANTASY] > **'fancily** *adv* > **'fanciness** *n*

fancy dress *n* a costume worn at masquerades, etc, representing a historical figure, etc **b** (*as modifier*): *a fancy-dress ball; fancy-dress costume*

fancy-free *adj* having no commitments

fancy goods *pl n* small decorative gifts

fancy man *n sl* **1** a woman's lover **2** a pimp

fancy woman *n sl* **1** a man's lover **2** a prostitute

fancywork ('fænsɪˌwɜːk) *n* any ornamental needlework, such as embroidery or crochet

fan dance *n* a dance in which large fans are manipulated in front of the body, partially revealing or suggesting nakedness

fandangle (fæn'dæŋgᵊl) *n inf* **1** elaborate ornament **2** nonsense [C19 ?from FANDANGO]

fandango (fæn'dæŋgəʊ) *n, pl* **fandangos 1** an old Spanish courtship dance in triple time **2** a piece of music composed for or in the rhythm of this dance [C18 from Sp., from ?]

fane (feɪn) *n arch or poetic* a temple or shrine [C14 from L *fānum*]

fanfare ('fænfɛə) *n* **1** a flourish or short tune played on brass instruments **2** an ostentatious flourish or display [C17 from F, back formation from *fanfarer*, from Sp, from *fanfarron* boaster, from Ar. *farfār* garrulous]

fang (fæŋ) *n* **1** the long pointed hollow or grooved tooth of a venomous snake through which venom is injected **2** any large pointed tooth, esp the canine tooth of a carnivorous mammal **3** the root of a tooth **4** (*usually pl*) *Brit inf* a tooth [OE *fang* what is caught, prey] > **fanged** *adj* > **'fangless** *adj*

Fangio (*Spanish* 'faŋxjo) *n* **Juan Manuel** (xwan ma'nwɛl) 1911–95, Argentinian racing driver who won the World Championship five times between 1951 and 1957

Fang Lizhi (fæŋ 'liː'ʒɪ) *n* born 1936, Chinese astrophysicist and human-rights campaigner, living in the US from 1990

fan heater *n* a space heater consisting of an electrically heated element with an electrically driven fan to disperse the heat

fanjet ('fænˌdʒɛt) *n* another name for **turbofan**

fanlight ('fænˌlaɪt) *n* **1** a semicircular window over a door or window, often having sash bars like the ribs of a fan **2** a small rectangular window over a door. US name: **transom**

fan mail *n* mail sent to a famous person, such as a pop musician or film star, by admirers

fanny ('fænɪ) *n, pl* **fannies** *sl* **1** *taboo, Brit* the female genitals **2** *chiefly US & Canad* the buttocks [C20 ?from *Fanny*, pet name from *Frances*]

fanny adams *n Brit sl* **1** (usually preceded by *sweet*) absolutely nothing at all **2** *chiefly naut* (formerly) tinned meat [C19 from the name of a young murder victim whose body was cut up into small pieces. For sense 1: a euphemism for *fuck all*]

fantail ('fænˌteɪl) *n* **1** a breed of domestic pigeon having a large tail that can be opened like a fan **2** an Old World flycatcher of Australia, New Zealand, and SE Asia, having a broad fan-shaped tail **3** a tail shaped like an outspread fan **4** an auxiliary sail on the upper portion of a windmill **5** *US* a part of the deck projecting aft of the sternpost of a ship > **'fan-ˌtailed** *adj*

fan-tan *n* **1** a Chinese gambling game **2** a card game played in sequence, the winner being the first to use up all his cards [C19 from Chinese (Cantonese) *fan t'an* repeated divisions, from *fan* times + *t'an* division]

fantasia (fæn'teɪzɪə) *n* **1** any musical composition of a free or improvisatory nature **2** a potpourri of popular tunes woven loosely together [C18 from It.: fancy; see FANTASY]

fantasist ('fæntəsɪst) *n* **1** a person who indulges in fantasies **2** a person who writes literary or musical fantasies

fantasize *or* **fantasise** ('fæntəˌsaɪz) *vb* **fantasizes, fantasizing, fantasized** *or* **fantasises, fantasising, fantasised 1** (when *tr*, takes a clause as object) to conceive extravagant or whimsical ideas, images, etc **2** (*intr*) to conceive pleasant mental images

fantastic (fæn'tæstɪk) *adj* also **fantastical** **1** strange or fanciful in appearance, conception, etc **2** created in the mind; illusory **3** unrealistic: *fantastic plans* **4** incredible or preposterous: *a fantastic verdict* **5** *inf* very large or extreme: *a fantastic fortune* **6** *inf* very good; excellent **7** of or characterized by fantasy **8** capricious; fitful [c14 *fantastik* imaginary, via LL from Gk *phantastikos* capable of imagining, from *phantazein* to make visible] > **fan,tasti'cality** *or* **fan'tasticalness** *n* > **fan'tastically** *adv*

fantasy *or* **phantasy** ('fæntəsɪ) *n, pl* **fantasies** *or* **phantasies** **1a** imagination unrestricted by reality **1b** (*as modifier*): *a fantasy world* **2** a creation of the imagination, esp a weird or bizarre one **3** *psychol* a series of pleasing mental images, usually serving to fulfil a need not gratified in reality **4** a whimsical or far-fetched notion **5** an illusion or phantom **6** a highly elaborate imaginative design or creation **7** *music* another word for **fantasia** **8** literature, etc, having a large fantasy content **9** (*modifier*) of or relating to a competition, often in a newspaper, in which a participant selects players for an imaginary ideal team, and points are awarded according to the actual performances of the chosen players: *fantasy football* ▷ *vb* **fantasies, fantasying, fantasied** *or* **phantasies, phantasying, phantasied** **10** a less common word for **fantasize** [c14 *fantasie*, from L, from Gk *phantazein* to make visible]

Fantin-Latour (*French* fɑ̃tɛ̃latur) *n* (**Ignace**) **Henri** (**Joseph Théodore**) (ɑ̃ri) 1836–1904, French painter, noted for his still lifes and portrait groups

fan vaulting *n archit* vaulting having ribs that radiate like those of a fan and spring from the top of a capital. Also called: **palm vaulting**

fanzine ('fæn,ziːn) *n* a magazine produced by amateurs for fans of a specific interest, pop group, etc [c20 from FAN² + (MAGA)ZINE]

FAO *abbrev for*: **1** Food and Agriculture Organization (of the United Nations) **2** for the attention of

FAQ *computing abbrev for* frequently asked question *or* questions; a question or set of questions with answers, designed to give basic information about a particular topic, esp when made available as a computer file or on a website

f.a.q. *abbrev for*: **1** *commerce* fair average quality **2** free alongside quay

far (fɑː) *adv* **farther** *or* **further, farthest** *or* **furthest** **1** at, to, or from a great distance **2** at or to a remote time: *far in the future* **3** to a considerable degree: *a far better plan* **4** **as far as** **4a** to the degree or extent that **4b** to the distance or place of **4c** *inf* with reference to; as for **5** **by far** by a considerable margin **6** **far and away** by a very great margin **7** **far and wide** everywhere **8** **far be it from me** on no account: *far be it from me to tell you what to do* **9** **go far** **9a** to be successful: *your son will go far* **9b** to be sufficient or last long: *the wine didn't go far* **10** **go too far** to exceed reasonable limits **11** **so far** **11a** up to the present moment **11b** up to a certain point, extent, degree, etc ▷ *adj* (*prenominal*) **12** remote in space or time: *in the far past* **13** extending a great distance **14** more distant: *the far end of the room* **15** **far from** in a degree, state, etc remote from: *he is far from happy* [OE *feorr*] > **'farness** *n*

farad ('færəd) *n physics* the derived SI unit of electric capacitance; the capacitance of a capacitor between the plates of which a potential of 1 volt is created by a charge of 1 coulomb. Symbol: F [c19 see FARADAY]

faraday ('færə,deɪ) *n* a quantity of electricity, used in electrochemical calculations, equivalent to unit amount of substance of electrons. Symbol: F [c20 after Michael FARADAY]

Faraday ('færə,deɪ) *n* **Michael** 1791–1867, English physicist and chemist who discovered electromagnetic induction, leading to the invention of the dynamo. He also carried out research into the principles of electrolysis

faradic (fə'rædɪk) *adj* of or concerned with an intermittent alternating current such as that induced in the secondary winding of an induction coil [c19 from F *faradique*; from Michael FARADAY]

farandole ('færən,dəʊl) *n* **1** a lively dance from Provence **2** a piece of music composed for or in the rhythm of this dance [c19 from F, from Provençal *farandoulo*, from ?]

faraway ('fɑːrə,weɪ) *adj* (**far away** *when postpositive*) **1** very distant **2** absent-minded

farce (fɑːs) *n* **1** a broadly humorous play based on the exploitation of improbable situations **2** the genre of comedy represented by works of this kind **3** a ludicrous situation or action **4** another name for **forcemeat** [c14 (in the sense: stuffing): from OF, from L *farcīre* to stuff, interpolate passages (in the mass, in religious plays, etc)]

farcical ('fɑːsɪkᵊl) *adj* **1** absurd **2** of or relating to farce > **,farci'cality** *n* > **'farcically** *adv*

fardel ('fɑːdᵊl) *n arch* a bundle or burden [c13 from OF *farde*, ult. from Ar. *fardah*]

fare (fɛə) *n* **1** the sum charged or paid for conveyance in a bus, train, etc **2** a paying passenger, esp when carried by taxi **3** a range of food and drink ▷ *vb* **fares, faring, fared** (*intr*) **4** to get on (as specified): *he fared well* **5** (with *it* as a subject) to happen as specified: *it fared badly with him* **6** *arch* to eat: *we fared sumptuously* **7** (often foll by *forth*) *arch* to travel [OE *faran*] > **'farer** *n*

Far East *n* **the** the countries of E Asia, including China, Japan, North and South Korea, E Siberia, Indonesia, Malaysia, and the Philippines: sometimes extended to include all territories east of Afghanistan

Far Eastern *adj* of or relating to the Far East (E Asia) or its inhabitants

fare stage *n* **1** a section of a bus journey for which a set charge is made **2** the bus stop marking the end of such a section

Ff

farewell (,fɛə'wɛl) *sentence substitute* **1** goodbye; adieu ▷ *n* **2** a parting salutation **3** an act of departure **4** (*modifier*) expressing leave-taking: *a farewell speech* ▷ *vb* (*tr*) **5** *Austral & NZ* to honour (a person) at his or her departure, retirement, etc

far-fetched *adj* unlikely

far-flung *adj* **1** widely distributed **2** far distant; remote

Fargo ('fɑːgəʊ) *n* **William** 1818–81, US businessman: founded (1852) with Henry Wells the express mail service Wells, Fargo and Company

Farhi ('fɑːhɪ) *n* **Nicole** born 1946, French fashion designer based in Britain: married to Sir David Hare

farina (fə'riːnə) *n* **1** flour or meal made from any kind of cereal grain **2** *chiefly Brit* starch [c18 from L *fār* spelt, coarse meal]

farinaceous (,færɪ'neɪʃəs) *adj* **1** consisting or made of starch **2** having a mealy texture or appearance **3** containing starch: *farinaceous seeds*

farm (fɑːm) *n* **1a** a tract of land, usually with house and buildings, cultivated as a unit or used to rear livestock **1b** (*as modifier*): *farm produce* **1c** (*in combination*): *farmland* **2** a unit of land or water devoted to the growing or rearing of some particular type of vegetable, fruit, animal, or fish: *a fish farm* **3** an installation for storage or disposal: *a sewage farm* ▷ *vb* **4** (*tr*) **4a** to cultivate (land) **4b** to rear (stock, etc) on a farm **5** (*intr*) to engage in agricultural work, esp as a way of life **6** (*tr*) to look after (a child) for a fixed sum **7** to collect the moneys due and retain the profits from (a tax district, business, etc) for a specified period ▷ See also **farm out** [c13 from OF *ferme* rented land, ult. from L *firmāre* to settle] > **'farmable** *adj*

farmed (fɑːmd) *adj* (of fish and game) reared on a farm rather than caught in the wild

farmer ('fɑːmə) *n* **1** a person who operates or manages a farm **2** a person who obtains the right to collect and retain a tax, rent, etc, on payment of a fee

Farmer ('fɑːmə) *n* **John** ?1565–1605, English madrigal composer and organist

farmer's lung *n* inflammation of the alveoli of the lungs caused by an allergic response to fungal spores in hay

farm hand *n* a person who is hired to work on a farm

farmhouse ('fɑːm,haʊs) *n* a house attached to a farm, esp the dwelling from which the farm is managed

farming ('fɑːmɪŋ) *n* **a** the business or skill of agriculture **b** (*as modifier*): *farming methods*

farm out *vb* (*tr, adv*) **1** to send (work) to be done by another person, firm, etc **2** to put (a child, etc) into the care of a private individual **3** to lease to another for a fee the right to collect (taxes)

farmstead ('fɑːm,stɛd) *n* a farm or the part of a farm comprising its main buildings together with adjacent grounds

farmyard ('fɑːm,jɑːd) *n* an area surrounded by or adjacent to farm buildings

Farnborough ('fɑːnbərə, -brə) *n* a town in S England, in NE Hampshire: military base, with an aeronautical research centre. Pop: 52 535 (1991)

Farnese (*Italian* far'neːse) *n* **1 Alesandro** (ales'sandro) original name of (Pope) **Paul III 2 Alessandro,** duke of Parma and Piacenza. 1545–92, Italian general, statesman, and diplomat in the service of Philip II of Spain. As governor of the Netherlands (1578–92), he successfully suppressed revolts against Spanish rule

Far North *n* **the** the Arctic and sub-Arctic regions of the world

faro ('fɛərəʊ) *n* a gambling game in which players bet against the dealer on what cards he or she will turn up [C18 prob. spelling var. of *Pharoah*]

Faroes ('fɛərəʊz) *pl n* a variant spelling of **Faeroes**

Faroese (,fɛərəʊ'iːz) *adj, n* a variant spelling of **Faeroese**

far-off *adj* (**far off** *when postpositive*) remote in space or time; distant

farouche *French* (faruʃ) *adj* sullen or shy [C18 from F, from OF, from LL *forasticus* from without, from L *foras* out of doors]

Farouk I *or* **Faruk I** (fə'ruːk) *n* 1920–65, last king of Egypt (1936–52). He was forced to abdicate (1952)

far-out *sl* ▷ *adj* (**far out** *when postpositive*) **1** bizarre or avant-garde **2** wonderful ▷ *interj* **far out 3** an expression of amazement or delight

Farquhar ('fɑːkwə, -kə) *n* **George** 1678–1707, Irish-born dramatist; author of comedies such as *The Recruiting Officer* (1706) and *The Beaux' Stratagem* (1707)

Farquhar Islands ('fɑːkwə, -kə) *pl n* an island group in the Indian Ocean: administratively part of the Seychelles

farrago (fə'rɑːgəʊ) *n, pl* **farragos** *or* **farragoes** a hotchpotch [C17 from L: mash for cattle (hence, a mixture), from *fār* spelt] > **farraginous** (fə'rædʒɪnəs) *adj*

far-reaching *adj* extensive in influence, effect, or range

Farrell ('færəl) *n* **1 Colin (James)** born 1976, Irish film actor; he appeared in the TV series *Ballykissangel* before starring in the films *Tigerland* (2000), *Minority Report* (2002), and *Alexander* (2004) **2 J(ames) G(ordon)** 1935–79, British novelist: author of *Troubles* (1970), *The Siege of Krishnapur* (1973), and *The Singapore Grip* (1978) **3 James T(homas)** 1904–79, US writer. His works include the trilogy *Young* (1932), *The Young Manhood of Studs Lonigan* (1934), and *Judgment Day* (1935)

farrier ('færɪə) *n chiefly Brit* **1** a person who shoes horses **2** *arch* another name for **veterinary surgeon** [C16 from OF, from L *ferrārius* smith, from *ferrum* iron] > '**farriery** *n*

farrow ('færəʊ) *n* **1** a litter of piglets ▷ *vb* **2** (of a sow) to give birth to (a litter) [OE *fearh*]

far-seeing *adj* having shrewd judgment

Farsi ('fɑːsɪ) *n* a language spoken in Iran

far-sighted *adj* **1** possessing prudence and foresight **2** another word for **long-sighted** > ,**far-'sightedly** *adv* > ,**far-'sightedness** *n*

fart (fɑːt) *sl* ▷ *n* **1** an emission of intestinal gas from the anus **2** a contemptible person ▷ *vb* (*intr*) **3** to break wind **4 fart about** *or* **around 4a** to behave foolishly **4b** to waste time [ME *farten*]

farther ('fɑːðə) *adv* **1** to or at a greater distance in space or time **2** in addition ▷ *adj* **3** more distant or remote in space or time **4** additional [C13 see FAR, FURTHER]

> USAGE *Farther, farthest, further,* and *furthest* can all be used to refer to literal distance, but *further* and *furthest* are used for figurative senses denoting greater or additional amount, time, etc: *further to my letter. Further* and *furthest* are also preferred for figurative distance

farthermost ('fɑːðə,məʊst) *adj* most distant or remote

farthest ('fɑːðɪst) *adv* **1** to or at the greatest distance in space or time ▷ *adj* **2** most distant in space or time **3** most extended [C14 *ferthest*, from *ferther* FURTHER]

farthing ('fɑːðɪŋ) *n* **1** a former British bronze coin worth a quarter of an old penny: withdrawn in 1961 **2** something of negligible value; jot [OE *fēorthing* from *fēortha* FOURTH + -ING[1]]

farthingale ('fɑːðɪŋ,geɪl) *n* a hoop or framework worn under skirts, esp in the Elizabethan period, to shape and spread them [C16 from F *verdugale*, from OSp. *verdugado*, from *verdugo* rod]

Faruk I (fə'ruːk) *n* a variant spelling of **Farouk I**

fasces ('fæsiːz) *pl n, sing* **fascis** (-sɪs) **1** (in ancient Rome) one or more bundles of rods containing an axe with its blade protruding; a symbol of a magistrate's power **2** (in modern Italy) such an object used as the symbol of Fascism [C16 from L, pl of *fascis* bundle]

fascia *or* **facia** ('feɪʃɪə) *n, pl* **fasciae** *or* **faciae** (-ʃɪ,iː) **1** the flat surface above a shop window **2** *archit* a flat band or surface, esp a part of an architrave **3** ('fæʃɪə) fibrous connective tissue occurring in sheets between muscles **4** *biol* a distinctive band of colour, as on an insect or plant **5** *Brit* the outer panel which covers the dashboard of a motor vehicle [C16 from L: band: rel. to *fascis* bundle] > '**fascial** *or* '**facial** *adj*

fasciate ('fæʃɪ,eɪt) *or* **fasciated** *adj* **1** *bot* (of stems and branches) abnormally flattened due to coalescence **2** (of birds, insects, etc) marked by bands of colour [C17 prob. from NL *fasciātus* (unattested) having bands; see FASCIA]

fascicle ('fæsɪk[ə]l) *n* **1** a bundle of branches, leaves, etc **2** Also called: **fasciculus** *anat* a small bundle of fibres, esp nerve fibres [C15 from L *fasciculus* a small bundle, from *fascis* a bundle] > '**fascicled** *adj* > **fascicular** (fə'sɪkjʊlə) *or* **fasciculate** (fə'sɪkjʊ,leɪt) *adj* > **fas,cicu'lation** *n*

fascicule ('fæsɪ,kjuːl) *n* one part of a printed work that is published in instalments. Also called: **fascicle, fasciculus**

fascinate ('fæsɪ,neɪt) *vb* **fascinates, fascinating, fascinated** (*mainly tr*) **1** to attract and delight by arousing interest: *his stories fascinated me for hours* **2** to render motionless, as by arousing terror or awe **3** *arch* to put under a spell [C16 from L, from *fascinum* a bewitching] > ,**fasci'nation** *n*

fascinating ('fæsɪ,neɪtɪŋ) *adj* **1** arousing great interest **2** enchanting or alluring

fascinator ('fæsɪ,neɪtə) *n rare* a lace or crocheted head covering for women

Fascism ('fæʃɪzəm) *n* **1** the political movement, doctrine, system, or regime of Benito Mussolini in Italy. Fascism encouraged militarism and nationalism, organizing the country along hierarchical authoritarian lines **2** (*sometimes not cap*) any ideology or movement modelled on or inspired by this **3** *inf* (*often not cap*) any doctrine, system, or practice, regarded as authoritarian, militaristic, chauvinistic, or extremely right-wing [C20 from It. *fascismo*, from *fascio* political

group, from L *fascis* bundle; see FASCES]
▷ www.fordham.edu/halshall/mod/modsbook42.html
▷ www.remember.org/hist.root.what.html

Fascist (ˈfæʃɪst) *n* **1** a supporter or member of a Fascist movement **2** (*sometimes not cap*) any person regarded as having right-wing authoritarian views ▷ *adj* **3** characteristic of or relating to Fascism

fashion (ˈfæʃən) *n* **1a** style in clothes, behaviour, etc, esp the latest style **1b** (*as modifier*): *a fashion magazine* **2** (*modifier*) designed to be in the current fashion **3a** manner of performance: *in a striking fashion* **3b** (*in combination*): *crab-fashion* **4** a way of life that revolves around the activities, dress, interests, etc, that are most fashionable **5** shape or form **6** sort; kind **7 after** *or* **in a fashion** in some manner, but not very well: *I mended it, after a fashion* **8 of fashion** of high social standing ▷ *vb* (*tr*) **9** to give a particular form to **10** to make suitable or fitting **11** *obs* to contrive [C13 *facioun* form, manner, from OF *faceon*, from L, from *facere* to make] > ˈ**fashioner** *n*
▷ www.fashionshowroom.com
▷ www.costumes.org
▷ www.fashion.net/sites/fashiondesigners

fashionable (ˈfæʃənəbᵊl) *adj* **1** conforming to fashion; in vogue **2** of or patronized by people of fashion: *a fashionable café* **3** (usually foll by *with*) patronized (by) > ˌ**fashionaˈbility** *or* ˈ**fashionableness** *n* > ˈ**fashionably** *adv*

fashionista (ˌfæʃəˈniːstə) *n inf* a person who follows trends in the fashion industry obsessively and strives continually to adopt the latest fashions [C20 from FASHION + -*ista* as in SANDINISTA]

fashion plate *n* **1** an illustration of the latest fashion in dress **2** a fashionably dressed person

fashion victim *n inf* a person who slavishly follows fashion

Fassbinder (*German* ˈfasbɪndər) *n* **Rainer Werner** (ˈrainər ˈvɛrnər) 1946–82, German film director. His films include *The Bitter Tears of Petra von Kant* (1972), *Fear Eats the Soul* (1974), and *The Marriage of Maria Braun* (1978)

fast¹ (fɑːst) *adj* **1** acting or moving or capable of acting or moving quickly **2** accomplished in or lasting a short time: *a fast visit* **3** (*prenominal*) adapted to or facilitating rapid movement: *the fast lane of a motorway* **4** (of a clock, etc) indicating a time in advance of the correct time **5** given to an active dissipated life **6** of or characteristic of such activity: *a fast life* **7** not easily moved; firmly fixed; secure **8** firmly fastened or shut **9** steadfast; constant (esp in **fast friends**) **10** *sport* (of a playing surface, running track, etc) conducive to rapid speed, as of a ball used on it or of competitors racing on it **11** that will not fade or change colour readily **12** proof against fading **13** *photog* **13a** requiring a relatively short time of exposure to produce a given density: *a fast film* **13b** permitting a short exposure time: *a fast shutter* **14 a fast one** *inf* a deceptive or unscrupulous trick (esp in **pull a fast one**) **15 fast worker** a person who achieves results quickly, esp in seductions ▷ *adv* **16** quickly; rapidly **17** soundly; deeply: *fast asleep* **18** firmly; tightly **19** in quick succession **20** in advance of the correct time: *my watch is running fast* **21** in a reckless or dissipated way **22 fast by** *or* **beside** *arch* close by **23 play fast and loose** *inf* to behave in an insincere or unreliable manner [OE *fæst* strong, tight]

fast² (fɑːst) *vb* **1** (*intr*) to abstain from eating all or certain foods or meals, esp as a religious observance ▷ *n* **2a** an act or period of fasting **2b** (*as modifier*): *a fast day* [OE *fæstan*] > ˈ**faster** *n*

fastback (ˈfɑːstˌbæk) *n* a car having a back that forms one continuous slope from roof to rear

fast-breeder reactor *n* a nuclear reactor that uses little or no moderator and produces more fissionable material than it consumes

fast casual *n* a style of fast food involving healthier, fresher, and more varied dishes than traditional fast food, served in more attractive surroundings

fasten (ˈfɑːsᵊn) *vb* **1** to make or become fast or secure **2** to make or become attached or joined **3** to close or become closed by fixing firmly in place, locking, etc **4** (*tr*; foll by *in* or *up*) to enclose or imprison **5** (*tr*; usually foll by *on*) to cause (blame, a nickname, etc) to be attached (to) **6** (usually foll by *on* or *upon*) to direct or be directed in a concentrated way **7** (*intr*; usually foll by *on*) to take a firm hold (of) [OE *fæstnian*; *see* FAST¹] > ˈ**fastener** *n*

fastening (ˈfɑːsᵊnɪŋ) *n* something that fastens, such as a clasp or lock

fast food *n* **a** food, esp hamburgers, fried chicken, etc, that is prepared and served very quickly **b** (*as modifier*): *a fast-food restaurant*
▷ http://can-do.com/uci/lessons98/Nutrition.html
▷ www.fatcalories.com
▷ www.slowfood.com

fast-forward *n* **1** (*sometimes not hyphenated*) the control on a tape deck or video recorder used to wind the tape or video forwards at speed **2** *inf* a state of urgency or rapid progress: *put the deal into fast-forward* ▷ *vb* (*tr*) **3** to wind (a tape, etc) forward using the fast-forward control **4** *inf* **4a** to deal with or dispatch (something) rapidly: *fast-forward this to the press* **4b** to skip (something): *fast-forward the small talk and get down to business*

fastidious (fæˈstɪdɪəs) *adj* **1** hard to please **2** excessively particular about details **3** exceedingly delicate [C15 from L *fastīdiōsus* scornful, from *fastīdium* loathing, from *fastus* pride + *taedium* weariness] > **fasˈtidiously** *adv* > **fasˈtidiousness** *n*

fastie (ˈfɑːstɪ) *n Austral slang* **1** a deceitful act **2 pull a fastie** to play a sly trick

fastigiate (fæˈstɪdʒɪɪt) *or* **fastigiated** *adj biol* (of parts or organs) united in a tapering group [C17 from Med. L *fastīgiātus* lofty, from L *fastīgium* height]

fast lane *n* **1** the outside lane on a motorway for vehicles overtaking or travelling at high speed **2** *inf* the quickest but most competitive route to success

Ff

fastness (ˈfɑːstnɪs) *n* **1** a stronghold; fortress **2** the state or quality of being firm or secure [OE *fæstnes*; see FAST¹]

fast track *n* **1a** the quickest or most direct route or system **1b** (*as modifier*): *fast-track executives*; *a fast-track procedure for libel claims* ▷ *vb* **fast-track** (*tr*) **2** to speed up the progress of (a project or person) > ˌ**fast-ˈtracker** *n*

fat (fæt) *n* **1** any of a class of naturally occurring soft greasy solids that are present in some plants and animals, and are used in making soap and paint and in the food industry **2** vegetable or animal tissue containing fat **3** corpulence, obesity, or plumpness **4** the best or richest part of something **5 the fat is in the fire** an irrevocable action has been taken from which dire consequences are expected **6 the fat of the land** the best that is obtainable ▷ *adj* **fatter, fattest 7** having much or too much flesh or fat **8** consisting of or containing fat; greasy **9** profitable; lucrative **10** affording great opportunities: *a fat part in the play* **11** fertile or productive: *a fat land* **12** thick, broad, or extended: *a fat log of wood* **13** *sl* very little or none (in **a fat chance, a fat lot of good,** etc) ▷ *vb* **fats, fatting, fatted 14** to make or become fat; fatten [OE *fǣtt*, p.p. of *fǣtan* to cram] > ˈ**fatless** *adj* > ˈ**fatly** *adv* > ˈ**fatness** *n* > ˈ**fattish** *adj*

fatal (ˈfeɪtᵊl) *adj* **1** resulting in death: *a fatal accident* **2** bringing ruin **3** decisively important **4** inevitable [C14 from OF or L from L *fātum*; see FATE] > ˈ**fatally** *adv*

fatalism (ˈfeɪtəˌlɪzəm) *n* **1** the philosophical doctrine that all events are predetermined so that man is powerless to alter his destiny **2** the acceptance of and submission to this doctrine > ˈ**fatalist** *n* > ˌ**fatalˈistic** *adj*

fatality (fəˈtælɪtɪ) *n, pl* **fatalities 1** an accident or disaster resulting in death **2** a person killed in an accident or disaster **3** the power of causing death or disaster; deadliness **4** the quality or condition of being fated

5 something caused or dictated by fate

fate (feɪt) *n* **1** the ultimate agency that predetermines the course of events **2** the inevitable fortune that befalls a person or thing **3** the end or final result **4** death, destruction, or downfall ▷ *vb* **fates, fating, fated 5** (*tr; usually passive*) to predetermine: *he was fated to lose* [C14 from L *fātum* oracular utterance, from *fārī* to speak]

fated (ˈfeɪtɪd) *adj* **1** destined **2** doomed to death or destruction

fateful (ˈfeɪtfʊl) *adj* **1** having important consequences **2** bringing death or disaster **3** controlled by or as if by fate **4** prophetic > ˈ**fatefully** *adv* > ˈ**fatefulness** *n*

Fates (feɪts) *pl n* **1** *Greek myth* the three goddesses who control the destinies of the lives of man, which are likened to skeins of thread that they spin, measure out, and at last cut. See **Atropos, Clotho, Lachesis 2** *Norse myth* another name for the **Norns** (see **Norn**[1])

fat farm *n sl* a health farm or similar establishment to which people go to lose weight

fathead (ˈfætˌhɛd) *n inf* a stupid person; fool > ˈ**fatˌheaded** *adj*

father (ˈfɑːðə) *n* **1** a male parent **2** a person who founds a line or family; forefather **3** any male acting in a paternal capacity **4** (*often cap*) a respectful term of address for an old man **5** a male who originates something: *the father of modern psychology* **6** a leader of an association, council, etc: *a city father* **7** *Brit* the eldest or most senior member in a union, profession, etc **8** (*often pl*) a senator in ancient Rome ▷ *vb* (*tr*) **9** to procreate or generate (offspring) **10** to create, found, etc **11** to act as a father to **12** to acknowledge oneself as father or originator of **13** (foll by *on* or *upon*) to impose or foist upon [OE *fæder*] > ˈ**fatherhood** *n* > ˈ**fatherless** *adj* > ˈ**father-ˌlike** *adj*

Father (ˈfɑːðə) *n* **1** God, esp when considered as the first person of the Christian Trinity **2** any of the early writers on Christian doctrine **3** a title used for Christian priests

father confessor *n* **1** *Christianity* a priest who hears confessions **2** any person to whom one tells private matters

father-in-law *n, pl* **fathers-in-law** the father of one's wife or husband

fatherland (ˈfɑːðəˌlænd) *n* **1** a person's native country **2** the country of a person's ancestors

fatherly (ˈfɑːðəlɪ) *adj* of, resembling, or suitable to a father, esp in kindliness, encouragement, etc > ˈ**fatherliness** *n*

Father of the House *n* (in Britain) the longest-serving member of the House of Commons

Father's Day *n* a day observed in honour of fathers; in Britain the third Sunday in June

fathom (ˈfæðəm) *n* **1** a unit of length equal to six feet (1.829 metres), used to measure depths of water ▷ *vb* (*tr*) **2** to measure the depth of, esp with a sounding line **3** to penetrate (a mystery, problem, etc) [OE *fæthm*] > ˈ**fathomable** *adj*

Fathometer (fəˈðɒmɪtə) *n trademark* a type of echo sounder used for measuring the depth of water

fathomless (ˈfæðəmlɪs) *adj* another word for **unfathomable** > ˈ**fathomlessness** *n*

fatigue (fəˈtiːg) *n* **1** physical or mental exhaustion due to exertion **2** a tiring activity or effort **3** *physiol* the temporary inability of an organ or part to respond to a stimulus because of overactivity **4** the weakening of a material subjected to alternating stresses, esp vibrations **5** the temporary inability to respond to a situation resulting from overexposure to it: *compassion fatigue* **6** any of the mainly domestic duties performed by military personnel, esp as a punishment **7** (*pl*) special clothing worn by military personnel to carry out such duties ▷ *vb* **fatigues, fatiguing, fatigued 8** to make or become weary or exhausted [C17 from F, from *fatiguer* to tire, from L *fatīgāre*] > **fatigable** *or* **fatiguable** (ˈfætɪgəbᵊl) *adj*

Fatima (ˈfætɪmə) *n* ?606–632 AD daughter of Mohammed; wife of Ali

Fátima (*Portuguese* ˈfatimə) *n* a village in central Portugal: Roman Catholic shrine and pilgrimage centre

Fatshan (ˈfɑːtˈʃɑːn) *n* a variant transliteration of the Chinese name for **Foshan**

fatshedera (fætsˈhɛdərə) *n* a hybrid plant with five-lobed leaves [from NL, from *Fatsia japonica* + *Hedera hibernica*]

fatsia (ˈfætsɪə) *n* an evergreen hardy shrub. Also known as the **false castor-oil plant** [from NL]

fatso (ˈfætsəʊ) *n, pl* **fatsos** *sl* a fat person

fat-soluble *adj* soluble in substances such as ether, chloroform, and oils. Fat-soluble compounds are often insoluble in water

fat stock *n* livestock fattened and ready for market

fatten (ˈfætᵊn) *vb* **1** to grow or cause to grow fat or fatter **2** (*tr*) to cause (an animal or fowl) to become fat by feeding it **3** (*tr*) to make fuller or richer **4** (*tr*) to enrich (soil) > ˈ**fattening** *adj*

fattism (ˈfætɪzəm) *n* discrimination on the basis of weight, esp prejudice against those considered to be overweight [C20 from FAT + -ISM, on the model of RACISM] > ˈ**fattist** *n, adj*

fatty (ˈfætɪ) *adj* **fattier, fattiest 1** containing or derived from fat **2** greasy; oily **3** (esp of tissues, organs, etc) characterized by the excessive accumulation of fat ▷ *n, pl* **fatties 4** *inf* a fat person > ˈ**fattily** *adv* > ˈ**fattiness** *n*

fatty acid *n* an aliphatic carboxylic acid, esp one found in lipids, such as palmitic acid, stearic acid, and oleic acid

fatty degeneration *n pathol* the abnormal formation of tiny globules of fat within the cytoplasm of a cell

fatuity (fəˈtjuːɪtɪ) *n, pl* **fatuities 1** inanity **2** a fatuous remark, act, sentiment, etc > **faˈtuitous** *adj*

fatuous (ˈfætjʊəs) *adj* complacently or inanely foolish [C17 from L *fatuus*; rel. to *fatiscere* to gape] > ˈ**fatuously** *adv* > ˈ**fatuousness** *n*

fatwa *or* **fatwah** (ˈfætwə) *n* a religious decree issued by a Muslim leader [Ar.]

fauces (ˈfɔːsiːz) *n, pl* **fauces** *anat* the area between the cavity of the mouth and the pharynx [C16 from L: throat] > **faucal** (ˈfɔːkᵊl) *or* **faucial** (ˈfɔːʃəl) *adj*

faucet (ˈfɔːsɪt) *n* **1** a tap fitted to a barrel **2** the US name for **tap**[2] (sense 1) [C14 from OF from Provençal *falsar* to bore]

Faulkner *or* **Falkner** (ˈfɔːknə) *n* **William** 1897–1962, US novelist and short-story writer. Most of his works portray the problems of the southern US, esp the novels set in the imaginary county of Yoknapatawpha in Mississippi. Other novels include *The Sound and the Fury* (1929) and *Light in August* (1932): Nobel prize for literature 1949

fault (fɔːlt) *n* **1** a failing or defect; flaw **2** a mistake or error **3** a misdeed **4** responsibility for a mistake or misdeed **5** *electronics* a defect in a circuit, component, or line, such as a short circuit **6** *geol* a fracture in the earth's crust resulting in the relative displacement of the rocks on either side of it **7** *tennis, squash, etc* an invalid serve **8** (in showjumping) a penalty mark given for failing to clear, or refusing, a fence, etc **9 at fault** guilty of error; culpable **10 find fault (with)** to seek out minor imperfections or errors (in) **11 to a fault** excessively ▷ *vb* **12** *geol* to undergo or cause to undergo a fault **13** (*tr*) to criticize or blame **14** (*intr*) to commit a fault [C13 from OF *faute* ult. from L *fallere* to fail]

fault-finding *n* **1** continual criticism ▷ *adj* **2** given to finding fault > ˈ**fault-ˌfinder** *n*

faultless (ˈfɔːltlɪs) *adj* perfect or blameless > ˈ**faultlessly** *adv* > ˈ**faultlessness** *n*

faulty ('fɔːltɪ) *adj* **faultier, faultiest** defective or imperfect > '**faultily** *adv* > '**faultiness** *n*

faun (fɔːn) *n* (in Roman legend) a rural deity represented as a man with a goat's ears, horns, tail, and hind legs [c14 back formation from *Faunes* (pl), from L *Faunus* deity of forests] > '**faun,like** *adj*

fauna ('fɔːnə) *n, pl* **faunas** *or* **faunae** (-niː) **1** all the animal life of a given place or time **2** a descriptive list of such animals [c18 from NL, from LL *Fauna* a goddess of living things] > '**faunal** *adj*

Faunus ('fɔːnəs) *n* an ancient Italian deity of pastures and forests, later identified with the Greek Pan

Fauré ('fɔːreɪ; *French* fore) *n* **Gabriel** (**Urbain**) (gabriɛl) 1845–1924, French composer and teacher, noted particularly for his song settings of French poems, esp those of Verlaine, his piano music, and his *Messe de Requiem* (1887)

Faust (faʊst) *or* **Faustus** ('faʊstəs) *n German legend* a magician and alchemist who sells his soul to the devil in exchange for knowledge and power > '**Faustian** *adj*

Fauvism ('fəʊvɪzəm) *n* a form of expressionist painting characterized by the use of bright colours and simplified forms [c20 from F, from *fauve* wild beast] > **Fauve** *n, adj* > '**Fauvist** *n, adj*
▷ www.ibiblio.org/wm/paint/glo/fauvism
▷ www.artlex.com/ArtLex/f/fauvism.html

faux pas (fəʊ pɑː) *n, pl* **faux pas** (fəʊ pɑːz) a social blunder [c17 from F: false step]

fava bean ('fɑːvə) *n* the US and Canadian name for **broad bean** [c20 Italian *fava* from Latin *faba* bean]

fave (feɪv) *adj, n inf* short for **favourite** (senses 1, 2)

favour *or US* **favor** ('feɪvə) *n* **1** an approving attitude; goodwill **2** an act performed out of goodwill or mercy **3** prejudice and partiality **4** a condition of being regarded with approval (esp in **in favour, out of favour**) **5** a token of love, goodwill, etc **6** a small gift or toy given to a guest at a party **7** *history* a badge or ribbon worn or given to indicate loyalty **8** **find favour with** to be approved of by someone **9** **in favour of** **9a** approving **9b** to the benefit of **9c** (of a cheque, etc) made out to **9d** in order to show preference for ▷ *vb* (*tr*) **10** to regard with especial kindness **11** to treat with partiality **12** to support; advocate **13** to oblige **14** to help; facilitate **15** *inf* to resemble: *he favours his father* **16** to wear habitually: *she favours red* **17** to treat gingerly: *a footballer favouring an injured leg* [c14 from L, from *favēre* to protect] > '**favourer** *or US* '**favorer** *n*

favourable *or US* **favorable** ('feɪvərəbᵊl) *adj* **1** advantageous, encouraging or promising **2** giving consent > '**favourably** *or US* '**favorably** *adv*

-favoured *or US* **-favored** *adj* (*in combination*) having an appearance (as specified): *ill-favoured*

favourite *or US* **favorite** ('feɪvərɪt) *adj* **1** (*prenominal*) most liked ▷ *n* **2** a person or thing regarded with especial preference or liking **3** *sport* a competitor thought likely to win **4** (*pl*) *computing* a place on certain browsers that enables Internet users to list the addresses of websites they find and like with a click of the mouse, so that they can revisit them merely by opening the list and clicking on the address [c16 from It., from *favorire* to favour, from L *favēre*]

favouritism *or US* **favoritism** ('feɪvərɪ,tɪzəm) *n* the practice of giving special treatment to a person or group

Fawcett ('fɔːsɪt) *n* Dame **Millicent Garrett** 1847–1929, British suffragette

Fawkes (fɔːks) *n* **Guy** 1570–1606, English conspirator, executed for his part in the Gunpowder Plot to blow up King James I and the Houses of Parliament (1605). Effigies of him (guys) are burnt in Britain on Guy Fawkes Day (Nov 5)

fawn¹ (fɔːn) *n* **1** a young deer of either sex aged under one year **2a** a light greyish-brown colour **2b** (*as adj*): *a fawn raincoat* ▷ *vb* **3** (of deer) to bear (young) [c14 from OF, from L *fētus* offspring; see FETUS] > '**fawn,like** *adj*

fawn² (fɔːn) *vb* (*intr*; often foll by *on* or *upon*) **1** to seek attention and admiration (from) by cringing and flattering **2** (of animals, esp dogs) to try to please by a show of extreme friendliness [OE *fægnian* to be glad, from *fægen* glad; see FAIN] > '**fawner** *n* > '**fawning** *adj*

fax (fæks) *n* **1** short for **facsimile transmission** **2** a message or document sent by facsimile transmission **3** Also called: **fax machine, facsimile machine** a machine which transmits and receives exact copies of documents ▷ *vb* **4** (*tr*) to send (a message or document) by facsimile transmission

fay (feɪ) *n* a fairy or sprite [c14 from OF *feie*, ult. from L *fātum* FATE]

Fayal (*Portuguese* fəˈial) *n* a variant spelling of **Faial**

Fayum (faɪ'juːm) *n* See **El Faiyûm**

faze (feɪz) *vb* **fazes, fazing, fazed** (*tr*) *inf* to disconcert; worry; disturb [c19 var. of arch. *feeze* to beat off]

FBA *abbrev for* Fellow of the British Academy

FBI (in the US) *abbrev for* Federal Bureau of Investigation; an agency responsible for investigating violations of Federal laws
▷ www.fbi.gov

FC *abbrev for*: **1** (in Britain) Football Club **2** (in Canada) Federal Court

fcap *abbrev for* foolscap

F clef *n* another name for **bass clef**

FD *abbrev for* Fidei Defensor [L: Defender of the Faith]

FDA (in the US) *abbrev for* Food and Drug Administration: a federal agency responsible for monitoring trading and safety standards in the food and drug industries

FDR *abbrev for* Franklin Delano Roosevelt

Fe *the chemical symbol for* iron [from NL *ferrum*]

fealty ('fiːəltɪ) *n, pl* **fealties** (in feudal society) the loyalty sworn to one's lord on becoming his vassal [c14 from OF, from L *fidēlitās* FIDELITY]

Ff

fear (fɪə) *n* **1** a feeling of distress, apprehension, or alarm caused by impending danger, pain, etc **2** a cause of this feeling **3** awe; reverence: *fear of God* **4** concern; anxiety **5** possibility; chance **6** **for fear of, that** *or* **lest** to forestall or avoid **7** **no fear** certainly not ▷ *vb* **8** to be afraid (to do something) or of (a person or thing) **9** (*tr*) to revere; respect **10** (*tr; takes a clause as object*) to be sorry: *I fear that you have not won* **11** (*intr*; foll by *for*) to feel anxiety about something [OE *fǣr*] > '**fearless** *adj* > '**fearlessly** *adv* > '**fearlessness** *n*

fearful ('fɪəfʊl) *adj* **1** afraid **2** causing fear **3** *inf* very unpleasant: *a fearful cold* > '**fearfully** *adv* > '**fearfulness** *n*

fearsome ('fɪəsəm) *adj* **1** frightening **2** timorous; afraid > '**fearsomely** *adv*

feasibility study *n* a study designed to determine the practicability of a system or plan

feasible ('fiːzəbᵊl) *adj* **1** able to be done or put into effect; possible **2** likely; probable [c15 from Anglo-F *faisable*, from *faire* to do, from L *facere*] > ,**feasi'bility** *n* > '**feasibly** *adv*

feast (fiːst) *n* **1** a large and sumptuous meal **2** a periodic religious celebration **3** something extremely pleasing: *a feast for the eyes* **4** **movable feast** a festival of variable date ▷ *vb* **5** (*intr*) **5a** to eat a feast **5b** (usually foll by *on*) to enjoy the eating (of): *to feast on cakes* **6** (*tr*) to give a feast to **7** (*intr*; foll by *on*) to take great delight (in): *to feast on beautiful paintings* **8** (*tr*) to regale or delight: *to feast one's eyes* [c13 from OF, from L *festa*, neuter pl (later assumed to be fem sing) of *festus* joyful; rel. to L *fānum* temple, *fēriae* festivals] > '**feaster** *n*

Feast of Dedication *n* a literal translation of **Chanukah**

Feast of Lights *n* an English name for **Chanukah**

Feast of Tabernacles *n* a literal translation of **Sukkoth**

Feast of Weeks *n* a literal translation of **Shavuot**

feat (fiːt) *n* a remarkable, skilful, or daring action [c14 from Anglo-F *fait*, from L *factum* deed; see FACT]

feather ('fɛðə) *n* **1** any of the flat light waterproof structures forming the plumage of birds, each consisting of a hollow shaft having a vane of barbs on either side **2** something resembling a feather, such as a tuft of hair or grass **3** *archery* **3a** a bird's feather or artificial substitute fitted to an arrow to direct its flight **3b** the feathered end of an arrow **4** *rowing* the position of an oar turned parallel to the water between strokes **5** condition of spirits; fettle: *in fine feather* **6** something of negligible value: *I don't care a feather* **7 feather in one's cap** a cause for pleasure at one's achievements ▷ *vb* **8** (*tr*) to fit, cover, or supply with feathers **9** *rowing* to turn (an oar) parallel to the water during recovery between strokes, in order to lessen wind resistance **10** to change the pitch of (an aircraft propeller) so that the chord lines of the blades are in line with the airflow **11** (*intr*) (of a bird) to grow feathers **12 feather one's nest** to provide oneself with comforts [OE *fether*] > **'feathering** *n* > **'feather-,like** *adj* > **'feathery** *adj*

feather bed *n* **1** a mattress filled with feathers or down ▷ *vb* **featherbed, featherbeds, featherbedding, featherbedded 2** (*tr*) to pamper; spoil

featherbedding ('fɛðə,bɛdɪŋ) *n* the practice of limiting production or of overmanning in order to prevent redundancies or create jobs

featherbrain ('fɛðə,breɪn) *or* **featherhead** *n* a frivolous or forgetful person > **'feather,brained** *or* **'feather,headed** *adj*

featheredge ('fɛðər,ɛdʒ) *n* a board or plank that tapers to a thin edge at one side

featherstitch ('fɛðə,stɪtʃ) *n* **1** a zigzag embroidery stitch ▷ *vb* **2** to decorate (cloth) with featherstitch

featherweight ('fɛðə,weɪt) *n* **1a** something very light or of little importance **1b** (*as modifier*): *featherweight considerations* **2a** a professional boxer weighing 118–126 pounds (53.5–57 kg) **2b** an amateur boxer weighing 54–57 kg (119–126 pounds) **3** an amateur wrestler weighing usually 127–137 pounds (58–62 kg)

feature ('fiːtʃə) *n* **1** any one of the parts of the face, such as the nose, chin, or mouth **2** a prominent or distinctive part, as of a landscape, book, etc **3** the principal film in a programme at a cinema **4** an item or article appearing regularly in a newspaper, magazine, etc: *a gardening feature* **5** Also called: **feature story** a prominent story in a newspaper, etc: *a feature on prison reform* **6** a programme given special prominence on radio or television **7** *arch* general form ▷ *vb* **features, featuring, featured 8** (*tr*) to have as a feature or make a feature of **9** to give prominence to (an actor, famous event, etc) in a film or (of an actor, etc) to have prominence in a film **10** (*tr*) *arch* to draw the main features or parts of [c14 from Anglo-F *feture*, from L *factūra* a making, from *facere* to make] > **'featureless** *adj*

-featured *adj* (*in combination*) having features as specified: *heavy-featured*

Feb. *abbrev for* February

febri- *combining form* indicating fever: *febrifuge* [from L *febris* fever]

febrifuge ('fɛbrɪ,fjuːdʒ) *n* **1** any drug or agent for reducing fever ▷ *adj* **2** serving to reduce fever [c17 from Med. L *febrifugia* feverfew; see FEBRI-, -FUGE] > **febrifugal** (fɪ'brɪfjʊgᵊl) *adj*

febrile ('fiːbraɪl) *adj* of or relating to fever; feverish [c17 from Medical L *febrīlis*, from L *febris* fever] > **febrility** (fɪ'brɪlɪtɪ) *n*

February ('fɛbrʊərɪ) *n, pl* **Februaries** the second month of the year, consisting of 28 or (in a leap year) 29 days [c13 from L *Februārius mēnsis* month of expiation, from *februa* Roman festival of purification held on February 15, from pl of *februum* a purgation]

feces ('fiːsiːz) *pl n* the usual US spelling of **faeces** > **fecal** ('fiːkᵊl) *adj*

Fechner (*German* 'fɛçnər) *n* **Gustav Theodor** ('gʊstaf 'teːodoːr) 1801–87, German physicist, philosopher, and psychologist, noted particularly for his work on psychophysics, *Elemente der Psychophysik* (1860)

feckless ('fɛklɪs) *adj* feeble; weak; ineffectual [c16 from obs. *feck* value, effect + -LESS] > **'fecklessly** *adv* > **'fecklessness** *n*

feculent ('fɛkjʊlənt) *adj* **1** filthy or foul **2** of or containing waste matter [c15 from L *faeculentus*; see FAECES] > **'feculence** *n*

fecund ('fiːkənd, 'fɛk-) *adj* **1** fertile **2** intellectually productive [c14 from L *fēcundus*] > **fecundity** (fɪ'kʌndɪtɪ) *n*

fecundate ('fiːkən,deɪt, 'fɛk-) *vb* **fecundates, fecundating, fecundated** (*tr*) **1** to make fruitful **2** to fertilize [c17 from L *fēcundāre* to fertilize] > **,fecun'dation** *n*

fed[1] (fɛd) *vb* **1** the past tense and past participle of **feed 2 fed to death** *or* **fed (up) to the (back) teeth** *inf* bored or annoyed

fed[2] (fɛd) *n US sl* an agent of the FBI

Fed (fɛd) *n* short for **Federal Reserve System**

Fed. *or* **fed.** *abbrev for:* **1** Federal **2** Federation **3** Federated

fedayee (fə'dɑːjiː) *n, pl* **fedayeen** (-jiːn) **a** (*sometimes cap*) (in Arab states) a commando, esp one fighting against Israel **b** (esp in Iran and Afghanistan) a member of a guerrilla organization [from Ar. *fidā'ī* one who risks his life in a cause, from *fidā'* redemption]

federal ('fɛdərəl) *adj* **1** of or relating to a form of government or a country in which power is divided between one central and several regional governments **2** of or relating to the central government of a federation [c17 from L *foedus* league] > **'federa,lism** *n* > **'federalist** *n, adj* > **'federally** *adv*

Federal ('fɛdərəl) *adj* **1** characteristic of or supporting the Union government during the American Civil War ▷ *n* **2** a supporter of the Union government during the American Civil War

Federal Government *n* the national government of a federated state, such as the Canadian national government located in Ottawa

federalize *or* **federalise** ('fɛdərə,laɪz) *vb* **federalizes, federalizing, federalized** *or* **federalises, federalising, federalised** (*tr*) **1** to unite in a federal union **2** to subject to federal control > **,federali'zation** *or* **,federali'sation** *n*

Federal Republic of Germany *n* the official name of Germany, formerly of West Germany

Federal Reserve System *n* (in the US) a banking system consisting of twelve **Federal Reserve Banks** and their member banks. It performs functions similar to those of the Bank of England

▷ www.federalreserve.gov

federate *vb* ('fɛdə,reɪt), **federates, federating, federated 1** to unite or cause to unite in a federal union ▷ *adj* ('fɛdərɪt) **2** federal; federated > **'federative** *adj*

Federated Malay States *pl n* See **Malay States**

federation (,fɛdə'reɪʃən) *n* **1** the act of federating **2** the union of several provinces, states, etc, to form a federal union **3** a political unit formed in such a way **4** any league, alliance, or confederacy

▷ www.nga.gov.au/federation

Federation of Rhodesia and Nyasaland *n* a federation (1953–63) of Northern Rhodesia, Southern Rhodesia, and Nyasaland

fedora (fɪ'dɔːrə) *n* a soft felt brimmed hat, usually with a band [c19 allegedly after *Fédora* (1882), play by Victorien Sardou (1831–1908)]

fed up *adj* (*usually postpositive*) *inf* annoyed or bored: *I'm fed up with your conduct*

fee (fiː) *n* **1** a payment asked by professional people or public servants for their services: *school fees* **2** a charge made for a privilege: *an entrance fee* **3** *property law* an interest in land capable of being inherited. The interest can be with unrestricted rights of disposal (**fee simple**) or with restricted rights to one class of heirs (**fee tail**)

4 (in feudal Europe) the land granted by a lord to his vassal 5 **in fee** *law* (of land) in absolute ownership ▷ *vb* **fees, feeing, feed** 6 *rare* to give a fee to 7 *chiefly Scot* to hire for a fee [C14 from OF *fie*, of Gmc origin; see FIEF]

feeble ('fiːbᵊl) *adj* 1 lacking in physical or mental strength 2 unconvincing: *feeble excuses* 3 easily influenced [C12 from OF *feble, fleible*, from L *flēbilis* to be lamented, from *flēre* to weep] > **'feebleness** *n* > **'feebly** *adv*

feeble-minded *adj* 1 lacking in intelligence 2 mentally defective

feed (fiːd) *vb* **feeds, feeding, fed** (*mainly tr*) 1 to give food to: *to feed the cat* 2 to give as food: *to feed meat to the cat* 3 (*intr*) to eat food: *the horses feed at noon* 4 to provide food for 5 to gratify; satisfy 6 (*also intr*) to supply (a machine, furnace, etc) with (the necessary materials or fuel) for its operation, or (of such materials) to flow or move forwards into a machine, etc 7 *theatre, inf* to cue (an actor, esp a comedian) with lines 8 *sport* to pass a ball to (a team-mate) 9 (*also intr; foll by on or upon*) to eat or cause to eat ▷ *n* 10 the act or an instance of feeding 11 food, esp that of animals or babies 12 the process of supplying a machine or furnace with a material or fuel 13 the quantity of material or fuel so supplied 14 *theatre, inf* a performer, esp a straight man, who provides cues 15 *inf* a meal [OE *fēdan*] > **'feedable** *adj*

feedback ('fiːd,bæk) *n* 1 information or an opinion in response to an inquiry, proposal, etc 2a the return of part of the output of an electronic circuit, device, or mechanical system to its input. In **negative feedback** a rise in output energy reduces the input energy; in **positive feedback** an increase in output energy reinforces the input energy 2b that part of the output signal fed back into the input 3 the return of part of the sound output of a loudspeaker to the microphone or pick-up, so that a high-pitched whistle is produced 4 the whistling noise so produced 5 the effect of a product of a biological pathway on the rate of an earlier step in that pathway

feeder ('fiːdə) *n* 1 a person or thing that feeds or is fed 2 a child's feeding bottle or bib 3 a person or device that feeds the working material into a system or machine 4 a tributary channel 5 a road, service, etc, that links secondary areas to the main traffic network 6 a power line for transmitting electrical power from a generating station to a distribution network

feeding bottle *n* a bottle fitted with a rubber teat from which infants suck liquids

feel (fiːl) *vb* **feels, feeling, felt** 1 to perceive (something) by touching 2 to have a physical or emotional sensation of (something): *to feel anger* 3 (*tr*) to examine (something) by touch 4 (*tr*) to find (one's way) by testing or cautious exploration 5 (*copula*) to seem in respect of the sensation given: *it feels warm* 6 to sense (esp in **feel (it) in one's bones**) 7 to consider; believe; think 8 (*intr; foll by for*) to show sympathy or compassion (towards): *I feel for you in your sorrow* 9 (*tr; often foll by up*) *sl* to pass one's hands over the sexual organs of 10 **feel like** to have an inclination (for something or doing something): *I don't feel like going to the pictures* 11 **feel up to** (*usually used with a negative or in a question*) to be fit enough for (something or doing something): *I don't feel up to going out* ▷ *n* 12 the act or an instance of feeling 13 the quality of or an impression from something perceived through feeling: *a homely feel* 14 the sense of touch 15 an instinctive aptitude; knack: *she's got a feel for this sort of work* [OE *fēlan*]

feeler ('fiːlə) *n* 1 a person or thing that feels 2 an organ in certain animals, such as an antenna, that is sensitive to touch 3 a remark designed to probe the reactions or intentions of others

feeler gauge *n* a thin metal strip of known thickness used to measure a narrow gap or to set a gap between two parts

feel-good *adj* causing or characterized by a feeling of self-satisfaction: *feel-good factor; a feel-good movie*

feeling ('fiːlɪŋ) *n* 1 the sense of touch 2a the ability to experience physical sensations, such as heat, etc 2b the sensation so experienced 3 a state of mind 4 a physical or mental impression: *a feeling of warmth* 5 fondness; sympathy: *to have a great deal of feeling for someone* 6 a sentiment: *a feeling that the project is feasible* 7 an emotional disturbance, esp anger or dislike: *a lot of bad feeling* 8 intuitive appreciation and understanding: *a feeling for words* 9 sensibility in the performance of something 10 (*pl*) emotional or moral sensitivity (esp in **hurt** *or* **injure the feelings of**) 11 **have feelings for** to be emotionally or sexually attracted to ▷ *adj* 12 sentient; sensitive 13 expressing or containing emotion > **'feelingly** *adv*

feet (fiːt) *n* 1 the plural of **foot** 2 **at (someone's) feet** as someone's disciple 3 **be run** *or* **rushed off one's feet** to be very busy 4 **carry** *or* **sweep off one's feet** to fill with enthusiasm 5 **feet of clay** a weakness that is not widely known 6 **have** (*or* **keep**) **one's feet on the ground** to be practical and reliable 7 **on one's** *or* **its feet** 7a standing up 7b in good health 8 **stand on one's own feet** to be independent

feign (feɪn) *vb* 1 to pretend: *to feign innocence* 2 (*tr*) to invent: *to feign an excuse* 3 (*tr*) to copy; imitate [C13 from OF, from L *fingere* to form, shape, invent] > **'feigningly** *adv*

feijoa (fiː'dʒəʊə) *n* 1 an evergreen shrub of South America 2 the fruit of this shrub [C19 NL, after J. da Silva *Feijo*, 19th-cent. Sp. botanist]

Feininger ('faɪnɪŋə) *n* **Lyonel** 1871–1956, US artist, who worked at the Bauhaus, noted for his use of superimposed translucent planes of colour

feint[1] (feɪnt) *n* 1 a mock attack or movement designed to distract an adversary, as in boxing, fencing, etc 2 a misleading action or appearance ▷ *vb* 3 (*intr*) to make a feint [C17 from F, from OF *feindre* to FEIGN]

feint[2] (feɪnt) *n printing* a narrow rule used in the production of ruled paper [C19 var. of FAINT]

Feisal ('faɪsᵊl) *n* a variant spelling of **Faisal**

feisty ('faɪstɪ) *adj* **feistier, feistiest** *inf* 1 lively, resilient, and self-reliant 2 *US & Canad* frisky 3 *US & Canad* irritable [C19 dialect *feist, fist* small dog]

felafel (fə'lɑːfəl) *n* a variant spelling of **falafel**

feldspar ('fɛld,spɑː, 'fɛl,spɑː) *or* **felspar** *n* any of a group of hard rock-forming minerals consisting of aluminium silicates of potassium, sodium, calcium, or barium: the principal constituents of igneous rocks [C18 from G, from *Feld* field + *Spat(h)* SPAR[3]] > **feldspathic** (fɛld'spæθɪk, fɛl'spæθ-) *or* **fel'spathic** *adj*

felicitate (fɪ'lɪsɪ,teɪt) *vb* **felicitates, felicitating, felicitated** to congratulate > **fe,lici'tation** *n* > **fe'lici,tator** *n*

felicitous (fɪ'lɪsɪtəs) *adj* 1 well-chosen; apt 2 possessing an agreeable style 3 marked by happiness > **fe'licitously** *adv*

felicity (fɪ'lɪsɪtɪ) *n, pl* **felicities** 1 happiness 2 a cause of happiness 3 an appropriate expression or style 4 the display of such expressions or style [C14 from L *fēlīcitās* happiness, from *fēlix* happy]

feline ('fiːlaɪn) *adj* 1 of, relating to, or belonging to a family of predatory mammals, including cats, lions, leopards, and cheetahs, having a round head and retractile claws 2 resembling or suggestive of a cat, esp in stealth or grace ▷ *n* 3 any member of the cat family; a cat [C17 from L, from *fēlēs* cat] > **'felinely** *adv* > **felinity** (fɪ'lɪnɪtɪ) *n*

Felixstowe ('fiːlɪk,stəʊ) *n* a port and resort in E England, in Suffolk: ferry connections to Rotterdam and Zeebrugge. Pop: 28 606 (1991)

fell[1] (fɛl) *vb* the past tense of **fall**

fell[2] (fɛl) *vb* (*tr*) 1 to cut or knock down: *to fell a tree* 2 *needlework* to fold under and sew flat (the edges of a seam) ▷ *n* 3 *US & Canad* the timber felled in one season

Ff

4 a seam finished by felling [OE *fellan*; cf. FALL] > **'feller** *n*

fell[3] (fɛl) *adj* 1 *arch* cruel or fierce 2 *arch* destructive or deadly 3 **one fell swoop** a single hasty action or occurrence [c13 *fel*, from OF: cruel, from Med. L *fellō* villain; see FELON[1]]

fell[4] (fɛl) *n* an animal skin or hide [OE]

fell[5] (fɛl) *n (often pl) Scot & N English* **a** a mountain, hill, or moor **b** *(in combination)*: *fell-walking* [c13 from ON *fjall*; rel. to OHG *felis* rock]

fellah ('fɛlə) *n, pl* **fellahs, fellahin,** *or* **fellaheen** (ˌfɛlə'hiːn) a peasant in Arab countries [c18 from Ar., dialect var. of *fallāh*, from *falaha* to cultivate]

fellatio (fɪ'leɪʃɪəʊ) *n* a sexual activity in which the penis is stimulated by the mouth [c19 NL, from L *fellāre* to suck]

Felling ('fɛlɪŋ) *n* a town in NE England, in Gateshead unitary authority, Tyne and Wear; formerly noted for coal mining. Pop: 35 053 (1991)

Fellini (*Italian* fɛl'liːnɪ) *n* **Federico** (fede'riko) 1920–93, Italian film director. His films include *La Dolce Vita* (1959), *8½* (1963), *Satyricon* (1969), and *Intervista* (1987)

felloe ('fɛləʊ) *or* **felly** ('fɛlɪ) *n, pl* **felloes** *or* **fellies** a segment or the whole rim of a wooden wheel to which the spokes are attached [OE *felge*]

fellow ('fɛləʊ) *n* 1 a man or boy 2 an informal word for **boyfriend** 3 *inf* one or oneself: *a fellow has to eat* 4 a person considered to be of little worth **5a** *(often pl)* a companion; associate **5b** *(as modifier)*: *fellow travellers* 6 a member of the governing body at any of various universities or colleges 7 a postgraduate student employed, esp for a fixed period, to undertake research **8a** a person in the same group, class, or condition: *the surgeon asked his fellows* **8b** *(as modifier)*: *a fellow sufferer* 9 one of a pair; counterpart; mate [OE *fēolaga*]

Fellow ('fɛləʊ) *n* a member of any of various learned societies: *Fellow of the British Academy*

fellow feeling *n* 1 mutual sympathy or friendship 2 an opinion held in common

fellowship ('fɛləʊˌʃɪp) *n* 1 the state of sharing mutual interests, activities, etc 2 a society of people sharing mutual interests, activities, etc 3 companionship; friendship 4 the state or relationship of being a fellow 5 *education* **5a** a financed research post providing study facilities, privileges, etc, often in return for teaching services **5b** an honorary title carrying certain privileges awarded to a postgraduate student

fellow traveller *n* 1 a companion on a journey 2 a non-Communist who sympathizes with Communism

felon[1] ('fɛlən) *n* 1 *criminal law* (formerly) a person who has committed a felony ▷ *adj* 2 *arch* evil [c13 from OF: villain, from Med. L *fellō*, from ?]

felon[2] ('fɛlən) *n* a purulent inflammation of the end joint of a finger [c12 from Med. L *fellō*, ?from L *fel* poison]

felonious (fɪ'ləʊnɪəs) *adj* 1 *criminal law* of, involving, or constituting a felony 2 *obs* wicked > **fe'loniously** *adv* > **fe'loniousness** *n*

felony ('fɛlənɪ) *n, pl* **felonies** *criminal law* (formerly) a serious crime, such as murder or arson

felspar ('fɛlˌspɑː) *n* a variant spelling (esp Brit) of **feldspar** > **felspathic** (fɛl'spæθɪk) *adj*

felt[1] (fɛlt) *vb* the past tense and past participle of **feel**

felt[2] (fɛlt) *n* 1 a matted fabric of wool, hair, etc, made by working the fibres together under pressure or by heat or chemical action 2 any material, such as asbestos, made by a similar process of matting ▷ *vb* 3 *(tr)* to make into or cover with felt 4 *(intr)* to become matted [OE]

felt-tip pen *n* a pen whose writing point is made from pressed fibres. Also called: **fibre-tip pen**

felucca (fɛ'lʌkə) *n* a narrow lateen-rigged vessel of the Mediterranean [c17 from It., prob. from obs. Sp. *faluca*, prob. from Ar. *fulūk* ships, from Gk, from *ephelkein* to tow]

fem. *abbrev for*: 1 female 2 feminine

female ('fiːmeɪl) *adj* 1 of, relating to, or designating the sex producing gametes (ova) that can be fertilized by male gametes (spermatozoa) 2 of or characteristic of a woman 3 for or composed of women or girls: *a female choir* 4 (of reproductive organs such as the ovary and carpel) capable of producing female gametes 5 (of flowers) lacking, or having nonfunctional, stamens 6 having an internal cavity into which a projecting male counterpart can be fitted: *a female thread* ▷ *n* 7 a female animal or plant [c14 from earlier *femelle* (infl by *male*), from L *fēmella* a young woman, from *fēmina* a woman] > **'femaleness** *n*

female impersonator *n* a male theatrical performer who acts as a woman

feminine ('fɛmɪnɪn) *adj* 1 suitable to or characteristic of a woman 2 possessing qualities or characteristics considered typical of or appropriate to a woman 3 effeminate; womanish 4 *grammar* **4a** denoting or belonging to a gender of nouns that includes all kinds of referents as well as some female animate referents **4b** *(as n)*: *German* Zeit *"time" and* Ehe *"marriage" are feminines* [c14 from L, from *fēmina* woman] > **'femininely** *adv* > **ˌfemi'ninity** *or* **'feminineness** *n*

feminism ('fɛmɪˌnɪzəm) *n* a doctrine or movement that advocates equal rights for women > **'feminist** *n, adj*

feminize *or* **feminise** ('fɛmɪˌnaɪz) *vb* **feminizes, feminizing, feminized** *or* **feminises, feminising, feminised** 1 to make or become feminine 2 to cause (a male animal) to develop female characteristics > **ˌfemini'zation** *or* **ˌfemini'sation** *n*

femme fatale *French* (fam fatal) *n, pl* ***femmes fatales*** (fam fatal) an alluring or seductive woman, esp one who causes men to love her to their own distress [fatal woman]

femto- *prefix* denoting 10^{-15}: *femtometer*. Symbol: f [from Danish or Norwegian *femten* fifteen]

femur ('fiːmə) *n, pl* **femurs** *or* **femora** ('fɛmərə) 1 the longest thickest bone of the human skeleton, with the pelvis above and the knee below. Nontechnical name: **thighbone** 2 the corresponding bone in other vertebrates or the corresponding segment of an insect's leg [c18 from L: thigh] > **'femoral** *adj*

fen (fɛn) *n* low-lying flat land that is marshy or artificially drained [OE *fenn*] > **'fenny** *adj*

fence (fɛns) *n* 1 a structure that serves to enclose an area such as a garden or field, usually made of posts of timber, concrete, or metal connected by wire netting, rails, or boards 2 *sl* a dealer in stolen property 3 an obstacle for a horse to jump in steeplechasing or showjumping 4 *machinery* a guard or guide, esp in a circular saw or plane 5 **(sit) on the fence** (to be) unable or unwilling to commit oneself ▷ *vb* **fences, fencing, fenced** 6 *(tr)* to construct a fence on or around (a piece of land, etc) 7 *(tr; foll by* in *or* off*)* to close (in) or separate (off) with or as if with a fence: *he fenced in the livestock* 8 *(intr)* to fight using swords or foils 9 *(intr)* to evade a question or argument 10 *(intr) sl* to receive stolen property [c14 *fens*, shortened from *defens* DEFENCE] > **'fenceless** *adj* > **'fencer** *n*

fencible ('fɛnsəbᵊl) *n* (formerly) a person who undertook military service in immediate defence of his homeland only

fencing ('fɛnsɪŋ) *n* 1 the practice, art, or sport of fighting with foils, épées, sabres, etc **2a** wire, stakes, etc, used as fences **2b** fences collectively

▷ www.fencing.net

▷ www.foilcommittee.pwp.blueyonder.co.uk

fend (fɛnd) *vb* 1 *(intr; foll by* for*)* to give support (to someone, esp oneself) 2 *(tr; usually foll by* off*)* to ward off or turn aside (blows, questions, etc) ▷ *n* 3 *Scot & N English dialect* a shift or effort [c13 *fenden*, shortened from *defenden* to DEFEND]

fender ('fɛndə) *n* 1 a low metal frame which confines falling coals to the hearth 2 *chiefly US* a metal frame fitted to the front of locomotives to absorb shock, etc **3** a cushion-like device, such as a car tyre hung over the side of a vessel to reduce damage resulting from collision **4** the US and Canad name for the wing of a car

Fénelon (*French* fenlõ) *n* **François de Salignac de La Mothe** (frɑ̃swa də saliɲak də la mɔt) 1651–1715, French theologian and writer; author of *Maximes des saints* (1697), a defence of quietism, and *Les aventures de Télémaque* (1699), which was construed as criticizing the government of Louis XIV

fenestra (fɪˈnɛstrə) *n, pl* **fenestrae** (-triː) **1** *biol* a small opening in or between bones, esp one of the openings between the middle and inner ears **2** *zool* a transparent marking or spot, as on the wings of moths **3** *archit* a window or window-like opening in the outside wall of a building [c19 via NL from L: wall opening, window]

fenestrated (fɪˈnɛstreɪtɪd, ˈfɛnɪˌstreɪtɪd) *or* **fenestrate** *adj* **1** *archit* having windows **2** *biol* perforated or having fenestrae

fenestration (ˌfɛnɪˈstreɪʃən) *n* **1** the arrangement of windows in a building **2** an operation to restore hearing by making an artificial opening into the labyrinth of the ear

feng shui (ˈfʌŋ ˈʃweɪ) *n* the Chinese art of determining the most propitious design and placement of a grave, building, room, etc, so that the maximum harmony is achieved between the flow of chi of the environment and that of the user, believed to bring good fortune [c20 from Chinese *feng* wind + *shui* water]

▷ http://www.wofs.com/
▷ http://www.fengshuisociety.org.uk/
▷ http://www.fengshui-magazine.com/

Fenian (ˈfiːnɪən, ˈfiːnjən) *n* **1** (formerly) a member of an Irish revolutionary organization founded in the US in the 19th century to fight for an independent Ireland ▷ *adj* **2** of or relating to the Fenians [c19 from Irish Gaelic *fēinne*, after *Fiann* Irish folk hero] > **ˈFenianism** *n*

fennec (ˈfɛnɛk) *n* a very small nocturnal fox inhabiting deserts of N Africa and Arabia, having enormous ears [c18 from Ar. *fenek* fox]

fennel (ˈfɛnᵊl) *n* a strong-smelling yellow-flowered umbelliferous plant whose seeds, feathery leaves, and bulbous aniseed-flavoured root are used in cookery [OE *fenol*]

Fenrir (ˈfɛnrɪə), **Fenris** (ˈfɛnrɪs), *or* **Fenriswolf** (ˈfɛnrɪsˌwʊlf) *n Norse myth* an enormous wolf, fathered by Loki, which killed Odin

Fens (fɛnz) *pl n* **the** a flat low-lying area of E England, west and south of the Wash: consisted of marshes until reclaimed in the 17th to 19th centuries

Fenton (ˈfɛntən) *n* **James (Martin)** born 1949, British poet, journalist, and critic. His poetry includes the collections *A German Requiem* (1980) and *Out of Danger* (1993)

fenugreek (ˈfɛnjʊˌgriːk) *n* an annual heavily scented Mediterranean leguminous plant with hairy stems and white flowers [OE *fēnogrēcum*]

feoff (fiːf) *history* ▷ *n* **1** a variant spelling of **fief** ▷ *vb* **2** *(tr)* to invest with a benefice or fief [c13 from Anglo-F: a FIEF] > **ˈfeoffee** *n* > **ˈfeoffment** *n* > **ˈfeoffor** *or* **ˈfeoffer** *n*

-fer *n combining form* indicating a person or thing that bears something specified: *crucifer; conifer* [from L, from *ferre* to bear]

feral (ˈfɪərəl) *adj* **1** (of animals and plants) existing in a wild or uncultivated state **2** savage; brutal [c17 from Med. L, from L, from *ferus* savage]

fer-de-lance (ˌfɛədəˈlɑːns) *n* a large highly venomous tropical American snake with a greyish-brown mottled coloration [c19 from F, lit.: iron (head) of a lance]

Ferdinand (ˈfɜːdɪˌnænd; *German* ˈfɛrdinant) *n* See **Franz Ferdinand**

Ferdinand I (ˈfɜːdɪˌnænd) *n* **1** known as *Ferdinand the Great*. ?1016–65, king of Castile (1035–65) and León (1037–65): achieved control of the Moorish kings of Saragossa, Seville, and Toledo **2** 1503–64, king of Hungary and Bohemia (1526–64); Holy Roman Emperor (1558–64), bringing years of religious warfare to an end **3** 1751–1825, king of the Two Sicilies (1816–25); king of Naples (1759–1806; 1815–25), as Ferdinand IV, being dispossessed by Napoleon (1806–15) **4** 1793–1875, king of Hungary (1830–48) and emperor of Austria (1835–48); abdicated after the Revolution of 1848 in favour of his nephew, Franz Josef I **5** 1861–1948, ruling prince of Bulgaria (1887–1908) and tsar from 1908 until his abdication in 1918 **6** 1865–1927, king of Romania (1914–27); sided with the Allies in World War I

Ferdinand II *n* **1** 1578–1637, Holy Roman Emperor (1619–37); king of Bohemia (1617–19; 1620–37) and of Hungary (1617–37). His anti-Protestant policies led to the Thirty Years' War **2** title as king of Aragon and Sicily of **Ferdinand V**

Ferdinand III *n* **1** 1608–57, Holy Roman Emperor (1637–57) and king of Hungary (1625–57); son of Ferdinand II **2** title as king of Naples of **Ferdinand V**

Ferdinand V *n* known as *Ferdinand the Catholic*. 1452–1516, king of Castile (1474–1504); as Ferdinand II, king of Aragon (1479–1516) and Sicily (1468–1516); as Ferdinand III, king of Naples (1504–16). His marriage to Isabella I of Castile (1469) led to the union of Aragon and Castile and his reconquest of Granada from the Moors (1492) completed the unification of Spain. He introduced the Inquisition (1478), expelled the Jews from Spain (1492), and financed Columbus' voyage to the New World

Ferdinand VII *n* 1784–1833, king of Spain (1808; 1814–33). He precipitated the Carlist Wars by excluding his brother Don Carlos as his successor

feretory (ˈfɛrɪtərɪ, -trɪ) *n, pl* **feretories** *chiefly RC Church* **1** a shrine, usually portable, for a saint's relics **2** the chapel in which a shrine is kept [c14 from MF *fiertre*, from L *feretrum* a bier, from Gk, from *pherein* to bear]

Fergana *or* **Ferghana** (fəˈgɑːnə) *n* **1** a region of W central Asia, surrounded by high mountains and accessible only from the west; mainly in Uzbekistan and partly in Tajikistan and Kyrgyzstan **2** the chief city of this region, in E Uzbekistan. Pop: 203 000 (1998 est)

Fergus (ˈfɜːgəs) *n* (in Irish legend) a warrior king of Ulster, who was supplanted by Conchobar

feria (ˈfɪərɪə) *n, pl* **ferias** *or* **feriae** (-rɪˌiː) *RC Church*. a weekday, other than Saturday, on which no feast occurs [c19 from LL: day of the week (as in *prīma fēria* Sunday), sing of L *fēriae* festivals] > **ˈferial** *adj*

Ferlinghetti (ˌfɜːlɪŋˈgɛtɪ) *n* **Lawrence** born 1920, US poet of the Beat Generation. His poetry includes the collections *Pictures of the Gone World* (1955) and *When I Look at Pictures* (1990)

Fermanagh (fəˈmænə) *n* a district and historical county of SW Northern Ireland: contains the Upper and Lower Lough Erne. Pop: 57 527 (2001). Area (excluding water): 1700 sq km (656 sq miles)

Fermat (fɜːˈmæt; *French* fɛrma) *n* **Pierre de** (pjɛr də) 1601–65, French mathematician, regarded as the founder of the modern theory of numbers. He studied the properties of whole numbers and, with Pascal, investigated the theory of probability

fermata (fəˈmɑːtə) *n, pl* **fermatas** *or* **fermate** (-tɪ) *music* another word for **pause** (sense 5) [from It., from *fermare* to stop, from L *firmāre* to establish]

ferment *n* (ˈfɜːmɛnt) **1** any agent or substance, such as a bacterium, mould, yeast, or enzyme, that causes fermentation **2** another word for **fermentation** **3** commotion; unrest ▷ *vb* (fəˈmɛnt) **4** to undergo or cause to undergo fermentation **5** to stir up or seethe with excitement [c15 from L *fermentum* yeast, from *fervēre* to seethe] > **ferˈmentable** *adj*

USAGE See at **foment**

fermentation (ˌfɜːmɛnˈteɪʃən) *n* a chemical reaction in

Ff

which an organic molecule splits into simpler substances, esp the conversion of sugar to ethyl alcohol by yeast > **fer'mentative** *adj*

fermentation lock *n* a valve placed on the top of bottles of fermenting wine to allow bubbles to escape

fermi ('fɜːmɪ) *n* a unit of length used in nuclear physics equal to 10^{-15} metre [C20 after Enrico FERMI]

Fermi ('fɜːmɪ; *Italian* 'fermi) *n* **Enrico** (en'riːko) 1901–54, Italian nuclear physicist, in the US from 1939. He was awarded a Nobel prize for physics in 1938 for his work on radioactive substances and nuclear bombardment and headed the group that produced the first controlled nuclear reaction (1942)

fermion ('fɜːmɪˌɒn) *n* any of a group of elementary particles, such as a nucleon, that has half-integral spin and obeys the Pauli exclusion principle ▷ Cf **boson** [C20 after Enrico FERMI; see -ON]

fermium ('fɜːmɪəm) *n* a transuranic element artificially produced by neutron bombardment of plutonium. Symbol: Fm; atomic no.: 100; half-life of most stable isotope, ^{257}Fm: 80 days (approx.). [C20 after Enrico FERMI]

Fermor ('fɜːmɔː) *n* **Patrick (Michael) Leigh** born 1915, British traveller and author, noted esp for the travel books *A Time of Gifts* (1977) and *Between the Woods and the Water* (1986)

fern (fɜːn) *n* **1** a plant having roots, stems, and fronds and reproducing by spores formed in structures (sori) on the fronds **2** any of certain similar but unrelated plants, such as the sweet fern [OE *fearn*] > **'ferny** *adj*

Fernandel (*French* fɛrnɑ̃dɛl) *n* real name *Fernand Joseph Désiré Contandin*. 1903–71, French comic film actor

Fernando de Noronha (*Portuguese* fer'nəndu di no'roɲa) *n* a volcanic island in the S Atlantic northeast of Cape São Roque: constitutes a federal territory of Brazil; a penal colony since the 18th century; inhabited by military personnel. Area: 26 sq km (10 sq miles)

Fernando Po (fə'nændəʊ pəʊ) *n* a former name (until 1973) of **Bioko**

fernbird ('fɜːnˌbɜːd) *n* a New Zealand swamp bird with a fernlike tail

ferocious (fə'rəʊʃəs) *adj* savagely fierce or cruel: *a ferocious tiger* [C17 from L *ferox* fierce, warlike] > **ferocity** (fə'rɒsɪtɪ) *n*

-ferous *adj combining form* bearing or producing: *coniferous* [from -FER + -OUS]

Ferrara (fə'rɑːrə; *Italian* fer'rara) *n* a city in N Italy, in Emilia-Romagna: a centre of the Renaissance under the House of Este; university (1391). Pop: 132 127 (2000 est)

Ferrari (*Italian* fɛr'raːrɪ) *n* **Enzo** ('ɛntso) 1898–1988, Italian designer and manufacturer of racing cars

ferrate ('fɛreɪt) *n* a salt containing the divalent ion, FeO_4^{2-} [C19 from L *ferrum* iron]

ferret ('fɛrɪt) *n* **1** a domesticated albino variety of the polecat bred for hunting rats, rabbits, etc **2** an assiduous searcher ▷ *vb* **ferrets, ferreting, ferreted 3** to hunt (rabbits, rats, etc) with ferrets **4** (*tr; usually foll by out*) to drive from hiding: *to ferret out snipers* **5** (*tr; usually foll by out*) to find by persistent investigation **6** (*intr*) to search around [C14 from OF *furet*, from L *fur* thief] > **'ferreter** *n* > **'ferrety** *adj*

ferri- *combining form* indicating the presence of iron, esp in the trivalent state: *ferricyanide; ferriferous* ▷ Cf **ferro-** [from L *ferrum* iron]

ferriage ('fɛrɪɪdʒ) *n* **1** transportation by ferry **2** the fee charged for passage on a ferry

ferric ('fɛrɪk) *adj* of or containing iron in the trivalent state; designating an iron(III) compound [C18 from L *ferrum* iron]

ferric oxide *n* a red crystalline insoluble oxide of iron that occurs as haematite and rust and is made by heating ferrous sulphate; it is used as a pigment and metal polish (**jeweller's rouge**), and as a sensitive coating on magnetic tape. Formula: Fe_2O_3. Systematic name: **iron(III) oxide**

Ferrier ('fɛrɪə) *n* **Kathleen** 1912–53, British contralto; noted for her expressive voice

ferrimagnetism (ˌfɛrɪ'mægnɪˌtɪzəm) *n* a phenomenon exhibited by certain substances, such as ferrites, in which the magnetic moments of neighbouring ions are nonparallel and unequal in magnitude > **ferrimagnetic** (ˌfɛrɪmæg'nɛtɪk) *adj*

Ferris wheel ('fɛrɪs) *n* a fairground wheel having seats freely suspended from its rim [C19 after G.W.G. *Ferris* (1859–96), American engineer]

ferrite ('fɛraɪt) *n* any of a class of nonconducting magnetic mixed-oxide ceramics

ferrite-rod aerial *n* a type of aerial, normally used in radio reception, consisting of a small coil of wire mounted on a ferromagnetic ceramic core, the coil serving as a tuning inductance

ferro- *combining form* **1** indicating a property of iron or the presence of iron: *ferromagnetism* **2** indicating the presence of iron in the divalent state: *ferrocyanide* ▷ Cf **ferri-** [from L *ferrum* iron]

ferrocene ('fɛrəʊˌsiːn) *n* a reddish-orange compound in which the molecules have an iron atom sandwiched between two cyclopentadiene rings. Formula: $Fe(C_5H_5)_2$ [C20 from FERRO- + C(YCLOPENTADI)ENE]

ferroconcrete (ˌfɛrəʊ'kɒŋkriːt) *n* another name for **reinforced concrete**

Ferrol (*Spanish* fɛ'rrɔl) *n* See **El Ferrol**

ferromagnetism (ˌfɛrəʊ'mægnɪˌtɪzəm) *n* the phenomenon exhibited by substances, such as iron, that have relative permeabilities much greater than unity and increasing magnetization with applied magnetizing field. Certain of these substances retain their magnetization in the absence of the applied field > **ferromagnetic** (ˌfɛrəʊmæg'nɛtɪk) *adj*

ferromanganese (ˌfɛrəʊ'mæŋgəˌniːz) *n* an alloy of iron and manganese, used in making additions of manganese to cast iron and steel

ferrous ('fɛrəs) *adj* of or containing iron in the divalent state; designating an iron(II) compound [C19 from FERRI- + -OUS]

ferrous sulphate *n* an iron salt usually obtained as greenish crystals: used in inks, tanning, etc. Formula: $FeSO_4$. Systematic name: **iron(II) sulphate.** Also called: **copperas**

ferruginous (fɛ'ruːdʒɪnəs) *adj* **1** (of minerals, rocks, etc) containing iron: *a ferruginous clay* **2** rust-coloured [C17 from L *ferrūgineus* of a rusty colour, from *ferrum* iron]

ferrule ('fɛruːl) *n* **1** a metal ring, tube, or cap placed over the end of a stick or post for added strength or to increase wear **2** a small length of tube, etc, esp one used for making a joint [C17 from ME *virole*, from OF, from L, from *viria* bracelet; infl. by L *ferrum* iron]

ferry ('fɛrɪ) *n, pl* **ferries 1** Also called: **ferryboat** a vessel for transporting passengers and usually vehicles across a body of water, esp as a regular service **2a** such a service **2b** (*in combination*): *a ferryman* **3** the delivering of aircraft by flying them to their destination ▷ *vb* **ferries, ferrying, ferried 4** to transport or go by ferry **5** to deliver (an aircraft) by flying it to its destination **6** (*tr*) to convey (passengers, goods, etc) [OE *ferian* to carry, bring]
▷ http://routesinternational.com/ships.htm

fertigate ('fɜːtɪˌgeɪt) *vb* **fertigates, fertigating, fertigated** to fertilize and irrigate at the same time, by adding fertilizers to the water supply [C20 from FERTILIZE + IRRIGATE] > **ˌferti'gation** *n*

fertile ('fɜːtaɪl) *adj* **1** capable of producing offspring **2a** (of land) capable of sustaining an abundant growth of plants **2b** (of farm animals) capable of breeding stock **3** *biol* capable of undergoing growth and development: *fertile seeds; fertile eggs* **4** producing many offspring; prolific **5** highly productive: *a fertile brain* **6** *physics* (of a substance) able to be transformed into fissile or fissionable material [C15 from L *fertilis*, from *ferre* to bear] > '**fertilely** *adv* > '**fertileness** *n*

Fertile Crescent *n* an area of fertile land in the Middle East, extending around the Rivers Tigris and Euphrates in a semicircle from Israel to the Persian Gulf

fertility (fɜː'tɪlɪtɪ) *n* **1** the ability to produce offspring **2** the state or quality of being fertile

fertility drug *n* any of a group of preparations used to stimulate ovulation in women hitherto infertile

fertilize *or* **fertilise** ('fɜːtɪˌlaɪz) *vb* **fertilizes, fertilizing, fertilized** *or* **fertilises, fertilising, fertilised** (*tr*) **1** to provide (an animal, plant, etc) with sperm or pollen to bring about fertilization **2** to supply (soil or water) with nutrients to aid the growth of plants **3** to make fertile > ˌ**fertili'zation** *or* ˌ**fertili'sation** *n*

fertilizer *or* **fertiliser** ('fɜːtɪˌlaɪzə) *n* **1** any substance, such as manure, added to soil or water to increase its productivity **2** an object or organism that fertilizes an animal or plant

ferula ('fɛrʊlə) *n, pl* **ferulas** *or* **ferulae** (-ˌliː) a large umbelliferous plant having thick stems and dissected leaves [C14 from L: giant fennel]

ferule ('fɛruːl) *n* **1** a flat piece of wood, such as a ruler, used in some schools to cane children on the hand ▷ *vb* **ferules, feruling, feruled 2** (*tr*) *rare* to punish with a ferule [C16 from L *ferula* giant fennel]

fervent ('fɜːvənt) *or* **fervid** ('fɜːvɪd) *adj* **1** intensely passionate; ardent **2** *arch or poetic* burning or glowing [C14 from L *fervēre* to boil, glow] > '**fervency** *n* > '**fervently** *or* '**fervidly** *adv*

> USAGE While both *fervent* and *fervid* come from the same root and share the meaning 'intense, ardent', the first has largely positive connotations, and is associated with *hopes, wishes, beliefs* and *admirers, supporters, fans*. The second, apart from being used less often than the first, is chiefly negative: *...in the fervid politics of New York City*. *A fervent kiss* from an admirer would probably be welcome; a *fervid* one would not

fervour *or US* **fervor** ('fɜːvə) *n* **1** great intensity of feeling or belief **2** *rare* intense heat [C14 from L *fervor* heat, from *fervēre* to glow, boil]

Fès (fɛs) *or* **Fez** *n* a city in N central Morocco, traditional capital of the north: became an independent kingdom in the 11th century, at its height in the 14th century; religious centre; university (850). Pop: 263 828 (1994)

fescue ('fɛskjuː) *or* **fescue grass** *n* a widely cultivated pasture and lawn grass, having stiff narrow leaves [C14 from OF *festu*, ult. from L *festūca* stem, straw]

fess (fɛs) *vb inf, chiefly US* to make a confession [C19 shortened from CONFESS]

fesse *or* **fess** (fɛs) *n heraldry* an ordinary consisting of a horizontal band across a shield [C15 from Anglo-F, from L *fascia* band, fillet]

fest (fɛst) *n* **a** a meeting or event at which the emphasis is on a particular activity: *a fashion fest* **b** (*in combination*): *schmaltz-fest; lovefest* [C19 from G *Fest* festival]

festal ('fɛstᵊl) *adj* another word for **festive** [C15 from L *festum* holiday] > '**festally** *adv*

fester ('fɛstə) *vb* **1** to form or cause to form pus **2** (*intr*) to become rotten; decay **3** to become or cause to become bitter, irritated, etc, esp over a long period of time ▷ *n* **4** a small ulcer or sore containing pus [C13 from OF *festre* suppurating sore, from L: FISTULA]

festival ('fɛstɪvᵊl) *n* **1** a day or period set aside for celebration or feasting, esp one of religious significance **2** any occasion for celebration **3** an organized series of special events and performances: *a festival of drama* **4** *arch* a time of revelry **5** (*modifier*) relating to or characteristic of a festival [C14 from Church L *fēstivālis* of a feast, from L *festīvus* FESTIVE]

Festival Hall *n* a concert hall in London, on the South Bank of the Thames: constructed for the 1951 Festival of Britain; completed 1964–65. Official name: **Royal Festival Hall**

▷ www.rfh.org.uk

festive ('fɛstɪv) *adj* appropriate to or characteristic of a holiday, etc [C17 from L *festīvus* joyful, from *festus* of a FEAST] > '**festively** *adv*

festivity (fɛs'tɪvɪtɪ) *n, pl* **festivities 1** merriment characteristic of a festival, etc **2** any festival or other celebration **3** (*pl*) celebrations

festoon (fɛ'stuːn) *n* **1** a decorative chain of flowers, ribbons, etc, suspended in loops **2** a carved or painted representation of this, as in architecture, furniture, or pottery ▷ *vb* (*tr*) **3** to decorate or join together with festoons **4** to form into festoons [C17 from F, from It. *festone* ornament for a feast, from *festa* FEAST]

festoon blind *n* a window blind consisting of vertical rows of horizontally gathered fabric that may be drawn up to form a series of ruches

feta ('fɛtə) *n* a white sheep or goat cheese popular in Greece [Mod. Gk, from the phrase *turi pheta*, from *turi* cheese + *pheta*, from It. *fetta* a slice]

fetal *or* **foetal** ('fiːtᵊl) *adj* of, relating to, or resembling a fetus

fetal alcohol syndrome *n* a condition in newborn babies caused by excessive intake of alcohol by the mother during pregnancy: characterized by various defects including mental retardation

fetch[1] (fɛtʃ) *vb* (*mainly tr*) **1** to go after and bring back: *to fetch help* **2** to cause to come; bring or draw forth **3** (*also intr*) to cost or sell for (a certain price): *the table fetched six hundred pounds* **4** to utter (a sigh, groan, etc) **5** *inf* to deal (a blow, slap, etc) **6** (used esp as a command to dogs) to retrieve (an object thrown, etc) **7 fetch and carry** to perform menial tasks or run errands ▷ *n* **8** the reach, stretch, etc, of a mechanism **9** a trick or stratagem [OE *feccan*] > '**fetcher** *n*

Ff

fetch[2] (fɛtʃ) *n* the ghost or apparition of a living person [C18 from ?]

fetching ('fɛtʃɪŋ) *adj inf* **1** attractively befitting **2** charming

fetch up *vb* (*adv*) **1** (*intr*; usually foll by *at* or *in*) *inf* to arrive (at) or end up (in): *to fetch up in New York* **2** *sl* to vomit (food, etc)

fête *or* **fete** (feɪt) *n* **1** a gala, bazaar, or similar entertainment, esp one held outdoors in aid of charity **2** a feast day or holiday, esp one of religious significance ▷ *vb* **fêtes, fêting, fêted** *or* **fetes, feting, feted 3** (*tr*) to honour or entertain with or as if with a fête [C18 from F: FEAST]

fetid *or* **foetid** ('fɛtɪd, 'fiː-) *adj* having a stale nauseating smell, as of decay [C16 from L, from *fētēre* to stink; rel. to *fūmus* smoke] > '**fetidly** *or* '**foetidly** *adv* > '**fetidness** *or* '**foetidness** *n*

fetish ('fɛtɪʃ, 'fiːtɪʃ) *n* **1** something, esp an inanimate object, that is believed to have magical powers **2a** a form of behaviour involving fetishism **2b** any object that is involved in fetishism **3** any object, activity, etc, to which one is excessively devoted [C17 from F, from Port. *feitiço* (n) sorcery, from adj: artificial, from L *factīcius* made by art, FACTITIOUS]

fetishism ('fɛtɪˌʃɪzəm, 'fiː-) *n* **1** a condition in which the handling of an inanimate object or a part of the body other than the sexual organs is a source of sexual satisfaction **2** belief in or recourse to a fetish for magical purposes > '**fetishist** *n* > ˌ**fetish'istic** *adj*

fetlock ('fɛtˌlɒk) *n* **1** a projection behind and above a horse's hoof **2** Also called: **fetlock joint** the joint at this part of the leg **3** the tuft of hair growing from this part [C14 *fetlak*]

fetor *or* **foetor** ('fiːtə) *n* an offensive stale or putrid odour [C15 from L, from *fētēre* to stink]

fetter ('fɛtə) *n* 1 (*often pl*) a chain or bond fastened round the ankle 2 (*usually pl*) a check or restraint ▷ *vb* (*tr*) 3 to restrict or confine 4 to bind in fetters [OE *fetor*]

fettle ('fɛtᵊl) *vb* **fettles, fettling, fettled** (*tr*) 1 to line or repair (the walls of a furnace) 2 *Brit dialect* 2a to prepare or arrange (a thing, oneself, etc) 2b to repair or mend (something) ▷ *n* 3 state of health, spirits, etc (esp in **in fine fettle**) [C14 (in the sense: to put in order): back formation from *fetled* girded up, from OE *fetel* belt]

fettler ('fɛtlə) *n* a person employed to maintain railway tracks

fetus *or* **foetus** ('fi:təs) *n, pl* **fetuses** *or* **foetuses** the embryo of a mammal in the later stages of development, esp a human embryo from the end of the second month of pregnancy until birth [C14 from L: offspring]

feu (fju:) *n* 1 *Scot legal history* 1a a feudal tenure of land for which rent was paid in money or grain instead of by the performance of military service 1b the land so held 2 *Scots law* a right to the use of land in return for a fixed annual payment (**feu duty**) [C15 from OF; see FEE]

Feuchtwanger (*German* 'fɔɪçtvaŋər) *n* **Lion** ('li:ɔn) 1884–1958, German novelist and dramatist, lived in the US (1940–58): noted for his historical novels, including *Die hässliche Herzogin* (1923) and *Jud Süss* (1925)

feud[1] (fju:d) *n* 1 long and bitter hostility between two families, clans, or individuals 2 a quarrel or dispute ▷ *vb* 3 (*intr*) to carry on a feud [C13 *fede*, from OF, from OHG *fēhida*; rel. to OE *fǣhth* hostility; see FOE] > '**feudist** *n*

feud[2] *or* **feod** (fju:d) *n Feudal law* land held in return for service [C17 from Med. L *feodum*, of Gmc origin; see FEE]

feudal ('fju:dᵊl) *adj* 1 of or characteristic of feudalism or its institutions 2 of or relating to a fief 3 *disparaging* old-fashioned [C17 from Med. L, from *feudum* FEUD[2]]

feudalism ('fju:də,lɪzəm) *n* the legal and social system that evolved in W Europe in the 8th and 9th centuries, in which vassals were protected and maintained by their lords, usually through the granting of fiefs, and were required to serve under them in war. Also called: **feudal system** > '**feudalist** *n* > ,**feudal'istic** *adj*

feudality (fju:'dælɪtɪ) *n, pl* **feudalities** 1 the state or quality of being feudal 2 a fief or fee

feudalize *or* **feudalise** ('fju:də,laɪz) *vb* **feudalizes, feudalizing, feudalized** *or* **feudalises, feudalising, feudalised** (*tr*) to create feudal institutions in (a society, etc) > ,**feudali'zation** *or* ,**feudali'sation** *n*

feudatory ('fju:dətərɪ) (in feudal Europe) ▷ *n, pl* **feudatories** 1 a person holding a fief; vassal ▷ *adj* 2 relating to or characteristic of the relationship between lord and vassal [C16 from Med. L *feudātor*]

Feuerbach (*German* 'fɔɪərbax) *n* **Ludwig Andreas** ('lu:tvɪç an'dre:as) 1804–72, German materialist philosopher: in *The Essence of Christianity* (1841), translated into English by George Eliot (1853), he maintained that God is merely an outward projection of man's inner self

feuilleton (*French* fœjtɔ̃) *n* 1 the part of a European newspaper carrying reviews, serialized fiction, etc 2 such a review or article [C19 from F, from *feuillet* sheet of paper, dim. of *feuille* leaf, from L *folium*]

fever ('fi:və) *n* 1 an abnormally high body temperature, accompanied by a fast pulse rate, dry skin, etc. Related adj: **febrile** 2 any of various diseases, such as yellow fever or scarlet fever, characterized by a high temperature 3 intense nervous excitement ▷ *vb* 4 (*tr*) to affect with or as if with fever [OE *fēfor*, from L *febris*] > '**fevered** *adj*

feverfew ('fi:və,fju:) *n* a bushy European strong-scented perennial plant with white flower heads, formerly used medicinally [OE *feferfuge*, from LL, from L *febris* fever + *fugāre* to put to flight]

feverish ('fi:vərɪʃ) *or* **feverous** *adj* 1 suffering from fever 2 in a state of restless excitement 3 of, caused by, or causing fever > '**feverishly** *or* '**feverously** *adv*

fever pitch *n* a state of intense excitement

fever therapy *n* a former method of treating disease by raising the body temperature

few (fju:) *determiner* 1a hardly any: *few men are so cruel* 1b (*as pronoun; functioning as pl*): *many are called but few are chosen* 2 (preceded by *a*) 2a a small number of: *a few drinks* 2b (*as pronoun; functioning as pl*): *a few of you* 3 **a good few** *inf* several 4 **few and far between** 4a widely spaced 4b scarce 5 **not** *or* **quite a few** *inf* several ▷ *n* 6 **the few** a small number of people considered as a class: *the few who fell at Thermopylae* [OE *fēawa*] > '**fewness** *n*

USAGE See at **less**

fey (feɪ) *adj* 1 interested in or believing in the supernatural 2 clairvoyant; visionary 3 *chiefly Scot* fated to die; doomed 4 *chiefly Scot* in a state of high spirits [OE *fǣge* marked out for death] > '**feyness** *n*

Feydeau (*French* fɛdo) *n* **Georges** (ʒɔrʒ) 1862–1921, French dramatist, noted for his farces, esp *La Dame de chez Maxim* (1899) and *Occupe-toi d'Amélie* (1908)

Feynman ('faɪnmən) *n* **Richard** 1918–88, US physicist, noted for his research on quantum electrodynamics; shared the Nobel prize for physics in 1965

fez (fɛz) *n, pl* **fezzes** an originally Turkish brimless felt or wool cap, shaped like a truncated cone [C19 via F from Turkish, from Fès]

Fez (fɛz) *n* a variant of **Fès**

Fezzan (fɛ'za:n) *n* a region of SW Libya, in the Sahara: a former province (until 1963)

ff *music symbol for* fortissimo

ff. 1 *abbrev for* folios 2 *symbol for* and the following (pages, lines, etc)

Ffestiniog (fɛs'tɪnjɒg) *n* a town in N Wales, in Gwynedd: tourist attractions include former slate quarries and a narrow-gauge railway at nearby Blaenau Ffestiniog. Pop: 800 (latest est)

FI *abbrev for* Falkland Islands

fiacre (fɪ'ɑ:krə) *n* a small four-wheeled horse-drawn carriage [C17 after the Hotel de St *Fiacre*, Paris, where these vehicles were first hired out]

fiancé *or* (*fem*) **fiancée** (fɪ'ɒnseɪ) *n* a person who is engaged to be married [C19 from F, from OF *fiancier* to promise, betroth, from *fiance* a vow, from *fier* to trust, from L *fīdere*]

Fianna ('fi:ənə) *pl n* a legendary band of Irish warriors noted for their heroic exploits, attributed to the 2nd and 3rd centuries AD. Also called: **Fenians**

fiasco (fɪ'æskəʊ) *n, pl* **fiascos** *or* **fiascoes** a complete failure, esp one that is ignominious or humiliating [C19 from It., lit.: FLASK; sense development obscure]

fiat ('faɪət) *n* 1 official sanction 2 an arbitrary order or decree [C17 from L, lit.: let it be done]

fib (fɪb) *n* 1 a trivial and harmless lie ▷ *vb* **fibs, fibbing, fibbed** 2 (*intr*) to tell such a lie [C17 ?from *fibble-fable* an unlikely story; see FABLE] > '**fibber** *n*

Fibonacci (*Italian* fibo'nattʃi) *n* **Leonardo** (leo'nardo), also called *Leonardo of Pisa*. ?1170–?1250, Italian mathematician: popularized the decimal system in Europe

Fibonacci sequence *or* **series** (,fɪbə'nɑ:tʃɪ) *n* the infinite sequence of numbers, 0, 1, 1, 2, 3, 5, 8, etc, in which each member (**Fibonacci number**) is the sum of the previous two [after Leonardo FIBONACCI]

fibre *or US* **fiber** ('faɪbə) *n* 1 a natural or synthetic filament that may be spun into yarn, such as cotton or nylon 2 cloth or other material made from such yarn 3 a long fine continuous thread or filament 4 the texture of any material or substance 5 essential substance or nature 6 strength of character (esp in **moral fibre**) 7 *bot* 7a a narrow elongated thick-walled cell 7b a very small root or twig 8 a fibrous substance, such as bran, as part of someone's diet: *dietary fibre* [C14 from L *fibra* filament, entrails] > '**fibred** *or US* '**fibered** *adj*

fibreboard *or US* **fiberboard** ('faɪbə,bɔ:d) *n* a building

material made of compressed wood or other plant fibres
fibreglass *or US* **fiberglass** ('faɪbə,glɑ:s) *n* 1 material consisting of matted fine glass fibres, used as insulation in buildings, etc 2 a light strong material made by bonding fibreglass with a synthetic resin; used for car bodies, etc
fibre optics *or US* **fiber optics** *n (functioning as sing)* the transmission of information modulated on light down very thin flexible fibres of glass. See also **optical fibre** > **,fibre-'optic** *or US* **,fiber-'optic** *adj*
fibrescope *or US* **fiberscope** ('faɪbə,skəʊp) *n* a medical instrument using fibre optics used to examine internal organs, such as the stomach
fibril ('faɪbrɪl) *or* **fibrilla** (faɪ'brɪlə) *n, pl* **fibrils** *or* **fibrillae** (-'brɪli:) 1 a small fibre or part of a fibre 2 *biol* a root hair [C17 from NL *fibrilla* a little FIBRE] > **fi'brillar** *or* **fi'brillose** *adj*
fibrillation (,faɪbrɪ'leɪʃən, ,fɪb-) *n* 1 a local and uncontrollable twitching of muscle fibres, esp of the heart 2 irregular twitchings of the muscular wall of the heart
fibrin ('fɪbrɪn) *n* a white insoluble elastic protein formed from fibrinogen when blood clots: forms a network that traps red cells and platelets
fibrinogen (fɪ'brɪnədʒən) *n* a soluble protein in blood plasma, converted to fibrin by the action of the enzyme thrombin when blood clots
fibro ('faɪbrəʊ) *n Austral inf* **a** short for **fibrocement** **b** *(as modifier): a fibro shack*
fibro- *combining form* 1 indicating fibrous tissue: *fibrosis* 2 indicating fibre: *fibrocement* [from L *fibra* FIBRE]
fibrocement (,faɪbrəʊsɪ'mɛnt) *n* cement combined with asbestos fibre, used esp in sheets for building
fibroid ('faɪbrɔɪd) *adj* 1 *anat* (of structures or tissues) containing or resembling fibres ▷ *n* 2 a benign tumour, composed of fibrous and muscular tissue, occurring in the wall of the uterus and often causing heavy menstruation
fibroin ('faɪbrəʊɪn) *n* a tough elastic protein that is the principal component of spiders' webs and raw silk
fibroma (faɪ'brəʊmə) *n, pl* **fibromata** (-mətə) *or* **fibromas** a benign tumour derived from fibrous connective tissue
fibrosis (faɪ'brəʊsɪs) *n* the formation of an abnormal amount of fibrous tissue in an organ or part
fibrositis (,faɪbrə'saɪtɪs) *n* inflammation of white fibrous tissue, esp that of muscle sheaths
fibrous ('faɪbrəs) *adj* consisting of or resembling fibres: *fibrous tissue* > **'fibrously** *adv*
fibula ('fɪbjʊlə) *n, pl* **fibulae** (-,li:) *or* **fibulas** 1 the outer and thinner of the two bones between the knee and ankle of the human leg ▷ Cf **tibia** 2 the corresponding bone in other vertebrates 3 a metal brooch resembling a safety pin [C17 from L: clasp, prob. from *figere* to fasten] > **'fibular** *adj*
-fic *suffix forming adjectives* making or producing: *honorific* [from L *-ficus*, from *facere* to do, make]
fiche (fi:ʃ) *n* See **microfiche, ultrafiche**
fichu ('fi:ʃu:) *n* a woman's shawl worn esp in the 18th century [C19 from F: small shawl, from *ficher* to fix with a pin, from L *figere* to fasten, FIX]
fickle ('fɪk^əl) *adj* changeable in purpose, affections, etc [OE *ficol* deceitful] > **'fickleness** *n*
fictile ('fɪktaɪl) *adj* 1 moulded or capable of being moulded from clay 2 made of clay by a potter [C17 from L *fictilis* that can be moulded, from *fingere* to shape]
fiction ('fɪkʃən) *n* 1 literary works invented by the imagination, such as novels or short stories 2 an invented story or explanation 3 the act of inventing a story 4 *law* something assumed to be true for the sake of convenience, though probably false [C14 from L *fictiō* a fashioning, hence something imaginary, from *fingere* to shape] > **'fictional** *adj* > **'fictionally** *adv* > **'fictive** *adj*
fictionalize *or* **fictionalise** ('fɪkʃənə,laɪz) *vb* **fictionalizes, fictionalizing, fictionalized** *or* **fictionalises, fictionalising, fictionalised** *(tr)* to make into fiction > **,fictionali'zation** *or* **,fictionali'sation** *n*
fictitious (fɪk'tɪʃəs) *adj* 1 not genuine or authentic: *to give a fictitious address* 2 of, related to, or characteristic of fiction > **fic'titiously** *adv* > **fic'titiousness** *n*
fid (fɪd) *n naut* 1 a spike for separating strands of rope in splicing 2 a wooden or metal bar for supporting the topmast [C17 from ?]
-fid *adj combining form* divided into parts or lobes: *bifid* [from L *-fidus*, from *findere* to split]
fiddle ('fɪd^əl) *n* 1 *inf or disparaging* the violin 2 a violin played as a folk instrument 3 *naut* a small railing around the top of a table to prevent objects from falling off it 4 *Brit inf* an illegal transaction or arrangement 5 *Brit inf* a manually delicate or tricky operation 6 **at** *or* **on the fiddle** *inf* engaged in an illegal or fraudulent undertaking 7 **fit as a fiddle** *inf* in very good health 8 **play second fiddle** *inf* to play a minor part ▷ *vb* **fiddles, fiddling, fiddled** 9 to play (a tune) on the fiddle 10 *(intr; often foll by with)* to make aimless movements with the hands 11 (when *intr*, often foll by *about* or *around*) *inf* to waste (time) 12 (often foll by *with*) *inf* to interfere (with) 13 *inf* to contrive to do (something) by illicit means or deception 14 *(tr) inf* to falsify (accounts, etc) [OE *fithele*; see VIOLA[1]]
fiddle-faddle ('fɪd^əl,fæd^əl) *n, interj* 1 trivial matter; nonsense ▷ *vb* **fiddle-faddles, fiddle-faddling, fiddle-faddled** 2 *(intr)* to fuss or waste time [C16 reduplication of FIDDLE] > **'fiddle-,faddler** *n*
fiddler ('fɪdlə) *n* 1 a person who plays the fiddle 2 See **fiddler crab** 3 *inf* a petty rogue
fiddler crab *n* any of various burrowing crabs of American coastal regions, the males of which have one of their pincer-like claws enlarged [C19 referring to the rapid fiddling movement of the enlarged anterior claw of the males, used to attract females]
fiddlestick ('fɪd^əl,stɪk) *n* 1 *inf* a violin bow 2 any trifle 3 **fiddlesticks!** an expression of annoyance or disagreement
fiddling ('fɪdlɪŋ) *adj* 1 trifling or insignificant 2 another word for **fiddly**
fiddly ('fɪdlɪ) *adj* **fiddlier, fiddliest** small and awkward to do or handle
Fidei Defensor *Latin* ('faɪdɪ,aɪ dɪ'fɛnsɔ:) *n* defender of the faith; a title given to Henry VIII by Pope Leo X, and appearing on British coins as FID DEF (before decimalization) or FD (after decimalization)
fidelity (fɪ'dɛlɪtɪ) *n, pl* **fidelities** 1 devotion to duties, obligations, etc 2 loyalty or devotion, as to a person or cause 3 faithfulness to one's spouse, lover, etc 4 accuracy in reporting detail 5 *electronics* the degree to which an amplifier or radio accurately reproduces the characteristics of the input signal [C15 from L, from *fidēs* faith, loyalty]
fidget ('fɪdʒɪt) *vb* 1 *(intr)* to move about restlessly 2 *(intr; often foll by with)* to make restless or uneasy movements (with something) 3 *(tr)* to cause to fidget ▷ *n* 4 *(often pl)* a state of restlessness or unease: *he's got the fidgets* 5 a person who fidgets [C17 from earlier *fidge*, prob. from ON *fikjast* to desire eagerly] > **'fidgety** *adj*
fiducial (fɪ'dju:ʃɪəl) *adj* 1 *physics, etc* used as a standard of reference or measurement: *a fiducial point* 2 of or based on trust or faith [C17 from LL *fīdūciālis*, from L *fīdūcia* confidence, from *fīdere* to trust]
fiduciary (fɪ'du:ʃɪərɪ) *law* ▷ *n, pl* **fiduciaries** 1 a person bound to act for another's benefit, as a trustee ▷ *adj* 2a having the nature of a trust 2b of or relating to a trust or trustee [C17 from L *fīdūciārius* relating to something held in trust, from *fīdūcia* trust]
fiduciary issue *n* an issue of banknotes not backed by gold
fie (faɪ) *interj obs or facetious* an exclamation of distaste or

Ff

mock dismay [c13 from OF *fi*, from L *fī*, exclamation of disgust]

fief *or* **feoff** (fiːf) *n* (in feudal Europe) the property or fee granted to a vassal for his maintenance by his lord in return for service [c17 from OF *fie*, of Gmc origin; cf. OE *fēo* cattle, money, L *pecus* cattle, *pecūnia* money, Gk *pokos* fleece]

fiefdom (ˈfiːfdəm) *n* **1** (in feudal Europe) the property owned by a lord **2** an area over which a person or organization exerts authority or influence: *treating the country as his own personal fiefdom*

field (fiːld) *n* **1** an open tract of uncultivated grassland; meadow **2** a piece of land cleared of trees and undergrowth used for pasture or growing crops: *a field of barley* **3** a limited or marked off area on which any of various sports, athletic competitions, etc, are held: *a soccer field* **4** an area that is rich in minerals or other natural resources: *a coalfield* **5** short for **battlefield** or **airfield** **6** the mounted followers that hunt with a pack of hounds **7a** all the runners in a race or competitors in a competition **7b** the runners in a race or competitors in a competition excluding the favourite **8** *cricket* the fielders collectively, esp with regard to their positions **9** a wide or open expanse: *a field of snow* **10a** an area of human activity: *the field of human knowledge* **10b** a sphere or division of knowledge, etc: *his field is physics* **11** a place away from the laboratory, office, library, etc, where practical work is done **12** the surface or background, as of a flag, coin, or heraldic shield, on which a design is displayed **13** Also called: **field of view** the area within which an object may be observed with a telescope, etc **14** *physics* See **field of force** **15** *maths* a set of entities, such as numbers, subject to two binary operations, addition and multiplication, such that the set is a commutative group under addition and the set, minus the zero, is a commutative group under multiplication **16** *computing* a set of one or more characters comprising a unit of information **17** **play the field** *inf* to disperse one's interests or attentions among a number of activities, people, or objects **18** **take the field** to begin or carry on activity, esp in sport or military operations **19** (*modifier*) *mil* of or relating to equipment, personnel, etc, specifically trained for operations in the field: *a field gun* ▷ *vb* **20** (*tr*) *sport* to stop, catch, or return (the ball) as a fielder **21** (*tr*) *sport* to send (a player or team) onto the field to play **22** (*intr*) *sport* (of a player or team) to act or take turn as a fielder or fielders **23** (*tr*) to enter (a person) in a competition: *each party fielded a candidate* **24** (*tr*) *inf* to deal with or handle: *to field a question* [OE *feld*]

Field (fiːld) *n* **John** 1782–1837, Irish composer and pianist, lived in Russia from 1803: invented the nocturne

field artillery *n* artillery capable of deployment in support of front-line troops, due mainly to its mobility

field day *n* **1** a day spent in some special outdoor activity, such as nature study **2** *mil* a day devoted to manoeuvres or exercises, esp before an audience **3** *inf* a day or time of exciting activity: *the children had a field day with their new toys*

field effect transistor *n* a unipolar transistor in which the transverse application of an electric field produces amplification

fielder (ˈfiːldə) *n* *cricket, etc* **a** a player in the field **b** a member of the fielding side

field event *n* a competition, such as the discus, etc, that takes place on a field or similar area as opposed to those on the running track

fieldfare (ˈfiːld,fɛə) *n* a large Old World thrush having a pale grey head, brown wings and back, and a blackish tail [OE *feldefare*; see FIELD, FARE]

field glasses *pl n* another name for **binoculars**

field goal *n* **1** *basketball* a goal scored while the ball is in normal play rather than from a free throw **2** *American & Canadian football* a score of three points made by kicking the ball through the opponent's goalposts above the crossbar

field hockey *n* *US & Canad* hockey played on a field, as distinguished from ice hockey

field hospital *n* a temporary hospital set up near a battlefield for emergency treatment

Fielding (ˈfiːldɪŋ) *n* **Henry** 1707–54, English novelist and dramatist, noted particularly for his picaresque novel *Tom Jones* (1749) and for *Joseph Andrews* (1742), which starts as a parody of Richardson's *Pamela*: also noted as an enlightened magistrate and a founder of the Bow Street runners (1749)

field magnet *n* a permanent magnet or an electromagnet that produces the magnetic field in a generator, electric motor, or similar device

field marshal *n* an officer holding the highest rank in certain armies

fieldmouse (ˈfiːld,maʊs) *n, pl* **fieldmice** a nocturnal mouse inhabiting woods, fields, and gardens of the Old World that has yellowish-brown fur

field officer *n* an officer holding the rank of major, lieutenant colonel, or colonel

field of force *n* the region of space surrounding a body, such as a charged particle or a magnet, within which it can exert a force on another similar body not in contact with it

Fields (fiːldz) *n* **1** Dame **Gracie** real name *Grace Stansfield.* 1898–1979, English popular singer and entertainer **2** **W C** real name *William Claude Dukenfield.* 1880–1946, US film actor, noted for his portrayal of comic roles

fieldsman (ˈfiːldzmən) *n, pl* **fieldsmen** *cricket* another name for **fielder**

field sports *pl n* sports carried on in the countryside, such as hunting or fishing

field tile *n* *Brit & NZ* an earthenware drain used in farm drainage

field trial *n* (*often pl*) a test to display performance, efficiency, or durability, as of a vehicle or invention

field trip *n* an expedition, as by a group of students, to study something at first hand

field winding (ˈwaɪndɪŋ) *n* the current-carrying coils on a field magnet that produce the magnetic field intensity required to set up the electrical excitation in a generator or motor

fieldwork (ˈfiːld,wɜːk) *n* *mil* a temporary structure used in fortifying a place or position

field work *n* an investigation or search for material, data, etc, made in the field as opposed to the classroom or laboratory > **field worker** *n*

fiend (fiːnd) *n* **1** an evil spirit **2** a cruel, brutal, or spiteful person **3** *inf* **3a** a person who is intensely interested in or fond of something: *a fresh-air fiend* **3b** an addict: *a drug fiend* [OE *fēond*]

fiendish (ˈfiːndɪʃ) *adj* **1** of or like a fiend **2** diabolically wicked or cruel **3** *inf* extremely difficult or unpleasant

Fiennes (faɪnz) *n* **1** **Ralph** (reɪf) (**Nathanial**) born 1962, British actor; his films include *Schindler's List* (1993), *The English Patient* (1997), and *The End of the Affair* (2000) **2** his cousin Sir **Ranulph** (**Twistleton-Wykeham-**) born 1944, British explorer; led the first surface journey around the earth's polar axis (1979–82); unsupported crossing of Antarctica (1992–93)

fierce (fɪəs) *adj* **1** having a violent and unrestrained nature: *a fierce dog* **2** wild or turbulent in force, action, or intensity: *a fierce storm* **3** intense or strong: *fierce competition* **4** *inf* very unpleasant [c13 from OF *fiers*, from L *ferus*] > **ˈfiercely** *adv* > **ˈfierceness** *n*

fiery (ˈfaɪərɪ) *adj* **fierier, fieriest** **1** of, containing, or composed of fire **2** resembling fire in heat, colour, ardour, etc: *a fiery speaker* **3** easily angered or aroused: *a fiery temper* **4** (of food) producing a burning sensation: *a fiery curry* **5** (of the skin or a sore) inflamed **6** flammable > **ˈfierily** *adv* > **ˈfieriness** *n*

Fiesole[1] (*Italian* 'fiɛ:zole) *n* a town in central Italy, in Tuscany near Florence: Etruscan and Roman remains. Pop: 4 000 (latest est). Ancient name: **Faesulae** ('fi:sʊli:)

Fiesole[2] (*Italian* 'fiɛ:zole) *n* **Giovanni da** (dʒo'vanni da) the monastic name of (Fra) **Angelico**

fiesta (fɪ'ɛstə) *n* (esp in Spain and Latin America) **1** a religious festival or celebration **2** a holiday or carnival [Sp., from L *festa;* see FEAST]

FIFA ('fi:fə) *n acronym for* Fédération Internationale de Football Association [from F]

▷ www.fifa.com

fife (faɪf) *n* **1** a small high-pitched flute similar to the piccolo, used esp in military bands ▷ *vb* **fifes, fifing, fifed** **2** to play (music) on a fife [c16 from OHG *pfīfa;* see PIPE[1]] > **'fifer** *n*

Fife[1] (faɪf) *n* a council area and historical county of E central Scotland, bordering on the North Sea between the Firths of Tay and Forth: coastal lowlands in the north and east, with several ranges of hills; mainly agricultural. Administrative centre: Glenrothes. Pop: 349 429 (2001 est). Area: 1323 sq km (511 sq miles)

Fife[2] (faɪf) *n* **Duncan** See **Phyfe, Duncan**

FIFO ('faɪfəʊ) *n acronym for* first in, first out (as an accounting principle in costing stock) ▷ Cf **LIFO**

fifteen ('fɪf'ti:n) *n* **1** the cardinal number that is the sum of ten and five **2** a numeral, 15, XV, etc, representing this number **3** something represented by, representing, or consisting of 15 units **4** a Rugby Union (football) team ▷ *determiner* **5a** amounting to fifteen: *fifteen jokes* **5b** (*as pronoun*): *fifteen of us danced* [OE *fīftēne*] > **'fif'teenth** *adj, n*

fifth (fɪfθ) *adj* (*usually prenominal*) **1a** coming after the fourth in order, position, etc. Often written 5th **1b** (*as n*): *he came on the fifth* ▷ *n* **2a** one of five equal parts of an object, quantity, etc **2b** (*as modifier*): *a fifth part* **3** the fraction equal to one divided by five (1/5) **4** *music* **4a** the interval between one note and another five notes away from it in a diatonic scale **4b** one of two notes constituting such an interval in relation to the other ▷ *adv* **5** Also: **fifthly** after the fourth person, position, event, etc ▷ *sentence connector* **6** Also: **fifthly** as the fifth point [OE *fīfta*]

fifth column *n* **1** (originally) a group of Falangist sympathizers in Madrid during the Spanish Civil War who were prepared to join the insurgents marching on the city **2** any group of hostile infiltrators > **fifth columnist** *n*

fifth wheel *n* **1** a spare wheel for a four-wheeled vehicle **2** a superfluous or unnecessary person or thing

fifty ('fɪftɪ) *n, pl* **fifties** **1** the cardinal number that is the product of ten and five **2** a numeral, 50, L, etc, representing this number **3** something represented by, representing, or consisting of 50 units ▷ *determiner* **4a** amounting to fifty: *fifty people* **4b** (*as pronoun*): *fifty should be sufficient* [OE *fīftig*] > **'fiftieth** *adj, n*

fifty-fifty *adj, adv inf* in equal parts

fig (fɪg) *n* **1** a tree or shrub in which the flowers are borne inside a pear-shaped receptacle **2** the fruit of any of these trees, which develops from the receptacle and has sweet flesh containing numerous seedlike structures **3** (*used with a negative*) something of negligible value: *I don't care a fig for your opinion* [c13 from OF, from *figa,* from L *ficus* fig tree]

fig. *abbrev for:* **1** figurative(ly) **2** figure

fight (faɪt) *vb* **fights, fighting, fought** **1** to oppose or struggle against (an enemy) in battle **2** to oppose or struggle against (a person, cause, etc) in any manner **3** (*tr*) to engage in or carry on (a battle, contest, etc) **4** (when *intr*, often foll by *for*) to uphold or maintain (a cause, etc) by fighting or struggling: *to fight for freedom* **5** (*tr*) to make or achieve (a way) by fighting **6** to engage (another or others) in combat **7** **fight it out** to contend until a decisive result is obtained **8** **fight shy** to keep aloof from ▷ *n* **9** a battle, struggle, or physical combat **10** a quarrel, dispute, or contest **11** resistance (esp in **put up a fight**) **12** a boxing match ▷ See also **fight off** [OE *feohtan*]

fighter ('faɪtə) *n* **1** a person who fights, esp a professional boxer **2** a person who has determination **3** *mil* an armed aircraft designed for destroying other aircraft

▷ www.fighter-planes.com

fighter-bomber *n* an aircraft that combines the roles of fighter and bomber

fighting chance *n* a slight chance of success dependent on a struggle

fighting cock *n* **1** a gamecock **2** a pugnacious person

fighting fish *n* any of various tropical fishes of the genus *Betta*, esp the Siamese fighting fish

fight off *vb* (*tr, adv*) **1** to repulse; repel **2** to struggle to avoid or repress: *to fight off a cold*

fight-or-flight *n* (*modifier*) involving or relating to an involuntary response to stress in which the hormone adrenaline is secreted into the blood in readiness for physical action, such as fighting or running away

figjam ('fɪg,dʒæm) *n Austral sl* a very conceited person [c20 from *f(uck)* I('*m*) *g(ood) j(ust) a(sk) m(e)*]

fig leaf *n* **1** a leaf from a fig tree **2** a representation of a fig leaf used in sculpture, etc to cover the genitals of nude figures **3** a device to conceal something regarded as shameful

figment ('fɪgmənt) *n* a fantastic notion or fabrication: *a figment of the imagination* [c15 from LL *figmentum* a fiction, from L *fingere* to shape]

figurant ('fɪgjʊrənt) *n* a ballet dancer who does group work but no solo roles [c18 from F, from *figurer* to represent, appear, FIGURE] > **figurante** (,fɪgjʊ'rɒnt) *fem n*

figuration (,fɪgə'reɪʃən) *n* **1** *music* **1a** the employment of characteristic patterns of notes, esp in variations on a theme **1b** florid ornamentation **2** the act or an instance of representing figuratively, as by means of allegory **3** a figurative representation **4** the act of decorating with a design

figurative ('fɪgərətɪv) *adj* **1** involving a figure of speech; not literal; metaphorical **2** using or filled with figures of speech **3** representing by means of an emblem, likeness, etc > **'figuratively** *adv* > **'figurativeness** *n*

figure ('fɪgə) *n* **1** any written symbol other than a letter, esp a whole number **2** another name for **digit** (sense 2) **3** an amount expressed numerically: *a figure of £1800 was suggested* **4** (*pl*) calculations with numbers: *he's good at figures* **5** visible shape or form; outline **6** the human form: *a girl with a slender figure* **7** a slim bodily shape (esp in **keep** *or* **lose one's figure**) **8** a character or personage: *a figure in politics* **9** the impression created by a person through behaviour (esp in **cut a fine, bold,** etc, **figure**) **10a** a person as impressed on the mind **10b** (*in combination*): *father-figure* **11** a representation in painting or sculpture, esp of the human form **12** an illustration or diagram in a text **13** a representative object or symbol **14** a pattern or design, as in wood **15** a predetermined set of movements in dancing or skating **16** *geom* any combination of points, lines, curves, or planes **17** *logic* one of four possible arrangements of the terms in the major and minor premises of a syllogism that give the same conclusion **18** *music* **18a** a numeral written above or below a note in a part **18b** a characteristic short pattern of notes ▷ *vb* **figures, figuring, figured** **19** (when *tr*, often foll by *up*) to calculate or compute (sums, amounts, etc) **20** (*tr; usually takes a clause as object*) *inf, US, Canad, & NZ* to consider **21** (*tr*) to represent by a diagram or illustration **22** (*tr*) to pattern or mark with a design **23** (*tr*) to depict or portray in a painting, etc **24** (*tr*) to imagine **25** (*tr*) *music* to decorate (a melody line or part) with ornamentation **26** (*intr;* usually foll by *in*) to be included: *his name figures in the article* **27** (*intr*) *inf* to accord

Ff

with expectation: *it figures that he wouldn't come* ▷ See also **figure out** [C13 from L *figūra* a shape, from *fingere* to mould] > **'figurer** *n*

figured ('fɪgəd) *adj* **1** depicted as a figure in painting or sculpture **2** decorated with a design **3** having a form **4** *music* **4a** ornamental **4b** (of a bass part) provided with numerals indicating accompanying harmonies

figured bass (beɪs) *n* a shorthand method of indicating a thorough-bass part in which each bass note is accompanied by figures indicating the intervals to be played in the chord above it

figurehead ('fɪgə,hɛd) *n* **1** a person nominally having a prominent position, but no real authority **2** a carved bust on the bow of some sailing vessels

figure of speech *n* an expression of language, such as metaphor, by which the literal meaning of a word is not employed

figure out *vb (tr, adv; may take a clause as object) inf* **1** to calculate **2** to understand

figure skating *n* **1** ice skating in which the skater traces outlines of selected patterns **2** the whole art of skating, as distinct from skating at speed > **figure skater** *n*

figurine (,fɪgə'riːn) *n* a small carved or moulded figure; statuette [C19 from F, from It. *figurina* a little FIGURE]

figwort ('fɪg,wɜːt) *n* a plant related to the foxglove having square stems and small brown or greenish flowers

Fiji ('fiːdʒiː, fiː'dʒiː) *n* **1** an independent republic, consisting of 844 islands (chiefly Viti Levu and Vanua Levu) in the SW Pacific: a British colony (1874–1970); a member of the Commonwealth (1970–87 and from 1997); the large islands are of volcanic origin, surrounded by coral reefs; smaller ones are of coral. Official language: English. Religion: Christian and Hindu. Currency: dollar. Capital: Suva. Pop: 827 000 (2001 est). Area: 18 272 sq km (7055 sq miles) ▷ *n, adj* **2** another word for **Fijian**
▷ www.fiji.gov.fj

Fijian (fiː'dʒiːən) *n* **1** a member of the indigenous people of mixed Melanesian and Polynesian descent inhabiting Fiji **2** the language of this people, belonging to the Malayo-Polynesian family ▷ *adj* **3** of, relating to, or characteristic of Fiji or its inhabitants ▷ Also **Fiji**

filagree ('fɪlə,griː) *n, adj* a less common spelling of **filigree**

filament ('fɪləmənt) *n* **1** the thin wire, usually tungsten, inside a light bulb that emits light when heated to incandescence by an electric current **2** *electronics* a high-resistance wire forming the cathode in some valves **3** a single strand of a natural or synthetic fibre **4** *bot* the stalk of a stamen **5** any slender structure or part [C16 from NL, from Med. L *fīlāre* to spin, from L *fīlum* thread] > **filamentary** (,fɪlə'mɛntərɪ) *or* **,fila'mentous** *adj*

filaria (fɪ'lɛərɪə) *n, pl* **filariae** (-ɪ,iː) a parasitic nematode worm that lives in the blood of vertebrates and is transmitted by insects: the cause of filariasis [C19 NL (former name of genus), from L *fīlum* thread] > **fi'larial** *adj*

filariasis (,fɪlə'raɪəsɪs, fɪ,lɛərɪ'eɪsɪs) *n* a disease common in tropical and subtropical countries resulting from infestation of the lymphatic system with nematode worms transmitted by mosquitoes: characterized by inflammation. See also **elephantiasis** [C19 from NL; see FILARIA]

filbert ('fɪlbət) *n* **1** any of several N temperate shrubs that have edible rounded brown nuts **2** Also called: **hazelnut, cobnut** the nut of any of these shrubs [C14 after St *Philbert*, 7th-century Frankish abbot, because the nuts are ripe around his feast day, Aug. 22]

filch (fɪltʃ) *vb (tr)* to steal or take in small amounts [C16 *filchen* to steal, attack, ?from OE *gefylce* band of men] > **'filcher** *n*

file[1] (faɪl) *n* **1** a folder, box, etc, used to keep documents or other items in order **2** the documents, etc, kept in this way **3** documents or information about a specific subject, person, etc **4** a line of people in marching formation, one behind another **5** any of the eight vertical rows of squares on a chessboard **6** *computing* a named collection of information, in the form of text, programs, graphics, etc, held on a permanent storage device, such as a magnetic disk **7** **on file** recorded or catalogued for reference, as in a file ▷ *vb* **files, filing, filed** **8** to place (a document, etc) in a file **9** *(tr)* to place (a legal document) on public or official record **10** *(tr)* to bring (a suit, esp a divorce suit) in a court of law **11** *(tr)* to submit (copy) to a newspaper **12** *(intr)* to march or walk in a file or files: *the ants filed down the hill* [C16 (in the sense: string on which documents are hung): from OF, from Med. L *fīlāre*; see FILAMENT] > **'filer** *n*

file[2] (faɪl) *n* **1** a hand tool consisting of a steel blade with small cutting teeth on some or all of its faces. It is used for shaping or smoothing ▷ *vb* **files, filing, filed** **2** *(tr)* to shape or smooth (a surface) with a file [OE *fīl*] > **'filer** *n*

filefish ('faɪl,fɪʃ) *n, pl* **filefish** *or* **filefishes** any tropical triggerfish having a narrow compressed body and a very long dorsal spine [C18 referring to its file-like scales]

filename ('faɪl,neɪm) *n* an arrangement of characters that enables a computer system to permit the user to have access to a particular file

file server *n computing* the central unit of a local area network that controls its operation and provides access to separately stored data files

filet ('fɪlɪt, 'fɪleɪ) *n* a variant spelling of **fillet** (senses 1–3) [C20 from F: net, from OF, from *fil* thread, from L *fīlum*]

filet mignon ('fɪleɪ 'miːnjɒn) *n* a small tender boneless cut of beef [from F, lit.: dainty fillet]

filial ('fɪljəl) *adj* **1** of, resembling, or suitable to a son or daughter: *filial affection* **2** *genetics* designating any of the generations following the parental generation [C15 from LL *fīliālis*, from L *fīlius* son] > **'filially** *adv*

filibeg *or* **philibeg** ('fɪlɪ,bɛg) *n* the kilt worn by Scottish Highlanders [C18 from Scot. Gaelic *fēileadhbeag*, from *fēileadh* kilt + *beag* small]

filibuster ('fɪlɪ,bʌstə) *n* **1** the process of obstructing legislation by means of delaying tactics **2** Also called: **filibusterer** a legislator who engages in such obstruction **3** a freebooter or military adventurer, esp in a foreign country ▷ *vb* **4** to obstruct (legislation) with delaying tactics **5** *(intr)* to engage in unlawful military action [C16 from Sp., from F *flibustier*, prob. from Du. *vrijbuiter* pirate, lit.: one plundering freely; see FREEBOOTER] > **'fili,busterer** *n*

filigree ('fɪlɪ,griː) *or* **filagree** *n* **1** delicate ornamental work of twisted gold, silver, or other wire **2** any fanciful delicate ornamentation ▷ *adj* **3** made of or as if with filigree [C17 from earlier *filigreen*, from F *filigrane*, from L *fīlum* thread + *grānum* GRAIN] > **'fili,greed** *adj*

filings ('faɪlɪŋz) *pl n* shavings or particles removed by a file: *iron filings*

Filipino (,fɪlɪ'piːnəʊ) *n* **1** *(pl* **Filipinos***)* Also (fem): **Filipina** a native or inhabitant of the Philippines **2** another name for **Tagalog** ▷ *adj* **3** of or relating to the Philippines or their inhabitants

fill (fɪl) *vb (mainly tr; often foll by up)* **1** *(also intr)* to make or become full: *to fill up a bottle* **2** to occupy the whole of: *the party filled the house* **3** to plug (a gap, crevice, etc) **4** to meet (a requirement or need) satisfactorily **5** to cover (a page or blank space) with writing, drawing, etc **6** to hold and perform the duties of (an office or position) **7** to appoint or elect an occupant to (an office or position) **8** *(also intr)* to swell or cause to swell with wind, as in manoeuvring the sails of a sailing vessel **9** *chiefly US & Canad* to put together the necessary materials for (a prescription or order) **10** **fill the bill** *inf* to serve or perform adequately ▷ *n* **11** material such as gravel, stones, etc, used to bring an area of ground up to a required level **12** **one's fill** the quantity needed to satisfy one ▷ See also **fill in, fill out,** etc [OE *fyllan*]

filler ('fɪlə) *n* **1** a person or thing that fills **2** an object or substance used to add weight or size to something or to fill in a gap **3** a paste, used for filling in cracks, holes, etc, in a surface before painting **4** the inner portion of a cigar **5** *journalism* articles, photographs, etc, to fill space between more important articles in a newspaper or magazine

fillet ('fɪlɪt) *n* **1a** Also called: **fillet steak** a strip of boneless meat **1b** the boned side of a fish **2** a narrow strip of any material **3** a thin strip of ribbon, lace, etc, worn in the hair or around the neck **4** a narrow flat moulding, esp one between other mouldings **5** a narrow band between flutings on the shaft of a column **6** *heraldry* a horizontal division of a shield **7** a narrow decorative line, impressed on the cover of a book ▷ *vb* **fillets, filleting, filleted** (*tr*) **8** to cut or prepare (meat or fish) as a fillet **9** to cut fillets from (meat or fish) **10** to bind or decorate with or as if with a fillet ▷ Also (for senses 1–3): **filet** [C14 from OF *filet*, from *fil* thread, from L *fīlum*]

fill in *vb* (*adv*) **1** (*tr*) to complete (a form, drawing, etc) **2** (*intr*) to act as a substitute **3** (*tr*) to put material into (a hole or cavity), esp so as to make it level with a surface **4** (*tr*) *inf* to inform with facts or news ▷ *n* **fill-in 5** a substitute

filling ('fɪlɪŋ) *n* **1** the substance or thing used to fill a space or container: *pie filling* **2** *dentistry* any of various substances (metal, plastic, etc) for inserting into the prepared cavity of a tooth **3** *chiefly US* the weft in weaving ▷ *adj* **4** (of food or a meal) substantial and satisfying

filling station *n* a place where petrol and other supplies for motorists are sold

fillip ('fɪlɪp) *n* **1** something that adds stimulation or enjoyment **2** the action of holding a finger towards the palm with the thumb and suddenly releasing it outwards to produce a snapping sound **3** a quick blow or tap made by this ▷ *vb* **4** (*tr*) to stimulate or excite **5** (*tr*) to strike or project sharply with a fillip **6** (*intr*) to make a fillip [C15 *philippe*, imit.]

Fillmore ('fɪlmɔː) *n* **Millard** 1800–74, 13th president of the US (1850–53); a leader of the Whig Party

fill out *vb* (*adv*) **1** to make or become fuller, thicker, or rounder **2** to make more substantial **3** (*tr*) *chiefly US & Canad* to fill in (a form, etc)

fill up *vb* (*adv*) **1** (*tr*) to complete (a form, application, etc) **2** to make or become full ▷ *n* **fill-up 3** the act of filling something completely, esp the petrol tank of a car

filly ('fɪlɪ) *n, pl* **fillies** a female horse or pony under the age of four [C15 from ON *fylja*; see FOAL]

film (fɪlm) *n* **1a** a sequence of images of moving objects photographed by a camera and providing the optical illusion of continuous movement when projected onto a screen **1b** a form of entertainment, etc, composed of such a sequence of images **1c** (*as modifier*): *film techniques* **2** a thin flexible strip of cellulose coated with a photographic emulsion, used to make negatives and transparencies **3** a thin coating or layer **4** a thin sheet of any material, as of plastic for packaging **5** a fine haze, mist, or blur **6** a gauzy web of filaments or fine threads ▷ *vb* **7a** to photograph with a cine camera **7b** to make a film of (a screenplay, event, etc) **8** (often foll by *over*) to cover or become covered or coated with a film [OE *filmen* membrane]

filmic ('fɪlmɪk) *adj* **1** of or relating to films or the cinema **2** suggestive of films or the cinema > '**filmically** *adv*

film noir (nwɑː) *n* a type of gangster thriller, made esp in the 1940s in Hollywood, characterized by stark lighting, an involved plot, and an atmosphere of cynicism and corruption [C20 F, lit.: black film]
▷ www.filmsite.org/filmnoir.html
▷ www.nyfavideo.com

filmography (fɪl'mɒgrəfɪ) *n, pl* **filmographies 1** a list of the films made by a particular director, actor, etc **2** any writing that deals with films or the cinema

filmset ('fɪlm,sɛt) *vb* **filmsets, filmsetting, filmset** (*tr*) *Brit* to set (type matter) by filmsetting > '**film,setter** *n*

filmsetting ('fɪlm,sɛtɪŋ) *n Brit, printing* typesetting by exposing type characters onto photographic film from which printing plates are made

film speed *n* **1** the sensitivity to light of a photographic film, specified in terms of the film's ISO rating **2** the rate at which the film passes through a motion picture camera or projector

film strip *n* a strip of film composed of different images projected separately as slides

filmy ('fɪlmɪ) *adj* **filmier, filmiest 1** transparent or gauzy **2** hazy; blurred > '**filmily** *adv* > '**filminess** *n*

filo ('fiːləʊ) *n* a type of Greek flaky pastry in very thin sheets [C20 Mod. Gk *phullon* leaf]

Filofax ('faɪləʊ,fæks) *n trademark* a type of loose-leaf ring binder with sets of different-coloured paper, used as a portable personal filing system, including appointments, addresses, etc

filter ('fɪltə) *n* **1** a porous substance, such as paper or sand, that allows fluid to pass but retains suspended solid particles **2** any device containing such a porous substance for separating suspensions from fluids **3** any of various porous substances built into the mouth end of a cigarette or cigar for absorbing impurities such as tar **4** any electronic, optical, or acoustic device that blocks signals or radiations of certain frequencies while allowing others to pass **5** any transparent disc of gelatine or glass used to eliminate or reduce the intensity of given frequencies from the light leaving a lamp, entering a camera, etc **6** *Brit* a traffic signal at a road junction which permits vehicles to turn either left or right when the main signals are red ▷ *vb* **7** (often foll by *out*) to remove or separate (suspended particles, etc) from (a liquid, gas, etc) by the action of a filter **8** (*tr*) to obtain by filtering **9** (*intr*; foll by *through*) to pass (through a filter or something like a filter) **10** (*intr*) to flow slowly; trickle [C16 *filtre*, from Med. L *filtrum* piece of felt used as a filter, of Gmc origin]

filterable ('fɪltərəbᵊl) *or* **filtrable** ('fɪltrəbᵊl) *adj* **1** capable of being filtered **2** (of most viruses and certain bacteria) capable of passing through the pores of a fine filter

filter bed *n* a layer of sand or gravel in a tank or reservoir through which a liquid is passed so as to purify it

filter feeding *n zool* a method of feeding in some aquatic animals, such as whalebone whales, in which minute food particles are filtered from the surrounding water > **filter feeder** *n*

filter out *or* **through** *vb* (*intr, adv*) to become known gradually; leak

filter paper *n* a porous paper used for filtering liquids

filter tip *n* **1** an attachment to the mouth end of a cigarette for trapping impurities such as tar during smoking **2** a cigarette having such an attachment > '**filter-,tipped** *adj*

filth (fɪlθ) *n* **1** foul or disgusting dirt; refuse **2** extreme physical or moral uncleanliness **3** vulgarity or obscenity **4 the filth** *derog sl* the police [OE *fȳlth*]

filthy ('fɪlθɪ) *adj* **filthier, filthiest 1** very dirty or obscene **2** offensive or vicious: *that was a filthy trick to play* **3** *inf, chiefly Brit* extremely unpleasant: *filthy weather* ▷ *adv* **4** extremely; disgustingly (esp in **filthy rich**) > '**filthily** *adv* > '**filthiness** *n*

filtrate ('fɪltreɪt) *n* **1** a liquid or gas that has been filtered ▷ *vb* **filtrates, filtrating, filtrated 2** to filter [C17 from Med. L *filtrāre* to FILTER]

filtration (fɪl'treɪʃən) *n* the act or process of filtering

fin (fɪn) *n* **1** any of the firm appendages that are the organs of locomotion and balance in fishes and some other aquatic animals **2** a part or appendage that resembles a fin **3a** *Brit* a vertical surface to which the

Ff

rudder is attached at the rear of an aeroplane **3b** a tail surface fixed to a rocket or missile to give stability **4** *naut* a fixed or adjustable blade projecting under water from the hull of a vessel to give it stability or control **5** a projecting rib to dissipate heat from the surface of an engine cylinder or radiator ▷ *vb* **fins, finning, finned** **6** (*tr*) to provide with fins [OE *finn*] > **'finless** *adj* > **finned** *adj*

fin. *abbrev for:* **1** finance **2** financial

Fin. *abbrev for:* **1** Finland **2** Finnish

finable *or* **fineable** ('faɪnəbᵊl) *adj* liable to a fine > **'finableness** *or* **'fineableness** *n*

finagle (fɪ'neɪgᵊl) *vb* **finagles, finagling, finagled** *inf* **1** (*tr*) to get or achieve by craftiness or persuasion **2** to use trickery on (a person) [c20 ?from dialect *fainaigue* cheat] > **fi'nagler** *n*

final ('faɪnᵊl) *adj* **1** of or occurring at the end; last **2** having no possibility of further discussion, action, or change: *a final decree of judgment* **3** relating to or constituting an end or purpose: *a final clause may be introduced by "in order to"* **4** *music* another word for **perfect** (sense 9b) ▷ *n* **5** a last thing; end **6** a deciding contest between the winners of previous rounds in a competition ▷ See also **finals** [c14 from L *fīnālis*, from *fīnis* limit, boundary]

finale (fɪ'nɑːlɪ) *n* **1** the concluding part of any performance or presentation **2** the closing section or movement of a musical composition [c18 from It., n use of adj *finale*, from L *fīnālis* FINAL]

finalist ('faɪnəlɪst) *n* a contestant who has reached the last stage of a competition

finality (faɪ'nælɪtɪ) *n, pl* **finalities** **1** the condition or quality of being final or settled: *the finality of death* **2** a final or conclusive act

finalize *or* **finalise** ('faɪnəˌlaɪz) *vb* **finalizes, finalizing, finalized** *or* **finalises, finalising, finalised** **1** (*tr*) to put into final form; settle: *to finalize plans for the merger* **2** to reach agreement on a transaction > **ˌfinali'zation** *or* **ˌfinali'sation** *n*

finally ('faɪnəlɪ) *adv* **1** at last; eventually **2** at the end or final point; lastly **3** completely; conclusively ▷ *sentence connector* **4** in the end; lastly: *finally, he put his tie on* **5** as the last or final point

finals ('faɪnᵊlz) *pl n* **1** the deciding part of a competition **2** *education* the last examinations in an academic or professional course

final-salary *adj* another name for **defined-benefit**

finance (fɪ'næns, 'faɪnæns) *n* **1** the system of money, credit, etc, esp with respect to government revenues and expenditures **2** funds or the provision of funds **3** (*pl*) financial condition ▷ *vb* **finances, financing, financed** **4** (*tr*) to provide or obtain funds or credit for [c14 from OF, from *finer* to end, settle by payment]

finance company *or* **house** *n* an enterprise engaged in the loan of money against collateral, esp one specializing in the financing of hire-purchase contracts

financial (fɪ'nænʃəl, faɪ-) *adj* **1** of or relating to finance or finances **2** of or relating to persons who manage money, capital, or credit **3** *Austral & NZ inf* having money; in funds **4** *Austral & NZ* (of a club member) fully paid-up > **fi'nancially** *adv*

financial futures *pl n* futures in a stock-exchange index, currency exchange rate, or interest rate enabling banks, building societies, brokers, and speculators to hedge their involvement in these markets

Financial Ombudsman *n* any of five British ombudsmen: the **Banking Ombudsman**, set up in 1986 to investigate complaints from banking customers; the **Building Society Ombudsman**, set up in 1987 to investigate complaints from building society customers; the **Insurance Ombudsman**, set up in 1981 to investigate complaints by policyholders (since 1988 this ombudsman has also operated a **Unit Trust Ombudsman** scheme); the **Investment Ombudsman**, set up in 1989 to investigate complaints by investors (the **Personal Investment Authority Ombudsman** is responsible for investigating complaints by personal investors); and the **Pensions Ombudsman**, set up in 1993 to investigate complaints regarding pension schemes

financial year *n Brit* **1** any annual period at the end of which a firm's accounts are made up **2** the annual period ending April 5, over which Budget estimates are made by the British Government ▷ US and Canad equivalent: **fiscal year**

financier (fɪ'nænsɪə, faɪ-) *n* a person who is engaged in large-scale financial operations

financing gap *n* the difference between a country's requirements for foreign exchange to finance its debts and imports and its income from overseas

finback ('fɪnˌbæk) *n* another name for **rorqual**

finch (fɪntʃ) *n* any of various songbirds having a short stout bill for feeding on seeds, such as the bullfinch, chaffinch, siskin, and canary [OE *finc*]

Finchley ('fɪntʃlɪ) *n* a residential district of N London, part of the Greater London borough of Barnet from 1965

find (faɪnd) *vb* **finds, finding, found** (*mainly tr*) **1** to meet with or discover by chance **2** to discover or obtain, esp by search or effort: *to find happiness* **3** (*may take a clause as object*) to realize: *he found that nobody knew* **4** (*may take a clause as object*) to consider: *I find this wine a little sour* **5** to look for and point out (something to be criticized) **6** (*also intr*) *law* to determine an issue and pronounce a verdict (upon): *the court found the accused guilty* **7** to regain (something lost or not functioning): *to find one's tongue* **8** to reach (a target): *the bullet found its mark* **9** to provide, esp with difficulty: *we'll find room for you too* **10** to be able to pay: *I can't find that amount of money* **11** **find oneself** to realize and accept one's true character; discover one's vocation **12** **find one's feet** to become capable or confident ▷ *n* **13** a person, thing, etc, that is found, esp a valuable discovery [OE *findan*]

finder ('faɪndə) *n* **1** a person or thing that finds **2** *physics* a small telescope fitted to a more powerful larger telescope **3** *photog* short for **viewfinder** **4** **finders keepers** *inf* whoever finds something has the right to keep it

fin de siècle *French* (fɛ̃ də sjɛklə) *n* **1** the end of the 19th century ▷ *adj* **fin-de-siècle** **2** of or relating to the close of the 19th century **3** decadent, esp in artistic tastes

finding ('faɪndɪŋ) *n* **1** a thing that is found or discovered **2** *law* the conclusion reached after a judicial inquiry; verdict

find out *vb* (*adv*) **1** to gain knowledge of (something); learn **2** to detect the crime, deception, etc, of (someone)

fine¹ (faɪn) *adj* **1** very good of its kind: *a fine speech* **2** superior in skill or accomplishment: *a fine violinist* **3** (of weather) clear and dry **4** enjoyable or satisfying: *a fine time* **5** (*postpositive*) *inf* quite well: *I feel fine* **6** satisfactory; acceptable: *that's fine by me* **7** of delicate composition or careful workmanship: *fine crystal* **8** (of precious metals) pure or having a high degree of purity: *fine silver* **9** discriminating: *a fine eye for antique brasses* **10** abstruse or subtle: *a fine point* **11** very thin or slender: *fine hair* **12** very small: *fine print* **13** (of edges, blades, etc) sharp; keen **14** ornate, showy, or smart **15** good-looking: *a fine young woman* **16** polished, elegant, or refined: *a fine gentleman* **17** *cricket* (of a fielding position) oblique to and behind the wicket: *fine leg* **18** (*prenominal*) *inf* disappointing or terrible: *a fine mess* ▷ *adv* **19** *inf* all right: *that suits me fine* **20** finely ▷ *vb* **fines, fining, fined** **21** to make or become finer; refine **22** (often foll by *down* or *away*) to make or become smaller [c13 from OF *fin*, from L *fīnis* end, boundary, as in *fīnis honōrum* the highest degree of honour] > **'finely** *adv* > **'fineness** *n*

fine² (faɪn) *n* **1** a certain amount of money exacted as a penalty: *a parking fine* **2** a payment made by a tenant at the start of his or her tenancy to reduce his or her subsequent rent; premium **3 in fine 3a** in short **3b** in conclusion ▷ *vb* **fines, fining, fined 4** (*tr*) to impose a fine on [C12 (in the sense: conclusion, settlement): from OF *fin*; see FINE[1]]

fine[3] ('fi:neɪ) *n music* the point at which a piece is to end [It., from L *finis* end]

fine art *n* **1** art produced chiefly for its aesthetic value **2** (*often pl*) any of the fields in which such art is produced, such as painting, sculpture, and engraving
▷ www.fine-art.com
▷ www.tate.org.uk
▷ www.vam.ac.uk
▷ www.royalacademy.org.uk
▷ www.nationalgallery.org.uk
▷ www.metmuseum.org
▷ www.louvre.fr/louvrea.htm
▷ www.rijksmuseum.nl
▷ www.guggenheim.org

fine-draw *vb* **fine-draws, fine-drawing, fine-drew, fine-drawn** (*tr*) to sew together so finely that the join is scarcely noticeable

fine-drawn *adj* **1** (of arguments, distinctions, etc) precise or subtle **2** (of wire, etc) drawn out until very fine

fine-grained *adj* **1** (of wood, leather, etc) having a fine smooth even grain **2** detailed, in-depth, or involving fine detail

finery[1] ('faɪnərɪ) *n* elaborate or showy decoration, esp clothing and jewellery

finery[2] ('faɪnərɪ) *n, pl* **fineries** a hearth for converting cast iron into wrought iron [C17 from OF *finerie*, from *finer* to refine; see FINE[1]]

fines herbes (*French* finz ɛrb) *pl n* a mixture of finely chopped herbs, used to flavour omelettes, salads, etc

finespun ('faɪn'spʌn) *adj* **1** spun or drawn out to a fine thread **2** excessively subtle or refined

finesse (fɪ'nɛs) *n* **1** elegant skill in style or performance **2** subtlety and tact in handling difficult situations **3** *bridge, whist* an attempt to win a trick when opponents hold a high card in the suit led by playing a lower card **4** a trick, artifice, or strategy ▷ *vb* **finesses, finessing, finessed 5** to bring about with finesse **6** to play (a card) as a finesse [C15 from OF, from *fin* fine, delicate; see FINE[1]]

fine-tooth comb *or* **fine-toothed comb** *n* **1** a comb with fine teeth set closely together **2 go over** (*or* **through**) **with a fine-tooth(ed) comb** to examine very thoroughly

fine-tune *vb* **fine-tunes, fine-tuning, fine-tuned** (*tr*) to make fine adjustments to (something) in order to obtain optimum performance

Fingal's Cave ('fɪŋgᵊlz) *n* a cave in W Scotland, on Staffa Island in the Inner Hebrides: basaltic pillars. Length: 69 m (227 ft). Height: 36 m (117 ft)

finger ('fɪŋgə) *n* **1a** any of the digits of the hand, often excluding the thumb **1b** (*as modifier*): *a finger bowl* **1c** (*in combination*): *a fingernail*. Related adj: **digital 2** the part of a glove made to cover a finger **3** something that resembles a finger in shape or function: *a finger of land* **4** the length or width of a finger used as a unit of measurement **5** a quantity of liquid in a glass, etc, as deep as a finger is wide **6 get** *or* **pull one's finger out** *Brit inf* to begin or speed up activity, esp after initial delay **7 have a** (*or* **one's**) **finger in the pie 7a** to have an interest in or take part in some activity **7b** to meddle or interfere **8 lay** *or* **put one's finger on** to indicate or locate accurately **9 not lift** (*or* **raise**) **a finger** (*foll by an infinitive*) not to make any effort (to do something) **10 twist** *or* **wrap around one's little finger** to have easy and complete control or influence over **11 put the finger on** *inf* to inform on or identify, esp for the police ▷ *vb* **12** (*tr*) to touch or manipulate with the fingers; handle **13** (*tr*) *inf, chiefly US* to identify as a criminal or suspect **14** to use one's fingers in playing (an instrument, such as a piano or clarinet) **15** to indicate on (a composition or part) the fingering required by a pianist, etc [OE] > '**fingerless** *adj*

fingerboard ('fɪŋgə,bɔ:d) *n* the long strip of hard wood on a violin, guitar, etc upon which the strings are stopped by the fingers

finger bowl *n* a small bowl filled with water for rinsing the fingers at the table after a meal

finger buffet ('bʊfeɪ) *n* a buffet meal at which food that may be picked up in the fingers (**finger food**), such as canapés or vol-au-vents, is served

fingered ('fɪŋgəd) *adj* **1** marked or dirtied by handling **2a** having a finger or fingers **2b** (*in combination*): *red-fingered* **3** (of a musical part) having numerals indicating the fingering

fingering ('fɪŋgərɪŋ) *n* **1** the technique or art of using one's fingers in playing a musical instrument, esp the piano **2** the numerals in a musical part indicating this

fingerling ('fɪŋgəlɪŋ) *n* a very young fish, esp the parr of salmon or trout

fingermark ('fɪŋgə,mɑ:k) *n* a mark left by dirty or greasy fingers on paintwork, walls, etc

fingernail ('fɪŋgə,neɪl) *n* a thin horny translucent plate covering part of the dorsal surface of the end joint of each finger

finger painting *n* the process or art of painting with **finger paints** of starch, glycerine, and pigments, using the fingers, hand, or arm

finger post *n* a signpost showing a pointing finger or hand

fingerprint ('fɪŋgə,prɪnt) *n* **1** an impression of the pattern of ridges on the surface of the end joint of each finger and thumb **2** any unique identifying characteristic ▷ *vb* (*tr*) **3** to take an inked impression of the fingerprints of (a person) **4** to take a sample of the DNA of (a person)

fingerstall ('fɪŋgə,stɔ:l) *n* a protective covering for a finger. Also called: **cot**

fingertip ('fɪŋgə,tɪp) *n* **1** the end joint or tip of a finger **2 at one's fingertips** readily available

finial ('faɪnɪəl) *n* **1** an ornament on top of a spire, etc, esp in the form of a fleur-de-lys **2** an ornament at the top of a piece of furniture, etc [C14 from *finial* (adj), var. of FINAL]

finicky ('fɪnɪkɪ) *or* **finicking** *adj* **1** excessively particular; fussy **2** overelaborate [C19 from *finical*, from FINE[1]]

finis ('fɪnɪs) *n* the end; finish: used at the end of books, films, etc [C15 from L]

finish ('fɪnɪʃ) *vb* (*mainly tr*) **1** to bring to an end; conclude or stop **2** (*intr; sometimes foll by up*) to be at or come to the end; use up **3** to bring to a desired or complete condition **4** to put a particular surface texture on (wood, cloth, etc) **5** (often foll by *off*) to destroy or defeat completely **6** to train (a person) in social graces and talents **7** (*intr; foll by with*) to end a relationship or association ▷ *n* **8** the final or last stage or part; end **9** the death or absolute defeat of a person or one side in a conflict: *a fight to the finish* **10** the surface texture or appearance of wood, cloth, etc: *a rough finish* **11** a thing, event, etc, that completes **12** completeness and high quality of workmanship **13** *sport* ability to sprint at the end of a race [C14 from OF, from L *fīnīre*; see FINE[1]] > '**finisher** *n*

finished ('fɪnɪʃt) *adj* **1** perfected **2** (*predicative*) at the end of a task, activity, etc: *they were finished by four* **3** (*predicative*) without further hope of success or continuation: *she was finished as a prima ballerina*

finishing school *n* a private school for girls that teaches social graces

Finistère (,fɪnɪ'stɛə; *French* finistɛr) *n* a department of NW France, at the tip of the Breton peninsula. Capital: Quimper. Pop: 852 418 (1999). Area: 7029 sq km (2741 sq miles)

Ff

Finisterre (ˌfɪnɪˈstɛə) *n* **1 Cape** a headland in NW Spain: the westernmost point of the Spanish mainland **2** an English name for **Finistère**

finite (ˈfaɪnaɪt) *adj* **1** bounded in magnitude or spatial or temporal extent **2** *maths, logic* having a countable number of elements **3** limited or restricted in nature: *human existence is finite* **4** denoting any form of a verb inflected for grammatical features such as person, number, and tense [c15 from L *fīnītus* limited, from *fīnīre* to limit, end] > **ˈfinitely** *adv* > **ˈfiniteness** *or* **finitude** (ˈfaɪnɪˌtjuːd) *n*

fink (fɪŋk) *n sl, chiefly US & Canad* **1** a strikebreaker **2** an unpleasant or contemptible person [c20 from ?]

Finland (ˈfɪnlənd) *n* **1** a republic in N Europe, on the Baltic Sea: ceded to Russia by Sweden in 1809; gained independence in 1917; Soviet invasion successfully withstood in 1939–40, with the loss of Karelia; a member of the European Union. It is generally low-lying, with about 50 000 lakes, extensive forests, and peat bogs. Official languages: Finnish and Swedish. Religion: Christian, Lutheran majority. Currency: euro. Capital: Helsinki. Pop: 5 185 000 (2001 est). Area: 337 000 sq km (130 120 sq miles). Finnish name: **Suomi 2 Gulf of** an arm of the Baltic Sea between Finland, Estonia, and Russia

▷ www.valtioneuvosto.fi/vn/liston/base.lsp?=en

▷ www.finland-tourism.com

Finlandization *or* **Finlandisation** (ˌfɪnləndaɪˈzeɪʃən) *n* neutralization of a small country by a superpower, using conciliation rather than confrontation, as the former Soviet Union did in relation to Finland

Finlay (ˈfɪnlɪ) *n* **Carlos Juan** (ˈkarlos xwan) 1833–1915, Cuban physician: discovered that the mosquito was the vector of yellow fever

Finn[1] (fɪn) *n* a native, inhabitant, or citizen of Finland [OE *Finnas* (pl)]

Finn[2] (fɪn) *n* known as *Finn MacCool*. (in Irish legend) chief of the Fianna, father of the heroic poet Ossian

finnan haddock (ˈfɪnən) *or* **haddie** (ˈhædɪ) *n* smoked haddock [c18 *finnan* after *Findon*, a village in NE Scotland]

Finney (ˈfɪnɪ) *n* **Albert** born 1936, British stage and film actor: films include *Tom Jones* (1963), *Murder on the Orient Express* (1974), *The Dresser* (1983), and *Erin Brockovich* (2000)

Finnic (ˈfɪnɪk) *n* **1** one of the two branches of the Finno-Ugric family of languages, including Finnish and several languages of NE Europe ▷ *adj* **2** of or relating to this group of languages or to the Finns

Finnish (ˈfɪnɪʃ) *adj* **1** of or characteristic of Finland, the Finns, or their language ▷ *n* **2** the official language of Finland, belonging to the Finno-Ugric family

Finnmark (ˈfɪnˌmɑːk) *n* a county of N Norway: the largest, northernmost, and least populated county; mostly a barren plateau. Capital: Vadsø. Pop: 74 059 (2000 est). Area: 48 649 sq km (18 779 sq miles)

Finno-Ugric (ˈfɪnəʊˈuːgrɪk, -ˈjuː-) *or* **Finno-Ugrian** *n* **1** a family of languages spoken in Scandinavia, E Europe, and W Asia, including Finnish, Estonian, and Hungarian ▷ *adj* **2** of, relating to, speaking, or belonging to this family of languages

finny (ˈfɪnɪ) *adj* **finnier, finniest 1** *poetic* relating to or containing many fishes **2** having or resembling a fin or fins

fino (ˈfiːnəʊ) *n, pl* **finos** a very dry sherry [Sp.: FINE[1]]

Finsen (*Danish* ˈfensən) *n* **Niels Ryberg** (neːls ˈryber) 1860–1904, Danish physician; founder of phototherapy: Nobel prize for physiology or medicine 1903

Finsteraarhorn (*German* ˌfɪnstərˈaːrhɔrn) *n* a mountain in S central Switzerland: highest peak in the Bernese Alps. Height: 4274 m (14 022 ft)

fiord (fjɔːd) *n* a variant spelling of **fjord**

fioriture (ˌfjɔːrɪˈtʊəreɪ) *pl n music* flourishes; embellishments [c19 It, from *fiorire* to flower]

fipple (ˈfɪpᵊl) *n* a wooden plug forming a flue in the end of a pipe, as the mouthpiece of a recorder [c17 from ?]

fipple flute *n* an end-blown flute provided with a fipple, such as the recorder or flageolet

fir (fɜː) *n* **1** any of a genus of pyramidal coniferous trees having single needle-like leaves and erect cones **2** any of various other related trees, such as the Douglas fir **3** the wood of any of these trees [OE *furh*]

Firbank (ˈfɜːbæŋk) *n* (**Arthur Annesley**) **Ronald** 1886–1926, English novelist, whose works include *Valmouth* (1919), *The Flower beneath the Foot* (1923), and *Concerning the Eccentricities of Cardinal Pirelli* (1926)

Firdausi (fɪəˈdaʊsɪ) *or* **Firdusi** (fɪəˈduːsɪ) *n* pen name of *Abul Qasim Mansur* ?935–1020 AD, Persian epic poet; author of *Shah Nama* (*The Book of Kings*), a chronicle of the legends and history of Persia

fire (ˈfaɪə) *n* **1** the state of combustion in which inflammable material burns, producing heat, flames, and often smoke **2a** a mass of burning coal, wood, etc, used esp in a hearth to heat a room **2b** (*in combination*): *firelighter* **3** a destructive conflagration, as of a forest, building, etc **4** a device for heating a room, etc **5** something resembling a fire in light or brilliance: *a diamond's fire* **6** the act of discharging weapons, artillery, etc **7** a burst or rapid volley: *a fire of questions* **8** intense passion; ardour **9** liveliness, as of imagination, etc **10** fever and inflammation **11** a severe trial or torment (esp in **go through fire and water**) **12 between two fires** under attack from two sides **13 catch fire** to ignite **14 on fire 14a** in a state of ignition **14b** ardent or eager **15 open fire** to start firing a gun, artillery, etc **16 play with fire** to be involved in something risky **17 set fire to** *or* **set on fire 17a** to ignite **17b** to arouse or excite **18 under fire** being attacked, as by weapons or by harsh criticism **19** (*modifier*) *astrol* of or relating to a group of three signs of the zodiac, Aries, Leo, and Sagittarius ▷ *vb* **fires, firing, fired 20** to discharge (a firearm or projectile), or (of a firearm, etc) to be discharged **21** to detonate (an explosive charge or device), or (of such a charge or device) to be detonated **22** (*intr*) (of an engine) to start working; ignite **23** (*tr*) *inf* to dismiss from employment **24** (*tr*) *ceramics* to bake in a kiln to harden the clay, etc **25** to kindle or be kindled **26** (*tr*) to provide with fuel: *oil fires the heating system* **27** (*tr*) to subject to heat **28** (*tr*) to heat slowly so as to dry **29** (*tr*) to arouse to strong emotion **30** to glow or cause to glow ▷ *sentence substitute* **31** a cry to warn others of a fire **32** the order to begin firing a gun, artillery, etc [OE *fȳr*] > **ˈfirer** *n*

fire alarm *n* a device to give warning of fire, esp a bell, siren, or hooter

fire appliance *n* another name for fire engine

firearm (ˈfaɪərˌɑːm) *n* a weapon from which a projectile can be discharged by an explosion caused by igniting gunpowder, etc

fireback (ˈfaɪəˌbæk) *n* an ornamental iron slab against the back wall of a hearth

fireball (ˈfaɪəˌbɔːl) *n* **1** a ball-shaped discharge of lightning **2** the region of hot ionized gas at the centre of a nuclear explosion **3** *astron* a large bright meteor **4** *sl* an energetic person

fire blight *n* a disease of apples, pears, and similar fruit trees, caused by a bacterium and characterized by blackening of the blossoms and leaves

fireboat (ˈfaɪəˌbəʊt) *n* a motor vessel equipped with fire-fighting apparatus

firebomb (ˈfaɪəˌbɒm) *n* another name for **incendiary** (sense 6)

firebox (ˈfaɪəˌbɒks) *n* the furnace chamber of a boiler in a steam locomotive

firebrand (ˈfaɪəˌbrænd) *n* **1** a piece of burning wood **2** a person who causes unrest

firebreak (ˈfaɪəˌbreɪk) *n* a strip of open land in forest or prairie, serving to arrest the advance of a fire

firebrick (ˈfaɪəˌbrɪk) *n* a refractory brick made of fire

clay, used for lining furnaces, flues, etc
fire brigade *n chiefly Brit* an organized body of firefighters
firebug ('faɪə,bʌg) *n inf* a person who deliberately sets fire to property
fire clay *n* a heat-resistant clay used in the making of firebricks, furnace linings, etc
fire company *n* **1** an insurance company selling policies relating to fire risk **2** *US* an organized body of firemen
fire control *n mil* the procedures by which weapons are brought to engage a target
firecracker ('faɪə,krækə) *n* a small cardboard container filled with explosive powder
firecrest ('faɪə,krɛst) *n* a small European warbler having a crown striped with yellow, black, and white
firedamp ('faɪə,dæmp) *n* an explosive mixture of hydrocarbons, chiefly methane, formed in coal mines. See also **afterdamp**
firedog ('faɪə,dɒg) *n* either of a pair of metal stands used to support logs in an open fire
fire door *n* **1** a door made of noncombustible material that prevents a fire spreading within a building **2** a similar door leading to the outside of a building that can be easily opened from inside; emergency exit
fire-eater *n* **1** a performer who simulates the swallowing of fire **2** a belligerent person
fire engine *n* a vehicle that carries firemen and fire-fighting equipment to a fire
fire escape *n* a means of evacuating persons from a building in the event of fire
fire-extinguisher *n* a portable device for extinguishing fires, usually consisting of a canister with a directional nozzle used to direct a spray of water, etc, onto the fire
firefighter ('faɪə,faɪtə) *n* a person who assists in extinguishing fires and rescuing those endangered by them, usually a public employee or trained volunteer > **'fire-,fighting** *n, adj*
firefly ('faɪə,flaɪ) *n, pl* **fireflies** a nocturnal beetle common in warm and tropical regions, having luminescent abdominal organs
fireguard ('faɪə,gɑːd) *n* a meshed frame put before an open fire to protect against falling logs, sparks, etc
fire hall *n Canad* a fire station
fire hydrant *n* a hydrant for use as an emergency supply for fighting fires
fire insurance *n* insurance covering damage or loss caused by fire or lightning
fire irons *pl n* metal fireside implements, such as poker, shovel, and tongs
firelock ('faɪə,lɒk) *n* **1** an obsolete type of gunlock with a priming mechanism ignited by sparks **2** a gun or musket having such a lock
fireman ('faɪəmən) *n, pl* **firemen** **1** a man who fights fires; firefighter **2a** (on steam locomotives) the man who stokes the fire **2b** (on diesel and electric locomotives) the driver's assistant **3** a man who tends furnaces; stoker
Firenze (fi'rɛntse) *n* the Italian name for **Florence**
fire opal *n* an orange-red translucent variety of opal, valued as a gemstone
fireplace ('faɪə,pleɪs) *n* **1** an open recess at the base of a chimney, etc, for a fire; hearth **2** *Austral* an authorized place or installation for outside cooking, esp by a roadside
fireplug ('faɪə,plʌg) *n* another name (esp US and NZ) for **fire hydrant**
fire power *n mil* **1** the amount of fire that can be delivered by a unit or weapon **2** the capability of delivering fire
fireproof ('faɪə,pruːf) *adj* **1** capable of resisting damage by fire ▷ *vb* **2** (*tr*) to make resistant to fire
fire raiser *n* a person who deliberately sets fire to property, etc > **fire raising** *n*
fire sale *n* **1** a sale of goods at reduced prices after a fire at a shop or factory **2** any instance of offering goods or assets at greatly reduced prices to ensure a quick sale
fire screen *n* **1** a decorative screen placed in the hearth when there is no fire **2** a screen placed before a fire to protect the face
fire ship *n* a vessel loaded with explosives and used, esp formerly, as a bomb by igniting it and directing it to drift among an enemy's warships
fireside ('faɪə,saɪd) *n* **1** the hearth **2** family life; the home
fire station *n* a building where fire-fighting vehicles and equipment are stationed and where firefighters on duty wait. Also called (US): **firehouse, station house**
firestorm ('faɪə,stɔːm) *n* an uncontrollable blaze sustained by violent winds that are drawn into the column of rising hot air over the burning area: often the result of heavy bombing
fire trail *n Austral* a permanent track cleared through the bush to provide access for fire-fighting
firetrap ('faɪə,træp) *n* a building that would burn easily or one without fire escapes
firewall ('faɪə,wɔːl) *n* **1** a fireproof wall or partition used to impede the progress of a fire **2** *computing* a computer system that isolates another computer from the Internet in order to prevent unauthorized access
firewater ('faɪə,wɔːtə) *n* any strong spirit, esp whisky
fireweed ('faɪə,wiːd) *n* **1** any of various plants that appear as first vegetation in burnt-over areas, esp rosebay willowherb **2** Also called: **pilewort** a weedy North American plant, *Erechtites hieracifolia*, having small white or greenish flowers: family *Asteraceae* (composites) ▷ *n* **3** an Australian rainforest tree, *Stenocarpus sinuatus*, having whorls of bright red flowers
firework ('faɪə,wɜːk) *n* a device, such as a Catherine wheel or rocket, in which combustible materials are ignited and produce coloured flames, sparks, and smoke
fireworks ('faɪə,wɜːks) *pl n* **1** a show in which large numbers of fireworks are let off **2** *inf* an exciting exhibition, as of musical virtuosity or wit **3** *inf* a burst of temper
firie ('faɪərɪ) *n Austral inf* a firefighter
firing ('faɪərɪŋ) *n* **1** the process of baking ceramics, etc, in a kiln **2** the act of stoking a fire or furnace **3** a discharge of a firearm **4** something used as fuel, such as coal or wood
firing line *n* **1** *mil* the positions from which fire is delivered **2** the leading or most advanced position in an activity
firkin ('fɜːkɪn) *n* **1** a small wooden barrel **2** *Brit* a unit of capacity equal to nine gallons [C14 *fir*, from MDu. *vierde* FOURTH + -KIN]
firm[1] (fɜːm) *adj* **1** not soft or yielding to a touch or pressure **2** securely in position; stable or stationary **3** decided; settled **4** enduring or steady **5** having determination or strength **6** (of prices, markets, etc) tending to rise ▷ *adv* **7** in a secure or unyielding manner: *he stood firm* ▷ *vb* **8** (sometimes foll by *up*) to make or become firm [C14 from L *firmus*] > **'firmly** *adv* > **'firmness** *n*
firm[2] (fɜːm) *n* **1** a business partnership **2** any commercial enterprise **3** a team of doctors and their assistants **4 the** (*often cap*) *sl* any organized group of people, such as intelligence agents, criminals, or football hooligans [C16 (in the sense: signature): from Sp. *firma* signature, from *firmar* to sign, from L *firmāre* to confirm, from *firmus* firm]
firmament ('fɜːməmənt) *n* the expanse of the sky; heavens [C13 from LL *firmāmentum* sky (considered as fixed above the earth), from L: prop, support, from *firmāre* to make FIRM[1]]
firmware ('fɜːm,wɛə) *n computing* a series of fixed instructions built into the hardware of a computer that

Ff

can be changed only if the hardware itself is modified in some way

first (fɜːst) *adj* (*usually prenominal*) **1a** coming before all others **1b** (*as n*): *I was the first to arrive* **2** preceding all others in numbering or counting order; the ordinal number of *one*. Often written: 1st **3** rated, graded, or ranked above all other levels **4** denoting the lowest forward ratio of a gearbox in a motor vehicle **5** *music* **5a** denoting the highest part assigned to one of the voice parts in a chorus or one of the sections of an orchestra: *the first violins* **5b** denoting the principal player in a specific orchestral section: *he plays first horn* **6** **first thing** as the first action of the day: *I'll see you first thing tomorrow* ▷ *n* **7** the beginning; outset: *I couldn't see at first because of the mist* **8** *education, chiefly Brit* an honours degree of the highest class. Full term: **first-class honours degree** **9** the lowest forward ratio of a gearbox in a motor vehicle **10** something that has not occurred before: *a first for the company* ▷ *adv* **11** Also: **firstly** before anything else in order, time, importance, etc: *do this first* **12** **first and last** on the whole **13** **from first to last** throughout **14** for the first time: *I've loved you since I first saw you* **15** (*sentence modifier*) in the first place or beginning of a series of actions [OE *fyrest*]

first aid *n* **a** immediate medical assistance given in an emergency **b** (*as modifier*): *first-aid box*

first-born *adj* **1** eldest of the children in a family ▷ *n* **2** the eldest child in a family

first class *n* **1** the class or grade of the best or highest value, quality, etc ▷ *adj* (**first-class** *when prenominal*) **2** of the best or highest class or grade: *a first-class citizen* **3** excellent **4** of or denoting the most comfortable class of accommodation in a hotel, aircraft, train, etc **5** (in Britain) of mail that is processed most quickly ▷ *adv* **first-class** **6** by first-class mail, means of transportation, etc

first-day cover *n philately* an envelope postmarked on the first day of the issue of its stamps

first-degree burn *n pathol* the least severe type of burn, in which the skin surface is red and painful

first-foot *chiefly Scot* ▷ *n also* **first-footer** **1** the first person to enter a household in the New Year ▷ *vb* **2** to enter (a house) as first-foot > **ˈfirst-ˈfooting** *n*

first fruits *pl n* **1** the first results or profits of an undertaking **2** fruit that ripens first

first-hand *adj, adv* **1** from the original source: *he got the news first-hand* **2** **at first hand** directly: *he saw at first hand how other children suffered*

first lady *n* (*often caps*) (in the US) the wife or official hostess of a state governor or a president

firstling (ˈfɜːstlɪŋ) *n* the first, esp the first offspring

first-loss policy *n* an insurance policy for goods in which a total loss is extremely unlikely and the insurer agrees to provide cover for a sum less than the total value of the property

firstly (ˈfɜːstlɪ) *adv* another word for **first**

first mate *n* an officer second in command to the captain of a merchant ship

First Minister *n* **1** the chief minister of the Northern Ireland Assembly **2** the chief minister of the Scottish Parliament

first mortgage *n* a mortgage that has priority over other mortgages on the same property

first name *n* a name given to a person at birth, as opposed to a surname. Also called: **Christian name, forename, given name**

First Nation *n Canad* a formally recognized group of Indians on a reserve

first night *n* **a** the first public performance of a play, etc **b** (*as modifier*): *first-night nerves*

first offender *n* a person convicted of a criminal offence for the first time

first officer *n* **1** another name for **first mate** **2** the member of an aircraft crew who is second in command to the captain

first-past-the-post *n* (*modifier*) of a voting system in which a candidate may be elected by a simple majority

First Peoples *pl n Canad* a collective term for the Native Canadian peoples, the Inuit, and the Métis

first person *n* a grammatical category of pronouns and verbs used by the speaker to refer to or talk about himself or herself

first-rate *adj* **1** of the best or highest rated class or quality **2** *inf* very good; excellent

first reading *n* the introduction of a bill into a legislative assembly

first refusal *n* the right to buy something before it is offered to others

First Secretary *n* the chief minister of the National Assembly for Wales

first-strike *adj* (of a nuclear missile) intended for use in an opening attack calculated to destroy the enemy's nuclear weapons

first water *n* **1** the finest quality of diamond or other precious stone **2** the highest grade or best quality

firth (fɜːθ) *or* **frith** *n* a narrow inlet of the sea, esp in Scotland [C15 from ON *fjörthr* FJORD]

fiscal (ˈfɪskᵊl) *adj* **1** of or relating to government finances, esp tax revenues **2** of or involving financial matters ▷ *n* **3a** (in some countries) a public prosecutor **3b** *Scot* short for **procurator fiscal** [C16 from L *fiscālis* concerning the state treasury, from *fiscus* public money] > **ˈfiscally** *adv*

fiscal year *n* the US and Canad term for **financial year**

Fischer (*German* ˈfɪʃər) *n* **1** **Emil Hermann** (ˈeːmiːl ˈhɛrman) 1852–1919, German chemist, noted particularly for his work on synthetic sugars and the purine group: Nobel prize for chemistry 1902 **2** **Ernst Otto** 1918–94, German chemist: shared the Nobel prize for chemistry in 1973 with Geoffrey Wilkinson for his work on inorganic complexes **3** **Hans** (hans) 1881–1945, German chemist, noted particularly for his work on chlorophyll, haemin, and the porphyrins: Nobel prize for chemistry 1930 **4** **Robert James**, known as *Bobby*. born 1943, US chess player; world champion 1972–75

Fischer-Dieskau (*German* -ˈdiːskau) *n* **Dietrich** (ˈdiːtrɪç) born 1925, German baritone, noted particularly for his interpretation of Schubert's song cycles

fish (fɪʃ) *n, pl* **fish** *or* **fishes** **1a** any of a large group of cold-blooded aquatic vertebrates having jaws, gills, and usually fins and a skin covered in scales: includes the sharks, rays, teleosts, lungfish, etc **1b** (*in combination*): *fishpond*. Related adj: **piscine** **2** any of various similar but jawless vertebrates, such as the hagfish and lamprey **3** (*not in technical use*) any of various aquatic invertebrates, such as the cuttlefish and crayfish **4** the flesh of fish used as food **5** *inf* a person of little emotion or intelligence: *a poor fish* **6** **drink like a fish** to drink (esp alcohol) to excess **7** **have other fish to fry** to have other activities to do, esp more important ones **8** **like a fish out of water** out of one's usual place **9** **make fish of one and flesh of another** *Irish* to discriminate unfairly between people **10** **neither fish, flesh, nor fowl** neither this nor that ▷ *vb* **11** (*intr*) to attempt to catch fish, as with a line and hook or with nets, traps, etc **12** (*tr*) to fish in (a particular area of water) **13** to search (a body of water) for something or to search for something, esp in a body of water **14** (*intr; foll by for*) to seek something indirectly ▷ See also **fish out** [OE *fisc*] > **ˈfishˌlike** *adj*

▷ http://recipe-fish-seafood.com

▷ http://fishing.about.com/cs/fishrecipes

▷ www.fish4fun.com/seafoodrecipes.htm

fish and brewis *n Canad* a Newfoundland dish of cooked salt cod and soaked hard bread

fish and chips *n* fish fillets coated with batter and deep-fried, eaten with potato chips

fishbone fern ('fɪʃ,bəʊn) *n* a common Australian fern, *Nephrolepsis cordifolia*, having fronds with many pinnae
fish cake *n* a fried flattened ball of flaked fish mixed with mashed potatoes
fisher ('fɪʃə) *n* 1 a fisherman 2 Also called: **pekan** 2a a large North American marten having dark brown fur 2b the fur of this animal
Fisher ('fɪʃə) *n* 1 **Andrew** 1862–1928, Australian statesman, born in Scotland: prime minister of Australia (1908–09; 1910–13; 1914–15) 2 **Saint John** ?1469–1535, English prelate and scholar: executed for refusing to acknowledge Henry VIII as supreme head of the church. Feast day: June 22 3 **John Arbuthnot**, 1st Baron Fisher of Kilverstone. 1841–1920, British admiral; First Sea Lord (1904–10; 1914–15); introduced the dreadnought
fisherman ('fɪʃəmən) *n, pl* **fishermen** 1 a person who fishes as a profession or for sport 2 a vessel used for fishing
fishery ('fɪʃərɪ) *n, pl* **fisheries** 1a the industry of catching, processing, and selling fish 1b a place where this is carried on 2 a place where fish are reared 3 a fishing ground
Fishes ('fɪʃɪz) *n* **the** the constellation Pisces, the twelfth sign of the zodiac
fisheye lens ('fɪʃ,aɪ) *n photog* a lens of small focal length, having a highly curved protruding front element that covers an angle of view of almost 180°
fishfinger ('fɪʃ'fɪŋgə) *or US & Canad* **fish stick** *n* an oblong piece of filleted or minced fish coated in breadcrumbs
Fishguard ('fɪʃ,gɑːd) *n* a port and resort in SW Wales, in Pembrokeshire: ferry connections to Cork and Rosslare. Pop: 2679 (1991)
fish hawk *n* another name for the **osprey**
fish-hook *n* a sharp hook used in angling, esp one with a barb
fishing ('fɪʃɪŋ) *n* **a** the occupation of catching fish **b** (*as modifier*): *a fishing match*
▷ www.fao.org/fi/defaultN.asp
▷ www.fishbase.org
fishing ground *n* an area of water that is good for fishing
fishing rod *n* a long tapered flexible pole for use with a fishing line and, usually, a reel
fish joint *n* a connection formed by fishplates at the meeting point of two rails, beams, etc
fishmeal ('fɪʃ,miːl) *n* ground dried fish used as feed for farm animals, as a fertilizer, etc
fishmonger ('fɪʃ,mʌŋgə) *n chiefly Brit* a retailer of fish
fishnet ('fɪʃ,nɛt) *n* **a** an open mesh fabric resembling netting **b** (*as modifier*): *fishnet tights*
fish out *vb (tr, adv)* to find or extract (something): *to fish keys out of a pocket*
fishplate ('fɪʃ,pleɪt) *n* a flat piece of metal joining one rail or beam to the next, esp on railway tracks
fishtail ('fɪʃ,teɪl) *n* 1 an aeroplane manoeuvre in which the tail is moved from side to side to reduce speed 2 a nozzle having a long narrow slot at the top, placed over a Bunsen burner to produce a thin fanlike flame
fishwife ('fɪʃ,waɪf) *n, pl* **fishwives** 1 a woman who sells fish 2 a coarse scolding woman
fishy ('fɪʃɪ) *adj* **fishier, fishiest** 1 of, involving, or suggestive of fish 2 abounding in fish 3 *inf* suspicious, doubtful, or questionable 4 dull and lifeless: *a fishy look* > **'fishily** *adv*
fissile ('fɪsaɪl) *adj* 1 *Brit* capable of undergoing nuclear fission 2 fissionable 3 tending to split or capable of being split [C17 from L, from *fissus* split]
fission ('fɪʃən) *n* 1 the act or process of splitting or breaking into parts 2 *biol* a form of asexual reproduction involving a division into two or more equal parts 3 short for **nuclear fission** [C19 from L *fissiō* a cleaving] > **'fissionable** *adj*
fission-track dating *n* the dating of samples of minerals by comparing the tracks in them made by fission fragments of the uranium nuclei they contain, before and after irradiation by neutrons
fissiparous (fɪ'sɪpərəs) *adj biol* reproducing by fission > **fis'siparously** *adv*
fissure ('fɪʃə) *n* 1 any long narrow cleft or crack, esp in a rock 2 a weakness or flaw 3 *anat* a narrow split or groove that divides an organ such as the brain, lung, or liver into lobes ▷ *vb* **fissures, fissuring, fissured** 4 to crack or split apart [C14 from Medical L *fissūra*, from L *fissus* split]
fist (fɪst) *n* 1 a hand with the fingers clenched into the palm, as for hitting 2 Also called: **fistful** the quantity that can be held in a fist or hand 3 *inf* handwriting 4 an informal word for **index** (sense 9) ▷ *vb* 5 (*tr*) to hit with the fist [OE *fȳst*]
fisticuffs ('fɪstɪ,kʌfs) *pl n* combat with the fists [C17 prob. from *fisty* with the fist + CUFF²]
fistula ('fɪstjʊlə) *n, pl* **fistulas** *or* **fistulae** (-,liː) *pathol* an abnormal opening between one hollow organ and another or between a hollow organ and the surface of the skin, caused by ulceration, malformation, etc [C14 from L: pipe, tube, hollow reed, ulcer] > **'fistulous** *or* **'fistular** *adj*
fit¹ (fɪt) *vb* **fits, fitting, fitted** *or US* **fit** 1 to be appropriate or suitable for (a situation, etc) 2 to be of the correct size or shape for (a container, etc) 3 (*tr*) to adjust in order to render appropriate 4 (*tr*) to supply with that which is needed 5 (*tr*) to try clothes on (someone) in order to make adjustments if necessary 6 (*tr*) to make competent or ready 7 (*tr*) to locate with care 8 (*intr*) to correspond with the facts or circumstances ▷ *adj* **fitter, fittest** 9 appropriate 10 having the right qualifications; qualifying 11 in good health 12 worthy or deserving 13 (*foll by an infinitive*) *inf* ready (to); strongly disposed (to): *she was fit to scream* ▷ *n* 14 the manner in which something fits 15 the act or process of fitting 16 *statistics* the correspondence between observed and predicted characteristics of a distribution or model ▷ See also **fit in, fit out** [C14 prob. from MDu. *vitten*; rel. to ON *fitja* to knit] > **'fitly** *adv* > **'fittable** *adj*
fit² (fɪt) *n* 1 *pathol* a sudden attack or convulsion, such as an epileptic seizure 2 a sudden spell of emotion: *a fit of anger* 3 an impulsive period of activity or lack of activity 4 **have** *or* **throw a fit** *inf* to become very angry 5 **in** *or* **by fits and starts** in spasmodic spells [OE *fitt* conflict]
fitch (fɪtʃ) *n* 1 a polecat 2 the fur of the polecat [C16 prob. from *ficheux*, from OF, from ?]
fitful ('fɪtfʊl) *adj* characterized by or occurring in irregular spells > **'fitfully** *adv*
fit in *vb* 1 (*tr*) to give a place or time to 2 (*intr, adv*) to belong or conform, esp after adjustment: *he didn't fit in with their plans*
fitment ('fɪtmənt) *n* 1 *machinery* an accessory attached to an assembly of parts 2 *chiefly Brit* a detachable part of the furnishings of a room
fitness ('fɪtnɪs) *n* 1 the state of being fit 2 *biol* 2a the degree of adaptation of an organism to its environment, determined by its genetic constitution 2b the ability of an organism to produce viable offspring capable of surviving to the next generation
fit out *vb (tr, adv)* to equip
fitted ('fɪtɪd) *adj* 1 designed for excellent fit: *a fitted suit* 2 (of a carpet) cut or sewn to cover a floor completely 3a (of furniture) built to fit a particular space: *a fitted cupboard* 3b (of a room) equipped with fitted furniture: *a fitted kitchen* 4 (of sheets) having ends that are elasticated and shaped to fit tightly over a mattress
fitter ('fɪtə) *n* 1 a person who fits a garment, esp when it is made for a particular person 2 a person who is skilled in the assembly and adjustment of machinery, esp of a specified sort
fitting ('fɪtɪŋ) *adj* 1 appropriate or proper ▷ *n* 2 an

Ff

accessory or part: *an electrical fitting* **3** (*pl*) furnishings or accessories in a building **4** work carried out by a fitter **5** the act of trying on clothes so that they can be adjusted to fit > **'fittingly** *adv*

Fittipaldi (ˌfɪtɪ'pældɪ) *n* **Emerson** born 1946, Brazilian motor-racing driver: world champion in 1972 and 1974

Fitzgerald (fɪts'dʒɛrəld) *n* **1 Edward** 1809–83, English poet, noted particularly for his free translation of the *Rubáiyát of Omar Khayyám* (1859) **2 Ella** 1918–96, US jazz singer, noted esp for her vocal range and scat singing **3 F(rancis) Scott (Key)** 1896–1940, US novelist and short-story writer, noted particularly for his portrayal of the 1920s in *The Great Gatsby* (1925) and *Tender is the Night* (1934) **4 Garret** born 1926, Irish politician; leader of Fine Gael party (1977–87); prime minister of the Republic of Ireland (1981–82; 1982–87)

Fitzgerald-Lorentz contraction *n physics* the contraction that a moving body exhibits when its velocity approaches that of light [c19 after G. F. *Fitzgerald* (1851–1901), Irish physicist, and H. A. LORENTZ]

Fitzpatrick (fɪts'pætrɪk) *n* **Sean** (ʃɔːn) born 1963, New Zealand Rugby Union footballer; captain of the All Blacks (1992–98)

Fitzrovia (fɪts'rəʊvɪə) *n inf* the district north of Oxford Street, London, around Fitzroy Square and its pubs, noted in the 1930s and 40s as a haunt of poets

Fitzsimmons (fɪt'sɪmənz) *n* **Bob** 1862–1917, New Zealand boxer, born in England: world middleweight (1891–97), heavyweight (1897–99), and light-heavyweight (1903–05) champion

Fiume ('fiuːme) *n* the Italian name for **Rijeka**

five (faɪv) *n* **1** the cardinal number that is the sum of four and one **2** a numeral, 5, V, etc, representing this number **3** the amount or quantity that is one greater than four **4** something representing, represented by, or consisting of five units, such as a playing card with five symbols on it **5 five o'clock** five hours after noon or midnight ▷ *determiner* **6a** amounting to five: *five nights* **6b** (*as pronoun*): *choose any five you like* ▷ See also **fives** [OE *fīf*]

five-a-side *n* a version of soccer with five players on each side

5BX *n* a fitness exercise programme originally devised in the Canadian Air Force [from *5 b(asic) (e)x(ercises)*]

five-eighth *n Austral & NZ* a rugby player positioned between the halfbacks and three-quarters

five-finger *n* any of various plants having five-petalled flowers or five lobed leaves, such as cinquefoil and Virginia creeper

fivefold ('faɪvˌfəʊld) *adj* **1** equal to or having five times as many or as much **2** composed of five parts ▷ *adv* **3** by or up to five times as many or as much

Five Nations *pl n* (formerly) a confederacy of N American Indian peoples consisting of the Cayugas, Mohawks, Oneidas, Onondagas, and Senecas. See also **Six Nations**

five-o'clock shadow *n* beard growth visible late in the day on a man's shaven face

fivepins ('faɪvˌpɪnz) *n* (*functioning as sing*) a bowling game using five pins, played esp in Canada > **'fiveˌpin** *adj*

fiver ('faɪvə) *n Brit inf* a five-pound note

fives (faɪvz) *n* (*functioning as sing*) a ball game similar to squash but played with bats or the hands
▷ www.etonfives.co.uk

Five Towns *pl n* **the** the name given in his fiction by Arnold Bennett to the Potteries towns (actually six in number) of Burslem, Fenton, Hanley, Longton, Stoke-upon-Trent, and Tunstall, now part of the city of Stoke-on-Trent

Five-Year Plan *n* (in socialist economies) a government plan for economic development over a period of five years

fix (fɪks) *vb* (*mainly tr*) **1** (*also intr*) to make or become firm, stable, or secure **2** to attach or place permanently **3** (often foll by *up*) to settle definitely; decide **4** to hold or direct (eyes, etc) steadily: *he fixed his gaze on the woman* **5** to call to attention or rivet **6** to make rigid: *to fix one's jaw* **7** to place or ascribe: *to fix the blame* **8** to mend or repair **9** *inf* to provide or be provided with: *how are you fixed for supplies?* **10** *inf* to influence (a person, etc) unfairly, as by bribery **11** *sl* to take revenge on **12** *inf* to give (someone) his or her just deserts: *that'll fix him* **13** *inf, chiefly US & Canad* to prepare: *to fix a meal* **14** *dialect or inf* to spay or castrate (an animal) **15** *photog* to treat (a film, plate, or paper) with fixer to make permanent the image rendered visible by developer **16a** to convert (atmospheric nitrogen) into nitrogen compounds, as in the manufacture of fertilizers or the action of bacteria in the soil **16b** to convert (carbon dioxide) into organic compounds, esp carbohydrates, as occurs in photosynthesis **17** to reduce (a substance) to a solid state or a less volatile state **18** (*intr*) *sl* to inject a narcotic drug ▷ *n* **19** *inf* a predicament; dilemma **20** the ascertaining of the navigational position, as of a ship, by radar, etc **21** *sl* an intravenous injection of a narcotic such as heroin ▷ See also **fix up** [c15 from Med. L *fixāre*, from L *fixus* fixed, from L *fīgere*] > **'fixable** *adj*

fixate (fɪk'seɪt) *vb* **fixates, fixating, fixated 1** to become or cause to become fixed **2** *psychol* to engage in fixation **3** (*tr; usually passive*) *inf* to obsess [c19 from L *fixus* fixed + -ATE[1]]

fixation (fɪk'seɪʃən) *n* **1** the act of fixing or the state of being fixed **2** a preoccupation or obsession **3** *psychol* **3a** the situation of being set in a certain way of thinking or acting **3b** a strong attachment of a person to another person or an object in early life **4** *chem* the conversion of nitrogen in the air into a compound, esp a fertilizer **5** the reduction of a substance to a nonvolatile or solid form

fixative ('fɪksətɪv) *adj* **1** serving or tending to fix ▷ *n* **2** a fluid sprayed over drawings to prevent smudging or one that fixes tissues and cells for microscopic study **3** a substance added to a liquid, such as a perfume, to make it less volatile

fixed (fɪkst) *adj* **1** attached or placed so as to be immovable **2** stable: *fixed prices* **3** steadily directed: *a fixed expression* **4** established as to relative position: *a fixed point* **5** always at the same time: *a fixed holiday* **6** (of ideas, etc) firmly maintained **7** (of an element) held in chemical combination: *fixed nitrogen* **8** (of a substance) nonvolatile **9** arranged **10** *inf* equipped or provided for, as with money, possessions, etc **11** *inf* illegally arranged: *a fixed trial* > **fixedly** ('fɪksɪdlɪ) *adv* > **'fixedness** *n*

fixed assets *pl n* nontrading business assets of a relatively permanent nature, such as plant, fixtures, or goodwill. Also called: **capital assets**

fixed oil *n* a natural animal or vegetable oil that is not volatile: a mixture of esters of fatty acids

fixed-point representation *n computing* the representation of numbers by a single set of digits such that the radix point has a predetermined location ▷ Cf **floating-point representation**

fixed satellite *n* a satellite revolving in a stationary orbit so that it appears to remain over a fixed point on the earth's surface

fixed star *n* an extremely distant star whose position appears to be almost stationary over a long period of time

fixer ('fɪksə) *n* **1** a person or thing that fixes **2** *photog* a solution used to dissolve unexposed silver halides after developing **3** *sl* a person who makes arrangements, esp by underhand or illegal means

fixing ('fɪksɪŋ) *n* a means of attaching one thing to another, as a pipe to a wall, a slate to a roof, etc

fixity ('fɪksɪtɪ) *n, pl* **fixities 1** the state or quality of being fixed **2** a fixture

fixture ('fɪkstʃə) *n* **1** an object firmly fixed in place, esp a household appliance **2** a person or thing regarded as fixed in a particular place or position **3** *property law* an article attached to land and regarded as part of it **4** *chiefly Brit* **4a** a sports match or social occasion **4b** the date of such an event [C17 from LL *fixūra* a fastening (with -t- by analogy with *mixture*)]

fix up *vb (tr, adv)* **1** to arrange: *let's fix up a date* **2** (often foll by *with*) to provide: *I'm sure we can fix you up with a room*

fizgig ('fɪzˌɡɪɡ) *n* **1** a frivolous or flirtatious girl **2** a firework that fizzes as it moves [C16 prob. from obs. *fise* a breaking of wind + *gig* girl]

fizz (fɪz) *vb (intr)* **1** to make a hissing or bubbling sound **2** (of a drink) to produce bubbles of carbon dioxide ▷ *n* **3** a hissing or bubbling sound **4** the bubbly quality of a drink; effervescence **5** any effervescent drink [C17 imit.] > **'fizzy** *adj* > **'fizziness** *n*

fizzle ('fɪzᵊl) *vb* **fizzles, fizzling, fizzled** *(intr)* **1** to make a hissing or bubbling sound **2** (often foll by *out*) *inf* to fail or die out, esp after a promising start ▷ *n* **3** a hissing or bubbling sound **4** *inf* a failure [C16 prob. from obs. *fist* to break wind]

fjord *or* **fiord** (fjɔːd) *n* a long narrow inlet of the sea between high steep cliffs, common in Norway [C17 from Norwegian, from ON *fjörthr*; see FIRTH, FORD]

FL *abbrev for:* **1** Flight Lieutenant **2** Florida

fl. *abbrev for* floruit

Fla. *abbrev for* Florida

flab (flæb) *n* unsightly or unwanted fat on the body [C20 back formation from FLABBY]

flabbergast ('flæbəˌɡɑːst) *vb (tr; usually passive) inf* to amaze utterly; astound [C18 from ?]

flabby ('flæbɪ) *adj* **flabbier, flabbiest 1** loose or yielding: *flabby muscles* **2** having flabby flesh, esp through being overweight **3** lacking vitality; weak [C17 alteration of *flappy* from FLAP + -Y¹; cf. Du. *flabbe* drooping lip] > **'flabbiness** *n*

flaccid ('flæksɪd) *adj* lacking firmness; soft and limp [C17 from L *flaccidus*, from *flaccus*] > **flac'cidity** *n*

flacon (*French* flakɔ̃) *n* a small stoppered bottle, esp used for perfume [C19 from F; see FLAGON]

flag¹ (flæɡ) *n* **1** a piece of cloth, esp bunting, often attached to a pole or staff, decorated with a design and used as an emblem, symbol, or standard or as a means of signalling **2** a small piece of paper, etc, sold on flag days **3** the conspicuously marked or shaped tail of a deer or of certain dogs **4** anything used like a flag to attract attention, esp a code inserted into a computer file to distinguish certain information **5** *Brit, Austral, & NZ* the part of a taximeter that is raised when a taxi is for hire **6 show the flag 6a** to assert a claim by military presence **6b** *inf* to make an appearance ▷ *vb* **flags, flagging, flagged** *(tr)* **7** to decorate or mark with a flag or flags **8** (often foll by *down*) to warn or signal (a vehicle) to stop **9** to send or communicate (messages, information, etc) by flag [C16 from ?] > **'flagger** *n*

flag² (flæɡ) *n* **1** any of various plants that have long swordlike leaves, esp an iris (**yellow flag**) **2** the leaf of any such plant [C14 prob. from ON]

flag³ (flæɡ) *vb* **flags, flagging, flagged** *(intr)* **1** to hang down; droop **2** to become weak or tired [C16 from ?]

flag⁴ (flæɡ) *n* **1** short for **flagstone** ▷ *vb* **flags, flagging, flagged 2** *(tr)* to furnish (a floor, etc) with flagstones

flag day *n Brit* a day on which money is collected by a charity and small flags or emblems are given to contributors

flagellant ('flædʒɪlənt, flə'dʒɛlənt) *or* **flagellator** ('flædʒɪˌleɪtə) *n* a person who whips himself or herself or others either as part of a religious penance or for sexual gratification [C16 from L *flagellāre* to whip, from FLAGELLUM]

flagellate *vb* ('flædʒɪˌleɪt), **flagellates, flagellating, flagellated 1** *(tr)* to whip; flog ▷ *adj* ('flædʒɪlɪt), *also* **flagellated 2** possessing one or more flagella **3** whiplike ▷ *n* ('flædʒɪlɪt) **4** a flagellate organism > ˌ**flagel'lation** *n*

flagellum (flə'dʒɛləm) *n, pl* **flagella** (-lə) *or* **flagellums 1** *biol* a long whiplike outgrowth from a cell that acts as an organ of locomotion: occurs in some protozoans, gametes, etc **2** *bot* a long thin shoot or runner [C19 from L: a little whip, from *flagrum* a whip, lash] > **fla'gellar** *adj*

flageolet¹ (ˌflædʒə'lɛt) *n* a high-pitched musical instrument of the recorder family [C17 from F, modification of OF *flajolet* a little flute, from Vulgar L *flabeolum* (unattested), from L *flāre* to blow]

flageolet² *or* **flageolet bean** (ˌflædʒə'lɛt) *n* the pale green immature seed of a haricot bean, cooked and eaten as a vegetable [C19 from F *fageolet*, from L *phaseolus* bean; ?infl. by FLAGEOLET¹]

flag fall *n Austral* the minimum charge for hiring a taxi, to which the rate per kilometre is added

flag of convenience *n* a national flag flown by a ship registered in that country to gain financial or legal advantage

flag of truce *n* a white flag indicating an invitation to an enemy to negotiate

flagon ('flæɡən) *n* **1** a large bottle of wine, cider, etc **2** a vessel having a handle, spout, and narrow neck [C15 from OF *flascon*, from LL *flascō*, prob. of Gmc origin; see FLASK]

flagpole ('flæɡˌpəʊl) *or* **flagstaff** ('flæɡˌstɑːf) *n, pl* **flagpoles, flagstaffs** *or* **flagstaves** (-ˌsteɪvz) a pole or staff on which a flag is hoisted and displayed

flagrant ('fleɪɡrənt) *adj* openly outrageous [C15 from L *flagrāre* to blaze, burn] > **'flagrancy** *n* > **'flagrantly** *adv*

flagrante delicto (flə'ɡræntɪ dɪ'lɪktəʊ) *adv* See **in flagrante delicto**

flagship ('flæɡˌʃɪp) *n* **1** a ship, esp in a fleet, aboard which the commander of the fleet is quartered **2** the most important ship belonging to a shipping company **3** the item in a group considered most important esp in establishing a public image: *costume drama is the flagship of the BBC*

Ff

Flagstad ('flæɡstæd; *Norwegian* 'flaksta) *n* **Kirsten** ('çirstən) 1895–1962, Norwegian operatic soprano, noted particularly for her interpretations of Wagner

flagstone ('flæɡˌstəʊn) *n* **1** a hard fine-textured rock that can be split up into slabs for paving **2** a slab of such a rock [C15 *flag* (in the sense: sod, turf), from ON *flaga* slab; cf. OE *flæcg* plaster, poultice]

flag-waving *n inf* an emotional appeal intended to arouse patriotic feeling > **'flag,waver** *n*

Flaherty ('flæhətɪ) *n* **Robert (Joseph)** 1884–1951, US film director, a pioneer of documentary film; his work includes *Nanook of the North* (1922) and *Elephant Boy* (1935)

flail (fleɪl) *n* **1** an implement used for threshing grain, consisting of a wooden handle with a free-swinging metal or wooden bar attached to it ▷ *vb* **2** *(tr)* to beat with or as if with a flail **3** to thresh about: *with arms flailing* [C12 *fleil*, ult. from LL *flagellum* flail, from L: whip]

flair (flɛə) *n* **1** natural ability; talent **2** perceptiveness **3** *inf* stylishness or elegance: *to dress with flair* [C19 from F, lit.: sense of smell, from OF: scent, ult. from L *frāgrāre* to smell sweet; see FRAGRANT]

flak (flæk) *n* **1** anti-aircraft fire or artillery **2** *inf* adverse criticism [C20 from G *Fl(ieger)a(bwehr)k(anone)*, lit.: aircraft defence gun]

flake¹ (fleɪk) *n* **1** a small thin piece or layer chipped off or detached from an object or substance **2** a small piece or particle: *a flake of snow* **3** *archaeol* a fragment removed by chipping from a larger stone used as a tool or weapon **4** *inf* an eccentric, crazy, or unreliable person ▷ *vb* **flakes, flaking, flaked 5** to peel or cause to peel off in flakes **6** to cover or become covered with or as with flakes **7** *(tr)* to form into flakes [C14 from ON]

flake² (fleɪk) *n* a rack or platform for drying fish [C14 from ON *flaki*; rel. to Du. *vlaak* hurdle]

flake out *vb (intr, adv) inf* to collapse or fall asleep as through extreme exhaustion

flake white *n* a pigment made from flakes of white lead

flak jacket *n* a reinforced jacket for protection against gunfire or shrapnel worn by soldiers, policemen, etc

flaky ('fleɪkɪ) *adj* **flakier, flakiest** 1 like or made of flakes 2 tending to break easily into flakes 3 Also spelt: **flakey** *inf* eccentric; crazy > '**flakily** *adv* > '**flakiness** *n*

flambé ('flɑːmbeɪ) *adj* 1 (of food, such as steak or pancakes) served in flaming brandy ▷ *vb* **flambés, flambéing, flambéed** 2 *(tr)* to serve (food) in such a manner [F, p.p. of *flamber* to FLAME]

flambeau ('flæmbəʊ) *n, pl* **flambeaux** (-bəʊ, -bəʊz) *or* **flambeaus** a burning torch, as used in night processions, etc [C17 from OF: torch, lit.: a little flame, from *flambe* FLAME]

Flamborough Head ('flæmbərə, -brə) *n* a chalk promontory in NE England, on the coast of the East Riding of Yorkshire

flamboyant (flæm'bɔɪənt) *adj* 1 elaborate or extravagant; showy 2 rich or brilliant in colour 3 exuberant or ostentatious 4 of the French Gothic style of architecture characterized by flamelike tracery and elaborate carving [C19 from F: flaming, from *flamboyer* to FLAME] > **flam'boyance** *or* **flam'boyancy** *n* > **flam'boyantly** *adv*

flame (fleɪm) *n* 1 a hot usually luminous body of burning gas emanating in flickering streams from burning material or produced by a jet of ignited gas 2 *(often pl)* the state or condition of burning with flames: *to burst into flames* 3 a brilliant light 4a a strong reddish-orange colour 4b *(as adj)*: *a flame carpet* 5 intense passion or ardour 6 *inf* a lover or sweetheart (esp in **an old flame**) 7 *inf* an abusive message sent by email ▷ *vb* **flames, flaming, flamed** 8 to burn or cause to burn brightly 9 *(intr)* to become red or fiery: *his face flamed with anger* 10 *(intr)* to become angry or excited 11 *(tr)* to apply a flame to (something) 12 *inf* to send an abusive message by email [C14 from Anglo-F, from OF *flambe*, from L *flammula* a little flame, from *flamma* flame] > '**flame,like** *adj* > '**flamy** *adj*

flame gun *n* a type of flame-thrower for destroying garden weeds, etc

flamen ('fleɪmɛn) *n, pl* **flamens** *or* **flamines** ('flæmɪ,niːz) (in ancient Rome) any of 15 priests who each served a particular deity [C14 from L; prob. rel. to OE *blōtan* to sacrifice, Gothic *blotan* to worship]

flamenco (flə'mɛŋkəʊ) *n, pl* **flamencos** 1 a type of dance music for vocal soloist and guitar, characterized by sad mood 2 the dance performed to such music [from Sp.: like a Gipsy, lit.: Fleming, from MDu. *Vlaminc* Fleming]

flameout ('fleɪm,aʊt) *n* the failure of an aircraft jet engine in flight due to extinction of the flame

flame-thrower *n* a weapon that ejects a stream or spray of burning fluid

flame tree *n* any of various tropical trees with red or orange flowers

flaming ('fleɪmɪŋ) *adj* 1 burning with or emitting flames 2 glowing brightly 3 intense or ardent: *a flaming temper* 4 *inf* (intensifier): *you flaming idiot*

flamingo (flə'mɪŋgəʊ) *n, pl* **flamingos** *or* **flamingoes** a large wading bird having a pink-and-red plumage and downward-bent bill and inhabiting brackish lakes [C16 from Port., from Provençal, from L *flamma* flame + Gmc suffix *-ing* denoting descent from; cf. -ING[3]]

Flaminian Way (flə'mɪnɪən) *n* an ancient road in Italy, extending north from Rome to Rimini: constructed in 220 BC by Gaius Flaminius. Length: over 322 km (200 miles). Latin name: **Via Flaminia**

Flamininus (,flæmɪ'naɪnəs) *n* **Titus Quinctius** ('taɪtəs 'kwɪŋktɪəs) ?230–?174 BC, Roman general and statesman: defeated Macedonia (197) and proclaimed the independence of the Greek states (196)

Flaminius (flə'mɪnɪəs) *n* **Gaius** ('gaɪəs) died 217 BC, Roman statesman and general: built the Flaminian Way; defeated by Hannibal at Trasimene (217)

flammable ('flæməbᵊl) *adj* readily combustible; inflammable > ,**flamma'bility** *n*

> USAGE *Flammable* and *inflammable* are interchangeable when used of the properties of materials. *Flammable* is, however, often preferred for warning labels as there is less likelihood of misunderstanding (*inflammable* being sometimes taken to mean *not flammable*). *Inflammable* is preferred in figurative contexts: *this could prove to be an inflammable situation*

Flamsteed ('flæm,stiːd) *n* **John** 1646–1719, English astronomer: the first Astronomer Royal and first director of the Royal Observatory, Greenwich (1675) He increased the accuracy of existing stellar catalogues, greatly aiding navigation

flan (flæn) *n* 1 an open pastry or sponge tart filled with fruit or a savoury mixture 2 a piece of metal ready to receive the die or stamp in the production of coins [C19 from F, from OF *flaon*, from LL *fladō* flat cake, of Gmc origin]

Flanders ('flɑːndəz) *n* a powerful medieval principality in the SW part of the Low Countries, now in the Belgian provinces of East and West Flanders, the Netherlands province of Zeeland, and the French department of the Nord; scene of battles in many wars

flange (flændʒ) *n* 1 a radially projecting collar or rim on an object for strengthening it or for attaching it to another object 2 a flat outer face of a rolled-steel joist ▷ *vb* **flanges, flanging, flanged** 3 *(tr)* to provide (a component) with a flange [C17 prob. changed from earlier *flaunche* curved segment at side of a heraldic field, from F *flanc* FLANK] > **flanged** *adj* > '**flangeless** *adj*

flank (flæŋk) *n* 1 the side of a man or animal between the ribs and the hip 2 a cut of beef from the flank 3 the side of anything, such as a mountain or building 4 the side of a naval or military formation ▷ *vb* 5 (when *intr*, often foll by *on* or *upon*) to be located at the side of (an object, etc) 6 *mil* to position or guard on or beside the flank of (a formation, etc) [C12 from OF *flanc*, of Gmc origin]

flanker ('flæŋkə) *n* 1 one of a detachment of soldiers detailed to guard the flanks 2 a fortification used to protect a flank 3 Also called: **flank forward** *rugby* another name for **winger**

flannel ('flænᵊl) *n* 1 a soft light woollen fabric with a slight nap, used for clothing, etc 2 *(pl)* trousers or other garments made of flannel 3 *Brit* a small piece of cloth used to wash the face and hands; face flannel. US and Canad equivalent: **washcloth** 4 *Brit inf* indirect or evasive talk ▷ *vb* **flannels, flannelling, flannelled** *or US* **flannels, flanneling, flanneled** *(tr)* 5 to cover or wrap with flannel 6 to rub or polish with flannel 7 *Brit inf* to flatter [C14 prob. var. of *flanen* sackcloth, from Welsh, from *gwlân* wool] > '**flannelly** *adj*

flannelette (,flænᵊ'lɛt) *n* a cotton imitation of flannel

flap (flæp) *vb* **flaps, flapping, flapped** 1 to move (wings or arms) up and down, esp in or as if in flying, or (of wings or arms) to move in this way 2 to move or cause to move noisily back and forth or up and down: *the curtains flapped in the breeze* 3 *(intr) inf* to become agitated or flustered 4 to deal (a person or thing) a blow with a broad flexible object ▷ *n* 5 the action, motion, or noise made by flapping: *with one flap of its wings the bird was off* 6 a piece of material, etc, attached at one edge and usually used to cover an opening, as on a tent, envelope, or pocket 7 a blow dealt with a flat object 8 a movable surface fixed to an aircraft wing that increases lift during takeoff and drag during landing 9 *inf* a state of

panic or agitation [c14 prob. imit.]
flapdoodle ('flæp,du:dᵊl) *n sl* foolish talk; nonsense [c19 from ?]
flapjack ('flæp,dʒæk) *n* **1** a chewy biscuit made with rolled oats **2** *chiefly US & Canad* another word for **pancake**
flapper ('flæpə) *n* (in the 1920s) a young woman, esp one flaunting her unconventional behaviour
flare (flɛə) *vb* **flares, flaring, flared 1** to burn or cause to burn with an unsteady or sudden bright flame **2** to burn off excess gas or oil **3** to spread or cause to spread outwards from a narrow to a wider shape ▷ *n* **4** an unsteady flame **5** a sudden burst of flame **6a** a blaze of light or fire used to illuminate, signal distress, alert, etc **6b** the device producing such a blaze **7** a spreading shape or anything with a spreading shape: *a skirt with a flare* **8** an open flame used to burn off unwanted gas at an oil well **9** *astron* short for **solar flare** [c16 (to spread out): from ?]
flares (flɛəz) *pl n inf* trousers with legs that widen below the knee
flare-up *n* **1** a sudden burst of fire or light **2** *inf* a sudden burst of emotion or violence ▷ *vb* **flare up** (*intr, adv*) **3** to burst suddenly into fire or light **4** *inf* to burst into anger
flash (flæʃ) *n* **1** a sudden short blaze of intense light or flame: *a flash of sunlight* **2** a sudden occurrence or display, esp one suggestive of brilliance: *a flash of understanding* **3** a very brief space of time: *over in a flash* **4** Also called: **newsflash** a short news announcement concerning a new event **5** Also called: **patch** *chiefly Brit* an insignia or emblem worn on a uniform, vehicle, etc, to identify its military formation **6** a sudden rush of water down a river or watercourse **7** *photog, inf* short for **flashlight** (sense 2) **8** (*modifier*) involving, using, or produced by a flash of heat, light, etc: *flash distillation* **9 flash in the pan** a project, person, etc, that enjoys only short-lived success ▷ *adj* **10** *inf* ostentatious or vulgar **11** sham or counterfeit **12** *inf* relating to or characteristic of the criminal underworld **13** brief and rapid: *flash freezing* ▷ *vb* **14** to burst or cause to burst suddenly or intermittently into flame **15** to emit or reflect or cause to emit or reflect light suddenly or intermittently **16** (*intr*) to move very fast: *he flashed by on his bicycle* **17** (*intr*) to come rapidly (into the mind or vision) **18** (*intr*; foll by *out* or *up*) to appear like a sudden light **19a** to signal or communicate very fast: *to flash a message* **19b** to signal by use of a light, such as car headlights **20** (*tr*) *inf* to display ostentatiously: *to flash money around* **21** (*tr*) *inf* to show suddenly and briefly **22** (*intr*) *Brit sl* to expose oneself indecently **23** to send a sudden rush of water down (a river, etc), or to carry (a vessel) down by this method [c14 (in the sense: to rush, as of water): from ?] > '**flasher** *n*
flashback ('flæʃ,bæk) *n* a transition in a novel, film, etc, to an earlier scene or event
flashboard ('flæʃ,bɔ:d) *n* a board or boarding that is placed along the top of a dam to increase its height and capacity
flashbulb ('flæʃ,bʌlb) *n photog* a small expendable glass light bulb formerly used to produce a bright flash of light
flashbulb memory *n psychol* the clear recollections that a person may have of the circumstances associated with a dramatic event
flash burn *n pathol* a burn caused by momentary exposure to intense radiant heat
flash card *n* a card on which are written or printed words for children to look at briefly, used as an aid to learning
flashcube ('flæʃ,kju:b) *n* a boxlike camera attachment, holding four flashbulbs, that turns so that each flashbulb can be used
flash flood *n* a sudden short-lived torrent, usually caused by a heavy storm, esp in desert regions
flashgun ('flæʃ,gʌn) *n* a type of electronic flash, attachable to or sometimes incorporated in a camera, that emits a very brief flash of light when the shutter is open
flashing ('flæʃɪŋ) *n* a weatherproof material, esp thin sheet metal, used to cover the valleys between the slopes of a roof, the junction between a chimney and a roof, etc
flashlight ('flæʃ,laɪt) *n* **1** another word (esp US and Canad) for **torch 2** *photog* the brief bright light emitted by an electronic flash unit. Often shortened to **flash**
flash mob *n* a group of people coordinated by email to meet to perform some predetermined action at a particular place and time and then disperse quickly > '**flash,mobbing** *n*
flash point *n* **1** the lowest temperature at which the vapour above a liquid can be ignited in air **2** a critical time or place beyond which a situation will inevitably erupt into violence
flashy ('flæʃɪ) *adj* **flashier, flashiest 1** brilliant and dazzling, esp for a short time or in a superficial way **2** cheap and ostentatious > '**flashily** *adv* > '**flashiness** *n*
flask (flɑ:sk) *n* **1** a bottle with a narrow neck, esp used in a laboratory or for wine, oil, etc **2** Also called: **hip flask** a small flattened container of glass or metal designed to be carried in a pocket, esp for liquor **3** See **vacuum flask** [c14 from OF, from Med. L *flasca, flasco*, ? of Gmc origin; cf. OE *flasce, flaxe*]
flat[1] (flæt) *adj* **flatter, flattest 1** horizontal; level: *a flat roof* **2** even or smooth, without projections or depressions: *a flat surface* **3** lying stretched out at full length: *he lay flat on the ground* **4** having little depth or thickness: *a flat dish* **5** (*postpositive*; often foll by *against*) having a surface or side in complete contact with another surface: *flat against the wall* **6** (of a tyre) deflated **7** (of shoes) having an unraised heel **8** *chiefly Brit* **8a** (of races, racetracks, or racecourses) not having obstacles to be jumped **8b** of, relating to, or connected with flat racing as opposed to steeplechasing and hurdling **9** without qualification; total: *a flat denial* **10** fixed: *a flat rate* **11** (*prenominal or immediately postpositive*) neither more nor less; exact: *he did the journey in 30 minutes flat* **12** unexciting: *a flat joke* **13** without variation or resonance; monotonous: *a flat voice* **14** (of beer, sparkling wines, etc) having lost effervescence, as by exposure to air **15** (of trade, business, etc) commercially inactive **16** (of a battery) fully discharged **17** (of a print, photograph, or painting) lacking contrast **18** (of paint) without gloss or lustre **19** (of lighting) diffuse **20** *music* **20a** (*immediately postpositive*) denoting a note of a given letter name (or the sound it represents) that has been lowered in pitch by one chromatic semitone: *B flat* **20b** (of an instrument, voice, etc) out of tune by being too low in pitch ▷ Cf **sharp** (sense 12) **21 flat** *phonetics* the vowel sound of *a* as in the usual US or S Brit pronunciation of *hand, cat* ▷ *adv* **22** in or into a prostrate, level, or flat state or position: *he held his hand out flat* **23** completely or utterly; absolutely **24** exactly; precisely: *in three minutes flat* **25** *music* **25a** lower than a standard pitch **25b** too low in pitch: *she sings flat* ▷ Cf **sharp** (sense 17) **26 fall flat (on one's face)** to fail to achieve a desired effect **27 flat out** *inf* **27a** with the maximum speed or effort **27b** totally exhausted ▷ *n* **28** a flat object, surface, or part **29** (*often pl*) a low-lying tract of land, esp a marsh or swamp **30** (*often pl*) a mud bank exposed at low tide **31** *music* **31a** an accidental that lowers the pitch of a note by one chromatic semitone. Usual symbol: ♭ **31b** a note affected by this accidental ▷ Cf **sharp** (sense 18) **32** *theatre* a wooden frame covered with painted canvas, etc, used to form part of a stage setting **33** a punctured car tyre **34** (*often cap*; preceded by *the*) *chiefly Brit* **34a** flat racing, esp as opposed to steeplechasing and hurdling **34b** the season of flat racing **35** *US & Canad* a shallow box used for holding

Ff

plants, etc ▷ *vb* **flats, flatting, flatted 36** to make or become flat [C14 from ON *flatr*] > **'flatly** *adv* > **'flatness** *n* > **'flattish** *adj*

flat² (flæt) *n* **1** a set of rooms comprising a residence entirely on one floor of a building. Usual US and Canad name: **apartment** ▷ *vb* **2** (*intr*) *Austral & NZ inf* to live in a flat with other people [OE *flett* floor, hall, house]

flatbed lorry ('flæt,bɛd) *n* a lorry with a flat platform for its body

flatbed scanner *n computing* a computer-controlled device that electronically scans images placed on its flat glass, to produce digitized images for use in desktop publishing, etc

flatboat ('flæt,bəʊt) *n* any boat with a flat bottom, usually for transporting goods on a canal

flatbread ('flæt,brɛd) *n* a type of thin unleavened bread

flatette (,flæt'ɛt) *n Austral* a very small flat

flatfish ('flæt,fɪʃ) *n, pl* **flatfish** *or* **flatfishes** any of an order of marine spiny-finned fish including the halibut, plaice, turbot, and sole, all of which have a flat body that has both eyes on the uppermost side

flatfoot ('flæt,fʊt) *n* **1** Also called: **splayfoot** a condition in which the instep arch of the foot is flattened **2** (*pl* **flatfoots** *or* **flatfeet**) a slang word (usually derogatory) for a **policeman**

flat-footed (,flæt'fʊtɪd) *adj* **1** having flatfoot **2** *inf* **2a** awkward **2b** downright **3** *inf* off guard (often in **catch flat-footed**) > ,**flat-'footedly** *adv* > ,**flat-'footedness** *n*

flathead ('flæt,hɛd) *n, pl* **flathead** *or* **flatheads** a Pacific food fish which resembles the gurnard

flatiron ('flæt,aɪən) *n* (formerly) an iron for pressing clothes that was heated by being placed on a stove, etc

flatlet ('flætlɪt) *n* a flat having only a few rooms

flatmate ('flæt,meɪt) *n* a person with whom one shares a flat

flat-pack *adj* (of a piece of furniture, equipment, or other construction) supplied in pieces packed into a flat box for assembly by the buyer

flat racing *n* **a** the racing of horses on racecourses without jumps **b** (*as modifier*): *the flat-racing season*

flat spin *n* **1** an aircraft spin in which the longitudinal axis is more nearly horizontal than vertical **2** *inf* a state of confusion; dither

flat spot *n* **1** *engineering* a region of poor acceleration over a narrow range of throttle openings, caused by a weak mixture in the carburettor **2** any narrow region of poor performance in a mechanical device

flatten ('flætᵊn) *vb* **1** (sometimes foll by *out*) to make or become flat or flatter **2** (*tr*) *inf* **2a** to knock down or injure **2b** to crush or subdue **3** (*tr*) *music* to lower the pitch of (a note) by one chromatic semitone > **'flattener** *n*

flatter ('flætə) *vb* **1** to praise insincerely, esp in order to win favour or reward **2** to show to advantage: *that dress flatters her* **3** (*tr*) to make appear more attractive, etc, than in reality **4** to gratify the vanity of (a person) **5** (*tr*) to encourage, esp falsely **6** (*tr*) to deceive (oneself): *I flatter myself that I am the best* [C13 prob. from OF *flater* to lick, fawn upon, of Frankish origin] > **'flatterable** *adj* > **'flatterer** *n*

flattery ('flætərɪ) *n, pl* **flatteries 1** the act of flattering **2** excessive or insincere praise

flattie ('flætɪ) *n NZ inf* a flounder or other flatfish

flatties ('flætɪz) *pl n* shoes with flat heels

flat top *n* a style of haircut in which the hair is cut shortest on the top of the head so that it stands up from the scalp and appears flat from the crown to the forehead

flatulent ('flætjʊlənt) *adj* **1** suffering from or caused by an excessive amount of gas in the alimentary canal **2** generating excessive gas in the alimentary canal **3** pretentious [C16 from NL *flātulentus*, from L *flatus*, from *flāre* to breathe, blow] > **'flatulence** *or* **'flatulency** *n* > **'flatulently** *adv*

flatus ('fleɪtəs) *n, pl* **flatuses** gas generated in the alimentary canal [C17 from L: a blowing, from *flāre* to breathe, blow]

flatworm ('flæt,wɜːm) *n* any parasitic or free-living invertebrate of the phylum *Platyhelminthes*, including flukes and tapeworms, having a flattened body

Flaubert ('fləʊbɛə; *French* flobɛr) *n* **Gustave** (gystav) 1821–80, French novelist and short-story writer, regarded as a leader of the 19th-century naturalist school. His most famous novel, *Madame Bovary* (1857), for which he was prosecuted (and acquitted) on charges of immorality, and *L'Éducation sentimentale* (1869) deal with the conflict of romantic attitudes and bourgeois society. His other major works include *Salammbô* (1862), *La Tentation de Saint Antoine* (1874), and *Trois contes* (1877)

flaunt (flɔːnt) *vb* **1** to display (possessions, oneself, etc) ostentatiously **2** to wave or cause to wave freely ▷ *n* **3** the act of flaunting [C16 ? of Scand. origin]

> **USAGE** *Flaunt* is sometimes wrongly used where *flout* is meant: *they must be prevented from flouting* (not *flaunting*) *the law*

flautist ('flɔːtɪst) *or US & Canad* **flutist** ('fluːtɪst) *n* a player of the flute [C19 from It. *flautista*, from *flauto* FLUTE]

flavescent (flə'vɛsᵊnt) *adj* turning yellow; yellowish [C19 from L *flāvēscere* to become yellow]

flavin *or* **flavine** ('fleɪvɪn) *n* **1** a heterocyclic ketone that forms the nucleus of certain natural yellow pigments, such as riboflavin **2** any yellow pigment based on flavin [C19 from L *flāvus* yellow]

flavine ('fleɪvɪn) *n* another name for **acriflavine hydrochloride**

flavone ('fleɪvəʊn) *n* **1** a crystalline compound occurring in plants **2** any of a class of yellow plant pigments derived from flavone [C19 from G, from L *flāvus* yellow + -ONE]

flavoprotein (,fleɪvəʊ'prəʊtiːn) *n* any of a group of enzymes that contain a derivative of riboflavin linked to a protein and catalyse oxidation in cells

flavour *or US* **flavor** ('fleɪvə) *n* **1** taste perceived in food or liquid in the mouth **2** a substance added to food, etc, to impart a specific taste **3** a distinctive quality or atmosphere **4** *physics* a property of quarks that distinguishes different types ▷ *vb* **5** (*tr*) to impart a flavour or quality to [C14 from OF *flaour*, from LL *flātor* (unattested) bad smell, breath, from L *flāre* to blow] > **'flavourless** *or US* **'flavorless** *adj* > **'flavourful** *or US* **'flavorful** *adj*

flavour enhancer *n* a food additive, such as monosodium glutamate, used to intensify the flavour of foods

flavouring *or US* **flavoring** ('fleɪvərɪŋ) *n* a substance used to impart a particular flavour to food

flaw¹ (flɔː) *n* **1** an imperfection or blemish **2** a crack or rift **3** *law* an invalidating defect in a document or proceeding ▷ *vb* **4** to make or become blemished or imperfect [C14 prob. from ON *flaga* stone slab] > **'flawless** *adj*

flaw² (flɔː) *n* a sudden short gust of wind; squall [C16 of Scand. origin]

flax (flæks) *n* **1** a herbaceous plant or shrub that has blue flowers and is cultivated for its seeds (flaxseed) and for the fibres of its stems **2** the fibre of this plant, made into thread and woven into linen fabrics **3** any of various similar plants **4** *NZ* a swamp plant producing a fibre that is used by Maoris for clothing, baskets, etc [OE *fleax*]

flaxen ('flæksən) *adj* **1** of or resembling flax **2** of a soft yellow colour: *flaxen hair*

Flaxman ('flæksmən) *n* **John** 1755–1826, English neoclassical sculptor and draughtsman, noted particularly for his monuments and his engraved illustrations for the *Iliad*, the *Odyssey*, and works by Dante and Aeschylus

flaxseed ('flæks,si:d) *n* the seed of the flax plant, which yields linseed oil. Also called: **linseed**

flay (fleɪ) *vb (tr)* **1** to strip off the skin or covering of, esp by whipping **2** to attack with savage criticism [OE *flēan*] > '**flayer** *n*

flaysome ('fleɪsəm) *adj Northern English dialect* frightening

flea (fli:) *n* **1** a small wingless parasitic blood-sucking jumping insect living on the skin of mammals and birds **2 flea in one's ear** *inf* a sharp rebuke [OE *flēah*]

fleabane ('fli:,beɪn) *n* any of several plants, including one having purplish tubular flower heads with orange centres and one having yellow daisy-like flower heads, that are reputed to ward off fleas

fleabite ('fli:,baɪt) *n* **1** the bite of a flea **2** a slight or trifling annoyance or discomfort

flea-bitten *adj* **1** bitten by or infested with fleas **2** *inf* shabby or decrepit

flea market *n* an open-air market selling cheap and often second-hand goods

fleapit ('fli:,pɪt) *n inf* a shabby cinema or theatre

fleawort ('fli:,wɜ:t) *n* **1** any of various plants with yellow daisy-like flowers and rosettes of downy leaves **2** a Eurasian plantain whose seeds were formerly used as a flea repellent

flèche (fleɪʃ, flɛʃ) *n* a slender spire, esp over the intersection of the nave and transept ridges of a church roof. Also called: **spirelet** [c18 from F: spire (lit.: arrow), prob. of Gmc origin]

fleck (flɛk) *n* **1** a small marking or streak **2** a speck: *a fleck of dust* ▹ *vb* **3** *(tr)* Also: **flecker** to speckle [c16 prob. from ON *flekkr* stain, spot]

Flecker ('flɛkə) *n* **James Elroy** 1884–1915, English poet and dramatist; author of *Hassan* (1922)

fled (flɛd) *vb* the past tense and past participle of **flee**

fledge (flɛdʒ) *vb* **fledges, fledging, fledged** *(tr)* **1** to feed and care for (a young bird) until it is able to fly **2** Also called: **fletch** to fit (something, esp an arrow) with a feather or feathers **3** to cover or adorn with or as if with feathers [OE *-flycge*, as in *unflycge* unfledged; see FLY[1]]

fledgling *or* **fledgeling** ('flɛdʒlɪŋ) *n* **1** a young bird that has grown feathers **2** a young and inexperienced person

flee (fli:) *vb* **flees, fleeing, fled** **1** to run away from (a place, danger, etc) **2** *(intr)* to run or move quickly [OE *flēon*] > '**fleer** *n*

fleece (fli:s) *n* **1** the coat of wool that covers the body of a sheep or similar animal **2** the wool removed from a single sheep **3** something resembling a fleece **4** sheepskin or a fabric with soft pile, used as a lining for coats, etc **5a** a warm polyester fabric with a brushed nap, used for outdoor garments **5b** a jacket or top made from such a fabric ▹ *vb* **fleeces, fleecing, fleeced** *(tr)* **6** to defraud or charge exorbitantly **7** another term for **shear** (sense 1) [OE *flēos*]

fleecie ('fli:sɪ) *n* NZ a person who collects fleeces after shearing and prepares them for baling. Also called: **fleece-oh**

fleecy ('fli:sɪ) *adj* **fleecier, fleeciest** of or resembling fleece > '**fleecily** *adv*

fleer (flɪə) *arch* ▹ *vb* **1** to scoff; sneer ▹ *n* **2** a derisory glance [c14 from ON; cf. Norwegian *flire* to snigger]

fleet[1] (fli:t) *n* **1** a number of warships organized as a tactical unit **2** all the warships of a nation **3** a number of aircraft, ships, buses, etc, operating together or under the same ownership [OE *flēot*]

fleet[2] (fli:t) *adj* **1** rapid in movement; swift **2** *poetic* fleeting ▹ *vb* **3** *(intr)* to move rapidly **4** *(tr) obs* to cause (time) to pass rapidly [prob. OE *flēotan* to float, glide rapidly] > '**fleetly** *adv* > '**fleetness** *n*

Fleet (fli:t) *n* **the 1** a stream that formerly ran into the Thames between Ludgate Hill and Fleet Street and is now a covered sewer **2** Also called: **Fleet Prison** (formerly) a London prison, esp used for holding debtors

Fleet Air Arm *n* the aviation branch of the Royal Navy

fleet chief petty officer *n* a noncommissioned officer in the Royal Navy comparable in rank to a warrant officer in the army or the Royal Air Force

fleeting ('fli:tɪŋ) *adj* rapid and transient: *a fleeting glimpse of the sea* > '**fleetingly** *adv*

fleet rate *or* **rating** *n* a reduced rate quoted by an insurance company to underwrite the risks to a fleet of vehicles, aircraft, etc

Fleet Street *n* **1** a street in central London in which many newspaper offices were formerly situated **2** British journalism or journalists collectively

Fleetwood ('fli:t,wʊd) *n* a fishing port in NW England, in Lancashire. Pop: 27 227 (1991)

Flémalle (*French* flemal) *n* **Master of** See (Robert) **Campin**

Fleming[1] ('flɛmɪŋ) *n* a native or inhabitant of Flanders or of Flemish-speaking Belgium

Fleming[2] ('flɛmɪŋ) *n* **1** Sir **Alexander** 1881–1955, Scottish bacteriologist: discovered lysozyme (1922) and penicillin (1928): shared the Nobel prize for physiology or medicine in 1945 **2 Ian** (**Lancaster**) 1908–64, English author of spy novels; creator of the secret agent James Bond **3** Sir **John Ambrose** 1849–1945, English electrical engineer: invented the thermionic valve (1904)

Flemish ('flɛmɪʃ) *n* **1** one of the two official languages of Belgium **2 the Flemish** *(functioning as pl)* the Flemings collectively ▹ *adj* **3** of or characteristic of Flanders, the Flemings, or their language

Flemish Brabant *n* a province of central Belgium, formed in 1995 from the N part of Brabant province: densely populated and intensively farmed, with large industrial centres. Pop: 1 041 704 (2000 est). Area: 2106 sq km (813 sq miles)

Flensburg (*German* 'flɛnsbʊrk) *n* a port in N Germany, in Schleswig-Holstein: taken from Denmark by Prussia in 1864; voted to remain German in 1920. Pop: 87 240 (1991)

flense (flɛns), **flench** (flɛntʃ), *or* **flinch** (flɪntʃ) *vb* **flenses, flensing, flensed** *or* **flenches, flenching, flenched** *or* **flinches, flinching, flinched** *(tr)* to strip (a whale, seal, etc) of (its blubber or skin) [c19 from Danish *flense*; rel. to Du. *flensen*]

flesh (flɛʃ) *n* **1** the soft part of the body of an animal or human, esp muscular tissue, as distinct from bone and viscera **2** *inf* excess weight; fat **3** *arch* the edible tissue of animals as opposed to that of fish or, sometimes, fowl **4** the thick soft part of a fruit or vegetable **5** the human body and its physical or sensual nature as opposed to the soul or spirit. Related adj: **carnal** **6** mankind in general **7** animate creatures in general **8** one's own family; kin (esp in **one's own flesh and blood**) **9a** a yellowish-pink colour **9b** *(as adj)*: *flesh tights* **10 in the flesh** in person; actually present **11 press the flesh** *inf* to shake hands, usually with large numbers of people, esp as a political campaigning ploy ▹ *vb* **12** *(tr) hunting* to stimulate the hunting instinct of (hounds or falcons) by giving them small quantities of raw flesh **13** *arch or poetic* to accustom or incite to bloodshed or battle by initial experience **14** to fatten; fill out [OE *flǣsc*]

fleshings ('flɛʃɪŋz) *pl n* flesh-coloured tights

fleshly ('flɛʃlɪ) *adj* **fleshlier, fleshliest** **1** relating to the body; carnal: *fleshly desire* **2** worldly as opposed to spiritual **3** fat > '**fleshliness** *n*

flesh out *vb (adv)* **1** *(tr)* to give substance to (an argument, description, etc) **2** *(intr)* to expand or become more substantial

fleshpots ('flɛʃ,pɒts) *pl n often facetious* **1** luxurious living **2** places where bodily desires are gratified [c16 from the Biblical use as applied to Egypt (Exodus 16:3)]

flesh wound (wu:nd) *n* a wound affecting superficial tissues

fleshy ('flɛʃɪ) *adj* **fleshier, fleshiest 1** plump **2** related to or resembling flesh **3** *bot* (of some fruits, etc) thick and pulpy > '**fleshiness** *n*

fletcher ('flɛtʃə) *n* a person who makes arrows [C14 from OF *flechier*, from *fleche* arrow; see FLÈCHE]

Fletcher ('flɛtʃə) *n* **John** 1579–1625, English Jacobean dramatist, noted for his romantic tragicomedies written in collaboration with Francis Beaumont, esp *Philaster* (1610) and *The Maid's Tragedy* (1611)

fleur-de-lys *or* **fleur-de-lis** (ˌflɜːdə'liː) *n, pl* **fleurs-de-lys** *or* **fleurs-de-lis** (ˌflɜːdə'liːz) **1** *heraldry* a charge representing a lily with three distinct petals **2** another name for **iris** (sense 2) [C19 from OF *flor de lis*, lit.: lily flower]

fleurette *or* **fleuret** (flʊə'rɛt) *n* an ornament or motif resembling a flower [C19 F, lit.: a small flower, from *fleur* flower]

Fleury (*French* flœri) *n* **André Hercule de** (ɑ̃dre ɛrkyl də) 1653–1743, French cardinal and statesman: Louis XV's chief adviser and virtual ruler of France (1726–43)

flew (fluː) *vb* the past tense of **fly**[1]

flews (fluːz) *pl n* the fleshy hanging upper lip of a bloodhound or similar dog [C16 from ?]

flex (flɛks) *n* **1** *Brit* a flexible insulated electric cable, used esp to connect appliances to mains. US and Canad name: **cord** ▷ *vb* **2** to bend or be bent: *he flexed his arm* **3** to contract (a muscle) or (of a muscle) to contract **4** (*intr*) to work flexitime [C16 from L *flexus* bent, winding, from *flectere* to bend, bow]

flexecutive (flɛg'zɛkjʊtɪv) *n* an executive to whom the employer allows flexibility about times and locations of working [C20 from FLEX(IBLE)+ (EX)ECUTIVE]

flexible ('flɛksɪbᵊl) *adj* **1** Also **flexile** ('flɛksaɪl) able to be bent easily without breaking **2** adaptable or variable: *flexible working hours* **3** able to be persuaded easily > ˌ**flexi'bility** *n* > '**flexibly** *adv*

flexion ('flɛkʃən) *or* **flection** *n* **1** the act of bending a joint or limb **2** the condition of the joint or limb so bent > '**flexional** *adj*

flexitime ('flɛksɪˌtaɪm) *n* a system permitting flexibility of working hours at the beginning or end of the day, provided an agreed period (**core time**) is spent at work. Also called: **flextime**

flexor ('flɛksə) *n* any muscle whose contraction serves to bend a joint or limb ▷ Cf **extensor** [C17 NL; see FLEX]

flexuous ('flɛksjʊəs) *adj* full of bends or curves; winding [C17 from L *flexuōsus* full of bends, tortuous, from *flexus* a bending; see FLEX] > '**flexuously** *adv*

flexure ('flɛkʃə) *n* **1** the act of flexing or the state of being flexed **2** a bend, turn, or fold

flex-wing *n* *aeronautics* a collapsible fabric delta wing, as used with hang-gliders

flibbert ('flɪbət) *n* *Southwest English dialect* a small piece or bit

flibbertigibbet ('flɪbətɪˌdʒɪbɪt) *n* an irresponsible, silly, or gossipy person [C15 from ?]

flick[1] (flɪk) *vb* **1** (*tr*) to touch with or as if with the finger or hand in a quick jerky movement **2** (*tr*) to propel or remove by a quick jerky movement, usually of the fingers or hand **3** to move or cause to move quickly or jerkily **4** (*intr; foll by through*) to read or look at (a book, etc) quickly or idly ▷ *n* **5** a tap or quick stroke with the fingers, a whip, etc **6** the sound made by such a stroke **7** a fleck or particle **8** **give (someone) the flick** to dismiss (someone) from consideration [C15 imit.; cf. F *flicflac*]

flick[2] (flɪk) *n sl* **1** a cinema film **2** **the flicks** the cinema: *what's on at the flicks tonight?*

flicker[1] ('flɪkə) *vb* **1** (*intr*) to shine with an unsteady or intermittent light **2** (*intr*) to move quickly to and fro **3** (*tr*) to cause to flicker ▷ *n* **4** an unsteady or brief light or flame **5** a swift quivering or fluttering movement [OE *flicorian*]

flicker[2] ('flɪkə) *n* a North American woodpecker which has a yellow undersurface to the wings and tail [C19 ? imit. of the bird's call]

flick knife *n* a knife with a retractable blade that springs out when a button is pressed

flier ('flaɪə) *n* a variant spelling of **flyer**

flight[1] (flaɪt) *n* **1** the act, skill, or manner of flying **2** a journey made by a flying animal or object **3** a group of flying birds or aircraft: *a flight of swallows* **4** the basic tactical unit of a military air force **5** a journey through space, esp of a spacecraft **6** an aircraft flying on a scheduled journey **7** a soaring mental journey above or beyond the normal everyday world: *a flight of fancy* **8** a single line of hurdles across a track in a race **9** a feather or plastic attachment fitted to an arrow or dart to give it stability in flight **10** a set of steps or stairs between one landing or floor and the next ▷ *vb* (*tr*) **11** *sport* to cause (a ball, dart, etc) to float slowly towards its target **12** to shoot (a bird) in flight **13** to fledge (an arrow or dart) [OE *flyht*]

flight[2] (flaɪt) *n* **1** the act of fleeing or running away, as from danger **2** **put to flight** to cause to run away **3** **take (to) flight** to run away; flee [OE *flyht* (unattested)]

flight attendant *n* a person who attends to the needs of passengers on a commercial flight

flight deck *n* **1** the crew compartment in an airliner **2** the upper deck of an aircraft carrier from which aircraft take off

flightless ('flaɪtlɪs) *adj* (of certain birds and insects) unable to fly. See also **ratite**

flight lieutenant *n* an officer holding a commissioned rank senior to a flying officer and junior to a squadron leader in the Royal Air Force

flight path *n* the course through the air of an aircraft, rocket, or projectile

flight recorder *n* an electronic device fitted to an aircraft for collecting and storing information concerning its performance in flight. It is often used to determine the cause of a crash. Also called: **black box**

flight sergeant *n* a noncommissioned officer in the Royal Air Force, junior in rank to that of master aircrew

flight simulator *n* a ground-training device that reproduces exactly the conditions experienced on the flight deck of an aircraft

flighty ('flaɪtɪ) *adj* **flightier, flightiest 1** frivolous and irresponsible **2** mentally erratic or wandering > '**flightiness** *n*

flim (flɪm) *n* *Northern English dialect* a five-pound note

flimflam ('flɪmˌflæm) *inf* ▷ *n* **1a** nonsense; rubbish; foolishness **1b** (*as modifier*): *flimflam arguments* **2** a deception; trick; swindle ▷ *vb* **flimflams, flimflamming, flimflammed 3** (*tr*) to deceive; trick; swindle; cheat [C16 prob. of Scand. origin] > '**flimˌflammer** *n*

flimsy ('flɪmzɪ) *adj* **flimsier, flimsiest 1** not strong or substantial: *a flimsy building* **2** light and thin: *a flimsy dress* **3** unconvincing; weak: *a flimsy excuse* ▷ *n* **4** thin paper used for making carbon copies of a letter, etc **5** a copy made on such paper [C17 from ?] > '**flimsiness** *n*

flinch (flɪntʃ) *vb* (*intr*) **1** to draw back suddenly, as from pain, shock, etc; wince **2** (often foll by *from*) to avoid contact (with): *he never flinched from his duty* [C16 from OF *flenchir*; rel. to MHG *lenken* to bend, direct] > '**flinchingly** *adv*

flinders ('flɪndəz) *pl n rare* small fragments or splinters (esp in **fly into flinders**) [C15 prob. from ON; cf. Norwegian *flindra* thin piece of stone]

Flinders Island *n* an island off the coast of NE Tasmania: the largest of the Furneaux Islands. Pop: 1100 (latest est). Area: 2077 sq km (802 sq miles)

Flinders Range *n* a mountain range in E South Australia, between Lake Torrens and Lake Frome. Highest peak: 1188 m (3898 ft)

fling (flɪŋ) *vb* **flings, flinging, flung** (*mainly tr*) **1** to throw, esp with force or abandon **2** to put or send without warning or preparation: *to fling someone into jail* **3** (*also intr*) to move (oneself or a part of the body) with abandon or speed **4** (usually foll by *into*) to apply (oneself) diligently and with vigour (to) **5** to cast aside: *she flung away her scruples* ▷ *n* **6** the act or an instance of flinging **7** a period or occasion of unrestrained or extravagant behaviour **8** any of various vigorous Scottish reels full of leaps and turns, such as the Highland fling **9** a trial; try: *to have a fling at something different* [C13 from ON] > '**flinger** *n*

flint (flɪnt) *n* **1** an impure greyish-black form of quartz that occurs in chalk. It produces sparks when struck with steel and is used in the manufacture of pottery and road-construction materials. Formula: SiO_2 **2** any piece of flint, esp one used as a primitive tool or for striking fire **3** a small cylindrical piece of an iron alloy, used in cigarette lighters **4** Also called: **flint glass** colourless glass other than plate glass [OE]

Flint (flɪnt) *n* **1** a town in NE Wales, in Flintshire, on the Dee estuary. Pop: 11 737 (1991) **2** a city in SE Michigan: closure of the car production plants led to a high level of unemployment. Pop: 124 943 (2000)

flintlock ('flɪntˌlɒk) *n* **1** an obsolete gunlock in which the charge is ignited by a spark produced by a flint in the hammer **2** a firearm having such a lock

Flintshire ('flɪntʃɪə, -ʃə) *n* a county of NE Wales, on the Irish Sea and the Dee estuary: became part of Clwyd in 1974, reinstated with reduced borders in 1996: includes the industrialized Deeside region in the E and the Clwydian Hills in the SW. Administrative centre: Mold. Pop: 148 565 (2001). Area: 437 sq km (169 sq miles)

flinty ('flɪntɪ) *adj* **flintier, flintiest 1** of or resembling flint **2** hard or cruel; unyielding > '**flintily** *adv* > '**flintiness** *n*

flip (flɪp) *vb* **flips, flipping, flipped 1** to throw (something light or small) carelessly or briskly **2** to throw or flick (an object such as a coin) so that it turns or spins in the air **3** to flick: *to flip a crumb across the room* **4** (foll by *through*) to read or look at (a book, etc) quickly, idly, or incompletely **5** (*intr*) to make a snapping movement or noise with the finger and thumb **6** (*intr*) *sl* to fly into a rage or an emotional outburst (also in **flip one's lid, flip one's top, flip out**) ▷ *n* **7** a snap or tap, usually with the fingers **8** a rapid jerk **9** any alcoholic drink containing beaten egg ▷ *adj* **10** *inf* flippant or pert [C16 prob. imit.; see FILLIP]

flip chart *n* a pad, containing large sheets of paper that can be easily turned over, mounted on a stand and used to present reports, data, etc

flip-flop *n* **1** a backward handspring **2** Also called: **bistable** an electronic device or circuit that can assume either of two states by the application of a suitable pulse **3** *inf, chiefly US* a complete change of opinion, policy, etc **4** a repeated flapping noise **5** Also called (esp US, Austral, and Canad): **thong** a rubber-soled sandal attached to the foot by a thong between the big toe and the next toe ▷ *vb* **flip-flops, flip-flopping, flip-flopped** (*intr*) **6** *inf, chiefly US* to have a complete change of opinion, policy, etc **7** to move with repeated flaps [C16 reduplication of FLIP]

flippant ('flɪpənt) *adj* **1** marked by inappropriate levity; frivolous **2** impertinent; saucy [C17 ?from FLIP] > '**flippancy** *n* > '**flippantly** *adv*

flipper ('flɪpə) *n* **1** the flat broad limb of seals, whales, etc, specialized for swimming **2** (*often pl*) either of a pair of rubber paddle-like devices worn on the feet as an aid in swimming

flip side *n* **1** another term for **B-side 2** another, less familiar, aspect of a person or thing

flirt (flɜːt) *vb* **1** (*intr*) to behave or act amorously without emotional commitment **2** (*intr;* usually foll by *with*) to deal playfully or carelessly (with something dangerous or serious): *the motorcyclist flirted with death* **3** (*intr;* usually foll by *with*) to toy (with): *to flirt with the idea of leaving* **4** (*intr*) to dart; flit **5** (*tr*) to flick or toss ▷ *n* **6** a person who acts flirtatiously [C16 from ?] > '**flirter** *n* > '**flirty** *adj*

flirtation (flɜːˈteɪʃən) *n* **1** behaviour intended to arouse sexual feelings or advances without emotional commitment **2** any casual involvement

flirtatious (flɜːˈteɪʃəs) *adj* **1** given to flirtation **2** expressive of playful sexual invitation: *a flirtatious glance* > **flir'tatiously** *adv*

flit (flɪt) *vb* **flits, flitting, flitted** (*intr*) **1** to move along rapidly and lightly **2** to fly rapidly and lightly **3** to pass quickly: *a memory flitted into his mind* **4** *Scot & N English dialect* to move house **5** *Brit inf* to depart hurriedly and stealthily in order to avoid obligations ▷ *n* **6** the act or an instance of flitting **7** *Brit inf* a hurried and stealthy departure in order to avoid obligations [C12 from ON *flytja* to carry] > '**flitter** *n*

flitch (flɪtʃ) *n* **1** a side of pork salted and cured **2** a piece of timber cut lengthways from a tree trunk [OE *flicce;* cf. FLESH]

flitter ('flɪtə) *vb* a less common word for **flutter**

flittermouse ('flɪtəˌmaʊs) *n, pl* **flittermice** a dialect name for **bat**[2] (sense 1) [C16 translation of G *Fledermaus*]

float (fləʊt) *vb* **1** to rest or cause to rest on the surface of a fluid or in a fluid or space without sinking: *oil floats on water* **2** to move or cause to move buoyantly, lightly, or freely across a surface or through air, water, etc **3** to move about aimlessly, esp in the mind: *thoughts floated before him* **4** (*tr*) **4a** to launch or establish (a commercial enterprise, etc) **4b** to offer for sale (stock or bond issues, etc) on the stock market **5** (*tr*) *finance* to allow (a currency) to fluctuate against other currencies in accordance with market forces **6** (*tr*) to flood, inundate, or irrigate (land) ▷ *n* **7** something that floats **8** *angling* an indicator attached to a baited line that sits on the water and moves when a fish bites **9** a small hand tool with a rectangular blade used for smoothing plaster, etc **10** Also called: **paddle** a blade of a paddle wheel **11** *Brit* a buoyant garment or device to aid a person in staying afloat **12** a structure fitted to the underside of an aircraft to allow it to land on water **13** a motor vehicle used to carry a tableau or exhibit in a parade, esp a civic parade **14** a small delivery vehicle, esp one powered by batteries: *a milk float* **15** *Austral & NZ* a vehicle for transporting horses **16** a sum of money used by shopkeepers to provide change at the start of the day's business **17** the hollow floating ball of a ballcock [OE *flotian;* see FLEET[2]] > '**floatable** *adj* > ˌ**floata'bility** *n* > '**floaty** *adj*

floatage ('fləʊtɪdʒ) *n* a variant spelling of **flotage**

floatation (fləʊˈteɪʃən) *n* a variant spelling of **flotation**

floatel (fləʊˈtɛl) *n* a variant spelling of **flotel**

floater ('fləʊtə) *n* **1** a person or thing that floats **2** a dark spot that appears in one's vision as a result of dead cells or cell fragments in the eye **3** *US & Canad* a person of no fixed political opinion **4** *US inf* a person who often changes employment, residence, etc

float glass *n* polished glass made by floating molten glass on liquid metal in a reservoir

floating ('fləʊtɪŋ) *adj* **1** having little or no attachment **2** (of an organ or part) displaced from the normal position or abnormally movable: *a floating kidney* **3** uncommitted or unfixed: *floating voters* **4** *finance* **4a** (of capital) available for current use **4b** (of debt) short-term and unfunded, usually raised to meet current expenses **4c** (of a currency) free to fluctuate against other currencies in accordance with market forces

floating-point representation *n computing* the representation of numbers by two sets of digits (*a, b*), the set *a* indicating the significant digits, the set *b* giving the position of the radix point. Also called: **floating decimal point representation** ▷ Cf **fixed-point representation**

Ff

floating rib *n* any rib of the lower two pairs of ribs in man, which are not attached to the breastbone

floats (fləʊts) *pl n theatre* another word for **footlights**

flob (flɒb) *vb* **flobs, flobbing, flobbed** (*intr*) *Brit sl* to spit [c20 from?]

flocculate ('flɒkjʊˌleɪt) *vb* **flocculates, flocculating, flocculated** to form or be formed into an aggregated flocculent mass > ˌ**floccu'lation** *n*

flocculent ('flɒkjʊlənt) *adj* **1** like wool; fleecy **2** *chem* aggregated in woolly cloudlike masses: *a flocculent precipitate* **3** *biol* covered with tufts or flakes [c19 from L *floccus* FLOCK[2] + -ULENT] > '**flocculence** *n*

flocculus ('flɒkjʊləs) *n, pl* **flocculi** (-ˌlaɪ) **1** Also called: **plage** a cloudy marking on the sun's surface. It consists of calcium when lighter than the surroundings and of hydrogen when darker **2** *anat* a tiny prominence on each side of the cerebellum

flock[1] (flɒk) *n* (*sometimes functioning as pl*) **1** a group of animals of one kind, esp sheep or birds **2** a large number of people **3** a body of Christians regarded as the pastoral charge of a priest, bishop, etc ▷ *vb* (*intr*) **4** to gather together or move in a flock **5** to go in large numbers: *people flocked to the church* [OE *flocc*]

flock[2] (flɒk) *n* **1** a tuft, as of wool, hair, cotton, etc **2** waste from fabrics such as cotton or wool used for stuffing mattresses, etc **3** Also called: **flocking** very small tufts of wool applied to fabrics, wallpaper, etc, to give a raised pattern [c13 from OF *floc*, from L *floccus*] > '**flocky** *adj*

Flodden ('flɒdᵊn) *n* a hill in Northumberland where invading Scots were defeated by the English in 1513 and James IV of Scotland was killed. Also called: **Flodden Field**

floe (fləʊ) *n* See **ice floe** [c19 prob. from Norwegian *flo* slab, layer, from ON; see FLAW[1]]

flog (flɒg) *vb* **flogs, flogging, flogged 1** (*tr*) to beat harshly, esp with a whip, strap, etc **2** *Brit sl* to sell **3** (*intr*) to make progress by painful work **4** *NZ* to steal **5** **flog a dead horse 5a** to harp on some long-discarded subject **5b** to pursue the solution of a problem long realized to be insoluble [c17 prob. from L *flagellāre*; see FLAGELLANT] > '**flogger** *n*

flong (flɒŋ) *n printing* a material used for making moulds in stereotyping [c20 var. of FLAN]

flood (flʌd) *n* **1a** the inundation of land that is normally dry through the overflowing of a body of water, esp a river **1b** the state of a river that is at an abnormally high level. Related adj: **diluvial 2** a great outpouring or flow: *a flood of words* **3a** the rising of the tide from low to high water **3b** (*as modifier*): *the flood tide* ▷ Cf **ebb** (sense 3) **4** *theatre* short for **floodlight** ▷ *vb* **5** (of water) to inundate or submerge (land) or (of land) to be inundated or submerged **6** to fill or be filled to overflowing, as with a flood **7** (*intr*) to flow; surge: *relief flooded through him* **8** to supply an excessive quantity of petrol to (a carburettor or petrol engine) or (of a carburettor, etc) to be supplied with such an excess **9** (*intr*) to overflow **10** (*intr*) to bleed profusely from the uterus, as following childbirth [OE *flōd*; see FLOW, FLOAT]

Flood (flʌd) *n Old Testament* **the** the flood from which Noah and his family and livestock were saved in the ark (Genesis 7–8)

floodgate ('flʌdˌgeɪt) *n* **1** Also called: **head gate, water gate** a gate in a sluice that is used to control the flow of water **2** (*often pl*) a control or barrier against an outpouring or flow

flooding ('flʌdɪŋ) *n* **1** *psychol* a method of eliminating anxiety in a given situation, by exposing a person to the situation until the anxiety subsides **2** *pathol* excessive bleeding from the uterus

floodlight ('flʌdˌlaɪt) *n* **1** a broad intense beam of artificial light, esp as used in the theatre or to illuminate the exterior of buildings **2** the lamp producing such light ▷ *vb* **floodlights, floodlighting, floodlit 3** (*tr*) to illuminate as by floodlight

flood plain *n* the flat area bordering a river, composed of sediment deposited during flooding

floor (flɔː) *n* **1** Also called: **flooring** the inner lower surface of a room **2** a storey of a building: *the second floor* **3** a flat bottom surface in or on any structure: *a dance floor* **4** the bottom surface of a tunnel, cave, sea, etc **5** that part of a legislative hall in which debate and other business is conducted **6** the right to speak in a legislative body (esp in **get, have,** *or* **be given the floor**) **7** the room in a stock exchange where trading takes place **8** the earth; ground **9** a minimum price charged or paid **10** **take the floor** to begin dancing on a dance floor ▷ *vb* **11** to cover with or construct a floor **12** (*tr*) to knock to the floor or ground **13** (*tr*) *inf* to disconcert, confound, or defeat [OE *flōr*]

floorboard ('flɔːˌbɔːd) *n* one of the boards forming a floor

flooring ('flɔːrɪŋ) *n* **1** the material used in making a floor **2** another word for **floor** (sense 1)

floor manager *n* **1** the stage manager of a television programme **2** a person in overall charge of one floor of a large shop

floor plan *n* a drawing to scale of the arrangement of rooms on one floor of a building

floor show *n* a series of entertainments, such as singing and dancing, performed in a nightclub

floozy, floozie, *or* **floosie** ('fluːzɪ) *n, pl* **floozies** *or* **floosies** *sl* a disreputable woman [c20 from ?]

flop (flɒp) *vb* **flops, flopping, flopped 1** (*intr*) to bend, fall, or collapse loosely or carelessly: *his head flopped backwards* **2** (when *intr*, often foll by *into, onto*, etc) to fall, cause to fall, or move with a sudden noise **3** (*intr*) *inf* to fail: *the scheme flopped* **4** (*intr*) to fall flat onto the surface of water **5** (*intr*; often foll by *out*) *sl* to go to sleep ▷ *n* **6** the act of flopping **7** *inf* a complete failure [c17 var. of FLAP]

floppy ('flɒpɪ) *adj* **floppier, floppiest 1** limp or hanging loosely ▷ *n, pl* **floppies 2** short for **floppy disk** > '**floppily** *adv* > '**floppiness** *n*

floppy disk *n* a flexible magnetic disk that stores information and can be used to store data in the memory of a digital computer

flops (flɒps) *n acronym for* (*sometimes caps*) floating-point operations per second: a measure of computer processing power

flora ('flɔːrə) *n, pl* **floras** *or* **florae** (-riː) **1** all the plant life of a given place or time **2** a descriptive list of such plants, often including a key for identification [c18 from NL, from FLORA]

Flora ('flɔːrə) *n* the Roman goddess of flowers [c16 from L, from *flōs* flower]

floral ('flɔːrəl) *adj* **1** decorated with or consisting of flowers or patterns of flowers **2** of or associated with flowers > '**florally** *adv*

Florence ('flɒrəns) *n* a city in central Italy, on the River Arno in Tuscany: became an independent republic in the 14th century; under Austrian and other rule intermittently from 1737 to 1859; capital of Italy 1865–70. It was the major cultural and artistic centre of the Renaissance and is still one of the world's chief art centres. Pop: 376 682 (2000 est). Ancient name: **Florentia** (flɒ'rɛntsɪə, -'rɛntɪə) Italian name: **Firenze**

Florentine ('flɒrənˌtaɪn) *adj* **1** of or relating to Florence, in Italy ▷ *n* **2** a native or inhabitant of Florence **3** a chocolate-covered biscuit with nuts and dried fruit

Flores ('flɔːrɛs) *n* **1** an island in Indonesia, one of the Lesser Sunda Islands, between the Flores Sea and the Savu Sea: mountainous, with active volcanoes and unexplored forests. Chief town: Ende. Area: 17 150 sq km (6622 sq miles) **2** (*also Portuguese* 'florɪʃ) an island in the Atlantic, the westernmost of the Azores. Chief town: Santa Cruz. Area: 142 sq km (55 sq miles)

florescence (flɔː'rɛsəns) *n* the process, state, or period of flowering [c18 from NL, from L *flōrēscere* to come into flower]

Flores Sea *n* a part of the Pacific Ocean in Indonesia between Celebes and the Lesser Sunda Islands

floret ('flɔːrɪt) *n* a small flower, esp one of many making up the head of a composite flower [c17 from OF, from *flor* FLOWER]

Florey ('flɔːrɪ) *n* **Howard Walter**, Baron Florey 1898–1968, British pathologist: shared the Nobel prize for physiology or medicine (1945) with E. B. Chain and Alexander Fleming for their work on penicillin

Florianópolis (*Portuguese* floriə'nɔpulis) *n* a port in S Brazil, capital of Santa Caterina state, on the W coast of Santa Caterina Island. Pop: 321 778 (2000)

floriated *or* **floreated** ('flɔːrɪˌeɪtɪd) *adj archit* having ornamentation based on flowers and leaves [c19 from L *flōs* FLOWER]

floribunda (ˌflɔːrɪ'bʌndə) *n* any of several varieties of cultivated hybrid roses whose flowers grow in large sprays [c19 from NL, fem of *flōribundus* flowering freely]

floriculture ('flɔːrɪˌkʌltʃə) *n* the cultivation of flowering plants > ˌ**flori'cultural** *adj* > ˌ**flori'culturist** *n*

florid ('flɒrɪd) *adj* **1** having a red or flushed complexion **2** excessively ornate; flowery: *florid architecture* [c17 from L *flōridus* blooming] > **flo'ridity** *n* > '**floridly** *adv*

Florida ('flɒrɪdə) *n* **1** a state of the southeastern US, between the Atlantic and the Gulf of Mexico: consists mostly of a low-lying peninsula ending in the **Florida Keys**, a chain of small islands off the coast of S Florida, extending southwest for over 160 km (100 miles) Capital: Tallahassee. Pop: 15 982 378 (2000). Area: 143 900 sq km (55 560 sq miles). Abbreviations: **Fla** or (with zip code) **FL** **2** **Straits of** a sea passage between the Florida Keys and Cuba, linking the Atlantic with the Gulf of Mexico

Floridian (flɒ'rɪdɪən) *n* **1** a native or inhabitant of Florida ▷ *adj* **2** of or relating to Florida or its inhabitants

floriferous (flɔː'rɪfərəs) *adj* bearing or capable of bearing many flowers

florin ('flɒrɪn) *n* **1** a former British coin, originally silver, equivalent to ten (new) pence **2** (formerly) another name for **guilder** (sense 1) [c14 from F, from OIt. *fiorino* Florentine coin, from *fiore* flower, from L *flōs*]

florist ('flɒrɪst) *n* a person who grows or deals in flowers

floristic (flɒ'rɪstɪk) *adj* of or relating to flowers or a flora > **flo'ristically** *adv*

-florous *adj combining form* indicating number or type of flowers: *tubuliflorous*

floruit *Latin* ('flɒruːɪt) *vb* (he or she) flourished: used to indicate the period when a figure, whose birth and death dates are unknown, was most active

floss (flɒs) *n* **1** the mass of fine silky fibres obtained from cotton and similar plants **2** any similar fine silky material **3** untwisted silk thread used in embroidery, etc **4** See **dental floss** ▷ *vb* **5** **to clean (between one's teeth) with dental floss** [c18 ?from OF *flosche* down]

flossy ('flɒsɪ) *adj* **flossier, flossiest** consisting of or resembling floss

flotage *or* **floatage** ('fləʊtɪdʒ) *n* **1** the act or state of floating **2** power or ability to float **3** flotsam

flotation *or* **floatation** (fləʊ'teɪʃən) *n* **1a** the launching or financing of a commercial enterprise by bond or share issues **1b** the raising of a loan or new capital by bond or share issues **2** power or ability to float **3** Also called: **froth flotation** a process to concentrate the valuable ore in low-grade ores by using induced differences in surface tension to carry the valuable fraction to the surface

flotel *or* **floatel** (fləʊ'tɛl) *n* a rig used for accommodation of workers in off-shore oil fields [c20 FLO(ATING) + (HO)TEL]

flotilla (flə'tɪlə) *n* a small fleet or a fleet of small vessels [c18 from Sp., from F *flotte*, ult. from ON *floti*]

flotsam ('flɒtsəm) *n* **1** wreckage from a ship found floating ▷ Cf **jetsam** **2** odds and ends (esp in **flotsam and jetsam**) **3** vagrants [c16 from Anglo-F *floteson*, from *floter* to FLOAT]

flounce[1] (flaʊns) *vb* **flounces, flouncing, flounced** **1** (*intr*; often foll by *about*, *away*, *out*, etc) to move or go with emphatic movements ▷ *n* **2** the act of flouncing [c16 of Scand. origin]

flounce[2] (flaʊns) *n* an ornamental gathered ruffle sewn to a garment by its top edge [c18 from OF, from *froncir* to wrinkle, of Gmc origin]

flounder[1] ('flaʊndə) *vb* (*intr*) **1** to move with difficulty, as in mud **2** to make mistakes ▷ *n* **3** the act of floundering [c16 prob. a blend of FOUNDER[2] + BLUNDER; ? infl. by FLOUNDER[2]]

> USAGE *Flounder* is sometimes wrongly used where *founder* is meant: *the project foundered* (not *floundered) because of lack of funds*

flounder[2] ('flaʊndə) *n, pl* **flounder** *or* **flounders** a European flatfish having a greyish-brown body covered with prickly scales: an important food fish [c14 from ON]

flour ('flaʊə) *n* **1** a powder, which may be either fine or coarse, prepared by grinding the meal of a grass, esp wheat **2** any finely powdered substance ▷ *vb* (*tr*) **3** to make (grain, etc) into flour **4** to dredge or sprinkle (food or utensils) with flour [c13 *flur* finer portion of meal, FLOWER] > '**floury** *adj*

flourish ('flʌrɪʃ) *vb* **1** (*intr*) to thrive; prosper **2** (*intr*) to be at the peak of condition **3** (*intr*) to be healthy: *plants flourish in the light* **4** to wave or cause to wave in the air with sweeping strokes **5** to display or make a display **6** to play (a fanfare, etc) on a musical intrument ▷ *n* **7** the act of waving or brandishing **8** a showy gesture: *he entered with a flourish* **9** an ornamental embellishment in writing **10** a display of ornamental language or speech **11** a grandiose passage of music [c13 from OF, ult. from L *flōrēre* to flower, from *flōs* a flower] > '**flourisher** *n*

flout (flaʊt) *vb* (when *intr*, usually foll by *at*) to show contempt (for) [c16 ?from ME *flouten* to play the flute, from OF *flauter*] > '**floutingly** *adv*

> USAGE See at **flaunt**

flow (fləʊ) *vb* (*mainly intr*) **1** (of liquids) to move or be conveyed as in a stream **2** (of blood) to circulate around the body **3** to move or progress freely as if in a stream: *the crowd flowed into the building* **4** to be produced continuously and effortlessly: *ideas flowed from her pen* **5** to be marked by smooth or easy movement **6** to hang freely or loosely: *her hair flowed down her back* **7** to be present in abundance: *wine flows at their parties* **8** (of tide water) to advance or rise ▷ Cf **ebb** (sense 1) **9** (of rocks such as slate) to yield to pressure so that the structure and arrangement of the constituent minerals are altered ▷ *n* **10** the act, rate, or manner of flowing: *a fast flow* **11** a continuous stream or discharge **12** continuous progression **13** the advancing of the tide **14** *Scot* **14a** a marsh or swamp **14b** an inlet or basin of the sea **14c** (*cap when part of a name*): *Scapa Flow* [OE *flōwan*]

flow chart *or* **sheet** *n* a diagrammatic representation of the sequence of operations in an industrial process, computer program, etc

Flow Country *n* an area of moorland and peat bogs in northern Scotland known for its wildlife, now partly afforested

flower ('flaʊə) *n* **1a** a bloom or blossom on a plant **1b** a plant that bears blooms or blossoms **2** the reproductive structure of angiosperm plants, consisting normally of stamens and carpels surrounded by petals and sepals. In some plants it is brightly coloured and attracts insects or other animals for pollination. Related adj: **floral** **3** any similar reproductive structure in other plants **4** the prime; peak: *in the flower of his youth* **5** the choice or

Ff

finest product, part, or representative **6** a decoration or embellishment **7** (*pl*) fine powder, usually produced by sublimation: *flowers of sulphur* ▷ *vb* **8** (*intr*) to produce flowers; bloom **9** (*intr*) to reach full growth or maturity **10** (*tr*) to deck or decorate with flowers or floral designs [C13 from OF *flor*, from L *flōs*] > **'flowerless** *adj* > **'flower-,like** *adj*
▷ www.garden.org
▷ www.ontariogardening.com/Tips/flowers.jsp
▷ www.bbc.co.uk/gardening/basics/techniques
▷ www.anbg.gov.au
▷ www.sis.agr.gc.ca/cansis/nsdb/climate/hardiness/intro.html

flowered ('flaʊəd) *adj* **1** having flowers **2** decorated with flowers or a floral design

floweret ('flaʊərɪt) *n* another name for **floret**

flower girl *n* a girl or woman who sells flowers in the street

flowering ('flaʊərɪŋ) *adj* (of certain species of plants) capable of producing conspicuous flowers

flowerpot ('flaʊə,pɒt) *n* a pot in which plants are grown

flower power *n inf* a youth cult of the late 1960s advocating peace and love; associated with drug-taking. Its adherents were known as **flower children** or **flower people**

flowery ('flaʊərɪ) *adj* **1** abounding in flowers **2** decorated with flowers or floral patterns **3** like or suggestive of flowers **4** (of language or style) elaborate > **'floweriness** *n*

flown (fləʊn) *vb* the past participle of **fly**[1]

flow-on *n Austral & NZ* **a** a wage or salary increase granted to one group of workers as a consequence of a similar increase granted to another group **b** (*as modifier*): *a flow-on effect*

fl. oz. *abbrev for* fluid ounce

flu (flu:) *n inf* **1** (often preceded by *the*) short for **influenza** **2** any of various viral infections, esp a respiratory or intestinal infection

fluctuate ('flʌktjʊ,eɪt) *vb* **fluctuates, fluctuating, fluctuated** **1** to change or cause to change position constantly **2** (*intr*) to rise and fall like a wave [C17 from L, from *fluctus* a wave, from *fluere* to flow] > **'fluctuant** *adj* > **,fluctu'ation** *n*

flue (flu:) *n* a shaft, tube, or pipe, esp as used in a chimney, to carry off smoke, gas, etc [C16 from ?]

fluent ('flu:ənt) *adj* **1** able to speak or write a specified foreign language with facility **2** spoken or written with facility **3** graceful in motion or shape **4** flowing or able to flow freely [C16 from L: flowing, from *fluere* to flow] > **'fluency** *n* > **'fluently** *adv*

flue pipe *or* **flue** *n* an organ pipe whose sound is produced by the passage of air across a fissure in the side, as distinguished from a **reed pipe**

fluff (flʌf) *n* **1** soft light particles, such as the down or nap of cotton or wool **2** any light downy substance **3** *inf* a mistake, esp in speaking or reading lines or performing music **4** *inf* a young woman (esp in **a bit of fluff**) ▷ *vb* **5** to make or become soft and puffy **6** *inf* to make a mistake in performing (an action, music, etc) [C18 ?from *flue* downy matter]

fluffy ('flʌfɪ) *adj* **fluffier, fluffiest** **1** of, resembling, or covered with fluff **2** soft and light > **'fluffily** *adv* > **'fluffiness** *n*

flugelhorn ('flu:gᵊl,hɔ:n) *n* a type of valved brass instrument consisting of a tube of conical bore with a cup-shaped mouthpiece, used esp in brass bands [G, from *Flügel* wing + *Horn* HORN]

fluid ('flu:ɪd) *n* **1** a substance, such as a liquid or gas, that can flow, has no fixed shape, and offers little resistance to an external stress ▷ *adj* **2** capable of flowing and easily changing shape **3** of or using a fluid or fluids **4** constantly changing or apt to change **5** flowing [C15 from L, from *fluere* to flow] > **flu'idity** *or* **'fluidness** *n*

fluidics (flu:'ɪdɪks) *n* (*functioning as sing*) the study and use of systems in which the flow of fluids in tubes simulates the flow of electricity in conductors > **flu'idic** *adj*

fluidize *or* **fluidise** ('flu:ɪ,daɪz) *vb* **fluidizes, fluidizing, fluidized** *or* **fluidises, fluidising, fluidised** (*tr*) to make fluid, esp to make (solids) fluid by pulverizing them so that they can be transported in gas as if they were liquids > **,fluidi'zation** *or* **,fluidi'sation** *n*

fluid mechanics *n* (*functioning as sing*) the study of the mechanical and flow properties of fluids, esp as they apply to practical engineering. Also called: **hydraulics**

fluid ounce *n* **1** *Brit* a unit of capacity equal to one twentieth of an Imperial pint **2** *US* a unit of capacity equal to one sixteenth of a US pint

fluke[1] (flu:k) *n* **1** a flat bladelike projection at the end of the arm of an anchor **2** either of the two lobes of the tail of a whale **3** the barb of a harpoon, arrow, etc [C16 ? a special use of FLUKE[3] (in the sense: a flounder)]

fluke[2] (flu:k) *n* **1** an accidental stroke of luck **2** any chance happening ▷ *vb* **flukes, fluking, fluked** **3** (*tr*) to gain, make, or hit by a fluke [C19 from ?]

fluke[3] (flu:k) *n* any parasitic flatworm, such as the blood fluke and liver fluke [OE *flōc*; rel. to ON *flōki* flounder]

fluky *or* **flukey** ('flu:kɪ) *adj* **flukier, flukiest** *inf* **1** done or gained by an accident, esp a lucky one **2** variable; uncertain > **'flukiness** *n*

flume (flu:m) *n* **1** a ravine through which a stream flows **2** a narrow artificial channel made for providing water for power, floating logs, etc **3** a slide in the form of a long and winding tube with a stream of water running through it that descends into a purpose-built pool ▷ *vb* **flumes, fluming, flumed** **4** (*tr*) to transport (logs) in a flume [C12 from OF, ult. from L *flūmen* stream, from *fluere* to flow]

flummery ('flʌmərɪ) *n, pl* **flummeries** **1** *inf* meaningless flattery **2** *chiefly Brit* a cold pudding of oatmeal, etc [C17 from Welsh *llymru*]

flummox ('flʌməks) *vb* (*tr*) to perplex or bewilder [C19 from ?]

flung (flʌŋ) *vb* the past tense and past participle of **fling**

flunitrazepam (,flu:naɪ'træzə,pæm) *n* a drug similar to diazepam, used in treating long-term insomnia

flunk (flʌŋk) *vb inf, US, Canad, & NZ* **1** to fail or cause to fail to reach the required standard in (an examination, course, etc) **2** (*intr*; foll by *out*) to be dismissed from a school [C19 ?from FLINCH + FUNK[1]]

flunky *or* **flunkey** ('flʌŋkɪ) *n, pl* **flunkies** *or* **flunkeys** **1** a servile person **2** a person who performs menial tasks **3** *usually derog* a manservant in livery [C18 from ?]

fluor ('flu:ɔ:) *n* another name for **fluorspar** [C17 from L: a flowing; so called from its use as a metallurgical flux]

fluor- *combining form* a variant of **fluoro-** before a vowel: *fluorine*

fluoresce (,flʊə'rɛs) *vb* **fluoresces, fluorescing, fluoresced** (*intr*) to exhibit fluorescence [C19 back formation from FLUORESCENCE]

fluorescence (,flʊə'rɛsəns) *n* **1** *physics* **1a** the emission of light or other radiation from atoms or molecules that are bombarded by particles, such as electrons, or by radiation from a separate source **1b** such an emission of photons that ceases as soon as the bombarding radiation is discontinued **2** the radiation emitted as a result of fluorescence ▷ Cf **phosphorescence** [C19 FLUOR + *-escence* (as in *opalescence*)] > **,fluo'rescent** *adj*

fluorescent lamp *n* a type of lamp in which ultraviolet radiation from an electrical gas discharge causes a thin layer of phosphor on a tube's inside surface to fluoresce

fluoridate ('flʊərɪ,deɪt) *vb* **fluoridates, fluoridating, fluoridated** to subject (water) to fluoridation

fluoridation (,flʊərɪ'deɪʃən) *n* the addition of fluorides to the public water supply as a protection against tooth decay

fluoride (ˈflʊəˌraɪd) *n* **1** any salt of hydrofluoric acid, containing the fluoride ion, F^- **2** any compound containing fluorine, such as methyl fluoride

fluorinate (ˈflʊərɪˌneɪt) *vb* **fluorinates, fluorinating, fluorinated** to treat or combine with fluorine > ˌ**fluoriˈnation** *n*

fluorine (ˈflʊəriːn) *n* a toxic pungent pale yellow gas of the halogen group that is the most electronegative and reactive of all the elements: used in the production of uranium, fluorocarbons, and other chemicals. Symbol: F; atomic no.: 9; atomic wt.: 18.998

fluorite (ˈflʊəraɪt) *n* the US and Canad name for **fluorspar**

fluoro- *or before a vowel* **fluor-** *combining form* **1** indicating the presence of fluorine: *fluorocarbon* **2** indicating fluorescence: *fluoroscope*

fluorocarbon (ˌflʊərəʊˈkɑːbᵊn) *n* any compound derived by replacing all or some of the hydrogen atoms in hydrocarbons by fluorine atoms. Many of them are used as lubricants, solvents, coatings, and aerosol propellants. See also **Freon, CFC**

fluorometer (ˌflʊəˈrɒmɪtə) *or* **fluorimeter** (ˌflʊəˈrɪmɪtə) *n* a device for detecting and measuring ultraviolet radiation by determining the amount of fluorescence that it produces from a phosphor

fluoroscope (ˈflʊərəˌskəʊp) *n* a device consisting of a fluorescent screen and an X-ray source that enables an X-ray image of an object, person, or part to be observed directly

fluoroscopy (flʊəˈrɒskəpɪ) *n, pl* **fluoroscopies** examination of a person or object by means of a fluoroscope

fluorosis (flʊəˈrəʊsɪs) *n* fluoride poisoning, due to ingestion of too much fluoride

fluorspar (ˈflʊəˌspɑː), **fluor,** *or US & Canad* **fluorite** *n* a white or colourless soft mineral, sometimes fluorescent or tinted by impurities, consisting of calcium fluoride (CaF) in crystalline form: the chief ore of fluorine

flurry (ˈflʌrɪ) *n, pl* **flurries 1** a sudden commotion **2** a light gust of wind or rain or fall of snow ▷ *vb* **flurries, flurrying, flurried 3** to confuse or bewilder or be confused or bewildered [C17 from obs. *flurr* to scatter, ? formed on analogy with HURRY]

flush[1] (flʌʃ) *vb* **1** to blush or cause to blush **2** to flow or flood or cause to flow or flood with or as if with water **3** to glow or shine or cause to glow or shine with a rosy colour **4** to send a volume of water quickly through (a pipe, etc) or into (a toilet) for the purpose of cleansing, etc **5** (*tr; usually passive*) to excite or elate ▷ *n* **6** a rosy colour, esp in the cheeks **7** a sudden flow or gush, as of water **8** a feeling of excitement or elation: *the flush of success* **9** freshness: *the flush of youth* **10** redness of the skin, as from the effects of a fever, alcohol, etc [C16 (in the sense: to gush forth): ?from FLUSH[3]] > ˈ**flusher** *n*

flush[2] (flʌʃ) *adj* (*usually postpositive*) **1** level or even with another surface **2** directly adjacent; continuous **3** *inf* having plenty of money **4** *inf* abundant or plentiful, as money **5** full to the brim ▷ *adv* **6** so as to be level or even **7** directly or squarely ▷ *vb* (*tr*) **8** to cause (surfaces) to be on the same level or in the same plane ▷ *n* **9** a period of fresh growth of leaves, shoots, etc [C18 prob. from FLUSH[1] (in the sense: spring out)] > ˈ**flushness** *n*

flush[3] (flʌʃ) *vb* (*tr*) to rouse (game, etc) and put to flight [C13 *flusshen*, ? imit.]

flush[4] (flʌʃ) *n* (in poker and similar games) a hand containing only one suit [C16 from OF, from L *fluxus* FLUX]

Flushing (ˈflʌʃɪŋ) *n* a port in the SW Netherlands, in Zeeland province, on Walcheren Island, at the mouth of the West Scheldt river: the first Dutch city to throw off Spanish rule (1572). Pop: 43 945 (latest est). Dutch name: **Vlissingen**

fluster (ˈflʌstə) *vb* **1** to make or become nervous or upset ▷ *n* **2** a state of confusion or agitation [C15 from ON]

flute (fluːt) *n* **1** a wind instrument consisting of an open cylindrical tube of wood or metal having holes in the side stopped either by the fingers or by pads controlled by keys. The breath is directed across a mouth hole cut in the side **2** *archit* a rounded shallow concave groove on the shaft of a column, pilaster, etc **3** a tall narrow wineglass ▷ *vb* **flutes, fluting, fluted 4** to produce or utter (sounds) in the manner or tone of a flute **5** (*tr*) to make grooves or furrows in [C14 from OF *flahute*, from Vulgar L *flabeolum* (unattested); ? also infl. by OF *laut* lute] > ˈ**fluteˌlike** *adj* > ˈ**fluty** *adj*

fluting (ˈfluːtɪŋ) *n* a design or decoration of flutes on a column, pilaster, etc

flutist (ˈfluːtɪst) *n now chiefly US & Canad* a variant spelling of **flautist**

flutter (ˈflʌtə) *vb* **1** to wave or cause to wave rapidly **2** (*intr*) (of birds, butterflies, etc) to flap the wings **3** (*intr*) to move, esp downwards, with an irregular motion **4** (*intr*) *pathol* (of the heart) to beat abnormally rapidly, esp in a regular rhythm **5** to be or make nervous or restless **6** (*intr*) to move about restlessly ▷ *n* **7** a quick flapping or vibrating motion **8** a state of nervous excitement or confusion **9** excited interest; stir **10** *Brit inf* a modest bet or wager **11** *pathol* an abnormally rapid beating of the heart, esp in a regular rhythm **12** *electronics* a slow variation in pitch in a sound-reproducing system, similar to wow but occurring at higher frequencies **13** a potentially dangerous oscillation of an aircraft, or part of an aircraft **14** Also called: **flutter tonguing** *music* a method of sounding a wind instrument, esp the flute, with a rolling movement of the tongue [OE *floterian* to float to and fro] > ˈ**flutterer** *n* > ˈ**fluttery** *adj*

fluvial (ˈfluːvɪəl) *adj* of or occurring in a river: *fluvial deposits* [C14 from L, from *fluvius* river, from *fluere* to flow]

flux (flʌks) *n* **1** a flow or discharge **2** continuous change; instability **3** a substance, such as borax or salt, that gives a low melting-point mixture with a metal oxide to assist in fusion **4** *metallurgy* a chemical used to increase the fluidity of refining slags **5** *physics* **5a** the rate of flow of particles, energy, or a fluid, such as that of neutrons (**neutron flux**) or of light energy (**luminous flux**) **5b** the strength of a field in a given area: *magnetic flux* **6** *pathol* an excessive discharge of fluid from the body, such as watery faeces in diarrhoea ▷ *vb* **7** to make or become fluid **8** (*tr*) to apply flux to (a metal, soldered joint, etc) [C14 from L *fluxus* a flow, from *fluere* to flow]

flux density *n physics* the amount of flux per unit of cross-sectional area

fluxion (ˈflʌkʃən) *n maths, obs* the rate of change of a function, especially the instantaneous velocity of a moving body; derivative [C16 from LL *fluxiō* a flowing]

fly[1] (flaɪ) *vb* **flies, flying, flew, flown 1** (*intr*) (of birds, aircraft, etc) to move through the air in a controlled manner using aerodynamic forces **2** to travel over (an area of land or sea) in an aircraft **3** to operate (an aircraft or spacecraft) **4** to float, flutter, or be displayed in the air or cause to float, etc, in this way: *they flew the flag* **5** to transport or be transported by or through the air by aircraft, wind, etc **6** (*intr*) to move or be moved very quickly, or suddenly: *the door flew open* **7** (*intr*) to pass swiftly: *time flies* **8** to escape from (an enemy, place, etc); flee **9** (*intr; may be foll by at or upon*) to attack a person **10 fly a kite 10a** to procure money by an accommodation bill **10b** to release information or take a step in order to test public opinion **11 fly high** *inf* **11a** to have a high aim **11b** to prosper or flourish **12 fly the coop.** See **coop**[1] (sense 4) **13 let fly** *inf* **13a** to lose one's temper (with a person): *she really let fly at him* **13b** to shoot or throw (an object) ▷ *n, pl* **flies 14** (*often pl*) Also called: **fly front** a closure that conceals a zip, buttons, or other

Ff

fastening, by having one side overlapping, as on trousers **15** Also called: **fly sheet** **15a** a flap forming the entrance to a tent **15b** a piece of canvas drawn over the ridgepole of a tent to form an outer roof **16** short for **flywheel** **17a** the outer edge of a flag **17b** the distance from the outer edge of a flag to the staff **18** *Brit* a light one-horse covered carriage formerly let out on hire **19** *(pl) Theatre.* the space above the stage out of view of the audience, used for storing scenery, etc **20** *rare* the act of flying [OE *flēogan*] > '**flyable** *adj*

fly[2] (flaɪ) *n, pl* **flies** **1** any dipterous insect, esp the housefly, characterized by active flight **2** any of various similar but unrelated insects, such as the caddis fly, firefly, and dragonfly **3** *angling* a lure made from a fish-hook dressed with feathers, tinsel, etc, to resemble any of various flies or nymphs: used in fly-fishing **4** **fly in the ointment** *inf* a slight flaw that detracts from value or enjoyment **5** **fly on the wall** **5a** a person who watches others, while not being noticed himself **5b** *(as modifier)*: *a fly-on-the-wall documentary* **6** **there are no flies on him, her,** etc *inf* he, she, etc, is no fool [OE *flēoge*] > '**flyless** *adj*

fly[3] (flaɪ) *adj sl, chiefly Brit* knowing and sharp; smart [c19 from ?]

fly agaric *n* a woodland fungus having a scarlet cap with white warts and white gills: poisonous but rarely fatal [so named from its use as a poison on flypaper]

fly ash *n* fine solid particles of ash carried into the air during combustion

flyaway ('flaɪəˌweɪ) *adj* **1** (of hair or clothing) loose and fluttering **2** frivolous or flighty; giddy

flyblow ('flaɪˌbləʊ) *vb* **flyblows, flyblowing, flyblew, flyblown** **1** *(tr)* to contaminate, esp with the eggs or larvae of the blowfly; taint ▷ *n* **2** *(usually pl)* the eggs or young larva of a blowfly

flyblown ('flaɪˌbləʊn) *adj* **1** covered with flyblows **2** contaminated; tainted

flybook ('flaɪˌbʊk) *n* a small case or wallet used by anglers for storing artificial flies

flyby ('flaɪˌbaɪ) *n, pl* **flybys** a flight past a particular position or target, esp the close approach of a spacecraft to a planet or satellite

fly-by-night *inf* ▷ *adj* **1** unreliable or untrustworthy, esp in finance ▷ *n* **2** an untrustworthy person, esp one who departs secretly or by night to avoid paying debts

flycatcher ('flaɪˌkætʃə) *n* **1** a small insectivorous songbird of the Old World having a small slender bill fringed with bristles **2** an American passerine bird

fly-drive *adj, adv* describing a type of package-deal holiday in which the price includes outward and return flights and car hire while away

flyer *or* **flier** ('flaɪə) *n* **1** a person or thing that flies or moves very fast **2** an aviator or pilot **3** *inf* a large flying leap **4** a rectangular step in a straight flight of stairs ▷ Cf **winder** (sense 5) **5** *athletics inf* a flying start **6** *chiefly US* a speculative business transaction **7** a small handbill

fly-fish *vb (intr) angling* to fish using artificial flies as lures > '**fly-ˌfishing** *n*

fly half *n rugby* another name for **stand-off half**

flying ('flaɪɪŋ) *adj* **1** *(prenominal)* hurried; fleeting: *a flying visit* **2** *(prenominal)* designed for fast action **3** *(prenominal)* moving or passing quickly on or as if on wings: *flying hours* **4** hanging, waving, or floating freely: *flying hair* ▷ *n* **5** the act of piloting, navigating, or travelling in an aircraft **6** *(modifier)* relating to, accustomed to, or adapted for flight: *a flying machine*

flying boat *n* a seaplane in which the fuselage consists of a hull that provides buoyancy

flying bridge *n* an auxiliary bridge of a vessel

flying buttress *n* a buttress consisting of an arch that transmits the thrust outwards and downwards

flying colours *pl n* conspicuous success; triumph: *he passed his test with flying colours*

flying doctor *n* (in areas of sparse or scattered population) a doctor who travels by aircraft to visit patients

flying fish *n* a fish common in warm and tropical seas, having enlarged winglike pectoral fins used for gliding above the surface of the water

flying fox *n* **1** any large fruit bat of tropical Africa and Asia **2** *Austral & NZ* a cable mechanism used for transportation across a river, gorge, etc

flying gurnard *n* a marine spiny-finned gurnard-like fish having enlarged fan-shaped pectoral fins used to glide above the surface of the sea

flying jib *n* the jib set furthest forward or outboard on a vessel with two or more jibs

flying lemur *n* either of the two arboreal mammals of S and SE Asia that resemble lemurs but have a fold of skin between the limbs enabling movement by gliding leaps

flying officer *n* an officer holding commissioned rank senior to a pilot officer but junior to a flight lieutenant in the British and certain other air forces

flying phalanger *n* a nocturnal arboreal phalanger of E Australia and New Guinea, moving with gliding leaps using folds of skin between the hind limbs and forelimbs

flying picket *n* (in industrial disputes) a member of a group of pickets organized to be able to move quickly from place to place

flying saucer *n* any unidentified disc-shaped flying object alleged to come from outer space

flying squad *n* a small group of police, soldiers, etc, ready to move into action quickly

flying squirrel *n* a nocturnal rodent of Asia and North America, related to the squirrel. Furry folds of skin between the forelegs and hind legs enable these animals to move by gliding leaps

flying start *n* **1** (in sprinting) a start by a competitor anticipating the starting signal **2** a start to a race in which the competitor is already travelling at speed as he passes the starting line **3** any promising beginning **4** an initial advantage

flying wing *n* **1** an aircraft consisting mainly of one large wing or tailplane and no fuselage **2** (in Canadian football) the twelfth player, who has a variable position behind the scrimmage line

flyleaf ('flaɪˌliːf) *n, pl* **flyleaves** the inner leaf of the endpaper of a book, pasted to the first leaf

Flynn (flɪn) *n* **1** **Errol** 1909–59, Australian-born Hollywood actor, who was noted for his swashbuckling roles; his films included *Captain Blood* (1935), *The Adventures of Robin Hood* (1938), and *Too Much Too Soon* (1958) **2** Rev. **John** 1880–1951, founder of the Australian flying doctor service

flyover ('flaɪˌəʊvə) *n* **1** *Brit* an intersection of two roads at which one is carried over the other by a bridge **2** the US name for **fly-past**

flypaper ('flaɪˌpeɪpə) *n* paper with a sticky and poisonous coating, usually hung from the ceiling to trap flies

fly-past *n* a ceremonial flight of aircraft over a given area

flyposting ('flaɪˌpəʊstɪŋ) *n* the posting of advertising or political posters, etc, in unauthorized places

flyscreen ('flaɪˌskriːn) *n* a wire-mesh screen over a window to prevent flies entering a room

fly sheet *n* **1** another term for **fly**[1] (sense 14) **2** a short handbill

flyspeck ('flaɪˌspɛk) *n* **1** the small speck of the excrement of a fly **2** a small spot or speck ▷ *vb* **3** *(tr)* to mark with flyspecks

fly spray *n* a liquid used to destroy flies and other insects, sprayed from an aerosol

fly-tipping *n* the deliberate dumping of rubbish in an unauthorized place

flytrap ('flaɪˌtræp) *n* **1** any of various insectivorous plants **2** a device for catching flies

fly way *n* the usual route used by birds when migrating

flyweight ('flaɪˌweɪt) *n* **1a** a professional boxer weighing not more than 112 pounds (51 kg) **1b** an amateur boxer weighing 48–51 kg (106–112 pounds) **2** an amateur wrestler weighing 107–115 pounds (49–52 kg)

flywheel ('flaɪˌwiːl) *n* a heavy wheel that stores kinetic energy and smooths the operation of a reciprocating engine by maintaining a constant speed of rotation over the whole cycle

fm *abbrev for:* **1** fathom **2** from

Fm *the chemical symbol for* fermium

FM *abbrev for:* **1** frequency modulation **2** Field Marshal

FMRI *abbrev for* functional magnetic resonance imaging: a technique that directly measures the blood flow in the brain, thereby providing information on brain activity

f-number, f number, f-stop, *or* **f stop** *n photog* the numerical value of the relative aperture. If the relative aperture is f8, 8 is the f-number

Fo (fəʊ) *n* **Dario** ('dærɪəʊ) born 1926, Italian playwright and actor. His plays include *The Accidental Death of an Anarchist* (1970), *Trumpets and Raspberries* (1984), and *The Tricks of the Trade* (1991): Nobel prize for literature 1997

FO *abbrev for:* **1** *Army* Field Officer **2** *Air Force* Flying Officer **3** Foreign Office

fo. *abbrev for* folio

foal (fəʊl) *n* **1** the young of a horse or related animal ▷ *vb* **2** to give birth to (a foal) [OE *fola*]

foam (fəʊm) *n* **1** a mass of small bubbles of gas formed on the surface of a liquid, such as the froth produced by a solution of soap or detergent in water **2** frothy saliva sometimes formed in and expelled from the mouth, as in rabies **3** the frothy sweat of a horse or similar animal **4a** any of a number of light cellular solids made by creating bubbles of gas in the liquid material: used as insulation and packaging **4b** (*as modifier*): *foam rubber; foam plastic* ▷ *vb* **5** to produce or cause to produce foam; froth **6** (*intr*) to be very angry (esp in **foam at the mouth**) [OE *fām*] > '**foamless** *adj*

foamy ('fəʊmɪ) *adj* **foamier, foamiest** of, resembling, consisting of, or covered with foam

fob[1] (fɒb) *n* **1** a chain or ribbon by which a pocket watch is attached to a waistcoat **2** any ornament hung on such a chain **3** a small pocket in a man's waistcoat, etc, for holding a watch [c17 prob. of Gmc origin]

fob[2] (fɒb) *vb* **fobs, fobbing, fobbed** (*tr*) *arch* to cheat [c15 prob. from G *foppen* to trick]

fob[3] (fɒb) *n NZ sl* a Pacific Islander who has newly arrived in New Zealand [c20 *f(resh) o(ff the) b(oat)*]

f.o.b. *or* **FOB** *commerce abbrev for* free on board

fob off *vb* (*tr, adv*) **1** to trick (a person) with lies or excuses **2** to dispose of (goods) by trickery

focal ('fəʊkᵊl) *adj* **1** of or relating to a focus **2** situated at or measured from the focus

focalize *or* **focalise** ('fəʊkəˌlaɪz) *vb* **focalizes, focalizing, focalized** *or* **focalises, focalising, focalised** a less common word for **focus** > ˌ**focali'zation** *or* ˌ**focali'sation** *n*

focal length *or* **distance** *n* the distance from the focal point of a lens or mirror to the reflecting surface of the mirror or the centre point of the lens

focal plane *n* the plane that is perpendicular to the axis of a lens or mirror and passes through the focal point

focal point *n* the point on the axis of a lens or mirror to which parallel rays of light converge or from which they appear to diverge after refraction or reflection. Also called: **focus**

Foch (*French* fɔʃ) *n* **Ferdinand** (fɛrdinɑ̃) 1851–1929, marshal of France; commander in chief of Allied armies on the Western front in World War I (1918)

fo'c's'le *or* **fo'c'sle** ('fəʊksᵊl) *n* a variant spelling of **forecastle**

focus ('fəʊkəs) *n, pl* **focuses** *or* **foci** (-saɪ) **1** a point of convergence of light or sound waves, etc, or a point from which they appear to diverge **2** another name for **focal point** or **focal length** **3** *optics* the state of an optical image when it is distinct and clearly defined or the state of an instrument producing this image: *the telescope is out of focus* **4** a point upon which attention, activity, etc, is concentrated **5** *geom* a fixed reference point on the concave side of a conic section, used when defining its eccentricity **6** the point beneath the earth's surface at which an earthquake originates **7** *pathol* the main site of an infection ▷ *vb* **focuses, focusing, focused** *or* **focusses, focussing, focussed** **8** to bring or come to a focus or into focus **9** (*tr; often foll by on*) to concentrate [c17 via NL from L: hearth, fireplace] > '**focuser** *n*

focus group *n* a group of people gathered by a market research company to discuss and assess a product or service

focus puller *n films* the member of a camera crew who adjusts the focus of the lens as the camera is tracked in or out

fodder ('fɒdə) *n* **1** bulk feed for livestock, esp hay, straw, etc ▷ *vb* **2** (*tr*) to supply (livestock) with fodder [OE *fōdor*]

foe (fəʊ) *n formal or literary* another word for **enemy** [OE *fāh* hostile]

FoE *or* **FOE** *abbrev for* Friends of the Earth

foehn (fɜːn; *German* føːn) *n meteorol* a variant spelling of **föhn**

foeman ('fəʊmən) *n, pl* **foemen** *arch & poetic* an enemy in war; foe

foetal ('fiːtᵊl) *adj* a variant spelling of **fetal**

foetid ('fɛtɪd, 'fiː-) *adj* a variant spelling of **fetid** > '**foetidly** *adv* > '**foetidness** *n*

foetus ('fiːtəs) *n, pl* **foetuses** a variant spelling of **fetus**

fog[1] (fɒg) *n* **1** a mass of droplets of condensed water vapour suspended in the air, often greatly reducing visibility **2** a cloud of any substance in the atmosphere reducing visibility **3** a state of mental uncertainty **4** *photog* a blurred area on a developed negative, print, or transparency ▷ *vb* **fogs, fogging, fogged** **5** to envelop or become enveloped with or as if with fog **6** to confuse or become confused **7** *photog* to produce fog on (a negative, print, or transparency) or (of a negative, print, or transparency) to be affected by fog **8** (*tr*) to treat (an infested area) with insecticide in the form of a spray [c16 ? back formation from *foggy* damp, boggy, from FOG[2]]

Ff

fog[2] (fɒg) *n* a second growth of grass after the first mowing [c14 prob. from ON]

Fogarty ('fɒgətɪ) *n* **Carl** (**George**) born 1965, British racing motorcyclist; Superbike world champion 1994, 1995, 1998, 1999

fog bank *n* a distinct mass of fog, esp at sea

fogbound ('fɒgˌbaʊnd) *adj* prevented from operation by fog: *the airport was fogbound*

fogbow ('fɒgˌbəʊ) *n* a faint arc of light sometimes seen in a fog bank

fogey *or* **fogy** ('fəʊgɪ) *n, pl* **fogeys** *or* **fogies** an extremely fussy or conservative person (esp in **old fogey**) [c18 from ?] > '**fogeyish** *or* '**fogyish** *adj*

Foggia (*Italian* 'fɔddʒa) *n* a city in SE Italy, in Apulia: seat of Emperor Frederick II; centre for Carbonari revolutionary societies in the revolts of 1820, 1848, and 1860. Pop: 154 891 (2000 est)

fogging machine *n Caribbean* a mechanical device, usually mounted on a tractor or other vehicle, used to spray an area with insecticide

foggy ('fɒgɪ) *adj* **foggier, foggiest** **1** thick with fog **2** obscure or confused **3** **not the foggiest** (**idea** *or* **notion**) no idea whatsoever: *I haven't the foggiest* > '**fogginess** *n*

foghorn ('fɒgˌhɔːn) *n* **1** a mechanical instrument sounded at intervals to serve as a warning to vessels in fog **2** *inf* a loud deep resounding voice

fog signal *n* a signal used to warn railway engine drivers

in fog, consisting of a detonator placed on the line
föhn *or* **foehn** (fɜːn; *German* føːn) *n* a warm dry wind blowing down the northern slopes of the Alps [G, from OHG, from L *favōnius*; rel. to *fovēre* to warm]
foible ('fɔɪbᵊl) *n* **1** a slight peculiarity or minor weakness; idiosyncrasy **2** the most vulnerable part of a sword's blade, from the middle to the tip [C17 from obs. F, from obs. adj: FEEBLE]
foie gras (*French* fwa grɑ) *n* See **pâté de foie gras**
foil¹ (fɔɪl) *vb* (*tr*) **1** to baffle or frustrate (a person, attempt, etc) **2** *hunting* (of hounds, hunters, etc) to obliterate the scent left by a hunted animal or (of a hunted animal) to run back over its own trail ▷ *n* **3** *arch* a setback or defeat [C13 *foilen* to trample, from OF, *fuler* tread down] > **'foilable** *adj*
foil² (fɔɪl) *n* **1** metal in the form of very thin sheets: *tin foil* **2** the thin metallic sheet forming the backing of a mirror **3** a thin leaf of shiny metal set under a gemstone to add brightness or colour **4** a person or thing that gives contrast to another **5** *archit* a small arc between cusps **6** short for **hydrofoil** ▷ *vb* (*tr*) **7** Also: **foliate** *archit* to ornament (windows, etc) with foils [C14 from OF, from L *folia* leaves]
foil³ (fɔɪl) *n* a light slender flexible sword tipped by a button [C16 from ?]
foist (fɔɪst) *vb* (*tr*) **1** (often foll by *off* or *on*) to sell or pass off (something, esp an inferior article) as genuine, valuable, etc **2** (usually foll by *in* or *into*) to insert surreptitiously or wrongfully [C16 prob. from obs. Du. *vuisten* to enclose in one's hand, from MDu. *vuist* fist]
Fokine (*Russian* 'fɔkin; *French* fɔkin) *n* **Michel** (miʃɛl) 1880–1942, US choreographer, born in Russia, regarded as the creator of modern ballet. He worked with Diaghilev as director of the Ballet Russe (1909–15), producing works such as *Les Sylphides* and *Petrushka*
Fokker ('fɒkə; *Dutch* 'fɔkər) *n* **Anthony Herman Gerard** (ɑn'toːniː 'hɛrman 'xeːrɑrt) 1890- -1939, Dutch designer and builder of aircraft, born in Java
fol. *abbrev for:* **1** folio **2** following
fold¹ (fəʊld) *vb* **1** to bend or be bent double so that one part covers another **2** (*tr*) to bring together and intertwine (the arms, legs, etc) **3** (*tr*) (of birds, insects, etc) to close (the wings) together from an extended position **4** (*tr*; often foll by *up* or *in*) to enclose in or as if in a surrounding material **5** (*tr*; foll by *in*) to clasp (a person) in the arms **6** (*tr*; usually foll by *round, about*, etc) to wind (around); entwine **7** Also: **fold in** (*tr*) to mix (a whisked mixture) with other ingredients by gently turning one part over the other with a spoon **8** (*intr*; often foll by *up*) *inf* to collapse; fail: *the business folded* ▷ *n* **9** a piece or section that has been folded: *a fold of cloth* **10** a mark, crease, or hollow made by folding **11** a hollow in undulating terrain **12** a bend in stratified rocks that results from movements within the earth's crust **13** a coil, as in a rope, etc [OE *fealdan*] > **'foldable** *adj*
fold² (fəʊld) *n* **1a** a small enclosure or pen for sheep or other livestock, where they can be gathered **1b** a flock of sheep **2** a church or the members of it ▷ *vb* **3** (*tr*) to gather or confine (sheep, etc) in a fold [OE *falod*]
-fold *suffix forming adjectives and adverbs* having so many parts or being so many times as much or as many: *three-hundredfold* [OE *-fald, -feald*]
foldaway ('fəʊldə,weɪ) *adj* (*prenominal*) (of a bed, etc) able to be folded away when not in use
folded dipole *n* a type of aerial consisting of two parallel dipoles connected together at their outer ends and fed at the centre of one of them. The length is usually half the operating wavelength
folder ('fəʊldə) *n* **1** a binder or file for holding loose papers, etc **2** a folded circular **3** a person or thing that folds
folderol ('fɒldə,rɒl) *n* a variant spelling of **falderal**
folding door *n* a door in the form of two or more vertical hinged leaves that can be folded one against another
folding money *n inf* paper money
foley *or* **foley artist** ('fəʊlɪ) *n films* the US name for **footsteps editor** [C20 after the inventor of the technique]
foliaceous (,fəʊlɪ'eɪʃəs) *adj* **1** having the appearance of the leaf of a plant **2** bearing leaves or leaflike structures **3** *geol* consisting of thin layers [C17 from L *foliāceus*]
foliage ('fəʊlɪɪdʒ) *n* **1** the green leaves of a plant **2** sprays of leaves used for decoration **3** an ornamental leaflike design [C15 from OF *fuellage*, from *fuelle* leaf; infl. in form by L *folium*]
foliar ('fəʊlɪə) *adj* of or relating to a leaf or leaves [C19 from F, from L *folium* leaf]
foliate *adj* ('fəʊlɪɪt, -,eɪt) **1a** relating to, possessing, or resembling leaves **1b** (*in combination*): *trifoliate* ▷ *vb* ('fəʊlɪ,eɪt), **foliates, foliating, foliated** **2** (*tr*) to ornament with foliage or with leaf forms such as foils **3** to hammer or cut (metal) into thin plates or foil **4** (*tr*) to number the leaves of (a book, etc) ▷ Cf **paginate** **5** (*intr*) (of plants) to grow leaves [C17 from L *foliātus* leaved, leafy]
foliation (,fəʊlɪ'eɪʃən) *n* **1** *bot* **1a** the process of producing leaves **1b** the state of being in leaf **1c** the arrangement of leaves in a leaf bud **2** *archit* ornamentation consisting of cusps and foils **3** the consecutive numbering of the leaves of a book **4** *geol* the arrangement of the constituents of a rock in leaflike layers, as in schists
folic acid ('fəʊlɪk) *n* any of a group of vitamins of the B complex, used in the treatment of anaemia. Also called: **folacin** [C20 from L *folium* leaf; so called because it may be obtained from green leaves]
folio ('fəʊlɪəʊ) *n, pl* **folios** **1** a sheet of paper folded in half to make two leaves for a book **2** a book of the largest common size made up of such sheets **3a** a leaf of paper numbered on the front side only **3b** the page number of a book **4** *law* a unit of measurement of the length of legal documents, determined by the number of words, generally 72 or 90 in Britain and 100 in the US ▷ *adj* **5** relating to or having the format of a folio: *a folio edition* [C16 from L phrase *in foliō* in a leaf, from *folium* leaf]
folk (fəʊk) *n, pl* **folk** *or* **folks** **1** (*functioning as pl; often pl in form*) people in general, esp those of a particular group or class: *country folk* **2** (*functioning as pl; usually pl in form*) *inf* members of a family **3** (*functioning as sing*) *inf* short for **folk music** **4** a people or tribe **5** (*modifier*) originating from or traditional to the common people of a country: *a folk song* [OE *folc*] > **'folkish** *adj*
folk dance *n* **1** any of various traditional rustic dances **2** a piece of music composed for or in the rhythm of such a dance > **folk dancing** *n*
Folkestone ('fəʊkstən) *n* a port and resort in SE England, in E Kent. Pop: 45 587 (1991)
folk etymology *n* the gradual change in the form of a word through the influence of a more familiar word or phrase with which it becomes associated, as for example *sparrow-grass* for *asparagus*
folkie *or* **folky** ('fəʊkɪ) *n, pl* **folkies** *inf* a devotee of folk music
folklore ('fəʊk,lɔː) *n* **1** the unwritten literature of a people as expressed in folk tales, songs, etc **2** the body of stories and legends attached to a particular place, group, etc: *rugby folklore* **3** study of folkloric materials > **'folk,loric** *adj* > **'folk,lorist** *n, adj*
folk medicine *n* medicine as practised among rustic communities and primitive peoples, consisting typically of the use of herbal remedies
folk music *n* **1** music that is passed on from generation to generation **2** any music composed in this idiom
▷ www.folkmusic.org
▷ www.allmusic.com
folk-rock *n* a style of rock music influenced by folk
folk song *n* **1** a song which has been handed down

among the common people **2** a modern song that reflects the folk idiom

folksy ('fəʊksɪ) *adj* **folksier, folksiest 1** of or like ordinary people; sometimes used derogatorily to describe affected simplicity **2** *inf, chiefly US* friendly; affable

folk tale *or* **story** *n* a tale or legend originating among a people and becoming part of an oral tradition

folk weave *n* a type of fabric with a loose weave

follicle ('fɒlɪkᵊl) *n* **1** any small sac or cavity in the body having an excretory, secretory, or protective function: *a hair follicle* **2** *bot* a dry fruit that splits along one side only to release its seeds [C17 from L *folliculus* small bag, from *follis* pair of bellows, leather money-bag] > **follicular** (fɒ'lɪkjʊlə), **folliculate** (fɒ'lɪkjʊ,leɪt), *or* **fol'licu,lated** *adj*

follow ('fɒləʊ) *vb* **1** to go or come after in the same direction **2** (*tr*) to accompany: *she followed her sister everywhere* **3** to come after as a logical or natural consequence **4** (*tr*) to keep to the course or track of: *she followed the towpath* **5** (*tr*) to act in accordance with: *to follow instructions* **6** (*tr*) to accept the ideas or beliefs of (a previous authority, etc): *he followed Donne in most of his teachings* **7** to understand (an explanation, etc): *the lesson was difficult to follow* **8** to watch closely or continuously: *she followed his progress* **9** (*tr*) to have a keen interest in: *to follow athletics* **10** (*tr*) to help in the cause of: *the men who followed Napoleon* [OE *folgian*]

follower ('fɒləʊə) *n* **1** a person who accepts the teachings of another: *a follower of Marx* **2** an attendant **3** a supporter, as of a sport or team **4** (esp formerly) a male admirer

following ('fɒləʊɪŋ) *adj* **1a** (*prenominal*) about to be mentioned, specified, etc: *the following items* **1b** (*as n*): *will the following please raise their hands?* **2** (of winds, currents, etc) moving in the same direction as a vessel ▷ *n* **3** a group of supporters or enthusiasts: *he attracted a large following* ▷ *prep* **4** as a result of: *he was arrested following a tip-off*

follow-on *cricket* ▷ *n* **1** an immediate second innings forced on a team scoring a prescribed number of runs fewer than its opponents in the first innings ▷ *vb* **follow on 2** (*intr, adv*) (of a team) to play a follow-on

follow out *vb* (*tr, adv*) to implement (an idea or action) to a conclusion

follow through *vb* (*adv*) **1** *sport* to complete (a stroke or shot) by continuing the movement to the end of its arc **2** (*tr*) to pursue (an aim) to a conclusion ▷ *n* **follow-through 3** the act of following through

follow up *vb* (*tr, adv*) **1** to pursue or investigate (a person, etc) closely **2** to continue (action) after a beginning, esp to increase its effect ▷ *n* **follow-up 3a** something done to reinforce an initial action **3b** (*as modifier*): *a follow-up letter* **4** *med* an examination of a patient at intervals after treatment

folly ('fɒlɪ) *n, pl* **follies 1** the state or quality of being foolish **2** a foolish action, idea, etc **3** a building in the form of a castle, temple, etc, built to satisfy a fancy or conceit **4** (*pl*) *theatre* an elaborately costumed revue [C13 from OF *folie* madness, from *fou* mad; see FOOL¹]

foment (fə'mɛnt) *vb* (*tr*) **1** to encourage or instigate (trouble, discord, etc) **2** *med* to apply heat and moisture to (a part of the body) to relieve pain [C15 from LL, from L *fōmentum* a poultice, ult. from *fovēre* to foster] > **fomentation** (,fəʊmɛn'teɪʃən) *n* > **fo'menter** *n*

> USAGE Both *foment* and *ferment* can be used to talk about stirring up trouble: *he was accused of fomenting/fermenting unrest*. Only *ferment* can be used intransitively or as a noun: *his anger continued to ferment* (not *foment*); *rural areas were unaffected by the ferment in the cities*

fond (fɒnd) *adj* **1** (*postpositive*; foll by *of*) having a liking (for) **2** loving; tender **3** indulgent: *a fond mother* **4** (of hopes, wishes, etc) cherished but unlikely to be realized: *he had fond hopes of starting his own firm* **5** *arch or dialect* **5a** foolish **5b** credulous [C14 *fonned*, from *fonne* a fool] > **'fondly** *adv* > **'fondness** *n*

Fonda ('fɒndə) *n* **Henry** 1905–82, US film actor. His many films include *Young Mr Lincoln* (1939), *The Grapes of Wrath* (1940), *Twelve Angry Men* (1957), and *On Golden Pond* (1981) for which he won an Oscar

fondant ('fɒndənt) *n* **1** a thick flavoured paste of sugar and water, used in sweets and icings **2** a sweet made of this mixture ▷ *adj* **3** (of a colour) soft, pastel [C19 from F, lit.: melting, from *fondre* to melt, from L *fundere*; see FOUND³]

fondle ('fɒndᵊl) *vb* **fondles, fondling, fondled** (*tr*) to touch or stroke tenderly [C17 from (obs.) vb *fond* to fondle; see FOND] > **'fondler** *n*

fondue ('fɒndjuː; *French* fɔ̃dy) *n* a Swiss dish, consisting of melted cheese into which small pieces of bread are dipped [C19 from F, fem of *fondu* melted; see FONDANT]

Fonseca (*Spanish* fɔn'seka) *n* **Gulf of** an inlet of the Pacific Ocean in W Central America

font¹ (fɒnt) *n* **1a** a large bowl for baptismal water **1b** a receptacle for holy water **2** the reservoir for oil in an oil lamp **3** *arch or poetic* a fountain or well [OE, from Church L *fons*, from L: fountain]

font² (fɒnt) *n* *printing* a complete set of type of one style and size [C16 from Old French *fonte* a founding, casting, from Vulgar Latin *funditus* (unattested) a casting, from Latin *fundere* to melt; see FOUND³]
▷ www.fontscape.com
▷ http://babel.uoregon.edu/yamada/altfonts.html

Fontainebleau ('fɒntɪn,bləʊ; *French* fɔ̃tɛnblo) *n* a town in N France, in the **Forest of Fontainebleau**: famous for its palace (now a museum), one of the largest royal residences in France, built largely by Francis I (16th century). Pop: 18 753 (latest est)
▷ www.bc.edu/bc_org/avp/cas/fnart/arch
▷ www.greatbuildings.com/buildings

fontanelle *or chiefly US* **fontanel** (,fɒntə'nɛl) *n* *anat* any of the soft membranous gaps between the bones of the skull in a fetus or infant [C16 (in the sense: hollow between muscles): from OF *fontanele*, lit.: a little spring, from *fontaine* FOUNTAIN]

Fonteyn (fɒn'teɪn) *n* Dame **Margot** real name *Margaret Hookham*. 1919–91, English classical ballerina

Foochow ('fuː'tʃaʊ) *n* a variant transliteration of the Chinese name for **Fuzhou**

food (fuːd) *n* **1** any substance that can be ingested by a living organism and metabolized into energy and body tissue. Related adj: **alimentary 2** nourishment in more or less solid form: *food and drink* **3** anything that provides mental nourishment or stimulus [OE *fōda*]

food additive *n* any of various natural or synthetic substances, such as salt or citric acid, used in the commercial processing of food as preservatives, antioxidants, emulsifiers, etc

food chain *n* *ecology* a sequence of organisms in an ecosystem in which each species is the food of the next member of the chain

food combining *n* the practice of keeping carbohydrates separate from proteins in one's daily diet, as a way of losing weight and also for some medical conditions

foodie *or* **foody** ('fuːdɪ) *n, pl* **foodies** a person having an enthusiastic interest in the preparation and consumption of good food

food poisoning *n* an acute illness caused by food that is either naturally poisonous or contaminated by bacteria

food processor *n* *cookery* an electric domestic appliance for automatic chopping, grating, blending, etc

foodstuff ('fuːd,stʌf) *n* any material, substance, etc, that can be used as food

food value *n* the relative degree of nourishment obtained from different foods

fool¹ (fuːl) *n* **1** a person who lacks sense or judgment **2** a

Ff

person who is made to appear ridiculous **3** (formerly) a professional jester living in a royal or noble household **4** *obs* an idiot or imbecile: *the village fool* **5 play** *or* **act the fool** to deliberately act foolishly ▷ *vb* **6** (*tr*) to deceive (someone), esp in order to make him or her look ridiculous **7** (*intr*; foll by *with*, *around with*, or *about with*) *inf* to act or play (with) irresponsibly or aimlessly **8** (*intr*) to speak or act in a playful or jesting manner **9** (*tr*; foll by *away*) to squander; fritter ▷ *adj* **10** *US inf* short for **foolish** [c13 from OF *fol* mad person, from LL *follis* empty-headed fellow, from L: bellows]

fool² (fu:l) *n chiefly Brit* a dessert made from a purée of fruit with cream [c16 ?from FOOL¹]

foolery (ˈfu:lərɪ) *n, pl* **fooleries 1** foolish behaviour **2** an instance of this

foolhardy (ˈfu:lˌhɑ:dɪ) *adj* **foolhardier, foolhardiest** heedlessly rash or adventurous [c13 from OF, from *fol* foolish + *hardi* bold] > ˈ**foolˌhardily** *adv* > ˈ**foolˌhardiness** *n*

foolish (ˈfu:lɪʃ) *adj* **1** unwise; silly **2** resulting from folly or stupidity **3** ridiculous or absurd **4** weak-minded; simple > ˈ**foolishly** *adv* > ˈ**foolishness** *n*

foolproof (ˈfu:lˌpru:f) *adj inf* **1** proof against failure **2** (esp of machines, etc) proof against human misuse, error, etc

foolscap (ˈfu:lzˌkæp) *n chiefly Brit* a size of writing or printing paper, 13½ by 17 inches [c17 see FOOL¹, CAP; so called from the watermark formerly used on this kind of paper]

fool's cap *n* **1** a hood or cap with bells or tassels, worn by court jesters **2** a dunce's cap

fool's errand *n* a fruitless undertaking

fool's gold *n* any of various yellow minerals, esp pyrite, that can be mistaken for gold

fool's paradise *n* illusory happiness

fool's-parsley *n* an evil-smelling Eurasian umbelliferous plant with small white flowers

foot (fʊt) *n, pl* **feet 1** the part of the vertebrate leg below the ankle joint that is in contact with the ground during standing and walking. Related adj: **pedal 2** the part of a garment covering a foot **3** any of various organs of locomotion or attachment in invertebrates, including molluscs **4** *bot* the lower part of some plants or plant structures **5** a unit of length equal to one third of a yard or 12 inches. 1 foot is equivalent to 0.3048 metre **6** any part resembling a foot in form or function: *the foot of a chair* **7** the lower part of something; bottom: *the foot of a hill* **8** the end of a series or group: *the foot of the list* **9** manner of walking or moving: *a heavy foot* **10a** infantry, esp in the British army **10b** (*as modifier*): *a foot soldier* **11** any of various attachments on a sewing machine that hold the fabric in position **12** *prosody* a group of two or more syllables in which one syllable has the major stress, forming the basic unit of poetic rhythm **13 my foot!** an expression of disbelief, often of the speaker's own preceding statement **14 of foot** *arch* in manner of movement: *fleet of foot* **15 one foot in the grave** *inf* near to death **16 on foot 16a** walking or running **16b** astir; afoot **17 put a foot wrong** to make a mistake **18 put one's best foot forward 18a** to try to do one's best **18b** to hurry **19 put one's foot down** *inf* to act firmly **20 put one's foot in it** *inf* to blunder **21 under foot** on the ground; beneath one's feet ▷ *vb* **22** to dance to music (esp in **foot it**) **23** (*tr*) to walk over or set foot on (esp in **foot it**) **24** (*tr*) to pay the entire cost of (esp in **foot the bill**) [OE *fōt*] ▷ See also **feet** > ˈ**footless** *adj*

> USAGE In front of another noun, the plural for the unit of length is *foot*: *a 20-foot putt*; *his 70-foot ketch*. *Foot* can also be used instead of *feet* when mentioning a quantity and in front of words like *tall*: *four foot of snow*; *he is at least six foot tall*

footage (ˈfʊtɪdʒ) *n* **1** a length or distance measured in feet **2** the extent of film material shot and exposed

foot-and-mouth disease *n* an acute highly infectious viral disease of cattle, pigs, sheep, and goats, characterized by the formation of vesicular eruptions in the mouth and on the feet

football (ˈfʊtˌbɔ:l) *n* **1a** any of various games played with a round or oval ball and usually based on two teams competing to kick, head, carry, or otherwise propel the ball into each other's goal, territory, etc **1b** (*as modifier*): *a football supporter* **2** the ball used in any of these games or their variants **3** a problem, issue, etc, that is continually passed from one group or person to another as a pretext for argument > ˈ**footˌballer** *n*
▷ www.fifa.com

footboard (ˈfʊtˌbɔ:d) *n* **1** a board for a person to stand or rest his or her feet on **2** a treadle or foot-operated lever on a machine **3** a vertical board at the foot of a bed

footbridge (ˈfʊtˌbrɪdʒ) *n* a narrow bridge for the use of pedestrians

-footed *adj* **1** having a foot or feet as specified: *four-footed* **2** having a tread as specified: *heavy-footed*

footer¹ (ˈfʊtə) *n* (*in combination*) a person or thing of a specified length or height in feet: *a six-footer*

footer² (ˈfʊtə) *n Brit inf* short for **football** (the game)

footfall (ˈfʊtˌfɔ:l) *n* the sound of a footstep

foot fault *n tennis* a fault that occurs when the server fails to keep both feet behind the baseline until he or she has served

foothill (ˈfʊtˌhɪl) *n* (*often pl*) a relatively low hill at the foot of a mountain

foothold (ˈfʊtˌhəʊld) *n* **1** a ledge or other place affording a secure grip, as during climbing **2** a secure position from which further progress may be made

footing (ˈfʊtɪŋ) *n* **1** the basis or foundation on which something is established: *the business was on a secure footing* **2** the relationship or status existing between two persons, groups, etc **3** a secure grip by or for the feet **4** the lower part of a foundation of a column, wall, building, etc

footle (ˈfu:tᵊl) *vb* **footles, footling, footled** (*intr*; often foll by *around* or *about*) *inf* to loiter aimlessly [c19 prob. from F *foutre* to copulate with, from L *futuere*]

footlights (ˈfʊtˌlaɪts) *pl n theatre* lights set in a row along the front of the stage floor

footling (ˈfu:tlɪŋ) *adj inf* silly, trivial, or petty

footloose (ˈfʊtˌlu:s) *adj* **1** free to go or do as one wishes **2** restless: *to feel footloose*

footman (ˈfʊtmən) *n, pl* **footmen 1** a male servant, esp one in livery **2** (formerly) a foot soldier

footnote (ˈfʊtˌnəʊt) *n* **1** a note printed at the bottom of a page, to which attention is drawn by means of a mark in the text ▷ *vb* **footnotes, footnoting, footnoted 2** (*tr*) to supply (a page, etc) with footnotes

footpad (ˈfʊtˌpæd) *n arch* a robber or highwayman, on foot rather than horseback

footpath (ˈfʊtˌpɑ:θ) *n* **1** a narrow path for walkers only **2** *chiefly Austral & NZ* another word for **pavement**

footplate (ˈfʊtˌpleɪt) *n chiefly Brit* a platform in the cab of a locomotive on which the crew stand to operate the controls

foot-pound-second *n* See **fps units**

footprint (ˈfʊtˌprɪnt) *n* **1** an indentation or outline of the foot of a person or animal on a surface **2** the shape and size of the area something occupies: *enlarging the footprint of the building; a computer with a small footprint* **3** *computing* the amount of resources, such as disk space and memory, that an application requires. See also **electronic footprint**

footrest (ˈfʊtˌrɛst) *n* something that provides a support for the feet, such as a low stool, rail, etc

foot rot *n vet science* See **rot** (sense 10)

footsie (ˈfʊtsɪ) *n inf* flirtation involving the touching together of feet, etc

Footsie (ˈfʊtsɪ) *n Brit inf* the Financial Times Stock

Exchange 100 index. See **FT Index** (sense 2)
foot soldier *n* an infantryman
footsore ('fʊt,sɔː) *adj* having sore or tired feet, esp from much walking > '**foot,soreness** *n*
footstep ('fʊt,stɛp) *n* **1** the action of taking a step in walking **2** the sound made by walking **3** the distance covered with a step **4** a footmark **5** a single stair **6 follow in someone's footsteps** to continue the example of another
footsteps editor *n Brit films* the technician who adds sound effects, such as doors closing, rain falling, etc, during the postproduction sound-dubbing process. US name: **foley** *or* **foley artist**
footstool ('fʊt,stuːl) *n* a low stool used for supporting or resting the feet of a seated person
footwear ('fʊt,wɛə) *n* anything worn to cover the feet
footwork ('fʊt,wɜːk) *n* **1** the use of the feet, esp in sports, dancing, etc **2** *inf* clever manoeuvring: *deft political footwork* **3** *inf* preliminary groundwork
footy *or* **footie** ('fʊtɪ) *n inf* **a** football **b** (*as modifier*): *footy boots*
fop (fɒp) *n* a man who is excessively concerned with fashion and elegance [C15 rel. to G *foppen* to trick] > '**foppery** *n* > '**foppish** *adj*
for (fɔː; *unstressed* fə) *prep* **1** directed or belonging to: *there's a phone call for you* **2** to the advantage of: *I only did it for you* **3** in the direction of: *heading for the border* **4** over a span of (time or distance): *working for six days* **5** in favour of: *vote for me* **6** in order to get or achieve: *I do it for money* **7** designed to meet the needs of: *these kennels are for puppies* **8** at a cost of: *I got it for hardly any money* **9** such as explains or results in: *his reason for changing his job was not given* **10** in place of: *a substitute for the injured player* **11** because of: *she wept for pure relief* **12** with regard or consideration to the usual characteristics of: *it's cool for this time of year* **13** concerning: *desire for money* **14** as being: *I know that for a fact* **15** at a specified time: *a date for the next evening* **16** to do or partake of: *an appointment for supper* **17** in the duty or task of: *that's for him to say* **18** to allow of: *too big a job for us to handle* **19** despite: *she's a good wife, for all her nagging* **20** in order to preserve, retain, etc: *to fight for survival* **21** as a direct equivalent to: *word for word* **22** in order to become or enter: *to train for the priesthood* **23** in recompense for: *I paid for it last week* **24 for it** *Brit inf* liable for punishment or blame: *you'll be for it if she catches you* ▷ *conj* **25** (*coordinating*) because; seeing that: *I couldn't stay, for the area was violent* [OE]
for- *prefix* **1** indicating rejection or prohibition: *forbid* **2** indicating falsity: *forswear* **3** used to give intensive force: *forlorn* [OE *for-*]
forage ('fɒrɪdʒ) *n* **1** food for horses or cattle, esp hay or straw **2** the act of searching for food or provisions ▷ *vb* **forages, foraging, foraged 3** to search (the countryside or a town) for food, etc **4** (*intr*) *mil* to carry out a raid **5** (*tr*) to obtain by searching about **6** (*tr*) to give food or other provisions to **7** (*tr*) to feed (cattle or horses) with such food [C14 from OF *fourrage*, prob. of Gmc origin] > '**forager** *n*
forage cap *n* a soldier's undress cap
foramen (fɒ'reɪmɛn) *n, pl* **foramina** (-'ræmɪnə) *or* **foramens** a natural hole, esp one in a bone [C17 from L, from *forāre* to bore, pierce]
foraminifer (,fɒrə'mɪnɪfə) *n* a protozoan of the phylum *Foraminifera*, having a shell with numerous openings through which the cytoplasmic processes protrude [C19 from NL, from FORAMEN + -FER]
forasmuch as (fərəz'mʌtʃ) *conj* (*subordinating*) *arch or legal* seeing that
foray ('fɒreɪ) *n* **1** a short raid or incursion ▷ *vb* **2** to raid or ravage (a town, district, etc) [C14 from *forrayen* to pillage, from OF, from *fuerre* fodder]
forbade (fə'bæd, -'beɪd) *or* **forbad** (fə'bæd) *vb* the past tense of **forbid**
forbear[1] (fɔː'bɛə) *vb* **forbears, forbearing, forbore, forborne 1** (when *intr*, often foll by *from* or an infinitive) to cease or refrain (from doing something) **2** *arch* to tolerate (misbehaviour, etc) [OE *forberan*]
forbear[2] ('fɔː,bɛə) *n* a variant spelling of **forebear**
forbearance (fɔː'bɛərəns) *n* **1** the act of forbearing **2** self-control; patience
Forbes (fɔːbz) *n* **George William** 1869–1947, New Zealand statesman; prime minister of New Zealand (1930–35)
forbid (fə'bɪd) *vb* **forbids, forbidding, forbade** *or* **forbad, forbidden** *or* **forbid** (*tr*) **1** to prohibit (a person) in a forceful or authoritative manner (from doing or having something) **2** to make impossible **3** to shut out or exclude [OE *forbēodan*; see FOR-, BID] > **for'bidder** *n*

> USAGE It was formerly considered incorrect to talk of *forbidding* someone *from* doing something, but in modern usage either *from* or *to* can be used: *he was forbidden from entering/to enter the building*

forbidden (fə'bɪdᵊn) *adj* **1** not permitted by order or law **2** *physics* involving a change in quantum numbers that is not permitted by certain rules derived from quantum mechanics
Forbidden City *n* **the 1** Lhasa, Tibet: once famed for its inaccessibility and hostility to strangers **2** a walled section of Beijing, China, enclosing the Imperial Palace and associated buildings of the former Chinese Empire
forbidden fruit *n* any pleasure or enjoyment regarded as illicit, esp sexual indulgence
forbidding (fə'bɪdɪŋ) *adj* **1** hostile or unfriendly: *the most forbidding terrain on earth* **2** dangerous or ominous: *a forbidding presence*
forbore (fɔː'bɔː) *vb* the past tense of **forbear**[1]
forborne (fɔː'bɔːn) *vb* the past participle of **forbear**[1]
force[1] (fɔːs) *n* **1** strength or energy; power: *the force of the blow* **2** exertion or the use of exertion against a person or thing that resists **3** *physics* **3a** a dynamic influence that changes a body from a state of rest to one of motion or changes its rate of motion **3b** a static influence that produces a strain in a body or system. Symbol: F **4a** intellectual, political, or moral influence or strength: *the force of his argument* **4b** a person or thing with such influence: *he was a force in the land* **5** vehemence or intensity: *she spoke with great force* **6** a group of persons organized for military or police functions: *armed forces* **7** (*sometimes cap*; preceded by *the*) *inf* the police force **8** a group of persons organized for particular duties or tasks: *a workforce* **9** *criminal law* violence unlawfully committed or threatened **10 in force 10a** (of a law) having legal validity **10b** in great strength or numbers ▷ *vb* **forces, forcing, forced** (*tr*) **11** to compel or cause (a person, group, etc) to do something through effort, superior strength, etc **12** to acquire or produce through effort, superior strength, etc: *to force a confession* **13** to propel or drive despite resistance **14** to break down or open (a lock, door, etc) **15** to impose or inflict: *he forced his views on them* **16** to cause (plants or farm animals) to grow or fatten artificially at an increased rate **17** to strain to the utmost: *to force the voice* **18** to rape **19** *cards* **19a** to compel a player by the lead of a particular suit to play (a certain card) **19b** (in bridge) to induce (a bid) from one's partner [C13 from OF, from Vulgar L *fortia* (unattested), from L *fortis* strong] > '**forceable** *adj* > '**forceless** *adj* > '**forcer** *n*
force[2] (fɔːs) *n* (in N England) a waterfall [C17 from ON *fors*]
forced (fɔːst) *adj* **1** done because of force: *forced labour* **2** false or unnatural: *a forced smile* **3** due to an emergency or necessity: *a forced landing*
force de frappe *French* (fɔrs də frap) *n* a military strike force, esp the independent nuclear strike force of France [C20 lit.: striking force]
force-feed *vb* **force-feeds, force-feeding, force-fed** (*tr*) to

force (a person or animal) to eat or swallow food
forceful ('fɔːsfʊl) *adj* **1** powerful **2** persuasive or effective > **'forcefully** *adv* > **'forcefulness** *n*
forcemeat ('fɔːs,miːt) *n* a mixture of chopped ingredients used for stuffing. Also called: **farce** [C17 from *force* (see FARCE) + MEAT]
forceps ('fɔːsɪps) *n, pl* **forceps** **1a** a surgical instrument in the form of a pair of pincers, used esp in the delivery of babies **1b** (*as modifier*): *a forceps baby* **2** any part of an organism shaped like a forceps [C17 from L, from *formus* hot + *capere* to seize]
force pump *n* a pump that ejects fluid under pressure ▷ Cf **lift pump**
Forces ('fɔːsɪz) *pl n* (usually preceded by *the*) the armed services of a nation
forcible ('fɔːsəbᵊl) *adj* **1** done by, involving, or having force **2** convincing or effective: *a forcible argument* > **'forcibly** *adv*
ford (fɔːd) *n* **1** a shallow area in a river that can be crossed by car, on horseback, etc ▷ *vb* **2** (*tr*) to cross (a river, brook, etc) over a shallow area [OE] > **'fordable** *adj*
Ford (fɔːd) *n* **1 Ford Maddox** ('mædəks) original name *Ford Madox Hueffer*. 1873–1939, English novelist, editor, and critic; works include *The Good Soldier* (1915) and the war tetralogy *Parade's End* (1924–28) **2 Gerald R(udolph)** born 1913, US politician; 38th president of the US (1974–77) **3 Harrison** born 1942, US film actor. His films include *Star Wars* (1977) and its sequels, *Raiders of the Lost Ark* (1981) and its sequels, *Bladerunner* (1982), *Clear and Present Danger* (1994), and *What Lies Beneath* (2000) **4 Henry** 1863–1947, US car manufacturer, who pioneered mass production **5 John** 1586–?1639, English dramatist; author of revenge tragedies such as *'Tis Pity She's a Whore* (1633) **6 John**, real name *Sean O'Feeney*. 1895–1973, US film director, esp of Westerns such as *Stagecoach* (1939) and *She Wore a Yellow Ribbon* (1949)
fore¹ (fɔː) *adj* **1** (*usually in combination*) located at, in, or towards the front: *the forelegs of a horse* ▷ *n* **2** the front part **3** something located at, or towards the front **4 fore and aft** located at both ends of a vessel: *a fore-and-aft rig* **5 to the fore** to the front or conspicuous position ▷ *adv* **6** at or towards a ship's bow **7** *obs* before ▷ *prep, conj* **8** a less common word for **before** [OE]
fore² (fɔː) *sentence substitute* (in golf) a warning shout made by a player about to make a shot [C19 prob. short for BEFORE]
fore- *prefix* **1** before in time or rank: *forefather* **2** at or near the front: *forecourt* [OE, from *fore* (adv)]
fore-and-after *n naut* **1** any vessel with a fore-and-aft rig **2** a double-ended vessel
forearm¹ ('fɔːr,ɑːm) *n* the part of the arm from the elbow to the wrist [C18 from FORE- + ARM¹]
forearm² (fɔːr'ɑːm) *vb* (*tr*) to prepare or arm (someone) in advance [C16 from FORE- + ARM²]
forebear *or* **forbear** ('fɔː,bɛə) *n* an ancestor
forebode (fɔː'bəʊd) *vb* **forebodes, foreboding, foreboded** **1** to warn of or indicate (an event, result, etc) in advance **2** to have a premonition of (an event)
foreboding (fɔː'bəʊdɪŋ) *n* **1** a feeling of impending evil, disaster, etc **2** an omen or portent ▷ *adj* **3** presaging something
forebrain ('fɔː,breɪn) *n* the nontechnical name for **prosencephalon**
forecast ('fɔː,kɑːst) *vb* **forecasts, forecasting, forecast** *or* **forecasted** **1** to predict or calculate (weather, events, etc) in advance **2** (*tr*) to serve as an early indication of ▷ *n* **3** a statement of probable future weather calculated from meteorological data **4** a prediction **5** the practice or power of forecasting > **'fore,caster** *n*
forecastle, fo'c's'le, *or* **fo'c'sle** ('fəʊksᵊl) *n* the part of a vessel at the bow where the crew is quartered
foreclose (fɔː'kləʊz) *vb* **forecloses, foreclosing, foreclosed** **1** *law* to deprive (a mortgagor, etc) of the right to redeem (a mortgage or pledge) **2** (*tr*) to shut out; bar **3** (*tr*) to prevent or hinder [C15 from OF, from *for-* out + *clore* to close, from L *claudere*] > **fore'closable** *adj* > **foreclosure** (fɔː'kləʊʒə) *n*
forecourt ('fɔː,kɔːt) *n* **1** a courtyard in front of a building, as one in a filling station **2** the section of the court in tennis, badminton, etc, between the service line and the net
foredoom (fɔː'duːm) *vb* (*tr*) to doom or condemn beforehand
forefather ('fɔː,fɑːðə) *n* an ancestor, esp a male > **'fore,fatherly** *adj*
forefinger ('fɔː,fɪŋgə) *n* the finger next to the thumb. Also called: **index finger**
forefoot ('fɔː,fʊt) *n, pl* **forefeet** either of the front feet of a quadruped
forefront ('fɔː,frʌnt) *n* **1** the extreme front **2** the position of most prominence or action
foregather *or* **forgather** (fɔː'gæðə) *vb* (*intr*) **1** to gather together **2** (foll by *with*) to socialize
forego¹ (fɔː'gəʊ) *vb* **foregoes, foregoing, forewent, foregone** to precede in time, place, etc [OE *foregān*]
forego² (fɔː'gəʊ) *vb* **foregoes, foregoing, forewent, foregone** (*tr*) a variant spelling of **forgo**
foregoing (fɔː'gəʊɪŋ) *adj* (*prenominal*) (esp of writing or speech) going before; preceding
foregone (fɔː'gɒn, 'fɔː,gɒn) *adj* gone or completed; past > **fore'goneness** *n*
foregone conclusion *n* an inevitable result or conclusion
foreground ('fɔː,graʊnd) *n* **1** the part of a scene situated towards the front or nearest to the viewer **2** a conspicuous position
forehand ('fɔː,hænd) *adj* (*prenominal*) **1** *tennis, squash, etc* (of a stroke) made with the palm of the hand facing the direction of the stroke ▷ *n* **2** *tennis, squash, etc* **2a** a forehand stroke **2b** the side on which such strokes are made **3** the part of a horse in front of the saddle
forehead ('fɒrɪd, 'fɔː,hɛd) *n* the part of the face between the natural hairline and the eyes. Related adj: **frontal** [OE *forhēafod*]
foreign ('fɒrɪn) *adj* **1** of, located in, or coming from another country, area, people, etc: *a foreign resident* **2** dealing or concerned with another country, area, people, etc: *a foreign office* **3** not pertinent or related: *a matter foreign to the discussion* **4** not familiar; strange **5** in an abnormal place or position: *foreign matter* [C13 from OF, from Vulgar L *forānus* (unattested) on the outside, from L *foris* outside] > **'foreignness** *n*
foreign affairs *pl n* matters abroad that involve the homeland, such as relations with another country
foreigner ('fɒrɪnə) *n* **1** a person from a foreign country **2** an outsider **3** something from a foreign country, such as a ship or product
foreign minister *or* **secretary** *n* (*often caps*) a cabinet minister who is responsible for a country's dealings with other countries. US equivalent: **secretary of state**
foreign office *n* the ministry of a country or state that is concerned with dealings with other states. US equivalent: **State Department**
foreknowledge (fɔː'nɒlɪdʒ) *n* knowledge of a thing before it exists or occurs; prescience > **fore'know** *vb* > **fore'knowable** *adj*
foreland ('fɔːlənd) *n* **1** a headland, cape, or coastal promontory **2** land lying in front of something, such as water
foreleg ('fɔː,lɛg) *n* either of the front legs of a horse, sheep, or other quadruped
forelimb ('fɔː,lɪm) *n* either of the front or anterior limbs of a four-limbed vertebrate
forelock ('fɔː,lɒk) *n* a lock of hair growing or falling over the forehead
foreman ('fɔːmən) *n, pl* **foremen** **1** a person, often

experienced, who supervises other workmen **2** *law* the principal juror, who presides at the deliberations of a jury

Foreman ('fɔːmən) *n* **George** born 1949, US boxer: WBA world heavyweight champion (1973–74); he regained the title in 1994 but refused to fight the WBA's top-ranked challenger and was stripped of the title in 1995; recognized as WBU champion until 1997

foremast ('fɔːˌmɑːst; *naut* 'fɔːməst) *n* the mast nearest the bow on vessels with two or more masts

foremost ('fɔːˌməʊst) *adj, adv* first in time, place, rank, etc [OE, from *forma* first]

forename ('fɔːˌneɪm) *n* another term for **first name**

forenamed ('fɔːˌneɪmd) *adj (prenominal)* named or mentioned previously; aforesaid

forenoon ('fɔːˌnuːn) *n* the daylight hours before or just before noon

forensic (fəˈrɛnsɪk) *adj* used in, or connected with a court of law: *forensic science* [C17 from L *forēnsis* public, from FORUM] > **fo'rensically** *adv*

forensic medicine *n* the use of medical knowledge, esp pathology, for the purposes of the law, as in determining the cause of death. Also called: **medical jurisprudence**

foreordain (ˌfɔːrɔːˈdeɪn) *vb (tr; may take a clause as object)* to determine (events, etc) in the future > **foreordination** (ˌfɔːrɔːdɪˈneɪʃən) *n*

forepaw ('fɔːˌpɔː) *n* either of the front feet of most land mammals that do not have hoofs

foreplay ('fɔːˌpleɪ) *n* mutual sexual stimulation preceding sexual intercourse

forequarter ('fɔːˌkwɔːtə) *n* the front portion, including the leg, of half of a carcass, as of beef

forequarters ('fɔːˌkwɔːtəz) *pl n* the part of the body of a horse, etc that consists of the forelegs, shoulders, and adjoining parts

forerun (fɔːˈrʌn) *vb* **foreruns, forerunning, foreran, forerun** *(tr)* **1** to serve as a herald for **2** to precede **3** to forestall

forerunner ('fɔːˌrʌnə) *n* **1** a person or thing that precedes another **2** a person or thing coming in advance to herald the arrival of someone or something **3** an omen; portent

foresail ('fɔːˌseɪl; *naut* 'fɔːsᵊl) *n naut* **1** the aftermost headsail of a fore-and-aft rigged vessel **2** the lowest sail set on the foremast of a square-rigged vessel

foresee (fɔːˈsiː) *vb* **foresees, foreseeing, foresaw, foreseen** *(tr; may take a clause as object)* to see or know beforehand: *he did not foresee that* > **fore'seeable** *adj* > **fore'seer** *n*

foreshadow (fɔːˈʃædəʊ) *vb (tr)* to show, indicate, or suggest in advance; presage

foreshank ('fɔːˌʃæŋk) *n* **1** the top of the front leg of an animal **2** a cut of meat from this part

foresheet ('fɔːˌʃiːt) *n* **1** the sheet of a foresail **2** *(pl)* the part forward of the foremost thwart of a boat

foreshock ('fɔːˌʃɒk) *n chiefly US* a relatively small earthquake heralding the arrival of a much larger one

foreshore ('fɔːˌʃɔː) *n* **1** the part of the shore that lies between the limits for high and low tides **2** the part of the shore that lies just above the high water mark

foreshorten (fɔːˈʃɔːtᵊn) *vb (tr)* to represent (a line, form, object, etc) as shorter than actual length in order to give an illusion of recession or projection

foreshow (fɔːˈʃəʊ) *vb* **foreshows, foreshowing, foreshowed; foreshown** *or* **foreshowed** *(tr) arch* to indicate in advance

foresight ('fɔːˌsaɪt) *n* **1** provision for or insight into future problems, needs, etc **2** the act or ability of foreseeing **3** the act of looking forward **4** *surveying* a reading taken looking forwards **5** the front sight on a firearm > ˌ**fore'sighted** *adj* > ˌ**fore'sightedly** *adv* > ˌ**fore'sightedness** *n*

foreskin ('fɔːˌskɪn) *n anat* the nontechnical name for **prepuce**

forest ('fɒrɪst) *n* **1** a large wooded area having a thick growth of trees and plants **2** the trees of such an area **3** NZ an area planted with pines or similar trees, not native trees ▷ Cf **bush**[1] (sense 4) **4** something resembling a large wooded area, esp in density: *a forest of telegraph poles* **5** *law* (formerly) an area of woodland, esp one owned by the sovereign and set apart as a hunting ground **6** *(modifier)* of, involving, or living in a forest or forests: *a forest glade* ▷ *vb* **7** *(tr)* to create a forest [C13 from OF, from Med. L *forestis* unfenced woodland, from L *foris* outside] > '**forested** *adj*

forestall (fɔːˈstɔːl) *vb (tr)* **1** to delay, stop, or guard against beforehand **2** to anticipate **3** to buy up merchandise for profitable resale [C14 *forestallen* to waylay, from OE, from *fore-* in front of + *steall* place] > **fore'staller** *n* > **fore'stalment** *n*

forestation (ˌfɒrɪˈsteɪʃən) *n* the planting of trees over a wide area

forestay ('fɔːˌsteɪ) *n naut* an adjustable stay leading from the truck of the foremast to the deck, for controlling the bending of the mast

forester ('fɒrɪstə) *n* **1** a person skilled in forestry or in charge of a forest **2** a person or animal that lives in a forest **3** *(cap)* a member of the Ancient Order of Foresters, a friendly society

Forester ('fɒrɪstə) *n* **C(ecil) S(cott)** 1899–1966, English novelist; creator of Captain Horatio Hornblower in a series of novels on the Napoleonic Wars

forest park *n* NZ a recreational reserve which may include bush and exotic trees

forestry ('fɒrɪstrɪ) *n* **1** the science of planting and caring for trees **2** the planting and management of forests **3** *rare* forest land

▷ www.metla.fi/info/vlib/Forestry

▷ www.forestry.gov.uk

foretaste ('fɔːˌteɪst) *n* an early but limited experience of something to come

foretell (fɔːˈtɛl) *vb* **foretells, foretelling, foretold** *(tr; may take a clause as object)* to tell or indicate (an event, a result, etc) beforehand

forethought ('fɔːˌθɔːt) *n* **1** advance consideration or deliberation **2** thoughtful anticipation of future events

foretoken *n* ('fɔːˌtəʊkən) **1** a sign of a future event ▷ *vb* (fɔːˈtəʊkən) **2** *(tr)* to foreshadow

foretop ('fɔːˌtɒp; *naut* 'fɔːtəp) *n naut* a platform at the top of the foremast

fore-topgallant (ˌfɔːtɒpˈgælənt; *naut* ˌfɔːtəˈgælənt) *adj naut* of, relating to, or being the topmost portion of a foremast

fore-topmast (fɔːˈtɒpˌmɑːst; *naut* fɔːˈtɒpməst) *n naut* a mast stepped above a foremast

fore-topsail (fɔːˈtɒpˌseɪl; *naut* fɔːˈtɒpsᵊl) *n naut* a sail set on a fore-topmast

forever (fɔːˈrɛvə, fə-) *adv* **1** Also: **for ever** without end; everlastingly **2** at all times **3** *inf* for a very long time: *he went on speaking forever* ▷ *n* **forever** **4** *(as object) inf* a very long time: *it took him forever to reply*

USAGE *Forever* and *for ever* can both be used to say that something is without end. For all other meanings, *forever* is the preferred form

for evermore *or* **forevermore** (fɔːˌrɛvəˈmɔː, fə-) *adv* a more emphatic or emotive term for **forever**

forewarn (fɔːˈwɔːn) *vb (tr)* to warn beforehand > **fore'warner** *n*

forewent (fɔːˈwɛnt) *vb* the past tense of **forego**

forewing ('fɔːˌwɪŋ) *n* either wing of the anterior pair of an insect's two pairs of wings

foreword ('fɔːˌwɜːd) *n* an introductory statement to a book [C19 literal translation of G *Vorwort*]

forfaiting ('fɔːˌfeɪtɪŋ) *n* the financial service of

Ff

discounting, without recourse, a promissory note, bill of exchange, letter of credit, etc, received from an overseas buyer by an exporter; a form of debt discounting [c20 from F *forfaire* to forfeit or surrender]

Forfar (ˈfɔːfər, -fɑː) *n* a market town in E Scotland, the administrative centre of Angus: site of a castle, residence of Scottish kings between the 11th and 14th centuries. Pop: 12 961 (1991)

forfeit (ˈfɔːfɪt) *n* **1** something lost or given up as a penalty for a fault, mistake, etc **2** the act of losing or surrendering something in this manner **3** *law* something confiscated as a penalty for an offence, etc **4** (*sometimes pl*) **4a** a game in which a player has to give up an object, perform a specified action, etc, if he commits a fault **4b** an object so given up ▷ *vb* (*tr*) **5** to lose or be liable to lose in consequence of a mistake, fault, etc **6** *law* to confiscate as punishment ▷ *adj* **7** surrendered or liable to be surrendered as a penalty [c13 from OF *forfet* offence, from *forfaire* to commit a crime, from Med. L, from L *foris* outside + *facere* to do] > **ˈforfeiter** *n*

forfeiture (ˈfɔːfɪtʃə) *n* **1** something forfeited **2** the act of forfeiting or paying a penalty

forfend *or* **forefend** (fɔːˈfɛnd) *vb* (*tr*) **1** US to protect or secure **2** *obs* to prevent

forgather (fɔːˈgæðə) *vb* a variant spelling of **foregather**

forgave (fəˈgeɪv) *vb* the past tense of **forgive**

forge[1] (fɔːdʒ) *n* **1** a place in which metal is worked by heating and hammering; smithy **2** a hearth or furnace used for heating metal ▷ *vb* **forges, forging, forged 3** (*tr*) to shape (metal) by heating and hammering **4** (*tr*) to form, make, or fashion (objects, etc) **5** (*tr*) to invent or devise (an agreement, etc) **6** to make a fraudulent imitation of (a signature, etc) or to commit forgery [c14 from OF *forgier* to construct, from L *fabricāre*, from *faber* craftsman] > **ˈforger** *n*

forge[2] (fɔːdʒ) *vb* **forges, forging, forged** (*intr*) **1** to move at a steady pace **2 forge ahead** to increase speed [c17 from ?]

forgery (ˈfɔːdʒərɪ) *n, pl* **forgeries 1** the act of reproducing something for a fraudulent purpose **2** something forged, such as an antique **3** *criminal law* **3a** the false making or altering of a document, such as a cheque, etc, or any tape or disk storing information, with intent to defraud **3b** something forged

forget (fəˈgɛt) *vb* **forgets, forgetting, forgot, forgotten** *or* (*arch or dialect*) **forgot 1** (when *tr, may take a clause as object or an infinitive*) to fail to recall (someone or something once known) **2** (*tr; may take a clause as object or an infinitive*) to neglect, either as the result of an unintentional error or intentionally **3** (*tr*) to leave behind by mistake **4 forget oneself 4a** to act in an improper manner **4b** to be unselfish **4c** to be deep in thought [OE *forgietan*] > **forˈgettable** *adj* > **forˈgetter** *n*

forgetful (fəˈgɛtfʊl) *adj* **1** tending to forget **2** (*often postpositive;* foll by *of*) inattentive (to) or neglectful (of) > **forˈgetfully** *adv* > **forˈgetfulness** *n*

forget-me-not *n* a temperate low-growing plant having clusters of small blue flowers

forgive (fəˈgɪv) *vb* **forgives, forgiving, forgave, forgiven 1** to cease to blame (someone or something) **2** to grant pardon for (a mistake, etc) **3** (*tr*) to free (someone) from penalty **4** (*tr*) to free from the obligation of (a debt, etc) [OE *forgiefan*] > **forˈgivable** *adj* > **forˈgiver** *n*

forgiveness (fəˈgɪvnɪs) *n* **1** the act of forgiving or the state of being forgiven **2** willingness to forgive

forgiving (fəˈgɪvɪŋ) *adj* willing to forgive

forgo *or* **forego** (fɔːˈgəʊ) *vb* **forgoes, forgoing, forwent, forgone** (*tr*) to give up or do without [OE *forgān*]

forgot (fəˈgɒt) *vb* **1** the past tense of **forget 2** *arch or dialect* a past participle of **forget**

forgotten (fəˈgɒtᵊn) *vb* a past participle of **forget**

forint (*Hungarian* ˈforint) *n* the standard monetary unit of Hungary [from Hungarian, from It. *fiorino* FLORIN]

fork (fɔːk) *n* **1** a small usually metal implement consisting of two, three, or four long thin prongs on the end of a handle, used for lifting food to the mouth, etc **2** a similar-shaped agricultural tool, used for lifting, digging, etc **3** a pronged part of any machine, device, etc **4** (of a road, river, etc) **4a** a division into two or more branches **4b** the point where the division begins **4c** such a branch ▷ *vb* **5** (*tr*) to pick up, dig, etc, with a fork **6** (*tr*) *chess* to place (two enemy pieces) under attack with one of one's own pieces **7** (*intr*) to be divided into two or more branches **8** to take one or other branch at a fork in a road, etc [OE *forca*, from L *furca*]

forked (fɔːkt) *adj* **1a** having a fork or forklike parts **1b** (*in combination*): *two-forked* **2** zigzag: *forked lightning* > **forkedly** (ˈfɔːkɪdlɪ) *adv*

fork-lift truck *n* a vehicle having two power-operated horizontal prongs that can be raised and lowered for transporting and unloading goods. Sometimes shortened to **fork-lift**

fork out, over, *or* **up** *vb* (*adv*) *sl* to pay (money, goods, etc), esp with reluctance

forlorn (fəˈlɔːn) *adj* **1** miserable or cheerless **2** forsaken **3** (*postpositive;* foll by *of*) bereft: *forlorn of hope* **4** desperate: *the last forlorn attempt* [OE *forloren* lost, from *forlēosan* to lose] > **forˈlornness** *n*

forlorn hope *n* **1** a hopeless enterprise **2** a faint hope **3** *obs* a group of soldiers assigned to an extremely dangerous duty [c16 (in the obs. sense): changed (by folk etymology) from Du. *verloren hoop* lost troop, from *verloren*, p.p. of *verliezen* to lose + *hoop* troop (lit.: heap)]

form (fɔːm) *n* **1** the shape or configuration of something as distinct from its colour, texture, etc **2** the particular mode, appearance, etc, in which a thing or person manifests itself: *water in the form of ice* **3** a type or kind: *imprisonment is a form of punishment* **4** a printed document, esp one with spaces in which to insert facts or answers: *an application form* **5** physical or mental condition, esp good condition, with reference to ability to perform: *off form* **6** the previous record of a horse, athlete, etc, esp with regard to fitness **7** *Brit sl* a criminal record **8** a fixed mode of artistic expression or representation in literary, musical, or other artistic works: *sonata form* **9** a mould, frame, etc, that gives shape to something **10** *education, chiefly Brit* a group of children who are taught together **11** behaviour or procedure, esp as governed by custom or etiquette: *good form* **12** formality or ceremony **13** a prescribed set or order of words, terms, etc, as in a religious ceremony or legal document **14** *philosophy* **14a** the structure of anything as opposed to its content **14b** essence as opposed to matter **15** See **logical form 16** *Brit, Austral, & NZ* a bench, esp one that is long, low, and backless **17** a hare's nest **18** any of the various ways in which a word may be spelt or inflected ▷ *vb* **19** to give shape or form to or to take shape or form, esp a particular shape **20** to come or bring into existence: *a scum formed* **21** to make or construct or be made or constructed **22** to construct or develop in the mind: *to form an opinion* **23** (*tr*) to train or mould by instruction or example **24** (*tr*) to acquire or develop: *to form a habit* **25** (*tr*) to be an element of or constitute: *this plank will form a bridge* **26** (*tr*) to organize: *to form a club* [c13 from OF, from L *forma* shape, model]

-form *adj combining form* having the shape or form of or resembling: *cruciform; vermiform* [from NL *-formis*, from L, from *fōrma* FORM]

formal (ˈfɔːməl) *adj* **1** of or following established forms, conventions, etc: *a formal document* **2** characterized by observation of conventional forms of ceremony, behaviour, etc: *a formal dinner* **3** methodical or stiff **4** suitable for occasions organized according to conventional ceremony: *formal dress* **5** denoting idiom, vocabulary, etc, used by educated speakers and writers of a language **6** acquired by study in academic institutions **7** symmetrical in form: *a formal garden* **8** of or relating to the appearance, form, etc, of something as distinguished from its substance **9** logically deductive: *formal proof* **10** denoting a second-person pronoun in some languages: *in French the pronoun 'vous' is formal, while 'tu' is informal* [C14 from L *formālis*] > **ˈformally** *adv* > **ˈformalness** *n*

formaldehyde (fɔːˈmældɪˌhaɪd) *n* a colourless poisonous irritating gas with a pungent characteristic odour, used as formalin and in the manufacture of synthetic resins. Formula: HCHO. Systematic name: **methanal** [C19 FORM(IC) + ALDEHYDE; on the model of G *Formaldehyd*]

formalin (ˈfɔːməlɪn) *n* a solution of formaldehyde in water, used as a disinfectant, preservative for biological specimens, etc

formalism (ˈfɔːməˌlɪzəm) *n* **1** scrupulous or excessive adherence to outward form at the expense of content **2** the mathematical or logical structure of a scientific argument as distinguished from its subject matter **3** *theatre* a stylized mode of production **4** (in Marxist criticism, etc) excessive concern with artistic technique at the expense of social values, etc > **ˈformalist** *n* > **ˌformalˈistic** *adj*

formality (fɔːˈmælɪtɪ) *n, pl* **formalities 1** a requirement of custom, etiquette, etc **2** the quality of being formal or conventional **3** strict or excessive observance of ceremony, etc

formalize *or* **formalise** (ˈfɔːməˌlaɪz) *vb* **formalizes, formalizing, formalized** *or* **formalises, formalising, formalised 1** to be or make formal **2** (*tr*) to make official or valid **3** (*tr*) to give a definite shape or form to > **ˌformaliˈzation** *or* **ˌformaliˈsation** *n*

formal language *n* any of various languages designed for use in fields such as mathematics, logic, or computer programming, the symbols and formulas of which stand in precisely specified syntactic and semantic relations to one another

formal logic *n* the study of systems of deductive argument in which symbols are used to represent precisely defined categories of expressions

Forman (ˈfɔːmən) *n* **Miloš** (ˈmiːləʊʃ) born 1932, Czech film director working in the USA. since 1968. His films include *One Flew over the Cuckoo's Nest* (1976), *Amadeus* (1985), and *The People vs Larry Flynt* (1996)

formant (ˈfɔːmənt) *n acoustics, phonetics* any of the constituents of a sound, esp a vowel sound, that impart to the sound its own special quality, tone colour, or timbre

format (ˈfɔːmæt) *n* **1** the general appearance of a publication, including type style, paper, binding, etc **2** style, plan, or arrangement, as of a television programme **3** *computing* **3a** the defined arrangement of data encoded in a file or, for example, on magnetic disk or CD-ROM, that is essential for the correct recording and recovery of data on different devices **3b** the arrangement of text on printed output or on a display screen ▷ *vb* **formats, formatting, formatted** (*tr*) **4** to arrange (a book, page, etc) into a specified format [C19 via F from G, from L *liber formātus* volume formed]

formation (fɔːˈmeɪʃən) *n* **1** the act of giving or taking form or existence **2** something that is formed **3** the manner in which something is arranged **4a** a formal arrangement of a number of persons or things acting as a unit, such as a troop of soldiers or a football team **4b** (*as modifier*): *formation dancing* **5** *geol* **5a** a series of rocks with certain characteristics in common **5b** the fundamental lithostratigraphic unit

formative (ˈfɔːmətɪv) *adj* **1** of or relating to formation, development, or growth: *formative years* **2** shaping; moulding: *a formative experience* **3** functioning in the formation of derived, inflected, or compound words ▷ *n* **4** an inflectional or derivational affix > **ˈformatively** *adv*

Formby (ˈfɔːmbɪ) *n* **George** real name *George Booth*. 1904–61, British comedian. He made many musical films in the 1930s, accompanying his songs on the ukulele

form class *n* **1** another term for **part of speech 2** a group of words distinguished by common inflections, such as the weak verbs of English

forme *or US* **form** (fɔːm) *n printing* type matter, blocks, etc, assembled in a chase and ready for printing [C15 from F: FORM]

former[1] (ˈfɔːmə) *adj* (*prenominal*) **1** belonging to or occurring in an earlier time: *former glory* **2** having been at a previous time: *a former colleague* **3** denoting the first or first mentioned of two ▷ *n* **4 the former** the first or first mentioned of two: distinguished from *latter*

former[2] (ˈfɔːmə) *n* **1** a person or thing that forms or shapes **2** *electrical engineering* a tool for giving a coil or winding the required shape

formerly (ˈfɔːməlɪ) *adv* at or in a former time; in the past

formic (ˈfɔːmɪk) *adj* **1** of, relating to, or derived from ants **2** of, containing, or derived from formic acid [C18 from L *formīca* ant; the acid occurs naturally in ants]

Formica (fɔːˈmaɪkə) *n trademark* any of various laminated plastic sheets used esp for heat-resistant surfaces, which can be easily cleaned

formic acid *n* a colourless corrosive liquid carboxylic acid found in some insects, esp ants, and many plants: used in the manufacture of insecticides. Formula: HCOOH. Systematic name: **methanoic acid**

formidable (ˈfɔːmɪdəbᵊl) *adj* **1** arousing or likely to inspire fear or dread **2** extremely difficult to defeat, overcome, manage, etc **3** tending to inspire awe or admiration because of great size, excellence, etc [C15 from L, from *formīdāre* to dread, from *formīdō* fear] > **ˈformidably** *adv*

formless (ˈfɔːmlɪs) *adj* without a definite shape or form; amorphous > **ˈformlessly** *adv*

form letter *n* a single copy of a letter that has been mechanically reproduced in large numbers for circulation

Formosa (fɔːˈməʊsə) *n* the former name of **Taiwan**

Formosa Strait *n* an arm of the Pacific between Taiwan and mainland China, linking the East and South China Seas. Also called: **Taiwan Strait**

formula (ˈfɔːmjʊlə) *n, pl* **formulas** *or* **formulae** (-ˌliː) **1** an established form or set of words, as used in religious ceremonies, legal proceedings, etc **2** *maths, physics* a general relationship, principle, or rule stated, often as an equation, in the form of symbols **3** *chem* a representation of molecules, radicals, ions, etc, expressed in the symbols of the atoms of their constituent elements **4a** a method, pattern, or rule for doing or producing something, often one proved to be successful **4b** (*as modifier*): *formula fiction* **5** *US & Canad* a prescription for making up a medicine, baby's food, etc **6** *motor racing* the category in which a type of car competes, judged according to engine size, weight, and fuel capacity [C17 from L: dim. of *forma* FORM] > **formulaic** (ˌfɔːmjʊˈleɪɪk) *adj*

Formula One *n* **1** the top class of professional motor racing **2** the most important world championship in motor racing

▷ www.formula1.com

▷ www.fia.com

formularize *or* **formularise** (ˈfɔːmjʊləˌraɪz) *vb* **formularizes, formularizing, formularized** *or* **formularises, formularising, formularised** a less common word for **formulate** (sense 1)

formulary (ˈfɔːmjʊlərɪ) *n, pl* **formularies 1** a book of prescribed formulas, esp relating to religious procedure or doctrine **2** a formula **3** *pharmacol* a book containing a list of pharmaceutical products with their formulas ▷ *adj* **4** of or relating to a formula

Ff

formulate ('fɔːmjʊˌleɪt) *vb* **formulates, formulating, formulated** *(tr)* **1** to put into or express in systematic terms; express in or as if in a formula **2** to devise > ˌ**formuˈlation** *n*

formwork ('fɔːmˌwɜːk) *n* an arrangement of wooden boards, etc, used to shape concrete while it is setting

fornicate ('fɔːnɪˌkeɪt) *vb* **fornicates, fornicating, fornicated** *(intr)* to commit fornication [c16 from LL *fornicārī*, from L *fornix* vault, brothel situated therein] > '**forniˌcator** *n*

fornication (ˌfɔːnɪ'keɪʃən) *n* **1** voluntary sexual intercourse outside marriage **2** *Bible* sexual immorality in general, esp adultery

Forrest ('fɒrɪst) *n* **John**, 1st Baron Forrest. 1847–1918, Australian statesman and explorer; first premier of Western Australia (1890–1901)

forsake (fə'seɪk) *vb* **forsakes, forsaking, forsook, forsaken** *(tr)* **1** to abandon **2** to give up (something valued or enjoyed) [OE *forsacan*] > **for'saker** *n*

forsaken (fə'seɪkən) *vb* **1** the past participle of **forsake** ▹ *adj* **2** completely deserted or helpless > **for'sakenly** *adv* > **for'sakenness** *n*

forsook (fə'sʊk) *vb* the past tense of **forsake**

forsooth (fə'suːθ) *adv arch* in truth; indeed [OE *forsōth*]

Forster ('fɔːstə) *n* **E(dward) M(organ)** 1879–1970, English novelist, short-story writer, and essayist. His best-known novels are *A Room with a View* (1908), *Howard's End* (1910), and *A Passage to India* (1924), in all of which he stresses the need for sincerity and sensitivity in human relationships and criticizes English middle-class values

forswear (fɔː'swɛə) *vb* **forswears, forswearing, forswore, forsworn** **1** *(tr)* to reject or renounce with determination or as upon oath **2** *(tr)* to deny or disavow absolutely or upon oath **3** to perjure (oneself) [OE *forswearian*] > **for'swearer** *n*

forsworn (fɔː'swɔːn) *vb* the past participle of **forswear** > **for'swornness** *n*

Forsyth ('fɔːsaɪθ) *n* **Frederick** born 1938, British thriller writer. His books include *The Day of the Jackal* (1970), *The Odessa File* (1972), and *The Fourth Protocol* (1984)

forsythia (fɔː'saɪθɪə) *n* a shrub native to China, Japan, and SE Europe but widely cultivated for its showy yellow bell-shaped flowers, which appear in spring before the foliage [c19 NL, after William *Forsyth* (1737–1804), E botanist]

fort (fɔːt) *n* **1** a fortified enclosure, building, or position able to be defended against an enemy **2** **hold the fort** *inf* to guard something temporarily [c15 from OF, from *fort* (adj) strong, from L *fortis*]

Fortaleza (*Portuguese* forta'leza) *n* a port in NE Brazil, capital of Ceará state. Pop: 2 138 234 (2000). Also called: **Ceará**

Fort-de-France (*French* fɔrdəfrɑ̃s) *n* the capital of Martinique, a port on the W coast: commercial centre of the French Antilles. Pop: 94 049 (1999 est)

forte[1] (fɔːt, 'fɔːteɪ) *n* **1** something at which a person excels: *cooking is my forte* **2** *fencing* the stronger section of a sword, between the hilt and the middle [c17 from F, from *fort* (adj) strong, from L *fortis*]

forte[2] ('fɔːtɪ) *music* ▹ *adj, adv* **1** loud or loudly. Symbol: f ▹ *n* **2** a loud passage in music [c18 from It., from L *fortis* strong]

forte-piano (ˌfɔːtɪ'pjɑːnəʊ) *music* ▹ *adj, adv* **1** loud and then immediately soft. Symbol: fp ▹ *n* **2** a note played in this way

forth (fɔːθ) *adv* **1** forward in place, time, order, or degree **2** out, as from concealment or inaction **3** away, as from a place or country **4** **and so forth** and so on ▹ *prep* **5** *arch* out of [OE]

Forth (fɔːθ) *n* **1** **Firth of** an inlet of the North Sea in SE Scotland: spanned by a cantilever railway bridge 1600 m (almost exactly 1 mile) long (1889), and by a road bridge (1964) **2** a river in S Scotland, flowing generally east to the Firth of Forth. Length: about 104 km (65 miles)

forthcoming (ˌfɔːθ'kʌmɪŋ) *adj* **1** approaching in time: *the forthcoming debate* **2** about to appear: *his forthcoming book* **3** available or ready **4** open or sociable

forthright *adj* ('fɔːθˌraɪt) **1** direct and outspoken ▹ *adv* (ˌfɔːθ'raɪt, 'fɔːθˌraɪt), *also* **forthrightly** **2** in a direct manner; frankly **3** at once > '**forthˌrightness** *n*

forthwith (ˌfɔːθ'wɪθ) *adv* at once

fortification (ˌfɔːtɪfɪ'keɪʃən) *n* **1** the act, art, or science of fortifying or strengthening **2a** a wall, mound, etc, used to fortify a place **2b** such works collectively

fortify ('fɔːtɪˌfaɪ) *vb* **fortifies, fortifying, fortified** *(mainly tr)* **1** *(also intr)* to make (a place) defensible, as by building walls, etc **2** to strengthen physically, mentally, or morally **3** to add alcohol to (wine), in order to produce sherry, port, etc **4** to increase the nutritious value of (a food), as by adding vitamins **5** to confirm: *to fortify an argument* [c15 from OF, from LL, from L *fortis* strong + *facere* to make] > '**fortiˌfiable** *adj* > '**fortiˌfier** *n*

fortissimo (fɔː'tɪsɪˌməʊ) *music* ▹ *adj, adv* **1** very loud. Symbol: ff ▹ *n* **2** a very loud passage in music [c18 from It., from L, from *fortis* strong]

fortitude ('fɔːtɪˌtjuːd) *n* strength and firmness of mind [c15 from L *fortitūdō* courage]

Fort Knox (nɒks) *n* a military reservation in N Kentucky: site of the US Gold Bullion Depository. Pop: 38 280 (latest est)

Fort Lamy ('fɔːt 'lɑːmɪ; *French* fɔr lami) *n* the former name (until 1973) of **Ndjamena**

fortnight ('fɔːtˌnaɪt) *n* a period of 14 consecutive days; two weeks [OE *fēowertīene niht* fourteen nights]

fortnightly ('fɔːtˌnaɪtlɪ) *chiefly Brit* ▹ *adj* **1** occurring or appearing once each fortnight ▹ *adv* **2** once a fortnight ▹ *n, pl* **fortnightlies** **3** a publication issued at intervals of two weeks

Fortran ('fɔːtræn) *n* a high-level computer programming language for mathematical and scientific purposes [c20 from *for(mula) tran(slation)*]

fortress ('fɔːtrɪs) *n* **1** a large fort or fortified town **2** a place or source of refuge or support ▹ *vb* **3** *(tr)* to protect [c13 from OF, from Med. L *fortalitia*, from L *fortis* strong]

Fort Sumter ('sʌmtə) *n* a fort in SE South Carolina, guarding Charleston Harbour. Its capture by Confederate forces (1861) was the first action of the Civil War

fortuitous (fɔː'tjuːɪtəs) *adj* happening by chance, esp by a lucky chance [c17 from L *fortuitus* happening by chance, from *fors* chance, luck] > **for'tuitously** *adv*

fortuity (fɔː'tjuːɪtɪ) *n, pl* **fortuities** **1** a chance or accidental occurrence **2** chance or accident

Fortuna (fɔː'tjuːnə) *n* the Roman goddess of fortune and good luck. Greek counterpart: **Tyche**

fortunate ('fɔːtʃənɪt) *adj* **1** having good luck **2** occurring by or bringing good fortune or luck > '**fortunately** *adv*

fortune ('fɔːtʃən) *n* **1** an amount of wealth or material prosperity, esp a great amount **2** **small fortune** a large sum of money **3** a power or force, often personalized, regarded as being responsible for human affairs **4** luck, esp when favourable **5** *(often pl)* a person's destiny ▹ *vb* **fortunes, fortuning, fortuned** **6** *(intr) arch* to happen by chance [c13 from OF, from L, from *fors* chance]

fortune-hunter *n* a person who seeks to secure a fortune, esp through marriage

fortune-teller *n* a person who makes predictions about the future as by looking into a crystal ball, etc > '**fortune-ˌtelling** *adj, n*

Fort William ('wɪljəm) *n* a town in W Scotland, in Highland at the head of Loch Linnhe: tourist centre; the fort itself, built in 1655 and renamed after William III in 1690, was demolished in 1866. Pop: 10 391 (1991)

Fort Worth (wɜːθ) *n* a city in N Texas, at the junction of the Clear and West forks of the Trinity River: aircraft works, electronics. Pop: 534 694 (2000)

forty (ˈfɔːtɪ) *n, pl* **forties** **1** the cardinal number that is the product of ten and four **2** a numeral, 40, XL, etc, representing this number **3** something representing, represented by, or consisting of 40 units ▷ *determiner* **4a** amounting to forty: *forty thieves* **4b** (*as pronoun*): *there were forty in the herd* [OE *fēowertig*] > **ˈfortieth** *adj, n*

forty-five *n* a gramophone record played at 45 revolutions per minute

Forty-Five *n* **the** *British history* another name for the **Jacobite Rebellion** of 1745–46. See **Young Pretender**

forty-niner *n* (*sometimes cap*) *US history* a prospector who took part in the California gold rush of 1849

forty-ninth parallel *n Canad* an informal name for the border with the USA, which is in part delineated by the parallel line of latitude at 49°

forty winks *n* (*functioning as sing or pl*) *inf* a short light sleep; nap

forum (ˈfɔːrəm) *n, pl* **forums** *or* **fora** (-rə) **1** a meeting for the open discussion of subjects of public interest **2** a medium for open discussion, such as a magazine **3** a public meeting place for open discussion **4** a court; tribunal **5** *S African* a pressure group of leaders or representatives, esp Black leaders or representatives **6** (in ancient Italy) an open space serving as a city's marketplace and centre of public business [c15 from L: public place]

Forum *or* **Forum Romanum** (rəʊˈmɑːnəm) *n* **the** the main forum of ancient Rome

forward (ˈfɔːwəd) *adj* **1** directed or moving ahead **2** lying or situated in or near the front part of something **3** presumptuous, pert, or impudent **4** well developed or advanced, esp in physical or intellectual development **5a** of or relating to the future or favouring change **5b** (*in combination*): *forward-looking* **6** (*often postpositive*) *arch* ready, eager, or willing **7** *commerce* relating to fulfilment at a future date ▷ *n* **8** an attacking player in any of various sports, such as soccer **9** an email that has been sent to one recipient and then forwarded to another ▷ *adv* **10** a variant of **forwards** **11** (ˈfɔːwəd; *naut* ˈfɒrəd) towards the front or bow of an aircraft or ship **12** into a position of being subject to public scrutiny: *the witness came forward* ▷ *vb* (*tr*) **13** to send forward or pass on to an ultimate destination: *the letter was forwarded* **14** to advance or promote: *to forward one's career* [OE *foreweard*] > **ˈforwarder** *n* > **ˈforwardly** *adv* > **ˈforwardness** *n*

forwards (ˈfɔːwədz) *or* **forward** *adv* **1** towards or at a place ahead or in advance, esp in space but also in time **2** towards the front

forwent (fɔːˈwɛnt) *vb* the past tense of **forgo**

forza (ˈfɔːtsə) *n music* force [c19 It., lit.: force]

Foshan (ˈfɔːˈʃɑːn) *or* **Fatshan** *n* a city in SE China, in W Guangdong province. Pop: 411 107 (1999 est). Also called: **Namhoi**

fossa (ˈfɒsə) *n, pl* **fossae** (-siː) an anatomical depression or hollow area [c19 from L: ditch, from *fossus* dug up, from *fodere* to dig up]

fosse *or* **foss** (fɒs) *n* a ditch or moat, esp one dug as a fortification [c14 from OF, from L *fossa*; see FOSSA]

Fosse Way (fɒs) *n* a Roman road in Britain between Lincoln and Exeter, with a fosse on each side

fossick (ˈfɒsɪk) *vb Austral & NZ* **1** (*intr*) to search for gold or precious stones in abandoned workings, rivers, etc **2** to rummage or search for (something): *to fossick around for* [c19 Austral, prob. from E dialect *fussock* to bustle about, from FUSS] > **ˈfossicker** *n*

fossil (ˈfɒsᵊl) *n* **1a** a relic or representation of an organism that existed in a past geological age, or of the activity of such an organism, occurring in the form of mineralized bones, shells, etc **1b** (*as modifier*): *fossil insects* **2** *inf, derog* a person, idea, thing, etc, that is outdated or incapable of change **3** *linguistics* a form once current but now appearing only in one or two special contexts [c17 from L *fossilis* dug up, from *fodere* to dig]

fossil fuel *n* any naturally occurring fuel, such as coal, and natural gas, formed by the decomposition of prehistoric organisms

fossiliferous (ˌfɒsɪˈlɪfərəs) *adj* (of sedimentary rocks) containing fossils

fossilize *or* **fossilise** (ˈfɒsɪˌlaɪz) *vb* **fossilizes, fossilizing, fossilized** *or* **fossilises, fossilising, fossilised** **1** to convert or be converted into a fossil **2** to become or cause to become antiquated or inflexible > ˌ**fossiliˈzation** *or* ˌ**fossiliˈsation** *n*

fossorial (fɒˈsɔːrɪəl) *adj* (of the forelimbs and skeleton of burrowing animals) adapted for digging [c19 from Med. L, from L *fossor* digger, from *fodere* to dig]

foster (ˈfɒstə) *vb* (*tr*) **1** to promote the growth or development of **2** to bring up (a child, etc) **3** to cherish (a plan, hope, etc) in one's mind **4** *chiefly Brit* **4a** to place (a child) in the care of foster parents **4b** to bring up under fosterage ▷ *adj* **5** indicating relationship through fostering and not through birth: *foster child, foster mother* **6** of or involved in the rearing of a child by persons other than his natural parents: *foster home* [OE *fōstrian* to feed, from *fōstor* FOOD] > **ˈfosterer** *n* > **ˈfostering** *n*

Foster (ˈfɒstə) *n* **1** **Jodie** born 1962, US film actress and director: her films include *Taxi Driver* (1976), *The Accused* (1988), *The Silence of the Lambs* (1990), *Little Man Tate* (1991; also directed), *Nell* (1995), and *The Panic Room* (2002) **2** **Norman**, Baron born 1935, British architect. His works include the Willis Faber building (1978) in Ipswich, Stansted Airport, Essex (1991), Chek Lap Kok Airport, Hong Kong (1998), the renovation of the Reichstag, Berlin (1999), and City Hall, London (2002) **3** **Stephen Collins** 1826–64, US composer of songs such as *The Old Folks at Home* and *Oh Susanna*

fosterage (ˈfɒstərɪdʒ) *n* **1** the act of caring for a foster child **2** the state of being a foster child **3** the act of encouraging

Fotheringhay (ˈfɒðərɪŋˌgeɪ) *n* a village in E England, in NE Northamptonshire: ruined castle, scene of the imprisonment and execution of Mary Queen of Scots (1587)

Foucault (*French* fuko) *n* **1** **Jean Bernard Léon** (ʒɑ̃ bɛrnar leɔ̃) 1819–68, French physicist. He determined the velocity of light and proved that light travels more slowly in water than in air (1850). He demonstrated by means of the pendulum named after him the rotation of the earth on its axis (1851) and invented the gyroscope (1852) **2** **Michel** 1926–84, French philosopher and historian of ideas. His publications include *Histoire de la folie* (1961) and *Les Mots et les choses* (1966)

Foucquet (*French* fukɛ) *n* a variant spelling of (Nicolas) **Fouquet**

fought (fɔːt) *vb* the past tense and past participle of **fight**

foul (faʊl) *adj* **1** offensive to the senses; revolting **2** stinking **3** charged with or full of dirt or offensive matter **4** (of food) putrid; rotten **5** morally or spiritually offensive **6** obscene; vulgar: *foul language* **7** unfair: *to resort to foul means* **8** (esp of weather) unpleasant or adverse **9** blocked or obstructed with dirt or foreign matter: *a foul drain* **10** (of the bottom of a vessel) covered with barnacles that slow forward motion **11** *inf* unsatisfactory; bad: *a foul book* ▷ *n* **12** *sport* **12a** a violation of the rules **12b** (*as modifier*): *a foul blow* **13** an entanglement or collision, esp in sailing or fishing ▷ *vb* **14** to make or become polluted **15** to become or cause to become entangled **16** (*tr*) to disgrace **17** to become or cause to become clogged **18** (*tr*) *naut* (of underwater growth) to cling to (the bottom of a vessel) so as to slow its motion **19** (*tr*) *sport* to commit a foul against (an opponent) **20** (*intr*) *sport* to infringe the rules **21** to collide (with a boat, etc) **22** to leave a dog's faeces in a public place ▷ *adv* **23** in a foul manner **24** **fall foul of** **24a** come into conflict with **24b** *naut* to come into

Ff

collision with [OE *fūl*] > **'foully** *adv* > **'foulness** *n*

foulard (fuːˈlɑːd) *n* a soft light fabric of plain-weave or twill-weave silk or rayon, usually with a printed design [c19 from F, from ?]

Foulness (faʊlˈnɛs) *n* a flat marshy island in SE England, in Essex north of the Thames estuary

foul play *n* **1** violent or treacherous conduct, esp murder **2** a violation of the rules in a game or sport

foul up *vb* (*adv*) **1** (*tr*) to bungle **2** (*tr*) to contaminate **3** to be or cause to be blocked, choked, or entangled ▷ *n* **foul-up 4** a state of confusion or muddle caused by bungling

found[1] (faʊnd) *vb* **1** the past tense and past participle of find ▷ *adj* **2** furnished or fitted out **3** *Brit* with meals, heating, etc, provided without extra charge

found[2] (faʊnd) *vb* **1** (*tr*) to bring into being or establish (something, such as an institution, etc) **2** (*tr*) to build or establish the foundation of **3** (*also intr; foll by on or upon*) to have a basis (in) [c13 from OF, from L, from *fundus* bottom]

found[3] (faʊnd) *vb* (*tr*) **1** to cast (a material, such as metal or glass) by melting and pouring into a mould **2** to make (articles) in this way [c14 from OF, from L *fundere* to melt]

foundation (faʊnˈdeɪʃən) *n* **1** that on which something is founded **2** (*often pl*) a construction below the ground that distributes the load of a building, wall, etc **3** the base on which something stands **4** the act of founding or establishing or the state of being founded or established **5** an endowment for the support of an institution such as a school **6** an institution supported by an endowment, often one that provides funds for charities, research, etc **7** a cosmetic used as a base for make-up > **founˈdational** *adj*

foundation garment *n* a woman's undergarment worn to shape and support the figure. Also called: **foundation**

foundation stone *n* a stone laid at a ceremony to mark the foundation of a new building

foundation subjects *pl n Brit education.* the subjects studied as part of the National Curriculum, including the compulsory core subjects

founder[1] (ˈfaʊndə) *n* a person who establishes an institution, society, etc [c14 see FOUND[2]]

founder[2] (ˈfaʊndə) *vb* (*intr*) **1** (of a ship, etc) to sink **2** to break down or fail: *the project foundered* **3** to sink into or become stuck in soft ground **4** to collapse **5** (of a horse) to stumble or go lame [c13 from OF *fondrer* to submerge, from L *fundus* bottom]

> USAGE *Founder* is sometimes wrongly used where *flounder* is meant: *this unexpected turn of events left him floundering* (not *foundering*)

founder[3] (ˈfaʊndə) *n* **a** a person who makes metal castings **b** (*in combination*): *an iron founder* [c15 see FOUND[3]]

foundling (ˈfaʊndlɪŋ) *n* an abandoned infant whose parents are not known [c13 *foundeling*; see FIND]

foundry (ˈfaʊndrɪ) *n, pl* **foundries** a place in which metal castings are produced [c17 from OF, from *fondre*; see FOUND[3]]

fount[1] (faʊnt) *n* **1** *poetic* a spring or fountain **2** source [c16 back formation from FOUNTAIN]

fount[2] (faʊnt, fɒnt) *n printing* another name for **font**[2]

fountain (ˈfaʊntɪn) *n* **1** a jet or spray of water or some other liquid **2** a structure from which such a jet or a number of such jets spurt **3** a natural spring of water, esp the source of a stream **4** a stream, jet, or cascade of sparks, lava, etc **5** a principal source **6** a reservoir, as for oil in a lamp [c15 from OF, from LL, from L *fons* spring, source] > **'fountained** *adj*

fountainhead (ˈfaʊntɪn,hɛd) *n* **1** a spring that is the source of a stream **2** a principal or original source

fountain pen *n* a pen the nib of which is supplied with ink from a cartridge or a reservoir in its barrel

Fouqué (*German* fuˈkeː) *n* **Friedrich Heinrich Karl** (ˈfriːdrɪç ˈhainrɪç karl), Baron de la Motte. 1777–1843, German romantic writer; author of *Undine* (1811)

Fouquet (*French* fukɛ) *n* **1 Jean** (ʒɑ̃) ?1420–?80, French painter and miniaturist **2** Also: **Foucquet Belle-Isle, Nicolas** (nikɔla), *Marquis de Belle-Isle*. 1615–80, French statesman; superintendent of finance (1653–61) under Louis XIV. He was imprisoned for embezzlement, having been denounced by Colbert

Fouquier-Tinville (*French* fukjetɛ̃vil) *n* **Antoine Quentin** (ɑ̃twan kɑ̃tɛ̃) 1746–95, French revolutionary; as public prosecutor (1793–94) during the Reign of Terror, he sanctioned the guillotining of Desmoulins, Danton, and Robespierre

four (fɔː) *n* **1** the cardinal number that is the sum of three and one **2** a numeral, 4, IV, etc, representing this number **3** something representing, represented by, or consisting of four units, such as a playing card with four symbols on it **4** Also called: **four o'clock** four hours after noon or midnight **5** *cricket* **5a** a shot that crosses the boundary after hitting the ground **5b** the four runs scored for such a shot **6** *rowing* **6a** a racing shell propelled by four oarsmen **6b** the crew of such a shell ▷ *determiner* **7a** amounting to four: *four times* **7b** (*as pronoun*): *four are ready* [OE *fēower*]

four-by-four *n* a vehicle equipped with four-wheel drive

four flush *n* a useless poker hand, containing four of a suit and one odd card

fourfold (ˈfɔː,fəʊld) *adj* **1** equal to or having four times as many or as much **2** composed of four parts ▷ *adv* **3** by or up to four times as many or as much

Fourier (ˈfʊərɪ,eɪ; *French* furje) *n* **1** (**François Marie**) **Charles** (ʃarl) 1772–1837, French social reformer: propounded a system of cooperatives known as Fourierism, esp in his work *Le Nouveau monde industriel* (1829–30) **2 Jean Baptiste Joseph** (ʒɑ̃ batist ʒozɛf) 1768–1830, French mathematician, Egyptologist, and administrator, noted particularly for his research on the theory of heat and the method of analysis named after him

four-in-hand *n* **1** a road vehicle drawn by four horses and driven by one driver **2** a four-horse team **3** *US* a long narrow tie tied in a flat slipknot with the ends dangling

four-leaf clover *or* **four-leaved clover** *n* a clover with four leaves rather than three, supposed to bring good luck

four-letter word *n* any of several short English words referring to sex or excrement: regarded generally as offensive or obscene

Fournier (*French* furnje) *n* See **Alain-Fournier**

four-o'clock *n* a tropical American plant, cultivated for its tubular yellow, red, or white flowers that open in late afternoon. Also called: **marvel-of-Peru**

four-poster *n* a bed with posts at each corner supporting a canopy and curtains

fourscore (,fɔːˈskɔː) *determiner* an archaic word for **eighty**

foursome (ˈfɔːsəm) *n* **1** a set or company of four **2** Also called: **four-ball** *golf* a game between two pairs of players

foursquare (,fɔːˈskwɛə) *adv* **1** squarely; firmly ▷ *adj* **2** solid and strong **3** forthright **4** a rare word for **square**

four-stroke *adj* designating an internal-combustion engine in which the piston makes four strokes for every explosion

fourteen (ˈfɔːˈtiːn) *n* **1** the cardinal number that is the sum of ten and four **2** a numeral, 14, XIV, etc, representing this number **3** something represented by or consisting of 14 units ▷ *determiner* **4a** amounting to fourteen: *fourteen cats* **4b** (*as pronoun*): *the fourteen who remained* [OE *fēowertīene*] > **'fourˈteenth** *adj, n*

fourth (fɔːθ) *adj* (*usually prenominal*) **1a** coming after the third in order, position, time, etc Often written: 4th **1b** (*as n*): *the fourth in succession* **2** denoting the highest forward ratio of a gearbox in most motor vehicles ▷ *n*

3 *music* **3a** the interval between one note and another four notes away from it in a diatonic scale **3b** one of two notes constituting such an interval in relation to the other **4** the fourth forward ratio of a gearbox in a motor vehicle, usually the highest gear in cars **5** a less common word for **quarter** (sense 2) ▷ *adv* **6** Also: **fourthly** after the third person, position, event, etc ▷ *sentence connector* **7** Also: **fourthly** as the fourth point

fourth dimension *n* **1** the dimension of time, which in addition to three spatial dimensions specifies the position of a point or particle **2** the concept in science fiction of a dimension in addition to three spatial dimensions > ˌ**fourth-diˈmensional** *adj*

fourth estate *n* (*sometimes caps*) journalists or their profession; the press

four-wheel drive *n* a system used in motor vehicles in which all four wheels are connected to the source of power

fovea (ˈfəʊvɪə) *n, pl* **foveae** (-vɪˌiː) *anat* any small pit or depression in the surface of a bodily organ or part [c19 from L: a small pit]

Fowey (fɔɪ) *n* a resort and fishing village in SW England, in Cornwall, linked administratively with St Austell in 1968. Pop: 1939 (1991)

fowl (faʊl) *n* **1** Also called: **domestic fowl** a domesticated gallinaceous bird occurring in many varieties **2** any other bird that is used as food or hunted as game **3** the flesh or meat of fowl, esp of chicken **4** an archaic word for any **bird** ▷ *vb* **5** (*intr*) to hunt or snare wildfowl [OE *fugol*] > ˈ**fowler** *n* > ˈ**fowling** *n, adj*

Fowler (ˈfaʊlə) *n* **Henry Watson** 1858–1933, English lexicographer and grammarian; compiler of *Modern English Usage* (1926)

Fowliang *or* **Fou-liang** (ˈfuːˈljæŋ) *n* a variant transliteration of the Chinese name for **Jingdezhen**

fowl pest *n* an acute and usually fatal viral disease of domestic fowl, characterized by discoloration of the comb and wattles

fox (fɒks) *n, pl* **foxes** *or* **fox** **1** any canine mammal of the genus *Vulpes* and related genera. They are mostly predators and have a pointed muzzle and a bushy tail **2** the fur of any of these animals, usually reddish-brown or grey in colour **3** a person who is cunning and sly ▷ *vb* **4** (*tr*) *inf* to perplex: *to fox a person with a problem* **5** to cause (paper, wood, etc) to become discoloured with spots, or (of paper, etc) to become discoloured **6** (*tr*) to trick; deceive **7** (*intr*) to act deceitfully or craftily [OE] > ˈ**foxˌlike** *adj*

Fox (fɒks) *n* **1** **Charles James** 1749–1806, British Whig statesman and orator. He opposed North over taxation of the American colonies and Pitt over British intervention against the French Revolution. He advocated parliamentary reform and the abolition of the slave trade **2** **George** 1624–91, English religious leader; founder (1647) of the Society of Friends (Quakers) **3** **Vicente** (*Spanish* viˈθente) born 1942, Mexican politician; president of Mexico from 2000 **4** Sir **William** 1812–93, New Zealand statesman, born in England: prime minister of New Zealand (1856; 1861–62; 1869–72; 1873)

Foxe (fɒks) *n* **John** 1516–87, English Protestant clergyman; author of *History of the Acts and Monuments of the Church* (1563), popularly known as the *Book of Martyrs*

Foxe Basin (fɒks) *n* an arm of the Atlantic in NE Canada, between Melville Peninsula and Baffin Island

foxfire (ˈfɒksˌfaɪə) *n* a luminescent glow emitted by certain fungi on rotting wood

foxglove (ˈfɒksˌglʌv) *n* a plant having spikes of purple or white thimble-like flowers. The soft wrinkled leaves are a source of digitalis [OE]

foxhole (ˈfɒksˌhəʊl) *n* *mil* a small pit dug to provide shelter against hostile fire

foxhound (ˈfɒksˌhaʊnd) *n* a breed of short-haired hound, usually kept for hunting foxes

fox hunt *n* **1a** the hunting of foxes with hounds **1b** an instance of this **2** an organization for fox-hunting within a particular area > ˈ**fox-ˌhunter** *n* > ˈ**fox-ˌhunting** *n*

foxtail (ˈfɒksˌteɪl) *n* any grass of Europe, Asia, and South America, having soft cylindrical spikes of flowers: cultivated as a pasture grass

Fox Talbot (ˈtɔːlbət) *n* **William Henry** 1800–77, English physicist; a pioneer of photography

fox terrier *n* either of two breeds of small tan-black-and-white terrier, the wire-haired and the smooth

foxtrot (ˈfɒksˌtrɒt) *n* **1** a ballroom dance in quadruple time, combining short and long steps in various sequences ▷ *vb* **foxtrots, foxtrotting, foxtrotted** **2** (*intr*) to perform this dance

foxy (ˈfɒksɪ) *adj* **foxier, foxiest** **1** of or resembling a fox, esp in craftiness **2** of a reddish-brown colour **3** (of paper, etc) spotted, esp by mildew **4** *sl* sexy; sexually attractive > ˈ**foxily** *adv* > ˈ**foxiness** *n*

foyer (ˈfɔɪeɪ, ˈfɔɪə) *n* a hall, lobby, or anteroom, as in a hotel, theatre, cinema, etc [c19 from F: fireplace, from Med. L, from L *focus* fire]

fp *music abbrev for* forte-piano

FP *abbrev for:* **1** fire plug **2** former pupil **3** Also: **fp** freezing point

FPA *abbrev for* Family Planning Association

fps *abbrev for:* **1** feet per second **2** foot-pound-second **3** *photog* frames per second

fps units *pl n* an Imperial system of units based on the foot, pound, and second as the units of length, mass, and time

Fr *abbrev for:* **1** *Christianity:* **1a** Father **1b** Frater [L: brother] **2** *the chemical symbol for* francium

fr. *abbrev for* franc

Fr. *abbrev for:* **1** France **2** French

Fra (frɑː) *n* brother: a title given to an Italian monk or friar [It., short for *frate* brother, from L *frāter* BROTHER]

fracas (ˈfrækɑː) *n* a noisy quarrel; brawl [c18 from F, from *fracasser* to shatter, from L *frangere* to break, infl. by *quassāre* to shatter]

fractal (ˈfræktəl) *n* any of various irregular and fragmented shapes or surfaces that are generated by a series of successive subdivisions [c20 from L *frāctus*, p.p. of *frangere* to break]

fraction (ˈfrækʃən) *n* **1** *maths* a ratio of two expressions or numbers other than zero **2** any part or subdivision **3** a small piece; fragment **4** *chem* a component of a mixture separated by fractional distillation **5** *Christianity* the formal breaking of the bread in Communion [c14 from LL, from L *fractus* broken, from *frangere* to break] > ˈ**fractional** *adj* > ˈ**fractionˌize** *or* ˈ**fractionˌise** *vb*

fractional crystallization *n* *chem* the process of separating the components of a solution on the basis of their different solubilities, by means of evaporating the solution until the least soluble component crystallizes out

fractional distillation *n* the process of separating the constituents of a liquid mixture by heating it and condensing separately the components according to their different boiling points. Sometimes shortened to **distillation**

fractionate (ˈfrækʃəˌneɪt) *vb* **fractionates, fractionating, fractionated** **1** to separate or cause to separate into constituents **2** (*tr*) *chem* to obtain (a constituent of a mixture) by a fractional process > ˌ**fractionˈation** *n*

fractious (ˈfrækʃəs) *adj* **1** irritable **2** unruly [c18 from (obs.) *fraction* discord + -OUS] > ˈ**fractiously** *adv* > ˈ**fractiousness** *n*

fracture (ˈfræktʃə) *n* **1** the act of breaking or the state of being broken **2a** the breaking or cracking of a bone or the tearing of a cartilage **2b** the resulting condition **3** a

Ff

division, split, or breach **4** *mineralogy* **4a** the characteristic appearance of the surface of a freshly broken mineral or rock **4b** the way in which a mineral or rock naturally breaks ▷ *vb* **fractures, fracturing, fractured** **5** to break or cause to break **6** to break or crack (a bone) or (of a bone) to become broken or cracked [c15 from OF, from L, from *frangere* to break] > **'fractural** *adj*

fraenum *or* **frenum** ('fri:nəm) *n, pl* **fraena** *or* **frena** (-nə) a fold of membrane or skin, such as the fold beneath the tongue [c18 from L: bridle]

fragile ('frædʒaɪl) *adj* **1** able to be broken easily **2** in a weakened physical state **3** delicate; light: *a fragile touch* **4** slight; tenuous [c17 from L *fragilis*, from *frangere* to break] > **'fragilely** *adv* > **fragility** (frə'dʒɪlɪtɪ) *n*

fragment *n* ('frægmənt) **1** a piece broken off or detached **2** an incomplete piece: *fragments of a novel* **3** a scrap; bit ▷ *vb* (fræg'mɛnt) **4** to break or cause to break into fragments [c15 from L *fragmentum*, from *frangere* to break] > **,fragmen'tation** *n*

fragmentary ('frægməntərɪ) *adj* made up of fragments; disconnected. Also: **fragmental**

Fragonard (*French* fragɔnar) *n* **Jean-Honoré** (ʒɑ̃ ɔnɔre) 1732–1806, French artist, noted for richly coloured paintings typifying the frivolity of 18th- century French court life

fragrance ('freɪgrəns) *or* **fragrancy** *n, pl* **fragrances** *or* **fragrancies** **1** a pleasant or sweet odour **2** the state of being fragrant

fragrant ('freɪgrənt) *adj* having a pleasant or sweet smell [c15 from L, from *frāgrāre* to emit a smell] > **'fragrantly** *adv*

frail[1] (freɪl) *adj* **1** physically weak and delicate **2** fragile: *a frail craft* **3** easily corrupted or tempted [c13 from OF *frele*, from L *fragilis*, FRAGILE]

frail[2] (freɪl) *n* **1** a rush basket for figs or raisins **2** a quantity of raisins or figs equal to between 50 and 75 pounds [c13 from OF *fraiel*, from ?]

frailty ('freɪltɪ) *n, pl* **frailties** **1** physical or moral weakness **2** (*often pl*) a fault symptomatic of moral weakness

framboesia *or US* **frambesia** (fræm'bi:zɪə) *n pathol* another name for **yaws** [c19 from NL, from F *framboise* raspberry; from its raspberry-like excrescences]

frame (freɪm) *n* **1** an open structure that gives shape and support to something, such as the ribs of a ship's hull or an aircraft's fuselage or the beams of a building **2** an enclosing case or border into which something is fitted: *the frame of a picture* **3** the system around which something is built up: *the frame of government* **4** the structure of the human body **5** a condition; state (esp in **frame of mind**) **6a** one of a series of exposures on film used in making motion pictures **6b** an exposure on a film used in still photography **7** a television picture scanned by one or more electron beams at a particular frequency **8** *snooker, etc* **8a** the wooden triangle used to set up the balls **8b** the balls when set up **8c** a single game finished when all the balls have been potted **9** (on a website) a self-contained section that functions independently from other parts; by using frames a designer can make some areas of a website remain constant while others change according to choices made by the user **10** short for **cold frame** **11** one of the sections of which a beehive is composed, esp one designed to hold a honeycomb **12** *statistics* an enumeration of a population for the purposes of sampling **13** *sl* another word for **frame-up** **14** *obs* shape; form ▷ *vb* **frames, framing, framed** (*mainly tr*) **15** to construct by fitting parts together **16** to draw up the plans or basic details for: *to frame a policy* **17** to compose or conceive: *to frame a reply* **18** to provide, support, or enclose with a frame: *to frame a picture* **19** to form (words) with the lips, esp silently **20** *sl* to conspire to incriminate (someone) on a false charge [OE *framiae* to avail] > **'frameless** *adj* > **'framer** *n*

Frame (freɪm) *n* **Janet** 1924–2004, New Zealand writer: author of the novels *Owls Do Cry* (1957) and *Faces in the Water* (1961), the collection of verse *The Pocket* (1967), and volumes of autobiography including *An Angel at My Table* (1984), which was made into a film in 1990

frame house *n* a house that has a timber framework and cladding

frame of reference *n* **1** *sociol* a set of standards that determines and sanctions behaviour **2** any set of planes or curves, such as the three coordinate axes, used to locate a point in space

frame-up *n sl* **1** a conspiracy to incriminate someone on a false charge **2** a plot to bring about a dishonest result, as in a contest

framework ('freɪm,wɜ:k) *n* **1** a structural plan or basis of a project **2** a structure or frame supporting or containing something

franc (fræŋk; *French* frɑ̃) *n* **1** the former standard monetary unit of France, most French dependencies, Andorra, and Monaco, divided into 100 centimes. Also called: **French franc** **2** the standard monetary unit, comprising 100 centimes, of various countries including Belgium, Benin, Burkina-Faso, Cameroon, the Central African Republic, Congo-Brazzaville, Gabon, Guinea, Guinea-Bissau, Liechtenstein, Luxembourg, Mauritania, Niger, Senegal, Switzerland, Togo, etc **3** a Moroccan monetary unit worth one hundredth of a dirham [c14 from OF; from L *Rex Francōrum* King of the Franks, inscribed on 14th-century francs]

France[1] (frɑ:ns) *n* a republic in W Europe, between the English Channel, the Mediterranean, and the Atlantic: the largest country wholly in Europe; became a republic in 1793 after the French Revolution and an empire in 1804 under Napoleon; reverted to a monarchy (1815–48), followed by the Second Republic (1848–52), the Second Empire (1852–70), the Third Republic (1870–1940), and the Fourth and Fifth Republics (1946 and 1958); a member of the European Union. It is generally flat or undulating in the north and west and mountainous in the south and east. Official language: French. Religion: Roman Catholic majority. Currency: euro. Capital: Paris. Pop: 59 090 000 (2001 est). Area: (including Corsica) 551 600 sq km (212 973 sq miles). Related adjs: **French, Gallic**

▷ www.assemblee-nationale.com/english/index.asp
▷ www.francetourism.com

France[2] (*French* frɑ̃s) *n* **Anatole** (anatɔl), real name *Anatole François Thibault*. 1844–1924, French novelist, short-story writer, and critic. His works include *Le Crime de Sylvestre Bonnard* (1881), *L'Île des Pingouins* (1908), and *La Révolte des anges* (1914): Nobel prize for literature 1921

Francesca (*Italian* fran'tʃeska) *n* See **Piero Della Francesca**

Franche-Comté (*French* frɑ̃ʃkɔ̃te) *n* a region of E France, covering the Jura and the low country east of the Saône: part of the Kingdom of Burgundy (6th cent. AD–1137); autonomous as the Free County of Burgundy (1137–1384); under Burgundian rule again (1384–1477) and Hapsburg rule (1493–1674); annexed by France (1678)

franchise ('fræntʃaɪz) *n* **1** (usually preceded by *the*) the right to vote, esp for representatives in a legislative body **2** any exemption, privilege, or right granted to an individual or group by a public authority **3** *commerce* authorization granted by a manufacturing enterprise to a distributor to market the manufacturer's products **4** the full rights of citizenship ▷ *vb* **franchises, franchising, franchised** **5** (*tr*) *commerce, chiefly US & Canad* to grant (a person, firm, etc) a franchise [c13 from OF, from *franchir* to set free, from *franc* free] > **,franchi'see** *n* > **franchisement** ('fræntʃɪzmənt) *n* > **'franchiser** *n*

Francis ('frɑ:nsɪs) *n* **1** **Dick**, full name *Richard Stanley*

Francis. born 1920, British thriller writer, formerly a champion jockey. His books include *Dead Cert* (1962), *The Edge* (1988), and *Come to Grief* (1995) **2** Sir **Philip** 1740–1818, British politician; probable author of the *Letters of Junius* (1769–72) He played an important part in the impeachment of Warren Hastings (1788–95)

Francis I *n* **1** 1494–1547, king of France (1515–47) His reign was dominated by his rivalry with Emperor Charles V for the control of Italy. He was a noted patron of the arts and learning **2** 1708–65, duke of Lorraine (1729–37), grand duke of Tuscany (1737–65), and Holy Roman Emperor (1745–65). His marriage (1736) to Maria Theresa led to the War of the Austrian Succession (1740–48) **3** title as emperor of Austria of **Francis II**

Francis II *n* **1** 1544–60, king of France (1559–60); son of Henry II and Catherine de' Medici; first husband of Mary, Queen of Scots **2** 1768–1835, last Holy Roman Emperor (1792–1806) and, as Francis I, first emperor of Austria (1804–35). The Holy Roman Empire was dissolved (1806) following his defeat by Napoleon at Austerlitz

Franciscan (fræn'sɪskən) *n* **a** a member of a Christian religious order of friars or nuns tracing their origins back to Saint Francis of Assisi **b** (*as modifier*): *a Franciscan friary*

Francis of Assisi *n* **Saint** original name *Giovanni di Bernardone.* ?1181–1226, Italian monk; founder of the Franciscan order of friars. He is remembered for his humility and love for all creation and was the first person to exhibit stigmata (1224). Feast day: Oct. 4

Francis of Sales (seɪlz; *French* sal) *n* **Saint** 1567–1622, French ecclesiastic and theologian; bishop of Geneva (1602–22) and an opponent of Calvinism; author of *Introduction to a Devout Life* (1609) and founder of the Order of the Visitation (1610). Feast day: Jan. 24

Francis Xavier ('zeɪvɪə) *n* **Saint** See (Saint Francis) **Xavier**

francium ('frænsɪəm) *n* an unstable radioactive element of the alkali-metal group, occurring in minute amounts in uranium ores. Symbol: Fr; atomic no.: 87; half-life of most stable isotope, ^{223}Fr: 22 minutes [c20 from NL, from FRANCE + -IUM; because first found in France]

francize *or* **francise** ('frænsaɪz) *vb* **francizes, francizing, francized** *or* **francises, francising, francised** *Canad* to make or become French-speaking > ˌ**franci'zation** *or* ˌ**franci'sation** *n*

Franck *n* **1** (*French* frɑ̃k) **César** (**Auguste**) (sezar) 1822–90, French composer, organist, and teacher, born in Belgium. His works, some of which make use of cyclic form, include a violin sonata, a string quartet, the *Symphony in D Minor* (1888), and much organ music **2** (fræŋk) **James** 1882–1964, US physicist, born in Germany: shared a Nobel prize for physics with Gustav Hertz (1925) for work on the quantum theory, particularly the effects of bombarding atoms with electrons

Franco ('fræŋkəʊ; *Spanish* 'fraŋko) *n* **Francisco** (fran'θisko), called *el Caudillo.* 1892–1975, Spanish general and statesman; head of state (1939–1975). He was commander-in- chief of the Falangists in the Spanish Civil War (1936–39), defeating the republican government and establishing a dictatorship (1939). He kept Spain neutral in World War II

Franco- ('fræŋkəʊ-) *combining form* indicating France or French: *Franco-Prussian* [from Med. L *Francus,* from LL: FRANK[1]]

francolin ('fræŋkəʊlɪn) *n* an African or Asian partridge [c17 from F, from OIt. *francolino,* from ?]

Franconia (fræŋ'kəʊnɪə) *n* a medieval duchy of Germany, inhabited by the Franks from the 7th century, now chiefly in Bavaria, Hesse, and Baden-Württemberg

Franconian (fræŋ'kəʊnɪən) *n* **1** a group of medieval Germanic dialects spoken by the Franks in an area from N Bavaria and Alsace to the mouth of the Rhine. **Low Franconian** developed into Dutch, while **Upper Franconian** contributed to High German, of which it remains a recognizable dialect. See also **Old Low German, Old High German, Frankish** ▷ *adj* **2** of or relating to Franconia, the Franks, or their languages

Francophobe ('fræŋkəʊˌfəʊb) *n* **1** a person who hates or fears France or its people **2** *Canad* a person who hates or fears Canadian Francophones

Francophone ('fræŋkəʊˌfəʊn) (*often not cap*) ▷ *n* **1** a person who speaks French, esp a native speaker ▷ *adj* **2** speaking French as a native language **3** using French as a lingua franca

frangible ('frændʒɪbᵊl) *adj* breakable or fragile [c15 from OF, ult. from L *frangere* to break] > ˌ**frangi'bility** *or* '**frangibleness** *n*

frangipane ('frændʒɪˌpeɪn) *n* **1** a pastry filled with cream and flavoured with almonds **2** a variant of **frangipani** (the perfume)

frangipani (ˌfrændʒɪ'pɑːnɪ) *n, pl* **frangipanis** *or* **frangipani** **1** a tropical American shrub cultivated for its waxy white or pink flowers, which have a sweet overpowering scent **2** a perfume prepared from this plant or resembling the odour of its flowers **3 native frangipani** *Austral* an Australian evergreen tree with large fragrant yellow flowers [c17 via F from It.: perfume for scenting gloves, after the Marquis Muzio *Frangipani,* 16th-century Roman nobleman who invented it]

Franglais ('frɒŋgleɪ; *French* frɑ̃glɛ) *n* informal French containing a high proportion of English [c20 from *français* French + *anglais* English]

frank (fræŋk) *adj* **1** honest and straightforward in speech or attitude: *a frank person* **2** outspoken or blunt **3** open and avowed: *frank interest* ▷ *vb* (*tr*) **4** *chiefly Brit* to put a mark on (a letter, etc), either cancelling the postage stamp or in place of a stamp, ensuring free carriage **5** to mark (a letter, etc) with an official mark or signature, indicating the right of free delivery **6** to facilitate or assist (a person) to enter easily **7** to obtain immunity for (a person) ▷ *n* **8** an official mark or signature affixed to a letter, etc, ensuring free delivery or delivery without stamps [c13 from OF, from Med. L *francus* free; identical with FRANK[1] (in Frankish Gaul only members of this people enjoyed full freedom)] > '**frankable** *adj* > '**franker** *n* > '**frankness** *n*

Ff

Frank[1] (fræŋk) *n* a member of a group of West Germanic peoples who spread from the east in the late 4th century AD, gradually conquering most of Gaul and Germany [OE *Franca;* ?from the name of a Frankish weapon (cf. OE *franca* javelin)]

Frank[2] (*Dutch* fraŋk) *n* **1 Anne** 1929–45, German Jewess, whose *Diary* (1947) recorded the experiences of her family while in hiding from the Nazis in Amsterdam (1942–44). They were betrayed and she died in a concentration camp **2 Robert** born 1924, US photographer and film maker, born in Switzerland; best known for his photographic book *The Americans* (1959)

Frankenstein ('fræŋkɪnˌstaɪn) *n* **1** a person who creates something that brings about his or her ruin **2** Also called: **Frankenstein's monster** a thing that destroys its creator [c19 after Baron *Frankenstein,* who created a destructive monster from parts of corpses in the novel by Mary Shelley (1818)] > ˌ**Franken'steinian** *adj*

Frankenstein food *n facetious* any foodstuff that has been genetically modified [c20 from FRANKENSTEIN, alluding to its unnatural origin]

Frankfort ('fræŋkfət) *n* **1** a city in N Kentucky: the state capital. Pop: 25 535 (1990) **2** *now rare* an English spelling of **Frankfurt**

Frankfurt (**am Main**) (*German* 'fraŋkfʊrt (am 'main)) *n* a city in central Germany, in Hesse on the Main River: a Roman settlement in the 1st century; a free imperial city (1372–1806); seat of the federal assembly (1815–66); university (1914); trade fairs since the 13th century. Pop: 644 700 (1999 est)

Frankfurt (**an der Oder**) (*German* 'fraŋkfʊrt (an der 'oːdər)) *n* a city in E Germany on the Polish border: member of the Hanseatic League (1368–1450). Pop: 85 360 (1991)

frankfurter ('fræŋk,fɜːtə) *n* a smoked sausage, made of finely minced pork or beef [c20 short for G *Frankfurter Wurst* sausage from FRANKFURT AM MAIN]

Frankfurter ('fræŋk,fɜːtə) *n* an inhabitant or native of Frankfurt

frankincense ('fræŋkɪn,sɛns) *n* an aromatic gum resin obtained from trees of the genus *Boswellia*, which occur in Asia and Africa [c14 from OF *franc* free, pure + *encens* INCENSE[1]; see FRANK]

Frankish ('fræŋkɪʃ) *n* **1** the ancient West Germanic language of the Franks ▷ *adj* **2** of or relating to the Franks or their language

franklin ('fræŋklɪn) *n* (in 14th- and 15th-century England) a substantial landholder of free but not noble birth [c13 from Anglo-F, from OF *franc* free, on the model of CHAMBERLAIN]

Franklin ('fræŋklɪn) *n* **1** **Aretha** (ə'riːθə) born 1942, US soul, pop, and gospel singer **2** **Benjamin** 1706–90, American statesman, scientist, and author. He helped draw up the Declaration of Independence (1776) and, as ambassador to France (1776–85), he negotiated an alliance with France and a peace settlement with Britain. As a scientist, he is noted particularly for his researches in electricity, esp his invention of the lightning conductor **3** Sir **John** 1786–1847, English explorer of the Arctic: lieutenant-governor of Van Diemen's Land (now Tasmania) (1836–43): died while on a voyage to discover the Northwest Passage **4** **Rosalind** 1920–58, British x-ray crystallographer. She contributed to the discovery of the structure of DNA, before her premature death from cancer

frankly ('fræŋklɪ) *adv* **1** (*sentence modifier*) to be honest **2** in a frank manner

frantic ('fræntɪk) *adj* **1** distracted with fear, pain, joy, etc **2** marked by or showing frenzy: *frantic efforts* [c14 from OF, from L *phrenēticus* mad] > **'frantically** *or* **'franticly** *adv*

Franz Ferdinand (*German* frants 'fɛrdinant) *n* English name *Francis Ferdinand*. 1863–1914, archduke of Austria; heir apparent of Franz Josef I. His assassination contributed to the outbreak of World War I

Franz Josef I (*German* frants 'joːzɛf) *n* English name *Francis Joseph I*. 1830–1916, emperor of Austria (1848–1916) and king of Hungary (1867–1916)

Franz Josef Land (*German* frants 'joːzɛf) *n* an archipelago of over 100 islands in the Arctic Ocean, administratively part of Russia. Area: about 21 000 sq km (8000 sq miles). Russian name: **Zemlya Frantsa Iosifa** (zji'mlja 'frantsə 'jɔsifə)

frappé ('fræpeɪ) *n* **1** a drink consisting of a liqueur, etc, poured over crushed ice ▷ *adj* **2** (*postpositive*) (esp of drinks) chilled [c19 from F, from *frapper* to strike, hence, chill]

Fraser[1] ('freɪzə) *n* a river in SW Canada, in S central British Columbia, flowing northwest, south, and west through spectacular canyons in the Coast Mountains to the Strait of Georgia. Length: 1370 km (850 miles)

Fraser[2] ('freɪzə) *n* **1** (**John**) **Malcolm** born 1930, Australian statesman; prime minister of Australia (1975–83) **2** **Peter** 1884–1950, New Zealand statesman, born in Scotland; prime minister (1940–49)

frater ('freɪtə) *n arch* a refectory [c13 from OF *fraiteur*, from *refreitor*, from LL *rēfectōrium* REFECTORY]

fraternal (frə'tɜːnᵊl) *adj* **1** of or suitable to a brother; brotherly **2** of a fraternity **3** designating twins of the same or opposite sex that developed from two separate fertilized ova ▷ Cf **identical** (sense 3) [c15 from L, from *frāter* brother] > **fra'ternalism** *n*

fraternity (frə'tɜːnɪtɪ) *n, pl* **fraternities** **1** a body of people united in interests, aims, etc: *the teaching fraternity* **2** brotherhood **3** *US & Canad* a secret society joined by male students, functioning as a social club

fraternize *or* **fraternise** ('frætə,naɪz) *vb* **fraternizes, fraternizing, fraternized** *or* **fraternises, fraternising, fraternised** (*intr; often foll by with*) to associate on friendly terms > **,fraterni'zation** *or* **,fraterni'sation** *n* > **'frater,nizer** *or* **'frater,niser** *n*

fratricide ('frætrɪ,saɪd, 'freɪ-) *n* **1** the act of killing one's brother **2** a person who kills his or her brother [c15 from L, from *frater* brother + -CIDE] > **,fratri'cidal** *adj*

Frau (fraʊ) *n, pl* **Frauen** ('fraʊən) *or* **Fraus** a married German woman: usually used as a title equivalent to *Mrs* [from OHG *frouwa*]

fraud (frɔːd) *n* **1** deliberate deception, trickery, or cheating intended to gain an advantage **2** an act or instance of such deception **3** *inf* a person who acts in a false or deceitful way [c14 from OF, from L *fraus* deception]

fraudster ('frɔːdstə) *n* a swindler

fraudulent ('frɔːdjʊlənt) *adj* **1** acting with or having the intent to deceive **2** relating to or proceeding from fraud [c15 from L *fraudulentus* deceitful] > **'fraudulence** *n* > **'fraudulently** *adv*

Frauenfeld (*German* 'frauənfɛlt) *n* a town in NE Switzerland, capital of Thurgau canton. Pop: 19 402 (1990)

fraught (frɔːt) *adj* **1** (*usually postpositive* and foll by *with*) filled or charged: *a venture fraught with peril* **2** *inf* showing or producing tension or anxiety [c14 from MDu. *vrachten*, from *vracht* FREIGHT]

Fräulein (*German* 'frɔylaɪn) *n, pl* **Fräulein** *or English* **Fräuleins** an unmarried German woman: often used as a title equivalent to *Miss* [from MHG *vrouwelīn*, dim. of *vrouwe* lady]

Fraunhofer (*German* 'fraunhoːfər) *n* **Joseph von** ('joːzɛf fɔn) 1787–1826, German physicist and optician, who investigated spectra of the sun, planets, and fixed stars, and improved telescopes and other optical instruments

Fraunhofer lines *pl n* a set of dark lines appearing in the continuous emission spectrum of the sun

fraxinella (,fræksɪ'nɛlə) *n* another name for **gas plant** [c17 from NL: a little ash tree, from L *frāxinus* ash]

fray[1] (freɪ) *n* **1** a noisy quarrel **2** a fight or brawl [c14 short for AFFRAY]

fray[2] (freɪ) *vb* **1** to wear or cause to wear away into loose threads, esp at an edge or end **2** to make or become strained or irritated **3** to rub or chafe (another object) [c14 from F *frayer* to rub, from L *fricāre* to rub]

Fray Bentos (,freɪ 'bɛntɒs) *n* a port in W Uruguay, on the River Uruguay: noted for meat-packing. Pop: 21 400 (1995 est)

Frazer ('freɪzə) *n* Sir **James George** 1854–1941, Scottish anthropologist; author of many works on primitive religion, and magic, esp *The Golden Bough* (1890)

Frazier ('freɪʒə) *n* **Joe** born 1944, US boxer: won the world heavyweight title in 1970 and was the first to beat Muhammad Ali professionally (1971)

frazil ('freɪzɪl) *n* small pieces of ice that form in water moving turbulently enough to prevent the formation of a sheet of ice [c19 from Canad F, from F *fraisil* cinders, ult. from L *fax* torch]

frazzle ('fræzᵊl) *inf* ▷ *vb* **frazzles, frazzling, frazzled** **1** to make or become exhausted or weary ▷ *n* **2** the state of being frazzled or exhausted **3** **to a frazzle** completely (esp in **burnt to a frazzle**) [c19 prob. from ME *faselen* to fray, from *fasel* fringe; infl. by FRAY[2]]

freak (friːk) *n* **1** a person, animal, or plant that is abnormal or deformed **2a** an object, event, etc, that is abnormal **2b** (*as modifier*): *a freak storm* **3** a personal whim or caprice **4** *inf* a person who acts or dresses in a markedly unconventional way **5** *inf* a person who is ardently fond of something specified: *a jazz freak* ▷ *vb* **6** See **freak out** [c16 from ?] > '**freakish** *adj* > '**freaky** *adj*

freak out *vb (adv) inf* to be or cause to be in a heightened emotional state

freckle ('frɛkᵊl) *n* **1** a small brownish spot on the skin developed by exposure to sunlight **2** any small area of discoloration ▷ *vb* **freckles, freckling, freckled 3** to mark or become marked with freckles or spots [c14 from ON *freknur*] > '**freckled** or '**freckly** *adj*

Fredericia (*Danish* freðə'redsja) *n* a port in Denmark, in E Jutland at the N end of the Little Belt. Pop: 28 000 (1990)

Frederick I ('frɛdrɪk) *n* **1** See **Frederick Barbarossa 2** 1657–1713, first king of Prussia (1701–13); son of Frederick William

Frederick II *n* **1** 1194–1250, Holy Roman Emperor (1220–50), king of Germany (1212–50), and king of Sicily (1198–1250) **2** See **Frederick the Great**

Frederick III *n* **1** 1415–93, Holy Roman Emperor (1452–93) and, as Frederick IV, king of Germany (1440–93) **2** called *the Wise*. 1463–1525, elector of Saxony (1486–1525). He protected Martin Luther in Wartburg Castle after the Diet of Worms (1521)

Frederick IV *n* See **Frederick III** (sense 1)

Frederick V *n* called *the Winter King*. 1596–1632, elector of the Palatinate (1610–23) and king of Bohemia (1619–20). He led the revolt of Bohemian Protestants at the beginning of the Thirty Years' War

Frederick IX *n* 1899–1972, king of Denmark (1947–72)

Frederick Barbarossa (ˌbɑːbə'rɒsə) *n* official title *Frederick I*. ?1123–90, Holy Roman Emperor (1155–90), king of Germany (1152–90). His attempt to assert imperial rights in Italy ended in his defeat at Legnano (1176) and the independence of the Lombard cities (1183)

Frederick the Great *n* official title *Frederick II*. 1712–86, king of Prussia (1740–86); son of Frederick William I. He gained Silesia during the War of Austrian Succession (1740–48) and his military genius during the Seven Years' War (1756–63) established Prussia as a European power. He was also a noted patron of the arts

Frederick William *n* called *the Great Elector*. 1620–88, elector of Brandenburg (1640–88)

Frederick William I *n* 1688–1740, king of Prussia (1713–40); son of Frederick I: reformed the Prussian army

Frederick William III *n* 1770–1840, king of Prussia (1797–1840)

Frederick William IV *n* 1795–1861, king of Prussia (1840–61). He submitted to the 1848 Revolution but refused the imperial crown offered by the Frankfurt Parliament (1849). In 1857 he became insane and his brother, William I, became regent (1858–61)

Fredericton ('frɛdrɪktən) *n* a city in SE Canada, capital of New Brunswick, on the St John River. Pop: 45 364 (1991)

Frederiksberg (*Danish* frɛðregs'bɛr) *n* a city in E Denmark, within the area of greater Copenhagen: founded in 1651 by King Frederick III. Pop: 88 002 (1995 est)

Fredrikstad (*Norwegian* 'frɛdrikstad) *n* a port in SE Norway at the entrance to Oslo Fjord. Pop: 26 546 (1990)

free (friː) *adj* **freer, freest 1** able to act at will; not under compulsion or restraint **2a** not enslaved or confined **2b** (*as n*): *land of the free* **3** (*often postpositive* and foll by *from*) not subject (to) or restricted (by some regulation, constraint, etc): *free from pain* **4** (of a country, etc) autonomous or independent **5** exempt from external direction: *free will* **6** not subject to conventional constraints: *free verse* **7** not exact or literal: *a free translation* **8** provided without charge: *free entertainment* **9** *law* (of property) **9a** not subject to payment of rent or performance of services; freehold **9b** not subject to any burden or charge; unencumbered **10** (*postpositive; often* foll by *of* or *with*) ready or generous in using or giving: *free with advice* **11** not occupied or in use; available: *a free cubicle* **12** (of a person) not busy **13** open or available to all **14** without charge to the subscriber or user: *freepost; freephone* **15** not fixed or joined; loose: *the free end of a chain* **16** without obstruction or impediment: *free passage* **17** *chem* chemically uncombined: *free nitrogen* **18** *logic* denoting an occurrence of a variable not bound by a quantifier ▷ Cf **bound**[1] (sense 8) **19** (of routines in figure skating competitions) chosen by the competitor **20** (of jazz) totally improvised **21 for free** *nonstandard* without charge or cost **22 free and easy** casual or tolerant; easy-going **23 make free with** to behave too familiarly towards ▷ *adv* **24** in a free manner; freely **25** without charge or cost **26** *naut* with the wind blowing from the quarter ▷ *vb* **frees, freeing, freed** (*tr*) **27** to set at liberty; release **28** to remove impediments from **29** (often foll by *of* or *from*) to relieve or rid (of obstacles, pain, etc) [OE *frēo*] > '**freely** *adv* > '**freeness** *n*

-free *adj combining form* free from: *trouble-free; lead-free petrol*

free alongside ship *adj* (of a shipment of goods) delivered to the dock without charge to the buyer, but excluding the cost of loading onto the vessel ▷ Cf **free on board**

free association *n psychoanal* a method of exploring a person's unconscious by eliciting words and thoughts that are associated with key words provided by a psychoanalyst

freebase ('friːˌbeɪs) *sl* ▷ *n* **1** cocaine that has been refined by heating it in ether or some other solvent ▷ *vb* **freebases, freebasing, freebased 2** (*tr*) to refine (cocaine) in this way **3** to smoke or inhale the fumes from (refined cocaine)

freebie ('friːbɪ) *n sl* something provided without charge

freeboard ('friːˌbɔːd) *n* the space or distance between the deck of a vessel and the waterline

freebooter ('friːˌbuːtə) *n* a person, such as a pirate, living from plunder [c16 from Du., from *vrijbuit* booty; see FILIBUSTER] > '**freeboot** *vb* (*intr*)

freeborn ('friːˌbɔːn) *adj* **1** not born in slavery **2** of or suitable for people not born in slavery

Free Church *n chiefly Brit* any Protestant Church, esp the Presbyterian, other than the Established Church

free city *n* a sovereign or autonomous city

freedman ('friːdˌmæn) *n, pl* **freedmen** a man who has been freed from slavery

freedom ('friːdəm) *n* **1** personal liberty, as from slavery, serfdom, etc **2** liberation, as from confinement or bondage **3** the quality or state of being free, esp to enjoy political and civil liberties **4** (usually foll by *from*) exemption or immunity: *freedom from taxation* **5** the right or privilege of unrestricted use or access: *the freedom of a city* **6** autonomy, self-government, or independence **7** the power or liberty to order one's own actions **8** *philosophy* the quality, esp of the will or the individual, of not being totally constrained **9** ease or frankness of manner: *she talked with complete freedom* **10** excessive familiarity of manner **11** ease and grace, as of movement [OE *frēodōm*]

freedom fighter *n* a militant revolutionary

free energy *n* a thermodynamic property that expresses the capacity of a system to perform work under certain conditions

free enterprise *n* an economic system in which commercial organizations compete for profit with little state control

free fall *n* **1** free descent of a body in which the gravitational force is the only force acting on it **2** the part of a parachute descent before the parachute opens

free flight *n* the flight of a rocket, missile, etc, when its engine has ceased to produce thrust

free-for-all *n inf* **1** a disorganized brawl or argument, usually involving all those present **2a** a contest, discussion, etc, that is open to everyone **2b** (*as modifier*): *a free-for-all contest*

free-form *adj arts* freely flowing, spontaneous

free hand *n* **1** unrestricted freedom to act (esp in **give (someone) a free hand**) ▷ *adj, adv* **freehand** **2** (done) by hand without the use of guiding instruments: *a freehand drawing*

free-handed *adj* generous or liberal; unstinting > ˌ**free-ˈhandedly** *adv*

freehold (ˈfriːˌhəʊld) *property law* ▷ *n* **1a** tenure by which land is held in fee simple, fee tail, or for life **1b** an estate held by such tenure ▷ *adj* **2** relating to or having the nature of freehold > ˈ**freeholder** *n*

free house *n Brit* a public house not bound to sell only one brewer's products

free kick *n soccer* a place kick awarded for a foul or infringement

freelance (ˈfriːˌlɑːns) *n* **1a** Also called: **freelancer** a self-employed person, esp a writer or artist, who is hired to do specific assignments **1b** (*as modifier*): *a freelance journalist* **2** (in medieval Europe) a mercenary soldier or adventurer ▷ *vb* **freelances, freelancing, freelanced** **3** to work as a freelance on (an assignment, etc) ▷ *adv* **4** as a freelance [c19 (in sense 2): later applied to politicians, writers, etc]

free-living *adj* **1** given to ready indulgence of the appetites **2** (of animals and plants) not parasitic > ˌ**free-ˈliver** *n*

freeloader (ˈfriːˌləʊdə) *n sl* a person who habitually depends on others for food, shelter, etc

free love *n* the practice of sexual relationships without fidelity to a single partner

freeman (ˈfriːmən) *n, pl* **freemen** **1** a person who is not a slave **2** a person who enjoys political and civil liberties **3** a person who enjoys a privilege, such as the freedom of a city

Freeman (ˈfriːmən) *n* **Cathy**, full name *Catherine Astrid Salome Freeman*. born 1973, Australian sprinter; winner of the 200m and 400m in the 1994 Commonwealth Games and the 400m in the 2000 Olympic Games

free market *n* **a** an economic system that allows supply and demand to regulate prices, wages, etc, rather than government policy **b** (*as modifier*): *a free-market economy*

freemartin (ˈfriːˌmɑːtɪn) *n* the female of a pair of twin calves of unlike sex that is imperfectly developed and sterile [c17 from ?]

Freemason (ˈfriːˌmeɪsᵊn) *n* a member of the widespread secret order, constituted in London in 1717, of **Free and Accepted Masons**, pledged to brotherly love, faith, and charity. Sometimes shortened to **Mason**

freemasonry (ˈfriːˌmeɪsᵊnrɪ) *n* natural or tacit sympathy and understanding

Freemasonry (ˈfriːˌmeɪsᵊnrɪ) *n* **1** the institutions, rites, practices, etc, of Freemasons **2** Freemasons collectively

free on board *adj* (of a shipment of goods) delivered on board ship or other carrier without charge to the buyer ▷ Cf **free alongside ship**

free port *n* **1** a port open to all commercial vessels on equal terms **2** a port that permits the duty-free entry of foreign goods intended for re-export

free radical *n* an atom or group of atoms containing at least one unpaired electron and existing for a brief period of time before reacting to produce a stable molecule

free-range *adj chiefly Brit* kept or produced in natural conditions: *free-range eggs*

free-select *vb* (*tr*) *Austral history* to select (areas of crown land) and acquire the freehold by a series of annual payments > ˈ**free-seˈlection** *n* > ˈ**free-seˈlector** *n*

freesia (ˈfriːzɪə) *n* a plant of Southern Africa, cultivated for its white, yellow, or pink tubular fragrant flowers [c19 NL, after F. H. T. *Freese* (died 1876), G physician]

free skating *n* either of two parts in a figure-skating competition in which the skater chooses the sequence of figures and the music and which are judged on technique and artistic presentation. The short programme consists of specified movements and the long programme is entirely the skater's own choice

free space *n* a region that has no gravitational and electromagnetic fields. It is used as an absolute standard and was formerly referred to as a vacuum

free-spoken *adj* speaking frankly or without restraint > ˌ**free-ˈspokenly** *adv*

freestanding (ˌfriːˈstændɪŋ) *adj* not attached to or supported by another object

Free State *n* a province of central South Africa; replaced Orange Free State in 1994. Capital: Bloemfontein. Pop: 2 782 500 (1995 est). Area: 129 480 sq km (49 992 sq miles)
▷ www.fs.gov.za
▷ www.fstourism.co.za

freestone (ˈfriːˌstəʊn) *n* **1** any fine-grained stone, esp sandstone or limestone, that can be worked in any direction without breaking **2** *bot* a fruit, such as a peach, in which the flesh separates readily from the stone

freestyle (ˈfriːˌstaɪl) *n* **1** a competition or race, as in swimming, in which each participant may use a style of his or her choice instead of a specified style **2a** **International freestyle** an amateur style of wrestling with an agreed set of rules **2b** Also called: **all-in wrestling** a style of professional wrestling with no internationally agreed set of rules

freethinker (ˌfriːˈθɪŋkə) *n* a person who forms his or her ideas and opinions independently of authority or accepted views, esp in matters of religion > **free thought** *n*

Freetown (ˈfriːˌtaʊn) *n* the capital and chief port of Sierra Leone: founded in 1787 for slaves freed and destitute in England. Pop: 822 000 (1999 est)

free trade *n* **1** international trade that is free of such government interference as protective tariffs **2** *arch* smuggling

free verse *n* unrhymed verse without a metrical pattern

freeware (ˈfriːˌwɛə) *n* computer software that may be distributed and used without payment

freeway (ˈfriːˌweɪ) *n US* **1** an expressway **2** a major road that can be used without paying a toll

freewheel (ˌfriːˈwiːl) *n* **1** a ratchet device in the rear hub of a bicycle wheel that permits the wheel to rotate freely while the pedals are stationary ▷ *vb* **2** (*intr*) to coast on a bicycle using the freewheel

free will *n* **1a** the apparent human ability to make choices that are not externally determined **1b** the doctrine that such human freedom of choice is not illusory ▷ Cf **determinism** **2** the ability to make a choice without outside coercion: *he left of his own free will*

Free World *n* **the** the non-Communist countries collectively

freeze (friːz) *vb* **freezes, freezing, froze, frozen** **1** to change (a liquid) into a solid as a result of a reduction in temperature, or (of a liquid) to solidify in this way **2** (when *intr*, sometimes foll by *over* or *up*) to cover, clog, or harden with ice, or become so covered, clogged, or hardened **3** to fix fast or become fixed (to something) because of the action of frost **4** (*tr*) to preserve (food) by subjection to extreme cold, as in a freezer **5** to feel or cause to feel the sensation or effects of extreme cold **6** to die or cause to die of extreme cold **7** to become or cause to become paralysed, fixed, or motionless, esp through fear, shock, etc **8** (*tr*) to cause (moving film) to stop at a particular frame **9** to make or become formal, haughty, etc, in manner **10** (*tr*) to fix (prices, incomes, etc) at a particular level **11** (*tr*) to forbid by law the exchange, liquidation, or collection of (loans, assets, etc) **12** (*tr*) to stop (a process) at a particular stage of development **13** (*intr*; foll by *onto*) *inf, chiefly US* to cling ▷ *n* **14** the act of freezing or state of being frozen **15** *meteorol* a spell of temperatures below freezing point, usually over a wide area **16** the fixing of incomes, prices, etc, by legislation ▷ *sentence substitute* **17** *chiefly US* a command to stop instantly or risk being shot [OE *frēosan*] > '**freezable** *adj*

freeze-dry *vb* **freeze-dries, freeze-drying, freeze-dried** (*tr*) to preserve (a substance) by rapid freezing and subsequently drying in a vacuum

freeze-frame *n* **1** *films, television* a single frame of a film repeated to give an effect like a still photograph **2** *video* a single frame of a video recording viewed as a still by stopping the tape ▷ *vb* **3** (*tr*) to make a freeze-frame of (an image)

freeze out *vb* (*tr, adv*) *inf* to exclude, as by unfriendly behaviour, etc

freezer ('fri:zə) *n* an insulated cold-storage cabinet for long-term storage of perishable foodstuffs. Also called: **deepfreeze**

freeze-up *n US & Canad inf* **a** the freezing of lakes, rivers, etc, in autumn or early winter **b** the time of year when this occurs

freezing ('fri:zɪŋ) *adj inf* extremely cold

freezing point *n* the temperature below which a liquid turns into a solid

freezing works *n Austral & NZ* a slaughterhouse at which animal carcasses are frozen for export

Frege (*German* 'fre:gə) *n* **Gottlob** 1848–1925, German logician and philosopher, who laid the foundations of modern formal logic and semantics in his *Begriffsschrift* (1879)

Freiburg (*German* 'fraibʊrk) *n* **1** a city in SW Germany, in SW Baden-Württemberg: under Austrian rule (1368–1805); university (1457). Pop: 201 000 (1999 est). Official name: **Freiburg im Breisgau** (ɪm 'braisgau) **2** the German name for **Fribourg**

freight (freɪt) *n* **1a** commercial transport that is slower and cheaper than express **1b** the price charged for such transport **1c** goods transported by this means **1d** (*as modifier*): *freight transport* **2** *chiefly Brit* a ship's cargo or part of it ▷ *vb* (*tr*) **3** to load with goods for transport [c16 from MDu *vrecht*, var. of *vracht*]

freightage ('freɪtɪdʒ) *n* **1** the commercial conveyance of goods **2** the goods so transported **3** the price charged for such conveyance

freighter ('freɪtə) *n* **1** a ship or aircraft designed for transporting cargo **2** a person concerned with the loading of a ship

freightliner ('freɪt,laɪnə) *n trademark* a type of goods train carrying containers that can be transferred onto lorries or ships

Fremantle ('fri:,mænt^əl) *n* a port in SW Western Australia, on the Indian Ocean. Pop: 24 000 (latest est)

French[1] (frɛntʃ) *n* **1** the official language of France: also an official language of Switzerland, Belgium, Canada, and certain other countries. It is the native language of approximately 70 million people; also used for diplomacy. Historically, French is an Indo-European language belonging to the Romance group. See also **Old French, Anglo-French** **2** **the French** (*functioning as plural*) the natives, citizens, or inhabitants of France collectively **3** See **French vermouth** ▷ *adj* **4** relating to, denoting, or characteristic of France, the French, or their language ▷ Related prefixes **Franco-, Gallo-** **5** (in Canada) of or relating to French Canadians [Old English *Frencisc* French, Frankish; see FRANK]
▷ www.institut-francais.org.uk
▷ www.alliancefrancaise.org.uk

French[2] (frɛntʃ) *n* Sir **John Denton Pinkstone**, 1st Earl of Ypres. 1852–1925, British field marshal in World War I: commanded the British Expeditionary Force in France and Belgium (1914–15); Lord Lieutenant of Ireland (1918–21)

French bread *n* white bread in a long slender loaf that has a crisp brown crust

French Cameroons *pl n* the part of Cameroon formerly administered by France (1919–60)

French Canada *n* the areas of Canada, esp in the province of Quebec, where French Canadians predominate

French Canadian *n* **1** a Canadian citizen whose native language is French ▷ *adj* **French-Canadian** **2** of or relating to French Canadians or their language

French chalk *n* a variety of talc used to mark cloth, remove grease stains, or as a dry lubricant

French doors *pl n* the US and Canad name for **French windows**

French dressing *n* a salad dressing made from oil and vinegar with seasonings; vinaigrette

French Equatorial Africa *n* the former French overseas territories of Chad, Gabon, Middle Congo, and Ubangi-Shari (1910–58)

French Foreign Legion *n* a unit of the French army formerly serving esp in French North African colonies
▷ www.foreignlegionlife.com

French fried potatoes *pl n* a more formal name for chips. Often shortened to **French fries, fries**

French Guiana *n* a French overseas region in NE South America, on the Atlantic: colonized by the French in about 1637; tropical forests. Capital: Cayenne. Pop: 168 000 (2001 est). Area: about 91 000 sq km (23 000 sq miles)

French Guianese *or* **Guianan** *adj* **1** of or relating to French Guiana or its inhabitants ▷ *n* **2** a native or inhabitant of French Guiana

French Guinea *n* a former French territory of French West Africa: became independent as Guinea in 1958

French horn *n music* a valved brass instrument with a funnel-shaped mouthpiece and a tube of conical bore coiled into a spiral

Frenchify ('frɛntʃɪ,faɪ) *vb* **Frenchifies, Frenchifying, Frenchified** *inf* to make or become French in appearance, etc

French India *n* a former French overseas territory in India, including Chandernagore and Pondicherry: restored to India between 1949 and 1954

French Indochina *n* the territories of SE Asia that were colonized by France and held mostly until 1954: included Cochin China, Annam, and Tonkin (now largely Vietnam), Cambodia, Laos, and Kuang-Chou Wan (returned to China in 1945, now Zhanjiang)

French kiss *n* a kiss involving insertion of the tongue into the partner's mouth

French knickers *pl n* women's wide-legged underpants

French leave *n* an unauthorized or unannounced absence or departure [c18 alluding to a custom in France of leaving without saying goodbye to one's host or hostess]

French letter *n Brit* a slang term for **condom**

Frenchman ('frɛntʃmən) *n, pl* **Frenchmen** a native, citizen, or inhabitant of France > '**French,woman** *fem n*

French Morocco *n* a former French protectorate in NW Africa, united in 1956 with Spanish Morocco and Tangier to form the kingdom of Morocco

French mustard *n* a mild mustard paste made with vinegar rather than water

French North Africa *n* the former French possessions of Algeria, French Morocco, and Tunisia

French Oceania *n* a former name (until 1958) of **French Polynesia**

French paradox *n* the theory that the lower incidence of heart disease in Mediterranean countries compared to that in the US is a consequence of the larger intake of flavonoids from red wine in these countries

French polish *n* **1** a varnish for wood consisting of shellac dissolved in alcohol **2** the gloss finish produced by this polish ▷ *vb* **French-polish** **3** to treat with French polish or give a French polish (to)

French Polynesia *n* a French overseas territory in the S Pacific Ocean, including the Society Islands, the Tuamotu group, the Gambier group, the Tubuai Islands, and the Marquesas Islands. Capital: Papeete, on Tahiti. Pop: 238 000 (2001 est). Area: about 4000 sq km (1500 sq miles). Former name (until 1958): **French Oceania**

French Revolutionary calendar *n* the calendar used in France between 1793 and 1805

French Revolutionary Calendar

- **Vendémiaire**
- **Brumaire**
- **Frimaire**
- **Nivôse**
- **Pluviôse**
- **Ventôse**
- **Germinal**
- **Floréal**
- **Prairial**
- **Messidor**
- **Thermidor** *or* **Fervidor**
- **Fructidor**

French seam *n* a seam in which the edges are not visible

French Somaliland *n* a former name (until 1967) of **Djibouti**

French Southern and Antarctic Territories *pl n* a French overseas territory, comprising Adélie Land in Antarctica and the islands of Amsterdam and St Paul and the Kerguelen and Crozet archipelagos in the S Indian Ocean

French Sudan *n* a former name (1898–1959) of **Mali**

French toast *n* **1** *Brit* toast cooked on one side only **2** bread dipped in beaten egg and lightly fried

French Togoland *n* a former United Nations Trust Territory in W Africa, administered by France (1946–60), now the independent republic of Togo

French West Africa *n* a former group (1895–1958) of French Overseas Territories: consisted of Senegal, Mauritania, French Sudan, Burkina-Faso, Niger, French Guinea, the Ivory Coast, and Dahomey

French windows *pl n* (*sometimes sing*) *Brit* a pair of casement windows extending to floor level and opening onto a balcony, garden, etc

frenetic (frɪˈnɛtɪk) *adj* distracted or frantic [c14 via OF, from L, from Gk, from *phrenitis* insanity, from *phrēn* mind] > **freˈnetically** *adv*

frenum (ˈfriːnəm) *n, pl* **frena** (-nə) a variant spelling (esp US) of **fraenum**

frenzy (ˈfrɛnzɪ) *n, pl* **frenzies** **1** violent mental derangement **2** wild excitement or agitation **3** a bout of wild or agitated activity: *a frenzy of preparations* ▷ *vb* **frenzies, frenzying, frenzied** **4** (*tr*) to drive into a frenzy [c14 from OF, from LL *phrēnēsis* madness, from LGk, ult. from Gk *phrēn* mind] > **ˈfrenzied** *adj*

Freon (ˈfriːˌɒn) *n trademark* any of a group of chemically unreactive gaseous or liquid derivatives of methane in which hydrogen atoms have been replaced by chlorine and fluorine atoms: used as aerosol propellants, refrigerants, and solvents

frequency (ˈfriːkwənsɪ) *n, pl* **frequencies** **1** the state of being frequent **2** the number of times that an event occurs within a given period **3** *physics* the number of times that a periodic function or vibration repeats itself in a specified time, often 1 second. It is usually measured in hertz **4** *statistics* **4a** the number of individuals in a class (**absolute frequency**) **4b** the ratio of this number to the total number of individuals under survey (**relative frequency**) **5** *ecology* the number of individuals of a species within a given area [c16 from L, from *frequēns* crowded]

frequency distribution *n statistics* the function of the distribution of a sample corresponding to the probability density function of the underlying population and tending to it as the sample size increases

frequency modulation *n* a method of transmitting information using a radio-frequency carrier wave. The frequency of the carrier wave is varied in accordance with the amplitude of the input signal, the amplitude of the carrier remaining unchanged ▷ Cf **amplitude modulation**

frequent *adj* (ˈfriːkwənt) **1** recurring at short intervals **2** habitual ▷ *vb* (frɪˈkwɛnt) **3** (*tr*) to visit repeatedly or habitually [c16 from L *frequēns* numerous] > **ˌfrequenˈtation** *n* > **freˈquenter** *n* > **ˈfrequently** *adv*

frequentative (frɪˈkwɛntətɪv) *grammar* ▷ *adj* **1** denoting an aspect of verbs in some languages used to express repeated or habitual action **2** (in English) denoting a verb or an affix meaning repeated action, such as the verb *wrestle*, from *wrest* ▷ *n* **3** a frequentative verb or affix

fresco (ˈfrɛskəʊ) *n, pl* **frescoes** *or* **frescos** **1** a very durable method of wall-painting using watercolours on wet plaster **2** a painting done in this way [c16 from It.: fresh plaster, from *fresco* (adj) fresh, cool, of Gmc origin]

Frescobaldi (*Italian* freskoˈbaldi) *n* **Girolamo** (dʒiˈrɔːlamo) 1583–1643, Italian organist and composer, noted esp for his organ and harpsichord music

fresh (frɛʃ) *adj* **1** newly made, harvested, etc: *fresh bread; fresh strawberries* **2** newly acquired, found, etc: *fresh publications* **3** novel; original: *a fresh outlook* **4** most recent: *fresh developments* **5** further; additional: *fresh supplies* **6** not canned, frozen, or otherwise preserved: *fresh fruit* **7** (of water) not salt **8** bright or clear: *a fresh morning* **9** chilly or invigorating: *a fresh breeze* **10** not tired; alert **11** not worn or faded: *fresh colours* **12** having a healthy or ruddy appearance **13** newly or just arrived: *fresh from the presses* **14** youthful or inexperienced **15** *inf* presumptuous or disrespectful; forward ▷ *n* **16** the fresh part or time of something **17** another name for **freshet** ▷ *adv* **18** in a fresh manner [OE *fersc* fresh, unsalted] > **ˈfreshly** *adv* > **ˈfreshness** *n*

fresh breeze *n* a wind of force 5 on the Beaufort scale, blowing at speeds between 19 and 24 mph

freshen (ˈfrɛʃən) *vb* **1** to make or become fresh or fresher **2** (often foll by *up*) to refresh (oneself), esp by washing **3** (*intr*) (of the wind) to increase

fresher (ˈfrɛʃə) *or* **freshman** (ˈfrɛʃmən) *n, pl* **freshers** *or* **freshmen** a first-year student at college or university

freshet (ˈfrɛʃɪt) *n* **1** the sudden overflowing of a river caused by heavy rain or melting snow **2** a stream of fresh water emptying into the sea

freshwater (ˈfrɛʃˌwɔːtə) *n* (*modifier*) **1** of or living in fresh water **2** (esp of a sailor who has not sailed on the sea) inexperienced **3** *US* little known: *a freshwater school*

fresnel (ˈfreɪnɛl) *n* a unit of frequency equivalent to 10^{12} hertz [c20 after A. J. FRESNEL]

Fresnel (*French* frɛnɛl) *n* **Augustin Jean** (ogystɛ̃ ʒɑ̃) 1788–1827, French physicist: worked on the interference of light, contributing to the wave theory of light

Fresno (ˈfrɛznəʊ) *n* a city in central California, in the San Joaquin Valley. Pop: 427 652 (2000)

fret[1] (frɛt) *vb* **frets, fretting, fretted** **1** to distress or be distressed **2** to rub or wear away **3** to feel or give annoyance or vexation **4** to eat away or be eaten away, as by chemical action **5** (*tr*) to make by wearing away; erode ▷ *n* **6** a state of irritation or anxiety [OE *fretan* to eat]

fret[2] (frɛt) *n* **1** a repetitive geometrical figure, esp one used as an ornamental border **2** such a pattern made in relief; fretwork ▷ *vb* **frets, fretting, fretted** **3** (*tr*) to ornament with fret or fretwork [c14 from OF *frete* interlaced design used on a shield, prob. of Gmc origin] > '**fretless** *adj*

fret[3] (frɛt) *n* any of several small metal bars set across the fingerboard of a musical instrument of the lute, guitar, or viol family at various points along its length so as to produce the desired notes [c16 from ?] > '**fretless** *adj*

fretboard ('frɛtbɔːd) *n* a fingerboard with frets on a stringed instrument

fretful ('frɛtfʊl) *adj* peevish, irritable, or upset > '**fretfully** *adv* > '**fretfulness** *n*

fret saw *n* a fine-toothed saw with a long thin narrow blade, used for cutting designs in thin wood or metal

fretwork ('frɛtˌwɜːk) *n* decorative geometrical carving

Freud (frɔɪd) *n* **1 Anna** 1895–1982, Austrian psychiatrist: daughter of Sigmund Freud and pioneer of child psychoanalysis **2 Lucian** born 1922, British painter, esp of nudes and portraits; grandson of Sigmund Freud **3 Sigmund** ('ziːkmʊnt) 1856–1939, Austrian psychiatrist; originator of psychoanalysis, based on free association of ideas and analysis of dreams. He stressed the importance of infantile sexuality in later development, evolving the concept of the Oedipus complex. His works include *The Interpretation of Dreams* (1900) and *The Ego and the Id* (1923)

Freudian ('frɔɪdɪən) *adj* **1** of or relating to Sigmund Freud or his ideas ▷ *n* **2** a person who follows or believes in the basic ideas of Sigmund Freud > '**Freudian,ism** *n*

Freudian slip *n* any action, such as a slip of the tongue, that may reveal an unconscious thought

Frey (freɪ) *or* **Freyr** (freɪə) *n Norse myth* the god of earth's fertility and dispenser of prosperity

Freya *or* **Freyja** ('freɪə) *n Norse myth* the goddess of love and fecundity, sister of Frey

Freytag (*German* 'fraitaːk) *n* **Gustav** ('gʊstaf) 1816–95, German novelist and dramatist; author of the comedy *Die Journalisten* (1853) and *Soll und Haben* (1855), a novel about German commercial life

Fri. *abbrev for* Friday

friable ('fraɪəbᵊl) *adj* easily broken up; crumbly [c16 from L, from *friāre* to crumble] > ˌ**fria'bility** *or* '**friableness** *n*

friar ('fraɪə) *n* a member of any of various chiefly mendicant religious orders of the Roman Catholic Church [c13 *frere*, from OF: brother, from L *frāter* BROTHER]

friar's balsam *n* a compound containing benzoin, mixed with hot water and used as an inhalant

friary ('fraɪərɪ) *n, pl* **friaries** *Christianity* a convent or house of friars

Fribourg (*French* fribur) *n* **1** a canton in W Switzerland. Capital: Fribourg. Pop: 234 300 (2000 est). Area: 1676 sq km (645 sq miles) **2** a town in W Switzerland, capital of Fribourg canton: university (1889). Pop: 35 000 (latest est). German name: **Freiburg**

fricandeau ('frɪkənˌdəʊ) *n, pl* **fricandeaus** *or* **fricandeaux** (-ˌdəʊz) a larded and braised veal fillet [c18 from OF, prob. based on FRICASSEE]

fricassee (ˌfrɪkə'siː, 'frɪkəsɪ) *n* **1** stewed meat, esp chicken or veal, served in a thick white sauce ▷ *vb* **fricassees, fricasseeing, fricasseed 2** (*tr*) to prepare (meat, etc) as a fricassee [c16 from OF, from *fricasser* to fricassee]

fricative ('frɪkətɪv) *n* **1** a consonant produced by partial occlusion of the airstream, such as (f) or (z) ▷ *adj* **2** relating to or denoting a fricative [c19 from NL, from L *fricāre* to rub]

friction ('frɪkʃən) *n* **1** a resistance encountered when one body moves relative to another body with which it is in contact **2** the act, effect, or an instance of rubbing one object against another **3** disagreement or conflict [c16 from F, from L *frictiō* a rubbing, from *fricāre* to rub] > '**frictional** *adj* > '**frictionless** *adj*

Friday ('fraɪdɪ) *n* **1** the sixth day of the week; fifth day of the working week **2** See **man Friday** [OE *Frīgedæg*]

fridge (frɪdʒ) *n* short for **refrigerator**

fried (fraɪd) *vb* the past tense and past participle of **fry**[1]

Friedan ('friːdən) *n* **Betty** born 1921, US feminist, founder and first president (1966–70) of the National Organization for Women. Her books include *The Feminine Mystique* (1963), *The Second Stage* (1982), and *The Fountain of Life* (1993)

Friedman ('friːdmən) *n* **Milton** born 1912. US economist, particularly associated with monetarism; a forceful advocate of free market capitalism

Friedrich (*German* 'friːdrɪç) *n* **Caspar David** ('kaspar 'daːfɪt) 1774–1840, German romantic landscape painter, noted for his skill in rendering changing effects of light

friend (frɛnd) *n* **1** a person known well to another and regarded with liking, affection, and loyalty **2** an acquaintance or associate **3** an ally in a fight or cause **4** a fellow member of a party, society, etc **5** a patron or supporter **6 be friends (with)** to be friendly (with) **7 make friends (with)** to become friendly (with) ▷ *vb* **8** (*tr*) an archaic word for **befriend** [OE *frēond*] > '**friendless** *adj* > '**friendship** *n*

Friend (frɛnd) *n* a member of the Religious Society of Friends; Quaker

friend at court *n* an influential acquaintance who can promote one's interests

friendly ('frɛndlɪ) *adj* **friendlier, friendliest 1** showing or expressing liking, goodwill, or trust **2** on the same side; not hostile **3** tending or disposed to help or support: *a friendly breeze helped them escape* ▷ *n, pl* **friendlies 4** Also: **friendly match** *sport* a match played for its own sake > '**friendlily** *adv* > '**friendliness** *n*

-friendly *adj combining form* helpful, easy, or good for the person or thing specified: *ozone-friendly*

friendly fire *n mil* firing by one's own side, esp when it harms one's own personnel

Friendly Islands *pl n* another name for **Tonga**[2]

friendly society *n Brit* an association of people who pay regular dues or other sums in return for old-age pensions, sickness benefits, etc

friend of Dorothy ('dɒrəθɪ) *n inf* a male homosexual [c20 after a character in the 1939 film *The Wizard of Oz* played by the US actress Judy Garland (1922–69), who has a large gay following]

Friends of the Earth *n* an organization of environmentalists and conservationists whose aim is to promote the sustainable use of the earth's resources

frier ('fraɪə) *n* a variant spelling of **fryer.** See **fry**[1]

fries (fraɪz) *pl n* short for **French fried potatoes**; chips

Friese-Greene (ˌfriːz'griːn) *n* **William** 1855–1921, British photographer. He invented (with Mortimer Evans) the first practicable motion-picture camera

Friesian ('friːʒən) *n* **1** *Brit* any of several breeds of black-and-white dairy cattle having a high milk yield **2** see **Frisian**

Friesland ('friːzlənd; *Dutch* 'friːslɑnt) *n* **1** a province of the N Netherlands, on the IJsselmeer and the North Sea: includes four of the West Frisian Islands; flat, with sand dunes and fens (under reclamation), canals, and lakes. Capital: Leeuwarden. Pop: 624 500 (2000 est). Area: 3319 sq km (1294 sq miles). Official and Frisian name: **Fryslân** **2** an area comprising the province of Friesland in the Netherlands along with the regions of **East Friesland** and **North Friesland** in Germany

frieze[1] (friːz) *n* **1** *archit* **1a** the horizontal band between the architrave and cornice of a classical entablature **1b** the upper part of the wall of a room, below the cornice **2** any ornamental band on a wall [c16 from F *frise*, ?from Med. L *frisium*, changed from L *Phrygium* Phrygian (work), from Phrygia, famous for embroidery in gold]

frieze[2] (friːz) *n* a heavy woollen fabric used for coats, etc

[c15 from OF, from MDu. ?from *Vriese* Frisian]
frigate (ˈfrɪɡɪt) *n* **1** a medium-sized square-rigged warship of the 18th and 19th centuries **2a** *Brit* a warship smaller than a destroyer **2b** *US* (formerly) a warship larger than a destroyer **2c** *US* a small escort vessel [c16 from F *frégate*, from It. *fregata*, from ?]
frigate bird *n* a bird of tropical and subtropical seas, having a long bill, a wide wingspan, and a forked tail
Frigg (frɪɡ) *or* **Frigga** (ˈfrɪɡə) *n Norse myth* the wife of Odin; goddess of the heavens and married love
fright (fraɪt) *n* **1** sudden fear or alarm **2** a sudden alarming shock **3** *inf* a horrifying or ludicrous person or thing: *she looks a fright* **4 take fright** to become frightened ▷ *vb* **5** a poetic word for **frighten** [OE *fryhto*]
frighten (ˈfraɪtᵊn) *vb* (*tr*) **1** to terrify; scare **2** to drive or force to go (away, off, out, in, etc) by making afraid > ˈ**frightener** *n* > ˈ**frighteningly** *adv*
frightful (ˈfraɪtfʊl) *adj* **1** very alarming or horrifying **2** unpleasant, annoying, or extreme: *a frightful hurry* > ˈ**frightfully** *adv* > ˈ**frightfulness** *n*
frigid (ˈfrɪdʒɪd) *adj* **1** formal or stiff in behaviour or temperament **2** (esp of women) lacking sexual responsiveness **3** characterized by physical coldness: *a frigid zone* [c15 from L *frigidus* cold, from *frīgēre* to be cold] > **friˈgidity** *or* ˈ**frigidness** *n* > ˈ**frigidly** *adv*
Frigid Zone *n arch* the cold region inside the Arctic or Antarctic Circle where the sun's rays are very oblique
frijol (*Spanish* friˈxol) *n, pl* **frijoles** (*Spanish* -ˈxoles) a variety of bean extensively cultivated for food in Mexico [c16 from Sp., ult. from L *phaseolus*, from Gk *phasēlos* bean with edible pod]
frill (frɪl) *n* **1** a gathered, ruched, or pleated strip of cloth sewn on at one edge only, as on garments, as ornament, or to give extra body **2** a ruff of hair or feathers around the neck of a dog or bird or a fold of skin around the neck of a reptile or amphibian **3** (*often pl*) *inf* a superfluous or pretentious thing or manner; affectation: *he made a plain speech with no frills* ▷ *vb* **4** (*tr*) to adorn or fit with a frill or frills **5** to form into a frill or frills [c14 ? of Flemish origin] > ˈ**frilliness** *n* > ˈ**frilly** *adj*
frill-necked lizard *or* **frilled lizard** *n* a large arboreal insectivorous Australian lizard, *Chlamydosaurus kingi*, having an erectile fold of skin around the neck: family *Agamidae* (agamas)
fringe (frɪndʒ) *n* **1** an edging consisting of hanging threads, tassels, etc **2a** an outer edge; periphery **2b** (*as modifier*): *a fringe area* **3** (*modifier*) unofficial; not conventional in form: *fringe theatre* **4** *chiefly Brit* a section of the front hair cut short over the forehead **5** an ornamental border **6** *physics* any of the light and dark bands produced by diffraction or interference of light ▷ *vb* **fringes, fringing, fringed** (*tr*) **7** to adorn with a fringe or fringes **8** to be a fringe for [c14 from OF *frenge*, ult. from L *fimbria* fringe, border] > ˈ**fringeless** *adj*
fringe benefit *n* an additional advantage, esp a benefit provided by an employer to supplement an employee's regular pay
fringing reef *n* a coral reef close to the shore to which it is attached, having a steep seaward edge
Frink (frɪŋk) *n* Dame **Elisabeth** 1930–93, British sculptor
frippery (ˈfrɪpərɪ) *n, pl* **fripperies** **1** ornate or showy clothing or adornment **2** ostentation **3** trifles; trivia [c16 from OF, from *frepe* frill, rag, from Med. L *faluppa* a straw, splinter, from ?]
Frisbee (ˈfrɪzbɪ) *n trademark* a light plastic disc thrown with a spinning motion for recreation or in competition
Frisch (frɪʃ) *n* **1 Karl von** 1886–1982, Austrian zoologist; studied animal behaviour, esp of bees; shared the Nobel prize for physiology or medicine 1973 **2 Max** (maks) 1911–91, Swiss dramatist and novelist. His works are predominantly satirical and include the plays *Biedermann und die Brandstifter* (1953) and *Andorra* (1961), and the novel *Stiller* (1954) **3 Otto** 1904–79, British nuclear physicist, born in Austria, who contributed to the development of the first atomic bomb **4 Ragnar** (**Anton Kittil**) 1895–1973, Norwegian economist, who pioneered the study of econometrics and greatly influenced the management of the Norwegian economy from 1945: shared the first Nobel prize for economics (1969) with Jan Tinbergen
Frisches Haff (ˈfrɪʃəs ˈhaf) *n* the German name for **Vistula** (sense 2)
Frisian (ˈfrɪʒən) *or* **Friesian** *n* **1** a language spoken in the NW Netherlands, parts of N Germany, and some of the adjacent islands **2** a speaker of this language or a native or inhabitant of Friesland ▷ *adj* **3** of or relating to this language, its speakers, or the peoples and culture of Friesland [c16 from L *Frīsīī* people of northern Germany]
Frisian Islands *pl n* a chain of islands in the North Sea along the coasts of the Netherlands, Germany, and Denmark: separated from the mainland by shallows
frisk (frɪsk) *vb* **1** (*intr*) to leap, move about, or act in a playful manner **2** (*tr*) (esp of animals) to whisk or wave briskly: *the dog frisked its tail* **3** (*tr*) *inf* to search (someone) by feeling for concealed weapons, etc ▷ *n* **4** a playful antic or movement **5** *inf* an instance of frisking a person [c16 from OF *frisque*, of Gmc origin] > ˈ**frisker** *n*
frisky (ˈfrɪskɪ) *adj* **friskier, friskiest** lively, high-spirited, or playful > ˈ**friskily** *adv*
frisson *French* (frisɔ̃) *n* a shiver; thrill [c18 (but in common use only from c20): lit.: shiver]
frit (frɪt) *n* **1a** the basic materials, partially or wholly fused, for making glass, glazes for pottery, enamel, etc **1b** a glassy substance used in some soft-paste porcelain ▷ *vb* **frits, fritting, fritted** **2** (*tr*) to fuse (materials) in making frit [c17 from It. *fritta*, lit.: fried, from *friggere* to fry, from L *frīgere*]
fritillary (frɪˈtɪlərɪ) *n, pl* **fritillaries** **1** a liliaceous plant having purple or white drooping bell-shaped flowers, typically marked in a chequered pattern **2** any of various butterflies having brownish wings chequered with black and silver [c17 from NL *fritillāria*, from L *fritillus* dice box; prob. with reference to the markings]
fritter[1] (ˈfrɪtə) *vb* (*tr*) **1** (usually foll by *away*) to waste: *to fritter away time* **2** to break into small pieces [c18 prob. from obs. *fitter* to break into small pieces, ult. from OE *fitt* a piece]
fritter[2] (ˈfrɪtə) *n* a piece of food, such as apple, that is dipped in batter and fried in deep fat [c14 from OF, from L *frictus* fried, from *frīgere* to fry]
Friuli (*Italian* friˈuːli) *n* a historic region of SW Europe, between the Carnic Alps and the Gulf of Venice: the W part (**Venetian Friuli**) was ceded by Austria to Italy in 1866 and **Eastern Friuli** in 1919; in 1947 Eastern Friuli (except Gorizia) was ceded to Yugoslavia
Friulian (frɪˈuːlɪən) *n* **1** the Rhaetian dialect spoken in parts of Friuli. See also **Ladin, Romansch** **2** an inhabitant of Friuli or a speaker of Friulian ▷ *adj* **3** of or relating to Friuli, its inhabitants, or their language
Friuli-Venezia Giulia (*Italian* ˈdʒuːlja) *n* a region of NE Italy, formed in 1947 from **Venetian Friuli** and part of **Eastern Friuli.** Capital: Trieste. Pop: 1 185 172 (2000 est) Area: 7851 sq km (3031 sq miles)
frivolous (ˈfrɪvələs) *adj* **1** not serious or sensible in content, attitude, or behaviour **2** unworthy of serious or sensible treatment: *frivolous details* [c15 from L *frīvolus*] > ˈ**frivolously** *adv* > ˈ**frivolousness** *or* **frivolity** (frɪˈvɒlɪtɪ) *n*
frizz (frɪz) *vb* **1** (of the hair, nap, etc) to form or cause (the hair, etc) to form tight curls or crisp tufts ▷ *n* **2** hair that has been frizzed **3** the state of being frizzed [c19 from F *friser* to curl]
frizzle[1] (ˈfrɪzᵊl) *vb* **frizzles, frizzling, frizzled** **1** to form (the hair) into tight crisp curls ▷ *n* **2** a tight curl [c16 prob. rel. to OE *frīs* curly]
frizzle[2] (ˈfrɪzᵊl) *vb* **frizzles, frizzling, frizzled** **1** to scorch or be scorched, esp with a sizzling noise **2** (*tr*) to fry

(bacon, etc) until crisp [c16 prob. blend of FRY[1] + SIZZLE]
frizzy ('frɪzɪ) *or* **frizzly** ('frɪzlɪ) *adj* **frizzier, frizziest** *or* **frizzlier, frizzliest** (of the hair) in tight crisp wiry curls > '**frizziness** *or* '**frizzliness** *n*
fro (frəʊ) *adv* back or from [c12 from ON *frā*]
Frobisher ('frəʊbɪʃə) *n* Sir **Martin** ?1535–94, English navigator and explorer: made three unsuccessful voyages in search of the Northwest Passage (1576; 1577; 1578), visiting Labrador and Baffin Island
Frobisher Bay *n* **1** an inlet of the Atlantic in NE Canada, in the SE coast of Baffin Island **2** the former name of **Iqaluit**
frock (frɒk) *n* **1** a girl's or woman's dress **2** a loose garment of several types, such as a peasant's smock **3** a wide-sleeved outer garment worn by members of some religious orders ▷ *vb* **4** (*tr*) to invest (a person) with the office of a cleric [c14 from OF *froc*]
frock coat *n* a man's single- or double-breasted skirted coat, as worn in the 19th century
Fröding (*Swedish* 'frø:dɪŋ) *n* **Gustaf** ('gʊstav) 1860–1911, Swedish poet. His popular lyric verse includes the collections *Guitar and Concertina* (1891), *New Poems* (1894), and *Splashes and Rags* (1896)
Froebel *or* **Fröbel** (*German* 'frø:bəl) *n* **1** **Friedrich (Wilhelm August)** ('fri:drɪç) 1782–1852, German educator: founded the first kindergarten (1840) ▷ *adj* **2** of, denoting, or relating to a system of kindergarten education developed by him or to the training and qualification of teachers to use this system
frog[1] (frɒg) *n* **1** an insectivorous amphibian, having a short squat tailless body with a moist smooth skin and very long hind legs specialized for hopping **2** any of various similar amphibians, such as the tree frog **3** any spiked object that is used to support plant stems in a flower arrangement **4** **a frog in one's throat** phlegm on the vocal cords that affects one's speech [OE *frogga*] > '**froggy** *adj*
frog[2] (frɒg) *n* **1** (*often pl*) a decorative fastening of looped braid or cord, as on a military uniform **2** an attachment on a belt to hold the scabbard of a sword, etc [c18 ? ult. from L *floccus* tuft of hair] > **frogged** *adj* > '**frogging** *n*
frog[3] (frɒg) *n* a tough elastic horny material in the centre of the sole of a horse's foot [c17 from ?]
frog[4] (frɒg) *n* a plate of iron or steel to guide train wheels over an intersection of railway lines [c19 from ?; ? a special use of FROG[1]]
Frog (frɒg) *or* **Froggy** ('frɒgɪ) *n, pl* **Frogs** *or* **Froggies** *Brit sl* a derogatory word for a French person
froghopper ('frɒg,hɒpə) *n* any small leaping insect whose larvae secrete a protective spittle-like substance around themselves
frogman ('frɒgmən) *n, pl* **frogmen** a swimmer equipped with a rubber suit, flippers, and breathing equipment for working underwater
frogmarch ('frɒg,mɑ:tʃ) *chiefly Brit* ▷ *n* **1** a method of carrying a resisting person in which each limb is held and the victim is carried horizontally and face downwards **2** any method of making a person move against his or her will ▷ *vb* **3** (*tr*) to carry in a frogmarch or cause to move forward unwillingly
frogmouth ('frɒg,maʊθ) *n* a nocturnal insectivorous bird of SE Asia and Australia, similar to the nightjars
frogspawn ('frɒg,spɔ:n) *n* a mass of fertilized frogs' eggs surrounded by a protective nutrient jelly
frog spit *or* **spittle** *n* **1** another name for **cuckoo spit** **2** a foamy mass of threadlike green algae floating on ponds
Froissart (*French* frwasar) *n* **Jean** (ʒɑ̃) ?1333–?1400, French chronicler and poet, noted for his *Chronique*, a vivid history of Europe from 1325 to 1400
frolic ('frɒlɪk) *n* **1** a light-hearted entertainment or occasion **2** light-hearted activity; gaiety; merriment ▷ *vb* **frolics, frolicking, frolicked** **3** (*intr*) to caper about; act playfully ▷ *adj* **4** *arch* full of fun; gay [c16 from Du. *vrolijk*, from MDu. *vro* happy] > '**frolicker** *n*
frolicsome ('frɒlɪksəm) *adj* merry and playful > '**frolicsomely** *adv*
from (frɒm; *unstressed* frəm) *prep* **1** used to indicate the original location, situation, etc: *from behind the bushes* **2** in a period of time starting at: *he lived from 1910 to 1970* **3** used to indicate the distance between two things or places: *a hundred miles from here* **4** used to indicate a lower amount: *from five to fifty pounds* **5** showing the model of: *painted from life* **6** used with the gerund to mark prohibition, etc: *nothing prevents him from leaving* **7** because of: *exhausted from his walk* [OE *fram*]
fromage frais ('frɒmɑ:ʒ 'freɪ; *French* frɔmaʒ frɛ) *n* a low-fat soft cheese with a smooth light texture [F, lit.: fresh cheese]
Frome (frəʊm) *n* **Lake** a shallow salt lake in NE South Australia: intermittently filled with water. Length: 100 km (60 miles). Width: 48 km (30 miles)
Fromm (frɒm) *n* **Erich** ('ɛrɪk) 1900–80, US psychologist and philosopher, born in Germany. His works include *The Art of Loving* (1956) and *To Have and To Be* (1976)
frond (frɒnd) *n* a large compound leaf, esp of a fern [c18 from L *frōns*]
front (frʌnt) *n* **1** that part or side that is forward, or most often seen or used **2** a position or place directly before or ahead: *a fountain stood at the front of the building* **3** the beginning, opening, or first part **4** the position of leadership: *in the front of scientific knowledge* **5** land bordering a lake, street, etc **6** land along a seashore or large lake, esp a promenade **7** *mil* **7a** the total area in which opposing armies face each other **7b** the space in which a military unit is operating: *to advance on a broad front* **8** *meteorol* the dividing line or plane between two air masses or water masses of different origins **9** outward aspect or bearing, as when dealing with a situation: *a bold front* **10** *inf* a business or other activity serving as a respectable cover for another, usually criminal, organization **11** Also called: **front man** a nominal leader of an organization etc; figurehead **12** *inf* outward appearance of rank or wealth **13** a particular field of activity: *on the wages front* **14** a group of people with a common goal: *a national liberation front* **15** a false shirt front; a dicky **16** *arch* the forehead or the face ▷ *adj* (*prenominal*) **17** of, at, or in the front: *a front seat* **18** *phonetics* of or denoting a vowel articulated with the tongue brought forward, as for the sound of *ee* in English *see* or *a* in English *hat* ▷ *vb* **19** (when *intr*, foll by *on* or *onto*) to face (onto): *this house fronts the river* **20** (*tr*) to be a front of or for **21** (*tr*) to appear as a presenter in (a television show) **22** (*tr*) to be the lead singer or player in (a band) **23** (*tr*) to confront **24** to supply a front for **25** (*intr*; often foll by *up*) *Austral inf* to appear (at): *to front up at the police station* [c13 (in the sense: forehead, face): from L *frōns* forehead, foremost part] > '**frontless** *adj*
frontage ('frʌntɪdʒ) *n* **1** the façade of a building or the front of a plot of ground **2** the extent of the front of a shop, plot of land, etc **3** the direction in which a building faces
frontal ('frʌntᵊl) *adj* **1** of, at, or in the front **2** of or relating to the forehead: *frontal artery* **3** of or relating to the anterior part of a body or organ ▷ *n* **4** a decorative hanging for the front of an altar [c14 (in the sense: adornment for forehead, altarcloth): via OF *frontel*, from L *frōns* forehead] > '**frontally** *adv*
frontal lobe *n* *anat* the anterior portion of each cerebral hemisphere
front bench *n* **1** *Brit* **1a** the foremost bench of either the Government or Opposition in the House of Commons **1b** the leadership (**frontbenchers**) of either group, who occupy this bench **2** the leadership of the government or opposition in various legislative assemblies
front-end *adj* (of money, costs, etc) required or incurred in advance of a project in order to get it under way

Ff

frontier ('frʌntɪə, frʌn'tɪə) *n* **1a** the region of a country bordering on another or a line, barrier, etc, marking such a boundary **1b** (*as modifier*): *a frontier post* **2** *US* the edge of the settled area of a country **3** (*often pl*) the limit of knowledge in a particular field: *the frontiers of physics have been pushed back* [c14 from OF, from *front* (in the sense: part which is opposite)]

frontiersman ('frʌntɪəzmən, frʌn'tɪəz-) *or* (*fem*) **frontierswoman** (-ˌwʊmən) *n, pl* **frontiersmen** *or* **frontierswomen** (formerly) a person living on a frontier, esp in a newly pioneered territory of the US

frontispiece ('frʌntɪsˌpiːs) *n* **1** an illustration facing the title page of a book **2** the principal façade of a building **3** a pediment over a door, window, etc [c16 *frontispice*, from F, from LL *frontispicium* façade, from L *frōns* forehead + *specere* to look at; infl. by PIECE]

frontlet ('frʌntlɪt) *n Judaism* a phylactery attached to the forehead [c15 from OF *frontelet* a little FRONTAL]

front line *n* **1** *military* **1a** the most advanced military units in a battle **1b** (*modifier*) of, relating to, or suitable for the military front line: *frontline troops* **2** (*modifier*) close to a hostile country or scene of armed conflict: *the frontline states*

front loader *n* a washing machine with a door at the front which opens one side of the drum into which washing is placed

front-page *n* (*modifier*) important enough to be put on the front page of a newspaper

frontrunner ('frʌntˌrʌnə) *n inf* the leader or a favoured contestant in a race, election, etc

frontrunning ('frʌntˌrʌnɪŋ) *n stock exchange* the practice by market makers of using advance information provided by their own investment analysts before it has been given to clients

frost (frɒst) *n* **1** a white deposit of ice particles, esp one formed on objects out of doors at night **2** an atmospheric temperature of below freezing point, characterized by the production of this deposit **3** **degrees of frost** degrees below freezing point **4** *inf* something given a cold reception; failure **5** *inf* coolness of manner **6** the act of freezing ▷ *vb* **7** to cover or be covered with frost **8** (*tr*) to give a frostlike appearance to (glass, etc), as by means of a fine-grained surface **9** (*tr*) *chiefly US & Canad* to decorate (cakes, etc) with icing or frosting **10** (*tr*) to kill or damage (crops, etc) with frost [OE *frost*]

Frost (frɒst) *n* **1** Sir **David** (**Paradine**) born 1939, British television presenter and executive, noted esp for political interviews **2** **Robert** (**Lee**) 1874–1963, US poet, noted for his lyrical verse on country life in New England. His books include *A Boy's Will* (1913), *North of Boston* (1914), and *New Hampshire* (1923)

frostbite ('frɒstˌbaɪt) *n* destruction of tissues, esp those of the fingers, ears, toes, and nose, by freezing > **'frostˌbitten** *adj*

frosted ('frɒstɪd) *adj* **1** covered or injured by frost **2** *chiefly US & Canad* covered with icing, as a cake **3** (of glass, etc) having a surface roughened to prevent clear vision through it

frost hollow *n* a depression in a hilly area in which cold air collects, becoming very cold at night

frosting ('frɒstɪŋ) *n* **1** another word (*chiefly* US and Canad) for **icing** **2** a rough or matt finish on glass, silver, etc

frosty ('frɒstɪ) *adj* **frostier, frostiest** **1** characterized by frost: *a frosty night* **2** covered by or decorated with frost **3** lacking warmth or enthusiasm: *the new plan had a frosty reception* > **'frostily** *adv* > **'frostiness** *n*

froth (frɒθ) *n* **1** a mass of small bubbles of air or a gas in a liquid, produced by fermentation, etc **2** a mixture of saliva and air bubbles formed at the lips in certain diseases, such as rabies **3** trivial ideas or entertainment ▷ *vb* **4** to produce or cause to produce froth **5** (*tr*) to give out in the form of froth [c14 from ON *frotha* or *frauth*] > **'frothy** *adj* > **'frothily** *adv*

Froude (fruːd) *n* **1** **James Anthony** 1818–94, English historian; author of a controversial biography (1882–84) of Carlyle **2** his brother **William** 1810–79, English civil engineer

froufrou ('fruːˌfruː) *n* a swishing sound, as made by a long silk dress [c19 from F, imit.]

froward ('frəʊəd) *adj arch* obstinate; contrary [c14 see FRO, -WARD] > **'frowardly** *adv* > **'frowardness** *n*

frown (fraʊn) *vb* **1** (*intr*) to draw the brows together and wrinkle the forehead, esp in worry, anger, or concentration **2** (*intr; foll by on or upon*) to look disapprovingly (upon) **3** (*tr*) to express (worry, etc) by frowning ▷ *n* **4** the act of frowning **5** a show of dislike or displeasure [c14 from OF *froigner*, of Celtic origin] > **'frowner** *n* > **'frowningly** *adv*

frowst (fraʊst) *n Brit inf* a hot and stale atmosphere; fug [c19 back formation from *frowsty* musty, stuffy, var. of FROWZY]

frowsty ('fraʊstɪ) *adj* **frowstier, frowstiest** ill-smelling; stale; musty > **'frowstiness** *n*

frowzy *or* **frowsy** ('fraʊzɪ) *adj* **frowzier, frowziest** *or* **frowsier, frowsiest** **1** untidy or unkempt in appearance **2** ill-smelling; frowsty [c17 from ?] > **'frowziness** *or* **'frowsiness** *n*

froze (frəʊz) *vb* the past tense of **freeze**

frozen ('frəʊzᵊn) *vb* **1** the past participle of **freeze** ▷ *adj* **2** turned into or covered with ice **3** killed or stiffened by extreme cold **4** (of a region or climate) icy or snowy **5** (of food) preserved by a freezing process **6a** (of prices, wages, etc) arbitrarily pegged at a certain level **6b** (of business assets) not convertible into cash **7** frigid or disdainful in manner **8** motionless or unyielding: *he was frozen with horror* > **'frozenly** *adv*

frozen shoulder *n pathol* painful stiffness in a shoulder joint

FRS (in Britain) *abbrev for* Fellow of the Royal Society

FRSNZ *abbrev for* Fellow of the Royal Society of New Zealand

fructify ('frʌktɪˌfaɪ) *vb* **fructifies, fructifying, fructified** **1** to bear or cause to bear fruit **2** to make or become fruitful [c14 from OF, from LL *frūctificāre*, from L *frūctus* fruit + *facere* to produce] > **ˌfructifi'cation** *n* > **fruc'tiferous** *adj* > **'fructiˌfier** *n*

fructose ('frʌktəʊs) *n* a white crystalline sugar occurring in many fruits. Formula: $C_6H_{12}O_6$ [c19 from L *frūctus* fruit + -OSE²]

frugal ('fruːgᵊl) *adj* **1** practising economy; thrifty **2** not costly; meagre [c16 from L, from *frūgī* useful, temperate, from *frux* fruit] > **fru'gality** *n* > **'frugally** *adv*

frugivorous (fruː'dʒɪvərəs) *adj* fruit-eating [c18 from *frugi-* (as in FRUGAL) + -VOROUS]

fruit (fruːt) *n* **1** *bot* the ripened ovary of a flowering plant, containing one or more seeds. It may be dry, as in the poppy, or fleshy, as in the peach **2** any fleshy part of a plant that supports the seeds and is edible, such as the strawberry **3** any plant product useful to man, including grain, vegetables, etc **4** (*often pl*) the result or consequence of an action or effort **5** *arch* offspring of man or animals **6** *inf, chiefly US & Canad* a male homosexual ▷ *vb* **7** to bear or cause to bear fruit [c12 from OF, from L *frūctus* enjoyment, fruit, from *fruī* to enjoy] > **'fruitˌlike** *adj*

▷ www.backyardgardener.com/plants/gfruittree.html
▷ www.doityourself.com/fruits
▷ www.ourbrisbane.com/home_garden/gardening/plants/fruit.htm
▷ www.gardentimeonline.com/Fruit.html

fruit bat *n* a large Old World bat occurring in tropical and subtropical regions and feeding on fruit

fruitcake ('fruːtˌkeɪk) *n* a rich cake containing mixed dried fruit, lemon peel, etc

fruit drop *n* **1** the premature shedding of fruit from a tree before fully ripe **2** a boiled sweet with a fruity flavour

fruiterer ('fruːtərə) *n chiefly Brit* a fruit dealer or seller

fruit fly *n* **1** a small dipterous fly which feeds on and lays its eggs in plant tissues **2** any dipterous fly of the genus *Drosophila*. See **drosophila**

fruitful ('fruːtfʊl) *adj* **1** bearing fruit in abundance **2** productive or prolific **3** producing results or profits: *a fruitful discussion* > '**fruitfully** *adv* > '**fruitfulness** *n*

fruition (fruː'ɪʃən) *n* **1** the attainment of something worked for or desired **2** enjoyment of this **3** the act or condition of bearing fruit [c15 from LL, from L *fruī* to enjoy]

fruitless ('fruːtlɪs) *adj* **1** yielding nothing or nothing of value; unproductive **2** without fruit > '**fruitlessly** *adv* > '**fruitlessness** *n*

fruit machine *n Brit* a gambling machine that pays out when certain combinations of diagrams, usually of fruit, appear on a dial

fruit salad *n* a dessert consisting of sweet fruits cut up and served in a syrup

fruit sugar *n* another name for **fructose**

fruit tree *n* any tree that bears edible fruit

fruity ('fruːtɪ) *adj* **fruitier, fruitiest 1** of or resembling fruit **2** (of a voice) mellow or rich **3** *inf, chiefly Brit* erotically stimulating; salacious **4** *inf, chiefly US & Canad* homosexual > '**fruitily** *adv* > '**fruitiness** *n*

frumenty ('fruːməntɪ) *or* **furmenty** *n Brit* a kind of porridge made from hulled wheat boiled with milk, sweetened, and spiced [c14 from OF, from *frument* grain, from L *frūmentum*]

frump (frʌmp) *n* a woman who is dowdy, drab, or unattractive [c16 (in the sense: to be sullen; c19 dowdy woman): from MDu. *verrompelen* to wrinkle] > '**frumpy** *or* '**frumpish** *adj*

Frunze (*Russian* 'frunzɪ) *n* the former name (until 1991) of **Bishkek**

frustrate (frʌ'streɪt) *vb* **frustrates, frustrating, frustrated** (*tr*) **1** to hinder or prevent (the efforts, plans, or desires) of **2** to upset, agitate, or tire ▷ *adj* **3** *arch* frustrated or thwarted [c15 from L *frustrāre* to cheat, from *frustrā* in error]

frustrated (frʌ'streɪtɪd) *adj* having feelings of dissatisfaction or lack of fulfilment

frustration (frʌ'streɪʃən) *n* **1** the condition of being frustrated **2** something that frustrates **3** *psychol* **3a** the prevention or hindering of a potentially satisfying activity **3b** the emotional reaction to such prevention that may involve aggression

frustum ('frʌstəm) *n, pl* **frustums** *or* **frusta** (-tə) *geom* **a** the part of a solid, such as a cone or pyramid, contained between the base and a plane parallel to the base that intersects the solid **b** the part of such a solid contained between two parallel planes intersecting the solid [c17 from L: piece]

fry[1] (fraɪ) *vb* **fries, frying, fried 1** (when *tr*, sometimes foll by *up*) to cook or be cooked in fat, oil, etc, usually over direct heat **2** *sl, chiefly US* to kill or be killed by electrocution ▷ *n, pl* **fries 3** a dish of something fried, esp the offal of a specified animal: *pig's fry* **4 fry-up** *Brit inf* the act of preparing a mixed fried dish or the dish itself [c13 from OF *frire*, from L *frīgere* to fry] > '**fryer** *or* '**frier** *n*

fry[2] (fraɪ) *pl n* **1** the young of various species of fish **2** the young of certain other animals, such as frogs [c14 (in the sense: young, offspring): from OF *freier* to spawn, from L *fricāre* to rub]

Fry (fraɪ) *n* **1 Christopher** born 1907, English dramatist; author of the verse dramas *A Phoenix Too Frequent* (1946), *The Lady's Not For Burning* (1948), and *Venus Observed* (1950) **2 Elizabeth** 1780–1845, English prison reformer and Quaker **3 Roger Eliot** 1866–1934, English art critic and painter who helped to introduce the postimpressionists to Britain. His books include *Vision and Design* (1920) and *Cézanne* (1927) **4 Stephen (John)** born 1957, British writer, actor, and comedian; his novels include *The Liar* (1991) and *The Stars' Tennis Balls* (2000)

frying pan *n* **1** a long-handled shallow pan used for frying **2 out of the frying pan into the fire** from a bad situation to a worse one

FSB *abbrev for* the Russian Federal Security Service, founded in 1995 [c20 from Russian *Federalnaya sluzhba bezopasnosti*]

f-stop ('ɛf,stɒp) *n* any of the settings for the f-number of a camera

ft. *abbrev for* foot *or* feet

FTAA *abbrev for* Free Trade Area of the Americas

fth. *or* **fthm.** *abbrev for* fathom

FT Index *abbrev for:* **1** Financial Times Industrial Ordinary Share Index: an index designed to show the general trend in share prices, produced daily by the *Financial Times* newspaper **2** Financial Times Stock Exchange 100 Index: an index produced by the *Financial Times* based on an average of 100 securities and giving the best indication of daily movements. Also: **FTSE Index** Informal name: **Footsie**

FTP *abbrev for* (*sometimes not caps*) file transfer protocol: the standard mechanism used to transfer files between computer systems or across the Internet

Fuad I (fuː'ɑːd) *n* original name *Ahmed Fuad Pasha*. 1868–1936, sultan of Egypt (1917–22) and king (1922–36)

Fu-chou ('fuː'tʃaʊ) *n* a variant transliteration of the Chinese name for **Fuzhou**

Fuchs (fʊks, fuːks) *n* **1 Klaus Emil** (klaus 'eːmiːl) 1911–88, East German physicist. He was born in Germany, became a British citizen (1942), and was imprisoned (1950–59) for giving secret atomic research information to the Soviet Union **2** Sir **Vivian Ernest** 1908–99, English explorer and geologist: led the Commonwealth Trans-Antarctic Expedition (1955–58)

fuchsia ('fjuːʃə) *n* **1** a shrub widely cultivated for its showy drooping purple, red, or white flowers **2a** a reddish-purple to purplish-pink colour **2b** (*as adj*): *a fuchsia dress* [c18 from NL, after Leonhard *Fuchs* (1501–66), G botanist]

fuchsin ('fuːksɪn) *or* **fuchsine** ('fuːksiːn, -sɪn) *n* an aniline dye forming a red solution in water: used as a textile dye and a biological stain [c19 from FUCHS(IA) + -IN; from its similarity in colour to the flower]

fuck (fʌk) *taboo* ▷ *vb* **1** to have sexual intercourse with (someone) ▷ *n* **2** an act of sexual intercourse **3** *sl* a partner in sexual intercourse **4 not care** *or* **give a fuck** not to care at all ▷ *interj* **5** *offens* an expression of strong disgust or anger [c16 of Gmc origin]

fuck off *offens taboo sl* ▷ *interj* **1** a forceful expression of dismissal or contempt ▷ *vb* **2** (*intr, adv*) to go away ▷ *adj* **3** (*prenominal*) very large or impressive: *a huge fuck-off cigar*

fucus ('fjuːkəs) *n, pl* **fuci** (-saɪ) *or* **fucuses** a seaweed of the genus *Fucus*, having greenish-brown slimy fronds [c16 from L: rock lichen, from Gk *phukos* seaweed, of Semitic origin]

fuddle ('fʌdᵊl) *vb* **fuddles, fuddling, fuddled 1** (*tr; often passive*) to cause to be confused or intoxicated ▷ *n* **2** a muddled or confused state [c16 from ?]

fuddy-duddy ('fʌdɪ,dʌdɪ) *n, pl* **fuddy-duddies** *inf* a person, esp an elderly one, who is extremely conservative or dull [c20 from ?]

fudge[1] (fʌdʒ) *n* a soft variously flavoured sweet made from sugar, butter, etc [c19 from ?]

fudge[2] (fʌdʒ) *n* **1** foolishness; nonsense ▷ *interj* **2** a mild exclamation of annoyance [c18 from ?]

fudge[3] (fʌdʒ) *n* **1** a small section of type matter in a box in a newspaper allowing late news to be included without the whole page having to be remade **2** the late news so inserted **3** an unsatisfactory compromise reached to evade a difficult problem or controversial

Ff

issue ▷ *vb* **fudges, fudging, fudged** **4** (*tr*) to make or adjust in a false or clumsy way **5** (*tr*) to misrepresent; falsify **6** to evade (a problem, issue, etc) [c19 ? rel. to arch. *fadge* to agree, succeed]

Fuegian (fjuː'iːdʒɪən, 'fweɪdʒ-) *adj* **1** of or relating to Tierra del Fuego or its indigenous Indians ▷ *n* **2** an Indian of Tierra del Fuego

fuel (fjʊəl) *n* **1** any substance burned as a source of heat or power, such as coal or petrol **2** the material, containing a fissile substance such as uranium-235, that produces energy in a nuclear reactor **3** something that nourishes or builds up emotion, action, etc ▷ *vb* **fuels, fuelling, fuelled** *or US* **fuels, fueling, fueled** **4** to supply with or receive fuel [c14 from OF, from *feu* fire, ult. from L *focus* hearth]

fuel air bomb *n* a type of bomb that spreads a cloud of gas, which is then detonated, over the target area, causing extensive destruction

fuel cell *n* a cell in which chemical energy is converted directly into electrical energy

fuel injection *n* a system for introducing fuel directly into the combustion chambers of an internal-combustion engine without the use of a carburettor

fuel oil *n* a liquid petroleum product used as a substitute for coal in industrial furnaces, ships, and locomotives

Fuentes ('fwɛnteɪs) *n* **Carlos** born 1928, Mexican novelist and writer. His novels include *A Change of Skin* (1967), *Terra Nostra* (1975), and *Cristóbal Nonato* (1987)

fug (fʌg) *n chiefly Brit* a hot, stale, or suffocating atmosphere [c19 ? var. of FOG[1]] > **'fuggy** *adj*

fugacity (fjuː'gæsɪtɪ) *n thermodynamics* a property of a gas that expresses its tendency to escape or expand

Fugard ('fuːgɑːd) *n* **Athol** ('æθɒl) born 1932, South African dramatist and theatre director. His plays include *The Blood-Knot* (1961), *Sizwe Bansi is Dead* (1972), *Statements after an Arrest under the Immorality Act* (1974), and *The Captain's Tiger* (1999)

-fuge *n combining form* indicating an agent or substance that expels or drives away: *vermifuge* [from L *fugāre* to expel]

fugitive ('fjuːdʒɪtɪv) *n* **1** a person who flees **2** a thing that is elusive or fleeting ▷ *adj* **3** fleeing, esp from arrest or pursuit **4** not permanent; fleeting [c14 from L, from *fugere* to take flight] > **'fugitively** *adv*

fugleman ('fjuːgəlmən) *n, pl* **fuglemen** **1** (formerly) a soldier used as an example for those learning drill **2** a leader or example [c19 from G *Flügelmann*, from *Flügel* wing + *Mann* MAN]

fugly ('fʌglɪ) *adj* **fuglier, fugliest** *chiefly US & Austral offens* extremely ugly [c20 FUCKING + UGLY]

fugue (fjuːg) *n* **1** a musical form consisting of a theme repeated a fifth above or a fourth below the continuing first statement **2** *psychiatry* a dreamlike altered state of consciousness, during which a person may lose his memory and wander away [c16 from F, from It. *fuga*, from L: a running away] > **'fugal** *adj*

Führer *or* ***Fuehrer*** *German* ('fyːrər) *n* a leader: applied esp to Adolf Hitler while he was Chancellor [G, from *führen* to lead]

Fuji ('fuːdʒɪ) *n* **Mount** an extinct volcano in central Japan, in S central Honshu: the highest mountain in Japan, famous for its symmetrical snow-capped cone. Height: 3776 m (12 388 ft) Also called: **Fujiyama, Fuji-san**

Fujian *or* **Fukien** ('fuː'kjɛn) *n* **1** a province of SE China: mountainous and forested, drained chiefly by the Min River; noted for the production of flower-scented teas. Capital: Fuzhou. Pop: 34 710 000 (2000 est). Area: 123 000 sq km (47 970 sq miles) **2** any of the Chinese dialects of this province. See also **Min**

Fukuoka (ˌfuːkuː'əʊkə) *n* an industrial city and port in SW Japan, in N Kyushu: an important port in ancient times; site of Kyushu university. Pop: 1 284 741 (1995)

-ful *suffix* **1** (*forming adjectives*) full of or characterized by: *painful; restful* **2** (*forming adjectives*) able or tending to: *useful* **3** (*forming nouns*) indicating as much as will fill the thing specified: *mouthful* [OE *-ful, -full*, from FULL[1]]

> USAGE Where the amount held by a spoon, etc, is used as a rough unit of measurement, the correct form is *spoonful*, etc: *take a spoonful of this medicine every day*. *Spoon full* is used in a sentence such as *he held out a spoon full of dark liquid*, where *full of* describes the spoon. A plural form such as *spoonfuls* is preferred by many speakers and writers to *spoonsful*

fulcrum ('fʊlkrəm, 'fʌl-) *n, pl* **fulcrums** *or* **fulcra** (-krə) **1** the pivot about which a lever turns **2** something that supports or sustains; prop [c17 from L: foot of a couch, from *fulcire* to prop up]

fulfil *or US* **fulfill** (fʊl'fɪl) *vb* **fulfils, fulfilling, fulfilled** *or US* **fulfills, fulfilling, fulfilled** (*tr*) **1** to bring about the completion or achievement of (a desire, promise, etc) **2** to carry out or execute (a request, etc) **3** to conform with or satisfy (regulations, etc) **4** to finish or reach the end of **5** **fulfil oneself** to achieve one's potential or desires [OE *fulfyllan*] > **ful'filment** *or US* **ful'fillment** *n*

fulgent ('fʌldʒənt) *adj poetic* shining brilliantly; gleaming [c15 from L *fulgēre* to shine]

fulgurate ('fʌlgjʊˌreɪt) *vb* **fulgurates, fulgurating, fulgurated** (*intr*) *rare* to flash like lightning [c17 from L, from *fulgur* lightning]

fulgurite ('fʌlgjʊˌraɪt) *n* glassy mineral matter found in sand and rock, formed by the action of lightning [c19 from L *fulgur* lightning]

Fulham ('fʊləm) *n* a district of the Greater London borough of Hammersmith and Fulham (since 1965): contains **Fulham Palace** (16th century), residence of the Bishop of London

fuliginous (fjuː'lɪdʒɪnəs) *adj* **1** sooty or smoky **2** of the colour of soot [c16 from LL *fūlīginōsus* full of soot, from L *fūlīgō* soot]

full[1] (fʊl) *adj* **1** holding or containing as much as possible **2** abundant in supply, quantity, number, etc: *full of energy* **3** having consumed enough food or drink **4** (esp of the face or figure) rounded or plump **5** (*prenominal*) complete: *a full dozen* **6** (*prenominal*) with all privileges, rights, etc: *a full member* **7** (*prenominal*) having the same parents: *a full brother* **8** filled with emotion or sentiment: *a full heart* **9** (*postpositive; foll by of*) occupied or engrossed (with): *full of his own projects* **10** *music* **10a** powerful or rich in volume and sound **10b** completing a piece or section; concluding: *a full close* **11** (of a garment, esp a skirt) containing a large amount of fabric **12** (of sails, etc) distended by wind **13** (of wine, such as a burgundy) having a heavy body **14** (of a colour) rich; saturated **15** *inf* drunk **16** **full of oneself** full of pride or conceit **17** **full up** filled to capacity **18** **in full swing** at the height of activity: *the party was in full swing* ▷ *adv* **19a** completely; entirely **19b** (*in combination*): *full-fledged* **20** directly; right: *he hit him full in the stomach* **21** very; extremely (esp in **full well**) ▷ *n* **22** the greatest degree, extent, etc **23** **in full** without omitting or shortening: *we paid in full for our mistake* **24** **to the full** thoroughly; fully ▷ *vb* **25** (*tr*) *needlework* to gather or tuck **26** (*intr*) (of the moon) to be fully illuminated [OE] > **'fullness** *or esp US* **'fulness** *n*

full[2] (fʊl) *vb* (of cloth, yarn, etc) to become or to make (cloth, yarn, etc) more compact during manufacture through shrinking and pressing [c14 from OF *fouler*, ult. from L *fullō* a FULLER]

fullback ('fʊlˌbæk) *n soccer, hockey, rugby* **a** a defensive player **b** the position held by this player

full-blooded *adj* **1** (esp of horses) of unmixed ancestry **2** having great vigour or health; hearty > **ˌfull-'bloodedness** *n*

full-blown *adj* 1 characterized by the fullest, strongest, or best development 2 in full bloom

full board *n* accommodation at a hotel, etc, that includes all meals

full-bodied *adj* having a full rich flavour or quality

full-court press *n basketball* the tactic of harrying the opposing team in all areas of the court, as opposed to the more usual practice of trying to defend one's own basket

full dress *n* **a** a formal style of dress, such as white tie and tails for a man **b** (*as modifier*): *full-dress uniform*

full employment *n* a state in which the labour force and other economic resources of a country are utilized to their maximum extent

fuller ('fʊlə) *n* a person who fulls cloth for a living [OE *fullere*]

Fuller ('fʊlə) *n* 1 (**Richard**) **Buckminster** 1895–1983, US architect and engineer: developed the geodesic dome 2 **Roy** (**Broadbent**) 1912–91, British poet and writer, whose collections include *The Middle of a War* (1942) and *A Lost Season* (1944), both of which are concerned with World War II, *Epitaphs and Occasions* (1949), and *Available for Dreams* (1989) 3 **Thomas** 1608–61, English clergyman and antiquarian; author of *The Worthies of England* (1662)

fullerene ('fʊləˌriːn) *n* short for **buckminsterfullerene**

fuller's earth *n* a natural absorbent clay used, after heating, for clarifying oils and fats, fulling cloth, etc

full face *adj* facing towards the viewer, with the entire face visible

full-fledged *adj* See **fully fledged**

full-frontal *inf* ▷ *adj* 1 (of a nude person or a photograph of a nude person) exposing the genitals to full view 2 all-out; unrestrained ▷ *n* **full frontal** 3 a full-frontal photograph

full house *n* 1 *poker* a hand with three cards of the same value and another pair 2 a theatre, etc, filled to capacity 3 (in bingo, etc) the set of numbers needed to win

full-length *n* (*modifier*) 1 showing the complete length 2 not abridged

full monty ('mɒntɪ) *n* **the** *inf* something in its entirety [from ?]

full moon *n* one of the four phases of the moon when the moon is visible as a fully illuminated disc

full nelson *n* a wrestling hold in which a wrestler places both arms under his opponent's arms from behind and exerts pressure on the back of the neck

full-on *adj inf* complete; unrestrained: *full-on military intervention; full-on hard rock*

full sail *adv* 1 at top speed ▷ *adj* (*postpositive*), *adv* 2 with all sails set

full-scale *n* (*modifier*) 1 (of a plan, etc) of actual size 2 using all resources; all-out

full stop *or* **full point** *n* the punctuation mark (.) used at the end of a sentence that is not a question or exclamation, after abbreviations, etc. Also called (esp US and Canad): **period**

full time *n* the end of a football or other match

full-time *adj* 1 for the entire time appropriate to an activity: *a full-time job* ▷ *adv* **full time** 2 on a full-time basis: *he works full time* ▷ Cf **part-time** > ˌ**full-'timer** *n*

full toss *or* **full pitch** *n cricket* a bowled ball that reaches the batsman without bouncing

fully ('fʊlɪ) *adv* 1 to the greatest degree or extent 2 amply; adequately: *they were fully fed* 3 at least: *it was fully an hour before she came*

fully fashioned *adj* (of stockings, knitwear, etc) shaped and seamed so as to fit closely

fully fledged *or* **full-fledged** *adj* 1 (of a young bird) having acquired adult feathers, enabling it to fly 2 developed to the fullest degree 3 of full rank or status

fulmar ('fʊlmə) *n* a heavily built short-tailed oceanic bird of polar regions [c17 of Scand. origin]

fulminate ('fʌlmɪˌneɪt) *vb* **fulminates, fulminating, fulminated** 1 (*intr; often foll by against*) to make severe criticisms or denunciations; rail 2 to explode with noise and violence ▷ *n* 3 any salt or ester of **fulminic acid**, an isomer of cyanic acid, which is used as a detonator [c15 from Med. L, from L, from *fulmen* lightning that strikes] > '**fulminant** *adj* > ˌ**fulmi'nation** *n* > '**fulmiˌnatory** *adj*

fulsome ('fʊlsəm) *adj* 1 excessive or insincere, esp in an offensive or distasteful way: *fulsome compliments* 2 *not standard* extremely complimentary 3 *inf* full, rich, or abundant: a *fulsome figure; a fulsome flavour; fulsome detail* > '**fulsomely** *adv* > '**fulsomeness** *n*

> USAGE The use of *fulsome* to mean 'extremely complimentary' or 'full, rich, or abundant' is common in journalism, but should be avoided in other kinds of writing

Fulton ('fʊltᵊn) *n* **Robert** 1765–1815, US engineer: designed the first successful steamboat (1807) and steam warship (1814)

fulvous ('fʌlvəs) *adj* of a dull brownish-yellow colour [c17 from L *fulvus* reddish yellow]

fumarole ('fjuːməˌrəʊl) *n* a vent in or near a volcano from which hot gases, esp steam, are emitted [c19 from F, from LL *fūmāriolum* smoke hole, from L *fūmus* smoke]

fumble ('fʌmbᵊl) *vb* **fumbles, fumbling, fumbled** 1 (*intr; often foll by for or with*) to grope about clumsily or blindly, esp in searching 2 (*intr; foll by at or with*) to finger or play with, esp in an absent-minded way 3 to say or do awkwardly: *he fumbled the introduction badly* 4 to fail to catch or grasp (a ball, etc) cleanly ▷ *n* 5 the act of fumbling [c16 prob. of Scand. origin] > '**fumbler** *n* > '**fumblingly** *adv*

fume (fjuːm) *vb* **fumes, fuming, fumed** 1 (*intr*) to be overcome with anger or fury 2 to give off (fumes) or (of fumes) to be given off, esp during a chemical reaction 3 (*tr*) to fumigate ▷ *n* 4 (*often pl*) a pungent or toxic vapour, gas, or smoke 5 a sharp or pungent odour [c14 from OF *fum*, from L *fūmus* smoke, vapour] > '**fumeless** *adj* > '**fumingly** *adv* > '**fumy** *adj*

fumed (fjuːmd) *adj* (of wood, esp oak) having a dark colour and distinctive grain from exposure to ammonia fumes

fumigant ('fjuːmɪgənt) *n* a substance used for fumigating

fumigate ('fjuːmɪˌgeɪt) *vb* **fumigates, fumigating, fumigated** to treat (something contaminated or infected) with fumes or smoke [c16 from L, from *fūmus* smoke + *agere* to drive] > ˌ**fumi'gation** *n* > '**fumiˌgator** *n*

fuming sulphuric acid *n* a mixture of acids, made by dissolving sulphur trioxide in concentrated sulphuric acid. Also called: **oleum**

fumitory ('fjuːmɪtərɪ) *n, pl* **fumitories** any plant of the genus *Fumaria* having spurred flowers and formerly used medicinally [c14 from OF, from Med. L *fūmus terrae*, lit.: smoke of the earth]

fun (fʌn) *n* 1 a source of enjoyment, amusement, diversion, etc 2 pleasure, gaiety, or merriment 3 jest or sport (esp in **in** *or* **for fun**) 4 **fun and games** *ironic or facetious* frivolous or hectic activity 5 **make fun of** *or* **poke fun at** to ridicule or deride 6 (*modifier*) full of amusement, diversion, gaiety, etc: *a fun sport* [c17 ?from obs. *fon* to make a fool of; see FOND]

funambulist (fjuːˈnæmbjʊlɪst) *n* a tightrope walker [c18 from L, from *fūnis* rope + *ambulāre* to walk] > **fu'nambulism** *n*

Funchal (*Portuguese* fũˈʃal) *n* the capital and chief port of the Madeira Islands, on the S coast of Madeira. Pop: 44 110 (latest est)

function ('fʌŋkʃən) *n* 1 the natural action of a person or thing: *the function of the kidneys is to filter waste products from the blood* 2 the intended purpose of a person or thing in a specific role: *the function of a hammer is to hit nails into wood* 3 an official or formal social gathering or ceremony 4 a factor dependent upon another or other factors 5 Also

Ff

called: **map, mapping** *maths, logic* a relation between two sets that associates a unique element (the value) of the second (the range) with each element (the argument) of the first (the domain). Symbol: f(x). The value of f(x) for x=2 is f(2) ▷ *vb (intr)* 6 to operate or perform as specified 7 (foll by *as*) to perform the action or role (of something or someone else): *a coin may function as a screwdriver* [c16 from L *functiō*, from *fungī* to perform]

functional (ˈfʌŋkʃənᵊl) *adj* 1 of, involving, or containing a function or functions 2 practical rather than decorative; utilitarian 3 capable of functioning; working 4 *med* affecting a function of an organ without structural change > ˈ**functionally** *adv*

functional food *n* food containing additives that provide extra nutritional value. Also called: **nutraceutical**

functionalism (ˈfʌŋkʃənəˌlɪzəm) *n* 1 the theory of design that the form of a thing should be determined by its use 2 any doctrine that stresses purpose > ˈ**functionalist** *n, adj*

functionality (ˌfʌŋkʃənˈælɪtɪ) *n, pl* **functionalities** 1 the quality of being functional 2 *computing* a function or range of functions in a computer, program, package, etc

functionary (ˈfʌŋkʃənərɪ) *n, pl* **functionaries** a person acting in an official capacity, as for a government; an official

fund (fʌnd) *n* 1 a reserve of money, etc, set aside for a certain purpose 2 a supply or store of something; stock: *it exhausted his fund of wisdom* ▷ *vb (tr)* 3 to furnish money to in the form of a fund 4 to place or store up in a fund 5 to convert (short-term floating debt) into long-term debt bearing fixed interest and represented by bonds 6 to accumulate a fund for the discharge of (a recurrent liability): *to fund a pension plan* ▷ See also **funds** [c17 from L *fundus* the bottom, piece of land] > ˈ**funder** *n*

fundament (ˈfʌndəmənt) *n euphemistic or facetious* the buttocks [c13 from L, from *fundāre* to FOUND²]

fundamental (ˌfʌndəˈmɛntᵊl) *adj* 1 of, involving, or comprising a foundation; basic 2 of, involving, or comprising a source; primary 3 *music* denoting or relating to the principal or lowest note of a harmonic series ▷ *n* 4 a principle, law, etc, that serves as the basis of an idea or system 5a the principal or lowest note of a harmonic series 5b the bass note of a chord in root position > ˌ**fundamenˈtality** *n* > ˌ**fundaˈmentally** *adv*

fundamental interaction *n* any of the four basic interactions that occur in nature: the gravitational, electromagnetic, strong, and weak interactions

fundamentalism (ˌfʌndəˈmɛntəˌlɪzəm) *n* 1 *Christianity* the view that the Bible is divinely inspired and is therefore literally true 2 *Islam* a movement favouring strict observance of the teachings of the Koran and Islamic law > ˌ**fundaˈmentalist** *n, adj*

fundamental particle *n* another name for **elementary particle**

fundamental unit *n* one of a set of unrelated units that form the basis of a system of units. For example, the metre, kilogram, and second are fundamental SI units

funded debt *n* that part of the British national debt that the government is not obliged to repay by a fixed date

fundholding (ˈfʌndˌhəʊldɪŋ) *n* (formerly, in the National Health Service in Britain) the system enabling general practitioners to receive a fixed budget from which to pay for primary care, drugs, and non-urgent hospital treatment for patients; abolished in 1999 > ˈ**fundˌholder** *n*

fundi (ˈfʊndiː) *n S African* an expert [c20 from Nguni *umfundisi* teacher]

fundie (ˈfʌndɪ) *n Austral derogatory sl* a fundamentalist Christian

fundraiser (ˈfʌndˌreɪzə) *n* 1 a person engaged in fundraising 2 an event held to raise money for a cause

fundraising (ˈfʌndˌreɪzɪŋ) *n* 1 the activity involved in raising money for a cause ▷ *adj* 2 of, for, or related to fundraising

funds (fʌndz) *pl n* 1 money that is readily available 2 British government securities representing national debt

fund supermarket *n* an online facility offering discounted investment opportunities and advice

fundus (ˈfʌndəs) *n, pl* **fundi** (-daɪ) *anat* the base of an organ or the part farthest away from its opening [c18 from L, lit.: the bottom]

Fundy (ˈfʌndɪ) *n* **Bay of** an inlet of the Atlantic in SE Canada, between S New Brunswick and W Nova Scotia: remarkable for its swift tides of up to 21 m (70 ft)

Funen (ˈfuːnən) *n* the second largest island of Denmark, between the Jutland peninsula and the island of Sjælland. Pop: 472 064 (2001 est). Area: 3481 sq km (1344 sq miles). Danish name: **Fyn** German name: **Fünen**

funeral (ˈfjuːnərəl) *n* 1a a ceremony at which a dead person is buried or cremated 1b (*as modifier*): *funeral service* 2 a procession of people escorting a corpse to burial 3 *inf* concern; affair: *it's your funeral* [c14 from Med. L, from LL, from L *fūnus* funeral] > ˈ**funerary** *adj*

funeral director *n* an undertaker

funeral parlour *n* a place where the dead are prepared for burial or cremation. Usual US name: **funeral home**

funereal (fjuːˈnɪərɪəl) *adj* suggestive of a funeral; gloomy or mournful. Also: **funebrial** [c18 from L *fūnereus*] > **fuˈnereally** *adv*

funfair (ˈfʌnˌfɛə) *n Brit* an amusement park or fairground

fungible (ˈfʌndʒɪbᵊl) *n* (*often pl*) *law* movable perishable goods of a sort that may be estimated by number or weight, such as grain, wine, etc [c18 from Med. L *fungibilis*, from L *fungī* to perform] > ˌ**fungiˈbility** *n*

fungicide (ˈfʌndʒɪˌsaɪd) *n* a substance or agent that destroys or is capable of destroying fungi > ˌ**fungiˈcidal** *adj*

fungoid (ˈfʌŋgɔɪd) *adj* resembling a fungus or fungi

fungous (ˈfʌŋgəs) *adj* appearing suddenly and spreading quickly like a fungus

fungus (ˈfʌŋgəs) *n, pl* **fungi** (ˈfʌŋgaɪ, ˈfʌndʒaɪ, ˈfʌndʒɪ) *or* **funguses** 1 any member of a kingdom of organisms, formerly classified as plants, that lack chlorophyll, leaves, true stems, and roots, reproduce by spores, and live as saprotrophs or parasites 2 something resembling a fungus, esp in suddenly growing 3 *pathol* any soft tumorous growth [c16 from L: mushroom, fungus] > ˈ**fungal** *adj*

▷ www.agarics.org/Index.jsp
▷ www.fungaljungal.org
▷ www.botanical.com
▷ www.ucmp.berkeley.edu/fungi/fungi.html
▷ www.elib.cs.berkeley.edu/photos/fungi

funicular (fjuːˈnɪkjʊlə) *n* 1 Also called: **funicular railway** a railway up the side of a mountain, consisting of two cars at either end of a cable passing round a driving wheel at the summit ▷ *adj* 2 relating to or operated by a rope, etc [c17 from L, from *fūnis* rope]

▷ www.funimag.com/Funimag-funio3.html

funk¹ (fʌŋk) *inf, chiefly Brit* ▷ *n* 1 Also called: **blue funk** a state of nervousness, fear, or depression 2 a coward ▷ *vb* 3 to flinch from (responsibility, etc) through fear 4 (*tr; usually passive*) to make afraid [c18 university sl, ? rel. to *funk* to smoke]

funk² (fʌŋk) *n* a type of polyrhythmic Black dance music with heavy syncopation [c20 back formation from FUNKY]

▷ www.soul-patrol.com/funk
▷ www.funk-station.co.uk

Funk (fʌŋk) *n* **Casimir** (ˈkæzɪˌmɪə) 1884–1967, US biochemist, born in Poland: studied and named vitamins

funky (ˈfʌŋkɪ) *adj* **funkier, funkiest** *inf* (of jazz, pop, etc) passionate; soulful [c20 from *funk* to smoke (tobacco), ? alluding to music that was smelly, that is, earthy]

funnel ('fʌnᵊl) *n* **1** a hollow utensil with a wide mouth tapering to a small hole, used for pouring liquids, etc, into a narrow-necked vessel **2** something resembling this in shape or function **3** a smokestack for smoke and exhaust gases, as on a steam locomotive ▷ *vb* **funnels, funnelling, funnelled** *or US* **funnels, funneling, funneled** **4** to move or cause to move or pour through or as if through a funnel [c15 from OProvençal *fonilh*, ult. from L *infundibulum*, from *infundere* to pour in] > '**funnel-,like** *adj*

funnel-web *n Austral* a large poisonous black spider that constructs funnel-shaped webs

funny ('fʌnɪ) *adj* **funnier, funniest** **1** causing amusement or laughter; humorous **2** peculiar; odd **3** suspicious or dubious (esp in **funny business**) **4** *inf* faint or ill ▷ *n, pl* **funnies** **5** *inf* a joke or witticism > '**funnily** *adv* > '**funniness** *n*

funny bone *n* the area near the elbow where the ulnar nerve is close to the surface of the skin: when it is struck, a sharp tingling sensation is experienced

fun run *n* a long run or part-marathon run for exercise and pleasure, often by large numbers of people, esp to raise money for charity

fuoco (fuː'əʊkəʊ) *n music* **1** fire **2** **con fuoco** in a fiery manner [c19 It., lit.: fire]

fur (fɜː) *n* **1** the dense coat of fine silky hairs on such mammals as the cat and mink **2a** the dressed skin of certain fur-bearing animals, with the hair left on **2b** (*as modifier*): *a fur coat* **3** a garment made of fur, such as a stole **4** a pile fabric made in imitation of animal fur **5** *heraldry* any of various stylized representations of animal pelts used in coats of arms **6** **make the fur fly** to cause a scene or disturbance **7** *inf* a whitish coating on the tongue, caused by excessive smoking, illness, etc **8** *Brit* a whitish-grey deposit precipitated from hard water onto the insides of pipes, kettles, etc ▷ *vb* **furs, furring, furred** **9** (*tr*) to line or trim a garment, etc, with fur **10** (often foll by *up*) to cover or become covered with a furlike lining or deposit [c14 from OF *forrer* to line a garment, from *fuerre* sheath, of Gmc origin] > '**furless** *adj*

fur. *abbrev for* furlong

furbelow ('fɜːbɪ,ləʊ) *n* **1** a flounce, ruffle, or other ornamental trim **2** (*often pl*) showy ornamentation ▷ *vb* **3** (*tr*) to put a furbelow on (a garment, etc) [c18 by folk etymology from F dialect *farbella* a frill]

furbish ('fɜːbɪʃ) *vb* (*tr*) **1** to make bright by polishing **2** (often foll by *up*) to renovate; restore [c14 from OF *fourbir* to polish, of Gmc origin] > '**furbisher** *n*

furcate ('fɜːkeɪt) *vb* **furcates, furcating, furcated** **1** to divide into two parts ▷ *adj* **2** forked: *furcate branches* [c19 from LL, from L *furca* a fork] > **fur'cation** *n*

furfuraceous (,fɜːfjʊ'reɪʃəs) *adj* **1** relating to or resembling bran **2** *med* resembling dandruff [c17 from L *furfur* bran, scurf + -ACEOUS]

Furies ('fjʊərɪz) *pl n, sing* **Fury** *classical myth* the snake-haired goddesses of vengeance, usually three in number, who pursued unpunished criminals. Also called: **Erinyes, Eumenides**

furioso (,fjʊərɪ'əʊsəʊ) *music* ▷ *adj, adv* **1** in a frantically rushing manner ▷ *n, pl* **furiosos** **2** a passage or piece to be performed in this way [c19 It., lit.: furious]

furious ('fjʊərɪəs) *adj* **1** extremely angry or annoyed **2** violent or unrestrained, as in speed, energy, etc > '**furiously** *adv* > '**furiousness** *n*

furl (fɜːl) *vb* **1** to roll up (an umbrella, flag, etc) neatly and securely or (of an umbrella, flag, etc) to be rolled up in this way ▷ *n* **2** the act or an instance of furling **3** a single rolled-up section [c16 from OF, from *ferm* tight (from L *firmus* FIRM¹) + *lier* to bind, from L *ligāre*] > '**furlable** *adj*

furlong ('fɜː,lɒŋ) *n* a unit of length equal to 220 yards (201.168 metres) [OE *furlang*, from *furh* furrow + *lang* long]

furlough ('fɜːləʊ) *n* **1** leave of absence from military duty ▷ *vb* (*tr*) **2** to grant a furlough to [c17 from Du. *verlof*, from *ver-* FOR- + *lof* leave, permission]

furnace ('fɜːnɪs) *n* **1** an enclosed chamber in which heat is produced to destroy refuse, smelt or refine ores, etc **2** a very hot place [c13 from OF, from L *fornax* oven, furnace]

Furness ('fɜːnɪs) *n* a region in NW England in Cumbria, forming a peninsula between the Irish Sea and Morecambe Bay

furnish ('fɜːnɪʃ) *vb* (*tr*) **1** to provide (a house, room, etc) with furniture, etc **2** to equip with what is necessary **3** to supply: *the records furnished the information* [c15 from OF *fournir*, of Gmc origin] > '**furnisher** *n*

furnishings ('fɜːnɪʃɪŋz) *pl n* furniture, carpets, etc, with which a room or house is furnished

furniture ('fɜːnɪtʃə) *n* **1** the movable articles that equip a room, house, etc **2** the equipment necessary for a ship, factory, etc **3** *printing* lengths of wood, plastic, or metal, used in assembling formes to surround the type ▷ See also **door furniture, street furniture** [c16 from F, from *fournir* to equip]

▷ www.furnituresociety.org
▷ www.iserv.net/~plucas
▷ www.robbstucky.com/furnglossary.htm
▷ www.first-furniture.com/glosary.asp

Furnivall ('fɜːnɪvᵊl) *n* **Frederick James** 1825–1910, English philologist: founder of the Early English Text Society and one of the founders of the *Oxford English Dictionary*

furore (fjʊ'rɔːrɪ) *or esp US* **furor** ('fjʊərɔː) *n* **1** a public outburst; uproar **2** a sudden widespread enthusiasm; craze **3** frenzy; rage [c15 from L: frenzy, from *furere* to rave]

furphy ('fɜːfɪ) *n, pl* **furphies** *Austral sl* a rumour or fictitious story [c20 from *Furphy* carts (used for water or sewage in World War I), made at a foundry established by the Furphy family]

Furphy ('fɜːfɪ) *n* **Joseph**, pen name *Tom Collins*. 1843–1912, Australian author. His works include the classic Australian novel *Such is Life* (1903) and *The Buln-Buln and the Brolga* (1948)

furred (fɜːd) *adj* **1** made of, lined with, or covered in fur **2** wearing fur **3** (of animals) having fur **4** another word for **furry** (sense 3) **5** provided with furring strips **6** (of a pipe, kettle, etc) lined with hard lime

furrier ('fʌrɪə) *n* a person whose occupation is selling, making, or repairing fur garments [c14 *furour*, from OF *fourrer* to trim with FUR] > '**furriery** *n*

furring ('fɜːrɪŋ) *n* **1** short for **furring strip** **2** the formation of fur on the tongue **3** trimming of animal fur, as on a coat

furring strip *n* a strip of wood or metal fixed to a wall, floor, or ceiling to provide a surface for the fixing of plasterboard, floorboards, etc

furrow ('fʌrəʊ) *n* **1** a long narrow trench made in the ground by a plough **2** any long deep groove, esp a deep wrinkle on the forehead ▷ *vb* **3** to develop or cause to develop furrows or wrinkles **4** to make a furrow or furrows in (land) [OE *furh*] > '**furrower** *n* > '**furrowless** *adj* > '**furrowy** *adj*

furry ('fɜːrɪ) *adj* **furrier, furriest** **1** covered with fur or something furlike **2** of, relating to, or resembling fur **3** Also: **furred** (of the tongue) coated with whitish cellular debris > '**furrily** *adv* > '**furriness** *n*

Fur Seal Islands *pl n* another name for the **Pribilof Islands**

further ('fɜːðə) *adv* **1** in addition; furthermore **2** to a greater degree or extent **3** to or at a more advanced point **4** to or at a greater distance in time or space ▷ *adj* **5** additional; more **6** more distant or remote in time or space ▷ *vb* **7** (*tr*) to assist the progress of ▷ See also **far, furthest** [OE *furthor*]

USAGE See at **farther**

Ff

furtherance ('fɜːðərəns) *n* **1** the act of furthering **2** something that furthers

further education *n* (in Britain) formal education beyond school other than at a university or polytechnic

furthermore ('fɜːðəˌmɔː) *adv* in addition; moreover

furthermost ('fɜːðəˌməʊst) *adj* most distant; furthest

furthest ('fɜːðɪst) *adv* **1** to the greatest degree or extent **2** to or at the greatest distance in time or space; farthest ▷ *adj* **3** most distant or remote in time or space; farthest

furtive ('fɜːtɪv) *adj* characterized by stealth; sly and secretive [C15 from L *furtīvus* stolen, from *furtum* a theft, from *fūr* a thief] > **'furtively** *adv* > **'furtiveness** *n*

Furtwängler (*German* 'fʊrtvɛŋlər) *n* **Wilhelm** ('vɪlhɛlm) 1886–1954, German conductor, noted for his interpretations of Wagner

furuncle ('fjʊərʌŋkᵊl) *n pathol* the technical name for **boil**[2] [C17 from L *fūrunculus* pilferer, sore, from *fūr* thief] > **furuncular** (fjʊ'rʌŋkjʊlə) *or* **fu'runculous** *adj*

furunculosis (fjʊˌrʌŋkjʊ'ləʊsɪs) *n* **1** a skin condition characterized by the presence of multiple boils **2** a disease of salmon and trout caused by a bacterium

fury ('fjʊərɪ) *n, pl* **furies** **1** violent or uncontrolled anger **2** an outburst of such anger **3** uncontrolled violence: *the fury of the storm* **4** a person, esp a woman, with a violent temper **5** See **Furies** **6** **like fury** *inf* violently; furiously [C14 from L, from *furere* to be furious]

furze (fɜːz) *n* another name for **gorse** [OE *fyrs*] > **'furzy** *adj*

fuscous ('fʌskəs) *adj* of a brownish-grey colour [C17 from L *fuscus* dark, swarthy, tawny]

fuse[1] *or chiefly US* **fuze** (fjuːz) *n* **1** a lead of combustible black powder (**safety fuse**), or a lead containing an explosive (**detonating fuse**), used to fire an explosive charge **2** any device by which an explosive charge is ignited ▷ *vb* **fuses, fusing, fused** *or chiefly US* **fuzes, fuzing, fuzed** **3** (*tr*) to equip with such a fuse [C17 from It. *fuso* spindle, from L *fūsus*] > **'fuseless** *adj*

fuse[2] (fjuːz) *vb* **fuses, fusing, fused** **1** to unite or become united by melting, esp by the action of heat **2** to become or cause to become liquid, esp by the action of heat **3** to join or become combined **4** (*tr*) to equip (a plug, etc) with a fuse **5** *Brit* to fail or cause to fail as a result of the blowing of a fuse: *the lights fused* ▷ *n* **6** a protective device for safeguarding electric circuits, etc, containing a wire that melts and breaks the circuit when the current exceeds a certain value [C17 from L *fūsus* melted, cast, from *fundere* to pour out; sense 5 infl. by FUSE[1]]

fusee *or* **fuzee** (fjuː'ziː) *n* **1** (in early clocks and watches) a spirally grooved spindle, functioning as an equalizing force on the unwinding of the mainspring **2** a friction match with a large head [C16 from F *fusée* spindleful of thread, from OF *fus* spindle, from L *fūsus*]

fuselage ('fjuːzɪˌlɑːʒ) *n* the main body of an aircraft [C20 from F, from *fuseler* to shape like a spindle, from OF *fusel* spindle]

fusel oil *or* **fusel** ('fjuːzᵊl) *n* a poisonous by-product formed in the distillation of fermented liquors and used as a source of amyl alcohols [C19 from G *Fusel* bad spirits]

Fushih *or* **Fu-shih** ('fuː'ʃiː) *n* another name for **Yanan**

Fushun ('fuː'ʃʌn) *n* a city in NE China, in central Liaoning province near Shenyang: situated on one of the richest coalfields in the world; site of the largest thermal power plant in NE Asia. Pop: 1 271 113 (1999 est)

fusible ('fjuːzəbᵊl) *adj* capable of being fused or melted > **ˌfusi'bility** *n* > **'fusibly** *adv*

fusiform ('fjuːzɪˌfɔːm) *adj* elongated and tapering at both ends [C18 from L *fūsus* spindle]

fusil ('fjuːzɪl) *n* a light flintlock musket [C16 (in the sense: steel for a tinderbox): from OF, from Vulgar L *focīlis* (unattested), from L *focus* fire]

fusilier (ˌfjuːzɪ'lɪə) *n* **1** (formerly) an infantryman armed with a light musket **2** Also: **fusileer** **2a** a soldier, esp a private, serving in any of certain British or other infantry regiments **2b** (*pl; cap when part of a name*): *the Royal Welch Fusiliers* [C17 from F; see FUSIL]

fusillade (ˌfjuːzɪ'leɪd) *n* **1** a rapid continual discharge of firearms **2** a sudden outburst, as of criticism ▷ *vb* **fusillades, fusillading, fusilladed** **3** (*tr*) to attack with a fusillade [C19 from F, from *fusiller* to shoot; see FUSIL]

fusion ('fjuːʒən) *n* **1** the act or process of fusing or melting together **2** the state of being fused **3** something produced by fusing **4** a kind of popular music that is a blend of two or more styles, such as jazz and funk **5** See **nuclear fusion** **6** a coalition of political parties **7** (*modifier*) relating to a style of cooking that combines traditional Western techniques and ingredients with those used in Eastern cuisine: *fusion cuisine; fusion food* [C16 from L *fūsiō* a pouring out, melting, from *fundere* to pour out, FOUND[3]]

fusion bomb *n* a type of bomb in which most of the energy is provided by nuclear fusion. Also called: **thermonuclear bomb, fission-fusion bomb**

fuss (fʌs) *n* **1** nervous activity or agitation, esp when unnecessary **2** complaint or objection: *he made a fuss over the bill* **3** an exhibition of affection or admiration: *they made a great fuss over the new baby* **4** a quarrel ▷ *vb* **5** (*intr*) to worry unnecessarily **6** (*intr*) to be excessively concerned over trifles **7** (when *intr*, usually foll by *over*) to show great or excessive concern, affection, etc (for) **8** (*tr*) to bother (a person) [C18 from ?] > **'fusser** *n*

fusspot ('fʌsˌpɒt) *n Brit inf* a person who fusses unnecessarily

fussy ('fʌsɪ) *adj* **fussier, fussiest** **1** inclined to fuss over minor points **2** very particular about detail **3** characterized by overelaborate detail > **'fussily** *adv* > **'fussiness** *n*

fustanella (ˌfʌstə'nɛlə) *n* a white knee-length pleated skirt worn by men in Greece and Albania [C19 from It., from Mod. Gk *phoustani*, prob. from It. *fustagno* FUSTIAN]

fustian ('fʌstɪən) *n* **1a** a hard-wearing fabric of cotton mixed with flax or wool **1b** (*as modifier*): *a fustian jacket* **2** pompous talk or writing ▷ *adj* **3** cheap; worthless **4** bombastic [C12 from OF, from Med. L *fustāneum*, from L *fustis* cudgel]

fustic ('fʌstɪk) *n* **1** Also called: **old fustic** a large tropical American tree **2** the yellow dye obtained from the wood of this tree **3** any of various trees or shrubs that yield a similar dye, esp a European sumach (**young fustic**) [C15 from F *fustoc*, from Sp., from Ar. *fustuq*, from Gk *pistakē* pistachio tree]

fusty ('fʌstɪ) *adj* **fustier, fustiest** **1** smelling of damp or mould **2** old-fashioned in attitude [C14 from *fust* wine cask, from OF: cask, from L *fūstis* cudgel] > **'fustily** *adv* > **'fustiness** *n*

futhark ('fuːθɑːk) *or* **futhorc, futhork** ('fuːθɔːk) *n* a phonetic alphabet consisting of runes [C19 from the first six letters: *f, u, th, a, r, k*]

futile ('fjuːtaɪl) *adj* **1** having no effective result; unsuccessful **2** pointless; trifling **3** inane or foolish [C16 from L *futtilis* pouring out easily, from *fundere* to pour out] > **'futilely** *adv* > **futility** (fjuː'tɪlɪtɪ) *n*

futon ('fuːˌtɒn) *n* a Japanese padded quilt, laid on the floor as a bed [C19 from Japanese]

futtock ('fʌtək) *n naut* one of the ribs in the frame of a wooden vessel [C13 ? var. of *foothook*]

future ('fjuːtʃə) *n* **1** the time yet to come **2** undetermined events that will occur in that time **3** the condition of a person or thing at a later date: *the future of the school is undecided* **4** likelihood of later improvement: *he has a future as a singer* **5** *grammar* **5a** a tense of verbs used when the action or event described is to occur after the time of utterance **5b** a verb in this tense **6** **in future** from now on ▷ *adj* **7** that is yet to come or be **8** of or expressing time yet to come **9** (*prenominal*) destined to become **10** *grammar* in or denoting the future as a tense of verbs ▷ See also **futures** [C14 from L

fūtūrus about to be, from *esse* to be] > '**futureless** *adj*
future perfect *grammar* ▷ *adj* **1** denoting a tense of verbs describing an action that will have been performed by a certain time ▷ *n* **2a** the future perfect tense **2b** a verb in this tense
future-proof *adj* (of a system, computer, program, etc) guaranteed not to be superseded by future versions, developments, etc
futures ('fjuːtʃəz) *pl n* **a** commodities or other financial products bought or sold at an agreed price for delivery at a specified future date. See also **financial futures** **b** (*as modifier*): *futures contract; futures market*
future value *n* the value that a sum of money invested at compound interest will have after a specified period
futurism ('fjuːtʃəˌrɪzəm) *n* an artistic movement that arose in Italy in 1909 to replace traditional aesthetic values with the characteristics of the machine age > '**futurist** *n, adj*
▷ www.unknown.nu/futurism
▷ www.futurism.org.uk/futurism.htm
futuristic (ˌfjuːtʃə'rɪstɪk) *adj* **1** denoting or relating to design, etc, that is thought likely to be fashionable at some future time **2** of or relating to futurism > ˌ**futur'istically** *adv*
futurity (fjuː'tjʊərɪtɪ) *n, pl* **futurities** **1** a less common word for **future** **2** the quality of being in the future **3** a future event
futurology (ˌfjuːtʃə'rɒlədʒɪ) *n* the study or prediction of the future of mankind > ˌ**futur'ologist** *n*
fuze (fjuːz) *n, vb* **fuzes, fuzing, fuzed** *chiefly US* a variant spelling of **fuse**[1]
fuzee (fjuː'ziː) *n* a variant spelling of **fusee**
Fuzhou ('fuː'ʒəʊ), **Foochow**, *or* **Fuchou** *n* a port in SE China, capital of Fujian province on the Min Jiang: one of the original five treaty ports (1842). Pop: 1 057 372 (1999 est)
fuzz[1] (fʌz) *n* **1** a mass or covering of fine or curly hairs, fibres, etc **2** a blur ▷ *vb* **3** to make or become fuzzy **4** to make or become indistinct; blur [C17 ?from Low G *fussig* loose]
fuzz[2] (fʌz) *n* a slang word for **police** or **policeman** [C20 from ?]
fuzzy ('fʌzɪ) *adj* **fuzzier, fuzziest** **1** of, resembling, or covered with fuzz **2** unclear or distorted **3** (of the hair) tightly curled or very wavy > '**fuzzily** *adv* > '**fuzziness** *n*
fuzzy logic *n* a branch of logic that allows degrees of imprecision in reasoning and knowledge to be represented in such a way that the information can be processed by computer
fuzzy-wuzzy ('fʌzɪˌwʌzɪ) *n, pl* **fuzzy-wuzzies** *offens arch sl* a Black fuzzy-haired native of any of various countries
fwd *abbrev for* forward
FWIW *text messaging abbrev for* for what it's worth
f-word *n* **the** (*sometimes cap*) a euphemistic way of referring to the word **fuck** [from F(UCK) + WORD]
FX *n* **1** *films inf* short for **special effects** **2** (in the US and Canad) *abbrev for* foreign exchange
-fy *suffix forming verbs* to make or become: *beautify* [from OF *-fier*, from L *-ficāre*, from *-ficus* -FIC]
FYI *text messaging abbrev for* for your information
Fylde (faɪld) *n* a region in NW England in Lancashire between the Wyre and Ribble estuaries
fylfot ('faɪlfɒt) *n* a rare word for **swastika** [C16 (apparently meaning: a sign or device for the lower part or foot of a painted window): from *fillen* to fill + *fot* foot]
Fyn (*Danish* fyːn) *n* the Danish name for **Funen**
FYROM *abbrev for* Former Yugoslav Republic of Macedonia

Gg

g *or* **G** (dʒiː) *n, pl* **g's, G's,** *or* **Gs** **1** the seventh letter of the English alphabet **2** a speech sound represented by this letter, usually either as in *grass*, or as in *page*

g *symbol for:* **1** gallon(s) **2** gram(s) **3** grav **4** acceleration of free fall (due to gravity)

G *symbol for:* **1** *music* **1a** the fifth note of the scale of C major **1b** the major or minor key having this note as its tonic **2** gauss **3** gravitational constant **4** *physics* conductance **5** *biochem* guanine **6** German **7** giga- **8** good **9** *sl, chiefly US* grand (a thousand dollars or pounds) **10** (in Australia) **10a** general exhibition (used to describe a category of film certified as suitable for viewing by anyone) **10b** *(as modifier)*: *a G film*

G. *or* **g.** *abbrev for:* **1** gauges **2** gelding **3** guilder(s) **4** guinea(s) **5** Gulf

2G *abbreviation for* second-generation; a system for mobile phones, characterized by digital technology, Internet access, and a short-message service

3G *abbreviation for* third-generation; a system for mobile phones allowing fast connection, Internet access, digital photography, graphics transmission and display, and other advanced features

4G *abbrev for* fourth generation; a system for mobile phones in which data can be provided more quickly and on broader bandwidths than previously

G3 *abbrev for* Group of Three

G5 *abbrev for* Group of Five

G7 *abbrev for* Group of Seven

G8 *abbrev for* Group of Eight

G10 *abbrev for* Group of Ten

G24 *abbrev for* Group of Twenty-Four

G77 *abbrev for* Group of Seventy-Seven

Ga *the chemical symbol for* gallium

GA *abbrev for:* **1** General Assembly (of the United Nations) **2** general average **3** Georgia

Ga. *abbrev for* Georgia

gab (gæb) *inf* ▷ *vb* **gabs, gabbing, gabbed** **1** *(intr)* to talk excessively or idly; gossip ▷ *n* **2** idle or trivial talk **3** **gift of the gab** ability to speak glibly or persuasively [C18 prob. from Irish Gaelic *gob* mouth] > **'gabber** *n*

gabardine *or* **gaberdine** ('gæbəˌdiːn, ˌgæbə'diːn) *n* **1** a twill-weave worsted, cotton, or spun-rayon fabric **2** an ankle-length loose coat or frock worn by men, esp by Jews, in the Middle Ages **3** any of various other garments made of gabardine, esp a child's raincoat [C16 from OF *gauvardine* pilgrim's garment, from MHG *wallewart* pilgrimage]

gabble ('gæbᵊl) *vb* **gabbles, gabbling, gabbled** **1** to utter (words, etc) rapidly and indistinctly; jabber **2** *(intr)* (of geese, etc) to utter rapid cackling noises ▷ *n* **3** rapid and indistinct speech or noises [C17 from MDu. *gabbelen*, imit.] > **'gabbler** *n*

gabbro ('gæbrəʊ) *n, pl* **gabbros** a dark coarse-grained igneous rock consisting of feldspar, pyroxene, and often olivine [C19 from It., prob. from L *glaber* smooth, bald]

gabby ('gæbɪ) *adj* **gabbier, gabbiest** *inf* inclined to chatter; talkative

Gaberones (ˌgæbə'rəʊnɛs) *n* the former name for **Gaborone**

Gabès ('gɑːbɛs; *French* gabɛs) *n* **1** a port in E Tunisia. Pop: 98 800 (1994) **2** **Gulf of** an inlet of the Mediterranean on the E coast of Tunisia. Ancient name: **Syrtis Minor** Arabic name: **Qabis**

gabfest ('gæbˌfɛst) *n inf, chiefly US & Canad* **1** prolonged gossiping or conversation **2** an informal gathering for conversation [C19 from GAB + FEST]

gabion ('geɪbɪən) *n* **1** a cylindrical metal container filled with stones, used in the construction of underwater foundations **2** a wickerwork basket filled with stones or earth, used (esp formerly) as part of a fortification [C16 from F: basket, from It., from *gabbia* cage, from L *cavea*; see CAGE]

gable ('geɪbᵊl) *n* **1** the triangular upper part of a wall between the sloping ends of a pitched roof (**gable roof**) **2** a triangular ornamental feature, esp as used over a door or window [c14 OF, prob. from ON *gafl*] > '**gabled** *adj*

Gable ('geɪbᵊl) *n* (**William**) **Clark** 1901–60, US film actor. His films include *It Happened One Night* (1934), *San Francisco* (1936), *Gone with the Wind* (1939), *Mogambo* (1953), and *The Misfits* (1960)

gable end *n* the end wall of a building on the side which is topped by a gable

Gabo ('gɑːbəʊ, -bə) *n* **Naum** (naʊm), original name *Naum Neemia Pevsner*. 1890–1977, US sculptor, born in Russia: a leading constructivist

Gabon (gə'bɒn; *French* gabɔ̃) *n* a republic in W central Africa, on the Atlantic: settled by the French in 1839; made part of the French Congo in 1888; became independent in 1960; almost wholly forested. Official language: French. Religion: Christian majority; significant animist minority. Currency: franc. Capital: Libreville. Pop: 1 221 000 (2001 est). Area: 267 675 sq km (103 350 sq miles)
▷ www.tourisme-gabon.com

Gabonese (ˌgæbə'niːz) *adj* **1** of or relating to Gabon or its inhabitants ▷ *n* **2** a native or inhabitant of Gabon

gaboon (gə'buːn) *n* a dark mahogany-like wood from an African tree, used in plywood, for furniture, and as a veneer [c20 altered from GABON]

gaboon viper *n* a large venomous viper of African rainforests. It has brown and purple markings and hornlike projections on its snout

Gabor (gə'bɔː) *n* **Dennis** 1900–79, British electrical engineer, born in Hungary. He invented holography: Nobel prize for physics 1971

Gaborone (ˌgæbə'rəʊnɪ) *n* the capital of Botswana (since 1964), in the extreme southeast. Pop: 183 487 (1997 est). Former name: **Gaberones**
▷ www.gov.bw/tourism/attractions/gaborone.html

Gabriel[1] ('geɪbrɪəl) *n Bible* one of the archangels, the messenger of good news (Daniel 8:16–26; Luke 1:11–20, 26–38)

Gabriel[2] (*French* gabriɛl) *n* **Jacques-Ange** (ʒakɑ̃ʒ) 1698–1782, French architect: designed the Petit Trianon at Versailles

Gabrieli (*Italian* gabrɪ'ɛli) *or* **Gabrielli** *n* **1** **Andrea** (an'drɛːa) 1520–86, Italian organist and composer; chief organist of St Mark's, Venice **2** his nephew, **Giovanni** (dʒo'vanni) 1558–1612, Italian organist and composer

gaby ('geɪbɪ) *n, pl* **gabies** *arch or dialect* a simpleton [c18 from ?]

gad (gæd) *vb* **gads, gadding, gadded** **1** (*intr*; often foll by *about* or *around*) to go out in search of pleasure; gallivant ▷ *n* **2** carefree adventure (esp in **on the gad**) [c15 back formation from obs. *gadling* companion, from OE, from *gæd* fellowship] > '**gadder** *n*

Gad (gæd) *n Old Testament* **1a** Jacob's sixth son, whose mother was Zilpah, Leah's maid **1b** the Israelite tribe descended from him **1c** the territory of this tribe, lying to the east of the Jordan and extending southwards from the Sea of Galilee **2** a prophet and admonisher of David (I Samuel 22; II Samuel 24)

gadabout ('gædəˌbaʊt) *n inf* a person who restlessly seeks amusement, etc

Gadarene ('gædəˌriːn) *adj* relating to or engaged in a headlong rush [c19 via LL from Gk *Gadarēnos*, of Gadara (Palestine), alluding to the Gadarene swine (Matthew 8:28ff.)]

Gaddafi *or* **Qaddafi** (gə'dɑːfɪ) *n* **Mu'ammar Muhammad al-** ('məʊəˌmɑː mʊ'hɑːmɑːd æl) born 1942, Libyan army officer and statesman; head of state from 1969

gadfly ('gædˌflaɪ) *n, pl* **gadflies** **1** any of various large dipterous flies, esp the horsefly, that annoy livestock by sucking their blood **2** a constantly irritating person [c16 from *gad* sting + FLY[2]]

gadget ('gædʒɪt) *n* **1** a small mechanical device or appliance **2** any object that is interesting for its ingenuity [c19 ?from F *gâchette* lock catch, dim. of *gâche* staple]

gadgetry ('gædʒɪtrɪ) *n* **1** gadgets collectively **2** use of or preoccupation with gadgets

gadoid ('geɪdɔɪd) *adj* **1** of or belonging to an order of marine soft-finned fishes typically having the pectoral and pelvic fins close together and small cycloid scales. The group includes cod and hake ▷ *n* **2** any gadoid fish [c19 from NL *Gadidae*, from *gadus* cod; see -OID]

gadolinium (ˌgædə'lɪnɪəm) *n* a ductile malleable silvery-white ferromagnetic element of the lanthanide series of metals. Symbol: Gd; atomic no.: 64; atomic wt.: 157.25 [c19 NL, after Johan *Gadolin* (1760–1852), Finnish mineralogist]

gadroon *or* **godroon** (gə'druːn) *n* a decorative moulding composed of a series of convex flutes and curves, used esp as an edge to silver articles [c18 from F *godron*, ?from OF *godet* cup, goblet]

Gadsden Purchase ('gædzdən) *n* an area of about 77 000 sq km (30 000 sq miles) in present-day Arizona and New Mexico, bought by the US from Mexico for 10 million dollars in 1853. The purchase was negotiated by James Gadsden (1788–1858), US diplomat

gadwall ('gædˌwɔːl) *n, pl* **gadwalls** *or* **gadwall** a duck related to the mallard. The male has a grey body and black tail [c17 from ?]

gadzooks (gæd'zuːks) *interj arch* a mild oath [c17 ?from *God's hooks* (the nails of the cross) from *Gad* arch euphemism for God]

Gaea ('dʒiːə), **Gaia**, *or* **Ge** *n Greek myth* the goddess of the earth, who bore Uranus and by him Oceanus, Cronus, and the Titans [from Gk *gaia* earth]

Gael (geɪl) *n* a person who speaks a Gaelic language, esp a Highland Scot or an Irishman [c19 from Gaelic *Gaidheal*] > '**Gaeldom** *n*

Gaelic ('geɪlɪk, 'gæ-) *n* **1** any of the closely related languages of the Celts in Ireland, Scotland, or the Isle of Man ▷ *adj* **2** of, denoting, or relating to the Celtic people of Ireland, Scotland, or the Isle of Man or their language or customs

Gaelic coffee *n* another name for **Irish coffee**

Gaeltacht ('gɛːltəxt) *n* any of the regions in Ireland in which Irish Gaelic is the vernacular speech [c20 from Irish Gaelic]

gaff[1] (gæf) *n* **1** *angling* a stiff pole with a stout prong or hook attached for landing large fish **2** *naut* a boom hoisted aft of a mast to support a fore-and-aft sail **3** a metal spur fixed to the leg of a gamecock ▷ *vb* **4** (*tr*) *angling* to hook or land (a fish) with a gaff [c13 from F *gaffe*, from Provençal *gaf* boat hook]

gaff[2] (gæf) *n* **1** *sl* nonsense **2** **blow the gaff** *Brit sl* to divulge a secret [c19 from ?]

gaffe (gæf) *n* a social blunder, esp a tactless remark [c19 from F]

gaffer ('gæfə) *n* **1** an old man: often used affectionately or patronizingly **2** *inf, chiefly Brit* a boss, foreman, or owner of a factory, etc **3** *inf* the senior electrician on a television or film set [c16 from GODFATHER]

gag[1] (gæg) *vb* **gags, gagging, gagged** **1** (*tr*) to stop up (a person's mouth), esp with a piece of cloth, etc, to prevent him or her from speaking or crying out **2** (*tr*) to suppress or censor (free expression, information, etc) **3** to retch or cause to retch **4** (*intr*) to struggle for breath; choke ▷ *n* **5** a piece of cloth, rope, etc, stuffed into or tied across the mouth **6** any restraint on or suppression of information, free speech, etc **7** *parliamentary procedure* another word for **closure** (sense 4) [c15 *gaggen*; ? imit. of a gasping sound]

gag[2] (gæg) *inf* ▷ *n* **1** a joke or humorous story, esp one

Gg

told by a professional comedian **2** a hoax, practical joke, etc ▷ *vb* **gags, gagging, gagged** **3** (*intr*) to tell jokes or funny stories, as comedians in nightclubs, etc [C19 ? special use of GAG[1]]

gaga ('gɑːgɑː) *adj inf* **1** senile; doting **2** slightly crazy [C20 from F, imit.]

Gagarin (*Russian* ga'garin) *n* **Yuri** ('jurɪ) 1934–68, Soviet cosmonaut: made the first manned space flight (1961)

gage[1] (geɪdʒ) *n* **1** something deposited as security against the fulfilment of an obligation; pledge **2** (formerly) a glove or other object thrown down to indicate a challenge to combat ▷ *vb* **gages, gaging, gaged** **3** (*tr*) *arch* to stake, pledge, or wager [C14 from OF, of Gmc origin]

gage[2] (geɪdʒ) *n* short for **greengage**

gage[3] (geɪdʒ) *n, vb* **gages, gaging, gaged** *US* a variant spelling (esp in technical senses) of **gauge**

Gage (geɪdʒ) *n* **Thomas** 1721–87, British general and governor in America; commander in chief of British forces at Bunker Hill (1775)

gaggle ('gægᵊl) *vb* **gaggles, gaggling, gaggled** **1** (*intr*) (of geese) to cackle ▷ *n* **2** a flock of geese **3** *inf* a disorderly group of people [C14 of Gmc origin; imit.]

Gaia ('gaɪə) *n* a variant of **Gaea**

Gaia hypothesis *or* **theory** *n* the theory that the earth and everything on it constitutes a single self-regulating living system

gaiety ('geɪətɪ) *n, pl* **gaieties** **1** the state or condition of being merry, bright, or lively **2** festivity; merrymaking **3** bright appearance.

USAGE See at **gay**

Gaillard Cut (gɪl'jɑːd, 'geɪlɑːd) *n* the SE section of the Panama Canal, cut through Culebra Mountain. Length: about 13 km (8 miles). Former name: **Culebra Cut** [C19 named after David Du Bose *Gaillard* (1859–1913), US army engineer in charge of the work]

gaillardia (geɪ'lɑːdɪə) *n* a plant of the composite family having ornamental flower heads with yellow or red rays and purple discs [C19 from NL, after *Gaillard* de Marentonneau, 18th-cent. F amateur botanist]

gaily ('geɪlɪ) *adv* **1** in a gay manner; merrily **2** with bright colours; showily

gain (geɪn) *vb* **1** (*tr*) to acquire (something desirable); obtain **2** (*tr*) to win in competition: *to gain the victory* **3** to increase, improve, or advance: *the car gained speed* **4** (*tr*) to earn (a wage, living, etc) **5** (*intr*; usually foll by *on* or *upon*) **5a** to get nearer (to) or catch up (on) **5b** to get farther away (from) **6** (*tr*) (esp of ships) to get to; reach: *the steamer gained port* **7** (of a timepiece) to operate too fast, so as to indicate a time ahead of the true time ▷ *n* **8** something won, acquired, earned, etc; profit; advantage **9** an increase in size, amount, etc **10** the act of gaining; attainment; acquisition **11** Also called: **amplification** *electronics* the ratio of the output signal of an amplifier to the input signal, usually measured in decibels [C15 from OF *gaaignier*, of Gmc origin]

gainer ('geɪnə) *n* **1** a person or thing that gains **2** a type of dive in which the diver leaves the board facing forward and completes a full backward somersault to enter the water feet first with his back to the diving board

gainful ('geɪnfʊl) *adj* profitable; lucrative > **'gainfully** *adv* > **'gainfulness** *n*

gainsay (geɪn'seɪ) *vb* **gainsays, gainsaying, gainsaid** (*tr*) *arch or literary* to deny (an allegation, statement, etc); contradict [C13 *gainsaien*, from *gain-* AGAINST + *saien* to SAY] > **gain'sayer** *n*

Gainsborough ('geɪnzbərə, -brə) *n* **Thomas** 1727–88, English painter, noted particularly for his informal portraits and for his naturalistic landscapes

'gainst *or* **gainst** (gɛnst, geɪnst) *prep poetic* short for against

Gaiseric ('gaɪzərɪk) *n* a variant of **Genseric**

gait (geɪt) *n* **1** manner of walking or running **2** (used esp of horses and dogs) the pattern of footsteps at a particular speed, as the walk, canter, etc ▷ *vb* **3** (*tr*) to teach (a horse) a particular gait [C16 var. of GATE]

gaiter ('geɪtə) *n* (*often pl*) **1** a cloth or leather covering for the leg or ankle **2** Also called: **spat** a similar covering extending from the ankle to the instep [C18 from F *guêtre*, prob. of Gmc origin]

Gaitskell ('geɪtskɪl) *n* **Hugh** (**Todd Naylor**) 1906–63, British politician; leader of the Labour Party (1955–63)

Gaius ('gaɪəs) *or* **Caius** *n* **1** ?110–?180 AD, Roman jurist. His *Institutes* were later used as the basis for those of Justinian **2** **Gaius Caesar** See **Caligula**

gal (gæl) *n sl* a girl

gal. *or* **gall.** *abbrev for* gallon

Gal. *Bible abbrev for* Galatians

gala ('gɑːlə, 'geɪlə) *n* **1a** a celebration; festive occasion **1b** (*as modifier*): *a gala occasion* **2** *chiefly Brit* a sporting occasion involving competitions in several events: *a swimming gala* [C17 from F or It., from OF *gale*, from *galer* to make merry, prob. of Gmc origin]

galactic (gə'læktɪk) *adj* **1** *astron* of or relating to a galaxy, esp the Galaxy **2** **galactic plane** the plane passing through the spiral arms of the Galaxy, contained by the great circle of the celestial sphere (**galactic equator**) and perpendicular to an imaginary line joining opposite points (**galactic poles**) on the celestial sphere **3** *med* of or relating to milk [C19 from Gk *galaktikos*; see GALAXY]

galactic halo *n astron* a spheroidal aggregation of globular clusters, individual stars, dust, and gas that surrounds the Galaxy

galago (gə'lɑːgəʊ) *n, pl* **galagos** another name for **bushbaby** [C19 from NL, ?from Wolof *golokh* monkey]

galah (gə'lɑː) *n* **1** an Australian cockatoo, having grey wings, back, and crest, and a pink body **2** *Austral sl* a fool or simpleton [C19 from Abor.]

Galahad ('gælə,hæd) *n* **1** **Sir** (in Arthurian legend) the most virtuous knight of the Round Table **2** a pure or noble man

galantine ('gælən,tiːn) *n* a cold dish of meat or poultry, which is boned, cooked, then pressed and glazed [C14 from OF, from Med. L *galatina*, prob. from L *gelātus* frozen, set]

Galápagos Islands (gə'læpəgəs; *Spanish* ga'lapaɣos) *pl n* a group of 15 islands in the Pacific west of Ecuador, of which they form a province: discovered (1535) by the Spanish; main settlement on San Cristóbal. Pop: 17 000 (2000 est). Area: 7844 sq km (3028 sq miles). Official Spanish name: **Archipiélago de Colón**

Galashiels (,gælə'ʃiːlz) *n* a town in SE Scotland, in central Scottish Borders. Pop: 13 753 (1997)

Galata ('gælətə) *n* a port in NW Turkey, a suburb and the chief business section of Istanbul

Galatea (,gælə'tɪə) *n Greek myth* a statue of a maiden brought to life by Aphrodite in response to the prayers of the sculptor Pygmalion, who had fallen in love with his creation

Galați (*Romanian* ga'latsj) *n* an inland port in SE Romania, on the River Danube. Pop: 331 360 (1997 est)

Galatia (gə'leɪʃə, -ʃɪə) *n* an ancient region in central Asia Minor, conquered by Gauls 278–277 BC: later a Roman province

Galatian (gə'leɪʃən, -ʃɪən) *adj* **1** of or relating to Galatia or its inhabitants ▷ *n* **2** a native or inhabitant of Galatia

galaxy ('gæləksɪ) *n, pl* **galaxies** **1** any of a vast number of star systems held together by gravitational attraction **2** a splendid gathering, esp one of famous or distinguished people [C14 (in the sense: the Milky Way): from Med. L *galaxia*, from L, from Gk, from *gala* milk]

Galaxy ('gæləksɪ) *n* **the** the spiral galaxy that contains the solar system about three fifths of the distance from its centre. Also called: the **Milky Way System**

galbanum ('gælbənəm) *n* a bitter aromatic gum resin

extracted from any of several Asian umbelliferous plants [c14 from L, from Gk, from Heb. *helbenāh*]

Galbraith (gæl'breɪθ) *n* **John Kenneth** born 1908, US economist and diplomat born in Canada; author of *The Affluent Society* (1958), *The New Industrial State* (1967), and *The Culture of Contentment* (1992)

gale (geɪl) *n* **1** a strong wind, specifically one of force 8 on the Beaufort scale or 39–46 mph **2** (*often pl*) a loud outburst, esp of laughter **3** *arch & poetic* a gentle breeze [c16 from ?]

galea ('geɪlɪə) *n, pl* **galeae** (-lɪ,iː) a part shaped like a helmet, such as the petals of certain flowers [c18 from L: helmet] > **'gale,ate** *or* **'gale,ated** *adj*

Galen ('geɪlən) *n* Latin name *Claudius Galenus*. ?130–?200 AD, Greek physician, anatomist, and physiologist. He codified existing medical knowledge and his authority continued until the Renaissance

galena (gə'liːnə) *or* **galenite** (gə'liːnaɪt) *n* a soft heavy bluish-grey or black mineral consisting of lead sulphide: the chief source of lead. Formula: PbS [c17 from L: lead ore]

Galenic (geɪ'lɛnɪk, gə-) *adj* of or relating to Galen or his teachings or methods

Galicia *n* **1** (gə'lɪʃɪə, -'lɪʃə) a region of E central Europe on the N side of the Carpathians, now in SE Poland and the Ukraine **2** (*Spanish* ga'liθja) an autonomous region and former kingdom of NW Spain, on the Bay of Biscay and the Atlantic. Pop: 2 731 900 (2000 est)

Galician (gə'lɪʃɪən, -ʃən) *adj* **1** of or relating to Galicia in E central Europe **2** of or relating to Galicia in NW Spain ▷ *n* **3** a native or inhabitant of either Galicia **4** the Romance language or dialect of Spanish Galicia, sometimes regarded as a dialect of Spanish, although historically it is more closely related to Portuguese

Galilean¹ (,gælɪ'liːən) *n* **1** a native or inhabitant of Galilee **2 the** an epithet of Jesus Christ ▷ *adj* **3** of Galilee

Galilean² (,gælɪ'leɪən) *adj* of or relating to Galileo

Galilee ('gælɪ,liː) *n* **1 Sea of** also called: Lake **Tiberias**, Lake **Kinneret** a lake in NE Israel, 209 m (686 ft) below sea level, through which the River Jordan flows. Area: 165 sq km (64 sq miles) **2** a northern region of Israel: scene of Christ's early ministry

Galileo¹ (,gælɪ'leɪəʊ) *n* full name *Galileo Galilei*. 1564–1642, Italian mathematician, astronomer, and physicist. He discovered the isochronism of the pendulum and demonstrated that falling bodies of different weights descend at the same rate. He perfected the refracting telescope, which led to his discovery of Jupiter's satellites, sunspots, and craters on the moon. He was forced by the Inquisition to recant his support of the Copernican system

galingale ('gælɪŋ,geɪl) *or* **galangal** (gə'læŋgᵊl) *n* a European plant with rough-edged leaves, reddish spikelets of flowers, and aromatic roots [c13 from OF, from Ar., from Chinese]

galiot *or* **galliot** ('gælɪət) *n* **1** a small swift galley formerly sailed on the Mediterranean **2** a ketch formerly used along the coasts of Germany and the Netherlands [c14 from OF, from It., from Med. L *galea* GALLEY]

galipot ('gælɪ,pɒt) *n* a resin obtained from several species of pine [c18 from F, from ?]

gall¹ (gɔːl) *n* **1** *inf* impudence **2** bitterness; rancour **3** something bitter or disagreeable **4** *physiol* an obsolete term for **bile**. See also **gall bladder** [from ON, replacing OE *gealla*]

gall² (gɔːl) *n* **1** a sore on the skin caused by chafing **2** something that causes vexation or annoyance **3** irritation; exasperation ▷ *vb* **4** to abrade (the skin, etc) as by rubbing **5** (*tr*) to irritate or annoy; vex [c14 of Gmc origin; rel. to OE *gealla* sore on a horse, & ? to GALL¹]

gall³ (gɔːl) *n* an abnormal outgrowth in plant tissue caused by certain parasitic insects, fungi, bacteria, or mechanical injury [c14 from OF, from L *galla*]

gall. *or* **gal.** *abbrev for* gallon

gallant *adj* ('gælənt) **1** brave and high-spirited; courageous and honourable: *a gallant warrior* **2** (gə'lænt, 'gælənt) (of a man) attentive to women; chivalrous **3** imposing; dignified; stately: *a gallant ship* **4** *arch* showy in dress ▷ *n* ('gælənt, gə'lænt) *arch* **5** a woman's lover or suitor **6** a dashing or fashionable young man, esp one who pursues women **7** a brave, high-spirited, or adventurous man ▷ *vb* (gə'lænt, 'gælənt) *rare* **8** (when *intr*, usually foll by *with*) to court or flirt (with) [c15 from OF, from *galer* to make merry, from *gale* enjoyment, of Gmc origin] > **'gallantly** *adv*

gallantry ('gæləntrɪ) *n, pl* **gallantries** **1** conspicuous courage, esp in war **2** polite attentiveness to women **3** a gallant action, speech, etc

gall bladder *n* a muscular pear-shaped sac, lying underneath the right lobe of the liver, that stores bile

Galle ('gɔːl) *n* a port in SW Sri Lanka. Pop: 123 616 (1997 est). Former name: **Point de Galle**

galleass ('gælɪ,æs) *n* a three-masted galley used as a warship in the Mediterranean from the 15th to the 18th centuries [c16 from F, from It., from Med. L *galea* GALLEY]

galleon ('gælɪən) *n* a large sailing ship having three or more masts, used as a warship or trader from the 15th to the 18th centuries [c16 from Sp. *galeón*, from F, from OF *galie* GALLEY]

gallery ('gælərɪ) *n, pl* **galleries** **1** a room or building for exhibiting works of art **2** a covered passageway open on one side or on both sides **3** a balcony running along or around the inside wall of a church, hall, etc **4** *theatre* **4a** an upper floor that projects from the rear and contains the cheapest seats **4b** the seats there **4c** the audience seated there **5** a long narrow room, esp one used for a specific purpose: *a shooting gallery* **6** an underground passage, as in a mine, etc **7** a small ornamental railing, esp one surrounding the top of a desk, table, etc **8** any group of spectators, as at a golf match **9** a glass-fronted soundproof room overlooking a television studio, used for lighting, etc **10 play to the gallery** to try to gain popular favour, esp by crude appeals [c15 from OF, from Med. L, prob. from *galilea* galilee, porch or chapel at entrance to medieval church] > **'galleried** *adj*

Gg

galley ('gælɪ) *n* **1** any of various kinds of ship propelled by oars or sails used in ancient or medieval times **2** the kitchen of a ship, boat, or aircraft **3** any of various long rowing boats **4** *printing* **4a** a tray for holding composed type **4b** short for **galley proof** [c13 from OF *galie*, from Med. L *galea*, from Gk *galaia*, from ?]

galley proof *n* a printer's proof, esp one taken from type in a galley, used to make corrections before the matter has been split into pages. Often shortened to **galley**

galley slave *n* **1** a criminal or slave condemned to row in a galley **2** *inf* a drudge

gallfly ('gɔːl,flaɪ) *n, pl* **gallflies** any of several small insects that produce galls in plant tissues

Gallia ('gælɪə) *n* the Latin name of **Gaul**

galliard ('gæljəd) *n* **1** a spirited dance in triple time for two persons, popular in the 16th and 17th centuries **2** a piece of music composed for or in the rhythm of this dance [c14 from OF *gaillard* valiant, ? of Celtic origin]

Gallic ('gælɪk) *adj* **1** of or relating to France **2** of or relating to ancient Gaul or the Gauls

gallic acid *n* a colourless crystalline compound obtained from tannin: used as a tanning agent and in making inks and paper [c18 from F *gallique*; see GALL³]

Gallicism ('gælɪ,sɪzəm) *n* a word or idiom borrowed from French

Gallicize *or* **Gallicise** ('gælɪ,saɪz) *vb* **Gallicizes, Gallicizing, Gallicized** *or* **Gallicises, Gallicising, Gallicised** to make or become French in attitude, language, etc

galligaskins (,gælɪ'gæskɪnz) *pl n* **1** loose wide breeches or hose, esp as worn by men in the 17th century **2** leather leggings, as worn in the 19th century [c16 from obs. F, from It. *grechesco* Greek, from L *Graecus*]

gallimaufry (ˌgælɪˈmɔːfrɪ) *n, pl* **gallimaufries** a jumble; hotchpotch [c16 from F *galimafrée* ragout, hash, from ?]

gallinacean (ˌgælɪˈneɪʃən) *n* any gallinaceous bird

gallinaceous (ˌgælɪˈneɪʃəs) *adj* of, relating to, or belonging to an order of birds, including domestic fowl, pheasants, grouse, etc, having a heavy rounded body, short bill, and strong legs [c18 from L, from *gallīna* hen]

Gallinas Point (gɑːˈjiːnəs) *n* a cape in NE Colombia: the northernmost point of South America. Spanish name: **Punta Gallinas** (ˈpunta gaˈʎinas)

galling (ˈgɔːlɪŋ) *adj* irritating, exasperating, or bitterly humiliating > ˈ**gallingly** *adv*

gallinule (ˈgælɪˌnjuːl) *n* any of various aquatic birds, typically having a dark plumage, red bill, and a red shield above the bill [c18 from NL *Gallīnula*, from L *gallīna* hen]

galliot (ˈgælɪət) *n* a variant spelling of **galiot**

Gallipoli (gəˈlɪpəlɪ) *n* **1** a peninsula in NW Turkey, between the Dardanelles and the Gulf of Saros: scene of a costly but unsuccessful Allied campaign in 1915 **2** a port in NW Turkey, at the entrance to the Sea of Marmara: historically important for its strategic position. Pop: 16 751 (latest est). Turkish name: **Gelibolu**

gallipot (ˈgælɪˌpɒt) *n* a small earthenware pot used by pharmacists as a container for ointments, etc [c16 prob. from GALLEY + POT[1]; because imported in galleys]

gallium (ˈgælɪəm) *n* a silvery metallic element that is liquid for a wide temperature range. It is used in high-temperature thermometers and low-melting alloys. **Gallium arsenide** is a semiconductor. Symbol: Ga; atomic no.: 31; atomic wt.: 69.72 [c19 from NL, from L *gallus* cock, translation of F *coq* in the name of its discoverer, *Lecoq* de Boisbaudran, 19th-cent. F chemist]

gallivant (ˈgælɪˌvænt) *vb* (*intr*) to go about in search of pleasure, etc; gad about [c19 ? whimsical from GALLANT]

Gällivare (*Swedish* ˈjɛlivɑːrə) *n* a town in N Sweden, within the Arctic Circle: iron mines. Pop: 22 400 (1990)

galliwasp (ˈgælɪˌwɒsp) *n* a lizard of the Caribbean [c18 from ?]

gallnut (ˈgɔːlˌnʌt) *or* **gall-apple** *n* a type of plant gall that resembles a nut

Gallo- (ˈgæləʊ) *combining form* denoting Gaul or France: *Gallo-Roman* [from L *Gallus* a Gaul]

gallon (ˈgælən) *n* **1** Also called: **imperial gallon** *Brit* a unit of capacity equal to 277.42 cubic inches. 1 Brit gallon is equivalent to 1.20 US gallons or 4.55 litres **2** *US* a unit of capacity equal to 231 cubic inches. 1 US gallon is equivalent to 0.83 imperial gallon or 3.79 litres **3** (*pl*) *inf* great quantities [c13 from ONorthern F *galon* (OF *jalon*), ? of Celtic origin]

gallonage (ˈgælənɪdʒ) *n* a capacity measured in gallons

galloon (gəˈluːn) *n* a narrow band of cord, embroidery, silver or gold braid, etc, used on clothes and furniture [c17 from F, from OF *galonner* to trim with braid, from ?]

gallop (ˈgæləp) *vb* **gallops, galloping, galloped 1** (*intr*) (of a horse or other quadruped) to run fast with a two-beat stride in which all four legs are off the ground at once **2** to ride (a horse, etc) at a gallop **3** (*intr*) to move, read, progress, etc, rapidly ▷ *n* **4** the fast two-beat gait of horses **5** an instance of galloping [c16 from OF *galoper*, from ?] > ˈ**galloper** *n*

Gallovidian (ˌgæləʊˈvɪdɪən) *n* **1** a native or inhabitant of Galloway ▷ *adj* **2** of or relating to Galloway ▷ Also **Galwegian**

Galloway (ˈgæləˌweɪ) *n* **1** an area of SW Scotland, on the Solway Firth: consists of the former counties of Kirkcudbright and Wigtown, now part of Dumfries and Galloway; in the west is a large peninsula, the **Rhinns of Galloway,** with the **Mull of Galloway,** a promontory, at the south end of it (the southernmost point of Scotland). Related adjs: **Gallovidian, Galwegian 2** a breed of hardy beef cattle, usually black, originally bred in Galloway

gallows (ˈgæləʊz) *n, pl* **gallowses** *or* **gallows 1** a wooden structure usually consisting of two upright posts with a crossbeam, used for hanging criminals **2** any timber structure resembling this **3 the gallows** execution by hanging [c13 from ON *galgi*, replacing OE *gealga*]

gallows bird *n inf* a person considered deserving of hanging

gallows humour *n* sinister and ironic humour

gallows tree *or* **gallow tree** *n* another name for gallows (sense 1)

gallsickness (ˈgɔːlˌsɪknɪs) *n* a disease of cattle and sheep, caused by infection with rickettsiae, resulting in anaemia and jaundice. Also called: **anaplasmosis**

gallstone (ˈgɔːlˌstəʊn) *n* a small hard concretion formed in the gall bladder or its ducts

Gallup (ˈgæləp) *n* **George Horace** 1901–84, US statistician: devised the Gallup Poll; founded the American Institute of Public Opinion (1935) and its British counterpart (1936)

Gallup Poll *n* a sampling of the views of a representative cross section of the population, used esp as a means of forecasting voting

gall wasp *n* any small solitary wasp that produces galls in plant tissue

galoot *or* **galloot** (gəˈluːt) *n sl, chiefly US* a clumsy or uncouth person [c19 from ?]

galop (ˈgæləp) *n* **1** a 19th-century dance in quick duple time **2** a piece of music for this dance [c19 from F; see GALLOP]

galore (gəˈlɔː) *determiner* (*immediately postpositive*) in great numbers or quantity: *there were daffodils galore in the park* [c17 from Irish Gaelic *go leór* to sufficiency]

galoshes *or* **goloshes** (gəˈlɒʃɪz) *pl n* (*sometimes sing*) a pair of waterproof overshoes [c14 (in the sense: wooden shoe): from OF, from LL *gallicula* Gallic shoe]

Galsworthy (ˈgɔːlzˌwɜːðɪ) *n* **John** 1867–1933, English novelist and dramatist, noted for *The Forsyte Saga* (1906–28): Nobel prize for literature 1932

Galton (ˈgɔːltən) *n* Sir **Francis** 1822–1911, English explorer and scientist, a cousin of Charles Darwin, noted for his researches in heredity, meteorology, and statistics. He founded the study of eugenics and the theory of anticyclones

galumph (gəˈlʌmpf, -ˈlʌmf) *vb* (*intr*) *inf* to leap or move about clumsily or joyfully [c19 (coined by Lewis Carroll): prob. a blend of GALLOP + TRIUMPH]

Galvani (*Italian* galˈvaːni) *n* **Luigi** (luˈiːdʒi) 1737–98, Italian physiologist: observed that muscles contracted on contact with dissimilar metals. This led to the galvanic cell and the electrical theory of muscle control by nerves

galvanic (gælˈvænɪk) *adj* **1** of, producing, or concerned with an electric current, esp a direct current produced chemically **2** *inf* resembling the effect of an electric shock; convulsive, startling, or energetic > **gal**ˈ**vanically** *adv*

galvanism (ˈgælvəˌnɪzəm) *n* **1** *obs* electricity, esp when produced by chemical means as in a cell or battery **2** *med* treatment involving the application of electric currents to tissues [c18 via F from It. *galvanismo*, after GALVANI]

galvanize *or* **galvanise** (ˈgælvəˌnaɪz) *vb* **galvanizes, galvanizing, galvanized** *or* **galvanises, galvanising, galvanised** (*tr*) **1** to stimulate to action; excite; startle **2** to cover (iron, steel, etc) with a protective zinc coating **3** to stimulate by application of an electric current > ˌ**galvani**ˈ**zation** *or* ˌ**galvani**ˈ**sation** *n*

galvanized iron *or* **galvanised iron** *n building trades* iron, esp a sheet of corrugated iron, covered with a protective coating of zinc

galvano- *combining form* indicating a galvanic current: *galvanometer*

galvanometer (ˌgælvəˈnɒmɪtə) *n* any sensitive instrument for detecting or measuring small electric currents > **galvanometric** (ˌgælvənəʊˈmɛtrɪk, gælˌvænəʊ-) *adj* > ˌ**galvaˈnometry** *n*

Galway (ˈgɔːlweɪ) *n* **1** a county of W Republic of Ireland, in S Connacht, on **Galway Bay** and the Atlantic: it has a deeply indented coastline and many offshore islands, including the Aran Islands. County town: Galway. Pop: 188 854 (1996). Area: 5939 sq km (2293 sq miles) **2** a port in W Republic of Ireland, county town of Co. Galway, on Galway Bay: important fisheries (esp for salmon). Pop: 57 241 (1996) **3** Former name: **Roscommon** a breed of sheep with long wool, originally from W Ireland

Galwegian (gælˈwiːdʒən) *n* **1** another word for **Gallovidian** (sense 1) **2** a native or inhabitant of the town or county of Galway in W Republic of Ireland ▷ *adj* **3** another word for **Gallovidian** (sense 2) [c18 influenced by *Norway, Norwegian*]

gam (gæm) *n sl* a leg [c18 from F *jambe* leg]

Gama (ˈgɑːmə) *n* **Vasco da** (ˈvæskəʊ də) ?1469–1524, Portuguese navigator, who discovered the sea route from Portugal to India around the Cape of Good Hope (1498)

Gambetta (gæmˈbɛtə; *French* gɑ̃bɛta) *n* **Léon** (leɔ̃) 1838–82, French statesman; prime minister (1881–82). He organized resistance during the Franco-Prussian War (1870–71) and was a founder of the Third Republic (1871)

Gambia (ˈgæmbɪə) *n* **The** a republic in W Africa, entirely surrounded by Senegal except for an outlet to the Atlantic: sold to English merchants by the Portuguese in 1588; became a British colony in 1843; gained independence and became a member of the Commonwealth in 1965; joined with Senegal to form the Confederation of Senegambia (1982–89); consists of a strip of land about 16 km (10 miles) wide, on both banks of the **Gambia River**, extending inland for about 480 km (300 miles). Official language: English. Religion: Muslim majority. Currency: dalasi. Capital: Banjul. Pop: 1 411 000 (2001 est). Area: 11 295 sq km (4361 sq miles)

▷ www.gambia.com

Gambian (ˈgæmbɪən) *adj* **1** of or relating to Gambia or its inhabitants ▷ *n* **2** a native or inhabitant of Gambia

gambier *or* **gambir** (ˈgæmbɪə) *n* an astringent resinous substance obtained from a tropical Asian plant: used as an astringent and tonic and in tanning [c19 from Malay]

Gambier Islands (ˈgæmbɪə) *pl n* a group of islands in the S Pacific Ocean, in French Polynesia. Chief settlement: Rikitéa. Pop: 580 (latest est) Area: 30 sq km (11 sq miles)

gambit (ˈgæmbɪt) *n* **1** *chess* an opening move in which a chessman, usually a pawn, is sacrificed to secure an advantageous position **2** an opening comment, manoeuvre, etc, intended to secure an advantage [c17 from F, from It. *gambetto* a tripping up, from *gamba* leg]

gamble (ˈgæmbᵊl) *vb* **gambles, gambling, gambled** **1** (*intr*) to play games of chance to win money, etc **2** to risk or bet (money, etc) on the outcome of an event, sport, etc **3** (*intr; often foll by on*) to act with the expectation of: *to gamble on its being a sunny day* **4** (often foll by *away*) to lose by or as if by betting; squander ▷ *n* **5** a risky act or venture **6** a bet or wager [c18 prob. var. of GAME¹] > ˈ**gambler** *n* > ˈ**gambling** *n*

▷ www.betinf.com

gamboge (gæmˈbəʊdʒ, -ˈbuːʒ) *n* **1a** a gum resin used as the source of a yellow pigment and as a purgative **1b** the pigment made from this resin **2** **gamboge tree** any of several tropical Asian trees that yield this resin [c18 from NL *gambaugium*, from CAMBODIA, where first found]

gambol (ˈgæmbᵊl) *vb* **gambols, gambolling, gambolled** *or US* **gambols, gamboling, gamboled** **1** (*intr*) to skip or jump about in a playful manner; frolic ▷ *n* **2** a playful antic; frolic [c16 from F *gambade*; see JAMB]

gambrel (ˈgæmbrəl) *n* **1** the hock of a horse or similar animal **2** short for **gambrel roof** [c16 from OF, from *gambe* leg]

gambrel roof *n* **1** *chiefly Brit* a hipped roof having a small gable at both ends **2** *chiefly US & Canad* a roof having two slopes on both sides, the lower slopes being steeper than the upper

game¹ (geɪm) *n* **1** an amusement or pastime; diversion **2** a contest with rules, the result being determined by skill, strength, or chance **3** a single period of play in such a contest, sport, etc **4** the score needed to win a contest **5** a single contest in a series; match **6** (*pl; often cap*) an event consisting of various sporting contests, esp in athletics: *Olympic Games* **7** equipment needed for playing certain games **8** short for **computer game** **9** style or ability in playing a game **10** a scheme, proceeding, etc, practised like a game: *the game of politics* **11** an activity undertaken in a spirit of levity; joke: *marriage is just a game to him* **12a** wild animals, including birds and fish, hunted for sport, food, or profit **12b** (*as modifier*): *game laws* **13** the flesh of such animals, used as food **14** an object of pursuit; quarry; prey (esp in **fair game**) **15** *inf* work or occupation **16** *inf* a trick, strategy, or device: *I can see through your little game* **17** *sl, chiefly Brit* prostitution (esp in **on the game**) **18** **give the game away** to reveal one's intentions or a secret **19** **make (a) game of** to make fun of; ridicule; mock **20** **play the game** to behave fairly or in accordance with the rules **21** **the game is up** there is no longer a chance of success ▷ *adj* **22** *inf* full of fighting spirit; plucky; brave **23** (usually foll by *for*) *inf* prepared or ready; willing: *I'm game for a try* ▷ *vb* **games, gaming, gamed** **24** (*intr*) to play games of chance for money, stakes, etc; gamble [OE *gamen*] > ˈ**gamely** *adv* > ˈ**gameness** *n*

game² (geɪm) *adj* a less common word for **lame** (esp in **game leg**) [c18 prob. from Irish *cam* crooked]

gamecock (ˈgeɪmˌkɒk) *n* a cock bred and trained for fighting. Also called: **fighting cock**

game fish *n* any fish providing sport for the angler

gamekeeper (ˈgeɪmˌkiːpə) *n* a person employed to take care of game, as on an estate

gamelan (ˈgæmɪˌlæn) *n* a type of percussion orchestra common in the East Indies [from Javanese]

game laws *pl n* laws governing the hunting and preservation of game

game plan *n* **1** a strategy **2** a plan of campaign, esp in politics

game point *n tennis, etc* a stage at which winning one further point would enable one player or side to win a game

gamer (ˈgeɪmə) *n* a person who plays a computer game or participates in a role-playing game

gamesmanship (ˈgeɪmzmənʃɪp) *n inf* the art of winning games or defeating opponents by cunning practices without actually cheating

gamesome (ˈgeɪmsəm) *adj* full of merriment; sportive > ˈ**gamesomeness** *n*

gamester (ˈgeɪmstə) *n* a person who habitually plays games for money; gambler

gametangium (ˌgæmɪˈtændʒɪəm) *n, pl* **gametangia** (-dʒɪə) *biol* an organ or cell in which gametes are produced, esp in algae and fungi [c19 NL, from GAMETO- + Gk *angeion* vessel]

gamete (ˈgæmiːt, gəˈmiːt) *n* a haploid germ cell that fuses with another during fertilization [c19 from NL, from Gk *gametē* wife, from *gamos* marriage] > **gametic** (gəˈmɛtɪk) *adj*

gamete intrafallopian transfer (ˌɪntrəfəˈləʊpɪən) *n* See **GIFT**

game theory *n* mathematical theory concerned with the optimum choice of strategy in situations involving a conflict of interest

Gg

gameto- *or sometimes before a vowel* **gamet-** *combining form* gamete: *gametophyte*

gametophyte (gəˈmiːtəʊˌfaɪt) *n* the plant body, in species showing alternation of generations, that produces the gametes > **gametophytic** (ˌɡæmɪtəʊˈfɪtɪk) *adj*

gamey *or* **gamy** (ˈɡeɪmɪ) *adj* **gamier, gamiest 1** having the smell or flavour of game, esp high game **2** *inf* spirited; plucky; brave > **ˈgamily** *adv* > **ˈgaminess** *n*

gamin (ˈɡæmɪn) *n* a street urchin [from F]

gamine (ˈɡæmiːn) *n* a slim and boyish girl or young woman; an elfish tomboy [from F]

gaming (ˈɡeɪmɪŋ) *n* **a** gambling on games of chance **b** (*as modifier*): *gaming house*

gamma (ˈɡæmə) *n* **1** the third letter in the Greek alphabet (Γ, γ) **2** the third in a group or series [c14 from Gk]

gamma distribution *n statistics* a continuous two-parameter distribution from which the chi-square and exponential distributions are derived

gamma globulin *n* any of a group of proteins in blood plasma that includes most known antibodies

gamma-hydroxybutyrate (ˌɡæməhaɪˌdrɒksɪˈbjuːtɪreɪt) *n* a substance that occurs naturally in the brain, used medically as a sedative but also as a recreational drug and alleged aphrodisiac: known as 'liquid ecstasy' when mixed with alcohol. Abbreviation: **GHB**

gamma knife *n* a machine that uses radiation with extreme accuracy to destroy abnormal tissue, esp in the brain

gamma radiation *n* electromagnetic radiation of shorter wavelength and higher energy than X-rays

gamma-ray astronomy *n* the investigation of cosmic gamma rays, such as those from quasars

gamma-ray burster *n astron* a distant event involving a very bright burst of light and gamma rays lasting a few seconds, possibly caused by a supernova or by the collision of neutron stars

gamma rays *pl n* streams of gamma radiation

gamma stock *n* any of the third rank of active securities on the London stock exchange. Prices displayed by market makers are given as an indication rather than an offer to buy or sell

gammer (ˈɡæmə) *n rare, chiefly Brit* a dialect word for an old woman: now chiefly humorous or contemptuous [c16 prob. from GODMOTHER or GRANDMOTHER]

gammon[1] (ˈɡæmən) *n* **1** a cured or smoked ham **2** the hindquarter of a side of bacon, cooked either whole or in rashers [c15 from OF *gambon*, from *gambe* leg]

gammon[2] (ˈɡæmən) *n* **1** a double victory in backgammon in which one player throws off all his pieces before his opponent throws any ▷ *vb* **2** (*tr*) to score such a victory over [c18 prob. special use of ME *gamen* GAME[1]]

gammon[3] (ˈɡæmən) *Brit inf* ▷ *n* **1** deceitful nonsense; humbug ▷ *vb* **2** to deceive (a person) [c18 ? special use of GAMMON[1]]

gammy (ˈɡæmɪ) *adj* **gammier, gammiest** *Brit sl* (esp of the leg) malfunctioning, injured, or lame; game [c19 dialect var. of GAME[2]]

gamo- *or before a vowel* **gam-** *combining form* **1** indicating sexual union or reproduction: *gamogenesis* **2** united or fused: *gamopetalous* [from Gk *gamos* marriage]

gamopetalous (ˌɡæməʊˈpɛtələs) *adj* (of flowers) having petals that are united or partly united, as the primrose

gamp (ɡæmp) *n Brit inf* an umbrella [c19 after Mrs Sarah *Gamp*, a nurse in Dickens' *Martin Chuzzlewit*, who carried a faded cotton umbrella]

gamut (ˈɡæmət) *n* **1** entire range or scale, as of emotions **2** *music* **2a** a scale, esp (in medieval theory) one starting on the G on the bottom line of the bass staff **2b** the whole range of notes **3** *physics* the range of chromaticities that can be obtained by mixing three colours [c14 from Med. L, from *gamma*, the lowest note of the hexachord as established by Guido d'Arezzo + *ut* (now, *doh*), the first of the notes of the scale *ut, re, mi, fa, sol, la, si*]

-gamy *n combining form* denoting marriage or sexual union: *bigamy* [from Gk, from *gamos* marriage] > **-gamous** *adj combining form*

Gance (*French* ɡɑ̃s) *n* **Abel** (abɛl) 1889–1981, French film director, whose works include *J'accuse* (1919, 1937) and *Napoléon* (1927), which introduced the split-screen technique

Gand (ɡɑ̃) *n* the French name for **Ghent**

gander (ˈɡændə) *n* **1** a male goose **2** *inf* a quick look (esp in **take** (*or* **have**) **a gander**) **3** *inf* a simpleton [OE *gandra, ganra*]

Gandhi (ˈɡændɪ) *n* **1 Indira** (**Priyadarshini**) (ɪnˈdɪərə, ˈɪndərə), daughter of Jawaharlal Nehru. 1917–84, Indian stateswoman; prime minister of India (1966–77; 1980–84); assassinated **2 Mohandas Karamchand** (ˌməʊhənˈdʌs ˌkʌrəmˈtʃʌnd), known as *Mahatma Gandhi*. 1869–1948, Indian political and spiritual leader and social reformer. He played a major part in India's struggle for home rule and was frequently imprisoned by the British for organizing acts of civil disobedience. He advocated passive resistance and hunger strikes as means of achieving reform, campaigned for the untouchables, and attempted to unite Muslims and Hindus. He was assassinated by a Hindu extremist **3 Rajiv** (ræˈdʒiːv), son of Indira Gandhi. 1944–91, Indian statesman; prime minister of India (1984–89); assassinated

Gandhian (ˈɡændɪən) *adj* **1** of or relating to Mahatma Gandhi or his ideas ▷ *n* **2** a follower of Gandhi or his ideas

G & S *abbrev for* Gilbert and Sullivan

Gandzha (*Russian* ɡanˈdʒa) *or* **Gäncä** *n* a city in NW Azerbaijan: annexed by the Russians in 1804; centre of a cotton-growing region. Pop: 291 900 (1997 est). Former names: **Yelisavetpol** (1813–1920), **Kirovabad** (1936–91)

Ganesa (ɡæˈniːsə) *n* the Hindu god of prophecy, represented as having an elephant's head

gang[1] (ɡæŋ) *n* **1** a group of people who associate together or act as an organized body, esp for criminal or illegal purposes **2** an organized group of workmen **3** a series of similar tools arranged to work simultaneously in parallel ▷ *vb* **4** to form into, become part of, or act as a gang ▷ See also **gang up** [OE: journey]

gang[2] (ɡæŋ) *n* a variant spelling of **gangue**

gang[3] (ɡæŋ) *vb* (*intr*) *Scot* to go or walk [OE *gangan*]

gangbang (ˈɡæŋˌbæŋ) *n sl* an instance of sexual intercourse between one woman and several men one after the other, esp against her will

gang-banger *n US sl* a member of a street gang > **ˈgang-ˌbanging** *n*

ganger (ˈɡæŋə) *n chiefly Brit* the foreman of a gang of labourers

Ganges (ˈɡændʒiːz) *n* the great river of N India and central Bangladesh: rises in two headstreams in the Himalayas and flows southeast to Allahabad, where it is joined by the Jumna; continues southeast into Bangladesh, where it enters the Bay of Bengal in a great delta; the most sacred river to Hindus, with many places of pilgrimage, esp Varanasi. Length: 2507 km (1557 miles). Hindi name: **Ganga** (ˈɡʌŋɡə, ˈɡɑːŋ-)

Gangetic (ɡænˈdʒɛtɪk) *adj* of or relating to the river Ganges

gangland (ˈɡæŋˌlænd, -lənd) *n* the criminal underworld

gangling (ˈɡæŋɡlɪŋ) *or* **gangly** *adj* tall, lanky, and awkward in movement [see GANG[3]]

ganglion (ˈɡæŋɡlɪən) *n, pl* **ganglia** (-ɡlɪə) *or* **ganglions** **1** an encapsulated collection of nerve-cell bodies, usually located outside the brain and spinal cord **2** any concentration or centre of energy, activity, or strength

3 a cystic tumour on a tendon sheath [c17 from LL: swelling, from Gk: cystic tumour] > **'gangliar** *adj* > **,gangli'onic** *or* **'gangli,ated** *adj*

gangplank ('gæŋ,plæŋk) *or* **gangway** *n naut* a portable bridge for boarding and leaving a vessel at dockside

gangrene ('gæŋgri:n) *n* **1** death and decay of tissue due to an interrupted blood supply, disease, or injury ▷ *vb* **gangrenes, gangrening, gangrened 2** to become or cause to become affected with gangrene [c16 from L, from Gk *gangraina* an eating sore] > **gangrenous** ('gæŋgrınəs) *adj*

gang-saw *n* a multiple saw used in a timber mill to cut planks from logs

gangsta rap ('gæŋstə) *n* a style of rap music, usually characterized by songs about Black street gangs in the US, with nihilistic and misogynistic lyrics [c20 phonetic rendering of GANGSTER] > **gangsta rapper** *n*
▷ www.bandhunt.com/genre/style.php/uro4

gangster ('gæŋstə) *n* a member of an organized gang of criminals

gangsterism ('gæŋstərızəm) *n* the culture of belonging to organized gangs of criminals, esp involving violence

Gangtok ('gʌŋtɒk) *n* a city in NE India: capital of Sikkim state. Pop: 24 970 (1991)

gangue *or* **gang** (gæŋ) *n* valueless and undesirable material in an ore [c19 from F, from G *Gang* vein of metal, course]

gang up *vb* (*intr, adv;* often foll by *on* or *against*) *inf* to combine in a group (against)

gangway ('gæŋ,weı) *n* **1** another word for **gangplank 2** an opening in a ship's side to take a gangplank **3** *Brit* an aisle between rows of seats **4** temporary planks over mud, as on a building site ▷ *sentence substitute* **5** clear a path!

ganister *or* **gannister** ('gænıstə) *n* a refractory siliceous sedimentary rock occurring beneath coal seams: used for lining furnaces [c20 from ?]

gannet ('gænıt) *n* **1** any of several heavily built marine birds having a long stout bill and typically white plumage with dark markings **2** *sl* a greedy person [OE *ganot*]

ganoid ('gænɔıd) *adj* **1** (of the scales of certain fishes) consisting of an inner bony layer and an outer layer of an enamel-like substance (**ganoin**) **2** denoting fishes, including the sturgeon, having such scales ▷ *n* **3** a ganoid fish [c19 from F, from Gk *ganos* brightness + -OID]

Gansu ('gæn'su:) *or* **Kansu** *n* a province of NW China, between Tibet and Inner Mongolia: mountainous, with desert regions; forms a corridor, the Old Silk Road, much used in early and medieval times for trade with Turkestan, India, and Persia. Capital: Lanzhou. Pop: 25 620 000 (2000 est). Area: 366 500 sq km (141 500 sq miles)

gantry ('gæntrı) *n, pl* **gantries 1** a bridgelike framework used to support a travelling crane, signals over a railway track, etc **2** Also called: **gantry scaffold** the framework tower used to attend to a large rocket on its launch pad **3** a supporting framework for a barrel **4a** the area behind a bar where bottles, esp spirit bottles mounted in optics, are kept **4b** the range or quality of the spirits on display there [c16 (in the sense: wooden platform for barrels): from OF *chantier*, from Med. L, from L *canthērius* supporting frame, pack ass]

Gantt chart (gænt) *n* a chart showing, in horizontal lines, activity planned to take place during specified periods, which are indicated in vertical bands [c20 named after Henry L. Gantt (1861–1919), US management consultant]

Ganymede ('gænı,mi:d) *n classical myth* a beautiful Trojan youth who was abducted by Zeus to Olympus and made the cupbearer of the gods

Gao ('gɑ:əʊ, gaʊ) *n* a town in E Mali, on the River Niger: a small river port. Pop: 54 875 (latest est)

gaol (dʒeıl) *n, vb* (*tr*) *Brit* a variant spelling of **jail** > **'gaoler** *n*

Gao Xingjian (jaʊ 'ʃıŋ'dʒjæn) *n* born 1940, Chinese dramatist, novelist, and dissident, living in France from 1987; his works include the play *Chezhan* (*Bus Stop*, 1983) and the novel *Lingshan* (*Soul Mountain*, 1989): Nobel prize for literature 2000

Gaoxiong (,jaʊə'ʃɒŋ) *n* a variant transliteration of the Chinese name for **Kaohsiung**

gap (gæp) *n* **1** a break or opening in a wall, fence, etc **2** a break in continuity; interruption; hiatus **3** a break in a line of hills or mountains affording a route through **4** *chiefly US* a gorge or ravine **5** a divergence or difference; disparity: *the generation gap* **6** *electronics* **6a** a break in a magnetic circuit that increases the inductance and saturation point of the circuit **6b** See **spark gap 7 bridge, close, fill,** *or* **stop a gap** to remedy a deficiency ▷ *vb* **gaps, gapping, gapped 8** (*tr*) to make a breach or opening in [c14 from ON *gap* chasm] > **'gappy** *adj*

gape (geıp) *vb* **gapes, gaping, gaped** (*intr*) **1** to stare in wonder, esp with the mouth open **2** to open the mouth wide, esp involuntarily, as in yawning **3** to be or become wide open: *the crater gaped under his feet* ▷ *n* **4** the act of gaping **5** a wide opening **6** the width of the widely opened mouth of a vertebrate **7** a stare of astonishment [c13 from ON *gapa*] > **'gaper** *n* > **'gaping** *adj*

gapes (geıps) *n* (*functioning as sing*) **1** a disease of young domestic fowl, characterized by gaping and caused by parasitic worms (**gapeworms**) **2** *inf* a fit of yawning

gap year *n* a year's break taken by a student between leaving school and starting further education

gar (gɑ:) *n, pl* **gar** *or* **gars** short for **garpike**

garage ('gærɑ:ʒ, -rıdʒ) *n* **1** a building used to house a motor vehicle **2** a commercial establishment in which motor vehicles are repaired, serviced, bought, and sold, and which usually also sells motor fuels ▷ *vb* **garages, garaging, garaged 3** (*tr*) to put into or keep in a garage [c20 from F, from OF: to protect, from OHG *warōn*]

garage band *n* a rough-and-ready amateurish rock group [?from the practice of such bands rehearsing in a garage]

garage sale *n* a sale of personal belongings or household effects held at a person's home, usually in the garage

garb (gɑ:b) *n* **1** clothes, esp the distinctive attire of an occupation: *clerical garb* **2** style of dress; fashion **3** external appearance, covering, or attire ▷ *vb* **4** (*tr*) to clothe; attire [c16 from OF: graceful contour, from OIt. *garbo* grace, prob. of Gmc origin]

garbage ('gɑ:bıdʒ) *n* **1** worthless, useless, or unwanted matter **2** another word (esp US and Canad) for **rubbish 3** *computing* invalid data **4** *inf* nonsense [c15 prob. from Anglo-F *garbelage* removal of discarded matter, from ?]

garbage collection *n* **1** the removal of household refuse **2** *computing* a system in which memory is automatically reallocated when data is no longer live

garble ('gɑ:bᵊl) *vb* **garbles, garbling, garbled** (*tr*) **1** to jumble (a story, quotation, etc), esp unintentionally **2** to distort the meaning of (an account, text, etc), as by making misleading omissions; corrupt ▷ *n* **3a** the act of garbling **3b** garbled matter [c15 from OIt. *garbellare* to strain, sift, from Ar., from LL *crībellum* small sieve] > **'garbler** *n*

Garbo ('gɑ:bəʊ) *n* **Greta** ('grɛtə), real name *Greta Lovisa Gustafson*. 1905–90, US film actress, born in Sweden. Her films include *Grand Hotel* (1932), *Queen Christina* (1933), *Anna Karenina* (1935), *Camille* (1936), and *Ninotchka* (1939)

garboard ('gɑ:,bɔ:d) *n naut* the bottommost plank of a vessel's hull. Also called: **garboard strake** [c17 from Du. *gaarboord*, prob. from MDu. *gaderen* to GATHER + *boord* BOARD]

garbology (gɑːˈbɒlədʒɪ) *n chiefly US* **1** analysis of refuse as a means of investigating the lifestyle of the person or people who produced it **2** the study of waste disposal [c20 from GARBAGE + -OLOGY] > **gar'bologist** *n*

García Lorca (*Spanish* garˈθia ˈlɔrka) *n* See (Federico García) **Lorca**

García Márquez (*Spanish* garˈsia ˈmarkes) *n* **Gabriel** born 1928, Colombian novelist and short-story writer. His novels include *One Hundred Years of Solitude* (1967), *The Autumn of the Patriarch* (1977), *Love in the Time of Cholera* (1984), and *News of a Kidnapping* (1996). Nobel prize for literature 1982

garçon (ˈgɑːsɒn; *French* garsɔ̃) *n* a waiter or male servant, esp if French [c19 from OF *gars* lad, prob. of Gmc origin]

Gard (*French* gar) *n* a department of S France, in Languedoc-Roussillon region. Capital: Nîmes. Pop: 623 125 (1999). Area: 5881 sq km (2294 sq miles)

garda (ˈgɑːrdə) *n, pl* **gardaí** (ˈgɑːrdɪ) a member of the **Garda Síochána,** the police force of the Republic of Ireland

Garda (ˈgɑːdə) *n* **Lake** a lake in N Italy: the largest lake in the country. Area: 370 sq km (143 sq miles)

garden (ˈgɑːdᵊn) *n* **1** *Brit* **1a** an area of land, usually planted with grass, trees, flowerbeds, etc, adjoining a house. US and Canad word: **yard 1b** (*as modifier*): *a garden chair* **2a** an area of land used for the cultivation of ornamental plants, herbs, fruit, vegetables, trees, etc **2b** (*as modifier*): *garden tools.* Related adj: **horticultural 3** (*often pl*) such an area of land that is open to the public, sometimes part of a park: *botanical gardens* **4** a fertile and beautiful region **5 lead (a person) up the garden path** *inf* to mislead or deceive ▷ *vb* **6** to work in, cultivate, or take care of (a garden, plot of land, etc) [c14 from OF *gardin*, of Gmc origin] > **'gardener** *n* > **'gardening** *n*

▷ www.garden.org
▷ www.gardenadvice.co.uk
▷ www.uk.gardenweb.com
▷ www.ngs.org.uk
▷ www.greenfingers.com
▷ www.bbc.co.uk/gardening
▷ www.abc.net.au/gardening
▷ www.bestgardening.co.nz/bgc/default.htm
▷ www.canadiangardening.com/home.shtml
▷ www.global-garden.com.au

garden centre *n* a place where gardening tools and equipment, plants, seeds, etc are sold

garden city *n Brit* a planned town of limited size surrounded by a rural belt

gardenia (gɑːˈdiːnɪə) *n* **1** any evergreen shrub or tree of the Old World tropical genus *Gardenia*, cultivated for their large fragrant waxlike typically white flowers **2** the flower of any of these shrubs [c18 NL, after Dr Alexander *Garden* (1730–91), American botanist]

gardening leave *or* **garden leave** *n Brit inf* a period during which an employee who is about to leave a company continues to receive a salary but does not work

Garden of Eden *n* the full name for **Eden**[1]

garderobe (ˈgɑːdˌrəʊb) *n arch* **1** a wardrobe or its contents **2** a private room **3** a privy [c14 from F, from *garder* to keep + *robe* dress, clothing; see WARDROBE]

Gardiner (ˈgɑːdnə) *n* **1** Sir **John Eliot** born 1943, British conductor, noted for performances using period instruments; founded the Monteverdi Choir in 1965 and the Orchestre Révolutionnaire et Romantique in 1990 **2 Stephen** ?1483–1555, English bishop and statesman; lord chancellor (1553–55) He opposed Protestantism, supporting the anti-Reformation policies of Mary I

Gardner (ˈgɑːdnə) *n* **Ava** 1922–90, US film actress. Her films include *The Killers* (1946), *The Sun also Rises* (1957), and *The Night of the Iguana* (1964)

Garfield (ˈgɑːˌfiːld) *n* **James Abram** 1831–81, 20th president of the US (1881); assassinated in office

garfish (ˈgɑːˌfɪʃ) *n, pl* **garfish** *or* **garfishes 1** another name for **garpike** (sense 1) **2** an elongated marine teleost fish with long toothed jaws: related to the flying fishes [OE *gār* spear + FISH]

garganey (ˈgɑːgənɪ) *n* a small Eurasian duck closely related to the mallard. The male has a white stripe over each eye [c17 from It. dialect *garganei*, imit.]

gargantuan (gɑːˈgæntjʊən) *adj* (*sometimes cap*) huge; enormous [after *Gargantua*, a giant in Rabelais' satire *Gargantua and Pantagruel* (1534)]

> **USAGE** Some people think that *gargantuan* should only be used to describe things connected with food: *a gargantuan meal; his gargantuan appetite*. Nevertheless, the word is now widely used as a synonym of 'colossal'

gargle (ˈgɑːgᵊl) *vb* **gargles, gargling, gargled 1** to rinse the mouth and throat with (a liquid, esp a medicinal fluid) by slowly breathing out through the liquid ▷ *n* **2** the liquid used for gargling **3** the sound produced by gargling [c16 from OF, from *gargouille* throat, ? imit.]

gargoyle (ˈgɑːgɔɪl) *n* **1** a waterspout carved in the form of a grotesque face or creature and projecting from a roof gutter **2** a person with a grotesque appearance [c15 from OF *gargouille* gargoyle, throat; see GARGLE]

garibaldi (ˌgærɪˈbɔːldɪ) *n Brit* a type of biscuit having a layer of currants in the centre

Garibaldi (ˌgærɪˈbɔːldɪ) *n* **Giuseppe** (dʒuˈzɛppe) 1807–82, Italian patriot; a leader of the Risorgimento. He fought against the Austrians and French in Italy (1848–49; 1859) and, with 1000 volunteers, conquered Sicily and Naples for the emerging kingdom of Italy (1860)

garish (ˈgɛərɪʃ) *adj* gay or colourful in a crude manner; gaudy [c16 from earlier *gaure* to stare + -ISH] > **'garishly** *adv* > **'garishness** *n*

garland (ˈgɑːlənd) *n* **1** a wreath of flowers, leaves, etc, worn round the head or neck or hung up **2** a collection of short literary pieces, such as poems; anthology ▷ *vb* **3** (*tr*) to adorn with a garland or garlands [c14 from OF *garlande*, ? of Gmc origin]

Garland (ˈgɑːlənd) *n* **Judy,** real name *Frances Gumm*. 1922–69, US singer and film actress. Already a child star, she achieved international fame with *The Wizard of Oz* (1939). Later films included *Meet Me in St Louis* (1944) and *A Star is Born* (1954)

garlic (ˈgɑːlɪk) *n* **1** a hardy widely cultivated Asian alliaceous plant having whitish flowers **2** the bulb of this plant, made up of small segments (cloves) that have a strong odour and pungent taste and are used in cooking [OE *gārlēac*, from *gār* spear + *lēac* LEEK] > **'garlicky** *adj*

garment (ˈgɑːmənt) *n* **1** (*often pl*) an article of clothing **2** outer covering ▷ *vb* **3** (*tr; usually passive*) to cover or clothe [c14 from OF *garniment*, from *garnir* to equip; see GARNISH]

garner (ˈgɑːnə) *vb* (*tr*) **1** to gather or store as in a granary ▷ *n* **2** an archaic word for **granary 3** *arch* a place for storage [c12 from OF: granary, from L *grānārium*, from *grānum* grain]

Garner (ˈgɑːnə) *n* **Erroll** 1921–77, US jazz pianist and composer

garnet (ˈgɑːnɪt) *n* any of a group of hard glassy red, yellow, or green minerals consisting of silicates in cubic crystalline form: used as a gemstone and abrasive [c13 from OF, from *grenat* (adj) red, from *pome grenate* POMEGRANATE]

garnish (ˈgɑːnɪʃ) *vb* (*tr*) **1** to decorate; trim **2** to add something to (food) in order to improve its appearance or flavour **3** *law* **3a** to serve with notice of proceedings; warn **3b** to attach (a debt) ▷ *n* **4** a decoration; trimming **5** something, such as parsley, added to a dish for its flavour or decorative effect [c14 from OF *garnir* to adorn, equip, of Gmc origin] > **'garnisher** *n*

garnishee (ˌgɑːnɪˈʃiː) *law* ▷ *n* **1** a person upon whom a garnishment has been served ▷ *vb* **garnishees,**

garnisheeing, garnisheed (*tr*) **2** to attach (a debt or other property) by garnishment **3** to serve (a person) with a garnishment

garnishment ('gɑːnɪʃmənt) *n* **1** decoration or embellishment **2** *law* **2a** a notice or warning **2b** *obs* a summons to court proceedings already in progress **2c** a notice warning a person holding money or property belonging to a debtor whose debt has been attached to hold such property until directed by the court to apply it

garniture ('gɑːnɪtʃə) *n* decoration or embellishment [c16 from F, from *garnir* to GARNISH]

Garonne (*French* garɔn) *n* a river in SW France, rising in the central Pyrenees in Spain and flowing northeast then northwest into the Gironde estuary. Length: 580 km (360 miles)

garpike ('gɑː,paɪk) *n* **1** Also called: **garfish, gar** any primitive freshwater elongated bony fish of North and Central America, having very long toothed jaws and a body covering of thick scales **2** another name for **garfish** (sense 2)

garret ('gærɪt) *n* another word for **attic** (sense 1) [c14 from OF: watchtower, from *garir* to protect, of Gmc origin]

Garrett ('gærət) *n* **1 Lesley** born 1955, British soprano; principal soprano with the English National Opera from 1984 **2 Peter** born 1953, Australian rock musician and environmental activist. The former lead singer of Midnight Oil (1976–2002), he is president of the Australian Conservation Foundation (1989–93; 1998–)

garret window *n* a skylight that lies along the slope of the roof

Garrick ('gærɪk) *n* **David** 1717–79, English actor and theatre manager

garrison ('gærɪsᵊn) *n* **1** the troops who maintain and guard a base or fortified place **2** the place itself ▷ *vb* **3** (*tr*) to station (troops) in (a fort, etc) [c13 from OF, from *garir* to defend, of Gmc origin]

garron ('gærən) *n* a small sturdy pony bred and used chiefly in Scotland and Ireland [c16 from Gaelic *gearran*]

garrotte *or* **garotte** (gə'rɒt) *n* **1** a Spanish method of execution by strangulation **2** the device, usually an iron collar, used in such executions **3** *obs* strangulation of one's victim while committing robbery ▷ *vb* **garrottes, garrotting, garrotted** *or* **garottes, garotting, garotted** (*tr*) **4** to execute by means of the garrotte **5** to strangle, esp in order to commit robbery [c17 from Sp. *garrote*, ?from OF *garrot* cudgel; from ?] > **gar'rotter** *or* **ga'rotter** *n*

garrulous ('gærʊləs) *adj* **1** given to constant chatter; talkative **2** wordy or diffuse [c17 from L, from *garrīre* to chatter] > **'garrulously** *adv* > **'garrulousness** *or* **garrulity** (gæ'ruːlɪtɪ) *n*

garryowen (,gærɪ'əʊɪn) *n* (in rugby union) another term for **up-and-under** [from *Garryowen* RFC, Ireland]

garter ('gɑːtə) *n* **1** a band, usually of elastic, worn round the leg to hold up a sock or stocking **2** the US and Canad word for **suspender** ▷ *vb* **3** (*tr*) to fasten or secure as with a garter [c14 from OF *gartier*, from *garet* bend of the knee, prob. of Celtic origin]

Garter ('gɑːtə) *n* **the 1 Order of the Garter** the highest order of British knighthood, open to women since 1987 **2** (*sometimes not cap*) **2a** the badge of this Order **2b** membership of this Order

garter snake *n* a nonvenomous North American snake, typically marked with longitudinal stripes

garter stitch *n* knitting in which all the rows are knitted in plain stitch

garth (gɑːθ) *n* **1** a courtyard surrounded by a cloister **2** *arch* a yard or garden [c14 from ON *garthr*]

Gary ('gærɪ) *n* a port in NW Indiana, on Lake Michigan: a major world steel producer. Pop: 102 746 (1996 est)

gas (gæs) *n, pl* **gases** *or* **gasses 1** a substance in a physical state in which it does not resist change of shape and will expand indefinitely to fill any container ▷ Cf **liquid** (sense 1), **solid** (sense 1) **2** any substance that is gaseous at room temperature and atmospheric pressure **3** any gaseous substance that is above its critical temperature and therefore not liquefiable by pressure alone ▷ Cf **vapour** (sense 2) **4a** a fossil fuel in the form of a gas, used as a source of domestic and industrial heat **4b** (*as modifier*): *a gas cooker; gas fire* **5** a gaseous anaesthetic, such as nitrous oxide **6** *mining* firedamp or the explosive mixture of firedamp and air **7** the usual US, Canad, Austral, and NZ word for **petrol**, a shortened form of **gasoline 8 step on the gas** *inf* **8a** to accelerate a motor vehicle **8b** to hurry **9** a toxic, etc, substance in suspension in air used against an enemy, etc **10** *inf* idle talk or boasting **11** *sl* a delightful or successful person or thing: *his latest record is a gas* **12** US an informal name for **flatus** ▷ *vb* **gases** *or* **gasses, gassing, gassed 13** (*tr*) to provide or fill with gas **14** (*tr*) to subject to gas fumes, esp so as to asphyxiate or render unconscious **15** (*intr; foll by to*) *inf* to talk in an idle or boastful way (to a person) [c17 (coined by J. B. van Helmont (1577–1644), Flemish chemist): from Gk *khaos* atmosphere]

gasbag ('gæs,bæg) *n inf* a person who talks in a voluble way, esp about unimportant matters

gas chamber *or* **oven** *n* an airtight room into which poison gas is introduced to kill people or animals

gas chromatography *n* a technique for analysing a mixture of volatile substances in which the mixture is carried by an inert gas through a column packed with a selective adsorbent or absorbent and a detector records on a moving strip the conductivity of the gas leaving the tube

Gascon ('gæskən) *n* **1** a native or inhabitant of Gascony **2** the dialect of French spoken in Gascony ▷ *adj* **3** of or relating to Gascony, its inhabitants, or their dialect of French

gasconade (,gæskə'neɪd) *rare* ▷ *n* **1** boastful talk or bluster ▷ *vb* **gasconades, gasconading, gasconaded 2** (*intr*) to boast, brag, or bluster [c18 from F, from *gasconner* to chatter, boast like a GASCON]

gas constant *n* **1** another name for **universal gas constant 2** the universal gas constant divided by the molar mass of a specified gas

Gascony ('gæskənɪ) *n* a former province of SW France. French name: **Gascogne** (gaskɔɲ)

gas-cooled reactor *n* a nuclear reactor using a gas as the coolant

gas-discharge tube *n electronics* any tube in which an electric discharge takes place through a gas

gaseous ('gæsɪəs, -ʃəs, -ʃɪəs, 'geɪ-) *adj* of, concerned with, or having the characteristics of a gas > **'gaseousness** *n*

gas equation *n* an equation relating the product of the pressure and the volume of an ideal gas to the product of its thermodynamic temperature and the gas constant

gas gangrene *n* gangrene resulting from infection of a wound by anaerobic bacteria that cause gas bubbles in the surrounding tissues

gas guzzler *n sl, chiefly US* a car that consumes large quantities of petrol

gash (gæʃ) *vb* **1** (*tr*) to make a long deep cut in; slash ▷ *n* **2** a long deep cut [c16 from OF *garser* to scratch, from Vulgar L, from Gk *kharassein*]

gasholder ('gæs,həʊldə) *n* **1** Also called: **gasometer** a large tank for storing coal gas or natural gas prior to distribution to users **2** any vessel for storing or measuring a gas

gasify ('gæsɪ,faɪ) *vb* **gasifies, gasifying, gasified** to make into or become a gas > **,gasifi'cation** *n*

Gaskell ('gæskᵊl) *n* **Mrs** married name of *Elizabeth Cleghorn Stevenson*. 1810–65, English novelist. Her novels include *Mary Barton* (1848), an account of industrial life in Manchester, and *Cranford* (1853), a social study of a country village

gasket ('gæskɪt) *n* **1** a compressible packing piece of

Gg

paper, rubber, asbestos, etc, sandwiched between the faces of a metal joint to provide a seal **2** *naut* a piece of line used as a sail stop [c17 (in the sense: rope lashing a furled sail): prob. from F *garcette* rope's end, lit.: little girl, from OF]

gaslight ('gæs,laɪt) *n* **1** a type of lamp in which the illumination is produced by an incandescent mantle heated by a jet of gas **2** the light produced by such a lamp

gasman ('gæs,mæn) *n, pl* **gasmen** a man employed to read household gas meters, supervise gas fittings, etc

gas mantle *n* a mantle for use in a gaslight. See **mantle** (sense 4)

gas mask *n* a mask fitted with a chemical filter to enable the wearer to breathe air free of poisonous or corrosive gases

gas meter *n* an apparatus for measuring and recording the amount of gas passed through it

gasoline *or* **gasolene** ('gæsə,liːn) *n* a US and Canad name for **petrol**

gasometer (gæs'ɒmɪtə) *n* a nontechnical name for **gasholder**

gasp (gɑːsp) *vb* **1** (*intr*) to draw in the breath sharply or with effort, esp in expressing awe, horror, etc **2** (*intr; foll by after or for*) to crave **3** (*tr; often foll by out*) to utter breathlessly ▷ *n* **4** a short convulsive intake of breath **5 at the last gasp 5a** at the point of death **5b** at the last moment [c14 from ON *geispa* to yawn]

Gaspar ('gæspə, 'gæspɑː) *n* a variant of **Caspar**

Gaspé Peninsula (gæ'speɪ; *French* gaspe) *n* a peninsula in E Canada, in SE Quebec between the St Lawrence River and New Brunswick: mountainous and wooded with many lakes and rivers. Area: about 29 500 sq km (11 400 sq miles). Also called: **the Gaspé**

gasper ('gɑːspə) *n* **1** a person who gasps **2** *Brit dated sl* a cheap cigarette

gaspereau ('gæspərəʊ) *n Canad* another name for **alewife** [from Canadian French]

gas plant *n* an aromatic white-flowered Eurasian plant that emits vapour capable of being ignited. Also called: **burning bush, dittany, fraxinella**

gas ring *n* a circular assembly of gas jets, used esp for cooking

Gasser ('gæsə) *n* **Herbert Spencer** 1888–1963, US physiologist: shared a Nobel prize for physiology or medicine (1944) with Erlanger for work on electrical signs of nervous activity

gassy ('gæsɪ) *adj* **gassier, gassiest 1** filled with, containing, or resembling gas **2** *inf* full of idle or vapid talk > **'gassiness** *n*

gasteropod ('gæstərə,pɒd) *n, adj* a variant spelling of **gastropod**

gas thermometer *n* a device for measuring temperature by observing the pressure of gas at a constant volume or the volume of a gas kept at a constant pressure

gastric ('gæstrɪk) *adj* of, relating to, near, or involving the stomach

gastric juice *n* a digestive fluid secreted by the stomach, containing hydrochloric acid, pepsin, rennin, etc

gastric ulcer *n* an ulcer of the mucous membrane lining the stomach

gastritis (gæs'traɪtɪs) *n* inflammation of the lining of the stomach

gastro- *or often before a vowel* **gastr-** *combining form* stomach: *gastroenteritis; gastritis* [from Gk *gastēr*]

gastrocolic (,gæstrəʊ'kɒlɪk) *adj* of or relating to the stomach and colon: *gastrocolic reflex*

gastroenteritis (,gæstrəʊ,entə'raɪtɪs) *n* inflammation of the stomach and intestines

gastrointestinal (,gæstrəʊɪn'tɛstɪnᵊl) *adj* of or relating to the stomach and intestinal tract
▷ www.ccfa.org

gastronome ('gæstrə,nəʊm), **gastronomer** (gæs'trɒnəmə), *or* **gastronomist** *n* less common words for **gourmet**

gastronomy (gæs'trɒnəmɪ) *n* the art of good eating [c19 from F, from Gk, from *gastēr* stomach; see -NOMY] > **gastronomic** (,gæstrə'nɒmɪk) *or* **,gastro'nomical** *adj* > **,gastro'nomically** *adv*
▷ www.1999hs2000.com/Such-n-Such/gastronome.htm

gastropod ('gæstrə,pɒd) *or* **gasteropod** *n* any of a class of molluscs typically having a flattened muscular foot for locomotion and a head that bears stalked eyes. The class includes the snails, whelks, and slugs > **gastropodan** (gæs'trɒpədᵊn) *adj, n*

gastroscope ('gæstrə,skəʊp) *n* a medical instrument for examining the interior of the stomach

gastrula ('gæstrʊlə) *n, pl* **gastrulas** *or* **gastrulae** (-,liː) a saclike animal embryo consisting of three layers of cells surrounding a central cavity with a small opening to the exterior [c19 NL: little stomach, from Gk *gastēr* belly]

gas turbine *n* an internal-combustion engine in which the expanding gases emerging from one or more combustion chambers drive a turbine

gasworks ('gæs,wɜːks) *n* (*functioning as sing*) a plant in which gas, esp coal gas, is made

gat (gæt) *vb arch* a past tense of **get**

gate (geɪt) *n* **1** a movable barrier, usually hinged, for closing an opening in a wall, fence, etc **2** an opening to allow passage into or out of an enclosed place **3** any means of entrance or access **4** a mountain pass or gap, esp one providing entry into another country or region **5a** the number of people admitted to a sporting event or entertainment **5b** the total entrance money received from them **6** *electronics* a logic circuit having one or more input terminals and one output terminal, the output being switched between two voltage levels determined by the combination of input signals **7** a component in a motion-picture camera or projector that holds each frame flat and momentarily stationary behind the lens **8** a slotted metal frame that controls the positions of the gear lever in a motor vehicle ▷ *vb* **gates, gating, gated 9** (*tr*) *Brit* to restrict (a student) to the school or college grounds as a punishment [OE *geat*]

gâteau ('gætəʊ) *n, pl* **gâteaux** (-təʊz) a rich cake usually layered with cream and elaborately decorated [F: cake]

gate-crash *vb inf* to gain entry to (a party, concert, etc) without invitation or payment > **'gate-,crasher** *n*

gatefold ('geɪt,fəʊld) *n* an oversize page in a book or magazine that is folded in. Also called: **foldout**

gatehouse ('geɪt,haʊs) *n* **1** a building at or above a gateway, used by a porter or guard, or, formerly, as a fortification **2** a small house at the entrance to the grounds of a country mansion

gatekeeper ('geɪt,kiːpə) *n* **1** a person who has charge of a gate and controls who may pass through it **2** a manager in a large organization who controls the flow of information, esp to parent and subsidiary companies **3** any of several Eurasian butterflies having brown-bordered orange wings

gate-leg table *or* **gate-legged table** *n* a table with one or two leaves supported by a hinged leg swung out from the frame

gatepost ('geɪt,pəʊst) *n* **1a** the post on which a gate is hung **1b** the post to which a gate is fastened when closed **2 between you, me, and the gatepost** confidentially

Gates (geɪts) *n* **1 Bill,** full name *William Henry Gates*. born 1955, US computer-software executive; founder (1976) of Microsoft Corporation **2 Henry Louis** born 1950, US scholar and critic, who pioneered African-American studies in such works as *Figures in Black* (1987) **3 Horatio** ?1728–1806, American Revolutionary general: defeated the British at Saratoga (1777)

Gateshead ('geɪts,hɛd) *n* **1** a port in NE England, in Gateshead unitary authority, Tyne and Wear: engineering works, cultural centre. Pop: 83 159 (1991) **2** a unitary authority in NE England, in Tyne and Wear. Pop: 191 151 (2001). Area: 142 sq km (55 sq miles)

gateway ('geɪt,weɪ) *n* **1** an entrance that may be closed by or as by a gate **2** a means of entry or access: *Bombay, gateway to India* **3** *computer technol* hardware and software that connect incompatible computer networks

Gath (gæθ) *n Old Testament* one of the five cities of the Philistines, from which Goliath came (I Samuel 17:4) and near which Saul fell in battle (II Samuel 1:20). Douay spelling: **Geth** (gɛθ)

gather ('gæðə) *vb* **1** to assemble or cause to assemble **2** to collect or be collected gradually; muster **3** (*tr*) to learn from information given; conclude or assume **4** (*tr*) to pick or harvest (flowers, fruit, etc) **5** (*tr*) to bring close (to) **6** to increase or cause to increase gradually, as in force, speed, intensity, etc **7** to contract (the brow) or (of the brow) to become contracted into wrinkles; knit **8** (*tr*) to assemble (sections of a book) in the correct sequence for binding **9** (*tr*) to prepare or make ready: *to gather one's wits* **10** to draw (material) into a series of small tucks or folds **11** (*intr*) (of a boil or other sore) to come to a head; form pus ▷ *n* **12a** the act of gathering **12b** the amount gathered **13** a small fold in material, as made by a tightly pulled stitch; tuck [OE *gadrian*] > '**gatherer** *n*

gathering ('gæðərɪŋ) *n* **1** a group of people, things, etc, that are gathered together; assembly **2** *sewing* a series of gathers in material **3** *inf* **3a** the formation of pus in a boil **3b** the pus so formed **4** *printing* an informal name for **section** (sense 16)

Gatling gun ('gætlɪŋ) *n* a machine gun equipped with a rotating cluster of barrels that are fired in succession [c19 after R. J. *Gatling* (1818–1903), its US inventor]

GATT (gæt) *n acronym for* General Agreement on Tariffs and Trade: a multilateral international treaty signed in 1947 to promote trade; replaced in 1995 by the World Trade Organization

Gatún Lake (*Spanish* ga'tun) *n* a lake in Panama, part of the Panama Canal: formed in 1912 on the completion of the **Gatún Dam** across the Chagres River. Area: 424 sq km (164 sq miles)

gauche (gəʊʃ) *adj* lacking ease of manner; tactless [c18 F: awkward, left, from OF *gauchir* to swerve, ult. of Gmc origin] > '**gauchely** *adv* > '**gaucheness** *n*

gaucherie (,gəʊʃə'riː, 'gəʊʃərɪ) *n* **1** the quality of being gauche **2** a gauche act

gaucho ('gaʊtʃəʊ) *n, pl* **gauchos** a cowboy of the South American pampas, usually one of mixed Spanish and Indian descent [c19 from American Sp., prob. from Quechuan *wáhcha* orphan, vagabond]

gaud (gɔːd) *n* an article of cheap finery [c14 prob. from OF *gaudir* to be joyful, from L *gaudēre*]

Gaudí ('gaʊdɪ; *Spanish* gau'ði) *n* **Antonio** (an'tonjo) 1852–1926, Spanish architect, regarded as one of the most original exponents of Art Nouveau in Europe and noted esp for the church of the Sagrada familia, Barcelona

Gaudier-Brzeska (*French* godjebʒɛska) *n* **Henri** (ɑ̃ri), original name *Henri Gaudier*. 1891–1915, French vorticist sculptor

gaudy[1] ('gɔːdɪ) *adj* **gaudier, gaudiest** bright or colourful in a crude or vulgar manner [c16 from GAUD] > '**gaudily** *adv* > '**gaudiness** *n*

gaudy[2] ('gɔːdɪ) *n, pl* **gaudies** *Brit* a celebratory feast held at some schools and colleges [c16 from L *gaudium* joy, from *gaudēre* to rejoice]

gauge *or* **gage** (geɪdʒ) *vb* **gauges, gauging, gauged** *or* **gages, gaging, gaged** (*tr*) **1** to measure or determine the amount, quantity, size, condition, etc, of **2** to estimate or appraise; judge **3** to check for conformity or bring into conformity with a standard measurement, etc ▷ *n* **4** a standard measurement, dimension, capacity, or quantity **5** any of various instruments for measuring a quantity: *a pressure gauge* **6** any of various devices used to check for conformity with a standard measurement **7** a standard or means for assessing; test; criterion **8** scope, capacity, or extent **9** the diameter of the barrel of a gun, esp a shotgun **10** the thickness of sheet metal or the diameter of wire **11** the distance between the rails of a railway track **12** the distance between two wheels on the same axle of a vehicle, truck, etc **13** *naut* the position of a vessel in relation to the wind and another vessel **14** a measure of the fineness of woven or knitted fabric **15** the width of motion-picture film or magnetic tape ▷ *adj* **16** (of a pressure measurement) measured on a pressure gauge that registers zero at atmospheric pressure [c15 from OF, prob. of Gmc origin] > '**gaugeable** *or* '**gageable** *adj*

gauge boson *n physics* a boson that mediates the interaction between elementary particles. There are four types: photons for electromagnetic interactions, gluons for strong interactions, intermediate vector bosons for weak interactions, and gravitons for gravitational interactions

gauge theory *n physics* a type of theory of elementary particles designed to explain the strong, weak, and electromagnetic interactions in terms of exchange of virtual particles

Gauguin (*French* gogɛ̃) *n* **Paul** (pɔl) 1848–1903, French postimpressionist painter, who worked in the South Pacific from 1891. Inspired by primitive art, his work is characterized by flat contrasting areas of pure colours

Gauhati (gaʊ'hɑːtɪ) *n* a city in NE India, in Assam on the River Brahmaputra: centre of British administration in Assam (1826–74). Pop: 584 342 (1991)

Gaul (gɔːl) *n* **1** an ancient region of W Europe corresponding to N Italy, France, Belgium, part of Germany, and the S Netherlands: divided into Cisalpine Gaul, which became a Roman province before 100 BC, and Transalpine Gaul, which was conquered by Julius Caesar (58–51 BC). Latin name: **Gallia** **2** a native of ancient Gaul **3** a Frenchman

Gauleiter ('gaʊ,laɪtə) *n* **1** a provincial governor in Germany under Hitler **2** (*sometimes not cap*) a person in a position of petty authority who behaves in an overbearing manner [G, from *Gau* district + *Leiter* leader]

Gaulish ('gɔːlɪʃ) *n* **1** the extinct Celtic language of the pre-Roman Gauls ▷ *adj* **2** of ancient Gaul, the Gauls, or their language

Gaulle (gəʊl, gɔːl; *French* gol) *n* **Charles de** See (Charles) **de Gaulle**

gaunt (gɔːnt) *adj* **1** bony and emaciated in appearance **2** (of places) bleak or desolate [c15 ?from ON] > '**gauntly** *adv* > '**gauntness** *n*

gauntlet[1] ('gɔːntlɪt) *n* **1** a medieval armoured leather glove **2** a heavy glove with a long cuff **3 take up** (*or* **throw down**) **the gauntlet** to accept (*or* offer) a challenge [c15 from OF *gantelet*, dim. of *gant* glove, of Gmc origin]

gauntlet[2] ('gɔːntlɪt) *n* **1** a punishment in which the victim is forced to run between two rows of men who strike at him as he passes: formerly a military punishment **2 run the gauntlet** **2a** to suffer this punishment **2b** to endure an onslaught, as of criticism **3** a testing ordeal [c15 changed (through infl. of GAUNTLET[1]) from earlier *gantlope*, from Swedish *gatlopp* passageway]

gaur ('gaʊə) *n* a large wild ox of mountainous regions of S Asia [c19 from Hindi, from Sansk. *gāura*]

gauss (gaʊs) *n, pl* **gauss** the cgs unit of magnetic flux density. 1 gauss is equivalent to 10^{-4} tesla [after K. F. GAUSS]

Gauss (*German* gaus) *n* **Karl Friedrich** (karl 'friːdrɪç) 1777–1855, German mathematician: developed the

Gg

theory of numbers and applied mathematics to astronomy, electricity and magnetism, and geodesy

Gaussian distribution *n* another name for **normal distribution**

Gauteng (xaʊˈtɛŋ) *n* a province of N South Africa; formed in 1994 from part of the former province of Transvaal: service industries, mining, and manufacturing. Capital: Johannesburg. Pop: 7 807 273 (1999 est). Area: 18 810 sq km (7262 sq miles)

Gautier (*French* gotje) *n* **Théophile** (teɔfil) 1811–72, French poet, novelist, and critic. His early extravagant romanticism gave way to a preoccupation with poetic form and expression that anticipated the Parnassians

gauze (gɔːz) *n* **1** a transparent cloth of loose weave **2** a surgical dressing of muslin or similar material **3** any thin openwork material, such as wire **4** a fine mist or haze [c16 from F *gaze*, ?from GAZA, where it was believed to originate]

gauzy (ˈgɔːzɪ) *adj* **gauzier, gauziest** resembling gauze; thin and transparent > **ˈgauzily** *adv* > **ˈgauziness** *n*

Gavaskar (gæˈvæskɑː) *n* **Sunil Manohar** (ˈsʊnɪl ˈmænəʊhɑː) born 1949, Indian cricketer. He captained India 1978–83 and 1984–85

gave (geɪv) *vb* the past tense of **give**

gavel (ˈgævᵊl) *n* a small hammer used by a chairman, auctioneer, etc, to call for order or attention [c19 from ?]

gavial (ˈgeɪvɪəl), **gharial,** *or* **garial** (ˈgærɪəl) *n* a large fish-eating Indian crocodile with a very long slender snout [c19 from F, from Hindi]

Gävle (*Swedish* ˈjɛːvlə) *n* a port in E Sweden, on an inlet of the Gulf of Bothnia. Pop: 90 270 (1994)

gavotte *or* **gavot** (gəˈvɒt) *n* **1** an old formal dance in quadruple time **2** a piece of music composed for or in the rhythm of this dance [c17 from F, from Provençal, from *gavot* mountaineer, dweller in the Alps (where the dance originated)]

gawk (gɔːk) *n* **1** a clumsy stupid person; lout ▷ *vb* **2** (*intr*) to stare in a stupid way; gape [c18 from ODanish *gaukr*; prob. rel. to GAPE]

gawky (ˈgɔːkɪ) *adj* **gawkier, gawkiest** clumsy or ungainly; awkward. Also: **gawkish** > **ˈgawkily** *adv* > **ˈgawkiness** *n*

gawp *or* **gaup** (gɔːp) *vb* (*intr*; often foll by *at*) *Brit sl* to stare stupidly; gape [c14 *galpen*; prob. rel. to OE *gielpan* to boast, YELP] > **ˈgawper** *n*

gay (geɪ) *adj* **1a** homosexual **1b** of or for homosexuals: *a gay club; gay rights* **2** carefree and merry: *a gay temperament* **3** brightly coloured; brilliant: *a gay hat* **4** given to pleasure, esp in social entertainment: *a gay life* ▷ *n* **5** a homosexual [c13 from OF *gai*, from OProvençal, of Gmc origin] > **ˈgayness** *n*

> USAGE *Gayness* is used in the great majority of cases to refer to the state of being homosexual. The noun which refers to the state of being carefree and merry is *gaiety*

Gay (geɪ) *n* **John** 1685–1732, English poet and dramatist; author of *The Beggar's Opera* (1728)

Gaya (ˈgɑːjə, ˈgaɪə) *n* a city in NE India, in Bihar: Hindu place of pilgrimage and one of the holiest sites of Buddhism. Pop: 291 675 (1991)

gaydar (ˈgeɪdɑː) *n inf* the ability of a homosexual person to recognize whether another person is homosexual [c20 from GAY + (RA)DAR]

Gay-Lussac (ˈgeɪˈluːsæk; *French* gɛlysak) *n* **Joseph Louis** (ʒozɛf lwi) 1778–1850, French physicist and chemist: discovered the law named after him (1808), investigated the effects of terrestrial magnetism, isolated boron and cyanogen, and discovered methods of manufacturing sulphuric and oxalic acids

Gaza (ˈgɑːzə) *n* a city in the Gaza Strip: a Philistine city in biblical times. It was under Egyptian administration from 1949 until occupied by Israel (1967). Pop: 388 031 (1999 est). Arabic name: **Ghazzah**

gazania (gæˈzeɪnɪə) *n* any of a genus of S African plants of the composite family, Asteraceae, having large showy flowers [? after Theodore of *Gaza* (1398–1478), who translated the botanical works of Theophrastus into Latin]

Gazankulu (ˌgazaŋˈkuːluː) *n* (formerly) a Bantu homeland in South Africa; abolished in 1993. Capital: Giyani

Gaza Strip *n* a coastal region on the SE corner of the Mediterranean: administered by Egypt from 1949; occupied by Israel from 1967; granted autonomy in 1993 and administered by the Palestinian National Authority from 1994. Pop: 1 147 000 (2000 est)

gaze (geɪz) *vb* **gazes, gazing, gazed** **1** (*intr*) to look long and fixedly, esp in wonder ▷ *n* **2** a fixed look [c14 from Swedish dialect *gasa* to gape at] > **ˈgazer** *n*

gazebo (gəˈziːbəʊ) *n, pl* **gazebos** *or* **gazeboes** a summerhouse, garden pavilion, or belvedere, sited to command a view [c18 ? a pseudo-Latin coinage based on GAZE]

gazelle (gəˈzɛl) *n, pl* **gazelles** *or* **gazelle** any small graceful usually fawn-coloured antelope of Africa and Asia [c17 from OF, from Ar. *ghazāl*]

gazette (gəˈzɛt) *n* **1** a newspaper or official journal **2** *Brit* an official document containing public notices, appointments, etc ▷ *vb* **gazettes, gazetting, gazetted** **3** (*tr*) *Brit* to announce or report (facts or an event) in a gazette [c17 from F, from It., from Venetian dialect *gazeta* news-sheet costing one *gazet*, small copper coin]

gazetteer (ˌgæzɪˈtɪə) *n* **1** a book or section of a book that lists and describes places **2** *arch* a writer for a gazette

Gaziantep (ˌgɑːziːɑːnˈtɛp) *n* a city in S Turkey: base for Ibrahim Pasha's campaign against the Turks (1839) and centre of Turkish resistance to French forces (1921). Pop: 712 800 (1997). Former name (until 1921): **Aintab**

gazillion (gəˈzɪljən) *inf n, pl* **gazillions** *or* **gazillion** **1** an extremely large but unspecified number, quantity, or amount: *gazillions of people turned up* ▷ *determiner* **2a** amounting to a gazillion: *a gazillion types to choose from* **2b** (*as pronoun*): *I found a gazillion under the sink* [c20 on the model of *million*]

gazillionaire (gəˈzɪljəˌnɛə) *n inf* a person who is enormously rich

gazpacho (gəzˈpɑːtʃəʊ, gæs-) *n* a Spanish soup made from tomatoes, peppers, etc, and served cold [from Sp.]

gazump (gəˈzʌmp) *Brit* ▷ *vb* **1** to raise the price of something, esp a house, after agreeing a price verbally with (an intending buyer) **2** (*tr*) to swindle or overcharge ▷ *n* **3** an instance of gazumping [c20 from ?] > **gaˈzumper** *n*

gazunder (gəˈzʌndə) *Brit* ▷ *vb* **1** to reduce an offer on a property immediately before exchanging contracts, having previously agreed to a higher price with (the seller) ▷ *n* **2** an act or instance of gazundering [c20 modelled on GAZUMP] > **gaˈzunderer** *n*

GB *abbrev for* Great Britain

GBE *abbrev for* (Knight or Dame) Grand Cross of the British Empire (a Brit title)

GBH *abbrev for* grievous bodily harm

GC *abbrev for* George Cross (a Brit award for bravery)

GCB *abbrev for* (Knight) Grand Cross of the Bath (a Brit title)

gcd *or* **GCD** *abbrev for* greatest common divisor

GCE *abbrev for* General Certificate of Education: a public examination in specified subjects taken in English and Welsh schools at the ages of 17 and 18. The GCSE has replaced the former GCE O level. See also **A level, AS level, S level**

GCHQ (in Britain) *abbrev for* Government Communications Headquarters

G clef *n* another name for **treble clef**

GCMG *abbrev for* (Knight or Dame) Grand Cross of the Order of St Michael and St George (a Brit title)

GCSE (in England and Wales) *abbrev for* General Certificate of Secondary Education: a public examination in specified subjects for 16-year-old schoolchildren. It replaced GCE O level and CSE
GCVO *abbrev for* (Knight or Dame) Grand Cross of the Royal Victorian Order (a Brit title)
Gd *the chemical symbol for* gadolinium
Gdańsk (*Polish* gdajinsk) *n* **1** the chief port of Poland, on the Baltic: a member of the Hanseatic league; under Prussian rule (1793–1807 and 1814–1919); a free city under the League of Nations from 1919 until annexed by Germany in 1939; returned to Poland in 1945. Pop: 445 988 (1999 est). German name: **Danzig 2 Bay of** a wide inlet of the Baltic Sea on the N coast of Poland
g'day *or* **gidday** (gə'daɪ) *sentence substitute* an Australian and NZ informal variant of **good day**
Gdns *abbrev for* Gardens
GDR *abbrev for* German Democratic Republic (East Germany; DDR)
Gdynia (*Polish* 'gdɪnja) *n* a port in N Poland, near Gdańsk: developed 1924–39 as the outlet for trade through the Polish Corridor; naval base. Pop: 253 521 (1999 est)
Ge[1] (dʒiː) *n* another name for **Gaea**
Ge[2] *the chemical symbol for* germanium
gean (giːn) *n* a white-flowered tree of the rose family of Europe, W Asia, and N Africa; the ancestor of the cultivated sweet cherries [c16 from OF *guine*]
gear (gɪə) *n* **1** a toothed wheel that engages with another toothed wheel or with a rack in order to change the speed or direction of transmitted motion **2** a mechanism for transmitting motion by gears **3** the engagement or specific ratio of a system of gears: *in gear; high gear* **4** personal belongings **5** equipment and supplies for a particular operation, sport, etc **6** *naut* all equipment or appurtenances belonging to a certain vessel, sailor, etc **7** short for **landing gear 8** *inf* up-to-date clothes and accessories **9** *sl* drugs of any type **10** a less common word for **harness** (sense 1) **11 out of gear** out of order; not functioning properly ▷ *vb* **12** (*tr*) to adjust or adapt (one thing) so as to fit in or work with another: *to gear our output to current demand* **13** (*tr*) to equip with or connect by gears **14** (*intr*) to be in or come into gear **15** (*tr*) to equip with a harness [c13 from ON *gervi*]
gearbox ('gɪə,bɒks) *n* **1** the metal casing within which a train of gears is sealed **2** this metal casing and its contents, esp in a motor vehicle
gearing ('gɪərɪŋ) *n* **1** an assembly of gears designed to transmit motion **2** the act or technique of providing gears to transmit motion **3** Also called: **capital gearing** *accounting, Brit* the ratio of a company's debt capital to its equity capital. US word: **leverage**
gear lever *or US & Canad* **gearshift** ('gɪə,ʃɪft) *n* a lever used to move gearwheels relative to each other, esp in a motor vehicle
gear train *n engineering* a system of gears that transmits power from one shaft to another
gearwheel ('gɪə,wiːl) *n* another name for **gear** (sense 1)
Geber ('dʒiːbə) *n* Latinized form of Jabir, assumed in honour of Jabir ibn Hayyan by a 14th-century alchemist, probably Spanish: he described the preparation of nitric and sulphuric acids
Gebrselassie (,gɛbrəsə'læsɪ) *n* **Haile** ('haɪlɪ) born 1973, Ethiopian athlete; Olympic gold medallist in the 10 000 metres in 1996 and 2000
gecko ('gɛkəʊ) *n, pl* **geckos** *or* **geckoes** a small insectivorous terrestrial lizard of warm regions [c18 from Malay *ge'kok*, imit.]
gee[1] (dʒiː) *interj* **1** Also: **gee up!** an exclamation, as to a horse or draught animal, to encourage it to turn to the right, go on, or go faster ▷ *vb* **gees, geeing, geed 2** (usually foll by *up*) to move (an animal, esp a horse) ahead; urge on **3** (foll by *up*) to encourage (someone) to greater effort or activity [c17 from ?]
gee[2] (dʒiː) *interj US & Canad inf* a mild exclamation of surprise, admiration, etc. Also: **gee whizz** [c20 euphemism for JESUS]
Gee (dʒiː) *n* **Maurice** born 1931, New Zealand novelist
geebung ('dʒiːbʌŋ) *n* **1** any of several Australian trees or shrubs with edible but tasteless fruit **2** the fruit of these trees [from Abor.]
geek (giːk) *n sl* **1** a boring or unattractive social misfit **2** a person who is preoccupied with or very knowledgeable about computing **3** a degenerate [c19 prob. from Scot. *geck* fool] > **'geeky** *adj*
geelbek ('xiːl,bɛk) *n S African* an edible marine fish with yellow jaws. Also called: **Cape salmon** [from Afrik. *geel* yellow + *bek* mouth]
Geelong (dʒə'lɒŋ) *n* a port in SE Australia, in S Victoria on Port Phillip Bay. Pop: 186 307 (1998 est)
geese (giːs) *n* the plural of **goose**[1]
geezer ('giːzə) *n inf* a man [c19 prob. from dialect pronunciation of GUISER]
Gehenna (gɪ'hɛnə) *n* **1** *Old Testament* the valley below Jerusalem, where children were sacrificed and, later, unclean things were burnt **2** *New Testament, Judaism* a place where the wicked are punished after death **3** a place or state of pain and torment [c16 from LL, from Gk, from Heb. *Gê' Hinnōm*, lit.: valley of Hinnom, symbolic of hell]
Gehry ('geɪrɪ) *n* **Frank O(wen)** born 1929, US architect and furniture designer, born in Canada; best known for the Guggenheim Museum in Bilbao, Spain (1997)
Geiger counter *or* **Geiger-Müller counter** ('gaɪgə 'mʊlə) *n* an instrument for detecting and measuring the intensity of ionizing radiation [c20 after Hans *Geiger* and W. *Müller* (20th-cent.), G physicists]
geisha ('geɪʃə) *n, pl* **geisha** *or* **geishas** a professional female companion for men in Japan, trained in music, dancing, and the art of conversation [c19 from Japanese, from Ancient Chinese]
Geissler tube ('gaɪslə) *n* a glass or quartz vessel for maintaining an electric discharge in a low-pressure gas as a source of visible or ultraviolet light for spectroscopy, etc [c19 after Heinrich *Geissler* (1814–79), G mechanic]
gel (dʒɛl) *n* **1** a semirigid jelly-like colloid in which a liquid is dispersed in a solid: *nondrip paint is a gel* **2** a jelly-like substance applied to the hair before styling in order to retain the style ▷ *vb* **gels, gelling, gelled 3** to become or cause to become a gel **4** a variant spelling of **jell** [c19 from GELATINE]
gelatine ('dʒɛlə,tiːn) *or* **gelatin** ('dʒɛlətɪn) *n* **1** a colourless or yellowish water-soluble protein prepared by boiling animal hides and bones: used in foods, glue, photographic emulsions, etc **2** an edible jelly made of this substance [c19 from F *gélatine*, from Med. L, from L *gelāre* to freeze]
gelatinize *or* **gelatinise** (dʒɪ'lætɪ,naɪz) *vb* **gelatinizes, gelatinizing, gelatinized** *or* **gelatinises, gelatinising, gelatinised 1** to make or become gelatinous **2** (*tr*) *photog* to coat (glass, paper, etc) with gelatine > **ge,latini'zation** *or* > **ge,latini'sation** *n*
gelatinous (dʒɪ'lætɪnəs) *adj* **1** consisting of or resembling jelly; viscous **2** of, containing, or resembling gelatine > **ge'latinously** *adv* > **ge'latinousness** *n*
gelation[1] (dʒɪ'leɪʃən) *n* the act or process of freezing a liquid [c19 from L *gelātiō* a freezing; see GELATINE]
gelation[2] (dʒɪ'leɪʃən) *n* the act or process of forming into a gel [c20 from GEL]
geld (gɛld) *vb* **gelds, gelding, gelded** *or* **gelt** (gɛlt) (*tr*) **1** to castrate (a horse or other animal) **2** to deprive of virility or vitality; emasculate; weaken [c13 from ON, from *geldr* barren]
Gelderland *or* **Guelderland** ('gɛldə,lænd; *Dutch* 'xɛldərlɑnt) *n* a province of the E Netherlands: formerly

Gg

a duchy, belonging successively to several different European powers. Capital: Arnhem. Pop: 1 919 200 (2000 est). Area: 5014 sq km (1955 sq miles). Also called: **Guelders**

gelding ('gɛldɪŋ) *n* a castrated male horse [c14 from ON *geldingr*; see GELD, -ING[1]]

Geldof ('gɛldɒf) *n* **Bob**, full name *Robert Frederick Zenon Geldof*. born 1954, Irish rock singer and philanthropist: formerly lead vocalist with the Boomtown Rats (1977–86); organizer of the Band Aid charity for famine relief in Africa. He received an honorary knighthood in 1986

Gelée (*French* ʒəle) *n* **Claude** (klod) the original name of **Claude Lorrain**

Gelibolu (gɛ'libɔlu) *n* the Turkish name for **Gallipoli**

gelid ('dʒɛlɪd) *adj* very cold, icy, or frosty [c17 from L *gelidus*, from *gelu* frost] > **ge'lidity** *n*

gelignite ('dʒɛlɪg,naɪt) *n* a type of dynamite in which the nitrogelatine is absorbed in a base of wood pulp and potassium or sodium nitrate. Also called (informal): **gelly** [c19 from GEL(ATINE) + L *ignis* fire + -ITE[1]]

Gelligaer (*Welsh* ,gɛhli:'gaɪr) *n* a town in S Wales, in Caerphilly county borough. Pop: 15 906 (1991)

Gell-Mann ('gɛl'mæn) *n* **Murray** born 1929, US physicist, noted for his research on the interaction and classification of elementary particles: Nobel prize for physics in 1969

Gelsenkirchen (*German* gɛlzən'kɪrçən) *n* an industrial city in W Germany, in North Rhine-Westphalia. Pop: 283 300 (1999 est)

gem (dʒɛm) *n* **1** a precious or semiprecious stone used in jewellery as a decoration; jewel **2** a person or thing held to be a perfect example; treasure ▷ *vb* **gems, gemming, gemmed 3** (*tr*) to set or ornament with gems [c14 from OF, from L *gemma* bud, precious stone] > **'gem,like** *adj* > **'gemmy** *adj*

▷ www.min.uni-bremen.de/sgmcol

Gemara (gɛ'mɑ:rə; *Hebrew* gɛma'ra) *n Judaism* the later main part of the Talmud, being a commentary on the Mishnah: the primary source of Jewish religious law [c17 from Aramaic *gemārā* completion]

gemclip ('dʒɛm,klɪp) *n S African* a paperclip

geminate *adj* ('dʒɛmɪnɪt, -,neɪt) *also* **geminated 1** combined in pairs; doubled: *a geminate leaf* ▷ *vb* ('dʒɛmɪ,neɪt), **geminates, geminating, geminated 2** to arrange or be arranged in pairs: *the "t"s in "fitted" are geminated* [c17 from L *gemināre* to double, from *geminus* twin] > **'geminately** *adv* > **,gemi'nation** *n*

Gemini ('dʒɛmɪ,naɪ, -,ni:) *n* **1** *astron* a zodiacal constellation in the N hemisphere containing the stars Castor and Pollux **2** *classical myth* another name for **Castor and Pollux 3** *astrol* Also called: the **Twins** the third sign of the zodiac. The sun is in this sign between about May 21 and June 20

gemma ('dʒɛmə) *n, pl* **gemmae** (-mi:) **1** a small asexual reproductive structure in mosses, etc, that becomes detached from the parent and develops into a new individual **2** *zool* another name for **gemmule** [c18 from L: bud, GEM]

gemmate ('dʒɛmeɪt) *adj* **1** (of some plants and animals) having or reproducing by gemmae ▷ *vb* **gemmates, gemmating, gemmated 2** (*intr*) to produce or reproduce by gemmae > **gem'mation** *n*

gemmiparous (dʒɛ'mɪpərəs) *adj* (of plants and animals) reproducing by gemmae or buds. Also: **gemmiferous**

gemmule ('dʒɛmju:l) *n* **1** *zool* a cell or mass of cells produced asexually by sponges and developing into a new individual; bud **2** *bot* a small gemma [c19 from F, from L *gemmula* a little bud; see GEM]

gemology *or* **gemmology** (dʒɛ'mɒlədʒɪ) *n* the branch of mineralogy concerned with gems and gemstones > **gemological** *or* **gemmological** (,dʒɛmə'lɒdʒɪkəl) *adj* > **gem'ologist** *or* **gem'mologist** *n*

gemsbok *or* **gemsbuck** ('gɛmz,bʌk) *n, pl* **gemsbok, gemsboks** *or* **gemsbuck, gemsbucks** an oryx of southern Africa, marked with a broad black band along its flanks [c18 from Afrik., from G *Gemsbock*, from *Gemse* chamois + *Bock* BUCK[1]]

gemstone ('dʒɛm,stəʊn) *n* a precious or semiprecious stone, esp one cut and polished

gen (dʒɛn) *n Brit, Austral, & NZ inf* information: *give me the gen on your latest project*. See also **gen up** [c20 from *gen(eral information)*]

Gen. *abbrev for:* **1** General **2** *Bible* Genesis

-gen *suffix forming nouns* **1** producing or that which produces: *hydrogen* **2** something produced: *carcinogen* [via F *-gène*, from Gk *-genēs* born]

Genck (*Flemish* xɛŋk) *n* a variant spelling of **Genk**

gendarme ('ʒɒndɑ:m) *n* **1** a member of the police force in France or in countries influenced or controlled by France **2** a sharp pinnacle of rock on a mountain ridge [c16 from F, from *gens d'armes* people of arms]

gendarmerie *or* **gendarmery** (ʒɒn'dɑ:mərɪ) *n* **1** the whole corps of gendarmes **2** the headquarters of a body of gendarmes

gender ('dʒɛndə) *n* **1** a set of two or more grammatical categories into which the nouns of certain languages are divided **2** any of the categories, such as masculine, feminine, neuter, or common, within such a set **3** *inf* the state of being male, female, or neuter **4** *inf* all the members of one sex: *the female gender* [c14 from OF, from L *genus* kind]

gender-bender *n inf* **1** a person who adopts an androgynous style of dress, hair, etc **2** a male-male or female-female adaptor, used esp for computer hardware

gene (dʒi:n) *n* a unit of heredity composed of DNA occupying a fixed position on a chromosome and transmitted from parent to offspring during reproduction. Some viral genes are composed of RNA [c20 from G *Gen*, shortened from *Pangen*; see PAN-, -GEN]

-gene *suffix forming nouns* a variant of **-gen**

genealogy (,dʒi:nɪ'ælədʒɪ) *n, pl* **genealogies 1** the direct descent of an individual or group from an ancestor **2** the study of the evolutionary development of animals and plants from earlier forms **3** a chart showing the relationships and descent of an individual, group, genes, etc [c13 from OF, from LL, from Gk, from *genea* race] > **genealogical** (,dʒi:nɪə'lɒdʒɪkəl) *adj* > **,genea'logically** *adv* > **,gene'alogist** *n*

gene bank *n bot* a collection of seeds, plants, tissue cultures, etc, of potentially useful species, esp species containing genes of significance to the breeding of crops

gene clone *n* See **clone** (sense 2)

genecology (,dʒɛnɪ'kɒlədʒɪ) *n* the study of the gene frequency of a species in relation to its population distribution within a particular environment

gene flow *n* the movement and exchange of genes between interbreeding populations

gene library *n* a collection of gene clones that represents the genetic material of an organism: used in genetic engineering

gene pool *n* the total of all the genes and their alleles in a population of a plant or animal species

genera ('dʒɛnərə) *n* a plural of **genus**

general ('dʒɛnərəl, 'dʒɛnrəl) *adj* **1** common; widespread **2** of, applying to, or participated in by all or most of the members of a group, category, or community **3** relating to various branches of an activity, profession, etc; not specialized: *general office work* **4** including various or miscellaneous items: *general knowledge; a general store* **5** not specific as to detail; overall: *a general description* **6** not definite; vague: *the general idea* **7** applicable or true in most cases; usual **8** (*prenominal or immediately postpositive*) having superior or extended authority or rank: *general manager; consul general* ▷ *n* **9** an officer of a rank senior to lieutenant general, esp one who commands a large military formation **10** any person acting as a leader and applying strategy or tactics **11** a general condition or principle: opposed to *particular* **12** a title for the head of a religious order, congregation, etc **13** *arch* the people; public **14 in general** generally; mostly or usually [c13 from L *generālis* of a particular kind, from *genus* kind]

general anaesthetic *n* See **anaesthesia**

General Assembly *n* **1** the deliberative assembly of the United Nations. Abbrev: **GA** **2** the supreme governing body of certain religious denominations, esp of the Presbyterian Church

general average *n insurance* loss or damage to a ship or its cargo that is shared among the shipowners and all the cargo owners. Abbrev: **GA** ▷ Cf **particular average**

General Certificate of Education *n* See **GCE**

General Certificate of Secondary Education *n* See **GCSE**

general election *n* **1** an election in which representatives are chosen in all constituencies of a state **2** *US* a final election from which successful candidates are sent to a legislative body **3** *US & Canad* a national, state, or provincial election

generalissimo (ˌdʒɛnərəˈlɪsɪˌməʊ, ˌdʒɛnrə-) *n, pl* **generalissimos** a supreme commander of combined military, naval, and air forces [c17 from It., sup. of *generale* GENERAL]

generality (ˌdʒɛnəˈrælɪtɪ) *n, pl* **generalities** **1** a principle or observation having general application **2** the state or quality of being general **3** *arch* the majority

generalization *or* **generalisation** (ˌdʒɛnrəlaɪˈzeɪʃən) *n* **1** a principle, theory, etc, with general application **2** the act or an instance of generalizing **3** *logic* the derivation of a general statement from a particular one, formally by prefixing a quantifier and replacing a subject term by a bound variable. If the quantifier is universal (**universal generalization**) the argument is not in general valid; if it is existential (**existential generalization**) it is valid

generalize *or* **generalise** (ˈdʒɛnrəˌlaɪz) *vb* **generalizes, generalizing, generalized** *or* **generalises, generalising, generalised** **1** to form (general principles or conclusions) from (detailed facts, experience, etc); infer **2** (*intr*) to think or speak in generalities, esp in a prejudiced way **3** (*tr; usually passive*) to cause to become widely used or known

generally (ˈdʒɛnrəlɪ) *adv* **1** usually; as a rule **2** commonly or widely **3** without reference to specific details or facts; broadly

general practitioner *n* a physician who does not specialize but has a medical practice (**general practice**) in which he deals with all illnesses. Informal name: **family doctor** Abbrev: **GP**

general-purpose *adj* having a range of uses; not restricted to one function

generalship (ˈdʒɛnrəlʃɪp) *n* **1** the art or duties of exercising command of a major military formation or formations **2** tactical or administrative skill

general staff *n* officers assigned to advise commanders in the planning and execution of military operations

general strike *n* a strike by all or most of the workers of a country, province, city, etc

General Synod *n* the governing body, under Parliament, of the Church of England, made up of the bishops and elected clerical and lay representatives

generate (ˈdʒɛnəˌreɪt) *vb* **generates, generating, generated** (*mainly tr*) **1** to produce or bring into being; create **2** (*also intr*) to produce (electricity) **3** to produce (a substance) by a chemical process **4** *maths, linguistics* to provide a precise criterion for membership in (a set) **5** *geom* to trace or form by moving a point, line, or plane in a specific way: *circular motion of a line generates a cylinder* [c16 from L *generāre* to beget, from *genus* kind]
> ˈ**generable** *adj*

generation (ˌdʒɛnəˈreɪʃən) *n* **1** the act or process of bringing into being; production or reproduction, esp of offspring **2a** a successive stage in natural descent of organisms: the time between when an organism comes into being and when it reproduces **2b** the individuals produced at each stage **3** the average time between two such generations of a species: about 35 years for humans **4** all the people of approximately the same age, esp when considered as sharing certain attitudes, etc **5** production of electricity, heat, etc **6** (*modifier, in combination*) **6a** belonging to a generation specified as having been born in or as having parents, grandparents, etc, born in a given country: *a third-generation American* **6b** belonging to a specified stage of development in manufacture: *a second-generation computer*

generation gap *n* the years separating one generation from the next, esp when regarded as representing the difference in outlook and the lack of understanding between them

Generation X *n* members of the generation of people born between the mid-1960s and the mid-1970s who are highly educated and underemployed, reject consumer culture, and have little hope for the future [c20 from the novel *Generation X: Tales for an Accelerated Culture* by Douglas Coupland]

generative (ˈdʒɛnərətɪv) *adj* **1** of or relating to the production of offspring, parts, etc **2** capable of producing or originating

generative grammar *n* a description of a language in terms of explicit rules that ideally generate all and only the grammatical sentences of the language

generator (ˈdʒɛnəˌreɪtə) *n* **1** *physics* **1a** any device for converting mechanical energy into electrical energy **1b** a device for producing a voltage electrostatically **2** an apparatus for producing a gas **3** a person or thing that generates

generatrix (ˈdʒɛnəˌreɪtrɪks) *n, pl* **generatrices** (ˈdʒɛnəˌreɪtrɪˌsiːz) a point, line, or plane moved in a specific way to produce a geometric figure

generic (dʒɪˈnɛrɪk) *adj* **1** applicable or referring to a whole class or group; general **2** *biol* of, relating to, or belonging to a genus: *the generic name* **3** denoting the nonproprietary name of a drug, food products, etc [c17 from F; see GENUS] > **geˈnerically** *adv*

generic advertising *n* advertising designed to promote a class of product rather than a particular brand

generosity (ˌdʒɛnəˈrɒsɪtɪ) *n, pl* **generosities** **1** willingness and liberality in giving away one's money, time, etc; magnanimity **2** freedom from pettiness in character and mind **3** a generous act **4** abundance; plenty

generous (ˈdʒɛnərəs, ˈdʒɛnrəs) *adj* **1** willing and liberal in giving away one's money, time, etc; munificent **2** free from pettiness in character and mind **3** full or plentiful: *a generous portion* **4** (of wine) rich in alcohol [c16 via OF from L *generōsus* nobly born, from *genus* race]
> ˈ**generously** *adv* > ˈ**generousness** *n*

genesis (ˈdʒɛnɪsɪs) *n, pl* **geneses** (-ˌsiːz) a beginning or origin of anything [OE: via L from Gk; rel. to Gk *gignesthai* to be born]

Genesis (ˈdʒɛnɪsɪs) *n* the first book of the Old Testament recounting the Creation of the world

-genesis *n combining form* indicating genesis, development, or generation: *parthenogenesis* [NL, from L: GENESIS] > **-genetic** *or* **-genic** *adj combining form*

genet[1] (ˈdʒɛnɪt) *or* **genette** (dʒɪˈnɛt) *n* **1** an agile catlike mammal of Africa and S Europe, having thick spotted fur and a very long tail **2** the fur of such an animal [c15 from OF, from Ar. *jarnayt*]

Gg

genet[2] (ˈdʒɛnɪt) *n* an obsolete spelling of **jennet**

Genet (*French* ʒənɛ) *n* **Jean** (ʒɑ̃) 1910–86, French dramatist and novelist; his novels include *Notre-Dame des Fleurs* (1944) and his plays *Les Bonnes* (1947) and *Le Balcon* (1956)

gene therapy *n* the replacement or alteration of defective genes in order to prevent the occurrence of such inherited diseases as haemophilia. Effected by genetic engineering techniques, it is still at an early stage of development

genetic (dʒɪˈnɛtɪk) *or* **genetical** *adj* of or relating to genetics, genes, or the origin of something [C19 from GENESIS] > **geˈnetically** *adv*

genetically modified *adj* denoting or derived from an organism whose DNA has been altered for the purpose of improvement or correction of defects: *genetically modified food. Abbrev:* **GM** > **genetic modification** *n*

genetic code *n biochem* the order in which the four nitrogenous bases of DNA are arranged in the molecule, which determines the type and amount of protein synthesized in the cell

genetic counselling *n* the provision of advice for couples with a history of inherited disorders who wish to have children, including the likelihood of having affected children and the course and management of the disorder, etc

genetic engineering *n* alteration of a genome for the purposes of research, commerce, or health

genetic fingerprint *n* the pattern of DNA unique to each individual, that can be analysed in a sample of blood, saliva, or tissue: used as a means of identification > **genetic fingerprinting** *n*

genetic map *n* a graphic representation of the order of genes within chromosomes by means of detailed analysis of the DNA. See also **chromosome map** > **genetic mapping** *n*

genetic marker *n* a gene with two or more alternative forms, producing readily identifiable variations in a particular character, used in studies of linkage, genetic mapping, and identification of the presence of other genes that are closely linked to, and therefore usually inherited with, it

genetics (dʒɪˈnɛtɪks) *n* **1** (*functioning as sing*) the branch of biology concerned with the study of heredity and variation in organisms **2** (*functioning as pl*) the genetic features and constitution of a single organism, species, or group > **geˈneticist** *n*

▹ www.geneticalliance.org
▹ www.ornl.gov/TechResources/Human_Genome/
▹ www.genetics.org
▹ http://ghr.nlm.nih.gov
▹ www.hgc.gov.uk

Geneva (dʒɪˈniːvə) *n* **1** a city in SW Switzerland, in the Rhône valley on Lake Geneva: centre of Calvinism; headquarters of the International Red Cross (1864), the International Labour Office (1925), the League of Nations (1929–46), the World Health Organization, and the European office of the United Nations; banking centre. Pop: 172 809 (1999 est) **2** a canton in SW Switzerland. Capital: Geneva. Pop: 403 100 (2000 est). Area: 282 sq km (109 sq miles) ▹ French name **Genève** German name: **Genf** **3** **Lake** a lake between SW Switzerland and E France: fed and drained by the River Rhône, it is the largest of the Alpine lakes; the surface is subject to considerable changes of level. Area: 580 sq km (224 sq miles). French name: **Lac Léman** German name: **Genfersee**

Geneva bands *pl n* a pair of white lawn or linen strips hanging from the front of the neck or collar of some ecclesiastical and academic robes [C19 after GENEVA, where orig. worn by Swiss Calvinist clergy]

Geneva Convention *n* the international agreement, first formulated in 1864 at Geneva, establishing a code for wartime treatment of the sick or wounded: revised and extended to cover maritime warfare and prisoners of war

Geneva gown *n* a black gown with wide sleeves worn by Protestant clerics [C19 after GENEVA; see GENEVA BANDS]

Genevan (dʒɪˈniːvᵊn) *or* **Genevese** (ˌdʒɛnəˈviːz) *adj* **1** of, relating to, or characteristic of Geneva **2** of, adhering to, or relating to the teachings of Calvin or the Calvinists ▹ *n, pl* **Genevans** *or* **Genevese** **3** a native or inhabitant of Geneva **4** a less common name for a **Calvinist**

Geneva protocol *n* the agreement in 1925 to ban the use of asphyxiating, poisonous, or other gases in war. It does not ban the development or manufacture of such gases

Genève (ʒənɛv) *n* the French name for **Geneva**

Geneviève (ˈdʒɛnɪˌviːv; *French* ʒənvjɛv) *n* **Saint** ?422–?512 AD, French nun; patron saint of Paris. Feast day: Jan. 3

Genf (gɛnf) *n* the German name for **Geneva** (sense 1, 2)

Genfersee (ˈgɛnfərzeː) *n* the German name for (Lake) **Geneva**

Genghis Khan (ˈdʒɛŋgɪs kɑːn) *n* original name *Temuchin* or *Temujin*. ?1162–1227, Mongol ruler, whose empire stretched from the Black Sea to the Pacific. Also called: **Jinghis Khan, Jenghis Khan**

genial[1] (ˈdʒiːnjəl, -nɪəl) *adj* **1** cheerful, easy-going, and warm in manner **2** pleasantly warm, so as to give life, growth, or health [C16 from L *geniālis* relating to birth or marriage, from *genius* tutelary deity; see GENIUS] > **geniality** (ˌdʒiːnɪˈælɪtɪ) *n* > **ˈgenially** *adv*

genial[2] (dʒɪˈniːəl) *adj anat* of or relating to the chin [C19 from Gk, from *genus* jaw]

genic (ˈdʒɛnɪk) *adj* of or relating to a gene or genes

-genic *adj combining form* **1** relating to production or generation: *carcinogenic* **2** suited to or suitable for: *photogenic* [from -GEN + -IC]

genie (ˈdʒiːnɪ) *n* **1** (in fairy tales and stories) a servant who appears by magic and fulfils a person's wishes **2** another word for **jinni** [C18 from F, from Ar. *jinni* demon, infl. by L *genius* attendant spirit; see GENIUS]

genista (dʒɪˈnɪstə) *n* any of a genus of leguminous deciduous shrubs, usually having yellow, often fragrant, flowers; broom [C17 from L]

genital (ˈdʒɛnɪtᵊl) *adj* **1** of or relating to the sexual organs or to reproduction **2** *psychoanal* relating to the mature stage of psychosexual development [C14 from L *genitālis* concerning birth, from *gignere* to beget]

genital herpes *n* a sexually transmitted disease caused by the herpes simplex virus, in which painful blisters occur in the genital region

genitals (ˈdʒɛnɪtᵊlz) *or* **genitalia** (ˌdʒɛnɪˈteɪlɪə, -ˈteɪljə) *pl n* the external sexual organs

genitive (ˈdʒɛnɪtɪv) *grammar* ▹ *adj* **1** denoting a case of nouns, pronouns, and adjectives in inflected languages used to indicate a relation of ownership or association ▹ *n* **2a** the genitive case **2b** a word or speech element in this case [C14 from L *genetīvus* relating to birth, from *gignere* to produce] > **genitival** (ˌdʒɛnɪˈtaɪvᵊl) *adj*

genitourinary (ˌdʒɛnɪtəʊˈjʊərɪnərɪ) *adj* of or relating to both the reproductive and excretory organs; urogenital: *genitourinary medicine*

genius (ˈdʒiːnɪəs, -njəs) *n, pl* **geniuses** *or* (*for senses 5, 6*) **genii** (ˈdʒiːnɪˌaɪ) **1** a person with exceptional ability, esp of a highly original kind **2** such ability **3** the distinctive spirit of a nation, era, language, etc **4** a person considered as exerting influence of a certain sort: *an evil genius* **5** *Roman myth* **5a** the guiding spirit who attends a person from birth to death **5b** the guardian spirit of a place **6** (*usually pl*) *Arabic myth* a demon; jinn [C16 from L, from *gignere* to beget]

genizah (gɛˈniːzə) *n, pl* **genizahs** *or* **genizoth** (gɛˈniːzəθ) *Judaism* a repository for sacred objects which can no longer be used but which may not be destroyed [C19 from Heb., lit.: a hiding place]

Genk *or* **Genck** (*Flemish* xɛŋk) *n* a town in NE Belgium, in Limburg province: coal-mining. Pop: 61 996 (1995 est)

genoa (ˈdʒɛnəʊə) *n yachting* a large jib sail

Genoa (ˈdʒɛnəʊə) *n* a port in NW Italy, capital of Liguria, on the **Gulf of Genoa:** Italy's main port; an independent commercial city with many colonies in the Middle Ages; university (1243); heavy industries. Pop: 636 104 (2000 est). Italian name: **Genova**

genocide (ˈdʒɛnəʊˌsaɪd) *n* the policy of deliberately killing a nationality or ethnic group [c20 from Gk *genos* race + -CIDE] > ˌ**genoˈcidal** *adj*

Genoese (ˌdʒɛnəʊˈiːz) *or* **Genovese** (ˌdʒɛnəˈviːz) *n, pl* **Genoese** *or* **Genovese** 1 a native or inhabitant of Genoa ▷ *adj* 2 of or relating to Genoa or its inhabitants

genome (ˈdʒiːˌnəʊm) *n* the full complement of genetic material within an organism [c20 from GEN(E) + (CHROMOS)OME] > ˌ**genomic** (dʒɪˈnɒmɪk) *adj*

genomics (dʒɪˈnɒmɪks) *n (functioning as singular)* the branch of molecular genetics concerned with the study of genomes, specifically the identification and sequencing of their constituent genes and the application of this knowledge in medicine, pharmacy, agriculture, etc

genotype (ˈdʒɛnəʊˌtaɪp) *n* 1 the genetic constitution of an organism 2 a group of organisms with the same genetic constitution > **genotypic** (ˌdʒɛnəʊˈtɪpɪk) *adj*

-genous *adj combining form* 1 yielding or generating: *erogenous* 2 generated by or issuing from: *endogenous* [from -GEN + -OUS]

Genova (ˈdʒɛːnova) *n* the Italian name for **Genoa**

genre (ˈʒɑːnrə) *n* 1a kind, category, or sort, esp of literary or artistic work 1b *(as modifier): genre fiction* 2 a category of painting in which incidents from everyday life are depicted [c19 from F, from OF *gendre;* see GENDER]

gens (dʒɛnz) *n, pl* **gentes** (ˈdʒɛntiːz) 1 (in ancient Rome) any of a group of families, having a common name and claiming descent from a common ancestor in the male line 2 *anthropol* a group based on descent in the male line [c19 from L: race]

Genseric (ˈgɛnsərɪk, ˈdʒɛn-) *or* **Gaiseric** *n* ?390–477 AD, king of the Vandals (428–77). He seized Roman lands, esp extensive parts of N Africa, and sacked Rome (455)

gent (dʒɛnt) *n inf* short for **gentleman**

Gent (xɛnt) *n* the Flemish name for **Ghent**

genteel (dʒɛnˈtiːl) *adj* 1 affectedly proper or refined; excessively polite 2 respectable, polite, and well-bred 3 appropriate to polite or fashionable society [c16 from F *gentil* well-born; see GENTLE] > **genˈteelly** *adv* > **genˈteelness** *n*

gentian (ˈdʒɛnʃən) *n* 1 any plant of the genera *Gentiana* or *Gentianella*, having blue, yellow, white, or red showy flowers 2 the bitter-tasting roots of the yellow gentian, which can be used as a tonic [c14 from L *gentiāna;* ? after *Gentius*, a second-century BC Illyrian king, reputedly the first to use it medicinally]

gentian violet *n* a greenish crystalline substance that forms a violet solution in water, used as an indicator, antiseptic, and in the treatment of burns

Gentile[1] (ˈdʒɛntaɪl) *n* 1 a person, esp a Christian, who is not a Jew 2 a Christian, as contrasted with a Jew 3 a person who is not a member of one's own church: used esp by Mormons 4 a heathen or pagan ▷ *adj* 5 of or relating to a race or religion that is not Jewish 6 Christian, as contrasted with Jewish 7 not being a member of one's own church: used esp by Mormons 8 pagan or heathen [c15 *gentil*, from LL *gentīlis*, from L: one belonging to the same tribe]

Gentile[2] (*Italian* dʒenˈtiːle) *n* **Giovanni** (dʒoˈvanni) 1875–1944, Italian Idealist philosopher and Fascist politician: minister of education (1922–24)

Gentile da Fabriano (*Italian* dʒenˈtiːle da fabriˈaːno) *n* original name *Niccolo di Giovanni di Massio*. ?1370–1427, Italian painter. His works, in the International Gothic style, include the *Adoration of the Magi* (1423)

gentility (dʒɛnˈtɪlɪtɪ) *n, pl* **gentilities** 1 respectability and polite good breeding 2 affected politeness 3 noble birth or ancestry 4 people of noble birth [c14 from OF, from L *gentīlitās* relationship of those belonging to the same tribe or family; see GENS]

gentle (ˈdʒɛntᵊl) *adj* 1 having a mild or kindly nature or character 2 soft or temperate; mild; moderate 3 gradual: *a gentle slope* 4 easily controlled; tame 5 *arch* of good breeding; noble: *gentle blood* 6 *arch* gallant; chivalrous ▷ *vb* **gentles, gentling, gentled** *(tr)* 7 to tame or subdue (a horse, etc) 8 to appease or mollify ▷ *n* 9 a maggot, esp when used as bait in fishing [c13 from OF *gentil* noble, from L *gentīlis* belonging to the same family; see GENS] > ˈ**gentleness** *n* > ˈ**gently** *adv*

gentle breeze *n* a wind of force 3 on the Beaufort scale, blowing at 8-12 mph

gentlefolk (ˈdʒɛntᵊlˌfəʊk) *or* **gentlefolks** *pl n* persons regarded as being of good breeding

gentleman (ˈdʒɛntᵊlmən) *n, pl* **gentlemen** 1 a man regarded as having qualities of refinement associated with a good family 2 a man who is cultured, courteous, and well-educated 3 a polite name for a man 4 the personal servant of a gentleman (esp in **gentleman's gentleman**) > ˈ**gentlemanly** *adj* > ˈ**gentlemanliness** *n*

gentleman-farmer *n, pl* **gentlemen-farmers** 1 a person who engages in farming but does not depend on it for his living 2 a person who owns farmland but does not farm it personally

gentlemen's agreement *or* **gentleman's agreement** *n* an understanding or arrangement based on honour and not legally binding

gentlewoman (ˈdʒɛntᵊlˌwʊmən) *n, pl* **gentlewomen** 1 *arch* a woman regarded as being of good family or breeding; lady 2 (formerly) a woman in personal attendance on a high-ranking lady

gentrification (ˌdʒɛntrɪfɪˈkeɪʃən) *n Brit* a process by which middle-class people take up residence in a traditionally working-class area, changing its character [c20 from *gentrify* (to become GENTRY)] > ˈ**gentriˌfier** *n*

gentry (ˈdʒɛntrɪ) *n* 1 *Brit* persons just below the nobility in social rank 2 people of a particular class, esp one considered to be inferior [c14 from OF *genterie*, from *gentil* GENTLE]

gents (dʒɛnts) *n (functioning as sing) Brit inf* a men's public lavatory

genuflect (ˈdʒɛnjʊˌflɛkt) *vb (intr)* 1 to act in a servile or deferential manner 2 *RC Church* to bend one or both knees as a sign of reverence [c17 from Med. L, from L *genu* knee + *flectere* to bend] > ˌ**genuˈflection** *or* (esp Brit) ˌ**genuˈflexion** *n* > ˈ**genuˌflector** *n*

genuine (ˈdʒɛnjʊɪn) *adj* 1 not fake or counterfeit; original; real; authentic 2 not pretending; frank; sincere 3 being of authentic or original stock [c16 from L *genuīnus* inborn, hence (in LL) authentic] > ˈ**genuinely** *adv* > ˈ**genuineness** *n*

gen up *vb* **gens, genning, genned** *(adv; often passive;* when *intr*, usually foll by *on) Brit inf* to make or become fully conversant (with)

genus (ˈdʒiːnəs) *n, pl* **genera** *or* **genuses** 1 *biol* any of the taxonomic groups into which a family is divided and which contains one or more species 2 *logic* a class of objects or individuals that can be divided into two or more groups or species 3 a class, group, etc, with common characteristics [c16 from L: race]

-geny *n combining form* origin or manner of development: *phylogeny* [from Gk, from *-genēs* born] > **-genic** *adj combining form*

geo- *combining form* indicating earth: *geomorphology* [from Gk, from *gē* earth]

geocentric (ˌdʒiːəʊˈsɛntrɪk) *adj* 1 having the earth at its centre: *a geocentric system* 2 measured from or relating to

Gg

the centre of the earth > ˌgeo'centrically *adv*

geochronology (ˌdʒiːəʊkrə'nɒlədʒɪ) *n* the branch of geology concerned with ordering and dating events in the earth's history > **geochronological** (ˌdʒiːəʊˌkrɒnə'lɒdʒɪkᵊl) *adj*

geode ('dʒiːəʊd) *n* a cavity, usually lined with crystals, within a rock mass or nodule [c17 from L *geōdēs* a precious stone, from Gk: earthlike; see GEO-, -ODE[1]] > **geodic** (dʒɪ'ɒdɪk) *adj*

geodesic (ˌdʒiːəʊ'dɛsɪk, -'diː-) *adj* **1** Also: **geodetic** relating to the geometry of curved surfaces ▷ *n* **2** Also called: **geodesic line** the shortest line between two points on a curved surface

geodesic dome *n* a light structural framework arranged as a set of polygons in the form of a shell

geodesy (dʒɪ'ɒdɪsɪ) *n* the branch of science concerned with determining the exact position of geographical points and the shape and size of the earth [c16 from F, from Gk *geōdaisia*, from GEO- + *daiein* to divide] > **ge'odesist** *n*

geodetic (ˌdʒiːəʊ'dɛtɪk) *adj* **1** of or relating to geodesy **2** another word for **geodesic** > ˌ**geo'detically** *adv*

Geoffrey of Monmouth ('dʒɛfrɪ) *n* ?1100–54, Welsh bishop and chronicler; author of *Historia Regum Britanniae*, the chief source of Arthurian legends

geog. *abbrev for:* **1** geographic(al) **2** geography

geographical mile *n* a former name for **nautical mile**

geography (dʒɪ'ɒgrəfɪ) *n, pl* **geographies 1** the study of the natural features of the earth's surface, including topography, climate, soil, vegetation, etc, and man's response to them **2** the natural features of a region > **ge'ographer** *n* > **geographical** (ˌdʒɪə'græfɪkᵊl) *or* ˌ**geo'graphic** *adj* > ˌ**geo'graphically** *adv*

▷ www.sosig.ac.uk/geography
▷ www.colorado.edu/geography/virtdept/resources/contents.htm
▷ http://oceanworld.tamu.edu/
▷ www.geoexplorer.co.uk
▷ http://plasma.nationalgeographic.com/mapmachine/
▷ www.library.wisc.edu/libraries/Geography/offcamp.htm

geoid ('dʒiːɔɪd) *n* **1** a hypothetical surface that corresponds to mean sea level and extends under the continents **2** the shape of the earth

geol. *abbrev for:* **1** geologic(al) **2** geology

geology (dʒɪ'ɒlədʒɪ) *n* **1** the scientific study of the origin, structure, and composition of the earth **2** the geological features of a district or country > **geological** (ˌdʒɪə'lɒdʒɪkᵊl) *or* ˌ**geo'logic** *adj* > ˌ**geo'logically** *adv* > **ge'ologist** *n*

▷ www.psigate.ac.uk/newsite/earth-gateway.html
▷ http://personal.cmich.edu/francım/homepage.htm
▷ www.earthquakes.bgs.ac.uk
▷ http://nsidc.org/glaciers/information.html
▷ http://pubs.usgs.gov/gip/fossils/

geom. *abbrev for:* **1** geometric(al) **2** geometry

geomagnetism (ˌdʒiːəʊ'mægnɪˌtɪzəm) *n* **1** the magnetic field of the earth **2** the branch of physics concerned with this > **geomagnetic** (ˌdʒiːəʊmæg'nɛtɪk) *adj*

geometric (ˌdʒɪə'mɛtrɪk) *or* **geometrical** *adj* **1** of, relating to, or following the methods and principles of geometry **2** consisting of, formed by, or characterized by points, lines, curves, or surfaces **3** (of design or ornamentation) composed predominantly of simple geometric forms, such as circles, triangles, etc > ˌ**geo'metrically** *adv*

geometric mean *n* the average value of a set of *n* integers, terms, or quantities, expressed as the *n*th root of their product

geometric progression *n* **1** a sequence of numbers, each of which differs from the succeeding one by a constant ratio, as 1, 2, 4, 8, ... ▷ Cf **arithmetic progression** **2** **geometric series** such numbers written as a sum

geometrid (dʒɪ'ɒmɪtrɪd) *n* any of a family of moths, the larvae of which are called measuring worms, inchworms, or loopers [c19 from NL, from L, from Gk *geometrēs* land measurer, from the looping gait of the larvae]

geometry (dʒɪ'ɒmɪtrɪ) *n* **1** the branch of mathematics concerned with the properties, relationships, and measurement of points, lines, curves, and surfaces **2** a shape, configuration, or arrangement [c14 from L, from Gk, from *geōmetrein* to measure the land] > **geˌome'trician** *n*

geomorphology (ˌdʒiːəʊmɔː'fɒlədʒɪ) *n* the branch of geology that is concerned with the structure, origin, and development of the topographical features of the earth's surface > **geomorphological** (ˌdʒiːəʊˌmɔːfə'lɒdʒɪkᵊl) *or* ˌ**geoˌmorpho'logic** *adj*

geophysics (ˌdʒiːəʊ'fɪzɪks) *n* (*functioning as sing*) the study of the earth's physical properties and of the physical processes acting upon, above, and within the earth. It includes seismology, meteorology, and oceanography > ˌ**geo'physical** *adj* > ˌ**geo'physicist** *n*

geopolitics (ˌdʒiːəʊ'pɒlɪtɪks) *n* **1** (*functioning as sing*) the study of the effect of geographical factors on politics **2** (*functioning as pl*) the combination of geographical and political factors affecting a country or area **3** (*functioning as pl*) politics as they affect the whole world; global politics > **geopolitical** (ˌdʒiːəʊpə'lɪtɪkᵊl) *adj*

Using the Internet to Find Information Concerning Countries, Governments, and International Organizations

The Internet has a vast amount of information on these subjects available to academics, students, researchers, and casual surfers alike. Finding reliable and freely accessible data should not be problematic as long as a few simple rules are followed.

The material should be up to date.
Small organizations and departments within academic institutions sometimes encounter funding or budgetary problems and are unable to continue with their researches. Make sure to look at the 'Last updated' section of the main website page before using any data. Try clicking on the links to make sure that they have been maintained properly and do not result in error messages.

The data, where possible, should be value-free and not driven by an agenda or ideology.
Information provided by political parties, pressure groups, individuals, profit-making bodies, think tanks, and religious organizations should be treated with healthy scepticism. Data provided by academic institutions, official organizations (such as the United Nations), and the statistical departments of democratically elected governments should be much more reliable.

A number of useful online sources for this type of information have been listed below.

ORGANIZATION: **United Nations Statistical Division**
WEBSITE: http://unstats.un.org/unsd/
INFORMATION: world, regional, and national statistics; trends and indicators. The UN also has useful geographical and political information organized and displayed in a way that is helpful to children and teachers at the following site:

▷ http://cyberschoolbus.un.org/index.asp

ORGANIZATION: **World Trade Organization**
WEBSITE: www.wto.org/english/res_e/statis_e/natl_e.pdf
INFORMATION: links to national statistical offices

ORGANIZATION: **The European Information Association**
WEBSITE: www.eia.org.uk/websites.htm
INFORMATION: a portal to websites concerned with the European Union and its agencies institutions, and information networks.

ORGANIZATION: **Keele University**
WEBSITE: www.psr.keele.ac.uk/const.htm
INFORMATION: links to governments, legislatures, central banks, and statistical offices. Also features constitutions, conventions, treaties, declarations, and election results.

ORGANIZATION: **Inter-Parliamentary Union**
WEBSITE: www.ipu.org/english/parlweb.htm
INFORMATION: links to websites of national parliaments

ORGANIZATION: **BBC**
WEBSITE: http://news.bbc.co.uk/1/hi/world/europe/country_profiles
INFORMATION: country profiles, brief histories, and guides to international organizations such as NATO, the United Nations, and the British Commonwealth.

ORGANIZATION: **University of Michigan**
WEBSITE: www.lib.umich.edu/govdocs/intl.html
INFORMATION: links to governments, international organizations, and embassies. Links and data on human rights, international relations, flags, maps, and national anthems.

ORGANIZATION: **UK Government**
WEBSITE: www.ukonline.gov.uk/Home/Homepage/fs/en

ORGANIZATION: **Her Majesty's Stationery Office**
WEBSITE: www.hmso.gov.uk

ORGANIZATION: **National Statistics Online**
WEBSITE: www.statistics.gov.uk

ORGANIZATION: **Foreign and Commonwealth Office**
WEBSITE: www.fco.gov.uk

ORGANIZATION: **Australian Government**
WEBSITE: www.fed.gov.au

ORGANIZATION: **Australian Bureau of Statistics**
WEBSITE: www.abs.gov.au

ORGANIZATION: **Foreign Affairs and Trade**
WEBSITE: www.dfat.gov.au

ORGANIZATION: **Canadian Government**
WEBSITE: http://canada.gc.ca/main_e.html

ORGANIZATION: **Statistics Canada**
WEBSITE: www.statcan.ca/start.html

ORGANIZATION: **Department of Foreign Affairs and International Trade**
WEBSITE: www.dfait-maeci.gc.ca/menu-en.asp

ORGANIZATION: **New Zealand Government**
WEBSITE: www.govt.nz

ORGANIZATION: **Statistics New Zealand**
WEBSITE: www.stats.govt.nz

ORGANIZATION: **New Zealand Ministry of Foreign Affairs and Trade**
WEBSITE: www.mfat.govt.nz

ORGANIZATION: **South African Government**
WEBSITE: www.gov.za

ORGANIZATION: **Statistics South Africa**
WEBSITE: www.statssa.gov.za

ORGANIZATION: **South African Department of Foreign Affairs**
WEBSITE: www.dfa.gov.za

Geordie ('dʒɔːdɪ) *Brit* ▷ *n* **1** a person who comes from or lives in Tyneside **2** the dialect spoken by these people ▷ *adj* **3** of or relating to these people or their dialect [C19 a dim. of *George*]

George (dʒɔːdʒ) *n* **1 David Lloyd** See **Lloyd George 2** Sir **Edward** (**Alan John**), known as *Eddie.* born 1938, British economist, governor of the Bank of England (1993–2003) **3 Henry** 1839–97, US economist: advocated a single tax on land values, esp in *Progress and Poverty* (1879) **4 Saint** died ?303 AD, Christian martyr, the patron saint of England; the hero of a legend in which he slew a dragon. Feast day: April 23 **5** (*German* geˈɔrgə) **Stefan** (**Anton**) ('ʃtɛfan) 1868–1933, German poet and aesthete. Influenced by the French Symbolists, esp Mallarmé and later by Nietzsche, he sought for an idealized purity of form in his verse. He refused Nazi honours and went into exile in 1933

George I *n* 1660–1727, first Hanoverian king of Great Britain and Ireland (1714–27) and elector of Hanover (1698–1727). His dependence in domestic affairs on his ministers led to the emergence of Walpole as the first prime minister

George II *n* **1** 1683–1760, king of Great Britain and Ireland and elector of Hanover (1727–60); son of George I. His victory over the French at Dettingen (1743) in the War of the Austrian Succession was the last appearance on a battlefield by a British king **2** 1890–1947, king of Greece (1922–24; 1935–47) He was overthrown by the republicans (1924) and exiled during the German occupation of Greece (1941–45)

George III *n* 1738–1820, king of Great Britain and Ireland (1760–1820) and of Hanover (1814–20). During his reign the American colonies were lost. He became insane in 1811, and his son acted as regent for the rest of the reign

George IV *n* 1762–1830, king of Great Britain and Ireland and also of Hanover (1820–30); regent (1811–20). His father (George III) disapproved of his profligate ways, which undermined the prestige of the crown, and of his association with the Whig opposition

George V *n* 1865–1936, king of Great Britain and Northern Ireland and emperor of India (1910–36)

George VI *n* 1895–1952, king of Great Britain and Northern Ireland (1936–52) and emperor of India (1936–47). The second son of George V, he succeeded to the throne after the abdication of his brother, Edward VIII

George Cross *n* a British award for bravery, esp of civilians. Abbrev: **GC**

Georgetown ('dʒɔːdʒˌtaʊn) *n* **1** the capital and chief port of Guyana, at the mouth of the Demerara River: became capital of the Dutch colonies of Essequibo and Demerara in 1784; seat of the University of Guyana. Pop:

275 000 (1999 est). Former name (until 1812): **Stabroek** **2** the capital of the Cayman Islands: a port on Grand Cayman Island. Pop: 16 600 (1995 est)

George Town *n* a port in NW Malaysia, capital of Penang state, in NE Penang Island: the first chartered city of the Malayan federation. Pop: 219 376 (1991). Also called: **Penang**

georgette *or* **georgette crepe** (dʒɔːˈdʒɛt) *n* a thin silk or cotton crepe fabric [c20 from Mme *Georgette*, a F modiste]

Georgia (ˈdʒɔːdʒjə) *n* **1** a republic in NW Asia, on the Black Sea: an independent kingdom during the middle ages, it was divided by Turkey and Persia in 1555; became part of Russia in 1918 and a separate Soviet republic in 1936; its independence was recognized internationally in 1992. It is rich in minerals and has hydroelectric resources. Official language: Georgian. Religion: believers are mainly Christian or Muslim. Currency: lari. Capital: Tbilisi. Pop: 4 989 000 (2001 est). Area: 69 493 sq km (26 831 sq miles) **2** a state of the southeastern US, on the Atlantic: consists of coastal plains with forests and swamps, rising to the Cumberland Plateau and the Appalachians in the northwest. Capital: Atlanta. Pop: 8 186 453 (2000). Area: 152 489 sq km (58 876 sq miles). Abbreviations: **Ga** or (with zip code) **GA**
▷ www.parliament.ge

Georgian (ˈdʒɔːdʒjən) *adj* **1** of or relating to any or all of the four kings who ruled Great Britain from 1714 to 1830, or to their reigns **2** of or relating to George V of Great Britain or his reign (1910–36): *the Georgian poets* **3** of or relating to Georgia, its people, or their language **4** of or relating to the American State of Georgia or its inhabitants **5** (of furniture, architecture, etc) in or imitative of the style prevalent in Britain during the 18th century ▷ *n* **6** the official language of Georgia, belonging to the South Caucasian family **7** a native or inhabitant of Georgia **8** a native or inhabitant of the American State of Georgia

Georgian Bay *n* a bay in S central Canada, in Ontario, containing many small islands: the NE part of Lake Huron. Area: 15 000 sq km (5800 sq miles)

geostatics (ˌdʒiːəʊˈstætɪks) *n* (*functioning as sing*) the branch of physics concerned with the statics of rigid bodies, esp the balance of forces within the earth

geostationary (ˌdʒiːəʊˈsteɪʃənərɪ) *adj* (of a satellite, etc) in a circular equatorial orbit in which it circles the earth once in 24 hours so that it appears stationary in relation to the earth's surface

geostrophic (ˌdʒiːəʊˈstrɒfɪk) *adj* of, relating to, or caused by the force produced by the rotation of the earth: *geostrophic wind*

geosynchronous (ˌdʒiːəʊˈsɪŋkrənəs) *n* (of a satellite) in an orbit in which it circles the earth once in 24 hours

geosyncline (ˌdʒiːəʊˈsɪŋklaɪn) *n* a broad elongated depression in the earth's crust

geotextile (ˌdʒiːəʊˈtɛkstaɪl) *n* any strong synthetic fabric used in civil engineering, as to retain an embankment

geothermal (ˌdʒiːəʊˈθɜːməl) *or* **geothermic** *adj* of or relating to the heat in the interior of the earth

geotropism (dʒɪˈɒtrəˌpɪzəm) *n* the response of a plant part to the stimulus of gravity. Plant stems, which grow upwards irrespective of the position in which they are placed, show **negative geotropism** > **geotropic** (ˌdʒiːəʊˈtrɒpɪk) *adj*

Ger. *abbrev for:* **1** German **2** Germany

Gera (*German* ˈgeːra) *n* an industrial city in E central Germany, in Thuringia. Pop: 115 800 (1999 est)

geranium (dʒɪˈreɪnɪəm) *n* **1** a cultivated plant of the genus *Pelargonium* having scarlet, pink, or white showy flowers. See also **pelargonium** **2** any plant such as cranesbill and herb Robert, having divided leaves and pink or purplish flowers [c16 from L: cranesbill, from Gk *geranion*, from *geranos* CRANE]

Gérard (*French* ʒerar) *n* **François** (**Pascal Simon**), Baron. 1770–1837, French painter, court painter to Napoleon I and Louis XVIII

gerbera (ˈdʒɜːbərə) *n* a genus of African or Asian plants belonging to the composite family, Asteraceae, esp the Transvaal daisy [c19 from NL, after T. *Gerber* (died 1743), G naturalist]

gerbil *or* **gerbille** (ˈdʒɜːbɪl) *n* a burrowing rodent inhabiting hot dry regions of Asia and Africa [c19 from F, from NL *gerbillus* a little JERBOA]

gerfalcon (ˈdʒɜːˌfɔːlkən, -ˌfɔːkən) *n* a variant spelling of **gyrfalcon**

Gergiev (ˈgɛədʒjɛf) *n* **Valery Abesalovich** born 1953, Russian conductor; musical director of the Kirov (now the Mariinsky) Opera from 1988

geriatric (ˌdʒɛrɪˈætrɪk) *adj* **1** of or relating to geriatrics or to elderly people **2** *inf* old, decrepit, or useless ▷ *n* **3** an elderly person [c20 from Gk *gēras* old age + IATRIC]

geriatrics (ˌdʒɛrɪˈætrɪks) *n* (*functioning as sing*) the branch of medical science concerned with the diagnosis and treatment of diseases affecting elderly people > ˌ**geriaˈtrician** *n*
▷ www.asaging.org

Géricault (*French* ʒeriko) *n* (**Jean Louis André**) **Théodore** (teɔdɔr) 1791–1824, French romantic painter, noted for his skill in capturing movement, esp of horses

Gerlachovka (*Czech* ˈgɛrlaxɔfka) *n* a mountain in N Slovakia, in the Tatra Mountains: the highest peak of the Carpathian Mountains. Height: 2663 m (8737 ft)

germ (dʒɜːm) *n* **1** a microorganism, esp one that produces disease **2** (*often pl*) the rudimentary or initial form of something: *the germs of revolution* **3** a simple structure that is capable of developing into a complete organism [c17 from F, from L *germen* sprout, seed]

german (ˈdʒɜːmən) *adj* **1** (used in combination) **1a** having the same parents as oneself: *a brother-german* **1b** having a parent that is a brother or sister of either of one's own parents: *cousin-german* **2** a less common word for **germane** [c14 via OF, from L *germānus* of the same race, from *germen* sprout, offshoot]

German (ˈdʒɜːmən) *n* **1** the official language of Germany and Austria and one of the official languages of Switzerland **2** a native, inhabitant, or citizen of Germany **3** a person whose native language is German ▷ *adj* **4** denoting, relating to, or using the German language **5** relating to, denoting, or characteristic of any German state or its people
▷ www.goethe.de/enindex.htm

German Democratic Republic *n* (formerly) the official name of **East Germany** Abbreviations: **GDR, DDR**

germander (dʒɜːˈmændə) *n* any of several plants of Europe, having two-lipped flowers with a very small upper lip [c15 from Med. L, ult. from Gk *khamai* on the ground + *drus* oak tree]

germane (dʒɜːˈmeɪn) *adj* (*postpositive*; usually foll by *to*) related (to the topic being considered); akin; relevant [var. of GERMAN] > **gerˈmanely** *adv* > **gerˈmaneness** *n*

German East Africa *n* a former German territory in E Africa, consisting of Tanganyika and Ruanda-Urundi: divided in 1919 between Great Britain and Belgium; now in Tanzania, Rwanda, and Burundi

Germanic (dʒɜːˈmænɪk) *n* **1** a branch of the Indo-European family of languages that includes English, Dutch, German, the Scandinavian languages, and Gothic. Abbrev: **Gmc** **2** Also called: **Proto-Germanic** the unrecorded language from which all of these languages developed ▷ *adj* **3** of, denoting, or relating to this group of languages **4** of, relating to, or characteristic of the German language or any people that speaks a Germanic language **5** (formerly) of the German people

Germanicus Caesar (dʒɜːˈmænɪkəs) *n* 15 BC–19 AD, Roman general; nephew of the emperor Tiberius; waged decisive campaigns against the Germans (14–16)

germanium (dʒɜːˈmeɪnɪəm) *n* a brittle crystalline grey element that is a semiconducting metalloid: used in transistors, and to strengthen alloys. Symbol: Ge; atomic no.: 32; atomic wt.: 72.59 [C19 NL, after GERMANY]

German measles *n (functioning as sing)* a nontechnical name for **rubella**

German Ocean *n* a former name for the **North Sea**

German shepherd dog *n* another name for **Alsatian**

German silver *n* another name for **nickel silver**

Germany (ˈdʒɜːmənɪ) *n* a country in central Europe: in the Middle Ages the centre of the Holy Roman Empire; dissolved into numerous principalities; united under the leadership of Prussia in 1871 after the Franco-Prussian War; became a republic with reduced size in 1919 after being defeated in World War I; under the dictatorship of Hitler from 1933 to 1945; defeated in World War II and divided by the Allied Powers into four zones, which became established as East and West Germany in the late 1940s; reunified in 1990: a member of the European Union. It is flat and low-lying in the north with plateaus and uplands (including the Black Forest and the Bavarian Alps) in the centre and south. Official language: German. Religion: Christianity, Protestant majority. Currency: euro. Capital: Berlin. Pop: 82 386 000 (2001 est). Area: 357 041 sq km (137 825 sq miles). German name: **Deutschland** Official name: **Federal Republic of Germany.** See also **East Germany, West Germany** Related adj: **Teutonic**
▹ http://eng.bundesregierung.de/frameset/index.jsp
▹ www.visits-to-germany.com

germ cell *n* a sexual reproductive cell

germicide (ˈdʒɜːmɪˌsaɪd) *n* any substance that kills germs > **ˌgermiˈcidal** *adj*

germinal (ˈdʒɜːmɪnᵊl) *adj* **1** of, relating to, or like germs or a germ cell **2** of or in the earliest stage of development [C19 from NL, from L *germen* bud; see GERM] > **ˈgerminally** *adv*

germinate (ˈdʒɜːmɪˌneɪt) *vb* **germinates, germinating, germinated 1** to cause (seeds or spores) to sprout or (of seeds or spores) to sprout **2** to grow or cause to grow; develop **3** to come or bring into existence; originate: *the idea germinated with me* [C17 from L *germināre* to sprout; see GERM] > **ˈgerminative** *adj* > **ˌgermiˈnation** *n* > **ˈgermiˌnator** *n*

Germiston (ˈdʒɜːmɪstən) *n* a city in South Africa, southeast of Johannesburg: industrial centre, with the world's largest gold refinery, serving the Witwatersrand mines. Pop: 134 005 (1991)

germ plasm *n* **a** the part of a germ cell that contains hereditary material **b** the germ cells collectively

germ warfare *n* the military use of disease-spreading bacteria against an enemy

Gerona (*Spanish* xeˈrona) *n* a city in NE Spain: city walls and 14th-century cathedral; often besieged, in particular by the French (1809). Pop: 67 580 (latest est). Ancient name: **Gerunda** (dʒəˈruːndə)

Geronimo (dʒəˈrɒnɪˌməʊ) *n* **1** 1829–1909, Apache Indian chieftain: led a campaign against the White settlers until his final capture in 1886 ▹ *interj* **2** *US* a shout given by paratroopers as they jump into battle

gerontology (ˌdʒɛrɒnˈtɒlədʒɪ) *n* the scientific study of ageing and the problems associated with elderly people > **gerontological** (ˌdʒɛrɒntəˈlɒdʒɪkᵊl) *adj* > **ˌgeronˈtologist** *n*

-gerous *adj combining form* bearing or producing: *armigerous* [from L *-ger* bearing + -OUS]

gerrymander (ˈdʒɛrɪˌmændə) *vb* **1** to divide the constituencies of (a voting area) so as to give one party an unfair advantage **2** to manipulate or adapt to one's advantage ▹ *n* **3** an act or result of gerrymandering [C19 from Elbridge *Gerry*, US politician + (SALA)MANDER; from the salamander-like outline of an electoral district reshaped (1812) for political purposes while Gerry was governor of Massachusetts]

Gers (*French* ʒɛr) *n* a department of SW France, in Midi-Pyrénées region. Capital: Auch. Pop: 172 335 (1999). Area: 6291 sq km (2453 sq miles)

Gershwin (ˈgɜːʃwɪn) *n* **1 George,** original name *Jacob Gershvin*. 1898–1937, US composer: incorporated jazz into works such as *Rhapsody in Blue* (1924) for piano and jazz band and the opera *Porgy and Bess* (1935) **2** his brother, **Ira,** original name *Israel Gershvin*. 1896–1983, US song lyricist, noted esp for his collaboration with George Gershwin

gerund (ˈdʒɛrənd) *n* a noun formed from a verb, ending in *-ing*, denoting an action or state: *the living is easy* [C16 from LL, from L *gerundum* something to be carried on, from *gerere* to wage] > **gerundial** (dʒɪˈrʌndɪəl) *adj*

gerundive (dʒɪˈrʌndɪv) *n* **1** (in Latin grammar) an adjective formed from a verb, expressing the desirability, etc, of the activity denoted by the verb ▹ *adj* **2** of or relating to the gerund or gerundive [C17 from LL, from *gerundium* GERUND] > **gerundival** (ˌdʒɛrənˈdaɪvᵊl) *adj*

Gervais (ˌdʒɜːˈveɪz) *n* **Ricky** born 1962, British comedian and actor, best known for his starring role in the TV series *The Office* (2001–02), which he also co-wrote and co-directed

Geryon (ˈgɛrɪən) *n Greek myth* a winged monster with three bodies joined at the waist, killed by Hercules, who stole the monster's cattle as his tenth labour

gesso (ˈdʒɛsəʊ) *n* **1** a white ground of plaster and size, used to prepare panels or canvas for painting or gilding **2** any white substance, esp plaster of Paris, that forms a ground when mixed with water [C16 from It.: chalk, GYPSUM]

gest *or* **geste** (dʒɛst) *n arch* **1** a notable deed or exploit **2** a tale of adventure or romance, esp in verse [C14 from OF, from L *gesta* deeds, from *gerere* to carry out]

Gg

Gestalt psychology (gəˈʃtælt) *n* a system of thought that regards all mental phenomena as being arranged in patterns or structures (**gestalts**) perceived as a whole and not merely as the sum of their parts [C20 from G *Gestalt* form]

Gestapo (gɛˈstɑːpəʊ) *n* the secret state police in Nazi Germany [from G *Ge(heime) Sta(ats)po(lizei)*, lit.: secret state police]

gestate (ˈdʒɛsteɪt) *vb* **gestates, gestating, gestated 1** (*tr*) to carry (developing young) in the uterus during pregnancy **2** (*tr*) to develop (a plan or idea) in the mind **3** (*intr*) to be in the process of gestating [C19 from L p.p. of *gestare*, from *gerere* to bear]

gestation (dʒɛˈsteɪʃən) *n* **1a** the development of the embryo of a viviparous mammal, between conception and birth: about 266 days in humans, 624 days in elephants, and 63 days in cats **1b** (*as modifier*): *gestation period* **2** the development of an idea or plan in the mind **3** the period of such a development

gesticulate (dʒɛˈstɪkjʊˌleɪt) *vb* **gesticulates, gesticulating, gesticulated** to express by or make gestures [C17 from L, from *gesticulus* (unattested except in LL) gesture, from *gerere* to bear, conduct] > **geˌsticuˈlation** *n* > **geˈsticulative** *adj* > **gesˈticuˌlator** *n* > **gesˈticulatory** *adj*

gesture (ˈdʒɛstʃə) *n* **1** a motion of the hands, head, or body to express or emphasize an idea or emotion **2** something said or done as a formality or as an indication of intention ▹ *vb* **gestures, gesturing, gestured 3** to express by or make gestures; gesticulate [C15 from Med. L *gestūra* bearing, from L *gestus*, p.p. of *gerere* to bear] > **ˈgestural** *adj*

get (gɛt) *vb* **gets, getting, got; got** *or esp US* **gotten** (*mainly tr*) **1** to come into possession of; receive or earn **2** to bring or fetch **3** to contract or be affected by: *he got a chill*

4 to capture or seize: *the police got him* **5** (*also intr*) to become or cause to become or act as specified: *to get one's hair cut; get wet* **6** (*intr;* foll by a preposition or adverbial particle) to succeed in going, coming, leaving, etc: *get off the bus* **7** (*takes an infinitive*) to manage or contrive: *how did you get to be captain?* **8** to make ready or prepare: *to get a meal* **9** to hear, notice, or understand: *I didn't get your meaning* **10** to learn or master by study **11** (*intr;* often foll by *to*) to come (to) or arrive (at): *we got home safely; to get to London* **12** to catch or enter: *to get a train* **13** to induce or persuade: *get him to leave* **14** to reach by calculation: *add 2 and 2 and you will get 4* **15** to receive (a broadcast signal) **16** to communicate with (a person or place), as by telephone **17** (*also intr;* foll by *to*) *inf* to have an emotional effect (on): *that music really gets me* **18** *inf* to annoy or irritate: *her voice gets me* **19** *inf* to bring a person into a difficult position from which he or she cannot escape **20** *inf* to puzzle; baffle **21** *inf* to hit: *the blow got him in the back* **22** *inf* to be revenged on, esp by killing **23** *inf* to have the better of: *your extravagant habits will get you in the end* **24** (*intr;* foll by present participle) *inf* to begin: *get moving* **25** (used as a command) *inf* go! leave now! **26** *arch* to beget or conceive **27** **get with child** *arch* to make pregnant ▹ *n* **28** *rare* the act of begetting **29** *rare* something begotten; offspring **30** *Brit sl* a variant of **git** ▹ See also **get about, get across,** etc [OE *gietan*] > '**getable** *or* '**gettable** *adj* > '**getter** *n*

USAGE See at **off**

GeT *abbrev for* Greenwich Electronic Time

get about *or* **around** *vb* (*intr, adv*) **1** to move around, as when recovering from an illness **2** to be socially active **3** (of news, rumour, etc) to become known; spread

get across *vb* **1** to cross or cause to cross **2** (*adv*) to be or cause to be understood

get at *vb* (*intr, prep*) **1** to gain access to **2** to mean or intend: *what are you getting at?* **3** to irritate or annoy persistently; criticize: *she is always getting at him* **4** to influence or seek to influence, esp illegally by bribery, intimidation, etc: *someone had got at the witness before the trial*

get away *vb* (*adv, mainly intr*) **1** to make an escape; leave **2** to make a start **3** **get away with 3a** to steal and escape with (money, goods, etc) **3b** to do (something wrong, illegal, etc) without being discovered or punished ▹ *interj* **4** an exclamation indicating mild disbelief ▹ *n* **getaway** **5** the act of escaping, esp by criminals **6** a start or acceleration **7** a short holiday away from home **8** (*modifier*) used for escaping: *a getaway car*

get back *vb* (*adv*) **1** (*tr*) to recover or retrieve **2** (*intr;* often foll by *to*) to return, esp to a former position or activity **3** (*intr;* foll by *at*) to retaliate (against); wreak vengeance (on) **4** **get one's own back** *inf* to obtain one's revenge

get by *vb* **1** to pass; go past or overtake **2** (*intr, adv*) *inf* to manage, esp in spite of difficulties **3** (*intr*) to be accepted or permitted: *that book will never get by the authorities*

Gethsemane (gɛθ'sɛmənɪ) *n* *New Testament* the garden in Jerusalem where Christ was betrayed on the night before his Crucifixion (Matthew 26:36–56)

get in *vb* (*mainly adv*) **1** (*intr*) to enter a car, train, etc **2** (*intr*) to arrive, esp at one's home or place of work **3** (*tr*) to bring in or inside: *get the milk in* **4** (*tr*) to insert or slip in: *he got his suggestion in before anyone else* **5** (*tr*) to gather or collect (crops, debts, etc) **6** to be elected or cause to be elected **7** (*intr*) to obtain a place at university, college, etc **8** (foll by *on*) to join or cause to join (an activity or organization)

get off *vb* **1** (*intr, adv*) to escape the consequences of an action: *he got off very lightly* **2** (*adv*) to be or cause to be acquitted: *a good lawyer got him off* **3** (*adv*) to depart or cause to depart: *to get the children off to school* **4** (*intr*) to descend (from a bus, train, etc); dismount: *she got off at the terminus* **5** to move or cause to move to a distance (from): *get off the field* **6** (*tr, adv*) to remove; take off: *get your coat off* **7** (*adv*) to go or send to sleep **8** (*adv*) to send (letters) or (of letters) to be sent **9** **get off with** *Brit inf* to establish an amorous or sexual relationship (with)

get on *vb* (*mainly adv*) **1** Also (*when prep*): **get onto** to board or cause or help to board (a bus, train, etc) **2** (*tr*) to dress in (clothes as specified) **3** (*intr*) to grow late or (of time) to elapse: *it's getting on and I must go* **4** (*intr*) (of a person) to grow old **5** (*intr;* foll by *for*) to approach (a time, age, amount, etc): *she is getting on for seventy* **6** (*intr*) to make progress, manage, or fare: *how did you get on in your exam?* **7** (*intr;* often foll by *with*) to establish a friendly relationship: *he gets on well with other people* **8** (*intr;* foll by *with*) to continue to do: *get on with your homework!*

get out *vb* (*adv*) **1** to leave or escape or cause to leave or escape: used in the imperative when dismissing a person **2** to make or become known; publish or be published **3** (*tr*) to express with difficulty **4** (*tr;* often foll by *of*) to extract (information or money) (from a person): *to get a confession out of a criminal* **5** (*tr*) to gain or receive something, esp something of significance or value **6** (foll by *of*) to avoid or cause to avoid: *she always gets out of swimming* **7** *cricket* to dismiss or be dismissed

get over *vb* **1** to cross or surmount (something) **2** (*intr, prep*) to recover from (an illness, shock, etc) **3** (*intr, prep*) to overcome or master (a problem) **4** (*intr, prep*) to appreciate fully: *I just can't get over seeing you again* **5** (*tr, adv*) to communicate effectively **6** (*tr, adv;* sometimes foll by *with*) to bring (something necessary but unpleasant) to an end: *let's get this job over with quickly*

get round *or* **around** *vb* (*intr*) **1** (*prep*) to circumvent or overcome **2** (*prep*) *inf* to have one's way with; cajole: *that girl can get round anyone* **3** (*prep*) to evade (a law or rules) **4** (*adv;* foll by *to*) to reach or come to at length: *I'll get round to that job in an hour*

get through *vb* **1** to succeed or cause or help to succeed in an examination, test, etc **2** to bring or come to a destination, esp after overcoming problems: *we got through the blizzards to the survivors* **3** (*intr, adv*) to contact, as by telephone **4** (*intr, prep*) to use, spend, or consume (money, supplies, etc) **5** to complete or cause to complete (a task, process, etc): *to get a bill through Parliament* **6** (*adv;* foll by *to*) to reach the awareness and understanding (of a person): *I just can't get the message through to him*

get-together *n* **1** *inf* a small informal meeting or social gathering ▹ *vb* **get together** (*adv*) **2** (*tr*) to gather or collect **3** (*intr*) (of people) to meet socially **4** (*intr*) to discuss, esp in order to reach an agreement

Getty ('gɛtɪ) *n* **J(ean) Paul** 1892–1976, US oil executive, millionaire, and art collector

Gettysburg ('gɛtɪz,bɜːg) *n* a small town in S Pennsylvania, southwest of Harrisburg: scene of a crucial battle (1863) during the American Civil War, in which Meade's Union forces defeated Lee's Confederate army; site of the national cemetery dedicated by President Lincoln. Pop: 7195 (latest est)

get up *vb* (*mainly adv*) **1** to wake and rise from one's bed or cause to wake and rise from bed **2** (*intr*) to rise to one's feet; stand up **3** (*also prep*) to ascend or cause to ascend **4** to increase or cause to increase in strength: *the wind got up at noon* **5** (*tr*) *inf* to dress (oneself) in a particular way, esp elaborately **6** (*tr*) *inf* to devise or create: *to get up an entertainment for Christmas* **7** (*tr*) *inf* to study or improve one's knowledge of: *I must get up my history* **8** (*intr;* foll by *to*) *inf* to be involved in: *he's always getting up to mischief* ▹ *n* **get-up** *inf* **9** a costume or outfit **10** the arrangement or production of a book, etc

get-up-and-go *n* *inf* energy or drive

Getz (gɛts) *n* **Stanley,** known as *Stan.* 1927–91, US jazz saxophonist: leader of his own group from 1949

geum ('dʒiːəm) *n* any herbaceous plant of the rose type, having compound leaves and red, orange, yellow, or white flowers [C19 NL, from L: herb bennet, avens]

gewgaw (ˈgjuːgɔː, ˈguː-) *n* a showy but valueless trinket [c15 from ?]

geyser (ˈgiːzə; *US* ˈgaɪzər) *n* **1** a spring that discharges steam and hot water **2** *Brit* a domestic gas water heater [c18 from Icelandic *Geysir*, from ON *geysa* to gush]

Gezira (dʒəˈzɪərə) *n* a region of the E central Sudan between the Blue and White Niles: site of a large-scale irrigation system

G-force *n* the force of gravity

Ghana (ˈgɑːnə) *n* a republic in W Africa, on the Gulf of Guinea: a powerful empire from the 4th to the 13th centuries; a major source of gold and slaves for Europeans after 1471; British colony of the Gold Coast established in 1874; united with British Togoland in 1957 and became a republic and a member of the Commonwealth in 1960. Official language: English. Religions: Christian, Muslim, and animist. Currency: cedi. Capital: Accra. Pop: 19 894 000 (2001 est). Area: 238 539 sq km (92 100 sq miles)
▷ www.ghana.gov.gh
▷ www.africaonline.com.gh/Tourism

Ghanaian (gɑːˈneɪən) *or* **Ghanian** (ˈgɑːnɪən) *adj* **1** of or relating to Ghana or its inhabitants ▷ *n* **2** a native or inhabitant of Ghana

gharry *or* **gharri** (ˈgærɪ) *n, pl* **gharries** a horse-drawn vehicle used in India [c19 from Hindi *gāṛī*]

ghastly (ˈgɑːstlɪ) *adj* **ghastlier, ghastliest 1** *inf* very bad or unpleasant **2** deathly pale; wan **3** *inf* extremely unwell; ill **4** terrifying; horrible ▷ *adv* **5** unhealthily; sickly: *ghastly pale* [OE *gāstlīc* spiritual] > ˈ**ghastliness** *n*

ghat (gɔːt) *n* (in India) **1** stairs or a passage leading down to a river **2** a mountain pass **3** a place of cremation [c17 from Hindi, from Sansk.]

Ghats (gɔːts) *pl n* See **Eastern Ghats** and **Western Ghats**

Ghazali (ˈgɑːzˌɑːlɪ) *n* **al-** 1058–1111, Muslim theologian, philosopher, and mystic

ghazi (ˈgɑːzɪ) *n, pl* **ghazis 1** a Muslim fighter against infidels **2** (*often cap*) a Turkish warrior of high rank [c18 from Ar., from *ghazā* he made war]

Ghazzah (ˈgɑːzə, ˈgʌzə) *n* transliteration of the Arabic name for **Gaza**

GHB *abbrev for* gamma-hydroxybutyrate

ghee (giː) *n* a clarified butter used in Indian cookery [c17 from Hindi *ghī*, from Sansk. *ghri* sprinkle]

Ghent (gɛnt) *n* an industrial city and port in NW Belgium, capital of East Flanders province, at the confluence of the Rivers Lys and Scheldt: formerly famous for its cloth industry; university (1816). Pop: 224 180 (2000 est). Flemish name: **Gent** French name: **Gand**

Gheorgiu (ˈdʒodʒju) *n* **Angela** born 1965, Romanian soprano: married to Roberto Alagna

gherkin (ˈgɜːkɪn) *n* **1** the small immature fruit of any of various cucumbers, used for pickling **2a** a tropical American climbing plant **2b** its small spiny edible fruit [c17 from Du., dim. of *gurk*, ult. from Gk *angourion*]

ghetto (ˈgɛtəʊ) *n, pl* **ghettos** *or* **ghettoes 1** a densely populated slum area of a city inhabited by a socially and economically deprived minority **2** an area or community that is segregated or isolated **3** an area in a European city in which Jews were formerly required to live [c17 from It., ?from *borghetto*, dim. of *borgo* settlement outside a walled city, or from *ghetto* foundry, because one occupied the site of the later Venetian ghetto]

ghettoblaster (ˈgɛtəʊˌblɑːstə) *n inf* a large portable cassette or CD recorder with built-in speakers

ghettoize *or* **ghettoise** (ˈgɛtəʊˌaɪz) *vb* **ghettoizes, ghettoizing, ghettoized** *or* **ghettoises, ghettoising, ghettoised** (*tr*) to confine or restrict to a particular area, activity, or category: *to ghettoize women as housewives* > ˌ**ghettoiˈzation** *or* ˌ**ghettoiˈsation** *n*

Ghiberti (*Italian* giˈbɛrti) *n* **Lorenzo** (loˈrɛntso) 1378–1455, Italian sculptor, painter, and goldsmith of the quattrocento: noted esp for the bronze doors of the baptistry of Florence Cathedral

ghillie (ˈgɪlɪ) *n* a variant spelling of **gillie**

Ghirlandaio *or* **Ghirlandajo** (*Italian* girlanˈdaːjo) *n* **Domenico** (doˈmeːniko) original name *Domenico Bigordi*. 1449–94, Italian painter of frescoes

ghost (gəʊst) *n* **1** the disembodied spirit of a dead person, supposed to haunt the living as a pale or shadowy vision; phantom. Related adj: **spectral 2** a haunting memory: *the ghost of his former life rose up before him* **3** a faint trace or possibility of something; glimmer: *a ghost of a smile* **4** the spirit; soul (archaic, except in **the Holy Ghost**) **5** *physics* **5a** a faint secondary image produced by an optical system **5b** a similar image on a television screen **6** (*modifier*) falsely recorded as doing a particular job or fulfilling a particular function in order that some benefit, esp money, may be obtained: *a ghost worker* **7 give up the ghost** to die ▷ *vb* **8** See **ghostwrite 9** (*tr*) to haunt **10** (*intr*) to move effortlessly and smoothly, esp unnoticed: *he ghosted into the penalty area* [OE *gāst*] > ˈ**ghostˌlike** *adj* > ˈ**ghostly** *adj*

ghost car *n Canad* an unmarked police car

ghost town *n* a deserted town, esp one in the western US that was formerly a boom town

ghost word *n* a word that has entered the language through the perpetuation, in dictionaries, etc, of an error

ghostwrite (ˈgəʊstˌraɪt) *vb* **ghostwrites, ghostwriting, ghostwrote, ghostwritten** to write (an article, etc) on behalf of a person who is then credited as the author. Often shortened to **ghost** > ˈ**ghostˌwriter** *n*

ghoul (guːl) *n* **1** a malevolent spirit or ghost **2** a person interested in morbid or disgusting things **3** a person who robs graves **4** (in Muslim legend) an evil demon thought to eat corpses [c18 from Ar. *ghūl*, from *ghāla* he seized] > ˈ**ghoulish** *adj* > ˈ**ghoulishly** *adv* > ˈ**ghoulishness** *n*

GHQ *mil abbrev for* General Headquarters

ghyll (gɪl) *n* a variant spelling of **gill**[3]

Gi *symbol for* gibi-

GI *US inf* ▷ *n* **1** (*pl* **GIs** *or* **GI's**) a soldier in the US Army, esp an enlisted man ▷ *adj* **2** conforming to US Army regulations [c20 abbrev of *government issue*]

Giacometti (*Italian* dʒakoˈmetti) *n* **Alberto** (alˈbɛrto) 1901–66, Swiss sculptor and painter, noted particularly for his long skeletal statues of isolated figures

Giambologna (*Italian* dʒamboˈlɔɲa) *n* original name *Giovanni da Bologna* or *Jean de Boulogne*. 1529–1608, Italian mannerist sculptor, born in Flanders: noted for his fountains and such works as *Samson Slaying a Philistine* (1565)

giant (ˈdʒaɪənt) *n* **1** Also (fem): **giantess** (ˈdʒaɪəntɪs) a mythical figure of superhuman size and strength, esp in folklore or fairy tales **2** a person or thing of exceptional size, reputation, etc ▷ *adj* **3** remarkably or supernaturally large [c13 from OF *geant*, from L *gigās*, *gigant-*, from Gk]

giant hogweed *n* a species of cow parsley that grows up to 3½ metres (10 ft) and whose irritant hairs and sap can cause a severe reaction

giantism (ˈdʒaɪənˌtɪzəm) *n* another term for **gigantism** (sense 1)

giant panda *n* See **panda** (sense 1)

Giant's Causeway *n* a promontory of columnar basalt on the N coast of Northern Ireland, in Antrim: consists of several thousand pillars, mostly hexagonal, that were formed by the rapid cooling of lava and the inward contraction of the lava flow

giant slalom *n skiing* a type of slalom in which the course is longer and the obstacles are further apart than in a standard slalom

giant star *n* any of a class of stars that have swelled and brightened considerably as they approach the end of their life, their energy supply having changed

giaour ('dʒaʊə) *n* a derogatory term for a non-Muslim, esp a Christian [C16 from Turkish: unbeliever, from Persian *gaur*]

gib (gɪb) *n* **1** a metal wedge, pad, or thrust bearing, esp a brass plate let into a steam engine crosshead ▷ *vb* **gibs, gibbing, gibbed 2** (*tr*) to fasten or supply with a gib [C18 from ?]

Gib (dʒɪb) *n* an informal name for **Gibraltar**

gibber[1] ('dʒɪbə) *vb* **1** to utter rapidly and unintelligibly; prattle **2** (*intr*) (of monkeys and related animals) to make characteristic chattering sounds [C17 imit.]

gibber[2] ('gɪbə) *n Austral* **1** a stone or boulder **2** (*modifier*) of or relating to a dry flat area of land covered with wind-polished stones: *gibber plains* [C19 from Abor.]

Gibberd ('gɪbəd) *n* Sir **Frederick** 1908–84, British architect and town planner. His buildings include the Liverpool Roman Catholic cathedral (1960–67) and the Regent's Park Mosque in London (1977). Harlow in the U.K. and Santa Teresa in Venezuela were built to his plans

gibberellin (ˌdʒɪbəˈrɛlɪn) *n* any of several plant hormones whose main action is to cause elongation of the stem [C20 from NL *Gibberella*, lit.: a little hump, from L *gibber* hump + -IN]

gibberish ('dʒɪbərɪʃ) *n* **1** rapid chatter **2** incomprehensible talk; nonsense

gibbet ('dʒɪbɪt) *n* **1a** a wooden structure resembling a gallows, from which the bodies of executed criminals were formerly hung to public view **1b** a gallows ▷ *vb* (*tr*) **2** to put to death by hanging on a gibbet **3** to hang (a corpse) on a gibbet **4** to expose to public ridicule [C13 from OF: gallows, lit.: little cudgel, from *gibe* cudgel; from ?]

gibbon ('gɪbᵊn) *n* a small agile arboreal anthropoid ape inhabiting forests in S Asia [C18 from F, prob. from an Indian dialect word]

Gibbon ('gɪbᵊn) *n* **1 Edward** 1737–94, English historian; author of *The History of the Decline and Fall of the Roman Empire* (1776–88), controversial in its historical criticism of Christianity **2 Lewis Grassic** ('græsɪk), real name *James Leslie Mitchell*. 1901–35, Scottish writer: best known for his trilogy of novels *Scots Quair* (1932–34)

Gibbons ('gɪbᵊnz) *n* **1 Grinling** 1648–1721, English sculptor and woodcarver, noted for his delicate carvings of fruit, flowers, birds, etc **2 Orlando** 1583–1625, English organist and composer, esp of anthems, motets, and madrigals

gibbous ('gɪbəs) *or* **gibbose** ('gɪbəʊs) *adj* **1** (of the moon or a planet) more than half but less than fully illuminated **2** hunchbacked **3** bulging [C17 from LL *gibbōsus* humpbacked, from L *gibba* hump] > **'gibbously** *adv* > **'gibbousness** *or* **gibbosity** (gɪˈbɒsɪtɪ) *n*

Gibbs (gɪbz) *n* **1 James** 1682–1754, British architect; his buildings include St Martin's-in-the-Fields, London (1722–26), and the Radcliffe Camera, Oxford (1737–49) **2 Josiah Willard** 1839–1903, US physicist and mathematician: founder of chemical thermodynamics

gibe[1] *or* **jibe** (dʒaɪb) *vb* **gibes, gibing, gibed** *or* **jibes, jibing, jibed 1** to make jeering or scoffing remarks (at); taunt ▷ *n* **2** a derisive or provoking remark [C16 ?from OF *giber* to treat roughly, from ?] > **'giber** *or* **'jiber** *n*

gibe[2] (dʒaɪb) *vb* **gibes, gibing, gibed,** *n naut* a variant spelling of **gybe**

Gibeon ('gɪbɪən) *n* an ancient town of Palestine: the excavated site thought to be its remains lies about 9 kilometres (6 miles) northwest of Jerusalem

gibi- ('gɪbɪ) *prefix computing.* denoting 2^{30}: *gibibyte*. Also: **giga-** Symbol: **Gi** [C20 from GI(GA-) + BI(NARY)]

USAGE See at **kilo-**

giblets ('dʒɪblɪts) *pl n* (*sometimes sing*) the gizzard, liver, heart, and neck of a fowl [C14 from OF *gibelet* stew of game birds, prob. from *gibier* game, of Gmc origin]

Gibraltar (dʒɪˈbrɔːltə) *n* **1 City of** a city on the **Rock of Gibraltar,** a limestone promontory at the tip of S Spain: settled by Moors in 711 and taken by Spain in 1462; ceded to Britain in 1713; a British crown colony (1830–1969), still politically associated with Britain; a naval and air base of strategic importance. Pop: 27 100 (1998 est). Area: 6.5 sq km (2.5 sq miles). Ancient name: **Calpe 2 Strait of** a narrow strait between the S tip of Spain and the NW tip of Africa, linking the Mediterranean with the Atlantic

Gibraltarian (ˌdʒɪbrɔːlˈtɛərɪən) *adj* **1** of or relating to Gibraltar or its inhabitants ▷ *n* **2** a native or inhabitant of Gibraltar

Gibran (dʒɪˈbrɑːn) *n* **Kahlil** ('kɑːliːl) 1883–1931, Syro-Lebanese poet, mystic, and painter, resident in the US after 1910; author of *The Prophet* (1923)

Gibson ('gɪbsᵊn) *n* **Mel** born 1956, Australian film actor and director: his films include *Mad Max* (1979), *Hamlet* (1990), *Braveheart* (1996; also directed), *What Women Want* (2000), and *The Passion of the Christ* (2004; director only)

Gibson Desert *n* a desert in W central Australia, between the Great Sandy Desert and the Victoria Desert: salt marshes, salt lakes, and scrub. Area: about 220 000 sq km (85 000 sq miles)

gidday (gəˈdaɪ) *sentence substitute* a variant spelling of **g'day**

giddy ('gɪdɪ) *adj* **giddier, giddiest 1** affected with a reeling sensation and feeling as if about to fall; dizzy **2** causing or tending to cause vertigo **3** impulsive; scatterbrained ▷ *vb* **giddies, giddying, giddied 4** to make or become giddy [OE *gydig* mad, frenzied, possessed by God; rel. to GOD] > **'giddily** *adv* > **'giddiness** *n*

Gide (*French* ʒid) *n* **André** (ɑ̃dre) 1869–1951, French novelist, dramatist, critic, diarist, and translator, noted particularly for his exploration of the conflict between self-fulfilment and conventional morality. His novels include *L'Immoraliste* (1902), *La Porte étroite* (1909), and *Les Faux-Monnayeurs* (1926): Nobel prize for literature 1947

Gideon ('gɪdɪən) *n Old Testament* a Hebrew judge who led the Israelites to victory over their Midianite oppressors (Judges 6:11–8:35)

gidgee *or* **gidjee** ('gɪdʒiː) *n Austral* **1** a small acacia tree yielding useful timber **2** a spear made of this [C19 from Abor.]

gie (giː) *vb* **gies, gi'ing, gi'ed** a Scot word for **give**

Gielgud ('giːlgʊd) *n* Sir **John** 1904–2000, English stage, film, and television actor and director

Giessen (*German* 'giːsən) *n* a city in central Germany, in Hesse: university (1607). Pop: 71 750 (latest est)

GIF (gɪf) *n computing* **a** a standard compressed file format used for pictures **b** a picture held in this format [C20 from *g(raphic) i(nterchange) f(ormat)*]

gift (gɪft) *n* **1** something given; a present **2** a special aptitude, ability, or power; talent **3** the power or right to give or bestow (esp in **in the gift of, in (someone's) gift**) **4** the act or process of giving **5 look a gift-horse in the mouth** (*usually negative*) to find fault with a free gift or chance benefit ▷ *vb* (*tr*) **6** to present (something) as a gift to (a person) [OE *gift* payment for a wife, dowry; see GIVE]

GIFT (gɪft) *n acronym for* gamete intrafallopian transfer: a technique, similar to IVF, that enables some women who cannot conceive to bear children

gifted ('gɪftɪd) *adj* having or showing natural talent or aptitude: *a tremendously gifted musician* > **'giftedly** *adv* > **'giftedness** *n*

gift of tongues *n* an utterance, partly or wholly unintelligible, believed by some to be produced under the influence of ecstatic religious emotion. Also called: **glossolalia**

giftwrap ('gɪftˌræp) *vb* **giftwraps, giftwrapping, giftwrapped** to wrap (a gift) attractively

Gifu ('giːfuː) *n* a city in Japan, on central Honshu: hot springs, textile and paper lantern manufacturing. Pop: 407 145 (1995)

gig[1] (gɪg) *n* **1** a light two-wheeled one-horse carriage without a hood **2** *naut* a light tender for a vessel **3** a long light rowing boat, used esp for racing ▷ *vb* **gigs, gigging, gigged 4** (*intr*) to travel in a gig [c13 (in the sense: flighty girl, spinning top): ?from ON]

gig[2] (gɪg) *n* **1** a cluster of barbless hooks drawn through a shoal of fish to try to impale them ▷ *vb* **gigs, gigging, gigged 2** to catch (fish) with a gig [c18 ? shortened from obs. *fishgig* or *fizgig* kind of harpoon]

gig[3] (gɪg) *n* **1** a job, esp a single booking for jazz or pop musicians **2** the performance itself ▷ *vb* **gigs, gigging, gigged 3** (*intr*) to perform at a gig or gigs [c20 from ?]

giga- (ˈgɪgə, ˈgaɪgə) *prefix* **1** denoting 10^9: *gigahertz* **2** Also: **gibi-** *computing* denoting 2^{30}: *gigabyte* ▷ Symbol: G [from Gk *gigas* GIANT]

USAGE See at **kilo-**

gigaflop (ˈgɪgəˌflɒp, ˈgaɪgə-) *n computing* a measure of processing speed, consisting of a thousand million floating-point operations a second [c20 from GIGA- + *flo(ating) p(oint)*]

gigantic (dʒaɪˈgæntɪk) *adj* **1** very large; enormous **2** Also: **gigantesque** (ˌdʒaɪgænˈtɛsk) of or suitable for giants [c17 from Gk *gigantikos*, from *gigas* GIANT] > **giˈgantically** *adv*

gigantism (ˈdʒaɪgænˌtɪzəm, dʒaɪˈgæntɪzəm) *n* **1** Also called: **giantism** excessive growth of the entire body, caused by overproduction of growth hormone by the pituitary gland **2** the state or quality of being gigantic

giggle (ˈgɪgᵊl) *vb* **giggles, giggling, giggled 1** (*intr*) to laugh nervously or foolishly ▷ *n* **2** such a laugh **3** *inf* something or someone that causes amusement [c16 imit.] > **ˈgiggler** *n* > **ˈgiggling** *adj, n* > **ˈgiggly** *adj*

Gigli (*Italian* ˈdʒiʎʎi) *n* **Beniamino** (benjaˈmiːno) 1890–1957, Italian operatic tenor

gigolo (ˈʒɪgəˌləʊ) *n, pl* **gigolos 1** a man who is kept by a woman, esp an older woman **2** a man who is paid to dance with or escort women [c20 from F, back formation from *gigolette* girl for hire as a dancing partner, prostitute, ult. from *gigue* a fiddle]

gigot (ˈdʒɪgət) *n* **1** a leg of lamb or mutton **2** a leg-of-mutton sleeve [c16 from OF: leg, a small fiddle, from *gigue* a fiddle, of Gmc origin]

gigue (ʒiːg) *n* a piece of music, usually in six-eight time, incorporated into the classical suite [c17 from F, from It. *giga*, lit.: a fiddle; see GIGOT]

Gijón (giːˈhəʊn; *Spanish* xiˈxɔn) *n* a port in NW Spain, on the Bay of Biscay: capital of the kingdom of Asturias until 791. Pop: 265 491 (1998 est). Ancient name: **Gigia**

Gila monster (ˈhiːlə) *n* a large venomous brightly coloured lizard inhabiting deserts of the southwestern US and Mexico [c19 after the *Gila*, a river in New Mexico and Arizona]

gilbert (ˈgɪlbət) *n* the cgs unit of magnetomotive force. Symbol: Gb, Gi [c19 after William GILBERT]

Gilbert (ˈgɪlbət) *n* **1 Grove Karl** 1843–1918, US geologist who pioneered the study of river development and valley erosion **2** Sir **Humphrey** ?1539–83, English navigator: founded the colony at St John's, Newfoundland (1583) **3 William** 1540–1603, English physician and physicist, noted for his study of terrestrial magnetism in *De Magnete* (1600) **4** Sir **W(illiam) S(chwenck)** 1836–1911, English dramatist, humorist, and librettist. He collaborated (1871–96) with Arthur Sullivan on the famous series of comic operettas, including *The Pirates of Penzance* (1879), *Iolanthe* (1882), and *The Mikado* (1885)

Gilbert Islands *pl n* a group of islands in the W Pacific: with Banaba, the Phoenix Islands, and three of the Line Islands they constitute the independent state of Kiribati; until 1975 they formed part of the British colony of **Gilbert and Ellice Islands;** achieved full independence in 1979. Pop: 71 757 (1995). Area: 295 sq km (114 sq miles)

gild[1] (gɪld) *vb* **gilds, gilding, gilded** *or* **gilt** (*tr*) **1** to cover with or as if with gold **2 gild the lily 2a** to adorn unnecessarily something already beautiful **2b** to praise someone inordinately **3** to give a falsely attractive or valuable appearance to [OE *gyldan*, from *gold* GOLD] > **ˈgilder** *n*

gild[2] (gɪld) *n* a variant spelling of **guild**

gilding (ˈgɪldɪŋ) *n* **1** the act or art of applying gilt to a surface **2** the surface so produced **3** another word for **gilt**[1] (sense 2)

Gilead[1] (ˈgɪlɪˌæd) *n* a historic mountainous region east of the River Jordan, rising over 1200 m (4000 ft)

Gilead[2] (ˈgɪlɪˌæd) *n Old Testament* a grandson of Manasseh; ancestor of the Coileadites (Numbers 26: 29–30)

Giles (dʒaɪlz) *n* **1 Saint** 7th century AD, Greek hermit in France; patron saint of cripples, beggars, and lepers. Feast day: Sept 1 **2 William Ernest Powell** 1835–97, Australian explorer, born in England. He was noted esp for his exploration of the western desert (1875–76)

gilet (ˈʒiːleɪ) *n* a garment resembling a waistcoat [c20 F, lit.: waistcoat]

gill[1] (gɪl) *n* **1** the respiratory organ in many aquatic animals **2** any of the radiating leaflike spore-producing structures on the undersurface of the cap of a mushroom [c14 from ON] > **gilled** *adj*

gill[2] (dʒɪl) *n* a unit of liquid measure equal to one quarter of a pint [c14 from OF *gille* vat, tub, from LL *gillō*, from ?]

gill[3] *or* **ghyll** (gɪl) *n dialect* **1** a narrow stream; rivulet **2** a wooded ravine [c11 from ON *gil* steep-sided valley]

Gill (gɪl) *n* (**Arthur**) **Eric** (**Rowton**) 1882–1940, British sculptor, engraver, and typographer: his sculptures include the *Stations of the Cross* in Westminster Cathedral, London

Gillespie (gɪˈlɛspɪ) *n* **Dizzy,** nickname of *John Birks Gillespie*. 1917–93, US jazz trumpeter

gillie, ghillie, *or* **gilly** (ˈgɪlɪ) *n, pl* **gillies** *or* **ghillies** *Scot* **1** an attendant or guide for hunting or fishing **2** (formerly) a Highland chieftain's male attendant [c17 from Scot. Gaelic *gille* boy, servant]

Gillingham (ˈdʒɪlɪŋəm) *n* a town in SE England, in Medway unitary authority, Kent, on the Medway estuary: former dockyards. Pop: 94 923 (1991)

Gillray (ˈgɪlreɪ) *n* **James** 1757–1815, English caricaturist

gills (gɪlz) *pl n* **1** (*sometimes sing*) the wattle of birds such as domestic fowl **2** the cheeks and jowls of a person **3 green about the gills** *inf* looking or feeling nauseated

gillyflower *or* **gilliflower** (ˈdʒɪlɪˌflaʊə) *n* **1** any of several plants having fragrant flowers, such as the stock and wallflower **2** an archaic name for **carnation** [c14 from *gilofre*, from OF *girofle*, from Med. L, from Gk: clove tree, from *karuon* nut + *phullon* leaf]

Gilolo (dʒaɪˈləʊləʊ, dʒɪ-) *n* See **Halmahera**

gilt[1] (gɪlt) *vb* **1** a past tense and past participle of **gild**[1] ▷ *n* **2** gold or a substance simulating it, applied in gilding **3** another word for **gilding** (senses 1, 2) **4** superficial or false appearance of excellence **5** a gilt-edged security **6 take the gilt off the gingerbread** to destroy the part of something that gives it its appeal ▷ *adj* **7** covered with or as if with gold or gilt; gilded

gilt[2] (gɪlt) *n* a young female pig, esp one that has not had a litter [c15 from ON *gyltr*]

gilt-edged *adj* **1** denoting government securities on which interest payments will certainly be met and that will certainly be repaid at par on the due date **2** of the highest quality: *the last track on the album is a gilt-edged classic* **3** (of books, papers, etc) having gilded edges

gimbals (ˈdʒɪmbᵊlz, ˈgɪm-) *pl n* a device, consisting of two or three pivoted rings at right angles to each other, that provides free suspension in all planes for a compass, chronometer, etc. Also called: **gimbal ring** [c16 var. of

Gg

earlier *gimmal*, from OF *gemel* double finger ring, from L *gemellus*, dim. of *geminus* twin]

gimcrack ('dʒɪmˌkræk) *adj* **1** cheap; shoddy ▷ *n* **2** a cheap showy trifle or gadget [c18 from c14 *gibecrake* little ornament, from ?] > **'gimˌcrackery** *n*

gimlet ('gɪmlɪt) *n* **1** a small hand tool consisting of a pointed spiral tip attached at right angles to a handle, used for boring small holes in wood **2** *US* a cocktail consisting of half gin or vodka and half lime juice ▷ *vb* **3** (*tr*) to make holes in (wood) using a gimlet ▷ *adj* **4** penetrating; piercing (esp in **gimlet-eyed**) [c15 from OF *guimbelet*, of Gmc origin, see WIMBLE]

gimmick ('gɪmɪk) *n inf* **1** something designed to attract extra attention, interest, or publicity **2** any clever device, gadget, or stratagem, esp one used to deceive [c20 orig. US sl, from ?] > **'gimmickry** *n* > **'gimmicky** *adj*

gimp *or* **guimpe** (gɪmp) *n* a tapelike trimming [c17 prob. from Du. *gimp*, from ?]

gin[1] (dʒɪn) *n* an alcoholic drink obtained by distillation of the grain of malted barley, rye, or maize, flavoured with juniper berries [c18 from Du. *genever*, via OF from L *jūniperus* JUNIPER]

▷ www.ginvodka.org

▷ www.webtender.com

gin[2] (dʒɪn) *n* **1** a primitive engine in which a vertical shaft is turned by horses driving a horizontal beam in a circle **2** Also called: **cotton gin** a machine of this type used for separating seeds from raw cotton **3** a trap for catching small mammals, consisting of a noose of thin strong wire ▷ *vb* **gins, ginning, ginned** (*tr*) **4** to free (cotton) of seeds with a gin **5** to trap or snare (game) with a gin [c13 *gyn*, from ENGINE]

gin[3] (gɪn) *vb* **gins, ginning, gan** (gæn), **gun** (gʌn) an archaic word for **begin**

gin[4] (dʒɪn) *n Austral offens sl* an Aboriginal woman [c19 from Abor.]

ginger ('dʒɪndʒə) *n* **1** any of several plants of the East Indies, cultivated throughout the tropics for their spicy hot-tasting underground stems **2** the underground stem of this plant, which is used fresh or powdered as a flavouring or crystallized as a sweetmeat **3a** a reddish-brown or yellowish-brown colour **3b** (*as adj*): *ginger hair* **4** *inf* liveliness; vigour [c13 from OF *gingivre*, ult. from Sansk. *śrñgaveram*, from *śrñga-* horn + *vera-* body, referring to its shape] > **'gingery** *adj*

ginger ale *n* a sweetened effervescent nonalcoholic drink flavoured with ginger extract

ginger beer *n* a slightly alcoholic drink made by fermenting a mixture of syrup and root ginger

gingerbread ('dʒɪndʒəˌbrɛd) *n* **1** a moist brown cake, flavoured with ginger and treacle **2a** a biscuit, similarly flavoured, cut into various shapes **2b** (*as modifier*): *gingerbread man* **3** an elaborate but unsubstantial ornamentation

ginger group *n chiefly Brit* a group within a party, association, etc, that enlivens its parent body

gingerly ('dʒɪndʒəlɪ) *adv* **1** in a cautious, reluctant, or timid manner ▷ *adj* **2** cautious, reluctant, or timid [c16 ?from OF *gensor* dainty, from *gent* of noble birth; see GENTLE]

ginger nut *or* **snap** *n* a crisp biscuit flavoured with ginger

gingham ('gɪŋəm) *n* a cotton fabric, usually woven of two coloured yarns in a checked or striped design [c17 from F, from Malay *ginggang* striped cloth]

gingili ('dʒɪndʒɪlɪ) *n* **1** the oil obtained from sesame seeds **2** another name for **sesame** [c18 from Hindi *jingalī*]

gingiva ('dʒɪndʒɪvə, dʒɪn'dʒaɪvə) *n, pl* **gingivae** (-dʒɪˌviː, -'dʒaɪviː) *anat* the technical name for the **gum**[2] [from L] > **'gingival** *adj*

gingivitis (ˌdʒɪndʒɪ'vaɪtɪs) *n* inflammation of the gums

ginglymus ('dʒɪŋglɪməs, 'gɪŋ-) *n, pl* **ginglymi** (-ˌmaɪ) *anat* a hinge joint [c17 NL, from Gk *ginglumos* hinge]

gink (gɪŋk) *n sl* a man or boy, esp one considered to be odd [c20 from ?]

ginkgo ('gɪŋkgəʊ) *or* **gingko** ('gɪŋkəʊ) *n, pl* **ginkgoes** *or* **gingkoes** a widely planted ornamental Chinese tree with fan-shaped deciduous leaves and fleshy yellow fruit. Also called: **maidenhair tree** [c18 from Japanese, from Ancient Chinese: silver + apricot]

ginormous (dʒaɪ'nɔːməs) *adj inf* very large [c20 blend of *giant* or *gigantic* & *enormous*]

gin palace (dʒɪn) *n* (formerly) a gaudy drinking house

gin rummy (dʒɪn) *n* a version of rummy in which a player may go out if the odd cards outside his sequences total less than ten points [c20 from GIN[1] + RUMMY]

Ginsberg ('gɪnzbɜːg) *n* **Allen** 1926–97, US poet of the Beat Generation. His poetry includes *Howl* (1956) and *Kaddish* (1960)

ginseng ('dʒɪnsɛŋ) *n* **1** either of two plants of China or of North America, whose forked aromatic roots are used medicinally **2** the root of either of these plants or a substance obtained from the roots, believed to possess tonic and energy-giving properties [c17 from Mandarin Chinese *jen shen*]

Ginzburg (*Italian* 'gindzburg) *n* **Natalia** (nata'liːa) 1916–91, Italian writer and dramatist. Her books include *The Road to the City* (1942), *Voices in the Evening* (1961), and *Family Sayings* (1963)

Gioconda (*Italian* dʒo'konda) *n* **1 La** Also called: **Mona Lisa** the portrait by Leonardo da Vinci of a young woman with an enigmatic smile **2** (*modifier*) mysterious or enigmatic [It.: the smiling (lady)]

giocoso (dʒə'kəʊzəʊ) *adj music* jocose [It.]

Giorgione (*Italian* dʒor'dʒoːne) *n* **Il** original name *Giorgio Barbarelli*. ?1478–1511, Italian painter of the Venetian school, who introduced a new unity between figures and landscape

Giotto (*Italian* 'dʒɔtto) *n* also known as *Giotto di Bondone*. ?1267–1337, Florentine painter, who broke away from the stiff linear design of the Byzantine tradition and developed the more dramatic and naturalistic style characteristic of the Renaissance: his work includes cycles of frescoes in Assisi, the Arena Chapel in Padua, and the Church of Santa Croce, Florence

gip (dʒɪp) *vb* **gips, gipping, gipped 1** a variant spelling of **gyp**[1] ▷ *n* **2** a variant spelling of **gyp**[2]

Gippsland ('gɪpsˌlænd) *n* a fertile region of SE Australia, in SE Victoria, extending east along the coast from Melbourne to the New South Wales border. Area: 35 200 sq km (13 600 sq miles)

gippy ('gɪpɪ) *n, pl* **-ies** *Northern English dialect* a starling

Gipsy ('dʒɪpsɪ) *n, pl* **Gipsies** (*sometimes not cap*) a variant spelling of **Gypsy**

gipsy moth *n* a variant spelling of **gypsy moth**

giraffe (dʒɪ'rɑːf, -'ræf) *n, pl* **giraffes** *or* **giraffe** a large ruminant mammal inhabiting savannas of tropical Africa: the tallest mammal, with very long legs and neck [c17 from It. *giraffa*, from Ar. *zarāfah*, prob. of African origin]

Giraldus Cambrensis (dʒɪ'rældəs kæm'brɛnsɪs) *n* literary name of *Gerald de Barri*. ?1146–?1223, Welsh chronicler and churchman, noted for his accounts of his travels in Ireland and Wales

girandole ('dʒɪrənˌdəʊl) *n* **1** a branched wall candleholder **2** an earring or pendant having a central gem surrounded by smaller ones **3** a revolving firework **4** *artillery* a group of connected mines [c17 from F, from It. *girandola*, from L *gȳrāre* to GYRATE]

girasol *or* **girasole** ('dʒɪrəˌsɒl, -ˌsəʊl) *n* a type of opal that has a red or pink glow; fire opal [c16 from It., from *girare* to revolve (see GYRATE) + *sole* the sun]

Giraud (*French* ʒiro) *n* **Henri Honoré** (ɑ̃ri ɔnɔre) 1879–1949, French general, who commanded French forces in North Africa (1942–43)

Giraudoux (*French* ʒirodu) *n* (**Hyppolyte**) **Jean** (ʒɑ̃)

1882–1944, French dramatist. His works include the novel *Suzanne et le Pacifique* (1921) and the plays *Amphitryon 38* (1929) and *La Guerre de Troie n'aura pas lieu* (1935)

gird[1] (gɜːd) *vb* **girds, girding, girded** *or* **girt** (*tr*) **1** to put a belt, girdle, etc, around (the waist or hips) **2** to bind or secure with or as if with a belt: *to gird on one's armour* **3** to surround; encircle **4** to prepare (oneself) for action (esp in **gird (up) one's loins**) [OE *gyrdan*, of Gmc origin]

gird[2] (gɜːd) *N English dialect* ▹ *vb* **1** (when *intr*, foll by *at*) to jeer (at someone); mock ▹ *n* **2** a taunt; gibe [C13 *girden* to strike, cut, from ?]

girder ('gɜːdə) *n* a large beam, esp one made of steel, used in the construction of bridges, buildings, etc

girdle[1] ('gɜːdəl) *n* **1** a woman's elastic corset covering the waist to the thigh **2** anything that surrounds or encircles **3** a belt or sash **4** *jewellery* the outer edge of a gem **5** *anat* any encircling structure or part **6** the mark left on a tree trunk after the removal of a ring of bark ▹ *vb* **girdles, girdling, girdled** (*tr*) **7** to put a girdle on or around **8** to surround or encircle **9** to remove a ring of bark from (a tree) [OE *gyrdel*, of Gmc origin; see GIRD[1]]

girdle[2] ('gɜːdəl) *n Scot & N English dialect* another word for **griddle**

Girgenti (*Italian* dʒir'dʒɛnti) *n* a former name (until 1927) of **Agrigento**

girl (gɜːl) *n* **1** a female child from birth to young womanhood **2** a young unmarried woman; lass; maid **3** *inf* a sweetheart or girlfriend **4** *inf* a woman of any age **5** a female employee, esp a female servant **6** *S African derog* a Black female servant [C13 from ?; ? rel. to Low G *Göre* boy, girl] > **'girlish** *adj*

girlfriend ('gɜːlˌfrɛnd) *n* **1** a female friend with whom a person is romantically or sexually involved **2** any female friend

Girl Guide *n* See **Guide**
▹ www.girlguiding.org.uk

girlhood ('gɜːlˌhʊd) *n* the state or time of being a girl

girlie *or* **girly** ('gɜːlɪ) *adj* **1** *inf* featuring nude or scantily dressed women: *a girlie magazine* **2** suited to or designed to appeal to young women: *a real girlie night out*

Girl Scout *n US* a member of the equivalent organization for girls to the Scouts
▹ www.wagggsworld.com

giro ('dʒaɪrəʊ) *n, pl* **giros 1** a system of transferring money within a financial organization, such as a bank or post office, directly from the account of one person into that of another **2** *Brit inf* an unemployment benefit or income support payment by giro cheque [C20 ult. from Gk *guros* circuit]

Gironde (*French* ʒirɔ̃d) *n* **1** a department of SW France, in Aquitaine region. Capital: Bordeaux. Pop: 1 287 334 (1999). Area: 10 726 sq km (4183 sq miles) **2** an estuary in SW France, formed by the confluence of the Rivers Garonne and Dordogne. Length: 72 km (45 miles)

girt[1] (gɜːt) *vb* a past tense and past participle of **gird**[1]

girt[2] (gɜːt) *vb* **1** (*tr*) to bind or encircle; gird **2** to measure the girth of (something)

girth (gɜːθ) *n* **1** the distance around something; circumference **2** a band around a horse's belly to keep the saddle in position ▹ *vb* **3** (usually foll by *up*) to fasten a girth on (a horse) **4** (*tr*) to encircle or surround [C14 from ON *gjörth* belt; see GIRD[1]]

GIS (in Canada) *abbrev for* guaranteed income supplement

Gisborne ('gɪzbən) *n* a port in N New Zealand, on E North Island on Poverty Bay. Pop: 31 700 (1994)
▹ www.gdc.govt.nz
▹ www.gisborne.govt.nz/events_calendar

Giscard d'Estaing (*French* ʒiskar dɛstɛ̃) *n* **Valéry** (valeri) born 1926, French politician; minister of finance and economic affairs (1962–66; 1969–74); president (1974–81)

Gish (gɪʃ) *n* **1 Dorothy** 1898–1968, US film actress, chiefly in silent films **2** her sister, **Lillian** 1896–1993, US film and stage actress, noted esp for her roles in such silent films as *The Birth of a Nation* (1915) and *Intolerance* (1916)

Gissing ('gɪsɪŋ) *n* **George (Robert)** 1857–1903, English novelist, noted for his depiction of middle-class poverty. His works include *Demos* (1886) and *New Grub Street* (1891)

gist (dʒɪst) *n* the point or substance of an argument, speech, etc [C18 from Anglo-F, as in *cest action gist en* this action consists in, lit.: lies in, from OF *gésir*, from L *jacēre*]

git (gɪt) *n Brit sl* **1** a contemptible person, often a fool **2** a bastard [C20 from GET (in the sense: *to beget*, hence a bastard, fool)]

gîte (ʒiːt) *n* a self-catering holiday cottage for let in France [C20 F]

gittern ('gɪtɜːn) *n* an obsolete medieval stringed instrument resembling the guitar [C14 from OF, ult. from OSp. *guitarra* GUITAR; see CITTERN]

Giulini (*Italian* dʒu'liːni) *n* **Carlo Maria** ('karlo ma'riːa) born 1914, Italian orchestral conductor, esp of opera

Giulio Romano (*Italian* 'dʒuːljo ro'maːno) *n* ?1499–1546, Italian architect and painter; a founder of mannerism

giusto ('dʒuːstəʊ) *adj music* (of tempo) exact; strict [It.]

give (gɪv) *vb* **gives, giving, gave, given** (*mainly tr*) **1** (*also intr*) to present or deliver voluntarily (something that is one's own) to another **2** (often foll by *for*) to transfer (something that is one's own, esp money) to the possession of another as part of an exchange: *to give fifty pounds for a painting* **3** to place in the temporary possession of another: *I gave him my watch while I went swimming* **4** (when *intr*, foll by *of*) to grant, provide, or bestow: *give me some advice* **5** to administer: *to give a reprimand* **6** to award or attribute: *to give blame, praise*, etc **7** to be a source of: *he gives no trouble* **8** to impart or communicate: *to give news* **9** to utter or emit: *to give a shout* **10** to perform, make, or do: *the car gave a jolt* **11** to sacrifice or devote: *he gave his life for his country* **12** to surrender: *to give place to others* **13** to concede or yield: *I will give you this game* **14** (*intr*) *inf* to happen: *what gives?* **15** (often foll by *to*) to cause; lead: *she gave me to believe that she would come* **16** to perform or present as an entertainment: *to give a play* **17** to act as a host of (a party, etc) **18** (*intr*) to yield or break under force or pressure: *this surface will give if you sit on it* **19 give as good as one gets** to respond to verbal or bodily blows to at least an equal extent as those received **20 give or take** plus or minus: *three thousand people came, give or take a few hundred* **21 give it up for (someone)** *sl* to applaud (someone) ▹ *n* **22** tendency to yield under pressure; resilience ▹ See also **give away, give in,** etc [OE *giefan*] > **'givable** *or* **'giveable** *adj* > **'giver** *n*

give-and-take *n* **1** mutual concessions, shared benefits, and cooperation **2** a smoothly flowing exchange of ideas and talk ▹ *vb* **give and take** (*intr*) **3** to make mutual concessions

give away *vb* (*tr, adv*) **1** to donate or bestow as a gift, prize, etc **2** to sell very cheaply **3** to reveal or betray **4** to fail to use (an opportunity) through folly or neglect **5** to present (a bride) formally to her husband in a marriage ceremony ▹ *n* **giveaway 6** a betrayal or disclosure esp when unintentional **7** (*modifier*) **7a** very cheap (esp in **giveaway prices**) **7b** free of charge: *a giveaway property magazine*

give in *vb* (*adv*) **1** (*intr*) to yield; admit defeat **2** (*tr*) to submit or deliver (a document)

given ('gɪvən) *vb* **1** the past participle of **give** ▹ *adj* **2** (*postpositive*; foll by *to*) tending (to); inclined or addicted (to) **3** specific or previously stated **4** assumed as a premise **5** *maths* known or determined independently: *a given volume* **6** (on official documents) issued or executed, as on a stated date

given name *n* another term (esp US) for **first name**

give off *vb* (*tr, adv*) to emit or discharge: *the mothballs gave off an acrid odour*

give out *vb* (*adv*) **1** (*tr*) to emit or discharge **2** (*tr*) to publish or make known: *the chairman gave out that he would*

Gg

resign **3** (*tr*) to hand out or distribute: *they gave out free chewing gum* **4** (*intr*) to become exhausted; fail: *the supply of candles gave out*

give over *vb* (*adv*) **1** (*tr*) to transfer, esp to the care or custody of another **2** (*tr*) to assign or resign to a specific purpose or function: *the day was given over to pleasure* **3** *inf* to cease (an activity): *give over fighting, will you!*

give up *vb* (*adv*) **1** to abandon hope (for) **2** (*tr*) to renounce (an activity, belief, etc): *I have given up smoking* **3** (*tr*) to relinquish or resign from: *he gave up the presidency* **4** (*tr; usually reflexive*) to surrender: *the escaped convict gave himself up* **5** (*intr*) to admit one's defeat or inability to do something **6** (*tr; often passive or reflexive*) to devote completely (to): *she gave herself up to caring for the sick*

gizmo *or* **gismo** ('gɪzməʊ) *n, pl* **gizmos** *or* **gismos** *sl* a device; gadget [C20 from ?]

gizzard ('gɪzəd) *n* **1** the thick-walled part of a bird's stomach, in which hard food is broken up **2** *inf* the stomach and entrails generally [C14 from OF *guisier* fowl's liver, from L *gigēria* entrails of poultry when cooked, from ?]

Gk *abbrev for* Greek

glabella (glə'bɛlə) *n, pl* **glabellae** (-liː) *anat* a smooth elevation of the frontal bone just above the bridge of the nose [C19 NL, from L, from *glaber* bald, smooth] > **gla'bellar** *adj*

glabrous ('gleɪbrəs) *adj biol* without hair or a similar growth; smooth [C17 from L *glaber*]

glacé ('glæsɪ) *adj* **1** crystallized or candied: *glacé cherries* **2** covered in icing **3** (of leather, silk, etc) having a glossy finish ▷ *vb* **glacés, glacéing, glacéed 4** (*tr*) to ice or candy (cakes, fruits, etc) [C19 from F *glacé*, lit.: iced, from *glacer* to freeze, from L *glaciēs* ice]

glacial ('gleɪsɪəl, -ʃəl) *adj* **1** characterized by the presence of masses of ice **2** relating to, caused by, or deposited by a glacier **3** extremely cold; icy **4** cold or hostile in manner **5** (of a chemical compound) of or tending to form crystals that resemble ice > **'glacially** *adv*

glacial acetic acid *n* pure acetic acid

glacial period *n* **1** any period of time during which a large part of the earth's surface was covered with ice, due to the advance of glaciers **2** (*often caps*) the Pleistocene epoch ▷ Also called: **glacial epoch, ice age**

glaciate ('gleɪsɪˌeɪt) *vb* **glaciates, glaciating, glaciated 1** to cover or become covered with glaciers or masses of ice **2** (*tr*) to subject to the effects of glaciers, such as denudation and erosion > **ˌglaci'ation** *n*

glacier ('glæsɪə, 'gleɪs-) *n* a slowly moving mass of ice originating from an accumulation of snow [C18 from F (dialect), from OF *glace* ice, from LL, from L *glaciēs* ice]

glaciology (ˌglæsɪ'ɒlədʒɪ, ˌgleɪ-) *n* the study of the distribution, character, and effects of glaciers > **glaciological** (ˌglæsɪə'lɒdʒɪkᵊl, ˌgleɪ-) *adj* > **ˌglaci'ologist** *n*

glacis ('glæsɪs, 'glæsɪ, 'gleɪ-) *n, pl* **glacises** *or* **glacis** (-iːz, -ɪz) **1** a slight incline; slope **2** an open slope in front of a fortified place [C17 from F, from OF *glacier* to freeze, slip, from L, from *glaciēs* ice]

glad¹ (glæd) *adj* **gladder, gladdest 1** happy and pleased; contented **2** causing happiness or contentment **3** (*postpositive; foll by to*) very willing: *he was glad to help* **4** (*postpositive; foll by of*) happy or pleased to have: *glad of her help* ▷ *vb* **glads, gladding, gladded 5** (*tr*) an archaic word for **gladden** [OE *glæd*] > **'gladly** *adv* > **'gladness** *n*

glad² (glæd) *n inf* short for **gladiolus**

Gladbeck (*German* 'glatbɛk) *n* a city in NW Germany, in North Rhine-Westphalia. Pop: 79 190 (latest est)

gladden ('glædᵊn) *vb* to make or become glad and joyful > **'gladdener** *n*

glade (gleɪd) *n* an open place in a forest; clearing [C16 from ?; ? rel. to GLAD¹ (in obs. sense: bright); see GLEAM]

glad eye *n inf* an inviting or seductive glance (esp in **give (someone) the glad eye**)

gladiator ('glædɪˌeɪtə) *n* **1** (in ancient Rome) a man trained to fight in arenas to provide entertainment **2** a person who supports and fights publicly for a cause [C16 from L: swordsman, from *gladius* sword] > **gladiatorial** (ˌglædɪə'tɔːrɪəl) *adj*

gladiolus (ˌglædɪ'əʊləs) *n, pl* **gladiolus, gladioli** (-laɪ), *or* **gladioluses** any plant of a widely cultivated genus having sword-shaped leaves and spikes of funnel-shaped brightly coloured flowers. Also called: **gladiola** [C16 from L: a small sword, sword lily, from *gladius* a sword]

glad rags *pl n inf* best clothes or clothes used on special occasions

gladsome ('glædsəm) *adj* an archaic word for **glad¹** > **'gladsomely** *adv* > **'gladsomeness** *n*

Gladstone ('glædstən) *n* **William Ewart** 1809–98, British statesman. He became leader of the Liberal Party in 1867 and was four times prime minister (1868–74; 1880–85; 1886; 1892–94) In his first ministry he disestablished the Irish Church (1869) and introduced educational reform (1870) and the secret ballot (1872). He succeeded in carrying the Reform Act of 1884 but failed to gain support for a Home Rule Bill for Ireland, to which he devoted much of the latter part of his career

Gladstone bag *n* a piece of hand luggage consisting of two equal-sized hinged compartments [C19 after W. E. GLADSTONE]

gladwrap ('glædˌræp) *n trademark NZ* **1** a thin polythene material that clings closely to any surface around which it is placed: used for wrapping food ▷ *vb* **gladwraps, gladwrapping, gladwrapped 2** to cover (food) with gladwrap

Glagolitic (ˌglægə'lɪtɪk) *adj* of, relating to, or denoting a Slavic alphabet whose invention is attributed to Saint Cyril [C19 from NL, from Serbo-Croat *glagolica* the Glagolitic alphabet]

glair (glɛə) *n* **1** white of egg, esp when used as a size or adhesive **2** any substance resembling this ▷ *vb* **3** (*tr*) to apply glair to (something) [C14 from OF *glaire*, from Vulgar L *clāria* (unattested) CLEAR, from L *clārus*] > **'glairy** *or* **'glaireous** *adj*

glam (glæm) *adj inf* short for **glamorous**

Glamorgan (glə'mɔːgən) *or* **Glamorganshire** (glə'mɔːgənˌʃɪə, -ʃə) *n* a former county of SE Wales: divided into West Glamorgan, Mid Glamorgan, and South Glamorgan in 1974; since 1996 administered by the county of Swansea and the county boroughs of Neath Port Talbot, Bridgend, Rhondda Cynon Taff, Vale of Glamorgan, Merthyr Tydfil, and part of Caerphilly

glamorize, glamorise, *or US* (*sometimes*) **glamourize** ('glæməˌraɪz) *vb* **glamorizes, glamorizing, glamorized; glamorises, glamorising, glamorised** *or US* (*sometimes*) **glamourizes, glamourizing, glamourized** (*tr*) to cause to be or seem glamorous; romanticize or beautify > **ˌglamori'zation** *or* **ˌglamori'sation** *n*

glamorous ('glæmərəs) *adj* **1** possessing glamour; alluring and fascinating **2** beautiful and smart, esp in a showy way: *a glamorous woman* > **'glamorously** *adv*

glamour *or US* (*sometimes*) **glamor** ('glæmə) *n* **1** charm and allure; fascination **2a** fascinating or voluptuous beauty **2b** (*as modifier*): *a glamour girl* **3** *arch* a magic spell; charm [C18 Scot. var. of GRAMMAR (hence a magic spell, because occult practices were popularly associated with learning)]

glance¹ (glɑːns) *vb* **glances, glancing, glanced 1** (*intr*) to look hastily or briefly **2** (*intr; foll by over, through, etc*) to look over briefly: *to glance through a report* **3** (*intr*) to reflect, glint, or gleam: *the sun glanced on the water* **4** (*intr; usually foll by off*) to depart (from an object struck) at an oblique angle: *the arrow glanced harmlessly off the tree* ▷ *n* **5** a hasty or brief look; peep **6** a flash or glint of light; gleam **7** the act or an instance of an object glancing off another **8** a brief allusion [C15 from *glacen* to strike obliquely, from

OF *glacier* to slide (see GLACIS)] > '**glancing** *adj* > '**glancingly** *adv*

> USAGE *Glance* is sometimes wrongly used where *glimpse* is meant: *he caught a glimpse* (not *glance*) *of her making her way through the crowd*

glance² (glɑːns) *n* any mineral having a metallic lustre [c19 from G *Glanz* brightness, lustre]

gland¹ (glænd) *n* **1** a cell or organ in man and other animals that synthesizes chemical substances and secretes them for the body to use or eliminate, either through a duct (exocrine gland) or directly into the bloodstream (endocrine gland) **2** a structure, such as a lymph node, that resembles a gland in form **3** a cell or organ in plants that synthesizes and secretes a particular substance [c17 from L *glāns* acorn]

gland² (glænd) *n* a device that prevents leakage of fluid along a rotating shaft or reciprocating rod passing between areas of high and low pressure. It often consists of a flanged metal sleeve bedding into a stuffing box [c19 from ?]

glanders ('glændəz) *n* (*functioning as sing*) a highly infectious bacterial disease of horses, sometimes transmitted to humans, characterized by inflammation and ulceration of the mucous membranes of the air passages, skin and lymph glands [c16 from OF *glandres*, from L *glandulae*, lit.: little acorns, from *glāns* acorn; see GLAND¹]

glandular ('glændjʊlə) *or* **glandulous** ('glændjʊləs) *adj* of, relating to, containing, functioning as, or affecting a gland [c18 from L *glandula*, lit.: a little acorn; see GLANDERS] > '**glandularly** *or* '**glandulously** *adv*

glandular fever *n* another name for **infectious mononucleosis**

glandule ('glændjuːl) *n* a small gland

glans (glænz) *n, pl* **glandes** ('glændiːz) *anat* any small rounded body or glandlike mass, such as the head of the penis (**glans penis**) [c17 from L: acorn; see GLAND¹]

glare (glɛə) *vb* **glares, glaring, glared 1** (*intr*) to stare angrily; glower **2** (*tr*) to express by glowering **3** (*intr*) (of light, colour, etc) to be very bright and intense **4** (*intr*) to be dazzlingly ornamented or garish ▷ *n* **5** an angry stare **6** a dazzling light or brilliance **7** garish ornamentation or appearance [c13 prob. from MLow G, MDu. *glaren* to gleam]

glaring ('glɛərɪŋ) *adj* **1** conspicuous: *a glaring omission* **2** dazzling or garish > '**glaringly** *adv* > '**glaringness** *n*

Glarus (*German* 'glaːrʊs) *n* **1** an Alpine canton of E central Switzerland. Capital: Glarus. Pop: 38 700 (2000 est). Area 684 sq km (264 sq miles) **2** a town in E central Switzerland, the capital of Glarus canton. Pop: 5541 (1990) ▷ French name **Glaris** (glari)

Glaser ('gleɪzə) *n* **Donald Arthur** born 1926, US physicist: invented the bubble chamber; Nobel prize for physics 1960

Glasgow ('glɑːzgəʊ, 'glæz-) *n* **1** a city in W central Scotland, in City of Glasgow council area on the River Clyde: the largest city in Scotland; centre of a major industrial region, formerly an important port; universities (1451, 1964, 1992). Pop: 662 954 (1991). Related adj: **Glaswegian 2 City of** a council area in W central Scotland. Pop: 577 869 (2001). Area: 175 sq km (68 sq miles)

glasnost ('glæsˌnɒst) *n* the policy of public frankness and accountability developed in the former Soviet Union under the leadership of Mikhail Gorbachov [c20 Russian, lit.: publicity, openness]

glass (glɑːs) *n* **1a** a hard brittle transparent or translucent noncrystalline solid, consisting of metal silicates or similar compounds. It is made from a fused mixture of oxides, such as lime, silicon dioxide, phosphorus pentoxide, etc **1b** (*as modifier*): *a glass bottle*. Related adj: **vitreous 2** something made of glass, esp a drinking vessel, a barometer, or a mirror **3** Also called: **glassful** the amount or volume contained in a drinking glass: *he drank a glass of wine* **4** glassware collectively **5** See **fibreglass** ▷ *vb* **6** (*tr*) to cover with, enclose in, or fit with glass [OE *glæs*] > '**glassless** *adj* > '**glass**ˌ**like** *adj*

Glass (glɑːs) *n* **Philip** born 1937, US avant-garde composer noted for his minimalist style: his works include *Music in Fifths* (1970), *Akhnaten* (1984), *The Voyage* (1992), and *Monsters of Grace* (1998)

glass-blowing *n* the process of shaping a mass of molten glass by blowing air into it through a tube > '**glass-**ˌ**blower** *n*

glass ceiling *n* a situation in which progress, esp promotion, appears to be possible but restrictions or discrimination create a barrier that prevents it

glasses ('glɑːsɪz) *pl n* a pair of lenses for correcting faulty vision, in a frame that rests on the bridge of the nose and hooks behind the ears. Also called: **spectacles, eyeglasses**

glass fibre *n* another name for **fibreglass**

glass harmonica *n* a musical instrument of the 18th century consisting of a set of glass bowls of graduated pitches, played by rubbing the fingers over the moistened rims or by a keyboard mechanism Sometimes shortened to **harmonica.** Also called: **musical glasses**

glasshouse ('glɑːsˌhaʊs) *n* **1** *Brit* a glass building, esp a greenhouse, used for growing plants in protected or controlled conditions **2** *inf, chiefly Brit* a military detention centre

glassine (glæ'siːn) *n* a glazed translucent paper

glass snake *n* any snakelike lizard of Europe, Asia, or North America, with vestigial hind limbs and a tail that breaks off easily

glassware ('glɑːsˌwɛə) *n* articles made of glass, esp drinking glasses

glass wool *n* fine spun glass massed into a wool-like bulk, used in insulation, filtering, etc

Gg

glasswort ('glɑːsˌwɜːt) *n* **1** any plant of salt marshes having fleshy stems and scalelike leaves: formerly used as a source of soda for glass-making **2** another name for **saltwort**

glassy ('glɑːsɪ) *adj* **glassier, glassiest 1** resembling glass, esp in smoothness or transparency **2** void of expression, life, or warmth: *a glassy stare* > '**glassily** *adv* > '**glassiness** *n*

Glastonbury ('glæstənbərɪ, -brɪ) *n* a town in SW England, in Somerset: remains of prehistoric lake villages; the reputed burial place of King Arthur; site of a ruined Benedictine abbey, probably the oldest in England. Pop: 7747 (1991)

Glaswegian (glæz'wiːdʒən) *adj* **1** of or relating to Glasgow or its inhabitants ▷ *n* **2** a native or inhabitant of Glasgow [c19 infl. by NORWEGIAN]

Glauber's salt ('glaʊbəz) *or* **Glauber salt** *n* the crystalline decahydrate of sodium sulphate: used in making glass, detergents, and pulp [c18 after J. R. *Glauber* (1604–68), G chemist]

Glauce ('glɔːsɪ) *n* *Greek myth* **1** the second bride of Jason, murdered on her wedding day by Medea, whom Jason had deserted **2** a sea nymph, one of the Nereids

glaucoma (glɔː'kəʊmə) *n* a disease of the eye in which increased pressure within the eyeball causes impaired vision, sometimes progressing to blindness [c17 from L, from Gk, from *glaukos*; see GLAUCOUS] > **glau'comatous** *adj*

glaucous ('glɔːkəs) *adj* **1** *bot* covered with a bluish waxy or powdery bloom **2** bluish-green [c17 from L *glaucus* silvery, bluish-green, from Gk *glaukos*]

glaze (gleɪz) *vb* **glazes, glazing, glazed 1** (*tr*) to fit or cover with glass **2** (*tr*) *ceramics* to cover with a vitreous solution, rendering impervious to liquid **3** (*tr*) to cover (foods) with a shiny coating by applying beaten egg, sugar, etc **4** (*tr*) to make glossy or shiny **5** (when *intr*, often foll by *over*) to become or cause to become glassy: *his eyes were glazing over* ▷ *n* **6** *ceramics* **6a** a vitreous coating **6b** the substance used to produce such a coating **7** a smooth lustrous finish on a fabric produced by applying various chemicals **8** something used to give a glossy surface to foods: *a syrup glaze* [C14 *glasen*, from *glas* GLASS] > **glazed** *adj* > **'glazer** *n*

glaze ice *n Brit* a thin clear layer of ice caused by the freezing of rain in the air or by refreezing after a thaw

glazier ('gleɪzɪə) *n* a person who fits windows, doors, etc, with glass > **'glaziery** *n*

glazing ('gleɪzɪŋ) *n* **1** the surface of a glazed object **2** glass fitted, or to be fitted, in a door, frame, etc

Glazunov ('glæzʊnɒf; *Russian* gləzu'nɔf) *n* **Aleksandr Konstantinovich** (alɪk'sandr kənstan'tinəvitʃ) 1865–1936, Russian composer, in France from 1928. A pupil of Rimsky-Korsakov, he wrote eight symphonies and concertos for piano and for violin among other works

GLC *abbrev for* Greater London Council; abolished 1986

gleam (gliːm) *n* **1** a small beam or glow of light, esp reflected light **2** a brief or dim indication: *a gleam of hope* ▷ *vb* (*intr*) **3** to send forth or reflect a beam of light **4** to appear, esp briefly [OE *glǣm*] > **'gleaming** *adj* > **'gleamingly** *adv* > **'gleamy** *adj*

glean (gliːn) *vb* **1** to gather (something) slowly and carefully in small pieces: *to glean information* **2** to gather (the useful remnants of a crop) from the field after harvesting [C14 from OF *glener*, from LL *glennāre*, prob. of Celtic origin] > **'gleaner** *n*

gleanings ('gliːnɪŋz) *pl n* the useful remnants of a crop that can be gathered from the field after harvesting

glebe (gliːb) *n* **1** *Brit history* land granted to a clergyman as part of his benefice **2** *poetic* land, esp for growing things [C14 from L *glaeba*]

glee (gliː) *n* **1** great merriment or delight, often caused by someone else's misfortune **2** a type of song originating in 18th-century England, sung by three or more unaccompanied voices [OE *gléo*]

glee club *n now chiefly US & Canad* a society organized for the singing of choral music

gleeful ('gliːfʊl) *adj* full of glee; merry > **'gleefully** *adv* > **'gleefulness** *n*

gleeman ('gliːmən) *n, pl* **gleemen** *obs* a minstrel

Gleiwitz ('glaɪvɪts) *n* the German name for **Gliwice**

glen (glɛn) *n* a narrow and deep mountain valley, esp in Scotland or Ireland [C15 from Scot. Gaelic *gleann*, from OIrish *glend*]

Glen Albyn ('ælbɪn, 'ɔːl-) *n* another name for the **Great Glen**

Glencoe (glɛn'kəʊ) *n* a glen in W Scotland, in S Highland: site of a massacre of Macdonalds by Campbells and English troops (1692)

Glendower (glɛn'daʊə) *n* **Owen,** Welsh name *Owain Glyndwr* ?1350–?1416, Welsh chieftain, who led a revolt against Henry IV's rule in Wales (1400–15)

glengarry (glɛn'gærɪ) *n, pl* **glengarries** a brimless Scottish cap with a crease down the crown, often with ribbons at the back. Also called: **glengarry bonnet** [C19 after *Glengarry*, Scotland]

Glen More (mɔː) *n* another name for the **Great Glen**

Glenn (glɛn) *n* **John** born 1921, US astronaut and politician. The first American to orbit the earth (Feb., 1962), he later became a senator (1975–99) and in 1998 returned to space at the age of 77

Glennie ('glɛnɪ) *n* **Evelyn (Elizabeth Ann)** born 1965, British percussionist

Glenrothes (glɛn'rɒθɪs) *n* a new town in E central Scotland, the administrative centre of Fife: founded in 1948. Pop: 38 650 (1991)

glia ('gliːə) *n* the delicate web of connective tissue that surrounds and supports nerve cells. Also called: **neuroglia** > **'glial** *adj*

glib (glɪb) *adj* **glibber, glibbest** fluent and easy, often in an insincere or deceptive way [C16 prob. from MLow G *glibberich* slippery] > **'glibly** *adv* > **'glibness** *n*

glib ice *n Canad* ice that is particularly smooth and slippery

glide (glaɪd) *vb* **glides, gliding, glided** **1** to move or cause to move easily without jerks or hesitations **2** (*intr*) to pass slowly or without perceptible change: *to glide into sleep* **3** to cause (an aircraft) to come in to land without engine power, or (of an aircraft) to land in this way **4** (*intr*) to fly a glider **5** (*intr*) *music* to execute a portamento from one note to another **6** (*intr*) *phonetics* to produce a glide ▷ *n* **7** a smooth easy movement **8a** any of various dances featuring gliding steps **8b** a step in such a dance **9** a manoeuvre in which an aircraft makes a gentle descent without engine power **10** the act or process of gliding **11** *music* a portamento or slur **12** *phonetics* a transitional sound as the speech organs pass from the articulatory position of one speech sound to that of the next [OE *glīdan*] > **'glidingly** *adv*

glide path *or* **glide slope** *n* the path of an aircraft as it descends to land

glider ('glaɪdə) *n* **1** an aircraft capable of gliding and soaring in air currents without the use of an engine **2** a person or thing that glides

▷ www.gliding.co.uk
▷ www.fai.org/gliding

glide time *n* the NZ term for **flexitime**

glimmer ('glɪmə) *vb* (*intr*) **1** (of a light) to glow faintly or flickeringly **2** to be indicated faintly: *hope glimmered in his face* ▷ *n* **3** a glow or twinkle of light **4** a faint indication [C14 cf. MHG *glimmern*] > **'glimmeringly** *adv*

glimpse (glɪmps) *n* **1** a brief or incomplete view: *to catch a glimpse of the sea* **2** a vague indication **3** *arch* a glimmer of light ▷ *vb* **glimpses, glimpsing, glimpsed** **4** (*tr*) to catch sight of momentarily [C14 of Gmc origin; cf. MHG *glimsen* to glimmer] > **'glimpser** *n*

> USAGE *Glimpse* is sometimes wrongly used where *glance* is meant: *he gave a quick glance* (not *glimpse*) *at his watch*

Glinka (*Russian* 'glinkə) *n* **Mikhail Ivanovich** (mixa'il i'vanəvitʃ) 1803–57, Russian composer who pioneered the Russian national school of music. His works include the operas *A Life for the Tsar* (1836) and *Russlan and Ludmilla* (1842)

glint (glɪnt) *vb* **1** to gleam or cause to gleam brightly ▷ *n* **2** a bright gleam or flash **3** brightness or gloss **4** a brief indication [C15 prob. from ON]

glioma (glaɪ'əʊmə) *n, pl* **gliomata** (-mətə) *or* **gliomas** a tumour of the brain and spinal cord, composed of glia cells and fibres [C19 from NL, from Gk *glia* glue + -OMA]

glissade (glɪ'sɑːd, -'seɪd) *n* **1** a gliding step in ballet **2** a controlled slide down a snow slope ▷ *vb* **glissades, glissading, glissaded** **3** (*intr*) to perform a glissade [C19 from F, from *glisser* to slip, from OF *glicier*, of Frankish origin]

glissando (glɪ'sændəʊ) *n, pl* **glissandi** (-diː) *or* **glissandos** a rapidly executed series of notes, each of which is discretely audible [C19 prob. It. var. of GLISSADE]

glisten ('glɪsᵊn) *vb* (*intr*) **1** (of a wet or glossy surface) to gleam by reflecting light **2** (of light) to reflect with brightness: *the sunlight glistens on wet leaves* ▷ *n* **3** *rare* a gleam or gloss [OE *glisnian*]

glister ('glɪstə) *vb, n* an archaic word for **glitter** [C14 prob. from MDu. *glisteren*]

glitch (glɪtʃ) *n* **1** a sudden instance of malfunctioning in an electronic system **2** a change in the rotation rate of a pulsar [C20 from ?]

glitter ('glɪtə) *vb* (*intr*) **1** (of a hard, wet, or polished surface) to reflect light in bright flashes **2** (of light) to be reflected in bright flashes **3** (usually foll by *with*) to be decorated or enhanced by the glamour (of): *the show glitters with famous actors* ▷ *n* **4** sparkle or brilliance

5 show and glamour 6 tiny pieces of shiny decorative material 7 *Canad* Also called: **silver thaw** ice formed from freezing rain [C14 from ON *glitra*] > '**glitteringly** *adv* > '**glittery** *adj*

glitterati (ˌglɪtəˈrɑːtiː) *pl n inf* the leaders of society, esp the rich and beautiful [C20 from GLITTER + *-ati* as in LITERATI]

glitzy (ˈglɪtsɪ) *adj* **glitzier, glitziest** *sl* showily attractive; flashy or glittery [C20 prob. via Yiddish from G *glitzern* to glitter]

Gliwice (*Polish* gliˈvitsɛ) *n* an industrial city in S Poland. Pop: 212 164 (1999 est). German name: **Gleiwitz**

gloaming (ˈgləʊmɪŋ) *n Scot or poetic* twilight or dusk [OE *glōmung*, from *glōm*]

gloat (gləʊt) *vb* **1** (*intr*; often foll by *over*) to dwell (on) with malevolent smugness or exultation ▷ *n* **2** the act of gloating [C16 prob. of Scand. origin; cf. ON *glotta* to grin, MHG *glotzen* to stare] > '**gloater** *n*

glob (glɒb) *n inf* a rounded mass of some thick fluid substance [C20 prob. from GLOBE, infl. by BLOB]

global (ˈgləʊbᵊl) *adj* **1** covering or relating to the whole world **2** comprehensive; total > '**globally** *adv*

globalization *or* **globalisation** (ˌgləʊbᵊlaɪˈzeɪʃən) *n* **1** the process enabling financial and investment markets to operate internationally, largely as a result of deregulation and improved communications **2** the emergence since the 1980s of a single world market dominated by multinational companies, leading to a diminishing capacity for national governments to control their economies **3** the process by which a company, etc, expands to operate internationally

globalize *or* **globalise** (ˈgləʊbᵊˌlaɪz) *vb* **globalizes, globalizing, globalized** *or* **globalises, globalising, globalised** (*tr*) to put into effect or spread worldwide

global product *n* a commercial product, such as Coca Cola, that is marketed throughout the world under the same brand name

global warming *n* an increase in the average temperature worldwide believed to be caused by the greenhouse effect

globe (gləʊb) *n* **1** a sphere on which a map of the world is drawn **2** **the globe** the world; the earth **3** a planet or some other astronomical body **4** an object shaped like a sphere, such as a glass lampshade or fishbowl **5** an orb, usually of gold, symbolic of sovereignty **6** *Austral, NZ, & S African* an electric light bulb ▷ *vb* **globes, globing, globed** **7** to form or cause to form into a globe [C16 from OF, from L *globus*] > '**globe,like** *adj*

globefish (ˈgləʊbˌfɪʃ) *n, pl* **globefish** *or* **globefishes** another name for **puffer**

globeflower (ˈgləʊbˌflaʊə) *n* a plant having pale yellow, white, or orange globe-shaped flowers

globetrotter (ˈgləʊbˌtrɒtə) *n* a habitual worldwide traveller, esp a tourist > '**globe,trotting** *n, adj*

globigerina (gləʊˌbɪdʒəˈraɪnə) *n, pl* **globigerinas** *or* **globigerinae** (-niː) **1** a marine protozoan having a rounded shell with spiny processes **2** **globigerina ooze** a deposit on the ocean floor consisting of the shells of these protozoans [C19 from NL, from L *globus* GLOBE + *gerere* to bear]

globoid (ˈgləʊbɔɪd) *adj* **1** shaped like a globe ▷ *n* **2** a globoid body

globose (ˈgləʊbəʊs, gləʊˈbəʊs) *or* **globous** (ˈgləʊbəs) *adj* spherical or approximately spherical [C15 from L *globōsus*; see GLOBE] > '**globosely** *adv*

globular (ˈglɒbjʊlə) *or* **globulous** *adj* **1** shaped like a globe or globule **2** having or consisting of globules

globule (ˈglɒbjuːl) *n* a small globe, esp a drop of liquid [C17 from L *globulus*, dim. of *globus* GLOBE]

globulin (ˈglɒbjʊlɪn) *n* any of a group of simple proteins that are generally insoluble in water but soluble in salt solutions

glockenspiel (ˈglɒkənˌspiːl, -ˌʃpiːl) *n* a percussion instrument consisting of a set of tuned metal plates played with a pair of small hammers [C19 G, from *Glocken* bells + *Spiel* play]

glom (glɒm) *vb slang* to attach oneself to [C20 from Scot. *glaum*]

glomerate (ˈglɒmərɪt) *adj* **1** gathered into a compact rounded mass **2** *anat* (esp of glands) conglomerate in structure [C18 from L *glomerāre*, from *glomus* ball] > ˌ**glomeˈration** *n*

glomerule (ˈglɒməˌruːl) *n bot* an inflorescence in the form of a ball-like cluster of flowers [C18 from NL *glomerulus*]

Glomma (*Norwegian* ˈglɔma) *n* a river in SE Norway, rising near the border with Sweden and flowing generally south to the Skagerrak: the largest river in Scandinavia; important for hydroelectric power and floating timber. Length: 588 km (365 miles)

gloom (gluːm) *n* **1** partial or total darkness **2** a state of depression or melancholy **3** an appearance or expression of despondency or melancholy **4** *poetic* a dim or dark place ▷ *vb* **5** (*intr*) to look sullen or depressed **6** to make or become dark or gloomy [C14 *gloumben* to look sullen]

gloomy (ˈgluːmɪ) *adj* **gloomier, gloomiest** **1** dark or dismal **2** causing depression or gloom: *gloomy news* **3** despairing; sad > '**gloomily** *adv* > '**gloominess** *n*

gloop (gluːp) *or esp US* **glop** (glɒp) *n inf* any messy sticky fluid or substance [C20 from ?] > '**gloopy** *or esp US* '**gloppy** *adj*

Glooscap, Gluscap, *or* **Gluskap** (ˈgluːskæp) *n* (among the Micmac and other Native North American peoples) a traditional trickster hero [of Algonquian origin]

grid road *n* (in Canada) a road that follows a surveyed division between areas of a township, municipality, etc

gloria (ˈglɔːrɪə) *n* a halo or nimbus, esp as represented in art [C16 from L: GLORY]

Gloria (ˈglɔːrɪə, -ˌɑː) *n* **1** any of several doxologies beginning with the word *Gloria* **2** a musical setting of one of these

glorify (ˈglɔːrɪˌfaɪ) *vb* **glorifies, glorifying, glorified** (*tr*) **1** to make glorious **2** to make more splendid; adorn **3** to worship, exalt, or adore **4** to extol **5** to cause to seem more splendid or imposing than reality > ˌ**glorifiˈcation** *n*

gloriole (ˈglɔːrɪˌəʊl) *n* another name for a **halo** [C19 from L *glōriola*, lit.: a small GLORY]

glorious (ˈglɔːrɪəs) *adj* **1** having or full of glory; illustrious **2** conferring glory or renown: *a glorious victory* **3** brilliantly beautiful **4** delightful or enjoyable > '**gloriously** *adv* > '**gloriousness** *n*

glory (ˈglɔːrɪ) *n, pl* **glories** **1** exaltation, praise, or honour **2** something that brings or is worthy of praise (esp in **crowning glory**) **3** thanksgiving, adoration, or worship: *glory be to God* **4** pomp; splendour: *the glory of the king's reign* **5** radiant beauty; resplendence: *the glory of the sunset* **6** the beauty and bliss of heaven **7** a state of extreme happiness or prosperity **8** another word for **halo** or **nimbus** ▷ *vb* **glories, glorying, gloried** **9** (*intr*; often foll by *in*) to triumph or exalt ▷ *interj* **10** *inf* a mild interjection to express pleasure or surprise (often **glory be!**) [C13 from OF *glorie*, from L *glōria*, from ?]

glory box *n Austral & NZ* (esp formerly) a box in which a young woman stores clothes, etc, in preparation for marriage

glory hole *n* **1** a cupboard or storeroom, esp one which is very untidy **2** *naut* another term for **lazaretto** (sense 1)

Glos *abbrev for* Gloucestershire

gloss[1] (glɒs) *n* **1a** lustre or sheen, as of a smooth surface **1b** (*as modifier*): *gloss paint* **2** a superficially attractive appearance **3** a cosmetic used to give a sheen ▷ *vb* **4** to give a gloss to or obtain a gloss **5** (*tr*; often foll by *over*) to hide under a deceptively attractive surface or appearance [C16 prob. of Scand. origin] > '**glosser** *n*

Gg

gloss² (glɒs) *n* **1** a short or expanded explanation or interpretation of a word, expression, or foreign phrase in the margin or text of a manuscript, etc **2** an intentionally misleading explanation **3** short for **glossary** ▷ *vb (tr)* **4** to add glosses to **5** (often foll by *over*) to give a false or misleading interpretation of [C16 from L *glōssa* unusual word requiring explanatory note, from Ionic Gk]

glossary (ˈglɒsərɪ) *n, pl* **glossaries** an alphabetical list of terms peculiar to a field of knowledge with explanations [C14 from LL *glossārium;* see GLOSS²] > **glossarial** (glɒˈsɛərɪəl) *adj* > ˈ**glossarist** *n*

glosseme (ˈglɒsiːm) *n* the smallest meaningful unit of a language, such as stress, form, etc [C20 from Gk; see GLOSS², -EME]

glossitis (glɒˈsaɪtɪs) *n* inflammation of the tongue > **glossitic** (glɒˈsɪtɪk) *adj*

glosso- *or before a vowel* **gloss-** *combining form* indicating a tongue or language: *glossolaryngeal* [from Gk *glossa* tongue]

glossolalia (ˌglɒsəˈleɪlɪə) *n* another term for **gift of tongues** [C19 NL, from GLOSSO- + Gk *lalein* to speak]

glossy (ˈglɒsɪ) *adj* **glossier, glossiest** **1** smooth and shiny; lustrous **2** superficially attractive; plausible **3** (of a magazine) lavishly produced on shiny paper ▷ *n, pl* **glossies** **4** Also called (US): **slick** an expensively produced magazine, printed on shiny paper and containing high-quality colour photography **5** a photograph printed on paper that has a smooth shiny surface > ˈ**glossily** *adv* > ˈ**glossiness** *n*

glottal (ˈglɒtᵊl) *adj* **1** of or relating to the glottis **2** *phonetics* articulated or pronounced at or with the glottis

glottal stop *n* a plosive speech sound produced by tightly closing the glottis and allowing the air pressure to build up before opening the glottis, causing the air to escape with force

glottis (ˈglɒtɪs) *n, pl* **glottises** *or* **glottides** (-tɪˌdiːz) the vocal apparatus of the larynx, consisting of the two true vocal cords and the opening between them [C16 from NL, from Gk, from Attic form of Ionic *glōssa* tongue; see GLOSS²]

Gloucester¹ (ˈglɒstə) *n* a city in SW England, administrative centre of Gloucestershire, on the River Severn; cathedral (founded 1100). Pop: 104 800 (1993 est). Latin name: **Glevum** (ˈgliːvʊm)

Gloucester² (ˈglɒstə) *n* **1** **Humphrey,** Duke of. 1391–1447, English soldier and statesman; son of Henry IV. He acted as protector during Henry VI's minority (1422–29) and was noted for his patronage of humanists **2** **Duke of** See **Richard III** **3** **Duke of** See **Thomas of Woodstock**

Gloucestershire (ˈglɒstəʃɪə, -ʃə) *n* a county of SW England, situated around the lower Severn valley: contains the Forest of Dean and the main part of the Cotswold Hills: the geographical and ceremonial county includes the unitary authority of South Gloucestershire (part of Avon county from 1974 to 1996). Administrative centre: Gloucester. Pop (excluding South Gloucestershire): 564 559 (1996 est). Area (excluding South Gloucestershire): 2643 sq km (1020 sq miles). Abbrev: **Glos**

glove (glʌv) *n* **1** (*often pl*) a shaped covering for the hand with individual sheaths for the fingers and thumb, made of leather, fabric, etc **2** any of various large protective hand covers worn in sports, such as a boxing glove ▷ *vb* **gloves, gloving, gloved** **3** (*tr*) to cover or provide with or as if with gloves [OE *glōfe*]

glove box *n* a closed box in which toxic or radioactive substances can be handled by an operator who places his hands through protective gloves sealed to the box

glove compartment *n* a small compartment in a car dashboard for the storage of miscellaneous articles

glover (ˈglʌvə) *n* a person who makes or sells gloves

glow (gləʊ) *n* **1** light emitted by a substance or object at a high temperature **2** a steady even light without flames **3** brilliance of colour **4** brightness of complexion **5** a feeling of wellbeing or satisfaction **6** intensity of emotion ▷ *vb (intr)* **7** to emit a steady even light without flames **8** to shine intensely, as if from great heat **9** to be exuberant, as from excellent health or intense emotion **10** to experience a feeling of wellbeing or satisfaction: *to glow with pride* **11** (esp of the complexion) to show a strong bright colour, esp red **12** to be very hot [OE *glōwan*]

glow discharge *n* a silent luminous discharge of electricity through a low-pressure gas

glower (ˈglaʊə) *vb* **1** (*intr*) to stare hard and angrily ▷ *n* **2** a sullen or angry stare [C16 prob. of Scand. origin] > ˈ**gloweringly** *adv*

glowing (ˈgləʊɪŋ) *adj* **1** emitting light without flames: *glowing embers* **2** warm and rich in colour: *glowing shades of gold and orange* **3** flushed and rosy: *glowing cheeks* **4** displaying or indicative of extreme pride or emotion: *a glowing account of his son's achievements*

glow-worm *n* a European beetle, the females and larvae of which bear luminescent organs producing a soft greenish light

gloxinia (glɒkˈsɪnɪə) *n* any of several tropical plants cultivated for their large white, red, or purple bell-shaped flowers [C19 after Benjamin P. *Gloxin*, 18th-cent. G physician & botanist]

gloze (gləʊz) *vb* **glozes, glozing, glozed** *arch* **1** (*tr;* often foll by *over*) to explain away; minimize the effect or importance of **2** to make explanatory notes or glosses on (a text) **3** to use flattery (on) [C13 from OF *glosser* to comment; see GLOSS²]

Gluck (*German* glʊk) *n* **Christoph Willibald von** (ˈkrɪstɔf ˈvɪlibalt fɔn) 1714–87, German composer, esp of operas, including *Orfeo ed Euridice* (1762) and *Alceste* (1767)

glucose (ˈgluːkəʊz, -kəʊs) *n* **1** a white crystalline sugar, the most abundant form being dextrose. Formula: $C_6H_{12}O_6$ **2** a yellowish syrup obtained by incomplete hydrolysis of starch: used in confectionery, fermentation, etc [C19 from F, from Gk *gleukos* sweet wine; rel. to Gk *glukus* sweet]

glucoside (ˈgluːkəʊˌsaɪd) *n biochem* any of a large group of glycosides that yield glucose on hydrolysis > **glucosidic** (ˌgluːkəʊˈsɪdɪk) *adj*

glue (gluː) *n* **1** any natural or synthetic adhesive, esp a sticky gelatinous substance prepared by boiling animal products such as bones, skin, and horns **2** any other sticky or adhesive substance ▷ *vb* **glues, gluing** *or* **glueing, glued** **3** (*tr*) to join or stick together as with glue [C14 from OF *glu*, from LL *glūs*] > ˈ**glueˌlike** *adj* > ˈ**gluer** *n* > ˈ**gluey** *adj*

glue ear *n* accumulation of fluid in the middle ear in children, caused by infection and resulting in deafness

glue-sniffing *n* the practice of inhaling the fumes of certain types of glue to produce intoxicating or hallucinatory effects > ˈ**glue-ˌsniffer** *n*

gluhwein (ˈgluːˌvaɪn) *n* mulled wine [G]

glum (glʌm) *adj* **glummer, glummest** silent or sullen, as from gloom [C16 var. of GLOOM] > ˈ**glumly** *adv* > ˈ**glumness** *n*

glume (gluːm) *n bot* one of a pair of dry membranous bracts at the base of the spikelet of grasses [C18 from L *glūma* husk of corn] > **gluˈmaceous** *adj*

gluon (ˈgluːɒn) *n* a hypothetical particle believed to be exchanged between quarks in order to bind them together to form particles [C20 coined from GLUE + -ON]

glurge (glɜːdʒ) *n* stories, often sent by email, that are supposed to be true and uplifting, but which are often fabricated and sentimental [C20 from ??]

glut (glʌt) *n* **1** an excessive amount, as in the production of a crop **2** the act of glutting or state of being glutted ▷ *vb* **gluts, glutting, glutted** (*tr*) **3** to feed or supply beyond capacity **4** to supply (a market, etc) with a commodity in excess of the demand for it [C14 prob. from OF *gloutir*, from L *gluttīre*; see GLUTTON[1]]

glutamic acid (gluː'tæmɪk) *n* an amino acid, occurring in proteins

gluten ('gluːtᵊn) *n* a protein present in cereal grains, esp wheat [C16 from L: GLUE] > '**glutenous** *adj*

gluteus (glʊ'tiːəs) *n, pl* **glutei** (-'tiːaɪ) any one of the three large muscles that form the human buttock [C17 from NL, from Gk *gloutos* buttock, rump] > **glu'teal** *adj*

glutinous ('gluːtɪnəs) *adj* resembling glue in texture; sticky > '**glutinously** *adv*

glutton[1] ('glʌtᵊn) *n* **1** a person devoted to eating and drinking to excess; greedy person **2** a person who has or appears to have a voracious appetite for something: *he's a real glutton for punishment* [C13 from OF *glouton*, from L from *gluttīre* to swallow] > '**gluttonous** *adj* > '**gluttonously** *adv*

glutton[2] ('glʌtᵊn) *n* another name for **wolverine** [C17 from GLUTTON[1], apparently translating G *Vielfrass* great eater]

gluttony ('glʌtənɪ) *n* the act or practice of eating to excess

glyceride ('glɪsəˌraɪd) *n* any fatty-acid ester of glycerol

glycerine ('glɪsəriːn, ˌglɪsə'riːn) *or* **glycerin** ('glɪsərɪn) *n* another name (not in technical usage) for **glycerol** [C19 from F, from Gk *glukeros* sweet + *-ine* -IN; rel. to Gk *glukus* sweet]

glycerol ('glɪsəˌrɒl) *n* a colourless odourless syrupy liquid: a by-product of soap manufacture, used as a solvent, antifreeze, plasticizer, and sweetener (**E422**). Formula: $CH_2OHCHOHCH_2OH$ [C19 from GLYCER(IN) + -OL[1]]

glycine ('glaɪsiːn, glaɪ'siːn) *n* a white sweet crystalline amino acid occurring in most proteins [C19 GLYCO- + -INE[2]]

glyco- *or before a vowel* **glyc-** *combining form* sugar: *glycogen* [from Gk *glukus* sweet]

glycogen ('glaɪkəʊdʒən) *n* a polysaccharide consisting of glucose units: the form in which carbohydrate is stored in animals > **glycogenic** (ˌglaɪkəʊ'dʒɛnɪk) *adj* > ˌ**glyco'genesis** *n*

glycol ('glaɪkɒl) *n* another name (not in technical usage) for **ethanediol**

glycolic acid (glaɪ'kɒlɪk) *n* a colourless crystalline compound found in sugar cane and sugar beet: used in the manufacture of pharmaceuticals, pesticides, and plasticizers

glycolysis (glaɪ'kɒlɪsɪs) *n biochem* the breakdown of glucose by enzymes with the liberation of energy

glycoside ('glaɪkəʊˌsaɪd) *n* any of a group of substances derived from simple sugars by replacing the hydroxyl group by another group > **glycosidic** (ˌglaɪkəʊ'sɪdɪk) *adj*

glycosuria (ˌglaɪkəʊ'sjʊərɪə) *n* the presence of excess sugar in the urine, as in diabetes [C19 from NL, from F *glycose* GLUCOSE + -URIA]

Glyndebourne ('glaɪndˌbɔːn) *n* an estate in SE England, in East Sussex: site of a famous annual festival of opera founded in 1934 by John Christie

glyph (glɪf) *n* **1** a carved channel or groove, esp a vertical one **2** *now rare* another word for **hieroglyphic** [C18 from F, from Gk, from *gluphein* to carve] > '**glyphic** *adj*

glyphosate ('glaɪfəʊˌseɪt) *n* a systemic nonselective herbicide used in certain commercial weedkillers

glyptic ('glɪptɪk) *adj* of or relating to engraving or carving, esp on precious stones [C19 from F, from Gk, from *gluphein* to carve]

glyptodont ('glɪptəˌdɒnt) *n* an extinct mammal of South America which resembled the giant armadillo [C19 from Gk *gluptos* carved + -ODONT]

GM *abbrev for:* **1** general manager **2** genetically modified **3** (in Britain) George Medal **4** Grand Master **5** grant-maintained

G-man *n, pl* **G-men** **1** *US sl* an FBI agent **2** *Irish* a political detective

Gmc *abbrev for* Germanic

GMDSS *abbrev for* Global Marine Distress and Safety System: a worldwide satellite communication system used for transmitting messages (esp distress messages) at sea

GMO *abbrev for* genetically modified organism

GMT *abbrev for* Greenwich Mean Time

GMTA *text messaging abbrev for* great minds think alike

gnarl (nɑːl) *n* **1** any knotty swelling on a tree ▷ *vb* **2** (*tr*) to knot or cause to knot [C19 back formation from *gnarled*]

gnarled (nɑːld) *adj* **1** having gnarls: *the gnarled trunk of the old tree* **2** (esp of hands) rough, twisted, and weather-beaten

gnarly ('nɑːlɪ) *adj* **gnarlier, gnarliest** **1** another word for **gnarled** **2** *NZ inf* good; great

gnash (næʃ) *vb* **1** to grind (the teeth) together, as in pain or anger **2** (*tr*) to bite or chew as by grinding the teeth ▷ *n* **3** the act of gnashing the teeth [C15 prob. from ON; cf. *gnastan* gnashing of teeth]

gnat (næt) *n* any of various small fragile biting two-winged insects [OE *gnætt*]

gnathic ('næθɪk) *adj anat* of or relating to the jaw [C19 from Gk *gnathos* jaw]

-gnathous *adj combining form* indicating or having a jaw of a specified kind: *prognathous* [from NL, from Gk *gnathos* jaw]

gnaw (nɔː) *vb* **gnaws, gnawing, gnawed; gnawed** *or* **gnawn** **1** (when *intr*, often foll by *at* or *upon*) to bite (at) or chew (upon) constantly so as to wear away little by little **2** (*tr*) to form by gnawing: *to gnaw a hole* **3** to cause erosion of (something) **4** (when *intr*, often foll by *at*) to cause constant distress or anxiety (to) ▷ *n* **5** the act or an instance of gnawing [OE *gnagan*]

gnawing ('nɔːɪŋ) *n* a dull persistent pang or pain, esp of hunger

gneiss (naɪs) *n* any coarse-grained metamorphic rock that is banded and foliated [C18 from G *Gneis*, prob. from MHG *ganeist* spark] > '**gneissic,** '**gneissoid,** *or* '**gneissose** *adj*

gnocchi ('nɒkɪ) *pl n* dumplings made of pieces of semolina pasta, or sometimes potato, served with sauce [It., pl of *gnocco* lump, prob. of Gmc origin]

gnome (nəʊm) *n* **1** one of a species of legendary creatures, usually resembling small misshapen old men, said to live in the depths of the earth and guard buried treasure **2** the statue of a gnome, esp in a garden **3** a very small or ugly person **4** *facetious or derog* an international banker or financier (esp in **gnomes of Zürich**) [C18 from F, from NL *gnomus*, coined by Paracelsus (1493-1541), Swiss alchemist, from ?] > '**gnomish** *adj*

gnomic ('nəʊmɪk, 'nɒm-) *adj* of or relating to aphorisms; pithy > '**gnomically** *adv*

gnomon ('nəʊmɒn) *n* **1** the stationary arm that projects the shadow on a sundial **2** a geometric figure remaining after a parallelogram has been removed from one corner of a larger parallelogram [C16 from L, from Gk: interpreter, from *gignōskein* to know] > **gno'monic** *adj*

-gnosis *n combining form* (esp in medicine) recognition or knowledge: *diagnosis* [via L from Gk: knowledge] > **-gnostic** *adj combining form*

gnostic ('nɒstɪk) *adj* of, relating to, or possessing knowledge, esp spiritual knowledge

Gnostic ('nɒstɪk) *n* **1** an adherent of Gnosticism ▷ *adj* **2** of or relating to Gnostics or to Gnosticism [C16 from LL, from Gk *gnōstikos* relating to knowledge]

Gnosticism ('nɒstɪˌsɪzəm) *n* a religious movement characterized by a belief in intuitive spiritual knowledge: regarded as a heresy by the Christian Church

gnotobiotic (ˌnəʊtəʊbaɪˈɒtɪk) *adj* of or pertaining to germ-free conditions, esp in a laboratory in which animals are injected with known strains of organisms [C20 from Gk *gnōtos*, from *gignōskein* to know + BIOTIC]

GNP *abbrev for* gross national product

gnu (nuː) *n, pl* **gnus** *or* **gnu** either of two sturdy antelopes inhabiting the savannas of Africa, having an oxlike head and a long tufted tail. Also called: **wildebeest** [C18 from Xhosa *nqu*]

GNVQ (in Britain) *abbrev for* general national vocational qualification: a qualification which rewards the development of skills likely to be of use to employers

go (gəʊ) *vb* **goes, going, went, gone** (*mainly intr*) **1** to move or proceed, esp to or from a point or in a certain direction: *go home* **2** (*tr; takes an infinitive*, often with *to* omitted or replaced by *and*) to proceed towards a particular person or place with some specified purpose: *I must go and get that book* **3** to depart: *we'll have to go at eleven* **4** to start, as in a race: often used in commands **5** to make regular journeys: *this train service goes to the east coast* **6** to operate or function effectively: *the radio won't go* **7** (*copula*) to become: *his face went red* **8** to make a noise as specified: *the gun went bang* **9** to enter into a specified state or condition: *to go into hysterics* **10** to be or continue to be in a specified state or condition: *to go in rags; to go in poverty* **11** to lead, extend, or afford access: *this route goes to the north* **12** to proceed towards an activity: *to go to sleep* **13** (*tr; takes an infinitive*) to serve or contribute: *this letter goes to prove my point* **14** to follow a course as specified; fare: *the lecture went badly* **15** to be applied or allotted to a particular purpose or recipient: *his money went on drink* **16** to be sold: *the necklace went for three thousand pounds* **17** to be ranked; compare: *this meal is good as my meals go* **18** to blend or harmonize: *these chairs won't go with the rest of your furniture* **19** (foll by *by* or *under*) to be known (by a name or disguise) **20** to have a usual or proper place: *those books go on this shelf* **21** (of music, poetry, etc) to be sounded; expressed, etc: *how does that song go?* **22** to fail or give way: *my eyesight is going* **23** to break down or collapse abruptly: *the ladder went at the critical moment* **24** to die: *the old man went at 2 a.m* **25** (often foll by *by*) **25a** (of time, etc) to elapse: *the hours go by so slowly* **25b** to travel past: *the train goes by her house* **25c** to be guided (by) **26** to occur: *happiness does not always go with riches* **27** to be eliminated, abolished, or given up: *this entry must go to save space* **28** to be spent or finished: *all his money has gone* **29** to attend: *go to school* **30** to join a stated profession: *go on the stage* **31** (foll by *to*) to have recourse (to); turn: *to go to arbitration* **32** (foll by *to*) to subject or put oneself (to): *she goes to great pains to please him* **33** to proceed, esp up to or beyond certain limits: *you will go too far one day and then you will be punished* **34** to be acceptable or tolerated: *anything goes* **35** to carry the weight of final authority: *what the boss says goes* **36** (*tr*) *nonstandard* to say: *Then she goes, "Give it to me!" and she just snatched it* **37** (foll by *into*) to be contained in: *four goes into twelve three times* **38** (often foll by *for*) to endure or last out: *we can't go for much longer without water* **39** (*tr*) *cards* to bet or bid: *I go two hearts* **40** **be going** to intend or be about to start (to do or be doing something): often used as an alternative future construction: *what's going to happen to us?* **41** **go and** *inf* to be so foolish or unlucky as to: *then she had to go and lose her hat* **42** **go it** *sl* to do something or move energetically **43** **go it alone** *inf* to act or proceed without allies or help **44** **go one better** *inf* to surpass or outdo (someone) **45** **let go** **45a** to relax one's hold (on); release **45b** to discuss or consider no further **46** **let oneself go** **46a** to act in an uninhibited manner **46b** to lose interest in one's appearance, manners, etc **47** **to go** **47a** remaining **47b** *US & Canad inf* (of food served by a restaurant) for taking away ▷ *n, pl* **goes** **48** the act of going **49a** an attempt or try: *he had a go at the stamp business* **49b** an attempt at stopping a person suspected of a crime: *the police are not always in favour of the public having a go* **49c** an attack, esp verbal: *she had a real go at them* **50** a turn: *it's my go next* **51** *inf* the quality of being active and energetic: *she has much more go than I have* **52** *inf* hard or energetic work: *it's all go* **53** *inf* a successful venture or achievement: *he made a go of it* **54** *inf* a bargain or agreement **55** **from the word go** *inf* from the very beginning **56** **no go** *inf* impossible; abortive or futile: *it's no go, I'm afraid* **57** **on the go** *inf* active and energetic ▷ *adj* **58** (*postpositive*) *inf* functioning properly and ready for action: esp used in astronautics: *all systems are go* ▷ See also **go about, go against,** etc [OE *gān*]

Goa (ˈgəʊə) *n* a state on the W coast of India: a Portuguese overseas territory from 1510 until annexed by India in 1961. Pop: 1 343 998 (2001). Area: 3702 sq km (1430 sq miles)

go about *vb* (*intr*) **1** (*prep*) to busy oneself with: *to go about one's duties* **2** (*prep*) to tackle (a problem or task) **3** to circulate (in): *there's a lot of flu going about* **4** (*adv*) (of a sailing ship) to change from one tack to another

goad (gəʊd) *n* **1** a sharp pointed stick for urging on cattle, etc **2** anything that acts as a spur or incitement ▷ *vb* **3** (*tr*) to drive as if with a goad; spur; incite [OE *gād*, of Gmc origin]

Goa, Daman, and Diu *n* a former Union Territory of India consisting of the widely separated districts of Goa and Daman and the island of Diu. Capital: Panaji. Area: 3814 sq km (1472 sq miles)

go against *vb* (*intr, prep*) **1** to be contrary to (principles or beliefs) **2** to be unfavourable to (a person): *the case went against him*

go-ahead *n* **1** (usually preceded by *the*) *inf* permission to proceed ▷ *adj* **2** enterprising or ambitious

goal (gəʊl) *n* **1** the aim or object towards which an endeavour is directed **2** the terminal point of a journey or race **3** (in various sports) the net, basket, etc, into or over which players try to propel the ball, puck, etc, to score **4** *sport* **4a** a successful attempt at scoring **4b** the score so made **5** (in soccer, hockey, etc) the position of goalkeeper [C16 ? rel. to ME *gol* boundary, OE *gǣlan* to hinder] > ˈ**goalless** *adj*

goalball (ˈgəʊlˌbɔːl) *n* **1** a game played by two teams who compete to score goals by throwing a ball that emits sound when in motion. Players are blindfolded during play **2** the ball used in this game

goalie (ˈgəʊlɪ) *n inf* short for **goalkeeper**

goalkeeper (ˈgəʊlˌkiːpə) *n sport* a player in the goal whose duty is to prevent the ball, puck, etc, from entering or crossing it

goal kick *n soccer* a kick taken from the six-yard line by the defending team after the ball has been put out of play by an opposing player

goal line *n sport* the line marking each end of the pitch, on which the goals stand

go along *vb* (*intr, adv;* often foll by *with*) to refrain from disagreement; assent

goalpost (ˈgəʊlˌpəʊst) *n* **1** either of two upright posts supporting the crossbar of a goal **2** **move the goalposts** to change the target required during negotiations, etc

goanna (gəʊˈænə) *n* any of various Australian monitor lizards [C19 from IGUANA]

goat (gəʊt) *n* **1** any sure-footed agile ruminant mammal with hollow horns, naturally inhabiting rough stony ground in Europe, Asia, and N Africa **2** *inf* a lecherous man **3** a foolish person **4** **get (someone's) goat** *sl* to cause annoyance to (someone) [OE *gāt*] > ˈ**goatish** *adj*

Goat (gəʊt) *n* **the** the constellation Capricorn, the tenth sign of the zodiac

go at *vb* (*intr, prep*) **1** to make an energetic attempt at (something) **2** to attack vehemently

goatee (gəʊˈtiː) *n* a pointed tuftlike beard on the chin [C19 from GOAT + *-ee* (see -Y[2])]

goatherd (ˈgəʊtˌhɜːd) *n* a person employed to tend or herd goats

goatsbeard *or* **goat's-beard** ('gəʊts,bɪəd) *n* **1** Also called: **Jack-go-to-bed-at-noon** a Eurasian plant of the composite family, Asteracea, with woolly stems and large heads of yellow rayed flowers **2** an American plant with long spikes of small white flowers

goatskin ('gəʊt,skɪn) *n* **1** the hide of a goat **2** something made from the hide of a goat, such as leather or a container for wine

goatsucker ('gəʊt,sʌkə) *n* the US and Canad name for **nightjar**

go-away bird *n S African* a common name for a grey-plumaged **lourie**

gob[1] (gɒb) *n* **1** a lump or chunk, esp of a soft substance **2** *(often pl) inf* a great quantity or amount **3** *inf* a globule of spittle or saliva **4** a lump of molten glass used to make a piece of glassware ▷ *vb* **gobs, gobbing, gobbed 5** *(intr) Brit inf* to spit [C14 from OF *gobe* lump, from *gober;* see GOBBET]

gob[2] (gɒb) *n* a slang word (esp Brit) for the **mouth** [C16 ?from Gaelic *gob*]

go back *vb (intr, adv)* **1** to return **2** (often foll by *to*) to originate (in): *the links with France go back to the Norman Conquest* **3** (foll by *on*) to change one's mind about; repudiate (esp in **go back on one's word**)

gobbet ('gɒbɪt) *n* a chunk, lump, or fragment, esp of raw meat [C14 from OF *gobet,* from *gober* to gulp down]

Gobbi (*Italian* 'gɔbbi) *n* **Tito** ('ti:to) 1915–84, Italian operatic baritone

gobble[1] ('gɒbᵊl) *vb* **gobbles, gobbling, gobbled 1** (when *tr*, often foll by *up*) to eat or swallow (food) hastily and in large mouthfuls **2** *(tr; often foll by up) inf* to snatch [C17 prob. from GOB[1]]

gobble[2] ('gɒbᵊl) *n* **1** the loud rapid gurgling sound made by male turkeys ▷ *vb* **gobbles, gobbling, gobbled 2** *(intr)* (of a turkey) to make this sound [C17 prob. imit.]

gobbledegook *or* **gobbledygook** ('gɒbᵊldɪ,gu:k) *n* pretentious or unintelligible jargon, such as that used by officials [C20 whimsical formation from GOBBLE[2]]

gobbler ('gɒblə) *n inf* a male turkey

Gobelin ('gəʊbəlɪn; *French* gɔblɛ̃) *adj* **1** of or resembling tapestry made at the Gobelins' factory in Paris, having vivid pictorial scenes ▷ *n* **2** a tapestry of this kind [C19 from the *Gobelin* family, who founded the factory]

go-between *n* a person who acts as agent or intermediary for two people or groups in a transaction or dealing

Gobi ('gəʊbɪ) *n* a desert in E Asia, mostly in Mongolia and the Inner Mongolian Autonomous Region of China: sometimes considered to include all the arid regions east of the Pamirs and north of the plateau of Tibet and the Great Wall of China: one of the largest deserts in the world. Length: about 1600 km (1000 miles). Width: about 1000 km (625 miles). Average height: 900 m (3000 ft). Chinese name: **Shamo** > **'Gobian** *adj*

Gobind Singh ('gəʊbɪnd sɪŋ) *or* **Govind Singh** *n* 1666–1708, tenth and last guru of the Sikhs (1675–1708): assassinated

goblet ('gɒblɪt) *n* **1** a vessel for drinking, with a base and stem but without handles **2** *arch* a large drinking cup [C14 from OF *gobelet* a little cup, ult. of Celtic origin]

goblin ('gɒblɪn) *n* (in folklore) a small grotesque supernatural creature, regarded as malevolent towards human beings [C14 from OF, from MHG *kobolt;* cf. COBALT]

gobo ('gəʊbəʊ) *n, pl* **gobos** *or* **goboes** a shield placed round a microphone to exclude unwanted sounds, or round a camera lens, etc, to reduce the incident light [C20 from ?]

gobshite ('gɒb,ʃaɪt) *n sl* a stupid person [C20 from GOB[2] + *shite* excrement; see SHIT]

gobsmacked ('gɒb,smækt) *adj Brit sl* astounded; astonished [C20 from GOB[2] + SMACK]

goby ('gəʊbɪ) *n, pl* **goby** *or* **gobies** a small spiny-finned fish of coastal or brackish waters, having a large head, an elongated tapering body, and the ventral fins modified as a sucker [C18 from L *gōbius* gudgeon from Gk *kōbios*]

go-by *n sl* a deliberate snub or slight (esp in **give (a person) the go-by**)

go by *vb (intr)* **1** to pass: *as the years go by* **2** *(prep)* to be guided by: *in the darkness we could only go by the stars* **3** *(prep)* to use as a basis for forming an opinion or judgment: *it's wise not to go only by appearances*

go-cart *n* See **kart**

god (gɒd) *n* **1** a supernatural being, who is worshipped as the controller of some part of the universe or some aspect of life in the world or is the personification of some force **2** an image, idol, or symbolic representation of such a deity **3** any person or thing to which excessive attention is given: *money was his god* **4** a man who has qualities regarded as making him superior to other men **5** *(pl)* the gallery of a theatre [OE *god*]

God (gɒd) *n* **1** the sole Supreme Being, eternal, spiritual, and transcendent, who is the Creator and ruler of all and is infinite in all attributes; the object of worship in monotheistic religions ▷ *interj* **2** an oath or exclamation used to indicate surprise, annoyance, etc (and in such expressions as **My God!** or **God Almighty!**)

Godard (*French* gɔdar) *n* **Jean-Luc** (ʒɑ̃lyk) born 1930, French film director and writer associated with the New Wave of the 1960s. His works include *À bout de souffle* (1960), *Weekend* (1967), *Sauve qui peut* (1980), *Nouvelle Vague* (1990), and *Éloge de l'amour* (2002)

Godavari (gəʊ'dɑ:vərɪ) *n* a river in central India, rising in the Western Ghats and flowing southeast to the Bay of Bengal: extensive delta, linked by canal with the Krishna delta; a sacred river to Hindus. Length: about 1500 km (900 miles)

God-botherer ('gɒd,bɒðərə) *n inf* an over-zealous Christian

godchild ('gɒd,tʃaɪld) *n, pl* **godchildren** a person who is sponsored by adults at baptism

Goddard ('gɒdɑ:d) *n* **Robert Hutchings** 1882–1945, US physicist. He made the first workable liquid-fuelled rocket

goddaughter ('gɒd,dɔ:tə) *n* a female godchild

goddess ('gɒdɪs) *n* **1** a female divinity **2** a woman who is adored or idealized, esp by a man

Gödel ('gɜ:dᵊl) *n* **Kurt** (kʊrt) 1906–78, US logician and mathematician, born in Austria-Hungary. He showed (**Gödel's proof**) that in a formal axiomatic system, such as logic or mathematics, it is impossible to prove consistency without using methods from outside the system

Goderich ('gəʊdrɪtʃ) *n* **Viscount,** title of *Frederick John Robinson,* 1st Earl of Ripon. 1782–1859, British statesman; prime minister (1827–28)

Godesberg (*German* 'go:dəsbɛrk) *n* a town and spa in W Germany, in North Rhine-Westphalia on the Rhine: a SE suburb of Bonn. Official name: **Bad Godesberg**

godetia (gə'di:ʃə) *n* any plant of the American genus *Godetia,* esp one grown as a showy-flowered annual garden plant [C19 after C. H. *Godet* (died 1879), Swiss botanist]

godfather ('gɒd,fɑ:ðə) *n* **1** a male godparent **2** the head of a Mafia family or other criminal ring **3** an originator or leading exponent: *the godfather of South African pop*

godfather offer *n inf* a takeover bid pitched so high that the management of the target company is unable to dissuade shareholders from accepting it [from the 1972 film *The Godfather,* in which a character was made an offer he could not refuse by a threatening mafioso]

God-fearing *adj* pious; devout

godforsaken ('gɒdfə,seɪkən) *adj (sometimes cap)* **1** *(usually prenominal)* desolate; dreary; forlorn **2** wicked

Godhead ('gɒd,hɛd) *n (sometimes not cap)* **1** the essential

Gg

nature and condition of being God **2 the Godhead** God

godhood ('gɒd,hʊd) *n* the state of being divine

Godiva (gə'daɪvə) *n* **Lady** ?1040–1080, wife of Leofric, Earl of Mercia. According to legend, she rode naked through Coventry in order to obtain remission for the townspeople from the heavy taxes imposed by her husband

godless ('gɒdlɪs) *adj* **1** wicked or unprincipled **2** lacking a god **3** refusing to acknowledge God > **'godlessly** *adv* > **'godlessness** *n*

godlike ('gɒd,laɪk) *adj* resembling or befitting a god or God; divine

godly ('gɒdlɪ) *adj* **godlier, godliest** having a religious character; pious; devout > **'godliness** *n*

godmother ('gɒd,mʌðə) *n* a female godparent

Godolphin (gə'dɒlfɪn) *n* **Sidney** 1st Earl of Godolphin. 1645–1712, English statesman; as Lord Treasurer, he managed the financing of Marlborough's campaigns in the War of the Spanish Succession

godown ('gəʊ,daʊn) *n* (in the East, esp in India) a warehouse [C16 from Malay *godong*]

go down *vb* (*intr, mainly adv*) **1** (*also prep*) to move or lead to or as if to a lower place or level; sink, decline, decrease, etc **2** to be defeated; lose **3** to be remembered or recorded (esp in **go down in history**) **4** to be received: *his speech went down well* **5** (of food) to be swallowed **6** *Brit* to leave a college or university at the end of a term **7** (usually foll by *with*) to fall ill; be infected **8** (of a celestial body) to sink or set **9** *US & Canad sl* to take place; happen **10 go down on** *sl* to perform cunnilingus or fellatio on

godparent ('gɒd,pɛərənt) *n* a person who stands sponsor to another at baptism

God's acre *n literary* a churchyard or burial ground [C17 translation of G *Gottesacker*]

godsend ('gɒd,sɛnd) *n* a person or thing that comes unexpectedly but is particularly welcome [C19 from C17 *God's send*, alteration of *goddes sand* God's message, from OE *sand*; see SEND]

godslot ('gɒd,slɒt) *n inf* a time in a television or radio schedule traditionally reserved for religious broadcasts

godson ('gɒd,sʌn) *n* a male godchild

Godspeed ('gɒd'spi:d) *sentence substitute, n* an expression of good wishes for a person's success and safety [C15 from *God spede* may God prosper (you)]

godsquad ('gɒd,skwɒd) *n inf, derog* any group of evangelical Christians, members of which are regarded as intrusive and exuberantly pious

Godthaab (*Danish* 'gɔdhɔ:b) *n* the former name for **Nuuk**

Godunov ('gɒdə,nɒf, 'gʊd-; *Russian* gədu'nɔf) *n* **Boris Fyodorovich** (ba'ris 'fjɔdərəvitʃ) ?1551–1605, Russian regent (1584–98) and tsar (1598–1605)

Godwin ('gɒdwɪn) *n* **1** died 1053, Earl of Wessex. He was chief adviser to Canute and Edward the Confessor. His son succeeded Edward to the throne as Harold II **2 Mary** See (Mary) **Wollstonecraft 3 William** 1756–1836, British political philospher and novelist. In *An Enquiry concerning Political Justice* (1793), he rejected government and social institutions, including marriage. His views greatly influenced English romantic writers

Godwin Austen *n* another name for **K2**

godwit ('gɒdwɪt) *n* a large shore bird of the sandpiper family having long legs and a long upturned bill [C16 from ?]

Godzone *n Austral inf* one's own country [from *God's own country*]

Goebbels (*German* 'gœbəls) *n* **Paul Joseph** (paul 'jo:zɛf) 1897–1945, German Nazi politician; minister of propaganda (1933–45)

goer ('gəʊə) *n* **1a** a person who attends something regularly **1b** (*in combination*): *filmgoer* **2** a person or thing that goes, esp one that goes very fast **3** an energetic person **4** *Austral inf* an acceptable or feasible idea, proposal, etc: *the resort could be a goer*

Goering (*German* 'gø:rɪŋ) *n* See (Hermann Wilhelm) **Göring**

Goethe (*German* 'gø:tə) *n* **Johann Wolfgang von** (jo'han 'vɔlfgaŋ fɔn) 1749–1832, German poet, novelist, and dramatist, who settled in Weimar in 1775. His early works of the *Sturm und Drang* period include the play *Götz von Berlichingen* (1773) and the novel *The Sorrows of Young Werther* (1774). After a journey to Italy (1786–88) his writings, such as the epic play *Iphigenie auf Tauris* (1787) and the epic idyll *Hermann und Dorothea* (1797), showed the influence of classicism. Other works include the *Wilhelm Meister* novels (1796–1829) and his greatest masterpiece *Faust* (1808; 1832)

go-faster stripe *n inf* a decorative line, often suggestive of high speed, on the bodywork of a car

gofer ('gəʊfə) *n sl* a person who runs errands [C20 from GO + FOR]

goffer ('gəʊfə) *vb* (*tr*) **1** to press pleats into (a frill) **2** to decorate (the edges of a book) ▷ *n* **3** an ornamental frill made by pressing pleats **4** the decoration formed by goffering books **5** the iron or tool used in making goffers [C18 from F *gaufrer* to impress a pattern, from *gaufre*, from MLow G *wāfel*; see WAFFLE[1], WAFER]

go for *vb* (*intr, prep*) **1** to go somewhere in order to have or fetch: *he went for a drink* **2** to seek to obtain: *I'd go for that job if I were you* **3** to prefer or choose; like: *I really go for that new idea of yours* **4** to make a physical or verbal attack on **5** to be considered to be of a stated importance or value: *his twenty years went for nothing when he was made redundant* **6 go for it** *inf* to make the maximum effort to achieve a particular goal

Gog and Magog (gɒg; 'meɪgɒg) *n* **1** *Old Testament* a hostile prince and the land from which he comes to attack Israel (Ezekiel 38) **2** *New Testament* two kings, who are to attack the Church in a climactic battle, but are then to be destroyed by God (Revelation 20:8–10) **3** *Brit folklore* two giants, the only survivors of a race of giants destroyed by Brutus, the legendary founder of Britain

go-getter *n inf* an ambitious enterprising person > **,go-'getting** *adj*

gogga ('xɒxə) *n S African inf* any small animal that crawls or flies, esp an insect [C20 from Khoikhoi *xoxon* insects collectively]

goggle ('gɒgᵊl) *vb* **goggles, goggling, goggled 1** (*intr*) to stare fixedly, as in astonishment **2** to cause (the eyes) to roll or bulge or (of the eyes) to roll or bulge ▷ *n* **3** a bulging stare **4** (*pl*) spectacles, often of coloured glass or covered with gauze: used to protect the eyes [C14 from *gogelen* to look aside, from ?; see AGOG] > **'goggle-,eyed** *adj*

gogglebox ('gɒgᵊl,bɒks) *n Brit sl* a television set

Gogh (gɒx; *Dutch* xɔx) *n* See (Vincent) **van Gogh**

Go-Go *n* a form of soul music originating in Washington, DC, characterized by the use of funk rhythms and a brass section

go-go dancer *n* a dancer, usually scantily dressed, who performs rhythmic and often erotic modern dance routines, esp in a nightclub

Gogol ('gəʊgɒl; *Russian* 'gɔgəlj) *n* **Nikolai Vasilievich** (nika'laj va'siljɪvitʃ) 1809–52, Russian novelist, dramatist, and short-story writer. His best-known works are *The Government Inspector* (1836), a comedy satirizing bureaucracy, and the novel *Dead Souls* (1842)

Gogra ('gɒgrə) *n* a river in N India, rising in Tibet, in the Himalayas, and flowing southeast through Nepal as the Karnali, then through Uttar Pradesh to join the Ganges. Length: about 1000 km (600 miles)

Goiânia (gɔɪ'ɑ:nɪə; *Portuguese* go'jənja) *n* a city in central Brazil, capital of Goiás state: planned in 1933 to replace the old capital, Goiás; two universities. Pop: 1 083 396 (2000)

Goiás (*Portuguese* gɔ'jas) *n* a state of central Brazil, in the Brazilian Highlands: contains Brasília, the capital of

Brazil. Capital: Goiânia. Pop: 4 994 897 (1995 est). Area: 341 289 sq km (131 772 sq miles)

Goidelic (gɔɪˈdɛlɪk) *n* **1** the N group of Celtic languages, consisting of Irish Gaelic, Scottish Gaelic, and Manx ▷ *adj* **2** of, relating to, or characteristic of this group of languages [C19 from OIrish *Goidel* a Celt, from OWelsh, from *gwydd* savage]

go in *vb (intr, adv)* **1** to enter **2** *(prep)* See **go into** **3** (of the sun) to become hidden behind a cloud **4** **go in for** **4a** to enter as a competitor or contestant **4b** to adopt as an activity, interest, or guiding principle: *she went in for nursing*

going (ˈgəʊɪŋ) *n* **1** a departure or farewell **2** the condition of a surface such as a road or field with regard to walking, riding, etc: *muddy going* **3** *inf* speed, progress, etc: *we made good going on the trip* ▷ *adj* **4** thriving (esp in **a going concern**) **5** current or accepted: *the going rate* **6** *(postpositive)* available: *the best going*

going-over *n, pl* **goings-over** *inf* **1** a check, examination, or investigation **2** a castigation or thrashing

goings-on *pl n inf* **1** actions or conduct, esp when regarded with disapproval **2** happenings or events, esp when mysterious or suspicious

go into *vb (intr, prep)* **1** to enter **2** to start a career in: *to go into publishing* **3** to investigate or examine **4** to discuss: *we won't go into that now* **5** to be admitted to, esp temporarily: *she went into hospital* **6** to enter a specified state: *she went into fits of laughter*

goitre *or US* **goiter** (ˈgɔɪtə) *n pathol* a swelling of the thyroid gland, in some cases nearly doubling the size of the neck [C17 from F, from OF *goitron* ult. from L *guttur* throat] > **ˈgoitred** *or US* **ˈgoitered** *adj* > **ˈgoitrous** *adj*

go-kart *or* **go-cart** *n* See **kart**

Golan Heights (ˈgəʊˌlæn) *pl n* a range of hills in the Middle East, possession of which is disputed between Israel and Syria: under Syrian control until 1967 when they were stormed by Israeli forces; Jewish settlements have since been established. Highest peak: 2224 m (7297 ft)

Golconda (gɒlˈkɒndə) *n* **1** a ruined town and fortress in S central India, in W Andhra Pradesh near Hyderabad city: capital of one of the five Muslim kingdoms of the Deccan from 1512 to 1687, then annexed to the Mogul empire; renowned for its diamonds **2** *(sometimes not capital)* a source of wealth or riches, esp a mine

gold (gəʊld) *n* **1a** a dense inert bright yellow element that is the most malleable and ductile metal, occurring in rocks and alluvial deposits: used as a monetary standard and in jewellery, dentistry, and plating. Symbol: Au; atomic no.: 79; atomic wt.: 196.97. Related adj: **auric** **1b** *(as modifier): a gold mine* **2** a coin or coins made of this metal **3** money; wealth **4** something precious, beautiful, etc, such as a noble nature (esp in **heart of gold**) **5a** a deep yellow colour, sometimes with a brownish tinge **5b** *(as adj): a gold carpet* **6** short for **gold medal** [OE *gold*]

Gold (gəʊld) *n* **Thomas** born 1920, Austrian-born astronomer, working in England and the US: with Bondi and Hoyle he proposed the steady-state theory of the universe

gold card *n* a credit card issued by credit-card companies to favoured clients, entitling them to high unsecured overdrafts, some insurance cover, etc

Gold Coast *n* **1** the former name (until 1957) of **Ghana** **2** a line of resort towns and beaches in E Australia, extending for over 30 km (20 miles) along the SE coast of Queensland and the NE coast of New South Wales

goldcrest (ˈgəʊldˌkrɛst) *n* a small Old World warbler having a greenish plumage and a bright yellow-and-black crown

gold-digger *n* **1** a person who prospects or digs for gold **2** *inf* a woman who uses her sexual attractions to accumulate gifts and wealth

gold disc *n* **1** (in Britain) an LP record certified to have sold 100 000 copies or a single certified to have sold 400 000 copies **2** (in the US) an LP record or single certified to have sold 500 000 copies

gold dust *n* gold in the form of small particles or powder

golden (ˈgəʊldən) *adj* **1** of the yellowish colour of gold: *golden hair* **2** made from or largely consisting of gold: *a golden statue* **3** happy or prosperous: *golden days* **4** *(sometimes cap)* (of anniversaries) the 50th in a series: *Golden Jubilee; golden wedding* **5** *inf* very successful or destined for success: *the golden girl of tennis* **6** extremely valuable or advantageous: *a golden opportunity* > **ˈgoldenly** *adv* > **ˈgoldenness** *n*

golden age *n* **1** *classical myth* the first and best age of mankind, when existence was happy, prosperous, and innocent **2** the most flourishing and outstanding period, esp in the history of an art or nation: *the golden age of poetry*

golden eagle *n* a large eagle of mountainous regions of the N hemisphere, having a plumage that is golden brown on the back

goldeneye (ˈgəʊldənˌaɪ) *n, pl* **goldeneyes** *or* **goldeneye** either of two black-and-white diving ducks of northern regions

Golden Fleece *n Greek myth* the fleece of a winged ram stolen by Jason and the Argonauts

Golden Gate *n* a strait between the Pacific and San Francisco Bay: crossed by the **Golden Gate Bridge**, with a central span of 1280 m (4200 ft)

golden goal *n soccer* (in certain matches) the first goal scored in extra time, which wins the match for the side scoring it

golden goose *n* a goose in folklore that laid a golden egg every day until its greedy owner killed it in an attempt to get all the gold at once

golden handcuffs *pl n* payments deferred over a number of years that induce a person to stay with a particular company or in a particular job

Gg

golden handshake *n inf* a sum of money given to an employee, either on retirement or as compensation for loss of employment

golden hello *n* a payment made to a sought-after recruit on signing a contract of employment with a company

Golden Horn *n* an inlet of the Bosporus in NW Turkey, forming the harbour of Istanbul. Turkish name: **Haliç**

golden hour *n* the first hour after a serious accident, when it is crucial that the victim receives medical treatment in order to have a chance of surviving

golden mean *n* **1** the middle course between extremes **2** another term for **golden section**

golden number *n* a number between 1 and 19, used to indicate the position of any year in the Metonic cycle: so called from its importance in fixing the date of Easter

golden parachute *n inf* a clause in the employment contract of a senior executive providing for special benefits if the executive's employment is terminated as a result of a takeover

golden retriever *n* a large breed of dog with a silky wavy coat of a golden colour

goldenrod (ˈgəʊldənˌrɒd) *n* a plant of the composite family (Asteraceae) of North America, Europe, and Asia, having spikes of minute yellow florets

golden rule *n* **1** any of a number of rules of fair conduct, such as *Whatsoever ye would that men should do to you, do ye even so to them* (Matthew 7:12) **2** any important principle: *a golden rule of sailing is to wear a life jacket* **3** another name for **rule of three**

golden section *or* **mean** *n* the proportion of the two divisions of a straight line such that the smaller is to the larger as the larger is to the sum of the two

golden share *n* a share in a company that controls at least 51% of the voting rights, esp one retained by the UK

government in some privatization issues
golden syrup *n Brit* a light golden-coloured treacle produced by the evaporation of cane sugar juice, used to flavour cakes, puddings, etc
Golden Triangle *n* **the** an opium-producing area of SE Asia, comprising parts of Myanmar, Laos, and Thailand
golden wattle *n* **1** an Australian yellow-flowered plant that yields a useful gum and bark **2** any of several similar and related Australian plants
goldfinch (ˈgəʊldˌfɪntʃ) *n* a common European finch, the adult of which has a red-and-white face and yellow-and-black wings
goldfish (ˈgəʊldˌfɪʃ) *n, pl* **goldfish** *or* **goldfishes** a freshwater fish of E Europe and Asia, esp China, widely introduced as a pond or aquarium fish. It resembles the carp and has a typically golden or orange-red coloration
gold foil *n* thin gold sheet that is thicker than gold leaf
Golding (ˈgəʊldɪŋ) *n* Sir **William (Gerald)** 1911–93, English novelist noted for his allegories of man's proclivity for evil. His novels include *Lord of the Flies* (1954), *Darkness Visible* (1979), *Rites of Passage* (1980), *Close Quarters* (1987), and *Fire Down Below* (1989). Nobel prize for literature 1983
gold leaf *n* very thin gold sheet produced by rolling or hammering gold and used for gilding woodwork, etc
gold medal *n* a medal of gold, awarded to the winner of a competition or race
Goldoni (*Italian* golˈdoːni) *n* **Carlo** (ˈkarlo) 1707–93, Italian dramatist; author of over 250 plays in Italian or French, including *La Locandiera* (1753). His work introduced realistic Italian comedy, superseding the commedia dell'arte
gold plate *n* **1** a thin coating of gold, usually produced by electroplating **2** vessels or utensils made of gold > **ˌgold-ˈplate** *vb (tr)*
gold reserve *n* the gold reserved by a central bank to support domestic credit expansion, to cover balance of payments deficits, and to protect currency
gold rush *n* a large-scale migration of people to a territory where gold has been found
Goldschmidt (ˈgəʊldʃmɪt) *n* **Richard Benedikt** 1878–1958, US geneticist, born in Germany. He advanced the theory that heredity is determined by the chemical configuration of the chromosome molecule rather than by the qualities of the individual genes
goldsmith (ˈgəʊldˌsmɪθ) *n* **1** a dealer in articles made of gold **2** an artisan who makes such articles
▷ www.gold.org/goldwork
Goldsmith (ˈgəʊldˌsmɪθ) *n* **Oliver** ?1730–74, Irish poet, dramatist, and novelist. His works include the novel *The Vicar of Wakefield* (1766), the poem *The Deserted Village* (1770), and the comedy *She Stoops to Conquer* (1773)
gold standard *n* **1** a monetary system in which the unit of currency is defined with reference to gold **2** the supreme example of something against which others are judged or measured: *the current gold standard for breast cancer detection*
Goldwyn (ˈgəʊldwɪn) *n* **Samuel,** original name *Samuel Goldfish.* 1882–1974, US film producer, born in Poland
golf (gɒlf) *n* **1** a game played on a large open course, the object of which is to hit a ball using clubs, with as few strokes as possible, into each of usually 18 holes ▷ *vb* **2** *(intr)* to play golf [C15 ?from MDu. *colf* CLUB] > **ˈgolfer** *n*
▷ www.pga.com
▷ www.randa.org
golf ball *n* **1** a small resilient, usually white, ball of either two-piece or three-piece construction, the former consisting of a solid inner core with a thick covering of toughened material, the latter consisting of a liquid centre, rubber-wound core, and a thin layer of balata **2** (in some electric typewriters) a small detachable metal sphere, around the surface of which type characters are arranged
golf club *n* **1** any of various long-shafted clubs with wood or metal heads used to strike a golf ball **2a** an association of golf players, usually having its own course and facilities **2b** the premises of such an association
golf course *or* **links** *n* an area of ground laid out for the playing of golf
Golgi (*Italian* ˈgɔldʒi) *n* **Camillo** (kaˈmillo) 1844–1926, Italian neurologist and histologist, noted for his work on the central nervous system and his discovery in animal cells of the bodies known by his name: shared the Nobel prize for physiology or medicine 1906
Golgotha (ˈgɒlgəθə) *n* **1** another name for **Calvary** **2** *(sometimes not cap) now rare* a place of burial [C17 from LL, from Gk, from Aramaic, based on Heb. *gulgōleth* skull]
Goliath (gəˈlaɪəθ) *n Bible* a Philistine giant who was killed by David with a stone from his sling (I Samuel 17)
golliwog (ˈgɒlɪˌwɒg) *n* a soft doll with a black face, usually made of cloth or rags [C19 from a doll in a series of American children's books]
gollop (ˈgɒləp) *vb* **gollops, golloping, golloped** to eat or drink quickly or greedily [dialect var. of GULP]
golly (ˈgɒlɪ) *interj* an exclamation of mild surprise [C19 orig. a euphemism for GOD]
goloshes (gəˈlɒʃɪz) *pl n* a less common spelling of **galoshes**
Gomel (*Russian* ˈgɔmɪlj) *n* an industrial city in SE Belarus, on the River Sozh; an industrial centre. Pop: 513 000 (1998 est)
Gomorrah *or* **Gomorrha** (gəˈmɒrə) *n* **1** *Old Testament* one of two ancient cities near the Dead Sea, the other being Sodom, that were destroyed by God as a punishment for the wickedness of their inhabitants (Genesis 19:24) **2** any place notorious for vice and depravity > **Goˈmorrean** *or* **Goˈmorrhean** *adj*
Gomulka (gəˈmʊlkə) *n* **Władysław** (vwaˈdiswaf) 1905–82, Polish statesman; first secretary of the Polish Communist Party (1956–70)
-gon *n combining form* indicating a figure having a specified number of angles: *pentagon* [from Gk *-gōnon*, from *gōnia* angle]
gonad (ˈgɒnæd) *n* an animal organ in which gametes are produced, such as a testis or an ovary [C19 from NL *gonas*, from Gk *gonos* seed] > **ˈgonadal** *adj*
gonadotrophin (ˌgɒnədəʊˈtrəʊfɪn) *or* **gonadotropin** (-ˈtrəʊpɪn) *n* any of several hormones that stimulate the gonads. See also **HCG** > **gonadotrophic** (ˌgɒnədəʊˈtrɒfɪk) *or* **ˌgonadoˈtropic** *adj*
Gonaïves (*French* gɔnaiv) *n* a port in W Haiti, on the **Gulf of Gonaïves**; scene of the proclamation of Haiti's independence (1804). Pop: 63 291 (1992)
Goncharov (ˌgʌntʃəˈrɒf) *n* **Ivan Aleksandrovich** (ɪˈvan alɛksanˈdrɔvɪtʃ) 1812–91, Russian novelist: his best-known work is *Oblomov* (1859)
Goncourt (*French* gɔ̃kur) *n* **Edmond Louis Antoine Huot de** (ɛdmɔ̃ lwi ɑ̃twan yo də), 1822–96, and his brother, **Jules Alfred Huot de** (ʒyl alfrɛd), 1830–70, French writers, noted for their collaboration, esp on their *Journal*, and for the Académie Goncourt founded by Edmond's will
Gondar (ˈgɒndɑː) *n* a city in NW Ethiopia: capital of Ethiopia from the 17th century until 1868. Pop: 112 249 (1999 est)
gondola (ˈgɒndələ) *n* **1** a long narrow flat-bottomed boat with a high ornamented stem: traditionally used on the canals of Venice **2a** a car or cabin suspended from an airship or balloon **2b** a moving cabin suspended from a cable across a valley, etc **3** a flat-bottomed barge used on canals and rivers of the US **4** *US & Canad* a low open flat-bottomed railway goods wagon **5** a set of island shelves in a self-service shop: used for displaying goods **6** *Canad* a broadcasting booth built close to the roof of an ice-hockey stadium [C16 from It. (dialect), from Med. L, ? ult. from Gk *kondu* drinking vessel]

gondolier (ˌgɒndəˈlɪə) *n* a man who propels a gondola

Gondwanaland (gɒndˈwɑːnəˌlænd) *n* one of the two ancient supercontinents comprising chiefly what are now Africa, South America, Australia, Antarctica, and the Indian subcontinent [c19 from *Gondwana*, region in central north India, where the rock series was orig. found]

gone (gɒn) *vb* **1** the past participle of **go** ▷ *adj* (*usually postpositive*) **2** ended; past **3** lost; ruined **4** dead **5** spent; consumed; used up **6** *inf* faint or weak **7** *inf* having been pregnant (for a specified time): *six months gone* **8** (usually foll by *on*) *sl* in love (with)

goner (ˈgɒnə) *n sl* a person or thing beyond help or recovery, esp a person who is about to die

gonfalon (ˈgɒnfələn) *n* **1** a banner hanging from a crossbar, used esp by certain medieval Italian republics **2** a battle flag suspended crosswise on a staff, usually having a serrated edge [c16 from OIt., from OF, of Gmc origin]

gong (gɒŋ) *n* **1** a percussion instrument consisting of a metal platelike disc struck with a soft-headed drumstick **2** a rimmed metal disc, hollow metal hemisphere, or metal strip, tube, or wire that produces a note when struck **3** a fixed saucer-shaped bell, as on an alarm clock, struck by a mechanically operated hammer **4** *Brit sl* a medal ▷ *vb* **5** (*intr*) to sound a gong **6** (*tr*) (of traffic police) to summon (a driver) to stop by sounding a gong [c17 from Malay, imit.]

goniometer (ˌgəʊnɪˈɒmɪtə) *n* **1** an instrument for measuring the angles between the faces of a crystal **2** an instrument used to determine the bearing of a distant radio station [c18 via F from Gk *gōnia* angle] > **goniometric** (ˌgəʊnɪəˈmɛtrɪk) *adj* > ˌ**goniˈometry** *n*

-gonium *n combining form* indicating a seed or reproductive cell: *archegonium* [from NL, from Gk *gonos* seed]

gonococcus (ˌgɒnəʊˈkɒkəs) *n, pl* **gonococci** (-ˈkɒkaɪ, -ˈkɒkiː) a spherical bacterium that causes gonorrhoea

gonorrhoea *or esp US* **gonorrhea** (ˌgɒnəˈrɪə) *n* an infectious venereal disease characterized by a discharge of mucus and pus from the urethra or vagina [c16 from L, from Gk *gonos* semen + *rhoia* flux] > ˌ**gonorˈrhoeal** *or esp US* ˌ**gonorˈrheal** *adj*

-gony *n combining form* genesis, origin, or production: *cosmogony* [from L, from Gk, from *gonos* seed, procreation]

gonzo (ˈgɒnzəʊ) *sl* ▷ *adj* **1** wild or crazy **2** (of journalism) focusing on the eccentric personality or lifestyle of the reporter as much as on the events reported ▷ *n, pl* **gonzos** **3** a wild or crazy person [c20 coined by Hunter S. Thompson, US journalist, ? from It., lit.: fool, or Sp. *ganso* idiot (lit.: goose)]
▷ www.gonzo.org

goo (guː) *n inf* **1** a sticky substance **2** coy or sentimental language or ideas [c20 from ?]

good (gʊd) *adj* **better, best** **1** having admirable, pleasing, superior, or positive qualities; not negative, bad, or mediocre: *a good teacher* **2a** morally excellent or admirable; virtuous; righteous: *a good man* **2b** (*as collective n; preceded by the*): *the good* **3** suitable or efficient for a purpose: *a good winter coat* **4** beneficial or advantageous: *vegetables are good for you* **5** not ruined or decayed: *the meat is still good* **6** kindly or generous: *you are good to him* **7** valid or genuine: *I would not do this without good reason* **8** honourable or held in high esteem: *a good family* **9** financially secure, sound, or safe: *a good investment* **10** (of a draft, etc) drawn for a stated sum **11** (of debts) expected to be fully paid **12** clever, competent, or talented: *he's good at science* **13** obedient or well-behaved: *a good dog* **14** reliable, safe, or recommended: *a good make of clothes* **15** affording material pleasure: *the good life* **16** having a well-proportioned or generally fine appearance: *a good figure* **17** complete; full: *I took a good look round the house* **18** propitious; opportune: *a good time to ask for a rise* **19** satisfying or gratifying: *a good rest* **20** comfortable: *did you have a good night?* **21** newest or of the best quality: *keep the good plates for guests* **22** fairly large, extensive, or long: *a good distance away* **23** sufficient; ample: *we have a good supply of food* **24** **a good one** **24a** an unbelievable assertion **24b** a very funny joke **25** **as good as** virtually; practically: *it's as good as finished* **26** **good and** *inf* (intensifier): *good and mad* ▷ *interj* **27** an exclamation of approval, agreement, pleasure, etc ▷ *n* **28** moral or material advantage or use; benefit or profit: *for the good of our workers; what is the good of worrying?* **29** positive moral qualities; goodness; virtue; righteousness; piety **30** (*sometimes cap*) moral qualities seen as an abstract entity: *we must pursue the Good* **31** a good thing **32** **for good** (**and all**) forever; permanently: *I have left them for good* **33** **good for** *or* **on you** well done, well said, etc: a term of congratulation **34** **make good** **34a** to recompense or repair damage or injury **34b** to be successful **34c** to prove the truth of (a statement or accusation) **34d** to secure and retain (a position) **34e** to effect or fulfil (something intended or promised) ▷ See also **goods** [OE *gōd*] > ˈ**goodish** *adj*

Good Book *n* a name for the **Bible**

goodbye (ˌgʊdˈbaɪ) *sentence substitute* **1** farewell: a conventional expression used at leave-taking or parting with people ▷ *n* **2** a leave-taking; parting: *they prolonged their goodbyes* **3** a farewell: *they said goodbyes to each other* [c16 from *God be with ye*]

good day *sentence substitute* a conventional expression of greeting or farewell used during the day

good-for-nothing *n* **1** an irresponsible or worthless person ▷ *adj* **2** irresponsible; worthless

Good Friday *n* the Friday before Easter, observed as a commemoration of the Crucifixion of Jesus

Good Hope *n* **Cape of** See **Cape of Good Hope**

good-humoured *adj* being in or expressing a pleasant, tolerant, and kindly state of mind > ˌ**good-ˈhumouredly** *adv*

goodies (ˈgʊdɪz) *pl n* any objects, rewards, etc, considered particularly desirable

good-looking *adj* handsome or pretty

goodly (ˈgʊdlɪ) *adj* **goodlier, goodliest** **1** considerable: *a goodly amount of money* **2** *obs* attractive, pleasing, or fine > ˈ**goodliness** *n*

goodman (ˈgʊdmən) *n, pl* **goodmen** *arch* **1** a husband **2** a man not of gentle birth: used as a title **3** a master of a household

Goodman (ˈgʊdmən) *n* **Benny,** full name *Benjamin David Goodman*. 1909–86, US jazz clarinetist and bandleader, whose treatment of popular songs created the jazz idiom known as swing

good morning *sentence substitute* a conventional expression of greeting or farewell used in the morning

good-natured *adj* of a tolerant and kindly disposition > ˌ**good-ˈnaturedly** *adv*

goodness (ˈgʊdnɪs) *n* **1** the state or quality of being good **2** generosity; kindness **3** moral excellence; piety; virtue **4** what is good in something; essence ▷ *interj* **5** a euphemism for **God**: used as an exclamation of surprise

goodness of fit *n statistics* the extent to which observed sample values of a variable approximate to values derived from a theoretical density

good night *sentence substitute* a conventional expression of farewell, used in the evening or at night, esp when departing to bed

good-oh *or* **good-o** (ˈgʊdˈəʊ) *interj Brit & Austral inf* an exclamation of pleasure, agreement, etc

good oil *n* (usually preceded by *the*) *Austral sl* true or reliable facts, information, etc

goods (gʊdz) *pl n* **1** possessions and personal property **2** (*sometimes sing*) *econ* commodities that are tangible, usually movable, and generally not consumed at the same time as they are produced **3** articles of commerce;

Gg

merchandise **4** *chiefly Brit* **4a** merchandise when transported, esp by rail; freight **4b** *(as modifier): a goods train* **5 the goods 5a** *inf* that which is expected or promised: *to deliver the goods* **5b** *sl* the real thing **5c** *US & Canad sl* incriminating evidence (esp in **have the goods on someone**)

Good Samaritan *n* **1** *New Testament* a figure in one of Christ's parables (Luke 10:30–37) who is an example of compassion towards those in distress **2** a kindly person who helps another in difficulty or distress

Good Shepherd *n New Testament* a title given to Jesus Christ in John 10:11–12

good-sized *adj* quite large

good-tempered *adj* of a kindly and generous disposition

good turn *n* a helpful and friendly act; favour

goodwife ('gʊd,waɪf) *n, pl* **goodwives** *arch* **1** the mistress of a household **2** a woman not of gentle birth: used as a title

goodwill (,gʊd'wɪl) *n* **1** benevolence, approval, and kindly interest **2** willingness or acquiescence **3** an intangible asset of an enterprise reflecting its commercial reputation, customer connections, etc

Goodwin Sands ('gʊdwɪn) *pl n* a dangerous stretch of shoals at the entrance to the Strait of Dover: separated from the E coast of Kent by the Downs roadstead

Goodwood ('gʊd,wʊd) *n* an area in SE England, in Sussex: site of a famous racecourse and of **Goodwood House,** built 1780–1800

goody[1] ('gʊdɪ) *interj* **1** a child's exclamation of pleasure ▷ *n, pl* **goodies 2** short for **goody-goody 3** *inf* the hero in a film, book, etc **4** See **goodies**

goody[2] ('gʊdɪ) *n, pl* **goodies** *arch or literary* a married woman of low rank: used as a title: *Goody Two-Shoes* [C16 from GOODWIFE]

Goodyear ('gʊd,jɪə) *n* **Charles** 1800–60, US inventor of vulcanized rubber

goody-goody *n, pl* **goody-goodies 1** *inf* a smugly virtuous or sanctimonious person ▷ *adj* **2** smug and sanctimonious

gooey ('gu:ɪ) *adj* **gooier, gooiest** *inf* **1** sticky, soft, and often sweet **2** oversweet and sentimental > **'gooily** *adv*

goof (gu:f) *inf* ▷ *n* **1** a foolish error **2** a stupid person ▷ *vb* **3** to bungle (something); botch **4** *(intr;* often foll by *about* or *around)* to fool (around); mess (about) [C20 prob. from (dialect) *goff* simpleton, from OF *goffe* clumsy, from It. *goffo*, from ?]

go off *vb (intr)* **1** *(adv)* (of power, a water supply, etc) to cease to be available or functioning: *the lights suddenly went off* **2** *(adv)* to explode **3** *(adv)* to occur as specified: *the meeting went off well* **4** to leave (a place): *the actors went off stage* **5** *(adv)* (of a sensation) to gradually cease to be felt **6** *(adv)* to fall asleep **7** *(adv)* (of concrete, mortar, etc) to harden **8** *(adv) Brit inf* (of food, etc) to become stale or rotten **9** *(prep) Brit inf* to cease to like

goofy ('gu:fɪ) *adj* **goofier, goofiest** *inf* foolish; silly > **'goofily** *adv* > **'goofiness** *n*

goog (gʊg) *n Austral sl* an egg [?from Du. *oog*]

google ('gu:gᵊl) *vb (tr)* **1** to search for (something on the Internet) using a search engine **2** to check (the credentials of someone) by searching for websites containing his or name [C20 from *Google*, a popular search engine on the World Wide Web]

googly ('gu:glɪ) *n, pl* **googlies** *cricket* an off break bowled with a leg break action [C20 Austral from ?]

Goolagong ('gu:lə,gɒŋ) *n* **Evonne** See (Evonne) **Cawley**

Goole (gu:l) *n* an inland port in NE England, in the East Riding of Yorkshire at the confluence of the Ouse and Don Rivers, 75 km (47 miles) from the North Sea. Pop: 19 410 (1991)

goolie *or* **gooly** ('gu:lɪ) *n, pl* **goolies** *sl* **1** *(usually pl)* a testicle **2** *Austral* a stone or pebble [from Hindi *goli* ball]

goon (gu:n) *n* **1** a stupid or deliberately foolish person **2** *US inf* a thug hired to commit acts of violence or intimidation, esp in an industrial dispute [C20 partly from dialect *gooney* fool, partly after the character Alice the *Goon*, created by E. C. Segar (1894–1938), American cartoonist]

go on *vb (intr, mostly adv)* **1** to continue or proceed **2** to happen: *there's something peculiar going on here* **3** *(prep)* to ride on, esp as a treat: *children love to go on donkeys at the seaside* **4** *theatre* to make an entrance on stage **5** to talk excessively; chatter **6** to continue talking, esp after a short pause **7** to criticize or nag: *stop going on at me all the time!* ▷ *sentence substitute* **8** I don't believe what you're saying

gooney bird ('gu:nɪ) *n* an informal name for **albatross,** esp the black-footed albatross [C19 *gony* (orig. sailors' sl), prob. from dialect *gooney* fool, from ?]

goop (gu:p) *n US & Canad sl* **1** a rude or ill-mannered person **2** any sticky or semiliquid substance [C20 coined by G. Burgess (1866–1951), American humorist] > **'goopy** *adj*

goorie *or* **goory** ('gu:rɪ) *n, pl* **goories** *NZ inf* a mongrel dog [from Maori *kuri*]

goosander (gu:'sændə) *n* a common merganser (a duck) of Europe and North America, having a dark head and white body in the male [C17 prob. from GOOSE[1] + ON *önd* (genitive *andar*) duck]

goose[1] (gu:s) *n, pl* **geese 1** any of various web-footed long-necked birds typically larger and less aquatic than ducks. They are gregarious and migratory **2** the female of such a bird, as opposed to the male (gander) **3** *inf* a silly person **4** *(pl* **gooses***)* a pressing iron with a long curving handle, used esp by tailors **5** the flesh of the goose, used as food **6 cook someone's goose** *inf* **6a** to spoil someone's chances or plans completely **6b** to bring about someone's downfall **7 kill the goose that lays the golden eggs** See **golden goose** [OE *gōs*]

goose[2] (gu:s) *sl* ▷ *vb* **gooses, goosing, goosed 1** *(tr)* to prod (a person) playfully in the bottom ▷ *n, pl* **gooses 2** such a prod [C19 from GOOSE[1], prob. from a comparison with the jabbing of a goose's bill]

gooseberry ('gʊzbərɪ, -brɪ) *n, pl* **gooseberries 1** a Eurasian shrub having ovoid yellow-green or red-purple berries **2a** the berry of this plant **2b** *(as modifier): gooseberry jam* **3** *Brit inf* an unwanted single person, esp a third person with a couple (often in **play gooseberry**)

goose flesh *n* the bumpy condition of the skin induced by cold, fear, etc, caused by contraction of the muscles at the base of the hair follicles with consequent erection of papillae. Also called: **goose bumps, goose pimples, goose skin**

goosefoot ('gu:s,fʊt) *n, pl* **goosefoots** any typically weedy plant having small greenish flowers and leaves shaped like a goose's foot

goosegog ('gʊzgɒg) *n Brit* a dialect or informal word for **gooseberry** [from *goose* in GOOSEBERRY + *gog*, var. of GOB[1]]

goosegrass ('gu:s,grɑ:s) *n* another name for **cleavers**

gooseneck ('gu:s,nɛk) *n* something, such as a jointed pipe, in the form of the neck of a goose

goose step *n* **1** a military march step in which the leg is swung rigidly to an exaggerated height ▷ *vb* **goose-step, goose-steps, goose-stepping, goose-stepped 2** *(intr)* to march in goose step

Goossens ('gu:sənz) *n* **1** Sir **Eugene** 1893–1962, British composer and conductor, born in Belgium **2** his brother, **Leon** 1896–1988, British oboist

go out *vb (intr, adv)* **1** to depart from a room, house, country, etc **2** to cease to illuminate, burn, or function: *the fire has gone out* **3** to cease to be fashionable or popular: *that style went out ages ago!* **4** (of a broadcast) to be transmitted **5** to go to entertainments, social functions, etc **6** (usually foll by *with* or *together*) to associate (with a person of the opposite sex) regularly **7** (of workers) to begin to strike **8** *card games, etc* to get rid of the last card, token, etc, in one's hand

go over *vb (intr)* 1 to be received in a specified manner: *the concert went over very well* 2 *(prep)* Also: **go through** to examine and revise as necessary: *he went over the accounts* 3 *(prep)* to check and repair: *can you go over my car, please?* 4 *(prep)* Also: **go through** to rehearse: *I'll go over my lines before the play*

gopak ('gəʊ,pæk) *n* a spectacular high-leaping Russian peasant dance for men [from Russian]

Go-Ped ('gəʊ,pɛd) *n trademark* a motorized vehicle consisting of a low footboard on wheels, steered by handlebars

gopher ('gəʊfə) *n* 1 Also called: **pocket gopher** a burrowing rodent of North and Central America, having a thickset body, short legs, and cheek pouches 2 another name for **ground squirrel** 3 a burrowing tortoise of SE North America [C19 from earlier *megopher* or *magopher*, from ?]

Gorakhpur ('gɔːrək,pʊə) *n* a city in N India, in SE Uttar Pradesh: formerly an important Muslim garrison. Pop: 505 566 (1991)

goral ('gɔːrəl) *n* a small goat antelope inhabiting mountainous regions of S Asia [C19 from Hindi, prob. from Sansk.]

Gorbachov *or* **Gorbachev** (gərba'tʃɒf) *n* **Mikhail Sergeevich** (mixa'il sir'gjejivitʃ) born 1931, Soviet statesman; general secretary of the Soviet Communist Party (1985–91): president (1988–91). Nobel peace prize 1990. His reforms ended the Communist monopoly of power and led to the break-up of the Soviet Union

Gorbals ('gɔːbᵊlz) *n* **the** a district of Glasgow, formerly known for its slums

Gordian knot ('gɔːdɪən) *n* 1 (in Greek legend) a complicated knot, tied by King Gordius of Phrygia, that Alexander the Great cut with a sword 2 a complicated and intricate problem (esp in **cut the Gordian knot**)

Gordimer ('gɔːdɪmə) *n* **Nadine** born 1923, South African novelist. Her books include *The Lying Days* (1952), *July's People* (1981), *The Conservationist* (1974), which won the Booker prize, *None to Accompany Me* (1994), and *The House Gun* (1998). Her works were banned in South Africa for their condemnation of apartheid. Nobel prize for literature 1991

Gordon ('gɔːdᵊn) *n* 1 **Adam Lindsay** 1833–70, Australian poet and horseman, born in the Azores, who developed the bush ballad as a literary form, esp in *Bush Ballads and Galloping Rhymes* (1870) 2 **Charles George,** known as *Chinese Gordon*. 1833–85, British general and administrator. He helped to crush the Taiping rebellion (1863–64), and was governor of the Sudan (1877–80), returning in 1884 to aid Egyptian forces against the Mahdi. He was killed in the siege of Khartoum 3 **Dexter (Keith)** 1923–90, US jazz tenor saxophonist 4 **Lord George** 1751–93, English religious agitator. He led the Protestant opposition to legislation relieving Roman Catholics of certain disabilities, which culminated in the Gordon riots (1780) 5 **George Hamilton** See (4th Earl of) **Aberdeen**

gore¹ (gɔː) *n* 1 blood shed from a wound, esp when coagulated 2 *inf* killing, fighting, etc [OE *gor* dirt]

gore² (gɔː) *vb* **gores, goring, gored** *(tr)* (of an animal, such as a bull) to pierce or stab (a person or another animal) with a horn or tusk [C16 prob. from OE *gār* spear]

gore³ (gɔː) *n* 1 a tapering or triangular piece of material used in making a shaped skirt, umbrella, etc ▷ *vb* **gores, goring, gored** 2 *(tr)* to make into or with a gore or gores [OE *gāra*] > **gored** *adj*

Gore (gɔː) *n* **Al(bert) Jr** born 1948, US Democrat politician; vice president of the US (1993–2001)

Górecki (gɔ'rɛkɪ) *n* **Henryk (Mikołaj)** born 1933, Polish composer, best known for his sombre third symphony (1979)

Gorey ('gɔːrɪ) *n* **Edward St John** 1925–2000, US illustrator and author, noted for his bizarre humour in such works as *The Unstrung Harp* (1953) and *The Wuggly Ump* (1963)

gorge (gɔːdʒ) *n* 1 a deep ravine, esp one through which a river runs 2 the contents of the stomach 3 feelings of disgust or resentment (esp in **one's gorge rises**) 4 an obstructing mass: *an ice gorge* 5 *fortifications* a narrow rear entrance to a work 6 *arch* the throat or gullet ▷ *vb* **gorges, gorging, gorged** 7 to swallow (food) ravenously 8 *(tr)* to stuff (oneself) with food [C14 from OF *gorger* to stuff, from *gorge* throat, from LL *gurga*, from L *gurges* whirlpool]

gorgeous ('gɔːdʒəs) *adj* 1 strikingly beautiful or magnificent: *a gorgeous array; a gorgeous girl* 2 *inf* extremely pleasing, fine, or good: *gorgeous weather* [C15 from OF *gorgias* elegant, from *gorge*; see GORGE] > **'gorgeously** *adv* > **'gorgeousness** *n*

gorget ('gɔːdʒɪt) *n* 1 a collar-like piece of armour worn to protect the throat 2 a part of a wimple worn by women to cover the throat and chest, esp in the 14th century 3 a band of distinctive colour on the throat of an animal, esp a bird [C15 from OF, from *gorge*; see GORGE]

Gorgio ('gɔːdʒɪəʊ) *n, pl* **Gorgios** the Gypsy name for a non-Gypsy [C19 from Romany]

Gorgon ('gɔːgən) *n* 1 *Greek myth* any of three winged monstrous sisters who had live snakes for hair, huge teeth, and brazen claws 2 *(often not cap) inf* a fierce or unpleasant woman [via L *Gorgō* from Gk, from *gorgos* terrible]

gorgonian (gɔː'gəʊnɪən) *n* any of various corals having a horny or calcareous branching skeleton, such as the sea fans and red corals

Gorgonzola (,gɔːgən'zəʊlə) *n* a semihard blue-veined cheese of sharp flavour, made from pressed milk [C19 after *Gorgonzola*, It. town where it originated]

Gorica ('gɔritsa) *n* the Serbo-Croat name for **Gorizia**

gorilla (gə'rɪlə) *n* 1 the largest anthropoid ape, inhabiting the forests of central W Africa. It is stocky with a short muzzle and coarse dark hair 2 *inf* a large, strong, and brutal-looking man [C19 NL, from Gk *Gorillai*, an African tribe renowned for their hirsute appearance]

Göring *or* **Goering** (*German* 'gøːrɪŋ) *n* **Hermann Wilhelm** ('hɛrman 'vɪlhɛlm) 1893–1946, German Nazi leader and field marshal. He commanded Hitler's storm troops (1923) and as Prussian prime minister and German commissioner for aviation (1933–45) he founded the Gestapo and mobilized Germany for war. Sentenced to death at Nuremberg, he committed suicide

Gorizia (*Italian* go'rittsja) *n* a city in NE Italy, in Friuli-Venezia Giulia, on the Isonzo River: cultural centre under the Hapsburgs. Pop: 39 230 (1990). German name: **Görz** Serbo-Croat name: **Gorica**

Gorki¹ *or* **Gorky** (*Russian* 'gɔrjkij) *n* the former name (until 1991) of **Nizhni Novgorod**

Gorki² *or* **Gorky** (*Russian* 'gɔrjkij) *n* **Maxim** (mak'sim), pen name of *Aleksey Maximovich Peshkov*. 1868–1936, Russian novelist, dramatist, and short-story writer, noted for his depiction of the outcasts of society. His works include the play *The Lower Depths* (1902), the novel *Mother* (1907), and an autobiographical trilogy (1913–23)

Gorky ('gɔːkɪ) *n* **Arshile** ('ɑːʃɪl) 1904–48, US abstract expressionist painter, born in Armenia. Influenced by Picasso and Miró, his style is characterized by fluid lines and resonant colours

Görlitz (*German* 'gœrlɪts) *n* a city in E Germany, in Saxony on the Neisse River: divided in 1945, the area on the E bank of the river becoming the Polish town of **Zgorzelec.** Pop: 70 450 (1991)

Gorlovka (*Russian* 'gɔrləfkə) *n* a city in SE Ukraine in the centre of the Donets Basin: a major coal-mining centre. Pop: 309 300 (1998 est)

gormand ('gɔːmənd) *n* a less common spelling of **gourmand**

Gg

gormandize *or* **gormandise** ('gɔːmən,daɪz) *vb* **gormandizes, gormandizing, gormandized** *or* **gormandises, gormandising, gormandised** to eat (food) greedily and voraciously > '**gormand,izer** *or* '**gormand,iser** *n*

gormless ('gɔːmlɪs) *adj Brit inf* stupid; dull [C19 var. of C18 *gaumless*, from dialect *gome*, from OE *gom, gome*, from ON *gaumr* heed]

Gorno-Altai Republic ('gɔːnəʊæl'taɪ, -'æltaɪ) *n* a constituent republic of S Russia: mountainous, rising over 4350 m (14 500 ft) in the Altai Mountains of the south. Capital: Gorno-Altaisk. Pop: 205 000 (2000 est). Area: 92 600 sq km (35 740 sq miles). Also called: **Altai Republic**

Gorno-Badakhshan Autonomous Republic (-bə'dækʃɑːn) *n* an administrative division of Tajikistan: generally mountainous and inaccessible. Capital: Khorog. Pop: 206 000 (1999 est). Area: 63 700 sq km (24 590 sq miles). Also called: **Badakhshan**

go round *vb (intr)* **1** *(adv)* to be sufficient: *are there enough sweets to go round?* **2** to circulate (in): *measles is going round the school* **3** to be long enough to encircle: *will that belt go round you?*

gorse (gɔːs) *n* an evergreen shrub which has yellow flowers and thick green spines instead of leaves. Also called: **furze, whin** [OE *gors*] > '**gorsy** *adj*

Gorton ('gɔːtᵊn) *n* Sir **John Grey** 1911–2002, Australian statesman; prime minister (1968–71)

gory ('gɔːrɪ) *adj* **gorier, goriest 1** horrific or bloodthirsty: *a gory story* **2** involving bloodshed and killing: *a gory battle* **3** covered in gore > '**gorily** *adv* > '**goriness** *n*

Görz (gœrts) *n* the German name for **Gorizia**

gosh (gɒʃ) *interj* an exclamation of mild surprise or wonder [C18 euphemistic for GOD]

goshawk ('gɒs,hɔːk) *n* a large hawk of Europe, Asia, and North America, having a bluish-grey back and wings and paler underparts: used in falconry [OE *gōshafoc*; see GOOSE[1], HAWK[1]]

Goshen ('gəʊʃən) *n* **1** a region of ancient Egypt, east of the Nile delta: granted to Jacob and his descendants by the king of Egypt and inhabited by them until the Exodus (Genesis 45:10) **2** a place of comfort and plenty

gosling ('gɒzlɪŋ) *n* **1** a young goose **2** an inexperienced or youthful person [C15 from ON *gæslingr*; rel. to Danish *gäsling*; see GOOSE[1], -LING[1]]

go-slow *n* **1** *Brit* a deliberate slackening of the rate of production by organized labour as a tactic in industrial conflict. US and Canad equivalent: **slowdown** ▷ *vb* **go slow 2** *(intr)* to work deliberately slowly as a tactic in industrial conflict

gospel ('gɒspᵊl) *n* **1** Also called: **gospel truth** an unquestionable truth: *to take someone's word as gospel* **2** a doctrine maintained to be of great importance **3** Black religious music originating in the churches of the Southern states of the United States **4** the message or doctrine of a religious teacher **5a** the story of Christ's life and teachings as narrated in the Gospels **5b** the good news of salvation in Jesus Christ **5c** *(as modifier)*: *the gospel story* [OE *gōdspell*, from *gōd* GOOD + *spell* message; see SPELL[2]]

▷ www.gospelmusic.org
▷ www.allmusic.com

Gospel ('gɒspᵊl) *n* **1** any of the first four books of the New Testament, namely Matthew, Mark, Luke, and John **2** a reading from one of these in a religious service

Gosport ('gɒs,pɔːt) *n* a town in S England, in Hampshire on Portsmouth harbour: naval base since the 16th century. Pop: 67 802 (1991)

goss (gɒs) *n inf* short for **gossip**

gossamer ('gɒsəmə) *n* **1** a gauze or silk fabric of the very finest texture **2** a filmy cobweb often seen on foliage or floating in the air **3** anything resembling gossamer in fineness or filminess [C14 (in sense 2): prob. from *gos* GOOSE[1] + *somer* SUMMER; the phrase refers to *St Martin's summer*, a period in November when goose was traditionally eaten; from the prevalence of the cobweb in the autumn] > '**gossamery** *adj*

Gosse (gɒs) *n* Sir **Edmund William** 1849–1928, English critic and poet, noted particularly for his autobiographical work *Father and Son* (1907)

gossip ('gɒsɪp) *n* **1** casual and idle chat **2** a conversation involving malicious chatter or rumours about other people **3** Also called: **gossipmonger** a person who habitually talks about others, esp maliciously **4** light easy communication: *to write a letter full of gossip* **5** *arch* a close woman friend ▷ *vb* **gossips, gossiping, gossiped 6** *(intr; often foll by about)* to talk casually or maliciously (about other people) [OE *godsibb* godparent, from GOD + SIB; came to be applied esp to a woman's female friends at the birth of a child, hence a woman fond of light talk] > '**gossiper** *n* > '**gossipy** *adj*

gossypol ('gɒsɪ,pɒl) *n* a toxic crystalline pigment that is a constituent of cottonseed oil [C19 from Mod. L *gossypium* cotton plant + -OL[1]]

got (gɒt) *vb* **1** the past tense and past participle of **get 2 have got 2a** to possess **2b** *(takes an infinitive)* used as an auxiliary to express compulsion: *I've got to get a new coat*

Göta *(Swedish* 'jøːta) *n* a river in S Sweden, draining Lake Vänern and flowing south-southwest to the Kattegat: forms part of the **Göta Canal,** which links Göteborg in the west with Stockholm in the east. Length: 93 km (58 miles)

Göteborg *(Swedish* jœtə'bɔrj) *or* **Gothenburg** *n* a port in SW Sweden, at the mouth of the Göta River: the largest port and second largest city in the country; developed through the Swedish East India Company and grew through Napoleon's continental blockade and with the opening of the Göta Canal (1832); university (1891). Pop: 462 470 (2000 est)

Goth (gɒθ) *n* **1** a member of an East Germanic people from Scandinavia who settled south of the Baltic early in the first millennium AD. They moved on to the Ukrainian steppes and raided and later invaded many parts of the Roman Empire from the 3rd to the 5th century **2** a rude or barbaric person **3** a fan of a style of rock music with mournful lyrics, who dresses in black and wears heavy make-up [C14 from LL (pl) *Gothī* from Gk *Gothoi*]

▷ www.fernweb.pwp.blueyonder.co.uk/mf/goths.htm
▷ www.wikipedia.org/wiki/Goths

Gotha ('gəʊθə; *German* 'goːta) *n* a town in central Germany, in Thuringia on the N edge of the Thuringian forest: capital of Saxe-Coburg-Gotha (1826–1918); noted for the *Almanach de Gotha* (a record of the royal and noble houses of Europe, first published in 1764). Pop: 57 360 (latest est)

Gothenburg ('gɒθən,bɜːg) *n* the English name for **Göteborg**

Gothic ('gɒθɪk) *adj* **1** denoting, relating to, or resembling the style of architecture that was used in W Europe from the 12th to the 16th centuries, characterized by the lancet arch, the ribbed vault, and the flying buttress. See also **Gothic Revival 2** of or relating to the style of sculpture, painting, or other arts as practised in W Europe from the 12th to the 16th centuries **3** *(sometimes not cap)* of or relating to a literary style characterized by gloom, the grotesque, and the supernatural, popular esp in the late 18th century: when used of modern literature, films, etc, sometimes spelt: **Gothick 4** of, relating to, or characteristic of the Goths or their language **5** *(sometimes not cap)* primitive and barbarous in style, behaviour, etc **6** of or relating to the Middle Ages ▷ *n* **7** Gothic architecture or art **8** the extinct language of the ancient Goths, known mainly from fragments of a translation of the Bible made in the 4th century by Bishop Wulfila **9** Also called (esp Brit): **black**

letter a family of heavy script typefaces > 'Gothically *adv*
▷ www.artlex.com/ArtLex/g/gothic.html
▷ www.greatbuildings.com/types/styles/gothic.html
▷ www.artcyclopedia.com/history/gothic.html

Gothic Revival *n* a Gothic style of architecture popular between the late 18th and late 19th centuries, exemplified by the Houses of Parliament in London (1840). Also called: **neogothic**
▷ www.building-history.pwp.blueyonder.co.uk
▷ www.bc.edu/bc_org/avp/cas/fnart/fa267/19house2.html
▷ www.britainexpress.com/architecture

go through *vb (intr)* **1** *(adv)* to be approved or accepted: *the amendment went through* **2** *(prep)* to consume; exhaust: *we went through our supplies in a day* **3** *(prep)* Also: **go over** to examine: *he went through the figures* **4** *(prep)* to suffer: *she went through tremendous pain* **5** *(prep)* Also: **go over** to rehearse: *let's just go through the details again* **6** *(prep)* to search: *she went through the cupboards* **7** *(adv; foll by with)* to come or bring to a successful conclusion, often by persistence

Gotland ('gɒtlənd; *Swedish* 'gɔtlant), **Gothland** ('gɒθlənd), *or* **Gottland** ('gɒtlənd) *n* an island in the Baltic Sea, off the SE coast of Sweden: important trading centre since the Bronze Age; long disputed between Sweden and Denmark, finally becoming Swedish in 1645; tourism and agriculture now important. Capital: Visby. Pop: (including associated islands) 57 313 (2001 est). Area: 3140 sq km (1212 sq miles)

go together *vb (intr, adv)* **1** to be mutually suited; harmonize: *the colours go well together* **2** *inf* (of two people) to have a romantic or sexual relationship: *they had been going together for two years*

gotten ('gɒtᵊn) *vb chiefly US* a past participle of **get**

Götterdämmerung (ˌgɒtə'dɛməˌrʊŋ) *n German myth* the twilight of the gods; their ultimate destruction in a battle with the forces of evil

Gottfried von Strassburg (*German* 'gɔtfriːt fɔn 'ʃtraːsbʊrk) *n* early 13th-century German poet; author of the incomplete epic *Tristan and Isolde*, the version of the legend that served as the basis of Wagner's opera

Göttingen ('gœtɪŋən) *n* a city in central Germany, in Lower Saxony: important member of the Hanseatic League (14th century); university, founded in 1734 by George II of England. Pop: 127 366 (1999 est)

gouache (gʊ'ɑːʃ) *n* **1** Also called: **body colour** a painting technique using opaque watercolour in which the pigments are bound with glue and lighter tones contain white **2** the paint used in this technique **3** a painting done by this method [c19 from F, from It. *guazzo* puddle, from L, from *aqua* water]

Gouda ('gaʊdə; *Dutch* 'xɔudaː) *n* **1** a town in the W Netherlands, in South Holland province: important medieval cloth trade; famous for its cheese. Pop: 69 917 (1994) **2** a large round Dutch cheese, mild and similar in taste to Edam

gouge (gaʊdʒ) *vb* **gouges, gouging, gouged** *(mainly tr)* **1** (usually foll by *out*) to scoop or force (something) out of its position **2** (sometimes foll by *out*) to cut (a hole or groove) in (something) with a sharp instrument or tool **3** *US & Canad inf* to extort from **4** *(also intr) Austral* to dig for (opal) ▷ *n* **5** a type of chisel with a blade that has a concavo-convex section **6** a mark or groove made as with a gouge **7** *US & Canad inf* extortion; swindling [c15 from F, from LL *gulbia* a chisel, of Celtic origin] > '**gouger** *n*

goujon ('guːʒɒn) *n* a small strip of fish or chicken, coated in breadcrumbs and deep-fried [F, lit.: gudgeon]

goulash ('guːlæʃ) *n* **1** Also called: **Hungarian goulash** a rich stew, originating in Hungary, made of beef, lamb, or veal highly seasoned with paprika **2** *bridge* a method of dealing in threes and fours without first shuffling the cards, to produce freak hands [c19 from Hungarian *gulyás hus* herdsman's meat, from *gulya* herd]

Gould (guːld) *n* **1** **Benjamin Apthorp** 1824–96, US astronomer: the first to use the telegraph to determine longitudes; founded the *Astronomical Journal* (1849) **2** **Glenn** 1932–82, Canadian pianist

go under *vb (intr, mainly adv)* **1** *(also prep)* to sink below (a surface) **2** to be overwhelmed: *the firm went under in the economic crisis*

Gounod ('guːnəʊ; *French* guno) *n* **Charles François** (ʃarl frɑ̃swa) 1818–93, French composer of the operas *Faust* (1859) and *Romeo and Juliet* (1867)

go up *vb (intr, mainly adv)* **1** *(also prep)* to move or lead as to a higher place or level; rise; increase: *prices are always going up* **2** to be destroyed: *the house went up in flames* **3** *Brit* to go or return (to college or university) at the beginning of a term or academic year

gourami ('gʊərəmɪ) *n, pl* **gourami** *or* **gouramis** **1** a large SE Asian labyrinth fish used for food **2** any of various other labyrinth fishes, many of which are brightly coloured and popular aquarium fishes [from Malay *gurami*]

gourd (gʊəd) *n* **1** the fruit of any of various plants of the cucumber family, esp the bottle gourd and some squashes, whose dried shells are used for ornament, drinking cups, etc **2** any plant that bears this fruit **3** a bottle or flask made from the dried shell of the bottle gourd [c14 from OF *gourde*, ult. from L *cucurbita*]

gourmand ('gʊəmənd) *or* **gormand** *n* a person devoted to eating and drinking, esp to excess [c15 from OF *gourmant*, from ?] > '**gourmandˌism** *n*

gourmet ('gʊəmeɪ) *n* a person who cultivates a discriminating palate for the enjoyment of good food and drink [c19 from F, from OF *gromet* serving boy]

gout (gaʊt) *n* **1** a metabolic disease characterized by painful inflammation of certain joints, esp of the big toe, caused by deposits of sodium urate **2** *arch* a drop or splash, esp of blood [c13 from OF, from L *gutta* a drop] > '**gouty** *adj* > '**goutily** *adv* > '**goutiness** *n*

Gov. *or* **gov.** *abbrev for* governor

govern ('gʌvᵊn) *vb (mainly tr)* **1** *(also intr)* to direct and control the actions, affairs, policies, functions, etc, of (an organization, nation, etc); rule **2** to exercise restraint over; regulate or direct: *to govern one's temper* **3** to decide or determine (something): *his injury governed his decision to avoid sports* **4** to control the speed of (an engine, machine, etc) using a governor **5** (of a word) to determine the inflection of (another word): *Latin nouns govern adjectives that modify them* [c13 from OF, from L *gubernāre* to steer, from Gk *kubernan*] > '**governable** *adj*

governance ('gʌvənəns) *n* **1** government, control, or authority **2** the action, manner, or system of governing

governess ('gʌvənɪs) *n* a woman teacher employed in a private household to teach and train the children

government ('gʌvənmənt, 'gʌvəmənt) *n* **1** the exercise of political authority over the actions, affairs, etc, of a political unit, people, etc; the action of governing; political rule and administration **2** the system or form by which a community, etc, is ruled: *tyrannical government* **3a** the executive policy-making body of a political unit, community, etc; ministry or administration **3b** *(cap when of a specific country)*: *the British Government* **4a** the state and its administration: *blame it on the government* **4b** *(as modifier)*: *a government agency* **5** regulation; direction **6** *grammar* the determination of the form of one word by another word > **governmental** (ˌgʌvən'mɛntᵊl, ˌgʌvə'mɛntᵊl) *adj* > ˌ**govern'mentally** *adv*
▷ www.lib.umich.edu/govdocs/index.html
▷ www.library.northwestern.edu/govpub/resource/internat
▷ www.wto.org/english/res_e/statis_e/natl_e.pdf
▷ www.politicalresources.net
▷ www.lib.berkeley.edu/doemoff/gov_intlgen.html
▷ www.psa.ac.uk/www/archives.htm

Gg

Government House *n* the official residence of a representative of the British Crown (such as a Canadian Lieutenant-Governor or an Australian Governor General) in a state or province that recognizes the British sovereign as Head of the Commonwealth

governor ('gʌvənə) *n* **1** a person who governs **2** the ruler or chief magistrate of a colony, province, etc **3** the representative of the Crown in a British colony **4** *Brit* the senior administrator of a society, prison, etc **5** the chief executive of any state in the US **6** a device that controls the speed of an engine, esp by regulating the supply of fuel **7** *Brit inf* a name or title of respect for a father, employer, etc > **'governor,ship** *n*

governor general *n, pl* **governors general** *or* **governor generals** **1** the representative of the Crown in a dominion of the Commonwealth or a British colony; vicegerent **2** *Brit* a governor with jurisdiction or precedence over other governors > **,governor-'general,ship** *n*

Govt *or* **govt** *abbrev for* government

Gower[1] ('gaʊə) *n* **the** a peninsula in S Wales, in Swansea county on the Bristol Channel: mainly agricultural with several resorts

Gower[2] ('gaʊə) *n* **John** ?1330–1408, English poet, noted particularly for his tales of love, the *Confessio Amantis*

go with *vb (intr, prep)* **1** to accompany **2** to blend or harmonize: *that new wallpaper goes well with the furniture* **3** to be a normal part of: *three acres of land go with the house* **4** (of two people of the opposite sex) to associate frequently with each other

go without *vb (intr) chiefly Brit* to be denied or deprived of (something, esp food): *if you don't like your tea you can go without*

gowk (gaʊk) *n Scot & N English dialect* **1** a fool **2** a cuckoo [from ON *gaukr* cuckoo]

gown (gaʊn) *n* **1** any of various outer garments, such as a woman's elegant or formal dress, a dressing robe, or a protective garment, esp one worn by surgeons during operations **2** a loose wide garment indicating status, such as worn by academics **3** the members of a university as opposed to the other residents of the university town ▷ *vb* **4** *(tr)* to supply with or dress in a gown [c14 from OF, from LL *gunna* garment made of leather or fur, of Celtic origin]

goy (gɔɪ) *n, pl* **goyim** ('gɔɪɪm) *or* **goys** a Jewish word for a **Gentile** [from Yiddish, from Heb. *goi* people] > **'goyish** *adj*

Goya ('gɔɪə; *Spanish* 'goja) *n* **Francisco de** (fran'θisko de), full name *Francisco José de Goya y Lucientes*. 1746–1828, Spanish painter and etcher; well known for his portraits, he became court painter to Charles IV of Spain (1799). He recorded the French invasion of Spain in a series of etchings *The Disasters of War* (1810–14) and two paintings *2 May 1808* and *3 May 1808* (1814)

GP *abbrev for:* **1** Gallup Poll **2** *music* general pause **3** general practitioner **4** (in Britain) graduated pension **5** Grand Prix

GPMU (in Britain) *abbrev for* Graphical, Paper and Media Union

GPO *abbrev for* general post office

GPRS *abbrev for* general packet radio service: a telecommunications system providing very fast internet connections for mobile phones

GPS *abbrev for* Global Positioning System: a satellite-based navigation system

Gr. *abbrev for:* **1** Grecian **2** Greece **3** Greek

Graafian follicle ('grɑːfɪən) *n* a fluid-filled vesicle in the mammalian ovary containing a developing egg cell [c17 after R. de *Graaf* (1641–73), Du. anatomist]

grab (græb) *vb* **grabs, grabbing, grabbed** **1** to seize hold of (something) **2** *(tr)* to seize illegally or unscrupulously **3** *(tr)* to arrest; catch **4** *(tr) inf* to catch the attention or interest of; impress ▷ *n* **5** the act or an instance of grabbing **6** a mechanical device for gripping objects, esp the hinged jaws of a mechanical excavator **7** something that is grabbed [c16 prob. from MLow G or MDu. *grabben*] > **'grabber** *n*

grab bag *n* **1** a collection of miscellaneous things **2** *US, Canad, & Austral* a bag or other container from which gifts are drawn at random

grabby ('grabɪ) *adj* **grabbier, grabbiest** **1** greedy or selfish **2** direct, stimulating, or attention-grabbing: *grabbier opening paragraphs*

Gracchus ('grækəs) *n* **Tiberius Sempronius** (taɪ'bɪərɪəs sɛm'prəʊnɪəs) ?163–133 BC, and his younger brother, **Gaius Sempronius** ('gaɪəs), 153–121 BC, known as *the Gracchi*. Roman tribunes and reformers. Tiberius attempted to redistribute public land among the poor but was murdered in the ensuing riot. Violence again occurred when the reform was revived by Gaius, and he too was killed

grace (greɪs) *n* **1** elegance and beauty of movement, form, expression, or proportion **2** a pleasing or charming quality **3** goodwill or favour **4** a delay granted for the completion of a task or payment of a debt **5** a sense of propriety and consideration for others **6** *(pl)* **6a** affectation of manner (esp in **airs and graces**) **6b in (someone's) good graces** regarded favourably and with kindness by (someone) **7** mercy; clemency **8** *Christian theol* **8a** the free and unmerited favour of God shown towards man **8b** the divine assistance given to man in spiritual rebirth **8c** the condition of being favoured or sanctified by God **8d** an unmerited gift, favour, etc, granted by God **9** a short prayer recited before or after a meal to give thanks for it **10** *music* a melodic ornament or decoration **11 with (a) bad grace** unwillingly or grudgingly **12 with (a) good grace** willingly or cheerfully ▷ *vb* **graces, gracing, graced** **13** *(tr)* to add elegance and beauty to: *flowers graced the room* **14** *(tr)* to honour or favour: *to grace a party with one's presence* **15** to ornament or decorate (a melody, part, etc) with nonessential notes [c12 from OF, from L *grātia*, from *grātus* pleasing]

Grace[1] (greɪs) *n* (preceded by *your, his,* or *her*) a title used to address or refer to a duke, duchess, or archbishop

Grace[2] (greɪs) *n* **W(illiam) G(ilbert)** 1848–1915, English cricketer

grace-and-favour *n (modifier) Brit* (of a house, flat, etc) owned by the sovereign and granted free of rent to a person to whom the sovereign wishes to express gratitude

graceful ('greɪsfʊl) *adj* characterized by beauty of movement, style, form, etc > **'gracefully** *adv* > **'gracefulness** *n*

graceless ('greɪslɪs) *adj* **1** lacking manners **2** lacking elegance > **'gracelessly** *adv* > **'gracelessness** *n*

grace note *n music* a note printed in small type to indicate that it is melodically and harmonically nonessential

Graces ('greɪsɪz) *pl n Greek myth.* three sister goddesses, givers of charm and beauty

gracious ('greɪʃəs) *adj* **1** characterized by or showing kindness and courtesy **2** condescendingly courteous, benevolent, or indulgent **3** characterized by or suitable for a life of elegance, ease, and indulgence: *gracious living* **4** merciful or compassionate ▷ *interj* **5** an expression of mild surprise or wonder > **'graciously** *adv* > **'graciousness** *n*

grackle ('græk^əl) *n* **1** an American songbird of the oriole family, having a dark iridescent plumage **2** any of various starlings, such as the Indian grackle or hill myna [c18 from NL, from L *grāculus* jackdaw]

grad. *abbrev for:* **1** *maths* gradient **2** *education* graduate(d)

gradate (grə'deɪt) *vb* **gradates, gradating, gradated** **1** to change or cause to change imperceptibly, as from one colour, tone, or degree to another **2** *(tr)* to arrange in grades or ranks

gradation (grəˈdeɪʃən) *n* **1** a series of systematic stages; gradual progression **2** (*often pl*) a stage or degree in such a series or progression **3** the act or process of arranging or forming in stages, grades, etc, or of progressing evenly **4** (in painting, drawing, or sculpture) transition from one colour, tone, or surface to another through a series of very slight changes **5** *linguistics* any change in the quality or length of a vowel within a word indicating certain distinctions, such as inflectional or tense differentiations. See **ablaut** > **graˈdational** *adj*

grade (greɪd) *n* **1** a position or degree in a scale, as of quality, rank, size, or progression: *high-grade timber* **2** a group of people or things of the same category **3** *chiefly US* a military or other rank **4** a stage in a course of progression **5** a mark or rating indicating achievement or the worth of work done, as at school **6** *US & Canad* a unit of pupils of similar age or ability taught together at school **7** **make the grade** *inf* **7a** to reach the required standard **7b** to succeed ▷ *vb* **grades, grading, graded** **8** (*tr*) to arrange according to quality, rank, etc **9** (*tr*) to determine the grade of or assign a grade to **10** (*intr*) to achieve or deserve a grade or rank **11** to change or blend (something) gradually; merge **12** (*tr*) to level (ground, a road, etc) to a suitable gradient [c16 from F, from L *gradus* step, from *gradī* to step]

-grade *adj combining form* indicating a kind or manner of movement or progression: *plantigrade; retrograde* [via F from L *-gradus*, from *gradus* a step, from *gradī* to walk]

grade inflation *n* an apparently continual increase in numbers of students attaining high examination grades, or the practice of awarding grades in this way

gradely (ˈgreɪdlɪ) *adj* **gradelier, gradeliest** *Midland English dialect* fine; excellent [c13 from ON *greidhligr*, from *greidhr* ready]

grader (ˈgreɪdə) *n* **1** a person or thing that grades **2** a machine that levels earth, rubble, etc, as in road construction

gradient (ˈgreɪdɪənt) *n* **1** Also called (esp US): **grade** a part of a railway, road, etc, that slopes upwards or downwards; inclination **2** Also called (esp US and Canad): **grade** a measure of such a slope, esp the ratio of the vertical distance between two points on the slope to the horizontal distance between them **3** *physics* a measure of the change of some physical quantity, such as temperature or electric potential, over a specified distance **4** *maths* (of a curve) the slope of the tangent at any point on a curve with respect to the horizontal axis ▷ *adj* **5** sloping uniformly [c19 from L *gradiēns* stepping, from *gradī* to go]

gradin (ˈgreɪdɪn) *or* **gradine** (grəˈdi:n) *n* **1** a ledge above or behind an altar for candles, etc, to stand on **2** one of a set of steps or seats arranged on a slope, as in an amphitheatre [c19 from F, from It. *gradino*, dim. of *grado* a step]

gradual (ˈgrædjʊəl) *adj* **1** occurring, developing, moving, etc, in small stages: *a gradual improvement in health* **2** not steep or abrupt: *a gradual slope* ▷ *n* **3** (*often cap*) *Christianity* **3a** an antiphon usually from the Psalms, sung or recited immediately after the epistle at Mass **3b** a book of plainsong containing the words and music of the parts of the Mass that are sung by the cantors and choir [c16 from Med. L: relating to steps, from L *gradus* a step] > **ˈgradually** *adv* > **ˈgradualness** *n*

gradualism (ˈgrædjʊəˌlɪzəm) *n* **1** the policy of seeking to change something gradually, esp in politics **2** the theory that explains major changes in fossils, rock strata, etc, in terms of gradual evolutionary processes rather than sudden violent catastrophes > **ˈgradualist** *n, adj* > **ˌgradualˈistic** *adj*

graduand (ˈgrædjʊˌænd) *n chiefly Brit* a person who is about to graduate [c19 from Med. L gerundive of *graduārī* to GRADUATE]

graduate *n* (ˈgrædjʊɪt) **1** a person who has been awarded a first degree from a university or college **2** *US & Canad* a student who has completed a course of studies at a high school and received a diploma ▷ *vb* (ˈgrædjʊˌeɪt), **graduates, graduating, graduated** **3** to receive or cause to receive a degree or diploma **4** *chiefly US & Canad* to confer a degree, diploma, etc, upon **5** (*tr*) to mark (a thermometer, flask, etc) with units of measurement; calibrate **6** (*tr*) to arrange or sort into groups according to type, quality, etc **7** (*intr; often foll by to*) to change by degrees (from something to something else) [c15 from Med. L *graduārī* to take a degree, from L *gradus* a step] > **ˈgraduˌator** *n*

graduated pension *n* (in Britain) a national pension scheme in which employees' contributions are scaled in accordance with their wage rate

graduation (ˌgrædjʊˈeɪʃən) *n* **1** the act of graduating or the state of being graduated **2** the ceremony at which school or college degrees and diplomas are conferred **3** a mark or division or all the marks or divisions that indicate measure on an instrument or vessel

Graeae (ˈgri:i:) *or* **Graiae** *pl n Greek myth* three aged sea deities, having only one eye and one tooth among them, guardians of their sisters, the Gorgons

Graecism *or esp US* **Grecism** (ˈgri:sɪzəm) *n* **1** Greek characteristics or style **2** admiration for or imitation of these, as in sculpture or architecture **3** a form of words characteristic of the idiom of the Greek language

Graeco- *or esp US* **Greco-** (ˈgri:kəʊ, ˈgrɛkəʊ) *combining form* Greek: *Graeco-Roman*

Graeco-Roman *or esp US* **Greco-Roman** *adj* of, characteristic of, or relating to Greek and Roman influences

Graf (græf) *n* **Steffi** born 1969, German tennis player: Wimbledon champion 1988, 1989, 1991, 1992, 1993, 1995, and 1996

graffiti (græˈfi:tɪ) *pl n* (*sometimes functioning as sing*) drawings, messages, etc, often obscene, scribbled on the walls of public lavatories, advertising posters, etc [c19 see GRAFFITO]

graffito (græˈfi:təʊ) *n, pl* **graffiti** (-tɪ) **1** *archaeol* any inscription or drawing scratched onto a surface, esp rock or pottery **2** See **graffiti** [c19 from It.: a little scratch, from L *graphium* stylus, from Gk *grapheion*; see GRAFT[1]]

graft[1] (grɑ:ft) *n* **1** *horticulture* **1a** a piece of plant tissue (the scion), normally a stem, that is made to unite with an established plant (the stock), which supports and nourishes it **1b** the plant resulting from the union of scion and stock **1c** the point of union between the scion and the stock **2** *surgery* a piece of tissue transplanted from a donor or from the patient's own body to an area of the body in need of the tissue **3** the act of joining one thing to another as by grafting ▷ *vb* **4** *horticulture* **4a** to induce (a plant or part of a plant) to unite with another part or (of a plant or part of a plant) to unite in this way **4b** to produce (fruit, flowers, etc) by this means or (of fruit, etc) to grow by this means **5** to transplant (tissue) or (of tissue) to be transplanted **6** to attach or incorporate or become attached or incorporated: *to graft a happy ending onto a sad tale* [c15 from OF *graffe*, from Med. L *graphium*, from L: stylus, from Gk *grapheion*, from *graphein* to write] > **ˈgrafting** *n*

graft[2] (grɑ:ft) *n* **1** *inf* work (esp in **hard graft**) **2a** the acquisition of money, power, etc, by dishonest or unfair means, esp by taking advantage of a position of trust **2b** something gained in this way **2c** a payment made to a person profiting by such a practice ▷ *vb* **3** (*intr*) *inf* to work, esp hard **4** to acquire by or practise graft [c19 from ?] > **ˈgrafter** *n*

Graham (ˈgreɪəm) *n* **1** **Martha** 1893–1991, US dancer and choreographer **2** **Thomas** 1805–69, British physicist: proposed **Graham's law** (1831) of gaseous diffusion and coined the terms osmosis, crystalloids, and colloids

Gg

3 **William Franklin,** known as *Billy Graham*. born 1918, US evangelist
Grahame ('greɪəm) *n* **Kenneth** 1859–1932, Scottish author, noted for the children's classic *The Wind in the Willows* (1908)
Graham Land *n* the N part of the Antarctic Peninsula: became part of the British Antarctic Territory in 1962 (formerly part of the Falkland Islands Dependencies)
Graiae ('greɪiː, 'graɪiː) *pl n* a variant of **Graeae**
Graian Alps ('greɪən, 'graɪ-) *pl n* the N part of the Western Alps, in France and NW Piedmont, Italy. Highest peak: Gran Paradiso, 4061 m (13 323 ft)
Grail (greɪl) *n* See **Holy Grail**
grain (greɪn) *n* **1** the small hard seedlike fruit of a grass, esp a cereal plant **2** a mass of such fruits, esp when gathered for food **3** the plants, collectively, from which such fruits are harvested **4** a small hard particle: *a grain of sand* **5a** the general direction or arrangement of the fibres, layers, or particles in wood, leather, stone, etc **5b** the pattern or texture resulting from such an arrangement **6** the relative size of the particles of a substance: *sugar of fine grain* **7** the granular texture of a rock, mineral, etc **8** the outer layer of a hide or skin from which the hair or wool has been removed **9** the smallest unit of weight in the avoirdupois, Troy, and apothecaries' systems: equal to 0.0648 gram **10** the threads or direction of threads in a woven fabric **11** *photog* any of a large number of particles in a photographic emulsion **12** cleavage lines in crystalline material **13** *chem* any of a large number of small crystals forming a solid **14** a very small amount: *a grain of truth* **15** natural disposition, inclination, or character (esp in **go against the grain**) **16** *astronautics* a homogenous mass of solid propellant in a form designed to give the required combustion characteristics for a particular rocket **17** (not in technical usage) kermes or a red dye made from this insect ▷ *vb (mainly tr)* **18** *(also intr)* to form grains or cause to form into grains; granulate; crystallize **19** to give a granular or roughened appearance or texture to **20** to paint, stain, etc, in imitation of the grain of wood or leather **21a** to remove the hair or wool from (a hide or skin) before tanning **21b** to raise the grain pattern on (leather) [C13 from OF, from L *grānum*]
grain alcohol *n* ethanol containing about 10 per cent of water, made by the fermentation of grain
grain elevator *n* a machine for raising grain to a higher level, esp one having an endless belt fitted with scoops
Grainger ('greɪndʒə) *n* **Percy Aldridge** 1882–1961, Australian pianist, composer, and collector of folk music on which many of his works are based
graining ('greɪnɪŋ) *n* **1** the pattern or texture of the grain of wood, leather, etc **2** the process of painting, printing, staining, etc, a surface in imitation of a grain **3** a surface produced by such a process
grainy ('greɪnɪ) *adj* **grainier, grainiest 1** resembling, full of, or composed of grain; granular **2** resembling the grain of wood, leather, etc **3** *photog* having poor definition because of large grain size > **'graininess** *n*
grallatorial (ˌgrælə'tɔːrɪəl) *adj* of or relating to long-legged wading birds [C19 from NL, from L *grallātor* one who walks on stilts, from *grallae* stilts]
gram¹ (græm) *n* a metric unit of mass equal to one thousandth of a kilogram. Symbol: g [C18 from F *gramme*, from LL *gramma*, from Gk: small weight, from *graphein* to write]
gram² (græm) *n* **1** any of several leguminous plants whose seeds are used as food in India **2** the seed of any of these plants [C18 from Port. *gram* (modern spelling: *grão*), from L *grānum* GRAIN]
gram. *abbrev for:* **1** grammar **2** grammatical
-gram *n combining form* indicating a drawing or something written or recorded: *hexagram; telegram* [from L *-gramma*, from Gk, from *gramma* letter & *grammē* line]
gram atom *or* **gram-atomic weight** *n* an amount of an element equal to its atomic weight expressed in grams: now replaced by the mole
gramineous (grə'mɪnɪəs) *adj* resembling a grass; grasslike ▷ Also: **graminaceous** (ˌgræmɪ'neɪʃəs) [C17 from L, from *grāmen* grass]
graminivorous (ˌgræmɪ'nɪvərəs) *adj* (of animals) feeding on grass [C18 from L *grāmen* grass + -VOROUS]
grammar ('græmə) *n* **1** the branch of linguistics that deals with syntax and morphology, sometimes also phonology and semantics **2** the abstract system of rules in terms of which a person's mastery of his native language can be explained **3** a systematic description of the grammatical facts of a language **4** a book containing an account of the grammatical facts of a language or recommendations as to rules for the proper use of a language **5** the use of language with regard to its correctness or social propriety, esp in syntax: *the teacher told him to watch his grammar* [C14 from OF, from L, from Gk *grammatikē (tekhnē)* the grammatical (art), from *grammatikos* concerning letters, from *gramma* letter]
▷ www.ucl.ac.uk/internet-grammar/home.htm
grammarian (grə'mɛərɪən) *n* **1** a person whose occupation is the study of grammar **2** the author of a grammar
grammar school *n* **1** *Brit* (esp formerly) a state-maintained secondary school providing an education with an academic bias **2** *US* another term for **elementary school 3** *Austral* a private school, esp one controlled by a church **4** *NZ* a secondary school forming part of the public education system
grammatical (grə'mætɪkᵊl) *adj* **1** of or relating to grammar **2** (of a sentence) well formed; regarded as correct > **gram'matically** *adv* > **gram'maticalness** *n*
gram molecule *or* **gram-molecular weight** *n* an amount of a compound equal to its molecular weight expressed in grams: now replaced by the mole. See **mole³**
Grammy ('græmɪ) *n, pl* **Grammys** *or* **Grammies** (in the US) one of the gold-plated discs awarded annually for outstanding achievement in the record industry [C20 from GRAM(OPHONE) + *-my* as in EMMY]
▷ www.grammy.com
gramophone ('græməˌfəʊn) *n* **1a** Also called: **record player** a device for reproducing the sounds stored on a record: now usually applied to the early type that uses an acoustic horn. US and Canad word: **phonograph 1b** *(as modifier)*: *a gramophone record* **2** the technique of recording sound on disc: *the gramophone has made music widely available* [C19 orig. a trademark, ? based on an inversion of *phonogram;* see PHONO-, -GRAM]
Grampian Mountains ('græmpɪən) *pl n* **1** a mountain system of central Scotland, extending from the southwest to the northeast and separating the Highlands from the Lowlands. Highest peak: Ben Nevis, 1343 m (4406 ft) **2** a mountain range in SE Australia, in W Victoria ▷ Also called **the Grampians**
Grampian Region *n* a former local government region in NE Scotland, formed in 1975 from Aberdeenshire, Kincardineshire, and most of Banffshire and Morayshire; replaced in 1996 by the council areas of Aberdeenshire, City of Aberdeen, and Moray
grampus ('græmpəs) *n, pl* **grampuses 1** a widely distributed slaty-grey dolphin with a blunt snout **2** another name for **killer whale** [C16 from OF *graspois*, from *gras* fat (from L *crassus*) + *pois* fish (from L *piscis*)]
Gram's method (græmz) *n bacteriol* **1** a technique used to classify bacteria by staining them with a violet iodine solution **2** **Gram-positive** *(or* **Gram-negative***)* *adj* denoting bacteria that do *(or* do not) retain this stain [C19 after H. C. J. *Gram* (1853–1938), Danish physician]
gran (græn) *n* an informal word for **grandmother**

Granada (grəˈnɑːdə) *n* **1** a former kingdom of S Spain, in Andalusia: founded in the 13th century and divided in 1833 into the present-day provinces of Granada, Almería, and Málaga, in Andalusia **2** a city in S Spain, in Andalusia: capital of the Moorish kingdom of Granada from 1238 to 1492 and a great commercial and cultural centre, containing the Alhambra palace (13th and 14th centuries); university (1531). Pop: 241 471 (1998 est) **3** a city in SW Nicaragua, on the NW shore of Lake Nicaragua: the oldest city in the country, founded in 1523 by Córdoba; attacked frequently by pirates in the 17th century. Pop: 74 396 (1995 est)

granadilla (ˌgrænəˈdɪlə) *n* **1** any of various passionflowers that have edible egg-shaped fleshy fruit **2** Also called: **passion fruit** the fruit of such a plant [C18 from Sp., dim. of *granada* pomegranate, from LL *grānātum*]

Granados (*Spanish* graˈnaðos) *n* **Enrique** (enˈrike), full name *Enrique Granados y Campina*. 1867–1916, Spanish composer, noted for the *Goyescas* (1911) for piano, which formed the basis for an opera of the same name

granary (ˈgrænərɪ; *US* ˈgreɪnərɪ) *n, pl* **granaries** **1** a building for storing threshed grain **2** a region that produces a large amount of grain ▷ *adj* **3** (*cap*) *trademark* (of bread, flour, etc) containing malted wheat grain [C16 from L *grānārium*, from *grānum* GRAIN]

Gran Canaria (graŋ kaˈnarja) *n* the Spanish name for **Grand Canary**

Gran Chaco (*Spanish* gran ˈtʃako) *n* a plain of S central South America, between the Andes and the Paraguay River in SE Bolivia, E Paraguay, and N Argentina: huge swamps and scrub forest. Area: about 780 000 sq km (300 000 sq miles). Often shortened to: **Chaco**

grand (grænd) *adj* **1** large or impressive in size, extent, or consequence: *grand mountain scenery* **2** characterized by or attended with magnificence or display; sumptuous: *a grand feast* **3** of great distinction or pretension; dignified or haughty **4** designed to impress: *grand gestures* **5** very good; wonderful **6** comprehensive; complete: *a grand total* **7** worthy of respect; fine: *a grand old man* **8** large or impressive in conception or execution: *grand ideas* **9** most important; chief: *the grand arena* ▷ *n* **10** See **grand piano** **11** (*pl* **grand**) *sl* a thousand pounds or dollars [C16 from OF, from L *grandis*] > ˈ**grandly** *adv* > ˈ**grandness** *n*

grand- *prefix* (in designations of kinship) one generation removed in ascent or descent: *grandson; grandfather* [from F *grand-*, on the model of L *magnus* in such phrases as *avunculus magnus* great-uncle]

grandad, granddad (ˈgrænˌdæd) *or* **grandaddy, granddaddy** (ˈgrænˌdædɪ) *n, pl* **grandads, granddads** *or* **grandaddies, granddaddies** informal words for **grandfather**

grandam (ˈgrændəm, -dæm) *or* **grandame** (ˈgrændeɪm, -dəm) *n* an archaic word for **grandmother** [C13 from Anglo-F *grandame*, from OF GRAND- + *dame* lady, mother]

grandaunt (ˈgrændˌɑːnt) *n* another name for **great-aunt**

Grand Bahama *n* an island in the Atlantic, in the W Bahamas. Pop: 40 898 (1990). Area: 1114 sq km (430 sq miles)

Grand Banks *pl n* a part of the continental shelf in the Atlantic, extending for about 560 km (350 miles) off the SE coast of Newfoundland: meeting place of the cold Labrador Current and the warm Gulf Stream, producing frequent fogs and rich fishing grounds

Grand Canal *n* **1** a canal in E China, extending north from Hangzhou to Tianjin: the longest canal in China, now partly silted up; central section, linking the Yangtze and Yellow Rivers, finished in 486 BC; north section finished by Kublai Khan between 1282 and 1292. Length: about 1600 km (1000 miles). Chinese name: **Da Yunhe** **2** a canal in Venice, forming the main water thoroughfare: noted for its bridges, the Rialto, and the fine palaces along its banks

Grand Canary *n* an island in the Atlantic, in the Canary Islands: part of the Spanish province of Las Palmas. Capital: Las Palmas. Pop: 631 000 (latest est). Area: 1533 sq km (592 sq miles). Spanish name: **Gran Canaria**

Grand Canyon *n* a gorge of the Colorado River in N Arizona, extending from its junction with the Little Colorado River to Lake Mead; cut by vertical river erosion through the multicoloured strata of a high plateau; partly contained in the **Grand Canyon National Park,** covering 2610 sq km (1008 sq miles). Length: 451 km (280 miles). Width: 6 km (4 miles) to 29 km (18 miles). Greatest depth: over 1.5 km (1 mile)

grandchild (ˈgrænˌtʃaɪld) *n, pl* **grandchildren** the son or daughter of one's child

Grand Coulee (ˈkuːlɪ) *n* a canyon in central Washington State, over 120 m (400 ft) deep, at the N end of which is situated the **Grand Coulee Dam,** on the Columbia River. Height of dam: 168 m (550 ft). Length of dam: 1310 m (4300 ft)

granddaughter (ˈgrænˌdɔːtə) *n* a daughter of one's son or daughter

grand duchess *n* **1** the wife or widow of a grand duke **2** a woman who holds the rank of grand duke in her own right

grand duchy *n* the territory, state, or principality of a grand duke or grand duchess

grand duke *n* **1** a prince or nobleman who rules a territory, state, or principality **2** a son or a male descendant in the male line of a Russian tsar **3** a medieval Russian prince who ruled over other princes

grande dame *French* (grɑ̃d dam) *n* a woman regarded as the most experienced, prominent, or venerable member of her profession, etc

grandee (grænˈdiː) *n* **1** a Spanish or Portuguese prince or nobleman of the highest rank **2** a person of high station [C16 from Sp. *grande*]

Grande-Terre (*French* grɑ̃dtɛr) *n* a French island in the Caribbean, in the Lesser Antilles: one of the two main islands which constitute Guadeloupe. Chief town: Pointe-à-Pitre

grandeur (ˈgrændʒə) *n* **1** personal greatness, esp when based on dignity, character, or accomplishments **2** magnificence; splendour **3** pretentious or bombastic behaviour

Grand Falls *pl n* the former name (until 1965) of **Churchill Falls**

grandfather (ˈgrænˌfɑːðə, ˈgrænd-) *n* **1** the father of one's father or mother **2** (*often pl*) a male ancestor **3** (*often cap*) a familiar term of address for an old man > ˈ**grandˌfatherly** *adj*

grandfather clock *n* a long-pendulum clock in a tall standing wooden case

Grand Guignol *French* (grɑ̃ giɲɔl) *n* **a** a brief sensational play intended to horrify **b** (*modifier*) of or like plays of this kind [C20 after *Le Grand Guignol*, a small theatre in Montmartre, Paris]

grandiloquent (grænˈdɪləkwənt) *adj* inflated, pompous, or bombastic in style or expression [C16 from L *grandiloquus*, from *grandis* great + *loquī* to speak] > **granˈdiloquence** *n* > **granˈdiloquently** *adv*

grandiose (ˈgrændɪˌəʊs) *adj* **1** pretentiously grand or stately **2** imposing in conception or execution [C19 from F, from It., from *grande* great; see GRAND] > ˈ**grandiˌosely** *adv* > **grandiosity** (ˌgrændɪˈɒsɪtɪ) *n*

grand jury *n law* (esp in the US and, now rarely, in Canada) a jury summoned to inquire into accusations of crime and ascertain whether the evidence is adequate to found an indictment. Abolished in Britain in 1948

grand larceny *n* **1** (formerly, in England) the theft of property valued at over 12 pence. Abolished in 1827 **2** (in some states of the US) the theft of property of which the value is above a specified figure

grandma (ˈgrænˌmɑː), **grandmama,** *or*

grandmamma ('grænmə,mɑː) *n* informal words for **grandmother**

grand mal (grɒn mæl) *n* a form of epilepsy characterized by loss of consciousness for up to five minutes and violent convulsions ▹ Cf **petit mal** [F: great illness]

Grandma Moses *n* the nickname of (Anna Mary Robertson) **Moses**

Grand Manan (mə'næn) *n* a Canadian island, off the SW coast of New Brunswick: separated from the coast of Maine by the **Grand Manan Channel** Area: 147 sq km (57 sq miles)

grandmaster ('grænd,mɑːstə) *n* **1** *chess* one of the top chess players of a particular country **2** a leading exponent of any of various arts

Grand Master *n* the title borne by the head of any of various societies, orders, and other organizations, such as the Templars, Freemasons, or the various martial arts

grandmother ('græn,mʌðə, 'grænd-) *n* **1** the mother of one's father or mother **2** (*often pl*) a female ancestor > **'grand,motherly** *adj*

Grand National *n* **the** an annual steeplechase run at Aintree, Liverpool, since 1839

grandnephew ('græn,nɛvjuː, -,nɛfjuː, 'grænd-) *n* another name for **great-nephew**

grandniece ('græn,niːs, 'grænd-) *n* another name for **great-niece**

grand opera *n* an opera that has a serious plot and is entirely in musical form, with no spoken dialogue

grandpa ('græn,pɑː) *or* **grandpapa** ('grænpə,pɑː) *n* informal words for **grandfather**

grandparent ('græn,pɛərənt, 'grænd-) *n* the father or mother of either of one's parents

grand piano *n* a form of piano in which the strings are arranged horizontally

Grand Pré (grɒn preɪ; *French* grɑ̃ pre) *n* a village in SE Canada, in W Nova Scotia: setting of Longfellow's *Evangeline*

Grand Prix (grɒn priː; *French* grɑ̃ pri) *n* **1** any of a series of formula motor races to determine the annual Driver's World Championship **2** a very important competitive event in various other sports, such as athletics, snooker, or powerboating [F: great prize]

Grand Rapids *n* (*functioning as singular*) a city in SW Michigan: electronics, car parts. Pop: 197 800 (2000)

grandsire ('græn,saɪə, 'grænd-) *n* an archaic word for **grandfather**

grand slam *n* **1** *bridge, etc* the winning of 13 tricks by one player or side or the contract to do so ▹ Cf **little slam** **2** the winning of all major competitions in a season, esp in tennis and golf **3** (*often caps*) *rugby union* the winning of all the games in the annual Six Nations Championship involving Scotland, England, Wales, Ireland, France, and Italy

grandson ('grænsʌn, 'grænd-) *n* a son of one's son or daughter

grandstand ('græn,stænd, 'grænd-) *n* **1** a terraced block of seats commanding the best view at racecourses, football pitches, etc **2** the spectators in a grandstand

grand tour *n* **1** (formerly) an extended tour through the major cities of Europe, esp one undertaken by a rich or aristocratic Englishman to complete his education **2** *inf* an extended sightseeing trip, tour of inspection, etc

granduncle ('grænd,ʌŋkᵊl) *n* another name for **great-uncle**

grand unified theory *n physics* any of a number of theories of elementary particles and fundamental interactions designed to explain the electromagnetic, strong, and weak interactions in terms of a single mathematical formalism. Abbrev: **GUT**

Grand Union Canal *n* a canal in S England linking London and the Midlands: opened in 1801

grange (greɪndʒ) *n* **1** *chiefly Brit* a farm, esp a farmhouse or country house with its various outbuildings **2** *arch* a granary or barn [c13 from Anglo-F *graunge*, from Med. L *grānica*, from L *grānum* GRAIN]

Grangemouth ('greɪndʒmaʊθ, -məθ) *n* a port in Scotland, in Falkirk council area: now Scotland's second port, with oil refineries, shipyards, and chemical industries. Pop: 18 739 (1991)

Granicus (grə'naɪkəs) *n* an ancient river in NW Asia Minor where Alexander the Great won his first major battle against the Persians (334 BC)

granita (grə'niːtə) *n* a type of Italian dessert, similar to a sorbet [from It. *granito* grainy]

granite ('grænɪt) *n* **1** a light-coloured coarse-grained acid plutonic igneous rock consisting of quartz and feldspars: widely used for building **2** great hardness, endurance, or resolution [c17 from It. *granito* grained, from *grano* grain, from L *grānum*] > **granitic** (grə'nɪtɪk) *adj*

graniteware ('grænɪt,wɛə) *n* **1** iron vessels coated with enamel of a granite-like appearance **2** a type of pottery with a speckled glaze

granivorous (græ'nɪvərəs) *adj* (of animals) feeding on seeds and grain > **granivore** ('grænɪ,vɔː) *n*

granny *or* **grannie** ('grænɪ) *n, pl* **grannies** **1** informal words for **grandmother** **2** *inf* an irritatingly fussy person **3** See **granny knot**

granny bond *n Brit inf* a savings scheme available originally only to people over retirement age

granny farm *n derog sl* an old people's home, esp one that charges high fees and offers poor care

granny flat *n* self-contained accommodation within or built onto a house, suitable for an elderly parent

granny knot *or* **granny's knot** *n* a reef knot with the ends crossed the wrong way, making it liable to slip or jam

Gran Paradiso (*Italian* gram para'diːzo) *n* a mountain in NW Italy, in NW Piedmont: the highest peak of the Graian Alps. Height: 4061 m (13 323 ft)

grant (grɑːnt) *vb* (*tr*) **1** to consent to perform or fulfil: *to grant a wish* **2** (*may take a clause as object*) to permit as a favour, indulgence, etc: *to grant an interview* **3** (*may take a clause as object*) to acknowledge the validity of; concede: *I grant what you say is true* **4** to bestow, esp in a formal manner **5** to transfer (property) to another, esp by deed; convey **6** **take for granted** **6a** to accept or assume without question: *one takes certain amenities for granted* **6b** to fail to appreciate the value, merit, etc, of (a person) ▹ *n* **7** a sum of money provided by a government, local authority, or public fund to finance educational study, building repairs, overseas aid, etc **8** a privilege, right, etc, that has been granted **9** the act of granting **10** a transfer of property by deed; conveyance [c13 from OF *graunter*, from Vulgar L *credentāre* (unattested), from L *crēdere* to believe] > **'grantable** *adj* > **'granter** *or* (*law*) **'grantor** *n*

Grant (grɑːnt) *n* **1** **Cary,** real name *Alexander Archibald Leach*. 1904–86, US film actor, born in England. His many films include *Bringing up Baby* (1938), *The Philadelphia Story* (1940), *Arsenic and Old Lace* (1944), and *Mr Blandings Builds his Dream House* (1948) **2** **Duncan (James Corrowr)** 1885–1978, British painter and designer **3** **Ulysses S(impson),** real name *Hiram Ulysses Grant*. 1822–85, 18th president of the US (1869–77); commander in chief of Union forces in the American Civil War (1864–65)

Granta ('græntə, 'grɑːntə) *n* the original name, still in use locally, for the River Cam

grantee (grɑːn'tiː) *n law* a person to whom a grant is made

Granth (grʌnt) *n* the sacred scripture of the Sikhs [from Hindi, from Sansk. *grantha* a book]
▹ www.srigranth.org

Grantham ('grænθəm) *n* a town in E England, in Lincolnshire: birthplace of Sir Isaac Newton and

Margaret Thatcher. Pop: 33 243 (1991)

grant-in-aid *n, pl* **grants-in-aid** a sum of money granted by one government to a lower level of government for a programme, etc

grant-maintained *adj* (**grant maintained** *when postpositive*) (of schools or educational institutions) funded directly by central government

gran turismo ('græn tʊə'rɪzməʊ) *n, pl* **gran turismos** See **GT** [c20 from It.]

granular ('grænjʊlə) *adj* **1** of, like, or containing granules **2** having a grainy surface > **granularity** (ˌgrænjʊ'lærɪtɪ) *n* > **'granularly** *adv*

granulate ('grænjʊˌleɪt) *vb* **granulates, granulating, granulated 1** (*tr*) to make into grains: *granulated sugar* **2** to make or become roughened in surface texture > **ˌgranu'lation** *n* > **'granulative** *adj* > **'granuˌlator** *or* **'granuˌlater** *n*

granule ('grænju:l) *n* a small grain [c17 from LL *grānulum* a small GRAIN]

granulocyte ('grænjʊləˌsaɪt) *n* any of a group of unpigmented blood cells having cytoplasmic granules that take up various dyes

Granville ('grænvɪl) *n* **1 1st Earl,** title of *John Carteret.* 1690–1763, British statesman: secretary of state (1742–44); a leading opponent of Walpole **2 2nd Earl,** title of *Granville George Leveson-Gower.* 1815–91, British Liberal politician: Gladstone's foreign secretary (1870–74; 1880–85) and a supporter of Irish Home Rule

Granville-Barker ('grænvɪl'bɑ:kə) *n* **Harley** 1877–1946, English dramatist, theatre director, and critic, noted particularly for his *Prefaces to Shakespeare* (1927–47)

grape (greɪp) *n* **1** the fruit of the grapevine, which has a purple or green skin and sweet flesh: eaten raw, dried to make raisins, currants, or sultanas, or used for making wine **2** See **grapevine** (sense 1) **3 the grape** *inf* wine **4** See **grapeshot** [c13 from OF *grape* bunch of grapes, of Gmc origin; rel. to CRAMP², GRAPPLE] > **'grapey** *or* **'grapy** *adj*

grapefruit ('greɪpˌfru:t) *n, pl* **grapefruit** *or* **grapefruits 1** a tropical or subtropical cultivated evergreen tree **2** the large round edible fruit of this tree, which has yellow rind and juicy slightly bitter pulp

grape hyacinth *n* any of various Eurasian bulbous plants of the lily family with clusters of rounded blue flowers resembling tiny grapes

grapeshot ('greɪpˌʃɒt) *n* ammunition for cannons consisting of a cluster of iron balls that scatter after firing

grape sugar *n* another name for **dextrose**

grapevine ('greɪpˌvaɪn) *n* **1** any of several vines of E Asia, widely cultivated for its fruit (grapes) **2** *inf* an unofficial means of relaying information, esp from person to person

graph (grɑ:f) *n* **1** Also called: **chart** a drawing depicting the relation between certain sets of numbers or quantities by means of a series of dots, lines, etc, plotted with reference to a set of axes **2** *maths* a drawing depicting a functional relation between two or three variables by means of a curve or surface containing only those points whose coordinates satisfy the relation **3** *linguistics* a symbol in a writing system not further subdivisible into other such symbols ▷ *vb* **4** (*tr*) to draw or represent in a graph [c19 short for *graphic formula*]

-graph *n combining form* **1** an instrument that writes or records: *telegraph* **2** a writing, record, or drawing: *autograph; lithograph* [via L from Gk, from *graphein* to write] > **-graphic** *or* **-graphical** *adj combining form* > **-graphically** *adv combining form*

grapheme ('græfi:m) *n linguistics* the complete class of letters or combinations of letters that represent one speech sound: for instance, the *f* in *full*, the *gh* in *cough*, and the *ph* in *photo* are members of the same grapheme [c20 from Gk *graphēma* a letter] > **gra'phemically** *adv*

-grapher *n combining form* **1** indicating a person skilled in a subject: *geographer; photographer* **2** indicating a person who writes or draws in a specified way: *stenographer; lithographer*

graphic ('græfɪk) *or* **graphical** *adj* **1** vividly or clearly described: *a graphic account of the disaster* **2** of or relating to writing: *graphic symbols* **3** *maths* using, relating to, or determined by a graph: *a graphic representation of the figures* **4** of or relating to the graphic arts **5** *geol* having or denoting a texture resembling writing: *graphic granite* [c17 from L *graphicus*, from Gk *graphikos*, from *graphein* to write] > **'graphically** *adv* > **'graphicness** *n*

graphicacy ('græfɪkəsɪ) *n* the ability to understand and use maps, symbols, etc [c20 formed on the model of *literacy*]

graphical user interface *n* an interface between a user and a computer system that allows the user to operate the system by means of pictorial devices, such as menus and icons

graphic arts *pl n* any of the fine or applied visual arts based on drawing or the use of line, esp illustration and printmaking of all kinds

graphic equalizer *n* a tone control that enables the output signal of an audio amplifier to be adjusted in each of a series of frequency bands by means of sliding contacts

graphic novel *n* a novel in the form of a comic strip

graphics ('græfɪks) *n* **1** (*functioning as sing*) the process or art of drawing in accordance with mathematical principles **2** (*functioning as sing*) the study of writing systems **3** (*functioning as pl*) the drawings, photographs, etc, in a magazine or book, or in a television or film production **4** (*functioning as pl*) *computing* information displayed in the form of diagrams, graphs, etc

graphics adapter *n computing* (on a computer) the hardware that controls the way graphics appear on the monitor

graphite ('græfaɪt) *n* a blackish soft form of carbon used in pencils, electrodes, as a lubricant, as a moderator in nuclear reactors, and, in carbon fibre form, for tough lightweight sports equipment [c18 from G *Graphit*, from Gk *graphein* to write + -ITE¹] > **graphitic** (grə'fɪtɪk) *adj*

graphology (græ'fɒlədʒɪ) *n* **1** the study of handwriting, esp to analyse the writer's character **2** *linguistics* the study of writing systems > **ˌgrapho'logical** *adj* > **gra'phologist** *n*

graph paper *n* paper printed with intersecting lines for drawing graphs, diagrams, etc

-graphy *n combining form* **1** indicating a form of writing, representing, etc: *calligraphy; photography* **2** indicating an art or descriptive science: *choreography; oceanography* [via L from Gk, from *graphein* to write]

grapnel ('græpnᵊl) *n* **1** a device with a multiple hook at one end and attached to a rope, which is thrown or hooked over a firm mooring to secure an object attached to the other end of the rope **2** a light anchor for small boats [c14 from OF *grapin*, from *grape* a hook; see GRAPE]

grappa ('græpə) *n* a spirit distilled from the fermented remains of grapes after pressing [It.: grape stalk, of Gmc origin; see GRAPE]

Grappelli *or* **Grappelly** (grə'pɛlɪ) *n* **Stéphane** ('stɛfᵊn) 1908–97, French jazz violinist: with Django Reinhardt, he led the Quintet of the Hot Club of France between 1934 and 1939

grapple ('græpᵊl) *vb* **grapples, grappling, grappled 1** to come to grips with (one or more persons), esp to struggle in hand-to-hand combat **2** (*intr; foll by with*) to cope or contend: *to grapple with a financial problem* **3** (*tr*) to secure with a grapple ▷ *n* **4** any form of hook or metal instrument by which something is secured, such as a grapnel **5a** the act of gripping or seizing, as in wrestling **5b** a grip or hold [c16 from OF *grappelle* a little

Gg

hook, from *grape* hook; see GRAPNEL] > **'grappler** *n*

grappling iron *or* **hook** *n* a grapnel, esp one used for securing ships

graptolite ('græptə,laɪt) *n* an extinct Palaeozoic colonial animal: a common fossil used to determine the age of sedimentary rocks [C19 from Gk *graptos* written, from *graphein* to write + -LITE]

Grasmere ('grɑːs,mɪə) *n* a village in NW England, in Cumbria at the head of **Lake Grasmere:** home of William Wordsworth and of Thomas de Quincey

grasp (grɑːsp) *vb* **1** to grip (something) firmly as with the hands **2** (when *intr*, often foll by *at*) to struggle, snatch, or grope (for) **3** (*tr*) to understand, esp with effort ▷ *n* **4** the act of grasping **5** a grip or clasp, as of a hand **6** total rule or possession **7** understanding; comprehension [C14 from Low G *grapsen;* rel. to OE *græppian* to seize] > **'graspable** *adj* > **'grasper** *n*

grasping ('grɑːspɪŋ) *adj* greedy; avaricious > **'graspingly** *adv* > **'graspingness** *n*

grass (grɑːs) *n* **1** any of a family of plants having jointed stems sheathed by long narrow leaves, flowers in spikes, and seedlike fruits. The family includes cereals, bamboo, etc **2** such plants collectively, in a lawn, meadow, etc. Related adj: **verdant 3** ground on which such plants grow; a lawn, field, etc **4** ground on which animals are grazed; pasture **5** a slang word for **marijuana 6** *Brit sl* a person who informs, esp on criminals **7** **let the grass grow under one's feet** to squander time or opportunity ▷ *vb* **8** to cover or become covered with grass **9** to feed or be fed with grass **10** (*tr*) to spread (cloth, etc) out on grass for drying or bleaching in the sun **11** (*intr;* usually foll by *on*) *Brit sl* to inform, esp to the police ▷ See also **grass up** [OE *græs*] > **'grass,like** *adj*
▷ www.doityourself.com/lawn
▷ www.grasses.co.uk
▷ http://forums.gardenweb.com/forums/grasses

Grass (*German* gras) *n* **Günter** (**Wilhelm**) ('gyntər) born 1927, German novelist, dramatist, and poet. His novels include *The Tin Drum* (1959), *Dog Years* (1963), *The Rat* (1986), *Toad Croaks* (1992), and *Crabwalk* (2002). Nobel prize for literature 1999

grass hockey *n* in W Canada, field hockey, as contrasted with ice hockey

grasshopper ('grɑːs,hɒpə) *n* an insect having hind legs adapted for leaping: typically terrestrial, feeding on plants, and producing a ticking sound by rubbing the hind legs against the leathery forewings

grassland ('grɑːs,lænd) *n* **1** land, such as a prairie, on which grass predominates **2** land reserved for natural grass pasture

grass roots *pl n* **1** ordinary people as distinct from the active leadership of a group or organization, esp a political party **2** the essentials

grass snake *n* **1** a harmless nonvenomous European snake having a brownish-green body with variable markings **2** any of several similar related European snakes

grass tree *n* **1** Also called: **blackboy** any plant of the Australian genus *Xanthorrhoea*, having a woody stem, stiff grasslike leaves, and a spike of small white flowers **2** any of several similar Australasian plants

grass up *vb* (*tr, adv*) *sl* to inform on (someone), esp to the police

grass widow *or* (*masc*) **grass widower** *n* a person whose spouse is regularly away for a short period [C16 ? an allusion to a grass bed as representing an illicit relationship]

grassy ('grɑːsɪ) *adj* **grassier, grassiest** covered with, containing, or resembling grass > **'grassiness** *n*

grate[1] (greɪt) *vb* **grates, grating, grated 1** (*tr*) to reduce to small shreds by rubbing against a rough or sharp perforated surface: *to grate carrots* **2** to scrape (an object) against something or (objects) together, producing a harsh rasping sound, or (of objects) to scrape with such a sound **3** (*intr;* foll by *on* or *upon*) to annoy [C15 from OF *grater* to scrape, of Gmc origin] > **'grater** *n*

grate[2] (greɪt) *n* **1** a framework of metal bars for holding fuel in a fireplace, stove, or furnace **2** a less common word for **fireplace 3** another name for **grating**[1] ▷ *vb* **4** (*tr*) to provide with a grate or grates [C14 from OF, from L *crātis* hurdle]

grateful ('greɪtfʊl) *adj* **1** thankful for gifts, favours, etc; appreciative **2** showing gratitude: *a grateful letter* **3** favourable or pleasant: *a grateful rest* [C16 from obs. *grate*, from L *grātus* + -FUL] > **'gratefully** *adv* > **'gratefulness** *n*

Gratian ('greɪʃɪən) *n* Latin name *Flavius Gratianus*. 359–383 AD, Roman emperor (367–383): ruled with his father Valentinian I (367–375); ruled the Western Roman Empire with his brother Valentinian II (375-83); appointed Theodosius I emperor of the Eastern Roman Empire (379)

graticule ('grætɪ,kjuːl) *n* **1** the grid of intersecting lines esp of latitude and longitude, on which a map is drawn **2** another name for **reticle** [C19 from F, from L *crāticula*, from *crātis* wickerwork]

gratify ('grætɪ,faɪ) *vb* **gratifies, gratifying, gratified** (*tr*) **1** to satisfy or please **2** to yield to or indulge (a desire, whim, etc) [C16 from L *grātificārī*, from *grātus* grateful + *facere* to make] > **,gratifi'cation** *n* > **'grati,fier** *n* > **'grati,fying** *adj* > **'grati,fyingly** *adv*

gratin (*French* gratɛ̃) See **au gratin**

grating[1] ('greɪtɪŋ) *n* a framework of metal bars in the form of a grille set into a wall, pavement, etc, serving as a cover or guard but admitting air and sometimes light. Also called: **grate**

grating[2] ('greɪtɪŋ) *adj* **1** (of sounds) harsh and rasping **2** annoying; irritating ▷ *n* **3** (*often pl*) something produced by grating > **'gratingly** *adv*

gratis ('greɪtɪs, 'grætɪs, 'grɑːtɪs) *adv, adj* (*postpositive*) without payment; free of charge [C15 from L: out of kindness, from *grātiīs*, ablative pl of *grātia* favour]

gratitude ('grætɪ,tjuːd) *n* a feeling of thankfulness, as for gifts or favours [C16 from Med. L *grātitūdō*, from L *grātus* GRATEFUL]

gratuitous (grə'tjuːɪtəs) *adj* **1** given or received without payment or obligation **2** without cause; unjustified [C17 from L *grātuītus* from *grātia* favour] > **gra'tuitously** *adv* > **gra'tuitousness** *n*

gratuity (grə'tjuːɪtɪ) *n, pl* **gratuities 1** a gift or reward, usually of money, for services rendered; tip **2** *mil* a financial award granted for long or meritorious service

gratulatory ('grætjʊlətərɪ) *adj* expressing congratulation [C16 from L *grātulārī* to congratulate]

Graubünden (*German* grau'byndən) *n* an Alpine canton of E Switzerland: the largest of the cantons, but sparsely populated. Capital: Chur. Pop: 186 000 (2000 est). Area: 7109 sq km (2773 sq miles). Italian name: **Grigioni** Romansch name: **Grishun** French name: **Grisons**

grav (græv) *n* a unit of acceleration equal to the standard acceleration of free fall. 1 grav is equivalent to 9.806 65 metres per second per second. Symbol: G

gravadlax ('grævəd,læks) *n* another name for **gravlax**

gravamen (grə'veɪmɛn) *n, pl* **gravamina** (-'væmɪnə) **1** *law* that part of an accusation weighing most heavily against an accused **2** *law* the substance or material grounds of a complaint **3** a rare word for **grievance** [C17 from LL: trouble, from L *gravis* heavy]

grave[1] (greɪv) *n* **1** a place for the burial of a corpse, esp beneath the ground and usually marked by a tombstone. Related adj: **sepulchral 2** something resembling a grave or resting place: *the ship went to its grave* **3** (often preceded by *the*) a poetic term for **death 4** **make** (**someone**) **turn in his grave** to do something that would have shocked or distressed a person now dead [OE *græf*]

grave² (greɪv) *adj* **1** serious and solemn: *a grave look* **2** full of or suggesting danger: *a grave situation* **3** important; crucial: *grave matters of state* **4** (of colours) sober or dull **5** (grɑːv) *phonetics* of or relating to an accent (`) over vowels, denoting a pronunciation with lower or falling musical pitch (as in ancient Greek), with certain special quality (as in French), or in a manner that gives the vowel status as a syllable (as in English *agèd*) ▷ *n* **6** (*also* grɑːv) a grave accent [c16 from OF, from L *gravis*] > ˈ**gravely** *adv* > ˈ**graveness** *n*

grave³ (greɪv) *vb* **graves, graving, graved; graved** *or* **graven** (*tr*) *arch* **1** to carve or engrave **2** to fix firmly in the mind [OE *grafan*]

grave⁴ (ˈgrɑːveɪ) *adj music* solemn [It.]

grave clothes (greɪv) *pl n* the wrappings in which a dead body is interred

gravel (ˈgrævᵊl) *n* **1** an unconsolidated mixture of rock fragments and pebbles that is coarser than sand **2** *pathol* small rough calculi in the kidneys or bladder ▷ *vb* **gravels, gravelling, gravelled** *or US* **gravels, graveling, graveled** (*tr*) **3** to cover with gravel **4** to confound or confuse **5** *US inf* to annoy or disturb [c13 from OF *gravele*, dim. of *grave*, ? of Celtic origin]

gravel-blind *adj literary* almost completely blind [c16 from GRAVEL + BLIND]

gravelly (ˈgrævəlɪ) *adj* **1** consisting of or abounding in gravel **2** of or like gravel **3** (esp of a voice) harsh and grating

graven (ˈgreɪvᵊn) *vb* **1** a past participle of **grave³** ▷ *adj* **2** strongly fixed

Gravenhage (xraːvənˈhaːxə) *n* **'s** a Dutch name for (The) **Hague**

graven image *n chiefly Bible* a carved image used as an idol

graver (ˈgreɪvə) *n* any of various engraving or sculpting tools, such as a burin

Graves¹ (grɑːv) *n* (*sometimes not cap*) a white or red wine from the district around Bordeaux, France

Graves² (greɪvz) *n* **Robert** (**Ranke**) 1895–1985, English poet, novelist, and critic, whose works include his World War I autobiography, *Goodbye to All That* (1929), and the historical novels *I, Claudius* (1934) and *Claudius the God* (1934)

Gravesend (ˌgreɪvzˈɛnd) *n* a river port in SE England, in NW Kent on the Thames. Pop: 51 435 (1991)

gravestone (ˈgreɪvˌstəʊn) *n* a stone marking a grave

graveyard (ˈgreɪvˌjɑːd) *n* a place for graves; a burial ground, esp a small one or one in a churchyard

graveyard shift *n US* the working shift between midnight and morning

graveyard slot *n television* the hours from late night until early morning when the number of people watching television is at its lowest

gravid (ˈgrævɪd) *adj* the technical word for **pregnant** [c16 from L *gravidus*, from *gravis* heavy]

gravimeter (grəˈvɪmɪtə) *n* **1** an instrument for measuring the earth's gravitational field at points on its surface **2** an instrument for measuring relative density [c18 from F *gravimètre*, from L *gravis* heavy] > graˈ**vimetry** *n*

gravimetric (ˌgrævɪˈmɛtrɪk) *adj* **1** of, concerned with, or using measurement by weight **2** *chem* of analysis of quantities by weight

graving dock *n* another term for **dry dock**

gravitas (ˈgrævɪˌtæs) *n* seriousness or solemnity, esp of conduct or demeanour; weight or authority [c20 from L *gravitās* weight, from *gravis* heavy]

gravitate (ˈgrævɪˌteɪt) *vb* **gravitates, gravitating, gravitated** (*intr*) **1** *physics* to move under the influence of gravity **2** (usually foll by *to* or *towards*) to be influenced or drawn, as by strong impulses **3** to sink or settle > ˈ**graviˌtater** *n* > ˈ**graviˌtative** *adj*

gravitation (ˌgrævɪˈteɪʃən) *n* **1** the force of attraction that bodies exert on one another as a result of their mass **2** any process or result caused by this interaction ▷ Also called: **gravity** > ˌ**graviˈtational** *adj* > ˌ**graviˈtationally** *adv*

gravitational constant *n* the factor relating force to mass and distance in Newton's law of gravitation. Symbol: G

gravitational field *n* the field of force surrounding a body of finite mass in which another body would experience an attractive force that is proportional to the product of the masses and inversely proportional to the square of the distance between them

gravitational mass *n* the mass of a body expressed in terms of the gravitational force between it and the earth ▷ Cf **inertial mass**

graviton (ˈgrævɪˌtɒn) *n* a postulated quantum of gravitational energy, usually considered to be a particle with zero charge and rest mass and a spin of 2

gravity (ˈgrævɪtɪ) *n, pl* **gravities 1** the force of attraction that moves or tends to move bodies towards the centre of a celestial body, such as the earth or moon **2** the property of being heavy or having weight **3** another name for **gravitation 4** seriousness or importance, esp as a consequence of an action or opinion **5** manner or conduct that is solemn or dignified **6** lowness in pitch **7** (*modifier*) of or relating to gravity or gravitation or their effects: *gravity feed* [c16 from L *gravitās* weight, from *gravis* heavy]

gravity wave *n physics* **1** a wave propagated in a gravitational field, predicted to occur as a result of an accelerating mass **2** a surface wave on water or other liquid propagated because of the weight of liquid in the crests ▷ Also called: **gravitational wave**

gravlax (ˈgrævˌlæks) *or* **gravadlax** *n* dry-cured salmon, marinated in salt, sugar, and spices, as served in Scandinavia [c20 from Norwegian, from *grav* grave (because the salmon is left to ferment) + *laks* or Swedish *lax* salmon]

gravure (grəˈvjʊə) *n* **1** a method of intaglio printing using a plate with many small etched recesses. See also **rotogravure 2** See **photogravure 3** matter printed by this process [c19 from F, from *graver* to engrave]

gravy (ˈgreɪvɪ) *n, pl* **gravies 1a** the juices that exude from meat during cooking **1b** the sauce made by thickening and flavouring such juices **2** *sl* money or gain acquired with little effort, esp above that needed for ordinary living [c14 from OF *gravé*, from ?]

gravy boat *n* a small often boat-shaped vessel for serving gravy or other sauces

gray¹ (greɪ) *adj, n, vb* a variant spelling (now esp US) of **grey**

gray² (greɪ) *n* the derived SI unit of the absorbed dose of ionizing radiation: equal to 1 joule per kilogram. Symbol: Gy [c20 after L. H. *Gray*, Brit radiobiologist]

Gray (greɪ) *n* **1 Simon** (**James Holiday**) born 1936, British writer: his plays include *Butley* (1971), *The Common Pursuit* (1988), and *Life Support* (1997) **2 Thomas** 1716–71, English poet, best known for his *Elegy written in a Country Churchyard* (1751)

grayling (ˈgreɪlɪŋ) *n, pl* **grayling** *or* **graylings 1** a freshwater food fish of the salmon family of the N hemisphere, having a long spiny dorsal fin, a silvery back, and greyish-green sides **2** any of various European butterflies having grey or greyish-brown wings

Graz (*German* graːts) *n* an industrial city in SE Austria, capital of Styria province: the second largest city in the country. Pop: 226 424 (2001)

graze¹ (greɪz) *vb* **grazes, grazing, grazed 1** to allow (animals) to consume the vegetation on (an area of land), or (of animals) to feed thus **2** (*tr*) to tend (livestock) while at pasture **3** (*intr*) *inf* to eat snacks throughout the day rather than formal meals **4** (*intr*) US to pilfer and eat sweets, vegetables, etc, from supermarket shelves while shopping [OE *grasian*, from *græs* GRASS]

graze² (greɪz) *vb* **grazes, grazing, grazed** **1** (when *intr*, often foll by *against* or *along*) to brush or scrape (against) gently, esp in passing **2** (*tr*) to break the skin of (a part of the body) by scraping ▷ *n* **3** the act of grazing **4** a scrape or abrasion made by grazing [c17 prob. special use of GRAZE¹]

grazier (ˈgreɪzɪə) *n* a rancher or farmer who rears or fattens cattle or sheep on grazing land

grazing (ˈgreɪzɪŋ) *n* **1** the vegetation on pastures that is available for livestock to feed upon **2** the land on which this is growing

grazioso (ˌgrɑːtsɪˈəʊsəʊ) *adj music* graceful [It.]

grease (griːs, griːz) *n* **1** animal fat in a soft or melted condition **2** any thick fatty oil, esp one used as a lubricant for machinery, etc ▷ *vb* **greases, greasing, greased** (*tr*) **3** to soil, coat, or lubricate with grease **4** **grease the palm** (*or* **hand**) **of** *sl* to bribe; influence by giving money to [c13 from OF *craisse*, from L *crassus* thick] > ˈ**greaser** *n*

grease gun *n* a device for forcing grease through nipples into bearings

grease monkey *n inf* a mechanic, esp one who works on cars or aircraft

grease nipple *n* a metal nipple designed to engage with a grease gun for injecting grease into a bearing, etc

greasepaint (ˈgriːsˌpeɪnt) *n* **1** a waxy or greasy substance used as make-up by actors **2** theatrical make-up

greaseproof paper (ˈgriːsˌpruːf) *n* any paper that is resistant to penetration by greases and oils

greasies (ˈgriːsɪz) *pl n NZ inf* fish and chips

greasy (ˈgriːsɪ, -zɪ) *adj* **greasier, greasiest** **1** coated or soiled with or as if with grease **2** composed of or full of grease **3** resembling grease **4** unctuous or oily in manner > ˈ**greasily** *adv* > ˈ**greasiness** *n*

greasy wool *n* untreated wool still retaining the lanolin; used for waterproof clothing

great (greɪt) *adj* **1** relatively large in size or extent; big **2** relatively large in number; having many parts or members: *a great assembly* **3** of relatively long duration: *a great wait* **4** of larger size or more importance than others of its kind: *the great auk* **5** extreme or more than usual: *great worry* **6** of significant importance or consequence: *a great decision* **7a** of exceptional talents or achievements; remarkable: *a great writer* **7b** (*as n*): *the great; one of the greats* **8** doing or exemplifying (something) on a large scale: *she's a great reader* **9** arising from or possessing idealism in thought, action, etc; heroic: *great deeds* **10** illustrious or eminent: *a great history* **11** impressive or striking: *a great show of wealth* **12** active or enthusiastic: *a great walker* **13** (often foll by *at*) skilful or adroit: *a great carpenter; you are great at singing* **14** *inf* excellent; fantastic ▷ *n* **15** Also called: **great organ** the principal manual on an organ [OE *grēat*] > ˈ**greatly** *adv* > ˈ**greatness** *n*

great- *prefix* **1** being the parent of a person's grandparent (in the combinations **great-grandfather, great-grandmother, great-grandparent**) **2** being the child of a person's grandchild (in the combinations **great-grandson, great-granddaughter, great-grandchild**)

great auk *n* a large flightless auk, extinct since the middle of the 19th century

great-aunt *or* **grandaunt** *n* an aunt of one's father or mother; sister of one's grandfather or grandmother

Great Australian Bight *n* a wide bay of the Indian Ocean, in S Australia, extending from Cape Pasley to the Eyre Peninsula: notorious for storms

Great Barrier Reef *n* a coral reef in the Coral Sea, off the NE coast of Australia, extending for about 2000 km (1250 miles) from the Torres Strait along the coast of Queensland; the largest coral reef in the world

Great Basin *n* a semiarid region of the western US, between the Wasatch and the Sierra Nevada Mountains, having no drainage to the ocean: includes Nevada, W Utah, and parts of E California, S Oregon, and Idaho. Area: about 490 000 sq km (189 000 sq miles)

Great Bear *n* **the** the English name for **Ursa Major**

Great Bear Lake *n* a lake in NW Canada, in the Northwest Territories: the largest freshwater lake entirely in Canada; drained by the **Great Bear River,** which flows to the Mackenzie River. Area: 31 792 sq km (12 275 sq miles)

Great Belt *n* a strait in Denmark, between Zealand and Funen islands, linking the Kattegat with the Baltic. Danish name: **Store Bælt**

Great Britain *n* England, Wales, and Scotland including those adjacent islands governed from the mainland (i.e. excluding the Isle of Man and the Channel Islands). The United Kingdom of Great Britain was formed by the Act of Union (1707), although the term Great Britain had been in use since 1603, when James VI of Scotland became James I of England (including Wales). Later unions created the United Kingdom of Great Britain and Ireland (1801) and the United Kingdom of Great Britain and Northern Ireland (1922). Pop: 57 103 927 (2001 est). Area: 229 523 sq km (88 619 sq miles). See also **United Kingdom**

great circle *n* a circular section of a sphere that has a radius equal to that of the sphere

greatcoat (ˈgreɪtˌkəʊt) *n* a heavy overcoat

Great Dane *n* one of a very large breed of dog with a short smooth coat

Great Dividing Range *pl n* a series of mountain ranges and plateaus roughly parallel to the E coast of Australia, in Queensland, New South Wales, and Victoria; the highest range is the Australian Alps, in the south

Greater (ˈgreɪtə) *adj* (of a city) considered with the inclusion of the outer suburbs: *Greater London*

Greater Antilles *pl n* **the** a group of islands in the Caribbean, including Cuba, Jamaica, Hispaniola, and Puerto Rico

Greater London *n* See **London** (sense 2)

Greater Manchester *n* a metropolitan county of NW England, administered since 1986 by the unitary authorities of Wigan, Bolton, Bury, Rochdale, Salford, Manchester, Oldham, Trafford, Stockport, and Tameside. Area: 1286 sq km (496 sq miles)

Greater Sunda Islands *pl n* a group of islands in the W Malay Archipelago, forming the larger part of the Sunda Islands: consists of Borneo, Sumatra, Java, and Sulawesi

Great Glen *n* **the** a fault valley across the whole of Scotland, extending southwest from the Moray Firth in the east to Loch Linnhe and containing Loch Ness and Loch Lochy. Also called: **Glen More, Glen Albyn**

great gross *n* a unit of quantity equal to one dozen gross (or 1728)

great-hearted *adj* benevolent or noble; magnanimous > ˌ**great-**ˈ**heartedness** *n*

Great Indian Desert *n* another name for the **Thar Desert**

Great Lakes *pl n* a group of five lakes in central North America with connecting waterways: the largest group of lakes in the world: consists of Lakes Superior, Huron, Erie, and Ontario, which are divided by the border between the US and Canada and Lake Michigan, which is wholly in the US; constitutes the most important system of inland waterways in the world, discharging through the St Lawrence into the Atlantic. Total length: 3767 km (2340 miles). Area: 246 490 sq km (95 170 sq miles)

great-nephew *or* **grandnephew** *n* a son of one's nephew or niece; grandson of one's brother or sister

great-niece *or* **grandniece** *n* a daughter of one's nephew or niece; grand-daughter of one's brother or sister

Great Ouse *n* See **Ouse** (sense 1)

Great Plains *pl n* a vast region of North America east of the Rocky Mountains, extending from the lowlands of the Mackenzie River (Canada), south to the Big Bend of the Rio Grande

Great Red Spot *n* a large long-lived oval feature, south of Jupiter's equator, that is an anticyclonic disturbance in the atmosphere

Great Rift Valley *n* the most extensive rift in the earth's surface, extending from the Jordan valley in Syria to Mozambique; marked by a chain of steep-sided lakes, volcanoes, and escarpments

Great Russian *n* **1** *linguistics* the technical name for **Russian** **2** a member of the chief East Slavonic people of Russia ▷ *adj* **3** of or relating to this people or their language

Greats (greɪts) *pl n* (at Oxford University) **1** the Honour School of Literae Humaniores, involving the study of Greek and Roman history and literature and philosophy **2** the final examinations at the end of this course

Great Saint Bernard Pass *n, usually abbreviated to* **Great St Bernard Pass** a pass over the W Alps, between SW central Switzerland and N Italy: noted for the hospice at the summit, founded in the 11th century. Height: 2469 m (8100 ft)

Great Salt Lake *n* a shallow salt lake in NW Utah, in the Great Basin at an altitude of 1260 m (4200 ft): the area has fluctuated from less than 2500 sq km (1000 sq miles) to over 5000 sq km (2000 sq miles)

Great Sandy Desert *n* **1** a desert in NW Australia. Area: about 415 000 sq km (160 000 sq miles) **2** the English name for the **Rub' al Khali**

great seal *n* (*often caps*) the principal seal of a nation, sovereign, etc, used to authenticate documents of the highest importance

Great Slave Lake *n* a lake in NW Canada, in the Northwest Territories: drained by the Mackenzie River into the Arctic Ocean. Area: 28 440 sq km (10 980 sq miles)

Great Slave River *n* another name for the **Slave River**

Great Smoky Mountains *or* **Great Smokies** *pl n* the W part of the Appalachians, in W North Carolina and E Tennessee. Highest peak: Clingman's Dome, 2024 m (6642 ft)

Great Stour *n* another name for **Stour** (sense 1)

great tit *n* a Eurasian tit with yellow-and-black underparts and a black-and-white head

Great Trek *n* **the** *S African history* the migration of Boer farmers from the Cape Colony to the north and east from about 1836 to 1845 to escape British authority

great-uncle *or* **granduncle** *n* an uncle of one's father or mother; brother of one's grandfather or grandmother

Great Victoria Desert *n* a desert in S Australia, in SE Western Australia and W South Australia. Area: 323 750 sq km (125 000 sq miles)

Great Wall of China *n* a defensive wall in N China, extending from W Gansu to the Gulf of Liaodong: constructed in the 3rd century BC as a defence against the Mongols; substantially rebuilt in the 15th century. Length: over 2400 km (1500 miles). Average height: 6 m (20 ft). Average width: 6 m (20 ft)

Great War *n* another name for **World War I**

Great Yarmouth ('jɑːməθ) *n* a port and resort in E England, in E Norfolk. Pop: 56 190 (1991)

greave (griːv) *n* (*often pl*) a piece of armour worn to protect the shin [c14 from OF *greve*, ?from *graver* to part the hair, of Gmc origin]

grebe (griːb) *n* an aquatic bird, such as the great crested grebe and little grebe, similar to the divers but with lobate rather than webbed toes and a vestigial tail [c18 from F *grèbe*, from ?]

Grecian ('griːʃən) *adj* **1** (esp of beauty or architecture) conforming to Greek ideals ▷ *n* **2** a scholar of Greek ▷ *adj, n* **3** another word for **Greek**

Grecism ('griːˌsɪzəm) *n* a variant spelling (esp US) of **Graecism**

Greco- ('griːkəʊ, 'grɛkəʊ) *combining form* a variant (esp US) of **Graeco-**

Greco ('grɛkəʊ) *n* **El** See **El Greco**

Greece (griːs) *n* a republic in SE Europe, occupying the S part of the Balkan Peninsula and many islands in the Ionian and Aegean Seas; site of two of Europe's earliest civilizations (the Minoan and Mycenaean); in the classical era divided into many small independent city-states, the most important being Athens and Sparta; part of the Roman and Byzantine Empires; passed under Turkish rule in the late Middle Ages; became an independent kingdom in 1827; taken over by a military junta (1967–74); the monarchy was abolished in 1973; became a republic in 1975; a member of the European Union. Official language: Greek. Official religion: Eastern (Greek) Orthodox. Currency: euro. Capital: Athens. Pop: 10 975 000 (2001 est). Area: 131 944 sq km (50 944 sq miles). Modern Greek name: **Ellás** Related adj: **Hellenic**

▷ www.parliament.gr/english/default.asp
▷ www.gnto.gr
▷ www.ancientgreece.com
▷ www.historylink101.com/ancient_greece.htm

greed (griːd) *n* **1** excessive consumption of or desire for food **2** excessive desire, as for wealth or power [c17 back formation from GREEDY]

greedy ('griːdɪ) *adj* **greedier, greediest** **1** excessively desirous of food or wealth, esp in large amounts; voracious **2** (*postpositive*; foll by *for*) eager (for): *a man greedy for success* [OE *grǣdig*] > '**greedily** *adv* > '**greediness** *n*

greegree ('griːgriː) *n* a variant spelling of **grigri**

Greek (griːk) *n* **1** the official language of Greece, constituting the Hellenic branch of the Indo-European family of languages. See **Ancient Greek, Late Greek, Medieval Greek, Modern Greek** **2** a native or inhabitant of Greece or a descendant of such a native **3** a member of the Greek Orthodox Church **4** *inf* anything incomprehensible (esp in the phrase **it's (all) Greek to me**) **5** **Greek meets Greek** equals meet ▷ *adj* **6** denoting, relating to, or characteristic of Greece, the Greeks, or the Greek language; Hellenic **7** of, relating to, or designating the Greek Orthodox Church [from Old English *Grēcas* (plural), or Latin *Graecus*, from Greek *Graikos*] > '**Greekness** *n*

GREEK ALPHABET

alpha	α	A
beta	β	B
gamma	γ	Γ
delta	δ	Δ
epsilon	ε	E
zêta	ζ	Z
êta	η	H
theta	θ	Θ
iota	ι	I
kappa	κ	K
lambda	λ	Λ
mu	μ	M
nu	ν	N
xi	ξ	Ξ
omicron	ο	O

pi	π	Π
rho	ρ	P
sigma	σ	Σ
tau	τ	T
upsilon	υ	Y
phi	φ	Φ
chi	χ	X
psi	ψ	Ψ
omega	ω	Ω

Greek cross *n* a cross with each of the four arms of the same length

Greek fire *n* a Byzantine weapon consisting of an unknown mixture that caught fire when wetted

Greek gift *n* a gift given with the intention of tricking and causing harm to the recipient [C19 in allusion to Virgil's *Aeneid* ii 49; see also TROJAN HORSE]

Greek Orthodox Church *n* 1 Also called: **Greek Church** the established Church of Greece, governed by the holy synod of Greece, in which the Metropolitan of Athens has primacy of honour 2 another name for **Orthodox Church**
▷ http://www.patriarchate.org

green (gri:n) *n* 1 any of a group of colours, such as that of fresh grass, that lie between yellow and blue in the visible spectrum. Related adj: **verdant** 2 a dye or pigment of or producing these colours 3 something of the colour green 4 a small area of grassland, esp in the centre of a village 5 an area of smooth turf kept for a special purpose: *a putting green* 6 (*pl*) 6a the edible leaves and stems of certain plants, eaten as a vegetable 6b freshly cut branches of ornamental trees, shrubs, etc, used as a decoration 7 (*sometimes cap*) a person, esp a politician, who supports environmentalist issues ▷ *adj* 8 of the colour green 9 greenish in colour or having parts or marks that are greenish 10 (*sometimes cap*) of or concerned with conservation of natural resources and improvement of the environment: used esp in a political context 11 vigorous; not faded: *a green old age* 12 envious or jealous 13 immature, unsophisticated, or gullible 14 characterized by foliage or green plants: *a green wood; a green salad* 15 (formerly) denoting a unit of account that is adjusted in accordance with fluctuations between the currencies of the EU nations and is used to make payments to agricultural producers within the EU: *green pound* 16 fresh, raw, or unripe: *green bananas* 17 unhealthily pale in appearance: *he was green after his boat trip* 18 (of meat) not smoked or cured: *green bacon* 19 (of timber) freshly felled; not dried or seasoned ▷ *vb* 20 to make or become green [OE *grēne*] > '**greenish** *or* '**greeny** *adj* > '**greenly** *adv* > '**greenness** *n*

Green (gri:n) *n* 1 **Henry,** real name *Henry Vincent Yorke.* 1905–73, British novelist: author of *Living* (1929), *Loving* (1945), and *Back* (1946) 2 **John Richard** 1837–83, British historian; author of *A Short History of the English People* (1874) 3 **T(homas) H(ill)** 1836–82, British idealist philosopher. His chief work, *Prolegomena to Ethics,* was unfinished at his death

Greenaway ('gri:nə,weɪ) *n* **Kate** 1846–1901, English painter, noted as an illustrator of children's books

greenback ('gri:n,bæk) *n US* 1 *inf* a legal-tender US currency note 2 *sl* a dollar bill

green ban *n Austral* a trade-union ban on any development that might be considered harmful to the environment

green bean *n* any bean plant, such as the French bean, having narrow green edible pods

green belt *n* a zone of farmland, parks, and open country surrounding a town or city

Green Cross Code *n Brit* a code for children giving rules for road safety

Greene (gri:n) *n* 1 **Graham** 1904–91, English novelist and dramatist; his works include the novels *Brighton Rock* (1938), *The Power and the Glory* (1940), *The End of the Affair* (1951), and *Our Man in Havana* (1958), and the film script *The Third Man* (1949) 2 **Robert** ?1558–92, English poet, dramatist, and prose writer, noted for his autobiographical tract *A Groatsworth of Wit bought with a Million of Repentance* (1592), which contains an attack on Shakespeare

greenery ('gri:nərɪ) *n, pl* **greeneries** green foliage, esp when used for decoration

green-eyed *adj* 1 jealous or envious 2 **the green-eyed monster** jealousy or envy

greenfield ('gri:n,fi:ld) *n* (*modifier*). denoting or located in a rural area which has not previously been built on

greenfinch ('gri:n,fɪntʃ) *n* a European finch the male of which has a dull green plumage with yellow patches on the wings and tail

green fingers *pl n* considerable talent or ability to grow plants

Green Flag *n* an award given to a bathing beach that meets EU standards of cleanliness but that does not provide facilities

greenfly ('gri:n,flaɪ) *n, pl* **greenflies** a greenish aphid commonly occurring as a pest on garden and crop plants

greengage ('gri:n,geɪdʒ) *n* 1 a cultivated variety of plum tree with edible green plumlike fruits 2 the fruit of this tree [C18 GREEN + *-gage,* after Sir W. *Gage* (1777–1864), E botanist who brought it from France]

greengrocer ('gri:n,grəʊsə) *n chiefly Brit* a retail trader in fruit and vegetables > '**green,grocery** *n*

Greenham Common ('gri:nəm) *n* a village in West Berkshire unitary authority, Berkshire; site of a US cruise missile base, and, from 1981, a camp of women protesters against nuclear weapons; although the base had closed by 1991 a small number of women remained until 2000

greenheart ('gri:n,hɑ:t) *n* 1 Also called: **bebeeru** a tropical American tree that has dark green durable wood 2 any of various similar trees 3 the wood of any of these trees

greenhorn ('gri:n,hɔ:n) *n* 1 an inexperienced person, esp one who is extremely gullible 2 *chiefly US* a newcomer [C17 orig. an animal with *green* (that is, young) horns]

greenhouse ('gri:n,haʊs) *n* 1 a building with glass walls and roof for the cultivation of plants under controlled conditions ▷ *adj* 2 relating to or contributing to the greenhouse effect: *greenhouse gases, such as carbon dioxide*

greenhouse effect *n* 1 an effect occurring in greenhouses, etc, in which ultraviolet radiation from the sun passes through the glass warming the contents, the infrared radiation from inside being trapped by the glass 2 the application of this effect to a planet's atmosphere, esp the warming up of the earth as man-made carbon dioxide in the atmosphere traps the infrared radiation emitted by the earth's surface as a result of exposure to solar radiation. The greenhouse effect is made more serious by damage to the ozone layer, which permits more ultraviolet radiation to reach the earth

greenie ('gri:nɪ) *n Austral inf* a conservationist

green-ink brigade *n inf* a collective term for people who write abusive or threatening letters to people in the public eye [C20 from the idea that only the eccentric would write in green ink]

greenkeeper ('gri:n,ki:pə) *n* a person responsible for maintaining a golf course or bowling green

Greenland ('gri:nlənd) *n* a large island, lying mostly within the Arctic Circle off the NE coast of North America: first settled by Icelanders in 986; resettled by Danes from 1721 onwards; integral part of Denmark (1953–79); granted internal autonomy 1979; mostly covered by an icecap up to 3300 m (11 000 ft) thick, with ice-free coastal strips and coastal mountains; the population is largely Inuit, with a European minority; fishing, hunting, and mining. Capital: Nuuk. Pop: 56 300 (2001 est). Area: 175 600 sq km (840 000 sq miles). Danish name: **Grønland** Greenlandic name: **Kalaallit Nunaat**

Greenlandic (griːnˈlændɪk) *adj* 1 of, relating to, or characteristic of Greenland, the Greenlanders, or the Inuit dialect spoken in Greenland ▷ *n* 2 the dialect of Inuktitut spoken in Greenland

Greenland Sea *n* the S part of the Arctic Ocean, off the NE coast of Greenland

Greenland whale *n* another name for **bowhead**

green leek *n* any of several Australian parrots with a green or mostly green plumage

green light *n* 1 a signal to go, esp a green traffic light 2 permission to proceed with a project, etc ▷ *vb* **greenlight, greenlights, greenlighting, greenlighted** (*tr*) 3 to permit (a project, etc) to proceed

green line *n* a line of demarcation between two hostile communities

greenmail (ˈɡriːnˌmeɪl) *n* (esp in the US) the practice of a company buying sufficient shares in another company to threaten takeover and making a quick profit as a result of the threatened company buying back its shares at a higher price

green monkey disease *n* another name for **Marburg disease**

Green Mountains *pl n* a mountain range in E North America, extending from Canada through Vermont into W Massachusetts: part of the Appalachian system. Highest peak: Mount Mansfield, 1338 m (4393 ft)

Greenock (ˈɡriːnək) *n* a port in SW Scotland, in Inverclyde on the Firth of Clyde: shipbuilding and other marine industries. Pop: 50 013 (1991)

Greenough (ˈɡriːnəʊ) *n* **George Bellas** 1778–1855, English geologist, founder of the Geological Society of London

green paper *n* (*often caps*) (in Britain) a government document containing policy proposals to be discussed, esp by Parliament

Green Party *n* a political party whose policies are based on concern for the environment

Greenpeace (ˈɡriːnˌpiːs) *n* a conservationist organization founded in 1971: members take active but nonviolent measures against what are regarded as threats to environmental safety, such as the dumping of nuclear waste at sea

green pepper *n* the green unripe fruit of the sweet pepper, eaten raw or cooked

green pound *n* a unit of account used in calculating Britain's contributions to and payments from the Community Agricultural Fund of the EU. See also **green** (sense 15)

Green River *n* a river in the western US, rising in W central Wyoming and flowing south into Utah, east through NW Colorado, re-entering Utah before joining the Colorado River. Length: 1175 km (730 miles)

greenroom (ˈɡriːnˌruːm, -ˌrʊm) *n* (esp formerly) a backstage room in a theatre where performers may rest or receive visitors [c18 prob. from its original colour]

greensand (ˈɡriːnˌsænd) *n* an olive-green sandstone consisting mainly of quartz and glauconite

Greensboro (ˈɡriːnzbərə, -brə) *n* a city in N central North Carolina. Pop: 223 891 (2000)

greenshank (ˈɡriːnˌʃæŋk) *n* a large European sandpiper with greenish legs and a slightly upturned bill

greensickness (ˈɡriːnˌsɪknɪs) *n* an informal name for **chlorosis**

greenstick fracture (ˈɡriːnˌstɪk) *n* a fracture in children in which the bone is partly bent and splinters only on the convex side of the bend [c20 alluding to the similar way in which a green stick splinters]

greenstone (ˈɡriːnˌstəʊn) *n* 1 any basic dark green igneous rock 2 a variety of jade formerly used in New Zealand by Maoris for ornaments and tools, now used for jewellery

greensward (ˈɡriːnˌswɔːd) *n* *arch or literary* fresh green turf or an area of such turf

green tea *n* a sharp tea made from tea leaves that have been dried quickly without fermenting

green turtle *n* a mainly tropical edible turtle, with greenish flesh

greenwash (ˈɡriːnˌwɒʃ) *n* a superficial or insincere display of concern for the environment that is shown by an organization

green-wellie *n* (*modifier*) characterizing or belonging to the upper-class set devoted to hunting, shooting, and fishing: *the green-wellie brigade*

Greenwich (ˈɡrɪnɪdʒ, -ɪtʃ, ˈɡrɛn-) *n* a Greater London borough on the Thames: site of a Royal Naval College and of the original Royal Observatory designed by Christopher Wren (1675), accepted internationally as the prime meridian of longitude since 1884, and the basis of Greenwich Mean Time; also site of the Millennium Dome. Pop: 214 540 (2001). Area: 46 sq km (18 sq miles)

Greenwich Electronic Time *n* an international time standard designed for electronic commerce on the Internet

Greenwich Mean Time *or* **Greenwich Time** *n* mean solar time on the 0° meridian passing through Greenwich, England, measured from midnight: formerly a standard time in Britain and a basis for calculating times throughout most of the world, it has been replaced by an atomic timescale. See **universal time** Abbrev: **GMT**

> USAGE The name *Greenwich Mean Time* is ambiguous, having been measured from mean midday in astronomy up to 1925, and is not used for scientific purposes. It is generally and incorrectly used in the sense of *universal coordinated time*, an atomic timescale available since 1972 from broadcast signals, in addition to the earliest sense of *universal time*, adopted internationally in 1928 as the name for GMT measured from midnight

Greenwich Village (ˈɡrɛnɪtʃ, ˈɡrɪn-) *n* a part of New York City in the lower west side of Manhattan; traditionally the home of many artists and writers

greenwood (ˈɡriːnˌwʊd) *n* a forest or wood when the leaves are green

Greer (ɡrɪə) *n* **Germaine** born 1939, Australian writer and feminist. Her books include *The Female Eunuch* (1970), *Sex and Destiny* (1984), and *The Whole Woman* (1998)

greet[1] (ɡriːt) *vb* (*tr*) 1 to meet or receive with expressions of gladness or welcome 2 to send a message of friendship to 3 to receive in a specified manner: *her remarks were greeted by silence* 4 to become apparent to: *the smell of bread greeted him* [OE *grētan*] > ˈ**greeter** *n*

greet[2] (ɡriːt) *Scot or dialect* ▷ *vb* 1 (*intr*) to weep; lament ▷ *n* 2 weeping; lamentation [from OE *grētan*, N dialect var. of *grætan*]

greeting (ˈɡriːtɪŋ) *n* 1 the act or an instance of welcoming or saluting on meeting 2 (*often pl*) 2a an expression of friendly salutation 2b (*as modifier*): *a greetings card*

gregarious (ɡrɪˈɡɛərɪəs) *adj* 1 enjoying the company of others 2 (of animals) living together in herds or flocks 3 (of plants) growing close together 4 of or characteristic of crowds or communities [c17 from L, from *grex* flock] > **gre**ˈ**gariously** *adv* > **gre**ˈ**gariousness** *n*

Gregorian calendar (ɡrɪˈɡɔːrɪən) *n* the revision of the Julian calendar introduced in 1582 by Pope Gregory XIII and still in force, whereby the ordinary year is made to consist of 365 days

Gregorian Calendar

January
February
March
April
May
June
July
August
September
October
November
December

Gregorian chant *n* another name for **plainsong**
Gregorian telescope *n* a type of reflecting astronomical telescope with a concave secondary mirror and the eyepiece set in the centre of the parabolic primary mirror [C18 after J. *Gregory* (died 1675), Scot. mathematician]
Gregory (ˈɡrɛɡərɪ) *n* Lady (**Isabella**) **Augusta** (**Persse**) 1852–1932, Irish dramatist; a founder and director of the Abbey Theatre, Dublin
Gregory I *n* **Saint,** known as *Gregory the Great*. ?540–604 AD, pope (590–604), who greatly influenced the medieval Church. He strengthened papal authority by centralizing administration, tightened discipline, and revised the liturgy. He appointed Saint Augustine missionary to England. Feast day: March 12 or Sept. 3
Gregory VII *n* **Saint,** monastic name *Hildebrand*. ?1020–85, pope (1073– 85), who did much to reform abuses in the Church. His assertion of papal supremacy and his prohibition (1075) of lay investiture was opposed by the Holy Roman Emperor Henry IV, whom he excommunicated (1076). He was driven into exile when Henry captured Rome (1084). Feast day: May 25
Gregory XIII *n* 1502–85, pope (1572–85). He promoted the Counter-Reformation and founded seminaries. His reformed (Gregorian) calendar was issued in 1582
Gregory of Tours *n* **Saint** ?538–?594 AD, Frankish bishop and historian. His *Historia Francorum* is the chief source of knowledge of 6th-century Gaul. Feast day: Nov. 17
gremial (ˈɡriːmɪəl) *n RC Church* a cloth spread upon the lap of a bishop when seated during Mass [C17 from L *gremium* lap]
gremlin (ˈɡrɛmlɪn) *n* **1** an imaginary imp jokingly said to be responsible for mechanical troubles in aircraft, esp in World War II **2** any mischievous troublemaker [C20 from ?]
Grenada (ɡrɛˈneɪdə) *n* an island state in the Caribbean, in the Windward Islands: formerly a British colony (1783–1967); since 1974 an independent state within the Commonwealth; occupied by US troops (1983–85); mainly agricultural. Official language: English. Religion: Christian majority. Currency: East Caribbean dollar. Capital: St George's. Pop: 102 000 (2001 est). Area: 344 sq km (133 sq miles)
▷ http://grenadagrenadines.com
grenade (ɡrɪˈneɪd) *n* **1** a small container filled with explosive thrown by hand or fired from a rifle **2** a sealed glass vessel that is thrown and shatters to release chemicals, such as tear gas [C16 from F, from Sp.: pomegranate, from LL, from L *grānātus* seedy; see GRAIN]
Grenadian (ɡrɛˈneɪdɪən) *adj* **1** of or relating to Grenada or its inhabitants ▷ *n* **2** a native or inhabitant of Grenada
grenadier (ˌɡrɛnəˈdɪə) *n* **1** *mil* **1a** (in the British Army) a member of the senior regiment of infantry in the Household Brigade **1b** (formerly) a member of a special formation, usually selected for strength and height **1c** (formerly) a soldier trained to throw grenades **2** any of various deep-sea fish, typically having a large head and a long tapering tail [C17 from F; see GRENADE]
grenadine[1] (ˌɡrɛnəˈdiːn) *n* a light thin fabric of silk, wool, rayon, or nylon, used for dresses, etc [C19 from F]
grenadine[2] (ˌɡrɛnəˈdiːn, ˈɡrɛnəˌdiːn) *n* a syrup made from pomegranate juice, used as a sweetening and colouring agent in various drinks [C19 from F: a little pomegranate; see GRENADE]
Grenadines (ˌɡrɛnəˈdiːnz, ˈɡrɛnəˌdiːnz) *pl n* **the** a chain of about 600 islets in the Caribbean, part of the Windward Islands, extending for about 100 km (60 miles) between St Vincent and Grenada and divided administratively between the two states. Largest island: Carriacou
Grendel (ˈɡrɛndᵊl) *n* (in Old English legend) a man-eating monster defeated by the hero Beowulf
Grenfell (ˈɡrɛnfəl) *n* **Joyce,** real name *Joyce Irene Phipps*. 1910–79, British comedy actress and writer
Grenoble (ɡrəˈnəʊbᵊl; *French* ɡrənɔblə) *n* a city in SE France, on the Isère River: university (1339). Pop: 153 317 (1999)
Grenville (ˈɡrɛnvɪl) *n* **1** **George** 1712–70, British statesman; prime minister (1763–65) His policy of taxing the American colonies precipitated the War of Independence **2** Sir **Richard** ?1541–91, English naval commander. He was fatally wounded aboard his ship, the *Revenge*, during a lone battle with a fleet of Spanish treasure ships **3** **William Wyndham,** Baron Grenville, son of George Grenville. 1759–1834, British statesman; prime minister (1806–07) of the coalition government known as the "ministry of all the talents"
Gresham (ˈɡrɛʃəm) *n* Sir **Thomas** ?1519–79, English financier, who founded the Royal Exchange in London (1568)
Gresham's law *or* **theorem** *n* the economic hypothesis that bad money drives good money out of circulation; the superior currency will tend to be hoarded and the inferior will thus dominate the circulation [C16 after Sir T. GRESHAM]
gressorial (ɡrɛˈsɔːrɪəl) *or* **gressorious** *adj* **1** (of the feet of certain birds) specialized for walking **2** (of birds, such as the ostrich) having such feet [C19 from NL, from *gressus* having walked, from *gradī* to step]
Gretna Green (ˈɡrɛtnə) *n* a village in S Scotland, in Dumfries and Galloway on the border with England: famous smithy where eloping couples were married by the blacksmith from 1754 until 1940, when such marriages became illegal. Pop: 3149 (1991)
Gretzky (ˈɡrɛtski) *n* **Wayne** born 1961, Canadian ice-hockey player, based in the U.S
Greville (ˈɡrɛvɪl) *n* **Fulke** (fʊlk), 1st Baron Brooke. 1554–1628, English poet, writer, politician, and diplomat: Chancellor of the Exchequer (1614–22); author of *The Life of the Renowned Sir Philip Sidney* (1652)
grew (ɡruː) *vb* the past tense of **grow**
grey *or US* **gray** (ɡreɪ) *adj* **1** of a neutral tone, intermediate between black and white, that has no hue and reflects and transmits only a little light **2** greyish in colour or having greyish marks **3** dismal or dark, esp from lack of light; gloomy **4** conventional or dull, esp in character or opinion **5** having grey hair **6** of or relating to people of middle age or above: *grey power* **7** ancient; venerable ▷ *n* **8** any of a group of grey tones **9** grey cloth or clothing **10** an animal, esp a horse, that is grey or whitish ▷ *vb* **11** to become or make grey [OE *grǣg*] > **ˈgreyish** *or US* **ˈgrayish** *adj* > **ˈgreyness** *or US* **ˈgrayness** *n*
Grey (ɡreɪ) *n* **1** **Charles,** 2nd Earl Grey. 1764–1845, British statesman. As Whig prime minister (1830–34), he carried the Reform Bill of 1832 and the bill for the abolition of slavery throughout the British Empire (1833) **2** Sir **Edward,** 1st Viscount Grey of Fallodon. 1862–1933, British statesman; foreign secretary (1905–16) **3** Sir **George** 1812–98, British statesman and colonial

administrator; prime minister of New Zealand (1877–79) **4** Lady **Jane** 1537–54, queen of England (July 9–19, 1553); great-granddaughter of Henry VII. Her father-in-law, the Duke of Northumberland, persuaded Edward VI to alter the succession in her favour, but after ten days as queen she was imprisoned and later executed **5 Zane** 1875–1939, US author of Westerns, including *Riders of the Purple Sage* (1912)

grey area *n* **1** an area or part of something existing between two extremes and having mixed characteristics of both **2** an area, situation, etc, lacking clearly defined characteristics

greybeard *or US* **graybeard** (ˈgreɪˌbɪəd) *n* **1** an old man, esp a sage **2** a large stoneware or earthenware jar or jug for spirits

grey eminence *n* the English equivalent of ***éminence grise***

Grey Friar *n* a Franciscan friar

greyhen (ˈgreɪˌhɛn) *n* the female of the black grouse

greyhound (ˈgreɪˌhaʊnd) *n* a tall slender fast-moving breed of dog
▷ www.thedogs.co.uk
▷ www.gra-america.org
▷ www.graq.org.au

grey knight *n inf* an ambiguous intervener in a takeover battle, who makes a counterbid for the shares of the target company without having made his intentions clear ▷ Cf **black knight, white knight**

greylag *or* **greylag goose** (ˈgreɪˌlæg) *n* a large grey Eurasian goose: the ancestor of many domestic breeds of goose. US spelling: **graylag** [C18 from GREY + LAG[1], from its migrating later than other species]

grey market *n* **1** trade in newly-issued shares before they have been formally listed and traded on the Stock Exchange **2** a practice in which supermarkets buy excess stock of branded goods from other retailers at a low margin and then sell them at discounted prices **3** the market for goods and services created by older people with a comfortable disposable income and increased opportunities for spending it

grey matter *n* **1** the greyish tissue of the brain and spinal cord, containing nerve cell bodies and fibres **2** *inf* brains or intellect

grey nurse shark *n* a common greyish Australian shark, *Odontaspis arenarius*

grey squirrel *n* a grey-furred squirrel, native to E North America but now widely established

Grey-Thompson (ˈgreɪˈtɒmpsən) *n* **Tanni** (**Carys Davina**) born 1969, British wheelchair athlete; nine gold medals in the Paralympics (1988–2000)

grey vote *n* the body of elderly people's votes, or elderly people regarded collectively as voters

greywacke (ˈgreɪˌwækə) *n* any dark sandstone or grit having a matrix of clay minerals [C19 partial translation of G *Grauwacke;* see WACKE]

grey water *n* water that has been used for one purpose but can be used again for another without repurification (e.g. bathwater, which can be used to water plants)

grey wolf *n* another name for **timber wolf**

grid (grɪd) *n* **1** See **gridiron 2** a network of horizontal and vertical lines superimposed over a map, building plan, etc, for locating points **3** a grating consisting of parallel bars **4 the grid** the national network of transmission lines, pipes, etc, by which electricity, gas, or water is distributed **5** Also called: **control grid** *electronics* an electrode usually consisting of a cylindrical mesh of wires, that controls the flow of electrons between the cathode and anode of a valve **6** See **starting grid 7** a plate in an accumulator that carries the active substance **8** any interconnecting system of links: *the bus service formed a grid across the country* [C19 back formation from GRIDIRON]

grid bias *n* the fixed voltage applied between the control grid and cathode of a valve

griddle (ˈgrɪdᵊl) *n* **1** Also called: **girdle** *Brit* a thick round iron plate with a half hoop handle over the top, for making scones, etc **2** any flat heated surface, esp on the top of a stove, for cooking food ▷ *vb* **griddles, griddling, griddled 3** (*tr*) to cook (food) on a griddle [C13 from OF *gridil*, from LL *crātīculum* (unattested) fine wickerwork; see GRILL]

griddlecake (ˈgrɪdᵊlˌkeɪk) *n* another name for **drop scone**

gridiron (ˈgrɪdˌaɪən) *n* **1** a utensil of parallel metal bars, used to grill meat, fish, etc **2** any framework resembling this utensil **3** a framework above the stage in a theatre from which suspended scenery, lights, etc, are manipulated **4a** the field of play in American football **4b** an informal name for **American football** ▷ Often shortened to **grid** [C13 *gredire*, ? a var. (through influence of *ire* IRON) of *gredile* GRIDDLE]

gridlock (ˈgrɪdˌlɒk) *chiefly US* ▷ *n* **1** obstruction of urban traffic caused by queues of vehicles forming across junctions and causing further queues to form in the intersecting streets **2** a point in a dispute at which no agreement can be reached: *political gridlock* ▷ *vb* **3** (*tr*) (of traffic) to block or obstruct (an area)

grid road *n* (in Canada) a road that follows a surveyed division between areas of a township, municipality, etc

grief (gri:f) *n* **1** deep or intense sorrow, esp at the death of someone **2** something that causes keen distress **3** *Brit & S African inf* trouble or annoyance: *I got grief for leaving early* **4 come to grief** *inf* to end unsuccessfully or disastrously [C13 from Anglo-F *gref*, from *grever* to GRIEVE]

grief tourism *n* the practice of travelling to a place specifically in order to take part in public mourning

Grieg (gri:g) *n* **Edvard** (**Hagerup**) (ˈɛdvard) 1843–1907, Norwegian composer. His works, often inspired by Norwegian folk music, include the incidental music for *Peer Gynt* (1876), a piano concerto, and many songs

Grierson (ˈgrɪəsᵊn) *n* **John** 1898–1972, Scottish film director. He coined the noun *documentary*, of which genre his *Industrial Britain* (1931) and *Song of Ceylon* (1934) are notable examples

grievance (ˈgri:vᵊns) *n* **1** a real or imaginary wrong causing resentment and regarded as grounds for complaint **2** a feeling of resentment or injustice at having been unfairly treated [C15 *grevance*, from OF, from *grever* to GRIEVE]

grieve (gri:v) *vb* **grieves, grieving, grieved** to feel or cause to feel great sorrow or distress, esp at the death of someone [C13 from OF *grever*, from L *gravāre* to burden, from *gravis* heavy] > ˈ**griever** *n* > ˈ**grieving** *n, adj*

grievous (ˈgri:vəs) *adj* **1** very severe or painful: *a grievous injury* **2** very serious; heinous: *a grievous sin* **3** showing or marked by grief **4** causing great pain or suffering > ˈ**grievously** *adv* > ˈ**grievousness** *n*

grievous bodily harm *n criminal law* serious injury caused by one person to another

griffin (ˈgrɪfɪn), **griffon,** *or* **gryphon** *n* a winged monster with an eagle-like head and the body of a lion [C14 from OF *grifon*, from L *grȳphus*, from Gk *grups*, from *grupos* hooked]

Griffith (ˈgrɪfɪθ) *n* **1 Arthur** 1872–1922, Irish journalist and nationalist: founder of Sinn Féin (1905); president of the Free State assembly (1922) **2 D**(**avid Lewelyn**) **W**(**ark**) 1875–1948, US film director and producer. He introduced several cinematic techniques, including the flashback and the fade-out, in his masterpiece *The Birth of a Nation* (1915)

Griffith-Joyner (ˌgrɪfɪθˈdʒɔɪnə) *n* **Florence,** known as *Flojo*. 1959–98, US sprinter, winner of two gold medals at the 1988 Olympic Games

griffon[1] (ˈgrɪfᵊn) *n* **1** any of various small wire-haired breeds of dog, originally from Belgium **2** a large vulture of Africa, S Europe, and SW Asia, having a pale plumage with black wings [C19 from F: GRIFFIN]

griffon² (ˈgrɪfᵊn) *n* a variant of **griffin**

grifter (ˈgrɪftə) *n sl, chiefly US* a petty criminal or gambler [C20 a blend of GR(AFT)² (sense 2) + DRIFTER (sense 2)]

Grigioni (griˈdʒoːni) *n* the Italian name for **Graubünden**

grigri, gris-gris, *or* **greegree** (ˈgriːgriː) *n, pl* **grigris, gris-gris** (-griːz) *or* **greegrees** an African talisman, amulet, or charm [of African origin]

grill (grɪl) *vb* **1** to cook (meat, etc) by direct heat, as under a grill or over a hot fire, or (of meat, etc) to be cooked in this way. Usual US and Canad word: **broil** **2** (*tr; usually passive*) to torment with or as if with extreme heat: *the travellers were grilled by the scorching sun* **3** (*tr*) *inf* to subject to insistent or prolonged questioning ▷ *n* **4** a device with parallel bars of thin metal on which meat, etc, may be cooked by a fire; gridiron **5** a device on a cooker that radiates heat downwards for grilling meat, etc **6** food cooked by grilling **7** See **grillroom** [C17 from F *gril* gridiron, from L *crātīcula* fine wickerwork; see GRILLE] > **grilled** *adj* > **ˈgriller** *n*

grillage (ˈgrɪlɪdʒ) *n* an arrangement of beams and crossbeams used as a foundation on soft ground [C18 from F, from *griller* to furnish with a grille]

grille *or* **grill** (grɪl) *n* **1** a framework, esp of metal bars arranged to form an ornamental pattern, used as a screen or partition **2** Also called: **radiator grille** a grating that admits cooling air to the radiator of a motor vehicle **3** a metal or wooden openwork grating used as a screen or divider **4** a protective screen, usually plastic or metal, in front of the loudspeaker in a radio, record player, etc [C17 from OF, from L *crātīcula* fine hurdlework, from *crātis* a hurdle]

grillroom (ˈgrɪlˌruːm, -ˌrʊm) *n* a restaurant where grilled steaks and other meat are served

grilse (grɪls) *n, pl* **grilses** *or* **grilse** a young salmon that returns to fresh water after one winter in the sea [C15 *grilles* (pl), from ?]

grim (grɪm) *adj* **grimmer, grimmest** **1** stern; resolute: *grim determination* **2** harsh or formidable in manner or appearance **3** harshly ironic or sinister: *grim laughter* **4** cruel, severe, or ghastly: *a grim accident* **5** *arch or poetic* fierce: *a grim warrior* **6** *inf* unpleasant; disagreeable [OE *grimm*] > **ˈgrimly** *adv* > **ˈgrimness** *n*

grimace (grɪˈmeɪs) *n* **1** an ugly or distorted facial expression, as of wry humour, disgust, etc ▷ *vb* **grimaces, grimacing, grimaced** **2** (*intr*) to contort the face [C17 from F, of Gmc origin; rel. to Sp. *grimazo* caricature] > **griˈmacer** *n*

Grimaldi² (grɪˈmɔːldɪ) *n* **Joseph** 1779–1837, English actor, noted as a clown in pantomime

grimalkin (grɪˈmælkɪn, -ˈmɔːl-) *n* **1** an old cat, esp an old female cat **2** a crotchety or shrewish old woman [C17 from GREY + *malkin*, dim. of female name *Maud*]

grime (graɪm) *n* **1** dirt, soot, or filth, esp when ingrained ▷ *vb* **grimes, griming, grimed** **2** (*tr*) to make dirty or coat with filth [C15 from MDu. *grime*] > **ˈgrimy** *adj* > **ˈgriminess** *n*

Grimm (grɪm) *n* **Jakob Ludwig Karl** (ˈjaːkɔp ˈluːtvɪç karl), 1785–1863, and his brother, **Wilhelm Karl** (ˈvɪlhɛlm karl), 1786–1859, German philologists and folklorists, who collaborated on *Grimm's Fairy Tales* (1812–22) and began a German dictionary. Jakob is noted also for his philological work *Deutsche Grammatik* (1819–37), in which he formulated the law named after him

Grimsby (ˈgrɪmzbɪ) *n* a port in E England, in North East Lincolnshire unitary authority, Lincolnshire, formerly important for fishing. Pop: 90 703 (1991)

grin (grɪn) *vb* **grins, grinning, grinned** **1** to smile with the lips drawn back revealing the teeth or express (something) by such a smile: *to grin a welcome* **2** (*intr*) to draw back the lips revealing the teeth, as in a snarl or grimace **3** **grin and bear it** *inf* to suffer trouble or hardship without complaint ▷ *n* **4** a broad smile **5** a snarl or grimace [OE *grennian*] > **ˈgrinning** *adj, n*

grinch (grɪntʃ) *n US inf* a person whose lack of enthusiasm or bad temper has a depressing effect on others [C20 from a character in the 1957 children's book *How the Grinch stole Christmas* by Dr Seuss (1904–91), US writer and illustrator, whose full name was Theodor Seuss Geisel]

grind (graɪnd) *vb* **grinds, grinding, ground** **1** to reduce or be reduced to small particles by pounding or abrading: *to grind corn* **2** (*tr*) to smooth, sharpen, or polish by friction or abrasion: *to grind a knife* **3** to scrape or grate together (two things, esp the teeth) with a harsh rasping sound or (of such objects) to be scraped together **4** (*tr; foll by out*) to speak or say something in a rough voice **5** (*tr; often foll by down*) to hold down; oppress; tyrannize **6** (*tr*) to operate (a machine) by turning a handle **7** (*tr; foll by out*) to produce in a routine or uninspired manner: *he ground out his weekly article for the paper* **8** (*intr*) *inf* to study or work laboriously ▷ *n* **9** *inf* laborious or routine work or study **10** a specific grade of pulverization, as of coffee beans: *coarse grind* **11** the act or sound of grinding [OE *grindan*] > **ˈgrindingly** *adv*

Grindelwald (*German* ˈgrɪndəlvalt) *n* a valley and resort in central Switzerland, in the Bernese Oberland: mountaineering centre, with the Wetterhorn and the Eiger nearby

grinder (ˈgraɪndə) *n* **1** a person who grinds, esp one who grinds cutting tools **2** a machine for grinding **3** a molar tooth

grindstone (ˈgraɪndˌstəʊn) *n* **1a** a machine having a circular block of stone rotated for sharpening tools or grinding metal **1b** the stone used in this machine **1c** any stone used for sharpening; whetstone **2** **keep** *or* **have one's nose to the grindstone** to work hard and perseveringly

gringo (ˈgrɪŋgəʊ) *n, pl* **gringos** a person from an English-speaking country: used as a derogatory term by Latin Americans [C19 from Sp.: foreigner, prob. from *griego* Greek, hence an alien]

grip (grɪp) *n* **1** the act or an instance of grasping and holding firmly: *he lost his grip on the slope* **2** Also called: **handgrip** the strength or pressure of such a grasp, as in a handshake **3** the style or manner of grasping an object, such as a tennis racket **4** understanding, control, or mastery of a subject, problem, etc **5** a person who manoeuvres the cameras in a film or television studio **6** **get** *or* **come to grips** (often foll by *with*) **6a** to deal with (a problem or subject) **6b** to tackle (an assailant) **7** Also called: **handgrip** a part by which an object is grasped; handle **8** Also called: **handgrip** a travelling bag or holdall **9** See **hairgrip** **10** any device that holds by friction, such as certain types of brake ▷ *vb* **grips, gripping, gripped** **11** to take hold of firmly or tightly, as by a clutch **12** to hold the interest or attention of: *the thrilling performance gripped the audience* [OE *gripe* grasp] > **ˈgripper** *n* > **ˈgripping** *adj*

gripe (graɪp) *vb* **gripes, griping, griped** **1** (*intr*) *inf* to complain, esp in a persistent nagging manner **2** to cause sudden intense pain in the intestines of (a person) or (of a person) to experience this pain **3** *arch* to clutch; grasp **4** (*tr*) *arch* to afflict ▷ *n* **5** (*usually pl*) a sudden intense pain in the intestines; colic **6** *inf* a complaint or grievance **7** *now rare* **7a** the act of gripping **7b** a firm grip **7c** a device that grips [OE *grīpan*] > **ˈgriper** *n*

Gripe Water *n Brit, trademark* a solution given to infants to relieve colic

grippe *or* **grip** (grɪp) *n* a former name for **influenza** [C18 from F *grippe*, from *gripper* to seize, of Gmc origin; see GRIP]

Griqualand East (ˈgriːkwəˌlænd, ˈgrɪk-) *n* an area of central South Africa: settled in 1861 by Griquas led by Adam Kok III; annexed to the Cape Colony in 1879; part of the Transkei in 1903–94. Chief town: Kokstad. Area: 17 100 sq km (6602 sq miles)

Griqualand West *n* an area of N South Africa, north of the Orange river: settled after 1803 by the Griquas; annexed by the British in 1871 following a dispute with the Orange Free State; became part of the Cape Colony in 1880. Chief town: Kimberley. Area: 39 360 sq km (15 197 sq miles)

Gris (*Spanish* gris) *n* **Juan** (xwan) 1887–1927, Spanish cubist painter, resident in France from 1906

grisaille (grɪˈzeɪl) *n* **1** a technique of monochrome painting in shades of grey, imitating the effect of relief **2** a painting, stained-glass window, etc, in this manner [c19 from F, from *gris* grey]

griseofulvin (ˌgrɪzɪəʊˈfʊlvɪn) *n* an antibiotic used to treat fungal infections of the skin and hair [c20 from NL, ult. from Med. L *griseus* grey + L *fulvus* reddish-yellow]

grisette (grɪˈzɛt) *n* (esp formerly) a French working girl [c18 from F, from grey fabric used for dresses, from *gris* grey]

gris-gris (ˈgriːgriː) *n, pl* **gris-gris** (-griːz) a variant spelling of **grigri**

Grisham (ˈgrɪʃəm) *n* **John** born 1955, US novelist and lawyer; his legal thrillers, many of which have been filmed, include *A Time to Kill* (1989), *The Pelican Brief* (1992), and *The Summons* (2002)

Grishun (griːˈʃʊn) *n* the Romansch name for **Graubünden**

grisly (ˈgrɪzlɪ) *adj* **grislier, grisliest** causing horror or dread; gruesome [OE *grislic*] > ˈ**grisliness** *n*

USAGE See at **grizzly**

Grisons (grizɔ̃) *n* the French name for **Graubünden**

grist (grɪst) *n* **1a** grain intended to be or that has been ground **1b** the quantity of such grain processed in one grinding **2** *brewing* malt grains that have been cleaned and cracked **3 grist to** (*or* **for**) **the** (*or* **one's**) **mill** anything that can be turned to profit or advantage [OE *grīst*]

gristle (ˈgrɪsᵊl) *n* cartilage, esp when in meat [OE *gristle*] > ˈ**gristly** *adj* > ˈ**gristliness** *n*

grit (grɪt) *n* **1** small hard particles of sand, earth, stone, etc **2** Also called: **gritstone** any coarse sandstone that can be used as a grindstone or millstone **3** indomitable courage, toughness, or resolution ▹ *vb* **grits, gritting, gritted 4** to clench or grind together (two objects, esp the teeth) **5** to cover (a surface, such as icy roads) with grit [OE *grēot*] > ˈ**gritter** *n*

Grit (grɪt) *n, adj Canad* an informal word for **Liberal**

grits (grɪts) *pl n* **1** hulled or coarsely ground grain **2** *US* See **hominy grits** [OE *grytt*]

gritty (ˈgrɪtɪ) *adj* **grittier, grittiest 1** courageous; hardy; resolute **2** of, like, or containing grit > ˈ**grittily** *adv* > ˈ**grittiness** *n*

grizzle¹ (ˈgrɪzᵊl) *vb* **grizzles, grizzling, grizzled 1** to make or become grey ▹ *n* **2** a grey colour **3** grey hair [c15 from OF *grisel*, from *gris*, of Gmc origin]

grizzle² (ˈgrɪzᵊl) *vb* **grizzles, grizzling, grizzled** (*intr*) *inf, chiefly Brit* (esp of a child) to fret; whine [c18 of Gmc origin] > ˈ**grizzler** *n*

grizzled (ˈgrɪzᵊld) *adj* **1** streaked or mixed with grey; grizzly **2** having grey hair

grizzly (ˈgrɪzlɪ) *adj* **grizzlier, grizzliest 1** somewhat grey; grizzled ▹ *n, pl* **grizzlies 2** See **grizzly bear**

USAGE *Grizzly* is sometimes wrongly used where *grisly* is meant: *a grisly* (not *grizzly*) *murder*

grizzly bear *n* a variety of the brown bear, formerly widespread in W North America; its brown fur has cream or white tips on the back, giving a grizzled appearance. Often shortened to **grizzly**

groan (grəʊn) *n* **1** a prolonged stressed dull cry expressive of agony, pain, or disapproval **2** a loud harsh creaking sound, as of a tree bending in the wind **3** *inf* a grumble or complaint, esp a persistent one ▹ *vb* **4** to utter (low inarticulate sounds) expressive of pain, grief, disapproval, etc **5** (*intr*) to make a sound like a groan **6** (*intr*; usually foll by *beneath* or *under*) to be weighed down (by) or suffer greatly (under) **7** (*intr*) *inf* to complain or grumble [OE *grānian*] > ˈ**groaner** *n* > ˈ**groaning** *adj, n* > ˈ**groaningly** *adv*

groat (grəʊt) *n* an obsolete English silver coin worth four pennies [c14 from MDu. *groot*, from MLow G *gros*, from Med. L (*denarius*) *grossus* thick (coin); see GROSCHEN]

groats (grəʊts) *pl n* the hulled and crushed grain of oats, wheat, or certain other cereals [OE *grot* particle]

grocer (ˈgrəʊsə) *n* a dealer in foodstuffs and other household supplies [c15 from OF *grossier*, from *gros* large; see GROSS]

groceries (ˈgrəʊsərɪz) *pl n* merchandise, esp foodstuffs, sold by a grocer

grocery (ˈgrəʊsərɪ) *n, pl* **groceries** the business or premises of a grocer

Grodno (*Russian* ˈgrɔdnə) *n* a city in W Belarus on the Neman River: part of Poland (1921–39); an industrial centre. Pop: 306 000 (1998 est)

Groening (ˈgrɜːnɪŋ) *n* **Matt(hew)** born 1954, US cartoonist and writer, creator and producer of *The Simpsons* television series from 1989

grog (grɒg) *n* **1** diluted spirit, usually rum, as an alcoholic drink **2** *Austral & NZ inf* alcoholic drink in general, esp spirits [c18 from Old *Grog*, nickname of Edward Vernon (1684–1757), Brit admiral, who in 1740 issued naval rum diluted with water; his nickname arose from his grogram cloak]

groggy (ˈgrɒgɪ) *adj* **groggier, groggiest** *inf* **1** dazed or staggering, as from exhaustion, blows, or drunkenness **2** faint or weak > ˈ**groggily** *adv* > ˈ**grogginess** *n*

grogram (ˈgrɒgrəm) *n* a coarse fabric of silk, wool, or silk mixed with wool or mohair, often stiffened with gum, formerly used for clothing [c16 from F *gros grain* coarse grain; see GROSGRAIN]

groin (grɔɪn) *n* **1** the depression or fold where the legs join the abdomen **2** *euphemistic* the genitals, esp the testicles **3** a variant spelling (esp US) of **groyne 4** *archit* a curved arris formed where two intersecting vaults meet ▹ *vb* **5** (*tr*) *archit* to provide or construct with groins [c15 ?from E *grynde* abyss]

grommet (ˈgrɒmɪt) *or* **grummet** *n* **1** a ring of rubber or plastic or a metal eyelet designed to line a hole to prevent a cable or pipe passed through it from chafing **2** *med* a small tube inserted into the eardrum in cases of glue ear in order to allow air to enter the middle ear **3** *Austral inf* a young or inexperienced surfer [c15 from obs. F *gourmette* chain linking the ends of a bit, from *gourmer* bridle, from ?]

Gromyko (*Russian* graˈmikə) *n* **Andrei Andreyevich** (anˈdrjej anˈdrjejɪvɪtʃ) 1909–89, Soviet statesman and diplomat; foreign minister (1957–85); president (1985–88)

Groningen (ˈgrəʊnɪŋən; *Dutch* ˈxroːnɪŋə) *n* **1** a province in the NE Netherlands: mainly agricultural. Capital: Groningen. Pop: 562 600 (2000 est). Area: 2336 sq km (902 sq miles) **2** a city in the NE Netherlands, capital of Groningen province. Pop: 171 193 (1999 est)

Grønland (ˈgrœnlan) *n* the Danish name for **Greenland**

groom (gruːm, grʊm) *n* **1** a person employed to clean and look after horses **2** See **bridegroom 3** any of various officers of a royal or noble household **4** *arch* a male servant ▹ *vb* (*tr*) **5** to make or keep (clothes, appearance, etc) clean and tidy **6** to rub down, clean, and smarten (a horse, dog, etc) **7** to train or prepare for a particular task, occupation, etc: *to groom someone for the Presidency* [c13 *grom* manservant; ? rel. to OE *grōwan* to GROW]

groomsman (ˈgruːmzmən, ˈgrʊmz-) *n, pl* **groomsmen** a man who attends the bridegroom at a wedding, usually the best man

groove (gruːv) *n* **1** a long narrow channel or furrow, esp

Gg

one cut into wood by a tool **2** the spiral channel in a gramophone record **3** a settled existence, routine, etc, to which one is suited or accustomed **4** *dated sl* an experience, event, etc, that is groovy **5** **in the groove** **5a** *jazz* playing well and apparently effortlessly, with a good beat, etc **5b** US fashionable ▷ *vb* **grooves, grooving, grooved** **6** (*tr*) to form or cut a groove in **7** (*intr*) *dated sl* to enjoy oneself or feel in rapport with one's surroundings **8** (*intr*) *jazz* to play well, with a good beat, etc [C15 from obs. Du. *groeve*, of Gmc origin]

groovy ('gru:vɪ) *adj* **groovier, grooviest** *sl, often jocular* attractive, fashionable, or exciting

grope (grəʊp) *vb* **gropes, groping, groped** **1** (*intr*; usually foll by *for*) to feel or search about uncertainly (for something) with the hands **2** (*intr*; usually foll by *for* or *after*) to search uncertainly or with difficulty (for a solution, answer, etc) **3** (*tr*) to find (one's way) by groping **4** (*tr*) *sl* to fondle the body of (someone) for sexual gratification ▷ *n* **5** the act of groping [OE *grāpian*] > '**gropingly** *adv*

groper ('grəʊpə) *or* **grouper** *n, pl* **groper, gropers** *or* **grouper, groupers** a large marine fish of warm and tropical seas [C17 from Port. *garupa*, prob. from a South American Indian word]

Gropius ('grəʊpɪəs) *n* **Walter** 1883–1969, US architect, designer, and teacher, born in Germany. He founded (1919) and directed (1919–28) the Bauhaus in Germany. His influence stemmed from his adaptation of architecture to modern social needs and his pioneering use of industrial materials, such as concrete and steel. His buildings include the Fagus factory at Alfeld (1911) and the Bauhaus at Dessau (1926)

Gros (*French* gro) *n* Baron **Antoine Jean** (ɑ̃twan ʒɑ̃) 1771–1835, French painter, noted for his battle scenes

grosbeak ('grəʊs,bi:k, 'grɒs-) *n* any of various finches that have a massive powerful bill [C17 from F *grosbec*, from OF *gros* large, thick + *bec* BEAK[1]]

groschen ('grəʊʃən) *n, pl* **groschen** **1** a former Austrian monetary unit worth one hundredth of a schilling **2** a former German coin worth ten pfennigs **3** a former German silver coin [C17 from G: alteration of MHG *grosse*, from Med. L (*denarius*) *grossus* thick (penny); see GROSS, GROAT]

grosgrain ('grəʊ,greɪn) *n* a heavy ribbed silk or rayon fabric or tape for trimming clothes, etc [C19 from F *gros grain* coarse grain; see GROSS, GRAIN]

gros point ('grəʊ 'pɔɪnt; *French* gro pwɛ̃) *n* **1** a needlepoint stitch covering two horizontal and two vertical threads **2** work done in this stitch [OF: large point]

gross (grəʊs) *adj* **1** repellently or excessively fat or bulky **2** with no deductions for expenses, tax, etc; total: *gross sales* ▷ Cf **net**[2] **3** (of personal qualities, tastes, etc) conspicuously coarse or vulgar **4** obviously or exceptionally culpable or wrong; flagrant: *gross inefficiency* **5** lacking in perception, sensitivity, or discrimination: *gross judgments* **6** (esp of vegetation) dense; thick; luxuriant ▷ *n* **7** (*pl* **gross**) a unit of quantity equal to 12 dozen **8** (*pl* **grosses**) **8a** the entire amount **8b** the great majority ▷ *interj* **9** *sl* an exclamation indicating disgust ▷ *vb* (*tr*) **10** to earn as total revenue, before deductions for expenses, tax, etc [C14 from OF *gros* large, from LL *grossus* thick] > '**grossly** *adv* > '**grossness** *n*

gross domestic product *n* the total value of all goods and services produced domestically by a nation during a year. It is equivalent to gross national product minus net investment incomes from foreign nations. Abbrev: **GDP**

Grosseteste ('grəʊs,tɛst) *n* **Robert** ?1175–1253, English prelate and scholar; bishop of Lincoln (1235–53) He attacked ecclesiastical abuses and wrote commentaries on Aristotle and treatises on theology, philosophy, and science

gross national product *n* the total value of all final goods and services produced annually by a nation. Abbrev: **GNP**

gross profit *n accounting* the difference between total revenue from sales and the total cost of purchases or materials, with an adjustment for stock

Grosswardein (gro:svar'dain) *n* the German name for **Oradea**

gross weight *n* total weight of an article inclusive of the weight of the container and packaging

Grosz (grəʊs; *German* grɔs) *n* **George** 1893–1959, German painter, in the US from 1932, whose works satirized German militarism and bourgeois society

grot (grɒt) *n sl* rubbish; dirt [C20 from GROTTY]

Grote (grəʊt) *n* **George** 1794–1871, English historian, noted particularly for his *History of Greece* (1846–56)

grotesque (grəʊ'tɛsk) *adj* **1** strangely or fantastically distorted; bizarre **2** of or characteristic of the grotesque in art **3** absurdly incongruous; in a ludicrous context ▷ *n* **4** a 16th-century decorative style in which parts of human, animal, and plant forms are distorted and mixed **5** a decorative device, as in painting or sculpture, in this style **6** *printing* the family of 19th-century sans serif display types **7** any grotesque person or thing [C16 from F, from OIt. (*pittura*) *grottesca* cave painting, from *grotta* cave; see GROTTO] > **gro'tesquely** *adv* > **gro'tesqueness** *n* > **gro'tesquery** *or* **gro'tesquerie** *n*

Grotius ('grəʊtɪəs) *n* **Hugo,** original name *Huig de Groot.* 1583–1645, Dutch jurist and statesman, whose *De Jure Belli ac Pacis* (1625) is regarded as the foundation of modern international law

grotto ('grɒtəʊ) *n, pl* **grottoes** *or* **grottos** **1** a small cave, esp one with attractive features **2** a construction in the form of a cave, esp as in landscaped gardens during the 18th century [C17 from OIt. *grotta*, from LL *crypta* vault; see CRYPT]

grotty ('grɒtɪ) *adj* **grottier, grottiest** *Brit sl* **1** nasty or unattractive **2** of poor quality or in bad condition [C20 from GROTESQUE]

grouch (graʊtʃ) *inf* ▷ *vb* (*intr*) **1** to complain; grumble ▷ *n* **2** a complaint, esp a persistent one **3** a person who is always grumbling [C20 from obs. *grutch*, from OF *grouchier* to complain; see GRUDGE] > '**grouchy** *adj* > '**grouchily** *adv* > '**grouchiness** *n*

ground[1] (graʊnd) *n* **1** the land surface **2** earth or soil **3** (*pl*) the land around a dwelling house or other building **4** (*sometimes pl*) an area of land given over to a purpose: *football ground* **5** land having a particular characteristic: *high ground* **6** matter for consideration or debate; field of research or inquiry: *the report covered a lot of ground* **7** a position or viewpoint, as in an argument or controversy (esp in **give ground, hold, stand,** *or* **shift one's ground**) **8** position or advantage, as in a subject or competition (esp in **gain ground, lose ground,** etc) **9** (*often pl*) reason; justification: *grounds for complaint* **10** *arts* **10a** the prepared surface applied to a wall, canvas, etc, to prevent it reacting with or absorbing the paint **10b** the background of a painting against which the other parts of a work of art appear superimposed **11a** the first coat of paint applied to a surface **11b** (*as modifier*): *ground colour* **12** the bottom of a river or the sea **13** (*pl*) sediment or dregs, esp from coffee **14** *chiefly Brit* the floor of a room **15** *cricket* the area from the popping crease back past the stumps, in which a batsman may legally stand **16** *electrical* the usual US and Canad word for **earth** (sense 8) **17** **break new ground** to do something that has not been done before **18** **common ground** an agreed basis for identifying issues in an argument **19** **cut the ground from under someone's feet** to anticipate someone's action or argument and thus make it irrelevant or meaningless **20** **(down) to the ground** *Brit inf* completely; absolutely: *it suited him down to the ground* **21** **home ground** a familiar area or topic

22 into the ground beyond what is requisite or can be endured; to exhaustion **23** *(modifier)* on or concerned with the ground: *ground frost; ground forces* ▷ *vb* **24** *(tr)* to put or place on the ground **25** *(tr)* to instruct in fundamentals **26** *(tr)* to provide a basis or foundation for; establish **27** *(tr)* to confine (an aircraft, pilot, etc) to the ground **28** *(tr)* to confine (a teenager) to the house as a punishment **29** the usual US and Canad word for **earth** (sense 13) **30** *(tr) naut* to run (a vessel) aground **31** *(intr)* to hit or reach the ground [OE *grund*]

ground² (graʊnd) *vb* **1** the past tense and past participle of **grind** ▷ *adj* **2** having the surface finished, thickness reduced, or an edge sharpened by grinding **3** reduced to fine particles by grinding

groundage ('graʊndɪdʒ) *n Brit* a fee levied on a vessel entering a port or anchored off a shore

groundbait ('graʊnd,beɪt) *n angling* bait, such as bread or maggots, thrown into an area of water to attract fish

ground bass (beɪs) *n music* a short melodic bass line that is repeated over and over again

ground-breaking *adj* innovative: *a ground-breaking novel*

ground control *n* **1** the personnel, radar, computers, etc, on the ground that monitor the progress of aircraft or spacecraft **2** a system for feeding radio messages to an aircraft pilot to enable him to make a blind landing

ground cover *n* dense low herbaceous plants and shrubs that grow over the surface of the ground

grounded ('graʊndɪd) *adj* sensible and down-to-earth; having one's feet on the ground

ground elder *n* a widely naturalized Eurasian umbelliferous plant with white flowers and creeping underground stems. Also called: **bishop's weed, goutweed**

ground floor *n* **1** the floor of a building level or almost level with the ground **2 get in on the ground floor** *inf* to be in a project, undertaking, etc, from its inception

ground frost *n* the condition resulting from a temperature reading of 0°C or below on a thermometer in contact with a grass surface

ground glass *n* **1** glass that has a rough surface produced by grinding, used for diffusing light **2** glass in the form of fine particles produced by grinding, used as an abrasive

groundhog ('graʊnd,hɒg) *n* another name for **woodchuck**

grounding ('graʊndɪŋ) *n* a foundation, esp the basic general knowledge of a subject

ground ivy *n* a creeping or trailing Eurasian aromatic herbaceous plant with scalloped leaves and purplish-blue flowers

groundless ('graʊndlɪs) *adj* without reason or justification: *his suspicions were groundless* > '**groundlessly** *adv* > '**groundlessness** *n*

groundling ('graʊndlɪŋ) *n* **1** any animal or plant that lives close to the ground or at the bottom of a lake, river, etc **2** (in Elizabethan theatre) a spectator standing in the yard in front of the stage and paying least **3** a person on the ground as distinguished from one in an aircraft

groundnut ('graʊnd,nʌt) *n* **1** a North American climbing leguminous plant with small edible underground tubers **2** the tuber of this plant **3** *Brit* another name for **peanut**

ground plan *n* **1** a drawing of the ground floor of a building, esp one to scale **2** a preliminary or basic outline

ground rule *n* a procedural or fundamental principle

groundsel ('graʊnsəl) *n* any of certain plants of the composite family, Asteraceae, esp a Eurasian weed with heads of small yellow flowers [OE, from *gundeswilge*, from *gund* pus + *swelgan* to swallow; after its use in poultices]

groundsheet ('graʊnd,ʃi:t) *n* a waterproof rubber, plastic, or polythene sheet placed on the ground in a tent, etc, to keep out damp

groundsill ('graʊnd,sɪl) *n* a joist forming the lowest member of a timber frame. Also called: **ground plate**

groundsman ('graʊndzmən) *n, pl* **groundsmen** a person employed to maintain a sports ground, park, etc

groundspeed ('graʊnd,spi:d) *n* the speed of an aircraft relative to the ground

ground squirrel *n* a burrowing rodent resembling a chipmunk and occurring in North America, E Europe, and Asia. Also called: **gopher**

groundswell ('graʊnd,swɛl) *n* **1** a considerable swell of the sea, often caused by a distant storm or earthquake **2** a rapidly developing general feeling or opinion

ground water *n* underground water that has come mainly from the seepage of surface water and is held in pervious rocks

groundwork ('graʊnd,wɜ:k) *n* **1** preliminary work as a foundation or basis **2** the ground or background of a painting, etc

ground zero *n* a point on the ground directly below the centre of a nuclear explosion

group (gru:p) *n* **1** a number of persons or things considered as a collective unit **2a** a number of persons bound together by common social standards, interests, etc **2b** *(as modifier)*: *group behaviour* **3** a small band of players or singers, esp of pop music **4** a number of animals or plants considered as a unit because of common characteristics, habits, etc **5** an association of companies under a single ownership and control **6** two or more figures or objects forming a design in a painting or sculpture **7** a military formation comprising complementary arms and services: *a brigade group* **8** an air force organization of higher level than a squadron **9** Also called: **radical** *chem* two or more atoms that are bound together in a molecule and behave as a single unit: *a methyl group* $-CH_3$ **10** a vertical column of elements in the periodic table that all have similar electronic structures, properties, and valencies: *the halogen group* **11** *maths* a set under an operation involving any two members of the set such that the set is closed, associative, and contains both an identity and the inverse of each member **12** See **blood group** ▷ *vb* **13** to arrange or place (things, people, etc) in or into a group, or (of things, etc) to form into a group [C17 from F *groupe*, of Gmc origin; cf. It. *gruppo*; see CROP]

group captain *n* an officer holding commissioned rank senior to a wing commander but junior to an air commodore in the RAF and certain other air forces

group dynamics *n (functioning as sing) psychol* a field of social psychology concerned with the nature of human groups, their development, and their interactions

grouper ('gru:pə) *n* a variant spelling of **groper**

groupie ('gru:pɪ) *n sl* **1** an ardent fan of a celebrity, esp a girl who follows the members of a pop group on tour in order to have sexual relations with them **2** an enthusiastic follower of some activity: *a political groupie*

Group of Eight *n* the Group of Seven nations and Russia, whose heads of government meet to discuss economic matters and international relations. Abbrev: **G8**

Group of Five *n* France, Japan, the UK, the US, and Germany acting as a group to stabilize their currency exchange rates. Abbrev: **G5**

Group of Seven *n* the seven leading industrial nations excepting Russia, i.e. Canada, France, Germany, Italy, Japan, the UK, and the US, whose heads of government and finance ministers meet regularly to coordinate economic policy. Abbrev: **G7**

Group of Seventy-Seven *n* the developing countries of the world. Abbrev: **G77**

Group of Ten *n* the ten nations who met in Paris in 1961 to arrange the special drawing rights of the IMF: Belgium, Canada, France, Italy, Japan, the Netherlands,

Sweden, the UK, the US, and Germany. Abbrev: **G10**
Group of Three *n* Japan, the US, and Germany, regarded as the largest industrialized nations. Abbrev: **G3**
Group of Twenty-Four *n* the twenty-four richest industrial countries of the world. Abbrev: **G24**
group practice *n* a group of doctors who together run a general practice
group therapy *n psychol* the simultaneous treatment of a number of individuals who are brought together to share their problems in group discussion
groupuscule (ˈgruːpəˌskjuːl) *n usually derog* a small group within a political party or movement [c20 a blend of GROUP + *corpuscule*; see CORPUSCLE]
groupware (ˈgruːpˌwɛə) *n* software that enables a group of computers to work together, so that users may access shared files, exchange messages, etc
grouse[1] (graʊs) *n, pl* **grouse** *or* **grouses** a game bird occurring mainly in the N hemisphere, having a stocky body and feathered legs and feet [c16 from ?]
grouse[2] (graʊs) *vb* **grouses, grousing, groused 1** (*intr*) to grumble; complain ▷ *n* **2** a persistent complaint [c19 from ?] > ˈ**grouser** *n*
grouse[3] (graʊs) *adj Austral & NZ sl* fine; excellent [from ?]
grout (graʊt) *n* **1** a thin mortar for filling joints between tiles, masonry, etc **2** a fine plaster used as a finishing coat **3** (*pl*) sediment or dregs ▷ *vb* **4** (*tr*) to fill (joints) or finish (walls, etc) with grout [OE *grūt*] > ˈ**grouter** *n*
grove (grəʊv) *n* **1** a small wooded area **2** a road lined with houses and trees, esp in a suburban area [OE *grāf*]
grovel (ˈgrɒvᵊl) *vb* **grovels, grovelling, grovelled** *or US* **grovels, groveling, groveled** (*intr*) **1** to humble or abase oneself, as in making apologies or showing respect **2** to lie or crawl face downwards, as in fear or humility **3** (often foll by *in*) to indulge or take pleasure (in sensuality or vice) [c16 back formation from obs. *groveling* (adv), from ME *on grufe* on the face, of Scand. origin; see -LING[2]] > ˈ**groveller** *or US* ˌ**groveler** *n*
Groves (grəʊvz) *n* Sir **Charles** 1915–92, English orchestral conductor
grow (grəʊ) *vb* **grows, growing, grew, grown 1** (of an organism or part of an organism) to increase in size or develop (hair, leaves, or other structures) **2** (*intr*; usually foll by *out of* or *from*) to originate, as from an initial cause or source: *the federation grew out of the Empire* **3** (*intr*) to increase in size, number, degree, etc: *the population is growing rapidly* **4** (*intr*) to change in length or amount in a specified direction: *some plants grow downwards* **5** (*copula; may take an infinitive*) (esp of emotions, physical states, etc) to develop or come into existence or being gradually: *to grow cold* **6** (*intr*; foll by *together*) to be joined gradually by or as by growth **7** (when *intr*, foll by *with*) to become covered with a growth: *the path grew with weeds* **8** to produce (plants) by controlling or encouraging their growth, esp for home consumption or on a commercial basis ▷ See also **grow into, grow on,** etc [OE *grōwan*] > ˈ**growable** *adj* > ˈ**grower** *n*
grow bag *n* a plastic bag containing a sterile growing medium that enables a plant to be grown to full size in it, usually for one season only [c20 from *Gro-bag*, trademark for the first ones marketed]
growing pains *pl n* **1** pains in muscles or joints sometimes experienced by growing children **2** difficulties besetting a new enterprise in its early stages
grow into *vb* (*intr, prep*) to become big or mature enough for: *clothes big enough for him to grow into*
growl (graʊl) *vb* **1** (of animals, esp when hostile) to utter (sounds) in a low inarticulate manner: *the dog growled* **2** to utter (words) in a gruff or angry manner **3** (*intr*) to make sounds suggestive of an animal growling: *the thunder growled* ▷ *n* **4** the act or sound of growling [c18 from earlier *grolle*, from OF *grouller* to grumble] > ˈ**growler** *n*
grown (grəʊn) *adj* **a** developed or advanced: *fully grown* **b** (*in combination*): *half-grown*
grown-up *adj* **1** having reached maturity; adult **2** suitable for or characteristic of an adult ▷ *n* **3** an adult
grow on *vb* (*intr, prep*) to become progressively more acceptable or pleasant to
grow out of *vb* (*intr, adv + prep*) to become too big or mature for: *she soon grew out of her girlish ways*
growth (grəʊθ) *n* **1** the process or act of growing **2** an increase in size, number, significance, etc **3** something grown or growing: *a new growth of hair* **4** a stage of development: *a full growth* **5** any abnormal tissue, such as a tumour **6** (*modifier*) of, relating to, causing, or characterized by growth: *a growth industry; growth hormone*
growth curve *n* a curve on a graph in which a variable is plotted against time to illustrate the growth of the variable
grow up *vb* (*intr, adv*) **1** to reach maturity; become adult **2** to come into existence; develop
groyne *or esp US* **groin** (grɔɪn) *n* a wall or jetty built out from a riverbank or seashore to control erosion. Also called: **spur, breakwater** [c16 ?from OF *groign* snout, promontory]
Grozny (*Russian* ˈgrɔznij) *n* a city in S Russia, capital of the Chechen Republic: a major oil centre: it was badly damaged during fighting between separatists and Russian troops (1994–95, 1999–2000). Pop: 186 000 (1999 est)
grub (grʌb) *vb* **grubs, grubbing, grubbed 1** (when *tr*, often foll by *up* or *out*) to search for and pull up (roots, stumps, etc) by digging in the ground **2** to dig up the surface of (ground, soil, etc), esp to clear away roots, stumps, etc **3** (*intr*; often foll by *in* or *among*) to search carefully **4** (*intr*) to work unceasingly, esp at a dull task ▷ *n* **5** the short legless larva of certain insects, esp beetles **6** *sl* food; victuals **7** a person who works hard, esp in a dull plodding way [c13 of Gmc origin; cf. OHG *grubilōn* to dig] > ˈ**grubber** *n*
grubby (ˈgrʌbɪ) *adj* **grubbier, grubbiest 1** dirty; slovenly **2** mean; beggarly **3** infested with grubs > ˈ**grubbily** *adv* > ˈ**grubbiness** *n*
grub screw *n* a small headless screw used to secure a sliding component in position
grubstake (ˈgrʌbˌsteɪk) *US & Canad inf* ▷ *n* **1** supplies provided for a prospector on the condition that the donor has a stake in any finds ▷ *vb* **grubstakes, grubstaking, grubstaked** (*tr*) **2** to furnish with such supplies **3** to supply (a person) with a stake in a gambling game > ˈ**grubˌstaker** *n*
Grub Street *n* **1** a former street in London frequented by literary hacks and needy authors **2** the world or class of literary hacks, etc ▷ *adj also* **Grubstreet 3** (*sometimes not cap*) relating to or characteristic of hack literature
grudge (grʌdʒ) *n* **1** a persistent feeling of resentment, esp one due to an insult or injury **2** (*modifier*) planned or carried out in order to settle a grudge: *a grudge fight* ▷ *vb* **grudges, grudging, grudged 3** (*tr*) to give unwillingly **4** to feel resentful or envious about (someone else's success, etc) [c15 from OF *grouchier* to grumble, prob. of Gmc origin] > ˈ**grudging** *adj* > ˈ**grudgingly** *adv*
gruel (ˈgruːəl) *n* a drink or thin porridge made by boiling meal, esp oatmeal, in water or milk [c14 from OF, of Gmc origin]
gruelling *or US* **grueling** (ˈgruːəlɪŋ) *adj* **1** extremely severe or tiring ▷ *n* **2** *inf* a severe or tiring experience, esp punishment [c19 from obs. *gruel* (vb) to punish]
gruesome (ˈgruːsəm) *adj* inspiring repugnance and horror; ghastly [c16 orig. Northern E and Scot., of Scand. origin] > ˈ**gruesomely** *adv* > ˈ**gruesomeness** *n*
gruff (grʌf) *adj* **1** rough or surly in manner, speech, etc: *he gave a gruff reply* **2** (of a voice, bark, etc) low and throaty [c16 orig. Scot., from Du. *grof*, of Gmc origin; rel. to OE

hrēof] > ˈ**gruffly** *adv* > ˈ**gruffness** *n*

grumble (ˈgrʌmbᵊl) *vb* **grumbles, grumbling, grumbled** 1 to utter (complaints) in a nagging way 2 (*intr*) to make low rumbling sounds ▷ *n* 3 a complaint 4 a low rumbling sound [c16 from MLow G *grommelen*, of Gmc origin] > ˈ**grumbler** *n* > ˈ**grumblingly** *adv* > ˈ**grumbly** *adj*

grumbling appendix *n inf* a condition in which the appendix causes intermittent pain or discomfort but appendicitis has not developed

grummet (ˈgrʌmɪt) *n* a variant of **grommet**

grump (grʌmp) *inf* ▷ *n* 1 a surly or bad-tempered person 2 (*pl*) a sulky or morose mood (esp in **have the grumps**) ▷ *vb* 3 (*intr*) to complain or grumble [c18 dialect: surly remark, prob. imit.]

grumpy (ˈgrʌmpɪ) *or* **grumpish** *adj* **grumpier, grumpiest** peevish; sulky [c18 from GRUMP + -Y[1]] > ˈ**grumpily** *or* ˈ**grumpishly** *adv* > ˈ**grumpiness** *or* ˈ**grumpishness** *n*

Grundy (ˈgrʌndɪ) *n* a narrow-minded person who keeps critical watch on the propriety of others [c18 after Mrs *Grundy*, the character in T. Morton's play *Speed the Plough* (1798)] > ˈ**Grundy**ˌ**ism** *n* > ˈ**Grundyist** *or* ˈ**Grundyite** *n*

Grünewald (*German* ˈgryːnəvalt) *n* **Matthias** (maˈtiːas), original name *Mathis Gothardt*. ?1470–1528, German painter, the greatest exponent of late Gothic art in Germany. The *Isenheim Altarpiece* is regarded as his masterpiece

grunge (grʌndʒ) *n* 1 *US sl* dirt or rubbish 2 a style of rock music originating in the US in the late 1980s, featuring a distorted guitar sound 3 a deliberately untidy and uncoordinated fashion style [c20 possibly a coinage imitating GRIME + SLUDGE]
▷ www.wikipedia.org/wiki/Grunge_music

grungy (ˈgrʌndʒɪ) *adj* **grungier, grungiest** 1 *sl, chiefly US & Canad* squalid, seedy, grotty 2 (of pop music) characterized by a loud fuzzy guitar sound

grunion (ˈgrʌnjən) *n* a Californian marine fish that spawns on beaches [c20 prob. from Sp. *gruñón* a grunter]

grunt (grʌnt) *vb* 1 (*intr*) (esp of pigs and some other animals) to emit a low short gruff noise 2 (when *tr, may take a clause as object*) to express something gruffly: *he grunted his answer* ▷ *n* 3 the characteristic low short gruff noise of pigs, etc, or a similar sound, as of disgust 4 any of various mainly tropical marine fishes that utter a grunting sound when caught [OE *grunnettan*, prob. imit.; cf. OHG *grunnizōn, grunni* moaning] > ˈ**grunter** *n*

Gruyère *or* **Gruyère cheese** (ˈgruːjɛə) *n* a hard flat whole-milk cheese, pale yellow in colour and with holes [c19 after *Gruyère*, Switzerland, where it originated]

gr. wt. *abbrev for* gross weight

gryphon (ˈgrɪfᵊn) *n* a variant of **griffin**

grysbok (ˈgraɪsˌbɒk) *n* either of two small antelopes of central and southern Africa, having small straight horns [c18 Afrik., from Du. *grijs* grey + *bok* BUCK[1]]

GS *abbrev for:* 1 General Secretary 2 General Staff

GSM *abbrev for* Global System for Mobile Communications

GST (in Australia, New Zealand, and Canada) *abbrev for* goods and services tax

G-string *n* 1 a piece of cloth worn by striptease artistes covering the pubic area and attached to a narrow waistband 2 a strip of cloth attached to the front and back of a waistband and covering the loins 3 *music* a string tuned to G

G-suit *n* a close-fitting garment that is worn by the crew of high-speed aircraft and can be pressurized to prevent blackout during manoeuvres [c20 from *g(ravity) suit*]

GSVQ (in Britain) *abbrev for* General Scottish Vocational Qualification: the Scottish equivalent of GNVQ

GT *abbrev for* gran turismo: a touring car; usually a fast sports car with a hard fixed roof

gtd *abbrev for* guaranteed

Guadalajara (ˌgwɑːdᵊləˈhɑːrə; *Spanish* gwaðalaˈxara) *n* 1 a city in W Mexico, capital of Jalisco state: the second largest city of Mexico: centre of the Indian slave trade until its abolition, declared here in 1810; two universities (1792 and 1935). Pop: 1 647 000 (2000 est) 2 a city in central Spain, in New Castile. Pop: 67 200 (1991)

Guadalcanal (ˌgwɑːdᵊlkəˈnæl; *Spanish* gwaðalkaˈnal) *n* a mountainous island in the SW Pacific, the largest of the Solomon Islands: under British protection until 1978; occupied by the Japanese (1942–43). Pop: 61 243 (1997 est). Area: 6475 sq km (2500 sq miles)

Guadalquivir (ˌgwɑːdᵊlkwɪˈvɪə; *Spanish* gwaðalkiˈβir) *n* the chief river of S Spain, rising in the Sierra de Segura and flowing west and southwest to the Gulf of Cádiz: navigable by ocean-going vessels to Seville. Length: 560 km (348 miles)

Guadalupe Hidalgo (ˌgwɑːdᵊˈluːp hɪˈdælgəʊ; *Spanish* gwaðaˈlupe iˈðalɣo) *n* a city in central Mexico, northwest of Mexico City: became a pilgrimage centre after an Indian convert had a vision of the Virgin Mary here in 1531. Pop: 668 500 (2000 est). Former name (1931–71): **Gustavo A Madero**

Guadeloupe (ˌgwɑːdᵊˈluːp) *n* an overseas region of France in the E Caribbean, in the Leeward Islands, formed by the islands of Basse Terre and Grande Terre and their five dependencies. Capital: Basse-Terre. Pop: 432 000 (2001 est). Area: 1780 sq km (687 sq miles)

Guadiana (*Spanish* gwaˈðjana; *Portuguese* gwəˈðjənə) *n* a river in SW Europe, rising in S central Spain and flowing west, then south as part of the border between Spain and Portugal, to the Gulf of Cádiz. Length: 578 km (359 miles)

guaiacum (ˈgwaɪəkəm) *n* 1 any of a family of tropical American evergreen trees such as the lignum vitae 2 the hard heavy wood of any of these trees 3 a brownish resin obtained from the lignum vitae, used medicinally and in making varnishes [c16 NL, from Sp. *guayaco*, of Amerind origin]

Guam (gwɑːm) *n* an island in the N Pacific, the largest and southernmost of the Marianas: belonged to Spain from the 17th century until 1898, when it was ceded to the US; site of naval and air force bases. Capital: Agaña. Pop: 158 000 (2001 est). Area: 541 sq km (209 sq miles)

Gg

Guamanian (gwɑːˈmeɪnɪən) *adj* 1 of or relating to Guam or its inhabitants ▷ *n* 2 a native or inhabitant of Guam

Guanabara (*Portuguese* gwənaˈbara) *n* (until 1975) a state of SE Brazil, on the Atlantic and **Guanabara Bay,** now amalgamated with the state of Rio de Janeiro

guanaco (gwɑːˈnɑːkəʊ) *n, pl* **guanacos** a cud-chewing South American mammal closely related to the domesticated llama [c17 from Sp., from Quechuan *huanacu*]

Guanajuato (*Spanish* gwanaˈxwato) *n* 1 a state of central Mexico, on the great central plateau: mountainous in the north, with fertile plains in the south; important mineral resources. Capital: Guanajuato. Pop: 4 656 761 (2000). Area: 30 588 sq km (11 810 sq miles) 2 a city in central Mexico, capital of Guanajuato state: founded in 1554, it became one of the world's richest silver-mining centres. Pop: 113 580 (1990)

Guangdong (ˈgwæŋˈdʊŋ) *or* **Kwangtung** *n* a province of SE China, on the South China Sea: includes the Leizhou Peninsula, with densely populated river valleys, Macao and Hong Kong; the only true tropical climate in China. Capital: Canton. Pop: 86 420 000 (2000 est). Area: 197 100 sq km (76 100 sq miles)

Guangxi Zhuang Autonomous Region (ˈgwæŋˈsiːˈdʒwæŋ) *or* **Kwangsi-Chuang Autonomous Region** *n* an administrative division of S China. Capital: Nanning. Pop: 44 890 000 (2000 est). Area: 220 400 sq km (85 100 sq miles)

Guangzhou (ˈgwæŋˈdzəʊ) *n* the Pinyin transliteration of the Chinese name for **Canton**

guanine (ˈgwɑːniːn, ˈguːəˌniːn) *n* a white almost insoluble compound: one of the purine bases in nucleic acids [C19 from GUANO + -INE[2]]

guano ('gwɑːnəʊ) *n, pl* **guanos** **1a** the dried excrement of fish-eating sea birds, deposited in rocky coastal regions of South America: used as a fertilizer **1b** the accumulated droppings of bats and seals **2** any similar but artificial substances used as a fertilizer [C17 from Sp., from Quechuan *huano* dung]

Guantánamo (*Spanish* gwan'tanamo) *n* a city in SE Cuba; nearby is **Guantánamo Bay**, site of a US naval base since 1903, now used to hold prisoners captured in the so-called war against terrorism in Afghanistan. Pop: 207 796 (1994 est)

Guaporé (*Portuguese* gwapo'rɛ) *n* **1** a river in W central South America, rising in SW Brazil and flowing northwest as part of the border between Brazil and Bolivia, to join the Mamoré River. Length: 1750 km (1087 miles). Spanish name: **Iténez** **2** the former name (until 1956) of **Rondônia**

Guarani (ˌgwɑːrə'niː) *n* **1** (*pl* **Guarani** *or* **Guaranis**) a member of a South American Indian people of Paraguay, S Brazil, and Bolivia **2** the language of this people

guarantee (ˌgærən'tiː) *n* **1** a formal assurance, esp in writing, that a product, service, etc, will meet certain standards or specifications **2** *law* a promise, esp a collateral agreement, to answer for the debt, default, or miscarriage of another **3a** a person, company, etc, to whom a guarantee is made **3b** a person, company, etc, who gives a guarantee **4** a person who acts as a guarantor **5** something that makes a specified condition or outcome certain **6** a variant spelling of **guaranty** ▷ *vb* **guarantees, guaranteeing, guaranteed** (*mainly tr*) **7** (*also intr*) to take responsibility for (someone else's debts, obligations, etc) **8** to serve as a guarantee for **9** to secure or furnish security for: *a small deposit will guarantee any dress* **10** (usually foll by *from* or *against*) to undertake to protect or keep secure, as against injury, loss, etc **11** to ensure: *good planning will guarantee success* **12** (*may take a clause as object or an infinitive*) to promise or make certain [C17 ?from Sp. *garante* or F *garant*, of Gmc origin; cf. WARRANT]

guarantor (ˌgærən'tɔː) *n* a person who gives or is bound by a guarantee or guaranty; surety

guaranty ('gærəntɪ) *n, pl* **guaranties** **1** a pledge of responsibility for fulfilling another person's obligations in case of that person's default **2** a thing given or taken as security for a guaranty **3** the act of providing security **4** a person who acts as a guarantor ▷ *vb* **guaranties, guarantying, guarantied** **5** a variant spelling of **guarantee** [C16 from OF *garantie*, var. of *warantie*, of Gmc origin; see WARRANTY]

guard (gɑːd) *vb* **1** to watch over or shield (a person or thing) from danger or harm; protect **2** to keep watch over (a prisoner or other potentially dangerous person or thing), as to prevent escape **3** (*tr*) to control: *to guard one's tongue* **4** (*intr*; usually foll by *against*) to take precautions **5** to control entrance and exit through (a gate, door, etc) **6** (*tr*) to provide (machinery, etc) with a device to protect the operator **7** (*tr*) **7a** *chess, cards* to protect or cover (a chessman or card) with another **7b** *curling, bowling* to protect or cover (a stone or bowl) by placing one's own stone or bowl between it and another player ▷ *n* **8** a person or group who keeps a protecting, supervising, or restraining watch or control over people, such as prisoners, things, etc. Related adj: **custodial** **9** a person or group of people, such as soldiers, who form a ceremonial escort **10** *Brit* the official in charge of a train **11a** the act or duty of protecting, restraining, or supervising **11b** (*as modifier*): *guard duty* **12** a device, part, or attachment on an object, such as a weapon or machine tool, designed to protect the user against injury **13** anything that provides or is intended to provide protection: *a guard against infection* **14** *sport* an article of light tough material worn to protect any of various parts of the body **15** the posture of defence or readiness in fencing, boxing, cricket, etc **16** **mount guard** **16a** (of a sentry, etc) to begin to keep watch **16b** (with *over*) to take a protective or defensive stance (towards something) **17** **off (one's) guard** having one's defences down; unprepared **18** **on (one's) guard** prepared to face danger, difficulties, etc **19** **stand guard** (of a sentry, etc) to keep watch [C15 from OF, from *garder* to protect, of Gmc origin; see WARD] > **'guarder** *n*

Guardafui (ˌgwɑːdə'fuːɪ) *n* **Cape** a cape at the NE tip of Somalia, extending into the Indian Ocean

guarded ('gɑːdɪd) *adj* **1** protected or kept under surveillance **2** prudent, restrained, or noncommittal: *a guarded reply* > **'guardedly** *adv* > **'guardedness** *n*

guard hair *n* any of the coarse hairs that form the outer fur in certain mammals

guardhouse ('gɑːdˌhaʊs) *or* **guardroom** ('gɑːdˌruːm, -rʊm) *n mil* a building serving as headquarters for military police and in which military prisoners are detained

Guardi (*Italian* 'gwardi) *n* **Francesco** (fran'tʃesko) 1712–93, Venetian landscape painter

guardian ('gɑːdɪən) *n* **1** one who looks after, protects, or defends: *the guardian of public morals* **2** *law* someone legally appointed to manage the affairs of a person incapable of acting for himself, as a minor or person of unsound mind ▷ *adj* **3** protecting or safeguarding > **'guardianˌship** *n*

Guardian Angels *pl n* vigilante volunteers who patrol the New York Underground and elsewhere, wearing red berets, to deter violent crime

guard ring *n* **1** Also called: **keeper ring** a ring worn to prevent another from slipping off the finger **2** an electrode used to counteract distortion of the electric fields at the edges of other electrodes

Guards (gɑːdz) *pl n* (esp in European armies) any of various regiments responsible for ceremonial duties and, formerly, the protection of the head of state: *the Life Guards*

guardsman ('gɑːdzmən) *n, pl* **guardsmen** **1** (in Britain) a member of a Guards battalion or regiment **2** (in the US) a member of the National Guard **3** a guard

guard's van *n railways, Brit & NZ* the van in which the guard travels, usually attached to the rear of a train. US and Canad equivalent: **caboose**

Guarneri (gwɑː'nɪərɪ; *Italian* gwar'nɛːri), **Guarnieri** (*Italian* gwar'njɛːri), *or* **Guarnerius** (gwɑː'nɛərɪəs) *n pl* **Guarneris, Guarnieris** *or* **Guarneriuses** **1** an Italian family of 17th- and 18th-century violin-makers **2** any violin made by a member of this family

Guat. *abbrev for* Guatemala

Guatemala (ˌgwɑːtə'mɑːlə) *n* a republic in Central America: original Maya Indians conquered by the Spanish in 1523; became the centre of Spanish administration in Central America; gained independence and was annexed to Mexico in 1821, becoming an independent republic in 1839. Official language: Spanish. Religion: Roman Catholic majority. Currency: quetzal and US dollar. Capital: Guatemala City. Pop: 11 687 000 (2001 est). Area: 108 889 sq km (42 042 sq miles)

▷ www.congreso.gob.gt

▷ www.terra.com.gt/turismogt

Guatemala City *n* the capital of Guatemala, in the southeast: founded in 1776 to replace the former capital, Antigua Guatemala, after an earthquake; university (1676). Pop: 2 578 526 (2000 est)

Guatemalan (ˌgwɑːtə'mɑːlən) *adj* **1** of or relating to Guatemala or its inhabitants ▷ *n* **2** a native or inhabitant of Guatemala

guava ('gwɑːvə) *n* **1** any of various tropical American trees, grown esp for their edible fruit **2** the fruit of such a tree, having yellow skin and pink pulp [c16 from Sp. *guayaba*, from a South American Indian word]

Guayaquil (*Spanish* gwaja'kil) *n* a port in W Ecuador: the largest city in the country and its chief port; university (1867). Pop: 1 973 880 (1997 est)

guayule (gwə'ju:lɪ) *n* **1** a bushy shrub of the southwestern US **2** rubber derived from the sap of this plant [from American Sp., from Nahuatl *cuauhuli*, from *cuahuitl* tree + *uli* gum]

gubbins ('gʌbɪnz) *n inf* **1** (*functioning as sing*) an object of little or no value **2** (*functioning as sing*) a small gadget **3** (*functioning as pl*) odds and ends; rubbish **4** (*functioning as sing*) a silly person [c16 (meaning: fragments): from obs. *gobbon*]

gubernatorial (ˌgju:bənə'tɔ:rɪəl, ˌgu:-) *adj chiefly US* of or relating to a governor [c18 from L *gubernātor* governor]

guddle ('gʌdᵊl) *Scot* ▷ *vb* **guddles, guddling, guddled** **1** to catch (fish) by groping with the hands under the banks or stones of a stream ▷ *n* **2** a muddle; confusion [c19 from ?]

gudgeon[1] ('gʌdʒən) *n* **1** a small slender European freshwater fish with a barbel on each side of the mouth: used as bait by anglers **2** any of various other fishes, such as the goby **3** *sl* a person who is easy to trick or cheat ▷ *vb* **4** (*tr*) *sl* to trick or cheat [c15 from OF *gougon*, prob. from L *gōbius*; see GOBY]

gudgeon[2] ('gʌdʒən) *n* **1** the female or socket portion of a pinned hinge **2** *naut* one of two or more looplike sockets, fixed to the transom of a boat, into which the pintles of a rudder are fitted [c14 from OF *goujon*, ?from LL *gulbia* chisel]

gudgeon pin *n Brit* the pin through the skirt of a piston in an internal-combustion engine, to which the little end of the connecting rod is attached. US and Canad name: **wrist pin**

Gudrun ('gʊdru:n), **Guthrun** ('gʊðru:n), *or* **Kudrun** ('kʊdru:n) *n Norse myth* the wife of Sigurd and, after his death, of Atli, whom she slew for his murder of her brother Gunnar. She corresponds to Kriemhild in the *Nibelungenlied*

guelder-rose ('gɛldəˌrəʊz) *n* a Eurasian shrub with clusters of white flowers and small red fruits [c16 from Du. *geldersche roos*, from *Gelderland* or *Gelders*, province of Holland]

Guelders ('gɛldəz) *n* another name for **Gelderland**

Guelph (gwɛlf) *n* a city in Canada, in SE Ontario. Pop: 95 821 (1996)

guenon (gə'nɒn) *n* a slender agile Old World monkey inhabiting wooded regions of Africa and having long hind limbs and tail and long hair surrounding the face [c19 from F, from ?]

guerdon ('gɜ:dᵊn) *poetic* ▷ *n* **1** a reward or payment ▷ *vb* **2** (*tr*) to give a guerdon to [c14 from OF *gueredon*, of Gmc origin; final element infl. by L *dōnum* gift]

Guernica (gɜ:'ni:kə, 'gɜ:nɪkə; *Spanish* gɛr'nika) *n* a town in N Spain: formerly the seat of a Basque parliament; destroyed in 1937 by German bombers during the Spanish Civil War, an event depicted in one of Picasso's most famous paintings. Pop: 16 380 (latest est)

Guernsey ('gɜ:nzɪ) *n* **1** an island in the English Channel: the second largest of the Channel Islands, which, with Alderney and Sark, Herm, Jethou, and some islets, forms the bailiwick of Guernsey; finance, market gardening, dairy farming, and tourism. Capital: St Peter Port. Pop: 64 300 (2001 est). Area: 63 sq km (24.5 sq miles) **2** a breed of dairy cattle producing rich creamy milk, originating from the island of Guernsey **3** (*sometimes not cap*) a seaman's knitted woollen sweater **4** (*not cap*) *Austral* a sleeveless woollen shirt or jumper worn by a football player **5** **get a guernsey** *Austral* to be selected or gain recognition for something

Guerrero (*Spanish* gɛ'rrɛro) *n* a mountainous state of S Mexico, on the Pacific: rich mineral resources. Capital: Chilpancingo. Pop: 3 075 083 (2000 est). Area: 63 794 sq km (24 631 sq miles)

guerrilla *or* **guerilla** (gə'rɪlə) *n* **a** a member of an irregular usually politically motivated armed force that combats stronger regular forces **b** (*as modifier*): *guerrilla warfare* [c19 from Sp., dim. of *guerra* WAR]

guess (gɛs) *vb* (*when tr, may take a clause as object*) **1** (*when intr*, often foll by *at* or *about*) to form or express an uncertain estimate or conclusion (about something), based on insufficient information: *guess what we're having for dinner* **2** to arrive at a correct estimate of (something) by guessing **3** *inf, chiefly US & Canad* to believe, think, or suppose (something): *I guess I'll go now* ▷ *n* **4** an estimate or conclusion arrived at by guessing: *a bad guess* **5** the act of guessing [c13 prob. from ON] > '**guesser** *n*

guesstimate *or* **guestimate** *inf* ▷ *n* ('gɛstɪmɪt) **1** an estimate calculated mainly or only by guesswork ▷ *vb* ('gɛstɪˌmeɪt), **guesstimates, guesstimating, guesstimated** (*tr*) **2** to form a guesstimate of

guesswork ('gɛsˌwɜ:k) *n* **1** a set of conclusions, estimates, etc, arrived at by guessing **2** the process of making guesses

guest (gɛst) *n* **1** a person who is entertained, taken out to eat, etc, and paid for by another **2a** a person who receives hospitality at the home of another **2b** (*as modifier*): *the guest room* **3a** a person who receives the hospitality of a government, establishment, or organization **3b** (*as modifier*): *a guest speaker* **4a** an actor, contestant, entertainer, etc, taking part as a visitor in a programme in which there are also regular participants **4b** (*as modifier*): *a guest appearance* **5** a patron of a hotel, boarding house, restaurant, etc ▷ *vb* **6** (*intr*) (in theatre and broadcasting) to be a guest: *to guest on a show* [OE *giest* guest, stranger, enemy]

guest beer *n* a draught beer stocked by a bar, often for a limited period, in addition to its usual range

guesthouse ('gɛstˌhaʊs) *n* a private home or boarding house offering accommodation

guest rope *n naut* any line trailed over the side of a vessel as a convenience for boats drawing alongside, as an aid in towing, etc

Guevara (gə'vɑ:rə; *Spanish* ge'βara) *n* **Ernesto** (ɛr'nesto), known as *Che Guevara*. 1928–67, Latin American politician and soldier, born in Argentina. He developed guerrilla warfare as a tool for revolution and was instrumental in Castro's victory in Cuba (1959), where he held government posts until 1965. He was killed while training guerrillas in Bolivia

guff (gʌf) *n sl* ridiculous or insolent talk [c19 imit. of empty talk]

guffaw (gʌ'fɔ:) *n* **1** a crude and boisterous laugh ▷ *vb* **2** to laugh or express (something) in this way [c18 imit.]

Guggenheim Museum ('gʊgənˌhaɪm) *n* a museum of modern art in New York: designed by Frank Lloyd Wright (1956–59)

▷ www.guggenheim.org

▷ www.guggenheimcollection.org

Guiana (gaɪ'ænə, gɪ'ɑ:nə) *or* **The Guianas** *n* a region of NE South America, including Guyana, Surinam, French Guiana, and the **Guiana Highlands** (largely in SE Venezuela and partly in N Brazil) Area: about 1 787 000 sq km (690 000 sq miles) > **Guianese** (ˌgaɪə'ni:z, ˌgɪə-) *or* **Guianan** (gaɪ'ænən, gɪ'ɑ:nən) *adj, n*

guidance ('gaɪdᵊns) *n* **1** leadership, instruction, or direction **2a** counselling or advice on educational, vocational, or psychological matters **2b** (*as modifier*): *the marriage-guidance counsellor* **3** something that guides **4** any process by which the flight path of a missile is controlled in flight

guide (gaɪd) *vb* **guides, guiding, guided** **1** to lead the way for (a person) **2** to control the movement or course of (an animal, vehicle, etc) by physical action; steer **3** to supervise or instruct (a person) **4** (*tr*) to direct the affairs

Gg

of (a person, company, nation, etc) **5** *(tr)* to advise or influence (a person) in his or her standards or opinions: *let truth guide you* ▹ *n* **6a** a person, animal, or thing that guides **6b** *(as modifier)*: *a guide dog* **7** a person, usually paid, who conducts tour expeditions, etc **8** a model or criterion, as in moral standards or accuracy **9** Also called: **guidebook** a handbook with information for visitors to a place **10** a book that instructs or explains the fundamentals of a subject or skill **11** any device that directs the motion of a tool or machine part **12** a mark, sign, etc, that points the way **13a** *naval* a ship in a formation used as a reference for manoeuvres **13b** *mil* a soldier stationed to one side of a column or line to regulate alignment, show the way, etc [C14 from (O)F *guider*, of Gmc origin] > **'guidable** *adj* > **'guider** *n*

Guide (gaɪd) *n (sometimes not cap)* a member of an organization for girls equivalent to the Scouts. US equivalent: **Girl Scout**

guided missile *n* a missile, esp one that is rocket-propelled, having a flight path controlled either by radio signals or by internal preset or self-actuating homing devices

guide dog *n* a dog that has been specially trained to accompany someone who is blind, enabling the blind person to move about safely

guideline ('gaɪd,laɪn) *n* a principle put forward to set standards or determine a course of action

guidepost ('gaɪd,pəʊst) *n* **1** a sign on a post by a road indicating directions **2** a principle or guideline

Guider ('gaɪdə) *n (sometimes not cap)* a woman leader of a company of Guides or of a pack of Brownie Guides

Guido d'Arezzo (*Italian* 'gwi:do da'rettso) *n* ?995–?1050 AD, Italian Benedictine monk and musical theorist: reputed inventor of solmization

guidon ('gaɪdᵊn) *n* **1** a small pennant, used as a marker or standard, esp by cavalry regiments **2** the man or vehicle that carries this [C16 from F, from OProvençal *guidoo*, from *guida* GUIDE]

Guienne *or* **Guyenne** (*French* gɥijɛn) *n* a former province of SW France: formed, with Gascony, the duchy of Aquitaine during the 12th century

guild *or* **gild** (gɪld) *n* **1** an organization, club, or fellowship **2** (esp in medieval Europe) an association of men sharing the same interests, such as merchants or artisans: formed for mutual aid and protection and to maintain craft standards [C14 from ON; cf. *gjald* payment, *gildi* guild; rel. to OE *gield* offering, OHG *gelt* money] > **'guildsman, 'gildsman** *or (fem)* **'guildswoman, 'gildswoman** *n*

guilder ('gɪldə) *or* **gulden** *n, pl* **guilders, guilder** *or* **guldens, gulden 1** Also: **gilder, florin** the former standard monetary unit of the Netherlands, divided into 100 cents; replaced by the euro in 2002 **2** any of various former gold or silver coins of Germany, Austria, or the Netherlands [C15 from MDu. *gulden*, lit.: GOLDEN]

Guildford ('gɪlfəd) *n* a city in S England, in Surrey: cathedral (1936–68); seat of the University of Surrey (1966). Pop: 65 998 (1991)

guildhall ('gɪld,hɔ:l) *n Brit* **a** the hall of a guild or corporation **b** a town hall

guile (gaɪl) *n* clever or crafty character or behaviour [C18 from OF *guile*, of Gmc origin; see WILE] > **'guileful** *adj* > **'guilefully** *adv* > **'guilefulness** *n* > **'guileless** *adj* > **'guilelessly** *adv* > **'guilelessness** *n*

Guilin ('gweɪ'lɪn), **Kweilin**, *or* **Kuei-lin** *n* a city in S China, in Guangxi Zhuang AR on the Li River: noted for the unusual caves and formations of the surrounding karst scenery; trade and manufacturing centre. Pop: 458 333 (1999 est)

Guillaume de Lorris (*French* gijom də lɔris) *n* 13th century, French poet who wrote the first 4058 lines of the allegorical romance, the *Roman de la rose*, continued by Jean de Meung

Guillem (*French* giɛm) *n* **Sylvie** born 1965, French ballet dancer based in Britain; with the Royal Ballet from 1989

guillemot ('gɪlɪ,mɒt) *n* a northern oceanic diving bird having a black-and-white plumage and long narrow bill [C17 from F, dim. of *Guillaume* William]

guilloche (gɪ'lɒʃ) *n* an ornamental border with a repeating pattern of two or more interwoven wavy lines, as in architecture [C19 from F: tool used in ornamental work, ?from *Guillaume* William]

guillotine *n* ('gɪlə,ti:n) **1a** a device for beheading persons, consisting of a weighted blade set between two upright posts **1b the guillotine** execution by this instrument **2** a device for cutting or trimming sheet material, such as paper or sheet metal, consisting of a slightly inclined blade that descends onto the sheet **3** a surgical instrument for removing tonsils, growths in the throat, etc **4** (in Parliament, etc) a form of closure under which a bill is divided into compartments, groups of which must be completely dealt with each day ▹ *vb* (,gɪlə'ti:n), **guillotines, guillotining, guillotined** *(tr)* **5** to behead (a person) by guillotine **6** (in Parliament, etc) to limit debate on (a bill, motion, etc) by the guillotine [C18 from F, after Joseph Ignace *Guillotin* (1738–1814), F physician, who advocated its use in 1789] > **,guillo'tiner** *n*

guilt (gɪlt) *n* **1** the fact or state of having done wrong or committed an offence **2** responsibility for a criminal or moral offence deserving punishment or a penalty **3** remorse or self-reproach caused by feeling that one is responsible for a wrong or offence **4** *arch* sin or crime [OE *gylt*, from ?]

guiltless ('gɪltlɪs) *adj* free of all responsibility for wrongdoing or crime; innocent > **'guiltlessly** *adv* > **'guiltlessness** *n*

guilty ('gɪltɪ) *adj* **guiltier, guiltiest 1** responsible for an offence or misdeed **2** *law* having committed an offence or adjudged to have done so: *the accused was found guilty* **3** of, showing, or characterized by guilt > **'guiltily** *adv* > **'guiltiness** *n*

guimpe (gɪmp) *n* a variant spelling of **gimp**

Guin. *abbrev for* Guinea

guinea ('gɪnɪ) *n* **1a** a British gold coin taken out of circulation in 1813, worth 21 shillings **1b** the sum of 21 shillings (£1.05), still used in quoting professional fees **2** See **guinea fowl** [C16 the coin was orig. made of gold from Guinea]

Guinea ('gɪnɪ) *n* **1** a republic in West Africa, on the Atlantic: established as the colony of French Guinea in 1890 and became an independent republic in 1958. Official language: French. Religion: Muslim majority and animist. Currency: franc. Capital: Conakry. Pop: 7 614 000 (2001 est). Area: 245 855 sq km (94 925 sq miles) **2** (formerly) the coastal region of West Africa, between Cape Verde and Namibe (formerly Moçâmedes; Angola): divided by a line of volcanic peaks into **Upper Guinea** (between The Gambia and Cameroon) and **Lower Guinea** (between Cameroon and S Angola) **3 Gulf of** a large inlet of the S Atlantic on the W coast of Africa, extending from Cape Palmas, Liberia, to Cape Lopez, Gabon: contains two large bays, the Bight of Biafra and the Bight of Benin, separated by the Niger delta
▹ www.guinee.gov.gn

Guinea-Bissau *n* a republic in West Africa, on the Atlantic: first discovered by the Portuguese in 1446 and of subsequent importance in the slave trade; made a colony in 1879; became an independent republic in 1974. Official language: Portuguese; Cape Verde creole is widely spoken. Religion: animist majority and Muslim. Currency: franc. Capital: Bissau. Pop: 1 316 000 (2001 est). Area: 36 125 sq km (13 948 sq miles). Former name (until 1974): **Portuguese Guinea**

guinea fowl *or* **guinea** *n* a domestic fowl of Africa and SW Asia, having a dark plumage mottled with white, a

naked head and neck, and a heavy rounded body
guinea hen *n* a guinea fowl, esp a female
guinea pig *n* 1 a domesticated cavy, commonly kept as a pet and used in scientific experiments 2 a person or thing used for experimentation [c17 from ?]
Guinevere ('gwɪnɪˌvɪə), **Guenevere** ('gwɛnɪˌvɪə), *or* **Guinever** ('gwɪnɪvə) *n* (in Arthurian legend) the wife of King Arthur and paramour of Lancelot
Guinness ('gɪnɪs) *n* Sir **Alec** 1914–2000, British stage and film actor. His films include *Kind Hearts and Coronets* (1949), *The Bridge on the River Kwai* (1957), for which he won an Oscar, and *Star Wars* (1977); TV roles include Le Carré's George Smiley
guipure (gɪ'pjʊə) *n* 1 Also called: **guipure lace** any of many types of heavy lace that have their pattern connected by threads, rather than supported on a net mesh 2 a heavy corded trimming; gimp [c19 from OF, from *guiper* to cover with cloth, of Gmc origin]
guise (gaɪz) *n* 1 semblance or pretence: *under the guise of friendship* 2 external appearance in general 3 *arch* manner or style of dress [c13 from OF *guise*, of Gmc origin]
guising ('gaɪzɪŋ) *n* (in Scotland and N England) the practice or custom of disguising oneself in fancy dress, often with mask, and visiting people's houses, esp at Halloween > '**guiser** *n*
guitar (gɪ'tɑː) *n* a plucked stringed instrument originating in Spain, usually having six strings, a flat sounding board with a circular sound hole in the centre, a flat back, and a fretted fingerboard [c17 from Sp. *guitarra*, from Ar. *qītār*, from Gk: CITHARA] > **gui'tarist** *n*
Guitry (*French* gitri) *n* **Sacha** (saʃa) 1885–1957, French actor, dramatist, and film director, born in Russia: plays include *Nono* (1905)
Guiyang ('gweɪ'jæŋ), **Kweiyang**, *or* **Kuei-yang** *n* a city in S China, capital of Guizhou province: reached by rail in 1959, with subsequent industrial growth. Pop: 1 320 566 (1999 est)
Guizhou ('gweɪ'dʒəʊ), **Kweichow**, *or* **Kueichou** *n* a province of SW China, between the Yangtze and Xi Rivers: a high plateau. Capital: Guiyang. Pop: 35 250 000 (2000 est). Area: 174 000 sq km (69 278 sq miles)
Guizot (*French* gizo) *n* **François Pierre Guillaume** (frɑ̃swa pjɛr gijom) 1787–1874, French statesman and historian. As chief minister (1840–48), his reactionary policies contributed to the outbreak of the revolution of 1848
Gujarat *or* **Gujerat** (ˌgʊdʒə'rɑːt) *n* 1 a state of W India: formed in 1960 from the N and W parts of Bombay State; one of India's most industrialized states. Capital: Gandhinagar. Pop: 50 596 992 (2001). Area: 196 024 sq km (75 268 sq miles) 2 a region of W India, north of the Narmada River: generally includes the areas north of Bombay city where Gujarati is spoken
Gujarati *or* **Gujerati** (ˌgʊdʒjə'rɑːtɪ) *n* 1 (*pl* **-ti**) a member of a people of India living chiefly in Gujarat 2 the state language of Gujarat, belonging to the Indic branch of the Indo-European family ▷ *adj* 3 of or relating to Gujarat, its people, or their language
Gujranwala (guːdʒ'rɑːnˌwʌlə) *n* a city in NE Pakistan: textile manufacturing. Pop: 1 124 799 (1998)
Gulag ('guːlæg) *n* 1 (formerly) the central administrative department of the Soviet security service, responsible for maintaining prisons and labour camps 2 (*not cap*) any system used to silence dissidents [c20 from Russian *G(lavnoye) U(pravleniye Ispravitelno-Trudovykh) Lag(erei)* Main Administration for Corrective Labour Camps]
Gulbenkian (gʊl'bɛŋkɪən) *n* 1 **Calouste Sarkis** (kæ'luːst 'sɑːkɪz) 1869–1955, British industrialist, born in Turkey. He endowed the international Gulbenkian Foundation for the advancement of the arts, science, and education 2 his son, **Nubar Sarkis** ('nuːbɑː 'sɑːkɪz) 1896–1972, British industrialist, diplomat, and philanthropist
gulch (gʌltʃ) *n US & Canad* a narrow ravine cut by a fast stream [c19 from ?]
gulden ('gʊldᵊn) *n, pl* **guldens** *or* **gulden** a variant of **guilder**
Gülek Boğaz (guː'lɛk bəʊ'gɑːz) *n* the Turkish name for the **Cilician Gates**
gules (gjuːlz) *adj* (*usually postpositive*), *n heraldry* red [c14 from OF *gueules* red fur worn around the neck, from *gole* throat, from L *gula* GULLET]
gulf (gʌlf) *n* 1 a large deep bay 2 a deep chasm 3 something that divides or separates, such as a lack of understanding 4 something that engulfs, such as a whirlpool ▷ *vb* 5 (*tr*) to swallow up; engulf [c14 from OF *golfe*, from It. *golfo*, from Gk *kolpos*]
Gulf (gʌlf) *n* **the** 1 the Persian Gulf 2 *Austral* **2a** the Gulf of Carpentaria **2b** (*modifier*) of, relating to, or adjoining the Gulf: *Gulf country* 3 NZ the Hauraki Gulf
Gulf States *pl n* **the** 1 the oil-producing states around the Persian Gulf: Iran, Iraq, Kuwait, Saudi Arabia, Bahrain, Qatar, the United Arab Emirates, and Oman 2 the states of the US that border on the Gulf of Mexico: Alabama, Florida, Louisiana, Mississippi, and Texas
Gulf Stream *n* a relatively warm ocean current flowing northeastwards from the Gulf of Mexico towards NW Europe. Also called: **North Atlantic Drift**
Gulf War *n* 1 the war (1991) between US-led UN forces and Iraq, following Iraq's invasion of Kuwait 2 See **Iran-Iraq War**
▷ www.ngwrc.org
Gulf War syndrome *n* a group of various debilitating symptoms experienced by many soldiers who served in the Gulf War of 1991. It is claimed to be associated with damage to the central nervous system, caused by exposure to pesticides containing organophosphates
gulfweed ('gʌlfˌwiːd) *n* a brown seaweed having air bladders and forming dense floating masses in tropical Atlantic waters, esp the Gulf Stream. Also called: **sargasso, sargasso weed**
gull¹ (gʌl) *n* an aquatic bird such as the common gull or mew having long pointed wings, short legs, and a mostly white plumage [c15 of Celtic origin]
gull² (gʌl) *arch* ▷ *n* 1 a person who is easily fooled or cheated ▷ *vb* 2 (*tr*) to fool, cheat, or hoax [c16 ?from dialect *gull* unfledged bird, prob. from *gul*, from ON *gulr* yellow]
gullet ('gʌlɪt) *n* 1 a less formal name for the **oesophagus** 2 the throat or pharynx [c14 from OF *goulet*, dim. of *goule*, from L *gula* throat]
gullible ('gʌlɪbᵊl) *adj* easily taken in or tricked > ˌ**gulli'bility** *n* > '**gullibly** *adv*
gully *or* **gulley** ('gʌlɪ) *n, pl* **gullies** *or* **gulleys** 1 a channel or small valley, esp one cut by heavy rainwater 2 NZ a bush-clad small valley 3 *cricket* **3a** a fielding position between the slips and point **3b** a fielder in this position ▷ *vb* **gullies, gullying, gullied** *or* **gulleys, gulleying, gulleyed** 4 (*tr*) to make channels in (the ground, sand, etc) [c16 from F *goulet* neck of a bottle; see GULLET]
gulp (gʌlp) *vb* 1 (*tr; often foll by down*) to swallow rapidly, esp in large mouthfuls 2 (*tr; often foll by back*) to stifle or choke: *to gulp back sobs* 3 (*intr*) to swallow air convulsively because of nervousness, surprise, etc 4 (*intr*) to make a noise, as when swallowing too quickly ▷ *n* 5 the act of gulping 6 the quantity taken in a gulp [c15 from MDu. *gulpen*, imit.] > '**gulper** *n* > '**gulpingly** *adv* > '**gulpy** *adj*
gum¹ (gʌm) *n* 1 any of various sticky substances that exude from certain plants, hardening on exposure to air and dissolving or forming viscous masses in water 2 any of various products, such as adhesives, that are made from such substances 3 any sticky substance used as an adhesive; mucilage; glue 4 See **chewing gum, bubble gum,** and **gumtree** 5 NZ See **kauri gum** 6 *chiefly Brit* a gumdrop ▷ *vb* **gums, gumming, gummed** 7 to cover or become covered, clogged, or stiffened as

Gg

with gum **8** (*tr*) to stick together or in place with gum **9** (*intr*) to emit or form gum ▷ See also **gum up** [c14 from OF *gomme*, from L *gummi*, from Gk *kommi*, from Egyptian *kemai*]

gum² (gʌm) *n* the fleshy tissue that covers the jawbones around the bases of the teeth. Technical name: **gingiva** Related adj: **gingival** [OE *gōma* jaw]

gum ammoniac *n* another name for **ammoniac**

gum arabic *n* a gum exuded by certain acacia trees, used in the manufacture of ink, food thickeners, pills, emulsifiers, etc. Also called: **gum acacia**

gumbo (ˈgʌmbəʊ) *n, pl* **gumbos** *US* **1** the mucilaginous pods of okra **2** another name for **okra 3** a soup or stew thickened with okra pods **4** a fine soil in the W prairies that becomes muddy when wet [c19 from Louisiana F *gombo*, of Bantu origin]

gumboil (ˈgʌm,bɔɪl) *n* an abscess on the gums

gumboots (ˈgʌm,buːts) *pl n* another name for **Wellington boots** (sense 1)

gum-digger *n NZ* a person who digs for fossilized kauri gum in a **gum-field,** an area where it is found buried

gumdrop (ˈgʌm,drɒp) *n* a small jelly-like sweet containing gum arabic and various colourings and flavourings. Also called (esp Brit): **gum**

gummy¹ (ˈgʌmɪ) *adj* **gummier, gummiest 1** sticky or tacky **2** consisting of, coated with, or clogged by gum or a similar substance **3** producing gum [c14 from GUM¹ + -Y¹] > **ˈgumminess** *n*

gummy² (ˈgʌmɪ) *adj* **gummier, gummiest 1** toothless ▷ *n, pl* **gummies 2** Also called: **gummy shark** *Austral* a small crustacean-eating shark with flat crushing teeth [c20 from GUM² + -Y¹]

gum nut *n Austral* the hardened seed container of the gumtree *Eucalyptus gummifera*

gumption (ˈgʌmpʃən) *n inf* **1** *Brit* common sense or resourcefulness **2** initiative or courage [c18 orig. Scot., from ?]

gum resin *n* a mixture of resin and gum obtained from various plants and trees

gumtree (ˈgʌm,triː) *n* **1** any of various trees that yield gum, such as the eucalyptus, sweet gum, and sour gum. Sometimes shortened to **gum 2 up a gumtree** *inf* in a very awkward position; in difficulties

gum up *vb* (*tr, adv*) **1** to cover, dab, or stiffen with gum **2** *inf* to make a mess of; bungle (often in **gum up the works**)

gun (gʌn) *n* **1a** a weapon with a metallic tube or barrel from which a missile is discharged, usually by force of an explosion. It may be portable or mounted **1b** (*as modifier*): *a gun barrel* **2** the firing of a gun as a salute or signal, as in military ceremonial **3** a member of or a place in a shooting party or syndicate **4** any device used to project something under pressure: *a spray gun* **5** *US sl* an armed criminal; gunman **6** *Austral & NZ sl* **6a** an expert **6b** (*as modifier*): *a gun shearer* **7 give it the gun** *sl* to increase speed, effort, etc, to a considerable or maximum degree **8 go great guns** *sl* to act or function with great speed, intensity, etc **9 jump** *or* **beat the gun 9a** (of a runner, etc) to set off before the starting signal is given **9b** *inf* to act prematurely **10 stick to one's guns** *inf* to maintain one's opinions or intentions in spite of opposition ▷ *vb* **guns, gunning, gunned 11** (when *tr*, often foll by *down*) to shoot (someone) with a gun **12** (*tr*) to press hard on the accelerator of (an engine): *to gun the engine* **13** (*intr*) to hunt with a gun ▷ See also **gun for** [c14 prob. from a female pet name, from the Scand. name *Gunnhildr* (from ON *gunnr* war + *hildr* war)]
▷ www.gunsmagazine.com

gunboat (ˈgʌn,bəʊt) *n* a small shallow-draft vessel carrying mounted guns and used by coastal patrols, etc

gunboat diplomacy *n* diplomacy conducted by threats of military intervention

guncotton (ˈgʌn,kɒtᵊn) *n* cellulose nitrate containing a relatively large amount of nitrogen: used as an explosive

gun dog *n* **1** a dog trained to work with a hunter or gamekeeper, esp in retrieving, pointing at, or flushing game **2** a dog belonging to any breed adapted to these activities

gunfight (ˈgʌn,faɪt) *n chiefly US* a fight between persons using firearms > **ˈgun,fighter** *n*

gunfire (ˈgʌn,faɪə) *n* **1** the firing of one or more guns, esp when done repeatedly **2** the use of firearms, as contrasted with other military tactics

gun for *vb* (*intr, prep*) **1** to search for in order to reprimand, punish, or kill **2** to try earnestly for: *he was gunning for promotion*

gunge (gʌndʒ) *inf* ▷ *n* **1** sticky, rubbery, or congealed matter ▷ *vb* **gunges, gunging, gunged 2** (*tr; usually passive;* foll by *up*) to block or encrust with gunge; clog [c20 imit., ? infl. by GOO & SPONGE] > **ˈgungy** *adj*

gunk (gʌŋk) *n inf* slimy, oily, or filthy matter [c20 ? imit.]

gunlock (ˈgʌn,lɒk) *n* the mechanism in some firearms that causes the charge to be exploded

gunman (ˈgʌnmən) *n, pl* **gunmen 1** a man armed with a gun, esp unlawfully **2** a man skilled with a gun

gunmetal (ˈgʌn,mɛtᵊl) *n* **1** a type of bronze containing copper, tin, and zinc **2a** a dark grey colour **2b** (*as adj*): *gunmetal chiffon*

Gunn (gʌn) *n* **Thom(son William)** born 1929, British poet resident in the USA. His works include *Fighting Terms* (1954), *My Sad Captains* (1961), *Jack Straw's Castle* (1976), and *The Man with Night Sweats* (1992)

Gunnar (ˈgʊnɑː) *n Norse myth* brother of Gudrun and husband of Brynhild, won for him by Sigurd. He corresponds to Gunther in the *Nibelungenlied*

gunnel¹ (ˈgʌnᵊl) *n* any eel-like fish occurring in coastal regions of northern seas [c17 from ?]

gunnel² (ˈgʌnᵊl) *n* a variant spelling of **gunwale**

gunner (ˈgʌnə) *n* **1** a serviceman who works with, uses, or specializes in guns **2** *naval* (formerly) a warrant officer responsible for the training of gun crews, their performance in action, and accounting for ammunition **3** (in the British Army) an artilleryman, esp a private **4** a person who hunts with a rifle or shotgun

gunnery (ˈgʌnərɪ) *n* **1** the art and science of the efficient design and use of ordnance, esp artillery **2** guns collectively **3** the use and firing of guns

gunny (ˈgʌnɪ) *n, pl* **gunnies** *chiefly US* **1** a coarse hard-wearing fabric usually made from jute and used for sacks, etc **2** Also called: **gunny sack** a sack made from this fabric [c18 from Hindi, from Sansk. *gōnī* sack, prob. of Dravidian origin]

gunplay (ˈgʌn,pleɪ) *n chiefly US* the use of firearms, as by criminals, etc

gunpoint (ˈgʌn,pɔɪnt) *n* **1** the muzzle of a gun **2 at gunpoint** being under or using the threat of being shot

gunpowder (ˈgʌn,paʊdə) *n* an explosive mixture of potassium nitrate, charcoal, and sulphur: used in time fuses and in fireworks

gun room *n* **1** (esp in the Royal Navy) the mess allocated to junior officers **2** a room where guns are stored

gunrunning (ˈgʌn,rʌnɪŋ) *n* the smuggling of guns and ammunition or other weapons of war into a country > **ˈgun,runner** *n*

gunshot (ˈgʌn,ʃɒt) *n* **1a** shot fired from a gun **1b** (*as modifier*): *gunshot wounds* **2** the range of a gun **3** the shooting of a gun

gunslinger (ˈgʌn,slɪŋə) *n sl* a gunfighter or gunman, esp in the Old West

gunsmith (ˈgʌn,smɪθ) *n* a person who makes or repairs firearms, esp portable guns

gunstock (ˈgʌn,stɒk) *n* the wooden handle or support to which is attached the barrel of a rifle

Gunter (ˈgʌntə) *n* **Edmund** 1581–1626, English mathematician and astronomer, who invented various measuring instruments, including Gunter's chain

Gunter's chain *n surveying* a measuring chain 22 yards in length, or this length as a unit [c17 after E. GUNTER]

Gunther ('gʊntə) *n* (in the *Nibelungenlied*) a king of Burgundy, allied with Siegfried, who won for him his wife Brunhild. He corresponds to Gunnar in Norse mythology

Guntur (gʊn'tʊə) *n* a city in E India, in central Andhra Pradesh: founded by the French in the 18th century; ceded to Britain in 1788. Pop: 471 051 (1991)

gunwale *or* **gunnel** ('gʌnᵊl) *n naut* the top of the side of a boat or ship [c15 from GUN + WALE from its use to support guns]

gunyah ('gʌnjə) *n Austral* a bush hut or shelter [c19 from Abor.]

guppy ('gʌpɪ) *n, pl* **guppies** a small brightly coloured freshwater fish of N South America and the Caribbean: a popular aquarium fish [c20 after R. J. L. *Guppy*, 19th-cent clergyman of Trinidad who first presented specimens to the British Museum]

Gurdjieff ('gɛːdjɛf) *n* **Georgei Ivanovitch** ('dʒɔːdʒɪ ɪ'vanəˌvitʃ) ?1877–1949, Russian mystic: founded a teaching centre in Paris (1922)

gurdwara ('gɜːdwɑːrə) *n* a Sikh place of worship [c20 from Punjabi *gurduārā*, from Sansk. *guru* teacher + *dvārā* door]

gurgle ('gɜːgᵊl) *vb* **gurgles, gurgling, gurgled** (*intr*) **1** (of liquids, esp of streams, etc) to make low bubbling noises when flowing **2** to utter low throaty bubbling noises, esp as a sign of contentment: *the baby gurgled with delight* ▷ *n* **3** the act or sound of gurgling [c16 ?from Vulgar L *gurgulāre*, from L *gurguliō* gullet]

Gurkha ('gɜːkə) *n* **1** a member of a Hindu people, descended from Brahmins and Rajputs, living chiefly in Nepal **2** a member of a Gurkha regiment in the Indian or British army

gurnard ('gɜːnəd) *or* **gurnet** ('gɜːnɪt) *n, pl* **gurnard, gurnards** *or* **gurnet, gurnets** a European marine fish having a heavily armoured head and finger-like pectoral fins [c14 from OF *gornard*, from *grognier* to grunt, from L *grunnīre*]

guru ('gʊruː, 'guːruː) *n* **1** a Hindu or Sikh religious teacher or leader, giving personal spiritual guidance to his disciples **2** *often derog* a leader or chief theoretician of a movement, esp a spiritual or religious cult **3** *often facetious* a leading authority in a particular field: *a cricketing guru* [c17 from Hindi *gurū*, from Sansk. *guruh* weighty]

gush (gʌʃ) *vb* **1** to pour out or cause to pour out suddenly and profusely, usually with a rushing sound **2** to act or utter in an overeffusive, affected, or sentimental manner ▷ *n* **3** a sudden copious flow or emission, esp of liquid **4** something that flows out or is emitted **5** an extravagant and insincere expression of admiration, sentiment, etc [c14 prob. imit.; cf. ON *gjósa*] > **'gushing** *adj* > **'gushingly** *adv*

gusher ('gʌʃə) *n* **1** a person who gushes, as in being effusive or sentimental **2** something, such as a spurting oil well, that gushes

gushy ('gʌʃɪ) *adj* **gushier, gushiest** *inf* displaying excessive admiration or sentimentality > **'gushily** *adv* > **'gushiness** *n*

gusset ('gʌsɪt) *n* **1** an inset piece of material used esp to strengthen or enlarge a garment **2** a triangular metal plate for strengthening a corner joist ▷ *vb* **3** (*tr*) to put a gusset in (a garment) [c15 from OF *gousset* a piece of mail, dim. of *gousse* pod, from ?] > **'gusseted** *adj*

gust (gʌst) *n* **1** a sudden blast of wind **2** a sudden rush of smoke, sound, etc **3** an outburst of emotion ▷ *vb* **4** (*intr*) to blow in gusts [c16 from ON *gustr*; rel. to *gjōsa* to GUSH; see GEYSER]

gustation (gʌ'steɪʃən) *n* the act of tasting or the faculty of taste [c16 from L *gustātiō*, from *gustāre* to taste] > **gustatory** ('gʌstətərɪ) *or* **'gustative** *adj*

Gustavo A. Madero (*Spanish* gus'taβo a ma'ðero) *n* the former name (1931–71) of **Guadalupe Hidalgo**

Gustavus I (gʊ'stɑːvəs) *n* called *Gustavus Vasa*. ?1496–1560, king of Sweden (1523–60). He was elected king after driving the Danes from Sweden (1520–23)

Gustavus II *n* See **Gustavus Adolphus**

Gustavus VI *n* title of *Gustaf Adolf*. 1882–1973, king of Sweden (1950–73)

Gustavus Adolphus (ə'dɒlfəs) *or* **Gustavus II** *n* 1594–1632, king of Sweden (1611–32). A brilliant general, he waged successful wars with Denmark, Russia, and Poland and in the Thirty Years' War led a Protestant army against the Catholic League and the Holy Roman Empire (1630–32). He defeated Tilly at Leipzig (1631) and Lech (1632) but was killed at the battle of Lützen

gusto ('gʌstəʊ) *n* vigorous enjoyment, zest, or relish: *the aria was sung with great gusto* [c17 from Sp.: taste, from L *gustus* a tasting]

gusty ('gʌstɪ) *adj* **gustier, gustiest** **1** blowing in gusts or characterized by blustery weather: *a gusty wind* **2** given to sudden outbursts, as of emotion > **'gustily** *adv* > **'gustiness** *n*

gut (gʌt) *n* **1a** the lower part of the alimentary canal; intestine **1b** the entire alimentary canal. Related adj: **visceral** **2** (*often pl*) the bowels or entrails, esp of an animal **3** *sl* the belly; paunch **4** See **catgut** **5** a silky fibrous substance extracted from silkworms, used in the manufacture of fishing tackle **6** a narrow channel or passage **7** (*pl*) *inf* courage, willpower, or daring; forcefulness **8** (*pl*) *inf* the essential part: *the guts of a problem* ▷ *vb* **guts, gutting, gutted** (*tr*) **9** to remove the entrails from (fish, etc) **10** (esp of fire) to destroy the inside of (a building) **11** to take out the central points of (an article, etc), esp in summary form ▷ *adj* **12** *inf* instinctive, basic, or fundamental: *a gut feeling; capital punishment is a gut issue* [OE *gutt*; rel. to *gēotan* to flow]

GUT (gʌt) *n acronym for* grand unified theory

Gutenberg ('guːtᵊnˌbɜːg; *German* 'guːtənbɛrk) *n* **Johann** (jo'han), original name *Johannes Gensfleisch*. ?1398–1468, German printer; inventor of printing by movable type

Gütersloh (*German* 'gyːtərsloː) *n* a town in NW Germany, in North Rhine-Westphalia. Pop: 83 400 (latest est)

Guthrie ('gʌθrɪ) *n* **1** **Samuel** 1782–1848, US chemist: invented percussion priming powder and a punch lock for exploding it, and discovered chloroform (1831) **2** **Sir (William) Tyrone** 1900–71, English theatrical director **3** **Woody**, full name *Woodrow Wilson Guthrie*. 1912–67, US folk singer and songwriter. His songs include "So Long, it's been Good to Know you" (1940) and "This Land is your Land" (1944)

Guthrun ('gʊðruːn) *n* a variant of **Gudrun**

gutless ('gʌtlɪs) *adj inf* lacking courage or determination

gut reaction *n* the first, instinctive, reaction to a situation

gutsy ('gʌtsɪ) *adj* **gutsier, gutsiest** *sl* **1** gluttonous; greedy **2** full of courage or boldness **3** passionate; lusty

gutta-percha ('gʌtə'pɜːtʃə) *n* **1** any of several tropical trees with leathery leaves **2** a whitish rubber substance derived from the coagulated milky latex of any of these trees: used in electrical insulation and dentistry [c19 from Malay *getah* gum + *percha* tree that produces it]

guttate ('gʌteɪt) *adj biol* (esp of plants) covered with small drops or droplike markings [c19 from L *guttātus* dappled, from *gutta* a drop]

gutted ('gʌtɪd) *adj inf* disappointed and upset

gutter ('gʌtə) *n* **1** a channel along the eaves or on the roof of a building, used to collect and carry away rainwater **2** a channel running along the kerb or the centre of a road to collect and carry away rainwater **3** either of the two channels running parallel to a tenpin bowling lane **4** *printing* the white space between the facing pages of an open book **5** *surfing* a dangerous deep channel formed by currents and waves **6 the gutter** a poverty-stricken, degraded, or criminal environment ▷ *vb* **7** (*tr*) to make gutters in **8** (*intr*) to flow in a stream **9** (*intr*) (of a candle) to melt away as the wax forms channels and runs down in drops **10** (*intr*) (of a flame) to flicker and be about to go out [c13 from Anglo-F *goutiere*, from OF *goute* a drop, from L *gutta*] > **'guttering** *n*

gutter press *n* the section of the popular press that seeks sensationalism in its coverage

guttersnipe ('gʌtəˌsnaɪp) *n* a child who spends most of his or her time in the streets, esp in a slum area

guttural ('gʌtərəl) *adj* **1** *anat* of or relating to the throat **2** *phonetics* pronounced in the throat or the back of the mouth **3** raucous ▷ *n* **4** *phonetics* a guttural consonant [c16 from NL *gutturālis*, from L *guttur* gullet] > **'gutturally** *adv*

gut-wrenching *adj inf* causing great distress or suffering: *gut-wrenching scenes*

guy[1] (gaɪ) *n* **1** *inf* a man or youth **2** *Brit* a crude effigy of Guy Fawkes, usually made of old clothes stuffed with straw or rags, that is burnt on top of a bonfire on Guy Fawkes Day **3** *Brit* a person in shabby or ludicrously odd clothes **4** (*pl*) *inf* persons of either sex ▷ *vb* **5** (*tr*) to make fun of; ridicule [c19 from Guy FAWKES]

guy[2] (gaɪ) *n* **1** a rope, chain, wire, etc, for anchoring an object in position or for steadying or guiding it ▷ *vb* **2** (*tr*) to anchor, steady, or guide with a guy or guys [c14 prob. from Low G; cf. OF *guie* guide, from *guier* to GUIDE]

Guy (gaɪ) *n* **Buddy,** real name *George Guy*. born 1936, U.S. blues singer and guitarist

Guyana (gaɪ'ænə) *n* a republic in NE South America, on the Atlantic: colonized chiefly by the Dutch in the 17th and 18th centuries; became a British colony in 1831 and an independent republic within the Commonwealth in 1966. Official language: English. Religions: Christian and Hindu. Currency: dollar. Capital: Georgetown. Pop: 776 000 (2001 est). Area: about 215 000 sq km (83 000 sq miles). Former name (until 1966): **British Guiana**

Guyanese (ˌgaɪə'ni:z) *or* **Guyanan** (gaɪ'ænən) *adj* **1** of or relating to Guyana or its inhabitants ▷ *n* **2** a native or inhabitant of Guyana

Guyenne (*French* gɥijɛn) *n* a variant spelling of **Guienne**

Guzmán Blanco (*Spanish* guθ'man 'blaŋko) *n* **Antonio** (an'tonjo) 1829–99, Venezuelan statesman; president (1873–77; 1879–84; 1886–87). He was virtual dictator of Venezuela from 1870 until his overthrow (1889)

guzzle ('gʌz^əl) *vb* **guzzles, guzzling, guzzled** to consume (food or drink) excessively or greedily [c16 from ?] > **'guzzler** *n*

Gwalior ('gwɑ:lɪˌɔ:) *n* **1** a city in N central India, in Madhya Pradesh: built around the fort, which dates from before 525; industrial and commercial centre. Pop: 690 765 (1991) **2** a former princely state of central India, established in the 18th century: merged with Madhya Bharat in 1948, which in turn merged with Madhya Pradesh in 1956

Gwent (gwɛnt) *n* a former county of SE Wales: formed in 1974 from most of Monmouthshire and part of Breconshire; replaced in 1996 by Monmouthshire and the county boroughs of Newport, Torfaen, Blaenau Gwent, and part of Caerphilly

Gweru ('gweɪru:) *n* a city in central Zimbabwe. Pop: 170 000 (1998 est). Former name (until 1982): **Gwelo** ('gwi:ləʊ)

Gwich'in ('gwɪtʃɪn) *n* **1** a member of a North American Indian people from NW Canada and NE Alaska **2** the language of these people

Gwyn (gwɪn) *n* **Nell,** original name *Eleanor Gwynne*. 1650–87, English actress; mistress of Charles II

Gwynedd ('gwɪnɛð) *n* a county of NW Wales, formed in 1974 from Anglesey, Caernarvonshire, part of Denbighshire, and most of Merionethshire; lost Anglesey and part of the NE in 1996: generally mountainous with many lakes, much of it lying in the Snowdonia National Park. Administrative centre: Caernarfon. Pop: 116 838 (2001). Area: 2550 sq km (869 sq miles)

gybe, gibe, *or* **jibe** (dʒaɪb) *Naut* ▷ *vb* **gybes, gybing, gybed, gibes, gibing, gibed** *or* **jibes, jibing, jibed 1** (*intr*) (of a fore-and-aft sail) to shift suddenly from one side of the vessel to the other when running before the wind **2** to cause (a sailing vessel) to gybe or (of a sailing vessel) to undergo gybing ▷ *n* **3** an instance of gybing [c17 from obs. Du. *gijben* (now *gijpen*), from ?]

gym (dʒɪm) *n, adj* short for **gymnasium, gymnastics, gymnastic**

▷ www.webaerobics.com

gym bunny *n inf* a person who spends a lot of time exercising at a gymnasium

gymkhana (dʒɪm'kɑ:nə) *n* **1** *chiefly Brit* an event in which horses and riders display skill and aptitude in various races and contests **2** (in Anglo-India) a place providing sporting and athletic facilities [c19 from Hindi *gend-khānā*, lit.: ball house]

gymnasium (dʒɪm'neɪzɪəm) *n, pl* **gymnasiums** *or* **gymnasia** (-zɪə) **1** a large room or hall equipped with bars, weights, ropes, etc, for physical training **2** (in various European countries) a secondary school that prepares pupils for university [c16 from L: school for gymnastics, from Gk *gumnasion*, from *gumnazein* to exercise naked]

gymnast ('dʒɪmnæst) *n* a person who is skilled or trained in gymnastics

gymnastic (dʒɪm'næstɪk) *adj* of, like, or involving gymnastics > **gym'nastically** *adv*

gymnastics (dʒɪm'næstɪks) *n* **1** (*functioning as sing*) practice or training in exercises that develop physical strength and agility or mental capacity **2** (*functioning as pl*) gymnastic exercises

▷ www.fig-gymnastics.com

gymno- *combining form* naked, bare, or exposed: *gymnosperm* [from Gk *gumnos* naked]

gymnosperm ('dʒɪmnəʊˌspɜ:m, 'gɪm-) *n* any seed-bearing plant in which the ovules are borne naked on open scales, which are often arranged in cones; any conifer or related plant ▷ Cf **angiosperm** > **ˌgymno'spermous** *adj*

gympie ('gɪmpɪ) *n* a tall Australian tree with stinging hairs on its leaves. Also: **nettle tree**

gym shoe *n* another name for **plimsoll**

gymslip ('dʒɪmˌslɪp) *n* a tunic or pinafore dress worn by schoolgirls, often part of a school uniform

gyn- *combining form* a variant of **gyno-** before a vowel

gynaeco- *or US* **gyneco-** *combining form* relating to women; female: *gynaecology* [from Gk, from *gunē*, *gunaik-* woman, female]

gynaecology *or US* **gynecology** (ˌgaɪnɪ'kɒlədʒɪ) *n* the branch of medicine concerned with diseases and conditions specific to women > **gynaecological** (ˌgaɪnɪkə'lɒdʒɪk^əl), **ˌgynaeco'logic** *or US* **ˌgyneco'logical, ˌgyneco'logic** *adj* > **ˌgynae'cologist** *or US* **ˌgyne'cologist** *n*

▷ http://omni.ac.uk/subject-listing/WP100.html
▷ www.obgyn.net

gynandromorph (dʒɪ'nændrəʊˌmɔ:f, gaɪ-) *n* an organism, esp an insect, that has both male and female physical characteristics

gynandrous (dʒaɪ'nændrəs, gaɪ-) *adj* (of flowers such as the orchid) having the stamens and styles united in a column [c19 from Gk *gunandros* of uncertain sex, from *gunē* woman + *anēr* man]

gyno- *or before a vowel* **gyn-** *combining form* **1** relating to women; female: *gynarchy* **2** denoting a female reproductive organ: *gynophore* [from Gk, from *gunē* woman]

gynoecium, gynaeceum, *or esp US* **gynecium**

(dʒaɪˈniːsɪəm, gaɪ-) *n, pl* **gynoecia, gynaecea** *or esp US* **gynecia** (-sɪə) the carpels of a flowering plant collectively [c18 NL, from Gk *gunaikeion* women's quarters, from *gunaik-, gunē* woman + *-eion*, suffix indicating place]

gynophore (ˈdʒaɪnəʊˌfɔː, ˈgaɪ-) *n* a stalk in some plants that bears the gynoecium above the level of the other flower parts

-gynous *adj combining form* **1** of or relating to women or females: *androgynous; misogynous* **2** relating to female organs: *epigynous* [from NL, from Gk, from *gunē* woman] > **-gyny** *n combining form*

Györ (*Hungarian* djøːr) *n* an industrial town in NW Hungary: medieval Benedictine abbey. Pop: 127 119 (2000 est)

gyp[1] *or* **gip** (dʒɪp) *Sl* ▷ *vb* **gyps, gypping, gypped** *or* **gips, gipping, gipped 1** (*tr*) to swindle, cheat, or defraud ▷ *n* **2** an act of cheating **3** a person who gyps [c18 back formation from GYPSY]

gyp[2] *or* **gip** (dʒɪp) *n Brit & NZ sl* severe pain; torture: *his arthritis gave him gyp* [c19 prob. a contraction of *gee up!*; see GEE[1]]

gyp[3] (dʒɪp) *n* a college servant at Cambridge University [c18 ?from obs. *gippo* scullion]

Gyprock (ˈdʒɪprɒk) *n trademark Austral* the brand name of a type of plasterboard [from GYPSUM + ROCK]

gypsophila (dʒɪpˈsɒfɪlə) *n* any of a Mediterranean genus of plants, having small white or pink fragrant flowers [c18 NL, from Gk *gupsos* chalk + *philos* loving]

gypsum (ˈdʒɪpsəm) *n* a mineral consisting of hydrated calcium sulphate that occurs in sedimentary rocks and clay and is used principally in making plasters and cements, esp plaster of Paris. Formula: $CaSO_4.2H_2O$ [c17 from L, from Gk *gupsos* chalk, plaster, cement, of Semitic origin] > **gypseous** (ˈdʒɪpsɪəs) *adj*

Gypsy *or* **Gipsy** (ˈdʒɪpsɪ) *n, pl* **Gypsies** *or* **Gipsies** (*sometimes not cap*) **1a** a member of a people scattered throughout Europe and North America, who maintain a nomadic way of life in industrialized societies. They migrated from NW India about the 9th century onwards **1b** (*as modifier*): *a Gypsy fortune-teller* **2** the language of the Gypsies; Romany **3** a person who looks or behaves like a Gypsy [c16 from EGYPTIAN, since they were thought to have come orig. from Egypt] > **ˈGypsyish** *or* **ˈGipsyish** *adj*

gypsy moth *or* **gipsy moth** *n* a European moth whose caterpillars are pests on deciduous trees

gyrate *vb* (dʒaɪˈreɪt), **gyrates, gyrating, gyrated 1** (*intr*) to rotate or spiral, esp about a fixed point or axis ▷ *adj* (ˈdʒaɪrɪt) **2** *biol* curved or coiled into a circle [c19 from LL *gȳrāre*, from L *gȳrus* circle, from Gk *guros*] > **gyˈration** *n* > **gyˈrator** *n* > **gyratory** (ˈdʒaɪrətərɪ) *adj*

gyre (ˈdʒaɪə) *chiefly literary* ▷ *n* **1** a circular or spiral movement or path **2** a ring, circle, or spiral ▷ *vb* **gyres, gyring, gyred 3** (*intr*) to whirl [c16 from L *gȳrus* circle, from Gk *guros*]

gyrfalcon *or* **gerfalcon** (ˈdʒɜːˌfɔːlkən, -ˌfɔːkən) *n* a very large rare falcon of northern and arctic regions [c14 from OF *gerfaucon*, ?from ON *geirfalki*, from *geirr* spear + *falki* falcon]

gyro (ˈdʒaɪrəʊ) *n, pl* **gyros 1** See **gyrocompass 2** See **gyroscope**

gyro- *or before a vowel* **gyr-** *combining form* **1** indicating rotating or gyrating motion: *gyroscope* **2** indicating a gyroscope: *gyrocompass* [via L from Gk, from *guros* circle]

gyrocompass (ˈdʒaɪrəʊˌkʌmpəs) *n* a nonmagnetic compass that uses a motor-driven gyroscope to indicate true north

gyrodyne (ˈdʒaɪrəʊˌdaɪn) *n* an aircraft that uses a powered rotor to take off and manoeuvre, but uses autorotation when cruising

gyromagnetic (ˌdʒaɪrəʊmægˈnɛtɪk) *adj* of or caused by magnetic properties resulting from the spin of a charged particle, such as an electron

gyroscope (ˈdʒaɪrəˌskəʊp) *n* a device containing a disc rotating on an axis that can turn freely in any direction so that the disc maintains the same orientation irrespective of the movement of the surrounding structure > **gyroscopic** (ˌdʒaɪrəˈskɒpɪk) *adj* > **ˌgyroˈscopically** *adv*

gyrostabilizer *or* **gyrostabiliser** (ˌdʒaɪrəʊˈsteɪbɪˌlaɪzə) *n* a gyroscopic device used to stabilize the rolling motion of a ship

gyve (dʒaɪv) *arch* ▷ *vb* **gyves, gyving, gyved 1** (*tr*) to shackle or fetter ▷ *n* **2** (*usually pl*) fetter [c13 from ?]

Gg

Hh

h *or* **H** (eɪtʃ) *n, pl* **h's, H's,** *or* **Hs** **1** the eighth letter of the English alphabet **2** a speech sound represented by this letter **3a** something shaped like an H **3b** (*in combination*): *an H-beam*

h *symbol for:* **1** *physics* Planck constant **2** hecto- **3** hour

H *symbol for:* **1** *chem* hydrogen **2** *physics* magnetic field strength **3** *electronics* henry **4** (on Brit pencils, signifying degree of hardness of lead) hard

h. *or* **H.** *abbrev for:* **1** harbour **2** height **3** hour **4** husband

ha[1] *or* **hah** (hɑː) *interj* **1** an exclamation expressing derision, triumph, surprise, etc **2** (*reiterated*) a representation of the sound of laughter

ha[2] *symbol for* hectare

Haakon VII *n* 1872–1957, king of Norway (1905–57). During the Nazi occupation of Norway (1940–45) he led Norwegian resistance from England

haar (hɑː) *n Eastern Brit* a cold sea mist or fog off the North Sea [C17 rel. to Du. dialect *harig* damp]

Haarlem (*Dutch* ˈhaːrlɛm) *n* a city in the W Netherlands, capital of North Holland province. Pop: 148 262 (1999 est)

Hab. *Bible abbrev for* Habakkuk

Habakkuk (ˈhæbəkək) *n Old Testament* **1** a Hebrew prophet **2** the book containing his oracles and canticle

Habana (aˈβana) *n* the Spanish name for **Havana**

habanera (ˌhæbəˈnɛərə) *n* **1** a slow Cuban dance in duple time **2** a piece of music for this dance [from Sp. *danza habanera* dance from Havana]

habeas corpus (ˈheɪbɪəs ˈkɔːpəs) *n law* a writ ordering a person to be brought before a court or judge, esp so that the court may ascertain whether his detention is lawful [C15 from the opening of the L writ, lit.: you may have the body]

haberdasher (ˈhæbəˌdæʃə) *n* **1** *Brit* a dealer in small articles for sewing, such as buttons, zips, and ribbons **2** *US* a men's outfitter [C14 from Anglo-F *hapertas* small items of merchandise, from ?]

haberdashery (ˈhæbəˌdæʃərɪ) *n, pl* **haberdasheries** the goods or business kept by a haberdasher

habergeon (ˈhæbədʒən) *n* a light sleeveless coat of mail worn in the 14th century under the plated hauberk [C14 from OF *haubergeon* a little HAUBERK]

Haber process (ˈhɑːbə) *n* an industrial process for producing ammonia by reacting atmospheric nitrogen with hydrogen at high pressure and temperature in the presence of a catalyst [after Fritz *Haber* (1868–1934), G chemist]

habiliment (həˈbɪlɪmənt) *n* (*often pl*) dress or attire [C15 from OF *habillement*, from *habiller* to dress]

habilitate (həˈbɪlɪˌteɪt) *vb* **habilitates, habilitating, habilitated** **1** (*tr*) *US* to equip and finance (a mine) **2** (*intr*) to qualify for office [C17 from Med. L *habilitāre* to make fit, from L *habilitās* aptness] > **haˌbiliˈtation** *n*

habit (ˈhæbɪt) *n* **1** a tendency or disposition to act in a particular way **2** established custom, usual practice, etc **3** *psychol* a learned behavioural response to a particular situation **4** mental disposition or attitude: *a good working habit of mind* **5a** a practice or substance to which a person is addicted: *drink has become a habit with him* **5b** the state of being dependent on something, esp a drug **6** *bot, zool* method of growth, type of existence, behaviour or general appearance: *a burrowing habit* **7** the customary apparel of a particular occupation, rank, etc, now esp the costume of a nun or monk **8** Also called: **riding habit** a woman's riding dress ▷ *vb* **habits, habiting, habited** (*tr*) **9** to clothe **10** an archaic word for **inhabit** [C13 from L *habitus* custom, from *habēre* to have]

habitable (ˈhæbɪtəbᵊl) *adj* able to be lived in > **ˌhabitaˈbility** *or* **ˈhabitableness** *n* > **ˈhabitably** *adv*

habitant (ˈhæbɪtᵊnt) *n* **1** a less common word for **inhabitant** **2a** an early French settler in Canada or

Louisiana **2b** a descendant of these settlers, esp a farmer

habitat ('hæbɪˌtæt) *n* **1** the environment in which an animal or plant normally lives or grows **2** the place in which a person, group, class, etc, is normally found [c18 from L: it inhabits, from *habitāre* to dwell, from *habēre* to have]

habitation (ˌhæbɪ'teɪʃən) *n* **1** a dwelling place **2** occupation of a dwelling place

habit-forming *adj* tending to become a habit or addiction

habitual (hə'bɪtjʊəl) *adj* **1** (*usually prenominal*) done or experienced regularly and repeatedly: *the habitual Sunday walk* **2** (*usually prenominal*) by habit: *a habitual drinker* **3** customary; usual > **ha'bitually** *adv* > **ha'bitualness** *n*

habituate (hə'bɪtjʊˌeɪt) *vb* **habituates, habituating, habituated** **1** to accustom; make used to **2** *US & Canad arch* to frequent > **haˌbitu'ation** *n*

habitude ('hæbɪˌtju:d) *n rare* habit; tendency

habitué (hə'bɪtjʊˌeɪ) *n* a frequent visitor to a place [c19 from F, from *habituer* to frequent]

Habsburg ('ha:psbʊrk) *n* the German name for **Hapsburg**

HAC *abbrev for* Honourable Artillery Company

hachure (hæ'ʃjʊə) *n* shading of short lines drawn on a relief map to indicate gradients [c19 from F, from *hacher* to chop up]

hacienda (ˌhæsɪ'ɛndə) *n* (in Spain or Spanish-speaking countries) **1a** a ranch or large estate **1b** any substantial manufacturing establishment in the country **2** the main house on such a ranch or establishment [c18 from Sp., from L *facienda* things to be done, from *facere* to do]

hack[1] (hæk) *vb* **1** (when *intr*, usually foll by *at* or *away*) to chop (at) roughly or violently **2** to cut and clear (a way), as through undergrowth **3** (in sport, esp rugby) to foul (an opposing player) by kicking his shins **4** (*intr*) to cough in short dry bursts **5** (*tr*) to cut (a story, article, etc) in a damaging way **6** (*intr*; usually foll by *into*) to manipulate a computer program skilfully, esp to gain unauthorized access to another computer system **7** (*tr*) *sl* to tolerate or cope with: *I joined the army but I couldn't hack it* ▷ *n* **8** a cut or gash **9** any tool used for shallow digging, such as a mattock or pick **10** a chopping blow **11** a dry spasmodic cough **12** a kick on the shins, as in rugby [OE *haccian*]

hack[2] (hæk) *n* **1** a horse kept for riding **2** an old or overworked horse **3** a horse kept for hire **4** *Brit* a country ride on horseback **5** a drudge **6** a person who produces mediocre literary work **7** *US inf* **7a** a cab driver **7b** a taxi ▷ *vb* **8** *Brit* to ride (a horse) cross-country for pleasure **9** (*tr*) *inf* to write (an article, etc) in the manner of a hack ▷ *adj* **10** (*prenominal*) banal, mediocre, or unoriginal: *hack writing* [c17 short for HACKNEY]

hack[3] (hæk) *n* **1** a rack used for fodder for livestock **2** a board on which meat is placed for a hawk **3** a pile or row of unfired bricks stacked to dry [c16 var. of HATCH[2]]

hackamore ('hækəˌmɔ:) *n US & NZ* a rope or rawhide halter used for unbroken foals [c19 from Sp. *jáquima* headstall, ult. from Ar. *shaqīmah*]

hackberry ('hækˌbɛrɪ) *n, pl* **hackberries** **1** an American tree having edible cherry-like fruits **2** the fruit [c18 var. of c16 *hagberry*, of Scand. origin]

hacker ('hækə) *n* **1** a person that hacks **2** *sl* a computer fanatic, esp one who through a personal computer breaks into the computer system of a company, government, etc

hackery ('hækərɪ) *n* **1** *ironic* journalism; hackwork **2** *inf* a variant of **hacking**[2]

hacking[1] ('hækɪŋ) *adj* (of a cough) harsh, dry, and spasmodic

hacking[2] ('hækɪŋ) *n* the practice of gaining illegal access to a computer system

hackle ('hækᵊl) *n* **1** any of the long slender feathers on the neck of poultry and other birds **2** *angling* parts of an artificial fly made from hackle feathers, representing the legs and sometimes the wings of a real fly **3** a feathered ornament worn in the headdress of some British regiments **4** a steel flax comb ▷ *vb* **hackles, hackling, hackled** (*tr*) **5** to comb (flax) using a hackle [c15 *hakell* prob. from OE]

hackles ('hækᵊlz) *pl n* **1** the hairs on the back of the neck and the back of a dog, cat, etc, which rise when the animal is angry or afraid **2** anger or resentment: *to make one's hackles rise*

Hackman ('hækmən) *n* **Gene** born 1930, U.S. film actor; his films include *The French Connection* (1971), *Mississippi Burning* (1988), and *Absolute Power* (1997)

hackney ('hæknɪ) *n* **1** a compact breed of harness horse with a high-stepping trot **2** a coach or carriage that is for hire **3** a popular term for **hack**[2] (sense 1) ▷ *vb* **4** (*tr*; *usually passive*) to make commonplace and banal by too frequent use [c14 prob. after HACKNEY, where horses were formerly raised]

Hackney ('hæknɪ) *n* a borough of NE Greater London: formed in 1965 from the former boroughs of Shoreditch, Stoke Newington, and Hackney; nearby are **Hackney Marshes**, the largest recreation ground in London. Pop: 202 819 (2001). Area: 19 sq km (8 sq miles)

hackneyed ('hæknɪd) *adj* used so often as to be trite, dull, and stereotyped

hack off *vb* (*tr, adv; often passive*) *inf* to annoy, irritate, or disappoint

hacksaw ('hækˌsɔ:) *n* a handsaw for cutting metal, with a blade in a frame under tension

hackwork ('hækˌwɜ:k) *n* undistinguished literary work produced to order

had (hæd) *vb* the past tense and past participle of **have**

haddock ('hædək) *n, pl* **haddocks** *or* **haddock** a North Atlantic gadoid food fish similar to but smaller than the cod [c14 from ?]

hade (heɪd) *geol* ▷ *n* **1** *obs* the angle made to the vertical by the plane of a fault or vein ▷ *vb* **hades, hading, haded** **2** (*intr*) to incline from the vertical [c18 from ?]

hadedah ('hɑ:dɪˌdɑ:) *n* a large grey-green S African ibis [imit.]

Haden ('heɪdən) *n* **Charles** (**Edward**) born 1937, U.S. jazz bassist

Hades ('heɪdi:z) *n* **1** *Greek myth* **1a** the underworld abode of the souls of the dead **1b** Pluto, the god of the underworld **2** (*often not cap*) hell

Hadhramaut *or* **Hadramaut** (ˌhɑ:drə'mɔ:t) *n* a plateau region of the S Arabian Peninsula, in SE Yemen on the Indian Ocean; formerly in South Yemen: corresponds roughly to the former East Aden Protectorate. Area: about 151 500 sq km (58 500 sq miles)

Hadith ('hædɪθ, hɑ:'di:θ) *n* the body of tradition about Mohammed and his followers [Ar.]

hadj (hædʒ) *n* a variant spelling of **hajj**

hadji ('hædʒɪ) *n, pl* **hadjis** a variant spelling of **hajji**

Hadlee ('hædlɪ) *n* Sir **Richard** (**John**) born 1951, New Zealand cricketer

hadn't ('hædᵊnt) *contraction of* had not

Hadrian ('heɪdrɪən) *or* **Adrian** *n* Latin name *Publius Aelius Hadrianus*. 76–138 AD, Roman emperor (117–138); adopted son and successor of Trajan. He travelled throughout the Roman Empire, strengthening its frontiers and encouraging learning and architecture, and in Rome he reorganized the army and codified Roman law

Hadrian's Wall *n* a fortified Roman wall, of which substantial parts remain, extending across N England from the Solway Firth in the west to the mouth of the River Tyne in the east. It was built in 120–123 AD on the orders of the emperor Hadrian as a defence against the N British tribes

hadron ('hædrɒn) *n* an elementary particle capable of taking part in a strong nuclear interaction [c20 from Gk *hadros* heavy, from *hadēn* enough + -ON] > **had'ronic** *adj*

hadst (hædst) *vb arch or dialect* (used with the pronoun *thou*) a singular form of the past tense (indicative mood) of **have**

haecceity (hɛk'siːɪtɪ, hiːk-) *n, pl* **haecceities** *philosophy* the property that uniquely identifies an object [c17 from Med. L *haecceitas*, lit.: thisness, from *haec*, fem. of *hic* this]

Haeckel (*German* 'hɛkəl) *n* **Ernst Heinrich** (ɛrnst 'hainrɪç) 1834–1919, German biologist and philosopher. He formulated the recapitulation theory of evolution and was an exponent of the philosophy of materialistic monism

haem *or US* **heme** (hiːm) *n biochem* a complex red organic pigment containing ferrous iron, present in haemoglobin [c20 from HAEMATIN]

haem- *combining form* a variant of **haemo-** before a vowel. Also (US): **hem-**

haemal *or US* **hemal** ('hiːməl) *adj* **1** of the blood **2** denoting or relating to the region of the body containing the heart

haematemesis *or US* **hematemesis** (ˌhiːmə'tɛmɪsɪs) *n* vomiting of blood, esp as the result of a bleeding ulcer [c19 from HAEMATO- + Gk *emesis* vomiting]

haematic *or US* **hematic** (hiː'mætɪk) *adj* relating to, acting on, having the colour of, or containing blood. Also: **haemic** *or US* **hemic**

haematin *or US* **hematin** ('hɛmətɪn, 'hiː-) *n biochem* a dark bluish or brownish pigment obtained by the oxidation of haem

haematite ('hiːməˌtaɪt, 'hɛm-) *n* a variant spelling of **hematite**

haemato- *or before a vowel* **haemat-** *combining form* indicating blood: *haematology*. Also: **haemo-** *or US* **hemato-, hemat-, hemo-** [from Gk *haima*, *haimat-* blood]

haematocrit *or US* **hematocrit** ('hɛmətəʊkrɪt, 'hiː-) *n* **1** a centrifuge for separating blood cells from plasma **2** the ratio of the volume occupied by these cells, esp the red cells, to the total volume of blood, expressed as a percentage [c20 from HAEMATO- + *-crit*, from Gk *kritēs* judge, from *krinein* to separate]

haematology *or US* **hematology** (ˌhiːmə'tɒlədʒɪ) *n* the branch of medical science concerned with diseases of the blood > **haematologic** (ˌhiːmətə'lɒdʒɪk), **ˌhaemato'logical** *or US* **ˌhemato'logic, ˌhemato'logical** *adj*

haematoma *or US* **hematoma** (ˌhiːmə'təʊmə) *n, pl* **haematomas, haematomata** *or US* **hematomas, hematomata** (-mətə) *Pathol.* a tumour of clotted blood

haematuria *or US* **hematuria** (ˌhiːmə'tjʊərɪə) *n pathol* the presence of blood or red blood cells in the urine

-haemia *or esp US* **-hemia** *n combining form* variants of **-aemia**

haemo-, haema-, *or before a vowel* **haem-** *combining form* denoting blood. Also: (US) **hemo-, hema-,** or **hem-** [from Gk *haima* blood]

haemocyanin *or US* **hemocyanin** (ˌhiːməʊ'saɪənɪn) *n* a blue copper-containing respiratory pigment in crustaceans and molluscs that functions as haemoglobin

haemocytometer *or US* **hemocytometer** (ˌhiːməʊsaɪ'tɒmɪtə) *n med* an apparatus for counting the number of cells in a quantity of blood

haemodialysis *or US* **hemodialysis** (ˌhiːməʊdaɪ'ælɪsɪs) *n, pl* **haemodialyses** *or US* **hemodialyses** (-ˌsiːz) *med* the filtering of circulating blood through a membrane in an apparatus (**haemodialyser** or **artificial kidney**) to remove waste products: performed in cases of kidney failure [c20 from HAEMO- + DIALYSIS]

haemoglobin *or US* **hemoglobin** (ˌhiːməʊ'gləʊbɪn) *n* a protein that gives red blood cells their characteristic colour. It combines reversibly with oxygen and is thus very important in the transportation of oxygen to tissues [c19 shortened from *haematoglobulin*: see HAEMATIN + GLOBULIN]

haemolysis (hɪ'mɒlɪsɪs), **haematolysis** (ˌhiːmə'tɒlɪsɪs) *or US* **hemolysis, hematolysis** *n, pl* **haemolyses, haematolyses** *or US* **hemolyses, hematolyses** (-ˌsiːz) the disintegration of red blood cells, with the release of haemoglobin > **haemolytic** *or US* **hemolytic** (ˌhiːməʊ'lɪtɪk) *adj*

haemophilia *or US* **hemophilia** (ˌhiːməʊ'fɪlɪə) *n* an inheritable disease, usually affecting only males, characterized by loss or impairment of the normal clotting ability of blood > **ˌhaemo'philiac** *or US* **ˌhemo'philiac** *n* > **ˌhaemo'philic** *or US* **ˌhemo'philic** *adj*
▷ www.hemophilia.org

haemoptysis *or US* **hemoptysis** (hɪ'mɒptɪsɪs) *n, pl* **haemoptyses** *or US* **hemoptyses** (-ˌsiːz) spitting or coughing up of blood, as in tuberculosis [c17 from HAEMO- + *-ptysis*, from Gk *ptyein* to spit]

haemorrhage *or US* **hemorrhage** ('hɛmərɪdʒ) *n* **1** profuse bleeding from ruptured blood vessels **2** a steady or severe loss or depletion of resources, staff, etc ▷ *vb* **haemorrhages, haemorrhaging, haemorrhaged** *or US* **hemorrhages, hemorrhaging, hemorrhaged 3** (*intr*) to bleed profusely [c17 from L *haemorrhagia*; see HAEMO-, -RRHAGIA]

haemorrhoids *or US* **hemorrhoids** ('hɛməˌrɔɪdz) *pl n pathol* swollen and twisted veins in the region of the anus. Nontechnical name: **piles** [c14 from L *haemorrhoidae* (pl), from Gk, from *haimorrhoos* discharging blood, from *haimo-* HAEMO- + *rhein* to flow] > **ˌhaemor'rhoidal** *or US* **ˌhemor'rhoidal** *adj*

haemostasis *or US* **hemostasis** (ˌhiːməʊ'steɪsɪs) *n* the stopping of bleeding or of blood circulation, as during a surgical operation [c18 from NL, from HAEMO- + Gk *stasis* a standing still] > **ˌhaemo'static** *or US* **ˌhemo'static** *adj*

haemostat *or US* **hemostat** ('hiːməʊˌstæt) *n* a surgical instrument or chemical agent that retards or stops bleeding

haeremai ('haɪrəˌmaɪ) *NZ* ▷ *sentence substitute* **1** an expression of greeting or welcome ▷ *n* **2** the act of saying "haeremai" [c18 Maori, lit.: come hither]

Ha-erh-pin ('hɑː'ɛə'pɪn) *n* transliteration of the Chinese name for **Harbin**

hafiz ('hɑːfɪz) *n Islam* **1** a title for a person who knows the Koran by heart **2** the guardian of a mosque [from Persian, from Ar., from *hafiza* to guard]

hafnium ('hæfnɪəm) *n* a bright metallic element found in zirconium ores. Symbol: Hf; atomic no.: 72; atomic wt.: 178.49 [c20 NL, after *Hafnia*, L name of Copenhagen + -IUM]

haft (hɑːft) *n* **1** the handle of an axe, knife, etc ▷ *vb* **2** (*tr*) to provide with a haft [OE *hæft*]

hag[1] (hæg) *n* **1** an unpleasant or ugly old woman **2** a witch **3** short for **hagfish** [OE *hægtesse* witch] > **'haggish** *adj*

hag[2] (hæg) *n Scot & N English dialect* **1** a firm spot in a bog **2** a soft place in a moor [c13 from ON]

Hag. *Bible abbrev for* Haggai

Hagar ('heɪgɑː, -gə) *n Old Testament* an Egyptian maid of Sarah, who bore Ishmael to Abraham, Sarah's husband

Hagen[1] ('hɑːgən) *n* (in the *Nibelungenlied*) Siegfried's killer, who in turn is killed by Siegfried's wife, Kriemhild

Hagen[2] (*German* 'haːgən) *n* an industrial city in NW Germany, in North Rhine-Westphalia. Pop: 206 400 (1999 est)

Hagen[3] ('heɪgən) *n* **Walter** 1892–1969, US golfer

hagfish ('hægˌfɪʃ) *n, pl* **hagfish** *or* **hagfishes** an eel-like marine vertebrate having a round sucking mouth and feeding on the tissues of other animals and on dead organic material

Haggadah *or* **Haggodoh** (hə'gɑːdə) *n, pl* **Haggadahs, Haggadas** *or* **Haggadoth** (ˌhægə'dəʊt) *Judaism* **a** a book containing the order of service of the traditional Passover meal **b** the narrative of the Exodus from Egypt that constitutes the main part of that service ▷ See also **Seder** [c19 from Heb.: story, from *hagged* to tell] > **haggadic** (hə'gædɪk, -'gɑː-) *adj*

Haggai ('hægeɪ,aɪ) *n Old Testament* **1** a Hebrew prophet, whose oracles are usually dated between August and December of 520 BC **2** the book in which these oracles are contained, chiefly concerned with the rebuilding of the Temple after the Exile. Douay spelling: **Aggeus** (ə'dʒiːəs)

haggard ('hægəd) *adj* **1** careworn or gaunt, as from anxiety or starvation **2** wild or unruly **3** (of a hawk) having reached maturity in the wild before being caught ▷ *n* **4** *falconry* a haggard hawk [c16 from OF *hagard*, ? rel. to HEDGE] > **'haggardly** *adv* > **'haggardness** *n*

Haggard ('hægəd) *n* Sir (**Henry**) **Rider** 1856–1925, British author of romantic adventure stories, including *King Solomon's Mines* (1885)

haggis ('hægɪs) *n* a Scottish dish made from sheep's or calf's offal, oatmeal, suet, and seasonings boiled in a skin made from the animal's stomach [c15 ?from *haggen* to HACK[1]]

haggle ('hæg^{ə}l) *vb* **haggles, haggling, haggled** (*intr; often foll by over*) to bargain or wrangle (over a price, terms of an agreement, etc); barter [c16 of Scand. origin] > **'haggler** *n*

hagio- *or before a vowel* **hagi-** *combining form* indicating a saint, saints, or holiness: *hagiography* [via LL from Gk, from *hagios* holy]

Hagiographa (,hægɪ'ɒgrəfə) *n* the third of the three main parts into which the books of the Old Testament are divided in Jewish tradition (the other two parts being the Law and the Prophets)

hagiographer (,hægɪ'ɒgrəfə) *or* **hagiographist** *n* **1** a person who writes about the lives of the saints **2** one of the writers of the Hagiographa

hagiography (,hægɪ'ɒgrəfɪ) *n, pl* **hagiographies** **1** the writing of the lives of the saints **2** a biography that idealizes or idolizes its subject > **hagiographic** (,hægɪə'græfɪk) *or* **,hagio'graphical** *adj*

hagiolatry (,hægɪ'ɒlətrɪ) *n* worship or veneration of saints

hagiology (,hægɪ'ɒlədʒɪ) *n, pl* **hagiologies** literature concerned with the lives and legends of saints > **hagiological** (,hægɪə'lɒdʒɪk^{ə}l) *adj* > **,hagi'ologist** *n*

hag-ridden *adj* tormented or worried, as if by a witch

Hague (heɪg) *n* **The** the seat of government of the Netherlands and capital of South Holland province, situated about 3 km (2 miles) from the North Sea. Pop: 440 743 (1999 est). Dutch names: **'s Gravenhage, Den Haag**

hah (hɑː) *interj* a variant spelling of **ha**[1]

ha-ha[1] ('hɑː'hɑː) *or* **haw-haw** ('hɔː'hɔː) *interj* **1** a representation of the sound of laughter **2** an exclamation expressing derision, mockery, etc

ha-ha[2] ('hɑːhɑː) *or* **haw-haw** ('hɔːhɔː) *n* a wall or other boundary marker that is set in a ditch so as not to interrupt the landscape [c18 from F *haha*, prob. based on *ha!*, ejaculation denoting surprise]

Hahn (*German* haːn) *n* **1 Kurt** 1886–1974, German educationalist. During the Nazi era he escaped to Britain, where he founded Gordonstoun School (1935) and helped to establish the Duke of Edinburgh's award scheme **2 Otto** ('ɔto) 1879–1968, German physicist: discovered the radioactive element protactinium with Meitner (1917); with Strassmann, demonstrated the nuclear fission of uranium, when it is bombarded with neutrons: Nobel prize for chemistry 1944

Hahnemann (*German* 'haːnəman) *n* (**Christian Friedrich**) **Samuel** ('zaːmueːl) 1755–1843, German physician; founder of homeopathy

hahnium ('hɑːnɪəm) *n* the former name for **hassium** [c20 after Otto HAHN]

Haidar Ali ('haɪdər 'ɑːlɪ) *n* a variant spelling of **Hyder Ali**

Haifa ('haɪfə) *n* a port in NW Israel, near Mount Carmel, on the Bay of Acre: Israel's chief port, with an oil refinery and other heavy industry. Pop: 265 700 (1999 est)

Haig (heɪg) *n* **Douglas,** 1st Earl Haig. 1861–1928, British field marshal; commander in chief of the British forces in France and Flanders (1915–18)

haik *or* **haick** (haɪk, heɪk) *n* a traditional Arabian outer garment for the head and body [c18 from Ar.]

haiku ('haɪkuː) *or* **hokku** ('hɒkuː) *n, pl* **haiku** *or* **hokku** an epigrammatic Japanese verse form in 17 syllables [from Japanese, from *hai* amusement + *ku* verse]

hail[1] (heɪl) *n* **1** small pellets of ice falling from cumulonimbus clouds when there are strong rising air currents **2** a storm of such pellets **3** words, ideas, missiles, etc, directed with force and in great quantity: *a hail of abuse* ▷ *vb* **4** (*intr; with it as subject*) to be the case that hail is falling **5** (often with *it* as subject) to fall or cause to fall as or like hail [OE *hægl*]

hail[2] (heɪl) *vb* (*mainly tr*) **1** to greet, esp enthusiastically: *the crowd hailed the actress with joy* **2** to acclaim or acknowledge: *they hailed him as their hero* **3** to attract the attention of by shouting or gesturing: *to hail a taxi* **4** (*intr; foll by from*) to be a native of: *she hails from India* ▷ *n* **5** the act or an instance of hailing **6** a distance across which one can attract attention (esp in **within hail**) ▷ *sentence substitute* **7** *poetic* an exclamation of greeting [c12 from ON *heill* healthy]

Haile Selassie ('haɪlɪ sə'læsɪ) *n* title of *Ras Tafari Makonnen*. 1892–1975, emperor of Ethiopia (1930–36; 1941–74). During the Italian occupation of Ethiopia (1936–41), he lived in exile in England. He was a prominent figure in the Pan-African movement: deposed 1974

hail-fellow-well-met *adj* genial and familiar, esp in an offensive or ingratiating way

Hail Mary *n* **1** Also called: **Ave Maria** *RC Church* a prayer to the Virgin Mary, based on the salutations of the angel Gabriel (Luke 1:28) and Elizabeth (Luke 1:42) to her **2** *American football sl* a very long high pass into the end zone, made in the final seconds of a half or of a game

hailstone ('heɪl,stəʊn) *n* a pellet of hail

hailstorm ('heɪl,stɔːm) *n* a storm during which hail falls

Hailwood ('heɪl,wʊd) *n* **Mike,** full name *Stanley Michael Bailey Hailwood*. 1940–81, English racing motorcyclist: world champion (250 cc) 1961 and 1966–67; (350 cc) 1966–67; and (500 cc) 1962–65

Hainan ('haɪ'næn) *or* **Hainan Tao** (taʊ) *n* an island and province in the South China Sea, separated from the mainland of S China by **Hainan Strait**: part of Guangdong province until 1988; China's second largest offshore island. Pop: 7 240 000 (1996 est) Area: 33 572 sq km (12 962 sq miles)

Hainaut *or* **Hainault** (*French* ɛno) *n* a province of SW Belgium: stretches from the Flanders Plain in the north to the Ardennes in the south. Capital: Mons. Pop: 1 279 467 (2000 est). Area: 3797 sq km (1466 sq miles)

Haiphong ('haɪ'fɒŋ) *n* a port in N Vietnam, on the Red River delta: a major industrial centre. Pop: 783 133 (1992 est)

hair (hɛə) *n* **1** any of the threadlike structures that grow from follicles beneath the skin of mammals **2** a growth of such structures, as on an animal's body, which helps prevent heat loss **3** *bot* any threadlike outgrowth, such as a root hair **4** a fabric made from the hair of some animals **5** another word for **hair's-breadth:** *to lose by a hair* **6 get in someone's hair** *inf* to annoy someone persistently **7 hair of the dog** (**that bit one**) an alcoholic drink taken as an antidote to a hangover **8 keep your hair on!** *Brit inf* keep calm **9 let one's hair down** to behave without reserve **10 not turn a hair** to show no surprise, anger, fear, etc **11 split hairs** to make petty and

Hh

unnecessary distinctions [OE *hær*] > **'hairless** *adj* > **'hair,like** *adj*
haircloth ('hɛə,klɒθ) *n* a cloth woven from horsehair, used (esp formerly) in upholstery, etc
haircut ('hɛə,kʌt) *n* **1** the act of cutting the hair **2** the style in which hair has been cut
hairdo ('hɛə,du:) *n, pl* **hairdos** the arrangement of a person's hair, esp after styling and setting
hairdresser ('hɛə,drɛsə) *n* **1** a person whose business is cutting, dyeing, and arranging hair **2** a hairdresser's establishment ▷ Related adj: **tonsorial** > **'hair,dressing** *n*
-haired *adj* having hair as specified: *long-haired*
hair gel *n* a preparation used in hair styling
hairgrip ('hɛə,grɪp) *n chiefly Brit* a small tightly bent metal hair clip. Also called (US, Canad, and NZ): **bobby pin** or (NZ) **hairclip**
hairline ('hɛə,laɪn) *n* **1** the natural margin formed by hair on the head **2a** a very narrow line **2b** (*as modifier*): *a hairline crack*
hairline fracture *n* a very fine crack in a bone
hairnet ('hɛə,nɛt) *n* any of several kinds of light netting worn over the hair to keep it in place
hairpiece ('hɛə,pi:s) *n* **1** a wig or toupee **2** a section of extra hair attached to a woman's real hair to give it greater bulk or length
hairpin ('hɛə,pɪn) *n* **1** a thin double-pronged pin used to fasten the hair **2** (*modifier*) (esp of a bend in a road) curving very sharply
hair-raising *adj* inspiring horror; terrifying
hair's-breadth *n* **a** a very short or imperceptible margin or distance **b** (*as modifier*): *a hair's-breadth escape*
hair shirt *n* **1** a shirt made of haircloth worn next to the skin as a penance **2** a secret trouble or affliction
hair slide *n* a hinged clip with a tortoiseshell, bone, or similar back, used to fasten a girl's hair
hairsplitting ('hɛə,splɪtɪŋ) *n* **1** the making of petty distinctions ▷ *adj* **2** occupied with or based on petty distinctions > **'hair,splitter** *n*
hairspring ('hɛə,sprɪŋ) *n* a fine spiral spring in some timepieces which, in combination with the balance wheel, controls the timekeeping
hairstreak ('hɛə,stri:k) *n* a small butterfly having fringed wings with narrow white streaks
hairstyle ('hɛə,staɪl) *n* a particular mode of arranging the hair > **'hair,stylist** *n*
▷ www.costumegallery.com/hairstyles.htm
hair trigger *n* **1** a trigger of a firearm that responds to very slight pressure **2** *inf* any mechanism, reaction, etc, set in operation by slight provocation
hairy ('hɛərɪ) *adj* **hairier, hairiest 1** covered with hair **2** *sl* **2a** difficult or problematic **2b** dangerous or exciting > **'hairiness** *n*
Haiti ('heɪtɪ, hɑ:'i:tɪ) *n* **1** a republic occupying the W part of the island of Hispaniola in the Caribbean, the E part consisting of the Dominican Republic: ceded by Spain to France in 1697 and became one of the richest colonial possessions in the world, with numerous plantations; slaves rebelled under Toussaint L'Ouverture in 1793 and defeated the French; taken over by the US (1915–41) after long political and economic chaos; under the authoritarian regimes of François Duvalier (1957–71) and his son Jean-Claude Duvalier (1971–86); returned to civilian rule in 1990, but another coup in 1991 brought military rule, which was ended in 1994 with US intervention. Official languages: French and Haitian creole. Religions: Roman Catholic and voodoo. Currency: gourde. Capital: Port-au-Prince. Pop: 6 965 000 (2001 est). Area: 27 749 sq km (10 714 sq miles) **2** a former name for **Hispaniola**
▷ www.port-haiti.com
▷ www.haititourism.org
Haitian *or* **Haytian** ('heɪʃɪən, hɑ:'i:ʃən) *adj* **1** relating to or characteristic of Haiti, its inhabitants, or their language ▷ *n* **2** a native, citizen, or inhabitant of Haiti **3** the creolized French spoken in Haiti
Haitink ('haɪ,tɪŋk) *n* **Bernard** born 1929, Dutch orchestral conductor; received an honorary knighthood in 1977
Haji-Ioannou (*Greek* ,hadʒijɔ'anu) *n* **Stelios** born 1967, British businessman, born in Greece; founder (1995) and chairman (until 2002) of the low-cost airline company Easyjet
hajj *or* **hadj** (hædʒ) *n* the pilgrimage to Mecca that every Muslim is required to make at least once [from Ar.]
hajji, hadji, *or* **haji** ('hædʒɪ) *n, pl* **hajjis, hadjis,** *or* **hajis 1** a Muslim who has made a pilgrimage to Mecca: also used as a title **2** a Christian who has visited Jerusalem
haka ('hɑ:kə) *n* NZ **1** a Maori war chant accompanied by gestures **2** a similar performance by, for instance, a rugby team
hake (heɪk) *n, pl* **hake** *or* **hakes 1** a gadoid food fish of the N hemisphere, having an elongated body with a large head and two dorsal fins **2** a similar North American fish [c15 ?from ON *haki* hook]
hakea ('hɑ:kɪə, 'heɪkɪə) *n* any shrub or tree of the Australian genus *Hakea*, having a hard woody fruit and often yielding a useful wood [c19 NL, after C. L. von *Hake* (died 1818), G botanist]
hakim *or* **hakeem** (hɑ:'ki:m) *n* **1** a Muslim judge, ruler, or administrator **2** a Muslim physician [c17 from Ar., from *hakama* to rule]
Hakluyt ('hæklu:t) *n* **Richard** ?1552–1616, English geographer, who compiled *The Principal Navigations, Voyages, and Discoveries of the English Nation* (1589)
Hakodate (,hɑ:kəʊ'dɑ:teɪ) *n* a port in N Japan, on S Hokkaido: fishing industry and shipbuilding. Pop: 298 868 (1995)
hakuna mathata (hə'ku:nə mə'tɑ:tə) *sentence substitute* no problem [from Swahili, there is no difficulty]
Halabja (hə'læbdʒə) *n* a Kurdish town in NE Iraq; in March 1998 Iraqi forces used poison gas on the population, killing hundreds of civilians. Pop: 80 000 (latest est)
Halakah *or* **Halacha** (,hɑ:lə'kɑ:, hə'lɑ:kə) *n* that part of traditional Jewish literature concerned with the law, as contrasted with Haggadah [c19 from Heb.: way, from *hālakh* to go] > **Halakic** *or* **Halachic** (hə'lækɪk) *adj*
halal *or* **hallal** (hɑ:'lɑ:l) *n* **1** meat from animals that have been killed according to Muslim law ▷ *adj* **2** of or relating to such meat: *a halal butcher* ▷ *vb* **halals, halalling, halalled** *or* **hallals, hallalling, hallalled** (*tr*) **3** to kill (animals) according to Muslim law [from Ar.: lawful]
halation (hə'leɪʃən) *n photog* fogging usually seen as a bright ring surrounding a source of light [c19 from HALO + -ATION]
halberd ('hælbəd) *or* **halbert** ('hælbət) *n* a weapon consisting of a long shaft with an axe blade and a pick, topped by a spearhead: used in 15th- and 16th-century warfare [c15 from OF *hallebarde*, from MHG *helm* handle + *barde* axe] > **,halber'dier** *n*
Halberstadt ('hælbə,ʃtæt) *n* a town in central Germany, in Saxony-Anhalt: industrial centre noted for its historic buildings. Pop: 47 500 (latest est)
halcyon ('hælsɪən) *adj* **1** peaceful, gentle, and calm **2 halcyon days 2a** a fortnight of calm weather during the winter solstice **2b** a period of peace and happiness ▷ *n* **3** *Greek myth* a fabulous bird associated with the winter solstice **4** a poetic name for the **kingfisher** [c14 from L *alcyon*, from Gk *alkuōn* kingfisher, from ?]
Haldane ('hɔ:ldeɪn) *n* **1 J**(ohn) **B**(urdon) **S**(anderson) 1892–1964, Scottish biochemist, geneticist, and writer on science **2** his father, **John Scott** 1860–1936, Scottish physiologist, noted particularly for his research into industrial diseases **3** his brother, **Richard Burdon, 1st** Viscount Haldane of Cloan. 1856–1928, British

statesman and jurist. As secretary of state for war (1905–12) he reorganized the army and set up the territorial reserve

hale[1] (heɪl) *adj* healthy and robust (esp in **hale and hearty**) [OE *hæl* WHOLE] > ˈ**haleness** *n*

hale[2] (heɪl) *vb* **hales, haling, haled** (*tr*) to pull or drag [C13 from OF *haler*, of Gmc origin] > ˈ**haler** *n*

Hale (heɪl) *n* **1 George Ellery** 1868–1938, US astronomer: undertook research into sunspots and invented the spectroheliograph **2** Sir **Matthew** 1609–76, English judge and scholar; Lord Chief Justice (1671–76)

Haleakala (ˌhɑːliːˌɑːkɑːˈlɑː) *n* a volcano in Hawaii, on E Maui Island. Height: 3057 m (10 032 ft). Area of crater: 49 sq km (19 sq miles). Depth of crater: 829 m (2720 ft)

Halesowen (heɪlzˈəʊɪn) *n* a town in W central England, in Dudley unitary authority, West Midlands. Pop: 57 918 (1991)

Haley (ˈheɪlɪ) *n* **Bill,** full name *William John Clifton Haley.* 1925–81, US rock and roll singer, best known for his recording of "Rock Around the Clock" (1955)

half (hɑːf) *n, pl* **halves** (hɑːvz) **1a** either of two equal or corresponding parts that together comprise a whole **1b** a quantity equalling such a part: *half a dozen* **2** half a pint, esp of beer **3** *Scot* a small drink of spirits, esp whisky **4** *football, hockey, etc* the half of the pitch regarded as belonging to one team **5** *golf* an equal score with an opponent **6** (in various games) either of two periods of play separated by an interval **7** a half-price ticket on a bus, etc **8** short for **half-hour 9** *sport* short for **halfback 10** *obs* a half-year period **11 by half** to an excessive degree: *he's too arrogant by half* **12 by halves** (*used with a negative*) without being thorough: *we don't do things by halves* **13 go halves** (often foll by *on, in,* etc) **13a** to share expenses **13b** to share the whole amount (of something): *to go halves on an orange* ▷ *determiner* **14a** being a half or approximately a half: *half the kingdom* **14b** (*as pron; functioning as sing or pl*): *half of them came* **15 have half a mind to** to have a vague intention to ▷ *adj* **16** not perfect or complete: *he only did a half job on it* ▷ *adv* **17** to the amount or extent of a half **18** to a great amount or extent **19** partially; to an extent **20 half two,** etc *inf* 30 minutes after two o'clock, etc **21 not half** *inf* **21a** not in any way: *he's not half clever enough* **21b** *Brit* very: *he isn't half stupid* **21c** yes, indeed [OE *healf*]

half- *prefix* **1** one of two equal parts: *half-moon* **2** related through one parent only: *half-brother* **3** not completely; partly: *half-hardy*

half-and-half *n* **1** a mixture of half one thing and half another thing **2** a drink consisting of equal parts of beer and stout, or equal parts of bitter and mild

halfback (ˈhɑːfˌbæk) *n* **1** *soccer* any of three players positioned behind the line of forwards and in front of the fullbacks **2** *rugby* either the scrum half or the stand-off half **3** any of certain similar players in other team sports

half-baked *adj* **1** insufficiently baked **2** *inf* foolish; stupid **3** *inf* poorly planned

halfbeak (ˈhɑːfˌbiːk) *n* a marine and freshwater teleost fish having an elongated body with a short upper jaw and a long protruding lower jaw

half-binding *n* a type of bookbinding in which the backs are bound in one material and the sides in another

half-blood *n* **1a** the relationship between individuals having only one parent in common **1b** an individual having such a relationship **2** a less common name for a **half-breed** > ˌ**half-ˈblooded** *adj*

half board *n* accommodation at a hotel, etc, that includes breakfast and one main meal. Also called: **demi-pension**

half-boot *n* a boot reaching to the midcalf

half-bottle *n* a bottle of spirits or wine that contains half the quantity of a standard bottle

half-breed *n* **1** *offens* a person whose parents are of different races, esp the offspring of a White person and an American Indian ▷ *adj also* **half-bred 2** of, relating to, or designating offspring of people or animals of different races or breeds

half-brother *n* the son of either of one's parents by another partner

half-butt *n* a snooker cue that is longer than an ordinary cue

half-caste *offens* ▷ *n* **1** a person having parents of different races, esp the offspring of a European and an Indian ▷ *adj* **2** of, relating to, or designating such a person

half-century *n* **1** a period of 50 years **2** a score or grouping of 50: *he scored his first half-century for England*

half-cock *n* **1** the halfway position of a firearm's hammer when the trigger is cocked by the hammer and the hammer cannot reach the primer to fire the weapon **2 go off at half-cock** *or* **half-cocked** to fail as a result of inadequate preparation or premature starting

half-crown *n* a former British coin worth two shillings and sixpence (12½p). Also called: **half-a-crown**

half-cut *adj Brit sl* rather drunk

half-dozen *n* six

half gainer *n* a type of dive in which the diver completes a half backward somersault to enter the water headfirst facing the diving board

half-hardy *adj* (of a cultivated plant) able to survive out of doors except during severe frost

half-hearted *adj* without enthusiasm or determination > ˌ**half-ˈheartedly** *adv*

half-hitch *n* a knot made by passing the end of a piece of rope around itself and through the loop thus made

half-hour *n* **1** a period of 30 minutes **2** the point of time 30 minutes after the beginning of an hour > ˌ**half-ˈhourly** *adv, adj*

half-hunter *n* a watch with a hinged lid in which a small circular opening or crystal allows the approximate time to be read

half landing *n* a landing halfway up a flight of stairs

half-life *n* the time taken for half of the atoms in a radioactive material to undergo decay

half-light *n* a dim light, as at dawn or dusk

half-mast *n* the lower than normal position to which a flag is lowered on a mast as a sign of mourning

half measure *n* (*often pl*) an inadequate measure or action; compromise

half-moon *n* **1** the moon at first or last quarter when half its face is illuminated **2** the time at which a half-moon occurs **3** something shaped like a half-moon

half-nelson *n* a wrestling hold in which a wrestler places an arm under one of his opponent's arms from behind and exerts pressure with his palm on the back of his opponent's neck

half-note *n* the usual US name for **minim** (sense 2)

halfpenny *or* **ha'penny** (ˈheɪpnɪ, *for sense 1* ˈhɑːfˌpɛnɪ) *n* **1** (*pl* **halfpennies** *or* **ha'pennies**) a small British coin worth half a new penny (withdrawn 1985) **2** (*pl* **halfpennies** *or* **ha'pennies**) an old British coin worth half an old penny **3** (*pl* **halfpence**) something of negligible value > **halfpennyworth** *or* **ha'p'orth** (ˈheɪpəθ) *n*

half-pie *adj NZ inf* ill planned; not properly thought out: *a half-pie scheme* [from Maori *pai* good]

half-pint *n sl* a small or insignificant person

half-pipe *n* a structure with a U-shaped cross-section, used in performing stunts in skateboarding, snowboarding, rollerblading, etc

half-plate *or* **half-print** *n photog* a size of plate measuring 6½ × 4¾ inches

half-rotten *adj* partially rotted or decomposed

half seas over *adj Brit inf* drunk

half-section *n engineering* a scale drawing of a section through a symmetrical object that shows only half the object

Hh

half-sister *n* the daughter of either of one's parents by another partner

half-size *n* any size, esp in clothing, that is halfway between two sizes

half-sole *n* a sole from the shank of a shoe to the toe

half term *n Brit education* a short holiday midway through an academic term

half-timbered *or* **half-timber** *adj* (of a building) having an exposed timber framework filled with brick, stone, or plastered laths, as in Tudor architecture > ˌ**half-ˈtimbering** *n*

half-time *n sport* **a** a rest period between the two halves of a game **b** (*as modifier*): *the half-time score*

half-title *n* **1** the short title of a book as printed on the right-hand page preceding the title page **2** a title on a separate page preceding a section of a book

halftone (ˈhɑːfˌtəʊn) *n* **1** a process used to reproduce an illustration by photographing it through a fine screen to break it up into dots **2** the print obtained **3** *music* the usual US and Canad name for **semitone**

half-track *n* a vehicle with caterpillar tracks on the wheels that supply motive power only

half-truth *n* a partially true statement intended to mislead > ˌ**half-ˈtrue** *adj*

half volley *n sport* a stroke or shot in which the ball is hit immediately after it bounces

halfway (ˌhɑːfˈweɪ) *adv, adj* **1** at or to half the distance **2** in or of an incomplete manner **3 meet halfway** to compromise with

halfway house *n* **1** a place to rest midway on a journey **2** the halfway point in any progression **3** a centre or hostel designed to facilitate the readjustment to private life of released prisoners, mental patients, etc

halfwit (ˈhɑːfˌwɪt) *n* **1** a feeble-minded person **2** a foolish or inane person > ˌ**halfˈwitted** *adj*

half-year *n* a period of six months

halibut (ˈhælɪbət) *n, pl* **halibuts** *or* **halibut** the largest flatfish: a dark green North Atlantic species that is a very important food fish [C15 from *hali* HOLY (because it was eaten on holy days) + *butte* flat-fish, from MDu.]

Haliç (haˈliːtʃ) *n* the Turkish name for the **Golden Horn**

Halicarnassian (ˌhælɪkɑːˈnæsɪən) *adj* of or relating to the ancient Greek city of Halicarnassus

Halicarnassus (ˌhælɪkɑːˈnæsəs) *n* a Greek colony on the SW coast of Asia Minor: one of the major Hellenistic cities

halide (ˈhælaɪd) *or* **halid** (ˈhælɪd) *n* a binary compound containing a halogen atom or ion in combination with a more electropositive element

Halifax[1] (ˈhælɪˌfæks) *n* **1** a port in SE Canada, capital of Nova Scotia, on the Atlantic: founded in 1749 as a British stronghold. Pop: 113 910 (1996) **2** a town in N England, in Calderdale unitary authority, West Yorkshire: textiles. Pop: 91 069 (1991)

Halifax[2] (ˈhælɪˌfæks) *n* **1 Charles Montagu,** Earl of Halifax. 1661–1715, British statesman; founder of the National Debt (1692) and the Bank of England (1694) **2 Edward Frederick Lindley Wood,** Earl of Halifax. 1881–1959, British Conservative statesman. He was viceroy of India (1926–31), foreign secretary (1938–40), and ambassador to the US (1941–46) **3 George Savile,** 1st Marquess of Halifax, known as *the Trimmer*. 1633–95, British politician, noted for his wavering opinions. He opposed the exclusion of the Catholic James II from the throne but later supported the Glorious Revolution

Haligonian (ˌhælɪˈgəʊnɪən) *n* **1** a native or inhabitant of Halifax, Canada ▷ *adj* **2** of or relating to Halifax, Canada

halite (ˈhælaɪt) *n* a mineral consisting of sodium chloride in cubic crystalline form, occurring in sedimentary beds and dried salt lakes: an important source of table salt. Also called: **rock salt** [C19 from NL *halītes*, from Gk *hals* salt + -ITE[2]]

halitosis (ˌhælɪˈtəʊsɪs) *n* the state or condition of having bad breath [C19 NL, from L *hālitus* breath, from *hālāre* to breathe]

hall (hɔːl) *n* **1** a room serving as an entry area **2** (*sometimes cap*) a building for public meetings **3** (*often cap*) the great house of an estate; manor **4** a large building or room used for assemblies, dances, etc **5** a residential building, esp in a university; hall of residence **6a** a large room, esp for dining, in a college or university **6b** a meal eaten in this room **7** the large room of a house, castle, etc **8** *US & Canad* a corridor into which rooms open **9** (*often pl*) *inf* short for **music hall** [OE *heall*]

Hall (hɔːl) *n* **1 Charles Martin** 1863–1914, US chemist: discovered the electrolytic process for producing aluminium **2** Sir **John** 1824–1907, New Zealand statesman, born in England: prime minister of New Zealand (1879–82) **3** Sir **Peter** born 1930, English stage director: director of the Royal Shakespeare Company (1960–73) and of the National Theatre (1973–88) **4** (**Marguerite**) **Radclyffe** 1883–1943, British novelist and poet. Her frank treatment of a lesbian theme in the novel *The Well of Loneliness* (1928) led to an obscenity trial

Halle (*German* ˈhalə) *n* a city in E central Germany, in Saxony-Anhalt, on the River Saale: early saltworks; a Hanseatic city in the late Middle Ages; university (1694). Pop: 258 500 (1999 est). Official name: **Halle an der Saale** (an der ˈzaːlə)

Hallé (ˈhæleɪ) *n* Sir **Charles,** original name *Karl Hallé*. 1819–95, German conductor and pianist, in Britain from 1848. In 1857 he founded the Hallé Orchestra in Manchester

hallelujah, halleluiah (ˌhælɪˈluːjə), *or* **alleluia** (ˌælɪˈluːjə) *interj* **1** an exclamation of praise to God ▷ *n* **2** an exclamation of "Hallelujah" **3** a musical composition that uses the word *Hallelujah* as its text [C16 from Heb. *hellēl* to praise + *yāh* the Lord]

Haller (*German* ˈhalər) *n* **Albrecht von** (ˈalbrɛçt fɔn) 1708–77, Swiss biologist: founder of experimental physiology

Halley (ˈhælɪ) *n* **Edmund** 1656–1742, English astronomer and mathematician. He predicted the return of the comet now known as **Halley's comet,** constructed charts of magnetic declination, and produced the first wind maps

halliard (ˈhæljəd) *n* a variant spelling of **halyard**

Hall-Jones (ˈhɔːlˈdʒəʊnz) *n* Sir **William** 1851–1936, New Zealand statesman, born in England: prime minister of New Zealand (1906)

hallmark (ˈhɔːlˌmɑːk) *n* **1** *Brit* an official series of marks stamped by the London Guild of Goldsmiths on gold, silver, or platinum articles to guarantee purity, date of manufacture, etc **2** a mark of authenticity or excellence **3** an outstanding feature ▷ *vb* **4** (*tr*) to stamp with or as if with a hallmark [C18 after Goldsmiths' *Hall* in London, where items were graded and stamped]

hallo (həˈləʊ) *sentence substitute, n* **1** a variant spelling of **hello** ▷ *sentence substitute, n, vb* **2** a variant spelling of **halloo**

halloo (həˈluː), **hallo,** *or* **halloa** (həˈləʊ) *sentence substitute* **1** a shout to attract attention, esp to call hounds at a hunt ▷ *n, pl* **halloos, hallos,** *or* **halloas** **2** a shout of "halloo" ▷ *vb* **halloos, hallooing, hallooed; hallos, halloing, halloed;** *or* **halloas, halloaing, halloaed** **3** to shout **4** (*tr*) to urge on (dogs) with shouts [C16 ? var. of *hallow* to encourage hounds by shouting]

halloumi *or* **haloumi** (həˈluːmɪ) *n* a salty white sheep's-milk cheese from Greece or Turkey, usually eaten grilled [probably from Arabic *haluma* be mild]

hallow (ˈhæləʊ) *vb* (*tr*) **1** to consecrate or set apart as being holy **2** to venerate as being holy [OE *hālgian*, from *hālig* HOLY] > ˈ**hallower** *n*

hallowed (ˈhæləʊd; *liturgical* ˈhæləʊɪd) *adj* **1** set apart as sacred **2** consecrated or holy

Halloween *or* **Hallowe'en** (ˌhæləʊˈiːn) *n* the eve of All

Saints' Day celebrated on Oct 31; Allhallows Eve [c18 see ALLHALLOWS, EVEN[2]]

hall stand *or esp US* **hall tree** *n* a piece of furniture for hanging coats, hats, etc, on

Hallstatt ('hælstæt) *adj* of a late Bronze Age culture extending from central Europe to Britain and lasting from the 9th to the 5th century BC [c19 after *Hallstatt*, Austrian village where remains were found]

hallucinate (hə'lu:sɪˌneɪt) *vb* **hallucinates, hallucinating, hallucinated** (*intr*) to experience hallucinations [c17 from L *ālūcinārī* to wander in mind] > **hal'luciˌnator** *n*

hallucination (həˌlu:sɪ'neɪʃən) *n* the alleged perception of an object when no object is present, occurring under hypnosis, in some mental disorders, etc > **hal'lucinatory** *adj*

hallucinogen (hə'lu:sɪnəˌdʒɛn) *n* any drug that induces hallucinations > **hallucinogenic** (həˌlu:sɪnə'dʒɛnɪk) *adj*

hallux ('hæləks) *n* the first digit on the hind foot of a mammal, bird, reptile, or amphibian; the big toe of man [c19 NL, from LL *allex* big toe]

hallway ('hɔ:lˌweɪ) *n* a hall or corridor

halm (hɔ:m) *n* a variant spelling of **haulm**

halma ('hælmə) *n* a board game in which players attempt to transfer their pieces from their own to their opponents' bases [c19 from Gk *halma* leap]

Halmahera (ˌhælmə'hɪərə) *n* an island in NE Indonesia, the largest of the Moluccas: consists of four peninsulas enclosing three bays; mountainous and forested. Area: 17 780 sq km (6865 sq miles). Dutch name: **Djailolo, Gilolo,** *or* **Jilolo**

Halmstad (*Swedish* 'halmstɑ:d) *n* a port in SW Sweden, on the Kattegat. Pop: 83 080 (1994)

halo ('heɪləʊ) *n, pl* **haloes** *or* **halos** **1** a disc or ring of light around the head of an angel, saint, etc, as in painting **2** the aura surrounding a famous or admired person, thing, or event **3** a circle of light around the sun or moon, caused by the refraction of light by particles of ice ▷ *vb* **haloes** *or* **halos, haloing, haloed** **4** to surround with or form a halo [c16 from Med. L, from L *halōs* circular threshing floor, from Gk]

halogen ('hæləˌdʒɛn) *n* any of the chemical elements fluorine, chlorine, bromine, iodine, and astatine. They are all monovalent and readily form negative ions [c19 from Swedish, from Gk *hals* salt + -GEN] > **halogenous** (hə'lɒdʒɪnəs) *adj*

halogenate ('hælədʒəˌneɪt) *vb* **halogenates, halogenating, halogenated** *chem* to treat or combine with a halogen > **ˌhalogen'ation** *n*

haloid ('hælɔɪd) *chem* ▷ *adj* **1** derived from a halogen: *a haloid salt* ▷ *n* **2** a compound containing halogen atoms in its molecules

halon ('hælɒn) *n* any of a class of chemical compounds derived from hydrocarbons by replacing one or more hydrogen atoms by bromine atoms and other hydrogen atoms by other halogen atoms (chlorine, fluorine, or iodine)

Hals (*Dutch* hɑls) *n* **Frans** (frɑns) ?1580–1666, Dutch portrait and genre painter: his works include *The Laughing Cavalier* (1624)

Hälsingborg (*Swedish* hɛlsiŋ'bɔrj) *n* the former name (until 1971) of **Helsingborg**

halt[1] (hɔ:lt) *n* **1** an interruption or end to movement or progress **2** *chiefly Brit* a minor railway station, without permanent buildings **3** **call a halt (to)** to put an end (to); stop ▷ *n, sentence substitute* **4** a command to halt, esp as an order when marching ▷ *vb* **5** to come or bring to a halt [c17 from *to make halt*, translation of G *halt machen*, from *halten* to stop]

halt[2] (hɔ:lt) *vb* (*intr*) **1** (esp of verse) to falter or be defective **2** to be unsure **3** *arch* to be lame ▷ *adj* **4** *arch* **4a** lame **4b** (*as collective n*; preceded by *the*): *the halt* [OE *healt* lame]

halter ('hɔ:ltə) *n* **1** headgear for a horse, usually with a rope for leading **2** Also: **halterneck** a style of woman's top fastened behind the neck and waist, leaving the back and arms bare **3** a rope having a noose for hanging a person **4** death by hanging ▷ *vb* (*tr*) **5** to put on a halter **6** to hang (someone) [OE *hælfter*]

haltere ('hæltɪə) *n, pl* **halteres** (hæl'tɪəri:z) one of a pair of short projections in dipterous insects that are modified hind wings, used for maintaining equilibrium during flight [c18 from Gk *haltēres* (pl) hand-held weights used as balancers or to give impetus in leaping, from *hallesthai* to leap]

halting ('hɔ:ltɪŋ) *adj* **1** hesitant: *halting speech* **2** lame > **'haltingly** *adv*

Halton ('hɔ:ltən) *n* a unitary authority in NW England, in N Cheshire. Pop: 118 215 (2001). Area: 75 sq km (29 sq miles)

halvah, halva ('hælvɑ:), *or* **halavah** ('hæləvɑ:) *n* an Eastern sweetmeat made of honey and containing sesame seeds, nuts, etc [from Yiddish *halva*, ult. from Ar. *halwā*]

halve (hɑ:v) *vb* **halves, halving, halved** (*mainly tr*) **1** to divide into two approximately equal parts **2** to share equally **3** (*also intr*) to reduce by half, as by cutting **4** *golf* to take the same number of strokes on (a hole or round) as one's opponent [OE *hielfan*]

halyard *or* **halliard** ('hæljəd) *n* *naut* a line for hoisting or lowering a sail, flag, or spar [c14 *halier*, infl. by YARD[1]; see HALE[2]]

ham[1] (hæm) *n* **1** the part of the hindquarters of a pig between the hock and the hip **2** the meat of this part **3** *inf* the back of the leg above the knee [OE *hamm*]

ham[2] (hæm) *n* **1** *theatre, inf* **1a** an actor who overacts or relies on stock gestures **1b** overacting or clumsy acting **1c** (*as modifier*): *a ham actor* **2** *inf* a licensed amateur radio operator ▷ *vb* **hams, hamming, hammed** **3** *inf* to overact [c19 special use of HAM[1]; in some senses prob. infl. by AMATEUR]

Hh

Hama ('hɑ:mɑ:) *n* a city in W Syria, on the Orontes River: an early Hittite settlement; famous for its huge water wheels, used for irrigation since the Middle Ages. Pop: 264 348 (1994). Biblical name: **Hamath**

Hamadān *or* **Hamedān** ('hæməˌdæn) *n* city in W central Iran, at an altitude of over 1830 m (6000 ft): changed hands several times from the 17th century between Iraq, Persia, and Turkey; trading centre. Pop: 401 281 (1998)

hamadryad (ˌhæmə'draɪəd) *n* **1** *classical myth* a nymph who inhabits a tree and dies with it **2** another name for **king cobra** [c14 from L *Hamādryas*, from Gk *Hamadruas*, from *hama* together with + *drus* tree]

hamadryas (ˌhæmə'draɪəs) *n* a baboon of Arabia and NE Africa, having long silvery hair on the head, neck, and chest [c19 via NL from L; see HAMADRYAD]

Hamamatsu (ˌhæmə'mætsu:) *n* a city in central Japan, in S central Honshu: cotton textiles and musical instruments. Pop: 561 568 (1995)

hamba ('hæmbə) *sentence substitute S African, usually offens* go away; be off [from a Bantu language, from *ukuttamba* to go]

Hamburg ('hæmbɜ:g) *n* a city-state and port in NW Germany, on the River Elbe: the largest port in Germany; a founder member of the Hanseatic League; became a free imperial city in 1510 and a state of the German empire in 1871; university (1919); extensive shipyards. Pop: 1 701 800 (1999 est)

hamburger ('hæmˌbɜ:gə) *n* a cake of minced beef, often served in a bread roll. Also called: **beefburger** [c20 from *Hamburger steak* (steak in the fashion of HAMBURG)]

hame (heɪm) *n* either of the two curved bars holding the traces of the harness, attached to the collar of a draught animal [c14 from MDu. *hame*]

Hameln (*German* 'ha:məln) *n* an industrial town in N

Germany, in Lower Saxony on the Weser River: famous for the legend of the Pied Piper (supposedly took place in 1284). Pop: 57 640 (latest est). English name: **Hamelin** ('hæməlɪn, 'hæmlɪn)

Hamersley Range ('hæməzlɪ) *n* a mountain range in N Western Australia: iron-ore deposits. Highest peak: 1236 m (4056 ft)

ham-fisted *or* **ham-handed** *adj inf* lacking dexterity or elegance; clumsy

Hamhung *or* **Hamheung** ('hɑːm'hʊŋ) *n* an industrial city in central North Korea: commercial and governmental centre of NE Korea during the Yi dynasty (1392–1910). Pop: 701 000 (latest est)

Hamilcar Barca (hæ'mɪlkɑː 'bɑːkə, 'hæmɪlˌkɑː) *n* died ?228 BC, Carthaginian general; father of Hannibal. He held command (247–41) during the first Punic War and established Carthaginian influence in Spain (237–?228)

Hamilton[1] ('hæməltən) *n* **1** a port in central Canada, in S Ontario on Lake Ontario: iron and steel industry. Pop: 322 352 (1996) **2** a city in New Zealand, on central North Island. Pop: 117 100 (1999 est) **3** a town in S Scotland, in South Lanarkshire near Glasgow. Pop: 49 991 (1991) **4** the capital and chief port of Bermuda. Pop: 1100 (1995 est) **5** the former name of the **Churchill** River in Labrador

Hamilton[2] ('hæməltən) *n* **1** **Alexander** ?1757–1804, American statesman. He was a leader of the Federalists and as first secretary of the Treasury (1789–95) established a federal bank **2** Lady **Emma** ?1765–1815, mistress of Nelson **3** **James**, 1st Duke of Hamilton. 1606–49, Scottish supporter of Charles I in the English Civil War: defeated by Cromwell at the Battle of Preston and executed **4** **Richard** born 1922, British artist: a pioneer of the pop art style **5** Sir **William Rowan** 1805–65, Irish mathematician: founded Hamiltonian mechanics and formulated the theory of quaternions

Hamitic (hæ'mɪtɪk, hə-) *n* **1** a group of N African languages related to Semitic ▷ *adj* **2** denoting or belonging to this group of languages **3** denoting or characteristic of the Hamites, a group of peoples of N Africa, including the ancient Egyptians, supposedly descended from Noah's son Ham

hamlet ('hæmlɪt) *n* a small village, esp (in Britain) one without its own church [C14 from OF *hamelet*, dim. of *hamel*, from *ham*, of Gmc origin]

Hamm (*German* ham) *n* an industrial city in NW Germany, in North Rhine-Westphalia: a Hanse town from 1417; severely damaged in World War II. Pop: 181 500 (1999 est)

Hammarskjöld ('hæməʃʊld; *Swedish* 'hamarʃœld) *n* **Dag (Hjalmar Agne Carl)** (dɑːg) 1905–61, Swedish statesman; secretary-general of the United Nations (1953–61): Nobel peace prize 1961

hammer ('hæmə) *n* **1** a hand tool consisting of a heavy usually steel head held transversely on the end of a handle, used for driving in nails, etc **2** any tool or device with a similar function, such as the striking head on a bell **3** a power-driven striking tool, esp one used in forging **4** a part of a gunlock that strikes the primer or percussion cap when the trigger is pulled **5** *athletics* **5a** a heavy metal ball attached to a flexible wire: thrown in competitions **5b** the sport of throwing the hammer **6** an auctioneer's gavel **7** a device on a piano that is made to strike a string or group of strings causing them to vibrate **8** *anat* the nontechnical name for **malleus** **9** **go under the hammer** to be offered for sale by an auctioneer **10** **hammer and tongs** with great effort or energy **11** **on someone's hammer** *Austral & NZ sl* persistently demanding and critical of someone ▷ *vb* **12** to strike or beat with or as if with a hammer **13** (*tr*) to shape with or as if with a hammer **14** (*tr; foll by in or into*) to force (facts, ideas, etc) into (someone) through constant repetition **15** (*intr*) to feel or sound like hammering **16** (*intr; often foll by away*) to work at constantly **17** (*tr*) *Brit* to criticize severely **18** (*tr*) *inf* to defeat **19** (*tr*) *stock exchange* **19a** to announce the default of (a member) **19b** to cause prices of (securities, the market, etc) to fall by bearish selling [OE *hamor*] > **'hammer-ˌlike** *adj*

hammer and sickle *n* the emblem on the flag of the former Soviet Union, representing the industrial workers and the peasants respectively

hammer beam *n* either of a pair of short horizontal beams that project from opposite walls to support arched braces and struts

Hammerfest (*Norwegian* 'hamərfɛst) *n* a port in N Norway, on the W coast of Kvalöy Island: the northernmost town in Europe, with uninterrupted daylight from May 17 to July 29 and no sun between Nov. 21 and Jan. 21; fishing and tourist centre. Pop: 6900 (1991)

hammerhead ('hæməˌhɛd) *n* **1** a shark having a flattened hammer-shaped head **2** a tropical African wading bird having a dark plumage and a long backward-pointing crest **3** a large African fruit bat with a hammer-shaped muzzle > **'hammerˌheaded** *adj*

hammerlock ('hæməˌlɒk) *n* a wrestling hold in which a wrestler twists his opponent's arm upwards behind his back

hammer out *vb* (*tr, adv*) **1** to shape or remove with or as if with a hammer **2** to settle or reconcile (differences, problems, etc)

Hammersmith and Fulham ('hæməˌsmɪθ) *n* a borough of Greater London on the River Thames: established in 1965 by the amalgamation of Fulham and Hammersmith. Pop: 165 243 (2001). Area: 16 sq km (6 sq miles)

Hammerstein II ('hæməˌstaɪn) *n* **Oscar** 1895–1960, US librettist and songwriter: collaborated with the composer Richard Rodgers in musicals such as *South Pacific* (1949) and *The Sound of Music* (1959)

hammertoe ('hæməˌtəʊ) *n* a deformity causing the toe to be bent in a clawlike arch

Hammett ('hæmət) *n* **Dashiell** 1894–1961, US writer of detective novels. His books include *The Maltese Falcon* (1930) and *The Thin Man* (1932)

hammock ('hæmək) *n* a length of canvas, net, etc, suspended at the ends and used as a bed [C16 from Sp. *hamaca*, from Amerind]

Hammond[1] ('hæmənd) *n* a city in NW Indiana, adjacent to Chicago. Pop: 83 048 (2000)

Hammond[2] ('hæmənd) *n* **Walter Reginald**, known as *Wally*. 1903–65, English cricketer. An all-rounder, he played for England 85 times between 1928 and 1946

Hammurabi (ˌhæmʊ'rɑːbɪ) *or* **Hammurapi** *n* ?18th century BC, king of Babylonia; promulgator of one of the earliest known codes of law

hammy ('hæmɪ) *adj* **hammier, hammiest** *inf* **1** (of an actor) tending to overact **2** (of a play, performance, etc) overacted or exaggerated

Hampden ('hæmpdən, 'hæmdən) *n* **John** 1594–1643, English statesman; one of the leaders of the Parliamentary opposition to Charles I

hamper[1] ('hæmpə) *vb* **1** (*tr*) to prevent the progress or free movement of ▷ *n* **2** *naut* gear aboard a vessel that, though essential, is often in the way [C14 from ?; ? rel. to OE *hamm* enclosure, *hemm* HEM[1]]

hamper[2] ('hæmpə) *n* **1** a large basket, usually with a cover **2** *Brit* a selection of food and drink packed in a hamper or other container [C14 var. of earlier *hanaper* a small basket, from OF, of Gmc origin]

Hampshire ('hæmpʃɪə, -ʃə) *n* a county of S England, on the English Channel: crossed by the **Hampshire Downs** and the South Downs, with the New Forest in the southwest and many prehistoric and Roman remains: the geographical and ceremonial county includes

Portsmouth and Southampton, which became independent unitary authorities in 1997. Administrative centre: Winchester. Pop (excluding unitary authorities): 1 240 032 (2001). Area (excluding unitary authorities): 3679 sq. km (1420 sq. miles). Abbrev: **Hants**

Hampstead (ˈhæmpstɪd) *n* a residential district in N London: part of the Greater London borough of Camden since 1965; nearby is **Hampstead Heath**, a popular recreation area

Hampton[1] (ˈhæmptən) *n* **1** a city in SE Virginia, on the harbour of **Hampton Roads** on Chesapeake Bay. Pop: 146 437 (2000) **2** a district of the Greater London borough of Richmond-upon-Thames, on the River Thames: famous for **Hampton Court Palace** (built in 1515 by Cardinal Wolsey)

Hampton[2] (ˈhæmptən) *n* **1** **Christopher James** born 1946, British playwright: his works include *When Did You Last See My Mother?* (1964), the screenplay for the film *Dangerous Liaisons* (1988), and the book for the musical *Sunset Boulevard* (1993) **2** **Lionel** 1913–2002, US jazz-band leader and vibraphone player

hamster (ˈhæmstə) *n* a Eurasian burrowing rodent having a stocky body, short tail, and cheek pouches: a popular pet [C17 from G, from OHG *hamustro*, of Slavic origin]

hamstring (ˈhæmˌstrɪŋ) *n* **1** any of the tendons at the back of the knee **2** the large tendon at the back of the hind leg of a horse, etc ▷ *vb* **hamstrings, hamstringing, hamstrung** (*tr*) **3** to cripple by cutting the hamstring of **4** to thwart [C16 HAM[1] + STRING]

Hamsun (*Norwegian* ˈhamsun) *n* **Knut,** (knuːt), pen name of *Knut Pedersen*. 1859–1952, Norwegian novelist, whose works include *The Growth of the Soil* (1917): Nobel prize for literature 1920

hamulus (ˈhæmjʊləs) *n, pl* **hamuli** (-ˌlaɪ) *biol* a hook or hooklike process, between the fore and hind wings of a bee [C18 from L: a little hook, from *hāmus* hook]

Han[1] (hæn) *n* **1** the imperial dynasty that ruled China for most of the time from 206 BC to 221 AD, expanding its territory and developing its bureaucracy **2** the Chinese people as contrasted to Mongols, Manchus, etc

Han[2] (hæn) *n* a river in E central China, rising in S Shaanxi and flowing southeast through Hubei to the Yangtze River at Wuhan. Length: about 1450 km (900 miles)

Hanau (*German* ˈhaːnau) *n* a city in central Germany, in Hesse east of Frankfurt am Main: a centre of the jewellery industry. Pop: 84 420 (latest est)

Han Cities *pl n* a group of three cities in E central China, in SE Hubei at the confluence of the Han and Yangtze Rivers: Hanyang, Hankow, and Wuchang; united in 1950 to form the conurbation of Wuhan, the capital of Hubei province

Hancock (ˈhænkɒk) *n* **1** **Anthony John,** known as *Tony*. 1924–68, British comedian, noted for his radio series *Hancock's Half Hour* **2** **John** 1737–93, American statesman; first signatory of the Declaration of Independence

hand (hænd) *n* **1** the prehensile part of the body at the end of the arm, consisting of a thumb, four fingers, and a palm. Related adj: **manual** **2** the corresponding part in animals **3** something resembling this in shape or function **4a** the cards dealt in one round of a card game **4b** a player holding such cards **4c** one round of a card game **5** agency or influence: *the hand of God* **6** a part in something done: *he had a hand in the victory* **7** assistance: *to give someone a hand* **8** a pointer on a dial, indicator, or gauge, esp on a clock **9** acceptance or pledge of partnership, as in marriage **10** a position indicated by its location to the side of an object or the observer: *on the right hand* **11** a contrastive aspect, condition, etc: *on the other hand* **12** source or origin: *a story heard at third hand* **13** a person, esp one who creates something: *a good hand at painting* **14** a manual worker **15** a member of a ship's crew: *all hands on deck* **16** a person's handwriting: *the letter was in his own hand* **17** a round of applause: *give him a hand* **18** a characteristic way of doing something: *the hand of a master* **19** a unit of length equalling four inches, used for measuring the height of horses **20** a cluster of bananas **21** (*modifier*) **21a** of or involving the hand: *a hand grenade* **21b** carried in or worn on the hand: *hand luggage* **21c** operated by hand: *a hand drill* **22** (*in combination*) made by hand rather than machine: *hand-sewn* **23** **a free hand** freedom to do as desired **24** **a hand's turn** (*usually used with a negative*) a small amount of work: *he hasn't done a hand's turn* **25** **a heavy hand** tyranny or oppression: *he ruled with a heavy hand* **26** **a high hand** a dictatorial manner **27** **by hand** **27a** by manual rather than mechanical means **27b** by messenger or personally: *the letter was delivered by hand* **28** **force someone's hand** to force someone to act **29** **from hand to mouth** **29a** in poverty: *living from hand to mouth* **29b** without preparation or planning **30** **hand and foot** in all ways possible; completely: *they waited on him hand and foot* **31** **hand in glove** in close association **32** **hand over fist** steadily and quickly: *he makes money hand over fist* **33** **hold one's hand** to stop or postpone a planned action or punishment **34** **hold someone's hand** to support, help, or guide someone, esp by giving sympathy **35** **in hand** **35a** under control **35b** receiving attention **35c** available in reserve **35d** with deferred payment: *he works a week in hand* **36** **keep one's hand in** to maintain a limited involvement in an activity so as to preserve one's proficiency at it **37** (**near**) **at hand** very close, esp in time **38** **on hand** close by; present **39** **out of hand** **39a** beyond control **39b** without reservation or deeper examination: *he condemned him out of hand* **40** **show one's hand** to reveal one's stand, opinion, or plans **41** **take in hand** to discipline; control **42** **throw one's hand in** to give up a venture, game, etc **43** **to hand** accessible **44** **try one's hand** to attempt to do something ▷ *vb* (*tr*) **45** to transmit or offer by the hand or hands **46** to help or lead with the hand **47** *naut* to furl (a sail) **48** **hand it to someone** to give credit to someone ▷ See also **hand down, hand in,** etc, **hands** [OE *hand*] > **ˈhandless** *adj*

Hh

HAND *text messaging abbrev for* have a nice day

handbag (ˈhændˌbæg) *n* **1** Also called: **bag, purse** (US and Canad), **pocketbook** (chiefly US) a woman's small bag carried to contain personal articles **2** a small suitcase that can be carried by hand

handball (ˈhændˌbɔːl) *n* **1** a game in which two teams of seven players try to throw a ball into their opponent's goal **2** a game in which two or four people strike a ball against a wall with the hand **3** *soccer* the offence committed when a player other than a goalkeeper in his or her own penalty area touches the ball with a hand ▷ *vb* **4** *Australian rules football* to pass (the ball) with a blow of the fist

▷ www.ihf.info

handbarrow (ˈhændˌbærəʊ) *n* a flat tray for transporting loads, usually carried by two men

handbill (ˈhændˌbɪl) *n* a small printed notice for distribution by hand

handbook (ˈhændˌbʊk) *n* a reference book listing brief facts on a subject or place or directions for maintenance or repair, as of a car

handbrake (ˈhændˌbreɪk) *n* **1** a brake operated by a hand lever **2** the lever that operates the handbrake

handbrake turn *n* a turn sharply reversing the direction of a vehicle by speedily applying the handbrake while turning the steering wheel

handbreadth (ˈhændˌbrɛtθ, -ˌbrɛdθ) *or* **hand's-breadth** *n* the width of a hand used as an indication of length

h and c *abbrev for* hot and cold (water)

handcart (ˈhændˌkɑːt) *n* a simple cart, usually with one or two wheels, pushed or drawn by hand

handcraft ('hænd,krɑːft) *n* **1** another word for **handicraft** ▷ *vb* **2** (*tr*) to make by handicraft
handcrafted ('hænd,krɑːftɪd) *adj* made by handicraft
handcuff ('hænd,kʌf) *vb* **1** (*tr*) to put handcuffs on (a person); manacle ▷ *n* **2** (*pl*) a pair of locking metal rings joined by a short bar or chain for securing prisoners, etc
hand down *vb* (*tr, adv*) **1** to bequeath **2** to pass (an outgrown garment) on from one member of a family to a younger one **3** *US & Canad law* to announce (a verdict)
-handed *adj* of, for, or using a hand or hands as specified: *left-handed; a four-handed game of cards*
Handel ('hændᵊl) *n* **George Frederick,** German name *Georg Friedrich Händel*. 1685–1759, German composer, resident in England, noted particularly for his oratorios, including the *Messiah* (1741) and *Samson* (1743). Other works include over 40 operas, 12 concerti grossi, organ concertos, chamber and orchestral music, esp *Water Music* (1717)
handful ('hændfʊl) *n, pl* **handfuls 1** the amount or number that can be held in the hand **2** a small number or quantity **3** *inf* a person or thing difficult to manage or control
handgun ('hænd,gʌn) *n US & Canad* a firearm that can be fired with one hand, such as a pistol
hand-held *adj* **1** held in position by the hand **2** (of a film camera) held rather than mounted, as in close-up action shots **3** (of a computer) able to be held in the hand ▷ *n* **4** a computer that can be held in the hand; a palmtop computer
handicap ('hændɪ,kæp) *n* **1** something that hampers or hinders **2a** a contest, esp a race, in which competitors are given advantages or disadvantages of weight, distance, etc, in an attempt to equalize their chances **2b** the advantage or disadvantage prescribed **3** *golf* the number of strokes by which a player's averaged score exceeds par for the course **4** any disability or disadvantage resulting from physical, mental, or social impairment or abnormality ▷ *vb* **handicaps, handicapping, handicapped** (*tr*) **5** to be a hindrance or disadvantage to **6** to assign a handicap to **7** to organize (a contest) by handicapping [c17 prob. from *hand in cap*, a lottery game in which players drew forfeits from a cap or deposited money in it] > **'handi,capper** *n*
handicapped ('hændɪ,kæpt) *adj* **1a** physically or mentally disabled **1b** (*as collective n; preceded by the*): *the handicapped* **2** (of a competitor) assigned a handicap
handicraft ('hændɪ,krɑːft) *n* **1** skill in working with the hands **2** a particular skill performed with the hands, such as weaving **3** the work so produced ▷ Also called: **handcraft** [c15 changed from HANDCRAFT through infl. of HANDIWORK]
hand in *vb* (*tr, adv*) to return or submit (something, such as an examination paper)
handism ('hænd,ɪzəm) *n* discriminination against people on the grounds of whether they are left-handed or right-handed
handiwork ('hændɪ,wɜːk) *n* **1** work produced by hand **2** the result of the action or endeavours of a person or thing [OE *handgeweorc*, from HAND + *ge-* (collective prefix) + *weorc* WORK]
handkerchief ('hæŋkətʃɪf, -tʃiːf) *n* a small square of soft absorbent material carried and used to wipe the nose, etc
handlanger ('hænd,læŋə) *n S African* an unskilled assistant to a tradesman [from Dutch]
handle ('hændᵊl) *n* **1** the part of a utensil, drawer, etc, designed to be held in order to move, use, or pick up the object **2** *sl* a person's name or title **3** *CB radio* a slang name for **call sign 4** an excuse for doing something: *his background served as a handle for their mockery* **5** the quality, as of textiles, perceived by feeling **6** *NZ* a glass beer mug with a handle **7 fly off the handle** *inf* to become suddenly extremely angry ▷ *vb* **handles, handling, handled** (*mainly tr*) **8** to hold, move, or touch with the hands **9** to operate using the hands: *the boy handled the reins well* **10** to control: *my wife handles my investments* **11** to manage successfully: *a secretary must be able to handle clients* **12** to discuss (a theme, subject, etc) **13** to deal with in a specified way: *I was handled with great tact* **14** to trade or deal in (specified merchandise) **15** (*intr*) to react in a specified way to operation: *the car handles well on bends* [OE] > **'handled** *adj*
handlebar moustache ('hændᵊl,bɑː) *n* a bushy extended moustache with curled ends
handlebars ('hændᵊl,bɑːz) *pl n* (*sometimes sing*) a metal tube having its ends curved to form handles, used for steering a bicycle, etc
handler ('hændlə) *n* **1** a person who trains and controls an animal, esp a police dog **2** the trainer or second of a boxer
Handler ('hændlə) *n* **Daniel** born 1970, US writer for older children, best known for the macabre humour of his *A Series of Unfortunate Events*, a sequence of books written in the persona of **Lemony Snicket**
Handley Page *n* Sir **Frederick** See (Sir Frederick Handley) **Page**
handling ('hændlɪŋ) *n* **1** the act or an instance of picking up, turning over, or touching something **2** treatment, as of a theme in literature **3a** the process by which a commodity is packaged, transported, etc **3b** (*as modifier*): *handling charges* **4** *law* the act of receiving property that one knows or believes to be stolen
handmade (,hænd'meɪd) *adj* made by hand, not by machine, esp with care or craftsmanship
handmaiden ('hænd,meɪdᵊn) *or* **handmaid** *n* **1** a person or thing that serves a useful but subordinate purpose **2** *arch* a female servant
hand-me-down *n inf* **1** something, esp an outgrown garment, passed down from one person to another **2** anything that has already been used by another
hand-off *rugby* ▷ *n* **1** the act of warding off an opposing player with the open hand ▷ *vb* **hand off 2** (*tr, adv*) to ward off thus
hand on *vb* (*tr, adv*) to pass to the next in a succession
hand organ *n* another name for **barrel organ**
hand-out *n* **1** clothing, food, or money given to a needy person **2** a leaflet, free sample, etc, given out to publicize something **3** a statement distributed to the press or an audience to confirm or replace an oral presentation ▷ *vb* **hand out 4** (*tr, adv*) to distribute
hand over *vb* **1** (*tr, adv*) to surrender possession of; transfer ▷ *n* **handover 2** a transfer; surrender
hand-pick *vb* (*tr*) to select with great care, as for a special job > **,hand-'picked** *adj*
handrail ('hænd,reɪl) *n* a rail alongside a stairway, etc, to provide support
hands (hændz) *pl n* **1** power or keeping: *your welfare is in his hands* **2** Also called: **handling** *soccer* the infringement of touching the ball with the hand or arm **3 change hands** to pass from the possession of one person to another **4 hands down** without effort; easily **5 have one's hands full 5a** to be completely occupied **5b** to be beset with problems **6 have one's hands tied** to be unable to act **7 lay hands on** *or* **upon 7a** to get possession of **7b** to beat up; assault **7c** to find **7d** *Christianity* to place hands on (someone) in order to confirm or ordain **8 off one's hands** for which one is no longer responsible **9 on one's hands 9a** for which one is responsible: *I've got too much on my hands to help* **9b** to spare: *time on my hands* **10 wash one's hands of** to have nothing more to do with; refuse to accept responsibility for
handsaw ('hænd,sɔː) *n* any saw for use in one hand only
hand's-breadth *n* another name for **handbreadth**
handsel *or* **hansel** ('hænsᵊl) *arch or dialect* ▷ *n* **1** a gift for good luck at the beginning of a new year, new venture, etc ▷ *vb* **handsels, handselling, handselled** *or* **hansels,**

hanselling, hanselled; *or US* **handsels, handseling, handseled** *or* **hansels, hanseling, hanseled** *(tr)* **2** to give a handsel to (a person) **3** to inaugurate [OE *handselen* delivery into the hand]

handset ('hænd,sɛt) *n* a telephone mouthpiece and earpiece mounted as a single unit

handshake ('hænd,ʃeɪk) *n* the act of grasping and shaking a person's hand, as when being introduced or agreeing on a deal

hands-off *adj* **1** (of a machine, device, etc) without need of manual operation **2** denoting a policy, etc, of deliberate noninvolvement: *a hands-off strategy towards industry*

handsome ('hænsəm) *adj* **1** (of a man) good-looking **2** (of a woman) fine-looking in a dignified way **3** well-proportioned; stately: *a handsome room* **4** liberal: *a handsome allowance* **5** gracious or generous: *a handsome action* [C15 *handsom* easily handled] > '**handsomely** *adv* > '**handsomeness** *n*

hands-on *adj* involving practical experience of equipment, etc: *hands-on training in computing*

handspring ('hænd,sprɪŋ) *n* a gymnastic feat in which a person starts from a standing position and leaps forwards or backwards into a handstand and then onto his feet

handstand ('hænd,stænd) *n* the act of supporting the body on the hands in an upside-down position

hand-to-hand *adj, adv* at close quarters

hand-to-mouth *adj, adv* with barely enough money or food to satisfy immediate needs

handwork ('hænd,wɜːk) *n* work done by hand rather than by machine > '**hand,worked** *adj*

handwriting ('hænd,raɪtɪŋ) *n* **1** writing by hand rather than by typing or printing **2** a person's characteristic writing style: *that is in my handwriting* > '**hand,written** *adj*

handy ('hændɪ) *adj* **handier, handiest 1** conveniently within reach **2** easy to handle or use **3** skilful with one's hands > '**handily** *adv* > '**handiness** *n*

Handy ('hændɪ) *n* **W**(**illiam**) **C**(**hristopher**) 1873–1958, US blues musician and songwriter, esp noted for the song "St Louis Blues"

handy dog *n NZ* a farm dog that can perform a number of different tasks

handyman ('hændɪ,mæn) *n, pl* **handymen** a man employed to do or skilled in odd jobs, etc

hanepoot ('hɑːnə,pɔːt) *n S African* a kind of grape for eating or wine making [from Du.]

hang (hæŋ) *vb* **hangs, hanging, hung 1** to fasten or be fastened from above, esp by a cord, chain, etc **2** to place or be placed in position as by a hinge so as to allow free movement: *to hang a door* **3** *(intr;* sometimes foll by *over)* to be suspended; hover: *a pall of smoke hung over the city* **4** *(intr;* sometimes foll by *over)* to threaten **5** *(intr)* to be or remain doubtful (esp in **hang in the balance**) **6** *(pt & pp* **hanged**) to suspend or be suspended by the neck until dead **7** *(tr)* to decorate, furnish, or cover with something suspended **8** *(tr)* to fasten to a wall: *to hang wallpaper* **9** to exhibit or be exhibited in an art gallery, etc **10** to droop or allow to droop: *to hang one's head* **11** (of cloth, clothing, etc) to drape, fall, or flow: *her skirt hangs well* **12** *(tr)* to suspend (game such as pheasant) so that it becomes slightly decomposed and therefore more tasty **13** (of a jury) to prevent or be prevented from reaching a verdict **14** *(pt & pp* **hanged**) *sl* to damn or be damned: used in mild curses or interjections **15** *(intr)* to pass slowly (esp in **time hangs heavily**) **16 hang fire** to be delayed or to procrastinate ▷ *n* **17** the way in which something hangs **18** *(usually used with a negative) sl* a damn: *I don't care a hang* **19 get the hang of** *inf* **19a** to understand the technique of doing something **19b** to perceive the meaning of ▷ See also **hang about, hang back,** etc [OE *hangian*]

hang about *or* **around** *vb (intr)* **1** to waste time; loiter **2** *(adv;* foll by *with)* to frequent the company (of someone)

hangar ('hæŋə) *n* a large building for storing and maintaining aircraft [C19 from F: shed, ?from Med. L *angārium* shed used as a smithy, from ?]

hang back *vb (intr, adv;* often foll by *from)* to be reluctant to go forward or carry on

Hangchow ('hæŋ'dʒəʊ) *n* a variant transliteration of the Chinese name for **Hangzhou**

hangdog ('hæŋ,dɒg) *adj* downcast, furtive, or guilty in appearance or manner

hanger ('hæŋə) *n* **1a** any support, such as a peg or loop, on or by which something may be hung **1b** See **coat hanger 2a** a person who hangs something **2b** *(in combination): paperhanger* **3** a type of dagger worn on a sword belt **4** *Brit* a wood on a steep hillside

hanger-on *n, pl* **hangers-on** a sycophantic follower or dependant

hang-glider *n* an unpowered aircraft consisting of a large wing made of cloth or plastic stretched over a light framework from which the pilot hangs in a harness > '**hang-,gliding** *n*

▷ www.bhpa.co.uk

▷ www.fai.org/hang-gliding

hangi ('hʌŋiː) *n NZ* **1** an open-air cooking pit **2** the food cooked in it **3** the social gathering at the resultant meal [from Maori]

hang in *vb (intr, prep) inf, chiefly US & Canad* to persist: *just hang in there for a bit longer*

hanging ('hæŋɪŋ) *n* **1a** the putting of a person to death by suspending the body by the neck **1b** *(as modifier): a hanging offence* **2** *(often pl)* a decorative drapery hung on a wall or over a window ▷ *adj* **3** not supported from below; suspended **4** undecided; still under discussion **5** projecting downwards; overhanging **6** situated on a steep slope **7** *(prenominal)* given to issuing death sentences: *a hanging judge*

Hanging Gardens of Babylon *pl n* (in ancient Babylon) gardens, probably planted on terraces of a ziggurat: one of the Seven Wonders of the World

hanging valley *n geog* a tributary valley entering a main valley at a much higher level because of overdeepening of the main valley, esp by glacial erosion

hangman ('hæŋmən) *n, pl* **hangmen** an official who carries out a sentence of hanging

hangnail ('hæŋ,neɪl) *n* a piece of skin torn away from, but still attached to, the base or side of a fingernail [C17 from OE *angnægl*, from *enge* tight + *nægl* nail; infl. by HANG]

hang on *vb (intr)* **1** *(adv)* to continue or persist, esp with effort or difficulty **2** *(adv)* to grasp or hold **3** *(prep)* to depend on: *everything hangs on this deal* **4** *(prep)* Also: **hang onto, hang upon** to listen attentively to **5** *(adv) inf* to wait: *hang on for a few minutes*

hang out *vb (adv)* **1** to suspend, be suspended, or lean **2** *(intr) inf* to frequent a place **3 let it all hang out** *inf, chiefly US* **3a** to relax completely in an unassuming way **3b** to act or speak freely ▷ *n* **hang-out 4** *inf* a place that one frequents

hangover ('hæŋ,əʊvə) *n* **1** the delayed aftereffects of drinking too much alcohol **2** a person or thing left over from or influenced by a past age

Hang Seng Index (hæŋ sɛŋ) *n* an index of share prices based on an average of 33 stocks quoted on the Hong Kong Stock Exchange [name of a Hong Kong bank]

hang together *vb (intr, adv)* **1** to be cohesive or united **2** to be consistent: *your statements don't quite hang together*

Hanguk ('hæn'gʊk) *n* the Korean name for **South Korea**

hang up *vb (adv)* **1** *(tr)* to put on a hook, hanger, etc **2** to replace (a telephone receiver) on its cradle at the end of a conversation **3** *(tr; usually passive;* usually foll by *on) inf* to cause to have an emotional or psychological preoccupation or problem: *he's really hung up on his mother* ▷ *n* **hang-up** *inf* **4** an emotional or psychological preoccupation or problem **5** a persistent cause of annoyance

Hangzhou ('hæŋ'ʒəʊ) *or* **Hangchow** *n* a port in E China, capital of Zhejiang province, on **Hangzhou Bay** (an inlet of the East China Sea), at the foot of the Eye of Heaven Mountains: regarded by Marco Polo as the finest city in the world; seat of two universities (1927, 1959). Pop: 1 346 148 (1999 est)

hank (hæŋk) *n* **1** a loop, coil, or skein, as of rope **2** *naut* a ringlike fitting that can be opened to admit a stay for attaching the luff of a sail **3** a unit of measurement of cloth, such as a length of 840 yards (767 m) of cotton or 560 yards (512 m) of worsted yarn [c13 from ON]

hanker ('hæŋkə) *vb* (foll by *for, after*, or an infinitive) to have a yearning [c17 prob. from Du. dialect *hankeren*] > **'hankering** *n*

Hankow *or* **Han-k'ou** ('hæn'kaʊ) *n* a former city in SE China, in SE Hubei at the confluence of the Han and Yangtze Rivers: one of the Han Cities; merged with Hanyang and Wuchang in 1950 to form the conurbation of Wuhan

Hanks (hæŋks) *n* **Tom** born 1956, US film actor: his films include *Splash* (1984), *Philadelphia* (1993), *Forrest Gump* (1994), *Saving Private Ryan* (1998), and *Catch Me If You Can* (2003)

hanky *or* **hankie** ('hæŋkɪ) *n, pl* **hankies** *inf* short for **handkerchief**

hanky-panky ('hæŋkɪ'pæŋkɪ) *n inf* **1** dubious or foolish behaviour **2** illicit sexual relations [c19 var. of HOCUS-POCUS]

Hanna ('hænə) *n* **William** 1910–2001, US animator and film producer, who, with **Joseph Barbera** (born 1911), created the cartoon characters Tom and Jerry in the 1940s; the Hanna-Barbera company later produced numerous cartoon series for television

Hannah ('hænə) *n Old Testament* the woman who gave birth to Samuel (I Samuel 1–2)

Hannibal ('hænɪbᵊl) *n* 247–182 BC, Carthaginian general; son of Hamilcar Barca. He commanded the Carthaginian army in the Second Punic War (218–201). After capturing Sagunto in Spain, he invaded Italy (218), crossing the Alps with an army of about 40 000 men and defeating the Romans at Trasimene (217) and Cannae (216). In 203 he was recalled to defend Carthage and was defeated by Scipio at Zama (202). He was later forced into exile and committed suicide to avoid capture

Hannover (*German* ha'no:fər) *n* a city in N Germany, capital of Lower Saxony: capital of the kingdom of Hannover (1815–66); situated on the Mittelland canal. Pop: 515 200 (1999 est). English spelling: **Hanover**

Hanoi (hæ'nɔɪ) *n* the capital of Vietnam, on the Red River: became capital of Tonkin in 1802, of French Indochina in 1887, of Vietnam in 1945, and of North Vietnam (1954–75); university (1917); industrial centre. Pop (urban area): 2 154 900 (1993 est)

Hanover[1] ('hænəʊvə) *n* the English spelling of **Hannover**

Hanover[2] ('hænəʊvə) *n* **1** a princely house of Germany (1692–1815), the head of which succeeded to the British throne as George I in 1714 **2** the royal house of Britain (1714–1901)

▷ www.royal.gov.uk/output/Page105.asp
▷ www.royalty.nu/Europe/England/Hanover

Hanoverian (ˌhænə'vɪərɪən) *adj* **1** of, relating to, or situated in Hannover **2** of or relating to the princely house of Hanover or to the monarchs of England or their reigns from 1714 to 1901 ▷ *n* **3** a member or supporter of the house of Hanover

Hansard ('hænsɑ:d) *n* **1** the official verbatim report of the proceedings of the British Parliament **2** a similar report kept by the Canadian, South African, Australian, or New Zealand parliament [c19 after an English printer L. *Hansard* (1752–1828) and his descendants, who compiled the reports until 1889]

Hanse (hæns) *n* **1** a medieval guild of merchants **2** a fee paid by the new members of a medieval trading guild **3** another name for the **Hanseatic League** [c12 of Gmc origin] > **Hanseatic** (ˌhænsɪ'ætɪk) *adj*

Hanseatic League *n* a commercial organization of towns in N Germany formed in the mid 14th century to protect and control trade

hansel ('hænsᵊl) *n, vb* a variant spelling of **handsel**

hansom ('hænsəm) *n* (*sometimes cap*) a two-wheeled one-horse carriage with a fixed hood. The driver sits on a high outside seat at the rear. Also called: **hansom cab** [c19 after its designer J. A. *Hansom* (1803–82)]

hantavirus ('hæntəˌvaɪrəs) *n* any member of a genus of viruses that infect rodents and can be transmitted to humans, in whom they can cause kidney damage or respiratory disease [c20 after the *Hantaan* river, South Korea]

Hants (hænts) *abbrev for* Hampshire

Hanukkah ('hɑ:nəkə, -nʊˌkɑ:) *n* a variant of **Chanukah**

Hanuman (ˌhʌnʊ'mɑ:n) *n* **1** (*pl* **Hanumans**) another word for **entellus** (the monkey) **2** the monkey chief of Hindu mythology [from Hindi, from Sansk. *hanumant* having (conspicuous) jaws, from *hanu* jaw]

Hanyang *or* **Han-yang** ('hæn'jæŋ) *n* a former city in SE China, in SE Hubei at the confluence of the Han and Yangtze Rivers: one of the Han Cities; merged with Hankow and Wuchang in 1950 to form the conurbation of Wuhan

hap (hæp) *arch* ▷ *n* **1** luck; chance **2** an occurrence ▷ *vb* **haps, happing, happed 3** (*intr*) to happen [c13 from ON *happ* good luck]

ha'penny ('heɪpnɪ) *n, pl* **ha'pennies** *Brit* a variant spelling of **halfpenny**

haphazard (hæp'hæzəd) *adv, adj* **1** at random ▷ *adj* **2** careless > **hap'hazardly** *adv* > **hap'hazardness** *n*

hapless ('hæplɪs) *adj* unfortunate; wretched > **'haplessly** *adv* > **'haplessness** *n*

haplography (hæp'lɒgrəfɪ) *n, pl* **haplographies** the accidental omission of a letter or syllable which recurs, as in spelling *endodontics* as *endontics* [c19 from Gk, from *haplous* single + -GRAPHY]

haploid ('hæplɔɪd) *biol* ▷ *adj* **1** (esp of gametes) having a single set of unpaired chromosomes ▷ *n* **2** a haploid cell or organism [c20 from Gk *haploeidēs*, from *haplous* single] > **'haploidy** *n*

haplology (hæp'lɒlədʒɪ) *n* omission of a repeated occurrence of a sound or syllable in fluent speech, as for example in the pronunciation of *library* as ('laɪbrɪ)

haply ('hæplɪ) *adv* (*sentence modifier*) an archaic word for **perhaps**

happen ('hæpᵊn) *vb* **1** (*intr*) to take place; occur **2** (*intr*; foll by *to*) (of some unforeseen event, esp death) to fall to the lot (of): *if anything happens to me it'll be your fault* **3** (*tr*) to chance (to be or do something): *I happen to know him* **4** (*tr*; *takes a clause as object*) to be the case, esp by chance: *it happens that I know him* ▷ *adv, sentence substitute* **5** N English *dialect* another word for **perhaps** [c14 see HAP, -EN[1]]

USAGE See at **occur**

happening ('hæpənɪŋ, 'hæpnɪŋ) *n* **1** an event **2** an improvised or spontaneous performance consisting of bizarre events ▷ *adj* **3** *inf* fashionable and up-to-the-minute

happen on *or* **upon** *vb* (*intr; prep*) to find by chance

happy ('hæpɪ) *adj* **happier, happiest 1** feeling or expressing joy; pleased **2** willing: *I'd be happy to show you around* **3** causing joy or gladness **4** fortunate: *the happy position of not having to work* **5** aptly expressed; appropriate: *a happy turn of phrase* **6** (*postpositive*) *inf* slightly intoxicated [c14 see HAP, -Y[1]] > **'happily** *adv* > **'happiness** *n*

happy event *n inf* the birth of a child

happy-go-lucky *adj* carefree or easy-going

happy hour *n* a period during which some public

houses, bars, restaurants, etc, charge reduced prices
happy hunting ground *n* **1** (in Amerind legend) the paradise to which a person passes after death **2** a productive or profitable area to explore
happy medium *n* a course or state that avoids extremes
Hapsburg ('hæps,bɜ:g) *n* a German princely family founded by Albert, count of Hapsburg (1153). From 1440 to 1806, the Hapsburgs wore the imperial crown of the Holy Roman Empire almost uninterruptedly. They also provided rulers for Austria, Spain, Hungary, Bohemia, etc The line continued as the royal house of **Hapsburg-Lorraine,** ruling in Austria (1806–48) and Austria-Hungary (1848–1918). German name: **Habsburg**
haptic ('hæptɪk) *adj* relating to or based on the sense of touch [C19 from Gk, from *haptein* to touch]
hapuka *or* **hapuku** (hə'pu:kə, 'hɑ:pʊkə) *n* NZ another name for **groper** [from Maori]
hara-kiri (,hærə'kɪrɪ) *or* **hari-kari** (,hærɪ'kɑ:rɪ) *n* (formerly, in Japan) ritual suicide by disembowelment when disgraced or under sentence of death. Also called: **seppuku** [C19 from Japanese, from *hara* belly + *kiri* cutting]
Harald I ('hærəld) *n* called *Harald Fairhair*. ?850–933, first king of Norway: his rule caused emigration to the British Isles
Harald III *n* surname *Hardraade*. 1015–66, king of Norway (1047–66); invaded England (1066) and died at the battle of Stamford Bridge
harangue (hə'ræŋ) *vb* **harangues, haranguing, harangued 1** to address (a person or crowd) in an angry, vehement, or forcefully persuasive way ▷ *n* **2** a loud, forceful, or angry speech [C15 from OF, from OIt. *aringa* public speech, prob. of Gmc origin] > **ha'ranguer** *n*
Harappa (hə'ræpə) *n* an ancient city in the Punjab in NW Pakistan: one of the centres of the Indus civilization that flourished from 2500 to 1700 BC; probably destroyed by Indo-European invaders
Harappan (hə'ræpən) *adj* **1** of or relating to Harappa (an ancient city in the Punjab) or its inhabitants ▷ *n* **2** a native or inhabitant of Harappa
Harar *or* **Harrer** ('hɑ:rə) *n* a city in E Ethiopia: former capital of the Muslim state of Adal. Pop: 122 932 (1994 est)
Harare (hə'rɑ:rɪ) *n* the capital of Zimbabwe, in the northeast: University of Zimbabwe (1957); industrial and commercial centre. Pop: 1 686 169 (1998 est). Former name (until 1982): **Salisbury**
▷ www.zimbabwetourism.co.zw/destzim/index.html
harass ('hærəs, hə'ræs) *vb* (*tr*) to trouble, torment, or confuse by continual persistent attacks, questions, etc [C17 from F *harasser*, var. of OF *harer* to set a dog on, of Gmc origin] > **'harassed** *adj* > **'harassment** *n*
Harbin (hɑ:'bi:n, -'bɪn) *n* a city in NE China, capital of Heilongjiang province on the Songhua River: founded by the Russians in 1897; centre of tsarist activities after the October Revolution in Russia (1917). Pop: 2 586 978 (1999 est). Also called: **Ha-erh-pin**
harbinger ('hɑ:bɪndʒə) *n* **1** a person or thing that announces or indicates the approach of something; forerunner ▷ *vb* **2** (*tr*) to announce the approach or arrival of [C12 from OF *herbergere*, from *herberge* lodging, from OSaxon]
harbour *or US* **harbor** ('hɑ:bə) *n* **1** a sheltered port **2** a place of refuge or safety ▷ *vb* **3** (*tr*) to give shelter to: *to harbour a criminal* **4** (*tr*) to maintain secretly: *to harbour a grudge* **5** to shelter (a vessel) in a harbour or (of a vessel) to seek shelter [OE *herebeorg*, from *here* army + *beorg* shelter]
harbourage *or US* **harborage** ('hɑ:bərɪdʒ) *n* shelter or refuge, as for a ship
harbour master *n* an official in charge of a harbour
hard (hɑ:d) *adj* **1** firm or rigid **2** toughened; not soft or smooth: *hard skin* **3** difficult to do or accomplish: *a hard task* **4** difficult to understand: *a hard question* **5** showing or requiring considerable effort or application: *hard work* **6** demanding: *a hard master* **7** harsh; cruel: *a hard fate* **8** inflicting pain, sorrow, or hardship: *hard times* **9** tough or violent: *a hard man* **10** forceful: *a hard knock* **11** cool or uncompromising: *we took a long hard look at our profit factor* **12** indisputable; real: *hard facts* **13** *chem* (of water) impairing the formation of a lather by soap **14** practical, shrewd, or calculating: *he is a hard man in business* **15** harsh: *hard light* **16a** (of currency) in strong demand, esp as a result of a good balance of payments situation **16b** (of credit) difficult to obtain; tight **17** (of alcoholic drink) being a spirit rather than a wine, beer, etc **18** (of a drug) highly addictive **19** *physics* (of radiation) having high energy and the ability to penetrate solids **20** *chiefly US* (of goods) durable **21** short for **hard-core 22** *phonetics* (not in technical usage) denoting the consonants *c* and *g* when they are pronounced as in *cat* and *got* **23a** heavily fortified **23b** (of nuclear missiles) located underground **24** politically extreme: *the hard left* **25** *Brit & NZ inf* incorrigible or disreputable (esp in **a hard case**) **26 a hard nut to crack 26a** a person not easily won over **26b** a thing not easily done or understood **27 hard by** close by **28 hard of hearing** slightly deaf **29 hard up** *inf* **29a** in need of money **29b** (foll by *for*) in great need (of): *hard up for suggestions* ▷ *adv* **30** with great energy, force, or vigour: *the team always played hard* **31** as far as possible: *hard left* **32** earnestly or intently: *she thought hard about the formula* **33** with great intensity: *his son's death hit him hard* **34** (foll by *on, upon, by,* or *after*) close; near: *hard on his heels* **35** (foll by *at*) assiduously; devotedly **36a** with effort or difficulty: *their victory was hard won* **36b** (*in combination*): *hard-earned* **37** slowly: *prejudice dies hard* **38 go hard with** to cause pain or difficulty to (someone) **39 hard put (to it)** scarcely having the capacity (to do something) ▷ *n* **40** *Brit* a roadway across a foreshore **41** *sl* hard labour **42** *sl* an erection of the penis (esp in **get** or **have a hard on**) [OE *heard*] > **'hardness** *n*
hard and fast *adj* (**hard-and-fast** *when prenominal*) (of rules, etc) invariable or strict
hardback ('hɑ:d,bæk) *n* **1** a book with covers of cloth, cardboard, or leather ▷ *adj* **2** Also: **casebound, hardbound, hardcover** of or denoting a hardback or the publication of hardbacks
hard-bitten *adj inf* tough and realistic
hardboard ('hɑ:d,bɔ:d) *n* a thin stiff sheet made of compressed sawdust and wood pulp bound together under heat and pressure
hard-boiled *adj* **1** (of an egg) boiled until solid **2** *inf* **2a** tough, realistic **2b** cynical
hard card *n* a hard disk, mounted on a card, that can be added to a personal computer
hard cash *n* money or payment in money, as opposed to payment by cheque, credit, etc
hard coal *n* another name for **anthracite**
hard copy *n* computer output printed on paper, as contrasted with machine-readable output such as magnetic tape
hardcore ('hɑ:d,kɔ:) *n* **1** a style of rock music characterized by short fast songs with minimal melody and aggressive delivery **2** a type of dance music with a very fast beat
hard core *n* **1** the members of a group who form an intransigent nucleus resisting change **2** material, such as broken stones, used to form a foundation for a road, etc ▷ *adj* **hard-core 3** (of pornography) describing or depicting sexual acts in explicit detail **4** extremely committed or fanatical: *a hard-core Communist*
hard disk *n computing* a disk of rigid magnetizable material that is used to store data for computers: it is permanently mounted in its disk drive and usually has a storage capacity of a few gigabytes
hard drive *or* **hard disk drive** *n computing* (on a

Hh

computer) the mechanism that handles the reading, writing, and storage of data on the hard disk

Hardecanute ('hɑːdɪkəˌnjuːt) *n* a variant of **Harthacanute**

harden ('hɑːdᵊn) *vb* **1** to make or become hard or harder; freeze, stiffen, or set **2** to make or become tough or unfeeling **3** to make or become stronger or firmer **4** *(intr) commerce* **4a** (of prices, a market, etc) to cease to fluctuate **4b** (of price) to rise higher > **'hardener** *n*

Hardenberg (*German* 'hardənbɛrk) *n* **Friedrich von** ('friːdrɪç fɔn) the original name of **Novalis**

hardened ('hɑːdᵊnd) *adj* **1** rigidly set, as in a mode of behaviour **2** toughened; seasoned

harden off *vb (tr, adv)* to cause (plants) to become resistant to cold, frost, etc, by gradually exposing them to such conditions

hard feeling *n (often pl; often used with a negative)* resentment; ill will: *no hard feelings?*

hard hat *n* **1** a hat made of a hard material for protection, worn esp by construction workers, equestrians, etc **2** *inf, chiefly US* a construction worker

hard-headed *adj* tough, realistic, or shrewd; not moved by sentiment

hardhearted (ˌhɑːd'hɑːtɪd) *adj* unkind or intolerant > **ˌhard'heartedness** *n*

Hardicanute ('hɑːdɪkəˌnjuːt) *n* a variant of **Harthacanute**

Hardie ('hɑːdɪ) *n* **(James) Keir** (kɪə) 1856–1915, British Labour leader and politician, born in Scotland; the first parliamentary leader of the Labour Party

hardihood ('hɑːdɪˌhʊd) *n* courage or daring

Harding ('hɑːdɪŋ) *n* **Warren G(amaliel)** 1865–1923, 29th president of the US (1921–23)

hard labour *n criminal law* (formerly) the penalty of compulsory physical labour imposed in addition to a sentence of imprisonment

hard landing *n* **1** a landing by a rocket or spacecraft in which the vehicle is destroyed on impact **2** a solution to a problem that involves hardship **3** a sudden economic slowdown followed by a recession

hard line *n* an uncompromising course or policy > **ˌhard'liner** *n*

hardly ('hɑːdlɪ) *adv* **1** scarcely; barely: *we hardly knew the family* **2** only just: *he could hardly hold the cup* **3** *often used ironically* not at all: *he will hardly incriminate himself* **4** with difficulty **5** *rare* harshly or cruelly.

USAGE See at **scarcely**

hard-nosed *adj inf* tough, shrewd, and practical

Hardouin Mansart (*French* ardwɛ̃ mɑ̃sar) *n* See (Jules Hardouin) **Mansart**

hard pad *n* (in dogs) an abnormal increase in the thickness of the foot pads: one of the clinical signs of canine distemper. See **distemper**[1]

hard palate *n* the anterior bony portion of the roof of the mouth

hardpan ('hɑːdˌpæn) *n* a hard impervious layer of clay below the soil

hard paste *n* **a** porcelain made with kaolin and petuntse, of Chinese origin and made in Europe from the early 18th century **b** *(as modifier): hard-paste porcelain*

hard-pressed *adj* **1** in difficulties **2** subject to severe competition or attack **3** closely pursued

hard rock *n* rhythmically simple rock music that is very loud

hard sauce *n* another name for **brandy butter**

hard science *n* one of the natural or physical sciences, such as physics, chemistry, biology, geology, or astronomy > **hard scientist** *n*

hard sell *n* an aggressive insistent technique of selling or advertising

hard-shell *adj also* **hard-shelled** **1** *zool* having a shell or carapace that is thick, heavy, or hard **2** *US* strictly orthodox

hardship ('hɑːdʃɪp) *n* **1** conditions of life difficult to endure **2** something that causes suffering or privation

hard shoulder *n Brit* a surfaced verge running along the edge of a motorway for emergency stops

hardtack ('hɑːdˌtæk) *n* a kind of hard saltless biscuit, formerly eaten esp by sailors as a staple aboard ship. Also called: **ship's biscuit, sea biscuit**

hardtop ('hɑːdˌtɒp) *n* a car with a metal or plastic roof that is sometimes detachable

hardware ('hɑːdˌwɛə) *n* **1** metal tools, implements, etc, esp cutlery or cooking utensils **2** *computing* the physical equipment used in a computer system, such as the central processing unit, peripheral devices, and memory ▷ Cf **software** **3** mechanical equipment, components, etc **4** heavy military equipment, such as tanks and missiles **5** *inf* a gun

hard-wired *adj* **1** (of a circuit or instruction) permanently wired into a computer, replacing separate software **2** (of human behaviour) innate; not learned: *humans have a hard-wired ability for acquiring language*

hardwood ('hɑːdˌwʊd) *n* **1** the wood of any of numerous broad-leaved trees, such as oak, beech, ash, etc, as distinguished from the wood of a conifer **2** any tree from which this wood is obtained

hardy ('hɑːdɪ) *adj* **hardier, hardiest** **1** having or demanding a tough constitution; robust **2** bold; courageous **3** foolhardy; rash **4** (of plants) able to live out of doors throughout the winter [c13 from OF *hardi*, pp of *hardir* to become bold, of Gmc origin; cf. OE *hierdan* to HARDEN, ON *hertha*, OHG *herten*] > **'hardily** *adv* > **'hardiness** *n*

Hardy ('hɑːdɪ) *n* **1 Oliver** See **Laurel and Hardy** **2 Thomas** 1840–1928, British novelist and poet. Most of his novels are set in his native Dorset (part of his fictional Wessex) and include *Far from the Madding Crowd* (1874), *The Return of the Native* (1878), *The Mayor of Casterbridge* (1886), *Tess of the d'Urbervilles* (1891), and *Jude the Obscure* (1895), after which his work consisted chiefly of verse **3** Sir **Thomas Masterman** 1769–1839, British naval officer, flag captain under Nelson (1799–1805): 1st Sea Lord (1830)

hare (hɛə) *n, pl* **hares** *or* **hare** **1** a solitary mammal which is larger than a rabbit, has longer ears and legs, and lives in a shallow nest (form) **2** **run with the hare and hunt with the hounds** to be on good terms with both sides **3** **start a hare** to raise a topic for conversation ▷ *vb* **hares, haring, hared** **4** *(intr; often foll by off, after, etc) Brit inf* to run fast or wildly [OE *hara*] > **'hareˌlike** *adj*

Hare (hɛə) *n* a member of a Dene Native Canadian people of northern Canada [of Athaspascan origin]

hare and hounds *n (functioning as sing)* a game in which certain players (**hares**) run across country scattering pieces of paper that the other players (**hounds**) follow in an attempt to catch the hares

harebell ('hɛəˌbɛl) *n* a N temperate plant having slender stems and leaves, and bell-shaped blue flowers

harebrained *or* **hairbrained** ('hɛəˌbreɪnd) *adj* rash, foolish, or badly thought out

Hare Krishna ('hɑːrɪ 'krɪʃnə) *n* **1** a Hindu sect devoted to a form of Hinduism (**Krishna Consciousness**) based on the worship of the god Krishna **2** *(pl* **Hare Krishnas***)* a member or follower of this sect [c20 from Hindi, literally: Lord Krishna (vocative): the opening words of a sacred verse often chanted in public by adherents of the movement]

harelip ('hɛəˌlɪp) *n* a congenital fissure in the midline of the upper lip, resembling the cleft upper lip of a hare, often occurring with cleft palate > **'hareˌlipped** *adj*

harem ('hɛərəm, hɑː'riːm) *or* **hareem** (hɑː'riːm) *n* **1** the part of an Oriental house reserved strictly for wives, concubines, etc **2** a Muslim's wives and concubines collectively **3** a group of female animals that are the mates of a single male [c17 from Ar. *harīm* forbidden (place)]

hare's-foot *n* a plant that grows on sandy soils in Europe and NW Asia and has downy heads of white or pink flowers
Harfleur ('hɑːflɜː; *French* arflœr) *n* a port in N France, in the Seine-Maritime department: important centre in the Middle Ages. Pop: 9700 (latest est)
Hargeisa (hɑː'geɪsə) *n* a city in NW Somalia: former capital of British Somaliland (1941–60); trading centre for nomadic herders. Pop: 400 000 (latest est)
Hargreaves ('hɑːgriːvz) *n* **James** died 1778, English inventor of the spinning jenny
haricot ('hærɪkəʊ) *n* a variety of French bean with light-coloured edible seeds, which can be dried and stored [c17 from F, ?from Amerind]
Harijan ('hʌrɪdʒən) *n* a member of certain classes in India, formerly considered inferior and untouchable [Hindi, lit.: man of God (so called by Mahatma Gandhi)]
hari-kari (ˌhærɪ'kɑːrɪ) *n* a non-Japanese variant spelling of **hara-kiri**
Haringey ('hærɪŋˌgeɪ) *n* a borough of N Greater London. Pop: 216 510 (2001 est). Area: 30 sq km (12 sq miles)
hark (hɑːk) *vb* (*intr; usually imperative*) to listen; pay attention [OE *heorcnian* to HEARKEN]
hark back *vb* (*intr, adv*) to return to an earlier subject in speech or thought
harken ('hɑːkən) *vb* a variant spelling (esp US) of **hearken** > '**harkener** *n*
harl (hɑːl) *n angling* a variant of **herl**
Harlech ('hɑːlɪk) *n* a town in N Wales, in Gwynedd: noted for its ruined 13th-century castle overlooking Cardigan Bay: tourism. Pop: 1233 (1991)
Harlem ('hɑːləm) *n* a district of New York City, in NE Manhattan: now largely a Black ghetto
harlequin ('hɑːlɪkwɪn) *n* **1** (*sometimes cap*) *theatre* a stock comic character originating in the commedia dell'arte; the foppish lover of Columbine in the English harlequinade. He is usually represented in diamond-patterned multicoloured tights, wearing a black mask **2** a clown or buffoon ▷ *adj* **3** varied in colour or decoration **4** (of certain animals) having a white coat with patches of a dark colour [c16 from OF *Herlequin, Hellequin* leader of band of demon horsemen]
harlequinade (ˌhɑːlɪkwɪ'neɪd) *n* **1** (*sometimes cap*) *theatre* a play in which harlequin has a leading role **2** buffoonery
Harley ('hɑːlɪ) *n* **Robert,** 1st Earl of Oxford. 1661–1724, British statesman; head of the government (1710–14), negotiated the treaty of Utrecht (1713).
Harley Street *n* a street in central London famous for its large number of medical specialists' consulting rooms
harlot ('hɑːlət) *n* a prostitute [c13 from OF *herlot* rascal, from ?] > '**harlotry** *n*
Harlow[1] ('hɑːləʊ) *n* a town in SE England, in W Essex: designated a new town in 1947, with a planned population of 80 000. Pop: 74 629 (1991)
Harlow[2] ('hɑːləʊ) *n* **Jean,** real name *Harlean Carpentier*. 1911–37, US film actress, whose films include *Hell's Angels* (1930), *Red Dust* (1932), and *Bombshell* (1933)
harm (hɑːm) *n* **1** physical or mental injury **2** moral wrongdoing ▷ *vb* **3** (*tr*) to injure physically, morally, or mentally [OE *hearm*]
harmattan (hɑː'mætᵊn) *n* a dry dusty wind from the Sahara blowing towards the W African coast [c17 from native African language *haramata*, ?from Ar. *harām* forbidden thing; see HAREM]
harmful ('hɑːmfʊl) *adj* causing or tending to cause harm; injurious > '**harmfully** *adv*
harmless ('hɑːmlɪs) *adj* **1** not causing or tending to cause harm **2** unlikely to annoy or worry people: *a harmless sort of man* > '**harmlessly** *adv*
harmonic (hɑː'mɒnɪk) *adj* **1** of, producing, or characterized by harmony; harmonious **2** *music* of or belonging to harmony **3** *maths* **3a** capable of expression in the form of sine and cosine functions **3b** of or relating to numbers whose reciprocals form an arithmetic progression **4** *physics* of or concerned with a harmonic or harmonics ▷ *n* **5** *physics, music* a component of a periodic quantity, such as a musical tone, with a frequency that is an integral multiple of the fundamental frequency **6** *music* (not in technical use) overtone ▷ See also **harmonics** [c16 from L *harmonicus* relating to HARMONY] > **har'monically** *adv*
harmonica (hɑː'mɒnɪkə) *n* **1** Also called: **mouth organ** a small wind instrument in which reeds of graduated lengths set into a metal plate enclosed in a narrow oblong box are made to vibrate by blowing and sucking **2** See **glass harmonica** [c18 from L *harmonicus* relating to HARMONY]
harmonic analysis *n* the representation of a periodic function by means of the summation and integration of simple trigonometric functions
harmonic mean *n* the reciprocal of the arithmetic mean of the reciprocals of a set of specified numbers: the harmonic mean of 2, 3, and 4 is $3(\frac{1}{2} + \frac{1}{3} + \frac{1}{4})^{-1} = 36/13$
harmonic minor scale *n music* a minor scale modified from the natural by the sharpening of the seventh degree
harmonic motion *n* a periodic motion in which the displacement is symmetrical about a point or a periodic motion that is composed of such motions
harmonic progression *n* a sequence of numbers whose reciprocals form an arithmetic progression, as 1, ½, ⅓, ...
harmonics (hɑː'mɒnɪks) *n* **1** (*functioning as sing*) the science of musical sounds and their acoustic properties **2** (*functioning as pl*) the overtones of a fundamental note, as produced by lightly touching the string of a stringed instrument at one of its node points while playing
harmonic series *n* **1** *maths* a series whose terms are in harmonic progression, as in $1 + \frac{1}{2} + \frac{1}{3} + \ldots$ **2** *acoustics* the series of tones with frequencies strictly related to one another and to the fundamental tone, as obtained by touching lightly the node points of a string while playing it
harmonious (hɑː'məʊnɪəs) *adj* **1** (esp of colours or sounds) fitting together well **2** having agreement **3** tuneful or melodious
harmonist ('hɑːmənɪst) *n* **1** a person skilled in the art and techniques of harmony **2** a person who combines and collates parallel narratives
harmonium (hɑː'məʊnɪəm) *n* a musical keyboard instrument in which air from pedal-operated bellows causes the reeds to vibrate [c19 from F, from *harmonie* HARMONY]
harmonize *or* **harmonise** ('hɑːməˌnaɪz) *vb* **harmonizes, harmonizing, harmonized** *or* **harmonises, harmonising, harmonised** **1** to make or become harmonious **2** (*tr*) *music* to provide a harmony for (a tune, etc) **3** (*intr*) to sing in harmony, as with other singers **4** to collate parallel narratives > ˌ**harmoni'zation** *or* ˌ**harmoni'sation** *n*
harmony ('hɑːmənɪ) *n, pl* **harmonies** **1** agreement in action, opinion, feeling, etc **2** order or congruity of parts to their whole or to one another **3** agreeable sounds **4** *music* **4a** any combination of notes sounded simultaneously **4b** the vertically represented structure of a piece of music ▷ Cf **melody** (sense 1b) **4c** the art or science concerned with combinations of chords **5** a collation of parallel narratives, esp of the four Gospels [c14 from L *harmonia* concord of sounds, from Gk: harmony, from *harmos* a joint]
Harmsworth ('hɑːmzwɜːθ) *n* **1** **Alfred Charles William** See (Viscount) **Northcliffe** **2** **Harold Sydney** See (1st Viscount) **Rothermere**
harness ('hɑːnɪs) *n* **1** an arrangement of straps fitted to a draught animal in order that the animal can be attached to and pull a cart **2** something resembling

Hh

this, esp for attaching something to the body: *a parachute harness* **3** *weaving* the part of a loom that raises and lowers the warp threads **4** *arch* armour **5** **in harness** at one's routine work ▷ *vb (tr)* **6** to put a harness on (a horse) **7** (usually foll by *to*) to attach (a draught animal) to (a cart, etc) **8** to control so as to employ the energy or potential power of: *to harness the atom* **9** to equip with armour [c13 from OF *harneis* baggage, prob. from ON *hernest* (unattested), from *herr* army + *nest* provisions] > **ˈharnesser** *n*

harness race *n horse racing* a trotting or pacing race for horses pulling sulkies

Harney Peak (ˈhɑːnɪ) *n* a mountain in SW South Dakota: the highest peak in the Black Hills. Height: 2207 m (7242 ft)

Harnoncourt (*French* arnɔ̃kur) *n* **Nikolaus** born 1929, Austrian conductor and cellist, noted for his performances using period instruments

Harold I (ˈhærəld) *n* surname *Harefoot*. died 1040, king of England (1037–40); son of Canute

Harold II *n* ?1022–66, king of England (1066); son of Earl Godwin and successor of Edward the Confessor. His claim to the throne was disputed by William the Conqueror, who defeated him at the Battle of Hastings (1066)

harp (hɑːp) *n* **1** a large triangular plucked stringed instrument consisting of a soundboard connected to an upright pillar by means of a curved crossbar from which the strings extend downwards ▷ *vb (intr)* **2** to play the harp **3** (foll by *on* or *upon*) to speak or write in a persistent and tedious manner [OE *hearpe*] > **ˈharper** *or* **ˈharpist** *n*

Harper's Ferry (ˈhɑːpəz) *n* a village in NE West Virginia, at the confluence of the Potomac and Shenandoah Rivers: site of an arsenal seized by John Brown (1859). Pop: 308 (1990)

harpoon (hɑːˈpuːn) *n* **1a** a barbed missile attached to a long cord and hurled or fired from a gun when hunting whales, etc **1b** *(as modifier): a harpoon gun* ▷ *vb* **2** *(tr)* to spear with or as if with a harpoon [c17 prob. from Du. *harpoen*, from OF *harpon* clasp, ? of Scand. origin] > **harˈpooner** *or* **ˌharpoonˈeer** *n*

harp seal *n* a brownish-grey North Atlantic and Arctic seal, having a dark mark on its back

harpsichord (ˈhɑːpsɪˌkɔːd) *n* a horizontally strung stringed keyboard instrument, triangular in shape, with strings plucked by pivoted plectra mounted on jacks [c17 from NL *harpichordium*, from LL *harpa* HARP + L *chorda* CHORD[1]] > **ˈharpsiˌchordist** *n*

harpy (ˈhɑːpɪ) *n, pl* **harpies** a cruel grasping woman [c16 from L *Harpyia*, from Gk *Harpuiai* the Harpies, lit.: snatchers, from *harpazein* to seize]

Harpy (ˈhɑːpɪ) *n, pl* **Harpies** *Greek myth* a ravenous creature with a woman's head and trunk and a bird's wings and claws

harquebus (ˈhɑːkwɪbəs) *n, pl* **harquebuses** a variant spelling of **arquebus**

Harrer (ˈhɑːrə) *n* a variant spelling of **Harar**

harridan (ˈhærɪdᵊn) *n* a scolding old woman; nag [c17 from ?; ? rel. to F *haridelle*, lit.: broken-down horse]

harrier[1] (ˈhærɪə) *n* **1** a person or thing that harries **2** a diurnal bird of prey having broad wings and long legs and tail

harrier[2] (ˈhærɪə) *n* **1** a smallish breed of hound used originally for hare-hunting **2** a cross-country runner [c16 from HARE + -ER[1]; infl. by HARRIER[1]]

Harriman (ˈhærɪmən) *n* **W(illiam) Averell** 1891–1986, US diplomat: negotiated the Nuclear Test Ban Treaty with the Soviet Union (1963); governor of New York (1955–58)

Harris[1] (ˈhærɪs) *n* the S part of the island of Lewis with Harris, in the Outer Hebrides. Pop: (including Lewis) 23 390 (latest est). Area: 500 sq km (193 sq miles)

Harris[2] (ˈhærɪs) *n* **1** Sir **Arthur Travers,** known as *Bomber Harris*. 1892–1984, British air marshal. He was commander-in-chief of Bomber Command of the RAF (1942–45) **2** **Frank** 1856–1931, British writer and journalist; his books include his autobiography *My Life and Loves* (1923–27) and *Contemporary Portraits* (1915–30) **3** **Joel Chandler** 1848–1908, US writer; creator of Uncle Remus **4** **Roy** 1898–1979, US composer, esp of orchestral and choral music incorporating American folk tunes

Harrisburg (ˈhærɪsˌbɜːg) *n* a city in S Pennsylvania, on the Susquehanna River: the state capital. Pop: 53 430 (1992 est)

Harrison (ˈhærɪsᵊn) *n* **1** **Benjamin** 1833–1901, 23rd president of the US (1889–93) **2** **George** 1943–2001, British rock singer, guitarist, and songwriter: a member of the Beatles (1962–70) His solo recordings include *All Things Must Pass* (1970) and *Cloud Nine* (1987) **3** **Rex** (**Carey**) 1908–90, British actor. His many films include *Major Barbara* (1940), *Blithe Spirit* (1945), and *My Fair Lady* (1964) **4** **Tony** born 1937, British poet, dramatist, and translator: best known for his poems for television and his translations for the stage **5** grandfather of Benjamin, **William Henry** 1773–1841, 9th president of the US (1841)

Harris Tweed *n trademark* a loose-woven tweed made in the Outer Hebrides

Harrogate (ˈhærəgɪt) *n* a town in N England, in North Yorkshire: a former spa, now a centre for tourism and conferences. Pop: 66 178 (1991)

harrow (ˈhærəʊ) *n* **1** any of various implements used to level the ground, stir the soil, break up clods, destroy weeds, etc, in soil ▷ *vb (tr)* **2** to draw a harrow over (land) **3** to distress; vex [c13 from ON] > **ˈharrower** *n* > **ˈharrowing** *adj*

Harrow (ˈhærəʊ) *n* a borough of NW Greater London; site of an English boys' public school founded in 1571 at **Harrow-on-the-Hill,** a part of this borough. Pop: 207 389 (2001). Area: 51 sq km (20 sq miles)

harrumph (həˈrʌmf) *vb (intr) chiefly US & Canad* to clear or make the noise of clearing the throat

harry (ˈhærɪ) *vb* **harries, harrying, harried** **1** *(tr)* to harass; worry **2** to ravage (a town, etc), esp in war [OE *hergian*; rel. to *here* army, ON *herja* to lay waste]

harsh (hɑːʃ) *adj* **1** rough or grating to the senses **2** stern, severe, or cruel [c16 prob. of Scand. origin] > **ˈharshly** *adv* > **ˈharshness** *n*

hart (hɑːt) *n, pl* **harts** *or* **hart** the male of the deer, esp the red deer aged five years or more [OE *heorot*]

Hart (hɑːt) *n* **1** **Lorenz** 1895–1943, US lyricist: collaborated with Richard Rodgers in writing musicals **2** **Moss** 1904–61, US dramatist: collaborated with George Kaufman on Broadway comedies and wrote libretti for musicals

hartal (hɑːˈtɑːl) *n* (in India) the act of closing shops or suspending work, esp in political protest [c20 from Hindi *hartāl*, from *hāt* shop + *tālā* bolt for a door, from Sansk.]

Harte (hɑːt) *n* (**Francis**) **Bret** 1836–1902, US poet and short-story writer, noted for his sketches of Californian gold miners, such as *The Luck of Roaring Camp* (1870)

hartebeest (ˈhɑːtɪˌbiːst) *or* **hartbeest** (ˈhɑːtˌbiːst) *n* either of two large African antelopes having an elongated muzzle, lyre-shaped horns, and a fawn-coloured coat [c18 via Afrik. from Du.; see HART, BEAST]

Hartford (ˈhɑːtfəd) *n* a port in central Connecticut, on the Connecticut River: the state capital. Pop: 121 578 (2000)

Harthacanute (ˈhɑːθəkəˌnjuːt), **Hardecanute**, *or* **Hardicanute** *n* ?1019–42, king of Denmark (1035–42) and of England (1040–42); son of Canute

Hartington (ˈhɑːtɪŋtən) *n* **Lord** See (8th Duke of) **Devonshire**

Hartlepool (ˈhɑːtlɪˌpuːl) *n* **1** a port in NE England, in Hartlepool unitary authority, Co. Durham, on the North

Sea: greatly enlarged in 1967 by its amalgamation with West Hartlepool; engineering, clothing, food processing. Pop: 87 310 (1991) **2** a unitary authority in NE England, in Co. Durham: formerly (1974–96) part of the county of Cleveland. Pop: 88 629 (2001). Area: 93 sq km (36 sq miles)

Hartley ('hɑːtlɪ) *n* **1 David** 1705–57, English philosopher and physician. In *Observations of Man* (1749) he introduced the theory of psychological associationism **2 L(eslie) P(oles)** 1895–1972, British novelist. His novels include the trilogy *The Shrimp and the Anemone* (1944), *The Sixth Heaven* (1946), and *Eustace and Hilda* (1947) as well as *The Go-Between* (1953)

Hartnell ('hɑːtnᵊl) *n* Sir **Norman** 1901–79, English couturier

hartshorn ('hɑːtsˌhɔːn) *n* an obsolete name for **sal volatile** [OE *heortes horn* hart's horn (formerly a chief source of ammonia)]

hart's-tongue *n* an evergreen Eurasian fern with narrow undivided fronds

harum-scarum ('hɛərəm'skɛərəm) *adj, adv* **1** in a reckless way or of a reckless nature ▷ *n* **2** a person who is impetuous or rash [C17 ?from *hare* (in obs. sense: harass) + *scare*, var. of STARE]

Harun al-Rashid (hæ'ruːn ælræ'ʃiːd) *n* ?763–809 AD, Abbasid caliph of Islam (786–809), whose court at Baghdad was idealized in the *Arabian Nights*

haruspex (hə'rʌspɛks) *n, pl* **haruspices** (hə'rʌspɪˌsiːz) (in ancient Rome) a priest who practised divination, esp by examining the entrails of animals [C16 from L, prob. from *hīra* gut + *specere* to look] > **haruspicy** (hə'rʌspɪsɪ) *n*

harvest ('hɑːvɪst) *n* **1** the gathering of a ripened crop **2** the crop itself **3** the season for gathering crops **4** the product of an effort, action, etc: *a harvest of love* ▷ *vb* **5** to gather (a ripened crop) from (the place where it has been growing) **6** (*tr*) to receive (consequences) [OE *hærfest*] > '**harvesting** *n*

harvester ('hɑːvɪstə) *n* **1** a person who harvests **2** a harvesting machine, esp a combine harvester

harvest home *n* **1** the bringing in of the harvest **2** *chiefly Brit* a harvest supper

harvestman ('hɑːvɪstmən) *n, pl* **harvestmen 1** a person engaged in harvesting **2** Also called (US and Canad): **daddy-longlegs** an arachnid having a small rounded body and very long thin legs

harvest moon *n* the full moon occurring nearest to the autumnal equinox

harvest mouse *n* a very small reddish-brown Eurasian mouse, *Micromys minutus*, inhabiting cornfields, hedgerows, etc, and feeding on grain and seeds

Harvey ('hɑːvɪ) *n* **William** 1578–1657, English physician who discovered the mechanism of blood circulation, expounded in *On the motion of the heart* (1628)

Harwell ('hɑːˌwɛl) *n* a village in S England, in Oxfordshire: atomic research station (1947)

Harwich ('hærɪtʃ) *n* a port in SE England, in NE Essex on the North Sea. Pop: 18 436 (1991)

Haryana (hɜː'jɑːnə) *n* a state of NE India, formed in 1966 from the Hindi-speaking parts of the state of Punjab. Capital: Chandigarh (shared with Punjab). Pop: 21 082 989 (2001 est). Area: 44 506 sq km (17 182 sq miles)

Harz *or* **Harz Mountains** (hɑːts) *pl n* a range of wooded hills in central Germany, between the Rivers Weser and Elbe: source of many legends. Highest peak: Brocken, 1142 m (3746 ft)

has (hæz) *vb* (used with *he, she, it*, or a singular noun) a form of the present tense (indicative mood) of **have**

has-been *n inf* a person or thing that is no longer popular, successful, effective, etc

hasbian ('hæzbɪən) *n* a former lesbian who has become heterosexual or bisexual [C20 HAS-BEEN + LESBIAN]

Hasdrubal ('hæzdrʊbᵊl) *n* died 207 BC, Carthaginian general: commanded the Carthaginian army in Spain (218–211); joined his brother Hannibal in Italy and was killed at the Metaurus

Hašek (*Czech* 'haʃɛk) *n* **Jaroslav** ('jarɔslaf) 1883–1923, Czech novelist and short-story writer; author of *The Good Soldier Schweik* (1923)

hash[1] (hæʃ) *n* **1** a dish of diced cooked meat, vegetables, etc, reheated in a sauce **2** a reuse or rework of old material **3 make a hash of** *inf* to mess up or destroy **4 settle someone's hash** *inf* to subdue or silence someone ▷ *vb (tr)* **5** to chop into small pieces **6** to mess up [C17 from OF *hacher* to chop up, from *hache* HATCHET]

hash[2] (hæʃ) *n sl* short for **hashish**

Hashemite Kingdom of Jordan ('hæʃɪˌmaɪt) *n* the official name of **Jordan**

hashish ('hæʃiːʃ, -ɪʃ) *or* **hasheesh** *n* a resinous extract of the dried flower tops of the female hemp plant, used as a hallucinogenic. See also **cannabis** [C16 from Ar. *hashīsh* hemp]

haslet ('hæzlɪt) *or* **harslet** *n* a loaf of cooked minced pig's offal, eaten cold [C14 from OF *hastelet* piece of spit-roasted meat, from *haste* spit, of Gmc origin]

hasn't ('hæzᵊnt) *contraction of* has not

hasp (hɑːsp) *n* **1** a metal fastening consisting of a hinged strap with a slot that fits over a staple and is secured by a pin, bolt, or padlock ▷ *vb* **2** (*tr*) to secure (a door, window, etc) with a hasp [OE *hæpse*]

Hassan II (hæ'sɑːn, 'hæsᵊn) *n* 1929–99, king of Morocco (1961–99)

Hasselt (*Flemish* 'hɑsəlt; *French* asɛlt) *n* a market town in E Belgium, capital of Limbourg province. Pop: 67 486 (1995 est)

Hassid ('hæsɪd) *n* a variant spelling of **Chassid**

hassium ('hæsɪəm) *n* a synthetic element produced in small quantities by high-energy ion bombardment. Symbol: Hs; atomic no. 108. Former name: **hahnium** [C20 from L, from HESSE[1], German state where it was discovered]

hassle ('hæsᵊl) *inf* ▷ *n* **1** a great deal of trouble **2** a prolonged argument ▷ *vb* **hassles, hassling, hassled 3** (*tr*) to cause annoyance or trouble to (someone); harass **4** (*intr*) to quarrel or wrangle [C20 from ?]

hassock ('hæsək) *n* **1** a firm upholstered cushion used for kneeling on, esp in church **2** a thick clump of grass [OE *hassuc* matted grass]

hast (hæst) *vb arch or dialect* (used with the pronoun *thou*) a singular form of the present tense (indicative mood) of **have**

hastate ('hæsteɪt) *adj* (of a leaf) having a pointed tip and two outward-pointing lobes at the base [C18 from L *hastātus*, from *hasta* spear]

haste (heɪst) *n* **1** speed, esp in an action **2** the act of hurrying in a careless manner **3** a necessity for hurrying; urgency **4 make haste** to hurry ▷ *vb* **hastes, hasting, hasted 5** a poetic word for **hasten** [C14 from OF *haste*, of Gmc origin]

hasten ('heɪsᵊn) *vb* **1** (*may take an infinitive*) to hurry or cause to hurry; rush **2** (*tr*) to be anxious (to say something) > '**hastener** *n*

Hastings[1] ('heɪstɪŋz) *n* **1** a port in SE England, in East Sussex on the English Channel: near the site of the **Battle of Hastings** (1066), in which William the Conqueror defeated King Harold; chief of the Cinque Ports. Pop: 81 139 (1991) **2** a town in New Zealand, on E North Island: centre of a rich agricultural and fruit-growing region. Pop (urban area): 58 700 (1995 est)

Hastings[2] ('heɪstɪŋz) *n* **1 Gavin** born 1962, Scottish Rugby Union footballer; played for Scotland 1986–95 **2 Warren** 1732–1818, British administrator in India; governor general of Bengal (1773–85) He implemented important reforms but was impeached by parliament (1788) on charges of corruption; acquitted in 1795

hasty ('heɪstɪ) *adj* **hastier, hastiest 1** rapid; swift; quick **2** excessively or rashly quick **3** short-tempered

Hh

4 showing irritation or anger: *hasty words* > 'hastily *adv* > 'hastiness *n*

hat (hæt) *n* 1 a head covering, esp one with a brim and a shaped crown 2 *inf* a role or capacity 3 **I'll eat my hat** *inf* I will be greatly surprised if (something that proves me wrong) happens 4 **keep (something) under one's hat** to keep (something) secret 5 **pass** (*or* **send**) **the hat round** to collect money, as for a cause 6 **take off one's hat to** to admire or congratulate 7 **talk through one's hat** 7a to talk foolishly 7b to deceive or bluff ▷ *vb* **hats, hatting, hatted** 8 (*tr*) to supply (a person, etc) with a hat or put a hat on (someone) [OE *hætt*] > '**hatless** *adj*

▷ www.thehatsite.com

▷ www.hatsuk.com

hatband ('hæt,bænd) *n* a band or ribbon around the base of the crown of a hat

hatbox ('hæt,bɒks) *n* a box or case for a hat

hatch[1] (hætʃ) *vb* 1 to cause (the young of various animals, esp birds) to emerge from the egg or (of young birds, etc) to emerge from the egg 2 to cause (eggs) to break and release the fully developed young or (of eggs) to break and release the young animal within 3 (*tr*) to contrive or devise (a scheme, plot, etc) ▷ *n* 4 the act or process of hatching 5 a group of newly hatched animals [C13 of Gmc origin]

hatch[2] (hætʃ) *n* 1 a covering for a hatchway 2a short for **hatchway** 2b a door in an aircraft or spacecraft 3 Also called: **serving hatch** an opening in a wall separating a kitchen from a dining area 4 the lower half of a divided door 5 a sluice in a dam, dyke, or weir 6 **down the hatch** *sl* (used as a toast) drink up! 7 **under hatches** 7a below decks 7b out of sight 7c dead [OE *hæcc*]

hatch[3] (hætʃ) *vb drawing, engraving, etc* to mark (a figure, etc) with fine parallel or crossed lines to indicate shading [C15 from OF *hacher* to chop, from *hache* HATCHET] > '**hatching** *n*

hatch[4] (hætʃ) *n inf* short for **hatchback**

hatchback ('hætʃ,bæk) *n* 1 a sloping rear end of a car having a single door that is lifted to open 2 a car having such a rear end

hatchery ('hætʃərɪ) *n, pl* **hatcheries** a place where eggs are hatched under artificial conditions

hatchet ('hætʃɪt) *n* 1 a short axe used for chopping wood, etc 2 a tomahawk 3 (*modifier*) of narrow dimensions and sharp features: *a hatchet face* 4 **bury the hatchet** to cease hostilities and become reconciled [C14 from OF *hachette*, from *hache* axe, of Gmc origin]

hatchet job *n inf* a malicious or devastating verbal or written attack

hatchet man *n inf* 1 a person carrying out unpleasant assignments for an employer or superior 2 a severe or malicious critic

hatchling ('hætʃlɪŋ) *n* a young animal that has newly emerged from the egg [C19 from HATCH[1] + -LING[1]]

hatchment ('hætʃmənt) *n heraldry* a diamond-shaped tablet displaying the coat of arms of a dead person [C16 changed from earlier use of *achievement* in this sense]

hatchway ('hætʃ,weɪ) *n* 1 an opening in the deck of a vessel to provide access below 2 a similar opening in a wall, floor, ceiling, or roof

hate (heɪt) *vb* **hates, hating, hated** 1 to dislike (something) intensely; detest 2 (*intr*) to be unwilling (to be or do something) ▷ *n* 3 intense dislike 4 *inf* a person or thing that is hated (esp in **pet hate**) 5 (*modifier*) expressing or arousing feelings of hatred: *hate mail* [OE *hatian*] > '**hateable** *or* '**hatable** *adj* > '**hater** *n*

hate crime *n* a crime, esp of violence, in which the victim is targeted because of his or her race, religion, sexuality, etc

hateful ('heɪtfʊl) *adj* 1 causing or deserving hate; loathsome; detestable 2 *arch* full of hate > '**hatefully** *adv* > '**hatefulness** *n*

Hatfield ('hæt,fi:ld) *n* a market town in S central England, in Hertfordshire, with a new town of the same name built on the outskirts: university (1992); site of **Hatfield House** (1607–11), the seat of the Cecil family. Pop: 31 104 (1991)

hath (hæθ) *vb arch or dialect* (used with the pronouns *he*, *she*, or *it* or a singular noun) a form of the present tense (indicative mood) of **have**

Hathaway ('hæθə,weɪ) *n* **Anne** ?1557–1623, wife of William Shakespeare

Hathor ('hæθɔ:) *n* (in ancient Egyptian religion) the mother of Horus and goddess of creation > **Hathoric** (hæ'θɔ:rɪk, -'θɒr-) *adj*

hatred ('heɪtrɪd) *n* intense dislike; enmity

Hatshepsut (hæt'ʃɛpsu:t) *or* **Hatshepset** *n* queen of Egypt of the 18th dynasty (?1512–1482 BC). She built a great mortuary temple at Deir el Bahri near Thebes

hat stand *or esp US* **hat tree** *n* a pole equipped with hooks for hanging up hats, etc

hatter ('hætə) *n* 1 a person who makes and sells hats 2 **mad as a hatter** eccentric

Hatteras ('hætərəs) *n* **Cape** a promontory off the E coast of North Carolina, on **Hatteras Island**, which is situated between Pamlico Sound and the Atlantic: known as the "Graveyard of the Atlantic" for its danger to shipping

Hattersley ('hætəzlɪ) *n* **Roy** (**Sydney George**), Baron Hattersley of Sparkbrook. born 1932, British Labour politician; deputy leader of the Labour Party (1983–92); shadow home secretary (1980–83; 1987–92)

hat trick *n* 1 *cricket* the achievement of a bowler in taking three wickets with three successive balls 2 any achievement of three successive points, victories, etc

hauberk ('hɔ:bɜ:k) *n* a long coat of mail, often sleeveless [C13 from OF *hauberc*, of Gmc origin; cf. OHG *halsberc*, OE *healsbeorg*, from *heals* neck + *beorg* protection]

Haughey ('hɔ:xɪ; *Irish* 'hʌhi:) *n* **Charles James** born 1925, Irish politician; leader of the Fianna Fáil party; prime minister of the Republic of Ireland (1979–81; 1982; 1987–92)

haughty ('hɔ:tɪ) *adj* **haughtier, haughtiest** having or showing arrogance [C16 from OF *haut* lofty, from L *altus* high] > '**haughtily** *adv* > '**haughtiness** *n*

haul (hɔ:l) *vb* 1 to drag (something) with effort 2 (*tr*) to transport, as in a lorry 3 *naut* to alter the course of (a vessel), esp so as to sail closer to the wind 4 (*intr*) *naut* (of the wind) to blow from a direction nearer the bow ▷ *n* 5 the act of dragging with effort 6 (esp of fish) the amount caught at a single time 7 something that is hauled 8 the goods obtained from a robbery 9 a distance of hauling or travelling 10 the amount of a contraband seizure: *arms haul*; *drugs haul* [C16 from OF *haler*, of Gmc origin] > '**hauler** *n*

haulage ('hɔ:lɪdʒ) *n* 1 the act or labour of hauling 2 a charge levied for the transport of goods, esp by rail

haulier ('hɔ:ljə) *n* 1 *Brit* a person or firm that transports goods by road 2 a mine worker who conveys coal from the workings to the foot of the shaft

haulm *or* **halm** (hɔ:m) *n* 1 the stalks of beans, peas, potatoes, grasses, etc, collectively 2 a single stem of such a plant [OE *healm*]

haul up *vb* (*adv*) 1 (*tr*) *inf* to call to account or criticize 2 *naut* to sail (a vessel) closer to the wind

haunch (hɔ:ntʃ) *n* 1 the human hip or fleshy hindquarter of an animal 2 the leg and loin of an animal, used for food 3 *archit* the part of an arch between the impost and apex [C13 from OF *hanche*; rel. to Sp., It. *anca*, of Gmc origin]

haunt (hɔ:nt) *vb* 1 to visit (a person or place) in the form of a ghost 2 (*tr*) to recur to (the memory, thoughts, etc): *he was haunted by the fear of insanity* 3 to visit (a place) frequently 4 to associate with (someone) frequently ▷ *n* 5 (*often pl*) a place visited frequently 6 a place to which animals habitually resort for food, drink, shelter, etc [C13 from OF *hanter*, of Gmc origin]

haunted ('hɔːntɪd) *adj* **1** frequented or visited by ghosts **2** (*postpositive*) obsessed or worried

haunting ('hɔːntɪŋ) *adj* **1** (of memories) poignant or persistent **2** poignantly sentimental; eerily evocative ▷ '**hauntingly** *adv*

Hauptmann (*German* 'haʊptman) *n* **Gerhart** ('geːrhart) 1862–1946, German naturalist, dramatist, novelist, and poet. His works include the historical drama *The Weavers* (1892): Nobel prize for literature 1912

Hauraki Gulf (haʊ'rækɪ) *n* an inlet of the Pacific in New Zealand, on the N coast of North Island

Hausa ('haʊsə) *n* **1** (*pl* **Hausas** *or* **Hausa**) a member of a Negroid people of W Africa, living chiefly in N Nigeria **2** the language of this people, widely used as a trading language throughout W Africa

hausfrau ('haʊsˌfraʊ) *n* a German housewife [G, from *Haus* house + *Frau* woman, wife]

Haussmann (*French* osman) *n* **Georges-Eugène,** Baron. 1809–91, French town planner, noted for his major rebuilding of Paris in the reign of Napoleon III

hautboy ('əʊbɔɪ) *n* **1** a strawberry with large fruit **2** an archaic word for **oboe** [c16 from F *hautbois*, from *haut* high + *bois* wood, of Gmc origin]

haute couture *French* (ot kutyr) *n* high fashion [lit.: high dressmaking]

haute cuisine *French* (ot kɥizin) *n* high-class cooking [lit.: high cookery]

haute école *French* (ot ekɔl) *n* the classical art of riding [lit.: high school]

Haute-Garonne (*French* otgarɔn) *n* a department of SW France, in Midi-Pyrénées region. Capital: Toulouse. Pop: 1 046 338 (1999). Area: 6367 sq km (2483 sq miles)

Haute-Loire (*French* otlwar) *n* a department of S central France, in Auvergne region. Capital: Le Puy. Pop: 209 113 (1999). Area: 5001 sq km (1950 sq miles)

Haute-Marne (*French* otmarn) *n* a department of NE France, in Champagne-Ardenne region. Capital: Chaumont. Pop: 194 873 (1999). Area: 6257 sq km (2440 sq miles)

Haute-Normandie (*French* otnɔrmɑ̃di) *n* a region of NW France, on the English Channel: generally fertile and flat

Hautes-Alpes (*French* otzalp) *n* a department of SE France in Provence-Alpes-Côte d'Azur region. Capital: Gap. Pop: 121 419 (1999). Area: 5643 sq km (2201 sq miles)

Haute-Saône (*French* otson) *n* a department of E France, in Franche-Comté region. Capital: Vesoul. Pop: 229 732 (1999). Area: 5375 sq km (2096 sq miles)

Haute-Savoie (*French* otsavwa) *n* a department of E France, in Rhône-Alpes region. Capital: Annecy. Pop: 631 679 (1999). Area: 4958 sq km (1934 sq miles)

Hautes-Pyrénées (*French* otpirene) *n* a department of SW France, in Midi-Pyrénées region. Capital: Tarbes. Pop: 222 368 (1999). Area: 4534 sq km (1768 sq miles)

hauteur (əʊ'tɜː) *n* pride; haughtiness [c17 from F, from *haut* high; see HAUGHTY]

Haute-Vienne (*French* otvjɛn) *n* a department of W central France, in Limousin region. Capital: Limoges. Pop: 353 893 (1999). Area: 5555 sq km (2166 sq miles)

haut monde *French* (o mɔ̃d) *n* high society [lit.: high world]

Haut-Rhin (*French* orɛ̃) *n* a department of E France in Alsace region. Capital: Colmar. Pop: 708 025 (1999). Area: 3566 sq km (1377 sq miles)

Hauts-de-Seine (*French* odəsɛn) *n* a department of N central France, in Île-de-France region just west of Paris: formed in 1964. Capital: Nanterre. Pop: 1 428 238 (1999). Area: 175 sq km (68 sq miles)

Havana (hə'vænə) *n* the capital of Cuba, a port in the northwest on the Gulf of Mexico: the largest city in the Caribbean; founded in 1514 as San Cristóbal de la Habana by Diego Velásquez. Pop: 2 198 392 (1994 est). Spanish name: **Habana** Related adjective: **Habanero**

Havana cigar *n* any of various cigars manufactured in Cuba, known esp for their high quality. Also: **Havana**

Havant ('hævᵊnt) *n* a market town in S England, in SE Hampshire. Pop: 46 510 (1991)

have (hæv) *vb* **has, having, had** (*mainly tr*) **1** to be in possession of; own: *he has two cars* **2** to possess as a quality or attribute: *he has dark hair* **3** to receive, take, or obtain: *she had a present; have a look* **4** to hold in the mind: *to have an idea* **5** to possess a knowledge of: *I have no German* **6** to experience: *to have a shock* **7** to suffer from: *to have a cold* **8** to gain control of or advantage over: *you have me on that point* **9** (*usually passive*) *sl* to cheat or outwit: *he was had by that dishonest salesman* **10** (foll by *on*) to exhibit (mercy, etc, towards) **11** to take part in: *to have a conversation* **12** to arrange or hold: *to have a party* **13** to cause, compel, or require to (be, do, or be done): *have my shoes mended* **14** (takes an infinitive with *to*) used as an auxiliary to express compulsion or necessity: *I had to run quickly to escape him* **15** to eat, drink, or partake of **16** *sl* to have sexual intercourse with **17** (*used with a negative*) to tolerate or allow: *I won't have all this noise* **18** to state or assert: *rumour has it that they will marry* **19** to place: *I'll have the sofa in this room* **20** to receive as a guest: *to have people to stay* **21** to be pregnant with or bear (offspring) **22** (*takes a past participle*) used as an auxiliary to form compound tenses expressing completed action: *I have gone; I had gone* **23** **had rather** *or* **sooner** to consider preferable that: *I had rather you left at once* **24** **have had it** *inf* **24a** to be exhausted, defeated, or killed **24b** to have lost one's last chance **24c** to become unfashionable **25** **have it away** *or* **off** *Brit sl* to have sexual intercourse **26** **have it so good** to have so many material benefits **27** **have to do with** **27a** to have dealings with **27b** to be of relevance to **28** **let someone have it** *sl* to launch an attack on someone ▷ *n* **29** (*usually pl*) *inf* a person or group in possession of wealth, security, etc: *the haves and the have-nots* ▷ See also **have at, have on,** etc [OE *habban*]

have-a-go *adj inf* (of members of the public at the scene of a crime) intervening physically in an attempt to catch or thwart a criminal, esp one who is armed: *a have-a-go pensioner*

have at *vb* (*intr, prep*) *arch* to make an opening attack on, esp in fencing

Havel[1] (*German* 'haːfəl) *n* a river in E Germany, flowing south to Berlin, then west and north to join the River Elbe. Length: about 362 km (225 miles)

Havel[2] (*Czech* 'havɛl) *n* **Václav** ('vʌtslav) born 1936, Czech dramatist and statesman: founder of the Civil Forum movement for political change: president of Czechoslovakia (1989–92); president of the Czech Republic (1993–2003). His plays include *The Garden Party* (1963) and *Redevelopment* (1989)

havelock ('hævlɒk) *n* a light-coloured cover for a service cap with a flap extending over the back of the neck to protect the head and neck from the sun [c19 after Sir H. *Havelock* (1795–1857), E general in India]

haven ('heɪvᵊn) *n* **1** a harbour or other sheltered place for shipping **2** a place of safety; shelter ▷ *vb* **3** (*tr*) to shelter as in a haven [OE *hæfen*, from ON *höfn*]

have-not *n* (*usually pl*) a person or group in possession of relatively little material wealth

haven't ('hævᵊnt) *contraction of* have not

have on *vb* (*tr*) **1** (*usually adv*) to wear **2** (*usually adv*) to have a commitment: *what does your boss have on this afternoon?* **3** (*adv*) *inf* to trick or tease (a person) **4** (*prep*) to have available (information, esp when incriminating) about (a person)

have out *vb* (*tr, adv*) **1** to settle (a matter) or come to (a final decision), esp by fighting or by frank discussion (often in **have it out**) **2** to have extracted or removed

haver ('heɪvə) *vb* (*intr*) **1** *Scot & N English dialect* to babble; talk nonsense **2** to dither ▷ *n* **3** (*usually pl*) *Scot* nonsense [c18 from ?]

Hh

Havering (ˈheɪvərɪŋ) *n* a borough of NE Greater London, formed in 1965 from Romford and Hornchurch (both previously in Essex). Pop: 224 248 (2001). Area: 120 sq km (46 sq miles)

haversack (ˈhævəˌsæk) *n* a canvas bag for provisions or equipment, carried on the back or shoulder [c18 from F *havresac*, from G *Habersack* oat bag, from OHG *habaro* oats + *Sack* SACK[1]]

haversine (ˈhævəˌsaɪn) *n* half the value of the versed sine [c19 combination of *half* + *versed* + *sine*[1]]

have up *vb* (*tr, adv; usually passive*) to cause to appear for trial: *he was had up for breaking and entering*

havildar (ˈhævɪlˌdɑː) *n* a noncommissioned officer in the Indian army, equivalent in rank to sergeant [c17 from Hindi, from Persian *hawāldār* one in charge]

havoc (ˈhævək) *n* **1** destruction; devastation; ruin **2** *inf* confusion; chaos **3** **cry havoc** *arch* to give the signal for pillage and destruction **4** **play havoc** (often foll by *with*) to cause a great deal of damage, distress, or confusion (to) [c15 from OF *havot* pillage, prob. of Gmc origin]

Havre (ˈhɑːvrə; *French* avrə) *n* See **Le Havre**

haw[1] (hɔː) *n* **1** the fruit of the hawthorn **2** another name for **hawthorn** [OE *haga*, identical with *haga* hedge]

haw[2] (hɔː) *n, interj* **1** an inarticulate utterance, as of hesitation, embarrassment, etc; hem ▷ *vb* **2** (*intr*) to make this sound [c17 imit.]

haw[3] (hɔː) *n* the nictitating membrane of a horse or other domestic animal [c15 from ?]

Hawaii (həˈwaɪɪ) *n* a state of the US in the central Pacific, consisting of over 20 volcanic islands and atolls, including Hawaii, Maui, Oahu, Kauai, and Molokai: discovered by Captain Cook in 1778; annexed by the US in 1898; naval base at Pearl Harbor attacked by the Japanese in 1941, a major cause of US entry into World War II; became a state in 1959. Capital: Honolulu. Pop: 1 211 537 (2000). Area: 16 640 sq km (6425 sq miles). Former name: **Sandwich Islands** Abbreviations: **Ha.** or (with zip code) **HI**

Hawaiian (həˈwaɪən) *adj* **1** of or relating to Hawaii, its people, or their language ▷ *n* **2** a native or inhabitant of Hawaii, esp one descended from Melanesian or Tahitian immigrants **3** a language of Hawaii belonging to the Malayo-Polynesian family

Hawaiki (ˈhɑːwaɪkiː) *n* NZ a legendary Pacific island from which the Maoris migrated to New Zealand by canoe [Maori]

Hawes Water (hɔːz) *n* a lake in NW England, in the Lake District: provides part of Manchester's water supply; extended by damming from 4 km (2.5 miles) to 6 km (4 miles)

hawfinch (ˈhɔːˌfɪntʃ) *n* an uncommon European finch having a very stout bill

Haw-Haw (ˈhɔːˌhɔː) *n* **Lord** See (William) **Joyce**

Hawick (ˈhɔːɪk) *n* a town in SE Scotland, in S central Scottish Borders: knitwear industry. Pop: 15 812 (1991)

hawk[1] (hɔːk) *n* **1** any of various diurnal birds of prey of the family Accipitridae, typically having short rounded wings and a long tail **2** a person who advocates or supports war or warlike policies ▷ Cf **dove** (sense 2) **3** a ruthless or rapacious person ▷ *vb* **4** (*intr*) to hunt with falcons, hawks, etc **5** (*intr*) (of falcons or hawks) to fly in quest of prey **6** to pursue or attack on the wing, as a hawk [OE *hafoc*] > ˈ**hawking** *n* > ˈ**hawkish** *adj* > ˈ**hawk**ˌ**like** *adj*

hawk[2] (hɔːk) *vb* **1** to offer (goods) for sale, as in the street **2** (*tr; often foll by about*) to spread (news, gossip, etc) [c16 back formation from HAWKER[1]]

hawk[3] (hɔːk) *vb* **1** (*intr*) to clear the throat noisily **2** (*tr*) to force (phlegm, etc) up from the throat [c16 imit.]

hawk[4] (hɔːk) *n* a small square board with a handle underneath, for carrying wet mortar. Also called: **mortarboard** [from ?]

Hawke (hɔːk) *n* **1** **Edward, 1st Baron.** 1705–81, British admiral. He destroyed the French fleet in Quiberon Bay (1759), preventing a French invasion of England **2** **Robert** (**James Lee**), known as *Bob*. born 1929, Australian statesman; prime minister of Australia (1983–91)

hawker[1] (ˈhɔːkə) *n* a person who travels from place to place selling goods [c16 prob. from MLow G *hōker*, from *hōken* to peddle; see HUCKSTER]

hawker[2] (ˈhɔːkə) *n* a person who hunts with hawks, falcons, etc [OE *hafecere*]

hawk-eyed *adj* **1** having extremely keen sight **2** vigilant, watchful, or observant

Hawking (ˈhɔːkɪŋ) *n* **Stephen William** born 1942, British physicist. Stricken with a progressive nervous disease since the 1960s, he has nevertheless been a leader in cosmological theory. His *A Brief History of Time* (1987) was a bestseller

Hawkins (ˈhɔːkɪnz) *n* **1** **Coleman** 1904–69, US pioneer of the tenor saxophone for jazz **2** Sir **John** 1532–95, English naval commander and slave trader, treasurer of the navy (1577–89); commander of a squadron in the fleet that defeated the Spanish Armada (1588)

hawk moth *n* any of various moths having long narrow wings and powerful flight, with the ability to hover over flowers when feeding from the nectar

Hawks (hɔːks) *n* **Howard** (**Winchester**) 1896–1977, US film director. His films include *Sergeant York* (1941) and *The Big Sleep* (1946)

hawksbill turtle *or* **hawksbill** (ˈhɔːksˌbɪl) *n* a small tropical turtle with a hooked beaklike mouth: a source of tortoiseshell

Hawksmoor (ˈhɔːksˌmɔː) *n* **Nicholas** 1661–1736, English architect. His designs include All Souls', Oxford, and a number of London churches, notably St Anne's, Limehouse

hawkweed (ˈhɔːkˌwiːd) *n* a hairy plant with clusters of dandelion-like flowers

Haworth[1] (ˈhaʊəθ) *n* a village in N England, in Bradford unitary authority, West Yorkshire: home of Charlotte, Emily, and Anne Brontë. Pop: 4956 (1991)

Haworth[2] (ˈhaʊəθ) *n* Sir **Walter Norman** 1883–1950, British biochemist, who shared the Nobel prize for chemistry (1937) for being the first to synthesize ascorbic acid (vitamin C)

hawse (hɔːz) *n* *naut* **1** the part of the bows of a vessel where the hawseholes are **2** short for **hawsehole** or **hawsepipe** **3** the distance from the bow of an anchored vessel to the anchor **4** the arrangement of port and starboard anchor ropes when a vessel is riding on both anchors [c14 from earlier *halse*, prob. from ON *háls* neck, ship's bow]

hawsehole (ˈhɔːzˌhəʊl) *n* *naut* one of the holes in the upper part of the bows of a vessel through which the anchor ropes pass

hawsepipe (ˈhɔːzˌpaɪp) *n* *naut* a strong metal pipe through which an anchor rope passes

hawser (ˈhɔːzə) *n* *naut* a large heavy rope [c14 from Anglo-F *hauceour*, from OF *haucier* to hoist, ult. from L *altus* high]

hawthorn (ˈhɔːˌθɔːn) *n* any of various thorny trees or shrubs of a N temperate genus, having white or pink flowers and reddish fruits (haws). Also called (in Britain): **may, may tree, mayflower** [OE *haguthorn*, from *haga* hedge + *thorn* thorn]

Hawthorne (ˈhɔːˌθɔːn) *n* **Nathaniel** 1804–64, US novelist and short-story writer: his works include the novels *The Scarlet Letter* (1850) and *The House of the Seven Gables* (1851), and the children's stories *Tanglewood Tales* (1853)

hay (heɪ) *n* **1a** grass, clover, etc, cut and dried as fodder **1b** (*in combination*): *a hayfield* **2** **hit the hay** *sl* to go to bed **3** **make hay of** to throw into confusion **4** **make hay while the sun shines** to take full advantage of an opportunity **5** **roll in the hay** *inf* sexual intercourse or heavy petting ▷ *vb* **6** to cut, dry, and store (grass, etc) as fodder [OE *hieg*]

Hay (heɪ) *n* **Will** 1888–1949, British music-hall comedian, who later starred in films, such as *Oh, Mr Porter!* (1937)

haybox (ˈheɪˌbɒks) *n* an airtight box full of hay used for cooking preheated food by retained heat

haycock (ˈheɪˌkɒk) *n* a small cone-shaped pile of hay left in the field until dry

Haydn (ˈhaɪdᵊn) *n* **1** (**Franz**) **Joseph** (ˈjoːzɛf) 1732–1809, Austrian composer, who played a major part in establishing the classical forms of the symphony and the string quartet. His other works include the oratorios *The Creation* (1796–98) and *The Seasons* (1798–1801) **2** his brother, **Johann Michael** (*German* joˈhan ˈmɪçaeːl) 1737–1806, Austrian composer, esp of church music

Hayek (ˈhaɪɛk) *n* **Friedrich August von** 1899–1992, British economist and political philosopher, born in Austria: noted for his advocacy of free-market ideas; shared the Nobel prize for economics 1974

Hayes (heɪz) *n* **Rutherford B(irchard)** 1822–93, 19th president of the US (1877–81)

hay fever *n* an allergic reaction to pollen, dust, etc, characterized by sneezing, runny nose, and watery eyes due to inflammation of the mucous membranes of the eyes and nose

haymaker (ˈheɪˌmeɪkə) *n* **1** a person who helps to cut, turn, or carry hay **2** either of two machines, one designed to crush stems of hay, the other to break and bend them, in order to cause more rapid and even drying **3** *boxing sl* a wild swinging punch > ˈ**hay**ˌ**making** *adj, n*

haymow (ˈheɪˌmaʊ) *n* **1** a part of a barn where hay is stored **2** a quantity of hay stored

hayseed (ˈheɪˌsiːd) *n* **1** seeds or fragments of grass or straw **2** *US & Canad inf, derog* a yokel

haystack (ˈheɪˌstæk) *or* **hayrick** *n* a large pile of hay, esp one built in the open air and covered with thatch

haywire (ˈheɪˌwaɪə) *adj (postpositive) inf* **1** (of things) not functioning properly **2** (of people) erratic or crazy [c20 from the disorderly tangle of wire removed from bales of hay]

hazard (ˈhæzəd) *n* **1** exposure or vulnerability to injury, loss, etc **2** **at hazard** at risk; in danger **3** a thing likely to cause injury, etc **4** *golf* an obstacle such as a bunker, a road, rough, water, etc **5** chance; accident **6** a gambling game played with two dice **7** *real tennis* **7a** the receiver's side of the court **7b** one of the winning openings **8** *billiards* a scoring stroke made either when a ball other than the striker's is pocketed (**winning hazard**) or the striker's cue ball itself (**losing hazard**) ▷ *vb (tr)* **9** to risk **10** to venture (an opinion, guess, etc) **11** to expose to danger [c13 from OF *hasard*, from Ar. *az-zahr* the die]

hazard lights *pl n* the indicator lights of a motor vehicle when flashing simultaneously to indicate that the vehicle is stationary and temporarily obstructing the traffic. Also called: **hazard warning lights, hazards**

hazardous (ˈhæzədəs) *adj* **1** involving great risk **2** depending on chance. > ˈ**hazardously** *adv* > ˈ**hazardousness** *n*

hazard warning device *n* an appliance fitted to a motor vehicle that operates the hazard lights

haze[1] (heɪz) *n* **1** *meteorol* reduced visibility in the air as a result of condensed water vapour, dust, etc, in the atmosphere **2** obscurity of perception, feeling, etc ▷ *vb* **hazes, hazing, hazed** **3** (when *intr*, often foll by *over*) to make or become hazy [c18 back formation from HAZY]

haze[2] (heɪz) *vb* **hazes, hazing, hazed** *(tr)* **1** *chiefly US & Canad* to subject (fellow students) to ridicule or abuse **2** *naut* to harass with humiliating tasks [c17 from ?]

hazel (ˈheɪzᵊl) *n* **1** Also called: **cob** any of several shrubs of a N temperate genus, having edible rounded nuts **2** the wood of any of these trees **3** short for **hazelnut** **4a** a light yellowish-brown colour **4b** *(as adj): hazel eyes* [OE *hæsel*]

hazelhen (ˈheɪzᵊlˌhɛn) *n* a European woodland gallinaceous bird with a speckled brown plumage and slightly crested crown

hazelnut (ˈheɪzᵊlˌnʌt) *n* the nut of a hazel shrub, having a smooth shiny hard shell. Also called: **filbert,** (Brit) **cobnut, cob**

Hazlitt (ˈhæzlɪt) *n* **William** 1778–1830, English critic and essayist: works include *Characters of Shakespeare's Plays* (1817), *Table Talk* (1821), and *The Plain Speaker* (1826)

hazy (ˈheɪzɪ) *adj* **hazier, haziest** misty; indistinct; vague [c17 from ?] > ˈ**hazily** *adv* > ˈ**haziness** *n*

Hb *symbol for* haemoglobin

HB (on Brit pencils) *symbol for* hard-black: denoting a medium-hard lead

HBC *abbrev for* Hudson's Bay Company

HBM (in Britain) *abbrev for* His (*or* Her) Britannic Majesty

H-bomb *n* short for **hydrogen bomb**

HC *abbrev for:* **1** Holy Communion **2** (in Britain) House of Commons

HCF *or* **hcf** *abbrev for* highest common factor

HCG *abbrev for* human chorionic gonadotrophin; a hormone produced by the placenta during pregnancy: its presence in the urine is used as the basis of most pregnancy tests

hcp *abbrev for* handicap

HD *abbrev for* heavy duty

HDD *abbrev for computing* hard disk drive

hdqrs *abbrev for* headquarters

HDTV *abbrev for* high definition television
▷ http://hdtvinfoport.com

he (hiː; *unstressed* iː) *pron (subjective)* **1** refers to a male person or animal **2** refers to an indefinite antecedent such as *whoever* or *anybody: everybody can do as he likes* **3** refers to a person or animal of unknown or unspecified sex: *a member may vote as he sees fit* ▷ *n* **4a** a male person or animal **4b** *(in combination): he-goat* **5** (in children's play) another name for **tag**[2] (sense 1), **it** (sense 7) [OE *hē*]

Hh

He *the chemical symbol for* helium

HE *abbrev for:* **1** high explosive **2** His Eminence **3** His (*or* Her) Excellency

head (hɛd) *n* **1** the upper or front part of the body in vertebrates, including man, that contains and protects the brain, eyes, mouth, nose, and ears. Related adj: **cephalic** **2** the corresponding part of an invertebrate animal **3** something resembling a head in form or function, such as the top of a tool **4a** the person commanding most authority within a group, organization, etc **4b** *(as modifier): head buyer* **4c** *(in combination): headmaster* **5** the position of leadership or command **6** the most forward part of a thing; front: *the head of a queue* **7** the highest part of a thing; upper end: *the head of the pass* **8** the froth on the top of a glass of beer **9** aptitude, intelligence, and emotions (esp in **over one's head, lose one's head,** etc): *she has a good head for figures* **10** (*pl* **head**) a person or animal considered as a unit: *the show was two pounds per head; six hundred head of cattle* **11** the head considered as a measure: *he's a head taller than his mother* **12** *bot* **12a** a dense inflorescence such as that of the daisy **12b** any other compact terminal part of a plant, such as the leaves of a cabbage **13** a culmination or crisis (esp in **bring** or **come to a head**) **14** the pus-filled tip or central part of a pimple, boil, etc **15** the source of a river or stream **16** *(cap when part of a name)* a headland or promontory **17** the obverse of a coin, usually bearing a portrait of the head of a monarch, etc **18** a main point of an argument, discourse, etc **19** *(often pl)* a headline or heading **20** *(often pl) naut* a lavatory **21** the taut membrane of a drum, tambourine, etc **22a** the height of the surface of liquid above a specific point, esp as a measure of the pressure at that point: *a* *head of four feet* **22b** pressure of water, caused by height or velocity, measured in terms of a vertical column of water **22c** any pressure: *a head of steam in the boiler* **23** *sl* **23a** a person who regularly takes drugs, esp LSD or cannabis **23b** (*in combination*): *an acidhead* **24** *mining* a road driven into the coalface **25a** the terminal point of a route **25b** (*in combination*): *railhead* **26** a device on a turning or boring machine equipped with one or more cutting tools held to the work by this device **27** **cylinder head** See **cylinder** (sense 4) **28** an electromagnet that can read, write, or erase information on a magnetic medium, used in computers, tape recorders, etc **29** *inf* short for **headmaster** *or* **headmistress** **30** a narrow margin of victory (esp in (**win**) **by a head**) **31** *inf* short for **headache** **32** **bite** *or* **snap someone's head off** to speak sharply to someone **33** **give someone** (*or* **something**) **his** (*or* **her** *or* **its**) **head** **33a** to allow a person greater freedom or responsibility **33b** to allow a horse to gallop by lengthening the reins **34** **go to one's head** **34a** to make one dizzy or confused, as might an alcoholic drink **34b** to make one conceited: *his success has gone to his head* **35** **head and shoulders above** greatly superior to **36** **head over heels** **36a** turning a complete somersault **36b** completely; utterly (esp in **head over heels in love**) **37** **hold up one's head** to be unashamed **38** **keep one's head** to remain calm **39** **keep one's head above water** to manage to survive difficulties, esp financial ones **40** **make head or tail of** (*used with a negative*) to attempt to understand (a problem, etc) **41** **off** (*or* **out of**) **one's head** *sl* insane or delirious **42** **on one's** (**own**) **head** at a one's (own) risk or responsibility **43** **over someone's head** **43a** without a person in the obvious position being considered: *the graduate was promoted over the heads of several of his seniors* **43b** without consulting a person in the obvious position but referring to a higher authority: *he went straight to the director, over the head of his immediate boss* **43c** beyond a person's comprehension **44** **put** (**our, their,** etc) **heads together** *inf* to consult together **45** **take it into one's head** to conceive a notion (to do something) **46** **turn someone's head** to make someone vain, conceited, etc ▷ *vb* **47** (*tr*) to be at the front or top of: *to head the field* **48** (*tr;* often foll by *up*) to be in the commanding or most important position **49** (often foll by *for*) to go or cause to go (towards): *where are you heading?* **50** to turn or steer (a vessel) as specified: *to head into the wind* **51** *soccer* to propel (the ball) by striking it with the head **52** (*tr*) to provide with or be a head or heading for **53** (*tr*) to cut the top branches or shoots off a tree or plant **54** (*intr*) to form a head, as a plant **55** (*intr;* often foll by *in*) (of streams, rivers, etc) to originate or rise ▷ See also **head off, heads** [OE *hēafod*] > **'headless** *adj* > **'head,like** *adj*

-head *n combining form* indicating a person having a preoccupation as specified: *breadhead*

Head (hɛd) *n* **Edith** 1907–81, US dress designer: won many Oscars for her Hollywood film costume designs

headache ('hɛd,eɪk) *n* **1** a continuous pain in the head **2** *inf* any cause of worry, difficulty, or annoyance > **'head,achy** *adj*

headband ('hɛd,bænd) *n* **1** a ribbon or band worn around the head **2** a narrow cloth band attached to the top of the spine of a book for protection or decoration

headbang ('hɛd,bæŋ) *vb* (*intr*) *sl* to nod one's head violently to the beat of heavy-metal rock music

head-banger *n sl* **1** a heavy-metal rock fan **2** a crazy or stupid person

headboard ('hɛd,bɔːd) *n* a vertical board or terminal at the head of a bed

head-butt *vb* (*tr*) **1** to strike (someone) deliberately with the head ▷ *n* **head butt** **2** an act or an instance of deliberately striking someone with the head

headdress ('hɛd,drɛs) *n* any head covering, esp an ornate one or one denoting a rank

headed ('hɛdɪd) *adj* **1a** having a head or heads **1b** (*in combination*): *two-headed; bullet-headed* **2** having a heading: *headed notepaper*

header ('hɛdə) *n* **1** a machine that trims the heads from castings, forgings, etc, or one that forms heads, as in wire, to make nails **2** a person who operates such a machine **3** Also called: **header tank** a reservoir that maintains a gravity feed or a static fluid pressure in an apparatus **4** a brick or stone laid across a wall so that its end is flush with the outer surface **5** the action of striking a ball with the head **6** *inf* a headlong fall or dive

headfirst ('hɛd'fɜːst) *adj, adv* **1** with the head foremost; headlong ▷ *adv* **2** rashly

headfuck ('hɛd,fʌk) *n taboo sl* an experience that is wildly exciting or impressive

headgear ('hɛd,gɪə) *n* **1** a hat **2** any part of a horse's harness that is worn on the head **3** the hoisting mechanism at the pithead of a mine

headguard ('hɛd,gɑːd) *n* a lightweight helmet-like piece of equipment worn to protect the head in various sports

head-hunting *n* **1** the practice among certain peoples of removing the heads of slain enemies and preserving them as trophies **2** *US sl* the destruction or neutralization of political opponents **3** (of a company or corporation) the recruitment of, or a drive to recruit, new high-level personnel, esp in management or in specialist fields > **'head-,hunter** *n*

heading ('hɛdɪŋ) *n* **1** a title for a page, chapter, etc **2** a main division, as of a speech **3** *mining* **3a** a horizontal tunnel **3b** the end of such a tunnel **4** the angle between the direction of an aircraft and a specified meridian, often due north **5** the compass direction parallel to the keel of a vessel **6** the act of heading

headland *n* **1** ('hɛdlənd) a narrow area of land jutting out into a sea, lake, etc **2** ('hɛd,lænd) a strip of land along the edge of an arable field left unploughed to allow space for machines

headlight ('hɛd,laɪt) *or* **headlamp** *n* a powerful light, equipped with a reflector and attached to the front of a motor vehicle, etc

headline ('hɛd,laɪn) *n* **1a** a phrase at the top of a newspaper or magazine article indicating the subject of the article, usually in larger and heavier type **1b** a line at the top of a page indicating the title, page number, etc **2** **hit the headlines** to become prominent in the news **3** (*usually pl*) the main points of a television or radio news broadcast, read out before the full broadcast ▷ *vb* **headlines, headlining, headlined** **4** (*tr*) to furnish (a story or page) with a headline **5** to have top billing (in)

headlong ('hɛd,lɒŋ) *adv, adj* **1** with the head foremost; headfirst **2** with great haste ▷ *adj* **3** *arch* (of slopes, etc) very steep; precipitous

headman ('hɛdmən) *n, pl* **headmen** **1** *anthropol* a chief or leader **2** a foreman or overseer

headmaster (,hɛd'mɑːstə) *or* (*fem*) **headmistress** *n* the principal of a school

headmost ('hɛd,məʊst) *adj* foremost

head off *vb* (*tr, adv*) **1** to intercept and force to change direction **2** to prevent or forestall

head-on *adv, adj* **1** front foremost: *a head-on collision* **2** with directness or without compromise: *in his usual head-on fashion*

headphones ('hɛd,fəʊnz) *pl n* an electrical device consisting of two earphones held in position by a flexible metallic strap passing over the head. Informal name: **cans**

headpiece ('hɛd,piːs) *n* **1** *printing* a decorative band at the top of a page, etc **2** a helmet **3** *arch* the intellect

headpin ('hɛd,pɪn) *n tenpin bowling* another word for **kingpin** (sense 2)

headquarters (,hɛd'kwɔːtəz) *pl n* (*sometimes functioning as sing*) **1** any centre from which operations are directed, as in the police **2** a military formation comprising the commander and his staff ▷ Abbrevs: **HQ, h.q.**

headrace ('hɛd,reɪs) *n* a channel that carries water to a water wheel, turbine, etc

headrest ('hɛd,rɛst) *n* a support for the head, as on a dentist's chair or car seat

head restraint *n* an adjustable support for the head, attached to a car seat, to prevent the neck from being jolted backwards sharply in the event of a crash or sudden stop

headroom ('hɛd,rʊm, -,ru:m) *or* **headway** *n* the height of a bridge, room, etc; clearance

heads (hɛdz) *interj, adv* with the obverse side of a coin uppermost, esp if it has a head on it: used as a call before tossing a coin

headscarf ('hɛd,skɑ:f) *n, pl* **headscarves** a scarf for the head, often worn tied under the chin

headset ('hɛd,sɛt) *n* a pair of headphones, esp with a microphone attached

headship ('hɛdʃɪp) *n* **1** the position or state of being a leader; command **2** *Brit* the position of headmaster or headmistress of a school

headshrinker ('hɛd,ʃrɪŋkə) *n* **1** a slang name for **psychiatrist** Often shortened to **shrink 2** a head-hunter who shrinks the heads of his victims

headsman ('hɛdzmən) *n, pl* **headsmen** (formerly) an executioner who beheaded condemned persons

headstall ('hɛd,stɔ:l) *n* the part of a bridle that fits round a horse's head

head start *n* an initial advantage in a competitive situation

headstock ('hɛd,stɒk) *n* the part of a machine that supports and transmits the drive

headstone ('hɛd,stəʊn) *n* **1** a memorial stone at the head of a grave **2** *archit* another name for **keystone**

headstream ('hɛd,stri:m) *n* a stream that is the source or a source of a river

headstrong ('hɛd,strɒŋ) *adj* **1** self-willed; obstinate **2** (of an action) heedless; rash

head-to-head *inf* ▷ *adj* **1** in direct competition ▷ *n* **2** a competition involving two people, teams, etc

head-up display *n* a projection of readings from instruments onto a windscreen, enabling a pilot or driver to see them without moving his or her eyes

head voice *or* **register** *n* the high register of the human voice, in which the vibrations of sung notes are felt in the head

headwaters ('hɛd,wɔ:təz) *pl n* the tributary streams of a river in the area in which it rises

headway ('hɛd,weɪ) *n* **1** motion forward: *the vessel made no headway* **2** progress: *he made no headway with the problem* **3** another name for **headroom 4** the interval between consecutive trains, buses, etc, on the same route

headwind ('hɛd,wɪnd) *n* a wind blowing directly against the course of an aircraft or ship

headword ('hɛd,wɜ:d) *n* a key word placed at the beginning of a line, paragraph, etc, as in a dictionary entry

headwork ('hɛd,wɜ:k) *n* **1** mental work **2** the ornamentation of the keystone of an arch

heady ('hɛdɪ) *adj* **headier, headiest 1** (of alcoholic drink) intoxicating **2** strongly affecting the senses; extremely exciting **3** rash; impetuous > '**headily** *adv* > '**headiness** *n*

heal (hi:l) *vb* **1** to restore or be restored to health **2** (*intr;* often foll by *over* or *up*) (of a wound) to repair by natural processes, as by scar formation **3** (*tr*) to cure (a disease or disorder) **4** to restore or be restored to friendly relations, harmony, etc [OE *hǣlan;* see HALE[1], WHOLE] > '**healer** *n* > '**healing** *n, adj*

health (hɛlθ) *n* **1** the state of being bodily and mentally vigorous and free from disease **2** the general condition of body and mind: *in poor health* **3** the condition of any unit, society, etc: *the economic health of a nation* **4** a toast to a person **5** (*modifier*) of or relating to food or other goods reputed to be beneficial to the health: *health food* **6** (*modifier*) of or relating to health: *health care; health service* [OE *hǣlth;* rel. to *hāl* HALE[1]]

Finding Reliable Health-related Information Online

Until the recent past most people had no way of sourcing up-to-date health-related information. The Internet has changed that drastically, with laypeople having potentially as much access to the latest medical research as health professionals. Although online medical resources can increase understanding of health problems they can also cause a number of problems.

People using the Internet to research their symptoms often misdiagnose themselves and bring their problems, as well as a mass of downloaded information, to their doctor. Cyberchondria, as it is sometimes known, adds to the burden of health professionals.

The Internet is unregulated and not all health-related websites offer patients and consumers reliable advice and approved treatments. Those concerned about a health problem sometimes seek a treatment or purchase a drug that is unsuitable, expensive, or of dubious medical benefit.

Some patients can have their expectations heightened by websites offering new treatments and drugs, only to have their hopes dashed when told by a health professional that the products and cures they want are available only in the US.

It is recommended that those with concerns about their own health or that of relatives should consult a local health professional first before exploring resources online. However, we can recommend a number of useful websites and portals that will provide information in addition to that offered by a general practitioner or health visitor. The online sources listed below offer advice and information to consumers, carers, and health professionals alike in the UK, Australia, New Zealand, Canada, and South Africa.

▷ www.ohn.gov.uk/gateway/gateway.htm
Useful information provided by the UK's Department of Health. The "Health Focus" page has links to many other sites including ones related to heart disease and stroke, food safety, nutrition, and smoking.

▷ www.hon.ch
The Health on the Net Foundation (HON) has drawn up a code of conduct for reliable medical and health websites. Sites that adhere to the HON code display the HON logo on their home page. This website is a large non-profit portal to good-quality online health-related information.

▷ www.nhsdirect.nhs.uk
As well as providing its own information, NHS Direct Online also acts as a gateway to quality-controlled information on health matters elsewhere on the Internet.

▷ www.nice.org.uk
The National Institute for Clinical Excellence (NICE) is the body set up by the UK government to evaluate the value of new treatments and products provided by the NHS.

▷ www.healthcentre.org.uk
A gateway with a directory of links to mainly UK health-related sites.

▷ www.cancerbacup.org.uk
Maintained by the British charity of the same name. A comprehensive resource for cancer patients, their families, and health professionals.

▷ www.surgerydoor.co.uk
A commercial portal with health information, discussion boards, and online shops.

▷ http://omni.ac.uk
OMNI (Organising Medical Network Information) is a database of over 4000 vetted medical and health links, aimed principally at the UK's medical and scientific communities, but also of much use to laypeople.

▷ www.healthinsite.gov.au
HealthInsite is an Australian Government initiative, funded by the Department of Health and Ageing. It aims to improve the health of Australians by providing easy access to quality information about human health. HealthInsite offers consumers information ranging from daily health needs, such as nutrition, to information related to life events, such as having a baby.

▷ www.mydr.com.au
myDr is a commercial healthcare website but it complies with the standards set by HealthInsite – an Australian Federal Government accreditation initiative designed to provide Quality Assurance for health information on the Internet. The website also abides by the HON Code principles of the Health on the Net Foundation.

▷ www.nzhis.govt.nz
The New Zealand Health Information Service (NZHIS) is a body within the Ministry of Health. It has responsibility for the collection, processing, maintenance, and dissemination of health data, health statistics, and health information.

▷ www.healthed.govt.nz
The Health Education Resources Database of the New Zealand government is a searchable database of over 350 health education titles covering a range of health topics. The database contained on this website allows health professionals, the education sector, and the general public to view and request copies of this information.

▷ www.hc-sc.gc.ca/english/index.html
Health Canada is the federal department responsible for helping the people of Canada maintain and improve their health. Health Canada "strives to improve the health of all Canada's people, while respecting individual choices and circumstances, and therefore seeks to put Canada among the countries with the healthiest people in the world."

▷ http://chp-pcs.gc.ca/CHP/index_e.jsp
The Canada Health Portal provides Canadians with an authoritative and integrated view of Canadian health information and services from various jurisdictions. The information found on the CHP originates from numerous reliable and trusted sources.

▷ www.doh.gov.za/index.html
The website maintained by the South African Department of Health. It provides health information and advice and has links to relevant provincial, national, and international websites.

▷ www.health24.co.za
This commercial South African site abides by the HON Code principles of the Health on the Net Foundation. Health24 information ranges from medical content through to general health & lifestyle issues.

health card *n Canad* an identity card required to obtain public health insurance services

health centre *n* (in Britain) premises, owned by a local authority, providing health care for a local community and usually housing a group practice, nursing staff, a child-health clinic, etc

health farm *n* a residential establishment, often in the country, visited by those who wish to improve their health by losing weight, eating healthy foods, taking exercise, etc

health food *n* **a** food eaten for its alleged benefits to health, esp fruit, vegetables, etc, that are organically grown, high in dietary fibre, and without additives **b** (*as modifier*): *a health-food shop*

healthful ('hɛlθfʊl) *adj* a less common word for **healthy** (senses 1–3)

health salts *pl n* magnesium sulphate or similar salts taken as a mild laxative

health visitor *n* (in Britain) a nurse employed by a district health authority to visit people in their homes and give help and advice on health and social welfare, esp to mothers of preschool children, and to handicapped and elderly people

healthy ('hɛlθɪ) *adj* **healthier, healthiest 1** enjoying good health **2** sound: *the company's finances are not very healthy* **3** conducive to health **4** indicating soundness of body or mind: *a healthy appetite* **5** *inf* considerable: *a healthy sum* > **'healthily** *adv* > **'healthiness** *n*

Heaney ('hi:nɪ) *n* **Seamus (Justin)** ('ʃeɪməs) born 1939, Irish poet and critic, born in Northern Ireland. His collections include *Death of a Naturalist* (1966), *North* (1975), *The Haw Lantern* (1987), *The Spirit Level* (1996), and *Electric Light* (2001). Nobel prize for literature 1995

heap (hi:p) *n* **1** a collection of articles or mass of material gathered in a pile **2** (*often pl; usually foll by of*) *inf* a large number or quantity **3 give it heaps** *NZ sl* to try very hard **4** *inf* a thing that is very old, unreliable, etc: *the car was a heap* ▷ *adv* **5 heaps** (intensifier): *he was heaps better* ▷ *vb* **6** (often foll by *up* or *together*) to collect or be collected into or as if into a pile **7** (*tr; often foll by with, on, or upon*) to load (with) abundantly: *to heap with riches* [OE *héap*] > **'heaper** *n*

hear (hɪə) *vb* **hears, hearing, heard** (hɜ:d) **1** (*tr*) to perceive (a sound) with the sense of hearing **2** (*tr; may take a clause as object*) to listen to: *did you hear what I said?* **3** (when *intr*, sometimes foll by *of* or *about*; when *tr*, *may take a clause as object*) to be informed (of); receive information (about) **4** *law* to give a hearing to (a case) **5** (when *intr*, usually foll by *of* and used with a negative) to listen (to) with favour, assent, etc: *she wouldn't hear of it* **6** (*intr; foll by from*) to receive a letter (from) **7 hear! hear!** an exclamation of approval **8 hear tell (of)** *dialect* to be told (about) [OE *hieran*] > **'hearer** *n*

Heard and McDonald Islands (hɜ:d, mək'dɒnəld) *pl n* a group of islands in the S Indian Ocean: an external territory of Australia from 1947. Area: 412 sq km (159 sq miles)

hearing ('hɪərɪŋ) *n* **1** the sense by which sound is perceived **2** an opportunity to be listened to **3** the range within which sound can be heard; earshot **4** the investigation of a matter by a court of law, esp the preliminary inquiry into an indictable crime by magistrates

hearing aid *n* a device for assisting the hearing of partially deaf people, typically a small battery-powered amplifier worn in or behind the ear. Also called: **deaf aid**

hearing dog *n* a dog that has been specially trained to help deaf or partially deaf people by alerting them to such sounds as a ringing doorbell, an alarm, etc

hearken *or US (sometimes)* **harken** (ˈhɑːkən) *vb arch* to listen to (something) [OE *heorcnian*]

hear out *vb (tr, adv)* to listen in regard to every detail and give a proper or full hearing to

hearsay (ˈhɪəˌseɪ) *n* gossip; rumour

hearsay evidence *n law* evidence based on what has been reported to a witness by others rather than what he or she has himself or herself observed

hearse (hɜːs) *n* a vehicle, such as a car or carriage, used to carry a coffin to the grave [C14 from OF *herce*, from L *hirpex* harrow]

Hearst (hɜːst) *n* **William Randolph** 1863–1951, US newspaper publisher, whose newspapers were noted for their sensationalism

heart (hɑːt) *n* **1** the hollow muscular organ in vertebrates whose contractions propel the blood through the circulatory system. Related adj: **cardiac** **2** the corresponding organ in invertebrates **3** this organ considered as the seat of emotions, esp love **4** emotional mood: *a change of heart* **5** tenderness or pity: *you have no heart* **6** courage or spirit **7** the most central part: *the heart of the city* **8** the most important part: *the heart of the matter* **9** (of vegetables, such as cabbage) the inner compact part **10** the breast: *she held him to her heart* **11** a dearly loved person: *dearest heart* **12** a conventionalized representation of the heart, having two rounded lobes at the top meeting in a point at the bottom **13a** a red heart-shaped symbol on a playing card **13b** a card with one or more of these symbols or (*when pl*) the suit of cards so marked **14** a fertile condition in land (esp in **in good heart**) **15** **after one's own heart** appealing to one's own disposition or taste **16** **break one's** (*or* **someone's**) **heart** to grieve (or cause to grieve) very deeply, esp through love **17** **by heart** by committing to memory **18** **eat one's heart out** to brood or pine with grief or longing **19** **from** (**the bottom of**) **one's heart** very sincerely or deeply **20** **have a change of heart** to experience a profound change of outlook, attitude, etc **21** **have one's heart in one's mouth** (*or* **throat**) to be full of apprehension, excitement, or fear **22** **have one's heart in the right place** to be kind, thoughtful, or generous **23** **have the heart** (*usually used with a negative*) to have the necessary will, callousness, etc (to do something): *I didn't have the heart to tell him* **24** **heart of hearts** the depths of one's conscience or emotions **25** **heart of oak** a brave person **26** **lose heart** to become despondent or disillusioned (over something) **27** **lose one's heart to** to fall in love with **28** **set one's heart on** to have as one's ambition to obtain; covet **29** **take heart** to become encouraged **30** **take to heart** to take seriously or be upset about **31** **wear one's heart on one's sleeve** to show one's feelings openly **32** **with all one's heart** very willingly ▷ *vb (intr)* **33** (of vegetables) to form a heart ▷ See also **hearts** [OE *heorte*]
▷ www.americanheart.org

heartache (ˈhɑːtˌeɪk) *n* intense anguish or mental suffering

heart attack *n* any sudden severe instance of abnormal heart functioning, esp coronary thrombosis

heartbeat (ˈhɑːtˌbiːt) *n* one complete pulsation of the heart

heart block *n* impaired conduction of the impulse that regulates the heartbeat, resulting in a lack of coordination between the beating of the atria and the ventricles

heartbreak (ˈhɑːtˌbreɪk) *n* intense and overwhelming grief, esp through disappointment in love > ˈ**heartˌbreaker** *n* > ˈ**heartˌbreaking** *adj*

heartburn (ˈhɑːtˌbɜːn) *n* a burning sensation beneath the breastbone caused by irritation of the oesophagus. Technical names: **cardialgia, pyrosis**

-hearted *adj (in combination)* having a heart or disposition as specified: *cold-hearted; heavy-hearted*

hearten (ˈhɑːtᵊn) *vb* to make or become cheerful

heartening (ˈhɑːtᵊnɪŋ) *adj* causing cheerfulness; encouraging

heart failure *n* **1** a condition in which the heart is unable to pump an adequate amount of blood to the tissues **2** sudden cessation of the heartbeat, resulting in death

heartfelt (ˈhɑːtˌfɛlt) *adj* sincerely and strongly felt

hearth (hɑːθ) *n* **1a** the floor of a fireplace, esp one that extends outwards into the room **1b** (*as modifier*): *hearth rug* **2** this as a symbol of the home, etc **3** the bottom part of a metallurgical furnace in which the molten metal is produced or contained [OE *heorth*]

hearthstone (ˈhɑːθˌstəʊn) *n* **1** a stone that forms a hearth **2** soft stone used (esp formerly) to clean and whiten floors, steps, etc

heartily (ˈhɑːtɪlɪ) *adv* **1** thoroughly or vigorously **2** in a sincere manner

heartland (ˈhɑːtˌlænd) *n* the central or most important region of a country or continent

heartless (ˈhɑːtlɪs) *adj* unkind or cruel > ˈ**heartlessly** *adv* > ˈ**heartlessness** *n*

heart-lung machine *n* a machine used to maintain the circulation and oxygenation of the blood during heart surgery

heart-rending *adj* causing great mental pain and sorrow > ˈ**heart-ˌrendingly** *adv*

hearts (hɑːts) *n (functioning as sing)* a card game in which players must avoid winning tricks containing hearts or the queen of spades. Also called: **Black Maria**

heart-searching *n* examination of one's feelings or conscience

heartsease *or* **heart's-ease** (ˈhɑːtsˌiːz) *n* **1** another name for the **wild pansy** **2** peace of mind

heartsick (ˈhɑːtˌsɪk) *adj* deeply despondent > ˈ**heartˌsickness** *n*

heartstrings (ˈhɑːtˌstrɪŋz) *pl n often facetious* deep emotions [C15 orig. referring to the tendons supposed to support the heart]

heart-throb *n* **1** an object of infatuation **2** a heartbeat

heart-to-heart *adj* **1** (esp of a conversation) concerned with personal problems or intimate feelings ▷ *n* **2** an intimate conversation

heart-warming *adj* **1** pleasing; gratifying **2** emotionally moving

heartwood (ˈhɑːtˌwʊd) *n* the central core of dark hard wood in tree trunks, consisting of nonfunctioning xylem tissue that has become blocked with resins, tannins, and oils

hearty (ˈhɑːtɪ) *adj* **heartier, heartiest** **1** warm and unreserved in manner **2** vigorous and heartfelt: *hearty dislike* **3** healthy and strong (esp in **hale and hearty**) **4** substantial and nourishing ▷ *n, pl* **hearties** *inf* **5** a comrade, esp a sailor **6** a vigorous sporting man: *a rugby hearty* > ˈ**heartiness** *n*

heat (hiːt) *n* **1** the energy transferred as a result of a difference in temperature. Related adjs: **thermal, calorific** **2** the sensation caused by heat energy; warmth **3** the state of being hot **4** hot weather: *the heat of summer* **5** intensity of feeling: *the heat of rage* **6** pressure: *the political heat on the government over the economy* **7** the most intense part: *the heat of the battle* **8** a period of sexual excitement in female mammals that occurs at oestrus

9 *sport* **9a** a preliminary eliminating contest in a competition **9b** a single section of a contest **10** *sl* police activity after a crime: *the heat is off* **11** *sl, chiefly US* criticism or abuse: *he took a lot of heat for that mistake* **12** **in the heat of the moment** without pausing to think **13** **on** *or* **in heat** **13a** Also: **in season** (of some female mammals) sexually receptive **13b** in a state of sexual excitement ▷ *vb* **14** to make or become hot or warm **15** to make or become excited or intense [OE *hǣtu*]

heat barrier *n* another name for **thermal barrier**

heat capacity *n* the heat required to raise the temperature of a substance by unit temperature interval under specified conditions

heat death *n thermodynamics* the condition of any closed system when its total entropy is a maximum and it has no available energy. If the universe is a closed system it should eventually reach this state

heated (ˈhiːtɪd) *adj* **1** made hot **2** impassioned or highly emotional > ˈ**heatedly** *adv*

heat engine *n* an engine that converts heat energy into mechanical energy

heater (ˈhiːtə) *n* **1** any device for supplying heat, such as a convector **2** *US sl* a pistol **3** *electronics* a conductor carrying a current that indirectly heats the cathode in some types of valve

heat exchanger *n* a device for transferring heat from one fluid to another without allowing them to mix

heat exhaustion *n* a condition resulting from exposure to intense heat, characterized by dizziness, abdominal cramp, and prostration

heath (hiːθ) *n* **1** *Brit* a large open area, usually with sandy soil and scrubby vegetation, esp heather **2** Also called: **heather** a low-growing evergreen shrub having small bell-shaped typically pink or purple flowers **3** any of several heathlike plants, such as sea heath [OE *hǣth*] > ˈ**heath,like** *adj* > ˈ**heathy** *adj*

Heath (hiːθ) *n* Sir **Edward** (**Richard George**) born 1916, British statesman; leader of the Conservative Party (1965–75); prime minister (1970–74)

heathen (ˈhiːðən) *n, pl* **heathens** *or* **heathen** **1** a person who does not acknowledge the God of Christianity, Judaism, or Islam; pagan **2** an uncivilized or barbaric person ▷ *adj* **3** irreligious; pagan **4** uncivilized; barbaric **5** of or relating to heathen peoples or their customs and beliefs [OE *hǣthen*] > ˈ**heathendom** *n* > ˈ**heathenism** *or* ˈ**heathenry** *n*

heathenize *or* **heathenise** (ˈhiːðə,naɪz) *vb* **heathenizes, heathenizing, heathenized** *or* **heathenises, heathenising, heathenised** to render or become heathen

heather (ˈhɛðə) *n* **1** Also called: **ling, heath** a low-growing evergreen Eurasian shrub that grows in dense masses on open ground and has clusters of small bell-shaped typically pinkish-purple flowers **2** a purplish-red to pinkish-purple colour ▷ *adj* **3** of a heather colour **4** of or relating to interwoven yarns of mixed colours: *heather mixture* [C14 orig. Scot. & N English, prob. from HEATH] > ˈ**heathery** *adj*

Heath Robinson *adj* (of a mechanical device) absurdly complicated in design and having a simple function [C20 after (William) *Heath Robinson* (1872–1944), British cartoonist]

heating (ˈhiːtɪŋ) *n* **1** a device or system for supplying heat, esp central heating, to a building **2** the heat supplied

heat pump *n* a device for extracting heat from a source and delivering it elsewhere at a higher temperature

heat rash *n* a nontechnical name for **miliaria**

heat-seeking *adj* (of a missile, detecting device, etc) able to detect a source of heat, as from an aircraft engine: *a heat-seeking missile* > **heat seeker** *n*

heat shield *n* a coating or barrier for shielding from excessive heat, such as that experienced by a spacecraft on re-entry into the earth's atmosphere

heat sink *n* **1** a metal plate designed to conduct and radiate heat from an electrical component **2** a layer within the outer skin of high-speed aircraft to absorb heat

heatstroke (ˈhiːt,strəʊk) *n* a condition resulting from prolonged exposure to intense heat, characterized by high fever

heat-treat *vb* (*tr*) to apply heat to (a metal or alloy) in one or more temperature cycles to give it desirable properties > **heat treatment** *n*

heat wave *n* **1** a continuous spell of abnormally hot weather **2** an extensive slow-moving air mass at a relatively high temperature

heave (hiːv) *vb* **heaves, heaving, heaved** *or* **hove** **1** (*tr*) to lift or move with a great effort **2** (*tr*) to throw (something heavy) with effort **3** to utter (sounds) noisily or unhappily: *to heave a sigh* **4** to rise and fall or cause to rise and fall heavily **5** (*pt & pp* **hove**) *naut* **5a** to move or cause to move in a specified direction: *to heave in sight* **5b** (*intr*) (of a vessel) to pitch or roll **6** (*tr*) to displace (rock strata, etc) in a horizontal direction **7** (*intr*) to retch ▷ *n* **8** the act of heaving **9** a horizontal displacement of rock strata at a fault ▷ See also **heave to, heaves** [OE *hebban*] > ˈ**heaver** *n*

heave-ho *interj* a sailors' cry, as when hoisting anchor

heaven (ˈhɛvᵊn) *n* **1** (*sometimes cap*) *Christianity* **1a** the abode of God and the angels **1b** a state of communion with God after death **2** (*usually pl*) the firmament surrounding the earth **3** (in various mythologies) a place, such as Elysium or Valhalla, to which those who have died in the gods' favour are brought to dwell in happiness **4** a place or state of happiness **5** (*sing or pl; sometimes cap*) God or the gods, used in exclamatory phrases: *for heaven's sake* **6** **move heaven and earth** to do everything possible (to achieve something) [OE *heofon*]

heavenly (ˈhɛvᵊnlɪ) *adj* **1** *inf* wonderful **2** of or occurring in space: *a heavenly body* **3** holy > ˈ**heavenliness** *n*

heavenward (ˈhɛvᵊnwəd) *adj* **1** directed towards heaven or the sky ▷ *adv* **2** Also **heavenwards** towards heaven or the sky

heaves (hiːvz) *n* (*functioning as sing or pl*) a chronic respiratory disorder of animals of the horse family, caused by allergies and dust. Also called: **broken wind**

heave to *vb* (*adv*) to stop (a vessel) or (of a vessel) to stop, as by trimming the sails, etc

Heaviside (ˈhɛvɪ,saɪd) *n* **Oliver** 1850–1925, English physicist. Independently of Kennelly, he predicted (1902) the existence of an ionized gaseous layer in the upper atmosphere (the **Heaviside layer**); he also contributed to telegraphy

Heaviside layer *n* another name for **E region** (of the ionosphere) [C20 after O. HEAVISIDE]

heavy (ˈhɛvɪ) *adj* **heavier, heaviest** **1** of comparatively great weight **2** having a relatively high density: *lead is a heavy metal* **3** great in yield, quality, or quantity: *heavy traffic* **4** considerable: *heavy emphasis* **5** hard to bear or fulfil: *heavy demands* **6** sad or dejected: *heavy at heart* **7** coarse or broad: *heavy features* **8** (of soil) having a high clay content; cloggy **9** solid or fat: *heavy legs* **10** (of an industry) engaged in the large-scale complex manufacture of capital goods or extraction of raw materials **11** serious; grave **12** *mil* **12a** equipped with large weapons, armour, etc **12b** (of guns, etc) of a large and powerful type **13** (of a syllable) having stress or accentuation **14** dull and uninteresting: *a heavy style* **15** prodigious: *a heavy drinker* **16** (of cakes, etc) insufficiently leavened **17** deep and loud: *a heavy thud* **18** (of music, literature, etc) **18a** dramatic and powerful **18b** not immediately comprehensible or appealing **19** *sl* (of rock music) having a powerful beat; hard **20** burdened: *heavy with child* **21** **heavy on** *inf* using large quantities of: *this car is very heavy on petrol* **22** clumsy and slow: *heavy going* **23** cloudy or overcast: *heavy skies* **24** not easily digestible: *a heavy meal* **25** (of an element or compound) being or containing an isotope with greater atomic weight than that of the naturally occurring element: *heavy water* **26** (of the going on a racecourse) soft and muddy **27** *sl* using, or prepared to use, violence or brutality ▷ *n, pl* **heavies 28a** a villainous role **28b** an actor who plays such a part **29** *mil* **29a** a large fleet unit, esp an aircraft carrier or battleship **29b** a large piece of artillery **30** (*usually pl; often preceded by the*) *inf* a serious newspaper: *the Sunday heavies* **31** *inf* a heavyweight boxer, wrestler, etc **32** *sl* a man hired to threaten violence or deter others by his presence ▷ *adv* **33a** in a heavy manner; heavily: *time hangs heavy* **33b** (*in combination*): *heavy-laden* [OE *hefig*] > **'heavily** *adv* > **'heaviness** *n*

heavy-duty *n* (*modifier*) made to withstand hard wear, bad weather, etc

heavy-handed *adj* **1** clumsy **2** harsh and oppressive > **ˌheavy-'handedly** *adv*

heavy-hearted *adj* sad; melancholy

heavy hitter *n inf* another name for **big hitter** (sense 2)

heavy hydrogen *n* another name for **deuterium**

heavy metal *n* a type of rock music characterized by high volume, a driving beat, and extended guitar solos, often with violent, nihilistic, and misogynistic lyrics
▷ www.heavymetal.about.com
▷ www.metal-rules.com

heavy middleweight *n* a professional wrestler weighing 177–187 pounds (81–85 kg)

heavy spar *n* another name for **barytes**

heavy water *n* water that has been electrolytically decomposed to reduce the amount of normal hydrogen present and enrich it in deuterium in the form D_2O or HDO. See also **deuterium oxide**

heavyweight ('hɛvɪˌweɪt) *n* **1** a person or thing that is heavier than average **2a** a professional boxer weighing more than 175 pounds (79 kg) **2b** an amateur boxer weighing more than 81 kg (179 pounds) **3a** a professional wrestler weighing over 209 pounds (95 kg) **3b** an amateur wrestler weighing over 220 pounds (100kg) **4** *inf* an important or highly influential person

Heb. *or* **Hebr.** *abbrev for:* **1** Hebrew (language) **2** *Bible* Hebrews

Hebbel (*German* 'hɛbəl) *n* **Christian Friedrich** ('krɪstian 'fri:drɪç) 1813–63, German dramatist and lyric poet, whose historical works were influenced by Hegel; his major plays are *Maria Magdalena* (1844), *Herodes und Marianne* (1850), and the trilogy *Die Nibelungen* (1862)

hebdomadal (hɛb'dɒmədᵊl) *adj* weekly [c18 from L, from Gk *hebdomas* seven (days), from *hepta* seven]

Hebe ('hi:bɪ) *n Greek myth* the goddess of youth and spring, daughter of Zeus and Hera and wife of Hercules

Hebei ('hʌ'beɪ), **Hopeh**, *or* **Hopei** *n* a province of NE China, on the Gulf of Chihli: important for the production of winter wheat, cotton, and coal. Capital: Shijiazhuang. Pop: 67 440 000 (2000 est). Area: 202 700 sq km (79 053 sq miles)

hebetate ('hɛbɪˌteɪt) *adj* **1** (of plant parts) having a blunt or soft point ▷ *vb* **hebetates, hebetating, hebetated** **2** *rare* to make or become blunted [c16 from L *hebetāre* to make blunt, from *hebes* blunt] > **ˌhebe'tation** *n*

Hebraic (hɪ'breɪɪk) *or* **Hebraical** *adj* of, relating to, or characteristic of the Hebrews or their language or culture > **He'braically** *adv*

Hebraism ('hi:breɪˌɪzəm) *n* a linguistic usage, custom, or other feature borrowed from or particular to the Hebrew language, or to the Jewish people or their culture > **'Hebraist** *n* > **'HebraˌIze** *or* **'HebraˌIse** *vb*

Hebrew ('hi:bru:) *n* **1** the ancient language of the Hebrews, revived as the official language of Israel **2** a member of an ancient Semitic people claiming descent from Abraham; an Israelite **3** *arch or offens* a Jew ▷ *adj* **4** of or relating to the Hebrews or their language **5** *arch or offens* Jewish [c13 from OF *Ebreu*, from *Hebraeus*, ult. from Heb. *'ibhrī* one from beyond (the river)]
▷ www.wsu.edu.8080/~dee/hebrews/hebrews.htm

Hebrew Alphabet

aleph	א
beth	ב
gimel	ג
daleth	ד
he	ה
vav	ו
zayin	ז
cheth	ח
teth	ט
yod	י
kaph	כ
lamed	ל
mem	מ
nun	נ
samekh	ס
ayin	ע
pe	פ
sadie	צ
koph	ק
resh	ר
shin	שׁ
sin	שׂ
tav	ת

Hebrews ('hi:bru:z) *n* (*functioning as sing*) a book of the New Testament

Hebridean (ˌhɛbrɪ'di:ən) *or* **Hebridian** (hɛ'brɪdɪən) *adj* **1** of or relating to the Hebrides or their inhabitants ▷ *n* **2** a native or inhabitant of the Hebrides

Hebrides ('hɛbrɪˌdi:z) *pl n* **the** a group of over 500 islands off the W coast of Scotland: separated by the North Minch, Little Minch, and the Sea of the Hebrides: the chief islands are Skye, Raasay, Rhum, Eigg, Coll, Tiree, Mull, Jura, Colonsay, and Islay (**Inner Hebrides**), and Lewis with Harris, North Uist, Benbecula, South Uist, and Barra (**Outer Hebrides**) Also called: **Western Isles**

Hebron ('hɛbrɒn, 'hi:-) *n* a city in the West Bank: famous for the Haram, which includes the cenotaphs of Abraham and Sarah, Isaac and Rebecca, and Jacob and Leah. Pop: 119 401 (1997). Arabic name: **El Khalil**

Hecate *or* **Hekate** ('hɛkətɪ) *n Greek myth* a goddess of the underworld

hecatomb ('hɛkəˌtəʊm, -ˌtu:m) *n* **1** (in ancient Greece or Rome) any great public sacrifice and feast, originally one in which 100 oxen were sacrificed **2** a great sacrifice [c16 from L *hecatombē*, from Gk, from *hekaton* hundred + *bous* ox]

heck (hɛk) *interj* a mild exclamation of surprise, irritation, etc [c19 euphemistic for *hell*]

heckelphone ('hɛkəlˌfəʊn) *n music* a type of bass oboe [c20 after W. *Heckel* (1856–1909), G inventor]

heckle ('hɛkᵊl) *vb* **heckles, heckling, heckled** **1** to interrupt (a public speaker, etc) by comments, questions, or taunts **2** (*tr*) Also: **hackle, hatchel** to comb (hemp or flax) ▷ *n* **3** an instrument for combing flax or hemp [c15 N English & East Anglian form of HACKLE] > **'heckler** *n*

hectare ('hɛktɑ:) *n* one hundred ares (10 000 sq metres or 2.471 acres). Symbol: ha [c19 from F; see HECTO-, ARE[2]]

hectic ('hɛktɪk) *adj* **1** characterized by extreme activity or excitement **2** associated with or symptomatic of tuberculosis (esp in **hectic fever, hectic flush**) ▷ *n* **3** a hectic fever or flush **4** *rare* a person who is consumptive [C14 from LL *hecticus*, from Gk *hektikos* habitual, from *hexis* state, from *ekhein* to have] > ˈ**hectically** *adv*

hecto- *or before a vowel* **hect-** *prefix* denoting 100: *hectogram*. Symbol: h [via F from Gk *hekaton* hundred]

hectog *abbrev for* hectogram

hectogram *or* **hectogramme** (ˈhɛktəʊˌɡræm) *n* one hundred grams (3.527 ounces). Symbol: hg

hectograph (ˈhɛktəʊˌɡrɑːf) *n* **1** a process for copying type or manuscript from a glycerine-coated gelatine master to which the original has been transferred **2** a machine using this process

hector (ˈhɛktə) *vb* **1** to bully or torment ▷ *n* **2** a blustering bully [C17 after HECTOR, in the sense: a bully]

Hector (ˈhɛktə) *n classical myth* a son of King Priam of Troy, who was killed by Achilles

Hecuba (ˈhɛkjʊbə) *n classical myth* the wife of King Priam of Troy, and mother of Hector and Paris

he'd (hiːd; *unstressed* iːd, hɪd, ɪd) *contraction of* he had *or* he would

heddle (ˈhɛdᵊl) *n* one of a set of frames of vertical wires on a loom, each wire having an eye through which a warp thread can be passed [OE *hefeld* chain]

hedera (ˈhɛdərə) *n* the genus name of **ivy** (sense 1) [L]

hedge (hɛdʒ) *n* **1** a row of shrubs, bushes, or trees forming a boundary **2** a barrier or protection against something **3** the act or a method of reducing the risk of loss on an investment, etc **4** a cautious or evasive statement **5** (*as modifier*) low, inferior, or illiterate: *hedge priest* ▷ *vb* **hedges, hedging, hedged 6** (*tr*) to enclose or separate with or as if with a hedge **7** (*intr*) to make or maintain a hedge **8** (*tr; often foll by* in, about, *or* around) to hinder or restrict **9** (*intr*) to evade decision, esp by making noncommittal statements **10** (*tr*) to guard against the risk of loss in (a bet, etc), esp by laying bets with other bookmakers **11** (*intr*) to protect against loss through future price fluctuations, as by investing in futures [OE *hecg*] > ˈ**hedger** *n* > ˈ**hedging** *n*

hedge fund *n* a largely unregulated speculative fund, which offers substantial returns for high-risk investments

hedgehog (ˈhɛdʒˌhɒɡ) *n* a small nocturnal Old World mammal having a protective covering of spines on the back

hedgehop (ˈhɛdʒˌhɒp) *vb* **hedgehops, hedgehopping, hedgehopped** (*intr*) (of an aircraft) to fly close to the ground, as in crop spraying > ˈ**hedgeˌhopping** *n, adj*

hedgerow (ˈhɛdʒˌrəʊ) *n* a hedge of shrubs or low trees, esp one bordering a field

hedge sparrow *n* a small brownish European songbird. Also called: **dunnock**

hedonics (hiːˈdɒnɪks) *n* (*functioning as sing*) **1** the branch of psychology concerned with the study of pleasant and unpleasant sensations **2** (in philosophy) the study of pleasure

hedonism (ˈhiːdᵊˌnɪzəm, ˈhɛd-) *n* **1** *ethics* **1a** the doctrine that moral value can be defined in terms of pleasure **1b** the doctrine that the pursuit of pleasure is the highest good **2** indulgence in sensual pleasures [C19 from Gk *hēdonē* pleasure] > ˌ**hedonˈistic** *adj* > ˈ**hedonist** *n*

-hedron *n combining form* indicating a solid having a specified number of surfaces: *tetrahedron* [from Gk *-edron* -sided, from *hedra* seat, base] > **-hedral** *adj combining form*

heebie-jeebies (ˈhiːbɪˈdʒiːbɪz) *pl n* **the** *sl* apprehension and nervousness [C20 coined by W. De Beck (1890–1942), American cartoonist]

heed (hiːd) *n* **1** careful attention; notice: *to take heed* ▷ *vb* **2** to pay close attention to (someone or something) [OE *hēdan*] > ˈ**heedful** *adj* > ˈ**heedfully** *adv* > ˈ**heedfulness** *n*

heedless (ˈhiːdlɪs) *adj* taking no notice; careless or thoughtless > ˈ**heedlessly** *adv* > ˈ**heedlessness** *n*

heehaw (ˌhiːˈhɔː) *interj* an imitation or representation of the braying sound of a donkey

heel[1] (hiːl) *n* **1** the back part of the human foot **2** the corresponding part in other vertebrates **3** the part of a stocking, etc, designed to fit the heel **4** the outer part of a shoe underneath the heel **5** the end or back section of something: *the heel of a loaf* **6** *horticulture* the small part of the parent plant that remains attached to a young shoot cut for propagation **7** the back part of a golf club head where it bends to join the shaft **8** *sl* a contemptible person **9 at** (*or* **on**) **one's heels** following closely **10 down at heel 10a** shabby or worn **10b** slovenly **11 kick** (*or* **cool**) **one's heels** to wait or be kept waiting **12 take to one's heels** to run off **13 to heel** under control, as a dog walking by a person's heel ▷ *vb* **14** (*tr*) to repair or replace the heel of (a shoe, etc) **15** (*tr*) *golf* to strike (the ball) with the heel of the club **16** to follow at the heels of (a person) [OE *hēla*] > ˈ**heelless** *adj*

heel[2] (hiːl) *vb* **1** (of a vessel) to lean over; list ▷ *n* **2** inclined position from the vertical [OE *hieldan*]

heelball (ˈhiːlˌbɔːl) *n* **a** a mixture of beeswax and lampblack used by shoemakers to blacken the edges of heels and soles **b** a similar substance used to take rubbings, esp brass rubbings

heeler (ˈhiːlə) *n* **1** *US* See **ward heeler 2** a person or thing that heels **3** *Austral & NZ* a dog that herds cattle, etc, by biting at their heels

heel in *vb* (*tr, adv*) to insert (cuttings, shoots, etc) into the soil before planting to keep them moist

heeltap (ˈhiːlˌtæp) *n* **1** a layer of leather, etc, in the heel of a shoe **2** a small amount of alcoholic drink left at the bottom of a glass

Heerlen (ˈhɪələn; *Dutch* ˈheːrlə) *n* a city in the SE Netherlands, in Limburg province: industrial centre of a coal-mining region. Pop: 95 794 (1994)

Hefei (ˈhʌˈfeɪ) *or* **Hofei** *n* a city in SE China, capital of Anhui province: administrative and commercial centre in a rice- and cotton-growing region. Pop: 1 000 655 (1999 est)

heft (hɛft) *vb* (*tr*) *Brit dialect & US inf* **1** to assess the weight of (something) by lifting **2** to lift ▷ *n* **3** weight **4** *US* the main part [C19 prob. from HEAVE, by analogy with *thieve, theft, cleave, cleft*]

hefty (ˈhɛftɪ) *adj* **heftier, heftiest** *inf* **1** big and strong **2** characterized by vigour or force: *a hefty blow* **3** bulky or heavy **4** sizable; involving a large amount of money: *a hefty bill* > ˈ**heftily** *adv*

Hegel (ˈheɪɡᵊl) *n* **Georg Wilhelm Friedrich** (ɡeˈɔrk ˈvɪlhɛlm ˈfriːdrɪç) 1770–1831, German philosopher, who created a fundamentally influential system of thought. His view of man's mind as the highest expression of the Absolute is expounded in *The Phenomenology of Mind* (1807). He developed his concept of dialectic, in which the contradiction between a proposition (thesis) and its antithesis is resolved at a higher level of truth (synthesis), in *Science of Logic* (1812–16)

hegemony (hɪˈɡɛmənɪ) *n, pl* **hegemonies** ascendancy or domination of one power or state within a league, confederation, etc [C16 from Gk *hēgemonia*, from *hēgemōn* leader, from *hēgeisthai* to lead] > **hegemonic** (ˌhɛɡəˈmɒnɪk) *adj*

Hegira *or* **Hejira** (ˈhɛdʒɪrə) *n* **1** the flight of Mohammed from Mecca to Medina in 622 AD; the starting point of the Muslim era **2** the Muslim era itself **3** (*often not cap*) an emigration, escape, or flight [C16 from Med. L, from Ar. *hijrah* emigration or flight]

Heidegger (*German* ˈhaidɛɡər) *n* **Martin** (ˈmartiːn) 1889–1976, German existentialist philosopher: he expounded his ontological system in *Being and Time* (1927)

Heidelberg (ˈhaɪdᵊlˌbɜːɡ; *German* ˈhaidəlbɛrk) *n* a city in SW Germany, in NW Baden-Württemberg on the River Neckar: capital of the Palatinate from the 13th century until 1719; famous castle (begun in the 12th century) and university (1386), the oldest in Germany. Pop: 139 400 (1999 est)

heifer ('hɛfə) *n* a young cow [OE *heahfore*]
Heifetz ('haɪfɪts) *n* **Jascha** ('jæʃə) 1901–87, US violinist, born in Russia
heigh-ho ('heɪ'həʊ) *interj* an exclamation of weariness, surprise, or happiness
height (haɪt) *n* **1** the vertical distance from the bottom of something to the top **2** the vertical distance of a place above sea level **3** relatively great altitude **4** the topmost point; summit **5** *astron* the angular distance of a celestial body above the horizon **6** the period of greatest intensity: *the height of the battle* **7** an extreme example: *the height of rudeness* **8** (*often pl*) an area of high ground [OE *hīehthu*; see HIGH]
heighten ('haɪtᵊn) *vb* to make or become higher or more intense > '**heightened** *adj*
height of land *n US & Canad* a watershed
Heilbronn (*German* hail'brɔn) *n* a city in SW Germany, in N Baden-Württemberg on the River Neckar. Pop: 119 900 (1999 est)
Heilongjiang ('heɪ'lʊŋdʒaɪ'æŋ) *or* **Heilungkiang** ('heɪ'lʊŋ'kjæŋ, -kaɪ'æŋ) *n* a province of NE China, in Manchuria: coal-mining, with placer gold in some rivers. Capital: Harbin. Pop: 36 890 000 (2000 est). Area: 464 000 sq km (179 000 sq miles)
Heilong Jiang ('heɪ'lʊŋ dʒaɪ'æŋ) *n* the Pinyin transliteration of the Chinese name for the **Amur**
Heiltsuk ('haɪl,tsʊk) *n* a member of a coastal Native Canadian people living in British Columbia. Formerly called: **Bella Bella** [of Wakashan origin]
Heimdall, Heimdal ('heɪm,dɑːl), *or* **Heimdallr** ('heɪm,dɑːlə) *n Norse myth* the god of light and the dawn, and the guardian of the rainbow bridge Bifrost
Heine (*German* 'hainə) *n* **Heinrich** ('hainrɪç) 1797–1856, German poet and essayist, whose chief poetic work is *Das Buch der Lieder* (1827). Many of his poems have been set to music, notably by Schubert and Schumann
Heinkel (*German* 'haink ᵊl) *n* **Ernst Heinrich** (ɛrnst 'hainrɪç) 1888–1958, German aircraft designer. His company provided many military aircraft in World Wars I and II, including the first jet-powered plane
heinous ('heɪnəs, 'hiː-) *adj* evil; atrocious [c14 from OF *haineus*, from *haine* hatred, of Gmc origin] > '**heinously** *adv*
heir (ɛə) *n* **1** the person legally succeeding to all property of a deceased person **2** any person or thing that carries on some tradition, circumstance, etc, from a forerunner [c13 from OF, from L *hērēs*] > '**heirdom** *or* '**heirship** *n*
heir apparent *n, pl* **heirs apparent** *property law* a person whose right to succeed to certain property cannot be defeated, provided such person survives his ancestor
heiress ('ɛərɪs) *n* **1** a woman who inherits or expects to inherit great wealth **2** a female heir
heirloom ('ɛə,luːm) *n* **1** an object that has been in a family for generations **2** an item of personal property inherited in accordance with the terms of a will [c15 from HEIR + *lome* tool; see LOOM[1]]
heir presumptive *n, pl* **heirs presumptive** *property law* a person who expects to succeed to an estate but whose right may be defeated by the birth of one nearer in blood to the ancestor
Heisenberg ('haɪzᵊn,bɜːg; *German* 'haizənbɛrk) *n* **Werner Karl** ('vɛrnər karl) 1901–76, German physicist. He contributed to quantum mechanics and formulated the uncertainty principle (1927): Nobel prize for physics 1932
heist (haɪst) *sl, chiefly US & Canad* ▷ *n* **1** a robbery ▷ *vb* **2** (*tr*) to steal [var. of HOIST]
Heitler (*German* 'haitlər) *n* **Walter** ('valtər) 1904–81, German physicist, noted for his work on chemical bonds
Hejaz *or* **Hijaz** (hiː'dʒæz) *n* a region of W Saudi Arabia, along the Red Sea and the Gulf of Aqaba: formerly an independent kingdom; united with Nejd in 1932 to form Saudi Arabia. Area: about 348 600 sq km (134 600 sq miles)
Hejira ('hɛdʒɪrə) *n* a variant spelling of **Hegira**
Hekate ('hɛkətɪ) *n* a variant spelling of **Hecate**
Hekla ('hɛklə) *n* a volcano in SW Iceland: several craters, with the last eruption in 1970. Height: 1491 m (4892 ft)
Hel (hɛl) *or* **Hela** ('hɛlɑː) *n Norse myth* **1** the goddess of the dead **2** the underworld realm of the dead
held (hɛld) *vb* the past tense and past participle of **hold**[1]
Helen ('hɛlɪn) *n Greek myth* the beautiful daughter of Zeus and Leda, whose abduction by Paris from her husband Menelaus caused the Trojan War
Helena[1] ('hɛlənə) *n* a city in W Montana: the state capital. Pop: 24 569 (1990)
Helena[2] (hɛlənə) *n* **Saint** ?248–?328 AD, Roman empress, mother of Constantine I. After converting to Christianity (313) she made a pilgrimage to the Holy Land (?326) where she supposedly discovered the cross on which Christ died. Feast day: May 21
helenium (hɛ'liːnɪəm) *n* a perennial garden plant with yellow, bronze, or crimson flowers [from Gk *helenion* name of a plant]
Helgoland ('hɛlgolant) *n* the German name for **Heligoland**
heliacal rising (hɪ'laɪəkᵊl) *n* **1** the rising of a celestial object at the same time as the sun **2** the date at which such a celestial object first becomes visible [c17 from LL *hēliacus* relating to the sun, from Gk, from *hēlios* sun]
helianthemum (hiːlɪ'ænθəməm) *n* any of a genus of dwarf shrubs with brightly coloured flowers: often grown in rockeries [from Gk *helios* sun + *anthemon* flower]
helianthus (,hiːlɪ'ænθəs) *n, pl* **helianthuses** a plant of the composite family having large yellow daisy-like flowers with yellow, brown, or purple centres [c18 NL, from Gk *hēlios* sun + *anthos* flower]
heli-boarding *n NZ* the sport of snowboarding on mountains or glaciers accessible only by helicopter or skiplane
helical ('hɛlɪkᵊl) *adj* of or like a helix; spiral
helical gear *n* a gearwheel having the tooth form generated on a helical path about the axis of the wheel
helices ('hɛlɪ,siːz) *n* a plural of **helix**
helichrysum (,hɛlɪ'kraɪzəm) *n* any plant of the genus *Helichrysum*, whose flowers retain their shape and colour when dried [c16 from L, from Gk, from *helix* spiral + *khrusos* gold]
helicoid ('hɛlɪ,kɔɪd) *adj* **1** *biol* shaped like a spiral: *a helicoid shell* ▷ *n* **2** *geom* any surface resembling that of a screw thread
helicon ('hɛlɪkən) *n* a bass tuba made to coil over the shoulder of a band musician [c19 prob. from HELICON; associated with Gk *helix* spiral]
Helicon ('hɛlɪkən) *n* a mountain in Greece, in Boeotia: location of the springs of Hippocrene and Aganippe, believed by the Ancient Greeks to be the source of poetic inspiration and the home of the Muses. Height: 1749 m (5738 ft). Modern Greek name: **Elikón**
helicopter ('hɛlɪ,kɒptə) *n* an aircraft capable of hover, vertical flight, and horizontal flight in any direction. Most get their lift and propulsion from overhead rotating blades [c19 from F, from Gk *helix* spiral + *pteron* wing]
▷ www.helicoptermuseum.org/museum/links.htm
▷ www.helikopter.li
helicopter gunship *n* a large heavily armed helicopter used for ground attack
helicopter view *n* an overview of a situation without any details
Heligoland ('hɛlɪgəʊ,lænd) *n* a small island in the North Sea, one of the North Frisian Islands, separated from the coast of NW Germany by **Heligoland Bight**: administratively part of the German state of Schleswig-Holstein: a large island in early medieval times, now eroded to an area of about 150 hectares (380 acres); ceded by Britain to Germany in 1890 in exchange

Hh

for Zanzibar. German name: **Helgoland**
helio- *or before a vowel* **heli-** *combining form* indicating the sun: *heliocentric* [from Gk, from *hēlios* sun]
heliocentric (ˌhiːlɪəʊˈsɛntrɪk) *adj* **1** having the sun at its centre **2** measured from or in relation to the sun > ˌ**helioˈcentrically** *adv*
Heliogabalus (ˌhiːlɪəʊˈɡæbələs) *or* **Elagabalus** *n* original name *Varius Avitus Bassianus*. ?204–222 AD, Roman emperor (218–222). His reign was notorious for debauchery and extravagance
heliograph (ˈhiːlɪəʊˌɡrɑːf) *n* **1** an instrument with mirrors and a shutter used for sending messages in Morse code by reflecting the sun's rays **2** a device used to photograph the sun > ˌ**heliˈography** *n*
heliometer (ˌhiːlɪˈɒmɪtə) *n* a refracting telescope used to determine angular distances between celestial bodies > ˌ**heliˈometry** *n*
heliopause (ˈhiːlɪəʊˌpɔːz) *n* the region of space beyond the sun's magnetic field
Heliopolis (ˌhiːlɪˈɒpəlɪs) *n* **1** (in ancient Egypt) a city near the apex of the Nile delta: a centre of sun worship. Ancient Egyptian name: **On** **2** the Ancient Greek name for **Baalbek**
heliopsis (ˌhɛlɪˈɒpsɪs) *n* a perennial plant with yellow daisy-like flowers
Helios (ˈhiːlɪˌɒs) *n Greek myth* the god of the sun, who drove his chariot daily across the sky. Roman counterpart: **Sol**
heliostat (ˈhiːlɪəʊˌstæt) *n* an astronomical instrument used to reflect the light of the sun in a constant direction > ˌ**helioˈstatic** *adj*
heliotrope (ˈhiːlɪəˌtrəʊp, ˈhɛljə-) *n* **1** any plant of the genus *Heliotropium*, esp the South American variety, cultivated for its small fragrant purple flowers **2a** a bluish-violet to purple colour **2b** *(as adj)*: *a heliotrope dress* **3** another name for **bloodstone** [C17 from L *hēliotropium*, from Gk, from *hēlios* sun + *trepein* to turn]
heliotropism (ˌhiːlɪˈɒtrəˌpɪzəm) *n* the growth of plants or plant parts (esp flowers) in response to the stimulus of sunlight > **heliotropic** (ˌhiːlɪəʊˈtrɒpɪk) *adj*
heliport (ˈhɛlɪˌpɔːt) *n* an airport for helicopters [C20 from HELI(COPTER) + PORT[1]]
heli-skiing *n* skiing in which skiers are transported by helicopter to remote slopes > ˈ**heli-ˌskier** *n*
helium (ˈhiːlɪəm) *n* a very light nonflammable colourless odourless element that is an inert gas, occurring in certain natural gases. Symbol: He; atomic no.: 2; atomic wt.: 4.0026 [C19 NL, from HELIO- + -IUM; because first detected in the solar spectrum]
helix (ˈhiːlɪks) *n, pl* **helices** *or* **helixes** **1** a spiral **2** the incurving fold that forms the margin of the external ear **3** another name for **volute** (sense 2) **4** any terrestrial mollusc of the genus *Helix*, including the garden snail [C16 from L, from Gk: spiral; prob. rel. to Gk *helissein* to twist]
hell (hɛl) *n* **1** *(sometimes cap) Christianity* **1a** the place or state of eternal punishment of the wicked after death **1b** forces of evil regarded as residing there **2** *(sometimes cap)* (in various religions and cultures) the abode of the spirits of the dead **3** pain, extreme difficulty, etc **4** *inf* a cause of such suffering: *war is hell* **5** *US & Canad* high spirits or mischievousness **6** *now rare* a gambling house **7** **(come) hell or high water** *inf* whatever difficulties may arise **8** **for the hell of it** *inf* for the fun of it **9** **from hell** *inf* denoting a person or thing that is particularly bad or alarming: *job from hell* **10** **give someone hell** *inf* **10a** to give someone a severe reprimand or punishment **10b** to be a source of torment to someone **11** **hell for leather** at great speed **12** **hell to pay** *inf* serious consequences, as of a foolish action **13** **the hell** *inf* **13a** (intensifier): used in such phrases as **what the hell** **13b** an expression of strong disagreement: *the hell I will* ▷ *interj* **14** *inf* an exclamation of anger, surprise, etc [OE *hell*]
he'll (hiːl; *unstressed* iːl, hɪl, ɪl) *contraction of* he will *or* he shall
hellacious (hɛˈleɪʃəs) *adj US sl* **1** remarkable; horrifying **2** wonderful; excellent [C20 from HELL + *-acious* as in AUDACIOUS]
Helladic (hɛˈlædɪk) *adj* of or relating to the Bronze Age civilization that flourished about 2900 to 1100 BC on the Greek mainland and islands
Hellas (ˈhɛləs) *n* transliteration of the Ancient Greek name for **Greece**
hellbent (ˌhɛlˈbɛnt) *adj (postpositive;* foll by *on) inf* strongly or rashly intent
hellcat (ˈhɛlˌkæt) *n* a spiteful fierce-tempered woman
Helle (ˈhɛlɪ) *n Greek myth* a daughter of King Athamas, who was borne away with her brother Phrixus on the golden winged ram. She fell from its back and was drowned in the Hellespont. See also **Phrixus, Golden Fleece**
hellebore (ˈhɛlɪˌbɔː) *n* **1** any plant of the Eurasian genus *Helleborus*, typically having showy flowers and poisonous parts. See also **Christmas rose** **2** any of various plants that yield alkaloids used in the treatment of heart disease [C14 from Gk *helleboros*, from ?]
Hellen (ˈhɛlɪn) *n* (in Greek legend) a Thessalian king and eponymous ancestor of the Hellenes
Hellene (ˈhɛliːn) *or* **Hellenian** (hɛˈliːnɪən) *n* another name for a **Greek**
Hellenic (hɛˈlɛnɪk, -ˈliː-) *adj* **1** of or relating to the ancient or modern Greeks or their language **2** of or relating to ancient Greece or the Greeks of the classical period (776–323 BC) ▷ Cf **Hellenistic** ▷ *n* **3** the Greek language in its various ancient and modern dialects
Hellenism (ˈhɛlɪˌnɪzəm) *n* **1** the principles, ideals, and pursuits associated with classical Greek civilization **2** the spirit or national character of the Greeks **3** imitation of or devotion to the culture of ancient Greece > ˈ**Hellenist** *n*
Hellenistic (ˌhɛlɪˈnɪstɪk) *or* **Hellenistical** *adj* **1** characteristic of or relating to Greek civilization in the Mediterranean world, esp from the death of Alexander the Great (323 BC) to the defeat of Antony and Cleopatra (30 BC) **2** of or relating to the Greeks or to Hellenism > ˌ**Hellenˈistically** *adv*
▷ www.isidore-of-seville.com/hellenistic
▷ www.hapcdt.plus.com/ebooks/hellenisticworld.html
Hellenize *or* **Hellenise** (ˈhɛlɪˌnaɪz) *vb* **Hellenizes, Hellenizing, Hellenized** *or* **Hellenises, Hellenising, Hellenised** to make or become like the ancient Greeks > ˌ**Helleniˈzation** *or* ˌ**Helleniˈsation** *n*
Heller (ˈhɛlə) *n* **Joseph** 1923–99, US novelist. His works include *Catch 22* (1961), *God Knows* (1984), *Picture This* (1988), and *Closing Time* (1994)
Helles (ˈhɛlɪs) *n* **Cape** a cape in NW Turkey, at the S end of the Gallipoli Peninsula
Hellespont (ˈhɛlɪˌspɒnt) *n* the ancient name for the **Dardanelles**
hellfire (ˈhɛlˌfaɪə) *n* **1** the torment of hell, envisaged as eternal fire **2** *(modifier)* characterizing sermons that emphasize this
hellion (ˈhɛljən) *n chiefly US inf* a rowdy person, esp a child; troublemaker [C19 prob. from dialect *hallion* rogue, from ?]
hellish (ˈhɛlɪʃ) *adj* **1** of or resembling hell **2** wicked; cruel **3** *inf* very unpleasant ▷ *adv* **4** *Brit inf* (intensifier): *a hellish good idea*
Hellman (ˈhɛlmən) *n* **Lillian** 1905–84, US dramatist. Her works include the plays *The Little Foxes* (1939), *The Searching Wind* (1944), and the autobiographical *Scoundrel Time* (1976)
hello, hallo, *or* **hullo** (hɛˈləʊ, hə-; ˈhɛləʊ) *sentence substitute* **1** an expression of greeting **2** a call used to attract attention **3** an expression of surprise ▷ *n, pl* **hellos, hallos,** *or* **hullos** **4** the act of saying or calling

"hello": *a quick round of hellos, the odd handshake, and he was ready* [C19 see HOLLO]

Hell's Angel *n* a member of a motorcycle gang who typically dress in Nazi-style paraphernalia and are noted for their lawless behaviour

helm[1] (hɛlm) *n* **1** *naut* **1a** the wheel or entire apparatus by which a vessel is steered **1b** the position of the helm: that is, on the side of the keel opposite from that of the rudder **2** a position of leadership or control (esp in **at the helm**) ▷ *vb* **3** (*tr*) to steer [OE *helma*] > **'helmsman** *n*

helm[2] (hɛlm) *n* an archaic or poetic word for **helmet** [OE *helm*]

Helmand ('hɛlmənd) *n* a river in S Asia, rising in E Afghanistan and flowing generally southwest to a marshy lake, Hamun Helmand, on the border with Iran. Length: 1400 km (870 miles)

helmer ('hɛlmə) *n* a film director

helmet ('hɛlmɪt) *n* **1** a piece of protective or defensive armour for the head worn by soldiers, policemen, firemen, divers, etc. See also **crash helmet, pith helmet** **2** *biol* a part or structure resembling a helmet, esp the upper part of the calyx of certain flowers [C15 from OF, dim. of *helme*, of Gmc origin] > **'helmeted** *adj*

Helmholtz (*German* 'hɛlmhɔlts) *n* Baron **Hermann Ludwig Ferdinand von** ('hɛrman 'lu:tvɪç 'fɛrdinant fɔn) 1821–94, German physiologist, physicist, and mathematician: helped to found the theory of the conservation of energy; invented the ophthalmoscope (1850); and investigated the mechanics of sight and sound

helminth ('hɛlmɪnθ) *n* any parasitic worm, esp a nematode or fluke [C19 from Gk *helmins* parasitic worm] > **hel'minthic** *or* **helminthoid** ('hɛlmɪn,θɔɪd, hɛl'mɪnθɔɪd) *adj*

helminthiasis (,hɛlmɪn'θaɪəsɪs) *n* infestation of the body with parasitic worms [C19 from NL, from Gk *helminthian* to be infested with worms]

Helmont (*Flemish* 'hɛlmɔnt) *n* **Jean Baptiste van** (ʒɑ̃ batist vɑn) 1577–1644, Flemish chemist and physician. He was the first to distinguish gases and claimed to have coined the word *gas*

Héloïse ('ɛləʊ,i:z; *French* elɔiz) *n* ?1101–64, pupil, mistress, and wife of Abelard

helot ('hɛlət, 'hi:-) *n* **1** (*cap*) (in ancient Sparta) a member of the class of serfs owned by the state **2** a serf or slave [C16 from L *Hēlotēs*, from Gk *Heilōtes*, alleged to have meant orig.: inhabitants of Helos, who, after its conquest, were serfs of the Spartans] > **'helotism** *n* > **'helotry** *n*

help (hɛlp) *vb* **1** to assist (someone to do something), esp by sharing the work, cost, or burden of something **2** to alleviate the burden of (someone else) by giving assistance **3** (*tr*) to assist (a person) to go in a specified direction: *help the old lady up* **4** to contribute to: *to help the relief operations* **5** to improve (a situation, etc): *crying won't help* **6** (*tr*; preceded by *can, could*, etc; *usually used with a negative*) **6a** to refrain from: *we can't help wondering who he is* **6b** (usually foll by *it*) to be responsible for: *I can't help it if it rains* **7** to alleviate (an illness, etc) **8** (*tr*) to serve (a customer) **9** (*tr*; foll by *to*) **9a** to serve (someone with food, etc) (usually in **help oneself**) **9b** to provide (oneself with) without permission **10** **cannot help but** to be unable to do anything else except: *I cannot help but laugh* **11** **so help me** **11a** on my honour **11b** no matter what: *so help me, I'll get revenge* ▷ *n* **12** the act of helping or being helped, or a person or thing that helps **13a** a person hired for a job, esp a farm worker or domestic servant **13b** (*functioning as sing*) several employees collectively **14** a remedy: *there's no help for it* ▷ *sentence substitute* **15** used to ask for assistance ▷ See also **help out** [OE *helpan*] > **'helper** *n*

helpful ('hɛlpfʊl) *adj* giving help > **'helpfully** *adv* > **'helpfulness** *n*

helping ('hɛlpɪŋ) *n* a single portion of food

helping hand *n* assistance: *many people lent a helping hand in making arrangements*

helpless ('hɛlplɪs) *adj* **1** unable to manage independently **2** made weak: *they were helpless from giggling* > **'helplessly** *adv* > **'helplessness** *n*

helpline ('hɛlp,laɪn) *n* a telephone line operated by a charitable organization for people in distress or by a commercial organization to provide information

Helpmann ('hɛlpmən) *n* Sir **Robert** 1909–86, Australian ballet dancer and choreographer: his ballets include *Miracle in the Gorbals* (1944), *Display* (1965), and *Yugen* (1965)

helpmate ('hɛlp,meɪt) *n* a companion and helper, esp a wife

helpmeet ('hɛlp,mi:t) *n* a less common word for **helpmate** [C17 from *an helpe meet* (suitable) *for him* Genesis 2:18]

help out *vb* (*adv*) to assist, esp by sharing the burden or cost of something with (another person)

Helsingborg (*Swedish* hɛlsiŋ'bɔrj) *n* a port in SW Sweden, on the Sound opposite Helsingør, Denmark: changed hands several times between Denmark and Sweden, finally becoming Swedish in 1710; shipbuilding. Pop: 116 870 (2000 est). Former name (until 1971): **Hälsingborg**

Helsingør (*Danish* hɛlseŋ'ø:r) *n* a port in NE Denmark, in NE Zealand: site of Kronborg Castle (16th century), famous as the scene of Shakespeare's *Hamlet*. Pop: 56 855 (1995). English name: **Elsinore**

Helsinki ('hɛlsɪŋkɪ, hɛl'sɪŋ-) *n* the capital of Finland, a port in the south on the Gulf of Finland: founded by Gustavus I of Sweden in 1550; replaced Turku as capital in 1812, while under Russian rule; university. Pop: 551 123 (2000 est). Swedish name: **Helsingfors** (hɛlsɪŋ'fɔrs)
▷ www.hel.fi/English

helter-skelter ('hɛltə'skɛltə) *adj* **1** haphazard or careless ▷ *adv* **2** in a helter-skelter manner ▷ *n* **3** *Brit* a high spiral slide, as at a fairground **4** disorder [C16 prob. imit.]

Hh

helve (hɛlv) *n* the handle of a hand tool such as an axe or pick [OE *hielfe*]

Helvellyn (hɛl'vɛlɪn) *n* a mountain in NW England, in the Lake District. Height: 950 m (3118 ft)

Helvetia (hɛl'vi:ʃə) *n* **1** the Latin name for Switzerland **2** a Roman province in central Europe (1st century BC to the 5th century AD), corresponding to part of S Germany and parts of W and N Switzerland

Helvetian (hɛl'vi:ʃən) *adj* **1** Swiss ▷ *n* **2** a native or citizen of Switzerland

Helvétius (hɛl'vi:ʃɪəs; *French* ɛlvesjys) *n* **Claude Adrien** (klod adriɛ̃) 1715–71, French philosopher. In his chief work *De l'Esprit* (1758), he asserted that the mainspring of human action is self-interest and that differences in human intellects are due only to differences in education

hem[1] (hɛm) *n* **1** an edge to a piece of cloth, made by folding the raw edge under and stitching it down **2** short for **hemline** ▷ *vb* **hems, hemming, hemmed** (*tr*) **3** to provide with a hem **4** (usually foll by *in, around*, or *about*) to enclose or confine [OE *hemm*] > **'hemmer** *n*

hem[2] (hɛm) *n, interj* **1** a representation of the sound of clearing the throat, used to gain attention, etc ▷ *vb* **hems, hemming, hemmed** **2** (*intr*) to utter this sound **3** **hem** (*or* **hum**) **and haw** to hesitate in speaking

he-man *n, pl* **he-men** *inf* a strongly built muscular man

hematite *or* **haematite** ('hɛmətaɪt, 'hi:m-) *n* a red, grey, or black mineral, found as massive beds and in veins and igneous rocks. It is the chief source of iron. Composition: iron (ferric) oxide. Crystal structure: hexagonal (rhombohedral) [C16 via L from Gk *haimatitēs* resembling blood, from *haima* blood] > **hematitic** *or* **haematitic** (,hɛmə'tɪtɪk, ,hi:-) *adj*

hemato- *or before a vowel* **hemat-** *combining form* US variants of **haemato-**

Hemel Hempstead ('hɛməl 'hɛmstɪd) *n* a town in SE England, in W Hertfordshire: designated a new town in 1947. Pop: 79 235 (1991)

hemeralopia (ˌhɛmərəˈləʊpɪə) *n* inability to see clearly in bright light. Nontechnical name: **day blindness** [c18 NL, from Gk, from *hēmera* day + *alaos* blind + *ōps* eye]

hemerocallis (ˌhɛmərəʊˈkælɪs) *n* a N temperate plant with large funnel-shaped orange flowers: each single flower lasts for only one day. Also called: **day lily** [c17 from Gk *hēmera* day + *kallos* beauty]

hemi- *prefix* half: *hemicycle; hemisphere* [from L, from Gk *hēmi-*]

-hemia *n combining form* a US variant of **-aemia**

hemidemisemiquaver (ˌhɛmɪˌdɛmɪˈsɛmɪˌkweɪvə) *n music* a note having the time value of one sixty-fourth of a semibreve. Usual US and Canad name: **sixty-fourth note**

Hemingway ('hɛmɪŋˌweɪ) *n* **Ernest** 1899–1961, US novelist and short-story writer. His novels include *The Sun Also Rises* (1926), *A Farewell to Arms* (1929), *For Whom the Bell Tolls* (1940), and *The Old Man and the Sea* (1952): Nobel prize for literature 1954

hemiplegia (ˌhɛmɪˈpliːdʒɪə) *n* paralysis of one side of the body > ˌ**hemiˈplegic** *adj*

hemipode ('hɛmɪˌpəʊd) *n* a small quail-like bird occurring in tropical and subtropical regions of the Old World. Also called: **button quail**

hemipteran (hɪˈmɪptərən) *n* any hemipterous insect [c19 from HEMI- + Gk *pteron* wing]

hemipterous (hɪˈmɪptərəs) *adj* of or belonging to a large order of insects having sucking or piercing mouthparts

hemisphere ('hɛmɪˌsfɪə) *n* **1** one half of a sphere **2a** half of the terrestrial globe, divided into **northern** and **southern hemispheres** by the equator or into **eastern** and **western hemispheres** by some meridians, usually 0° and 180° **2b** a map or projection of one of the hemispheres **3** *anat* short for **cerebral hemisphere,** a half of the cerebrum > **hemispheric** (ˌhɛmɪˈsfɛrɪk) *or* ˌ**hemiˈspherical** *adj*

hemistich ('hɛmɪˌstɪk) *n prosody* a half line of verse

hemline ('hɛmˌlaɪn) *n* the level to which the hem of a skirt or dress hangs

hemlock ('hɛmˌlɒk) *n* **1** an umbelliferous poisonous Eurasian plant having finely divided leaves, spotted stems, and small white flowers **2** a poisonous drug derived from this plant **3** Also called: **hemlock spruce** a coniferous tree of North America and Asia [OE *hymlic*]

hemo- *combining form* a US variant of **haemo-**

hemp (hɛmp) *n* **1** Also called: **cannabis, marijuana** an Asian plant having tough fibres, deeply lobed leaves, and small greenish flowers. See also **Indian hemp** **2** the fibre of this plant, used to make canvas, rope, etc **3** any of several narcotic drugs obtained from some varieties of this plant, esp from Indian hemp [OE *hænep*] > ˈ**hempen** *or* ˈ**hempˌlike** *adj*

hemstitch ('hɛmˌstɪtʃ) *n* **1** a decorative edging stitch, usually for a hem, in which the cross threads are stitched in groups ▷ *vb* **2** to decorate (a hem, etc) with hemstitches

hen (hɛn) *n* **1** the female of any bird, esp of the domestic fowl **2** the female of certain other animals, such as the lobster **3** *Scot dialect* a term of address used to women [OE *henn*]

Henan ('hʌˈnæn) *or* **Honan** *n* a province of N central China: the chief centre of early Chinese culture; mainly agricultural (the largest wheat-producing province in China). Capital: Zhengzhou. Pop: 95 560 000 (2000 est)

henbane ('hɛnˌbeɪn) *n* a poisonous European plant with sticky hairy leaves: yields the drug hyoscyamine

hence (hɛns) *sentence connector* **1** for this reason; therefore ▷ *adv* **2** from this time: *a year hence* **3** *arch* from here; away ▷ *sentence substitute* **4** *arch* begone! away! [OE *hionane*]

henceforth (ˌhɛnsˈfɔːθ), **henceforwards,** *or* **henceforward** *adv* from now on

henchman ('hɛntʃmən) *n, pl* **henchmen** **1** a faithful attendant or supporter **2** *arch* a squire; page [c14 *hengestman*, from OE *hengest* stallion + MAN]

hendeca- *combining form* eleven: *hendecagon; hendecasyllable* [from Gk *hendeka*, from *hen*, neuter of *heis* one + *deka* ten]

hendecagon (hɛnˈdɛkəgən) *n* a polygon having 11 sides > **hendecagonal** (ˌhɛndɪˈkægənᵊl) *adj*

hendecasyllable ('hɛndɛkəˌsɪləbᵊl) *n prosody* a verse line of 11 syllables [c18 from Gk]

Henderson ('hɛndəsən) *n* **Arthur** 1863–1935, British Labour politician. As foreign secretary (1929–31) he supported the League of Nations and international disarmament; Nobel peace prize 1934

hendiadys (hɛnˈdaɪədɪs) *n* a rhetorical device by which two nouns joined by a conjunction are used instead of a noun and a modifier, as in *to run with fear and haste* instead of *to run with fearful haste* [c16 from Med. L, from Gk *hen dia duoin*, lit.: one through two]

Hendra ('hɛndrə) *n* a virus that affects humans and horses, causing a fatal, influenza-like illness [c20 after the suburb of Brisbane, the location of the outbreak during which the virus was first isolated]

Hendrix ('hɛndrɪks) *n* **Jimi,** full name *James Marshall Hendrix*. 1942–70, US rock guitarist, singer, and songwriter, noted for his innovative guitar technique. His recordings include "Purple Haze" (1967) and *Are you Experienced?* (1967)

Hendry ('hɛndrɪ) *n* **Stephen** born 1969, British snooker player: world champion 1990, 1992–96, and 1999

henequen, henequin, *or* **heniquen** ('hɛnɪkɪn) *n* **1** an agave plant native to Mexico **2** the fibre of this plant, used in making rope, twine, and fabrics [c19 from American Sp. *henequén*, prob. of Amerind origin]

henge (hɛndʒ) *n* a circular monument, often containing a circle of stones, dating from the Neolithic and Bronze Ages [back formation from *Stonehenge*, site of important megalithic ruins on Salisbury Plain, S England]

Hengelo (*Dutch* 'hɛŋəloː) *n* a city in the E Netherlands, in Overijssel province on the Twente Canal: industrial centre, esp for textiles. Pop: 77 514 (1994)

Hengist ('hɛŋgɪst) *n* died ?488 AD, a leader, with his brother Horsa, of the first Jutish settlers in Britain; he is thought to have conquered Kent (?455)

Hengyang ('hɛŋˈjæŋ) *n* a city in SE central China, in Hunan province on the Xiang River. Pop: 584 346 (1999 est)

hen harrier *n* a common harrier that nests in marshes and open land

henhouse ('hɛnˌhaʊs) *n* a coop for hens

Henie ('hɛnɪ) *n* **Sonja** ('sɒnjə) 1912–69, Norwegian figure-skater

Henley-on-Thames ('hɛnlɪ-) *n* a town in S England, in SE Oxfordshire on the River Thames: a riverside resort with an annual regatta. Pop: 10 558 (1991). Often shortened to: **Henley**

henna ('hɛnə) *n* **1** a shrub or tree of Asia and N Africa **2** a reddish dye obtained from the powdered leaves of this plant, used as a cosmetic and industrial dye **3a** a reddish-brown colour **3b** (*as adj*): *henna tresses* ▷ *vb* **hennas, hennaing, hennaed** **4** (*tr*) to dye with henna [c16 from Ar. *hinnā'*; see ALKANET]

hen night *n inf* a party for women only, esp held for a woman shortly before she is married ▷ Cf **hen party, stag night**

henotheism ('hɛnəʊθiːˌɪzəm) *n* the worship of one deity (of several) as the special god of one's family, clan, or tribe [c19 from Gk *heis* one + *theos* god] > ˌ**henotheˈistic** *adj*

hen party *n inf* a party at which only women are present ▷ Cf **hen night, stag night**

henpeck ('hɛn,pɛk) *vb (tr)* (of a woman) to harass or torment (a man, esp her husband) by persistent nagging

henpecked ('hɛn,pɛkt) *adj* (of a man) continually harassed or tormented by the persistent nagging of a woman (esp his wife)

Henrietta Maria (,hɛnrɪ'ɛtə mə'riːə) *n* 1609–69, queen of England (1625–49), the wife of Charles I; daughter of Henry IV of France. Her Roman Catholicism contributed to the unpopularity of the crown in the period leading to the Civil War

henry ('hɛnrɪ) *n, pl* **henry, henries,** *or* **henrys** the derived SI unit of electric inductance; the inductance of a closed circuit in which an emf of 1 volt is produced when the current varies uniformly at the rate of 1 ampere per second. Symbol: H [C19 after Joseph HENRY]

Henry ('hɛnrɪ) *n* **1 Prince,** known as **Harry** born 1984, second son of Charles, Prince of Wales, and Diana, Princess of Wales **2 Joseph** 1797–1878, US physicist. He discovered the principle of electromagnetic induction independently of Faraday and constructed the first electromagnetic motor (1829) He also discovered self-induction and the oscillatory nature of electric discharges (1842) **3 O** See **O Henry 4 Patrick** 1736–99, American statesman and orator, a leading opponent of British rule during the War of American Independence

Henry I *n* **1** known as *Henry the Fowler.* ?876–936 AD, duke of Saxony (912–36) and king of Germany (919–36): founder of the Saxon dynasty (918–1024) **2** 1068–1135, king of England (1100–35) and duke of Normandy (1106–35); son of William the Conqueror: crowned in the absence of his elder brother, Robert II, duke of Normandy; conquered Normandy (1106)

Henry II *n* **1** known as *Henry the Saint.* 973–1024, king of Germany and Holy Roman Emperor (1014–24): canonized in 1145 **2** 1133–89, first Plantagenet king of England (1154–89): extended his Anglo-French domains and instituted judicial and financial reforms. His attempts to control the church were opposed by Becket **3** 1519–59, king of France (1547–59); husband of Catherine de' Medici. He recovered Calais from the English (1558) and suppressed the Huguenots

Henry III *n* **1** 1017–56, king of Germany and Holy Roman Emperor (1046–56) He increased the power of the Empire but his religious policy led to rebellions **2** 1207–72, king of England (1216–72); son of John. His incompetent rule provoked the Barons' War (1264–67), during which he was captured by Simon de Montfort **3** 1551–89, king of France (1574–89). He plotted the massacre of Huguenots on St Bartholomew's Day (1572) with his mother Catherine de' Medici, thus exacerbating the religious wars in France

Henry IV *n* **1** 1050–1106, Holy Roman Emperor (1084–1105) and king of Germany (1056–1105). He was excommunicated by Pope Gregory VII, whom he deposed (1084) **2** surnamed *Bolingbroke.* 1367–1413, first Lancastrian king of England (1399–1413); son of John of Gaunt: deposed Richard II (1399) and suppressed rebellions led by Owen Glendower and the Earl of Northumberland **3** known as *Henry of Navarre.* 1553–1610, first Bourbon king of France (1589–1610). He obtained toleration for the Huguenots with the Edict of Nantes (1598) and restored prosperity to France following the religious wars (1562–98)

Henry V *n* **1** 1081–1125, king of Germany (1089–1125) and Holy Roman Emperor (1111–25) **2** 1387–1422, king of England (1413–22); son of Henry IV. He defeated the French at the Battle of Agincourt (1415), conquered Normandy (1419), and was recognized as heir to the French throne (1420)

Henry VI *n* **1** 1165–97, king of Germany (1169–97) and Holy Roman Emperor (1190–97): added Sicily to the Empire **2** 1421–71, last Lancastrian king of England (1422–61; 1470–71); son of Henry V. His weak rule was blamed for the loss by 1453 of all his possessions in France except Calais; from 1454 he suffered periods of insanity which contributed to the outbreak of the Wars of the Roses (1455–85). He was deposed by Edward IV (1461) but was briefly restored to the throne (1470)

Henry VII *n* **1** ?1275–1313, Holy Roman Emperor (1312–13) and, as Henry VI, count of Luxembourg (1288–1313). He became king of the Lombards in 1313 **2** 1457–1509, first Tudor king of England (1485–1509). He came to the throne (1485) after defeating Richard III at the Battle of Bosworth Field, ending the Wars of the Roses. Royal power and the prosperity of the country greatly increased during his reign

Henry VIII *n* 1491–1547, king of England (1509–47); second son of Henry VII. The declaration that his marriage to Catherine of Aragon was invalid and his marriage to Anne Boleyn (1533) precipitated the Act of Supremacy, making Henry supreme head of the Church in England. Anne Boleyn was executed (1536) and Henry subsequently married Jane Seymour, Anne of Cleves, Catherine Howard, and Catherine Parr. His reign is also noted for the fame of his succession of advisers, Cardinal Wolsey, Sir Thomas More, and Thomas Cromwell

Henryson ('hɛnrɪsᵊn) *n* **Robert** ?1430–?1506, Scottish poet. His works include *Testament of Cresseid* (1593), a sequel to Chaucer's *Troilus and Cressida*, the 13 *Moral Fables of Esope the Phrygian*, and the pastoral dialogue *Robene and Makyne*

Henry the Navigator *n* 1394–1460, prince of Portugal, noted for his patronage of Portuguese voyages of exploration of the W coast of Africa

Henslowe ('hɛnzləʊ) *n* **Philip** died 1616, English theatre manager, noted also for his diary

Henze (*German* 'hɛntsə) *n* **Hans Werner** (hans 'vɛrnər) born 1926, German composer, whose works, in many styles, include the operas *The Stag King* (1956), *The Bassarids* (1965), *The English Cat* (1983), and *Das verratene Meer* (1990) and the oratorio *The Raft of the Medusa* (1968)

hep (hɛp) *adj* **hepper, heppest** *sl* an earlier word for **hip**[4]

heparin ('hɛpərɪn) *n* a polysaccharide, containing sulphate groups, present in most body tissues: an anticoagulant used in the treatment of thrombosis [C20 from Gk *hēpar* the liver + -IN]

hepatic (hɪ'pætɪk) *adj* **1** of the liver **2** having the colour of liver ▷ *n* **3** *obs* any of various drugs for use in treating diseases of the liver [C15 from L *hēpaticus*, from Gk *hēpar* liver]

hepatica (hɪ'pætɪkə) *n* a woodland plant of a N temperate genus, having three-lobed leaves and white, mauve, or pink flowers [C16 from Med. L: liverwort, from L *hēpaticus* of the liver]

hepatitis (,hɛpə'taɪtɪs) *n* inflammation of the liver

hepatitis A *n* a form of hepatitis caused by a virus transmitted in contaminated food or drink

hepatitis B *n* a form of hepatitis caused by a virus transmitted by infected blood (as in transfusions), contaminated hypodermic needles, sexual contact, or by contact with any other body fluid. Former name: **serum hepatitis**

hepatitis C *n* a form of hepatitis caused by a virus that is transmitted in the same ways as that responsible for hepatitis B. Former name: **non-A, non-B hepatitis**

Hepburn ('hɛp,bɜːn) *n* **1 Audrey** 1929–93, US actress, born in Belgium. Her films include *Roman Holiday* (1955), *Funny Face* (1957), and *My Fair Lady* (1964) **2 Katharine** 1907–2003, US film actress, whose films include *The Philadelphia Story* (1940), *Adam's Rib* (1949), *The African Queen* (1951), *The Lion in Winter* (1968) for which she won an Oscar, and *On Golden Pond* (1981)

Hephaestus (hɪ'fiːstəs) *or* **Hephaistos** (hɪ'faɪstɒs) *n Greek myth* the lame god of fire and metal-working. Son

Hh

of Zeus and Hera. Roman counterpart: **Vulcan**

Hepplewhite (ˈhɛpəlˌwaɪt) *adj* of or in a style of ornamental and carved 18th-century English furniture [c18 after George *Hepplewhite* (1727–86), E cabinetmaker]

hepta- *or before a vowel* **hept-** *combining form* seven: *heptameter* [from Gk]

heptad (ˈhɛptæd) *n* a group or series of seven [c17 from Gk *heptas* seven]

heptagon (ˈhɛptəgən) *n* a polygon having seven sides > **heptagonal** (hɛpˈtægənəl) *adj*

heptahedron (ˌhɛptəˈhiːdrən) *n* a solid figure having seven plane faces > ˌ**heptaˈhedral** *adj*

heptameter (hɛpˈtæmɪtə) *n prosody* a verse line of seven metrical feet > **heptametrical** (ˌhɛptəˈmɛtrɪkəl) *adj*

heptane (ˈhɛpteɪn) *n* an alkane which is found in petroleum and used as an anaesthetic [c19 from HEPTA- + -ANE, because it has seven carbon atoms]

heptarchy (ˈhɛptɑːkɪ) *n, pl* **heptarchies** 1 government by seven rulers 2 the seven kingdoms into which Anglo-Saxon England is thought to have been divided from about the 7th to the 9th centuries AD > ˈ**heptarch** *n* > **hepˈtarchic** *or* **hepˈtarchal** *adj*

heptathlon (hɛpˈtæθlɒn) *n* an athletic contest for women in which each athlete competes in seven different events [c20 from HEPTA- + Gk *athlon* contest] > **hepˈtathlete** *n*

heptavalent (hɛpˈtævələnt, ˌhɛptəˈveɪlənt) *adj chem* having a valency of seven

Hepworth (ˈhɛpwəθ) *n* Dame **Barbara** 1903–75, British sculptor of abstract works

her (hɜː; *unstressed* hə, ə) *pron (objective)* 1 refers to a female person or animal: *he loves her* 2 refers to things personified as feminine or traditionally to ships and nations ▷ *determiner* 3 of, belonging to, or associated with her: *her hair* [OE *hire*, genitive & dative of *hēo* SHE, fem. of *hē* HE]

USAGE See at **me**

Hera *or* **Here** (ˈhɪərə) *n Greek myth* the queen of the Olympian gods and sister and wife of Zeus. Roman counterpart: **Juno**

Heraclea (ˌhɛrəˈkliːə) *n* any of several ancient Greek colonies. The most famous is the S Italian site where Pyrrhus of Epirus defeated the Romans (280 BC)

Heracleides *or* **Heraclides of Pontus** (ˌhɛrəˈklaɪdiːz, ˈpɒntəs) *n* ?390–?322 BC, Greek astronomer and philosopher: the first to state that the earth rotates on its axis

Heracles *or* **Herakles** (ˈhɛrəˌkliːz) *n* the usual name (in Greek) for **Hercules** > ˌ**Heraˈclean** *or* ˌ**Heraˈklean** *adj*

Heraclitus (ˌhɛrəˈklaɪtəs) *n* ?535–?475 BC, Greek philosopher, who held that fire is the primordial substance of the universe and that all things are in perpetual flux

Heraclius (hɛˈræklɪəs) *n* ?575–641 AD, Byzantine emperor, who restored the Holy Cross to Jerusalem (629)

Herakleion *or* **Heraklion** (*Greek* heˈraːkliɔn) *n* variants of **Iráklion**

herald (ˈhɛrəld) *n* 1 a person who announces important news 2 *often literary* a forerunner; harbinger 3 the intermediate rank of heraldic officer, between king-of-arms and pursuivant 4 (in the Middle Ages) an official at a tournament ▷ *vb (tr)* 5 to announce publicly 6 to precede or usher in [c14 from OF *herault*, of Gmc origin]

heraldic (hɛˈrældɪk) *adj* of or relating to heraldry or heralds > **heˈraldically** *adv*

heraldry (ˈhɛrəldrɪ) *n, pl* **heraldries** 1 the study concerned with the classification of armorial bearings, the tracing of genealogies, etc 2 armorial bearings, insignia, etc 3 the show and ceremony of heraldry > ˈ**heraldist** *n*

▷ www.college-of-arms.gov.uk
▷ www.heraldica.org

Herat (hɛˈræt) *n* a city in NW Afghanistan, on the Hari Rud River: on the site of several ancient cities; at its height as a cultural centre in the 15th century. Pop: 186 800 (1990 est)

Hérault (*French* ero) *n* a department of S France, in Languedoc-Roussillon region. Capital: Montpellier. Pop: 896 441 (1999). Area: 6224 sq km (2427 sq miles)

herb (hɜːb; *US* ɜːrb) *n* 1 a plant whose aerial parts do not persist above ground at the end of the growing season; herbaceous plant 2 any of various usually aromatic plants, such as parsley and rosemary, that are used in cookery and medicine [c13 from OF *herbe*, from L *herba* grass, green plants] > ˈ**herbˌlike** *adj* > ˈ**herby** *adj*

▷ www.culinarycafe.com/Spices_Herbs
▷ www.herbs.org
▷ www.herbsforafrica.co.za
▷ www.theherbcottage.com/herbs.html

herbaceous (hɜːˈbeɪʃəs) *adj* 1 designating or relating to plants that are fleshy as opposed to woody: *a herbaceous plant* 2 (of petals and sepals) green and leaflike

herbaceous border *n* a flower bed that contains nonwoody perennials rather than annuals

herbage (ˈhɜːbɪdʒ) *n* 1 herbaceous plants collectively, esp the edible parts on which cattle, sheep, etc, graze 2 the vegetation of pasture land; pasturage

herbal (ˈhɜːbəl) *adj* 1 of or relating to herbs, usually culinary or medicinal herbs ▷ *n* 2 a book describing the properties of plants

herbalist (ˈhɜːbəlɪst) *n* 1 a person who grows or specializes in the use of herbs, esp medicinal herbs 2 (formerly) a descriptive botanist

herbarium (hɜːˈbɛərɪəm) *n, pl* **herbariums** *or* **herbaria** (-ɪə) 1 a collection of dried plants that are mounted and classified systematically 2 a room, etc, in which such a collection is kept

herb bennet (ˈbɛnɪt) *n* a Eurasian and N African plant with yellow flowers. Also called: **wood avens, bennet** [from OF *herbe benoite*, lit.: blessed herb, from Med. L *herba benedicta*]

Herbert (ˈhɜːbət) *n* 1 **Edward,** 1st Baron Herbert of Cherbury. 1583–1648, English philosopher and poet, noted for his deistic views 2 his brother, **George** 1593–1633, English Metaphysical poet. His chief work is *The Temple: Sacred Poems and Private Ejaculations* (1633) 3 **Zbigniew** (ᵊzˈbɪgnɪəf), 1924–98, Polish poet and dramatist, noted esp for his dramatic monologues

herbicide (ˈhɜːbɪˌsaɪd) *n* a chemical that destroys plants, esp one used to control weeds

herbivore (ˈhɜːbɪˌvɔː) *n* 1 an animal that feeds on grass and other plants 2 *inf* a liberal, idealistic, or nonmaterialistic person [c19 from NL *herbivora* grass-eaters] > **herˈbivorous** *adj*

herb Paris (ˈpærɪs) *n, pl* **herbs Paris** a Eurasian woodland plant with a whorl of four leaves and a solitary yellow flower [c16 from Med. L *herba paris*, lit.: herb of a pair: because the four leaves on the stalk look like a true lovers' knot]

herb Robert (ˈrɒbət) *n, pl* **herbs Robert** a low-growing N temperate plant with strongly scented divided leaves and small pink flowers [c13 from Med. L *herba Roberti* herb of Robert, prob. after St *Robert*, 11th-cent. F ecclesiastic]

Hercegovina (*Serbo-Croat* ˈhɛrtsɛgɔvina) *n* a variant of **Herzegovina**

Herculaneum (ˌhɜːkjʊˈleɪnɪəm) *n* an ancient city in SW Italy, of marked Greek character, on the S slope of Vesuvius: buried along with Pompeii by an eruption of the volcano (79 AD). Excavation has uncovered well-preserved streets, houses, etc

herculean (ˌhɜːkjʊˈliːən) *adj* 1 requiring tremendous effort, strength, etc 2 (*sometimes cap*) resembling Hercules in strength, courage, etc

Hercules (ˈhɜːkjʊˌliːz), **Heracles,** *or* **Herakles** *n* 1 Also called: **Alcides** *classical myth* a hero noted for his great strength, courage, and for the performance of twelve immense labours **2** a man of outstanding strength or size

herd[1] (hɜːd) *n* **1** a large group of mammals living and feeding together, esp cattle **2** *often disparaging* a large group of people ▷ *vb* **3** to collect or be collected into or as if into a herd [OE *heord*]

herd[2] (hɜːd) *n* **1a** *arch or dialect* a man who tends livestock; herdsman **1b** (*in combination*): *goatherd* ▷ *vb* (*tr*) **2** to drive forwards in a large group **3** to look after (livestock) [OE *hirde*: see HERD[1]]

herd instinct *n psychol* the inborn tendency to associate with others and follow the group's behaviour

herdsman (ˈhɜːdzmən) *n, pl* **herdsmen** *chiefly Brit* a person who breeds or cares for cattle or (rarely) other livestock. US equivalent: **herder**

here (hɪə) *adv* **1** in, at, or to this place, point, case, or respect: *we come here every summer; here comes Roy* **2 here and there** at several places in or throughout an area **3 here's to** a formula used in proposing a toast to someone or something **4 neither here nor there** of no relevance or importance ▷ *n* **5** this place or point: *they leave here tonight* [OE *hēr*]

hereabouts (ˈhɪərəˌbaʊts) *or* **hereabout** *adv* in this region or neighbourhood

hereafter (ˌhɪərˈɑːftə) *adv* **1** *formal or law* in a subsequent part of this document, matter, case, etc **2** a less common word for **henceforth** **3** at some time in the future **4** in a future life after death ▷ *n* (usually preceded by *the*) **5** life after death **6** the future

hereat (ˌhɪərˈæt) *adv arch* because of this

hereby (ˌhɪəˈbaɪ) *adv* (used in official statements, etc) by means of or as a result of this

hereditable (hɪˈrɛdɪtəbᵊl) *adj* a less common word for **heritable** > **heˌreditaˈbility** *n*

hereditament (ˌhɛrɪˈdɪtəmənt) *n property law* any kind of property capable of being inherited

hereditary (hɪˈrɛdɪtərɪ, -trɪ) *adj* **1** of or denoting factors that can be transmitted genetically from one generation to another **2** *law* **2a** descending to succeeding generations by inheritance **2b** transmitted according to established rules of descent **3** derived from one's ancestors; traditional: *hereditary feuds* > **heˈreditarily** *adv* > **heˈreditariness** *n*

heredity (hɪˈrɛdɪtɪ) *n, pl* **heredities** **1** the transmission from one generation to another of genetic factors that determine individual characteristics **2** the sum total of the inherited factors in an organism [C16 from OF *heredite*, from L *hērēditās* inheritance; see HEIR]

Hereford (ˈhɛrɪfəd) *n* **1** a city in W England, in Herefordshire on the River Wye: trading centre for agricultural produce; cathedral (begun 1079). Pop: 54 326 (1991) **2** a hardy breed of beef cattle characterized by a red body, red and white head, and white markings

Hereford and Worcester *n* a former county of the W Midlands of England, created in 1974 from the historic counties of Herefordshire and (most of) Worcestershire: abolished in 1998 when Herefordshire became an independent unitary authority

Herefordshire (ˈhɛrɪfədʃɪə, -ʃə) *n* a county of W England: from 1974 to 1998 part of Hereford and Worcester: drained chiefly by the River Wye; agricultural (esp fruit and cattle). Administrative centre: Hereford. Pop: 174 844 (2001). Area: 2180 sq km (842 sq miles)

herein (ˌhɪərˈɪn) *adv* **1** *formal or law* in or into this place, thing, document, etc **2** *rare* in this respect, circumstance, etc

hereinafter (ˌhɪərɪnˈɑːftə) *adv formal or law* from this point on in this document, etc

hereinto (ˌhɪərˈɪntuː) *adv formal or law* into this place, circumstance, etc

hereof (ˌhɪərˈɒv) *adv formal or law* of or concerning this

hereon (ˌhɪərˈɒn) *adv* an archaic word for **hereupon**

heresiarch (hɪˈriːzɪˌɑːk) *n* the leader or originator of a heretical movement or sect

heresy (ˈhɛrəsɪ) *n, pl* **heresies** **1a** an opinion contrary to the orthodox tenets of a religious body **1b** the act of maintaining such an opinion **2** any belief that is or is thought to be contrary to official or established theory **3** adherence to unorthodox opinion [C13 from OF *eresie*, from LL, from L: sect, from Gk, from *hairein* to choose]

heretic (ˈhɛrətɪk) *n* **1** *now chiefly RC Church* a person who maintains beliefs contrary to the established teachings of his Church **2** a person who holds unorthodox opinions in any field > **heretical** (hɪˈrɛtɪkᵊl) *adj* > **heˈretically** *adv*

hereto (ˌhɪəˈtuː) *adv formal or law* to this place, thing, matter, document, etc

heretofore (ˌhɪətʊˈfɔː) *adv formal or law* until now; before this time

hereunder (ˌhɪərˈʌndə) *adv formal or law* **1** (in documents, etc) below this; subsequently; hereafter **2** under the terms or authority of this

hereupon (ˌhɪərəˈpɒn) *adv* **1** following immediately after this; at this stage **2** *formal or law* upon this thing, point, subject, etc

Hereward (ˈhɛrɪwəd) *n* called *Hereward the Wake*. 11th-century Anglo-Saxon rebel, who defended the Isle of Ely against William the Conqueror (1070–71): a subject of many legends

herewith (ˌhɪəˈwɪð, -ˈwɪθ) *adv formal* together with this: *we send you herewith your statement of account*

heriot (ˈhɛrɪət) *n* (in medieval England) a death duty paid by villeins and free tenants to their lord, often consisting of the dead man's best beast or chattel [OE *heregeatwa*, from *here* army + *geatwa* equipment]

Herisau (*German* ˈheːrizau) *n* a town in NE Switzerland, capital of Appenzell Outer Rhodes demicanton. Pop: 14 955 (latest est)

heritable (ˈhɛrɪtəbᵊl) *adj* **1** capable of being inherited; inheritable **2** *chiefly law* capable of inheriting [C14 from OF, from *heriter* to INHERIT] > **ˌheritaˈbility** *n* > **ˈheritably** *adv*

heritage (ˈhɛrɪtɪdʒ) *n* **1** something inherited at birth **2** anything that has been transmitted from the past or handed down by tradition **3** the evidence of the past, such as historical sites, and the unspoilt natural environment, considered as the inheritance of present-day society **4** *law* any property, esp land, that by law has descended or may descend to an heir [C13 from OF; see HEIR]

herl (hɜːl) *or* **harl** *n angling* **1** the barb or barbs of a feather, used to dress fishing flies **2** an artificial fly dressed with such barbs [C15 from MLow G *herle*, from ?]

Hermannstadt (ˈhɛrmanʃtat) *n* the German name for **Sibiu**

hermaphrodite (hɜːˈmæfrəˌdaɪt) *n* **1** *biol* an animal or flower that has both male and female reproductive organs **2** a person having both male and female sexual characteristics **3** a person or thing in which two opposite qualities are combined ▷ *adj* **4** having the characteristics of a hermaphrodite [C15 from L *hermaphrodītus*, from Gk, after HERMAPHRODITUS] > **herˌmaphroˈditic** *or* **herˌmaphroˈditical** *adj* > **herˈmaphroditˌism** *n*

hermaphrodite brig *n* a sailing vessel with two masts, rigged square on the foremast and fore-and-aft on the aftermast

Hermaphroditus (hɜːˌmæfrəˈdaɪtəs) *n Greek myth* a son of Hermes and Aphrodite who merged with the nymph Salmacis to form one body

hermeneutic (ˌhɜːmɪˈnjuːtɪk) *or* **hermeneutical** *adj* **1** of or relating to the interpretation of Scripture **2** interpretive > **ˌhermeˈneutically** *adv*

Hh

hermeneutics (ˌhɜːmɪˈnjuːtɪks) *n (functioning as sing)* **1** the science of interpretation, esp of Scripture **2** *philosophy* **2a** the study and interpretation of human behaviour and social institutions **2b** (in existentialist thought) discussion of the purpose of life [C18 from Gk *hermēneutikos* expert in interpretation, from *hermēneuein* to interpret, from ?]

Hermes (ˈhɜːmiːz) *n Greek myth* the messenger and herald of the gods; the divinity of commerce, cunning, theft, travellers, and rascals. He was represented as wearing winged sandals. Roman counterpart: **Mercury**

Hermes Trismegistus (ˌtrɪsməˈdʒɪstəs) *n* a Greek name for the Egyptian god Thoth, credited with various works on mysticism and magic [Gk: Hermes thrice-greatest]

hermetic (hɜːˈmɛtɪk) *or* **hermetical** *adj* **1a** (of a seal) airtight **1b** (of a vessel, etc) sealed so as to be airtight **2** of or relating to alchemy or other forms of ancient science: *the hermetic arts* **3** esoteric or recondite **4** hidden or protected from the outside world: *the hermetic world of Vatican politics* [C17 from Med. L *hermēticus* belonging to HERMES TRISMEGISTUS, traditionally the inventor of a magic seal] > **herˈmetically** *adv*

hermit (ˈhɜːmɪt) *n* **1** one of the early Christian recluses **2** any person living in solitude [C13 from OF *hermite*, from LL, from Gk *erēmitēs* living in the desert, from *erēmos* lonely] > **herˈmitic** *or* **herˈmitical** *adj*

hermitage (ˈhɜːmɪtɪdʒ) *n* **1** the abode of a hermit **2** any retreat

hermit crab *n* a small soft-bodied crustacean living in and carrying about the empty shells of whelks or similar molluscs

Hermon (ˈhɜːmən) *n* **Mount** a mountain on the border between Lebanon and SW Syria, in the Anti-Lebanon Range: represented the NE limits of Israeli conquests under Moses and Joshua. Height: 2814 m (9232 ft)

Hermosillo (*Spanish* ɛrmoˈsiʎo) *n* a city in NW Mexico, capital of Sonora state, on the Sonora River: university (1938); winter resort and commercial centre for an agricultural and mining region. Pop: 544 889 (2000)

Hermoupolis (hɜːˈmuːpəlɪs) *n* a port in Greece, capital of Cyclades department, on the E coast of Syros Island. Pop: 14 115 (latest est)

Herne (*German* ˈhɛrnə) *n* an industrial city in W Germany, in North Rhine-Westphalia, in the Ruhr on the Rhine-Herne Canal. Pop: 176 200 (1999 est)

hernia (ˈhɜːnɪə) *n, pl* **hernias** *or* **herniae** (-nɪˌiː) the projection of an organ or part through the lining of the cavity in which it is normally situated, esp the intestine through the front wall of the abdominal cavity. Also called: **rupture** [C14 from L] > **ˈhernial** *adj* > **ˈherniˌated** *adj*

hero (ˈhɪərəʊ) *n, pl* **heroes** **1** a man distinguished by exceptional courage, nobility, etc **2** a man who is idealized for possessing superior qualities in any field **3** *classical myth* a being of extraordinary strength and courage, often the offspring of a mortal and a god **4** the principal male character in a novel, play, etc [C14 from L *hērōs*, from Gk]

Hero[1] (ˈhɪərəʊ) *n Greek myth* a priestess of Aphrodite, who killed herself when her lover Leander drowned while swimming the Hellespont to visit her

Hero[2] (ˈhɪərəʊ) *or* **Heron** *n* 1st century AD, Greek mathematician and inventor

Herod (ˈhɛrəd) *n* called *the Great*. ?73–4 BC, king of Judaea (37–4). The latter part of his reign was notable for his cruelty: according to the New Testament he ordered the Massacre of the Innocents

Herod Agrippa I *n* 10 BC–44 AD, king of Judaea (41–44), grandson of Herod (the Great). A friend of Caligula and Claudius, he imprisoned Saint Peter and executed Saint James

Herod Agrippa II *n* died ?93 AD, king of territories in N Palestine (50–?93 AD), son of Herod Agrippa. He presided (60) at the trial of Saint Paul and sided with the Roman authorities in the Jewish rebellion of 66

Herod Antipas (ˈæntɪˌpæs) *n* died ?40 AD, tetrarch of Galilee and Peraea (4 BC–40 AD); son of Herod the Great. At the instigation of his wife Herodias, he ordered the execution of John the Baptist

Herodias (hɛˈrəʊdɪˌæs) *n* ?14 BC–?40 AD, niece and wife of Herod Antipas and mother of Salome, whom she persuaded to ask for the head of John the Baptist. Her ambition led to the banishment of her husband

Herodotus (hɪˈrɒdətəs) *n* called *the Father of History*. ?485–?425 BC, Greek historian, famous for his *History*, dealing with the causes and events of the wars between the Greeks and the Persians (490–479)

heroic (hɪˈrəʊɪk) *or* **heroical** *adj* **1** of, like, or befitting a hero **2** courageous but desperate **3** treating of heroes and their deeds **4** of or resembling the heroes of classical mythology **5** (of language, manner, etc) extravagant **6** *prosody* of or resembling heroic verse **7** (of the arts, esp sculpture) larger than life-size; smaller than colossal > **heˈroically** *adv*

heroic age *n* the period in an ancient culture, when legendary heroes are said to have lived

heroic couplet *n prosody* a verse form consisting of two rhyming lines in iambic pentameter

heroics (hɪˈrəʊɪks) *pl n* **1** *prosody* short for **heroic verse** **2** extravagant or melodramatic language, behaviour, etc

heroic verse *n prosody* a type of verse suitable for epic or heroic subjects, such as the classical hexameter or the French Alexandrine

heroin (ˈhɛrəʊɪn) *n* a white bitter-tasting crystalline powder related to morphine: a highly addictive narcotic [C19 coined in G as a trademark, prob. from HERO, referring to its aggrandizing effect on the personality]

heroine (ˈhɛrəʊɪn) *n* **1** a woman possessing heroic qualities **2** a woman idealized for possessing superior qualities **3** the main female character in a novel, play, film, etc

heroism (ˈhɛrəʊˌɪzəm) *n* the state or quality of being a hero

heron (ˈhɛrən) *n* any of various wading birds having a long neck, slim body, and a plumage that is commonly grey or white [C14 from OF *hairon*, of Gmc origin]

Heron (ˈhɪərɒn) *n* **1** a variant of **Hero** **2** **Patrick** 1920–99, British abstract painter and art critic

heronry (ˈhɛrənrɪ) *n, pl* **heronries** a colony of breeding herons

Herophilus (hɪəˈrɒfɪləs) *n* died ?280 BC, Greek anatomist in Alexandria. He was the first to distinguish sensory from motor nerves

hero worship *n* **1** admiration for heroes or idealized persons **2** worship by the ancient Greeks and Romans of heroes ▷ *vb* **hero-worship, hero-worships, hero-worshipping, hero-worshipped** *or US* **hero-worships, hero-worshiping, hero-worshiped** **3** *(tr)* to feel admiration or adulation for > **ˈhero-ˌworshipper** *or US* **ˈhero-ˌworshiper** *n*

herpes (ˈhɜːpiːz) *n* any of several inflammatory diseases of the skin, esp herpes simplex [C17 via L from Gk, from *herpein* to creep] > **herpetic** (hɜːˈpɛtɪk) *adj, n*

herpes simplex (ˈsɪmplɛks) *n* an acute viral disease characterized by formation of clusters of watery blisters, esp on the lips or the genitals. See **cold sore, genital herpes** [NL: simple herpes]

herpes zoster (ˈzɒstə) *n* a technical name for **shingles** [NL: girdle herpes, from HERPES + Gk *zōstēr* girdle]

herpetology (ˌhɜːpɪˈtɒlədʒɪ) *n* the study of reptiles and amphibians [C19 from Gk *herpeton* creeping animal] > **herpetologic** (ˌhɜːpɪtəˈlɒdʒɪk) *or* **ˌherpetoˈlogical** *adj*

Herr (*German* hɛr) *n, pl* **Herren** (ˈhɛrən) a German man: used before a name as a title equivalent to *Mr* [G, from OHG *herro* lord]

Herrenvolk *German* (ˈhɛrənfɔlk) *n* a race, nation, or group, such as the Germans or Nazis as viewed by Hitler, believed by themselves to be superior to other races. Also called: **master race** [lit.: master race, from *Herren*, pl. of HERR + *Volk* folk]

Herrick ('hɛrɪk) *n* **Robert** 1591–1674, English poet. His chief work is the *Hesperides* (1648), a collection of short, delicate, sacred, and pastoral lyrics

herring ('hɛrɪŋ) *n, pl* **herrings** *or* **herring** an important food fish of northern seas, having an elongated body covered with large silvery scales [OE *hǣring*]

herringbone ('hɛrɪŋ,bəʊn) *n* **1a** a pattern consisting of two or more rows of short parallel strokes slanting in alternate directions to form a series of zigzags **1b** (*as modifier*): *a herringbone pattern* **2** *skiing* a method of ascending a slope by walking with the skis pointing outwards and one's weight on the inside edges ▷ *vb* **herringbones, herringboning, herringboned 3** to decorate (textiles, brickwork, etc) with herringbone **4** (*intr*) *skiing* to ascend a slope in herringbone fashion

herring gull *n* a common gull that has a white plumage with black-tipped wings

Herriot *n* **1** (*French* ɛrjo) **Édouard** (edwar) 1872–1957, French Radical statesman and writer; premier (1924–25; 1932) **2** ('hɛrɪət) **James** real name *James Alfred Wight*. 1916–95, British veterinary surgeon and writer. His books based on his experiences in Yorkshire have been adapted for television and films

hers (hɜːz) *pron* **1** something or someone belonging to her: *hers is the nicest dress; that cat is hers* **2** **of hers** belonging to her [c14 *hires*; see HER]

Herschel ('hɜːʃəl) *n* **1** **Caroline Lucretia** 1750–1848, British astronomer, born in Germany, noted for her catalogue of nebulae and star clusters: sister of Sir William Herschel **2** Sir **John Frederick William** 1792–1871, British astronomer. He discovered and catalogued over 525 nebulae and star clusters **3** his father, Sir (**Frederick**) **William**, original name *Friedrich Wilhelm Herschel*. 1738–1822, British astronomer, born in Germany. He constructed a reflecting telescope, which led to his discovery of the planet Uranus (1781), two of its satellites, and two of the satellites of Saturn. He also discovered the motions of binary stars

herself (hə'sɛlf) *pron* **1a** the reflexive form of *she* or *her* **1b** (intensifier): *the queen herself signed* **2** (*preceded by a copula*) her normal self: *she looks herself again*

Herstmonceux *or* **Hurstmonceux** ('hɜːstmən,suː, -,səʊ) *n* a village in S England, in E Sussex north of Eastbourne: 15th-century castle, site of the Royal Observatory, which was transferred from Greenwich between 1948 and 1958, until 1990

Hertford ('hɑːtfəd) *n* a town in SE England, administrative centre of Hertfordshire. Pop: 21 665 (1991)

Hertfordshire ('hɑːtfəd,ʃɪə, -ʃə) *n* a county of S England, bordering on Greater London in the south: mainly low-lying, with the Chiltern Hills in the northwest; largely agricultural; expanding light industries, esp in the new towns. Administrative centre: Hertford. Pop: 1 033 977 (2001). Area: 1634 sq km (631 sq miles)

Hertogenbosch (*Dutch* hɛrtoːxən'bɔs) *n* **'s** See **'s Hertogenbosch**

Herts (hɑːts) *abbrev for* Hertfordshire

hertz (hɜːts) *n, pl* **hertz** the derived SI unit of frequency; the frequency of a periodic phenomenon that has a periodic time of 1 second; 1 cycle per second. Symbol: Hz [c20 after H. R. HERTZ]

Hertz (hɜːts; *German* hɛrts) *n* **1** **Gustav** ('gʊstaf) 1887–1975, German atomic physicist. He provided evidence for the quantum theory by his research with Franck on the effects produced by bombarding atoms with electrons: they shared the Nobel prize for physics (1925) **2** **Heinrich Rudolph** ('hainrɪç 'ruːdɔlf) 1857–94, German physicist. He was the first to produce electromagnetic waves artificially

Hertzian wave ('hɜːtsɪən) *n* an electromagnetic wave with a frequency in the range from about 3×10^{10} hertz to about 1.5×10^{5} hertz [c19 after H. R. HERTZ]

Hertzog ('hɜːtsɒg) *n* **James Barry Munnik** 1866–1942, South African statesman; prime minister (1924–39): founded the Nationalist Party (1913), advocating complete South African independence from Britain; opposed South African participation in World Wars I and II

Hertzsprung-Russell diagram ('hɜːtsprʌŋ'rʌsᵊl) *n* a graph in which the spectral types of stars are plotted against their absolute magnitudes. Stars fall into different groupings in different parts of the graph [c20 after E. *Hertzsprung* (1873–1967), Danish astronomer, and H. N. *Russell* (1877–1957), US astronomer]

Herzegovina (,hɜːtsəgəʊ'viːnə) *or* **Hercegovina** *n* a region in Bosnia-Herzegovina: originally under Austro-Hungarian rule; became part of the province of Bosnia-Herzegovina (1878), which was a constituent republic of Yugoslavia (1946–92)

Herzl (*German* 'hɛrtsəl) *n* **Theodor** ('teːodoːr) 1860–1904, Austrian writer, born in Hungary; founder of the Zionist movement. In *The Jewish State* (1896), he advocated resettlement of the Jews in a state of their own

Herzog (*German* 'hɛrtsoːk) *n* **Werner** ('vɛrnər) born 1942, German film director. His films include *Signs of Life* (1967), *Fata Morgana* (1970), *Fitzcarraldo* (1982), and *Little Dieter Needs to Fly* (1997)

he's (hiːz) *contraction of* he is *or* he has

Heseltine ('hɛzəl,taɪn) *n* **Philip Arnold** See (Peter) **Warlock**

Hesiod ('hɛsɪ,ɒd) *n* 8th century BC, Greek poet and the earliest author of didactic verse. His two complete extant works are the *Works and Days*, dealing with the agricultural seasons, and the *Theogony*, concerning the origin of the world and the genealogies of the gods

Hesione (hɪ'saɪənɪ) *n Greek myth* daughter of King Laomedon, rescued by Hercules from a sea monster

hesitant ('hɛzɪtᵊnt) *adj* wavering, hesitating, or irresolute > **'hesitantly** *adv*

hesitate ('hɛzɪ,teɪt) *vb* **hesitates, hesitating, hesitated** (*intr*) **1** to be slow in acting; be uncertain **2** to be reluctant (to do something) **3** to stammer or pause in speaking [c17 from L *haesitāre*, from *haerēre* to cling to] > **hesitancy** ('hɛzɪtᵊnsɪ) *or* **,hesi'tation** *n* > **'hesi,tatingly** *adv*

Hesperia (hɛ'spɪərɪə) *n* a poetic name used by the ancient Greeks for Italy and by the Romans for Spain or beyond [Latin, from Greek: land of the west, from *hesperos* western]

Hesperian (hɛ'spɪərɪən) *adj* **1** *poetic* western **2** of or relating to the Hesperides or Islands of the Blessed

Hesperides (hɛ'spɛrɪ,diːz) *pl n Greek myth* **1** the daughters of Hesperus, nymphs who kept watch with a dragon over the garden of the golden apples in the Islands of the Blessed **2** (*functioning as sing*) the gardens themselves **3** another name for the **Islands of the Blessed** > **Hesperidian** (,hɛspə'rɪdɪən) *or* **,Hesper'idean** *adj*

hesperidium (,hɛspə'rɪdɪəm) *n bot* the fruit of citrus plants, in which the flesh consists of fluid-filled hairs and is protected by a tough rind [c19 NL; alluding to the fruit in the garden of the HESPERIDES]

Hesperus ('hɛspərəs) *n* an evening star, esp Venus [from L, from Gk, from *hesperos* western]

Hess (hɛs) *n* **1** Dame **Myra** 1890–1965, English pianist **2** (**Walther Richard**) **Rudolf** ('ruːdɔlf) 1894–1987, German Nazi leader. He made a secret flight to Scotland (1941) to negotiate peace with Britain but was held as a prisoner of war; later sentenced to life imprisonment at the Nuremberg trials (1946); committed suicide **3** **Victor Francis** 1883–1964, US physicist, born in Austria: pioneered the investigation of cosmic rays: shared the

Nobel prize for physics (1936)

Hesse[1] (hɛs; *German* 'hɛsə) *n* a state of central Germany, formed in 1945 from the former Prussian province of Hesse-Nassau and part of the former state of Hesse; part of West Germany until 1990. Capital: Wiesbaden. Pop: 6 052 000 (2000 est). Area: 21 111 sq km (8151 sq miles). German name: **Hessen** ('hɛsᵊn)

Hesse[2] (hɛs; *German* 'hɛsə) *n* **Hermann** ('hɛrman) 1877–1962, German novelist, short-story writer, and poet. His novels include *Der Steppenwolf* (1927) and *Das Glasperlenspiel* (1943): Nobel prize for literature 1946

Hesse-Nassau *n* a former province of Prussia, now part of the state of Hesse, Germany; part of West Germany until 1990

hessian ('hɛsɪən) *n* a coarse jute fabric similar to sacking [C18 from HESSIAN]

Hessian ('hɛsɪən) *n* **1** a native or inhabitant of Hesse **2** a Hessian soldier in any of the mercenary units of the British Army in the War of American Independence or the Napoleonic Wars ▷ *adj* **3** of Hesse or its inhabitants

Hessian fly *n* a small dipterous fly whose larvae damage wheat, barley, and rye [C18 thought to have been introduced into America by Hessian soldiers]

hest (hɛst) *n* an archaic word for **behest** [OE *hǣs*]

Hestia ('hɛstɪə) *n Greek myth* the goddess of the hearth. Roman counterpart: **Vesta**

hetaera (hɪ'tɪərə) *or* **hetaira** (hɪ'taɪrə) *n, pl* **hetaerae** (-'tɪəriː) *or* **hetairai** (-'taɪraɪ) (esp in ancient Greece) a prostitute, esp an educated courtesan [C19 from Gk *hetaira* concubine]

hetaerism (hɪ'tɪərɪzəm) *or* **hetairism** (hɪ'taɪrɪzəm) *n* **1** the state of being a concubine **2** *sociol, anthropol* a social system attributed to some primitive societies, in which women are communally shared

hetero- *combining form* other, another, or different: *heterosexual* [from Gk *heteros* other]

heteroclite ('hɛtərə,klaɪt) *adj also* **heteroclitic** (,hɛtərə'klɪtɪk) **1** (esp of the form of a word) irregular or unusual ▷ *n* **2** an irregularly formed word [C16 from LL *heteroclitus* declining irregularly, from Gk, from HETERO- + *klinein* to inflect]

heterocyclic (,hɛtərəʊ'saɪklɪk, -'sɪk-) *adj* (of an organic compound) containing a closed ring of atoms, at least one of which is not a carbon atom

heterodox ('hɛtərəʊ,dɒks) *adj* **1** at variance with established or accepted doctrines or beliefs **2** holding unorthodox opinions [C17 from Gk *heterodoxos*, from HETERO- + *doxa* opinion] > **'hetero,doxy** *n*

heterodyne ('hɛtərəʊ,daɪn) *electronics* ▷ *vb* **heterodynes, heterodyning, heterodyned 1** to combine by modulation (two alternating signals) to produce two signals having frequencies corresponding to the sum and the difference of the original frequencies ▷ *adj* **2** produced by, operating by, or involved in heterodyning two signals

heteroecious (,hɛtə'riːʃəs) *adj* (of parasites) undergoing different stages of the life cycle on different host species [from HETERO- + *-oecious*, from Gk *oikia* house] > **heteroecism** (,hɛtə'riː,sɪzəm) *n*

heterogamete (,hɛtərəʊgæ'miːt) *n* a gamete that differs in size and form from the one with which it unites in fertilization

heterogamy (,hɛtə'rɒgəmɪ) *n* **1** a type of sexual reproduction in which the gametes differ in both size and form **2** a condition in which different types of reproduction occur in successive generations of an organism **3** the presence of both male and female flowers in one inflorescence > **,heter'ogamous** *adj*

heterogeneous (,hɛtərəʊ'dʒiːnɪəs) *adj* **1** composed of unrelated parts **2** not of the same type [C17 from Med. L *heterogeneus*, from Gk, from HETERO- + *genos* sort] > **heterogeneity** (,hɛtərəʊdʒɪ'niːɪtɪ) *or* **,hetero'geneousness** *n*

heterogony (,hɛtə'rɒgənɪ) *n* **1** *biol* the alternation of parthenogenetic and sexual generations in rotifers and similar animals **2** the condition in plants, such as the primrose, of having flowers that differ from each other in the length of their stamens and styles > **,heter'ogonous** *adj*

heterologous (,hɛtə'rɒləgəs) *adj* **1** *pathol* designating cells or tissues not normally present in a particular part of the body **2** differing in structure or origin > **,heter'ology** *n*

heteromerous (,hɛtə'rɒmərəs) *adj biol* having parts that differ, esp in number

heteromorphic (,hɛtərəʊ'mɔːfɪk) *or* **heteromorphous** *adj biol* **1** differing from the normal form **2** (esp of insects) having different forms at different stages of the life cycle > **,hetero'morphism** *n*

heteronomous (,hɛtə'rɒnəməs) *adj* **1** subject to an external law **2** (of parts of an organism) differing in the manner of growth, development, or specialization > **,heter'onomy** *n*

heteronym ('hɛtərəʊ,nɪm) *n* one of two or more words pronounced differently but spelt alike: *the two English words spelt "bow" are heteronyms* ▷ Cf **homograph** [C17 from LGk *heteronumos*, from Gk HETERO- + *onoma* name]

heterophyllous (,hɛtərəʊ'fɪləs, ,hɛtə'rɒfɪləs) *adj* having more than one type of leaf on the same plant > **'hetero,phylly** *n*

heteropterous (,hɛtə'rɒptərəs) *or* **heteropteran** *adj* of or belonging to a suborder of hemipterous insects, including bedbugs, water bugs, etc, in which the forewings are membranous but have leathery tips [C19 from NL *Heteroptera*, from HETERO- + Gk *pteron* wing]

heterosexism (,hɛtərəʊ'sɛk,sɪzəm) *n* discrimination on the basis of sexual orientation, practised by heterosexuals against homosexuals > **hetero'sexist** *adj, n*

heterosexual (,hɛtərəʊ'sɛksjʊəl) *n* **1** a person who is sexually attracted to the opposite sex ▷ *adj* **2** of or relating to heterosexuality > **,hetero,sexu'ality** *n*

heterosocial (,hɛtərəʊ'səʊʃəl) *adj* relating to or denoting mixed-sex social relationships ▷ Cf **homosocial** > **heterosociality** (,hɛtərəʊ,səʊʃɪ'ælɪtɪ) *n*

heterotaxis (,hɛtərəʊ'tæksɪs) *or* **heterotaxy** *n* an abnormal or asymmetrical arrangement of parts, as of the organs of the body

heterotrophic (,hɛtərəʊ'trɒfɪk) *adj* (of organisms, such as animals) obtaining carbon for growth and energy from complex organic compounds [C20 from HETERO- + Gk *trophikos* concerning food, from *trophē* nourishment] > **'hetero,troph** *n*

heterozygote (,hɛtərəʊ'zaɪgəʊt) *n* an animal or plant that is heterozygous; a hybrid

heterozygous (,hɛtərəʊ'zaɪgəs) *adj genetics* (of an organism) having different alleles for any one gene: *heterozygous for eye colour*

hetman ('hɛtmən) *n, pl* **hetmans** an elected leader of the Cossacks. Also called: **ataman** [C18 from Polish, from G *Hauptmann* headman]

het up *adj inf* angry; excited: *don't get het up* [C19 from dialect pp of HEAT]

heuchera ('hɔɪkərə) *n* a North American shrub with red or pink flowers and ornamental foliage [after J. H. *Heucher* (1677–1747), G botanist]

heuristic (hjʊə'rɪstɪk) *adj* **1** helping to learn; guiding in investigation **2** (of a method of teaching) allowing pupils to learn things for themselves **3a** *maths, science, philosophy* using or obtained by exploration of possibilities rather than by following set rules **3b** *computing* denoting a rule of thumb for solving a problem without the exhaustive application of an algorithm: *a heuristic solution* ▷ *n* **4** (*pl*) the science of heuristic procedure [C19 from NL *heuristicus*, from Gk *heuriskein* to discover] > **heu'ristically** *adv*

Hevesy (*Hungarian* 'hɛvɛʃi) *n* **Georg von** ('geːɔrg fɔn) 1885–1966, Hungarian chemist. He worked on radioactive tracing and, with D Coster, discovered the element hafnium (1923): Nobel prize for chemistry 1943

hew (hjuː) *vb* **hews, hewing, hewed, hewed** *or* **hewn 1** to strike (something, esp wood) with cutting blows, as with an axe **2** (*tr; often foll by out*) to carve from a substance **3** (*tr; often foll by away, off*, etc) to sever from a larger portion **4** (*intr; often foll by to*) *US & Canad* to conform [OE *hēawan*] > '**hewer** *n*

Hewish ('hjuːɪʃ) *n* **Antony** born 1924, British radio astronomer, noted esp for his role in the discovery of pulsars (1967): shared the Nobel prize for physics 1974

Hewitt ('hjuːɪt) *n* **Lleyton** ('leɪtən) born 1981, Australian tennis player; US Open champion 2001, Wimbledon singles champion 2002

hex[1] (hɛks) *n* **a** short for **hexadecimal (notation) b** (*as modifier*): *hex code*

hex[2] (hɛks) *US & Canad inf* ▷ *vb* **1** (*tr*) to bewitch ▷ *n* **2** an evil spell **3** a witch [c19 via Pennsylvania Du. from G *Hexe* witch, from MHG *hecse*, ?from OHG *hagzissa*]

hexa- *or before a vowel* **hex-** *combining form* six: *hexachord; hexameter* [from Gk, from *hex* SIX]

hexachlorophene (ˌhɛksəˈklɔːrəfiːn) *n* an insoluble white bactericidal substance used in antiseptic soaps, deodorants, etc Formula: $(C_6HCl_3OH)_2CH_2$

hexachord ('hɛksəˌkɔːd) *n* (in medieval musical theory) any of three diatonic scales based upon C, F, and G, each consisting of six notes, from which solmization was developed

hexad ('hɛksæd) *n* a group or series of six [c17 from Gk *hexas*, from *hex* six]

hexadecane ('hɛksədɛˌkeɪn, ˌhɛksəˈdɛkeɪn) *n* the systematic name for **cetane**

hexadecanoic acid (ˌhɛksəˌdɛkəˈnəʊɪk) *n* the systematic name for **palmitic acid**

hexadecimal notation *or* **hexadecimal** (ˌhɛksəˈdɛsɪməl) *n* a number system having a base 16; the symbols for the numbers 0 – 9 are the same as those used in the decimal system, and the numbers 10 – 15 are usually represented by the letters A – F. The system is used as a convenient way of representing the internal binary code of a computer

hexagon ('hɛksəgən) *n* a polygon having six sides > **hex'agonal** *adj*

hexagram ('hɛksəˌgræm) *n* a star-shaped figure formed by extending the sides of a regular hexagon to meet at six points

hexahedron (ˌhɛksəˈhiːdrən) *n* a solid figure having six plane faces > ˌ**hexa'hedral** *adj*

hexameter (hɛkˈsæmɪtə) *n prosody* **1** a verse line consisting of six metrical feet **2** (in Greek and Latin epic poetry) a verse line of six metrical feet, of which the first four are usually dactyls or spondees, the fifth almost always a dactyl, and the sixth a spondee or trochee > **hexametric** (ˌhɛksəˈmɛtrɪk) *or* ˌ**hexa'metrical** *adj*

hexane ('hɛkseɪn) *n* a liquid alkane found in petroleum and used as a solvent. Formula: C_6H_{14} [c19 from HEXA- + -ANE]

hexapla ('hɛksəplə) *n* an edition of the Old Testament compiled by Origen (?185–?254 AD), Christian theologian, containing six versions of the text [c17 from Gk *hexaploos* sixfold] > '**hexaplar** *adj*

hexapod ('hɛksəˌpɒd) *n* an insect

hexavalent (ˌhɛksəˈveɪlənt) *adj chem* having a valency of six. Also: **sexivalent**

hexose ('hɛksəʊs, -əʊz) *n* a monosaccharide, such as glucose, that contains six carbon atoms per molecule

hey (heɪ) *interj* **1** an expression indicating surprise, dismay, discovery, etc **2 hey presto!** an exclamation used by conjurors to herald the climax of a trick [c13 imit.]

heyday ('heɪˌdeɪ) *n* the time of most power, popularity, vigour, etc [c16 prob. based on HEY]

Heyer ('heɪə) *n* **Georgette** 1902–74, British historical novelist and writer of detective stories, noted esp for her romances of the Regency period

Heyerdahl (*Norwegian* 'hɛiərdaːl) *n* **Thor** (tɔː) 1914–2002, Norwegian anthropologist. In 1947 he demonstrated that the Polynesians could originally have been migrants from South America, by sailing from Peru to the Pacific Islands of Tuamotu in the *Kon-Tiki*, a raft made of balsa wood. DNA testing in the late 1990s indicated that such a migration did not actually take place

Heysham ('heɪʃəm) *n* a port in NW England, in NW Lancashire. Pop (with Morecambe): 46 657 (1991)

Heywood[1] ('heɪˌwʊd) *n* a town in NW England, in Rochdale unitary authority, Greater Manchester, near Bury. Pop: 29 286 (1991)

Heywood[2] ('heɪˌwʊd) *n* **1 John** ?1497–?1580, English dramatist, noted for his comic interludes **2 Thomas** ?1574–1641, English dramatist, noted esp for his domestic drama *A Woman Killed with Kindness* (1607)

Hezekiah (ˌhɛzəˈkaɪə) *n* a king of Judah ?715–?687 BC, noted for his religious reforms (II Kings 18–19). Douay spelling: **Ezechias** [from Heb. *hizqīyyāhū* God has strengthened]

hf *abbrev for* half

Hf *the chemical symbol for* hafnium

HF *or* **h.f.** *abbrev for* high frequency

HFEA (in Britain) *abbrev for* Human Fertilization and Embryology Authority

hg *abbrev for* hectogram

Hg *the chemical symbol for* mercury [from NL *hydrargyrum*]

HG *abbrev for* His (or Her) Grace

hgt *abbrev for* height

HGV (formerly, in Britain) *abbrev for* heavy goods vehicle

HH *abbrev for:* **1** His (or Her) Highness **2** His Holiness (title of the Pope) ▷ **3** (on Brit pencils) *symbol for* double hard

hi (haɪ) *sentence substitute* an informal word for **hello** [c20 prob. from *how are you?*]

HI *abbrev for:* **1** Hawaii (state) **2** Hawaiian Islands

Hialeah (ˌhaɪəˈliːə) *n* a city in SE Florida, near Miami: racetrack. Pop: 226 419 (2000)

hiatus (haɪˈeɪtəs) *n, pl* **hiatuses** *or* **hiatus 1** (esp in manuscripts) a break or interruption in continuity **2** a break between adjacent vowels in the pronunciation of a word [c16 from L: gap, cleft, from *hiāre* to gape]

hiatus hernia *n* protrusion of part of the stomach through the diaphragm at the oesophageal opening

Hiawatha (ˌhaɪəˈwɒθə) *n* a 16th-century Onondaga Indian chief: credited with the organization of the Five Nations

Hib (hɪb) *n acronym for* Haemophilus influenzae type b: a vaccine against a type of bacterial meningitis

hibachi (hɪˈbɑːtʃɪ) *n* a portable brazier for heating and cooking food [from Japanese, from *hi* fire + *bachi* bowl]

hibakusha (hɪˈbɑːkʊʃə) *n, pl* **hibakusha** *or* **hibakushas** a survivor of either of the atomic-bomb attacks on Hiroshima and Nagasaki in 1945 [c20 from Japanese, from *hibaku* bombed + *-sha* -person]

hibernal (haɪˈbɜːnᵊl) *adj* of or occurring in winter [c17 from L *hībernālis*, from *hiems* winter]

hibernate ('haɪbəˌneɪt) *vb* **hibernates, hibernating, hibernated** (*intr*) **1** (of some animals) to pass the winter in a dormant condition with metabolism greatly slowed down **2** to cease from activity [c19 from L *hībernāre* to spend the winter, from *hībernus* of winter] > ˌ**hiber'nation** *n* > '**hiberˌnator** *n*

Hibernia (haɪˈbɜːnɪə) *n* the Roman name for **Ireland**: used poetically in later times > **Hi'bernian** *adj, n*

Hibernicism (haɪˈbɜːnɪˌsɪzəm) *n* an Irish expression, idiom, trait, custom, etc

Hiberno- (haɪˈbɜːnəʊ) *combining form* denoting Irish or

Hh

Ireland: *Hiberno-English; Hiberno-Latin*
hibiscus (hɪˈbɪskəs) *n, pl* **hibiscuses** any plant of the chiefly tropical and subtropical genus *Hibiscus*, cultivated for its large brightly coloured flowers [c18 from L, from Gk *hibiskos* marsh mallow]
hiccup (ˈhɪkʌp) *n* **1** a spasm of the diaphragm producing a sudden breathing in of air resulting in a characteristic sharp sound **2** (*pl*) the state of having such spasms **3** *inf* a minor difficulty ▷ *vb* **hiccups, hiccuping, hiccuped** *or* **hiccups, hiccupping, hiccupped 4** (*intr*) to make a hiccup or hiccups **5** (*tr*) to utter with a hiccup ▷ Also: **hiccough** (ˈhɪkʌp) [c16 imit.]
hic jacet *Latin* (hɪk ˈjækɛt) (on gravestones, etc) here lies
hick (hɪk) *n inf* **a** a country person; bumpkin **b** (*as modifier*): *hick ideas* [c16 after *Hick*, familiar form of *Richard*]
Hickok (ˈhɪkɒk) *n* **James Butler**, known as *Wild Bill Hickok*. 1837–76, US frontiersman and marshal
hickory (ˈhɪkərɪ) *n, pl* **hickories 1** a tree of a chiefly North American genus having nuts with edible kernels and hard smooth shells **2** the hard tough wood of this tree [c17 ult. from Algonquian *pawcohiccora* food made from ground hickory nuts]
Hickox (ˈhɪkɒks) *n* **Richard (Sidney)** born 1948, British conductor; musical director of the City of London Sinfonia and Singers since 1971
hid (hɪd) *vb* the past tense and a past participle of **hide**[1]
hidalgo (hɪˈdælgəʊ) *n, pl* **hidalgos** a member of the lower nobility in Spain [c16 from Sp., from OSp. *fijo dalgo* nobleman, from L *filius* son + *dē* of + *aliquid* something]
Hidalgo (hɪˈdælgəʊ; *Spanish* iˈðalɣo) *n* a state of central Mexico: consists of a high plateau, with the Sierra Madre Oriental in the north and east; ancient remains of Teltec culture (at Tula); rich mineral resources. Capital: Pachuca. Pop: 2 231 392 (2000). Area: 20 987 sq km (8103 sq miles)
hidden (ˈhɪdᵊn) *vb* **1** a past participle of **hide**[1] ▷ *adj* **2** concealed or obscured: *a hidden cave; a hidden meaning*
hidden agenda *n* a hidden motive or intention behind an overt action, policy, etc
hide[1] (haɪd) *vb* **hides, hiding, hid, hidden** *or* **hid 1** to conceal (oneself or an object) from view or discovery: *to hide a pencil; to hide from the police* **2** (*tr*) to obscure: *clouds hid the sun* **3** (*tr*) to keep secret **4** (*tr*) to turn (one's eyes, etc) away ▷ *n* **5** *Brit* a place of concealment, usually disguised to appear as part of the natural environment, used by hunters, birdwatchers, etc. US and Canad equivalent: **blind** [OE *hȳdan*] > ˈ**hider** *n*
hide[2] (haɪd) *n* **1** the skin of an animal, either tanned or raw **2** *inf* the human skin ▷ *vb* **hides, hiding, hided 3** (*tr*) *inf* to flog [OE *hȳd*]
hide[3] (haɪd) *n* an obsolete Brit land measure, varying from about 60 to 120 acres [OE *hīgid*]
hide-and-seek *or US, Canad, & Scot* **hide-and-go-seek** *n* a game in which one player covers his or her eyes while the others hide, and this player then tries to find them
hideaway (ˈhaɪdəˌweɪ) *n* a hiding place or secluded spot
hidebound (ˈhaɪdˌbaʊnd) *adj* **1** restricted by petty rules, a conservative attitude, etc **2** (of cattle, etc) having the skin closely attached to the flesh as a result of poor feeding
hideous (ˈhɪdɪəs) *adj* **1** extremely ugly; repulsive **2** terrifying and horrific [c13 from OF *hisdos*, from *hisde* fear; from ?] > ˈ**hideously** *adv* > ˈ**hideousness** *n*
hide-out *n* a hiding place, esp a remote place used by outlaws, etc; hideaway
hiding[1] (ˈhaɪdɪŋ) *n* **1** the state of concealment: *in hiding* **2 hiding place** a place of concealment
hiding[2] (ˈhaɪdɪŋ) *n inf* a flogging; beating
hidrosis (hɪˈdrəʊsɪs) *n* a technical word for **perspiration** or **sweat** [c18 via NL from Gk, from *hidrōs* sweat] > **hidrotic** (hɪˈdrɒtɪk) *adj*
hidy-hole *or* **hidey-hole** *n inf* a hiding place
hie (haɪ) *vb* **hies, hieing** *or* **hying, hied** *arch or poetic* to hurry; speed [OE *hīgian* to strive]
hieland (ˈhiːlənd) *adj Scot dialect* **1** a variant of **Highland 2** characteristic of Highlanders, esp alluding to their supposed gullibility or foolishness in towns or cities
hierarch (ˈhaɪəˌrɑːk) *n* **1** a high priest **2** a person at a high level in a hierarchy > ˌ**hierˈarchal** *adj*
hierarchy (ˈhaɪəˌrɑːkɪ) *n, pl* **hierarchies 1** a system of persons or things arranged in a graded order **2** a body of persons in holy orders organized into graded ranks **3** the collective body of those so organized **4** a series of ordered groupings within a system, such as the arrangement of plants into classes, orders, etc **5** government by a priesthood [c14 from Med. L *hierarchia*, from LGk, from *hierarkhēs* high priest; see HIERO-, -ARCHY] > ˌ**hierˈarchical** *or* ˌ**hierˈarchic** *adj* > ˈ**hierˌarchism** *n*
hieratic (ˌhaɪəˈrætɪk) *adj* **1** of priests **2** of a cursive form of hieroglyphics used by priests in ancient Egypt **3** of styles in art that adhere to certain fixed types, as in ancient Egypt ▷ *n* **4** the hieratic script of ancient Egypt [c17 from L *hierāticus*, from Gk, from *hiereus* priest] > ˌ**hierˈatically** *adv*
hiero- *or before a vowel* **hier-** *combining form* holy or divine: *hierarchy* [from Gk, from *hieros* holy]
hieroglyphic (ˌhaɪərəˈglɪfɪk) *adj also* **hieroglyphical 1** of or relating to a form of writing using picture symbols, esp as used in ancient Egypt **2** difficult to decipher ▷ *n also* **hieroglyph 3** a picture or symbol representing an object, concept, or sound **4** a symbol that is difficult to decipher [c16 from LL *hieroglyphicus*, from Gk, from HIERO- + *gluphē*, from *gluphein* to carve] > ˌ**hieroˈglyphically** *adv*
hieroglyphics (ˌhaɪərəˈglɪfɪks) *n (functioning as sing or pl)* **1** a form of writing, esp as used in ancient Egypt, in which pictures or symbols are used to represent objects, concepts, or sounds **2** difficult or indecipherable writing
Hieronymus (ˌhaɪəˈrɒnɪməs) *n* **Eusebius** (juːˈsiːbɪəs) the Latin name of (Saint) **Jerome**
hierophant (ˈhaɪərəˌfænt) *n* **1** (in ancient Greece) a high priest of religious mysteries **2** a person who interprets esoteric mysteries [c17 from LL *hierophanta*, from Gk, from HIERO- + *phainein* to reveal] > ˌ**hieroˈphantic** *adj*
hi-fi (ˈhaɪˌfaɪ) *n inf* **1a** short for **high fidelity 1b** (*as modifier*): *hi-fi equipment* **2** a set of high-quality sound-reproducing equipment
Higgins (ˈhɪgɪnz) *n* **Jack**, real name *Harry Patterson*. born 1929, British novelist; his thrillers include *The Eagle Has Landed* (1975), *Confessional* (1985), and *Midnight Runner* (2002)
higgledy-piggledy (ˈhɪgᵊldɪˈpɪgᵊldɪ) *inf* ▷ *adj, adv* **1** in a jumble ▷ *n* **2** a muddle
high (haɪ) *adj* **1** being a relatively great distance from top to bottom; tall: *a high building* **2** situated at a relatively great distance above sea level: *a high plateau* **3** (*postpositive*) being a specified distance from top to bottom: *three feet high* **4** extending from or performed at an elevation: *a high dive* **5** (*in combination*) coming up to a specified level: *knee-high* **6** being at its peak: *high noon* **7** of greater than average height: *a high collar* **8** greater than normal in intensity or amount: *a high wind; high mileage* **9** (of sound) acute in pitch **10** (of latitudes) relatively far north or south from the equator **11** (of meat) slightly decomposed, regarded as enhancing the flavour of game **12** very important: *the high priestess* **13** exalted in style or character: *high drama* **14** expressing contempt or arrogance: *high words* **15** elated; cheerful: *high spirits* **16** *inf* being in a state of altered consciousness induced by alcohol, narcotics, etc **17** *inf* overexcited: *by Christmas the children are high* **18** luxurious or extravagant: *high life* **19** advanced in complexity: *high finance* **20** (of a gear) providing a relatively great forward speed for a given engine speed **21** *phonetics* denoting a vowel whose

articulation is produced by raising the tongue, such as for the *ee* in *see* or *oo* in *moon* **22** (*cap when part of a name*) formal and elaborate: *High Mass* **23** (*usually cap*) relating to the High Church **24** *cards* having a relatively great value in a suit **25** **high and dry** stranded; destitute **26** **high and mighty** *inf* arrogant **27** **high opinion** a favourable opinion ▷ *adv* **28** at or to a height: *he jumped high* **29** in a high manner **30** *naut* close to the wind with sails full ▷ *n* **31** a high place or level **32** *inf* a state of altered consciousness induced by alcohol, narcotics, etc **33** another word for **anticyclone** **34** **on high** **34a** at a height **34b** in heaven [OE *hēah*]

High Arctic *n* the regions of Canada, esp the northern islands, within the Arctic Circle

highball ('haɪ,bɔːl) *n chiefly US* a long iced drink consisting of spirits with soda water, etc

highborn ('haɪ,bɔːn) *adj* of noble birth

highboy ('haɪ,bɔɪ) *n US & Canad* a tallboy

highbrow ('haɪ,braʊ) *often disparaging* ▷ *n* **1** a person of scholarly and erudite tastes ▷ *adj also* **highbrowed** **2** appealing to highbrows

highchair ('haɪ,tʃɛə) *n* a long-legged chair for a child, esp one with a table-like tray

High Church *n* **1** the party or movement within the Church of England stressing continuity with Catholic Christendom, the authority of bishops, and the importance of sacraments ▷ *adj* **High-Church** **2** of or relating to this party or movement > **'High-'Churchman** *n*

high-class *adj* **1** of very good quality: *a high-class grocer* **2** belonging to or exhibiting the characteristics of an upper social class

high-coloured *adj* (of the complexion) deep red or purplish; florid

high comedy *n* comedy set largely among cultured and articulate people and featuring witty dialogue

high commissioner *n* the senior diplomatic representative sent by one Commonwealth country to another instead of an ambassador

high-context *adj* preferring to communicate in person, rather than by electronic methods such as email ▷ Cf **low-context**

high country *n* (often preceded by *the*) NZ sheep pastures in the foothills of the Southern Alps, New Zealand

High Court *n* **1** Also called: **High Court of Justice** (in England) the supreme court dealing with civil law cases **2** (in Australia) the highest court of appeal, deciding esp constitutional issues **3** (in New Zealand) a court of law that is superior to a District Court. Former name: **Supreme Court**

high definition television *n* a television system using 1000 or more scanning lines and a higher field repetition rate. Abbrev: **HDTV**

high-dependency *adj* needing or providing a more than usually high level of health care: *a shortage of high-dependency beds*

high-energy physics *n* (*functioning as sing*) another name for **particle physics**

higher ('haɪə) *adj* **1** the comparative of **high** ▷ *n* (*usually cap*) (in Scotland) **2a** the advanced level of the Scottish Certificate of Education **2b** (*as modifier*): *Higher Latin* **3** a pass in a subject at Higher level: *she has four Highers*

higher education *n* education and training at colleges, universities, etc

higher mathematics *n* (*functioning as sing*) mathematics that is more abstract than normal arithmetic, algebra, geometry, and trigonometry

higher rate *n* (in Britain) a rate of income tax that is higher than the basic rate and becomes payable on taxable income in excess of a specified limit

Higher Still *n* a system of courses and qualifications introduced in Scotland to replace Highers and National Certificate modules, covering both academic and vocational subjects

higher-up *n inf* a person of higher rank or in a superior position

highest common factor *n* the largest number or quantity that is a factor of each member of a group of numbers or quantities

high explosive *n* an extremely powerful chemical explosive, such as TNT or gelignite

highfalutin (,haɪfə'luːtɪn) *or* **highfaluting** *adj inf* pompous or pretentious [C19 from HIGH + *-falutin*, ? var. of *fluting*, from FLUTE]

high fidelity *n* **a** the reproduction of sound using electronic equipment that gives faithful reproduction with little or no distortion **b** (*as modifier*): *a high-fidelity amplifier* ▷ Often shortened to **hi-fi**

high-five *n sl* a gesture of greeting or congratulation in which two people slap raised right palms together

high-flown *adj* extravagant or pretentious in conception or intention: *high-flown ideas*

high-flyer *or* **high-flier** *n* **1** a person who is extreme in aims, ambition, etc **2** a person of great ability, esp in a career > **,high-'flying** *adj, n*

high frequency *n* a radio frequency lying between 30 and 3 megahertz. Abbrev: **HF**

High German *n* the standard German language, historically developed from the form of West Germanic spoken in S Germany

high-handed *adj* tactlessly overbearing and inconsiderate > **,high-'handedness** *n*

high-hat *inf* ▷ *adj* **1** snobbish and arrogant ▷ *vb* **high-hats, high-hatting, high-hatted** (*tr*) **2** *chiefly US & Canad* to treat in a snobbish or offhand way ▷ *n* **3** a snobbish person

high hurdles *n* (*functioning as sing*) a race in which competitors leap over hurdles 42 inches (107 cm) high

high-impact *adj* (*prenominal*) **1** (of a plastic or other material) able to withstand great force or shock **2** (of aerobic or other exercise) placing great stress on various areas of the body **3** *inf* having great effect: *high-impact sound*

highjack ('haɪ,dʒæk) *vb, n* a less common spelling of **hijack** > **'high,jacker** *n*

high jump *n* **1** (usually preceded by *the*) an athletic event in which a competitor has to jump over a high bar **2** **be for the high jump** *Brit inf* to be liable to receive a severe reprimand or punishment > **high jumper** *n* > **high jumping** *n*

high-key *adj* (of a painting, etc) having a predominance of light tones or colours ▷ Cf **low-key** (sense 3)

highland ('haɪlənd) *n* **1** relatively high ground **2** (*modifier*) of or relating to a highland > **'highlander** *n*

Highland ('haɪlənd) *n* **1** a council area in N Scotland, formed in 1975 (as Highland Region) from Caithness, Sutherland, Nairnshire, most of Inverness-shire, and Ross and Cromarty except for the Outer Hebrides. Administrative centre: Inverness. Pop: 208 914 (2001). Area: 25 149 sq km (9710 sq miles) **2** (*modifier*) of, relating to, or denoting the Highlands of Scotland

Highland cattle *n* a breed of cattle with shaggy reddish-brown hair and long horns

Highland dress *n* **1** the historical costume including the plaid and kilt, of Highland clansmen and soldiers **2** a modern version of this worn for formal occasions
▷ www.myclan.com/clanship/tartan/history.asp

Highland fling *n* a vigorous Scottish solo dance

Highland Games *n* (*functioning as sing or pl*) a meeting in which competitions in sport, piping, and dancing are held: originating in the Highlands of Scotland
▷ www.albagames.co.uk
▷ www.st-andrews.ac.uk/~ig2/SGA

Highlands ('haɪləndz) *n* **the** **1a** the part of Scotland that lies to the northwest of the great fault that runs from

Hh

Dumbarton to Stonehaven **1b** a smaller area consisting of the mountainous north of Scotland: distinguished by Gaelic culture **2** (*often not cap*) the highland region of any country

high-level *adj* (of conferences, talks, etc) involving very important people

high-level language *n computing* a programming language that resembles natural language or mathematical notation and is designed to reflect the requirements of a problem

high-level waste *n* high-activity radioactive waste, such as spent nuclear fuel, needing cooling for several decades before disposal ▷ Cf **intermediate-level waste, low-level waste**

highlight ('haɪ,laɪt) *n* **1** an area of the lightest tone in a painting, photograph, etc **2** Also called: **high spot** the most exciting or memorable part or time **3** (*pl*) a lightened or brightened effect produced in the hair by bleaching selected strands ▷ *vb* (*tr*) **4** *painting, photog, etc* to mark with light tone **5** to bring emphasis to **6** to produce highlights in (the hair)

highlighter ('haɪ,laɪtə) *n* **1** a cosmetic cream or powder applied to the face to highlight the cheekbones, eyes, etc **2** a fluorescent felt-tip pen used as a marker to emphasize a section of text without obscuring it

highly ('haɪlɪ) *adv* **1** (intensifier): *highly disappointed* **2** with great approbation: *we spoke highly of it* **3** in a high position: *placed highly in class* **4** at or for a high cost

highly strung *or US & Canad* **high-strung** *adj* tense and easily upset; excitable; nervous

High Mass *n* a solemn and elaborate sung Mass

high-minded *adj* **1** having or characterized by high moral principles **2** *arch* arrogant; haughty > ,**high-'mindedness** *n*

highness ('haɪnɪs) *n* the condition of being high

Highness ('haɪnɪs) *n* (preceded by *Your, His,* or *Her*) a title used to address or refer to a royal person

high-octane *adj* **1** (of petrol) having a high octane number **2** *inf* dynamic, forceful, or intense: *high-octane drive and efficiency*

high-pass filter *n electronics* a filter that transmits all frequencies above a specified value, attenuating frequencies below this value

high-pitched *adj* **1** pitched high in tone **2** (of a roof) having steeply sloping sides **3** (of an argument, style, etc) lofty or intense

high-powered *adj* **1** (of an optical instrument or lens) having a high magnification **2** dynamic and energetic; highly capable

high-pressure *adj* **1** having, using, or designed to withstand pressure above normal **2** *inf* (of selling) persuasive in an aggressive and persistent manner

high priest *n* **1** *Bible* the priest of highest rank who alone was permitted to enter the holy of holies of the Temple **2** Also (fem): **high priestess** the head of a cult > **high priesthood** *n*

high profile *n* a position or attitude characterized by a deliberate seeking of prominence or publicity

high-rise *adj* **1** (*prenominal*) of or relating to a building that has many storeys, esp one used for flats or offices: *a high-rise block* ▷ *n* **2** a high-rise building

high-risk *adj* (*prenominal*) denoting a group, part, etc, that is particularly subject to a danger

highroad ('haɪ,rəʊd) *n* **1** a main road; highway **2** (usually preceded by *the*) the sure way: *the highroad to fame*

high school *n* **1** *Brit* another term for **grammar school** **2** *US, Canad, NZ, & Scot* a secondary school

high seas *pl n* (*sometimes sing*) the open seas, outside the jurisdiction of any one nation

high season *n* the most popular time of year at a holiday resort, etc

Highsmith ('haɪ,smɪθ) *n* **Patricia** 1921–95, US author of crime fiction. Her novels include *Strangers on a Train* (1950) and *Ripley's Game* (1974)

high-sounding *adj* another term for **high-flown**

high-spirited *adj* vivacious, bold, or lively > ,**high-'spiritedness** *n*

High Street *n* (*often not cap; usually preceded by the*) *Brit* the main street of a town, usually where the principal shops are situated

high table *n* (*sometimes cap*) the table in the dining hall of a school, college, etc, at which the principal teachers, fellows, etc, sit

hightail ('haɪ,teɪl) *vb* (*intr*) *inf, chiefly US & Canad* to go or move in a great hurry

High Tatra *n* another name for the **Tatra Mountains**

high tea *n Brit* See **tea** (sense 4b)

high tech (tɛk) *n* a variant spelling of **hi tech**

high technology *n* any type of sophisticated industrial process, esp electronic

high-tension *n* (*modifier*) carrying or operating at a relatively high voltage

high tide *n* **1** the tide at its highest level **2** a culminating point

high time *inf* ▷ *adv* **1** the latest possible time: *it's high time you left* ▷ *n* **2** Also: **high old time** an enjoyable and exciting time

high-toned *adj* **1** having a superior social, moral, or intellectual quality **2** affectedly superior **3** high in tone

high tops *pl n* training shoes that reach to above the ankles

high treason *n* an act of treason directly affecting a sovereign or state

high-up *n inf* a person who holds an important or influential position

highveld ('haɪ,fɛlt) *n* **the** the high grassland region of NE South Africa

high water *n* **1** another name for **high tide** **2** the state of any stretch of water at its highest level, as during a flood ▷ Abbrev: **HW**

high-water mark *n* **1** the level reached by sea water at high tide or by other stretches of water in flood **2** the highest point

highway ('haɪ,weɪ) *n* **1** a public road that all may use **2** *now chiefly US & Canad except in legal contexts* a main road, esp one that connects towns **3** a direct path or course

Highway Code *n* (in Britain) an official booklet giving guidance to users of public roads

highwayman ('haɪweɪmən) *n, pl* **highwaymen** (formerly) a robber, usually on horseback, who held up travellers on public roads

high wire *n* a tightrope stretched high in the air for balancing acts

High Wycombe ('wɪkəm) *n* a town in S central England, in S Buckinghamshire: furniture industry. Pop: 71 718 (1991)

HIH *abbrev for* His (*or* Her) Imperial Highness

hijack *or* **highjack** ('haɪ,dʒæk) *vb* **1** (*tr*) to seize or divert (a vehicle or the goods it carries) while in transit: *to hijack an aircraft* ▷ *n* **2** the act or an instance of hijacking [c20 from ?] > **'hi,jacker** *or* **'high,jacker** *n*

Hijaz (hiː'dʒæz) *n* a variant spelling of **Hejaz**

hike (haɪk) *vb* **hikes, hiking, hiked** **1** (*intr*) to walk a long way, usually for pleasure, esp in the country **2** (usually foll by *up*) to pull or be pulled; hitch **3** (*tr*; usually foll by *up*) to raise (prices) ▷ *n* **4** a long walk **5** a rise in price [c18 from ?] > **'hiker** *n*

hikoi ('hiːkɔɪ) *n NZ* a walk or march, esp a Maori protest march [Maori]

hilarious (hɪ'lɛərɪəs) *adj* very funny [c19 from L *hilaris* glad, from Gk *hilaros*] > **hi'lariously** *adv* > **hi'lariousness** *n*

hilarity (hɪ'lærɪtɪ) *n* mirth and merriment

Hilary of Poitiers ('hɪlərɪ) *n* **Saint** ?315–?367 AD, French bishop, an opponent of Arianism. Feast day: Jan. 13 or 14

Hilary term *n* the spring term at Oxford University, the

Inns of Court, and some other educational establishments [c16 after Saint HILARY of Poitiers]

Hilbert (ˈhɪlbət) *n* **David** (ˈdaːfɪt) 1862–1943, German mathematician, who made outstanding contributions to the theories of number fields and invariants and to geometry

Hildebrand (ˈhɪldəˌbrænd) *n* the monastic name of **Gregory VII**

Hildegard of Bingen (ˈhɪldəgaːd, ˈbɪŋən) *n* **Saint** 1098–1179, German abbess, poet, composer, and mystic

Hildesheim (*German* ˈhɪldəshaim) *n* a city in N central Germany, in Lower Saxony: a member of the Hanseatic League. Pop: 105 405 (1999 est)

hill (hɪl) *n* **1a** a natural elevation of the earth's surface, less high or craggy than a mountain **1b** (*in combination*): *a hillside* **2a** a heap or mound **2b** (*in combination*): *a dunghill* **3** an incline; slope **4 over the hill 4a** *inf* beyond one's prime **4b** *mil sl* absent without leave or deserting ▷ *vb* (*tr*) **5** to form into a hill **6** to cover or surround with a heap of earth [OE *hyll*] > ˈ**hilly** *adj*

Hill (hɪl) *n* **1 Archibald Vivian** 1886–1977, British biochemist, noted for his research into heat loss in muscle contraction: shared the Nobel prize for physiology or medicine (1922) **2 David Octavius** 1802–70, Scottish painter and portrait photographer, noted esp for his collaboration with the chemist Robert Adamson (1821–48) **3 Geoffrey** (**William**) born 1932, British poet: his books include *For the Unfallen* (1959), *Mercian Hymns* (1971), *The Mystery of the Charity of Charles Péguy* (1983), and *The Orchards of Syon* (2002) **4 Graham** 1929–75, British motor-racing driver: world champion (1962, 1968) **5 Octavia** 1838–1912, British housing reformer; a founder of the National Trust **6** Sir **Rowland** 1795–1879, British originator of the penny postage **7 Susan** (**Elizabeth**) born 1942, British novelist and writer of short stories: her books include *I'm the King of the Castle* (1970) *The Woman in Black* (1983), and *Felix Derby* (2002)

Hilla (ˈhɪlə) *n* a market town in central Iraq, on a branch of the Euphrates: built partly of bricks from the nearby site of Babylon. Pop: 268 834 (latest est). Also called: **Al Hillah**

Hillary (ˈhɪlərɪ) *n* Sir **Edmund** born 1919, New Zealand explorer and mountaineer. He and his Sherpa guide, Tenzing Norgay, were the first to reach the summit of Mount Everest (1953); New Zealand ambassador to India (1984–89)

hillbilly (ˈhɪlˌbɪlɪ) *n, pl* **hillbillies 1** *usually disparaging* an unsophisticated person, esp from the mountainous areas in the southeastern US **2** another name for **country and western** [c20 from HILL + *Billy* (the nickname)]

Hillel (ˈhɪlɛl, -ləl) *n* ?60 BC–?9 AD, rabbi, born in Babylonia; president of the Sanhedrin. He was the first to formulate principles of biblical interpretation

Hilliard (ˈhɪlɪəd) *n* **Nicholas** 1537–1619, English miniaturist, esp of portraits

Hillingdon (ˈhɪlɪŋdən) *n* a residential borough of W Greater London. Pop: 242 435 (2001). Area: 110 sq km (43 sq miles)

hillock (ˈhɪlək) *n* a small hill or mound [c14 *hilloc*] > ˈ**hillocked** *or* ˈ**hillocky** *adj*

hills (hɪlz) *pl n* **1 the** a hilly and often remote region **2 as old as the hills** very old

hill station *n* (in northern India, etc) a settlement or resort at a high altitude

hilt (hɪlt) *n* **1** the handle or shaft of a sword, dagger, etc **2 to the hilt** to the full [OE]

hilum (ˈhaɪləm) *n, pl* **hila** (-lə) **1** *bot* a scar on a seed marking its point of attachment to the seed stalk **2** *anat* a deep fissure or depression on the surface of a bodily organ around the point of entrace or exit of vessels, nerves, or ducts [c17 from L: trifle]

Hilversum (ˈhɪlvəsəm; *Dutch* ˈhɪlvərsym) *n* a city in the central Netherlands, in North Holland province: Dutch radio and television centre. Pop: 84 213 (1994)

him (hɪm; *unstressed* ɪm) *pron* (*objective*) refers to a male person or animal: *they needed him; she baked him a cake; not him again!* [OE *him*, dative of *hē* HE]

USAGE See at **me**

HIM *abbrev for* His (*or* Her) Imperial Majesty

Himachal Pradesh (hɪˈmaːtʃəl praːˈdɛʃ) *n* a state of N India, in the W Himalayas: rises to about 6700 m (22 000 ft) and is densely forested. Capital: Simla. Pop: 6 077 248 (2001). Area: 55 658 sq km (21 707 sq miles)

Himalayan (ˌhɪməˈleɪən) *adj* of or relating to the Himalayas or their inhabitants

Himalayas (ˌhɪməˈleɪəz, hɪˈmaːljəz) *pl n* **the** a vast mountain system in S Asia, extending 2400 km (1500 miles) from Kashmir (west) to Assam (east), between the valleys of the Rivers Indus and Brahmaputra: covers most of Nepal, Sikkim, Bhutan, and the S edge of Tibet; the highest range in the world, with several peaks over 7500 m (25 000 ft). Highest peak: Mount Everest, 8848 m (29 028 ft)

himation (hɪˈmætɪˌɒn) *n, pl* **himatia** (-ɪə) (in ancient Greece) a cloak draped around the body [c19 from Gk, from *heima* dress, from *hennunai* to clothe]

himbo (ˈhɪmbəʊ) *n, pl* **himbos** *sl, usually derog* an attractive, but empty-headed man [c20 from HIM + (BIM)BO]

Himeji (ˈhiːmɛˌdʒiː) *n* a city in central Japan, on W Honshu: cotton textile centre. Pop: 470 986 (1995)

Himmler (*German* ˈhɪmlər) *n* **Heinrich** (ˈhainrɪç) 1900–45, German Nazi leader, head of the SS and the Gestapo (1936–45); committed suicide

Hims (hɪmz) *n* a former name of **Homs**

himself (hɪmˈsɛlf; *medially often* ɪmˈsɛlf) *pron* **1a** the reflexive form of *he* or *him* **1b** (intensifier): *the king himself waved to me* **2** (*preceded by a copula*) his normal self: *he seems himself once more* [OE *him selfum*, dative sing of *hē self*; see HE, SELF]

Himyarite (ˈhɪmjəˌraɪt) *n* **1** a member of an ancient people of SW Arabia, sometimes regarded as including the Sabeans ▷ *adj* **2** of or relating to this people or their culture [c19 named after *Himyar* legendary king in ancient Yemen]

Hinayana (ˌhiːnəˈjaːnə) *n* any of various early forms of Buddhism [from Sansk., from *hīna* lesser + *yāna* vehicle]

Hinckley (ˈhɪŋklɪ) *n* a town in central England, in Leicestershire. Pop: 40 608 (1991 est)

hind[1] (haɪnd) *adj* **hinder, hindmost** *or* **hindermost** (*prenominal*) (esp of parts of the body) situated at the back: *a hind leg* [OE *hindan* at the back, rel. to G *hinten*]

hind[2] (haɪnd) *n, pl* **hinds** *or* **hind 1** the female of the deer, esp the red deer when aged three years or more **2** any of several marine fishes related to the groper [OE *hind*]

hind[3] (haɪnd) *n* (formerly) **1** a simple peasant **2** (in Scotland and N England) a skilled farm worker **3** a steward [OE *hīne*, from *hīgna*, genitive pl of *hīgan* servants]

Hindemith (*German* ˈhɪndəmɪt) *n* **Paul** (paul) 1895–1963, German composer and musical theorist, who opposed the twelve-tone technique. His works include the song cycle *Das Marienleben* (1923) and the opera *Mathis der Maler* (1938)

Hindenburg[1] (ˈhɪndənbʊrk) *n* the German name for **Zabrze**

Hindenburg[2] (ˈhɪndənˌbɜːg; *German* ˈhɪndənbʊrk) *n* **Paul von Beneckendorff und von** (paul fɔn ˈbɛnəkəndɔrf ʊnt fɔn) 1847–1934, German field marshal and statesman; president (1925–34). During World War I he directed German strategy together with Ludendorff (1916–18)

hinder[1] (ˈhɪndə) *vb* **1** to be or get in the way of (someone or something); hamper **2** (*tr*) to prevent [OE *hindrian*]

hinder[2] (ˈhaɪndə) *adj* (*prenominal*) situated at or further towards the back; posterior [OE]

Hindi (ˈhɪndɪ) *n* **1** a language or group of dialects of N

Hh

central India. See also **Hindustani** 2 a formal literary dialect of this language, the official language of India 3 a person whose native language is Hindi [c18 from Hindi, from *Hind* India, from OPersian *Hindu* the river Indus]

hindmost ('haɪnd,məʊst) *or* **hindermost** ('hɪndə,məʊst) *adj* furthest back; last

Hindoo ('hɪndu:, hɪn'du:) *n, pl* **Hindoos,** *adj* an older spelling of **Hindu** > '**Hindoo,ism** *n*

hindquarter ('haɪnd,kwɔ:tə) *n* 1 one of the two back quarters of a carcass of beef, lamb, etc 2 (*pl*) the rear, esp of a four-legged animal

hindrance ('hɪndrəns) *n* 1 an obstruction or snag; impediment 2 the act of hindering

hindsight ('haɪnd,saɪt) *n* 1 the ability to understand, after something has happened, what should have been done 2 a firearm's rear sight

Hindu ('hɪndu:, hɪn'du:) *n, pl* **Hindus** 1 a person who adheres to Hinduism 2 an inhabitant or native of Hindustan or India ▷ *adj* 3 relating to Hinduism, Hindus, or India [c17 from Persian *Hindū*, from *Hind* India; see HINDI]

Hinduism ('hɪndʊ,ɪzəm) *n* the complex of beliefs and customs comprising the dominant religion of India, characterized by the worship of many gods, a caste system, belief in reincarnation, etc
▷ www.himalayanacademy.com
▷ www.hindunet.org

Hindu Kush (kʊʃ, ku:ʃ) *pl n* a mountain range in central Asia, extending about 800 km (500 miles) east from the Koh-i-Baba Mountains of central Afghanistan to the Pamirs. Highest peak: Tirich Mir, 7690 m (25 230 ft)

Hindustan (,hɪndʊ'stɑ:n) *n* 1 the land of the Hindus, esp India north of the Deccan and excluding Bengal 2 the general area around the Ganges where Hindi is the predominant language 3 the areas of India where Hinduism predominates, as contrasted with those areas where Islam predominates

Hindustani, Hindoostani (,hɪndʊ'stɑ:nɪ), *or* **Hindostani** (,hɪndəʊ'stɑ:nɪ) *n* 1 the dialect of Hindi spoken in Delhi: used as a lingua franca throughout India 2 a group of languages or dialects consisting of all spoken forms of Hindi and Urdu considered together ▷ *adj* 3 of or relating to these languages or Hindustan

Hines (haɪnz) *n* **Earl,** known as *Earl "Fatha" Hines*. 1905–83, US jazz pianist, conductor, and songwriter

hinge (hɪndʒ) *n* 1 a device for holding together two parts such that one can swing relative to the other 2 a natural joint, such as the knee joint, that functions in only one plane 3 a similar structure in invertebrate animals, such as the joint between the two halves of a bivalve shell 4 something on which events, opinions, etc, turn 5 Also called: **mount** *philately* a small transparent strip of gummed paper for affixing a stamp to a page ▷ *vb* **hinges, hinging, hinged** 6 (*tr*) to fit a hinge to (something) 7 (*intr*; usually foll by *on* or *upon*) to depend (on) 8 (*intr*) to hang or turn on or as if on a hinge [c13 prob. of Gmc origin] > **hinged** *adj*

hinny¹ ('hɪnɪ) *n, pl* **hinnies** the sterile hybrid offspring of a male horse and a female donkey [c19 from L *hinnus*, from Gk *hinnos*]

hinny² ('hɪnɪ) *n Scot & N English dialect* a term of endearment, esp for a woman [var. of HONEY]

Hi-NRG (,haɪ'ɛnədʒɪ) *n* a type of dance music, originating in the late 1980s, that has a very fast tempo and a strong beat [c20 from HIGH + ENERGY]

hint (hɪnt) *n* 1 a suggestion given in an indirect or subtle manner 2 a helpful piece of advice 3 a small amount; trace ▷ *vb* 4 (when *intr*, often foll by *at*; when *tr*, *takes a clause as object*) to suggest indirectly [c17 from ?]

hinterland ('hɪntə,lænd) *n* 1 land lying behind something, esp a coast or the shore of a river 2 remote or undeveloped areas 3 an area near and dependent on a large city, esp a port [c19 from G, from *hinter* behind + *Land* LAND]

hip¹ (hɪp) *n* 1 (*often pl*) either side of the body below the waist and above the thigh 2 another name for **pelvis** (sense 1) 3 short for **hip joint** 4 the angle formed where two sloping sides of a roof meet [OE *hype*] > '**hipless** *adj*

hip² (hɪp) *n* the berry-like brightly coloured fruit of a rose plant. Also called: **rosehip** [OE *héopa*]

hip³ (hɪp) *interj* an exclamation used to introduce cheers (in **hip, hip, hurrah**) [c18 from ?]

hip⁴ (hɪp) *adj* **hipper, hippest** *sl* 1 aware of or following the latest trends 2 (*often postpositive*; foll by *to*) informed (about) [var. of earlier *hep*]

hip bath *n* a portable bath in which the bather sits

hipbone ('hɪp,bəʊn) *n* the nontechnical name for **innominate bone**

hip flask *n* a small metal flask for spirits, etc

hip-hop ('hɪp,hɒp) *n* a US pop culture movement originating in the 1980s comprising rap music, graffiti, and break dancing
▷ www.hiphop-directory.com
▷ www.hiphop-elements.com

hip joint *n* the ball-and-socket joint that connects each leg to the trunk of the body

Hipparchus (hɪ'pɑ:kəs) *n* 1 2nd century BC, Greek astronomer. He discovered the precession of the equinoxes, calculated the length of the solar year, and developed trigonometry 2 died 514 BC, tyrant of Athens (527–514)

hippeastrum (,hɪpɪ'æstrəm) *n* any plant of a South American genus cultivated for their large funnel-shaped typically red flowers [c19 NL, from Gk *hippeus* knight + *astron* star]

hipped¹ (hɪpt) *adj* 1a having a hip or hips 1b (*in combination*): *broad-hipped* 2 (esp of cows, sheep, etc) having an injury to the hip, such as a dislocation 3 *archit* having a hip or hips: *hipped roof*

hipped² (hɪpt) *adj* (*often postpositive*; foll by *on*) *US & Canad dated sl* very enthusiastic [c20 from HIP⁴]

hippie *n, pl* **hippies** a variant of **hippy¹**

hippo ('hɪpəʊ) *n, pl* **hippos** *inf* short for **hippopotamus**

hippocampus (,hɪpəʊ'kæmpəs) *n, pl* **hippocampi** (-paɪ) 1 a mythological sea creature with the forelegs of a horse and the tail of a fish 2 any of various small sea fishes with a horselike head; sea horse 3 an area of cerebral cortex that forms a ridge in the floor of the brain, which in cross section has the shape of a sea horse. It functions as part of the limbic system [c16 from L, from Gk *hippos* horse + *kampos* a sea monster]

hippocras ('hɪpəʊ,kræs) *n* an old English drink of wine flavoured with spices [c14 *ypocras*, from OF: HIPPOCRATES, prob. referring to a filter called *Hippocrates' sleeve*]

Hippocrates (hɪ'pɒkrə,ti:z) *n* ?460–?377 BC, Greek physician, commonly regarded as the father of medicine

Hippocratic oath (,hɪpə'krætɪk) *n* an oath taken by a doctor to observe a code of medical ethics, supposedly derived from that of Hippocrates

Hippocrene ('hɪpəʊ,kri:n, ,hɪpəʊ'kri:nɪ) *n* a spring on Mount Helicon in Greece, said to engender poetic inspiration [c17 via L from Gk *hippos* horse + *krēnē* spring] > ,**Hippo'crenian** *adj*

hippodrome ('hɪpə,drəʊm) *n* 1 a music hall, variety theatre, or circus 2 (in ancient Greece or Rome) an open-air course for horse and chariot races [c16 from L *hippodromos*, from Gk *hippos* horse + *dromos* race]

hippogriff *or* **hippogryph** ('hɪpəʊ,grɪf) *n* a monster with a griffin's head, wings, and claws and a horse's body [c17 from It. *ippogrifo*, from *ippo-* horse (from Gk) + *grifo* GRIFFIN]

Hippolyta (hɪ'pɒlɪtə) *or* **Hippolyte** (hɪ'pɒlɪ,ti:) *n Greek myth* a queen of the Amazons, slain by Hercules in battle for her belt, which he obtained as his ninth labour

Hippolytus (hɪ'pɒlɪtəs) *n Greek myth* a son of Theseus, killed after his stepmother Phaedra falsely accused him of raping her > **Hip'polytan** *adj*

Hippomenes (hɪ'pɒmɪˌniːz) *n Greek myth* the husband, in some traditions, of Atalanta

hippopotamus (ˌhɪpə'pɒtəməs) *n, pl* **hippopotamuses** *or* **hippopotami** (-ˌmaɪ) a very large gregarious mammal living in or around the rivers of tropical Africa [c16 from L, from Gk: river horse, from *hippos* horse + *potamos* river]

Hippo Regius ('hɪpəʊ 'riːdʒɪəs) *n* an ancient Numidian city, adjoining present-day Annaba, Algeria. Often shortened to: **Hippo**

hippy[1] *or* **hippie** ('hɪpɪ) *n, pl* **hippies** (esp during the 1960s) a person whose behaviour, dress, use of drugs, etc, implies a rejection of conventional values [c20 see HIP[4]]

hippy[2] ('hɪpɪ) *adj* **hippier, hippiest** *inf* (esp of a woman) having large hips

hip roof *n* a roof having sloping ends and sides

hipster ('hɪpstə) *n* **1** *sl, now rare* **1a** an enthusiast of modern jazz **1b** an outmoded word for **hippy**[1] **2** (*modifier*) (of trousers) cut so that the top encircles the hips

hipsters ('hɪpstəz) *pl n Brit* trousers cut so that the top encircles the hips. Usual US word: **hip-huggers**

Hiram ('haɪərəm) *n* 10th century BC, king of Tyre, who supplied Solomon with materials and craftsmen for the building of the Temple (II Samuel 5:11; I Kings 5:1–18)

hircine ('hɜːsaɪn, -sɪn) *adj* **1** *arch* of or like a goat **2** *literary* lascivious [c17 from L *hircīnus*, from *hircus* goat]

hire ('haɪə) *vb* **hires, hiring, hired** (*tr*) **1** to acquire the temporary use of (a thing) or the services of (a person) in exchange for payment **2** to employ (a person) for wages **3** (often foll by *out*) to provide (something) or the services of (oneself or others) for payment, usually for an agreed period **4** (foll by *out*) *chiefly Brit* to pay independent contractors for (work to be done) ▷ *n* **5a** the act of hiring or the state of being hired **5b** (*as modifier*): *a hire car* **6** the price for a person's services or the temporary use of something **7 for** *or* **on hire** available for hire [OE *hȳrian*] > **'hirable** *or* **'hireable** *adj* > **'hirer** *n*

hireling ('haɪəlɪŋ) *n derog* a person who works only for money [OE *hȳrling*]

hire-purchase *n Brit* a system in which a buyer takes possession of merchandise on payment of a deposit and completes the purchase by paying a series of instalments while the seller retains ownership until the final instalment is paid. Abbrev: **HP, h.p.** US and Canad equivalents: **installment plan, instalment plan**

Hirohito (ˌhɪərəʊ'hiːtəʊ) *n* 1901–89, emperor of Japan 1926–89. In 1946 he became a constitutional monarch

Hiroshige (ˌhɪərəʊ'ʃiːgeɪ) *n* **Ando** ('ɑːndəʊ) 1797–1858, Japanese artist, esp of colour wood-block prints

Hiroshima (ˌhɪrɒ'ʃiːmə, hɪ'rɒʃɪmə) *n* a port in SW Japan, on SW Honshu on the delta of the Ota River: largely destroyed on August 6, 1945, by the first atomic bomb to be used in warfare, dropped by the US, which killed over 75 000 of its inhabitants. Pop: 1 108 868 (1995)
▷ www.lclark.edu/~history/HIROSHIMA

Hirst (hɜːst) *n* **Damien** born 1965, British artist, noted for his works featuring dead animals preserved in tanks of formaldehyde

hirsute ('hɜːsjuːt) *adj* **1** covered with hair **2** (of plants) covered with long but not stiff hairs **3** (of a person) having long, thick, or untrimmed hair [c17 from L *hirsūtus* shaggy] > **'hirsuteness** *n*

his (hɪz; *unstressed* ɪz) *determiner* **1a** of, belonging to, or associated with him: *his knee; I don't like his being out so late* **1b** (*as pron*): *his is on the left; that book is his* **2 his and hers** for a man and woman respectively ▷ *pron* **3 of his** belonging to him [OE *his*, genitive of *hē* HE & of *hit* IT]

Hispania (hɪ'spænɪə) *n* the Iberian peninsula in the Roman world

Hispanic (hɪ'spænɪk) *adj* **1** of or derived from Spain or the Spanish ▷ *n* **2** *US* a US citizen of Latin-American descent > **His'panicism** *n*

Hispaniola (ˌhɪspən'jəʊlə; *Spanish* ispa'ɲola) *n* the second largest island in the Caribbean, in the Greater Antilles: divided politically into Haiti and the Dominican Republic; discovered in 1492 by Christopher Columbus, who named it La Isla Española. Area: 18 703 sq km (29 418 sq miles). Former name: **Santo Domingo**

hispid ('hɪspɪd) *adj biol* covered with stiff hairs or bristles [c17 from L *hispidus* bristly]

hiss (hɪs) *n* **1** a sound like that of a prolonged *s* **2** such a sound as an exclamation of derision, contempt, etc ▷ *vb* **3** (*intr*) to produce or utter a hiss **4** (*tr*) to express with a hiss **5** (*tr*) to show derision or anger towards (a speaker, performer, etc) by hissing [c14 imit.]

Hiss (hɪs) *n* **Alger** 1904–96, US government official: imprisoned (1950–54) for perjury in connection with alleged espionage activities

hissy fit ('hɪsɪ) *n inf* a childish temper tantrum

hist (hɪst) *interj* an exclamation used to attract attention or as a warning to be silent

histamine ('hɪstəˌmiːn) *n* an amine released by the body tissues in allergic reactions, causing irritation [c20 from HIST- + AMINE] > **histaminic** (ˌhɪstə'mɪnɪk) *adj*

histo- *or before a vowel* **hist-** *combining form* indicating animal or plant tissue: *histology; histochemistry* [from Gk, from *histos* web]

histogenesis (ˌhɪstəʊ'dʒɛnɪsɪs) *n* the formation of tissues and organs from undifferentiated cells > **histogenetic** (ˌhɪstəʊdʒə'nɛtɪk) *or* ˌ**histo'genic** *adj*

histogram ('hɪstəˌgræm) *n* a statistical graph that represents the frequency of values of a quantity by vertical rectangles of varying heights and widths [c20 ?from HISTO(RY) + -GRAM]

histology (hɪ'stɒlədʒɪ) *n* the study of the tissues of an animal or plant > **histological** (ˌhɪstə'lɒdʒɪkᵊl) *or* ˌ**histo'logic** *adj*

histolysis (hɪ'stɒlɪsɪs) *n* the disintegration of organic tissues > **histolytic** (ˌhɪstə'lɪtɪk) *adj*

historian (hɪ'stɔːrɪən) *n* a person who writes or studies history, esp one who is an authority on it

historic (hɪ'stɒrɪk) *adj* **1** famous in history; significant **2** *linguistics* (of Latin, Greek, or Sanskrit verb tenses) referring to past time.

> **USAGE** A distinction is usually made between *historic* (important, significant) and *historical* (pertaining to history): *a historic decision; a historical perspective*

historical (hɪ'stɒrɪkᵊl) *adj* **1** belonging to or typical of the study of history: *historical methods* **2** concerned with events of the past: *historical accounts* **3** based on or constituting factual material as distinct from legend or supposition **4** based on history: *a historical novel* **5** occurring in history > **his'torically** *adv*

> **USAGE** See at **historic**

historical-cost accounting *n* a method of accounting that values assets at the original cost. In times of high inflation profits can be overstated ▷ Cf **current-cost accounting**

historical linguistics *n* (*functioning as sing*) the study of language as it changes in the course of time

historical present *n* the present tense used to narrate past events, employed for effect or in informal use, as in *a week ago I see this accident*

historicism (hɪ'stɒrɪˌsɪzəm) *n* **1** the belief that natural laws govern historical events **2** the doctrine that each period of history has its own beliefs and values inapplicable to any other **3** excessive emphasis on history, past styles, etc > **his'toricist** *n, adj*

historicity (ˌhɪstə'rɪsɪtɪ) *n* historical authenticity

historiographer (hɪˌstɔːrɪ'ɒgrəfə) *n* **1** a historian, esp one concerned with historical method **2** a historian

Hh

employed to write the history of a group or public institution > **hiˌstoriˈography** *n*

history (ˈhɪstərɪ) *n, pl* **histories** **1** a record or account of past events, developments, etc **2** all that is preserved of the past, esp in written form **3** the discipline of recording and interpreting past events **4** past events, esp when considered as an aggregate **5** an event in the past, esp one that has been reduced in importance: *their quarrel was just history* **6** the past, previous experiences, etc, of a thing or person: *the house had a strange history* **7** a play that depicts historical events **8** a narrative relating the events of a character's life: *the history of Joseph Andrews* [c15 from L *historia*, from Gk: inquiry, from *historein* to narrate, from *histōr* judge]
▷ www.hyperhistory.com
▷ www.historychannel.com

histrionic (ˌhɪstrɪˈɒnɪk) *adj* **1** excessively dramatic or artificial: *histrionic gestures* **2** *now rare* dramatic ▷ *n* **3** (*pl*) melodramatic displays of temperament **4** *rare* (*pl; functioning as sing*) dramatics [c17 from LL *histriōnicus*, from L *histriō* actor] > ˌ**histriˈonically** *adv*

hit (hɪt) *vb* **hits, hitting, hit** (*mainly tr*) **1** (*also intr*) to deal (a blow) to (a person or thing); strike **2** to come into violent contact with: *the car hit the tree* **3** to strike with a missile: *to hit a target* **4** to knock or bump: *I hit my arm on the table* **5** to propel by striking: *to hit a ball* **6** *cricket* to score (runs) **7** to affect (a person, place, or thing), esp suddenly or adversely: *his illness hit his wife very hard* **8** to reach: *unemployment hit a new high* **9** to experience: *I've hit a slight snag here* **10** *sl* to murder (a rival criminal) in fulfilment of an underworld vendetta **11** *inf* to set out on: *let's hit the road* **12** *inf* to arrive: *he will hit town tomorrow* **13** *inf, chiefly US & Canad* to demand or request from: *he hit me for a pound* **14** **hit the bottle** *sl* to drink an excessive amount of alcohol ▷ *n* **15** an impact or collision **16** a shot, blow, etc, that reaches its object **17** an apt, witty, or telling remark **18** *inf* **18a** a person or thing that gains wide appeal: *she's a hit with everyone* **18b** (*as modifier*): *a hit record* **19** *inf* a stroke of luck **20** *sl* **20a** a murder carried out as the result of an underworld vendetta **20b** (*as modifier*): *a hit squad* **21** *computing* a single visit to a website **22** **make a hit with** *inf* to make a favourable impression on ▷ See also **hit off, hit on, hit out** [OE *hittan*, from ON *hitta*] > ˈ**hitter** *n*

Hitachi (hɪˈtætʃɪ) *n* a city in Japan, in E Honshu: a centre of the electronics industry. Pop: 199 241 (1995)

hit-and-miss *adj inf* random; haphazard: *a hit-and-miss affair; the technique is very hit and miss.* Also: **hit or miss**

hit-and-run *adj* (*prenominal*) **1** denoting a motor-vehicle accident in which the driver leaves the scene without stopping to give assistance, inform the police, etc **2** (of an attack, raid, etc) relying on surprise allied to a rapid departure from the scene of operations: *hit-and-run tactics*

hitch (hɪtʃ) *vb* **1** to fasten or become fastened with a knot or tie **2** (*tr; often foll by up*) to pull up (the trousers, etc) with a quick jerk **3** (*intr*) *chiefly US* to move in a halting manner **4** (*tr; passive*) *sl* to marry (esp in **get hitched**) **5** *inf* to obtain (a ride) by hitchhiking ▷ *n* **6** an impediment or obstacle, esp one that is temporary or minor **7** a knot that can be undone by pulling against the direction of the strain that holds it **8** a sudden jerk: *he gave it a hitch and it came loose* **9** *inf* a ride obtained by hitchhiking [c15 from ?] > ˈ**hitcher** *n*

Hitchcock (ˈhɪtʃˌkɒk) *n* Sir **Alfred (Joseph)** 1899–1980, English film director, noted for his mastery in creating suspense. His films include *The Thirty-Nine Steps* (1935), *Rebecca* (1940), *North by Northwest* (1959), *Psycho* (1960), and *The Birds* (1963)

hitchhike (ˈhɪtʃˌhaɪk) *vb* **hitchhikes, hitchhiking, hitchhiked** (*intr*) to travel by obtaining free lifts in motor vehicles > ˈ**hitchˌhiker** *n*

hi tech *or* **high tech** (tɛk) *n* **1** short for **high technology** **2** a style of interior design using features of industrial equipment ▷ *adj* **hi-tech** *or* **high-tech** **3** designed for or using high technology **4** of or in the interior design style ▷ Cf. **low tech**

hither (ˈhɪðə) *adv* **1** to or towards this place (esp in **come hither**) **2** **hither and thither** this way and that, as in confusion ▷ *adj* **3** *arch or dialect* (of a side or part) nearer; closer [OE *hider*]

hithermost (ˈhɪðəˌməʊst) *adj now rare* nearest to this place or in this direction

hitherto (ˌhɪðəˈtuː) *adv, adj* until this time: *hitherto, there have been no problems; hitherto private aristocratic homes*

Hitler (ˈhɪtlə) *n* **1** **Adolf** (ˈaːdɔlf), grandmother's maiden name and father's original surname *Schicklgrüber*, 1889–1945, German dictator, born in Austria. After becoming president of the National Socialist German Workers' Party (Nazi party), he attempted to overthrow the government of Bavaria (1923). While in prison he wrote *Mein Kampf*, expressing his philosophy of the superiority of the Aryan race and the inferiority of the Jews. He was appointed chancellor of Germany (1933), transforming it from a democratic republic into the totalitarian Third Reich, of which he became Führer in 1934. He established concentration camps to exterminate the Jews, rearmed the Rhineland (1936), annexed Austria (1938) and Czechoslovakia, and invaded Poland (1939), which precipitated World War II. He committed suicide **2** a person who displays dictatorial characteristics

Hitlerism (ˈhɪtləˌrɪzəm) *n* the policies, principles, and methods of the Nazi party as developed by Adolf Hitler

hit list *n inf* **1** a list of people to be murdered: *a terrorist hit list* **2** a list of targets to be eliminated in some way: *a hit list of pits to be closed*

hit man *n* a hired assassin

hit off *vb* **1** (*tr, adv*) to represent or mimic accurately **2** **hit it off with** *inf* to have a good relationship with

hit on *vb* (*intr, prep*) **1** to discover unexpectedly or guess correctly. Also: **hit upon** **2** *US & Canad* to make sexual advances to

hit out *vb* (*intr, adv; often foll by at*) **1** to direct blows forcefully and vigorously **2** to make a verbal attack (upon someone)

Hittite (ˈhɪtaɪt) *n* **1** a member of an ancient people of Anatolia, who built a great empire in N Syria and Asia Minor in the second millennium BC **2** the extinct language of this people ▷ *adj* **3** of or relating to this people, their civilization, or their language
▷ www.crystalinks.com/hittites.html

hit wicket *n cricket* an instance of a batsman breaking the wicket with the bat or a part of the body while playing a stroke and so being out

HIV *abbrev for* human immunodeficiency virus; the cause of AIDS

hive (haɪv) *n* **1** a structure in which social bees live **2** a colony of social bees **3** a place showing signs of great industry (esp in **a hive of activity**) **4** a teeming multitude ▷ *vb* **hives, hiving, hived** **5** to cause (bees) to collect or (of bees) to collect inside a hive **6** to live or cause to live in or as if in a hive **7** (*tr; often foll by up or away*) to store, esp for future use [OE *hӯf*]

hive off *vb* (*adv*) **1** to transfer or be transferred from a larger group or unit **2** (*usually tr*) to transfer (profitable activities of a nationalized industry) back to private ownership

hives (haɪvz) *n* (*functioning as sing or pl*) *pathol* a nontechnical name for **urticaria** [c16 from ?]

hiya (ˈhaɪjə, ˌhaɪˈjɑː) *sentence substitute* an informal term of greeting [c20 shortened from *how are you?*]

hl *abbrev for* hectolitre

HL (in Britain) *abbrev for* House of Lords

hm *symbol for* hectometre

h'm (*spelling pron* hmmm) *interj* used to indicate hesitation, doubt, assent, pleasure, etc

HM *abbrev for:* **1** His (*or* Her) Majesty **2** headmaster; headmistress

HMAS *abbrev for* His (*or* Her) Majesty's Australian Ship

HMCS *abbrev for* His (*or* Her) Majesty's Canadian Ship

HMI (in Britain) *abbrev for* His (*or* Her) Majesty's Inspector; a government official who examines and supervises schools

Hmong (hmɒŋ) *n, pl* **Hmongs** or **Hmong** **1** a member of a people living in mountain villages in parts of SE Asia **2** the language of this people

H.M.S. *or* **HMS** *abbrev for:* **1** His (*or* Her) Majesty's Service **2** His (*or* Her) Majesty's Ship

HMSO (in Britain) *abbrev for* (the former) His (*or* Her) Majesty's Stationery Office, now The Stationery Officer (TSO)

HNC (in Britain) *abbrev for* Higher National Certificate; a qualification recognized by many national technical and professional institutions

HND (in Britain) *abbrev for* Higher National Diploma; a qualification in technical subjects equivalent to a degree

ho[1] (həʊ) *interj* **1** Also: **ho-ho** an imitation or representation of a deep laugh **2** an exclamation used to attract attention, etc [c13 imit.]

ho[2] (həʊ) *n US Black sl* a derogatory term for a woman [c20 from Black or Southern US pronunciation of WHORE]

Ho *the chemical symbol for* holmium

hoar (hɔː) *n* **1** short for **hoarfrost** ▷ *adj* **2** *rare* covered with hoarfrost **3** *arch* a poetic variant of **hoary** [OE *hār*]

hoard (hɔːd) *n* **1** an accumulated store hidden away for future use **2** a cache of ancient coins, etc ▷ *vb* **3** to accumulate (a hoard) [OE *hord*] > **'hoarder** *n*

hoarding ('hɔːdɪŋ) *n* **1** Also called (esp US and Canad): **billboard** a large board used for displaying advertising posters, as by a road **2** a temporary wooden fence erected round a building or demolition site [c19 from c15 *hoard* fence, from OF *hourd* palisade, of Gmc origin]

hoarfrost ('hɔːˌfrɒst) *n* a deposit of needle-like ice crystals formed on the ground by direct condensation at temperatures below freezing point. Also called: **white frost**

hoarhound ('hɔːˌhaʊnd) *n* a variant spelling of **horehound**

hoarse (hɔːs) *adj* **1** gratingly harsh in tone **2** having a husky voice, as through illness, shouting, etc [c14 from ON] > **'hoarsely** *adv* > **'hoarseness** *n*

hoarsen ('hɔːsᵊn) *vb* to make or become hoarse

hoary ('hɔːrɪ) *adj* **hoarier, hoariest** **1** having grey or white hair **2** white or whitish-grey in colour **3** ancient or venerable > **'hoariness** *n*

hoatzin (həʊ'ætsɪn) *n* a unique South American bird with clawed wing digits in the young [c17 from American Sp., from Nahuatl *uatzin* pheasant]

hoax (həʊks) *n* **1** a deception, esp a practical joke ▷ *vb* **2** (*tr*) to deceive or play a joke on (someone) [c18 prob. from HOCUS] > **'hoaxer** *n*

hob[1] (hɒb) *n* **1** the flat top part of a cooking stove, or a separate flat surface, containing hotplates or burners **2** a shelf beside an open fire, for keeping kettles, etc, hot **3** a steel pattern used in forming a mould or die in cold metal [c16 var. of obs. *hubbe*; ? rel. to HUB]

hob[2] (hɒb) *n* **1** a hobgoblin or elf **2** **raise** *or* **play hob** *US inf* to cause mischief **3** a male ferret [c14 var. of *Rob*, short for *Robin* or *Robert*]

Hobart ('həʊbɑːt) *n* a port in Australia, capital of the island state of Tasmania on the estuary of the Derwent: excellent natural harbour; University of Tasmania (1890). Pop: 194 700 (1995 est)

Hobbema ('hɒbɪmə; *Dutch* 'hɔbəmaː) *n* **Meindert** ('maɪndərt) 1638–1709, Dutch painter of peaceful landscapes, usually including a watermill

Hobbes (hɒbz) *n* **Thomas** 1588–1679, English political philosopher. His greatest work is the *Leviathan* (1651), which contains his defence of absolute sovereignty

hobbit ('hɒbɪt) *n* one of an imaginary race of half-size people living in holes [c20 coined by J. R. R. Tolkien, with the meaning "hole-builder"]

hobble ('hɒbᵊl) *vb* **hobbles, hobbling, hobbled** **1** (*intr*) to walk with a lame awkward movement **2** (*tr*) to fetter the legs of (a horse) in order to restrict movement **3** (*intr*) to progress with difficulty ▷ *n* **4** a strap, rope, etc, used to hobble a horse **5** a limping gait ▷ Also (for senses 2, 4): **hopple** [c14 prob. from Low G] > **'hobbler** *n*

hobbledehoy (ˌhɒbᵊldɪ'hɔɪ) *n* a clumsy or bad-mannered youth [c16 from earlier *hobbard de hoy*, from ?]

Hobbs (hɒbz) *n* Sir **John Berry**, known as *Jack Hobbs*. 1882–1963, English cricketer: scored 197 centuries

hobby[1] ('hɒbɪ) *n, pl* **hobbies** **1** an activity pursued in spare time for pleasure or relaxation **2** *arch* a small horse **3** short for **hobbyhorse** (sense 1) **4** an early form of bicycle, without pedals [c14 *hobyn*, prob. var. of name *Robin*] > **'hobbyist** *n*

hobby[2] ('hɒbɪ) *n, pl* **hobbies** any of several small Old World falcons [c15 from OF *hobet*, from *hobe* falcon]

hobbyhorse ('hɒbɪˌhɔːs) *n* **1** a toy consisting of a stick with a figure of a horse's head at one end **2** a rocking horse **3** a figure of a horse attached to a performer's waist in a morris dance, etc **4** a favourite topic (esp in **on one's hobbyhorse**) [c16 from HOBBY[1], orig. a small horse; then generalized to apply to any pastime]

hobgoblin (ˌhɒb'gɒblɪn) *n* **1** a mischievous goblin **2** a bogey; bugbear [c16 from HOB[2] + GOBLIN]

hobnail ('hɒbˌneɪl) *n* **a** a short nail with a large head for protecting the soles of heavy footwear **b** (*as modifier*): *hobnail boots* [c16 from HOB[1] (in archaic sense: peg) + NAIL] > **'hobˌnailed** *adj*

hobnob ('hɒbˌnɒb) *vb* **hobnobs, hobnobbing, hobnobbed** (*intr*; *often foll by with*) **1** to socialize or talk informally **2** *obs* to drink (with) [c18 from *hob or nob* to drink to one another in turns, ult. from OE *habban* to HAVE + *nabban* not to have]

Hh

hobo ('həʊbəʊ) *n, pl* **hobos** *or* **hoboes** *chiefly US & Canad* **1** a tramp; vagrant **2** a migratory worker [c19 (US): from ?] > **'hoboism** *n*

Hoboken ('həʊbəʊkən) *n* a city in N Belgium, in Antwerp province, on the River Scheldt. Pop: 35 000 (latest est)

Hobson's choice ('hɒbsᵊnz) *n* the choice of taking what is offered or nothing at all [c16 after Thomas *Hobson* (1544–1631), E liveryman who gave his customers no choice but had them take the nearest horse]

Hochhuth (*German* 'hoːxhuːt) *n* **Rolf** (rɔlf) born 1933, Swiss dramatist. His best-known works are the controversial documentary drama *The Representative* (1963), on the papacy's attitude to the Jews in World War II, *Soldiers* (1967), *German Love Story* (1980), and *Wessis in Weimar* (1992)

Ho Chi Minh ('həʊ 'tʃiː 'mɪn) *n* original name *Nguyen That Tan*. 1890–1969, Vietnamese statesman; president of North Vietnam (1954–69). He headed the Vietminh (1941), which won independence for Vietnam from the French (1954)

Ho Chi Minh City *n* a port in S Vietnam, 97 km (60 miles) from the South China Sea, on the Saigon River: captured by the French in 1859; merged with adjoining Cholon in 1932; capital of the former Republic of Vietnam (South Vietnam) from 1954 to 1976; university (1917); US headquarters during the Vietnam War. Pop: 4 322 300 (1993 est). Former name (until 1976): **Saigon**

hock[1] (hɒk) *n* **1** the joint at the tarsus of a horse or similar animal, corresponding to the human ankle ▷ *vb* **2** another word for **hamstring** [c16 short for *hockshin*, from OE *hōhsinu* heel sinew]

hock[2] (hɒk) *n* any of several white wines from the

German Rhine [c17 short for obs. *hockamore* from G *Hochheimer*]

hock³ (hɒk) *inf, chiefly US & Canad* ▷ *vb* **1** *(tr)* to pawn or pledge ▷ *n* **2** the state of being in pawn **3 in hock 3a** in prison **3b** in debt **3c** in pawn [c19 from Du. *hok* prison, debt]

hockey ('hɒkɪ) *n* **1** Also called (esp US and Canad): **field hockey** a game played on a field by two opposing teams of 11 players each, who try to hit a ball into their opponents' goal using long sticks curved at the end **2** See **ice hockey** [c19 from earlier *hawkey*, from ?] ▷ www.fihockey.org

Hockney ('hɒknɪ) *n* **David** born 1937, English painter, best known for his etchings, such as those to Cavafy's poems (1966), naturalistic portraits such as *Mr and Mrs Clark and Percy* (1971), and for paintings of water, swimmers, and swimming pools

hocus ('həʊkəs) *vb* **hocuses, hocusing, hocused** *or* **hocusses, hocussing, hocussed** *(tr) now rare* **1** to trick **2** to stupefy, esp with a drug **3** to drug (a drink)

hocus-pocus ('həʊkəs'pəʊkəs) *n* **1** trickery or chicanery **2** an incantation used by conjurors or magicians **3** conjuring skill ▷ *vb* **hocus-pocuses, hocus-pocusing, hocus-pocused** *or* **hocus-pocusses, hocus-pocussing, hocus-pocussed 4** to deceive or trick (someone) [c17 ? dog Latin invented by jugglers]

hod (hɒd) *n* **1** an open wooden box attached to a pole, for carrying bricks, mortar, etc **2** a tall narrow coal scuttle [c14 ?from c13 dialect *hot*, from OF *hotte* pannier, prob. of Gmc origin]

Hodeida (hɒ'deɪdə) *n* a port in N Yemen, on the Red Sea; formerly in North Yemen. Pop: 298 500 (1994)

hodgepodge ('hɒdʒ,pɒdʒ) *n* a variant spelling (esp US and Canad) of **hotchpotch**

Hodgkin ('hɒdʒkɪn) *n* **1** Sir **Alan Lloyd** 1914–98, English physiologist. With A F Huxley, he explained the conduction of nervous impulses in terms of the physical and chemical changes involved: shared the Nobel prize for physiology or medicine (1963) **2 Dorothy Crowfoot** 1910–94, English chemist and crystallographer, who determined the three-dimensional structure of insulin: Nobel prize for chemistry (1964) **3** Sir **Howard** born 1932, British painter, noted for his brightly coloured semi-abstract works

Hodgkin's disease *n* a malignant disease, a form of lymphoma, characterized by painful enlargement of the lymph nodes, spleen, and liver [c19 after Thomas *Hodgkin* (1798–1866), London physician, who first described it]

hodograph ('hɒdə,grɑːf) *n* a curve of which the radius vector represents the velocity of a moving particle [c19 from Gk *hodos* way + -GRAPH]

hodometer (hɒ'dɒmɪtə) *n* another name for **odometer** > **ho'dometry** *n*

hoe (həʊ) *n* **1** any of several kinds of long-handled hand implement used to till the soil, weed, etc ▷ *vb* **hoes, hoeing, hoed 2** to dig, scrape, weed, or till (surface soil) with or as if with a hoe [c14 via OF *houe*, of Gmc origin] > **'hoer** *n*

hoedown ('həʊ,daʊn) *n US & Canad* **1** a boisterous square dance **2** a party at which hoedowns are danced

Hoek van Holland ('huːk fɑn 'hɔlɑnt) *n* the Dutch name for the **Hook of Holland**

Hofei ('həʊ'feɪ) *n* a variant transliteration of the Chinese name for **Hefei**

Hoffman ('hɒfmən) *n* **Dustin (Lee)** ('dʌstɪn) born 1937, US stage and film actor. His films include *The Graduate* (1967), *Midnight Cowboy* (1969), *All the President's Men* (1976), *Kramer vs Kramer* (1979), *Rain Man* (1989), *Wag the Dog* (1998), and *Moonlight Mile* (2002)

Hofmannsthal (*German* 'hoːfmanstaːl) *n* **Hugo von** ('huːgo fɔn) 1874–1929, Austrian lyric poet and dramatist, noted as the librettist for Richard Strauss's operas, esp *Der Rosenkavalier* (1911), *Elektra* (1909), and *Ariadne auf Naxos* (1912)

Hofuf (hʊ'fuːf) *n* another name for **Al Hufuf**

hog (hɒg) *n* **1** a domesticated pig, esp a castrated male **2** *US & Canad* any mammal of the family Suidae; pig **3** Also: **hogg** *Austral dialect* another name for **hogget 4** *inf* a greedy person **5 go the whole hog** *sl* to do something thoroughly or unreservedly ▷ *vb* **hogs, hogging, hogged** *(tr)* **6** *sl* to take more than one's share of **7** to arch (the back) like a hog **8** to cut (the mane) of (a horse) very short [OE *hogg*, of Celtic origin] > **'hogger** *n* > **'hog,like** *adj*

hogan ('həʊgən) *n* a wooden dwelling covered with earth, typical of the Navaho Indians of North America [of Amerind origin]

Hogan ('həʊgən) *n* **Ben,** full name *William Benjamin Hogan.* 1912–97, US golfer

Hogarth ('həʊgɑːθ) *n* **William** 1697–1764, English engraver and painter. He is noted particularly for his series of engravings satirizing the vices and affectations of his age, such as *A Rake's Progress* (1735) and *Marriage à la Mode* (1745)

hogback ('hɒg,bæk) *n* **1** Also called: **hog's back** a narrow ridge with steep sides **2** *archaeol* a tomb with sloping sides

hogfish ('hɒg,fɪʃ) *n, pl* **hogfish** *or* **hogfishes** a wrasse that occurs in the Atlantic. The head of the male resembles a pig's snout

Hogg (hɒg) *n* **1 James,** known as *the Ettrick Shepherd.* 1770–1835, Scottish poet and writer. His works include the volume of poems *The Queen's Wake* (1813) and the novel *The Confessions of a Justified Sinner* (1824) **2 Quintin** See (1st Baron) **Hailsham of St Marylebone**

hogget ('hɒgɪt) *n dialect, Austral & NZ* a young sheep that has yet to be sheared. Also: **hog, hogg**

hoggish ('hɒgɪʃ) *adj* selfish, gluttonous, or dirty

Hogmanay (,hɒgmə'neɪ) *n (sometimes not cap)* New Year's Eve in Scotland [c17 ?from Norman F *hoguinane*, from OF *aguillanneuf* a New Year's Eve gift]

hognose snake ('hɒg,nəʊz) *n* an American nonvenomous snake with a trowel-shaped snout. It inflates its body when alarmed. Also called: **puff adder**

hogshead ('hɒgz,hɛd) *n* **1** a unit of capacity, used esp for alcoholic beverages. It has several values **2** a large cask [c14 from ?]

hogtie ('hɒg,taɪ) *vb* **hogties, hogtying, hogtied** *(tr) chiefly US* **1** to tie together the legs or the arms and legs of **2** to impede, hamper, or thwart

Hogtown ('hɒg,taʊn) *n Canad* a slang name for **Toronto**

hogwash ('hɒg,wɒʃ) *n* **1** *inf* nonsense **2** pigswill

hogweed ('hɒg,wiːd) *n* any of several coarse weedy plants

Hogwood ('hɒgwʊd) *n* **Christopher (Jarvis Haley)** born 1941, British harpsichordist, conductor, and musicologist; founder and director of the Academy of Ancient Music from 1973

Hohenlohe ('həʊən,ləʊə; *German* hoːən'loːə) *n* **Chlodwig** ('kloːtvɪç), Prince of Hohenlohe-Schillingsfürst. 1819–1901, Prussian statesman; chancellor of the German empire (1894–1900)

Hohenstaufen ('həʊən,ʃtaʊfən; *German* hoːən'ʃtaufən) *n* a German princely family that provided rulers of Germany (1138–1208, 1215–54), Sicily (1194–1268), and the Holy Roman Empire (1138–1254)

Hohenzollern ('həʊən,zɒlən; *German* hoːən'tsɔlərn) *n* a German noble family, the younger (Franconian) branch of which provided rulers of Brandenburg (1417–1701) and Prussia (1701–1918). The last kings of Prussia (1871–1918) were also emperors of Germany

Hohhot ('hɒ'hɒt), **Huhehot,** *or* **Hu-ho-hao-t'e** *n* a city in N China, capital of Inner Mongolia Autonomous Region (since 1954); previously capital of the former Suiyüan province; Inner Mongolia University (1957). Pop: 754 749 (1999 est)

ho-hum (ˌhəʊˈhʌm) *adj inf* lacking interest or inspiration; dull; mediocre: *a ho-hum collection of new releases*
hoick *or* **hoik** (hɔɪk) *vb* to rise or raise abruptly and sharply [C20 prob. from HIKE]
hoi polloi (ˈhɔɪ pəˈlɔɪ) *pl n* **the** *often derog* the masses; common people [Gk, lit.: the many]
hoist (hɔɪst) *vb* **1** *(tr)* to raise or lift up, esp by mechanical means ▷ *n* **2** any apparatus or device for hoisting **3** the act of hoisting **4** *naut* a group of signal flags **5** the inner edge of a flag next to the staff [C16 var. of *hoise*, prob. from Low G] > ˈ**hoister** *n*
hoity-toity (ˌhɔɪtɪˈtɔɪtɪ) *adj inf* arrogant or haughty [C17 rhyming compound based on C16 *hoit* to romp, from ?]
hokey cokey (ˌhəʊkɪ ˈkəʊkɪ) *n* a dance routine performed to a cockney song of the same name
hokey-pokey (ˌhəʊkɪˈpəʊkɪ) *n NZ* a brittle toffee sold in lumps
Hokkaido (hɒˈkaɪdəʊ) *n* the second largest and northernmost of the four main islands of Japan, separated from Honshu by the Tsugaru Strait and from the island of Sakhalin, Russia, by La Pérouse Strait: constitutes an autonomous administrative division. Capital: Sapporo. Pop: 5 683 000 (2000 est). Area: 78 508 sq km (30 312 sq miles)
hokonui (ˌhəʊkəˈnuːiː) *n NZ* illicit whisky [from *Hokonui*, district of Southland region, NZ]
hokum (ˈhəʊkəm) *n sl, chiefly US & Canad* **1** claptrap; bunk **2** obvious or hackneyed material of a sentimental nature in a play, film, etc [C20 prob. a blend of HOCUS-POCUS & BUNKUM]
Hokusai (ˈhəʊkʊˌsaɪ, ˌhəʊkʊˈsaɪ) *n* **Katsushika** (ˌkætsuːˈʃiːkə) 1760–1849, Japanese artist, noted for the draughtsmanship of his colour wood-block prints, which influenced the impressionists
Holarctic (həʊˈlɑːktɪk) *adj* of or denoting a zoogeographical region consisting of the entire arctic regions [C19 from HOLO- + ARCTIC]
Holbein (*German* ˈhɔlbain) *n* **1 Hans** (hans), known as *Holbein the Elder*. 1465–1524, German painter **2** his son, **Hans,** known as *Holbein the Younger*. 1497–1543, German painter and engraver; court painter to Henry VIII of England (1536–43). He is noted particularly for his portraits, such as those of Erasmus (1524; 1532) and Sir Thomas More (1526)
hold[1] (həʊld) *vb* **holds, holding, held 1** to have or keep (an object) with or within the hands, arms, etc; clasp **2** *(tr)* to support: *to hold a drowning man's head above water* **3** to maintain or be maintained in a specified state: *to hold firm* **4** *(tr)* to set aside or reserve: *they will hold our tickets until tomorrow* **5** (when *intr, usually used in commands*) to restrain or be restrained from motion, action, departure, etc: *hold that man until the police come* **6** *(intr)* to remain fast or unbroken: *that cable won't hold much longer* **7** *(intr)* (of the weather) to remain dry and bright **8** *(tr)* to keep the attention of **9** *(tr)* to engage in or carry on: *to hold a meeting* **10** *(tr)* to have the ownership, possession, etc, of: *he holds a law degree; who's holding the ace?* **11** *(tr)* to have the use of or responsibility for: *to hold office* **12** *(tr)* to have the capacity for: *the carton will hold eight books* **13** *(tr)* to be able to control the outward effects of drinking (beer, spirits, etc) **14** (often foll by *to* or *by*) to remain or cause to remain committed (to): *hold him to his promise* **15** *(tr; takes a clause as object)* to claim: *he holds that the theory is incorrect* **16** *(intr)* to remain relevant, valid, or true: *the old philosophies don't hold nowadays* **17** *(tr)* to consider in a specified manner: *I hold him very dear* **18** *(tr)* to defend successfully: *hold the fort against the attack* **19** (sometimes foll by *on*) *music* to sustain the sound of (a note) throughout its specified duration **20** *(tr) computing* to retain (data) in a storage device after copying onto another storage device or location **21 hold (good) for** to apply or be relevant to: *the same rules hold for everyone* **22 there is no holding him** *or* **her** this person is so spirited that he or she cannot be restrained ▷ *n* **23** the act or method of holding fast or grasping **24** something to hold onto, as for support or control **25** an object or device that holds fast or grips something else **26** controlling influence: *she has a hold on him* **27** a short pause **28** a prison or a cell in a prison **29** *wrestling* a way of seizing one's opponent **30** *music* a pause or fermata **31a** a tenure, esp of land **31b** *(in combination)*: *freehold* **32** *arch* a fortified place **33 no holds barred** all limitations removed ▷ See also **hold back, hold down,** etc [OE *healdan*] > ˈ**holdable** *adj*
hold[2] (həʊld) *n* the space in a ship or aircraft for storing cargo [C16 var. of HOLE]
holdall (ˈhəʊldˌɔːl) *n Brit* a large strong bag or basket. Usual US and Canad name: **carryall**
hold back *vb (adv)* **1** to restrain or be restrained **2** *(tr)* to withhold: *he held back part of the payment*
hold down *vb (tr, adv)* **1** to restrain or control **2** *inf* to manage to retain or keep possession of: *to hold down two jobs at once*
holder (ˈhəʊldə) *n* **1** a person or thing that holds **2a** a person who has possession or control of something **2b** *(in combination)*: *householder* **3** *law* a person who has possession of a bill of exchange, cheque, or promissory note that he is legally entitled to enforce
Hölderlin (*German* ˈhœldərliːn) *n* **Friedrich** (ˈfriːdrɪç) 1770–1843, German lyric poet, whose works include the poems *Menon's Lament for Diotima* and *Bread and Wine* and the novel *Hyperion* (1797–99)
holdfast (ˈhəʊldˌfɑːst) *n* **1** the act of gripping strongly **2** any device used to secure an object, such as a hook, clamp, etc **3** the organ of attachment of a seaweed or related plant
hold forth *vb (adv)* **1** *(intr)* to speak for a long time or in public **2** *(tr)* to offer (an attraction or enticement)
hold in *vb (tr, adv)* **1** to curb, control, or keep in check **2** to conceal (feelings)
holding (ˈhəʊldɪŋ) *n* **1** land held under a lease **2** *(often pl)* property to which the holder has legal title, such as land, stocks, shares, and other investments **3** *sport* the obstruction of an opponent with the hands or arms, esp in boxing ▷ *adj* **4** *Austral inf* in funds; having money
holding company *n* a company with controlling shareholdings in one or more other companies
holding operation *n* a plan or procedure devised to prolong the existing situation
holding paddock *n Austral & NZ* a paddock in which cattle or sheep are kept temporarily, as before shearing, etc
holding pattern *n* the oval or circular path of an aircraft flying around an airport awaiting permission to land
hold off *vb (adv)* **1** *(tr)* to keep apart or at a distance **2** *(intr; often foll by from)* to refrain (from doing something)
hold on *vb (intr, adv)* **1** to maintain a firm grasp **2** to continue or persist **3** (foll by *to*) to keep or retain: *hold on to those stamps as they'll soon be valuable* **4** *inf* to keep a telephone line open ▷ *sentence substitute* **5** *inf* stop! wait!
hold out *vb (adv)* **1** *(tr)* to offer **2** *(intr)* to last or endure **3** *(intr)* to continue to stand firm, as a person refusing to succumb to persuasion **4** *chiefly US* to withhold (something due) **5 hold out for** to wait patiently for (the fulfilment of one's demands) **6 hold out on** *inf* to keep from telling (a person) some important information
hold over *vb (tr, mainly adv)* **1** to defer or postpone **2** *(prep)* to intimidate (a person) with (a threat)
hold-up *n* **1** a robbery, esp an armed one **2** a delay; stoppage ▷ *vb* **hold up** *(tr, adv)* **3** to delay; hinder **4** to support **5** to waylay in order to rob, esp using a weapon **6** to exhibit or present
hold with *vb (intr, prep)* to support; approve of
hole (həʊl) *n* **1** an area hollowed out in a solid **2** an opening in or through something **3** an animal's burrow

Hh

4 *inf* an unattractive place, such as a town 5 a fault (esp in **pick holes in**) 6 *sl* a difficult and embarrassing situation 7 the cavity in various games into which the ball must be thrust 8 (on a golf course) 8a each of the divisions of a course (usually 18) represented by the distance between the tee and a green 8b the score made in striking the ball from the tee into the hole 9 *physics* a vacancy in a nearly full band of quantum states of electrons in a semiconductor or an insulator. Under the action of an electric field holes behave as carriers of positive charge 10 **in holes** so worn as to be full of holes 11 **make a hole in** to consume or use a great amount of (food, drink, money, etc) ▷ *vb* **holes, holing, holed** 12 to make a hole or holes in (something) 13 (when *intr*, often foll by *out*) *golf* to hit (the ball) into the hole [OE *hol*] > '**holey** *adj*

hole-and-corner *adj* (*usually prenominal*) *inf* furtive or secretive

hole in one *n golf* a shot from the tee that finishes in the hole. Also (esp US): **ace**

hole in the heart *n* a defect of the heart in which there is an abnormal opening in any of the walls dividing the four heart chambers

hole in the wall *n inf* 1 *chiefly Brit* another name for **cash dispenser** 2 a small dingy place, esp one that is difficult to find

hole up *vb* (*intr, adv*) 1 (of an animal) to hibernate 2 *inf* to hide or remain secluded

Holguín (*Spanish* ɔl'ɣin) *n* a city in NE Cuba, in Holguín province: trading centre. Pop: 242 085 (1994 est)

Holi ('həʊlɪ) *n* a Hindu spring festival, celebrated for two to five days, commemorating Krishna's dalliance with the cowgirls. Bonfires are lit and coloured powder and water thrown over celebrants [after *Holika*, legendary female demon]

-holic *suffix forming nouns* indicating desire for or dependence on; *workaholic; chocoholic* [c20 abstracted from (*alco*)*holic*]

holiday ('hɒlɪˌdeɪ) *n* 1 (*often pl*) *chiefly Brit* a period in which a break is taken from work or studies for rest, travel, or recreation. US and Canad word: **vacation** 2 a day on which work is suspended by law or custom, such as a religious festival, bank holiday, etc. Related adj: **ferial** ▷ *vb* 3 (*intr*) *chiefly Brit* to spend a holiday [OE *hāligdæg*, lit.: holy day]

Holiday ('hɒlɪˌdeɪ) *n* **Billie** real name *Eleanora Fagan;* known as *Lady Day*. 1915–59, US jazz singer

holiday camp *n Brit* a place, esp one at the seaside, providing accommodation, recreational facilities, etc, for holiday-makers

holiday-maker *n Brit* a person who goes on holiday. US and Canad equivalents: **vacationer, vacationist**

holily ('həʊlɪlɪ) *adv* in a holy, devout, or sacred manner

holiness ('həʊlɪnɪs) *n* the state or quality of being holy

Holiness ('həʊlɪnɪs) *n* (preceded by *His* or *Your*) a title reserved for the pope

Holinshed ('hɒlɪnʃɛd) *or* **Holingshed** *n* **Raphael** died ?1580, English chronicler. His *Chronicles of England, Scotland, and Ireland* (1577) provided material for Shakespeare's historical and legendary plays

holism ('həʊlɪzəm) *n* 1 any doctrine that a system may have properties over and above those of its parts and their organization 2 (in medicine) the consideration of the complete person in the treatment of disease [c20 from HOLO- + -ISM]

holistic (həʊ'lɪstɪk) *adj* 1 of or relating to a doctrine of holism 2 of or relating to the the medical consideration of the complete person, physically and psychologically, in the treatment of a disease: *holistic medicine* > **ho'listically** *adv*

Holkar State (hɒl'kɑː) *n* a former state of central India, ruled by the Holkar dynasty of Maratha rulers of Indore (18th century until 1947)

holland ('hɒlənd) *n* a coarse linen cloth [c15 after HOLLAND, where it was made]

Holland[1] ('hɒlənd) *n* 1 another name for the **Netherlands** 2 a county of the Holy Roman Empire, corresponding to the present-day North and South Holland provinces of the Netherlands 3 **Parts of** an area in E England constituting a former administrative division of Lincolnshire

Holland[2] ('hɒlənd) *n* 1 **Henry** 1745–1806, British neoclassical architect. His work includes Brooks's Club (1776) and Carlton House (1783), both in London 2 Sir **Sidney George** 1893–1961, New Zealand statesman; prime minister of New Zealand (1949–57)

hollandaise sauce (ˌhɒlən'deɪz, 'hɒlənˌdeɪz) *n* a rich sauce of egg yolks, butter, vinegar, etc [c19 from F *sauce hollandaise* Dutch sauce]

Hollandia (hɒ'lændɪə) *n* a former name of **Jayapura**

Hollands ('hɒləndz) *n* (*functioning as sing*) Dutch gin, often sold in stone bottles [c18 from Du. *hollandsch genever*]

holler ('hɒlə) *inf* ▷ *vb* 1 to shout or yell (something) ▷ *n* 2 a shout; call [var. of c16 *hollow*, from *holla*, from F *holà* stop! (lit.: ho there!)]

hollo ('hɒləʊ) *or* **holla** ('hɒlə) *n, pl* **hollos** *or* **hollas**, *interj* 1 a cry for attention, or of encouragement ▷ *vb* 2 (*intr*) to shout [c16 from F *holà* ho there!]

hollow ('hɒləʊ) *adj* 1 having a hole or space within; not solid 2 having a sunken area; concave 3 deeply set: *hollow cheeks* 4 (of sounds) as if resounding in a hollow place 5 without substance or validity 6 hungry or empty 7 insincere; cynical ▷ *adv* 8 **beat (someone) hollow** *Brit inf* to defeat thoroughly ▷ *n* 9 a cavity, opening, or space in or within something 10 a depression in the land ▷ *vb* (often foll by *out*, usually when *tr*) 11 to make or become hollow 12 to form (a hole, cavity, etc) or (of a hole, etc) to be formed [c12 from *holu*, inflected form of OE *holh* cave] > '**hollowly** *adv* > '**hollowness** *n*

hollow-eyed *adj* with the eyes appearing to be sunk into the face, as from excessive fatigue

holly ('hɒlɪ) *n, pl* **hollies** 1 a tree or shrub having bright red berries and shiny evergreen leaves with prickly edges 2 its branches, used for Christmas decorations 3 **holly oak** another name for **holm oak** [OE *holegn*]

Holly ('hɒlɪ) *n* **Buddy** real name *Charles Harden Holley*. 1936–59, US rock-and-roll singer, guitarist, and songwriter. His hits (all 1956–59) include "That'll be the Day", "Maybe Baby", "Peggy Sue", "Oh, Boy", "Think it over", and "It doesn't Matter anymore"

hollyhock ('hɒlɪˌhɒk) *n* a tall plant with stout hairy stems and spikes of white, yellow, red, or purple flowers. Also called (US): **rose mallow** [c16 from HOLY + *hock*, from OE *hoc* mallow]

Hollywood ('hɒlɪˌwʊd) *n* 1 a NW suburb of Los Angeles, California: centre of the American film industry. Pop: 250 000 (latest est) 2a the American film industry 2b (*as modifier*): *a Hollywood star*

holm[1] (həʊm) *n dialect, chiefly Northwestern English* 1 an island in a river, lake, or estuary 2 low flat land near a river [OE *holm* sea, island]

holm[2] (həʊm) *n* 1 short for **holm oak** 2 *chiefly Brit* a dialect word for **holly** [c14 var. of obs. *holin*, from OE *holegn* holly]

Holmes (həʊmz) *n* 1 **Oliver Wendell** 1809–94, US author, esp of humorous essays, such as *The Autocrat of the Breakfast Table* (1858) and its sequels 2 his son, **Oliver Wendell** 1841–1935, US jurist, noted for his liberal judgments

holmium ('hɒlmɪəm) *n* a malleable silver-white metallic element of the lanthanide series. Symbol: Ho; atomic no.: 67; atomic wt.: 164.93 [c19 from NL *Holmia* Stockholm]

holm oak *n* an evergreen Mediterranean oak tree with prickly leaves resembling holly in young plants, which become smooth-edged with age. Also called: **holm, holly oak, ilex**

holo- *or before a vowel* **hol-** *combining form* whole or wholly: *holograph* [from Gk *holos*]

holocaust ('hɒləˌkɔːst) *n* **1** great destruction or loss of life or the source of such destruction, esp fire **2** (*usually cap*) **the** the mass murder of some six million European Jews by the Germans during World War II **3** a rare word for **burnt offering** [c13 from LL *holocaustum* whole burnt offering, from Gk, from HOLO- + *kaiein* to burn]

▷ www.holocaust-history.org

▷ www.nizkor.org

Holocene ('hɒləˌsiːn) *adj* **1** of, denoting, or formed in the second and most recent epoch of the Quaternary period, which began 10 000 years ago ▷ *n* **2 the** the Holocene epoch or rock series ▷ Also: **Recent**

Holofernes (ˌhɒlə'fɜːniːz, hə'lɒfəˌniːz) *n* the Assyrian general, who was killed by the biblical heroine Judith

hologram ('hɒləˌgræm) *n* a photographic record produced by illuminating the object with coherent light (as from a laser) and, without using lenses, exposing a film to light reflected from this object and to a direct beam of coherent light. When interference patterns on the film are illuminated by the coherent light a three-dimensional image is produced

holograph ('hɒləˌgrɑːf) *n* a book or document handwritten by its author; original manuscript; autograph

holography (hɒ'lɒgrəfɪ) *n* the science or practice of producing holograms > **holographic** (ˌhɒlə'græfɪk) *adj* > ˌ**holo'graphically** *adv*

holohedral (ˌhɒlə'hiːdrəl) *adj* (of a crystal) exhibiting all the planes required for the symmetry of the crystal system

holophytic (ˌhɒlə'fɪtɪk) *adj* (of plants) capable of synthesizing their food from inorganic molecules, esp by photosynthesis

holothurian (ˌhɒlə'θjʊərɪən) *n* **1** an echinoderm of the class *Holothuroidea*, having a leathery elongated body with a ring of tentacles around the mouth ▷ *adj* **2** of the *Holothuroidea* [c19 from NL *Holothūria*, name of type genus, from L: water polyp, from Gk, from ?]

hols (hɒlz) *pl n Brit school sl* holidays

Holst (həʊlst) *n* **1 Alison** born 1938, New Zealand chef **2 Gustav (Theodore)** 1874–1934, English composer. His works include operas, choral music, and orchestral music such as the suite *The Planets* (1917)

Holstein (*German* 'hɔlʃtain) *n* a region of N Germany, in S Schleswig-Holstein: in early times a German duchy of Saxony; became a duchy of Denmark in 1474; finally incorporated into Prussia in 1866

holster ('həʊlstə) *n* a sheathlike leather case for a pistol, attached to a belt or saddle [c17 via Du., of Gmc origin]

holt[1] (həʊlt) *n arch or poetic* a wood or wooded hill [OE *holt*]

holt[2] (həʊlt) *n* the lair of an animal, esp an otter [c16 from HOLD[1]]

Holt (həʊlt) *n* **Harold Edward** 1908–67, Australian statesman; prime minister (1966–67); believed drowned

holy ('həʊlɪ) *adj* **holier, holiest 1** of or associated with God or a deity; sacred **2** endowed or invested with extreme purity **3** devout or virtuous **4 holier-than-thou** offensively sanctimonious or self-righteous ▷ *n, pl* **holies 5** a sacred place [OE *hālig, hǣlig*]

Holy Communion *n* **1** the celebration of the Eucharist **2** the consecrated elements

holy day *n* a day on which a religious festival is observed

▷ www.bbc.co.uk/religion/religions

▷ www.calendarzone.com/Religious/

Holy Father *n RC Church* the pope

Holy Ghost *n* another name for the **Holy Spirit**

Holy Grail *n* **1** Also called: **Grail, Sangraal** (in medieval legend) the bowl used by Jesus at the Last Supper. It was brought to Britain by Joseph of Arimathea, where it became the quest of many knights **2** *inf* any desired ambition or goal: *the Holy Grail of infrared astronomy* [c14 *grail* from OF *graal*, from Med. L *gradālis* bowl, from ?]

Holyhead ('hɒlɪˌhɛd) *n* a town in NW Wales, in Anglesey, the chief town of Holy Island: a port on the N coast. Pop: 11 796 (1991)

Holy Island *n* **1** an island off the NE coast of Northumberland, linked to the mainland by road but accessible only at low water: site of a monastery founded by St Aidan in 635. Also called: **Lindisfarne 2** an island off the NW coast of Anglesey. Area: about 62 sq km (24 sq miles)

Holy Land *n* **the** another name for **Palestine** (sense 1)

Holyoake ('həʊlɪˌəʊk) *n* Sir **Keith Jacka** ('dʒækə) 1904–83, New Zealand politician; prime minister (1957; 1960–72); governor general (1977–80)

holy of holies *n* **1** any place of special sanctity **2** (*cap*) the innermost compartment of the Jewish tabernacle, where the Ark was enshrined

holy orders *pl n* **1** the sacrament whereby a person is admitted to the Christian ministry **2** the grades of the Christian ministry **3** the status of an ordained Christian minister

Holy Roman Empire *n* the complex of European territories under the rule of the Frankish or German king who bore the title of Roman emperor, beginning with the coronation of Charlemagne in 800 AD

▷ www.heraldica.org/topics/national/hre.htm

Holy Scripture *n* another term for **Scripture**

Holy See *n RC Church* **1** the see of the pope as bishop of Rome **2** the Roman curia

Holy Spirit *n Christianity* the third person of the Trinity. Also called: **Holy Ghost**

holystone ('həʊlɪˌstəʊn) *n* **1** a soft sandstone used for scrubbing the decks of a vessel ▷ *vb* **holystones, holystoning, holystoned 2** (*tr*) to scrub (a vessel's decks) with a holystone [c19 ?from its being used in a kneeling position]

holy synod *n* the governing body of any of the Orthodox Churches

holy water *n* water that has been blessed by a priest for use in symbolic rituals of purification

Holy Week *n* the week preceding Easter Sunday

Holy Willie ('wɪlɪ) *n* a person who is hypocritically pious [c18 from Burns's "Holy Willie's Prayer"]

Holy Writ *n* another term for **Scripture**

homage ('hɒmɪdʒ) *n* **1** a public show of respect or honour towards someone or something (esp in **pay** *or* **do homage to**) **2** (in feudal society) the act of respect and allegiance made by a vassal to his lord [c13 from OF, from *home* man, from L *homo*]

homburg ('hɒmbɜːg) *n* a man's hat of soft felt with a dented crown and a stiff upturned brim [c20 after *Homburg*, in Germany, where orig. made]

home (həʊm) *n* **1** the place where one lives **2** a house or other dwelling **3** a family or other group living in a house **4** a person's country, city, etc, esp viewed as a birthplace or a place dear to one **5** the habitat of an animal **6** the place where something is invented, founded, or developed **7** a building or organization set up to care for people in a certain category, such as orphans, the aged, etc **8** *sport* one's own ground: *the match is at home* **9a** the objective towards which a player strives in certain sports **9b** an area where a player is safe from attack **10 a home from home** a place other than one's own home where one can be at ease **11 at home 11a** in one's own home or country **11b** at ease **11c** giving an informal party at one's own home **12 at home in, on,** *or* **with** familiar with **13 home and dry** *Brit sl* definitely safe or successful. Austral and NZ equivalent: **home and hosed 14 near home** concerning one deeply ▷ *adj* (*usually prenominal*) **15** of one's home, country, etc; domestic **16** (of an activity) done in one's house: *home*

Hh

taping **17** *sport* relating to one's own ground: *a home game* **18** *US* central; principal: *the company's home office* ▷ *adv* **19** to or at home: *I'll be home tomorrow* **20** to or on the point **21** to the fullest extent: *hammer the nail home* **22 bring home to 22a** to make clear to **22b** to place the blame on **23 nothing to write home about** *inf* of no particular interest: *the film was nothing to write home about* ▷ *vb* **homes, homing, homed 24** (*intr*) (of birds and other animals) to return home accurately from a distance **25** (often foll by *in on* or *onto*) to direct or be directed onto a point or target, esp by automatic navigational aids **26** to send or go home **27** (*tr*) to furnish with a home **28** (*intr;* often foll by *in* or *in on*) to be directed towards a goal, target, etc [OE *hām*]

USAGE See at **hone**

Home (hju:m) *n* **Baron** See (Baron) **Home of the Hirsel**

home-alone *adj inf* (esp of a young child) left in a house, flat, etc, unattended

home banking *n* a system whereby a person at home or in an office can use a computer with a modem to call up information from a bank or to transfer funds electronically

homeboy ('həʊm,bɔɪ) *n sl, chiefly US* **1** a close friend **2** a person from one's home town or neighbourhood **3** a member of a neighbourhood gang [c20 US rap-music usage] > **'home,girl** *fem n*

home brand *n* an Australian term for **own brand**

home-brew *n* **1** a beer or other alcoholic drink brewed at home rather than commercially **2** *Canad inf* a professional football player who was born in Canada and is not an import > **,home-'brewed** *adj*

homecoming ('həʊm,kʌmɪŋ) *n* **1** the act of coming home **2** *US* an annual celebration held by a university, college, or school for former students

Home Counties *pl n* the counties surrounding London

home economics *n* (*functioning as sing or pl*) the study of diet, budgeting, child care, and other subjects concerned with running a home

home farm *n Brit* (esp formerly) a farm attached to and providing food for a large country house

Home Guard *n* a volunteer part-time military force recruited to defend the United Kingdom in World War II

home help *n Brit* a woman employed, esp by a local authority, to do housework in a person's home. NZ equivalent: **home aid**

home invasion *n Austral & NZ* aggravated burglary

homeland ('həʊm,lænd) *n* **1** the country in which one lives or was born **2** the official name for a **Bantustan**

homeless ('həʊmlɪs) *adj* **a** having nowhere to live **b** (*as collective n*; preceded by *the*): *the homeless* > **'homelessness** *n*

homely ('həʊmlɪ) *adj* **homelier, homeliest** **1** characteristic of or suited to the ordinary home; unpretentious **2** (of a person) **2a** *Brit* warm and domesticated **2b** *chiefly US & Canad* plain > **'homeliness** *n*

home-made *adj* **1** (esp of foods) made at home or on the premises, esp of high quality ingredients **2** crudely fashioned

homeo-, homoeo-, *or* **homoio-** *combining form* like or similar: *homeomorphism* [from L *homoeo-*, from Gk *homoio-*, from *homos* same]

Home Office *n Brit government* the department responsible for the maintenance of law and order, and all other domestic affairs not assigned to another department

Home of the Hirsel (hju:m, 'hɜ:səl) *n* Baron, title of *Sir Alec Douglas-Home*, formerly 14th Earl of Home. 1903–95, British Conservative statesman: he renounced his earldom to become prime minister of Great Britain and Northern Ireland (1963–64); foreign secretary (1970–74)

homeopathy *or* **homoeopathy** (,həʊmɪ'ɒpəθɪ) *n* a method of treating disease by the use of small amounts of a drug that, in healthy persons, produces symptoms similar to those of the disease being treated > **homeopathic** *or* **homoeopathic** (,həʊmɪə'pæθɪk) *adj* > **homeopathist, homoeopathist** (,həʊmɪ'ɒpəθɪst) *or* **homeopath, homoeopath** ('həʊmɪə,pæθ) *n*

▷ www.homeopathy.org

homeostasis *or* **homoeostasis** (,həʊmɪəʊ'steɪsɪs) *n* **1** the maintenance of metabolic equilibrium within an animal by a tendency to compensate for disrupting changes **2** the maintenance of equilibrium within a social group, person, etc

homeowner ('həʊm,əʊnə) *n* a person who owns the house in which he or she lives > **,home'ownership** *n*

home page *n computing* (on a website) the main document relating to an individual or an institution that provides introductory information about a website with links to the actual details of services or information provided

homer ('həʊmə) *n* a homing pigeon

Homer ('həʊmə) *n* c. 800 BC, Greek poet to whom are attributed the *Iliad* and the *Odyssey*: it is thought that he was born on the island of Chios and was blind

Homeric (həʊ'mɛrɪk) *adj* **1** of, relating to, or resembling Homer or his poems **2** imposing or heroic

homeroom ('həʊm,ru:m, -,rʊm) *n US* **1** a room in a school used by a particular group of students as a base for registration, notices, etc **2** a group of students who use the same room as a base in school

home rule *n* **1** self-government, esp in domestic affairs **2** the partial autonomy sometimes granted to a national minority or a colony

Home Secretary *n Brit government* the head of the Home Office

homesick ('həʊm,sɪk) *adj* depressed or melancholy at being away from home and family > **'home,sickness** *n*

homespun ('həʊm,spʌn) *adj* **1** having plain or unsophisticated character **2** woven or spun at home ▷ *n* **3** cloth made at home or made of yarn spun at home

homestead ('həʊm,stɛd, -stɪd) *n* **1** a house or estate and the adjoining land, buildings, etc, esp a farm **2** (in the US) a house and adjoining land designated by the owner as his fixed residence and exempt under the homestead laws from seizure and forced sale for debts **3** (in western Canada) a piece of land granted to a settler by the federal government **4** *Austral & NZ* (on a sheep or cattle station) the owner's or manager's residence; in New Zealand, the term includes all outbuildings

Homestead Act *n* **1** an act passed by the US Congress in 1862 making available to settlers 160-acre tracts of public land for cultivation **2** (in Canada) a similar act passed by the Canadian Parliament in 1872

homesteader ('həʊm,stɛdə) *n US & Canad* a person who possesses land under a homestead law

homestead law *n* (in the US and Canada) any of various laws conferring privileges on owners of homesteads

home straight *n* **1** *horse racing* the section of a racecourse forming the approach to the finish **2** the final stage of an undertaking ▷ Also (chiefly US): **home stretch**

home truth *n* (*often pl*) an unpleasant fact told to a person about himself or herself

home unit *n Austral & NZ* a self-contained residence which is part of a series of similar residences. Often shortened to **unit**

homeward ('həʊmwəd) *adj* **1** going home **2** (of a voyage, etc) returning to the home port ▷ *adv also* **homewards 3** towards home

homeware ('həʊmwɛə) *n* crockery, furniture, and furnishings with which a house, room, etc, is furnished [c20 HOME + WARE[1]]

homework ('həʊm,wɜ:k) *n* **1** school work done at home **2** any preparatory study **3** work done at home for pay

homey ('həʊmɪ) *adj* **homier, homiest** a variant spelling (esp US) of **homy** > **'homeyness** *n*

homicide ('hɒmɪ,saɪd) *n* **1** the killing of one human being by another **2** a person who kills another [c14 from OF, from L *homo* man + *caedere* to slay] > ˌ**homiˈcidal** *adj*

homiletics (ˌhɒmɪˈlɛtɪks) *n (functioning as sing)* the art of preaching or writing sermons [c17 from Gk *homilētikos* cordial, from *homilein*; see HOMILY] > ˌ**homiˈletic** *adj*

homily (ˈhɒmɪlɪ) *n, pl* **homilies** **1** a sermon **2** moralizing talk or writing [c14 from Church L *homīlia*, from Gk: discourse, from *homilein* to converse with, from *homilos* crowd, from *homou* together + *ilē* crowd] > ˈ**homilist** *n*

homing (ˈhəʊmɪŋ) *n (modifier)* **1** *zool* relating to the ability to return home after travelling great distances **2** (of an aircraft, missile, etc) capable of guiding itself onto a target

homing pigeon *n* any breed of pigeon developed for its homing instinct, used for racing. Also called: **homer**

hominid (ˈhɒmɪnɪd) *n* **1** any primate of the family Hominidae, which includes modern man (*Homo sapiens*) and the extinct precursors of man ▷ *adj* **2** of or belonging to the Hominidae [c19 via NL from L *homo* man + -ID[1]]

hominoid (ˈhɒmɪˌnɔɪd) *adj* **1** of or like man; manlike **2** of or belonging to the primate family, which includes the anthropoid apes and man ▷ *n* **3** a hominoid animal [c20 from L *homin-*, *homo* man + -OID]

hominy (ˈhɒmɪnɪ) *n chiefly US* coarsely ground maize prepared as a food by boiling in milk or water [c17 prob. of Algonquian origin]

hominy grits *pl n US* finely ground hominy

homo[1] (ˈhəʊməʊ) *n, pl* **homos** *inf, derog* short for **homosexual**

homo[2] (ˈhəʊməʊ) *n Canad inf* short for **homogenized milk**

Homo (ˈhəʊməʊ) *n* a genus of hominids including modern man (see ***Homo sapiens***) and several extinct species of primitive man [L: man]

homo- *combining form* same or like: *homologous*; *homosexual* [via L from Gk *homos* same]

homocyclic (ˌhəʊməʊˈsaɪklɪk) *adj* (of a chemical compound) containing a closed ring of atoms of the same kind, esp carbon atoms

homocysteine (ˌhəʊməʊˈsɪstɪˌiːn) *n* an amino acid occurring as an intermediate in the metabolism of methionine. Elevated levels in the blood may indicate increased risk of cardiovascular disease

homoeo- *combining form* a variant of **homeo-**

homogamy (hɒˈmɒgəmɪ) *n* **1** a condition in which all the flowers of an inflorescence are either of the same sex or hermaphrodite **2** the maturation of the anthers and stigmas at the same time, ensuring self-pollination > **hoˈmogamous** *adj*

homogeneous (ˌhəʊməˈdʒiːnɪəs, ˌhɒm-) *adj* **1** composed of similar or identical parts or elements **2** of uniform nature **3** similar in kind or nature **4** *maths* containing terms of the same degree with respect to all the variables, as in $x^2 + 2xy + y^2$ > **homogeneity** (ˌhəʊməʊdʒɪˈniːɪtɪ, ˌhɒm-) *n* > ˌ**homoˈgeneousness** *n*

homogenize *or* **homogenise** (hɒˈmɒdʒɪˌnaɪz) *vb* **homogenizes, homogenizing, homogenized** *or* **homogenises, homogenising, homogenised** **1** *(tr)* to break up the fat globules in (milk or cream) so that they are evenly distributed **2** to make or become homogeneous > **hoˌmogeniˈzation** *or* **hoˌmogeniˈsation** *n* > **hoˈmogeˌnizer** *or* **hoˈmogeˌniser** *n*

homogenous (həˈmɒdʒɪnəs) *adj* of, relating to, or exhibiting homogeny

homogeny (hɒˈmɒdʒɪnɪ) *n biol* similarity in structure because of common ancestry [c19 from Gk *homogeneia* community of origin, from *homogenēs* of the same kind]

homograph (ˈhɒməˌgrɑːf) *n* one of a group of words spelt in the same way but having different meanings > ˌ**homoˈgraphic** *adj*

homoiothermic (həʊˌmɔɪəˈθɜːmɪk) *or* **homothermal** (ˌhəʊməʊˈθɜːməl, ˌhɒm-) *adj* having a constant body temperature, usually higher than the temperature of the surroundings; warm-blooded > **hoˈmoioˌthermy** *or* ˈ**homoˌthermy** *n*

homologize *or* **homologise** (hɒˈmɒləˌdʒaɪz) *vb* **homologizes, homologizing, homologized** *or* **homologises, homologising, homologised** to be, show to be, or make homologous

homologous (həʊˈmɒləgəs, hɒ-), **homological** (ˌhəʊməˈlɒdʒɪkəl, ˌhɒm-), *or* **homologic** *adj* **1** having a related or similar position, structure, etc **2** *biol* (of organs and parts) having the same evolutionary origin but different functions: *the wing of a bat and the paddle of a whale are homologous* > ˌ**homoˈlogically** *adv* > ˈ**homoˌlogue** *or US (sometimes)* ˈ**homoˌlog** *n*

homology (həʊˈmɒlədʒɪ) *n, pl* **homologies** the condition of being homologous [c17 from Gk *homologia* agreement, from *homologos* agreeing, from HOMO- + *legein* to speak]

homolosine projection (hɒˈmɒləˌsaɪn) *n* a map projection of the world on which the oceans are distorted to allow for greater accuracy in representing the continents [c20 from Gk *homologos* agreeing + SINE[1]]

homomorphism (ˌhəʊməʊˈmɔːfɪzəm, ˌhɒm-) *or* **homomorphy** *n biol* similarity in form > ˌ**homoˈmorphic** *or* ˌ**homoˈmorphous** *adj*

homonym (ˈhɒmənɪm) *n* **1** one of a group of words spelt in the same way but having different meanings ▷ Cf **homograph, homophone** **2** *biol* a name for a species or genus that should be unique but has been used for two or more different organisms [c17 from L *homōnymum*, from Gk, from *homōnumos* of the same name; see HOMO-, -ONYM] > ˌ**homoˈnymic** *or* **hoˈmonymous** *adj*

homophobia (ˌhəʊməʊˈfəʊbɪə) *n* intense hatred or fear of homosexuals or homosexuality [c20 from HOMO(SEXUAL) + -PHOBIA] > ˈ**homoˌphobe** *n* > ˌ**homoˈphobic** *adj*

homophone (ˈhɒməˌfəʊn) *n* **1** one of a group of words pronounced in the same way but differing in meaning or spelling or both, as *bear* and *bare* **2** a written letter or combination of letters that represents the same speech sound as another: *"ph" is a homophone of "f"*

homophonic (ˌhɒməˈfɒnɪk) *adj* of or relating to music in which the parts move together rather than exhibit individual rhythmic independence

homopterous (həʊˈmɒptərəs) *or* **homopteran** *adj* of or belonging to a suborder of hemipterous insects having wings of a uniform texture held over the back at rest [c19 from Gk *homopteros*, from HOMO- + *pteron* wing]

Homo sapiens (ˈsæpɪˌɛnz) *n* the specific name of modern man; the only extant species of the genus *Homo*. This species also includes some extinct types of primitive man, such as Cro-Magnon man [NL, from L *homo* man + *sapiens* wise]

homosexual (ˌhəʊməʊˈsɛksjʊəl, ˌhɒm-) *n* **1** a person who is sexually attracted to members of the same sex ▷ *adj* **2** of or relating to homosexuals or homosexuality **3** of or relating to the same sex

homosexuality (ˌhəʊməʊˌsɛksjʊˈælɪtɪ, ˌhɒm-) *n* sexual attraction to or sexual relations with members of the same sex

homosocial (ˌhəʊməʊˈsəʊʃəl) *adj* relating to or denoting same-sex social relationships ▷ Cf. **heterosocial** > **homosociality** (ˌhəʊməʊˌsəʊʃɪˈælɪtɪ) *n*

homozygote (ˌhəʊməʊˈzaɪgəʊt) *n* an animal or plant that is homozygous and breeds true to type > **homozygotic** (ˌhəʊməʊzaɪˈgɒtɪk) *adj*

homozygous (ˌhəʊməʊˈzaɪgəs) *adj genetics* (of an organism) having identical alleles for any one gene: *these two fruit flies are homozygous for red eye colour*

Homs (hɒms) *or* **Hums** (hʊms) *n* a city in W Syria, near the Orontes River: important in Roman times as the capital of Phoenicia-Lebanesia. Pop: 644 204 (1994 est). Ancient name: **Emesa** (ˈɛmɛsə). Former name: **Hims**

homunculus (hɒˈmʌŋkjʊləs) *n, pl* **homunculi** (-ˌlaɪ) a

Hh

miniature man; midget. Also called: **homuncule** (həʊˈmʌŋkjuːl) [c17 from L, dim. of *homo* man] > **hoˈmuncular** *adj*

homy *or esp US* **homey** (ˈhəʊmɪ) *adj* **homier, homiest** like a home; cosy > **ˈhominess** *or esp US* **ˈhomeyness** *n*

hon. *abbrev for:* **1** honorary **2** honourable

Hon. *abbrev for* Honourable (title)

Honan (ˈhəʊˈnæn) *n* a variant transliteration of the Chinese name for **Henan**

honcho (ˈhɒntʃəʊ) *n, pl* **honchos** *inf, chiefly US* the person in charge; the boss [c20 from Japanese *han'chō* group leader]

Hond. *abbrev for* Honduras

Hondo (ˈhɒndəʊ) *n* another name for **Honshu**

Honduran (hɒnˈdjʊərən) *adj* **1** of or relating to Honduras or its inhabitants ▷ *n* **2** a native or inhabitant of Honduras

Honduras (hɒnˈdjʊərəs) *n* **1** a republic in Central America: an early centre of Mayan civilization; colonized by the Spanish from 1524 onwards; gained independence in 1821. Official language: Spanish; English is also widely spoken. Religion: Roman Catholic majority. Currency: lempira. Capital: Tegucigalpa. Pop: 6 626 000 (2001 est). Area: 112 088 sq km (43 277 sq miles) **2 Gulf of** an inlet of the Caribbean, on the coasts of Honduras, Guatemala, and Belize
▷ www.letsgohonduras.com/web

hone (həʊn) *n* **1** a fine whetstone for sharpening ▷ *vb* **hones, honing, honed 2** *(tr)* to sharpen or polish with or as if with a hone [OE *hān* stone]

USAGE *Hone* is sometimes wrongly used where *home* is meant: *this device makes it easier to home in on* (not *hone in on*) *the target*

Honecker (*German* ˈhɒnɛkər) *n* **Erich** (ˈeːrɪç) 1912–94, German statesman; head of state of East Germany (1976–89)

Honegger (ˈhɒnɪɡə; *French* ɔnɛɡɛr) *n* **Arthur** (artyr) 1892–1955, French composer, one of Les Six. His works include the oratorios *King David* (1921) and *Joan of Arc at the Stake* (1935), and *Pacific 231* (1924) for orchestra

honest (ˈɒnɪst) *adj* **1** not given to lying, cheating, stealing, etc; trustworthy **2** not false or misleading; genuine **3** just or fair: *honest wages* **4** characterized by sincerity: *an honest appraisal* **5** without pretensions: *honest farmers* **6** *arch* (of a woman) respectable **7 honest broker** a mediator in disputes, esp international ones **8 make an honest woman of** to marry (a woman, esp one who is pregnant) to prevent scandal [c13 from OF *honeste*, from L *honestus* distinguished, from *honōs* HONOUR]

honestly (ˈɒnɪstlɪ) *adv* **1** in an honest manner **2** (intensifier): *I honestly don't believe it*

honesty (ˈɒnɪstɪ) *n, pl* **honesties 1** the condition of being honest **2** *arch* virtue or respect **3** Also called: **moonwort, satinpod** a purple-flowered European plant cultivated for its flattened silvery pods, which are used for indoor decoration

honey (ˈhʌnɪ) *n* **1** a sweet viscid substance made by bees from nectar and stored in their nests or hives as food **2** anything that is sweet or delightful **3** *(often cap) chiefly US & Canad* a term of endearment **4** *inf, chiefly US & Canad* something very good of its kind ▷ *vb* **honeys, honeying, honeyed 5** *(tr)* to sweeten with or as if with honey **6** (often foll by *up*) to talk to (someone) in a flattering way [OE *huneg*] > **ˈhoney-ˌlike** *adj*

honey badger *n* another name for **ratel**

honeybee (ˈhʌnɪˌbiː) *n* any of various social bees widely domesticated as a source of honey and beeswax. Also called: **hive bee**

honey buzzard *n* a common European bird of prey having broad wings and a typically dull brown plumage with white-streaked underparts

honeycomb (ˈhʌnɪˌkəʊm) *n* **1** a waxy structure, constructed by bees in a hive, that consists of adjacent hexagonal cells in which honey is stored, eggs are laid, and larvae develop **2** something resembling this in structure **3** *zool* another name for **reticulum** (sense 2) ▷ *vb (tr)* **4** to pierce with holes, cavities, etc **5** to permeate: *honeycombed with spies*

honey creeper *n* a small tropical American songbird having a slender downward-curving bill and feeding on nectar

honeydew (ˈhʌnɪˌdjuː) *n* **1** a sugary substance excreted by aphids and similar insects **2** a similar substance exuded by certain plants

honeydew melon *n* a variety of muskmelon with a smooth greenish-white rind and sweet greenish flesh

honey-eater (ˈhʌnɪˌiːtə) *n* a small Australasian songbird having a downward-curving bill and a brushlike tongue specialized for extracting nectar from flowers

honeyed *or* **honied** (ˈhʌnɪd) *adj poetic* **1** flattering or soothing **2** made sweet or agreeable: *honeyed words* **3** full of honey

honey guide *n* a small bird inhabiting tropical forests of Africa and Asia and feeding on beeswax, honey, and insects

honeymoon (ˈhʌnɪˌmuːn) *n* **1** a holiday taken by a newly married couple **2** a holiday considered to resemble a honeymoon: *a second honeymoon* **3** the early, usually calm period of a relationship or enterprise ▷ *vb* **4** *(intr)* to take a honeymoon [c16 traditionally explained as an allusion to the feelings of married couples as changing with the phases of the moon] > **ˈhoneyˌmooner** *n*

honeypot (ˈhʌnɪˌpɒt) *n* **1** a container for honey **2** something that attracts in great numbers: *Cornwall is a honeypot for tourists*

honeysuckle (ˈhʌnɪˌsʌkəl) *n* **1** a temperate climbing shrub with fragrant white, yellow, or pink tubular flowers **2** any of various Australian trees or shrubs of the genus *Banksia*, having flowers in dense spikes [OE *hunigsūce*, from HONEY + SUCK]

honeytrap (ˈhʌnɪˌtræp) *n inf* a scheme in which a victim is lured into a compromising sexual situation that provides the opportunity for blackmail

hongi (ˈhɒŋiː) *n NZ* a form of salutation expressed by touching noses [Maori]

Hong Kong (ˌhɒŋ ˈkɒŋ) *n* **1** a Special Administrative Region of S China, with some autonomy; formerly a British Crown Colony: consists of Hong Kong Island, leased by China to Britain from 1842 until 1997, Kowloon Peninsula, Stonecutters Island, the New Territories (mainland), leased by China in 1898 for a 99-year period, and over 230 small islands; important entrepôt trade and manufacturing centre, esp for textiles and other consumer goods; university (1912). Administrative centre: Victoria. Pop: 6 732 000 (2001 est). Area: 1046 sq km (404 sq miles) **2** an island in Hong Kong region, south of Kowloon Peninsula: contains the capital, Victoria. Pop: 1 337 800 (2001). Area: 75 sq km (29 sq miles)

Hong-wu (ˈhɒŋˈwuː) *or* **Hung-wu** *n* title of *Chu Yuan-Zhang* (or *Chu Yüan-Chang*), 1328–98, first emperor (1368–98) of the Ming dynasty, uniting China under his rule by 1382

Hong Xiu Quan (ˈhɒŋ ˈʃjuː ˈtʃwɑːn) *or* **Hung Hsiu-Ch'uan** *n* 1814–64, Chinese religious leader and revolutionary. Claiming (1851) to be Christ's brother, he led the Taiping rebellion; committed suicide when it was defeated

Honiara (ˌhəʊnɪˈɑːrə) *n* the capital of the Solomon Islands, on NW Guadalcanal Island. Pop: 50 100 (2000 est)

honk (hɒŋk) *n* **1** a representation of the sound made by a goose **2** any sound resembling this, esp a motor horn **3** *Brit & Austral sl* a bad smell ▷ *vb* **4** to make or cause (something) to make such a sound **5** *(intr) Brit sl* to vomit

6 (intr) *Brit & Austral sl* to have a bad smell

honky ('hɒŋkɪ) *n, pl* **honkies** *derog sl, chiefly US* a White man or White men collectively [c20 from ?]

honky-tonk ('hɒŋkɪˌtɒŋk) *n* **1** *US & Canad sl* a cheap disreputable nightclub, bar, etc **2a** a style of ragtime piano-playing, esp on a tinny-sounding piano **2b** (*as modifier*): *honky-tonk music* [c19 rhyming compound based on HONK]

Honolulu (ˌhɒnə'luːluː) *n* a port in Hawaii, on S Oahu Island: the state capital. Pop: 371 657 (2000)

honorarium (ˌɒnə'rɛərɪəm) *n, pl* **honorariums** *or* **honoraria** (-ɪə) a fee paid for a nominally free service [c17 from L: something presented on being admitted to a post of HONOUR]

honorary ('ɒnərərɪ) *adj* (*usually prenominal*) **1a** held or given only as an honour, without the normal privileges or duties: *an honorary degree* **1b** (of a secretary, treasurer, etc) unpaid **2** having such a position or title **3** depending on honour rather than legal agreement

honorific (ˌɒnə'rɪfɪk) *adj* **1** showing respect **2a** (of a pronoun, verb inflection, etc) indicating the speaker's respect for the addressee **2b** (*as n*): *a Japanese honorific* > ˌ**honor'ifically** *adv*

honour *or US* **honor** ('ɒnə) *n* **1** personal integrity; allegiance to moral principles **2a** fame or glory **2b** a person who wins this for his or her country, school, etc **3** (*often pl*) great respect, esteem, etc, or an outward sign of this **4** (*often pl*) high or noble rank **5** a privilege or pleasure: *it is an honour to serve you* **6** a woman's chastity **7a** *bridge, etc* any of the top five cards in a suit or any of the four aces at no trumps **7b** *whist* any of the top four cards **8** *golf* the right to tee off first **9 in honour bound** under a moral obligation **10 in honour of** out of respect for **11 on one's honour** on the pledge of one's word or good name ▷ *vb* (*tr*) **12** to hold in respect **13** to show courteous behaviour towards **14** to worship **15** to confer a distinction upon **16** to accept and then pay when due (a cheque, draft, etc) **17** to keep (one's promise); fulfil (a previous agreement) **18** to bow or curtsy to (one's dancing partner) [c12 from OF *onor*, from L *honor* esteem]

Honour ('ɒnə) *n* (preceded by *Your, His,* or *Her*) a title used to or of certain judges

honourable *or US* **honorable** ('ɒnərəbᵊl) *adj* **1** possessing or characterized by high principles **2** worthy of honour or esteem **3** consistent with or bestowing honour > '**honourably** *or US* '**honorably** *adv*

Honourable *or US* **Honorable** ('ɒnərəbᵊl) *adj* (*prenominal*) **the** a title of respect placed before a name: used of various officials in the English-speaking world, as a courtesy title in Britain for the children of certain peers, and in Parliament by one member speaking of another. Abbrev: **Hon**

honours *or US* **honors** ('ɒnəz) *pl n* **1** observances of respect **2** (*often cap*) **2a** (in a university degree course) a rank of the highest academic standard **2b** (*as modifier*): *an honours degree*. Abbrev: **Hons** **3** a high mark awarded for an examination; distinction **4 do the honours** to serve as host or hostess **5 last** (*or* **funeral**) **honours** observances of respect at a funeral **6 military honours** ceremonies performed by troops in honour of royalty, at the burial of an officer, etc

honours of war *pl n mil* the honours granted by the victorious to the defeated, esp as of marching out with all arms and flags flying

Honshu ('hɒnʃuː) *n* the largest of the four main islands of Japan, between the Pacific and the Sea of Japan; regarded as the Japanese mainland; includes a number of offshore islands and contains most of the main cities. Pop: 100 995 000 (1995). Area: 230 448 sq km (88 976 sq miles). Also called: **Hondo**

hooch *or* **hootch** (huːtʃ) *n inf, chiefly US & Canad* alcoholic drink, esp illicitly distilled spirits [c20 of Amerind origin, *Hootchinoo*, name of a tribe that distilled a type of liquor]

Hooch *or* **Hoogh** (huːtʃ; *Dutch* hoːx) *n* **Pieter de** ('piːtər də) 1629–?1684, Dutch genre painter, noted esp for his light effects

hood[1] (hʊd) *n* **1** a loose head covering either attached to a cloak or coat or made as a separate garment **2** something resembling this in shape or use **3** the US and Canad name for **bonnet** (of a car) **4** the folding roof of a convertible car **5** a hoodlike garment worn over an academic gown, indicating its wearer's degree and university **6** *biol* a hoodlike structure, such as the fold of skin on the head of a cobra ▷ *vb* **7** (*tr*) to cover with or as if with a hood [OE *hōd*] > '**hood,like** *adj*

hood[2] (hʊd) *n sl* short for **hoodlum**

Hood (hʊd) *n* **1 Robin** See **Robin Hood** **2 Samuel,** 1st Viscount. 1724–1816, British admiral. He fought successfully against the French during the American Revolution and the French Revolutionary Wars **3 Thomas** 1799–1845, British poet and humorist: his work includes protest poetry, such as *The Song of the Shirt* (1843) and *The Bridge of Sighs* (1844)

-hood *suffix forming nouns* **1** indicating state or condition: *manhood* **2** indicating a body of persons: *knighthood; priesthood* [OE *-hād*]

hooded ('hʊdɪd) *adj* **1** covered with, having, or shaped like a hood **2** (of eyes) having heavy eyelids that appear to be half closed

hooded crow *n* a crow that has a grey body and black head, wings, and tail. Also called (Scot): **hoodie** ('hʊdɪ), **hoodie crow**

hoodlum ('huːdləm) *n* **1** a petty gangster **2** a lawless youth [c19 ?from Southern G *Haderlump* ragged good-for-nothing]

hoodman-blind (ˌhʊdmən'blaɪnd) *n Brit, arch* blind man's buff

hoodoo ('huːduː) *n, pl* **hoodoos** **1** a variant of **voodoo** **2** *inf* a person or thing that brings bad luck **3** *inf* bad luck ▷ *vb* **hoodoos, hoodooing, hoodooed** **4** (*tr*) *inf* to bring bad luck to

hoodwink ('hʊdˌwɪŋk) *vb* (*tr*) **1** to dupe; trick **2** *obs* to cover or hide [c16 orig., to cover the eyes with a hood, blindfold]

hooey ('huːɪ) *n, interj sl* nonsense [c20 from ?]

hoof (huːf) *n, pl* **hooves** *or* **hoofs** **1a** the horny covering of the end of the foot in the horse, deer, and all other ungulate mammals **1b** (*in combination*): *a hoofbeat*. Related adj: **ungular** **2** the foot of an ungulate mammal **3** a hoofed animal **4** *facetious* a person's foot **5 on the hoof** **5a** (of livestock) alive **5b** in an impromptu manner: *he did his thinking on the hoof* ▷ *vb* **6 hoof it** *sl* **6a** to walk **6b** to dance [OE *hōf*] > **hoofed** *adj*

hoofer ('huːfə) *n sl* a professional dancer

Hoogh (*Dutch* hoːx) *n* See (Pieter de) **Hooch**

Hooghly ('huːglɪ) *n* a river in NE India, in West Bengal: the westernmost and commercially most important channel by which the River Ganges enters the Bay of Bengal. Length: 232 km (144 miles)

hoo-ha ('huːˌhɑː) *n* a noisy commotion or fuss [c20 from ?]

hook (hʊk) *n* **1** a curved piece of material, usually metal, used to suspend, hold, or pull something **2** short for **fish-hook** **3** a trap or snare **4** something resembling a hook in design or use **5a** a sharp bend, esp in a river **5b** a sharply curved spit of land **6** *boxing* a short swinging blow delivered with the elbow bent **7** *cricket* a shot in which the ball is hit square on the leg side with the bat held horizontally **8** *golf* a shot that causes the ball to go to the player's left **9** a hook-shaped stroke used in writing, such as a part of a letter extending above or below the line **10** *music* a stroke added to the stem of a note to indicate time values shorter than a crotchet **11** a sickle **12** *naut* an anchor **13 by hook or** (**by**)

crook by any means **14 hook, line, and sinker** *inf* completely: *he fell for it hook, line, and sinker* **15 off the hook** *sl* free from obligation or guilt **16 sling one's hook** *Brit sl* to leave ▷ *vb* **17** (often foll by *up*) to fasten or be fastened with or as if with a hook or hooks **18** (*tr*) to catch (something, such as a fish) on a hook **19** to curve like or into the shape of a hook **20** (*tr*) to make (a rug) by hooking yarn through a stiff fabric backing with a special instrument **21** *boxing* to hit (an opponent) with a hook **22** *cricket, etc* to play (a ball) with a hook **23** *rugby* to obtain and pass (the ball) backwards from a scrum, using the feet **24** (*tr*) *sl* to steal [OE *hōc*] > **'hook,like** *adj*

hookah *or* **hooka** ('hʊkə) *n* an oriental pipe for smoking marijuana, tobacco, etc, consisting of one or more long flexible stems connected to a container of water or other liquid through which smoke is drawn and cooled. Also called: **hubble-bubble, water pipe** [c18 from Ar. *huqqah*]

Hooke (hʊk) *n* **Robert** 1635–1703, English physicist, chemist, and inventor. He formulated Hooke's law (1678), built the first Gregorian telescope, and invented a balance spring for watches

hooked (hʊkt) *adj* **1** bent like a hook **2** having a hook or hooks **3** caught or trapped **4** a slang word for **married** **5** *sl* addicted to a drug **6** (often foll by *on*) obsessed (with)

hooker ('hʊkə) *n* **1** a person or thing that hooks **2** *sl* a prostitute **3** *rugby* the central forward in the front row of a scrum

Hooker *n* **John Lee** 1917–2001, US blues singer and guitarist

Hooke's law *n* the principle that the stress imposed on a solid is directly proportional to the strain produced, within the elastic limit [c18 after R. HOOKE]

Hook of Holland *n* **the 1** a cape on the SW coast of the Netherlands, in South Holland province **2** a port on this cape ▷ Dutch name: **Hoek van Holland**

hook-up *n* **1** the contact of an aircraft in flight with the refuelling hose of a tanker aircraft **2** an alliance or relationship **3** the linking of broadcasting equipment or stations to transmit a special programme ▷ *vb* **hook up** (*adv*) **4** to connect (two or more people or things)

hookworm ('hʊk,wɜːm) *n* any of various parasitic bloodsucking worms which cause disease. They have hooked mouthparts and enter their hosts by boring through the skin ▷ Cf **ancylostomiasis**

hooky *or* **hookey** ('hʊkɪ) *n inf, chiefly US, Canad, & NZ* truancy, usually from school (esp in **play hooky**) [c20 ?from *hook it* to escape]

hooligan ('huːlɪgən) *n sl* a rough lawless young person [c19 ? var. of *Houlihan*, Irish surname] > **'hooliganism** *n*

hoon (huːn) *n Austral & NZ inf* a hooligan [of unknown origin]

hoop[1] (huːp) *n* **1** a rigid circular band of metal or wood **2** something resembling this **3** a band of iron that holds the staves of a barrel together **4** a child's toy shaped like a hoop and rolled on the ground or whirled around the body **5** *croquet* any of the iron arches through which the ball is driven **6a** a light curved frame to spread out a skirt **6b** (*as modifier*): *a hoop skirt* **7** *basketball* the round metal frame to which the net is attached to form the basket **8** a large ring through which performers or animals jump **9 go** *or* **be put through the hoop** to be subjected to an ordeal ▷ *vb* **10** (*tr*) to surround with or as if with a hoop [OE *hōp*] > **hooped** *adj*

hoop[2] (huːp) *n, vb* a variant spelling of **whoop**

hoopla ('huːplɑː) *n* **1** *Brit* a fairground game in which a player tries to throw a hoop over an object and so win it **2** *US & Canad sl* **2a** noise; bustle **2b** nonsense; ballyhoo [c20 see WHOOP, LA[2]]

hoopoe ('huːpuː) *n* an Old World bird having a pinkish-brown plumage with black-and-white wings and an erectile crest [c17 from earlier *hoopoop*, imit.]

hoop pine *n* a fast-growing timber tree of Australia, *Araucaria cunninghamii*, having rough bark with hooplike cracks around the trunk and branches

hooray (huː'reɪ) *interj, n, vb* **1** a variant spelling of **hurrah** ▷ *sentence substitute* **2** Also: **hooroo** (huː'ruː) *Austral inf* cheerio

Hooray Henry ('huː,reɪ 'hɛnrɪ) *n, pl* **Hooray Henries** *or* **Hooray Henrys** a young upper-class man, often with affectedly hearty voice and manners. Sometimes shortened to **Hooray**

hoosegow *or* **hoosgow** ('huːsgaʊ) *n US* a slang word for **jail** [c20 from Mexican Sp. *jusgado* prison, from Sp.: court of justice, ult. from L *judex* a JUDGE]

hoot[1] (huːt) *n* **1** the mournful wavering cry of some owls **2** a similar sound, such as that of a train whistle **3** a jeer of derision **4** *inf* an amusing person or thing ▷ *vb* **5** (often foll by *at*) to jeer or yell (something) contemptuously (at someone) **6** (*tr*) to drive (speakers, actors on stage, etc) off by hooting **7** (*intr*) to make a hoot **8** (*intr*) *Brit* to blow a horn [c13 *hoten*, imit.]

hoot[2] (huːt) *n Austral & NZ* a slang word for **money** [from Maori *utu* price]

hootenanny ('huːtᵊ,nænɪ) *or* **hootnanny** ('huːt,nænɪ) *n, pl* **hootenannies** *or* **hootnannies** *US & Canad* an informal performance by folk singers [c20 from ?]

hooter ('huːtə) *n chiefly Brit* **1** a person or thing that hoots, esp a car horn **2** *sl* a nose

Hoover[1] ('huːvə) *n* **1** *trademark* a type of vacuum cleaner ▷ *vb* (*usually not cap*) **2** to vacuum-clean (a carpet, etc) **3** (*tr*; often foll by *up*) to consume or dispose of (something) quickly and completely: *he hoovered up his grilled fish*

Hoover[2] ('huːvə) *n* **1 Herbert** (**Clark**) 1874–1964, US statesman; 31st president of the US (1929–33). He organized relief for Europe during and after World War I, but as president he lost favour after his failure to alleviate the effects of the Depression **2 J**(**ohn**) **Edgar** 1895–1972, US lawyer: director of the FBI (1924–72). He used new scientific methods to combat crime, including the first fingerprint file

Hoover Dam *n* a dam in the western US, on the Colorado River on the border between Nevada and Arizona; forms Lake Mead. Height: 222 m (727 ft). Length: 354 m (1180 ft). Former name (1933–47): **Boulder Dam**

hooves (huːvz) *n* a plural of **hoof**

hop[1] (hɒp) *vb* **hops, hopping, hopped 1** (*intr*) to jump forwards or upwards on one foot **2** (*intr*) (esp of frogs, birds, etc) to move forwards in short jumps **3** (*tr*) to jump over **4** (*intr*) *inf* to move quickly (in, on, out of, etc): *hop on a bus* **5** (*tr*) *inf* to cross (an ocean) in an aircraft **6** (*tr*) *US & Canad inf* to travel by means of: *he hopped a train to Chicago* **7** (*intr*) another word for **limp[1]** (senses 1 and 2) **8 hop it** (*or* **off**) *Brit sl* to go away ▷ *n* **9** the act or an instance of hopping **10** *inf* an informal dance **11** *inf* a trip, esp in an aircraft **12 on the hop** *inf* **12a** active or busy **12b** *Brit* unawares or unprepared [OE *hoppian*]

hop[2] (hɒp) *n* **1** a climbing plant which has green conelike female flowers and clusters of small male flowers **2 hop garden** a field of hops **3** *obs sl* opium or any other narcotic drug ▷ See also **hops** [c15 from MDu. *hoppe*]

hope (həʊp) *n* **1** (*sometimes pl*) a feeling of desire for something and confidence in the possibility of its fulfilment: *his hope for peace was justified* **2** a reasonable ground for this feeling: *there is still hope* **3** a person or thing that gives cause for hope **4** a thing, situation, or event that is desired: *my hope is that prices will fall* **5 not a hope** *or* **some hope** used ironically to express little confidence that expectations will be fulfilled ▷ *vb* **hopes, hoping, hoped 6** (*tr*; *takes a clause as object or an infinitive*) to desire (something) with some possibility of fulfilment: *I hope to tell you* **7** (*intr*; often foll by *for*) to have a wish **8** (*tr*; *takes a clause as object*) to trust or believe: *we hope that this is satisfactory* [OE *hopa*]

Hope (həʊp) *n* **1 Anthony**, real name *Sir Anthony Hope*

Hawkins. 1863–1933, English novelist; author of *The Prisoner of Zenda* (1894) **2 Bob**, real name *Leslie Townes Hope*. (1903–2003), US comedian and comic actor, born in England. His films include *The Cat and the Canary* (1939), *Road to Morocco* (1942), and *The Paleface* (1947). He was awarded an honorary knighthood in 1998 **3 David (Michael)** born 1940, British churchman, Archbishop of York from 1995

hope chest *n* the US and Canad name for **bottom drawer**

hopeful ('həʊpfʊl) *adj* **1** having or expressing hope **2** inspiring hope; promising ▷ *n* **3** a person considered to be on the brink of success (esp in **a young hopeful**) > '**hopefulness** *n*

hopefully ('həʊpfʊlɪ) *adv* **1** in a hopeful manner **2** *inf* it is hoped: *hopefully they will be married soon.*

> USAGE Objecting to the use of *hopefully* to mean *it is hoped that* is one of the great shibboleths of recent debate on correct usage. It first came into current use in America in the 1960s and rapidly established itself elsewhere, presumably because it filled a useful structural gap, replacing as it does a complete clause. In this way it is no different from other sentence adverbials of the kind *unfortunately*, which can be paraphrased as a clause containing the adjective and modifying the whole sentence

Hopeh *or* **Hopei** ('həʊ'peɪ) *n* a variant transliteration of the Chinese name for **Hebei**

hopeless ('həʊplɪs) *adj* **1** having or offering no hope **2** impossible to solve **3** unable to learn, function, etc **4** *inf* without skill or ability > '**hopelessly** *adv* > '**hopelessness** *n*

Hopi ('həʊpɪ) *n* **1** (*pl* **Hopis** *or* **Hopi**) a member of a North American Indian people of NE Arizona **2** the language of this people [from Hopi *Hópi* peaceful]

Hopkins ('hɒpkɪnz) *n* **1** Sir **Anthony** born 1937, US actor born in Wales: his films include *Bounty* (1984), *The Silence of the Lambs* (1991), *Shadowlands* (1994), and *Hannibal* (2000) **2** Sir **Frederick Gowland** ('gaʊlənd) 1861–1947, British biochemist, who pioneered research into what came to be called vitamins: shared the Nobel prize for physiology or medicine (1929) **3 Gerald Manley** 1844–89, British poet and Jesuit priest, who experimented with sprung rhythm in his highly original poetry **4 Harry L(loyd)** 1890–1946, US administrator. During World War II he was a personal aide to President Roosevelt and administered the lend-lease programme

hoplite ('hɒplaɪt) *n* (in ancient Greece) a heavily armed infantryman [C18 from Gk *hoplitēs*, from *hoplon* weapon, from *hepein* to prepare]

hopper ('hɒpə) *n* **1** a person or thing that hops **2** a funnel-shaped reservoir from which solid materials can be discharged into a receptacle below, esp for feeding fuel to a furnace, loading a truck, etc **3** a machine used for picking hops **4** any of various long-legged hopping insects **5** an open-topped railway truck for loose minerals, etc, unloaded through doors on the underside **6** *S African* another name for **cocopan** **7** *computing* a device for holding punched cards and feeding them to a card reader

hopping ('hɒpɪŋ) *adv* **hopping mad** in a terrible rage

hops (hɒps) *pl n* the dried flowers of the hop plant, used to give a bitter taste to beer

hopsack ('hɒp,sæk) *n* **1** a roughly woven fabric of wool, cotton, etc, used for clothing **2** Also called: **hopsacking** a coarse fabric used for bags, etc, made generally of hemp or jute

hopscotch ('hɒp,skɒtʃ) *n* a children's game in which a player throws a small stone or other object to land in one of a pattern of squares marked on the ground and then hops over to it to pick it up [C19 HOP[1] + SCOTCH[1]]

Horace ('hɒrɪs) *n* Latin name *Quintus Horatius Flaccus*. 65–8 BC, Roman poet and satirist: his verse includes the lyrics in the *Epodes* and the *Odes*, the *Epistles* and *Satires*, and the *Ars Poetica*

Horae ('hɔːriː) *pl n* *Classical myth* the goddesses of the seasons. Also called: **the Hours** [L: hours]

horary ('hɔːrərɪ) *adj arch* **1** relating to the hours **2** hourly [C17 from Med. L *hōrārius*, from L *hora*]

Horatian (hə'reɪʃən) *adj* of, relating to, or characteristic of Horace or his poetry

Horatius Cocles (hɒ'reɪʃɪəs 'kəʊkliːz) *n* a legendary Roman hero of the 6th century BC, who defended a bridge over the Tiber against Lars Porsena

horde (hɔːd) *n* **1** a vast crowd; throng; mob **2** a nomadic group of people, esp an Asiatic group **3** a large moving mass of animals, esp insects [C16 from Polish *horda*, from Turkish *ordū* camp]

Horeb ('hɔːrɛb) *n* *Bible* a mountain, probably Mount Sinai

horehound *or* **hoarhound** ('hɔː,haʊnd) *n* a downy herbaceous Old World plant with small white flowers that contain a bitter juice formerly used as a cough medicine and flavouring [OE *hārhūne*, from *hār* grey + *hūne* horehound, from ?]

horizon (hə'raɪzᵊn) *n* **1** Also called: **visible horizon, apparent horizon** the apparent line that divides the earth and the sky **2** *astron* **2a** Also called: **sensible horizon** the circular intersection with the celestial sphere of the plane tangential to the earth at the position of the observer **2b** Also called: **celestial horizon** the great circle on the celestial sphere, the plane of which passes through the centre of the earth and is parallel to the sensible horizon **3** the range or limit of scope, interest, knowledge, etc **4** a thin layer of rock within a stratum that has a distinct composition by which the stratum may be dated [C14 from L, from Gk *horizōn kuklos* limiting circle, from *horizein* to limit]

horizontal (,hɒrɪ'zɒntᵊl) *adj* **1** parallel to the plane of the horizon; level; flat **2** of or relating to the horizon **3** in a plane parallel to that of the horizon **4** applied uniformly to all members of a group **5** *econ* relating to identical stages of commercial activity: *horizontal integration* ▷ *n* **6** a horizontal plane, position, line, etc > ,**horizon'tality** *n* > ,**hori'zontally** *adv*

horizontal bar *n* *gymnastics* a raised bar on which swinging and vaulting exercises are performed

horlicks ('hɔːlɪks) *n* **make a horlicks** *Brit inf* to make a mistake or a mess: *his boss is making a horlicks of his job* [C20 from *Horlicks*, a drink meant to induce sleep]

hormone ('hɔːməʊn) *n* **1** a chemical substance produced in an endocrine gland and transported in the blood to a certain tissue, on which it exerts a specific effect **2** an organic compound produced by a plant that is essential for growth **3** any synthetic substance having the same effects [C20 from Gk *hormōn*, from *horman* to stir up, from *hormē* impulse] > **hor'monal** *adj*

hormone replacement therapy *n* treatment with oestrogens (and usually progestogens) to control menopausal symptoms and in the prevention of osteoporosis. Abbrev: **HRT**

Hormuz (hɔː'muːz, 'hɔːmʌz) *or* **Ormuz** *n* an island off the SE coast of Iran, in the **Strait of Hormuz**: ruins of the ancient city of Hormuz, a major trading centre in the Middle Ages. Area: about 41 sq km (16 sq miles)

horn (hɔːn) *n* **1** either of a pair of permanent bony outgrowths on the heads of cattle, antelopes, etc **2** the outgrowth from the nasal bone of a rhinoceros, consisting of a mass of fused hairs **3** any hornlike projection, such as the eyestalk of a snail **4** the antler of a deer **5a** the constituent substance, mainly keratin, of horns, hooves, etc **5b** (*in combination*): *horn-rimmed spectacles* **6** a container or device made from this substance or an artificial substitute: *a drinking horn* **7** an object resembling a horn in shape, such as a cornucopia **8** a primitive musical wind instrument made from horn **9** any musical instrument consisting of a pipe or tube of brass fitted with a mouthpiece. See **French horn, cor anglais** **10** *jazz sl* any wind instrument **11a** a device for producing a warning or signalling noise **11b** (*in combination*): *a foghorn* **12** (*usually pl*) the imaginary hornlike parts formerly supposed to appear on the forehead of a cuckold **13a** a hollow conical device coupled to a gramophone to control the direction and quality of the sound **13b** a similar device attached to an electrical loudspeaker, esp in a public-address system **14** a stretch of land or water shaped like a horn **15** *Brit sl* an erection of the penis ▷ *vb* (*tr*) **16** to provide with a horn or horns **17** to gore or butt with a horn **18** to remove or shorten the horns of (cattle, etc) ▷ See also **horn in** [OE] > **horned** *adj* > **'hornless** *adj*

Horn (hɔːn) *n* **Cape** See **Cape Horn**

hornbag ('hɔːnˌbæg) *n Austral sl* a good-looking promiscuous woman [c20 from HORNY]

hornbeam ('hɔːnˌbiːm) *n* **1** a tree of Europe and Asia having smooth grey bark and hard white wood **2** its wood ▷ Also called: **ironwood** [c14 from HORN + BEAM, referring to its tough wood]

hornbill ('hɔːnˌbɪl) *n* a bird of tropical Africa and Asia, having a very large bill with a basal bony protuberance

hornblende ('hɔːnˌblɛnd) *n* a mineral of the amphibole group consisting of the aluminium silicates of calcium, sodium, magnesium, and iron: varies in colour from green to black [c18 from G *Horn* horn + BLENDE]

hornbook ('hɔːnˌbʊk) *n* a page bearing a religious text or the alphabet, held in a frame with a thin window of horn over it

Hornby ('hɔːnbɪ) *n* **Nick** born 1958, British writer; his books include the memoir *Fever Pitch* (1992; filmed 1997) and the bestselling novels *About a Boy* (1998; filmed 2002) and *How to Be Good* (2001)

horned toad *or* **lizard** *n* a small insectivorous burrowing lizard inhabiting desert regions of America, having a flattened toadlike body covered with spines

horned viper *n* a venomous snake that occurs in desert regions of N Africa and SW Asia and has a small horny spine above each eye

hornet ('hɔːnɪt) *n* **1** any of various large social wasps that can inflict a severe sting **2** **hornet's nest** a strongly unfavourable reaction (often in **stir up a hornet's nest**) [OE *hyrnetu*]

horn in *vb* (*intr, adv; often foll by on*) *sl* to interrupt or intrude

Horn of Africa *n* a region of NE Africa, comprising Somalia and adjacent territories

horn of plenty *n* another term for **cornucopia**

hornpipe ('hɔːnˌpaɪp) *n* **1** an obsolete reed instrument with a mouthpiece made of horn **2** an old British solo dance to a hornpipe accompaniment, traditionally performed by sailors **3** a piece of music for such a dance

hornswoggle ('hɔːnˌswɒgᵊl) *vb* **hornswoggles, hornswoggling, hornswoggled** (*tr*) *sl* to cheat or trick; bamboozle [c19 from ?]

horny ('hɔːnɪ) *adj* **hornier, horniest** **1** of, like, or hard as horn **2** having a horn or horns **3** *sl* **3a** sexually aroused **3b** provoking or intended to provoke sexual arousal **3c** sexually eager or lustful > **'horniness** *n*

horologe ('hɒrəˌlɒdʒ) *n* a rare word for **timepiece** [c14 from L *hōrologium*, from Gk *hōrologion*, from *hōra* HOUR + *-logos* from *legein* to tell]

horologist (hɒ'rɒlədʒɪst) *or* **horologer** *n* a person skilled in horology

horology (hɒ'rɒlədʒɪ) *n* the art or science of making timepieces or of measuring time > **horologic** (ˌhɒrə'lɒdʒɪk) *or* **ˌhoro'logical** *adj*
▷ www.horology.com/vir-lib-horology.htm

horoscope ('hɒrəˌskəʊp) *n* **1** the prediction of a person's future based on zodiacal data for the time of birth **2** the configuration of the planets, sun, and moon in the sky at a particular moment **3** a diagram showing the positions of the planets, sun, moon, etc, at a particular time and place [OE *horoscopus*, from L, from Gk *hōroskopos*, from *hōra* HOUR + -SCOPE] > **horoscopic** (ˌhɒrə'skɒpɪk) *adj* > **horoscopy** (hɒ'rɒskəpɪ) *n*

Horowitz ('hɒrəvɪts) *n* **Vladimir** 1904–89, Russian virtuoso pianist, in the US from 1928

horrendous (hɒ'rɛndəs) *adj* another word for **horrific** [c17 from L *horrendus* fearful, from *horrēre* to bristle, shudder, tremble; see HORROR] > **hor'rendously** *adv*

horrible ('hɒrɪbᵊl) *adj* **1** causing horror; dreadful **2** disagreeable **3** *inf* cruel or unkind [c14 via OF from L *horribilis*, from *horrēre* to tremble] > **'horribleness** *n* > **'horribly** *adv*

horrid ('hɒrɪd) *adj* **1** disagreeable; unpleasant: *a horrid meal* **2** repulsive or frightening **3** *inf* unkind [c16 (in the sense: bristling, shaggy): from L *horridus* prickly, from *horrēre* to bristle] > **'horridly** *adv* > **'horridness** *n*

horrific (hɒ'rɪfɪk, hə-) *adj* provoking horror; horrible > **hor'rifically** *adv*

horrified ('hɒrɪˌfaɪd) *adj* **1** terrified; frightened **2** dismayed or shocked

horrify ('hɒrɪˌfaɪ) *vb* **horrifies, horrifying, horrified** (*tr*) **1** to cause feelings of horror in; terrify **2** to shock greatly > **ˌhorrifi'cation** *n*

horrifying ('hɒrɪˌfaɪɪŋ) *adj* **1** causing feelings of horror; awful; terrifying; **2** dismaying or greatly shocking; dreadful > **'horriˌfyingly** *adv*

horripilation (hɒˌrɪpɪ'leɪʃən) *n physiol* a technical name for **goose flesh** [c17 from LL *horripilātiō* a bristling, from L *horrēre* to stand on end + *pilus* hair]

horror ('hɒrə) *n* **1** extreme fear; terror; dread **2** intense hatred **3** (*often pl*) a thing or person causing fear, loathing, etc **4** (*modifier*) having a frightening subject: *a horror film* [c14 from L: a trembling with fear]

horrors ('hɒrəz) *pl n* **1** *sl* a fit of depression or anxiety **2** *inf* See **delirium tremens** ▷ *interj* **3** an expression of dismay, sometimes facetious

Horsa ('hɔːsə) *n* died ?455 AD, leader, with his brother Hengist, of the first Jutish settlers in Britain. See also **Hengist**

hors de combat *French* (ɔr də kɔ̃ba) *adj* (*postpositive*), *adv* disabled or injured [lit.: out of (the) fight]

hors d'oeuvre (ɔː 'dɜːvr) *n, pl* **hors d'oeuvre** *or* **hors d'oeuvres** ('dɜːvr) an appetizer, usually served before the main meal [c18 from F, lit.: outside the work]

horse (hɔːs) *n* **1** a solid-hoofed, herbivorous, domesticated mammal used for draught work and riding. Related adj: **equine** **2** the adult male of this species; stallion **3** **wild horse** another name for **Przewalski's horse** **4** (*functioning as pl*) horsemen, esp cavalry: *a regiment of horse* **5** Also called: **buck** *gymnastics* a padded apparatus on legs, used for vaulting, etc **6** a narrow board supported by a pair of legs at each end, used as a frame for sawing or as a trestle, barrier, etc **7** a contrivance on which a person may ride and exercise **8** a slang word for **heroin** **9** *mining* a mass of rock within a vein of ore **10** *naut* a rod, rope, or cable, fixed at the ends, along which something may slide; traveller **11** *inf* short for **horsepower** **12** (*modifier*) drawn by a horse or horses: *a horse cart* **13** **a horse of another** *or* **a different colour** a completely different topic, argument, etc **14** **be** (*or* **get**) **on one's high horse** *inf* to act disdainfully aloof **15** **hold one's horses** to restrain oneself **16** **horses for courses** a policy, course of action, etc modified slightly to take account of special circumstances without departing in essentials from the original **17** **the horse's mouth** the most reliable source ▷ *vb* **horses, horsing, horsed** **18** (*tr*) to provide with a horse or horses **19** to put or be put on horseback [OE *hors*] > **'horseˌlike** *adj*
▷ www.horseracing.com

▷ www.bhb.co.uk
▷ www.thejockeyclub.co.uk

horse around *or* **about** *vb (intr, adv) inf* to indulge in horseplay

horseback ('hɔːsˌbæk) *n* **a** a horse's back (esp in **on horseback**) **b** *chiefly US (as modifier)*: *horseback riding*

horsebox ('hɔːsˌbɒks) *n Brit* a van or trailer used for carrying horses

horse brass *n* a decorative brass ornament, originally attached to a horse's harness

horse chestnut *n* **1** a tree having palmate leaves, erect clusters of white, pink, or red flowers, and brown shiny inedible nuts enclosed in a spiky bur **2** Also called: **conker** the nut of this tree [C16 from its having been used in the treatment of respiratory disease in horses]

horseflesh ('hɔːsˌflɛʃ) *n* **1** horses collectively **2** the flesh of a horse, esp edible horse meat

horsefly ('hɔːsˌflaɪ) *n, pl* **horseflies** a large stout-bodied dipterous fly, the female of which sucks the blood of mammals, esp horses, cattle, and man. Also called: **gadfly, cleg**

horsehair ('hɔːsˌhɛə) *n* hair taken chiefly from the tail or mane of a horse, used in upholstery and for fabric, etc

horsehide ('hɔːsˌhaɪd) *n* **1** the hide of a horse **2** leather made from this hide

horse latitudes *pl n naut* the latitudes near 30°N or 30°S at sea, characterized by baffling winds, calms, and high barometric pressure [C18 referring either to the high mortality of horses on board ship in these latitudes or to *dead horse* (nautical slang: advance pay), which sailors expected to work off by this stage of a voyage]

horse laugh *n* a coarse or raucous laugh

horseleech ('hɔːsˌliːtʃ) *n* **1** any of several large carnivorous freshwater leeches **2** an archaic name for a **veterinary surgeon**

horse mackerel *n* **1** Also called: **scad** a mackerel-like fish of European Atlantic waters, with a row of bony scales along the lateral line. Sometimes called (US): **saurel** **2** any of various large tunnies or related fishes

horseman ('hɔːsmən) *n, pl* **horsemen** **1** a person skilled in riding **2** a person who rides a horse > **'horsemanˌship** *n* > **'horseˌwoman** *fem n*

horse mushroom *n* a large edible mushroom, with a white cap and greyish gills

Horsens (*Danish* 'hɔrsəns) *n* a port in Denmark, in E Jutland at the head of **Horsens Fjord.** Pop: 55 252 (1995)

horse pistol *n* a large holstered pistol formerly carried by horsemen

horseplay ('hɔːsˌpleɪ) *n* rough or rowdy play

horsepower ('hɔːsˌpaʊə) *n* an fps unit of power, equal to 550 foot-pounds per second (equivalent to 745.7 watts). Abbrev: **HP, h.p.**

horseradish ('hɔːsˌrædɪʃ) *n* a coarse Eurasian plant cultivated for its thick white pungent root, which is ground and combined with vinegar, etc, to make a sauce

horse sense *n* another term for **common sense**

horseshoe ('hɔːsˌʃuː) *n* **1** a piece of iron shaped like a U nailed to the underside of the hoof of a horse to protect the soft part of the foot: commonly thought to be a token of good luck **2** an object of similar shape

horseshoe bat *n* any of numerous large-eared Old World bats with a fleshy growth around the nostrils, used in echolocation

horseshoe crab *n* a marine arthropod of North America and Asia, having a rounded heavily armoured body with a long pointed tail. Also called: **king crab**

horsetail ('hɔːsˌteɪl) *n* **1** a plant having jointed stems with whorls of small dark toothlike leaves and producing spores within conelike structures at the tips of the stems **2** a stylized horse's tail formerly used as the emblem of a pasha

horse trading *n* shrewd bargaining

horsewhip ('hɔːsˌwɪp) *n* **1** a whip, usually with a long thong, used for managing horses ▷ *vb* **horsewhips, horsewhipping, horsewhipped** **2** *(tr)* to flog with such a whip > **'horseˌwhipper** *n*

horsey *or* **horsy** ('hɔːsɪ) *adj* **horsier, horsiest** **1** of or relating to horses: *a horsey smell* **2** dealing with or devoted to horses **3** like a horse: *a horsey face* > **'horsily** *adv* > **'horsiness** *n*

horst (hɔːst) *n* a ridge of land that has been forced upwards between two parallel faults [C20 from G *Horst* thicket]

Horta (*Portuguese* 'ɔrtə) *n* a port in the Azores, on the SE coast of Fayal Island

hortatory ('hɔːtətərɪ) *or* **hortative** ('hɔːtətɪv) *adj* tending to exhort; encouraging [C16 from LL *hortātōrius*, from L *hortārī* to EXHORT] > **hor'tation** *n* > **'hortatorily** *or* **'hortatively** *adv*

Hortense (*French* ɔrtɑ̃s) *n* See (Eugénie Hortense de) **Beauharnais**

Horthy (*Hungarian* 'horti) *n* **Miklós** ('mikloːʃ), full name *Horthy de Nagybánya*. 1868–1957, Hungarian admiral: suppressed Kun's Communist republic (1919); regent of Hungary (1920–44)

horticulture ('hɔːtɪˌkʌltʃə) *n* the art or science of cultivating gardens [C17 from L *hortus* garden + CULTURE; cf. AGRICULTURE] > **ˌhorti'cultural** *adj* > **ˌhorti'culturalist** *or* **ˌhorti'culturist** *n*

▷ www.horticulture.org.uk/IoHLinks.htm
▷ www.ishs.org/

Horus ('hɔːrəs) *n* a solar god of Egyptian mythology, usually depicted with a falcon's head [via LL from Gk *Hōros*, from Egyptian *Hur* hawk]

Hos. *Bible abbrev for* Hosea

hosanna (həʊ'zænə) *interj* an exclamation of praise, esp one to God [OE *osanna*, via LL from Gk, from Heb. *hōshi 'āh nnā* save now, we pray]

hose[1] (həʊz) *n* **1** a flexible pipe, for conveying a liquid or gas ▷ *vb* **hoses, hosing, hosed** **2** (sometimes foll by *down*) to wash, water, or sprinkle (a person or thing) with or as if with a hose [C15 later use of HOSE[2]]

hose[2] (həʊz) *n, pl* **hose** *or* **hosen** ('həʊzᵊn) **1** stockings, socks, and tights collectively **2** *history* a man's garment covering the legs and reaching up to the waist **3** **half-hose** socks [OE *hosa*]

Hosea (həʊ'zɪə) *n Old Testament* **1** a Hebrew prophet of the 8th century BC **2** the book containing his oracles

hoser ('həʊzə) *n Canad sl* a gauche or uncouth person [C20 ?from N American slang *hose* to trick, copulate]

hosier ('həʊzɪə) *n* a person who sells stockings, etc

hosiery ('həʊzɪərɪ) *n* stockings, socks, and knitted underclothing collectively

hospice ('hɒspɪs) *n* **1** a nursing home that specializes in caring for the terminally ill **2** *arch* a place of shelter for travellers, esp one kept by a monastic order [C19 from F, from L *hospitium* hospitality, from *hospes* guest]

hospitable ('hɒspɪtəbᵊl, hɒ'spɪt-) *adj* **1** welcoming to guests or strangers **2** fond of entertaining [C16 from Med. L *hospitāre* to receive as a guest, from L *hospes* guest] > **'hospitableness** *n* > **'hospitably** *adv*

hospital ('hɒspɪtᵊl) *n* **1** an institution for the medical or psychiatric care and treatment of patients **2** *(modifier)* having the function of a hospital: *a hospital ship* **3** a repair shop for something specified: *a dolls' hospital* **4** *arch* a charitable home, hospice, or school [C13 from Med. L *hospitāle* hospice, from L, from *hospes* guest]

Hospitalet (*Spanish* ɔspita'lɛt) *n* a city in NE Spain, a SW suburb of Barcelona. Pop: 248 521 (1998 est)

hospitality (ˌhɒspɪ'tælɪtɪ) *n, pl* **hospitalities** kindness in welcoming strangers or guests

hospitality suite *n* a room or suite, as at a conference, where free drinks are offered

hospitalization *or* **hospitalisation** (ˌhɒspɪtəlaɪ'zeɪʃən) *n* **1** the act or an instance of being hospitalized **2** the

Hh

duration of a stay in a hospital

hospitalize *or* **hospitalise** ('hɒspɪtəˌlaɪz) *vb* **hospitalizes, hospitalizing, hospitalized** *or* **hospitalises, hospitalising, hospitalised** (*tr*) to admit or send (a person) into a hospital

hospitaller *or US* **hospitaler** ('hɒspɪtələ) *n* a person, esp a member of certain religious orders, dedicated to hospital work, ambulance services, etc [C14 from OF *hospitalier*, from Med. L, from *hospitāle* hospice; see HOSPITAL]

Hospitaller *or US* **Hospitaler** ('hɒspɪtələ) *n* a member of the order of the Knights Hospitallers

hospital pass *n inf* **1** *sport* a pass made to a team-mate who is in a position such that he or she will be tackled heavily as soon as the ball is received **2** a task or project that will inevitably result in heavy criticism for the person to whom it has been assigned

host[1] (həʊst) *n* **1** a person who receives or entertains guests, esp in his or her own home **2a** a country or organization that provides facilities for and receives visitors to an event **2b** (*as modifier*): *the host nation* **3** the compere of a show or television programme **4** *biol* **4a** an animal or plant that supports a parasite **4b** an animal into which tissue is experimentally grafted **5** *computing* a computer that is connected to others on a network **6** the owner or manager of an inn ▷ *vb* **7** to be the host of (a party, programme, etc): *to host one's own show* [C13 from F *hoste*, from L *hospes* guest]

host[2] (həʊst) *n* **1** a great number; multitude **2** an archaic word for **army** [C13 from OF *hoste*, from L *hostis* stranger]

Host (həʊst) *n Christianity* the wafer of unleavened bread consecrated in the Eucharist [C14 from OF *oiste*, from L *hostia* victim]

hosta ('hɒstə) *n* a plant cultivated esp for its ornamental foliage [C19 NL, after N. T. *Host* (1761–1834), Austrian physician]

hostage ('hɒstɪdʒ) *n* **1** a person held as a security or pledge or to be ransomed, exchanged for prisoners, etc **2** the state of being held as a hostage **3** any security or pledge **4** **give hostages to fortune** to place oneself in a position in which misfortune may strike through the loss of what one values most [C13 from OF, from *hoste* guest]

hostel ('hɒstᵊl) *n* **1** a building providing overnight accommodation for homeless people **2** a building providing cheap accommodation and meals for tourists, hikers, etc **3** See **youth hostel** **4** *Brit* a supervised lodging house for nurses, workers, etc **5** *arch* another word for **hostelry** [C13 from OF, from Med. L *hospitāle* hospice; see HOSPITAL]

hosteller *or US* **hosteler** ('hɒstələ) *n* **1** a person who stays at youth hostels **2** an archaic word for **innkeeper**

hostelling *or US* **hosteling** ('hɒstəlɪŋ) *n* the practice of staying at youth hostels when travelling

hostelry ('hɒstəlrɪ) *n, pl* **hostelries** *arch or facetious* an inn

hostess ('həʊstɪs) *n* **1** a woman acting as host **2** a woman who receives and entertains patrons of a club, restaurant, etc **3** See **air hostess**

hostile ('hɒstaɪl) *adj* **1** antagonistic; opposed **2** of or relating to an enemy **3** unfriendly [C16 from L *hostīlis*, from *hostis* enemy] > **'hostilely** *adv*

hostility (hɒ'stɪlɪtɪ) *n, pl* **hostilities** **1** enmity **2** an act expressing enmity **3** (*pl*) fighting; warfare

hostler ('ɒslə) *n* a variant (esp Brit) of **ostler**

hot (hɒt) *adj* **hotter, hottest** **1** having a relatively high temperature **2** having a temperature higher than desirable **3** causing a sensation of bodily heat **4** causing a burning sensation on the tongue: *a hot curry* **5** expressing or feeling intense emotion, such as anger or lust **6** intense or vehement **7** recent; new: *hot from the press* **8** *ball games* (of a ball) thrown or struck hard, and so difficult to respond to **9** much favoured: *a hot favourite* **10** *inf* having a dangerously high level of radioactivity **11** *sl* stolen or otherwise illegally obtained **12** *sl* (of people) being sought by the police **13** (of a colour) intense; striking: *hot pink* **14** following closely: *hot on the scent* **15** *inf* at a dangerously high electric potential **16** *sl* good (esp in **not so hot**) **17** *jazz sl* arousing great excitement by inspired improvisation, strong rhythms, etc **18** *inf* dangerous or unpleasant (esp in **make it hot for someone**) **19** (in various games) very near the answer **20** *metallurgy* (of a process) at a sufficiently high temperature for metal to be in a soft workable state **21** *Austral inf* (of a price, etc) excessive **22** **hot on** *inf* **22a** very severe: *the police are hot on drunk drivers* **22b** particularly knowledgeable about **23** **hot under the collar** *inf* aroused with anger, annoyance, etc **24** **in hot water** *inf* in trouble ▷ *adv* **25** in a hot manner; hotly ▷ See also **hots, hot up** [OE *hāt*] > **'hotly** *adv* > **'hotness** *n* > **'hottish** *adj*

hot air *n inf* empty and usually boastful talk

Hotan ('həʊ'tæn), **Hotien**, *or* **Ho-t'ien** ('həʊ'tjɛn) *n* **1** an oasis in W China, in the Taklimakan Shamo desert of central Xinjiang Uygur Autonomous Region, around the seasonal Hotan River **2** the chief town of this oasis, situated at the foot of the Kunlun Mountains. Pop: 71 600 (latest est). Also called: **Khotan, Hetian**

hotbed ('hɒtˌbɛd) *n* **1** a glass-covered bed of soil, usually heated, for propagating plants, forcing early vegetables, etc **2** a place offering ideal conditions for the growth of an idea, activity, etc, esp one considered bad

hot-blooded *adj* **1** passionate or excitable **2** (of a horse) being of thoroughbred stock

hot button *n inf* **a** a controversial subject or issue that is likely to arouse strong emotions **b** (*as modifier*): *the hot-button issue of abortion*

hotchpotch ('hɒtʃˌpɒtʃ) *or esp US & Canad* **hodgepodge** *n* **1** a jumbled mixture **2** a thick soup or stew [C15 var. of *hotchpot* from OF, from *hocher* to shake + POT[1]]

hot cross bun *n* a yeast bun marked with a cross and traditionally eaten on Good Friday

hot desking ('dɛskɪŋ) *n* the practice of not assigning permanent desks in a workplace, so that employees may work at any available desk

hot dog[1] *n* a sausage, esp a frankfurter, usually served hot in a long roll split lengthways [C20 from the supposed resemblance of the sausage to a dachshund]

hot dog[2] *n* **1** *chiefly US* a person who performs showy acrobatic manoeuvres when skiing or surfing ▷ *vb* **hot-dog, hot-dogs, hot-dogging, hot-dogged** **2** (*intr*) to perform a series of manoeuvres in skiing, surfing, etc

hotel (həʊ'tɛl) *n* a commercially run establishment providing lodging and usually meals for guests and often containing a public bar [C17 from F *hôtel*, from OF *hostel*; see HOSTEL]

hotelier (hɒ'tɛljeɪ) *n* an owner or manager of one or more hotels

hotel ship *n* an accommodation barge anchored near an oil production rig

Hotere (həʊ'tɛərɪ) *n* **Ralph** born 1931, New Zealand artist of Maori origin, noted esp for his minimalist *Black Paintings*

hot flush *or US* **hot flash** *n* a sudden unpleasant hot feeling experienced by menopausal women

hotfoot ('hɒtˌfʊt) *adv* with all possible speed

hothead ('hɒtˌhɛd) *n* an excitable person

hot-headed *adj* impetuous, rash, or hot-tempered > **ˌhot-'headedness** *n*

hothouse ('hɒtˌhaʊs) *n* **1a** a greenhouse in which the temperature is maintained at a fixed level **1b** (*as modifier*): *a hothouse plant* **2a** an environment that encourages rapid development **2b** (*as modifier*): *a hothouse atmosphere* **3** (*modifier*) *inf, often disparaging* sensitive or delicate: *a hothouse temperament*

Hotien *or* **Ho-t'ien** ('həʊ'tjɛn) *n* a variant transliteration of the Chinese name for **Hotan**
hot key *n computing* a single key on the keyboard of a computer which carries out a series of commands
hotline ('hɒt,laɪn) *n* **1** a direct telephone, teletype, or other communications link between heads of government, etc, for emergency use **2** any such direct line kept for urgent use
hot link *n computing* a word or phrase in a hypertext document that can be selected to access additional information
hot money *n* capital that is transferred from one financial centre to another seeking the best opportunity for short-term gain
hotplate ('hɒt,pleɪt) *n* **1** an electrically heated plate on a cooker or one set into a working surface **2** a portable device on which food can be kept warm
hot pool *n* a pool or spring that is heated geothermally
hotpot ('hɒt,pɒt) *n* **1** *Brit* a casserole covered with a layer of potatoes **2** *Austral sl* a heavily backed horse
hot potato *n sl* a delicate or awkward matter
hot-press *n* **1** a machine for applying a combination of heat and pressure to give a smooth surface to paper, to express oil from it, etc ▷ *vb* **2** *(tr)* to subject (paper, cloth, etc) to such a process
hot rod *n* a car with an engine that has been radically modified to produce increased power
hots (hɒts) *pl n* **the** *sl* intense sexual desire; lust (esp in the phrase **have the hots for** (**someone**))
hot seat *n* **1** *inf* a difficult or dangerous position **2** *US* a slang term for **electric chair**
hot spot *n* **1** an area of potential violence **2** a lively nightclub **3** any local area of high temperature in a part of an engine, etc **4** *med* **4a** a small area on the surface or within a body with an exceptionally high level of radioactivity or of some chemical or mineral considered harmful **4b** a similar area that generates an abnormal amount of heat, as revealed by thermography **5** *computing* a company that provides wireless access to the Internet for users of portable computers, or a place from which the Internet can be accessed in this manner
hot spring *n* a natural spring of mineral water at 21°C (70°F) or above, found in areas of volcanic activity. Also called: **thermal spring**
hotspur ('hɒt,spɜː) *n* an impetuous or fiery person [C15 from HOTSPUR]
Hotspur ('hɒt,spɜː) *n* **Harry** nickname of (Sir Henry) **Percy**
hot stuff *n inf* **1** a person, object, etc, considered important, attractive, etc **2** a pornographic or erotic book, play, film, etc
hot-swappable *adj computing* (of devices, disks, etc) capable of being inserted or removed from a computer system that is running, without causing damage or affecting performance
hot swapping *n computing* the insertion or removal of peripheral devices, disks, etc while a computer is still running without either causing damage to the system or affecting performance
Hottentot ('hɒtᵊn,tɒt) *n* another name for **Khoikhoi**
hotting ('hɒtɪŋ) *n inf* the practice of stealing fast cars and putting on a show of skilful but dangerous driving > **'hotter** *n*
hot up *vb* **hots, hotting, hotted** *(adv) inf* **1** to make or become more exciting, active, or intense **2** *(tr)* another term for **soup up**
hot-water bottle *n* a receptacle now usually made of rubber, designed to be filled with hot water and used for warming a bed
hot-wire *vb* **hot-wires, hot-wiring, hot-wired** *(tr) sl* to start the engine of (a motor vehicle) by bypassing the ignition switch
Houdini (huː'diːnɪ) *n* **Harry**, real name *Ehrich Weiss*. 1874–1926, US magician and escapologist
Houdon (*French* udɔ̃) *n* **Jean Antoine** (ʒɑ̃ ɑ̃twan) 1741–1828, French neoclassical portrait sculptor
hough (hɒk) *Brit* ▷ *n* **1** a variant of **hock**[1] ▷ *vb (tr)* **2** to hamstring (cattle, horses, etc) [C14 from OE *hōh* heel]
Houghton-le-Spring ('haʊtᵊnlə'sprɪŋ) *n* a town in N England, in Sunderland unitary authority, Tyne and Wear: coal-mining. Pop: 35 100 (1991)
hound (haʊnd) *n* **1a** any of several breeds of dog used for hunting **1b** *(in combination)*: *a deerhound* **2** a dog, esp one regarded as annoying **3** a despicable person **4** (in hare and hounds) a runner who pursues a hare **5** *sl, chiefly US & Canad* an enthusiast **6 ride to hounds** *or* **follow the hounds** to take part in a fox hunt **7 the hounds** a pack of foxhounds, etc ▷ *vb (tr)* **8** to pursue relentlessly **9** to urge on [OE *hund*] > **'hounder** *n*
hound's-tongue *n* a plant which has small reddish-purple flowers and spiny fruits. Also called: **dog's-tongue** [OE *hundestunge*, translation of L *cynoglōssos*, from Gk, from *kuōn* dog + *glōssa* tongue; referring to the shape of its leaves]
hound's-tooth check *n* a pattern of broken or jagged checks, esp on cloth. Also called: **dog's-tooth check, dogtooth check**
Hounslow ('haʊnzləʊ) *n* a borough of Greater London, on the River Thames: site of London's first civil airport (1919). Pop: 212 344 (2001). Area: 59 sq km (23 sq miles)
Houphouet-Boigny (*French* ufwɛbwaɲi) *n* **Félix** (feliks) 1905–93, Côte d'Ivoire statesman; president of the Côte d'Ivoire (1960–93)
hour ('aʊə) *n* **1** a period of time equal to 3600 seconds; 1/24 of a calendar day. Related adj: **horary** **2** any of the points on the face of a timepiece that indicate intervals of 60 minutes **3** the time **4** the time allowed for or used for something: *lunch hour* **5** a special moment: *our finest hour* **6** the distance covered in an hour: *we live an hour away* **7** *astron* an angular measurement of right ascension equal to 15° or a 24th part of the celestial equator **8 one's last hour** the time of one's death **9 the hour** an exact number of complete hours: *the bus leaves on the hour* ▷ See also **hours** [C13 from OF *hore*, from L *hōra*, from Gk: season]
hour circle *n* a great circle on the celestial sphere passing through the celestial poles and a specified point, such as a star
hourglass ('aʊə,glɑːs) *n* **1** a device consisting of two transparent chambers linked by a narrow channel, containing a quantity of sand that takes a specified time to trickle from one chamber to the other **2** *(modifier)* well-proportioned with a small waist: *an hourglass figure*
hour hand *n* the pointer on a timepiece that indicates the hour
houri ('hʊərɪ) *n, pl* **houris** **1** (in Muslim belief) any of the nymphs of Paradise **2** any alluring woman [C18 from F, from Persian, from Ar. *hūr*, pl. of *haurā'* woman with dark eyes]
hourly ('aʊəlɪ) *adj* **1** of, occurring, or done every hour **2** done in or measured by the hour: *an hourly rate* **3** continual or frequent ▷ *adv* **4** every hour **5** at any moment
hours ('aʊəz) *pl n* **1** a period regularly appointed for work, etc **2** one's times of rising and going to bed: *he keeps late hours* **3 till all hours** until very late **4** an indefinite time **5** *RC Church* Also called: **canonical hours** **5a** the seven times of the day laid down for the recitation of the prayers of the divine office **5b** the prayers recited at these times
Hours (aʊəz) *pl n* another word for the **Horae**
house *n* (haʊs), *pl* **houses** ('haʊzɪz) **1a** a building used as a home; dwelling **1b** *(as modifier)*: *house dog* **2** the people present in a house **3a** a building for some specific purpose **3b** *(in combination)*: *a schoolhouse* **4** *(often cap)* a family or dynasty: *the House of York* **5a** a commercial

Hh

company: *a publishing house* **5b** (*as modifier*): *a house journal* **6** a legislative body **7** a quorum in such a body (esp in **make a house**) **8** a dwelling for a religious community **9** *astrol* any of the 12 divisions of the zodiac **10** any of several divisions of a large school **11** a hotel, restaurant, club, etc, or the management of such an establishment **12** (*modifier*) (of wine) sold unnamed by a restaurant, at a lower price than wines specified on the wine list: *the house red* **13** the audience in a theatre or cinema **14** an informal word for **brothel** **15** a hall in which a legislative body meets **16** See **full house** **17** *naut* any structure or shelter on the weather deck of a vessel **18** **bring the house down** *theatre* to win great applause **19** **like a house on fire** *inf* very well **20** **on the house** (usually of drinks) paid for by the management of the hotel, bar, etc **21** **put one's house in order** to settle or organize one's affairs **22** **safe as houses** *Brit* very secure ▷ *vb* (haʊz), **houses, housing, housed** **23** (*tr*) to provide with or serve as accommodation **24** to give or receive lodging **25** (*tr*) to contain or cover; protect **26** (*tr*) to fit (a piece of wood) into a mortise, etc [OE *hūs*] > **ˈhouseless** *adj*

house agent *n Brit* another name for **estate agent**

house arrest *n* confinement to one's own home rather than in prison

houseboat (ˈhaʊsˌbəʊt) *n* a stationary boat or barge used as a home

housebound (ˈhaʊsˌbaʊnd) *adj* unable to leave one's house because of illness, injury, etc

housebreaking (ˈhaʊsˌbreɪkɪŋ) *n criminal law* the act of entering a building as a trespasser for an unlawful purpose. Assimilated with burglary (1968) > **ˈhouseˌbreaker** *n*

housecoat (ˈhaʊsˌkəʊt) *n* a woman's loose robelike informal garment

house-craft *n* skill in domestic management

housefly (ˈhaʊsˌflaɪ) *n, pl* **houseflies** a common dipterous fly that frequents human habitations, spreads disease, and lays its eggs in carrion, decaying vegetables, etc

household (ˈhaʊsˌhəʊld) *n* **1** the people living together in one house **2** (*modifier*) relating to the running of a household: *household management*

householder (ˈhaʊsˌhəʊldə) *n* a person who owns or rents a house > **ˈhouseˌholderˌship** *n*

household name *or* **word** *n* a person or thing that is very well known

housekeeper (ˈhaʊsˌkiːpə) *n* a person, esp a woman, employed to run a household

housekeeping (ˈhaʊsˌkiːpɪŋ) *n* **1** the running of a household **2** money allotted for this **3** general maintenance as of records, data, etc, in an organization

houseleek (ˈhaʊsˌliːk) *n* an Old World plant which has a rosette of succulent leaves and pinkish flowers: grows on walls

house lights *pl n* the lights in the auditorium of a theatre, cinema, etc

housemaid (ˈhaʊsˌmeɪd) *n* a girl or woman employed to do housework, esp one who is resident in the household

housemaid's knee *n* inflammation and swelling of the bursa in front of the kneecap, caused esp by constant kneeling on a hard surface. Technical name: **prepatellar bursitis**

house martin *n* a Eurasian swallow with a forked tail

house mouse *n* any of various greyish mice, a common household pest in most parts of the world

House music *or* **House** *n* a type of disco music of the late 1980s, based on funk, with fragments of other recordings edited in electronically

▷ www.house-music-inyourface.com

House of Assembly *n* a legislative assembly or the lower chamber of such an assembly

house of cards *n* **1** a tiered structure created by balancing playing cards on their edges **2** an unstable situation, etc: *the property market is a house of cards*

House of Commons *n* (in Britain, Canada, etc) the lower chamber of Parliament

house of correction *n* (formerly) a place of confinement for persons convicted of minor offences

house officer *or* **houseman** (ˈhaʊsmən) *n, pl* **housemen** *med* a doctor who is the most junior member of the medical staff of a hospital. US and Canad equivalent: **intern**

house of ill repute *or* **ill fame** *n* a euphemistic name for **brothel**

House of Keys *n* the lower chamber of the legislature of the Isle of Man

House of Lords *n* (in Britain) the upper chamber of Parliament, composed of the peers of the realm

House of Representatives *n* **1** (in the US) the lower chamber of Congress, or of many state legislatures **2** (in Australia) the lower chamber of Parliament **3** the sole chamber of New Zealand's Parliament

houseparent (ˈhaʊsˌpɛərənt) *n* a person in charge of the welfare of a group of children in an institution

house party *n* **1** a party, usually in a country house, at which guests are invited to stay for several days **2** the guests who are invited

house plant *n* a plant that can be grown indoors

house-proud *adj* proud of the appearance, cleanliness, etc, of one's house, sometimes excessively so

houseroom (ˈhaʊsˌrʊm, -ˌruːm) *n* **1** room for storage or lodging **2** **give (something) houseroom** (*used with a negative*) to have or keep (something) in one's house

house-sit *vb* **house-sits, house-sitting, house-sat** (*intr*) to live in and look after a house during the absence of its owner or owners > **ˈhouse-ˌsitter** *n*

Houses of Parliament *pl n* (in Britain) **1** the building in which the House of Commons and the House of Lords assemble **2** these two chambers considered together

house sparrow *n* a small Eurasian bird, now established in North America and Australia. It has a brown plumage with grey underparts. Also called (US): **English sparrow**

housetop (ˈhaʊsˌtɒp) *n* **1** the roof of a house **2** **proclaim from the housetops** to announce (something) publicly

house-train *vb* (*tr*) *Brit* to train (pets) to urinate and defecate outside the house, or in a litter tray > **ˈhouse-ˌtrained** *adj*

house-warming *n* a party given after moving into a new home

housewife *n, pl* **housewives** **1** (ˈhaʊsˌwaɪf) a woman who keeps house **2** (ˈhʌzɪf) Also called: **hussy, huswife** *chiefly Brit* a small sewing kit > **housewifery** (ˈhaʊsˌwɪfərɪ) *n* > **ˈhousewifely** *adj*

housework (ˈhaʊsˌwɜːk) *n* the work of running a home, such as cleaning, cooking, etc

housey-housey (ˈhaʊsɪˈhaʊsɪ) *n* another name for **bingo** or **lotto** [C20 from the cry of "house!" shouted by the winner, prob. from FULL HOUSE]

housing¹ (ˈhaʊzɪŋ) *n* **1a** houses collectively **1b** (*as modifier*): *a housing problem* **2** the act of providing with accommodation **3** a hole or slot made in one wooden member to receive another **4** a part designed to contain or support a component or mechanism: *a wheel housing*

housing² (ˈhaʊzɪŋ) *n* (*often pl*) *arch* another word for **trappings** (sense 2) [C14 from OF *houce* covering, of Gmc origin]

housing estate *n* a planned area of housing, often with its own shops and other amenities

housing scheme *n* a local-authority housing estate. Often shortened to **scheme**

Housman (ˈhaʊsmən) *n* **A(lfred) E(dward)** 1859–1936, English poet and classical scholar, author of *A Shropshire Lad* (1896) and *Last Poems* (1922)

Houston (ˈhjuːstən) *n* an inland port in SE Texas, linked by the **Houston Ship Canal** to the Gulf of Mexico and the

Gulf Intracoastal Waterway: capital of the Republic of Texas (1837–39; 1842–45); site of the Manned Spacecraft Center (1964). Pop: 1 953 631 (2000)

hove (həʊv) *vb chiefly naut* a past tense and past participle of **heave**

Hove (həʊv) *n* a town and coastal resort in S England, in Brighton and Hove unitary authority, East Sussex. Pop: 67 602 (1991)

hovel (ˈhɒvᵊl) *n* **1** a ramshackle dwelling place **2** an open shed for livestock, carts, etc **3** the conical building enclosing a kiln [c15 from ?]

hover (ˈhɒvə) *vb (intr)* **1** to remain suspended in one place **2** (of certain birds, esp hawks) to remain in one place in the air by rapidly beating the wings **3** to linger uncertainly **4** to be in a state of indecision ▷ *n* **5** the act of hovering [c14 *hoveren*, var. of *hoven*, from ?] > ˈ**hoverer** *n*

hovercraft (ˈhɒvəˌkrɑːft) *n* a vehicle that is able to travel across both land and water on a cushion of air

hover fly *n* a dipterous fly with a hovering flight

hoverport (ˈhɒvəˌpɔːt) *n* a port for hovercraft

hovertrain (ˈhɒvəˌtreɪn) *n* a train that moves over a concrete track and is supported by a cushion of air supplied by powerful fans

how (haʊ) *adv* **1** in what way? by what means?: *how did it happen?* Also used in indirect questions: *tell me how he did it* **2** to what extent?: *how tall is he?* **3** how good? how well? what...like?: *how did she sing?* **4 and how!** (intensifier) very much so! **5 how about?** used to suggest something: *how about a cup of tea?* **6 how are you?** what is your state of health? **7 how come?** *inf* what is the reason (that)?: *how come you told him?* **8 how's that? 8a** what is your opinion? **8b** *cricket* Also written: **howzat** (haʊˈzæt) (an appeal to the umpire) is the batsman out? **9 how now?** *or* **how so?** *arch* what is the meaning of this? **10** in whatever way: *do it how you wish* ▷ *n* **11** the way a thing is done: *the how of it* [OE *hu*]

Howard (ˈhaʊəd) *n* **1 Catherine** ?1521–42, fifth wife of Henry VIII of England; beheaded **2 Charles,** Lord Howard of Effingham and 1st Earl of Nottingham. 1536–1624, Lord High Admiral of England (1585–1618). He commanded the fleet that defeated the Spanish Armada (1588) **3** Sir **Ebenezer** 1850–1928, English town planner, who introduced garden cities **4 Henry** See (Earl of) **Surrey 5 John** 1726–90, English prison reformer **6 John Winston** born 1939, Australian politician; prime minister of Australia from 1996 **7 Leslie** real name *Leslie Howard Stainer.* 1890–1943, British actor of Hungarian descent. His many films included *The Scarlet Pimpernel* (1938), *Pygmalion* (1938), and *Gone With the Wind* (1939) **8 Michael** born 1941, British politician; leader of the Conservative party from 2003 **9 Trevor** 1916–88, British actor. His many films include *Brief Encounter* (1946), *The Third Man* (1949), *Ryan's Daughter* (1970), and *White Mischief* (1987)

howbeit (haʊˈbiːɪt) *arch* ▷ *sentence connector* **1** however ▷ *conj* **2** *(subordinating)* though; although

howdah (ˈhaʊdə) *n* a seat for riding on an elephant's back, esp one with a canopy [c18 from Hindi *haudah*, from Ar. *haudaj* load carried by elephant or camel]

how do you do *sentence substitute* **1** a formal greeting said by people who are being introduced to each other ▷ *n* **how-do-you-do 2** *inf* a difficult situation

howdy (ˈhaʊdɪ) *sentence substitute chiefly US* an informal word for **hello** [c16 from *how d'ye do*]

Howe (haʊ) *n* **1 Elias** 1819–67, US inventor of the sewing machine (1846) **2 Gordon,** known as *Gordie.* born 1928, US ice-hockey player, who scored a record 1071 goals in a professional career lasting 32 years **3 Richard,** 4th Viscount Howe. 1726–99, British admiral: served (1776–78) in the War of American Independence and commanded the Channel fleet against France, winning the Battle of the Glorious First of June (1794) **4** his brother, **William,** 5th Viscount Howe. 1729–1814, British general; commander in chief (1776–78) of British forces in the War of American Independence

Howel Dda (ˈhaʊəl ˈdɑː) *n* See **Hywel Dda**

however (haʊˈɛvə) *sentence connector* **1** still; nevertheless **2** on the other hand; yet ▷ *adv* **3** by whatever means **4** *(used with adjectives of quantity or degree)* no matter how: *however long it takes, finish it* **5** an emphatic form of **how** (sense 1)

howitzer (ˈhaʊɪtsə) *n* a cannon having a short barrel with a low muzzle velocity and a steep angle of fire [c16 from Du. *houwitser*, from G, from Czech *houfnice* stone-sling]

howl (haʊl) *n* **1** a long plaintive cry characteristic of a wolf or hound **2** a similar cry of pain or sorrow **3** a prolonged outburst of laughter **4** *electronics* an unwanted high-pitched sound produced by a sound-producing system as a result of feedback ▷ *vb* **5** to express in a howl or utter such cries **6** *(intr)* (of the wind, etc) to make a wailing noise **7** *(intr) inf* to shout or laugh [c14 *houlen*]

Howland Island (ˈhaʊlənd) *n* a small island in the central Pacific, near the equator northwest of Phoenix Island: US airfield. Area: 2.6 sq km (1 sq mile)

howl down *vb (tr, adv)* to prevent (a speaker) from being heard by shouting disapprovingly

howler (ˈhaʊlə) *n* **1** Also called: **howler monkey** a large New World monkey inhabiting tropical forests in South America and having a loud howling cry **2** *inf* a glaring mistake **3** a person or thing that howls

howling (ˈhaʊlɪŋ) *adj (prenominal) inf* (intensifier): *a howling success; a howling error*

Howlin' Wolf (ˈhaʊlɪn) *n* real name *Chester Burnett.* 1910–76, US blues singer and songwriter

Howrah (ˈhaʊrə) *n* an industrial city in E India, in West Bengal on the Hooghly River opposite Calcutta. Pop: 950 435 (1991)

howsoever (ˌhaʊsəʊˈɛvə) *sentence connector, adv* a less common word for **however**

how-to *adj* (of a book or guide) giving basic instructions to the lay person on how to do or make something: *a how-to book on carpentry*

howzit (ˈhaʊzɪt) *sentence substitute S African* an informal term of greeting [c20 from *how is it?*]

Hoxha (*Albanian* ˈhodʒa) *n* **Enver** (ˈɛmvɛr) 1908–85, Albanian statesman: founded the Albanian Communist Party in 1941 and was its first secretary (1954–85)

hoy[1] (hɔɪ) *n naut* **1** a freight barge **2** a coastal fishing and trading vessel used during the 17th and 18th centuries [c15 from MDu. *hoei*]

hoy[2] (hɔɪ) *interj* a cry used to attract attention or drive animals [c14 var. of HEY]

hoya (ˈhɔɪə) *n* any plant of the genus *Hoya*, of E Asia and Australia, esp the waxplant [c19 after Thomas *Hoy* (died 1821), E gardener]

hoyden *or* **hoiden** (ˈhɔɪdᵊn) *n* a wild boisterous girl; tomboy [c16 ?from MDu. *heidijn* heathen] > ˈ**hoydenish** *or* ˈ**hoidenish** *adj*

Hoylake (ˈhɔɪˌleɪk) *n* a town and resort in NW England, in Wirral unitary authority, Merseyside, on the Irish Sea. Pop: 25 554 (1991)

Hoyle (hɔɪl) *n* Sir **Fred** 1915–2001, English astronomer and writer: his books include *The Nature of the Universe* (1950) and *Frontiers of Astronomy* (1955), and science-fiction writings

HP *abbrev for:* **1** *Brit* hire-purchase **2** horsepower **3** high pressure **4** (in Britain) Houses of Parliament ▷ Also (for senses 1–3): **h.p.**

HPV *abbrev for* human papilloma virus

HQ *or* **h.q.** *abbrev for* headquarters

hr *abbrev for* hour

Hradec Králové (*Czech* ˈhradɛts ˈkraːlɔvɛː) *n* a town in the N Czech Republic, on the Elbe River. Pop: 100 528 (1996 est). German name: **Königgrätz**

HRH *abbrev for* His (*or* Her) Royal Highness
HRT *abbrev for* hormone replacement therapy
Hrvatska ('hrva:tska:) *n* the Serbo-Croat name for **Croatia**
HS (in Britain) *abbrev for* Home Secretary
HSE (in Britain) *abbrev for* Health and Safety Executive
HSH *abbrev for* His (*or* Her) Serene Highness
Hsia Kuei ('ʃjɑ: 'kweɪ) *n* See **Xia Gui**
Hsia-men ('ʃjɑ:'mɛn) *n* a transliteration of the modern Chinese name for **Amoy**
Hsian (ʃjɑ:n) *n* a variant transliteration of the Chinese name for **Xi An**
Hsiang (ʃjɑ:ŋ) *n* a variant transliteration of the Chinese name for **Xiang**
Hsin-hai-lien ('ʃɪn 'haɪ 'ljɛn) *n* a variant transliteration of the Chinese name for **Lianyungang**
Hsining ('ʃi:'nɪŋ) *n* a variant transliteration of the Chinese name for **Xining**
Hsinking ('ʃɪn'kɪŋ) *n* the former name (1932–45) of **Changchun**
Hsüan T'ung ('ʃwɑ:n 'tʊŋ) *n* a variant transliteration of the Chinese name for **Xuan-tong**
Hsü-chou ('ʃu:'tʃaʊ) *n* a variant transliteration of the Chinese name for **Xuzhou**
ht *abbrev for* height
HT *physics abbrev for* high tension
HTLV *abbrev for* human T-cell lymphotropic virus: any one of a family of viruses that cause certain rare human diseases in the T-cells. HTLV-III was an early name for the AIDS virus
HTML *abbrev for* hypertext markup language: a text description language that is used for electronic publishing, esp on the World Wide Web
HTTP *abbrev for* hypertext transfer protocol, used esp on the World Wide Web. See also **hypertext**
Hua Guo Feng ('hwɑ: gwəʊ 'fɛŋ) *or* **Hua Kuo-feng** ('hwɑ: kwəʊ 'fɛŋ) *n* born *c.* 1920, Chinese Communist statesman; prime minister of China 1976–80
Huainan ('hwaɪ'næn) *n* a city in E China, in Anhui province north of Hefei. Pop: 1 200 000 (1991 est)
Huambo (*Portuguese* 'wambu) *n* a town in central Angola: designated by the Portuguese as the future capital of the country. Pop: 400 000 (1999 est). Former name (1928–73): **Nova Lisboa**
Huang Hai ('hwæŋ 'haɪ) *n* the Pinyin transliteration of the Chinese name for the **Yellow Sea**
Huang Ho ('hwæŋ 'həʊ) *n* the Pinyin transliteration of the Chinese name for the **Yellow River**
Huáscar (*Spanish* uaskar) *n* died 1533, Inca ruler (1525–33): murdered by his half-brother Atahualpa
Huascarán (*Spanish* uaska'ran) *or* **Huascán** (*Spanish* uas'kan) *n* an extinct volcano in W Peru, in the Peruvian Andes: the highest peak in Peru; avalanche in 1962 killed over 3000 people. Height: 6768 m (22 205 ft)
hub (hʌb) *n* **1** the central portion of a wheel, propeller, fan, etc, through which the axle passes **2** the focal point **3** *computing* a device for connecting computers in a network [c17 prob. var. of HOB[1]]
hub-and-spoke *n* (*modifier*) denoting a method of organizing intercontinental air traffic in which one major airport is used as a feeder for local airports. Sometimes shortened to **hub**
Hubble ('hʌbᵊl) *n* **Edwin Powell** 1889–1953, US astronomer, noted for his investigations of nebulae and the recession of the galaxies
hubble-bubble ('hʌbᵊl'bʌbᵊl) *n* **1** another name for **hookah** **2** turmoil **3** a gargling sound [c17 rhyming jingle based on BUBBLE]
Hubble's law *n astron* a law stating that the velocity of recession of a galaxy is proportional to its distance from the observer [c20 after E. P. HUBBLE]
Hubble telescope *n* a telescope launched into orbit around the earth in 1990 to provide information about the universe. Also called: **Hubble space telescope**
▷ http://hubblesite.org
▷ www.gsfc.nasa.gov
▷ www.aura-astronomy.org/nv/transition.pdf
hubbub ('hʌbʌb) *n* **1** a confused noise of many voices **2** tumult; uproar [c16 prob. from Irish *hooboobbes*]
hubby ('hʌbɪ) *n, pl* **hubbies** an informal word for **husband** [c17 by shortening and altering]
hubcap ('hʌb,kæp) *n* a cap fitting over the hub of a wheel
Hubei ('hu:'beɪ), **Hupeh**, *or* **Hupei** *n* a province of central China: largely low-lying with many lakes. Capital: Wuhan. Pop: 60 280 000 (2000 est). Area: 187 500 sq km (72 394 sq miles)
Hubli ('hu:blɪ) *n* a city in W India, in NW Mysore: incorporated with Dharwar in 1961; educational and trading centre. Pop (with Dharwar): 648 298 (1991)
hubris ('hju:brɪs) *n* **1** pride or arrogance **2** (in Greek tragedy) ambition, arrogance, etc, ultimately causing the transgressor's ruin [c19 from Gk] > **hu'bristic** *adj*
huckaback ('hʌkə,bæk) *n* a coarse absorbent linen or cotton fabric used for towels, etc. Also: **huck** (hʌk) [c17 from ?]
huckleberry ('hʌkᵊl,bɛrɪ) *n, pl* **huckleberries** **1** an American shrub having edible dark blue berries **2** the fruit of this shrub **3** a Brit name for **whortleberry** (sense 1,2) [c17 prob. var. of *hurtleberry*, from ?]
huckster ('hʌkstə) *n* **1** a person who uses aggressive or questionable methods of selling **2** *now rare* a person who sells small articles or fruit in the street **3** *US* a person who writes for radio or television advertisements ▷ *vb* **4** (*tr*) to peddle **5** (*tr*) to sell or advertise aggressively or questionably **6** to haggle (over) [c12 ?from MDu. *hoekster*, from *hoeken* to carry on the back]
Huddersfield ('hʌdəz,fi:ld) *n* a town in N England, in Kirklees unitary authority, West Yorkshire, on the River Colne: former textile centre, now with varied manufacturing and services; university 1992. Pop: 143 726 (1991)
huddle ('hʌdᵊl) *n* **1** a heaped or crowded mass of people or things **2** *inf* a private or impromptu conference (esp in **go into a huddle**) ▷ *vb* **huddles, huddling, huddled** **3** to crowd or nestle closely together **4** (often foll by *up*) to hunch (oneself), as through cold **5** (*intr*) *inf* to confer privately **6** (*tr*) *chiefly Brit* to do (something) in a careless way **7** (*tr*) *rare* to put on (clothes) hurriedly [c16 from ?; cf. ME *hoderen* to wrap up] > **'huddler** *n*
Hudson ('hʌdsən) *n* **1** **Henry** died 1611, English navigator: he explored the Hudson River (1609) and Hudson Bay (1610), where his crew mutinied and cast him adrift to die **2** **W(illiam) H(enry)** 1841–1922, British naturalist and novelist, born in Argentina, noted esp for his romance *Green Mansions* (1904) and the autobiographical *Far Away and Long Ago* (1918)
Hudson Bay *n* an inland sea in NE Canada: linked with the Atlantic by **Hudson Strait;** the S extension forms James Bay; discovered in 1610 by Henry Hudson. Area (excluding James Bay): 647 500 sq km (250 000 sq miles)
Hudson's Bay blanket *n Canad* a woollen blanket with wide stripes [c19 from a type of blanket originally sold by the Hudson's Bay Company]
Hudson River *n* a river in E New York State, flowing generally south into Upper New York Bay: linked to the Great Lakes, the St Lawrence Seaway, and Lake Champlain by the New York State Barge Canal and the canalized Mohawk River. Length: 492 km (306 miles)
hue (hju:) *n* **1** the attribute of colour that enables an observer to classify it as red, blue, etc, and excludes white, black, and grey **2** a shade of a colour **3** aspect: *a different hue on matters* [OE *hīw* beauty] > **hued** *adj*
Hué (*French* ɥe) *n* a port in central Vietnam, on the delta of the **Hué River** near the South China Sea: former

capital of the kingdom of Annam, of French Indochina (1883–1946), and of Central Vietnam (1946–54). Pop: 219 149 (1992 est)

hue and cry *n* **1** (formerly) the pursuit of a suspected criminal with loud cries in order to raise the alarm **2** any loud public outcry [C16 from Anglo-F *hu et cri*, from OF *hue* outcry, from *hu!* shout of warning + *cri* CRY]

Huelva (*Spanish* 'uɛlβa) *n* a port in SW Spain, between the estuaries of the Odiel and Tinto Rivers: exports copper and other ores. Pop: 139 991 (1998 est)

Huesca (*Spanish* 'ueska) *n* a city in NE Spain: Roman town, site of Quintus Sertorius's school (76 BC); 15th-century cathedral and ancient palace of Aragonese kings. Pop: 50 020 (1991). Latin name: **Osca** ('ɒskə)

huff (hʌf) *n* **1** a passing mood of anger or pique (esp in **in a huff**) ▷ *vb* **2** to make or become angry or resentful **3** (*intr*) to blow or puff heavily **4** Also: **blow** *draughts* to remove (an opponent's draught) from the board for failure to make a capture **5** (*tr*) *obs* to bully **6 huffing and puffing** empty threats or objections: bluster [C16 imit.; cf. PUFF] > **'huffy** *or* **'huffish** *adj* > **'huffily** *or* **'huffishly** *adv*

Hufuf (hʊ'fuːf) *n* See **Al Hufuf**

hug (hʌg) *vb* **hugs, hugging, hugged** (*mainly tr*) **1** (*also intr*) to clasp tightly, usually with affection; embrace **2** to keep close to a shore, kerb, etc **3** to cling to (beliefs, etc); cherish **4** to congratulate (oneself) ▷ *n* **5** a tight or fond embrace [C16 prob. of Scand. origin] > **'huggable** *adj*

huge (hjuːdʒ) *adj* extremely large [C13 from OF *ahuge*, from ?] > **'hugely** *adv* > **'hugeness** *n*

hugger-mugger ('hʌgəˌmʌgə) *n* **1** confusion **2** *rare* secrecy ▷ *adj, adv arch* **3** with secrecy **4** in confusion ▷ *vb obs* **5** (*tr*) to keep secret **6** (*intr*) to act secretly [C16 from ?]

Huggins ('hʌgɪnz) *n* Sir **William** 1824–1910, British astronomer. He pioneered the use of spectroscopy in astronomy and discovered the red shift in the lines of a stellar spectrum

huggy ('hʌgɪ) *adj* **huggier, huggiest** *inf* sensitive and caring: *a soft, lovely, huggy person*

Hugh Capet ('hjuː 'kæpɪt, 'keɪpɪt) *n* See (Hugh) **Capet**

Hughes (hjuːz) *n* **1 Howard** 1905–76, US industrialist, aviator, and film producer. He became a total recluse during the last years of his life **2** (**James Mercer**) **Langston** 1902–67, US Black poet and writer. His collections include *The Weary Blues* (1926) and *The Panther and the Lash* (1967) **3 Richard** (**Arthur Warren**) 1900–76, British novelist. He wrote *A High Wind in Jamaica* (1929), *In Hazard* (1938), and *The Fox in the Attic* (1961) **4 Robert** (**Studley Forrest**) born 1938, Australian art critic, writer, and broadcaster; his work includes the television series *The Shock of the New* (1981) and the book *The Culture of Complaint* (1993) **5 Ted,** full name *Edward James Hughes.* 1930–98, British poet: his works include *The Hawk in the Rain* (1957), *Crow* (1970), and *Birthday Letters* (1998). Poet laureate (1984–98) **6 Thomas** 1822–96, British novelist; author of *Tom Brown's Schooldays* (1857) **7 William Morris** 1864–1952, Australian statesman, born in England: prime minister of Australia (1915–23)

Hughie ('hjuːɪ) *n Austral & NZ inf* the god of rain and of surf (esp in the phrases **send her down, Hughie!, send 'em up, Hughie!**)

Hugo ('hjuːgəʊ; *French* ygo) *n* **Victor** (**Marie**) (viktɔr) 1802–85, French poet, novelist, and dramatist; leader of the romantic movement in France. His works include the volumes of verse *Les Feuilles d'automne* (1831) and *Les Contemplations* (1856), the novels *Notre-Dame de Paris* (1831) and *Les Misérables* (1862), and the plays *Hernani* (1830) and *Ruy Blas* (1838)

Huguenot ('hjuːgəˌnəʊ, -ˌnɒt) *n* **1** a French Calvinist, esp of the 16th or 17th centuries ▷ *adj* **2** designating the French Protestant Church [C16 from F, from Genevan dialect *eyguenot* one who opposed annexation by Savoy, ult. from Swiss G *Eidgenoss* confederate]

huh (*spelling pron* hʌ) *interj* an exclamation of derision, bewilderment, inquiry, etc

Huhehot (ˌhuːhɪ'hɒt ˌhuːɪ-) *or* **Hu-ho-hao-t'e** (ˌhuːhəʊhaʊ'teɪ) *n* a variant transliteration of the Chinese name for **Hohhot**

huhu ('huːhuː) *n* a New Zealand beetle with a hairy body [from Maori]

hui ('huːɪ) *n, pl* **huies** NZ a conference, meeting, or other gathering [Maori]

huia ('hʊɪjə) *n* an extinct New Zealand bird, prized by early Maoris for its distinctive tail feathers [from Maori]

hula ('huːlə) *or* **hula-hula** *n* a Hawaiian dance performed by a woman [from Hawaiian]

Hula Hoop *n trademark* a light hoop that is whirled around the body by movements of the waist and hips

hulk (hʌlk) *n* **1** the body of an abandoned vessel **2** *disparaging* a large or unwieldy vessel **3** *disparaging* a large ungainly person or thing **4** (*often pl*) the hull of a ship, used as a storehouse, etc, or (esp in 19th-century Britain) as a prison [OE *hulc*, from Med. L *hulca*, from Gk *holkas* barge, from *helkein* to tow]

hulking ('hʌlkɪŋ) *adj* big and ungainly

hull (hʌl) *n* **1** the main body of a vessel, tank, etc **2** the outer covering of a fruit or seed **3** the calyx at the base of a strawberry, raspberry, or similar fruit **4** the outer casing of a missile, rocket, etc ▷ *vb* **5** to remove the hulls from (fruit or seeds) **6** (*tr*) to pierce the hull of (a vessel, tank, etc) [OE *hulu*]

Hull[1] (hʌl) *n* **1** a city and port in NE England, in Kingston upon Hull unitary authority, East Riding of Yorkshire: fishing, food processing; two universities. Pop: 310 636 (1991). Official name: **Kingston upon Hull 2** a city in SE Canada, in SW Quebec on the River Ottawa: a centre of the timber trade and associated industries. Pop: 60 707 (1991)

Hull[2] (hʌl) *n* **Cordell** 1871–1955, US statesman; secretary of state (1933–44) He helped to found the UN: Nobel peace prize 1945

Hh

hullabaloo *or* **hullaballoo** (ˌhʌləbə'luː) *n, pl* **hullabaloos** *or* **hullaballoos** loud confused noise; commotion [C18 ?from HALLO + Scot. *baloo* lullaby]

hullo (hʌ'ləʊ) *sentence substitute, n* a variant spelling of **hello**

hum (hʌm) *vb* **hums, humming, hummed** (*intr*) **1** to make a low continuous vibrating sound **2** (of a person) to sing with the lips closed **3** to utter an indistinct sound, as in hesitation; hem **4** *inf* to be in a state of feverish activity **5** *Brit & Irish sl* to smell unpleasant **6 hum and haw** See **hem**[2] (sense 3) ▷ *n* **7** a low continuous murmuring sound **8** *electronics* an undesired low-frequency noise in the output of an amplifier or receiver ▷ *interj, n* **9** an indistinct sound of hesitation, embarrassment, etc; hem [C14 imit.]

human ('hjuːmən) *adj* **1** of or relating to mankind: *human nature* **2** consisting of people: *a human chain* **3** having the attributes of man as opposed to animals, divine beings, or machines: *human failings* **4a** kind or considerate **4b** natural ▷ *n* **5** a human being; person [C14 from L *hūmānus*; rel. to L *homō* man] > **'humanness** *n*

human being *n* a member of any of the races of *Homo sapiens*; person; man, woman, or child

humane (hjuː'meɪn) *adj* **1** characterized by kindness, sympathy, etc **2** inflicting as little pain as possible: *a humane killing* **3** civilizing or liberal: *humane studies* [C16 var. of HUMAN] > **hu'manely** *adv* > **hu'maneness** *n*

Human Genome Project *n* a 15-year international project to produce a map of all the human genes on their chromosomes: completed in April 2003

human immunodeficiency virus *n* the full name for **HIV**

human interest *n* (in a newspaper story, etc) reference to individuals and their emotions, sometimes from exploitative motives

humanism (ˈhjuːməˌnɪzəm) *n* **1** the rejection of religion in favour of a belief in the advancement of humanity by its own efforts **2** (*often cap*) a cultural movement of the Renaissance, based on classical studies **3** interest in the welfare of people > ˈ**humanist** *n* > ˌ**humanˈistic** *adj*

humanitarian (hjuːˌmænɪˈtɛərɪən) *adj* **1** having the interests of mankind at heart ▷ *n* **2** a philanthropist > **huˌmaniˈtarianism** *n*

humanity (hjuːˈmænɪtɪ) *n, pl* **humanities** **1** the human race **2** the quality of being human **3** kindness or mercy **4** (*pl; usually preceded by the*) the study of literature, philosophy, and the arts, esp study of Ancient Greece and Rome

humanize *or* **humanise** (ˈhjuːməˌnaɪz) *vb* **humanizes, humanizing, humanized** *or* **humanises, humanising, humanised** **1** to make or become human **2** to make or become humane > ˌ**humaniˈzation** *or* ˌ**humaniˈsation** *n*

humankind (ˌhjuːmənˈkaɪnd) *n* the human race; humanity

USAGE See at **mankind**

humanly (ˈhjuːmənlɪ) *adv* **1** by human powers or means **2** in a human or humane manner

human nature *n* the qualities common to humanity, esp with reference to human weakness

humanoid (ˈhjuːməˌnɔɪd) *adj* **1** like a human being in appearance ▷ *n* **2** a being with human rather than anthropoid characteristics **3** (in science fiction) a robot or creature resembling a human being

human papilloma virus *n* any of a class of viruses that cause tumours, including warts, in humans. Certain strains have been implicated as a cause of cervical cancer. Abbrev: **HPV**

human rights *pl n* the rights of individuals to liberty, justice, etc

▷ www.unhchr.ch

▷ www.echr.coe.int

Humber (ˈhʌmbə) *n* an estuary in NE England, into which flow the Rivers Ouse and Trent: flows east into the North Sea; navigable for large ocean-going ships as far as Hull; crossed by the **Humber Bridge** (1981), a single-span suspension bridge with a main span of 1410 m (4626 ft). Length: 64 km (40 miles)

Humberside (ˈhʌmbəˌsaɪd) *n* a former county of N England around the Humber estuary, formed in 1974 from parts of the East and West Ridings of Yorkshire and N Lincolnshire: replaced in 1996 by the unitary authorities of East Riding of Yorkshire, Kingston upon Hull, North Lincolnshire, and North East Lincolnshire

humble (ˈhʌmbᵊl) *adj* **1** conscious of one's failings **2** unpretentious; lowly: *a humble cottage; my humble opinion* **3** deferential or servile ▷ *vb* **humbles, humbling, humbled** (*tr*) **4** to cause to become humble; humiliate **5** to lower in status [c13 from OF, from L *humilis* low, from *humus* the ground] > ˈ**humbleness** *n* > ˈ**humbly** *adv*

humblebee (ˈhʌmbᵊlˌbiː) *n* another name for the **bumblebee** [c15 rel. to MDu. *hommel* bumblebee, OHG *humbal*]

humble pie *n* **1** (formerly) a pie made from the heart, entrails, etc, of a deer **2** **eat humble pie** to be forced to behave humbly; be humiliated [c17 earlier *an umble pie*, by mistaken word division from *a numble pie*, from *numbles* offal of a deer, ult. from L *lumbulus* a little loin]

Humboldt (ˈhʌmbəʊlt; *German* ˈhʊmbɔlt) *n* **1** Baron (**Friedrich Heinrich**) **Alexander von** (alɛˈksandər fɔn) 1769–1859, German scientist, who made important scientific explorations in Central and South America (1799–1804). In *Kosmos* (1845–62), he provided a comprehensive description of the physical universe **2** his brother, Baron (**Karl**) **Wilhelm von** (ˈvɪlhɛlm fɔn) 1767–1835, German philologist and educational reformer

humbug (ˈhʌmˌbʌɡ) *n* **1** a person or thing that deceives **2** nonsense **3** *Brit* a hard boiled sweet, usually having a striped pattern ▷ *vb* **humbugs, humbugging, humbugged** **4** to cheat or deceive (someone) [c18 from ?] > ˈ**humˌbugger** *n* > ˈ**humˌbuggery** *n*

humdinger (ˈhʌmˌdɪŋə) *n sl* an excellent person or thing [c20 from ?]

humdrum (ˈhʌmˌdrʌm) *adj* **1** ordinary; dull ▷ *n* **2** a monotonous routine, task, or person [c16 rhyming compound, prob. based on HUM]

Hume (hjuːm) *n* **1** (**George**) **Basil** 1923–99, English Roman Catholic Benedictine monk and cardinal; archbishop of Westminster (1976–99) **2** **David** 1711–76, Scottish empiricist philosopher, economist, and historian, whose sceptic philosophy restricted human knowledge to that which can be perceived by the senses. His works include *A Treatise of Human Nature* (1740), *An Enquiry concerning the Principles of Morals* (1751), *Political Discourses* (1752), and *History of England* (1754–62) **3** **John** born 1937, Northern Ireland politician; leader of the Social Democratic and Labour Party (SDLP) (1979–2001). Nobel peace prize jointly with David Trimble in 1998

humectant (hjuːˈmɛktənt) *adj* **1** producing moisture ▷ *n* **2** a substance added to another to keep it moist [c17 from L *ūmectāre* to wet, from *ūmēre* to be moist]

humerus (ˈhjuːmərəs) *n, pl* **humeri** (ˈhjuːməˌraɪ) **1** the bone that extends from the shoulder to the elbow in man **2** the corresponding bone in other vertebrates [c17 from L *umerus*; rel. to Gothic *ams* shoulder, Gk *ōmos*] > ˈ**humeral** *adj*

humid (ˈhjuːmɪd) *adj* moist; damp [c16 from L *ūmidus*, from *ūmēre* to be wet] > ˈ**humidly** *adv* > ˈ**humidness** *n*

humidex (ˈhjuːmɪˌdɛks) *n Canad* an index of discomfort showing the combined effect of humidity and temperature

humidifier (hjuːˈmɪdɪˌfaɪə) *n* a device for increasing or controlling the water vapour in a room, building, etc

humidify (hjuːˈmɪdɪˌfaɪ) *vb* **humidifies, humidifying, humidified** (*tr*) to make (air, etc) humid or damp > **huˌmidifiˈcation** *n*

humidity (hjuːˈmɪdɪtɪ) *n* **1** dampness **2** a measure of the amount of moisture in the air

humidor (ˈhjuːmɪˌdɔː) *n* a humid place or container for storing cigars, tobacco, etc

humify (ˈhjuːmɪˌfaɪ) *vb* **humifies, humifying, humified** to convert or be converted into humus > ˌ**humifiˈcation** *n*

humiliate (hjuːˈmɪlɪˌeɪt) *vb* **humiliates, humiliating, humiliated** (*tr*) to lower or hurt the dignity or pride of [c16 from LL *humiliāre*, from L *humilis* HUMBLE] > **huˈmiliˌatingly** *adv* > **huˌmiliˈation** *n* > **huˈmiliˌator** *n*

humility (hjuːˈmɪlɪtɪ) *n, pl* **humilities** the state or quality of being humble

Hummel (ˈhʊməl) *n* **Johann Nepomuk** (joˈhan ˈneːpomʊk) 1778–1837, German composer and pianist

hummingbird (ˈhʌmɪŋˌbɜːd) *n* a very small American bird having a brilliant iridescent plumage, long slender bill, and wings specialized for very powerful vibrating flight

hummock (ˈhʌmək) *n* **1** a hillock; knoll **2** a ridge or mound of ice in an ice field **3** *chiefly southern US* a wooded area lying above the level of an adjacent marsh [c16 from ?; cf. HUMP] > ˈ**hummocky** *adj*

hummus *or* **houmous** (ˈhʊməs) *n* a creamy dip originating in the Middle East, made from puréed chickpeas [from Turkish *humus*]

USAGE Avoid confusion with **humus**

humoral (ˈhjuːmərəl) *adj* **1** *immunol* denoting or relating to a type of immunity caused by free antibodies circulating in the blood **2** *obs* of or relating to the four bodily fluids (humours)

humoresque (ˌhjuːməˈrɛsk) *n* a short lively piece of music [c19 from G *Humoreske*, ult. from E HUMOUR]

humorist (ˈhjuːmərɪst) *n* a person who acts, speaks, or writes in a humorous way

humorous (ˈhjuːmərəs) *adj* **1** funny; comical; amusing **2** displaying or creating humour **3** *arch* another word for **capricious** > '**humorously** *adv* > '**humorousness** *n*

humour *or US* **humor** ('hjuːmə) *n* **1** the quality of being funny **2** Also called: **sense of humour** the ability to appreciate or express that which is humorous **3** situations, speech, or writings that are humorous **4a** a state of mind; mood **4b** (*in combination*): *good humour* **5** temperament or disposition **6** a caprice or whim **7** any of various fluids in the body: *aqueous humour* **8** Also called: **cardinal humour** *arch* any of the four bodily fluids (blood, phlegm, choler or yellow bile, melancholy or black bile) formerly thought to determine emotional and physical disposition **9** **out of humour** in a bad mood ▷ *vb* (*tr*) **10** to gratify; indulge: *he humoured the boy's whims* **11** to adapt oneself to: *to humour someone's fantasies* [c14 from L *humor* liquid; rel. to L *ūmēre* to be wet] > '**humourless** *or US* '**humorless** *adj*

hump (hʌmp) *n* **1** a rounded protuberance or projection **2** a rounded deformity of the back, consisting of a spinal curvature **3** a rounded protuberance on the back of a camel or related animal **4** **the hump** *Brit inf* a fit of sulking ▷ *vb* **5** to form or become a hump; hunch; arch **6** (*tr*) *sl* to carry or heave **7** *sl* to have sexual intercourse with (someone) [c18 prob. from earlier *humpbacked*] > '**humpy** *adj*

humpback ('hʌmp,bæk) *n* **1** another word for **hunchback** **2** Also called: **humpback whale** a large whalebone whale with a humped back and long flippers **3** a Pacific salmon, the male of which has a humped back **4** Also: **humpback bridge** *Brit* a road bridge having a sharp incline and decline and usually a narrow roadway [c17 alteration of earlier *crumpbacked*, ? infl. by HUNCHBACK] > '**hump,backed** *adj*

Humperdinck (*German* 'hʊmpərdɪŋk) *n* **Engelbert** ('ɛŋəlbɛrt) 1854–1921, German composer, esp of operas, including *Hansel and Gretel* (1893)

humph (*spelling pron* hʌmf) *interj* an exclamation of annoyance, indecision, etc

Humphrey ('hʌmfrɪ) *n* **1** **Duke** See (Humphrey, Duke of) **Gloucester** **2** **Hubert Horatio** 1911–78, US statesman; vice-president of the US under President Johnson (1965–69)

Humphreys Peak ('hʌmfrɪz) *n* a mountain in N central Arizona, in the San Francisco Peaks: the highest peak in the state. Height: 3862 m (12 670 ft)

Humphries ('hʌmfrɪz) *n* (**John**) **Barry** born 1934, Australian comic actor and writer, best known for creating the character Dame Edna Everage

humpty dumpty ('hʌmptɪ 'dʌmptɪ) *n, pl* **humpty dumpties** *chiefly Brit* **1** a short fat person **2** a person or thing that once broken cannot be mended [c18 from the nursery rhyme *Humpty Dumpty*]

humpy ('hʌmpɪ) *n, pl* **humpies** *Austral* a primitive hut [c19 from Abor.]

Hums (hʊms) *n* a variant of **Homs**

humus ('hjuːməs) *n* a dark brown or black colloidal mass of partially decomposed organic matter in the soil. It improves the fertility and water retention of the soil [c18 from L: soil]

USAGE Avoid confusion with **hummus**

Hun (hʌn) *n, pl* **Huns** *or* **Hun** **1** a member of any of several Asiatic nomadic peoples who dominated much of Asia and E Europe from before 300 BC, invading the Roman Empire in the 4th and 5th centuries AD **2** *inf* (esp in World War I) a derogatory name for a **German** **3** *inf* a vandal [OE *Hūnas*, from LL *Hūnī*, from Turkish *Hun-yū*] > '**Hunnish** *adj* > '**Hun,like** *adj*

Hunan ('huː'næn) *n* a province of S China, between the Yangtze River and the Nan Ling Mountains: drained chiefly by the Xiang and Yüan Rivers; valuable mineral resources. Capital: Changsha. Pop: 64 400 000 (2000 est). Area: 210 500 sq km (82 095 sq miles)

hunch (hʌntʃ) *n* **1** an intuitive guess or feeling **2** another word for **hump** **3** a lump or large piece ▷ *vb* **4** to draw (oneself or a part of the body) up or together **5** (*intr*; usually foll by *up*) to sit in a hunched position [c16 from ?]

hunchback ('hʌntʃ,bæk) *n* **1** a person having an abnormal curvature of the spine **2** such a curvature ▷ Also called: **humpback** [c18 from earlier *hunchbacked*] > '**hunch,backed** *adj*

hundred ('hʌndrəd) *n, pl* **hundreds** *or* **hundred** **1** the cardinal number that is the product of ten and ten; five score **2** a numeral, 100, C, etc, representing this number **3** (*often pl*) a large but unspecified number, amount, or quantity **4** (*pl*) the 100 years of a specified century: *in the sixteen hundreds* **5** something representing, represented by, or consisting of 100 units **6** *maths* the position containing a digit representing that number followed by two zeros: *in 4376, 3 is in the hundred's place* **7** an ancient division of a county ▷ *determiner* **8** amounting to or approximately a hundred: *a hundred reasons for that* [OE] > '**hundredth** *adj, n*

hundreds and thousands *pl n* tiny beads of coloured sugar, used in decorating cakes, etc

hundredweight ('hʌndrəd,weɪt) *n, pl* **hundredweights** *or* **hundredweight** **1** Also called: **long hundredweight** *Brit* a unit of weight equal to 112 pounds (50.802 kg) **2** Also called: **short hundredweight** *US & Canad* a unit of weight equal to 100 pounds (45.359 kg) **3** Also called: **metric hundredweight** a metric unit of weight equal to 50 kilograms ▷ Abbrev (for senses 1, 2): **cwt**

hung (hʌŋ) *vb* **1** the past tense and past participle of **hang** (except in the sense of *to execute*) ▷ *adj* **2** (of a political party, jury, etc) not having a majority: *a hung parliament* **3** **hung over** *inf* suffering from the effects of a hangover **4** **hung up** *sl* **4a** impeded by some difficulty or delay **4b** emotionally disturbed **5** **hung up on** *sl* obsessively interested in

Hung. *abbrev for:* **1** Hungarian **2** Hungary

Hungarian (hʌŋ'gɛərɪən) *n* **1** the official language of Hungary, also spoken in Romania and elsewhere, belonging to the Finno-Ugric family **2** a native, inhabitant, or citizen of Hungary ▷ *adj* **3** of or relating to Hungary, its people, or their language ▷ Cf **Magyar**

Hungary ('hʌŋgərɪ) *n* a republic in central Europe: Magyars first unified under Saint Stephen, the first Hungarian king (1001–38); taken by the Hapsburgs from the Turks at the end of the 17th century; gained autonomy with the establishment of the dual monarchy of Austria-Hungary (1867) and became a republic in 1918; passed under Communist control in 1949; a popular rising in 1956 was suppressed by Soviet troops; a multi-party democracy replaced Communism in 1989 after mass protests; joined the EU in 2004. It consists chiefly of the Middle Danube basin and plains. Official language: Hungarian. Religion: Christian majority. Currency: forint. Capital: Budapest. Pop: 10 190 000 (2001 est). Area: 93 030 sq km (35 919 sq miles). Hungarian name: **Magyarország**

▷ www.mkogy.hu

▷ www.gotohungary.com

hunger ('hʌŋgə) *n* **1** a feeling of emptiness or weakness induced by lack of food **2** desire or craving: *hunger for a woman* ▷ *vb* **3** (*intr*; usually foll by *for* or *after*) to have a great appetite or desire (for) [OE]

hunger march *n* a procession of protest or demonstration, esp by the unemployed

hunger strike *n* a voluntary fast undertaken, usually by a prisoner, as a means of protest > **hunger striker** *n*

Hung Hsiu-ch'uan ('hʌŋ 'ʃjuː 'tʃwɑːn) *n* See **Hong Xiu Quan**

Hungnam (,hʊŋ'næm) *n* a port in E North Korea, on the Sea of Japan southeast of Hamhung. Pop: 260 000 (latest est)

hungry ('hʌŋgrɪ) *adj* **hungrier, hungriest** **1** desiring food **2** (*postpositive*; foll by *for*) having a craving, desire, or need

Hh

(for) **3** expressing or appearing to express greed, craving, or desire **4** lacking fertility; poor **5** *Austral & NZ* greedy; mean **6** NZ (of timber) dry and bare > '**hungrily** *adv* > '**hungriness** *n*

Hung-wu ('hʌŋ 'wuː) *n* See **Hong-wu**

hunk (hʌŋk) *n* **1** a large piece **2** *sl* a sexually attractive man [c19 prob. rel. to Flemish *hunke*]

hunkers ('hʌŋkəz) *pl n* haunches [c18 from ?]

hunky-dory (ˌhʌŋkɪ'dɔːrɪ) *adj inf* very satisfactory; fine [c20 from ?]

hunt (hʌnt) *vb* **1** to seek out and kill (animals) for food or sport **2** (*intr; often foll by for*) to search (for): *to hunt for a book* **3** (*tr*) to use (hounds, horses, etc) in the pursuit of wild animals, game, etc: *to hunt a pack of hounds* **4** (*tr*) to search (country) to hunt game, etc: *to hunt the parkland* **5** (*tr; often foll by down*) to track diligently so as to capture: *to hunt down a criminal* **6** (*tr; usually passive*) to persecute; hound **7** (*intr*) (of a gauge indicator, etc) to oscillate about a mean value or position **8** (*intr*) (of an aircraft, rocket, etc) to oscillate about a flight path or its course axis ▹ *n* **9** the act or an instance of hunting **10** chase or search, esp of animals **11** the area of a hunt **12** a party or institution organized for the pursuit of wild animals, esp for sport **13** the members of such a party or institution **14 in the hunt** *inf* having a chance of success: *that result keeps us in the hunt* [OE *huntian*]

Hunt (hʌnt) *n* **1 Henry,** known as *Orator Hunt.* 1773–1835, British radical, who led the mass meeting that ended in the Peterloo Massacre (1819) **2** (**William**) **Holman** 1827–1910, British painter; a founder of the Pre-Raphaelite Brotherhood (1848) **3 James** 1947–93, British motor-racing driver: world champion 1976 **4** (**Henry Cecil**) **John,** Baron. 1910–98, British army officer and mountaineer. He planned and led the expedition that first climbed Mount Everest (1953) **5** (**James Henry**) **Leigh** (liː) 1784–1859, British poet and essayist: a founder of *The Examiner* (1808), in which he promoted the work of Keats and Shelley

huntaway ('hʌntəˌweɪ) *n* NZ a sheepdog trained to drive sheep forward by barking on command and able to respond to commands from a distance

hunted ('hʌntɪd) *adj* harassed: *a hunted look*

hunter ('hʌntə) *n* **1** a person or animal that seeks out and kills or captures game. Fem: **huntress** ('hʌntrɪs) **2a** a person who looks diligently for something **2b** (*in combination*): *a fortune-hunter* **3** a specially bred horse used in hunting, characterized by strength and stamina **4** a watch with a hinged metal lid or case (**hunting case**) to protect the crystal

hunter-killer *adj* denoting a type of submarine designed and equipped to pursue and destroy enemy craft

hunter's moon *n* the full moon following the harvest moon

hunting ('hʌntɪŋ) *n* **a** the pursuit and killing or capture of wild animals, regarded as a sport **b** (*as modifier*): *hunting lodge*

▹ www.hunting.net

▹ www.has.enviroweb.org/has.shtml

Huntingdon[1] ('hʌntɪŋdən) *n* a town in E central England, in Cambridgeshire: birthplace of Oliver Cromwell. Pop (with Godmanchester): 15 575 (1991)

Huntingdon[2] ('hʌntɪŋdən) *n* **Selina,** Countess of Huntingdon. 1707–91, English religious leader, who founded a Calvinistic Methodist sect

Huntingdonshire ('hʌntɪŋdənʃɪə, -ʃə) *n* (until 1974) a former county of E England, now part of Cambridgeshire

hunting horn *n* a long straight metal tube with a flared end, used in giving signals in hunting

Huntington's disease ('hʌntɪŋtənz) *n* a hereditary form of chorea associated with progressive dementia. Former name: **Huntington's chorea** [after G. *Huntington* (1850–1916), US physician]

huntsman ('hʌntsmən) *n, pl* **huntsmen 1** a person who hunts **2** a person who trains hounds, beagles, etc, and manages them during a hunt

Huntsville ('hʌntsvɪl) *n* a city in NE Alabama: space-flight and guided-missile research centre. Pop: 152 216 (2000)

Huon pine ('hjuːɒn) *n* a Tasmanian coniferous tree, with scalelike leaves and cup-shaped berry-like fruits [after the *Huon* River, Tasmania]

Hupeh *or* **Hupei** ('xuː'peɪ) *n* a variant transliteration of the Chinese name for **Hubei**

hurdle ('hɜːdᵊl) *n* **1a** *athletics* one of a number of light barriers over which runners leap in certain events **1b** a low barrier used in certain horse races **2** an obstacle: *the next hurdle in his career* **3** a light framework of interlaced osiers, etc, used as a temporary fence **4** a sledge on which criminals were dragged to their executions ▹ *vb* **hurdles, hurdling, hurdled 5** to jump (a hurdle) **6** (*tr*) to surround with hurdles **7** (*tr*) to overcome [OE *hyrdel*] > '**hurdler** *n*

hurdy-gurdy ('hɜːdɪ'gɜːdɪ) *n, pl* **hurdy-gurdies** any mechanical musical instrument, such as a barrel organ [c18 rhyming compound, prob. imit.]

hurl (hɜːl) *vb* (*tr*) **1** to throw with great force **2** to utter with force; yell: *to hurl insults* ▹ *n* **3** the act of hurling [c13 prob. imit.]

hurling ('hɜːlɪŋ) *or* **hurley** *n* a traditional Irish game resembling hockey, played with sticks and a ball between two teams of 15 players

▹ www.gaa.ie/sports/hurling

hurly-burly ('hɜːlɪ'bɜːlɪ) *n, pl* **hurly-burlies** confusion or commotion [c16 from earlier *hurling and burling,* rhyming phrase based on *hurling,* in obs. sense of uproar]

Huron ('hjʊərən) *n* **1 Lake** a lake in North America, between the US and Canada: the second largest of the Great Lakes. Area: 59 570 sq km (23 000 sq miles) **2** (*pl* **Hurons** *or* **Huron**) a member of a North American Indian people formerly living in the region east of Lake Huron **3** the Iroquoian language of this people

hurrah (hʊ'rɑː), **hooray** (huː'reɪ), *or* **hurray** (hʊ'reɪ) *interj, n* **1** a cheer of joy, victory, etc ▹ *vb* **2** to shout "hurrah" [c17 prob. from G *hurra;* cf. HUZZAH]

hurricane ('hʌrɪkᵊn) *n* **1** a severe, often destructive storm, esp a tropical cyclone **2** a wind of force 12 on the Beaufort scale, with speeds over 72 mph [c16 from Sp. *huracán,* of Amerind origin, from *hura* wind]

hurricane deck *n* a ship's deck that is covered by a light deck as a sunshade

hurricane lamp *n* a paraffin lamp with a glass covering. Also called: **storm lantern**

hurried ('hʌrɪd) *adj* performed with great or excessive haste > '**hurriedly** *adv* > '**hurriedness** *n*

hurry ('hʌrɪ) *vb* **hurries, hurrying, hurried 1** (*intr; often foll by up*) to hasten; rush **2** (*tr; often foll by along*) to speed up the completion, progress, etc, of ▹ *n* **3** haste **4** urgency or eagerness **5 in a hurry** *inf* **5a** easily: *you won't beat him in a hurry* **5b** willingly: *we won't go there again in a hurry* [c16 *horyen,* prob. imit.]

hurst (hɜːst) *n arch* **1** a wood **2** a sandbank [OE *hyrst*]

Hurstmonceux ('hɜːstmənˌsuː, -ˌsəʊ) *n* a variant spelling of **Herstmonceux**

hurt (hɜːt) *vb* **hurts, hurting, hurt 1** (*tr*) to cause physical pain to (someone or something) **2** (*tr*) to cause emotional pain or distress to (someone) **3** to produce a painful sensation in (someone): *the bruise hurts* **4** (*intr*) *inf* to feel pain ▹ *n* **5** physical or mental pain or suffering **6** a wound, cut, or sore **7** damage or injury; harm ▹ *adj* **8** injured or pained: *a hurt knee; a hurt look* [c12 *hurten* to hit, from OF *hurter* to knock against, prob. of Gmc origin]

hurtful ('hɜːtfʊl) *adj* causing distress or injury: *to say hurtful things* > '**hurtfully** *adv*

hurtle ('hɜːtᵊl) *vb* **hurtles, hurtling, hurtled** to project or be projected very quickly, noisily, or violently [c13

hurtlen, from *hurten* to strike; see HURT]
Hus (*Czech* hʊs) *n* **Jan** (jan) the Czech name of (John) **Huss**
Husain (hʊ'seɪn, -'saɪn) *n* **1** ?629–680 AD, Islamic caliph, the son of Ali and Fatima and the grandson of Mohammed **2** a variant of **Hussein**
husband ('hʌzbənd) *n* **1** a woman's partner in marriage **2** *arch* a manager of an estate ▷ *vb* **3** to manage or use (resources, finances, etc) thriftily **4** (*tr*) *arch* to find a husband for **5** (*tr*) *obs* to till (the soil) [OE *hūsbonda*, from ON *hūsbōndi*, from *hūs* house + *bōndi* one who has a household] > '**husbander** *n*
husbandman ('hʌzbəndmən) *n*, *pl* **husbandmen** *arch* a farmer
husbandry ('hʌzbəndrɪ) *n* **1** farming, esp when regarded as a science, skill, or art **2** management of affairs and resources
Husein ibn-Ali (hʊ'seɪn 'ɪbᵊn'ɑːlɪ, 'ælɪ, hʊ'saɪn) *n* 1856–1931, first king of Hejaz (1916–24): initiated the Arab revolt against the Turks (1916–18); forced to abdicate by ibn-Saud
hush (hʌʃ) *vb* **1** to make or become silent; quieten; soothe ▷ *n* **2** stillness; silence ▷ *interj* **3** a plea or demand for silence [c16 prob. from earlier *husht* quiet!, the *-t* being thought to indicate a past participle] > **hushed** *adj*
hushaby ('hʌʃəˌbaɪ) *interj* **1** used in quietening a baby or child to sleep ▷ *n*, *pl* **hushabies** **2** a lullaby [c18 from HUSH + *by*, as in BYE-BYES]
hush-hush *adj inf* (esp of official work, documents, etc) secret; confidential
hush money *n sl* money given to a person to ensure that something is kept secret
hush up *vb* (*tr, adv*) to suppress information or rumours about
husk (hʌsk) *n* **1** the external green or membranous covering of certain fruits and seeds **2** any worthless outer covering ▷ *vb* **3** (*tr*) to remove the husk from [c14 prob. based on MDu. *huusken* little house, from *hūs* house]
husky[1] ('hʌskɪ) *adj* **huskier, huskiest** **1** (of a voice, utterance, etc) slightly hoarse or rasping **2** of or containing husks **3** *inf* big and strong [c19 prob. from HUSK, from the toughness of a corn husk] > '**huskily** *adv* > '**huskiness** *n*
husky[2] ('hʌskɪ) *n*, *pl* **huskies** **1** a breed of Arctic sled dog with a thick dense coat, pricked ears, and a curled tail **2** *Canad sl* **2a** a member of the Inuit people **2b** their language [c19 prob. based on ESKIMO]
Huss (hʌs) *n* **John,** Czech name *Jan Hus*. ?1372–1415, Bohemian religious reformer. Influenced by Wycliffe, he anticipated the Reformation in denouncing doctrines and abuses of the Church. His death at the stake precipitated the Hussite wars in Bohemia and Moravia
hussar (hʊ'zɑː) *n* **1** a member of any of various light cavalry regiments, renowned for their elegant dress **2** a Hungarian horseman of the 15th century [c15 from Hungarian *huszár* hussar, formerly freebooter, ult. from OIt. *corsaro* CORSAIR]
Hussein (hʊ'seɪn) *n* **1** Also: **Husain** 1935–99, king of Jordan (1952–99) **2** **Saddam** (sæ'dæm) born 1937, Iraqi politician: president (1979–2003) and prime minister (1994–2003) of Iraq. He led Iraq into the Iran-Iraq War (1980–88) and the Gulf War (1991) and was deposed in the US-led invasion of 2003
Husserl (*German* 'hʊsərl) *n* **Edmund** ('ɛtmʊnt) 1859–1938, German philosopher; founder of phenomenology
Hussite ('hʌsaɪt) *n* **1** an adherent of the ideas of John Huss or a member of the movement initiated by him ▷ *adj* **2** of or relating to John Huss, his teachings, followers, etc > '**Hussitism** *n*
hussy ('hʌsɪ, -zɪ) *n*, *pl* **hussies** *contemptuous* a shameless or promiscuous woman [c16 (in the sense: housewife): from *hussif* HOUSEWIFE]
hustings ('hʌstɪŋz) *n* (*functioning as pl or sing*) **1** *Brit* (before 1872) the platform on which candidates were nominated for Parliament and from which they addressed the electors **2** the proceedings at a parliamentary election [c11 from ON *hūsthing*, from *hūs* HOUSE + *thing* assembly]
hustle ('hʌsᵊl) *vb* **hustles, hustling, hustled** **1** to shove or crowd (someone) roughly **2** to move hurriedly or furtively: *he hustled her out of sight* **3** (*tr*) to deal with hurriedly: *to hustle legislation through* **4** *sl* to obtain (something) forcefully **5** *US & Canad sl* (of procurers and prostitutes) to solicit ▷ *n* **6** an instance of hustling [c17 from Du. *husselen* to shake, from MDu. *hutsen*] > '**hustler** *n*
Huston ('hjuːstən) *n* **John** 1906–87, US film director. His films include *The Treasure of the Sierra Madre* (1947), for which he won an Oscar, *The African Queen* (1951), *The Man Who Would Be King* (1975), *Prizzi's Honor* (1985), and *The Dead* (1987)
hut (hʌt) *n* **1** a small house or shelter ▷ *vb* **huts, hutting, hutted** **2** to furnish with or live in a hut [c17 from F *hutte*, of Gmc origin] > '**hut,like** *adj*
hutch (hʌtʃ) *n* **1** a cage, usually of wood and wire mesh, for small animals **2** *inf, derog* a small house **3** a cart for carrying ore [c14 *hucche*, from OF *huche*, from Med. L *hutica*, from ?]
hutment ('hʌtmənt) *n chiefly mil* a number or group of huts
Hutterite ('hʌtəˌraɪt) *n* a member of an Anabaptist Christian sect founded in Moravia, branches of which established farming communities in western Canada and the northwest US [c19 after Jacob *Hutter* (died 1536), Moravian Anabaptist]
Hutton ('hʌtᵊn) *n* **1** (**James**) **Brian** (**Edward**), Baron. born 1931, Northern Irish lawyer; Lord Chief Justice of Northern Ireland (1988–97) He headed the **Hutton Inquiry** (2003–04) into the events leading up to the suicide of the British weapons expert, Dr David Kelly **2** **James** 1726–97, Scottish geologist, regarded as the founder of modern geology **3** Sir **Leonard,** known as *Len Hutton*. 1916–90, English cricketer; the first professional captain of England (1953)
Huxley ('hʌkslɪ) *n* **1** **Aldous** (**Leonard**) ('ɔːldəs) 1894–1963, British novelist and essayist, noted particularly for his novel *Brave New World* (1932), depicting a scientifically controlled civilization of human robots **2** his half-brother, Sir **Andrew Fielding,** born 1917, English biologist: noted for his research into nerve cells and the mechanism by which nerve impulses are transmitted; Nobel prize for physiology or medicine shared with Alan Hodgkin and John Eccles 1963; president of the Royal Society (1980–85) **3** brother of Aldous, Sir **Julian** (**Sorrel**) 1887–1975, English biologist; first director-general of UNESCO (1946–48). His works include *Essays of a Biologist* (1923) and *Evolution: the Modern Synthesis* (1942) **4** their grandfather, **Thomas Henry** 1825–95, English biologist, the leading British exponent of Darwin's theory of evolution; his works include *Man's Place in Nature* (1863) and *Evolution and Ethics* (1893)
Hu Yaobang (xuː jaʊ'bɑːŋ) *n* 1915–89, Chinese statesman; leader of the Chinese Communist Party (1981–87)
Huygens ('haɪgənz; *Dutch* 'hœixəns) *n* **Christiaan** ('kristiːˌaːn) 1629–95, Dutch physicist: first formulated the wave theory of light
Huysmans (*French* ɥismɑ̃s) *n* **Joris Karl** (ʒɔris karl) 1848–1907, French novelist of the Decadent school, whose works include *À Rebours* (1884)
huzzah (hə'zɑː) *interj, n, vb* an archaic word for **hurrah** [c16 from ?]
HV *or* **h.v.** *abbrev for* high voltage
Hwange ('hwæŋgeɪ) *n* a town in W Zimbabwe: coal mines. Pop: 40 000 (latest est). Former name (until 1982): **Wankie**

Hh

Hwang Hai ('wæŋ 'haɪ) *n* a variant transliteration of the Chinese name for the **Yellow Sea**

Hwang Ho ('wæŋ 'həʊ) *n* a variant transliteration of the Chinese name for the **Yellow River**

HWM *abbrev for* high-water mark

hwyl ('huːɪl) *n* emotional fervour, as in the recitation of poetry [c19 Welsh]

hyacinth ('haɪəsɪnθ) *n* **1** any plant of the Mediterranean genus *Hyacinthus*, esp a cultivated variety having a thick flower stalk bearing bell-shaped fragrant flowers **2** the flower or bulb of such a plant **3** any similar plant, such as the grape hyacinth **4** Also called: **jacinth** a reddish transparent variety of the mineral zircon, used as a gemstone **5a** any of the varying colours of the hyacinth flower or stone **5b** *(as adj)*: *hyacinth eyes* [c16 from L *hyacinthus*, from Gk *huakinthos*] > ˌ**hya'cinthine** *adj*

Hyacinthus (ˌhaɪə'sɪnθəs) *n Greek myth* a youth beloved of Apollo and inadvertently killed by him. At the spot where the youth died, Apollo caused a flower to grow

Hyades[1] ('haɪəˌdiːz) *pl n* an open cluster of stars in the constellation Taurus, formerly believed to bring rain when they rose with the sun [c16 via L from Gk *huades*, ?from *huein* to rain]

Hyades[2] ('haɪəˌdiːz) *pl n Greek myth* seven nymphs, daughters of Atlas, whom Zeus placed among the stars after death

hyaena (haɪ'iːnə) *n* a variant spelling of **hyena**

hyaline ('haɪəlɪn) *adj biol* clear and translucent, as a common type of cartilage [c17 from LL *hyalinus*, from Gk, from *hualos* glass]

hyalite ('haɪəˌlaɪt) *n* a clear and colourless variety of opal in globular form

hyaloid ('haɪəˌlɔɪd) *adj anat, zool* clear and transparent; hyaline [c19 from Gk *hualoeidēs*]

hyaloid membrane *n* the delicate transparent membrane enclosing the vitreous humour of the eye

hybrid ('haɪbrɪd) *n* **1** an animal or plant resulting from a cross between genetically unlike individuals; usually sterile **2** anything of mixed ancestry **3** a word, part of which is derived from one language and part from another, such as *monolingual* ▷ *adj* **4** denoting or being a hybrid; of mixed origin [c17 from L *hibrida* offspring of a mixed union (human or animal)] > '**hybridism** *n* > **hy'bridity** *n*

hybrid computer *n* a computer that uses both analogue and digital techniques

hybridize *or* **hybridise** ('haɪbrɪˌdaɪz) *vb* **hybridizes, hybridizing, hybridized** *or* **hybridises, hybridising, hybridised** to produce or cause to produce hybrids; crossbreed > ˌ**hybridi'zation** *or* ˌ**hybridi'sation** *n*

hybridoma (ˌhaɪbrɪ'dəʊmə) *n* a hybrid cell formed by the fusion of two different types of cell, esp one capable of producing antibodies fused with an immortal tumour cell [c20 from HYBRID + -OMA]

hybrid vigour *n biol* the increased size, strength, etc, of a hybrid as compared to either of its parents. Also called: **heterosis**

hydatid ('haɪdətɪd) *n* **1** a large bladder containing encysted larvae of the tapeworm *Echinococcus*: causes serious disease in man **2** Also called: **hydatid cyst** a sterile fluid-filled cyst produced in man and animals during infestation by *Echinococcus* larval forms [c17 from Gk *hudatis* watery vesicle, from *hudōr*, *hudat-* water]

Hyde[1] (haɪd) *n* a town in NW England, in Tameside unitary authority, Greater Manchester; textiles, footwear, engineering. Pop: 30 666 (1991)

Hyde[2] (haɪd) *n* **1 Douglas** 1860–1949, Irish scholar and author; first president of Eire (1938–45) **2 Edward** See (1st Earl of) **Clarendon**

Hyde Park *n* a park in W central London: popular for open-air meetings

Hyderabad ('haɪdərəˌbɑːd, -ˌbæd, 'haɪdrə-) *n* **1** a city in S central India, capital of Andhra Pradesh state and capital of former Hyderabad state; university (1918). Pop: 3 145 939 (1991) **2** a former state of S India: divided in 1956 between the states of Andhra Pradesh, Mysore, and Maharashtra **3** a city in SW Pakistan, on the River Indus: seat of the University of Sind (1947). Pop: 1 151 271 (1998)

Hyder Ali *or* **Haidar Ali** ('haɪdər 'ɑːlɪ) *n* 1722–82, Indian ruler of Mysore (1766–82), who waged two wars against the British in India (1767–69; 1780–82)

hydr- *combining form* a variant of **hydro-** before a vowel

hydra ('haɪdrə) *n, pl* **hydras** *or* **hydrae** (-driː) **1** a freshwater coelenterate in which the body is a slender polyp with tentacles around the mouth **2** a persistent trouble or evil [c16 from L, from Gk *hudra* water serpent]

Hydra ('haɪdrə) *n Greek myth* a monster with nine heads, each of which, when struck off, was replaced by two new ones

hydracid (haɪ'dræsɪd) *n* an acid, such as hydrochloric acid, that does not contain oxygen

hydrangea (haɪ'dreɪndʒə) *n* a shrub or tree of an Asian and American genus cultivated for their large clusters of white, pink, or blue flowers [c18 from NL, from Gk *hudōr* water + *angeion* vessel: prob. from the cup-shaped fruit]

hydrant ('haɪdrənt) *n* an outlet from a water main, usually an upright pipe with a valve attached, from which water can be tapped for fighting fires, etc [c19 from HYDRO- + -ANT]

hydrate ('haɪdreɪt) *n* **1** a chemical compound containing water that is chemically combined with a substance **2** a crystalline chemical compound containing weakly bound water molecules ▷ *vb* **hydrates, hydrating, hydrated 3** to undergo or cause to undergo treatment or impregnation with water > **hy'dration** *n* > '**hydrator** *n*

hydrated ('haɪdreɪtɪd) *adj* (of a compound) chemically bonded to water molecules

hydraulic (haɪ'drɒlɪk) *adj* **1** operated by pressure transmitted through a pipe by a liquid, such as water or oil **2** of or employing liquids in motion **3** of hydraulics **4** hardening under water: *hydraulic cement* [c17 from L *hydraulicus*, from Gk *hudraulikos*, from *hudraulos* water organ, from HYDRO- + *aulos* pipe] > **hy'draulically** *adv*

hydraulic brake *n* a type of brake, used in motor vehicles, in which the braking force is transmitted from the brake pedal to the brakes by a liquid under pressure

hydraulic coupling *n* another name for **torque converter**

hydraulic press *n* a press that utilizes liquid pressure to enable a small force applied to a small piston to produce a large force on a larger piston

hydraulic ram *n* **1** the larger or working piston of a hydraulic press **2** a form of water pump utilizing the kinetic energy of running water to provide static pressure to raise water to a reservoir higher than the source

hydraulics (haɪ'drɒlɪks) *n (functioning as sing)* another name for **fluid mechanics**

hydraulic suspension *n* a system of motor-vehicle suspension using hydraulic members, often with hydraulic compensation between front and rear systems (**hydroelastic suspension**)

hydrazine ('haɪdrəˌziːn, -zɪn) *n* a colourless liquid made from sodium hypochlorite and ammonia: used as a rocket fuel. Formula: N_2H_4 [c19 from HYDRO- + AZO + -INE[2]]

hydric ('haɪdrɪk) *adj* **1** of or containing hydrogen **2** containing or using moisture

hydride ('haɪdraɪd) *n* any compound of hydrogen with another element

hydrilla (haɪ'drɪlə) *n* a type of underwater aquatic weed that was introduced from Asia into the south US, where it has become a serious problem, choking fish and hindering navigation [c20 NL, prob. from L *hydra*: see HYDRA]

hydriodic acid (ˌhaɪdrɪˈɒdɪk) *n* a solution of hydrogen iodide in water: a strong acid [c19 from HYDRO- + IODIC]

hydro¹ (ˈhaɪdrəʊ) *n, pl* **hydros** *Brit* (esp formerly) a hotel or resort, often near a spa, offering facilities for hydropathic treatment

hydro² (ˈhaɪdrəʊ) *adj* 1 short for **hydroelectric** ▷ *n* 2 a Canadian name for **electricity**

Hydro (ˈhaɪdrəʊ) *n* (esp in Canada) a hydroelectric power company or board

hydro- *or sometimes before a vowel* **hydr-** *combining form* 1 indicating water or fluid: *hydrodynamics* 2 indicating hydrogen in a chemical compound: *hydrochloric acid* 3 indicating a hydroid: *hydrozoan* [from Gk *hudōr* water]

hydrobromic acid (ˌhaɪdrəʊˈbrəʊmɪk) *n* a solution of hydrogen bromide in water: a strong acid

hydrocarbon (ˌhaɪdrəʊˈkɑːbᵊn) *n* any organic compound containing only carbon and hydrogen

hydrocele (ˈhaɪdrəʊˌsiːl) *n* an abnormal collection of fluid in any saclike space

hydrocephalus (ˌhaɪdrəʊˈsɛfələs) *or* **hydrocephaly** (ˌhaɪdrəʊˈsɛfəlɪ) *n* accumulation of cerebrospinal fluid within the ventricles of the brain because its normal outlet has been blocked by congenital malformation or disease. Nontechnical name: **water on the brain** > **hydrocephalic** (ˌhaɪdrəʊsɛˈfælɪk) *or* ˌ**hydroˈcephalous** *adj*

hydrochloric acid (ˌhaɪdrəˈklɒrɪk) *n* a solution of hydrogen chloride in water: a strong acid used in many industrial and laboratory processes

hydrochloride (ˌhaɪdrəˈklɔːraɪd) *n* a quaternary salt formed by the addition of hydrochloric acid to an organic base

hydrocyanic acid (ˌhaɪdrəʊsaɪˈænɪk) *n* another name for **hydrogen cyanide**

hydrodynamics (ˌhaɪdrəʊdaɪˈnæmɪks, -dɪ-) *n (functioning as sing)* the branch of science concerned with the mechanical properties of fluids, esp liquids. Also called: **hydromechanics**

hydroelastic suspension (ˌhaɪdrəʊɪˈlæstɪk) *n* See **hydraulic suspension**

hydroelectric (ˌhaɪdrəʊɪˈlɛktrɪk) *adj* 1 generated by the pressure of falling water: *hydroelectric power* 2 of the generation of electricity by water pressure: *a hydroelectric scheme* > **hydroelectricity** (ˌhaɪdrəʊɪlɛkˈtrɪsɪtɪ) *n*

hydrofluoric acid (ˌhaɪdrəʊfluːˈɒrɪk) *n* a solution of hydrogen fluoride in water: a strong acid that attacks glass

hydrofoil (ˈhaɪdrəˌfɔɪl) *n* 1 a fast light vessel the hull of which is raised out of the water on one or more pairs of fixed vanes 2 any of these vanes

hydroforming (ˈhaɪdrəʊˌfɔːmɪŋ) *n* 1 *chem* the catalytic reforming of petroleum to increase the proportion of aromatic and branched-chain hydrocarbons 2 *engineering* a forming process in which a metal is shaped by a punch forced against a die, consisting of a flexible bag containing a fluid

hydrogen (ˈhaɪdrədʒən) *n* **a** a flammable colourless gas that is the lightest and most abundant element in the universe. It occurs in water and in most organic compounds. Symbol: H; atomic no.: 1; atomic wt.: 1.007 94 **b** *(as modifier)*: *hydrogen bomb* [c18 from F *hydrogène*, from HYDRO- + -GEN; because its combustion produces water] > **hydrogenous** (haɪˈdrɒdʒɪnəs) *adj*

hydrogenate (ˈhaɪdrədʒɪˌneɪt, haɪˈdrɒdʒɪˌneɪt) *vb* **hydrogenates, hydrogenating, hydrogenated** to undergo or cause to undergo a reaction with hydrogen: *to hydrogenate ethylene* > ˌ**hydrogenˈation** *n*

hydrogen bomb *n* a type of bomb in which energy is released by fusion of hydrogen nuclei to give helium nuclei. The energy required to initiate the fusion is provided by the detonation of an atomic bomb, which is surrounded by a hydrogen-containing substance. Also called: **H-bomb**

hydrogen bond *n* a weak chemical bond between an electronegative atom, such as fluorine, oxygen, or nitrogen, and a hydrogen atom bound to another electronegative atom

hydrogen bromide *n* 1 a colourless pungent gas used in organic synthesis. Formula: HBr 2 an aqueous solution of hydrogen bromide; hydrobromic acid

hydrogen carbonate *n* another name for **bicarbonate**

hydrogen chloride *n* 1 a colourless pungent corrosive gas obtained by the action of sulphuric acid on sodium chloride: used in making vinyl chloride and other organic chemicals. Formula: HCl 2 an aqueous solution of hydrogen chloride; hydrochloric acid

hydrogen cyanide *n* a colourless poisonous liquid with a faint odour of bitter almonds. It forms prussic acid in aqueous solution and is used for making plastics and as a war gas. Formula: HCN. Also called: **hydrocyanic acid**

hydrogen fluoride *n* 1 a colourless poisonous corrosive gas or liquid made by reaction between calcium fluoride and sulphuric acid: used as a fluorinating agent and catalyst. Formula: HF 2 an aqueous solution of hydrogen fluoride; hydrofluoric acid

hydrogen iodide *n* 1 a colourless poisonous corrosive gas obtained by a catalysed reaction between hydrogen and iodine vapour: used in making iodides. Formula HI 2 an aqueous solution of this gas; hydriodic acid

hydrogen ion *n* an ionized hydrogen atom, occurring in aqueous solutions of acids; proton. Formula: H^+

hydrogenize *or* **hydrogenise** (ˈhaɪdrədʒɪˌnaɪz, haɪˈdrɒdʒɪˌnaɪz) *vb* **hydrogenizes, hydrogenizing, hydrogenized** *or* **hydrogenises, hydrogenising, hydrogenised** a variant of **hydrogenate**

hydrogen peroxide *n* a colourless oily unstable liquid used as a bleach and as an oxidizer in rocket fuels. Formula: H_2O_2

hydrogen sulphide *n* a colourless poisonous gas with an odour of rotten eggs. Formula: H_2S. Also called: **sulphuretted hydrogen**

hydrography (haɪˈdrɒgrəfɪ) *n* the study, surveying, and mapping of the oceans, seas, and rivers > **hyˈdrographer** *n* > **hydrographic** (ˌhaɪdrəˈgræfɪk) *adj*

▷ www.imo.org/home.asp

hydroid (ˈhaɪdrɔɪd) *adj* 1 of or relating to the *Hydroida*, an order of hydrozoan coelenterates that have the polyp phase dominant 2 having or consisting of hydra-like polyps ▷ *n* 3 a hydroid colony or individual

hydrokinetics (ˌhaɪdrəʊkɪˈnɛtɪks, -kaɪ-) *n (functioning as sing)* the branch of science concerned with the behaviour and properties of fluids in motion. Also called: **hydrodynamics**

hydrolase (ˈhaɪdrəˌleɪz) *n* an enzyme that controls hydrolysis

hydrology (haɪˈdrɒlədʒɪ) *n* the study of the distribution, conservation, use, etc, of the water of the earth and its atmosphere, particularly at the land surface > **hydrological** (ˌhaɪdrəˈlɒdʒɪkᵊl) *adj* > **hyˈdrologist** *n*

hydrolyse *or US* **hydrolyze** (ˈhaɪdrəˌlaɪz) *vb* **hydrolyses, hydrolysing, hydrolysed** *or US* **hydrolyzes, hydrolyzing, hydrolyzed** to subject to or undergo hydrolysis

hydrolysis (haɪˈdrɒlɪsɪs) *n* a chemical reaction in which a compound reacts with water to produce other compounds > **hydrolytic** (ˌhaɪdrəˈlɪtɪk) *adj*

hydrolyte (ˈhaɪdrəˌlaɪt) *n* a substance subjected to hydrolysis

hydromel (ˈhaɪdrəʊˌmɛl) *n arch* another word for **mead** (the drink) [c15 from L, from Gk *hudromeli*, from HYDRO- + *meli* honey]

hydrometer (haɪˈdrɒmɪtə) *n* an instrument for measuring the relative density of a liquid > **hydrometric** (ˌhaɪdrəʊˈmɛtrɪk) *or* ˌ**hydroˈmetrical** *adj*

hydronaut (ˈhaɪdrəʊˌnɔːt) *n US Navy* a person trained to

Hh

operate deep submergence vessels [C20 from Gk, from HYDRO- + *-naut*, as in *astronaut*]
hydropathy (haɪˈdrɒpəθɪ) *n* a pseudoscientific method of treating disease by the use of large quantities of water both internally and externally > **hydropathic** (ˌhaɪdrəʊˈpæθɪk) *adj*
hydrophilic (ˌhaɪdrəʊˈfɪlɪk) *adj chem* tending to dissolve in, mix with, or be wetted by water: *a hydrophilic colloid* > **hydrophile** (ˈhaɪdrəʊˌfaɪl) *n*
hydrophobia (ˌhaɪdrəˈfəʊbɪə) *n* **1** another name for **rabies** **2** a fear of drinking fluids, esp that of a person with rabies, because of painful spasms when trying to swallow > ˌ**hydroˈphobic** *adj*
hydrophone (ˈhaɪdrəˌfəʊn) *n* an electroacoustic transducer that converts sound travelling through water into electrical oscillations
hydrophyte (ˈhaɪdrəʊˌfaɪt) *n* a plant that grows only in water or very moist soil
hydroplane (ˈhaɪdrəʊˌpleɪn) *n* **1** a motorboat equipped with hydrofoils or with a shaped bottom that raises its hull out of the water at high speeds **2** an attachment to an aircraft to enable it to glide along the surface of the water **3** another name for a **seaplane** **4** a horizontal vane on the hull of a submarine for controlling its vertical motion ▷ *vb* **hydroplanes, hydroplaning, hydroplaned** **5** (*intr*) (of a boat) to rise out of the water in the manner of a hydroplane
hydroponics (ˌhaɪdrəʊˈpɒnɪks) *n* (*functioning as sing*) a method of cultivating plants by growing them in gravel, etc, through which water containing dissolved inorganic nutrient salts is pumped [C20 from HYDRO- + (*geo*)*ponics* science of agriculture] > ˌ**hydroˈponic** *adj* > ˌ**hydroˈponically** *adv*
hydropower (ˈhaɪdrəʊˌpaʊə) *n* hydroelectric power
hydroquinone (ˌhaɪdrəʊkwɪˈnəʊn) *or* **hydroquinol** (ˌhaɪdrəʊˈkwɪnɒl) *n* a white crystalline soluble phenol used as a photographic developer
hydrosphere (ˈhaɪdrəˌsfɪə) *n* the watery part of the earth's surface, including oceans, lakes, water vapour in the atmosphere, etc
hydrostatics (ˌhaɪdrəʊˈstætɪks) *n* (*functioning as sing*) the branch of science concerned with the mechanical properties and behaviour of fluids that are not in motion > ˌ**hydroˈstatic** *adj*
hydrotherapeutics (ˌhaɪdrəʊˌθɛrəˈpjuːtɪks) *n* (*functioning as sing*) the branch of medical science concerned with hydrotherapy
hydrotherapy (ˌhaɪdrəʊˈθɛrəpɪ) *n med* the treatment of certain diseases by the application of water, esp by exercising in water to mobilize stiff joints or strengthen weak muscles
hydrothermal (ˌhaɪdrəʊˈθɜːməl) *adj* of or relating to the action of water under conditions of high temperature, esp in forming rocks
hydrotropism (haɪˈdrɒtrəˌpɪzəm) *n* the directional growth of plants in response to the stimulus of water
hydrous (ˈhaɪdrəs) *adj* containing water
hydrovane (ˈhaɪdrəʊˌveɪn) *n* a vane on a seaplane conferring stability on water (a sponson) or facilitating takeoff (a hydrofoil)
hydroxide (haɪˈdrɒksaɪd) *n* **1** a base or alkali containing the ion OH^- **2** any compound containing an -OH group
hydroxy (haɪˈdrɒksɪ) *adj* (of a chemical compound) containing one or more hydroxyl groups [C19 HYDRO- + OXY(GEN)]
hydroxyl (haɪˈdrɒksɪl) *n* (*modifier*) of, consisting of, or containing the monovalent group -OH or the ion OH^-: *a hydroxyl group or radical*
hydroxytryptamine (haɪˌdrɒksɪˈtrɪptəˌmiːn) *n* 5-hydroxytryptamine: another name for **serotonin** Abbrev: **5HT**
hydrozoan (ˌhaɪdrəʊˈzəʊən) *n* **1** any coelenterate of the class *Hydrozoa*, which includes the hydra and the Portuguese man-of-war ▷ *adj* **2** of the *Hydrozoa*
hyena *or* **hyaena** (haɪˈiːnə) *n* any of several long-legged carnivorous doglike mammals such as the spotted or laughing hyena, of Africa and S Asia [C16 from Med. L, from L *hyaena*, from Gk, from *hus* hog] > **hyˈenic** *or* **hyˈaenic** *adj*
Hygeia (haɪˈdʒiːə) *n* the Greek goddess of health > **Hyˈgeian** *adj*
hygiene (ˈhaɪdʒiːn) *n* **1** Also called: **hygienics** the science concerned with the maintenance of health **2** clean or healthy practices or thinking: *personal hygiene* [C18 from NL *hygiēna*, from Gk *hugieinē*, from *hugiēs* healthy]
hygienic (haɪˈdʒiːnɪk) *adj* promoting health or cleanliness; sanitary > **hyˈgienically** *adv*
hygienics (haɪˈdʒiːnɪks) *n* (*functioning as sing*) another word for **hygiene** (sense 1)
hygienist (ˈhaɪdʒiːnɪst) *n* a person skilled in the practice of hygiene
hygro- *or before a vowel* **hygr-** *combining form* indicating moisture: *hygrometer* [from Gk *hugros* wet]
hygrometer (haɪˈgrɒmɪtə) *n* any of various instruments for measuring humidity > **hygrometric** (ˌhaɪgrəˈmɛtrɪk) *adj*
hygrophyte (ˈhaɪgrəˌfaɪt) *n* any plant that grows in wet or waterlogged soil > **hygrophytic** (ˌhaɪgrəˈfɪtɪk) *adj*
hygroscope (ˈhaɪgrəˌskəʊp) *n* any device that indicates the humidity of the air without necessarily measuring it
hygroscopic (ˌhaɪgrəˈskɒpɪk) *adj* (of a substance) tending to absorb water from the air > ˌ**hygroˈscopically** *adv*
hying (ˈhaɪɪŋ) *vb* a present participle of **hie**
hyla (ˈhaɪlə) *n* a tree frog of tropical America [C19 from NL, from Gk *hulē* forest]
hylomorphism (ˌhaɪləˈmɔːfɪzəm) *n* the philosophical doctrine that identifies matter with the first cause of the universe
hylozoism (ˌhaɪləˈzəʊɪzəm) *n* the philosophical doctrine that life is one of the properties of matter [C17 from Gk *hulē* wood, matter + *zōē* life]
hymen (ˈhaɪmɛn) *n anat* a fold of mucous membrane that partly covers the entrance to the vagina and is usually ruptured when sexual intercourse takes place for the first time [C17 from Gk: membrane] > ˈ**hymenal** *adj*
Hymen (ˈhaɪmɛn) *n* the Greek and Roman god of marriage
hymeneal (ˌhaɪmɛˈniːəl) *adj* **1** *chiefly poetic* of or relating to marriage ▷ *n* **2** a wedding song or poem
hymenopteran (ˌhaɪmɪˈnɒptərən) *or* **hymenopteron** *n, pl* **hymenopterans, hymenoptera** (-tərə), *or* **hymenopterons** any hymenopterous insect
hymenopterous (ˌhaɪmɪˈnɒptərəs) *adj* of or belonging to an order of insects, including bees, wasps, and ants, having two pairs of membranous wings [C19 from Gk *humenopteros* membrane wing; see HYMEN, -PTEROUS]
Hymettian (haɪˈmɛtɪən) *or* **Hymettic** (haɪˈmɛtɪk) *adj* of or relating to Hymettus, a mountain in SE Greece
Hymettus (haɪˈmɛtəs) *n* a mountain in SE Greece, in Attica, east of Athens: famous for its marble and for honey. Height: 1032 m (3386 ft). Modern Greek name: **Imittós**
hymn (hɪm) *n* **1** a Christian song of praise sung to God or a saint **2** a similar song praising other gods, a nation, etc ▷ *vb* **3** to express (praises, thanks, etc) by singing hymns [C13 from L *hymnus*, from Gk *humnos*] > **hymnic** (ˈhɪmnɪk) *adj*
hymnal (ˈhɪmnᵊl) *n* **1** Also: **hymn book** a book of hymns ▷ *adj* **2** of, relating to, or characteristic of hymns
hymnody (ˈhɪmnədɪ) *n* **1** the composition or singing of hymns **2** hymns collectively ▷ Also called: **hymnology** [C18 from Med. L *hymnōdia*, from Gk, from *humnōidein*, from HYMN + *aeidein* to sing]

hymnology (hɪm'nɒlədʒɪ) *n* **1** the study of hymn composition **2** another word for **hymnody** > **hym'nologist** *n*

hyoid ('haɪɔɪd) *adj* of or relating to the **hyoid bone**, the horseshoe-shaped bone that lies at the base of the tongue [C19 from NL *hyoïdes*, from Gk *huoeidēs* having the shape of the letter UPSILON, from *hu* upsilon + -OID]

hyoscine ('haɪə,si:n) *n* another name for **scopolamine** [C19 from *huosc(yamus)* a medicinal plant + -INE[2]; see HYOSCYAMINE]

hyoscyamine (,haɪə'saɪə,mi:n) *n* a poisonous alkaloid occurring in henbane and related plants: used in medicine [C19 from NL, from Gk *huoskuamos* (from *hus* pig + *kuamos* bean) + AMINE]

hyp. *abbrev for:* **1** hypotenuse **2** hypothetical

hypaethral *or US* **hypethral** (hɪ'pi:θrəl, haɪ-) *adj* (esp of a classical temple) having no roof [C18 from L *hypaethrus* uncovered, from Gk, from HYPO- + *aithros* clear sky]

hypallage (haɪ'pælə,dʒi:) *n rhetoric* a figure of speech in which the natural relations of two words in a statement are interchanged, as in *the fire spread the wind* [C16 via LL from Gk *hupallagē*, from HYPO- + *allassein* to exchange]

Hypatia (haɪ'peɪʃɪə) *n* died 415 AD, Neo-Platonist philosopher and politician, who lectured at Alexandria. She was murdered by a Christian mob

hype[1] (haɪp) *sl* ▷ *n* **1** an intensive or exaggerated publicity or sales promotion **2** a deception or racket ▷ *vb* **hypes, hyping, hyped 3** (*tr*) to market or promote (a product) using intensive or exaggerated publicity [C20 from ?]

hype[2] (haɪp) *sl* ▷ *n* **1** a hypodermic needle or injection ▷ *vb* **hypes, hyping, hyped 2** (*intr; usually foll by up*) to inject oneself with a drug **3** (*tr*) to stimulate artificially or excite [C20 shortened from HYPODERMIC]

hyped up *adj sl* stimulated or excited by or as if by the effect of a stimulating drug

hyper ('haɪpə) *adj inf* overactive; overexcited [C20 prob. independent use of HYPER-]

hyper- *prefix* **1** above, over, or in excess: *hypercritical* **2** denoting an abnormal excess: *hyperacidity* **3** indicating that a chemical compound contains a greater than usual amount of an element: *hyperoxide* [from Gk *huper* over]

hyperacidity (,haɪpərə'sɪdɪtɪ) *n* excess acidity of the gastrointestinal tract, esp the stomach, producing a burning sensation

hyperactive (,haɪpər'æktɪv) *adj* abnormally active > ,**hyperac'tivity** *n*

hyperaemia *or US* **hyperemia** (,haɪpər'i:mɪə) *n pathol* an excessive amount of blood in an organ or part

hyperaesthesia *or US* **hyperesthesia** (,haɪpəri:s'θi:zɪə) *n pathol* increased sensitivity of any of the sense organs > **hyperaesthetic** *or US* **hyperesthetic** (,haɪpəri:s'θɛtɪk) *adj*

hyperbaton (haɪ'pɜ:bə,tɒn) *n rhetoric* a figure of speech in which the normal order of words is reversed, as in *cheese I love* [C16 via L from Gk, lit.: an overstepping, from HYPER- + *bainein* to step]

hyperbola (haɪ'pɜ:bələ) *n, pl* **hyperbolas** *or* **hyperbole** (-,li:) a conic section formed by a plane that cuts both bases of a cone: it consists of two branches asymptotic to two intersecting fixed lines [C17 from Gk *huperbolē*, lit.: excess, extravagance, from HYPER- + *ballein* to throw]

hyperbole (haɪ'pɜ:bəlɪ) *n* a deliberate exaggeration used for effect: *he embraced her a thousand times* [C16 from Gk, from HYPER- + *bolē*, from *ballein* to throw] > **hy'perbolism** *n*

hyperbolic (,haɪpə'bɒlɪk) *or* **hyperbolical** *adj* **1** of a hyperbola **2** *rhetoric* of a hyperbole > ,**hyper'bolically** *adv*

hyperbolic function *n* any of a group of functions of an angle expressed as a relationship between the distances of a point on a hyperbola to the origin and to the coordinate axes

hyperbolize *or* **hyperbolise** (haɪ'pɜ:bə,laɪz) *vb* **hyperbolizes, hyperbolizing, hyperbolized** *or* **hyperbolises, hyperbolising, hyperbolised** to express (something) by means of hyperbole

hyperboloid (haɪ'pɜ:bə,lɔɪd) *n* a geometric surface consisting of one sheet, or of two sheets separated by a finite distance, whose sections parallel to the three coordinate planes are hyperbolas or ellipses

Hyperborean (,haɪpə'bɔ:rɪən) *n* **1** *Greek myth* one of a people believed to have lived beyond the North Wind in a sunny land **2** an inhabitant of the extreme north ▷ *adj* **3** (*sometimes not cap*) of or relating to the extreme north [C16 from L *hyperboreus*, from Gk, from HYPER- + *Boreas* the north wind]

hypercharge ('haɪpə,tʃɑ:dʒ) *n* a property of baryons that is used to account for the absence of certain strong interaction decays

hypercholesterolaemia *or US* **hypercholesterolemia** (,haɪpəkə,lɛstərɒl'i:mɪə) *n* the condition of having a high concentration of cholesterol in the blood, predisposing to atherosclerosis of the coronary arteries

hypercorrect (,haɪpəkə'rɛkt) *adj* **1** excessively correct or fastidious **2** resulting from or characterized by hypercorrection

hypercorrection (,haɪpəkə'rɛkʃən) *n* a mistaken correction to text or speech made through a desire to avoid nonstandard pronunciation or grammar: *"between you and I" is a hypercorrection of "between you and me"*

hypercritical (,haɪpə'krɪtɪkᵊl) *adj* excessively or severely critical > ,**hyper'critically** *adv*

hyperfocal distance (,haɪpə'fəʊkᵊl) *n* the distance from a camera lens to the point beyond which all objects appear sharp and clearly defined

hyperglycaemia *or US* **hyperglycemia** (,haɪpəglaɪ'si:mɪə) *n pathol* an abnormally large amount of sugar in the blood [C20 from HYPER- + GLYCO- + -AEMIA] > ,**hypergly'caemic** *or US* ,**hypergly'cemic** *adj*

hypergolic (,haɪpə'gɒlɪk) *adj* (of a rocket fuel) able to ignite spontaneously on contact with an oxidizer [C20 from G *Hypergol* (?from HYP(ER-) + ERG[1] + -OL[2]) + -IC]

hypericum (haɪ'pɛrɪkəm) *n* any herbaceous plant or shrub of the temperate genus *Hypericum*. See **rose of Sharon, Saint John's wort** [C16 via L from Gk *hupereikon*, from HYPER- + *ereikē* heath]

hyperinflation (,haɪpərɪn'fleɪʃən) *n* an extremely high level of inflation (with price rises of 50 per cent per month), often involving social disorder

Hyperion (haɪ'pɪərɪən) *n Greek myth* a Titan, son of Uranus and Gaea, father of Helios (sun), Selene (moon), and Eos (dawn)

hyperlink ('haɪpə,lɪŋk) *n* **1** a word, phrase, picture, icon, etc, in a computer document on which a user may click to move to another part of the document or to another document ▷ *vb* **2** (*tr*) to link (files) in this way ▷ Often shortened to **link**

hypermarket ('haɪpə,mɑ:kɪt) *n Brit* a huge self-service store, usually built on the outskirts of a town [C20 translation of F *hypermarché*]

hypermedia ('haɪpə,mi:dɪə) *n* computer software and hardware that allows users to interact with text, graphics, sound, and video, each of which can be accessed from within any of the others ▷ Cf **hypertext**

hypermetropia (,haɪpəmɪ'trəʊpɪə) *or* **hypermetropy** (,haɪpə'mɛtrəpɪ) *n pathol* a variant of **hyperopia** [C19 from Gk *hupermetros* beyond measure (from HYPER- + *metron* measure) + -OPIA]

hyperon ('haɪpə,rɒn) *n physics* any baryon that is not a nucleon [C20 from HYPER- + -ON]

hyperopia (,haɪpə'rəʊpɪə) *n* inability to see near objects clearly because the images received by the eye are focused behind the retina; long-sightedness > **hyperopic** (,haɪpə'rɒpɪk) *adj*

Hh

hyperphysical (ˌhaɪpəˈfɪzɪkᵊl) *adj* beyond the physical; supernatural or immaterial

hyperpyrexia (ˌhaɪpəpaɪˈrɛksɪə) *n pathol* an extremely high fever, with a temperature of 41°C (106°F) or above

hyperreal (ˌhaɪpəˈrɪəl) *adj* **1** involving or characterized by particularly realistic graphic representation **2** distorting or exaggerating reality **3** pertaining to or creating a hyperreality ▹ *n* **4** **the hyperreal** that which constitutes hyperreality **5** short for **hyperreal number**

hyperreal number *n* any of a set of numbers formed by the addition of infinite numbers and infinitesimal numbers to the set of real numbers

hypersensitive (ˌhaɪpəˈsɛnsɪtɪv) *adj* **1** having unduly vulnerable feelings **2** abnormally sensitive to an allergen, a drug, or other agent > **ˌhyperˈsensitiveness** *or* **ˌhyperˌsensiˈtivity** *n*

hypersonic (ˌhaɪpəˈsɒnɪk) *adj* concerned with or having a velocity of at least five times that of sound in the same medium under the same conditions > **ˌhyperˈsonics** *n*

hyperspace (ˌhaɪpəˈspeɪs) *n* **1** *maths* space having more than three dimensions **2** (in science fiction) a theoretical dimension within which conventional space-time relationship does not apply

hypersthene (ˈhaɪpəˌsθiːn) *n* a green, brown, or black pyroxene mineral [C19 from HYPER- + Gk *sthenos* strength]

hypertension (ˌhaɪpəˈtɛnʃən) *n pathol* abnormally high blood pressure > **hypertensive** (ˌhaɪpəˈtɛnsɪv) *adj, n*

hypertext (ˈhaɪpəˌtɛkst) *n* computer software and hardware that allows users to create, store, and view text and move between related items easily and in a nonsequential way

hypertext markup language *n* the full name for **HTML**

hyperthermia (ˌhaɪpəˈθɜːmɪə) *or* **hyperthermy** (ˈhaɪpəˌθɜːmɪ) *n pathol* a variant of **hyperpyrexia** > **ˌhyperˈthermal** *adj*

hyperthermophile (ˌhaɪpəˈθɜːməʊˌfaɪl) *n* an organism, esp a bacterium, that lives at high temperatures (above 80°C), found in some hot springs > **hyperthermophilic** (ˌhaɪpəˌθɜːməʊˈfɪlɪk) *adj*

hyperthyroidism (ˌhaɪpəˈθaɪrɔɪˌdɪzəm) *n* overproduction of thyroid hormone by the thyroid gland, causing nervousness, insomnia, and sensitivity to heat > **ˌhyperˈthyroid** *adj, n*

hypertonic (ˌhaɪpəˈtɒnɪk) *adj* **1** (esp of muscles) being in a state of abnormally high tension **2** (of a solution) having a higher osmotic pressure than that of a specified solution

hypertrophy (haɪˈpɜːtrəfɪ) *n, pl* **hypertrophies** **1** enlargement of an organ or part resulting from an increase in the size of the cells ▹ *vb* **hypertrophies, hypertrophying, hypertrophied** **2** to undergo or cause to undergo this condition

hyperventilation (ˌhaɪpəˌvɛntɪˈleɪʃən) *n* an increase in the rate of breathing, sometimes resulting in cramp and dizziness > **ˌhyperˈventiˌlate** *vb*

hypha (ˈhaɪfə) *n, pl* **hyphae** (-fiː) any of the filaments that constitute the body (mycelium) of a fungus [C19 from NL, from Gk *huphē* web] > **ˈhyphal** *adj*

hyphen (ˈhaɪfᵊn) *n* **1** the punctuation mark (-), used to separate parts of compound words, to link the words of a phrase, and between syllables of a word split between two consecutive lines ▹ *vb* **2** (*tr*) another word for **hyphenate** [C17 from LL (meaning: the combining of two words), from Gk *huphen* (adv) together, from HYPO- + *heis* one]

hyphenate (ˈhaɪfᵊˌneɪt) *vb* **hyphenates, hyphenating, hyphenated** (*tr*) to separate (words, etc) with a hyphen > **ˌhyphenˈation** *n*

hyphenated (ˈhaɪfᵊˌneɪtɪd) *adj* **1** containing or linked with a hyphen **2** *chiefly US* having a nationality denoted by a hyphenated word: *Irish-American*

hypno- *or before a vowel* **hypn-** *combining form* **1** indicating sleep: *hypnopaedia* **2** relating to hypnosis: *hypnotherapy* [from Gk *hupnos* sleep]

hypnoid (ˈhɪpˌnɔɪd) *or* **hypnoidal** (hɪpˈnɔɪdᵊl) *adj psychol* of or relating to a state resembling sleep or hypnosis

hypnology (hɪpˈnɒlədʒɪ) *n psychol* the study of sleep and hypnosis > **hypˈnologist** *n*

hypnopaedia (ˌhɪpnəʊˈpiːdɪə) *n* the learning of lessons heard during sleep [C20 from HYPNO- + Gk *paideia* education]

hypnopompic (ˌhɪpnəʊˈpɒmpɪk) *adj psychol* relating to the state existing between sleep and full waking, characterized by the persistence of dreamlike imagery [C20 from HYPNO- + Gk *pompē* a sending forth, escort + -IC]

Hypnos (ˈhɪpnɒs) *n Greek myth* the god of sleep. Roman counterpart: **Somnus** ▹ Cf **Morpheus** [Gk: sleep]

hypnosis (hɪpˈnəʊsɪs) *n, pl* **hypnoses** (-siːz) an artificially induced state of relaxation and concentration in which deeper parts of the mind become more accessible

hypnotherapy (ˌhɪpnəʊˈθɛrəpɪ) *n* the use of hypnosis in the treatment of emotional and psychogenic problems > **ˌhypnoˈtherapist** *n*

hypnotic (hɪpˈnɒtɪk) *adj* **1** of or producing hypnosis or sleep **2** (of a person) susceptible to hypnotism ▹ *n* **3** a drug that induces sleep **4** a person susceptible to hypnosis [C17 from LL *hypnōticus*, from Gk, from *hupnoun* to put to sleep, from *hupnos* sleep] > **hypˈnotically** *adv*

hypnotism (ˈhɪpnəˌtɪzəm) *n* **1** the scientific study and practice of hypnosis **2** the process of inducing hypnosis > **ˈhypnotist** *n*

hypnotize *or* **hypnotise** (ˈhɪpnəˌtaɪz) *vb* **hypnotizes, hypnotizing, hypnotized** *or* **hypnotises, hypnotising, hypnotised** (*tr*) **1** to induce hypnosis in (a person) **2** to charm or beguile; fascinate > **ˌhypnotiˈzation** *or* **ˌhypnotiˈsation** *n* > **ˈhypnoˌtizer** *or* **ˈhypnoˌtiser** *n*

hypo¹ (ˈhaɪpəʊ) *n* short for **hyposulphite** [C19]

hypo² (ˈhaɪpəʊ) *n, pl* **hypos** *inf* short for **hypodermic syringe**

hypo- *or before a vowel* **hyp-** *prefix* **1** beneath or below: *hypodermic* **2** lower: *hypogastrium* **3** less than; denoting a deficiency: *hypoglycaemia, hypothyroid* **4** indicating that a chemical compound contains an element in a lower oxidation state than usual: *hypochlorous acid* [from Gk, from *hupo* under]

hypoallergenic (ˌhaɪpəʊˌæləˈdʒɛnɪk) *adj* (of cosmetics, earrings, etc) not likely to cause an allergic reaction

hypoblast (ˈhaɪpəˌblæst) *n embryol* the inner layer of an embryo at an early stage of development that becomes the endoderm

hypocaust (ˈhaɪpəˌkɔːst) *n* an ancient Roman heating system in which hot air circulated under the floor and between double walls [C17 from L *hypocaustum*, from Gk, from *hupokaiein* to light a fire beneath, from HYPO- + *kaiein* to burn]

hypocentre (ˈhaɪpəʊˌsɛntə) *n* the point immediately below the centre of explosion of a nuclear bomb. Also called: **ground zero**

hypochlorite (ˌhaɪpəˈklɔːraɪt) *n* any salt or ester of hypochlorous acid

hypochlorous acid (ˌhaɪpəˈklɔːrəs) *n* an unstable acid known only in solution and in the form of its salts: a strong oxidizing and bleaching agent. Formula: HOCl

hypochondria (ˌhaɪpəˈkɒndrɪə) *n* chronic abnormal anxiety concerning the state of one's health. Also called: **hypochondriasis** (ˌhaɪpəkɒnˈdraɪəsɪs) [C18 from LL: abdomen, supposedly the seat of melancholy, from Gk, from *hupokhondrios*, from HYPO- + *khondros* cartilage]

hypochondriac (ˌhaɪpəˈkɒndrɪˌæk) *n* **1** a person suffering from hypochondria ▹ *adj also* **hypochondriacal** (ˌhaɪpəkɒnˈdraɪəkᵊl) **2** relating to or suffering from hypochondria

hypocorism (haɪˈpɒkəˌrɪzəm) *n* a pet name, esp one using a diminutive affix: *"Sally" is a hypocorism for "Sarah"* [c19 from Gk *hupokorisma*, from *hupokorizesthai* to use pet names, from *hypo-* beneath + *korizesthai*, from *korē* girl, *koros* boy] > **hypocoristic** (ˌhaɪpəkɔːˈrɪstɪk) *adj*

hypocotyl (ˌhaɪpəˈkɒtɪl) *n* the part of an embryo plant between the cotyledons and the radicle [c19 from HYPO- + COTYL(EDON)]

hypocrisy (hɪˈpɒkrəsɪ) *n, pl* **hypocrisies** **1** the practice of professing standards, beliefs, etc, contrary to one's real character or actual behaviour **2** an act or instance of this

hypocrite (ˈhɪpəkrɪt) *n* a person who pretends to be what he or she is not [c13 from OF *ipocrite*, via LL from Gk *hupokritēs* one who plays a part, from *hupokrinein* to feign, from *krinein* to judge] > ˌ**hypoˈcritical** *adj* > ˌ**hypoˈcritically** *adv*

hypocycloid (ˌhaɪpəˈsaɪklɔɪd) *n* a curve described by a point on the circumference of a circle as the circle rolls around the inside of a fixed coplanar circle > ˌ**hypocyˈcloidal** *adj*

hypodermic (ˌhaɪpəˈdɜːmɪk) *adj* **1** of or relating to the region of the skin beneath the epidermis **2** injected beneath the skin ▷ *n* **3** a hypodermic syringe or needle **4** a hypodermic injection > ˌ**hypoˈdermically** *adv*

hypodermic syringe *n med* a type of syringe consisting of a hollow cylinder, usually of glass or plastic, a tightly fitting piston, and a hollow needle (**hypodermic needle**), used for withdrawing blood samples, etc

hypodermis (ˌhaɪpəˈdɜːmɪs) *or* **hypoderm** *n* **1** *bot* a layer of thick-walled supportive or water-storing cells beneath the epidermis in some plants **2** *zool* the epidermis of arthropods, annelids, etc [c19 from HYPO- + EPIDERMIS]

hypogastrium (ˌhaɪpəˈgæstrɪəm) *n, pl* **hypogastria** (-trɪə) *anat* the lower front central region of the abdomen [c17 from NL, from Gk *hupogastrion*, from HYPO- + *gastrion*, dim. of *gastēr* stomach]

hypogeal (ˌhaɪpəˈdʒiːəl) *or* **hypogeous** *adj* occurring or living below the surface of the ground [c19 from L *hypogēus*, from Gk, from HYPO- + *gē* earth]

hypogene (ˈhaɪpəˌdʒiːn) *adj* formed or originating beneath the surface of the earth

hypogeum (ˌhaɪpəˈdʒiːəm) *n, pl* **hypogea** (-ˈdʒiːə) an underground vault, esp one used for burials [c18 from L, from Gk *hupogeion*; see HYPOGEAL]

hypoid gear (ˈhaɪpɔɪd) *n* a gear having a tooth form generated by a hypocycloidal curve [c20 *hypoid*, shortened from HYPOCYCLOID]

hyponasty (ˈhaɪpəˌnæstɪ) *n* increased growth of the lower surface of a plant part, resulting in an upward bending of the part > ˌ**hypoˈnastic** *adj*

hypophosphate (ˌhaɪpəˈfɒsfeɪt) *n* any salt or ester of hypophosphoric acid

hypophosphite (ˌhaɪpəˈfɒsfaɪt) *n* any salt of hypophosphorous acid

hypophosphoric acid (ˌhaɪpəfɒsˈfɒrɪk) *n* a tetrabasic acid produced by the slow oxidation of phosphorus in moist air. Formula: $H_4P_2O_6$

hypophosphorous acid (ˌhaɪpəˈfɒsfərəs) *n* a monobasic acid and a reducing agent. Formula: H_3PO_2

hypophysis (haɪˈpɒfɪsɪs) *n, pl* **hypophyses** (-ˌsiːz) the technical name for **pituitary gland** [c18 from Gk: outgrowth, from HYPO- + *phuein* to grow] > **hypophyseal** *or* **hypophysial** (ˌhaɪpəˈfɪzɪəl, haɪˌpɒfɪˈsɪəl) *adj*

hypostasis (haɪˈpɒstəsɪs) *n, pl* **hypostases** (-ˌsiːz) **1** *metaphysics* the essential nature of a substance **2** *Christianity* **2a** any of the three persons of the Godhead **2b** the one person of Christ in which the divine and human natures are united **3** the accumulation of blood in an organ or part under the influence of gravity as the result of poor circulation [c16 from LL: substance, from Gk *hupostasis* foundation, from *huphistasthai*, from HYPO- + *histanai* to cause to stand] > **hypostatic** (ˌhaɪpəˈstætɪk) *or* ˌ**hypoˈstatical** *adj*

hypostyle (ˈhaɪpəʊˌstaɪl) *adj* **1** having a roof supported by columns ▷ *n* **2** a building constructed in this way

hyposulphite (ˌhaɪpəˈsʌlfaɪt) *n* another name for **sodium thiosulphate**, esp when used as a photographic fixer. Often shortened to **hypo**

hyposulphurous acid (ˌhaɪpəˈsʌlfərəs) *n* an unstable acid known only in solution: a powerful reducing agent. Formula $H_2S_2O_4$

hypotension (ˌhaɪpəʊˈtɛnʃən) *n pathol* abnormally low blood pressure > **hypotensive** (ˌhaɪpəʊˈtɛnsɪv) *adj*

hypotenuse (haɪˈpɒtɪˌnjuːz) *n* the side in a right-angled triangle that is opposite the right angle. Abbrev: **hyp** [c16 from L *hypotēnūsa*, from Gk *hupoteinousa grammē* subtending line, from HYPO- + *teinein* to stretch]

hypothalamus (ˌhaɪpəˈθæləməs) *n, pl* **hypothalami** (-ˌmaɪ) a neural control centre at the base of the brain, concerned with hunger, thirst, satiety, and other autonomic functions > **hypothalamic** (ˌhaɪpəθəˈlæmɪk) *adj*

hypothec (haɪˈpɒθɪk) *n Roman & Scots law* a charge on property in favour of a creditor [c16 from LL *hypotheca*, from Gk *hupothēkē* pledge, from *hupotithenai* to deposit as a security, from HYPO- + *tithenai* to place]

hypothecate (haɪˈpɒθɪˌkeɪt) *vb* **hypothecates, hypothecating, hypothecated** (*tr*) **1** *law* to pledge (personal property or a ship) as security for a debt without transferring possession or title **2** to reserve (the proceeds) from (a tax or duty) for use in a particular way: *we intend to hypothecate the penny on income tax for education* > **hyˌpotheˈcation** *n* > **hyˈpotheˌcator** *n*

hypothermia (ˌhaɪpəʊˈθɜːmɪə) *n* **1** *pathol* an abnormally low body temperature, as induced in the elderly by exposure to cold weather **2** *med* the intentional reduction of normal body temperature to reduce the patient's metabolic rate

hypothesis (haɪˈpɒθɪsɪs) *n, pl* **hypotheses** (-ˌsiːz) **1** a suggested explanation for a group of facts or phenomena, either accepted as a basis for further verification (**working hypothesis**) or accepted as likely to be true **2** an assumption used in an argument; supposition [c16 from Gk, from *hupotithenai* to propose, lit.: put under; see HYPO-, THESIS] > **hyˈpothesist** *n*

hypothesize *or* **hypothesise** (haɪˈpɒθɪˌsaɪz) *vb* **hypothesizes, hypothesizing, hypothesized** *or* **hypothesises, hypothesising, hypothesised** to form or assume as a hypothesis > **hyˈpotheˌsizer** *or* **hyˈpotheˌsiser** *n*

hypothetical (ˌhaɪpəˈθɛtɪkᵊl) *or* **hypothetic** *adj* **1** having the nature of a hypothesis **2** assumed or thought to exist **3** *logic* another word for **conditional** (sense 3) > ˌ**hypoˈthetically** *adv*

hypothyroidism (ˌhaɪpəʊˈθaɪrɔɪˌdɪzəm) *n pathol* **1** insufficient production of thyroid hormones by the thyroid gland **2** any disorder, such as cretinism or myxoedema, resulting from this > ˌ**hypoˈthyroid** *n, adj*

hypotonic (ˌhaɪpəˈtɒnɪk) *adj* **1** *pathol* (of muscles) lacking normal tone or tension **2** (of a solution) having a lower osmotic pressure than that of a specified solution

hypoxia (haɪˈpɒksɪə) *n* deficiency in the amount of oxygen delivered to the body tissues [c20 from HYPO- + OXY-² + -IA] > **hypoxic** (haɪˈpɒksɪk) *adj*

Hypsilantis *or* **Hypsilantes** (*Greek* ˌipsiˈlandis) *n* variants of **Ypsilanti**

hypso- *or before a vowel* **hyps-** *combining form* indicating height: *hypsometry* [from Gk *hupsos*]

hypsography (hɪpˈsɒgrəfɪ) *n* the scientific study and mapping of the earth's topography above sea level

hypsometer (hɪpˈsɒmɪtə) *n* **1** an instrument for measuring altitudes by determining the boiling point of water at a given altitude **2** any instrument used to calculate the heights of trees by triangulation

hypsometry (hɪpˈsɒmɪtrɪ) *n* (in mapping) the

Hh

establishment of height above sea level

hyrax (ˈhaɪræks) *n, pl* **hyraxes** *or* **hyraces** (ˈhaɪrəˌsiːz) any of various agile herbivorous mammals of Africa and SW Asia. They resemble rodents but have feet with hooflike toes. Also called: **dassie** [C19 from NL, from Gk *hurax* shrewmouse]

Hyrcania (hɜːˈkeɪnɪə) *n* an ancient district of Asia, southeast of the Caspian Sea > **Hyrˈcanian** *adj*

hyssop (ˈhɪsəp) *n* **1** a widely cultivated Asian plant with spikes of small blue flowers and aromatic leaves, used as a condiment and in perfumery and folk medicine **2** a Biblical plant, used for sprinkling in the ritual practices of the Hebrews [OE *ysope*, from L *hyssōpus*, from Gk *hussōpos*, of Semitic origin]

hysterectomy (ˌhɪstəˈrɛktəmɪ) *n, pl* **hysterectomies** surgical removal of the uterus

hysteresis (ˌhɪstəˈriːsɪs) *n physics* the lag in a variable property of a system with respect to the effect producing it as this effect varies, esp the phenomenon in which the magnetic induction of a ferromagnetic material lags behind the changing external field [from Gk *husterēsis*, from *husteros* coming after] > **hysteretic** (ˌhɪstəˈrɛtɪk) *adj*

hysteresis loop *n* a closed curve showing the variation of the magnetic induction of a ferromagnetic material with the external magnetic field producing it, when this field is changed through a complete cycle

hysteria (hɪˈstɪərɪə) *n* **1** a mental disorder characterized by emotional outbursts and, often, symptoms such as paralysis **2** any frenzied emotional state, esp of laughter or crying [C19 from NL, from L *hystericus* HYSTERIC]

hysteric (hɪˈstɛrɪk) *n* **1** a hysterical person ▷ *adj* **2** hysterical [C17 from L *hystericus*, lit.: of the womb, from Gk, from *hustera* womb; from the belief that hysteria in women originated in disorders of the womb]

hysterical (hɪˈstɛrɪkᵊl) *adj* **1** suggesting hysteria: *hysterical cries* **2** suffering from hysteria **3** *inf* wildly funny > **hysˈterically** *adv*

hysterics (hɪˈstɛrɪks) *n (functioning as pl or sing)* **1** an attack of hysteria **2** *inf* wild uncontrollable bursts of laughter

hystero- *or before a vowel* **hyster-** *combining form* the uterus: *hysterectomy* [from Gk *hustera* womb]

hysteron proteron (ˈhɪstəˌrɒn ˈprɒtəˌrɒn) *n* **1** *logic* a fallacious argument in which the proposition to be proved is assumed as a premise **2** *rhetoric* a figure of speech in which the normal order of two sentences, clauses, etc, is reversed: *bred and born* (for *born and bred*) [C16 from LL, from Gk *husteron proteron* the latter (placed as) former]

hystricomorph (hɪˈstraɪkəʊˌmɔːf) *n* **1** any rodent of the suborder *Hystricomorpha*, which includes porcupines, cavies, agoutis, and chinchillas ▷ *adj also* **hystricomorphic** (hɪˌstraɪkəʊˈmɔːfɪk) **2** of the *Hystricomorpha* [C19 from L *hystrix* porcupine, from Gk *hustrix*]

Hywel Dda *or* **Howel Dda** (ˈhaʊəl ˈdɑː) *n* known as *Hywel the Good*. died 950 AD, Welsh prince. He united S and N Wales and codified Welsh law

Hz *symbol for* hertz

Ii

i *or* **I** (aɪ) *n, pl* **i's, I's,** *or* **Is** **1** the ninth letter and third vowel of the English alphabet **2** any of several speech sounds represented by this letter **3a** something shaped like an I **3b** (*in combination*): *an I-beam*

i *symbol for* the imaginary number √–1

I[1] (aɪ) *pron* (*subjective*) refers to the speaker or writer [C12 from OE *ic*; cf. OSaxon *ik*, OHG *ih*, Sansk. *ahám*]

I[2] *symbol for:* **1** *chem* iodine **2** *physics* current **3** *physics* isospin ▷ **4** *the Roman numeral for* one. See **Roman numerals**

I. *abbrev for:* **1** Independence **2** Independent **3** Institute **4** International **5** Island; Isle

Ia. *or* **IA** *abbrev for* Iowa

-ia *suffix forming nouns* **1** in place names: *Columbia* **2** in names of diseases: *pneumonia* **3** in words denoting condition or quality: *utopia* **4** in names of botanical genera and zoological classes: *Reptilia* **5** in collective nouns borrowed from Latin: *regalia* [(for senses 1–4) NL, from L & Gk, suffix of fem nouns; (for sense 5) from L, neuter pl suffix]

IAA *abbrev for* indoleacetic acid

IAEA *abbrev for* International Atomic Energy Agency ▷ www.iaea.org

-ial *suffix forming adjectives* of or relating to: *managerial* [from L *-iālis*, adj. suffix; cf. -AL[1]]

iamb ('aɪæm, 'aɪæmb) *or* **iambus** (aɪ'æmbəs) *n, pl* **iambs, iambi** (aɪ'æmbaɪ), *or* **iambuses** *prosody* **1** a metrical foot of two syllables, a short one followed by a long one **2** a line of verse of such feet [C19 *iamb*, from C16 *iambus*, from L, from Gk *iambos*]

iambic (aɪ'æmbɪk) *prosody* ▷ *adj* **1** of, relating to, or using an iamb **2** (in Greek literature) denoting a satirical verse written in iambs ▷ *n* **3** a metrical foot, line, or stanza consisting of iambs **4** an ancient Greek satirical verse written in iambs

-ian *suffix* a variant of **-an**: *Etonian* [from L *-iānus*]

-iana *suffix forming nouns* a variant of **-ana**

IAP *abbrev for* Internet access provider

Iaşi (*Romanian* 'iaʃj) *n* a city in NE Romania: capital of Moldavia (1565–1859); university (1860). Pop: 348 399 (1997 est). German name: **Jassy**

-iasis *or* **-asis** *n combining form* (in medicine) indicating a diseased condition: *psoriasis* ▷ Cf **-osis** (sense 2) [from NL, from Gk, suffix of action]

IATA (aɪ'ɑːtə, iː'ɑːtə) *n acronym for* International Air Transport Association

-iatrics *n combining form* indicating medical care or treatment: *paediatrics* [C19 from Gk, from *iasthai* to heal]

iatrogenic (aɪˌætrəʊ'dʒɛnɪk) *adj med* (of an illness) induced in a patient as the result of a physician's actions, esp as a consequence of taking a drug prescribed by the physician > **iatrogenicity** (aɪˌætrəʊdʒɪ'nɪsɪtɪ) *n*

-iatry *n combining form* indicating healing or medical treatment: *psychiatry* ▷ Cf **-iatrics** [from NL *-iatria*, from Gk *iatreia* the healing art, from *iatros* healer, physician] > **-iatric** *adj combining form*

IBA (in Britain) *abbrev for* Independent Broadcasting Authority

Ibadan (ɪ'bædᵊn) *n* a city in SW Nigeria, capital of Oyo state: university (1948). Pop: 1 432 000 (1996 est)

Ibagué (*Spanish* iβa'ɣe) *n* a city in W central Colombia. Pop: 393 664 (1999 est)

Ibarruri (*Spanish* i'βarruri) *n* **Dolores** (do'lores) real name of (La) **Pasionaria**

I-beam *n* a rolled steel joist or a girder with a cross section in the form of a capital I

Iberia (aɪ'bɪərɪə) *n* **1** the Iberian Peninsula **2** an ancient region in central Asia, south of the Caucasus corresponding approximately to present-day Georgia

Iberian (aɪˈbɪərɪən) *n* **1** a member of a group of ancient Caucasoid peoples who inhabited the Iberian Peninsula, in classical times **2** a native or inhabitant of the Iberian Peninsula; a Spaniard or Portuguese **3** a native or inhabitant of ancient Iberia ▷ *adj* **4** relating to the pre-Roman peoples of the Iberian Peninsula or of Caucasian Iberia **5** of or relating to the Iberian Peninsula, its inhabitants, or any of their languages
Iberian Peninsula *n* a peninsula of SW Europe, occupied by Spain and Portugal
iberis (aɪˈbɪərɪs) *n* any of various Mediterranean plants with white, lilac, or purple flowers. Also called: **candytuft** [from Gk *ibēris* pepperwort]
Ibert (*French* ibɛr) *n* **Jacques** (**François Antoine**) (ʒak) 1890–1962, French composer; his works include the humorous orchestral *Divertissement* (1930)
ibex (ˈaɪbɛks) *n, pl* **ibexes, ibices** (ˈɪbɪˌsiːz, ˈaɪ-), *or* **ibex** any of three species of wild goat of mountainous regions of Europe, Asia, and North Africa, having large backward-curving horns [C17 from L: chamois]
IBF *abbrev for* International Boxing Federation
ibid. *or* **ib.** (referring to a book, etc, previously cited) *abbrev for* ibidem [L: in the same place]
ibis (ˈaɪbɪs) *n, pl* **ibises** *or* **ibis** any of various wading birds such as the sacred ibis, that occur in warm regions and have a long thin down-curved bill [C14 via L from Gk, from Egyptian *hby*]
Ibiza (*Spanish* iˈβiθa) *n* **1** a Spanish island in the W Mediterranean, one of the Balearic Islands: hilly, with a rugged coast; tourism. Pop: 45 000 (latest est). Area: 541 sq km (209 sq miles) **2** the capital of Ibiza, a port on the south of the island. Pop: 16 000 (latest est)
-ible *suffix forming adjectives* a variant of **-able** > **-ibly** *suffix forming adverbs* > **-ibility** *suffix forming nouns*
ibn-Rushd (ˌɪbᵊnˈrʊʃt) *n* the Arabic name of **Averroës**
ibn-Saud (ˌɪbᵊnˈsaʊd) *n* **Abdul-Aziz** (æbˈdʊlæˈziːz) 1880–1953, first king of Saudi Arabia (1932–53)
ibn-Sina (ˌɪbᵊnˈsiːnə) *n* the Arabic name of **Avicenna**
Ibo *or* **Igbo** (ˈiːbəʊ) *n* **1** (*pl* **Ibos** *or* **Ibo**) a member of a Negroid people of W Africa, living in S Nigeria **2** their language, belonging to the Niger-Congo family
Ibrahim Pasha (ˌɪbrəˈhiːm ˈpɑːʃə) *n* 1789–1848, Albanian general; son of Mehemet Ali, whom he succeeded as viceroy of Egypt (1848)
IBRD *abbrev for* International Bank for Reconstruction and Development (the World Bank)
Ibsen (ˈɪbsən) *n* **Henrik** (ˈhɛnrɪk) 1828–1906, Norwegian dramatist and poet. After his early verse plays *Brand* (1866) and *Peer Gynt* (1867), he began the series of social dramas in prose, including *A Doll's House* (1879), *Ghosts* (1881), and *The Wild Duck* (1886), which have had a profound influence on modern drama. His later plays, such as *Hedda Gabler* (1890) and *The Master Builder* (1892), are more symbolic
ibuprofen (aɪˈbjuːprəʊˌfɛn) *n* a drug that relieves pain and reduces inflammation: used to treat arthritis and muscular strains
i/c *abbrev for:* **1** in charge (of) **2** internal combustion
-ic *suffix forming adjectives* **1** of, relating to, or resembling: *periodic* See also **-ical** **2** (in chemistry) indicating that an element is chemically combined in the higher of two possible valence states: *ferric* ▷ Cf **-ous** (sense 2) [from L *-icus* or Gk *-ikos*; *-ic* also occurs in nouns that represent a substantive use of adjectives (*magic*) and in nouns borrowed directly from L or Gk (*critic, music*)]
Içá (ˈiːsɑː; *Portuguese* iˈsa) *n* the Brazilian part of the **Putumayo River**
ICA *abbrev for:* **1** (in Britain) Institute of Contemporary Arts **2** Institute of Chartered Accountants
-ical *suffix forming adjectives* a variant of **-ic**, but having a less literal application than corresponding adjectives ending in *-ic: economical* [from L *-icālis*] > **-ically** *suffix forming adverbs*
ICAO *abbrev for* International Civil Aviation Organization
Icaria (aɪˈkɛərɪə, ɪ-) *n* a Greek island in the Aegean Sea, in the Southern Sporades group. Area: 256 sq km (99 sq miles). Modern Greek name: **Ikaría** Also called: **Nikaria**
Icarian Sea *n* the part of the Aegean Sea between the islands of Patmos and Leros and the coast of Asia Minor, where, according to legend, Icarus fell into the sea
Icarus (ˈɪkərəs, ˈaɪ-) *n Greek myth* the son of Daedalus, with whom he escaped from Crete, flying with wings made of wax and feathers. Heedless of his father's warning he flew too near the sun, causing the wax to melt, and fell into the Aegean and drowned
ICBM *abbrev for* intercontinental ballistic missile: a missile with a range greater than 5550 km
ice (aɪs) *n* **1** water in the solid state, formed by freezing liquid water. Related adj: **glacial** **2** a portion of ice cream **3** *sl* a diamond or diamonds **4** *sl* a concentrated and highly potent form of methamphetamine with dangerous side effects **5** **break the ice** **5a** to relieve shyness, etc, esp between strangers **5b** to be the first of a group to do something **6** **on ice** in abeyance; pending **7** **on thin ice** unsafe; vulnerable **8** **the Ice** *NZ inf* Antarctica ▷ *vb* **ices, icing, iced** **9** (often foll by *up, over,* etc) to form ice; freeze **10** (*tr*) to mix with ice or chill (a drink, etc) **10** (*tr*) to cover (a cake, etc) with icing [OE *īs*] > **iced** *adj*
ICE (in Britain) *abbrev for* Institution of Civil Engineers
Ice. *abbrev for* Iceland(ic)
ice age *n* another name for **glacial period**
ice axe *n* a light axe used by mountaineers for cutting footholds in ice
ice bag *n* a waterproof bag used as an ice pack
iceberg (ˈaɪsbɜːg) *n* **1** a large mass of ice floating in the sea **2** **tip of the iceberg** the small visible part of something, esp a problem, that is much larger **3** *sl, chiefly US* a person considered to have a cold or reserved manner [C18 prob. part translation of MDu. *ijsberg* ice mountain; cf. Norwegian *isberg*]
iceberg lettuce *n* a type of lettuce with very crisp pale leaves tightly enfolded
iceblink (ˈaɪsˌblɪŋk) *n* a reflected glare in the sky over an ice field. Also called: **blink**
icebound (ˈaɪsˌbaʊnd) *adj* covered or made immobile by ice; frozen in: *an icebound ship*
icebox (ˈaɪsˌbɒks) *n* **1** a compartment in a refrigerator for storing or making ice **2** an insulated cabinet packed with ice for storing food **3** a US and Canad name for **refrigerator**
icebreaker (ˈaɪsˌbreɪkə) *n* **1** Also called: **iceboat** a vessel with a reinforced bow for breaking up the ice in bodies of water **2** a device for breaking ice into smaller pieces **3** something intended to relieve shyness between strangers
ice bridge *n Canad* a body of ice that forms across the width of a river and is strong enough to bear traffic
icecap (ˈaɪsˌkæp) *n* a thick mass of glacial ice that permanently covers an area, such as the polar regions or the peak of a mountain
ice cream *n* a sweetened frozen liquid, made from cream, milk, or a custard base, flavoured in various ways
▷ www.ice-cream-recipes.com
▷ www.foodsci.uoguelph.ca/dairyedu/ichist.html
▷ www.freerecipe.org/Dessert/Frozen/Ice_Cream
ice dance *n* any of a number of dances, mostly based on ballroom dancing, performed by a couple skating on ice > **ice dancer** *n* > **ice dancing** *n*
▷ www.isu.org
icefall (ˈaɪsˌfɔːl) *n* a steep part of a glacier that resembles a frozen waterfall
ice field *n* **1** a large ice floe **2** a large mass of ice permanently covering an extensive area of land
ice floe *n* a sheet of ice, of variable size, floating in the

sea ▷ See also **ice field** (sense 1)

ice hockey *n* a game played on ice by two teams wearing skates, who try to propel a flat puck into their opponents' goal with long sticks
▷ www.iihf.com
▷ www.nhl.com

ice house *n* a building for storing ice

Içel (iː'tʃɛl) *n* another name for **Mersin**

Iceland ('aɪslənd) *n* an island republic in the N Atlantic, regarded as part of Europe: settled by Norsemen, who established a legislative assembly in 930; under Danish rule (1380–1918); gained independence in 1918 and became a republic in 1944; contains large areas of glaciers, snowfields, and lava beds with many volcanoes and hot springs (the chief source of domestic heat); inhabited chiefly along the SW coast. The economy is based largely on fishing and tourism. Official language: Icelandic. Official religion: Evangelical Lutheran. Currency: króna. Capital: Reykjavik. Pop: 284 000 (2001 est). Area: 102 828 sq km (39 702 sq miles)
▷ http://government.is
▷ www.icetourist.is

Icelander ('aɪslændə, 'aɪsləndə) *n* a native or inhabitant of Iceland

Icelandic (aɪs'lændɪk) *adj* **1** of or relating to Iceland, its people, or their language ▷ *n* **2** the official language of Iceland

Iceland poppy *n* any of various arctic poppies with white or yellow nodding flowers

Iceland spar *n* a pure transparent variety of calcite with double-refracting crystals

ice lolly *n Brit inf* a water ice or an ice cream on a stick. Also called: **lolly**

ice pack *n* **1** a bag or folded cloth containing ice, applied to a part of the body to reduce swelling, etc **2** another name for **pack ice** **3** a sachet containing a gel that retains its temperature for an extended period of time, used esp in cool bags

ice pick *n* a pointed tool used for breaking ice

ice plant *n* a low-growing plant of southern Africa, with fleshy leaves covered with icelike hairs and pink or white rayed flowers

ice point *n* the temperature at which a mixture of ice and water are in equilibrium at a pressure of one atmosphere. It is 0° on the Celsius scale and 32° on the Fahrenheit scale ▷ Cf **steam point**

ice sheet *n* a thick layer of ice covering a large area of land for a long time, esp those in Antarctica and Greenland

ice shelf *n* a thick mass of ice that is permanently attached to the land but projects into and floats on the sea

ice skate *n* **1** a boot having a steel blade fitted to the sole to enable the wearer to glide over ice **2** the steel blade on such a boot ▷ *vb* **ice-skate, ice-skates, ice-skating, ice-skated** **3** (*intr*) to glide over ice on ice skates > **'ice-,skater** *n*

ice station *n* a scientific research station in polar regions, where ice movement, weather, and environmental conditions are monitored

icewine ('aɪswaɪn) *n Canad* a dessert wine made from grapes that have frozen before being harvested

Ichang *or* **I-ch'ang** ('iː'tʃæŋ) *n* a variant transliteration of the Chinese name of **Yichang**

IChemE *abbrev for* Institution of Chemical Engineers

I Ching ('iː 'tʃɪŋ) *n* an ancient Chinese book of divination and a source of Confucian and Taoist philosophy
▷ http://www.zhouyi.com/

ichneumon (ɪk'njuːmən) *n* a mongoose of Africa and S Europe, having greyish-brown speckled fur [C16 via L from Gk, lit.: tracker, hunter, from *ikhneuein* to track, from *ikhnos* a footprint; so named from the animal's alleged ability to locate the eggs of crocodiles]

ichneumon fly *or* **wasp** *n* any hymenopterous insect whose larvae are parasitic in caterpillars and other insect larvae

ichnography (ɪk'nɒgrəfɪ) *n* **1** the art of drawing ground plans **2** the ground plan of a building [C16 from L, from Gk, from *ikhnos* trace, track] > **ichnographic** (,ɪknə'græfɪk) *or* **,ichno'graphical** *adj*

ichor ('aɪkɔː) *n* **1** *Greek myth* the fluid said to flow in the veins of the gods **2** *pathol* a foul-smelling watery discharge from a wound or ulcer [C17 from Gk *ikhōr*, from ?] > **'ichorous** *adj*

ichthyo- *or before a vowel* **ichthy-** *combining form* indicating or relating to fishes: *ichthyology* [from L, from Gk *ikhthus* fish]

ichthyoid ('ɪkθɪ,ɔɪd) *adj* **1** Also: **ichthyoidal** resembling a fish ▷ *n* **2** a fishlike vertebrate

ichthyology (,ɪkθɪ'ɒlədʒɪ) *n* the study of fishes > **ichthyologic** (,ɪkθɪə'lɒdʒɪk) *or* **,ichthyo'logical** *adj* > **,ichthy'ologist** *n*

ichthyosaur ('ɪkθɪə,sɔː) *or* **ichthyosaurus** (,ɪkθɪə'sɔːrəs) *n, pl* **ichthyosaurs, ichthyosauruses,** *or* **ichthyosauri** (-'sɔːraɪ) an extinct marine Mesozoic reptile which had a porpoise-like body with dorsal and tail fins and paddle-like limbs. See also **plesiosaur**

ichthyosis (,ɪkθɪ'əʊsɪs) *n* a congenital disease in which the skin is coarse, dry, and scaly > **ichthyotic** (,ɪkθɪ'ɒtɪk) *adj*

ICI *abbrev for* Imperial Chemical Industries

-ician *suffix forming nouns* indicating a person skilled or involved in a subject or activity: *physician; beautician* [from F *-icien*; see -IC, -IAN]

icicle ('aɪsɪkᵊl) *n* a hanging spike of ice formed by the freezing of dripping water [C14 from ICE + *ickel*, from OE *gicel* icicle, rel. to ON *jökull* glacier]

icing ('aɪsɪŋ) *n* **1** Also (esp US and Canad): **frosting** a sugar preparation, variously flavoured and coloured, for coating and decorating cakes, etc **2** **icing on the cake** any unexpected extra or bonus **3** the formation of ice, as on a ship, due to the freezing of moisture in the atmosphere

icing sugar *n Brit* a very finely ground sugar used for icings, confections, etc. US term: **confectioners' sugar**

icky ('ɪkɪ) *adj* **ickier, ickiest** *inf, chiefly US* **1** sticky **2** excessively sentimental or emotional > **'ickiness** *n*

icon *or* **ikon** ('aɪkɒn) *n* **1** a representation of Christ or a saint, esp one painted in oil on a wooden panel in a traditional Byzantine style and venerated in the Eastern Church **2** an image, picture, etc **3** a symbol resembling or analogous to the thing it represents **4** a person regarded as a sex symbol or as a symbol of a belief or cultural movement **5** a pictorial representation of a facility available on a computer that can be implemented by a cursor rather than by a textual instruction [C16 from L, from Gk *eikōn* image, from *eikenai* to be like]

Iconium (aɪ'kəʊnɪəm) *n* the ancient name for **Konya**

icono- *or before a vowel* **icon-** *combining form* indicating an image or likeness: *iconology*

iconoclast (aɪ'kɒnə,klæst) *n* **1** a person who attacks established or traditional concepts, principles, etc **2a** a destroyer of religious images or objects **2b** an adherent of a heretical iconoclastic movement within the Greek Orthodox Church from 725 to 842 AD [C16 from LL, from LGk *eikonoklastes*, from *eikōn* icon + *klastes* breaker] > **i,cono'clastic** *adj* > **i'cono,clasm** *n*

iconography (,aɪkɒ'nɒgrəfɪ) *n, pl* **iconographies** **1a** the symbols used in a work of art **1b** the conventional significance attached to such symbols **2** a collection of pictures of a particular subject **3** the representation of the subjects of icons or portraits, esp on coins > **,ico'nographer** *n* > **iconographic** (aɪ,kɒnə'græfɪk) *or* **i,cono'graphical** *adj*

Ii

iconolatry (ˌaɪkɒˈnɒlətrɪ) *n* the worship of icons as idols > ˌicoˈ**nolater** *n* > ˌicoˈ**nolatrous** *adj*

iconology (ˌaɪkɒˈnɒlədʒɪ) *n* **1** the study of icons **2** icons collectively **3** the symbolic representation of icons > **iconological** (aɪˌkɒnəˈlɒdʒɪkᵊl) *adj* > ˌicoˈ**nologist** *n*

iconoscope (aɪˈkɒnəˌskəʊp) *n* a television camera tube in which an electron beam scans a surface, converting an optical image into electrical pulses

iconostasis (ˌaɪkəʊˈnɒstəsɪs) *or* **iconostas** (aɪˈkɒnəˌstæs) *n, pl* **iconostases** (ˌaɪkəʊˈnɒstəˌsiːz *or* aɪˈkɒnəˌstæsɪz) *Eastern Church* a screen with doors and with icons set in tiers, which separates the sanctuary from the nave [C19 Church L, from LGk *eikonostasion* shrine, lit.: area where images are placed, from *icono-* + *histanai* to stand]

icosahedron (ˌaɪkəsəˈhiːdrən) *n, pl* **icosahedrons** *or* **icosahedra** (-drə) a solid figure having 20 faces [C16 from Gk, from *eikosi* twenty + *-edron* -HEDRON] > ˌ**icosaˈhedral** *adj*

-ics *suffix forming nouns (functioning as sing)* **1** indicating a science, art, or matters relating to a particular subject: *politics* **2** indicating certain activities: *acrobatics* [pl. of *-ic*, representing L *-ica*, from Gk *-ika*]

ICT *abbrev for* Information and Communications Technology

Ictinus (ɪkˈtaɪnəs) *n* 5th century BC, Greek architect, who designed the Parthenon with Callicrates

ictus (ˈɪktəs) *n, pl* **ictuses** *or* **ictus** **1** *prosody* metrical or rhythmic stress in verse feet, as contrasted with the stress accent on words **2** *med* a sudden attack or stroke [C18 from L *icere* to strike] > ˈ**ictal** *adj*

ICU *abbrev for* intensive care unit

icy (ˈaɪsɪ) *adj* **icier, iciest** **1** made of, covered with, or containing ice **2** resembling ice **3** freezing or very cold **4** cold or reserved in manner; aloof > ˈ**icily** *adv* > ˈ**iciness** *n*

id (ɪd) *n psychoanal* the primitive instincts and energies in the unconscious mind that, modified by the ego and the superego, underlie all psychic activity [C20 NL, from L: it; used to render G *Es*]

ID *abbrev for:* **1** Idaho **2** identification **3** Also: **i.d.** intradermal(ly)

id. *abbrev for* idem

Id. *abbrev for* Idaho

I'd (aɪd) *contraction of* I had *or* I would

-id¹ *suffix forming nouns and adjectives* indicating members of a zoological family: *cyprinid* [from NL *-idae* or *-ida*, from Gk *-idēs* suffix indicating offspring]

-id² *suffix forming nouns* a variant of **-ide**

Ida (ˈaɪdə) *n* **Mount** **1** a mountain in central Crete: the highest on the island; in ancient times associated with the worship of Zeus. Height: 2456 m (8057 ft). Modern Greek name: **Idhi** **2** a mountain in NW Turkey, southeast of the site of ancient Troy. Height: 1767 m (5797 ft). Turkish name: **Kaz Dağ** i

IDA *abbrev for* International Development Association

-idae *suffix forming plural proper nouns* indicating names of zoological families: *Felidae* [NL, from L, from Gk *-idai*, suffix indicating offspring]

Idaho (ˈaɪdəˌhəʊ) *n* a state of the northwestern US: consists chiefly of ranges of the Rocky Mountains, with the Snake River basin in the south; important for agriculture (**Idaho potatoes**), livestock, and silver-mining. Capital: Boise. Pop: 1 293 953 (2000) Area: 216 413 sq km (83 557 sq miles). Abbreviations: **Id, Ida,** or (with zip code) **ID**

-ide *or* **-id** *suffix forming nouns* **1** *(added to the combining form of the nonmetallic or electronegative elements)* indicating a binary compound: *sodium chloride* **2** indicating an organic compound derived from another: *acetanilide* **3** indicating one of a class of compounds or elements: *peptide* [from G *-id*, from F *oxide* OXIDE, based on the suffix of *acide* ACID]

idea (aɪˈdɪə) *n* **1** any product of mental activity; thought **2** the thought of something: *the idea appals me* **3** a belief; opinion **4** a scheme, intention, plan, etc **5** a vague notion; inkling: *he had no idea of the truth* **6** a person's conception of something: *her idea of honesty is not the same as mine* **7** significance or purpose: *the idea of the game is to discover the murderer* **8** *philosophy* **8a** an immediate object of thought or perception **8b** *(sometimes cap)* (in Plato) the universal essence or archetype of any class of things or concepts **9** **get ideas** to become ambitious, restless, etc **10** **not one's idea of** not what one regards as (hard work, a holiday, etc) **11** **that's an idea** that is worth considering **12** **the very idea!** that is preposterous, unreasonable, etc [C16 via LL from Gk: model, notion, from *idein* to see]

> USAGE It is usually considered correct to say that someone has *the idea of doing* something, rather than *the idea to do it*: *he had the idea of taking* (not *the idea to take*) *a short holiday*

idea hamster *or* **ideas hamster** *n sl* a person who is employed as a source of new ideas

ideal (aɪˈdɪəl) *n* **1** a conception of something that is perfect **2** a person or thing considered to represent perfection **3** something existing only as an idea **4** a pattern or model, esp of ethical behaviour ▷ *adj* **5** conforming to an ideal **6** of, involving, or existing in the form of an idea **7** *philosophy* **7a** of or relating to a highly desirable and possible state of affairs **7b** of or relating to idealism > **iˈdeally** *adv* > **iˈdealness** *n*

ideal element *n* any element added to a mathematical theory in order to eliminate special cases. The ideal element i = √−1 allows all algebraic equations to be solved

ideal gas *n* a hypothetical gas which obeys Boyle's law exactly at all temperatures and pressures, and which has internal energy that depends only upon the temperature

idealism (aɪˈdɪəˌlɪzəm) *n* **1** belief in or pursuance of ideals **2** the tendency to represent things in their ideal forms, rather than as they are **3** *philosophy* the doctrine that material objects and the external world do not exist in reality, but are creations of the mind ▷ Cf **materialism** > **iˈdealist** *n* > **iˌdealˈistic** *adj* > **iˌdealˈistically** *adv*

▷ http://www.stfx.ca/arpa/BI-RP.html

▷ http://pratt.edu/~arch543p/help/idealism.html

idealize *or* **idealise** (aɪˈdɪəˌlaɪz) *vb* **idealizes, idealizing, idealized** *or* **idealises, idealising, idealised** **1** to consider or represent (something) as ideal **2** *(tr)* to portray as ideal; glorify **3** *(intr)* to form an ideal or ideals > **iˌdealiˈzation** *or* **iˌdealiˈsation** *n* > **iˈdealˌizer** *or* **iˈdealˌiser** *n*

idée fixe *French* (ide fiks) *n, pl* ***idées fixes*** (ide fiks) a fixed idea; obsession

idem *Latin* (ˈaɪdɛm, ˈɪdɛm) *pron, adj* the same: used to refer to an article, chapter, etc, previously cited

identic (aɪˈdɛntɪk) *adj diplomacy* (esp of opinions expressed by two or more governments) having the same wording or intention regarding another power

identical (aɪˈdɛntɪkᵊl) *adj* **1** being the same: *we got the identical hotel room as last year* **2** exactly alike or equal **3** designating either or both of a pair of twins of the same sex who developed from a single fertilized ovum that split into two ▷ Cf **fraternal** (sense 3) [C17 from Med. L *identicus*, from L *idem* the same] > **iˈdentically** *adv*

identification (aɪˌdɛntɪfɪˈkeɪʃən) *n* **1** the act of identifying or the state of being identified **2a** something that identifies a person or thing **2b** *(as modifier)*: *an identification card* **3** *psychol* **3a** the process of recognizing specific objects as the result of remembering **3b** the process by which one incorporates aspects of another person's personality **3c** the transferring of a response from one situation to another because the two bear similar features

identification parade *n* a group of persons, including one suspected of a crime, assembled for the purpose of discovering whether a witness can identify the suspect

identify (aɪˈdɛntɪˌfaɪ) *vb* **identifies, identifying, identified** (*mainly tr*) **1** to prove or recognize as being a certain person or thing; determine the identity of **2** to consider as the same or equivalent **3** (*also intr; often foll by with*) to consider (oneself) as similar to another **4** to determine the taxonomic classification of (a plant or animal) **5** (*intr; usually foll by with*) *psychol* to engage in identification > **iˈdentiˌfiable** *adj* > **iˈdentiˌfiableness** *n* > **iˈdentiˌfier** *n*

Identikit (aɪˈdɛntɪˌkɪt) *n* **1** *trademark* (formerly) **1a** a set of transparencies of typical facial characteristics that can be superimposed on one another to build up a picture of a person sought by the police **1b** (*as modifier*): *an Identikit picture* **2** (*modifier*) artificially created by copying different elements in an attempt to form a whole: *an Identikit pop group*

identity (aɪˈdɛntɪtɪ) *n, pl* **identities 1** the state of having unique identifying characteristics **2** the individual characteristics by which a person or thing is recognized **3** the state of being the same in nature, quality, etc: *linked by the identity of their tastes* **4** the state of being the same as a person or thing described or known: *the identity of the stolen goods was soon established* **5** *maths* **5a** an equation that is valid for all values of its variables, as in $(x-y)(x+y) = x^2 - y^2$. Often denoted by the symbol ≡ **5b** Also called: **identity element** a member of a set that when operating on another member, *x*, produces that member *x*: the identity for multiplication of numbers is 1 since $x.1 = 1.x = x$ **6** *logic* the relationship between an object and itself **7** *Austral inf* **7a** a well-known local person; figure: *a Barwidgee identity* **7b** an eccentric; character: *an old identity in the town* **8** NZ a well-known person [C16 from LL *identitās*, from L *idem* the same]

identity card *n* a card that establishes a person's identity, esp one issued to all members of the population in wartime, to the staff of an organization, etc

identity theft *n* the crime of setting up and using bank accounts and credit facilities fraudulently in another person's name without his or her knowledge

ideo- *combining form* of or indicating idea or ideas: *ideology* [from F *idéo-*, from Gk *idea* IDEA]

ideogram (ˈɪdɪəʊˌɡræm) *or* **ideograph** (ˈɪdɪəʊˌɡrɑːf) *n* **1** a sign or symbol, used in a writing system such as that of China, that directly represents a concept or thing, rather than a word for it **2** any graphic sign or symbol, such as % or &

ideography (ˌɪdɪˈɒɡrəfɪ) *n* the use of ideograms to communicate ideas

ideology (ˌaɪdɪˈɒlədʒɪ) *n, pl* **ideologies 1** a body of ideas that reflects the beliefs of a nation, political system, class, etc **2** speculation that is imaginary or visionary **3** the study of the nature and origin of ideas > **ideological** (ˌaɪdɪəˈlɒdʒɪkᵊl) *or* **ˌideoˈlogic** *adj* > **ˌideoˈlogically** *adv* > **ˌideˈologist** *or* **ˈideoˌlogue** *n*

ides (aɪdz) *n* (*functioning as sing*) (in the Roman calendar) the 15th day in March, May, July, and October and the 13th day of each other month [C15 from OF, from L *īdūs* (pl), from ?]

id est *Latin* (ˈɪd ˈɛst) the full form of **i.e.**

Idhi (ˈiðɪ) *n* a transliteration of the Modern Greek name for (Mount) **Ida** (sense 1)

idiocy (ˈɪdɪəsɪ) *n, pl* **idiocies 1** (*not in technical usage*) severe mental retardation **2** foolishness; stupidity **3** a foolish act or remark

idiom (ˈɪdɪəm) *n* **1** a group of words whose meaning cannot be predicted from the constituent words: (*it was raining*) *cats and dogs* **2** linguistic usage that is grammatical and natural to native speakers **3** the characteristic vocabulary or usage of a specific human group or subject **4** the characteristic artistic style of an individual, school, etc [C16 from L *idiōma* peculiarity of language, from Gk *idios* private, separate] > **idiomatic** (ˌɪdɪəˈmætɪk) *adj* > **ˌidioˈmatically** *adv*

idiosyncrasy (ˌɪdɪəʊˈsɪŋkrəsɪ) *n, pl* **idiosyncrasies 1** a tendency, type of behaviour, etc, of a person; quirk **2** the composite physical or psychological make-up of a person **3** an abnormal reaction of an individual to specific foods, drugs, etc [C17 from Gk, from *idios* private, separate + *sunkrasis* mixture, temperament]

idiosyncratic (ˌɪdɪəʊsɪŋˈkrætɪk) *adj* of or relating to idiosyncrasy; characteristic of a specific person > **ˌidiosynˈcratically** *adv*

idiot (ˈɪdɪət) *n* **1** a person with severe mental retardation **2** a foolish or senseless person [C13 from L *idiōta* ignorant person, from Gk *idiōtēs* private person, ignoramus]

idiot board *n* a slang name for **Autocue**

idiot box *n sl* a television set

idiotic (ˌɪdɪˈɒtɪk) *adj* of or resembling an idiot; foolish; senseless > **ˌidiˈotically** *adv*

idiot savant (ˈiːdjəʊ sæˈvɑ̃, ˈɪdɪət ˈsævənt) *n, pl* **idiots savants** (ˈiːdjəʊ sæˈvɑ̃) *or* **idiot savants** a person of limited mental or social capabilities who performs brilliantly at some specialized intellectual task

idiot strings *pl n Canad inf* strings attached to children's mittens to prevent the wearer from losing them

idiot tape *n computing* a tape that prints out information in a continuous stream, with no line breaks

idle (ˈaɪdᵊl) *adj* **1** unemployed or unoccupied; inactive **2** not operating or being used **3** (of money) not used to earn interest, etc **4** not wanting to work; lazy **5** (*usually prenominal*) frivolous or trivial: *idle pleasures* **6** ineffective or powerless; vain **7** without basis; unfounded ▷ *vb* **idles, idling, idled 8** (when *tr*, often foll by *away*) to waste or pass (time) fruitlessly or inactively **9** (*intr*) (of a shaft, etc) to turn without doing useful work **10** (*intr*) (of an engine) to run at low speed with the transmission disengaged [OE *īdel*] > **ˈidleness** *n* > **ˈidly** *adv*

idle pulley *or* **idler pulley** *n* a freely rotating pulley used to control the tension or direction of a belt. Also called: **idler**

idler (ˈaɪdlə) *n* **1** a person who idles **2** another name for **idle pulley** or **idle wheel**

idle wheel *n* a gearwheel interposed between two others to transmit torque without changing the direction of rotation or the velocity ratio. Also called: **idler**

idol (ˈaɪdᵊl) *n* **1** a material object that is worshipped as a god **2** *Christianity, Judaism* any being (other than the one God) to which divine honour is paid **3** a person who is revered, admired, or highly loved [C13 from LL, from L: image, from Gk, from *eidos* shape, form]

idolatry (aɪˈdɒlətrɪ) *n* **1** the worship of idols **2** great devotion or reverence > **iˈdolater** *n or* **iˈdolatress** *fem n* > **iˈdolatrous** *adj*

idolize *or* **idolise** (ˈaɪdəˌlaɪz) *vb* **idolizes, idolizing, idolized** *or* **idolises, idolising, idolised 1** (*tr*) to admire or revere greatly **2** (*tr*) to worship as an idol **3** (*intr*) to worship idols > **ˌidoliˈzation** *or* **ˌidoliˈsation** *n* > **ˈidolˌizer** *or* **ˈidolˌiser** *n*

idolum (ɪˈdəʊləm) *n* **1** a mental picture; idea **2** a false idea; fallacy [C17 from L: IDOL]

Idomeneus (aɪˈdɒmɪˌnjuːs) *n Greek myth* a king of Crete who fought on the Greek side in the Trojan War

IDP *abbrev for* integrated data processing

Idun (ˈiːdʊn) *or* **Ithunn** *n Norse myth* the goddess of spring who guarded the apples that kept the gods eternally young; wife of Bragi

idyll *or US* (*sometimes*) **idyl** (ˈɪdɪl) *n* **1** a poem or prose work describing an idealized rural life, pastoral scenes, etc **2** a charming or picturesque scene or event **3** a piece of music with a calm or pastoral character [C17 from L *īdyllium*, from Gk *eidullion*, from *eidos* shape, (literary)

form] > **i'dyllic** *adj* > **i'dyllically** *adv*
IE *abbrev for* Indo-European (languages)
i.e. *abbrev for* id est [L: that is (to say); in other words]
USAGE See at **e.g.**
-ie *suffix forming nouns* a variant of **-y²**: *groupie*
IEA *abbrev for* International Energy Agency
IEE *abbrev for* Institution of Electrical Engineers
Ieper ('i:pər) *n* the Flemish name for **Ypres**
-ier *suffix forming nouns* a variant of **-eer**: *brigadier* [from OE *-ere* -ER¹ or (in some words) from OF *-ier*, from L *-ārius* -ARY]
Ieyasu (ˌi:jɛ'jɑ:su:) *n* a variant spelling of (Tokugawa) **Iyeyasu**
if (ɪf) *conj (subordinating)* **1** in case that, or on condition that: *if you try hard it might work* **2** used to introduce an indirect question. In this sense, *if* approaches the meaning of *whether* **3** even though: *an attractive if awkward girl* **4a** used to introduce expressions of desire, with *only*: *if I had only known* **4b** used to introduce exclamations of surprise, dismay, etc: *if this doesn't top everything!* ▷ *n* **5** an uncertainty or doubt: *the big if is whether our plan will work* **6** a condition or stipulation: *I won't have any ifs or buts* [OE *gif*]
IF *or* **i.f.** *electronics abbrev for* intermediate frequency
IFA *abbrev for* independent financial adviser
IFAD *abbrev for* International Fund for Agricultural Development
IFC *abbrev for* International Finance Corporation
Ife ('i:fɪ) *n* a town in W central Nigeria: one of the largest and oldest Yoruba towns; university (1961); centre of the cocoa trade. Pop: 296 800 (1996 est)
-iferous *suffix forming adjectives* containing or yielding: *carboniferous*
iffy ('ɪfɪ) *adj* **iffier, iffiest** *inf* uncertain or subject to contingency [c20 from IF + -Y¹]
Ifni (*Spanish* 'ifni) *n* a former Spanish province in S Morocco, on the Atlantic: returned to Morocco in 1969
IFP *abbrev for* Inkatha Freedom Party
IFS *abbrev for* Irish Free State (now called Republic of Ireland)
-ify *suffix forming verbs* a variant of **-fy**: *intensify* > **-ification** *suffix forming nouns*
Igbo ('i:bəʊ) *n, pl* **igbo** *or* **igbos** a variant spelling of **Ibo**
IGC *abbrev for* intergovernmental conference (esp in the European Union)
Igdrasil ('ɪgdrəsɪl) *n* a variant spelling of **Yggdrasil**
igloo *or* **iglu** ('ɪglu:) *n, pl* **igloos** *or* **iglus 1** a dome-shaped Inuit house, built of blocks of solid snow **2** a hollow made by a seal in the snow over its breathing hole in the ice [c19 from Inuktitut *igdlu* house]
Ignatius (ɪg'neɪʃɪəs) *n* **Saint**, surnamed *Theophorus*. died ?110 AD, bishop of Antioch. His seven letters, written on his way to his martyrdom in Rome, give valuable insight into the early Christian Church. Feast day: Oct. 17 or Dec. 17 or 20
Ignatius Loyola (lɔɪ'əʊlə) *n* **Saint** 1491–1556, Spanish ecclesiastic. He founded the Society of Jesus (1534) and was its first general (1541–56). His *Spiritual Exercises* (1548) remains the basic manual for the training of Jesuits. Feast day: July 31
igneous ('ɪgnɪəs) *adj* **1** (of rocks) derived by solidification of magma or molten lava emplaced on or below the earth's surface **2** of or relating to fire [c17 from L *igneus* fiery, from *ignis* fire]
ignis fatuus ('ɪgnɪs 'fætjʊəs) *n, pl* **ignes fatui** ('ɪgni:z 'fætjʊˌaɪ) another name for **will-o'-the-wisp** [c16 from Med. L, lit.: foolish fire]
ignite (ɪg'naɪt) *vb* **ignites, igniting, ignited 1** to catch fire or set fire to; burn or cause to burn **2** *(tr) chem* to heat strongly **3** *(tr)* to stimulate or provoke [c17 from L, from *ignis* fire] > **ig'nitable** *or* **ig'nitible** *adj* > **igˌnita'bility** *or* **igˌniti'bility** *n* > **ig'niter** *n*
ignition (ɪg'nɪʃən) *n* **1** the act or process of initiating combustion **2** the process of igniting the fuel in an internal-combustion engine **3** (preceded by *the*) the devices used to ignite the fuel in an internal-combustion engine
ignition coil *n* an induction coil that supplies the high voltage to the sparking plugs on an internal-combustion engine
ignition key *n* the key used in a motor vehicle to turn the switch that connects the battery to the ignition system
ignitron (ɪg'naɪtrɒn, 'ɪgnɪˌtrɒn) *n* a rectifier controlled by a subsidiary electrode, the igniter, partially immersed in a mercury cathode. A current passed between igniter and cathode forms a hot spot sufficient to strike an arc between cathode and anode [c20 from *igniter* + ELECTRON]
ignoble (ɪg'nəʊbᵊl) *adj* **1** dishonourable; base; despicable **2** of low birth or origins; humble; common **3** of low quality; inferior [c16 from L, from IN-¹ + OL *gnōbilis* NOBLE] > ˌ**igno'bility** *or* **ig'nobleness** *n* > **ig'nobly** *adv*
ignominy ('ɪgnəˌmɪnɪ) *n, pl* **ignominies 1** disgrace or public shame; dishonour **2** a cause of disgrace; a shameful act [c16 from L *ignōminia* disgrace, from *ig-* (see IN-²) + *nōmen* name, reputation] > ˌ**igno'minious** *adj* > ˌ**igno'miniously** *adv* > ˌ**igno'miniousness** *n*
ignoramus (ˌɪgnə'reɪməs) *n, pl* **ignoramuses** an ignorant person; fool [c16 from legal L, lit.: we have no knowledge of, from L *ignōrāre* to be ignorant of; see IGNORE; modern usage originated from use of *Ignoramus* as the name of an unlettered lawyer in a play by G Ruggle, 17th-century E dramatist]
ignorance ('ɪgnərəns) *n* lack of knowledge, information, or education; the state of being ignorant
ignorant ('ɪgnərənt) *adj* **1** lacking in knowledge or education; unenlightened **2** *(postpositive; often foll by of)* lacking in awareness or knowledge (of): *ignorant of the law* **3** resulting from or showing lack of knowledge or awareness: *an ignorant remark* > **'ignorantly** *adv*
ignore (ɪg'nɔ:) *vb* **ignores, ignoring, ignored** *(tr)* to fail or refuse to notice; disregard [c17 from L *ignōrāre* not to know, from *ignārus* ignorant of] > **ig'norer** *n*
Iguaçú *or* **Iguassú** (*Portuguese* igua'su) *n* a river in SE South America, rising in S Brazil and flowing west to join the Paraná River, forming part of the border between Brazil and Argentina. Length: 1200 km (745 miles)
Iguaçú Falls *n* a waterfall on the border between Brazil and Argentina, on the Iguaçú River: divided into hundreds of separate falls by forested rocky islands. Width: about 4 km (2.5 miles). Height: 82 m (269 ft)
iguana (ɪ'gwɑ:nə) *n* either of two large tropical American arboreal herbivorous lizards, esp the common iguana, having a greyish-green body with a row of spines along the back [c16 from Sp., from S Amerind *iwana*] > **i'guanian** *n, adj*
iguanodon (ɪ'gwɑ:nəˌdɒn) *n* a massive herbivorous long-tailed bipedal dinosaur common in Europe and N Africa in Jurassic and Cretaceous times [c19 NL, from IGUANA + Gk *odōn* tooth]
IHC (in New Zealand) *abbrev for* intellectually handicapped child
Ihimaera (ɪhɪ'mɑ:rə) *n* **Witi** ('wɪtɪ), full name *Witi Tame Ihimaera-Smiler*. born 1944, New Zealand Maori novelist and short-story writer; his novels include *The Whale Rider* (1987) and *The Uncle's Story* (2002)
IHS the first three letters of the name Jesus in Greek (ΙΗΣΟΥΣ), often used as a Christian emblem
IJssel ('aɪsᵊl; *Dutch* 'ɛisəl) *n* a river in the central Netherlands: a distributary of the Rhine, flowing north to the IJsselmeer. Length: 116 km (72 miles)
Ikaría (ika'ria) *n* a transliteration of the Modern Greek name for **Icaria**
ikat ('i:kæt) *n* a method of creating patterns in fabric by

tie-dyeing the yarn before weaving [c20 from Malay, lit.: to tie, bind]
▷ www.kasuridyeworks.com/fabexplan/kdlkat.html

ikebana (ˌiːkəˈbɑːnə) *n* the Japanese decorative art of flower arrangement
▷ www.jinjapan.org
▷ www.ikebana.com.au/history

Ikeja (ɪˈkeɪjə) *n* a town in SW Nigeria, capital of Lagos state: residential and industrial suburb of Lagos. Pop: 63 870 (latest est)

Ikhnaton (ɪkˈnɑːtən) *n* a variant of **Akhenaten**

ikon (ˈaɪkɒn) *n* a variant spelling of **icon**

IL *abbrev for* Illinois

il- *prefix* a variant of **in-**[1] and **in-**[2] before *l*

-ile *or* **-il** *suffix forming adjectives and nouns* indicating capability, liability, or a relationship with something: *agile; juvenile* [via F from L or directly from L *-ilis*] > **-ility** *suffix forming nouns*

Île-de-France (*French* ildəfrɑ̃s) *n* **1** a region of N France, in the Paris Basin: part of the duchy of France in the 10th century **2** a former name (1715–1810) for **Mauritius**

Île du Diable (il dy djɑblə) *n* the French name for **Devil's Island**

ileitis (ˌɪlɪˈaɪtɪs) *n* inflammation of the ileum

ileostomy (ˌɪlɪˈɒstəmɪ) *n, pl* **ileostomies** the surgical formation of a permanent opening through the abdominal wall into the ileum

Îles Comores (il kɔmɔr) *pl n* the French name for the **Comoros**

Îles du Salut (il dy saly) *pl n* the French name for the **Safety Islands**

Ilesha (ɪˈleɪʃə) *n* a town in W Nigeria. Pop: 378 400 (1996 est)

Îles Mascareignes (il maskarɛɲ) *pl n* the French name for the **Mascarene Islands**

Îles sous le Vent (il su lə vɑ̃) *pl n* the French name for the **Leeward Islands** (sense 3)

ileum (ˈɪlɪəm) *n* the part of the small intestine between the jejunum and the caecum [c17 NL, from L *īlium, īleum* flank, groin, from ?] > **ˈileˌac** *adj*

ilex (ˈaɪlɛks) *n* **1** any of a genus of trees or shrubs such as the holly and inkberry **2** another name for the **holm oak** [c16 from L]

Ilia (ˈɪlɪə) *n* (in Roman legend) the daughter of Aeneas and Lavinia, who, according to some traditions, was the mother of Romulus and Remus. See also **Rhea Silvia**

Ilía (iˈlia) *n* a transliteration of the Modern Greek name for **Elia**[1]

Iliamna (ˌɪlɪˈæmnə) *n* **1** a lake in SW Alaska: the largest lake in Alaska. Length: about 130 km (80 miles). Width: 40 km (25 miles) **2** a volcano in SW Alaska, northwest of Iliamna Lake. Height: 3076 m (10 092 ft)

Iligan (ɪˈliːgən) *n* a city in the Philippines, a port on the N coast of Mindanao. Pop: 209 639 (1994 est)

Ilion (ˈɪlɪən) *n* a transliteration of the Greek name for ancient **Troy**

ilium (ˈɪlɪəm) *n, pl* **ilia** (-ɪə) the uppermost and widest of the three sections of the hipbone

Ilium (ˈɪlɪəm) *n* the Latin name for ancient **Troy**

ilk (ɪlk) *n* **1** a type; class; sort (esp in **of that, his,** etc, **ilk**): *people of that ilk should not be allowed here* **2** **of that ilk** *Scot* of the place of the same name: to indicate that the person is laird of the place named: *Moncrieff of that ilk* [OE *ilca* the same family, same kind]

> **USAGE** Although the use of *ilk* to mean 'a type or class' is sometimes condemned as being the result of a misunderstanding of the Scottish expression *of that ilk*, it is nevertheless well established and generally acceptable

Ilkeston (ˈɪlkɪstən) *n* a town in N central England, in SE Derbyshire. Pop: 35 134 (1991)

Ilkley (ˈɪlklɪ) *n* a town in N England, in Bradford unitary authority, West Yorkshire: nearby is **Ilkley Moor** (to the south) Pop: 13 530 (1991)

ill (ɪl) *adj* **worse, worst** **1** (*usually postpositive*) not in good health; sick **2** characterized by or intending harm, etc; hostile: *ill deeds* **3** causing pain, harm, adversity, etc **4** ascribing or imputing evil to something referred to: *ill repute* **5** promising an unfavourable outcome; unpropitious: *an ill omen* **6** harsh; lacking kindness: *ill will* **7** not up to an acceptable standard; faulty: *ill manners* **8** **ill at ease** unable to relax; uncomfortable ▷ *n* **9** evil or harm; misfortune; trouble **10** a mild disease ▷ *adv* **11** badly: *the title ill befits him* **12** with difficulty; hardly: *he can ill afford the money* **13** not rightly: *he ill deserves such good fortune* [c11 (in the sense: evil): from ON *illr* bad]

Ill. *abbrev for* Illinois

I'll (aɪl) *contraction of* I will *or* I shall

ill-advised *adj* **1** acting without reasonable care or thought: *you would be ill-advised to sell your house now* **2** badly thought out; not or insufficiently considered: *an ill-advised plan of action* > **ill-advisedly** (ˌɪlədˈvaɪzɪdlɪ) *adv*

ill-affected *adj* (often foll by *towards*) not well disposed; disaffected

Illampu (*Spanish* iʎamˈpu) *n* one of the two peaks of Mount **Sorata**

ill-assorted *adj* badly matched; incompatible

illative (ɪˈleɪtɪv) *adj* **1** relating to inference; inferential **2** *grammar* denoting a word or morpheme used to signal inference, for example *so* or *therefore* **3** (esp in Finnish grammar) denoting a case of nouns expressing a relation of motion or direction, usually translated by *into* or *towards* ▷ *n* **4** *grammar* **4a** the illative case **4b** an illative word or speech element [c16 from LL *illātīvus* inferring, concluding] > **ilˈlatively** *adv*

Illawarra (ˌɪləˈwɒrə) *n* **1** a coastal district of E Australia, in S New South Wales. Pop: 342 700 (1991) **2** an Australian breed of shorthorn dairy cattle noted for its high milk yield and ability to survive on poor pastures

ill-bred *adj* badly brought up; lacking good manners > **ˌill-ˈbreeding** *n*

ill-considered *adj* done without due consideration; not thought out: *an ill-considered decision*

ill-defined *adj* imperfectly defined; having no clear outline

ill-disposed *adj* (often foll by *towards*) not kindly disposed

Ille-et-Vilaine (*French* ilevilɛn) *n* a department of NW France, in E Brittany. Capital: Rennes. Pop: 867 533 (1999). Area: 6992 sq km (2727 sq miles)

illegal (ɪˈliːgᵊl) *adj* **1** forbidden by law; unlawful; illicit **2** unauthorized or prohibited by a code of official or accepted rules ▷ *n* **3** a person who has entered or attempted to enter a country illegally > **ilˈlegally** *adv* > **ˌilleˈgality** *n*

illegible (ɪˈlɛdʒɪbᵊl) *adj* unable to be read or deciphered > **ilˌlegiˈbility** *or* **ilˈlegibleness** *n* > **ilˈlegibly** *adv*

illegitimate (ˌɪlɪˈdʒɪtɪmɪt) *adj* **1a** born of parents who were not married to each other at the time of birth; bastard **1b** occurring outside marriage: *of illegitimate birth* **2** illegal; unlawful **3** contrary to logic; incorrectly reasoned ▷ *n* **4** an illegitimate person; bastard > **ˌilleˈgitimacy** *or* **ˌilleˈgitimateness** *n* > **ˌilleˈgitimately** *adv*

ill-fated *adj* doomed or unlucky

ill-favoured *adj* **1** unattractive or repulsive in appearance; ugly **2** disagreeable or objectionable > **ˌill-ˈfavouredly** *adv* > **ˌill-ˈfavouredness** *n*

ill feeling *n* hostile feeling; animosity

ill-founded *adj* not founded on true or reliable premises; unsubstantiated

ill-gotten *adj* obtained dishonestly or illegally (esp in **ill-gotten gains**)

ill humour *n* a disagreeable or sullen mood; bad temper > **ˌill-ˈhumoured** *adj* > **ˌill-ˈhumouredly** *adv*

illiberal (ɪˈlɪbərəl) *adj* **1** narrow-minded; prejudiced;

Ii

bigoted; intolerant **2** not generous; mean **3** lacking in culture or refinement > **il,liber'ality** *n* > **il'liberally** *adv*
Illich ('ılıtʃ) *n* **Ivan** 1926–2002, US teacher and writer, born in Austria. His books include *Deschooling Society* (1971), *Medical Nemesis* (1975), and *In the Mirror of the Past* (1991)
illicit (ı'lısıt) *adj* **1** another word for **illegal** **2** not allowed or approved by common custom, rule, or standard: *illicit sexual relations* > **il'licitly** *adv* > **il'licitness** *n*
Illimani (*Spanish* iʎi'mani) *n* a mountain in W Bolivia, in the Andes near La Paz. Height: 6882 m (22 580 ft)
illimitable (ı'lımıtəbᵊl) *adj* limitless; boundless > **il,limita'bility** *or* **il'limitableness** *n*
Illinois (,ılı'nɔı) *n* **1** a state of the N central US, in the Midwest: consists of level prairie crossed by the Illinois and Kaskaskia Rivers; mainly agricultural. Capital: Springfield. Pop: 12 419 293 (2000). Area: 144 858 sq km (55 930 sq miles). Abbreviations: **Ill** or (with zip code) **IL** **2** a river in Illinois, flowing SW to the Mississippi. Length: 439 km (273 miles)
illiterate (ı'lıtərıt) *adj* **1** unable to read and write **2** violating accepted standards in reading and writing: *an illiterate scrawl* **3** uneducated, ignorant, or uncultured: *scientifically illiterate* ▷ *n* **4** an illiterate person > **il'literacy** *or* **il'literateness** *n* > **il'literately** *adv*
ill-judged *adj* rash; ill-advised
ill-mannered *adj* having bad manners; rude; impolite > **,ill-'manneredly** *adv*
ill-natured *adj* naturally unpleasant and mean > **,ill-'naturedly** *adv* > **,ill-'naturedness** *n*
illness ('ılnıs) *n* **1** a disease or indisposition; sickness **2** a state of ill health
illogical (ı'lɒdʒıkᵊl) *adj* **1** characterized by lack of logic; senseless or unreasonable **2** disregarding logical principles > **illogicality** (ı,lɒdʒı'kælıtı) *or* **il'logicalness** *n* > **il'logically** *adv*
ill-starred *adj* unlucky; unfortunate; ill-fated
ill temper *n* bad temper; irritability > **,ill-'tempered** *adj* > **,ill-'temperedly** *adv*
ill-timed *adj* occurring at or planned for an unsuitable time
ill-treat *vb* (*tr*) to behave cruelly or harshly towards; misuse; maltreat > **,ill-'treatment** *n*
illuminance (ı'lu:mınəns) *n* the luminous flux incident on unit area of a surface. Sometimes called: **illumination** ▷ Cf **irradiance**
illuminant (ı'lu:mınənt) *n* **1** something that provides or gives off light ▷ *adj* **2** giving off light; illuminating
illuminate *vb* (ı'lu:mı,neıt), **illuminates, illuminating, illuminated** **1** (*tr*) to throw light in or into; light up **2** (*tr*) to make easily understood; clarify **3** to adorn, decorate, or be decorated with lights **4** (*tr*) to decorate (a letter, etc) by the application of colours, gold, or silver **5** (*intr*) to become lit up ▷ *adj* (ı'lu:mınıt, -,neıt) **6** *arch* made clear or bright with light ▷ *n* (ı'lu:mınıt, -,neıt) **7** a person who claims to have special enlightenment [c16 from L *illūmināre* to light up, from *lūmen* light] > **il'lumi,nating** *adj* > **il'luminative** *adj* > **il'lumi,nator** *n*
illuminati (ı,lu:mı'nɑ:ti:) *pl n, sing* **illuminato** (-təʊ) **1** a group of persons claiming exceptional enlightenment on some subject, esp religion **2** (*cap*) any of several groups of illuminati, esp in 18th-century France and Bavaria or 16th-century Spain [c16 from L, lit.: the enlightened ones, from *illūmināre* to ILLUMINATE]
illumination (ı,lu:mı'neıʃən) *n* **1** the act of illuminating or the state of being illuminated **2** a source of light **3** (*often pl*) *chiefly Brit* a light or lights used as decoration in streets, parks, etc **4** spiritual or intellectual enlightenment; insight or understanding **5** the act of making understood; clarification **6** decoration in colours, gold, or silver used on some manuscripts **7** *physics* another name (not in technical usage) for **illuminance**
illumine (ı'lu:mın) *vb* **illumines, illumining, illumined** a literary word for **illuminate** [c14 from L *illūmināre* to make light] > **il'luminable** *adj*
ill-use *vb* ('ıl'ju:z), **ill-uses, ill-using, ill-used** **1** to use badly or cruelly; abuse; maltreat ▷ *n* ('ıl'ju:s) **2** Also: **ill-usage** harsh or cruel treatment; abuse
illusion (ı'lu:ʒən) *n* **1** a false appearance or deceptive impression of reality **2** a false or misleading perception or belief; delusion **3** *psychol* a perception that is not true to reality, having been altered subjectively in the mind of the perceiver. See also **hallucination** [c14 from L *illūsiō* deceit, from *illūdere* to sport with, from *ludus* game] > **il'lusionary** *or* **il'lusional** *adj*
illusionism (ı'lu:ʒə,nızəm) *n* **1** *philosophy* the doctrine that the external world exists only in illusory sense perceptions **2** the use of highly illusory effects in art
illusionist (ı'lu:ʒənıst) *n* **1** a person given to illusions; visionary; dreamer **2** *philosophy* a person who believes in illusionism **3** an artist who practises illusionism **4** a conjuror; magician > **il,lusion'istic** *adj*
illusory (ı'lu:sərı) *or* **illusive** (ı'lu:sıv) *adj* producing or based on illusion; deceptive or unreal > **il'lusorily** *adv* > **il'lusoriness** *n*

> USAGE *Illusive* is sometimes wrongly used where *elusive* is meant: *they fought hard, but victory remained elusive* (not *illusive*)

illust. *or* **illus.** *abbrev for:* **1** illustrated **2** illustration
illustrate ('ılə,streıt) *vb* **illustrates, illustrating, illustrated** **1** to clarify or explain by use of examples, analogy, etc **2** (*tr*) to be an example of **3** (*tr*) to explain or decorate (a book, text, etc) with pictures [c16 from L, from *lustrāre* to purify, brighten; see LUSTRUM] > **'illus,trative** *adj* > **'illus,trator** *n*
illustration (,ılə'streıʃən) *n* **1** pictorial matter used to explain or decorate a text **2** an example: *an illustration of his ability* **3** the act of illustrating or the state of being illustrated > **,illus'trational** *adj*
illustrious (ı'lʌstrıəs) *adj* **1** of great renown; famous and distinguished **2** glorious or great: *illustrious deeds* [c16 from L *illustris* bright, famous, from *illustrāre* to make light; see ILLUSTRATE] > **il'lustriously** *adv* > **il'lustriousness** *n*
ill will *n* hostile feeling; enmity; antagonism
Illyria (ı'lıərıə) *n* an ancient region of uncertain boundaries on the E shore of the Adriatic Sea, including parts of present-day Croatia, Montenegro, and Albania > **I'llyrian** *adj, n*
Illyricum (ı'lıərıkəm) *n* a Roman province founded after 168 BC, based on the coastal area of Illyria
Ilmen ('ılmən) *n* **Lake** a lake in NW Russia, in the Novgorod Region: drains through the Volkhov River into Lake Ladoga. Area: between 780 sq km (300 sq miles) and 2200 sq km (850 sq miles), according to the season
ILO *abbrev for* International Labour Organisation ▷ www.ilo.org
Iloilo (,i:ləʊ'i:ləʊ) *n* a port in the W central Philippines, on SE Panay Island. Pop: 365 820 (2000)
Ilorin (ı'lɒrın) *n* a city in W Nigeria, capital of Kwara state: agricultural trade centre. Pop: 475 800 (1996 est)
ILU *text messaging abbrev for* I love you
Ilyushin (*Russian* il'ju:ʃın) *n* **Sergei Vladimirovich** (sɛr'gɛi vladi'mi:rovıtʃ) 1894–1977, Soviet aircraft designer. He designed the dive bomber Il-2 Stormovik and the jet airliner Il-62
IM *or* **i.m.** *abbrev for:* **1** intramuscular(ly) **2** instant messaging
I'm (aım) *contraction of* I am
im- *prefix* a variant of **in-**[1] and **in-**[2] before *b*, *m*, and *p*
image ('ımıdʒ) *n* **1** a representation or likeness of a person or thing, esp in sculpture **2** an optically formed reproduction of an object, such as one formed by a lens or mirror **3** a person or thing that resembles another closely; double or copy **4** a mental picture; idea

produced by the imagination **5** the personality presented to the public by a person, organization, etc: *a politician's image* **6** the pattern of light that is focused onto the retina **7** *psychol* the mental experience of something that is not immediately present to the senses, often involving memory. See also **imagery** **8** a personification of a specified quality; epitome: *the image of good breeding* **9** a mental picture or association of ideas evoked in a literary work **10** a figure of speech such as a simile or metaphor ▷ *vb* **images, imaging, imaged** (*tr*) **11** to picture in the mind; imagine **12** to make or reflect an image of **13** to project or display on a screen, etc **14** to portray or describe **15** to be an example or epitome of; typify [C13 from OF *imagene*, from L *imāgō* copy, representation; rel. to L *imitārī* to IMITATE] > **'imageable** *adj* > **'imageless** *adj*

image converter *or* **tube** *n* an electronic device that converts an invisible image, esp one formed by X-rays, into an image that is visible on a fluorescent screen

image enhancement *n* a method of improving the definition of a video picture by a computer program which reduces the lowest grey values to black and the highest to white: used for pictures from microscopes, surveillance cameras, and scanners

image intensifier *or* **tube** *n* any of various devices for amplifying the intensity of an optical image, sometimes used in conjunction with an image converter

image orthicon *n* a television camera tube in which electrons, emitted from a surface in proportion to the intensity of the incident light, are focused onto the target causing secondary emission of electrons

image processing *n* the manipulation or modification of a digitized image, esp to improve its quality

imagery ('ɪmɪdʒrɪ, -dʒərɪ) *n, pl* **imageries** **1** figurative or descriptive language in a literary work **2** images collectively **3** *psychol* **3a** the materials or general processes of the imagination **3b** the characteristic kind of mental images formed by a particular individual. See also **image** (sense 7), **imagination** (sense 1)

image tube *n* another name for **image converter** or **image intensifier**

imaginary (ɪ'mædʒɪnərɪ, -dʒɪnrɪ) *adj* **1** existing in the imagination; unreal; illusory **2** *maths* involving or containing imaginary numbers > **im'aginarily** *adv*

imaginary number *n* any complex number of the form *a* + i*b*, where *b* is not zero and i = √−1

imagination (ɪˌmædʒɪ'neɪʃən) *n* **1** the faculty or action of producing ideas, esp mental images of what is not present or has not been experienced **2** mental creative ability **3** the ability to deal resourcefully with unexpected or unusual problems, circumstances, etc

imaginative (ɪ'mædʒɪnətɪv) *adj* **1** produced by or indicative of a creative imagination **2** having a vivid imagination > **im'aginatively** *adv* > **im'aginativeness** *n*

imagine (ɪ'mædʒɪn) *vb* **imagines, imagining, imagined** **1** (*when tr, may take a clause as object*) to form a mental image of **2** (*when tr, may take a clause as object*) to think, believe, or guess **3** (*tr; takes a clause as object*) to suppose; assume: *I imagine he'll come* **4** (*tr; takes a clause as object*) to believe without foundation: *he imagines he knows the whole story* [C14 from L *imāginārī* to fancy, picture mentally, from *imāgō* likeness; see IMAGE] > **im'aginable** *adj* > **im'aginably** *adv* > **im'aginer** *n*

imagism ('ɪmɪˌdʒɪzəm) *n* an early 20th-century poetic movement, advocating the use of ordinary speech and the precise presentation of images > **'imagist** *n, adj* > **ˌimag'istic** *adj*

imago (ɪ'meɪgəʊ) *n, pl* **imagoes** *or* **imagines** (ɪ'mædʒəˌniːz) **1** an adult sexually mature insect **2** *psychoanal* an idealized image of another person, usually a parent, carried in the unconscious [C18 NL, from L: likeness]

imam (ɪ'mɑːm) *or* **imaum** (ɪ'mɑːm, ɪ'mɔːm) *n Islam* **1** a leader of congregational prayer in a mosque **2** a caliph, as leader of a Muslim community **3** any of a succession of Muslim religious leaders regarded by their followers as divinely inspired [C17 from Ar.: leader]

imamate (ɪ'mɑːmeɪt) *n Islam* **1** the region or territory governed by an imam **2** the office, rank, or period of office of an imam

IMAX ('aɪmæks) *n trademark* a process of film projection using a giant screen on which an image approximately ten times larger than standard is projected

imbalance (ɪm'bæləns) *n* a lack of balance, as in emphasis, proportion, etc: *the political imbalance of the programme*

imbecile ('ɪmbɪˌsiːl, -ˌsaɪl) *n* **1** *psychol* a person of very low intelligence (IQ of 25 to 50) **2** *inf* an extremely stupid person; dolt ▷ *adj also* **imbecilic** (ˌɪmbɪ'sɪlɪk) **3** of or like an imbecile; mentally deficient; feeble-minded **4** stupid or senseless: *an imbecile thing to do* [C16 from L *imbēcillus* feeble (physically or mentally)] > **'imbeˌcilely** *or* **ˌimbe'cilically** *adv* > **ˌimbe'cility** *n*

imbed (ɪm'bɛd) *vb* **imbeds, imbedding, imbedded** a less common spelling of **embed**

imbibe (ɪm'baɪb) *vb* **imbibes, imbibing, imbibed** **1** to drink (esp alcoholic drinks) **2** *literary* to take in or assimilate (ideas, etc): *to imbibe the spirit of the Renaissance* **3** (*tr*) to take in as if by drinking: *to imbibe fresh air* **4** to absorb or cause to absorb liquid or moisture; assimilate or saturate [C14 from L *imbibere*, from *bibere* to drink] > **im'biber** *n*

imbizo (ɪm'biːzɒ) *n, pl* **imbizos** *S African* a meeting, esp a gathering of the Zulu people called by the king or a traditional leader [from Zulu *biza* to call or summon]

imbricate *adj* ('ɪmbrɪkɪt, -ˌkeɪt) Also: **imbricated** **1** *archit* relating to or having tiles, shingles, or slates that overlap **2** (of leaves, scales, etc) overlapping each other ▷ *vb* ('ɪmbrɪˌkeɪt), **imbricates, imbricating, imbricated** **3** (*tr*) to decorate with a repeating pattern resembling scales or overlapping tiles [C17 from L *imbricāre* to cover with overlapping tiles, from *imbrex* pantile] > **'imbricately** *adv* > **ˌimbri'cation** *n*

imbroglio (ɪm'brəʊlɪˌəʊ) *n, pl* **imbroglios** **1** a confused or perplexing political or interpersonal situation **2** *obs* a confused heap; jumble [C18 from It., from *imbrogliare* to confuse, EMBROIL]

Imbros ('ɪmbrəs) *n* a Turkish island in the NE Aegean Sea, west of the Gallipoli Peninsula: occupied by Greece (1912–14) and Britain (1914–23). Area: 280 sq km (108 sq miles). Turkish name: **Imroz**

imbrue (ɪm'bruː) *vb* **imbrues, imbruing, imbrued** (*tr*) *rare* **1** to stain, esp with blood **2** to permeate or impregnate [C15 from OF *embreuver*, from L *imbibere* to IMBIBE] > **im'bruement** *n*

imbue (ɪm'bjuː) *vb* **imbues, imbuing, imbued** (*tr; usually foll by with*) **1** to instil or inspire (with ideals, principles, etc) **2** *rare* to soak, esp with dye, etc [C16 from L *imbuere* to stain, accustom] > **im'buement** *n*

IMechE *abbrev for* Institution of Mechanical Engineers

IMF *abbrev for* International Monetary Fund
▷ www.imf.org

IMHO *text messaging abbrev for* in my humble *or* honest opinion

Imhotep (ɪm'həʊtɛp) *n* c. 2600 BC, Egyptian physician and architect. After his death he was worshipped as a god; the Greeks identified him with Asclepius

imitate ('ɪmɪˌteɪt) *vb* **imitates, imitating, imitated** (*tr*) **1** to try to follow the manner, style, etc, of or take as a model: *many writers imitated the language of Shakespeare* **2** to pretend to be or to impersonate, esp for humour; mimic **3** to make a copy or reproduction of; duplicate [C16 from L *imitārī*; see IMAGE] > **imitable** ('ɪmɪtəbᵊl) *adj* > **ˌimita'bility** *n* > **'imiˌtator** *n*

imitation (ˌɪmɪ'teɪʃən) *n* **1** the act or practice of imitating; mimicry **2** an instance or product of

Ii

imitating, such as a copy of the manner of a person; impression **3a** a copy of a genuine article; counterfeit **3b** (*as modifier*): *imitation jewellery* **4** *music* the repetition of a phrase or figure in one part after its appearance in another, as in a fugue > ˌ**imiˈtational** *adj*

imitative (ˈɪmɪtətɪv) *adj* **1** imitating or tending to copy **2** characterized by imitation **3** copying or reproducing an original, esp in an inferior manner: *imitative painting* **4** another word for **onomatopoeic** > ˈ**imitatively** *adv* > ˈ**imitativeness** *n*

Imittós (ˌimiˈtɔs) *n* a transliteration of the Modern Greek name for **Hymettus**

immaculate (ɪˈmækjʊlɪt) *adj* **1** completely clean; extremely tidy: *his clothes were immaculate* **2** completely flawless, etc: *an immaculate rendering of the symphony* **3** morally pure; free from sin or corruption **4** *biol* with no spots or markings [C15 from L, from IM- (not) + *macula* blemish] > **imˈmaculacy** *or* **imˈmaculateness** *n* > **imˈmaculately** *adv*

Immaculate Conception *n Christian theol, RC Church* the doctrine that the Virgin Mary was conceived without any stain of original sin

immanent (ˈɪmənənt) *adj* **1** existing, operating, or remaining within; inherent **2** (of God) present throughout the universe [C16 from L *immanēre* to remain in] > ˈ**immanence** *or* ˈ**immanency** *n* > ˈ**immanently** *adv* > ˈ**immanenˌtism** *n*

Immanuel *or* **Emmanuel** (ɪˈmænjʊəl) *n Bible* the child whose birth was foretold by Isaiah (Isaiah 7:14) and who in Christian tradition is identified with Jesus [from Heb. *ʿimmānūʾel*, lit.: God with us]

immaterial (ˌɪməˈtɪərɪəl) *adj* **1** of no real importance; inconsequential **2** not formed of matter; incorporeal; spiritual > ˌ**immaˌteriˈality** *n* > ˌ**immaˈterially** *adv*

immaterialism (ˌɪməˈtɪərɪəˌlɪzəm) *n philosophy* the doctrine that the material world exists only in the mind > ˌ**immaˈterialist** *n*

immature (ˌɪməˈtjʊə, -ˈtʃʊə) *adj* **1** not fully grown or developed **2** deficient in maturity; lacking wisdom, insight, emotional stability, etc > ˌ**immaˈturely** *adv* > ˌ**immaˈturity** *or* ˌ**immaˈtureness** *n*

immeasurable (ɪˈmɛʒərəbᵊl) *adj* incapable of being measured, esp by virtue of great size; limitless > **imˌmeasuraˈbility** *or* **imˈmeasurableness** *n* > **imˈmeasurably** *adv*

immediate (ɪˈmiːdɪət) *adj* (*usually prenominal*) **1** taking place or accomplished without delay: *an immediate reaction* **2** closest or most direct in effect or relationship: *the immediate cause of his downfall* **3** having no intervening medium; direct in effect: *an immediate influence* **4** contiguous in space, time, or relationship: *our immediate neighbour* **5** present; current: *the immediate problem is food* **6** *philosophy* of or relating to a concept that is directly known or intuited [C16 from Med. L, from L IM- (not) + *mediāre* to be in the middle; see MEDIATE] > **imˈmediacy** *or* **imˈmediateness** *n*

immediately (ɪˈmiːdɪətlɪ) *adv* **1** without delay or intervention; at once; instantly **2** very closely or directly: *this immediately concerns you* **3** near or close by: *somewhere immediately in this area* ▷ *conj* **4** (*subordinating*) *chiefly Brit* as; as soon as: *immediately he opened the door, there was a gust of wind*

immemorial (ˌɪmɪˈmɔːrɪəl) *adj* originating in the distant past; ancient (postpositive in **time immemorial**) [C17 from Med. L, from L IM- (not) + *memoria* MEMORY] > ˌ**immeˈmorially** *adv*

immense (ɪˈmɛns) *adj* **1** unusually large; huge; vast **2** without limits; immeasurable **3** *inf* very good; excellent [C15 from L *immensus*, lit.: unmeasured, from IM- (not) + *mētīrī* to measure] > **imˈmensely** *adv* > **imˈmenseness** *n*

immensity (ɪˈmɛnsɪtɪ) *n, pl* **immensities** **1** the state of being immense; vastness; enormity **2** enormous expanse, distance, or volume **3** *inf* a huge amount: *an immensity of wealth*

immerse (ɪˈmɜːs) *vb* **immerses, immersing, immersed** (*tr*) **1** (often foll by *in*) to plunge or dip into liquid **2** (*often passive; often foll by in*) to involve deeply; engross: *to immerse oneself in a problem* **3** to baptize by dipping the whole body into water [C17 from L *immergere*, from IM- (in) + *mergere* to dip] > **imˈmersible** *adj* > **imˈmersion** *n*

immerser (ɪˈmɜːsə) *n* an informal term for **immersion heater**

immersion heater *n* an electrical device, usually thermostatically controlled, for heating the liquid in which it is immersed, esp as a fixture in a domestic hot-water tank

immersive (ɪˈmɜːsɪv) *adj* providing information or stimulation for a number of senses, not only sight and sound: *immersive television sets*

immigrant (ˈɪmɪɡrənt) *n* **1a** a person who immigrates **1b** (*as modifier*): *an immigrant community* **2** *Brit* a person who has been settled in a country of which he or she is not a native for less than ten years

immigrate (ˈɪmɪˌɡreɪt) *vb* **immigrates, immigrating, immigrated** **1** (*intr*) to come to a place or country of which one is not a native in order to settle there **2** (*tr*) to introduce or bring in as an immigrant [C17 from L *immigrāre* to go into] > ˈ**immiˌgrator** *n* > ˈ**immiˌgratory** *adj*

immigration (ˌɪmɪˈɡreɪʃən) *n* **1** the movement of non-native people into a country in order to settle there **2** the part of a port, airport, etc where government employees examine the passports, visas, etc of foreign nationals entering the country

imminent (ˈɪmɪnənt) *adj* **1** liable to happen soon; impending **2** *obs* overhanging [C16 from L *imminēre* to project over; rel. to *mons* mountain] > ˈ**imminence** *n* > ˈ**imminently** *adv*

Immingham (ˈɪmɪŋəm) *n* a port in NE England, in North East Lincolnshire unitary authority, Lincolnshire: docks opened in 1912, principally for the exporting of coal; now handles chiefly bulk materials, esp imported iron ore. Pop: 12 278 (1991)

immiscible (ɪˈmɪsɪbᵊl) *adj* (of liquids) incapable of being mixed: *oil and water are immiscible* > **imˌmisciˈbility** *n* > **imˈmiscibly** *adv*

immitigable (ɪˈmɪtɪɡəbᵊl) *adj rare* unable to be mitigated > **imˌmitigaˈbility** *n* > **imˈmitigably** *adv*

immobile (ɪˈməʊbaɪl) *adj* **1** not moving; motionless **2** not able to move or be moved; fixed > **immobility** (ˌɪməʊˈbɪlɪtɪ) *n*

immobilize *or* **immobilise** (ɪˈməʊbɪˌlaɪz) *vb* **immobilizes, immobilizing, immobilized** *or* **immobilises, immobilising, immobilised** (*tr*) **1** to make immobile: *to immobilize a car* **2** *finance* to convert (circulating capital) into fixed capital > **imˌmobiliˈzation** *or* **imˌmobiliˈsation** *n* > **imˈmobiˌlizer** *or* **imˈmobiˌliser** *n*

immoderate (ɪˈmɒdərɪt, ɪˈmɒdrɪt) *adj* lacking in moderation; excessive: *immoderate demands* > **imˈmoderately** *adv* > **imˌmoderˈation** *or* **imˈmoderateness** *n*

immodest (ɪˈmɒdɪst) *adj* **1** indecent, esp with regard to sexual propriety; improper **2** bold, impudent, or shameless > **imˈmodestly** *adv* > **imˈmodesty** *n*

immolate (ˈɪməʊˌleɪt) *vb* **immolates, immolating, immolated** (*tr*) **1** to kill or offer as a sacrifice, esp by fire **2** *literary* to sacrifice (something highly valued) [C16 from L *immolāre* to sprinkle an offering with sacrificial meal, sacrifice; see MILL] > ˌ**immoˈlation** *n* > ˈ**immoˌlator** *n*

immoral (ɪˈmɒrəl) *adj* **1** transgressing accepted moral rules; corrupt **2** sexually dissolute; profligate or promiscuous **3** unscrupulous or unethical: *immoral trading* **4** tending to corrupt or resulting from corruption: *immoral earnings* > **imˈmorally** *adv*

USAGE See at **amoral**

immorality (ˌɪməˈrælɪtɪ) *n, pl* **immoralities** **1** the quality or state of being immoral **2** immoral behaviour, esp in sexual matters; licentiousness; promiscuity **3** an immoral act

immortal (ɪˈmɔːtᵊl) *adj* **1** not subject to death or decay; having perpetual life **2** having everlasting fame; remembered throughout time **3** everlasting; perpetual; constant **4** of or relating to immortal beings or concepts ▷ *n* **5** an immortal being **6** (*often pl*) a person who is remembered enduringly, esp an author > ˌ**immorˈtality** *n* > **imˈmortally** *adv*

immortalize *or* **immortalise** (ɪˈmɔːtəˌlaɪz) *vb* **immortalizes, immortalizing, immortalized** *or* **immortalises, immortalising, immortalised** (*tr*) **1** to give everlasting fame to, as by treating in a literary work: *Macbeth was immortalized by Shakespeare* **2** to give immortality to > **imˌmortaliˈzation** *or* **imˌmortaliˈsation** *n* > **imˈmortalˌizer** *or* **imˈmortalˌiser** *n*

immortelle (ˌɪmɔːˈtɛl) *n* any of various composite plants that retain their colour when dried. Also called: **everlasting** [C19 from F (*fleur*) *immortelle* everlasting (flower)]

immovable *or* **immoveable** (ɪˈmuːvəbᵊl) *adj* **1** unable to move or be moved; immobile **2** unable to be diverted from one's intentions; steadfast **3** unaffected by feeling; impassive **4** unchanging; unalterable **5** (of feasts, etc) on the same date every year **6** *law* **6a** (of property) not liable to be removed; fixed **6b** of or relating to immovable property > **imˌmovaˈbility, imˌmoveaˈbility** *or* **imˈmovableness, imˈmoveableness** *n* > **imˈmovably** *or* **imˈmoveably** *adv*

immune (ɪˈmjuːn) *adj* **1** protected against a specific disease by inoculation or as the result of innate or acquired resistance **2** relating to or conferring immunity: *an immune body* (see **antibody**) **3** (*usually postpositive*; foll by *to*) unsusceptible (to) or secure (against): *immune to inflation* **4** exempt from obligation, penalty, etc ▷ *n* **5** an immune person or animal [C15 from L *immūnis* exempt from a public service]

immune response *n* the reaction of an organism's body to foreign materials (antigens), including the production of antibodies

immunity (ɪˈmjuːnɪtɪ) *n, pl* **immunities** **1** the ability of an organism to resist disease, either through the activities of specialized blood cells or antibodies produced by them in response to natural exposure or inoculation (**active immunity**) or by the injection of antiserum or the transfer of antibodies from a mother to her baby via the placenta or breast milk (**passive immunity**) See also **acquired immunity, natural immunity** **2** freedom from obligation or duty, esp exemption from tax, legal liability, etc

immunize *or* **immunise** (ˈɪmjʊˌnaɪz) *vb* **immunizes, immunizing, immunized** *or* **immunises, immunising, immunised** (*tr*) to make immune, esp by inoculation > ˌ**immuniˈzation** *or* ˌ**immuniˈsation** *n* > ˈ**immuˌnizer** *or* ˈ**immuˌniser** *n*

immuno- *or before a vowel* **immun-** *combining form* indicating immunity or immune: *immunology*

immunoassay (ˌɪmjʊnəʊˈæseɪ) *n immunol* a technique of identifying a substance by its ability to bind to an antibody

immunocompromised (ˌɪmjʊnəʊˈkɒmprəˌmaɪzd) *adj* having an impaired immune system and therefore incapable of an effective immune response, usually as a result of disease, such as AIDS, that damages the immune system

immunodeficiency (ˌɪmjʊnəʊdɪˈfɪʃənsɪ) *n* a deficiency in or breakdown of a person's immune system

immunogenic (ˌɪmjʊnəʊˈdʒɛnɪk) *adj* causing or producing immunity or an immune response > ˌ**immunoˈgenically** *adv*

immunoglobulin (ˌɪmjʊnəʊˈglɒbjʊlɪn) *n* any of five classes of proteins, all of which show antibody activity

immunology (ˌɪmjʊˈnɒlədʒɪ) *n* the branch of biological science concerned with the study of immunity > **immunologic** (ˌɪmjʊnəˈlɒdʒɪk) *or* ˌ**immunoˈlogical** *adj* > ˌ**immunoˈlogically** *adv* > ˌ**immuˈnologist** *n*

immunoreaction (ɪˌmjuːnəʊrɪˈækʃən) *n* the reaction between an antigen and its antibody

immunosuppression (ˌɪmjʊnəʊsəˈprɛʃən) *n* medical suppression of the body's immune system, esp in order to reduce the likelihood of rejection of a transplanted organ > ˌ**immunosupˈpressant** *n, adj*

immunosuppressive (ˌɪmjʊnəʊsəˈprɛsɪv) *n* **1** any drug that lessens the body's rejection, esp of a transplanted organ ▷ *adj* **2** of or relating to such a drug

immunotherapy (ˌɪmjʊnəʊˈθɛrəpɪ) *n* the treatment of disease by stimulating or modifying the immune response > **immunotherapeutic** (ˌɪmjʊnəʊˌθɛrəˈpjuːtɪk) *adj*

immure (ɪˈmjʊə) *vb* **immures, immuring, immured** (*tr*) **1** *arch or literary* to enclose within or as if within walls; imprison **2** to shut (oneself) away from society [C16 from Med. L, from L IM- (in) + *mūrus* wall] > **imˈmurement** *n*

immutable (ɪˈmjuːtəbᵊl) *adj* unchanging through time; unalterable; ageless: *immutable laws* > **imˌmutaˈbility** *or* **imˈmutableness** *n*

Imo (ˈiːməʊ) *n* a state of SE Nigeria, formed in 1976 from part of East-Central State. Capital: Owerri. Pop: 2 779 028 (1995 est). Area: 5530 sq km (2135 sq miles)

IMO *abbrev for* International Maritime Organization

imp (ɪmp) *n* **1** a small demon or devil; mischievous sprite **2** a mischievous child ▷ *vb* **3** (*tr*) *falconry* to insert new feathers in order to repair (the wing of a falcon) [OE *impa* bud, graft, hence offspring, child, from *impian* to graft]

imp. *abbrev for:* **1** imperative **2** imperfect **3** imperial

impact *n* (ˈɪmpækt) **1** the act of one body, etc, striking another; collision **2** the force with which one thing hits another **3** the impression made by an idea, social group, etc ▷ *vb* (ɪmˈpækt) **4** to drive or press (an object) firmly into (another object, thing, etc) or (of two objects) to be driven or pressed firmly together **5** to have an impact or strong effect (on) [C18 from L *impactus* pushed against, fastened on, from *impingere* to thrust at, from *pangere* to drive in] > **imˈpaction** *n*

Ii

impacted (ɪmˈpæktɪd) *adj* **1** (of a tooth) unable to erupt, esp because of being wedged against another tooth below the gum **2** (of a fracture) having the jagged broken ends wedged into each other

impair (ɪmˈpɛə) *vb* (*tr*) to reduce or weaken in strength, quality, etc: *his hearing was impaired by an accident* [C14 from OF *empeirer* to make worse, from LL, from L *pēior* worse; see PEJORATIVE] > **imˈpairable** *adj* > **imˈpairer** *n* > **imˈpairment** *n*

impala (ɪmˈpɑːlə) *n, pl* **impalas** *or* **impala** an antelope of southern and eastern Africa, having lyre-shaped horns and able to move with enormous leaps [from Zulu]

impale *or* **empale** (ɪmˈpeɪl) *vb* **impales, impaling, impaled** (*tr*) **1** (often foll by *on, upon,* or *with*) to pierce with a sharp instrument: *they impaled his severed head on a spear* **2** *heraldry* to charge (a shield) with two coats of arms placed side by side [C16 from Med. L, from L IM- (in) + *pālus* PALE²] > **imˈpalement** *or* **emˈpalement** *n*

impalpable (ɪmˈpælpəbᵊl) *adj* **1** imperceptible, esp to the touch: *impalpable shadows* **2** difficult to understand; abstruse > **imˌpalpaˈbility** *n* > **imˈpalpably** *adv*

impanel (ɪmˈpænᵊl) *vb* **impanels, impanelling, impanelled** *or US* **impanels, impaneling, impaneled** a variant spelling (esp US) of **empanel** > **imˈpanelment** *n*

impart (ɪmˈpɑːt) *vb* (*tr*) **1** to communicate (information, etc); relate **2** to give or bestow (an abstract quality): *to impart wisdom* [C15 from OF, from L, from IM- (in) + *partīre* to share, from *pars* part] > **imˈpartable** *adj* > ˌ**imparˈtation** *or* **imˈpartment** *n*

impartial (ɪmˈpɑːʃəl) *adj* not prejudiced towards or

against any particular side; fair; unbiased > **im,parti'ality** *or* **im'partialness** *n* > **im'partially** *adv*

impartible (ɪm'pɑːtəbᵊl) *adj law* (of land, an estate, etc) incapable of partition; indivisible > **im,parti'bility** *n* > **im'partibly** *adv*

impassable (ɪm'pɑːsəbᵊl) *adj* (of terrain, roads, etc) not able to be travelled through or over > **im,passa'bility** *or* **im'passableness** *n* > **im'passably** *adv*

impasse (æm'pɑːs, 'æmpɑːs) *n* a situation in which progress is blocked; an insurmountable difficulty; stalemate [C19 from F; see IM-, PASS]

impassible (ɪm'pæsəbᵊl) *adj rare* **1** not susceptible to pain or injury **2** impassive or unmoved > **im,passi'bility** *or* **im'passibleness** *n* > **im'passibly** *adv*

impassion (ɪm'pæʃən) *vb (tr)* to arouse the passions of; inflame

impassioned (ɪm'pæʃənd) *adj* filled with passion; fiery; inflamed: *an impassioned appeal* > **im'passionedly** *adv* > **im'passionedness** *n*

impassive (ɪm'pæsɪv) *adj* **1** not revealing or affected by emotion; reserved **2** calm; serene; imperturbable > **im'passively** *adv* > **im'passiveness** *or* **impassivity** (,ɪmpæ'sɪvɪtɪ) *n*

impasto (ɪm'pæstəʊ) *n* **1** paint applied thickly, so that brush marks are evident **2** the technique of painting in this way [C18 from It., from *impastare*, from *pasta* PASTE]

impatience (ɪm'peɪʃəns) *n* **1** lack of patience; intolerance of or irritability with anything that impedes or delays **2** restless desire for change and excitement

impatiens (ɪm'peɪʃɪ,ɛnz) *n, pl* **impatiens** a plant with explosive pods, such as balsam, touch-me-not, and busy Lizzie [C18 NL from L: impatient; from the fact that the ripe pods burst open when touched]

impatient (ɪm'peɪʃənt) *adj* **1** lacking patience; easily irritated at delay, etc **2** exhibiting lack of patience **3** *(postpositive;* foll by *of)* intolerant (of) or indignant (at): *impatient of indecision* **4** *(postpositive;* often foll by *for)* restlessly eager (for *or* to do something) > **im'patiently** *adv*

impeach (ɪm'piːtʃ) *vb (tr)* **1** *criminal law* to bring a charge or accusation against **2** *Brit criminal law* to accuse of a crime against the state **3** *chiefly US* to charge (a public official) with an offence committed in office **4** to challenge or question (a person's honesty, etc) [C14 from OF, from LL *impedicāre* to entangle, catch, from L IM- (in) + *pedica* a fetter, from *pēs* foot] > **im'peachable** *adj* > **im'peachment** *n*

impeccable (ɪm'pɛkəbᵊl) *adj* **1** without flaw or error; faultless: *an impeccable record* **2** *rare* incapable of sinning [C16 from LL *impeccābilis* sinless, from L IM- (not) + *peccāre* to sin] > **im,pecca'bility** *n* > **im'peccably** *adv*

impecunious (,ɪmpɪ'kjuːnɪəs) *adj* without money; penniless [C16 from IM- (not) + from L *pecūniōsus* wealthy, from *pecūnia* money] > **,impe'cuniously** *adv* > **,impe'cuniousness** *or* **impecuniosity** (,ɪmpɪkjuːnɪ'ɒsɪtɪ) *n*

impedance (ɪm'piːdᵊns) *n* **1** a measure of the opposition to the flow of an alternating current equal to the square root of the sum of the squares of the resistance and the reactance, expressed in ohms **2** the ratio of the sound pressure in a medium to the rate of alternating flow through a specified surface due to the sound wave **3** the ratio of the mechanical force to the velocity of the resulting vibration

impede (ɪm'piːd) *vb* **impedes, impeding, impeded** *(tr)* to restrict or retard in action, progress, etc; obstruct [C17 from L *impedīre* to hinder, lit.: shackle the feet, from *pēs* foot] > **im'peder** *n* > **im'pedingly** *adv*

impediment (ɪm'pɛdɪmənt) *n* **1** a hindrance or obstruction **2** a physical defect, esp one of speech, such as a stammer **3** *(pl* **impediments** *or* **impedimenta** (-'mɛntə)) *law* an obstruction to the making of a contract, esp one of marriage > **im,pedi'mental** *or* **im,pedi'mentary** *adj*

impedimenta (ɪm,pɛdɪ'mɛntə) *pl n* **1** any objects that impede progress, esp the baggage and equipment carried by an army **2** a plural of **impediment** (sense 3) [C16 from L, pl of *impedīmentum* hindrance; see IMPEDE]

impel (ɪm'pɛl) *vb* **impels, impelling, impelled** *(tr)* **1** to urge or force (a person) to an action; constrain or motivate **2** to push, drive, or force into motion [C15 from L *impellere* to push against, drive forward] > **im'pellent** *n, adj*

impeller (ɪm'pɛlə) *n* the vaned rotating disc of a centrifugal pump, compressor, etc

impend (ɪm'pɛnd) *vb (intr)* **1** (esp of something threatening) to be imminent **2** (foll by *over*) *Rare.* to be suspended; hang [C16 from L *impendēre* to overhang, from *pendēre* to hang] > **im'pendence** *or* **im'pendency** *n*

impending (ɪm'pɛndɪŋ) *adj* about to happen; imminent

impenetrable (ɪm'pɛnɪtrəbᵊl) *adj* **1** incapable of being pierced through or penetrated: *an impenetrable forest* **2** incapable of being understood; incomprehensible **3** incapable of being seen through: *impenetrable gloom* **4** not susceptible to ideas, influence, etc: *impenetrable ignorance* **5** *physics* (of a body) incapable of occupying the same space as another body > **im,penetra'bility** *n* > **im'penetrableness** *n* > **im'penetrably** *adv*

impenitent (ɪm'pɛnɪtənt) *adj* not sorry or penitent; unrepentant > **im'penitence, im'penitency,** *or* **im'penitentness** *n* > **im'penitently** *adv*

imperative (ɪm'pɛrətɪv) *adj* **1** extremely urgent or important; essential **2** peremptory or authoritative: *an imperative tone of voice* **3** Also: **imperatival** (ɪm,pɛrə'taɪvᵊl) *grammar* denoting a mood of verbs used in giving orders, making requests, etc ▷ *n* **4** something that is urgent or essential **5** an order or command **6** *grammar* **6a** the imperative mood **6b** a verb in this mood [C16 from LL, from L *imperāre* to command] > **im'peratively** *adv* > **im'perativeness** *n*

imperator (,ɪmpə'rɑːtɔː) *n* (in ancient Rome) a title bestowed upon generals and, later, emperors [C16 from L: commander, from *imperāre* to command] > **imperatorial** (ɪm,pɛrə'tɔːrɪəl) *adj* > **,impe'rator,ship** *n*

imperceptible (,ɪmpə'sɛptɪbᵊl) *adj* too slight, subtle, gradual, etc, to be perceived > **,imper,cepti'bility** *or* **,imper'ceptibleness** *n* > **,imper'ceptibly** *adv*

imperceptive (,ɪmpə'sɛptɪv) *adj, also* **impercipient** (,ɪmpə'sɪpɪənt) lacking in perception; obtuse > **,imper'ception** *n* > **,imper'ceptively** *adv* > **,imper'ceptiveness** *or* **,imper'cipience** *n*

imperf. *abbrev for:* **1** Also: **impf** imperfect **2** (of stamps) imperforate

imperfect (ɪm'pɜːfɪkt) *adj* **1** exhibiting or characterized by faults, mistakes, etc; defective **2** not complete or finished; deficient **3** *grammar* denoting a tense of verbs used most commonly in describing continuous or repeated past actions or events **4** *law* legally unenforceable **5** *music* **5a** proceeding to the dominant from the tonic, subdominant, or any chord other than the dominant **5b** of or relating to all intervals other than the fourth, fifth, and octave ▷ Cf **perfect** (sense 9) ▷ *n* **6** *grammar* **6a** the imperfect tense **6b** a verb in this tense > **im'perfectly** *adv* > **im'perfectness** *n*

imperfection (,ɪmpə'fɛkʃən) *n* **1** the condition or quality of being imperfect **2** a fault or defect

imperfective (,ɪmpə'fɛktɪv) *grammar* ▷ *adj* **1** denoting an aspect of the verb to indicate that the action is in progress without regard to its completion ▷ Cf **perfective** ▷ *n* **2a** the imperfective aspect of a verb **2b** a verb in this aspect > **,imper'fectively** *adv*

imperforate (ɪm'pɜːfərɪt, -,reɪt) *adj* **1** not perforated **2** (of a postage stamp) not provided with perforation or any other means of separation **3** *anat* without the normal opening > **im,perfo'ration** *n*

imperial (ɪmˈpɪərɪəl) *adj* **1** of or relating to an empire, emperor, or empress **2** characteristic of an emperor; majestic; commanding **3** exercising supreme authority; imperious **4** (esp of products) of a superior size or quality **5** (*usually prenominal*) (of weights, measures, etc) conforming to standards legally established in Great Britain ▷ *n* **6** a book size, esp 7½ by 11 inches or 11 by 15 inches **7** a size of writing paper, 23 by 31 inches (US and Canad) or 22 by 30 inches (Brit) **8** *US* **8a** the top of a carriage **8b** a luggage case carried there **9** a small tufted beard popularized by the French emperor Napoleon III **10** a wine bottle holding the equivalent of eight normal bottles [c14 from LL, from L *imperium* command, authority, empire] > **imˈperially** *adv* > **imˈperialness** *n*

imperialism (ɪmˈpɪərɪəˌlɪzəm) *n* **1** the policy or practice of extending a state's rule over other territories **2** the extension or attempted extension of authority, influence, power, etc, by any person, country, institution, etc: *cultural imperialism* **3** a system of imperial government or rule by an emperor **4** the spirit, character, authority, etc, of an empire > **imˈperialist** *adj, n* > **imˌperialˈistic** *adj* > **imˌperialˈistically** *adv*

imperil (ɪmˈpɛrɪl) *vb* **imperils, imperilling, imperilled** *or US* **imperils, imperiling, imperiled** (*tr*) to place in danger or jeopardy; endanger > **imˈperilment** *n*

imperious (ɪmˈpɪərɪəs) *adj* **1** domineering; overbearing **2** *rare* urgent [c16 from L, from *imperium* command, power] > **imˈperiously** *adv* > **imˈperiousness** *n*

imperishable (ɪmˈpɛrɪʃəbᵊl) *adj* **1** not subject to decay or deterioration **2** not likely to be forgotten: *imperishable truths* > **imˌperishaˈbility** *or* **imˈperishableness** *n* > **imˈperishably** *adv*

impermanent (ɪmˈpɜːmənənt) *adj* not permanent; fleeting > **imˈpermanence** *or* **imˈpermanency** *n* > **imˈpermanently** *adv*

impermeable (ɪmˈpɜːmɪəbᵊl) *adj* (of a substance) not allowing the passage of a fluid through interstices; not permeable > **imˌpermeaˈbility** *or* **imˈpermeableness** *n* > **imˈpermeably** *adv*

impermissible (ˌɪmpəˈmɪsɪbᵊl) *adj* not permissible; not allowed > **ˌimperˌmissiˈbility** *n*

impersonal (ɪmˈpɜːsənᵊl) *adj* **1** without reference to any individual person; objective: *an impersonal assessment* **2** devoid of human warmth or sympathy; cold: *an impersonal manner* **3** not having human characteristics: *an impersonal God* **4** *grammar* (of a verb) having no logical subject: *it is raining* **5** *grammar* (of a pronoun) not denoting a person > **imˌpersonˈality** *n* > **imˈpersonally** *adv*

impersonalize *or* **impersonalise** (ɪmˈpɜːsənəˌlaɪz) *vb* **impersonalizes, impersonalizing, impersonalized** *or* **impersonalises, impersonalising, impersonalised** (*tr*) to make impersonal, esp to rid of such human characteristics as sympathy, etc; dehumanize > **imˌpersonaliˈzation** *or* **imˌpersonaliˈsation** *n*

impersonate (ɪmˈpɜːsəˌneɪt) *vb* **impersonates, impersonating, impersonated** (*tr*) **1** to pretend to be (another person) **2** to imitate the character, mannerisms, etc, of (another person) **3** *rare* to play the part or character of **4** an archaic word for **personify** > **imˌpersonˈation** *n* > **imˈpersonˌator** *n*

impertinence (ɪmˈpɜːtɪnəns) *or* **impertinency** *n* **1** disrespectful behaviour or language; rudeness; insolence **2** an impertinent act, gesture, etc **3** *rare* lack of pertinence; irrelevance; inappropriateness

impertinent (ɪmˈpɜːtɪnənt) *adj* **1** rude; insolent; impudent **2** irrelevant or inappropriate [c14 from L *impertinēns* not belonging, from L IM- (not) + *pertinēre* to be relevant; see PERTAIN] > **imˈpertinently** *adv*

imperturbable (ˌɪmpɜːˈtɜːbəbᵊl) *adj* not easily perturbed; calm; unruffled > **ˌimperˌturbaˈbility** *or* **ˌimperˈturbableness** *n* > **ˌimperˈturbably** *adv*

impervious (ɪmˈpɜːvɪəs) *or* **imperviable** *adj* **1** not able to be penetrated, as by water, light, etc; impermeable **2** (*often postpositive*; foll by *to*) not able to be influenced (by) or not receptive (to): *impervious to argument* > **imˈperviously** *adv* > **imˈperviousness** *n*

impetigo (ˌɪmpɪˈtaɪgəʊ) *n* a contagious pustular skin disease [c16 from L: scabby eruption, from *impetere* to assail; see IMPETUS; for form, cf. VERTIGO] > **impetiginous** (ˌɪmpɪˈtɪdʒɪnəs) *adj*

impetuous (ɪmˈpɛtjʊəs) *adj* **1** liable to act without consideration; rash; impulsive **2** resulting from or characterized by rashness or haste **3** *poetic* moving with great force or violence; rushing: *the impetuous stream hurtled down the valley* [c14 from LL *impetuōsus* violent; see IMPETUS] > **imˈpetuously** *adv* > **imˈpetuousness** *or* **impetuosity** (ɪmˌpɛtjʊˈɒsɪtɪ) *n*

impetus (ˈɪmpɪtəs) *n, pl* **impetuses 1** an impelling movement or force; incentive or impulse; stimulus **2** *physics* the force that sets a body in motion or that tends to resist changes in a body's motion [c17 from L: attack, from *impetere* to assail, from IM- (in) + *petere* to make for, seek out]

Imphal (ɪmˈfɑːl, ˈɪmfəl) *n* a city in NE India, capital of Manipur Territory, on the Manipur River: formerly the seat of the Manipur kings: site of a major Anglo-Indian victory over the Japanese (1944), which was a turning point in the British recovery of Burma (now called Myanmar). Pop: 198 535 (1991)

impi (ˈɪmpɪ) *n, pl* **impi** *or* **impies** a group of Bantu warriors [c19 from Zulu]

impiety (ɪmˈpaɪɪtɪ) *n, pl* **impieties 1** lack of reverence or proper respect for a god **2** any lack of proper respect **3** an impious act

impinge (ɪmˈpɪndʒ) *vb* **impinges, impinging, impinged 1** (*intr; usually foll by on or upon*) to encroach or infringe; trespass: *to impinge on someone's time* **2** (*intr; usually foll by on, against, or upon*) to collide (with); strike [c16 from L *impingere* to drive at, dash against, from *pangere* to fasten, drive in] > **imˈpingement** *n* > **imˈpinger** *n*

Ii

impious (ˈɪmpɪəs) *adj* **1** lacking piety or reverence for a god **2** lacking respect; undutiful > **ˈimpiously** *adv* > **ˈimpiousness** *n*

impish (ˈɪmpɪʃ) *adj* of or like an imp; mischievous > **ˈimpishly** *adv* > **ˈimpishness** *n*

implacable (ɪmˈplækəbᵊl) *adj* **1** incapable of being placated or pacified; unappeasable **2** inflexible; intractable > **imˌplacaˈbility** *n* > **imˈplacably** *adv*

implant *vb* (ɪmˈplɑːnt) (*tr*) **1** to inculcate; instil: *to implant sound moral principles* **2** to plant or embed; infix; entrench **3** *surgery* to graft or insert (a tissue, hormone, etc) into the body ▷ *n* (ˈɪmplɑːnt) **4** anything implanted, esp surgically, such as a tissue graft or hormone > **ˌimplanˈtation** *n*

implausible (ɪmˈplɔːzəbᵊl) *adj* not plausible; provoking disbelief; unlikely > **imˌplausiˈbility** *or* **imˈplausibleness** *n* > **imˈplausibly** *adv*

implement *n* (ˈɪmplɪmənt) **1** a piece of equipment; tool or utensil: *gardening implements* **2** a means to achieve a purpose; agent ▷ *vb* (ˈɪmplɪˌmɛnt) (*tr*) **3** to carry out; put into action: *to implement a plan* **4** *rare* to supply with tools [c17 from LL *implēmentum*, lit.: a filling up, from L *implēre* to fill up, satisfy, fulfil] > **ˌimpleˈmental** *adj* > **ˌimplemenˈtation** *n*

implicate (ˈɪmplɪˌkeɪt) *vb* **implicates, implicating, implicated** (*tr*) **1** to show to be involved, esp in a crime **2** to imply: *his protest implicated censure by the authorities* **3** *rare* to entangle [c16 from L *implicāre* to involve, from *plicāre* to fold] > **implicative** (ɪmˈplɪkətɪv) *adj* > **imˈplicatively** *adv*

implication (ˌɪmplɪˈkeɪʃən) *n* **1** the act of implicating **2** something that is implied **3** *logic* a relation between two propositions, such that the second can be logically deduced from the first

implicit (ɪmˈplɪsɪt) *adj* **1** not explicit; implied; indirect

2 absolute and unreserved; unquestioning: *implicit trust* 3 (when *postpositive*, foll by *in*) contained or inherent: *to bring out the anger implicit in the argument* [C16 from L *implicitus*, var. of *implicātus* interwoven; see IMPLICATE] > **im'plicitly** *adv* > **im'plicitness** *n*

implied (ɪm'plaɪd) *adj* hinted at or suggested; not directly expressed: *an implied criticism*

implode (ɪm'pləʊd) *vb* **implodes, imploding, imploded** to collapse inwards ▷ Cf **explode** [C19 from IM- + (EX)PLODE]

implore (ɪm'plɔː) *vb* **implores, imploring, implored** (*tr*) to beg or ask (someone) earnestly (to do something); plead with; beseech; supplicate [C16 from L *implōrāre*, from IM- + *plōrāre* to bewail] > ,**implo'ration** *n* > **im'ploratory** *adj* > **im'ploringly** *adv*

imply (ɪm'plaɪ) *vb* **implies, implying, implied** (*tr; may take a clause as object*) 1 to express or indicate by a hint; suggest 2 to suggest or involve as a necessary consequence [C14 from OF *emplier*, from L; see IMPLICATE]

USAGE See at **infer**

impolder (ɪm'pəʊldə) *or* **empolder** *vb rare* to make into a polder; reclaim (land) from the sea [C19 from Du. *inpolderen*, see IN-², POLDER]

impolite (,ɪmpə'laɪt) *adj* discourteous; rude > ,**impo'litely** *adv* > ,**impo'liteness** *n*

impolitic (ɪm'pɒlɪtɪk) *adj* not politic or expedient; unwise > **im'politicly** *adv*

imponderable (ɪm'pɒndərəbᵊl, -drəbᵊl) *adj* 1 unable to be weighed or assessed ▷ *n* 2 something difficult or impossible to assess > **im,pondera'bility** *or* **im'ponderableness** *n* > **im'ponderably** *adv*

import *vb* (ɪm'pɔːt, 'ɪmpɔːt) 1 to buy or bring in (goods or services) from a foreign country 2 (*tr*) to bring in from an outside source: *to import foreign words into the language* 3 *rare* to signify; mean: *to import doom* ▷ *n* ('ɪmpɔːt) 4 (*often pl*) 4a goods or services that are bought from foreign countries 4b (*as modifier*): *an import licence* 5 importance: *a man of great import* 6 meaning 7 *inf* a sportsman or -woman who is not native to the country in which he or she plays [C15 from L *importāre* to carry in] > **im'portable** *adj* > **im'porter** *n*

importance (ɪm'pɔːtᵊns) *n* 1 the state of being important; significance 2 social status; standing; esteem: *a man of importance* 3 *obs* 3a meaning or signification 3b an important matter 3c importunity

important (ɪm'pɔːtᵊnt) *adj* 1 of great significance or value; outstanding 2 of social significance; notable; eminent; esteemed: *an important man in the town* 3 (when *postpositive*, usually foll by *to*) of great concern (to); valued highly (by): *your wishes are important to me* [C16 from OIt., from Med. L *importāre* to signify, be of consequence, from L: to carry in] > **im'portantly** *adv*

USAGE The use of *more importantly* as in *more importantly, the local council is opposed to this proposal* has become very common, but many people still prefer to use *more important*

importation (,ɪmpɔː'teɪʃən) *n* 1 the act, business, or process of importing goods or services 2 an imported product or service

importunate (ɪm'pɔːtjʊnɪt) *adj* 1 persistent or demanding; insistent 2 *rare* troublesome; annoying > **im'portunately** *adv* > **im'portunateness** *n*

importune (ɪm'pɔːtjuːn, ,ɪmpɔː'tjuːn) *vb* **importunes, importuning, importuned** (*tr*) 1 to harass with persistent requests; demand of (someone) insistently 2 to beg for persistently; request with insistence [C16 from L *importūnus* tiresome, from *im-* IN-¹ + *-portūnus* as in *opportūnus* OPPORTUNE] > **im'portunely** *adv* > **im'portuner** *n* > ,**impor'tunity** *or* **im'portunacy** *n*

impose (ɪm'pəʊz) *vb* **imposes, imposing, imposed** (usually foll by *on* or *upon*) 1 (*tr*) to establish as something to be obeyed or complied with; enforce 2 to force (oneself, one's presence, etc) on others; obtrude 3 (*intr*) to take advantage, as of a person or quality: *to impose on someone's kindness* 4 (*tr*) *printing* to arrange (pages, type, etc) in a chase so that the pages will be in the correct order 5 (*tr*) to pass off deceptively; foist [C15 from OF, from L *impōnere* to place upon, from *pōnere* to place, set] > **im'posable** *adj* > **im'poser** *n*

imposing (ɪm'pəʊzɪŋ) *adj* grand or impressive: *an imposing building* > **im'posingly** *adv* > **im'posingness** *n*

imposition (,ɪmpə'zɪʃən) *n* 1 the act of imposing 2 something imposed unfairly on someone 3 a task set as a school punishment 4 the arrangement of pages for printing

impossibility (ɪm,pɒsə'bɪlɪtɪ, ,ɪmpɒs-) *n, pl* **impossibilities** 1 the state or quality of being impossible 2 something that is impossible

impossible (ɪm'pɒsəbᵊl) *adj* 1 incapable of being done, undertaken, or experienced 2 incapable of occurring or happening 3 absurd or inconceivable; unreasonable 4 *inf* intolerable; outrageous: *those children are impossible* > **im'possibleness** *n* > **im'possibly** *adv*

impossible figure *n* a picture of an object that at first sight looks three-dimensional but cannot be a two-dimensional projection of a real three-dimensional object, for example a picture of a staircase that re-enters itself while appearing to ascend continuously

impost[1] ('ɪmpəʊst) *n* 1 a tax, esp a customs duty 2 the weight that a horse must carry in a handicap race ▷ *vb* 3 (*tr*) *US* to classify (imported goods) according to the duty payable on them [C16 from Med. L *impostus* tax, from L *impositus* imposed; see IMPOSE] > **'imposter** *n*

impost[2] ('ɪmpəʊst) *n archit* a member at the top of a column that supports an arch [C17 from F *imposte*, from L *impositus* placed upon; see IMPOSE]

impostor *or* **imposter** (ɪm'pɒstə) *n* a person who deceives others, esp by assuming a false identity; charlatan [C16 from LL: deceiver; see IMPOSE]

imposture (ɪm'pɒstʃə) *n* the act or an instance of deceiving others, esp by assuming a false identity [C16 from F, from LL, from L *impōnere*; see IMPOSE] > **impostrous** (ɪm'pɒstrəs) *or* **impostorous** (ɪm'pɒstərəs) *adj*

impotent ('ɪmpətənt) *adj* 1 (when *postpositive*, often takes an infinitive) lacking sufficient strength; powerless 2 (esp of males) unable to perform sexual intercourse > **'impotence** *or* **'impotency** *n* > **'impotently** *adv*

impound (ɪm'paʊnd) *vb* (*tr*) 1 to confine (animals, etc) in a pound 2 to take legal possession of (a document, evidence, etc) 3 to collect (water) in a reservoir or dam > **im'poundable** *adj* > **im'poundage** *or* **im'poundment** *n* > **im'pounder** *n*

impoverish (ɪm'pɒvərɪʃ) *vb* (*tr*) 1 to make poor or diminish the quality of: *to impoverish society by cutting the grant to the arts* 2 to deprive (soil, etc) of fertility [C15 from OF *empovrir*, from *povre* POOR] > **im'poverishment** *n*

impracticable (ɪm'præktɪkəbᵊl) *adj* 1 incapable of being put into practice or accomplished; not feasible 2 unsuitable for a desired use; unfit > **im,practica'bility** *or* **im'practicableness** *n* > **im'practicably** *adv*

impractical (ɪm'præktɪkᵊl) *adj* 1 not practical or workable: *an impractical solution* 2 not given to practical matters or gifted with practical skills > **im,practi'cality** *or* **im'practicalness** *n* > **im'practically** *adv*

imprecate ('ɪmprɪ,keɪt) *vb* **imprecates, imprecating, imprecated** 1 (*intr*) to swear or curse 2 (*tr*) to invoke or bring down (evil, a curse, etc) [C17 from L *imprecārī* to invoke, from *im-* IN-² + *precārī* to PRAY] > **'impre,catory** *adj*

imprecation (,ɪmprɪ'keɪʃən) *n* 1 the act of imprecating 2 a malediction; curse

imprecise (,ɪmprɪ'saɪs) *adj* not precise; inexact or inaccurate > ,**impre'cisely** *adv* > **imprecision** (,ɪmprɪ'sɪʒən) *or* ,**impre'ciseness** *n*

impregnable[1] (ɪm'prɛgnəbᵊl) *adj* 1 unable to be broken into or taken by force: *an impregnable castle* 2 unshakable: *impregnable self-confidence* 3 incapable of being refuted: *an* *impregnable argument* [C15 *imprenable*, from OF, from IM- (not) + *prenable* able to be taken, from *prendre* to take] > **im,pregna'bility** *n* > **im'pregnably** *adv*

impregnable² (ɪm'prɛgnəb°l) *or* **impregnatable** (,ɪmprɛg'neɪtəb°l) *adj* able to be impregnated; fertile

impregnate *vb* ('ɪmprɛg,neɪt), **impregnates, impregnating, impregnated** (*tr*) **1** to saturate, soak, or infuse **2** to imbue or permeate; pervade **3** to cause to conceive; make pregnant; fertilize **4** to make (land, soil, etc) fruitful ▷ *adj* (ɪm'prɛgnɪt, -,neɪt) **5** pregnant or fertilized [C17 from LL, from L *im-* IN-² + *praegnans* PREGNANT] > ,**impreg'nation** *n* > **im'pregnator** *n*

impresario (,ɪmprə'sɑːrɪ,əʊ) *n, pl* **impresarios** the director or manager of an opera, ballet, etc [C18 from It., lit.: one who undertakes]

imprescriptible (,ɪmprɪ'skrɪptəb°l) *adj law* immune or exempt from prescription > ,**impre,scripti'bility** *n* > ,**impre'scriptibly** *adv*

impress¹ *vb* (ɪm'prɛs) (*tr*) **1** to make an impression on; have a strong, lasting, or favourable effect on: *I am impressed by your work* **2** to produce (an imprint, etc) by pressure in or on (something): *to impress a seal in wax* **3** (often foll by *on*) to stress (something to a person); urge; emphasize **4** to exert pressure on; press ▷ *n* ('ɪmprɛs) **5** the act or an instance of impressing **6** a mark, imprint, or effect produced by impressing [C14 from L *imprimere* to press into, imprint] > **im'presser** *n* > **im'pressible** *adj*

impress² *vb* (ɪm'prɛs) **1** to commandeer or coerce (men or things) into government service; press-gang ▷ *n* ('ɪmprɛs) **2** the act of commandeering or coercing into government service [C16 see *im-* IN-², PRESS²]

impression (ɪm'prɛʃən) *n* **1** an effect produced in the mind by a stimulus; sensation: *he gave the impression of wanting to help* **2** an imprint or mark produced by pressing **3** a vague idea, consciousness, or belief: *I had the impression we had met before* **4** a strong, favourable, or remarkable effect **5** the act of impressing or the state of being impressed **6** *printing* **6a** the act, process, or result of printing from type, plates, etc **6b** the total number of copies of a publication printed at one time **7** an imprint of the teeth and gums for preparing crowns, dentures, etc **8** an imitation or impersonation > **im'pressional** *adj* > **im'pressionally** *adv*

impressionable (ɪm'prɛʃənəb°l, -'prɛʃnə-) *adj* easily influenced or characterized by susceptibility to influence: *an impressionable age* > **im,pressiona'bility** *or* **im'pressionableness** *n*

impressionism (ɪm'prɛʃə,nɪzəm) *n* (*often cap*) a 19th-century movement in French painting, having the aim of objectively recording experience by a system of fleeting impressions, esp of natural light > **im'pressionist** *n*

▷ www.artcyclopedia.com/history/impressionism.html

▷ www.artlex.com/ArtLex/ij/impressionism.html

impressive (ɪm'prɛsɪv) *adj* capable of impressing, esp by size, magnificence, etc; awe-inspiring; commanding > **im'pressively** *adv* > **im'pressiveness** *n*

imprest (ɪm'prɛst) *n* **1** a fund of cash from which a department, etc, pays incidental expenses, topped up periodically from central funds **2** *chiefly Brit* an advance from government funds for some public business or service [C16 prob. from It. *imprestare* to lend, from L *in-* towards + *praestāre* to pay, from *praestō* at hand; see PRESTO]

imprimatur (,ɪmprɪ'meɪtə, -'mɑː-) *n* **1** sanction or approval for something to be printed **2** *RC Church* a licence certifying the Church's approval [C17 NL, lit.: let it be printed]

imprint *n* ('ɪmprɪnt) **1** a mark or impression produced by pressure, printing, or stamping **2** a characteristic mark or indication; stamp: *the imprint of great sadness on his face* **3a** the publisher's name and address, often with the date of publication, printed in a book, usually on the title page or the verso title page **3b** the printer's name and address on any printed matter ▷ *vb* (ɪm'prɪnt) (*tr*) **4** to produce (a mark, impression, etc) on (a surface) by pressure, printing, or stamping: *to imprint a seal on wax* **5** to establish firmly; impress: *to imprint the details on one's mind* **6** to cause (a young animal) to undergo the process of imprinting: *chicks can be imprinted on human beings*

imprinting (ɪm'prɪntɪŋ) *n* the development in young animals of recognition of and attraction to members of their own species or surrogates

imprison (ɪm'prɪzən) *vb* (*tr*) to confine in or as if in prison > **im'prisonment** *n*

improbable (ɪm'prɒbəb°l) *adj* not likely or probable; doubtful; unlikely > **im,proba'bility** *or* **im'probableness** *n* > **im'probably** *adv*

improbity (ɪm'prəʊbɪtɪ) *n, pl* **improbities** dishonesty, wickedness, or unscrupulousness

impromptu (ɪm'prɒmptjuː) *adj* **1** unrehearsed; spontaneous **2** produced or done without care or planning; improvised ▷ *adv* **3** in a spontaneous or improvised way: *he spoke impromptu* ▷ *n* **4** something that is impromptu **5** a short piece of instrumental music, sometimes improvisatory in character [C17 from F, from L *in promptū* in readiness, from *promptus* (adj) ready, PROMPT]

improper (ɪm'prɒpə) *adj* **1** lacking propriety; not seemly **2** unsuitable for a certain use or occasion; inappropriate **3** irregular or abnormal > **im'properly** *adv* > **im'properness** *n*

improper fraction *n* a fraction in which the numerator is greater than the denominator, as 7/6

impropriate *vb* (ɪm'prəʊprɪ,eɪt), **impropriates, impropriating, impropriated** **1** (*tr*) to transfer (property, rights, etc) from the Church into lay hands ▷ *adj* (ɪm'prəʊprɪɪt, -,eɪt) **2** transferred in this way [C16 from Med. L *impropriāre* to make one's own, from L *im-* IN-² + *propriāre* to APPROPRIATE] > **im,propri'ation** *n* > **im'propri,ator** *n*

impropriety (,ɪmprə'praɪɪtɪ) *n, pl* **improprieties** **1** lack of propriety; indecency; indecorum **2** an improper act or use **3** the state of being improper

improve (ɪm'pruːv) *vb* **improves, improving, improved** **1** to make or become better in quality; ameliorate **2** (*tr*) to make (buildings, land, etc) more valuable by additions or betterment **3** (*intr*; usually foll by *on* or *upon*) to achieve a better standard or quality in comparison (with): *to improve on last year's crop* [C16 from Anglo-F *emprouer* to turn to profit, from LL *prōde* beneficial, from L *prōdesse* to be advantageous] > **im'provable** *adj* > **im,prova'bility** *or* **im'provableness** *n* > **im'prover** *n*

improvement (ɪm'pruːvmənt) *n* **1** the act of improving or the state of being improved **2** something that improves, esp an addition or alteration **3** (*usually pl*) *Austral inf* a building, etc, on a piece of land, adding to its value

improvident (ɪm'prɒvɪdənt) *adj* **1** not provident; thriftless, imprudent, or prodigal **2** heedless or incautious; rash > **im'providence** *n* > **im'providently** *adv*

improvise ('ɪmprə,vaɪz) *vb* **improvises, improvising, improvised** **1** to perform or make quickly from materials and sources available, without previous planning **2** to perform (a poem, play, piece of music, etc), composing as one goes along [C19 from F, from It., from L *imprōvīsus* unforeseen, from *prōvidēre* to foresee; see PROVIDE] > **'impro,viser** *n* > ,**improvi'sation** *n* > **improvisatory** (,ɪmprə'vaɪzətərɪ, -'vɪz-, ,ɪmprəvaɪz'eɪtərɪ) *adj*

imprudent (ɪm'pruːd°nt) *adj* not prudent; rash, heedless, or indiscreet > **im'prudence** *n* > **im'prudently** *adv*

impudence ('ɪmpjʊdəns) *or* **impudency** *n* **1** the quality of being impudent; disrespect **2** an impudent act or

Ii

statement [c14 from L *impudēns* shameless]

impudent (ˈɪmpjʊdənt) *adj* 1 mischievous, impertinent, or disrespectful 2 *obs* immodest > **ˈimpudently** *adv* > **ˈimpudentness** *n*

impugn (ɪmˈpjuːn) *vb* (*tr*) to challenge or attack as false; criticize [c14 from OF, from L *impugnāre* to fight against, attack] > **imˈpugnable** *adj* > **imˈpugnment** *n* > **imˈpugner** *n*

impulse (ˈɪmpʌls) *n* 1 an impelling force or motion; thrust; impetus 2 a sudden desire, whim, or inclination 3 an instinctive drive; urge 4 tendency; current; trend 5 *physics* 5a the product of the average magnitude of a force acting on a body and the time for which it acts 5b the change in the momentum of a body as a result of a force acting upon it 6 *physiol* See **nerve impulse** 7 **on impulse** spontaneously or impulsively [c17 from L *impulsus* a pushing against, incitement, from *impellere* to strike against; see IMPEL]

impulse buying *n* the buying of merchandise prompted by a whim > **impulse buyer** *n*

impulsion (ɪmˈpʌlʃən) *n* 1 the act of impelling or the state of being impelled 2 motion produced by an impulse; propulsion 3 a driving force; compulsion

impulsive (ɪmˈpʌlsɪv) *adj* 1 characterized by actions based on sudden desires, whims, or inclinations: *an impulsive man* 2 based on emotional impulses or whims; spontaneous 3 forceful, inciting, or impelling 4 (of physical forces) acting for a short time; not continuous 5 (of a sound) brief, loud, and having a wide frequency range > **imˈpulsively** *adv* > **imˈpulsiveness** *n*

impunity (ɪmˈpjuːnɪtɪ) *n, pl* **impunities** 1 exemption or immunity from punishment, recrimination, or other unpleasant consequences 2 **with impunity** with no care or heed for such consequences [c16 from L, from *impūnis* unpunished, from IM- (not) + *poena* punishment]

impure (ɪmˈpjʊə) *adj* 1 not pure; combined with something else; tainted or sullied 2 (in certain religions) ritually unclean 3 (of a colour) mixed with another colour 4 of more than one origin or style, as of architecture > **imˈpurely** *adv* > **imˈpureness** *n*

impurity (ɪmˈpjʊərɪtɪ) *n, pl* **impurities** 1 the quality of being impure 2 an impure thing, constituent, or element: *impurities in the water* 3 *electronics* a small quantity of an element added to a pure semiconductor crystal to control its electrical conductivity

impute (ɪmˈpjuːt) *vb* **imputes, imputing, imputed** (*tr*) 1 to attribute or ascribe (something dishonest or dishonourable) to a person 2 to attribute to a source or cause: *I impute your success to nepotism* 3 *commerce* to give (a notional value) to goods, etc, when the real value is unknown [c14 from L, from IM- + *putāre* to think, calculate] > **ˌimpuˈtation** *n* > **imˈputative** *adj* > **imˈputer** *n* > **imˈputable** *adj*

Imroz (ˈimrɔz) *n* the Turkish name for **Imbros**

IMunE *abbrev for* Institution of Municipal Engineers

in (ɪn) *prep* 1 inside; within: *no smoking in the auditorium* 2 at a place where there is: *in the shade* 3 indicating a state, situation, or condition: *in silence* 4 when (a period of time) has elapsed: *return in one year* 5 using: *written in code* 6 concerned with, esp as an occupation: *in journalism* 7 while or by performing the action of: *in crossing the street he was run over* 8 used to indicate purpose: *in honour of the king* 9 (of certain animals) pregnant with: *in calf* 10 a variant of **into**: *she fell in the water* 11 **have it in one** (often foll by an infinitive) to have the ability (to do something) 12 **in that** *or* **in so far as** (*conj*) because or to the extent that: *I regret my remark in that it upset you* 13 **nothing in it** no difference or interval between two things ▷ *adv* (*particle*) 14 in or into a particular place; inward or indoors: *come in* 15 so as to achieve office or power: *Labour got in at the last election* 16 so as to enclose: *block in* 17 (in certain games) so as to take one's turn of the play: *you have to get the other side out before you go in* 18 NZ competing: *you've got to be in to win* 19 Brit (of a fire) alight 20 (*in combination*) indicating an activity or gathering: *teach-in; work-in* 21 **in at** present at (the beginning, end, etc) 22 **in for** about to be affected by (something, esp something unpleasant): *you're in for a shock* 23 **in on** acquainted with or sharing in: *I was in on all his plans* 24 **in with** associated with; friendly with; regarded highly by 25 **have (got) it in for** to wish or intend harm towards ▷ *adj* 26 (*stressed*) fashionable; modish: *the in thing to do* ▷ *n* 27 **ins and outs** intricacies or complications; details [OE]

In *the chemical symbol for* indium

in. *abbrev for* inch(es)

in-[1]**, il-, im-,** *or* **ir-** *prefix* a not; non-: *incredible; illegal; imperfect; irregular* b lack of: *inexperience* ▷ Cf **un-** [from L *in-*; rel. to *ne-*, *nōn* not]

in-[2]**, il-, im-,** *or* **ir-** *prefix* 1 in; into; towards; within; on: *infiltrate; immigrate* 2 having an intensive or causative function: *inflame; imperil* [from IN (prep, adv)]

-in *suffix forming nouns* 1 indicating a neutral organic compound, including proteins, glucosides, and glycerides: *insulin; tripalmitin* 2 indicating an enzyme in certain nonsystematic names: *pepsin* 3 indicating a pharmaceutical substance: *penicillin; aspirin* 4 indicating a chemical substance in certain nonsystematic names: *coumarin* [from NL *-ina*; cf. -INE[2]]

in absentia *Latin* (ɪn æbˈsɛntɪə) *adv* in the absence of (someone indicated)

inaccessible (ˌɪnækˈsɛsəbᵊl) *adj* not accessible; unapproachable > **ˌinacˌcessiˈbility** *or* **ˌinacˈcessibleness** *n* > **ˌinacˈcessibly** *adv*

inaccuracy (ɪnˈækjʊrəsɪ) *n, pl* **inaccuracies** 1 lack of accuracy; imprecision 2 an error, mistake, or slip > **inˈaccurate** *adj*

inaction (ɪnˈækʃən) *n* lack of action; idleness; inertia

inactivate (ɪnˈæktɪˌveɪt) *vb* **inactivates, inactivating, inactivated** (*tr*) to render inactive > **inˌactiˈvation** *n*

inactive (ɪnˈæktɪv) *adj* 1 idle or inert; not active 2 sluggish or indolent 3 *mil* of or relating to persons or equipment not in active service 4 *chem* (of a substance) having little or no reactivity > **inˈactively** *adv* > **ˌinacˈtivity** *n*

inadequate (ɪnˈædɪkwɪt) *adj* 1 not adequate; insufficient 2 not capable; lacking > **inˈadequacy** *n* > **inˈadequately** *adv*

inadvertence (ˌɪnədˈvɜːtᵊns) *or* **inadvertency** *n* 1 lack of attention; heedlessness 2 an oversight; slip

inadvertent (ˌɪnədˈvɜːtᵊnt) *adj* 1 failing to act carefully or considerately; inattentive 2 resulting from heedless action; unintentional > **ˌinadˈvertently** *adv*

-inae *suffix forming plural proper nouns* occurring in names of zoological subfamilies: *Felinae* [NL, from L, fem pl of *-īnus* -INE[1]]

inalienable (ɪnˈeɪljənəbᵊl) *adj* not able to be transferred to another; not alienable: *the inalienable rights of the citizen* > **inˌalienaˈbility** *or* **inˈalienableness** *n* > **inˈalienably** *adv*

inalterable (ɪnˈɔːltərəbᵊl) *adj* not alterable; unalterable > **inˌalteraˈbility** *or* **inˈalterableness** *n* > **inˈalterably** *adv*

inamorata (ɪnˌæməˈrɑːtə, ˌɪnæmə-) *or* (*masc*) **inamorato** (ɪnˌæməˈrɑːtəʊ, ˌɪnæmə-) *n, pl* **inamoratas** *or* (*masc*) **inamoratos** a person with whom one is in love; lover [c17 from It., from *innamorare* to cause to fall in love, from *amore* love, from L *amor*]

inane (ɪˈneɪn) *adj* 1 senseless, unimaginative, or empty; unintelligent: *inane remarks* ▷ *n* 2 *arch* something empty or vacant, esp the void of space [c17 from L *inānis* empty] > **inˈanely** *adv*

inanimate (ɪnˈænɪmɪt) *adj* 1 lacking the qualities of living beings; not animate: *inanimate objects* 2 lacking any sign of life or consciousness; appearing dead 3 lacking vitality; dull > **inˈanimately** *adv* > **inˈanimateness** *or* **inanimation** (ɪnˌænɪˈmeɪʃən) *n*

inanition (ˌɪnəˈnɪʃən) *n* 1 exhaustion resulting from lack of food **2** mental, social, or spiritual weakness or lassitude [C14 from LL *inānītio* emptiness, from L *inānis* empty; see INANE]

inanity (ɪˈnænɪtɪ) *n, pl* **inanities** **1** lack of intelligence or imagination; senselessness; silliness **2** a senseless action, remark, etc **3** an archaic word for **emptiness**

inapposite (ɪnˈæpəzɪt) *adj* not appropriate or pertinent; unsuitable > **inˈappositely** *adv* > **inˈappositeness** *n*

inapt (ɪnˈæpt) *adj* **1** not apt or fitting; inappropriate **2** lacking skill; inept > **inˈaptiˌtude** *or* **inˈaptness** *n* > **inˈaptly** *adv*

inarch (ɪnˈɑːtʃ) *vb* (*tr*) to graft (a plant) by uniting stock and scion while both are still growing independently

inasmuch as (ˌɪnəzˈmʌtʃ) *conj* (*subordinating*) **1** in view of the fact that; seeing that; since **2** to the extent or degree that; in so far as

inaugural (ɪnˈɔːgjʊrəl) *adj* **1** characterizing or relating to an inauguration ▷ *n* **2** a speech made at an inauguration, esp by a president of the US

inaugurate (ɪnˈɔːgjʊˌreɪt) *vb* **inaugurates, inaugurating, inaugurated** (*tr*) **1** to commence officially or formally; initiate **2** to place in office formally and ceremonially; induct **3** to open ceremonially; dedicate formally: *to inaugurate a factory* [C17 from L *inaugurāre*, lit.: to take omens, practise augury, hence to install in office after taking auguries; see IN-[2], AUGUR] > **inˌauguˈration** *n* > **inˈauguˌrator** *n* > **inauguratory** (ɪnˈɔːgjʊrətərɪ, -trɪ) *adj*

in-between *adj* intermediate: *he's at the in-between stage, neither a child nor an adult*

inboard (ˈɪnˌbɔːd) *adj* **1** (esp of a boat's motor or engine) situated within the hull **2** situated between the wing tip of an aircraft and its fuselage: *an inboard engine* ▷ *adv* **3** towards the centre line of or within a vessel, aircraft, etc

inborn (ˈɪnˈbɔːn) *adj* existing from birth; congenital; innate

inbred (ˈɪnˈbrɛd) *adj* **1** produced as a result of inbreeding **2** deeply ingrained; innate: *inbred good manners*

inbreed (ˈɪnˈbriːd) *vb* **inbreeds, inbreeding, inbred** **1** to breed from unions between closely related individuals, esp over several generations **2** (*tr*) to develop within; engender > **ˈinˈbreeding** *n, adj*

in-built *adj* built-in, integral

inc. *abbrev for* including

Inc. (esp US) *abbrev for* incorporated

Inca (ˈɪŋkə) *n, pl* **Inca** *or* **Incas** **1** a member of a South American Indian people whose empire centred on Peru lasted from about 1100 AD to the Spanish conquest in the early 1530s **2** the language of the Incas. See also **Quechua** [C16 from Sp., from Quechua *inka* king] > **Incan** *adj*

▷ www.wsu.edu/~dee/CIVAMRCA/INCAS.HTM
▷ www.incaconquest.com

incalculable (ɪnˈkælkjʊləbᵊl) *adj* beyond calculation; unable to be predicted or determined > **inˌcalculaˈbility** *n* > **inˈcalculably** *adv*

incandesce (ˌɪnkænˈdɛs) *vb* **incandesces, incandescing, incandesced** (*intr*) to make or become incandescent

incandescent (ˌɪnkænˈdɛsᵊnt) *adj* **1** emitting light as a result of being heated; red-hot or white-hot **2** *inf* extremely angry [C18 from L *incandescere* to become hot, glow, from *candēre* to be white; see CANDID] > **ˌincanˈdescently** *adv* > **ˌincanˈdescence** *n*

incandescent lamp *n* a source of light that contains a heated solid, such as an electrically heated filament

incantation (ˌɪnkænˈteɪʃən) *n* **1** ritual recitation of magic words or sounds **2** the formulaic words or sounds used; a magic spell [C14 from LL *incantātiō* an enchanting, from *incantāre* to repeat magic formulas, from L, from IN-[2] + *cantāre* to sing; see ENCHANT] > **ˌincanˈtational** *or* **inˈcantatory** *adj*

incapacitate (ˌɪnkəˈpæsɪˌteɪt) *vb* **incapacitates, incapacitating, incapacitated** (*tr*) **1** to deprive of power, strength, or capacity; disable **2** to deprive of legal capacity or eligibility > **ˌincaˌpaciˈtation** *n*

incapacity (ˌɪnkəˈpæsɪtɪ) *n, pl* **incapacities** **1** lack of power, strength, or capacity; inability **2** *law* legal disqualification or ineligibility

in-car *adj* (of hi-fi equipment, etc) installed inside a car

incarcerate (ɪnˈkɑːsəˌreɪt) *vb* **incarcerates, incarcerating, incarcerated** (*tr*) to confine or imprison [C16 from Med. L, from L IN-[2] + *carcer* prison] > **inˌcarcerˈation** *n* > **inˈcarcerˌator** *n*

incarnadine (ɪnˈkɑːnəˌdaɪn) *arch or literary* ▷ *vb* **incarnadines, incarnadining, incarnadined** **1** (*tr*) to tinge or stain with red ▷ *adj* **2** of a pinkish or reddish colour similar to that of flesh or blood [C16 from F *incarnadin* flesh-coloured, from It., from LL *incarnātus* made flesh, INCARNATE]

incarnate *adj* (ɪnˈkɑːnɪt, -neɪt) (*usually immediately postpositive*) **1** possessing bodily form, esp the human form: *a devil incarnate* **2** personified or typified: *stupidity incarnate* ▷ *vb* (ɪnˈkɑːneɪt), **incarnates, incarnating, incarnated** (*tr*) **3** to give a bodily or concrete form to **4** to be representative or typical of [C14 from LL *incarnāre* to make flesh, from L IN-[2] + *carō* flesh]

incarnation (ˌɪnkɑːˈneɪʃən) *n* **1** the act of manifesting or state of being manifested in bodily form, esp human form **2** a bodily form assumed by a god, etc **3** a person or thing that typifies or represents some quality, idea, etc

Incarnation (ˌɪnkɑːˈneɪʃən) *n Christian theol* the assuming of a human body by the Son of God

incarvillea (ˌɪnkɑːˈvɪlɪə) *n* any of various perennials with pink flowers and pinnate leaves. Also called: **Chinese trumpet flower** [C18 after Pierre d'*Incarville*, F missionary in China]

incase (ɪnˈkeɪs) *vb* **incases, incasing, incased** a variant spelling of **encase** > **inˈcasement** *n*

incautious (ɪnˈkɔːʃəs) *adj* not careful or cautious > **inˈcautiously** *adv* > **inˈcautiousness** *or* **inˈcaution** *n*

incendiary (ɪnˈsɛndɪərɪ) *adj* **1** of or relating to the illegal burning of property, goods, etc **2** tending to create strife, violence, etc **3** (of a substance) capable of catching fire or burning readily ▷ *n, pl* **incendiaries** **4** a person who illegally sets fire to property, goods, etc; arsonist **5** (esp formerly) a person who stirs up civil strife, violence, etc; agitator **6** Also called: **incendiary bomb** a bomb that is designed to start fires **7** an incendiary substance, such as phosphorus [C17 from L, from *incendium* fire, from *incendere* to kindle] > **inˈcendiaˌrism** *n*

incense[1] (ˈɪnsɛns) *n* **1** any of various aromatic substances burnt for their fragrant odour, esp in religious ceremonies **2** the odour or smoke so produced **3** any pleasant fragrant odour; aroma ▷ *vb* **incenses, incensing, incensed** **4** to burn incense in honour of (a deity) **5** (*tr*) to perfume or fumigate with incense [C13 from OF *encens*, from Church L *incensum*, from L *incendere* to kindle]

incense[2] (ɪnˈsɛns) *vb* **incenses, incensing, incensed** (*tr*) to enrage greatly [C15 from L *incensus* set on fire, from *incendere* to kindle] > **inˈcensement** *n*

incensory (ˈɪnsɛnsərɪ) *n, pl* **incensories** a less common name for **censer** [C17 from Med. L *incensorium*]

incentive (ɪnˈsɛntɪv) *n* **1** a motivating influence; stimulus **2a** an additional payment made to employees to increase production **2b** (*as modifier*): *an incentive scheme* ▷ *adj* **3** serving to incite to action [C15 from LL, from L: striking up, setting the tune, from *incinere* to sing]

incentivize *or* **incentivise** (ɪnˈsɛntɪˌvaɪz) *vb* **a** to provide (someone) with a good reason for wanting to do something: *why not incentivize companies to relocate?* **b** to promote (something) with a particular incentive: *an incentivized share option scheme*

incept (ɪnˈsɛpt) *vb* (*tr*) **1** (of organisms) to ingest (food) **2** *Brit* (formerly) to take a master's or doctor's degree at a

Ii

university [c19 from L *inceptus* begun, attempted, from *incipere* to begin, take in hand] > **in'ceptor** *n*

inception (ɪn'sɛpʃən) *n* the beginning, as of a project or undertaking

inceptive (ɪn'sɛptɪv) *adj* **1** beginning; incipient; initial **2** Also called: **inchoative** *grammar* denoting a verb used to indicate the beginning of an action ▷ *n* **3** *grammar* an inceptive verb > **in'ceptively** *adv*

incertitude (ɪn'sɜːtɪˌtjuːd) *n* **1** uncertainty; doubt **2** a state of mental or emotional insecurity

incessant (ɪn'sɛsᵊnt) *adj* not ceasing; continual [c16 from LL, from L IN-¹ + *cessāre* to CEASE] > **in'cessancy** *n* > **in'cessantly** *adv*

incest ('ɪnsɛst) *n* sexual intercourse between two persons who are too closely related to marry [c13 from L, from IN-¹ + *castus* CHASTE]

incestuous (ɪn'sɛstjʊəs) *adj* **1** relating to or involving incest: *an incestuous union* **2** guilty of incest **3** resembling incest in excessive or claustrophobic intimacy > **in'cestuously** *adv* > **in'cestuousness** *n*

inch¹ (ɪntʃ) *n* **1** a unit of length equal to one twelfth of a foot or 0.0254 metre **2** *meteorol* **2a** an amount of precipitation that would cover a surface with water one inch deep **2b** a unit of pressure equal to a mercury column one inch high in a barometer **3** a very small distance, degree, or amount **4** **every inch** in every way; completely: *every inch an aristocrat* **5** **inch by inch** gradually; little by little **6** **within an inch of one's life** almost to death ▷ *vb* **7** to move or be moved very slowly or in very small steps: *the car inched forward* **8** (*tr*; foll by *out*) to defeat (someone) by a very small margin [OE *ynce*; see OUNCE¹]

inch² (ɪntʃ) *n Scot & Irish* a small island [c15 from Gaelic *innis* island; cf. Welsh *ynys*]

inchoate *adj* (ɪn'kəʊeɪt, -'kəʊɪt) **1** just beginning; incipient **2** undeveloped; immature; rudimentary ▷ *vb* (ɪn'kəʊeɪt), **inchoates, inchoating, inchoated** (*tr*) **3** to begin [c16 from L *incohāre* to make a beginning, lit.: to hitch up, from IN-² + *cohum* yokestrap] > **in'choately** *adv* > **in'choateness** *n* > **ˌincho'ation** *n* > **inchoative** (ɪn'kəʊətɪv) *adj*

Inchon *or* **Incheon** ('ɪn'tʃɒn) *n* a port in W South Korea, on the Yellow Sea: the chief port for Seoul: site of a major strategic amphibious assault by UN troops, liberating Seoul (Sept. 15, 1950). Pop: 2 307 618 (1995). Former name: **Chemulpo**

inchworm ('ɪntʃˌwɜːm) *n* another name for **measuring worm**

incidence ('ɪnsɪdəns) *n* **1** degree, extent, or frequency of occurrence; amount: *a high incidence of death from pneumonia* **2** the act or manner of impinging on or affecting by proximity or influence **3** *physics* the arrival of a beam of light or particles at a surface. See also **angle of incidence** **4** *geom* the partial coincidence of two configurations, such as a point on a circle

incident ('ɪnsɪdənt) *n* **1** a definite occurrence; event **2** a minor, subsidiary, or related event **3** a relatively insignificant event that might have serious consequences **4** a public disturbance **5** the occurrence of something interesting or exciting: *the trip was not without incident* ▷ *adj* **6** (*postpositive*; foll by *to*) related (to) or dependent (on) **7** (when *postpositive*, often foll by *to*) having a subsidiary or minor relationship (with) **8** (esp of a beam of light or particles) arriving at or striking a surface [c15 from Med. L, from L *incidere*, lit.: to fall into, hence befall, happen]

incidental (ˌɪnsɪ'dɛntᵊl) *adj* **1** happening in connection with or resulting from something more important; casual or fortuitous **2** (*postpositive*; foll by *to*) found in connection (with); related (to) **3** (*postpositive*; foll by *upon*) caused (by) **4** occasional or minor: *incidental expenses* ▷ *n* **5** (*often pl*) a minor expense, event, or action > **ˌinci'dentalness** *n*

incidentally (ˌɪnsɪ'dɛntəlɪ) *adv* **1** as a subordinate or chance occurrence **2** (*sentence modifier*) by the way

incidental music *n* background music for a film, etc

incinerate (ɪn'sɪnəˌreɪt) *vb* **incinerates, incinerating, incinerated** to burn up completely; reduce to ashes [c16 from Med. L, from L IN-² + *cinis* ashes] > **inˌciner'ation** *n*

incinerator (ɪn'sɪnəˌreɪtə) *n* a furnace or apparatus for incinerating something, esp refuse

incipient (ɪn'sɪpɪənt) *adj* just starting to be or happen; beginning [c17 from L, from *incipere* to begin, take in hand] > **in'cipience** *or* **in'cipiency** *n* > **in'cipiently** *adv*

incise (ɪn'saɪz) *vb* **incises, incising, incised** (*tr*) to produce (lines, a design, etc) by cutting into the surface of (something) with a sharp tool [c16 from L *incīdere* to cut into]

incision (ɪn'sɪʒən) *n* **1** the act of incising **2** a cut, gash, or notch **3** a cut made with a knife during a surgical operation

incisive (ɪn'saɪsɪv) *adj* **1** keen, penetrating, or acute **2** biting or sarcastic; mordant: *an incisive remark* **3** having a sharp cutting edge: *incisive teeth* > **in'cisively** *adv* > **in'cisiveness** *n*

incisor (ɪn'saɪzə) *n* a chisel-edged tooth at the front of the mouth

incite (ɪn'saɪt) *vb* **incites, inciting, incited** (*tr*) to stir up or provoke to action [c15 from L, from IN-² + *citāre* to excite] > **ˌinci'tation** *n* > **in'citement** *n* > **in'citer** *n* > **in'citingly** *adv*

incivility (ˌɪnsɪ'vɪlɪtɪ) *n, pl* **incivilities** **1** lack of civility or courtesy; rudeness **2** an impolite or uncivil act or remark

incl. *abbrev for:* **1** including **2** inclusive

inclement (ɪn'klɛmənt) *adj* **1** (of weather) stormy, severe, or tempestuous **2** severe or merciless > **in'clemency** *n* > **in'clemently** *adv*

inclination (ˌɪnklɪ'neɪʃən) *n* **1** (often foll by *for, to, towards*, or an infinitive) a particular disposition, esp a liking; tendency: *I've no inclination for such dull work* **2** the degree of deviation from a particular plane, esp a horizontal or vertical plane **3** a sloping or slanting surface; incline **4** the act of inclining or the state of being inclined **5** the act of bowing or nodding the head **6** another name for **dip** (sense 24) > **ˌincli'national** *adj*

incline *vb* (ɪn'klaɪn), **inclines, inclining, inclined** **1** to deviate from a particular plane, esp a vertical or horizontal plane; slope or slant **2** (when *tr*, may take an infinitive) to be disposed or cause to be disposed (towards some attitude or to do something) **3** to bend or lower (part of the body, esp the head), as in a bow or in order to listen **4** **incline one's ear** to listen favourably (to) ▷ *n* ('ɪnklaɪn, ɪn'klaɪn) **5** an inclined surface or slope; gradient [c13 from L *inclīnāre* to cause to lean, from *clīnāre* to bend; see LEAN¹] > **in'cliner** *n*

inclined (ɪn'klaɪnd) *adj* **1** (*postpositive*; often foll by *to*) having a disposition; tending **2** sloping or slanting

inclined plane *n* a plane whose angle to the horizontal is less than a right angle

inclinometer (ˌɪnklɪ'nɒmɪtə) *n* an aircraft instrument that indicates the angle an aircraft makes with the horizontal

inclose (ɪn'kləʊz) *vb* **incloses, inclosing, inclosed** a less common spelling of **enclose** > **in'closure** *n*

include (ɪn'kluːd) *vb* **includes, including, included** (*tr*) **1** to have as contents or part of the contents; be made up of or contain **2** to add as part of something else; put in as part of a set, group, or category **3** to contain as a secondary or minor ingredient or element [c15 (in the sense: to enclose): from L, from IN-² + *claudere* to close] > **in'cludable** *or* **in'cludible** *adj*

include out *vb* (*tr, adv*) *inf* to exclude: *you can include me out of that deal*

inclusion (ɪn'kluːʒən) *n* **1** the act of including or the state of being included **2** something included

inclusion body *n pathol* any of the small particles found in the nucleus and cytoplasm of cells infected with certain viruses

inclusive (ɪn'kluːsɪv) *adj* 1 (*postpositive; foll by of*) considered together (with): *capital inclusive of profit* 2 (*postpositive*) including the limits specified: *Monday to Friday inclusive* 3 comprehensive 4 *logic* (of a disjunction) true if at least one of its component propositions is true > **in'clusively** *adv* > **in'clusiveness** *n*

inclusive language *n* language that avoids the use of expressions or words that might be considered to exclude particular groups of people, esp gender-specific words, such as "man", "mankind", and masculine pronouns, in contexts that could exclude women

incognito (ˌɪnkɒg'niːtəʊ, ɪn'kɒgnɪtəʊ) *or* (*fem*) **incognita** *adv, adj* (*postpositive*) 1 under an assumed name or appearance; in disguise ▷ *n, pl* **incognitos** *or* (*fem*) **incognitas** 2 a person who is incognito 3 the assumed name or disguise of such a person [C17 from It., from L *incognitus* unknown]

incognizant (ɪn'kɒgnɪzənt) *adj* (when *postpositive*, often foll by *of*) unaware (of) > **in'cognizance** *n*

incoherent (ˌɪnkəʊ'hɪərənt) *adj* 1 lacking in clarity or organization; disordered 2 unable to express oneself clearly; inarticulate 3 *physics* (of two or more waves) having the same frequency but not the same phase: *incoherent light* > **ˌinco'herently** *adv* > **ˌinco'herence** *or* **ˌinco'herency** *n*

income ('ɪnkʌm, 'ɪnkəm) *n* 1 the amount of monetary or other returns, either earned or unearned, accruing over a given period of time 2 receipts; revenue [C13 (in the sense: arrival, entrance): from OE *incumen* a coming in]

incomer ('ɪnkʌmə) *n* a person who comes to live in a place in which he or she was not born

incomes policy *n* an economic policy that attempts to reduce or control inflation by limiting incomes

income support *n* (in Britain, formerly) a social security payment for people on very low incomes

income tax *n* a personal tax levied on annual income subject to certain deductions

incoming ('ɪnˌkʌmɪŋ) *adj* 1 coming in; entering 2 about to come into office; succeeding 3 (of interest, dividends, etc) being received; accruing ▷ *n* 4 the act of coming in; entrance 5 (*usually pl*) income or revenue

incommensurable (ˌɪnkə'mɛnʃərəbᵊl) *adj* 1 incapable of being judged, measured, or considered comparatively 2 (*postpositive; foll by with*) not in accordance; incommensurate 3 *maths* not having a common factor other than 1, such as 2 and √−5 ▷ *n* 4 something incommensurable > **ˌincomˌmensura'bility** *n* > **ˌincom'mensurably** *adv*

incommensurate (ˌɪnkə'mɛnʃərɪt) *adj* 1 (when *postpositive*, often foll by *with*) not commensurate; disproportionate 2 incommensurable > **ˌincom'mensurately** *adv* > **ˌincom'mensurateness** *n*

incommode (ˌɪnkə'məʊd) *vb* **incommodes, incommoding, incommoded** (*tr*) to bother, disturb, or inconvenience [C16 from L *incommodāre* to be troublesome, from *incommodus* inconvenient; see COMMODE]

incommodious (ˌɪnkə'məʊdɪəs) *adj* 1 insufficiently spacious; cramped 2 troublesome or inconvenient > **ˌincom'modiously** *adv*

incommodity (ˌɪnkə'mɒdɪtɪ) *n, pl* **incommodities** anything that causes inconvenience

incommunicado (ˌɪnkəˌmjuːnɪ'kɑːdəʊ) *adv, adj* (*postpositive*) deprived of communication with other people, as while in solitary confinement [C19 from Sp., from *incomunicar* to deprive of communication; see IN-[1], COMMUNICATE]

incomparable (ɪn'kɒmpərəbᵊl, -prəbᵊl) *adj* 1 beyond or above comparison; matchless; unequalled 2 lacking a basis for comparison; not having qualities or features that can be compared > **inˌcompara'bility** *or* **in'comparableness** *n* > **in'comparably** *adv*

incompatible (ˌɪnkəm'pætəbᵊl) *adj* 1 incapable of living or existing together in harmony; conflicting 2 opposed in nature or quality; inconsistent 3 *med* (esp of two drugs or two types of blood) incapable of being combined or used together; antagonistic 4 *logic* (of two propositions) unable to be both true at the same time 5 (of plants) incapable of fertilizing each other ▷ *n* 6 (*often pl*) a person or thing that is incompatible with another > **ˌincomˌpati'bility** *or* **ˌincom'patibleness** *n* > **ˌincom'patibly** *adv*

incompetent (ɪn'kɒmpɪtənt) *adj* 1 not possessing the necessary ability, skill, etc, to do or carry out a task; incapable 2 marked by lack of ability, skill, etc 3 *law* not legally qualified: *an incompetent witness* ▷ *n* 4 an incompetent person > **in'competence** *or* **in'competency** *n* > **in'competently** *adv*

incomplete (ˌɪnkəm'pliːt) *adj* 1 not complete or finished 2 not completely developed; imperfect > **ˌincom'pletely** *adv* > **ˌincom'pleteness** *or* **ˌincom'pletion** *n*

incomprehensible (ˌɪnkɒmprɪ'hɛnsəbᵊl, ɪnˌkɒm-) *adj* 1 incapable of being understood; unintelligible 2 *arch* limitless; boundless > **ˌincompreˌhensi'bility** *or* **ˌincompre'hensibleness** *n* > **ˌincompre'hensibly** *adv*

inconceivable (ˌɪnkən'siːvəbᵊl) *adj* incapable of being conceived, imagined, or considered > **ˌinconˌceiva'bility** *or* **ˌincon'ceivableness** *n* > **ˌincon'ceivably** *adv*

inconclusive (ˌɪnkən'kluːsɪv) *adj* not conclusive or decisive; not finally settled; indeterminate > **ˌincon'clusively** *adv* > **ˌincon'clusiveness** *n*

incongruous (ɪn'kɒŋgrʊəs) *or* **incongruent** *adj* 1 (when *postpositive*, foll by *with* or *to*) incompatible with (what is suitable); inappropriate 2 containing disparate or discordant elements or parts > **in'congruously** *adv* > **in'congruousness** *or* **incongruity** (ˌɪnkɒŋ'gruːɪtɪ) *n*

inconnu ('ɪnkənjuː, 'ɪnkənuː) *n Canad* a whitefish of Far Northern waters [C19 from F, lit: unknown]

inconsequential (ˌɪnkɒnsɪ'kwɛnʃəl, ɪnˌkɒn-) *or* **inconsequent** (ɪn'kɒnsɪkwənt) *adj* 1 not following logically as a consequence 2 trivial or insignificant 3 not in a logical sequence; haphazard > **ˌinconseˌquenti'ality, ˌinconse'quentialness,** *or* **in'consequence** *n* > **ˌinconse'quentially** *or* **in'consequently** *adv*

inconsiderable (ˌɪnkən'sɪdərəbᵊl) *adj* 1 relatively small 2 not worthy of consideration; insignificant > **ˌincon'siderableness** *n* > **ˌincon'siderably** *adv*

inconsiderate (ˌɪnkən'sɪdərɪt) *adj* lacking in care or thought for others; thoughtless > **ˌincon'siderately** *adv* > **ˌincon'siderateness** *or* **ˌinconˌsider'ation** *n*

inconsistency (ˌɪnkən'sɪstənsɪ) *n, pl* **inconsistencies** 1 lack of consistency or agreement; incompatibility 2 an inconsistent feature or quality

inconsistent (ˌɪnkən'sɪstənt) *adj* 1 lacking in consistency, agreement, or compatibility; at variance 2 containing contradictory elements 3 irregular or fickle in behaviour or mood 4 *logic* (of a set of propositions) enabling an explicit contradiction to be validly derived > **ˌincon'sistently** *adv*

inconsolable (ˌɪnkən'səʊləbᵊl) *adj* incapable of being consoled or comforted; disconsolate > **ˌinconˌsola'bility** *or* **ˌincon'solableness** *n* > **ˌincon'solably** *adv*

inconsonant (ɪn'kɒnsənənt) *adj* lacking in harmony or compatibility; discordant > **in'consonance** *n* > **in'consonantly** *adv*

inconspicuous (ˌɪnkən'spɪkjʊəs) *adj* not easily noticed or seen; not prominent or striking > **ˌincon'spicuously** *adv* > **ˌincon'spicuousness** *n*

incontinent[1] (ɪn'kɒntɪnənt) *adj* 1 relating to or exhibiting involuntary urination or defecation 2 lacking in restraint or control, esp sexually 3 (foll by *of*) having little or no control (over) 4 unrestrained;

Ii

uncontrolled [C14 from OF, from L, from IN-[1] + *continere* to hold, restrain] > **in'continence** *n* > **in'continently** *adv*

incontinent² (ɪn'kɒntɪnənt) *or* **incontinently** *adv* obsolete words for **immediately** [C15 from LL *in continentī tempore*, lit.: in continuous time, that is, with no interval]

incontrovertible (ˌɪnkɒntrə'vɜːtəbᵊl, ɪnˌkɒn-) *adj* incapable of being contradicted or disputed; undeniable > ˌ**incontroˌverti'bility** *n* > ˌ**incontro'vertibly** *adv*

inconvenience (ˌɪnkən'viːnjəns, -'viːnɪəns) *n* **1** the state or quality of being inconvenient **2** something inconvenient; a hindrance, trouble, or difficulty ▷ *vb* **3** (*tr*) to cause inconvenience to; trouble or harass

inconvenient (ˌɪnkən'viːnjənt, -'viːnɪənt) *adj* not convenient; troublesome, awkward, or difficult > ˌ**incon'veniently** *adv*

incorporate *vb* (ɪn'kɔːpəˌreɪt), **incorporates, incorporating, incorporated** **1** to include or be included as a part or member of a united whole **2** to form a united whole or mass; merge or blend **3** to form into a corporation or other organization with a separate legal identity ▷ *adj* (ɪn'kɔːpərɪt, -prɪt) **4** combined into a whole; incorporated **5** formed into or constituted as a corporation [C14 (in the sense: put into the body of something else): from LL *incorporāre* to embody, from L IN-[2] + *corpus* body] > **in'corpoˌrated** *adj* > **inˌcorpo'ration** *n* > **in'corporative** *adj*

incorporeal (ˌɪnkɔː'pɔːrɪəl) *adj* **1** without material form, body, or substance **2** spiritual or metaphysical **3** *law* having no material existence but existing by reason of its annexation of something material: *an incorporeal hereditament* > ˌ**incor'poreally** *adv* > **incorporeity** (ɪnˌkɔːpə'riːɪtɪ) *or* ˌ**incorpore'ality** *n*

incorrect (ˌɪnkə'rekt) *adj* **1** false; wrong: *an incorrect calculation* **2** not fitting or proper: *incorrect behaviour* > ˌ**incor'rectly** *adv* > ˌ**incor'rectness** *n*

incorrigible (ɪn'kɒrɪdʒəbᵊl) *adj* **1** beyond correction, reform, or alteration **2** firmly rooted; ineradicable ▷ *n* **3** a person or animal that is incorrigible > **inˌcorrigi'bility** *or* **in'corrigibleness** *n* > **in'corrigibly** *adv*

incorruptible (ˌɪnkə'rʌptəbᵊl) *adj* **1** incapable of being corrupted; honest; just **2** not subject to decay or decomposition > ˌ**incorˌrupti'bility** *n* > ˌ**incor'ruptibly** *adv*

incrassate *adj* (ɪn'kræsɪt, -eɪt), *also* **incrassated** **1** *biol* thickened or swollen ▷ *vb* (ɪn'kræseɪt), **incrassates, incrassating, incrassated** **2** *obs* to make or become thicker [C17 from LL, from L *crassus* thick, dense] > ˌ**incras'sation** *n*

increase *vb* (ɪn'kriːs), **increases, increasing, increased** **1** to make or become greater in size, degree, frequency, etc; grow or expand ▷ *n* ('ɪnkriːs) **2** the act of increasing; augmentation **3** the amount by which something increases **4** **on the increase** increasing, esp becoming more frequent [C14 from OF *encreistre*, from L, from IN-[2] + *crēscere* to grow] > **in'creasable** *adj* > **increasedly** (ɪn'kriːsɪdlɪ) *or* **in'creasingly** *adv* > **in'creaser** *n*

incredible (ɪn'krɛdəbᵊl) *adj* **1** beyond belief or understanding; unbelievable **2** *inf* marvellous; amazing > **inˌcredi'bility** *or* **in'credibleness** *n* > **in'credibly** *adv*

incredulity (ˌɪnkrɪ'djuːlɪtɪ) *n* lack of belief; scepticism

incredulous (ɪn'krɛdjʊləs) *adj* (often foll by *of*) not prepared or willing to believe (something); unbelieving > **in'credulously** *adv* > **in'credulousness** *n*

increment ('ɪnkrɪmənt) *n* **1** an increase or addition, esp one of a series **2** the act of increasing; augmentation **3** *maths* a small positive or negative change in a variable or function [C15 from L *incrēmentum* growth, INCREASE] > **incremental** (ˌɪnkrɪ'mɛntᵊl) *adj*

incremental plotter *n* a device that plots graphs on paper from computer-generated instructions

incriminate (ɪn'krɪmɪˌneɪt) *vb* **incriminates, incriminating, incriminated** (*tr*) **1** to imply or suggest the guilt or error of (someone) **2** to charge with a crime or fault [C18 from LL *incrīmināre* to accuse, from L *crīmen* accusation; see CRIME] > **inˌcrimi'nation** *n* > **in'crimiˌnator** *n* > **in'criminatory** *adj*

incrust (ɪn'krʌst) *vb* a variant spelling of **encrust** > **in'crustant** *n, adj* > ˌ**incrus'tation** *n*

incubate ('ɪnkjʊˌbeɪt) *vb* **incubates, incubating, incubated** **1** (of birds) to supply (eggs) with heat for their development, esp by sitting on them **2** to cause (bacteria, etc) to develop, esp in an incubator or culture medium **3** (*intr*) (of embryos, etc) to develop in favourable conditions, esp in an incubator **4** (*intr*) (of disease germs) to remain inactive in an animal or human before causing disease **5** to develop gradually; foment or be fomented [C18 from L *incubāre* to lie upon, hatch, from IN-[2] + *cubāre* to lie down] > ˌ**incu'bation** *n* > ˌ**incu'bational** *adj* > '**incuˌbative** *or* '**incuˌbatory** *adj*

incubation period *n med* the time between exposure to an infectious disease and the appearance of the first signs or symptoms

incubator ('ɪnkjʊˌbeɪtə) *n* **1** *med* an apparatus for housing prematurely born babies until they are strong enough to survive **2** a container in which, for example, birds' eggs can be artificially hatched or bacterial cultures grown **3** a person, animal, or thing that incubates

incubus ('ɪnkjʊbəs) *n, pl* **incubi** (-ˌbaɪ) *or* **incubuses** **1** a demon believed in folklore to have sexual intercourse with sleeping women ▷ Cf **succubus** **2** something that oppresses or disturbs greatly, esp a nightmare or obsession [C14 from LL, from L *incubāre* to lie upon; see INCUBATE]

inculcate ('ɪnkʌlˌkeɪt, ɪn'kʌlkeɪt) *vb* **inculcates, inculcating, inculcated** (*tr*) to instil by insistent repetition [C16 from L *inculcāre* to tread upon, ram down, from IN-[2] + *calcāre* to trample, from *calx* heel] > ˌ**incul'cation** *n* > '**inculˌcator** *n*

inculpate ('ɪnkʌlˌpeɪt, ɪn'kʌlpeɪt) *vb* **inculpates, inculpating, inculpated** (*tr*) to incriminate; cause blame to be imputed to [C18 from LL, from L *culpāre* to blame, from *culpa* fault, blame] > ˌ**incul'pation** *n* > **inculpative** (ɪn'kʌlpətɪv) *or* **inculpatory** (ɪn'kʌlpətərɪ, -trɪ) *adj*

incumbency (ɪn'kʌmbənsɪ) *n, pl* **incumbencies** **1** the state or quality of being incumbent **2** the office, duty, or tenure of an incumbent

incumbent (ɪn'kʌmbənt) *adj* **1** *formal* (often *postpositive* and foll by *on* or *upon* and an infinitive) morally binding; obligatory: *it is incumbent on me to attend* **2** (usually *postpositive* and foll by *on*) resting or lying (on) **3** (usually *prenominal*) occupying or holding an office ▷ *n* **4** a person who holds an office, esp a clergyman holding a benefice [C16 from L *incumbere* to lie upon, devote one's attention to]

incunabula (ˌɪnkjʊ'næbjʊlə) *pl n, sing* **incunabulum** (-ləm) **1** any book printed before 1500 **2** the earliest stages of something; beginnings [C19 from L, orig.: swaddling clothes, hence beginnings, from IN-[2] + *cūnābula* cradle] > ˌ**incu'nabular** *adj*

incur (ɪn'kɜː) *vb* **incurs, incurring, incurred** (*tr*) **1** to make oneself subject to (something undesirable); bring upon oneself **2** to run into or encounter [C16 from L *incurrere* to run into, from *currere* to run] > **in'currable** *adj*

incurable (ɪn'kjʊərəbᵊl) *adj* **1** (esp of a disease) not curable; unresponsive to treatment ▷ *n* **2** a person having an incurable disease > **inˌcura'bility** *or* **in'curableness** *n* > **in'curably** *adv*

incurious (ɪn'kjʊərɪəs) *adj* not curious; indifferent or uninterested > **incuriosity** (ɪnˌkjʊərɪ'ɒsɪtɪ) *or* **in'curiousness** *n* > **in'curiously** *adv*

incursion (ɪn'kɜːʃən) *n* **1** a sudden invasion, attack, or raid **2** the act of running or leaking into; penetration [C15 from L *incursiō* onset, attack, from *incurrere* to run into; see INCUR] > **incursive** (ɪn'kɜːsɪv) *adj*

incus (ˈɪŋkəs) *n, pl* **incudes** (ɪnˈkjuːdiːz) the central of the three small bones in the middle ear of mammals ▷ Cf **malleus, stapes** [C17 from L: anvil, from *incūdere* to forge]
incuse (ɪnˈkjuːz) *n* **1** a design stamped or hammered onto a coin ▷ *vb* **incuses, incusing, incused** **2** to impress (a coin) with a design by hammering or stamping ▷ *adj* **3** stamped or hammered onto a coin [C19 from L *incūsus* hammered; see INCUS]
Ind (ɪnd) *n* **1** a poetic name for **India** **2** an obsolete name for the **Indies**
Ind. *abbrev for:* **1** Independent **2** India **3** Indian
indaba (ɪnˈdɑːbə) *n* **1** (among Bantu peoples of southern Africa) a meeting to discuss a serious topic **2** *S African inf* a matter of concern or for discussion [C19 from Zulu: topic]
indebted (ɪnˈdɛtɪd) *adj (postpositive)* **1** owing gratitude for help, favours, etc; obligated **2** owing money
indebtedness (ɪnˈdɛtɪdnɪs) *n* **1** the state of being indebted **2** the total of a person's debts
indecency (ɪnˈdiːsənsɪ) *n, pl* **indecencies** **1** the state or quality of being indecent **2** an indecent act, etc
indecent (ɪnˈdiːsᵊnt) *adj* **1** offensive to standards of decency, esp in sexual matters **2** unseemly or improper (esp in **indecent haste**) > **inˈdecently** *adv*
indecent assault *n* the offence of subjecting a person to a form of sexual activity, other than rape, against his or her will
indecent exposure *n* the offence of indecently exposing one's body in public, esp the genitals
indecisive (ˌɪndɪˈsaɪsɪv) *adj* **1** (of a person) vacillating; irresolute **2** not decisive or conclusive > **ˌindeˈcision** *or* **ˌindeˈcisiveness** *n* > **ˌindeˈcisively** *adv*
indecorous (ɪnˈdɛkərəs) *adj* improper or ungraceful; unseemly > **inˈdecorously** *adv*
indecorum (ˌɪndɪˈkɔːrəm) *n* lack of decorum; unseemliness
indeed (ɪnˈdiːd) *(sentence connector)* **1** certainly; actually: *indeed, it may never happen* ▷ *adv* **2** (intensifier): *that is indeed amazing* **3** or rather; what is more: *a comfortable, indeed wealthy family* ▷ *interj* **4** an expression of doubt, surprise, etc
indef. *abbrev for* indefinite
indefatigable (ˌɪndɪˈfætɪɡəbᵊl) *adj* unable to be tired out; unflagging [C16 from L, from *fatīgāre* to tire] > **ˌindeˌfatigaˈbility** *n* > **ˌindeˈfatigably** *adv*
indefeasible (ˌɪndɪˈfiːzəbᵊl) *adj law* not liable to be annulled or forfeited > **ˌindeˌfeasiˈbility** *n* > **ˌindeˈfeasibly** *adv*
indefensible (ˌɪndɪˈfɛnsəbᵊl) *adj* **1** not justifiable or excusable **2** capable of being disagreed with; untenable **3** incapable of defence against attack > **ˌindeˌfensiˈbility** *n* > **ˌindeˈfensibly** *adv*
indefinite (ɪnˈdɛfɪnɪt) *adj* **1** not certain or determined; unsettled **2** without exact limits; indeterminate: *an indefinite number* **3** vague or unclear **4** in traditional logic, a proposition in which it is not stated whether the subject is universal or particular, as in *men are mortal* > **inˈdefinitely** *adv* > **inˈdefiniteness** *n*
indefinite article *n grammar* a determiner that expresses nonspecificity of reference, such as *a, an,* or *some*
indehiscent (ˌɪndɪˈhɪsᵊnt) *adj* (of fruits, etc) not dehiscent; not opening to release seeds, etc > **ˌindeˈhiscence** *n*
indelible (ɪnˈdɛlɪbᵊl) *adj* **1** incapable of being erased or obliterated **2** making indelible marks: *indelible ink* [C16 from L, from IN-¹ + *dēlēre* to destroy] > **inˌdeliˈbility** *or* **inˈdelibleness** *n* > **inˈdelibly** *adv*
indelicate (ɪnˈdɛlɪkɪt) *adj* **1** coarse, crude, or rough **2** offensive, embarrassing, or tasteless > **inˈdelicacy** *or* **inˈdelicateness** *n* > **inˈdelicately** *adv*
indemnify (ɪnˈdɛmnɪˌfaɪ) *vb* **indemnifies, indemnifying, indemnified** *(tr)* **1** to secure against future loss, damage, or liability; give security for; insure **2** to compensate for loss, etc; reimburse > **inˌdemnifiˈcation** *n* > **inˈdemniˌfier** *n*
indemnity (ɪnˈdɛmnɪtɪ) *n, pl* **indemnities** **1** compensation for loss or damage; reimbursement **2** protection or insurance against future loss or damage **3** legal exemption from penalties incurred through one's acts or defaults **4** *Canad* the annual salary paid by the government to a member of Parliament or of a provincial legislature [C15 from LL, from *indemnis* uninjured, from L IN-¹ + *damnum* damage]
indene (ˈɪndiːn) *n* a colourless liquid hydrocarbon obtained from coal tar and used in making synthetic resins. Formula: C_9H_8 [C20 from INDOLE + -ENE]
indent¹ *vb* (ɪnˈdɛnt) *(mainly tr)* **1** to place (written matter, etc) in from the margin **2** to cut (a document in duplicate) so that the irregular lines may be matched **3** *chiefly Brit* (in foreign trade) to place an order for (foreign goods) **4** (when *intr*, foll by *for, on,* or *upon*) *chiefly Brit* to make an order on (a source or supply) or for (something) **5** to notch (an edge, border, etc); make jagged **6** to bind (an apprentice, etc) by indenture ▷ *n* (ˈɪnˌdɛnt) *chiefly Brit* **7** (in foreign trade) an order for foreign merchandise **8** an official order for goods [C14 from OF *endenter*, from EN-¹ + *dent* tooth, from L *dēns*] > **inˈdenter** *or* **inˈdentor** *n*
indent² *vb* (ɪnˈdɛnt) **1** *(tr)* to make a dent or depression in ▷ *n* (ˈɪnˌdɛnt) **2** a dent or depression [C15 from IN-² + DENT]
indentation (ˌɪndɛnˈteɪʃən) *n* **1** a hollowed, notched, or cut place, as on an edge or on a coastline **2** a series of hollows, notches, or cuts **3** the act of indenting or the condition of being indented **4** Also: **indention, indent** the leaving of space or the amount of space left between a margin and the start of an indented line
indention (ɪnˈdɛnʃən) *n* another word for **indentation** (sense 4)
indenture (ɪnˈdɛntʃə) *n* **1** any deed, contract, or sealed agreement between two or more parties **2** (formerly) a deed drawn up in duplicate, each part having correspondingly indented edges for identification and security **3** *(often pl)* a contract between an apprentice and his or her master **4** a less common word for **indentation** ▷ *vb* **indentures, indenturing, indentured** **5** *(intr)* to enter into an agreement by indenture **6** *(tr)* to bind (an apprentice, servant, etc) by indenture > **inˈdentureˌship** *n*
independence (ˌɪndɪˈpɛndəns) *n* the state or quality of being independent. Also: **independency**
Independence (ˌɪndɪˈpɛndəns) *n* a city in W Missouri, near Kansas City: starting point for the Santa Fe, Oregon, and California Trails (1831–44). Pop: 113 288 (2000)
independency (ˌɪndɪˈpɛndənsɪ) *n, pl* **independencies** **1** a territory or state free from the control of any other power **2** another word for **independence**
independent (ˌɪndɪˈpɛndənt) *adj* **1** free from control in action, judgment, etc; autonomous **2** not dependent on anything else for function, validity, etc; separate **3** not reliant on the support, esp financial support, of others **4** capable of acting for oneself or on one's own: *a very independent little girl* **5** providing a large unearned sum towards one's support (esp in **independent income, independent means**) **6** living on an unearned income **7** *maths* (of a system of equations) not linearly dependent. See also **independent variable** **8** *logic* (of two or more propositions) unrelated ▷ *n* **9** an independent person or thing **10** a person who is not affiliated to or who acts independently of a political party > **ˌindeˈpendently** *adv*
Independent (ˌɪndɪˈpɛndənt) *Christianity* ▷ *n* **1** (in England) a member of the Congregational Church ▷ *adj* **2** of or relating to the Congregational Church
independent clause *n grammar* a main or coordinate

Ii

clause ▷ Cf **dependent clause**

independent school *n* **1** (in Britain) a school that is neither financed nor controlled by the government or local authorities **2** (in Australia) a school that is not part of the state system

independent variable *n* a variable in a mathematical equation or statement whose value determines that of the dependent variable: in *y* = f(*x*), *x* is the independent variable

in-depth *adj* detailed and thorough: *an in-depth study*

indescribable (ˌɪndɪˈskraɪbəbᵊl) *adj* beyond description; too intense, extreme, etc, for words > **ˌindeˌscribaˈbility** *n* > **ˌindeˈscribably** *adv*

indestructible (ˌɪndɪˈstrʌktəbᵊl) *adj* incapable of being destroyed; very durable > **ˌindeˌstructiˈbility** *or* **ˌindeˈstructibleness** *n* > **ˌindeˈstructibly** *adv*

indeterminate (ˌɪndɪˈtɜːmɪnɪt) *adj* **1** uncertain in extent, amount, or nature **2** not definite; inconclusive: *an indeterminate reply* **3** unable to be predicted, calculated, or deduced **4** *maths* **4a** having no numerical meaning, as 0/0 **4b** (of an equation) having more than one variable and an unlimited number of solutions > **ˌindeˈterminacy** *or* **ˌindeˈterminateness** *n* > **ˌindeˈterminately** *adv*

indeterminism (ˌɪndɪˈtɜːmɪˌnɪzəm) *n* the philosophical doctrine that behaviour is not entirely determined by motives > **ˌindeˈterminist** *n, adj* > **ˌindeˌterminˈistic** *adj*

index (ˈɪndɛks) *n, pl* **indexes** *or* **indices** (-dɪˌsiːz) **1** an alphabetical list of persons, subjects, etc, mentioned in a printed work, usually at the back, and indicating where they are referred to **2** See **thumb index** **3** *library science* a systematic list of book titles or authors' names, giving cross-references and the location of each book; catalogue **4** an indication, sign, or token **5** a pointer, needle, or other indicator, as on an instrument **6** *maths* **6a** another name for **exponent** (sense 4) **6b** a number or variable placed as a superscript to the left of a radical sign indicating the root to be extracted, as in $\sqrt[3]{8} = 2$ **7** a numerical scale by means of which levels of the cost of living can be compared with some base number **8** a number or ratio indicating a specific characteristic, property, etc: *refractive index* **9** Also called: **fist** a printer's mark, ☛ used to indicate notes, paragraphs, etc ▷ *vb* (*tr*) **10** to put an index in (a book) **11** to enter (a word, item, etc) in an index **12** to point out; indicate **13** to make index-linked **14** to move (a machine, etc) so that an operation will be repeated at certain defined intervals [C16 from L: pointer, hence forefinger, title, index, from *indicāre* to disclose, show; see INDICATE] > **ˈindexer** *n*

indexation (ˌɪndɛkˈseɪʃən) *or* **index-linking** *n* the act of making wages, interest rates, etc, index-linked

index case *n med* the first case of a disease, or the primary case referred to in a report

index finger *n* the finger next to the thumb. Also called: **forefinger**

index fossil *n* a fossil species that characterizes and is used to delimit a geological zone. Also called: **zone fossil**

index futures *pl n* a form of financial futures based on projected movements of a share price index, such as the Financial Times Stock Exchange 100 Share Index

indexical (ɪnˈdɛksɪkᵊl) *adj* **1** arranged as or relating to an index or indexes ▷ *n* **2** Also called: **deictic** *logic, linguistics* a term whose reference depends on the context of utterance, such as *I, you, here, now,* or *tomorrow*

Index Librorum Prohibitorum *Latin* (ˈɪndɛks laɪˈbrɔːrʊm prəʊˌhɪbɪˈtɔːrʊm) *n RC Church* (formerly) an official list of proscribed books. Often called: **the Index** [C17, lit.: list of forbidden books]

index-linked *adj* (of wages, interest rates, etc) directly related to the cost-of-living index and rising or falling accordingly

index number *n statistics* a statistic indicating the relative change occurring in the price or value of a commodity or in a general economic variable, with reference to a previous base period conventionally given the number 100

India (ˈɪndɪə) *n* **1** a republic in S Asia: history dates from the Indus Valley civilization (3rd millennium BC); came under British supremacy in 1763 and passed to the British Crown in 1858; nationalist movement arose under Gandhi (1869–1948); Indian subcontinent divided into Pakistan (Muslim) and India (Hindu) in 1947; became a republic within the Commonwealth in 1950. It consists chiefly of the Himalayas, rising over 7500 m (25 000 ft) in the extreme north, the Ganges plain in the north, the Thar Desert in the northwest, the Chota Nagpur plateau in the northeast, and the Deccan Plateau in the south. Official and administrative languages: Hindi and English; each state has its own language. Religion: Hindu majority, Muslim minority. Currency: rupee. Capital: New Delhi. Pop: 1 029 991 000 (2001 est). Area: 3 268 100 sq km (1 261 813 sq miles). Hindi name: **Bharat** **2** *communications* a code word for the letter *i*
▷ http://goidirectory.nic.in
▷ http://goidirectory.nic.in/tourism.htm

Indiaman (ˈɪndɪəmən) *n, pl* **Indiamen** (formerly) a merchant ship engaged in trade with India

Indian (ˈɪndɪən) *n* **1** a native or inhabitant of the Republic of India or a descendant of one **2** an American Indian **3** (*not in scholarly usage*) any of the languages of the American Indians ▷ *adj* **4** of or relating to India, its inhabitants, or any of their languages **5** of or relating to the American Indians or any of their languages

Indiana (ˌɪndɪˈænə) *n* a state of the N central US, in the Midwest: consists of an undulating plain, with sand dunes and lakes in the north and limestone caves in the south. Capital: Indianapolis. Pop: 6 080 485 (2000). Area: 93 491 sq km (36 097 sq miles). Abbreviations: **Ind** or (with zip code) **IN**

Indianapolis (ˌɪndɪəˈnæpəlɪs) *n* a city in central Indiana: the state capital. Pop: 791 926 (2000)

Indian club *n* a bottle-shaped club, usually used in pairs by gymnasts, jugglers, etc

Indian corn *n* another name for **maize** (sense 1)

Indian Desert *n* another name for the **Thar Desert**

Indian Empire *n* British India and the Indian states under indirect British control, which gained independence as India and Pakistan in 1947

Indian file *n* another term for **single file**

Indian hemp *n* another name for **hemp,** esp the variety *Cannabis indica*, from which several narcotic drugs are obtained

Indian ink *or esp US & Canad* **India ink** *n* **1** a black pigment made from a mixture of lampblack and a binding agent such as gelatine or glue: usually formed into solid cakes and sticks **2** a black liquid ink made from this pigment ▷ Also called: **China ink, Chinese ink**

Indian list *n inf* (in Canada) a list of persons to whom spirits may not be sold

Indian meal *n* another name for **corn meal**

Indian Ocean *n* an ocean bordered by Africa in the west, Asia in the north, and Australia in the east and merging with the Antarctic Ocean in the south. Average depth: 3900 m (13 000 ft). Greatest depth (off the Sunda Islands): 7450 m (24 442 ft). Area: about 73 556 000 sq km (28 400 000 sq miles)

Indian rope-trick *n* the supposed Indian feat of climbing an unsupported rope

Indian States and Agencies *pl n* another name for the **Native States**

Indian summer *n* **1** a period of unusually warm weather in the late autumn **2** a period of tranquillity or of renewed productivity towards the end of something, esp a person's life [orig. US: prob. so named because it was first noted in Amerind regions]

Indian Territory *n* the territory established in the early 19th century in present-day Oklahoma, where Indians were forced to settle by the US government. The last remnant was integrated into the new state of Oklahoma in 1907

Indian tobacco *n* a poisonous North American plant with small pale bell-shaped blue flowers and rounded inflated seed capsules

India paper *n* a thin soft opaque printing paper originally made in the Orient

India rubber *n* another name for **rubber**[1] (sense 1)

Indic ('ɪndɪk) *adj* **1** denoting, belonging to, or relating to a branch of Indo-European consisting of certain languages of India, including Sanskrit, Hindi, and Urdu ▷ *n* **2** this group of languages ▷ Also: **Indo-Aryan**

indicate ('ɪndɪˌkeɪt) *vb* **indicates, indicating, indicated** (*tr*) **1** (*may take a clause as object*) to be or give a sign or symptom of; imply: *cold hands indicate a warm heart* **2** to point out or show **3** (*may take a clause as object*) to state briefly; suggest **4** (of instruments) to show a reading of **5** (*usually passive*) to recommend or require: *surgery seems to be indicated for this patient* [C17 from L *indicāre* to point out, from IN-[2] + *dicāre* to proclaim; cf. INDEX] > **'indiˌcatable** *adj* > **indicatory** (ɪn'dɪkətərɪ, -trɪ) *adj*

indication (ˌɪndɪ'keɪʃən) *n* **1** something that serves to indicate or suggest; sign: *an indication of foul play* **2** the degree or quantity represented on a measuring instrument or device **3** the action of indicating **4** something that is indicated as advisable, necessary, or expedient

indicative (ɪn'dɪkətɪv) *adj* **1** (*usually postpositive*; foll by *of*) serving as a sign; suggestive: *indicative of trouble ahead* **2** *grammar* denoting a mood of verbs used chiefly to make statements ▷ *n* **3** *grammar* **3a** the indicative mood **3b** a verb in the indicative mood ▷ Abbrev: **indic** > **in'dicatively** *adv*

indicator ('ɪndɪˌkeɪtə) *n* **1** something that provides an indication, esp of trends. See **economic indicator** **2** a device to attract attention, such as the pointer of a gauge or a warning lamp **3** an instrument that displays certain operating conditions in a machine, such as a gauge showing temperature, etc **4** a device that registers something, such as the movements of a lift, or that shows information, such as train departure times **5** Also called: **blinker** a device for indicating that a motor vehicle is about to turn left or right, esp two pairs of lights that flash **6** a delicate measuring instrument used to determine small differences in the height of mechanical components **7** *chem* a substance used to indicate the completion of a chemical reaction, usually by a change of colour **8** Also called: **indicator species** *ecology* a plant or animal species that thrives only under particular environmental conditions and therefore indicates these conditions where it is found

indices ('ɪndɪˌsiːz) *n* a plural of **index**

indicia (ɪn'dɪʃɪə) *pl n, sing* **indicium** (-ʃɪəm) distinguishing markings or signs; indications [C17 from L, pl of *indicium* a notice, from INDEX] > **in'dicial** *adj*

indict (ɪn'daɪt) *vb* (*tr*) to charge (a person) with crime, esp formally in writing; accuse [C14 alteration of *enditen* to INDITE] > **ˌindict'ee** *n* > **in'dicter** *or* **in'dictor** *n* > **in'dictable** *adj*

USAGE See at **indite**

indictment (ɪn'daɪtmənt) *n* *criminal law* **1** a formal written charge of crime formerly referred to and presented on oath by a grand jury **2** any formal accusation of crime **3** the act of indicting or the state of being indicted

indie ('ɪndɪ) *n* *inf* **a** an independent film or record company **b** (*as modifier*): *an indie producer; the indie charts*

▷ www.indie-music.com

▷ www.dotmusic.com

Indies ('ɪndɪz) *n* **the** **1** the territories of S and SE Asia included in the East Indies, India, and Indochina **2** See **East Indies** **3** See **West Indies**

indifference (ɪn'dɪfrəns, -fərəns) *n* **1** the fact or state of being indifferent; lack of care or concern **2** lack of quality; mediocrity **3** lack of importance; insignificance

indifferent (ɪn'dɪfrənt, -fərənt) *adj* **1** (often foll by *to*) showing no care or concern; uninterested: *he was indifferent to my pleas* **2** unimportant; immaterial **3a** of only average or moderate size, extent, quality, etc **3b** not at all good; poor **4** showing or having no preferences; impartial [C14 from L *indifferēns* making no distinction] > **in'differently** *adv*

indifferentism (ɪn'dɪfrənˌtɪzəm, -fərən-) *n* systematic indifference, esp in matters of religion > **in'differentist** *n*

indigenous (ɪn'dɪdʒɪnəs) *adj* (when *postpositive*, foll by *to*) **1** originating or occurring naturally (in a country, etc); native **2** innate (to); inherent (in) [C17 from L *indigenus*, from *indi-* in + *gignere* to beget] > **in'digenously** *adv* > **in'digenousness** *n*

indigent ('ɪndɪdʒənt) *adj* **1** so poor as to lack even necessities; very needy **2** (usually foll by *of*) *arch* lacking (in) or destitute (of) ▷ *n* **3** an impoverished person [C14 from L *indigēre* to need, from *egēre* to lack] > **'indigence** *n* > **'indigently** *adv*

indigestible (ˌɪndɪ'dʒɛstəb[ə]l) *adj* **1** incapable of being digested or difficult to digest **2** difficult to understand or absorb mentally: *an indigestible book* > **ˌindiˌgesti'bility** *n* > **ˌindi'gestibly** *adv*

indigestion (ˌɪndɪ'dʒɛstʃən) *n* difficulty in digesting food, accompanied by abdominal pain, heartburn, and belching

indignant (ɪn'dɪgnənt) *adj* feeling or showing indignation [C16 from L *indignārī* to be displeased with] > **in'dignantly** *adv*

indignation (ˌɪndɪg'neɪʃən) *n* anger aroused by something felt to be unfair, unworthy, or wrong

indignity (ɪn'dɪgnɪtɪ) *n, pl* **indignities** injury to one's self-esteem or dignity; humiliation

indigo ('ɪndɪˌgəʊ) *n, pl* **indigos** *or* **indigoes** **1** a blue vat dye originally obtained from plants but now made synthetically **2** any of various leguminous tropical plants, such as the anil, that yield this dye **3a** any of a group of colours that have the same blue-violet hue; a spectral colour **3b** (*as adj*): *an indigo rug* [C16 from Sp. *indico*, via L from Gk *Indikos* of India] > **indigotic** (ˌɪndɪ'gɒtɪk) *adj*

indigo blue *n, adj* (**indigo-blue** *when prenominal*) the full name for **indigo** (the colour and the dye)

indirect (ˌɪndɪ'rɛkt) *adj* **1** deviating from a direct course or line; roundabout; circuitous **2** not coming as a direct effect or consequence; secondary: *indirect benefits* **3** not straightforward, open, or fair; devious or evasive > **ˌindi'rectly** *adv* > **ˌindi'rectness** *n*

indirect costs *pl n* another name for **overheads**

indirection (ˌɪndɪ'rɛkʃən) *n* **1** indirect procedure, courses, or methods **2** lack of direction or purpose; aimlessness **3** indirect dealing; deceit

indirect lighting *n* reflected or diffused light from a concealed source

indirect object *n* *grammar* a noun, pronoun, or noun phrase indicating the recipient or beneficiary of the action of a verb and its direct object, as *John* in the sentence *I bought John a newspaper*

indirect proof *n* *logic, maths* proof of a conclusion by showing its negation to be self-contradictory ▷ Cf **direct** (sense 17)

indirect question *n* a question reported in indirect speech, as in *She asked why you came*

indirect speech *or esp US* **indirect discourse** *n* the reporting of something said or written by conveying what was meant rather than repeating the exact words, as in the sentence *He said I looked happy* as opposed to *He said to me, "You look happy."* Also called: **reported speech**

Ii

indirect tax *n* a tax levied on goods or services rather than on individuals or companies

indiscreet (ˌɪndɪˈskriːt) *adj* not discreet; imprudent or tactless > ˌ**indisˈcreetly** *adv* > ˌ**indisˈcreetness** *n*

indiscrete (ˌɪndɪˈskriːt) *adj* not divisible or divided into parts

indiscretion (ˌɪndɪˈskrɛʃən) *n* **1** the characteristic or state of being indiscreet **2** an indiscreet act, remark, etc

indiscriminate (ˌɪndɪˈskrɪmɪnɪt) *adj* **1** lacking discrimination or careful choice; random or promiscuous **2** jumbled; confused > ˌ**indisˈcriminately** *adv* > ˌ**indisˈcriminateness** *n* > ˌ**indisˌcrimiˈnation** *n*

indispensable (ˌɪndɪˈspɛnsəbᵊl) *adj* **1** absolutely necessary; essential **2** not to be disregarded or escaped: *an indispensable role* ▷ *n* **3** an indispensable person or thing > ˌ**indisˌpensaˈbility** *or* ˌ**indisˈpensableness** *n* > ˌ**indisˈpensably** *adv*

indispose (ˌɪndɪˈspəʊz) *vb* **indisposes, indisposing, indisposed** (*tr*) **1** to make unwilling or opposed; disincline **2** to cause to feel ill **3** to make unfit (for something or to do something)

indisposed (ˌɪndɪˈspəʊzd) *adj* **1** sick or ill **2** unwilling [C15 from L *indispositus* disordered] > **indisposition** (ˌɪndɪspəˈzɪʃən) *n*

indisputable (ˌɪndɪˈspjuːtəbᵊl) *adj* beyond doubt; not open to question > ˌ**indisˌputaˈbility** *or* ˌ**indisˈputableness** *n* > ˌ**indisˈputably** *adv*

indissoluble (ˌɪndɪˈsɒljʊbᵊl) *adj* incapable of being dissolved or broken; permanent > ˌ**indisˈsolubly** *adv*

indistinct (ˌɪndɪˈstɪŋkt) *adj* incapable of being clearly distinguished, as by the eyes, ears, or mind; not distinct > ˌ**indisˈtinctly** *adv* > ˌ**indisˈtinctness** *n*

indistinguishable (ˌɪndɪˈstɪŋgwɪʃəbᵊl) *adj* **1** (*often postpositive*; foll by *from*) identical or very similar (to): *twins indistinguishable from one another* **2** not easily perceptible; indiscernible > ˌ**indisˌtinguishaˈbility** *or* ˌ**indisˈtinguishableness** *n* > ˌ**indisˈtinguishably** *adv*

indite (ɪnˈdaɪt) *vb* **indites, inditing, indited** (*tr*) *arch* to write [C14 from OF *enditer*, from L *indīcere* to declare, from IN-[2] + *dīcere* to say] > **inˈditement** *n* > **inˈditer** *n*

> USAGE *Indite* and *inditement* are sometimes wrongly used where *indict* and *indictment* are meant: *he was indicted* (not *indited*) *for fraud*

indium (ˈɪndɪəm) *n* a rare soft silvery metallic element associated with zinc ores: used in alloys, electronics, and electroplating. Symbol: In; atomic no.: 49; atomic wt.: 114.82 [C19 NL, from INDIGO + -IUM]

individual (ˌɪndɪˈvɪdjʊəl) *adj* **1** of, relating to, characteristic of, or meant for a single person or thing **2** separate or distinct, esp from others of its kind; particular: *please mark the individual pages* **3** characterized by unusual and striking qualities; distinctive **4** *obs* indivisible; inseparable ▷ *n* **5** a single person, esp when regarded as distinct from others **6** *biol* a single animal or plant, esp as distinct from a species **7** *inf* a person: *a most obnoxious individual* [C15 from Med. L, from L *indīviduus* indivisible, from IN-[1] + *dīvidere* to DIVIDE] > ˌ**indiˈvidually** *adv*

individualism (ˌɪndɪˈvɪdjʊəˌlɪzəm) *n* **1** the principle of asserting one's independence and individuality; egoism **2** an individual quirk **3** another word for **laissez faire** (sense 1) **4** *philosophy* the doctrine that only individual things exist > ˌ**indiˈvidualist** *n*

individuality (ˌɪndɪˌvɪdjʊˈælɪtɪ) *n, pl* **individualities** **1** distinctive or unique character or personality: *a work of great individuality* **2** the qualities that distinguish one person or thing from another; identity **3** the state or quality of being a separate entity; discreteness

individualize *or* **individualise** (ˌɪndɪˈvɪdjʊəˌlaɪz) *vb* **individualizes, individualizing, individualized** *or* **individualises, individualising, individualised** (*tr*) **1** to make or mark as individual or distinctive in character **2** to consider or treat individually; particularize **3** to make or modify so as to meet the special requirements of a person > ˌ**indiˌvidualiˈzation** *or* ˌ**indiˌvidualiˈsation** *n* > ˌ**indiˈvidualˌizer** *or* ˌ**indiˈvidualˌiser** *n*

individuate (ˌɪndɪˈvɪdjʊˌeɪt) *vb* **individuates, individuating, individuated** (*tr*) **1** to give individuality or an individual form to **2** to distinguish from others of the same species or group; individualize > ˌ**indiˈviduˌator** *n*

indivisible (ˌɪndɪˈvɪzəbᵊl) *adj* **1** unable to be divided **2** *maths* leaving a remainder when divided by a given number > ˌ**indiˌvisiˈbility** *n* > ˌ**indiˈvisibly** *adv*

Indo- (ˈɪndəʊ) *combining form* denoting India or Indian: *Indo-European*

Indo-Canadian *n* **1** a Canadian of Indian descent ▷ *adj* **2** of or relating to Canadians of Indian descent

Indo-Caribbean *adj* **1** denoting or relating to Caribbean people of Indian descent or their culture ▷ *n* a Caribbean of Indian descent ▷ Also: **East Indian**

Indochina *or* **Indo-China** *n* (ˈɪndəʊˈtʃaɪnə) **1** Also called: **Farther India** a peninsula in SE Asia, between India and China: consists of Myanmar, Thailand, Laos, Cambodia, Vietnam, and Malaysia **2** the former French colonial possessions of Cochin China, Annam, Tonkin, Laos, and Cambodia

indoctrinate (ɪnˈdɒktrɪˌneɪt) *vb* **indoctrinates, indoctrinating, indoctrinated** (*tr*) **1** to teach (a person or group of people) systematically to accept doctrines, esp uncritically **2** *rare* to instruct > **inˌdoctriˈnation** *n* > **inˈdoctriˌnator** *n*

Indo-European *adj* **1** denoting, belonging to, or relating to a family of languages that includes English: characteristically marked, esp in the older languages, such as Latin, by inflection showing gender, number, and case **2** denoting or relating to the hypothetical parent language of this family, primitive Indo-European **3** denoting, belonging to, or relating to any of the peoples speaking these languages ▷ *n* **4** the Indo-European family of languages **5** the reconstructed hypothetical parent language of this family ▷ Also (*obs*): **Indo-Germanic**

Indo-Iranian *adj* **1** of or relating to the Indic and Iranian branches of the Indo-European family of languages ▷ *n* **2** this group of languages, sometimes considered as forming a single branch of Indo-European

indole (ˈɪndəʊl) *or* **indol** (ˈɪndəʊl, -dɒl) *n* a white or yellowish crystalline heterocyclic compound extracted from coal tar and used in perfumery, medicine, and as a flavouring agent [C19 from IND(IGO) + -OLE[1]]

indolent (ˈɪndələnt) *adj* **1** disliking work or effort; lazy; idle **2** *pathol* causing little pain: *an indolent tumour* **3** (esp of a painless ulcer) slow to heal [C17 from L *indolēns* not feeling pain, from IN-[1] + *dolēre* to grieve, cause distress] > ˈ**indolence** *n* > ˈ**indolently** *adv*

indomitable (ɪnˈdɒmɪtəbᵊl) *adj* (of courage, pride, etc) difficult or impossible to defeat or subdue [C17 from LL, from L *indomitus* untameable, from *domāre* to tame] > **inˌdomitaˈbility** *or* **inˈdomitableness** *n* > **inˈdomitably** *adv*

Indonesia (ˌɪndəʊˈniːzɪə) *n* a republic in SE Asia, in the Malay Archipelago, consisting of the main islands of Sumatra, Java and Madura, Bali, Sulawesi (Celebes), Lombok, Sumbawa, Flores, the Moluccas, part of Timor, part of Borneo (Kalimantan), Irian Jaya, and over 3000 small islands in the Indian and Pacific Oceans: became the Dutch East Indies in 1798; declared independence in 1945; became a republic in 1950; East Timor (illegally annexed in 1975) became independent in 2002; Official language: Bahasa Indonesia. Religion: Muslim majority. Currency: rupiah. Capital: Jakarta. Pop: 212 195 000 (2001 est). Area: 1 919 317 sq km (741 052 sq miles). Former names (1798–1945): **Dutch East Indies, Netherlands East Indies**

▷ www.indonesia.go.id

▷ www.indonesiatourism.com

Indonesian (ˌɪndəʊˈniːzɪən) *adj* **1** of or relating to Indonesia, its people, or their language ▷ *n* **2** a native or inhabitant of Indonesia

indoor (ˈɪnˌdɔː) *adj (prenominal)* of, situated in, or appropriate to the inside of a house or other building: *an indoor pool; indoor amusements*

indoors (ˌɪnˈdɔːz) *adv, adj (postpositive)* inside or into a house or other building

Indore (ɪnˈdɔː) *n* **1** a city in central India, in W Madhya Pradesh. Pop: 1 091 674 (1991) **2** a former state of central India: became part of Madhya Bharat in 1948, which in turn became part of Madhya Pradesh in 1956

indorse (ɪnˈdɔːs) *vb* **indorses, indorsing, indorsed** a variant spelling of **endorse**

Indra (ˈɪndrə) *n Hinduism* the most celebrated god of the Rig-Veda, governing the weather and dispensing rain

indraught *or US* **indraft** (ˈɪnˌdrɑːft) *n* **1** the act of drawing or pulling in **2** an inward flow, esp of air

indrawn (ˌɪnˈdrɔːn) *adj* **1** drawn or pulled in **2** inward-looking or introspective

Indre (*French* ɛ̃drə) *n* a department of central France in the Centre region. Capital: Châteauroux. Pop: 231 139 (1999). Area: 6906 sq km (2693 sq miles)

Indre-et-Loire (*French* ɛ̃drelwar) *n* a department of W central France in the Centre region: contains many famous châteaux along the Loire. Capital: Tours. Pop: 554 003 (1999). Area: 6158 sq km (2402 sq miles)

indris (ˈɪndrɪs) *or* **indri** (ˈɪndrɪ) *n, pl* **indris** **1** a large Madagascan arboreal lemuroid primate with thick silky fur patterned in black, white, and fawn **2** **woolly indris** a related nocturnal Madagascan animal with thick grey-brown fur and a long tail [C19 from F: lemur, from native word *indry!* look! mistaken for the animal's name]

indubitable (ɪnˈdjuːbɪtəbᵊl) *adj* incapable of being doubted; unquestionable [C18 from L, from IN-[1] + *dubitāre* to doubt] > **inˈdubitably** *adv*

induce (ɪnˈdjuːs) *vb* **induces, inducing, induced** *(tr)* **1** (often foll by an infinitive) to persuade or use influence on **2** to cause or bring about **3** *med* to initiate or hasten (labour), as by administering a drug to stimulate uterine contractions **4** *logic, obs* to assert or establish (a general proposition, etc) by induction **5** to produce (an electromotive force or electrical current) by induction **6** to transmit (magnetism) by induction [C14 from L *indūcere* to lead in] > **inˈducer** *n* > **inˈducible** *adj*

inducement (ɪnˈdjuːsmənt) *n* **1** the act of inducing **2** a means of inducing; persuasion; incentive **3** *law* the introductory part that leads up to and explains the matter in dispute

induct (ɪnˈdʌkt) *vb (tr)* **1** to bring in formally or install in an office, place, etc; invest **2** (foll by *to* or *into*) to initiate in knowledge (of) **3** *US* to enlist for military service **4** *physics* another word for **induce** (senses 5, 6) [C14 from L *inductus* led in, p.p. of *indūcere* to introduce; see INDUCE]

inductance (ɪnˈdʌktəns) *n* **1** the property of an electric circuit as a result of which an electromotive force is created by a change of current in the same or in a neighbouring circuit **2** a component, such as a coil, in an electrical circuit, the main function of which is to produce inductance

induction (ɪnˈdʌkʃən) *n* **1** the act of inducting or state of being inducted **2** the act of inducing **3** (in an internal-combustion engine) the drawing in of mixed air and fuel from the carburettor to the cylinder **4** *logic* **4a** a process of reasoning by which a general conclusion is drawn from a set of premises, based mainly on experience or experimental evidence **4b** a conclusion reached by this process of reasoning **5** the process by which electrical or magnetic properties are transferred, without physical contact, from one circuit or body to another. See also **inductance** **6** *maths* a method of proving a proposition P(*n*) by showing that it is true for all preceding values of *n* and for *n* + 1 **7a** a formal introduction or entry into an office or position **7b** *(as modifier)*: *induction course* **8** *US* the enlistment of a civilian into military service > **inˈductional** *adj*

induction coil *n* **1** any coil of wire used to introduce inductance into a circuit **2** another name for **ignition coil**

induction heating *n* the heating of a conducting material as a result of the electric currents induced in it by an externally applied alternating magnetic field

induction loop system *n* an electronic system enabling partially deaf people to hear dialogue and sound in theatres, cinemas, etc. Often shortened to **induction loop**

induction motor *n* a type of electric motor in which an alternating supply fed to the windings of the stator creates a magnetic field that induces a current in the windings of the rotor. Rotation of the rotor results from the interaction of the magnetic field created by the rotor current with the field of the stator

inductive (ɪnˈdʌktɪv) *adj* **1** relating to or operated by electrical or magnetic induction: *an inductive reactance* **2** *logic, maths* of, relating to, or using induction: *inductive reasoning* **3** serving to induce or cause > **inˈductively** *adv* > **inˈductiveness** *n*

inductor (ɪnˈdʌktə) *n* **1** a person or thing that inducts **2** another name for an **inductance** (sense 2)

indue (ɪnˈdjuː) *vb* **indues, induing, indued** a variant spelling of **endue**

indulge (ɪnˈdʌldʒ) *vb* **indulges, indulging, indulged** **1** (when *intr*, often foll by *in*) to yield to or gratify (a whim or desire for): *to indulge in new clothes* **2** *(tr)* to yield to the wishes of; pamper: *to indulge a child* **3** *(tr)* to allow (oneself) the pleasure of something: *he indulged himself* **4** *(intr) inf* to take alcoholic drink, esp to excess [C17 from L *indulgēre* to concede] > **inˈdulger** *n* > **inˈdulgingly** *adv*

indulgence (ɪnˈdʌldʒəns) *n* **1** the act of indulging or state of being indulgent **2** a pleasure, habit, etc, indulged in; extravagance **3** liberal or tolerant treatment **4** something granted as a favour or privilege **5** *RC Church* a remission of the temporal punishment for sin after its guilt has been forgiven **6** Also called: **Declaration of Indulgence** a royal grant during the reigns of Charles II and James II of England giving Nonconformists and Roman Catholics a measure of religious freedom

indulgent (ɪnˈdʌldʒənt) *adj* showing or characterized by indulgence > **inˈdulgently** *adv*

induna (ɪnˈduːnə) *n* (in South Africa) a Black African overseer in a factory, mine, etc [C20 from Zulu *nduna* an official]

indurate *vb* (ˈɪndjʊˌreɪt), **indurates, indurating, indurated** **1** to make or become hard or callous **2** to make or become hardy ▷ *adj* (ˈɪndjʊrɪt) **3** hardened, callous, or unfeeling [C16 from L *indūrāre* to make hard; see ENDURE] > ˌ**induˈration** *n* > ˈ**induˌrative** *adj*

Indus (ˈɪndəs) *n* a river in S Asia, rising in SW Tibet in the Kailas Range of the Himalayas and flowing northwest through Kashmir, then southwest across Pakistan to the Arabian Sea: important throughout history, esp for the Indus Civilization (about 3000 to 1500 BC), and for irrigation. Length: about 2900 km (1800 miles)

indusium (ɪnˈdjuːzɪəm) *n, pl* **indusia** (-zɪə) **1** a membranous outgrowth on the undersurface of fern leaves that protects the developing sporangia **2** an enveloping membrane, such as the amnion [C18 NL, from L: tunic, from *induere* to put on] > **inˈdusial** *adj*

industrial (ɪnˈdʌstrɪəl) *adj* **1** of, relating to, or derived from industry **2** employed in industry: *the industrial workforce* **3** relating to or concerned with workers in industry: *industrial conditions* **4** used in industry: *industrial chemicals* > **inˈdustrially** *adv*

Ii

industrial action *n Brit* any action, such as a strike or go-slow, taken by employees in industry to protest against working conditions, etc

industrial archaeology *n* the study of industrial machines, works, etc of the past

industrial design *n* the art or practice of designing any object for manufacture > **industrial designer** *n*

industrial diamond *n* a small often synthetic diamond, valueless as a gemstone, used in cutting tools, abrasives, etc

industrial disease *n* any disease to which workers in a particular industry are prone

industrial espionage *n* attempting to obtain trade secrets by dishonest means, as by telephone- or computer-tapping, infiltration of a competitor's workforce, etc

industrial estate *n Brit* another name for **trading estate** US equivalent: **industrial park**

industrialism (ɪnˈdʌstrɪəˌlɪzəm) *n* an organization of society characterized by large-scale mechanized manufacturing industry rather than trade, farming, etc

industrialist (ɪnˈdʌstrɪəlɪst) *n* a person who has a substantial interest in the ownership or control of industrial enterprise

industrialize *or* **industrialise** (ɪnˈdʌstrɪəˌlaɪz) *vb* **industrializes, industrializing, industrialized** *or* **industrialises, industrialising, industrialised** **1** (*tr*) to develop industry on an extensive scale in (a country, region, etc) **2** (*intr*) (of a country, region, etc) to undergo the development of industry on an extensive scale > **inˌdustrialiˈzation** *or* **inˌdustrialiˈsation** *n*

industrial medicine *n* the study and practice of the health care of employees of large organizations

industrial relations *n* **1** (*functioning as pl*) relations between the employers and employees in an industrial enterprise **2** (*functioning as sing*) the management of such relations

Industrial Revolution *n* **the** the transformation in the 18th and 19th centuries of Britain and other countries into industrial nations
▹ http://members.aol.com/TeacherNet/Industrial.html
▹ www.bergen.org/technology/industrial

industrial tribunal *n* (in Northern Ireland and formerly elsewhere in the UK) a tribunal that rules on disputes between employers and employees regarding unfair dismissal, redundancy, etc

industrious (ɪnˈdʌstrɪəs) *adj* hard-working, diligent, or assiduous > **inˈdustriously** *adv* > **inˈdustriousness** *n*

industry (ˈɪndəstrɪ) *n, pl* **industries** **1** organized economic activity concerned with manufacture, processing of raw materials, or construction **2** a branch of commercial enterprise concerned with the output of a specified product: *the steel industry* **3a** industrial ownership and management interests collectively **3b** manufacturing enterprise collectively, as opposed to agriculture **4** diligence; assiduity [C15 from L *industria* diligence, from *industrius* active, from ?]

indwell (ɪnˈdwɛl) *vb* **indwells, indwelling, indwelt** **1** (*tr*) (of a spirit, principle, etc) to inhabit; suffuse **2** (*intr*) to dwell; exist > **inˈdweller** *n*

Indy, d' (*French* dɛ̃di) *n* **Vincent** (vɛ̃sɑ̃) See (Vincent) **d'Indy**

-ine[1] *suffix forming adjectives* **1** of, relating to, or belonging to: *saturnine* **2** consisting of or resembling: *crystalline* [from L *-īnus*, from Gk *-inos*]

-ine[2] *suffix forming nouns* **1** indicating a halogen: *chlorine* **2** indicating a nitrogenous organic compound, including amino acids, alkaloids, and certain other bases: *nicotine* **3** Also: **-in** indicating a chemical substance in certain nonsystematic names: *glycerine* **4** indicating a mixture of hydrocarbons: *benzine* **5** indicating feminine form: *heroine* [via F from L *-ina* (from *-inus*) and Gk *-inē*]

Ine (ˈɪnə, ˈɪnɪ) *n* died after 726, king of Wessex (688–726)

inebriate *vb* (ɪnˈiːbrɪˌeɪt), **inebriates, inebriating, inebriated** (*tr*) **1** to make drunk; intoxicate **2** to arouse emotionally; make excited ▹ *n* (ɪnˈiːbrɪɪt) **3** a person who is drunk, esp habitually ▹ *adj* (ɪnˈiːbrɪɪt), *also* **inebriated** **4** drunk, esp habitually [C15 from L, from IN-[2] + *ēbriāre* to intoxicate, from *ēbrius* drunk] > **inˌebriˈation** *n* > **inebriety** (ˌɪnɪˈbraɪɪtɪ) *n*

inedible (ɪnˈɛdɪbᵊl) *adj* not fit to be eaten > **inˌediˈbility** *n*

ineducable (ɪnˈɛdjʊkəbᵊl) *adj* incapable of being educated, esp on account of mental retardation > **inˌeducaˈbility** *n*

ineffable (ɪnˈɛfəbᵊl) *adj* **1** too great or intense to be expressed in words; unutterable **2** too sacred to be uttered **3** indescribable; indefinable [C15 from L, from IN-[1] + *effābilis*, from *fārī* to speak] > **inˌeffaˈbility** *or* **inˈeffableness** *n* > **inˈeffably** *adv*

ineffective (ˌɪnɪˈfɛktɪv) *adj* **1** having no effect **2** incompetent or inefficient > **ˌineffectively** *adv* > **ˌineffectiveness** *n*

ineffectual (ˌɪnɪˈfɛktʃʊəl) *adj* **1** having no effect or an inadequate effect **2** lacking in power or forcefulness; impotent: *an ineffectual ruler* > **ˌinefˌfectuˈality** *or* **ˌineffectualness** *n* > **ˌineffectually** *adv*

inefficacious (ˌɪnɛfɪˈkeɪʃəs) *adj* failing to produce the desired effect > **ˌineffiˈcaciously** *adv* > **inefficacy** (ɪnˈɛfɪkəsɪ), **ˌineffiˈcaciousness,** *or* **inefficacity** (ˌɪnɛfɪˈkæsɪtɪ) *n*

inefficient (ˌɪnɪˈfɪʃənt) *adj* **1** unable to perform a task or function to the best advantage; wasteful or incompetent **2** unable to produce the desired result > **ˌinefficiency** *n* > **ˌinefficiently** *adv*

ineligible (ɪnˈɛlɪdʒəbᵊl) *adj* **1** (often foll by *for* or an infinitive) not fit or qualified: *ineligible for a grant; ineligible to vote* ▹ *n* **2** an ineligible person > **inˌeligiˈbility** *or* **inˈeligibleness** *n* > **inˈeligibly** *adv*

ineluctable (ˌɪnɪˈlʌktəbᵊl) *adj* (esp of fate) incapable of being avoided; inescapable [C17 from L, from IN-[1] + *ēluctārī* to escape, from *luctārī* to struggle] > **ˌineˌluctaˈbility** *n* > **ˌineˈluctably** *adv*

inept (ɪnˈɛpt) *adj* **1** awkward, clumsy, or incompetent **2** not suitable, appropriate, or fitting; out of place [C17 from L *ineptus*, from IN-[1] + *aptus* fitting] > **inˈeptiˌtude** *n* > **inˈeptly** *adv* > **inˈeptness** *n*

inequable (ɪnˈɛkwəbᵊl) *adj* **1** uneven **2** not uniform **3** changeable

inequality (ˌɪnɪˈkwɒlɪtɪ) *n, pl* **inequalities** **1** the state or quality of being unequal; disparity **2** an instance of disparity **3** lack of smoothness or regularity **4** social or economic disparity **5** *maths* **5a** a statement indicating that the value of one quantity or expression is not equal to another **5b** the relation of being unequal **6** *astron* a departure from uniform orbital motion

inert (ɪnˈɜːt) *adj* **1** having no inherent ability to move or to resist motion **2** inactive, lazy, or sluggish **3** having only a limited ability to react chemically; unreactive [C17 from L *iners* unskilled, from IN-[1] + *ars* skill; see ART[1]] > **inˈertly** *adv* > **inˈertness** *n*

inert gas *n* **1** any of the unreactive gaseous elements helium, neon, argon, krypton, xenon, and radon **2** (loosely) any gas, such as carbon dioxide, that is nonoxidizing

inertia (ɪnˈɜːʃə, -ʃɪə) *n* **1** the state of being inert; disinclination to move or act **2** *physics* **2a** the tendency of a body to preserve its state of rest or uniform motion unless acted upon by an external force **2b** an analogous property of other physical quantities that resist change: *thermal inertia* > **inˈertial** *adj*

inertial guidance *or* **navigation** *n* a method of controlling the flight path of a missile by instruments contained within it

inertial mass *n* the mass of a body as determined by its momentum, as opposed to the extent to which it responds to the force of gravity ▷ Cf **gravitational mass**

inertia-reel seat belt *n* a type of car seat belt in which the belt is free to unwind from a metal drum except when the drum locks as a result of rapid change of velocity

inertia selling *n* the illegal practice of sending unrequested goods to householders, followed by a bill for the goods if they do not return them

inescapable (ˌɪnɪˈskeɪpəbᵊl) *adj* incapable of being escaped or avoided > ˌ**inesˈcapably** *adv*

inestimable (ɪnˈɛstɪməbᵊl) *adj* **1** not able to be estimated; immeasurable **2** of immeasurable value > **inˌestimaˈbility** *or* **inˈestimableness** *n* > **inˈestimably** *adv*

inevitable (ɪnˈɛvɪtəbᵊl) *adj* **1** unavoidable **2** sure to happen; certain ▷ *n* **3** (often preceded by *the*) something that is unavoidable [C15 from L, from IN-¹ + *ēvītāre* to shun, from *vītāre* to avoid] > **inˌevitaˈbility** *or* **inˈevitableness** *n* > **inˈevitably** *adv*

inexcusable (ˌɪnɪkˈskjuːzəbᵊl) *adj* not able to be excused or justified > ˌ**inexˌcusaˈbility** *or* ˌ**inexˈcusableness** *n* > ˌ**inexˈcusably** *adv*

inexhaustible (ˌɪnɪɡˈzɔːstəbᵊl) *adj* **1** incapable of being used up; endless **2** incapable or apparently incapable of becoming tired; tireless > ˌ**inexˌhaustiˈbility** *n* > ˌ**inexˈhaustibly** *adv*

inexorable (ɪnˈɛksərəbᵊl) *adj* **1** not able to be moved by entreaty or persuasion **2** relentless [C16 from L, from IN-¹ + *exōrāre* to prevail upon, from *ōrāre* to pray] > **inˌexoraˈbility** *n* > **inˈexorably** *adv*

inexpensive (ˌɪnɪkˈspɛnsɪv) *adj* not expensive; cheap > ˌ**inexˈpensively** *adv* > ˌ**inexˈpensiveness** *n*

inexperience (ˌɪnɪkˈspɪərɪəns) *n* lack of experience or of the knowledge and understanding derived from experience > ˌ**inexˈperienced** *adj*

inexpiable (ɪnˈɛkspɪəbᵊl) *adj* **1** incapable of being expiated; unpardonable **2** *arch* implacable > **inˈexpiableness** *n*

inexplicable (ˌɪnɪkˈsplɪkəbᵊl, ɪnˈɛksplɪkəbᵊl) *adj* not capable of explanation; unexplained > ˌ**inexplicaˈbility** *n* > ˌ**inexˈplicably** *adv*

in extenso *Latin* (ɪn ɪkˈstɛnsəʊ) *adv* at full length

in extremis *Latin* (ɪn ɪkˈstriːmɪs) *adv* **1** in extremity; in dire straits **2** at the point of death [lit.: in the furthest reaches]

inextricable (ˌɪnɛksˈtrɪkəbᵊl) *adj* **1** not able to be escaped from: *an inextricable dilemma* **2** not able to be disentangled, etc: *an inextricable knot* **3** extremely involved or intricate > ˌ**inextricaˈbility** *or* ˌ**inexˈtricableness** *n* > ˌ**inexˈtricably** *adv*

inf. *abbrev for:* **1** Also: **Inf** infantry **2** infinitive **3** informal

infallible (ɪnˈfæləbᵊl) *adj* **1** not fallible; not liable to error **2** not liable to failure; certain; sure: *an infallible cure* ▷ *n* **3** a person or thing that is incapable of error or failure > **inˌfalliˈbility** *or* **inˈfallibleness** *n* > **inˈfallibly** *adv*

infamous (ˈɪnfəməs) *adj* **1** having a bad reputation; notorious **2** causing or deserving a bad reputation; shocking: *infamous conduct* > **ˈinfamously** *adv* > **ˈinfamousness** *n*

infamy (ˈɪnfəmɪ) *n, pl* **infamies** **1** the state or condition of being infamous **2** an infamous act or event [C15 from L *infāmis* of evil repute, from IN-¹ + *fāma* FAME]

infancy (ˈɪnfənsɪ) *n, pl* **infancies** **1** the state or period of being an infant; childhood **2** an early stage of growth or development **3** infants collectively **4** the period of life prior to attaining legal majority; minority nonage

infant (ˈɪnfənt) *n* **1** a child at the earliest stage of its life; baby **2** *law* another word for **minor** (sense 9) **3** *Brit* a young schoolchild **4** a person who is beginning or inexperienced in an activity **5** (*modifier*) **5a** of or relating to young children or infancy **5b** designed or intended for young children ▷ *adj* **6** in an early stage of development; nascent: *an infant science* **7** *law* of or relating to the legal status of infancy [C14 from L *infāns*, lit.: speechless, from IN-¹ + *fārī* to speak] > **ˈinfantˌhood** *n*

infanta (ɪnˈfæntə) *n* (formerly) **1** a daughter of a king of Spain or Portugal **2** the wife of an infante [C17 from Sp. or Port., fem of INFANTE]

infante (ɪnˈfæntɪ) *n* (formerly) a son of a king of Spain or Portugal, esp one not heir to the throne [C16 from Sp. or Port., lit.: INFANT]

infanticide (ɪnˈfæntɪˌsaɪd) *n* **1** the killing of an infant **2** the practice of killing newborn infants, still prevalent in some primitive tribes **3** a person who kills an infant > **inˌfantiˈcidal** *adj*

infantile (ˈɪnfənˌtaɪl) *adj* **1** like a child in action or behaviour; childishly immature; puerile **2** of, relating to, or characteristic of infants or infancy **3** in an early stage of development > **infantility** (ˌɪnfənˈtɪlɪtɪ) *n*

infantile paralysis *n* a former name for **poliomyelitis**

infantilism (ɪnˈfæntɪˌlɪzəm) *n* **1** *psychol* a condition in which an older child or adult is mentally or physically undeveloped **2** childish speech; baby talk

infantry (ˈɪnfəntrɪ) *n, pl* **infantries** **a** soldiers or units of soldiers who fight on foot with small arms **b** (*as modifier*): *an infantry unit* [C16 from It. *infanteria*, from *infante* boy, foot soldier; see INFANT]

infantryman (ˈɪnfəntrɪmən) *n, pl* **infantrymen** a soldier belonging to the infantry

infant school *n* (in England and Wales) a school for children aged between 5 and 7

infarct (ɪnˈfɑːkt) *n* a localized area of dead tissue resulting from obstruction of the blood supply to that part. Also called: **infarction** [C19 via NL from L *infarctus* stuffed into, from *farcīre* to stuff] > **inˈfarcted** *adj*

infatuate *vb* (ɪnˈfætjʊˌeɪt), **infatuates, infatuating, infatuated** (*tr*) **1** to inspire or fill with foolish, shallow, or extravagant passion **2** to cause to act foolishly ▷ *n* (ɪnˈfætjʊɪt, -ˌeɪt) **3** *literary* a person who is infatuated [C16 from L *infatuāre*, from IN-² + *fatuus* FATUOUS] > **inˌfatuˈation** *n*

infatuated (ɪnˈfætjʊˌeɪtɪd) *adj* (often foll by *with*) possessed by a foolish or extravagant passion, esp for another person

infatuation (ɪnˌfætjʊˈeɪʃən) *n* **1** the act of infatuating or state of being infatuated **2** foolish or extravagant passion **3** an object of foolish or extravagant passion

infect (ɪnˈfɛkt) *vb* (*mainly tr*) **1** to cause infection in; contaminate (an organism, wound, etc) with pathogenic microorganisms **2** (*also intr*) to affect or become affected with a communicable disease **3** to taint, pollute, or contaminate **4** to affect, esp adversely, as if by contagion **5** (*also intr*) *computing* to affect or become affected with a computer virus ▷ *adj* **6** *arch* contaminated or polluted with or as if with a disease; infected [C14 from L *inficere* to dip into, stain, from *facere* to make] > **inˈfector** *or* **inˈfecter** *n*

infection (ɪnˈfɛkʃən) *n* **1** invasion of the body by pathogenic microorganisms **2** the resulting condition in the tissues **3** an infectious disease **4** the act of infecting or state of being infected **5** an agent or influence that infects **6** persuasion or corruption, as by ideas, perverse influences, etc

infectious (ɪnˈfɛkʃəs) *adj* **1** (of a disease) capable of being transmitted **2** (of a disease) caused by microorganisms, such as bacteria, viruses, or protozoa **3** causing or transmitting infection **4** tending or apt to spread, as from one person to another: *infectious mirth* > **inˈfectiously** *adv* > **inˈfectiousness** *n*

infectious hepatitis *n* any form of hepatitis caused by viruses. See **hepatitis A, hepatitis B, hepatitis C**

infectious mononucleosis *n* an acute infectious disease, caused by a virus (**Epstein-Barr virus**), characterized by fever, sore throat, swollen and painful lymph nodes, and abnormal lymphocytes in the blood. Also called: **glandular fever**

infective (ɪnˈfɛktɪv) *adj* **1** capable of causing infection

Ii

2 a less common word for **infectious** > **in'fectively** *adv* > **in'fectiveness** *n*

infelicity (ˌɪnfɪˈlɪsɪtɪ) *n, pl* **infelicities** **1** unhappiness; misfortune **2** an instance of bad luck or mischance **3** something, esp a remark or expression, that is inapt or inappropriate > **ˌinfe'licitous** *adj*

infer (ɪnˈfɜː) *vb* **infers, inferring, inferred** (when *tr*, *may take a clause as object*) **1** to conclude (a state of affairs, supposition, etc) by reasoning from evidence; deduce **2** (*tr*) to have or lead to as a necessary or logical consequence; indicate **3** (*tr*) to hint or imply [C16 from L *inferre* to bring into, from *ferre* to bear, carry] > **in'ferable** *or* **in'ferrable** *adj* > **in'ferrer** *n*

> USAGE The use of *infer* to mean *imply* is becoming more and more common in both speech and writing. There is nevertheless a useful distinction between the two which many people would be in favour of maintaining. To *infer* means 'to deduce', and is used in the construction *to infer something from something: I inferred from what she said that she had not been well.* To *imply* (sense 1) means 'to suggest, to insinuate' and is normally followed by a clause: *are you implying that I was responsible for the mistake?*

inference (ˈɪnfərəns, -frəns) *n* **1** the act or process of inferring **2** an inferred conclusion, deduction, etc **3** any process of reasoning from premises to a conclusion **4** *logic* the specific mode of reasoning used

inferential (ˌɪnfəˈrɛnʃəl) *adj* of, relating to, or derived from inference > **ˌinfer'entially** *adv*

inferior (ɪnˈfɪərɪə) *adj* **1** lower in value or quality **2** lower in rank, position, or status; subordinate **3** not of the best; mediocre; commonplace **4** lower in position; situated beneath **5** (of a plant ovary) situated below the other floral parts **6** *astron* **6a** orbiting between the sun and the earth: *an inferior planet* **6b** lying below the horizon **7** *printing* (of a character) printed at the foot of an ordinary character ▷ *n* **8** an inferior person **9** *printing* an inferior character [C15 from L: lower, from *inferus* low] > **inferiority** (ɪnˌfɪərɪˈɒrɪtɪ) *n* > **in'feriorly** *adv*

inferiority complex *n psychiatry* a disorder arising from the conflict between the desire to be noticed and the fear of being humiliated, characterized by aggressiveness or withdrawal into oneself

infernal (ɪnˈfɜːnᵊl) *adj* **1** of or relating to an underworld of the dead **2** deserving or befitting hell; diabolic; fiendish **3** *inf* irritating; confounded [C14 from LL, from *infernus* hell, from L (adj): lower, hellish; rel. to L *inferus* low] > **ˌinfer'nality** *n* > **in'fernally** *adv*

infernal machine *n arch* an explosive device (usually disguised) or booby trap

inferno (ɪnˈfɜːnəʊ) *n, pl* **infernos** **1** (*sometimes cap;* usually preceded by *the*) hell; the infernal region **2** any place or state resembling hell, esp a conflagration [C19 from It., from LL *infernus* hell]

infertile (ɪnˈfɜːtaɪl) *adj* **1** not capable of producing offspring; sterile **2** (of land) not productive; barren > **in'fertilely** *adv* > **infertility** (ˌɪnfəˈtɪlɪtɪ) *n*

infest (ɪnˈfɛst) *vb* (*tr*) **1** to inhabit or overrun in unpleasantly large numbers **2** (of parasites such as lice) to invade and live on or in (a host) [C15 from L *infestāre* to molest, from *infestus* hostile] > **ˌinfes'tation** *n* > **in'fester** *n*

infeudation (ˌɪnfjʊˈdeɪʃən) *n history* **1** (in feudal society) the act of putting a vassal in possession of a fief **2** the granting of tithes to laymen

infidel (ˈɪnfɪdᵊl) *n* **1** a person who has no religious belief; unbeliever ▷ *adj* **2** rejecting a specific religion, esp Christianity or Islam **3** of or relating to unbelievers or unbelief [C15 from Med. L, from L (adj): unfaithful, from IN-[1] + *fidēlis* faithful; see FEALTY]

infidelity (ˌɪnfɪˈdɛlɪtɪ) *n, pl* **infidelities** **1** lack of faith or constancy, esp sexual faithfulness **2** lack of religious faith; disbelief **3** an act or instance of disloyalty

infield (ˈɪnˌfiːld) *n* **1** *cricket* the area of the field near the pitch ▷ Cf **outfield** (sense 1) **2** *baseball* the area of the playing field enclosed by the base lines **3** *agriculture* the part of a farm nearest to the farm buildings > **'inˌfielder** *n*

infighting (ˈɪnˌfaɪtɪŋ) *n* **1** *boxing* combat at close quarters in which proper blows are inhibited **2** intense competition, as between members of an organization > **'inˌfighter** *n*

infill (ˈɪnfɪl) *or* **infilling** (ˈɪnfɪlɪŋ) *n* **1** the act of filling or closing gaps, etc, in something, such as a row of buildings **2** material used to fill a cavity, gap, hole, etc

infiltrate (ˈɪnfɪlˌtreɪt) *vb* **infiltrates, infiltrating, infiltrated** **1** to undergo the process in which a fluid passes into the pores or interstices of a solid; permeate **2** *mil* to pass undetected through (an enemy-held line or position) **3** to gain or cause to gain entrance or access surreptitiously: *they infiltrated the party structure* ▷ *n* **4** something that infiltrates [C18 from IN-[2] + FILTRATE] > **ˌinfil'tration** *n* > **'infilˌtrative** *adj* > **'infilˌtrator** *n*

infin. *abbrev for* infinitive

infinite (ˈɪnfɪnɪt) *adj* **1a** having no limits or boundaries in time, space, extent, or magnitude **1b** (*as n;* preceded by *the*): *the infinite* **2** extremely or immeasurably great or numerous: *infinite wealth* **3** all-embracing, absolute, or total: *God's infinite wisdom* **4** *maths* having an unlimited or uncountable number of digits, factors, terms, etc > **'infinitely** *adv* > **'infiniteness** *n*

infinitesimal (ˌɪnfɪnɪˈtɛsɪməl) *adj* **1** infinitely or immeasurably small **2** *maths* of, relating to, or involving a small change in the value of a variable that approaches zero as a limit ▷ *n* **3** *maths* an infinitesimal quantity > **ˌinfini'tesimally** *adv*

infinitesimal calculus *n* another name for **calculus** (sense 1)

infinitive (ɪnˈfɪnɪtɪv) *n grammar* a form of the verb not inflected for grammatical categories such as tense and person and used without an overt subject. In English, the infinitive usually consists of the word *to* followed by the verb > **infinitival** (ˌɪnfɪnɪˈtaɪvᵊl) *adj* > **in'finitively** *or* **ˌinfini'tivally** *adv*

infinitude (ɪnˈfɪnɪˌtjuːd) *n* **1** the state or quality of being infinite **2** an infinite extent, quantity, degree, etc

infinity (ɪnˈfɪnɪtɪ) *n, pl* **infinities** **1** the state or quality of being infinite **2** endless time, space, or quantity **3** an infinitely or indefinitely great number or amount **4** *maths* **4a** the concept of a value greater than any finite numerical value **4b** the reciprocal of zero **4c** the limit of an infinite sequence of numbers

infirm (ɪnˈfɜːm) *adj* **1a** weak in health or body, esp from old age **1b** (*as collective n;* preceded by *the*): *the infirm* **2** lacking moral certainty; indecisive or irresolute **3** not stable, sound, or secure: *an infirm structure* **4** *law* (of a law, etc) lacking legal force; invalid > **in'firmly** *adv* > **in'firmness** *n*

infirmary (ɪnˈfɜːmərɪ) *n, pl* **infirmaries** a place for the treatment of the sick or injured; hospital

infirmity (ɪnˈfɜːmɪtɪ) *n, pl* **infirmities** **1** the state or quality of being infirm **2** physical weakness or debility; frailty **3** a moral flaw or failing

infix *vb* (ɪnˈfɪks, ˈɪnˌfɪks) **1** (*tr*) to fix firmly in **2** (*tr*) to instil or inculcate **3** *grammar* to insert (an affix) into the middle of a word ▷ *n* (ˈɪnˌfɪks) **4** *grammar* an affix inserted into the middle of a word > **ˌinfix'ation** *or* **infixion** (ɪnˈfɪkʃən) *n*

in flagrante delicto (ɪn fləˈgræntɪ dɪˈlɪktəʊ) *adv chiefly law* while committing the offence; red-handed. Also: **flagrante delicto** [L, lit.: with the crime still blazing]

inflame (ɪnˈfleɪm) *vb* **inflames, inflaming, inflamed** **1** to arouse or become aroused to violent emotion **2** (*tr*) to increase or intensify; aggravate **3** to produce inflammation in (a tissue, organ, or part) or (of a tissue, etc) to become inflamed **4** to set or be set on fire **5** (*tr*) to cause to redden > **in'flamer** *n*

inflammable (ɪn'flæməbᵊl) *adj* **1** liable to catch fire; flammable **2** readily aroused to anger or passion ▷ *n* **3** something that is liable to catch fire > **in,flamma'bility** *or* **in'flammableness** *n* > **in'flammably** *adv*

USAGE See at **flammable**

inflammation (,ɪnflə'meɪʃən) *n* **1** the reaction of living tissue to injury or infection, characterized by heat, redness, swelling, and pain **2** the act of inflaming or the state of being inflamed

inflammatory (ɪn'flæmətərɪ, -trɪ) *adj* **1** characterized by or caused by inflammation **2** tending to arouse violence, strong emotion, etc > **in'flammatorily** *adv*

inflatable (ɪn'fleɪtəbᵊl) *n* **1** any of various large air-filled objects made of strong plastic or rubber ▷ *adj* **2** capable of being inflated

inflate (ɪn'fleɪt) *vb* **inflates, inflating, inflated** **1** to expand or cause to expand by filling with gas or air **2** (*tr*) to cause to increase excessively; puff up; swell: *to inflate one's opinion of oneself* **3** (*tr*) to cause inflation of (prices, money, etc) **4** (*tr*) to raise in spirits; elate **5** (*intr*) to undergo economic inflation [C16 from L *inflāre* to blow into, from *flāre* to blow] > **in'flatedly** *adv* > **in'flatedness** *n* > **in'flater** *or* **in'flator** *n*

inflation (ɪn'fleɪʃən) *n* **1** the act of inflating or state of being inflated **2** *econ* a progressive increase in the general level of prices brought about by an expansion in demand or the money supply or by autonomous increases in costs ▷ Cf **reflation** **3** *inf* the rate of increase of prices **4** *astron* a very fast expansion of the universe occurring immediately after the big bang, postulated in certain models of the universe (**inflationary universes**) to account for the present distribution of matter > **in'flationary** *adj*

inflationary spiral *n* a self-sustaining form of inflation in which a rise in prices generates a wage demand, causing a further price rise and a further wage demand

inflationary universe *n* a variation of the cosmological big-bang theory in which the early stage of the evolution of the universe is postulated to include a period of accelerated expansion

inflationism (ɪn'fleɪʃə,nɪzəm) *n* the policy of inflation through expansion of the supply of money and credit > **in'flationist** *n, adj*

inflect (ɪn'flɛkt) *vb* **1** *grammar* to change (the form of a word) by inflection **2** (*tr*) to change (the voice) in tone or pitch; modulate **3** (*tr*) to cause to deviate from a straight or normal line or course; bend [C15 from L *inflectere* to curve round, alter, from *flectere* to bend] > **in'flectedness** *n* > **in'flective** *adj* > **in'flector** *n*

inflection *or* **inflexion** (ɪn'flɛkʃən) *n* **1** modulation of the voice **2** *grammar* a change in the form of a word, signalling change in such grammatical functions as tense, person, gender, number, or case **3** an angle or bend **4** the act of inflecting or the state of being inflected **5** *maths* a change in curvature from concave to convex or vice versa > **in'flectional** *or* **in'flexional** *adj* > **in'flectionally** *or* **in'flexionally** *adv* > **in'flectionless** *or* **in'flexionless** *adj*

inflexible (ɪn'flɛksəbᵊl) *adj* **1** not flexible; rigid; stiff **2** obstinate; unyielding **3** without variation; unalterable; fixed [C14 from L *inflexibilis*; see INFLECT] > **in,flexi'bility** *or* **in'flexibleness** *n* > **in'flexibly** *adv*

inflict (ɪn'flɪkt) *vb* (*tr*) **1** (often foll by *on* or *upon*) to impose (something unwelcome, such as pain, oneself, etc) **2** to deal out (blows, lashes, etc) [C16 from L *inflīgere* to strike (something) against, dash against, from *flīgere* to strike] > **in'flictable** *adj* > **in'flicter** *or* **in'flictor** *n* > **in'fliction** *n*

in-flight *adj* provided during flight in an aircraft: *in-flight entertainment*

inflorescence (,ɪnflɔː'rɛsəns) *n* **1** the part of a plant that consists of the flower-bearing stalks **2** the arrangement of the flowers on the stalks **3** the process of flowering; blossoming [C16 from NL, from LL, from *flōrescere* to bloom] > **,inflo'rescent** *adj*

inflow ('ɪn,fləʊ) *n* **1** something, such as a liquid or gas, that flows in **2** Also called: **inflowing** the act of flowing in; influx

influence ('ɪnflʊəns) *n* **1** an effect of one person or thing on another **2** the power of a person or thing to have such an effect **3** power resulting from ability, wealth, position, etc **4** a person or thing having influence **5** *astrol* an ethereal fluid regarded as emanating from the stars and affecting a person's future **6** **under the influence** *inf* drunk ▷ *vb* **influences, influencing, influenced** (*tr*) **7** to persuade or induce **8** to have an effect upon (actions, events, etc); affect [C14 from Med. L *influentia* emanation of power from the stars, from L *influere* to flow into, from *fluere* to flow] > **'influenceable** *adj* > **'influencer** *n*

influent ('ɪnflʊənt) *adj also* **inflowing** **1** flowing in ▷ *n* **2** something flowing in, esp a tributary **3** *ecology* an organism that has a major effect on its community

influential (,ɪnflʊ'ɛnʃəl) *adj* having or exerting influence > **,influ'entially** *adv*

influenza (,ɪnflʊ'ɛnzə) *n* a highly contagious viral disease characterized by fever, muscular aches and pains, and inflammation of the respiratory passages [C18 from It., lit.: INFLUENCE, hence, incursion, epidemic (first applied to influenza in 1743)] > **,influ'enzal** *adj*

influx ('ɪn,flʌks) *n* **1** the arrival or entry of many people or things **2** the act of flowing in; inflow **3** the mouth of a stream or river [C17 from LL *influxus*, from *influere*; see INFLUENCE]

info ('ɪnfəʊ) *n inf* short for **information**

infold (ɪn'fəʊld) *vb* (*tr*) a variant of **enfold**

inform (ɪn'fɔːm) *vb* **1** (*tr*; often foll by *of* or *about*) to give information to; tell **2** (*tr*; often foll by *of* or *about*) to make conversant (with) **3** (*intr*; often foll by *against* or *on*) to give information regarding criminals, to the police, etc **4** (*tr*) to give form to **5** (*tr*) to impart some essential or formative characteristic to **6** (*tr*) to animate or inspire [C14 from L *informāre* to give form to, describe, from *formāre* to FORM] > **in'formable** *adj*

informal (ɪn'fɔːməl) *adj* **1** not of a formal, official, or stiffly conventional nature **2** appropriate to everyday life or use **3** denoting or characterized by idiom, vocabulary, etc, appropriate to conversational language rather than to formal written language **4** denoting a second-person pronoun in some languages used when the addressee is regarded as a friend or social inferior > **in'formally** *adv*

informality (,ɪnfɔː'mælɪtɪ) *n, pl* **informalities** **1** the condition or quality of being informal **2** an informal act

informal settlement *n S African euphemistic* a squatter camp or shanty town

informal vote *n Austral & NZ* an invalid vote or ballot

informant (ɪn'fɔːmənt) *n* a person who gives information

information (,ɪnfə'meɪʃən) *n* **1** knowledge acquired through experience or study **2** knowledge of specific and timely events or situations; news **3** the act of informing or the condition of being informed **4a** an office, agency, etc, providing information **4b** (*as modifier*): *information service* **5** a charge or complaint made before justices of the peace, usually on oath, to institute summary criminal proceedings **6** *computing* **6a** the meaning given to data by the way it is interpreted **6b** another word for **data** (sense 2) > **,infor'mational** *adj*

information retrieval *n computing* the process of recovering information from stored data

information superhighway *n* **1** the concept of a worldwide network of computers capable of

Ii

transferring all types of digital information at high speed **2** another name for the **Internet** ▷ Also called: **information highway**

information technology *n* the production, storage, and communication of information using computers, etc

▷ www.itmweb.com/cgi-bin/dclinks/dclinks.cgi

▷ www.crito.uci.edu

information theory *n* a collection of mathematical theories concerned with coding, transmitting, storing, retrieving, and decoding information

information warfare *n* the use of electronic communciations and the Internet to disrupt a country's telecommunications, power supply, transport system, etc

informative (ɪnˈfɔːmətɪv) *or* **informatory** *adj* providing information; instructive > **inˈformatively** *adv* > **inˈformativeness** *n*

informed (ɪnˈfɔːmd) *adj* **1** having much knowledge or education; learned or cultured **2** based on information: an informed judgment

informer (ɪnˈfɔːmə) *n* **1** a person who informs against someone, esp a criminal **2** a person who provides information

infotainment (ˌɪnfəʊˈteɪnmənt) *n* (in television) the practice of presenting serious or instructive subjects in a style designed primarily to be entertaining [C20 from INFO + (ENTER)TAINMENT]

infra- *prefix* below; beneath; after: *infrasonic* [from L *infrā*]

infract (ɪnˈfrækt) *vb (tr)* to violate or break (a law, etc) [C18 from L *infractus* broken off; see INFRINGE] > **inˈfraction** *n* > **inˈfractor** *n*

infra dig (ˈɪnfrə ˈdɪɡ) *adj (postpositive) inf* beneath one's dignity [C19 from L *infrā dignitātem*]

infrangible (ɪnˈfrændʒɪbᵊl) *adj* **1** incapable of being broken **2** not capable of being violated or infringed [C16 from LL, from L IN-[1] + *frangere* to break] > **inˌfrangiˈbility** *or* **inˈfrangibleness** *n* > **inˈfrangibly** *adv*

infrared (ˌɪnfrəˈrɛd) *n* **1** the part of the electromagnetic spectrum with a longer wavelength than light but a shorter wavelength than radio waves ▷ *adj* **2** of, relating to, using, or consisting of radiation lying within the infrared

infrared astronomy *n* the study of radiations from space in the infrared region of the electromagnetic spectrum

infrared photography *n* photography using film with an emulsion that is sensitive to infrared light, enabling it to be used in dark or misty conditions

infrasound (ˈɪnfrəˌsaʊnd) *n* soundlike waves having a frequency below the audible range, i.e. below about 16 Hz > **infrasonic** (ˌɪnfrəˈsɒnɪk) *adj*

infrastructure (ˈɪnfrəˌstrʌktʃə) *n* **1** the basic structure of an organization, system, etc **2** the stock of fixed capital equipment in a country, including factories, roads, schools, etc, considered as a determinant of economic growth

infrequent (ɪnˈfriːkwənt) *adj* rarely happening or present; only occasional > **inˈfrequency** *or* **inˈfrequence** *n* > **inˈfrequently** *adv*

infringe (ɪnˈfrɪndʒ) *vb* **infringes, infringing, infringed** **1** *(tr)* to violate or break (a law, agreement, etc) **2** *(intr; foll by on or upon)* to encroach or trespass [C16 from L *infringere* to break off, from *frangere* to break] > **inˈfringement** *n* > **inˈfringer** *n*

infundibular (ˌɪnfʌnˈdɪbjʊlə) *adj* funnel-shaped [C18 from L *infundibulum* funnel]

infuriate *vb* (ɪnˈfjʊərɪˌeɪt), **infuriates, infuriating, infuriated** **1** *(tr)* to anger; annoy ▷ *adj* (ɪnˈfjʊərɪɪt) **2** *arch* furious [C17 from Med. L *infuriāre* (vb); see IN-[2], FURY] > **inˈfuriˌating** *adj* > **inˈfuriˌatingly** *adv*

infuse (ɪnˈfjuːz) *vb* **infuses, infusing, infused** **1** *(tr; often foll by into)* to instil or inculcate **2** *(tr; foll by with)* to inspire; emotionally charge **3** to soak or be soaked so as to extract flavour or other properties **4** *rare (foll by into)* to pour [C15 from L *infundere* to pour into] > **inˈfuser** *n*

infusible[1] (ɪnˈfjuːzəbᵊl) *adj* not fusible; not easily melted; having a high melting point [C16 from IN-[1] + FUSIBLE] > **inˌfusiˈbility** *or* **inˈfusibleness** *n*

infusible[2] (ɪnˈfjuːzəbᵊl) *adj* capable of being infused [C17 from INFUSE + -IBLE] > **inˌfusiˈbility** *or* **inˈfusibleness** *n*

infusion (ɪnˈfjuːʒən) *n* **1** the act of infusing **2** something infused **3** an extract obtained by soaking > **infusive** (ɪnˈfjuːsɪv) *adj*

infusorian (ˌɪnfjʊˈzɔːrɪən) *obs* ▷ *n* **1** any of the microscopic organisms, such as protozoans, found in infusions of organic material ▷ *adj* **2** of or relating to infusorians [C18 from NL *Infusoria* former class name; see INFUSE] > ˌ**infuˈsorial** *adj*

-ing[1] *suffix forming nouns* **1** *(from verbs)* the action of, process of, result of, or something connected with the verb: *meeting; winnings* **2** *(from other nouns)* something used in, consisting of, involving, etc: *tubing; soldiering* **3** *(from other parts of speech): an outing* [OE *-ing, -ung*]

-ing[2] *suffix* **1** forming the present participle of verbs: *walking; believing* **2** forming participial adjectives: *a sinking ship* **3** forming adjectives not derived from verbs: *swashbuckling* [ME *-ing, -inde*, from OE *-ende*]

-ing[3] *suffix forming nouns* a person or thing having a certain quality or being of a certain kind: *sweeting; whiting* [OE *-ing*; rel. to ON *-ingr*]

ingather (ɪnˈɡæðə) *vb (tr)* to gather together or in (a harvest, etc) > **inˈgatherer** *n*

Inge (ɪŋ) *n* **William Ralph,** known as *the Gloomy Dean.* 1860–1954, English theologian, noted for his pessimism; dean of St Paul's Cathedral (1911–34)

ingeminate (ɪnˈdʒɛmɪˌneɪt) *vb* **ingeminates, ingeminating, ingeminated** *(tr) rare* to repeat; reiterate [C16 from L *ingemināre* to redouble, from IN-[2] + *gemināre* to GEMINATE]

Ingenhousz (ˈɪŋɡənˌhaʊs) *n* **Jan** (jɑn) 1730–99, Dutch plant physiologist and physician, who discovered photosynthesis

ingenious (ɪnˈdʒiːnjəs, -nɪəs) *adj* possessing or done with ingenuity; skilful or clever [C15 from L, from *ingenium* natural ability; see ENGINE] > **inˈgeniously** *adv* > **inˈgeniousness** *n*

ingénue (ˌænʒeɪˈnjuː) *n* an artless, innocent, or inexperienced girl or young woman [C19 from F, fem of *ingénu* INGENUOUS]

ingenuity (ˌɪndʒɪˈnjuːɪtɪ) *n, pl* **ingenuities** **1** inventive talent; cleverness **2** an ingenious device, act, etc **3** *arch* frankness; candour [C16 from L *ingenuitās* a freeborn condition, outlook consistent with such a condition, from *ingenuus* native, freeborn (see INGENUOUS); meaning infl. by INGENIOUS]

ingenuous (ɪnˈdʒɛnjʊəs) *adj* **1** naive, artless, or innocent **2** candid; frank; straightforward [C16 from L *ingenuus* freeborn, virtuous, from IN-[2] + *gignere* to beget] > **inˈgenuously** *adv* > **inˈgenuousness** *n*

ingest (ɪnˈdʒɛst) *vb (tr)* to take (food or liquid) into the body [C17 from L *ingerere* to put into, from IN-[2] + *gerere* to carry; see GEST] > **inˈgestible** *adj* > **inˈgestion** *n* > **inˈgestive** *adj*

ingle (ˈɪŋɡᵊl) *n arch or dialect* a fire in a room or a fireplace [C16 prob. from Scot. Gaelic *aingeal* fire]

Ingleborough (ˈɪŋɡᵊlbərə, -brə) *n* a mountain in N England, in North Yorkshire: potholes. Height: 723 m (2373 ft)

inglenook (ˈɪŋɡᵊlˌnʊk) *n Brit* a corner by a fireplace; chimney corner

ingoing (ˈɪnˌɡəʊɪŋ) *adj* going in; entering

Ingolstadt (*German* ˈɪŋɡɔlʃtat) *n* a city in S central Germany, in Bavaria on the River Danube: oil-refining. Pop: 114 500 (1999 est)

ingot (ˈɪŋɡət) *n* a piece of cast metal obtained from a mould in a form suitable for storage, etc [C14 ?from IN-[2] + OE *goten*, p.p. of *geotan* to pour]

ingraft (ɪnˈɡrɑːft) *vb* a variant spelling of **engraft** > **inˈgraftment** *or* **ˌingrafˈtation** *n*

ingrain *or* **engrain** *vb* (ɪnˈɡreɪn) (*tr*) **1** to impress deeply on the mind or nature; instil **2** *arch* to dye into the fibre of (a fabric) ▷ *adj* (ˈɪnˌɡreɪn) **3** (of woven or knitted articles) made of dyed yarn or of fibre that is dyed before being spun into yarn ▷ *n* (ˈɪnˌɡreɪn) **4** a carpet made from ingrained yarn [C18 from *dyed in grain* dyed with kermes through the fibre]

ingrained *or* **engrained** (ɪnˈɡreɪnd) *adj* **1** deeply impressed or instilled **2** (*prenominal*) complete or inveterate; utter **3** (esp of dirt) worked into or through the fibre, pores, etc > **ingrainedly** *or* **engrainedly** (ɪnˈɡreɪnɪdlɪ) *adv* > **inˈgrainedness** *or* **enˈgrainedness** *n*

ingrate (ˈɪnɡreɪt, ɪnˈɡreɪt) *arch* ▷ *n* **1** an ungrateful person ▷ *adj* **2** ungrateful [C14 from L *ingrātus* (adj), from IN-[1] + *grātus* GRATEFUL] > **ˈingrately** *adv*

ingratiate (ɪnˈɡreɪʃɪˌeɪt) *vb* **ingratiates, ingratiating, ingratiated** (*tr*; often foll by *with*) to place (oneself) purposely in the favour (of another) [C17 from L, from IN-[2] + *grātia* grace, favour] > **inˈgratiˌating** *or* **inˈgratiatory** *adj* > **inˈgratiˌatingly** *adv* > **inˌgratiˈation** *n*

ingredient (ɪnˈɡriːdɪənt) *n* a component of a mixture, compound, etc, esp in cooking [C15 from L *ingrediēns* going into, from *ingredī* to enter; see INGRESS]

Ingres (*French* ɛ̃ɡrə) *n* **Jean Auguste Dominique** (ʒɑ̃ oɡyst dɔminik) 1780–1867, French classical painter, noted for his draughtsmanship

ingress (ˈɪnɡrɛs) *n* **1** the act of going or coming in; an entering **2** a way in; entrance **3** the right or permission to enter [C15 from L *ingressus*, from *ingredī* to go in, from *gradī* to step, go] > **ingression** (ɪnˈɡrɛʃən) *n*

in-group *n sociol* a highly cohesive and relatively closed social group characterized by the preferential treatment reserved for its members

ingrowing (ˈɪnˌɡrəʊɪŋ) *adj* **1** (esp of a toenail) growing abnormally into the flesh **2** growing within or into > **ˈinˌgrowth** *n*

ingrown (ˈɪnˌɡrəʊn, ɪnˈɡrəʊn) *adj* **1** (esp of a toenail) grown abnormally into the flesh; covered by adjacent tissues **2** grown within; native; innate

inguinal (ˈɪŋɡwɪnᵊl) *adj anat* of or relating to the groin [C17 from L *inguinālis*, from *inguen* groin]

ingulf (ɪnˈɡʌlf) *vb* (*tr*) a variant of **engulf**

ingurgitate (ɪnˈɡɜːdʒɪˌteɪt) *vb* **ingurgitates, ingurgitating, ingurgitated** to swallow (food, etc) greedily or in excess [C16 from L *ingurgitāre* to flood, from IN-[2] + *gurges* abyss] > **inˌgurgiˈtation** *n*

Ingush Republic *n* a constituent republic of S Russia: part of the Checheno-Ingush Autonomous Republic from 1936 until 1992. Capital: Nazran. Also called: **Ingushetia** (ˌɪnɡuːˈʃɛtɪə)

inhabit (ɪnˈhæbɪt) *vb* **inhabits, inhabiting, inhabited** (*tr*) to live or dwell in; occupy [C14 from L *inhabitāre*, from *habitāre* to dwell] > **inˈhabitable** *adj* > **inˌhabitaˈbility** *n* > **inˌhabiˈtation** *n*

inhabitant (ɪnˈhæbɪtənt) *n* a person or animal that is a permanent resident of a particular place or region > **inˈhabitancy** *or* **inˈhabitance** *n*

inhalant (ɪnˈheɪlənt) *adj* **1** (esp of a medicinal formulation) inhaled for its therapeutic effect **2** inhaling ▷ *n* **3** an inhalant medicinal formulation

inhale (ɪnˈheɪl) *vb* **inhales, inhaling, inhaled** to draw (breath, etc) into the lungs; breathe in [C18 from IN-[2] + L *halāre* to breathe] > **ˌinhaˈlation** *n*

inhaler (ɪnˈheɪlə) *n* **1** a device for breathing in therapeutic vapours, esp one for relieving nasal congestion or asthma **2** a person who inhales

Inhambane (ˌɪnjəmˈbɑːnə) *n* a port in SE Mozambique on an inlet of the Mozambique Channel (**Inhambane Bay**). Pop: 64 274 (latest est)

inhere (ɪnˈhɪə) *vb* **inheres, inhering, inhered** (*intr*; foll by *in*) to be an inseparable part (of) [C16 from L *inhaerēre* to stick in, from *haerēre* to stick]

inherent (ɪnˈhɪərənt, -ˈhɛr-) *adj* existing as an inseparable part; intrinsic > **inˈherently** *adv*

inherit (ɪnˈhɛrɪt) *vb* **inherits, inheriting, inherited** **1** to receive (property, etc) by succession or under a will **2** (*intr*) to succeed as heir **3** (*tr*) to possess (a characteristic) through genetic transmission **4** (*tr*) to receive (a position, etc) from a predecessor [C14 from OF *enheriter*, from LL *inhērēditāre* to appoint an heir, from L *hērēs* HEIR] > **inˈherited** *adj* > **inˈheritor** *n* > **inˈheritress** *or* **inˈheritrix** *fem n*

inheritable (ɪnˈhɛrɪtəbᵊl) *adj* **1** capable of being transmitted by heredity from one generation to a later one **2** capable of being inherited **3** *rare* having the right to inherit > **inˌheritaˈbility** *or* **inˈheritableness** *n* > **inˈheritably** *adv*

inheritance (ɪnˈhɛrɪtəns) *n* **1** *law* **1a** hereditary succession to an estate, title, etc **1b** the right of an heir to succeed on the death of an ancestor **1c** something that may legally be transmitted to an heir **2** the act of inheriting **3** something inherited; heritage **4** the derivation of characteristics of one generation from an earlier one by heredity

inheritance tax *n* **1** (in Britain) a tax introduced in 1986 to replace capital transfer tax, consisting of a percentage levied on that part of an inheritance exceeding a specified allowance **2** (in the US) a state tax imposed on an inheritance according to its size and the relationship of the beneficiary to the deceased

inhibit (ɪnˈhɪbɪt) *vb* **inhibits, inhibiting, inhibited** (*tr*) **1** to restrain or hinder (an impulse, desire, etc) **2** to prohibit, forbid, or prevent **3** to stop, prevent, or decrease the rate of (a chemical reaction) [C15 from L *inhibēre* to restrain, from IN-[2] + *habēre* to have] > **inˈhibitable** *adj* > **inˈhibitive** *or* **inˈhibitory** *adj*

inhibition (ˌɪnɪˈbɪʃən, ˌɪnhɪ-) *n* **1** the act of inhibiting or the condition of being inhibited **2** *psychol* a mental state or condition in which the varieties of expression and behaviour of an individual become restricted **3** the process of stopping or retarding a chemical reaction **4** *physiol* the suppression of the function or action of an organ or part, as by stimulation of its nerve supply

inhibitor (ɪnˈhɪbɪtə) *n* **1** Also: **inhibiter** a person or thing that inhibits **2** a substance that retards or stops a chemical reaction **3** *biochem* **3a** a substance that inhibits the action of an enzyme **3b** a substance that inhibits a metabolic or physiological process: *a plant growth inhibitor*

inhospitable (ɪnˈhɒspɪtəbᵊl, ˌɪnhɒˈspɪt-) *adj* **1** not hospitable; unfriendly **2** (of a region, an environment, etc) lacking a favourable climate, terrain, etc > **inˈhospitableness** *n* > **inˈhospitably** *adv*

in-house *adj, adv* within an organization or group: *an in-house job; the job was done in-house*

inhuman (ɪnˈhjuːmən) *adj* **1** Also: **inhumane** (ˌɪnhjuːˈmeɪn) lacking humane feelings, such as sympathy, understanding, etc; cruel; brutal **2** not human > **ˌinhuˈmanely** *adv* > **inˈhumanly** *adv* > **inˈhumanness** *n*

inhumanity (ˌɪnhjuːˈmænɪtɪ) *n, pl* **inhumanities** **1** lack of humane qualities **2** an inhumane act, decision, etc

inhume (ɪnˈhjuːm) *vb* **inhumes, inhuming, inhumed** (*tr*) to inter; bury [C17 from L, from IN-[2] + *humus* ground] > **ˌinhuˈmation** *n* > **inˈhumer** *n*

inimical (ɪˈnɪmɪkᵊl) *adj* **1** adverse or unfavourable **2** not friendly; hostile [C17 from LL, from *inimīcus*, from IN-[1] + *amīcus* friendly; see ENEMY] > **inˈimically** *adv* > **inˈimicalness** *or* **inˌimiˈcality** *n*

inimitable (ɪˈnɪmɪtəbᵊl) *adj* incapable of being duplicated or imitated; unique > **inˌimitaˈbility** *or* **inˈimitableness** *n* > **inˈimitably** *adv*

Ii

iniquity (ɪˈnɪkwɪtɪ) *n, pl* **iniquities** 1 lack of justice or righteousness; wickedness; injustice 2 a wicked act; sin [C14 from L, from *inīquus* unfair, from IN-[1] + *aequus* even, level; see EQUAL] > **inˈiquitous** *adj* > **inˈiquitously** *adv* > **inˈiquitousness** *n*

initial (ɪˈnɪʃəl) *adj* 1 of, at, or concerning the beginning ▷ *n* 2 the first letter of a word, esp a person's name 3 *printing* a large letter set at the beginning of a chapter or work 4 *bot* a cell from which tissues and organs develop by division and differentiation ▷ *vb* **initials, initialling, initialled** *or US* **initials, initialing, initialed** 5 (*tr*) to sign with one's initials, esp to indicate approval; endorse [C16 from L *initiālis* of the beginning, from *initium* beginning, lit.: an entering upon, from *inīre* to go in] > **inˈitialer** *or* **inˈitialler** *n* > **inˈitially** *adv*

initialize *or* **initialise** (ɪˈnɪʃəˌlaɪz) *vb* **initializes, initializing, initialized** *or* **initialises, initialising, initialised** (*tr*) to assign an initial value to (a variable or storage location) in a computer program > **inˌitialiˈzation** *or* **inˌitialiˈsation** *n*

initiate *vb* (ɪˈnɪʃɪˌeɪt), **initiates, initiating, initiated** (*tr*) 1 to begin or originate 2 to accept (new members) into an organization such as a club, through often secret ceremonies 3 to teach fundamentals to ▷ *adj* (ɪˈnɪʃɪɪt, -ˌeɪt) 4 initiated; begun ▷ *n* (ɪˈnɪʃɪɪt, -ˌeɪt) 5 a person who has been initiated, esp recently 6 a beginner; novice [C17 from L *initiāre* (vb), from *initium*; see INITIAL] > **inˈitiatory** *adj*

initiation (ɪˌnɪʃɪˈeɪʃən) *n* 1 the act of initiating or the condition of being initiated 2 the ceremony, often secret, initiating new members into an organization

initiative (ɪˈnɪʃɪətɪv, -ˈnɪʃətɪv) *n* 1 the first step or action of a matter; commencing move: *a peace initiative* 2 the right or power to begin or initiate something: *he has the initiative* 3 the ability or attitude required to begin or initiate something 4 *government* the right of citizens to introduce legislation, etc, in a legislative body, as in Switzerland 5 **on one's own initiative** without being prompted ▷ *adj* 6 of or concerning initiation or serving to initiate; initiatory > **inˈitiatively** *adv*

initiator (ɪˈnɪʃɪˌeɪtə) *n* 1 a person or thing that initiates 2 *chem* a substance that starts a chain reaction 3 *chem* a very sensitive explosive used in detonators

inject (ɪnˈdʒɛkt) *vb* (*tr*) 1 *med* to introduce (a fluid) into the body (of a person or animal) by means of a syringe 2 (foll by *into*) to introduce (a new aspect or element): *to inject humour into a scene* 3 to interject (a comment, idea, etc) [C17 from *injicere* to throw in, from *jacere* to throw] > **inˈjectable** *adj* > **inˈjector** *n*

injection (ɪnˈdʒɛkʃən) *n* 1 fluid injected into the body, esp for medicinal purposes 2 something injected 3 the act of injecting 4a the act or process of introducing fluid under pressure, such as fuel into the combustion chamber of an engine 4b (*as modifier*): *injection moulding* > **inˈjective** *adj*

injunction (ɪnˈdʒʌŋkʃən) *n* 1 *law* an instruction or order issued by a court to a party to an action, esp to refrain from some act 2 a command, admonition, etc 3 the act of enjoining [C16 from LL, from L *injungere* to ENJOIN] > **inˈjunctive** *adj* > **inˈjunctively** *adv*

injure (ˈɪndʒə) *vb* **injures, injuring, injured** (*tr*) 1 to cause physical or mental harm or suffering to; hurt or wound 2 to offend, esp by an injustice [C16 back formation from INJURY] > **ˈinjurable** *adj* > **ˈinjured** *adj* > **ˈinjurer** *n*

injurious (ɪnˈdʒʊərɪəs) *adj* 1 causing damage or harm; deleterious; hurtful 2 abusive, slanderous, or libellous > **inˈjuriously** *adv* > **inˈjuriousness** *n*

injury (ˈɪndʒərɪ) *n, pl* **injuries** 1 physical damage or hurt: *playing on terrible pitches which may cause injury* 2 a specific instance of this: *a leg injury* 3 harm done to a reputation 4 *law* a violation or infringement of another person's rights that causes him or her harm and is actionable at law [C14 from L *injūria* injustice, wrong, from *injūriōsus* acting unfairly, wrongful, from IN-[1] + *jūs* right]

injury list *n* the people who are unable to participate in a sport as expected, due to illness or injury

injury time *n soccer, rugby, etc* extra playing time added on to compensate for time spent attending to injured players during the match. Also called: **stoppage time**

injustice (ɪnˈdʒʌstɪs) *n* 1 the condition or practice of being unjust or unfair 2 an unjust act

ink (ɪŋk) *n* 1 a fluid or paste used for printing, writing, and drawing 2 a dark brown fluid ejected into the water for self-concealment by an octopus or related mollusc ▷ *vb* (*tr*) 3 to mark with ink 4 to coat (a printing surface) with ink [C13 from OF *enque*, from LL *encaustum* a purplish-red ink, from Gk *enkauston* purple ink, from *enkaustos* burnt in, from *enkaiein* to burn in; see EN-[2], CAUSTIC] > **ˈinker** *n*

Inkatha (ɪnˈkɑːtə) *n* a South African political party; originally a Zulu organization founded in 1975 as a paramilitary group seeking nonracial democracy; won four seats in democratic multiracial elections in 1994 [C20 Zulu name for the grass coil used by Zulu women carrying loads on their heads]

inkblot (ˈɪŋkˌblɒt) *n* a patch of ink accidentally or deliberately spilled. Ten such patches, of different shapes, are used in the Rorschach test

ink-cap *n* any of several saprotrophic fungi whose caps disintegrate into a black inky fluid after the spores mature

Inkerman (ˈɪŋkəmən; *Russian* inkɪrˈman) *n* a village in the Ukraine, in the S Crimea east of Sevastopol: scene of a battle during the Crimean War in which British and French forces defeated the Russians (1854)

inkhorn (ˈɪŋkˌhɔːn) *n* (formerly) a small portable container for ink, usually made from horn

ink in *vb* (*adv*) 1 (*tr*) to use ink to go over pencil lines in (a drawing) 2 to apply ink to (a printing surface) in preparing to print from it 3 to arrange or confirm definitely

inkling (ˈɪŋklɪŋ) *n* a slight intimation or suggestion; suspicion [C14 prob. from *inclen* to hint at]

inkstand (ˈɪŋkˌstænd) *n* a stand or tray on which are kept writing implements and containers for ink

inkwell (ˈɪŋkˌwɛl) *n* a small container for pen ink, often let into the surface of a desk

inky (ˈɪŋkɪ) *adj* **inkier, inkiest** 1 resembling ink, esp in colour; dark or black 2 of, containing, or stained with ink > **ˈinkiness** *n*

INLA *abbrev for* Irish National Liberation Army

inlaid (ˈɪnˌleɪd, ɪnˈleɪd) *adj* 1 set in the surface, as a design in wood 2 having such a design or inlay: *an inlaid table*

inland *adj* (ˈɪnlənd) 1 of or located in the interior of a country or region away from a sea or border 2 *chiefly Brit* operating within a country or region; domestic; not foreign ▷ *n* (ˈɪnˌlænd, -lənd) 3 the interior of a country or region ▷ *adv* (ˈɪnˌlænd, -lənd) 4 towards or into the interior of a country or region > **ˈinlander** *n*

Inland Revenue *n* (in Britain and New Zealand) a government board that administers and collects major direct taxes, such as income tax

Inland Sea *n* a sea in SW Japan, between the islands of Honshu, Shikoku, and Kyushu. Japanese name: **Seto Naikai**

in-law *n* 1 a relative by marriage ▷ *adj* 2 (*postpositive; in combination*) related by marriage: *a father-in-law* [C19 back formation from *father-in-law*, etc]

inlay *vb* (ɪnˈleɪ), **inlays, inlaying, inlaid** (*tr*) 1 to decorate (an article, esp of furniture) by inserting pieces of wood, ivory, etc, into slots in the surface ▷ *n* (ˈɪnˌleɪ) 2 *dentistry* a filling inserted into a cavity and held in position by cement 3 decoration made by inlaying 4 an inlaid article, surface, etc > **ˈinˌlayer** *n*

inlet *n* (ˈɪnˌlɛt) 1 a narrow inland opening of the

coastline **2** an entrance or opening **3** the act of letting someone or something in **4** something let in or inserted **5a** a passage or valve through which a substance, esp a fluid, enters a machine **5b** *(as modifier): an inlet valve* ▷ *vb* (ɪnˈlɛt), **inlets, inletting, inlet** **6** *(tr)* to insert or inlay
inlier (ˈɪnˌlaɪə) *n* an outcrop of rocks that is entirely surrounded by younger rocks
in-line skate *n* another name for **Rollerblade**
in loco parentis *Latin* (ɪn ˈləʊkəʊ pəˈrɛntɪs) in place of a parent: said of a person acting in a parental capacity
inly (ˈɪnlɪ) *adv poetic* inwardly; intimately
inmate (ˈɪnˌmeɪt) *n* a person who is confined to an institution such as a prison or hospital
in medias res *Latin* (ɪn ˈmiːdɪˌæs ˈreɪs) in or into the middle of events or a narrative [lit.: into the midst of things, taken from a passage in Horace's *Ars Poetica*]
in memoriam (ɪn mɪˈmɔːrɪəm) in memory of: used in obituaries, epitaphs, etc [L]
inmost (ˈɪnˌməʊst) *adj* another word for **innermost**
inn (ɪn) *n* a pub or small hotel providing food and accommodation
Inn (ɪn) *n* a river in central Europe, rising in Switzerland in Graubünden and flowing northeast through Austria and Bavaria to join the River Danube at Passau: forms part of the border between Austria and Germany. Length: 514 km (319 miles)
innards (ˈɪnədz) *pl n inf* **1** the internal organs of the body, esp the viscera **2** the interior parts of anything, esp the working parts [c19 colloquial var. of *inwards*]
innate (ɪˈneɪt, ˈɪneɪt) *adj* **1** existing from birth; congenital; inborn **2** being an essential part of the character of a person or thing **3** instinctive; not learned: *innate capacities* **4** *philosophy* (of ideas) present in the mind before any experience and knowable by pure reason [c15 from L, from *innascī* to be born in, from *nascī* to be born] > **inˈnately** *adv* > **inˈnateness** *n*
inner (ˈɪnə) *adj (prenominal)* **1** being or located further inside: *an inner room* **2** happening or occurring inside **3** relating to the soul, mind, spirit, etc **4** more profound or obscure; less apparent: *the inner meaning* **5** exclusive or private: *inner regions of the party* ▷ *n* **6** *archery* **6a** the red innermost ring on a target **6b** a shot which hits this ring > **ˈinnerly** *adv* > **ˈinnerness** *n*
inner bar *n* **the** *Brit* all Queen's or King's Counsel collectively
inner child *n psychol* the part of the psyche that retains feelings as they were experienced in childhood
inner city *n* **a** the parts of a city in or near its centre, esp when associated with poverty, substandard housing, etc **b** *(as modifier): inner-city schools*
Inner Hebrides *pl n* See **Hebrides**
inner man *or (fem)* **inner woman** *n* **1** the mind or soul **2** *jocular* the stomach or appetite
Inner Mongolia *n* an autonomous region of NE China: consists chiefly of the Mongolian plateau, with the Gobi Desert in the north and the Great Wall of China in the south. Capital: Hohhot. Pop: 23 760 000 (2000 est). Area: 1 177 500 sq km (459 225 sq miles)
innermost (ˈɪnəˌməʊst) *adj* **1** being or located furthest within; central **2** intimate; private
inner tube *n* an inflatable rubber tube that fits inside a pneumatic tyre casing
innervate (ˈɪnɜːˌveɪt) *vb* **innervates, innervating, innervated** *(tr)* **1** to supply nerves to (a bodily organ or part) **2** to stimulate (a bodily organ or part) with nerve impulses > **ˌinnerˈvation** *n*
innings (ˈɪnɪŋz) *n* **1** *(functioning as sing) cricket, etc* **1a** the batting turn of a player or team **1b** the runs scored during such a turn **2** *(sometimes sing)* a period of opportunity or action
Inniskilling (ˌɪnɪsˈkɪlɪŋ) *n* the former name of **Enniskillen**
innkeeper (ˈɪnˌkiːpə) *n* an owner or manager of an inn
innocence (ˈɪnəsəns) *n* the quality or state of being innocent. Archaic word: **innocency** (ˈɪnəsənsɪ) [c14 from L *innocentia* harmlessness, from *innocēns* blameless, from IN-[1] + *nocēre* to hurt]
innocent (ˈɪnəsənt) *adj* **1** not corrupted or tainted with evil; sinless; pure **2** not guilty of a particular crime; blameless **3** *(postpositive; foll by of)* free (of); lacking: *innocent of all knowledge of history* **4a** harmless or innocuous: *an innocent game* **4b** not cancerous: *an innocent tumour* **5** credulous, naive, or artless **6** simple-minded; slow-witted ▷ *n* **7** an innocent person, esp a young child or an ingenuous adult **8** a simple-minded person; simpleton > **ˈinnocently** *adv*
Innocent II *n* original name *Gregorio Papareschi*. died 1143, pope (1130–43). He condemned Abelard's teachings
Innocent III *n* original name *Giovanni Lotario de' Conti*. ?1161–1216, pope (1198–1216), under whom the temporal power of the papacy reached its height. He instituted the Fourth Crusade (1202) and a crusade against the Albigenses (1208), and called the fourth Lateran Council (1215)
Innocent IV *n* original name *Sinibaldo de' Fieschi*. died 1254, pope (1243–54); an unrelenting enemy of Emperor Frederick II and his heirs
innocuous (ɪˈnɒkjʊəs) *adj* having little or no adverse or harmful effect; harmless [c16 from L *innocuus* harmless, from IN-[1] + *nocēre* to harm] > **inˈnocuously** *adv* > **inˈnocuousness** *or* **innocuity** (ˌɪnəˈkjuːɪtɪ) *n*
innominate bone (ɪˈnɒmɪnɪt) *n* either of the two bones that form the sides of the pelvis, consisting of the ilium, ischium, and pubis. Nontechnical name: **hipbone**
innovate (ˈɪnəˌveɪt) *vb* **innovates, innovating, innovated** to invent or begin to apply (methods, ideas, etc) [c16 from L *innovāre* to renew, from IN-[2] + *novāre* to make new, from *novus* new] > **ˈinnoˌvative** *or* **ˈinnoˌvatory** *adj* > **ˈinnoˌvator** *n*
innovation (ˌɪnəˈveɪʃən) *n* **1** something newly introduced, such as a new method or device **2** the act of innovating > **ˌinnoˈvational** *adj* > **ˌinnoˈvationist** *n*
Innsbruck (ˈɪnzbrʊk) *n* a city in W Austria, on the River Inn at the foot of the Brenner Pass: tourist centre. Pop: 113 826 (2001)
Innu (ˈɪnuː) *n* **1** a member of an Algonquian people living in Labrador and northern Quebec **2** the Algonquian language of this people
innuendo (ˌɪnjʊˈɛndəʊ) *n, pl* **innuendos** *or* **innuendoes** **1** an indirect or subtle reference, esp one made maliciously or indicating criticism or disapproval; insinuation **2** *law* (in an action for defamation) an explanation of the construction put upon words alleged to be defamatory where this meaning is not apparent [c17 from L, lit.: by hinting, from *innuere* to convey by a nod, from IN-[2] + *nuere* to nod]
Innuit (ˈɪnjuːɪt) *n* a variant spelling of **Inuit**
innumerable (ɪˈnjuːmərəbᵊl, ɪˈnjuːmrəbᵊl) *or* **innumerous** *adj* so many as to be uncountable; extremely numerous > **inˌnumeraˈbility** *or* **inˈnumerableness** *n* > **inˈnumerably** *adv*
innumerate (ɪˈnjuːmərɪt) *adj* **1** having neither knowledge nor understanding of mathematics or science ▷ *n* **2** an innumerate person > **inˈnumeracy** *n*
inoculate (ɪˈnɒkjʊˌleɪt) *vb* **inoculates, inoculating, inoculated** **1** to introduce (the causative agent of a disease) into the body in order to induce immunity **2** *(tr)* to introduce (microorganisms, esp bacteria) into (a culture medium) **3** *(tr)* to cause to be influenced or imbued, as with ideas [c15 from L *inoculāre* to implant, from IN-[2] + *oculus* eye, bud] > **inˌocuˈlation** *n* > **inˈoculative** *adj* > **inˈocuˌlator** *n*
inoculum (ɪˈnɒkjʊləm) *or* **inoculant** *n, pl* **inocula** (-lə) *or* **inoculants** *med* the substance used in giving an inoculation [c20 NL; see INOCULATE]

Ii

in-off *n billiards* a shot that goes into a pocket after striking another ball

Inönü ('iːnɜːˌnʊ, ˌɪnɜː'nuː) *n* **Ismet** (ɪs'mɛt, 'ɪsmɛt) 1884–1973, Turkish statesman; president of Turkey (1938–50) and prime minister (1923–37; 1961–65)

inoperable (ɪn'ɒpərəbᵊl, -'ɒprə-) *adj* **1** incapable of being implemented or operated **2** *surgery* not suitable for operation without risk, esp because of metastasis > **inˌopera'bility** *or* **in'operableness** *n* > **in'operably** *adv*

inordinate (ɪn'ɔːdɪnɪt) *adj* **1** exceeding normal limits; immoderate **2** unrestrained, as in behaviour or emotion; intemperate **3** irregular or disordered [C14 from L *inordinātus* disordered, from IN-[1] + *ordināre* to put in order] > **in'ordinacy** *or* **in'ordinateness** *n* > **in'ordinately** *adv*

inorganic (ˌɪnɔː'gænɪk) *adj* **1** not having the structure or characteristics of living organisms; not organic **2** relating to or denoting chemical compounds that do not contain carbon **3** not having a system, structure, or ordered relation of parts; amorphous **4** not resulting from or produced by growth; artificial > **ˌinor'ganically** *adv*

inorganic chemistry *n* the branch of chemistry concerned with the elements and all their compounds except those containing carbon

inosculate (ɪn'ɒskjʊˌleɪt) *vb* **inosculates, inosculating, inosculated 1** *physiol* (of small blood vessels) to communicate by anastomosis **2** to unite or be united so as to be continuous; blend **3** to intertwine or cause to intertwine [C17 from IN-[2] + L *ōsculāre* to equip with an opening, from *ōsculum*, dim. of *ōs* mouth] > **inˌoscu'lation** *n*

inositol (ɪ'nəʊsɪˌtɒl) *n* a cyclic alcohol, one isomer of which (*i*-inositol) is present in yeast and is a growth factor for some organisms [C19 from Gk *in-*, *is* sinew + -OSE[2] + -ITE[1] + -OL[1]]

inpatient ('ɪnˌpeɪʃənt) *n* a hospital patient who occupies a bed for at least one night in the course of treatment, examination, or observation

in perpetuum *Latin* (ɪn pɜː'pɛtjʊəm) forever

input ('ɪnˌpʊt) *n* **1** the act of putting in **2** that which is put in **3** (*often pl*) a resource required for industrial production, such as capital goods, etc **4** *electronics* the signal or current fed into a component or circuit **5** *computing* the data fed into a computer from a peripheral device **6** (*modifier*) of or relating to electronic, computer, or other input: *input program* ▷ *vb* **inputs, inputting, input 7** (*tr*) to insert (data) into a computer

input/output *n computing* **1** the data or information passed into or out of a computer **2** (*modifier*) concerned with or relating to such passage of data or information

inquest ('ɪnˌkwɛst) *n* **1** an inquiry, esp into the cause of an unexplained, sudden, or violent death, held by a coroner, in certain cases with a jury **2** *inf* any inquiry or investigation [C13 from Med. L, from L IN-[2] + *quaesītus* investigation, from *quaerere* to examine]

inquietude (ɪn'kwaɪɪˌtjuːd) *n* restlessness, uneasiness, or anxiety > **inquiet** (ɪn'kwaɪət) *adj* > **in'quietly** *adv*

inquiline ('ɪnkwɪˌlaɪn) *n* **1** an animal that lives in close association with another animal without harming it. See also **commensal** (sense 1) ▷ *adj* **2** of or living as an inquiline [C17 from L *inquilīnus* lodger, from IN-[2] + *colere* to dwell] > **inquilinous** (ˌɪnkwɪ'laɪnəs) *adj*

inquire *or* **enquire** (ɪn'kwaɪə) *vb* **inquires, inquiring, inquired** *or* **enquires, enquiring, enquired 1a** to seek information (about); ask: *she inquired his age; she inquired about rates of pay* **1b** (*intr*; foll by *of*) to ask (a person) for information: *I'll inquire of my aunt when she is coming* **2** (*intr*; often foll by *into*) to make a search or investigation [C13 from L *inquīrere*, from IN-[2] + *quaerere* to seek] > **in'quirer** *or* **en'quirer** *n*

inquiry *or* **enquiry** (ɪn'kwaɪərɪ) *n, pl* **inquiries** *or* **enquiries 1** a request for information; a question **2** an investigation, esp a formal one conducted into a matter of public concern by a body constituted for that purpose by a government, local authority, or other organization

inquisition (ˌɪnkwɪ'zɪʃən) *n* **1** the act of inquiring deeply or searchingly; investigation **2** a deep or searching inquiry, esp a ruthless official investigation in order to suppress revolt or root out the unorthodox **3** an official inquiry, esp one held by a jury before an officer of the Crown [C14 from legal L *inquīsītiō*, from *inquīrere* to seek for; see INQUIRE] > **ˌinqui'sitional** *adj* > **ˌinqui'sitionist** *n*

Inquisition (ˌɪnkwɪ'zɪʃən) *n history* a judicial institution of the Roman Catholic Church (1232–1820) founded to suppress heresy
▷ www.fordham.edu/halsall/source/inquisition1.html
▷ www.catholic.com/library/inquisition.asp
▷ http://bibletopics.com/biblestudy/64.htm

inquisitive (ɪn'kwɪzɪtɪv) *adj* **1** excessively curious, esp about the affairs of others; prying **2** eager to learn; inquiring > **in'quisitively** *adv* > **in'quisitiveness** *n*

inquisitor (ɪn'kwɪzɪtə) *n* **1** a person who inquires, esp deeply, searchingly, or ruthlessly **2** (*often cap*) an official of the ecclesiastical court of the Inquisition

inquisitorial (ɪnˌkwɪzɪ'tɔːrɪəl) *adj* **1** of, relating to, or resembling inquisition or an inquisitor **2** offensively curious; prying **3** *law* denoting criminal procedure in which one party is both prosecutor and judge, or in which the trial is held in secret ▷ Cf **accusatorial** (sense 2) > **inˌquisi'torially** *adv* > **inˌquisi'torialness** *n*

inquorate (ɪn'kwɔːˌreɪt) *adj Brit* not consisting of or being a quorum: *this meeting is inquorate*

in re (ɪn 'reɪ) *prep* in the matter of: used esp in bankruptcy proceedings [C17 from L]

INRI *abbrev for* Iesus Nazarenus Rex Iudaeorum (the inscription placed over Christ's head during the Crucifixion) [L: Jesus of Nazareth, King of the Jews]

inro ('ɪnrəʊ) *n, pl* **inro** a set of small lacquer boxes formerly worn hung from the belt by Japanese men and used to carry medicines, seals, etc

inroad ('ɪnˌrəʊd) *n* **1** an invasion or hostile attack; raid or incursion **2** an encroachment or intrusion

inrush ('ɪnˌrʌʃ) *n* a sudden usually overwhelming inward flow or rush; influx > **'inˌrushing** *n, adj*

ins. *abbrev for* inches

insane (ɪn'seɪn) *adj* **1a** mentally deranged; crazy; of unsound mind **1b** (*as collective n; preceded by the*): *the insane* **2** characteristic of a person of unsound mind: *an insane stare* **3** irresponsible; very foolish; stupid > **in'sanely** *adv* > **in'saneness** *n*

insanitary (ɪn'sænɪtərɪ, -trɪ) *adj* not sanitary; dirty or infected

insanity (ɪn'sænɪtɪ) *n, pl* **insanities 1** relatively permanent disorder of the mind; state or condition of being insane **2** utter folly; stupidity

insatiable (ɪn'seɪʃəbᵊl, -ʃɪə-) *or* **insatiate** (ɪn'seɪʃɪɪt) *adj* not able to be satisfied; greedy or unappeasable > **inˌsatia'bility** *or* **in'satiateness** *n* > **in'satiably** *or* **in'satiately** *adv*

inscape ('ɪnskeɪp) *n* the essential inner nature of a person, object, etc [C19 from IN-[2] + *-scape*, as in LANDSCAPE; coined by Gerard Manley HOPKINS]

inscribe (ɪn'skraɪb) *vb* **inscribes, inscribing, inscribed** (*tr*) **1** to make, carve, or engrave (writing, letters, etc) on (a surface such as wood, stone, or paper) **2** to enter (a name) on a list or in a register **3** to sign one's name on (a book, etc) before presentation to another person **4** to draw (a geometric construction) inside another construction so that the two are in contact but do not intersect [C16 from L *inscrībere*; see INSCRIPTION] > **in'scribable** *adj* > **in'scribableness** *n* > **in'scriber** *n*

inscription (ɪn'skrɪpʃən) *n* **1** something inscribed, esp words carved or engraved on a coin, tomb, etc **2** a signature or brief dedication in a book or on a work of art **3** the act of inscribing [C14 from L *inscriptiō* a writing upon, from *inscrībere* to write upon, from IN-[2] + *scrībere* to write] > **in'scriptional** *or* **in'scriptive** *adj* > **in'scriptively** *adv*

inscrutable (ɪn'skruːtəbᵊl) *adj* mysterious or enigmatic; incomprehensible [C15 from LL, from L IN-[1] + *scrūtārī* to examine] > **in,scruta'bility** *or* **in'scrutableness** *n* > **in'scrutably** *adv*

insect ('ɪnsɛkt) *n* **1** any of a class of small air-breathing arthropods, having a body divided into head, thorax, and abdomen, three pairs of legs, and (in most species) two pairs of wings **2** (loosely) any similar invertebrate, such as a spider, tick, or centipede **3** a contemptible, loathsome, or insignificant person [C17 from L *insectum* (animal that has been) cut into, insect, from *insecāre*, from IN-[2] + *secāre* to cut] > **in'sectile** *adj* > **'insect-,like** *adj*

insectarium (,ɪnsɛk'tɛərɪəm) *or* **insectary** (ɪn'sɛktərɪ) *n*, *pl* **insectariums, insectaria** (-'tɛərɪə), *or* **insectaries** a place where living insects are kept, bred, and studied

insecticide (ɪn'sɛktɪ,saɪd) *n* a substance used to destroy insect pests > **in,secti'cidal** *adj*

insectivore (ɪn'sɛktɪ,vɔː) *n* **1** any of an order of placental mammals, being typically small, with simple teeth, and feeding on invertebrates. The group includes shrews, moles, and hedgehogs **2** any animal or plant that derives nourishment from insects

insectivorous (,ɪnsɛk'tɪvərəs) *adj* **1** feeding on or adapted for feeding on insects: *insectivorous plants* **2** of or relating to the order *Insectivora*

insecure (,ɪnsɪ'kjʊə) *adj* **1** anxious or afraid; not confident or certain **2** not adequately protected: *an insecure fortress* **3** unstable or shaky > **,inse'curely** *adv* > **,inse'cureness** *n* > **,inse'curity** *n*

inselberg ('ɪnzᵊl,bɜːg) *n* an isolated rocky hill rising abruptly from a flat plain [from G, from *Insel* island + *Berg* mountain]

inseminate (ɪn'sɛmɪ,neɪt) *vb* **inseminates, inseminating, inseminated** (*tr*) **1** to impregnate (a female) with semen **2** to introduce (ideas or attitudes) into the mind of (a person or group) [C17 from L *insēmināre*, from IN-[2] + *sēmināre* to sow, from *sēmen* seed] > **in,semi'nation** *n* > **in'semi,nator** *n*

insensate (ɪn'sɛnseɪt, -sɪt) *adj* **1** lacking sensation or consciousness **2** insensitive; unfeeling **3** foolish; senseless > **in'sensately** *adv* > **in'sensateness** *n*

insensible (ɪn'sɛnsəbᵊl) *adj* **1** lacking sensation or consciousness **2** (foll by *of* or *to*) unaware (of) or indifferent (to): *insensible to suffering* **3** thoughtless or callous **4** a less common word for **imperceptible** > **in,sensi'bility** *or* **in'sensibleness** *n* > **in'sensibly** *adv*

insensitive (ɪn'sɛnsɪtɪv) *adj* **1** lacking sensitivity; unfeeling **2** lacking physical sensation **3** (*postpositive*; foll by *to*) not sensitive (to) or affected (by): *insensitive to radiation* > **in'sensitively** *adv* > **in'sensitiveness** *or* **in,sensi'tivity** *n*

insentient (ɪn'sɛnʃɪənt) *adj* lacking consciousness or senses; inanimate > **in'sentience** *n*

inseparable (ɪn'sɛpərəbᵊl, -'sɛprə-) *adj* incapable of being separated or divided > **in,separa'bility** *or* **in'separableness** *n* > **in'separably** *adv*

insert *vb* (ɪn'sɜːt) (*tr*) **1** to put in or between; introduce **2** to introduce into text, as in a newspaper; interpolate ▷ *n* ('ɪnsɜːt) **3** something inserted **4** Also called: **inset** **4a** a folded section placed in another for binding in with a book **4b** a printed sheet, esp one bearing advertising, placed loose between the leaves of a book, periodical, etc [C16 from L *inserere* to plant in, from IN-[2] + *serere* to join] > **in'sertable** *adj* > **in'serter** *n*

insertion (ɪn'sɜːʃən) *n* **1** the act of inserting or something that is inserted **2** a word, sentence, correction, etc, inserted into text, such as a newspaper **3** a strip of lace, embroidery, etc, between two pieces of material **4** *anat* the point or manner of attachment of a muscle to the bone that it moves > **in'sertional** *adj*

in-service *adj* denoting training that is given to employees during the course of employment: *an in-service course*

insessorial (,ɪnsɛ'sɔːrɪəl) *adj* **1** (of feet or claws) adapted for perching **2** (of birds) having insessorial feet [C19 from NL *Insessōrēs* birds that perch, from L: perchers, from *insidēre* to sit upon]

inset *vb* (ɪn'sɛt), **insets, insetting, inset** **1** (*tr*) to set or place in or within; insert ▷ *n* ('ɪn,sɛt) **2** something inserted **3** *printing* **3a** a small map or diagram set within the borders of a larger one **3b** another name for **insert** (sense 4) **4** a piece of fabric inserted into a garment, as to shape it or for decoration > **'in,setter** *n*

inshallah (ɪn'ʃælə) *sentence substitute Islam* if Allah wills it [C19 from Ar.]

inshore ('ɪn'ʃɔː) *adj* **1** in or on the water, but close to the shore: *inshore weather* ▷ *adv, adj* **2** towards the shore from the water: *an inshore wind; we swam inshore*

inside *n* ('ɪn'saɪd) **1** the interior; inner or enclosed part or surface **2** the side of a path away from the road or adjacent to a wall **3** (*also pl*) *inf* the internal organs of the body, esp the stomach and bowels **4** **inside of** in a period of time less than; within **5** **inside out** with the inside facing outwards **6** **know (something) inside out** to know thoroughly or perfectly ▷ *prep* (,ɪn'saɪd) **7** in or to the interior of; within or to within; on the inside of ▷ *adj* ('ɪn,saɪd) **8** on or of an interior; on the inside: *an inside door* **9** (*prenominal*) arranged or provided by someone within an organization or building, esp illicitly: *the raid was an inside job; inside information* ▷ *adv* (,ɪn'saɪd) **10** within or to within a thing or place; indoors **11** *sl* in or into prison.

USAGE See at **outside**

inside job *n inf* a crime committed with the assistance of someone associated with the victim

inside lane *n athletics* the inside, and therefore the shortest, route around a circular or oval multi-lane running track

insider (,ɪn'saɪdə) *n* **1** a member of a specified group **2** a person with access to exclusive information

insider dealing *or* **trading** *n* the illegal practice of a person on the Stock Exchange or in some branches of the Civil Service taking advantage of early confidential information in order to deal in shares for personal profit > **insider dealer** *or* **trader** *n*

insidious (ɪn'sɪdɪəs) *adj* **1** stealthy, subtle, cunning, or treacherous **2** working in a subtle or apparently innocuous way, but nevertheless deadly: *an insidious illness* [C16 from L *insidiōsus* cunning, from *insidiae* an ambush, from *insidēre* to sit in] > **in'sidiously** *adv* > **in'sidiousness** *n*

insight ('ɪn,saɪt) *n* **1** the ability to perceive clearly or deeply; penetration **2** a penetrating and often sudden understanding, as of a complex situation or problem **3** *psychol* the capacity for understanding one's own or another's mental processes **4** *psychiatry* the ability to understand one's own problems > **'in,sightful** *adj*

insignia (ɪn'sɪgnɪə) *n*, *pl* **insignias** *or* **insignia** **1** a badge or emblem of membership, office, or dignity **2** a distinguishing sign or mark [C17 from L: badges, from *insignis* distinguished by a mark, prominent, from IN-[2] + *signum* mark]

insignificant (,ɪnsɪg'nɪfɪkənt) *adj* **1** having little or no importance; trifling **2** almost or relatively meaningless **3** small or inadequate: *an insignificant wage* **4** not distinctive in character, etc > **,insig'nificance** *or* **,insig'nificancy** *n* > **,insig'nificantly** *adv*

insincere (,ɪnsɪn'sɪə) *adj* lacking sincerity; hypocritical > **,insin'cerely** *adv* > **insincerity** (,ɪnsɪn'sɛrɪtɪ) *n*

insinuate (ɪn'sɪnjʊ,eɪt) *vb* **insinuates, insinuating, insinuated** **1** (*may take a clause as object*) to suggest by indirect allusion, hints, innuendo, etc **2** (*tr*) to introduce subtly or deviously **3** (*tr*) to cause (someone,

Ii

esp oneself) to be accepted by gradual approaches or manoeuvres [C16 from L *insinuāre* to wind one's way into, from IN-[2] + *sinus* curve] > **in'sinuative** *or* **in'sinuatory** *adj* > **in'sinu,ator** *n*

insinuation (ɪn,sɪnjʊ'eɪʃən) *n* **1** an indirect or devious hint or suggestion **2** the act or practice of insinuating

insipid (ɪn'sɪpɪd) *adj* **1** lacking spirit or interest; boring **2** lacking taste; unpalatable [C17 from L, from IN-[1] + *sapidus* full of flavour, SAPID] > **,insi'pidity** *or* **in'sipidness** *n* > **in'sipidly** *adv*

insist (ɪn'sɪst) *vb* (when *tr, takes a clause as object;* when *intr,* usually foll by *on* or *upon*) **1** to make a determined demand (for): *he insisted on his rights* **2** to express a convinced belief (in) or assertion (of) [C16 from L *insistere* to stand upon, urge, from IN-[2] + *sistere* to stand] > **in'sister** *n* > **in'sistingly** *adv*

insistent (ɪn'sɪstənt) *adj* **1** making continual and persistent demands **2** demanding notice or attention; compelling: *the insistent cry of a bird* > **in'sistence** *or* **in'sistency** *n* > **in'sistently** *adv*

in situ *Latin* (ɪn 'sɪtju:) *adv, adj (postpositive)* in the natural, original, or appropriate position

in so far as *or* **insofar as** (,ɪnsəʊ'fɑ:) *adv* to the degree or extent that

insolation (,ɪnsəʊ'leɪʃən) *n* **1** the quantity of solar radiation falling upon a body or planet, esp per unit area **2** exposure to the sun's rays **3** former name for **sunstroke**

insole ('ɪn,səʊl) *n* **1** the inner sole of a shoe or boot **2** a loose additional inner sole used to give extra warmth or to make a shoe fit

insolent ('ɪnsələnt) *adj* impudent or disrespectful [C14 from L, from IN-[1] + *solēre* to be accustomed] > **'insolence** *n* > **'insolently** *adv*

insoluble (ɪn'sɒljʊbᵊl) *adj* **1** incapable of being dissolved; incapable of forming a solution, esp in water **2** incapable of being solved > **in,solu'bility** *or* **in'solubleness** *n* > **in'solubly** *adv*

insolvent (ɪn'sɒlvənt) *adj* **1** having insufficient assets to meet debts and liabilities; bankrupt **2** of or relating to bankrupts or bankruptcy ▷ *n* **3** a person who is insolvent; bankrupt > **in'solvency** *n*

insomnia (ɪn'sɒmnɪə) *n* chronic inability to fall asleep or to enjoy uninterrupted sleep [C18 from L, from *insomnis* sleepless, from *somnus* sleep] > **in'somni,ac** *n, adj* > **in'somnious** *adj*

insomuch (,ɪnsəʊ'mʌtʃ) *adv* **1** (foll by *as* or *that*) to such an extent or degree **2** (foll by *as*) because of the fact (that); inasmuch (as)

insouciant (ɪn'su:sɪənt) *adj* carefree or unconcerned; light-hearted [C19 from F, from IN-[1] + *souciant* worrying, from *soucier* to trouble, from L *sollicitāre*] > **in'souciance** *n* > **in'souciantly** *adv*

inspan (ɪn'spæn) *vb* **inspans, inspanning, inspanned** *(tr) chiefly S African* **1** to harness (animals) to (a vehicle); yoke **2** to press (people) into service [C19 from Afrik., from MDu. *inspannen,* from *spannen* to stretch]

inspect (ɪn'spɛkt) *vb (tr)* **1** to examine closely, esp for faults or errors **2** to scrutinize officially (a document, military personnel on ceremonial parade, etc) [C17 from L *inspicere,* from *specere* to look] > **in'spectable** *adj* > **in'spection** *n* > **in'spective** *adj*

inspector (ɪn'spɛktə) *n* **1** a person who inspects, esp an official who examines for compliance with regulations, standards, etc **2** a police officer ranking below a superintendent and above a sergeant > **in'spectoral** *or* **inspectorial** (,ɪnspɛk'tɔ:rɪəl) *adj* > **in'spector,ship** *n*

inspectorate (ɪn'spɛktərɪt) *n* **1** the office, rank, or duties of an inspector **2** a body of inspectors **3** a district under an inspector

inspiration (,ɪnspɪ'reɪʃən) *n* **1** stimulation or arousal of the mind, feelings, etc, to special activity or creativity **2** the state or quality of being so stimulated or aroused **3** someone or something that causes this state **4** an idea or action resulting from such a state **5** the act or process of inhaling; breathing in

inspiratory (ɪn'spaɪərətərɪ, -trɪ) *adj* of or relating to inhalation or the drawing in of air

inspire (ɪn'spaɪə) *vb* **inspires, inspiring, inspired** **1** to exert a stimulating or beneficial effect upon (a person, etc); animate or invigorate **2** *(tr;* foll by *with* or *to; may take an infinitive)* to arouse (with a particular emotion or to a particular action); stir **3** *(tr)* to prompt or instigate; give rise to **4** *(tr; often passive)* to guide or arouse by divine influence or inspiration **5** to take or draw (air, gas, etc) into the lungs; inhale **6** *(tr) arch* to breathe into or upon [C14 (in the sense: to breathe upon, blow into): from L *inspīrāre,* from *spīrāre* to breathe] > **in'spirable** *adj* > **in'spirative** *adj* > **in'spirer** *n* > **in'spiringly** *adv*

inspirit (ɪn'spɪrɪt) *vb (tr)* to fill with vigour; inspire > **in'spiriter** *n* > **in'spiriting** *adj* > **in'spiritment** *n*

inspissate (ɪn'spɪseɪt) *vb* **inspissates, inspissating, inspissated** *arch* to thicken, as by evaporation [C17 from LL *inspissātus* thickened, from L, from *spissus* thick] > **,inspis'sation** *n* > **'inspis,sator** *n*

Inst. *abbrev for:* **1** Institute **2** Institution

instability (,ɪnstə'bɪlɪtɪ) *n, pl* **instabilities** **1** lack of stability or steadiness **2** tendency to variable or unpredictable behaviour

install *or* **instal** (ɪn'stɔ:l) *vb* **installs** *or* **instals, installing, installed** *(tr)* **1** to place (equipment) in position and connect and adjust for use **2** to transfer (computer software) from a distribution file to a permanent location on disk, and prepare it for its particular environment and application **3** to put in a position, rank, etc **4** to settle (a person, esp oneself) in a position or state: *she installed herself in an armchair* [C16 from Med. L *installāre,* from IN-[2] + *stallum* STALL[1]] > **in'staller** *n*

installation (,ɪnstə'leɪʃən) *n* **1** the act of installing or the state of being installed **2** a large device, system, or piece of equipment that has been installed

installment plan *or esp Canad* **instalment plan** *n* the US and Canad name for **hire-purchase**

instalment *or US* **installment** (ɪn'stɔ:lmənt) *n* **1** one of the portions into which a debt is divided for payment at specified intervals over a fixed period **2** a portion of something that is issued, broadcast, or published in parts [C18 from obs. *estallment,* prob. from OF *estaler* to fix, from *estal* something fixed, from OHG *stal* STALL[1]]

instance ('ɪnstəns) *n* **1** a case or particular example **2 for instance** for or as an example **3** a specified stage in proceedings; step (in **in the first, second,** etc, **instance**) **4** urgent request or demand (esp in **at the instance of**) ▷ *vb* **instances, instancing, instanced** *(tr)* **5** to cite as an example [C14 (in the sense: case, example): from Med. L *instantia* example, (in the sense: urgency) from L: a being close upon, from *instāns* urgent; see INSTANT]

instant ('ɪnstənt) *n* **1** a very brief time; moment **2** a particular moment or point in time: *at the same instant* **3 on the instant** immediately; without delay ▷ *adj* **4** immediate; instantaneous **5** (esp of foods) prepared or designed for preparation with very little time and effort: *instant coffee* **6** urgent or imperative **7** *(postpositive)* of the present month: *a letter of the 7th instant.* Abbrev: **inst** [C15 from L *instāns,* from *instāre* to be present, press closely, from IN-[2] + *stāre* to stand]

instantaneous (,ɪnstən'teɪnɪəs) *adj* **1** occurring with almost no delay; immediate **2** happening or completed within a moment: *instantaneous death* > **,instan'taneously** *adv* > **,instan'taneousness** *or* **instantaneity** (ɪn,stæntə'ni:ɪtɪ) *n*

instanter (ɪn'stæntə) *adv law* without delay; the same day or within 24 hours [C17 from L: urgently, from *instans* INSTANT]

instantly ('ɪnstəntlɪ) *adv* **1** immediately; at once **2** *arch* urgently or insistently

instant messaging *n* a form of electronic communication that enables two or more people to communicate with each other instantaneously via the Internet. Abbrev: **IM**
instar (ˈɪnstɑː) *n* the stage in the development of an insect between any two moults [C19 NL from L: image]
instate (ɪnˈsteɪt) *vb* **instates, instating, instated** (*tr*) to place in a position or office; install > **inˈstatement** *n*
instead (ɪnˈstɛd) *adv* **1** as a replacement, substitute, or alternative **2 instead of** (*prep*) in place of or as an alternative to [C13 from *in stead* in place]
instep (ˈɪnˌstɛp) *n* **1** the middle section of the human foot, forming the arch between the ankle and toes **2** the part of a shoe, stocking, etc, covering this [C16 prob. from IN-[2] + STEP]
instigate (ˈɪnstɪˌgeɪt) *vb* **instigates, instigating, instigated** (*tr*) **1** to bring about, as by incitement: *to instigate rebellion* **2** to urge on to some drastic or unadvisable action [C16 from L *instīgāre* to incite] > ˌ**instiˈgation** *n* > ˈ**instiˌgative** *adj* > ˈ**instiˌgator** *n*
instil *or US* **instill** (ɪnˈstɪl) *vb* **instils** *or US* **instills, instilling, instilled** (*tr*) **1** to introduce gradually; implant or infuse **2** *rare* to pour in or inject in drops [C16 from L *instillāre* to pour in a drop at a time, from *stillāre* to drip] > **inˈstiller** *n* > **inˈstilment,** *US* **inˈstillment,** *or* ˌ**instilˈlation** *n*
instinct *n* (ˈɪnstɪŋkt) **1** the innate capacity of an animal to respond to a given stimulus in a relatively fixed way **2** inborn intuitive power ▷ *adj* (ɪnˈstɪŋkt) **3** (*postpositive; often foll by with*) *rare* **3a** animated or impelled (by) **3b** imbued or infused (with) [C15 from L *instinctus* roused, from *instinguere* to incite]
instinctive (ɪnˈstɪŋktɪv) *adj* **1** of, relating to, or resulting from instinct **2** conditioned so as to appear innate: *an instinctive movement in driving* > **inˈstinctively** *adv*
instinctual (ɪnˈstɪŋktjʊəl) *adj* of or pertaining to instinct > **inˈstinctually** *adv*
institute (ˈɪnstɪˌtjuːt) *vb* **institutes, instituting, instituted** (*tr*) **1** to organize; establish **2** to initiate: *to institute a practice* **3** to establish in a position or office; induct ▷ *n* **4** an organization founded for particular work, such as education, promotion of the arts, or scientific research **5** the building where such an organization is situated **6** something instituted, esp a rule, custom, or precedent [C16 from L *instituere*, from *statuere* to place] > ˈ**instiˌtutor** *or* ˈ**instiˌtuter** *n*
institutes (ˈɪnstɪˌtjuːts) *pl n* a digest or summary, esp of laws
institution (ˌɪnstɪˈtjuːʃən) *n* **1** the act of instituting **2** an organization or establishment founded for a specific purpose, such as a hospital or college **3** the building where such an organization is situated **4** an established custom, law, or relationship in a society or community **5** Also called: **institutional investor** a large organization, such as an insurance company or pension fund, that has substantial sums to invest on a stock exchange **6** *inf* a constant feature or practice: *Jones's drink at the bar was an institution* **7** the appointment of an incumbent to an ecclesiastical office or pastoral charge > ˌ**instiˈtutionary** *adj*
institutional (ˌɪnstɪˈtjuːʃənᵊl) *adj* **1** of, relating to, or characteristic of institutions **2** dull, routine, and uniform: *institutional meals* **3** relating to principles or institutes, esp of law > ˌ**instiˈtutionally** *adv* > ˌ**instiˈtutionaˌlism** *n*
institutionalize *or* **institutionalise** (ˌɪnstɪˈtjuːʃənəˌlaɪz) *vb* **institutionalizes, institutionalizing, institutionalized** *or* **institutionalises, institutionalising, institutionalised** **1** (*tr; often passive*) to subject to the deleterious effects of confinement in an institution **2** (*tr*) to place in an institution **3** to make or become an institution > ˌ**instiˌtutionaliˈzation** *or* ˌ**instiˌtutionaliˈsation** *n*
in-store *adj* available within a supermarket or other large shop: *in-store banking facilities*
instruct (ɪnˈstrʌkt) *vb* (*tr*) **1** to direct to do something; order **2** to teach (someone) how to do (something) **3** to furnish with information; apprise **4** *law, chiefly Brit* (esp of a client to his or her solicitor or a solicitor to a barrister) to give relevant facts or information to [C15 from L *instruere* to construct, equip, teach, from *struere* to build] > **inˈstructible** *adj*
instruction (ɪnˈstrʌkʃən) *n* **1** a direction; order **2** the process or act of imparting knowledge; teaching; education **3** *computing* a part of a program consisting of a coded command to the computer to perform a specified function > **inˈstructional** *adj*
instructions (ɪnˈstrʌkʃənz) *pl n* **1** directions, orders, or recommended rules for guidance, use, etc **2** *law* the facts and details relating to a case given by a client to his solicitor or by a solicitor to a barrister
instructive (ɪnˈstrʌktɪv) *adj* serving to instruct or enlighten; conveying information > **inˈstructively** *adv* > **inˈstructiveness** *n*
instructor (ɪnˈstrʌktə) *n* **1** someone who instructs; teacher **2** *US & Canad* a university teacher ranking below assistant professor > **inˈstructorship** *n* > **instructress** (ɪnˈstrʌktrɪs) *fem n*
instrument *n* (ˈɪnstrəmənt) **1** a mechanical implement or tool, esp one used for precision work **2** *music* any of various contrivances or mechanisms that can be played to produce musical tones or sounds **3** an important factor or agency in something: *her evidence was an instrument in his arrest* **4** *inf* a person used by another to gain an end; dupe **5** a measuring device, such as a pressure gauge **6a** a device or system for use in navigation or control, esp of aircraft **6b** (*as modifier*): *instrument landing* **7** a formal legal document ▷ *vb* (ˈɪnstrəˌmɛnt) (*tr*) **8** another word for **orchestrate** (sense 1) **9** to equip with instruments [C13 from L *instrūmentum* tool, from *instruere* to erect, furnish; see INSTRUCT]
instrumental (ˌɪnstrəˈmɛntᵊl) *adj* **1** serving as a means or influence; helpful **2** of, relating to, or characterized by an instrument **3** played by or composed for musical instruments **4** *grammar* denoting a case of nouns, etc indicating the instrument used in performing an action, usually using the prepositions *with* or *by means of* ▷ *n* **5** a piece of music composed for instruments rather than for voices **6** *grammar* the instrumental case > ˌ**instrumenˈtality** *n* > ˌ**instruˈmentally** *adv*
instrumentalist (ˌɪnstrəˈmɛntəlɪst) *n* a person who plays a musical instrument
instrumentation (ˌɪnstrəmɛnˈteɪʃən) *n* **1** the instruments specified in a musical score or arrangement **2** another word for **orchestration** **3** the study of the characteristics of musical instruments **4** the use of instruments or tools
instrument panel *or* **board** *n* **1** a panel on which instruments are mounted, as on a car. See also **dashboard** **2** an array of instruments, gauges, etc, mounted to display the condition or performance of a machine
insubordinate (ˌɪnsəˈbɔːdɪnɪt) *adj* **1** not submissive to authority; disobedient or rebellious **2** not in a subordinate position or rank ▷ *n* **3** an insubordinate person > ˌ**insubˈordinately** *adv* > ˌ**insubˌordiˈnation** *n*
insubstantial (ˌɪnsəbˈstænʃəl) *adj* **1** not substantial; flimsy, tenuous, or slight **2** imaginary; unreal > ˌ**insubˌstantiˈality** *n* > ˌ**insubˈstantially** *adv*
insufferable (ɪnˈsʌfərəbᵊl) *adj* intolerable; unendurable > **inˈsufferableness** *n* > **inˈsufferably** *adv*
insufficiency (ˌɪnsəˈfɪʃənsɪ) *n* **1** Also: ˌ**insufˈficience** the state of being insufficient **2** *pathol* failure in the functioning of an organ, tissue, etc: *cardiac insufficiency*
insufficient (ˌɪnsəˈfɪʃənt) *adj* not sufficient; inadequate or deficient > ˌ**insufˈficiently** *adv*

insufflate ('ɪnsʌˌfleɪt) *vb* **insufflates, insufflating, insufflated** **1** (*tr*) to breathe or blow (something) into (a room, area, etc) **2** *med* to blow (air, medicated powder, etc) into a body cavity **3** (*tr*) to breathe or blow upon (someone or something) as a ritual or sacramental act > ˌ**insufˈflation** *n* > ˈ**insufˌflator** *n*

insular ('ɪnsjʊlə) *adj* **1** of, relating to, or resembling an island **2** remote, detached, or aloof **3** illiberal or narrow-minded **4** isolated or separated [C17 from LL, from L *insula* island] > ˈ**insularism** *or* **insularity** (ˌɪnsjʊ'lærɪtɪ) *n* > ˈ**insularly** *adv*

insulate ('ɪnsjʊˌleɪt) *vb* **insulates, insulating, insulated** (*tr*) **1** to prevent the transmission of electricity, heat, or sound to or from (a body or device) by surrounding with a nonconducting material **2** to isolate or detach [C16 from LL *insulātus* made into an island]

insulation (ˌɪnsjʊ'leɪʃən) *n* **1** Also: **insulant** material used to insulate a body or device **2** the act or process of insulating

insulator ('ɪnsjʊˌleɪtə) *n* any material or device that insulates, esp a material with a very low electrical conductivity or thermal conductivity

insulin ('ɪnsjʊlɪn) *n* a protein hormone, secreted in the pancreas by the islets of Langerhans, that controls the concentration of glucose in the blood [C20 from NL *insula* islet (of the pancreas) + -IN]

insult *vb* (ɪn'sʌlt) (*tr*) **1** to treat, mention, or speak to rudely; offend; affront ▷ *n* ('ɪnsʌlt) **2** an offensive or contemptuous remark or action; affront; slight **3** a person or thing producing the effect of an affront: *some television is an insult to intelligence* **4** *med* an injury or trauma [C16 from L *insultāre* to jump upon] > **inˈsulter** *n*

insuperable (ɪn'suːpərəbᵊl, -prəbᵊl, -'sjuː-) *adj* incapable of being overcome; insurmountable > **inˌsuperaˈbility** *n* > **inˈsuperably** *adv*

insupportable (ˌɪnsə'pɔːtəbᵊl) *adj* **1** incapable of being endured; intolerable; insufferable **2** incapable of being supported or justified; indefensible > ˌ**insupˈportableness** *n* > ˌ**insupˈportably** *adv*

insurance (ɪn'ʃʊərəns, -'ʃɔː-) *n* **1a** the act, system, or business of providing financial protection against specified contingencies, such as death, loss, or damage **1b** the state of having such protection **1c** Also called: **insurance policy** the policy providing such protection **1d** the pecuniary amount of such protection **1e** the premium payable in return for such protection **1f** (*as modifier*): *insurance agent; insurance broker; insurance company* **2** a means of protecting or safeguarding against risk or injury

insure (ɪn'ʃʊə, -'ʃɔː) *vb* **insures, insuring, insured** **1** (often foll by *against*) to guarantee or protect (against risk, loss, etc) **2** (often foll by *against*) to issue (a person) with an insurance policy or take out an insurance policy (on): *his house was heavily insured against fire* **3** a variant spelling (esp US) of **ensure** ▷ Also (rare) (for senses 1, 2): **ensure** > **inˈsurable** *adj* > **inˌsuraˈbility** *n*

insured (ɪn'ʃʊəd, -'ʃɔːd) *adj* **1** covered by insurance: *an insured risk* ▷ *n* **2** the person, persons, or organization covered by an insurance policy

insurer (ɪn'ʃʊərə, -'ʃɔː-) *n* **1** a person or company offering insurance policies in return for premiums **2** a person or thing that insures

insurgence (ɪn'sɜːdʒəns) *n* rebellion, uprising, or riot

insurgent (ɪn'sɜːdʒənt) *adj* **1** rebellious or in revolt, as against a government in power or the civil authorities ▷ *n* **2** a person who takes part in an uprising or rebellion; insurrectionist [C18 from L *insurgēns* rising upon or against, from *surgere* to rise] > **inˈsurgency** *n*

insurmountable (ˌɪnsə'maʊntəbᵊl) *adj* incapable of being overcome; insuperable > ˌ**insurˌmountaˈbility** *or* ˌ**insurˈmountableness** *n* > ˌ**insurˈmountably** *adv*

insurrection (ˌɪnsə'rɛkʃən) *n* the act or an instance of rebelling against a government in power or the civil authorities; insurgency [C15 from LL *insurrectiō*, from *insurgere* to rise up] > ˌ**insurˈrectional** *adj* > ˌ**insurˈrectionary** *n, adj* > ˌ**insurˈrectionist** *n, adj*

intact (ɪn'tækt) *adj* untouched or unimpaired; left complete or perfect [C15 from L *intactus* not touched, from *tangere* to touch] > **inˈtactness** *n*

intaglio (ɪn'tɑːlɪˌəʊ) *n, pl* **intaglios** *or* **intagli** (-ljiː) **1** a seal, gem, etc, ornamented with a sunken or incised design **2** the art or process of incised carving **3** a design, figure, or ornamentation carved, engraved, or etched into the surface of the material used **4** any of various printing techniques using an etched or engraved plate **5** an incised die used to make a design in relief [C17 from It., from *intagliare* to engrave, from *tagliare* to cut, from LL *tāliāre*; see TAILOR] > **intagliated** (ɪn'tɑːlɪˌeɪtɪd) *adj*

intake ('ɪnˌteɪk) *n* **1** a thing or a quantity taken in: *an intake of students* **2** the act of taking in **3** the opening through which fluid enters a duct or channel, esp the air inlet of a jet engine **4** a ventilation shaft in a mine **5** a contraction or narrowing: *an intake in a garment*

intangible (ɪn'tændʒɪbᵊl) *adj* **1** incapable of being perceived by touch; impalpable **2** imprecise or unclear to the mind: *intangible ideas* **3** (of property or a business asset) saleable though not possessing intrinsic productive value ▷ *n* **4** something that is intangible > **inˌtangiˈbility** *n* > **inˈtangibly** *adv*

intarsia (ɪn'tɑːsɪə) *or* **tarsia** *n* **1** a decorative mosaic of inlaid wood of a style developed in the Italian Renaissance **2** (in knitting) **2a** an individually worked motif **2b** the method of knitting blocks of colour in place to create such a pattern [C19 changed from It. *intarsio*]

integer ('ɪntɪdʒə) *n* **1** any rational number that can be expressed as the sum or difference of a finite number of units, as 1, 2, 3, etc **2** an individual entity or whole unit [C16 from L: untouched, from *tangere* to touch]

integral ('ɪntɪgrəl, ɪn'tɛgrəl) *adj* **1** (often foll by *to*) being an essential part (of); intrinsic (to) **2** intact; entire **3** formed of constituent parts; united **4** *maths* **4a** of or involving an integral **4b** involving or being an integer ▷ *n* **5** *maths* the sum of a large number of infinitesimally small quantities, summed either between stated limits (**definite integral**) or in the absence of limits (**indefinite integral**) **6** a complete thing; whole > **integrality** (ˌɪntɪ'grælɪtɪ) *n* > ˈ**integrally** *adv*

integral calculus *n* the branch of calculus concerned with the determination of integrals (**integration**) and their application to the solution of differential equations

integrand ('ɪntɪˌgrænd) *n* a mathematical function to be integrated [C19 from L: to be integrated]

integrant ('ɪntəgrənt) *adj* **1** part of a whole; integral; constituent ▷ *n* **2** an integrant part

integrate *vb* ('ɪntɪˌgreɪt), **integrates, integrating, integrated** **1** to make or be made into a whole; incorporate or be incorporated **2** (*tr*) to designate (a school, park, etc) for use by all races or groups; desegregate **3** to amalgamate or mix (a racial or religious group) with an existing community **4** *maths* to determine the integral of a function or variable ▷ *adj* ('ɪntɪgrɪt) **5** made up of parts; integrated [C17 from L *integrāre*; see INTEGER] > **integrable** ('ɪntəgrəbᵊl) *adj* > ˌ**integraˈbility** *n* > ˌ**inteˈgration** *n* > ˈ**inteˌgrative** *adj*

integrated circuit *n* a very small electronic circuit consisting of an assembly of elements made from a chip of semiconducting material

integrity (ɪn'tɛgrɪtɪ) *n* **1** adherence to moral principles; honesty **2** the quality of being unimpaired; soundness **3** unity; wholeness [C15 from L *integritās*; see INTEGER]

integument (ɪn'tɛgjʊmənt) *n* any outer protective layer or covering, such as skin, a cuticle, seed coat, rind, or shell [C17 from L *integumentum*, from *tegere* to cover] > **inˌteguˈmental** *or* **inˌteguˈmentary** *adj*

intellect (ˈɪntɪˌlɛkt) *n* **1** the capacity for understanding, thinking, and reasoning **2** a mind or intelligence, esp a brilliant one: *his intellect is wasted on that job* **3** *inf* a person possessing a brilliant mind; brain [C14 from L *intellectus* comprehension, from *intellegere* to understand; see INTELLIGENCE] > ˌ**intelˈlective** *adj* > ˌ**intelˈlectively** *adv*

intellection (ˌɪntɪˈlɛkʃən) *n* **1** mental activity; thought **2** an idea or thought

intellectual (ˌɪntɪˈlɛktʃʊəl) *adj* **1** of or relating to the intellect **2** appealing to or characteristic of people with a developed intellect: *intellectual literature* **3** expressing or enjoying mental activity ▷ *n* **4** a person who enjoys mental activity and has highly developed tastes in art, etc **5** a person who uses his or her intellect **6** a highly intelligent person > ˌ**intelˌlectuˈality** *or* ˌ**intelˈlectualness** *n* > ˌ**intelˈlectualˌize** *or* ˌ**intelˈlectualˌise** *vb* > ˌ**intelˈlectually** *adv*

intellectualism (ˌɪntɪˈlɛktʃʊəˌlɪzəm) *n* **1** development and exercise of the intellect **2** *philosophy* the doctrine that reason is the ultimate criterion of knowledge > ˌ**intelˈlectualist** *n, adj* > ˌ**intelˌlectualˈistic** *adj*

intellectually handicapped *adj Austral* mentally handicapped

intellectual property *n* an intangible asset, such as a copyright or patent

▷ www.wipo.int/treaties/convention/index.html

intelligence (ɪnˈtɛlɪdʒəns) *n* **1** the capacity for understanding; ability to perceive and comprehend meaning **2** *old-fashioned* news; information **3** military information about enemies, spies, etc **4** a group or department that gathers or deals with such information **5** (*often cap*) an intelligent being, esp one that is not embodied **6** (*modifier*) of or relating to intelligence: *an intelligence network* [C14 from L *intellegentia*, from *intellegere* to discern, lit.: to choose between, from INTER- + *legere* to choose] > **inˌtelliˈgential** *adj*

intelligence quotient *n* a measure of the intelligence of an individual. The quotient is derived by dividing an individual's mental age by his chronological age and multiplying the result by 100. Abbrev: **IQ**

intelligence test *n* any of a number of tests designed to measure a person's mental skills

intelligent (ɪnˈtɛlɪdʒənt) *adj* **1** having or indicating intelligence; clever **2** indicating high intelligence; perceptive: *an intelligent guess* **3** (of computerized functions, weapons, etc) able to initiate or modify action in the light of ongoing events **4** (*postpositive; foll by of*) *arch* having knowledge or information > **inˈtelligently** *adv*

intelligent card *n* another name for **smart card**

intelligentsia (ɪnˌtɛlɪˈdʒɛntsɪə) *n* (usually preceded by *the*) the educated or intellectual people in a society or community [C20 from Russian *intelligentsiya*, from L *intellegentia* INTELLIGENCE]

intelligible (ɪnˈtɛlɪdʒəbᵊl) *adj* **1** able to be understood; comprehensible **2** *philosophy* capable of being apprehended by the mind or intellect alone [C14 from L *intellegibilis*; see INTELLECT] > **inˌtelligiˈbility** *n* > **inˈtelligibly** *adv*

intemperate (ɪnˈtɛmpərɪt, -prɪt) *adj* **1** consuming alcoholic drink habitually or to excess; immoderate **2** unrestrained: *intemperate rage* **3** extreme or severe: *an intemperate climate* > **inˈtemperance** *or* **inˈtemperateness** *n* > **inˈtemperately** *adv*

intend (ɪnˈtɛnd) *vb* **1** (*may take a clause as object*) to propose or plan (something or to do something); have in mind; mean **2** (*tr; often foll by for*) to design or destine (for a certain purpose, person, etc) **3** (*tr*) to mean to express or indicate: *what do his words intend?* **4** (*intr*) to have a purpose as specified; mean: *he intends well* [C14 from L *intendere* to stretch forth, give one's attention to, from *tendere* to stretch] > **inˈtender** *n*

intendancy (ɪnˈtɛndənsɪ) *n* **1** the position or work of an intendant **2** intendants collectively

intendant (ɪnˈtɛndənt) *n* a senior administrator; superintendent or manager

intended (ɪnˈtɛndɪd) *adj* **1** planned or future ▷ *n* **2** *inf* a person whom one is to marry; fiancé or fiancée

intense (ɪnˈtɛns) *adj* **1** of extreme force, strength, degree, or amount: *intense heat* **2** characterized by deep or forceful feelings: *an intense person* [C14 from L *intensus* stretched, from *intendere* to stretch out] > **inˈtensely** *adv* > **inˈtenseness** *n*

> USAGE *Intense* is sometimes wrongly used where *intensive* is meant: *the land is under intensive* (not *intense*) *cultivation*. *Intensely* is sometimes wrongly used where *intently* is meant: *he listened intently* (not *intensely*)

intensifier (ɪnˈtɛnsɪˌfaɪə) *n* **1** a person or thing that intensifies **2** a word, esp an adjective or adverb, that serves to intensify the meaning of the word or phrase that it modifies **3** a substance, esp one containing silver or uranium, used to increase the density of a photographic film or plate

intensify (ɪnˈtɛnsɪˌfaɪ) *vb* **intensifies, intensifying, intensified** **1** to make or become intense or more intense **2** (*tr*) to increase the density of (a photographic film or plate) > **inˌtensifiˈcation** *n*

intension (ɪnˈtɛnʃən) *n logic* the set of characteristics or properties that distinguish the referent or referents of a given word > **inˈtensional** *adj*

intensity (ɪnˈtɛnsɪtɪ) *n, pl* **intensities** **1** the state or quality of being intense **2** extreme force, degree, or amount **3** *physics* **3a** a measure of field strength or of the energy transmitted by radiation **3b** (of sound in a specified direction) the average rate of flow of sound energy for one period through unit area at right angles to the specified direction

intensive (ɪnˈtɛnsɪv) *adj* **1** of, relating to, or characterized by intensity: *intensive training* **2** (*usually in combination*) using one factor of production proportionately more than others, as specified: *capital-intensive; labour-intensive* **3** *agriculture* involving or farmed using large amounts of capital or labour to increase production from a particular area ▷ Cf **extensive** (sense 3) **4** denoting or relating to a grammatical intensifier **5** denoting or belonging to a class of pronouns used to emphasize a noun or personal pronoun **6** of or relating to intension ▷ *n* **7** an intensifier or intensive pronoun or grammatical construction > **inˈtensively** *adv* > **inˈtensiveness** *n*

> USAGE See at **intense**

intensive care *n* **1** extensive and continuous care provided for an acutely ill patient in a hospital **2** the unit in which this care is provided; intensive-care unit

intent (ɪnˈtɛnt) *n* **1** something that is intended; aim; purpose; design **2** the act of intending **3** *law* the will or purpose with which one does an act **4** implicit meaning; connotation **5** **to all intents and purposes** for all practical purposes; virtually ▷ *adj* **6** firmly fixed; determined; concentrated: *an intent look* **7** (*postpositive; usually foll by on or upon*) having the fixed intention (of); directing one's mind or energy (to): *intent on committing a crime* [C13 (in the sense: intention): from LL *intentus* aim, from L: a stretching out; see INTEND] > **inˈtently** *adv* > **inˈtentness** *n*

> USAGE See at **intense**

intention (ɪnˈtɛnʃən) *n* **1** a purpose or goal; aim: *it is his intention to reform* **2** *med* a natural healing process in which the edges of a wound cling together with no tissue between (**first intention**), or in which the edges adhere with tissue between (**second intention**) **3** (*usually pl*) design or purpose with respect to a proposal of marriage (esp in **honourable intentions**)

intentional (ɪnˈtɛnʃənᵊl) *adj* **1** performed by or expressing intention; deliberate **2** of or relating to

Ii

intention or purpose > **in,tention'ality** *n* > **in'tentionally** *adv*

inter (ɪn'tɜː) *vb* **inters, interring, interred** (*tr*) to place (a body, etc) in the earth; bury, esp with funeral rites [C14 from OF *enterrer*, from L IN-[2] + *terra* earth]

inter- *prefix* **1** between or among: *international* **2** together, mutually, or reciprocally: *interdependent; interchange* [from L]

interact (,ɪntər'ækt) *vb* (*intr*) to act on or in close relation with each other

Interact ('ɪntər,ækt) *n Canad* a system of electronic bank payments or withdrawals

interaction (,ɪntə'ækʃən) *n* **1** a mutual or reciprocal action **2** *physics* the transfer of energy between elementary particles, between a particle and a field, or between fields. See **fundamental interaction**

interactive (,ɪntər'æktɪv) *adj* **1** allowing or relating to continuous two-way transfer of information between a user and the central point of a communication system, such as a computer or television **2** (of two or more persons, forces, etc) acting upon or in close relation with each other; interacting

inter alia *Latin* ('ɪntər 'eɪlɪə) *adv* among other things

interbreed (,ɪntə'briːd) *vb* **interbreeds, interbreeding, interbred 1** to breed within a single family or strain so as to produce particular characteristics in the offspring **2** another term for **crossbreed** (sense 1)

interbroker dealer (,ɪntə'brəʊkə) *n stock exchange* a specialist who matches the needs of different market makers and facilitates dealings between them

intercalary (ɪn'tɜːkələrɪ) *adj* **1** (of a day, month, year, etc) inserted in the calendar **2** (of a particular year) having one or more days inserted **3** inserted, introduced, or interpolated [C17 from L *intercalārius*; see INTERCALATE]

intercalate (ɪn'tɜːkə,leɪt) *vb* **intercalates, intercalating, intercalated** (*tr*) **1** to insert (one or more days) into the calendar **2** to interpolate or insert [C17 from L *intercalāre* to insert, proclaim that a day has been inserted, from INTER- + *calāre* to proclaim] > **in,terca'lation** *n* > **in'tercalative** *adj*

intercede (,ɪntə'siːd) *vb* **intercedes, interceding, interceded** (*intr*; often foll by *in*) to come between parties or act as mediator or advocate: *to intercede in the strike* [C16 from L *intercēdere*, from INTER- + *cēdere* to move] > **,inter'ceder** *n*

intercensal (,ɪntə'sɛnsəl) *adj* (of population figures, etc) estimated at a time between official censuses [C19 from INTER- + *censal*, irregularly formed from CENSUS]

intercept *vb* (,ɪntə'sɛpt) (*tr*) **1** to stop, deflect, or seize on the way from one place to another; prevent from arriving or proceeding **2** *sport* to seize or cut off (a pass) on its way from one opponent to another **3** *maths* to cut off, mark off, or bound (some part of a line, curve, plane, or surface) ▷ *n* ('ɪntə,sɛpt) **4** *maths* **4a** a point at which two figures intersect **4b** the distance from the origin to the point at which a line, curve, or surface cuts a coordinate axis **5** *sport, US & Canad* the act of intercepting an opponent's pass [C16 from L *intercipere* to seize before arrival, from INTER- + *capere* to take] > **,inter'ception** *n* > **,inter'ceptive** *adj*

interceptor *or* **intercepter** (,ɪntə'sɛptə) *n* **1** a person or thing that intercepts **2** a fast highly manoeuvrable fighter aircraft used to intercept enemy aircraft

intercession (,ɪntə'sɛʃən) *n* **1** the act or an instance of interceding **2** the act of interceding or offering petitionary prayer to God on behalf of others **3** such petitionary prayer [C16 from L *intercessio*; see INTERCEDE] > **,inter'cessional** *or* **,inter'cessory** *adj* > **,inter'cessor** *n* > **,interces'sorial** *adj*

interchange *vb* (,ɪntə'tʃeɪndʒ), **interchanges, interchanging, interchanged 1** to change places or cause to change places; alternate; exchange; switch ▷ *n* ('ɪntə,tʃeɪndʒ) **2** the act of interchanging; exchange or alternation **3** a motorway junction of interconnecting roads and bridges designed to prevent streams of traffic crossing one another > **,inter'changeable** *adj* > **,inter,changea'bility** *or* **,inter'changeableness** *n* > **,inter'changeably** *adv*

Intercity (,ɪntə'sɪtɪ) *adj* (in Britain) *trademark* denoting a fast train or passenger rail service, esp between main towns

intercom ('ɪntə,kɒm) *n inf* an internal telephone system for communicating within a building, aircraft, etc [C20 short for INTERCOMMUNICATION]

intercommunicate (,ɪntəkə'mjuːnɪ,keɪt) *vb* **intercommunicates, intercommunicating, intercommunicated** (*intr*) **1** to communicate mutually **2** to interconnect, as two rooms, etc > **,intercom'municable** *adj* > **,intercom,muni'cation** *n* > **,intercom'municative** *adj*

intercommunion (,ɪntəkə'mjuːnjən) *n* association between Churches, involving esp mutual reception of Holy Communion

intercontinental (,ɪntə,kɒntɪ'nɛntᵊl) *adj* travelling between or linking continents

interconvertible (,ɪntəkən'vɜːtɪbᵊl) *adj* (of two or more things) capable of being converted into each other

intercostal (,ɪntə'kɒstᵊl) *adj anat* between the ribs: *intercostal muscles* [C16 via NL from L INTER- + *costa* rib]

intercourse ('ɪntə,kɔːs) *n* **1** See **sexual intercourse** **2** communication or exchange between individuals; mutual dealings [C15 from Med. L *intercursus* business, from L *intercurrere* to run between]

intercurrent (,ɪntə'kʌrənt) *adj* **1** occurring during or in between; intervening **2** *pathol* (of a disease) occurring during the course of another disease > **,inter'currence** *n*

interdependent (,ɪntədɪ'pɛndənt) *adj* (of two or more things) dependent on each other

interdict *n* ('ɪntə,dɪkt) **1** *RC Church* the exclusion of a person in a particular place from certain sacraments, although not from communion **2** *civil law* any order made by a court or official prohibiting an act **3** *Scots law* an order having the effect of an injunction ▷ *vb* (,ɪntə'dɪkt) (*tr*) **4** to place under legal or ecclesiastical sanction; prohibit; forbid **5** *mil* to destroy (an enemy's lines of communication) by firepower [C13 from L *interdictum* prohibition, from *interdīcere* to forbid, from INTER- + *dīcere* to say] > **,inter'diction** *n* > **,inter'dictive** *or* **,inter'dictory** *adj* > **,inter'dictively** *adv* > **,inter'dictor** *n*

interdigitate (,ɪntə'dɪdʒɪ,teɪt) *vb* **interdigitates, interdigitating, interdigitated** (*intr*) to interlock like the fingers of clasped hands [C19 from INTER- + L *digitus* (see DIGIT) + -ATE[1]]

interdisciplinary (,ɪntə'dɪsɪ,plɪnərɪ) *adj* involving two or more academic disciplines

interest ('ɪntrɪst, -tərɪst) *n* **1** the sense of curiosity about or concern with something or someone **2** the power of stimulating such a sense: *to have great interest* **3** the quality of such stimulation **4** something in which one is interested; a hobby or pursuit **5** (*often pl*) benefit; advantage: *in one's own interest* **6** (*often pl*) a right, share, or claim, esp in a business or property **7a** a charge for the use of credit or borrowed money **7b** such a charge expressed as a percentage per time unit of the sum borrowed or used **8** (*often pl*) a section of a community, etc, whose members have common aims: *the landed interest* **9** **declare an interest** to make known one's connection, esp a prejudicial connection, with an affair ▷ *vb* (*tr*) **10** to arouse or excite the curiosity or concern of **11** to cause to become involved in something; concern [C15 from L: it concerns, from *interesse*, from INTER- + *esse* to be]

interested ('ɪntrɪstɪd, -tərɪs-) *adj* **1** showing or having interest **2** (*usually prenominal*) personally involved or implicated: *the interested parties met to discuss the business* > **'interestedly** *adv* > **'interestedness** *n*

interesting ('ɪntrɪstɪŋ, -tərɪs-) *adj* inspiring interest; absorbing > **'interestingly** *adv* > **'interestingness** *n*

interest-rate futures *pl n* financial futures based on projected movements of interest rates

interface *n* ('ɪntəˌfeɪs) **1** *physical chem* a surface that forms the boundary between two liquids or chemical phases **2** a common point or boundary between two things **3** an electrical circuit linking one device, esp a computer, with another ▷ *vb* (ˌɪntə'feɪs), **interfaces, interfacing, interfaced** **4** (*tr*) to design or adapt the input and output configurations of (two electronic devices) so that they may work together compatibly **5** to be an interface (with) **6** to be interactive (with) > **interfacial** (ˌɪntə'feɪʃəl) *adj* > **ˌinter'facially** *adv*

interfacing ('ɪntəˌfeɪsɪŋ) *n* **1** a piece of fabric sewn beneath the facing of a garment, usually at the inside of the neck, armholes, etc, to give shape and firmness **2** another name for **interlining**

interfere (ˌɪntə'fɪə) *vb* **interferes, interfering, interfered** (*intr*) **1** (often foll by *in*) to interpose, esp meddlesomely or unwarrantedly; intervene **2** (often foll by *with*) to come between or into opposition; hinder **3** (foll by *with*) *euphemistic* to assault sexually **4** to strike one against the other, as a horse's legs **5** *physics* to cause or produce interference [c16 from OF *s'entreferir* to collide, from *entre-* INTER- + *ferir* to strike, from L *ferīre*] > **ˌinter'fering** *adj*

interference (ˌɪntə'fɪərəns) *n* **1** the act or an instance of interfering **2** *physics* the process in which two or more coherent waves combine to form a resultant wave in which the displacement at any point is the vector sum of the displacements of the individual waves **3** any undesired signal that tends to interfere with the reception of radio waves > **interferential** (ˌɪntəfə'rɛnʃəl) *adj*

interferometer (ˌɪntəfə'rɒmɪtə) *n* *physics* any acoustic, optical, or microwave instrument that uses interference patterns to make accurate measurements of wavelength, distance, etc > **interferometric** (ˌɪntəˌfɛrə'mɛtrɪk) *adj* > **ˌinterˌfero'metrically** *adv* > **ˌinterfer'ometry** *n*

interferon (ˌɪntə'fɪərɒn) *n* *biochem* any of a family of proteins made by cells in response to virus infection that prevent the growth of the virus [c20 from INTERFERE + -ON]

interfuse (ˌɪntə'fjuːz) *vb* **interfuses, interfusing, interfused** **1** to diffuse or mix throughout or become so diffused or mixed; intermingle **2** to blend or fuse or become blended or fused > **ˌinter'fusion** *n*

intergovernmental (ˌɪntəˌɡʌvən'mɛntᵊl) *adj* conducted between or involving two or more governments

interim ('ɪntərɪm) *adj* **1** (*prenominal*) temporary, provisional, or intervening: *interim measures to deal with the emergency* ▷ *n* **2** (usually preceded by *the*) the intervening time; the meantime (esp in **in the interim**) ▷ *adv* **3** *rare* meantime [c16 from L: meanwhile]

interior (ɪn'tɪərɪə) *n* **1** a part, surface, or region that is inside or on the inside: *the interior of Africa* **2** inner character or nature **3** a film or scene shot inside a building, studio, etc **4** a picture of the inside of a room or building, as in a painting or stage design **5** the inside of a building or room, with respect to design and decoration ▷ *adj* **6** of, situated on, or suitable for the inside; inner **7** coming or acting from within; internal **8** of or involving a nation's domestic affairs; internal **9** (esp of one's spiritual or mental life) secret or private; not observable [c15 from L (adj), comp. of *inter* within] > **in'teriorly** *adv*

interior angle *n* an angle of a polygon contained between two adjacent sides

interior decoration *n* **1** the colours, furniture, etc, of the interior of a house, etc **2** Also called: **interior design** the art or business of planning the interiors of houses, etc > **interior decorator** *n*

interiorize *or* **interiorise** (ɪn'tɪərɪəˌraɪz) *vb* **interiorizes, interiorizing, interiorized** *or* **interiorises, interiorising, interiorised** (*tr*) another word for **internalize**

interj. *abbrev for* interjection

interject (ˌɪntə'dʒɛkt) *vb* (*tr*) to interpose abruptly or sharply; interrupt with; throw in: *she interjected clever remarks* [c16 from L *interjicere* to place between, from *jacere* to throw] > **ˌinter'jector** *n*

interjection (ˌɪntə'dʒɛkʃən) *n* **1** the act of interjecting **2** a word or phrase that is used in syntactic isolation and that expresses sudden emotion; expletive. Abbrev: **interj** > **ˌinter'jectional** *or* **ˌinter'jectory** *adj* > **ˌinter'jectionally** *adv*

Interlaken ('ɪntəˌlɑːkən) *n* a town and resort in central Switzerland, situated between Lakes Brienz and Thun on the River Aar. Pop: 4900 (latest est)

interlard (ˌɪntə'lɑːd) *vb* (*tr*) **1** to scatter thickly in or between; intersperse: *to interlard one's writing with foreign phrases* **2** to occur frequently in; be scattered in or through: *foreign phrases interlard his writings*

interlay (ˌɪntə'leɪ) *vb* **interlays, interlaying, interlaid** (*tr*) to insert (layers) between; interpose

interleaf ('ɪntəˌliːf) *n, pl* **interleaves** a blank leaf inserted between the leaves of a book

interleave (ˌɪntə'liːv) *vb* **interleaves, interleaving, interleaved** (*tr*) **1** (often foll by *with*) to intersperse (with), esp alternately, as the illustrations in a book (with protective leaves) **2** to provide (a book) with blank leaves for notes, etc, or to protect illustrations

interleukin (ˌɪntə'luːkɪn) *n* a substance extracted from white blood cells that stimulates their activity against infection and may be used to combat some forms of cancer

interline¹ (ˌɪntə'laɪn) *or* **interlineate** (ˌɪntə'lɪnɪˌeɪt) *vb* **interlines, interlining, interlined** *or* **interlineates, interlineating, interlineated** (*tr*) to write or print (matter) between the lines of (a text, book, etc) > **'interˌlining** *or* **ˌinterˌline'ation** *n*

Ii

interline² (ˌɪntə'laɪn) *vb* **interlines, interlining, interlined** (*tr*) to provide (a part of a garment) with a second lining, esp of stiffened material > **'interˌliner** *n*

interlinear (ˌɪntə'lɪnɪə) *or* **interlineal** *adj* **1** written or printed between lines of text **2** written or printed with the text in different languages or versions on alternate lines > **ˌinter'linearly** *or* **ˌinter'lineally** *adv*

interlining ('ɪntəˌlaɪnɪŋ) *n* the material used to interline parts of garments, now often made of reinforced paper

interlock *vb* (ˌɪntə'lɒk) **1** to join or be joined firmly, as by a mutual interconnection of parts ▷ *n* ('ɪntəˌlɒk) **2** the act of interlocking or the state of being interlocked **3** a device, esp one operated electromechanically, used in a logic circuit to prevent an activity being initiated unless preceded by certain events **4** a closely knitted fabric ▷ *adj* **5** closely knitted > **'interˌlocker** *n*

interlocutor (ˌɪntə'lɒkjʊtə) *n* **1** a person who takes part in a conversation **2** the man in the centre of a troupe of minstrels who engages the others in talk or acts as announcer **3** *Scots law* a decree by a judge > **ˌinter'locutress, ˌinter'locutrice,** *or* **ˌinter'locutrix** *fem n*

interlocutory (ˌɪntə'lɒkjʊtərɪ, -trɪ) *adj* **1** *law* pronounced during the course of proceedings; provisional: *an interlocutory injunction* **2** interposed, as into a conversation, narrative, etc **3** of, relating to, or characteristic of dialogue > **ˌinter'locutorily** *adv*

interloper ('ɪntəˌləʊpə) *n* **1** an intruder **2** a person who introduces himself or herself into professional or social circles where he or she does not belong **3** a person who interferes in matters that are not his or her concern [c17 from INTER- + *loper*, from MDu. *loopen* to leap] > **ˌinter'lope** *vb* (*intr*)

interlude ('ɪntəˌluːd) *n* **1** a period of time or different activity between longer periods, processes, or events; episode or interval **2** *theatre* a short dramatic piece played separately or as part of a longer entertainment, common in 16th-century England **3** a brief piece of music, dance, etc, given between the sections of another performance [C14 from Med. L, from L INTER- + *lūdus* play]

intermarry (ˌɪntəˈmærɪ) *vb* **intermarries, intermarrying, intermarried** (*intr*) **1** (of different races, religions, etc) to become connected by marriage **2** to marry within one's own family, clan, group, etc > ˌ**interˈmarriage** *n*

intermediary (ˌɪntəˈmiːdɪərɪ) *n, pl* **intermediaries** **1** a person who acts as a mediator or agent between parties **2** something that acts as a medium or means ▷ *adj* **3** acting as an intermediary **4** situated, acting, or coming between

intermediate *adj* (ˌɪntəˈmiːdɪɪt) **1** occurring or situated between two points, extremes, places, etc; in between **2** (of a class, course, etc) suitable for learners with some degree of skill or competence ▷ *n* (ˌɪntəˈmiːdɪɪt) **3** something intermediate **4** a substance formed during one of the stages of a chemical process before the desired product is obtained ▷ *vb* (ˌɪntəˈmiːdɪˌeɪt), **intermediates, intermediating, intermediated** **5** (*intr*) to act as an intermediary or mediator [C17 from Med. L *intermediāre* to intervene, from L INTER- + *medius* middle] > ˌ**interˈmediacy** *or* ˌ**interˈmediateness** *n* > ˌ**interˈmediately** *adv* > ˌ**interˌmediˈation** *n* > ˌ**interˈmediˌator** *n*

intermediate-acting *adj* (of a drug) intermediate in its effects between long- and short-acting drugs ▷ Cf **long-acting, short-acting**

intermediate frequency *n electronics* the frequency to which the signal carrier frequency is changed in a superheterodyne receiver and at which most of the amplification takes place

intermediate-level waste *n* radioactive waste material, such as reactor components, that can be mixed with concrete and safely stored in steel drums in deep mines or beneath the seabed in concrete chambers ▷ Cf **high-level waste, low-level waste**

intermediate technology *n* technology that implements sophisticated technical ideas using readily available cheap materials and resources, esp for use in developing countries

intermediate vector boson *n physics* a hypothetical particle believed to mediate the weak interaction between elementary particles

interment (ɪnˈtɜːmənt) *n* burial, esp with ceremonial rites

intermezzo (ˌɪntəˈmɛtsəʊ) *n, pl* **intermezzos** *or* **intermezzi** (-tsiː) **1** a short piece of instrumental music composed for performance between the acts or scenes of an opera, drama, etc **2** an instrumental piece either inserted between two longer movements in an extended composition or intended for independent performance [C19 from It., from LL *intermedium* interval; see INTERMEDIATE]

interminable (ɪnˈtɜːmɪnəbᵊl) *adj* endless or seemingly endless because of monotony or tiresome length > **inˈterminableness** *n* > **inˈterminably** *adv*

intermission (ˌɪntəˈmɪʃən) *n* **1** an interval, as between parts of a film, etc **2** a period between events or activities; pause **3** the act of intermitting or the state of being intermitted [C16 from L, from *intermittere* to INTERMIT] > ˌ**interˈmissive** *adj*

intermit (ˌɪntəˈmɪt) *vb* **intermits, intermitting, intermitted** to suspend (activity) or (of activity) to be suspended temporarily or at intervals [C16 from L *intermittere* to leave off, from INTER- + *mittere* to send] > ˌ**interˈmittor** *n*

intermittent (ˌɪntəˈmɪtᵊnt) *adj* occurring occasionally or at regular or irregular intervals; periodic > ˌ**interˈmittence** *or* ˌ**interˈmittency** *n* > ˌ**interˈmittently** *adv*

intermix (ˌɪntəˈmɪks) *vb* **1** (*tr*) to mix (ingredients, liquids, etc) together **2** (*intr*) to become or have the capacity to become combined, joined, etc

intermixture (ˌɪntəˈmɪkstʃə) *n* **1** the act of intermixing or state of being intermixed **2** an additional ingredient

intern *vb* **1** (ɪnˈtɜːn) (*tr*) to detain or confine within a country or a limited area, esp during wartime **2** (ˈɪntɜːn) (*intr*) *chiefly US* to serve or train as an intern ▷ *n* (ˈɪntɜːn) **3** another word for **internee** **4** Also: **interne** the approximate US and Canad equivalent of **house officer** **5** Also: **interne** *chiefly US* a student teacher **6** Also: **interne** *chiefly US* a student or recent graduate undergoing practical training in a working environment [C19 from L *internus* internal] > **inˈternment** *n* > ˈ**internship** *or* ˈ**interneship** *n*

internal (ɪnˈtɜːnᵊl) *adj* **1** of, situated on, or suitable for the inside; inner **2** coming or acting from within; interior **3** involving the spiritual or mental life; subjective **4** of or involving a nation's domestic as opposed to foreign affairs **5** situated within, affecting, or relating to the inside of the body ▷ *n* **6** *euphemistic* a medical examination of the vagina, uterus, or rectum [C16 from Med. L, from LL *internus* inward] > ˌ**interˈnality** *or* **inˈternalness** *n* > **inˈternally** *adv*

internal-combustion engine *n* a heat engine in which heat is supplied by burning the fuel in the working fluid (usually air)

internal energy *n* the thermodynamic property of a system that changes by an amount equal to the work done on the system when it suffers an adiabatic change

internalize *or* **internalise** (ɪnˈtɜːnəˌlaɪz) *vb* **internalizes, internalizing, internalized** *or* **internalises, internalising, internalised** (*tr*) *psychol, sociol* to make internal, esp to incorporate within oneself (values, attitudes, etc) through learning or socialization. Also: **interiorize** > **inˌternaliˈzation** *or* **inˌternaliˈsation** *n*

internal market *n* a system in which goods and services are sold by the provider to a range of purchasers within the same organization, who compete to establish the price of the product

internal medicine *n* the branch of medical science concerned with the diagnosis and nonsurgical treatment of disorders of the internal structures of the body

international (ˌɪntəˈnæʃənᵊl) *adj* **1** of, concerning, or involving two or more nations or nationalities **2** established by, controlling, or legislating for several nations: *an international court* **3** available for use by all nations: *international waters* ▷ *n* **4** *sport* **4a** a contest between two national teams **4b** a member of a national team > ˌ**interˌnationˈality** *n* > ˌ**interˈnationally** *adv*

International (ˌɪntəˈnæʃənᵊl) *n* **1** any of several international socialist organizations, esp **First International** (1864–76) and **Second International** (1889 until World War I) **2** a member of any of these organizations

International Atomic Time *n* the scientific standard of time based on the SI unit, the second, used to synchronize the time standards of the major nations. Abbrev: **TAI**

International Bank for Reconstruction and Development *n* the official name for the **World Bank**

International Court of Justice *n* a court established in the Hague, in the Netherlands, to settle disputes brought by nations that are parties to the Statute of the Court. Also called: **World Court**
▷ www.icj-cij.org

International Date Line *n* the line approximately following the 180° meridian from Greenwich on the east side of which the date is one day earlier than on the west

internationalism (ˌɪntəˈnæʃənəˌlɪzəm) *n* **1** the ideal or practice of cooperation and understanding between nations **2** the state or quality of being international > ˌ**interˈnationalist** *n*

internationalize *or* **internationalise** (ˌɪntəˈnæʃənəˌlaɪz) *vb* **internationalizes, internationalizing, internationalized** *or* **internationalises, internationalising, internationalised** (*tr*) **1** to make international **2** to put under international control > ˌ**interˌnationaliˈzation** *or* ˌ**interˌnationaliˈsation** *n*

international law *n* the body of rules generally recognized by civilized nations as governing their conduct towards each other

▹ www.icj-cij.org
▹ www.un.org/law/ilc/index.htm
▹ www.hcch.net/e/index.html
▹ http://europa.eu.int/eur-lex/en/index.html
▹ www.pca-cpa.org
▹ www.echr.coe.int
▹ www.oceanlaw.org/index.html

International Modernism *n* See **International Style**

International Phonetic Alphabet *n* a series of signs and letters for the representation of human speech sounds. It is based on the Roman alphabet but supplemented by modified signs or symbols from other writing systems

International Practical Temperature Scale *n* a temperature scale adopted by international agreement in 1968 based on thermodynamic temperature and using experimental values to define 11 fixed points

International Space Station Alpha *n* an orbiting space station constructed between 1998 and 2001 with the cooperation of 16 nations, used for scientific and space research

▹ www.scipoc.msfc.nasa.gov

International Style *or* **Modernism** *n* an architectural style of the 1920s that used cubic forms, large windows, and modern materials

International Telecommunications Union *n* a special agency of the United Nations, founded in 1947, that is responsible for the international allocation and registration of frequencies for communications and the regulation of telegraph, telephone, and radio services

interne (ˈɪntɜːn) *n* a variant spelling of **intern** (senses 4, 5, 6)

internecine (ˌɪntəˈniːsaɪn) *adj* **1** mutually destructive or ruinous; maiming both or all sides: *internecine war* **2** of or relating to slaughter or carnage; bloody **3** of or involving conflict within a group or organization [C17 from L, from *internecāre* to destroy, from *necāre* to kill]

internee (ˌɪntɜːˈniː) *n* a person who is interned, esp an enemy citizen in wartime or a terrorism suspect

Internet (ˈɪntəˌnɛt) *n* **the** (*also not cap*) the single worldwide computer network that interconnects other computer networks, on which end-user services, such as World Wide Web sites or data archives, are located, enabling data and other information to be exchanged. Also called: **the Net**

INTERNET DOMAIN NAMES

ac	Ascension Island
ad	Andorra
ae	United Arab Emirates
af	Afghanistan
ag	Antigua and Barbuda
ai	Anguilla
al	Albania
am	Armenia
an	Netherlands Antilles
ao	Angola
aq	Antarctica
ar	Argentina
as	American Samoa
at	Austria
au	Australia
aw	Aruba
az	Azerbaijan
ba	Bosnia and Herzegovina
bb	Barbados
bd	Bangladesh
be	Belgium
bf	Burkina Faso
bg	Bulgaria
bh	Bahrain
bi	Burundi
bj	Benin
bm	Bermuda
bn	Brunei Darussalam
bo	Bolivia
br	Brazil
bs	Bahamas
bt	Bhutan
bv	Bouvet Island
bw	Botswana
by	Belarus
bz	Belize
ca	Canada
cc	Cocos Islands
cd	Democratic Republic of Congo
cf	Central African Republic
cg	Republic of Congo
ch	Switzerland
ci	Côte d'Ivoire
ck	Cook Islands
cl	Chile
cm	Cameroon
cn	China
co	Colombia
cr	Costa Rica
cu	Cuba
cv	Cap Verde
cx	Christmas Island
cz	Czech Republic
de	Germany
dj	Djibouti
dk	Denmark
dm	Dominica
do	Dominican Republic
dz	Algeria
ec	Ecuador
ee	Estonia
eg	Egypt
eh	Western Sahara
er	Eritrea
es	Spain
et	Ethiopia
eu	the European Union
fi	Finland
fj	Fiji
fk	Falkland Islands
fm	Micronesia
fo	Faeroe Islands
fr	France
ga	Gabon
gd	Grenada
ge	Georgia
gf	French Guiana
gg	Guernsey
gh	Ghana
gi	Gibraltar
gl	Greenland

- **gm** The Gambia
- **gn** Guinea
- **gp** Guadeloupe
- **gq** Equatorial Guinea
- **gr** Greece
- **gs** South Georgia and the South Sandwich Islands
- **gt** Guatemala
- **gu** Guam
- **gw** Guinea-Bissau
- **gy** Guyana
- **hk** Hong Kong
- **hm** Heard and McDonald Islands
- **hn** Honduras
- **hr** Croatia
- **ht** Haiti
- **hu** Hungary
- **id** Indonesia
- **ie** Ireland
- **il** Israel
- **im** Isle of Man
- **in** India
- **io** British Indian Ocean Territory
- **iq** Iraq
- **ir** Iran
- **is** Iceland
- **it** Italy
- **je** Jersey
- **jm** Jamaica
- **jo** Jordan
- **jp** Japan
- **ke** Kenya
- **kg** Kyrgyzstan
- **kh** Cambodia
- **ki** Kiribati
- **km** Comoros
- **kn** St Kitts and Nevis
- **kp** Democratic Republic of Korea
- **kr** Republic of Korea
- **kw** Kuwait
- **ky** Cayman Islands
- **kz** Kazakhstan
- **la** Lao People's Democratic Republic
- **lb** Lebanon
- **lc** St Lucia
- **li** Liechtenstein
- **lk** Sri Lanka
- **lr** Liberia
- **ls** Lesotho
- **lt** Lithuania
- **lu** Luxembourg
- **lv** Latvia
- **ly** Libyan Arab Jamahiriya
- **ma** Morocco
- **mc** Monaco
- **md** Moldova
- **mg** Madagascar
- **mh** Marshall Islands
- **mk** Macedonia
- **ml** Mali
- **mm** Myanmar
- **mn** Mongolia
- **mo** Macau
- **mp** Northern Mariana Islands
- **mq** Martinique
- **ms** Montserrat
- **mt** Malta
- **mu** Mauritius
- **mv** Maldives
- **mw** Malawi
- **mx** Mexico
- **my** Malaysia
- **mz** Mozambique
- **na** Namibia
- **nc** New Caledonia
- **ne** Niger
- **nf** Norfolk Island
- **ng** Nigeria
- **ni** Nicaragua
- **nl** the Netherlands
- **no** Norway
- **np** Nepal
- **nr** Nauru
- **nu** Niue
- **nz** New Zealand
- **om** Oman
- **pa** Panama
- **pe** Peru
- **pf** French Polynesia
- **pg** Papua New Guinea
- **ph** Philippines
- **pk** Pakistan
- **pl** Poland
- **pm** St Pierre and Miquelon
- **pn** Pitcairn Island
- **pr** Puerto Rico
- **ps** Palestinian Territories
- **pt** Portugal
- **pw** Palau
- **py** Paraguay
- **qa** Qatar
- **re** Reunion Island
- **ro** Romania
- **ru** Russian Federation
- **rw** Rwanda
- **sa** Saudi Arabia
- **sb** Solomon Islands
- **sc** Seychelles
- **sd** Sudan
- **se** Sweden
- **sg** Singapore
- **sh** St Helena
- **si** Slovenia
- **sj** Svalbard and Jan Mayen Islands
- **sk** Slovak Republic
- **sl** Sierra Leone
- **sm** San Marino
- **sn** Senegal
- **so** Somalia
- **sr** Suriname
- **st** São Tomé and Principe
- **sv** El Salvador
- **sy** Syrian Arab Republic
- **sz** Swaziland
- **tc** Turks and Caicos Islands
- **td** Chad
- **tf** French Southern Territories
- **tg** Togo
- **th** Thailand
- **tj** Tajikistan
- **tk** Tokelau
- **tm** Turkmenistan
- **tn** Tunisia
- **to** Tonga
- **tp** East Timor
- **tr** Turkey
- **tt** Trinidad and Tobago
- **tv** Tuvalu
- **tw** Taiwan
- **tz** Tanzania
- **ua** Ukraine
- **ug** Uganda
- **uk** United Kingdom
- **um** US Minor Outlying Islands
- **us** United States
- **uy** Uruguay

uz	Uzbekistan
va	Holy See (Vatican State)
vc	St Vincent and the Grenadines
ve	Venezuela
vg	British Virgin Islands
vi	US Virgin Islands
vn	Vietnam
vu	Vanuatu
wf	Wallis and Futuna Islands
ws	Western Samoa
ye	Yemen
yt	Mayotte
yu	Yugoslavia
za	South Africa
zm	Zambia
zw	Zimbabwe

▷ www.iana.org/cctld/cctld-whois.htm

internist (ˈɪntɜːnɪst, ɪnˈtɜːnɪst) *n chiefly US* a physician who specializes in internal medicine

interoperable (ˌɪntərˈɒpərəbᵊl) *adj* of or relating to the ability to share data between different computer systems, esp on different machines: *interoperable network management systems* > **ˌinterˌoperaˈbility** *n*

interpellate (ɪnˈtɜːpɛˌleɪt) *vb* **interpellates, interpellating, interpellated** (*tr*) *parliamentary procedure* (in European legislatures) to question (a member of the government) on a point of government policy, often interrupting the business of the day [C16 from L *interpellāre* to disturb, from INTER- + *pellere* to push] > **inˌterpelˈlation** *n* > **inˈterpelˌlator** *n*

interpenetrate (ˌɪntəˈpɛnɪˌtreɪt) *vb* **interpenetrates, interpenetrating, interpenetrated** **1** to penetrate (something) thoroughly; pervade **2** to penetrate each other or one another mutually > **ˌinterˈpenetrable** *adj* > **ˌinterˈpenetrant** *adj* > **ˌinterˌpeneˈtration** *n* > **ˌinterˈpenetrative** *adj* > **ˌinterˈpenetratively** *adv*

interplay (ˈɪntəˌpleɪ) *n* reciprocal and mutual action and reaction, as in circumstances, events, or personal relations

interpleader (ˌɪntəˈpliːdə) *n law* **1** a process by which a person holding money claimed by two or more parties and having no interest in it himself can require the claimants to litigate with each other **2** a person who interpleads

Interpol (ˈɪntəˌpɒl) *n acronym for* International Criminal Police Organization, an association of over 100 national police forces, devoted to fighting international crime

▷ www.interpol.int

interpolate (ɪnˈtɜːpəˌleɪt) *vb* **interpolates, interpolating, interpolated** **1** to insert or introduce (a comment, passage, etc) into (a conversation, text, etc) **2** to falsify or alter (a text, manuscript, etc) by the later addition of (material, esp spurious passages) **3** (*intr*) to make additions, interruptions, or insertions **4** *maths* to estimate (a value of a function) between the values already known or determined ▷ Cf **extrapolate** (sense 1) [C17 from L *interpolāre* to give a new appearance to] > **inˈterpoˌlater** *or* **inˈterpoˌlator** *n* > **inˈterpolative** *adj*

interpose (ˌɪntəˈpəʊz) *vb* **interposes, interposing, interposed** **1** to put or place between or among other things **2** to introduce (comments, questions, etc) into a speech or conversation; interject **3** to exert or use influence or action in order to alter or intervene in (a situation) [C16 from OF, from L *interpōnere*, from INTER- + *pōnere* to put] > **ˌinterˈposal** *n* > **ˌinterˈposer** *n* > **ˌinterpoˈsition** *n*

interpret (ɪnˈtɜːprɪt) *vb* **1** (*tr*) to clarify or explain the meaning of; elucidate **2** (*tr*) to construe the significance or intention of **3** (*tr*) to convey the spirit or meaning of (a poem, song, etc) in performance **4** (*intr*) to act as an interpreter; translate orally [C14 from L *interpretārī*, from *interpres* negotiator, one who explains] > **inˈterpretable** *adj* > **inˌterpretaˈbility** *or* **inˈterpretableness** *n* > **inˈterpretably** *adv* > **inˈterpretive** *adj*

interpretation (ɪnˌtɜːprɪˈteɪʃən) *n* **1** the act or process of interpreting or explaining; elucidation **2** the result of interpreting; an explanation **3** a particular view of an artistic work, esp as expressed by stylistic individuality in its performance **4** explanation, as of a historical site, provided by the use of original objects, visual display material, etc > **inˌterpreˈtational** *adj*

interpreter (ɪnˈtɜːprɪtə) *n* **1** a person who translates orally from one language into another **2** a person who interprets the work of others **3** *computing* a program that translates a statement in a source program to machine code and executes it before translating and executing the next statement > **inˈterpretership** *n* > **inˈterpretress** *fem n*

interpretive centre *n* (at a historical site, etc) a building that provides interpretation of the site through a variety of media, such as video displays and exhibitions, and, often, includes facilities such as refreshment rooms

interregnum (ˌɪntəˈrɛgnəm) *n, pl* **interregnums** *or* **interregna** (-nə) **1** an interval between two reigns, governments, etc **2** any period in which a state lacks a ruler, government, etc **3** a period of absence of some control, authority, etc **4** a gap in a continuity [C16 from L, from INTER- + *regnum* REIGN] > **ˌinterˈregnal** *adj*

interrelate (ˌɪntərɪˈleɪt) *vb* **interrelates, interrelating, interrelated** to place in or come into a mutual or reciprocal relationship > **ˌinterreˈlation** *n* > **ˌinterreˈlationˌship** *n*

interrogate (ɪnˈtɛrəˌgeɪt) *vb* **interrogates, interrogating, interrogated** to ask questions (of), esp to question (a witness in court, spy, etc) closely [C15 from L *interrogāre*, from *rogāre* to ask] > **inˈterroˌgator** *n*

interrogation (ɪnˌtɛrəˈgeɪʃən) *n* **1** the technique, practice, or an instance of interrogating **2** a question or query **3** *telecomm* the transmission of one or more triggering pulses to a transponder > **inˌterroˈgational** *adj*

interrogation mark *n* a less common term for **question mark**

interrogative (ˌɪntəˈrɒgətɪv) *adj* **1** asking or having the nature of a question **2** denoting a form or construction used in asking a question **3** denoting or belonging to a class of words, such as *which* and *whom*, that serve to question which individual referent is intended ▷ *n* **4** an interrogative word, phrase, sentence, or construction **5** a question mark > **ˌinterˈrogatively** *adv*

interrogatory (ˌɪntəˈrɒgətərɪ, -trɪ) *adj* **1** expressing or involving a question ▷ *n, pl* **interrogatories** **2** a question or interrogation

interrupt (ˌɪntəˈrʌpt) *vb* **1** to break the continuity of (an action, event, etc) or hinder (a person) by intrusion **2** (*tr*) to cease to perform (some action) **3** (*tr*) to obstruct (a view, etc) **4** to prevent or disturb (a conversation, discussion, etc) by questions, interjections, or comment [C15 from L *interrumpere*, from INTER- + *rumpere* to break] > **ˌinterˈruptible** *adj* > **ˌinterˈruptive** *adj* > **ˌinterˈruptively** *adv* > **ˌinterˈrupted** *adj*

interrupted screw *n* a screw with a slot cut into the thread, esp one used in the breech of some guns permitting both engagement and release of the block by a partial turn of the screw

interrupter *or* **interruptor** (ˌɪntəˈrʌptə) *n* **1** a person or thing that interrupts **2** an electromechanical device for opening and closing an electric circuit

interruption (ˌɪntəˈrʌpʃən) *n* **1** something that interrupts, such as a comment, question, or action **2** an interval or intermission **3** the act of interrupting or the state of being interrupted

interscholastic (ˌɪntəskəˈlæstɪk) *adj* **1** (of sports events,

competitions, etc) occurring between two or more schools **2** representative of various schools
intersect (ˌɪntəˈsɛkt) *vb* **1** to divide, cut, or mark off by passing through or across **2** (esp of roads) to cross (each other) **3** *maths* (often foll by *with*) to have one or more points in common (with another configuration) [C17 from L *intersecāre* to divide, from INTER- + *secāre* to cut]
intersection (ˌɪntəˈsɛkʃən, ˈɪntəˌsɛk-) *n* **1** a point at which things intersect, esp a road junction **2** the act of intersecting or the state of being intersected **3** *maths* **3a** a point or set of points common to two or more geometric configurations **3b** Also called: **product** the set of elements that are common to two sets **3c** the operation that yields that set from a pair of given sets > ˌ**interˈsectional** *adj*
intersex (ˈɪntəˌsɛks) *n* an individual with characteristics intermediate between those of a male and a female
intersexual (ˌɪntəˈsɛksjʊəl) *adj* **1** occurring or existing between the sexes **2** relating to or being an intersex > ˌ**interˌsexuˈality** *n* > ˌ**interˈsexually** *adv*
interspace *vb* (ˌɪntəˈspeɪs), **interspaces, interspacing, interspaced 1** (*tr*) to make or occupy a space between ▷ *n* (ˈɪntəˌspeɪs) **2** space between or among things > **interspatial** (ˌɪntəˈspeɪʃəl) *adj* > ˌ**interˈspatially** *adv*
intersperse (ˌɪntəˈspɜːs) *vb* **intersperses, interspersing, interspersed** (*tr*) **1** to scatter or distribute among, between, or on **2** to diversify (something) with other things scattered here and there [C16 from L *interspargere*, from INTER- + *spargere* to sprinkle] > **interspersedly** (ˌɪntəˈspɜːsɪdlɪ) *adv* > **interspersion** (ˌɪntəˈspɜːʃən) *or* ˌ**interˈspersal** *n*
interstate (ˈɪntəˌsteɪt) *n US* a motorway crossing between states
interstellar (ˌɪntəˈstɛlə) *adj* between or among stars
interstice (ɪnˈtɜːstɪs) *n* (*usually pl*) **1** a minute opening or crevice between things **2** *physics* the space between adjacent atoms in a crystal lattice [C17 from L *interstitium* interval, from *intersistere*, from INTER- + *sistere* to stand]
interstitial (ˌɪntəˈstɪʃəl) *adj* **1** of or relating to an interstice or interstices **2** *physics* forming or occurring in an interstice: *an interstitial atom* **3** *anat, zool* occurring in the spaces between organs, tissues, etc: *interstitial cells* ▷ *n* **4** *chem* an atom or ion situated in the interstices of a crystal lattice > ˌ**interˈstitially** *adv*
intertrigo (ˌɪntəˈtraɪɡəʊ) *n* chafing between two skin surfaces, as under the breasts or at the armpit [C18 from INTER- + *-trigo*, from L *terere* to rub]
interval (ˈɪntəvəl) *n* **1** the period of time between two events, instants, etc **2** the distance between two points, objects, etc **3** a pause or interlude, as between periods of intense activity **4** *Brit* a short period between parts of a play, etc; intermission **5** *music* the difference of pitch between two notes, either sounded simultaneously or in succession as in a musical part **6** the ratio of the frequencies of two sounds **7 at intervals 7a** occasionally or intermittently **7b** with spaces between [C13 from L *intervallum*, lit.: space between two palisades, from INTER- + *vallum* palisade] > **intervallic** (ˌɪntəˈvælɪk) *adj*
intervene (ˌɪntəˈviːn) *vb* **intervenes, intervening, intervened** (*intr*) **1** (often foll by *in*) to take a decisive or intrusive role (in) in order to determine events **2** (foll by *in* or *between*) to come or be (among or between) **3** (of a period of time) to occur between events or points in time **4** (of an event) to disturb or hinder a course of action **5** *econ* to take action to affect the market forces of an economy, esp to maintain the stability of a currency **6** *law* to interpose and become a party to a legal action between others, esp in order to protect one's interests [C16 from L *intervenīre* to come between] > ˌ**interˈvener** *or* ˌ**interˈvenor** *n*
intervention (ˌɪntəˈvɛnʃən) *n* **1** an act of intervening **2** any interference in the affairs of others, esp by one state in the affairs of another **3** *econ* the action of a central bank in supporting the international value of a currency by buying large quantities of the currency to keep the price up **4** *commerce* the action of the EU in buying up surplus produce when the market price drops to a certain value
interventionist (ˌɪntəˈvɛnʃənɪst) *adj* **1** of, relating to, or advocating intervention, esp in order to achieve a policy objective ▷ *n* **2** a person or state that pursues a policy of intervention
intervertebral disc (ˌɪntəˈvɜːtɪbrəl) *n* any of the cartilaginous discs between individual vertebrae, acting as shock absorbers
interview (ˈɪntəˌvjuː) *n* **1** a conversation with or questioning of a person, usually conducted for television or a newspaper **2** a formal discussion, esp one in which an employer assesses a job applicant ▷ *vb* **3** to conduct an interview with (someone) [C16 from OF *entrevue*] > ˌ**interviewˈee** *n* > ˈ**interˌviewer** *n*
inter vivos *Latin* (ˈɪntə ˈviːvɒs) *adj law* between living people: *an inter vivos gift*
interwar (ˌɪntəˈwɔː) *adj* of or happening in the period between World War I and World War II
intestate (ɪnˈtɛsteɪt, -tɪt) *adj* **1a** (of a person) not having made a will **1b** (of property) not disposed of by will ▷ *n* **2** a person who dies without having made a will [C14 from L *intestātus*, from IN-[1] + *testārī* to bear witness, make a will, from *testis* a witness] > **inˈtestacy** *n*
intestine (ɪnˈtɛstɪn) *n* the part of the alimentary canal between the stomach and the anus. See **large intestine, small intestine** [C16 from L *intestīnum* gut, from *intestīnus* internal, from *intus* within] > **intestinal** (ɪnˈtɛstɪnᵊl, ˌɪntɛsˈtaɪnᵊl) *adj*
inti (ˈɪntɪ) *n* a former monetary unit of Peru [C20 from Quechua]
intifada (ˌɪntɪˈfɑːdə) *n* a Palestinian uprising against Israel in the West Bank and Gaza Strip. Two uprisings have occurred, one starting in 1987 and the other in 2000 [C20 from Ar., lit.: uprising]
intimacy (ˈɪntɪməsɪ) *n, pl* **intimacies 1** close or warm friendship or understanding; personal relationship **2** (*often pl*) *euphemistic* sexual relations
intimate[1] (ˈɪntɪmɪt) *adj* **1** characterized by a close or warm personal relationship: *an intimate friend* **2** deeply personal, private, or secret **3** (*often postpositive; foll by with*) *Euphemistic*. having sexual relations (with) **4** (*postpositive*; foll by *with*) having a deep or unusual knowledge (of) **5** having a friendly, warm, or informal atmosphere: *an intimate nightclub* **6** of or relating to the essential part or nature of something; intrinsic ▷ *n* **7** a close friend [C17 from L *intimus* very close friend, from (adj): innermost, from *intus* within] > ˈ**intimately** *adv* > ˈ**intimateness** *n*
intimate[2] (ˈɪntɪˌmeɪt) *vb* **intimates, intimating, intimated** (*tr; may take a clause as object*) **1** to hint; suggest **2** to proclaim; make known [C16 from LL *intimāre* to proclaim, from L *intimus* innermost] > ˈ**intiˌmater** *n* > ˌ**intiˈmation** *n*
intimidate (ɪnˈtɪmɪˌdeɪt) *vb* **intimidates, intimidating, intimidated** (*tr*) **1** to make timid or frightened; scare **2** to discourage, restrain, or silence unscrupulously, as by threats [C17 from Med. L *intimidāre*, from L IN-[2] + *timidus* fearful, from *timor* fear] > ˌ**inˈtimiˌdating** *adj* > **inˌtimiˈdation** *n* > **inˈtimiˌdator** *n*
intinction (ɪnˈtɪŋkʃən) *n Christianity* the practice of dipping the Eucharistic bread into the wine at Holy Communion [C16 from LL *intinctiō* a dipping in, from L *intingere*, from *tingere* to dip]
intitule (ɪnˈtɪtjuːl) *vb* **intitules, intituling, intituled** (*tr*) *parliamentary procedure* (in Britain) to entitle (an Act) [C15 from OF *intituler*, from L *titulus* TITLE]
intl *abbrev for* international

into ('ɪntuː; *unstressed* 'ɪntə) *prep* **1** to the interior or inner parts of: *to look into a case* **2** to the middle or midst of so as to be surrounded by: *into the bushes* **3** against; up against: *he drove into a wall* **4** used to indicate the result of a change: *he changed into a monster* **5** *maths* used to indicate a dividend: *three into six is two* **6** *inf* interested or enthusiastically involved in: *I'm really into Freud*

intonation (ˌɪntəʊ'neɪʃən) *n* **1** the sound pattern of phrases and sentences produced by pitch variation in the voice **2** the act or manner of intoning **3** an intoned, chanted, or monotonous utterance; incantation **4** *music* the opening of a piece of plainsong, sung by a soloist **5** *music* the capacity to play or sing in tune > ˌ**into'national** *adj*

intone (ɪn'təʊn) *or* **intonate** *vb* **intones, intoning, intoned** *or* **intonates, intonating, intonated** **1** to utter, recite, or sing (a chant, prayer, etc) in a monotonous or incantatory tone **2** (*intr*) to speak with a particular or characteristic intonation or tone **3** to sing (the opening phrase of a psalm, etc) in plainsong [C15 from Med. L *intonare*, from IN-[2] + TONE] > **in'toner** *n*

in toto *Latin* (ɪn 'təʊtəʊ) *adv* totally; entirely

intoxicant (ɪn'tɒksɪkənt) *n* **1** anything that causes intoxication ▷ *adj* **2** causing intoxication

intoxicate (ɪn'tɒksɪˌkeɪt) *vb* **intoxicates, intoxicating, intoxicated** (*tr*) **1** (of an alcoholic drink) to produce in (a person) a state ranging from euphoria to stupor; make drunk; inebriate **2** to stimulate, excite, or elate so as to overwhelm **3** (of a drug, etc) to poison [C16 from Med. L, from *intoxicāre* to poison, from L *toxicum* poison; see TOXIC] > **in'toxicable** *adj*

intoxicating (ɪn'tɒksɪˌkeɪtɪŋ) *adj* **1** (of an alcoholic drink) producing in a person a state ranging from euphoria to stupor, usually accompanied by loss of inhibitions and control; inebriating **2** stimulating, exciting, or producing great elation > **in'toxiˌcatingly** *adv*

intoxication (ɪnˌtɒksɪ'keɪʃən) *n* **1** drunkenness; inebriation **2** great elation **3** the act of intoxicating **4** poisoning

intr *abbrev for* intransitive

intra- *prefix* within; inside: *intrastate; intravenous* [from L *intrā* within; see INTERIOR]

Intracoastal Waterway (ˌɪntrə'kəʊstəl) *n* short for **Atlantic Intracoastal Waterway**

intractable (ɪn'træktəbəl) *adj* **1** difficult to influence or direct: *an intractable disposition* **2** (of a problem, illness, etc) difficult to solve, alleviate, or cure > **inˌtracta'bility** *or* **in'tractableness** *n* > **in'tractably** *adv*

intradermal (ˌɪntrə'dɜːməl) *adj* within the skin: *an intradermal injection*. Abbrevs (esp of an injection): **ID, i.d** > ˌ**intra'dermally** *adv*

intrados (ɪn'treɪdɒs) *n, pl* **intrados** *or* **intradoses** *archit* the inner curve or surface of an arch [C18 from F, from INTRA- + *dos* back, from L *dorsum*]

intramural (ˌɪntrə'mjʊərəl) *adj* *education, chiefly US & Canad* operating within or involving those in a single establishment > ˌ**intra'murally** *adv*

intramuscular (ˌɪntrə'mʌskjʊlə) *adj* within a muscle: *an intramuscular injection*. Abbrevs. (esp of an injection): **IM, i.m.** > ˌ**intra'muscularly** *adv*

intranet ('ɪntrəˌnɛt) *n* *computing* an internal network in a company or other organization that makes use of Internet technology [C20 INTRA- + NET(WORK) (sense 5), modelled on INTERNET]

intrans. *abbrev for* intransitive

intransigent (ɪn'trænsɪdʒənt) *adj* **1** not willing to compromise; obstinately maintaining an attitude: *government's intransigent attitude* ▷ *n* **2** an intransigent person, esp in politics [C19 from Sp. *los intransigentes* the uncompromising (ones), a name adopted by certain political extremists, from IN-[1] + *transigir* to compromise, from L *transigere* to settle; see TRANSACT] > **in'transigence** *or* **in'transigency** *n* > **in'transigently** *adv*

intransitive (ɪn'trænsɪtɪv) *adj* **1a** denoting a verb that does not require a direct object: *"to faint" is an intransitive verb* **1b** (*as n*) such a verb **2** denoting an adjective or noun that does not require any particular noun phrase as a referent **3** having the property that if it holds between one argument and a second, and between the second and a third, it must fail to hold between the first and third: *"being the mother of" is an intransitive relation* ▷ Cf **transitive** > **in'transitively** *adv* > **inˌtransi'tivity** *or* **in'transitiveness** *n*

intrapreneur (ˌɪntrəprə'nɜː) *n* a person who while remaining within a larger organization uses entrepreneurial skills to develop a new product or line of business as a subsidiary of the organization [C20 from INTRA- + (ENTRE)PRENEUR]

intrauterine (ˌɪntrə'juːtəraɪn) *adj* within the womb

intrauterine device *n* a metal or plastic device, in the shape of a loop, coil, or ring, inserted into the uterus to prevent conception. Abbrev: **IUD**

intravenous (ˌɪntrə'viːnəs) *adj* *anat* within a vein: *an intravenous injection*. Abbrevs (esp of an injection): **IV, i.v.** > ˌ**intra'venously** *adv*

in-tray *n* a tray for incoming papers, etc, requiring attention

intrench (ɪn'trɛntʃ) *vb* a less common spelling of **entrench** > **in'trencher** *n* > **in'trenchment** *n*

intrepid (ɪn'trɛpɪd) *adj* fearless; daring; bold [C17 from L *intrepidus*, from IN-[1] + *trepidus* fearful] > ˌ**intre'pidity** *n* > **in'trepidly** *adv*

intricate ('ɪntrɪkɪt) *adj* **1** difficult to understand; obscure; complex; puzzling **2** entangled or involved: *intricate patterns* [C15 from L *intrīcāre* to entangle, perplex, from IN-[2] + *trīcae* trifles, perplexities] > **'intricacy** *or* **'intricateness** *n* > **'intricately** *adv*

intrigue *vb* (ɪn'triːg), **intrigues, intriguing, intrigued** **1** (*tr*) to make interested or curious **2** (*intr*) to make secret plots or employ underhand methods; conspire **3** (*intr; often foll by with*) to carry on a clandestine love affair ▷ *n* (ɪn'triːg, 'ɪntriːg) **4** the act or an instance of secret plotting, etc **5** a clandestine love affair **6** the quality of arousing interest or curiosity; beguilement [C17 from F *intriguer*, from It., from L *intrīcāre*; see INTRICATE] > **in'triguer** *n* > **in'triguingly** *adv*

Ii

intrinsic (ɪn'trɪnsɪk) *or* **intrinsical** *adj* **1** of or relating to the essential nature of a thing; inherent **2** *anat* situated within or peculiar to a part: *intrinsic muscles* [C15 from LL *intrinsecus* from L, inwardly, from *intrā* within + *secus* alongside] > **in'trinsically** *adv*

intro ('ɪntrəʊ) *n, pl* **intros** *inf* short for **introduction**

intro. *or* **introd.** *abbrev for:* **1** introduction **2** introductory

intro- *prefix* in, into, or inward: *introvert* [from L *intrō* inwardly, within]

introduce (ˌɪntrə'djuːs) *vb* **introduces, introducing, introduced** (*tr*) **1** (often foll by *to*) to present (someone) by name (to another person) **2** (foll by *to*) to cause to experience for the first time: *to introduce a visitor to beer* **3** to present for consideration or approval, esp before a legislative body: *to introduce a bill in parliament* **4** to bring in; establish: *to introduce decimal currency* **5** to present (a radio or television programme, etc) verbally **6** (foll by *with*) to start: *he introduced his talk with some music* **7** (often foll by *into*) to insert or inject: *he introduced the needle into his arm* **8** to place (members of a plant or animal species) in a new environment with the intention of producing a resident breeding population [C16 from L *intrōdūcere* to bring inside] > ˌ**intro'ducer** *n* > ˌ**intro'ducible** *adj*

introduction (ˌɪntrə'dʌkʃən) *n* **1** the act of introducing or fact of being introduced **2** a presentation of one person to another or others **3** a means of presenting a person to another person, such as a letter of introduction or reference **4** a preliminary part, as of a book **5** *music* an opening passage in a movement or composition that precedes the main material **6** a basic or elementary work of instruction, reference, etc

introductory (ˌɪntrəˈdʌktərɪ, -trɪ) *adj* serving as an introduction; preliminary; prefatory

introit (ˈɪntrɔɪt) *n RC Church, Church of England* a short prayer said or sung as the celebrant is entering the sanctuary to celebrate Mass or Holy Communion [c15 from Church L *introitus* introit, from L: entrance, from *introīre* to go in] > **inˈtroital** *adj*

intromit (ˌɪntrəˈmɪt) *vb* **intromits, intromitting, intromitted** (*tr*) *rare* to enter or insert [c15 from L *intrōmittere* to send in] > **ˌintroˈmissible** *adj* > **ˌintroˈmission** *n* > **ˌintroˈmittent** *adj*

introspection (ˌɪntrəˈspɛkʃən) *n* the examination of one's own thoughts, impressions, and feelings [c17 from L *intrōspicere* to look within] > **ˌintroˈspective** *adj* > **ˌintroˈspectively** *adv*

introversion (ˌɪntrəˈvɜːʃən) *n psychol* the directing of interest inwards towards one's own thoughts and feelings rather than towards the external world or making social contacts > **ˌintroˈversive** *or* **ˌintroˈvertive** *adj*

introvert *n* (ˈɪntrəˌvɜːt) **1** *psychol* a person prone to introversion ▷ *adj* (ˈɪntrəˌvɜːt) **2** Also: **introverted** characterized by introversion ▷ *vb* (ˌɪntrəˈvɜːt) **3** (*tr*) *pathol* to turn (a hollow organ or part) inside out [c17 see INTRO-, INVERT]

intrude (ɪnˈtruːd) *vb* **intrudes, intruding, intruded** **1** (often foll by *into*, *on*, or *upon*) to put forward or interpose (oneself, one's views, something) abruptly or without invitation **2** *geol* to force or thrust (molten magma) between solid rocks [c16 from L *intrūdere* to thrust in] > **inˈtruder** *n* > **inˈtrudingly** *adv*

intrusion (ɪnˈtruːʒən) *n* **1** the act or an instance of intruding; an unwelcome visit, etc: *an intrusion on one's privacy* **2a** the movement of magma into spaces in the overlying strata to form igneous rock **2b** any igneous rock formed in this way **3** *property law* an unlawful entry onto land by a stranger after determination of a particular estate of freehold > **inˈtrusional** *adj*

intrusive (ɪnˈtruːsɪv) *adj* **1** characterized by intrusion or tending to intrude **2** (of igneous rocks) formed by intrusion **3** *phonetics* relating to or denoting a speech sound that is introduced into a word or piece of connected speech for a phonetic reason > **inˈtrusively** *adv* > **inˈtrusiveness** *n*

intrust (ɪnˈtrʌst) *vb* a less common spelling of **entrust**

intubate (ˈɪntjʊˌbeɪt) *vb* **intubates, intubating, intubated** (*tr*) *med* to insert a tube into (a hollow organ) > **ˌintuˈbation** *n*

intuit (ɪnˈtjuːɪt) *vb* **intuits, intuiting, intuited** to know or discover by intuition > **inˈtuitable** *adj*

intuition (ˌɪntjʊˈɪʃən) *n* **1** knowledge or belief obtained neither by reason nor perception **2** instinctive knowledge or belief **3** a hunch or unjustified belief [c15 from LL *intuitiō* a contemplation, from L *intuērī* to gaze upon, from *tuērī* to look at] > **ˌintuˈitional** *adj* > **ˌintuˈitionally** *adv*

intuitionism (ˌɪntjʊˈɪʃəˌnɪzəm) *or* **intuitionalism** *n philosophy* **1** the doctrine that knowledge is acquired primarily by intuition **2** the theory that the solution to moral problems can be discovered by intuition **3** the doctrine that external objects are known to be real by intuition > **ˌintuˈitionist** *or* **ˌintuˈitionalist** *n*

intuitive (ɪnˈtjuːɪtɪv) *adj* **1** resulting from intuition: *an intuitive awareness* **2** of, characterized by, or involving intuition > **inˈtuitively** *adv* > **inˈtuitiveness** *n*

intumesce (ˌɪntjʊˈmɛs) *vb* **intumesces, intumescing, intumesced** (*intr*) to swell [c18 from L *intumescere*, from *tumescere* to begin to swell, from *tumēre* to swell] > **ˌintuˈmescence** *n*

intussusception (ˌɪntəssəˈsɛpʃən) *n* **1** *pathol* the telescoping of one section of the intestinal tract into a lower section **2** *biol* growth in the surface area of a cell by the deposition of new material between the existing components of the cell wall [c18 from L *intus* within + *susceptiō* a taking up]

Inuit *or* **Innuit** (ˈɪnjuːɪt) *n, pl* **Inuit, Inuits** *or* **Innuit, Innuits** **1** a member of a group of peoples inhabiting N Canada, Greenland, Alaska, and E Siberia **2** the language of these peoples; Inuktitut [from Inuktitut *inuit* people, pl of *inuk* a man]

Inuk (ˈɪnʊk) *n Canad* a member of the Inuit [from Inuktitut *inuk* a man]

inukshuk (ˈɪnʊkˌʃʊk) *n pl* **inukshuks** *or* **inukshuit** a stone used by the Inuit to mark a location [from Inuktitut, lit.: something in the shape of a man]

Inuktitut (ɪˈnʊktɪˌtʊt) *n Canad* the language of the Inuit [from Inuktitut *inuk* man + *titut* speech]

inunction (ɪnˈʌŋkʃən) *n* **1** the application of an ointment to the skin, esp by rubbing **2** the ointment so used **3** the act of anointing; anointment [c15 from L *inunguere* to anoint, from *unguere*; see UNCTION]

inundate (ˈɪnʌnˌdeɪt) *vb* **inundates, inundating, inundated** (*tr*) **1** to cover completely with water; overflow; flood; swamp **2** to overwhelm, as if with a flood: *to be inundated with requests* [c17 from L *inundāre*, from *unda* wave] > **ˈinundant** *or* **inˈundatory** *adj* > **ˌinunˈdation** *n* > **ˈinunˌdator** *n*

inure *or* **enure** (ɪˈnjʊə) *vb* **inures, inuring, inured** *or* **enures, enuring, enured** **1** (*tr; often passive*; often foll by *to*) to cause to accept or become hardened to; habituate **2** (*intr*) (esp of a law, etc) to come into operation; take effect [c15 *enuren* to accustom, from *ure* use, from OF *euvre* custom, work, from L *opera* works] > **inˈurement** *or* **enˈurement** *n*

in utero *Latin* (ɪn ˈjuːtərəʊ) *adv, adj* in the uterus

in vacuo *Latin* (ɪn ˈvækjʊˌəʊ) *adv* in a vacuum

invade (ɪnˈveɪd) *vb* **invades, invading, invaded** **1** to enter (a country, territory, etc) by military force **2** (*tr*) to occupy in large numbers; overrun; infest **3** (*tr*) to trespass or encroach upon (privacy, etc) **4** (*tr*) to enter and spread throughout, esp harmfully; pervade [c15 from L *invādere*, from *vādere* to go] > **inˈvadable** *adj* > **inˈvader** *n*

invaginate *vb* (ɪnˈvædʒɪˌneɪt), **invaginates, invaginating, invaginated** **1** *pathol* to push one section of (a tubular organ or part) back into itself so that it becomes ensheathed **2** (*intr*) (of the outer layer of an organism or part) to undergo this process ▷ *adj* (ɪnˈvædʒɪnɪt, -ˌneɪt) **3** (of an organ or part) folded back upon itself [c19 from Med. L *invāgīnāre*, from L IN-[2] + *vāgīna* sheath] > **inˈvaginable** *adj* > **inˌvagiˈnation** *n*

invalid[1] (ˈɪnvəˌliːd, -lɪd) *n* **1a** a person suffering from disablement or chronic ill health **1b** (*as modifier*): *an invalid chair* ▷ *adj* **2** suffering from or disabled by injury, sickness, etc ▷ *vb* (*tr*) **3** to cause to become an invalid; disable **4** (*often passive*; usually foll by *out*) *chiefly Brit* to require (a member of the armed forces) to retire from active service through wounds or illness [c17 from L *invalidus* infirm, from IN-[1] + *validus* strong] > **invalidity** (ˌɪnvəˈlɪdɪtɪ) *n*

invalid[2] (ɪnˈvælɪd) *adj* **1** not valid; having no cogency or legal force **2** *logic* (of an argument) having a conclusion that does not follow from the premises [c16 from Med. L *invalidus* without legal force; see INVALID[1]] > **ˌinvaˈlidity** *or* **inˈvalidness** *n* > **inˈvalidly** *adv*

invalidate (ɪnˈvælɪˌdeɪt) *vb* **invalidates, invalidating, invalidated** (*tr*) **1** to render weak or ineffective (an argument) **2** to take away the legal force or effectiveness of; annul (a contract) > **inˌvaliˈdation** *n* > **inˈvaliˌdator** *n*

invaluable (ɪnˈvæljʊəbᵊl) *adj* having great value that is impossible to calculate; priceless > **inˈvaluableness** *n* > **inˈvaluably** *adv*

Invar (ɪnˈvɑː) *n trademark* an alloy containing iron, nickel, and carbon. It has a very low coefficient of expansion and is used for the balance springs of watches, etc [c20 shortened from INVARIABLE]

invariable (ɪnˈvɛərɪəbᵊl) *adj* **1** not subject to alteration; unchanging ▷ *n* **2** a mathematical quantity having an unchanging value; a constant > **inˌvariaˈbility** *or* **inˈvariableness** *n*

invariably (ɪnˈvɛərɪəblɪ) *adv* always; without exception

invariant (ɪnˈvɛərɪənt) *maths* ▷ *n* **1** an entity, quantity, etc, that is unaltered by a particular transformation of coordinates ▷ *adj* **2** (of a relationship or a property of a function, configuration, or equation) unaltered by a particular transformation of coordinates > **inˈvariance** *or* **inˈvariancy** *n*

invasion (ɪnˈveɪʒən) *n* **1** the act of invading with armed forces **2** any encroachment or intrusion: *an invasion of rats* **3** the onset or advent of something harmful, esp of a disease **4** *pathol* the spread of cancer from its point of origin into surrounding tissues **5** the movement of plants to a new area or to an area to which they are not native

invasive (ɪnˈveɪsɪv) *adj* **1** of or relating to an invasion, intrusion, etc **2** (of surgery) involving making a relatively large incision in the body to gain access to the target of the surgery

invective (ɪnˈvɛktɪv) *n* **1** vehement accusation or denunciation, esp of a bitterly abusive or sarcastic kind ▷ *adj* **2** characterized by or using abusive language, bitter sarcasm, etc [c15 from LL *invectīvus* reproachful, from L *invectus* carried in; see INVEIGH] > **inˈvectively** *adv* > **inˈvectiveness** *n*

inveigh (ɪnˈveɪ) *vb* (*intr;* foll by *against*) to speak with violent or invective language; rail [c15 from L *invehī*, lit.: to be carried in, hence, assail physically or verbally] > **inˈveigher** *n*

inveigle (ɪnˈviːgᵊl, -ˈveɪ-) *vb* **inveigles, inveigling, inveigled** (*tr;* often foll by *into* or an infinitive) to lead (someone into a situation) or persuade (to do something) by cleverness or trickery; cajole [c15 from OF *avogler* to blind, deceive, from *avogle* blind, from Med. L *ab oculis* without eyes] > **inˈveiglement** *n* > **inˈveigler** *n*

invent (ɪnˈvɛnt) *vb* **1** to create or devise (new ideas, machines, etc) **2** to make up (falsehoods, etc); fabricate [c15 from L *invenīre* to find, come upon] > **inˈventable** *adj*

invention (ɪnˈvɛnʃən) *n* **1** the act or process of inventing **2** something that is invented **3** *patent law* the discovery or production of some new or improved process or machine **4** creative power or ability; inventive skill **5** *euphemistic* a fabrication; lie **6** *music* a short piece consisting of two or three parts usually in imitative counterpoint > **inˈventional** *adj* > **inˈventionless** *adj*

inventive (ɪnˈvɛntɪv) *adj* **1** skilled or quick at contriving; ingenious; resourceful **2** characterized by inventive skill: *an inventive programme of work* **3** of or relating to invention > **inˈventively** *adv* > **inˈventiveness** *n*

inventor (ɪnˈvɛntə) *n* a person who invents, esp as a profession > **inˈventress** *fem n*

inventory (ˈɪnvəntərɪ, -trɪ) *n, pl* **inventories 1** a detailed list of articles, goods, property, etc **2** (*often pl*) *accounting, chiefly US* **2a** the amount or value of a firm's current assets that consist of raw materials, work in progress, and finished goods; stock **2b** such assets individually ▷ *vb* **inventories, inventorying, inventoried 3** (*tr*) to enter (items) in an inventory; make a list of [c16 from Med. L *inventōrium;* see INVENT] > **ˈinventoriable** *adj* > **ˌinvenˈtorial** *adj* > **ˌinvenˈtorially** *adv*

Inveraray (ˌɪnvəˈrɛərɪ) *n* a town in W Scotland, in Argyll and Bute: Inveraray Castle is the seat of the Dukes of Argyll. Pop: 512 (1991)

Invercargill (ˌɪnvəˈkɑːgɪl) *n* a city in New Zealand, on South Island: regional trading centre for sheep and agricultural products. Pop: 51 600 (1995 est)

Inverclyde (ˌɪnvəˈklaɪd) *n* a council area of W central Scotland: created in 1996 from part of Strathclyde region. Administrative centre: Greenock. Pop: 84 203 (2001). Area: 162 sq km (63 sq miles)

Inverness (ˌɪnvəˈnɛs) *n* **1** a city in N Scotland, administrative centre of Highland: tourism and specialized engineering. Pop: 41 234 (1991) **2** (*sometimes not cap*) an overcoat with a removable cape

Inverness-shire (ˌɪnvəˈnɛsʃɪə, -ʃə) *n* (until 1975) a county of NW Scotland, now part of Highland

inverse (ɪnˈvɜːs, ˈɪnvɜːs) *adj* **1** opposite or contrary in effect, sequence, direction, etc **2** *maths* **2a** (of a relationship) containing two variables such that an increase in one results in a decrease in the other **2b** (of an element) operating on a specified member of a set to produce the identity of the set: *the additive inverse element of x is –x* **3** (*usually prenominal*) upside-down; inverted: *in an inverse position* ▷ *n* **4** *maths* an inverse element [c17 from L *inversus*, from *invertere* to INVERT] > **inˈversely** *adv*

inverse function *n* a function whose independent variable is the dependent variable of a given trigonometric or hyperbolic function: *the inverse function of* sin *x is* arcsin *y* (*also written* $\sin^{-1}y$)

inversion (ɪnˈvɜːʃən) *n* **1** the act of inverting or state of being inverted **2** something inverted, esp a reversal of order, mutual functions, etc: *an inversion of their previous relationship* **3** Also: **anastrophe** *rhetoric* the reversal of a normal order of words, as in the phrase *weeping left she sorrowfully* **4** *chem* **4a** the conversion of a dextrorotatory solution of sucrose into a laevorotatory solution of glucose and fructose by hydrolysis **4b** any similar reaction in which the optical properties of the reactants are opposite to those of the products **5** *music* **5a** the process or result of transposing the notes of a chord such that the root, originally in the bass, is placed in an upper part **5b** the modification of an interval in which the higher note becomes the lower or the lower one the higher **6** *pathol* abnormal positioning of an organ or part, as in being upside down or turned inside out **7** *psychiatry* **7a** the adoption of the role or characteristics of the opposite sex **7b** another word for **homosexuality 8** *meteorol* an abnormal condition in which the layer of air next to the earth's surface is cooler than an overlying layer **9** *computing* an operation by which each digit of a binary number is changed to the alternative digit, as 10110 to 01001 > **inˈversive** *adj*

invert *vb* (ɪnˈvɜːt) **1** to turn or cause to turn upside down or inside out **2** (*tr*) to reverse in effect, sequence, direction, etc **3** (*tr*) *phonetics* to turn (the tip of the tongue) up and back to pronounce (a speech sound) ▷ *n* (ˈɪnvɜːt) **4** *psychiatry* **4a** a person who adopts the role of the opposite sex **4b** another word for **homosexual 5** *archit* **5a** the lower inner surface of a drain, sewer, etc **5b** an arch that is concave upwards, esp one used in foundations [c16 from L *invertere*, from IN-[2] + *vertere* to turn] > **inˈvertible** *adj* > **inˌvertiˈbility** *n*

invertase (ɪnˈvɜːteɪz) *n* an enzyme, occurring in the intestinal juice of animals and in yeasts, that hydrolyses sucrose to glucose and fructose

invertebrate (ɪnˈvɜːtɪbrɪt, -ˌbreɪt) *n* **1** any animal lacking a backbone, including all species not classified as vertebrates ▷ *adj also* **invertebral 2** of, relating to, or designating invertebrates

inverted comma *n* another term for **quotation mark**

inverted mordent *n music* a melodic ornament consisting of the rapid alternation of a principal note with a note one degree higher

inverter *or* **invertor** (ɪnˈvɜːtə) *n* any device for converting a direct current into an alternating current

invert sugar *n* a mixture of fructose and glucose obtained by the inversion of sucrose

invest (ɪnˈvɛst) *vb* **1** (often foll by *in*) to lay out (money or capital in an enterprise) with the expectation of profit

2 (*tr; often foll by in*) to devote (effort, resources, etc, to a project) 3 (*tr; often foll by in or with*) *arch or ceremonial* to clothe or adorn (in some garment, esp the robes of an office) 4 (*tr; often foll by in*) to install formally or ceremoniously (in an official position, rank, etc) 5 (*tr; foll by in or with*) to place (power, authority, etc, in) or provide (with power or authority): *to invest new rights in the monarchy* 6 (*tr; usually passive; foll by in or with*) to provide or endow (a person with qualities, characteristics, etc) 7 (*tr; foll by with*) *usually poetic* to cover or adorn, as if with a coat or garment: *when spring invests the trees with leaves* 8 (*tr*) *rare* to surround with military forces; besiege 9 (*intr; foll by in*) *inf* to purchase; buy [C16 from Med. L *investīre* to clothe, from L, from *vestīre*, from *vestis* a garment] > **in'vestable** *or* **in'vestible** *adj* > **in'vestor** *n*

investigate (ɪn'vɛstɪˌgeɪt) *vb* **investigates, investigating, investigated** to inquire into (a situation or problem, esp a crime or death) thoroughly; examine systematically, esp in order to discover the truth [C16 from L *investīgāre* to search after, from IN-² + *vestīgium* track; see VESTIGE] > **in'vestiˌgative** *or* **in'vestigatory** *adj* > **in'vestiˌgator** *n*

investigation (ɪnˌvɛstɪ'geɪʃən) *n* the act or process of investigating; a careful search or examination in order to discover facts, etc

investiture (ɪn'vɛstɪtʃə) *n* 1 the act of presenting with a title or with the robes and insignia of an office or rank 2 (in feudal society) the formal bestowal of the possessory right to a fief > **in'vestitive** *adj*

investment (ɪn'vɛstmənt) *n* **1a** the act of investing money **1b** the amount invested **1c** an enterprise, asset, etc, in which money is or can be invested **2a** the act of investing effort, resources, etc **2b** the amount invested 3 *biol* the outer layer or covering of an organ, part, or organism 4 a less common word for **investiture** (sense 1) 5 the act of investing or state of being invested, as with an official robe, specific quality, etc 6 *rare* the act of besieging with military forces, works, etc

investment analyst *n* a specialist in forecasting the prices of stocks and shares

investment bond *n* a single-premium life-assurance policy in which a fixed sum is invested in an asset-backed fund

investment trust *n* a financial enterprise that invests its subscribed capital in securities for its investors' benefit

inveterate (ɪn'vɛtərɪt) *adj* 1 long established, esp so as to be deep-rooted or ingrained: *an inveterate feeling of hostility* 2 (*prenominal*) confirmed in a habit or practice, esp a bad one; hardened [C16 from L *inveterātus* of long standing, from *inveterāre* to make old, from IN-² + *vetus* old] > **in'veteracy** *n* > **in'veterately** *adv*

invidious (ɪn'vɪdɪəs) *adj* 1 incurring or tending to arouse resentment, unpopularity, etc: *an invidious task* 2 (of comparisons or distinctions) unfairly or offensively discriminating [C17 from L *invidiōsus* full of envy, from *invidia* ENVY] > **in'vidiously** *adv* > **in'vidiousness** *n*

invigilate (ɪn'vɪdʒɪˌleɪt) *vb* **invigilates, invigilating, invigilated** (*intr*) 1 *Brit* to watch examination candidates, esp to prevent cheating. US word: **proctor** 2 *arch* to keep watch [C16 from L *invigilāre* to watch over; see VIGIL] > **inˌvigi'lation** *n* > **in'vigiˌlator** *n*

invigorate (ɪn'vɪgəˌreɪt) *vb* **invigorates, invigorating, invigorated** (*tr*) to give vitality and vigour to; animate; brace; refresh: *to be invigorated by fresh air* [C17 from IN-² + L *vigor* VIGOUR] > **in'vigorˌating** *adj* > **inˌvigor'ation** *n* > **in'vigorative** *adj* > **in'vigorˌator** *n*

invincible (ɪn'vɪnsəbᵊl) *adj* incapable of being defeated; unconquerable [C15 from LL *invincibilis*, from L IN-¹ + *vincere* to conquer] > **inˌvinci'bility** *or* **in'vincibleness** *n* > **in'vincibly** *adv*

inviolable (ɪn'vaɪələbᵊl) *adj* that must not or cannot be transgressed, dishonoured, or broken; to be kept sacred: *an inviolable oath* > **inˌviola'bility** *n* > **in'violably** *adv*

inviolate (ɪn'vaɪəlɪt, -ˌleɪt) *adj* 1 free from violation, injury, disturbance, etc 2 a less common word for **inviolable** > **in'violacy** *or* **in'violateness** *n* > **in'violately** *adv*

invisible (ɪn'vɪzəbᵊl) *adj* 1 not visible; not able to be perceived by the eye: *invisible rays* 2 concealed from sight; hidden 3 not easily seen or noticed: *invisible mending* 4 kept hidden from public view; secret 5 *econ* of or relating to services, such as insurance and freight, rather than goods: *invisible earnings* ▷ *n* 6 *econ* an invisible item of trade; service > **inˌvisi'bility** *or* **in'visibleness** *n* > **in'visibly** *adv*

invitation (ˌɪnvɪ'teɪʃən) *n* **1a** the act of inviting, such as an offer of entertainment or hospitality **1b** (*as modifier*): *an invitation race* 2 the act of enticing or attracting; allurement

invite *vb* (ɪn'vaɪt), **invites, inviting, invited** (*tr*) 1 to ask (a person) in a friendly or polite way (to do something, attend an event, etc) 2 to make a request for, esp publicly or formally: *to invite applications* 3 to bring on or provoke; give occasion for: *you invite disaster by your actions* 4 to welcome or tempt ▷ *n* ('ɪnvaɪt) 5 *inf* an invitation [C16 from L *invītāre* to invite, entertain] > **in'viter** *n*

inviting (ɪn'vaɪtɪŋ) *adj* tempting; alluring; attractive > **in'vitingness** *n*

in vitro (ɪn 'viːtrəʊ) *adv, adj* (of biological processes or reactions) made to occur outside the living organism in an artificial environment, such as a culture medium [NL, lit.: in glass]

in vitro fertilization *n* a technique enabling some women who are unable to conceive to bear children. Egg cells removed from a woman's ovary are fertilized by sperm in vitro; some of the resulting fertilized egg cells are then implanted into her uterus. Abbrev: **IVF**

in vivo (ɪn 'viːvəʊ) *adv, adj* (of biological processes or experiments) occurring or carried out in the living organism [NL, lit.: in a living (thing)]

invocation (ˌɪnvə'keɪʃən) *n* 1 the act of invoking or calling upon some agent for assistance 2 a prayer asking God for help, forgiveness, etc 3 an appeal for inspiration from a Muse or deity at the beginning of a poem **4a** the act of summoning a spirit from another world by ritual incantation or magic **4b** the incantation used in this act > **ˌinvo'cational** *adj* > **invocatory** (ɪn'vɒkətərɪ, -trɪ) *adj*

invoice ('ɪnvɔɪs) *n* 1 a document issued by a seller to a buyer listing the goods or services supplied and stating the sum of money due 2 *rare* a consignment of invoiced merchandise ▷ *vb* **invoices, invoicing, invoiced** 3 (*tr*) **3a** to present (a customer, etc) with an invoice **3b** to list (merchandise sold) on an invoice [C16 from earlier *invoyes*, from OF *envois*, pl. of *envoi* message; see ENVOY¹]

invoke (ɪn'vəʊk) *vb* **invokes, invoking, invoked** (*tr*) 1 to call upon (an agent, esp God or another deity) for help, inspiration, etc 2 to put (a law, penalty, etc) into use: *the union invoked the dispute procedure* 3 to appeal to (an outside authority) for confirmation, corroboration, etc 4 to implore or beg (help, etc) 5 to summon (a spirit, etc); conjure up [C15 from L *invocāre* to appeal to, from *vocāre* to call] > **in'vocable** *adj* > **in'voker** *n*

> **USAGE** *Invoke* is sometimes wrongly used where *evoke* is meant: *this proposal evoked* (not *invoked*) *a strong reaction*

involucre ('ɪnvəˌluːkə) *or* **involucrum** (ˌɪnvə'luːkrəm) *n, pl* **involucres** *or* **involucra** (-krə) a ring of bracts at the base of an inflorescence [C16 (in the sense: envelope): from NL *involucrum*, from L: wrapper, from *involvere* to wrap] > **ˌinvo'lucral** *adj* > **ˌinvo'lucrate** *adj*

involuntary (ɪn'vɒləntərɪ, -trɪ) *adj* 1 carried out without one's conscious wishes; not voluntary; unintentional 2 *physiol* (esp of a movement or muscle) performed or acting without conscious control: *involuntary spasms*

> **in'voluntarily** *adv* > **in'voluntariness** *n*

involute *adj* ('ɪnvə,luːt), *also* **involuted 1** complex, intricate, or involved **2** *bot* (esp of petals, leaves, etc, in bud) having margins that are rolled inwards **3** (of certain shells) closely coiled so that the axis is obscured ▷ *n* ('ɪnvə,luːt) **4** *geom* the curve described by the free end of a thread as it is wound around another curve, the **evolute**, such that its normals are tangential to the evolute ▷ *vb* (,ɪnvə'luːt), **involutes, involuting, involuted 5** (*intr*) to become involute [C17 from L *involūtus*, from *involvere*; see INVOLVE] > **'invo,lutely** *adv* > **,invo'lutedly** *adv*

involution (,ɪnvə'luːʃən) *n* **1** the act of involving or complicating or the state of being involved or complicated **2** something involved or complicated **3** *zool* degeneration or structural deformation **4** *biol* an involute formation or structure **5** *physiol* reduction in size of an organ or part, as of the uterus following childbirth or as a result of ageing **6** an algebraic operation in which a number, expression, etc, is raised to a specified power > **,invo'lutional** *adj*

involve (ɪn'vɒlv) *vb* **involves, involving, involved** (*tr*) **1** to include or contain as a necessary part **2** to have an effect on; spread to: *the investigation involved many innocent people* **3** (*often passive; usually foll by* in *or* with) to concern or associate significantly: *many people were involved in the crime* **4** (*often passive*) to make complicated; tangle **5** *rare, often poetic* to wrap or surround **6** *maths, obs* to raise to a specified power [C14 from L *involvere* to surround, from IN-[2] + *volvere* to roll] > **in'volvement** *n* > **in'volver** *n*

invulnerable (ɪn'vʌlnərəbəl, -'vʌlnrəbəl) *adj* **1** incapable of being wounded, hurt, damaged, etc **2** incapable of being damaged or captured: *an invulnerable fortress* > **in,vulnera'bility** *or* **in'vulnerableness** *n* > **in'vulnerably** *adv*

inward ('ɪnwəd) *adj* **1** going or directed towards the middle of or into something **2** situated within; inside **3** of, relating to, or existing in the mind or spirit: *inward meditation* **4** of one's own country or a specific country: *inward investment* ▷ *adv* **5** a variant of **inwards** ▷ *n* **6** the inward part; inside > **'inwardness** *n*

inwardly ('ɪnwədlɪ) *adv* **1** within the private thoughts or feelings; secretly **2** not aloud: *to laugh inwardly* **3** with reference to the inside or inner part; internally

inwards *adv* ('ɪnwədz), *also* **inward 1** towards the interior or middle of something **2** in, into, or towards the mind or spirit ▷ *pl n* ('ɪnədz) **3** a variant of **innards** (sense 1)

inweave (ɪn'wiːv) *vb* **inweaves, inweaving, inwove** *or* **inweaved; inwoven** *or* **inweaved** (*tr*) to weave together into or as if into a design, fabric, etc

inwrap (ɪn'ræp) *vb* **inwraps, inwrapping, inwrapped** a less common spelling of **enwrap**

inwrought (,ɪn'rɔːt) *adj* **1** worked or woven into material, esp decoratively **2** *rare* blended with other things

in-your-face *adj sl* aggressive and confrontational: *provocative in-your-face activism*

Io[1] ('aɪəʊ) *n Greek myth* a maiden loved by Zeus and turned into a white heifer by either Zeus or Hera

Io[2] *the chemical symbol for* ionium

Ioánnina (*Greek* jɔ'anina) *or* **Yanina** *n* a city in NW Greece: belonged to the Serbs (1349–1430) and then the Turks (until 1913); seat of Ali Pasha, the "Lion of Janina", from 1788 to 1822. Pop: 56 496 (1991 est). Serbian name: **Janina**

IOC *abbrev for* International Olympic Committee

iodic (aɪ'ɒdɪk) *adj* of or containing iodine, esp in the pentavalent state

iodide ('aɪə,daɪd) *n* **1** a salt of hydriodic acid, containing the iodide ion, I^- **2** a compound containing an iodine atom, such as methyl iodide (iodomethane)

iodine ('aɪə,diːn) *n* a bluish-black element of the halogen group that sublimates into a violet irritating gas. Its compounds are used in medicine and photography and in dyes. The radioisotope **iodine-131** is used in the treatment of thyroid disease. Symbol: I; atomic no.: 53; atomic wt.: 126.90 [C19 from F *iode*, from Gk *iōdēs* rust-coloured, but mistaken as violet-coloured, from *ion* violet]

iodize *or* **iodise** ('aɪə,daɪz) *vb* **iodizes, iodizing, iodized** *or* **iodises, iodising, iodised** (*tr*) to treat or react with iodine or an iodine compound. Also: **iodate** > **,iodi'zation** *or* **,iodi'sation** *n* > **'io,dizer** *or* **'io,diser** *n*

iodoform (aɪ'ɒdə,fɔːm) *n* a yellow crystalline solid made by heating alcohol with iodine and an alkali: used as an antiseptic. Formula: CHI_3. Systematic name: **triiodomethane**

iodopsin (,aɪə'dɒpsɪn) *n* a violet light-sensitive pigment in the cones of the retina of the eye that is responsible for colour vision. See also **rhodopsin**

IOM *abbrev for* Isle of Man

ion ('aɪən, -ɒn) *n* an electrically charged atom or group of atoms formed by the loss or gain of one or more electrons. See also **cation, anion** [C19 from Gk, lit.: going, from *ienai* to go]

-ion *suffix forming nouns* indicating an action, process, or state: *creation; objection* ▷ Cf **-ation, -tion** [from L *-iōn-*, *-io*]

Iona (aɪ'əʊnə) *n* an island off the W coast of Scotland, in the Inner Hebrides: site of St Columba's monastery (founded in 563) and an important early centre of Christianity. Area: 854 ha (2112 acres)

Ionesco (,iːə'nɛskəʊ; *French* jɔnɛsko) *n* **Eugène** (øʒɛn) 1912–94, French dramatist, born in Romania; a leading exponent of the theatre of the absurd. His plays include *The Bald Prima Donna* (1950) and *Rhinoceros* (1960)

ion exchange *n* the process in which ions are exchanged between a solution and an insoluble solid, usually a resin. It is used to soften water

Ionia (aɪ'əʊnɪə) *n* an ancient region of W central Asia Minor, including adjacent Aegean islands: colonized by Greeks in about 1100 BC > **I'onian** *adj, n*

Ionian Islands *pl n* a group of Greek islands in the Ionian Sea, consisting of Corfu, Cephalonia, Zante, Levkas, Ithaca, Cythera, and Paxos: ceded to Greece in 1864. Pop: 214 274 (2001). Area: 2307 sq km (891 sq miles)

Ionian Sea *n* the part of the Mediterranean Sea between SE Italy, E Sicily, and Greece

ionic (aɪ'ɒnɪk) *adj* of, relating to, or occurring in the form of ions

Ionic (aɪ'ɒnɪk) *adj* **1** of, denoting, or relating to one of the five classical orders of architecture, characterized by fluted columns and capitals with scroll-like ornaments **2** of or relating to Ionia, on the coast of Asia Minor, its inhabitants or their dialect of Ancient Greek ▷ *n* **3** one of four chief dialects of Ancient Greek; the dialect spoken in Ionia

▷ www.hellenism.net/eng/arts.htm

ionium (aɪ'əʊnɪəm) *n obs* a naturally occurring radioisotope of thorium with a mass number of 230. Symbol: Io [C20 from NL]

ionization *or* **ionisation** (,aɪənaɪ'zeɪʃən) *n* **a** the formation of ions as a result of a chemical reaction, high temperature, electrical discharge, or radiation **b** (*as modifier*): *ionization temperature*

ionize *or* **ionise** ('aɪə,naɪz) *vb* **ionizes, ionizing, ionized** *or* **ionises, ionising, ionised** to change or become changed into ions > **'ion,izable** *or* **'ion,isable** *adj* > **'ion,izer** *or* **'ion,iser** *n*

ionosphere (aɪ'ɒnə,sfɪə) *n* a region of the earth's atmosphere, extending from about 60 to 1000 km above the earth's surface, in which there is a high concentration of free electrons formed as a result of ionizing radiation entering the atmosphere from space > **ionospheric** (aɪ,ɒnə'sfɛrɪk) *adj*

iota (aɪ'əʊtə) *n* **1** the ninth letter in the Greek alphabet (Ι, ι), a vowel or semivowel **2** (*usually used with a negative*) a very small amount; jot (esp in **not one** *or* **an iota**) [c16 via L from Gk, of Semitic origin]

IOU *n* a written promise or reminder to pay a debt [c17 representing *I owe you*]

-ious *suffix forming adjectives from nouns* characterized by or full of: *suspicious* [from L *-ius* & *-iōsus* full of]

IOW *abbrev for* Isle of Wight

Iowa (ˈaɪəʊə) *n* a state of the N central US, in the Midwest: consists of rolling plains crossed by many rivers, with the Missouri forming the western border and the Mississippi the eastern. Capital: Des Moines. Pop: 2 926 324 (2000). Area: 144 887 sq km (55 941 sq miles). Abbreviations: **Ia** or (with zip code) **IA**

IPA *abbrev for* International Phonetic Alphabet

IP address *n computing* Internet protocol address: the numeric code that identifies all computers that are connected to the Internet

ipecacuanha (ˌɪpɪˌkækjʊˈænə) *or* **ipecac** (ˈɪpɪˌkæk) *n* **1** a low-growing South American shrub **2** a drug prepared from the dried roots of this plant, used as a purgative and emetic [c18 from Port., from Amerind *ipekaaguéne*, from *ipeh* low + *kaa* leaves + *guéne* vomit]

Iphigenia (ˌɪfɪdʒɪˈnaɪə) *n Greek myth* the daughter of Agamemnon, taken by him to be sacrificed to Artemis, who saved her life and made her a priestess

I-pin (ɪˈpɪn) *n* a variant transliteration of the Chinese name for **Yibin**

IPO *stock exchange abbrev for* initial public offering

IPOC *abbrev for* independent publicly owned company

Ipoh (ˈiːpəʊ) *n* a city in Malaysia, capital of Perak state: tin-mining centre. Pop: 382 633 (1991)

ipomoea (ˌɪpəˈmɪə, ˌaɪ-) *n* **1** any tropical or subtropical plant, such as the morning-glory, sweet potato, and jalap, having trumpet-shaped flowers **2** the dried root of a Mexican species which yields a cathartic resin [c18 NL, from Gk *ips* worm + *homoios* like]

ippon (ˈɪpɒn) *n judo & karate* a winning point awarded in a sparring competition for a perfectly executed technique [c20 Japanese, lit.: one point]

Ipsambul (ˌɪpsæmˈbuːl) *n* another name for **Abu Simbel**

ipse dixit *Latin* (ˈɪpseɪ ˈdɪksɪt) *n* an arbitrary and unsupported assertion [c16, lit.: he himself said it]

ipso facto (ˈɪpsəʊ ˈfæktəʊ) *adv* by that very fact or act [from L]

Ipsus (ˈɪpsəs) *n* an ancient town in Asia Minor, in S Phrygia: site of a decisive battle (301 BC) in the Wars of the Diadochi in which Lysimachus and Seleucus defeated Antigonus and Demetrius

Ipswich (ˈɪpswɪtʃ) *n* a town in E England, administrative centre of Suffolk, a port at the head of the Orwell estuary: financial services, telecommunications. Pop: 130 157 (1991)

IQ *abbrev for* intelligence quotient

Iqaluit (ɪˈkælʊɪt) *n* a town in N Canada, capital of Nunavut. Pop: 3700 (1999 est). Former name: **Frobisher Bay**

Iqbal (ˈɪkbal) *n* Sir **Muhammad** (mʊˈhæməd) 1875–1938, Indian Muslim poet, philosopher, and political leader, who advocated the establishment of separate nations for Indian Hindus and Muslims and is generally regarded as the originator of Pakistan

Iquique (*Spanish* iˈkike) *n* a port in N Chile: oil refineries. Pop: 159 815 (1999 est)

Iquitos (*Spanish* iˈkitɔs) *n* an inland port in NE Peru, on the Amazon 3703 km (2300 miles) from the Atlantic: head of navigation for large steamers. Pop: 334 613 (1998 est)

Ir *the chemical symbol for* iridium

Ir. *abbrev for*: **1** Ireland **2** Irish

ir- *prefix* a variant of **in-**[1] and **in-**[2] before *r*

IRA *abbrev for* Irish Republican Army

irade (ɪˈrɑːdɛ) *n* a written edict of a Muslim ruler [c19 from Turkish: will, from Ar. *irādah*]

Iráklion (*Greek* iˈrakliɔn) *n* a port in Greece, in N Crete: former capital of Crete (until 1841); ruled by Venetians (13th–17th centuries). Pop: 117 167 (1991). Italian name: **Candia** Also called: **Heraklion, Herakleion**

Iran (ɪˈrɑːn) *n* a republic in SW Asia, between the Caspian Sea and the Persian Gulf: consists chiefly of a high central desert plateau almost completely surrounded by mountains, a semitropical fertile region along the Caspian coast, and a hot and dry area beside the Persian Gulf. Oil is the most important export. Official language: Farsi (Persian). Official religion: Muslim majority. Currency: rial. Capital: Tehran. Pop: 63 442 000 (2001 est). Area: 1 647 050 sq km (635 932 sq miles). Former name (until 1935): **Persia** Official name: **Islamic Republic of Iran** See also **Persian Empire**

▹ www.president.ir

▹ www.itto.org

Iranian (ɪˈreɪnɪən) *n* **1** a native or inhabitant of Iran **2** a branch of the Indo-European family of languages, including Persian **3** the modern Persian language ▹ *adj* **4** relating to or characteristic of Iran, its inhabitants, or their language; Persian **5** belonging to or relating to the Iranian branch of Indo-European

Iran-Iraq War *n* the indecisive war (1980–88) fought by Iran and Iraq, following the Iraqi invasion of disputed border territory in Iran. Also called: **Gulf War**

▹ www.wikipedia.org/wiki/Iran-Iraq_War

▹ http://users.erols.com/mwhite28/iraniraq.htm

Iraq (ɪˈrɑːk) *n* a republic in SW Asia, on the Persian Gulf: coextensive with ancient Mesopotamia; became a British mandate in 1920, independent in 1932, and a republic in 1958. The Iraqi invasion of Kuwait (1990) led to their defeat in the first Gulf War (1991) by US-led UN forces. Iraq's refusal to destroy their weapons of mass destruction resulted in defeat in the second Gulf War (2003) by a coalition of US and UK forces. Iraq consists chiefly of the mountains of Kurdistan in the northeast, part of the Syrian Desert, and the lower basin of the Rivers Tigris and Euphrates. Oil is the major export. Official language: Arabic; Kurdish is official in the Kurdish Autonomous Region only. Official religion: Muslim. Currency: dinar. Capital: Baghdad. Pop: 23 332 000 (2001 est). Area: 438 446 sq km (169 284 sq miles) > **Iˈraqui** (ɪˈrɑːkɪ) *adj, n*

▹ www.iraq.net

irascible (ɪˈræsɪbᵊl) *adj* **1** easily angered; irritable **2** showing irritability: *an irascible action* [c16 from LL *īrascibilis*, from L *īra* anger] > **iˌrasciˈbility** *or* **iˈrascibleness** *n* > **iˈrascibly** *adv*

irate (aɪˈreɪt) *adj* **1** incensed with anger; furious **2** marked by extreme anger: *an irate letter* [c19 from L *īrātus* enraged, from *īrascī* to be angry] > **iˈrately** *adv*

Irbid (ˈɪrbɪd) *n* a town in NW Jordan. Pop: 208 201 (1994)

Irbil (ˈɪəbɪl) *n* a variant of **Erbil**

IRBM *abbrev for* intermediate-range ballistic missile

IRC *abbrev for*: **1** International Red Cross **2** International Red Crescent

IRD (in New Zealand) *abbrev for* Inland Revenue Department

ire (ˈaɪə) *n literary* anger; wrath [c13 from OF, from L *īra*] > **ˈireful** *adj* > **ˈirefulness** *n*

Ire. *abbrev for* Ireland

Ireland[1] (ˈaɪələnd) *n* **1** an island off NW Europe: part of the British Isles, separated from Britain by the North Channel, the Irish Sea, and St George's Channel; contains large areas of peat bog, with mountains that rise over 900 m (3000 ft) in the southwest and several large lakes. It was conquered by England in the 16th and early 17th centuries and ruled as a dependency until 1801, when it was united with Great Britain until its division in 1921 into the Irish Free State and Northern Ireland. Latin name: **Hibernia** **2** **Republic of Ireland** Also called: **Irish Republic, Southern Ireland** a republic in NW

Europe occupying most of Ireland: established as the Irish Free State (a British dominion) in 1921 and declared a republic in 1949; joined the European Community (now the European Union) in 1973. Official languages: Irish (Gaelic) and English. Currency: euro. Capital: Dublin. Pop: 3 823 000 (2001 est). Area: 70 285 sq km (27 137 sq miles). Gaelic name: **Eire** ▹ See also **Northern Ireland**
▹ www.irlgov.ie
▹ www.ireland.travel.ie

Ireland² ('aɪələnd) *n* **John** (**Nicholson**) 1879–1962, English composer, esp of songs

irenic, eirenic (aɪ'riːnɪk, -'rɛn-) *or* **irenical, eirenical** *adj* tending to conciliate or promote peace [c19 from Gk *eirēnikos*, from *eirēnē* peace] > **i'renically** *or* **ei'renically** *adv*

Ireton ('aɪətᵊn) *n* **Henry** 1611–51, English Parliamentarian general in the Civil War; son-in-law of Oliver Cromwell. His plan for a constitutional monarchy was rejected by Charles I (1647), whose death warrant he signed; lord deputy of Ireland (1650–51)

Irian Barat ('ɪərɪən 'bærɑːt) *n* the former Indonesian name for **Irian Jaya**

Irian Jaya *n* the W part of the island of New Guinea: formerly under Dutch rule, becoming a province of Indonesia in 1963. Capital: Jayapura. Pop: 2 165 300 (1999 est). Area: 416 990 sq km (161 000 sq miles). Former names (until 1963): **Dutch New Guinea, Netherlands New Guinea**. English name: **West Irian**

iridaceous (ˌɪrɪ'deɪʃəs, ˌaɪ-) *adj* of, relating to, or belonging to the family of monocotyledonous plants, including the iris, having swordlike leaves and showy flowers

iridescent (ˌɪrɪ'dɛsᵊnt) *adj* displaying a spectrum of colours that shimmer and change due to interference and scattering as the observer's position changes [c18 from L *irid-* iris + -ESCENT] > ˌ**iri'descence** *n* > ˌ**iri'descently** *adv*

iridium (aɪ'rɪdɪəm, ɪ'rɪd-) *n* a very hard yellowish-white transition element that is the most corrosion-resistant metal known. It occurs in platinum ores and is used as an alloy with platinum. Symbol: Ir; atomic no.: 77; atomic wt.: 192.2 [c19 NL, from L *irid-* iris + -IUM; from its colourful appearance when dissolving in certain acids]

iris ('aɪrɪs) *n, pl* **irises** *or* **irides** ('aɪrɪˌdiːz, 'ɪrɪ-) **1** the coloured muscular diaphragm that surrounds and controls the size of the pupil of the eye **2** Also called: **fleur-de-lys** any iridaceous plant having brightly coloured flowers composed of three petals and three drooping sepals **3** a poetic word for **rainbow** **4** short for **iris diaphragm** [c14 from L: rainbow, iris (flower), crystal, from Gk]

Iris ('aɪrɪs) *n* the goddess of the rainbow along which she travelled to earth as a messenger of the gods

iris diaphragm *n* an adjustable diaphragm that regulates the amount of light entering an optical instrument, esp a camera

Irish ('aɪrɪʃ) *adj* **1** of, relating to, or characteristic of Ireland, its people, their Celtic language, or their dialect of English **2** *inf offens* ludicrous or illogical ▹ *n* **3** **the Irish** (*functioning as pl*) the natives or inhabitants of Ireland **4** another name for **Irish Gaelic** **5** the dialect of English spoken in Ireland

Irish coffee *n* hot coffee mixed with Irish whiskey and topped with double cream

Irish Free State *n* a former name for the (Republic of) **Ireland** (1921–37)

Irish Gaelic *n* the Goidelic language of the Celts of Ireland, now spoken mainly along the west coast; an official language of the Republic of Ireland since 1921

Irishman ('aɪrɪʃmən) *or* (*fem*) **Irishwoman** *n, pl* **Irishmen** *or* **Irishwomen** a native or inhabitant of Ireland

Irish pipes *pl n* another name for **uillean pipes**

Irish Republic *n* See **Ireland¹** (sense 2)

Irish Republican Army *n* a militant organization of Irish nationalists founded with the aim of striving for a united independent Ireland by means of guerrilla warfare. Abbrev: **IRA**

Irish Sea *n* an arm of the North Atlantic Ocean between Great Britain and Ireland

Irish stew *n* a stew made of mutton, lamb, or beef, with potatoes, onions, etc

Irish wolfhound *n* a very large breed of hound with a rough thick coat

iritis (aɪ'raɪtɪs) *n* inflammation of the iris of the eye > **iritic** (aɪ'rɪtɪk) *adj*

irk (ɜːk) *vb* (*tr*) to irritate, vex, or annoy [c13 *irken* to grow weary]

irksome ('ɜːksəm) *adj* causing vexation, annoyance, or boredom; troublesome or tedious > **'irksomely** *adv* > **'irksomeness** *n*

Irkutsk (*Russian* ir'kutsk) *n* a city in S Russia; situated on the Trans-Siberian railway; university (1918); one of the largest industrial centres in Siberia, esp for heavy engineering. Pop: 596 400 (1999 est)

IRO *abbrev for*: **1** (in Britain) Inland Revenue Office **2** International Refugee Organization

iron ('aɪən) *n* **1a** a malleable ductile silvery-white ferromagnetic metallic element. It is widely used for structural and engineering purposes. Symbol: Fe; atomic no.: 26; atomic wt.: 55.847. Related adjs: **ferric, ferrous**. Related prefix: **ferro-** **1b** (*as modifier*): *iron railings* **2** any of certain tools or implements made of iron or steel, esp for use when hot: *a grappling iron; a soldering iron* **3** an appliance for pressing fabrics using dry heat or steam, esp a small electrically heated device with a handle and a weighted flat bottom **4** any of various golf clubs with metal heads, numbered from 1 to 10 according to the slant of the face **5** a splintlike support for a malformed leg **6** great hardness, strength, or resolve: *a will of iron* **7** **strike while the iron is hot** to act at an opportune moment ▹ *adj* **8** very hard, immovable, or implacable: *iron determination* **9** very strong; extremely robust: *an iron constitution* **10** cruel or unyielding: *he ruled with an iron hand* ▹ *vb* **11** to smooth (clothes or fabric) by removing (creases or wrinkles) using a heated iron; press **12** (*tr*) to furnish or clothe with iron **13** (*tr*) *rare* to place (a prisoner) in irons ▹ See also **iron out, irons** [OE *īrēn*] > **'ironer** *n* > **'ironless** *adj* > **'iron,like** *adj*

Ii

Iron Age *n* **a** the period following the Bronze Age characterized by the extremely rapid spread of iron tools and weapons **b** (*as modifier*): *an Iron-Age weapon*

ironbark ('aɪənˌbɑːk) *n* any of several Australian eucalyptus trees that have hard rough bark

ironbound ('aɪənˌbaʊnd) *adj* **1** bound with iron **2** unyielding; inflexible **3** (of a coast) rocky; rugged

Iron Chancellor *n* **the** nickname of (Prince Otto Eduard Leopold von) **Bismarck**

ironclad *adj* (ˌaɪən'klæd) **1** covered or protected with iron: *an ironclad warship* **2** inflexible; rigid: *an ironclad rule* ▹ *n* ('aɪənˌklæd) **3** a large wooden 19th-century warship with armoured plating

Iron Curtain *n* **1** (formerly) **1a** the guarded border between the countries of the Soviet bloc and the rest of Europe **1b** (*as modifier*): *Iron Curtain countries* **2** (*sometimes not caps*) any barrier that separates communities or ideologies

Iron Gate *or* **Iron Gates** *n* a gorge of the River Danube on the border between Romania and Serbia and Montenegro. Length: 3 km (2 miles). Romanian name: **Porţile de Fier**

iron hand *n* harsh or rigorous control; overbearing or autocratic force

iron horse *n arch* a steam-driven railway locomotive

ironic (aɪ'rɒnɪk) *or* **ironical** *adj* of, characterized by, or using irony > **i'ronically** *adv* > **i'ronicalness** *n*

ironing ('aɪənɪŋ) *n* 1 the act of ironing washed clothes 2 clothes, etc, that are to be or that have been ironed
ironing board *n* a board, usually on legs, with a suitable covering on which to iron clothes
iron lung *n* an airtight metal cylinder enclosing the entire body up to the neck and providing artificial respiration
iron maiden *n* a medieval instrument of torture, consisting of a hinged case (often shaped in the form of a woman) lined with iron spikes, which was forcibly closed on the victim
iron man *n Austral* 1 an event at a surf carnival in which contestants compete at swimming, surfing, running, etc 2 a participant in such an event
ironmaster ('aɪən,mɑːstə) *n Brit* a manufacturer of iron
ironmonger ('aɪən,mʌŋɡə) *n Brit* a dealer in metal utensils, hardware, locks, etc. US and Canad equivalent: **hardware dealer** > **'iron,mongery** *n*
iron out *vb (tr, adv)* 1 to smooth, using a heated iron 2 to put right or settle (a problem or difficulty) as a result of negotiations or discussions 3 *Austral inf* to knock unconscious
iron pyrites ('paɪraɪts) *n* another name for **pyrite**
iron rations *pl n* emergency food supplies, esp for military personnel in action
irons ('aɪənz) *pl n* 1 fetters or chains (often in **in** *or* **into irons**) 2 **have several irons in the fire** to be involved in many projects, etc
Ironside ('aɪən,saɪd) *n* nickname of **Edmund II** of England
ironsides ('aɪən,saɪdz) *n* 1 a person with great stamina or resistance 2 an ironclad ship 3 *(often cap)* (in the English Civil War) 3a the cavalry regiment trained and commanded by Oliver Cromwell 3b Cromwell's entire army
ironstone ('aɪən,stəʊn) *n* 1 any rock consisting mainly of an iron-bearing ore 2 a tough durable earthenware
ironware ('aɪən,wɛə) *n* domestic articles made of iron
ironwood ('aɪən,wʊd) *n* 1 any of various trees, such as hornbeam, that have very hard wood 2 a Californian rosaceous tree with very hard wood 3 any of various other trees with hard wood, such as the mopani 4 the wood of any of these trees
ironwork ('aɪən,wɜːk) *n* 1 work done in iron, esp decorative work 2 the craft or practice of working in iron
ironworks ('aɪən,wɜːks) *n (sometimes functioning as sing)* a building in which iron is smelted, cast, or wrought
irony[1] ('aɪrənɪ) *n, pl* **ironies** 1 the humorous or mildly sarcastic use of words to imply the opposite of what they normally mean 2 an instance of this, used to draw attention to some incongruity or irrationality 3 incongruity between what is expected to be and what actually is, or a situation or result showing such incongruity 4 See **dramatic irony** 5 *philosophy* See **Socratic irony** [C16 from L, from Gk *eirōneia*, from *eirōn* dissembler, from *eirein* to speak]
irony[2] ('aɪənɪ) *adj* of, resembling, or containing iron
Iroquois ('ɪrə,kwɔɪ) *n* 1 *(pl* **Iroquois**) a member of a confederacy of North American Indian tribes formerly living in and around New York State 2 any of the languages of these people > **,Iro'quoian** *adj*
irradiance (ɪ'reɪdɪəns) *n* the radiant flux incident on unit area of a surface. Also: **irradiation** ▷ Cf **illuminance**
irradiate (ɪ'reɪdɪ,eɪt) *vb* **irradiates, irradiating, irradiated** 1 *(tr) physics* to subject to or treat with light or other electromagnetic radiation or with beams of particles 2 *(tr)* to expose (food) to electromagnetic radiation to kill bacteria and retard deterioration 3 *(tr)* to make clear or bright intellectually or spiritually; illumine 4 a less common word for **radiate** (sense 1) 5 *(intr) obs* to become radiant > **ir'radi,ation** *n* > **ir'radiative** *adj* > **ir'radi,ator** *n*
irrational (ɪ'ræʃən[ə]l) *adj* 1 inconsistent with reason or logic; illogical; absurd 2 incapable of reasoning 3a *maths* (of an equation, etc) containing one or more variables in irreducible radical form or raised to a fractional power: $\sqrt{(x^2+1)} = x^{5/3}$ 3b *(as n): an irrational* > **ir,ration'ality** *n* > **ir'rationally** *adv*
irrational number *n* any real number that cannot be expressed as the ratio of two integers, such as π
Irrawaddy (,ɪrə'wɒdɪ) *n* the main river in Myanmar, rising in the north in two headstreams and flowing south through the whole length of Myanmar, to enter the Andaman Sea by nine main mouths. Length: 2100 km (1300 miles)
irreclaimable (,ɪrɪ'kleɪməb[ə]l) *adj* not able to be reclaimed > **,irre,claima'bility** *or* **,irre'claimableness** *n* > **,irre'claimably** *adv*
irreconcilable (ɪ'rɛk[ə]n,saɪləb[ə]l, ɪ,rɛk[ə]n'saɪ-) *adj* 1 not able to be reconciled; uncompromisingly conflicting; incompatible ▷ *n* 2 a person or thing that is implacably hostile or uncompromisingly opposed 3 *(usually pl)* one of various principles, ideas, etc, that are incapable of being brought into agreement > **ir,recon,cila'bility** *or* **ir'recon,cilableness** *n* > **ir'recon,cilably** *adv*
irrecoverable (,ɪrɪ'kʌvərəb[ə]l, -'kʌvrə-) *adj* 1 not able to be recovered or regained 2 not able to be remedied or rectified > **,irre'coverableness** *n* > **,irre'coverably** *adv*
irrecusable (,ɪrɪ'kjuːzəb[ə]l) *adj* not able to be rejected or challenged, as evidence, etc
irredeemable (,ɪrɪ'diːməb[ə]l) *adj* 1 (of bonds, shares, etc) without a date of redemption of capital; incapable of being bought back directly or paid off 2 (of paper money) not convertible into specie 3 (of a loss) not able to be recovered; irretrievable 4 not able to be improved or rectified; irreparable > **,irre,deema'bility** *or* **,irre'deemableness** *n* > **,irre'deemably** *adv*
irredentist (,ɪrɪ'dɛntɪst) *n* 1 *(sometimes cap)* a person, esp a member of a 19th-century Italian association, who favours the acquisition of territory that was once part of his country or is considered to have been ▷ *adj* 2 of or relating to irredentists or their policies [C19 from It. *irredentista*, from *ir-* IN-[1] + *redento* redeemed, from L *redemptus* bought back; see REDEEM] > **,irre'dentism** *n*
irreducible (,ɪrɪ'djuːsɪb[ə]l) *adj* 1 not able to be reduced or lessened 2 not able to be brought to a simpler or reduced form 3 *maths* (of a polynomial) unable to be factorized into polynomials of lower degree, as (x^2+1) > **,irre,duci'bility** *n* > **,irre'ducibly** *adv*
irrefragable (ɪ'rɛfrəɡəb[ə]l) *adj* not able to be denied or refuted [C16 from LL *irrefrāgābilis*, from L *ir-* + *refrāgārī* to resist] > **ir,refraga'bility** *or* **ir'refragableness** *n* > **ir'refragably** *adv*
irrefrangible (,ɪrɪ'frændʒəb[ə]l) *adj* 1 not to be broken or transgressed; inviolable 2 *physics* incapable of being refracted > **,irre,frangi'bility** *or* **,irre'frangibleness** *n* > **,irre'frangibly** *adv*
irrefutable (ɪ'rɛfjʊtəb[ə]l, ,ɪrɪ'fjuːtəb[ə]l) *adj* impossible to deny or disprove; incontrovertible > **ir,refuta'bility** *n* > **ir'refutably** *adv*
irreg. *abbrev for* irregular(ly)
irregular (ɪ'rɛɡjʊlə) *adj* 1 lacking uniformity or symmetry; uneven in shape, position, arrangement, etc 2 not occurring at expected or equal intervals: *an irregular pulse* 3 differing from the normal or accepted practice or routine; unconventional 4 (of the formation, inflections, or derivations of a word) not following the usual pattern of formation in a language 5 of or relating to guerrillas or volunteers not belonging to regular forces: *irregular troops* 6 (of flowers) having any of their petals differing in size, shape, etc 7 *US* (of merchandise) not up to the manufacturer's standards or specifications; imperfect ▷ *n* 8 a soldier not in a regular army 9 *(often pl) US* imperfect or flawed merchandise > **ir,regu'larity** *n* > **ir'regularly** *adv*
irrelevant (ɪ'rɛləvənt) *adj* not relating or pertinent to

the matter at hand > **ir'relevance** *or* **ir'relevancy** *n* > **ir'relevantly** *adv*

irreligion (ˌɪrɪˈlɪdʒən) *n* **1** lack of religious faith **2** indifference or opposition to religion > **ˌirre'ligionist** *n* > **ˌirre'ligious** *adj* > **ˌirre'ligiously** *adv* > **ˌirre'ligiousness** *n*

irremediable (ˌɪrɪˈmiːdɪəbᵊl) *adj* not able to be remedied; incurable or irreparable > **ˌirre'mediableness** *n* > **ˌirre'mediably** *adv*

irremissible (ˌɪrɪˈmɪsəbᵊl) *adj* **1** unpardonable; inexcusable **2** that must be done, as through duty or obligation > **ˌirreˌmissi'bility** *or* **ˌirre'missibleness** *n* > **ˌirre'missibly** *adv*

irremovable (ˌɪrɪˈmuːvəbᵊl) *adj* not able to be removed > **ˌirreˌmova'bility** *n* > **ˌirre'movably** *adv*

irreparable (ɪˈrɛpərəbᵊl, ɪˈrɛprəbᵊl) *adj* not able to be repaired or remedied; beyond repair > **irˌrepara'bility** *or* **ir'reparableness** *n* > **ir'reparably** *adv*

irreplaceable (ˌɪrɪˈpleɪsəbᵊl) *adj* not able to be replaced: *an irreplaceable antique* > **ˌirre'placeably** *adv*

irrepressible (ˌɪrɪˈprɛsəbᵊl) *adj* not capable of being repressed, controlled, or restrained > **ˌirreˌpressi'bility** *or* **ˌirre'pressibleness** *n* > **ˌirre'pressibly** *adv*

irreproachable (ˌɪrɪˈprəʊtʃəbᵊl) *adj* not deserving reproach; blameless > **ˌirreˌproacha'bility** *or* **ˌirre'proachableness** *n* > **ˌirre'proachably** *adv*

irresistible (ˌɪrɪˈzɪstəbᵊl) *adj* **1** not able to be resisted or refused; overpowering: *an irresistible impulse* **2** very fascinating or alluring: *an irresistible woman* > **ˌirreˌsisti'bility** *or* **ˌirre'sistibleness** *n* > **ˌirre'sistibly** *adv*

irresolute (ɪˈrɛzəˌluːt) *adj* lacking resolution; wavering; hesitating > **ir'resoˌlutely** *adv* > **ir'resoˌluteness** *or* **irˌreso'lution** *n*

irrespective (ˌɪrɪˈspɛktɪv) *adj* **1 irrespective of** without taking account of; regardless of ▷ *adv* **2** *inf* regardless; without due consideration: *he carried on with his plan irrespective* > **ˌirre'spectively** *adv*

irresponsible (ˌɪrɪˈspɒnsəbᵊl) *adj* **1** not showing or done with due care for the consequences of one's actions or attitudes; reckless **2** not capable of bearing responsibility > **ˌirreˌsponsi'bility** *or* **ˌirre'sponsibleness** *n* > **ˌirre'sponsibly** *adv*

irresponsive (ˌɪrɪˈspɒnsɪv) *adj* not responsive > **ˌirre'sponsively** *adv* > **ˌirre'sponsiveness** *n*

irretrievable (ˌɪrɪˈtriːvəbᵊl) *adj* not able to be retrieved, recovered, or repaired > **ˌirreˌtrieva'bility** *n* > **ˌirre'trievably** *adv*

irreverence (ɪˈrɛvərəns, ɪˈrɛvrəns) *n* **1** lack of due respect or veneration; disrespect **2** a disrespectful remark or act > **ir'reverent** *or* **irˌreve'rential** *adj* > **ir'reverently** *adv*

irreversible (ˌɪrɪˈvɜːsəbᵊl) *adj* **1** not able to be reversed: *the irreversible flow of time* **2** not able to be revoked or repealed; irrevocable **3** *chem, physics* capable of changing or producing a change in one direction only: *an irreversible reaction* > **ˌirreˌversi'bility** *n* > **ˌirre'versibly** *adv*

irrevocable (ɪˈrɛvəkəbᵊl) *adj* not able to be revoked, changed, or undone > **irˌrevoca'bility** *or* **ir'revocableness** *n* > **ir'revocably** *adv*

irrigate (ˈɪrɪˌɡeɪt) *vb* **irrigates, irrigating, irrigated 1** to supply (land) with water by means of artificial canals, etc, esp to promote the growth of food crops **2** *med* to bathe or wash out (a bodily part, cavity, or wound) **3** *(tr)* to make fertile, fresh, or vital by or as if by watering [C17 from L *irrigāre*, from *rigāre* to moisten, conduct water] > **'irrigable** *adj* > **ˌirri'gation** *n* > **'irriˌgative** *adj* > **'irriˌgator** *n*

irritable (ˈɪrɪtəbᵊl) *adj* **1** quickly irritated; easily annoyed; peevish **2** (of all living organisms) capable of responding to such stimuli as heat, light, and touch **3** *pathol* abnormally sensitive > **ˌirrita'bility** *n* > **'irritableness** *n* > **'irritably** *adv*

irritable bowel syndrome *n med* a chronic condition of recurring abdominal pain with constipation or diarrhoea or both

irritant (ˈɪrɪtənt) *adj* **1** causing irritation; irritating ▷ *n* **2** something irritant > **'irritancy** *n*

irritate (ˈɪrɪˌteɪt) *vb* **irritates, irritating, irritated 1** to annoy or anger (someone) **2** *(tr) biol* to stimulate (an organism or part) to respond in a characteristic manner **3** *(tr) pathol* to cause (a bodily organ or part) to become excessively stimulated, resulting in inflammation, tenderness, etc [C16 from L *irrītāre* to provoke] > **'irriˌtator** *n*

irritation (ˌɪrɪˈteɪʃən) *n* **1** something that irritates **2** the act of irritating or the condition of being irritated > **'irriˌtative** *adj*

irrupt (ɪˈrʌpt) *vb (intr)* **1** to enter forcibly or suddenly **2** (of a plant or animal population) to enter a region suddenly and in very large numbers **3** (of a population) to increase suddenly and greatly [C19 from L *irrumpere* to rush into, invade, from *rumpere* to break, burst] > **ir'ruption** *n* > **ir'ruptive** *adj*

Irtysh *or* **Irtish** (ɪəˈtɪʃ) *n* a river in central Asia, rising in China in the Altai Mountains and flowing west through Kazakhstan, then northwest into Russia to join the Ob River as its chief tributary. Length: 4444 km (2760 miles)

Irvine[1] (ˈɜːvɪn) *n* a town on the W coast of Scotland, the administrative centre of North Ayrshire: designated a new town in 1966. Pop: 32 988 (1991)

Irvine[2] (ˈɜːvaɪn) *n* **Alexander Andrew Mackay,** Baron, known as *Derry*. born 1940, British lawyer and Labour politician; Lord Chancellor 1997–2003

Irving (ˈɜːvɪŋ) *n* **1** Sir **Henry** real name *John Henry Brodribb*. 1838–1905, English actor and manager of the Lyceum Theatre in London (1878–1902) **2 Washington** 1783–1859, US essayist and short-story writer, noted for *The Sketch Book of Geoffrey Crayon* (1820), which contains the stories *Rip Van Winkle* and *The Legend of Sleepy Hollow*

is (ɪz) *vb* (used with *he, she, it*, and with singular nouns) a form of the present tense (indicative mood) of **be** [OE]

Is. *abbrev for:* **1** Also: **Isa** *Bible* Isaiah **2** Island(s) *or* Isle(s)

is- *combining form* a variant of **iso-** before a vowel: *isentropic*

ISA (ˈaɪsə) *n acronym for* individual savings account: a tax-free savings scheme that was introduced in the UK in 1999

Isaac (ˈaɪzək) *n* an Old Testament patriarch, the son of Abraham and Sarah and father of Jacob and Esau (Genesis 17; 21–27)

Isabella (ˌɪzəˈbɛlə) *n* original name *Elizabeth Farnese*. 1692–1766, second wife (1714–46) of Philip V of Spain and mother of Charles III of Spain

Isabella I *n* known as *Isabella the Catholic*. 1451–1504, queen of Castile (1474–1504) and, with her husband, Ferdinand V, joint ruler of Castile and Aragon (1479–1504)

Isabella II *n* 1830–1904, queen of Spain (1833–68), whose accession precipitated the first Carlist war (1833–39). She was deposed in a revolution

Isabella of France *n* 1292–1358, wife (1308–27) of Edward II of England, whom, aided by her lover, Roger de Mortimer, she deposed; mother of Edward III

isagogics (ˌaɪsəˈɡɒdʒɪks) *n* introductory studies, esp in the history of the Bible [C19 from L, from Gk, from *eisagein* to introduce, from *eis-* into + *agein* to lead]

Isaiah (aɪˈzaɪə) *n Old Testament* **1** the first of the major Hebrew prophets, who lived in the 8th century BC **2** the book of his and others' prophecies

isallobar (aɪˈsæləˌbɑː) *n* a line on a map connecting places with equal pressure changes

Isar (ˈiːzɑː) *n* a river in central Europe, rising in W Austria and flowing generally northeast through S Germany into the Danube. Length: over 260 km (160 miles)

isatin (ˈaɪsətɪn) *or* **isatine** (ˈaɪsəˌtiːn) *n* a yellowish-red crystalline compound soluble in hot water, used for the preparation of vat dyes [C19 from L *isatis* woad + -IN] > **ˌisa'tinic** *adj*

Isauria (aɪ'sɔːrɪə) *n* an ancient district of S central Asia Minor, chiefly on the N slopes of the W Taurus Mountains > **I'saurian** *adj, n*

ISBN *abbrev for* International Standard Book Number ▹ www.isbn.org

Iscariot (ɪ'skærɪət) *n* See **Judas** (Iscariot)

ischaemia *or* **ischemia** (ɪ'skiːmɪə) *n pathol* an inadequate supply of blood to an organ or part, as from an obstructed blood flow [c19 from Gk *iskhein* to restrict, + -AEMIA] > **ischaemic** *or* **ischemic** (ɪ'skɛmɪk) *adj*

Ischia ('iːskjɑː, 'ɪskɪə) *n* a volcanic island in the Tyrrhenian Sea, at the N end of the Bay of Naples. Area: 47 sq km (18 sq miles)

ischium ('ɪskɪəm) *n, pl* **ischia** (-kɪə) one of the three sections of the hipbone, situated below the ilium [c17 from L: hip joint, from Gk *iskhion*] > **'ischial** *adj*

-ise *suffix forming verbs* a variant of **-ize**

USAGE See at **-ize**

isentropic (ˌaɪsɛn'trɒpɪk) *adj* having or taking place at constant entropy

Isère (*French* izɛr) *n* **1** a department of SE France, in Rhône-Alpes region. Capital: Grenoble. Pop: 1 094 006 (1999). Area: 7904 sq km (3083 sq miles) **2** a river in SE France, rising in the Graian Alps and flowing west and southwest to join the River Rhône near Valence. Length: 290 km (180 miles)

Iseult, Yseult (ɪ'suːlt), *or* **Isolde** (ɪ'zəʊldə) *n* (in Arthurian legend) **1** an Irish princess wed to Mark, king of Cornwall, but in love with his knight Tristan **2** (in another account) the daughter of the king of Brittany, married to Tristan

Isfahan (ˌɪsfə'hɑːn) *or* **Eşfahān** *n* a city in central Iran: the second largest city in the country; capital of Persia in the 11th century and from 1598 to 1722. Pop: 1 266 765 (1996). Ancient name: **Aspadana** (ˌæspə'dɑːnə)

-ish *suffix forming adjectives* **1** of or belonging to a nationality: *Scottish* **2** *often derog* having the manner or qualities of; resembling: *slavish; boyish* **3** somewhat; approximately: *yellowish; sevenish* **4** concerned or preoccupied with: *bookish* [OE -*isc*]

Isherwood ('ɪʃəˌwʊd) *n* **Christopher,** full name *Christopher William Bradshaw-Isherwood*. 1904–86, US novelist and dramatist, born in England. His works include the novel *Goodbye to Berlin* (1939) and three verse plays written in collaboration with WH Auden

Ishiguro (ˌɪʃɪ'gʊrəʊ) *n* **Kazuo** (kæt'zuːəʊ) born 1954, British novelist, born in Japan. His novels include *An Artist of the Floating World* (1986), the Booker-prizewinning *The Remains of the Day* (1989), and *When We Were Orphans* (2000)

Ishmael ('ɪʃmeɪəl) *n* **1** the son of Abraham and Hagar, Sarah's handmaid: the ancestor of 12 Arabian tribes (Genesis 21:8–21; 25:12–18) **2** a bandit chieftain, who defied the Babylonian conquerors of Judah and assassinated the governor appointed by Nebuchadnezzar (II Kings 25:25; Jeremiah 40:13–41:18) **3** *rare* an outcast

Ishtar ('ɪʃtɑː) *n* the principal goddess of the Babylonians and Assyrians; divinity of love, fertility, and war

Isidore of Seville ('ɪzɪdɔː) *n* **Saint,** Latin name *Isidorus Hispalensis*. ?560–636 AD, Spanish archbishop and scholar, noted for his *Etymologies*, an encyclopedia. Feast day: April 4

isinglass ('aɪzɪŋˌglɑːs) *n* a gelatine made from the air bladders of freshwater fish, used as a clarifying agent and adhesive [c16 from MDu. *huysenblase*, lit.: sturgeon bladder; infl. by E GLASS]

Isis[1] ('aɪsɪs) *n* the local name for the River Thames at Oxford

Isis[2] ('aɪsɪs) *n* an ancient Egyptian fertility goddess, usually depicted as a woman with a cow's horns, between which was the disc of the sun; wife and sister of Osiris

Iskenderun (ɪs'kɛndəˌruːn) *n* a port in S Turkey, on the **Gulf of Iskenderun.** Pop: 161 728 (1997). Former name: **Alexandretta**

Isl. *abbrev for:* **1** Island **2** Isle

Islam ('ɪzlɑːm) *n* **1** Also called: **Islamism** the religion of Muslims, teaching that there is only one God and that Mohammed is his prophet; Mohammedanism **2a** Muslims collectively and their civilization **2b** the countries where the Muslim religion is predominant [c19 from Ar.: surrender (to God), from *aslama* to surrender] > **Is'lamic** *adj*

▹ http://www.islamworld.net/

Islamabad (ɪz'lɑːməˌbɑːd) *n* the capital of Pakistan, in the north on the Potwar Plateau: site chosen in 1959; surrounded by the Capital Territory of Islamabad for 909 sq km (351 sq miles). Pop: 524 500 (1998)

Islamist ('ɪzləmɪst) *adj* **1** supporting or advocating Islamic fundamentalism ▹ *n* **2** a supporter or advocate of Islamic fundamentalism

Islamize *or* **Islamise** ('ɪzləˌmaɪz) *vb* **Islamizes, Islamizing, Islamized** *or* **Islamises, Islamising, Islamised** (*tr*) to convert or subject to the influence of Islam > **ˌIslami'zation** *or* **ˌIslami'sation** *n*

island ('aɪlənd) *n* **1** a mass of land that is surrounded by water and is smaller than a continent **2** something isolated, detached, or surrounded: *a traffic island* **3** *anat* a part, structure, or group of cells distinct in constitution from its immediate surroundings ▹ Related adj: **insular** ▹ *vb* (*tr*) *rare* **4** to cause to become an island **5** to intersperse with islands **6** to place on an island; insulate; isolate [OE *īgland*] > **'island-ˌlike** *adj*

islander ('aɪləndə) *n* **1** a native or inhabitant of an island **2** (*cap*) NZ a native or inhabitant of the Pacific Islands

Islands ('aɪləndz) *pl n* **the** NZ the islands of the South Pacific

Islands of the Blessed *pl n Greek myth* lands where the souls of heroes and good men were taken after death. Also called: **Hesperides**

island universe *n* a former name for **galaxy**

Islay ('aɪlə, 'aɪleɪ) *n* an island off the W coast of Scotland: the southernmost of the Inner Hebrides; separated from the island of Jura by the **Sound of Islay.** Pop: 3500 (latest est) Area: 606 sq km (234 sq miles)

isle (aɪl) *n poetic except when cap and part of place name* an island, esp a small one [c13 from OF, from L *insula* island]

Isle of Dogs *n* See (Isle of) **Dogs**

Isle of Man *n* See (Isle of) **Man**

Isle of Pines *n* the former name of the (Isle of) **Youth**

Isle of Sheppey *n* See (Isle of) **Sheppey**

Isle of Wight *n* See (Isle of) **Wight**

Isle of Youth *n* See (Isle of) **Youth**

Isle Royale ('rɔɪəl) *n* an island in the northeast US, in NW Lake Superior: forms, with over 100 surrounding islands, **Isle Royale National Park.** Area: 541 sq km (209 sq miles)

islet ('aɪlɪt) *n* a small island [c16 from OF *islette*; see ISLE]

islets *or* **islands of Langerhans** ('læŋəˌhæns) *pl n* small groups of endocrine cells in the pancreas that secrete insulin [c19 after Paul *Langerhans* (1847–88), G physician]

Islington ('ɪzlɪŋtən) *n* a borough of N Greater London. Pop: 175 787 (2001). Area: 16 sq km (6 sq miles)

ism ('ɪzəm) *n inf, often derog* an unspecified doctrine, system, or practice

-ism *suffix forming nouns* **1** indicating an action, process, or result: *criticism* **2** indicating a state or condition: *paganism* **3** indicating a doctrine, system, or body of principles and practices: *Leninism; spiritualism* **4** indicating behaviour or a characteristic quality: *heroism* **5** indicating a characteristic usage, esp of a language: *Scotticism* **6** indicating prejudice on the basis specified: *sexism; ageism* [from OF -*isme*, from L -*ismus*, from Gk -*ismos*]

Ismaili *or* **Isma'ili** (ˌɪzmɑː'iːlɪ) *n Islam* **1** a Shiah sect whose adherents believe that Ismail, son of the sixth imam, was the rightful seventh imam **2** a member of this sect

Ismailia (ˌɪzmaɪˈlɪə) *n* a city in NE Egypt, on the Suez Canal: founded in 1863 by the former Suez Canal Company; devastated by Israeli troops in the October War (1973). Pop: 254 477 (1996)

Ismail Pasha (ˌɪzmɑːˈiːl ˈpɑːʃə) *n* 1830–95, viceroy (1863–66) and khedive (1867–79) of Egypt, who brought his country close to bankruptcy. He was forced to submit to Anglo-French financial control (1876) and to abdicate (1879)

isn't (ˈɪzᵊnt) *contraction of* is not

ISO[1] (ˈaɪˈɛsˈəʊ) *n* International Organization for Standardization [from Gk *isos* equal; often wrongly thought to be an abbreviation for *International Standards Organization*]

▷ www.iso.ch

ISO[2] *abbrev for* Imperial Service Order (a Brit decoration)

iso- *or before a vowel* **is-** *combining form* **1** equal or identical: *isomagnetic* **2** indicating that a chemical compound is an isomer of a specified compound: *isobutane* [from Gk *isos* equal]

isobar (ˈaɪsəʊˌbɑː) *n* **1** a line on a map connecting places of equal atmospheric pressure, usually reduced to sea level for purposes of comparison, at a given time or period **2** *physics* any of two or more atoms that have the same mass number but different atomic numbers ▷ Cf **isotope** [c19 from Gk *isobarēs* of equal weight] > ˌ**isoˈbaric** *adj* > ˈ**isobarˌism** *n*

isobutene (ˌaɪsəʊˈbjuːtiːn) *n* a colourless gas used in the manufacture of synthetic rubber

isocheim *or* **isochime** (ˈaɪsəʊˌkaɪm) *n* a line on a map connecting places with the same mean winter temperature ▷ Cf **isothere** [c19 from ISO- + Gk *kheima* winter weather] > ˌ**isoˈcheimal** *or* ˌ**isoˈchimal** *adj*

isochronal (aɪˈsɒkrənᵊl) *or* **isochronous** *adj* **1** having the same duration; equal in time **2** occurring at equal time intervals; having a uniform period of vibration [c17 from NL, from Gk *isokhronos*, from ISO- + *khronos* time] > **iˈsochronally** *or* **iˈsochronously** *adv* > **iˈsochroˌnism** *n*

isoclinal (ˌaɪsəʊˈklaɪnᵊl) *or* **isoclinic** (ˌaɪsəʊˈklɪnɪk) *adj* **1** sloping in the same direction and at the same angle **2** *geol* (of folds) having limbs that are parallel to each other ▷ *n* **3** Also: **isocline, isoclinal line** an imaginary line connecting points on the earth's surface having equal angles of magnetic dip

isocline (ˈaɪsəʊˌklaɪn) *n* **1** a series of rock strata with isoclinal folds **2** another name for **isoclinal** (sense 3)

Isocrates (aɪˈsɒkrəˌtiːz) *n* 436–338 BC, Athenian rhetorician and teacher

isodynamic (ˌaɪsəʊdaɪˈnæmɪk) *adj physics* **1** having equal force or strength **2** of or relating to an imaginary line on the earth's surface connecting points of equal magnetic intensity

isogeotherm (ˌaɪsəʊˈdʒiːəʊˌθɜːm) *n* an imaginary line below the surface of the earth connecting points of equal temperature > ˌ**isoˌgeoˈthermal** *or* ˌ**isoˌgeoˈthermic** *adj*

isogloss (ˈaɪsəʊˌglɒs) *n* a line drawn on a map around the area in which a linguistic feature is to be found > ˌ**isoˈglossal** *or* ˌ**isoˈglottic** *adj*

isogonic (ˌaɪsəʊˈgɒnɪk) *or* **isogonal** (aɪˈsɒgənᵊl) *adj* **1** *maths* having, making, or involving equal angles ▷ *n* **2** Also called: **isogonic line, isogonal line, isogone** *physics* an imaginary line connecting points on the earth's surface having equal magnetic declination

isohel (ˈaɪsəʊˌhɛl) *n* a line on a map connecting places with an equal period of sunshine [c20 from ISO- + Gk *hēlios* sun]

isohyet (ˌaɪsəʊˈhaɪɪt) *n* a line on a map connecting places having equal rainfall [c19 from ISO- + *-hyet*, from Gk *huetos* rain]

isolate *vb* (ˈaɪsəˌleɪt), **isolates, isolating, isolated** (*tr*) **1** to place apart; cause to be alone **2** *med* to quarantine (a person or animal) having a contagious disease **3** to obtain (a compound) in an uncombined form **4** to obtain pure cultures of (bacteria, esp those causing a particular disease) **5** *electronics* to prevent interaction between (circuits, components, etc); insulate ▷ *n* (ˈaɪsəlɪt) **6** an isolated person or group [c19 back formation from *isolated*, via It. from L *insulātus*, lit.: made into an island] > ˈ**isolable** *adj* > ˌ**isolaˈbility** *n* > ˈ**isoˌlator** *n* > ˌ**isoˈlation** *n*

ISO Latin-1 *or* **ISO-8859-1** *n computing* a standard set of characters for Western European languages put together by the International Organization for Standardization

isolationism (ˌaɪsəˈleɪʃəˌnɪzəm) *n* **1** a policy of nonparticipation in or withdrawal from international affairs **2** an attitude favouring such a policy > ˌ**isoˈlationist** *n, adj*

Isolde (iˈzɔldə) *n* the German name of **Iseult**

isomer (ˈaɪsəmə) *n* **1** *chem* a compound that exhibits isomerism with one or more other compounds **2** *physics* a nuclide that exhibits isomerism with one or more other nuclides > **isomeric** (ˌaɪsəˈmɛrɪk) *adj*

isomerism (aɪˈsɒməˌrɪzəm) *n* **1** the existence of two or more compounds having the same molecular formula but a different arrangement of atoms **2** the existence of two or more nuclides having the same atomic numbers and mass numbers but different energy states

isomerous (aɪˈsɒmərəs) *adj* (of flowers) having floral whorls with the same number of parts

isometric (ˌaɪsəʊˈmɛtrɪk) *adj also* **isometrical** **1** having equal dimensions or measurements **2** *physiol* of or relating to muscular contraction that does not produce shortening of the muscle **3** (of a crystal or system of crystallization) having three mutually perpendicular equal axes **4** (of a method of projecting a drawing in three dimensions) having the three axes equally inclined and all lines drawn to scale ▷ *n* **5** Also called: **isometric drawing** a drawing made in this way [c19 from Gk *isometria*] > ˌ**isoˈmetrically** *adv*

isometrics (ˌaɪsəʊˈmɛtrɪks) *n* (*functioning as sing*) physical exercise involving isometric contraction of muscles

isomorphism (ˌaɪsəʊˈmɔːˌfɪzəm) *n* **1** *biol* similarity of form, as in different generations of the same life cycle **2** *chem* the existence of two or more substances of different composition in a similar crystalline form **3** *maths* a one-to-one correspondence between the elements of two or more sets, such as those of Arabic and Roman numerals > ˈ**isoˌmorph** *n* > ˌ**isoˈmorphic** *or* ˌ**isoˈmorphous** *adj*

isophote (ˈaɪsəˌfəʊt) *n astron* a line on a diagram or image of a galaxy, nebula, or other celestial object joining points of equal surface brightness

isopleth (ˈaɪsəʊˌplɛθ) *n* a line on a map connecting places registering the same amount or ratio of some geographical, etc phenomenon [c20 from Gk *isoplēthēs* equal in number, from ISO- + *plēthos* multitude]

isopod (ˈaɪsəʊˌpɒd) *n* a crustacean, such as the woodlouse, in which the body is flattened > **isopodan** (aɪˈsɒpədən) *or* **iˈsopodous** *adj*

isoprene (ˈaɪsəʊˌpriːn) *n* a colourless volatile liquid with a penetrating odour: used in making synthetic rubbers. Formula: CH_2:C(CH_3)CH:CH_2. Systematic name: **methylbuta-1,3-diene** [c20 from ISO- + PR(OPYL) + -ENE]

isopteran (aɪˈsɒptərən) *n, pl* **isopterans** *or* **isoptera** (-tərə) **1** any of an order of insects having two pairs of wings equal in size: comprises the termites ▷ *adj also* **isopterous** **2** of, relating to, or belonging to this order [c19 from NL, from ISO- + Gk *pteron* wing]

ISO rating *n photog* a classification of film speed in which a doubling of the ISO number represents a doubling in sensitivity; for example, ISO 400 film

Ii

requires half the exposure of ISO 200 under the same conditions. The system uses identical numbers to the obsolete ASA rating [c20 from ISO[1]]

isosceles (aɪˈsɒsɪˌliːz) *adj* (of a triangle) having two sides of equal length [c16 from LL, from Gk, from ISO- + *skelos* leg]

isoseismal (ˌaɪsəʊˈsaɪzməl) *adj* **1** of or relating to equal intensity of earthquake shock ▷ *n* **2** a line on a map connecting points at which earthquake shocks are of equal intensity ▷ Also: **isoseismic**

isostasy (aɪˈsɒstəsɪ) *n* the state of balance which sections of the earth's lithosphere are thought ultimately to achieve when the vertical forces upon them remain unchanged. If a section is loaded as by ice, it slowly subsides. If a section is reduced in mass, as by erosion, it slowly rises [c19 ISO- + -*stasy*, from Gk *stasis* a standing] > **isostatic** (ˌaɪsəʊˈstætɪk) *adj*

isothere (ˈaɪsəʊˌθɪə) *n* a line on a map linking places of equal mean summer temperature ▷ Cf **isocheim** [c19 from ISO- + Gk *theros* summer] > **isotheral** (aɪˈsɒθərəl) *adj*

isotherm (ˈaɪsəʊˌθɜːm) *n* **1** a line on a map linking places of equal temperature **2** *physics* a curve on a graph that connects points of equal temperature ▷ Also called: **isothermal, isothermal line**

isothermal (ˌaɪsəʊˈθɜːməl) *adj* **1** (of a process or change) taking place at constant temperature **2** of or relating to an isotherm ▷ *n* **3** another word for **isotherm** > ˌ**isoˈthermally** *adv*

isotonic (ˌaɪsəʊˈtɒnɪk) *adj* **1** *physiol* (of two or more muscles) having equal tension **2** (of a drink) designed to replace the fluid and salts lost from the body during strenuous exercise **3** Also: **isosmotic** (of two solutions) having the same osmotic pressure, commonly having physiological osmotic pressure ▷ Cf **hypertonic, hypotonic** > **isotonicity** (ˌaɪsəʊtəʊˈnɪsɪtɪ) *n*

isotope (ˈaɪsəˌtəʊp) *n* one of two or more atoms with the same atomic number that contain different numbers of neutrons [c20 from ISO- + Gk *topos* place] > **isotopic** (ˌaɪsəˈtɒpɪk) *adj* > ˌ**isoˈtopically** *adv* > **isotopy** (aɪˈsɒtəpɪ) *n*

isotropic (ˌaɪsəʊˈtrɒpɪk) *or* **isotropous** (aɪˈsɒtrəpəs) *adj* **1** having uniform physical properties in all directions **2** *biol* not having predetermined axes: *isotropic eggs* > ˌ**isoˈtropically** *adv* > **iˈsotropy** *n*

ISP *abbrev for* Internet service provider

I-spy *n* a game in which one player specifies the initial letter of the name of an object that he or she can see, which the other players then try to guess

Israel (ˈɪzreɪəl, -rɪəl) *n* **1** a republic in SW Asia, on the Mediterranean Sea: established in 1948, in the former British mandate of Palestine, as a primarily Jewish state; eight disputes with Arab neighbours (who did not recognize the state of Israel), erupted into full-scale wars in 1948, 1956, 1967 (the Six Day War), and 1973 (the Yom Kippur War). In 1993 Israel agreed to grant autonomous status to the Gaza Strip and the West Bank, according to the terms of a peace agreement with the PLO. Official languages: Hebrew and Arabic. Religion: Jewish majority, Muslim and Christian minorities. Currency: shekel. Capital: Jerusalem (international recognition withheld as East Jerusalem was annexed (1967) by Israel: UN recognized capital: Tel Aviv). Pop: 6 258 000 (2001 est). Area (including Golan Heights and East Jerusalem): 21 946 sq km (8473 sq miles) **2a** the ancient kingdom of the 12 Hebrew tribes at the SE end of the Mediterranean **2b** the kingdom in the N part of this region formed by the ten northern tribes of Israel in the 10th century BC and destroyed by the Assyrians in 721 BC **3** *inf* the Jewish community throughout the world

▷ www.mfa.gov.il

▷ www.goisrael.com

Israeli (ɪzˈreɪlɪ) *n, pl* **Israelis** *or* **Israeli** **1** a citizen or inhabitant of the state of Israel ▷ *adj* **2** of or relating to the state of Israel or its inhabitants

Israelite (ˈɪzrɪəˌlaɪt, -rə-) *n* **1** *Bible* a member of the ethnic group claiming descent from Jacob; a Hebrew **2** a member of any of various Christian sects who regard themselves as God's chosen people **3** an archaic word for a **Jew**

Issachar (ˈɪsəˌkɑː) *n Old Testament* **1** the fifth son of Jacob by his wife Leah (Genesis 30:17–18) **2** the tribe descended from this patriarch **3** the territory of this tribe

Isserlis (ˈɪsəlɪs) *n* **Steven** (**John**) born 1958, British cellist

Issigonis (ˌɪsɪˈɡəʊnɪs) *n* Sir **Alec** (**Arnold Constantine**) 1906–88, British car designer born in Smyrna. He is noted for his designs for the Morris Minor (1948) and the Mini (1959)

ISSN *abbrev for* International Standard Serial Number

issuance (ˈɪʃʊəns) *n* the act of issuing

issue (ˈɪʃjuː) *n* **1** the act of sending or giving out something; supply; delivery **2** something issued; an edition of stamps, a magazine, etc **3** the number of identical items, such as banknotes or shares in a company, that become available at a particular time **4** the act of emerging; outflow; discharge **5** something flowing out, such as a river **6** a place of outflow; outlet **7** the descendants of a person; offspring; progeny **8** a topic of interest or discussion **9** an important subject requiring a decision **10** an outcome or consequence; result **11** *pathol* discharge from a wound **12** *law* the matter remaining in dispute between the parties to an action after the pleadings **13** the yield from or profits arising out of land or other property **14 at issue** **14a** under discussion **14b** in disagreement **15 force the issue** to compel decision on some matter **16 join issue** to join in controversy **17 take issue** to disagree ▷ *vb* **issues, issuing, issued** **18** to come forth or emerge or cause to come forth or emerge **19** to publish or deliver (a newspaper, magazine, etc) **20** (*tr*) to make known or announce **21** (*intr*) to originate or proceed **22** (*intr*) to be a consequence; result **23** (*intr; foll by in*) to end or terminate **24** (*tr foll by with*) to supply officially (with) [c13 from OF *eissue* way out, from *eissir* to go out, from L *exīre*] > ˈ**issuable** *adj* > ˈ**issuer** *n*

issue price *n stock exchange* the price at which a new issue of shares is offered to the public

Issus (ˈɪsəs) *n* an ancient town in S Asia Minor, in Cilicia north of present-day Iskenderun: scene of a battle (333 BC) in which Alexander the Great defeated the Persians

Issyk-Kul (*Russian* isˈsikˈkulj) *n* a lake in NE Kyrgyzstan in the Tian Shan mountains, at an altitude of 1609 m (5280 ft): one of the largest mountain lakes in the world. Area: 6200 sq km (2390 sq miles)

-ist *suffix* **1** (*forming nouns*) a person who performs a certain action or is concerned with something specified: *motorist; soloist* **2** (*forming nouns*) a person who practises in a specific field: *physicist* **3** (*forming nouns and adjectives*) a person who advocates a particular doctrine, system, etc, or relating to such a person or the doctrine advocated: *socialist* **4** (*forming nouns and adjectives*) a person characterized by a specified trait, tendency, etc, or relating to such a person or trait: *purist* **5** (*forming nouns and adjectives*) a person who is prejudiced on the basis specified: *sexist* [via OF from L -*ista*, -*istēs*, from Gk -*istēs*]

Istanbul (ˌɪstænˈbuːl) *n* a port in NW Turkey, on the western (European) shore of the Bosporus: the largest city in Turkey; founded in about 660 BC by Greeks; refounded by Constantine the Great in 330 AD as the capital of the Eastern Roman Empire; taken by the Turks in 1453 and remained capital of the Ottoman Empire until 1922; industrial centre for shipbuilding, textiles, etc Pop: 8 260 438 (1997). Ancient name: **Byzantium** Former name (330–1926): **Constantinople**

isthmian (ˈɪsθmɪən) *adj* relating to or situated in an isthmus

isthmus (ˈɪsməs) *n, pl* **isthmuses** *or* **isthmi** (-maɪ) **1** a narrow strip of land connecting two relatively large land areas **2** *anat* **2a** a narrow band of tissue connecting two larger parts of a structure **2b** a narrow passage connecting two cavities [c16 from L, from Gk *isthmos*] > ˈ**isthmoid** *adj*

-istic *suffix forming adjectives* equivalent to a combination of **-ist** and **-ic** but in some words having a less specific or literal application and sometimes a mildly pejorative force, as compared with corresponding adjectives ending in **-ist**: *communistic; impressionistic* [from L *-isticus*, from Gk *istikos*]

istle (ˈɪstlɪ) *or* **ixtle** *n* a fibre obtained from various tropical American agave and yucca trees used in making carpets, cord, etc [c19 from Mexican Sp. *ixtle*, from Amerind *ichtli*]

Istria (ˈɪstrɪə) *n* a peninsula in the N Adriatic Sea: passed from Italy to Yugoslavia (except for Trieste) in 1947 and to Croatia in 1991 > ˈ**Istrian** *n, adj*

it (ɪt) *pron (subjective or objective)* **1** refers to a nonhuman, animal, plant, or inanimate thing, or sometimes to a small baby: *it looks dangerous; give it a bone* **2** refers to an unspecified or implied antecedent or to a previous or understood clause, phrase, etc: *it is impossible; I knew it* **3** used to represent human life or experience in respect of the present situation: *how's it going? I've had it; to brazen it out* **4** used as a formal subject (or object), referring to a following clause, phrase, or word: *it helps to know the truth; I consider it dangerous to go on* **5** used in the nominative as the formal grammatical subject of impersonal verbs: *it is raining; it hurts* **6** (used as complement with *be*) *inf* the crucial or ultimate point: *the steering failed and I thought that was it* ▷ *n* **7** (in children's games) the player whose turn it is to try to touch another **8** *inf* **8a** sexual intercourse **8b** sex appeal **9** *inf* a desirable quality or ability: *he's really got it* [OE *hit*]

IT *abbrev for* information technology

It. *abbrev for:* **1** Italian **2** Italy

i.t.a. *or* **ITA** *abbrev for* initial teaching alphabet, a partly phonetic alphabet used to teach reading

ital. *abbrev for* italic

Ital. *abbrev for:* **1** Italian **2** Italy

Italia (iˈtaːlja) *n* the Italian name for **Italy**

Italian (ɪˈtæljən) *n* **1** the official language of Italy and one of the official languages of Switzerland **2** a native or inhabitant of Italy or a descendant of one ▷ *adj* **3** relating to, denoting, or characteristic of Italy, its inhabitants, or their language

Italianate (ɪˈtæljənɪt, -ˌneɪt) *or* **Italianesque** *adj* Italian in style or character

Italian East Africa *n* a former Italian territory in E Africa, formed in 1936 from the possessions of Eritrea, Italian Somaliland, and Ethiopia: taken by British forces in 1941

Italian Somaliland *n* a former Italian colony in E Africa, united with British Somaliland in 1960 to form the independent republic of Somalia

italic (ɪˈtælɪk) *adj* **1** Also: **Italian** of, relating to, or denoting a style of handwriting with the letters slanting to the right **2** of, relating to, or denoting a style of printing type modelled on this, chiefly used to indicate emphasis, a foreign word, etc ▷ Cf **roman** ▷ *n* **3** *(often pl)* italic type or print [c16 (after an edition of Virgil (1501) printed in Venice and dedicated to Italy): from L *Italicus* of Italy, from Gk *Italikos*]

Italic (ɪˈtælɪk) *n* **1** a branch of the Indo-European family of languages that includes many of the ancient languages of Italy ▷ *adj* **2** denoting, relating to, or belonging to this group of languages, esp the extinct ones

italicize *or* **italicise** (ɪˈtælɪˌsaɪz) *vb* **italicizes, italicizing, italicized** *or* **italicises, italicising, italicised 1** to print (textual matter) in italic type **2** *(tr)* to underline (words, etc) with a single line to indicate italics > **iˌtaliciˈzation** *or* **iˌtaliciˈsation** *n*

Italy (ˈɪtəlɪ) *n* a republic in S Europe, occupying a peninsula in the Mediterranean between the Tyrrhenian and the Adriatic Seas, with the islands of Sardinia and Sicily to the west: first united under the Romans but became fragmented into numerous political units in the Middle Ages; united kingdom proclaimed in 1861; under the dictatorship of Mussolini (1922–43); became a republic in 1946; a member of the European Union. It is generally mountainous, with the Alps in the north and the Apennines running the length of the peninsula. Official language: Italian. Religion: Roman Catholic majority. Currency: euro. Capital: Rome. Pop: 57 892 000 (2001 est). Area: 301 247 sq km (116 312 sq miles). Italian name: **Italia**

▷ www.italiantourism.com

▷ www.governo.it

ITC (in Britain) *abbrev for* Independent Television Commission

▷ www.itc.org.uk

itch (ɪtʃ) *n* **1** an irritation or tickling sensation of the skin causing a desire to scratch **2** a restless desire **3** any skin disorder, such as scabies, characterized by intense itching ▷ *vb (intr)* **4** to feel or produce an irritating or tickling sensation **5** to have a restless desire (to do something) **6 have itchy feet** to be restless; have a desire to travel **7 itching palm** a grasping nature; avarice [OE *gīccean*] > ˈ**itchy** *adj* > ˈ**itchiness** *n*

-ite[1] *suffix forming nouns* **1** a native or inhabitant of: *Israelite* **2** a follower or advocate of; a supporter of a group: *Luddite; labourite* **3** (in biology) indicating a division of a body or organ: *somite* **4** indicating a mineral or rock: *nephrite; peridotite* **5** indicating a commercial product: *vulcanite* [via L *-ita* from Gk *-itēs* or directly from Gk]

-ite[2] *suffix forming nouns* indicating a salt or ester of an acid having a name ending in *-ous*: *a nitrite is a salt of nitrous acid* [from F, arbitrary alteration of -ATE[1]]

item *n* (ˈaɪtəm) **1** a thing or unit, esp included in a list or collection **2** *book-keeping* an entry in an account **3** a piece of information, detail, or note: *a news item* **4** *inf* two people having a romantic or sexual relationship ▷ *vb* (ˈaɪtəm) **5** *(tr) arch* to itemize ▷ *adv* (ˈaɪtɛm) **6** likewise; also [c14 (adv) from L: in like manner]

itemize *or* **itemise** (ˈaɪtəˌmaɪz) *vb* **itemizes, itemizing, itemized** *or* **itemises, itemising, itemised** *(tr)* to put on a list or make a list of > ˌ**itemiˈzation** *or* ˌ**itemiˈsation** *n* > ˈ**itemˌizer** *or* ˈ**itemˌiser** *n*

Iténez (iˈteneθ) *n* the Spanish name for the **Guaporé**

iterate (ˈɪtəˌreɪt) *vb* **iterates, iterating, iterated** *(tr)* to say or do again [c16 from L *iterāre*, from *iterum* again] > ˈ**iterant** *adj* > ˌ**iterˈation** *n* > ˈ**iterative** *adj*

Ithaca (ˈɪθəkə) *n* a Greek island in the Ionian Sea, the smallest of the Ionian Islands: regarded as the home of Homer's Odysseus. Area: 93 sq km (36 sq miles). Modern Greek name: **Itháki** (iˈθaki) > ˈ**Ithacan** *n, adj*

Ithunn (ˈiːðʊn) *n* a variant of **Idun**

itinerancy (ɪˈtɪnərənsɪ, aɪ-) *or* **itineracy** *n* **1** the act of itinerating **2** *chiefly Methodist Church* the system of appointing a minister to a circuit of churches or chapels **3** itinerants collectively

itinerant (ɪˈtɪnərənt, aɪ-) *adj* **1** itinerating **2** working for a short time in various places, esp as a casual labourer ▷ *n* **3** an itinerant worker or other person [c16 from LL *itinerārī* to travel, from L *iter* a journey] > **iˈtinerantly** *adv*

itinerary (aɪˈtɪnərərɪ, ɪ-) *n, pl* **itineraries 1** a plan or line of travel; route **2** a record of a journey **3** a guidebook for travellers ▷ *adj* **4** of or relating to travel or routes of travel

itinerate (aɪˈtɪnəˌreɪt, ɪ-) *vb* **itinerates, itinerating, itinerated** *(intr)* to travel from place to place > **iˌtinerˈation** *n*

-itis *suffix forming nouns* **1** indicating inflammation of a

Ii

specified part: *tonsillitis* **2** *inf* indicating a preoccupation with or imaginary condition of illness caused by: *computeritis; telephonitis* [NL, from Gk, fem of *-itēs* belonging to]

it'll ('ɪtᵊl) *contraction of* it will *or* it shall

ITN (in Britain) *abbrev for* Independent Television News

Ito ('iːtəʊ) *n* Prince **Hirobumi** (ˌhɪərə'buːmɪ) 1841–1909, Japanese statesman; premier (1884–88; 1892–96; 1898; 1900–01). He led the movement to modernize Japan and helped to draft the Meiji constitution (1889); assassinated

ITO *abbrev for* International Trade Organization

-itol *suffix forming nouns* indicating that certain chemical compounds are alcohols containing two or more hydroxyl groups: *inisitol; sorbitol* [from -ITE² + -OL¹]

its (ɪts) *determiner* **a** of, belonging to, or associated in some way with it: *its left rear wheel; I can see its logical consequence* **b** (*as pronoun*): *each town claims its is the best*

it's (ɪts) *contraction of* it is *or* it has

> **USAGE** One of the commonest mistakes made in written English is the confusion of *its* and *it's*. You can see examples of this every day in books, magazines, and newspapers: *its good for us; a smart black case with it's own mirror* and even *Cheng and its' subsidiaries*. Here are the rules about when to use *its* and when to use *it's*. *Its* refers to something belonging to or relating to a thing that has already been mentioned: *the baby threw its rattle out of the pram*. *It's* is a shortened way of saying *it is* or *it has* (the apostrophe indicates that a letter has been omitted): *it's a lovely day; it's been a great weekend*

itself (ɪt'sɛlf) *pron* **1a** the reflexive form of **it** **1b** (intensifier): *even the money itself won't convince me* **2** (*preceded by a copula*) its normal or usual self: *my cat doesn't seem itself these days*

itsy-bitsy ('ɪtsɪ'bɪtsɪ) *or* **itty-bitty** ('ɪtɪ'bɪtɪ) *adj inf* very small; tiny [c20 baby talk alteration of *little bit*]

ITU *abbrev for:* **1** intensive therapy unit **2** International Telecommunications Union

ITV (in Britain) *abbrev for* Independent Television ▹ www.itv.co.uk

-ity *suffix forming nouns* indicating state or condition: *technicality* [from OF *-ite*, from L *-itās*]

IU *abbrev for:* **1** immunizing unit **2** international unit

IU(C)D *abbrev for* intrauterine (contraceptive) device

Iulus (aɪ'juːləs) *n Roman myth* **1** another name for **Ascanius** **2** the son of Ascanius, founder of the Julian gens or clan

-ium *or sometimes* **-um** *suffix forming nouns* **1** indicating a metallic element: *platinum; barium* **2** (in chemistry) indicating groups forming positive ions: *ammonium chloride; hydroxonium ion* **3** indicating a biological structure: *syncytium* [NL, from L, from Gk *-ion*, dim. suffix]

i.v. *or* **I.V.** *abbrev for* intravenous(ly)

Ivan III ('aɪvən) *n* known as *Ivan the Great*. 1440–1505, grand duke of Muscovy (1462–1505). He expanded Muscovy, defeated the Tatars (1480), and assumed the title of Ruler of all Russia (1472)

Ivan IV *n* known as *Ivan the Terrible*. 1530–84, grand duke of Muscovy (1533–47) and first tsar of Russia (1547–84). He conquered Kazan (1552), Astrakhan (1556), and Siberia (1581), but was defeated by Poland in the Livonian War (1558–82) after which his rule became increasingly oppressive

Ivanovo (*Russian* ɪ'vanəvə) *n* a city in W central Russia, on the Uvod River: textile centre. Pop: 463 400 (1999 est). Former name (1871–1932): **Ivanovo-Voznesensk** (-vəznɪ'sjɛnsk)

I've (aɪv) *contraction of* I have

-ive *suffix* **1** (*forming adjectives*) indicating a tendency, inclination, character, or quality: *divisive; festive; massive* **2** (*forming nouns of adjectival origin*): *detective; expletive* [from L *-īvus*]

Ives (aɪvz) *n* **1** **Charles Edward** 1874–1954, US composer, noted for his innovative use of polytonality, polyrhythms, and quarter tones. His works include *Second Piano Sonata: Concord* (1915), five symphonies, chamber music, and songs **2** **Frederick Eugene** 1856–1937, US inventor of halftone photography

IVF *abbrev for* in vitro fertilization

ivied ('aɪvɪd) *adj* covered with ivy

Ivorian (aɪ'vɔːrɪən) *n* **1** a native or inhabitant of the Côte d'Ivoire ▹ *adj* **2** of or relating to the Côte d'Ivoire or its inhabitants

ivories ('aɪvərɪz, -vrɪz) *pl n Sl* **1** the keys of a piano **2** billiard balls **3** another word for **teeth** **4** another word for **dice**

ivory ('aɪvərɪ, -vrɪ) *n, pl* **ivories** **1a** a hard smooth creamy white variety of dentine that makes up a major part of the tusks of elephants and walruses **1b** (*as modifier*): *ivory ornaments* **2** a tusk made of ivory **3a** a yellowish-white colour; cream **3b** (*as adj*): *ivory shoes* **4** a substance resembling elephant tusk **5** an ornament, etc, made of ivory **6** **black ivory** *obs* Black slaves collectively [c13 from OF, from L *evoreus* made of ivory, from *ebur* ivory] > **'ivory-ˌlike** *adj*

Ivory ('aɪvərɪ) *n* **James** born 1928, US film director. With the producer Ismael Merchant, his films include *Shakespeare Wallah* (1964), *Heat and Dust* (1983), *A Room With a View* (1986), and *The Golden Bowl* (2000)

ivory black *n* a black pigment obtained by grinding charred scraps of ivory in oil

Ivory Coast *n* **the** the former name (until 1986) of **Côte d'Ivoire**

ivory nut *n* **1** the seed of the ivory palm, which contains an ivory-like substance used to make buttons, etc **2** any similar seed from other palms ▹ Also called: **vegetable ivory**

ivory tower ('taʊə) *n* **a** seclusion or remoteness of attitude regarding problems, everyday life, etc **b** (*as modifier*): *ivory-tower aestheticism* > **ˌivory-'towered** *adj*

ivorywood ('aɪvərɪˌwʊd) *n* **1** the yellowish-white wood of an Australian tree, used for engraving, inlaying, and turnery **2** the tree itself

IVR *abbrev for* International Vehicle Registration

ivy ('aɪvɪ) *n, pl* **ivies** **1** a woody climbing or trailing plant having lobed evergreen leaves and black berry-like fruits **2** any of various other climbing or creeping plants, such as poison ivy and ground ivy [OE *īfig*] > **'ivy-ˌlike** *adj*

iwi ('iːwɪː) *n NZ* a Maori tribe [Maori, literally: bone(s)]

Iwo ('iːwəʊ) *n* a city in SW Nigeria. Pop: 362 000 (1996 est)

Iwo Jima ('dʒiːmə) *n* an island in the W Pacific, about 1100 km (700 miles) south of Japan: one of the Volcano Islands; scene of prolonged fighting between US and Japanese forces until taken by the US in 1945; returned to Japan in 1968. Area: 20 sq km (8 sq miles)

IWW *abbrev for* Industrial Workers of the World

ixia ('ɪksɪə) *n* an iridaceous plant of southern Africa, having showy ornamental funnel-shaped flowers [c18 NL from Gk *ixos* mistletoe]

Ixion (ɪk'saɪən) *n Greek myth* a Thessalian king punished by Zeus for his love of Hera by being bound to a perpetually revolving wheel > **Ixionian** (ˌɪksɪ'əʊnɪən) *adj*

Ixtaccihuatl *or* **Iztaccihuatl** (ˌiːstæk'siːwætᵊl) *n* a dormant volcano in central Mexico, southeast of Mexico City. Height: (central peak) 5286 m (17 342 ft)

ixtle ('ɪkstlɪ, 'ɪst-) *n* a variant spelling of **istle**

Iyeyasu *or* **Ieyasu** (ˌiːjeɪ'jɑːsuː) *n* **Tokugawa** (ˌtɒkuː'gɑːwə) 1542–1616, Japanese statesman and general; founder of the Tokugawa shogunate (1603–1867)

IYKWIMAITYD *text messaging abbrev for* if you know what I mean and I think you do

izard ('ɪzəd) *n* (esp in the Pyrenees) another name for **chamois**

-ize *or* **-ise** *suffix forming verbs* **1** to cause to become, resemble, or agree with: *legalize* **2** to become; change into: *crystallize* **3** to affect in a specified way; subject to: *hypnotize* **4** to act according to some practice, principle, policy, etc: *economize* [from OF *-iser*, from LL *-izāre*, from Gk *-izein*]

> **USAGE** In Britain and the US *-ize* is the preferred ending for many verbs, but *-ise* is equally acceptable in British English. Certain words (chiefly those not formed by adding the suffix to an existing word) are, however, always spelt with *-ise* in both Britain and the US: *advertise, revise*

Izetbegović (ˌɪzət'bɛgəvɪtʃ) *n* **Alija** ('æljə) 1925–2003, Bosnia and Herzegovinian politician: president (1992–2000; from 1996 as part of a tripartite presidency); he led the country to independence and during the subsequent civil war

Izhevsk (*Russian* i'ʒɛfsk) *n* an industrial city in central Russia, capital of the Udmurt Republic. Pop: 655 000 (1999 est)

Izmir ('ɪzmɪə) *n* a port in W Turkey, situated on the **Gulf of Izmir**: the third largest city in the country; university (1955). Pop: 2 081 556 (1997). Former name: **Smyrna**

Izmit ('ɪzmɪt) *n* a town in NW Turkey, on the **Gulf of Izmit**. Pop: 198 200 (1997)

Iznik (ɪz'nɪk) *n* the modern Turkish name of **Nicaea**

Iztaccihuatl (ˌiːstək'siːwət^{ə}l) *n* a variant spelling of **Ixtaccihuatl**

Ii

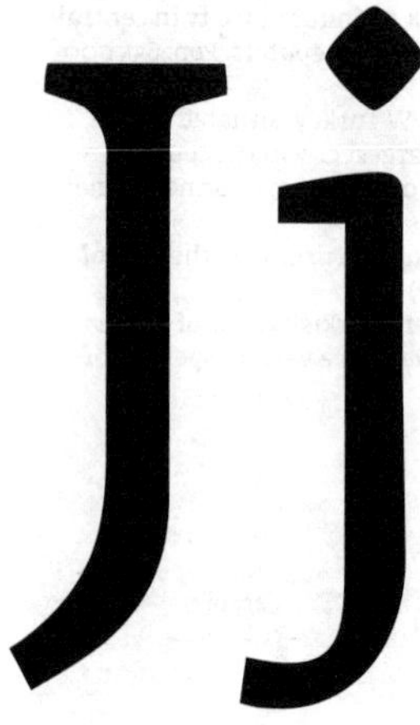

j *or* **J** (dʒeɪ) *n, pl* **j's, J's,** *or* **Js** **1** the tenth letter of the English alphabet **2** a speech sound represented by this letter

j *symbol for:* **1** *maths* the unit vector along the *y*-axis **2** the imaginary number √−1

J *symbol for:* **1** current density **2** *cards* jack **3** joule(s)

ja (jɑː) *sentence substitute S African* yes [Afrik.]

jab (dʒæb) *vb* **jabs, jabbing, jabbed** **1** to poke or thrust sharply **2** to strike with a quick short blow or blows ▷ *n* **3** a sharp poke or stab **4** a quick short blow **5** *inf* an injection: *polio jabs* [C19 orig. Scot. var. of JOB] > **'jabbing** *adj*

Jabalpur (ˌdʒʌbəl'pʊə) *n* a city in central India, in central Madhya Pradesh. Pop: 741 927 (1991)

jabber ('dʒæbə) *vb* **1** to speak or say rapidly, incoherently, and without making sense; chatter ▷ *n* **2** such talk [C15 imit.]

jabberwocky ('dʒæbəˌwɒkɪ) *n* nonsensical writing or speech [C19 coined by Lewis Carroll as the title of a poem in *Through the Looking Glass* (1871)]

Jabir ibn Hayyan ('dʒɑːbɪə ˌiːbᵊn hɑː'jɑːn) *n* ?721–?815. Arab alchemist, whose many works enjoyed enormous esteem among later alchemists, such as Geber

jabiru ('dʒæbɪˌruː) *n* **1** a large white tropical American stork with a dark naked head and a dark bill **2** Also called: **black-necked stork, policeman bird** a large Australian stork, having a white plumage, dark green back and tail, and red legs **3** another name for **saddlebill** [C18 via Port., of Amerind origin]

jabot ('ʒæbəʊ) *n* a frill or ruffle on the breast or throat of a garment [C19 from F: bird's crop, jabot]

jaçana (ˌʒɑːsə'nɑː, ˌdʒæ-) *n* a bird of tropical and subtropical marshy regions, having long legs and very long toes that enable walking on floating plants [C18 from Port., of Amerind origin, from *jasaná*]

jacaranda (ˌdʒækə'rændə) *n* **1** a tropical American tree having fernlike leaves and pale purple flowers and widely cultivated in temperate areas of Australia **2** the fragrant ornamental wood of this tree **3** any of several related or similar trees or their wood [C18 from Port., of Amerind origin, from *yacarandá*]

jacaré ('dʒækəˌreɪ) *n* another name for **cayman** [C18 from Port., of Amerind origin]

jacinth ('dʒæsɪnθ) *n* another name for **hyacinth** (sense 4) [C13 from Med. L *jacinthus*, from L *hyacinthus* plant, precious stone; see HYACINTH]

jack (dʒæk) *n* **1** a man or fellow **2** a sailor **3** the male of certain animals, esp of the ass or donkey **4** a mechanical or hydraulic device for exerting a large force, esp to raise a heavy weight such as a motor vehicle **5** any of several mechanical devices that replace manpower, such as a contrivance for rotating meat on a spit **6** one of four playing cards in a pack, one for each suit; knave **7** *bowls* a small usually white bowl at which the players aim with their own bowls **8** *electrical engineering* a female socket with two or more terminals designed to receive a male plug (**jack plug**) that either makes or breaks the circuit or circuits **9** a flag, esp a small flag flown at the bow of a ship indicating the ship's nationality **10** a part of the action of a harpsichord, consisting of a fork-shaped device on the end of a pivoted lever on which a plectrum is mounted **11a** any of various tropical and subtropical fishes **11b** an immature pike **12** Also called: **jackstone** one of the pieces used in the game of jacks **13** *US* a slang word for **money** **14** **every man jack** everyone without exception **15** **the jack** *Austral sl* syphilis ▷ *adj* **16** *Austral sl* tired or fed up (esp in **be jack of something**) ▷ *vb* **17** *(tr)* to lift or push (an object) with a jack ▷ See also **jack in, jack up** [C16 *jakke*, var. of *Jankin*, dim. of *John*]

Jack (dʒæk) *n* **I'm all right, Jack** *Brit inf* a remark indicating smug and complacent selfishness

jackal ('dʒækɔːl) *n* **1** any of several African or S Asian mammals closely related to the dog, having long legs and pointed ears and muzzle: they are predators and carrion-eaters **2** a person who does menial tasks for another [C17 from Turkish, from Persian, from Sansk. *srgāla*]

jackanapes ('dʒækəˌneɪps) *n (functioning as sing)* **1** a conceited impertinent person **2** a mischievous child **3** *arch* a monkey [C16 var. of *Jakken-apes*, lit.: Jack of the ape, nickname of William de la Pole (1396–1450), first Duke of Suffolk, whose badge showed an ape's ball and chain]

jackass ('dʒækˌæs) *n* **1** a male donkey **2** a fool [C18 from JACK (male) + ASS[1]]

jackboot ('dʒækˌbuːt) *n* **1** an all-leather military boot, extending up to or above the knee **2** authoritarian rule or behaviour > **'jackˌbooted** *adj*

jackdaw ('dʒækˌdɔː) *n* a large Eurasian bird, related to the crow, having a black and dark grey plumage: noted for its thieving habits [C16 from JACK + *daw*, obs. name for jackdaw]

jackeroo *or* **jackaroo** (ˌdʒækə'ruː) *n, pl* **jackeroos** *or* **jackaroos** *Austral inf* a novice on a sheep or cattle station [C19 from JACK + (KANG)AROO]

jacket ('dʒækɪt) *n* **1** a short coat, esp one that is hip-length and has a front opening and sleeves **2** something that resembles this: *a life jacket* **3** any exterior covering or casing, such as the insulating cover of a boiler **4** See **dust jacket** **5a** the skin of a baked potato **5b** *(as modifier)*: *jacket potatoes* **6** *oil industry* the support structure, esp the legs, of an oil platform ▷ *vb* **7** *(tr)* to put a jacket on (someone or something) [C15 from OF *jaquet* short jacket, from *jacque* peasant, from *Jacques* James] > **'jacketed** *adj*

Jack Frost *n* a personification of frost

Jackie *or* **Jacky** ('dʒækɪ) *n, pl* **Jackies** *Austral offens sl* **1** a native Australian **2** native Australians collectively **3** **sit up like Jackie** to sit bolt upright, esp cheekily

jack in *vb (tr, adv) sl* to abandon or leave (an attempt or enterprise)

jack-in-office *n* a self-important petty official

jack-in-the-box *n, pl* **jack-in-the-boxes** *or* **jacks-in-the-box** a toy consisting of a figure on a compressed spring in a box, which springs out when the lid is opened

Jack Ketch (kɛtʃ) *n Brit arch* a hangman [C18 after *John Ketch* (died 1686), public executioner in England]

jackknife ('dʒækˌnaɪf) *n, pl* **jackknives** **1** a knife with the blade pivoted to fold into a recess in the handle **2** a former name for a type of dive in which the diver bends at the waist in midair; forward pike dive ▷ *vb* **jackknifes, jackknifing, jackknifed** *(intr)* **3** (of an articulated lorry) to go out of control in such a way that the trailer swings round at an angle to the tractor

jack of all trades *n, pl* **jacks of all trades** a person who undertakes many different kinds of work

jack-o'-lantern *n* **1** a lantern made from a hollowed pumpkin, which has holes cut in it to represent a human face **2** a will-o'-the-wisp

jack plane *n* a carpenter's plane, usually with a wooden body, used for rough planing of timber

jack plug *n* See **jack** (sense 8)

jackpot ('dʒækˌpɒt) *n* **1** any large prize, kitty, or accumulated stake that may be won in gambling **2** **hit the jackpot** **2a** to win a jackpot **2b** *inf* to achieve great success, esp through luck [C20 prob. from JACK (playing card) + POT[1]]

jack rabbit *n* any of various W North American hares having long hind legs and large ears [C19 shortened from *jackass-rabbit*, referring to its long ears]

Jack Robinson ('rɒbɪnsən) *n* **before you could** (*or* **can**) **say Jack Robinson** extremely quickly or suddenly

Jack Russell ('rʌsəl) *n* a small short-legged terrier having a white coat with tan, black, or lemon markings [after John *Russell* (1795–1883), E clergyman who developed the breed]

jacks (dʒæks) *n (functioning as sing)* a game in which bone, metal, or plastic pieces (**jackstones**) are thrown and then picked up between bounces of a small ball or throws of another piece (the **jack**) [C19 shortened from *jackstones*, var. of *checkstones* pebbles]

jacksie *or* **jacksy** ('dʒæksɪ) *n, pl* **jacksies** *Brit sl* the buttocks or anus. Also: **jaxie, jaxy** [C19 ? from JACK]

jacksnipe ('dʒækˌsnaɪp) *n, pl* **jacksnipe** *or* **jacksnipes** a small Eurasian short-billed snipe

Jackson[1] ('dʒæksən) *n* a city in and state capital of Mississippi, on the Pearl River. Pop: 184 256 (2000)

Jackson[2] ('dʒæksən) *n* **1** **Andrew** 1767–1845, US statesman, general, and lawyer; seventh president of the US (1829–37) He became a national hero after successfully defending New Orleans from the British (1815). During his administration the spoils system was introduced and the national debt was fully paid off **2** **Colin** (**Ray**) born 1967, British athlete, broke world record for 110 m hurdles in 1993 (12.91 seconds) and for the 60 m hurdles in 1994 (7.3 seconds) **3** **Jesse** (**Louis**) born 1941, US Democrat politician and clergyman; Black campaigner for minority rights **4** **Michael** (**Joe**) born 1958, US pop singer, lead vocalist with the Jacksons (originally the Jackson 5) (1969–86). His solo albums include *Thriller* (1982), *Bad* (1989), and *Invincible* (2001) **5** **Peter** born 1961,New Zealand film director, screenwriter, and producer; his films include *Heavenly Creatures* (1994) and *The Lord of the Rings* trilogy (2001–03) **6** **Thomas Jonathan,** known as *Stonewall Jackson*. 1824–63, Confederate general in the American Civil War, noted particularly for his command at the first Battle of Bull Run (1861)

Jacksonville ('dʒæksənˌvɪl) *n* a port in NE Florida: the leading commercial centre of the southeast. Pop: 735 617 (2000)

Jj

jackstraws ('dʒækˌstrɔːz) *n (functioning as sing)* another name for **spillikins**

Jack Tar *n now chiefly literary* a sailor

Jack the Ripper *n* an unidentified murderer who killed at least seven prostitutes in London's East End between August and November 1888

jack up *vb (adv)* **1** *(tr)* to increase (prices, salaries, etc) **2** *(tr)* to raise an object, such as a car, with or as with a jack **3** *(intr) sl* to inject oneself with a drug **4** *(intr) Austral inf* to refuse to comply **5** *(tr)* NZ to organize or procure, esp through unorthodox channels ▷ *n* **jack-up** **7** NZ something that has been contrived or achieved by dishonest means

Jacob ('dʒeɪkəb) *n Old Testament* the son of Isaac, twin brother of Esau, and father of the twelve patriarchs of Israel

Jacobean (ˌdʒækə'bɪən) *adj* **1** *history* relating to James I of England or to the period of his rule (1603–25) **2** of or relating to the style of furniture current at this time, characterized by the use of dark brown carved oak **3** relating to or having the style of architecture used in England during this period [C18 from NL, from *Jacōbus* James]

▷ www.building-history.pwp.blueyonder.co.uk

▷ www.probertencyclopaedia.com/T8.HTM

Jacobi *n* (*German* ja'koːbi) **Karl Gustav Jacob** (karl 'gʊstaf 'jaːkɔp) 1804–51, German mathematician. Independently of N H Abel, he discovered elliptic functions (1829). He also made important contributions to the study of determinants and differential equations

Jacobin ('dʒækəbɪn) *n* **1** a member of the most radical club founded during the French Revolution, which instituted the Reign of Terror **2** an extreme political radical **3** a French Dominican friar ▷ *adj* **4** of or relating to the Jacobins or their policies [c14 from OF, from Med. L *Jacōbīnus*, from LL *Jacōbus* James; the political club orig. met in the convent near the church of *St Jacques* in 1789] > ˌ**Jacoˈbinic** *or* ˌ**Jacoˈbinical** *adj* > ˈ**Jacobinism** *n*

Jacobite (ˈdʒækəˌbaɪt) *n Brit history* an adherent of James II after his overthrow in 1688, or of his descendants in their attempts to regain the throne [c17 from LL *Jacōbus* James + -ITE[1]] > **Jacobitic** (ˌdʒækəˈbɪtɪk) *adj*

Jacobsen (*Danish* ˈjakɔbsən) *n* **Arne** (ˈarnə) 1902–71, Danish architect and designer. His buildings include the Town Hall at Rodovre (1955)

Jacob's ladder *n* **1** *Old Testament* the ladder reaching up to heaven that Jacob saw in a dream (Genesis 28:12–17) **2** a ladder made of wooden or metal steps supported by ropes or chains **3** a North American plant with blue flowers and a ladder-like arrangement of leaves

Jacob's staff *n* a medieval instrument for measuring heights and distances

jaconet (ˈdʒækənɪt) *n* a light cotton fabric used for clothing, etc [c18 from Urdu *jagannāthī*, from *Jagannāthpūrī*, India, where orig. made]

Jacquard (ˈdʒækɑːd, dʒəˈkɑːd) *n* **1** Also called: **Jacquard weave** a fabric in which the design is incorporated into the weave **2** Also called: **Jacquard loom** the loom that produces this fabric [c19 after Joseph M. *Jacquard* (1752–1834), F inventor]

jactation (dʒækˈteɪʃən) *n* **1** *rare* the act of boasting **2** *pathol* another word for **jactitation** [c16 from L *jactātiō* bragging, from *jactāre* to flourish, from *jacere* to throw]

jactitation (ˌdʒæktɪˈteɪʃən) *n* **1** the act of boasting **2** a false assertion that one is married to another, formerly actionable at law **3** *pathol* restless tossing in bed, characteristic of severe fevers [c17 from Med. L, from L *jacitāre* to utter publicly, from *jactitāre* to toss about; see JACTATION]

Jacuzzi (dʒəˈkuːzɪ) *n trademark* **1** a device which swirls water in a bath **2** a bath containing such a device [c20 from Candido and Roy *Jacuzzi*, who developed and marketed it]

jade[1] (dʒeɪd) *n* **1** a semiprecious stone which varies in colour from white to green and is used for making ornaments and jewellery **2a** the green colour of jade **2b** (*as adj*): *a jade skirt* [c18 from F, from It. *giada*, from obs. Sp. *piedra de ijada* colic stone (lit.: stone of the flank, because it was believed to cure renal colic)]

jade[2] (dʒeɪd) *n* **1** an old overworked horse **2** *derog, facetious* a woman considered to be disreputable ▷ *vb* **jades, jading, jaded 3** to exhaust or make exhausted from work or use [c14 from ?] > ˈ**jadish** *adj*

jaded (ˈdʒeɪdɪd) *adj* **1** exhausted or dissipated **2** satiated > ˈ**jadedly** *adv* > ˈ**jadedness** *n*

jadeite (ˈdʒeɪdaɪt) *n* a green or white mineral, a variety of jade, consisting of sodium aluminium silicate in monoclinic crystalline form

Jadotville (*French* ʒadovil) *n* the former name of **Likasi**

j'adoube *French* (ʒadub) *interj chess* an expression of an intention to touch a piece in order to adjust its placement rather than to make a move [lit.: I adjust]

jaeger (ˈjeɪgə) *n US & Canad* any of several skuas [c18 from G *Jäger* hunter]

Jael (ˈdʒeɪəl) *n Old Testament* the woman who killed Sisera when he took refuge in her tent (Judges 4:17–21)

Jaén (xaˈen) *n* a city in S Spain. Pop: 107 184 (1998 est)

Jaffa (ˈdʒæfə, ˈdʒɑː-) *n* **1** a port in W Israel, on the Mediterranean: incorporated into Tel Aviv in 1950; an old Canaanite city. Biblical name: **Joppa**. Hebrew name: **Yafo 2** a large variety of orange, having a thick skin

Jaffna (ˈdʒæfnə) *n* a port in N Sri Lanka: for many centuries the capital of a Tamil kingdom. Pop: 145 600 (1997 est)

jag[1] (dʒæg) *vb* **jags, jagging, jagged 1** (*tr*) to cut unevenly **2** *Austral* to catch (fish) by impaling them on an unbaited hook ▷ *n* **3** *Scot* an informal word for **jab** (senses 3, 5) **4** a jagged notch or projection [c14 from ?]

jag[2] (dʒæg) *n sl* **1a** intoxication from drugs or alcohol **1b** a bout of drinking or drug taking **2** a period of uncontrolled activity: *a crying jag* [of unknown origin]

jagged (ˈdʒægɪd) *adj* having sharp projecting notches > ˈ**jaggedly** *adv*

Jagger (ˈdʒægə) *n* Sir **Mick**, full name *Michael Philip Jagger*. born 1943, English rock singer and songwriter: lead vocalist with the Rolling Stones

jaggy (ˈdʒægɪ) *adj* **jaggier, jaggiest 1** a less common word for **jagged 2** *Scot* prickly

jaguar (ˈdʒægjʊə) *n* a large feline mammal of S North America, Central America, and N South America, similar to the leopard but with larger spots on its coat [c17 from Port., from Guarani *yaguara*]

Jahwism (ˈjɑːˌwɪzəm) *or* **Jahvism** (ˈjɑːˌvɪzəm) *n* a variant of **Yahwism** or **Yahvism** > **Jahˈwistic** *or* **Jahˈvistic** *adj*

jai alai (ˈhaɪ ˈlaɪ, ˈhaɪ əˌlaɪ) *n* a version of pelota played by two or four players [via Sp. from Basque, from *jai* game + *alai* merry]

jail *or* **gaol** (dʒeɪl) *n* **1** a place for the confinement of persons convicted and sentenced to imprisonment or of persons awaiting trial ▷ *vb* **2** (*tr*) to confine in prison [c13 from OF *jaiole* cage, from Vulgar L *caveola* (unattested), from L *cavea* enclosure]

jailbait (ˈdʒeɪlˌbeɪt) *n inf* a young person, or young persons collectively, considered sexually attractive but below the age of consent

jailbird *or* **gaolbird** (ˈdʒeɪlˌbɜːd) *n* a person who is or has been confined to jail, esp repeatedly; convict

jailbreak *or* **gaolbreak** (ˈdʒeɪlˌbreɪk) *n* an escape from jail

jailer, jailor, *or* **gaoler** (ˈdʒeɪlə) *n* a person in charge of prisoners in a jail

Jain (dʒaɪn) *or* **Jaina** (ˈdʒaɪnə) *n* **1** an adherent of Jainism ▷ *adj* **2** of or relating to Jainism [c19 from Hindi *jaina* saint, lit.: overcomer, from Sansk.]

Jainism (ˈdʒaɪˌnɪzəm) *n* an ancient Hindu religion, characterized by the belief that the material world is progressing endlessly in a series of cycles > ˈ**Jainist** *n, adj*

Jaipur (dʒaɪˈpʊə) *n* a city of great beauty in N India, capital of Rajasthan state: University of Rajasthan (1947). Pop: 1 458 183 (1991)

Jakarta *or* **Djakarta** (dʒəˈkɑːtə) *n* the capital of Indonesia, in N West Java: founded in 1619 and ruled by the Dutch until 1945; the chief trading centre of the East in the 17th century; University of Indonesia (1947). Pop: 9 160 500 (1995 est). Former name (until 1949): **Batavia** ▷ www.jakarta.go.id

jake (dʒeɪk) *adj Austral & NZ sl* all right; fine: *she's jake* [from ?]

Jalalabad (dʒəˈlæləbæd) *n* a city in NE Afghanistan, capital of Nangarhar province; a trading, military, and tourist centre on the main route between Kabul and the Khyber Pass. Pop: 60 000 (latest est)

Jalandhar (ˈdʒælænˌdɑː) *n* a city in NW India, in central Punjab. Pop: 509 510 (1991)

jalap *or* **jalop** (ˈdʒæləp) *n* **1** a Mexican climbing plant **2** the dried and powdered root of any of these plants, used as a purgative [c17 from F, from Mexican Sp. *jalapa*] > **jalapic** (dʒəˈlæpɪk) *adj*

Jalapa (*Spanish* xaˈlapa) *n* a city in E central Mexico, capital of Veracruz State, at an altitude of 1427 m (4681 ft): resort. Pop: 375 000 (2000 est)

jalapeño (dʒæləˈpiːnəʊ; *Spanish* xalaˈpeɲo) *n, pl* **jalapeños** a type of red capsicum with a hot taste used in Mexican cookery [Mexican Sp.]

Jalisco (*Spanish* xaˈlisko) *n* a state of W Mexico, on the Pacific: crossed by the Sierra Madre; valuable mineral resources. Capital: Guadalajara. Pop: 6 321 278 (2000). Area: 80 137 sq km (30 934 sq miles)

jalopy *or* **jaloppy** (dʒəˈlɒpɪ) *n, pl* **jalopies** *or* **jaloppies** *inf* a dilapidated old car [c20 from ?]

jalousie ('ʒælʊˌziː) *n* **1** a window blind or shutter constructed from angled slats of wood, etc **2** a window made of angled slats of glass [c19 from OF *gelosie* latticework screen]

jam[1] (dʒæm) *vb* **jams, jamming, jammed** **1** (*tr*) to cram or wedge into or against something: *to jam paper into an incinerator* **2** (*tr*) to crowd or pack: *cars jammed the roads* **3** to make or become stuck or locked **4** (*tr*; often foll by *on*) to activate suddenly (esp in **jam on the brakes**) **5** (*tr*) to block; congest **6** (*tr*) to crush or squeeze **7** *radio* to prevent the clear reception of (radio communications) by transmitting other signals on the same frequency **8** (*intr*) *sl* to play in a jam session ▷ *n* **9** a crowd or congestion in a confined space: *a traffic jam* **10** the act of jamming or the state of being jammed **11** *inf* a predicament: *to help a friend out of a jam* **12** See **jam session** [c18 prob. imit.] > **'jammer** *n*

jam[2] (dʒæm) *n* **1** a preserve containing fruit, which has been boiled with sugar until the mixture sets **2** *sl* something desirable: *you want jam on it* [c18 ?from JAM[1] (the act of squeezing)]

Jam *abbrev for:* **1** Jamaica **2** *Bible* James

Jamaica (dʒə'meɪkə) *n* an island and state in the Caribbean: colonized by the Spanish from 1494 onwards, large numbers of Black slaves being imported; captured by the British in 1655 and established as a colony in 1866; gained full independence in 1962; a member of the Commonwealth. Exports: chiefly bauxite and alumina, sugar, and bananas. Official language: English. Religion: Protestant majority. Currency: Jamaican dollar. Capital: Kingston. Pop: 2 624 000 (2001 est). Area: 10 992 sq km (4244 sq miles) > **Ja'maican** *n, adj*
▷ www.cabinet.gov.jm
▷ www.conferencejamaica.com/tourist-board.htm

jamb *or* **jambe** (dʒæm) *n* a vertical side member of a doorframe, window frame, or lining [c14 from OF *jambe* leg, jamb, from LL *gamba* hoof, from Gk *kampē* joint]

Jambi ('dʒæmbɪ) *n* a port in W Indonesia, in SE Sumatra on the Hari River. Pop: 410 400 (1995 est). Also called: **Telanaipura**

jamboree (ˌdʒæmbə'riː) *n* **1** a large and often international gathering of Scouts **2** a party or celebration [c19 from ?]

James (dʒeɪmz) *n* **1** **Henry** 1843–1916, British novelist, short-story writer, and critic, born in the US Among his novels are *Washington Square* (1880), *The Portrait of a Lady* (1881), *The Bostonians* (1886), *The Wings of the Dove* (1902), *The Ambassadors* (1903), and *The Golden Bowl* (1904) **2** **Jesse (Woodson)** 1847–82, US outlaw **3** **P(hyllis) D(orothy)**, Baroness James of Holland Park. born 1920, British detective novelist. Her books include *Death of an Expert Witness* (1977), *Original Sin* (1994), and *Death in Holy Orders* (2001) **4** **William**, brother of Henry James. 1842–1910, US philosopher and psychologist, whose theory of pragmatism is expounded in *Essays in Radical Empiricism* (1912) His other works include *The Will to Believe* (1897), *The Principles of Psychology* (1890), and *The Varieties of Religious Experience* (1902) **5** *New Testament* **5a** known as *James the Great*. one of the twelve apostles, a son of Zebedee and brother to John the apostle (Matthew 4:21). Feast day: July 25 or April 30 **5b** known as *James the Less*. one of the twelve apostles, son of Alphaeus (Matthew 10:3). Feast day: May 3 or Oct. 9 **5c** known as *James the brother of the Lord*. a brother or close relative of Jesus (Mark 6:3; Galatians 1:19). Feast day: Oct. 23 **5d** the book ascribed to his authorship (in full **The Epistle of James**)

James I *n* **1** called *the Conqueror*. 1208–76, king of Aragon (1216–76). He captured the Balearic Islands and Valencia from the Muslims, thus beginning Aragonese expansion in the Mediterranean **2** 1394–1437, king of Scotland (1406–37), second son of Robert III **3** 1566–1625, king of England and Ireland (1603–25) and, as James VI, king of Scotland (1567–1625), in succession to Elizabeth I of England and his mother, Mary Queen of Scots, respectively. He alienated Parliament by his assertion of the divine right of kings, his favourites, esp the Duke of Buckingham, and his subservience to Spain

James II *n* **1** 1430–60, king of Scotland (1437–60), son of James I **2** 1633–1701, king of England, Ireland, and, as James VII, of Scotland (1685–88); son of Charles I. His pro-Catholic sympathies and arbitrary rule caused the Whigs and Tories to unite in inviting his eldest surviving daughter, Mary, and her husband, William of Orange, to take the throne as joint monarchs. James was defeated at the Boyne (1690) when he attempted to regain the throne

James III *n* 1451–88, king of Scotland (1460–88), son of James II

James IV *n* 1473–1513, king of Scotland (1488–1513), son of James III; he invaded England (1496) in support of Perkin Warbeck; he was killed at Flodden

James V *n* 1512–42, king of Scotland (1513–42), son of James IV

James VI *n* title as king of Scotland of **James I** of England and Ireland

James VII *n* title as king of Scotland of **James II** of England and Ireland

James Bay *n* the S arm of Hudson Bay, in central Canada. Area: 108 780 sq km (42 000 sq miles)

Jameson ('dʒeɪmsᵊn) *n* Sir **Leander Starr** 1853–1917, British administrator in South Africa, who led an expedition into the Transvaal in 1895 in an unsuccessful attempt to topple its Boer regime (the **Jameson Raid**); prime minister of Cape Colony (1904–08)

Jamestown ('dʒeɪmzˌtaʊn) *n* a ruined village in E Virginia, on **Jamestown Island** (a peninsula in the James River): the first permanent settlement by the English in America (1607); capital of Virginia (1607–98); abandoned in 1699

Jammu ('dʒʌmuː) *n* a city in N India, winter capital of the state of Jammu and Kashmir. Pop: 206 135 (1991)

Jammu and Kashmir *n* the official name for the part of **Kashmir** under Indian control

jammy ('dʒæmɪ) *adj* **jammier, jammiest** *Brit sl* **1** pleasant; desirable **2** lucky

Jamnagar (ˌdʒæmnə'gɑː) *n* a city in India, in Gujarat: noted for its palaces and temples: cement, pottery, textiles. Pop: 341 637 (1991)

jam-packed *adj* packed or filled to capacity

jam session *n sl* an unrehearsed or improvised performance by jazz or rock musicians [c20 prob. from JAM[1]]

Jamshedpur (ˌdʒʌmʃɛd'pʊə) *n* a city in NE India, in Jharkand: large iron and steel works (1907–11); a major industrial centre. Pop: 478 950 (1991)

Jamshid *or* **Jamshyd** (dʒæm'ʃiːd) *n Persian myth* a ruler of the peris who was punished for bragging that he was immortal by being changed into human form. He then became a great king of Persia. See also **peri**

Jan. *abbrev for* January

Janáček (*Czech* 'janaːtʃɛk) *n* **Leoš** ('lɛɔʃ) 1854–1928, Czech composer. His music is influenced by Czech folksong and speech rhythms and is remarkable for its integration of melody and language. His works include the operas *Jenufa* (1904) and *The Cunning Little Vixen* (1924), the *Glagolitic Mass* (1927), as well as orchestral and chamber music and songs

Jandal ('dʒændᵊl) *n NZ trademark* a kind of sandal with a strip of material between the big toe and the other toes and over the foot

Janet (*French* ʒanɛ) *n* **Pierre Marie Félix** (pjɛr mari feliks) 1859–1947, French psychologist and neurologist, noted particularly for his work on the origins of hysteria

jangle ('dʒæŋgᵊl) *vb* **jangles, jangling, jangled** **1** to sound or cause to sound discordantly, harshly, or unpleasantly

2 (*tr*) to produce a jarring effect on: *the accident jangled his nerves* **3** *arch* to wrangle ▷ *n* **4** a harsh unpleasant ringing noise **5** an argument or quarrel [c13 from OF *jangler*, of Gmc origin] > **'jangler** *n*

Janiculum (dʒə'nɪkjʊləm) *n* a hill in Rome across the River Tiber from the Seven Hills

Janina ('jani:na) *n* the Serbian name for **Ioánnina**

janissary ('dʒænɪsərɪ) *or* **janizary** ('dʒænɪzərɪ) *n, pl* **janissaries** *or* **janizaries** an infantryman in the Turkish army, originally a member of the sovereign's personal guard, from the 14th to the early 19th century [c16 from F, from It., from Turkish *yeniçeri*, from *yeni* new + *çeri* soldiery]

janitor ('dʒænɪtə) *n* **1** *Scot, US, & Canad* the caretaker of a building, esp a school **2** *chiefly US & Canad* a person employed to clean and maintain a building [c17 L: doorkeeper, from *jānua* door, from *jānus* covered way] > **janitorial** (,dʒænɪ'tɔ:rɪəl) *adj*

Jan Mayen ('jæn 'maɪən) *n* an island in the Arctic Ocean, between Greenland and N Norway: volcanic, with large glaciers; former site of Dutch whaling stations; annexed to Norway in 1929. Area: 373 sq km (144 sq miles)

Jansen ('dʒænsᵊn) *n* **Cornelis** (kɔ:'ni:lɪs) Latin name *Cornelius Jansenius*. 1585–1638, Dutch Roman Catholic theologian. In *Augustinus* (1640) he defended the teachings of St. Augustine, esp on free will, grace, and predestination

Jansenism ('dʒænsə,nɪzəm) *n* *RC Church* the doctrine of Cornelis Jansen and his disciples, who believed in predestination and denied free will > **'Jansenist** *n, adj* > **,Jansen'istic** *adj*

jansky ('dʒænskɪ) *n, pl* **janskys** (in radio astronomy) a unit used to measure the intensity of radio waves. Also called: **flux unit** [c20 after Karl G. *Jansky* (1905–50), US electrical engineer]

January ('dʒænjʊərɪ) *n, pl* **Januaries** the first month of the year, consisting of 31 days [c14 from L *Jānuārius*]

Janus ('dʒeɪnəs) *n* the Roman god of doorways, passages, and bridges. In art he is depicted with two heads facing opposite ways [c16 from L, from *jānus* archway]

Jap. *abbrev for* Japan(ese)

japan (dʒə'pæn) *n* **1** a glossy black lacquer originally from the Orient, used on wood, metal, etc **2** work decorated and varnished in the Japanese manner ▷ *vb* **japans, japanning, japanned** **3** (*tr*) to lacquer with japan or any similar varnish

Japan (dʒə'pæn) *n* an archipelago and empire in E Asia, extending for 3200 km (2000 miles) between the Sea of Japan and the Pacific and consisting of the main islands of Hokkaido, Honshu, Shikoku, and Kyushu and over 3000 smaller islands: feudalism abolished in 1871, followed by industrialization and expansion of territories, esp during World Wars I and II, when most of SE Asia came under Japanese control; dogma of the emperor's divinity abolished in 1946 under a new democratic constitution; rapid economic growth has made Japan the most industrialized nation in the Far East. Official language: Japanese. Religion: Shintoist majority, large Buddhist minority. Currency: yen. Capital: Tokyo. Pop: 127 100 000 (2001 est). Area: 369 660 sq km (142 726 sq miles). Japanese names: **Nippon, Nihon**
▷ http://jin.jcic.or.jp
▷ www.jnto.go.jp

Japan Current *n* a warm ocean current flowing northeastwards off the E coast of Japan towards the North Pacific. Also called: **Kuroshio**

Japanese (,dʒæpə'ni:z) *adj* **1** of or characteristic of Japan, its people, or their language ▷ *n* **2** (*pl* **Japanese**) a native or inhabitant of Japan **3** the official language of Japan

Japanese stranglehold *n* a wrestling hold in which an opponent's arms exert pressure on his own windpipe

jape (dʒeɪp) *n* **1** a jest or joke ▷ *vb* **japes, japing, japed** **2** to joke or jest (about) [c14 ?from OF *japper* to yap, imit.] > **'japer** *n* > **'japery** *n*

Japheth ('dʒeɪfɛθ) *n* *Old Testament* the second son of Noah, traditionally regarded as the ancestor of a number of non-Semitic nations (Genesis 10:1–5)

Japlish ('dʒæplɪʃ) *n* the adoption and adaptation of English words into the Japanese language [c20 from a blend of JAPANESE + ENGLISH]

japonica (dʒə'pɒnɪkə) *n* **1** Also called: **Japanese quince** a Japanese shrub cultivated for its red flowers and yellowish fruit **2** another name for the **camellia** [c19 from NL, fem of *japonicus* Japanese, from *Japonia* JAPAN]

Japurá (*Portuguese* ʒapu'ra) *n* a river in NW South America, rising in SW Colombia and flowing southeast across Colombia and Brazil to join the Amazon near Tefé: known as the Caquetá in Colombia. Length: about 2800 km (1750 miles). Spanish name: **Yapurá**

Jaques-Dalcroze (*French* ʒakdalkroz) *n* **Émile** (emil) 1865–1950, Swiss composer and teacher: invented eurythmics

jar[1] (dʒɑ:) *n* **1** a wide-mouthed container that is usually cylindrical, made of glass or earthenware, and without handles **2** Also: **jarful** the contents or quantity contained in a jar **3** *Brit inf* a glass of beer [c16 from OF *jarre, jarra*, from Ar. *jarrah* large earthen vessel]

jar[2] (dʒɑ:) *vb* **jars, jarring, jarred** **1** to vibrate or cause to vibrate **2** to make or cause to make a harsh discordant sound **3** (often foll by *on*) to have a disturbing or painful effect (on the nerves, mind, etc) **4** (*intr*) to disagree; clash ▷ *n* **5** a jolt or shock **6** a harsh discordant sound [c16 prob. imit.] > **'jarring** *adj* > **'jarringly** *adv*

jar[3] (dʒɑ:) *n* **on a** (*or* **the**) **jar** (of a door) slightly open; ajar [c17 (in the sense: turn): from earlier *char*, from OE *cierran* to turn]

jardinière (,ʒɑ:dɪ'njɛə) *n* **1** an ornamental pot or trough for plants **2** a garnish of fresh vegetables for a dish of meat [c19 from F, fem of *jardinier* gardener, from *jardin* GARDEN]

jargon ('dʒɑ:gən) *n* **1** specialized language concerned with a particular subject, culture, or profession **2** language characterized by pretentious vocabulary or meaning **3** gibberish [c14 from OF, ? imit.]

jarl (jɑ:l) *n* *medieval history* a Scandinavian chieftain or noble [c19 from ON] > **'jarldom** *n*

Jarman ('jɑ:mən) *n* **Derek** 1942–94, British film director and writer; his films include *Jubilee* (1977), *Caravaggio* (1986), and *Wittgenstein* (1993)

jarrah ('dʒærə) *n* an Australian eucalyptus tree that yields a valuable timber [from Abor.]

Jarrett ('dʒærɪt) *n* **Keith** born 1945, US jazz pianist and composer

Jarrow ('dʒærəʊ) *n* a port in NE England, in South Tyneside unitary authority, Tyne and Wear: ruined monastery where the Venerable Bede lived and died; its unemployed marched on London in the 1930s; shipyards, oil installations, iron and steel works. Pop: 29 325 (1991 est)

Jarry (*French* ʒari) *n* **Alfred** (alfrɛd) 1873–1907, French dramatist and poet, who anticipated the theatre of the absurd with his play *Ubu Roi* (1896)

Jaruzelski (*Polish* jaru:'ʒɛlski) *n* **Wojciech** ('vɔɪtʃɛk) born 1923, Polish statesman and soldier; prime minister (1981–85); head of state 1985–90 (as president from 1989)

Jas. *abbrev for* James

jasmine ('dʒæsmɪn, 'dʒæz-) *n* **1** Also called: **jessamine** any tropical or subtropical oleaceous shrub or climbing plant widely cultivated for their white, yellow, or red fragrant flowers **2** any of several other shrubs with fragrant flowers, such as the Cape jasmine, yellow jasmine, and frangipani (**red jasmine**) [c16 from OF *jasmin*, from Ar., from Persian *yāsmīn*]

Jason ('dʒeɪsᵊn) *n* *Greek myth* the hero who led the Argonauts in quest of the Golden Fleece. He became the husband of Medea, whom he later abandoned for Glauce

jaspé (ˈdʒæspeɪ) *adj* resembling jasper; variegated [c19 from F, from *jasper* to marble]

jasper (ˈdʒæspə) *n* **1** an opaque impure form of quartz, red, yellow, brown, or dark green in colour, used as a gemstone and for ornamental decoration **2** Also called: **jasper ware** a dense hard stoneware [c14 from OF *jaspe*, from L *jaspis*, from Gk *iaspis*, of Semitic origin]

Jasper National Park (ˈdʒæspə) *n* a national park in SW Canada, in W Alberta in the Rockies: wildlife sanctuary. Area: 10 900 sq km (4200 sq miles)

Jaspers (*German* ˈjaspərs) *n* **Karl** (karl) 1883–1969, German existentialist philosopher

Jassy (ˈjasi) *n* the German name for **Iași**

jato (ˈdʒeɪtəʊ) *n, pl* **jatos** *aeronautics* jet-assisted takeoff [c20 from *j(et-)a(ssisted) t(ake)o(ff)*]

jaundice (ˈdʒɔːndɪs) *n* **1** Also called: **icterus** yellowing of the skin due to the abnormal presence of bile pigments in the blood, as in hepatitis **2** jealousy, envy, and ill humour ▷ *vb* **jaundices, jaundicing, jaundiced** **3** to distort (the judgment, etc) adversely: *jealousy had jaundiced his mind* **4** (*tr*) to affect with or as if with jaundice [c14 from OF *jaunisse*, from *jaune* yellow, from L *galbinus* yellowish]

jaunt (dʒɔːnt) *n* **1** a short pleasurable excursion; outing ▷ *vb* **2** (*intr*) to go on such an excursion [c16 from ?]

jaunty (ˈdʒɔːntɪ) *adj* **jauntier, jauntiest** **1** sprightly and cheerful: *a jaunty step* **2** smart; trim: *a jaunty hat* [c17 from F *gentil* noble; see GENTEEL] > **ˈjauntily** *adv* > **ˈjauntiness** *n*

Jaurès (*French* ʒɔrɛs) *n* **Jean Léon** (ʒɑ̃ leɔ̃) 1859–1914, French politician and writer, who founded the socialist paper *l'Humanité* (1904), and united the French socialist movement into a single party (1905); assassinated

Java[1] (ˈdʒɑːvə) *n* an island of Indonesia, south of Borneo, from which it is separated by the **Java Sea**: politically the most important island of Indonesia; it consists chiefly of active volcanic mountains and is densely forested. It came under Dutch control in 1596 and became part of Indonesia in 1949. It is one of the most densely populated areas in the world. Capital: Jakarta. Pop (with Madura): 121 193 000 (1999 est). Area: 132 174 sq km (51 032 sq miles) > **ˈJavan** *n, adj*

Java[2] (ˈdʒɑːvə) *n trademark* a programming language especially applicable to the World Wide Web [c20 named after *Java* coffee, said to have been consumed in large quantities by the language's creators]

Java man *n* a type of primitive man, *Homo erectus*, that lived in the middle Palaeolithic Age in Java

Javanese (ˌdʒɑːvəˈniːz) *adj* **1** of or relating to the island of Java ▷ *n* **2** (*pl* **Javanese**) a native or inhabitant of Java **3** the Malayo-Polynesian language of Java

Javari *or* **Javary** (*Portuguese* ʒavaˈri) *n* a river in South America, flowing northeast as part of the border between Peru and Brazil to join the Amazon. Length: about 1050 km (650 miles). Spanish name: **Yavarí**

javelin (ˈdʒævlɪn) *n* **1** a long pointed spear thrown as a weapon or in competitive field events **2** **the javelin** the event or sport of throwing the javelin [c16 from OF *javeline*, var. of *javelot*, of Celtic origin]

javelin fish *n* a fish of the genus *Pomadasys* of semitropical Australian seas with a long spine on its anal fin

jaw (dʒɔː) *n* **1** the part of the skull of a vertebrate that frames the mouth and holds the teeth **2** the corresponding part of an invertebrate, esp an insect **3** a pair or either of a pair of hinged or sliding components of a machine or tool designed to grip an object **4** *sl* **4a** impudent talk **4b** idle conversation **4c** a lecture ▷ *vb* **5** (*intr*) *sl* **5a** to chat; gossip **5b** to lecture [c14 prob. from OF *joue* cheek]

jawbone (ˈdʒɔːˌbəʊn) *n* a nontechnical name for **mandible** or (less commonly) **maxilla**

jawbreaker (ˈdʒɔːˌbreɪkə) *n* **1** a device having hinged jaws for crushing rocks and ores **2** *inf* a word that is hard to pronounce > **ˈjawˌbreaking** *adj*

jaw-dropping *adj inf* amazing > **ˈjaw-ˌdroppingly** *adv*

ja well no fine *sentence substitute S African* used to indicate reluctant acceptance.

jaws (dʒɔːz) *pl n* **1** the narrow opening of some confined place such as a gorge **2** **the jaws** a dangerously close position: *the jaws of death*

Jaxartes (dʒækˈsɑːtiːz) *n* the ancient name for **Syr Darya**

jay (dʒeɪ) *n* **1** a passerine bird related to the crow having a pinkish-brown body, blue-and-black wings, and a black-and-white crest **2** a foolish or gullible person [c13 from OF *jai*, from LL *gāius*, ?from name *Gāius*]

Jay (dʒeɪ) *n* **John** 1745–1829, American statesman, jurist, and diplomat; first chief justice of the Supreme Court (1789–95) He negotiated the treaty with Great Britain (**Jay's treaty**, 1794), that settled outstanding disputes

Jaya (ˈdʒɑːjə) *n* **Mount** a mountain in E Indonesia, in Irian Jaya in the Sudirman Range: the highest mountain in New Guinea. Height: 5039 m (16 532 ft). Former names: (Mount) Carstensz, **Sukarno Peak**

Jayapura (ˌdʒɑːjɑːˈpʊərə) *n* a port in NE Indonesia, capital of Irian Jaya, on the N coast. Pop: 180 400 (1995 est). Former names: **Sukarnapura, Kotabaru, Hollandia**

Jayawardene (ˌdʒeɪəˈwɑːdɪnə) *n* **Junius Richard** 1906–96, Sri Lankan statesman; prime minister (1977–78) and first president of Sri Lanka (1978–89)

Jaycee (ˈdʒeɪˈsiː) *n US, Canad, Austral, & NZ* a young person who belongs to a junior chamber of commerce [c20 from *J(unior) C(hamber)*]

jaywalk (ˈdʒeɪˌwɔːk) *vb* (*intr*) to cross or walk in a street recklessly or illegally [c20 from JAY (sense 2)] > **ˈjayˌwalker** *n* > **ˈjayˌwalking** *n*

jazz (dʒæz) *n* **1a** music of US Black origin, characterized by syncopated rhythms, solo and group improvisation, and a variety of harmonic idioms and instrumental techniques **1b** (*as modifier*): *a jazz band* **1c** (*in combination*): *a jazzman* **2** *sl* rigmarole: *legal papers and all that jazz* ▷ *vb* **3** (*intr*) to play or dance to jazz music [c20 from ?] > **ˈjazzy** *adj* > **ˈjazzily** *adv* > **ˈjazziness** *n*

▷ www.apassion4jazz.net
▷ www.jazzreview.com
▷ www.allmusic.com
▷ www.jazzonln.com
▷ www.jazzinamerica.org

jazz up *vb* (*tr, adv*) *inf* **1** to imbue (a piece of music) with jazz qualities, esp by playing at a quicker tempo **2** to make more lively or appealing

JC *abbrev for:* **1** Jesus Christ **2** Julius Caesar

JCB *n trademark* a type of construction machine with a hydraulically operated shovel on the front and an excavator arm on the back [from the initials of J(oseph) C(yril) B(amford) (born 1916), its Brit manufacturer]

jealous (ˈdʒɛləs) *adj* **1** suspicious or fearful of being displaced by a rival **2** (often *postpositive* and foll by *of*) resentful (of) or vindictive (towards) **3** (often *postpositive* and foll by *of*) possessive and watchful in the protection (of): *jealous of one's reputation* **4** characterized by or resulting from jealousy **5** *obsolete except in Biblical use* demanding exclusive loyalty: *a jealous God* [c13 from OF *gelos*, from Med. L, from LL *zēlus* emulation, from Gk *zēlos* ZEAL] > **ˈjealously** *adv*

jealousy (ˈdʒɛləsɪ) *n, pl* **jealousies** the state or quality of being jealous

jean (dʒiːn) *n* a tough twill-weave cotton fabric used for hard-wearing trousers, overalls, etc [c16 short for *jean fustian*, from *Gene* GENOA]

Jean (*French* ʒɑ̃) *n* born 1921, grand duke of Luxembourg from 1964

Jean Baptiste (*French* ʒɑ̃batist) *n Canad sl* a French Canadian [F: John the Baptist, traditional patron saint of French Canada]

Jean de Meung (*French* ʒɑ̃ də mœ̃) *n* real name *Jean Clopinel*. ?1250–?1305, French poet, who continued Guillaume de Lorris' *Roman de la Rose*. His portion of the poem consists of some 18 000 lines and contains satirical attacks on women and the Church

Jeanne d'Arc (ʒan dark) *n* the French name of **Joan of Arc**

Jean Paul (*French* ʒɑ̃ pɔl) *n* real name *Johann Paul Friedrich Richter*. 1763–1825, German novelist

jeans (dʒiːnz) *pl n* trousers for casual wear, made esp of denim or corduroy [pl. of JEAN]

Jeans (dʒiːnz) *n* Sir **James Hopwood** 1877–1946, English astronomer, physicist, and mathematician, best known for his popular books on astronomy. He made important contributions to the kinetic theory of gases and the theory of stellar evolution

Jebel Musa (ˈdʒɛbᵊl ˈmuːsə) *n* a mountain in NW Morocco, near the Strait of Gibraltar: one of the Pillars of Hercules. Height: 850 m (2790 ft)

Jedda (ˈdʒɛdə) *n* another name for **Jidda**

Jeep (dʒiːp) *n trademark* a small road vehicle with four-wheel drive [c20 ?from GP, for *general-purpose* (*vehicle*), infl. by Eugene the *Jeep*, creature in a comic strip by E C Segar]

jeepers *or* **jeepers creepers** (ˈdʒiːpəz ˈkriːpəz) *interj US sl* a mild exclamation of surprise [c20 euphemism for *Jesus*]

jeer (dʒɪə) *vb* **1** (often foll by *at*) to laugh or scoff (at a person or thing) ▷ *n* **2** a remark or cry of derision [c16 from ?] > **ˈjeerer** *n* > **ˈjeering** *adj*, *n* > **ˈjeeringly** *adv*

Jefferson (ˈdʒɛfəsᵊn) *n* **Thomas** 1743–1826, US statesman: secretary of state (1790–93); third president (1801–09). He was the chief drafter of the Declaration of Independence (1776), the chief opponent of the centralizing policies of the Federalists under Hamilton, and effected the Louisiana Purchase (1803)

Jefferson City *n* a city in central Missouri, the state capital, on the Missouri River. Pop: 35 481 (1990)

Jeffrey (ˈdʒɛfrɪ) *n* **Francis,** Lord. 1773–1850, Scottish judge and literary critic. As editor of the *Edinburgh Review* (1803–29), he was noted for the severity of his criticism of the romantic poets, esp Wordsworth

Jeffreys (ˈdʒɛfrɪz) *n* **George,** 1st Baron Jeffreys of Wem. ?1645–89, English judge, notorious for his brutality at the "Bloody Assizes" (1685), where those involved in Monmouth's rebellion were tried

jehad (dʒɪˈhæd) *n* a variant spelling of **jihad**

Jehol (dʒəˈhɒl) *n* **1** a former province of NE China, north of the Great Wall: divided among Hebei, Liaoning, and Inner Mongolia in 1956. Area: 192 380 sq km (74 278 sq miles) **2** a region of NE China, in Hebei and Liaoning provinces: mountainous

Jehoshaphat (dʒɪˈhɒʃəˌfæt, -ˈhɒs-) *n Old Testament* **1** the king of Judah (?873–?849 BC) (I Kings 22:41–50) **2 Valley of Jehoshaphat** the site of Jehovah's apocalyptic judgment upon the nations (Joel 4:14)

Jehovah (dʒɪˈhəʊvə) *n Old Testament* the personal name of God, revealed to Moses on Mount Horeb (Exodus 3) [c16 from Med. L, from Heb. YHVH YAHWEH]

Jehovah's Witness *n* a member of a Christian Church of American origin, the followers of which believe that the end of the present world system of government is near ▷ http://watchtower.org/

Jehu (ˈdʒiːhjuː) *n* **1** *Old Testament* the successor to Ahab as king of Israel **2** *humorous* a reckless driver

jejune (dʒɪˈdʒuːn) *adj* **1** naive; unsophisticated **2** insipid; dull **3** lacking nourishment [c17 from L *jējūnus* hungry, empty] > **jeˈjunely** *adv* > **jeˈjuneness** *n*

jejunum (dʒɪˈdʒuːnəm) *n* the part of the small intestine between the duodenum and the ileum [c16 from L, from *jējūnus* empty; from the belief that the jejunum is empty after death]

Jekyll (ˈdʒɛkᵊl) *n* **Gertrude** 1843–1932, British landscape gardener: noted for her simplicity of design and use of indigenous plants

Jekyll and Hyde *n* **a** a person with two distinct personalities, one good, the other evil **b** (*as modifier*): *a Jekyll-and-Hyde personality* [c19 after the principal character of Robert Louis Stevenson's novel *The Strange Case of Dr Jekyll and Mr Hyde* (1886)]

jell *or* **gel** (dʒɛl) *vb* **1** to make or become gelatinous; congeal **2** (*intr*) to assume definite form: *his ideas have jelled* [c19 back formation from JELLY¹]

jellaba *or* **jellabah** (ˈdʒɛləbə) *n* variant spellings of **djellaba**

Jellicoe (ˈdʒɛlɪˌkəʊ) *n* **John Rushworth,** 1st Earl Jellicoe. 1859–1935, British admiral, who commanded the Grand Fleet at the Battle of Jutland (1916), which incapacitated the German fleet for the rest of World War I

jellies (ˈdʒɛlɪz) *pl n Brit sl* **1** gelatine capsules of temazepam, dissolved and injected as a recreational drug **2** Also called: **jelly shoes** shoes made from brightly coloured transparent plastic [c20 shortened from GELATINE]

jellify (ˈdʒɛlɪˌfaɪ) *vb* **jellifies, jellifying, jellified** to make into or become jelly > **ˌjellifiˈcation** *n*

jelly¹ (ˈdʒɛlɪ) *n*, *pl* **jellies** **1** a fruit-flavoured clear dessert set with gelatine **2** a preserve made from the juice of fruit boiled with sugar and used as jam **3** a savoury food preparation set with gelatine or with gelatinous stock: *calf's-foot jelly* ▷ *vb* **jellies, jellying, jellied** **4** to jellify [c14 from OF *gelee* frost, jelly, from *geler* to set hard, from L, from *gelu* frost] > **ˈjellied** *adj* > **ˈjelly-ˌlike** *adj*

jelly² (ˈdʒɛlɪ) *n Brit* a slang name for **gelignite**

jelly baby *n Brit* a small sweet made from a gelatinous substance formed to resemble a baby

jellyfish (ˈdʒɛlɪˌfɪʃ) *n*, *pl* **jellyfish** *or* **jellyfishes** **1** any marine coelenterate having a gelatinous umbrella-shaped body with trailing tentacles **2** *inf* a weak indecisive person

jelly fungus *n* a fungus that grows on trees and has a jelly-like consistency when wet

Jemappes (*French* ʒəmap) *n* a town in SW Belgium, in Hainaut province west of Mons: scene of a battle (1792) during the French Revolutionary Wars, in which the French defeated the Austrians. Pop: 18 100 (latest est)

jemmy (ˈdʒɛmɪ) *or US* **jimmy** *n*, *pl* **jemmies** *or US* **jimmies** **1** a short steel crowbar used, esp by burglars, for forcing doors and windows ▷ *vb* **jemmies, jemmying, jemmied** *or US* **jimmies, jimmying, jimmied** **2** (*tr*) to prise (something) open with a jemmy [c19 from the pet name for *James*]

Jena (*German* ˈjeːna) *n* a city in E central Germany, in Thuringia: university (1558), at which Hegel and Schiller taught; site of the battle (1806) in which Napoleon Bonaparte defeated the Prussians; optical and precision instrument industry. Pop: 101 061 (1996 est)

Jenghis Khan (ˈdʒɛŋgɪs ˈkɑːn) *n* See **Genghis Khan**

Jenner (ˈdʒɛnə) *n* **1 Edward** 1749–1823, English physician, who discovered vaccination by showing that injections of cowpox virus produce immunity against smallpox (1796) **2** Sir **William** 1815–98, English physician and pathologist, who differentiated between typhus and typhoid fevers (1849)

jennet, genet, *or* **gennet** (ˈdʒɛnɪt) *n* a small Spanish riding horse [c15 from OF *genet*, from Catalan *ginet*, horse used by the *Zenete*, from Ar. *Zanātah* the Zenete, a Moorish people renowned for their horsemanship]

jenny (ˈdʒɛnɪ) *n*, *pl* **jennies** **1** a machine for turning up the edge of a piece of sheet metal in preparation for making a joint **2** the female of certain animals or birds, esp a donkey, ass, or wren **3** short for **spinning jenny** **4** *billiards, etc* an in-off [c17 from name *Jenny*, dim. of *Jane*]

Jensen (*Danish* ˈjɛnsən) *n* **Johannes Vilhelm** (joˈhanəs ˈvɪlhelm) 1873–1950, Danish novelist, poet, and essayist: best known for his novel sequence about the origins of mankind *The Long Journey* (1908–22). Nobel prize for literature 1944

jeopardize *or* **jeopardise** ('dʒɛpəˌdaɪz) *vb* **jeopardizes, jeopardizing, jeopardized** *or* **jeopardises, jeopardising, jeopardised** (*tr*) **1** to risk; hazard: *he jeopardized his job by being persistently unpunctual* **2** to put in danger

jeopardy ('dʒɛpədɪ) *n* (usually preceded by *in*) **1** danger of injury, loss, death, etc: *his health was in jeopardy* **2** *law* danger of being convicted and punished for a criminal offence [c14 from OF *jeu parti*, lit.: divided game, hence uncertain issue, from *jeu* game, from L *jocus* joke, game + *partir* to divide]

Jephthah ('dʒɛfθə) *n Old Testament* a judge of Israel, who sacrificed his daughter in fulfilment of a vow (Judges 11:12–40). Douay spelling: **Jephte** ('dʒɛftə)

jequirity (dʒɪ'kwɪrɪtɪ) *n, pl* **jequirities** a tropical climbing plant with scarlet black-spotted seeds used as beads, and roots used as a substitute for liquorice. Also called: **Indian liquorice** [c19 from Port. *jequiriti*, of Amerind origin, from *jekiriti*]

Jer. *Bible abbrev for* Jeremiah

jerbil ('dʒɜːbɪl) *n* a variant spelling of **gerbil**

jerboa (dʒɜː'bəʊə) *n* any small nocturnal burrowing rodent inhabiting dry regions of Asia and N Africa, having long hind legs specialized for jumping [c17 from NL, from Ar. *yarbūʻ*]

jeremiad (ˌdʒɛrɪ'maɪəd) *n* a long mournful lamentation or complaint [c18 from F *jérémiade*, referring to the Lamentations of Jeremiah in the Old Testament]

Jeremiah (ˌdʒɛrɪ'maɪə) *n* **1** *Old Testament* **1a** a major prophet of Judah from about 626 to 587 BC **1b** the book containing his oracles **2** a person who habitually prophesies doom or denounces contemporary society

jerepigo (ˌdʒɛrɪ'pɪgəʊ) *n S African* a sweet white or red sherry-type wine [from Port. *cheripiga* an adulterant of port wine]

Jerez (*Spanish* xe'rɛθ) *n* a town in SW Spain: famous for the making of sherry. Pop: 181 602 (1998 est). Official name: **Jerez de la Frontera** (xe'rɛð ðe la frɔn'tera). Former name: **Xeres**

Jericho ('dʒɛrɪˌkəʊ) *n* a village in the West Bank near the N end of the Dead Sea, 251 m (825 ft) below sea level: on the site of an ancient city, the first place to be taken by the Israelites under Joshua after entering the Promised Land in the 14th century BC (Joshua 6)

jerk[1] (dʒɜːk) *vb* **1** to move or cause to move with an irregular or spasmodic motion **2** to throw, twist, pull, or push (something) abruptly or spasmodically **3** (*tr*; often foll by *out*) to utter (words, etc) in a spasmodic or breathless manner ▷ *n* **4** an abrupt or spasmodic movement **5** an irregular jolting motion **6** (*pl*) Also called: **physical jerks** *Brit inf* physical exercises **7** *sl, chiefly US & Canad* a stupid or ignorant person [c16 prob. var. of *yerk* to pull stitches tight] > **'jerker** *n*

jerk[2] (dʒɜːk) *vb* (*tr*) **1** to preserve beef, etc, by cutting into thin strips and drying in the sun ▷ *n* **2** Also called: **jerky** jerked meat [c18 back formation from *jerky*, from Sp. *charqui*, from Quechuan]

jerkin ('dʒɜːkɪn) *n* **1** a sleeveless short jacket worn by men or women **2** a man's sleeveless fitted jacket, often made of leather, worn in the 16th and 17th centuries [c16 from ?]

jerk off *or US* **jack off** *vb* (*adv, often reflexive*) *sl* (of a male) to masturbate

jerky ('dʒɜːkɪ) *adj* **jerkier, jerkiest** characterized by jerks > **'jerkily** *adv* > **'jerkiness** *n*

jeroboam (ˌdʒɛrə'bəʊəm) *n* a wine bottle holding the equivalent of four normal bottles [c19 allusion to JEROBOAM, a "mighty man of valour" (I Kings 11:28) who "made Israel to sin" (I Kings 14:16)]

Jeroboam (ˌdʒɛrə'bəʊəm) *n Old Testament* **1** the first king of the northern kingdom of Israel (?922–?901 BC) **2** king of the northern kingdom of Israel (?786–?746 BC)

Jerome (dʒə'rəʊm) *n* **1** Latin name *Eusebius Hieronymus*. ?347–?420 AD, Christian monk and scholar, whose outstanding work was the production of the Vulgate. Feast day: Sept. 30 **2** **Jerome K(lapka)** 1859–1927, English humorous writer; author of *Three Men in a Boat* (1889)

jerry ('dʒɛrɪ) *n, pl* **jerries** *Brit* an informal word for **chamber pot**

Jerry ('dʒɛrɪ) *n, pl* **Jerries** *Brit sl* **1** a German, esp a German soldier **2** the Germans collectively

jerry-build *vb* **jerry-builds, jerry-building, jerry-built** (*tr*) to build (houses, flats, etc) badly using cheap materials > **'jerry-ˌbuilder** *n*

jerry can *n* a flat-sided can with a capacity of between 4.5 and 5 gallons used for storing or transporting liquids, esp motor fuel [c20 from JERRY]

jersey ('dʒɜːzɪ) *n* **1** a knitted garment covering the upper part of the body **2a** a machine-knitted slightly elastic cloth of wool, silk, nylon, etc, used for clothing **2b** (*as modifier*): *a jersey suit* **3** a football shirt [c16 from JERSEY, from the woollen sweaters worn by the fishermen]

Jersey ('dʒɜːzɪ) *n* **1** an island in the English Channel, the largest of the Channel Islands: forms, with two other islands, the bailiwick of Jersey; colonized from Normandy in the 11th century and still officially French-speaking; noted for finance, market gardening, dairy farming, and tourism. Capital: St Helier. Pop: 89 400 (2001 est). Area: 116 sq km (45 sq miles) **2** a breed of dairy cattle producing milk with a high butterfat content, originating from the island of Jersey

Jersey City *n* an industrial city in NE New Jersey, opposite Manhattan on a peninsula between the Hudson and Hackensack Rivers: part of the Port of New York; site of one of the greatest railway terminals in the world. Pop: 240 055 (2000)

Jerusalem (dʒə'ruːsələm) *n* **1** the de facto capital of Israel (recognition of this has been withheld by the United Nations), situated in the Judaean hills: became capital of the Hebrew kingdom after its capture by David around 1000 BC; destroyed by Nebuchadnezzar of Babylon in 586 BC; taken by the Romans in 63 BC; devastated in 70 AD and 135 AD during the Jewish rebellions against Rome; fell to the Arabs in 637 and to the Seljuk Turks in 1071; ruled by Crusaders from 1099 to 1187 and by the Egyptians and Turks until conquered by the British (1917); centre of the British mandate of Palestine from 1920 to 1948, when the Arabs took the old city and the Jews held the new city; unified after the Six Day War (1967) under the Israelis; the holy city of Jews, Christians, and Muslims. Pop: 633 700 (1999 est) **2a the New Jerusalem** *Christianity* Heaven **2b** any ideal city
▷ www.jerusalem.muni.il

Jerusalem artichoke *n* **1** a North American sunflower widely cultivated for its underground edible tubers **2** the tuber of this plant, which is eaten as a vegetable [c17 by folk etymology from It. *girasole articiocco*; see GIRASOL]

Jervis Bay ('dʒɑːvɪs) *n* an inlet of the Pacific in SE Australia, on the coast of S New South Wales: part of the Australian Capital Territory: site of the Royal Australian Naval College

Jespersen ('jɛspəsᵊn, 'dʒɛs-) *n* **(Jens) Otto (Harry)** 1860–1943, Danish philologist: author of *Modern English Grammar* (1909–31)

jess (dʒɛs) *n falconry* a short leather strap, one end of which is permanently attached to the leg of a hawk or falcon [c14 from OF *ges*, from L *jactus* a throw, from *jacere* to throw] > **jessed** *adj*

jessamine ('dʒɛsəmɪn) *n* another name for **jasmine** (sense 1)

Jesse ('dʒɛsɪ) *n Old Testament* the father of David (I Samuel 16)

Jesselton ('dʒɛsəltən) *n* the former name of **Kota Kinabalu**

Jj

jessie ('dʒɛsɪ) *n Brit sl* an effeminate, weak, or cowardly boy or man

jest (dʒɛst) *n* **1** something done or said for amusement; joke **2** playfulness; fun: *to act in jest* **3** a jeer or taunt **4** an object of derision ▷ *vb* **5** to act or speak in an amusing or frivolous way **6** to make fun of (a person or thing) [C13 var. of GEST] > **'jesting** *adj, n* > **'jestingly** *adv*

jester ('dʒɛstə) *n* a professional clown employed by a king or nobleman during the Middle Ages

Jesu ('dʒi:zju:) *n* a poetic name for or vocative form of **Jesus** [C17 from LL, vocative of JESUS]

Jesuit ('dʒɛzjʊɪt) *n* **1** a member of a Roman Catholic religious order (the **Society of Jesus**) founded by Ignatius Loyola in 1534 with the aim of defending Catholicism against the Reformation **2** (*sometimes not cap*) *inf, offens* a person given to subtle and equivocating arguments [C16 from NL *Jēsuita*, from LL *Jēsus* + *-ita* -ITE[1]] > ,**Jesu'itical** *adj*

Jesus ('dʒi:zəs) *n* **1** Also called: **Jesus Christ, Jesus of Nazareth** ?4 BC–?29 AD, founder of Christianity, born in Bethlehem and brought up in Nazareth as a Jew. He is believed by Christians to be the Son of God and to have been miraculously conceived by the Virgin Mary, wife of Joseph. With 12 disciples, he undertook two missionary journeys through Galilee, performing miracles, teaching, and proclaiming the coming of the Kingdom of God. His revolutionary Sermon on the Mount (Matthew 5–8), which preaches love, humility, and charity, the essence of his teaching, aroused the hostility of the Pharisees. After the Last Supper with his disciples, he was betrayed by Judas and crucified. He is believed by Christians to have risen from his tomb after three days, appeared to his disciples several times, and ascended to Heaven after 40 days **2** *Son of Sirach.* 3rd century BC, author of the Apocryphal book of Ecclesiasticus ▷ *interj also* **Jesus wept 3** *taboo slang* used to express intense surprise, dismay, etc [via Latin from Greek *Iēsous*, from Hebrew *Yeshūa'*, shortened from *Yehōshūa'* God is help, JOSHUA]

Jesus freak *n inf* a vociferous Christian, esp one who is evangelical and belongs to a community

jet[1] (dʒɛt) *n* **1** a thin stream of liquid or gas forced out of a small aperture **2** an outlet or nozzle for emitting such a stream **3** a jet-propelled aircraft ▷ *vb* **jets, jetting, jetted 4** to issue or cause to issue in a jet: *water jetted from the hose* **5** to transport or be transported by jet aircraft [C16 from OF *jeter* to throw, from L *jactāre* to toss about]

jet[2] (dʒɛt) *n* **a** a hard black variety of coal that takes a brilliant polish and is used for jewellery, etc **b** (*as modifier*): *jet earrings* [C14 from OF *jaiet*, from L, from Gk *lithos gagatēs* stone of *Gagai*, a town in Lycia, Asia Minor]

jet black *n* **a** a deep black colour **b** (*as adj*): *jet-black hair*

jet-boat *n* a power boat that is powered and steered by a jet of water under pressure

jeté (ʒə'teɪ) *n ballet* a step in which the dancer springs from one leg and lands on the other [F, lit.: thrown, from *jeter*; see JET[1]]

jet engine *n* a gas turbine, esp one fitted to an aircraft

jetfoil ('dʒɛt,fɔɪl) *n* a type of hydrofoil that is propelled by water jets [C20 from a blend of JET[1] + (HYDRO)FOIL]

Jethro ('dʒɛθrəʊ) *n Old Testament* a Midianite priest, the father-in-law of Moses (Exodus 3:1; 4:18)

jet lag *n* a general feeling of fatigue, disorientation, or nausea often experienced by air travellers after long journeys

jet-propelled *adj* **1** driven by jet propulsion **2** *inf* very fast

jet propulsion *n* **1** propulsion by means of a jet of fluid **2** propulsion by means of a gas turbine, esp when the exhaust gases provide the propulsive thrust

jetsam ('dʒɛtsəm) *n* **1** that portion of the cargo of a vessel thrown overboard to lighten her, as during a storm ▷ Cf **flotsam** (sense 1) **2** another word for **flotsam** (sense 2) [C16 shortened from JETTISON]

jet set *n* **a** a rich and fashionable social set, the members of which travel widely for pleasure **b** (*as modifier*): *jet-set travellers* > **'jet-,setter** *n* > **'jet-,setting** *n, adj*

jet ski *n trademark* **1** a small self-propelled vehicle for one person resembling a scooter, which skims across water on a flat keel, and is steered by means of handlebars ▷ *vb* **jet-ski, jet-skis, jet-skiing, jet-skied** *or* **jet ski'd** (*intr*) **2** to ride a jet ski > **jet skier** *n* > **jet skiing** *n*

jet stream *n* **1** *meteorol* a narrow belt of high-altitude winds moving east at high speeds **2** the jet of exhaust gases produced by a gas turbine, etc

jettison ('dʒɛtɪsᵊn, -zᵊn) *vb* **jettisons, jettisoning, jettisoned** (*tr*) **1** to abandon: *to jettison old clothes* **2** to throw overboard ▷ *n* **3** another word for **jetsam** (sense 1) [C15 from OF, ult. from L *jactātiō* a tossing about]

jetton ('dʒɛtᵊn) *n* a counter or token, esp a chip used in such gambling games as roulette [C18 from F *jeton*, from *jeter* to cast up (accounts); see JET[1]]

jetty ('dʒɛtɪ) *n, pl* **jetties 1** a structure built from a shore out into the water to direct currents or protect a harbour **2** a landing pier; dock [C15 from OF *jetee* projecting part, lit.: something thrown out, from *jeter* to throw]

jeu d'esprit *French* (ʒø dɛspri) *n, pl* ***jeux d'esprit*** (ʒø dɛspri). a light-hearted display of wit or cleverness, esp in literature [lit.: play of spirit]

Jevons ('dʒɛvᵊnz) *n* **William Stanley** 1835–82, English economist and logician: introduced the concept of final or marginal utility in *The Theory of Political Economy* (1871)

Jew (dʒu:) *n* **1** a member of the Semitic people who are descended from the ancient Israelites **2** a person whose religion is Judaism [C12 from OF *juiu*, from L *jūdaeus*, from Gk *ioudaios*, from Heb., from *yehūdāh* JUDAH]

JEWISH CALENDAR

Tishri (Sept/Oct)
Cheshvan *or* **Heshvan** (Oct/Nov)
Kislev (Nov/Dec)
Tevet (Dec/Jan)
Shevat *or* **Shebet** (Apr/May)
Adar (Feb/Mar)
Nisan (Mar/Apr)
Iyar *or* **Iyyar** (Apr/May)
Sivan (May/June)
Tammuz (June/July)
Av *or* **Ab** (July/Aug)
Elul (Aug/Sept)

jewel ('dʒu:əl) *n* **1** a precious or semiprecious stone; gem **2** a person or thing resembling a jewel in preciousness, brilliance, etc **3** a gemstone used as a bearing in a watch **4** a piece of jewellery ▷ *vb* **jewels, jewelling, jewelled** *or US* **jewels, jeweling, jeweled 5** (*tr*) to fit or decorate with a jewel or jewels [C13 from OF *jouel*, ?from *jeu* game, from L *jocus*]

jewelfish ('dʒu:əl,fɪʃ) *n, pl* **jewelfish** *or* **jewelfishes** a beautifully coloured and popular aquarium fish native to Africa

jeweller *or US* **jeweler** ('dʒu:ələ) *n* a person whose business is the cutting or setting of gemstones or the making or selling of jewellery

jeweller's rouge *n* a finely powdered form of ferric oxide used as a metal polish

jewellery *or US* **jewelry** ('dʒu:əlrɪ) *n* objects that are worn for personal adornment, such as rings, necklaces, etc, considered collectively

▷ www.mondera.com/learn/antiques.asp
▷ www.add.gr/jewel/elka/index.html

▷ www.vam.ac.uk/exploring/galleries/metalwork/jewellery
▷ www.nationalmuseumindia.org/jew_ill.html
▷ www.tiffany.com

Jewess ('dʒuːɪs) *n offens* a Jewish girl or woman

jewfish ('dʒuːˌfɪʃ) *n, pl* **jewfish** *or* **jewfishes** **1** any of various large dark fishes of warm or tropical seas **2** *Austral* a freshwater catfish [c17 from ?]

jewie ('dʒuːɪ) *n Austral inf* a jewfish

Jewish ('dʒuːɪʃ) *adj* of or characteristic of Jews > '**Jewishly** *adv* > '**Jewishness** *n*

Jewish Autonomous Region *n* an administrative division of SE Russia, in E Siberia: colonized by Jews in 1928; largely agricultural. Capital: Birobidzhan. Pop: 216 000 (1995 est). Area: 36 000 sq km (13 895 sq miles). Also called: **Birobidzhan, Birobijan**

Jew lizard *n* a large Australian lizard with spiny scales round its neck

Jewry ('dʒʊərɪ) *n, pl* **Jewries** **1a** Jews collectively **1b** the Jewish religion or culture **2** a quarter of a town inhabited by Jews

jew's-ear *n* a pinky-red fungus

jew's-harp *n* a musical instrument consisting of a small lyre-shaped metal frame held between the teeth, with a steel tongue plucked with the finger

Jezebel ('dʒɛzəˌbɛl) *n* **1** *Old Testament* the wife of Ahab, king of Israel **2** (*sometimes not cap*) a shameless or scheming woman

Jezreel ('dʒɛzrɪəl) *n* **Plain of** another name for **Esdraelon**

JFK *abbrev for* John Fitzgerald Kennedy

Jhansi ('dʒɑːnsɪ) *n* a city in central India, in SW Uttar Pradesh: scene of a mutiny against the British in 1857. Pop: 300 850 (1991)

Jharkand ('dʒɑːkʌnd) *n* a state of NE India, created in 2000 from the S part of Bihar: consists of part of the Chota Nagpur plateau; mineral extraction, including coal and mica. Capital: Ranchi. pop: 26 909 428 (2001). Area 74 677 sq km (28 833 sq miles)

Jhelum ('dʒiːləm) *n* a river in Pakistan and Kashmir, rising in W central Kashmir and flowing northwest through the Vale of Kashmir, then southwest into N West Punjab to join the Chenab River: important for irrigation, having the Mangla Dam (Pakistan), completed in 1967. Length: about 720 km (450 miles)

JHVH *or* **JHWH** *Old Testament* a variant of **YHVH**

Jiang Qing ('dʒjæŋ 'tʃɪŋ) *or* **Chiang Ch'ing** *n* 1913–91, Chinese Communist actress and politician; widow of Mao Tse-tung. She was a leading member of the Gang of Four

Jiangsu ('dʒjæŋ'suː) *or* **Kiangsu** *n* a province of E China, on the Yellow Sea: consists mostly of the marshy delta of the Yangtze River, with some of China's largest cities and most densely populated areas. Capital: Nanjing. Pop: 74 380 000 (2000 est). Area: 102 200 sq km (39 860 sq miles)

Jiangxi ('dʒjæŋ'ʃiː) *or* **Kiangsi** *n* a province of SE central China, in the basins of the Kan River and the Poyang Lake: mineral resources include coal and tungsten. Capital: Nanchang. Pop: 41 400 000 (2000 est). Area: 164 800 sq km (64 300 sq miles)

Jiang Zemin ('dʒjæŋ ʒeɪ'mɪn) *n* born 1926, Chinese Communist politician: president (1993–2003)

Jiazhou ('dʒjæ'dʒəʊ) *or* **Kiaochow** *n* a territory of NE China, in SE Shandong province, surrounding **Jiazhou Bay** (an inlet of the Yellow Sea): leased to Germany from 1898 to 1914. Area: about 520 sq km (200 sq miles)

jib[1] (dʒɪb) *n* **1** *naut* any triangular sail set forward of the foremast of a vessel **2** **cut of someone's jib** someone's manner, style, etc [c17 from ?]

jib[2] (dʒɪb) *vb* **jibs, jibbing, jibbed** (*intr*) *chiefly Brit* **1** (often foll by *at*) to be reluctant (to) **2** (of an animal) to stop short and refuse to go forwards **3** *naut* a variant of **gybe** [c19 from ?] > '**jibber** *n*

jib[3] (dʒɪb) *n* the projecting arm of a crane or the boom of a derrick [c18 prob. based on GIBBET]

jib boom *n naut* a spar forming an extension of the bowsprit

jibe[1] (dʒaɪb) *or* **jib** (dʒɪb) *vb* **jibes, jibing, jibed** *or* **jibs, jibbing, jibbed** *n naut* a variant of **gybe**

jibe[2] (dʒaɪb) *vb* **jibes, jibing, jibed** a variant spelling of **gibe**[1]

jibe[3] (dʒaɪb) *vb* **jibes, jibing, jibed** (*intr*) *inf* to agree; accord; harmonize [c19 from ?]

Jibouti *or* **Jibuti** (dʒɪ'buːtɪ) *n* variant spellings of **Djibouti**

Jidda ('dʒɪdə) *or* **Jedda** *n* a port in W Saudi Arabia, on the Red Sea: the diplomatic capital and the port of entry for Mecca, 80 km (50 miles) east. Pop: 2 046 000 (1991 est)

jiffy ('dʒɪfɪ) *or* **jiff** *n, pl* **jiffies** *or* **jiffs** *inf* a very short time: *wait a jiffy* [c18 from ?]

Jiffy bag *n trademark* a large padded envelope

jig (dʒɪg) *n* **1** any of several old rustic kicking and leaping dances **2** a piece of music composed for or in the rhythm of this dance **3** a mechanical device designed to hold and locate a component during machining **4** *angling* any of various spinning lures that wobble when drawn through the water **5** Also called: **jigger** *mining* a device for separating ore from waste material by agitation in water ▷ *vb* **jigs, jigging, jigged** **6** to dance (a jig) **7** to jerk or cause to jerk up and down rapidly **8** (often foll by *up*) to fit or be fitted in a jig **9** (*tr*) to drill or cut (a workpiece) in a jig **10** (*tr*) *mining* to separate ore or coal from waste material using a jig [c16 from ?]

Jigawa (ˌdʒɪ'gɑːwə) *n* a state of N Nigeria. Capital: Dutse. Pop: 3 164 134 (1995 est). Area (including Kano state): 43 285 sq km (16 712 sq miles)

jigger[1] ('dʒɪgə) *n* **1** a person or thing that jigs **2** *golf* (formerly) a club, an iron, usually No. 4 **3** any of a number of mechanical devices having a vibratory motion **4** a light lifting tackle used on ships **5** a small glass, esp for whisky **6** *billiards* another word for **bridge**[1] (sense 11) **7** NZ a light hand- or power-propelled vehicle used on railway lines

jigger[2] *or* **jigger flea** ('dʒɪgə) *n* another name for the **chigoe** (sense 1)

jiggered ('dʒɪgəd) *adj* (*postpositive*) *inf* damned; blowed [c19 prob. euphemism for *buggered;* see BUGGER]

jiggermast ('dʒɪgəˌmɑːst) *n naut* any small mast on a sailing vessel

jiggery-pokery ('dʒɪgərɪ'pəʊkərɪ) *n inf, chiefly Brit* dishonest or deceitful behaviour [c19 from Scot. dialect *joukery-pawkery*]

jiggle ('dʒɪgᵊl) *vb* **jiggles, jiggling, jiggled** **1** to move or cause to move up and down or to and fro with a short jerky motion ▷ *n* **2** a short jerky motion [c19 frequentative of JIG] > '**jiggly** *adj*

jigsaw ('dʒɪgˌsɔː) *n* **1** a mechanical saw with a fine steel blade for cutting intricate curves in sheets of material **2** See **jigsaw puzzle** [c19 from JIG (to jerk up and down rapidly) + SAW[1]]

jigsaw puzzle *n* a puzzle in which the player has to reassemble a picture that has been cut into irregularly shaped interlocking pieces

jihad *or* **jehad** (dʒɪ'hæd) *n Islam* a holy war against infidels undertaken by Muslims [c19 from Ar. *jihād* a conflict]

Jilin ('dʒiː'lɪn) *or* **Kirin** *n* **1** a province of NE China, in central Manchuria. Capital: Changchun. Pop: 27 280 000 (2000 est). Area: 187 000 sq km (72 930 sq miles) **2** Also called: **Chi-lin** ('tʃiː'lɪn) a river port in NE China, in N central Jilin province on the Songhua River. Pop: 1 165 418 (1999 est)

Jilong ('dʒiː'lʊŋ) *n* the Pinyin transliteration of the Chinese name for **Chilung**

jilt (dʒɪlt) *vb* **1** (*tr*) to leave or reject (a lover), esp without previous warning ▷ *n* **2** a woman who jilts a lover [c17 from dialect *jillet* flighty girl, dim. of name *Gill*]

jim crow ('dʒɪm 'krəʊ) *n (often caps) US* **1a** the policy or practice of segregating Blacks **1b** *(as modifier)*: *jim-crow laws* **2** a derogatory term for **Black**[1] **3** an implement for bending iron bars or rails [c19 from *Jim Crow*, name of song used as the basis of an act by Thomas Rice (1808–60), US entertainer] > **'jim-'crowism** *n*

Jiménez (*Spanish* xi'meneθ) *n* **Juan Ramón** (xwan ra'mɔn) 1881–1958, Spanish lyric poet. His most famous work is *Platero y yo* (1917), a prose poem: Nobel prize for literature 1956

Jiménez de Cisneros (*Spanish* xi'meneð ðe θiz'nerɔs) *n* **Francisco** (fran'θisko) 1436–1517, Spanish cardinal and statesman; regent of Castile (1506–07) and Spain (1516–17) and grand inquisitor for Castile and León (1507–17). Also called: **Ximenez de Cisneros**

jimjams ('dʒɪm,dʒæmz) *pl n* **1** *sl* delirium tremens **2** a state of nervous tension or anxiety **3** *inf* pyjamas [c19 whimsical formation based on JAM[1]]

jimmy ('dʒɪmɪ) *n, pl* **jimmies**, *vb* **jimmies, jimmying, jimmied** a US variant of **jemmy**

Jinan ('dʒiː'næn), **Chinan**, *or* **Tsinan** *n* an industrial city in NE China, capital of Shandong province; probably over 3000 years old. Pop: 1 713 036 (1999 est)

Jingdezhen ('dʒɪŋ'dɛdʒɛn), **Fowliang**, *or* **Fou-liang** *n* a city in SE China, in NE Jiangxi province east of Lake Poyang: famous for its porcelain industry, established in the sixth century. Pop: 315 036 (1999 est)

Jinghis Khan ('dʒɪŋgɪs 'kɑːn) *n* See **Genghis Khan**

jingle ('dʒɪŋgᵊl) *vb* **jingles, jingling, jingled 1** to ring or cause to ring lightly and repeatedly **2** *(intr)* to sound in a manner suggestive of jingling: *a jingling verse* ▷ *n* **3** a sound of metal jingling **4** a rhythmic verse, etc, esp one used in advertising [c16 prob. imit.] > **'jingly** *adj*

jingo ('dʒɪŋgəʊ) *n, pl* **jingoes 1** a loud and bellicose patriot **2** jingoism **3 by jingo** an exclamation of surprise [c17 orig. ? euphemism for *Jesus*; applied to bellicose patriots after the use of *by Jingo!* in a 19th-cent. song]

jingoism ('dʒɪŋgəʊ,ɪzəm) *n* the belligerent spirit or foreign policy of jingoes > **'jingoist** *n, adj* > **jingo'istic** *adj*

Jinja ('dʒɪndʒə) *n* a town in Uganda, on the N shore of Lake Victoria. Pop: 60 979 (1991)

Jinjiang ('dʒɪn'dʒjæŋ), **Chinkiang**, *or* **Cheng-chiang** *n* a port in E China, in S Jiangsu at the confluence of the Yangtze River and the Grand Canal. Pop: 136 204 (1999 est)

jink (dʒɪŋk) *vb* **1** *(intr)* to move swiftly or turn in order to dodge ▷ *n* **2** a jinking movement [c18 of Scot. origin, imit. of swift movement]

jinker ('dʒɪŋkə) *n Austral* a vehicle for transporting timber, consisting of a tractor and two sets of wheels for supporting the logs [from ?]

jinks (dʒɪŋks) *pl n* boisterous or mischievous play (esp in **high jinks**) [c18 from ?]

jinn (dʒɪn) *n (often functioning as sing)* the plural of **jinni**

Jinnah ('dʒɪnə) *n* **Mohammed Ali** 1876–1948, Indian Muslim statesman. He campaigned for the partition of India into separate Hindu and Muslim states, becoming first governor general of Pakistan (1947–48)

jinni, jinnee, *or* **djinni** (dʒɪ'niː) *n, pl* **jinn** *or* **djinn** (dʒɪn) a being or spirit in Muslim belief who could assume human or animal form and influence man by supernatural powers [c17 from Ar.]

jinrikisha, jinricksha, *or* **jinrickshaw** (dʒɪn'rɪkʃɔː) *n* another name for **rickshaw** [c19 from Japanese, from *jin* man + *riki* power + *sha* carriage]

jinx (dʒɪŋks) *n* **1** an unlucky force, person, or thing ▷ *vb* **2** *(tr)* to be or put a jinx on [c20 ?from NL *Jynx*, genus name of the wryneck, from Gk *iunx* wryneck, a bird used in magic]

Jinzhou ('dʒɪn'dʒəʊ), **Chin-Chou**, *or* **Chin-chow** *n* a city in NE China, in SW Liaoning province. Pop: 596 860 (1990 est). Former name (1913–47): **Chin-hsien**

JIT *abbrev for* just-in-time

jitter ('dʒɪtə) *inf* ▷ *vb* **1** *(intr)* to be anxious or nervous ▷ *n* **2 the jitters** nervousness and anxiety [c20 from ?]

jitterbug ('dʒɪtə,bʌg) *n* **1** a fast jerky American dance, usually to a jazz accompaniment, that was popular in the 1940s **2** a person who dances the jitterbug ▷ *vb* **jitterbugs, jitterbugging, jitterbugged 3** *(intr)* to perform such a dance

jittery ('dʒɪtərɪ) *adj inf* nervous and anxious > **'jitteriness** *n*

jiujitsu *or* **jiujutsu** (dʒuː'dʒɪtsuː) *n* a variant spelling of **jujitsu**

jive (dʒaɪv) *n* **1** a style of lively and jerky dance, popular esp in the 1940s and 1950s **2** *sl, chiefly US* **2a** misleading or deceptive talk **2b** *(as modifier)*: *jive talk* ▷ *vb* **jives, jiving, jived 3** *(intr)* to dance the jive **4** *sl, chiefly US* to mislead; tell lies (to) [c20 from ?] > **'jiver** *n*

Joab ('dʒəʊæb) *n Old Testament* the successful commander of King David's forces and the slayer of Abner and Absalom (II Samuel 2:18–23; 3:24–27; 18:14–15)

Joachim *n* **1** ('joːaxɪm) **Joseph** ('joːzɛf) 1831–1907, Hungarian violinist and composer **2** ('dʒəʊəkɪm) **Saint** 1st century BC, traditionally the father of the Virgin Mary; feast day: July 25 or Sept. 9

Joan (dʒəʊn) *n* **1** known as *the Fair Maid of Kent*. 1328–85, wife of Edward the Black Prince; mother of Richard II **2 Pope** legendary female pope, first mentioned in the 13th century: said to have been elected while disguised as a man and to have died in childbirth

Joan of Arc *n* **Saint** known as *the Maid of Orléans*; French name *Jeanne d'Arc*. ?1412–31, French national heroine, who led the army that relieved Orléans in the Hundred Years' War, enabling Charles VII to be crowned at Reims (1429). After being captured (1430), she was burnt at the stake as a heretic. She was canonized in 1920. Feast day: May 30

João Pessoa (*Portuguese* 'ʒuəum pe'soa) *n* a port in NE Brazil, capital of Paraíba state. Pop: 594 922 (2000)

job (dʒɒb) *n* **1** an individual piece of work or task **2** an occupation **3** an object worked on or a result produced from working **4** a duty or responsibility: *his job was to cook the dinner* **5** *inf* a difficult task or problem: *I had a job to contact him* **6** a state of affairs: *make the best of a bad job* **7** *inf* a particular type of something: *a four-wheel drive job* **8** *inf* a crime, esp a robbery **9** *computing* a unit of work for a computer **10 jobs for the boys** jobs given to or created for allies or favourites **11 just the job** exactly what was required **12 on the job** actively engaged in one's employment ▷ *vb* **jobs, jobbing, jobbed 13** *(intr)* to work by the piece or at casual jobs **14** to make a private profit out of (a public office, etc) **15** *(intr; usually foll by in)* **15a** to buy and sell (goods or services) as a middleman: *she jobs in government surplus* **15b** *Brit* to buy and sell stocks and shares as a stockjobber **16** *Austral sl* to punch [c16 from ?] > **'jobless** *adj*

Job (dʒəʊb) *n* **1** *Old Testament* **1a** a Jewish patriarch, who maintained his faith in spite of the afflictions sent by God to test him **1b** the book containing Job's pleas to God under these afflictions, attempted explanations of them by his friends, and God's reply to him **2** any person who withstands great suffering without despairing

jobber ('dʒɒbə) *n* **1** *Brit* short for **stockjobber** (sense 1) See also **market maker 2** a person who jobs

jobbery ('dʒɒbərɪ) *n* the practice of making private profit out of a public office

jobbing ('dʒɒbɪŋ) *adj* working by the piece, not regularly employed: *a jobbing gardener*

Jobcentre ('dʒɒb,sɛntə) *n Brit* any of a number of government offices usually having premises situated in or near the main shopping area of a town in which people seeking jobs can consult displayed advertisements

Jobclub ('dʒɒb,klʌb) *n* a group of unemployed people

organized through a Jobcentre, which meets every weekday and is given advice on job seeking to increase its members' chances of finding employment

job description *n* a formal description of the duties and responsibilities involved in a job, esp as given to applicants for the job

job lot *n* **1** a miscellaneous collection of articles sold as a lot **2** a collection of cheap or trivial items

job satisfaction *n* the extent to which the desires and hopes of a worker are fulfilled as a result of his or her work

Job's comforter *n* a person who, while purporting to give sympathy, succeeds only in adding to distress

jobseeker's allowance ('dʒɒb,siːkəz) *n* (in Britain) a National Insurance or social security payment for unemployed people; replaced unemployment benefit in 1996. Abbrev: **JSA**

job sharing *n* the division of a job between two or more people such that each covers the same job for complementary parts of the day or week > **job share** *n*

jobsworth ('dʒɒbz,wɜːθ) *n inf* a person in a position of minor authority who invokes the letter of the law in order to avoid any action requiring initiative, cooperation, etc [c20 from *it's more than my job's worth to...*]

Joburg ('dʒəʊ,bɜːg) *n inf* Johannesburg

Jocasta (dʒəʊ'kæstə) *n Greek myth* a queen of Thebes, the wife of Laius, who married Oedipus without either of them knowing he was her son

Jochum (*German* 'jɔxʊm) *n* **Eugen** ('ɔygeːn) 1902–87, German orchestral conductor

jock (dʒɒk) *n inf* **1** short for **disc jockey** **2** short for **jockey** **3** short for **jockstrap**

Jock (dʒɒk) *n* a slang word or term of address for a **Scot**

jockey ('dʒɒkɪ) *n* **1** a person who rides horses in races, esp as a profession ▹ *vb* **2a** (*tr*) to ride (a horse) in a race **2b** (*intr*) to ride as a jockey **3** (*intr*: often foll by *for*) to try to obtain an advantage by manoeuvring (esp in **jockey for position**) **4** to trick or cheat (a person) [c16 (in the sense: lad): from name *Jock* + -EY]

jockstrap ('dʒɒk,stræp) *n* an elasticated belt with a pouch worn by men, esp athletes, to support the genitals. Also called: **athletic support** [c20 from sl *jock* penis + STRAP]

jocose (dʒə'kəʊs) *adj* characterized by humour [c17 from L *jocōsus* given to jesting, from *jocus* joke] > **jo'cosely** *adv* > **jocosity** (dʒə'kɒsɪtɪ) *n*

jocular ('dʒɒkjʊlə) *adj* **1** characterized by joking and good humour **2** meant lightly or humorously [c17 from L *joculāris*, from *joculus* little JOKE] > **jocularity** (,dʒɒkjʊ'lærɪtɪ) *n* > **'jocularly** *adv*

jocund ('dʒɒkənd) *adj* of a humorous temperament; merry [c14 from LL *jocundus*, from L *jūcundus* pleasant, from *juvāre* to please] > **jocundity** (dʒəʊ'kʌndɪtɪ) *n* > **'jocundly** *adv*

Jodhpur (,dʒɒd'pʊə) *n* **1** a former state of NW India, one of the W Rajputana states: now part of Rajasthan **2** a walled city in NW India, in W Rajasthan: university (1962). Pop: 666 279 (1991) > **Jodhpuri** ('dʒɒdpʊrɪ) *adj*

jodhpurs ('dʒɒdpəz) *pl n* riding breeches, loose-fitting around the thighs and tight-fitting from the knees to the ankles [c19 from JODHPUR]

Jodl (*German* 'jodəl) *n* **Alfred** ('alfreːt) 1890–1946, German general, largely responsible for German strategy during World War II: executed as a war criminal

Joe Blake (,dʒəʊ 'bleɪk) *n Austral sl* **1** a snake **2 the Joe Blakes** the DT's

Joe Bloggs ('blɒgz) *n Brit sl* an average or typical man. US, Canad, and Austral equivalent: **Joe Blow**. See also **Joe Six-Pack**

Joel ('dʒəʊəl) *n Old Testament* **1** a Hebrew prophet **2** the book containing his oracles

Joe Public *n sl* the general public

joes (dʒəʊz) *pl n* **the** *Austral inf* a fit of depression or deep unhappiness; the blues [short for *the Joe Blakes*]

Joe Six-Pack *n US sl* an average or typical man

joey ('dʒəʊɪ) *n Austral inf* **1** a young kangaroo **2** a young animal or child [c19 from Abor.]

Joffre (*French* ʒɔfrə) *n* **Joseph Jacques Césaire** (ʒozɛf ʒak sezɛr) 1852–1931, French marshal. He commanded the French army (1914–16) and was largely responsible for the Allies' victory at the Marne (1914), which halted the German advance on Paris

jog (dʒɒg) *vb* **jogs, jogging, jogged** **1** (*intr*) to run or move slowly or at a jog trot, esp for physical exercise **2** (*intr*; foll by *on* or *along*) to continue in a plodding way **3** (*tr*) to jar or nudge slightly **4** (*tr*) to remind: *jog my memory* ▹ *n* **5** the act of jogging **6** a slight jar or nudge **7** a jogging motion; trot [c14 prob. var. of *shog* to shake]

jogger ('dʒɒgə) *n* **1** a person who runs at a jog trot over some distance for exercise **2** NZ a cart with rubber tyres used on farms

jogger's nipple *n inf* painful inflammation of the nipple, caused by friction with a garment when running for long distances

jogging ('dʒɒgɪŋ) *n* a slow run or trot, esp as a keep-fit exercise

joggle ('dʒɒgᵊl) *vb* **joggles, joggling, joggled** **1** to shake or move (someone or something) with a slightly jolting motion **2** (*tr*) to join or fasten (two pieces of building material) by means of a joggle ▹ *n* **3** the act of joggling **4** a slight irregular shake **5** a joint between two pieces of building material by means of a projection on one piece that fits into a notch in the other [c16 frequentative of JOG] > **'joggler** *n*

Jogjakarta (,dʒəʊgjɑː'kɑːtɑː, ,dʒɒg-) *n* a variant spelling of **Yogyakarta**

jog trot *n* **1** an easy bouncy gait, esp of a horse, midway between a walk and a trot **2** a regular way of living or doing something

Johannesburg (dʒəʊ'hænɪs,bɜːg) *n* a city in N South Africa, in Gauteng province: South Africa's largest city and chief industrial centre; grew with the establishment in 1886 of the gold-mining industry; University of Witwatersrand (1922). Pop: 1 480 530 (1996)

john (dʒɒn) *n* **1** *chiefly US & Canad* a slang word for **lavatory** **2** *sl, chiefly US* a prostitute's client [c20 special use of the name]

John (dʒɒn) *n* **1** *New Testament* **1a** the apostle John, the son of Zebedee, identified with the author of the fourth Gospel, three epistles, and the book of Revelation. Feast day: Dec. 27 or Sept. 26 **1b** the fourth Gospel **1c** any of three epistles (in full **The First, Second, and Third Epistles of John**) **2** See **John the Baptist** **3** known as *John Lackland*. 1167–1216, king of England (1199–1216); son of Henry II. He succeeded to the throne on the death of his brother Richard I, having previously tried to usurp the throne. War with France led to the loss of most of his French possessions. After his refusal to recognize Stephen Langton as archbishop of Canterbury an interdict was imposed on England (1208–14). In 1215 he was compelled by the barons to grant the Magna Carta **4** called *the Fearless*. 1371–1419, duke of Burgundy (1404–19). His attempt to control the mad king Charles VI and his murder of the king's brother led to civil war: assassinated **5 Augustus** (**Edwin**) 1878–1961, British painter, esp of portraits **6 Sir Elton** (**Hercules**) original name *Reginald Dwight*. born 1947, British rock pianist, composer, and singer; his hits include "Goodbye Yellow Brick Road" (1973) and "Candle in the Wind 1997" (1997), a tribute to Diana, Princess of Wales **7 Gwen**, sister of Augustus John. 1876–1939, British painter, working in France: noted esp for her portraits of women

John I *n* **1** surnamed *Tzimisces*. 925–976 AD, Byzantine emperor (969–976): extended Byzantine power into Bulgaria and Syria **2** called *the Great*. 1357–1433, king of Portugal (1385–1433). He secured independence for

Jj

Portugal by his victory over Castile (1385) and initiated Portuguese overseas expansion

John II *n* 1 called *the Good.* 1319–64, king of France (1350–64): captured by the English at Poitiers (1356) and forced to sign treaties (1360) surrendering SW France to England 2 called *the Perfect.* 1455–95, king of Portugal (1481–95): sponsored Portuguese expansion in the New World and reduced the power of the aristocracy 3 surnamed *Casimir Vasa.* 1609–72, king of Poland (1648–68), who lost much territory to neighbouring countries: abdicated

John III *n* 1 1507–57, king of Portugal (1521–57): his reign saw the expansion of the Portuguese empire overseas but the start of economic decline at home 2 surnamed *Sobieski.* 1624–96, king of Poland (1674–96). He raised the Turkish siege of Vienna (1683)

John IV *n* called *the Fortunate.* 1604–56, king of Portugal (1640–56). As duke of Braganza he led a revolt against Spanish rule and became king: lost most of Portugal's Asian possessions to the Dutch

John XXII *n* original name *Jacques Duèse.* ?1244–1334, pope (1316–34), residing at Avignon; involved in a long conflict with the Holy Roman Emperor Louis IV and opposed the Franciscan Spirituals

John XXIII *n* original name *Angelo Giuseppe Roncalli.* 1881–1963, pope (1958–63). He promoted ecumenism and world peace and summoned the second Vatican Council (1962–65)

John Barleycorn *n usually humorous* the personification of alcoholic drink

John Bull *n* 1 a personification of England or the English people 2 a typical Englishman [c18 name of a character intended to be representative of the English nation in *The History of John Bull* (1712) by John Arbuthnot]

John Chrysostom ('krɪsəstəm) *n* **Saint** ?345–407 AD, Greek bishop and theologian; one of the Fathers of the Greek Church, noted for his eloquence. Feast day: Sept 13

John Doe *n* See **Doe**

John Dory ('dɔːrɪ) *n* 1 a European dory (the fish), *Zeus faber*, having a deep compressed body, spiny dorsal fins, and massive mobile jaws 2 a related fish, *Zeus australis*, which is a valued food fish of Australia [c18 from proper name *John* + DORY[1]; on the model of DOE]

John Hop *n Austral sl* a policeman [rhyming sl for COP[1]]

johnny ('dʒɒnɪ) *n, pl* **johnnies** *Brit inf (often cap)* a man or boy; chap

Johnny Canuck ('dʒɒnɪ kə'nʌk) *n Canad* 1 an informal name for a **Canadian** 2 a personification of Canada

Johnny-come-lately *n, pl* **Johnny-come-latelies** *or* **Johnnies-come-lately** *sl* a brash newcomer, novice, or recruit

John of Austria *n* called *Don John.* 1547–78, Spanish general: defeated the Turks at Lepanto (1571)

John of Damascus *n* **Saint** ?675–749 AD, Syrian theologian, who defended the veneration of icons and images against the iconoclasts. Feast day: Dec. 4

John of Gaunt (gɔːnt) *n* Duke of Lancaster. 1340–99, son of Edward III: virtual ruler of England during the last years of his father's reign and during Richard II's minority [*Gaunt*, variant of GHENT, where he was born]

John of Leyden ('laɪdᵊn) *n* original name *Jan Bockelson.* ?1509–36, Dutch Anabaptist leader. He established a theocracy in Münster (1534) but was tortured to death after the city was recaptured (1535) by its prince bishop

John of Salisbury *n* died 1180, English ecclesiastic and scholar; bishop of Chartres (1176–80). He supported Thomas à Becket against Henry II

John of the Cross *n* **Saint** original name *Juan de Yepis y Alvarez.* 1542–91, Spanish Carmelite monk, poet, and mystic. He founded the Discalced Carmelites with Saint Teresa (1568). Feast day: Dec. 14

John o'Groats (ə'grəʊts) *n* a village at the northeasternmost tip of the Scottish mainland: considered to be the northernmost point of the mainland of Great Britain although Dunnet Head, slightly to the west, lies further north. See also **Land's End**

John Paul I *n* original name *Albino Luciani.* 1912–78, pope (1978) whose brief 33-day reign was characterized by a simpler papal style and anticipated an emphasis on pastoral rather than administrative priorities

John Paul II *n* original name *Karol Wojtyla.* born 1920, pope from 1978, born in Poland: the first non-Italian to be elected since 1522

Johns (dʒɒnz) *n* **Jasper** born 1930, US artist, noted for his collages and constructions

Johnson ('dʒɒnsᵊn) *n* 1 **Amy** 1903–41, British aviator, who made several record flights, including those to Australia (1930) and to Cape Town and back (1936) 2 **Andrew** 1808–75, US Democrat statesman who was elected vice president under the Republican Abraham Lincoln; 17th president of the US (1865–69), became president after Lincoln's assassination. His lenience towards the South after the American Civil War led to strong opposition from radical Republicans, who tried to impeach him 3 **Earvin** ('ɜːvɪn), known as *Magic.* born 1959, US basketball player 4 **Eyvind** ('evɪnt) 1900–76, Swedish novelist and writer, whose novels include the *Krilon* trilogy (1941–43): joint winner of the Nobel prize for literature 1974 5 **Jack** 1878–1946, US boxer; world heavyweight champion (1908–15) 6 **Lionel** (**Pigot**) 1867–1902, British poet and critic, best known for his poems "Dark Angel" and "By the Statue of King Charles at Charing Cross" 7 **Lyndon Baines** known as *LBJ.* 1908–73, US Democrat statesman; 36th president of the US (1963–69). His administration carried the Civil Rights Acts of 1964 and 1965, but he lost popularity by increasing US involvement in the Vietnam war 8 **Martin** born 1970, English Rugby Union footballer; captain of the England team that won the World Cup in 2003 9 **Philip** (**Cortelyou**) born 1906, US architect and writer; his buildings include the New York State Theater (1964) and the American Telephone and Telegraph building (1978–83), both in New York 10 **Robert** ?1898–1937, US blues singer and guitarist 11 **Samuel** known as *Dr Johnson.* 1709–84, British lexicographer, critic, and conversationalist, whose greatest works are his *Dictionary* (1755), his edition of Shakespeare (1765), and his *Lives of the Most Eminent English Poets* (1779–81). His fame, however, rests as much on Boswell's biography of him as on his literary output

Johnsonian (dʒɒn'səʊnɪən) *adj* of, relating to, or characteristic of Samuel Johnson, his works, or his style of writing

John the Baptist *n* **Saint** *New Testament* the son of Zacharias and Elizabeth and the cousin and forerunner of Jesus, whom he baptized. He was beheaded by Herod (Matthew 14:1–2). Feast day: June 24

John Thomas *n sl* a euphemistic name for **penis**

Johore (dʒəʊ'hɔː) *n* a state of Malaysia, on the S Malay Peninsula: mostly forested, with large swamps; bauxite- and iron-mining. Capital: Johore Bahru. Pop: 2 565 701 (2000). Area: 18 984 sq km (7330 sq miles)

Johore Bahru ('bɑːruː) *n* a city in S Malaysia, capital of Johore state: important trading centre, situated at the sole crossing point of **Johore Strait** (between Malaya and Singapore Island) Pop: 328 646 (1991)

joie de vivre *French* (ʒwa də vivrə) *n* joy of living; enjoyment of life; ebullience

join (dʒɔɪn) *vb* 1 to come or bring together 2 to become a member of (a club, etc) 3 (*intr; often foll by with*) to become associated or allied 4 (*intr; usually foll by in*) to take part 5 (*tr*) to meet (someone) as a companion 6 (*tr*) to become part of 7 (*tr*) to unite (two people) in marriage 8 (*tr*) *geom* to connect with a straight line or a curve

9 join hands 9a to hold one's own hands together **9b** (of two people) to hold each other's hands **9c** (usually foll by *with*) to work together in an enterprise ▷ *n* **10** a joint; seam **11** the act of joining ▷ See also **join up** [c13 from OF, from L *jungere* to yoke]

joinder (ˈdʒɔɪndə) *n* **1** the act of joining, esp in legal contexts **2** *law* **2a** (in pleading) the stage at which the parties join issue (**joinder of issue**) **2b** the joining of two or more persons as coplaintiffs or codefendants (**joinder of parties**) [c17 from F *joindre* to JOIN]

joined-up *adj* **1** with all departments or sections communicating efficiently with each other and acting together purposefully and effectively: *joined-up government* **2a** focusing on or producing an integrated and coherent result, strategy, etc: *joined-up thinking* **2b** forming an integrated and coherent whole: *joined-up policies*

joiner (ˈdʒɔɪnə) *n* **1** *chiefly Brit* a person skilled in making finished woodwork, such as windows and stairs **2** a person or thing that joins **3** *inf* a person who joins many clubs, etc

joinery (ˈdʒɔɪnərɪ) *n* **1** the skill or craft of a joiner **2** work made by a joiner

joint (dʒɔɪnt) *n* **1** a junction of two or more parts or objects **2** *anat* the junction between two or more bones **3** the point of connection between movable parts in invertebrates **4** the part of a plant stem from which a branch or leaf grows **5** one of the parts into which a carcass of meat is cut by the butcher, esp for roasting **6** *geol* a crack in a rock along which no displacement has occurred **7** *sl* **7a** a bar or nightclub **7b** *often facetious* a dwelling or meeting place **8** *sl* a cannabis cigarette **9 out of joint 9a** dislocated **9b** out of order ▷ *adj* **10** shared by or belonging to two or more: *joint property* **11** created by combined effort **12** sharing with others or with one another: *joint rulers* ▷ *vb* (*tr*) **13** to provide with or fasten by a joint or joints **14** to plane the edge of (a board, etc) into the correct shape for a joint **15** to cut or divide (meat, etc) into joints > ˈ**jointed** *adj* > ˈ**jointly** *adv*

joint account *n* a bank account registered in the name of two or more persons, any of whom may make deposits and withdrawals

joint stock *n* capital funds held in common and usually divided into shares

joint-stock company *n* **1** *Brit* a business enterprise characterized by the sharing of ownership between shareholders, whose liability is limited **2** *US* a business enterprise whose owners are issued shares of transferable stock but do not enjoy limited liability

jointure (ˈdʒɔɪntʃə) *n* *law* **a** provision made by a husband for his wife by settling property upon her at marriage for her use after his death **b** the property so settled [c14 from OF, from L *junctūra* a joining]

join up *vb* (*adv*) **1** (*intr*) to become a member of a military or other organization; enlist **2** (often foll by *with*) to unite or connect

Joinville (*French* ʒwɛ̃vil) *n* **Jean de** (ʒɑ̃ də) ?1224–1317, French chronicler, noted for his *Histoire de Saint Louis* (1309)

joist (dʒɔɪst) *n* a beam made of timber, steel, or reinforced concrete, used in the construction of floors, roofs, etc [c14 from OF *giste* beam supporting a bridge, from Vulgar L *jacitum* (unattested) support, from *jacēre* to lie]

jojoba (həʊˈhəʊbə) *n* a shrub or small tree of SW North America having edible seeds containing a valuable oil that is used in cosmetics

joke (dʒəʊk) *n* **1** a humorous anecdote **2** something that is said or done for fun **3** a ridiculous or humorous circumstance **4** a person or thing inspiring ridicule or amusement **5 no joke** something very serious ▷ *vb* **jokes, joking, joked 6** (*intr*) to tell jokes **7** (*intr*) to speak or act facetiously **8** to make fun of (someone) **9 joking apart** seriously: said after there has been joking in a discussion [c17 from L *jocus* a jest] > ˈ**jokey** *or* ˈ**joky** *adj* > ˈ**jokingly** *adv*

joker (ˈdʒəʊkə) *n* **1** a person who jokes, esp in an obnoxious manner **2** *sl, often derog* a person: *who does that joker think he is?* **3** an extra playing card in a pack, which in many card games can rank above any other card

Jokjakarta (ˌdʒəʊkjɑːˈkɑːtɑː, ˌdʒɒk-) *n* a variant spelling of **Yogyakarta**

jol (dʒɒl) *S African sl* ▷ *n* **1** a party ▷ *vb* **jols, jolling, jolled 2** (*intr*) to have a good time [from Du.]

Joliot-Curie (*French* ʒɔljokyri) *n* **Jean-Frédéric** (ʒɑ̃frederik), 1900–58, and his wife, **Irène** (irɛn), 1897–1956, French physicists: shared the Nobel prize for chemistry in 1935 for discovering artificial radioactivity

jollification (ˌdʒɒlɪfɪˈkeɪʃən) *n* a merry festivity

jollify (ˈdʒɒlɪˌfaɪ) *vb* **jollifies, jollifying, jollified** to be or cause to be jolly

jollity (ˈdʒɒlɪtɪ) *n, pl* **jollities** the condition of being jolly

jolly (ˈdʒɒlɪ) *adj* **jollier, jolliest 1** full of good humour **2** having or provoking gaiety and merrymaking **3** pleasing ▷ *adv* **4** *Brit* (intensifier): *you're jolly nice* ▷ *vb* **jollies, jollying, jollied** (*tr*) *inf* **5** (often foll by *up* or *along*) to try to make or keep (someone) cheerful **6** to make good-natured fun of [c14 from OF *jolif*, prob. from ON *jōl* YULE] > ˈ**jolliness** *n*

jolly boat *n* a small boat used as a utility tender for a vessel [c18 *jolly* prob. from Danish *jolle* YAWL]

Jolly Jumper *n* *Canad trademark* a type of fixed sprung baby harness in which an infant may be placed and allowed to bounce up and down for exercise.

Jolly Roger *n* the traditional pirate flag, consisting of a white skull and crossbones on a black field

Jolo (həʊˈləʊ) *n* an island in the SW Philippines: the main island of the Sulu Archipelago. Pop: 360 590 (latest est). Area: 893 sq km (345 sq miles)

Jolson (ˈdʒəʊlsən) *n* **Al**, real name *Asa Yoelson*. 1886–1950, US singer and film actor, born in Russia; star of the first talking picture *The Jazz Singer* (1927)

jolt (dʒəʊlt) *vb* **1** (*tr*) to bump against with a jarring blow **2** to move in a jolting manner **3** (*tr*) to surprise or shock ▷ *n* **4** a sudden jar or blow **5** an emotional shock [c16 prob. blend of dialect *jot* to jerk & dialect *joll* to bump]

Jon. *Bible abbrev for* Jonah

Jonah (ˈdʒəʊnə) *or* **Jonas** (ˈdʒəʊnəs) *n* **1** *Old Testament* a Hebrew prophet who, having been thrown overboard from a ship was swallowed by a great fish and vomited onto dry land **2** a person believed to bring bad luck to those around him

Jonathan *n* *Old Testament* the son of Saul and David's close friend, who was killed in battle (I Samuel 31; II Samuel 1:19–26)

Jones (dʒəʊnz) *n* **1 Daniel** 1881–1967, British phonetician **2 Daniel** 1912–93, Welsh composer. He wrote nine symphonies and much chamber music **3 David** 1895–1974, British artist and writer: his literary works, which combine poetry and prose, include *In Parenthesis* (1937), an account of World War I, and *The Anathemata* (1952) **4 Digby** (**Marritt**) born 1956, British businessman; director-general of the Confederation of British Industry from 2000 **5 Inigo** (ˈɪnɪgəʊ) 1573–1652, English architect and theatrical designer, who introduced Palladianism to England. His buildings include the Banqueting Hall of Whitehall. He also designed the settings for court masques, being the first to use the proscenium arch and movable scenery in England **6 John Paul**, original name *John Paul*. 1747–92, US naval commander, born in Scotland: noted for his part in the War of American Independence **7** (**Everett**) **Le Roi** (ˈliːrɔɪ), Muslim name *Imanu Amīri Baraka*. born 1934, US Black poet, dramatist, and political figure **8 Quincy** born 1933, U.S. composer, arranger, conductor, record producer, and trumpeter, noted esp for his film scores **9 Robert Tyre,** known as *Bobby Jones*. 1902–71, US golfer

jong (jɒŋ) *n S African inf* a friend, often used in direct address [Afrik.]

Jongkind (*Dutch* ˈjɔŋkɪnt) *n* **Johann Barthold** (joːˈhɑn ˈbartɔlt) 1819–91, Dutch landscape painter and etcher, working in Paris: best known for his atmospheric seascapes

jongleur (*French* ʒɔ̃glœr) *n* (in medieval France) an itinerant minstrel [c18 from OF *jogleour*, from L *joculātor* jester]

Jönköping (*Swedish* ˈjœntçøːpiŋ) *n* a city in S Sweden, on the S shore of Lake Vättern: scene of the conclusion of peace between Sweden and Denmark in 1809. Pop: 116 344 (2000 est)

jonquil (ˈdʒɒŋkwɪl) *n* **1** a Eurasian variety of narcissus with long fragrant yellow or white short-tubed flowers **2** any of various other small daffodil-like plants [c17 from F *jonquille*, from Sp. *junquillo*, dim. of *junco* reed]

Jonson (ˈdʒɒnsᵊn) *n* **Ben** 1572–1637, English dramatist and poet, who developed the "comedy of humours", in which each character is used to satirize one particular humour or temperament. His plays include *Volpone* (1606), *The Alchemist* (1610), and *Bartholomew Fair* (1614), and he also wrote court masques

jook (dʒʊk) *vb Caribbean inf* **1** *(tr)* to poke or puncture ▷ *n* **2** a jab or the resulting wound [c20 of W African origin]

Joplin (ˈdʒɒplɪn) *n* **1 Janis** 1943–70, US rock singer, noted for her hoarse and passionate style. Her albums include *Cheap Thrills* (1968) and *Pearl* (1971) **2 Scott** 1868–1917, US pianist and composer: creator of ragtime

Joppa (ˈdʒɒpə) *n* the biblical name of **Jaffa,** the port from which Jonah embarked (Jonah 1:3)

Jordaens (*Flemish* jɔrˈdaːns) *n* **Jacob** (ˈjaːkɔp) 1593–1678, Flemish painter, noted for his naturalistic depiction of peasant scenes

Jordan[1] (ˈdʒɔːdᵊn) *n* **1** a kingdom in SW Asia: coextensive with the biblical Moab, Gilead, and Edom; made a League of Nations mandate and emirate under British control in 1922 and became an independent kingdom in 1946; territories west of the River Jordan and the Jordanian part of Jerusalem (intended to be part of an autonomous Palestine) were occupied by Israel after the war of 1967. It contains part of the Great Rift Valley and consists mostly of desert. Official language: Arabic. Official religion: (Sunni) Muslim. Currency: dinar. Capital: Amman. Pop: 5 132 000 (2001 est). Area: 89 185 sq km (34 434 sq miles). Official name: **Hashemite Kingdom of Jordan** Former name (1922–49): **Trans-Jordan** **2** the chief and only perennial river of Israel and Jordan, rising in several headstreams in Syria and Lebanon, and flowing south through the Sea of Galilee to the Dead Sea: occupies the N end of the Great Rift Valley system and lies mostly below sea level. Length: over 320 km (200 miles) > **Jordanian** (dʒɔːˈdeɪnɪən) *adj, n*
▷ www.kinghussein.gov.jo/government.html
▷ www.see-jordan.com

Jordan[2] (ˈdʒɔːdᵊn) *n* **Neil** born 1950, Irish film director and writer; his films include *The Company of Wolves* (1984), *Mona Lisa* (1986), *The Crying Game* (1992), *Michael Collins* (1996), and *The End of the Affair* (2000)

jorum (ˈdʒɔːrəm) *n* a large drinking bowl or vessel or its contents [c18 prob. after *Jorum*, who brought vessels of silver, gold, and brass to King David (II Samuel 8:10)]

Jos (dʒɒs) *n* a city in central Nigeria, capital of Plateau state on the **Jos Plateau:** major centre of the tin-mining industry. Pop: 206 300 (1996 est)

Joseph (ˈdʒəʊzɪf) *n* **1** *Old Testament* **1a** the eleventh son of Jacob and one of the 12 patriarchs of Israel (Genesis 30:2–24) **1b** either or both of two tribes descended from his sons Ephraim and Manasseh **2 Saint** *New Testament* the husband of Mary the mother of Jesus (Matthew 1:16–25). Feast day: Mar. 19

Joseph II *n* 1741–90, Holy Roman emperor (1765–90); son of Francis I. He ruled Austria jointly with his mother, Maria Theresa, until her death (1780). He reorganized taxation, abolished serfdom, curtailed the feudal power of the nobles, and asserted his independence from the pope

Joseph Bonaparte Gulf *n* an inlet of the Timor Sea in N Australia. Width: 360 km (225 miles)

Josephine (ˈdʒəʊzəˌfiːn) *n* **Empress,** previous name *Joséphine de Beauharnais;* real name *Marie Joséphine Tascher de la Pagerie*. 1763–1814, empress of France as wife of Napoleon Bonaparte (1796–1809)

Joseph of Arimathea (ˌærɪməˈθiːə) *n* **Saint** *New Testament* a wealthy member of the Sanhedrin, who obtained the body of Jesus after the Crucifixion and laid it in his own tomb (Matthew 27:57–60). Feast day: Mar. 17 or July 31

Josephus (dʒəʊˈsiːfəs) *n* **Flavius** (ˈfleɪvɪəs) real name *Joseph ben Matthias*. ?37–?100 AD, Jewish historian and general; author of *History of the Jewish War* and *Antiquities of the Jews*

josh (dʒɒʃ) *sl, chiefly US & Canad* ▷ *vb* **1** to tease (someone) in a bantering way ▷ *n* **2** a teasing joke [c19 ?from JOKE, infl. by BOSH] > ˈ**josher** *n*

Josh. *Bible abbrev for* Joshua

Joshua (ˈdʒɒʃʊə) *n Old Testament* **1** Moses' successor, who led the Israelites in the conquest of Canaan **2** the book recounting his deeds. Douay spelling: **Josue** (ˈdʒɒsjʊiː)

Josi (ˈdʒəʊsɪ) *n S African inf* Johannesburg

Josiah (dʒəʊˈsaɪə) *n* died ?609 BC, king of Judah (?640–?609). After the discovery of a book of law (probably Deuteronomy) in the Temple he began a programme of religious reform. Douay spelling: **Josias** (dʒəʊˈsaɪəs)

Josquin des Prés (*French* ʒɔskɛ̃ de pre) *n* See **des Prés**

joss (dʒɒs) *n* a Chinese deity worshipped in the form of an idol [c18 from pidgin E, from Port. *deos* god, from L *deus*]

joss house *n* a Chinese temple or shrine where an idol or idols are worshipped

joss stick *n* a stick of dried perfumed paste, giving off a fragrant odour when burnt as incense

jostle (ˈdʒɒsᵊl) *vb* **jostles, jostling, jostled** **1** to bump or push (someone) roughly **2** to come or bring into contact **3** to force (one's way) by pushing ▷ *n* **4** the act of jostling **5** a rough bump or push [c14 see JOUST]

jot (dʒɒt) *vb* **jots, jotting, jotted** **1** *(tr; usually foll by down)* to write a brief note of ▷ *n* **2** *(used with a negative)* a little bit (in **not care** (*or* **give**) **a jot**) [c16 from L *jota*, from Gk *iōta*, of Semitic origin]

jota (*Spanish* ˈxɔta) *n* a Spanish dance in fast triple time [Sp., prob. from OSp. *sota*, from *sotar* to dance, from L *saltāre*]

jotter (ˈdʒɒtə) *n* a small notebook

jotting (ˈdʒɒtɪŋ) *n* something jotted down

Jotun *or* **Jotunn** (ˈjɔːtʊn) *n Norse myth* any of a race of giants [from ON *jötunn* giant; related to EAT]

Jotunheim *or* **Jotunnheim** (ˈjɔːtʊnˌheɪm) *n Norse myth* the home of the giants in the northeast of Asgard [from ON, from *jötunn* giant + *heimr* world, HOME]

joual (ʒwɑːl) *n* nonstandard Canadian French dialect, esp as associated with ill-educated speakers [from the pronunciation in this dialect of F *cheval* horse]

joule (dʒuːl) *n* the derived SI unit of work or energy; the work done when the point of application of a force of 1 newton is displaced through a distance of 1 metre in the direction of the force. Symbol: J [c19 after J. P. JOULE]

Joule (dʒuːl) *n* **James Prescott** 1818–89, English physicist, who evaluated the mechanical equivalent of heat and contributed to the study of heat and electricity

jounce (dʒaʊns) *vb* **jounces, jouncing, jounced** **1** to shake or jolt or cause to shake or jolt ▷ *n* **2** a shake; bump [c15 prob. from dialect *joll* to bump + BOUNCE]

journal (ˈdʒɜːnᵊl) *n* **1** a newspaper or periodical **2** a book in which a daily record of happenings, etc, is kept **3** an official record of the proceedings of a legislative body **4** *book-keeping* one of several books in which transactions are initially recorded to facilitate subsequent entry in the ledger **5** *machinery* the part of a shaft or axle in contact with or enclosed by a bearing [c14 from OF: daily, from L *diurnālis*; see DIURNAL]

journal box *n machinery* a case enclosing or supporting a journal

journalese (ˌdʒɜːnəˈliːz) *n derog* a superficial style of writing regarded as typical of newspapers, etc

journalism (ˈdʒɜːnəˌlɪzəm) *n* **1** the profession or practice of reporting about, photographing, or editing news stories for one of the mass media **2** newspapers and magazines collectively
▷ www.ifj.org
▷ www.icfj.org

journalist (ˈdʒɜːnəlɪst) *n* **1** a person whose occupation is journalism **2** *rare* a person who keeps a journal > ˌ**journaˈlistic** *adj* > ˌ**journaˈlistically** *adv*

journalize *or* **journalise** (ˈdʒɜːnəˌlaɪz) *vb* **journalizes, journalizing, journalized** *or* **journalises, journalising, journalised** to record (daily events) in a journal > ˌ**journaliˈzation** *or* ˌ**journaliˈsation** *n*

journey (ˈdʒɜːnɪ) *n* **1** a travelling from one place to another **2a** the distance travelled in a journey **2b** the time taken to make a journey ▷ *vb* **3** (*intr*) to make a journey [c13 from OF *journee* a day, a day's travelling, from L *diurnum* day's portion] > ˈ**journeyer** *n*

journeyman (ˈdʒɜːnɪmən) *n, pl* **journeymen** **1** a worker trained in a particular trade who is qualified to work at this trade in the employment of someone else **2** a competent workman [c15 from JOURNEY (in obs. sense: a day's work) + MAN]

joust (dʒaʊst) *history* ▷ *n* **1** a combat between two mounted knights tilting against each other with lances ▷ *vb* **2** (*intr*; often foll by *against* or *with*) to encounter or engage in such a tournament: *he jousted with five opponents* [c13 from OF, from *jouster* to fight on horseback, from Vulgar L *juxtāre* (unattested) to come together, from L *juxtā* close] > ˈ**jouster** *n*

Jove (dʒəʊv) *n* **1** another name for **Jupiter**[1] **2** **by Jove** an exclamation of surprise or excitement [c14 from OL *Jovis* Jupiter] > ˈ**Jovian** *n*

jovial (ˈdʒəʊvɪəl) *adj* having or expressing convivial humour [c16 from L *joviālis* of (the planet) Jupiter, considered by astrologers to foster good humour] > **joviality** (ˌdʒəʊvɪˈælɪtɪ) *n* > ˈ**jovially** *adv*

Jovian (ˈdʒəʊvɪən) *n* full name *Flavius Claudius Jovianus.* ?331–364 AD, Roman emperor (363–64): he made peace with Persia, relinquishing Roman provinces beyond the Tigris, and restored privileges to the Christians

Jowett (ˈdʒaʊɪt) *n* **Benjamin** 1817–93, British classical scholar and educator: translated the works of Plato

jowl[1] (dʒaʊl) *n* **1** the jaw, esp the lower one **2** (*often pl*) a cheek **3** **cheek by jowl** See **cheek** [OE *ceafl* jaw] > **jowled** *adj*

jowl[2] (dʒaʊl) *n* **1** fatty flesh hanging from the lower jaw **2** a similar fleshy part in animals, such as the dewlap of a bull [OE *ceole* throat]

joy (dʒɔɪ) *n* **1** a deep feeling or condition of happiness or contentment **2** something causing such a feeling **3** an outward show of pleasure or delight **4** *Brit inf* success; satisfaction: *I went for a loan, but got no joy* ▷ *vb chiefly poetic* **5** (*intr*) to feel joy **6** (*tr*) to gladden [c13 from OF, from L *gaudium* joy, from *gaudēre* to be glad]

Joyce (dʒɔɪs) *n* **1** **James (Augustine Aloysius)** 1882–1941, Irish novelist and short-story writer. He profoundly influenced the development of the modern novel by his use of complex narrative techniques, esp stream of consciousness and parody, and of compound and coined words. His works include the novels *Ulysses* (1922) and *Finnegans Wake* (1939) and the short stories *Dubliners* (1914) **2** **William,** known as *Lord Haw-Haw.* 1906–46, British broadcaster of Nazi propaganda to Britain, who was executed for treason

Joycean (ˈdʒɔɪsɪən) *adj* **1** of, relating to, or like, James Joyce or his works ▷ *n* **2** a student or admirer of Joyce or his works

joyful (ˈdʒɔɪfʊl) *adj* **1** full of joy; elated **2** expressing or producing joy: *a joyful look; a joyful occasion* > ˈ**joyfully** *adv* > ˈ**joyfulness** *n*

joyless (ˈdʒɔɪlɪs) *adj* having or producing no joy or pleasure > ˈ**joylessly** *adv* > ˈ**joylessness** *n*

joyous (ˈdʒɔɪəs) *adj* **1** having a happy nature or mood **2** joyful > ˈ**joyously** *adv*

joyride (ˈdʒɔɪˌraɪd) *n* **1** a ride taken for pleasure in a car, esp in a stolen car driven recklessly ▷ *vb* **joy-ride, joy-rides, joy-riding, joy-rode, joy-ridden** **2** (*intr*) to take such a ride > ˈ**joyˌrider** *n* > ˈ**joyˌriding** *n*

joystick (ˈdʒɔɪˌstɪk) *n* **1** *inf* the control stick of an aircraft, machine, etc **2** *computing* a lever for controlling the movement of a cursor on a screen

JP *abbrev for* Justice of the Peace

JPEG (ˈdʒeɪˌpɛg) *n computing* **a** a standard compressed file format used for pictures **b** a picture held in this file format **c** (*as modifier*): *a JPEG image* [c20 technique devised by the *J(oint) P(hotographic) E(xperts) G(roup)*]

J/psi particle *n* a type of elementary particle thought to be formed from charmed quarks

Jr *or* **jr** *abbrev for* junior

JSA (in Britain) *abbrev for* **jobseeker's allowance**

Juan de Fuca (ˈdʒuːən dɪ ˈfjuːkə; *Spanish* xwan de ˈfuka) *n* **Strait of** a strait between Vancouver Island (Canada) and NW Washington (US). Length: about 129 km (80 miles). Width: about 24 km (15 miles)

Juan Fernández Islands (ˈdʒuːən fəˈnændɛz; *Spanish* xwan fɛrˈnandɛθ) *pl n* a group of three islands in the S Pacific Ocean, administered by Chile: volcanic and wooded. Area: about 180 sq km (70 sq miles)

Juárez[1] (*Spanish* ˈxwarɛθ) *n* short for **Ciudad Juárez**

Juárez[2] (*Spanish* ˈxwarɛθ) *n* **Benito Pablo** (beˈnito ˈpaβlo) 1806–72, Mexican statesman. As president (1861–65; 1867–72) he thwarted Napoleon III's attempt to impose an empire under Maximilian and introduced many reforms

Juba (ˈdʒuːbə) *n* a river in NE Africa, rising in S central Ethiopia and flowing south across Somalia to the Indian Ocean: the chief river of Somalia. Length: about 1660 km (1030 miles)

Jubal (ˈdʒuːbəl) *n Old Testament* the alleged inventor of musical instruments (Genesis 4:21)

jubbah (ˈdʒʊbə) *n* a long loose outer garment with wide sleeves, worn by Muslim men and women, esp in India [c16 from Ar.]

jube (dʒuːb) *n Austral & NZ inf* any jelly-like sweet [c20 shortened from JUJUBE]

jubilant (ˈdʒuːbɪlənt) *adj* feeling or expressing great joy [c17 from L, from *jūbilāre* to give a joyful cry, from *jūbilum* a shout] > ˈ**jubilance** *n* > ˈ**jubilantly** *adv*

jubilate (ˈdʒuːbɪˌleɪt) *vb* **jubilates, jubilating, jubilated** (*intr*) **1** to have or express great joy; rejoice **2** to celebrate a jubilee [c17 from L *jūbilāre*; see JUBILANT]

jubilation (ˌdʒuːbɪˈleɪʃən) *n* a feeling of great joy and celebration

jubilee (ˈdʒuːbɪˌliː) *n* **1** a time or season for rejoicing **2** a special anniversary, esp a 25th or 50th one **3** *RC Church* a specially appointed period in which special indulgences are granted **4** *Old Testament* a year that was to be observed every 50th year, during which Hebrew slaves were to be liberated, etc **5** a less common word for **jubilation** [c14 from OF *jubile*, from LL *jubilaeus*, from LGk, from Heb. *yōbhēl* ram's horn, used for the proclamation of the year of jubilee]

Jud. *Bible abbrev for:* **1** Also: **Judg** Judges **2** Judith

Judaea *or* **Judea** (dʒuːˈdɪə) *n* the S division of ancient

Jj

Palestine, succeeding the kingdom of Judah: a Roman province during the time of Christ > **Ju'daean** *or* **Ju'dean** (dʒuː'dɪən) *adj, n*

Judah ('dʒuːdə) *n Old Testament* **1** the fourth son of Jacob, one of whose descendants was to be the Messiah (Genesis 29:35; 49:8–12) **2** the tribe descended from him **3** the tribal territory of his descendants which became the nucleus of David's kingdom and, after the kingdom had been divided into Israel and Judah, the southern kingdom of Judah, with Jerusalem as its centre. Douay spelling: **Juda**

Judah ha-Levi (hɑː'liːvaɪ) *n* ?1075–1141, Jewish poet and philosopher, born in Spain; his major works include the collection in *Diwan* and the prose work *Sefer ha-Kuzari*, which presented his philosophy of Judaism in dialogue form

Judah ha-Nasi (hɑːnɑː'siː) *n* ?135–?220 AD, rabbi and patriarch of the Sanhedrin, who compiled the Mishnah

Judaic (dʒuː'deɪɪk) *adj* of or relating to the Jews or Judaism > **Ju'daically** *adv*

Judaism ('dʒuːdeɪˌɪzəm) *n* **1** the religion of the Jews, based on the Old Testament and the Talmud and having as its central point a belief in one God **2** the religious and cultural traditions of the Jews > ˌ**Juda'istic** *adj*
▷ http://jewfaq.org/
▷ http://judaism.about.com/

Judaize *or* **Judaise** ('dʒʊdeɪˌaɪz) *vb* **Judaizes, Judaizing, Judaized** *or* **Judaises, Judaising, Judaised** **1** to conform or bring into conformity with Judaism **2** (*tr*) to convert to Judaism > ˌ**Judai'zation** *or* ˌ**Judai'sation** *n*

Judas ('dʒuːdəs) *n* **1** *New Testament* the apostle who betrayed Jesus to his enemies for 30 pieces of silver (Luke 22:3–6, 47–48). Full name: **Judas Iscariot** **2** a person who betrays a friend; traitor **3** a brother or relative of James and also of Jesus (Matthew 13:55)

Judas Maccabaeus (ˌmækə'biːəs) *n* Jewish leader, whose revolt (166–161 BC) against the Seleucid kingdom of Antiochus IV (Epiphanes) enabled him to recapture Jerusalem and rededicate the Temple

Judas tree *n* small Eurasian leguminous tree with pinkish-purple flowers that bloom before the leaves appear

judder ('dʒʌdə) *inf, chiefly Brit* ▷ *vb* **1** (*intr*) to shake or vibrate ▷ *n* **2** abnormal vibration in a mechanical system **3** a juddering motion [prob. blend of JAR² + SHUDDER]

judder bar *n* a NZ name for **sleeping policeman**

Jude (dʒuːd) *n* **1** a book of the New Testament (in full **The Epistle of Jude**) **2** **Saint** Also called: **Judas** the author of this, stated to be the brother of James (Jude 1) and almost certainly identical with Thaddaeus (Matthew 10:2–4). Feast day: June 19 or Oct. 28

Judea (dʒuː'dɪə) *n* a variant spelling of **Judaea**

judge (dʒʌdʒ) *n* **1** a public official with authority to hear cases in a court of law and pronounce judgment upon them **2** a person who is appointed to determine the result of contests or competitions **3** a person qualified to comment critically: *a good judge of antiques* **4** a leader of the peoples of Israel from Joshua's death to the accession of Saul ▷ *vb* **judges, judging, judged** **5** to hear and decide upon (a case at law) **6** (*tr*) to pass judgment on **7** (when *tr, may take a clause as object or an infinitive*) to decide (something) after inquiry **8** to determine the result of (a contest or competition) **9** to appraise (something) critically **10** (*tr; takes a clause as object*) to believe something to be the case [C14 from OF, from L *jūdicāre* to pass judgment, from *jūdex* a judge] > '**judgeˌlike** *adj* > '**judger** *n* > '**judgeship** *n*

judge advocate *n, pl* **judge advocates** an officer who superintends proceedings at a military court martial

judges' rules *pl n* (in English law) a set of rules, not legally binding, governing the behaviour of police towards suspects

judgment *or* **judgement** ('dʒʌdʒmənt) *n* **1** the faculty of being able to make critical distinctions and achieve a balanced viewpoint **2a** the verdict pronounced by a court of law **2b** an obligation arising as a result of such a verdict, such as a debt **2c** (*as modifier*): *a judgment debtor* **3** the formal decision of one or more judges at a contest or competition **4** a particular decision formed in a case in dispute or doubt **5** an estimation: *a good judgment of distance* **6** criticism or censure **7** **against one's better judgment** contrary to a preferred course of action **8** **in someone's judgment** in someone's opinion **9** **sit in judgment** **9a** to preside as judge **9b** to assume the position of critic

Judgment ('dʒʌdʒmənt) *n* **1** the estimate by God of the ultimate worthiness or unworthiness of the individual or of all mankind **2** God's subsequent decision determining the final destinies of all individuals

judgmental *or* **judgemental** (dʒʌdʒ'mɛntᵊl) *adj* of or denoting an attitude in which judgments about other people's conduct are made

Judgment Day *n* the occasion of the Last Judgment by God at the end of the world. Also called: **Day of Judgment.** See **Last Judgment**

judicatory ('dʒuːdɪkətərɪ) *adj* **1** of or relating to the administration of justice ▷ *n* **2** a court of law **3** the administration of justice

judicature ('dʒuːdɪkətʃə) *n* **1** the administration of justice **2** the office, function, or power of a judge **3** the extent of authority of a court or judge **4** a body of judges; judiciary **5** a court of justice or such courts collectively

judicial (dʒuː'dɪʃəl) *adj* **1** of or relating to the administration of justice **2** of or relating to judgment in a court of law or to a judge exercising this function **3** allowed or enforced by a court of law: *judicial separation* **4** having qualities appropriate to a judge **5** giving or seeking judgment [C14 from L *jūdiciālis* belonging to the law courts, from *jūdicium* judgment, from *jūdex* a judge] > **ju'dicially** *adv*

judiciary (dʒuː'dɪʃɪərɪ) *adj* **1** of or relating to courts of law, judgment, or judges ▷ *n, pl* **judiciaries** **2** the branch of the central authority in a state concerned with the administration of justice **3** the system of courts in a country **4** the judges collectively

judicious (dʒuː'dɪʃəs) *adj* having or proceeding from good judgment > **ju'diciously** *adv* > **ju'diciousness** *n*

Judith ('dʒuːdɪθ) *n* **1** the heroine of one of the books of the Apocrypha, who saved her native town by decapitating Holofernes **2** the book recounting this episode

judo ('dʒuːdəʊ) *n* **a** the modern sport derived from jujitsu, in which the object is to force an opponent to submit using the minimum of physical effort **b** (*as modifier*): *a judo throw* [Japanese, from *jū* gentleness + *dō* way] > '**judoist** *n*
▷ www.ijf.org
▷ http://worldjudo.org

Judy ('dʒuːdɪ) *n, pl* **Judies** **1** the wife of Punch in the children's puppet show *Punch and Judy*. See **Punch** **2** (*often not cap*) *Brit sl* a girl

jug (dʒʌg) *n* **1** a vessel for holding or pouring liquids, usually having a handle and a lip. US equivalent: **pitcher** **2** *Austral & NZ* a container in which water is boiled, esp an electric kettle **3** *US* a large vessel with a narrow mouth **4** Also called: **jugful** the amount of liquid held by a jug **5** *Brit inf* a glass of beer **6** *sl* jail ▷ *vb* **jugs, jugging, jugged** **7** to stew or boil (meat, esp hare) in an earthenware container **8** (*tr*) *sl* to put in jail [C16 prob. from *Jug*, nickname from name *Joan*]

jugate ('dʒuːgeɪt, -gɪt) *adj* (esp of compound leaves) having parts arranged in pairs [C19 from NL *jugātus* (unattested), from L *jugum* a yoke]

juggernaut ('dʒʌgəˌnɔːt) *n* **1** any terrible force, esp one that demands complete self-sacrifice **2** *Brit* a very large heavy lorry [C17 from Hindi, from Sansk. *Jagannātha* lord of the world: devotees supposedly threw themselves under a cart carrying *Juggernaut*, an idol of Krishna]

juggins ('dʒʌgɪnz) *n* (*functioning as sing*) *Brit inf* a silly person [C19 special use of the surname *Juggins*]

juggle ('dʒʌgᵊl) *vb* **juggles, juggling, juggled 1** to throw and catch (several objects) continuously so that most are in the air all the time **2** to manipulate (facts, etc) so as to give a false picture **3** (*tr*) to keep (several activities) in progress, esp with difficulty ▷ *n* **4** an act of juggling [C14 from OF *jogler* to perform as a jester, from L, from *jocus* a jest] > '**juggler** *n*

Jugoslav ('ju:gəʊˌslɑ:v) *or* **Jugoslavian** (ˌju:gəʊ'slɑ:vɪən) *adj*, *n* a variant spelling of **Yugoslav** or **Yugoslavian**

Jugoslavia (ˌju:gəʊ'slɑ:vɪə) *n* a variant spelling of **Yugoslavia**

jugular ('dʒʌgjʊlə) *adj* **1** of, relating to, or situated near the throat or neck ▷ *n* **2** Also called: **jugular vein** any of the large veins in the neck carrying blood to the heart from the head [C16 from LL, from L *jugulum* throat]

Jugurtha (dʒu:'gɜ:θə) *n* died 104 BC, king of Numidia (?112–104), who waged war against the Romans (the **Jugurthine War**, 112–105) and was defeated and executed

juice (dʒu:s) *n* **1** any liquid that occurs naturally in or is secreted by plant or animal tissue: *the juice of an orange* **2** *inf* **2a** petrol **2b** electricity **2c** alcoholic drink **3** vigour or vitality [C13 from OF *jus*, from L] > '**juiceless** *adj*

juice up *vb* (*tr*, *adv*) *US sl* to make lively: *to juice up a party*

juicy ('dʒu:sɪ) *adj* **juicier, juiciest 1** full of juice **2** provocatively interesting; spicy: *juicy gossip* **3** profitable: *a juicy contract* > '**juicily** *adv* > '**juiciness** *n*

Juiz de Fora (*Portuguese* ʒu'iʃ di 'fɔra) *n* a city in SE Brazil, in Minas Gerais state on the Rio de Janeiro–Belo Horizonte railway: textiles. Pop: 443 359 (2000)

jujitsu, jujutsu, *or* **jiujutsu** (dʒu:'dʒɪtsu:) *n* the traditional Japanese system of unarmed self-defence perfected by the samurai. See also **judo** [C19 from Japanese, from *jū* gentleness + *jutsu* art]

juju ('dʒu:dʒu:) *n* **1** an object superstitiously revered by certain West African peoples and used as a charm or fetish **2** the power associated with a juju **3** a taboo effected by a juju [C19 prob. from Hausa *djudju* evil spirit, fetish]

jujube ('dʒu:dʒu:b) *n* **1** any of several Old World spiny trees that have small yellowish flowers and dark red edible fruits **2** the fruit of any of these trees **3** a chewy sweet made of flavoured gelatine and sometimes medicated to soothe sore throats [C14 from Med. L *jujuba*, modification of L *zīzyphum*, from Gk *zizuphon*]

jukebox ('dʒu:kˌbɒks) *n* a coin-operated machine, usually found in pubs, clubs, etc, that contains records, CDs, or videos, which are played when selected by a customer [C20 from Gullah (an African-American language) *juke* bawdy (as in *juke house* brothel) + BOX[1]]

jukskei ('jʊkˌskeɪ) *n* a South African game in which a peg is thrown over a fixed distance at a stake driven into the ground [from Afrik. *juk* yoke + *skei* pin]

julep ('dʒu:lɪp) *n* **1** a sweet drink, variously prepared and sometimes medicated **2** *chiefly US* short for **mint julep** [C14 from OF, from Ar. *julāb*, from Persian, from *gul* rose + *āb* water]

Julian[1] ('dʒu:ljən, -lɪən) *n* known as *Julian the Apostate*; Latin name *Flavius Claudius Julianus*. 331–363 AD, Roman emperor (361–363), who attempted to revive paganism in the Roman empire while remaining tolerant to Christians and Jews

Julian[2] ('dʒu:ljən, -lɪən) *adj* **1** of or relating to Julius Caesar **2** denoting or relating to the Julian calendar

Julian Alps *pl n* a mountain range in Slovenia: an E range of the Alps

Julian calendar *n* the calendar introduced by Julius Caesar in 46 BC, in which leap years occurred every fourth year and in every centenary year ▷ Cf **Gregorian calendar**

Julian of Norwich *n* ?1342–?1413, English mystic and anchoress: best known for the *Revelations of Divine Love* describing her visions

julienne (ˌdʒu:lɪ'ɛn) *adj* **1** (of vegetables) cut into thin shreds ▷ *n* **2** a clear consommé to which such vegetables have been added [F, from name *Jules*, *Julien*, or *Julienne*]

Julius II ('dʒu:ljəs, -lɪəs) *n* original name *Guiliano della Rovere*. 1443–1513, pope (1503–13). He completed the restoration of the Papal States to the Church, began the building of St Peter's, Rome (1506), and patronized Michelangelo, Raphael, and Bramante

Julius Caesar *n* See **Caesar**

Jullundur ('dʒʌləndə) *n* the former name of **Jalandhar**

July (dʒu:'laɪ) *n*, *pl* **Julies** the seventh month of the year, consisting of 31 days [C13 from Anglo-F *julie*, from L *Jūlius*, after Gaius *Julius* CAESAR, after whom it was named]

jumble ('dʒʌmbᵊl) *vb* **jumbles, jumbling, jumbled 1** to mingle (objects, etc) in a state of disorder **2** (*tr*; *usually passive*) to remember in a confused form ▷ *n* **3** a disordered mass, state, etc **4** *Brit* articles donated for a jumble sale [C16 from ?] > '**jumbly** *adj*

jumble sale *n* a sale of miscellaneous articles, usually second-hand, in aid of charity. US and Canad equivalent: **rummage sale**

jumbo ('dʒʌmbəʊ) *n*, *pl* **jumbos 1** *inf* **1a** a very large person or thing **1b** (*as modifier*): *a jumbo box of detergent* **2** See **jumbo jet** [C19 after a famous elephant exhibited by P T Barnum, from Swahili *jumbe* chief]

jumbo jet *n inf* a type of large jet-propelled airliner that carries several hundred passengers

jumbo pack *n* **1** the promotion of bulk sales of small unit items, such as confectionery, by packing several in one wrapping, usually with a unit price reduction **2** such a package of items

jumbuck ('dʒʌmˌbʌk) *n Austral* an informal word for **sheep** [C19 from Abor.]

Jumna ('dʒʌmnə) *n* a river in N India, rising in Uttaranchal in the Himalayas and flowing south and southeast to join the Ganges just below Allahabad (a confluence held sacred by Hindus). Length: 1385 km (860 miles)

jump (dʒʌmp) *vb* **1** (*intr*) to leap or spring clear of the ground or other surface by using the muscles in the legs and feet **2** (*tr*) to leap over or clear (an obstacle): *to jump a gap* **3** (*tr*) to cause to leap over an obstacle: *to jump a horse over a hedge* **4** (*intr*) to move or proceed hastily (into, onto, out of, etc): *she jumped into a taxi* **5** (*tr*) *inf* to board so as to travel illegally on: *he jumped the train as it was leaving* **6** (*intr*) to parachute from an aircraft **7** (*intr*) to jerk or start, as with astonishment, surprise, etc **8** to rise or cause to rise suddenly or abruptly **9** to pass or skip over (intervening objects or matter): *she jumped a few lines and then continued reading* **10** (*intr*) to change from one thing to another, esp from one subject to another **11** *draughts* to capture (an opponent's piece) by moving one of one's own pieces over it to an unoccupied square **12** (*intr*) *bridge* to bid in response to one's partner at a higher level than is necessary, to indicate a strong hand **13** (*tr*) to come off (a track, etc): *the locomotive jumped the rails* **14** (*intr*) (of the stylus of a record player) to be jerked out of the groove **15** (*intr*) *sl* to be lively: *the party was jumping* **16** (*tr*) *inf* to attack without warning: *thieves jumped the old man* **17** (*tr*) *inf* (of a driver or a motor vehicle) to pass through (a red traffic light) or move away from (traffic lights) before they change to green **18 jump down someone's throat** *inf* to address or reply to someone sharply **19 jump ship** to desert, esp to leave a ship in which one is legally bound to serve **20 jump the queue** *inf* to obtain some advantage out of turn or unfairly **21 jump to it** *inf* to begin something quickly and efficiently ▷ *n* **22** an act or

Jj

instance of jumping **23** a space, distance, or obstacle to be jumped or that has been jumped **24** a descent by parachute from an aircraft **25** *sport* any of several contests involving a jump: *the high jump* **26** a sudden rise: *the jump in prices last month* **27** a sudden or abrupt transition **28** a sudden jerk or involuntary muscular spasm, esp as a reaction of surprise **29** a step or degree: *one jump ahead* **30** *draughts* a move that captures an opponent's piece by jumping over it **31** *films* **31a** a break in continuity in the normal sequence of shots **31b** (*as modifier*): *a jump cut* **32** **on the jump** *inf, chiefly US & Canad* **32a** in a hurry **32b** busy **33** **take a running jump** *Brit inf* a contemptuous expression of dismissal ▷ See also **jump at, jump-off,** etc [c16 prob. imit.]

jump at *vb* (*intr, prep*) to be glad to accept: *I would jump at the chance of going*

jumped-up *adj inf* suddenly risen in significance, esp when appearing arrogant

jumper[1] ('dʒʌmpə) *n* **1** *chiefly Brit* a knitted or crocheted garment covering the upper part of the body **2** the US and Canad term for **pinafore dress** [c19 from obs. *jump* man's loose jacket, var. of *jupe*, from OF, from Ar. *jubbah* long cloth coat]

jumper[2] ('dʒʌmpə) *n* **1** a boring tool that works by repeated impact, such as a steel bit in a drill used in boring rock **2** Also called: **jumper cable, jumper lead** a short length of wire used to make a connection, usually temporarily **3** a person or animal that jumps

jumping bean *n* a seed of any of several Mexican plants that contains a moth caterpillar whose movements cause it to jerk about

jumping jack *n* a toy figure of a man with jointed limbs that can be moved by pulling attached strings

jump jet *n inf* a fixed-wing jet aircraft that is capable of landing and taking off vertically

jump jockey *n Brit inf* a jockey riding in a steeplechase, as opposed to racing on the flat

jump leads (li:dz) *pl n* two heavy cables fitted with crocodile clips used to start a motor vehicle with a discharged battery by connecting the battery to an external battery

jump-off *n* **1** an extra round in a showjumping contest when two or more horses are equal first, deciding the winner ▷ *vb* **jump off** **2** (*intr, adv*) to engage in a jump-off

jump on *vb* (*intr, prep*) *inf* to reprimand or attack suddenly and forcefully

jump seat *n* **1** a folding seat on some aircraft for an additional crew member **2** *Brit* a folding seat in a motor vehicle

jump-start *vb* **1** to start the engine of (a car) by pushing or rolling it and then engaging the gears or (of a car) to start in this way ▷ *n* **2** the act of starting a car in this way ▷ Also called (Brit): **bump-start**

jump suit *n* a one-piece garment of combined trousers and jacket or shirt

jumpy ('dʒʌmpɪ) *adj* **jumpier, jumpiest** **1** nervous or apprehensive **2** moving jerkily or fitfully > '**jumpily** *adv* > '**jumpiness** *n*

Jun. *abbrev for:* **1** June **2** Also: **jun** junior

Junagadh (ˌdʒu:nəˈgæd) *n* a town in India, in Gujarat: noted for its Buddhist caves and temples. Pop: 130 484 (1991)

junco ('dʒʌŋkəʊ) *n, pl* **juncos** *or* **juncoes** a North American bunting having a greyish plumage [c18 from Sp.: a rush, from L *juncus* rush]

junction ('dʒʌŋkʃən) *n* **1** a place where several routes, lines, or roads meet, link, or cross each other: *a railway junction* **2** a point on a motorway where traffic may leave or join it **3** *electronics* **3a** a contact between two different metals or other materials: *a thermocouple junction* **3b** a transition region in a semiconductor **4** the act of joining or the state of being joined [c18 from L *junctiō* a joining, from *jungere* to join]

junction box *n* an earthed enclosure within which wires or cables can be safely connected

junction transistor *n* a bipolar transistor consisting of two p-n junctions combined to form either an n-p-n or a p-n-p transistor

juncture ('dʒʌŋktʃə) *n* **1** a point in time, esp a critical one (often in **at this juncture**) **2** *linguistics* the set of phonological features signalling a division between words, such as those that distinguish *a name* from *an aim* **3** a less common word for **junction**

Jundiaí (*Portuguese* ʒundia'i) *n* an industrial city in SE Brazil, in São Paulo state. Pop: 299 669 (2000)

June (dʒu:n) *n* the sixth month of the year, consisting of 30 days [OE *iunius*, from L *junius*, prob. from *Junius* name of Roman gens]

Juneau ('dʒu:nəʊ) *n* a port in SE Alaska: state capital. Pop: 26 751 (1990)

Jung (jʊŋ) *n* **Carl Gustav** (karl 'gʊstaf) 1875–1961, Swiss psychologist. His criticism of Freud's emphasis on the sexual instinct ended their early collaboration. He went on to found analytical psychology, developing the concepts of the collective unconscious and its archetypes and of the extrovert and introvert as the two main psychological types

Jungfrau (*German* 'jʊŋfrau) *n* a mountain in S Switzerland, in the Bernese Alps south of Interlaken. Height: 4158 m (13 642 ft)

Junggar Pendi ('dʒʊŋ'gɛər 'pɛn'di:), **Dzungaria,** *or* **Zungaria** *n* an arid region of W China, in N Xinjiang Uygur between the Altai Mountains and the Tian Shan

jungle ('dʒʌŋgᵊl) *n* **1** an equatorial forest area with luxuriant vegetation **2** any dense or tangled thicket or growth **3** a place of intense or ruthless struggle for survival: *the concrete jungle* **4** a type of fast electronic dance music, originating in the early 1990s, which combines elements of techno and ragga [c18 from Hindi, from Sansk. *jāngala* wilderness] > '**jungly** *adj*

jungle fever *n* a serious malarial fever occurring in the East Indies

jungle fowl *n* **1** any small gallinaceous bird of S and SE Asia, the males of which (**junglecock**) have an arched tail and a combed and wattled head **2** *Austral* any of several megapodes

jungle juice *n sl* alcoholic liquor

junior ('dʒu:njə) *adj* **1** lower in rank or length of service; subordinate **2** younger in years **3** of or relating to youth or childhood **4** *Brit* of schoolchildren between the ages of 7 and 11 approximately **5** *US* of or designating the third year of a four-year course at college or high school ▷ *n* **6** *law* (in England) any barrister below the rank of Queen's Counsel **7** a junior person **8** *Brit* a junior schoolchild **9** *US* a junior student [c17 from L: younger, from *juvenis* young]

Junior ('dʒu:njə) *adj* being the younger: usually used after a name to distinguish the son from the father: *Charles Parker, Junior.* Abbrev: **Jnr, Jr, Jun., Junr**

junior common room *n* (in certain universities and colleges) a common room for the use of students

junior lightweight *n* **a** a professional boxer weighing 126–130 pounds (57–59 kg) **b** (*as modifier*): *a junior-lightweight bout*

junior middleweight *n* **a** a professional boxer weighing 147–154 pounds (66.5–70 kg) **b** (*as modifier*): *the junior-middleweight championship*

junior school *n* (in England and Wales) a school for children aged between 7 and 11

junior technician *n* a rank in the Royal Air Force comparable to that of private in the army

junior welterweight *n* **a** a professional boxer weighing 135–140 pounds (61–63.5 kg) **b** (*as modifier*): *a junior-welterweight fight*

juniper ('dʒu:nɪpə) *n* a coniferous shrub or small tree of the N hemisphere having purple berry-like cones. The cones of the **common** or **dwarf juniper** are used as a flavouring in making gin [c14 from L *jūniperus*, from ?]

junk[1] (dʒʌŋk) *n* **1** discarded objects, etc, collectively **2** *inf* **2a** rubbish generally **2b** nonsense: *the play was absolute junk* **3** *sl* any narcotic drug, esp heroin ▷ *vb* **4** (*tr*) *inf* to discard as junk [c15 *jonke* old useless rope]

junk[2] (dʒʌŋk) *n* a sailing vessel used in Chinese waters and characterized by a very high poop, flat bottom, and square sails supported by battens [c17 from Port. *junco*, from Javanese *jon*]

junk bond *n finance* a security that offers a high yield but often involves a high risk of default

Junker (ˈjʊŋkə) *n* **1** *history* any of the aristocratic landowners of Prussia **2** an arrogant German army officer or official **3** (formerly) a young German nobleman [c16 from G, from OHG *junchērro* young lord] > **ˈJunkerdom** *n*

Junkers (ˈjʊŋkəz) *n* **Hugo** 1859–1935, German aircraft designer. His military aircraft were used in both World Wars

junket (ˈdʒʌŋkɪt) *n* **1** a sweet dessert made of flavoured milk set to a curd with rennet **2** a feast **3** an excursion, esp one made for pleasure at public expense ▷ *vb* **4** to have or entertain with a feast **5** (*intr*) (of a public official, etc) to go on a junket [c14 (in the sense: rush basket, hence custard served on rushes): from OF (dialect) *jonquette*, from *jonc* rush, from L *juncus* reed] > **ˈjunketing** *n*

junk food *n* food which is eaten in addition to or instead of regular meals, and which often has a low nutritional value

junkie *or* **junky** (ˈdʒʌŋkɪ) *n, pl* **junkies** an informal word for **drug addict**

junk mail *n* unsolicited mail advertising goods or services

junk shop *n* a shop selling miscellaneous second-hand goods and sometimes antiques

Juno (ˈdʒuːnəʊ) *n* **1** (in Roman tradition) the queen of the Olympian gods. Greek counterpart: **Hera** **2** a woman of stately bearing and regal beauty

junta (ˈdʒʌntə, ˈhʊntə) *n* (*functioning as sing or pl*) **1** a group of military officers holding the power in a country, esp after a coup d'état **2** Also called: **junto** a small group of men **3** a legislative or executive council in some parts of Latin America [c17 from Sp.: council, from L, from *jungere* to join]

junto (ˈdʒʊntəʊ) *n, pl* **juntos** a variant of **junta** (sense 2) [c17]

Jupiter[1] (ˈdʒuːpɪtə) *n* (in Roman tradition) the king and ruler of the Olympian gods. Also called: **Jove**

Jupiter[2] (ˈdʒuːpɪtə) *n* the largest of the planets and the fifth from the sun
▷ www.solarviews.com/eng/jupiter.htm
▷ http://nssdc.gsfc.nasa.gov/planetary/planets/

Jura (ˈdʒʊərə) *n* **1** a department of E France, in Franche-Comté region. Capital: Lons-le-Saunier. Pop: 250 857 (1999). Area: 5055 sq km (1971 sq miles) **2** a canton of Switzerland, bordering the French frontier: formed in 1979 from part of Bern. Capital: Delémont. Pop: 68 800 (2000 est). Area: 838 sq km (323 sq miles) **3** an island off the W coast of Scotland, in the Inner Hebrides, separated from the mainland by the **Sound of Jura**. Pop (with Colonsay): 250 (latest est). Area: 381 sq km (147 sq miles) **4** a mountain range in W central Europe, between the Rivers Rhine and Rhône: mostly in E France, extending into W Switzerland **5** a range of mountains in the NE quadrant of the moon lying on the N border of the Mare Imbrium

Jurassic (dʒʊˈræsɪk) *adj* **1** of or formed in the second period of the Mesozoic era, lasting for 55 million years, during which dinosaurs and ammonites flourished ▷ *n* **2 the** the Jurassic period or rock system [c19 from F *jurassique*, after the JURA (Mountains)]

jurat (ˈdʒʊəræt) *n* **1** *law* a statement at the foot of an affidavit, naming the parties, stating when, where, and before whom it was sworn, etc **2** (in England) a municipal officer of the Cinque Ports **3** (in France and the Channel Islands) a magistrate [c16 from Med. L *jūrātus* one who has been sworn, from L *jūrāre* to swear]

juridical (dʒʊˈrɪdɪkᵊl) *adj* of or relating to law or to the administration of justice; legal [c16 from L, from *iūs* law + *dicere* to say] > **juˈridically** *adv*

jurisdiction (ˌdʒʊərɪsˈdɪkʃən) *n* **1** the right or power to administer justice and to apply laws **2** the exercise or extent of such right or power **3** authority in general [c13 from L *jūrisdictiō* administration of justice, from *jus* law + DICTION] > **ˌjurisˈdictional** *adj*

jurisprudence (ˌdʒʊərɪsˈpruːdᵊns) *n* **1** the science or philosophy of law **2** a system or body of law **3** a branch of law: *medical jurisprudence* [c17 from L *jūris prūdentia*, from *jus* law + PRUDENCE] > **jurisprudential** (ˌdʒʊərɪspruːˈdɛnʃəl) *adj*
▷ www.iisj.es

jurist (ˈdʒʊərɪst) *n* a person versed in the science of law, esp Roman or civil law [c15 from F *juriste*, from Med. L *jūrista*]

juristic (dʒʊˈrɪstɪk) *or* **juristical** *adj* **1** of or relating to jurists **2** of or characteristic of the study of law or the legal profession

juror (ˈdʒʊərə) *n* **1** a member of a jury **2** a person who takes an oath [c14 from Anglo-F *jurour*, from OF *jurer* to take an oath, from L *jūrāre*]

Juruá (*Portuguese* ʒuˈrua) *n* a river in South America, rising in E central Peru and flowing northeast across NW Brazil to join the Amazon. Length: 1900 km (1200 miles)

jury[1] (ˈdʒʊərɪ) *n, pl* **juries** **1** a group of, usually, twelve people sworn to deliver a true verdict according to the evidence upon a case presented in a court of law **2** a body of persons appointed to judge a competition and award prizes [c14 from OF *juree*, from *jurer* to swear]

Jj

jury[2] (ˈdʒʊərɪ) *adj chiefly naut* (*in combination*) makeshift: *jury-rigged* [c17 from ?]

jury box *n* an enclosure where the jury sits in court

juryman (ˈdʒʊərɪmən) *or* (*fem*) **jurywoman** *n, pl* **jurymen** *or* **jurywomen** a member of a jury

jury-rigged *adj chiefly naut* set up in a makeshift manner

jus (ʒuː; *French* ʒy) *n* a sauce [French: literally, juice]

just *adj* (dʒʌst) **1a** fair or impartial in action or judgment **1b** (*as collective n; preceded by the*): *the just* **2** conforming to high moral standards; honest **3** consistent with justice: *a just action* **4** rightly applied or given: *a just reward* **5** legally valid; lawful: *a just inheritance* **6** well-founded: *just criticism* **7** correct or true: *a just account* ▷ *adv* (dʒʌst; *unstressed* dʒəst) **8** used with forms of *have* to indicate an action performed in the very recent past: *I have just closed the door* **9** at this very instant: *he's just coming in to land* **10** no more than; only: *just an ordinary car* **11** exactly: *that's just what I mean* **12** barely: *he just got there in time* **13 just about** **13a** at the point of starting (to do something) **13b** almost: *I've just about had enough* **14 just a moment, second,** *or* **minute** an expression requesting the hearer to wait or pause for a brief period of time **15 just now** **15a** a very short time ago **15b** at this moment **15c** *S African inf* in a little while **16 just so** arranged with precision [c14 from L *jūstus* righteous, from *jūs* justice] > **ˈjustly** *adv* > **ˈjustness** *n*

USAGE The use of *just* with *exactly* (*it's just exactly what they want*) is redundant and should be avoided: *it's exactly what they want*

justice (ˈdʒʌstɪs) *n* **1** the quality or fact of being just **2** *ethics* the principle of fairness that like cases should be treated alike **3** the administration of law according to prescribed and accepted principles **4** conformity to the law **5** a judge of the Supreme Court of Judicature **6** short for **justice of the peace** **7** good reason (esp in with justice) **8** **bring to justice** to capture, try, and usually punish (a criminal, etc) **9** **do justice to** **9a** to show to full advantage **9b** to show full appreciation of by action **9c** to treat or judge fairly **10** **do oneself justice** to make full use of one's abilities [C12 from OF, from L *jūstitia*, from *justus* JUST] > **'justice,ship** *n*

justice of the peace *n* **1** (in Britain) a lay magistrate, appointed by the crown or acting *ex officio*, whose function is to preserve the peace in his or her area, try summarily such cases as are within his or her jurisdiction, and perform miscellaneous administrative duties **2** (in Australia and New Zealand) a person authorised to administer oaths, attest instruments, and take declarations

justiciar (dʒʌ'stɪʃɪ,ɑː) *n English legal history* the chief political and legal officer from the time of William I to that of Henry III, who deputized for the king in his absence. Also called: **justiciary** > **jus'ticiar,ship** *n*

justiciary (dʒʌ'stɪʃɪərɪ) *adj* **1** of or relating to the administration of justice ▷ *n, pl* **justiciaries** **2** an officer or administrator of justice; judge

justifiable ('dʒʌstɪ,faɪəbᵊl) *adj* capable of being justified > **justi,fia'bility** *n* > **'justi,fiably** *adv*

justifiable homicide *n* lawful killing, as in the execution of a death sentence

justification (,dʒʌstɪfɪ'keɪʃən) *n* **1** reasonable grounds for complaint, defence, etc **2** proof, vindication, or exculpation **3** *Christian theol* **3a** the act of justifying **3b** the process of being justified or the condition of having been justified > **'justifi,catory** *adj*

justify ('dʒʌstɪ,faɪ) *vb* **justifies, justifying, justified** (*mainly tr*) **1** (*often passive*) to prove or see to be just or valid; vindicate **2** to show to be reasonable: *his behaviour justifies our suspicion* **3** to declare or show to be free from blame or guilt **4** *law* to show good reason in court for (some action taken) **5** (*also intr*) *printing, computing* to adjust the spaces between words in (a line of type or data) so that it is of the required length or (of a line of type or data) to fit exactly **6a** *Protestant theol* to declare righteous by the imputation of Christ's merits to the sinner **6b** *RC theol* to change from sinfulness to righteousness by the transforming effects of grace **7** (*also intr*) *law* to prove (a person) to have sufficient means to act as surety, etc, or (of a person) to qualify to provide bail or surety [C14 from OF *justifier*, from L *justificāre*, from *jūstus* JUST + *facere* to make] > **'justi,fier** *n*

Justinian I (dʒʌ'stɪnɪən) *n* called *the Great*; Latin name *Flavius Anicius Justinianus*. 483–565 AD, Byzantine emperor (527–565). He recovered North Africa, SE Spain, and Italy, largely owing to the brilliance of generals such as Belisarius. He sponsored the Justinian Code

Justinian Code *n* a compilation of Roman imperial law made by order of Justinian I (483–565 AD), Byzantine emperor. *n* a compilation of Roman imperial law made by order of Justinian I

Justin Martyr ('dʒʌstɪn) *n* **Saint** ?100–?165 AD, Christian apologist and philosopher. Feast day: June 1

just-in-time *adj* denoting or relating to an industrial method in which waste, queues, bottlenecks, etc, are eliminated or reduced by producing production-line components, etc, and by delivering materials just before they are needed. Abbrev: **JIT**

justle ('dʒʌsᵊl) *vb* **justles, justling, justled** a less common word for **jostle**

jut (dʒʌt) *vb* **juts, jutting, jutted** **1** (*intr; often foll by out*) to stick out or overhang beyond the surface or main part ▷ *n* **2** something that juts out [C16 var. of JET[1]] > **'jutting** *adj*

jute (dʒuːt) *n* **1** either of two Old World tropical yellow-flowered herbaceous plants, cultivated for their strong fibre **2** this fibre, used in making sacks, rope, etc [C18 from Bengali *jhuto*, from Sansk. *jūta* braid of hair]

Jutland ('dʒʌtlənd) *n* a peninsula of N Europe: forms the continental portion of Denmark and geographically includes the N part of the German province of Schleswig-Holstein, while politically it includes only the mainland of Denmark and the islands north of Limfjorden; a major but inconclusive naval battle was fought off its NW coast in 1916 between the British and German fleets. Danish name: **Jylland**

juv. *abbrev for* juvenile

Juvenal ('dʒuːvɪnᵊl) *n* Latin name *Decimus Junius Juvenalis*. ?60–?140 AD, Roman satirist. In his 16 verse satires, he denounced the vices of imperial Rome

juvenescence (,dʒuːvɪ'nɛsəns) *n* **1** youth or immaturity **2** the act or process of growing from childhood to youth > **,juve'nescent** *adj*

juvenile ('dʒuːvɪ,naɪl) *adj* **1** young, youthful, or immature **2** suitable or designed for young people: *juvenile pastimes* ▷ *n* **3** a juvenile person, animal, or plant **4** an actor who performs youthful roles **5** a book intended for young readers [C17 from L *juvenīlis* youthful, from *juvenis* young] > **'juve,nilely** *adv*

juvenile court *n* a court that deals with juvenile offenders and children beyond parental control or in need of care

juvenile delinquency *n* antisocial or criminal conduct by juvenile delinquents

juvenile delinquent *n* a child or young person guilty of some offence, act of vandalism, or antisocial behaviour and who may be brought before a juvenile court

juvenilia (,dʒuːvɪ'nɪlɪə) *n* works of art, literature, or music produced in youth, before the artist, author, or composer has formed a mature style [C17 from L, lit.: youthful things]

juxtapose (,dʒʌkstə'pəʊz) *vb* **juxtaposes, juxtaposing, juxtaposed** (*tr*) to place close together or side by side [C19 back formation from *juxtaposition*, from L *juxta* next to + POSITION] > **,juxtapo'sition** *n* > **,juxtapo'sitional** *adj*

Jylland ('jylan) *n* the Danish name for **Jutland**

Kk

k *or* **K** (keɪ) *n, pl* **k's, K's,** *or* **Ks 1** the 11th letter and 8th consonant of the English alphabet **2** a speech sound represented by this letter, usually a voiceless velar stop, as in *kitten*

k *symbol for:* **1** kilo(s) **2** *maths* the unit vector along the z-axis

K *symbol for:* **1** kelvin(s) **2** *chess* king **3** *chem* potassium [from NL *kalium*] **4** *physics* kaon **5** *currency* **5a** kina **5b** kip **5c** kopeck **5d** kwacha **5e** kyat **6** one thousand [from KILO-] **7** *computing* **7a** a unit of 1024 words, bits, or bytes **7b** (not in technical usage) 1000

K *or* **K.** *abbrev for* Köchel: indicating the serial number in the catalogue of the works of Mozart made by Ludwig von Köchel, 1800–77

K2 *n* a mountain in the Karakoram Range on the Kashmir-Xinjiang Uygur AR border: the second highest mountain in the world. Height: 8611 m (28 250 ft). Also called: **Godwin Austen, Dapsang**

Kaaba *or* **Caaba** ('kɑːbə) *n* a cube-shaped building in Mecca, the most sacred Muslim pilgrim shrine, into which is built the black stone believed to have been given by Gabriel to Abraham [from Ar. *ka'bah*, from *ka'b* cube]

kaal ('kɑːl) *or* **kaal gat** ('kɑːl gæt) *adj S African inf* naked [from Afrik., lit.: bare (arsed)]

kabaddi (kə'bɑːdɪ) *n* a game played between two teams of seven players, in which individuals take turns to chase and try to touch members of the opposing team without being captured by them [Tamil]

▹ http://punjabsportsclub.com

Kabalega Falls (ˌkɑːbə'leɪgə) *pl n* rapids on the lower Victoria Nile, about 35 km (22 miles) east of Lake Albert, where the Nile drops 120 m (400 ft)

Kabardino-Balkar Republic (ˌkæbə'diːnəʊˌbælkə) *n* a constituent republic of S Russia, on the N side of the Caucasus Mountains. Capital: Nalchik. Pop: 792 000 (2000 est). Area: 12 500 sq km (4825 sq miles). Also called: **Kabardino-Balkaria** (kæbəˌdiːnəʊbæl'kɑːrɪə)

kabbala *or* **kabala** (kə'bɑːlə) *n* variant spellings of **cabbala**

kabeljou ('kɑːbəlˌjəʊ) *n S African* a large marine fish that is an important food fish of South African waters [c18 from Afrik., from Dutch, cod]

Kabila (kæ'biːlə) *n* **Laurent** (*French* lorã) 1940–2001, Congolese politician and guerrilla leader: he overthrew the Mobutu regime in Zaïre, becoming president of the renamed Democratic Republic of Congo (1997–2001): assassinated **2** his son, **Joseph** born 1972, Congolese soldier and politician, who became president (2001) of the Democratic Republic of Congo in succession to his father

Kabloona (kə'bluːnə) *n* (in Canada) a person who is not of Inuit ancestry, esp a White person [from Inuktitut]

kabuki (kæ'buːkɪ) *n* a form of Japanese drama based on legends and characterized by elaborate costumes and the use of male actors [Japanese, from *ka* singing + *bu* dancing + *ki* art]

▹ www.theatrelinks.com/

▹ www.inic.utexas.edu/asnic/countries/japan/kabuki.html

▹ www.japan-guide.com/e/e2090.html

Kabul (kə'bʊl, 'kɔːbᵊl) *n* **1** the capital of Afghanistan, in the northeast of the country at an altitude of 1800 m (5900 ft) on the **Kabul River**: over 3000 years old, with a strategic position commanding passes through the Hindu Kush and main routes to the Khyber Pass; destroyed and rebuilt many times; capital of the Mogul Empire from 1504 until 1738 and of Afghanistan from 1773; university (1932) Pop: 700 000 (1993 est) **2** a river in Afghanistan and Pakistan, rising in the Hindu Kush and flowing east into the Indus at Attock, Pakistan. Length: 700 km (435 miles)

Kabyle (kəˈbaɪl) *n* **1** (*pl* **Kabyles** *or* **Kabyle**) a member of a Berber people in Tunisia and Algeria **2** the dialect of Berber spoken by this people [c19 from Ar. *qabā'il*, pl. of *qabīlah* tribe]

Kádár (ˈkɑːdɑːr) *n* **János** (ˈjaːnoʃ) 1912–89, Hungarian statesman; Communist prime minister of Hungary (1956–58; 1961–65) and first secretary of the Communist Party (1956–88)

kadi (ˈkɑːdɪ, ˈkeɪdɪ) *n, pl* **kadis** a variant spelling of **cadi**

Kaduna (kəˈduːnə) *n* **1** a state of N Nigeria. Capital: Kaduna. Pop: 4 438 007 (1995 est). Area: 46 053 sq km (17 781 sq miles). Former name (until 1976): **North-Central State** **2** a city in N central Nigeria, capital of Kaduna state on the **Kaduna River** (a principal tributary of the Niger) Pop: 342 200 (1996 est)

Kaesŏng (ˌkeɪˈsɑŋ) *n* a city in SW North Korea: former capital of Korea (938–1392). Pop: 120 000 (latest est)

Kaffir *or* **Kafir** (ˈkæfə) *n, pl* **Kaffirs** *or* **Kaffir, Kafirs** *or* **Kafir** **1** *offens* **1a** (in southern Africa) any Black African **1b** (*as modifier*): *Kaffir farming* **2** a former name for the **Xhosa** language [c19 from Ar. *kāfir* infidel, from *kafara* to deny]

> **USAGE** This word is considered deeply offensive in South Africa and using it can be grounds for prosecution for crimen injuria

kaffir beer *n S African* beer made from sorghum (kaffir corn) or millet

kaffirboom (ˈkæfəˌbʊəm) *n* a S African deciduous flowering tree [from KAFFIR + Afrik. *boom* tree]

kaffir corn *n* a southern African variety of sorghum, cultivated in dry regions for its grain and as fodder. Sometimes shortened to **kaffir**

Kaffraria (kæˈfrɛərɪə) *n* a former region of S central South Africa: inhabited chiefly by the Kaffirs; British Kaffraria was a crown colony established in 1853 in the southwest of the region and annexed to Cape Colony in 1865 > **Kafˈfrarian** *adj, n*

Kafir (ˈkæfə) *n, pl* **Kafirs** *or* **Kafir** **1** a member of a people inhabiting E Afghanistan **2** a variant spelling of **Kaffir** [c19 from Ar.; see KAFFIR]

Kafiristan (ˌkæfɪrɪˈstɑːn) *n* the former name of **Nuristan**

Kafka (ˈkæfkə; *Czech* ˈkafka) *n* **Franz** (frants) 1883–1924, Czech novelist writing in German. In his two main novels *The Trial* (1925) and *The Castle* (1926), published posthumously against his wishes, he portrays man's fear, isolation, and bewilderment in a nightmarish dehumanized world

kaftan *or* **caftan** (ˈkæftæn) *n* **1** a long coatlike garment, usually with a belt, worn in the East **2** an imitation of this, worn esp by women, consisting of a loose dress with long wide sleeves [c16 from Turkish *qaftān*]

Kagera (kæˈgɛrə) *n* a river in E Africa, rising in headstreams on the border between Tanzania and Rwanda and flowing east to Lake Victoria: the most remote headstream of the Nile and largest tributary of Lake Victoria. Length: about 480 km (300 miles)

Kagoshima (ˌkægɒˈʃiːmə) *n* a port in SW Japan, on S Kyushu. Pop: 546 294 (1995)

kagoul (kəˈguːl) *n* a variant spelling of **cagoule**

kahawai (ˈkɑːhəwaɪ, ˈkɑːwaɪ) *n* a New Zealand food and game fish [from Maori]

Kahn (kɑːn) *n* **1** **Herman** 1922–83, US mathematician and futurologist; director of the Hudson Institute (1961–83) **2** **Louis I(sadore)** 1901–74, US architect, noted for his art museums at Yale (1951–53), Fort Worth (1966–72), and New Haven (1969–74)

kai (kaɪ) *n NZ inf* food [from Maori]

kaiak (ˈkaɪæk) *n* a variant spelling of **kayak**

Kaieteur Falls (ˌkaɪəˈtʊə) *pl n* a waterfall in Guyana, on the Potaro River. Height: 226 m (741 ft). Width: about 107 m (350 ft)

Kaifeng (ˈkaɪˈfɛŋ) *n* a city in E China, in N Henan on the Yellow River: one of the oldest cities in China and its capital (as Pien-liang) from 907 to 1126. Pop: 569 300 (1999 est)

kail (keɪl) *n* a variant spelling of **kale**

kai moana (məʊˈænə) *n NZ* seafood [Maori, from KAI + *moana* sea]

kainite (ˈkaɪnaɪt) *n* a white mineral consisting of potassium chloride and magnesium sulphate: a fertilizer and source of potassium salts [c19 from G *Kainit*, from Gk *kainos* new + -ITE[1]]

Kairouan (*French* kɛrwɑ̃), **Kairwan**, *or* **Qairwan** (kaɪəˈwɑːn) *n* a city in NE Tunisia: one of the holy cities of Islam; pilgrimage and trading centre. Pop: 102 600 (1994).

Kaiser[1] (ˈkaɪzə) *n* (*sometimes not cap*) *history* **1** any of the three German emperors **2** *obs* any Austro-Hungarian emperor [c16 from G, ult. from L *Caesar* emperor]

Kaiser[2] (*German* ˈkaizər) *n* **Georg** (ˈgeːɔrk) 1878–1945, German expressionist dramatist

Kaiserslautern (*German* kaizərsˈlautərn) *n* a city in W Germany, in S Rhineland-Palatinate. Pop: 100 300 (1999 est)

kaizen *Japanese* (kaɪˈzɛn) *n* a philosophy of continuous improvement of working practices that underlies total quality management and just-in-time business techniques [lit.: improvement]

kak (kʌk) *n S African taboo sl* **1** faeces **2** rubbish [Afrik.]

kaka (ˈkɑːkə) *n* a New Zealand parrot with a long compressed bill [c18 from Maori, ? imit. of its call]

kaka beak *n* a New Zealand shrub with beaklike red flowers [from KAKA]

kakapo (ˈkɑːkəˌpəʊ) *n, pl* **kakapos** a ground-living nocturnal parrot of New Zealand, resembling an owl [c19 from Maori, lit.: night kaka]

kakemono (ˌkækɪˈməʊnəʊ) *n, pl* **kakemonos** a Japanese paper or silk wall hanging, usually long and narrow, with a picture or inscription on it [c19 from Japanese, from *kake* hanging + *mono* thing]

Kalaalit Nunaat (kəˈlɑːlɪt ˈnuːnɑːt) *n* the Greenlandic name for **Greenland**

kala-azar (ˌkɑːləəˈzɑː) *n* a tropical infectious disease caused by a protozoan in the liver, spleen, etc [c19 from Assamese *kālā* black + *āzār* disease]

Kalahari (ˌkæləˈhɑːrɪ) *n* **the** an extensive arid plateau of South Africa, Namibia, and Botswana. Area: 260 000 sq km (100 000 sq miles). Also called: **Kalahari Desert**

Kalamazoo (ˌkæləməˈzuː) *n* a city in SW Michigan, midway between Detroit and Chicago: aircraft, missile parts. Pop: 77 145 (2000)

Kalashnikov (kəˈlæʃnɪˌkɒf) *n* a Russian-made automatic rifle. See also **AK-47** [c20 after Mikhail *Kalashnikov* (born 1919), its designer]

Kalat (kəˈlɑːt) *n* a region of SW Pakistan, in S Baluchistan: formerly a princely state ruled by the Khan of Kalat, which joined Pakistan in 1948

kale *or* **kail** (keɪl) *n* **1** a cultivated variety of cabbage with crinkled leaves **2** *Scot* a cabbage ▷ Cf **sea kale** [OE *cāl*]

kaleidoscope (kəˈlaɪdəˌskəʊp) *n* **1** an optical toy for producing symmetrical patterns by multiple reflections in inclined mirrors enclosed in a tube. Loose pieces of coloured glass, paper, etc, are placed between transparent plates at the far end of the tube, which is rotated to change the pattern **2** any complex pattern of frequently changing shapes and colours [c19 from Gk *kalos* beautiful + *eidos* form + -SCOPE] > **kaleidoscopic** (kəˌlaɪdəˈskɒpɪk) *adj*

kalends (ˈkælɪndz) *pl n* a variant spelling of **calends**

Kalevala (ˌkɑːləˈvɑːlə) *n Finnish legend* **1** the land of the hero Kaleva, who performed legendary exploits **2** the Finnish national epic in which these exploits are recounted [Finnish, from *kaleva* of a hero + *-la* home]

kaleyard *or* **kailyard** ('keɪlˌjɑːd; *Scot.* -ˌjard) *n Scot* a vegetable garden [c19 lit.: cabbage garden]
kaleyard school *or* **kailyard school** *n* a group of writers who depicted the homely aspects of life in the Scottish Lowlands. The best-known contributor was J. M. Barrie
Kalgan ('kɑːl'gɑːn) *n* a former name of **Zhangjiakou**
Kalgoorlie (kæl'gʊəlɪ) *n* a city in Western Australia, adjoining the town of Boulder: a centre of the Coolgardie gold rushes of the early 1890s; declining gold resources superseded by the discovery of nickel ore in 1966. Pop: 26 079 (including Boulder) (1991)
Kali ('kɑːlɪ) *n* the Hindu goddess of destruction, consort of Siva. Her cult was characterized by savagery and cannibalism
Kalidasa (ˌkælɪ'dɑːsə) *n* ?5th century AD, Indian dramatist and poet, noted for his romantic verse drama *Sakuntala*
kalied ('keɪlaɪd) *adj N English dialect* drunk
Kalimantan (ˌkælɪ'mæntən) *n* the Indonesian name for Borneo: applied to the Indonesian part of the island only, excluding the Malaysian states of Sabah and Sarawak and the sultanate of Brunei. Pop: 11 396 100 (1999 est)
Kalinin[1] (*Russian* ka'linin) *n* the former name (until 1991) of **Tver**
Kalinin[2] (*Russian* ka'linin) *n* **Mikhail Ivanovich** (mixa'il i'vanəvitʃ) 1875–1946, Soviet statesman: titular head of state (1919–46); a founder of *Pravda* (1912)
Kaliningrad (*Russian* kəlinin'grat) *n* a port in W Russia, on the Pregolya River: severely damaged in World War II as the chief German naval base on the Baltic; ceded to the Soviet Union in 1945 and is now Russia's chief Baltic naval base. Pop: 427 200 (1999 est). Former name (until 1946): **Königsberg**
Kalisz (*Polish* 'kaliʃ) *n* a town in central Poland, on an island in the Prosna River: textile industry. Pop: 106 641 (1999 est). Ancient name: **Calissia** (kə'lɪsɪə)
Kalmar (*Swedish* 'kalmar) *n* a port in SE Sweden, partly on the mainland and partly on a small island in the **Sound of Kalmar** opposite Öland: scene of the signing of the Union of Kalmar, which united Sweden, Denmark, and Norway into a single monarchy (1397–1523). Pop: 58 070 (1994)
kalmia ('kælmɪə) *n* an evergreen North American ericaceous shrub having showy clusters of white or pink flowers [c18 after Peter *Kalm* (1715–79), Swedish botanist and pupil of Linnaeus]
Kalmuck ('kælmʌk) *or* **Kalmyk** ('kælmɪk) *n* **1** (*pl* **Kalmucks, Kalmuck** *or* **Kalmyks, Kalmyk**) a member of a Mongoloid people of Buddhist tradition, who migrated from W China to Russia in the 17th century **2** the language of this people
Kalmuck Republic *or* **Kalmyk Republic** *n* a constituent republic of S Russia, on the Caspian Sea: became subject to Russia in 1646. Capital: Elista. Pop: 316 000 (2000 est). Area: 76 100 sq km (29 382 sq miles). Also called: **Kalmykia**
kalong ('kɑːlɒŋ) *n* a fruit bat of the Malay Archipelago; a flying fox [Javanese]
kalpa ('kælpə) *n* (in Hindu cosmology) a period in which the universe experiences a cycle of creation and destruction [c18 Sansk.]
Kaluga (*Russian* ka'lugə) *n* a city in central Russia, on the Oka River. Pop: 342 400 (1999 est)
Kama[1] (*Russian* 'kamə) *n* a river in central Russia, rising in the Ural Mountains and flowing to the River Volga. Length: 2030 km (1260 miles)
Kama[2] ('kɑːmə) *n* the Hindu god of love [from Sansk.]
Kamakura (ˌkæmə'kʊərə) *n* a city in central Japan, on S Honshu: famous for its Great Buddha (Daibutsu), a 13th-century bronze, 15 m (49 ft) high. Pop: 170 319 (1995 est)
Kamasutra (ˌkɑːmə'suːtrə) *n* **the** an ancient Hindu text on erotic pleasure [Sansk.: book on love, from *kāma* love + *sūtra* thread]
Kamchatka (*Russian* kam'tʃatkə) *n* a peninsula in E Russia, between the Sea of Okhotsk and the Bering Sea. Length: about 1200 km (750 miles) > **Kam'chatkan** *adj, n*
kame (keɪm) *n* an irregular mound or ridge of gravel, sand, etc, deposited by water derived from melting glaciers [c19 Scot & N English var. of COMB]
kameez (kə'miːz) *n, pl* **kameez** *or* **kameezes** a long tunic worn in the Indian subcontinent, often with a shalwar [Urdu *kamis*, from Ar. *gamīs*]
Kamensk-Uralski (*Russian* 'kamɪnsku'raljskij) *n* an industrial city in S Russia. Pop: 192 000 (1999 est)
Kamerlingh-Onnes (*Dutch* 'kamərlɪŋ 'onəs) *n* **Heike** ('haɪkə) 1853–1926, Dutch physicist: a pioneer of the physics of low-temperature materials and discoverer (1911) of superconductivity. Nobel prize for physics 1913
Kamerun ('kaməruːn) *n* the German name for **Cameroon**
Kamet ('kɑːmɛt, 'kʌmeɪt) *n* a mountain in N India, in Uttar Pradesh in the Himalayas. Height: 7756 m (25 447 ft)
kamik ('kɑːmɪk) *n Canad* a traditional Inuit boot made of caribou hide or sealskin [from Inuktitut]
kamikaze (ˌkæmɪ'kɑːzɪ) *n* **1** (*often cap*) (in World War II) one of a group of Japanese pilots who performed suicidal missions **2** (*modifier*) (of an action) undertaken or (of a person) undertaking an action in the knowledge that it will result in the death of the person performing it in order to inflict maximum damage on an enemy: *a kamikaze attack* **3** (*modifier*) extremely foolhardy and possibly self-defeating: *the Alliance had engaged in kamikaze politics by supporting him* [c20 from Japanese, from *kami* divine + *kaze* wind]
kamilaroi ('kæmələˌrɔɪ) *n* an Australian Aboriginal language formerly used in NW New South Wales
Kamloops trout ('kæmluːps) *n* a variety of rainbow trout common in British Columbia
Kampala (kæm'pɑːlə) *n* the capital and largest city of Uganda, in Central region on Lake Victoria: Makerere University (1961). Pop: 1 154 000 (1999 est)
▷ www.visituganda.com/uganda/cities_n_towns/index.htm
▷ www.destinationplanner.com/africa/uganda/kampala.html
kampong ('kæmpɒŋ) *n* (in Malaysia) a village [c19 from Malay]
Kampuchea (ˌkæmpʊ'tʃɪə) *n* the name of **Cambodia** from 1976 until 1989 > ˌ**Kampu'chean** *adj, n*
Kan. *abbrev for* Kansas
Kanak (kə'næk) *n* a native or inhabitant of New Caledonia who seeks independence from France [c20 from Hawaiian: man]
Kanaka (kə'nækə) *n* **1** a native Hawaiian **2** (*often not cap*) *Austral* any native of the South Pacific islands, esp (formerly) one abducted to work in Australia [c19 from Hawaiian: man]
Kananga (kə'næŋgə) *n* a city in the SW Democratic Republic of Congo (formerly Zaïre): a commercial centre on the railway from Lubumbashi to Port Francqui. Pop: 393 030 (1994 est). Former name (until 1966): **Luluabourg**
Kanara *or* **Canara** (kə'nɑːrə) *n* a region of SW India, in Karnataka on the Deccan Plateau and the W Coast. Area: about 155 000 sq km (60 000 sq miles)
Kanarese *or* **Canarese** (ˌkænə'riːz) *n* **1** (*pl* **Kanarese** *or* **Canarese**) a member of a people of S India living chiefly in Kanara **2** the language of this people
Kanazawa (ˌkænə'zɑːwə) *n* a port in central Japan, on W Honshu: textile and porcelain industries. Pop: 453 977 (1995)
kanban *Japanese* ('kænbæn) *n* **1** a just-in-time manufacturing process in which the movements of

Kk

materials through a process are recorded on specially designed cards **2** any of the cards used for ordering materials in such a system [lit.: advertisement hoarding]

Kanchenjunga (ˌkæntʃən'dʒʌŋgə) *n* a variant spelling of **Kangchenjunga**

Kanchipuram (kɑːn'tʃiːpərəm) *n* a city in SE India, in Tamil Nadu: a sacred Hindu town known as "the Benares of the South"; textile industries. Pop: 144 955 (1991)

Kandahar (ˌkændə'hɑː) *n* a city in S Afghanistan: an important trading centre, built by Ahmad Shah Durrani (1724–73) as his capital on the site of several former cities. Pop: 237 500 (1990 est)

Kandinsky (*Russian* kan'dinskij) *n* **Vasili** (va'silij) 1866–1944, Russian expressionist painter and theorist, regarded as the first to develop an entirely abstract style: a founder of *der Blaue Reiter*

Kandy ('kændɪ) *n* a city in central Sri Lanka: capital of the kingdom of Kandy from 1480 until 1815, when occupied by the British; sacred Buddhist temple; University of Sri Lanka. Pop: 150 532 (1997 est)

kanga *or* **khanga** ('kæŋgə) *n* a piece of gaily decorated thin cotton cloth used as a woman's garment, originally in E Africa [from Swahili]

kangaroo (ˌkæŋgə'ruː) *n, pl* **kangaroos 1** a large herbivorous marsupial of Australia and New Guinea, having large powerful hind legs used for leaping, and a long thick tail **2** (*usually pl*) *stock exchange* an Australian share, esp in mining, land, or a tobacco company [C18 prob. from Abor.] > ˌ**kanga'roo-**ˌ**like** *adj*

kangaroo closure *n parliamentary procedure* a form of closure in which the chairman or speaker selects certain amendments for discussion and excludes others

kangaroo court *n* an irregular court, esp one set up by strikers to judge strikebreakers

Kangaroo Island *n* an island in the Indian Ocean, off South Australia. Area: 4350 sq km (1680 sq miles)

kangaroo paw *n* any of various Australian plants having green-and-red hairy flowers

kangaroo rat *n* **1** a small leaping rodent related to the squirrels and inhabiting desert regions of North America, having a stocky body and very long hind legs and tail **2** Also called: **kangaroo mouse** any of several leaping Australian rodents

Kangchenjunga, Kanchenjunga (ˌkæntʃən'dʒʌŋgə), *or* **Kinchinjunga** *n* a mountain on the border between Nepal and Sikkim, in the Himalayas: the third highest mountain in the world. Height: 8598 m (28 208 ft)

kanji ('kændʒɪ) *n, pl* **kanji** *or* **kanjis 1** a Japanese writing system using characters mainly derived from Chinese ideograms **2** a character in this system [Japanese, from Chinese *han* Chinese + *zi* character]

Kano ('kɑːnəʊ, 'keɪnəʊ) *n* **1** a state of N Nigeria: consists of wooded savanna in the south and scrub vegetation in the north. Capital: Kano. Pop: 6 297 165 (1995 est). Area: 20 131 sq km (7773 sq miles) **2** a city in N Nigeria, capital of Kano state: transport and market centre. Pop: 674 100 (1996 est)

Kanpur (kɑːn'pʊə) *n* an industrial city in NE India, in S Uttar Pradesh on the River Ganges: scene of the massacre by Nana Sahib of British soldiers and European families and his later defeat by British forces in 1857. Pop: 1 874 409 (1991). Former name: **Cawnpore**

Kansas ('kænzəs) *n* a state of the central US: consists of undulating prairie, drained chiefly by the Arkansas, Kansas, and Missouri Rivers; mainly agricultural. Capital: Topeka. Pop: 2 688 418 (2000). Area: 213 096 sq km (82 277 sq miles). Abbreviations: **Kan, Kans** or (with zip code) **KS**

Kansas City *n* **1** a city in W Missouri, at the confluence of the Missouri and Kansas Rivers: important centre of livestock and meat-packing industry. Pop: 441 545 (2000) **2** a city in NE Kansas, adjacent to Kansas City, Missouri. Pop: 146 866 (2000)

Kansu ('kæn'suː) *n* a variant transliteration of the Chinese name for **Gansu**

Kant (kænt; *German* kant) *n* **Immanuel** (ɪ'maːnueːl) 1724–1804, German idealist philosopher. He sought to determine the limits of man's knowledge in *Critique of Pure Reason* (1781) and propounded his system of ethics as guided by the categorical imperative in *Critique of Practical Reason* (1788)

KANU ('kɑːnuː) *n acronym for* Kenya African National Union

Kaohsiung, Kao-hsiung ('kaʊ'ʃjʊŋ), *or* **Gaoxiong** *n* a port in SW Taiwan, on the South China Sea: the chief port of the island. Pop: 1 475 505 (2000 est). Japanese name: **Takao**

Kaolack ('kɑːəʊˌlæk, 'kaʊlæk) *n* a port in SW Senegal, on the Saloum River. Pop: 200 000 (1998 est)

kaolin ('keɪəlɪn) *n* a fine white clay used for the manufacture of hard-paste porcelain and bone china and in medicine as a poultice. Also called: **china clay** [C18 from F, from Chinese *Kaoling* Chinese mountain where supplies for Europe were first obtained] > ˌ**kao'linic** *adj* > '**kaolin**ˌ**ize** *or* '**kaolin**ˌ**ise** *vb*

kaon ('keɪɒn) *n* a meson that has a rest mass of about 996 or 964 electron masses. Also called: **K-meson** [C20 *ka* representing the letter *k* + (MES)ON]

kapa haka ('kɑːpə 'hɑːkə) *n NZ* the traditional Maori performing arts, often performed competitively [Maori, literally: traditional dance performed by groups in a line]

ka pai (ˌkə 'paɪ) *sentence substitute NZ* good! well done! [Maori]

kapellmeister (kæ'pɛlˌmaɪstə) *n* a variant spelling of **capellmeister**

Kapfenberg (*German* 'kapfənbɛrk) *n* an industrial town in E Austria, in Styria. Pop: 23 490 (1991)

Kapil Dev ('kæpɪl 'dɛv) *n* (**Ramlal**) **Nikhanj** (nɪ'kændʒ) born 1959, Indian cricketer: captain of India (1983–84)

Kapitza (kə'pitsa) *n* **Piotr Leonidovich** ('pjɔtᵊr liɔ'nidovitʃ) 1894–1984, Russian physicist. He worked in England and the USSR, doing research in several areas, particularly cryogenics; Nobel prize for physics in 1978

kapok ('keɪpɒk) *n* a silky fibre obtained from the hairs covering the seeds of a tropical tree (**kapok tree**): used for stuffing pillows, etc [C18 from Malay]

Kaposi's sarcoma (kæ'pəʊsɪz) *n* a form of skin cancer found in Africans and more recently in victims of AIDS [C20 after Moritz Kohn *Kaposi* (1837–1902), Austrian dermatologist who first described the sores that characterize the disease]

kappa ('kæpə) *n* the tenth letter in the Greek alphabet (Κ, κ) [Gk, of Semitic origin]

kaput (kæ'pʊt) *adj* (*postpositive*) *inf* ruined, broken, or not functioning [C20 from G *kaputt* done for]

karabiner (ˌkærə'biːnə) *n mountaineering* a metal clip with a spring for attaching to a piton, belay, etc. Also called: **snaplink, krab** [shortened from G *Karabinerhaken*, lit.: carbine hook]

Karachai-Cherkess Republic (kərʌ'tʃaɪtʃɛə'kɛs) *or* **Karachayevo-Cherkess Republic** (kərʌ'tʃaɪɛvəʊtʃɛə'kɛs) *n* a constituent republic of W Russia, on the N side of the Caucasus Mountains. Capital: Cherkessk. Pop: 435 000 (2000 est). Area: 14 100 sq km (5440 sq miles). Also called: **Karachai-Cherkessia** (kærəˌtʃaɪtʃɛə'kɛsɪə)

Karachi (kə'rɑːtʃɪ) *n* a port in S Pakistan, on the Arabian Sea: capital of Pakistan (1947–60); university (1950); chief port: commercial and industrial centre. Pop: 9 269 265 (1998)

Karadžić ('kærədzjɪtʃ) *n* **Radovan** ('rædəvæn) born 1945, Bosnian Serb political leader and psychiatrist; charged with genocide by the International War Crimes

Tribunal for his role in the Bosnian civil war of 1992–95; in hiding

Karafuto (ˌkɑːrɑːˈfuːtɔ) *n* transliteration of the Japanese name for **Sakhalin**

Karaganda (*Russian* kərəganˈda) *n* a city in E central Kazakhstan, founded in 1857: a major coal-mining and industrial centre. Pop: 436 900 (1999). Also called: **Qaraghandy**

Karajan (*German* ˈkaːrajan) *n* **Herbert von** (ˈhɛrbɛrt fɔn) 1908–89, Austrian conductor

Kara-Kalpak Autonomous Republic (kəˈrɑːkəlˈpɑːk) *n* an administrative division in NW Uzbekistan, on the Aral Sea: came under Russian rule by stages from 1873 until Uzbekistan became independent in 1991. Capital: Nukus. Pop: 1 343 000 (1993 est). Area: 165 600 sq km (63 900 sq miles). Also called: **Kara-Kalpakia** (kəˈrɑːkəlˈpɑːkɪə), **Kara-Kalpakstan** (kəˈrɑːkəlˌpɑːkˌstæn, -ˈstɑːn)

karakia (ˌkɑːrəˈkiːə) *n* NZ a prayer [Maori]

Karakoram *or* **Karakorum** (ˌkærəˈkɔːrəm) *n* a mountain system in N Kashmir, extending for about 480 km (300 miles) from northwest to southeast: contains the second highest peak in the world (K2); crossed by several high passes, notably the **Karakoram Pass** 5575 m (18 290 ft)

Karakorum (ˌkærəˈkɔːrəm) *n* a ruined city in Mongolia: founded in 1220 by Ghenghis Khan; destroyed by Kublai Khan when his brother rebelled against him, after Kublai Khan had moved his capital to Peking (now Beijing)

karakul *or* **caracul** (ˈkærəkᵊl) *n* **1** a breed of sheep of central Asia having coarse black, grey, or brown hair: the lambs have soft curled hair **2** the fur prepared from these lambs ▹ See also **Persian lamb** [c19 from Russian, from the name of a region in Bukhara where the sheep originated]

Kara Kum (*Russian* kəra ˈkum) *n* a desert in Turkmenistan, covering most of the country: extensive areas now irrigated. Area: about 300 000 sq km (120 000 sq miles)

Karamanlis (*Greek* karamanˈlis) *n* **Konstantinos** (kɔnstanˈtinɔs) 1907–98, Greek statesman; prime minister of Greece (1955–58; 1958–61; 1961–63; 1974–80): president of Greece (1980–85; 1990–95)

Karan (ˈkærən) *n* **Donna** born 1948, US fashion designer

karanga (kəˈræŋə) *n* NZ a call or chant of welcome, sung by a female elder [Maori]

karaoke (ˌkɑːrəˈəʊkɪ) *n* **a** an entertainment of Japanese origin in which people take it in turns to sing well-known songs over a prerecorded backing tape **b** (*as modifier*): *a karaoke bar* [from Japanese, from *kara* empty + *ōkesutora* orchestra]

Kara Sea (ˈkɑːrə) *n* a shallow arm of the Arctic Ocean off the N coast of Russia: ice-free for about three months of the year

karat (ˈkærət) *n* the usual US and Canad spelling of **carat** (sense 2)

karate (kəˈrɑːtɪ) *n* **a** a traditional Japanese system of unarmed combat, employing smashes, chops, kicks, etc, made with the hands, feet, elbows, or legs **b** (*as modifier*): *karate chop* [Japanese, lit.: empty hand]
▹ www.wkf.net
▹ www.itkf.org

karateka (kəˈrɑːtɪˌkɑː) *n* a competitor or expert in karate [Japanese; see KARATE]

Karbala (ˈkɑːbələ) *or* **Kerbela** *n* a town in central Iraq: the chief holy city of Iraq and centre of Shiah Muslim pilgrimage; burial place of Mohammed's grandson Husain. Pop: 296 705 (latest est)

Karelia (kəˈriːlɪə; *Russian* kaˈreljə) *n* **1** a region of NE Europe, formerly in Finland but annexed in several stages by the former Soviet Union: corresponds roughly to the Karelian Republic in Russia **2** another name for the **Karelian Republic** > **Kaˈrelian** *adj, n*

Karelian Isthmus *n* a strip of land, now in Russia, between the Gulf of Finland and Lake Ladoga: annexed by the former Soviet Union after the Russo-Finnish War (1939–40)

Karelian Republic *n* a constituent republic of NW Russia between the White Sea and Lakes Onega and Ladoga. Capital: Petrozavodsk. Pop: 766 000 (2000 est). Area: 172 400 sq km (66 560 sq miles). Also called: **Karelia**

Kariba (kəˈriːbə) *n* **Lake** a lake on the Zambia-Zimbabwe border, created by the building of the **Kariba Dam** across the Zambezi for hydroelectric power. Length: 282 km (175 miles)

Karitane (ˌkærɪˈtɑːnɛ) *n* NZ a nurse for babies; nanny [from former child-care hospital at *Karitane*, New Zealand]

Karl-Marx-Stadt (*German* karlˈmarksʃtat) *n* the former name (1953–90) of **Chemnitz**

Karloff (ˈkɑːlɒf) *n* **Boris**, real name *William Pratt* 1887–1969, English film actor, famous for his roles in horror films, esp *Frankenstein* (1931)

Karlovy Vary (*Czech* ˈkarlɔvi ˈvari) *n* a city in the W Czech Republic, at the confluence of the Tepla and Ohře Rivers: warm mineral springs. Pop: 56 290 (1991). German name: **Karlsbad** *or* **Carlsbad** (ˈkarlsbaːt)

Karlskrona (ˈkɑːlsˌkrəʊnə) *n* a port in S Sweden: Sweden's main naval base since 1680. Pop: 60 642 (1994)

Karlsruhe (*German* ˈkarlsruːə) *n* a city in SW Germany, in Baden-Württemberg: capital of the former Baden state. Pop: 276 700 (1999 est)

karma (ˈkɑːmə) *n* **1** *Hinduism, Buddhism* the principle of retributive justice determining a person's state of life and the state of his reincarnations as the effect of his past deeds **2** destiny or fate **3** *inf* an aura or quality that a person, place, or thing is felt to have [c19 from Sansk.: action, effect, from *karoti* he does] > ˈ**karmic** *adj*

Karnak (ˈkɑːnæk) *n* a village in E Egypt, on the Nile: site of the N part of the ruins of ancient Thebes

Karnataka (kəˈnɑːtəkə) *n* a state of S India, on the Arabian Sea: consists of a narrow coastal plain rising to the South Deccan plateau; mainly agricultural. Capital: Bangalore. Pop: 52 733 958 (2001). Area: 191 791 sq km (74 051 sq miles). Former name (1956–73): **Mysore**

Kärnten (ˈkɛrntən) *n* the German name for **Carinthia**

Karoo *or* **Karroo** (kəˈruː) *n pl* **-roos** (*often not capital*) **1** any of several high arid plateaus in South Africa, esp the **Central Karoo** and the **Little Karoo** The highveld, north of the Central Karoo, is sometimes called the **Northern Karoo** **2** a period or rock system in Southern Africa equivalent to the period or system extending from the Upper Carboniferous to the Lower Jurassic: divided into **Lower** and **Upper Karoo** ▹ *adj* **3** of, denoting, or formed in the Karoo period [c18 from Afrikaans *karo*, probably from Khoikhoi *garo* desert]

kaross (kəˈrɒs) *n* a garment of skins worn by indigenous peoples in southern Africa [c18 from Afrik. *karos*, ?from Du., from F *cuirasse* CUIRASS]

Karpov (*Russian* ˈkarpəf) *n* **Anatoly** (anaˈtɔlij) born 1951, Russian chess player: world champion (1975–85); FIDE world champion (1993–1999)

karri (ˈkɑːrɪ) *n, pl* **karris** **1** an Australian eucalyptus tree **2** the durable dark red wood of this tree, used for construction, etc [from Abor.]

karst (kɑːst) *n* (*modifier*) denoting the characteristic scenery of a limestone region, including underground streams, gorges, etc [c19 G, from *Karst*, limestone plateau near Trieste]

kart (kɑːt) *n* a light low-framed vehicle with small wheels and engine used for recreational racing (**karting**) Also called: **go-cart, go-kart**

karyo- *or* **caryo-** *combining form* indicating the nucleus of a cell [from NL, from Gk *karuon* kernel]

karyotype (ˈkærɪəˌtaɪp) *n* **1** the appearance of the

Kk

chromosomes in a somatic cell of an individual or species, with reference to their number, size, shape, etc ▷ *vb* **karyotypes, karyotyping, karyotyped** (*tr*) **2** to determine the karyotype of (a cell) > **karyotypic** (ˌkærɪəˈtɪpɪk) *or* ˌ**karyo'typical** *adj*

Karzai (ˈkɑːzaɪ) *n* **Hamid** born 1957, Afghan military and political leader: president from 2002

Kasai (kɑːˈsaɪ) *n* a river in southwestern Africa, rising in central Angola and flowing east then north as part of the border between Angola and the Democratic Republic of Congo (formerly Zaïre), continuing northwest through the Democratic Republic of Congo to the River Congo. Length: 2154 km (1338 miles)

kasbah *or* **casbah** (ˈkæzbɑː) *n* (*sometimes cap*) **1** the citadel of any of various North African cities **2** the quarter in which a kasbah is located [from Ar. *kûsbû* citadel]

kasha (ˈkɑːʃə) *n* a dish originating in Eastern Europe, consisting of boiled or baked buckwheat [from Russian]

Kashi (ˈkɑːˈʃiː) *or* **Kashgar** (ˈkɑːʃˈgɑː) *n* an oasis city in W China, in W Xinjiang Uygur AR. Pop: 205 056 (1999 est)

Kashmir (kæʃˈmɪə) *n* a region of SW central Asia: from the 16th century ruled by the Moguls, Afghanis, Sikhs, and British successively; since 1947 disputed between India, Pakistan, and China; 84 000 sq km (33 000 sq miles) in the northwest are held by Pakistan and known as Azad Kashmir (Free Kashmir); 42 735 sq km (16 496 sq miles) in the east are held by China; the remainder was in 1956 officially incorporated into India as the state of Jammu and Kashmir; traversed by the Himalaya and Karakoram mountain ranges and the Rivers Jhelum and Indus; a fruit-growing and cattle-grazing region, with a woollen industry. Capitals: (Azad Kashmir) Muzaffarabad; (Jammu and Kashmir) Srinagar (summer), Jammu (winter) > **Kash'miri** *adj, n* > **Kash'mirian** *adj, n*

kashruth *or* ***kashrut*** *Hebrew* (kaʃˈruːt) *n* **1** the condition of being fit for ritual use in general **2** the system of dietary laws that requires ritual slaughter, the complete separation of milk and meat, and the prohibition of such foods as pig meat and shell fish ▷ See also **kosher** (sense 1) [lit.: appropriateness]

Kasparov (ˈkæspərɒf) *n* **Garry** (ˈgærɪ), real name *Garik Weinstein.* born 1963, Armenian-Jewish chess player, born in Azerbaijan: world champion (1985–93); PCA world champion (1993–2000)

Kassa (ˈkɔʃʃɔ) *n* the Hungarian name for **Košice**

Kassala (kəˈsɑːlə) *n* a city in the E Sudan: founded as a fort by the Egyptians in 1834. Pop: 234 270 (1993)

Kassel (*German* ˈkasəl) *n* a city in central Germany, in Hesse; capital of Westphalia (1807–13) and of the Prussian province of Hesse-Nassau (1866–1945). Pop: 196 700 (1999 est)

kata (ˈkætə) *n* an exercise consisting of a sequence of the specific movements of a martial art, used in training and designed to show skill in technique [c20 Japanese, lit.: shape, pattern]

kata- *prefix* a variant spelling of **cata-**

katabatic (ˌkætəˈbætɪk) *adj* (of winds) blowing downhill through having become denser with cooling

Katanga (kəˈtæŋgə) *n* the former name (until 1972) of **Shaba**

Katar (kæˈtɑː) *n* a variant spelling of **Qatar**

Kathiawar (ˌkætɪəˈwɑː) *n* a large peninsula of W India, in Gujarat between the Gulf of Kutch and the Gulf of Cambay. Area: about 60 690 sq km (23 430 sq miles)

katipo (ˈkætɪˌpəʊ, ˈkɑːdɪ-) *n, pl* **katipos** a small venomous spider of New Zealand, commonly black with a red or orange stripe on the abdomen [Maori]

Katmai (ˈkætmaɪ) *n* **Mount** a volcano in SW Alaska, in the Aleutian Range: erupted in 1912 forming the Valley of Ten Thousand Smokes, a region with numerous fumaroles; established as **Katmai National Monument**, 10 917 sq km (4215 sq miles), in 1918. Height: 2100 m (7000 ft). Depth of crater: 1130 m (3700 ft). Width of crater: about 4 km (2.5 miles)

Katmandu *or* **Kathmandu** (ˌkætmænˈduː) *n* the capital of Nepal, in the east at the confluence of the Baghmati and Vishnumati Rivers. Pop: 701 499 (2000 est) ▷ www.welcomenepal.com/destinationKTM.asp?ID=1

Katowice (*Polish* katɔˈvitsɛ) *n* an industrial city in S Poland. Pop: 345 934 (1999 est). Former name (1953–56): **Stalinogrod**

Katrine (ˈkætrɪn) *n* **Loch** a lake in central Scotland, east of Loch Lomond: noted for its associations with Sir Walter Scott's *Lady of the Lake.* Length: about 13 km (8 miles)

Katsina (kætˈsiːnə) *n* a city in N Nigeria, in Kaduna state: a major intellectual and cultural centre of the Hausa people (16th–18th centuries). Pop: 206 500 (1996 est)

Kattegat *or* **Cattegat** (ˈkætɪˌgæt) *n* a strait between Denmark and Sweden: linked by the Sound, the Great Belt, and the Little Belt with the Baltic Sea and by the Skagerrak with the North Sea

katydid (ˈkeɪtɪˌdɪd) *n* a green long-horned grasshopper living on the foliage of trees in North America [c18 imit.]

Katz (ˈkæts) *n* Sir **Bernard** born 1911, British neurophysiologist, born in Germany. Shared the Nobel prize for physiology or medicine (1970) with Julius Axelrod and Ulf von Euler

Kauai (kɑːˈwɑːiː) *n* a volcanic island in NW Hawaii, northwest of Oahu. Chief town: Lihue. Pop: 50 947 (1990). Area: 1433 sq km (553 sq miles)

Kauffmann (ˈkaʊfmən) *n* **Angelica** (andʒeˈlikə) 1741–1807, Swiss painter, who worked chiefly in England

Kaufman (ˈkaʊfmən) *n* **George S**(**imon**) 1889–1961, US dramatist who, with Moss Hart, collaborated on many Broadway comedy hits

kaumatua (kaʊˈmɑːtuːə) *n NZ* a senior member of a tribe; elder [Maori]

Kaunas (ˈkaʊnəs) *n* a city in central Lithuania at the confluence of the Neman and Viliya Rivers: ceded by Poland to Russia in 1795; became the provisional capital of Lithuania (1920–40); incorporated into the Soviet Union 1944–91; university (1922). Pop: 412 614 (2000 est). Russian name: **Kovno**

Kaunda (kɑːˈʊndə) *n* **Kenneth** (**David**) born 1924, Zambian statesman. He became Zambia's first president (1964–91)

kaupapa (kaʊˈpɑːpə) *n NZ* a strategy, policy, or cause [Maori]

kauri (ˈkaʊrɪ) *n, pl* **kauris 1** a New Zealand coniferous tree with oval leaves and round cones **2** the wood or resin of this tree [c19 from Maori]

kauri gum *n* the fossil resin of the kauri tree

kava (ˈkɑːvə) *n* **1** a Polynesian shrub **2** a drink prepared from the aromatic roots of this shrub [c18 from Polynesian: bitter]

Kavála (kəˈvælə; *Greek* kaˈvala) *n* a port in E Greece, in Macedonia East and Thrace region on the **Bay of Kavála** an important Macedonian fortress of the Byzantine empire; ceded to Greece by Turkey after the Balkan War (1912–13). Pop: 58 576 (1991). Ancient name: **Neapolis**

Kavir Desert (kæˈvɪə) *n* another name for the **Dasht-i-Kavir**

Kawabata (ˌkæwəˈbɑːtə) *n* **Yasunari** (ˌjæsʊˈnɑːrɪ) 1899–1972, Japanese novelist, author of *Yukiguni* (*Snow Country*, 1948) and *Yama no oto* (*The Sound of the Mountain*, 1954): Nobel prize for literature 1968

Kawasaki (ˌkɑːwəˈsɑːkɪ) *n* an industrial port in central Japan, on SE Honshu, between Tokyo and Yokohama. Pop: 1 202 811 (1995)

Kawasaki's disease *n* a disease of children that causes a rash, fever, and swelling of the lymph nodes and often damages the heart muscle [c20 after T. *Kawasaki*, Japanese physician who first described it]

Kay (keɪ) *n* **Sir** (in Arthurian legend) the braggart foster brother and steward of King Arthur

kayak *or* **kaiak** (ˈkaɪæk) *n* **1** a canoe-like boat used by Inuit people, consisting of a frame covered with animal skins **2** a fibreglass or canvas-covered canoe of similar design [c18 from Inuktitut]

kayo *or* **KO** (ˈkeɪˈəʊ) *n, pl* **kayos**, *vb* **kayos, kayoing, kayoed** *boxing, sl* another term for **knockout** or **knock out** [c20 from the initial letters of *knock out*]

Kayseri (ˌkaɪsɛˈriː; *Turkish* ˈkɑisɛri) *n* a city in central Turkey: trading centre since ancient times as the chief city of Cappadocia. Pop: 498 233 (1997). Ancient name: **Caesarea Mazaca**

Kazakh *or* **Kazak** (kəˈzɑːk, kɑː-) *n* **1** (*pl* **Kazakhs** *or* **Kazaks**) a member of a Mongoloid people of Kazakhstan **2** the official language of Kazakhstan

Kazakhstan *or* **Kazakstan** (ˌkɑːzɑːkˈstæn, -ˈstɑːn) *n* a republic in central Asia: conquered by Mongols in the 13th century; came under Russian control in the 18th and 19th centuries; was a Soviet republic from 1936 until it gained independence in 1991. It has rich mineral deposits and agriculture is important. Official language: Kazakh. Religion: nonreligious, Muslim, and Christian. Official currency: tenge. Capital: Akmola. Pop: 14 868 000 (2001 est). Area: 2 715 100 sq km (1 048 030 sq miles)
▷ www.president.kz
▷ www.kazconsul.ca

Kazan[1] (kəˈzæn, -ˈzɑːn; *Russian* kaˈzanj) *n* a city in W Russia, capital of the Tatar Autonomous Republic on the River Volga: capital of an independent khanate in the 15th century; university (1804); a major industrial centre. Pop: 1 100 800 (1999 est)

Kazan[2] (kəˈzɑːn) *n* **Elia** (ˈiːljə), real name *Elia Kazanjoglous*. 1909–2003, US stage and film director and writer, born in Turkey. His films include *Gentleman's Agreement* (1947) and *On the Waterfront* (1954) for both of which he won Oscars, and *East of Eden* (1955)

Kazan Retto (kɑːˈzɑːn ˈrɛtəʊ) *n* transliteration of the Japanese name for the **Volcano Islands**

Kazantzakis (*Greek* kazanˈdzakis) *n* **Nikos** (ˈnikɔs) 1885–1957, Greek novelist, poet, and dramatist, noted esp for his novels *Zorba the Greek* (1946) and *Christ Recrucified* (1954) and his epic poem *The Odyssey* (1938)

Kazbek (kɑːzˈbɛk) *n* **Mount** an extinct volcano in N Georgia in the central Caucasus Mountains. Height: 5047 m (16 558 ft)

Kaz Daği (ˈkɑz ˈdɑj) *n* the Turkish name for (Mount) **Ida** (sense 2)

kazoo (kəˈzuː) *n, pl* **kazoos** a cigar-shaped musical instrument of metal or plastic with a membranous diaphragm of thin paper that vibrates with a nasal sound when the player hums into it [c20 prob. imit. of sound produced]

KB (in Britain) *abbrev for:* **1** King's Bench **2** *computing* kilobyte

KBE *abbrev for* Knight (Commander of the Order) of the British Empire

kbyte *computing abbrev for* kilobyte

kc *abbrev for* kilocycle

KC (in Britain) *abbrev for:* **1** King's Counsel **2** Kennel Club

kcal *abbrev for* kilocalorie

KCB *abbrev for* Knight Commander of the Bath (a Brit title)

KCMG *abbrev for* Knight Commander (of the Order) of St Michael and St George (a Brit title)

KE *abbrev for* kinetic energy

kea (ˈkeɪə) *n* a large New Zealand parrot with a brownish-green plumage [c19 from Maori, imit. of its call]

Kéa (ˈkɛa) *n* transliteration of the Modern Greek name for **Keos**

Kean (kiːn) *n* **Edmund** ?1789–1833, English actor, noted for his Shakespearean roles

Keating (ˈkiːtɪŋ) *n* **Paul** born 1944, Australian Labor politician; prime minister of Australia (1991–96)

Keaton (ˈkiːtᵊn) *n* **Buster**, real name *Joseph Francis Keaton* 1895–1966, US film comedian who starred in silent films such as *The Navigator* (1924), *The General* (1926), and *Steamboat Bill Junior* (1927)

Keats (kiːts) *n* **John** 1795–1821, English poet. His finest poetry is contained in *Lamia and other Poems* (1820), which includes *The Eve of St Agnes*, *Hyperion*, and the odes *On a Grecian Urn*, *To a Nightingale*, *To Autumn*, and *To Psyche*

kebab (kəˈbæb) *n* a dish consisting of small pieces of meat, tomatoes, onions, etc, grilled on skewers. Also called: **shish kebab** [c17 from Ar. *kabāb* roast meat]

Keble (ˈkiːbᵊl) *n* **John** 1792–1866, English clergyman. His sermon on national apostasy (1833) is considered to have inspired the Oxford Movement

kecks *or* **keks** (kɛks) *pl n N English dialect* trousers [c19 from obs. *kicks* breeches]

Kecskemét (*Hungarian* ˈkɛtʃkɛmeːt) *n* a city in central Hungary: vineyards and fruit farms. Pop: 105 606 (2000 est)

Kedah (ˈkɛdə) *n* a state of NW Malaysia: under Thai control until it came under the British in 1909; the chief exports are rice, tin, and rubber. Capital: Alor Star. Pop: 1 572 107 (2000 est). Area: 9425 sq km (3639 sq miles)

kedge (kɛdʒ) *naut* ▷ *vb* **kedges, kedging, kedged 1** to draw (a vessel) along by hauling in on the cable of a light anchor, or (of a vessel) to be drawn in this fashion ▷ *n* **2** a light anchor, used esp for kedging [c15 from *caggen* to fasten]

kedgeree (ˌkɛdʒəˈriː) *n chiefly Brit* a dish consisting of rice, cooked flaked fish, and hard-boiled eggs [c17 from Hindi, from Sansk. *khiccā*]

Kk

Kediri (kɪˈdɪərɪ) *n* a city in Indonesia, in E Java: commercial centre. Pop: 261 300 (1995 est)

Kedron (ˈkɛdrɒn) *or* **Kidron** *n Bible* a ravine under the eastern wall of Jerusalem

keek (kiːk) *n, vb* a Scot. word for **peep**[1] [c18 prob. from MDu. *kīken* to look]

keel[1] (kiːl) *n* **1** one of the main longitudinal structural members of a vessel to which the frames are fastened **2 on an even keel** well-balanced; steady **3** any structure corresponding to or resembling the keel of a ship **4** *biol* a ridgelike part; carina ▷ *vb* **5** to capsize ▷ See also **keel over** [c14 from ON *kjölr*]

keel[2] (kiːl) *n eastern English dialect* **1** a flat-bottomed vessel, esp one used for carrying coal **2** a measure of coal [c14 *kele*, from MDu. *kiel*]

keelage (ˈkiːlɪdʒ) *n* a fee charged by certain ports to allow a ship to dock

keelhaul (ˈkiːlˌhɔːl) *vb* (*tr*) **1** to drag (a person) by a rope from one side of a vessel to the other through the water under the keel **2** to rebuke harshly [c17 from Du. *kielhalen*; see KEEL[1], HAUL]

Keeling Islands (ˈkiːlɪŋ) *pl n* another name for the **Cocos Islands**

keel over *vb* (*adv*) **1** to turn upside down; capsize **2** (*intr*) *inf* to collapse suddenly

keelson (ˈkɛlsən, ˈkiːl-) *or* **kelson** *n* a longitudinal beam fastened to the keel of a vessel for strength and stiffness [c17 prob. from Low G *kielswin* keel swine, ult. of Scand. origin]

Keelung (ˈkiːˈlʊŋ) *n* another name for **Chilung**

keen[1] (kiːn) *adj* **1** eager or enthusiastic **2** (*postpositive*; foll by *on*) fond (of); devoted (to): *keen on golf* **3** intellectually acute: *a keen wit* **4** (of sight, smell, hearing, etc) capable of recognizing fine distinctions **5** having a sharp cutting edge or point **6** extremely cold and penetrating: *a keen wind* **7** intense or strong: *a keen desire* **8** *chiefly Brit* extremely low so as to be competitive: *keen prices* [OE *cēne*] > **'keenly** *adv* > **'keenness** *n*

keen² (ki:n) *vb* (*intr*) **1** to lament the dead ▷ *n* **2** a dirge or lament for the dead [c19 from Irish Gaelic *caoine*, from OIrish *coīnim* I wail] > **'keener** *n*

keener ('ki:nə) *n Canad inf* a person, esp a student, who is keen, enthusiastic, or zealous

keep (ki:p) *vb* **keeps, keeping, kept** **1** (*tr*) to have or retain possession of **2** (*tr*) to have temporary possession or charge of: *keep my watch for me* **3** (*tr*) to store in a customary place: *I keep my books in the desk* **4** to remain or cause to remain in a specified state or condition: *keep ready* **5** to continue or cause to continue: *keep in step* **6** (*tr*) to have or take charge or care of: *keep the shop for me till I return* **7** (*tr*) to look after or maintain for use, pleasure, etc: *to keep chickens* **8** (*tr*) to provide for the upkeep or livelihood of **9** (*tr*) to support financially, esp in return for sexual favours **10** to confine or detain or be confined or detained **11** to withhold or reserve or admit of withholding or reserving: *your news will keep* **12** (*tr*) to refrain from divulging or violating: *to keep a secret* **13** to preserve or admit of preservation **14** (*tr; sometimes foll by up*) to observe with due rites or ceremonies **15** (*tr*) to maintain by writing regular records in: *to keep a diary* **16** (when *intr*, foll by *in, on, to*, etc) to stay in, on, or at (a place or position): *keep to the path* **17** (*tr*) to associate with (esp in **keep bad company**) **18** (*tr*) to maintain in existence: *to keep court in the palace* **19** (*tr*) *chiefly Brit* to have habitually in stock: *this shop keeps all kinds of wool* **20** **how are you keeping?** how are you? ▷ *n* **21** living or support **22** *arch* charge or care **23** Also called: **dungeon, donjon** the main tower within the walls of a medieval castle or fortress **24** **for keeps** *inf* **24a** permanently **24b** for the winner or possessor to keep permanently ▷ See also **keep at, keep away**, etc [OE *cēpan* to observe]

keep at *vb* (*prep*) **1** (*intr*) to persist in **2** (*tr*) to constrain (a person) to continue doing (a task)

keep away *vb* (*adv; often foll by from*) to refrain or prevent from coming (near)

keep back *vb* (*adv; often foll by from*) **1** (*tr*) to refuse to reveal or disclose **2** to prevent or be prevented from advancing, entering, etc

keep down *vb* (*adv, mainly tr*) **1** to repress **2** to restrain or control: *he had difficulty keeping his anger down* **3** to cause not to increase or rise **4** (*intr*) to lie low **5** not to vomit

keeper ('ki:pə) *n* **1** a person in charge of animals, esp in a zoo **2** a person in charge of a museum, collection, or section of a museum **3** a person in charge of other people, such as a warder in a jail **4** See **goalkeeper, wicketkeeper, gamekeeper, park keeper** **5** a person who keeps something **6** a bar placed across the poles of a permanent magnet to close the magnetic circuit when it is not in use

keep fit *n* exercises designed to promote physical fitness if performed regularly

keep from *vb* (*prep*) **1** (foll by a gerund) to prevent or restrain (oneself or another); refrain or cause to refrain **2** (*tr*) to protect or preserve from

keeping ('ki:pɪŋ) *n* **1** conformity or harmony (esp in **in** *or* **out of keeping**) **2** charge or care: *valuables in the keeping of a bank*

keepnet ('ki:pˌnɛt) *n* a net strung on wire hoops and sealed at one end, suspended in water by anglers to keep alive the fish they have caught

keep off *vb* **1** to stay or cause to stay at a distance (from) **2** (*prep*) not to eat or drink or to prevent from eating or drinking **3** (*prep*) to avoid or cause to avoid (a topic)

keep on *vb* (*adv*) **1** to continue or persist in (doing something): *keep on running* **2** (*tr*) to continue to wear **3** (*tr*) to continue to employ: *the firm kept on only ten men* **4** (*intr; foll by about*) to persist in talking (about) **5** (*intr; foll by at*) to nag (a person)

keep out *vb* (*adv*) **1** to remain or cause to remain outside **2** **keep out of** **2a** to remain or cause to remain unexposed to **2b** to avoid or cause to avoid

keepsake ('ki:pˌseɪk) *n* a gift that evokes memories of a person or event

keep to *vb* (*prep*) **1** to adhere to or stand by or cause to adhere to or stand by **2** to confine or be confined to **3** **keep oneself to oneself** to avoid the society of others **4** **keep to oneself** **4a** (*intr*) to avoid the society of others **4b** (*tr*) to refrain from sharing or disclosing

keep up *vb* (*adv*) **1** (*tr*) to maintain (prices, one's morale) at the present level **2** (*intr; often foll by with*) to maintain a pace or rate set by another **3** (*intr; often foll by with*) to remain informed: *to keep up with developments* **4** (*tr*) to maintain in good condition **5** (*tr*) to hinder (a person) from going to bed at night **6** **keep it up** to continue a good performance **7** **keep up with** to remain in contact with, esp by letter **8** **keep up with (the Joneses)** *inf* to compete with (one's neighbours) in material possessions, etc

Keewatin (ki:'weɪtɪn) *n* a former administrative district of the Northwest Territories of Canada stretching from the district of Mackenzie to Hudson Bay; became part of Nunavut in 1999: mostly tundra

kef (kɛf) *n* a variant spelling of **kif**

keffiyeh (kɛ'fi:jə), **kaffiyeh,** *or* **kufiyah** *n* a cotton headdress worn by Arabs [c19 from Ar., ?from LL *cofea* COIF]

Keflavík ('kɛfləˌvɪk) *n* a port in SW Iceland: Nato airbase, fishing. Pop: 7627 (1994)

keg (kɛg) *n* **1** a small barrel with a capacity of between five and ten gallons **2** *Brit, Austral, & NZ* an aluminium container in which beer is transported and stored [c17 var. of ME *kag*, of Scand. origin]

Keighley ('ki:θlɪ) *n* a town in N England, in Bradford unitary authority, West Yorkshire, on the River Aire: textile industry. Pop: 49 567 (1991)

Keijo (ˌkeɪ'dʒəʊ) *n* transliteration of the Japanese name for **Seoul**

Keitel ('kaɪtᵊl) *n* **Wilhelm** ('vɪlhɛlm) 1882–1946, German field marshal; chief of the supreme command of the armed forces (1938–45). He was convicted at the Nuremberg trials and executed

Kekkonen (*Finnish* 'kɛkkɔnɛn) *n* **Urho** ('urhɔ) (1900–86), Finnish statesman; president (1956–81)

keks (kɛks) *pl n* a variant spelling of **kecks**

Kekulé von Stradonitz (*German* 'kekule fɔn 'ʃtradonɪts) *n* (**Friedrich**) **August** ('ogyst) 1829–96, German chemist. His elucidation of the concepts of valence and single, double, and triple bonds enabled him to suggest the structure of many molecules, notably benzene (**Kekulé structure**)

Kelantan (kɛ'læntən, kɪˌlæn'tæn) *n* a state of NE Malaysia: under Thai control until it came under the British in 1909; produces rice and rubber. Capital: Kota Bharu. Pop: 1 289 199 (2000 est). Area: 14 930 sq km (5765 sq miles)

Keller ('kɛlə) *n* **1** **Gottfried** 1819–90, Swiss novelist and short-story writer, who wrote in German: noted esp for the novel *Der Grüne Heinrich* (1855, rewritten 1880) **2** **Helen (Adams)** 1880–1968, US author and lecturer. Blind and deaf from infancy, she was taught to read, write, and speak and became noted for her work for the handicapped

Kells (kɛlz) *n* a town in the Republic of Ireland, in Co. Meath: *The Book of Kells*, an illuminated manuscript of the Gospels, was produced at the monastery here in the 8th century. Pop: 2187 (1991)

Kelly ('kɛlɪ) *n* **1** **Gene,** full name *Eugene Curran Kelly.* 1912–96, US dancer, choreographer, film actor, and director. His many films include *An American in Paris* (1951) and *Singin' in the Rain* (1952) **2** **Grace** 1929–82, US film actress. Her films include *High Noon* (1952) and *High Society* (1956). She married Prince Rainier III of Monaco in

1956 and died following a car crash **3 Ned** 1855–80, Australian horse and cattle thief and bushranger, active in Victoria: captured by the police and hanged **4 (as) game as Ned Kelly**. See **game**[1] (sense 25)

Kelman ('kɛlmən) *n* **James** born 1946, Scottish novelist; his novels include the Booker prizewinner *How Late It Was, How Late* (1994)

keloid ('kiːlɔɪd) *n pathol* a hard raised growth of scar tissue at the site of an injury [c19 from Gk *khēlē* claw]

kelp (kɛlp) *n* **1** any large brown seaweed **2** the ash of such seaweed, used as a source of iodine and potash [c14 from ?]

kelpie[1] *or* **kelpy** ('kɛlpɪ) *n, pl* **kelpies** an Australian breed of sheepdog having a coat of various colours and erect ears [named after a particular specimen of the breed, c. 1870]

kelpie[2] ('kɛlpɪ) *n* (in Scottish folklore) a water spirit in the form of a horse [c18 prob. rel. to Scot. Gaelic *cailpeach* heifer, from ?]

kelson ('kɛlsən) *n* a variant spelling of **keelson**

kelt (kɛlt) *n* a salmon that has recently spawned [c14 from ?]

Kelt (kɛlt) *n* a variant spelling of **Celt**

kelter ('kɛltə) *n* a variant of **kilter**

kelvin ('kɛlvɪn) *n* the basic SI unit of thermodynamic temperature; the fraction 1/273.16 of the thermodynamic temperature of the triple point of water. Symbol: K

Kelvin ('kɛlvɪn) *n* **William Thomson,** 1st Baron Kelvin. 1824–1907, British physicist, noted for his work in thermodynamics, inventing the Kelvin scale, and in electricity, pioneering undersea telegraphy

Kelvin scale *n* a thermodynamic temperature scale in which the zero is absolute zero. Originally the degree was equal to that on the Celsius scale but it is now defined so that the triple point of water is exactly 273.16 kelvins

Kemal Atatürk (kɛ'mɑːl 'ætəˌtɜːk) *n* See **Atatürk**

kembla ('kɛmblə) *n Austral sl* small change [from rhyming slang *Kembla Grange*]

Kemerovo (*Russian* 'kjemɪrəvə) *n* a city in S Russia: a major coal-mining centre of the Kuznetsk Basin, with important chemical plants. Pop: 496 300 (1999 est). Former name (until 1932): **Shcheglovsk**

Kempe (kɛmp) *n* **1 Margery** ?1373–?1440, English mystic. Her autobiography, *The Book of Margery Kempe*, describes her mystical experiences and pilgrimages in Europe and Palestine **2** (*German* 'kɛmpə) **Rudolf** ('ruːdɔlf) 1910–76, German orchestral conductor, noted esp for his interpretations of Wagner

Kempis ('kɛmpɪs) *n* **Thomas à** ?1380–1471, German Augustinian monk, generally regarded as the author of the devotional work *The Imitation of Christ*

kempt (kɛmpt) *adj* (of hair) tidy; combed. See also **unkempt** [c20 back formation from *unkempt*; orig. p.p. of dialect *kemb* to COMB]

ken (kɛn) *n* **1** range of knowledge (esp in **beyond** *or* **in one's ken**) ▷ *vb* **kens, kenning, kenned** *or* **kent 2** *Scot & northern English dialect* to know **3** *Scot & northern English dialect* to understand [OE *cennan*]

Ken. *abbrev for* Kentucky

Kendal ('kɛndᵊl) *n* a town in NW England, in Cumbria: a gateway town to the Lake District, with an ancient woollen industry. Pop: 25 461 (1991)

Kendall ('kɛndəl) *n* **Edward Calvin** 1886–1972, US biochemist, who isolated the hormone thyroxine (1916) He shared the Nobel prize for physiology or medicine (1950) with Phillip Hench and Tadeus Reichstein for their work on hormones

kendo ('kɛndəʊ) *n* the Japanese art of fencing with pliable bamboo staves or, sometimes, real swords [Japanese, lit.: way of the sword, from *ken* sword + *do* way]

Kendrew ('kɛndruː) *n* Sir **John Cowdery** 1917–97, British biochemist. Using X-ray diffraction he discovered the structure of myoglobin, for which he shared a Nobel Prize (1962) with Max Perutz

Keneally (kə'nælɪ) *n* **Thomas** (**Michael**) born 1935, Australian writer. His novels include the Booker prizewinner *Schindler's Ark* (1982); other works are *The Playmaker* (1987), *The Great Shame* (1998), and *The Office of Innocence* (2002)

Kenilworth ('kɛnɪlˌwɜːθ) *n* a town in central England, in Warwickshire: ruined 12th-century castle, subject of Sir Walter Scott's novel *Kenilworth*. Pop: 21 623 (1991)

Kénitra (*French* kenitra) *n* another name for **Mina Hassan Tani**

Kennedy[1] ('kɛnɪdɪ) *n* **Cape** a former name (1963–73) of (Cape) **Canaveral**

Kennedy[2] ('kɛnɪdɪ) *n* **1 Charles Peter** born 1959, British politician, leader of the Liberal Democrats from 1999 **2 Edward** (**Moore**), known as *Ted.* born 1932, US Democrat politician; senator since 1962 **3** his brother, **John** (**Fitzgerald**), known as *JFK.* 1917–63, US Democrat statesman; 35th president of the US (1961–63), the first Roman Catholic and the youngest man ever to be president. He demanded the withdrawal of Soviet missiles from Cuba (1962) and prepared civil rights reforms; assassinated **4 Robert** (**Francis**), known as *Bobby*, brother of John Kennedy. 1925–68, US Democrat statesman; attorney general (1961–64) and senator for New York (1965–68); assassinated

kennel ('kɛnᵊl) *n* **1** a hutlike shelter for a dog. US name: **doghouse 2** (*usually pl*) an establishment where dogs are bred, trained, boarded, etc **3** a hovel **4** a pack of hounds ▷ *vb* **kennels, kennelling, kennelled** *or US* **kennels, kenneling, kenneled 5** to keep or stay in a kennel [c14 from OF, from Vulgar L *canīle* (unattested), from L *canis* dog]

Kennelly ('kɛnəlɪ) *n* **Arthur Edwin** 1861–1939, US electrical engineer: independently of Heaviside, he predicted the existence of an ionized layer in the upper atmosphere, known as the Kennelly-Heaviside layer or E region

Kenneth I ('kɛnɪθ) *n* surnamed *MacAlpine.* died 858, king of the Scots of Dalriada and of the Picts (?844–858): considered the first Scottish king

kennett ('kɛnɪt) *vb Austral sl* another word for **jeff**

kenning ('kɛnɪŋ) *n* a conventional metaphoric name for something, esp in Old Norse and Old English poetry [c14 from ON, from *kenna;* see KEN]

Kenny ('kɛnɪ) *n* **Brett** born 1961, Australian rugby league player

Kensington and Chelsea ('kɛnzɪŋtən) *n* a borough of Greater London, on the River Thames: **Kensington Palace** (17th century) and gardens. Pop: 158 922 (2001). Area: 12 sq km (5 sq miles)

kenspeckle ('kɛnˌspɛkᵊl) *adj Scot* easily seen or recognized [c18 from dialect *kenspeck*, of Scand. origin]

Kent[1] (kɛnt) *n* a county of SE England, on the English Channel: the first part of Great Britain to be colonized by the Romans; one of the seven kingdoms of Anglo-Saxon England until absorbed by Wessex in the 9th century AD. Apart from the Downs it is mostly low-lying and agricultural, specializing in fruit and hops. The Medway towns (Rochester and Gillingham) became an independent unitary authority in 1998. Administrative centre: Maidstone. Pop (excluding Medway): 1 329 653 (2001). Area (excluding Medway): 3526 sq km (1361 sq miles) > '**Kentish** *adj*

Kent[2] (kɛnt) *n* **William** ?1685–1748, English architect, landscape gardener, and interior designer

Kentucky (kɛn'tʌkɪ) *n* **1** a state of the S central US: consists of an undulating plain in the west, the Bluegrass region in the centre, the Tennessee and Ohio River basins in the southwest, and the Appalachians in

Kk

the east. Capital: Frankfort. Pop: 4 041 769 (2000). Area: 102 693 sq km (39 650 sq miles). Abbreviations: **Ken, Ky.** or (with zip code) **KY** **2** a river in central Kentucky, rising in the Cumberland Mountains and flowing northwest to the Ohio River. Length: 417 km (259 miles) > **Ken'tuckian** *adj, n*

Kenya ('kɛnjə, 'kiːnjə) *n* **1** a republic in E Africa, on the Indian Ocean: became a British protectorate in 1895 and a colony in 1920; gained independence in 1963 and is a member of the Commonwealth. Tea and coffee constitute about a third of the total exports. Official languages: Swahili and English. Religions: Christian majority, animist minority. Currency: shilling. Capital: Nairobi. Pop: 30 766 000 (2001 est). Area: 582 647 sq km (224 960 sq miles) **2 Mount** an extinct volcano in central Kenya: the second highest mountain in Africa; girth at 2400 m (8000 ft) is about 150 km (95 miles). The regions above 3200 m (10 500 ft) constitute **Mount Kenya National Park.** Height: 5200 m (17 058 ft) > **'Kenyan** *adj, n*
▷ http://kenya.go.ke
▷ www.magicalkenya.com

Kenyatta (kɛn'jætə) *n* **Jomo** ('dʒəʊməʊ) ?1891–1978, Kenyan statesman: imprisoned as a suspected leader of the Mau Mau revolt (1953–59); elected president of the Kenya African National Union (1961); prime minister of independent Kenya (1963) and president (1964–78)

Keos ('keɪɒs) *n* an island in the Aegean Sea, in the NW Cyclades. Pop: 1700 (latest est). Area: 174 sq km (67 sq miles). Italian name: **Zea** Modern Greek name: **Kéa**

Kephallinía (ˌkɛfali'nia; *English* ˌkɛfə'liːnɪə) *n* transliteration of the Modern Greek name for **Cephalonia**

kepi ('keɪpiː) *n, pl* **kepis** a military cap with a circular top and a horizontal peak [C19 from F *képi*, from G (Swiss dialect) *käppi* a little cap, from *kappe* CAP]

Kepler ('kɛplə) *n* **Johannes** (jo'hanəs) 1571–1630, German astronomer. As discoverer of Kepler's laws of planetary motion he is regarded as one of the founders of modern astronomy

Kepler's laws *pl n* three laws of planetary motion published by Johannes Kepler between 1609 and 1619. They deal with the shape of a planet's orbit, the constant velocity of the planet in orbit, and the relationship between the length of a planetary year and the distance from the sun

kept (kɛpt) *vb* **1** the past tense and past participle of **keep** **2 kept woman** *derog* a woman maintained by a man as his mistress

Kerala ('kɛrələ, kə'rɑːlə) *n* a state of SW India, on the Arabian Sea: formed in 1956, it includes the former state of Travancore-Cochin; has the highest population density of any Indian state. Capital: Trivandrum. Pop: 31 838 619 (2001). Area: 38 863 sq km (15 005 sq miles)

keratin ('kɛrətɪn) *n* a fibrous protein that occurs in the outer layer of the skin and in hair, nails, hooves, etc

keratose ('kɛrəˌtəʊs, -ˌtəʊz) *adj* (esp of certain sponges) having a horny skeleton [C19 from Gk *keras* horn + -OSE[1]]

kerb *or US & Canad* **curb** (kɜːb) *n* a line of stone or concrete forming an edge between a pavement and a roadway [C17 from OF *courbe* bent, from L *curvus*; see CURVE] > **'kerbing** *n*

kerb crawling *n* the act of driving slowly beside the pavement seeking to entice someone into the car for sexual purposes > **kerb crawler** *n*

kerb drill *n* a pedestrian's procedure for crossing a road safely, esp as taught to children

Kerbela ('kɜːbələ) *n* a variant of **Karbala**

kerbstone *or US & Canad* **curbstone** ('kɜːbˌstəʊn) *n* one of a series of stones that form a kerb

Kerch (*Russian* kjertʃ) *n* a port in the S Ukraine on the **Kerch Peninsula** and the **Strait of Kerch** (linking the Black Sea with the Sea of Azov): founded as a Greek colony in the 6th century BC; ceded to Russia in 1774; iron-mining, steel production, and fishing. Pop: 167 400 (1998 est)

kerchief ('kɜːtʃɪf) *n* a piece of cloth worn over the head [C13 from OF, from *covrir* to COVER + *chef* head] > **'kerchiefed** *adj*

kerel ('kɛərəl) *n S African* a young man [from Afrik. *kêrel*; cf. OE *ceorl*]

Kerenski *or* **Kerensky** (kə'rɛnskɪ; *Russian* 'kjerɪnskij) *n* **Aleksandr Fyodorovich** (alɪk'sandr 'fjɔdərəvitʃ) 1881–1970, Russian liberal revolutionary leader; prime minister (July–October 1917): overthrown by the Bolsheviks

kerf (kɜːf) *n* the cut made by a saw, an axe, etc [OE *cyrf* a cutting]

kerfuffle (kə'fʌfᵊl) *n inf, chiefly Brit* commotion; disorder [from Scot. *curfuffle, carfuffle*, from Scot. Gaelic *car* twist, turn + *fuffle* to disarrange]

Kerguelen ('kɜːgɪlɪn) *n* an archipelago in the S Indian Ocean: consists of one large volcanic island (Kerguelen or Desolation Island) and 300 small islands; part of the French Southern and Antarctic Territories

Kerkrade (*Dutch* 'kɛrkraːdə) *n* a town in the SE Netherlands, in Limburg: one of the oldest coal-mining centres in Europe. Pop: 52 848 (1994)

Kérkyra ('kɛrkira) *n* transliteration of the Modern Greek name for **Corfu**

Kerman (kə'mɑːn) *n* a city in SE Iran: carpet-making centre. Pop: 384 991 (1996)

Kermanshah (ˌkɜːmæn'ʃɑː) *n* the former name (until 1987) of **Bakhtaran**

kermes ('kɜːmɪz) *n* **1** the dried bodies of female scale insects used as a red dyestuff **2** a small evergreen Eurasian oak tree: the host plant of kermes scale insects [C16 from F, from Ar. *qirmiz*, from Sansk. *krmija-* red dye, lit.: produced by a worm]

kermis *or* **kirmess** ('kɜːmɪs) *n* **1** (formerly, esp in Holland and northern Germany) an annual country festival **2** *US & Canad* a similar event held to collect money for charity [C16 from MDu., from *kerc* church + *misse* MASS; orig. a festival held to celebrate the dedication of a church]

kern[1] *or* **kerne** (kɜːn) *n* the part of the character on a piece of printer's type that projects beyond the body [C17 from F *carne* corner of type, ult. from L *cardō* hinge]

kern[2] (kɜːn) *n* **1** a lightly armed foot soldier in medieval Ireland or Scotland **2** *arch* a loutish peasant [C14 from MIrish *cethern* band of foot soldiers, from *cath* battle]

Kern (kɜːn) *n* **Jerome** (**David**) 1885–1945, US composer of musical comedies, esp *Show Boat* (1927)

kernel ('kɜːnᵊl) *n* **1** the edible central part of a seed, nut, or fruit within the shell or stone **2** the grain of a cereal, esp wheat, consisting of the seed in a hard husk **3** the central or essential part of something [OE *cyrnel* a little seed, from *corn* seed] > **'kernel-less** *adj*

kerosene *or* **kerosine** ('kɛrəˌsiːn) *n* **1** another name (esp US, Canad, Austral, & NZ) for **paraffin** (sense 1) **2** the general name for paraffin as a fuel for jet aircraft [C19 from Gk *kēros* wax + -ENE]

> **USAGE** The spelling *kerosine* is now the preferred form in technical and industrial usage

Kerouac ('kɛrʊˌæk) *n* **Jack,** real name *Jean-Louis Lebris de Kérouac*. 1922–69, US novelist and poet of the Beat Generation. His works include *On the Road* (1957) and *Big Sur* (1962)

Kerr (kɜː) *n* Sir **John Robert** 1914–91, Australian public servant. As governor general of Australia (1974–77), he dismissed the Labor prime minister Gough Whitlam (1975) amid great controversy

Kerry[1] ('kɛrɪ) *n* **1** a county of SW Republic of Ireland, in W Munster province: mostly mountainous (including the highest peaks in Ireland), with a deeply indented coast and many offshore islands. County town: Tralee.

Pop: 126 130 (1996). Area: 4701 sq km (1815 sq miles) **2** a small black breed of dairy cattle, originally from Kerry

Kerry[2] ('kɛrɪ) *n* **John Forbes** born 1943, US politician; Democratic Party candidate in the presidential election of 2004

kersey ('kɜ:zɪ) *n* a twilled woollen cloth with a cotton warp [C14 prob. from *Kersey*, village in Suffolk]

kerseymere ('kɜ:zɪˌmɪə) *n* a fine soft woollen cloth of twill weave [C18 from KERSEY + (*cassi*)*mere*, var. of CASHMERE]

Kesey ('ki:sɪ) *n* **Ken** 1935–2001, US novelist, best-known for *One Flew Over the Cuckoo's Nest* (1962)

Kesselring ('kɛsᵊlrɪŋ) *n* **Albert** ('albɛrt) 1885–1960, German field marshal. He commanded the Luftwaffe attacks on Poland, France, and Britain (1939–40), and was supreme commander in Italy (1943–45) and on the western front (1945)

Kesteven ('kɛstɪvᵊn, kɛ'sti:vᵊn) *n* **Parts of** an area in E England constituting a former administrative division of Lincolnshire

kestrel ('kɛstrəl) *n* any of several small falcons that feed on small mammals and tend to hover against the wind [C15 changed from OF *cresserele*, from *cressele* rattle, from Vulgar L *crepicella* (unattested), from L, from *crepāre* to rustle]

Keswick ('kɛzɪk) *n* a market town in NW England, in Cumbria in the Lake District: tourist centre. Pop: 4836 (1991)

ketch (kɛtʃ) *n* a two-masted sailing vessel, fore-and-aft rigged, with a tall mainmast [C15 *cache*, prob. from *cacchen* to hunt; see CATCH]

ketchup ('kɛtʃəp), **catchup,** *or* **catsup** *n* any of various sauces containing vinegar: *tomato ketchup* [C18 from Chinese *kōetsiap* brine of pickled fish, from *kōe* seafood + *tsiap* sauce]

ketone ('ki:təʊn) *n* any of a class of compounds with the general formula R'COR, where R and R' are alkyl or aryl groups [C19 from G, from *Aketon* ACETONE] > **ketonic** (kɪ'tɒnɪk) *adj*

ketone body *n biochem* any of three compounds produced when fatty acids are broken down in the liver to provide a source of energy. Excess ketone bodies are present in the blood and urine of people unable to use glucose as an energy source, as in diabetes

Kettering ('kɛtərɪŋ) *n* a town in central England, in Northamptonshire: footwear industry. Pop: 47 186 (1991)

kettle ('kɛtᵊl) *n* **1** a metal container with a handle and spout for boiling water **2** any of various metal containers for heating liquids, cooking fish, etc **3** a large metal vessel designed to withstand high temperatures, used in various industrial processes such as refining and brewing [C13 from ON *ketill*, ult. from L *catillus* a little pot, from *catīnus* pot]

kettledrum ('kɛtᵊlˌdrʌm) *n* a percussion instrument of definite pitch, consisting of a hollow bowl-like hemisphere covered with a skin or membrane, supported on a tripod. The pitch may be adjusted by means of screws, which alter the tension of the skin > **'kettleˌdrummer** *n*

kettle hole *n* a round hollow formed by the melting of a mass of buried ice

kettle of fish *n* **1** a situation; state of affairs (often used ironically in **a pretty** *or* **fine kettle of fish**) **2** case; matter for consideration: *that's quite a different kettle of fish*

Kevlar ('kɛvˌlɑ:) *n trademark* a synthetic fibre, consisting of long-chain polyamides, having high tensile strength and temperature resistance

Kew (kju:) *n* part of the Greater London borough of Richmond-upon-Thames, on the River Thames: famous for **Kew Gardens** (the Royal Botanic Gardens), established in 1759 and given to the nation in 1841

kewl (ku:l) *adj inf* a nonstandard variant spelling of **cool** (sense 11)

key[1] (ki:) *n* **1** a metal instrument, usually of a specifically contoured shape, that is made to fit a lock and, when rotated, operates the lock's mechanism **2** any instrument that is rotated to operate a valve, clock winding mechanism, etc **3** a small metal peg or wedge inserted to prevent relative motion **4** any of a set of buttons operating a typewriter, computer, etc **5** any of the visible parts of the lever mechanism of a musical keyboard instrument that when depressed cause the instrument to sound **6a** Also called: **tonality** any of the 24 major and minor diatonic scales considered as a corpus of notes upon which a piece of music draws for its tonal framework **6b** the main tonal centre in an extended composition: *a symphony in the key of F major* **7** something that is crucial in providing an explanation or interpretation **8** (*modifier*) of great importance: *a key issue* **9** a means of achieving a desired end: *the key to happiness* **10** a means of access or control: *Gibraltar is the key to the Mediterranean* **11** a list of explanations of symbols, codes, etc **12** a text that explains or gives information about a work of literature, art, or music **13** *electrical engineering* a hand-operated switch that is pressed to transmit coded signals, esp Morse code **14** the grooving or scratching of a surface or the application of a rough coat of plaster, etc, to provide a bond for a subsequent finish **15** pitch: *he spoke in a low key* **16** a mood or style: *a poem in a melancholic key* **17** short for **keystone** (sense 1) **18** *bot* any dry winged fruit, esp that of the ash ▷ *vb* (*mainly tr*) **19** (foll by *to*) to harmonize (with): *to key one's actions to the prevailing mood* **20** to adjust or fasten with a key or some similar device **21** to provide with a key or keys **22** (*also intr*) another word for **keyboard** (sense 3) **23** to include a distinguishing device in (an advertisement, etc), so that responses to it can be identified **24** (*also intr*) to groove, scratch, or apply a rough coat of plaster, etc, to (a surface) to provide a bond for a subsequent finish ▷ See also **key in, key up** [OE *cǣg*] > **'keyless** *adj*

Kk

key[2] (ki:) *n* a variant spelling of **cay**

keyboard ('ki:ˌbɔ:d) *n* **1a** a set of keys, usually hand-operated, as on a piano, typewriter, or typesetting machine **1b** (*as modifier*): *a keyboard instrument* **2** (*pl*) electronic keyboard instruments: *John plays keyboards for the band* ▷ *vb* **3** (*tr*) to set (a text) in type by using a keyboard machine > **'keyˌboarder** *n*

key drive *n computing* a very small, portable storage device that plugs into a computer and facilitates moving data between machines. Also: **pen drive**

key grip *n chiefly US* the person in charge of moving and setting up camera tracks and scenery in a film or television studio

keyhole ('ki:ˌhəʊl) *n* an aperture in a door or a lock case through which a key may be passed to engage the lock mechanism

keyhole surgery *n* surgery carried out through a very small incision

key in *vb* (*tr, adv*) to enter (information or instructions) in a computer or other device by means of a keyboard or keypad

key-man assurance *n* an assurance policy taken out, esp by a small company, on the life of a senior executive whose death would create a serious loss

key money *n* a fee payment required from a new tenant of a house or flat before he moves in

Keynes (keɪnz) *n* **John Maynard,** 1st Baron Keynes. 1883–1946, English economist. In *The General Theory of Employment, Interest and Money* (1936) he argued that unemployment was characteristic of an unregulated market economy and therefore to achieve a high level of employment it was necessary for governments to manipulate the overall level of demand through monetary and fiscal policies (including, when appropriate, deficit financing). He helped to found the

International Monetary Fund and the World Bank > **'Keynesian** *adj n*
▷ http://campus.northpark.edu/history/WebChron/Glossary/KeynesEc.CP.html
▷ www.econlib.org/library/Enc/NewKeynesianEconomics.html

keynote ('ki:ˌnəʊt) *n* **1a** a central or determining principle in a speech, literary work, etc **1b** *(as modifier)*: *a keynote speech* **2** the note upon which a scale or key is based; tonic ▷ *vb* **keynotes, keynoting, keynoted** *(tr)* **3** to deliver a keynote address to (a political convention, etc)

keypad ('ki:ˌpæd) *n* a small panel with a set of buttons for operating a teletext system, electronic calculator, etc

key punch *n* **1** Also called: **card punch** a device having a keyboard that is operated manually to transfer data onto punched cards, paper tape, etc ▷ *vb* **key-punch** **2** to transfer (data) by using a key punch

keyring drive *n computing* another name for **pocket drive**

key signature *n music* a group of sharps or flats appearing at the beginning of each stave line to indicate the key in which a piece, section, etc, is to be performed

key stage *n Brit education* any one of four broad age-group divisions (5–7; 7–11; 11–14; 14–16) to which each level of the National Curriculum applies

keystone ('ki:ˌstəʊn) *n* **1** the central stone at the top of an arch or the top stone of a dome or vault **2** something that is necessary to connect other related things

key up *vb (tr, adv)* to raise the intensity, excitement, tension, etc, of

key worker *n* a social or mental health worker assigned to an individual case or patient

kg **1** *abbrev. for* keg ▷ **2** *symbol for* kilogram

KG *abbrev for* Knight of the Order of the Garter (a Brit title)

KGB *abbrev for* the former Soviet secret police, founded in 1954 [from Russian *Komitet gosudarstvennoi bezopasnosti* State Security Committee]

Khabarovsk (*Russian* xa'barəfsk) *n* a port in E Russia, on the Amur River: it was the administrative centre of the whole Soviet Far Eastern territory until 1938; a major industrial centre. Pop: 614 000 (1999 est)

Khachaturian (ˌka:tʃə'tʊərɪən, xətʃətu'rjan) *n* **Aram Ilich** ('arəm ilj'jitʃ) 1903–78, Russian composer. His works, which often incorporate Armenian folk tunes, include a piano concerto and the ballets *Gayaneh* (1942) and *Spartacus* (1954)

khaddar ('ka:də) *or* **khadi** ('ka:dɪ) *n* a cotton cloth of plain weave, produced in India [from Hindi *khādar*]

Khakass Republic (kə'kæs) *n* a constituent republic of S central Russia, in the Krasnoyarsk Territory: formed in 1930. Capital: Abakan. Pop: 581 000 (2000 est). Area: 61 900 sq km (23 855 sq miles). Also called: **Khakassia** (kə'kæsɪə; *Russian* xə'kasɪjə)

khaki ('ka:kɪ) *n, pl* **khakis** **1** a dull yellowish-brown colour **2a** a hard-wearing fabric of this colour, used esp for military uniforms **2b** *(as modifier)*: *a khaki jacket* [c19 from Urdu, from Persian: dusty, from *khāk* dust]

Khalid ibn Abdul Aziz ('ka:lɪd 'ɪbᵊn 'æbdʊl ə'zi:z) *n* 1913–82, king and President of the Council of Ministers of Saudi Arabia (1975–82)

khalif ('keɪlɪf) *n* a variant spelling of **caliph**

Khalkidíki (xalkiði'ki) *n* transliteration of the Modern Greek name for **Chalcidice**

Khalkís (xal'kis) *n* transliteration of the Modern Greek name for **Chalcis**

Khalsa ('kælsə) *n* an order of the Sikh religion, founded (1699) by Guru Gobind Singh

Khama ('ka:mə) *n* Sir **Seretse** (sə'rɛtsɪ) 1921–80, Botswana statesman; the first president of Botswana (1966–80)

Khamenei (ˌxamə'nɪ) *n* Ayatollah **Seyed Ali** ('seɪjət) born 1940, Iranian political and religious leader: president of Iran (1981–89); leader of the Islamic Republic from 1989

khan¹ (ka:n) *n* **1a** (formerly) a title borne by medieval Chinese emperors and Mongol and Turkic rulers **1b** such a ruler **2** a title of respect borne by important personages in Afghanistan and central Asia [c14 from OF, from Med. L, from Turkish *khān*, contraction of *khāqān* ruler] > **'khanate** *n*

khan² (ka:n) *n* an inn in Turkey, etc; caravanserai [c14 via Ar. from Persian]

Khaniá (xa'nja) *n* transliteration of the Modern Greek name for **Chania**

Kharkov (*Russian* 'xarjkəf) *n* a city in the E Ukraine: capital of the Ukrainian Soviet Socialist Republic (1917–34); university (1805). Pop: 1 521 400 (1998 est)

Khartoum *or* **Khartum** (ka:'tu:m) *n* the capital of the Sudan, at the junction of the Blue and the White Nile: with adjoining Khartoum North and Omdurman, the largest conurbation in the country; destroyed by the Mahdists in 1885 when General Gordon was killed; seat of the Anglo-Egyptian government of the Sudan until 1954, then capital of the new republic. Pop: 924 505 (1993)
▷ www.sudan.net

Khatami (kə'ta:mɪ) *n* **Seyed Mohammad** ('seɪjət) born 1943, Iranian politician: president of Iran from 1997

Khayyám (kaɪ'a:m) *n* **Omar.** See **Omar Khayyám**

khedive (kɪ'di:v) *n* the viceroy of Egypt under Ottoman suzerainty (1867–1914) [c19 from F, from Turkish, from Persian *khidīw* prince] > **khe'dival** *or* **khe'divial** *adj*

Kherson (*Russian* xɪr'sɔn) *n* a port in the S Ukraine on the Dnieper River near the Black Sea: shipyards. Pop: 358 700 (1998 est)

Khingan Mountains ('ʃɪŋ'a:n) *pl n* a mountain system of NE China, in W Manchuria. Highest peak: 2034 m (6673 ft)

Khíos ('çiɔs) *n* transliteration of the Modern Greek name for **Chios**

Khirbet Qumran ('kɪəbɛt 'kʊmra:n) *n* an archaeological site in NW Jordan, near the NW shore of the Dead Sea: includes the caves where the Dead Sea Scrolls were found

Khmer (kmɛə) *n* **1** a member of a people of Cambodia, noted for a civilization that flourished from about 800 AD to about 1370 **2** the language of this people: the official language of Cambodia ▷ *adj* **3** of or relating to this people or their language > **'Khmerian** *adj*
▷ www.khmerclub.com/History.htm
▷ www.persoanl.psu.edu/users/h/x/hxt144/history.htm

Khmer Republic *n* the former official name (1970–76) of **Cambodia**

Khoikhoi (kɔɪ'kɔɪ, xɔɪ'xɔɪ) *n* **1** a member of a Southern African people who formerly occupied the region around the Cape of Good Hope and are now almost extinct **2** any of the languages of this people

Khomeini ('ɔxmeɪ'ni:) *n* **Ruholla** ('ruhɒ'la:), known as *Ayatollah Khomeini*. 1900–89, Iranian Shiite Muslim religious and political leader. Following the overthrow of the shah of Iran (1979) he returned from exile and instituted an Islamic republic. His rule saw deteriorating relations with the West and war (1980–88) with Iraq

Khotan ('kəʊ'ta:n) *n* another name for **Hotan**

Khrushchev (kru:s'tʃɒf, 'krʊstʃɒf; *Russian* xru'ʃtʃɔf) *n* **Nikita Sergeyevich** (ni'kitə sɪr'gjejɪvitʃ) 1894–1971, Soviet statesman; premier of the Soviet Union (1958–64). After Stalin's death he became first secretary of the Soviet Communist Party (1953–64) and initiated a policy to remove the influence of Stalin (1956). As premier, he pursued a policy of peaceful coexistence with the West, but alienated Communist China

Khufu ('ku:fu:) *n* the original name of **Cheops**

Khulna ('kʊlna:) *n* a city in S Bangladesh. Pop: 731 000 (1991)

Khyber Pass ('kaɪbə) *n* a narrow pass over the Safed Koh Range between Afghanistan and Pakistan, over which came the Persian, Greek, Tatar, Mogul, and Afghan invasions of India; scene of bitter fighting between the British and Afghans (1838–42, 1878–80). Length: about 53 km (33 miles). Highest point: 1072 m (3518 ft)

kHz *symbol for* kilohertz

kia kaha (ˌkɪə 'kɑːhə) *sentence substitute* NZ be strong! [Maori]

kiang (kɪ'æŋ) *n* a variety of the wild ass that occurs in Tibet and surrounding regions [c19 from Tibetan *rkyan*]

Kiangsi ('kjæŋ'siː) *n* a variant transliteration of the Chinese name for **Jiangxi**

Kiangsu ('kjæŋ'suː) *n* a variant transliteration of the Chinese name for **Jiangsu**

Kiaochow ('kjaʊ'tʃaʊ) *n* a variant transliteration of the Chinese name for **Jiazhou**

kia ora (ˌkɪə 'ɔːrə) *sentence substitute* NZ greetings! good luck! [Maori, lit.: be well!]

kibble[1] ('kɪbᵊl) *n Brit* a bucket used in wells or in mining for hoisting [c17 from G *kübel*, ult. from Med. L *cuppa* CUP]

kibble[2] ('kɪbᵊl) *vb* **kibbles, kibbling, kibbled** *(tr)* to grind into small pieces [c18 from ?]

kibbutz (kɪ'bʊts) *n, pl* **kibbutzim** (ˌkɪbʊt'siːm) a collective agricultural settlement in modern Israel, owned and administered communally by its members [c20 from Mod. Heb. *qibbūs* gathering, from Heb. *qibbūtz*]

kibe (kaɪb) *n* a chilblain, esp an ulcerated one on the heel [c14 prob. from Welsh *cibi*, from ?]

kibi- ('kɪbɪ) *prefix computing* denoting 2^{10}: *kibibyte*. Symbol: Ki [c20 from KI(LO-) + BI(NARY)]

USAGE See at **kilo-**

kiblah ('kɪblɑː) *n Islam* the direction of Mecca, to which Muslims turn in prayer [c18 from Ar. *qiblah* that which is placed opposite]

kibosh ('kaɪˌbɒʃ) *n* **put the kibosh on** *sl* to put a stop to; prevent from continuing; halt [c19 from ?]

kick (kɪk) *vb* **1** *(tr)* to drive or impel with the foot **2** *(tr)* to hit with the foot or feet **3** *(intr)* to strike out or thrash about with the feet, as in fighting or swimming **4** *(intr)* to raise a leg high, as in dancing **5** (of a gun, etc) to recoil or strike in recoiling when fired **6** *(tr) rugby* to make (a conversion or a drop goal) by means of a kick **7** *(tr) soccer* to score (a goal) by a kick **8** *(intr) athletics* to put on a sudden spurt **9** *(intr)* to make a sudden violent movement **10** *(intr; sometimes foll by against) inf* to object or resist **11** *(intr) inf* to be active and in good health (esp in **alive and kicking**) **12** *inf* to change gear in (a car): *he kicked into third* **13** *(tr) inf* to free oneself of (an addiction, etc): *he tried to kick the habit* **14 kick up one's heels** *inf* to enjoy oneself without inhibition ▷ *n* **15** a thrust or blow with the foot **16** any of certain rhythmic leg movements used in swimming **17** the recoil of a gun or other firearm **18** *inf* exciting quality or effect (esp in **get a kick out of, for kicks**) **19** *athletics* a sudden spurt, acceleration, or boost **20** a sudden violent movement **21** *inf* the sudden stimulating effect of strong alcoholic drink or certain drugs **22** *inf* power or force **23 kick in the teeth** *sl* a humiliating rebuff ▷ See also **kick about, kickback**, etc [c14 *kiken*, ?from ON] > **'kickable** *adj*

kick about *or* **around** *vb (mainly adv) Inf* **1** *(tr)* to treat harshly **2** *(tr)* to discuss (ideas, etc) informally **3** *(intr)* to wander aimlessly **4** *(intr)* to lie neglected or forgotten

kick ass *slang* ▷ *vb (intr)* **1** to be impressive, esp in a forceful way: *pop music that kicks ass* ▷ *adj* **kick-ass** **2** forceful, aggressive, and impressive

kickback ('kɪkˌbæk) *n* **1** a strong reaction **2** part of an income paid to a person in return for an opportunity to make a profit, often by some illegal arrangement ▷ *vb* **kick back** *(adv)* **3** *(intr)* to have a strong reaction **4** *(intr)* (esp of a gun) to recoil **5** to pay a kickback to (someone)

kick boxing *n* a martial art that resembles boxing but permits blows with the feet as well as punches

kickdown ('kɪkˌdaʊn) *n* a method of changing gear in a car with automatic transmission, by fully depressing the accelerator

kicker ('kɪkə) *n* **1** a person or thing that kicks **2** *US & Canad sl* a hidden and disadvantageous factor

kick in *vb (adv)* **1** *(intr)* to start or become activated **2** *(tr) chiefly Austral & NZ inf* to contribute

kick off *vb (intr, adv)* **1** to start play in a game of football by kicking the ball from the centre of the field **2** *inf* to commence (a discussion, job, etc) ▷ *n* **kickoff** **3a** a place kick from the centre of the field in a game of football **3b** the time at which the first such kick is due to take place

kick on *vb (adv) inf* to continue

kick out *vb (tr, adv) inf* to eject or dismiss

kickshaw ('kɪkˌʃɔː) *or* **kickshaws** *n* **1** a valueless trinket **2** *arch* a small exotic delicacy [c16 back formation from *kickshaws*, by folk etymology from F *quelque chose* something]

kickstand ('kɪkˌstænd) *n* a short metal bar attached to the frame of a motorcycle or bicycle, which when kicked into a vertical position holds the stationary vehicle upright

kick-start ('kɪkˌstɑːt) *vb (tr)* **1** to start (an engine, esp of a motorcycle) by means of a pedal that is kicked downwards **2** *inf* to make (something) active, functional, or productive again ▷ *n* **3** an action or event resulting in the reactivation of something > **'kick-ˌstarter** *n*

kick up *vb (adv) inf* to cause (trouble, etc)

kick upstairs *vb (tr, adv) inf* to promote to a higher but effectively powerless position

kid[1] (kɪd) *n* **1** the young of a goat or of a related animal, such as an antelope **2** soft smooth leather made from the hide of a kid **3** *inf* **3a** a young person; child **3b** *(modifier)* younger or being still a child: *kid brother* ▷ *vb* **kids, kidding, kidded** **4** (of a goat) to give birth to (young) [c12 from ON] > **'kiddishness** *n* > **'kidˌlike** *adj*

kid[2] (kɪd) *vb* **kids, kidding, kidded** *inf* (sometimes foll by *on* or *along*) **1** *(tr)* to tease or deceive for fun **2** *(intr)* to behave or speak deceptively for fun **3** *(tr)* to fool (oneself) into believing (something): *don't kid yourself that no-one else knows* [c19 prob. from KID[1]] > **'kidder** *n* > **'kiddingly** *adv*

Kid (kɪd) *n* **Thomas** a variant spelling of (Thomas) **Kyd**

Kidd (kɪd) *n* **William**, known as *Captain Kidd*. 1645–1701, Scottish privateer, pirate, and murderer; hanged

Kidderminster ('kɪdəˌmɪnstə) *n* **1** a town in W central England, in N Worcestershire on the River Stour: carpet industry. Pop: 54 644 (1991 est) **2** a type of ingrain reversible carpet originally made at Kidderminster

kiddy *or* **kiddie** ('kɪdɪ) *n, pl* **kiddies** *inf* an affectionate word for **child**

kid glove *n* **1** a glove made of kidskin **2 handle with kid gloves** to treat with great tact or caution ▷ *adj* **kidglove** **3** overdelicate or overrefined **4** diplomatic; tactful: *a kidglove approach*

Kidman ('kɪdmən) *n* **Nicole** born 1967, Australian film actress, born in Hawaii. Her films include *Far and Away* (1992), *To Die For* (1995), *Eyes Wide Shut* (1999), and *The Hours* (2002): formerly married to Tom Cruise

kidnap ('kɪdnæp) *vb* **kidnaps, kidnapping, kidnapped** *or US* **kidnaps, kidnaping, kidnaped** *(tr)* to carry off and hold (a person), usually for ransom [c17 KID[1] + obs. *nap* to steal; see NAB] > **'kidnapper** *n*

kidney ('kɪdnɪ) *n* **1** either of two bean-shaped organs at the back of the abdominal cavity in man. They filter waste products from the blood, which are excreted as urine. Related adj: **renal** **2** the corresponding organ in other animals **3** the kidneys of certain animals used as food **4** class, type, or disposition (esp in **of the same** *or* **a different kidney**) [c14 from ?]

▷ www.kidney.org

kidney bean *n* **1** any of certain bean plants having

Kk

kidney-shaped seeds, esp the scarlet runner **2** the seed of any of these beans

kidney machine *n* a machine carrying out the functions of a kidney, esp used in haemodialysis

kidney stone *n* **1** *pathol* a hard mass formed in the kidney, usually composed of oxalates, phosphates, and carbonates **2** *mineralogy* another name for **nephrite**

kidology (kɪˈdɒlədʒɪ) *n Brit inf* the practice of bluffing or deception [c20 from KID² + *ology* a science]

Kidron (ˈkiːdrən) *n* a variant of **Kedron**

kidskin (ˈkɪdˌskɪn) *n* a soft smooth leather made from the hide of a young goat. Often shortened to **kid**

kids' stuff *n sl* **1** something considered fit only for children **2** something considered easy

kidstakes (ˈkɪdˌsteɪks) *pl n Austral inf* pretence; nonsense: *cut the kidstakes!*

kie kie (ˈkiːɛ kiːɛ) *n* a New Zealand climbing plant with edible bracts [from Maori]

Kiel (kiːl) *n* a port in N Germany, capital of Schleswig-Holstein state, on the **Kiel Canal** (connecting the North Sea with the Baltic): joined the Hanseatic League in 1284; became part of Denmark in 1773 and passed to Prussia in 1866; an important naval base in World Wars I and II; shipbuilding and engineering industries. Pop: 235 500 (1999 est)

Kielce (*Polish* ˈkjɛltsɛ) *n* an industrial city in S Poland. Pop: 212 383 (1999 est)

Kierkegaard (ˈkɪəkəˌgaːd; *Danish* ˈkirgəgɔːr) *n* **Søren Aabye** (ˈsøːrən ˈɔːby) 1813–55, Danish philosopher and theologian. He rejected organized Christianity and anticipated the existentialists in emphasizing man's moral responsibility and freedom of choice. His works include *Either/Or* (1843), *The Concept of Dread* (1844), and *The Sickness unto Death* (1849)

kieselguhr (ˈkiːzəlˌgʊə) *n* an unconsolidated form of diatomite [c19 from G *Kieselgur*, from *Kiesel* flint + *Gur* loose earthy deposit]

Kieślowski (kiˈʃlɔfskɪ) *n* **Krzysztof** (ˈkrɪʃtɔf) 1941–96, Polish film director, whose later films were made in France; his work includes the television series *Decalogue* (1988–89) and the film trilogy *Three Colours* (1993–94)

Kiev (ˈkiːɛf; *Russian* ˈkijɪf) *n* the capital of the Ukraine, on the Dnieper River: formed the first Russian state by the late 9th century; university (1834). Pop: 2 620 900 (1998 est)

▷ www.uazone.net/Kiev.html
▷ www.kiev.info

kif (kɪf, kiːf), **kef**, *or* **kief** (kiːf) *n* **1** another name for **marijuana** **2** any drug that when smoked is capable of producing a euphoric condition **3** the euphoric condition produced by smoking marijuana [c20 from Ar. *kayf* pleasure]

Kigali (kɪˈgaːlɪ) *n* the capital of Rwanda, in the central part. Pop: 256 000 (1996 est)

kike (kaɪk) *n US & Canad sl* an offensive word for **Jew** [c20 prob. var. of *kiki*, reduplication of *-ki*, common name-ending among Jews from Slavic countries]

Kikládhes (kiˈklaðɛs) *n* transliteration of the Modern Greek name for **Cyclades**

Kilauea (ˌkiːlaːuːˈeɪə) *n* a crater on the E side of Mauna Loa volcano, on SE Hawaii Island: the world's largest active crater. Height: 1247 m (4090 ft). Width: 3 km (2 miles)

Kildare (kɪlˈdɛə) *n* a county of E Republic of Ireland, in Leinster province: mostly low-lying and fertile. County town: Naas. Pop: 134 992 (1996). Area: 1694 sq km (654 sq miles)

kilderkin (ˈkɪldəkɪn) *n* **1** an obsolete unit of liquid capacity equal to 16 or 18 Imperial gallons or of dry capacity equal to 16 or 18 wine gallons **2** a cask capable of holding a kilderkin [c14 from MDu. *kindekijn*, from *kintal* hundredweight, from Med. L *quintale*]

kilim (kɪˈliːm, ˈkiːlɪm) *n* a pileless woven rug of intricate design made in the Middle East [c19 from Turkish, from Persian *kilīm*]

Kilimanjaro (ˌkɪlɪmənˈdʒaːrəʊ) *n* a volcanic massif in N Tanzania: the highest peak in Africa; extends from east to west for 80 km (50 miles). Height: 5895 m (19 340 ft)

Kilkenny (kɪlˈkɛnɪ) *n* **1** a county of SE Republic of Ireland, in Leinster province: mostly agricultural. County town: Kilkenny. Pop: 75 336 (1996). Area: 2062 sq km (796 sq miles) **2** a market town in SE Republic of Ireland, county town of Co. Kilkenny: capital of the ancient kingdom of Ossory. Pop: 9500 (latest est)

kill (kɪl) *vb (mainly tr)* **1** *(also intr; when tr, sometimes foll by off)* to cause the death of (a person or animal) **2** to put an end to: *to kill someone's interest* **3** to occupy (time) by doing something unimportant, esp while waiting for something **4** to deaden (sound) **5** *inf* to tire out: *the effort killed him* **6** *inf* to cause to suffer pain or discomfort: *my shoes are killing me* **7** *inf* to quash or veto: *the bill was killed in the House of Lords* **8** *inf* to switch off; stop **9** *(also intr) inf* to overcome with attraction, laughter, surprise, etc: *she was dressed to kill* **10** *tennis, squash, etc* to hit (a ball) so hard or so accurately that the opponent cannot return it **11** *soccer* to bring (a moving ball) under control **12** **kill oneself** *inf* to overexert oneself: *don't kill yourself* **13** **kill two birds with one stone** to achieve two results with one action ▷ *n* **14** the act of causing death, esp at the end of a hunt, bullfight, etc **15** the animal or animals killed during a hunt **16** *NZ* a seasonal tally of the number of stock killed at a meatworks **17** the destruction of a battleship, tank, etc **18** **in at the kill** present at the end of some undertaking [c13 *cullen*; see QUELL]

Killarney (kɪˈlaːnɪ) *n* a town in SW Republic of Ireland, in Co. Kerry: a tourist centre near the **Lakes of Killarney**. Pop: 7250 (1991)

killdeer (ˈkɪlˌdɪə) *n, pl* **killdeer** *or* **killdeers** a large brown-and-white North American plover with two black breast bands [c18 imit.]

killer (ˈkɪlə) *n* **1a** a person or animal that kills, esp habitually **1b** *(as modifier)*: *a killer shark* **2** something, esp a task or activity, that is particularly taxing or exhausting **3** *Austral & NZ* a farm animal selected to be killed for food

killer application *n* a highly innovative, very powerful, or extremely useful computer application; esp one sufficiently important as to justify purchase of the equipment or software

killer bee *n* an African honeybee, or one of its hybrids originating in Brazil, that is extremely aggressive when disturbed

killer cell *n* a type of white blood cell that is able to kill cells, such as cancer cells and cells infected with viruses

killer whale *n* a predatory black-and-white toothed whale most common in cold seas

killick (ˈkɪlɪk) *or* **killock** (ˈkɪlək) *n naut* a small anchor, esp one made of a heavy stone [c17 from ?]

Killiecrankie (ˌkɪlɪˈkræŋkɪ) *n* a pass in central Scotland, in the Grampians: scene of a battle (1689) in which the Jacobites defeated William III's forces but lost their leader, Viscount Dundee

killifish (ˈkɪlɪˌfɪʃ) *n, pl* **killifish** *or* **killifishes** any of various chiefly American minnow-like fishes of fresh and brackish waters: used to control mosquitoes and as anglers' bait [c19 from MDu. *kille* river + FISH]

killing (ˈkɪlɪŋ) *adj* **1** *inf* very tiring: *a killing pace* **2** *inf* extremely funny **3** causing death; fatal ▷ *n* **4** the act of causing death; slaying **5** *inf* a sudden stroke of success, usually financial, as in speculations on the stock market (esp in **make a killing**)

killjoy (ˈkɪlˌdʒɔɪ) *n* a person who spoils other people's pleasure

Kilmarnock (kɪlˈmaːnək) *n* a town in SW Scotland, the administrative centre of East Ayrshire: associations with Robert Burns; engineering and textile industries; whisky blending. Pop: 44 307 (1991)

kiln (kɪln) *n* a large oven for burning, drying, or processing something, such as porcelain or bricks [OE *cylen*, from LL *culīna* kitchen, from L *coquere* to COOK]

kilo ('kiːləʊ) *n, pl* **kilos** short for **kilogram** or **kilometre**

kilo- *prefix* **1** denoting 10^3 (1000): *kilometre*. Symbol: k **2** Also: **kibi-** *computing* denoting 2^{10} (1024): *kilobyte*. Symbol Ki [from F, from Gk *khilioi* thousand]

> USAGE In general and scientific use *kilo-* means 10^{33} (i.e. 1000). However, in computing it denotes 2^{1010} (1024) but only for words connected with amounts of data (e.g. *kilobit*). In other computer contexts it retains its common meaning of 1000 (e.g. *kilohertz*). A recommended new prefix *kibi-* has been introduced to denote the specific computing use of 2^{1010}. Other metric prefixes, *mega-*, *giga-*, *tera-*, *peta-*, and *exa-*, behave in a similar way and the equivalent prefixes for binary multiples are *mebi-*, *gibi-*, *tebi-*, *pebi-*, and *exbi-*

kilobyte ('kɪləˌbaɪt) *n computing* 1024 bytes. Abbrev: **KB, kbyte** See also **kilo-** (sense 2)

kilocalorie ('kɪləʊˌkælərɪ) *n* another name for **Calorie**

kilocycle ('kɪləʊˌsaɪkᵊl) *n* short for kilocycle per second: a former unit of frequency equal to 1 kilohertz

kilogram ('kɪləʊˌɡræm) *n* **1** one thousand grams **2** the basic SI unit of mass, equal to the mass of the international prototype held by the *Bureau International des Poids et Mesures*. Symbol: kg

kilohertz ('kɪləʊˌhɜːts) *n* one thousand hertz; one thousand cycles per second. Symbol: kHz

kilolitre ('kɪləˌliːtə) *n* one thousand litres. Symbol: kl

kilometre *or US* **kilometer** ('kɪləˌmiːtə, kɪ'lɒmɪtə) *n* one thousand metres. Symbol: km > **kilometric** (ˌkɪləʊ'mɛtrɪk) *adj*

kiloton ('kɪləʊˌtʌn) *n* **1** one thousand tons **2** an explosive power, esp of a nuclear weapon, equal to the power of 1000 tons of TNT. Abbrev: **kt**

kilovolt ('kɪləʊˌvəʊlt) *n* one thousand volts. Symbol: kV

kilowatt ('kɪləʊˌwɒt) *n* one thousand watts. Symbol: kW

kilowatt-hour *n* a unit of energy equal to the work done by a power of 1000 watts in one hour. Symbol: kWh

kilt (kɪlt) *n* **1** a knee-length pleated skirt, esp one in tartan, as worn by men in Highland dress ▹ *vb (tr)* **2** to tuck (the skirt) up around one's body **3** to put pleats in (cloth, etc) [c18 of Scand. origin] > **'kilted** *adj*
▹ www.scotlandonline.com/heritage
▹ www.myclan.com/clanship/tartan/history.asp

kilter ('kɪltə) *or* **kelter** *n* working order (esp in **out of kilter**) [c17 from ?]

Kilung ('kiː'lʊŋ) *n* another name for **Chilung**

Kilvert ('kɪlvət) *n* **Francis** 1840–79, British clergyman and diarist. His diary (published 1938–40) gives a vivid account of life in the Welsh Marches in the 1870s

Kimberley ('kɪmbəlɪ) *n* **1** a city in central South Africa, in Northern Cape province: besieged (1899–1900) for 126 days during the Boer War; diamond-mining and -marketing centre, with heavy engineering works. Pop: 170 432 (1996) **2** Also called: **the Kimberleys** a plateau region of NW Australia, in N Western Australia: consists of rugged mountains surrounded by grassland. Area: about 360 000 sq km (140 000 sq miles)

kimberlite ('kɪmbəˌlaɪt) *n* an intrusive igneous rock consisting largely of olivine and phlogopite and often containing diamonds [c19 from KIMBERLEY + -ITE[1]]

Kim Il Sung (kim il sʌŋ) *n* 1912–94, North Korean statesman and marshal; prime minister (1948–72) and president (1972–94) of North Korea

Kim Jong Il (kɪm dʒɔŋ iːl) *n* born 1942, Korean politician; ruler of North Korea from 1994, official head of state from 1998: son of Kim Il Sung

kimono (kɪ'məʊnəʊ) *n, pl* **kimonos** a loose sashed ankle-length garment with wide sleeves, worn in Japan [c19 from Japanese: clothing, from *kiru* to wear + *mono* thing] > **ki'monoed** *adj*
▹ www.jinjapan.org/kidsweb/virtual/kimono/top.html

kin (kɪn) *n* **1** a person's relatives collectively **2** a class or group with similar characteristics **3** See **next of kin** ▹ *adj* **4** *(postpositive)* related by blood [OE *cyn*]

-kin *suffix forming nouns* small: *lambkin* [from MDu., of West Gmc origin]

Kinabalu (ˌkɪnəbə'luː) *n* a mountain in Malaysia, on N Borneo in central Sabah: the highest peak in Borneo. Height: 4125 m (13 533 ft)

kinaesthesia (ˌkɪnɪs'θiːzɪə) *or US* **kinesthesia** *n* the sensation by which bodily position, weight, muscle tension, and movement are perceived [c19 from NL, from Gk *kinein* to move + AESTHESIA] > **kinaesthetic** *or US* **kinesthetic** (ˌkɪnɪs'θɛtɪk) *adj*

Kincardineshire (kɪn'kɑːdɪnˌʃɪə, -ʃə) *n* a former county of E Scotland: became part of Grampian region in 1975 and part of Aberdeenshire in 1996. Also called: **the Mearns**

Kinchinjunga (ˌkɪntʃɪn'dʒʌŋɡə) *n* a variant of **Kangchenjunga**

kincob ('kɪŋkɒb) *n* a fine silk fabric embroidered with threads of gold or silver, of a kind made in India [c18 from Urdu *kimkhāb*]

kind[1] (kaɪnd) *adj* **1** having a friendly nature or attitude **2** helpful to others or to another: *a kind deed* **3** considerate or humane **4** cordial; courteous (esp in **kind regards**) **5** pleasant; mild: *a kind climate* **6** *inf* beneficial or not harmful [OE *gecynde* natural, native]

kind[2] (kaɪnd) *n* **1** a class or group having characteristics in common; sort; type: *two of a kind* **2** an instance or example of a class or group, esp a rudimentary one: *heating of a kind* **3** essential nature or character: *the difference is one of kind rather than degree* **4** *arch* nature; the natural order **5 in kind 5a** (of payment) in goods or produce rather than in money **5b** with something of the same sort: *to return an insult in kind* [OE *gecynd* nature] Kk

> USAGE The mixture of plural and singular, although often used informally with *kind* and *sort*, should be avoided in serious writing: *children enjoy those kinds* (not *those kind*) *of stories*; *these sorts* (not *these sort*) *of distinctions are becoming blurred*

kindergarten ('kɪndəˌɡɑːtᵊn) *n* a class or small school for young children, usually between the ages of four and six [c19 from G, lit.: children's garden]

kind-hearted *adj* kindly, readily sympathetic > ˌ**kind-'heartedly** *adv* > ˌ**kind-'heartedness** *n*

kindle ('kɪndᵊl) *vb* **kindles, kindling, kindled 1** to set alight or start to burn **2** to arouse or be aroused: *this project kindled his interest in the theatre* **3** to make or become bright [c12 from ON *kynda*, infl. by ON *kyndill* candle] > **'kindler** *n*

kindling ('kɪndlɪŋ) *n* material for starting a fire, such as dry wood, straw, etc

kindly ('kaɪndlɪ) *adj* **kindlier, kindliest 1** having a sympathetic or warm-hearted nature **2** motivated by warm and sympathetic feelings **3** pleasant: *a kindly climate* **4** *arch* natural; normal ▹ *adv* **5** in a considerate or humane way **6** with tolerance: *he kindly forgave my rudeness* **7** cordially: *he greeted us kindly* **8** please (often used to express impatience or formality): *will you kindly behave yourself!* **9** *arch* appropriately **10 not take kindly to** to react unfavourably towards > **'kindliness** *n*

kindness ('kaɪndnɪs) *n* **1** the practice or quality of being kind **2** a kind or helpful act

kindred ('kɪndrɪd) *adj* **1** having similar or common qualities, origin, etc **2** related by blood or marriage **3 kindred spirit** a person with whom one has something in common ▹ *n* **4** relationship by blood **5** similarity in character **6** a person's relatives collectively [c12 *kinred*, from KIN + *-red*, from OE *rǣden* rule, from *rǣdan* to rule]

kine (kaɪn) *n (functioning as pl)* an archaic word for cows or cattle [OE *cȳna* of cows, from *cū* cow[1]]

kinematics (ˌkɪnɪˈmætɪks) *n (functioning as sing)* the study of the motion of bodies without reference to mass or force [c19 from Gk *kinēma* movement; see CINEMA, -ICS] > ˌ**kineˈmatic** *adj* > ˌ**kineˈmatically** *adv*

kinematograph (ˌkɪnɪˈmætəˌgrɑːf) *n* a variant spelling of **cinematograph**

kinesics (kɪˈniːsɪks) *n (functioning as sing)* the study of the role of body movements, such as winking, shrugging, etc, in communication

kinesis (kɪˈniːsɪs, kaɪ-) *n biol* the nondirectional movement of an organism or cell in response to a stimulus, the rate of movement being dependent on the strength of the stimulus

kinesthesia (ˌkɪnɪsˈθiːzɪə) *n* the usual US spelling of **kinaesthesia**

kinetic (kɪˈnɛtɪk) *adj* relating to or caused by motion [c19 from Gk *kinētikos*, from *kinein* to move] > **kiˈnetically** *adv*

kinetic art *n* art, esp sculpture, that moves or has moving parts

kinetic energy *n* the energy of motion of a body equal to the work it would do if it were brought to rest. It is equal to the product of the increase of mass caused by motion times the square of the speed of light

kinetics (kɪˈnɛtɪks, kaɪ-) *n (functioning as sing)* **1** another name for **dynamics** (sense 2) **2** the branch of mechanics, including both dynamics and kinematics, concerned with the study of bodies in motion **3** the branch of dynamics that excludes the study of bodies at rest

kinetic theory (of gases) *n* **the** a theory of gases postulating that they consist of particles moving at random and undergoing elastic collisions

kinfolk (ˈkɪnˌfəʊk) *pl n chiefly US & Canad* another word for **kinsfolk**

king (kɪŋ) *n* **1** a male sovereign prince who is the official ruler of an independent state; monarch. Related adjs: **royal, regal 2a** a ruler or chief: *king of the fairies* **2b** *(in combination): the pirate king* **3** a person, animal, or thing considered as the best or most important of its kind **4** any of four playing cards in a pack, one for each suit, bearing the picture of a king **5** the most important chess piece **6** *draughts* a piece that has moved entirely across the board and has been crowned, after which it may move backwards as well as forwards **7** *(cap) Caribbean.* a man who wins a nationally recognized festive or costume competition **8 king of kings 8a** God **8b** a title of any of various oriental monarchs ▷ *vb (tr)* **9** to make (someone) a king **10 king it** to act in a superior fashion [OE *cyning*] > ˈ**kingˌhood** *n* > ˈ**kingˌlike** *adj*

King (kɪŋ) *n* **1 B.B.**, real name *Riley B. King*. born 1925, US blues singer and guitarist **2 Billie Jean** (née *Moffitt*) born 1943, US tennis player: Wimbledon champion 1966–68, 1972–73, and 1975; US champion 1967, 1971–72, and 1974 **3 Martin Luther** 1929–68, US Baptist minister and civil-rights leader. He advocated nonviolence in his campaigns against the segregation of Blacks in the South: assassinated: Nobel Peace Prize 1964 **4 Stephen (Edwin)** born 1947, US writer esp of horror novels; his books, many of which have been filmed, include *Carrie* (1974), *The Shining* (1977), *Misery* (1988), and *Everything's Eventual* (2002) **5 William Lyon Mackenzie** 1874–1950, Canadian Liberal statesman; prime minister (1921–26; 1926–30; 1935–48)

kingbird (ˈkɪŋˌbɜːd) *n* any of several large American flycatchers

kingbolt (ˈkɪŋˌbəʊlt) *or* **king rod** *n* **a** the pivot bolt that connects the body of a horse-drawn carriage to the front axle and provides the steering joint **b** a similar bolt placed between a railway carriage and the bogies

King Charles spaniel *n* a toy breed of spaniel with a short turned-up nose and a domed skull [c17 after Charles II of England, who popularized the breed]

king cobra *n* a very large venomous tropical Asian snake that extends its neck into a hood when alarmed. Also called: **hamadryad**

King Country *n* **the** an area in the centre of North Island, New Zealand: home of the King Movement, a nineteenth-century Maori separatist movement

king crab *n* another name for the **horseshoe crab**

kingcup (ˈkɪŋˌkʌp) *n Brit* any of several yellow-flowered plants, esp the marsh marigold

kingdom (ˈkɪŋdəm) *n* **1** a territory, state, people, or community ruled or reigned over by a king or queen **2** any of the three groups into which natural objects may be divided: the animal, plant, and mineral kingdoms **3** *biol* any of the major categories into which living organisms are classified. Modern systems recognize five kingdoms: *Prokaryotae* (bacteria), *Protoctista* (algae, protozoans, etc), *Fungi, Plantae*, and *Animalia*. See also **domain** (sense 12) **4** *theol* the eternal sovereignty of God **5** an area of activity: *the kingdom of the mind*

kingdom come *n* **1** the next world **2** *inf* the end of the world (esp in **until kingdom come**) **3** *inf* unconsciousness

kingfish (ˈkɪŋˌfɪʃ) *n, pl* **kingfish** *or* **kingfishes 1** a marine food and game fish occurring in warm American Atlantic coastal waters **2** *Austral* any of various types of trevally, mulloway, and barracouta **3** any of various other large food fishes, esp the Spanish mackerel

kingfisher (ˈkɪŋˌfɪʃə) *n* a bird which has a greenish-blue and orange plumage, a large head, short tail, and long sharp bill, tends to live near water, and feeds on fish [c15 orig. *king's fisher*]

King James Version *or* **Bible** *n* **the** another name for the **Authorized Version**

kingklip (ˈkɪŋˌklɪp) *n* an edible eel-like marine fish [from Afrik., from Du. *koning* king + *klip* rock]

kinglet (ˈkɪŋlɪt) *n* **1** *often derog* the king of a small or insignificant territory **2** *US & Canad* any of various small warblers having a black-edged yellow crown

kingly (ˈkɪŋlɪ) *adj* **kinglier, kingliest 1** appropriate to a king **2** royal ▷ *adv* **3** *poetic or arch* in a manner appropriate to a king > ˈ**kingliness** *n*

kingmaker (ˈkɪŋˌmeɪkə) *n* a person who has control over appointments to positions of authority

king-of-arms *n, pl* **kings-of-arms 1** the highest rank of heraldic officer **2** a person holding this rank

king of the castle *n chiefly Brit* a children's game in which each child attempts to stand alone on a mound by pushing other children off it

king penguin *n* a large New Zealand subantarctic penguin

kingpin (ˈkɪŋˌpɪn) *n* **1** the most important person in an organization **2** Also called (Brit): **swivel pin** a pivot pin that provides a steering joint in a motor vehicle by securing the stub axle to the axle beam **3** *tenpin bowling* the front pin in the triangular arrangement of the ten pins **4** (in ninepins) the central pin in the diamond pattern of the nine pins

king post *n* a vertical post connecting the apex of a triangular roof truss to the tie beam

King's Bench *n* (when the sovereign is male) another name for **Queen's Bench**

King's Counsel *n* (when the sovereign is male) another name for **Queen's Counsel**

King's English *n* (esp when the British sovereign is male) standard Southern British English

king's evidence *n* (when the sovereign is male) another name for **queen's evidence**

king's evil *n* **the** *pathol* a former name for **scrofula** [c14 from the belief that the king's touch would heal scrofula]

Kingsford-Smith (ˈkɪŋzfədˈsmɪθ) *n* Sir **Charles (Edward)** 1897–1935, Australian aviator and pioneer (with Charles Ulm) of trans-Pacific and trans-Tasman flights

king's highway *n* (in Britain, esp when the sovereign is male) any public road or right of way

kingship (ˈkɪŋʃɪp) *n* **1** the position or authority of a king **2** the skill of ruling as a king

king-size *or* **king-sized** *adj* larger or longer than a standard size

Kingsley (ˈkɪŋzlɪ) *n* **1** Sir **Ben** born 1943, British actor. He won an Oscar for his performance in the title role of the film *Gandhi* (1982) **2** **Charles** 1819–75, British clergyman and author. His works include the historical romances *Westward Ho!* (1855) and *Hereward the Wake* (1866) and the children's story *The Water Babies* (1863) **3** his brother, **Henry** 1830–76, British novelist, editor, and journalist, who spent some time in Australia. His works include *Ravenshoe* (1861) and the Anglo-Australian novels *The Recollections of Geoffrey Hamlyn* (1859) and *The Hillyars and the Burtons* (1865)

King's Lynn (ˈkɪŋz ˈlɪn) *n* a market town in E England, in Norfolk on the estuary of the Great Ouse near the Wash: a leading port in the Middle Ages. Pop: 41 281 (1991). Also called: **Lynn, Lynn Regis**

King-Smith (ˈkɪŋˈsmɪθ) *n* **Ronald Gordon**, known as *Dick*. born 1922, British writer for children; his numerous books include *The Sheep Pig* (1984) and the *Sophie* series

Kingston (ˈkɪŋstən) *n* **1** the capital and chief port of Jamaica, on the SE coast: University of the West Indies. Pop: 103 771 (1991) **2** a port in SE Canada, in SE Ontario: the chief naval base of Lake Ontario and a large industrial centre; university (1841). Pop: 56 597 (1991) **3** short for **Kingston upon Thames**
▷ www.jamaicatravelnet.com/info/kingston.html

Kingston upon Hull *n* **1** the official name of **Hull**[1] **2** a unitary authority in NE England, in the East Riding of Yorkshire: formerly (1974–96) part of the county of Humberside. Pop: 243 595 (2001). Area: 71 sq km (27 sq miles)

Kingston upon Thames *n* a borough of SW Greater London, on the River Thames: formed in 1965 by the amalgamation of several former boroughs of Surrey; administrative centre of Surrey. Pop: 147 295 (2001). Area: 38 sq km (15 sq miles)

Kingstown (ˈkɪŋzˌtaʊn) *n* the capital of St Vincent and the Grenadines: a port and resort. Pop: 16 175 (1999 est)

kinin (ˈkaɪnɪn) *n* **1** any of a group of polypeptides in the blood that cause dilation of the blood vessels **2** *bot* another name for **cytokinin** [c20 from Gk *kin(ēma)* motion + -IN]

kink (kɪŋk) *n* **1** a sharp twist or bend in a wire, rope, hair, etc **2** a crick in the neck or similar muscular spasm **3** a flaw or minor difficulty in some undertaking **4** a flaw or idiosyncrasy of personality [c17 from Du.: a curl in a rope]

kinkajou (ˈkɪŋkəˌdʒuː) *n* an arboreal fruit-eating mammal of Central and South America, with a long prehensile tail. Also called: **honey bear** [c18 from F *quincajou*, from Algonquian]

kinky (ˈkɪŋkɪ) *adj* **kinkier, kinkiest** **1** *sl* given to unusual, abnormal, or deviant sexual practices **2** *inf* exhibiting unusual idiosyncrasies of personality **3** *inf* attractive or provocative in a bizarre way: *kinky clothes* **4** tightly looped, as a wire or rope **5** tightly curled, as hair > ˈ**kinkily** *adv* > ˈ**kinkiness** *n*

Kinnock (ˈkɪnək) *n* **Neil** (**Gordon**) born 1942, British Labour politician, born in Wales; leader of the Labour Party (1983–92); European Commissioner (1994–99); vice president of the European Commission from 1999

kino (ˈkiːnəʊ) *n* a dark red resin obtained from various tropical plants, esp an Indian leguminous tree, used as an astringent and in tanning [c18 of West African origin]

Kinross-shire (kɪnˈrɒsʃɪə, -ʃə) *n* a former county of E central Scotland: became part of Tayside region in 1975 and part of Perth and Kinross in 1996

kin selection *n biol* natural selection resulting from altruistic behaviour by animals towards members of the same species, esp their offspring or other relatives

Kinsey (ˈkɪnzɪ) *n* **Alfred Charles** 1894–1956, US zoologist, who directed a survey of human sexual behaviour

kinsfolk (ˈkɪnzˌfəʊk) *pl n* one's family or relatives

Kinshasa (kɪnˈʃɑːzə, -ˈʃɑːsə) *n* the capital of the Democratic Republic of Congo (formerly Zaïre), on the River Congo opposite Brazzaville: became capital of the Belgian Congo in 1929 and of Zaïre in 1960; university (1954). Pop: 4 655 313 (1994 est). Former name (until 1966): **Léopoldville**

kinship (ˈkɪnʃɪp) *n* **1** blood relationship **2** the state of having common characteristics

kinsman (ˈkɪnzmən) *n, pl* **kinsmen** a blood relation or a relation by marriage > ˈ**kinsˌwoman** *fem n*

kiosk (ˈkiːɒsk) *n* **1** a small sometimes movable booth from which cigarettes, newspapers, sweets, etc, are sold **2** *chiefly Brit* a telephone box **3** (in Turkey, Iran, etc) a light open-sided pavilion [c17 from F *kiosque* bandstand, from Turkish, from Persian *kūshk* pavilion]

kip[1] (kɪp) *Brit sl* ▷ *n* **1** sleep or slumber: *to get some kip* **2** a bed or lodging ▷ *vb* **kips, kipping, kipped** (*intr*) **3** to sleep or take a nap **4** (foll by *down*) to prepare for sleep [c18 from ?]

kip[2] (kɪp) *or* **kipskin** *n* the hide of a young animal, esp a calf or lamb [c16 from MDu. *kipp*]

kip[3] (kɪp) *n Austral* a small board used to spin the coins in two-up [c19 from Brit dialect *kep* to catch]

Kipling (ˈkɪplɪŋ) *n* (**Joseph**) **Rudyard** (ˈrʌdjəd) 1865–1936, English poet, short-story writer, and novelist, born in India. His works include *Barrack-Room Ballads* (1892), the two *Jungle Books* (1894, 1895), *Stalky and Co.* (1899), *Kim* (1901), and the *Just So Stories* (1902): Nobel prize for literature 1907

kipper (ˈkɪpə) *n* **1** a fish, esp a herring, that has been cleaned, salted, and smoked **2** a male salmon during the spawning season ▷ *vb* **3** (*tr*) to cure (herrings or other fish) by salting and smoking [OE *cypera*, ?from *coper* COPPER[1], referring to its colour]

kir (kɜː; *French* kir) *n* a drink made from dry white wine and cassis [after Canon F. *Kir* (1876–1968), mayor of Dijon, who is said to have invented it]

kirby grip (ˈkɜːbɪ) *n trademark* a type of hairgrip with one straight and one wavy side

Kirchhoff (*German* ˈkɪrçhɔf) *n* **Gustav Robert** (ˈgʊstaf ˈroːbɛrt) 1824–87, German physicist. With Bunsen he developed the method of spectrum analysis that led to their discovery of caesium (1860) and rubidium (1861): also worked on electrical networks

Kirghiz *or* **Kirgiz** (ˈkɜːgɪz) *n* variant spellings of **Kyrgyz**

Kirghizia *or* **Kirgizia** (kɜːˈgɪzɪə) *n* the former Russian name for **Kyrgyzstan**

Kiribati (ˌkɪrɪˈbætɪ) *n* an independent republic in the W Pacific: comprises 33 islands including Banaba (Ocean Island), the Gilbert and Phoenix Islands, and eight of the Line Islands; part of the British colony of the Gilbert and Ellice Islands until 1975; became self-governing in 1977 and gained full independence in 1979 as the Republic of Kiribati; a member of the Commonwealth. Official languages: English, I-Kiribati (Gilbertese) is widely spoken. Religion: Christian majority. Currency: Australian dollar. Capital: Bairiki islet, in Tarawa atoll. Pop: 94 000 (2001 est). Area: 684 sq km (264 sq miles)
▷ www.tskl.net.ki/Kiribati/tourism/index.htm

Kirin (ˈkiːˈrɪn) *n* a variant transliteration of the Chinese name for **Jilin**

Kiritimati (ˈkɪrɪtɪˈmɑːtɪ) *n* an island in the central Pacific, in Kiribati: one of the Line Islands; the largest atoll in the world. Pop: 3225 (1995). Former name: **Christmas Island**

kirk (kɜːk) *n* **1** a Scottish word for **church** **2** a Scottish church [c12 from ON *kirkja*, from OE *cirice* CHURCH]

Kk

Kirk (kɜːk) *n* **Norman** 1923–74, prime minister of New Zealand (1972–74)

Kirkby (ˈkɜːbɪ) *n* a town in NW England, in Knowsley unitary authority, Merseyside. Pop: 43 017 (1991)

Kirkcaldy (kɜːˈkɔːdɪ) *n* a port in E Scotland, in SE Fife on the Firth of Forth. Pop: 47 155 (1991)

Kirkcudbrightshire (kɜːˈkuːbrɪʃɪə, -ʃə) *n* a former county of SW Scotland, part of Dumfries and Galloway since 1975

Kirklees (ˌkɜːkˈliːz) *n* a unitary authority in N England, in West Yorkshire. Pop: 388 576 (2001). Area: 410 sq km (158 sq miles)

Kirkpatrick (kɜːkˈpætrɪk) *n* **Mount** a mountain in Antarctica, in S Victoria Land in the Queen Alexandra Range. Height: 4528 m (14 856 ft)

kirk session *n* the lowest court of the Presbyterian Church

Kirkuk (kɜːˈkʊk, ˈkɜːkʊk) *n* a city in NE Iraq: centre of a rich oilfield with pipelines to the Mediterranean. Pop: 418 625 (latest est)

Kirkwall (ˈkɜːkˌwɔːl) *n* a town on the N coast of Mainland in the Orkney Islands: administrative centre of the island authority of Orkney: cathedral built by Norsemen (begun in 1137). Pop: 6469 (1991)

kirmess (ˈkɜːmɪs) *n* a variant spelling of **kermis**

Kirov[1] (*Russian* ˈkirəf) *n* a city in NW Russia, on the Vyatka River: an early trading centre; engineering industries. Pop: 466 100 (1995 est). Former name (1780–1934): **Vyatka**

Kirov[2] (*Russian* ˈkirəf) *n* **Sergei Mironovich** (sɪrˈgjej miˈrɔnəvitʃ) 1888–1934, Soviet politician; one of Stalin's chief aides. His assassination was the starting point for Stalin's purge of the Communist Party (1934–38)

Kirovabad (*Russian* kirəvaˈbat) *n* See **Gandzha**

Kirovograd (*Russian* kirəvaˈgrat) *n* a city in the S central Ukraine on the Ingul River: manufacturing centre of a rich agricultural area. Pop: 270 200 (1999 est). Former names: **Yelisavetgrad** (until 1924), **Zinovievsk** (1924–36)

Kirribilli House (ˈkɪrɪˌbɪlɪ) *n* the official Sydney residence of the Australian prime minister

Kirsch (kɪəʃ) *or* **Kirschwasser** (ˈkɪəʃˌvɑːsə) *n* a brandy distilled from cherries, made chiefly in the Black Forest in Germany [G *Kirschwasser* cherry water]

kirtle (ˈkɜːtᵊl) *n arch* **1** a woman's skirt or dress **2** a man's coat [OE *cyrtel*, prob. from *cyrtan* to shorten, ult. from L *curtus* cut short]

Kiruna (*Swedish* ˈkiːruna) *n* a town in N Sweden: iron-mining centre. Pop: 26 150 (1990)

Kisangani (ˌkɪsæŋˈgɑːnɪ) *n* a city in the N Democratic Republic of Congo (formerly Zaïre), at the head of navigation of the River Congo below Stanley Falls: Université Libre du Congo (1963). Pop: 417 517 (1994 est). Former name (until 1966): **Stanleyville**

Kishinev (*Russian* kiʃiˈnjɔf) *n* the capital of Moldova on the Byk River: manufacturing centre of a rich agricultural region; university (1945). Pop: 655 000 (1999 est). Romanian name: **Chişinău**
▷ www.chisinau.md/pmc/en/home.htm
▷ www.turism.md/eng/content/42

Kismayu (kɪsˈmɑːjuː) *n* another name for **Chisimaio**

kismet (ˈkɪzmɛt, ˈkɪs-) *n* **1** *Islam* the will of Allah **2** fate or destiny [c19 from Turkish, from Persian *qismat*, from Ar. *qasama* he divided]

kiss (kɪs) *vb* **1** (*tr*) to touch with the lips or press the lips against as an expression of love, greeting, respect, etc **2** (*intr*) to join lips with another person in an act of love or desire **3** to touch (each other) lightly **4** *billiards, snooker* (of balls) to touch (each other) lightly while moving ▷ *n* **5** a caress with the lips **6** a light touch ▷ See also **kiss off** [OE *cyssan*, from *coss*] > ˈ**kissable** *adj*

KISS *text messaging abbrev for* keep it simple, stupid

kissagram (ˈkɪsəˌgræm) *n* a greetings service in which a person is employed to present greetings by kissing the person celebrating [c20 blend of *kiss* and *telegram*]

kiss-and-tell *n* (*modifier*) denoting the practice of publicizing one's former sexual relationship with a celebrity, esp in the tabloid press: *a kiss-and-tell interview*

kiss curl *n Brit* a circular curl of hair pressed flat against the cheek or forehead

kisser (ˈkɪsə) *n* **1** a person who kisses, esp in a way specified **2** a slang word for **mouth** or **face**

Kissinger (ˈkɪsɪndʒə) *n* **Henry** (**Alfred**) born 1923, US academic and diplomat, born in Germany; assistant to President Nixon for national security affairs (1969–75); Secretary of State (1973–77): shared the Nobel peace prize 1973

kissing gate *n* a gate set in a U- or V-shaped enclosure, allowing only one person to pass through at a time

kiss off *US & Canad sl* ▷ *vb* **1** (*tr, adv*) to ignore or dismiss (a person) rudely or abruptly ▷ *n* **kiss-off** **2** a rude or abrupt dismissal

kiss of life *n* **the** mouth-to-mouth or mouth-to-nose resuscitation in which a person blows gently into the mouth or nose of an unconscious person, allowing the lungs to deflate after each blow

kist (kɪst) *n S African* a large wooden chest in which linen is stored, esp one used to store a bride's trousseau [from Afrik., from Du.: CHEST]

Kistna (ˈkɪstnə) *n* another name for the (River) **Krishna**

Kisumu (kɪˈsuːmuː) *n* a port in W Kenya, in Nyanza province on the NE shore of Lake Victoria: fishing and trading centre. Pop: 201 100 (1991 est)

kit[1] (kɪt) *n* **1** a set of tools, supplies, etc, for use together or for a purpose: *a first-aid kit* **2** the case or container for such a set **3** a set of pieces of equipment sold ready to be assembled **4a** clothing and other personal effects, esp those of a traveller or soldier: *safari kit* **4b** *inf* clothing in general (esp in the phrase **get one's kit off**) **5** *NZ* a flax basket ▷ See also **kit out** [c14 from MDu. *kitte* tankard]

kit[2] (kɪt) *n NZ old-fashioned* a string bag for shopping [from Maori *kete* flax basket]

KIT *text messaging abbrev for* keep in touch

Kitaj (ˈkaɪteɪ) *n* **R B** born 1932, US painter working in Britain, noted for such large figurative works as *If Not, Not* (1976)

Kitakyushu (ˌkiːtəˈkjuːʃuː) *n* a port in Japan, on N Kyushu: formed in 1963 by the amalgamation of the cities of Wakamatsu, Yahata, Tobata, Kokura, and Moji; one of Japan's largest industrial centres. Pop: 1 019 562 (1995)

kitbag (ˈkɪtˌbæg) *n* a canvas or other bag for a serviceman's kit

kitchen (ˈkɪtʃɪn) *n* **a** a room or part of a building equipped for preparing and cooking food **b** (*as modifier*): *a kitchen table* [OE *cycene*, ult. from LL *coquīna*, from L *coquere* to COOK]

kitchen cabinet *n* a group of unofficial advisers to a political leader, esp when considered to be more influential than the offical cabinet

Kitchener[1] (ˈkɪtʃɪnə) *n* an industrial town in SE Canada, in S Ontario: founded in 1806 as Dutch Sand Hills, it was renamed Berlin in 1830 and Kitchener in 1916. Pop: 178 420 (1996)

Kitchener[2] (ˈkɪtʃɪnə) *n* **Horatio Herbert,** 1st Earl Kitchener of Khartoum. 1850–1916, British field marshal. As head of the Egyptian army (1892–98), he expelled the Mahdi from the Sudan (1898), occupying Khartoum; he also commanded British forces (1900–02) in the Boer War and (1902–09) in India. He conducted the mobilization of the British army for World War I as war minister (1914–16); he was drowned on his way to Russia

kitchenette (ˌkɪtʃɪˈnɛt) *n* a small kitchen or part of a room equipped for use as a kitchen

kitchen garden *n* a garden where vegetables and sometimes also fruit are grown

kitchen midden *n archaeol* the site of a large mound of domestic refuse marking a prehistoric settlement; usually including bones, potsherds, etc

kitchen police *pl n inf* US soldiers who have been detailed to work in the kitchen, esp as a punishment

kitchen sink *n* **1** a sink in a kitchen for washing dishes, vegetables, etc **2** (*modifier*) denoting a type of drama or painting of the 1950s depicting sordid reality

kitchen tea *n Austral & NZ old-fashioned* a party held before a wedding to which guests bring items of kitchen equipment as wedding presents

kitchenware ('kɪtʃɪn,wɛə) *n* pots and pans, knives, forks, spoons, etc, used in the kitchen

kite (kaɪt) *n* **1** a light frame covered with a thin material flown in the wind at the end of a length of string **2** *Brit sl* an aeroplane **3** (*pl*) *naut* any of various light sails set in addition to the working sails of a vessel **4** a bird of prey having a long forked tail and long broad wings and usually preying on small mammals and insects **5** *arch* a person who preys on others **6** *commerce* a negotiable paper drawn without any actual transaction or assets and designed to obtain money on credit, give an impression of affluence, etc ▷ *vb* **kites, kiting, kited 7** to issue (fictitious papers) to obtain credit or money **8** (*intr*) to soar and glide [OE *cȳta*]
▷ www.kiteflyers.org

Kite mark *n Brit* the official mark of quality and reliability, in the form of a kite, on articles approved by the British Standards Institution

kitesurfing ('kaɪt,sɜːfɪŋ) *n* the sport of sailing standing up on a surfboard while being pulled along by a large kite > '**kite,surfer** *n*

kith (kɪθ) *n* **kith and kin** one's friends and relations [OE *cȳthth*, from *cūth*; see UNCOUTH]

Kíthira ('kiθira) *n* transliteration of the Modern Greek name for **Cythera**

kit out *or* **up** *vb* **kits, kitting, kitted** (*tr, adv*) *chiefly Brit* **1** to provide with (a kit of personal effects and necessities) **2** to provide with (an outfit of clothes)

kitsch (kɪtʃ) *n* tawdry, vulgarized, or pretentious art, literature, etc, usually with popular appeal [C20 from G] > '**kitschy** *adj*

kitset ('kɪt,sɛt) *n* NZ **a** a piece of furniture supplied in pieces for the purchaser to assemble himself or herself **b** (*as modifier*): *a kitset kitchen*

kitten ('kɪtᵊn) *n* **1** a young cat **2** **have kittens** *Brit inf* to react with disapproval, anxiety, etc: *she had kittens when she got the bill* ▷ *vb* **3** (of cats) to give birth to (young) [C14 from OF *caton*, from CAT; prob. infl. by ME *kiteling*]

kitten heel *n* **1** a low stiletto heel on a woman's shoe **2** a woman's shoe with a low stiletto heel

kittenish ('kɪtᵊnɪʃ) *adj* **1** like a kitten; lively **2** (of a woman) flirtatious, esp coyly flirtatious

kittiwake ('kɪtɪ,weɪk) *n* either of two oceanic gulls having pale grey black-tipped wings and a square-cut tail [C17 imit.]

kitty[1] ('kɪtɪ) *n, pl* **kitties** a diminutive or affectionate name for a **kitten** or **cat** [C18]

kitty[2] ('kɪtɪ) *n, pl* **kitties 1** the pool of bets in certain gambling games **2** any shared fund of money **3** (in bowls) the jack [C19 see KIT[1]]

kitty-cornered *adj* a variant of **cater-cornered**

Kitty Hawk ('kɪtɪ hɔːk) *n* a village in NE North Carolina, near Kill Devil Hill, where the Wright brothers made the first aeroplane flight in the US (1903)

Kitwe ('kɪtweɪ) *n* a city in N Zambia: commercial centre of the Copper Belt. Pop: 338 207 (1990)

Kitzbühel ('kɪtsbuəl) *n* a town in W Austria, in the Tirol: centre for winter sports. Pop: 8223 (1991)

Kivu ('kiːvuː) *n* **Lake** a lake in central Africa, between the Democratic Republic of Congo (formerly Zaïre) and Rwanda at an altitude of 1460 m (4790 ft). Area: 2698 sq km (1042 sq miles). Depth: (maximum) 475 m (1558 ft)

Kiwano (kɪ'wɑːnəʊ) *n, pl* **Kiwanos** *trademark* an edible oval fruit of the passionflower family, having a golden spiky skin, juicy green pulp and many seeds

kiwi ('kiːwiː) *n, pl* **kiwis 1** a nocturnal flightless New Zealand bird having a long beak, stout legs, and weakly barbed feathers **2** *inf except in NZ* a New Zealander **3** NZ *inf* a lottery [C19 from Maori, imit.: NZ sense from the *Golden Kiwi Lottery*]

Kiwiana (,kiːwɪ'ɑːnə) *pl n Austral and NZ* collectable objects, ornaments, etc, esp dating from the 1950s or 1960s, relating to the history or popular culture of New Zealand

kiwi fruit *n* the fuzzy edible fruit of an Asian climbing plant. Also called: **Chinese gooseberry**

Kizil Irmak (kɪ'zɪl ɪə'mɑːk) *n* a river in Turkey, rising in the Kizil Dag and flowing southwest, northwest, and northeast to the Black Sea: the longest river in Asia Minor. Length: about 1150 km (715 miles). Ancient name: **Halys** ('heɪlɪs)

KKK *abbrev for* Ku Klux Klan

Klagenfurt (*German* 'klaːgənfurt) *n* a city in S Austria, capital of Carinthia province: tourist centre. Pop: 89 415 (1991)

Klaipeda (*Russian* 'klajpɪdə) *n* a port in Lithuania on the Baltic: shipbuilding and fish canning. Pop: 202 484 (2000 est). German name: **Memel**

Klan (klæn) *n* (usually preceded by *the*) short for **Ku Klux Klan** > '**Klanism** *n*

klaxon ('klæksᵊn) *n* a type of loud horn formerly used on motor vehicles [C20 former trademark]

Kléber (*French* klebɛr) *n* **Jean Baptiste** (ʒɑ̃ batist) 1753–1800, French general, who succeeded Napoleon as commander in Egypt (1799); assassinated

Klee (*German* kleː) *n* **Paul** (paul) 1879–1940, Swiss painter and etcher. A founder member of *der Blaue Reiter*, he subsequently evolved an intensely personal style of unusual fantasy and wit

Kk

Kleenex ('kliːnɛks) *n, pl* **Kleenex** *or* **Kleenexes** *trademark* a kind of soft paper tissue, used esp as a handkerchief

Klein (klaɪn) *n* **Melanie** 1882–1960, Austrian psychoanalyst resident in England (from 1926), noted for her work on child behaviour

Klein bottle (klaɪn) *n maths* a three-dimensional surface formed by inserting the smaller end of an open tapered tube through the surface of the tube and making this end stretch to fit the other end [after Felix *Klein* (1849–1925), G mathematician]

kleinhuisie ('kleɪn,heɪsɪ) *n S African* an outside lavatory [C20 Afrik. lit.: little house]

Kleist (klaɪst) *n* (**Bernd**) **Heinrich** (**Wilhelm**) **von** ('hainrɪç fɔn) 1777–1811, German dramatist, poet, and short-story writer. His plays include *The Broken Pitcher* (1808), *Penthesilea* (1808), and *The Prince of Homburg* (published 1821)

Klemperer ('klɛmpərə) *n* **Otto** 1885–1973, orchestral conductor, born in Germany. He was best known for his interpretations of Beethoven

kleptocratic (,klɛptəʊ'krætɪk) *adj* (of a government, state, etc) characterized by corruption amongst those in power

kleptomania (,klɛptəʊ'meɪnɪə) *n psychol* a strong impulse to steal, esp when there is no obvious motivation [C19 *klepto-* from Gk, from *kleptein* to steal + -MANIA] > ,**klepto'mani,ac** *n*

klieg light (kliːg) *n* an intense carbon-arc light used in producing films [C20 after John H. *Kliegl* (1869–1959) & his brother Anton (1872–1927), German-born American inventors]

Kline (klaɪn) *n* **Franz** (frænts) 1910–62, US abstract expressionist painter. His works are characterized by heavy black strokes on a white or grey background

klipspringer ('klɪp,sprɪŋə) *n* a small agile antelope inhabiting rocky regions of Africa south of the Sahara

[c18 from Afrik., from Du. *klip* rock + *springer*, from *springen* to SPRING]

Klondike ('klɒndaɪk) *n* **1** a region of NW Canada, in the Yukon in the basin of the Klondike River: site of rich gold deposits, discovered in 1896 but largely exhausted by 1910. Area: about 2100 sq km (800 sq miles) **2** a river in NW Canada, rising in the Yukon and flowing west to the Yukon River. Length: about 145 km (90 miles)

kloof (klu:f) *n* a mountain pass or gorge in southern Africa [c18 from Afrik., from MDu. *clove* a cleft]

klystron ('klɪstrɒn) *n* an electron tube for the amplification or generation of microwaves [c20 *klys-*, from Gk *kluzein* to wash over + -TRON]

km *symbol for* kilometre

K-meson *n* another name for **kaon**

km/h *abbrev for* kilometres per hour

knack (næk) *n* **1** a skilful, ingenious, or resourceful way of doing something **2** a particular talent or aptitude, esp an intuitive one [c14 prob. var. of *knak* sharp knock, imit.]

knacker ('nækə) *Brit* ▷ *n* **1** a person who buys up old horses for slaughter **2** a person who buys up old buildings and breaks them up for scrap **3** *Irish sl* a despicable person ▷ *vb* **4** (*tr; usually passive*) *sl* to tire [c16 prob. from *nacker* saddler, prob. of Scand. origin] > **'knackery** *n*

knacker's yard *n Brit* **1** a slaughterhouse for horses **2** *inf* destruction because of being beyond all usefulness (esp in the phrase **ready for the knacker's yard**)

knag (næg) *n* **1** a knot in wood **2** a wooden peg [c15 ?from Low G *knagge*]

knap (næp) *vb* **knaps, knapping, knapped** (*tr*) *dialect* to hit or chip [c15 (in the sense: to strike with a sharp sound): imit] > **'knapper** *n*

knapping hammer *n* a hammer used for breaking and shaping stones

knapsack ('næp,sæk) *n* a canvas or leather bag carried strapped on the back or shoulder [c17 from Low G, prob. from *knappen* to bite + *sack* bag]

knapweed ('næp,wi:d) *n* any of several plants having purplish thistle-like flowers [c15 *knopwed*, from *knop* of Gmc origin + WEED]

knar (nɑ:) *n* a variant of **knur** [c14 *knarre* rough stone, knot on a tree]

knave (neɪv) *n* **1** *arch* a dishonest man **2** another word for **jack** (the playing card) **3** *obs* a male servant [OE *cnafa*] > **'knavish** *adj*

knavery ('neɪvərɪ) *n, pl* **knaveries 1** a deceitful or dishonest act **2** dishonest conduct; trickery

knead (ni:d) *vb* (*tr*) **1** to work and press (a soft substance, such as bread dough) into a uniform mixture with the hands **2** to squeeze or press with the hands **3** to make by kneading [OE *cnedan*] > **'kneader** *n*

knee (ni:) *n* **1** the joint of the human leg connecting the tibia and fibula with the femur and protected in front by the patella. Technical name: **genu 2a** the area surrounding and above this joint **2b** (*modifier*) reaching or covering the knee: *knee socks* **3** the upper surface of a sitting person's thigh: *the child sat on her mother's knee* **4** a corresponding or similar part in other vertebrates **5** the part of a garment that covers the knee **6** anything resembling a knee in action or shape **7** any of the hollow rounded protuberances that project upwards from the roots of the swamp cypress **8 bend** *or* **bow the knee** to kneel or submit **9 bring someone to his** (*or* **her**) **knees** to force someone into submission ▷ *vb* **knees, kneeing, kneed 10** (*tr*) to strike, nudge, or push with the knee [OE *cnēow*]

kneecap ('ni:,kæp) *n* **1** *anat* a nontechnical name for **patella** ▷ *vb* **kneecaps, kneecapping, kneecapped** (*tr*) **2** (esp of certain terrorist groups) to shoot (a person) in the kneecap

knee-deep *adj* **1** so deep as to reach or cover the knees **2** (*postpositive; often foll by in*) **2a** sunk or covered to the knees: *knee-deep in sand* **2b** deeply involved: *knee-deep in work*

knee-high *adj* another word for **knee-deep** (sense 1)

kneehole ('ni:,həʊl) *n* a space for the knees, esp under a desk

knee jerk *n* **1** *physiol* an outward reflex kick of the lower leg caused by a sharp tap on the quadriceps tendon just below the kneecap ▷ *modifier*. **kneejerk 2** made or occurring as a predictable and automatic response, without thought: *a kneejerk reaction*

kneel (ni:l) *vb* **kneels, kneeling, knelt** *or* **kneeled 1** (*intr*) to rest, fall, or support oneself on one's knees ▷ *n* **2** the act or position of kneeling [OE *cnēowlian*; see KNEE] > **'kneeler** *n*

knees-up *n, pl* **knees-ups** *Brit inf* a lively party [c20 after popular song *Knees up, Mother Brown!*]

knell (nɛl) *n* **1** the sound of a bell rung to announce a death or a funeral **2** something that precipitates or indicates death or destruction ▷ *vb* **3** (*intr*) to ring a knell **4** (*tr*) to proclaim by or as if by a tolling bell [OE *cnyll*]

Kneller ('nɛlə) *n* Sir **Godfrey** ?1646–1723, portrait painter at the English court, born in Germany

knelt (nɛlt) *vb* a past tense and past participle of **kneel**

Knesset ('knɛsɪt) *n* the representative assembly of Israel [c20 Heb., lit.: gathering]

knew (nju:) *vb* the past tense of **know**

knickerbocker glory ('nɪkə,bɒkə) *n* a rich confection consisting of layers of ice cream, jelly, cream, and fruit, served in a tall glass

knickerbockers ('nɪkə,bɒkəz) *pl n* baggy breeches fastened with a band at the knee or above the ankle. Also called (US): **knickers** [c19 regarded as the traditional dress of the Du. settlers in America; after Diedrich *Knickerbocker*, fictitious author of Washington Irving's *History of New York* (1809)]

knickers ('nɪkəz) *pl n* an undergarment for women covering the lower trunk and sometimes the thighs and having separate legs or leg-holes [c19 contraction of KNICKERBOCKERS]

knick-knack *or* **nick-nack** ('nɪk,næk) *n* **1** a cheap ornament **2** an ornamental article of furniture, dress, etc [c17 by reduplication from *knack*, in obs. sense: toy]

knife (naɪf) *n, pl* **knives** (naɪvz) **1** a cutting instrument consisting of a sharp-edged blade of metal fitted into a handle or onto a machine **2** a similar instrument used as a weapon **3 have one's knife in someone** to have a grudge against someone **4 under the knife** undergoing a surgical operation ▷ *vb* **knifes, knifing, knifed** (*tr*) **5** to stab or kill with a knife **6** to betray or depose in an underhand way [OE *cnīf*] > **'knife,like** *adj*

knife edge *n* **1** the sharp cutting edge of a knife **2** any sharp edge, esp an arête **3** a sharp-edged wedge of hard material on which the beam of a balance pivots **4** a critical point

knight (naɪt) *n* **1** (in medieval Europe) **1a** (originally) a person who served his lord as a mounted and heavily armed soldier **1b** (later) a gentleman with the military and social standing of this rank **2** (in modern times) a person invested by a sovereign with a nonhereditary rank and dignity usually in recognition of personal services, achievements, etc **3** a chess piece, usually shaped like a horse's head **4** a heroic champion of a lady or of a cause or principle **5** a member of the Roman class below the senators ▷ *vb* **6** (*tr*) to make (a person) a knight [OE *cniht* servant]

Knight (naɪt) *n* Dame **Laura** 1887–1970, British painter, noted for her paintings of Gypsies, the ballet, and the circus

knight errant *n, pl* **knights errant** (esp in medieval romance) a knight who wanders in search of deeds of courage, chivalry, etc > **knight errantry** *n*

knighthood ('naɪthʊd) *n* **1** the order, dignity, or rank of

a knight **2** the qualities of a knight
knightly ('naɪtlɪ) *adj* of, relating to, resembling, or befitting a knight > '**knightliness** *n*
knight of the road *n inf or facetious* **1** a tramp **2** a commercial traveller **3** a lorry driver
Knights Hospitallers *pl n* a military Christian religious order founded about the time of the first crusade (1096–99)
Knight Templar *n, pl* **Knights Templars** *or* **Knights Templar** another term for **Templar**
kniphofia (nɪf'əʊfɪə) *n* the Latin name for **red-hot poker** [C19 after Johann Hieronymus *Kniphof* (1704–63), G professor of medicine]
knit (nɪt) *vb* **knits, knitting, knitted** *or* **knit 1** to make (a garment, etc) by looping and entwining (wool) by hand by means of long eyeless needles (**knitting needles**) or by machine (**knitting machine**) **2** to join or be joined together closely **3** to draw (the brows) together or (of the brows) to come together, as in frowning or concentrating **4** (of a broken bone) to join together; heal ▷ *n* **5a** a fabric made by knitting **5b** (*in combination*): *a heavy knit* [OE *cnyttan* to tie in] > '**knitter** *n*
knitting ('nɪtɪŋ) *n* knitted work or the process of producing it
▷ wwww.woolworks.org
▷ www.tkga.com
▷ www.knitting-and-crochet-guild.org.uk
knitwear ('nɪt,wɛə) *n* knitted clothes, esp sweaters
knives (naɪvz) *n* the plural of **knife**
knob (nɒb) *n* **1** a rounded projection from a surface, such as a lump on a tree trunk **2** a handle of a door, drawer, etc, esp one that is rounded **3** a round hill or knoll ▷ *vb* **knobs, knobbing, knobbed 4** (*tr*) to supply or ornament with knobs **5** (*intr*) to bulge [C14 from MLow G *knobbe* knot in wood] > '**knobbly** *adj* > '**knobby** *adj* > '**knob,like** *adj*
knobkerrie ('nɒb,kɛrɪ), **knobkierie,** *or* **knobstick** *n* a stick with a round knob at the end, used as a club or missile by South African tribesmen [C19 from Afrik., from *knop* knob, from MDu. *cnoppe* + *kierie* stick, from Khoikhoi *kīrri*]
knock (nɒk) *vb* **1** (*tr*) to give a blow or push to **2** (*intr*) to rap sharply with the knuckles, a hard object, etc: *to knock at the door* **3** (*tr*) to make or force by striking: *to knock a hole in the wall* **4** (*intr; usually foll by against*) to collide (with) **5** (*tr*) to bring into a certain condition by hitting: *to knock someone unconscious* **6** (*tr*) *inf* to criticize adversely **7** (*intr*) Also: **pink** (of an internal-combustion engine) to emit a metallic noise as a result of faulty combustion **8** (*intr*) (of a bearing, esp one in an engine) to emit a regular characteristic sound as a result of wear **9** *Brit sl* to have sexual intercourse with (a person) **10 knock (a person) into the middle of next week** *inf* to hit (a person) with a very heavy blow **11 knock on the head 11a** to daze or kill (a person) by striking on the head **11b** to prevent the further development of (a plan) ▷ *n* **12a** a blow, push, or rap: *he gave the table a knock* **12b** the sound so caused **13** the sound of knocking in an engine or bearing **14** *inf* a misfortune, rebuff, or setback **15** *inf* criticism ▷ See also **knock about, knock back,** etc [OE *cnocian*, imit.]
knock about *or* **around** *vb* **1** (*intr, adv*) to wander about aimlessly **2** (*intr, prep*) to travel about, esp as resulting in varied experience: *he's knocked about the world* **3** (*intr, adv; foll by with*) to associate **4** (*tr, adv*) to treat brutally: *he knocks his wife about* **5** (*tr, adv*) to consider or discuss informally ▷ *adj* **knockabout 6** tough; boisterous: *knockabout farce*
knock back *vb* (*tr, adv*) *inf* **1** to drink, esp quickly **2** to cost **3** to reject or refuse **4** to shock; disconcert ▷ *n* **knock-back 5** *sl* a refusal or rejection **6** *prison sl* failure to obtain parole
knock down *vb* (*tr, adv*) **1** to strike to the ground with a blow, as in boxing **2** (in auctions) to declare (an article) sold **3** to demolish **4** to dismantle for ease of transport **5** *inf* to reduce (a price, etc) **6** *Austral sl* to spend (a cheque) **7** *Austral sl* to drink ▷ *adj* **knockdown** (*prenominal*) **8** powerful: *a knockdown blow* **9** *chiefly Brit* cheap: *a knockdown price* **10** easily dismantled: *knockdown furniture*
knocker ('nɒkə) *n* **1** an object, usually made of metal, attached to a door by a hinge and used for knocking **2** *inf* a person who finds fault or disparages **3** (*usually pl*) *sl* a female breast **4** a person or thing that knocks **5 on the knocker** *inf* promptly: *you pay on the knocker here*
knocking copy *n* publicity material designed to denigrate a competing product
knocking-shop *n Brit* a slang word for **brothel**
knock-knee *n* a condition in which the legs are bent inwards causing the knees to touch when standing > ,**knock-'kneed** *adj*
knock off *vb* (*mainly adv*) **1** (*intr, also prep*) *inf* to finish work: *we knocked off an hour early* **2** (*tr*) *inf* to make or do hastily or easily: *to knock off a novel in a week* **3** (*tr; also prep*) *inf* to reduce the price of (an article) **4** (*tr*) *sl* to kill **5** (*tr*) *sl* to rob or steal: *to knock off a bank* **6** (*tr*) *sl* to stop doing something, used as a command: *knock it off!* ▷ *n* **knockoff 7** *inf* **7a** an illegal imitation of a well-known product **7b** (*as modifier*): *knockoff merchandise*
knock-on *rugby* ▷ *n* **1** the infringement of playing the ball forward with the hand or arm ▷ *vb* **knock on** (*adv*) **2** to play (the ball) forward with the hand or arm
knock-on effect *n* the indirect result of an action: *the number of redundancies was not great but there were as many again from the knock-on effect*
knockout ('nɒk,aʊt) *n* **1** the act of rendering unconscious **2** a blow that renders an opponent unconscious **3a** a competition in which competitors are eliminated progressively **3b** (*as modifier*): *a knockout contest* **4** *inf* a person or thing that is overwhelmingly impressive or attractive: *she's a knockout* ▷ *vb* **knock out** (*tr, adv*) **5** to render unconscious, esp by a blow **6** *boxing* to defeat (an opponent) by a knockout **7** to destroy or injure badly **8** to eliminate, esp in a knockout competition **9** *inf* to overwhelm or amaze: *I was knocked out by that new song* **10 knock the bottom out of** *inf* to invalidate (an argument)

knockout drops *pl n sl* a drug secretly put into someone's drink to cause stupefaction. See also **Mickey Finn**
knock up *vb* (*adv, mainly tr*) **1** Also: **knock together** *inf* to assemble quickly: *to knock up a set of shelves* **2** *Brit inf* to waken; rouse: *to knock someone up early* **3** *sl* to make pregnant **4** *Brit inf* to exhaust **5** *cricket* to score (runs) **6** (*intr*) *tennis, squash, etc* to practise, esp before a match ▷ *n* **knock-up 7** a practice session at tennis, squash, etc
knoll (nəʊl) *n* a small rounded hill [OE *cnoll*] > '**knolly** *adj*
Knossos *or* **Cnossus** ('nɒsəs, 'knɒs-) *n* a ruined city in N central Crete: remains of the Minoan Bronze Age civilization
knot[1] (nɒt) *n* **1** any of various fastenings formed by looping and tying a piece of rope, cord, etc, in upon itself or to another piece of rope **2** a prescribed method of tying a particular knot **3** a tangle, as in hair or string **4** a decorative bow, as of ribbon **5** a small cluster or huddled group **6** a tie or bond: *the marriage knot* **7** a difficult problem **8a** a hard mass of wood where a branch joins the trunk of a tree **8b** a cross section of this visible on a piece of timber **9** a sensation of constriction, caused by tension or nervousness: *his stomach was tying itself in knots* **10** *pathol* a lump of vessels or fibres formed in a part, as in a muscle **11** a unit of velocity used by ships and aircraft, being one nautical mile (about 1.15 statute miles or 1.85 km) per hour **12 at a rate of knots** very fast **13 tie (someone) in knots** to completely perplex (someone) ▷ *vb* **knots, knotting, knotted 14** (*tr*) to tie or fasten in a knot **15** to form or cause to form into a knot **16** (*tr*) to entangle or become entangled **17** (*tr*) to make (an article or design) by tying

thread in ornamental knots [OE *cnotta*] > **'knotted** *adj* > **'knotter** *n* > **'knotless** *adj*
▷ www.realknots.com/

knot² (nɒt) *n* a small northern sandpiper with a short bill and grey plumage [c15 from ?]

knot garden *n* (esp formerly) a formal garden of intricate design

knotgrass ('nɒt,grɑːs) *n* **1** Also called: **allseed** a weed whose small green flowers produce numerous seeds **2** any of several related plants

knothole ('nɒt,həʊl) *n* a hole in a piece of wood where a knot has been

knotty ('nɒtɪ) *adj* **knottier, knottiest 1** (of wood, rope, etc) full of or characterized by knots **2** extremely difficult or intricate

knout (naʊt) *n* a stout whip used formerly in Russia as an instrument of punishment [c17 from Russian *knut*, of Scand. origin]

know (nəʊ) *vb* **knows, knowing, knew, known** (*mainly tr*) **1** (*also intr; may take a clause as object*) to be or feel certain of the truth or accuracy of (a fact, etc) **2** to be acquainted or familiar with: *she's known him five years* **3** to have a familiarity or grasp of: *he knows French* **4** (*also intr; may take a clause as object*) to understand, be aware of, or perceive (facts, etc): *he knows the answer now* **5** (foll by *how*) to be sure or aware of (how to be or do something) **6** to experience, esp deeply: *to know poverty* **7** to be intelligent, informed, or sensible enough (to do something) **8** (*may take a clause as object*) to be able to distinguish or discriminate **9** *arch* to have sexual intercourse with **10 know what's what** to know how one thing or things in general work **11 you never know** things are uncertain ▷ *n* **12 in the know** *inf* aware or informed [OE *gecnāwan*] > **'knowable** *adj* > **'knower** *n*

know-all *n inf, disparaging* a person who pretends or appears to know a great deal

know-how *n inf* **1** ingenuity, aptitude, or skill **2** commercial and saleable knowledge of how to do a particular thing

knowing ('nəʊɪŋ) *adj* **1** suggesting secret knowledge **2** wise, shrewd, or clever **3** deliberate ▷ *n* **4 there is no knowing** one cannot tell > **'knowingly** *adv* > **'knowingness** *n*

knowledge ('nɒlɪdʒ) *n* **1** the facts or experiences known by a person or group of people **2** the state of knowing **3** consciousness or familiarity gained by experience or learning **4** erudition or informed learning **5** specific information about a subject **6 to my knowledge 6a** as I understand it **6b** as I know

knowledgeable *or* **knowledgable** ('nɒlɪdʒəbᵊl) *adj* possessing or indicating much knowledge > **'knowledgeably** *or* **'knowledgably** *adv*

knowledge-based system *n computing* an expert system. Abbrev: **KBS**

knowledge economy *n* an economy in which information services are dominant as an area of growth

knowledge worker *n* a person employed to produce or analyse ideas and information

Knowles (nəʊəlz) *n* **Beyoncé** (beɪ'jɒnseɪ) born 1981, US singer, songwriter, and actress. A member of the hugely successful Destiny's Child, she later found solo success with *Dangerously in Love* (2003) and the single "Crazy in Love" (2003)

known (nəʊn) *vb* **1** the past participle of **know** ▷ *adj* **2** identified: *a known criminal*

Knowsley ('nəʊzlɪ) *n* a unitary authority of NW England, in Merseyside. Pop: 150 468 (2001). Area: 97 sq km (38 sq miles)

Knox (nɒks) *n* **1 John** ?1514–72, Scottish theologian and historian. After exile in England and on the Continent (1547–59), he returned to Scotland in 1559 and established the Presbyterian Church of Scotland (1560). His chief historical work was the *History of the Reformation in Scotland* (1586) **2 Ronald (Arbuthnott)** 1888–1957, British priest and author. A convert to Roman Catholicism, he is noted for his translation of the Vulgate (1945–49)

Knox-Johnston (,nɒks'dʒɒnstən) *n* Sir **Robin (William Robert Patrick)** born 1939, British yachtsman. He was the first to sail round the world alone nonstop (1968–69)

Knoxville ('nɒksvɪl) *n* an industrial city in E Tennessee, on the Tennessee River: state capital (1796–1812; 1817–19). Pop: 173 890 (2000)

knuckle ('nʌkᵊl) *n* **1** a joint of a finger, esp that connecting a finger to the hand **2** a joint of veal, pork, etc, consisting of the part of the leg below the knee joint **3 near the knuckle** *inf* approaching indecency ▷ *vb* **knuckles, knuckling, knuckled 4** (*tr*) to rub or press with the knuckles **5** (*intr*) to keep the knuckles on the ground while shooting a marble ▷ See also **knuckle down, knuckle under** [c14] > **'knuckly** *adj*

knucklebones ('nʌkᵊl,bəʊnz) *n* (*functioning as sing*) a less common name for **jacks** (the game)

knuckle down *vb* (*intr, adv*) *inf* to apply oneself diligently: *to knuckle down to some work*

knuckle-duster *n* (*often pl*) a metal bar fitted over the knuckles, often with holes for the fingers, for inflicting injury by a blow with the fist

knucklehead ('nʌkᵊl,hɛd) *n inf* a fool; idiot > **'knuckle,headed** *adj*

knuckle under *vb* (*intr, adv*) to give way under pressure or authority; yield

knur, knurr (nɜː), *or* **knar** *n* a knot or protuberance in a tree trunk or in wood [c16 *knor*; cf. KNAR]

knurl *or* **nurl** (nɜːl) *vb* (*tr*) **1** to impress with a series of fine ridges or serrations ▷ *n* **2** a small ridge, esp one of a series [c17 prob. from KNUR]

Knut (kə'njuːt) *n* a variant spelling of **Canute**

KO *or* **k.o.** ('keɪ'əʊ) *vb* **KO's, KO'ing, KO'd** *or* **k.o.'s, k.o.'ing, k.o.'d,** *n, pl* **KO's** *or* **k.o.'s** a slang term for **knockout** or **knock out**

koala *or* **koala bear** (kəʊ'ɑːlə) *n* a slow-moving Australian arboreal marsupial, having dense greyish fur and feeding on eucalyptus leaves. Also called (Austral): **native bear** [from Abor.]

koan ('kəʊæn) *n* (in Zen Buddhism) a problem that admits no logical solution [from Japanese]

Kobarid ('kəʊbə,riːd; *Serbo-Croat* 'kɔba,rid) *n* a village in Slovenia on the Isonzo River: part of Italy until 1947; scene of the defeat of the Italians by Austro-German forces (1917). Italian name: **Caporetto**

Kobe ('kəʊbɪ) *n* a port in S Japan, on S Honshu on Osaka Bay: formed in 1889 by the amalgamation of Hyogo and Kobe; a major industrial complex, producing ships, steel, and rubber goods. Pop: 1 423 830 (1995)

København (købən'haun) *n* the Danish name for **Copenhagen**

Koblenz *or* **Coblenz** (*German* 'koːblɛnts) *n* a city in W central Germany, in the Rhineland-Palatinate at the confluence of the Rivers Moselle and Rhine: ruled by the archbishop-electors of Trier from 1018 until occupied by the French in 1794; passed to Prussia in 1815, becoming capital of the Rhine Province (1824–1945) and of the Rhineland-Palatinate (1946–50); wine trade centre. Pop: 108 700 (1999 est). Latin name: **Confluentes** (,kɒnflʊ'ɛntiːz)

kobold ('kɒbəʊld) *n German myth* **1** a mischievous household sprite **2** a spirit that haunts mines [c19 from G; see COBALT]

Koch (*German* kɔx) *n* **Robert** ('roːbɛrt) 1843–1910, German bacteriologist, who isolated the anthrax bacillus (1876), the tubercle bacillus (1882), and the cholera bacillus (1883): Nobel prize for physiology or medicine 1905

Kochi (kəʊ'tʃiː) *n* a port in SW Japan, on central Shikoku on Urado Bay. Pop: 322 077 (1995 est)

kochia ('kɒ'ʃiːə) *n* an annual plant with ornamental

foliage that turns purple-red in late summer [c19 after W.D.J. *Koch*, G botanist]

Kodály (*Hungarian* 'koda:j) *n* **Zoltán** ('zolta:n) 1882–1967, Hungarian composer. His works were often inspired by native folk songs and include the comic opera *Háry János* (1926) and *Psalmus Hungaricus* (1923) for chorus and orchestra

Kodiak ('kəʊdɪ,æk) *n* an island in S Alaska, in the Gulf of Alaska: site of the first European settlement in Alaska, made by Russians in 1784. Pop: 13 309 (1990). Area: 8974 sq km (3465 sq miles)

Kodiak bear *or* **Kodiak** *n* a large variety of the brown bear inhabiting the W coast of Alaska and neighbouring islands, esp Kodiak

koeksister ('kʊk,sɪstə) *n S African* a plaited doughnut deep-fried and soaked in syrup [Afrik. but possibly of Malay origin]

koel ('kəʊəl) *n* any of several parasitic cuckoos of S and SE Asia and Australia [c19 from Hindi, from Sansk. *kokila*]

Koestler ('kɜ:stlə) *n* **Arthur** 1905–83, British writer, born in Hungary. Of his early antitotalitarian novels *Darkness at Noon* (1940) is outstanding. His later works, *The Sleepwalkers* (1959), *The Act of Creation* (1964), and *The Ghost in the Machine* (1967) reflect his interest in science, philosophy, and psychology. He committed suicide

Kofu ('kəʊfu:) *n* a city in central Japan, on S Honshu: textiles. Pop: 201 123 (1995 est)

Kogi ('kəʊgɪ) *n* a state of W Nigeria. Capital: Lokoja. Pop: 2 346 946 (1995 est)

koha ('kəʊhə) *n NZ* a gift or donation [Maori]

kohanga reo ('kɔ:hɑ:ŋɑ: 'reɪɔ:) *n NZ* an infant class in which the lessons are conducted in Maori [Maori, lit.: language nest]

Kohima ('kəʊhɪ,mɑ:) *n* a city in NE India, capital of Nagaland, near the Burmese border: centre of fierce fighting in World War II, when it was surrounded by the Japanese but not captured (1944). Pop: 21 545 (latest est)

kohl (kəʊl) *n* a cosmetic powder used, originally esp in Muslim and Asian countries, to darken the area around the eyes [c18 from Ar. *kohl*; see ALCOHOL]

Kohl (kəʊl) *n* **Helmut** ('hɛlmu:t) born 1930, German statesman: chancellor of West Germany (1982–90) and of Germany (1990–98)

Köhler (*German* 'kø:lər) *n* **Wolfgang** ('vɔlfgaŋ) 1887–1967, German psychologist, a leading exponent of Gestalt psychology

kohlrabi (kəʊl'rɑ:bɪ) *n, pl* **kohlrabies** a cultivated variety of cabbage whose thickened stem is eaten as a vegetable. Also called: **turnip cabbage** [c19 from G, from It. *cavoli rape* (pl), from *cavolo* cabbage (from L *caulis*) + *rapa* turnip (from L)]

koi (kɔɪ) *n* any of various ornamental forms of the common carp [Japanese]

koine ('kɔɪni:) *n* a common language among speakers of different languages; lingua franca [from Gk *koinē dialektos* common language]

Koine ('kɔɪni:) *n* (*sometimes not cap*) **the** the ancient Greek dialect that was the lingua franca of the empire of Alexander the Great and in Roman times

Koizumi (,kɔɪ'zu:mɪ) *n* **Junichiro** (,junɪ'kiro) born 1941, Japanese politician; prime minister from 2001

Kokand (*Russian* ka'kant) *n* a city in NE Uzbekistan, in the Fergana valley. Pop: 184 000 (1998 est)

kokanee (kəʊ'kænɪ) *n* a landlocked salmon of lakes in W North America: a variety of sockeye [prob. from *Kokanee* Creek, in SE British Columbia]

Koko Nor ('kəʊ'kəʊ 'nɔ:) *or* **Kuku Nor** *n* a lake in W China, in Qinghai province in the NE Tibetan Highlands at an altitude of about 3000 m (10 000 ft): the largest lake in China. Area: about 4100 sq km (1600 sq miles). Chinese name: **Qinghai**

Kokoschka (*German* ko'kɔʃka, 'kɔkɔʃka) *n* **Oskar** ('ɔskar) 1886–1980, Austrian expressionist painter and dramatist, noted for his landscapes and portraits

Kokura (,kəʊkə'rɑ:) *n* a former city in SW Japan, on N Kyushu: merged with adjacent townships in 1963 to form the new city of **Kitakyushu**

kola ('kəʊlə) *n* a variant spelling of **cola**

kola nut *n* a variant spelling of **cola nut**

Kola Peninsula ('kəʊlə) *n* a peninsula in NW Russia, between the Barents and White Seas: forms most of the Murmansk region. Area: about 130 000 sq km (50 000 sq miles)

Kolar Gold Fields (kəʊ'lɑ:) *n* a city in S India, in SE Karnataka: a major gold-mining centre since 1881. Pop: 83 219 (1991 est)

Kolding (*Danish* 'kɔleŋ) *n* a port in Denmark, in E Jutland at the head of **Kolding Fjord** (an inlet of the Little Belt) Pop: 59 558 (1995)

Kolhapur (,kəʊlhɑ:'pʊə) *n* a city in W India, in S Maharashtra: university (1963). Pop: 406 370 (1991)

kolinsky (kə'lɪnskɪ) *n, pl* **kolinskies** **1** any of various Asian minks **2** the rich tawny fur of this animal [c19 from Russian *kolinski* of Kola: see KOLA PENINSULA]

kolkhoz (kɒl'hɔ:z) *n* a Russian collective farm [c20 from Russian, short for *kollektivnoe khozyaistvo* collective farm]

Kolmar ('kɔlmar) *n* the German name for **Colmar**

Kolmogorov (,kɒlmɒ'gɔ:rɒf) *n* **Andrei Nikolaevich** (an'drjej nika'lajəvitʃ) (1903–87), Soviet mathematician, who made important contributions to the theoretical foundations of probability

Köln (kœln) *n* the German name for **Cologne**

Kol Nidre (kɔ:l 'nɪdreɪ) *n Judaism* **1** the evening service with which Yom Kippur begins **2** the opening prayer of that service [Aramaic *kōl nidhrē* all the vows; the prayer's opening words]

Kolomna (*Russian* ka'lɔmnə) *n* a city in the W central Russia, at the confluence of the Moskva and Oka Rivers: railway engineering centre. Pop: 151 500 (1999 est)

Kolyma (*Russian* kəli'ma) *n* a river in NE Russia, rising in the Kolyma Mountains north of the Sea of Okhotsk and flowing generally north to the East Siberian Sea. Length: 2600 km (1615 miles)

Kolyma Range *n* a mountain range in NE Russia, in NE Siberia, extending about 1100 km (700 miles) between the Kolyma River and the Sea of Okhotsk. Highest peak: 1862 m (6109 ft)

Komati (kə'mɑ:tɪ, 'kəʊmətɪ) *n* a river in southern Africa, rising in E South Africa and flowing east through Swaziland and Mozambique to the Indian Ocean at Delagoa Bay. Length: about 800 km (500 miles)

komatik ('kəʊmætɪk) *n* a sledge having wooden runners and crossbars bound with rawhide, used by Inuit [c20 from Inuktitut]

Komi Republic ('kəʊmɪ) *n* a constituent republic of NW Russia: annexed by the princes of Moscow in the 14th century. Capital: Syktyvkar. Pop: 1 135 000 (2000 est). Area: 415 900 sq km (160 540 sq miles)

Kommunarsk (*Russian* kəmu'narsk) *n* the former name (until 1992) of **Alchevsk**

Kommunizma Peak (*Russian* kəmu'njizmə) *n* a mountain in SE Tajikistan in the Pamirs: the highest mountain in the former Soviet Union. Height: 7495 m (24 590 ft). Former name: **Stalin Peak**

Komsomolsk (*Russian* kəmsa'mɔljsk) *n* an industrial city in W Russia, on the Amur River: built by members of the Komsomol (Communist youth league) in 1932. Pop: 295 100 (1999 est)

Konakry *or* **Konakri** (*French* kɔnakri) *n* variant spellings of **Conakry**

Kongur Shan ('kʊnguə 'ʃæn), **Kungur**, *or* **Qungur** *n* a mountain in China, in W Xinjiang Uygur: the highest peak in the Pamirs. Height: 7719 m (25 325 ft)

Kong Zi ('kʊŋ ziː) *n* the Pinyin transliteration of the Chinese name for **Confucius**

Königgrätz (køːnɪç'grɛːts) *n* the German name for **Hradec Králové**

Königsberg ('kɜːnɪgz,bɜːg; *German* 'køːnɪçsbɛrk) *n* the former name (until 1946) of **Kaliningrad**

Königshütte ('køːnɪçshytə) *n* the German name for **Chorzów**

Konstanz ('kɔnstants) *n* the German name for **Constance**

Konya *or* **Konia** ('kɔːnjɑː) *n* a city in SW central Turkey: in ancient times a Phrygian city and capital of Lycaonia. Pop: 623 333 (1997). Ancient name: **Iconium**

koodoo ('kuːduː) *n* a variant spelling of **kudu**

kook (kuːk) *n US & Canad inf* an eccentric or foolish person [c20 prob. from CUCKOO] > '**kooky** *or* '**kookie** *adj*

kookaburra ('kʊkə,bʌrə) *n* **1** Also called: **laughing jackass** a large arboreal Australian kingfisher, *Dacelo novaeguineae* (or *gigas*), with a cackling cry **2** Also called: **blue-winged kookaburra** a related smaller bird *D. Leachii*, of tropical Australia and New Guinea [c19 from a native Australian language]

Koolhaas (*Dutch* 'kulhɑs) *n* **Rem** Dutch architect and theorist, co-founder of the Office for Metropolitan Architecture (1975); buildings include the Grand Palais and associated developments in Lille, France (1989–96); books include *S, M, L, XL* (1996)

Kooning ('kuːnɪŋ) *n* **Willem de** ('wɪləm də) 1904–97, US abstract expressionist painter, born in Holland

Kootenay *or* **Kootenai** ('kuːtᵊniː, 'kuːtneɪ) *n* a river in W North America, rising in SE British Columbia and flowing south into NW Montana, then north into Idaho before re-entering British Columbia, broadening into **Kootenay Lake**, then flowing to the Columbia River. Length: 655 km (407 miles)

kopeck *or* **copeck** ('kəʊpɛk) *n* a monetary unit of Russia and Belarus worth one hundredth of a rouble: coins are still used as tokens for coin-operated machinery although the kopeck itself is virtually valueless [Russian *kopeika*, from *kopye* lance]

Kopeisk *or* **Kopeysk** (*Russian* ka'pjejsk) *n* a city in SW central Russia, in Chelyabinsk province: lignite mining. Pop: 78 300 (1991 est). Former name: **Kopi** ('kɔpi)

koppie *or* **kopje** ('kɒpɪ) *n* (in southern Africa) a small isolated hill [c19 from Afrik., from Du. *kopje*, lit.: a little head, from *kop* head]

kora ('kɔːrə) *n* a West African instrument with twenty-one strings, combining features of the harp and the lute

Koran (kɔː'rɑːn) *n* the sacred book of Islam, believed by Muslims to be the infallible word of God dictated to Mohammed. Also: **Qur'an** [c17 from Ar. *qur'ān* reading, book] > **Ko'ranic** *adj*
▷ http://www.quran.org.uk/

Korbut (*Russian* 'kɔrbʊt) *n* **Olga** ('ɔljgə) born 1955, Soviet gymnast: noted for her highly individualistic style, which greatly increased the popularity of the sport, esp following her performance in the 1972 Olympic Games

Korçë (*Albanian* 'kortʃə) *n* a market town in SE Albania. Pop: 67 100 (1991 est)

Korchnoi ('kɔːtʃ,nɔɪ) *n* **Victor** born 1931, Soviet-born chess player: Soviet champion 1960, 1962, and 1964: defected to the West in 1976

Korda ('kɔːdə) *n* Sir **Alexander**, real name *Sandor Kellner*. 1893–1956, British film producer and director, born in Hungary: his films include *The Scarlet Pimpernel* (1934), *Anna Karenina* (1948), and *The Third Man* (1949)

Kordofan (,kɔːdəʊ'fæn) *n* a region of the central Sudan: consists of a plateau with rugged uplands (the Nuba Mountains). Area: 380 548 sq km (146 930 sq miles)

Korea (kə'riːə) *n* a former country in E Asia, now divided into two separate countries, North Korea and South Korea. Korea occupied the peninsula between the Sea of Japan and the Yellow Sea: an isolated vassal of Manchu China for three centuries until the opening of ports to Japanese trade in 1876; gained independence in 1895; annexed to Japan in 1910 and divided in 1945 into two occupation zones (Russian in the north, American in the south), which became North Korea and South Korea in 1948. Japanese name (1910–45): **Chosen.** See **North Korea, South Korea** > **Ko'rean** *adj, n*

Korea Strait *n* a strait between South Korea and SW Japan, linking the Sea of Japan with the East China Sea

korfball ('kɔːf,bɔːl) *n* a game similar to basketball, in which each team consists of six men and six women [c20 from Du. *korfbal* basketball]

Kórinthos ('kɔrinθɔs) *n* transliteration of the Modern Greek name for **Corinth**

korma ('kɔːmə) *n* an Indian dish consisting of meat or vegetables braised with stock, yogurt, or cream [from Urdu]

Korsakoffian (,kɔːsə'kɒfɪən) *adj* **1** relating to or suffering from **Korsakoff's psychosis**, a mental illness involving severe confusion and inability to retain recent memories, usually caused by alcoholism ▷ *n* **2** a person suffering from Korsakoff's psychosis [c19 after Sergei *Korsakoff* (1854–1900), Russian neuropsychiatrist]

Korzybski (kɔː'zɪbskɪ) *n* **Alfred** (**Habdank Skarbek**) 1879–1950, US originator of the theory and study of general semantics, born in Poland

Kos *or* **Cos** (kɒs) *n* an island in the SE Aegean Sea, in the Greek Dodecanese Islands: separated from SW Turkey by the **Kos Channel**; settled in ancient times by Dorians and became famous for literature and medicine. Pop: 21 000 (latest est) Area: 282 sq km (109 sq miles)

Kosciusko (,kɒsɪ'ʌskəʊ) *n* **Mount** a mountain in SE New South Wales in the Australian Alps: the highest peak in Australia. Height: 2230 m (7316 ft)

kosher ('kəʊʃə) *adj* **1** *Judaism* conforming to religious law; fit for use: esp (of food) prepared in accordance with the dietary laws **2** *inf* **2a** genuine or authentic **2b** legitimate [c19 from Yiddish, from Heb. *kāshēr* proper]

Košice (*Czech* 'kɔʃitsɛ) *n* a city in E Slovakia: passed from Hungary to Czechoslovakia in 1920 and to Slovakia in 1993. Pop: 241 874 (2000 est). Hungarian name: **Kassa**

Kosovo (*Serbo-Croat* 'kɔsɔvɔ) *n* an autonomous province of Serbia and Montenegro, in SW Serbia: chiefly Albanian in population since the 13th century, it declared independence in 1990; Serb suppression of separatists escalated to a policy of ethnic cleansing in 1998, provoking NATO air strikes against Serbia in 1999: now under UN administration: mainly a plateau. Capital: Priština. Pop: 2 227 742 (1997 est). Area: 10 887 sq km (4203 sq miles). Full name: **Kosovo-Metohija** (*Serbo-Croat* 'kɔsɔvɔmɛ,tɔhija) > '**Kosovar** *or* '**Kosovan** *adj, n*

Kossoff ('kɒsɒf) *n* **Leon** born 1926, British painter, esp of London scenes

Kossuth (*Hungarian* 'koʃuːt) *n* **Lajos** ('lɔjoʃ) 1802–94, Hungarian statesman. He led the revolution against Austria (1848) and was provisional governor (1849), but he fled when the revolt was suppressed (1849)

Kostroma (*Russian* kəstra'ma) *n* a city in W central Russia, on the River Volga: fought over bitterly by Novgorod, Tver, and Moscow, until annexed by Moscow in 1329; textile centre. Pop: 289 300 (1999 est)

Kostunica (,kɒstjʊ'niːkə) *n* **Vojislav** ('vɒjɪslæf) born 1944, Serbian politician; president of the Federal Republic of Yugoslavia (2000–03)

Kosygin (*Russian* ka'sigin) *n* **Aleksei Nikolayevich** (alɪk'sjej nika'lajɪvitʃ) 1904–80, Soviet statesman; premier of the Soviet Union (1964–80)

Kota *or* **Kotah** ('kəʊtə) *n* a city in NW India, in Rajasthan on the Chambal River: textile industry. Pop: 537 371 (1991)

Kotabaru (ˈkəʊtəˈbɑːruː) *n* a former name of **Jayapura**

Kota Bharu *or* **Bahru** (ˈkəʊtə ˈbɑːruː) *n* a port in NE Peninsular Malaysia: capital of Kelantan state on the delta of the Kelantan River. Pop: 219 713 (1991)

Kota Kinabalu (ˈkəʊtə ˌkɪnəbəˈluː) *n* a port in Malaysia, capital of Sabah state on the South China Sea: exports timber and rubber. Pop: 208 484 (1991). Former name: **Jesselton**

koto (ˈkəʊtəʊ) *n, pl* **kotos** a Japanese stringed instrument [Japanese]

kotuku (ˈkəʊtʊkuː) *n, pl* **kotuku** NZ a white heron having brilliant white plumage, black legs and yellow eyes and bill [Maori]

kouprey (ˈkuːpreɪ) *n* a large wild member of the cattle tribe, of SE Asia, having a blackish-brown body and white legs: an endangered species [c20 from F, from Cambodian, from Pali *gō* cow + Khmer *brai* forest]

Kouro (ˈkuːrəʊ) *n* a town in N central French Guiana; site of the European Space Agency's launch and research base. Pop: 8000 (latest est)

Kovno (ˈkɔvnə) *n* transliteration of the Russian name for **Kaunas**

Kovrov (*Russian* kavˈrɔf) *n* a city in W central Russia, on the Klyazma River: textiles and heavy engineering. Pop: 161 200 (1999 est)

Koweit (kəʊˈweɪt) *n* a variant of **Kuwait**

kowhai (ˈkoːwaɪ) *n, pl* **kowhais** NZ a small leguminous tree of New Zealand and Chile with clusters of yellow flowers [c19 from Maori]

Kowloon (ˈkaʊˈluːn) *n* **1** a peninsula of SE China, opposite Hong Kong Island: part of the former British colony of Hong Kong. Area: 10 sq km (3.75 sq miles) **2** a port in Hong Kong, on Kowloon Peninsula. Pop: 2 025 800 (2001)

kowtow (ˌkaʊˈtaʊ) *vb (intr)* **1** to touch the forehead to the ground as a sign of deference: a former Chinese custom **2** (often foll by *to*) to be servile (towards) ▷ *n* **3** the act of kowtowing [c19 from Chinese, from *k'o* to strike, knock + *t'ou* head]

Kozhikode (ˌkəʊʒɪˈkəʊd) *n* a port in SW India, in W Kerala on the Malabar coast: important European trading post (1511–1765): formerly calico-manufacturing. Pop: 420 000 (1991). Former name: **Calicut**

Kr **1** *currency symbol for:* **1a** krona **1b** krone **2** *the chemical symbol for* krypton

kr. *abbrev for:* **1** krona **2** krone

Kra (krɑː) *n* **Isthmus of** an isthmus of SW Thailand, between the Bay of Bengal and the Gulf of Siam: the narrowest part of the Malay Peninsula. Width: about 56 km (35 miles)

kraal (krɑːl) *n S African* **1** a hut village in southern Africa, esp one surrounded by a stockade **2** an enclosure for livestock [c18 from Afrik., from Port. *curral* pen]

Krafft-Ebing (*German* ˈkraftˈeːbɪŋ) *n* **Richard** (ˈrɪçart), Baron von Krafft-Ebing. 1840–1902, German neurologist and psychiatrist who pioneered the systematic study of sexual behaviour in *Psychopathia Sexualis* (1886)

kraft (krɑːft) *n* strong wrapping paper [G: force]

Kragujevac (*Serbo-Croat* ˈkragujɛvats) *n* a town in E central Serbia and Montenegro, in Serbia; capital of Serbia (1818–39); automobile industry. Pop: 154 489 (2000 est)

krait (kraɪt) *n* any nonaggressive brightly coloured venomous snake of S and SE Asia [c19 from Hindi *karait*, from ?]

Krakatoa (ˌkrɑːkəˈtəʊə, ˌkrækəˈtəʊə) *or* **Krakatau** (ˌkrɑːkəˈtaʊ, ˌkrækəˈtaʊ) *n* a volcanic island in Indonesia, in the Sunda Strait between Java and Sumatra: partially destroyed by its eruption in 1883, the greatest in recorded history. Further eruptions 44 years later formed a new island, **Anak Krakatau** ("Child of Krakatau") Also called: **Rakata**

Krakau (ˈkraːkau) *n* the German name for **Cracow**

kraken (ˈkrɑːkən) *n* a legendary sea monster of gigantic size believed to dwell off the coast of Norway [c18 from Norwegian, from ?]

Kraków (ˈkrakuf) *n* the Polish name for **Cracow**

Kramatorsk (*Russian* krəmaˈtɔrsk) *n* a city in the E Ukraine: a major industrial centre of the Donets Basin. Pop: 190 800 (1998 est)

Kranj (kraːnj) *n* the Slovene name for **Carniola**

krans (krɑːns) *n S African* a sheer rock face; precipice [c18 from Afrik.]

Krasnodar (*Russian* krəsnaˈdar) *n* an industrial city in SW Russia, on the Kuban River. Pop: 643 400 (1999 est). Former name (until 1920): **Yekaterinodar**

Krasnoyarsk (*Russian* krəsnaˈjarsk) *n* a city in E central Russia, on the Yenisei River: the country's largest hydroelectric power station is nearby. Pop: 877 800 (1999 est)

Krebs (krɛbz) *n* Sir **Hans Adolf** 1900–81, British biochemist, born in Germany, who shared a Nobel prize for physiology or medicine (1953) for the discovery of the **Krebs cycle**

Krefeld (ˈkreɪfɛld; *German* ˈkreːfɛlt) *n* a city in Germany, in W North Rhine-Westphalia: textile industries. Pop: 242 800 (1999 est)

Kreisler (*German* ˈkraislər) *n* **Fritz** (frɪts) 1875–1962, US violinist, born in Austria

Kremenchug (*Russian* krɪmɪnˈtʃuk) *n* an industrial city in the E central Ukraine on the Dnieper River. Pop: 240 700 (1998 est)

Kremer (ˈkreɪmə) *n* **Gidon** born 1947, Latvian violinist, now based in the US

kremlin (ˈkrɛmlɪn) *n* the citadel of any Russian city [c17 from obs. G *Kremelin*, from Russian *kreml*]

Kremlin (ˈkrɛmlɪn) *n* **1** the 12th-century citadel in Moscow, containing the former Imperial Palace, three Cathedrals, and the offices of the Russian government **2** (formerly) the central government of the Soviet Union

Krems (*German* krɛms) *n* a town in NE Austria, in Lower Austria on the River Danube. Pop: 22 830 (1991)

Kriemhild (ˈkriːmhɪlt) *or* **Kriemhilde** (ˈkriːmˌhɪldə) *n* (in the *Nibelungenlied*) the wife of Siegfried. She corresponds to Gudrun in Norse mythology

krill (krɪl) *n, pl* **krill** any small shrimplike marine crustacean: the principal food of whalebone whales [c20 from Norwegian *kril* young fish]

krimmer (ˈkrɪmə) *n* a tightly curled light grey fur obtained from the skins of lambs from Crimea in Ukraine [c20 from G, from *Krim* Crimea]

Kriol (ˈkriːɒl) *n* a creole language used by Aboriginal communities in the northern regions of Australia, developed from Northern Territory pidgin

kris (krɪs) *n* a Malayan and Indonesian stabbing or slashing knife with a scalloped edge. Also called: **crease, creese** [c16 from Malay]

Krishna[1] (ˈkrɪʃnə) *n* a river in S India, rising in the Western Ghats and flowing generally southeast to the Bay of Bengal. Length: 1300 km (800 miles). Also called: **Kistna**

Krishna[2] (ˈkrɪʃnə) *n Hinduism* the most celebrated of the Hindu deities, whose life story is told in the *Mahabharata* [via Hindi from Sansk., lit.: dark, black] > ˈ**Krishnaism** *n*

Krishna Menon (ˈkriːʃnə ˈmɛnən) *n* **Vengalil Krishnan** (ˈvɛŋgəlɪl ˈkriːʃnən) See (Vengalil Krishnan Krishna) **Menon**

Kristiania (ˌkrɪstɪˈɑːnɪə) *n* a former name (1877–1924) of **Oslo**

Kristiansand *or* **Christiansand** (ˈkrɪstʃənˌsænd; *Norwegian* kristianˈsan) *n* a port in S Norway, on the Skagerrak: shipbuilding. Pop: 65 543 (1990)

Kristiansen (ˈkrɪstʃənsən) *n* **Ingrid** born 1956, Norwegian long-distance runner: former London

Kk

marathon winner: world 10 000 metres record holder (1986–93)

Kristianstad ('krɪstʃən,stɑːd; *Swedish* kri'ʃanstɑːd) *n* a town in S Sweden: founded in 1614 as a Danish fortress, it was finally acquired by Sweden in 1678. Pop: 73 543 (1994)

Kríti ('kriti) *n* transliteration of the Modern Greek name for **Crete**

Krivoy Rog (*Russian* kri'vɔj 'rɔk) *n* a city in the SE Ukraine: founded in the 17th century by Cossacks; iron-mining centre; iron- and steelworks. Pop: 715 400 (1998 est)

krona ('krəʊnə) *n, pl* **kronor** (-nə) the standard monetary unit of Sweden

króna ('krəʊnə) *n, pl* **krónur** (-nə) the standard monetary unit of Iceland

krone ('krəʊnə) *n, pl* **kroner** (-nə) **1** the standard monetary unit of Denmark, the Faroe Islands, and Greenland **2** the standard monetary unit of Norway [C19 from Danish or Norwegian, ult. from L *corōna* CROWN]

Kronos ('krəʊnɒs) *n* a variant of **Cronus**

Kronstadt *n* **1** (*Russian* kran'ʃtat) a port in NW Russia, on Kotlin island in the Gulf of Finland: naval base. Pop: 44 400 (1994 est) **2** ('kroːnʃtat) the German name for **Braşov**

Kropotkin (*Russian* kra'pɔtkin) *n* Prince **Peter**, Russian name *Pyotr Alexeyevich*. 1842–1921, Russian anarchist: his books include *Mutual Aid* (1902) and *Modern Science and Anarchism* (1903)

Kroto ('krəʊtəʊ) *n* Sir **Harold (Walter)** born 1939, British chemist who discovered buckminsterfullerene; Nobel prize for chemistry 1996

Kruger ('kruːgə) *n* **Stephanus Johannes Paulus** ('stɛfənʊs jəʊ'hænɪs 'pɔːlʊs), known as *Oom Paul*. 1825–1904, Boer statesman; president of the Transvaal (1883–1900). His opposition to Cecil Rhodes and his denial of civil rights to the Uitlanders led to the Boer War (1899–1902)

Kruger National Park *n* a wildlife sanctuary in NE South Africa: the world's largest game reserve. Area: over 21 700 sq km (8400 sq miles)

Krugerrand ('kruːgə,rænd) *n* a one-ounce gold coin minted in South Africa for investment only [C20 from Paul KRUGER + RAND[1]]

Krugersdorp ('kruːgəz,dɔːp) *n* a city in NE South Africa, on the Witwatersrand, at an altitude of 1722 m (5650 ft): a gold-, manganese-, and uranium-mining centre. Pop (urban area): 203 168 (1996)

krummhorn ('krʌm,hɔːn) *or* **crumhorn** *n* a medieval wind instrument consisting of an upward-curving tube blown through a double reed [C17 *krumhorn, cromorne*, from G *Krummhorn* curved horn]

Krupp (krʊp, krʌp) *n* a German family of steel and armaments manufacturers, including **Alfred,** 1812–87, his son **Friedrich Alfred,** 1854–1902, and the latter's son-in-law, **Gustav Krupp von Bohlen und Halbach,** 1870–1950

Krušné Hory ('krʊʃne 'hɔrɪ) *n* the Czech name for the **Erzgebirge**

Krym *or* **Krim** (krɪm) *n* transliteration of the Russian name for **Crimea**

krypton ('krɪptɒn) *n* an inert gaseous element occurring in trace amounts in air and used in fluorescent lights and lasers. Symbol: Kr; atomic no.: 36; atomic wt.: 83.80 [C19 from Gk, from *kruptos* hidden]

krytron ('kraɪtrɒn) *n electronics* a type of fast electronic gas-discharge switch, used as a trigger in nuclear weapons

KS *abbrev for* Kansas

Kshatriya ('kʃætrɪə) *n* a member of the second of the four main Hindu castes, the warrior caste [C18 from Sansk., from *kshatra* rule]

kt *abbrev for:* **1** karat **2** *naut* knot

Kt **1** Also: **knt** *abbrev for* Knight **2** Also: **N** *chess symbol for* knight

Kuala Lumpur ('kwɑːlə 'lʊmpʊə, -pə) *n* a city in Malaysia, in the SW Malay Peninsula: formerly (until 1999) the capital of Malaysia; became capital of the Federated Malay States in 1895, and of Malaysia in 1963; capital of Selangor state from 1880 to 1973, when it was made a federal territory. Pop: 1 145 075 (1991)
▷ www.visitmalaysia.com/kualalumpur.html

Kuban (*Russian* ku'banj) *n* a river in SW Russia, rising in the Caucasus Mountains and flowing north and northwest to the Sea of Azov. Length: 906 km (563 miles)

Kubelik (*Czech* 'kubɛliːk) *n* **Raphael** ('raːfaɛl) 1914–96, Czech conductor and composer

Kublai Khan ('kuːblaɪ 'kɑːn) *n* ?1216–94, Mongol emperor of China: grandson of Genghis Khan. He completed his grandfather's conquest of China by overthrowing the Sung dynasty (1279) and founded the Yuan dynasty (1279–1368)

Kubrick ('kjuːbrɪk) *n* **Stanley** 1928–99, US film writer, director, and producer. He directed *Lolita* (1962), *Dr Strangelove* (1963), *2001: A Space Odyssey* (1968), *A Clockwork Orange* (1971), *The Shining* (1980), *Full Metal Jacket* (1987), and *Eyes Wide Shut* (1999)

Kuching ('kuːtʃɪŋ) *n* a port in E Malaysia, capital of Sarawak state, on the Sarawak River 24 km (15 miles) from its mouth. Pop: 147 729 (1991)

kudlik ('kuːdlɪk) *n Canad* an Inuit soapstone seal-oil lamp [Inuktitut]

kudos ('kjuːdɒs) *n* (*functioning as sing*) acclaim, glory, or prestige [C18 from Gk]

kudu *or* **koodoo** ('kuːduː) *n* either of two spiral-horned antelopes (**greater kudu** or **lesser kudu**), which inhabit the bush of Africa [C18 from Afrik. *koedoe*, prob. from Khoi]

kuia ('kuːjə) *n NZ* a Maori female elder or elderly woman [Maori]

Kuibyshev *or* **Kuybyshev** (*Russian* 'kujbɪʃəf) *n* the former name (until 1991) of **Samara**

Ku Klux Klan (,kuː klʌks 'klæn) *n* **1** a secret organization of White Southerners formed after the US Civil War to fight Black emancipation **2** a secret organization of White Protestant Americans, mainly in the South, who use violence against Blacks, Jews, etc [C19 *Ku Klux*, prob. based on Gk *kuklos* CIRCLE + *Klan* CLAN] > **Ku Klux Klanner** ('klænə) *n*

kukri ('kʊkrɪ) *n, pl* **kukris** a knife with a curved blade that broadens towards the point, esp as used by Gurkhas [from Hindi]

Kuku Nor ('kuː'kuː 'nɔː) *n* a variant of **Koko Nor**

kulak ('kuːlæk) *n* (in Russia after 1906) a member of the class of peasants who became proprietors of their own farms. In 1929 Stalin initiated their liquidation [C19 from Russian: fist, hence, tightfisted person]

kulfi ('kʊlfɪ) *n* an Indian dessert that resembles ice cream flavoured with nuts and cardamom seeds

Kulun ('kuː'luːn) *n* the Chinese name for **Ulan Bator**

Kum (kʊm) *n* a variant spelling of **Qom**

Kumamoto (,kʊmə'məʊtəʊ) *n* a city in SW Japan, on W central Kyushu: Kumamoto Medical University (1949). Pop: 650 322 (1995)

Kumasi (kuː'mæsɪ) *n* a city in S Ghana: seat of Ashanti kings since 1663; university (1961); market town for a cocoa-producing region. Pop: 578 000 (1998 est)

Kumayri (*Russian* ,kʊmaɪ'rɪ) *n* a city in NW Armenia: textile centre. Pop: 120 000 (1995 est). Former names: **Aleksandropol** (1840–1924), **Leninakan** (1924–91)

Kumbh Mela (kʊm 'mɛlə) *n* a Hindu religious festival held every 12 years at Allahabad, India

kumera *or* **kumara** ('kuːmərə) *n NZ* the sweet potato [from Maori]

kumiss *or* **koumiss** ('kuːmɪs) *n* a drink made from fermented mare's or other milk, drunk by certain Asian tribes [c17 from Russian *kumys*]

kumite ('ku:mɪˌteɪ) *n karate, etc* freestyle sparring or fighting [c20 Japanese, lit.: sparring]

kümmel ('kʊməl) *n* a German liqueur flavoured with aniseed and cumin [c19 from G, from OHG *kumil*, prob. var. of *kumin* CUMIN]

kumquat *or* **cumquat** ('kʌmkwɒt) *n* **1** a small Chinese citrus tree **2** the small round orange fruit of such a tree, with a sweet rind, used in preserves and confections [c17 from Mandarin Chinese *chin chü* golden orange]

Kun (ku:n) *n* **Béla** ('be:lɔ) 1886–?1937, Hungarian Communist leader, president of the short-lived Communist republic in Hungary (1919). He was forced into exile and died in a Stalinist purge

Kundera ('kʌndərə) *n* **Milan** born 1929, Czech novelist living in France. His novels include *The Book of Laughter and Forgetting* (1979), *The Unbearable Lightness of Being* (1984), and *Ignorance* (2002)

kung fu ('kʌŋ 'fu:) *n* a Chinese martial art combining principles of karate and judo [from Chinese: martial art]

K'ung Fu-tse ('kʊŋ 'fu:'tseɪ) *n* the Chinese name of **Confucius**

Kungur ('kʊngʊə) *n* a variant transliteration of the Chinese name for **Kongur Shan**

Kunlun ('kʊn'lʊn) *or* **Kwenlun** *n* a mountain range in China, between the Tibetan plateau and the Tarim Basin, extending over 1600 km (1000 miles) east from the Pamirs: the largest mountain system of Asia. Highest peak: Ulugh Muztagh, 7723 m (25 338 ft)

Kunming *or* **K'un-ming** ('kʊn'mɪŋ) *n* a city in SW China, capital of Yunnan province, near Lake Tien: important during World War II as a Chinese military centre, American air base, and transport terminus for the Burma Road; Yunnan University (1934). Pop: 1 350 640 (1999 est)

Kuopio (*Finnish* 'kwɔpjɔ) *n* a city in S central Finland. Pop: 83 955 (1994)

Kura (kʊ'rɑ:) *n* a river in W Asia, rising in NE Turkey and flowing across Georgia and Azerbaijan to the Caspian Sea. Length: 1515 km (941 miles)

kura kaupapa Maori ('ku:rɑ: 'kɑ:u:pɑ:pɑ:) *n NZ* a primary school in which the lessons are conducted in Maori and the teaching is based on Maori culture [from Maori *kura* school + *kaupapa* scheme]

kurchatovium (ˌkɜ:tʃə'təʊvɪəm) *n* another name for **rutherfordium,** esp as used in the former Soviet Union [c20 from Russian, after I. V. *Kurchatov* (1903–60), Soviet physicist]

Kurd (kɜ:d) *n* a member of a nomadic people living chiefly in E Turkey, N Iraq, and W Iran

Kurdish ('kɜ:dɪʃ) *n* **1** the language of the Kurds ▷ *adj* **2** of or relating to the Kurds or their language

Kurdistan, Kurdestan, *or* **Kordestan** (ˌkɜ:dɪ'stɑ:n) *n* a large plateau and mountainous region, between the Caspian Sea and the Black Sea, south of the Caucasus. Area: over 29 000 sq km (74 000 sq miles)

Kure (ku:'reɪ) *n* a port in SW Japan, on SW Honshu: a naval base; shipyards. Pop: 209 477 (1995 est)

Kurgan (*Russian* kur'gan) *n* a city in W Russia, on the Tobol River: industrial centre for an agricultural region. Pop: 367 200 (1999 est)

kuri ('ku:rɪ) *n, pl* **kuris** *NZ* a mongrel dog. Also called: **goorie** [Maori]

Kuril Islands *or* **Kurile Islands** (kʊ'ri:l) *pl n* a chain of 56 volcanic islands off the NE coast of Asia, extending for 1200 km (750 miles) from the S tip of the Kamchatka Peninsula to NE Hokkaido. Area: 14 990 sq km (6020 sq miles). Japanese name: **Chishima**

Kurosawa (ˌkʊərə'sɑ:wə) *n* **Akira** (ə'kɪərə) 1910–99, Japanese film director. His works include *Rashomon* (1950), *The Seven Samurai* (1954), *The Throne of Blood* (1957), *Kagemusha* (1980), *Ran* (1985), and *Madadayo* (1993)

Kuroshio (kə'rəʊʃɪˌəʊ) *n* another name for **Japan Current**

kurrajong *or* **currajong** ('kʌrəˌdʒɒŋ) *n* any of various Australian trees or shrubs, esp one that yields a tough durable fibre [c19 from Abor.]

kursaal ('kɜ:zəl) *n* a public room at a health resort [from G, lit.: cure room]

Kursk (*Russian* kursk) *n* a city in W Russia: industrial centre of an agricultural region: scene of a major Soviet victory (1943). Pop: 445 400 (1999 est)

kurtosis (kə'təʊsɪs) *n statistics* a measure of the concentration of a distribution around its mean [from Gk, from *kurtos* arched]

kuru ('kʊru:) *n* a degenerative disease of the nervous system, restricted to certain tribes in New Guinea, marked by loss of muscular control and thought to be caused by a slow virus [c20 from a native name]

Kush (kʌʃ, kʊʃ) *n* a variant spelling of **Cush**

Kuskokwim ('kʌskəˌkwɪm) *n* a river in SW Alaska, rising in the Alaska Range and flowing generally southwest to **Kuskokwim Bay** an inlet of the Bering Sea. Length: about 970 km (600 miles)

Kutaisi (*Russian* kuta'isi) *n* an industrial city in W Georgia on the Rioni River: one of the oldest towns of the Caucasus. Pop: 240 000 (1997 est)

Kutch (kʌtʃ) *n* **1** a former state of W India, on the **Gulf of Kutch** (an inlet of the Arabian Sea): part of Gujarat state since 1960 **2 Rann of** an extensive salt waste in W central India, and S Pakistan: consists of the Great Rann in the north and the Little Rann in the southeast; seasonal alternation between marsh and desert; some saltworks. In 1968 an international tribunal awarded about 10 per cent of the border area to Pakistan. Area: 23 000 sq km (9000 sq miles)

Kutuzov (*Russian* ku'tuzəf) *n* Prince **Mikhail Ilarionovich** (mixa'il iləri'ɔnəvitʃ) 1745–1813, Russian field marshal, who harried the French army under Napoleon throughout their retreat from Moscow (1812–13)

Kuwait (kʊ'weɪt) *or* **Koweit** *n* **1** a state on the NW coast of the Persian Gulf: came under British protection in 1899 and gained independence in 1961; invaded by Iraq in 1990; liberated by US-led UN forces 1991 in the Gulf War: mainly desert. The economy is dependent on oil. Official language: Arabic. Official religion: Muslim. Currency: dinar. Capital: Kuwait. Pop: 2 275 000 (2001 est). Area: 24 280 sq km (9375 sq miles) **2** the capital of Kuwait: a port on the Persian Gulf. Pop: 28 859 (1995)
> **Ku'waiti** *or* **Ko'weiti** *adj, n*
▷ www.kems.net
▷ www.kuwaitiah.net/tourism.html

Kuznets ('kʊznɪts) *n* **Simon** 1901–85, US economist born in Russia. His books include *National Income and its Composition (1919–1938)* (1941) and *Economic Growth of Nations* (1971). He was awarded the Nobel Prize for economics in 1971

Kuznetsk Basin (*Russian* kuz'njɛtsk) *or* **Kuzbass** (*Russian* kuz'bas) *n* a region of S Russia, in the Kemerovo Region of W Siberia: the richest coalfield in the country, with reserves of iron ore. Chief industrial centre: Novokuznetsk. Area: about 69 900 sq km (27 000 sq miles)

Kvaløy (*Norwegian* 'kva:lœj) *n* two islands in the Arctic Ocean, off the N coast of Norway: **North Kvaløy,** 329 sq km (127 sq miles), and **South Kvaløy,** 735 sq km (284 sq miles)

kvass (kvɑ:s) *n* an alcoholic drink of low strength made in Russia and E Europe from cereals and stale bread [c16 from Russian *kvas*]

kvetch (kvɛtʃ) *vb (intr) sl, chiefly US* to complain or grumble, esp incessantly [c20 from Yiddish *kvetshn*, lit.: to squeeze, press]

kW *abbrev for* kilowatt

kwacha ('kwɑ:tʃɑ:) *n* **1** the standard monetary unit of Zambia **2** the standard monetary unit of Malawi [from a native word in Zambia]

Kk

kwaito ('kwaɪ,təʊ) *n* a type of South African pop music with lyrics spoken over an instrumental backing [c20 from *Amakwaito*, a gang in Sophiatown, South Africa, in the 1950s]

Kwajalein ('kwɑːdʒə,leɪn) *n* an atoll in the W Pacific, in the W Marshall Islands, in the central part of the Ralik Chain. Length: about 125 km (78 miles)

Kwangchow ('kwæŋ'tʃaʊ) *n* a variant transliteration of the Chinese name for **Canton**

Kwangchowan ('kwæŋ'tʃaʊ'wɑːn) *n* a territory of SE China, in SW Kwantung province: leased to France as part of French Indochina from 1898 to 1945. Area: 842 sq km (325 sq miles)

Kwangju ('kwæŋ'dʒuː) *n* a city in SW South Korea: an important military base during the Korean War; cotton textile industry. Pop: 1 257 504 (1995)

Kwangsi-Chuang Autonomous Region ('kwæŋ'siː'tʃwæŋ) *n* a variant transliteration of the Chinese name for **Guangxi Zhuang Autonomous Region**

Kwangtung ('kwæŋ'tʊŋ) *n* a variant transliteration of the Chinese name for **Guangdong**

Kwantung Leased Territory (,kwæn'tʊŋ) *n* a strategic territory of NE China, at the S tip of the Liaotung Peninsula of Manchuria: leased forcibly by Russia in 1898; taken over by Japan in 1905; occupied by the Soviet Union in 1945 and subsequently returned to China on the condition of shared administration; made part of Liaoning province by China in 1954. Area: about 3400 sq km (1300 sq miles). Also called: **Kuan-tung**

Kwara ('kwɑːrə) *n* a state of W Nigeria: mainly wooded savanna. Capital: Ilorin. Pop: 1 751 464 (1995 est). Area: 36 825 sq km (14 218 sq miles)

kwashiorkor (,kwæʃɪ'ɔːkə) *n* severe malnutrition of infants and young children, resulting from dietary deficiency of protein [c20 from native word in Ghana]

KwaZulu/Natal (kwɑː,zuːluːnə'tæl, -'tɑːl) *n* a province of NE South Africa; replaced the former province of Natal in 1994: service industries. Capital: Pietermaritzburg. Pop: 8 924 643 (1999 est). Area: 92 180 sq km (35 591 sq miles)
▷ www.kwazulunatal.gov.za
▷ www.kzn.org.za

Kweichow *or* **Kueichou** ('kweɪ'tʃaʊ) *n* a variant transliteration of the Chinese name for **Guizhou**

Kweilin *or* **Kuei-lin** ('kweɪ'lɪn) *n* a variant transliteration of the Chinese name for **Guilin**

Kweisui ('kweɪ'sweɪ) *n* the former name of **Hohhot**

Kweiyang *or* **Kuei-yang** ('kweɪ'jæŋ) *n* a variant transliteration of the Chinese name for **Guiyang**

kWh *abbrev for* kilowatt-hour

KWIC (kwɪk) *n acronym for* key word in context (esp in **KWIC index**)

KWOC (kwɒk) *n acronym for* key word out of context

Ky (kiː) *n* **Nguyen Kao** (ᵊŋ'guːjɛn 'kaʊ) born 1930, Vietnamese military and political leader: premier of South Vietnam (1965–67); vice president (1967–71)

Ky. *or* **KY** *abbrev for* Kentucky

kyanite ('kaɪə,naɪt) *or* **cyanite** *n* a grey, green, or blue mineral consisting of aluminium silicate in crystalline form > **kyanitic** (,kaɪə'nɪtɪk) *adj*

kyanize *or* **kyanise** ('kaɪə,naɪz) *vb* **kyanizes, kyanizing, kyanized** *or* **kyanises, kyanising, kyanised** (*tr*) to treat (timber) with corrosive sublimate to make it resistant to decay [c19 after J.H. *Kyan* (died 1850), Brit inventor of the process] > ,**kyani'zation** *or* ,**kyani'sation** *n*

Kyd *or* **Kid** (kɪd) *n* **Thomas** 1558–94, English dramatist, noted for his revenge play *The Spanish Tragedy* (1586)

kyle (kaɪl) *n Scot* (esp in place names) a narrow strait or channel: *Kyle of Lochalsh* [c16 from Gaelic *caol* narrow]

kylie *or* **kiley** ('kaɪlɪ) *n Austral* a boomerang that is flat on one side and convex on the other [c19 from Abor.]

kyloe ('kaɪləʊ) *n* a breed of small long-horned long-haired beef cattle from NW Scotland [c19 from ?]

kymograph ('kaɪmə,grɑːf) *n* a rotatable drum for holding paper on which a tracking stylus continuously records variations in sound waves, blood pressure, respiratory movements, etc [c20 from Gk *kuma* wave + -GRAPH] > ,**kymo'graphic** *adj*

Kymric ('kɪmrɪk) *n, adj* a variant spelling of **Cymric**

Kymry ('kɪmrɪ) *pl n* a variant spelling of **Cymry**

Kynewulf ('kɪnə,wʊlf) *n* a variant spelling of **Cynewulf**

Kyongsong ('kjɔːŋ'sɔːŋ) *n* another name for **Seoul**

Kyoto (kɪ'əʊtəʊ, 'kjəʊ-) *n* a city in central Japan, on S Honshu: the capital of Japan from 794 to 1868; cultural centre, with two universities (1875, 1897). Pop: 1 463 601 (1995)

kyphosis (kaɪ'fəʊsɪs) *n pathol* backward curvature of the thoracic spine, of congenital origin or resulting from injury or disease [c19 from NL, from Gk *kuphōsis*, from *kuphos* humpbacked] > **kyphotic** (kaɪ'fɒtɪk) *adj*

Kyrgyz ('kɪəgɪz) *n* **1** (*pl* **Kyrgyz**) a member of a Mongoloid people of central Asia, inhabiting Kyrgyzstan and a vast area of central Siberia **2** the language of this people, belonging to the Turkic branch of the Altaic family. Also: **Kirghiz, Kirgiz**

Kyrgyzstan ('kɪəgɪz,stɑːn, -,stæn), **Kirghizstan**, *or* **Kirgizstan** *n* a republic in central Asia: came under Russian rule in the 19th century, became a Soviet republic in 1936 and gained independence in 1991; it has deposits of minerals, oil, and gas. Official languages: Kyrgyz and Russian. Religion: nonreligious, Muslim. Currency: som. Capital: Bishkek. Pop: 4 934 000 (2001 est). Area: 198 500 sq km (76 460 sq miles)

Kyrgyz Steppe *n* a vast steppe region in central Kazakhstan. Also called: **the Steppes**

Kyrie eleison ('kɪrɪɪ ə'leɪsᵊn) *n* **1** a formal invocation used in the liturgies of the Roman Catholic, Greek Orthodox, and Anglican Churches **2** a musical setting of this. Often shortened to **Kyrie** [c14 via LL from LGk *kurie, eleēson* Lord, have mercy]

Kythera ('kɪθɪrə) *n* a variant spelling of **Cythera**

kyu (kjuː) *n judo* one of the student grades for inexperienced competitors [from Japanese]

Kyushu ('kjuːʃuː) *n* an island of SW Japan: the southernmost of Japan's four main islands, with over 300 surrounding small islands; coalfield and chemical industries. Chief cities: Fukuoka, Kitakyushu, and Nagasaki. Pop: 13 446 000 (2001 est). Area: 35 659 sq km (13 768 sq miles)

Kyzyl Kum (*Russian* ki'zil 'kum) *n* a desert in Kazakhstan and Uzbekistan

KZN (in South Africa) *abbrev for* KwaZulu/Natal

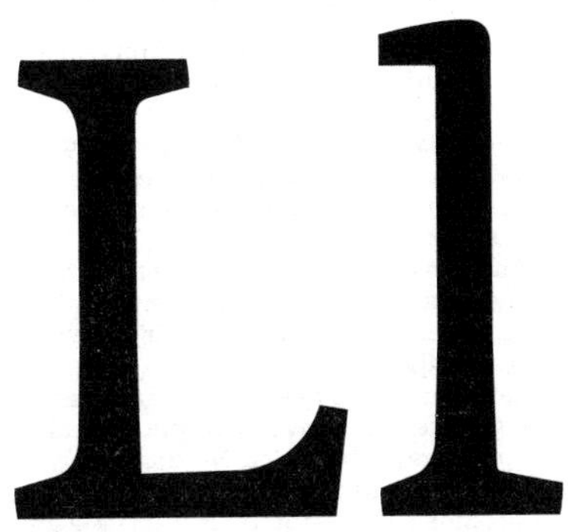

l *or* **L** (ɛl) *n, pl* **l's, L's,** *or* **Ls** **1** the 12th letter of the English alphabet **2** a speech sound represented by this letter **3a** something shaped like an L **3b** (*in combination*): *an L-shaped room*

l *symbol for* litre

L *symbol for:* **1** lambert(s) **2** large **3** Latin **4** (on British motor vehicles) learner driver **5** *physics* length **6** live **7** Usually written: £, pound [L *libra*] **8** lire **9** *electronics* inductor (in circuit diagrams) **10** *physics* **10a** latent heat **10b** self-inductance **11** the Roman numeral for 50. See **Roman numerals**

L. *or* **l.** *abbrev for:* **1** lake **2** left **3** length

la[1] (lɑː) *n music* the syllable used in the fixed system of solmization for the note A [C14 see GAMUT]

la[2] (lɔː) *interj* an exclamation of surprise or emphasis [OE *lā* lo]

La *the chemical symbol for* lanthanum

laager (ˈlɑːɡə) *n* **1** (in Africa) a camp, esp one defended by a circular formation of wagons **2** *mil* a place where armoured vehicles are parked ▷ *vb* **3** to form (wagons) into a laager **4** (*tr*) to park (armoured vehicles) in a laager [C19 from Afrik. *lager*, via G from OHG *legar* bed, lair]

lab (læb) *n inf* short for **laboratory**

lab. *abbrev for:* **1** laboratory **2** labour

Lab. *abbrev for:* **1** *politics* Labour **2** Labrador

Laban (ˈleɪbᵊn) *n Old Testament* the father-in-law of Jacob, father of Leah and Rachel (Genesis 29:16)

Labe (*Czech* ˈlabɛ) *n* the Czech name for the (River) **Elbe**

label (ˈleɪbᵊl) *n* **1** a piece of paper, card, or other material attached to an object to identify it or give instructions or details concerning its ownership, use, nature, destination, etc; tag **2** a brief descriptive phrase or term given to a person, group, school of thought, etc: *the label "Romantic" is applied to many different kinds of poetry* **3** a word or phrase heading a piece of text to indicate or summarize its contents **4** a trademark or company or brand name on certain goods, esp on gramophone records **5** *computing* a group of characters appended to a statement in a program to allow it to be identified **6** *chem* a radioactive element used in a compound to trace the mechanism of a chemical reaction ▷ *vb* **labels, labelling, labelled** *or US* **labels, labeling, labeled** (*tr*) **7** to fasten a label to **8** to mark with a label **9** to describe or classify in a word or phrase: *to label someone a liar* **10** to make (one or more atoms in a compound) radioactive, for use in determining the mechanism of a reaction [C14 from OF, from Gmc] > ˈ**labeller** *n*

labia (ˈleɪbɪə) *n* the plural of **labium**

labial (ˈleɪbɪəl) *adj* **1** of, relating to, or near lips or labia **2** *music* producing sounds by the action of an air stream over a narrow liplike fissure, as in a flue pipe of an organ **3** *phonetics* relating to a speech sound whose articulation involves movement or use of the lips ▷ *n* **4** Also called: **labial pipe** *music* an organ pipe with a liplike fissure **5** *phonetics* a speech sound such as English *p* or *m*, whose articulation involves movement or use of the lips [C16 from Med. L *labiālis*, from L *labium* lip] > ˈ**labially** *adv*

labiate (ˈleɪbɪˌeɪt, -ɪt) *n* **1** any plant of the family Lamiaceae (formerly *Labiatae*), having square stems, aromatic leaves, and a two-lipped corolla: includes mint, thyme, sage, rosemary, etc ▷ *adj* **2** of, relating to, or belonging to the family *Labiatae* [C18 from NL *labiātus*, from L *labium* lip]

Labiche (*French* labiʃ) *n* **Eugène Marin** (øʒɛn marɛ̃) 1815–88, French dramatist, noted for his farces of middle-class life, which include *Le Chapeau de paille d'Italie* (1851) and *Le Voyage de Monsieur Perrichon* (1860)

labile (ˈleɪbɪl) *adj* **1** *chem* (of a compound) prone to chemical change **2** liable to change or move [C15 via LL *lābilis*, from L *lābī* to slide] > **lability** (ləˈbɪlɪtɪ) *n*

labiodental (ˌleɪbɪəʊˈdɛntᵊl) *phonetics* ▷ *adj* **1** pronounced by bringing the bottom lip into contact with the upper teeth, as for *f* in *fat, puff* ▷ *n* **2** a labiodental consonant [C17 from L LABIUM + DENTAL]

labium (ˈleɪbɪəm) *n, pl* **labia** (-bɪə) **1** a lip or liplike structure **2** any one of the four lip-shaped folds of the female vulva, comprising an outer pair (**labia majora**) and an inner pair (**labia minora**) [C16 NL, from L.: lip]

laboratory (ləˈbɒrətərɪ, -trɪ; *US* ˈlæbrəˌtɔːrɪ) *n, pl* **laboratories 1a** a building or room equipped for conducting scientific research or for teaching practical science **1b** (*as modifier*): *laboratory equipment* **2** a place where chemicals or medicines are manufactured. Often shortened to **lab** [C17 from Med. L *labōrātōrium* workshop, from L *labōrāre* to LABOUR]

Labor Day *n* **1** a public holiday in the US and Canada in honour of labour, held on the first Monday in September **2** a public holiday in Australia, observed on different days in different states

laborious (ləˈbɔːrɪəs) *adj* **1** involving great exertion or long effort **2** given to working hard **3** (of literary style, etc) not fluent > **laˈboriously** *adv* > **laˈboriousness** *n*

Labor Party *n* one of the chief political parties of Australia, generally supporting the interests of organized labour

labour *or US & sometimes Canad* **labor** (ˈleɪbə) *n* **1** productive work, esp physical toil done for wages **2a** the people, class, or workers involved in this, esp in contrast to management, capital, etc **2b** (*as modifier*): *labour relations* **3a** difficult or arduous work or effort **3b** (*in combination*): *labour-saving* **4** a particular job or task, esp of a difficult nature **5a** the process or effort of childbirth or the time during which this takes place **5b** (*as modifier*): *labour pain; labour ward* ▷ *vb* **6** (*intr*) to perform labour; work **7** (*intr; foll by for, etc*) to strive or work hard (for something) **8** (*intr;* usually foll by *under*) to be burdened (by) or be at a disadvantage (because of): *to labour under a misapprehension* **9** (*intr*) to make one's way with difficulty **10** (*tr*) to deal with too persistently: *to labour a point* **11** (*intr*) (of a woman) to be in labour **12** (*intr*) (of a ship) to pitch and toss [C13 via OF from L *labor*]

labour camp *n* **1** a penal colony involving forced labour **2** a camp for migratory labourers

Labour Day *n* a public holiday in many countries in honour of labour, usually held on May 1

laboured *or US & sometimes Canad* **labored** (ˈleɪbəd) *adj* **1** (of breathing) performed with difficulty **2** showing effort; contrived; lacking grace or fluency

labourer *or US & sometimes Canad* **laborer** (ˈleɪbərə) *n* a person engaged in physical work, esp unskilled work

labour exchange *n Brit* a former name for the **employment office**

labour-intensive *adj* of or denoting a task, organization, industry, etc, in which a high proportion of the costs are due to wages, salaries, etc

Labourite (ˈleɪbəˌraɪt) *n* an adherent of the Labour Party

Labour Party *n* **1** a British political party, formed in 1900 as an amalgam of various trade unions and socialist groups, generally supporting the interests of organized labour and advocating democratic socialism and social equality **2** any similar party in any of various other countries

Labrador (ˈlæbrəˌdɔː) *n* **1** Also called: **Labrador-Ungava** a large peninsula of NE Canada, on the Atlantic, the Gulf of St. Lawrence, Hudson Strait, and Hudson Bay: contains most of the province of Quebec and the mainland part of Newfoundland; geologically part of the Canadian Shield. Area: 1 619 000 sq km (625 000 sq miles) **2** Also called: **Coast of Labrador** a region of NE Canada, on the Atlantic and consisting of the mainland part of Newfoundland province **3** (*often not capital*) short for **Labrador retriever**

Labrador retriever *n* a powerfully-built variety of retriever with a short dense usually black or golden-brown coat. Often shortened to **Labrador**

labret (ˈleɪbrɛt) *n* a piece of bone, shell, etc, inserted into the lip as an ornament by certain peoples [C19 from L *labrum* lip]

labrum (ˈleɪbrəm, ˈlæb-) *n, pl* **labra** (-brə) a lip or liplike part, such as the cuticular plate forming the upper lip of insects [C19 NL, from L]

La Bruyère (*French* la bryjɛr) *n* **Jean de** (ʒɑ̃ də) 1645–96, French moralist, noted for his *Caractères* (1688), satirical character studies, including portraits of contemporary public figures

Labuan (ləˈbuːən) *n* an island in Malaysia, off the NW coast of Borneo: part of the Straits Settlements until 1946, when transferred to North Borneo. Chief town: Victoria. Area: 98 sq km (38 sq miles)

laburnum (ləˈbɜːnəm) *n* any tree or shrub of a Eurasian genus having clusters of yellow drooping flowers: all parts of the plant are poisonous [C16 NL, from L]

labyrinth (ˈlæbərɪnθ) *n* **1** a mazelike network of tunnels, chambers, or paths, either natural or man-made **2** any complex or confusing system of streets, passages, etc **3** a complex or intricate situation **4** any system of interconnecting cavities, esp those comprising the internal ear **5** *electronics* an enclosure behind a high-performance loudspeaker, consisting of a series of air chambers designed to absorb unwanted sound waves [C16 via L from Gk *laburinthos*, from ?]

labyrinthine (ˌlæbəˈrɪnθaɪn) *adj* **1** of or relating to a labyrinth **2** resembling a labyrinth in complexity

lac[1] (læk) *n* a resinous substance secreted by certain insects (**lac insects**), used in the manufacture of shellac [C16 from Du. *lak* or F *laque*, from Hindi *lākh* resin, ult. from Sansk. *lākshā*]

lac[2] (lɑːk) *n* a variant spelling of **lakh**

Lacan (*French* lakɑ̃) *n* **Jacques** (ʒak) 1901–81, French psychoanalyst, who reinterpreted Freud in terms of structural linguistics: an important influence on poststructuralist thought

Laccadive, Minicoy, and Amindivi Islands (ˈlækədɪv, ˈmɪnɪˌkɔɪ, ˌʌmənˈdiːviː) *pl n* the former name (until 1973) of the **Lakshadweep Islands**

laccolith (ˈlækəlɪθ) *or* **laccolite** (ˈlækəˌlaɪt) *n* a dome-shaped body of igneous rock between two layers of older sedimentary rock ▷ Cf **lopolith** [C19 from Gk *lakkos* cistern + -LITH]

lace (leɪs) *n* **1** a delicate decorative fabric made from cotton, silk, etc, woven in an open web of different symmetrical patterns and figures **2** a cord or string drawn through eyelets or around hooks to fasten a shoe or garment **3** ornamental braid often used on military uniforms, etc ▷ *vb* **laces, lacing, laced** (*tr*) **4** to fasten (shoes, etc) with a lace **5** to draw (a cord or thread) through holes, eyes, etc, as when tying shoes **6** to compress the waist of (someone), as with a corset **7** to add a small amount of alcohol or drugs to (food or drink) **8** (*usually passive* and foll by *with*) to streak or mark with lines or colours: *the sky was laced with red* **9** to intertwine; interlace **10** *inf* to give a sound beating to [C13 *las*, from OF *laz*, from L *laqueus* noose]

▷ www.legacyoflace.com

▷ www.laceguild.demon.co.uk

lacebark (ˈleɪsbɑːk) *n* another name for **ribbonwood**

Lacedaemon (ˌlæsɪˈdiːmən) *n* another name for **Sparta** or **Laconia** > **Lacedaeˈmonian** *adj, n*

lacerate *vb* (ˈlæsəˌreɪt), **lacerates, lacerating, lacerated** (*tr*) **1** to tear (the flesh, etc) jaggedly **2** to hurt or harrow (the feelings, etc) ▷ *adj* (ˈlæsəˌreɪt, -rɪt) **3** having edges that are jagged: *lacerate leaves* [C16 from L *lacerāre* to tear, from *lacer* mangled] > ˌ**laceˈration** *n*

lace up *vb* **1** (*tr, adv*) to tighten or fasten (clothes or footwear) with laces ▷ *adj* **lace-up 2** (of footwear) to be

fastened with laces ▷ *n* **lace-up** **3** a lace-up shoe or boot
lacewing ('leɪs,wɪŋ) *n* any of various insects, esp the green lacewings and brown lacewings, having lacy wings and preying on aphids and similar pests
laches ('lætʃɪz) *n law* negligence or unreasonable delay in pursuing a legal remedy [C14 *lachesse*, via OF *lasche* slack, from L *laxus* LAX]
Lachesis ('lækɪsɪs) *n Greek myth* one of the three Fates [via L from Gk, from *lakhesis* destiny, from *lakhein* to befall by lot]
Lachlan ('lɒklən) *n* a river in SE Australia, rising in central New South Wales and flowing northwest then southwest to the Murrumbidgee River. Length: about 1450 km (900 miles) [named after *Lachlan* Macquarie, governor of New South Wales (1809–21)]
lachrymal ('lækrɪməl) *adj* a variant spelling of **lacrimal**
lachrymatory ('lækrɪmətərɪ, -trɪ) *n, pl* **lachrymatories** **1** a small vessel found in ancient tombs, formerly thought to hold the tears of mourners ▷ *adj* **2** a variant spelling of **lacrimatory**
lachrymose ('lækrɪ,məʊs) *adj* **1** given to weeping; tearful **2** mournful; sad [C17 from L, from *lacrima* a tear] > **'lachry,mosely** *adv*
lacing ('leɪsɪŋ) *n* **1** *chiefly Brit* a course of bricks, stone, etc, for strengthening a rubble or flint wall **2** another word for **lace** (senses 2, 3) **3** *inf* a severe beating
laciniate (lə'sɪnɪ,eɪt, -ɪt) *or* **laciniated** *adj* **1** *biol* jagged: *a laciniate leaf* **2** having a fringe [C17 from L *lacinia* flap] > **la,cini'ation** *n*
lack (læk) *n* **1** an insufficiency, shortage, or absence of something required or desired **2** something that is required but is absent or in short supply ▷ *vb* **3** (when *intr*, often foll by *in* or *for*) to be deficient (in) or have need (of) [C12 rel. to MDu. *laken* to be wanting]
lackadaisical (,lækə'deɪzɪkᵊl) *adj* **1** lacking vitality and purpose **2** lazy, esp in a dreamy way [C18 from earlier *lackadaisy*] > **,lacka'daisically** *adv*
lackey ('lækɪ) *n* **1** a servile follower; hanger-on **2** a liveried male servant or valet **3** a person who is treated like a servant ▷ *vb* **4** (when *intr*, often foll by *for*) to act as a lackey (to) [C16 via F *laquais*, from OF, ?from Catalan *lacayo, alacayo*]
lacklustre *or US* **lackluster** ('læk,lʌstə) *adj* lacking force, brilliance, or vitality
Laclos (*French* laklo) *n* **Pierre Choderlos de** (pjɛr ʃɔdɛrlo də) 1741–1803, French soldier and writer, noted for his novel in epistolary form *Les Liaisons dangereuses* (1782)
Laconia (lə'kəʊnɪə) *n* an ancient country of S Greece, in the SE Peloponnese, of which Sparta was the capital: corresponds to the present-day department of Lakonia > **La'conian** *n, adj*
laconic (lə'kɒnɪk) *adj* (of a person's speech) using few words; terse [C16 via L from Gk *Lakōnikos*, from *Lakōn* Laconian, Spartan; referring to the Spartans' terseness of speech] > **la'conically** *adv*
La Coruña (*Spanish* la ko'ruɲa) *n* a port in NW Spain, on the Atlantic: point of departure for the Spanish Armada (1588); site of the defeat of the French by the British under Sir John Moore in the Peninsular War (1809). Pop: 243 134 (1998 est). English name: **Corunna**
lacquer ('lækə) *n* **1** a hard glossy coating made by dissolving cellulose derivatives or natural resins in a volatile solvent **2** a black resinous substance, obtained from certain trees (**lacquer trees**), used to give a hard glossy finish to wooden furniture **3** Also called: **hair lacquer** a mixture of shellac and alcohol for spraying onto the hair to hold a style in place **4** *art* decorative objects coated with such lacquer, often inlaid ▷ *vb (tr)* **5** to apply lacquer to [C16 from obs. F *lacre* sealing wax, from Port. *laca* LAC[1]] > **'lacquerer** *n*
lacrimal, lachrymal, *or* **lacrymal** ('lækrɪməl) *adj* of or relating to tears or to the glands that secrete tears [C16 from Med. L, from L *lacrima* a tear]
lacrimation (,lækrɪ'meɪʃən) *n* the secretion of tears
lacrimatory, lachrymatory, *or* **lacrymatory** ('lækrɪmətərɪ, -trɪ) *adj* of, causing, or producing tears
lacrosse (lə'krɒs) *n* a ball game invented by American Indians, now played by two teams who try to propel a ball into each other's goal by means of long-handled pouched sticks (**lacrosse sticks**) [C19 Canad F: the hooked stick, crosier]
▷ www.lacrosse.ca
lactam ('læktæm) *n chem* any of a group of cyclic amides, derived from amino acids, having the characteristic group -CONH- [C20 from LACTO- + AM(IDE)]
lactate[1] ('lækteɪt) *n* an ester or salt of lactic acid [C18]
lactate[2] (læk'teɪt) *vb* **lactates, lactating, lactated** *(intr)* (of mammals) to produce or secrete milk
lactation (læk'teɪʃən) *n* **1** the secretion of milk from the mammary glands after parturition **2** the period during which milk is secreted
lacteal ('læktɪəl) *adj* **1** of, relating to, or resembling milk **2** (of lymphatic vessels) conveying or containing chyle ▷ *n* **3** any of the lymphatic vessels conveying chyle from the small intestine to the thoracic duct [C17 from L *lacteus* of milk, from *lac* milk]
lactescent (læk'tɛsᵊnt) *adj* **1** (of plants and certain insects) secreting a milky fluid **2** milky or becoming milky [C18 from L, from *lactescĕre* to become milky, from *lact-*, *lac* milk] > **lac'tescence** *n*
lactic ('læktɪk) *adj* relating to or derived from milk [C18 from L *lact-*, *lac* milk]
lactic acid *n* a colourless syrupy carboxylic acid found in sour milk and many fruits and used as a preservative (E270) for foodstuffs. Formula: $CH_3CH(OH)COOH$. Systematic name: **2-hydroxypropanoic acid**
lactiferous (læk'tɪfərəs) *adj* producing, conveying, or secreting milk or a milky fluid [C17 from L *lactifer*, from *lact-*, *lac* milk]
lacto- ('læktəʊ) *or before a vowel* **lact-** *combining form* indicating milk: *lactobacillus* [from L *lact-*, *lac* milk]
lactose ('læktəʊs, -təʊz) *n* a white crystalline sugar occurring in milk and used in pharmaceuticals and baby foods. Formula: $C_{12}H_{22}O_{11}$
lacto-vegetarian *n* a vegetarian whose diet includes dairy produce
La Cumbre (lə 'ku:mbreɪ) *n* another name for the **Uspallata Pass**
lacuna (lə'kju:nə) *n, pl* **lacunae** (-ni:) *or* **lacunas** **1** a gap or space, esp in a book or manuscript **2** *biol* a cavity or depression, such as any of the spaces in the matrix of bone [C17 from L *lacūna* pool, cavity, from *lacus* lake] > **la'cunose, la'cunal, la'cunar,** *or* **la'cunary** *adj*
lacustrine (lə'kʌstraɪn) *adj* **1** of or relating to lakes **2** living or growing in or on the shores of a lake [C19 from It. *lacustre*, from L *lacus* lake]
lacy ('leɪsɪ) *adj* **lacier, laciest** made of or resembling lace > **'lacily** *adv* > **'laciness** *n*
lad (læd) *n* **1** a boy or young man **2** *inf* a familiar form of address for any male **3** a lively or dashing man or youth (esp in **a bit of a lad**) **4** a young man whose behaviour is characteristic of male adolescents, esp in being rowdy, macho, or immature **5** *Brit* a boy or man who looks after horses [C13 *ladde*; ?from ON]
ladanum ('lædənəm) *n* a dark resinous juice obtained from various rockroses: used in perfumery [C16 L from Gk, from *lēdon* rockrose]
ladder ('lædə) *n* **1** a portable framework of wood, metal, rope, etc, in the form of two long parallel members connected by rungs or steps fixed to them at right angles, for climbing up or down **2** any hierarchy conceived of as having a series of ascending stages, levels, etc: *the social ladder* **3** Also called: **run** *chiefly Brit* a line of connected stitches that have come undone in knitted material, esp stockings ▷ *vb* **4** *chiefly Brit* to cause a line of interconnected stitches in (stockings, etc) to

Ll

undo, as by snagging, or (of a stocking) to come undone in this way [OE *hlǣdder*]

ladder back *n* a type of chair in which the back is constructed of horizontal slats between two uprights

laddie (ˈlædɪ) *n chiefly Scot* a familiar term for a male, esp a boy; lad

laddish (ˈlædɪʃ) *adj inf, usually derog.* characteristic of male adolescents or young men, esp by being rowdy, macho, or immature: *laddish behaviour*

lade (leɪd) *vb* **lades, lading, laded; laden** *or* **laded 1** to put cargo or freight on board (a ship, etc) or (of a ship, etc) to take on cargo or freight **2** (*tr; usually passive* and foll by *with*) to burden or oppress **3** (*tr; usually passive* and foll by *with*) to fill or load **4** to remove (liquid) with or as if with a ladle [OE *hladen* to load]

laden (ˈleɪdᵊn) *vb* **1** a past participle of **lade** ▷ *adj* **2** weighed down with a load; loaded **3** encumbered; burdened

ladette (ˌlædˈɛt) *n inf* a young woman whose social behaviour is similar to that of male adolescents or young men

la-di-da, lah-di-dah, *or* **la-de-da** (ˌlɑːdiːˈdɑː) *adj inf* affecting exaggeratedly genteel manners or speech [c19 mockingly imit. of affected speech]

ladies *or* **ladies' room** *n* (*functioning as sing*) *inf* a women's public lavatory

lading (ˈleɪdɪŋ) *n* a load; cargo; freight

Ladislaus I (ˈlædɪsˌlɔːs) *or* **Ladislas** (ˈlædɪsˌlæs) *n* **Saint** 1040–95, king of Hungary (1077–95) He extended his country's boundaries and suppressed paganism. Feast day: June 27

ladle (ˈleɪdᵊl) *n* **1** a long-handled spoon having a deep bowl for serving or transferring liquids **2** a large bucket-shaped container for transferring molten metal ▷ *vb* **ladles, ladling, ladled 3** (*tr*) to serve out as with a ladle [OE *hlædel*, from *hladan* to draw out] > **ˈladleful** *n*

ladle out *vb* (*tr, adv*) *inf* to distribute (money, gifts, etc) generously

Ladoga (*Russian* ˈladəgə) *n* **Lake** a lake in NW Russia, in the SW Karelian Republic: the largest lake in Europe; drains through the River Neva into the Gulf of Finland. Area: about 18 000 sq km (7000 sq miles). Russian name: **Ladozhskoye Ozero** (ˈladəʃskəjə ˈɔzɪrə)

Ladrone Islands (ləˈdrəʊn) *pl n* the former name (1521–1668) of the **Mariana Islands**

lady (ˈleɪdɪ) *n, pl* **ladies 1** a woman regarded as having the characteristics of a good family and high social position **2a** a polite name for a woman **2b** (*as modifier*): *a lady doctor* **3** an informal name for **wife 4 lady of the house** the female head of the household **5** *history* a woman with proprietary rights and authority, as over a manor [OE *hlǣfdīge*, from *hlāf* bread + *dīge* kneader, rel. to *dāh* dough]

Lady (ˈleɪdɪ) *n, pl* **Ladies 1** (in Britain) a title of honour borne by various classes of women of the peerage **2 my lady** a term of address to holders of the title Lady **3 Our Lady** a title of the Virgin Mary

ladybird (ˈleɪdɪˌbɜːd) *n* any of various small brightly coloured beetles, esp one having red elytra with black spots [c18 after Our *Lady*, the Virgin Mary]

lady bountiful *n* an ostentatiously charitable woman [c19 after a character in George Farquhar's play *The Beaux' Stratagem* (1707)]

ladyboy (ˈleɪdɪˌbɔɪ) *n inf* a man who dresses as a woman, esp one from the Far East

Lady Chapel *n* a chapel within a church or cathedral, dedicated to the Virgin Mary

Lady Day *n* March 25, the feast of the Annunciation of the Virgin Mary. Also called: **Annunciation Day**

lady-in-waiting *n, pl* **ladies-in-waiting** a lady who attends a queen or princess

lady-killer *n inf* a man who is, or believes he is, irresistibly fascinating to women

ladylike (ˈleɪdɪˌlaɪk) *adj* like or befitting a lady in manners and bearing; refined and fastidious

ladylove (ˈleɪdɪˌlʌv) *n now rare* a beloved woman

Lady Macbeth strategy *n* a strategy in a takeover battle in which a third party makes a bid acceptable to the target company, appearing to act as a white knight but subsequently joining forces with the original (unwelcome) bidder [c20 after *Lady Macbeth* in Shakespeare's *Macbeth* (1605)]

lady mayoress *n Brit* the wife of a lord mayor

Lady of the Lake *n* (in Arthurian legend) a mysterious supernatural being sometimes identified with **Vivian**

lady's bedstraw *n* a Eurasian plant with clusters of small yellow flowers

lady's finger *n* another name for **bhindi**

Ladyship (ˈleɪdɪʃɪp) *n* (preceded by *your* or *her*) a title used to address or refer to any peeress except a duchess

Ladysmith (ˈleɪdɪˌsmɪθ) *n* a city in E South Africa: besieged by Boers for four months (1899–1900) during the Boer War. Pop: 56 600 (latest est)

lady's-slipper *n* any of various orchids having reddish or purple flowers

lady's-smock *n* a N temperate plant with white or rose-pink flowers. Also called: **cuckooflower**

Laënnec (*French* laɛnɛk) *n* **René Théophile Hyacinthe** (rəne teɔfil jasɛ̃t) 1781–1826, French physician, who invented the stethoscope

Laertes (leɪˈɜːtiːz) *n Greek myth* the father of Odysseus

laevo- *or US* **levo-** *combining form* **1** on or towards the left: *laevorotatory* **2** (in chemistry) denoting a laevorotatory compound [from L *laevus* left]

laevorotation (ˌliːvəʊrəʊˈteɪʃən) *n* **1** a rotation to the left **2** an anticlockwise rotation of the plane of polarization of plane-polarized light as a result of its passage through a crystal, liquid, or solution ▷Cf **dextrorotation** > **laevorotatory** (ˌliːvəʊˈrəʊtətərɪ) *adj*

Lafayette *or* **La Fayette** (*French* lafajɛt) *n* **1 Marie Joseph Paul Yves Roch Gilbert du Motier** (mari ʒozɛf pɔl iv rɔk ʒilbɛr dy mɔtje), Marquis de Lafayette. 1757–1834, French general and statesman. He fought on the side of the colonists in the War of American Independence and, as commander of the National Guard (1789–91; 1830), he played a leading part in the French Revolution and the revolution of 1830 **2 Marie-Madeleine** (marimadlɛn), Comtesse de Lafayette. 1634–93, French novelist, noted for her historical romance *La Princesse de Clèves* (1678)

Laffer curve (ˈlæfə) *n econ* a graph showing government tax revenue plotted against percentage tax rates; it illustrates that a cut in a high tax rate can increase government revenue [c20 after Arthur *Laffer* (born 1940), US economist]

La Fontaine (*French* la fɔ̃tɛn) *n* **Jean de** (ʒɑ̃ də) 1621–95, French poet, famous for his *Fables* (1668–94)

Laforgue (*French* lafɔrg) *n* **Jules** (ʒyl) 1860–87, French symbolist poet. An originator of free verse, he had a considerable influence on modern poetry

LAFTA (ˈlæftə) *n acronym for* Latin American Free Trade Area, the name before 1981 of the Latin American Integration Association. See **LAIA**

▷ www-personal.umich.edu/alandear/glossary/l.html
▷ www.sice.oas.org/geograph/papers/iie/hufbauer0998.asp

lag¹ (læg) *vb* **lags, lagging, lagged** (*intr*) **1** (often foll by *behind*) to hang (back) or fall (behind) in movement, progress, development, etc **2** to fall away in strength or intensity ▷ *n* **3** the act or state of slowing down or falling behind **4** the interval of time between two events, esp between an action and its effect [c16 from ?]

lag² (læg) *sl* ▷ *n* **1** a convict or ex-convict (esp in **old lag**) **2** a term of imprisonment ▷ *vb* **lags, lagging, lagged 3** (*tr*) to arrest or put in prison [c19 from ?]

lag³ (læg) *vb* **lags, lagging, lagged 1** (*tr*) to cover (a pipe, cylinder, etc) with lagging to prevent loss of heat ▷ *n* **2** the insulating casing of a steam cylinder, boiler, etc **3** a stave [C17 of Scand. origin]

lagan ('lægᵊn) *n* goods or wreckage on the sea bed, sometimes attached to a buoy to permit recovery [C16 from OF *lagan*, prob. of Gmc origin]

lager ('lɑːgə) *n* a light-bodied effervescent beer, fermented in a closed vessel using yeasts that sink to the bottom of the brew [C19 from G *Lagerbier* beer for storing, from *Lager* storehouse]

Lagerfeld ('lɑːgə,fɛlt) *n* **Karl (Otto)** born 1938, German fashion designer working mainly in Paris

Lagerkvist (*Swedish* 'lɑːgərkvist) *n* **Pär (Fabian)** (pæːr) 1891–1974, Swedish novelist and dramatist. His works include the novels *The Dwarf* (1944) and *Barabbas* (1950): Nobel prize for literature 1951

Lagerlöf (*Swedish* 'lɑːgərløːv) *n* **Selma** ('sɛlma) 1858–1940, Swedish novelist, noted esp for her children's classic *The Wonderful Adventures of Nils* (1906–07): Nobel prize for literature 1909

lager lout *n* a rowdy or aggressive young drunk male

laggard ('lægəd) *n* **1** a person who lags behind ▷ *adj* **2** *rare* sluggish, slow, or dawdling > **'laggardly** *adj, adv* > **'laggardness** *n*

lagging ('lægɪŋ) *n* **1** insulating material wrapped around pipes, boilers, etc, or laid in a roof loft, to prevent loss of heat **2** the act or process of applying lagging

lagomorph ('lægəʊ,mɔːf) *n* any placental mammal having two pairs of upper incisors specialized for gnawing, such as rabbits and hares [C19 via NL from Gk *lagōs* hare; see -MORPH]

lagoon (lə'guːn) *n* **1** a body of water cut off from the open sea by coral reefs or sand bars **2** any small body of water, esp one adjoining a larger one [C17 from It. *laguna*, from L *lacūna* pool; see LACUNA]

Lagoon Islands *pl n* a former name of **Tuvalu**

Lagos ('leɪgɒs) *n* **1** the former capital and chief port of Nigeria, on the Bight of Benin: first settled in the sixteenth century; a slave market until the nineteenth century; ceded to Britain (1861); university (1962). Pop: 1 484 000 (1995 est) **2** a state of SW Nigeria. Capital: Ikeja. Pop: 6 357 253 (1995 est). Area: 3345 sq km (1292 sq miles)

Lagrange (*French* lagrɑ̃ʒ) *n* Comte **Joseph Louis** (ʒozɛf lwi) 1736–1813, French mathematician and astronomer, noted particularly for his work on harmonics, mechanics, and the calculus of variations

Lagrangian point (lə'greɪndʒɪən) *n astron* one of five points in the plane of revolution of two bodies in orbit around their common centre of gravity, at which a third body of negligible mass can remain in equilibrium with respect to the other two bodies [after J. L. LAGRANGE]

La Granja (*Spanish* la 'graŋxa) *n* another name for **San Ildefonso**

La Guaira *or* **La Guayra** (*Spanish* la 'gwaira) *n* the chief seaport of Venezuela, on the Caribbean. Pop: 26 669 (1990 est)

La Guardia (lə'gwɑːdɪə) *n* **Fiorello H(enry)** (,fɪə'rɛləʊ) 1882–1947, US politician. As mayor of New York (1933–45), he organized slum-clearance and labour safeguard schemes and suppressed racketeering

lah (lɑː) *n music* (in tonic sol-fa) the sixth note of any major scale; submediant [C14 later variant of *la*; see GAMUT]

lahar ('lɑːhɑː) *n* a landslide of volcanic debris mixed with water down the sides of a volcano, usually precipitated by heavy rainfall [C20 from Javanese: lava]

lah-di-dah (,lɑːdiː'dɑː) *adj, n inf* a variant spelling of **la-di-da**

Lahore (lə'hɔː) *n* **1** a city in NE Pakistan: capital of the former province of West Pakistan (1955–70); University of the Punjab (1882). Pop: 5 063 499 (1998) **2** a variety of large domestic fancy pigeon having a black-and-white plumage

Lahti (*Finnish* 'lɑhti) *n* a town in S Finland: site of the main Finnish radio and television stations; furniture industry. Pop: 94 706 (1994)

LAIA *abbrev for* Latin American Integration Association (before 1981, known as the Latin American Free Trade Area). An economic group, its members are Argentina, Bolivia, Brazil, Chile, Colombia, Ecuador, Mexico, Paraguay, Peru, Uruguay, and Venezuela
▷ www.itcilo.it/english/actrav/telearn/global/ilo/blokit/aladi.htm

Laibach ('laibax) *n* the German name for **Ljubljana**

laic ('leɪɪk) *adj also* **laical** **1** of or involving the laity; secular ▷ *n* **2** a rare word for **layman** [C15 from LL *lāicus* LAY³] > **'laically** *adv*

laicize *or* **laicise** ('leɪɪ,saɪz) *vb* **laicizes, laicizing, laicized** *or* **laicises, laicising, laicised** (*tr*) to withdraw clerical or ecclesiastical character or status from (an institution, building, etc) > **,laici'zation** *or* **,laici'sation** *n*

laid (leɪd) *vb* the past tense and past participle of **lay¹**

laid-back *adj* relaxed in style or character; easy-going and unhurried

laid paper *n* paper with a regular mesh impressed upon it

Lailat-ul-Qadr (,leɪlætʊl'kɑːdə) *n* a night of study and prayer observed annually by Muslims to mark the communication of the Koran: it usually follows the 27th day of Ramadan [from Ar.: night of determination]

lain (leɪn) *vb* the past participle of **lie²**

Laing (læŋ) *n* **R(onald) D(avid)** 1927–89, Scottish psychiatrist; his best known books include *The Divided Self* (1960), *The Politics of Experience and the Bird of Paradise* (1967), and *Knots* (1970)

Laingian ('læŋɪən) *adj* **1** of or based on R. D. Laing's theory that mental illnesses can be responses to stress in family and social situations ▷ *n* **2** a follower or adherent of Laing's teaching

lair¹ (lɛə) *n* **1** the resting place of a wild animal **2** *inf* a place of seclusion or hiding ▷ *vb* **3** (*intr*) (esp of a wild animal) to retreat to or rest in a lair **4** (*tr*) to drive or place (an animal) in a lair [OE *leger*]

lair² (lɛə) *Austral sl* ▷ *n* **1** a flashy man who shows off ▷ *vb* **2** (*intr*; foll by *up* or *around*) to behave or dress like a lair [?from LEER]

laird (lɛəd) *n Scot* a landowner, esp of a large estate [C15 Scot. var. of LORD]

laissez faire *or* **laisser faire** (,lɛseɪ 'fɛə) *n* **1a** Also called: **individualism** the doctrine of unrestricted freedom in commerce, esp for private interests **1b** (*as modifier*): *a laissez-faire economy* **2** indifference or noninterference, esp in the affairs of others [F, lit.: let (them) act]

laissez passer *French* (lese pase) *n* a permit allowing someone to pass, cross a frontier, etc [F, lit.: let (them) pass]

laity ('leɪɪtɪ) *n* **1** laymen, as distinguished from clergymen **2** all people not of a specific occupation [C16 from LAY³]

Laius ('laɪəs) *n Greek myth* a king of Thebes, killed by his son Oedipus, who did not know of their relationship

lake¹ (leɪk) *n* **1** an expanse of water entirely surrounded by land and unconnected to the sea except by rivers or streams. Related adj: **lacustrine** **2** anything resembling this **3** a surplus of a liquid commodity: *a wine lake* [C13 *lac*, via OF from L *lacus* basin]

lake² (leɪk) *n* **1** a bright pigment produced by the combination of an organic colouring matter with an inorganic compound, usually a metallic salt, oxide, or hydroxide **2** a red dye obtained by combining a metallic compound with cochineal [C17 var. of LAC¹]

Lake District *n* a region of lakes and mountains in NW England, in Cumbria: includes England's largest lake (Windermere) and highest mountain (Scafell Pike);

national park; literary associations (the Lake Poets); tourist region. Also called: **Lakeland**

lake dwelling *n* a dwelling, esp in prehistoric villages, constructed on platforms supported by wooden piles driven into the bottom of a lake > **lake dweller** *n*

Lakeland ('leɪk,lænd) *n* **1** another name for the **Lake District** *adj* **2** of or relating to the Lake District

Lakeland terrier *n* a wire-haired breed of terrier, originally from the Lake District

Lake of the Woods *n* a lake in N central North America, mostly in W Northern Ontario, Canada: fed chiefly by the Rainy River; drains into Lake Winnipeg by the Winnipeg River; many islands; tourist region. Area: 3846 sq km (1485 sq miles)

Lake Poets *pl n* the English poets Wordsworth, Coleridge, and Southey, who lived in and drew inspiration from the Lake District at the beginning of the 19th century

Lake Success *n* a village in SE New York State, on W Long Island: headquarters of the United Nations Security Council from 1946 to 1951. Pop: 2450 (1990 est)

lake trout *n* a yellow-spotted char of the Great Lakes region of Canada

lakh *or* **lac** (lɑːk) *n* (in India and Pakistan) the number 100 000, esp referring to this sum of rupees [C17 from Hindi *lākh*, ult. from Sansk. *lakshā* a sign]

Lakshadweep Islands (læk'ʃædwiːp) *pl n* a group of 26 coral islands and reefs in the Arabian Sea, off the SW coast of India: a union territory of India since 1956. Administrative centre: Kavaratti Island. Pop: 60 595 (2001). Area: 28 sq km (11 sq miles). Former name (until 1973): **Laccadive, Minicoy, and Amindivi Islands**

-lalia *n combining form* indicating a speech defect or abnormality: *echolalia* [NL, from Gk *lalia* chatter, from *lalein* to babble]

La Línea (*Spanish* la 'linea) *n* a town in SW Spain, on the Bay of Gibraltar. Pop: 57 000 (latest est). Official name: **La Línea de la Concepción** (ðe la ,konθep'θjon)

Lalique (*French* lalik) *n* **René (Jules)** (rəne) 1860–1945, French Art-Nouveau jeweller, glass-maker, and designer: noted esp for his frosted glassware

Lallans ('lælənz) *or* **Lallan** ('lælən) *n* **1** a literary version of the variety of English spoken and written in the Lowlands of Scotland **2** (*modifier*) of or relating to the Lowlands of Scotland or their dialects [Scot. var. of *Lowlands*]

lallation (læ'leɪʃən) *n phonetics* a defect of speech consisting of the pronunciation of (r) as (l) [C17 from L *lallāre* to sing lullaby, imit.]

Lalo ('lɑːləʊ) *n* **(Victor-Antoine-)Édouard** (edwar) 1823–92, French composer of Spanish descent. His works include the *Symphonie espagnole* (1873) and the ballet *Namouna* (1882)

lam[1] (læm) *vb* **lams, lamming, lammed** *sl* **1** (*tr*) to thrash or beat **2** (*intr*; usually foll by *into* or *out*) to make a sweeping stroke or blow [C16 from Scand.]

lam[2] (læm) *n US & Canad sl* **1** a sudden flight or escape, esp to avoid arrest **2 on the lam** making an escape [C19 ? from LAM[1] (hence, to be off)]

Lam. *Bible abbrev for* Lamentations

lama ('lɑːmə) *n* a priest or monk of Lamaism [C17 from Tibetan *blama*]

Lamaism ('lɑːmə,ɪzəm) *n* the Mahayana form of Buddhism of Tibet and Mongolia > **'Lamaist** *n, adj* > **,Lama'istic** *adj*

La Mancha (*Spanish* la 'mantʃa) *n* a plateau of central Spain, between the mountains of Toledo and the hills of Cuenca: traditionally associated with episodes in *Don Quixote*. Average height: 600 m (2000 ft)

La Manche (*French* la mɑ̃ʃ) *n* See **Manche** (sense 2)

Lamarck (*French* lamark) *n* **Jean Baptiste Pierre Antoine de Monet** (ʒɑ̃ batist pjɛr ɑ̃twan də mɔnɛ), Chevalier de Lamarck. 1744–1829, French naturalist. He outlined his theory of organic evolution (Lamarckism) in *Philosophie zoologique* (1809)

Lamarckism (lɑː'mɑːkɪzəm) *n* the theory of organic evolution proposed by Lamarck, based on the principle, now discredited, that characteristics of an organism modified during its lifetime are inheritable

Lamartine (*French* lamartin) *n* **Alphonse Marie Louis de Prat de** (alfɔ̃s mari lwi də pra də) 1790–1869, French romantic poet, historian, and statesman: his works include *Méditations poétiques* (1820) and *Histoire des Girondins* (1847)

lamasery ('lɑːməsərɪ) *n, pl* **lamaseries** a monastery of lamas [C19 from F *lamaserie*, from LAMA + F *-serie*, from Persian *serāī* palace]

lamb (læm) *n* **1** the young of a sheep **2** the meat of a young sheep **3** a person, esp a child, who is innocent, meek, good, etc **4** a person easily deceived ▷ *vb* **5** (*intr*) (of a ewe) to give birth **6** (*intr*) (of a shepherd) to tend the ewes and newborn lambs at lambing time [OE *lamb*, from Gmc] > **'lamb,like** *adj* (læm) *n*

Lamb[1] (læm) *n* **the** a title given to Christ in the New Testament

Lamb[2] (læm) *n* **1 Charles,** pen name *Elia*. 1775–1834, English essayist and critic. He collaborated with his sister Mary on *Tales from Shakespeare* (1807). His other works include *Specimens of English Dramatic Poets* (1808) and the largely autobiographical essays collected in *Essays of Elia* (1823; 1833) **2 William** See (2nd Viscount) **Melbourne** **3 Willis Eugene** born 1913, US physicist. He detected the small difference in energy between two states of the hydrogen atom (**Lamb shift**). Nobel prize for physics 1955

lambada (læm'bɑːdə) *n* **1** an erotic dance, originating in Brazil, performed by two people who hold each other closely and gyrate their hips in synchronized movements **2** the music that accompanies the lambada, combining salsa, calypso, and reggae [C20 from Port., lit.: the snapping of a whip]

Lambaréné (*French* lɑ̃barene) *n* a town in W Gabon on the Ogooué River: site of the hospital built by Albert Schweitzer, who died and was buried there (1965). Pop: 50 000 (latest est)

lambast (læm'bæst) *or* **lambaste** (læm'beɪst) *vb* **lambasts, lambasting, lambasted** *or* **lambastes, lambasting, lambasted** (*tr*) **1** to beat or whip severely **2** to reprimand or scold [C17 ?from LAM[1] + BASTE[3]]

lambda ('læmdə) *n* the 11th letter of the Greek alphabet (Λ, λ) [C14 from Gk, from Semitic]

lambent ('læmbənt) *adj* **1** (esp of a flame) flickering softly over a surface **2** glowing with soft radiance **3** (of wit or humour) light or brilliant [C17 from the present participle of L *lambere* to lick] > **'lambency** *n* > **'lambently** *adv*

lambert ('læmbət) *n* the cgs unit of illumination, equal to 1 lumen per square centimetre. Symbol: L [C20 after J. H. *Lambert* (1728–77), G mathematician & physicist]

Lambert ('læmbət) *n* **Constant** 1905–51, English composer and conductor. His works include much ballet music and *The Rio Grande* (1929), a work for chorus, orchestra, and piano, using jazz idioms

Lambeth ('læmbəθ) *n* **1** a borough of S Greater London, on the Thames: contains **Lambeth Palace** (the London residence of the Archbishop of Canterbury) Pop: 266 170 (2001). Area: 27 sq km (11 sq miles) **2** the Archbishop of Canterbury in his official capacity

lambing ('læmɪŋ) *n* **1** the birth of lambs **2** the shepherd's work of tending the ewes and newborn lambs at this time

lambkin ('læmkɪn) *n* **1** a small lamb **2** a term of affection for a small endearing child

Lamb of God *n* a title given to Christ in the New Testament, probably with reference to his sacrificial death

lambrequin ('læmbrɪkɪn, 'læmbə-) *n* **1** an ornamental hanging covering the edge of a shelf or the upper part of a window or door **2** (*often pl*) a scarf worn over a helmet [c18 from F, from Du. *lamperkin* (unattested), dim. of *lamper* veil]

Lambrusco (læm'brʊskəʊ) *n* **1** a red grape grown in Italy **2** a sparkling red wine made in Italy from this grape **3** a much less common white variety of this grape or wine

lambskin ('læm,skɪn) *n* **1** the skin of a lamb, esp with the wool still on **2** a material or garment prepared from this skin

lamb's lettuce *n* another name for **corn salad**

lamb's tails *pl n* the pendulous catkins of the hazel tree

lame (leɪm) *adj* **1** disabled or crippled in the legs or feet **2** painful or weak: *a lame back* **3** weak; unconvincing: *a lame excuse* **4** not effective or enthusiastic: *a lame try* **5** *sl* conventional or uninspiring ▷ *vb* **lames, laming, lamed** **6** (*tr*) to make lame [OE *lama*] > **'lamely** *adv* > **'lameness** *n*

lamé ('lɑːmeɪ) *n* a fabric of silk, cotton, or wool interwoven with threads of metal [c20 from F, from OF *lame* gold or silver thread, thin plate, from L *lāmina* thin plate]

lame duck *n* **1** a person or thing that is disabled or ineffectual **2** *stock exchange* a speculator who cannot discharge his liabilities **3** *US* an elected official or body of officials remaining in office in the interval between the election and inauguration of a successor

lamella (lə'mɛlə) *n, pl* **lamellae** (-liː) *or* **lamellas** a thin layer, plate, or membrane, esp any of the calcified layers of which bone is formed [c17 NL, from L, dim. of *lāmina* thin plate] > **la'mellar, lamellate** ('læmɪ,leɪt, -lɪt), *or* **lamellose** (lə'mɛləʊs, 'læmɪ,ləʊs) *adj*

lamellibranch (lə'mɛlɪ,bræŋk) *n, adj* another word for **bivalve** [c19 from NL *lamellibranchia* plate-gilled (animals)]

lamellicorn (lə'mɛlɪ,kɔːn) *n* **1** any beetle having flattened terminal plates to the antennae, such as the scarabs and stag beetles ▷ *adj* **2** designating antennae with platelike terminal segments [c19 from NL *Lamellicornia* plate-horned (animals)]

lament (lə'mɛnt) *vb* **1** to feel or express sorrow, remorse, or regret (for or over) ▷ *n* **2** an expression of sorrow **3** a poem or song in which a death is lamented [c16 from L *lāmentum*] > **la'menter** *n* > **la'mentingly** *adv*

lamentable ('læməntəbᵊl) *adj* **1** wretched, deplorable, or distressing **2** an archaic word for **mournful** > **'lamentably** *adv*

lamentation (,læmɛn'teɪʃən) *n* **1** a lament; expression of sorrow **2** the act of lamenting

lamented (lə'mɛntɪd) *adj* grieved for or regretted (often in **late lamented**): *our late lamented employer* > **la'mentedly** *adv*

lamina ('læmɪnə) *n, pl* **laminae** (-,niː) *or* **laminas** **1** a thin plate or layer, esp of bone or mineral **2** *bot* the flat blade of a leaf [c17 NL, from L: thin plate] > **'laminar** *or* **laminose** ('læmɪ,nəʊs, -,nəʊz) *adj*

laminar flow *n* nonturbulent motion of a fluid in which parallel layers have different velocities relative to each other

laminate *vb* ('læmɪ,neɪt), **laminates, laminating, laminated** **1** (*tr*) to make (material in sheet form) by bonding together two or more thin sheets **2** to split or be split into thin sheets **3** (*tr*) to beat, form, or press (material, esp metal) into thin sheets **4** (*tr*) to cover or overlay with a thin sheet of material ▷ *n* ('læmɪ,neɪt, -nɪt) **5** a material made by bonding together two or more sheets ▷ *adj* ('læmɪ,neɪt, -nɪt) **6** having or composed of lamina; laminated [c17 from NL *lāminātus* plated] > **'laminable** *adj* > **,lami'nation** *n* > **'lami,nator** *n*

laminated ('læmɪ,neɪtɪd) *adj* **1** composed of many layers of plastic, wood, etc, bonded together **2** covered with a thin protective layer of plastic, etc

lamington ('læmɪŋtən) *n Austral & NZ* a cube of sponge cake coated in chocolate or red jelly and dried coconut [c20 (in the earlier sense: a homburg hat): after Lady *Lamington*, wife of Baron Lamington, governor of Queensland (1896–1901)]

Lammas ('læməs) *n* **1** *RC Church* Aug 1, held as a feast, commemorating St Peter's miraculous deliverance from prison **2** Also called: **Lammas Day** the same day formerly observed in England as a harvest festival [OE *hlāfmæsse* loaf mass]

lammergeier *or* **lammergeyer** ('læmə,gaɪə) *n* a rare vulture of S Europe, Africa, and Asia, with dark wings, a pale breast, and black feathers around the bill [c19 from G *Lämmergeier*, from *Lämmer* lambs + *Geier* vulture]

lamp (læmp) *n* **1a** any of a number of devices that produce illumination: *an electric lamp; a gas lamp; an oil lamp* **1b** (*in combination*): *lampshade* **2** a device for holding one or more electric light bulbs: *a table lamp* **3** a vessel in which a liquid fuel is burned to supply illumination **4** any of a variety of devices that produce radiation, esp for therapeutic purposes: *an ultraviolet lamp* [c13 *lampe*, via OF from L *lampas*, from Gk, from *lampein* to shine]

lampblack ('læmp,blæk) *n* a finely divided form of almost pure carbon produced by the incomplete combustion of organic compounds, such as natural gas, used in making carbon electrodes and dynamo brushes and as a pigment

lamp chimney *n* a glass tube that surrounds the wick in an oil lamp

Lampedusa[1] (,læmpɪ'djuːzə) *n* an island in the Mediterranean, between Malta and Tunisia. Area: about 21 sq km (8 sq miles)

Lampedusa[2] (,læmpɪ'djuːzə) *n* **Giuseppe Tomasi di** 1896–1957, Italian novelist: author of the historical novel *The Leopard* (1958)

lamplight ('læmp,laɪt) *n* the light produced by a lamp or lamps

lamplighter ('læmp,laɪtə) *n* **1** (formerly) a person who lit and extinguished street lamps, esp gas ones **2** *chiefly US & Canad* any of various devices used to light lamps

lampoon (læm'puːn) *n* **1** a satire in prose or verse ridiculing a person, literary work, etc ▷ *vb* **2** (*tr*) to attack or satirize in a lampoon [c17 from F *lampon*, ?from *lampons* let us drink (frequently used as a refrain in poems)] > **lam'pooner** *or* **lam'poonist** *n* > **lam'poonery** *n*

lamppost ('læmp,pəʊst) *n* a post supporting a lamp, esp in a street

lamprey ('læmprɪ) *n* any eel-like vertebrate having a round sucking mouth for clinging to and feeding on the blood of other animals. Also called: **lamper eel** [c13 from OF *lamproie*, from LL *lamprēda*, from ?]

Lanai (lɑː'nɑːɪ, lə'naɪ) *n* an island in central Hawaii, west of Maui Island. Pop: 2426 (1990). Area: 363 sq km (140 sq miles)

Lanarkshire ('lænək,ʃɪə, -ʃə) *n* a historical county of S Scotland: became part of Strathclyde region in 1975; since 1996 administered by the council areas of North Lanarkshire, South Lanarkshire, and Glasgow

Lancashire ('læŋkə,ʃɪə, -ʃə) *n* **1** a county of NW England, on the Irish Sea: became a county palatine in 1351 and a duchy attached to the Crown; much reduced in size after the 1974 boundary changes, losing the Furness district to Cumbria and much of the south to Greater Manchester, Merseyside, and Cheshire: Blackburn with Darwen and Blackpool became independent unitary authorities in 1998. It was traditionally a cotton textiles manufacturing region. Administrative centre: Preston. Pop (excluding unitary authorities): 1 134 974 (2001). Area (excluding unitary authorities): 2889 sq km (1115 sq miles). Abbreviation: **Lancs** **2** a mild whitish-coloured cheese with a crumbly texture

Lancaster[1] ('læŋkəstə, 'læŋ,kæstə) *n* the English royal house that reigned from 1399 to 1461
▷ www.compapp.dcu.ie/humphrys/FamTree/Royal/lancaster.html

Ll

▷ www.nationmaster.com/encyclopedia/House-of-Lancaster

Lancaster² ('læŋkəstə) *n* a city in NW England, former county town of Lancashire, on the River Lune: castle (built on the site of a Roman camp); university (1964). Pop: 44 497 (1991)

Lancastrian (læŋ'kæstrıən) *n* **1** a native or resident of Lancashire or Lancaster **2** an adherent of the house of Lancaster in the Wars of the Roses ▷ *adj* **3** of or relating to Lancashire or Lancaster **4** of or relating to the house of Lancaster

lance (lɑːns) *n* **1** a long weapon with a pointed head used by horsemen **2** a similar weapon used for hunting, whaling, etc **3** *surgery* another name for **lancet** ▷ *vb* **lances, lancing, lanced** (*tr*) **4** to pierce (an abscess or boil) with a lancet **5** to pierce with or as with a lance [C13 *launce*, from OF *lance*, from L *lancea*]

lance corporal *n* a noncommissioned army officer of the lowest rank

lancelet ('lɑːnslıt) *n* any of several marine animals closely related to the vertebrates: they burrow in sand. Also called: **amphioxus** [C19 referring to the slender shape]

Lancelot ('lɑːnslət) *n* (in Arthurian legend) one of the Knights of the Round Table; the lover of Queen Guinevere

lanceolate ('lɑːnsıəˌleıt, -lıt) *adj* narrow and tapering to a point at each end: *lanceolate leaves* [C18 from LL *lanceolātus*, from *lanceola* small LANCE]

lancer ('lɑːnsə) *n* **1** (formerly) a cavalryman armed with a lance **2** a member of a regiment retaining such a title

lancers ('lɑːnsəz) *n* (*functioning as sing*) **1** a quadrille for eight or sixteen couples **2** a piece of music composed for or in the rhythm of this dance

lancet ('lɑːnsıt) *n* **1** Also called: **lance** a pointed surgical knife with two sharp edges **2** short for **lancet arch** or **lancet window** [C15 *lancette*, from OF: small LANCE]

lancet arch *n* a narrow acutely pointed arch

lancet window *n* a narrow window having a lancet arch

lancewood ('lɑːnsˌwʊd) *n* a New Zealand tree with slender leaves showing different configurations in youth and maturity

Lanchow *or* **Lan-chou** ('læn'tʃaʊ) *n* a variant transliteration of the Chinese name for **Lanzhou**

Lancs (læŋks) *abbrev for* Lancashire

land (lænd) *n* **1** the solid part of the surface of the earth as distinct from seas, lakes, etc. Related adj: **terrestrial** **2** ground, esp with reference to its use, quality, etc **3** rural or agricultural areas as contrasted with urban ones **4** farming as an occupation or way of life **5** *law* any tract of ground capable of being owned as property **6a** a country, region, or area **6b** the people of a country, etc **7** *econ* the factor of production consisting of all natural resources ▷ *vb* **8** to transfer (something) or go from a ship or boat to the shore: *land the cargo* **9** (*intr*) to come to or touch shore **10** (*intr*) (in Canada) to be legally admitted to the country, as an immigrant or **landed** immigrant **11** to come down or bring (something) down to earth after a flight or jump **12** to come or bring to some point, condition, or state **13** (*tr*) *angling* to retrieve (a hooked fish) from the water **14** (*tr*) *inf* to win or obtain: *to land a job* **15** (*tr*) *inf* to deliver (a blow) ▷ See also **land up** [OE] > **'landless** *adj*

Land (lænd) *n* **Edwin Herbert** 1909–91, US inventor of the Polaroid Land camera

Land *German* (lant) *n, pl* ***Länder*** ('lɛndər) **1** any of the federal states of Germany **2** any of the provinces of Austria

land agent *n* **1** a person who administers a landed estate and its tenancies **2** a person who acts as an agent for the sale of land > **land agency** *n*

landau ('lændɔː) *n* a four-wheeled carriage, usually horse-drawn, with two folding hoods over the passenger compartment [C18 after *Landau* (a town in Germany), where first made]

Landau (*Russian* lan'dau) *n* **Lev Davidovich** (ljɛf da'vidəvitʃ) 1908–68, Soviet physicist, noted for his researches on quantum theory and his work on the theories of solids and liquids: Nobel prize for physics 1962

landaulet (ˌlændɔː'lɛt) *n* **1** a small landau **2** *US* an early type of car with a folding hood over the passenger seats

landed ('lændıd) *adj* **1** owning land: *landed gentry* **2** consisting of or including land: *a landed estate* **3** *Canad* having been formally admitted into Canada as an immigrant

Landes (*French* lɑ̃d) *n* **1** a department of SW France, in Aquitaine region. Capital: Mont-de-Marsan. Pop: 327 334 (1999). Area: 9364 sq km (3652 sq miles) **2** a region of SW France, on the Bay of Biscay: occupies most of the Landes department and parts of Gironde and Lot-et-Garonne; consists chiefly of the most extensive forest in France. Area: 14 000 sq km (5400 sq miles)

landfall ('lændˌfɔːl) *n* **1** the act of sighting or nearing land, esp from the sea **2** the land sighted or neared

landfill ('lændˌfıl) *adj* of or denoting low-lying sites or tips being filled up with alternate layers of rubbish and earth

landform ('lændˌfɔːm) *n* *geol* any natural feature of the earth's surface

land girl *n* a girl or woman who does farm work, esp in wartime

landgrave ('lændˌgreıv) *n* *German history* **1** (from the 13th century to 1806) a count who ruled over a specified territory **2** (after 1806) the title of any of various sovereign princes [C16 via G, from MHG *lantgrāve*, from *lant* land + *grāve* count]

land-holder *n* a person who owns or occupies land > **'land-ˌholding** *adj, n*

landing ('lændıŋ) *n* **1a** the act of coming to land, esp after a flight or a sea voyage **1b** (*as modifier*): *landing place* **2** a place of disembarkation **3** the floor area at the top of a flight of stairs

landing craft *n* *mil* any small vessel designed for the landing of troops and equipment on beaches

landing field *n* an area of land on which aircraft land and from which they take off

landing gear *n* another name for **undercarriage**

landing net *n* *angling* a loose long-handled net for lifting hooked fish from the water

landing stage *n* a platform used for landing goods and passengers from a vessel

landing strip *n* another name for **airstrip**

landlady ('lændˌleıdı) *n, pl* **landladies** **1** a woman who owns and leases property **2** a woman who owns or runs a lodging house, pub, etc

ländler (*German* 'lɛntlər) *n* **1** an Austrian country dance in which couples spin and clap **2** a piece of music composed for or in the rhythm of this dance, in three-four time [G, from dialect *Landl* Upper Austria]

land line *n* a telecommunications wire or cable laid over land

landlocked ('lændˌlɒkt) *adj* **1** (esp of lakes) completely surrounded by land **2** (esp of certain salmon) living in fresh water that is permanently isolated from the sea

landlord ('lændˌlɔːd) *n* **1** a man who owns and leases property **2** a man who owns or runs a lodging house, pub, etc

landlubber ('lændˌlʌbə) *n* *naut* any person having no experience at sea

landmark ('lændˌmɑːk) *n* **1** a prominent or well-known object in or feature of a particular landscape **2** an important or unique decision, event, fact, discovery, etc **3** a boundary marker

landmass ('lændˌmæs) *n* a large continuous area of land, as opposed to seas or islands

land mine *n mil* an explosive charge placed in the ground, usually detonated by stepping or driving on it
land of milk and honey *n* **1** *Old Testament* the fertile land promised to the Israelites by God (Ezekiel 20:6) **2** any fertile land, state, etc
land of Nod *n* **1** *Old Testament* a region to the east of Eden to which Cain went after he had killed Abel (Genesis 4:14) **2** an imaginary land of sleep
Landor ('lændɔː) *n* **Walter Savage** 1775–1864, English poet, noted also for his prose works, including *Imaginary Conversations* (1824–29)
landowner ('lænd,əʊnə) *n* a person who owns land > **'land,owner,ship** *n* > **'land,owning** *n, adj*
Landowska (*Polish* lan'dɔfska) *n* **Wanda** ('vanda) 1877–1959, US harpsichordist, born in Poland
land rail *n* another name for **corncrake**
land reform *n* the redistributing of large agricultural holdings among the landless
landscape ('lænd,skeɪp) *n* **1** an extensive area of land regarded as being visually distinct **2** a painting, drawing, photograph, etc, depicting natural scenery **3** the genre including such pictures **4** the distinctive features of a given area of intellectual activity, regarded as an integrated whole ▷ *adj* **5** *printing* **5a** (of an illustration in a book, magazine, etc) of greater width than depth ▷ Cf **portrait** (sense 3) **5b** (of a page) carrying an illustration or table printed at right angles to the normal text ▷ *vb* **landscapes, landscaping, landscaped 6** (*tr*) to improve the natural features of (a garden, park, etc), as by creating contoured features and planting trees **7** (*intr*) to work as a landscape gardener [c16 *landskip* (orig. a term in painting), from MDu. *lantscap* region]
landscape gardening *n* the art of laying out grounds in imitation of natural scenery. Also called: **landscape architecture** > **landscape gardener** *n*
▷ www.landscaping.about.com
▷ http://panther.bsc.edu/~jtatter/glossary.html
▷ www.thegardenhelper.com/gardeningguides.html
landscapist ('lænd,skeɪpɪst) *n* a painter of landscapes
Landseer ('lænsɪə) *n* Sir **Edwin Henry** 1802–73, English painter, noted for his studies of animals
Land's End *n* a granite headland in SW England, on the SW coast of Cornwall: the westernmost point of England
Landshut (*German* 'lantshuːt) *n* a city in SE Germany, in Bavaria: Trausnitz castle (13th century); manufacturing centre for machinery and chemicals. Pop: 59 670 (1991)
landside ('lænd,saɪd) *n* **1** the part of an airport farthest from the aircraft, the boundary of which is the security check, customs, passport control, etc ▷ Cf **airside 2** the part of a plough that slides along the face of the furrow wall on the opposite side to the mouldboard
landslide ('lænd,slaɪd) *n* **1** Also called: **landslip 1a** the sliding of a large mass of rock material, soil, etc, down the side of a mountain or cliff **1b** the material dislodged in this way **2** an overwhelming electoral victory
landsman ('lændzmən) *n, pl* **landsmen** a person who works or lives on land, as distinguished from a seaman
Landsteiner (*German* 'lantʃtaɪnər) *n* **Karl** (karl) 1868–1943, Austrian immunologist, who discovered (1900) human blood groups and introduced the ABO classification system. He also discovered (1940) the Rhesus (Rh) factor in blood and researched into poliomyelitis. Nobel prize for physiology or medicine (1930)
land up *vb* (*adv, usually intr*) to arrive or cause to arrive at a final point or condition
landward ('lændwəd) *adj* **1** lying, facing, or moving towards land **2** in the direction of the land ▷ *adv* **3** a variant of **landwards**
landwards ('lændwədz) *or* **landward** *adv* towards land
lane (leɪn) *n* **1** a narrow road or way between buildings, hedges, fences, etc **2a** any of the parallel strips into which the carriageway of a major road or motorway is divided **2b** any narrow well-defined route or course for ships or aircraft **3** one of the parallel strips into which a running track or swimming bath is divided for races **4** the long strip of wooden flooring down which balls are bowled in a bowling alley [OE *lane, lanu*]
Lanfranc ('lænfræŋk) *n* ?1005–89, Italian ecclesiastic and scholar; archbishop of Canterbury (1070–89) and adviser to William the Conqueror. He instituted many reforms in the English Church
Lang (læŋ) *n* **1 Cosmo Gordon,** 1st Baron Lang of Lambeth. 1864–1945, British churchman; archbishop of Canterbury (1928–42) **2 Fritz** 1890–1976, Austrian film director, later in the US, most notable for his silent films, such as *Metropolis* (1926), *M* (1931), and *The Testament of Dr. Mabuse* (1932) **3 Jack (John Thomas)** 1876–1975, controversial Labor premier of New South Wales from 1925–27 and from 1930–32, who introduced much social welfare legislation and was dismissed by the governor, Sir Philip Game, in 1932 for acting unconstitutionally
Lange ('lɒŋɪ) *n* **David (Russell)** born 1942, New Zealand statesman: leader of the Labour Party from 1983: prime minister (1984–89)
Langerhans islets *or* **islands** ('læŋə,hæns) *pl n anat* See **islets of Langerhans**
Langland ('læŋlənd) *n* **William** ?1332–?1400, English poet. The allegorical religious poem in alliterative verse, *The Vision of William concerning Piers the Plowman*, is attributed to him
langlauf ('læŋ,laʊf) *n* cross-country skiing [G, lit.: long run] > **langläufer** ('læŋ,lɔɪfə) *n* > **langläufing** ('læŋ,lɔɪfɪŋ) *n*
Langley ('læŋlɪ) *n* **Samuel Pierpont** 1834–1906, US astronomer and physicist: invented the bolometer (1878) and pioneered the construction of heavier-than-air flying machines
Langmuir ('læŋmjʊə) *n* **Irving** 1881–1957, US chemist. He developed the gas-filled tungsten lamp and the atomic hydrogen welding process: Nobel prize for chemistry 1932
langouste ('lɒŋguːst, lɒŋ'guːst) *n* another name for the **spiny lobster** [F, from OProvençal *langosta*, ? from L *lōcusta* lobster, locust]
langoustine (,lɒŋguː'stiːn) *n* a large prawn or small lobster [from F, dim. of LANGOUSTE]
Langres Plateau (*French* lɑ̃grə) *n* a calcareous plateau of E France north of Dijon between the Seine and the Saône, reaching over 580 m (1900 ft): forms a watershed between rivers flowing to the Mediterranean and to the English Channel
langsam ('læŋzæm) *adj music* slow [G]
langsyne (,læŋ'saɪn) *Scot* ▷ *adv* **1** long ago; long since ▷ *n* **2** times long past, esp those fondly remembered [c16 Scot.: long since]
Langton ('læŋtən) *n* **Stephen** ?1150–1228, English cardinal; archbishop of Canterbury (1213–28) He was consecrated archbishop by Pope Innocent III in 1207 but was kept out of his see by King John until 1213. He was partly responsible for the Magna Carta (1215)
Langtry ('læŋtrɪ) *n* **Lillie,** known as *the Jersey Lily*, real name *Émilie Charlotte le Breton*. 1852–1929, English actress, noted for her beauty and for her friendship with Edward VII
language ('læŋgwɪdʒ) *n* **1** a system for the expression of thoughts, feelings, etc, by the use of spoken sounds or conventional symbols **2** the faculty for the use of such systems, which is a distinguishing characteristic of man as compared with other animals **3** the language of a particular nation or people **4** any other means of communicating, such as gesture or animal sounds: *the language of love* **5** the specialized vocabulary used by a particular group: *medical language* **6** a particular manner

7 *computing* See **programming language** [c13 from OF *language*, ult. from L *lingua* tongue]
▹ www.britac.ac.uk/portal/
▹ www.ilovelanguages.com
▹ http://babel.uoregon.edu/yamada/guides.html
▹ www.languagelearn.co.uk
▹ www.languages-on-the-web.com
▹ www.arels.org.uk
▹ www.iatefl.org/newhome.asp

language laboratory *n* a room equipped with tape recorders, etc, for learning foreign languages

langue (lɑːŋg) *n linguistics* language considered as an abstract system or a social institution, being the common possession of a speech community [c19 from F: language]

Languedoc (*French* lɑ̃gdɔk) *n* **1** a former province of S France, lying between the foothills of the Pyrenees and the River Rhône: formed around the countship of Toulouse in the 13th century; important production of bulk wines **2** a wine from this region

langue d'oc *French* (lɑ̃g dɔk) *n* the group of medieval French dialects spoken in S France: often regarded as including Provençal [lit.: language of *oc* (form for the Provençal *yes*), ult. from L *hoc* this]

Languedoc-Roussillon (*French* lɑ̃gdɔkrusijɔ̃) *n* a region of S France, on the Gulf of Lions: consists of the departments of Lozère, Gard, Hérault, Aude, and Pyrénées-Orientales; mainly mountainous with a coastal plain

langue d'oïl *French* (lɑ̃g dɔj) *n* the group of medieval French dialects spoken in France north of the Loire; the medieval basis of modern French [lit.: language of *oïl* (the northern form for *yes*), ult. from L *hoc ille (fecit)* this he (did)]

languid (ˈlæŋgwɪd) *adj* **1** without energy or spirit **2** without interest or enthusiasm **3** sluggish; inactive [c16 from L *languidus*, from *languēre* to languish] > ˈ**languidly** *adv* > ˈ**languidness** *n*

languish (ˈlæŋgwɪʃ) *vb (intr)* **1** to lose or diminish in strength or energy **2** (often foll by *for*) to be listless with desire; pine **3** to suffer deprivation, hardship, or neglect: *to languish in prison* **4** to put on a tender, nostalgic, or melancholic expression [c14 *languishen*, from OF *languiss-*, stem of *languir*, ult. from L *languēre*] > ˈ**languishing** *adj* > ˈ**languishingly** *adv* > ˈ**languishment** *n*

languor (ˈlæŋgə) *n* **1** physical or mental laziness or weariness **2** a feeling of dreaminess and relaxation **3** oppressive silence or stillness [c14 *langour*, via OF from L *languor*, from *languēre* to languish; the modern spelling is directly from L] > ˈ**languorous** *adj*

langur (lʌŋˈgʊə) *n* any of various agile arboreal Old World monkeys of S and SE Asia having a long tail and long hair surrounding the face [Hindi]

laniard (ˈlænjəd) *n* a variant spelling of **lanyard**

laniary (ˈlænɪərɪ) *adj* **1** (esp of canine teeth) adapted for tearing ▹ *n, pl* **laniaries 2** a tooth adapted for tearing [c19 from L *lanius* butcher, from *laniāre* to tear]

laniferous (ləˈnɪfərəs) *or* **lanigerous** (ləˈnɪdʒərəs) *adj biol* bearing wool or fleecy hairs resembling wool [c17 from L *lānifer*, from *lāna* wool]

La Niña (lə ˈniːnjə) *n meteorol* a cooling of the eastern tropical Pacific, occurring in certain years [from Sp.: The Little Girl, to distinguish it from El Niño]

lank (læŋk) *adj* **1** long and limp **2** thin or gaunt [OE *hlanc* loose] > ˈ**lankly** *adv* > ˈ**lankness** *n*

Lankester (ˈlæŋkɪstə) *n* **Sir Edwin Ray** 1847–1929, English zoologist, noted particularly for his work in embryology and study of protozoans

lanky (ˈlæŋkɪ) *adj* **lankier, lankiest** tall, thin, and loose-jointed > ˈ**lankily** *adv* > ˈ**lankiness** *n*

lanner (ˈlænə) *n* **1** a large falcon of Mediterranean regions, N Africa, and S Asia **2** *falconry* the female of this falcon. The male is called **lanneret** [c15 from OF *(faucon) lanier* cowardly (falcon), from L *lanārius* wool worker, coward; referring to its sluggish flight and timid nature]

lanolin (ˈlænəlɪn) *or* **lanoline** (ˈlænəlɪn, -ˌliːn) *n* a yellowish viscous substance extracted from wool: used in some ointments [c19 via G from L *lāna* wool + *oleum* oil; see -in]

Lansbury (ˈlænzbərɪ) *n* **George** 1859–1940, British Labour politician, who led the Labour Party in opposition (1931–35). A committed pacifist, he resigned over the party's reaction to Mussolini's seizure of Ethiopia

Lansing (ˈlænsɪŋ) *n* a city in S Michigan, on the Grand River: the state capital. Pop: 119 128 (2000)

lantern (ˈlæntən) *n* **1** a light with a transparent protective case **2** a structure on top of a dome or roof having openings or windows to admit light or air **3** the upper part of a lighthouse that houses the light [c13 from L *lanterna*, from Gk *lamptēr* lamp, from *lampein* to shine]

lantern jaw *n* (when *pl*, refers to upper and lower jaw; when *sing*, usually to lower jaw) a long hollow jaw that gives the face a drawn appearance > ˈ**lantern-jawed** *adj*

lantern slide *n* (formerly) a photographic slide for projection, used in a magic lantern

lanthanide (ˈlænθəˌnaɪd) *or* **lanthanoid** (ˈlænθəˌnɔɪd) *n* any of a class of 15 chemically related elements with atomic numbers from 57 (lanthanum) to 71 (lutetium)

lanthanum (ˈlænθənəm) *n* a silvery-white ductile metallic element of the lanthanide series: used in pyrophoric alloys, electronic devices, and in glass manufacture. Symbol: La; atomic no.: 57; atomic wt.: 138.91 [c19 NL, from Gk *lanthanein* to lie unseen]

lanthorn (ˈlæntˌhɔːn, ˈlæntən) *n* an archaic word for **lantern**

lanugo (ləˈnjuːgəʊ) *n, pl* **lanugos** a layer of fine hairs, esp the covering of the human fetus before birth [c17 from L: down, from *lāna* wool]

Lanús (*Spanish* laˈnus) *n* a city in E Argentina: a S suburb of Buenos Aires. Pop: 466 755 (1991)

lanyard *or* **laniard** (ˈlænjəd) *n* **1** a cord, esp one worn around the neck, to hold a whistle, knife, etc **2** a cord used in firing certain types of cannon **3** *naut* a line for extending or tightening standing rigging [c15 *lanyer*, from F *lanière*, from *lasne* strap, prob. of Gmc origin]

Lanzarote (ˌlænzəˈrɒtɪ) *n* the most easterly of the Canary Islands; mountainous, with a volcanic landscape; tourism, fishing. Pop: 58 000 (latest est). Area: 795 sq km (307 sq miles)

Lanzhou, Lanchow, *or* **Lan-chou** (ˈlænˈdʒəʊ) *n* a city in N China, capital of Gansu province, on the Yellow River: situated on the main route between China and the West. Pop: 1 429 673 (1999 est)

Laoag (lɑːˈwɑːg) *n* a city in the N Philippines, on NW Luzon: trade centre for an agricultural region. Pop: 84 000 (1990 est)

Laocoon (leɪˈɒkəʊˌɒn) *n Greek myth* a priest of Apollo at Troy who warned the Trojans against the wooden horse left by the Greeks; killed with his twin sons by two sea serpents

Laodicea (ˌleɪəʊdɪˈsɪə) *n* the ancient name of several Greek cities in W Asia, notably of **Latakia**

laodicean (ˌleɪəʊdɪˈsɪən) *adj* **1** lukewarm and indifferent, esp in religious matters ▹ *n* **2** a person having a lukewarm attitude towards religious matters [c17 referring to the early Christians of Laodicea (Revelation 3:14–16)]

Laoighis (liːʃ) *n* a variant spelling of **Laois**

Laois (liːʃ) *n* a county of central Republic of Ireland, in Leinster province: formerly boggy but largely reclaimed for agriculture. County town: Portlaoise. Pop: 52 945 (1996). Area: 1719 sq km (664 sq miles). Also called: **Laoighis, Leix**. Former name: **Queen's County**

Laomedon (leɪˈɒmɪˌdɒn) *n Greek myth* the founder and

ruler of Troy, who cheated Apollo and Poseidon of their wage for constructing the city's walls; the father of Priam

Laos (laʊz, laʊs) *n* a republic in SE Asia: first united as the kingdom of Lan Xang ("million elephants") in 1353, after being a province of the Khmer Empire for about four centuries; made part of French Indochina in 1893 and gained independence in 1949; became a republic in 1975. It is generally forested and mountainous, with the Mekong River running almost the whole length of the W border. Official language: Laotian. Religion: Buddhist majority, tribal religions. Currency: kip. Capital: Vientiane. Pop: 5 636 000 (2001 est). Area: 236 800 sq km (91 429 sq miles). Official name: **People's Democratic Republic of Laos** > **Laotian** ('laʊʃɪən) *adj, n*
▷ www.global.lao.net/laovl/gov.htm
▷ www.visit-mekong.com/laos

Lao Zi ('laʊ'zɪə) *or* **Lao-tzu** ('laʊ'tsuː) *n* ?604–?531 BC, Chinese philosopher, traditionally regarded as the founder of Taoism and the author of the *Tao-te Ching*

lap[1] (læp) *n* **1** the area formed by the upper surface of the thighs of a seated person **2** Also called: **lapful** the amount held in one's lap **3** a protected place or environment: *in the lap of luxury* **4** the part of one's clothing that covers the lap **5 drop in someone's lap** give someone the responsibility of [OE *læppa* flap; see LOBE]

lap[2] (læp) *n* **1** one circuit of a racecourse or track **2** a stage or part of a journey, race, etc **3a** an overlapping part or projection **3b** the extent of overlap **4** the length of material needed to go around an object **5** a rotating disc coated with fine abrasive for polishing gemstones ▷ *vb* **laps, lapping, lapped 6** (*tr*) to wrap or fold (around or over): *he lapped a bandage around his wrist* **7** (*tr*) to enclose or envelop in: *he lapped his wrist in a bandage* **8** to place or lie partly or completely over or project beyond **9** (*tr; usually passive*) to envelop or surround with comfort, love, etc: *lapped in luxury* **10** (*intr*) to be folded **11** (*tr*) to overtake (an opponent) in a race so as to be one or more circuits ahead **12** (*tr*) to polish or cut (a workpiece, gemstone, etc) with a fine abrasive [C13 (in the sense: to wrap): prob. from LAP[1]] > **'lapper** *n*

lap[3] (læp) *vb* **laps, lapping, lapped 1** (of small waves) to wash against (a shore, boat, etc), usually with light splashing sounds **2** (often foll by *up*) (esp of animals) to scoop (a liquid) into the mouth with the tongue ▷ *n* **3** the act or sound of lapping **4** a thin food for dogs or other animals ▷ See also **lap up** [OE *lapian*] > **'lapper** *n*

La Palma (*Spanish* la 'palma) *n* an island in the N Atlantic, in the NW Canary Islands: administratively part of Spain. Chief town: Santa Cruz de la Palma. Pop: 77 000 (latest est). Area: 725 sq km (280 sq miles)

laparoscope ('læpərəˌskəʊp) *n* a medical instrument consisting of a tube that is inserted through the abdominal wall and illuminated to enable a doctor to view the internal organs [C19 (applied to various instruments used to examine the abdomen) and C20 (in the specific modern sense): from Gk *lapara* (see LAPAROTOMY) + -SCOPE] > **ˌlapa'roscopy** *n*

laparotomy (ˌlæpə'rɒtəmɪ) *n, pl* **laparotomies** surgical incision through the abdominal wall [C19 from Gk *lapara* flank, from *laparos* soft + -TOMY]

La Paz (læ 'pæz; *Spanish* la 'paθ) *n* a city in W Bolivia, at an altitude of 3600 m (12 000 ft): seat of government since 1898 (though Sucre is still the official capital); the country's largest city; founded in 1548 by the Spaniards; university (1830). Pop (urban area): 1 000 899 (2000 est)

lap dancing *n* a form of entertainment in which scantily dressed women dance erotically for individual members of the audience

lap dissolve *n films* the technique of allowing the end of one scene to overlap the beginning of the next scene by fading out the former while fading in the latter

lapdog ('læpˌdɒg) *n* a pet dog small and docile enough to be cuddled in the lap

lapel (lə'pɛl) *n* the continuation of the turned or folded back collar on a suit, coat, jacket, etc [C18 from LAP[1]] > **la'pelled** *adj*

lapheld ('læpˌhɛld) *adj* (esp of a personal computer) small enough to be used on one's lap; portable

lapidary ('læpɪdərɪ) *n, pl* **lapidaries 1** a person whose business is to cut, polish, set, or deal in gemstones ▷ *adj* **2** of or relating to gemstones or the work of a lapidary **3** Also: **lapidarian** (ˌlæpɪ'dɛərɪən) engraved, cut, or inscribed in a stone or gemstone **4** of sufficiently high quality to be engraved on a stone: *a lapidary inscription* [C14 from L *lapidārius*, from *lapid-*, *lapis* stone]

lapillus (lə'pɪləs) *n, pl* **lapilli** (-laɪ) a small piece of lava thrown from a volcano [C18 L: little stone]

lapis lazuli ('læpɪs 'læzjʊˌlaɪ) *n* **1** a brilliant blue mineral used as a gemstone **2** the deep blue colour of lapis lazuli [C14 from L *lapis* stone + Med. L *lazulī*, from Ar. *lāzaward*, from Persian *lāzhuward*, from ?]

Lapith ('læpɪθ) *n, pl* **Lapithae** ('læpɪˌθiː) *or* **Lapiths** *Greek myth* a member of a people in Thessaly who at the wedding of their king, Pirithoüs, fought the drunken centaurs

lap joint *n* a joint made by placing one member over another and fastening them together. Also called: **lapped joint** > **'lap-jointed** *adj*

Laplace (*French* laplas) *n* **Pierre Simon** (pjɛr simɔ̃), Marquis de Laplace. 1749–1827, French mathematician, physicist, and astronomer. He formulated the nebular hypothesis (1796). He also developed the theory of probability

Laplace operator *n maths* the operator $\partial^2/\partial x^2 + \partial^2/\partial y^2 + \partial^2/\partial z^2$, used in differential analysis. Symbol: ∇^2

Lapland ('læpˌlænd) *n* an extensive region of N Europe, mainly within the Arctic Circle: consists of the N parts of Norway, Sweden, Finland, and the Kola Peninsula of the extreme NW of Russia. Also called (informal): **Land of the Midnight Sun** > **'Lapˌlander** *n*

La Plata (*Spanish* la 'plata) *n* **1** a port in E Argentina, near the Río de la Plata estuary: founded in 1882 and modelled on Washington DC; university (1897). Pop: 556 308 (1999 est) **2** See (Río de la) **Plata**

lap of honour *n* a ceremonial circuit of a racing track, etc, by the winner of a race

Lapp (læp) *n* **1** Also **Laplander** a member of a nomadic people living chiefly in N Scandinavia and the Kola Peninsula of Russia **2** the language of this people ▷ *adj* **3** of or relating to this people or their language > **'Lappish** *adj, n*

USAGE The indigenous people of Lapland prefer to be called *Sami*, although *Lapp* is still in widespread use

lappet ('læpɪt) *n* **1** a small hanging flap or piece of lace, etc **2** *zool* a lobelike hanging structure, such as the wattle on a bird's head [C16 from LAP[1] + -ET]

lapse (læps) *n* **1** a drop in standard of an isolated or temporary nature: *a lapse of justice* **2** a break in occurrence, usage, etc: *a lapse of five weeks between letters* **3** a gradual decline or a drop to a lower degree, condition, or state: *a lapse from high office* **4** a moral fall **5** *law* the termination of some right, interest, or privilege, as by neglecting to exercise it or through failure of some contingency **6** *insurance* the termination of coverage following a failure to pay the premiums ▷ *vb* **lapses, lapsing, lapsed** (*intr*) **7** to drop in standard or fail to maintain a norm **8** to decline gradually or fall in status, condition, etc **9** to be discontinued, esp through negligence or other failure **10** (usually foll by *into*) to drift or slide (into a condition): *to lapse into sleep* **11** (often foll by *from*) to turn away (from beliefs or norms) **12** (of time) to slip away [C15 from L *lāpsus* error, from *lābī* to glide] > **'lapsable** *or* **'lapsible** *adj* > **lapsed** *adj* > **'lapser** *n*

Ll

lapse rate *n* the rate of change of any meteorological factor with altitude, esp atmospheric temperature
Laptev Sea ('læptɪf) *n* a shallow arm of the Arctic Ocean, along the N coast of Russia between the Taimyr Peninsula and the New Siberian Islands. Former name: **Nordenskjöld Sea**
laptop ('læpˌtɒp) *or* **laptop computer** *n* a personal computer that is small and light enough to be operated on the user's lap ▷ Cf **palmtop computer**
lap up *vb (tr, adv)* **1** to eat or drink **2** to relish or delight in: *he laps up horror films* **3** to believe or accept eagerly and uncritically: *he laps up stories*
lapwing ('læpˌwɪŋ) *n* any of several plovers, typically having a crested head, wattles, and spurs. Also called: **green plover, peewit** [c17 altered form of OE *hlēapewince* plover]
Lara ('lɑːrə) *n* **Brian Charles** born 1970, Trinidadian cricketer: holder of records for highest individual score in first-class cricket and for highest Test innings score
larboard ('lɑːbəd) *n, adj naut* a former word for **port²** [c14 *laddeborde* (changed to *larboard* by association with *starboard*), from *laden* to load + *borde* BOARD]
larceny ('lɑːsɪnɪ) *n, pl* **larcenies** *law* (formerly) a technical word for **theft** [c15 from OF *larcin*, from L *lātrocinium* robbery, from *latrō* robber] > **'larcenist** *or* **'larcener** *n* > **'larcenous** *adj*
larch (lɑːtʃ) *n* **1** any coniferous tree having deciduous needle-like leaves and egg-shaped cones **2** the wood of any of these trees [c16 from G *Lärche*, ult. from L *larix*]
lard (lɑːd) *n* **1** the rendered fat from a pig, used in cooking ▷ *vb (tr)* **2** to prepare (lean meat, poultry, etc) by inserting small strips of bacon or fat before cooking **3** to cover or smear (foods) with lard **4** to add extra material to (speech or writing); embellish [c15 via OF from L *lāridum* bacon fat] > **'lardy** *adj*
larder ('lɑːdə) *n* a room or cupboard, used as a store for food [c14 from OF *lardier*, from LARD]
Lardner ('lɑːdnə) *n* **Ring(old Wilmer)** 1885–1933, US short-story writer and journalist, whose best-known works are collected in *How to Write Short Stories* (1924) and *The Love Nest* (1926)
lardon ('lɑːdᵊn) *or* **lardoon** (lɑː'duːn) *n* a strip of fat or piece of bacon used in larding meat [c15 from OF, from LARD]
lardy ('lɑːdɪ) *adj* **lardier, lardiest** *inf* fat; obese
lardy cake ('lɑːdɪ) *n Brit* a rich sweet cake made of bread dough, lard, sugar, and dried fruit
Laredo (lə'reɪdəʊ) *n* a city in the US, in Texas, on the Mexican border: founded by the Spanish in 1755 on the Rio Grande. Pop: 176 576 (2000)
lares and penates ('lɛəriːz, 'lɑː-) *pl n* **1** *Roman myth* **1a** household gods **1b** statues of these gods kept in the home **2** the valued possessions of a household [from L]
large (lɑːdʒ) *adj* **1** having a relatively great size, quantity, extent, etc; big **2** of wide or broad scope, capacity, or range; comprehensive **3** having or showing great breadth of understanding ▷ *n* **4** **at large** **4a** (esp of a dangerous criminal or wild animal) free; not confined **4b** roaming freely, as in a foreign country **4c** as a whole; in general **4d** in full detail; exhaustively **4e** **ambassador at large.** See **ambassador** (sense 4) ▷ *vb* **larges, larging, larged** **5** **large it** *Brit sl* to enjoy oneself or celebrate in an extravagant way [c12 (orig.: generous): via OF from L *largus* ample] > **'largeness** *n*
large intestine *n* the part of the alimentary canal consisting of the caecum, colon, and rectum
largely ('lɑːdʒlɪ) *adv* **1** principally; to a great extent **2** on a large scale or in a large manner
larger-than-life *adj* exceptionally striking or colourful
large-scale *adj* **1** wide-ranging or extensive **2** (of maps and models) constructed or drawn to a big scale
largesse *or* **largess** (lɑː'dʒɛs) *n* **1** the generous bestowal of gifts, favours, or money **2** the things so bestowed **3** generosity of spirit or attitude [c13 from OF, from LARGE]
larghetto (lɑː'gɛtəʊ) *music* ▷ *adj, adv* **1** to be performed moderately slowly ▷ *n, pl* **larghettos** **2** a piece or passage to be performed in this way [It.: dim. of LARGO]
largish ('lɑːdʒɪʃ) *adj* fairly large
largo ('lɑːgəʊ) *music* ▷ *adj, adv* **1** to be performed slowly and broadly ▷ *n, pl* **largos** **2** a piece or passage to be performed in this way [c17 from It., from L *largus* large]
Lariam ('lærɪəm) *n trademark* a brand of mefloquine, used in the treatment and prevention of malaria
lariat ('lærɪət) *n US & Canad* **1** another word for **lasso** **2** a rope for tethering animals [c19 from Sp. *la reata* the LASSO]
Larisa *or* **Larissa** (lə'rɪsə; *Greek* 'larisa) *n* a city in E Greece, in E Thessaly: fortified by Justinian; annexed to Greece in 1881. Pop: 113 426 (1991)
lark¹ (lɑːk) *n* **1** any brown bird of a predominantly Old World family of songbirds, esp the skylark: noted for their singing **2** short for **titlark** [OE *lāwerce, lǣwerce*, of Gmc origin]
lark² (lɑːk) *inf* ▷ *n* **1** a carefree adventure or frolic **2** a harmless piece of mischief ▷ *vb (intr)* **3** (often foll by *about*) to have a good time by frolicking **4** to play a prank [c19 orig. sl] > **'larkish** *or* **'larky** *adj*
Larkin ('lɑːkɪn) *n* **Philip** 1922–85, English poet: his verse collections include *The Less Deceived* (1955), *The Whitsun Weddings* (1964), and *High Windows* (1974)
larkspur ('lɑːkˌspɜː) *n* any of various plants related to the delphinium, with spikes of blue, pink, or white irregular spurred flowers [c16 LARK¹ + SPUR]
larn (lɑːn) *vb not standard* **1** *facetious* to learn **2** *(tr)* to teach (someone) a lesson: *that'll larn you!* [c18 from a dialect form of LEARN]
Larne (lɒːn) *n* a district of NE Northern Ireland, in Co. Antrim. Pop: 30 832 (2001). Area: 336 sq km (130 sq miles)
larney ('lɑːnɪ) *adj S African* (of clothes) smart [c20 prob. from an Indian language]
La Rochefoucauld (*French* la rɔʃfuko) *n* **François** (frɑ̃swa), Duc de La Rochefoucauld. 1613–80, French writer. His best-known work is *Réflexions ou sentences et maximes morales* (1665), a collection of epigrammatic and cynical observations on human nature
La Rochelle (*French* la rɔʃɛl) *n* a port in W France, on the Bay of Biscay: a Huguenot stronghold until its submission through famine to Richelieu's forces after a long siege (1627–28). Pop: 71 094 (1990)
Larousse (*French* larus) *n* **Pierre Athanase** (pjɛr atanaz) 1817–75, French grammarian, lexicographer, and encyclopedist. He edited and helped to compile the *Grand Dictionnaire universel du XIX siècle* (1866–76)
larrigan ('lærɪgən) *n* a knee-high oiled leather moccasin boot worn by trappers, etc [c19 from ?]
larrikin ('lærɪkɪn) *Austral & NZ sl* ▷ *n* **1** a mischievous person **2** a hooligan ▷ *adj* **3** mischievous: *larrikin wit* [c19 from E dialect: a mischievous youth]
larrup ('lærəp) *vb (tr) dialect* to beat or flog [c19 from ?]
Larry ('lærɪ) *n* **happy as Larry** *inf* very happy
larva ('lɑːvə) *n, pl* **larvae** (-viː) an immature free-living form of many animals that develops into a different adult form by metamorphosis [c18 (c17 in the orig. L sense: ghost): NL] > **'larval** *adj*
laryngeal (ˌlærɪn'dʒiːəl, lə'rɪndʒɪəl) *or* **laryngal** (lə'rɪŋgᵊl) *adj* **1** of or relating to the larynx **2** *phonetics* articulated at the larynx; glottal [c18 from NL *laryngeus* of the LARYNX]
laryngitis (ˌlærɪn'dʒaɪtɪs) *n* inflammation of the larynx > **laryngitic** (ˌlærɪn'dʒɪtɪk) *adj*
laryngo- *or before a vowel* **laryng-** *combining form* indicating the larynx: *laryngoscope*
laryngoscope (lə'rɪŋgəˌskəʊp) *n* a medical instrument for examining the larynx > **ˌlaryn'goscopy** *n*
laryngotomy (ˌlærɪŋ'gɒtəmɪ) *n, pl* **laryngotomies**

surgical incision into the larynx to facilitate breathing

larynx ('lærɪŋks) *n, pl* **larynges** (lə'rɪndʒi:z) *or* **larynxes** a cartilaginous and muscular hollow organ forming part of the air passage to the lungs: in higher vertebrates it contains the vocal cords [c16 from NL, from Gk *larunx*]

lasagne *or* **lasagna** (lə'zænjə, -'sæn-) *n* **1** a form of pasta consisting of wide flat sheets **2** any of several dishes made from layers of lasagne and meat, cheese, etc [from It. *lasagna*, from L *lasanum* cooking pot]

La Salle[1] (lə 'sæl) *n* a city in SE Canada, in Quebec: a S suburb of Montreal. Pop: 73 804 (1991)

La Salle[2] (*French* la sal) *n* Sieur **Robert Cavelier de** (rɔbɛr kavəlje də) 1643–87, French explorer and fur trader in North America; founder of Louisiana (1682)

La Scala (la 'ska:la) *n* the chief opera house in Italy, in Milan (opened 1776)

lascar ('læskə) *n* a sailor from the East Indies [c17 from Urdu *lashkar* soldier, from Persian: the army]

Lascaux (*French* lasko) *n* the site of a cave in SW France, in the Dordogne: contains Palaeolithic wall drawings and paintings

lascivious (lə'sɪvɪəs) *adj* **1** lustful; lecherous **2** exciting sexual desire [c15 from LL *lascīviōsus*, from L *lascīvia* wantonness, from *lascīvus*] > **las'civiously** *adv* > **las'civiousness** *n*

Lasdun ('læzdən) *n* Sir **Denys** 1914–2001, British architect, best known for the University of East Anglia (1968) and the National Theatre in London (1976)

lase (leɪz) *vb* **lases, lasing, lased** (*intr*) (of a substance, such as carbon dioxide or ruby) to be capable of acting as a laser

laser ('leɪzə) *n* **1** a source of high-intensity optical, infrared, or ultraviolet radiation produced as a result of stimulated emission maintained within a solid, liquid, or gaseous medium. The photons involved in the emission process all have the same energy and phase so that the laser beam is monochromatic and coherent, allowing it to be brought to a fine focus **2** any similar source producing a beam of any electromagnetic radiation, such as infrared or microwave radiation [c20 from *l*ight *a*mplification by *s*timulated *e*mission of *r*adiation]

laserdisc *or* (esp US) **laserdisk** ('leɪzə,dɪsk) *n* a disk similar in size to a long-playing record, on which data is stored in pits in a similar way to data storage on a compact disk, used esp for storing high-quality video

laser printer *n* a quiet high-quality computer printer that uses a laser beam shining on a photoconductive drum to produce characters, which are then transferred to paper

lash[1] (læʃ) *n* **1** a sharp cutting blow from a whip or other flexible object **2** the flexible end or ends of a whip **3** a cutting or hurtful blow to the feelings, as one caused by ridicule or scolding **4** a forceful beating or impact, as of wind, rain, or waves against something **5** **have a lash at** *Austral & NZ inf* to make an attempt at or take part in (something) **6** See **eyelash** ▷ *vb* (*tr*) **7** to hit (a person or thing) sharply with a whip, rope, etc, esp as punishment **8** (of rain, waves, etc) to beat forcefully against **9** to attack with words, ridicule, etc **10** to flick or wave sharply to and fro: *the panther lashed his tail* **11** to urge or drive as with a whip: *to lash the audience into a violent mood* ▷ See also **lash out** [c14 ? imit.] > **'lasher** *n*

lash[2] (læʃ) *vb* (*tr*) to bind or secure with rope, string, etc [c15 from OF *lachier*, ult. from L *laqueāre* to ensnare, from *laqueus* noose]

-lashed *adj* having eyelashes as specified: *long-lashed*

lashing[1] ('læʃɪŋ) *n* **1** a whipping; flogging **2** a scolding **3** (*pl; usually foll by of*) *Brit inf* large amounts; lots

lashing[2] ('læʃɪŋ) *n* rope, cord, etc, used for binding or securing

Lashio ('læʃɪ,əʊ) *n* a town in NE central Myanmar: starting point of the Burma Road to Chongqing, China

Lashkar ('lʌʃkə) *n* a former city in N India, in Madhya Pradesh: capital of the former states of Gwalior and Madhya Bharat; now part of the city of Gwalior

lash out *vb* (*intr, adv*) **1** to burst into or resort to verbal or physical attack **2** *Brit inf* to be extravagant, as in spending

lash-up *n* a temporary connection of equipment for experimental or emergency use

LASIK surgery ('leɪsɪk) *n* laser surgery to correct short sight [c20 from *L*aser-*A*ssisted *I*n *S*itu *K*eratomileusis]

Lasker ('læskə) *n* **Emanuel** 1868–1941, German chess player: world champion (1894–1921)

Laski ('læskɪ) *n* **Harold (Joseph)** 1893–1950, English political scientist and socialist leader

Las Palmas (*Spanish* las 'palmas) *n* a port in the central Canary Islands, on NE Grand Canary: a major fuelling port on the main shipping route between Europe and South America. Pop: 352 641 (1998 est)

La Spezia (*Italian* la 'spɛttsia) *n* a port in NW Italy, in Liguria, on the **Gulf of Spezia**: the chief naval base in Italy. Pop: 100 458 (1992)

lass (læs) *n* **1** a girl or young woman **2** *inf* a familiar form of address for any female [c13 from ?]

Lassa ('lɑ:sə) *n* a variant spelling of **Lhasa**

Lassa fever ('læsə) *n* a serious viral disease of Central West Africa, characterized by high fever and muscular pains [from *Lassa*, the Nigerian village where it was first identified]

Lassalle (*German* la'sal) *n* **Ferdinand** ('fɛrdinant) 1825–64, German socialist and writer: a founder of the first German workers' political party (1863), which later became the Social Democratic Party

Lassen Peak ('læsᵊn) *n* a volcano in S California, in the S Cascade Range. An area of 416 sq km (161 sq miles) was established as **Lassen Volcanic National Park** in 1916. Height: 3187 m (10 457 ft)

lassi ('læsɪ) *n* a cold drink made with yoghurt or buttermilk and flavoured with sugar, salt, or a mild spice [from Hindi]

lassie ('læsɪ) *n inf* a little lass; girl

lassitude ('læsɪ,tju:d) *n* physical or mental weariness [c16 from L *lassitūdō*, from *lassus* tired]

lasso (læ'su:, 'læsəʊ) *n, pl* **lassos** *or* **lassoes** **1** a long rope or thong with a running noose at one end, used (esp in America) for roping horses, cattle, etc; lariat ▷ *vb* **lassos, lassoing, lassoed** **2** (*tr*) to catch as with a lasso [c19 from Sp. *lazo*, ult. from L *laqueus* noose] > **las'soer** *n*

Lassus ('læsəs) *n* **Roland de** Italian name *Orlando di Lasso.* ?1532–94, Flemish composer, noted for his mastery in both sacred and secular music

last[1] (lɑ:st) *adj* (*often prenominal*) **1** being, happening, or coming at the end or after all others: *the last horse in the race* **2** being or occurring just before the present; most recent: *last Thursday* **3** only remaining: *one's last cigarette* **4** most extreme; utmost **5** least suitable, appropriate, or likely: *he was the last person I would have chosen* **6** (esp relating to the end of a person's life or of the world) final or ultimate: *last rites* ▷ *adv* **7** after all others; at or in the end: *he came last* **8** most recently: *he was last seen in the mountains* **9** (*sentence modifier*) as the last or latest item ▷ *n* **10** **the last** **10a** a person or thing that is last **10b** the final moment; end **11** one's last moments before death **12** the final appearance, mention, or occurrence: *we've seen the last of him* **13** **at last** in the end; finally **14** **at long last** finally, after difficulty, delay, or irritation [var. of OE *latest*, *lætest*, sup. of LATE]

> USAGE Since *last* can mean either *after all others* or *most recent*, it is better to avoid using this word where ambiguity might arise, as in *her last novel*. *Final* or *latest* should be used in such contexts to avoid any possible confusion

last[2] (lɑ:st) *vb* **1** (when *intr*, often foll by *for*) to remain in

Ll

being (for a length of time); continue: *his hatred lasted for several years* **2** to be sufficient for the needs of (a person) for (a length of time): *it will last us until Friday* **3** (when *intr*, often foll by *for*) to remain fresh, uninjured, or unaltered (for a certain time) ▷ See also **last out** [OE *lǣstan*] > **'laster** *n*

last³ (lɑːst) *n* **1** the wooden or metal form on which a shoe or boot is fashioned or repaired ▷ *vb* **2** (*tr*) to fit (a shoe or boot) on a last [OE *lǣste*, from *lāst* footprint] > **'laster** *n*

last-ditch *n* **a** a last resort or place of last defence **b** (*as modifier*): *a last-ditch effort*

last-gasp *n* (*modifier*) done in desperation at the last minute: *a last-gasp attempt to save the talks*

lasting ('lɑːstɪŋ) *adj* permanent or enduring > **'lastingly** *adv* > **'lastingness** *n*

Last Judgment *n* **the** the occasion, after the resurrection of the dead at the end of the world, when, according to biblical tradition, God will decree the final destinies of all men according to the good and evil in their earthly lives. Also called: **the Last Day, Doomsday, Judgment Day**

lastly ('lɑːstlɪ) *adv* **1** at the end or at the last point ▷ *sentence connector* **2** finally

last name *n* another term for **surname**

last out *vb* (*intr, adv*) **1** to be sufficient for one's needs: *how long will our supplies last out?* **2** to endure or survive: *some old people don't last out the winter*

last post *n* (in the British military services) **1** a bugle call that orders men to retire for sleep **2** a similar call sounded at military funerals

last rites *pl n Christianity* religious rites prescribed for those close to death

Last Supper *n* **the** the meal eaten by Christ with his disciples on the night before his Crucifixion

Las Vegas (læs 'veɪgəs) *n* a city in SE Nevada: famous for luxury hotels and casinos. Pop: 478 434 (2000)

lat. *abbrev for* latitude

Lat. *abbrev for* Latin

latah ('lɑːtə) *n* a psychological condition, observed esp in Malaysian cultures, in which an individual, after experiencing a shock, becomes anxious and suggestible, often imitating the actions of another person [c19 from Malay]

Latakia *or* **Lattakia** (ˌlætə'kiːə) *n* the chief port of Syria, in the northwest: tobacco industry. Pop: 306 535 (1994 est). Latin name: **Laodicea ad Mare**

latch (lætʃ) *n* **1** a fastening for a gate or door that consists of a bar that may be slid or lowered into a groove, hole, etc **2** a spring-loaded door lock that can be opened by a key from outside **3** Also called: **latch circuit** *electronics* a logic circuit that transfers the input states to the output states when signalled ▷ *vb* **4** to fasten, fit, or be fitted as with a latch [OE *læccan* to seize, of Gmc origin]

latchkey ('lætʃˌkiː) *n* **1** a key for an outside door or gate, esp one that lifts a latch **2** a supposed freedom from restrictions

latchkey child *n* a child who has to let himself or herself in at home on returning from school, as his or her parents are out at work

latch on *vb* (*intr, adv*; often foll by *to*) *inf* **1** to attach oneself (to) **2** to understand

latchstring ('lætʃˌstrɪŋ) *n* a length of string fastened to a latch and passed through a hole in the door so that it can be opened from the other side

late (leɪt) *adj* **1** occurring or arriving after the correct or expected time: *the train was late* **2** (*prenominal*) occurring at, scheduled for, or being at a relatively advanced time: *a late marriage* **3** (*prenominal*) towards or near the end: *the late evening* **4** at an advanced time in the evening or at night: *it was late* **5** (*prenominal*) occurring or being just previous to the present time: *his late remarks on industry* **6** (*prenominal*) having died, esp recently: *my late grandfather* **7** (*prenominal*) just preceding the present or existing person or thing; former: *the late manager of this firm* **8** **of late** recently; lately ▷ *adv* **9** after the correct or expected time: *he arrived late* **10** at a relatively advanced age: *she married late* **11** recently; lately: *as late as yesterday he was selling books* **12** **late in the day** **12a** at a late or advanced stage **12b** too late [OE *læt*] > **'lateness** *n*

lateen (lə'tiːn) *adj naut* denoting a rig with a triangular sail (**lateen sail**) bent to a yard hoisted to the head of a low mast, used esp in the Mediterranean [c18 from F *voile latine* Latin sail]

Late Greek *n* the Greek language from about the 3rd to the 8th centuries AD

Late Latin *n* the form of written Latin used from the 3rd to the 7th centuries AD

lately ('leɪtlɪ) *adv* in recent times; of late

La Tène (læ 'tɛn) *adj* of or relating to a Celtic culture in Europe from about the 5th to the 1st centuries BC, characterized by a distinctive type of curvilinear decoration [c20 from *La Tène*, a part of Lake Neuchâtel, Switzerland, where remains of this culture were first discovered]

latent ('leɪtᵊnt) *adj* **1** potential but not obvious or explicit **2** (of buds, spores, etc) dormant **3** *pathol* (esp of an infectious disease) not yet revealed or manifest **4** (of a virus) inactive in the host cell **5** *psychoanal* relating to that part of a dream expressive of repressed desires: *latent content* ▷ Cf **manifest** (sense 2) [c17 from L *latēnt-*, from *latēre* to lie hidden] > **'latency** *n* > **'latently** *adv*

latent heat *n* (*no longer in technical usage*) the heat evolved or absorbed by unit mass (**specific latent heat**) or unit amount of substance (**molar latent heat**) when it changes phase without change of temperature

latent image *n photog* the invisible image produced by the action of light, etc, on silver halide crystals suspended in the emulsion of a photographic material. It becomes visible after development

later ('leɪtə) *adj, adv* **1** the comparative of **late** ▷ *adv* **2** afterwards; subsequently

lateral ('lætərəl) *adj* **1** of or relating to the side or sides: *a lateral blow* ▷ *n* **2** a lateral object, part, passage, or movement [c17 from L *laterālis*, from *latus* side] > **'laterally** *adv*

lateral thinking *n* a way of solving problems by employing unorthodox and apparently illogical means

laterite ('lætəˌraɪt) *n* any of a group of residual insoluble deposits of ferric and aluminium oxides: formed by weathering of rocks in tropical regions [c19 from L *later* brick]

latest ('leɪtɪst) *adj, adv* **1** the superlative of **late** ▷ *adj* **2** most recent, modern, or new: *the latest fashions* ▷ *n* **3** **at the latest** no later than the time specified **4** **the latest** *inf* the most recent fashion or development

latex ('leɪtɛks) *n, pl* **latexes** *or* **latices** ('lætɪˌsiːz) **1** a whitish milky fluid containing protein, starch, alkaloids, etc, that is produced by many plants. Latex from the rubber tree is used in the manufacture of rubber **2** a suspension of synthetic rubber or plastic in water, used in the manufacture of synthetic rubber products, etc [c19 NL, from L: liquid]

lath (lɑːθ) *n, pl* **laths** (lɑːðz, lɑːθs) **1** one of several thin narrow strips of wood used to provide a supporting framework for plaster, tiles, etc **2** expanded sheet metal, wire mesh, etc, used to provide backing for plaster or rendering **3** any thin strip of wood ▷ *vb* **4** (*tr*) to attach laths to (a ceiling, roof, floor, etc) [OE *lætt*]

lathe (leɪð) *n* **1** a machine for shaping or boring metal, wood, etc, in which the workpiece is turned about a horizontal axis against a fixed tool ▷ *vb* **lathes, lathing, lathed** **2** (*tr*) to shape or bore (a workpiece) on a lathe [? c15 *lath* a support, from ON]

lather ('lɑːðə) *n* **1** foam formed by the action of soap or a detergent in water **2** foam formed by other liquid, such as the sweat of a horse **3** *inf* a state of agitation ▷ *vb* **4** to coat or become coated with lather **5** (*intr*) to form a lather [OE *lēathor* soap] > **'lathery** *adj*

lathi ('lɑːtɪ) *n, pl* **lathis** a long heavy wooden stick used as a weapon in India, esp by the police [Hindi]

Latimer ('lætɪmə) *n* **Hugh** ?1485–1555, English Protestant bishop: burnt at the stake for refusing to disavow his Protestant beliefs when Mary I assumed the throne

Latin ('lætɪn) *n* **1** the language of ancient Rome and the Roman Empire and of the educated in medieval Europe. Having originally been the language of Latium in W central Italy, belonging to the Italic branch of the Indo-European family, it later formed the basis of the Romance group **2** a member of any of those peoples whose languages are derived from Latin **3** an inhabitant of ancient Latium ▷ *adj* **4** of or relating to the Latin language, the ancient Latins, or Latium **5** characteristic of or relating to those peoples in Europe and Latin America whose languages are derived from Latin **6** of or relating to the Roman Catholic Church [OE *latin* and *læden* Latin, language, from L *Latīnus* of Latium]

Latin-1 *n computing* another name for **ISO Latin-1**

Latina (*Italian* la'tiːna) *n* a city in W central Italy, in Lazio: built as a planned town in 1932 on reclaimed land of the Pontine Marshes. Pop: 114 099 (2000 est). Former name (until 1947): **Littoria**

Latin America *n* those areas of America whose official languages are Spanish and Portuguese, derived from Latin: South America, Central America, Mexico, and certain islands in the Caribbean > **Latin American** *n, adj*

Latinate ('lætɪˌneɪt) *adj* (of writing, vocabulary, etc) imitative of or derived from Latin

Latinism ('lætɪˌnɪzəm) *n* a word, idiom, or phrase borrowed from Latin

Latinist ('lætɪnɪst) *n* a person who studies or is proficient in Latin

Latinize *or* **Latinise** ('lætɪˌnaɪz) *vb* **Latinizes, Latinizing, Latinized** *or* **Latinises, Latinising, Latinised** (*tr*) **1** to translate into Latin or Latinisms **2** to cause to acquire Latin style or customs **3** to bring Roman Catholic influence to bear upon (the form of religious ceremonies, etc) > **ˌLatiniˈzation** *or* **ˌLatiniˈsation** *n* > **ˈLatinˌizer** *or* **ˈLatinˌiser** *n*

Latin Quarter *n* an area of Paris, on the S bank of the River Seine: contains the city's main educational establishments; centre for students and artists

latish ('leɪtɪʃ) *adj, adv* rather late

latitude ('lætɪˌtjuːd) *n* **1a** an angular distance measured in degrees north or south of the equator (latitude 0°) **1b** (*often pl*) a region considered with regard to its distance from the equator **2** scope for freedom of action, thought, etc; freedom from restriction: *his parents gave him a great deal of latitude* [C14 from L *lātitūdō*, from *lātus* broad] > **ˌlatiˈtudinal** *adj* > **ˌlatiˈtudinally** *adv*

latitudinarian (ˌlætɪˌtjuːdɪˈnɛərɪən) *adj* **1** permitting or marked by freedom of attitude or behaviour, esp in religious matters ▷ *n* **2** a person with latitudinarian views [C17 from L *lātitūdō* breadth, infl. in form by TRINITARIAN] > **ˌlatiˌtudiˈnarianism** *n*

Latium ('leɪʃɪəm) *n* an ancient territory in W central Italy, in modern Lazio, on the Tyrrhenian Sea: inhabited by the Latin people from the 10th century BC until dominated by Rome (4th century BC). Italian name: **Lazio**

Latona (lə'təʊnə) *n* the Roman name of **Leto**

Latour (*French* latur) *n* **Maurice Quentin de** (mɔris kɑ̃tɛ̃ də) 1704–88, French pastelist noted for the vivacity of his portraits

La Tour (*French* la tur) *n* **Georges de** (ʒɔrʒ də) ?1593–1652, French painter, esp of candlelit religious scenes

latria (lə'traɪə) *n RC Church, theol* the adoration that may be offered to God alone [C16 via L from Gk *latreia* worship]

latrine (lə'triːn) *n* a lavatory, as in a barracks, camp, etc [C17 from F, from L *lātrīna*, shortened form of *lavātrīna* bath, from *lavāre* to wash]

-latry *n combining form* indicating worship of or excessive veneration of: *idolatry; Mariolatry* [from Gk *-latria*, from *latreia* worship] > **-latrous** *adj combining form*

latter ('lætə) *adj* (*prenominal*) **1a** denoting the second or second mentioned of two: distinguished from *former* **1b** (*as n; functioning as sing or pl*): *the latter is not important* **2** near or nearer the end: *the latter part of a film* **3** more advanced in time or sequence; later [OE *lætra*]

> USAGE *The latter* should only be used to refer to the second of two items: *many people choose to go by hovercraft rather than use the ferry, but I prefer the latter.* The last of three or more items can be referred to as *the last-named*

latter-day *adj* present-day; modern

Latter-day Saint *n* a more formal name for a **Mormon**

latterly ('lætəlɪ) *adv* recently; lately

lattice ('lætɪs) *n* **1** Also called: **latticework** an open framework of strips of wood, metal, etc, arranged to form an ornamental pattern **2a** a gate, screen, etc, formed of such a framework **2b** (*as modifier*): *a lattice window* **3** something, such as a decorative or heraldic device, resembling such a framework **4** an array of objects or points in a periodic pattern in two or three dimensions, esp an array of atoms, ions, etc, in a crystal or an array of points indicating their positions in space ▷ *vb* **lattices, latticing, latticed** **5** to make, adorn, or supply with a lattice or lattices [C14 from OF *lattis*, from *latte* LATH] > **ˈlatticed** *adj*

Latvia ('lætvɪə) *n* a republic in NE Europe, on the Gulf of Riga and the Baltic Sea: ruled by Poland, Sweden, and Russia since the 13th century, Latvia was independent from 1919 until 1940 and was a Soviet republic (1940–91), gaining its independence after conflict with Soviet forces; it joined the EU in 2004. Latvia is mostly forested. Official language: Latvian. Religion: nonreligious, Christian. Currency: lats. Capital: Riga. Pop: 2 358 000 (2001 est). Area: 63 700 sq km (25 590 sq miles)
▷ www.saeima.lv/index_eng.html
▷ www.latviatourism.com

Latvian ('lætvɪən) *adj* **1** of or relating to Latvia, its people, or their language ▷ *n* **2** Also called: **Lettish** the official language of Latvia **3** a native or inhabitant of Latvia

laud (lɔːd) *literary* ▷ *vb* **1** (*tr*) to praise or glorify ▷ *n* **2** praise or glorification [C14 vb from L *laudāre*; n from *laudēs*, pl. of L *laus* praise]

Laud (lɔːd) *n* **William** 1573–1645, English prelate; archbishop of Canterbury (1633–45) His persecution of Puritans and his High Church policies in England and Scotland were a cause of the Civil War; he was impeached by the Long Parliament (1640) and executed

laudable ('lɔːdəbᵊl) *adj* deserving or worthy of praise; admirable; commendable > **ˈlaudableness** *or* **ˌlaudaˈbility** *n* > **ˈlaudably** *adv*

laudanum ('lɔːdᵊnəm) *n* **1** a tincture of opium **2** (formerly) any medicine of which opium was the main ingredient [C16 NL, name chosen by Paracelsus for a preparation prob. containing opium]

laudation (lɔː'deɪʃən) *n* a formal word for **praise**

laudatory ('lɔːdətərɪ, -trɪ) *or* **laudative** *adj* expressing or containing praise; eulogistic

Lauder ('lɔːdə) *n* Sir **Harry** real name *Hugh MacLennan.* 1870–1950, Scottish ballad singer and music-hall comedian

lauds (lɔːdz) *n* (*functioning as sing or pl*) *chiefly RC Church* the traditional morning prayer, constituting with matins the first of the seven canonical hours [C14 see LAUD]

Laue (*German* 'lauə) *n* **Max Theodor Felix von** (maks 'teːodoːr 'feːlɪks fɔn) 1879–1960, German physicist. He

Ll

pioneered the technique of measuring the wavelengths of X-rays by their diffraction by crystals and contributed to the theory of relativity: Nobel prize for physics 1914

laugh (lɑːf) *vb* 1 (*intr*) to express or manifest emotion, esp mirth or amusement, typically by expelling air from the lungs in short bursts to produce an inarticulate voiced noise, with the mouth open 2 (*intr*) (esp of certain mammals or birds) to make a noise resembling a laugh 3 (*tr*) to utter or express with laughter: *he laughed his derision at the play* 4 (*tr*) to bring or force (someone, esp oneself) into a certain condition by laughter: *he laughed himself sick* 5 (*intr*; foll by *at*) to make fun (of); jeer (at) 6 **laugh up one's sleeve** to laugh or have grounds for amusement, self-satisfaction, etc, secretly 7 **laugh on the other side of one's face** to show sudden disappointment or shame after appearing cheerful or confident ▷ *n* 8 the act or an instance of laughing 9 a manner of laughter 10 *inf* a person or thing that causes laughter: *that holiday was a laugh* 11 **the last laugh** the final success in an argument, situation, etc, after previous defeat ▷ See also **laugh off** [OE *læhan, hliehhen*] > **'laugher** *n* > **'laughing** *n, adj* > **'laughingly** *adv*

laughable ('lɑːfəbᵊl) *adj* 1 producing scorn; ludicrous: *he offered me a laughable sum for the picture* 2 arousing laughter > **'laughableness** *n* > **'laughably** *adv*

laughing gas *n* another name for **nitrous oxide**

laughing jackass *n* another name for the **kookaburra**

laughing stock *n* an object of humiliating ridicule

laugh off *vb* (*tr, adv*) to treat or dismiss lightly, esp with stoicism

laughter ('lɑːftə) *n* 1 the action of or noise produced by laughing 2 the experience or manifestation of mirth, amusement, scorn, or joy [OE *hleahtor*]

Laughton ('lɔːtᵊn) *n* **Charles** 1899–1962, US actor, born in England: noted esp for his films of the 1930s, such as *The Private Life of Henry VIII* (1933), for which he won an Oscar, and *Mutiny on the Bounty* (1935)

Launceston ('lɔːnsəstən) *n* a city in Australia, the chief port of the island state of Tasmania on the Tamar River, 64 km (40 miles) from Bass Strait. Pop: 93 347 (1991)

launch[1] (lɔːntʃ) *vb* 1 to move (a vessel) into the water 2 to move (a newly built vessel) into the water for the first time 3 (*tr*) 3a to start off or set in motion: *to launch a scheme* 3b to put (a new product) on the market 4 (*tr*) to propel with force 5 to involve (oneself) totally and enthusiastically: *to launch oneself into work* 6 (*tr*) to set (a missile, spacecraft, etc) into motion 7 (*intr*; foll by *into*) to start talking or writing (about): *he launched into a story* 8 (*intr*; usually foll by *out*) to start (out) on a fresh course ▷ *n* 9 an act or instance of launching [C14 from Anglo-F *lancher*, from LL *lanceāre* to use a lance, hence, to set in motion. See LANCE] > **'launcher** *n*

launch[2] (lɔːntʃ) *n* 1 a motor-driven boat used chiefly as a transport boat 2 the largest of the boats of a man-of-war [C17 via Sp. *lancha* and Port. from Malay *lancharan* boat, from *lanchar* speed]

launch pad *or* **launching pad** *n* 1 a platform from which a spacecraft, rocket, etc, is launched 2 an effective starting point for a career, enterprise, or campaign

launch window *n* the limited period during which a spacecraft can be launched on a particular mission

launder ('lɔːndə) *vb* 1 to wash and often also iron (clothes, linen, etc) 2 (*intr*) to be capable of being laundered without shrinking, fading, etc 3 (*tr*) to make (money illegally obtained) appear to be legally gained by passing it through foreign banks or legitimate enterprises [C14 (n, meaning: a person who washes linen): changed from *lavender* washerwoman, from OF *lavandiere*, ult. from L *lavāre* to wash] > **'launderer** *n*

Launderette (ˌlɔːndəˈrɛt, lɔːnˈdrɛt) *Brit & NZ trademark* a commercial establishment where clothes can be washed and dried, using coin-operated machines. Also called (US, Canad, and NZ): **Laundromat**

laundress ('lɔːndrɪs) *n* a woman who launders clothes, sheets, etc, for a living

laundry ('lɔːndrɪ) *n, pl* **laundries** 1 a place where clothes and linen are washed and ironed 2 the clothes or linen washed and ironed 3 the act of laundering [C16 changed from C14 *lavendry*; see LAUNDER]

laundryman ('lɔːndrɪmən) *or* (*fem*) **laundrywoman** *n, pl* **laundrymen** *or* **laundrywomen** 1 a person who collects or delivers laundry 2 a person who works in a laundry

Laurasia (lɔːˈreɪʃə) *n* one of the two ancient supercontinents produced by the first split of the even larger supercontinent Pangaea about 200 million years ago, comprising what are now North America, Greenland, Europe, and Asia (excluding India). See also **Gondwanaland, Pangaea** [C20 from New Latin *Laur(entia)* (referring to the ancient N American landmass, from *Laurentian* strata of the Canadian Shield) + *(Eur)asia*]

laureate ('lɔːrɪɪt) *adj* (*usually immediately postpositive*) 1 *literary* crowned with laurel leaves as a sign of honour ▷ *n* 2 short for **poet laureate** 3 a person honoured with an award for art or science: *a Nobel laureate* 4 *rare* a person honoured with the laurel crown or wreath [C14 from L *laureātus*, from *laurea* LAUREL] > **'laureate,ship** *n*

laurel ('lɒrəl) *n* 1 Also called: **laurel** any lauraceous tree of the genus *Laurus*, such as the bay tree (see bay[4]) and *L. canariensis*, of the Canary Islands and Azores 2 any lauraceous plant 3 short for **mountain laurel** 4 **spurge laurel** a European evergreen shrub, *Daphne laureola*, with glossy leaves and small green flowers 5 (*pl*) a wreath of true laurel, worn on the head as an emblem of victory or honour in classical times 6 (*pl*) honour, distinction, or fame 7 **look to one's laurels** to be on guard against one's rivals 8 **rest on one's laurels** to be satisfied with distinction won by past achievements and cease to strive for further achievements ▷ *vb* **laurels, laurelling, laurelled** *or US* **laurels, laureling, laureled** 9 (*tr*) to crown with laurels [C13 *lorer*, from OF *lorier* laurel tree, ult. from L *laurus*]

Laurel and Hardy ('lɒrəl, 'hɑːdɪ) *n* a team of US film comedians, **Stan Laurel,** 1890–1965, born in Britain, the thin one, and his partner, **Oliver Hardy,** 1892–1957, the fat one

Lauren ('lɔːrən) *n* **Ralph** born 1939, US fashion designer

Laurentian (lɔːˈrɛnʃən) *adj* 1 Also: **Lawrentian** of or resembling the style of D. H. or T. E. Lawrence 2 of, relating to, or situated near the St Lawrence River

Laurentian Mountains *pl n* a range of low mountains in E Canada, in Quebec between the St Lawrence River and Hudson Bay. Highest point: 1191 m (3905 ft). Also called: **Laurentides** ('lɔːrən,taɪdz)

Laurentian Shield *n* another name for the **Canadian Shield.** Also called: **Laurentian Plateau**

Laurier ('lɒrɪə) *n* Sir **Wilfrid** 1841–1919, Canadian Liberal statesman; the first French-Canadian prime minister (1896–1911)

laurustinus (ˌlɔːrəˈstaɪnəs) *n* a Mediterranean shrub with glossy evergreen leaves and white or pink fragrant flowers [C17 from NL, from L *laurus* laurel]

Lausanne (ləʊˈzæn; *French* lozan) *n* a city in W Switzerland, capital of Vaud canton, on Lake Geneva; cultural and commercial centre; university (1537). Pop: 114 161 (1999 est)

Lautrec (*French* loˈtrɛk) *n* See (Henri de) **Toulouse-Lautrec**

lav (læv) *n Brit inf* short for **lavatory**

lava ('lɑːvə) *n* 1 magma emanating from volcanoes 2 any extrusive igneous rock formed by the solidification of molten lava [C18 from It., from L *lavāre* to wash]

lavabo (ləˈveɪbəʊ) *n, pl* **lavaboes** *or* **lavabos** *chiefly RC Church* 1a the ritual washing of the celebrant's hands after the offertory at Mass 1b (*as modifier*): *lavabo basin;*

lavabo towel **2** another name for **washbasin** **3** a trough for washing in a convent or monastery [C19 from L: I shall wash, the opening of Psalm 26:6]

lavage ('lævɪdʒ, læ'vɑːʒ) *n med* the washing out of a hollow organ by flushing with a fluid, such as water [C19 via F, from L *lavāre* to wash]

Laval[1] (lə'væl) *n* a city in SE Canada, in Quebec: a NW suburb of Montreal. Pop: 330 343 (1996)

Laval[2] (*French* laval) *n* **Pierre** (pjɛr) 1883–1945, French statesman. He was premier of France (1931–32; 1935–36) and premier of the Vichy government (1942–44). He was executed for collaboration with Germany

lavatorial (ˌlævə'tɔːrɪəl) *adj* characterized by excessive mention of the excretory functions; vulgar or scatological: *lavatorial humour*

lavatory ('lævətərɪ, -trɪ) *n, pl* **lavatories** **a** a sanitary installation for receiving and disposing of urine and faeces, consisting of a bowl fitted with a water-flushing device and connected to a drain **b** a room containing such an installation. Also called: **toilet, water closet, WC** [C14 from LL *lavātōrium*, from L *lavāre* to wash]

lavatory paper *n Brit* another name for **toilet paper**

lave (leɪv) *vb* **laves, laving, laved** an archaic word for **wash** [OE *lafian*, ?from L *lavāre* to wash]

lavender ('lævəndə) *n* **1** any of various perennial shrubs or herbaceous plants of the labiate family, esp *Lavandula vera*, cultivated for its mauve or blue flowers and as the source of a fragrant oil (**oil of lavender**) **2** the dried parts of *L. vera*, used to perfume clothes **3** a pale or light bluish-purple colour **4** perfume scented with lavender [C13 *lavendre*, via F from Med. L *lavendula*, from ?]

laver ('leɪvə) *n Old Testament* a large basin of water used by priests for ritual ablutions [C14 from OF *laveoir*, from LL *lavātōrium* washing place]

Laver ('leɪvə) *n* **Rod**(**ney**) (**George**) born 1938, Australian tennis player: Wimbledon champion 1961, 1962, 1968, 1969; US champion 1962, 1969

lavish ('lævɪʃ) *adj* **1** prolific, abundant, or profuse **2** generous; unstinting; liberal **3** extravagant; prodigal; wasteful: *lavish expenditure* ▷ *vb* **4** (*tr*) to give, expend, or apply abundantly, generously, or in profusion [C15 adj use of *lavas* profusion, from OF *lavasse* torrent, from L *lavāre* to wash] > **'lavisher** *n* > **'lavishly** *adv* > **'lavishness** *n*

Lavoisier (*French* lavwazje) *n* **Antoine Laurent** (ɑ̃twan lɔrɑ̃) 1743–94, French chemist; one of the founders of modern chemistry. He disproved the phlogiston theory, named oxygen, and discovered its importance in respiration and combustion

law (lɔː) *n* **1** a rule or set of rules, enforceable by the courts regulating the relationship between the state and its subjects, and the conduct of subjects towards one another **2a** a rule or body of rules made by the legislature. See **statute law** **2b** a rule or body of rules made by a municipal or other authority. See **bylaw** **3a** the condition and control enforced by such rules **3b** (*in combination*): *lawcourt* **4** **law and order** **4a** the policy of strict enforcement of the law, esp against crime and violence **4b** (*as modifier*): *law-and-order candidate* **5** a rule of conduct: *a law of etiquette* **6** one of a set of rules governing a particular field of activity: *the laws of tennis* **7** **the law** **7a** the legal or judicial system **7b** the profession or practice of law **7c** *inf* the police or a policeman **8** Also called: **law of nature** a generalization based on a recurring fact or event **9** the science or knowledge of law; jurisprudence **10** the principles originating and formerly applied only in courts of common law ▷ Cf **equity** (sense 3) **11** a general principle, formula, or rule describing a phenomenon in mathematics, science, philosophy, etc: *the laws of thermodynamics* **12** Also called: **Law of Moses** (*often cap*; preceded by *the*) the body of laws contained in the first five books of the Old Testament **13** **go to law** to resort to legal proceedings on some matter **14** **lay down the law** to speak in an authoritative or dogmatic manner. Related adjs: **judicial, juridical, legal** [OE *lagu*, from ON]

▷ www.worldlii.org
▷ www.britac.ac.uk/portal/bysection.asp?section=S1
▷ www.lcd.gov.uk/rlinksfr.htm
▷ www.llrx.com/features/uk2.htm
▷ www.law.gla.ac.uk/scot_guide/guide.html
▷ www.llrx.com/features/canadian3.htm
▷ www.llrx.com/features/australian2.htm
▷ www.llrx.com/features/newzealand.htm
▷ www.llrx.com/features/southafrica.htm

Law (lɔː) *n* **1** **Andrew Bonar** ('bɒnə) 1858–1923, British Conservative statesman, born in Canada; prime minister (1922–23) **2** **Denis** born 1940, Scottish footballer and television and radio commentator on the sport **3** **John** 1671–1729, Scottish financier. He founded the first bank in France (1716) and the Mississippi Scheme for the development of Louisiana (1717), which collapsed due to excessive speculation **4** **Jude** born 1972, British film actor, who starred in *The Talented Mr Ripley* (1999) and *Cold Mountain* (2003) **5** **William** 1686–1761, British Anglican divine, best known for *A Serious Call to a Holy and Devout Life* (1728)

law-abiding *adj* adhering more or less strictly to the laws: *a law-abiding citizen*

law agent *n* (in Scotland) a solicitor entitled to appear for a client in any Sheriff Court

lawbreaker ('lɔːˌbreɪkə) *n* a person who breaks the law > **'lawˌbreaking** *n, adj*

law centre *n Brit* an independent service financed by a local authority, which provides free legal advice and information to the general public

Lawes (lɔːz) *n* **1** **Henry** 1596–1662, English composer, noted for his music for Milton's masque *Comus* (1634) and for his settings of some of Robert Herrick's poems **2** his brother, **William** 1602–45, English composer, noted for his harmonically experimental instrumental music

Ll

lawful ('lɔːfʊl) *adj* allowed, recognized, or sanctioned by law; legal > **'lawfully** *adv* > **'lawfulness** *n*

lawgiver ('lɔːˌgɪvə) *n* **1** the giver of a code of laws **2** Also called: **lawmaker** a maker of laws > **'lawˌgiving** *n, adj*

lawks (lɔːks) *interj Brit* an expression of surprise or dismay [C18 var. of *Lord!*, prob. infl. in form by ALACK]

lawless ('lɔːlɪs) *adj* **1** without law **2** disobedient to the law **3** contrary to or heedless of the law **4** uncontrolled; unbridled: *lawless rage* > **'lawlessly** *adv* > **'lawlessness** *n*

Law Lords *pl n* (in Britain) members of the House of Lords who sit as the highest court of appeal

lawn[1] (lɔːn) *n* a flat and usually level area of mown and cultivated grass [C16 changed form of C14 *launde*, from OF *lande*, of Celtic origin] > **'lawny** *adj*

lawn[2] (lɔːn) *n* a fine linen or cotton fabric, used for clothing [C15 prob. from *Laon*, town in France where made] > **'lawny** *adj*

lawn mower *n* a hand-operated or power-operated machine for cutting grass on lawns

lawn mower racing *n* the sport of racing modified versions of the type of lawn mower that has a seated driver

lawn tennis *n* **1** tennis played on a grass court **2** the formal name for **tennis**

law of averages *n* (popularly) the expectation that a possible event is bound to occur regularly with a frequency approximating to its probability

law of supply and demand *n* the theory that the price of an article or service is determined by the interaction of supply and demand

law of the jungle *n* a state of ruthless competition or self-interest

law of thermodynamics *n* any of three principles governing the relationships between different forms of energy. The **first law** (conservation of energy) states that energy can be transformed but not destroyed. The **second law** states that in any irreversible process entropy always increases. The **third law** states that it is impossible to reduce the temperature of a system to absolute zero in a finite number of steps

Lawrence ('lɒrəns) *n* **1** **Saint** died 258 AD, Roman martyr: according to tradition he was roasted to death on a gridiron. Feast day: Aug 10 **2** **D(avid) H(erbert)** 1885–1930, British novelist, poet, and short-story writer. Many of his works deal with the destructiveness of modern industrial society, contrasted with the beauty of nature and instinct, esp the sexual impulse. His novels include *Sons and Lovers* (1913), *The Rainbow* (1915), *Women in Love* (1920), and *Lady Chatterley's Lover* (1928) **3** **Ernest Orlando** 1901–58, US physicist, who invented the cyclotron (1931): Nobel prize for physics 1939 **4** **Gertrude** 1898–1952, British actress, noted esp for her roles in comedies such as Noël Coward's *Private Lives* (1930) **5** Sir **Thomas** 1769–1830, British portrait painter **6** **T(homas) E(dward)**, known as *Lawrence of Arabia*. 1888–1935, British soldier and writer. He took a major part in the Arab revolt against the Turks (1916–18), proving himself an outstanding guerrilla leader. He described his experiences in *The Seven Pillars of Wisdom* (1926)

lawrencium (lɒ'rɛnsɪəm) *n* an element artificially produced from californium. Symbol: Lr; atomic no.: 103; half-life of most stable isotope, ^{256}Lr: 35 seconds [c20 after Ernest O. LAWRENCE]

Lawrentian (lɔː'rɛnʃən) *adj* a variant spelling of **Laurentian** (sense 1)

Lawson ('lɔːsən) *n* **Henry Archibald** 1867–1922, Australian poet and short-story writer, whose work is taken as being most representative of the Australian outback, esp in *While the Billy Boils* (1896) and *Joe Wilson and his Mates* (1901) **2** **Nigel**, Baron, born 1932, British Conservative politician; Chancellor of the Exchquer (1983–89) **3** his daughter, **Nigella** (naɪ'dʒɛlə) born 1959, British journalist, broadcaster, and cookery writer **4** **William** 1774–1850, Australian explorer and pioneer, born in Britain. With Gregory Blaxland and William Wentworth he led the first European passage through the Blue Mountains (1813), thus opening up the Australian interior for settlement

lawsuit ('lɔːˌsuːt) *n* a proceeding in a court of law brought by one party against another, esp a civil action

law term *n* **1** an expression or word used in law **2** any of various periods of time appointed for the sitting of law courts

lawyer ('lɔːjə, 'lɔɪə) *n* a member of the legal profession, esp a solicitor [c14 from LAW]

lax (læks) *adj* **1** lacking firmness; not strict **2** lacking precision or definition **3** not taut **4** *phonetics* (of a speech sound) pronounced with little muscular effort [c14 (orig. used with reference to the bowels): from L *laxus* loose] > **'laxly** *adv* > **'laxity** *or* **'laxness** *n*

laxative ('læksətɪv) *n* **1** an agent stimulating evacuation of faeces ▷ *adj* **2** stimulating evacuation of faeces [c14 (orig.: relaxing): from Med. L *laxātīvus*, from L *laxāre* to loosen]

Laxness ('laxsnɛs) *n* **Halldór (Kiljan)** (haldəʊr) 1902–98, Icelandic novelist, noted for his treatment of rural working life in Iceland. His works include *Salka Valka* (1932) and *Independent People* (1935). Nobel prize for literature 1955

lay¹ (leɪ) *vb* **lays, laying, laid** (*mainly tr*) **1** to put in a low or horizontal position; cause to lie: *to lay a cover on a bed* **2** to place, put, or be in a particular state or position: *he laid his finger on his lips* **3** (*intr*) *dialect or not standard* to be in a horizontal position; lie: *he often lays in bed all the morning* **4** (sometimes foll by *down*) to establish as a basis: *to lay a foundation for discussion* **5** to place or dispose in the proper position: *to lay a carpet* **6** to arrange (a table) for eating a meal **7** to prepare (a fire) for lighting by arranging fuel in the grate **8** (*also intr*) (of birds, esp the domestic hen) to produce (eggs) **9** to present or put forward: *he laid his case before the magistrate* **10** to impute or attribute: *all the blame was laid on him* **11** to arrange, devise, or prepare: *to lay a trap* **12** to place, set, or locate: *the scene is laid in London* **13** to make (a bet) with (someone): *I lay you five to one on Prince* **14** to cause to settle: *to lay the dust* **15** to allay; suppress: *to lay a rumour* **16** to bring down forcefully: *to lay a whip on someone's back* **17** *sl* to have sexual intercourse with **18** to press down or make smooth: *to lay the nap of cloth* **19** (*intr*) *naut* to move or go, esp into a specified position or direction: *to lay close to the wind* **20** **lay bare** to reveal or explain: *he laid bare his plans* **21** **lay hold of** to seize or grasp **22** **lay oneself open** to make oneself vulnerable (to criticism, attack, etc) **23** **lay open** to reveal or disclose ▷ *n* **24** the manner or position in which something lies or is placed **25** *taboo sl* **25a** an act of sexual intercourse **25b** a sexual partner ▷ See also **lay aside, lay-by,** etc [OE *lecgan*]

> USAGE In standard English, the verb *lay* can only be used with an object, and *lie* can only be used without one: *the Queen laid a wreath; he was lying on the floor*

lay² (leɪ) *vb* the past tense of **lie²**

lay³ (leɪ) *adj* **1** of, involving, or belonging to people who are not clergy **2** nonprofessional or nonspecialist; amateur [c14 from OF *lai*, from LL *lāicus*, ult. from Gk *laos* people]

lay⁴ (leɪ) *n* **1** a ballad or short narrative poem, esp one intended to be sung **2** a song or melody [c13 from OF *lai*, ? of Gmc origin]

layabout ('leɪəˌbaʊt) *n* a lazy person; loafer

Layamon ('laɪəmən) *or* **Lawman** ('lɔːmən) *n* 12th-century English poet and priest; author of the *Brut*, a chronicle providing the earliest version of the Arthurian story in English

lay analyst *n* a person without medical qualifications who practises psychoanalysis

Layard (lɛəd) *n* Sir **Austen Henry** 1817–94, English archaeologist, noted for his excavations at Nimrud and Nineveh

lay aside *vb* (*tr, adv*) **1** to abandon or reject **2** to store or reserve for future use

lay brother *or* (*fem*) **lay sister** *n* a person who has taken the vows of a religious order but is not ordained and not bound to divine office

lay-by *n* **1** *Brit* a place for drivers to stop at the side of a main road **2** *naut* an anchorage in a narrow waterway, away from the channel **3** a small railway siding where rolling stock may be stored or parked **4** *Austral & NZ* a system of payment whereby a buyer pays a deposit on an article, which is reserved for him until he has paid the full price ▷ *vb* **lay by** (*tr, adv*) **5** to set aside or save for future needs

lay days *pl n* **1** *commerce* the number of days permitted for the loading or unloading of a ship without payment of demurrage **2** *naut* the time during which a ship is kept from sailing because of loading, bad weather, etc

lay down *vb* (*tr, adv*) **1** to place on the ground, etc **2** to relinquish or discard: *to lay down one's life* **3** to formulate (a rule, principle, etc) **4** to build or begin to build: *the railway was laid down as far as Chester* **5** to record (plans) on paper **6** to convert (land) into pasture **7** to store or stock: *to lay down wine* **8** *inf* to wager or bet **9** *inf* to record (tracks) in a studio

layer ('leɪə) *n* **1** a thickness of some homogeneous substance, such as a stratum or a coating on a surface **2** a laying hen **3** *horticulture* a shoot or branch rooted during layering ▷ *vb* **4** to form or make a layer of (something) **5** to take root or cause to take root by layering [c14 *leyer, legger*, from LAY¹ + -ER¹]

layering ('leɪərɪŋ) *n* **1** *horticulture* a method of propagation that induces a shoot to take root while it is still attached to the parent plant **2** *geol* the banded appearance of certain igneous and metamorphic rocks, each band being of a different mineral composition

layette (leɪ'ɛt) *n* a complete set of articles, including clothing, bedclothes, and other accessories, for a newborn baby [C19 from F, from OF, from *laie*, from MDu. *laege* box]

lay figure *n* **1** an artist's jointed dummy, used in place of a live model, esp for studying effects of drapery **2** a person considered to be subservient or unimportant [C18 from obs. *layman*, from Du. *leeman*, lit.: joint-man]

lay in *vb (tr, adv)* to accumulate and store: *we must lay in food for the party*

lay into *vb (intr, prep) inf* **1** to attack forcefully **2** to berate severely

layman ('leɪmən) *or (fem)* **laywoman** *n, pl* **laymen** *or* **laywomen** **1** a person who is not a member of the clergy **2** a person who does not have specialized or professional knowledge of a subject: *science for the layman*

lay off *vb* **1** *(tr, adv)* to suspend from work with the intention of re-employing later: *the firm had to lay off 100 men* **2** *(intr) inf* to leave (a person, thing, or activity) alone: *lay off me, will you!* **3** *(tr, adv)* to mark off the boundaries of ▷ *n* **lay-off** **4** the act of suspending employees **5** a period of imposed unemployment

lay on *vb (tr, adv)* **1** to provide or supply: *to lay on entertainment* **2** *Brit* to install: *to lay on electricity* **3** **lay it on** *sl* **3a** to exaggerate, esp when flattering **3b** to charge an exorbitant price **3c** to punish or strike harshly

lay out *vb (tr, adv)* **1** to arrange or spread out **2** to prepare (a corpse) for burial or cremation **3** to plan or contrive **4** *inf* to spend (money), esp lavishly **5** *inf* to knock unconscious ▷ *n* **layout** **6** the arrangement or plan of something, such as a building **7** the arrangement of written material, photographs, or other artwork on an advertisement or page in a book, newspaper, etc **8** a preliminary plan indicating this **9** a drawing showing the relative disposition of parts in a machine, etc **10** the act of laying out **11** something laid out

lay over *US* ▷ *vb (adv)* **1** *(tr)* to postpone for future action **2** *(intr)* to make a temporary stop in a journey ▷ *n* **layover** **3** a break in a journey, esp in waiting for a connection

lay person *or* **layperson** *n pl* **lay persons** *or* **laypersons** *or* **lay people** *or* **laypeople** **1** a person who is not a member of the clergy **2** a person who does not have specialized or professional knowledge of a subject: *a lay person's guide to conveyancing*

lay reader *n* **1** *Church of England* a person licensed by a bishop to conduct religious services other than the Eucharist **2** *RC Church* a layman chosen from among the congregation to read the epistle at Mass

lay up *vb (tr, adv)* **1** to store or reserve for future use **2** *(usually passive) inf* to incapacitate or confine through illness

lazar ('læzə) *n* an archaic word for **leper** [C14 via OF and Med. L, after LAZARUS]

lazaretto (,læzə'rɛtəʊ), **lazaret,** *or* **lazarette** (,læzə'rɛt) *n, pl* **lazarettos, lazarets,** *or* **lazarettes** **1** Also called: **glory hole** *naut* a small locker at the stern of a boat or a storeroom between decks of a ship **2** Also called: **lazar house, pesthouse** (formerly) a hospital for persons with infectious diseases, esp leprosy [C16 It., from *lazzaro* LAZAR]

Lazarus ('læzərəs) *n New Testament* **1** the brother of Mary and Martha, whom Jesus restored to life (John 11–12) **2** the beggar who lay at the gate of the rich man Dives in Jesus' parable (Luke 16:19–31)

laze (leɪz) *vb* **lazes, lazing, lazed** **1** *(intr)* to be indolent or lazy **2** *(tr; often foll by away)* to spend (time) in indolence ▷ *n* **3** the act or an instance of idling [C16 back formation from LAZY]

Lazio ('lattsjo) *n* **1** a region of W central Italy, on the Tyrrhenian Sea: includes the plain of the lower Tiber, the reclaimed Pontine Marshes, and Campagna. Capital: Rome. Pop: 5 264 077 (2000 est) **2** the Italian name for **Latium**

lazy ('leɪzɪ) *adj* **lazier, laziest** **1** not inclined to work or exertion **2** conducive to or causing indolence **3** moving in a languid or sluggish manner: *a lazy river* [C16 from ?] > **'lazily** *adv* > **'laziness** *n*

lazybones ('leɪzɪ,bəʊnz) *n inf* a lazy person

lazy Susan *n* a revolving tray, often divided into sections, for holding condiments, etc

lb *abbrev for:* **1** pound (weight) [L *libra*] **2** *cricket* leg bye

LBD *inf abbrev for* little black dress

LBJ *abbrev for* Lyndon Baines Johnson

LBO *abbrev for* leveraged buyout

lbw *cricket abbrev for* leg before wicket

lc *abbrev for:* **1** left centre (of a stage, etc) **2** loco citato [L: in the place cited] **3** *printing* lower case

L/C, l/c, *or* **lc** *abbrev for* letter of credit

LCD *abbrev for:* **1** liquid-crystal display **2** Also: **lcd** lowest common denominator

LCJ (in Britain) *abbrev for* Lord Chief Justice

lcm *or* **LCM** *abbrev for* lowest common multiple

L/Cpl *abbrev for* lance corporal

LD *abbrev for* lethal dose (esp in LD_{50}). See **median lethal dose**

LDL *abbrev for* low-density lipoprotein

L-dopa (,ɛl'dəʊpə) *n* a substance occurring naturally in the body and used to treat Parkinson's disease. Also called: **levodopa** [C20 from *L-d(ihydr)o(xy)p(henyl)a(lanine)*]

LDS *abbrev for:* **1** Latter-day Saints **2** laus Deo semper [L: praise be to God forever] **3** (in Britain) Licentiate in Dental Surgery

lea (liː) *n* **1** *poetic* a meadow or field **2** land that has been sown with grass seed [OE *lēah*]

LEA (in Britain) *abbrev for* Local Education Authority

leach (liːtʃ) *vb* **1** to remove or be removed from a substance by a percolating liquid **2** to lose or cause to lose soluble substances by the action of a percolating liquid ▷ *n* **3** the act or process of leaching **4** a substance that is leached or the constituents removed by leaching **5** a porous vessel for leaching [C17 var. of obs. *letch* to wet, ?from OE *leccan* to water] > **'leacher** *n*

Leach (liːtʃ) *n* **Bernard (Howell)** 1887–1979, British potter, born in Hong Kong

Leacock ('liːkɒk) *n* **Stephen Butler** 1869–1944, Canadian humorist and economist: his comic works include *Literary Lapses* (1910) and *Frenzied Fiction* (1917)

lead[1] (liːd) *vb* **leads, leading, led** **1** to show the way to (an individual or a group) by going with or ahead: *lead the party into the garden* **2** to guide or be guided by holding, pulling, etc: *he led the horse by its reins* **3** *(tr)* to cause to act, feel, think, or behave in a certain way; induce; influence: *he led me to believe that he would go* **4** (when *intr*, foll by *to*) (of a road, route, etc) to serve as the means of reaching a place **5** *(tr)* to go ahead so as to indicate (esp in **lead the way**) **6** to guide, control, or direct: *to lead an army* **7** *(tr)* to direct the course of or conduct (water, a rope, or wire, etc) along or as if along a channel **8** to initiate the action of (something); have the principal part in (something): *to lead a discussion* **9** to go at the head of or have the top position in (something): *he leads his class in geography* **10** *(intr;* foll by *with)* to have as the first or principal item: *the newspaper led with the royal birth* **11** *music Brit* to play first violin in (an orchestra) **12** to direct and guide (one's partner) in a dance **13** *(tr)* **13a** to pass or spend: *I lead a miserable life* **13b** to cause to pass a life of a particular kind: *to lead a person a dog's life* **14** *(intr;* foll by *to)* to tend (to) or result (in): *this will only lead to misery* **15** to initiate a round of cards by putting down (the first card) or to have the right to do this: *she led a diamond* **16** *(intr) boxing* to make an offensive blow, esp as one's habitual

Ll

attacking punch ▷ *n* **17a** the first, foremost, or most prominent place **17b** (*as modifier*): *lead singer* **18** example, precedence, or leadership: *the class followed the teacher's lead* **19** an advance or advantage held over others: *the runner had a lead of twenty yards* **20** anything that guides or directs; indication; clue **21** another name for **leash** **22** the act or prerogative of playing the first card in a round of cards or the card so played **23** the principal role in a play, film, etc, or the person playing such a role **24a** the principal news story in a newspaper: *the scandal was the lead in the papers* **24b** (*as modifier*): *lead story* **25** *music* an important entry assigned to one part **26** a wire, cable, or other conductor for making an electrical connection **27** *boxing* **27a** one's habitual attacking punch **27b** a blow made with this **28** a deposit of metal or ore; lode ▷ See also **lead off, lead on,** etc [OE *lǣdan*; rel. to *līthan* to travel]

lead² (lɛd) *n* **1** a heavy toxic bluish-white metallic element that is highly malleable: used in alloys, accumulators, cable sheaths, paints, and as a radiation shield. Symbol: Pb; atomic no.: 82; atomic wt.: 207.2 **2** a lead weight suspended on a line used to take soundings of the depth of water **3** lead weights or shot, as used in cartridges, fishing lines, etc **4** a thin grooved strip of lead for holding small panes of glass or pieces of stained glass **5** (*pl*) **5a** thin sheets or strips of lead used as a roof covering **5b** a flat or low-pitched roof covered with such sheets **6** Also called: **leading** *printing* a thin strip of type metal used for spacing between lines **7a** graphite used for drawing **7b** a thin stick of this material, esp the core of a pencil **8** (*modifier*) of, consisting of, relating to, or containing lead ▷ *vb* (*tr*) **9** to fill or treat with lead **10** to surround, cover, or secure with lead or leads **11** *printing* to space (type) by use of leads [OE]

lead acetate (lɛd) *n* a white crystalline toxic solid used in dyeing cotton and in making varnishes and enamels. Formula: $Pb(CH_3COOH)_2$. Systematic name: **lead ethanoate**

Leadbelly (ˈlɛdˌbɛlɪ) *n* real name *Huddie Ledbetter*. 1888–1949, US blues singer and guitarist

lead chromate (lɛd) *n chem* a yellow solid used as a pigment, as in chrome yellow. Formula: $PbCrO_4$

leaded (ˈlɛdɪd) *adj* (of windows) composed of small panes of glass held in place by thin grooved strips of lead: *leaded lights*

leaden (ˈlɛdᵊn) *adj* **1** heavy and inert **2** laboured or sluggish: *leaden steps* **3** gloomy, spiritless, or lifeless **4** made partly or wholly of lead **5** of a dull greyish colour: *a leaden sky* > **ˈleadenly** *adv* > **ˈleadenness** *n*

leader (ˈliːdə) *n* **1** a person who rules, guides, or inspires others; head **2** *music* **2a** Also called (esp US and Canad): **concertmaster** the principal first violinist of an orchestra, who plays solo parts, and acts as the conductor's deputy and spokesman for the orchestra **2b** *US* a conductor or director of an orchestra or chorus **3a** the leading horse or dog in a team **3b** the first man on a climbing rope **4** *chiefly Brit* the leading editorial in a newspaper. Also: **leading article** **5** *angling* another word for **trace²** (sense 2) **6** a strip of blank film or tape used to facilitate threading a projector, developing machine, etc **7** (*pl*) *printing* rows of dots or hyphens used to guide the reader's eye across a page, as in a table of contents **8** *bot* any of the long slender shoots that grow from the stem or branch of a tree **9** *Brit* a member of the Government having primary authority in initiating legislative business (esp in **Leader of the House of Commons** and **Leader of the House of Lords**) > **ˈleaderless** *adj*

leaderboard (ˈliːdəˌbɔːd) *n* a board displaying the names and current scores of the leading competitors, esp in a golf tournament

leadership (ˈliːdəʃɪp) *n* **1** the position or function of a leader **2** the period during which a person occupies the position of leader: *during her leadership very little was achieved* **3a** the ability to lead **3b** (*as modifier*): *leadership qualities* **4** the leaders as a group of a party, union, etc: *the union leadership is now very reactionary*

lead-free (ˌlɛdˈfriː) *adj* See **unleaded**

lead glass (lɛd) *n* glass that contains lead oxide as a flux

lead-in (ˈliːdˌɪn) *n* **1** an introduction to a subject **2** the connection between a radio transmitter, receiver, etc, and the aerial or transmission line

leading¹ (ˈliːdɪŋ) *adj* **1** guiding, directing, or influencing **2** (*prenominal*) principal or primary **3** in the first position

leading² (ˈlɛdɪŋ) *n printing* **1** the spacing between lines of photocomposed or digitized type **2** another name for **lead²** (sense 6). Also called: **interlinear spacing**

leading aircraftman (ˈliːdɪŋ) *n Brit airforce* the rank above aircraftman > **leading aircraftwoman** *fem n*

leading edge (ˈliːdɪŋ) *n* **1** the forward edge of a propeller blade, wing, or aerofoil ▷ Cf **trailing edge** **2** *electrical engineering* the part of a pulse signal that has an increasing amplitude **3a** the leading position in any field **3b** (*as modifier*) *leading-edge technology*

leading light (ˈliːdɪŋ) *n* an important or outstanding person, esp in an organization

leading note (ˈliːdɪŋ) *n music* **1** another word for **subtonic** **2** (esp in cadences) a note that tends most naturally to resolve to the note lying one semitone above it

leading question (ˈliːdɪŋ) *n* a question phrased in a manner that tends to suggest the desired answer, such as *What do you think of the horrible effects of pollution?*

leading rating (ˈliːdɪŋ) *n* a rank in the Royal Navy comparable but junior to that of a corporal in the army

leading reins *or US & Canad* **leading strings** (ˈliːdɪŋ) *pl n* **1** straps or a harness and strap used to assist and control a child who is learning to walk **2** excessive guidance or restraint

lead monoxide (lɛd) *n* a poisonous insoluble oxide of lead existing in red and yellow forms: used in making glass, glazes, and cements, and as a pigment. Formula: PbO. Systematic name: **lead(II) oxide**

lead off (liːd) *vb* (*adv*) **1** to initiate the action of (something); begin ▷ *n* **lead-off** **2** an initial move or action

lead on (liːd) *vb* (*tr, adv*) to lure or entice, esp into trouble or wrongdoing

lead pencil (lɛd) *n* a pencil containing a thin stick of a graphite compound

lead poisoning (lɛd) *n* **1** acute or chronic poisoning by lead, characterized by abdominal pain, vomiting, convulsions, and coma **2** *US sl* death or injury resulting from being shot with bullets

lead screw (liːd) *n* a threaded rod that drives the tool carriage in a lathe

lead tetraethyl (lɛd) *n* another name for **tetraethyl lead**

lead time (liːd) *n* **1** *manufacturing, chiefly US* the time between the design of a product and its production **2** *commerce* the time from the placing of an order to the delivery of the goods

lead up to (liːd) *vb* (*intr, adv + prep*) **1** to act as a preliminary or introduction to **2** to approach (a topic) gradually or cautiously

leaf (liːf) *n, pl* **leaves** (liːvz) **1** the main organ of photosynthesis and transpiration in higher plants, usually consisting of a flat green blade attached to the stem directly or by a stalk **2** foliage collectively **3** **in leaf** (of shrubs, trees, etc) having a full complement of foliage leaves **4** one of the sheets of paper in a book **5** a hinged, sliding, or detachable part, such as an extension to a table **6** metal in the form of a very thin flexible sheet: *gold leaf* **7** **take a leaf out of** (*or* **from**) **someone's book** to imitate someone, esp in one particular course of action **8** **turn over a new leaf** to begin a new and improved course of behaviour ▷ *vb*

9 (when *intr*, usually foll by *through*) to turn (through pages, sheets, etc) cursorily 10 (*intr*) (of plants) to produce leaves [OE] > 'leafless *adj* > 'leaf,like *adj*

leafage ('li:fɪdʒ) *n* a less common word for **foliage**

leaflet ('li:flɪt) *n* 1 a printed and usually folded sheet of paper for distribution, usually free, esp for advertising, giving information about a charity, etc 2 any of the subdivisions of a compound leaf such as a fern leaf 3 (loosely) any small leaf or leaflike part ▷ *vb* **leaflets, leafleting, leafleted** 4 to distribute leaflets (to)

leaf miner *n* 1 any of various insect larvae that bore into and feed on leaf tissue 2 the adult insect of any of these larvae

leaf mould *n* 1 a nitrogen-rich material consisting of decayed leaves, etc, used as a fertilizer 2 any of various fungus diseases affecting the leaves of certain plants

leaf spring *n* 1 one of a number of metal strips bracketed together in length to form a spring 2 the compound spring so formed

leafstalk ('li:f,stɔ:k) *n* the stalk attaching a leaf to a stem or branch. Technical name: **petiole**

leafy ('li:fɪ) *adj* **leafier, leafiest** 1 covered with or having leaves 2 resembling a leaf or leaves > '**leafiness** *n*

league[1] (li:g) *n* 1 an association or union of persons, nations, etc, formed to promote the interests of its members 2 an association of sporting clubs that organizes matches between member teams 3 a class, category, or level: *he is not in the same league* 4 **in league** (**with**) working or planning together with 5 (*modifier*) of, involving, or belonging to a league: *a league game; a league table* ▷ *vb* **leagues, leaguing, leagued** 6 to form or be formed into a league [C15 from OF *ligue*, from It. *liga*, ult. from L *ligāre* to bind]

league[2] (li:g) *n* an obsolete unit of distance of varying length. It is commonly equal to 3 miles [C14 *leuge*, from LL *leuga, leuca*, of Celtic origin]

league football *n* 1 Also called: **league** *chiefly Austral* rugby league football ▷ Cf **rugby union** 2 *Austral* an Australian Rules competition conducted within a league

leaguer ('li:gə) *n chiefly US & Canad* a member of a league

league table *n* 1 a list of sports clubs ranked in order according to their performance 2 a comparison of performance in any sphere

Leah ('lɪə) *n Old Testament* the first wife of Jacob and elder sister of Rachel, his second wife (Genesis 29)

leak (li:k) *n* 1a a crack, hole, etc, that allows the accidental escape or entrance of fluid, light, etc 1b such escaping or entering fluid, light, etc 2 **spring a leak** to develop a leak 3 something resembling this in effect: *a leak in the defence system* 4 the loss of current from an electrical conductor because of faulty insulation, etc 5 a disclosure of secret information 6 the act or an instance of leaking 7 a slang word for **urination** ▷ *vb* 8 to enter or escape or allow to enter or escape through a crack, hole, etc 9 (when *intr*, often foll by *out*) to disclose (secret information) or (of secret information) to be disclosed 10 (*intr*) a slang word for **urinate** [C15 from ON] > '**leaker** *n*

leakage ('li:kɪdʒ) *n* 1 the act or an instance of leaking 2 something that escapes or enters by a leak 3 *physics* an undesired flow of electric current, neutrons, etc

Leakey ('li:kɪ) *n* 1 **Louis Seymour Bazett** ('bæzɪt) 1903–72, British anthropologist and archaeologist, settled in Kenya. He discovered fossil remains of manlike apes in E Africa 2 his son **Richard** born 1944, Kenyan anthropologist, who discovered the remains of primitive man over 2 million years old in E Africa

leaky ('li:kɪ) *adj* **leakier, leakiest** leaking or tending to leak > '**leakiness** *n*

leal (li:l) *adj arch or Scot* loyal; faithful [C13 from OF *leial*, from L *lēgālis* LEGAL; rel. to LOYAL] > '**leally** *adv* > **lealty** ('li:əltɪ) *n*

Leamington Spa ('lɛmɪŋtən) *n* a town in central England, in central Warwickshire: saline springs. Pop: 55 396 (1991). Official name: **Royal Leamington Spa**

lean[1] (li:n) *vb* **leans, leaning, leaned** *or* **leant** 1 (foll by *against, on*, or *upon*) to rest or cause to rest against a support 2 to incline or cause to incline from a vertical position 3 (*intr; foll by to or towards*) to have or express a tendency or leaning ▷ *n* 4 the condition of inclining from a vertical position [OE *hleonian, hlinian*]

lean[2] (li:n) *adj* 1 (esp of a person or animal) having no surplus flesh or bulk; not fat 2 not bulky or full 3 (of meat) having little or no fat 4 not rich, abundant, or satisfying 5 (of mixture of fuel and air) containing insufficient fuel and too much air ▷ *n* 6 the part of meat that contains little or no fat [OE *hlǣne*, of Gmc origin] > '**leanly** *adv* > '**leanness** *n*

Lean (li:n) *n* Sir **David** 1908–91, English film director. His films include *In Which We Serve* (1942), *Blithe Spirit* (1945), *Brief Encounter* (1946), *Great Expectations* (1946), *Oliver Twist* (1948), *The Bridge on the River Kwai* (1957), *Lawrence of Arabia* (1962), *Dr Zhivago* (1965), and *A Passage to India* (1984)

lean-burn *adj* (esp of an internal-combustion engine) designed to use a lean mixture of fuel and air in order to reduce petrol consumption and exhaust emissions

Leander (lɪ'ændə) *n* (in Greek legend) a youth of Abydos, who drowned in the Hellespont in a storm on one of his nightly visits to Hero, his beloved. See also **Hero**[1]

leaning ('li:nɪŋ) *n* a tendency or inclination

leant (lɛnt) *vb* a past tense and past participle of **lean**[1]

lean-to *n, pl* **lean-tos** 1 a roof that has a single slope adjoining a wall or building 2 a shed or outbuilding with such a roof

leap (li:p) *vb* **leaps, leaping, leapt** *or* **leaped** 1 (*intr*) to jump suddenly from one place to another 2 (*intr; often foll by at*) to move or react quickly 3 (*tr*) to jump over 4 to come into prominence rapidly: *the thought leapt into his mind* 5 (*tr*) to cause (an animal, esp a horse) to jump a barrier ▷ *n* 6 the act of jumping 7 a spot from which a leap was or may be made 8 an abrupt change or increase 9 **a leap in the dark** an action performed without knowledge of the consequences 10 **by leaps and bounds** with unexpectedly rapid progress [OE *hlēapan*] > '**leaper** *n*

leapfrog ('li:p,frɒg) *n* 1 a children's game in which each player in turn leaps over the others' bent backs ▷ *vb* **leapfrogs, leapfrogging, leapfrogged** 2a (*intr*) to play leapfrog 2b (*tr*) to leap in this way over (something) 3 to advance or cause to advance by jumps or stages

leap second *n* a second added to or removed from a scale for reckoning time on one particular occasion, to synchronize it with another scale

leapt (lɛpt, li:pt) *vb* a past tense and past participle of **leap**

leap year *n* a calendar year of 366 days, February 29 (**leap day**) being the additional day, that occurs every four years (those whose number is divisible by four) except for century years whose number is not divisible by 400

Lear (lɪə) *n* **Edward** 1812–88, English humorist and painter, noted for his illustrated nonsense poems and limericks

learn (lɜ:n) *vb* **learns, learning, learned** (lɜ:nd) *or* **learnt** 1 (when *tr, may take a clause as object*) to gain knowledge of (something) or acquire skill in (some art or practice) 2 (*tr*) to commit to memory 3 (*tr*) to gain by experience, example, etc 4 (*intr; often foll by of or about*) to become informed; know 5 *not standard* to teach [OE *leornian*] > '**learnable** *adj* > '**learner** *n*

learned ('lɜ:nɪd) *adj* 1 having great knowledge or erudition 2 involving or characterized by scholarship 3 (*prenominal*) a title applied in referring to a member of the legal profession, esp to a barrister: *my learned friend* > '**learnedly** *adv* > '**learnedness** *n*

learning ('lɜ:nɪŋ) *n* 1 knowledge gained by study; instruction or scholarship: *a man of science and learning*

2 the act of gaining knowledge

learning curve *n* a graphical representation of progress in learning: *I'm still only halfway up the learning curve*

learnt (lɜːnt) *vb* a past tense and past participle of **learn**

lease (liːs) *n* **1** a contract by which property is conveyed to a person for a specified period, usually for rent **2** the instrument by which such property is conveyed **3** the period of time for which it is conveyed **4** a prospect of renewed health, happiness, etc: *a new lease of life* ▷ *vb* **leases, leasing, leased** (*tr*) **5** to grant possession of (land, buildings, etc) by lease **6** to take a lease of (property); hold under a lease [C15 via Anglo-F from OF *lais* (n), from *laissier* to let go, from L *laxāre* to loosen] > **'leasable** *adj* > **'leaser** *n*

leaseback ('liːs,bæk) *n* a transaction in which the buyer leases the property to the seller

leasehold ('liːs,həʊld) *n* **1** land or property held under a lease **2** the tenure by which such property is held **3** (*modifier*) held under a lease > **'lease,holder** *n*

leash (liːʃ) *n* **1** a line or rope used to walk or control a dog or other animal; lead **2** something resembling this in function: *he kept a tight leash on his emotions* **3 straining at the leash** eagerly impatient to begin something ▷ *vb* **4** (*tr*) to control or secure as by a leash [C13 from OF *laisse*, from *laissier* to loose (hence, to let a dog run on a leash), ult. from L *laxus* lax]

least (liːst) *determiner* **1a the** the superlative of **little**: *you have the least talent of anyone* **1b** (*as pronoun; functioning as sing*): *least isn't necessarily worst* **2 at least 2a** if nothing else: *you should at least try* **2b** at the least **3 at the least** Also: **at least** at the minimum: *at the least you should earn a hundred pounds* **4 in the least** (*usually used with a negative*) in the slightest degree; at all: *I don't mind in the least* ▷ *adv* **5 the least** superlative of **little**: *they travel the least* ▷ *adj* **6** of very little importance [OE *lǣst*, sup. of *lǣssa* less]

least common denominator *n* another name for **lowest common denominator**

least common multiple *n* another name for **lowest common multiple**

least squares *n* a method for determining the best value of an unknown quantity relating one or more sets of observations or measurements, esp to find a curve that best fits a set of data

leastways ('liːst,weɪz) *or US & Canad* **leastwise** *adv inf* at least; anyway; at any rate

least-worst *adj inf* bad but better than any available alternative: *a least-worst scenario*

leather ('lɛðə) *n* **1a** a material consisting of the skin of an animal made smooth and flexible by tanning, removing the hair, etc **1b** (*as modifier*): *leather goods* **2** (*pl*) leather clothes, esp as worn by motorcyclists ▷ *vb* (*tr*) **3** to cover with leather **4** to whip as with a leather strap [OE *lether-* (in compound words)]
▷ www.leathertown.com/info_hist_leather.htm

Leatherhead ('lɛðə,hɛd) *n* a town in S England, in Surrey. Pop: 42 903 (1991)

leatherjacket ('lɛðə,dʒækɪt) *n* **1** any of various tropical fishes having a leathery skin **2** the greyish-brown tough-skinned larva of certain craneflies, which destroy the roots of grasses, etc

leathern ('lɛðən) *adj arch* made of or resembling leather

leatherneck ('lɛðə,nɛk) *n sl* a member of the US Marine Corps [from the custom of facing the neckband of their uniform with leather]

leathery ('lɛðərɪ) *adj* having the appearance or texture of leather, esp in toughness > **'leatheriness** *n*

leave¹ (liːv) *vb* **leaves, leaving, left** (*mainly tr*) **1** (*also intr*) to go or depart (from a person or place) **2** to cause to remain behind, often by mistake, in a place: *he often leaves his keys in his coat* **3** to cause to be or remain in a specified state: *paying the bill left him penniless* **4** to renounce or abandon: *to leave a political movement* **5** to refrain from consuming or doing something: *the things we have left undone* **6** to result in; cause: *childhood problems often leave emotional scars* **7** to entrust or commit: *leave the shopping to her* **8** to pass in a specified direction: *flying out of the country, we left the cliffs on our left* **9** to be survived by (members of one's family): *he leaves a wife and two children* **10** to bequeath: *he left his investments to his children* **11** (*tr*) to have as a remainder: *37 – 14 leaves 23* **12** *not standard* to permit; let **13 leave (someone) alone 13a** Also: **let alone** See **let¹** (sense 6) **13b** to permit to stay or be alone [OE *lǣfan*; rel. to *belīfan* to be left as a remainder] ▷ See also **leave off, leave out** > **'leaver** *n*

leave² (liːv) *n* **1** permission to do something: *he was granted leave to speak* **2 by** *or* **with your leave** with your permission **3** permission to be absent, as from a place of work: *leave of absence* **4** the duration of such absence: *ten days' leave* **5** a farewell or departure (esp in **take (one's) leave**) **6 on leave** officially excused from work or duty **7 take leave (of)** to say farewell (to) [OE *lēaf*; rel. to *alȳfan* to permit]

leave³ (liːv) *vb* **leaves, leaving, leaved** (*intr*) to produce or grow leaves

leaved (liːvd) *adj* **a** having a leaf or leaves; leafed **b** (*in combination*): *a five-leaved stem*

leaven ('lɛvᵊn) *n also* **leavening 1** any substance that produces fermentation in dough or batter, such as yeast, and causes it to rise **2** a piece of such a substance kept to ferment a new batch of dough **3** an agency or influence that produces a gradual change ▷ *vb* (*tr*) **4** to cause fermentation in (dough or batter) **5** to pervade, causing a gradual change, esp with some moderating or enlivening influence [C14 via OF ult. from L *levāmen* relief, (hence, raising agent), from *levāre* to raise]

Leavenworth ('lɛvᵊn,wɜːθ, -wəθ) *n* a city in NE Kansas, on the Missouri River: the state's oldest city, founded in 1854 by proslavery settlers from Missouri. Pop: 38 495 (1990)

leave off *vb* **1** (*intr*) to stop; cease **2** (*tr, adv*) to stop wearing or using

leave out *vb* (*tr, adv*) **1** to cause to remain in the open **2** to omit or exclude

leaves (liːvz) *n* the plural of **leaf**

leave-taking *n* the act of departing; a farewell

leavings ('liːvɪŋz) *pl n* something remaining, such as food on a plate, residue, refuse, etc

Leavis ('liːvɪs) *n* **F(rank) R(aymond)** 1895–1978, English literary critic. He edited *Scrutiny* (1932–53) and his books include *The Great Tradition* (1948) and *The Common Pursuit* (1952)

Lebanon ('lɛbənən) *n* (sometimes preceded by *the*) a republic in W Asia, on the Mediterranean: an important centre of the Phoenician civilization in the third millennium BC; part of the Ottoman Empire from 1516 until 1919; gained independence in 1941 (effective by 1945). Official language: Arabic; French and English are also widely spoken. Religion: Muslim and Christian. Currency: Lebanese pound. Capital: Beirut. Pop: 3 628 000 (2001 est). Area: 10 400 sq km (4015 sq miles) > **Lebanese** (,lɛbə'niːz) *adj, n*
▷ www.presidency.gov.lb
▷ www.lebanon-tourism.gov.lb

Lebanon Mountains *pl n* a mountain range in central Lebanon, extending across the whole country parallel with the Mediterranean coast. Highest peak: 3104 m (10 184 ft). Arabic name: **Jebel Liban** ('dʒɛbᵊl 'liːbɑːn)

Lebensraum ('leɪbənz,raʊm) *n* territory claimed by a nation or state as necessary for survival or growth [G, lit.: living space]

Leblanc (*French* ləblɑ̃) *n* **Nicolas** (nikɔla) ?1742–1806, French chemist, who invented a process for the manufacture of soda from common salt

Lebrun (*French* ləbrœ̃) *n* **1 Albert** (albɛr) 1871–1950, French statesman; president (1932–40) **2** Also: **Le Brun Charles** (ʃarl) 1619–90, French historical painter. He was court painter to Louis XIV and executed much of the decoration of the palace of Versailles

LEC (lɛk) *n acronym for* Local Enterprise Company. See **Training Agency**

Le Carré (lə ˈkæreɪ) *n* **John,** real name *David John Cornwell.* born 1931, English novelist, esp of spy thrillers such as *The Spy who came in from the Cold* (1963), *Tinker, Tailor, Soldier, Spy* (1974), *Smiley's People* (1980), *The Tailor of Panama* (1996), and *Absolute Friends* (2003)

Lecce (*Italian* ˈlettʃe) *n* a walled city in SE Italy, in Puglia: Greek and Roman remains. Pop: 100 046 (1996 est)

lech (lɛtʃ) *inf* ▷ *vb* **1** (*intr; usually foll by after*) to behave lecherously (towards); lust (after) ▷ *n* **2** a lecherous act or indulgence [c19 back formation from LECHER]

Lech (lɛk; *German* lɛç) *n* a river in central Europe, rising in SW Austria and flowing generally north through S Germany to the River Danube. Length: 285 km (177 miles)

lecher (ˈlɛtʃə) *n* a promiscuous or lewd man [c12 from OF *lecheor,* from *lechier* to lick, of Gmc origin]

lecherous (ˈlɛtʃərəs) *adj* characterized by or inciting lechery > ˈ**lecherously** *adv*

lechery (ˈlɛtʃərɪ) *n, pl* **lecheries** unrestrained and promiscuous sexuality

lecithin (ˈlɛsɪθɪn) *n biochem* any of a group of phospholipids that are found in many plant and animal tissues, esp egg yolk: used in making candles, cosmetics, and inks, and as an emulsifier and stabilizer (**E322**) in foods. Systematic name: **phosphatidycholine** [c19 from Gk *lekithos* egg yolk]

lecky (ˈlɛkɪ) *n Brit sl* short for **electricity**

Lecky (ˈlɛkɪ) *n* **William Edward Hartpole** (ˈhɑːtˌpəʊl) 1838–1903, Irish historian; author of *The History of England in the 18th Century* (1878–90)

Leclanché cell (ləˈklɑːnʃeɪ) *n electrical engineering* a primary cell with a carbon anode, surrounded by crushed carbon and manganese dioxide in a porous container in an electrolyte of aqueous ammonium chloride into which a zinc cathode dips [c19 after Georges *Leclanché* (1839–82), F engineer]

Leconte de Lisle (*French* ləkɔ̃t də lil) *n* **Charles Marie René** (ʃarl mari rəne) 1818–94, French Parnassian poet

Le Corbusier (*French* lə kɔrbyzje) *n* real name *Charles Édouard Jeanneret.* 1887–1965, French architect and town planner, born in Switzerland. He is noted for his use of reinforced concrete and for his modular system, which used units of a standard size. His works include Unité d'Habitation at Marseilles (1946–52) and the city of Chandigarh, India (1954)

Le Creusot (*French* lə krøzo) *n* a town in E central France: metal, machinery, and armaments industries. Pop: 33 275 (latest est)

lectern (ˈlɛktən) *n* **1** a reading desk in a church **2** any similar desk or support [c14 from OF *lettrun,* from LL *lectrum,* ult. from *legere* to read]

lectionary (ˈlɛkʃənərɪ) *n, pl* **lectionaries** a book containing readings appointed to be read at divine services [c15 from Church L *lectiōnārium,* from *lectio* a reading, from *legere* to read]

lector (ˈlɛktɔː) *n* **1** a lecturer or reader in certain universities **2** *RC Church* **2a** a person appointed to read lessons at certain services **2b** (in convents or monastic establishments) a member of the community appointed to read aloud during meals [c15 from L, from *legere* to read]

lecture (ˈlɛktʃə) *n* **1** a discourse on a particular subject given or read to an audience **2** the text of such a discourse **3** a method of teaching by formal discourse **4** a lengthy reprimand or scolding ▷ *vb* **lectures, lecturing, lectured 5** to give or read a lecture (to an audience or class) **6** (*tr*) to reprimand at length [c14 from Med. L *lectūra* reading, from *legere* to read] > ˈ**lecturer** *n* > ˈ**lectureship** *n*

led (lɛd) *vb* the past tense and past participle of **lead**[1]

LED *electronics abbrev for* light-emitting diode

Leda (ˈliːdə) *n Greek myth* a queen of Sparta who was the mother of Helen and Pollux by Zeus, who visited her in the form of a swan

Lederberg (ˈlɛdəˌbɜːg) *n* **Joshua** born 1925, US geneticist, who discovered the phenomenon of transduction in bacteria. Nobel prize for physiology or medicine 1958 with George Beadle and Edward Tatum

lederhosen (ˈleɪdəˌhəʊzᵊn) *pl n* leather shorts with H-shaped braces, worn by men in Austria, Bavaria, etc [G]

ledge (lɛdʒ) *n* **1** a narrow horizontal surface resembling a shelf and projecting from a wall, window, etc **2** a layer of rock that contains an ore; vein **3** a ridge of rock that lies beneath the surface of the sea **4** a narrow shelflike projection on a cliff or mountain [c14 *legge,* ?from *leggen* to LAY[1]] > ˈ**ledgy** *or* **ledged** *adj*

ledger (ˈlɛdʒə) *n* **1** *book-keeping* the principal book in which the commercial transactions of a company are recorded **2** *angling* a wire trace that allows the weight to rest on the bottom and the bait to float freely ▷ *vb* **3** (*intr*) *angling* to fish using a ledger [c15 *legger* book retained in a specific place, prob. from *leggen* to LAY[1]]

ledger line *n music* a short line placed above or below the staff to accommodate notes representing pitches above or below the staff

Led Zeppelin (ˈlɛd ˈzɛpəlɪn) *n* British rock group (1968–80); comprised Jimmy Page (born 1944), Robert Plant (born 1948), John Paul Jones (born 1946), and John Bonham (1948–80): recordings include *Led Zeppelin I* (1969), *Led Zeppelin IV* (1971), and *Physical Graffiti* (1975)

lee (liː) *n* **1** a sheltered part or side; the side away from the direction from which the wind is blowing ▷ *adj* **2** (*prenominal*) *naut* on, at, or towards the side or part away from the wind: *on a lee shore* ▷ Cf **weather** (sense 4) [OE *hlēow* shelter]

Lee[1] (liː) *n* a river in SW Republic of Ireland, flowing east into Cork Harbour. Length: about 80 km (50 miles)

Lee[2] (liː) *n* **1 Ang** (æŋ) born 1954, Taiwanese film director; his films include *Sense and Sensibility* (1995), *The Ice Storm* (1997), *Crouching Tiger, Hidden Dragon* (2000), and *Hulk* (2003) **2 Bruce,** original name *Lee Yuen Kam.* 1940–73, US film actor and kung fu expert who starred in such films as *Enter the Dragon* (1973) **3 Gypsy Rose,** original name *Rose Louise Hovick.* 1914–70, US striptease and burlesque artiste, who appeared in the Ziegfeld Follies (1936) and in films **4 Laurie** (ˈlɒrɪ) 1914–97, British poet and writer, best known for the autobiographical *Cider with Rosie* (1959) **5 Richard Henry** 1732–94, American Revolutionary statesman, who moved the resolution in favour of American independence (1776) **6 Robert E(dward)** 1807–70, American general; commander-in-chief of the Confederate armies in the Civil War **7 Spike,** real name *Shelton Jackson Lee.* born 1957, US film director: his films include *She's Gotta Have It* (1985), *Malcolm X* (1992), and *25th Hour* (2002) **8 T(sung)-D(ao)** (tsuːŋ daʊ) born 1926, US physicist, born in China. With Yang he disproved the principle that that parity is always conserved and shared the Nobel prize for physics in 1957

leech[1] (liːtʃ) *n* **1** an annelid worm which has a sucker at each end of the body and feeds on the blood or tissues of other animals **2** a person who clings to or preys on another person **3a** an archaic word for **physician 3b** (*in combination*): *leechcraft* ▷ *vb* (*tr*) **4** to use leeches to suck the blood of (a person), as a method of medical treatment [OE *lǣce, lœce*]

leech[2] (liːtʃ) *n naut* the after edge of a fore-and-aft sail or either of the vertical edges of a square sail [c15 of Gmc origin]

Leeds (liːdz) *n* **1** a city in N England, in Leeds unitary authority, West Yorkshire on the River Aire: linked with

LI

Liverpool and Goole by canals; a former centre of the clothing industry; two universities (1904, 1992). Pop: 424 194 (1991) **2** a unitary authority in N England, in West Yorkshire. Pop: 715 404 (2001). Area 562 sq km (217 sq miles)

leek (liːk) *n* **1** a vegetable with a slender white bulb, cylindrical stem, and broad flat overlapping leaves **2** a leek, or a representation of one, as a national emblem of Wales [OE *lēac*]

leer (lɪə) *vb* **1** (*intr*) to give an oblique, sneering, or suggestive look or grin ▷ *n* **2** such a look [C16 ? verbal use of obs. *leer* cheek, from OE *hlēor*] > **'leering** *adj, n* > **'leeringly** *adv*

leery ('lɪərɪ) *adj* **leerier, leeriest** **1** *now chiefly dialect* knowing or sly **2** *sl* (foll by *of*) suspicious or wary [C18 ?from obs. sense (to look askance) of LEER] > **'leeriness** *n*

lees (liːz) *pl n* the sediment from an alcoholic drink [C14 pl of obs. *lee*, from OF, prob. from Celtic]

leet (liːt) *n* *Scot* a list of candidates for an office [C15 ?from Anglo-F *litte*, var. of LIST[1]]

Leeuwarden (*Dutch* 'leːwardə) *n* a city in the N Netherlands, capital of Friesland province. Pop: 87 464 (1994)

Leeuwenhoek ('leɪvᵊn,huːk; *Dutch* 'leːwənhuːk) *n* **Anton van** ('antɔn van) 1632–1723, Dutch microscopist, whose microscopes enabled him to give the first accurate description of blood corpuscles, spermatozoa, and microbes

leeward ('liːwəd; *naut* 'luːəd) *chiefly naut* ▷ *adj* **1** of, in, or moving to the quarter towards which the wind blows ▷ *n* **2** the point or quarter towards which the wind blows **3** the side towards the lee ▷ *adv* **4** towards the lee ▷ Cf **windward**

Leeward Islands ('liːwəd) *pl n* **1** a group of islands in the Caribbean, in the N Lesser Antilles between Puerto Rico and Martinique **2** a former British colony in the E Caribbean (1871–1956), consisting of Antigua, Barbuda, Redonda, Saint Kitts, Nevis, Anguilla, Montserrat, and the British Virgin Islands **3** a group of islands in the S Pacific, in French Polynesia in the W Society Archipelago: Huahiné, Raiatéa, Tahaa, Bora-Bora, and Maupiti. Pop: 26 838 (1996). French name: **Îles sous le Vent**

lee wave *n* *meteorol* a stationary wave sometimes formed in an air stream on the leeward side of a hill or mountain range

leeway ('liː,weɪ) *n* **1** room for free movement within limits, as in action or expenditure **2** sideways drift of a boat or aircraft

Le Fanu ('lɛfənjuː) *n* (**Joseph**) **Sheridan** 1814–73, Irish writer, best known for his stories of mystery and the supernatural, esp *Uncle Silas* (1864) and the collection *In a Glass Darkly* (1872)

Lefkoşa (lef'koʃə) *n* the Turkish name for **Nicosia**

left[1] (lɛft) *adj* **1** (*usually prenominal*) of or designating the side of something or someone that faces west when the front is turned towards the north **2** (*usually prenominal*) worn on a left hand, foot, etc **3** (*sometimes cap*) of or relating to the political left **4** (*sometimes cap*) radical or progressive ▷ *adv* **5** on or in the direction of the left ▷ *n* **6** a left side, direction, position, area, or part. Related adjs: **sinister, sinistral** **7** (*often cap*) the supporters or advocates of varying degrees of social, political, or economic change, reform, or revolution **8** *boxing* **8a** a blow with the left hand **8b** the left hand [OE *left* idle, weak, var. of *lyft-* (in *lyftādl* palsy, lit.: left-disease)]

left[2] (lɛft) *vb* the past tense and past participle of **leave**[1]

Left Bank *n* a district of Paris, on the S bank of the River Seine; frequented by artists, students, etc

left brain *n* **a** the left hemisphere of the human brain, which is believed to control linear and analytical thinking, decision-making, and language **b** (*as modifier*): *a left-brain activity*

left-hand *adj* (*prenominal*) **1** of, relating to, located on, or moving towards the left **2** for use by the left hand; left-handed

left-handed *adj* **1** using the left hand with greater ease than the right **2** performed with the left hand **3** designed or adapted for use by the left hand **4** awkward or clumsy **5** ironically ambiguous: *a left-handed compliment* **6** turning from right to left; anticlockwise ▷ *adv* **7** with the left hand > **,left-'handedly** *adv* > **,left-'handedness** *n* > **,left-'hander** *n*

leftist ('lɛftɪst) *adj* **1** of, tending towards, or relating to the political left or its principles ▷ *n* **2** a person who supports or belongs to the political left > **'leftism** *n*

left-luggage office *n* *Brit* a place at a railway station, etc, where luggage may be left for a small charge. US and Canad name: **checkroom**

leftover ('lɛft,əʊvə) *n* **1** (*often pl*) an unused portion or remnant, as of material or of cooked food ▷ *adj* **2** left as an unused portion

leftward ('lɛftwəd) *adj* **1** on or towards the left ▷ *adv* **2** a variant of **leftwards**

leftwards ('lɛftwədz) *or* **leftward** *adv* towards or on the left

left wing *n* **1** (*often cap*) the leftist faction of an assembly, party, group, etc; the radical or progressive wing **2** *sport* **2a** the left-hand side of the field of play from the point of view of either team facing its opponents' goal **2b** a player positioned in this area in certain games ▷ *adj* **left-wing** **3** of, belonging to, or relating to the political left wing > **,left-'winger** *n*

lefty ('lɛftɪ) *n, pl* **lefties** *inf* **1** a left-winger **2** *chiefly US & Canad* a left-handed person

leg (lɛg) *n* **1** either of the two lower limbs in humans, or any similar or analogous structure in animals that is used for locomotion or support **2** this part of an animal, esp the thigh, used for food: *leg of lamb* **3** something similar to a leg in appearance or function, such as one of the four supporting members of a chair **4** a branch, limb, or part of a forked or jointed object **5** the part of a garment that covers the leg **6** a section or part of a journey or course **7** a single stage, lap, length, etc, in a relay race **8** either the opposite or adjacent side of a right-angled triangle **9** one of a series of games, matches, or parts of games **10** either one of two races on which a cumulative bet has been placed **11** *cricket* **11a** the side of the field to the left of a right-handed batsman as he or she faces the bowler **11b** (*as modifier*): *a leg slip; leg stump* **12** **have legs** *inf* to be successful or show the potential to succeed **13** **not have a leg to stand on** *inf* to have no reasonable or logical basis for an opinion or argument **14** **on his, its,** etc, **last legs** (of a person or thing) worn out; exhausted **15** **pull (someone's) leg** *inf* to tease, fool, or make fun of (someone) **16** **shake a leg** *inf* to hurry up: usually used in the imperative **17** **stretch one's legs** to stand up or walk around, esp after sitting for some time ▷ *vb* **legs, legging, legged** **18** **leg it** *inf* to walk, run, or hurry [C13 from ON *leggr*, from ?]

leg. *abbrev for* legato

legacy ('lɛgəsɪ) *n, pl* **legacies** **1** a gift by will, esp of money or personal property **2** something handed down or received from an ancestor or predecessor [C14 (meaning: office of a legate), C15 (meaning: bequest): from Med. L *lēgātia* commission; see LEGATE]

legal ('liːgᵊl) *adj* **1** established by or founded upon law; lawful **2** of or relating to law **3** recognized, enforceable, or having a remedy at law rather than in equity **4** relating to or characteristic of the profession of law [C16 from L *lēgālis*, from *lēx* law] > **'legally** *adv*

legal aid *n* financial assistance available to persons unable to meet the full cost of legal proceedings

legalese (,liːgə'liːz) *n* the conventional language in which legal documents are written

legalism (ˈliːɡəˌlɪzəm) *n* strict adherence to the law, esp the letter of the law rather than its spirit > **ˈlegalist** *n, adj* > **ˌlegalˈistic** *adj*

legality (lɪˈɡælɪtɪ) *n, pl* **legalities** 1 the state or quality of being legal or lawful 2 adherence to legal principles

legalize *or* **legalise** (ˈliːɡəˌlaɪz) *vb* **legalizes, legalizing, legalized** *or* **legalises, legalising, legalised** (*tr*) to make lawful or legal > **ˌlegaliˈzation** *or* **ˌlegaliˈsation** *n*

legal tender *n* currency that a creditor must by law accept in redemption of a debt

Legaspi (lɛˈɡæspɪ) *n* a port in the Philippines, on SE Luzon on the Gulf of Albay. Pop: 125 128 (1994 est)

legate (ˈlɛɡɪt) *n* 1 a messenger, envoy, or delegate 2 RC *Church* an emissary representing the Pope [OE, via OF from L *lēgātus* deputy, from *lēgāre* to delegate; rel. to *lēx* law] > **ˈlegateˌship** *n*

legatee (ˌlɛɡəˈtiː) *n* a person to whom a legacy is bequeathed

legation (lɪˈɡeɪʃən) *n* 1 a diplomatic mission headed by a minister 2 the official residence and office of a diplomatic minister 3 the act of sending forth a diplomatic envoy 4 the mission of a diplomatic envoy 5 the rank or office of a legate [C15 from L *lēgātiō*, from *lēgātus* LEGATE]

legato (lɪˈɡɑːtəʊ) *music* ▷ *adj, adv* 1 to be performed smoothly and connectedly ▷ *n, pl* **legatos** 2a a style of playing with no perceptible gaps between notes 2b (*as modifier*): *a legato passage* [C19 from It., lit.: bound]

leg before wicket *n cricket* a manner of dismissal on the grounds that a batsman has been struck on the leg by a bowled ball that otherwise would have hit the wicket. Abbrev: **lbw**

leg break *n cricket* a bowled ball that spins from leg to off on pitching

legend (ˈlɛdʒənd) *n* 1 a popular story handed down from earlier times whose truth has not been ascertained 2 a group of such stories: *the Arthurian legend* 3 a modern story that has the characteristics of a traditional tale 4 a person whose fame or notoriety makes him or her a source of exaggerated or romanticized tales 5 an inscription or title, as on a coin or beneath a coat of arms 6 explanatory matter accompanying a table, map, chart, etc [C14 (in the sense: a saint's life): from Med. L *legenda* passages to be read, from L *legere* to read]

legendary (ˈlɛdʒəndərɪ, -drɪ) *adj* 1 of or relating to legend 2 celebrated or described in a legend or legends 3 very famous or notorious

Legendre (*French* ləʒɑ̃drə) *n* **Adrien Marie** (adriɛ̃ mari) 1752–1833, French mathematician, noted for his work on the theory of numbers, the theory of elliptical functions, and the method of least squares

Léger (*French* leʒe) *n* **Fernand** (fɛrnɑ̃) 1881–1955, French cubist painter, influenced by industrial technology

legerdemain (ˌlɛdʒədəˈmeɪn) *n* 1 another name for **sleight of hand** 2 cunning deception or trickery [C15 from OF: light of hand]

leger line (ˈlɛdʒə) *n* a variant spelling of **ledger line**

legged (ˈlɛɡɪd, lɛɡd) *adj* **a** having a leg or legs **b** (*in combination*): *three-legged; long-legged*

leggiero (lɛdʒˈɛərəʊ) *adj, adv music* to be performed lightly and nimbly [It.]

leggings (ˈlɛɡɪŋz) *pl n* 1 an extra outer covering for the lower legs 2 children's closefitting trousers, usually with a strap under the instep, worn for warmth in winter 3 a fashion garment for women consisting of closefitting trousers

leggy (ˈlɛɡɪ) *adj* **leggier, leggiest** 1 having unusually long legs 2 (of a woman) having long and shapely legs 3 (of a plant) having an unusually long and weak stem > **ˈlegginess** *n*

leghorn (ˈlɛɡˌhɔːn) *n* 1 a type of Italian wheat straw that is woven into hats 2 any hat made from this straw [C19 after LEGHORN (Livorno)]

Leghorn *n* 1 (ˈlɛɡˌhɔːn) the English name for **Livorno** 2 (lɛˈɡɔːn) a breed of domestic fowl laying white eggs

legible (ˈlɛdʒəbᵊl) *adj* (of handwriting, print, etc) able to be read or deciphered [C14 from LL *legibilis*, from L *legere* to read] > **ˌlegiˈbility** *n* > **ˈlegibly** *adv*

legion (ˈliːdʒən) *n* 1 a unit in the ancient Roman army of infantry with supporting cavalry of three to six thousand men 2 any large military force: *the French Foreign Legion* 3 (*usually cap*) an association of ex-servicemen: *the British Legion* 4 (*often pl*) any very large number ▷ *adj* 5 (*usually postpositive*) very numerous [C13 from OF, from L *legio*, from *legere* to choose]

legionary (ˈliːdʒənərɪ) *adj* 1 of a legion ▷ *n, pl* **legionaries** 2 a soldier belonging to a legion

legionnaire (ˌliːdʒəˈnɛə) *n* (*often cap*) a member of certain military forces or associations

legionnaire's *or* **legionnaires' disease** *n* a serious, sometimes fatal, infection caused by a bacterium (**legionella**) which has symptoms similar to those of pneumonia [C20 after the outbreak at a meeting of the American Legion in Philadelphia in 1976]

legislate (ˈlɛdʒɪsˌleɪt) *vb* **legislates, legislating, legislated** 1 (*intr*) to make or pass laws 2 (*tr*) to bring into effect by legislation [C18 back formation from LEGISLATOR]

legislation (ˌlɛdʒɪsˈleɪʃən) *n* 1 the act or process of making laws 2 the laws so made

legislative (ˈlɛdʒɪslətɪv) *adj* 1 of or relating to legislation 2 having the power or function of legislating: *a legislative assembly* 3 of or relating to a legislature > **ˈlegislatively** *adv*

legislative assembly *n* (*often caps*) 1 the bicameral legislature in 28 states of the US 2 the chamber of the bicameral state legislatures in several Commonwealth countries, such as Australia 3 the unicameral legislature in most Canadian provinces 4 any assembly with legislative powers

legislative council *n* (*often caps*) 1 the upper chamber of certain bicameral legislatures, such as those of the Indian and Australian states (except Queensland) 2 the unicameral legislature of certain colonies or dependent territories 3 (in the US) a committee of members of both chambers of a state legislature that discusses problems, constructs a legislative programme, etc

Ll

legislator (ˈlɛdʒɪsˌleɪtə) *n* 1 a person concerned with the making of laws 2 a member of a legislature [C17 from L *lēgis lātor*, from *lēx* law + *lātor* from *lātus*, p.p. of *ferre* to bring]

legislature (ˈlɛdʒɪsˌleɪtʃə) *n* a body of persons vested with power to make and repeal laws

legit (lɪˈdʒɪt) *sl* ▷ *adj* 1 short for **legitimate** ▷ *n* 2 legitimate drama

legitimate *adj* (lɪˈdʒɪtɪmɪt) 1 born in lawful wedlock 2 conforming to established standards of usage, behaviour, etc 3 based on correct or acceptable principles of reasoning 4 authorized by or in accordance with law 5 of, relating to, or ruling by hereditary right: *a legitimate monarch* 6 of or relating to a body of famous long-established plays as distinct from films, television, vaudeville, etc ▷ *vb* (lɪˈdʒɪtɪˌmeɪt) **legitimates, legitimating, legitimated** 7 (*tr*) to make, pronounce, or show to be legitimate [C15 from Med. L *lēgitimātus* made legal, from *lēx* law] > **leˈgitimacy** *n* > **leˈgitimately** *adv* > **leˌgitiˈmation** *n*

legitimist (lɪˈdʒɪtɪmɪst) *n* a monarchist who supports the rule of a legitimate dynasty or of its senior branch > **leˈgitimism** *n*

legitimize, legitimise (lɪˈdʒɪtɪˌmaɪz) *or* **legitimatize, legitimatise** (lɪˈdʒɪtɪməˌtaɪz) *vb* **legitimizes, legitimizing, legitimized; legitimises, legitimising, legitimised** *or* **legitimatizes, legitimatizing, legitimatized; legitimatises, legitimatising,**

legitimatised (*tr*) to make legitimate; legalize > **le,gitimi'zation, le,gitimi'sation** *or* **le,gitimati'zation, le,gitimati'sation** *n*
legless ('lɛglɪs) *adj* **1** without legs **2** *inf* very drunk
Legnica (*Polish* lɛg'nitsa) *n* an industrial town in SW Poland. Pop: 109 335 (1999 est). German name: **Liegnitz**
Lego ('lɛgəʊ) *n trademark* a construction toy consisting of plastic bricks and other components that fit together [c20 from Danish *leg godt* play well]
leg-of-mutton *or* **leg-o'-mutton** *n* (*modifier*) (of a sail, sleeve, etc) tapering sharply
leg-pull *n Brit inf* a practical joke or mild deception
legroom ('lɛg,ru:m) *n* room to move one's legs comfortably, as in a car
leg rope *n Austral & NZ* a rope used to secure an animal by its hind leg
leguan ('lɛgʊ,ɑ:n) *n* a large amphibious S African lizard [c19 Du., from F *l'iguane* the iguana]
legume ('lɛgju:m, lɪ'gju:m) *n* **1** the long dry fruit produced by leguminous plants; a pod **2** any of various table vegetables, esp beans or peas **3** any leguminous plant [c17 from F *légume*, from L *legūmen* bean, from *legere* to pick (a crop)]
leguminous (lɪ'gju:mɪnəs) *adj* of, relating to, or belonging to any family of flowering plants having pods (or legumes) as fruits and (in most species) root nodules containing bacteria that fix nitrogen from the atmosphere [c17 from L *legūmen*; see LEGUME]
legwarmer ('lɛg,wɔ:mə) *n* one of a pair of garments resembling stockings without feet, often worn over jeans, tights, etc, or during exercise
legwork ('lɛg,wɜ:k) *n inf* work that involves travelling on foot or as if on foot
Lehár ('leɪhɑ:, lɪ'hɑ:) *n* **Franz** (frants) 1870–1948, Hungarian composer of operettas, esp *The Merry Widow* (1905)
Le Havre (lə 'hɑ:vrə; *French* lə ɑvrə) *n* a port in N France, on the English Channel at the mouth of the River Seine: transatlantic trade; oil refining. Pop: 190 651 (1999)
Lehmann ('leɪmən) *n* **1 Lilli** ('lɪlɪ) 1848–1929, German soprano **2 Lotte** ('lɒtə) 1888–1976, US soprano, born in Germany **3 Rosamond (Nina)** 1903–90, British novelist. Her books include *Dusty Answer* (1927), *Invitation to the Waltz* (1932), and *The Echoing Grove* (1953)
Lehmbruck (*German* 'le:mbrʊk) *n* **Wilhelm** ('vɪlhɛlm) 1881–1919, German sculptor and graphic artist
lei (leɪ) *n* (in Hawaii) a garland of flowers, worn around the neck [from Hawaiian]
Leibnitz *or* **Leibniz** ('laɪbnɪts) *n* Baron **Gottfried Wilhelm von** ('gɔtfri:t 'vɪlhɛlm fɔn) 1646–1716, German rationalist philosopher and mathematician. He conceived of the universe as a hierarchy of independent units or monads, synchronized by pre-established harmony. His works include *Théodicée* (1710) and *Monadologia* (1714). He also devised a system of calculus, independently of Newton
Leibovitz ('laɪbəvɪtz) *n* **Annie** born 1949, US photographer, known for her portraits of celebrities
Leicester[1] ('lɛstə) *n* **1** a city in central England, in Leicester unitary authority, on the River Soar: administrative centre of Leicestershire: Roman remains and a ruined Norman castle; two universities (1957, 1992); light engineering, hosiery, and footwear industries. Pop: 293 400 (1994 est) **2** a unitary authority in central England, in Leicestershire. Pop: 279 923 (2001). Area: 73 sq km (28 sq miles) **3** short for **Leicestershire** **4** a breed of sheep with long wool, originally from Leicestershire **5** a fairly mild dark orange whole-milk cheese, similar to Cheddar
Leicester[2] ('lɛstə) *n* **Earl of** title of *Robert Dudley*. ?1532–88, English courtier; favourite of Elizabeth I. He led an unsuccessful expedition to the Netherlands (1585–87)
Leicestershire ('lɛstəʃɪə, -ʃə) *n* a county of central England: absorbed the small historical county of Rutland in 1974; Rutland and Leicester city became independent unitary authorities in 1997: largely agricultural. Administrative centre: Leicester. Pop (excluding Leicester city): 609 579 (2001). Area (excluding Leicester city): 2084 sq km (804 sq miles). Shortened form: **Leicester.** Abbreviation: **Leics**
Leichhardt ('laɪk,hɑ:t; *German* 'laiçhart) *n* **Friedrich Wilhelm Ludwig** ('fri:drɪç 'vɪlhɛlm 'lu:tvɪç) 1813–48, Australian explorer, born in Prussia. He disappeared during an attempt to cross Australia from East to West
Leics *abbrev for* Leicestershire
Leiden *or* **Leyden** ('laɪdᵊn; *Dutch* 'lɛidə) *n* a city in the W Netherlands, in South Holland province: residence of the Pilgrim Fathers for 11 years before they sailed for America in 1620; university (1575). Pop: 117 389 (1999 est)
Leif Ericson ('li:f 'ɛrɪksən) *n* See **Ericson**
Leigh[1] (li:) *n* a town in NW England, in Wigan unitary authority, Greater Manchester: engineering industries. Pop: 43 150 (1991)
Leigh[2] (li:) *n* **1 Mike** born 1943, British dramatist and theatre, film, and television director, noted for his use of improvisation. His plays include *Abigail's Party* (1977), and his films include *High Hopes* (1988), *Secrets and Lies* (1996), and *All or Nothing* (2002) **2 Vivien,** real name *Vivian Hartley*. 1913–67, English stage and film actress. Her films include *Gone with the Wind* (1939) and *A Streetcar Named Desire* (1951), for both of which she won Oscars
Leighton ('leɪtən) *n* **Frederic,** 1st Baron Leighton of Stretton. 1830–96, British painter and sculptor of classical subjects: president of the Royal Academy (1878)
Leinster ('lɛnstə) *n* a province of E and SE Republic of Ireland: it consists of the counties of Carlow, Dublin, Kildare, Kilkenny, Laois, Longford, Louth, Meath, Offaly, Westmeath, Wexford, and Wicklow. Pop: 1 924 702 (1996). Area: 19 632 sq km (7580 sq miles)
Leipzig ('laɪpsɪg; *German* 'laiptsɪç) *n* a city in E central Germany, in Saxony: famous fairs, begun about 1170; publishing and music centre; university (1409); scene of a decisive defeat for Napoleon Bonaparte in 1813. Pop: 490 000 (1999 est)
Leiria (*Portuguese* lei'riə) *n* a city in central Portugal: site of the first printing press in Portugal (1466). Pop: 96 585 (latest est)
leishmaniasis (,li:ʃmə'naɪəsɪs) *or* **leishmaniosis** (li:ʃ,meɪnɪ'əʊsɪs, -,mæn-) *n* any disease, such as kala-azar, caused by protozoa of the genus *Leishmania* [c20 NL, after Sir W. B. *Leishman* (1865–1926), Scot. bacteriologist]
leister ('li:stə) *n* **1** a spear with three or more prongs for spearing fish, esp salmon ▷ *vb* **2** (*tr*) to spear (a fish) with a leister [c16 from Scand.]
leisure ('lɛʒə) *n* **1a** time or opportunity for ease, relaxation, etc **1b** (*as modifier*): *leisure activities* **2** ease or leisureliness **3 at leisure** **3a** having free time **3b** not occupied or engaged **3c** without hurrying **4 at one's leisure** when one has free time [c14 from OF *leisir*; ult. from L *licēre* to be allowed] > **'leisured** *adj*
leisure centre *n* a building designed to provide such leisure facilities as a library, sports hall, café, and rooms for meetings
leisurely ('lɛʒəlɪ) *adj* **1** unhurried; relaxed: *a leisurely stroll* ▷ *adv* **2** without haste; in a relaxed way: *we motored leisurely from Rome* > **'leisureliness** *n*
leisure sickness *n* a medical condition in which people who have been working become ill with symptoms such as fatigue or muscular pains at a weekend or while on holiday
Leith (li:θ) *n* a port in SE Scotland, on the Firth of Forth: part of Edinburgh since 1920
leitmotif *or* **leitmotiv** ('laɪtməʊ,ti:f) *n* **1** *music* a recurring short melodic phrase used, esp in Wagnerian music dramas, to suggest a character, thing, etc **2** an

often repeated image or theme in a literary work [c19 from G: leading motif]

Leitrim ('li:trɪm) *n* a county of N Republic of Ireland in Connacht province, on Donegal Bay: agricultural. County town: Carrick-on-Shannon. Pop: 25 057 (1996). Area: 1525 sq km (589 sq miles)

Leix (li:ʃ) *n* another name for **Laois**

Leizhou ('leɪ'dʒəʊ) *or* **Luichow Peninsula** *n* a peninsula of SE China, in SW Guangdong province, separated from Hainan Island by Hainan Strait

lek (lɛk) *n* a small area in which birds of certain species, notably the black grouse, gather for sexual display and courtship [c19 ?from dialect *lake* (vb) from OE *lácan* to frolic, fight, or ?from Swedish *leka* to play]

lekgotla (lɛ'xɒtlə) *or* **kgotla** ('xɒtlə) *n S African* a meeting place for village assemblies, court cases, and meetings of village leaders [from Sotho and Tswana *lekgotla* courtyard or court]

lekker ('lɛkə) *adj S African sl* **1** pleasing, enjoyable, or likeable **2** tasty [from Afrik., from Du.]

Lely ('li:lɪ) *n* Sir **Peter** Dutch name *Pieter van der Faes.* 1618–80, Dutch portrait painter in England

LEM (lɛm) *n acronym for* lunar excursion module

Lemaître (*French* ləmɛtr) *n* Abbé **Georges** (**Édouard**) (ʒɔrʒ) 1894–1966, Belgian astronomer and priest, who first proposed the big-bang theory of the universe (1927)

Lemalu (lə'mɑ:lu:) *n* **Jonathan** (**Fa'afetai**) born 1976, New Zealand singer of Samoan descent; a bass-baritone noted esp for his lieder recitals

Léman (lemã) *n* **Lac** the French name for (Lake) **Geneva**

Le Mans (*French* lə mã) *n* a city in NW France: scene of the first experiments in motoring and flying; annual motor race. Pop: 146 405 (1999)

Lemberg ('lɛmbɛrk) *n* the German name for **Lviv**

lemma ('lɛmə) *n, pl* **lemmas** *or* **lemmata** (-mətə) **1** a subsidiary proposition, assumed to be valid, that is used in the proof of another proposition **2** an argument or theme, esp when used as the subject or title of a composition **3** *linguistics* a word considered as its citation form together with all the inflected forms [c16 (meaning: proposition), c17 (meaning: title, theme): via L from Gk: premise, from *lambanein* to take (for granted)]

lemming ('lɛmɪŋ) *n* **1** any of various volelike rodents of northern and arctic regions of Europe, Asia, and North America **2** a member of any group following an unthinking course towards destruction [c17 from Norwegian] > **'lemming-,like** *adj*

Lemnos ('lɛmnɒs) *n* a Greek island in the N Aegean Sea: famous for its medicinal earth (**Lemnian seal**). Chief town: Kastron. Pop: 16 000 (latest est). Area: 477 sq km (184 sq miles). Modern Greek name: **Límnos** > **Lemnian** ('lɛmnɪən) *adj, n*

lemon ('lɛmən) *n* **1** a small Asian evergreen tree widely cultivated in warm and tropical regions for its edible fruits. Related adjs: **citric, citrine, citrous** **2a** the yellow oval fruit of this tree, having juicy acidic flesh **2b** (*as modifier*): *a lemon jelly* **3** Also called: **lemon yellow** **3a** a greenish-yellow or pale yellow colour **3b** (*as adj*): *lemon wallpaper* **4** a distinctive tart flavour made from or in imitation of the lemon **5** *sl* a person or thing considered to be useless or defective [c14 from Med. L *lemōn-*, from Ar. *laymūn*] > **'lemony** *adj*

lemonade (,lɛmə'neɪd) *n* a drink made from lemon juice, sugar, and water or from carbonated water, citric acid, etc

lemon balm *n* the full name of **balm**

lemon cheese *or* **curd** *n* a soft spread made from lemons, sugar, eggs, and butter

lemon grass *n* a perennial grass with a large flower spike: used in cooking and grown in tropical regions as the source of an aromatic oil (**lemon grass oil**)

lemon sole *n* a European flatfish with a variegated brown body: highly valued as a food fish

lemon squash *n Brit* a drink made from a sweetened lemon concentrate and water

Lemper ('lɜmpə) *n* **Ute** ('u:tɪ) born 1963, German singer and actress, noted esp for her performances of songs by Kurt Weill

lemur ('li:mə) *n* **1** any of a family of Madagascan prosimian primates such as the ring-tailed lemur. They are typically arboreal, having foxy faces and long tails **2** any similar or closely related animal, such as a loris or indris [c18 NL, adapted from L *lemurēs* ghosts; so named for its ghost-like face and nocturnal habits]

Lena ('li:nə; *Russian* 'ljɛnə) *n* a river in Russia, rising in S Siberia and flowing generally north through the Sakha Republic to the Laptev Sea by an extensive delta: the longest river in Russia. Length: 4271 km (2653 miles)

lend (lɛnd) *vb* **lends, lending, lent** **1** (*tr*) to permit the use of (something) with the expectation of its return **2** to provide (money) temporarily, often at interest **3** (*intr*) to provide loans, esp as a profession **4** (*tr*) to impart or contribute (something, esp some abstract quality): *her presence lent beauty* **5** **lend an ear** to listen **6** **lend oneself** *or* **itself** to possess the right characteristics or qualities for: *the novel lends itself to serialization* [c15 *lende* (orig. the past tense), from OE *lǣnan*, from *lǣn* loan] > **'lender** *n*

lending library *n* **1** Also called (esp US): **circulating library** the department of a public library providing books for use outside the building **2** a small commercial library

lend-lease *n* (during World War II) the system organized by the US in 1941 by which equipment and services were provided for countries fighting Germany

Lenglen (*French* lãglã) *n* **Suzanne** (syzan) 1899–1938, French tennis player: Wimbledon champion (1919-25)

length (lɛŋkθ, lɛŋθ) *n* **1** the linear extent or measurement of something from end to end, usually being the longest dimension **2** the extent of something from beginning to end, measured in some more or less regular units or intervals: *the book was 600 pages in length* **3** a specified distance, esp between two positions: *the length of a race* **4** a period of time, as between specified limits or moments **5** a piece or section of something narrow and long: *a length of tubing* **6** the quality, state, or fact of being long rather than short **7** (*usually pl*) the amount of trouble taken in pursuing or achieving something (esp in **to great lengths**) **8** (*often pl*) the extreme or limit of action (esp in **to any length(s)**) **9** *prosody, phonetics* the metrical quantity or temporal duration of a vowel or syllable **10** the distance from one end of a rectangular swimming bath to the other **11** **at length** **11a** in depth; fully **11b** eventually **11c** interminably [OE *lengthu*]

lengthen ('lɛŋkθən, 'lɛŋθən) *vb* to make or become longer > **'lengthener** *n*

lengthways ('lɛŋkθ,weɪz, 'lɛŋθ-) *or* **lengthwise** *adv, adj* in, according to, or along the direction of length

lengthy ('lɛŋkθɪ, 'lɛŋθɪ) *adj* **lengthier, lengthiest** of relatively great or tiresome extent or duration > **'lengthily** *adv* > **'lengthiness** *n*

lenient ('li:nɪənt) *adj* showing or characterized by mercy or tolerance [c17 from L *lēnīre* to soothe, from *lēnis* soft] > **'leniency** *or* **'lenience** *n* > **'leniently** *adv*

Lenin ('lɛnɪn) *n* **Vladimir Ilyich** (vla'dimir ilj'jitʃ), original surname *Ulyanov.* 1870–1924, Russian statesman and Marxist theoretician; first premier of the Soviet Union. He formed the Bolsheviks (1903) and led them in the October Revolution (1917), which established the Soviet Government. He adopted the New Economic Policy (1921) after the Civil War had led to the virtual collapse of the Russian economy, formed the Comintern (1919), and was the originator of the guiding doctrine of the Soviet Union, Marxism-Leninism. After the Soviet Union broke up in 1991, many statues of Lenin were demolished

Leninabad (*Russian* lınina'bat) *n* the former name (1937–91) of **Khojent**

Leninakan (*Russian* lınina'kan) *n* the former name (1925–91) of **Kumayri**

Leningrad ('lɛnın,græd; *Russian* lınin'grat) *n* the former name (1937–91) of **Saint Petersburg**

Leninism ('lɛnı,nızəm) *n* the political and economic theories of Lenin > **'Leninist** *n, adj*

Lenin Peak *n* a mountain in Tajikistan; the highest peak in the Trans Alai Range. Height: 7134 m (23 406 ft)

lenitive ('lɛnıtıv) *adj* 1 soothing or alleviating pain or distress ▷ *n* 2 *obsolete* a lenitive drug [c16 from Med. L *lēnītīvus*, from L *lēnīre* to soothe]

lenity ('lɛnıtı) *n, pl* **lenities** the state or quality of being lenient [c16 from L *lēnitās* gentleness, from *lēnis* soft]

Lennon ('lɛnən) *n* **John (Ono)**, original name *John Winston Lennon*. 1940–80, English rock guitarist, singer, and songwriter: member of the Beatles (1962–70). His subsequent recordings, many in collaboration with his wife Yoko Ono, include "Instant Karma" (1970), *Imagine* (1971), and *Double Fantasy* (1980). He was assassinated by a demented fan

leno ('li:nəʊ) *n, pl* **lenos** 1 (in textiles) a weave in which the warp yarns are twisted together in pairs between the weft or filling yarns 2 a fabric of this weave [c19 prob. from F *linon* lawn, from *lin* flax, from L *līnum*]

Leno ('li:nəʊ) *n* **Dan**, original name *George Galvin*. 1860–1904, British music-hall entertainer, noted esp for his pantomime performances: he died insane

lens (lɛnz) *n* 1 a piece of glass or other transparent material, used to converge or diverge transmitted light and form optical images 2 Also called: **compound lens** a combination of such lenses for forming images or concentrating a beam of light 3 a device that diverges or converges a beam of electromagnetic radiation, sound, or particles 4 *anat* See **crystalline lens** [c17 from L *lēns* lentil, referring to the similarity of a lens to the shape of a lentil]

lent (lɛnt) *vb* the past tense and past participle of **lend**

Lent (lɛnt) *n* *Christianity* the period of forty weekdays lasting from Ash Wednesday to Holy Saturday, observed as a time of penance and fasting commemorating Jesus' fasting in the wilderness [OE *lencten*, *lengten* spring, lit.: lengthening (of hours of daylight)]

lentamente (,lɛntə'mɛnteı) *adv music* slowly [It.]

lenten ('lɛntən) *adj* 1 (*often cap*) of or relating to Lent 2 *arch or literary* spare, plain, or meagre: *lenten fare*

lenticel ('lɛntı,sɛl) *n* any of numerous pores in the stem of a woody plant allowing exchange of gases between the plant and the exterior [c19 from NL *lenticella*, from L *lenticula* dim. of *lēns* lentil]

lenticular (lɛn'tıkjʊlə) *adj* 1 shaped like a biconvex lens 2 of or concerned with a lens or lenses 3 shaped like a lentil seed [c17 from L *lenticulāris* like a LENTIL]

lentil ('lɛntıl) *n* 1 a small annual leguminous plant of the Mediterranean region and W Asia, having edible convex seeds 2 any of the seeds of this plant, which are cooked and eaten in soups, etc [c13 from OF *lentille*, from L *lenticula*, dim. of *lēns* lentil]

lentivirus ('lɛntı,vaırəs) *n* another name for **slow virus** [c20 NL, from L *lentus* slow + VIRUS]

lent lily *n* another name for the **daffodil**

lento ('lɛntəʊ) *music* ▷ *adj, adv* 1 to be performed slowly ▷ *n, pl* **lentos** 2 a movement or passage performed in this way [c18 It., from L *lentus* slow]

Lent term *n* the spring term at Cambridge University and some other educational establishments

Lenya ('lɛnjə) *n* **Lotte** ('lɒtı), original name *Caroline Blamauer*. 1900–81, Austrian singer and actress, associated esp with the songs of her husband Kurt Weill

Leo ('li:əʊ) *n*, *Latin genitive* **Leonis** (li:'əʊnıs) 1 *astron* a zodiacal constellation in the N hemisphere, lying between Cancer and Virgo 2 *astrol* Also called: the **Lion** the fifth sign of the zodiac. The sun is in this sign between about July 23 and Aug 22

Leo I ('li:əʊ) *n* **Saint**, known as *Leo the Great*. ?390–461 AD, pope (440–461). He extended the authority of the papacy in the West and persuaded Attila not to attack Rome (452). Feast day: Nov 10 or Feb 18

Leo III *n* 1 called *the Isaurian*. ?675–741 AD, Byzantine emperor (717–41): he checked Arab expansionism and began the policy of iconoclasm, which divided the empire for the next century 2 **Saint** ?750–816 AD, pope (795–816) He crowned Charlemagne emperor of the Romans (800). Feast day: June 12

Leo X *n* original name *Giovanni de' Medici*. 1475–1521, pope (1513–21): noted for his patronage of Renaissance art and learning; excommunicated Luther (1521)

Leo XIII *n* original name *Gioacchino Pecci*. 1810–1903, pope (1878–1903). His many important encyclicals include *Rerum novarum* (1891) on the need for Roman Catholics to take action on various social problems

Leoben (*German* le'o:bən) *n* a city in E central Austria, in Styria on the Mur River: lignite mining. Pop: 28 504 (1991)

León (*Spanish* le'ɔn) *n* 1 a region and former kingdom of NW Spain, which united with Castile in 1230 2 a city of NW Spain: capital of the kingdom of León (10th century). Pop: 139 809 (1998 est) 3 a city in central Mexico, in W Guanajuato state: commercial centre of a rich agricultural region. Pop: 1 019 510 (2000 est). Official name: **León de los Aldamas** (de los 'aldamas) 4 a city in W Nicaragua: one of the oldest towns of Central America, founded in 1524; capital of Nicaragua until 1855; university (1812). Pop: 123 865 (1995)

Leonardo da Vinci (,li:ə'nɑ:dəʊ də 'vıntʃı) *n* 1452–1519, Italian painter, sculptor, architect, and engineer: the most versatile talent of the Italian Renaissance. His most famous paintings include *The Virgin of the Rocks* (1483–85), the *Mona Lisa* (or *La Gioconda*, 1503), and the *Last Supper* (?1495–97). His numerous drawings, combining scientific precision in observation with intense imaginative power, reflect the breadth of his interests, which ranged over biology, physiology, hydraulics, and aeronautics. He invented the first armoured tank and foresaw the invention of aircraft and submarines

Leonardo of Pisa *n* See (Leonardo) **Fibonacci**

Leoncavallo (*Italian* leoŋka'vallo) *n* **Ruggiero** (rud'dʒɛ:ro) 1858–1919, Italian composer of operas, notably *I Pagliacci* (1892)

Leonid ('li:ənıd) *n, pl* **Leonids** *or* **Leonides** (lı'ɒnı,di:z) any member of a meteor shower appearing to radiate from the constellation Leo [c19 from NL *Leōnidēs*, from *leō* lion]

Leonidas (lı'ɒnı,dæs) *n* died 480 BC, king of Sparta (?490–480), hero of the Battle of Thermopylae, in which he was killed by the Persians under Xerxes

leonine ('li:ə,naın) *adj* of, characteristic of, or resembling a lion [c14 from L *leōnīnus*, from *leō* lion]

Leonine ('li:ə,naın) *adj* 1 connected with one of the popes called Leo: an epithet applied to a district of Rome fortified by Pope Leo IV (**Leonine City**) 2 **Leonine verse** 2a a type of medieval hexameter or elegiac verse having internal rhyme 2b a type of English verse with internal rhyme

leopard ('lɛpəd) *n* 1 Also called: **panther** a large feline mammal of forests of Africa and Asia, usually having a tawny yellow coat with black rosette-like spots 2 any of several similar felines, such as the snow leopard and cheetah 3 *heraldry* a stylized leopard, painted as a lion with the face turned towards the front [c13 from OF *lepart*, from LL, from LGk *leópardos*, from *leōn* lion + *pardos* PARD (the leopard was thought to be the result of cross-breeding)] > **'leopardess** *fem n*

Leopardi (*Italian* leo'pardi) *n* Count **Giacomo** ('dʒa:komo) 1798–1837, Italian poet and philosopher, noted esp for his lyrics, collected in *I Canti* (1831)

Leopold I ('lɪəˌpəʊld) *n* **1** 1640–1705, Holy Roman Emperor (1658–1705). His reign was marked by wars with Louis XIV of France and with the Turks **2** 1790–1865, first king of the Belgians (1831–65)

Leopold II *n* **1** 1747–92, Holy Roman Emperor (1790–92). He formed an alliance with Prussia against France (1792) after the downfall of his brother-in-law Louis XVI **2** 1835–1909, king of the Belgians (1865–1909); son of Leopold I. He financed Stanley's explorations in Africa, becoming first sovereign of the Congo Free State (1885)

Leopold III *n* 1901–83, king of the Belgians (1934–51); son of Albert I. His surrender to the Nazis (1940) forced his eventual abdication in favour of his son, Baudouin

Léopoldville ('lɪəpəʊldˌvɪl; *French* leɔpɔlvil) *n* the former name (until 1966) of **Kinshasa**

leotard ('lɪəˌtɑːd) *n* **1** a tight-fitting garment covering the body from the shoulders down to the thighs and worn by acrobats, ballet dancers, etc **2** (*pl*) *US & Canad* another name for **tights** (sense 1b) [c19 after Jules *Léotard*, F acrobat]

Lepanto *n* **1** (lɪ'pæntəʊ) a port in W Greece, between the Gulfs of Corinth and Patras: scene of a naval battle (1571) in which the Turkish fleet was defeated by the fleets of the Holy League. Pop: 8170 (latest est). Greek name: **Návpaktos** **2** **Gulf of** another name for the (Gulf of) **Corinth**

Lepaya (lɪ'pɑːjə) *n* a variant spelling of **Liepāja**

Le Pen (*French* lə pɛ̃) *n* **Jean-Marie** (ʒɑ̃məri) born 1928, French politician; leader of the extreme right-wing Front National from 1972; runner-up in the presidential election of 2002

leper ('lɛpə) *n* **1** a person who has leprosy **2** a person who is ignored or despised [c14 via LL from Gk *lepra*, n. use of *lepros* scaly, from *lepein* to peel]

lepido- *or before a vowel* **lepid-** *combining form* scale or scaly: *lepidopterous* [from Gk *lepis* scale; see LEPER]

lepidopteran (ˌlɛpɪ'dɒptərən) *n, pl* **lepidopterans** *or* **lepidoptera** (-tərə) **1** any of a large order of insects typically having two pairs of wings covered with fragile scales: comprises the butterflies and moths ▷ *adj also* **lepidopterous** **2** of, relating to, or belonging to this order [c19 from NL, from LEPIDO- + Gk *pteron* wing]

lepidopterist (ˌlɛpɪ'dɒptərɪst) *n* a person who studies or collects moths and butterflies

Lepidus ('lɛpɪdəs) *n* **Marcus Aemilius** ('mɑːkəs iː'mɪlɪəs) died ?13 BC, Roman statesman: formed the Second Triumvirate with Octavian (later Augustus) and Mark Antony

Lepontine Alps (lɪ'pɒntaɪn) *pl n* a range of the S central Alps, in S Switzerland and N Italy. Highest peak: Monte Leone, 3553 m (11 657 ft)

leprechaun ('lɛprəˌkɔːn) *n* (in Irish folklore) a mischievous elf, often believed to have a treasure hoard [c17 from Irish Gaelic *leipreachān*, from MIrish *lūchorpān*, from *lū* small + *corp* body, from L *corpus* body]

leprosy ('lɛprəsɪ) *n pathol* a chronic infectious disease occurring mainly in tropical and subtropical regions, characterized by the formation of painful inflamed nodules beneath the skin and disfigurement and wasting of affected parts [c16 from LEPROUS + -Y[3]]

leprous ('lɛprəs) *adj* **1** having leprosy **2** relating to or resembling leprosy [c13 from OF, from LL *leprosus*, from *lepra* LEPER]

-lepsy *or sometimes* **-lepsia** *n combining form* indicating a seizure: *catalepsy* [from NL *-lepsia*, from Gk, from *lēpsis* a seizure, from *lambanein* to seize] > **-leptic** *adj combining form*

leptodactylous (ˌlɛptəʊ'dæktɪləs) *adj zool* having slender digits

lepton[1] ('lɛptɒn) *n, pl* **lepta** (-tə) **1** a former Greek monetary unit worth one hundredth of a drachma **2** a small coin of ancient Greece [from Gk *lepton* (*nomisma*) small (coin)]

lepton[2] ('lɛptɒn) *n physics* any of a group of elementary particles and their antiparticles, such as an electron, muon, or neutrino, that participate in electromagnetic and weak interactions [c20 from Gk *leptos* thin, from *lepein* to peel + -ON]

lepton number *n physics* a quantum number describing the behaviour of elementary particles, equal to the number of leptons present minus the number of antileptons. It is thought to be conserved in all processes

leptospirosis (ˌlɛptəʊspaɪ'rəʊsɪs) *n* any of several infectious diseases caused by bacteria, transmitted to man by animals and characterized by jaundice, meningitis, and kidney failure. Also called: **Weil's disease** [c20 from NL *Leptospira* (from Gk *leptos* thin + *speira* coil + -OSIS)]

Lérida (*Spanish* 'leriða) *n* a city in NE Spain, in Catalonia: commercial centre of an agricultural region. Pop: 112 207 (1998 est)

Lermontov (*Russian* 'ljɛrmәntәf) *n* **Mikhail Yurievich** (mixa'il 'jurjɪvitʃ) 1814–41, Russian novelist and poet: noted esp for the novel *A Hero of Our Time* (1840)

Lerner ('lɜːnə) *n* **Alan Jay** 1914–86, US songwriter and librettist. With Frederick Loewe he wrote *My Fair Lady* (1956) and *Camelot* (1960) as well as a number of film scripts, including *Gigi* (1958)

Lerwick ('lɜːwɪk) *n* a town in Shetland, administrative centre of the island authority of Shetland, on the island of Mainland: the most northerly town in the British Isles; knitwear, oil refining. Pop: 7336 (1991 est)

Le Sage *or* **Lesage** (*French* lə saʒ) *n* **Alain-René** (alɛ̃rəne) 1668–1747, French novelist and dramatist, author of the picaresque novel *Gil Blas* (1715–35)

lesbian ('lɛzbɪən) *n* **1** a female homosexual ▷ *adj* **2** of or characteristic of lesbians [c19 from the homosexuality attributed to SAPPHO] > **'lesbianism** *n*

Lesbos ('lɛzbɒs) *n* an island in the E Aegean, off the NW coast of Turkey: a centre of lyric poetry, led by Alcaeus and Sappho (6th century BC); annexed to Greece in 1913. Chief town: Mytilene. Pop: 105 082 (1991). Area: 1630 sq km (630 sq miles). Modern Greek name: **Lésvos**. Former name: **Mytilene**

Les Cayes (leɪ 'keɪ; *French* le kaj) *n* a port in SW Haiti, on the S Tiburon Peninsula. Pop: 45 904 (1992). Also called: **Cayes**. Former name: **Aux Cayes**

lese-majesty ('liːz'mædʒɪstɪ) *n* **1** any of various offences committed against the sovereign power in a state; treason **2** an attack on authority or position [c16 from F *lèse majesté*, from L *laesa mājestās* wounded majesty]

lesion ('liːʒən) *n* **1** any structural change in a bodily part resulting from injury or disease **2** an injury or wound [c15 via OF from LL *laesiō* injury, from L *laedere* to hurt]

Lesotho (lɪ'suːtʊ, lə'səʊtəʊ) *n* a kingdom in southern Africa, forming an enclave in the Republic of South Africa: annexed to British Cape Colony in 1871; made a protectorate in 1884; gained independence in 1966; a member of the Commonwealth. It is generally mountainous, with temperate grasslands throughout. Languages: Sesotho and English. Religion: Christian majority. Currency: loti. Capital: Maseru. Pop: 2 177 000 (2001 est). Area: 30 344 sq km (11 716 sq miles). Former name (1884–1966): **Basutoland**

▷ www.lesotho.gov.ls

▷ www.lesotho.gov.ls/mnsports.htm

less (lɛs) *determiner* **1a** the comparative of **little** (sense 1): *less sugar; less spirit than before* **1b** (*as pronoun; functioning as sing or pl*): *she has less than she needs; the less you eat, the less you want* **2** (usually preceded by *no*) lower in rank or importance: *no less a man than the president* **3** **less of** to a smaller extent or degree: *we see less of John these days; less of a success than I'd hoped* ▷ *adv* **4** the comparative of **little** (sense 10): *she walks less than she should; less quickly; less beautiful* ▷ *prep* **5** subtracting; minus: *three weeks less a day* [OE *lǣssa* (adj), *lǣs* (adv, n)]

Ll

USAGE *Less* should not be confused with *fewer*. *Less* refers strictly only to quantity and not to number: *there is less water than before*. *Fewer* means smaller in number: *there are fewer people than before*

-less *suffix forming adjectives* **1** without; lacking: *speechless* **2** not able to (do something) or not able to be (done, performed, etc): *countless* [OE *-lās*, from *lēas* lacking]

lessee (lɛˈsiː) *n* a person to whom a lease is granted; a tenant under a lease [c15 via Anglo-F from OF *lessé*, from *lesser* to LEASE]

lessen (ˈlɛsᵊn) *vb* **1** to make or become less **2** (*tr*) to make little of

Lesseps (ˈlɛsəps; *French* lɛsɛps) *n* Vicomte **Ferdinand Marie de** (fɛrdinɑ̃ mari də) 1805–94, French diplomat: directed the construction of the Suez Canal (1859–69) and the unsuccessful first attempt to build the Panama Canal (1881–89)

lesser (ˈlɛsə) *adj* not as great in quantity, size, or worth

Lesser Antilles *pl n* **the** a group of islands in the Caribbean, including the Leeward Islands, the Windward Islands, Barbados, and the Netherlands Antilles. Also called: **Caribbees**

lesser celandine *n* a Eurasian plant, related to the buttercup, having yellow flowers and heart-shaped leaves

lesser panda *n* See **panda** (sense 2)

Lesser Sunda Islands *pl n* the former name of **Nusa Tenggara**

Lessing (ˈlɛsɪŋ) *n* **1 Doris (May)** born 1919, English novelist and short-story writer, brought up in Rhodesia: her novels include the five-novel sequence *Children of Violence* (1952–69), *The Golden Notebook* (1962), *Memoirs of a Survivor* (1974), a series of science-fiction works (1979–83), *The Good Terrorist* (1985), and *The Sweetest Dream* (2001) **2 Gotthold Ephraim** (ˈɡɔthɔlt ˈeːfraɪm) 1729–81, German dramatist and critic. His plays include *Miss Sara Sampson* (1755), the first German domestic tragedy, and *Nathan der Weise* (1779). He is noted for his criticism of French classical dramatists, and for his treatise on aesthetics *Laokoon* (1766)

lesson (ˈlɛsᵊn) *n* **1a** a unit, or single period of instruction in a subject; class: *an hour-long music lesson* **1b** the content of such a unit **2** material assigned for individual study **3** something from which useful knowledge or principles can be learned; example **4** the principles, knowledge, etc, gained **5** a reprimand or punishment intended to correct **6** a portion of Scripture appointed to be read at divine service [c13 from OF *leçon*, from L *lēctiō*, from *legere* to read]

lessor (ˈlɛsɔː, lɛˈsɔː) *n* a person who grants a lease of property

lest (lɛst) *conj* (*subordinating; takes a subjunctive vb*) **1** so as to prevent any possibility that: *keep down lest anyone see us* **2** (*after vbs or phrases expressing fear, worry, anxiety, etc*) for fear that; in case: *he was alarmed lest she should find out* [OE *the lǣste*, earlier *thӯ lǣs the*, lit.: whereby less that]

Lésvos (ˈlɛzvɔs) *n* transliteration of the Modern Greek name for **Lesbos**

let¹ (lɛt) *vb* **lets, letting, let** (*tr*; usually takes an infinitive without *to* or an implied infinitive) **1** to permit; allow: *she lets him roam around* **2** (*imperative or dependent imperative*) **2a** used as an auxiliary to express a request, proposal, or command, or to convey a warning or threat: *let's get on; just let me catch you here again!* **2b** (in mathematical or philosophical discourse) used as an auxiliary to express an assumption or hypothesis: *let "a" equal "b"* **2c** used as an auxiliary to express resigned acceptance of the inevitable: *let the worst happen* **3a** to allow the occupation of (accommodation) in return for rent **3b** to assign (a contract for work) **4** to allow or cause the movement of (something) in a specified direction: *to let air out of a tyre* **5 let alone** (*conj*) much less; not to mention: *I can't afford wine, let alone champagne* **6 let** *or* **leave alone** *or* **be** refrain from annoying or interfering with: *let the poor cat alone* **7 let go** See **go** (sense 45) **8 let loose 8a** to set free **8b** *inf* to make (a sound or remark) suddenly: *he let loose a hollow laugh* **8c** *inf* to discharge (rounds) from a gun or guns: *they let loose a couple of rounds of ammunition* ▷ *n* **9** *Brit* the act of letting property or accommodation ▷ See also **let down, let in,** etc [OE *lǣtan* to permit]

let² (lɛt) *n* **1** an impediment or obstruction (esp in **without let or hindrance**) **2** *tennis, squash, etc* **2a** a minor infringement or obstruction of the ball, requiring a point to be replayed **2b** the point so replayed ▷ *vb* **lets, letting, letted** *or* **let 3** (*tr*) *arch* to hinder; impede [OE *lettan* to hinder, from *læt* late]

-let *suffix forming nouns* **1** small or lesser: *booklet* **2** an article of attire or ornament worn on a specified part of the body: *anklet* [from OF *-elet*, from L *-āle*, from L *-ellus*, dim. suffix]

Letchworth (ˈlɛtʃwəθ, -ˌwɜːθ) *n* a town in SE England, in N Hertfordshire: the first garden city in Great Britain (founded in 1903). Pop: 31 418 (1991)

let down *vb* (*tr, mainly adv*) **1** (*also prep*) to lower **2** to fail to fulfil the expectations of (a person); disappoint **3** to undo, shorten, and resew (the hem) so as to lengthen (a dress, skirt, etc) **4** to untie (long hair that is bound up) and allow to fall loose **5** to deflate: *to let down a tyre* ▷ *n* **letdown 6** a disappointment

lethal (ˈliːθəl) *adj* **1** able to cause or causing death **2** of or suggestive of death [c16 from L *lēthālis*, from *lētum* death] > **lethality** (liːˈθælɪtɪ) *n* > **ˈlethally** *adv*

lethargy (ˈlɛθədʒɪ) *n, pl* **lethargies 1** sluggishness, slowness, or dullness **2** an abnormal lack of energy [c14 from LL *lēthargīa*, from Gk *lēthargos* drowsy, from *lēthē* forgetfulness] > **lethargic** (lɪˈθɑːdʒɪk) *adj* > **leˈthargically** *adv*

Lethbridge (ˈlɛθbrɪdʒ) *n* a city in Canada, in S Alberta: coal-mining. Pop: 60 974 (1991)

Lethe (ˈliːθɪ) *n* **1** *Greek myth* a river in Hades that caused forgetfulness in those who drank its waters **2** forgetfulness [c16 via L from Gk, from *lēthē* oblivion] > **Lethean** (lɪˈθiːən) *adj*

let in *vb* (*tr, adv*) **1** to allow to enter **2 let in for** to involve (oneself or another) in (something more than is expected) **3 let in on** to allow (someone) to know about

Leto (ˈliːtəʊ) *n* the mother by Zeus of Apollo and Artemis. Roman name: **Latona**

let off *vb* (*tr, mainly adv*) **1** (*also prep*) to allow to disembark or leave **2** to explode or fire (a bomb, gun, etc) **3** (*also prep*) to excuse from (work or other responsibilities): *I'll let you off for a week* **4** *inf* to allow to get away without the expected punishment, work, etc **5** to let (accommodation) in portions **6** to release (liquid, air, etc)

let on *vb* (*adv; when tr, takes a clause as object*) *inf* **1** to allow (something, such as a secret) to be known; reveal: *he never let on that he was married* **2** (*tr*) to cause or encourage to be believed; pretend

let out *vb* (*adv, mainly tr*) **1** to give vent to; emit: *to let out a howl* **2** to allow to go or run free; release **3** (*may take a clause as object*) to reveal (a secret) **4** to make available to tenants, hirers, or contractors **5** to permit to flow out: *to let air out of the tyres* **6** to make (a garment) larger, as by unpicking (the seams) and sewing nearer the outer edge ▷ *n* **let-out 7** a chance to escape

let's (lɛts) *contraction of* let us: used to express a suggestion, command, etc, by the speaker to himself and his hearers

Lett (lɛt) *n* a former name for a **Latvian**

letter (ˈlɛtə) *n* **1** any of a set of conventional symbols used in writing or printing a language, each symbol being associated with a group of phonetic values; character of the alphabet **2** a written or printed communication addressed to a person, company, etc, usually sent by post **3** (often preceded by *the*) the strict legalistic or pedantic interpretation of the meaning of an agreement, document, etc; exact wording as distinct from actual intention (esp in **the letter of the law**) **4 to the letter 4a** following the literal interpretation or wording exactly **4b** attending to every detail ▷ *vb* **5** to write or mark letters on (a sign, etc), esp by hand **6** (*tr*) to set down or print using letters [C13 from OF *lettre*, from L *littera* letter of the alphabet] > **'letterer** *n*

letter bomb *n* an explosive device in an envelope, detonated when the envelope is opened

letter box *n chiefly Brit* **1a** a slot through which letters, etc, are delivered to a building **1b** a private box into which letters, etc, are delivered **2** Also: **postbox** a public box into which letters, etc, are put for collection

lettered ('lɛtəd) *adj* **1** well educated in literature, the arts, etc **2** literate **3** of or characterized by learning or culture **4** printed or marked with letters

letterhead ('lɛtəˌhɛd) *n* a sheet of writing paper printed with one's address, name, etc

lettering ('lɛtərɪŋ) *n* **1** the act, art, or technique of inscribing letters on to something **2** the letters so inscribed

letter of credit *n* a letter issued by a bank entitling the bearer to draw funds up to a specified maximum from that bank or its agencies

letter of intent *n* a letter indicating that the writer has the serious intention of doing something, such as signing a contract, in the circumstances specified. It does not constitute either a promise or a contract

letter of marque *or* **letters of marque** *n* (formerly) a licence granted by a state to a private citizen to arm a ship and seize merchant vessels of another nation. Also called: **letter of marque and reprisal**

letter-perfect *adj* another term (esp US) for **word-perfect**

letterpress ('lɛtəˌprɛs) *n* **1a** a method of printing in which ink is transferred from raised surfaces to paper by pressure **1b** matter so printed **2** text matter as distinct from illustrations

letters ('lɛtəz) *n* (*functioning as sing or pl*) **1** literary knowledge, ability, or learning: *a man of letters* **2** literary culture in general **3** an official title, degree, etc, indicated by an abbreviation: *letters after one's name*

letters patent *pl n* See **patent** (senses 1, 4)

Lettish ('lɛtɪʃ) *n* another name for **Latvian** (sense 2)

lettuce ('lɛtɪs) *n* **1** any of various plants of the composite family cultivated in many varieties for their large edible leaves **2** the leaves of any of these varieties, which are eaten in salads **3** any of various plants that resemble true lettuce, such as lamb's lettuce [C13 prob. from OF *laitues*, from L *lactūca*, from *lac-* milk, because of its milky juice]

let up *vb* (*intr, adv*) **1** to diminish, slacken, or stop **2** (foll by *on*) *inf* to be less harsh (towards someone) ▷ *n* **let-up** **3** *inf* a lessening or abatement

Leucas ('lu:kəs) *n* a variant spelling of **Leukas**

Leucippus (lu:'sɪpəs) *n* 5th century BC Greek philosopher, who originated the atomist theory of matter, developed by his disciple, Democritus

leuco-, leuko- *or before a vowel* **leuc-, leuk-** *combining form* white or lacking colour: *leucocyte; leukaemia* [from Gk *leukos* white]

leucoblast *or esp US* **leukoblast** ('lu:kəʊˌblæst) *n* an immature leucocyte

leucocyte *or esp US* **leukocyte** ('lu:kəˌsaɪt) *n* any of the various large unpigmented cells in the blood of vertebrates. Also called: **white blood cell, white** (**blood**) **corpuscle**. See also **lymphocyte, granulocyte** > **leucocytic** *or esp US* **leukocytic** (ˌlu:kə'sɪtɪk) *adj*

leucoma (lu:'kəʊmə) *n pathol* a white opaque scar of the cornea

leucotomy (lu:'kɒtəmɪ) *n, pl* **leucotomies** the surgical operation of cutting some of the nerve fibres in the frontal lobes of the brain for treating intractable mental disorders

Leuctra ('lu:ktrə) *n* an ancient town in Greece southwest of Thebes in Boeotia: site of a victory of Thebes over Sparta (371 BC), which marked the end of Spartan military supremacy in Greece

leukaemia *or esp US* **leukemia** (lu:'ki:mɪə) *n* an acute or chronic disease characterized by a gross proliferation of leucocytes, which crowd into the bone marrow, spleen, lymph nodes, etc, and suppress the blood-forming apparatus [C19 from LEUCO- + Gk *haima* blood]

Leukas *or* **Leucas** ('lu:kəs) *n* another name for **Levkás**

Leuven ('lø:və) *n* the Flemish name for **Louvain**

Lev. *Bible abbrev for* Leviticus

levant (lɪ'vænt) *n* a type of leather made from the skins of goats, sheep, or seals, having a pattern of irregular creases [C19 shortened from *Levant morocco* (type of leather)]

Levant (lɪ'vænt) *n* **the** a former name for the area of the E Mediterranean now occupied by Lebanon, Syria, and Israel [C15 from Old French, from the present participle of *lever* to raise (referring to the rising of the sun in the east), from Latin *levāre*] > **Levantine** ('lɛvənˌtaɪn) *adj, n*

levanter (lɪ'væntə) *n* (*sometimes cap*) **1** an easterly wind in the W Mediterranean area **2** an inhabitant of the Levant

levator (lɪ'veɪtə, -tɔ:) *n anat* any of various muscles that raise a part of the body [C17 NL, from L *levāre* to raise]

levee[1] ('lɛvɪ) *n US* **1** an embankment alongside a river, produced naturally by sedimentation or constructed by man to prevent flooding **2** an embankment that surrounds a field that is to be irrigated **3** a landing place on a river; quay [C18 from F, from Med. L *levāta* from L *levāre* to raise]

levee[2] ('lɛvɪ, 'lɛveɪ) *n* **1** a formal reception held by a sovereign just after rising from bed **2** (in Britain) a public court reception for men **3** *Canad* a reception held on New Year's Day [C17 from F, var. of *lever* a rising, from L *levāre* to raise]

level ('lɛvᵊl) *adj* **1** on a horizontal plane **2** having a surface of completely equal height **3** being of the same height as something else **4** (of quantities to be measured, as in recipes) even with the top of the cup, spoon, etc **5** equal to or even with (something or someone else) **6** not having or showing inconsistency or irregularities **7** Also: **level-headed** even-tempered; steady **8 one's level best** the best one can do ▷ *vb* **levels, levelling, levelled** *or US* **levels, leveling, leveled** **9** (*tr; sometimes foll by off*) to make (a surface) horizontal, level, or even **10** to make (two or more people or things) equal, as in position or status **11** (*tr*) to raze to the ground **12** (*tr*) to knock (a person) down as by a blow **13** (*tr*) to direct (a gaze, criticism, etc) emphatically at someone **14** (*intr; often foll by with*) *inf* to be straightforward and frank **15** (*intr; foll by off or out*) to manoeuvre an aircraft into a horizontal flight path after a dive, climb, or glide **16** (often foll by *at*) to aim (a weapon) horizontally ▷ *n* **17** a horizontal datum line or plane **18** a device, such as a spirit level, for determining whether a surface is horizontal **19** a surveying instrument used for measuring relative heights of land **20** position or status in a scale of values **21** amount or degree of progress; stage **22** a specified vertical position; altitude **23** a horizontal line or plane with respect to which measurement of elevation is based: *sea level* **24** a flat even surface or area of land **25** *physics* the ratio of the magnitude of a physical quantity to an arbitrary magnitude: *sound-pressure level* **26 on the level** *inf* sincere or genuine [C14 from OF *livel*, from Vulgar L *lībellum* (unattested), from L *lībella*, dim. of *lībra* scales] > **'leveller** *or US* **'leveler** *n* > **'levelly** *adv* > **'levelness** *n*

level crossing *n Brit, Canad, Austral, & NZ* a point at which

Ll

a railway and a road cross, esp one with barriers that close the road when a train is due to pass

level-headed *adj* even-tempered, balanced, and reliable; steady > ˌ**level-'headedly** *adv* > ˌ**level-'headedness** *n*

level of attainment *n Brit education* one of ten groupings, each with its own attainment criteria based on pupil age and ability, within which a pupil is assessed

level pegging *Brit inf* ▷ *n* **1** equality between two contestants ▷ *adj* **2** (of two contestants) equal

level playing field *n* a situation in which none of the competing parties has an advantage at the outset of a competitive activity

Leven ('liːvᵊn) *n* **Loch 1** a lake in E central Scotland: one of the shallowest of Scottish lochs, with seven islands, on one of which Mary, Queen of Scots was imprisoned (1567–8). Length: 6 km (3.7 miles). Width: 4 km (2.5 miles) **2** a sea loch in W Scotland, extending for about 14 km (9 miles) east from Loch Linnhe

lever ('liːvə) *n* **1** a rigid bar pivoted about a fulcrum, used to transfer a force to a load and usually to provide a mechanical advantage **2** any of a number of mechanical devices employing this principle **3** a means of exerting pressure in order to accomplish something ▷ *vb* **4** to prise or move (an object) with a lever [C13 from OF *leveour*, from *lever* to raise, from L *levāre* from *levis* light]

leverage ('liːvərɪdʒ, -vrɪdʒ) *n* **1** the action of a lever **2** the mechanical advantage gained by employing a lever **3** strategic advantage **4** power or influence: *the supermarket chains have greater leverage than single-outlet enterprises* **5** the US word for **gearing** (sense 3) **6** the use made by a company of its limited assets to guarantee the substantial loans required to finance its business

leveraged buyout ('liːvərɪdʒd, -vrɪdʒd) *n* a takeover bid in which a small company makes use of its limited assets, and those of the usually larger target company, to raise the loans required to finance the takeover. Abbrev: **LBO**

leveret ('lɛvərɪt, -vrɪt) *n* a young hare, esp one less than one year old [C15 from Norman F *levrete*, dim. of *levre*, from L *lepus* hare]

Leverhulme ('liːvəˌhjuːm) *n* **William Hesketh,** 1st Viscount. 1851–1925, English soap manufacturer and philanthropist, who founded (1881) the model industrial town Port Sunlight

Leverkusen (*German* 'leːvərˌkuːzən) *n* a town in NW Germany, in North Rhine-Westphalia on the Rhine: chemical industries. Pop: 161 100 (1999 est)

Leverrier (*French* ləvɛrje) *n* **Urbain Jean Joseph** (yrbɛ̃ ʒɑ̃ ʒozɛf) 1811–77, French astronomer: calculated the existence and position of the planet Neptune

Levi[1] ('liːvaɪ) *n* **1** *Old Testament* **1a** the third son of Jacob and Leah and the ancestor of the tribe of Levi (Genesis 29:34) **1b** the priestly tribe descended from this patriarch (Numbers 18:21–24) **2** *New Testament* another name for **Matthew** (the apostle)

Levi[2] (*Italian* 'lɛːvi) *n* **1 Carlo** 1902–75, Italian physician, painter, and writer. Best known for his novel *Christ Stopped at Eboli* (1947), his other works include *The Watch* (1952) and *Words are Stones* (1958) **2 Primo** ('priːməʊ) 1919–87, Italian novelist. His book *If This is a Man* (1947) relates his experiences in Auschwitz. Other books include *The Periodic Table* (1956) and *The Drowned and the Saved* (1988), published after his suicide

leviable ('lɛvɪəbᵊl) *adj* **1** (of taxes, etc) liable to be levied **2** (of goods, etc) liable to bear a levy; taxable

leviathan (lɪ'vaɪəθən) *n* **1** *Bible* a monstrous beast, esp a sea monster **2** any huge or powerful thing [C14 from LL, ult. from Heb. *liwyāthān*, from ?]

levigate ('lɛvɪˌgeɪt) *vb* **levigates, levigating, levigated** *chem* **1** (*tr*) to grind into a fine powder or a smooth paste **2** to form or cause to form a homogeneous mixture, as in the production of gels **3** (*tr*) to suspend (fine particles) by grinding in a liquid, esp as a method of separating fine from coarse particles [C17 from L *lēvigāre*, from *lēvis* smooth] > ˌ**levi'gation** *n*

Levis ('liːvaɪz) *pl n trademark* jeans, usually blue and made of denim

Lévi-Strauss ('lɛvɪ'straʊs; *French* levistros) *n* **Claude** (klod) born 1908, French anthropologist, leading exponent of structuralism. His books include *The Elementary Structures of Kinship* (1969), *Totemism* (1962), *The Savage Mind* (1966), *Mythologies* (1964–71), and *Saudades do Brazil* (Memories of Brazil; 1994)

levitate ('lɛvɪˌteɪt) *vb* **levitates, levitating, levitated** to rise or cause to rise and float in the air, without visible agency, usually attributed, esp formerly, to supernatural intervention [C17 from L *levis* light + *-tate*, as in *gravitate*] > ˌ**levi'tation** *n* > '**leviˌtator** *n*

levity ('lɛvɪtɪ) *n, pl* **levities 1** inappropriate lack of seriousness **2** fickleness or instability **3** *arch* lightness in weight [C16 from L *levitās* lightness, from *levis* light]

Levkás (lɛf'kæs), **Leukas,** *or* **Leucas** *n* a Greek island in the Ionian Sea, in the Ionian Islands. Pop: 22 000 (latest est). Area: 295 sq km (114 sq miles). Italian name: **Santa Maura**

Levkosia (lɛf'kəʊsɪə) *or* **Leukosia** *n* the Greek name for **Nicosia**

levodopa (ˌliːvəʊ'dəʊpə) *n* another name for **L-dopa**

levy ('lɛvɪ) *vb* **levies, levying, levied** (*tr*) **1** to impose and collect (a tax, tariff, fine, etc) **2** to conscript troops for service **3** to seize or attach (property) in accordance with the judgment of a court ▷ *n, pl* **levies 4a** the act of imposing and collecting a tax, tariff, etc **4b** the money so raised **5a** the conscription of troops for service **5b** a person conscripted in this way [C15 from OF *levée* a raising, from *lever*, from L *levāre* to raise]

Lévy-Bruhl (levibrul) *n* **Lucien** (lysjɛ̃) 1857–1939, French anthropologist and philosopher, noted for his study of the psychology of primitive peoples

lewd (luːd) *adj* characterized by or intended to excite crude sexual desire; obscene [C14 from OE *lǣwde* ignorant] > '**lewdly** *adv* > '**lewdness** *n*

Lewes ('luːɪs) *n* a market town in S England, administrative centre of East Sussex, on the River Ouse: site of a battle (1264) in which Henry III was defeated by Simon de Montfort. Pop: 15 376 (1991)

lewis ('luːɪs) *n* a lifting device for heavy stone blocks consisting of a number of curved pieces of metal fitting into a dovetailed recess cut into the stone [C18 ?from the name of the inventor]

Lewis[1] ('luːɪs) *n* the N part of the island of Lewis with Harris, in the Outer Hebrides. Area: 1634 sq km (631 sq miles)

Lewis[2] ('luːɪs) *n* **1 Carl** full name *Frederick Carleton Lewis.* born 1961, US athlete; winner of the long jump, 100 metres, 200 metres, and 4×100 metres relay at the 1984 Olympic Games; winner of the 100 metres in the 1988 Olympic Games; winner of the long jump in the 1992 and 1996 Olympic Games **2** See (Cecil) **Day-Lewis** **3 C(live) S(taples)** 1898–1963, English novelist, critic, and Christian apologist, noted for his critical work, *Allegory of Love* (1936), his theological study, *The Screwtape Letters* (1942), and for his children's books chronicling the land of Narnia **4 Lennox** born 1965, British boxer; undisputed world heavyweight champion 2000–2001 **5 Matthew Gregory,** known as *Monk Lewis.* 1775–1818, English novelist and dramatist, noted for his Gothic horror story *The Monk* (1796) **6 Meriwether** 1774–1807, American explorer who, with William Clark, led an overland expedition from St. Louis to the Pacific Ocean (1804–06) **7 (John) Saunders** ('sɔːndəz) 1893–1985, Welsh poet, dramatist, critic, and politician: founder (1926) and president (1926–39) of the Welsh Nationalist Party **8 (Harry) Sinclair** 1885–1951, US novelist. He satirized the complacency and philistinism of American small-town life, esp in *Main Street* (1920) and *Babbitt* (1922): Nobel prize for literature 1930 **9 Wally** born 1959, Australian rugby league player **10 (Percy) Wyndham** 1884–1957, British painter, novelist, and critic, born in the US: a founder of vorticism. His writings include *Time and Western Man* (1927), *The Apes of God* (1930), and the trilogy *The Human Age* (1928–55)

Lewis acid *n* a substance capable of accepting a pair of electrons from a base to form a covalent bond ▷ Cf **Lewis base** [C20 after G. N. *Lewis* (1875–1946), US chemist]

Lewis base *n* a substance capable of donating a pair of electrons to an acid to form a covalent bond ▷ Cf **Lewis acid** [C20 after G. N. *Lewis*; see LEWIS ACID]

Lewis gun *n* a light air-cooled gas-operated machine gun used chiefly in World Wars I and II [C20 after I. N. *Lewis* (1858–1931), US soldier]

Lewisham ('luːɪʃəm) *n* a borough of S Greater London, on the River Thames. Pop: 248 924 (2001). Area: 35 sq km (13 sq miles)

lewisite ('luːɪˌsaɪt) *n* a colourless oily poisonous liquid having a powerful blistering action and used as a war gas. Formula: $ClCH:CHAsCl_2$. Systematic name: **1-chloro-2-dichloroarsinoethene** [C20 after W. L. *Lewis* (1878–1943), US chemist]

Lewis with Harris *or* **Lewis and Harris** *n* an island in the Outer Hebrides, separated from the NW coast of Scotland by the Minch: consists of Lewis in the north and Harris in the south; many lakes and peat moors; economy based chiefly on the Harris tweed industry, with some fishing. Chief town: Stornoway. Pop: 23 500 (latest est). Area: 2134 sq km (824 sq miles)

lexeme ('lɛksiːm) *n linguistics* a minimal meaningful unit that cannot be understood from the meanings of its component morphemes [C20 from LEX(ICON) + -EME]

lexical ('lɛksɪkᵊl) *adj* **1** of or relating to items of vocabulary in a language **2** of or relating to a lexicon > **'lexically** *adv*

lexicography (ˌlɛksɪ'kɒgrəfɪ) *n* the process or profession of writing or compiling dictionaries > **ˌlexi'cographer** *n* > **lexicographic** (ˌlɛksɪkə'græfɪk) *or* **ˌlexico'graphical** *adj*
▷ www.ims.uni-stuttgart.de/euralex
▷ http://australex.anu.edu.au/

lexicon ('lɛksɪkən) *n* **1** a dictionary, esp one of an ancient language such as Greek or Hebrew **2** a list of terms relating to a particular subject **3** the vocabulary of a language or of an individual **4** *linguistics* the set of all the morphemes of a language [C17 NL, from Gk *lexikon*, n use of *lexikos* relating to words, from Gk *lexis* word, from *legein* to speak]

lexigraphy (lɛk'sɪgrəfɪ) *n* a system of writing in which each word is represented by a sign [C19 from Gk *lexis* word + -GRAPHY]

Lexington ('lɛksɪŋtən) *n* **1** a city in NE central Kentucky, in the bluegrass region: major centre for horse-breeding. Pop: 260 512 (2000) **2** a city in Massachusetts, northwest of Boston: site of the first action (1775) of the War of American Independence. Pop: 28 974 (1990)

lexis ('lɛksɪs) *n* the totality of vocabulary items in a language [C20 from Gk *lexis* word]

ley (leɪ, liː) *n* **1** arable land temporarily under grass **2** Also: **ley line** a line joining two prominent points in the landscape, thought to be the line of a prehistoric track [C14 var. of LEA]

Leyden[1] ('laɪdᵊn; *Dutch* 'lɛidə) *n* a variant spelling of **Leiden**

Leyden[2] ('laɪdᵊn) *n* See **Lucas van Leyden**

Leyden jar *n physics* an early type of capacitor consisting of a glass jar with the lower part of the inside and outside coated with tin foil [C18 first made in Leiden]

Leyland cypress ('leɪlənd) *n* a hybrid coniferous tree that is widely grown for hedging because it grows quickly. Also called: **Leylandii** (leɪ'lændɪˌaɪ) [C20 named after C. J. *Leyland* (1849–1926), Brit horticulturalist]

Leyte ('leɪteɪ) *n* an island in the central Philippines, in the Visayan Islands. Chief town: Tacloban. Pop: 1 362 050 (1990). Area: 7215 sq km (2786 sq miles)

Leyte Gulf *n* an inlet of the Pacific in the E Philippines, east of Leyte and south of Samar: scene of a battle (Oct 23–26, 1944) during World War II, in which the Americans defeated almost the entire Japanese navy, thereby ensuring ultimate Allied victory

lezzie ('lɛzɪ) *or* **lezza** ('lezə) *n sl* a lesbian

lf *printing abbrev for* light face

LF *radio abbrev for* low frequency

LG *abbrev for* Low German

LGV (in Britain) *abbrev for* large goods vehicle

lh *or* **LH** *abbrev for* left hand

Lhasa *or* **Lassa** ('lɑːsə) *n* a city in SW China, capital of Tibet AR, at an altitude of 3606 m (11 830 ft): for centuries the sacred city of Lamaism and residence of the Dalai Lamas from the 17th century until 1950; known as the Forbidden City because it was closed to Westerners until the beginning of the 20th century; annexed by China in 1951. The Dalai Lama fled after an unsuccessful revolt against Chinese rule in 1959. Pop: 121 568 (1999 est)

Li *the chemical symbol for* lithium

LI *abbrev for*: **1** Long Island **2** Light Infantry

liabilities (ˌlaɪə'bɪlɪtɪz) *pl n accounting* business obligations not discharged and shown as balanced against assets on the balance sheet

liability (ˌlaɪə'bɪlɪtɪ) *n, pl* **liabilities** **1** the state of being liable **2** a financial obligation **3** a hindrance or disadvantage

liable ('laɪəbᵊl) *adj (postpositive)* **1** legally obliged or responsible; answerable **2** susceptible or exposed; subject **3** probable or likely: *it's liable to happen soon* [C15 ? via Anglo-F, from OF *lier* to bind, from L *ligāre*]

USAGE The use of *liable* to mean *probable* or *likely* was formerly considered incorrect, but is now acceptable

LI

liaise (lɪ'eɪz) *vb* **liaises, liaising, liaised** *(intr; usually foll by with)* to communicate and maintain contact (with) [C20 back formation from LIAISON]

liaison (lɪ'eɪzɒn) *n* **1** communication and contact between groups or units **2** a secretive or adulterous sexual relationship **3** the relationship between military units necessary to ensure unity of purpose **4** one who acts as an agent between parties; intermediary **5** (esp in French) the pronunciation of a normally silent consonant at the end of a word immediately before another word commencing with a vowel, in such a way that the consonant is taken over as the initial sound of the following word, as in *ils ont* (ilzɔ̃) **5** any thickening for soups, sauces, etc, such as egg yolks or cream [C17 via F from OF, from *lier* to bind, from L *ligāre*]

Liákoura ('ljakura) *n* transliteration of the Modern Greek name for (Mount) **Parnassus**

liana (lɪ'ɑːnə) *or* **liane** (lɪ'ɑːn) *n* any of various woody climbing plants mainly of tropical forests [C19 changed from earlier *liane* (through infl. of F *lier* to bind), from F, from ?]

Lianyungang ('ljæn'jʊŋ'gæŋ), **Sinhailien**, *or* **Hsin-hai-lien** *n* a city in E China, near the coast of Jiangsu. Pop: 447 918 (1997 est)

Liao (ljaʊ) *n* a river in NE China, rising in SE Inner Mongolia and flowing northeast then southwest to the Gulf of Liaodong. Length: about 1100 km (700 miles)

Liaodong ('ljaʊ'dʊŋ) *or* **Liaotung** ('ljaʊ'tʊŋ) *n* **1** a peninsula of NE China, in S Manchuria extending south into the Yellow Sea: forms the S part of Liaoning province **2** **Gulf of** the N part of the Gulf of Chihli, west of the peninsula of Liaodong

Liaoning ('ljaʊ'nɪŋ) *n* a province of NE China, in S Manchuria. Capital: Shenyang. Pop: 42 380 000 (2000

est). Area: 150 000 sq km (58 500 sq miles)

Liaoyang ('ljaʊ'jæŋ) *n* a city in NE China, in S Manchuria, in Liaoning province: a regional capital in the early dynasties. Pop: 570 483 (1999 est)

liar ('laɪə) *n* a person who tells lies

Liard ('li:ɑ:d, li:'ɑ:d, -'ɑ:) *n* a river in W Canada, rising in the SE Yukon and flowing east and then northwest to the Mackenzie River. Length: 885 km (550 miles)

Lias ('laɪəs) *n* the lowest series of rocks of the Jurassic system [C15 (referring to a kind of limestone), C19 (geological sense): from OF *liois*, ?from *lie* dregs, so called from its appearance] > **Liassic** (laɪ'æsɪk) *adj*

lib (lɪb) *n inf, sometimes derog* short for **liberation**

lib. *abbrev for:* **1** librarian **2** library

Lib. *abbrev for* Liberal

libation (laɪ'beɪʃən) *n* **1a** the pouring-out of wine, etc, in honour of a deity **1b** the liquid so poured out **2** *usually facetious* an alcoholic drink [C14 from L *lībātiō*, from *lībāre* to pour an offering of drink]

Libau ('li:bau) *n* the German name for **Liepāja**

Libava (lɪ'bavə) *n* transliteration of the Russian name for **Liepāja**

Libby ('lɪbɪ) *n* **Willard Frank** 1908–80, US chemist, who devised the technique of radiocarbon dating: Nobel prize for chemistry 1960

libel ('laɪbᵊl) *n* **1** *law* **1a** the publication of defamatory matter in permanent form, as by a written or printed statement, picture, etc **1b** the act of publishing such matter **2** any defamatory or unflattering representation or statement **3** *Scots law* the formal statement of a charge ▷ *vb* **libels, libelling, libelled** *or US* **libels, libeling, libeled** (*tr*) **4** *law* to make or publish a defamatory statement or representation about (a person) **5** to misrepresent injuriously [C13 (in the sense: written statement), hence C14 legal sense: a plaintiff's statement, via OF from L *libellus* a little book] > **'libeller** *or* **'libelist** *n* > **'libellous** *or* **'libelous** *adj*

liberal ('lɪbərəl, 'lɪbrəl) *adj* **1** relating to or having social and political views that favour progress and reform **2** relating to or having policies or views advocating individual freedom **3** giving and generous in temperament or behaviour **4** tolerant of other people **5** abundant; lavish: *a liberal helping of cream* **6** not strict; free: *a liberal translation* **7** of or relating to an education that aims to develop general cultural interests and intellectual ability ▷ *n* **8** a person who has liberal ideas or opinions [C14 from L *līberālis* of freedom, from *līber* free] > **'liberally** *adv* > **'liberalness** *n*

Liberal ('lɪbərəl, 'lɪbrəl) *n* **1** a member or supporter of a Liberal Party or Liberal Democrat party ▷ *adj* **2** of or relating to a Liberal Party

liberal arts *pl n* the fine arts, humanities, sociology, languages, and literature. Often shortened to **arts**

Liberal Democrat *n* a member or supporter of the Liberal Democrats

Liberal Democrats *pl n* (in Britain) a political party with centrist policies; established in 1988 as the Social and Liberal Democrats when the Liberal Party merged with the Social Democratic Party; renamed Liberal Democrats in 1989

liberalism ('lɪbərə,lɪzəm, 'lɪbrə-) *n* liberal opinions, practices, or politics

liberality (,lɪbə'rælɪtɪ) *n, pl* **liberalities** **1** generosity; bounty **2** the quality or condition of being liberal

liberalize *or* **liberalise** ('lɪbərə,laɪz, 'lɪbrə-) *vb* **liberalizes, liberalizing, liberalized** *or* **liberalises, liberalising, liberalised** to make or become liberal > **,liberali'zation** *or* **,liberali'sation** *n* > **'liberal,izer** *or* **'liberal,iser** *n*

Liberal Party *n* **1** one of the former major political parties in Britain; in 1988 it merged with the Social Democratic Party to form the Social and Liberal Democrats; renamed the Liberal Democrats in 1989 **2** one of the major political parties in Australia, a conservative party, generally opposed to the Labor Party **3** any other party supporting liberal policies

liberal studies *n* (*functioning as sing*) *Brit* a supplementary arts course for those specializing in scientific, technical, or professional studies

liberate ('lɪbə,reɪt) *vb* **liberates, liberating, liberated** (*tr*) **1** to give liberty to; make free **2** to release (something, esp a gas) from chemical combination **3** to release from occupation or subjugation by a foreign power **4** to free from social prejudices or injustices **5** *euphemistic or facetious* to steal > **'liber,ator** *n*

liberated ('lɪbə,reɪtɪd) *adj* **1** given liberty; freed; released **2** released from occupation or subjugation by a foreign power **3** (esp in feminist theory) not bound by traditional sexual and social roles

liberation (,lɪbə'reɪʃən) *n* **1** a liberating or being liberated **2** the seeking of equal status or just treatment for or on behalf of any group believed to be discriminated against: *women's liberation; animal liberation* > **,liber'ationist** *n, adj*

liberation theology *n* the belief that Christianity involves not only faith in the Church but a commitment to change social and political conditions where it is considered exploitation and oppression exist: applied esp to South America

Liberec (*Czech* 'libɛrɛts) *n* a city in the N Czech Republic, on the Neisse River: a centre of the German Sudeten movement in 1938. Pop: 100 604 (1996 est). German name: **Reichenberg**

Liberia (laɪ'bɪərɪə) *n* a republic in W Africa, on the Atlantic: originated in 1822 as a home for freed Afro-American slaves, with land purchased by the American Colonization Society; republic declared in 1847; exports are predominantly rubber and iron ore. Official language: English. Religion: Christian majority, also animist. Currency: dollar. Capital: Monrovia. Pop: 3 226 000 (2001 est). Area: 111 400 sq km (43 000 sq miles) > **Li'berian** *adj, n*

libertarian (,lɪbə'tɛərɪən) *n* **1** a believer in freedom of thought, expression, etc **2** a believer in the doctrine of free will ▷ Cf **determinism** ▷ *adj* **3** of, relating to, or characteristic of a libertarian [C18 from LIBERTY] > **,liber'tarianism** *n*

libertine ('lɪbə,ti:n, -,taɪn) *n* **1** a morally dissolute person ▷ *adj* **2** morally dissolute [C14 (in the sense: freedman, dissolute person): from L *lībertīnus* freedman, from *lībertus* freed, from *līber* free] > **'liber,tinage** *or* **'libertin,ism** *n*

liberty ('lɪbətɪ) *n, pl* **liberties** **1** the power of choosing, thinking, and acting for oneself; freedom from control or restriction **2** the right or privilege of access to a particular place; freedom **3** (*often pl*) a social action regarded as being familiar, forward, or improper **4** (*often pl*) an action that is unauthorized: *he took liberties with the translation* **5a** authorized leave granted to a sailor **5b** (*as modifier*): *liberty man; liberty boat* **6** **at liberty** free, unoccupied, or unrestricted **7** **take liberties** (**with**) to be overfamiliar or overpresumptuous [C14 from OF *liberté*, from L *lībertās*, from *līber* free]

Liberty bodice *n trademark* a sleeveless vestlike undergarment covering the upper part of the body, formerly worn esp by young children

liberty hall *n* (*sometimes caps*) *inf* a place or condition of complete liberty

Liberty Island *n* a small island in upper New York Bay: site of the Statue of Liberty. Area: 5 hectares (12 acres). Former name (until 1956): **Bedloe's Island**

Libeskind ('li:bəskɪnd) *n* **Daniel** born 1946, US architect, born in Poland. Based in Berlin, he designed the Jewish Museum there (1999), the Imperial War Museum in Manchester (2000), the proposed spiral extension to London's Victoria and Albert Museum, and the Freedom Tower that will replace the World Trade Center in New York

Libia ('li:bja) *n* the Italian name for **Libya**
libidinous (lɪ'bɪdɪnəs) *adj* characterized by excessive sexual desire > **li'bidinously** *adv* > **li'bidinousness** *n*
libido (lɪ'bi:dəʊ) *n, pl* **libidos** **1** *psychoanal* psychic energy emanating from the id **2** sexual urge or desire [c20 (in psychoanalysis): from L: desire] > **libidinal** (lɪ'bɪdɪnᵊl) *adj* > **li'bidinally** *adv*
libra ('laɪbrə) *n, pl* **librae** (-bri:) an ancient Roman unit of weight corresponding to 1 pound [c14 from L, lit.: scales]
Libra ('li:brə) *n, Latin genitive* **Librae** ('li:bri:) **1** *astron* a small faint zodiacal constellation in the S hemisphere, lying between Virgo and Scorpius **2** Also called: the **Scales,** the **Balance** *astrol* the seventh sign of the zodiac. The sun is in this sign between about Sept 23 and Oct 22
librarian (laɪ'brɛərɪən) *n* a person in charge of or assisting in a library > **li'brarian,ship** *n*
library ('laɪbrərɪ) *n, pl* **libraries** **1** a room or set of rooms where books and other literary materials are kept **2** a collection of literary materials, films, CDs, etc, kept for borrowing or reference **3** the building or institution that houses such a collection: *a public library* **4** a set of books published as a series, often in a similar format **5** *computing* a collection of standard programs and subroutines, usually stored on disk **6** a collection of specific items for reference or checking against: *a library of genetic material* [c14 from OF *librairie*, from Med. L *librāris*, n. use of L *librārius* relating to books, from *liber* book]
▹ http://sunsite.berkeley.edu/Libweb/
▹ www.bl.uk/index.shtml
▹ www.loc.gov
libration (laɪ'breɪʃən) *n* **1** the act of oscillating **2** a real or apparent oscillation of the moon enabling approximately nine per cent of the surface facing away from earth to be seen [c17 from L, from *librāre* to balance]
librettist (lɪ'brɛtɪst) *n* the author of a libretto
libretto (lɪ'brɛtəʊ) *n, pl* **librettos** *or* **libretti** (-ti:) a text written for and set to music in an opera, etc [c18 from It., dim. of *libro* book]
Libreville (*French* librəvil) *n* the capital of Gabon, in the west on the estuary of the Gabon River: founded as a French trading post in 1843 and expanded with the settlement of freed slaves in 1848. Pop: 362 386 (1993)
Librium ('lɪbrɪəm) *n trademark* a brand of the drug chlordiazepoxide used as a tranquillizer. See also **benzodiazepine**
Libya ('lɪbɪə) *n* a republic in N Africa, on the Mediterranean: became an Italian colony in 1912; divided after World War II into Tripolitania and Cyrenaica (under British administration) and Fezzan (under French); gained independence in 1951; monarchy overthrown by a military junta in 1969. It consists almost wholly of desert and is a major exporter of oil. Official language: Arabic. Official religion: (Sunni) Muslim. Currency: Libyan dinar. Capital: Tripoli. Pop: 5 241 000 (2001 est). Area: 1 760 000 sq km (680 000 sq miles). Official name: **Al-Jumhuria al-Arabia allibya** > **'Libyan** *adj, n*
▹ www.libyaonline.com
Libyan Desert *n* a desert in N Africa, in E Libya, W Egypt, and the NW Sudan: the NE part of the Sahara
lice (laɪs) *n* the plural of **louse**
licence *or US* **license** ('laɪsəns) *n* **1** a certificate, tag, document, etc, giving official permission to do something **2** formal permission or exemption **3** liberty of action or thought; freedom **4** intentional disregard of conventional rules to achieve a certain effect: *poetic licence* **5** excessive freedom [c14 via OF and Med. L *licentia* permission, from L: freedom, from *licet* it is allowed]
license ('laɪsəns) *vb* **licenses, licensing, licensed** (*tr*) **1** to grant or give a licence for (something, such as the sale of alcohol) **2** to give permission to or for > **'licensable** *adj* > **'licenser** *or* **'licensor** *n*
licensee (ˌlaɪsən'si:) *n* a person who holds a licence, esp one permitting him or her to sell alcoholic drink
licentiate (laɪ'sɛnʃɪɪt) *n* **1** a person who holds a formal attestation of competence to practise a certain profession **2** a higher degree awarded by certain, chiefly European, universities **3** a person who holds this degree **4** *chiefly Presbyterian Church* a person holding a licence to preach [c15 from Med. L *licentiātus*, from *licentiāre* to permit] > **li'centiate,ship** *n*
licentious (laɪ'sɛnʃəs) *adj* **1** sexually unrestrained or promiscuous **2** *now rare* showing disregard for convention [c16 from L *licentiōsus* capricious, from *licentia* LICENCE] > **li'centiously** *adv* > **li'centiousness** *n*
lichee (ˌlaɪ'tʃi:) *n* a variant spelling of **litchi**
lichen ('laɪkən, 'lɪtʃən) *n* an organism that is formed by the symbiotic association of a fungus and an alga or cyanobacterium and occurs as crusty patches or bushy growths on tree trunks, bare ground, etc. Lichens are now classified as a phylum of fungi [c17 via L from Gk *leikhēn*, from *leikhein* to lick] > **'lichened** *adj* > **'lichenous** *adj*
Lichfield ('lɪtʃˌfi:ld) *n* a city in central England, in SE Staffordshire: cathedral with three spires (13th–14th century); birthplace of Samuel Johnson, during whose lifetime the **Lichfield Group** (a literary circle) flourished. Pop: 28 666 (1991)
lich gate (lɪtʃ) *n* a variant spelling of **lych gate**
Lichtenstein ('lɪktənˌstaɪn) *n* **Roy** 1923–97, US pop artist
licit ('lɪsɪt) *adj* a less common word for **lawful** [c15 from L *licitus*, from *licēre* to be permitted] > **'licitly** *adv* > **'licitness** *n*
lick (lɪk) *vb* **1** (*tr*) to pass the tongue over, esp in order to taste or consume **2** to flicker or move lightly over or round (something): *the flames licked around the door* **3** (*tr*) *inf* **3a** to defeat or vanquish **3b** to flog or thrash **3c** to be or do much better than **4** **lick into shape** to put into a satisfactory condition **5** **lick one's wounds** to retire after a defeat ▹ *n* **6** an instance of passing the tongue over something **7** a small amount: *a lick of paint* **8** short for **salt lick** **9** *inf* a hit; blow **10** *sl* a short musical phrase, usually on one instrument **11** *inf* rate of movement; speed **12** **a lick and a promise** something hastily done, esp a hurried wash [OE *liccian*] > **'licker** *n*

LI

lickerish *or* **liquorish** ('lɪkərɪʃ) *adj arch* **1** lecherous or lustful **2** greedy; gluttonous **3** appetizing or tempting [c16 changed from c13 *lickerous*, from OF *lechereus* lecherous; see LECHER]
lickety-split ('lɪkɪtɪ'splɪt) *adv US & Canad inf* very quickly; speedily [c19 from LICK + SPLIT]
licking ('lɪkɪŋ) *n inf* **1** a beating **2** a defeat
lickspittle ('lɪkˌspɪtᵊl) *n* a flattering or servile person
licorice ('lɪkərɪs) *n* the usual US and Canad spelling of **liquorice**
lictor ('lɪktə) *n* one of a group of ancient Roman officials, usually bearing fasces, who attended magistrates, etc [c16 *lictor*, c14 *littour*, from L *ligāre* to bind]
lid (lɪd) *n* **1** a cover, usually removable or hinged, for a receptacle: *a saucepan lid; a desk lid* **2** short for **eyelid** **3** **put the lid on** *inf* **3a** *Brit* to be the final blow to **3b** to curb, prevent, or discourage [OE *hlid*] > **'lidded** *adj* > **'lidless** *adj*
Liddell Hart ('lɪdᵊl hɑ:t) *n* Sir **Basil Henry** 1895–1970, British military strategist and historian: he advocated the development of mechanized warfare before World War II
Lidice (*Czech* 'lidjtsɛ) *n* a mining village in the Czech Republic: destroyed by the Germans in 1942 in reprisal for the assassination of Reinhard Heydrich; rebuilt as a national memorial
lido ('li:dəʊ) *n, pl* **lidos** *Brit* a public place of recreation, including a swimming pool [c20 after the *Lido*, island bathing beach near Venice, from L *litus* shore]
lie[1] (laɪ) *vb* **lies, lying, lied** **1** (*intr*) to speak untruthfully with intent to mislead or deceive **2** (*intr*) to convey a false impression or practise deception: *the camera does not lie* ▹ *n* **3** an untrue or deceptive statement deliberately

used to mislead **4** something that is deliberately intended to deceive **5 give the lie to 5a** to disprove **5b** to accuse of lying. Related adj: **mendacious** [OE *lyge* (n), *lēogan* (vb)]

lie[2] (laɪ) *vb* **lies, lying, lay, lain** (*intr*) **1** (often foll by *down*) to place oneself or be in a prostrate position, horizontal to the ground **2** to be situated, esp on a horizontal surface: *the pencil is lying on the desk; India lies to the south of Russia* **3** to be buried: *here lies Jane Brown* **4** (*copula*) to be and remain (in a particular state or condition): *to lie dormant* **5** to stretch or extend: *the city lies before us* **6** (usually foll by *on* or *upon*) to rest or weigh: *my sins lie heavily on my mind* **7** (usually foll by *in*) to exist or consist inherently: *strength lies in unity* **8** (foll by *with*) **8a** to be or rest (with): *the ultimate decision lies with you* **8b** *arch* to have sexual intercourse (with) **9** (of an action, claim, appeal, etc) to subsist; be maintainable or admissible **10** *arch* to stay temporarily ▷ *n* **11** the manner, place, or style in which something is situated **12** the hiding place or lair of an animal **13 lie of the land 13a** the topography of the land **13b** the way in which a situation is developing ▷ See also **lie down, lie in,** etc [OE *licgan* akin to OHG *ligen* to lie, L *lectus* bed]

USAGE See at **lay**

Lie (liː) *n* **Trygve Halvdan** ('trygvə 'halðan) 1896–1968, Norwegian statesman; first secretary-general of the United Nations (1946–52)

Liebig (*German* 'liːbɪç) *n* **Justus** ('jʊstʊs), Baron von Liebig. 1803–73, German chemist, who founded agricultural chemistry. He also contributed to organic chemistry, esp to the concept of radicals, and discovered chloroform

Liebig condenser ('liːbɪg) *n chem* a laboratory condenser consisting of a glass tube surrounded by a glass envelope through which cooling water flows

Liebknecht (*German* 'liːpknɛçt) *n* **1 Karl** (karl) 1871–1919, German socialist leader: with Rosa Luxemburg he led an unsuccessful Communist revolt (1919) and was assassinated **2** his father, **Wilhelm** ('vɪlhɛlm) 1826–1900, German socialist leader and journalist, a founder (1869) of what was to become (1891) the German Social Democratic Party

Liechtenstein ('lɪktən,staɪn; *German* 'lɪçtənʃtain) *n* a small mountainous principality in central Europe on the Rhine: formed in 1719 by the uniting of the lordships of Schellenburg and Vaduz, which had been purchased by the Austrian family of Liechtenstein; customs union formed with Switzerland in 1924. Official language: German. Religion: Roman Catholic majority. Currency: Swiss franc. Capital: Vaduz. Pop: 33 000 (2001 est). Area: 160 sq km (62 sq miles)
▷ www.liechtenstein.li
▷ www.tourismus.li

lied (liːd; *German* liːt) *n, pl* **lieder** ('liːdə; *German* 'liːdər) *music* any of various musical settings for solo voice and piano of a romantic or lyrical poem [from G: song]

lie detector *n inf* a polygraph used esp by a police interrogator to detect false or devious answers to questions, a sudden change in one or more involuntary physiological responses being considered a manifestation of guilt, fear, etc

lie down *vb* (*intr, adv*) **1** to place oneself or be in a prostrate position in order to rest **2** to accept without protest or opposition (esp in **take something lying down**) ▷ *n* **lie-down 3** a rest

lief (liːf) *adv* **1** *now rare* gladly; willingly: *I'd as lief go today as tomorrow* ▷ *adj* **2** *arch* **2a** ready; glad **2b** dear; beloved [OE *leof*; rel. to *lufu* love]

liege (liːdʒ) *adj* **1** (of a lord) owed feudal allegiance (esp in **liege lord**) **2** (of a vassal or servant) owing feudal allegiance: *a liege subject* **3** faithful; loyal ▷ *n* **4** a liege lord **5** a liegeman or true subject [c13 from OF *lige*, from Med. L *līticus*, from *lītus*, *laetus* serf, of Gmc origin]

Liège (lɪ'eɪʒ; *French* ljɛʒ) *n* **1** a province of E Belgium: formerly a principality of the Holy Roman Empire, much larger than the present-day province. Pop: 1 019 442 (2000 est). Area: 3877 sq km (1497 sq miles) **2** a city in E Belgium, capital of Liège province: the largest French-speaking city in Belgium; river port and industrial centre. Pop: 185 638 (2000 est). Flemish name **Luik**

liegeman ('liːdʒ,mæn) *n, pl* **liegemen 1** (formerly) a vassal **2** a loyal follower

Liegnitz ('liːgnɪts) *n* the German name for **Legnica**

lie in *vb* (*intr, adv*) **1** to remain in bed late in the morning **2** to be confined in childbirth ▷ *n* **lie-in 3** a long stay in bed in the morning

lien ('liːən, liːn) *n law* a right to retain possession of another's property pending discharge of a debt [c16 via OF from L *ligāmen* bond, from *ligāre* to bind]

Liepāja *or* **Lepaya** (lɪ'pɑːjə) *n* a port in W Latvia on the Baltic Sea; founded by the Teutonic Knights in 1263: a naval and industrial centre, with a fishing fleet. Pop: 100 271 (1995 est). Russian name: **Libava**. German name: **Libau**

lierne (lɪ'ɜːn) *n archit* a short rib that connects the intersections of the primary ribs, esp in Gothic vaulting [c19 from F, ? rel. to *lier* to bind]

Liestal (*German* 'liːstaːl) *n* a city in NW Switzerland, capital of Basel-Land demicanton. Pop: 12 160 (latest est)

lie to *vb* (*intr, adv*) *naut* (of a vessel) to be hove to with little or no swinging

Lietuva (lɪə'tuːvə) *n* the Lithuanian name for **Lithuania**

lieu (ljuː, luː) *n* stead; place (esp in **in lieu, in lieu of**) [c13 from OF, ult. from L *locus* place]

lieutenant (lɛf'tɛnənt; *US* luː'tɛnənt) *n* **1** a military officer holding commissioned rank immediately junior to a captain **2** a naval officer holding commissioned rank immediately junior to a lieutenant commander **3** *US* an officer in a police or fire department ranking immediately junior to a captain **4** a person who holds an office in subordination to or in place of a superior [c14 from OF, lit.: place-holding] > **lieu'tenancy** *n*

lieutenant colonel *n* an officer holding commissioned rank immediately junior to a colonel in certain armies, air forces, and marine corps

lieutenant commander *n* an officer holding commissioned rank in certain navies immediately junior to a commander

lieutenant general *n* an officer holding commissioned rank in certain armies, air forces, and marine corps immediately junior to a general

lieutenant governor *n* **1** a deputy governor **2** (in the US) an elected official who acts as deputy to a state governor **3** (in Canada) the representative of the Crown in a province: appointed by the federal government

Lifar (*Russian* lji'far) *n* **Serge** (sɛrʒ) 1905–86, Russian ballet dancer and choreographer: ballet master at the Paris Opera Ballet (1932–58). His ballets include *Prométhée* (1929), *Icare* (1935), and *Phèdre* (1950)

life (laɪf) *n, pl* **lives** (laɪvz) **1** the state or quality that distinguishes living beings or organisms from dead ones and from inorganic matter, characterized chiefly by metabolism, growth, and the ability to reproduce and respond to stimuli. Related adj: **animate 2** the period between birth and death **3** a living person or being: *to save a life* **4** the time between birth and the present time **5a** the remainder or extent of one's life **5b** (*as modifier*): *a life sentence; life membership; life work* **6** *inf* short for **life imprisonment 7** the amount of time that something is active or functioning: *the life of a battery* **8** a present condition, state, or mode of existence: *my life is very dull here* **9a** a biography **9b** (*as modifier*): *a life story* **10** a characteristic state or mode of existence: *town life* **11** the sum or course of human events and activities **12** liveliness or high spirits: *full of life* **13** a source of strength, animation, or vitality: *he was the life of the show* **14** all living things, taken as a whole: *there is no life on Mars; plant life* **15** *(modifier) arts* drawn or taken from a living model: *life drawing* **16** (in certain games) one of a number of opportunities for participation **17 a matter of life and death** a matter of extreme urgency **18 as large as life** *inf* real and living **19 for the life of me (him, her,** etc) though trying desperately **20 not on your life** *inf* certainly not **21 the life and soul** *inf* a person regarded as the main source of merriment and liveliness: *the life and soul of the party* **22 to the life** (of a copy or image) resembling the original exactly **23 true to life** faithful to reality [OE *līf*]

life assurance *n* a form of insurance providing for the payment of a specified sum to a named beneficiary on the death of the policyholder. Also called: **life insurance**

life belt *n* a buoyant ring used to keep a person afloat when in danger of drowning

lifeblood ('laɪf,blʌd) *n* **1** the blood, considered as vital to life **2** the essential or animating force

lifeboat ('laɪf,bəʊt) *n* **1** a boat used for rescuing people at sea, escaping from a sinking ship, etc **2** *inf* a fund set up by the dealers in a market to rescue any member who may become insolvent as a result of a collapse in market prices

life buoy *n* any of various kinds of buoyant device for keeping people afloat in an emergency

life coach *n* a person whose job is to improve the quality of his or her client's life, by offering advice on professional and personal matters, such as career, health, personal relationships, etc

life cycle *n* the series of changes occurring in an animal or plant between one stage and the identical stage in the next generation

life expectancy *n* the statistically determined average number of years of life remaining after a specified age

lifeguard ('laɪf,gɑːd) *n* a person at a beach or pool to guard people against the risk of drowning

life imprisonment *n* an indeterminate sentence always given for murder and as a maximum sentence in several other crimes. There is no remission, although the Home Secretary may order the prisoner's release on licence

life jacket *n* an inflatable sleeveless jacket worn to keep a person afloat when in danger of drowning

lifeless ('laɪflɪs) *adj* **1** without life; inanimate; dead **2** not sustaining living organisms **3** having no vitality or animation **4** unconscious > **'lifelessly** *adv* > **'lifelessness** *n*

lifelike ('laɪf,laɪk) *adj* closely resembling or representing life > **'life,likeness** *n*

lifeline ('laɪf,laɪn) *n* **1** a line thrown or fired aboard a vessel for hauling in a hawser for a breeches buoy **2** a line by which a deep-sea diver is raised or lowered **3** a single means of contact, communication, or support on which a person or an area, etc, relies

lifelong ('laɪf,lɒŋ) *adj* lasting for or as if for a lifetime

lifelong learning *n* the provision or use of both formal and informal learning opportunities throughout people's lives in order to foster the continuous development and improvement of the knowledge and skills needed for employment and personal fulfilment

life partner *n* either member of a couple in a long-term relationship

life peer *n Brit* a peer whose title lapses at his or her death

life preserver *n* **1** *Brit* a club or bludgeon, esp one kept for self-defence **2** *US & Canad* a life belt or life jacket

lifer ('laɪfə) *n inf* a prisoner sentenced to imprisonment for life

life raft *n* a raft for emergency use at sea

life-saver *n* **1** the saver of a person's life **2** *Austral* an expert swimmer, esp a member of a surf life-saving club at a surfing beach, who rescues surfers or swimmers from drowning **3** *inf* a person or thing that gives help in time of need > **'life-,saving** *adj, n*

life science *n* any one of the branches of science concerned with the structure and behaviour of living organisms, such as biology, botany, zoology, physiology, or biochemistry

▷ www.vlib.org/Biosciences.html
▷ www.sciencekomm.at/
▷ www.biologybrowser.org
▷ http://biotech.icmb.utexas.edu

life-size *or* **life-sized** *adj* representing actual size

life span *n* the period of time during which a human being, animal, machine, etc, may be expected to live or function

lifestyle ('laɪf,staɪl) *n* **1** a set of attitudes, habits, or possessions associated with a particular person or group **2** such attitudes, etc, regarded as fashionable or desirable **3** *NZ* **3a** a luxurious semirural manner of living **3b** *(as modifier)*: *a lifestyle property* **4** *(modifier)* suggestive of a fashionable or desirable lifestyle: *a lifestyle café* **5** *(modifer)* (of a drug) designed to treat problems, such as impotence, that affect a person's quality of life rather than his or her health

lifestyle block *n NZ* a semirural property comprising a house and land for small-scale farming

lifestyle business *n* a small business in which the owners are more anxious to pursue interests that reflect their lifestyle than to make more than a comfortable living

lifestyler ('laɪf,staɪlə) *n inf* a person who adopts a particular lifestyle: *new lifestyler; vampire lifestyler*

life-support *adj* of, providing, or relating to the equipment or treatment necessary to keep a person alive

lifetime ('laɪf,taɪm) *n* **1a** the length of time a person or animal is alive **1b** *(as modifier)*: *a lifetime supply* **2** the length of time that something functions, is useful, etc **3** Also called: **life** *physics* the average time of existence of an unstable or reactive entity

Liffey ('lɪfɪ) *n* a river in E Republic of Ireland, rising in the Wicklow Mountains and flowing west, then northeast through Dublin into Dublin Bay. Length: 80 km (50 miles)

Lifford ('lɪfərd) *n* the county town of Donegal, Republic of Ireland; market town. Pop: 1460 (latest est)

LIFO ('laɪfəʊ) *n acronym for* last in, first out (as an accounting principle in sorting stock) ▷ Cf **FIFO**

lift (lɪft) *vb* **1** to rise or cause to rise upwards from the ground or another support to a higher place: *to lift a sack* **2** to move or cause to move upwards: *to lift one's eyes* **3** (tr) to take hold of in order to carry or remove: *to lift something down from a shelf* **4** (tr) to raise in status, spirituality, estimation, etc: *his position lifted him from the common crowd* **5** (tr) to revoke or rescind: *to lift tax restrictions* **6** (tr) to take (plants or underground crops) out of the ground for transplanting or harvesting **7** (intr) to disappear by lifting or as if by lifting: *the fog lifted* **8** (tr) *inf* to take unlawfully or dishonourably; steal **9** (tr) *inf* to plagiarize **10** (tr) *sl* to arrest **11** (tr) to perform a face-lift on ▷ *n* **12** the act or an instance of lifting **13** the power or force available or used for lifting **14a** *Brit* a platform, compartment, or cage raised or lowered in a vertical shaft to transport persons or goods in a building. US and Canad word: **elevator 14b** See **chairlift, ski lift 15** the distance or degree to which something is lifted **16** a ride in a car or other vehicle for part or all of a passenger's journey **17** a rise in the height of the ground **18** a rise in morale or feeling of cheerfulness usually caused by some specific thing or event **19** the force required to lift an object **20** a layer inserted in the heel of a shoe, etc, to give the wearer added height **21** aid; help **22** the component of the aerodynamic forces acting on a wing, etc, at right angles to the

airflow and opposing gravity [c13 from ON] > 'lifter *n*
liftoff ('lɪft,ɒf) *n* 1 the initial movement of a rocket from its launch pad 2 the instant at which this occurs ▷ *vb* **lift off** 3 (*intr, adv*) (of a rocket) to leave its launch pad
lift pump *n* a pump that raises a fluid to a higher level ▷ Cf **force pump**
lig (lɪg) *Brit sl* ▷ *n* 1 (esp in the media) a function at which free entertainment and refreshments are available ▷ *vb* **ligs, ligging, ligged** 2 (*intr*) to attend such a function; freeload [c20 from ?] > '**ligger** *n* > '**ligging** *n*
ligament ('lɪgəmənt) *n* 1 *anat* any one of the bands of tough fibrous connective tissue that restrict movement in joints, connect various bones or cartilages, support muscles, etc 2 any physical or abstract bond [c14 from Med. L *ligāmentum*, from L (in the sense: bandage), from *ligāre* to bind]
ligand ('lɪgənd, 'laɪ-) *n chem* an atom, molecule, radical, or ion forming a complex with a central atom [c20 from L *ligandum*, from *ligāre* to bind]
ligate ('laɪgeɪt) *vb* **ligates, ligating, ligated** (*tr*) to tie up or constrict (something) with a ligature [c16 from L *ligātus*, from *ligāre* to bind] > **li'gation** *n*
ligature ('lɪgətʃə, -,tʃʊə) *n* 1 the act of binding or tying up 2 something used to bind 3 a link, bond, or tie 4 *surgery* a thread or wire for tying around a vessel, duct, etc, as for constricting the flow of blood 5 *printing* a character of two or more joined letters, such as ff, fl, fi, ffi 6 *music* a slur or the group of notes connected by it ▷ *vb* **ligatures, ligaturing, ligatured** 7 (*tr*) to bind with a ligature; ligate [c14 from LL *ligātūra*, ult. from L *ligāre* to bind]
liger ('laɪgə) *n* the hybrid offspring of a female tiger and a male lion
Ligeti (*Hungarian* 'ligɛti) *n* **György** (djørdj) born 1923, Hungarian composer, resident in Vienna. His works, noted for their experimentalism, include *Atmospheres* (1961) for orchestra, *Volumina* (1962) for organ, and a requiem mass (1965)
light[1] (laɪt) *n* 1 the medium of illumination that makes sight possible 2 Also called: **visible radiation** electromagnetic radiation that is capable of causing a visual sensation. See also **speed of light** 3 (*not in technical usage*) electromagnetic radiation that has a wavelength outside this range, esp ultraviolet radiation: *ultraviolet light* 4 the sensation experienced when electromagnetic radiation within the visible spectrum falls on the retina of the eye 5 anything that illuminates, such as a lamp or candle 6 See **traffic light** 7 a particular quality or type of light: *a good light for reading* 8a illumination from the sun during the day; daylight 8b the time this appears; daybreak; dawn 9 anything that allows the entrance of light, such as a window or compartment of a window 10 the condition of being visible or known (esp in **bring** *or* **come to light**) 11 an aspect or view: *he saw it in a different light* 12 mental understanding or spiritual insight 13 a person considered to be an authority or leader 14 brightness of countenance, esp a sparkle in the eyes 15a the act of igniting or kindling something, such as a cigarette 15b something that ignites or kindles, esp in a specified manner, such as a spark or flame 15c something used for igniting or kindling, such as a match 16 See **lighthouse** 17 **in (the) light of** in view of; taking into account; considering 18 **see the light** to acquire insight 19 **see the light (of day)** 19a to come into being 19b to come to public notice 20 **strike a light** 20a (*vb*) to ignite something, esp a match, by friction 20b (*interj*) *Brit* an exclamation of surprise ▷ *adj* 21 full of light; well-lighted 22 (of a colour) reflecting or transmitting a large amount of light: *light yellow* ▷ *vb* **lights, lighting, lit** *or* **lighted** 23 to ignite or cause to ignite 24 (often foll by *up*) to illuminate or cause to illuminate 25 to make or become cheerful or animated 26 (*tr*) to guide or lead by light ▷ See also **lights**[1], **light up** [OE *lēoht*] > '**lightish** *adj* > '**lightless** *adj*
light[2] (laɪt) *adj* 1 not heavy; weighing relatively little 2 having relatively low density: *magnesium is a light metal* 3 lacking sufficient weight; not agreeing with standard or official weights 4 not great in degree, intensity, or number: *light rain* 5 without burdens, difficulties, or problems; easily borne or done: *a light heart; light work* 6 graceful, agile, or deft: *light fingers* 7 not bulky or clumsy 8 not serious or profound; entertaining: *light music; light verse* 9 without importance or consequence; insignificant: *no light matter* 10 frivolous or capricious 11 loose in morals 12 dizzy or unclear: *a light head* 13 (of bread, cake, etc) spongy or well leavened 14 easily digested: *a light meal* 15 relatively low in alcoholic content: *a light wine* 16 (of a soil) having a crumbly texture 17 (of a vessel, lorry, etc) 17a designed to carry light loads 17b not loaded 18 carrying light arms or equipment: *light infantry* 19 (of an industry) engaged in the production of small consumer goods using light machinery 20 *aeronautics* (of an aircraft) having a maximum take-off weight less than 5670 kilograms (12 500 pounds) 21 *chem* (of an oil fraction obtained from coal tar) having a boiling range between about 100° and 210°C 22 (of a railway) having a narrow gauge, or in some cases a standard gauge with speed or load restrictions not applied to a main line 23 *phonetics, prosody* (of a syllable, vowel, etc) unaccented or weakly stressed; short 24 **light on** *inf* lacking a sufficient quantity of (something) 25 **make light of** to treat as insignificant or trifling ▷ *adv* 26 a less common word for lightly 27 with little equipment, baggage, etc: *to travel light* ▷ *vb* **lights, lighting, lit** *or* **lighted** (*intr*) 28 (esp of birds) to settle or land after flight 29 to get down from a horse, vehicle, etc 30 (foll by *on* or *upon*) to come upon unexpectedly 31 to strike or fall on: *the choice lighted on me* ▷ See also **light into, light out, lights**[2] [OE *lēoht*] > '**lightish** *adj* > '**lightly** *adv* > '**lightness** *n*
light air *n* very light air movement of force one (1–3 mph) on the Beaufort scale
light box *n* a light source contained in a box and covered with a diffuser, used for viewing photographic transparencies, negatives, etc
light breeze *n* a very light wind of force two (4–7 mph) on the Beaufort scale
light bulb *n* a glass bulb containing a gas at low pressure and enclosing a thin metal filament that emits light when an electric current is passed through it. Sometimes shortened to **bulb**
light bulb moment *n inf* a moment of sudden inspiration, revelation, or recognition [c20 from the cartoon image of a light bulb lighting up above a character's head when he or she has an idea]
light-emitting diode *n* a semiconductor that emits light when an electric current is applied to it: used in electronic calculators, digital watches, etc
lighten[1] ('laɪtᵊn) *vb* 1 to become or make light 2 (*intr*) to shine; glow 3 (*intr*) (of lightning) to flash 4 (*tr*) *arch* to cause to flash
lighten[2] ('laɪtᵊn) *vb* 1 to make or become less heavy 2 to make or become less burdensome or oppressive; mitigate 3 to make or become more cheerful or lively
lightening ('laɪtᵊnɪŋ) *n obstetrics* the sensation, experienced by many women late in pregnancy when the head of the fetus enters the pelvis, of a reduction in pressure on the diaphragm, making it easier to breathe
lighter[1] ('laɪtə) *n* 1 a small portable device for providing a naked flame to light cigarettes, etc 2 a person or thing that ignites something
lighter[2] ('laɪtə) *n* a flat-bottomed barge used for transporting cargo, esp in loading or unloading a ship [c15 prob. from MDu.]
lighterage ('laɪtərɪdʒ) *n* 1 the conveyance or loading and unloading of cargo by means of a lighter 2 the charge for this service

light face *n* **1** *printing* a weight of type characterized by light thin lines ▷ *adj also* **light-faced** **2** (of type) having this weight

light-fingered *adj* having nimble or agile fingers, esp for thieving or picking pockets

light flyweight *n* **1** an amateur boxer weighing not more than 48 kg (106 pounds) **2** an amateur wrestler weighing not more than 48 kg (106 pounds)

light-footed *adj* having a light or nimble tread > ˌ**light-ˈfootedly** *adv*

light-headed *adj* **1** frivolous **2** giddy; feeling faint or slightly delirious > ˌ**light-ˈheadedly** *adv* > ˌ**light-ˈheadedness** *n*

light-hearted *adj* cheerful or carefree in mood or disposition: *a light-hearted remark* > ˌ**light-ˈheartedly** *adv* > ˌ**light-ˈheartedness** *n*

light heavyweight *n* **1** Also (in Britain): **cruiserweight** **1a** a professional boxer weighing 160–175 pounds (72.5–79.5 kg) **1b** an amateur boxer weighing 75–81 kg (165–179 pounds) **2a** a professional wrestler weighing not more than 198 pounds (90 kg) **2b** an amateur wrestler weighing not more than 90 kg (198 pounds)

lighthouse (ˈlaɪtˌhaʊs) *n* a fixed structure in the form of a tower equipped with a light visible to mariners for warning them of obstructions, etc

lighting (ˈlaɪtɪŋ) *n* **1** the act or quality of illumination or ignition **2** the apparatus for supplying artificial light effects to a stage, film, or television set **3** the distribution of light on an object or figure, as in painting, photography, etc

lighting cameraman *n films* the person who designs and supervises the lighting of scenes to be filmed

lighting-up time *n* the time when vehicles are required by law to have their lights on

light into *vb (tr, prep) inf* to assail physically or verbally

light middleweight *n* an amateur boxer weighing 67–71 kg (148–157 pounds)

lightness (ˈlaɪtnɪs) *n* the attribute of an object or colour that enables an observer to judge the extent to which the object or colour reflects or transmits incident light

lightning (ˈlaɪtnɪŋ) *n* **1** a flash of light in the sky, occurring during a thunderstorm and caused by a discharge of electricity, either between clouds or between a cloud and the earth **2** (*modifier*) fast and sudden: *a lightning raid* [C14 var. of *lightening*]

lightning conductor *or* **rod** *n* a metal strip terminating in sharp points, attached to the highest part of a building, etc, to discharge the electric field before it can reach a dangerous level and cause a lightning strike

light opera *n* another term for **operetta**

light out *vb (intr, adv) inf* to depart quickly, as if being chased

light pen *n computer technol* **a** a rodlike device which, when applied to the screen of a cathode-ray tube, can detect the time of passage of the illuminated spot across that point thus enabling a computer to determine the position on the screen being pointed at **b** a penlike device, used to read bar codes, that emits light and determines the intensity of that light as reflected from a small area of an adjacent surface

light pollution *n* the glow from street and domestic lighting that obscures the night sky and hinders the observation of faint stars

light rail *n* a transport system using small trains or trams, often serving parts of a large metropolitan area
▷ www.lrta.org
▷ http://routesinternational.com/rail.htm#light

lights¹ (laɪts) *pl n* a person's ideas, knowledge, or understanding: *he did it according to his lights*

lights² (laɪts) *pl n* the lungs, esp of sheep, bullocks, and pigs, used esp for feeding pets [C13 pl n use of LIGHT², referring to the light weight of the lungs]

light-sensitive *adj physics* (of a surface) having a photoelectric property, such as the ability to generate a current, change its electrical resistance, etc, when exposed to light

lightship (ˈlaɪtˌʃɪp) *n* a ship equipped as a lighthouse and moored where a fixed structure would prove impracticable

light show *n* a kaleidoscopic display of moving lights, etc, projected onto a screen, esp during pop concerts

lightsome (ˈlaɪtsəm) *adj arch or poetic* **1** light-hearted or gay **2** airy or buoyant **3** not serious; frivolous

lights out *n* **1** the time when those resident at an institution, such as soldiers in barracks or children at a boarding school, are expected to retire to bed **2** a signal indicating this

light table *n printing* a translucent surface of ground glass or a similar substance, illuminated from below and used for the examination of film, pages, etc

light trap *n* any mechanical arrangement that allows some form of movement to take place while excluding light, such as a light-proof door or the lips of a film cassette

light up *vb (adv)* **1** to light a cigarette, pipe, etc **2** to illuminate or cause to illuminate **3** to make or become cheerful or animated

lightweight (ˈlaɪtˌweɪt) *adj* **1** of a relatively light weight **2** not serious; trivial ▷ *n* **3** a person or animal of a relatively light weight **4a** a professional boxer weighing 130–135 pounds (59–61 kg) **4b** an amateur boxer weighing 57–60 kg (126–132 pounds) **5a** a professional wrestler weighing not more than 154 pounds (70 kg) **5b** an amateur wrestler weighing not more than 68 kg (150 pounds) **6** *inf* a person of little importance or influence

light welterweight *n* an amateur boxer weighing 60–63.5 kg (132–140 pounds)

light year *n* a unit of distance used in astronomy, equal to the distance travelled by light in one year, i.e. 9.4607×10^{12} kilometres or 0.3066 parsecs

LI

ligneous (ˈlɪɡnɪəs) *adj* of or resembling wood [C17 from L *ligneus*, from *lignum* wood]

lignin (ˈlɪɡnɪn) *n* a complex polymer occurring in certain plant cell walls making the plant rigid [C19 from L *lignum* wood + -IN]

lignite (ˈlɪɡnaɪt) *n* a brown carbonaceous sedimentary rock with woody texture that consists of accumulated layers of partially decomposed vegetation: used as a fuel. Also called: **brown coal** > **lignitic** (lɪɡˈnɪtɪk) *adj*

lignum vitae (ˈlɪɡnəm ˈvaɪtɪ) *n* **1** either of two tropical American trees having blue or purple flowers **2** the heavy resinous wood of either of these trees ▷ See also **guaiacum** [NL, from LL, lit.: wood of life]

ligroin (ˈlɪɡrəʊɪn) *n* a volatile fraction of petroleum: used as a solvent [from ?]

Liguria (lɪˈɡjʊərɪə) *n* a region of NW Italy, on the **Ligurian Sea** (an arm of the Mediterranean): the third smallest of the regions of Italy. Pop: 1 625 870 (2000 est). Area: 5410 sq km (2089 sq miles) > **Liˈgurian** *adj, n*

likable *or* **likeable** (ˈlaɪkəbᵊl) *adj* easy to like; pleasing > ˈ**likableness** *or* ˈ**likeableness** *n*

Likasi (lɪˈkɑːsɪ) *n* a city in the S Democratic Republic of Congo (formerly Zaïre): a centre of copper and cobalt production. Pop: 299 118 (1994 est). Former name: **Jadotville**

like¹ (laɪk) *adj* **1** (*prenominal*) similar; resembling ▷ *prep* **2** similar to; similarly to; in the manner of: *acting like a maniac; he's so like his father* **3** used correlatively to express similarity: *like mother, like daughter* **4** such as: *there are lots of games — like draughts, for instance* ▷ *adv* **5** a dialect word for **likely** ▷ *conj* **6** *not standard* as though; as if: *you look like you've just seen a ghost* **7** in the same way as; in the same way that: *she doesn't dance like you do* ▷ *n* **8** the equal or counterpart of a person or thing **9** **the like** similar things: *dogs, foxes, and the like* **10** **the likes** (*or* **like**) **of** people or things similar to (someone or something specified): *we don't want the likes of you around here* [shortened from OE *gelīc*; compare ON *glīkr* and *līkr* like]

> **USAGE** The use of *like* to mean *such as* was formerly thought to be undesirable in formal writing, but has now become acceptable. It was also thought that *as* rather than *like* should be used to mean *in the same way that*, but now both *as* and *like* are acceptable: *they hunt and catch fish as/like their ancestors used to*. The use of *look like* and *seem like* before a clause, although very common, is thought by many people to be incorrect or nonstandard: *it looks as though he won't come* (not *it looks like he won't come*)

like² (laɪk) *vb* **likes, liking, liked 1** (*tr*) to find (something) enjoyable or agreeable or find it enjoyable or agreeable (to do something): *he likes boxing; he likes to hear music* **2** (*tr*) to be fond of **3** (*tr*) to prefer or wish (to do something): *we would like you to go* **4** (*tr*) to feel towards; consider; regard: *how did she like it?* **5** (*intr*) to feel disposed or inclined; choose; wish ▷ *n* **6** (*usually pl*) a favourable feeling, desire, preference, etc (esp in **likes and dislikes**) [OE *līcian*]

-like *suffix forming adjectives* **1** resembling or similar to: *lifelike* **2** having the characteristics of: *childlike* [from LIKE¹ (prep)]

likelihood (ˈlaɪklɪˌhʊd) *or* **likeliness** *n* **1** the condition of being likely or probable; probability **2** something that is probable

likely (ˈlaɪklɪ) *adj* **1** (usually foll by an infinitive) tending or inclined; apt: *likely to rain* **2** probable: *a likely result* **3** believable or feasible; plausible **4** appropriate for a purpose or activity **5** having good possibilities of success: *a likely candidate* ▷ *adv* **6** probably or presumably **7 as likely as not** very probably [c14 from ON *līkligr*]

> **USAGE** *Likely* as an adverb is preceded by another, intensifying, adverb, as in *it will very likely rain* or *it will most likely rain*. Its use without an intensifier, as in *it will likely rain*, is regarded as nonstandard by most users of British English, though it is common in colloquial US English

like-minded *adj* agreeing in opinions, goals, etc > ˌ**like-ˈmindedly** *adv* > ˌ**like-ˈmindedness** *n*

liken (ˈlaɪkən) *vb* (*tr*) to see or represent as the same or similar; compare [c14 from LIKE¹ (adj)]

likeness (ˈlaɪknɪs) *n* **1** the condition of being alike; similarity **2** a painted, carved, moulded, or graphic image of a person or thing **3** an imitative appearance; semblance

likewise (ˈlaɪkˌwaɪz) *adv* **1** in addition; moreover; also **2** in like manner; similarly

liking (ˈlaɪkɪŋ) *n* **1** the feeling of a person who likes; fondness **2** a preference, inclination, or pleasure

lilac (ˈlaɪlək) *n* **1** any of various Eurasian shrubs or small trees of the olive family which have large sprays of purple or white fragrant flowers **2a** a light or moderate purple colour **2b** (*as adj*): *a lilac carpet* [c17 via F from Sp., from Ar. *līlak*, changed from Persian *nīlak* bluish, from *nīl* blue]

Lilburne (ˈlɪlˌbɜːn) *n* **John** ?1614–57, English Puritan pamphleteer and leader of the Levellers, a radical group prominent during the Civil War

liliaceous (ˌlɪlɪˈeɪʃəs) *adj* of, relating to, or belonging to a family of plants having showy flowers and a bulb or bulblike organ: includes the lily, tulip, and bluebell [c18 from LL *līliāceus*, from *līlium* lily]

Lilienthal (*German* ˈliːliəntaːl) *n* **Otto** (ˈɔto) 1848–96, German aeronautical engineer, a pioneer of glider design

Lilith (ˈlɪlɪθ) *n* **1** (in the Old Testament and in Jewish folklore) a female demon, who attacks children **2** (in Talmudic literature) Adam's first wife **3** a witch notorious in medieval demonology

Liliuokalani (liːˌliːʊəʊkɑːˈlɑːniː) *n* **Lydia Kamekeha** (ˌkɑːmeɪˈkeɪhɑː) 1838–1917, queen and last sovereign of the Hawaiian Islands (1891–95)

Lille (*French* lil) *n* an industrial city in N France: the medieval capital of Flanders; forms with Roubaix and Tourcoing one of the largest conurbations in France. Pop: 182 228 (1999)

Lille Bælt (ˈlilə ˈbɛld) *n* the Danish name for the **Little Belt**

Lillee (ˈlɪlɪ) *n* **Dennis** (**Keith**) born 1949, Australian cricketer who, by the end of the 1982–83 season, had taken what was the then world record total of 355 wickets in 65 tests

Lilliputian (ˌlɪlɪˈpjuːʃɪən) *n* **1** a tiny person or being ▷ *adj* **2** tiny; very small **3** petty or trivial [c18 from *Lilliput*, an imaginary country of tiny inhabitants in Swift's *Gulliver's Travels* (1726)]

Lilo (ˈlaɪˌləʊ) *n*, *pl* **Lilos** *trademark* a type of inflatable plastic or rubber mattress

Lilongwe (lɪˈlɒŋwɪ) *n* the capital of Malawi, in the central part west of Lake Malawi. Pop: 435 964 (1998 est)
▷ www.tourismmalawi.com

lilt (lɪlt) *n* **1** (in music) a jaunty rhythm **2** a buoyant motion ▷ *vb* (*intr*) **3** (of a melody) to have a lilt **4** to move in a buoyant manner [c14 *lulten*, from ?] > ˈ**lilting** *adj*

lily (ˈlɪlɪ) *n*, *pl* **lilies 1** any perennial plant of a N temperate genus, such as the tiger lily, having scaly bulbs and showy typically pendulous flowers **2** the bulb or flower of any of these plants **3** any of various similar or related plants, such as the water lily [OE, from L *līlium*; rel. to Gk *leirion* lily] > ˈ**lily-**ˌ**like** *adj*

lily-livered *adj* cowardly; timid

lily of the valley *n*, *pl* **lilies of the valley** a small liliaceous plant of Eurasia and North America cultivated for its spikes of fragrant white bell-shaped flowers

lily-white *adj* **1** of a pure white: *lily-white skin* **2** *inf* pure; irreproachable

Lima (ˈliːmə) *n* **1** the capital of Peru, near the Pacific coast on the Rímac River: the centre of Spanish colonization in South America; university founded in 1551 (the oldest in South America); an industrial centre with a port at nearby Callao. Pop (city): 316 322 (1998 est), with a conurbation of 6 022 213 (1995) **2** *communications* a code word for the letter L.
▷ www.peru-travel.net/lima/lima.html

lima bean (ˈlaɪmə, ˈliː-) *n* **1** any of several varieties of the bean plant native to tropical America, cultivated for its flat pods containing pale green edible seeds **2** the seed of such a plant [c19 after LIMA]

Limassol (ˈlɪməˌsɒl) *n* a port in S Cyprus: trading centre. Pop: 152 900 (1998 est). Ancient name: **Lemessus** (ləˈmɛsəs)

Limavady (ˌlɪməˈvædɪ) *n* a district of N Northern Ireland, in Co Londonderry. Pop: 32 422 (2001). Area: 586 sq km (226 sq miles)

limb¹ (lɪm) *n* **1** an arm or leg, or the analogous part on an animal, such as a wing **2** any of the main branches of a tree **3** a branching or projecting section or member; extension **4** a person or thing considered to be a member, part, or agent of a larger group or thing **5** *chiefly Brit* a mischievous child (esp in **limb of Satan**, etc) **6 out on a limb 6a** in a precarious or questionable position **6b** *Brit* isolated, esp because of unpopular opinions [OE *lim*] > ˈ**limbless** *adj*

limb² (lɪm) *n* **1** the edge of the apparent disc of the sun, a moon, or a planet **2** a graduated arc attached to instruments, such as the sextant, used for measuring angles **3** *bot* the expanded part of a leaf, petal, or sepal **4** Also called: **fold limb** either of the sides of a geological fold [c15 from L *limbus* edge]

limbed (lɪmd) *adj* **a** having limbs **b** (*in combination*):

short-limbed; strong-limbed; loose-limbed

limber[1] ('lɪmbə) *adj* **1** capable of being easily bent or flexed; pliant **2** able to move or bend freely; agile [c16 from ?] > **'limberness** *n*

limber[2] ('lɪmbə) *n* **1** part of a gun carriage, consisting of an axle, pole, and two wheels ▷ *vb* **2** (usually foll by *up*) to attach the limber (to a gun, etc) [c15 *lymour* shaft of a gun carriage, from ?]

limber up *vb (intr, adv)* (esp in sports) to exercise in order to be limber and agile

limbic system ('lɪmbɪk) *n* the part of the brain concerned with basic emotion, hunger, and sex [c19 *limbic*, from F, from *limbe*, from NL *limbus*, from L: border]

limbo[1] ('lɪmbəʊ) *n, pl* **limbos** **1** *(often cap) Christianity* the supposed abode of infants dying without baptism and the just who died before Christ **2** an imaginary place for lost, forgotten, or unwanted persons or things **3** an unknown intermediate place or condition between two extremes: *in limbo* [c14 from Med. L *in limbo* on the border (of hell)]

limbo[2] ('lɪmbəʊ) *n, pl* **limbos** a Caribbean dance in which dancers pass, while leaning backwards, under a bar [c20 from ?]

Limburg ('lɪmbɜːg; *Dutch* 'lɪmbyrx) *n* **1** a medieval duchy of W Europe: divided between the Netherlands and Belgium in 1839 **2** a province of the SE Netherlands: contains a coalfield and industrial centres. Capital: Maastricht. Pop: 1 141 200 (2000 est). Area: 2253 sq km (809 sq miles) **3** a province of NE Belgium: contains the industrial regions of the Kempen coalfield. Capital: Hassett. Pop: 1 019 442 (2000 est). Area: 2422 sq km (935 sq miles). French name: **Limbourg**

Limburger ('lɪm,bɜːgə) *n* a semihard white cheese of very strong smell and flavour. Also called: **Limburg cheese**

lime[1] (laɪm) *n* **1** short for **quicklime, birdlime, slaked lime** **2** *agriculture* any of certain calcium compounds, esp calcium hydroxide, spread as a dressing on lime-deficient land ▷ *vb* **limes, liming, limed** *(tr)* **3** to spread (twigs, etc) with birdlime **4** to spread a calcium compound upon (land) to improve plant growth **5** to catch (animals, esp birds) as with birdlime **6** to whitewash (a wall, ceiling, etc) with a mixture of lime and water (**limewash**) [OE *līm*]

lime[2] (laɪm) *n* **1** a small Asian citrus tree with stiff sharp spines and small round or oval greenish fruits **2a** the fruit of this tree, having acid fleshy pulp rich in vitamin C **2b** *(as modifier): lime juice* ▷ *adj* **3** having the flavour of lime fruit [c17 from F, from Ar. *līmah*]

lime[3] (laɪm) *n* any linden tree planted in many varieties for ornament [c17 changed from obs. *line*, from OE *lind* LINDEN]

limeade (,laɪm'eɪd) *n* a drink made from sweetened lime juice and plain or carbonated water

lime green *n* **a** a moderate greenish-yellow colour **b** *(as adj): a lime-green dress*

limekiln ('laɪm,kɪln) *n* a kiln in which calcium carbonate is calcined to produce quicklime

limelight ('laɪm,laɪt) *n* **1** **the** a position of public attention or notice (esp in **in the limelight**) **2a** a type of lamp, formerly used in stage lighting, in which light is produced by heating lime to white heat **2b** Also called: **calcium light** brilliant white light produced in this way

limerick ('lɪmərɪk) *n* a form of comic verse consisting of five anapaestic lines [c19 allegedly from *will you come up to Limerick?*, a refrain sung between nonsense verses at a party]

Limerick ('lɪmərɪk) *n* **1** a county of SW Republic of Ireland, in N Munster province: consists chiefly of an undulating plain with rich pasture and mountains in the south. County town: Limerick. Pop: 165 042 (1996). Area: 2686 sq km (1037 sq miles) **2** a port in SW Republic of Ireland, county town of Limerick, at the head of the Shannon estuary. Pop: 52 039 (1996)

limescale ('laɪm,skeɪl) *n* a flaky deposit left in containers such as kettles by the precipitation of calcium salts from water. Often shortened to **scale**

limestone ('laɪm,stəʊn) *n* a sedimentary rock consisting mainly of calcium carbonate: used as a building stone and in making cement, lime, etc

limewater ('laɪm,wɔːtə) *n* **1** a clear colourless solution of calcium hydroxide in water, formerly used in medicine as an antacid **2** water that contains dissolved lime or calcium salts, esp calcium carbonate or calcium sulphate

limey ('laɪmɪ) *US, Canad, & Austral sl* ▷ *n* **1** a British person **2** a British sailor or ship ▷ *adj* **3** British [abbrev. from c19 *lime-juicer*, because British sailors drank lime juice as a protection against scurvy]

limit ('lɪmɪt) *n* **1** *(sometimes pl)* the ultimate extent, degree, or amount of something: *the limit of endurance* **2** *(often pl)* the boundary or edge of a specific area: *the city limits* **3** *(often pl)* the area of premises within specific boundaries **4** the largest quantity or amount allowed **5** *maths* **5a** a value to which a function approaches as the independent variable approaches a specified value or infinity **5b** a value to which a sequence a_n approaches as n approaches infinity **5c** the limit of a sequence of partial sums of a convergent infinite series **6** *maths* one of the two specified values between which a definite integral is evaluated **7** **the limit** *inf* a person or thing that is intolerably exasperating ▷ *vb* **limits, limiting, limited** *(tr)* **8** to restrict or confine, as to area, extent, time, etc [c14 from L *līmes* boundary] > **'limitable** *adj* > **'limitless** *adj* > **'limitlessly** *adv* > **'limitlessness** *n*

limitary ('lɪmɪtərɪ, -trɪ) *adj* **1** of, involving, or serving as a limit **2** restricted or limited

limitation (,lɪmɪ'teɪʃən) *n* **1** something that limits a quality or achievement **2** the act of limiting or the condition of being limited **3** *law* a certain period of time, legally defined, within which an action, claim, etc, must be commenced

limited ('lɪmɪtɪd) *adj* **1** having a limit; restricted; confined **2** without fullness or scope; narrow **3** (of governing powers, sovereignty, etc) restricted or checked, by or as if by a constitution, laws, or an assembly: *limited government* **4** *chiefly Brit* (of a business enterprise) owned by shareholders whose liability for the enterprise's debts is restricted > **'limitedly** *adv* > **'limitedness** *n*

limited liability *n Brit* liability restricted to the unpaid portion (if any) of the par value of the shares of a limited company

limiter ('lɪmɪtə) *n* an electronic circuit that produces an output signal whose positive or negative amplitude, or both, is limited to some predetermined value above which the peaks become flattened. Also called: **clipper**

limn (lɪm) *vb (tr)* **1** to represent in drawing or painting **2** *arch* to describe in words [c15 from OF *enluminer* to illumine (a manuscript) from L *inlūmināre* to brighten, from *lūmen* light] > **limner** ('lɪmnə) *n*

limnology (lɪm'nɒlədʒɪ) *n* the study of bodies of fresh water with reference to their plant and animal life, physical properties, geographical features, etc [c20 from Gk *limnē* lake] > **limnological** (,lɪmnə'lɒdʒɪkᵊl) *adj* > **lim'nologist** *n*

Límnos ('limnɔs) *n* transliteration of the Modern Greek name for **Lemnos**

Limoges (lɪ'məʊʒ; *French* limɔʒ) *n* a city in S central France, on the Vienne River: a centre of the porcelain industry since the 18th century. Pop: 133 960 (1990)

Limousin (*French* limuzɛ̃) *n* a region and former province of W central France, in the W part of the Massif Central

limousine ('lɪmə,ziːn, ,lɪmə'ziːn) *n* any large and luxurious car, esp one that has a glass division between the driver and passengers [c20 from F, lit.: cloak (orig.

Ll

one worn by shepherds in *Limousin*), hence later applied to the car]

limp[1] (lɪmp) *vb (intr)* **1** to walk with an uneven step, esp with a weak or injured leg **2** to advance in a labouring or faltering manner ▷ *n* **3** an uneven walk or progress [c16 prob. a back formation from obs. *limphalt* lame, from OE *lempheal t*] > **'limper** *n* > **'limping** *adj, n*

limp[2] (lɪmp) *adj* **1** not firm or stiff **2** not energetic or vital **3** (of the binding of a book) not stiffened with boards [c18 prob. of Scand. origin] > **'limply** *adv* > **'limpness** *n*

limpet ('lɪmpɪt) *n* **1** any of numerous marine gastropods, such as the common limpet and keyhole limpet, that have a conical shell and are found clinging to rocks **2** (*modifier*) relating to or denoting certain weapons that are attached to their targets by magnetic or adhesive properties and resist removal: *limpet mines* [OE *lempedu*, from L *lepas*, from Gk]

limpid ('lɪmpɪd) *adj* **1** clear or transparent **2** (esp of writings, style, etc) free from obscurity **3** calm; peaceful [c17 from F *limpide*, from L *limpidus* clear] > **lim'pidity** *or* **'limpidness** *n* > **'limpidly** *adv*

Limpopo (lɪm'pəʊpəʊ) *n* **1** a province of NE South Africa, comprising the N part of the former province of Transvaal: agriculture and service industries. Capital: Polokwane (formerly Pietersburg). Pop: 5 337 267 (1999 est). Area: 123 910 sq km (47 842 sq miles). Former name (1994–2002): **Northern Province** **2** a river in SE Africa, rising in E South Africa and flowing northeast, then southeast as the border between South Africa and Zimbabwe and through Mozambique to the Indian Ocean. Length: 1770 km (1100 miles)
▷ www.limpopo.gov.za
▷ www.tourismboard.org.za

limp-wristed *adj* ineffectual; effete

limy[1] ('laɪmɪ) *adj* **limier, limiest** of, like, or smeared with birdlime > **'liminess** *n*

limy[2] ('laɪmɪ) *adj* **limier, limiest** of or tasting of lime (the fruit)

Linacre ('lɪnəkə) *n* **Thomas** ?1460–1524, English humanist and physician: founded the Royal College of Physicians (1518)

linage ('laɪnɪdʒ) *n* **1** the number of lines in a piece of written or printed matter **2** payment for written material calculated according to the number of lines

Linares (*Spanish* li'nares) *n* a city in S Spain: site of Scipio Africanus' defeat of the Carthaginians (208 BC); lead mines. Pop: 57 210 (1991)

Lin Biao ('lɪn 'bjaʊ) *n* See **Lin Piao**

linchpin *or* **lynchpin** ('lɪntʃˌpɪn) *n* **1** a pin placed transversely through an axle to keep a wheel in position **2** a person or thing regarded as an essential or coordinating element: *the linchpin of the company* [c14 *lynspin*, from OE *lynis*]

Lincoln[1] ('lɪŋkən) *n* **1** a city in E central England, administrative centre of Lincolnshire: an important ecclesiastical and commercial centre in the Middle Ages; Roman ruins, a castle (founded by William the Conqueror) and a famous cathedral (begun in 1086). Pop: 80 281 (1991). Latin name: **Lindum** ('lɪndəm) **2** a city in SE Nebraska: state capital; University of Nebraska (1869). Pop: 225 581 (2000) **3** short for **Lincolnshire** **4** a breed of long-woolled sheep, originally from Lincolnshire

Lincoln[2] ('lɪŋkən) *n* **Abraham** 1809–65, US Republican statesman; 16th president of the US His fame rests on his success in saving the Union in the Civil War (1861–65) and on his emancipation of slaves (1863); assassinated by Booth

Lincoln green *n* **1a** a yellowish-green or brownish-green colour **1b** (*as adj*): *a Lincoln-green suit* **2** a cloth of this colour [c16 after a green fabric formerly made at LINCOLN in England]

Lincolnshire ('lɪŋkənˌʃɪə, -ʃə) *n* a county of E England, on the North Sea and the Wash: mostly low-lying and fertile, with fenland around the Wash and hills (the **Lincoln Wolds**) in the east; one of the main agricultural counties of Great Britain: the geographical and ceremonial county includes the unitary authorities of North Lincolnshire and North East Lincolnshire (both part of Humberside county from 1974 to 1996) Administrative centre: Lincoln. Pop (excluding unitary authorities): 646 646 (2001). Area (excluding unitary authorities): 5880 sq km (2270 sq miles). Abbreviation: **Lincs**

Lincs (lɪŋks) *abbrev for* Lincolnshire

linctus ('lɪŋktəs) *n, pl* **linctuses** a syrupy medicinal formulation taken to relieve coughs and sore throats [c17 (in the sense: medicine to be licked with the tongue): from L, p.p. of *lingere* to lick]

Lind (lɪnd) *n* **1 James** 1716–94, British physician. He demonstrated (1754) that citrus fruits can cure and prevent scurvy, a remedy adopted by the British navy in 1796 **2 Jenny,** original name *Johanna Maria Lind Goldschmidt* 1820–87, Swedish coloratura soprano

lindane ('lɪndeɪn) *n* a white poisonous crystalline powder: used as an insecticide and weedkiller [c20 after T. van der *Linden*, Du. chemist]

Lindbergh ('lɪndbɜːg, 'lɪnbɜːg) *n* **Charles Augustus** 1902–74, US aviator, who made the first solo nonstop flight across the Atlantic (1927)

Lindemann ('lɪndəmən) *n* **Frederick Alexander,** 1st Viscount Cherwell. 1886–1957, British physicist, born in Germany; Churchill's scientific adviser during World War II

linden ('lɪndən) *n* any of various deciduous trees of a N temperate genus having heart-shaped leaves and small fragrant yellowish flowers: cultivated for timber and as shade trees. See also **lime**[3] [c16 n use of obs. adj *linden*, from OE *linde* lime tree]

Lindesnes ('lɪndɪsˌnɛs) *n* a cape at the S tip of Norway, projecting into the North Sea. Also called: **the Naze**

Lindisfarne ('lɪndɪsˌfɑːn) *n* another name for **Holy Island**

Lindsay ('lɪndzɪ) *n* **1** See (Sir David) **Lyndsay** **2** (**Nicholas**) **Vachel** ('veɪtʃəl) 1879–1931, US poet; best known for *General William Booth* (1913) and *The Congo* (1914) **3 Norman Alfred William** 1879–1969, Australian artist and writer

Lindsey ('lɪndzɪ) *n* **Parts of** an area in E England constituting a former administrative division of Lincolnshire

Lindwall ('lɪndˌwɔːl) *n* **Ray**(**mond Russell**) 1921–96, Australian cricketer. A fast bowler, he played for Australia 61 times between 1946 and 1958

line[1] (laɪn) *n* **1** a narrow continuous mark, as one made by a pencil, pen, or brush across a surface **2** such a mark cut into or raised from a surface **3** a thin indented mark or wrinkle **4** a straight or curved continuous trace having no breadth that is produced by a moving point **5** *maths* **5a** any straight one-dimensional geometrical element whose identity is determined by two points. A **line segment** lies between any two points on a line **5b** a set of points (x, y) that satisfies the equation $y = mx + c$, where m is the gradient and c is the intercept with the y-axis **6** a border or boundary: *the county line* **7** *sport* **7a** a white or coloured band indicating a boundary or division on a field, track, etc **7b** a mark or imaginary mark at which a race begins or ends **8** *American football* **8a** See **line of scrimmage** **8b** the players arranged in a row on either side of the line of scrimmage at the start of each play **9** a specified point of change or limit: *the dividing line between sanity and madness* **10a** the edge or contour of a shape **10b** the sum or type of such contours, characteristic of a style or design: *the line of a building* **11** anything long, flexible, and thin, such as a wire or string: *a washing line; a fishing line* **12** a telephone connection: *a direct line to New York* **13** a conducting wire, cable, or circuit for making connections between pieces of electrical apparatus, such as a cable for electric-power transmission, telecommunications, etc **14** a system of travel or transportation, esp over agreed routes: *a shipping line* **15** a company operating such a system **16** a route between two points on a railway **17** *chiefly Brit* a railway track, including the roadbed, sleepers, etc **18** a course or direction of movement or advance: *the line of flight of a bullet* **19** a course or method of action, behaviour, etc: *take a new line with him* **20** a policy or prescribed course of action or way of thinking (often in **bring** *or* **come into line**) **21** a field of study, interest, occupation, trade, or profession: *this book is in your line* **22** alignment; true (esp in **in line, out of line**) **23** one kind of product or article: *a nice line in hats* **24** a row of persons or things: *a line of cakes on the conveyor belt* **25** a chronological or ancestral series, esp of people: *a line of prime ministers* **26** a row of words printed or written across a page or column **27** a unit of verse consisting of the number of feet appropriate to the metre being used and written or printed with the words in a single row **28** a short letter; note: *just a line to say thank you* **29** a piece of useful information or hint about something: *give me a line on his work* **30** one of a number of narrow horizontal bands forming a television picture **31** *physics* a narrow band in an electromagnetic spectrum, resulting from a transition in an atom of a gas **32** *music* **32a** any of the five horizontal marks that make up the stave **32b** the musical part or melody notated on one such set **32c** a discernible shape formed by sequences of notes or musical sounds: *a meandering melodic line* **32d** (in polyphonic music) a set of staves that are held together with a bracket or brace **33** a defensive or fortified position, esp one that marks the most forward position in war or a national boundary: *the front line* **34** a formation adopted by a body or a number of military units when drawn up abreast **35** the combatant forces of certain armies and navies, excluding supporting arms **36a** the equator (esp in **crossing the line**) **36b** any circle or arc on the terrestrial or celestial sphere **37** a US and Canad word for **queue** **38** *sl* a portion of a powdered drug for snorting **39** *sl* something said for effect, esp to solicit for money, sex, etc **40** **all along the line** **40a** at every stage in a series **40b** in every detail **41** **draw the line (at)** to object (to) or set a limit (on): *her father draws the line at her coming in after midnight* **42** **get a line on** *inf* to obtain information about **43** **hold the line** **43a** to keep a telephone line open **43b** *football* to prevent the opponents from taking the ball forward **43c** (of soldiers) to keep formation, as when under fire **44** **in line for** in the running for; a candidate for: *he's in line for a directorship* **45** **in line with** conforming to **46** **lay** *or* **put on the line** **46a** to pay money **46b** to speak frankly and directly **46c** to risk (one's career, reputation, etc) on something ▷ *vb* **lines, lining, lined** **47** (*tr*) to mark with a line or lines **48** (*tr*) to draw or represent with a line or lines **49** (*tr*) to be or put as a border to: *tulips lined the lawns* **50** to place in or form a row, series, or alignment ▷ See also **lines, line-up** [C13 partly from OF *ligne*, ult. from L *līnea*, n. use of *līneus* flaxen, from *līnum* flax; partly from OE *līn*, ult. also from L *līnum* flax] > **'linable** *or* **'lineable** *adj* > **lined** *adj*

line² (laɪn) *vb* **lines, lining, lined** (*tr*) **1** to attach an inside covering to (a garment, curtain, etc), as for protection, to hide the seaming, or so that it should hang well **2** to cover or fit the inside of: *to line the walls with books* **3** to fill plentifully: *a purse lined with money* [C14 ult. from L *līnum* flax, since linings were often of linen]

lineage¹ ('lɪnɪɪdʒ) *n* direct descent from an ancestor, esp a line of descendants from one ancestor [C14 from OF *lignage*, from L *līnea* LINE¹]

lineage² ('laɪnɪdʒ) *n* a variant spelling of **linage**

lineal ('lɪnɪəl) *adj* **1** being in a direct line of descent from an ancestor **2** of, involving, or derived from direct descent **3** a less common word for **linear** [C14 via OF from LL *līneālis*, from L *līnea* LINE¹] > **'lineally** *adv*

lineament ('lɪnɪəmənt) *n* (*often pl*) **1** a facial outline or feature **2** a distinctive feature [C15 from L: line, from *līneāre* to draw a line]

linear ('lɪnɪə) *adj* **1** of, in, along, or relating to a line **2** of or relating to length **3** resembling, represented by, or consisting of a line or lines **4** having one dimension **5** designating a style in the arts, esp painting, that obtains its effects through line rather than colour or light **6** *maths* of or relating to the first degree: *a linear equation* **7** narrow and having parallel edges: *a linear leaf* **8** *electronics* **8a** (of a circuit, etc) having an output that is directly proportional to input: *linear amplifier* **8b** having components arranged in a line [C17 from L *līneāris* of lines] > **linearity** (ˌlɪnɪ'ærɪtɪ) *n* > **'linearly** *adv*

linear accelerator *n* an accelerator in which charged particles are accelerated along a linear path by potential differences applied to a number of electrodes along their path

Linear B *n* an ancient system of writing found on clay tablets and jars of the second millennium BC excavated in Crete and on the Greek mainland. The script is apparently a modified form of the earlier and hitherto undeciphered **Linear A** and is generally accepted as being an early representation of Mycenaean Greek

linear measure *n* a unit or system of units for the measurement of length

linear motor *n* a form of electric motor in which the stator and the rotor are linear and parallel. It can be used to drive a train, one part of the motor being in the locomotive, the other in the track

linear programming *n* *maths* a technique used in economics, etc, for determining the maximum or minimum of a linear function of non-negative variables subject to constraints expressed as linear equalities or inequalities

lineation (ˌlɪnɪ'eɪʃən) *n* **1** the act of marking with lines **2** an arrangement of or division into lines

line dancing *n* a form of dancing performed by rows of people to country and western music
▷ www.knowledgehound.com/topics/linedanc.htm
▷ www.ourworld.compuserve.com/homepages/jgothard
▷ www.uk250.co.uk/linedancing

line drawing *n* a drawing made with lines only

Line Islands *pl n* a group of coral islands in the central Pacific, including Tabuaeran, Teraina, and Kiritimati: part of Kiribati, with Palmyra and Jarvis administered by the US

lineman ('laɪnmən) *n, pl* **linemen** **1** another name for **platelayer** **2** a person who does the marking of points for a surveyor **3** *Austral & NZ* (formerly) the member of a beach life-saving team who controlled the line used to help drowning swimmers and surfers **4** *American football* a member of the row of players who start each down, positioned on either side of the line of scrimmage **5** *US & Canad* another word for **linesman** (sense 2)

line management *n* the managers in charge of specific functions and concerned in the day-to-day operations of a company > **line manager** *n*

linen ('lɪnɪn) *n* **1a** a hard-wearing fabric woven from the spun fibres of flax **1b** (*as modifier*): *a linen tablecloth* **2** yarn or thread spun from flax fibre **3** clothes, sheets, tablecloths, etc, made from linen cloth or from cotton [OE *linnen*, ult. from L *līnum* flax]
▷ www.irishlinen.co.uk
▷ www.ulsterlinen.com/2.htm

line of battle *n* a formation adopted by a military or naval force when preparing for action

line of fire *n* the flight path of a missile discharged or to be discharged from a firearm

LI

line of force *n* a line in a field of force, such as an electric or magnetic field, for which the tangent at any point is the direction of the force at that point

line of scrimmage *n American football* an imaginary line, parallel to the goal lines, on which the ball is placed at the start of a down and on either side of which the offense and defense line up

line-out *n rugby union* the method of restarting play when the ball goes into touch, the forwards forming two parallel lines at right angles to the touchline and jumping for the ball when it is thrown in

line printer *n* an electromechanical device that prints a line of characters at a time: used in printing and in computer systems

liner[1] ('laɪnə) *n* **1** a passenger ship or aircraft, esp one that is part of a commercial fleet **2** See **freightliner** **3** Also called: **eyeliner** a cosmetic used to outline the eyes **4** a person or thing that uses lines, esp in drawing or copying

liner[2] ('laɪnə) *n* **1** a material used as a lining **2** a person who supplies or fits linings

lines (laɪnz) *pl n* **1** general appearance or outline: *a car with fine lines* **2** a plan of procedure or construction: *built on traditional lines* **3a** the spoken words of a theatrical presentation **3b** the words of a particular role: *he forgot his lines* **4** *inf, chiefly Brit* a marriage certificate: *marriage lines* **5** a defensive position, row of trenches, or other fortification: *we broke through the enemy lines* **6** a school punishment of writing the same sentence or phrase out a specified number of times **7 read between the lines** to understand or find an implicit meaning in addition to the obvious one

linesman ('laɪnzmən) *n, pl* **linesmen** **1** an official who helps the referee or umpire in various sports, esp by indicating when the ball has gone out of play **2** *chiefly Brit* a person who installs, maintains, or repairs telephone or electric-power lines. US and Canad name: **lineman**

line-up *n* **1** a row or arrangement of people or things assembled for a particular purpose: *the line-up for the football match* **2** the members of such a row or arrangement **3** *US* an identity parade ▷ *vb* **line up** (*adv*) **4** to form, put into, or organize a line-up **5** (*tr*) to produce, organize, and assemble: *they lined up some questions* **6** (*tr*) to align

ling[1] (lɪŋ) *n, pl* **ling** *or* **lings** **1** any of several northern coastal food fishes having an elongated body with long fins **2** another name for **burbot** (a fish) [c13 prob. from Low G]

ling[2] (lɪŋ) *n* another name for **heather** [c14 from ON *lyng*]

ling. *abbrev for* linguistics

-ling[1] *suffix forming nouns* **1** *often disparaging* a person or thing belonging to or associated with the group, activity, or quality specified: *nestling; underling* **2** used as a diminutive: *duckling* [OE *-ling*, of Gmc origin]

-ling[2] *suffix forming adverbs* in a specified condition, manner, or direction: *darkling* [OE *-ling*, adv. suffix]

lingam ('lɪŋgəm) *or* **linga** ('lɪŋgə) *n* the Hindu phallic image of the god Siva [c18 from Sansk.]

Lingayen Gulf (ˌlɪŋgɑːˈjɛn) *n* a large inlet of the South China Sea in the Philippines, on the NW coast of Luzon: site of the Japanese landing in the 1941 invasion

linger ('lɪŋgə) *vb* (*mainly intr*) **1** to delay or prolong departure **2** to go in a slow or leisurely manner; saunter **3** to remain just alive for some time prior to death **4** to persist or continue, esp in the mind **5** to be slow to act; dither [c13 (northern dialect) *lengeren* to dwell, from *lengen* to prolong, from OE *lengan*] > **'lingerer** *n* > **'lingering** *adj* > **'lingeringly** *adv*

lingerie ('lænʒərɪ) *n* women's underwear and nightwear [c19 from F, from *linge*, from L *līneus* linen, from *līnum* flax]

lingo ('lɪŋgəʊ) *n, pl* **lingoes** *inf* any foreign or unfamiliar language, jargon, etc [c17 ?from LINGUA FRANCA]

lingua franca ('lɪŋgwə 'fræŋkə) *n, pl* **lingua francas** *or* **linguae francae** ('lɪŋgwiː 'frænsiː) **1** a language used for communication among people of different mother tongues **2** a hybrid language containing elements from several different languages used in this way **3** any system of communication providing mutual understanding [c17 It., lit.: Frankish tongue]

Lingua Franca *n* a particular lingua franca spoken from the Crusades to the 18th century in the ports of the Mediterranean, based on Italian, Spanish, French, Arabic, Greek, and Turkish

lingual ('lɪŋgwəl) *adj* **1** *anat* of or relating to the tongue **2a** *rare* of or relating to language or languages **2b** (*in combination*): *polylingual* **3** articulated with the tongue ▷ *n* **4** a lingual consonant, such as Scots (r) > **'lingually** *adv*

linguiform ('lɪŋgwɪˌfɔːm) *adj* shaped like a tongue

linguist ('lɪŋgwɪst) *n* **1** a person who is skilled in foreign languages **2** a person who studies linguistics [c16 from L *lingua* tongue]

linguistic (lɪŋ'gwɪstɪk) *adj* **1** of or relating to language **2** of or relating to linguistics > **lin'guistically** *adv*

linguistic atlas *n* an atlas showing the distribution of distinctive linguistic features

linguistics (lɪŋ'gwɪstɪks) *n* (*functioning as sing*) the scientific study of language

▷ www.britac.ac.uk/portal/
▷ http://linguistlist.org/sp/LangAnalysis.html
▷ www-nlp.stanford.edu/links/linguistics.html
▷ www.phil.uni-passau.de/linguistik/linguistik_urls

liniment ('lɪnɪmənt) *n* a medicated liquid, usually containing alcohol, camphor, and an oil, applied to the skin to relieve pain, stiffness, etc [c15 from LL *linīmentum*, from *linere* to smear]

lining ('laɪnɪŋ) *n* **1** material used to line a garment, curtain, etc **2** any material used as an interior covering

link[1] (lɪŋk) *n* **1** any of the separate rings, loops, or pieces that connect or make up a chain **2** something that resembles such a ring, loop, or piece **3** a road, rail, air, or sea connection, as between two main routes **4** a connecting part or episode **5** a connecting piece in a mechanism **6** Also called: **radio link** a system of transmitters and receivers that connect two locations by means of radio and television signals **7** a unit of length equal to one hundredth of a chain. 1 link of a Gunter's chain is equal to 7.92 inches, and of an engineer's chain to 1 foot **8** *computing* short for **hyperlink** ▷ *vb* **9** (*often foll by up*) to connect or be connected with or as if with links **10** (*tr*) to connect by association, etc [c14 from ON]

link[2] (lɪŋk) *n* (formerly) a torch used to light dark streets [c16 ?from L *lychnus*, from Gk *lukhnos* lamp]

linkage ('lɪŋkɪdʒ) *n* **1** the act of linking or the state of being linked **2** a system of interconnected levers or rods for transmitting or regulating the motion of a mechanism **3** *electronics* the product of the total number of lines of magnetic flux and the number of turns in a coil or circuit through which they pass **4** *genetics* the occurrence of two genes close together on the same chromosome so that they tend to be inherited as a single unit

linkman ('lɪŋkmən) *n, pl* **linkmen** a presenter of a television or radio programme, esp a sports transmission, consisting of a number of outside broadcasts from different locations

Linköping (*Swedish* 'lintçøːpiŋ) *n* a city in S Sweden: a political and ecclesiastical centre in the Middle Ages; engineering industry. Pop: 132 500 (2000 est)

links (lɪŋks) *pl n* **1a** short for **golf links** **1b** (*as modifier*): *a links course*. See **golf course** **2** *chiefly Scot* undulating sandy ground near the shore [OE *hlincas* pl. of *hlinc* ridge]

link-up *n* a joining or linking together of two factions, objects, etc

Linlithgow (lɪnˈlɪθgəʊ) *n* **1** a town in SE Scotland, in West Lothian: ruined palace, residence of Scottish kings and birthplace of Mary, Queen of Scots. Pop: 11 866 (1991) **2** the former name of **West Lothian**

linn (lɪn) *n chiefly Scot* **1** a waterfall or a pool at the foot of it **2** a ravine or precipice [c16 prob. from a confusion of two words, Scot. Gaelic *linne* pool and OE *hlynn* torrent]

Linnaeus (lɪˈniːəs, -ˈneɪ-) *n* **Carolus** (ˈkærələs), original name *Carl von Linné* 1707–78, Swedish botanist, who established the binomial system of biological nomenclature that forms the basis of modern classification

linnet (ˈlɪnɪt) *n* a brownish Old World finch: the male has a red breast and forehead [c16 from OF *linotte*, ult. from L *līnum* flax (because the bird feeds on flaxseeds)]

Linnhe (ˈlɪnɪ) *n* **Loch** a sea loch of W Scotland, at the SW end of the Great Glen. Length: about 32 km (20 miles)

lino (ˈlaɪnəʊ) *n* short for **linoleum**

linocut (ˈlaɪnəʊˌkʌt) *n* **1** a design cut in relief on linoleum mounted on a wooden block **2** a print made from such a design

linoleum (lɪˈnəʊlɪəm) *n* a sheet material made of hessian, jute, etc, coated with a mixture of powdered cork, linseed oil, rosin, and pigment, used as a floor covering. Often shortened to **lino** [c19 from L *līnum* flax + *oleum* oil]

Linotype (ˈlaɪnəʊˌtaɪp) *n* **1** *trademark* a typesetting machine, operated by a keyboard, that casts an entire line on one solid slug of metal **2** type produced by such a machine

Lin Piao (ˈlɪn ˈpjaʊ) *or* **Lin Biao** *n* 1908–71, Chinese Communist general and statesman. He became minister of defence (1959) and second in rank to Mao Tse-tung (1966). He fell from grace and is reported to have died in an air crash while attempting to flee to the Soviet Union

linseed (ˈlɪnˌsiːd) *n* another name for **flaxseed** [OE *līnsǣd*, from *līn* flax + *sǣd* seed]

linseed oil *n* a yellow oil extracted from seeds of the flax plant. It is used in making oil paints, printer's ink, linoleum, etc

linsey-woolsey (ˈlɪnzɪˈwʊlzɪ) *n* **1** a thin rough fabric of linen warp and coarse wool or cotton filling **2** a strange nonsensical mixture or confusion [c15 prob. from *Lindsey*, village in Suffolk where first made + WOOL (with rhyming suffix *-sey*)]

lint (lɪnt) *n* **1** an absorbent cotton or linen fabric with the nap raised on one side, used to dress wounds, etc **2** shreds of fibre, yarn, etc [c14 prob. from L *linteus* made of linen, from *līnum* flax] > ˈ**linty** *adj*

lintel (ˈlɪntᵊl) *n* a horizontal beam, as over a door or window [c14 via OF prob. from LL *līmitāris* (unattested) of the boundary, infl. by *līminaris* of the threshold]

linter (ˈlɪntə) *n* **1** a machine for stripping the short fibres of ginned cotton seeds **2** (*pl*) the fibres so removed

Linz (lɪnts) *n* a port in N Austria, capital of Upper Austria, on the River Danube: cultural centre; steelworks. Pop: 186 298 (2001). Latin name: **Lentia** (ˈlɛntɪə, ˈlɛnsɪə)

LINZ (lɪnz) *n acronym for* Land Information New Zealand

lion (ˈlaɪən) *n* **1** a large gregarious predatory feline mammal of open country in parts of Africa and India, having a tawny yellow coat and, in the male, a shaggy mane. Related adj: **leonine** **2** a conventionalized lion, the principal beast used as an emblem in heraldry **3** a courageous, strong, or bellicose person **4** a celebrity or idol who attracts much publicity and a large following **5** **the lion's share** the largest portion [OE *līo*, *lēo* (ME *lioun*, from Anglo-F *liun*), both from L *leo*, Gk *leōn*] > ˈ**lioness** *fem n*

Lion (ˈlaɪən) *n* **the** the constellation Leo, the fifth sign of the zodiac

lion-hearted *adj* very brave; courageous

lionize *or* **lionise** (ˈlaɪəˌnaɪz) *vb* **lionizes, lionizing, lionized** *or* **lionises, lionising, lionised** (*tr*) to treat as or make into a celebrity > ˌ**lioniˈzation** *or* ˌ**lioniˈsation** *n* > ˈ**lionˌizer** *or* ˈ**lionˌiser** *n*

Lions (ˈlaɪənz) *n* **Gulf of** a wide bay of the Mediterranean off the S coast of France, between the Spanish border and Toulon. French name: **Golfe du Lion** (gɔlf dy ljɔ̃)

lip (lɪp) *n* **1** *anat* **1a** either of the two fleshy folds surrounding the mouth. Related adj: **labial** **1b** (*as modifier*): *lip salve* **2** the corresponding part in animals, esp mammals **3** any structure resembling a lip, such as the rim of a crater, the margin of a gastropod shell, etc **4** a nontechnical word for **labium** **5** *sl* impudent talk or backchat **6** **bite one's lip** **6a** to stifle one's feelings **6b** to be annoyed or irritated **7** **keep a stiff upper lip** to maintain one's courage or composure during a time of trouble **8** **lick** *or* **smack one's lips** to anticipate or recall something with glee or relish ▷ *vb* **lips, lipping, lipped** **9** (*tr*) to touch with the lip or lips **10** (*tr*) to form or be a lip or lips for **11** (*tr*) *rare* to murmur or whisper **12** (*intr*) to use the lips in playing a wind instrument [OE *lippa*] > ˈ**lipless** *adj* > ˈ**lipˌlike** *adj*

Lipari Islands (ˈlɪpərɪ) *pl n* a group of volcanic islands under Italian administration off the N coast of Sicily: remains that form a continuous record from Neolithic times. Chief town: Lipari. Pop: 10 300 (latest est). Area: 114 sq km (44 sq miles). Also called: **Aeolian Islands.** Italian name: **Isole Eolie** (ˈiːzole eˈɔːlje)

lipase (ˈlaɪpeɪs, ˈlɪpeɪs) *n* any of a group of fat-digesting enzymes produced in the stomach, pancreas, and liver [c19 from Gk *lipos* fat + -ASE]

Lipchitz (ˈlɪpʃɪts) *n* **Jacques** (ʒɑːk) 1891–1973, US sculptor, born in Lithuania: he pioneered cubist sculpture

Lipetsk (*Russian* ˈlipɪtsk) *n* a city in central Russia, on the Voronezh River: steelworks. Pop: 521 600 (1999 est)

lip gloss *n* a cosmetic applied to the lips to give a sheen

lipid *or* **lipide** (ˈlaɪpɪd, ˈlɪpɪd) *n biochem* any of a large group of organic compounds that are esters of fatty acids or closely related substances. They are important structural materials in living organisms. Former name: **lipoid** [c20 from F *lipide*, from Gk *lipos* fat]

Lipizzaner *or* **Lippizaner** (ˌlɪpɪtˈsɑːnə) *n* a breed of riding and carriage horse used by the Spanish Riding School in Vienna and nearly always grey in colour [G, after *Lipizza*, near Trieste, where these horses were bred]

Li Po *or* **Li T'ai-po** (ˈliː ˈtaɪ ˈpəʊ) *n* ?700–762 AD, Chinese poet. His lyrics deal mostly with wine, nature, and women and are remarkable for their imagery

lipo- *or before a vowel* **lip-** *combining form* fat or fatty: *lipoprotein* [from Gk *lipos* fat]

lipogram (ˈlɪpəʊˌgræm) *n* a piece of writing from which all words containing a particular letter have been deliberately omitted

lipography (lɪˈpɒgrəfɪ) *n* the accidental omission of words or letters in writing [c19 from Gk *lip-*, stem of *leipein* to omit + -GRAPHY]

lipoid (ˈlɪpɔɪd, ˈlaɪ-) *adj also* **lipoidal** **1** resembling fat; fatty ▷ *n* **2** a fatlike substance, such as wax **3** *biochem* a former name for **lipid**

lipoprotein (ˌlɪpəʊˈprəʊtiːn, ˌlaɪ-) *n* any of a group of proteins to which a lipid molecule is attached, important in the transport of lipids in the bloodstream. See also **low-density lipoprotein**

liposuction (ˈlɪpəʊˌsʌkʃən) *n* a cosmetic surgical operation in which subcutaneous fat is removed from the body by suction

Lippe (ˈlɪpə) *n* **1** a former state of NW Germany, now part of the German state of North Rhine-Westphalia: part of West Germany until 1990 **2** a river in NW Germany, flowing west to the Rhine. Length: about 240 km (150 miles)

-lipped *adj* having a lip or lips as specified: *tight-lipped*

Lippi (*Italian* ˈlippi) *n* **1** **Filippino** (filipˈpiːno) ?1457–1504, Italian painter of the Florentine school **2** his father, **Fra**

Filippo (fra fi'lippo) ?1406–69, Italian painter of the Florentine school, noted particularly for his frescoes at Prato Cathedral (1452–64)
Lippizaner (ˌlɪpɪt'sɑːnə) *n* a variant spelling of **Lipizzaner**
Lippmann ('lɪpmən; *French* lipman) *n* **Gabriel** (gabriɛl) 1845–1921, French physicist. He devised the earliest process of colour photography: Nobel prize for physics 1908
lip-read ('lɪpˌriːd) *vb* **lip-reads, lip-reading, lip-read** (-'rɛd) to interpret (words) by lip-reading
lip-reading *n* a method used by deaf people to comprehend spoken words by interpreting movements of the speaker's lips. Also called: **speech-reading** > **'lip-ˌreader** *n*
lip service *n* insincere support or respect expressed but not practised
lipstick ('lɪpˌstɪk) *n* a cosmetic for colouring the lips, usually in the form of a stick
lip-synch *or* **lip-sync** ('lɪpˌsɪŋk) *vb* to mouth (prerecorded words) on television or film
liq. *abbrev for* liquid
liquefacient (ˌlɪkwɪ'feɪʃənt) *n* **1** a substance that liquefies or that causes liquefaction ▷ *adj* **2** becoming or causing to become liquid [c19 from L *liquefacere* to make LIQUID]
liquefied natural gas *n* a mixture of various gases, esp methane, liquefied under pressure for transportation and used as an engine fuel. Abbrev: **LNG**
liquefied petroleum gas *n* a mixture of various petroleum gases, esp propane and butane, stored as a liquid under pressure and used as an engine fuel. Abbrev: **LPG** *or* **LP gas**
liquefy ('lɪkwɪˌfaɪ) *vb* **liquefies, liquefying, liquefied** (esp of a gas) to become or cause to become liquid [c15 via OF from L *liquefacere* to make liquid] > **liquefaction** (ˌlɪkwɪ'fækʃən) *n* > **'liqueˌfiable** *adj* > **'liqueˌfier** *n*
liquescent (lɪ'kwɛsᵊnt) *adj* (of a solid or gas) becoming or tending to become liquid [c18 from L *liquescere*] > **li'quescence** *or* **li'quescency** *n*
liqueur (lɪ'kjʊə; *French* likœr) *n* **1a** any of several highly flavoured sweetened spirits, such as Kirsch or Cointreau, intended to be drunk after a meal **1b** (*as modifier*): *liqueur glass* **2** a small hollow chocolate sweet containing liqueur [c18 from F; see LIQUOR]
▷ www.liqueurweb.com
▷ www.thatsthespirit.com/mixology/liqueurs.asp
▷ www.webtender.com
liquid ('lɪkwɪd) *n* **1** a substance in a physical state in which it does not resist change of shape but does resist change of size ▷ Cf **gas** (sense 1), **solid** (sense 1) **2** a substance that is a liquid at room temperature and atmospheric pressure **3** *phonetics* a frictionless continuant, esp (l) or (r) ▷ *adj* **4** of, concerned with, or being a liquid or having the characteristic state of liquids: *liquid wax* **5** shining, transparent, or brilliant **6** flowing, fluent, or smooth **7** (of assets) in the form of money or easily convertible into money [c14 via OF from L *liquidus*, from *liquēre* to be fluid] > **li'quidity** *or* **'liquidness** *n* > **'liquidly** *adv*
liquid air *n* air that has been liquefied by cooling: used in the production of pure oxygen, nitrogen, and as a refrigerant
liquidambar (ˌlɪkwɪd'æmbə) *n* **1** a deciduous tree of Asia and North and Central America, with star-shaped leaves, and exuding a yellow aromatic balsam **2** the balsam of this tree, used in medicine [c16 NL, from L *liquidus* liquid + Med. L *ambar* AMBER]
liquidate ('lɪkwɪˌdeɪt) *vb* **liquidates, liquidating, liquidated** **1** to settle or pay off (a debt, claim, etc) **2a** to terminate the operations of (a commercial firm, bankrupt estate, etc) by assessment of liabilities and appropriation of assets for their settlement **2b** (of a commercial firm, etc) to terminate operations in this manner **3** (*tr*) to convert (assets) into cash **4** (*tr*) to eliminate or kill > **'liquiˌdator** *n*
liquidation (ˌlɪkwɪ'deɪʃən) *n* **1a** the process of terminating the affairs of a business firm, etc, by realizing its assets to discharge its liabilities **1b** the state of a business firm, etc, having its affairs so terminated (esp in **to go into liquidation**) **2** destruction; elimination
liquid-crystal display *n* a flat-screen display used, for example, in portable computers, digital watches, and calculators, in which an array of liquid-crystal elements can be selectively activated to generate an image, by means of an electric field, which when applied to an element alters its optical properties
liquid ecstasy *n* another name for **GHB**
liquidize *or* **liquidise** ('lɪkwɪˌdaɪz) *vb* **liquidizes, liquidizing, liquidized** *or* **liquidises, liquidising, liquidised** **1** to make or become liquid; liquefy **2** (*tr*) to pulverize (food) in a liquidizer so as to produce a fluid
liquidizer *or* **liquidiser** ('lɪkwɪˌdaɪzə) *n* a kitchen appliance with blades for puréeing vegetables, blending liquids, etc. Also called: **blender**
liquid measure *n* a unit or system of units for measuring volumes of liquids or their containers
liquid oxygen *n* the clear pale blue liquid state of oxygen produced by liquefying air and allowing the nitrogen to evaporate: used in rocket fuels. Also called: **lox**
liquid paraffin *n* an oily liquid obtained by petroleum distillation and used as a laxative. Also called (esp US and Canad): **mineral oil**
liquor ('lɪkə) *n* **1** any alcoholic drink, esp spirits, or such drinks collectively **2** any liquid substance, esp that in which food has been cooked **3** *pharmacol* a solution of a pure substance in water **4** **in liquor** drunk [c13 via OF from L, from *liquēre* to be liquid]
liquorice *or US & Canad* **licorice** ('lɪkərɪs, -ərɪʃ) *n* **1** a perennial Mediterranean leguminous shrub **2** the dried root of this plant, used as a laxative and in confectionery **3** a sweet having a liquorice flavour [c13 via Anglo-Norman and OF from LL *liquirītia*, from L *glycyrrhīza*, from Gk *glukurrhiza*, from *glukus* sweet + *rhiza* root]
liquor store *n US & Canad* a store where alcoholic drinks are sold for consumption elsewhere
lira ('lɪərə; *Italian* 'liːra) *n, pl* **lire** ('lɪərɪ; *Italian* 'liːre) *or* **liras** **1** the former standard monetary unit of Italy, San Marino, and the Vatican City, replaced by the euro in 2002 **2** Also called: **pound** the standard monetary unit of Turkey **3** the standard monetary unit of Malta [It., from L *lībra* pound]
liriodendron (ˌlɪrɪəʊ'dɛndrən) *n, pl* **liriodendrons** *or* **liriodendra** (-drə) a deciduous tulip tree of North America or a similar Chinese tree [c18 NL, from Gk *leiron* lily + *dendron* tree]
Lisbon ('lɪzbən) *n* the capital and chief port of Portugal, in the southwest on the Tagus estuary: became capital in 1256; subject to earthquakes and severely damaged in 1755; university (1911). Pop (urban area): 3 754 000 (2001). Portuguese name: **Lisboa** (liʒ'boə)
▷ www.atl-turismolisboa.pt
▷ www.explore-lisbon.com
Lisburn ('lɪzbɜːn) *n* **1** a city in Northern Ireland in Lisburn district, Co Antrim, noted for its linen industry: headquarters of the British Army in Northern Ireland. Pop: 42 110 (1991) **2** a district of S Northern Ireland, in Co Antrim and Co Down. Pop: 108 694 (2001). Area: 446 sq km (172 sq miles)
Lisieux (*French* lizjø) *n* a town in NW France: Roman Catholic pilgrimage centre, for its shrine of St Thérèse, who lived there. Pop: 24 506 (1990)
lisle (laɪl) *n* **a** a strong fine cotton thread or fabric **b** (*as modifier*): *lisle stockings* [c19 after *Lisle* (now Lille), town in

France where this thread was orig. manufactured]

lisp (lɪsp) *n* **1** the articulation of *s* and *z* like or nearly like the *th* sounds in English *thin* and *then* respectively **2** the habit or speech defect of pronouncing *s* and *z* in this manner **3** the sound of a lisp in pronunciation ▷ *vb* **4** to use a lisp in the pronunciation of (speech) **5** to speak or pronounce imperfectly or haltingly [OE *āwlispian*, from *wlisp* lisping (adj), imit.] > **ˈlisper** *n* > **ˈlisping** *adj, n* > **ˈlispingly** *adv*

lissom *or* **lissome** (ˈlɪsəm) *adj* **1** supple in the limbs or body; lithe; flexible **2** agile; nimble [c19 var. of *lithesome*, LITHE + -SOME[1]] > **ˈlissomly** *or* **ˈlissomely** *adv* > **ˈlissomness** *or* **ˈlissomeness** *n*

list[1] (lɪst) *n* **1** an item-by-item record of names or things, usually written or printed one under the other **2** *computing* a linearly ordered data structure ▷ *vb* **3** (*tr*) to make a list of **4** (*tr*) to include in a list **5** (*tr*) *Brit* to declare to be a listed building **6** (*tr*) *stock exchange* to obtain an official quotation for (a security) so that it may be traded on the recognized market **7** an archaic word for **enlist** [c17 from F, ult. rel. to LIST[2]] > **ˈlistable** *adj* > **ˈlisting** *n*

list[2] (lɪst) *n* **1** a border or edging strip, esp of cloth **2** a less common word for **selvage** ▷ *vb* (*tr*) **3** to border with or as if with a list or lists ▷ See also **lists** [OE *līst*]

list[3] (lɪst) *vb* **1** (esp of ships) to lean over or cause to lean over to one side ▷ *n* **2** the act or an instance of leaning to one side [c17 from ?]

list[4] (lɪst) *arch* ▷ *vb* **1** to be pleasing to (a person) **2** (*tr*) to desire or choose ▷ *n* **3** a liking or desire [OE *lystan*]

list[5] (lɪst) *vb* an archaic or poetic word for **listen** [OE *hlystan*]

listed building *n* (in Britain) a building officially recognized as having special historical or architectural interest and therefore protected from demolition or alteration

listed company *n stock exchange* a company whose shares are quoted on the main market of the London stock exchange

listed security *n stock exchange* a security that is quoted on the main market of the London stock exchange and appears in its *Official List of Securities* ▷ Cf **Third Market, Unlisted Securities Market**

listen (ˈlɪsᵊn) *vb* (*intr*) **1** to concentrate on hearing something **2** to take heed; pay attention: *I warned you but you wouldn't listen* [OE *hlysnan*] > **ˈlistener** *n*

listenership (ˈlɪsnəˌʃɪp) *n* all the listeners collectively of a particular radio programme, station, or broadcaster

listen in *vb* (*intr, adv; often foll by* to) **1** to listen to the radio **2** to intercept radio communications **3** to listen but not contribute (to a discussion), esp surreptitiously

listening post *n* **1** *mil* a forward position set up to obtain early warning of enemy movement **2** any strategic position for obtaining information about another country or area

lister (ˈlɪstə) *n US & Canad agriculture* a plough with a double mouldboard designed to throw soil to either side of a central furrow [c19 from LIST[2]]

Lister (ˈlɪstə) *n* **Joseph,** 1st Baron Lister. 1827–1912, British surgeon, who introduced the use of antiseptics

listeriosis (lɪˌstɪərɪˈəʊsɪs) *n* a serious form of food poisoning, caused by a bacterium (**listeria**). Its symptoms can include meningitis and in pregnant women it may cause damage to the fetus [after Joseph LISTER]

listless (ˈlɪstlɪs) *adj* having or showing no interest; lacking vigour or energy [c15 from *list* desire + -LESS] > **ˈlistlessly** *adv* > **ˈlistlessness** *n*

Liston (ˈlɪstən) *n* **Sonny,** real name *Charles.* 1922–70, US boxer: former world heavyweight champion

list price *n* the selling price of merchandise as quoted in a catalogue or advertisement

list renting *n* the practice of renting a list of potential customers to a direct-mail seller of goods or to the fund-raisers of a charity

lists (lɪsts) *pl n* **1** *history* **1a** the enclosed field of combat at a tournament **1b** the barriers enclosing the field at a tournament **2** any arena or scene of conflict, controversy, etc **3** **enter the lists** to engage in a conflict, controversy, etc [c14 pl of LIST[2] (border)]

listserv (ˈlɪstˌsɜːv) *n* a service on the Internet that provides an electronic mailing to subscribers with similar interests

Liszt (lɪst) *n* **Franz** (frants) 1811–86, Hungarian composer and pianist. The greatest piano virtuoso of the 19th century, he originated the symphonic poem, pioneered the one-movement sonata form, and developed new harmonic combinations. His works include the symphonies *Faust* (1861) and *Dante* (1867), piano compositions and transcriptions, songs, and church music

lit (lɪt) *vb* **1** a past tense and past participle of **light[1]** (senses 23–26) **2** a past tense and past participle of **light[2]** (senses 28–31)

lit. *abbrev for:* **1** literal(ly) **2** literary **3** literature **4** litre

Li T'ai-po (ˈliː ˈtaɪˈpəʊ) *n* See **Li Po**

litany (ˈlɪtənɪ) *n, pl* **litanies** **1** *Christianity* **1a** a form of prayer consisting of a series of invocations, each followed by an unvarying response **1b** **the Litany** the general supplication in this form in the Book of Common Prayer **2** any tedious recital [c13 via OF from Med. L *litanīa* from LGk *litaneia* prayer, ult. from Gk *litē* entreaty]

litchi, lichee, *or* **lychee** (ˌlaɪˈtʃiː) *n* **1** a Chinese tree cultivated for its round edible fruits **2** the fruit of this tree, which has whitish juicy edible aril [c16 from Cantonese *lai chi*]

lite (ˈlaɪt) *adj* **1** (of food and drink) containing few calories or little alcohol or fat **2** denoting a more restrained or less extreme version of a person or thing: *reggae lite* [c20 var. spelling of LIGHT[2]]

-lite *n combining form* (in names of minerals) stone: *chrysolite* [from F *-lite* or *-lithe*, from Gk *lithos* stone]

liter (ˈliːtə) *n* the US spelling of **litre**

literacy (ˈlɪtərəsɪ) *n* **1** the ability to read and write **2** the ability to use language proficiently

literacy hour *n* (in England and Wales) a daily reading and writing lesson that was introduced into the national primary school curriculum in 1998 to raise standards of literacy

literal (ˈlɪtərəl) *adj* **1** in exact accordance with or limited to the primary or explicit meaning of a word or text **2** word for word **3** dull, factual, or prosaic **4** consisting of, concerning, or indicated by letters **5** true; actual ▷ *n* **6** Also called: **literal error** a misprint or misspelling in a text [c14 from LL *litterālis* concerning letters, from L *littera* letter] > **ˈliteralness** *or* **literality** (ˌlɪtəˈrælɪtɪ) *n*

literalism (ˈlɪtərəˌlɪzəm) *n* **1** the disposition to take words and statements in their literal sense **2** literal or realistic portrayal in art or literature > **ˈliteralist** *n* > **ˌliteralˈistic** *adj*

literally (ˈlɪtərəlɪ) *adv* **1** in a literal manner **2** (*intensifier*): *there were literally thousands of people.*

> USAGE The use of *literally* as an intensifier is common, esp in informal contexts. In some cases, it provides emphasis without adding to the meaning: *the house was literally only five minutes walk away.* Often, however, its use results in absurdity: *the news was literally an eye-opener to me.* It is therefore best avoided in formal contexts

literary (ˈlɪtərərɪ, ˈlɪtrərɪ) *adj* **1** of, relating to, concerned with, or characteristic of literature or scholarly writing: *a literary style* **2** versed in or knowledgeable about literature: *a literary woman* **3** (of a word) formal; not colloquial [c17 from L *litterārius* concerning reading &

writing; see LETTER] > **'literarily** *adv* > **'literariness** *n*
literate ('lɪtərɪt) *adj* **1** able to read and write **2** educated; learned ▷ *n* **3** a literate person [c15 from L *litterātus* learned; see LETTER] > **'literately** *adv*
literati (ˌlɪtə'rɑːtiː) *pl n* literary or scholarly people [c17 from L]
literature ('lɪtərɪtʃə, 'lɪtrɪ-) *n* **1** written material such as poetry, novels, essays, etc **2** the body of written work of a particular culture or people: *Scandinavian literature* **3** written or printed matter of a particular type or genre: *scientific literature* **4** the art or profession of a writer **5** *inf* printed matter on any subject [c14 from L *litterātūra* writing; see LETTER]
▷ www.britac.ac.uk/portal/
▷ http://etext.lib.virginia.edu/modeng/modeng0.browse.html
▷ www.lib.virginia.edu/wess/etexts.html
▷ www.themodernword.com/themodword.cfm
Lith. *abbrev for* Lithuania(n)
-lith *n combining form* indicating stone or rock: *megalith* [from Gk *lithos* stone]
litharge ('lɪθɑːdʒ) *n* another name for **lead monoxide** [c14 via OF from L *lithargyrus*, from Gk, from *lithos* stone + *arguros* silver]
lithe (laɪð) *adj* flexible or supple [OE (in the sense: gentle; c15 supple)] > **'lithely** *adv* > **'litheness** *n*
lithia ('lɪθɪə) *n* **1** another name for **lithium oxide** **2** lithium present in mineral waters as lithium salts [c19 NL, ult. from Gk *lithos* stone]
lithic ('lɪθɪk) *adj* **1** of, relating to, or composed of stone **2** *geol* containing fragments of previously formed rock **3** *pathol* of or relating to a calculus or calculi **4** of or containing lithium [c18 from Gk *lithikos* stony]
-lithic *n and adj combining form* relating to the use of stone implements in a specified cultural period: *Neolithic* [from Gk *lithikos*, from *lithos* stone]
lithium ('lɪθɪəm) *n* a soft silvery element of the alkali metal series: the lightest known metal, used as an alloy hardener, as a reducing agent, and in batteries. Symbol: Li; atomic no.: 3; atomic wt.: 6.941 [c19 NL, from LITHO- + -IUM]
lithium carbonate *n* a white crystalline solid used in the treatment of manic-depressive illness and mania. Formula: Li_2CO_3
lithium oxide *n* a white crystalline compound. It absorbs carbon dioxide and water vapour. Formula: Li_2O
litho ('laɪθəʊ) *n, pl* **lithos**, *adj, adv* short for **lithography, lithograph, lithographic,** or **lithographically**
litho- *or before a vowel* **lith-** *combining form* stone: *lithograph* [from L, from Gk, from *lithos* stone]
lithograph ('lɪθəˌgrɑːf) *n* **1** a print made by lithography ▷ *vb* **2** (*tr*) to reproduce (pictures, text, etc) by lithography > **lithographic** (ˌlɪθə'græfɪk) *adj* > **ˌlitho'graphically** *adv*
lithography (lɪ'θɒgrəfɪ) *n* a method of printing from a metal or stone surface on which the printing areas are not raised but made ink-receptive as opposed to ink-repellent [c18 from NL *lithographia*] > **li'thographer** *n*
lithology (lɪ'θɒlədʒɪ) *n* **1** the physical characteristics of a rock, including colour, composition, and texture **2** the study of rocks
lithophyte ('lɪθəˌfaɪt) *n* **1** a plant that grows on stony ground **2** an organism, such as a coral, that is partly composed of stony material
lithosphere ('lɪθəˌsfɪə) *n* the rigid outer layer of the earth, comprising the earth's crust and the solid upper part of the mantle
lithotomy (lɪ'θɒtəmɪ) *n, pl* **lithotomies** the surgical removal of a calculus, esp one in the urinary bladder [c18 via LL from Gk]
lithotripsy ('lɪθəʊˌtrɪpsɪ) *n, pl* **-sies** the use of ultrasound to pulverize kidney stones and gallstones *in situ* [c20 from LITHO- + Gk *thruptein* to crush]
Lithuania (ˌlɪθjʊ'eɪnɪə) *n* a republic in NE Europe, on the Baltic Sea: a grand duchy in medieval times; united with Poland in 1569; occupied by Russia in 1795 and by Germany during World War I; independent Lithuania formed in 1918, but occupied by Soviet troops in 1919 and then by Poland; became a Soviet republic in 1940; unilaterally declared independence from the Soviet Union in 1990; recognized as independent in 1991; joined the EU in 2004. Official language: Lithuanian. Religion: Roman Catholic majority. Currency: litas. Capital: Vilnius. Pop: 3 691 000 (2001 est). Area: 65 200 sq km (25 174 sq miles). Also called: **Lithuanian Republic.** Lithuanian name: **Lietuva**
▷ www.lrv.lt/main_en.php
▷ www.tourism.lt
▷ www.on.lt/travel.htm
Lithuanian (ˌlɪθjʊ'eɪnɪən) *adj* **1** of, relating to, or characteristic of Lithuania, its people, or their language ▷ *n* **2** the official language of Lithuania **3** a native or inhabitant of Lithuania
litigable ('lɪtɪgəbᵊl) *adj law* that may be the subject of litigation
litigant ('lɪtɪgənt) *n* **1** a party to a lawsuit ▷ *adj* **2** engaged in litigation
litigate ('lɪtɪˌgeɪt) *vb* **litigates, litigating, litigated** **1** to bring or contest (a claim, action, etc) in a lawsuit **2** (*intr*) to engage in legal proceedings [c17 from L *lītigāre*, from *līt-*, stem of *līs* lawsuit + *agere* to carry on] > **'litiˌgator** *n*
litigation (ˌlɪtɪ'geɪʃən) *n* **1** the act or process of bringing or contesting a lawsuit **2** a judicial proceeding or contest
litigious (lɪ'tɪdʒəs) *adj* **1** excessively ready to go to law **2** of or relating to litigation **3** inclined to dispute or disagree [c14 from L *lītigiōsus* quarrelsome, from *lītigium* strife] > **li'tigiously** *adv* > **li'tigiousness** *n*
litmus ('lɪtməs) *n* a soluble powder obtained from certain lichens. It turns red under acid conditions and blue under basic conditions. Absorbent paper treated with it (**litmus paper**) is used as an indicator [c16 ?from Scand.]
litotes ('laɪtəʊˌtiːz) *n, pl* **litotes** understatement for rhetorical effect, esp using negation with a term in place of using an antonym of that term, as in "She was not a little upset" for "She was extremely upset" [c17 from Gk, from *litos* small]
litre *or US* **liter** ('liːtə) *n* **1** one cubic decimetre **2** (formerly) the volume occupied by 1 kilogram of pure water. This is equivalent to 1.000 028 cubic decimetres or about 1.76 pints [c19 from F, from Med. L *litra*, from Gk: a unit of weight]
LittD *or* **LitD** *abbrev for* Doctor of Letters *or* Doctor of Literature [L: *Litterarum Doctor*]
litter ('lɪtə) *n* **1a** small refuse or waste materials carelessly dropped, esp in public places **1b** (*as modifier*): *litter bin* **2** a disordered or untidy condition or a collection of objects in this condition **3** a group of offspring produced at one birth by a mammal such as a sow **4** a layer of partly decomposed leaves, twigs, etc, on the ground in a wood or forest **5** straw, hay, or similar material used as bedding, protection, etc, by animals or plants **6** a means of conveying people, esp sick or wounded people, consisting of a light bed or seat held between parallel sticks **7** See **cat litter** ▷ *vb* **8** to make (a place) untidy by strewing (refuse) **9** to scatter (objects, etc) about or (of objects) to lie around or upon (anything) in an untidy fashion **10** (of pigs, cats, etc) to give birth to (offspring) **11** (*tr*) to provide (an animal or plant) with straw or hay for bedding, protection, etc [c13 (in the sense: bed): via Anglo-F, ult. from L *lectus* bed]
littérateur (ˌlɪtərə'tɜː; *French* literatœr) *n* an author, esp a professional writer [c19 from F from L *litterātor* a grammarian]
litter lout *or US & Canad* **litterbug** ('lɪtəˌbʌg) *n sl* a person

who tends to drop refuse in public places

little (ˈlɪtᵊl) *determiner* **1** (often preceded by *a*) **1a** a small quantity, extent, or duration of: *the little hope there is left; very little milk* **1b** (*as pronoun*): *save a little for me* **2** not much: *little damage was done* **3 make little of** to regard or treat as insignificant; dismiss **4 not a little 4a** very **4b** a lot **5 think little of** to have a low opinion of ▹ *adj* **6** of small or less than average size **7** young: *a little boy* **8** endearingly familiar; dear: *my husband's little ways* **9** contemptible, mean, or disagreeable: *your filthy little mind* ▹ *adv* **10** (usually preceded by *a*) in a small amount; to a small extent or degree; not a lot: *to laugh a little* **11** (*used preceding a verb*) not at all, or hardly: *he little realized his fate* **12** not much or often: *we go there very little now* **13 little by little** by small degrees ▹ See also **less, lesser, least** [OE *lȳtel*]

Little Bear *n* **the** the English name for **Ursa Minor**

Little Belt *n* a strait in Denmark, between Jutland and Funen Island, linking the Kattegat with the Baltic. Length: about 48 km (30 miles). Width: up to 29 km (18 miles). Danish name: **Lille Bælt**

Little Bighorn *n* a river in the W central US, rising in N Wyoming and flowing north to the Bighorn River. Its banks were the scene of the defeat (1876) and killing of General Custer and his command by Indians

Little Diomede *n* the smaller of the two Diomede Islands in the Bering Strait: administered by the US Area: about 10 sq km (4 sq miles)

Little Dipper *n* **the** a US name for **Ursa Minor**

Little John *n* one of Robin Hood's companions, noted for his great size and strength

little people *pl n folklore* small supernatural beings, such as elves or leprechauns

Little Rock *n* a city in central Arkansas, on the Arkansas River: state capital. Pop: 183 133 (2000)

Little Russia *n* a region of the former SW Soviet Union, consisting chiefly of the Ukraine

Little St Bernard Pass *n* a pass over the Savoy Alps, between Bourg-Saint-Maurice, France, and La Thuile, Italy: 11th-century hospice. Height: 2187 m (7177 ft)

little slam *n bridge, etc* the winning of all tricks except one ▹ Cf **grand slam.** Also called: **small slam**

Littlewood (ˈlɪtᵊlwʊd) *n* **(Maud) Joan** 1914–2002, British theatre director, who founded the Theatre Workshop Company (1945) with the aim of bringing theatre to the working classes: noted esp for her production of *Oh, What a Lovely War!* (1963)

littlie (ˈlɪtlɪ) *n Austral inf* a young child

littoral (ˈlɪtərəl) *adj* **1** of or relating to the shore of a sea, lake, or ocean ▹ *n* **2** a coastal or shore region [c17 from LL *littorālis*, from *lītus* shore]

Littoria (*Italian* litˈtɔːrja) *n* the former name (until 1947) of **Latina**

liturgical (lɪˈtɜːdʒɪkᵊl) *adj* **1** of or relating to public worship **2** of or relating to the liturgy > **liˈturgically** *adv*

liturgy (ˈlɪtədʒɪ) *n, pl* **liturgies 1** the forms of public services officially prescribed by a Church **2** (*often cap*) Also called: **Divine Liturgy** *chiefly Eastern Churches* the Eucharistic celebration **3** a particular order or form of public service laid down by a Church [c16 via Med. L, from Gk *leitourgia*, from *leitourgos* minister, from *leit-* people + *ergon* work]

Liturgy of the Hours *n Christianity* another name for **divine office**

Liu Shao Qi *or* **Liu Shao-ch'i** (ˈljuː ˈʃauˈtʃiː) *n* 1898–1974, Chinese Communist statesman; chairman of the People's Republic of China (1959–68); deposed during the Cultural Revolution

livable *or* **liveable** (ˈlɪvəbᵊl) *adj* **1** (of a room, house, etc) suitable for living in **2** worth living; tolerable **3** (foll by *with*) pleasant to live (with) > **ˈlivableness, ˈliveableness** *or* **ˌlivaˈbility, ˌliveaˈbility** *n*

live¹ (lɪv) *vb* **lives, living, lived** (*mainly intr*) **1** to show the characteristics of life; be alive **2** to remain alive or in existence **3** to exist in a specified way: *to live poorly* **4** (usually foll by *in* or *at*) to reside or dwell: *to live in London* **5** (often foll by *on*) to continue or last: *the pain still lives in her memory* **6** (usually foll by *by*) to order one's life (according to a certain philosophy, religion, etc) **7** (foll by *on, upon,* or *by*) to support one's style of life; subsist: *to live by writing* **8** (foll by *with*) to endure the effects (of a crime, mistake, etc) **9** (foll by *through*) to experience and survive: *he lived through the war* **10** (*tr*) to pass or spend (one's life, etc) **11** to enjoy life to the full: *he knows how to live* **12** (*tr*) to put into practice in one's daily life; express: *he lives religion every day* **13 live and let live** to refrain from interfering in others' lives; be tolerant ▹ See also **live down, live in,** etc [OE *libban, lifian*]

live² (laɪv) *adj* **1** (*prenominal*) showing the characteristics of life **2** (*usually prenominal*) of, relating to, or abounding in life: *the live weight of an animal* **3** (*usually prenominal*) of current interest; controversial: *a live issue* **4** actual: *a real live cowboy* **5** *inf* full of life and energy **6** (of a coal, ember, etc) glowing or burning **7** (esp of a volcano) not extinct **8** loaded or capable of exploding: *a live bomb* **9** *radio, television, etc* transmitted or present at the time of performance, rather than being a recording: *a live show* **10** (of a record) **10a** recorded in concert **10b** recorded in one studio take **11** connected to a source of electric power: *a live circuit* **12** being in a state of motion or transmitting power **13** acoustically reverberant ▹ *adv* **14** during, at, or in the form of a live performance [c16 from *on live* ALIVE]

-lived (-lɪvd) *adj* having or having had a life as specified: *short-lived*

live data *n computing* data that is still relevant

lived-in *adj* having a comfortable, natural, or homely appearance

live down (lɪv) *vb* (*tr, adv*) to withstand the effects of (a crime, mistake, etc) by waiting until others forget or forgive it

live in (lɪv) *vb* (*intr, adv*) **1** (of an employee) to dwell at one's place of employment, as in a hotel, etc ▹ *adj* **live-in 2** resident: *a live-in nanny; a live-in lover*

livelihood (ˈlaɪvlɪˌhʊd) *n* occupation or employment

livelong (ˈlɪvˌlɒŋ) *adj chiefly poetic* **1** (of time) long or seemingly long (esp in **all the livelong day**) **2** whole; entire

lively (ˈlaɪvlɪ) *adj* **livelier, liveliest 1** full of life or vigour **2** vivacious or animated, esp when in company **3** busy; eventful **4** characterized by mental or emotional intensity; vivid **5** having a striking effect on the mind or senses **6** refreshing or invigorating: *a lively breeze* **7** springy or bouncy or encouraging springiness: *a lively ball* ▹ *adv* also **livelily 8** in a brisk or lively manner: *step lively* > **ˈliveliness** *n*

liven (ˈlaɪvᵊn) *vb* (usually foll by *up*) to make or become lively; enliven > **ˈlivener** *n*

live oak (laɪv) *n* a hard-wooded evergreen oak of S North America: used for shipbuilding

live out (lɪv) *vb* (*intr, adv*) (of an employee, as in a hospital or hotel) to dwell away from one's place of employment

liver¹ (ˈlɪvə) *n* **1** a large highly vascular reddish-brown glandular organ in the human abdominal cavity. Its main function is the metabolic transformation of nutrients. It also secretes bile, stores glycogen, and detoxifies certain poisons. Related adj: **hepatic 2** the corresponding organ in animals **3** the liver of certain animals used as food **4** a reddish-brown colour [OE *lifer*]
▹ www.liverfoundation.org

liver² (ˈlɪvə) *n* a person who lives in a specified way: *a fast liver*

liveried (ˈlɪvərɪd) *adj* (esp of servants or footmen) wearing livery

liverish (ˈlɪvərɪʃ) *adj* **1** *inf* having a disorder of the liver **2** disagreeable; peevish > **ˈliverishness** *n*

liver opal *n* a form of opal having a reddish-brown coloration

Liverpool[1] ('lɪvə,pu:l) *n* **1** a city in NW England, in Liverpool unitary authority, Merseyside, on the Mersey estuary: second largest seaport in Great Britain; developed chiefly in the 17th century with the industrialization of S Lancashire; Liverpool University (1881) and John Moore's University (1992). Pop: 474 000 (1994 est) **2** a unitary authority in NW England, in Merseyside. Pop: 439 476 (2001). Area: 113 sq km (44 sq miles)

Liverpool[2] ('lɪvə,pu:l) *n* **Robert Banks Jenkinson,** 2nd Earl of Liverpool. 1770–1828, British Tory statesman; prime minister (1812–27) His government was noted for its repressive policies until about 1822, when more liberal measures were introduced by such men as Peel and Canning

Liverpudlian (,lɪvə'pʌdlɪən) *n* **1** a native or inhabitant of Liverpool ▷ *adj* **2** of or relating to Liverpool [c19 from LIVERPOOL, with humorous alteration of *pool* to *puddle*]

liver salts *pl n* a preparation of mineral salts used to treat indigestion

liver sausage *or esp US* **liverwurst** ('lɪvə,wɜ:st) *n* a sausage containing liver

liverwort ('lɪvə,wɜ:t) *n* any of a class of bryophyte plants growing in wet places and resembling green seaweeds or leafy mosses [late OE *liferwyrt*]

livery ('lɪvərɪ) *n, pl* **liveries** **1** the identifying uniform, badge, etc, of a member of a guild or one of the servants of a feudal lord **2** a uniform worn by some menservants **3** an individual or group that wears such a uniform **4** distinctive dress or outward appearance **5a** the stabling, keeping, or hiring out of horses for money **5b** (*as modifier*): *a livery horse* **6 at livery** being kept in a livery stable [c14 via Anglo-F from OF *livrée* allocation, from *livrer* to hand over, from L *līberāre* to set free]

livery company *n Brit* one of the chartered companies of the City of London originating from the craft guilds

liveryman ('lɪvərɪmən) *n, pl* **liverymen** **1** *Brit* a member of a livery company **2** a worker in a livery stable

livery stable *n* a stable where horses are accommodated and from which they may be hired out

lives (laɪvz) *n* the plural of **life**

livestock ('laɪv,stɒk) *n* (*functioning as sing or pl*) cattle, horses, and similar animals kept for domestic use but not as pets, esp on a farm

live together (lɪv) *vb* (*intr, adv*) (esp of an unmarried couple) to dwell in the same house or flat; cohabit

live up (lɪv) *vb* **1** (*intr, adv; foll by to*) to fulfil (an expectation, obligation, principle, etc) **2 live it up** *inf* to enjoy oneself, esp flamboyantly

live wire (laɪv) *n* **1** *inf* an energetic or enterprising person **2** a wire carrying an electric current

live with (lɪv) *vb* (*tr, prep*) to dwell with (a person to whom one is not married)

liveyer *or* **liveyere** ('lɪvjə) *n Canad* (in Newfoundland) a full-time resident [altered from LIVER, a dweller]

Livia Drusilla ('lɪvɪə dru:'sɪlə) *n* 58 BC–29 AD, Roman noblewoman: wife (from 39 BC) of Emperor Augustus and mother of Emperor Tiberius

livid ('lɪvɪd) *adj* **1** (of the skin) discoloured, as from a bruise or contusion **2** of a greyish tinge or colour **3** *inf* angry or furious [c17 via F from L *līvidus*, from *līvēre* to be black and blue] > **'lividly** *adv* > **'lividness** *or* **li'vidity** *n*

living ('lɪvɪŋ) *adj* **1a** possessing life; not dead **1b** (*as collective n preceded by the*): *the living* **2** having the characteristics of life (used esp to distinguish organisms from nonliving matter) **3** currently in use or valid: *living language* **4** seeming to be real: *a living image* **5** (of animals or plants) existing in the present age **6** presented by actors before a live audience: *living theatre* **7** (*prenominal*) (intensifier): *the living daylights* ▷ *n* **8** the condition of being alive **9** the manner in which one conducts one's life: *fast living* **10** the means, esp the financial means, whereby one lives **11** *Church of England* another term for **benefice** **12** (*modifier*) of, involving, or characteristic of everyday life: *living area* **13** (*modifier*) of or involving those now alive (esp in **living memory**)

living death *n* a life or lengthy experience of constant misery

living history *n* any of various activities involving the re-enactment of historical events or the recreation of living conditions of the past

living room *n* a room in a private house or flat used for relaxation and entertainment

Livingston ('lɪvɪŋstən) *n* a town in SE Scotland, the administrative centre of West Lothian: founded as a new town in 1962. Pop: 41 647 (1991)

Livingstone ('lɪvɪŋstən) *n* **1 David** 1813–73, Scottish missionary and explorer in Africa. After working as a missionary in Botswana, he led a series of expeditions and was the first European to discover Lake Ngami (1849), the Zambezi River (1851), the Victoria Falls (1855), and Lake Malawi (1859). In 1866 he set out to search for the source of the Nile and was found in dire straits and rescued (1871) by the journalist H. M. Stanley **2 Kenneth Robert,** known as *Ken*, born 1945, mayor of London from 2000; Labour leader of the Greater London Council (1981–86)

living wage *n* a wage adequate to maintain a person and his family in reasonable comfort

living will *n* a document that states that a person who becomes terminally ill does not wish his or her life to be prolonged by artificial means such as a life-support machine

Livonia (lɪ'vəʊnɪə) *n* **1** a former Russian province on the Baltic, north of Lithuania: became Russian in 1721; divided between Estonia and Latvia in 1918 **2** a city in SE Michigan, west of Detroit. Pop: 100 545 (2000) > **Li'vonian** *adj, n*

Livorno (*Italian* li'vorno) *n* a port in W central Italy, in Tuscany on the Ligurian Sea: shipyards; oil-refining. Pop: 161 673 (2000 est). English name: **Leghorn**

Livy ('lɪvɪ) *n* Latin name *Titus Livius*. 59 BC–17 AD, Roman historian; of his history of Rome in 142 books, only 35 survive

lizard ('lɪzəd) *n* any of a group of reptiles typically having an elongated body, four limbs, and a long tail: includes the geckos, iguanas, chameleons, monitors, and slowworms [c14 via OF from L *lacerta*]

Lizard ('lɪzəd) *n* **the** a promontory in SW England, in SW Cornwall: the southernmost point in Great Britain. Also called: **Lizard Head, Lizard Peninsula**

LJ (in Britain) *abbrev for* Lord Justice

Ljubljana (lu:'bljɑ:nə) *n* the capital of Slovenia: capital of Illyria (1816–49); part of Yugoslavia (1918–91); university (1595). Pop: 270 986 (2000 est). German name: **Laibach**

▷ www.ljubljana.si/generalinformation

▷ www.slovenia-tourism.si

LL *abbrev for:* **1** Late Latin **2** Low Latin **3** Lord Lieutenant

ll. *abbrev for* lines (of written matter)

llama ('lɑ:mə) *n* **1** a domesticated South American cud-chewing mammal of the camel family, that is used as a beast of burden and is valued for its hair, flesh, and hide **2** the cloth made from the wool of this animal [c17 via Sp. from Amerind]

Llandaff ('lændəf, -dæf) *or* **Llandaf** (*Welsh* hlan'dav) *n* a town in SE Wales, now a suburb of Cardiff; the oldest bishopric in Wales (6th century)

Llandudno (læn'dɪdnəʊ; *Welsh* hlan'dɪdnɔ) *n* a town and resort in NW Wales, in Conwy county borough on the Irish Sea. Pop: 14 576 (1991)

Llanelli *or* **Llanelly** (θlæ'nɛθlɪ; *Welsh* hla'nɛhli:) *n* an industrial town in S Wales, in SE Carmarthenshire on an inlet of Carmarthen Bay. Pop: 44 953 (1991)

Llanfairpwllgwyngyll (*Welsh* hlan,vaɪrpʊhl'gwɪŋgɪhl), **Llanfairpwll**, *or* **Llanfair P. G.** *n* a village in NW Wales, in SE Anglesey: reputed to be the longest place name in Great Britain when unabbreviated; means: St. Mary's Church in the hollow of the white hazel near the rapid whirlpool of Llandysilio of the red cave. Full name: **Llanfairpwllgwyngyllgogerychwyrndrobwll-llantysiliogogogoch** (*Welsh* hlan'vaɪrpʊhl'gwɪŋgɪhlgɔ-'gɛrəxwɪrn'drɔbʊhl'hlantə'sɪljɔ'gɔgɔ'gɔx)

Llangollen (*Welsh* hlan'gɒhlɛn) *n* a town in NE Wales, in Denbighshire on the River Dee: International Musical Eisteddfod held annually since 1946. Pop: 3267 (1991)

llano ('lɑːnəʊ; *Spanish* 'ʎano) *n, pl* **llanos** (-nəʊz; *Spanish* -nɔs) an extensive grassy treeless plain, esp in South America [c17 Sp., from L *plānum* level ground]

Llano Estacado ('lɑːnəʊ ,ɛstə'kɑːdəʊ) *n* the S part of the Great Plains of the US, extending over W Texas and E New Mexico: oil and natural gas resources. Chief towns: Lubbock and Amarillo. Area: 83 700 sq km (30 000 sq miles). Also called: **Staked Plain**

LLB *abbrev for* Bachelor of Laws [L: *Legum Baccalaureus*]

LLD *abbrev for* Doctor of Laws [L: *Legum Doctor*]

Llewelyn II *n* See **Llywelyn ap Gruffudd**

Lleyn Peninsula (*Welsh* hliːn) *n* a peninsula in NW Wales between Cardigan Bay and Caernarvon Bay

LLM *abbrev for* Master of Laws [L: *Legum Magister*]

Lloyd (lɔɪd) *n* **1** **Clive** (**Hubert**) born 1944, West Indian (Guyanese) cricketer; captained the West Indies (1974–88) **2** **Harold** (**Clayton**) 1893–1971, US comic film actor **3** **Marie,** real name *Matilda Alice Victoria Wood.* 1870–1922, English music-hall entertainer

Lloyd George *n* **David,** 1st Earl Lloyd George of Dwyfor. 1863–1945, British Liberal statesman: prime minister (1916–22). As chancellor of the exchequer (1908–15) he introduced old age pensions (1908), a radical budget (1909), and an insurance scheme (1911)

Lloyd's (lɔɪdz) *n* an association of London underwriters, set up in the late 17th century. Originally concerned with marine insurance, it now underwrites a variety of insurance policies and publishes a daily list (**Lloyd's List**) of shipping information [c17 after Edward *Lloyd* (died ?1726) at whose coffee house in London the underwriters orig. carried on their business]
▷ www.lloydsoflondon.co.uk

Lloyd Webber ('wɛbə) *n* **Andrew,** Baron Lloyd-Webber. born 1948, English composer. His musicals include *Joseph and the Amazing Technicolour Dreamcoat* (1968), *Jesus Christ Superstar* (1970), and *Evita* (1978), all with lyrics by Tim Rice, and *Cats* (1981), *Phantom of the Opera* (1986), *Sunset Boulevard* (1993), and *The Beautiful Game* (2000) **2** his brother, **Julian** born 1951, British cellist

Llywelyn ap Gruffudd ('hləwɛlɪn æp 'grɪfɪθ) *n* died 1282, prince of Wales (1258–82): the only Welsh ruler to be recognized as such by the English

lm *symbol for* lumen

LMS (in Britain) *abbrev for* local management of schools: the system of making each school responsible for controlling its total budget, after the budget has been calculated by the Local Education Authority

LNG *abbrev for* liquefied natural gas

lo (ləʊ) *interj* look! see! (now often in **lo and behold**) [OE *lā*]

loach (ləʊtʃ) *n* a carplike freshwater fish of Eurasia and Africa, having a long narrow body with barbels around the mouth [c14 from OF *loche*, from ?]

Loach (ləʊtʃ) *n* **Ken**(**neth**) born 1936, British television and film director; his works for television include *Cathy Come Home* (1966) and his films include *Kes* (1970), *Riff-Raff* (1991), *Bread and Roses* (2000), and *Ae Fond Kiss* (2004)

load (ləʊd) *n* **1** something to be borne or conveyed; weight **2a** the usual amount borne or conveyed **2b** (*in combination*): *a carload* **3** something that weighs down, oppresses, or burdens: *that's a load off my mind* **4** a single charge of a firearm **5** the weight that is carried by a structure **6** *electrical engineering, electronics* **6a** a device that receives or dissipates the power from an amplifier, oscillator, generator, or some other source of signals **6b** the power delivered by a machine, generator, circuit, etc **7** the resistance overcome by an engine or motor when it is driving a machine, etc **8** an external force applied to a component or mechanism **9** **a load of** *inf* a quantity of: *a load of nonsense* **10** **get a load of** *inf* pay attention to **11** **have a load on** *US & Canad sl* to be intoxicated ▷ *vb* (*mainly tr*) **12** (*also intr*) to place or receive (cargo, goods, etc) upon (a ship, lorry, etc) **13** to burden or oppress **14** to supply in abundance: *load with gifts* **15** to cause to be biased: *to load a question* **16** (*also intr*) to put an ammunition charge into (a firearm) **17** *photog* to position (a film, cartridge, or plate) in (a camera) **18** to weight or bias (a roulette wheel, dice, etc) **19** *insurance* to increase (a premium) to cover expenses, etc **20** *computing* to transfer (a program) to a memory **21** **load the dice** **21a** to add weights to dice in order to bias them **21b** to arrange to have a favourable or unfavourable position ▷ See also **loads** [OE *lād* course; in meaning, infl. by LADE] > '**loader** *n*

loaded ('ləʊdɪd) *adj* **1** carrying a load **2** (of dice, a roulette wheel, etc) weighted or otherwise biased **3** (of a question or statement) containing a hidden trap or implication **4** charged with ammunition **5** (of concrete) containing heavy metals, esp iron or lead, for use in making radiation shields **6** *sl* wealthy **7** (*postpositive*) *sl, chiefly US & Canad* **7a** drunk **7b** drugged

loading ('ləʊdɪŋ) *n* **1** a load or burden; weight **2** the addition of an inductance to electrical equipment, such as a transmission line or aerial, to improve its performance **3** *Austral & NZ* a payment made in addition to a basic wage or salary to reward special skills, compensate for unfavourable conditions, etc

load line *n* a pattern of lines painted on the hull of a ship, approximately midway between the bow and the stern, indicating the various levels that the water line should reach if the ship is properly loaded in different conditions

loads (ləʊdz) *inf* ▷ *pl n* **1** (often foll by *of*) a lot ▷ *adv* **2** (intensifier): *loads better*

loadstar ('ləʊd,stɑː) *n* a variant spelling of **lodestar**

loadstone ('ləʊd,stəʊn) *n* a variant spelling of **lodestone**

loaf[1] (ləʊf) *n, pl* **loaves** (ləʊvz) **1** a shaped mass of baked bread **2** any shaped or moulded mass of food, such as sugar, cooked meat, etc **3** *sl* the head; sense: *use your loaf!* [OE *hlāf*]

loaf[2] (ləʊf) *vb* **1** (*intr*) to loiter or lounge around in an idle way **2** (*tr*; foll by *away*) to spend (time) idly: *he loafed away his life* [c19 ? back formation from LOAFER]

loafer ('ləʊfə) *n* **1** a person who avoids work; idler **2** *chiefly US & Canad* a moccasin-like shoe [c19 ?from G *Landläufer* vagabond]

loam (ləʊm) *n* **1** rich soil consisting of a mixture of sand, clay, and decaying organic material **2** a paste of clay and sand used for making moulds in a foundry, plastering walls, etc ▷ *vb* **3** (*tr*) to cover, treat, or fill with loam [OE *lām*] > '**loamy** *adj* > '**loaminess** *n*

loan (ləʊn) *n* **1** the act of lending: *the loan of a car* **2** property lent, esp money lent at interest for a period of time **3** the adoption by speakers of one language of a form current in another language **4** short for **loan word** **5** **on loan** lent out; borrowed ▷ *vb* **6** to lend (something, esp money) [c13 *loon, lan*, from ON *lān*] > '**loaner** *n*

loanback ('ləʊn,bæk) *n* **1** a facility offered by some life-assurance companies in which an individual can borrow from his pension fund ▷ *vb* **loan back** **2** to make use of this facility

Loan Council *n* (in Australia) a statutory body that controls borrowing by the states

Ll

Loanda (ləʊ'ændə) *n* a variant spelling of **Luanda**
loan shark *n inf* a person who lends funds at illegal or exorbitant rates of interest
loan translation *n* the adoption by one language of a phrase or compound word whose components are literal translations of the components of a corresponding phrase or compound in a foreign language: *English "superman" from German "Übermensch"*. Also called: **calque**
loan word *n* a word adopted, often in a modified form, from one language into another
loath *or* **loth** (ləʊθ) *adj* **1** (usually foll by *to*) reluctant or unwilling **2** **nothing loath** willing [OE *lāth* (in the sense: hostile)]
loathe (ləʊð) *vb* **loathes, loathing, loathed** (*tr*) to feel strong hatred or disgust for [OE *lāthiān*, from LOATH] > **'loather** *n*
loathing ('ləʊðɪŋ) *n* abhorrence; disgust
loathly[1] ('ləʊθlɪ) *adv* with reluctance; unwillingly
loathly[2] ('ləʊðlɪ) *adj* an archaic word for **loathsome**
loathsome ('ləʊðsəm) *adj* causing loathing; abhorrent > **'loathsomely** *adv* > **'loathsomeness** *n*
loaves (ləʊvz) *n* the plural of **loaf**[1]
lob (lɒb) *sport* ▷ *n* **1** a ball struck in a high arc **2** *cricket* a ball bowled in a slow high arc ▷ *vb* **lobs, lobbing, lobbed** **3** to hit or kick (a ball) in a high arc **4** to throw, esp in a high arc [C14 prob. from Low G, orig. in the sense: something dangling]
Lobachevsky (*Russian* ləba'tʃɛfskij) *n* **Nikolai Ivanovich** (nika'laj i'vanəvitʃ) 1793–1856, Russian mathematician; a founder of non-Euclidean geometry
lobar ('ləʊbə) *adj* of, relating to, or affecting a lobe
lobate ('ləʊbeɪt) *adj* **1** having or resembling lobes **2** (of birds) having separate toes that are each fringed with a weblike lobe > **'lobately** *adv* > **lo'bation** *n*
lobby ('lɒbɪ) *n, pl* **lobbies** **1** a room or corridor used as an entrance hall, vestibule, etc **2** *chiefly Brit* a hall in a legislative building used for meetings between the legislators and members of the public **3** Also called: **division lobby** *chiefly Brit* one of two corridors in a legislative building in which members vote **4** a group of persons who attempt to influence legislators on behalf of a particular interest ▷ *vb* **lobbies, lobbying, lobbied** **5** to attempt to influence (legislators, etc) in the formulation of policy **6** (*intr*) to act in the manner of a lobbyist **7** (*tr*) to apply pressure for the passage of (a bill, etc) [C16 from Med. L *lobia* portico, from OHG *lauba* arbor, from *laub* leaf] > **'lobbyer** *n*
lobbyist ('lɒbɪɪst) *n* a person employed by a particular interest to lobby > **'lobby,ism** *n*
lobe (ləʊb) *n* **1** any rounded projection forming part of a larger structure **2** any of the subdivisions of a bodily organ or part, delineated by shape or connective tissue **3** Also called: **ear lobe** the fleshy lower part of the external ear **4** any of the parts, not entirely separate from each other, into which a flattened plant part, such as a leaf, is divided [C16 from LL *lobus*, from Gk *lobos* lobe of the ear or of the liver]
lobectomy (ləʊ'bɛktəmɪ) *n, pl* **lobectomies** surgical removal of a lobe from any organ or gland in the body
lobelia (ləʊ'bi:lɪə) *n* any of a genus of plants having red, blue, white, or yellow five-lobed flowers with the three lower lobes forming a lip [C18 from NL, after Matthias de *Lobel* (1538–1616), Flemish botanist]
Lobengula (,ləʊbən'gju:lə) *n* ?1836–94, last Matabele king (1870–93); his kingdom was destroyed by the British
Lobito (*Portuguese* lu'βitu) *n* the chief port in Angola, in the west on **Lobito Bay**: terminus of the railway through Benguela to Mozambique. Pop: 70 000 (latest est)
loblolly ('lɒb,lɒlɪ) *n, pl* **loblollies** a southern US pine tree with bright reddish-brown bark, green needle-like leaves, and reddish-brown cones [C16 ?from dialect *lob* to boil + obs. dialect *lolly* thick soup]
lobola *or* **lobolo** (lɔ:'bɔ:lə, lə'bəʊ-) *n* (in southern Africa) an African custom by which a bridegroom's family makes a payment in cattle or cash to the bride's family shortly before the marriage [from Nguni *ukulobola* to give the bride price]
lobotomy (ləʊ'bɒtəmɪ) *n, pl* **lobotomies** **1** surgical incision into a lobe of any organ **2** Also called: **prefrontal leucotomy** surgical interruption of one or more nerve tracts in the frontal lobe of the brain: used in the treatment of intractable mental disorders [C20 from LOBE + -TOMY]
lobscouse ('lɒb,skaʊs) *n* a sailor's stew of meat, vegetables, and hardtack [C18 ?from dialect *lob* to boil + *scouse* broth]
lobster ('lɒbstə) *n, pl* **lobsters** *or* **lobster** **1** any of several large marine decapod crustaceans occurring on rocky shores and having the first pair of limbs modified as large pincers **2** any of several similar crustaceans, esp the spiny lobster **3** the flesh of any of these crustaceans, eaten as a delicacy [OE *loppestre*, from *loppe* spider]
lobster pot *or* **trap** *n* a round basket or trap made of open slats used to catch lobsters
lobule ('lɒbju:l) *n* a small lobe or a subdivision of a lobe [C17 from NL *lobulus*, from LL *lobus* LOBE] > **lobular** ('lɒbjʊlə) *or* **lobulate** ('lɒbjʊlɪt) *adj*
lobworm ('lɒb,wɜ:m) *n* **1** another name for **lugworm** **2** a large earthworm used as bait in fishing [C17 from obs. *lob* lump + WORM]
local ('ləʊk[ə]l) *adj* **1** characteristic of or associated with a particular locality or area **2** of, concerned with, or relating to a particular place or point in space **3** *med* of, affecting, or confined to a limited area or part **4** (of a train, bus, etc) stopping at all stations or stops ▷ *n* **5** a train, bus, etc, that stops at all stations or stops **6** an inhabitant of a specified locality **7** *Brit inf* a pub close to one's home or place of work **8** *med* short for **local anaesthetic.** See **anaesthesia** **9** *US & Canad* an item of local interest in a newspaper [C15 via OF from LL *locālis*, from L *locus* place] > **'locally** *adv* > **'localness** *n*
local anaesthetic *n med* See **anaesthesia**
local authority *n Brit & NZ* the governing body of a county, district, etc. US equivalent: **local government**
locale (ləʊ'kɑ:l) *n* a place or area, esp with reference to events connected with it [C18 from F *local* (n use of adj); see LOCAL]
local government *n* **1** government of the affairs of counties, towns, etc, by locally elected political bodies **2** the US equivalent of **local authority**
Local Group *n astron* the cluster of galaxies to which the Galaxy and the Andromeda Galaxy belong
localism ('ləʊkə,lɪzəm) *n* **1** a pronunciation, phrase, etc, peculiar to a particular locality **2** another word for **provincialism**
locality (ləʊ'kælɪtɪ) *n, pl* **localities** **1** a neighbourhood or area **2** the site or scene of an event **3** the fact or condition of having a location or position in space
localize *or* **localise** ('ləʊkə,laɪz) *vb* **localizes, localizing, localized** *or* **localises, localising, localised** **1** to make or become local in attitude, behaviour, etc **2** (*tr*) to restrict or confine (something) to a particular area or part **3** (*tr*) to assign or ascribe to a particular region > **'local,izable** *or* **'local,isable** *adj* > **,locali'zation** *or* **,locali'sation** *n*
local loan *n* (in Britain) a loan issued by a local government authority
local option *n* (esp in Scotland, New Zealand, and the US) the privilege of a municipality, county, etc, to determine by referendum whether a particular activity, esp the sale of liquor, shall be permitted there
Locarno (*Italian* lo'karno) *n* a town in S Switzerland, in Ticino canton at the N end of Lake Maggiore: tourist resort. Pop: 14 150 (1990 est)

locate (ləʊˈkeɪt) *vb* **locates, locating, located** **1** (*tr*) to discover the position, situation, or whereabouts of; find **2** (*tr; often passive*) to situate or place: *located on the edge of the city* **3** (*intr*) to become established or settled > **loˈcater** *n*

location (ləʊˈkeɪʃən) *n* **1** a site or position; situation **2** the act or process of locating or the state of being located **3** a place outside a studio where filming is done: *shot on location* **4** (in South Africa) **4a** a Black African or Coloured township, usually located near a small town **4b** (formerly) a Black African tribal reserve **5** *computing* a position in a memory capable of holding a unit of information, such as a word, and identified by its address [C16 from L *locātiō*, from *locāre* to place]

locative (ˈlɒkətɪv) *grammar* ▷ *adj* **1** (of a word or phrase) indicating place or direction **2** denoting a case of nouns, etc, that refers to the place at which the action described by the verb occurs ▷ *n* **3a** the locative case **3b** a word or speech element in this case [C19 LOCATE + -IVE, on the model of *vocative*]

loc. cit. (in textual annotation) *abbrev for* loco citato [L: in the place cited]

loch (lɒx, lɒk) *n* **1** a Scot word for **lake**[1] (senses 1 and 2) **2** Also: **sea loch** a long narrow bay or arm of the sea in Scotland [C14 from Gaelic]

lochia (ˈlɒkɪə) *n* a vaginal discharge of cellular debris, mucus, and blood following childbirth [C17 NL from Gk *lokhia*, from *lokhos* childbirth] > **ˈlochial** *adj*

loci (ˈləʊsaɪ) *n* the plural of **locus**

lock[1] (lɒk) *n* **1** a device fitted to a gate, door, drawer, lid, etc, to keep it firmly closed **2** a similar device attached to a machine, vehicle, etc **3a** a section of a canal or river that may be closed off by gates to control the water level and the raising and lowering of vessels that pass through it **3b** (*as modifier*): *a lock gate; a lock keeper* **4** the jamming, fastening, or locking together of parts **5** *Brit* the extent to which a vehicle's front wheels will turn to the right or left: *this car has a good lock* **6** a mechanism that detonates the charge of a gun **7** **lock, stock, and barrel** completely; entirely **8** any wrestling hold in which a wrestler seizes a part of his opponent's body **9** Also called: **lock forward** *rugby* **9a** a player in the second row of the scrum **9b** this position **10** a gas bubble in a hydraulic system or a liquid bubble in a pneumatic system that stops the fluid flow in a pipe, capillary, etc: *an air lock* ▷ *vb* **11** to fasten (a door, gate, etc) or (of a door, etc) to become fastened with a lock, bolt, etc, so as to prevent entry or exit **12** (*tr*) to secure (a building) by locking all doors, windows, etc **13** to fix or become fixed together securely or inextricably **14** to become or cause to become rigid or immovable: *the front wheels of the car locked* **15** (when *tr, often passive*) to clasp or entangle (someone or each other) in a struggle or embrace **16** (*tr*) to furnish (a canal) with locks **17** (*tr*) to move (a vessel) through a system of locks ▷ See also **lock out, lock up** [OE *loc*] > **ˈlockable** *adj*

lock[2] (lɒk) *n* **1** a strand, curl, or cluster of hair **2** a tuft or wisp of wool, cotton, etc **3** (*pl*) *chiefly literary* hair, esp when curly or fine [OE *loc*]

lockdown (ˈlɒkˌdaʊn) *n US* a security measure in which those inside a building such as a prison, school, or hospital are required to remain confined in it for a time: *many schools remained under lockdown yesterday*

Locke (lɒk) *n* **1** **John** 1632–1704, English philosopher, who discussed the concept of empiricism in his *Essay Concerning Human Understanding* (1690). He influenced political thought, esp in France and America, with his *Two Treatises on Government* (1690), in which he sanctioned the right to revolt **2** **Matthew** ?1630–77, English composer, esp of works for the stage

locked-in syndrome *n* a condition in which a person is conscious but unable to move any part of the body except the eyes: results from damage to the brainstem

locker (ˈlɒkə) *n* **1a** a small compartment or drawer that may be locked, as one of several in a gymnasium, etc, for clothes and valuables **1b** (*as modifier*): *a locker room* **2** a person or thing that locks

Lockerbie (ˈlɒkəbɪ) *n* a town in SW Scotland, in Dumfries and Galloway: scene (1988) of the UK's worst air disaster when a jumbo jet was brought down by a terrorist bomb, killing 270 people, including eleven residents of the town

locket (ˈlɒkɪt) *n* a small ornamental case, usually on a necklace or chain, that holds a picture, keepsake, etc [C17 from F *loquet* latch, dim. of *loc* LOCK[1]]

lockjaw (ˈlɒkˌdʒɔː) *n pathol* a nontechnical name for **trismus** and (often) **tetanus**

lock out *vb* (*tr, adv*) **1** to prevent from entering by locking a door **2** to prevent (employees) from working during an industrial dispute, as by closing a factory ▷ *n* **lockout** **3** the closing of a place of employment by an employer, in order to bring pressure on employees to agree to terms

locksmith (ˈlɒkˌsmɪθ) *n* a person who makes or repairs locks

lockstep (ˈlɒkˌstɛp) *n* **1** a method of marching such that the marchers follow one another as closely as possible **2** **in lockstep with** progressing at exactly the same speed and in the same direction as (other people or things), esp as a matter of course rather than by choice

lock up *vb* (*adv*) **1** (*tr*) Also: **lock in, lock away** to imprison or confine **2** to lock or secure the doors, windows, etc, of (a building) **3** (*tr*) to keep or store securely: *secrets locked up in history* **4** (*tr*) to invest (funds) so that conversion into cash is difficult ▷ *n* **lockup** **5** the action or time of locking up **6** a jail or block of cells **7** *Brit* a small shop with no attached quarters for the owner **8** *Brit* a garage or storage place separate from the main premises **9** *stock exchange* an investment that is intended to be held for a relatively long period ▷ *adj* **lock-up** **10** *Brit & NZ* (of premises) without living quarters: *a lock-up shop*

Lockyer (ˈlɒkjə) *n* Sir **Joseph Norman** 1836–1920, English astronomer: a pioneer in solar spectroscopy, he was the first to observe helium in the sun's atmosphere (1868)

loco[1] (ˈləʊkəʊ) *n, pl* **locos** *inf* short for **locomotive**

loco[2] (ˈləʊkəʊ) *adj* **1** *sl, chiefly US* insane **2** (of an animal) affected with loco disease ▷ *n, pl* **locos** **3** *US* short for **locoweed** ▷ *vb* **locos, locoing, locoed** (*tr*) **4** to poison with locoweed **5** *US sl* to make insane [C19 via Mexican Sp. from Sp.: crazy]

loco[3] (ˈləʊkəʊ) *adj* denoting a price for goods, esp goods to be exported, that are in a place specified or known, the buyer being responsible for all transport charges from that place: *loco Bristol; a loco price* [C20 from L *locō* from a place]

loco disease *n* a disease of cattle, sheep, and horses characterized by paralysis and faulty vision, caused by ingestion of locoweed

locomotion (ˌləʊkəˈməʊʃən) *n* the act, fact, ability, or power of moving [C17 from L *locō* from a place, ablative of *locus* place + MOTION]

locomotive (ˌləʊkəˈməʊtɪv) *n* **1a** Also called: **locomotive engine** a self-propelled engine driven by steam, electricity, or diesel power and used for drawing trains along railway tracks **1b** (*as modifier*): *a locomotive shed; a locomotive works* ▷ *adj* **2** of or relating to locomotion **3** moving or able to move, as by self-propulsion

locomotor (ˌləʊkəˈməʊtə) *adj* of or relating to locomotion [C19 from L *locō* from a place + MOTOR (mover)]

locomotor ataxia *n pathol* another name for **tabes dorsalis**

locoweed (ˈləʊkəʊˌwiːd) *n* any of several perennial leguminous plants of W North America that cause loco disease in horses, cattle, and sheep

Locris *or* **Lokris** (ˈləʊkrɪs, ˈlɒk-) *n* an ancient region of

Ll

central Greece > 'Locrian or 'Lokrian *adj, n*

loculus ('lɒkjʊləs) *n, pl* **loculi** ('lɒkjʊˌlaɪ) **1** *bot* any of the chambers of an ovary or anther **2** *biol* any small cavity or chamber [c19 NL, from L: compartment, from *locus* place] > '**locular** *adj*

locum tenens ('ləʊkəm 'tiːnɛnz) *n, pl* **locum tenentes** (tə'nɛntiːz) *chiefly Brit* a person who stands in temporarily for another member of the same profession, esp for a physician, chemist, or clergyman. Often shortened to **locum** [c17 Med. L: (someone) holding the place (of another)]

locus ('ləʊkəs) *n, pl* **loci** **1** (in many legal phrases) a place or area, esp the place where something occurred **2** *maths* a set of points or lines whose location satisfies or is determined by one or more specified conditions: *the locus of points equidistant from a given point is a circle* **3** *genetics* the position of a particular gene on a chromosome [c18 L]

locust ('ləʊkəst) *n* **1** any of numerous insects, related to the grasshopper, of warm and tropical regions of the Old World, which travel in vast swarms, stripping large areas of vegetation **2** Also called: **locust tree** a North American leguminous tree having prickly branches, hanging clusters of white fragrant flowers, and reddish-brown seed pods **3** the yellowish durable wood of this tree **4** any of several similar trees, such as the honey locust and carob [c13 (the insect): from L *locusta*; applied to the tree (c17) because the pods resemble locusts]

locution (ləʊ'kjuːʃən) *n* **1** a word, phrase, or expression **2** manner or style of speech [c15 from L *locūtiō* an utterance, from *loquī* to speak]

Lod (lɒd) *n* a town in central Israel, southeast of Tel Aviv: Israel's chief airport. Pop: 42 000 (latest est). Also called: **Lydda**

lode (ləʊd) *n* **1** a deposit of valuable ore occurring between definite limits in the surrounding rock; vein **2** a deposit of metallic ore filling a fissure in the surrounding rock [OE *lād* course]

loden ('ləʊdᵊn) *n* **1** a thick heavy waterproof woollen cloth with a short pile, used for coats **2** a dark bluish-green colour, in which the cloth is often made [G, from OHG *lodo* thick cloth]

lodestar *or* **loadstar** ('ləʊdˌstɑː) *n* **1** a star, esp the North Star, used in navigation or astronomy as a point of reference **2** something that serves as a guide or model [c14 lit.: guiding star]

lodestone *or* **loadstone** ('ləʊdˌstəʊn) *n* **1a** magnetite that is naturally magnetic **1b** a piece of this, which can be used as a magnet **2** a person or thing regarded as a focus of attraction [c16 lit.: guiding stone]

lodge (lɒdʒ) *n* **1** *chiefly Brit* a small house at the entrance to the grounds of a country mansion, usually occupied by a gatekeeper or gardener **2** a house or cabin used occasionally, as for some seasonal activity **3** (*cap when part of a name*) a large house or hotel **4** a room for the use of porters in a university, college, etc **5** a local branch or chapter of certain societies **6** the building used as the meeting place of such a society **7** the dwelling place of certain animals, esp beavers **8** a hut or tent of certain North American Indian peoples ▷ *vb* **lodges, lodging, lodged** **9** to provide or be provided with accommodation or shelter, esp rented accommodation **10** (*intr*) to live temporarily, esp in rented accommodation **11** to implant, embed, or fix or be implanted, embedded, or fixed **12** (*tr*) to deposit or leave for safety, storage, etc **13** (*tr*) to bring (a charge or accusation) against someone **14** (*tr; often foll by in or with*) to place (authority, power, etc) in the control (of someone) [c15 from OF *loge*, ?from OHG *louba* porch]

Lodge[1] (lɒdʒ) *n* **the** the official Canberra residence of the Australian prime minister

Lodge[2] (lɒdʒ) *n* **1** **David (John)** born 1935, British novelist and critic. His books include *Changing Places* (1975), *Small World* (1984), *Nice Work* (1988), *Therapy* (1995), and *Thinks* (2001) **2** Sir **Oliver (Joseph)** 1851–1940, British physicist, who made important contributions to electromagnetism and radio reception, and attempted to detect the ether. He also studied allegedly psychic phenomena **3** **Thomas** ?1558–1625, English writer. His romance *Rosalynde* (1590) supplied the plot for Shakespeare's *As You Like It*

lodger ('lɒdʒə) *n* a person who pays rent in return for accommodation in someone else's house

lodging ('lɒdʒɪŋ) *n* **1** a temporary residence **2** (*sometimes pl*) sleeping accommodation

lodging house *n* a private home providing accommodation and meals for lodgers

lodgings ('lɒdʒɪŋz) *pl n* a rented room or rooms, esp in another person's house

lodgment *or* **lodgement** ('lɒdʒmənt) *n* **1** the act of lodging or the state of being lodged **2** a blockage or accumulation **3** a small area gained and held in enemy territory

Lodi (*Italian* 'lɔːdi) *n* a town in N Italy, in Lombardy: scene of Napoleon's defeat of the Austrians in 1796. Pop: 42 277 (1993 est)

Łódź (*Polish* wudʒ) *n* a city in central Poland: the country's second largest city; major centre of the textile industry; university (1945). Pop: 806 728 (1999 est)

loess ('ləʊɪs) *n* a light-coloured fine-grained accumulation of clay and silt deposited by the wind [c19 from G *Löss*, from Swiss G dialect *lösch* loose] > **loessial** (ləʊ'ɛsɪəl) *adj*

Loewe **1** (ləʊ) *n* **Frederick** 1904–88, US composer of such musical comedies as *Brigadoon* (1947), *My Fair Lady* (1956), and *Camelot* (1960), all with librettos by Alan Jay Lerner **2** Also: **Löwe** (*German* 'løːvə) *n* **(Johann) Karl (Gottfried)** 1796–1869, German composer, esp of songs, such as *Der Erlkönig* (1818)

Loewi ('ləʊɪ) *n* **Otto** 1873–1961, US pharmacologist, born in Germany. He shared a Nobel prize for physiology or medicine (1936) with Dale for their work on the chemical transmission of nerve impulses

Lofoten and Vesterålen (*Norwegian* 'luːfutən, 'vɛstəroːlən) *pl n* a group of islands off the NW coast of Norway, within the Arctic Circle. Largest island: Hinny. Pop: 66 600 (latest est). Area: about 5130 sq km (1980 sq miles)

loft (lɒft) *n* **1** the space inside a roof, used for storage or converted into living space **2** a gallery, esp one for the choir in a church **3** a room over a stable used to store hay **4** an upper storey of a warehouse or factory, esp when converted into living space **5** a raised house or coop in which pigeons are kept **6** *sport* **6a** (in golf) the angle from the vertical made by the club face to give elevation to a ball **6b** elevation imparted to a ball **6c** a lofting stroke or shot ▷ *vb* (*tr*) **7** *sport* to strike or kick (a ball) high in the air **8** to store or place in a loft **9** *golf* to slant (the face of a golf club) [OE, from ON *lopt* air, ceiling]

lofty ('lɒftɪ) *adj* **loftier, loftiest** **1** of majestic or imposing height **2** exalted or noble in character or nature **3** haughty or supercilious **4** elevated, eminent, or superior > '**loftily** *adv* > '**loftiness** *n*

log[1] (lɒg) *n* **1a** a section of the trunk or a main branch of a tree, when stripped of branches **1b** (*modifier*) constructed out of logs: *a log cabin* **2a** a detailed record of a voyage of a ship or aircraft **2b** a record of the hours flown by pilots and aircrews **2c** a book in which these records are made; logbook **3** a written record of information about transmissions kept by radio stations, amateur radio operators, etc **4** Also called: **chip log** a device consisting of a float with an attached line, formerly used to measure the speed of a ship **5** **like a log** without stirring or being disturbed (in **sleep like a log**) ▷ *vb* **logs, logging, logged** **6** (*tr*) to fell the trees of (a forest, area, etc) for timber **7** (*tr*) to saw logs from (trees) **8** (*intr*) to work at the felling of timber **9** (*tr*) to enter (a distance, event, etc) in a logbook or log **10** (*tr*) to travel (a specified distance or time) or move at (a specified speed) [C14 from ?]

log² (lɒg) *n* short for **logarithm**

-log *n combining form* a US variant of **-logue**

logan ('ləʊgən) *n Canad* another name for **bogan** (a backwater)

Logan ('ləʊgən) *n* **Mount** a mountain in NW Canada, in SW Yukon in the St. Elias Range: the highest peak in Canada and the second highest in North America. Height: 6050 m (19 850 ft)

loganberry ('ləʊgənbərɪ, -brɪ) *n, pl* **loganberries** **1** a trailing prickly hybrid plant of the rose family, cultivated for its edible fruit **2** the purplish-red acid fruit of this plant [C19 after James H. *Logan* (1841–1928), American judge and horticulturalist who first grew it (1881)]

logarithm ('lɒgə,rɪðəm) *n* the exponent indicating the power to which a fixed number, the base, must be raised to obtain a given number or variable. It is used esp to simplify multiplication and division. Often shortened to **log** [C17 from NL *logarithmus*, coined 1614 by John NAPIER, from Gk *logos* ratio + *arithmos* number] > **logarithmic** (,lɒgə'rɪðmɪk) *adj*

logarithmic function *n* **a** the mathematical function $y = \log x$ **b** a function that can be expressed in terms of this function

logbook ('lɒg,bʊk) *n* **1** a book containing the official record of trips made by a ship or aircraft **2** *Brit* a former name for **registration document**

log chip *n naut* the wooden chip or float of a chip log. See **log¹** (sense 4)

loge (ləʊʒ) *n* a small enclosure or box in a theatre or opera house [C18 F; see LODGE]

logger ('lɒgə) *n* another word for **lumberjack**

loggerhead ('lɒgə,hɛd) *n* **1** Also called: **loggerhead turtle** a large-headed turtle occurring in most seas **2** a tool consisting of a large metal sphere attached to a long handle, used for warming liquids, melting tar, etc **3** *arch or dialect* a blockhead; dunce **4** **at loggerheads** engaged in dispute or confrontation [C16 prob. from dialect *logger* wooden block + HEAD]

loggia ('lɒdʒə, 'lɒdʒɪə) *n, pl* **loggias** *or* **loggie** (-dʒɛ) a covered area on the side of a building [C17 It., from F *loge*. See LODGE]

logging ('lɒgɪŋ) *n* the work of felling, trimming, and transporting timber

logic ('lɒdʒɪk) *n* **1** the branch of philosophy concerned with analysing the patterns of reasoning by which a conclusion is properly drawn from a set of premises, without reference to meaning or context **2** any formal system in which are defined axioms and rules of inference **3** the system and principles of reasoning used in a specific field of study **4** a particular method of argument or reasoning **5** force or effectiveness in argument or dispute **6** reasoned thought or argument, as distinguished from irrationality **7** the relationship and interdependence of a series of events, facts, etc **8** *electronics, computers* the principles underlying the units in a computer system that perform arithmetical and logical operations. See also **logic circuit** [C14 from OF *logique* from Med. L *logica*, from Gk *logikos* concerning speech or reasoning]

▹ http://pvspade.com/Logic/

▹ http://www.philosophypages.com/lg/

logical ('lɒdʒɪkᵊl) *adj* **1** relating to, used in, or characteristic of logic: *logical connective* **2** using, according to, or deduced from the principles of logic: *a logical conclusion* **3** capable of or characterized by clear or valid reasoning **4** reasonable or necessary because of facts, events, etc: *the logical candidate* **5** *computing* of, performed by, used in, or relating to the logic circuits in a computer > ,**logi'cality** *or* '**logicalness** *n* > '**logically** *adv*

logical form *n* the structure of an argument by virtue of which it can be shown to be formally valid

logical positivism *or* **empiricism** *n* a philosophical theory holding that the only meaningful statements are those that are analytic or can be tested empirically. It therefore rejects theology, metaphysics, etc, as meaningless

logic bomb *n computing* an unauthorized program that is inserted into a computer system; when activated it interferes with the operation of the computer

logic cell *n* a logic circuit forming part of a chip

logic circuit *n* an electronic circuit used in computers to perform a logical operation on its two or more input signals

logician (lɒ'dʒɪʃən) *n* a person who specializes in or is skilled at logic

logic programming *n* the study or implementation of computer programs capable of discovering or checking proofs of formal expressions or segments

Logie ('ləʊgɪ) *n* (in Australia) one of the awards made annually for outstanding television performances [C20 after (John) *Logie* Baird (1888–1946), the Scottish inventor of the television]

log in *computing* ▹ *vb* **1** Also: **log on** to enter (an identification number, password, etc) from a remote terminal to gain access to a multiaccess system ▹ *n* **login** **2** the process by which a computer user logs in

logistics (lɒ'dʒɪstɪks) *n* (*functioning as sing or pl*) **1** the science of the movement and maintenance of military forces **2** the management of materials flow through an organization **3** the detailed planning and organization of any large complex operation [C19 from F *logistique*, from *loger* to LODGE] > **lo'gistical** *adj*

log jam *n chiefly US & Canad* **1** blockage caused by the crowding together of a number of logs floating in a river **2** a deadlock; standstill

loglog ('lɒglɒg) *n* the logarithm of a logarithm (in equations, etc)

logo ('ləʊgəʊ, 'lɒg-) *n, pl* **logos** short for **logotype** (sense 2)

logo- *combining form* indicating word or speech: *logogram* [from Gk *logos* word, from *legein* to speak]

logogram ('lɒgə,græm) *n* single symbol representing an entire morpheme, word, or phrase, as for example the symbol (%) meaning *per cent*

logorrhoea *or esp US* **logorrhea** (,lɒgə'rɪə) *n* uncontrollable or incoherent talkativeness

logos (lɒgɒs) *n* **1** *philosophy* reason, regarded as the controlling principle of the universe **2** (*cap*) the divine Word; the second person of the Trinity [C16 Gk: word, reason]

logotype ('lɒgəʊ,taɪp) *n* **1** *printing* a piece of type with several uncombined characters cast on it **2** Also called: **logo** a trademark, company emblem, or similar device

log out *computing* ▹ *vb* **1** Also: **log off** to disconnect a remote terminal from a multiaccess system by entering (an identification number, password, etc) ▹ *n* **2** Also: **logout** the process by which a computer user logs out

logroll ('lɒg,rəʊl) *vb chiefly US* to use logrolling in order to procure the passage of (legislation) > '**log,roller** *n*

logrolling ('lɒg,rəʊlɪŋ) *n* **1** *US* the practice of undemocratic agreements between politicians involving mutual favours, the trading of votes, etc **2** another name for **birling**. See **birl**

Logroño (*Spanish* lo'ɣroɲo) *n* a walled city in N Spain, on the Ebro River: trading centre of an agricultural region noted for its wine. Pop: 125 617 (1998 est)

-logue *or US* **-log** *n combining form* indicating speech or discourse of a particular kind: *travelogue; monologue* [from F, from Gk *-logos*]

logwood ('lɒg,wʊd) *n* **1** a leguminous tree of the Caribbean and Central America **2** the heavy

Ll

reddish-brown wood of this tree, yielding a dye

-logy *n combining form* **1** indicating the science or study of: *musicology* **2** indicating writing, discourse, or body of writings: *trilogy; phraseology; martyrology* [from L *-logia*, from Gk, from *logos* word] > **-logical** *or* **-logic** *adj combining form* > **-logist** *n combining form*

Lohengrin ('ləʊɪŋgrɪn) *n* (in German legend) a son of Parzival and knight of the Holy Grail

loin (lɔɪn) *n* **1** *anat* the lower back and sides between the pelvis and the ribs. Related adj: **lumbar** **2** a cut of meat from this part of an animal ▷ See also **loins** [c14 from OF *loigne*, ?from Vulgar L *lumbra* (unattested), from L *lumbus* loin]

loincloth ('lɔɪn,klɒθ) *n* a piece of cloth worn round the loins. Also called: **breechcloth**

loins (lɔɪnz) *pl n* **1** the hips and the inner surface of the legs where they join the trunk of the body; crotch **2** *euphemistic* the reproductive organs

Loire (*French* lwar) *n* **1** a department of E central France, in Rhône-Alpes region. Capital: St. Étienne. Pop: 728 524 (1999). Area: 4799 sq km (1872 sq miles) **2** a river in France, rising in the Massif Central and flowing north and west in a wide curve to the Bay of Biscay: the longest river in France. Its valley is famous for its wines and châteaux. Length: 1020 km (634 miles). Ancient name: **Liger**

Loire-Atlantique (*French* lwaratlɑ̃tik) *n* a department of W France, in Pays de la Loire region. Capital: Nantes. Pop: 1 134 266 (1999). Area: 6980 sq km (2722 sq miles)

Loiret (*French* lwarɛ) *n* a department of central France, in Centre region. Capital: Orléans. Pop: 618 126 (1999). Area: 6812 sq km (2657 sq miles)

Loir-et-Cher (*French* lwareʃɛr) *n* a department of N central France, in Centre region. Capital: Blois. Pop: 314 968 (1999). Area: 6422 sq km (2505 sq miles)

loiter ('lɔɪtə) *vb* (*intr*) to stand or act aimlessly or idly [c14 ?from MDu. *löteren* to wobble] > **'loiterer** *n* > **'loitering** *n, adj*

Loki ('ləʊkɪ) *n Norse myth* the god of mischief and destruction

LOL *text messaging abbrev for* laughing out loud

loll (lɒl) *vb* **1** (*intr*) to lie, lean, or lounge in a lazy or relaxed manner **2** to hang or allow to hang loosely ▷ *n* **3** an act or instance of lolling [c14 ? imit.] > **'loller** *n* > **'lolling** *adj*

Lolland (*Danish* 'lɔlan) *n* an island of Denmark in the Baltic Sea, south of Sjælland. Pop: 80 500 (latest est). Area: 1240 sq km (480 sq miles)

Lollard ('lɒləd) *n English history* a follower of John Wycliffe during the 14th, 15th, and 16th centuries [c14 from MDu.; mutterer, from *lollen* to mumble (prayers)] > **'Lollardism** *n*

lollipop ('lɒlɪ,pɒp) *n* **1** a boiled sweet or toffee stuck on a small wooden stick **2** *Brit* another word for **ice lolly** [c18 ?from N. English dialect *lolly* the tongue + POP[1]]

lollipop man *or* **lady** *n Brit inf* a person who stops traffic by holding up a circular sign on a pole, to enable children to cross the road safely

lollop ('lɒləp) *vb* **lollops, lolloping, lolloped** (*intr*) *chiefly Brit* **1** to walk or run with a clumsy or relaxed bouncing movement **2** a less common word for **lounge** [c18 prob. from LOLL + *-op* as in GALLOP, to emphasize the contrast in meaning]

lollo rosso ('lɒləʊ 'rɒsəʊ) *n* a variety of lettuce originating in Italy, having curly red-tipped leaves and a slightly bitter taste

lolly ('lɒlɪ) *n, pl* **lollies** **1** an informal word for **lollipop** **2** *Brit* short for **ice lolly** **3** *Brit, Austral & NZ* a slang word for **money** **4** *Austral & NZ inf* a sweet, esp a boiled one **5** **do the** (*or* **one's**) **lolly** *Austral inf* to lose one's temper [shortened from LOLLIPOP]

Lomax ('ləʊmæks) *n* **Alan** born 1915, and his father **John Avery** ('eɪvərɪ) (1867–1948), US folklorists

Lombard[1] ('lɒmbəd, -bɑːd, 'lʌm-) *n* **1** a native or inhabitant of Lombardy **2** a member of an ancient Germanic people who settled in N Italy after 568 AD ▷ *adj also* **Lombardic** **3** of or relating to Lombardy or the Lombards

Lombard[2] ('lɒmbəd, -bɑːd, 'lʌm-) *n* **Peter** ?1100–?60, Italian theologian, noted for his *Sententiarum libri quatuor*

Lombard Street *n* the British financial and banking world [c16 from a street in London once occupied by Lombard bankers]

Lombardy ('lɒmbədɪ, 'lʌm-) *n* a region of N central Italy, bordering on the Alps: dominated by prosperous lordships and city-states during the Middle Ages; later ruled by Spain and then by Austria before becoming part of Italy in 1859; intensively cultivated and in parts highly industrialized. Pop: 9 065 440 (2000 est). Area: 23 804 sq km (9284 sq miles). Italian name: **Lombardia** (,lombar'diːa)

Lombardy poplar *n* an Italian poplar tree with upwardly pointing branches giving it a columnar shape

Lombok ('lɒmbɒk) *n* an island of Indonesia, in the Nusa Tenggara Islands east of Java: came under Dutch rule in 1894; important biologically as being transitional between Asian and Australian in flora and fauna, the line of demarcation beginning at **Lombok Strait** (a channel between Lombok and Bali, connecting the Flores Sea with the Indian Ocean) Chief town: Mataram. Pop: 2 500 000 (1991). Area: 4730 sq km (1826 sq miles)

Lomé (*French* lɔme) *n* the capital and chief port of Togo, on the Bight of Benin. Pop: 790 000 (1999 est)

Lomond ('ləʊmənd) *n* **1** **Loch** a lake in W Scotland, north of Glasgow: the largest Scottish lake; designated a national park in 2002. Length: about 38 km (24 miles). Width: up to 8 km (5 miles) **2** See **Ben Lomond**

Lomu ('ləʊmuː) *n* **Jonah** born 1975, New Zealand Rugby Union football player

London[1] ('lʌndən) *n* **1** the capital of the United Kingdom, a port in S England on the River Thames near its estuary on the North Sea: consists of the **City** (the financial quarter), the **West End** (the entertainment and major shopping centre), the **East End** (the industrial and former dock area), and extensive suburbs. Latin name: **Londinium.** See also **City** **2** **Greater** the administrative area of London, consisting of the City of London and 32 boroughs (13 Inner London boroughs and 19 Outer London boroughs): formed in 1965 from the City, parts of Surrey, Kent, Essex, and Hertfordshire, and almost all of Middlesex: a Mayor of London and a London Assembly took office in 2000. Pop: 7 172 036 (2001). Area: 1579 sq km (610 sq miles) **3** a city in SE Canada, in SE Ontario on the Thames River: University of Western Ontario (1878). Pop: 325 646 (1996) > **'Londoner** *n*

London[2] ('lʌndən) *n* **Jack**, full name *John Griffith London.* 1876–1916, US novelist, short-story writer, and adventurer. His works include *Call of the Wild* (1903), *The Sea Wolf* (1904), *The Iron Heel* (1907), and the semiautobiographical *John Barleycorn* (1913)

▷ www.cityoflondon.gov.uk
▷ www.uktravel.com/london.htm
▷ www.londontourist.org

Londonderry ('lʌndən,dɛrɪ) *or* **Derry** *n* **1** a historical county of NW Northern Ireland, on the Atlantic: in 1973 replaced for administrative purposes by the districts of Coleraine, Derry, Limavady, and Magherafelt. Area: 2108 sq km (814 sq miles) **2** a port in N Northern Ireland, second city of Northern Ireland: given to the City of London in 1613 to be colonized by Londoners; besieged by James II's forces (1688–89). Pop: 72 334 (1991) ▷ See also **Derry**

London Eye *n* the world's largest Ferris wheel (diameter 132 m), opened on London's South Bank in 2000 and providing passengers with unique views of London. Also called: **Millennium Wheel**

London pride *n* a type of saxifrage plant having a basal rosette of leaves and pinkish-white flowers

Londrina (*Portuguese* lon'drina) *n* a city in S Brazil, in Paraná: centre of a coffee-growing area. Pop: 433 264 (2000)

lone (ləʊn) *adj* (*prenominal*) **1** unaccompanied; solitary **2** single or isolated: *a lone house* **3** a literary word for **lonely** **4** unmarried or widowed [C14 from the mistaken division of ALONE into *a lone*] > '**loneness** *n*

lonely ('ləʊnlɪ) *adj* **lonelier, loneliest** **1** unhappy as a result of being without companions **2** causing or resulting from the state of being alone **3** isolated, unfrequented, or desolate **4** without companions; solitary > '**loneliness** *n*

lonely hearts *adj* (*often caps*) of or for people who wish to meet a congenial companion or marriage partner: *a lonely hearts advertisement*

loner ('ləʊnə) *n inf* a person who avoids the company of others or prefers to be alone

lonesome ('ləʊnsəm) *adj* **1** *chiefly US & Canad* another word for **lonely** ▷ *n* **2** **on** *or US* **by one's lonesome** *inf* on one's own > '**lonesomely** *adv* > '**lonesomeness** *n*

long[1] (lɒŋ) *adj* **1** having relatively great extent in space or duration in time **2a** (*postpositive*) of a specified number of units in extent or duration: *three hours long* **2b** (*in combination*): *a two-foot-long line* **3** having or consisting of a relatively large number of items or parts: *a long list* **4** having greater than the average or expected range, extent, or duration: *a long match* **5** seeming to occupy a greater time than is really so: *she spent a long afternoon waiting* **6** (of drinks) containing a large quantity of nonalcoholic beverage **7** (of a garment) reaching to the wearer's ankles **8** *inf* (foll by *on*) plentifully supplied or endowed (with): *long on good ideas* **9** *phonetics* (of a speech sound, esp a vowel) **9a** of relatively considerable duration **9b** (in popular usage) denoting the qualities of the five English vowels in such words as *mate, mete, mite, moat, moot*, and *mute* **10** from end to end; lengthwise **11** unlikely to win, happen, succeed, etc: *a long chance* **12** *prosody* **12a** denoting a vowel of relatively great duration **12b** denoting a syllable containing such a vowel **12c** carrying the emphasis **13** *finance* having or characterized by large holdings of securities or commodities in anticipation of rising prices **14** *cricket* (of a fielding position) near the boundary: *long leg* **15** **in the long run** ultimately; after or over a period of time ▷ *adv* **16** for a certain time or period: *how long will it last?* **17** for or during an extensive period of time: *long into the next year* **18** at a distant time; quite a bit of time: *long before I met you; long ago* **19** *finance* into a position with more security or commodity holdings than are required by sale contracts and therefore dependent on rising prices for profit: *to go long* **20** **as** (*or* **so**) **long as** **20a** for or during just the length of time that **20b** inasmuch as; since **20c** provided that; if **21** **no longer** not any more; formerly but not now ▷ *n* **22** a long time (esp in **for long**) **23** a relatively long thing, such as a dash in Morse code **24** *phonetics* a long vowel or syllable **25** *finance* a person with large holdings of a security or commodity in expectation of a rise in its price; bull **26** **before long** soon **27** **the long and the short of it** the essential points or facts ▷ See also **longs** [OE *lang*]

long[2] (lɒŋ) *vb* (*intr*; foll by *for* or an infinitive) to have a strong desire [OE *langian*]

Long (lɒŋ) *n* **Crawford Williamson** 1815–78, US surgeon. He was the first to use ether as an anaesthetic

long. *abbrev for* longitude

long- *adv* (*in combination*) for or lasting a long time: *long-awaited; long-established; long-lasting*

long-acting *adj* (of a drug) slowly effective after initial dosage, but maintaining its effects over a long period of time ▷ Cf **intermediate-acting, short-acting**

Long Beach *n* a city in SW California, on San Pedro Bay: resort and naval base; oil-refining. Pop: 461 522 (2000)

Longbenton (ˌlɒŋ'bɛntən) *n* a town in N England, in North Tyneside unitary authority, Tyne and Wear. Pop: 34 630 (1991)

longboard ('lɒŋˌbɔːd) *n* **1** a type of surfboard **2** a type of skateboard

longboat ('lɒŋˌbəʊt) *n* the largest boat carried aboard a commercial sailing vessel

longbow ('lɒŋˌbəʊ) *n* a large powerful hand-drawn bow, esp as used in medieval England

longcase clock ('lɒŋˌkeɪs) *n* another name for **grandfather clock**

longcloth ('lɒŋˌklɒθ) *n* a fine plain-weave cotton cloth made in long strips

long-dated *adj* (of a gilt-edged security) having more than 15 years to run before redemption ▷Cf **medium-dated, short-dated**

long-day *adj* (of certain plants) able to mature and flower only if exposed to long periods of daylight ▷ Cf **short-day**

long-distance *n* **1** (*modifier*) covering relatively long distances: *a long-distance driver* **2** (*modifier*) (of telephone calls, lines, etc) connecting points a relatively long way apart **3** *chiefly US & Canad* a long-distance telephone call **4** a long-distance telephone system or its operator ▷ *adv* **5** by a long-distance telephone line: *he phoned long-distance*

long-drawn-out *adj* overprolonged or extended

Long Eaton ('iːtᵊn) *n* a town in N central England, in SE Derbyshire. Pop: 44 826 (1991)

longeron ('lɒndʒərən) *n* a main longitudinal structural member of an aircraft [C20 from F: side support, ult. from L *longus* LONG[1]]

longevity (lɒn'dʒɛvɪtɪ) *n* **1** long life **2** relatively long duration of employment, service, etc [C17 from LL *longaevitās*, from L *longaevus* long-lived, from *longus* LONG[1] + *aevum* age]

long face *n* a disappointed, solemn, or miserable facial expression > ˌ**long-'faced** *adj*

Longfellow ('lɒŋˌfɛləʊ) *n* **Henry Wadsworth** 1807–82, US poet, noted particularly for his long narrative poems *Evangeline* (1847) and *The Song of Hiawatha* (1855)

Longford ('lɒŋfəd) *n* **1** a county of N Republic of Ireland, in Leinster province. County town: Longford. Pop: 30 166 (1996). Area: 1043 sq km (403 sq miles) **2** a town in N Republic of Ireland, county town of Co Longford. Pop: 6800 (1995 est)

longhand ('lɒŋˌhænd) *n* ordinary handwriting in which letters, words, etc, are set down in full, as opposed to typing or to shorthand

long haul *n* **1** a journey over a long distance, esp one involving the transport of goods **2** a lengthy job

long-headed *adj* astute; shrewd; sagacious > ˌ**long-'headedly** *adv* > ˌ**long-'headedness** *n*

longhorn ('lɒŋˌhɔːn) *n* **1** a long-horned breed of beef cattle, formerly common in the southwestern US **2** *now rare* a British breed of beef cattle with long curved horns

longing ('lɒŋɪŋ) *n* **1** a prolonged unfulfilled desire or need ▷ *adj* **2** having or showing desire or need: *a longing look* > '**longingly** *adv*

Longinus (lɒn'dʒaɪnəs) *n* **Dionysius** (ˌdaɪə'nɪsɪəs) ?2nd century AD, supposed author of the famous Greek treatise on literary criticism, *On the Sublime*

longish ('lɒŋɪʃ) *adj* rather long

Long Island *n* an island in SE New York State, separated from the S shore of Connecticut by **Long Island Sound** (an arm of the Atlantic): contains the New York City boroughs of Brooklyn and Queens in the west, many resorts (notably Coney Island), and two large airports (La Guardia and John F. Kennedy). Area: 4462 sq km (1723 sq miles)

longitude ('lɒndʒɪ,tju:d, 'lɒŋgɪ-) *n* distance in degrees east or west of the prime meridian at 0° measured by the angle between the plane of the prime meridian and that of the meridian through the point in question, or by the time difference [C14 from L *longitūdō* length, from *longus* LONG[1]]

longitudinal (,lɒndʒɪ'tju:dɪn[ə]l, ,lɒŋgɪ-) *adj* **1** of or relating to longitude or length **2** placed or extended lengthways > ,**longi'tudinally** *adv*

longitudinal wave *n* a wave that is propagated in the same direction as the displacement of the transmitting medium

long johns *pl n inf* underpants with long legs

long jump *n* an athletic contest in which competitors try to cover the farthest distance possible with a running jump from a fixed board or mark. US and Canad equivalent: **broad jump**

long leg *n cricket* **a** a fielding position on the leg side near the boundary almost directly behind the batsman's wicket **b** a fielder in this position

long list *chiefly Brit* ▷ *n* **1** a list of suitable applicants for a job, post, etc, from which a short list will be selected ▷ *vb* **long-list** (*tr*) **2** to put (someone) on a long list

long-lived *adj* having long life, existence, or currency > ,**long-'livedness** *n*

long-off *n cricket* **a** a fielding position on the off side near the boundary almost directly behind the bowler **b** a fielder in this position

long-on *n cricket* **a** a fielding position on the leg side near the boundary almost directly behind the bowler **b** a fielder in this position

long-playing *adj* of or relating to an LP (long player)

long-range *adj* **1** of or extending into the future: *a long-range weather forecast* **2** (of vehicles, aircraft, etc) capable of covering great distances without refuelling **3** (of weapons) made to be fired at a distant target

longs (lɒŋz) *pl n* **1** full-length trousers **2** long-dated gilt-edged securities **3** unsold securities or commodities held in anticipation of rising prices

longship ('lɒŋ,ʃɪp) *n* a narrow open vessel with oars and a square sail, used esp by the Vikings

longshore ('lɒŋ,ʃɔ:) *adj* situated on, relating to, or along the shore [C19 short form of *alongshore*]

longshore drift *n* the process whereby beach material is gradually shifted laterally

longshoreman ('lɒŋ,ʃɔ:mən) *n, pl* **longshoremen** a US and Canad word for **docker**

long shot *n* **1** a competitor, as in a race, considered to be unlikely to win **2** a bet against heavy odds **3** an undertaking, guess, or possibility with little chance of success **4** *films, television* a shot where the camera is or appears to be distant from the object to be photographed **5 by a long shot** by any means: *he still hasn't finished by a long shot*

long-sighted *adj* **1** related to or suffering from hyperopia **2** able to see distant objects in focus **3** another term for **far-sighted** > ,**long-'sightedly** *adv* > ,**long-'sightedness** *n*

Longs Peak *n* a mountain in N Colorado, in the Front Range of the Rockies: the highest peak in the Rocky Mountain National Park. Height: 4345 m (14 255 ft)

long-standing *adj* existing for a long time

long-suffering *adj* **1** enduring pain, unhappiness, etc, without complaint ▷ *n* **2** long and patient endurance > ,**long-'sufferingly** *adv*

long suit *n* **1a** the longest suit in a hand of cards **1b** a holding of four or more cards of a suit **2** *inf* an outstanding advantage, personal quality, or talent

long-term *adj* **1** lasting or extending over a long time: *long-term prospects* **2** *finance* maturing after a long period: *a long-term bond*

long-termism *n* the tendency to focus attention on long-term gains

longtime ('lɒŋ,taɪm) *adj* of long standing

long ton *n* the full name for **ton[1]** (sense 1)

Longueuil (lɒŋ'geɪl; *French* lɔ̃gœj) *n* a city in SE Canada, in S Quebec: a suburb of Montreal. Pop: 127 977 (1996)

longueur (*French* lɔ̃gœr) *n* a period of boredom or dullness [lit.: length]

Longus ('lɒŋgəs) *n* ?3rd century AD, Greek author of the prose romance *Daphnis and Chloe*

long vacation *n* the long period of holiday in the summer during which universities, law courts, etc, are closed

long wave *n* **a** a radio wave with a wavelength greater than 1000 metres **b** (*as modifier*): *a long-wave broadcast*

longways ('lɒŋ,weɪz) *or US & Canad* **longwise** *adv* another word for **lengthways**

long weekend *n* a weekend holiday extended by a day or days on either side

long-winded (,lɒŋ'wɪndɪd) *adj* **1** tiresomely long **2** capable of energetic activity without becoming short of breath > ,**long-'windedly** *adv* > ,**long-'windedness** *n*

Longyearbyen ('lɒŋjɪə,bjɛn) *n* a village on Spitsbergen island, administrative centre of the Svalbard archipelago: coal-mining

lonicera (lɒ'nɪsərə) *n* See **honeysuckle**

Lons-le-Saunier (*French* lɔ̃ləsonje) *n* a town in E France: saline springs; manufactures sparkling wines. Pop (conurbation): 210 140 (1990)

loo[1] (lu:) *n, pl* **loos** *Brit* an informal word for **lavatory** [C20 ?from F *lieux d'aisance* water closet]

loo[2] (lu:) *n, pl* **loos** **1** a gambling card game **2** a stake used in this game [C17 shortened from *lanterloo*, via Du. from F *lanterelu*, orig. a nonsense word from the refrain of a popular song]

loofah ('lu:fə) *n* the fibrous interior of the fruit of a type of gourd, which is dried and used as a bath sponge or for scrubbing. Also (esp US): **loofa, luffa** [C19 from NL *luffa*, from Ar. *lūf*]

look (lʊk) *vb* (*mainly intr*) **1** (often foll by *at*) to direct the eyes (towards): *to look at the sea* **2** (often foll by *at*) to direct one's attention (towards): *let's look at the circumstances* **3** (often foll by *to*) to turn one's interests or expectations (towards): *to look to the future* **4** (*copula*) to give the impression of being by appearance to the eye or mind; seem: *that looks interesting* **5** to face in a particular direction: *the house looks north* **6** to expect, hope, or plan (to do something): *I look to hear from you soon; he's looking to get rich* **7** (foll by *for*) **7a** to search or seek: *I looked for you everywhere* **7b** to cherish the expectation (of); hope (for): *I look for success* **8** (foll by *to*) **8a** to be mindful (of): *to look to the promise one has made* **8b** to have recourse (to): *look to your swords, men!* **9** (foll by *into*) to carry out an investigation **10** (*tr*) to direct a look at (someone) in a specified way: *she looked her rival up and down* **11** (*tr*) to accord in appearance with (something): *to look one's age* **12 look alive, lively, sharp,** *or* **smart** to hurry up; get busy **13 look here** an expression used to attract someone's attention, add emphasis to a statement, etc ▷ *n* **14** the act or an instance of looking: *a look of despair* **15** a view or sight (of something): *let's have a look* **16** (*often pl*) appearance to the eye or mind; aspect: *the look of innocence; I don't like the looks of this place* **17** style; fashion: *the new look for spring* ▷ *sentence connector* **18** an expression demanding attention or showing annoyance, determination, etc: *look, I've had enough of this* ▷ See also **look after, look back,** etc [OE *lōcian*] > '**looker** *n*

USAGE See at **like**

look after *vb* (*intr, prep*) **1** to take care of; be responsible for **2** to follow with the eyes

lookalike ('lʊkə,laɪk) *n* **a** a person or thing that is the double of another, often well-known, person or thing **b** (*as modifier*): *a lookalike Minister; a lookalike newspaper*

look back *vb* (*intr, adv*) **1** to cast one's mind to the past **2 never look back**: to become increasingly successful:

after his first book was published, he never looked back
look down *vb* (*intr, adv; foll by on or upon*) to express or show contempt or disdain (for)
look forward to *vb* (*intr, adv + prep*) to wait or hope for, esp with pleasure
look-in *inf* ▷ *n* **1** a chance to be chosen, participate, etc **2** a short visit ▷ *vb* **look in** **3** (*intr, adv; often foll by on*) to pay a short visit
looking glass *n* a mirror
look on *vb* (*intr*) **1** (*adv*) to be a spectator at an event or incident **2** (*prep*) Also: **look upon** to consider or regard: *she looked on the whole affair as a joke* > ˌ**looker-ˈon** *n*
lookout (ˈlʊkˌaʊt) *n* **1** the act of keeping watch against danger, etc **2** a person or persons instructed or employed to keep such a watch, esp on a ship **3** a strategic point from which a watch is kept **4** *inf* worry or concern: *that's his lookout* **5** *chiefly Brit* outlook, chances, or view ▷ *vb* **look out** (*adv, mainly intr*) **6** to heed one's behaviour; be careful **7** to be on the watch: *look out for my mother at the station* **8** (*tr*) to search for and find **9** (*foll by on or over*) to face in a particular direction: *the house looks out over the moor*
look over *vb* **1** (*intr, prep*) to inspect by making a tour of (a factory, house, etc) **2** (*tr, adv*) to examine (a document, letter, etc) ▷ *n* **look-over** **3** an inspection
look-see *n sl* a brief inspection or look
look up *vb* (*adv*) **1** (*tr*) to discover (something required to be known) by resorting to a work of reference, such as a dictionary **2** (*intr*) to increase, as in quality or value: *things are looking up* **3** (*intr; foll by to*) to have respect (for): *I've always wanted a girlfriend I could look up to* **4** (*tr*) to visit or make contact with (a person): *I'll look you up when I'm in town*
loom[1] (luːm) *n* an apparatus, worked by hand or mechanically (**power loom**), for weaving yarn into a textile [c13 (meaning any kind of tool): var. of OE *gelōma* tool]
loom[2] (luːm) *vb* (*intr*) **1** to come into view indistinctly with an enlarged and often threatening aspect **2** (of an event) to seem ominously close **3** (*often foll by over*) (of large objects) to dominate or overhang ▷ *n* **4** a rising appearance, as of something far away [c16 ?from East Frisian *lomen* to move slowly]
loon[1] (luːn) *n* the US and Canad name for **diver** (the bird) [c17 of Scand. origin]
loon[2] (luːn) *n* **1** *inf* a simple-minded or stupid person **2** *arch* a person of low rank or occupation [c15 from ?]
loonie (ˈluːnɪ) *n Canad sl* **a** a Canadian dollar coin with a loon bird on one of its faces **b** the Canadian currency
loony *or* **looney** (ˈluːnɪ) *Sl* ▷ *adj* **loonier, looniest** **1** lunatic; insane **2** foolish or ridiculous ▷ *n, pl* **loonies** *or* **looneys** **3** a foolish or insane person > ˈ**looniness** *n*
loony bin *n sl* a mental hospital or asylum
loop (luːp) *n* **1** the round or oval shape formed by a line, string, etc, that curves around to cross itself **2** any round or oval-shaped thing that is closed or nearly closed **3** an intrauterine contraceptive device in the shape of a loop **4** *electronics* a closed electric or magnetic circuit through which a signal can circulate, as in a feedback control system **5** a flight manoeuvre in which an aircraft flies one complete circle in the vertical plane **6** Also called: **loop line** *chiefly Brit* a railway branch line which leaves the main line and rejoins it after a short distance **7** *maths, physics* a closed curve on a graph: *hysteresis loop* **8** a continuous strip of cinematographic film **9** *computing* a series of instructions in a program, performed repeatedly until some specified condition is satisfied **10** a group of people to whom information is circulated (esp in **in** *or* **out of the loop**) ▷ *vb* **11** (*tr*) to make a loop in or of (a line, string, etc) **12** (*tr*) to fasten or encircle with a loop or something like a loop **13** Also: **loop the loop** to cause (an aircraft) to perform a loop or (of an aircraft) to perform a loop **14** (*intr*) to move in loops or in a path like a loop [c14 *loupe*, from ?] > ˈ**looper** *n*
loophole (ˈluːpˌhəʊl) *n* **1** an ambiguity, omission, etc, as in a law, by which one can avoid a penalty or responsibility **2** a small gap or hole in a wall, esp one in a fortified wall ▷ *vb* **loopholes, loopholing, loopholed** **3** (*tr*) to provide with loopholes
loopy (ˈluːpɪ) *adj* **loopier, loopiest** **1** full of loops; curly or twisted **2** *inf* slightly mad, crazy
Loos (*German* luːs) *n* **Adolf** (ˈadɔlf) 1870–1933, Austrian architect: a pioneer of modern architecture, noted for his plain austere style in such buildings as Steiner House, Vienna (1910)
loose (luːs) *adj* **1** free or released from confinement or restraint **2** not close, compact, or tight in structure or arrangement **3** not fitted or fitting closely: *loose clothing* **4** not bundled, packaged, fastened, or put in a container: *loose nails* **5** inexact; imprecise: *a loose translation* **6** (of funds, cash, etc) not allocated or locked away; readily available: *loose change* **7a** (esp of women) promiscuous or easy **7b** (of attitudes, ways of life, etc) immoral or dissolute **8a** lacking a sense of responsibility or propriety: *loose talk* **8b** (*in combination*): *loosetongued* **9a** (of the bowels) emptying easily, esp excessively **9b** (of a cough) accompanied by phlegm, mucus, etc **10** *inf, chiefly US & Canad* very relaxed; easy ▷ *n* **11** **the loose** *rugby* the part of play when the forwards close round the ball in a ruck or loose scrum **12** **on the loose** **12a** free from confinement or restraint **12b** *inf* on a spree ▷ *adv* **13a** in a loose manner; loosely **13b** (*in combination*): *loose-fitting* ▷ *vb* **looses, loosing, loosed** **14** (*tr*) to set free or release, as from confinement, restraint, or obligation **15** (*tr*) to unfasten or untie **16** to make or become less strict, tight, firmly attached, compact, etc **17** (*when intr, often foll by off*) to let fly (a bullet, arrow, or other missile) [c13 (in the sense: not bound): from ON *lauss* free] > ˈ**loosely** *adv* > ˈ**looseness** *n*
loosebox (ˈluːsˌbɒks) *n* an enclosed stall with a door in which an animal can be confined
loose cannon *n* a person or thing that appears to be beyond control and is potentially a source of unintentional damage
loose cover *n* a fitted but easily removable cloth cover for a chair, sofa, etc
loose end *n* **1** a detail that is left unsettled, unexplained, or incomplete **2** **at a loose end** without purpose or occupation
loose head *n rugby* the prop on the hooker's left in the front row of a scrum ▷ Cf **tight head**
loose-jointed *adj* **1** supple and easy in movement **2** loosely built; with ill-fitting joints > ˌ**loose-ˈjointedness** *n*
loose-leaf *adj* (of a binder, album, etc) capable of being opened to allow removal and addition of pages
loosen (ˈluːsᵊn) *vb* **1** to make or become less tight, fixed, etc **2** (*often foll by up*) to make or become less firm, compact, or rigid **3** (*tr*) to untie **4** (*tr*) to let loose; set free **5** (*often foll by up*) to make or become less strict, severe, etc **6** (*tr*) to rid or relieve (the bowels) of constipation [c14 from LOOSE] > ˈ**loosener** *n*
loosestrife (ˈluːsˌstraɪf) *n* **1** any of a genus of plants, esp the yellow-flowered yellow loosestrife **2** **purple loosestrife** a purple-flowered marsh plant [c16 LOOSE + STRIFE, an erroneous translation of L *lysimachia*, as if from Gk *lusimakhos* ending strife, instead of from the name of the supposed discoverer, *Lusimakhos*]
loot (luːt) *n* **1** goods stolen during pillaging, as in wartime, during riots, etc **2** goods, money, etc, obtained illegally **3** *inf* money or wealth ▷ *vb* **4** to pillage (a city, etc) during war or riots **5** to steal (money or goods), esp during pillaging [c19 from Hindi *lūt*] > ˈ**looter** *n*
lop[1] (lɒp) *vb* **lops, lopping, lopped** (*tr; usually foll by off*) **1** to sever (parts) from a tree, body, etc, esp with swift

strokes **2** to cut out or eliminate from as excessive ▷ *n* **3** a part or parts lopped off, as from a tree [c15 *loppe* branches cut off] > **'lopper** *n*

lop² (lɒp) *vb* **lops, lopping, lopped 1** to hang or allow to hang loosely **2** (*intr*) to slouch about or move awkwardly [c16 ? rel. to LOP¹]

lope (ləʊp) *vb* **lopes, loping, loped 1** (*intr*) (of a person) to move or run with a long swinging stride **2** (*intr*) (of four-legged animals) to run with a regular bounding movement **3** to cause (a horse) to canter with a long easy stride or (of a horse) to canter in this manner ▷ *n* **4** a long steady gait or stride [c15 from ON *hlaupa* to LEAP]

lop-eared *adj* (of animals) having ears that droop

Lope de Vega (*Spanish* 'lope ðe 'βeɣa) *n* full name *Lope Felix de Vega Carpio*. 1562–1635, Spanish dramatist, novelist, and poet. He established the classic form of Spanish drama and was a major influence on European, esp French, literature. Some 500 of his 1800 plays are extant

Lopez ('ləʊpɛz) *n* **Jennifer** born 1970, US singer and film actress born in Puerto Rico, known as *J-Lo*; her films include *Selena* (1997) and *The Wedding Planner* (2001) and her records include *On the 6* (1999) and *This is Me.Then* (2002)

lopolith *n* a saucer- or lens-shaped body of intrusive igneous rock formed by the penetration of magma between the beds or layers of existing rock and subsequent subsidence beneath the intrusion ▷ Cf **laccolith** [c20 from Greek *lopas* dish + LITH]

lopsided (ˌlɒp'saɪdɪd) *adj* **1** leaning to one side **2** greater in weight, height, or size on one side > ˌ**lop'sidedly** *adv* > ˌ**lop'sidedness** *n*

loquacious (lɒ'kweɪʃəs) *adj* characterized by or showing a tendency to talk a great deal [c17 from L *loquāx* from *loquī* to speak] > **lo'quaciously** *adv* > **loquacity** (lɒ'kwæsɪtɪ) *or* **lo'quaciousness** *n*

loquat ('ləʊkwɒt, -kwət) *n* **1** an ornamental evergreen tree of China and Japan, having reddish woolly branches, white flowers, and small yellow edible plumlike fruits **2** the fruit of this tree [c19 from Chinese (Cantonese) *lō kwat*, lit.: rush orange]

lor (lɔ:) *interj not standard* an exclamation of surprise or dismay [from LORD (interj.)]

loran ('lɔ:rən) *n* a radio navigation system operating over long distances. Synchronized pulses are transmitted from widely spaced radio stations to aircraft or shipping, the time of arrival of the pulses being used to determine position [c20 *lo(ng-)ra(nge) n(avigation)*]

Lorca¹ (*Spanish* 'lɔrka) *n* a town in SE Spain, on the Guadalentín River. Pop: 66 940 (1991)

Lorca² (*Spanish* 'lɔrka) *n* **Federico García** (feðe'riko gar'θia) 1898–1936, Spanish poet and dramatist. His poetry, such as *Romancero gitano* (1928), shows his debt to Andalusian folk poetry. His plays include the trilogy *Bodas de sangre* (1933), *Yerma* (1934), and *La Casa de Bernarda Alba* (1936)

lord (lɔ:d) *n* **1** a person who has power or authority over others, such as a monarch or master **2** a male member of the nobility, esp in Britain **3** (in medieval Europe) a feudal superior, esp the master of a manor **4** a husband considered as head of the household (archaic except in the facetious phrase **lord and master**) **5 my lord** a respectful form of address used to a judge, bishop, or nobleman ▷ *vb* **6** (*tr*) *now rare* to make a lord of (a person) **7** to act in a superior manner towards (esp in **lord it over**) [OE *hlāford* bread keeper] > **'lordless** *adj* > **'lordˌlike** *adj*

Lord (lɔ:d) *n* **1** a title given to God or Jesus Christ **2** *Brit* **2a** a title given to men of high birth, specifically to an earl, marquess, baron, or viscount **2b** a courtesy title given to the younger sons of a duke or marquess **2c** the ceremonial title of certain high officials or of a bishop or archbishop: *Lord Mayor* ▷ *interj* **3** (*sometimes not cap*) an exclamation of dismay, surprise, etc: *Good Lord!*

Lord Chancellor *n Brit government* the cabinet minister who is head of the judiciary in England and Wales, and Speaker of the House of Lords

Lord Chief Justice *n* the judge who is second only to the Lord Chancellor in the English legal hierarchy; president of one division of the High Court of Justice

Lord High Chancellor *n* another name for the **Lord Chancellor**

Lord Howe Island (haʊ) *n* an island in the Tasman Sea, southeast of Australia: part of New South Wales. Area: 17 sq km (6 sq miles). Pop: 300 (latest est)

Lord Lieutenant *n* **1** (in Britain) the representative of the Crown in a county **2** (formerly) the British viceroy in Ireland

lordly ('lɔ:dlɪ) *adj* **lordlier, lordliest 1** haughty; arrogant; proud **2** of or befitting a lord ▷ *adv* **3** *arch* in the manner of a lord > **'lordliness** *n*

Lord Mayor *n* the mayor in the City of London and in certain other important boroughs and large cities

Lord of Misrule *n* (formerly, in England) a person appointed master of revels at a Christmas celebration

Lord of the Flies *n* a name for **Beelzebub** [translation of Heb.: see BEELZEBUB]

lordosis (lɔ:'dəʊsɪs) *n pathol* forward curvature of the lumbar spine [c18 NL from Gk, from *lordos* bent backwards] > **lordotic** (lɔ:'dɒtɪk) *adj*

Lord President of the Council *n* (in Britain) the cabinet minister who presides at meetings of the Privy Council

Lord Privy Seal *n* (in Britain) the senior cabinet minister without official duties

Lord Protector *n* See **Protector**

Lord Provost *n* the provost of one of the five major Scottish cities

Lords (lɔ:dz) *n* **the** short for **House of Lords**

Lord's (lɔ:dz) *n* a cricket ground in N London; headquarters of the MCC

lords-and-ladies *n* (*functioning as sing*) another name for **cuckoopint**

Lord's Day *n* **the** the Christian Sabbath; Sunday

lordship ('lɔ:dʃɪp) *n* the position or authority of a lord

Lordship ('lɔ:dʃɪp) *n* (preceded by *Your* or *His*) *Brit* a title used to address or refer to a bishop, a judge of the high court, or any peer except a duke

Lord's Prayer *n* **the** the prayer taught by Jesus Christ to his disciples, as in Matthew 6:9–13, Luke 11:2–4. Also called: **Our Father, Paternoster** (esp Latin version)

Lords Spiritual *pl n* the Anglican archbishops and senior bishops of England and Wales who are members of the House of Lords

Lord's Supper *n* **the** another term for **Holy Communion** (I Corinthians 11:20)

Lords Temporal *pl n* **the** (in Britain) peers other than bishops in their capacity as members of the House of Lords

lore (lɔ:) *n* **1** collective knowledge or wisdom on a particular subject, esp of a traditional nature **2** knowledge or learning [OE *lār*; rel. to *leornian* to LEARN]

Lorelei ('lɒrəˌlaɪ) *n* (in German legend) a siren, said to dwell on a rock at the edge of the Rhine south of Koblenz, who lures boatmen to destruction [c19 from G *Lurlei* name of the rock; from a poem by Clemens Brentano (1778–1842)]

Lorentz (*Dutch* 'lo:rənts) *n* **Hendrik Antoon** ('hɛndrɪk 'anto:n) 1853–1928, Dutch physicist: shared the Nobel prize for physics (1902) with Zeeman for their work on electromagnetic theory

Lorenz (*German* 'lo:rɛnts) *n* **Konrad Zacharias** ('kɔnra:t tsaxa'ri:as) 1903–89, Austrian zoologist, who founded ethology. His works include *On Aggression* (1966): shared the Nobel prize for physiology or medicine (1973)

lorgnette (lɔ:'njɛt) *n* a pair of spectacles or opera glasses mounted on a handle [c19 from F, from *lorgner* to squint, from OF *lorgne* squinting]

Lorient (*French* lɔrjɑ̃) *n* a port in W France, on the Bay of Biscay. Pop: 59 437 (1990)

lorikeet ('lɒrɪˌkiːt, ˌlɒrɪ'kiːt) *n* any of various small lories, such as the varied lorikeet or rainbow lorikeet [c18 from LORY + -*keet*, as in PARAKEET]

loris ('lɔːrɪs) *n, pl* **loris** any of several omnivorous nocturnal slow-moving prosimian primates of S and SE Asia, esp the slow loris and slender loris, having vestigial digits and no tails [c18 from F; from ?]

lorn (lɔːn) *adj poetic* forsaken or wretched [OE *loren*, p.p. of -*lēosan* to lose]

Lorrain (*French* lɔrɛ̃) *n* See **Claude Lorrain**

Lorraine (lɒ'reɪn; *French* lɔrɛn) *n* **1** a region and former province of E France; ceded to Germany in 1871 after the Franco-Prussian war and regained by France in 1919; rich iron-ore deposits. German name: **Lothringen** **2 Kingdom of** an early medieval kingdom on the Meuse, Moselle, and Rhine rivers: later a duchy **3** a former duchy in E France, once the S half of this kingdom

Lorris (*French* lɔris) *n* See **Guillaume de Lorris**

lorry ('lɒrɪ) *n, pl* **lorries** **1** a large motor vehicle designed to carry heavy loads, esp one with a flat platform. US and Canad name: **truck** **2 off the back of a lorry** *Brit inf* a phrase used humorously to indicate that something has been dishonestly acquired **3** any of various vehicles with a flat load-carrying surface, esp one designed to run on rails [c19 ? rel. to northern English dialect *lurry* to pull]

lory ('lɔːrɪ), **lowry,** *or* **lowrie** ('laʊrɪ) *n, pl* **lories** *or* **lowries** any of various small brightly coloured parrots of Australia and Indonesia, having a brush-tipped tongue with which to feed on nectar and pollen [c17 via Du. from Malay *lūrī*, var. of *nūrī*]

Los Alamos (lɒs 'æləmɒs) *n* a town in the US, in New Mexico: the first atomic bomb was developed here. Pop: 11 455 (1990)

Los Angeles (lɒs 'ændʒɪˌliːz) *n* a city in SW California, on the Pacific: the second largest city in the US, having absorbed many adjacent townships; industrial centre and port, with several universities. Pop: 3 694 820 (2000). Abbreviation: **LA**

lose (luːz) *vb* **loses, losing, lost** (*mainly tr*) **1** to part with or come to be without, as through theft, accident, negligence, etc **2** to fail to keep or maintain: *to lose one's balance* **3** to suffer the loss or deprivation of: *to lose a parent* **4** to cease to have or possess **5** to fail to get or make use of: *to lose a chance* **6** (*also intr*) to fail to gain or win (a contest, game, etc): *to lose the match* **7** to fail to see, hear, perceive, or understand: *I lost the gist of his speech* **8** to waste: *to lose money gambling* **9** to wander from so as to be unable to find: *to lose one's way* **10** to cause the loss of: *his delay lost him the battle* **11** to allow to go astray or out of sight: *we lost him in the crowd* **12** (*usually passive*) to absorb or engross: *he was lost in contemplation* **13** (*usually passive*) to cause the death or destruction of: *two men were lost in the attack* **14** to outdistance or elude: *he soon lost his pursuers* **15** (*intr*) to decrease or depreciate in value or effectiveness: *poetry always loses in translation* **16** (*also intr*) (of a timepiece) to run slow (by a specified amount) **17** (of a woman) to fail to give birth to (a viable baby), esp as the result of a miscarriage **18 lose it** *sl* to lose control of oneself or one's temper [OE *losian* to perish] > **'losable** *adj*

lose out *vb inf* **1** (*intr, adv*) to be defeated or unsuccessful **2 lose out on** to fail to secure or make use of: *we lost out on the sale*

loser ('luːzə) *n* **1** a person or thing that loses **2** *inf* a person or thing that seems destined to be taken advantage of, fail, etc: *a born loser*

Losey ('ləʊsɪ) *n* **Joseph** 1909–84, US film director, in Britain from 1952. His films include *The Servant* (1963), *The Go-Between* (1971), and *Don Giovanni* (1979)

losing ('luːzɪŋ) *adj* unprofitable; failing: *the business was a losing concern*

losings ('luːzɪŋz) *pl n* losses, esp in gambling

loss (lɒs) *n* **1** the act or an instance of losing **2** the disadvantage or deprivation resulting from losing: *a loss of reputation* **3** the person, thing, or amount lost: *a large loss* **4** (*pl*) military personnel lost by death or capture **5** (*sometimes pl*) the amount by which the costs of a business transaction or operation exceed its revenue **6** *insurance* **6a** an occurrence of something that has been insured against, thus giving rise to a claim by a policyholder **6b** the amount of the resulting claim **7 at a loss** **7a** uncertain what to do; bewildered **7b** rendered helpless (for lack of something): *at a loss for words* **7c** with income less than outlay: *the firm was running at a loss* [c14 n prob. formed from *lost*, p.p. of *losen* to perish, from OE *lōsian* to be destroyed, from *los* destruction]

loss adjuster *n insurance* a person qualified to adjust losses incurred through fire, theft, natural disaster, etc, to agree the loss and the compensation to be paid

loss leader *n* an article offered below cost to attract customers

lost (lɒst) *adj* **1** unable to be found or recovered **2** unable to find one's way or ascertain one's whereabouts **3** confused, bewildered, or helpless: *he is lost in discussions of theory* **4** (sometimes foll by *on*) not utilized, noticed, or taken advantage of (by): *rational arguments are lost on her* **5** no longer possessed or existing because of defeat, misfortune, or the passage of time: *a lost art* **6** destroyed physically: *the lost platoon* **7** (foll by *to*) no longer available or open (to) **8** (foll by *to*) insensible or impervious (to a sense of shame, justice, etc) **9** (foll by *in*) engrossed (in): *he was lost in his book* **10** morally fallen: *a lost woman* **11** damned: *a lost soul*

Lost Generation *n* (*sometimes not cap*) **1** the large number of talented young men killed in World War I **2** the generation of writers, esp American authors, active after World War I

lot (lɒt) *pron* **1** (*functioning as sing or pl; preceded by a*) a great number or quantity: *a lot to do; a lot of people* ▷ *n* **2** a collection of objects, items, or people: *a nice lot of youngsters* **3** portion in life; destiny; fortune: *it falls to my lot to be poor* **4** any object, such as a straw or slip of paper, drawn from others at random to make a selection or choice (esp in **draw** *or* **cast lots**) **5** the use of lots in making a selection or choice (esp in **by lot**) **6** an assigned or apportioned share **7** an item or set of items for sale in an auction **8** *chiefly US & Canad* an area of land: *a parking lot* **9** *chiefly US & Canad* a film studio **10 a bad lot** an unpleasant or disreputable person **11 cast** *or* **throw in one's lot with** to join with voluntarily and share the fortunes of **12 the lot** the entire amount or number ▷ *adv* (preceded by *a*) *inf* **13** to a considerable extent, degree, or amount; very much: *to delay a lot* **14** a great deal of the time or often: *to sing madrigals a lot* ▷ *vb* **lots, lotting, lotted** **15** to draw lots for (something) **16** (*tr*) to divide (land, etc) into lots **17** (*tr*) another word for **allot** ▷ See also **lots** [OE *hlot*]

Lot[1] (lɒt) *n* **1** a department of S central France, in Midi-Pyrénées region. Capital: Cahors. Pop: 160 197 (1999). Area: 5226 sq km (2038 sq miles) **2** a river in S France, rising in the Cevennes and flowing west into the Garonne River. Length: about 483 km (300 miles)

Lot[2] (lɒt) *n Old Testament* Abraham's nephew: he escaped the destruction of Sodom, but his wife was changed into a pillar of salt for looking back as they fled (Genesis 19)

Lot-et-Garonne (*French* lɔtegarɔn) *n* a department of SW France, in Aquitaine. Capital: Agen. Pop: 305 380 (1999). Area: 5385 sq km (2100 sq miles)

loth (ləʊθ) *adj* a variant spelling of **loath**

Lothair I (ləʊ'θɛə) *n* ?795–855 AD, Frankish ruler and Holy

Ll

Roman Emperor (823–30, 833–34, 840–55); son of Louis I, whom he twice deposed from the throne

Lothair II *n* called *the Saxon*. ?1070–1137, German king (1125–37) and Holy Roman Emperor (1133–37). He was elected German king over the hereditary Hohenstaufen claimant

Lothario (ləʊˈθɑːrɪ,əʊ) *n, pl* **Lotharios** (*sometimes not cap*) a rake, libertine, or seducer [c18 after a seducer in Nicholas Rowe's tragedy *The Fair Penitent* (1703)]

Lothian Region (ˈləʊðɪən) *n* a former local government region in SE central Scotland, formed in 1975 from East Lothian, most of Midlothian, and West Lothian; replaced in 1996 by the council areas of East Lothian, Midlothian, West Lothian, and Edinburgh

Lothians (ˈləʊðɪənz) *pl n* **the** three historic counties of SE central Scotland (now council areas): East Lothian, West Lothian, and Midlothian (including Edinburgh)

Lothringen (ˈloːtrɪŋən) *n* the German name for **Lorraine**

lotion (ˈləʊʃən) *n* a liquid preparation having a soothing, cleansing, or antiseptic action, applied to the skin, eyes, etc [c14 via OF from L *lōtiō* a washing, from *lōtus* p.p. of *lavāre* to wash]

lots (lɒts) *inf* ▷ *pl n* **1** (often foll by *of*) great numbers or quantities: *lots of people; to eat lots* ▷ *adv* **2** a great deal **3** (intensifier): *the journey is lots quicker by train*

lottery (ˈlɒtərɪ) *n, pl* **lotteries 1** a game of chance in which tickets are sold, which may later qualify the holder for a prize **2** an endeavour, the success of which is regarded as a matter of luck [c16 from OF *loterie*, from MDu. *loterije*]

lotto (ˈlɒtəʊ) *n* **1** Also called: **housey-housey** a children's game in which numbered discs are drawn at random and called out, while the players cover the corresponding numbers on cards, the winner being the first to cover all the numbers, a particular row, etc ▷ Cf **bingo 2** *Austral* a lottery with cash prizes based on this principle [c18 from It., from OF *lot*, from Gmc]

lotus (ˈləʊtəs) *n* **1** (in Greek mythology) a fruit that induces forgetfulness and a dreamy languor in those who eat it **2** any of several water lilies of tropical Africa and Asia, esp the **white lotus**, which was regarded as sacred in ancient Egypt **3** a similar plant which is the sacred lotus of India, China, Egypt, and Tibet **4** a representation of such a plant, common in Hindu, Buddhist, and ancient Egyptian art **5** any of a genus of leguminous plants of the legume family of the Old World and North America, having yellow, pink, or white pealike flowers ▷ Also (rare): **lotos** [c16 via L from Gk *lōtos*, from Semitic]

lotus-eater *n Greek myth* one of a people encountered by Odysseus in North Africa who lived in indolent forgetfulness, drugged by the fruit of the legendary lotus

lotus position *n* a seated cross-legged position used in yoga, meditation, etc

loud (laʊd) *adj* **1** (of sound) relatively great in volume: *a loud shout* **2** making or able to make sounds of relatively great volume: *a loud voice* **3** clamorous, insistent, and emphatic: *loud protests* **4** (of colours, designs, etc) offensive or obtrusive to look at **5** characterized by noisy, vulgar, and offensive behaviour ▷ *adv* **6** in a loud manner **7 out loud** audibly, as distinct from silently [OE *hlud*] > **ˈloudish** *adj* > **ˈloudly** *adv* > **ˈloudness** *n*

louden (ˈlaʊdᵊn) *vb* to make or become louder

loud-hailer *n* a portable loudspeaker having a built-in amplifier and microphone. Also (US and Canad): **bullhorn**

loudmouth (ˈlaʊd,maʊθ) *n inf* a person who brags or talks too loudly > **loudmouthed** (ˈlaʊd,maʊðd, -,maʊθt) *adj*

loudspeaker (,laʊdˈspiːkə) *n* a device for converting audio-frequency signals into sound waves. Often shortened to **speaker**

Lou Gehrig's disease (luː ˈɡɛrɪɡ) *n* another name for **amyotrophic lateral sclerosis** [c20 named after *Lou Gehrig* (1903–41), US baseball player who suffered from it]

lough (lɒx, lɒk) *n* **1** an Irish word for **lake**[1] (senses 1 and 2) **2** a long narrow bay or arm of the sea in Ireland [c14 from Irish *loch* lake]

Loughborough (ˈlʌfbərə, -brə) *n* a town in central England, in N Leicestershire: university (1966). Pop: 46 867 (1991)

Louis (ˈluːɪs) *n* **Joe,** real name *Joseph Louis Barrow*, nicknamed *the Brown Bomber*. 1914–81, US boxer; world heavyweight champion (1937–49)

Louis I (ˈluːɪ; *French* lwi) *n* known as *Louis the Pious* or *Louis the Debonair*. 778–840 AD, king of France and Holy Roman Emperor (814–23, 830–33, 834–40): he was twice deposed by his sons

Louis II *n* **1** known as *Louis the German*. ?804–876 AD, king of Germany (843–76); son of Louis I **2** 1845–86, king of Bavaria (1864–86): noted for his extravagant castles and his patronage of Wagner. Declared insane (1886), he drowned himself **3 de Bourbon.** See (Prince de) **Condé**

Louis IV *n* known as *Louis the Bavarian*. ?1287–1347, king of Germany (1314–47) and Holy Roman Emperor (1328–47)

Louis V *n* known as *Louis le Fainéant*. ?967–987 AD, last Carolingian king of France (986–87)

Louis VIII *n* known as *Coeur-de-Lion*. 1187–1226, king of France (1223–26). He was offered the English throne by opponents of King John but his invasion failed (1216)

Louis IX *n* known as *Saint Louis*. 1214–70, king of France (1226–70): led the Sixth Crusade (1248–54) and was held to ransom (1250); died at Tunis while on another crusade

Louis XI *n* 1423–83, king of France (1461–83); involved in a struggle with his vassals, esp the duke of Burgundy, in his attempt to unite France under an absolute monarchy

Louis XII *n* 1462–1515, king of France (1498–1515), who fought a series of unsuccessful wars in Italy

Louis XIII *n* 1601–43, king of France (1610–43). His mother (Marie de Médicis) was regent until 1617; after 1624 he was influenced by his chief minister Richelieu

Louis XIV *n* known as *le roi soleil* (the Sun King). 1638–1715, king of France (1643–1715); son of Louis XIII and Anne of Austria. Effective ruler from 1661, he established an absolute monarchy. His attempt to establish French supremacy in Europe, waging almost continual wars from 1667 to 1714, ultimately failed. But his reign is regarded as a golden age of French literature and art

▷ www.parisdigest.com/monument/chateaudeversailles.htm
▷ www.kfki.hu/~arthp/html/l/le_brun
▷ www.encyclopedia.com/html/section/louisper_louisxiv.asp

Louis XV *n* 1710–74, king of France (1715–74); great-grandson of Louis XIV. He engaged France in a series of wars, esp the disastrous Seven Years' War (1756–63), which undermined the solvency and authority of the crown

▷ www.encyclopedia.com/browse/browse-Log.asp

Louis XVI *n* 1754–93, king of France (1774–92); grandson of Louis XV. He married Marie Antoinette in 1770 and they were guillotined during the French Revolution

Louis XVII *n* 1785–95, titular king of France (1793–95) during the Revolution, after the execution of his father Louis XVI; he died in prison

Louis XVIII *n* 1755–1824, king of France (1814–24); younger brother of Louis XVI. He became titular king after the death of Louis XVII (1795) and ascended the throne at the Bourbon restoration in 1814. He was forced to flee during the Hundred Days

Louisbourg (ˈluːɪs,bɜːɡ) *n* a fortress in Canada, in Nova Scotia on SE Cape Breton Island: founded in 1713 by the French and strongly fortified (1720–40); captured by the

British (1758) and demolished; reconstructed as a historic site

louis d'or (ˌluːɪ ˈdɔː) *n, pl* **louis d'or** (ˌluːɪz ˈdɔː) **1** a former French gold coin worth 20 francs **2** an old French coin minted in the reign of Louis XIII. Often shortened to **louis** [c17 from F: golden louis, after Louis XIII]

Louisiana (luːˌiːzɪˈænə) *n* a state of the southern US, on the Gulf of Mexico: originally a French colony; bought by the US in 1803 as part of the Louisiana Purchase; chiefly low-lying. Capital: Baton Rouge. Pop: 4 468 976 (2000). Area: 116 368 sq km (44 930 sq miles). Abbreviations: **La.** or (with zip code) **LA**

Louis Napoleon *n* the original name of **Napoleon III**

Louis Philippe (*French* filip) *n* known as the *Citizen King*. 1773–1850, king of the French (1830–48). His régime became excessively identified with the bourgeoisie and he was forced to abdicate by the revolution of 1848

Louisville (ˈluːɪˌvɪl) *n* a port in N Kentucky, on the Ohio River: site of the annual Kentucky Derby; university (1837). Pop: 256 231 (2000)
▷ www.encyclopedia.com/browse/browse-Log.asp

lounge (laʊndʒ) *vb* **lounges, lounging, lounged 1** (*intr; often foll by about or around*) to sit, lie, walk, or stand in a relaxed manner **2** to pass (time) lazily or idly ▷ *n* **3** a communal room in a hotel, ship, etc, used for waiting or relaxing in **4** *chiefly Brit* a living room in a private house **5** Also called: **lounge bar, saloon** *Brit* a more expensive bar in a pub or hotel **6** a sofa or couch **7** the act or an instance of lounging [c16 from ?]

lounger (ˈlaʊndʒə) *n* **1** a comfortable couch or extending chair designed for someone to relax on **2** a loose comfortable leisure garment **3** a person who lounges

lounge suit *n* a man's suit of matching jacket and trousers worn for the normal business day

loupe (luːp) *n* a small magnifying glass used by jewellers, horologists, etc, worn in the eye socket [c20 from F (formerly an imperfect precious stone), from OF, from ?]

lour *or* **lower** (ˈlaʊə) *vb* (*intr*) **1** (esp of the sky, weather, etc) to be overcast, dark, and menacing **2** to scowl or frown ▷ *n* **3** a menacing scowl or appearance [c13 *louren* to scowl] > ˈ**louring** *or* ˈ**lowering** *adj*

Lourdes (*French* lurd) *n* a town in SW France: a leading place of pilgrimage for Roman Catholics after a peasant girl, Bernadette Soubirous, had visions of the Virgin Mary in 1858. Pop: 17 100 (1995 est)

Lourenço Marques (ləˈrɛnsəʊ ˈmɑːk, ˈmɑːks; *Portuguese* loˈrẽsu ˈmarkɪʃ) *n* the former name (until 1975) of **Maputo**

lourie *or* **loerie** (ˈlaʊrɪ) *n* a type of African bird with bright plumage [from Malay *luri*]

louse (laʊs) *n, pl* **lice 1** a wingless bloodsucking insect, such as the head louse, body louse, and crab louse, all of which infest man **2 biting** *or* **bird louse** a wingless insect, such as the chicken louse: external parasites of birds and mammals, with biting mouthparts **3** any of various similar but unrelated insects **4** (*pl* **louses**) *sl* an unpleasant or mean person ▷ *vb* **louses, lousing, loused** (*tr*) **5** to remove lice from **6** (*foll by up*) *sl* to ruin or spoil [OE *lūs*]

lousewort (ˈlaʊsˌwɜːt) *n* any of various N temperate plants having spikes of white, yellow, or mauve flowers

lousy (ˈlaʊzɪ) *adj* **lousier, lousiest 1** *sl* very mean or unpleasant **2** *sl* inferior or bad **3** infested with lice **4** (*foll by with*) *sl* provided with an excessive amount (of): *he's lousy with money* > ˈ**lousily** *adv* > ˈ**lousiness** *n*

lout (laʊt) *n* a crude or oafish person; boor [c16 ? from OE *lūtan* to stoop] > ˈ**loutish** *adj*

Louth (laʊθ) *n* a county of NE Republic of Ireland, in Leinster province on the Irish Sea: the smallest of the counties. County town: Dundalk. Pop: 92 166 (1996). Area: 821 sq km (317 sq miles)

Louvain (*French* luvɛ̃) *n* a town in central Belgium, in Flemish Brabant province: capital of the duchy of Brabant (11th–15th centuries) and centre of the cloth trade; university (1426). Pop: 87 165 (1995 est). Flemish name: **Leuven**

louvre *or US* **louver** (ˈluːvə) *n* **1a** any of a set of horizontal parallel slats in a door or window, sloping outwards to throw off rain and admit air **1b** Also called: **louvre boards** the slats and frame supporting them **2** *archit* a turret that allows smoke to escape [c14 from OF *lovier*, from ?] > ˈ**louvred** *or US* ˈ**louvered** *adj*

Louvre (*French* luvrə) *n* the national museum and art gallery of France, in Paris: formerly a royal palace, begun in 1546; used for its present purpose since 1793
▷ www.louvre.fr/louvrea.htm
▷ www.paris.org/Musees/Louvre

lovable *or* **loveable** (ˈlʌvəbᵊl) *adj* attracting or deserving affection > ˌ**lovaˈbility**, ˌ**loveaˈbility** *or* ˈ**lovableness**, ˈ**loveableness** *n* > ˈ**lovably** *or* ˈ**loveably** *adv*

lovage (ˈlʌvɪdʒ) *n* a European umbelliferous plant with greenish-white flowers and aromatic fruits, which are used for flavouring food [c14 *loveache*, from OF *luvesche*, from LL *levisticum*, from L *ligusticum*, lit.: Ligurian (plant)]

love (lʌv) *vb* **loves, loving, loved 1** (*tr*) to have a great attachment to and affection for **2** (*tr*) to have passionate desire, longing, and feelings for **3** (*tr*) to like or desire (to do something) very much **4** (*tr*) to make love to **5** (*intr*) to be in love ▷ *n* **6a** an intense emotion of affection, warmth, fondness, and regard towards a person or thing **6b** (*as modifier*): *love story* **7** a deep feeling of sexual attraction and desire **8** wholehearted liking for or pleasure in something **9** *Christianity* God's benevolent attitude towards man **10** Also: **my love** a beloved person: used esp as an endearment **11** *Brit inf* a term of address, not necessarily for a person regarded as likable **12** (in tennis, squash, etc) a score of zero **13 fall in love** to become in love **14 for love** without payment **15 for love or money** (*used with a negative*) in any circumstances: *I would not eat a snail for love or money* **16 for the love of** for the sake of **17 in love** in a state of strong emotional attachment and usually sexual attraction **18 make love (to) 18a** to have sexual intercourse (with) **18b** *now arch* to court [OE *lufu*]

love affair *n* a romantic or sexual relationship, esp temporary, between two people

love apple *n* an archaic name for **tomato**

lovebird (ˈlʌvˌbɜːd) *n* any of several small African parrots often kept as cagebirds

lovebite (ˈlʌvˌbaɪt) *n* a temporary red mark left on a person's skin by a partner's biting or sucking it during lovemaking

love child *n euphemistic* an illegitimate child; bastard

loved-up *adj sl* experiencing feelings of love, through or as if through taking a drug, esp the drug ecstasy

love-in-a-mist *n* an erect S European plant, cultivated as a garden plant, having finely cut leaves and white or pale blue flowers

Lovelace (ˈlʌvˌleɪs) *n* **1 Countess of,** title of *Ada Augusta King*. 1815–52, English mathematician and personal assistant to Charles Babbage: daughter of Lord Byron. She wrote the first computer program **2 Richard** 1618–58, English Cavalier poet, noted for *To Althea from Prison* (1642) and *Lucasta* (1649)

loveless (ˈlʌvlɪs) *adj* **1** without love: *a loveless marriage* **2** receiving or giving no love > ˈ**lovelessly** *adv* > ˈ**lovelessness** *n*

love-lies-bleeding *n* any of several plants having drooping spikes of small red flowers

Lovell (ˈlʌvəl) *n* Sir **Bernard** born 1913, English radio astronomer; founder (1951) and director of Jodrell Bank

lovelock (ˈlʌvˌlɒk) *n* a long lock of hair worn on the forehead

lovelorn (ˈlʌvˌlɔːn) *adj* miserable because of unrequited love or unhappiness in love

Ll

lovely (ˈlʌvlɪ) *adj* **lovelier, loveliest 1** very attractive or beautiful **2** highly pleasing or enjoyable: *a lovely time* **3** inspiring love; lovable ▷ *n, pl* **lovelies 4** *sl* a lovely woman > ˈ**loveliness** *n*

lovemaking (ˈlʌvˌmeɪkɪŋ) *n* **1** sexual play and activity between lovers, esp including sexual intercourse **2** an archaic word for **courtship**

love potion *n* any drink supposed to arouse sexual love in the one who drinks it

lover (ˈlʌvə) *n* **1** a person, now esp a man, who has an extramarital or premarital sexual relationship with another person **2** (*often pl*) either of the two people involved in a love affair **3a** someone who loves a specified person or thing: *a lover of music* **3b** (*in combination*): *a music-lover; a cat-lover*

love seat *n* a small upholstered sofa for two people

lovesick (ˈlʌvˌsɪk) *adj* pining or languishing because of love > ˈ**loveˌsickness** *n*

lovey-dovey (ˌlʌvɪˈdʌvɪ) *adj* making an excessive or ostentatious display of affection

loving (ˈlʌvɪŋ) *adj* feeling or showing love and affection > ˈ**lovingly** *adv* > ˈ**lovingness** *n*

loving cup *n* **1** a large vessel, usually two-handled, out of which people drink in turn at a banquet **2** a similar cup awarded to the winner of a competition

low[1] (ləʊ) *adj* **1** having a relatively small distance from base to top; not tall or high: *a low hill; a low building* **2a** situated at a relatively short distance above the ground, sea level, the horizon, or other reference position: *low cloud* **2b** (*in combination*): *low-lying* **3** of less than usual height, depth, or degree: *low temperature* **4a** (of numbers) small **4b** (of measurements) expressed in small numbers **5a** involving or containing a relatively small amount of something: *a low supply* **5b** (*in combination*): *low-pressure* **6a** having little value or quality **6b** (*in combination*): *low-grade* **7** coarse or vulgar: *a low conversation* **8a** inferior in culture or status **8b** (*in combination*): *low-class* **9** in a physically or mentally depressed or weakened state **10** low-necked: *a low dress* **11** with a hushed tone; quiet or soft: *a low whisper* **12** of relatively small price or monetary value: *low cost* **13** *music* relating to or characterized by a relatively low pitch **14** (of latitudes) situated not far north or south of the equator **15** having little or no money **16** abject or servile **17** unfavourable: *a low opinion* **18** not advanced in evolution: *a low form of plant life* **19** deep: *a low bow* **20** *phonetics* of, relating to, or denoting a vowel whose articulation is produced by moving the back of the tongue away from the soft palate, such as for the *a* in English *father* **21** (of a gear) providing a relatively low forward speed for a given engine speed **22** (*usually cap*) of or relating to the Low Church ▷ *adv* **23** in a low position, level, degree, intensity, etc: *to bring someone low* **24** at a low pitch; deep: *to sing low* **25** at a low price; cheaply: *to buy low* **26 lay low 26a** to cause to fall by a blow **26b** to overcome, defeat, or destroy **27 lie low 27a** to keep or be concealed or quiet **27b** to wait for a favourable opportunity ▷ *n* **28** a low position, level, or degree: *an all-time low* **29** an area of relatively low atmospheric pressure, esp a depression [C12 *lāh*, from ON *lāgr*] > ˈ**lowness** *n*

low[2] (ləʊ) *n also* **lowing 1** the sound uttered by cattle; moo ▷ *vb* **2** to make or express by a low or moo [OE *hlōwan*]

Low (ləʊ) *n* Sir **David** 1891–1963, British political cartoonist, born in New Zealand: created Colonel Blimp. See **blimp**[2]

low-alcohol *adj* (of beer or wine) containing only a small amount of alcohol ▷ Cf **alcohol-free**

lowan (ˈləʊən) *n* another name for **mallee fowl** [from Abor.]

Low Archipelago *n* another name for the **Tuamotu Archipelago**

lowborn (ˌləʊˈbɔːn) *or* **lowbred** (ˌləʊˈbrɛd) *adj now rare* of ignoble or common parentage

lowbrow (ˈləʊˌbraʊ) *disparaging* ▷ *n* **1** a person who has uncultivated or nonintellectual tastes ▷ *adj also* **lowbrowed 2** of or characteristic of such a person

Low Church *n* **1** the school of thought in the Church of England stressing evangelical beliefs and practices ▷ *adj* **Low-Church 2** of or relating to this school

low comedy *n* comedy characterized by slapstick and physical action

low-context *adj* tending to communicate by electronic methods such as e-mail, rather than in person ▷ Cf **high-context**

Low Countries *pl n* the lowland region of W Europe, on the North Sea: consists of Belgium, Luxembourg, and the Netherlands

low-density lipoprotein *n* a lipoprotein that is the form in which cholesterol is transported in the bloodstream. High levels in the blood are associated with atheroma. Abbrev: **LDL**

low-down *inf* ▷ *adj* **1** mean, underhand, or despicable ▷ *n* **lowdown 2 the** information

Löwe (*German* ˈløːvə) *n* See (Karl) **Loewe**

Lowell (ˈləʊəl) *n* **1 Amy** (**Lawrence**) 1874–1925, US imagist poet and critic **2 James Russell** 1819–91, US poet, essayist, and diplomat, noted for his series of poems in Yankee dialect, *Biglow Papers* (1848; 1867) **3 Robert** (**Traill Spence**) 1917–77, US poet. His volumes of verse include *Lord Weary's Castle* (1946), *Life Studies* (1959), *For the Union Dead* (1964), and a book of free translations of European poems, *Imitations* (1961)

lower[1] (ˈləʊə) *adj* **1** being below one or more other things: *the lower shelf* **2** reduced in amount or value: *a lower price* **3** *maths* (of a limit or bound) less than or equal to one or more numbers or variables **4** (*sometimes cap*) *geol* denoting the early part of a period, formation, etc: *Lower Silurian* ▷ *vb* **5** (*tr*) to cause to become low or on a lower level; bring, put, or cause to move down **6** (*tr*) to reduce or bring down in estimation, dignity, value, etc: *to lower oneself* **7** to reduce or be reduced: *to lower one's confidence* **8** (*tr*) to make quieter: *to lower the radio* **9** (*tr*) to reduce the pitch of **10** (*intr*) to diminish or become less [C12 (comp. of LOW[1]); C17 (vb)]

lower[2] (ˈlaʊə) *vb* a variant of **lour**

Lower Austria *n* a state of NE Austria: the largest Austrian province, containing most of the Vienna basin. Capital: Sankt Pölten. Pop: 1 549 640 (2001). Area: 19 170 sq km (7476 sq miles). German name: **Niederösterreich**

Lower California *n* a mountainous peninsula of NW Mexico, between the Pacific and the Gulf of California: administratively divided into the states of Baja California and Baja California Sur. Spanish name: **Baja California**

Lower Canada *n* (from 1791 to 1841) the official name of the S region of the present-day province of Quebec ▷ Cf **Upper Canada**

lower case *n* **1** the bottom half of a compositor's type case, in which the small letters are kept ▷ *adj* **lower-case 2** of or relating to small letters ▷ *vb* **lower-case, lower-cases, lower-casing, lower-cased 3** (*tr*) to print with lower-case letters

lower chamber *n* another name for a **lower house**

lower class *n* **1** the social stratum having the lowest position in the social hierarchy ▷ *adj* **lower-class 2** of or relating to the lower class **3** inferior or vulgar.

lowerclassman (ˌləʊˈklɑːsmən) *n, pl* **lowerclassmen** *US* a freshman or sophomore. Also called: **underclassman**

lower deck *n* **1** the deck of a ship situated immediately above the hold **2** *inf* the petty officers and seamen of a ship collectively

Lower Egypt *n* one of the two main administrative districts of Egypt: consists of the Nile Delta

lower house *n* one of the houses of a bicameral legislature: usually the larger and more representative. Also called: **lower chamber**

Lower Hutt (hʌt) *n* an industrial town in New Zealand on the S coast of North Island. Pop: 62 900 (latest est)

Lower Lakes *pl n chiefly Canad* Lakes Erie and Ontario

lowermost ('ləʊə,məʊst) *adj* lowest

lower regions *pl n* (usually preceded by *the*) hell

Lower Saxony *n* a state of N Germany, on the North Sea and including the E Frisian Islands; formerly in West Germany: a leading European producer of petroleum. Capital: Hanover. Pop: 7 898 800 (2000 est). Area: 47 408 sq km (18 489 sq miles). German name: **Niedersachsen**

lower world *n* **1** the earth as opposed to heaven **2** another name for **hell**

lowest common denominator *n* the smallest integer or polynomial that is exactly divisible by each denominator of a set of fractions. Abbrevs: **lcd, LCD.** Also called: **least common denominator**

lowest common multiple *n* the smallest number or quantity that is exactly divisible by each member of a set of numbers or quantities. Abbrevs: **lcm, LCM.** Also called: **least common multiple**

Lowestoft ('ləʊstɒft) *n* a fishing port and resort in E England, in NE Suffolk on the North Sea. Pop: 62 907 (1991)

low frequency *n* a radio-frequency band or a frequency lying between 300 and 30 kilohertz

Low German *n* a language of N Germany, spoken esp in rural areas: more closely related to Dutch than to standard High German. Abbrev: **LG.** Also called: **Plattdeutsch**

low-key *or* **low-keyed** *adj* **1** having a low intensity or tone **2** restrained or subdued **3** (of a photograph, painting, etc) having a predominance of dark grey tones or dark colours with few highlights ▷ Cf **high-key**

lowland ('ləʊlənd) *n* **1** relatively low ground **2** (*often pl*) a low generally flat region ▷ *adj* **3** of or relating to a lowland or lowlands > '**lowlander** *n*

Lowland ('ləʊlənd) *adj* of or relating to the Lowlands of Scotland or the dialects of English spoken there

Lowlands ('ləʊləndz) *pl n* **the** a low, generally flat region of S central Scotland, around the Forth and Clyde valleys, separating the Southern Uplands from the Highlands > '**Lowlander** *n*

Low Latin *n* any form of Latin other than the classical, such as Medieval Latin

low-level language *n* a computer programming language that is closer to machine language than to human language

low-level waste *n* waste material contaminated by traces of radioactivity that can be disposed of in steel drums in concrete-lined trenches ▷ Cf **high-level waste, intermediate-level waste**

lowlife ('ləʊ,laɪf) *n, pl* **lowlifes** *sl* a member or members of the criminal underworld

low-loader *n* a road or rail vehicle with a low platform for ease of access

lowly ('ləʊlɪ) *adj* **lowlier, lowliest 1** humble or low in position, rank, status, etc **2** full of humility; meek **3** simple, unpretentious, or plain ▷ *adv* **4** in a low or lowly manner > '**lowliness** *n*

Low Mass *n* a Mass that has a simplified ceremonial form and is spoken rather than sung

low-minded *adj* having a vulgar or crude mind and character > ,**low-'mindedly** *adv* > ,**low-'mindedness** *n*

low-pass filter *n electronics* a filter that transmits all frequencies below a specified value, attenuating frequencies above this value

low-pitched *adj* **1** pitched low in tone **2** (of a roof) having sides with a shallow slope

low-pressure *adj* **1** having, using, or involving a pressure below normal: *a low-pressure gas* **2** relaxed or calm: *a job in a low-pressure environment*

low profile *n* **1** a position or attitude characterized by a deliberate avoidance of prominence or publicity ▷ *adj* **low-profile 2** (of a tyre) wide in relation to its height

low-rise *adj* **1** of or relating to a building having only a few storeys ▷ *n* **2** such a building

lowry *or* **lowrie** ('laʊrɪ) *n* variant spellings of **lory**

Lowry ('laʊrɪ) *n* **1 L(awrence) S(tephen)** 1887–1976, English painter, noted for his bleak northern industrial scenes, often containing primitive or stylized figures **2 (Clarence) Malcolm** 1909–57, British novelist and writer, best known for his semiautobiographical novel *Under the Volcano* (1947)

low-spirited *adj* depressed or dejected > ,**low-'spiritedly** *adv* > ,**low-'spiritedness** *n*

low tech *n* **1** short for **low technology 2** a style of interior design using items associated with low technology ▷ *adj* **low-tech 3** of or using low technology **4** of or in the interior design style ▷ Cf **hi tech**

low technology *n* simple unsophisticated technology that is limited to the production of basic necessities

low-tension *adj* subjected to, carrying, or operating at a low voltage. Abbrev: **LT**

low tide *n* **1** the tide when it is at its lowest level or the time at which it reaches this **2** a lowest point

Lowveld ('ləʊ,fɛlt, -,vɛlt) *n* **the** another name for **Bushveld**

low water *n* **1** another name for **low tide 2** the state of any stretch of water at its lowest level

low-water mark *n* **1** the level reached at low tide **2** the lowest point or level; nadir

lox[1] (lɒks) *n* a kind of smoked salmon [C19 from Yiddish *laks*, from MHG *lahs* salmon]

lox[2] (lɒks) *n* short for **liquid oxygen,** esp when used as an oxidizer for rocket fuels

loyal ('lɔɪəl) *adj* **1** showing allegiance **2** faithful to one's country, government, etc **3** of or expressing loyalty [C16 from OF *loial, leial*, from L *lēgālis* LEGAL] > '**loyally** *adv*

loyalist ('lɔɪəlɪst) *n* a patriotic supporter of his or her sovereign or government > '**loyalism** *n*

Loyalist ('lɔɪəlɪst) *n* **1** (in Northern Ireland) any of the Protestants wishing to retain Ulster's link with Britain **2** (in North America) an American colonist who supported Britain during the War of American Independence **3** (in Canada) short for **United Empire Loyalist 4** (during the Spanish Civil War) a supporter of the republican government

loyalty ('lɔɪəltɪ) *n, pl* **loyalties 1** the state or quality of being loyal **2** (*often pl*) allegiance

loyalty card *n* a swipe card issued by a supermarket or chain store to a customer, used to record credit points awarded for money spent in the store

Loyang ('ləʊ'jæŋ) *n* a variant transliteration of the Chinese name for **Luoyang**

Loyola (lɔɪ'əʊlə) *n* See (Saint) **Ignatius Loyola**

lozenge ('lɒzɪndʒ) *n* **1** *med* a medicated tablet held in the mouth until it has dissolved **2** *geom* another name for **rhombus 3** *heraldry* a diamond-shaped charge [C14 from OF *losange* of Gaulish origin] > '**lozenged** *or* '**lozengy** *adj*

Lozère (*French* lɔzɛr) *n* a department of S central France, in Languedoc-Roussillon region. Capital: Mende. Pop: 73 509 (1999). Area: 5180 sq km (2020 sq miles)

LP[1] *n* **1a** a long-playing gramophone record, usually 12 inches (30 cm) in diameter, designed to rotate at 33⅓ revolutions per minute **1b** (*as modifier*): *an LP sleeve* **2** long play: a slow-recording facility on a VCR which allows twice the length of material to be recorded on a tape from that of standard play

LP[2] *abbrev for*: **1** (in Britain) Lord Provost **2** Also: **lp** low pressure

L/P *printing abbrev for* letterpress

Ll

LPG *or* **LP gas** *abbrev for* liquefied petroleum gas
L-plate *n Brit* a white rectangle with an "L" sign fixed to the back and front of a motor vehicle; a red "L" sign shows that the driver has not passed the driving test; a green "L" sign may be displayed by new drivers for up to a year after passing the driving test
Lr *the chemical symbol for* lawrencium
LSD *n* lysergic acid diethylamide; a crystalline compound prepared from lysergic acid, used in experimental medicine and taken illegally as a hallucinogenic drug. Informal name: **acid**
L.S.D., £.s.d., *or* **l.s.d.** (in Britain, esp formerly) *abbrev for* librae, solidi, denarii [L: pounds, shillings, pence]
LSE *abbrev for* London School of Economics
LSO *abbrev for* London Symphony Orchestra
Lt *abbrev for* Lieutenant
Ltd *or* **ltd** *abbrev for* limited (liability). US equivalent: **Inc**
LTNS *text messaging abbrev for* long time no see
LTSA (in New Zealand) *abbrev for* Land Transport Safety Authority
Lu *the chemical symbol for* lutetium
Lualaba (ˌluːəˈlɑːbə) *n* a river in the SE Democratic Republic of Congo (formerly Zaïre), rising in Shaba province and flowing north as the W headstream of the River Congo. Length: about 1800 km (1100 miles)
Luanda *or* **Loanda** (lʊˈændə) *n* the capital of Angola, a port in the west, on the Atlantic: founded in 1576, it became a centre of the slave trade to Brazil in the 17th and 18th centuries; oil refining. Pop: 2 255 000 (1999 est). Official name: **São Paulo de Loanda**
▹ www.angola.org/referenc/luanda.html
Luang Prabang (luːˈæŋ prɑːˈbæŋ) *n* a market town in N Laos, on the Mekong River: residence of the monarch of Laos (1946–75). Pop: 59 800 (1995 est)
luau (luːˈaʊ, ˈluːaʊ) *n* a feast of Hawaiian food [from Hawaiian *lu'au*]
lubber (ˈlʌbə) *n* **1** a big, awkward, or stupid person **2** short for **landlubber** [c14 *lobre*, prob. from ON] > ˈ**lubberly** *adj, adv* > ˈ**lubberliness** *n*
lubber line *n* a mark on a ship's compass that designates the fore-and-aft axis of the vessel. Also called: **lubber's line**
Lubbock (ˈlʌbək) *n* a city in NW Texas: cotton market. Pop: 199 564 (2000)
Lübeck (*German* ˈlyːbɛk) *n* a port in N Germany, in Schleswig-Holstein on the Baltic: the leading member of the Hanseatic League, and a major European commercial centre until the 15th century. Pop: 213 800 (1999 est)
Lublin (*Polish* ˈlublin) *n* an industrial city in E Poland: provisional seat of the government in 1918 and 1944. Pop: 356 251 (1999 est). Russian name: **Lyublin**
lubra (ˈluːbrə) *n Austral* an Aboriginal woman [c19 from Abor.]
lubricant (ˈluːbrɪkənt) *n* **1** a lubricating substance, such as oil ▹ *adj* **2** serving to lubricate [c19 from L *lūbricāns*, present participle of *lūbricāre*]
lubricate (ˈluːbrɪˌkeɪt) *vb* **lubricates, lubricating, lubricated 1** (*tr*) to cover or treat with an oily substance so as to lessen friction **2** (*tr*) to make greasy, slippery, or smooth **3** (*intr*) to act as a lubricant [c17 from L *lūbricāre*, from *lūbricus* slippery] > ˌ**lubriˈcation** *n* > ˈ**lubriˌcative** *adj* > ˈ**lubriˌcator** *n*
lubricity (luːˈbrɪsɪtɪ) *n* **1** *formal or literary* lewdness or salaciousness **2** *rare* smoothness or slipperiness [c15 (lewdness), c17 (slipperiness): from OF *lubricité*, from Med. L *lubricitās*, from L, from *lūbricus* slippery] > **lubricious** (luːˈbrɪʃəs) *or* **lubricous** (ˈluːbrɪkəs) *adj*
Lubumbashi (ˌluːbʊmˈbæʃɪ) *n* a city in the S Democratic Republic of Congo (formerly Zaïre): founded in 1910 as a copper-mining centre; university (1955). Pop: 851 381 (1994 est). Former name (until 1966): **Elisabethville**
Lucan (ˈluːkən) *n* Latin name *Marcus Annaeus Lucanus*. 39–65 AD, Roman poet. His epic poem *Pharsalia* describes the civil war between Caesar and Pompey
Lucania (luːˈkeɪnɪə) *n* the Latin name for **Basilicata**
Lucas (ˈluːkəs) *n* **George** born 1944, US film director, producer, and writer of screenplays. Films as director include *American Graffiti* (1973) and *Star Wars* (1977) and its prequels *The Phantom Menace* (1999) and *Attack of the Clones* (2002)
Lucas van Leyden (ˈluːkəs væn ˈlaɪdᵊn) *n* ?1494–1533, Dutch painter and engraver
Lucca (*Italian* ˈlukka) *n* a city in NW Italy, in Tuscany: centre of a rich agricultural region, noted for the production of olive oil. Pop: 86 676 (1990 est). Ancient name: **Luca** (ˈluːkə)
luce (luːs) *n* another name for the **pike** (the fish) [c14 from OF *lus*, from LL *lūcius* pike]
lucent (ˈluːsᵊnt) *adj* brilliant, shining, or translucent [c16 from L *lūcēns*, present participle of *lūcēre* to shine] > ˈ**lucency** *n* > ˈ**lucently** *adv*
lucerne (luːˈsɜːn) *n Brit* another name for **alfalfa**
Lucerne (luːˈsɜːn; *French* lysɛrn) *n* **1** a canton in central Switzerland, northwest of Lake Lucerne: joined the Swiss Confederacy in 1332. Pop: 345 400 (2000 est). Area: 1494 sq km (577 sq miles) **2** a city in central Switzerland, capital of Lucerne canton, on Lake Lucerne: tourist centre. Pop: 60 600 (latest est) **3 Lake** a lake in central Switzerland: fed and drained chiefly by the River Reuss. Area: 115 sq km (44 sq miles). German name: **Vierwaldstättersee.** German name (for senses 1 and 2): **Luzern**
Lucian (ˈluːsɪən) *n* 2nd century AD, Greek writer, noted esp for his satirical *Dialogues of the Gods* and *Dialogues of the Dead*
lucid (ˈluːsɪd) *adj* **1** readily understood; clear **2** shining or glowing **3** of or relating to a period of normality between periods of insane behaviour [c16 from L *lūcidus* full of light, from *lūx* light] > **luˈcidity** *or* ˈ**lucidness** *n* > ˈ**lucidly** *adv*
lucifer (ˈluːsɪfə) *n* a friction match: originally a trade name
Lucifer (ˈluːsɪfə) *n* **1** the leader of the rebellion of the angels; Satan **2** the planet Venus when it rises as the morning star [OE, from L *Lūcifer* light-bearer, from *lūx* light + *ferre* to bear]
Lucilius (luːˈsɪlɪəs) *n* **Gaius** (ˈgaɪəs) ?180–102 BC, Roman satirist, regarded as the originator of poetical satire
Lucina (luːˈsaɪnə) *n Roman myth* a title or name given to Juno as goddess of childbirth [c14 from L *lūcīnus* bringing to the light, from *lūx* light]
luck (lʌk) *n* **1** events that are beyond control and seem subject to chance; fortune **2** success or good fortune **3** something considered to bring good luck **4 down on one's luck** having little or no good luck to the point of suffering hardships **5 no such luck** *inf* unfortunately not **6 try one's luck** to attempt something that is uncertain [c15 from MDu. *luc*]
luckless (ˈlʌklɪs) *adj* having no luck; unlucky > ˈ**lucklessly** *adv* > ˈ**lucklessness** *n*
Lucknow (ˈlʌknaʊ) *n* a city in N India, capital of Uttar Pradesh: capital of Oudh (1775–1856); the British residency was besieged (1857) during the Indian Mutiny. Pop: 1 619 115 (1991)
luck out *vb* (*intr, adv*) to have good fortune; be lucky: *he'd lucked out by marrying Serena*
lucky (ˈlʌkɪ) *adj* **luckier, luckiest 1** having or bringing good fortune **2** happening by chance, esp as desired > ˈ**luckily** *adv* > ˈ**luckiness** *n*
Lucky Country *n Austral sl* a jocular name for **Australia**
lucky dip *n Brit, Austral, & NZ* **1** a box filled with sawdust containing small prizes for which children search **2** *inf* an undertaking of uncertain outcome
lucrative (ˈluːkrətɪv) *adj* producing a profit; profitable [c15 from OF *lucratif*; see LUCRE] > ˈ**lucratively** *adv*

lucre ('lu:kə) *n usually facetious* money or wealth (esp in **filthy lucre**) [c14 from L *lūcrum* gain]
Lucretia (lu:'kri:ʃɪə) *n* (in Roman legend) a Roman woman who killed herself after being raped by a son of Tarquin the Proud
Lucretius (lu:'kri:ʃɪəs) *n* full name *Titus Lucretius Carus*. ?96–55 BC, Roman poet and philosopher. In his didactic poem *De rerum natura*, he expounds Epicurus' atomist theory of the universe
lucubrate ('lu:kjʊˌbreɪt) *vb* **lucubrates, lucubrating, lucubrated** (*intr*) to write or study, esp at night [c17 from L *lūcubrāre* to work by lamplight] > **'lucuˌbrator** *n*
lucubration (ˌlu:kjʊ'breɪʃən) *n* **1** laborious study, esp at night **2** (*often pl*) a solemn literary work
Lucullus (lu:'kʌləs) *n* **Lucius Licinius** ('lu:sɪəs lɪ'sɪnɪəs) ?110–56 BC, Roman general and consul, famous for his luxurious banquets. He fought Mithradates VI (74–66) > **Lu'cullan, Lucullean** (ˌlu:kʌ'lɪən), *or* **ˌLucul'lian** *adj*
Lucy ('lu:sɪ) *n* **Saint** died ?303 AD, a virgin martyred by Diocletian in Syracuse. Feast day: Dec 13
lud (lʌd) *n Brit* lord (in **my lud, m'lud**): used when addressing a judge in court
Lüda ('lu:'dɑ:) *or* **Lü-ta** *n* a port in NE China, in S Liaoning province, comprising the two cities of Lü-shun and Dalian at the S end of the Liaodong peninsula: the chief northern port. Pop: 2 400 000 (1991 est)
Luddite ('lʌdaɪt) *n Brit history* **1** any of the textile workers opposed to mechanization, believing that its use led to unemployment, who organized machine-breaking between 1811 and 1816 **2** any opponent of industrial change or innovation ▷ *adj* **3** of or relating to the Luddites [c19 alleged to be after Ned *Ludd*, an 18th-century Leicestershire workman, who destroyed industrial machinery]
Ludendorff (*German* 'lu:dəndɔrf) *n* **Erich Friedrich Wilhelm von** ('e:rɪç 'fri:drɪç 'vɪlhɛlm fɔn) 1865–1937, German general, Hindenburg's aide in World War I
Lüdenscheid (*German* 'ly:dənʃait) *n* a city in W Germany, in North Rhine-Westphalia: manufacturing centre for aluminium and plastics. Pop: 76 110 (latest est)
Lüderitz (*German* 'ly:dərɪts) *n* a port in Namibia: diamond-mining centre. Pop: 6000 (1990)
Ludhiana (ˌlʊdɪ'ɑ:nə) *n* a city in N India, in the central Punjab: Punjab Agricultural University (1962). Pop: 1 042 740 (1991)
ludicrous ('lu:dɪkrəs) *adj* absurd or incongruous to the point of provoking laughter [c17 from L *lūdicrus* done in sport, from *lūdus* game] > **'ludicrously** *adv* > **'ludicrousness** *n*
Ludlow ('lʌdləʊ) *n* a market town in W central England, in Shropshire: castle (11th–16th century). Pop: 9040 (1991)
ludo ('lu:dəʊ) *n Brit* a simple board game in which players advance their counters by throwing dice [c19 from L: I play]
Ludwigsburg (*German* 'lu:tvɪçsbʊrk) *n* a city in SW Germany, in Baden-Württemberg north of Stuttgart: expanded in the 18th century around the palace of the dukes of Württemberg. Pop: 79 340 (latest est)
Ludwigshafen (*German* 'lu:tvɪçsha:fən) *n* a city in SW Germany, in the Rhineland-Palatinate, on the Rhine: chemical industry. Pop: 164 200 (1999 est)
luff (lʌf) *n* **1** *naut* the leading edge of a fore-and-aft sail ▷ *vb* **2** *naut* to head (a sailing vessel) into the wind so that her sails flap **3** (*intr*) *naut* (of a sail) to flap when the wind is blowing equally on both sides **4** to move the jib of (a crane) in order to shift a load [c13 (in the sense: steering gear): from OF *lof*, ?from MDu. *loef* peg of a tiller]
lug[1] (lʌg) *vb* **lugs, lugging, lugged** **1** to carry or drag (something heavy) with great effort **2** (*tr*) to introduce (an irrelevant topic) into a conversation or discussion ▷ *n* **3** the act or an instance of lugging [c14 prob. from ON]
lug[2] (lʌg) *n* **1** a projecting piece by which something is connected, supported, or lifted **2** a box or basket for vegetables or fruit **3** *inf or Scot* another word for **ear**[1] **4** *sl* a man, esp a stupid or awkward one [c15 (Scots dialect) *lugge* ear]
lug[3] (lʌg) *n naut* short for **lugsail**
Lugano (lʊ'gɑ:nəʊ) *n* a town in S Switzerland, on Lake Lugano: a financial centre and tourist resort. Pop: 26 800 (1995 est)
Lugansk (*Russian* lu'gansk) *n* an industrial city in the E Ukraine, in the Donbass mining region: established in 1795 as an iron-founding centre. Pop: 475 300 (1998 est). Former name (1935–91): **Voroshilovgrad**
luge (lu:ʒ) *n* **1** a racing toboggan on which riders lie on their backs, descending feet first ▷ *vb* **luges, luging, luged** **2** (*intr*) to ride or race on a luge [c20 from F]
▷ www.fil-luge.org
Luger ('lu:gə) *n trademark* a German 9 mm calibre automatic pistol
luggage ('lʌgɪdʒ) *n* suitcases, trunks, etc [c16 ? from LUG[1], infl. in form by BAGGAGE]
luggage van *n Brit* a railway carriage used to transport passengers' luggage, bicycles, etc
lugger ('lʌgə) *n naut* a small working boat rigged with a lugsail [c18 from LUGSAIL]
lughole ('lʌgˌhəʊl) *n Brit* an informal word for **ear**[1]. See also **lug**[2] (sense 3)
Lugo (*Spanish* 'luɣo) *n* a city in NW Spain: Roman walls; Romanesque cathedral. Pop: 86 658 (1991). Latin name: **Lucus Augusti** ('lu:kəs aʊ'gu:sti:, ɔ:'gʌsti:)
lugsail ('lʌgsəl) *n naut* a four-sided sail bent and hoisted on a yard [c17 ?from ME (now dialect) *lugge* pole, or from *lugge* ear]
lug screw *n* a small screw without a head
lugubrious (lʊ'gu:brɪəs) *adj* excessively mournful; doleful [c17 from L *lūgubris* mournful, from *lūgēre* to grieve] > **lu'gubriously** *adv* > **lu'gubriousness** *n*
lugworm ('lʌgˌwɜ:m) *n* a worm living in burrows on sandy shores and having tufted gills: much used as bait. Sometimes shortened to **lug** [c17 from ?]
Luhrmann ('lʊəmən) *n* **Baz** (**Mark Anthony**) born 1962, Australian film director and screenwriter; his films include *Strictly Ballroom* (1992), *Romeo and Juliet* (1996), and *Moulin Rouge* (2001)
Luichow Peninsula ('lu:'tʃaʊ) *n* a variant transliteration of the Chinese name for **Leizhou Peninsula**
Luik (lœik) *n* the Flemish name for **Liège**
Lukács ('lu:kætʃ) *n* **Georg** ('geɪɔ:k), original name *György*. 1885–1971, Hungarian Marxist philosopher and literary critic, whose works include *History and Class Consciousness* (1923), *Studies in European Realism* (1946), and *The Historical Novel* (1955)
Luke (lu:k) *n New Testament* **1** **Saint** a fellow worker of Paul and a physician (Colossians 4:14). Feast day: Oct 18 **2** the third Gospel, traditionally ascribed to Luke. Related adj: **Lucan**
lukewarm (ˌlu:k'wɔ:m) *adj* **1** (esp of water) moderately warm; tepid **2** having or expressing little enthusiasm or conviction [c14 *luke* prob. from OE *hlēow* warm] > **ˌluke'warmly** *adv* > **ˌluke'warmness** *n*
Luleå (*Swedish* 'lu:ləo:) *n* a port in N Sweden, on the Gulf of Bothnia: industrial and shipbuilding centre; icebound in winter. Pop: 70 694 (1994)
lull (lʌl) *vb* (*tr*) **1** to soothe (a person or animal) by soft sounds or motions (esp in **lull to sleep**) **2** to calm (someone or someone's fears, suspicions, etc), esp by deception: *people have been lulled into complacency* ▷ *n* **3** a short period of calm or diminished activity [c14 ? imit. of crooning sounds; rel. to MLow G *lollen* to soothe, MDu. *lollen* to talk drowsily, mumble]
lullaby ('lʌləˌbaɪ) *n, pl* **lullabies** **1** a quiet song to lull a child to sleep ▷ *vb* **lullabies, lullabying, lullabied** **2** (*tr*) to

Ll

quiet or soothe as with a lullaby [C16 ? a blend of LULL + GOODBYE]

Lully *n* **1** (*French* lyli) **Jean Baptiste** (ʒɑ̃ batist), Italian name *Giovanni Battista Lulli.* 1632–87, French composer, born in Italy; founder of French opera. With Philippe Quinault as librettist, he wrote operas such as *Alceste* (1674) and *Armide* (1686); as superintendent of music at the court of Louis XIV, he wrote incidental music to comedies by Molière **2** ('lʌlɪ) Also: **Lull** (*Spanish* lul) **Raymond** *or* **Ramón** (ra'mɔn) ?1235–1315, Spanish philosopher, mystic, and missionary. His chief works are *Ars generalis sive magna* and the Utopian novel *Blaquerna*

Luluabourg (luː'luːə,bʊə) *n* the former name (until 1966) of **Kananga**

lumbago (lʌm'beɪgəʊ) *n* pain in the lower back; backache [C17 from LL, from L *lumbus* loin]

lumbar ('lʌmbə) *adj* of, near, or relating to the part of the body between the lowest ribs and the hipbones [C17 from NL *lumbāris,* from L *lumbus* loin]

lumbar puncture *n med* insertion of a hollow needle into the lower spinal cord to withdraw cerebrospinal fluid, introduce drugs, etc

lumber[1] ('lʌmbə) *n* **1** *chiefly US & Canad* **1a** logs; sawn timber **1b** (*as modifier*): *the lumber trade* **2** *Brit* **2a** useless household articles that are stored away **2b** (*as modifier*): *lumber room* ▷ *vb* **3** (*tr*) to pile together in a disorderly manner **4** (*tr*) to fill up or encumber with useless household articles **5** *chiefly US & Canad* to convert (the trees) of (a forest) into marketable timber **6** (*tr*) *Brit inf* to burden with something unpleasant, tedious, etc [C17 ?from a n use of LUMBER[2]] > '**lumberer** *n* > '**lumbering** *n*

lumber[2] ('lʌmbə) *vb* (*intr*) **1** to move or proceed in an awkward heavy manner **2** an obsolete word for **rumble** [C14 *lomeren*] > '**lumbering** *adj*

lumberjack ('lʌmbə,dʒæk) *n* (esp in North America) a person whose work involves felling trees, transporting the timber, etc [C19 from LUMBER[1] + JACK (man)]

lumberjacket ('lʌmbə,dʒækɪt) *n* a boldly coloured, usually checked jacket in warm cloth

lumberyard ('lʌmbə,jɑːd) *n* the US and Canad word for **timberyard**

lumen ('luːmɪn) *n, pl* **lumens** *or* **lumina** (-mɪnə) **1** the derived SI unit of luminous flux; the flux emitted in a solid angle of 1 steradian by a point source having a uniform intensity of 1 candela. Symbol: lm **2** *anat* a passage, duct, or cavity in a tubular organ **3** a cavity within a plant cell [C19 NL, from L: light, aperture] > '**luminal** *adj*

Lumière (*French* lymjɛr) *n* **Auguste Marie Louis Nicolas** (ogyst mari lwi nikɔla) 1862–1954, and his brother, **Louis Jean** (lwi ʒɑ̃), 1864–1948, French chemists and cinema pioneers, who invented a cinematograph and a process of colour photography

luminance ('luːmɪnəns) *n* **1** a state or quality of radiating or reflecting light **2** a measure (in candelas per square metre) of the brightness of a point on a surface that is radiating or reflecting light. Symbol: *L* [C19 from L *lūmen* light]

luminary ('luːmɪnərɪ) *n, pl* **luminaries** **1** a person who enlightens or influences others **2** a famous person **3** *literary* something, such as the sun or moon, that gives off light [C15 via OF, from L *lūmināre* lamp, from *lūmen* light]

luminesce (,luːmɪ'nɛs) *vb* **luminesces, luminescing, luminesced** (*intr*) to exhibit luminescence [back formation from LUMINESCENT]

luminescence (,luːmɪ'nɛsəns) *n physics* the emission of light at low temperatures by any process other than incandescence [C19 from L *lūmen* light] > ,**lumi'nescent** *adj*

luminous ('luːmɪnəs) *adj* **1** radiating or reflecting light; shining; glowing: *luminous colours* **2** (*not in technical use*) exhibiting luminescence: *luminous paint* **3** full of light; well-lit **4** (of a physical quantity in photometry) evaluated according to the visual sensation produced in an observer rather than by absolute energy measurements: *luminous intensity* **5** easily understood; lucid; clear **6** enlightening or wise [C15 from L *lūminōsus* full of light, from *lūmen* light] > **luminosity** (,luːmɪ'nɒsɪtɪ) *n* > '**luminously** *adv* > '**luminousness** *n*

luminous flux *n* a measure of the rate of flow of luminous energy, evaluated according to its ability to produce a visual sensation. It is measured in lumens

luminous intensity *n* a measure of the amount of light that a point source radiates in a given direction

lumme *or* **lummy** ('lʌmɪ) *interj Brit* an exclamation of surprise or dismay [C19 alteration of *Lord love me*]

lummox ('lʌməks) *n inf* a clumsy or stupid person [C19 from ?]

lump[1] (lʌmp) *n* **1** a small solid mass without definite shape **2** *pathol* any small swelling or tumour **3** a collection of things; aggregate **4** *inf* an awkward, heavy, or stupid person **5** **the lump** *Brit* self-employed workers in the building trade considered collectively **6** (*modifier*) in the form of a lump or lumps: *lump sugar* **7** **a lump in one's throat** a tight dry feeling in one's throat, usually caused by great emotion **8** **in the lump** collectively; en masse ▷ *vb* **9** (*tr; often foll by together*) to collect into a mass or group **10** (*intr*) to grow into lumps or become lumpy **11** (*tr*) to consider as a single group, often without justification **12** (*tr*) to make or cause lumps in or on **13** (*intr; often foll by along*) to move in a heavy manner [C13 prob. rel. to early Du. *lompe* piece, Scand. dialect *lump* block, MHG *lumpe* rag]

lump[2] (lʌmp) *vb* (*tr*) *inf* to tolerate or put up with; endure (in **lump it**) [C16 from ?]

lumpectomy (lʌm'pɛktəmɪ) *n, pl* **lumpectomies** the surgical removal of a tumour in a breast [C20 from LUMP[1] + -ECTOMY]

lumpen ('lʌmpᵊn) *adj inf* stupid or unthinking [from G *Lump* vagabond, infl. by *Lumpen* rags, as in LUMPENPROLETARIAT]

lumpenproletariat (,lʌmpən,prəʊlɪ'tɛərɪət) *n* (esp in Marxist theory) the urban social group below the proletariat, consisting of criminals, tramps, etc [G, lit.: ragged proletariat]

lumpfish ('lʌmp,fɪʃ) *n, pl* **lumpfish** *or* **lumpfishes** a North Atlantic fish having a globular body covered with tubercles, pelvic fins fused into a sucker, and an edible roe. Also called: **lumpsucker** [C16 *lump* (now obs.) lumpfish, from MDu. *lumpe,* ? rel. to LUMP[1]]

lumpish ('lʌmpɪʃ) *adj* **1** resembling a lump **2** stupid, clumsy, or heavy > '**lumpishly** *adv* > '**lumpishness** *n*

lump sum *n* a relatively large sum of money, paid at one time, esp in cash

lumpy ('lʌmpɪ) *adj* **lumpier, lumpiest** **1** full of or having lumps **2** (esp of the sea) rough **3** (of a person) heavy or bulky > '**lumpily** *adv* > '**lumpiness** *n*

Lumumba (lʊ'mʊmbə) *n* **Patrice** (pə'triːs) 1925–61, Congolese statesman; first prime minister of the Democratic Republic of Congo (1960); assassinated

Luna ('luːnə) *n* the Roman goddess of the moon [from L: moon]

lunacy ('luːnəsɪ) *n, pl* **lunacies** **1** (formerly) any severe mental illness **2** foolishness

luna moth *n* a large American moth having light green wings with a yellow crescent-shaped marking on each forewing [C19 from the markings on its wings]

lunar ('luːnə) *adj* **1** of or relating to the moon **2** occuring on or used on the moon: *lunar module* **3** relating to, caused by, or measured by the position or orbital motion of the moon [C17 from L *lūnāris,* from *lūna* the moon]

lunar eclipse *n* See **eclipse**

lunar module *n* the module used to carry astronauts on a spacecraft to the surface of the moon and back to the spacecraft

lunar month *n* See **month** (sense 6)
lunar year *n* See **year** (sense 6)
lunate ('lu:neɪt) *or* **lunated** *adj anat, bot* shaped like a crescent [c18 from L *lūnātus* crescent-shaped, from *lūna* moon]
lunatic ('lu:nətɪk) *adj* **1** an archaic word for **insane** **2** foolish; eccentric ▷ *n* **3** a person who is insane [c13 (adj): via OF from LL *lūnāticus* crazy, moonstruck, from L *lūna* moon]
lunatic asylum *n offens* an institution for the mentally ill
lunatic fringe *n* the members of a society who adopt views regarded as fanatical
lunch (lʌntʃ) *n* **1** a meal eaten during the middle of the day ▷ *vb* **2** *(intr)* to eat lunch **3** *(tr)* to provide or buy lunch for [c16 prob. short form of LUNCHEON] > '**luncher** *n*
luncheon ('lʌntʃən) *n* a lunch, esp a formal one [c16 prob. var. of *nuncheon*, from ME *noneschench*, from *none* NOON + *schench* drink]
luncheon meat *n* a ground mixture of meat (often pork) and cereal, usually tinned
luncheon voucher *n* a voucher worth a specified amount issued to employees and redeemable at a restaurant for food. Abbrev: **LV**
lunchroom ('lʌntʃ,ru:m, -,rʊm) *n US & Canad* a room where lunch is served or where students, employees, etc, may eat lunches they bring
Lund (lʊnd) *n* a city in SE Sweden, northeast of Malmö: founded in about 1020 by the Danish King Canute; the archbishopric for all Scandinavia in the Middle Ages; university (1668). Pop: 95 895 (1994)
Lundy ('lʌndɪ) *n* an island in SW England, in Devon, in the Bristol Channel: now a bird sanctuary. Pop: 50 (latest est)
Lüneburg (*German* 'ly:nəbʊrk) *n* a city in N Germany, in Lower Saxony: capital of the duchy of Brunswick-Lüneburg from 1235 to 1369; prominent Hanse town; saline springs. Pop: 61 000 (1990 est)
lunette (lu:'nɛt) *n* **1** anything that is shaped like a crescent **2** an oval or circular opening to admit light in a dome **3** a semicircular panel containing a window, mural, or sculpture **4** a type of fortification like a detached bastion **5** Also called: **lune** *RC Church* a case fitted with a bracket to hold the consecrated host [c16 from F: crescent, from *lune* moon, from L *lūna*]
Lunéville (*French* lynevil) *n* a city in NE France: scene of the signing of the **Peace of Lunéville** between France and Austria (1801). Pop: 22 393 (1990)
lung (lʌŋ) *n* **1** either one of a pair of spongy saclike respiratory organs within the thorax of higher vertebrates, which oxygenate the blood and remove its carbon dioxide **2** **at the top of one's lungs** in one's loudest voice; yelling [OE *lungen*]
lunge[1] (lʌndʒ) *n* **1** a sudden forward motion **2** *fencing* a thrust made by advancing the front foot and straightening the back leg, extending the sword arm forwards ▷ *vb* **lunges, lunging, lunged** **3** to move or cause to move with a lunge **4** *(intr) fencing* to make a lunge [c18 short form of obs. c17 *allonge*, from F *allonger* to stretch out (one's arm) from LL *ēlongāre* to lengthen] > '**lunger** *n*
lunge[2] (lʌndʒ) *n* **1** a rope used in training or exercising a horse ▷ *vb* **lunges, lunging, lunged** **2** to exercise or train (a horse) on a lunge [c17 from OF *longe*, shortened from *allonge*, ult. from L *longus* long]
lungfish ('lʌŋ,fɪʃ) *n, pl* **lungfish** *or* **lungfishes** a freshwater bony fish having an air-breathing lung, fleshy paired fins, and an elongated body
Lungki *or* **Lung-chi** ('lʊŋ'ki:) *n* the former name of **Zhangzhou**
lungwort ('lʌŋ,wɜ:t) *n* **1** any of several Eurasian plants which have spotted leaves and clusters of blue or purple flowers: formerly used to treat lung diseases **2** See **oyster plant**
lunula ('lu:njʊlə) *n, pl* **lunulae** (-njʊ,li:) the white crescent-shaped area at the base of the human fingernail. Nontechnical name: **half-moon** [c16 from L: small moon, from *lūna*]
Luoyang *or* **Loyang** ('ləʊ'jæŋ) *n* a city in E China, in N Henan province on the Luo River near its confluence with the Yellow River; an important Buddhist centre in the 5th and 6th centuries; a commercial and industrial centre. Pop: 1 002 178 (1999 est)
Lupercalia (,lu:pɜ:'keɪlɪə) *n, pl* **Lupercalia** *or* **Lupercalias** an ancient Roman festival of fertility, celebrated on Feb 15 [L, from *Lupercālis* belonging to *Lupercus*, a Roman god of the flocks] > ,**Luper'calian** *adj*
lupin *or US* **lupine** ('lu:pɪn) *n* a leguminous plant of North America, Europe, and Africa, with large spikes of brightly coloured flowers and flattened pods [c14 from L *lupīnus* wolfish (see LUPINE); from the belief that the plant ravenously exhausted the soil]
lupine ('lu:paɪn) *adj* of, relating to, or resembling a wolf [c17 from L *lupīnus*, from *lupus* wolf]
lupus ('lu:pəs) *n* any of various ulcerative skin diseases [c16 via Med. L from L: wolf; so called because it rapidly eats away the affected part]
lupus vulgaris (vʌl'gɛərɪs) *n* tuberculosis of the skin, esp of the face. Sometimes shortened to **lupus**
lurch[1] (lɜ:tʃ) *vb (intr)* **1** to lean or pitch suddenly to one side **2** to stagger ▷ *n* **3** the act or an instance of lurching [c19 from ?]
lurch[2] (lɜ:tʃ) *n* **1** **leave (someone) in the lurch** to desert (someone) in trouble **2** *cribbage* the state of a losing player with less than 30 points at the end of a game [c16 from F *lourche* a game similar to backgammon, from *lourche* (adj) deceived, prob. of Gmc origin]
lurch[3] (lɜ:tʃ) *vb (intr) arch or dialect* to prowl suspiciously [c15 ? a var. of LURK]
lurcher ('lɜ:tʃə) *n* **1** a crossbred hunting dog, esp one trained to hunt silently **2** *arch* a person who prowls or lurks [c16 from LURCH[3]]
lure (lʊə) *vb* **lures, luring, lured** *(tr)* **1** (sometimes foll by *away* or *into*) to tempt or attract by the promise of some type of reward **2** *falconry* to entice (a hawk or falcon) from the air to the falconer by a lure ▷ *n* **3** a person or thing that lures **4** *angling* any of various types of brightly coloured artificial spinning baits **5** *falconry* a feathered decoy to which small pieces of meat can be attached [c14 from OF *loirre* falconer's lure, from Gmc] > '**lurer** *n*
Lurex ('lʊərɛks) *n* **1** *trademark* a thin metallic thread coated with plastic **2** fabric containing such thread, which makes it glitter
lurgy ('lɜ:gɪ) *n, pl* **lurgies** *facetious* any undetermined illness [c20 from ?]
lurid ('lʊərɪd) *adj* **1** vivid in shocking detail; sensational **2** horrible in savagery or violence **3** pallid in colour; wan **4** glowing with an unnatural glare [c17 from L *lūridus* pale yellow] > '**luridly** *adv* > '**luridness** *n*
lurk (lɜ:k) *vb (intr)* **1** to move stealthily or be concealed, esp for evil purposes **2** to be present in an unobtrusive way; be latent **3** to read messages posted on an electronic network without contributing messages oneself ▷ *n* **4** *Austral & NZ sl* a scheme for success [c13 prob. frequentative of LOUR] > '**lurker** *n*
lurking ('lɜ:kɪŋ) *adj* lingering but almost unacknowledged: *a lurking suspicion*
Lusaka (lu:'zɑ:kə, -'sɑ:kə) *n* the capital of Zambia, in the southeast at an altitude of 1280 m (4200 ft): became capital of Northern Rhodesia in 1932 and of Zambia in 1964; University of Zambia (1966). Pop: 982 362 (1990) ▷ www.zambiatourism.com
Lusatia (lu:'seɪʃɪə) *n* a region of central Europe, lying between the upper reaches of the Elbe and Oder Rivers:

Ll

now mostly in E Germany, extending into SW Poland; inhabited chiefly by Sorbs > **Lu'satian** *adj, n*

luscious ('lʌʃəs) *adj* **1** extremely pleasurable, esp to the taste or smell **2** very attractive **3** *arch* cloying [c15 *lucius, licius*, ? short for DELICIOUS] > **'lusciously** *adv* > **'lusciousness** *n*

lush[1] (lʌʃ) *adj* **1** (of vegetation) abounding in lavish growth **2** (esp of fruits) succulent and fleshy **3** luxurious, elaborate, or opulent [c15 prob. from OF *lasche* lazy, from L *laxus* loose] > **'lushly** *adv* > **'lushness** *n*

lush[2] (lʌʃ) *sl* ▷ *n* **1** a heavy drinker, esp an alcoholic **2** alcoholic drink ▷ *vb* **3** *US & Canad* to drink (alcohol) to excess [c19 from ?]

Lüshun ('lu:'ʃʊn) *n* a port in NE China, in S Liaoning province, at the S end of the Liaodong peninsula; together with the city of Dalian it comprises the port complex of Lüda: jointly held by China and the Soviet Union (1945–55). Former name: **Port Arthur**

Lusitania (,lu:sɪ'teɪnɪə) *n* an ancient region of the W Iberian Peninsula: a Roman province from 27 BC to the late 4th century AD; corresponds to most of present-day Portugal and the Spanish provinces of Salamanca and Cáceres

lust (lʌst) *n* **1** a strong desire for sexual gratification **2** a strong desire or drive ▷ *vb* **3** (*intr; often foll by after or for*) to have a lust (for) [OE] > **'lustful** *adj* > **'lustfully** *adv* > **'lustfulness** *n*

lustral ('lʌstrəl) *adj* of or relating to a ceremony of purification [c16 from L *lūstrālis* (adj) from LUSTRUM]

lustrate ('lʌstreɪt) *vb* **lustrates, lustrating, lustrated** (*tr*) to purify by means of religious rituals or ceremonies [c17 from L *lūstrāre* to brighten] > **lus'tration** *n*

lustre *or US* **luster** ('lʌstə) *n* **1** reflected light; sheen; gloss **2** radiance or brilliance of light **3** great splendour of accomplishment, beauty, etc **4** a dress fabric of cotton and wool with a glossy surface **5** a vase or chandelier from which hang cut-glass drops **6** a drop-shaped piece of cut glass or crystal used as such a decoration **7** a shiny metallic surface on some pottery and porcelain **8** *mineralogy* the way in which light is reflected from the surface of a mineral ▷ *vb* **lustres, lustring, lustred** *or US* **lusters, lustering, lustered** **9** to make, be, or become lustrous [c16 from OF, from OIt. *lustro*, from L *lustrāre* to make bright] > **'lustreless** *or US* **'lusterless** *adj* > **'lustrous** *adj*

lustreware *or US* **lusterware** ('lʌstə,wɛə) *n* pottery with lustre decoration

lustrum ('lʌstrəm) *or* **lustre** *n, pl* **lustrums, lustra** (-trə), *or* **lustres** *rare* a period of five years [c16 from L: ceremony of purification, from *lustrāre* to brighten, purify]

lusty ('lʌstɪ) *adj* **lustier, lustiest** **1** having or characterized by robust health **2** strong or invigorating > **'lustily** *adv* > **'lustiness** *n*

Lü-ta ('lu:'tɑ:) *n* a variant transliteration of the Chinese name for **Lüda**

lute[1] (lu:t) *n* an ancient plucked stringed instrument with a long fretted fingerboard and a body shaped like a sliced pear [c14 from OF *lut*, from Ar. *al 'ūd*, lit.: the wood]

lute[2] (lu:t) *n* **1** a mixture of cement and clay used to seal the joints between pipes, etc **2** *dentistry* a thin layer of cement used to fix a crown or inlay in place on a tooth ▷ *vb* **lutes, luting, luted** **3** (*tr*) to seal (a joint or surface) with lute [c14 via OF ult. from L *lutum* clay]

lutein ('lu:tɪɪn) *n* a xanthophyll pigment, occurring in plants, that has a light-absorbing function in photosynthesis [c20 from L *lūteus* yellow + -IN]

luteinizing hormone ('lu:tɪɪ,naɪzɪŋ) *n* a hormone secreted by the anterior lobe of the pituitary gland. In female vertebrates it stimulates ovulation, and in mammals it also induces corpus luteum formation. In male vertebrates it promotes maturation of the interstitial cells of the testes and stimulates androgen secretion [c19 from L *lūteum* egg yolk, from *lūteus* yellow]

lutenist, lutanist, ('lu:tənɪst) *or US & Canad* (*sometimes*) **lutist** ('lu:tɪst) *n* a person who plays the lute [c17 from Med. L *lūtānista*, from *lūtāna*, apparently from OF *lut* LUTE[1]]

Lutetia *or* **Lutetia Parisiorum** (lu:'ti:ʃə pə,rɪzɪ'ɔ:rəm) *n* an ancient name for **Paris** (the French city)

lutetium *or* **lutecium** (lʊ'ti:ʃɪəm) *n* a silvery-white metallic element of the lanthanide series. Symbol: Lu; atomic no.: 71; atomic wt.: 174.97 [c19 NL, from L *Lūtētia* ancient name of Paris, home of G. Urbain (1872–1938), F chemist, who discovered it]

Luther ('lu:θə) *n* **Martin** 1483–1546, German leader of the Protestant Reformation. As professor of biblical theology at Wittenberg University from 1511, he began preaching the crucial doctrine of justification by faith rather than by works, and in 1517 he nailed 95 theses to the church door at Wittenberg, attacking Tetzel's sale of indulgences. He was excommunicated and outlawed by the Diet of Worms (1521) as a result of his refusal to recant, but he was protected in Wartburg Castle by Frederick III of Saxony (1521–22). He translated the Bible into German (1521–34) and approved Melanchthon's Augsburg Confession (1530), defining the basic tenets of Lutheranism

Lutheran ('lu:θərən) *n* **1** a follower of Luther or a member of a Lutheran Church ▷ *adj* **2** of or relating to Luther or his doctrines **3** of or denoting any of the Protestant Churches that follow Luther's doctrines > **'Lutheranism** *n*
▷ http://www.lhm.org/

Luthuli *or* **Lutuli** (lu:'tu:lɪ) *n* Chief **Albert John** 1899–1967, South African political leader. As president of the African National Congress (1952–60), he campaigned for nonviolent resistance to apartheid: Nobel peace prize 1961

Lutine bell ('lu:ti:n, lu:'ti:n) *n* a bell, taken from the ship *Lutine*, kept at Lloyd's in London and rung before important announcements, esp the loss of a vessel

Luton ('lu:tᵊn) *n* **1** a town in SE central England, in Luton unitary authority, S Bedfordshire: airport; motor-vehicle industries; university (1993). Pop: 171 671 (1991) **2** a unitary authority in SE central England, in Bedfordshire. Pop: 184 390 (2001). Area: 43 sq km (17 sq miles)

Lutyens ('lʌtʃəns) *n* **1** Sir **Edwin** 1869–1944, British architect, noted for his neoclassical country houses and his planning of New Delhi, India **2** his daughter, **Elisabeth** 1906–83, British composer

Lützen (*German* 'lytsən) *n* a town near Leipzig in E Germany, in Saxony; site of a battle (1632) in the Thirty Years' War in which the army of the Holy Roman Empire under Wallenstein was defeated by the Swedes under Gustavus Adolphus, who died in the battle

Lützow-Holm Bay ('lʊtsəʊ'həʊm) *n* an inlet of the Indian Ocean on the coast of Antarctica, between Enderby Land and Queen Maud Land

luvvie *or* **luvvy** ('lʌvɪ) *n, pl* **luvvies** *facetious* a person who is involved in the acting profession or the theatre, esp one with a tendency to affectation

lux[1] (lʌks) *n, pl* **lux** the derived SI unit of illumination equal to a luminous flux of 1 lumen per square metre [c19 from L: light]

lux[2] (lʌks) *vb NZ inf* to clean with a vacuum cleaner [c20 from *Electrolux*, a vacuum-cleaner manufacturer]

Lux. *abbrev for* Luxembourg

luxate ('lʌkseɪt) *vb* **luxates, luxating, luxated** (*tr*) *pathol* to dislocate (a shoulder, knee, etc) [c17 from L *luxāre* to displace, from *luxus* dislocated] > **lux'ation** *n*

luxe (lʌks, lʊks; *French* lyks) *n* See **de luxe** [c16 from F from L *luxus* extravagance]

Luxembourg ('lʌksəm,bɜ:g; *French* lyksābur) *n* **1** a grand duchy in W Europe: formed the Benelux customs union with Belgium and the Netherlands in 1948 and is now a

member of the European Union. Languages: French, German, and Luxemburgish. Religion: Roman Catholic majority. Currency: euro. Capital: Luxembourg. Pop: 444 000 (2001 est). Area: 2586 sq km (999 sq miles) **2** the capital of Luxembourg, on the Alzette River: an industrial centre. Pop: 79 800 (1999 est) **3** a province in SE Belgium, in the Ardennes. Capital: Arlon. Pop: 246 820 (2000 est). Area: 4416 sq km (1705 sq miles)
▷ www.luxembourg-city.lu/touristinfo
▷ www.ont.lu
▷ www.luxembourg.co.uk

Luxemburg (*German* 'lʊksəmbʊrk) *n* **Rosa** ('ro:za) 1871–1919, German socialist leader, led an unsuccessful Communist revolt (1919) with Karl Liebknecht and was assassinated

Luxor ('lʌksɔ:) *n* a town in S Egypt, on the River Nile: the southern part of the site of ancient Thebes; many ruins and tombs, notably the temple built by Amenhotep III (about 1411–1375 BC). Pop: 360 503 (1996)

luxuriant (lʌg'zjʊərɪənt) *adj* **1** rich and abundant; lush **2** very elaborate or ornate **3** extremely productive or fertile [c16 from L *luxuriāns*, present participle of *luxuriāre* to abound to excess] > **lux'uriance** *n* > **lux'uriantly** *adv*

USAGE See at **luxurious**

luxuriate (lʌg'zjʊərɪ,eɪt) *vb* **luxuriates, luxuriating, luxuriated** (*intr*) **1** (foll by *in*) to take voluptuous pleasure; revel **2** to flourish profusely **3** to live in a sumptuous way [c17 from L *luxuriāre*] > **lux,uri'ation** *n*

luxurious (lʌg'zjʊərɪəs) *adj* **1** characterized by luxury **2** enjoying or devoted to luxury [c14 via OF from L *luxuriōsus* excessive] > **lux'uriously** *adv* > **lux'uriousness** *n*

USAGE *Luxurious* is sometimes wrongly used where *luxuriant* is meant: *he had a luxuriant* (not *luxurious*) *moustache; the walls were covered with a luxuriant growth of wisteria*

luxury ('lʌkʃərɪ) *n, pl* **luxuries** **1** indulgence in and enjoyment of rich and sumptuous living **2** (*sometimes pl*) something considered an indulgence rather than a necessity **3** something pleasant and satisfying: *the luxury of independence* **4** (*modifier*) relating to, indicating, or supplying luxury [c14 (in the sense: lechery): via OF from L *luxuria* excess, from *luxus* extravagance]

Luzern (lu'tsɛrn) *n* the German name for **Lucerne**

Luzon (lu:'zɒn) *n* the main and largest island of the Philippines, in the N part of the archipelago, separated from the other islands by the Sibuyan Sea: important agriculturally, producing most of the country's rice, with large forests and rich mineral resources; industrial centres at Manila and Batangas. Capital: Quezon City. Pop: 32 558 000 (1995 est). Area: 108 378 sq km (41 845 sq miles)

LV *abbrev for* luncheon voucher

Lviv (lvif) *n* an industrial city in the W Ukraine: it has belonged to Poland (1340–1772; 1919–39), Austria (1772–1918), Germany (1939–45), and the Soviet Union (1945–91); Ukrainian cultural centre, with a university (1661). Pop: 793 700 (1998 est). Russian name: **Lvov**. Polish name: **Lwów**. German name: **Lemberg**

LW *abbrev for*: **1** *radio* long wave **2** low water

Lwów (lvuf) *n* the Polish name for **Lviv**

lx *physics symbol for* lux

LXX *symbol for* Septuagint

-ly[1] *suffix forming adjectives* **1** having the nature or qualities of: *godly* **2** occurring at certain intervals; every: *daily* [OE *-lic*]

-ly[2] *suffix forming adverbs* in a certain manner; to a certain degree: *quickly; recently; chiefly* [OE *-lice*, from *-lic* -LY[1]]

Lyallpur (,laɪəl'pʊə) *n* the former name (until 1979) of **Faisalabad**

lyase ('laɪeɪz) *n* any enzyme that catalyses the separation of two parts of a molecule by the formation of a double bond between them [c20 from Gk *lusis* a loosening + -ASE]

lycanthropy (laɪ'kænθrəpɪ) *n* **1** the supposed magical transformation of a human being into a wolf **2** *psychiatry* a delusion in which a person believes that he or she is a wolf [c16 from Gk *lukānthropía*, from *lukos* wolf + *anthrōpos* man] > **lycanthrope** ('laɪkən,θrəʊp) *n* > **lycanthropic** (,laɪkən'θrɒpɪk) *adj*

Lycaon (laɪ'keɪɒn) *n Greek myth* a king of Arcadia said to have offered Zeus a plate of human flesh to learn whether the god was omniscient

Lycaonia (,lɪkə'əʊnɪə) *n* an ancient region of S Asia Minor, north of the Taurus Mountains; corresponds to present-day S central Turkey

lycée ('li:seɪ) *n, pl* **lycées** (-seɪz) *chiefly French* a secondary school [c19 F, from L: *Lyceum* a school in ancient Athens]

lyceum (laɪ'sɪəm) *n* (now chiefly in the names of buildings) **1** a public building for concerts, lectures, etc **2** *US* a cultural organization responsible for presenting concerts, lectures, etc

lychee (,laɪ'tʃi:) *n* a variant spelling of **litchi**

lych gate *or* **lich gate** (lɪtʃ) *n* a roofed gate to a churchyard, formerly used as a temporary shelter for the bier [c15 *lich*, from OE *līc* corpse]

lychnis ('lɪknɪs) *n* any of a genus of plants having red, pink, or white five-petalled flowers: includes ragged robin [c17 NL, via L, from Gk *lukhnis* a red flower]

Lycia ('lɪsɪə) *n* an ancient region on the coast of SW Asia Minor: a Persian, Rhodian, and Roman province > **'Lycian** *adj, n*

lycopodium (,laɪkə'pəʊdɪəm) *n* **1** any of a genus of club moss resembling moss but having vascular tissue and spore-bearing cones **2** a flammable yellow powder from the spores of this plant, used in medicine and in making fireworks [c18 NL, from Gk, from *lukos* wolf + *pous* foot]

Lycra ('laɪkrə) *n trademark* a type of synthetic elastic fabric and fibre used for tight-fitting garments, such as swimming costumes

Lycurgus (laɪ'kɜ:gəs) *n* 9th century BC, Spartan lawgiver. He is traditionally regarded as the founder of the Spartan constitution, military institutions, and educational system

Lydda ('lɪdə) *n* another name for **Lod**

lyddite ('lɪdaɪt) *n* an explosive consisting chiefly of fused picric acid [c19 after *Lydd*, town in Kent near which the first tests were made]

Lydgate ('lɪd,geɪt) *n* **John** ?1370–?1450, English poet and monk. His vast output includes devotional works and translations, such as that of a French version of Boccaccio's *The Fall of Princes* (1430–38)

Lydia ('lɪdɪə) *n* an ancient region on the coast of W Asia Minor: a powerful kingdom in the century and a half before the Persian conquest (546 BC). Chief town: Sardis > **'Lydian** *adj, n*

lye (laɪ) *n* **1** any solution obtained by leaching, such as the caustic solution obtained by leaching wood ash **2** a concentrated solution of sodium hydroxide or potassium hydroxide [OE *lēag*]

Lyell ('laɪəl) *n* Sir **Charles** 1797–1875, Scottish geologist. In *Principles of Geology* (1830–33) he advanced the theory of uniformitarianism, refuting the doctrine of catastrophism

lying[1] ('laɪɪŋ) *vb* the present participle and gerund of **lie**[1]

lying[2] ('laɪɪŋ) *vb* the present participle and gerund of **lie**[2]

lying-in *n, pl* **lyings-in** **a** confinement in childbirth **b** (*as modifier*): a lying-in hospital

lyke-wake ('laɪk,weɪk) *n Brit* a watch held over a dead person, often with festivities [c16 ?from ON]

Lyly ('lɪlɪ) *n* **John** ?1554–1606, English dramatist and novelist, noted for his two romances, *Euphues, or the Anatomy of Wit* (1578) and *Euphues and his England* (1580), written in an elaborate style. See also **euphuism**

Lyme disease (laɪm) *n* a disease of domestic animals and humans, caused by a spirochaete and transmitted by ticks, and affecting the joints, heart, and brain [c20 after *Lyme*, Connecticut, the town where it was first identified in humans]

Lyme Regis (laɪm ˈriːdʒɪs) *n* a resort in S England, in Dorset, on the English Channel: noted for finds of prehistoric fossils. Pop: 3851 (1991)

Lymington (ˈlɪmɪŋtən) *n* a market town in S England, in SW Hampshire, on the Solent: yachting centre and holiday resort. Pop: 13 508 (1991)

lymph (lɪmf) *n* the almost colourless fluid, containing chiefly white blood cells, that is collected from the tissues of the body and transported in the lymphatic system [c17 from L *lympha* water, from earlier *limpa*, infl. in form by Gk *numphē* nymph]

lymphatic (lɪmˈfætɪk) *adj* **1** of, relating to, or containing lymph **2** of or relating to the lymphatic system **3** sluggish or lacking vigour ▷ *n* **4** a lymphatic vessel [c17 (meaning: mad): from L *lymphāticus*. Original meaning ?from a confusion between *nymph* and LYMPH]

lymphatic system *n* an extensive network of capillary vessels that transports the interstitial fluid of the body as lymph to the venous blood circulation

lymphatic tissue *n* tissue, such as the lymph nodes, tonsils, spleen, and thymus, that produces lymphocytes

lymph gland *n* a former name for **lymph node**

lymph node *n* any of numerous bean-shaped masses of tissue, situated along the course of lymphatic vessels, that help to protect against infection and are a source of lymphocytes

lympho- *or before a vowel* **lymph-** *combining form* indicating lymph or the lymphatic system: *lymphocyte*

lymphocyte (ˈlɪmfəʊˌsaɪt) *n* a type of white blood cell formed in lymphatic tissue > **lymphocytic** (ˌlɪmfəʊˈsɪtɪk) *adj*

lymphoid (ˈlɪmfɔɪd) *adj* of or resembling lymph, or relating to the lymphatic system

lymphoma (lɪmˌfəʊmə) *n* cancer of the lymph nodes. Also called: **lymphosarcoma** (ˌlɪmfəʊsɑːˈkəʊmə)

Lynagh (ˈlaɪnə) *n* **Michael** born 1963, Australian Rugby Union football player; captain of Australia 1987, 1992–95

lynch (lɪntʃ) *vb* (*tr*) (of a mob) to punish (a person) for some supposed offence by hanging without a trial [orig. *Lynch's law*; ? after Capt. William *Lynch* (1742–1820) of Virginia, USA] > **ˈlyncher** *n* > **ˈlynching** *n*

Lynch (lɪntʃ) *n* **1 David** born 1946, US film director; his work includes the films *Eraserhead* (1977), *Blue Velvet* (1986), *Wild at Heart* (1990), and *Mulholland Drive* (2001) and the television series *Twin Peaks* (1990) **2 John,** known as *Jack Lynch*. 1917–99, Irish statesman; prime minister of the Republic of Ireland (1966–73; 1977–79)

lynchet (ˈlɪntʃɪt) *n* a terrace or ridge formed in prehistoric or medieval times by ploughing a hillside [OE *hlinc* ridge]

lynch law *n* the practice of punishing a person by mob action without a proper trial

lynchpin (ˈlɪntʃˌpɪn) *n* a variant spelling of **linchpin**

Lynn[1] (lɪn) *n* another name for **King's Lynn.** Also called: **Lynn Regis** (ˈriːdʒɪs)

Lynn[2] (lɪn) *n* Dame **Vera,** original name *Vera Margaret Lewis*. born 1917, British singer popular during World War II and known as "the forces' sweetheart". Her best-known songs are "We'll Meet Again" and "White Cliffs of Dover"

lynx (lɪŋks) *n, pl* **lynxes** *or* **lynx 1** a feline mammal of Europe and North America, with grey-brown mottled fur, tufted ears, and a short tail **2** the fur of this animal **3 bay lynx** another name for **bobcat 4 desert lynx** another name for **caracal** [c14 via L from Gk *lunx*] > **ˈlynx,like** *adj*

lynx-eyed *adj* having keen sight

Lyon (*French* ljɔ̃) *n* a city in SE central France, capital of Rhône department, at the confluence of the Rivers Rhône and Saône: the third largest city in France; a major industrial centre and river port. Pop: 445 257 (1999). English name: **Lyons** (ˈlaɪənz) Ancient name: **Lugdunum** (lʊgˈduːnəm)

Lyon King of Arms (ˈlaɪən) *n* the chief herald of Scotland. Also called: **Lord Lyon** [c14 archaic spelling of LION, referring to the figure on the royal shield]

Lyonnais (*French* ljɔnɛ) *n* a former province of E central France, on the Rivers Rhône and Saône: occupied by the present-day departments of Rhône and Loire. Chief town: Lyon

Lyonnesse (ˌlaɪəˈnɛs) *n* (in Arthurian legend) the mythical birthplace of Sir Tristram, situated in SW England and believed to have been submerged by the sea

Lyons (ˈlaɪənz) *n* **Joseph Aloysius** 1879–1939, Australian statesman; prime minister of Australia (1931–39)

lyrate (ˈlaɪərɪt) *adj* **1** shaped like a lyre **2** (of leaves) having a large terminal lobe and smaller lateral lobes [c18 from NL *lyrātus, from* L *lyra* LYRE]

lyre (ˈlaɪə) *n* an ancient Greek stringed instrument consisting of a resonating tortoise shell to which a crossbar was attached by two projecting arms. It was plucked with a plectrum and used for accompanying songs [c13 via OF from L *lyra*, from Gk *lura*]

lyrebird (ˈlaɪəˌbɜːd) *n* either of two pheasant-like Australian birds: during courtship displays, the male spreads its tail into the shape of a lyre

lyric (ˈlɪrɪk) *adj* **1** (of poetry) **1a** expressing the writer's personal feelings and thoughts **1b** having the form and manner of a song **2** of or relating to such poetry **3** (of music) having songlike qualities **4** (of a singing voice) having a light quality and tone **5** intended for singing, esp (in classical Greece) to the accompaniment of the lyre ▷ *n* **6** a short poem of songlike quality **7** (*pl*) the words of a popular song. Also (for senses 1–4): **lyrical** [c16 from L *lyricus*, from Gk *lurikos*, from *lura* lyre] > **ˈlyrically** *adv* > **ˈlyricalness** *n*

lyrical (ˈlɪrɪkᵊl) *adj* **1** another word for **lyric** (senses 1–4) **2** enthusiastic; effusive

lyricism (ˈlɪrɪˌsɪzəm) *n* **1** the quality or style of lyric poetry **2** emotional outpouring

lyricist (ˈlɪrɪsɪst) *n* **1** a person who writes the words for a song, opera, or musical play **2** Also called: **lyrist** a lyric poet

Lysander (laɪˈsændə) *n* died 395 BC, Spartan naval commander of the Peloponnesian War

lyse (laɪs, laɪz) *vb* **lyses, lysing, lysed** to undergo or cause to undergo lysis

Lysenko (lɪˈsɛŋkəʊ; *Russian* liˈsjɛnkə) *n* **Trofim Denisovich** (traˈfim dɪˈnisəvitʃ) 1898–1976, Russian biologist and geneticist

lysergic acid diethylamide (lɪˈsɜːdʒɪk; daɪˌɛθɪlˈeɪmaɪd) *n* See **LSD**

Lysias (ˈlɪsɪˌæs) *n* ?450–?380 BC, Athenian orator

Lysimachus (laɪˈsɪməkəs) *n* ?360–281 BC, Macedonian general under Alexander the Great; king of Thrace (323–281); killed in battle by Seleucus I

lysin (ˈlaɪsɪn) *n* any of a group of antibodies that cause dissolution of cells

Lysippus (laɪˈsɪpəs) *n* 4th century BC, Greek sculptor. He introduced a new naturalism into Greek sculpture

lysis (ˈlaɪsɪs) *n, pl* **lyses** (-siːz) **1** the destruction of cells by the action of a particular lysin **2** *med* the gradual reduction in the symptoms of a disease [c19 NL, from Gk, from *luein* to release]

-lysis *n combining form* indicating a loosening, decomposition, or breaking down: *electrolysis; paralysis* [from Gk, from *lusis* a loosening; see LYSIS]

Lysol (ˈlaɪsɒl) *n trademark* a solution containing a mixture of cresols in water, used as an antiseptic and disinfectant

-lyte *n combining form* indicating a substance that can be decomposed or broken down: *electrolyte; hydrolyte* [from

Gk *lutos* soluble, from *luein* to loose]

Lytham Saint Anne's (ˈlɪðəm sənt ˈænz) *n usually abbreviated to* **Lytham St Anne's** a resort in NW England, in Lancashire on the Irish Sea. Pop: 40 866 (1991)

-lytic *adj combining form* indicating a loosening or dissolving: *paralytic* [from Gk, from *lusis*; see -LYSIS]

Lytton (ˈlɪtᵊn) *n* **1st Baron,** title of *Edward George Earle Lytton Bulwer-Lytton*. 1803–73, British novelist, dramatist, and statesman, noted particularly for his historical romances

Lyublin (ˈljublɪn) *n* transliteration of the Russian name for **Lublin**

Ll

Mm

m *or* **M** (ɛm) *n, pl* **m's, M's,** *or* **Ms** **1** the 13th letter of the English alphabet **2** a speech sound represented by this letter, as in *mat*

m *symbol for:* **1** metre(s) **2** mile(s) **3** milli- **4** minute(s)

M *symbol for:* **1** mach **2** *currency* mark(s) **3** medium **4** mega- **5** million **6** (in Britain) motorway **7** *the Roman numeral for* 1000

M8 *text messaging abbrev for* mate

m. *abbrev for:* **1** *cricket* maiden (over) **2** male **3** mare **4** married **5** masculine

M. *abbrev for:* **1** Majesty **2** Master **3** (in titles) Member **6** million **7** (*pl* **MM** *or* **MM**) Also: **M** *French* Monsieur [F equivalent of *Mr*]

m- *prefix* short for **meta-** (sense 4)

M'- *prefix* a variant of **Mac-**

ma (mɑː) *n* an informal word for **mother**

MA *abbrev for:* **1** Massachusetts **2** Master of Arts **3** Military Academy

ma'am (mæm, mɑːm; *unstressed* məm) *n* short for **madam**: used as a title of respect, esp for female royalty

Maarianhamina ('mɑːrianhamina) *n* the Finnish name for **Mariehamn**

maas (mɑːs) *n S African* thick soured milk [from Nguni *amasi* milk]

Maas (mɑːs) *n* the Dutch name for the **Meuse**

Maastricht *or* **Maestricht** ('mɑːstrɪxt; *Dutch* maː'strɪxt) *n* a city in the SE Netherlands near the Belgian and German borders: capital of Limburg province, on the River Maas (Meuse); a European Community treaty (**Maastricht Treaty**) was signed here in 1992, setting out the terms for the creation of the European Union. Pop: 121 479 (1999 est)

Mab (mæb) *n* (in English and Irish folklore) a fairy queen said to create and control men's dreams

Mabuse (mə'bjuːz; *French* mabyz) *n* **Jan** (jɑn) original name *Jan Gossaert*. ?1478– ?1533, Flemish painter

mac *or* **mack** (mæk) *n Brit inf* short for **mackintosh**

Mac (mæk) *n chiefly US & Canad* an informal term of address to a man [c20 abstracted from MAC-]

Mac-, Mc-, *or* **M'-** *prefix* (in surnames of Scottish or Irish Gaelic origin) son of: *MacDonald* [from Goidelic *mac* son of]

macabre (mə'kɑːbə, -brə) *adj* gruesome; ghastly; grim [c15 from OF *danse macabre* dance of death, prob. from *macabé* relating to the Maccabees, who were associated with death because of the doctrines and prayers for the dead in II Macc (12:43–46)]

macadam (mə'kædəm) *n* a road surface made of compressed layers of small broken stones, esp one that is bound together with tar or asphalt [c19 after John *McAdam* (1756–1836), Scot engineer, the inventor]

macadamia (ˌmækə'deɪmɪə) *n* **1** an Australian tree having clusters of small white flowers and edible nutlike seeds **2** **macadamia nut** the seed [c19 NL, after John *Macadam* (died 1865), Australian chemist]

macadamize *or* **macadamise** (mə'kædəˌmaɪz) *vb* **macadamizes, macadamizing, macadamized** *or* **macadamises, macadamising, macadamised** (*tr*) to construct or surface (a road) with macadam
> **macˌadami'zation** *or* **macˌadami'sation** *n*
> **mac'adamˌizer** *or* **mac'adamˌiser** *n*

Macao (mə'kaʊ) *n* a special administrative region of S China, across the estuary of the Zhu Jiang from Hong Kong: chief centre of European trade with China in the 18th century; attained partial autonomy in 1976; formerly (until 1999) a Portuguese overseas province; transit trade with China; tourism and financial services. Pop: 445 000 (2001 est). Area: 16 sq km (6 sq miles). Portuguese name: **Macáu**

Macapá (*Portuguese* maka'pa) *n* a town in NE Brazil,

capital of the federal territory of Amapá, on the Canal do Norte of the Amazon delta. Pop (urban): 270 077 (2000)

Macapagal Arroyo (ˌmækəˈpeɪgəl əˈrɔɪjəʊ) *n* **Gloria** See **Arroyo (Gloria Macapagal)**

macaque (məˈkɑːk) *n* any of various Old World monkeys of Asia and Africa. Typically the tail is short or absent and cheek pouches are present [c17 from F, from Port. *macaco*, from W African *makaku*, from *kaku* monkey]

macaroni *or* **maccaroni** (ˌmækəˈrəʊnɪ) *n*, *pl* **macaronis, macaronies** *or* **maccaronis, maccaronies** **1** pasta tubes made from wheat flour **2** (in 18th-century Britain) a dandy who affected foreign manners and style [c16 from It. (dialect) *maccarone*, prob. from Gk *makaria* food made from barley]

macaroon (ˌmækəˈruːn) *n* a kind of sweet biscuit made of ground almonds, sugar, and egg whites [c17 via F *macaron* from It. *maccarone* MACARONI]

Macarthur (məˈkɑːθə) *n* **John** 1767–1834, Australian military officer, pastoralist, and entrepreneur, born in England. He established the breeding of merino sheep in Australia and was influential in founding the Australian wool industry

MacArthur (məˈkɑːθə) *n* **Douglas** 1880–1964, US general. During World War II he became commanding general of US armed forces in the Pacific (1944) and accepted the surrender of Japan, the Allied occupation of which he commanded (1945–51). He was commander in chief of United Nations forces in Korea (1950–51) until dismissed by President Truman

Macassar (məˈkæsə) *n* a variant spelling of **Makasar**

Macassar oil *n* an oily preparation formerly put on the hair to make it smooth and shiny [c19 from MAKASAR]

Macáu (məˈkau) *n* the Portuguese name for **Macao**

Macaulay (məˈkɔːlɪ) *n* **1** Dame **Rose** 1881–1958, British novelist. Her books include *Dangerous Ages* (1921) and *The Towers of Trebizond* (1956) **2 Thomas Babington,** 1st Baron. 1800–59, English historian, essayist, and statesman. His *History of England from the Accession of James the Second* (1848–61) is regarded as a classic of the Whig interpretation of history

macaw (məˈkɔː) *n* a large tropical American parrot having a long tail and brilliant plumage [c17 from Port. *macau*, from ?]

Macbeth (məkˈbɛθ, mæk-) *n* died 1057, king of Scotland (1040–57): succeeded Duncan, whom he killed in battle; defeated and killed by Duncan's son Malcolm III

MacBride (məkˈbraɪd) *n* **Sean** (ʃɔːn) 1904–88, Irish statesman; minister for external affairs (1948–51); chairman of Amnesty International (1961–75); Nobel peace prize 1974

Macc. *abbrev for* Maccabees (books of the Apocrypha)

McCarthy (məˈkɑːθɪ) *n* **1 Joseph R(aymond)** 1908-57, US Republican senator, who led (1950-54) the notorious investigations of alleged Communist infiltration into the US government **2 Mary (Therese)** 1912–89, US novelist and critic; her works include *The Group* (1963)

McCarthyism (məˈkɑːθɪˌɪzəm) *n chiefly US* **1** the practice of making unsubstantiated accusations of disloyalty or Communist leanings **2** the use of unsupported accusations for any purpose [c20 after Senator Joseph MCCARTHY] > **McˈCarthyist** *n, adj*

McCartney (məˈkɑːtnɪ) *n* **1** Sir **Paul** born 1942, English rock musician and songwriter; member of the Beatles (1961–70); leader of Wings (1971–81). His recordings include *Band on the Run* (1973), "Mull of Kintyre" (1977), *Flowers in the Dirt* (1989), and *Driving Rain* (2001). See also **Beatles** **2** his daughter, **Stella** born 1971, British fashion designer

macchiato (ˌmækɪˈɑːtəʊ) *n*, *pl* **macchiatos** espresso coffee served with a dash of hot or cold milk [Italian, literally: stained]

Macclesfield (ˈmækəlzˌfiːld) *n* a market town in NW England, in Cheshire: former centre of the silk industry; pharmaceuticals, services. Pop: 50 270 (1991)

McConnell (məˈkɒnəl) *n* **Jack** born 1960, Scottish Labour politician; first minister of the Scottish parliament from 2001

McCormack (məˈkɔːmæk) *n* **John** 1884–1945, Irish tenor: became US citizen 1919

McCoy[1] (məˈkɔɪ) *n sl* the genuine person or thing (esp in **the real McCoy**) [c20 ? after Kid *McCoy*, professional name of Norman Selby (1873–1940), American boxer, who was called "the real McCoy" to distinguish him from another boxer of that name]

McCoy[2] (məˈkɔɪ) *n* **Tony,** full name *Anthony Peter McCoy*. born 1974, Northern Irish jockey; winner of seven consecutive riders' titles in 2001–02

McCullers (məˈkʌləz) *n* **Carson** 1917–67, US writer, whose novels include *The Heart is a Lonely Hunter* (1940)

McDiarmid (məkˈdɜːmɪd) *n* **Hugh,** pen name of *Christopher Murray Grieve*. 1892–1978, Scottish poet; a founder of the Scottish National Party. His poems include *A Drunk Man Looks at the Thistle* (1926)

Macdonald (məkˈdɒnəld) *n* **1 Flora** 1722–90, Scottish heroine, who helped the Young Pretender to escape to Skye after his defeat at the battle of Culloden (1746) **2** Sir **John Alexander** 1815–91, Canadian statesman, born in Scotland, who was the first prime minister of the Dominion of Canada (1867–73; 1878–91)

MacDonald (məkˈdɒnəld) *n* **(James) Ramsay** 1866–1937, British statesman, who led the first and second Labour Governments (1924 and 1929–31) He also led a coalition (1931–35), which the majority of the Labour Party refused to support

McDonald (məkˈdɒnəld) *n* Sir **Trevor** born 1939, British broadcasting journalist, born in Trinidad; presenter of ITV's *News at Ten* (1990–99)

Macdonnell Ranges (məkˈdɒnəl) *pl n* a mountain system of central Australia, in Northern Territory, extending about 160 km (100 miles) east and west of Alice Springs. Highest peak: Mount Ziel, 1510 m (4955 ft)

Mm

mace[1] (meɪs) *n* **1** a club, usually having a spiked metal head, used esp in the Middle Ages **2** a ceremonial staff carried by certain officials **3** See **macebearer** **4** an early form of billiard cue [c13 from OF, prob. from Vulgar L *mattea* (unattested); apparently rel. to L *mateola* mallet]

mace[2] (meɪs) *n* a spice made from the dried aril round the nutmeg seed [c14 formed as a singular from OF *macis* (wrongly assumed to be pl), from L *macir* a spice]

macebearer (ˈmeɪsˌbɛərə) *n* a person who carries a mace in processions or ceremonies

Maced. *abbrev for* Macedonia(n)

macedoine (ˌmæsɪˈdwɑːn) *n* **1** a mixture of diced vegetables **2** a mixture of fruit in a syrup or in jelly **3** any mixture; medley [c19 from F, lit.: Macedonian, alluding to the mixture of nationalities in Macedonia]

Macedon (ˈmæsɪˌdɒn) *or* **Macedonia** *n* a region of the S Balkans, now divided among Greece, Bulgaria, and Macedonia (Former Yugoslav Republic of Macedonia). As a kingdom in the ancient world it achieved prominence under Philip II (359–336 BC) and his son Alexander the Great

Macedonia (ˌmæsɪˈdəʊnɪə) *n* **1** a country in SE Europe, comprising the NW half of ancient Macedon: it became part of the kingdom of Serbs, Croats, and Slovenes (subsequently Yugoslavia) in 1913; it declared independence in 1992, but Greece objected to the use of the historical name Macedonia; in 1993 it was recognized by the UN under its current official name. Official language: Macedonian. Religion: Christian majority, Muslim, nonreligious, and Jewish minorities. Currency: denar. Capital: Skopje. Pop: 2 046 000 (2001 est). Area: 25 713 sq km (10 028 sq miles). Serbian name: **Makedonija** Official name: **Former Yugoslav Republic of Macedonia** (FYROM) **2** an area of N Greece, comprising the regions of Macedonia Central, Macedonia West, and part of Macedonia East and Thrace. Modern Greek name: **Makedhonia** **3** a district of SW Bulgaria, now occupied by Blagoevgrad province. Area: 6465 sq km (2496 sq miles) > ˌ**Mace**ˈ**donian** *adj, n*

▷ www.gov.mk/English/index.htm

▷ www.macedonia.co.uk/mcic

▷ www.b-info.com/places/Macedonia/republic

Maceió (maseˈjɔ) *n* a port in NE Brazil, capital of Alagôas state, on the Atlantic. Pop: 794 894 (2000)

McEnroe (ˈmækᵊnˌrəʊ) *n* **John** (**Patrick Jr**) born 1959, US tennis player: US singles champion (1979–81; 1984) and doubles champion (1979; 1981; 1989): Wimbledon singles champion (1981; 1983; 1984) and doubles champion (1979; 1981; 1983; 1984; 1992)

macerate (ˈmæsəˌreɪt) *vb* **macerates, macerating, macerated** **1** to soften or separate or be softened or separated as a result of soaking **2** to become or cause to become thin [c16 from L *mācerāre* to soften] > ˌ**macer**ˈ**ation** *n* > ˈ**macer**ˌ**ator** *n*

McEwan (məˈkjuːən) *n* **Ian** (**Russell**) born 1948, British novelist and short-story writer. His books include *First Love, Last Rites* (1975), *The Child in Time* (1987), *The Innocent* (1990), *Amsterdam* (1998), and *Atonement* (2001)

McGonagall (məˈgɒnəgəl) *n* **William** 1830–?1902, Scottish writer of doggerel, noted for its bathos, repetitive rhymes, poor scansion, and ludicrous effect

McGrath (məˈgræθ) *n* **Glenn** (**Donald**) born 1970, Australian cricketer; played for Australia from 1993

MacGregor *n* **Joanna** (**Clare**) born 1959, British concert pianist and broadcaster; recordings include the "crossover" album *Play* (2001)

MacGuffin (məˈgʌfɪn) *n* an object or event in a book or a film that serves as the impetus for the plot [c20 coined (c. 1935) by Sir Alfred HITCHCOCK]

McGwire (məˈgwɪə) *n* **Mark** (**David**) born 1963, US baseball player

Mach[1] (mæk) *n* short for **Mach number**

Mach[2] (*German* max) *n* **Ernst** (ɛrnst) 1838–1916, Austrian physicist and philosopher. He devised the system of speed measurement using the Mach number. He also founded logical positivism, asserting that the validity of a scientific law is proved only after empirical testing

Machado (*Portuguese* maˈʃadu) *n* **Joaquim Maria** (ʒuaˈkɪ maˈria) 1839–1908, Brazilian author of novels and short stories, whose novels include *Epitaph of a Small Winner* (1881) and *Dom Casmurro* (1899)

machair (ˈmæxər) *n Scot* (in the western Highlands and islands of Scotland) a strip of sandy grassy land just above the shore: used for grazing, etc [c17 from Scot Gaelic]

Machel (məˈʃɛl) *n* **Samora** (**Moises**) (səˈmɔːrə) 1933–86, Mozambique statesman; president of Mozambique from 1975–86

machete (məˈʃɛtɪ, -ˈtʃeɪ-) *n* a broad heavy knife used for cutting or as a weapon, esp in parts of Central and South America [c16 *macheto*, from Sp. *machete*, from *macho* club, ?from Vulgar L *mattea* (unattested) club]

Machiavelli (ˌmækɪəˈvɛlɪ) *n* **Niccolò** (nikkoˈlɔ) 1469–1527, Florentine statesman and political philosopher; secretary to the war council of the Florentine republic (1498–1512). His most famous work is *Il Principe* (*The Prince*, 1532)

Machiavellian (ˌmækɪəˈvɛlɪən) *adj* **1** of or relating to the alleged political principles of Machiavelli; cunning, amoral, and opportunist ▷ *n* **2** a cunning, amoral, and opportunist person, esp a politician > ˌ**Machia**ˈ**vellian**ˌ**ism** *n*

machicolate (məˈtʃɪkəʊˌleɪt) *vb* **machicolates, machicolating, machicolated** (*tr*) to construct machicolations at the top of (a wall) [c18 from OF *machicoller*, ult. from Provençal *machacol*, from *macar* to crush + *col* neck]

machicolation (məˌtʃɪkəʊˈleɪʃən) *n* **1** (esp in medieval castles) a projecting gallery or parapet having openings through which missiles could be dropped **2** any such opening

machinate (ˈmækɪˌneɪt) *vb* **machinates, machinating, machinated** (*usually tr*) to contrive, plan, or devise (schemes, plots, etc) [c17 from L *māchinārī* to plan, from *māchina* MACHINE] > ˈ**machi**ˌ**nator** *n*

machination (ˌmækɪˈneɪʃən) *n* **1** a plot or scheme **2** the act of devising plots or schemes

machine (məˈʃiːn) *n* **1** an assembly of interconnected components arranged to transmit or modify force in order to perform useful work **2** a device for altering the magnitude or direction of a force, such as a lever or screw **3** a mechanically operated device or means of transport, such as a car or aircraft **4** any mechanical or electrical device that automatically performs tasks or assists in performing tasks **5** any intricate structure or agency **6** a mechanically efficient, rigid, or obedient person **7** an organized body of people that controls activities, policies, etc ▷ *vb* **machines, machining, machined** **8** (*tr*) to shape, cut, or remove (excess material) from (a workpiece) using a machine tool **9** to use a machine to carry out a process on (something) [c16 via F from L *māchina* machine, from Doric Gk *makhana* pulley] > **ma**ˈ**chinable** *or* **ma**ˈ**chineable** *adj* > **ma**ˌ**china**ˈ**bility** *n*

machine code *or* **language** *n* instructions for the processing of data in a binary, octal, or hexadecimal code that can be understood and executed by a computer

machine-down time *n* a period during which a machine, computer, etc, is out of service, because it is out of order or being serviced

machine gun *n* **1a** a rapid-firing automatic gun, using small-arms ammunition **1b** (*as modifier*): *machine-gun fire* ▷ *vb* **machine-gun, machine-guns, machine-gunning, machine-gunned** **2** (*tr*) to shoot or fire at with a machine gun > **machine gunner** *n*

machine learning *n* a branch of artificial intelligence in which a computer generates rules underlying or based on raw data that has been fed into it

machinery (məˈʃiːnərɪ) *n, pl* **machineries** **1** machines, machine parts, or machine systems collectively **2** a particular machine system or set of machines **3** a system similar to a machine

machine shop *n* a workshop in which machine tools are operated

machine tool *n* a power-driven machine, such as a lathe, for cutting, shaping, and finishing metals, etc > **ma**ˈ**chine-**ˌ**tooled** *adj*

machinist (məˈʃiːnɪst) *n* **1** a person who operates machines to cut or process materials **2** a maker or repairer of machines

machismo (mæˈkɪzməʊ, -ˈtʃɪz-) *n* strong or exaggerated masculinity [Mexican Sp., from Sp. *macho* male, from L *masculus* MASCULINE]

> **USAGE** This word is still in the process of being naturalized in English, and consequently pronunciation of the *ch* varies between a *k* and the standard pronunciation of *ch* at the beginning of a word, as in *chief*. The adjective *macho* is nearly always pronounced in the second way in English, and it would be more in keeping with the pronunciation of *ch* in general, and more in line with Spanish pronunciation, to pronounce *machismo* in the same way

Mach number *n* (*often not cap*) the ratio of the speed of a body in a particular medium to the speed of sound in that medium. Mach number 1 corresponds to the speed of sound [c19 after Ernst MACH]

macho (ˈmætʃəʊ) *adj* **1** strongly or exaggeratedly

masculine ▷ *n, pl* **machos** **2** a strong virile man.
USAGE See at **machismo**

Machu Picchu ('mɑːtʃuː 'piːktʃuː) *n* a ruined Incan city in S Peru

Macías Nguema (mə'siːəs ᵊŋ'gweɪmə) *n* the former name (until 1979) of **Bioko**

mack (mæk) *n Brit inf* short for **mackintosh**

Mackay (mə'kaɪ) *n* a port in E Australia, in Queensland: artificial harbour. Pop: 55 772 (1993)

Mackellar (mə'kɛlə) *n* **Dorothea** 1885–1968, Australian poet, who wrote "My Country", Australia's best known poem

McKellen (mə'kɛlən) *n* Sir **Ian** (**Murray**) born 1939, British actor, noted esp for his Shakespearean roles: films include *The Lord of the Rings* trilogy (2001–03)

McKenna (mə'kɛnə) *n* **Siobhán** (ʃə'vɔːn) 1923–86, Irish actress, whose notable roles included Pegeen Mike in Synge's *The Playboy of the Western World* and Shaw's Saint Joan

Mackenzie[1] (mə'kɛnzɪ) *n* a river in NW Canada, in the Northwest Territories and Nunavut, flowing northwest from Great Slave Lake to the Beaufort Sea: the longest river in Canada; navigable in summer. Length: 1770 km (1100 miles)

Mackenzie[2] (mə'kɛnzɪ) *n* **1** Sir **Alexander** ?1755–1820, Scottish explorer and fur trader in Canada. He explored the Mackenzie River (1789) and was the first European to cross America north of Mexico (1793) **2** **Alexander** 1822–92, Canadian statesman; first Liberal prime minister (1873–78) **3** Sir **Compton** 1883–1972, English author. His works include *Sinister Street* (1913–14) and the comic novel *Whisky Galore* (1947) **4** Sir **Thomas** 1854–1930, New Zealand statesman born in Scotland: prime minister of New Zealand (1912) **5** **William Lyon** 1795–1861, Canadian journalist and politician, born in Scotland. He led an unsuccessful rebellion against the oligarchic Family Compact (1837)

mackerel ('mækrəl) *n, pl* **mackerel** *or* **mackerels** **1** a spiny-finned food fish occurring in northern coastal regions of the Atlantic and in the Mediterranean. It has a deeply forked tail and a greenish-blue body marked with wavy dark bands on the back **2** any of various related fishes [c13 from Anglo-F, from OF *maquerel*, from ?]

mackerel sky *n* a sky patterned with cirrocumulus or small altocumulus clouds [from similarity to pattern on mackerel's back]

Mackerras (mə'kɛrəs) *n* **Charles** born 1925, Australian conductor, esp of opera; resident in England

Mackinac ('mækɪˌnɔː, -ˌnæk) *n* a wooded island in N Michigan, in the **Straits of Mackinac** (a channel between the lower and upper peninsulas of Michigan): an ancient Indian burial ground; state park. Length: 5 km (3 miles)

McKinley[1] (mə'kɪnlɪ) *n* **Mount** a mountain in S central Alaska, in the Alaska Range: the highest peak in North America. Height: 6194 m (20 320 ft)

McKinley[2] (mə'kɪnlɪ) *n* **William** 1843–1901, 25th president of the US (1897–1901) His administration was marked by high tariffs and by expansionist policies. He was assassinated

McKinnon (mə'kɪnən) *n* **Don**(**ald**) (**Charles**) born 1939, New Zealand politician; secretary-general of the Commonwealth from 2000; deputy prime minister of New Zealand (1990–96)

mackintosh *or* **macintosh** ('mækɪnˌtɒʃ) *n* **1** a waterproof raincoat made of rubberized cloth **2** such cloth **3** any raincoat [c19 after Charles *Macintosh* (1760–1843), who invented it]

Mackintosh ('mækɪnˌtɒʃ) *n* **1** Sir **Cameron (Anthony)** born 1946, British producer of musicals and theatre owner; his productions include *Cats* (1981), *Les Misérables* (1985), *Miss Saigon* (1987), and *My Fair Lady* (2001) **2** **Charles Rennie** 1868–1928, Scottish architect and artist, exponent of the Art Nouveau style; designer of the Glasgow School of Art (1896)

McIntosh ('mækɪnˌtɒʃ) *or* **McIntosh red** *n* a Canadian variety of red-skinned eating apple [c19 named after John *McIntosh*, (1777–c. 1845), US-born Canadian farmer on whose property the variety was first found growing wild]

Maclean (mə'kleɪn) *n* **1** **Donald** 1913–83, British civil servant, who spied for the Russians: fled to the former Soviet Union (with Guy Burgess) in 1951 **2** **Sorley** ('sɔːlɪ) 1911–96, Scottish Gaelic poet. His works include *Dàin do Eimhir agus Dàin Eile* (1943) and *Spring Tide and Neap Tide* (1977)

McLeish (mə'kliːʃ) *n* **Henry** born 1948, Scottish Labour politician: first minister of the Scottish parliament from 2000

Macleod (mə'klaʊd) *n* **John James Rickard** 1876–1935, Scottish physiologist: shared the Nobel prize for physiology or medicine (1923) with Banting for their part in discovering insulin

McLuhan (mə'kluːən) *n* (**Herbert**) **Marshall** 1911–80, Canadian author of works analysing the mass media, including *Understanding Media* (1964) and *The Medium is the Message* (1967)

Macmahon (*French* makmaɔ̃) *n* **Marie Edme Patrice Maurice** (mari ɛdmə patris mɔris), Comte de Macmahon. 1808–93, French military commander. He commanded the troops that suppressed the Paris Commune (1871) and was elected president of the Third Republic (1873–79)

McMahon (mək'mɑːən) *n* Sir **William** 1908–88, Australian statesman; prime minister of Australia (1971–72)

Macmillan (mək'mɪlən) *n* (**Maurice**) **Harold,** 1st Earl of Stockton. 1894–1986, British statesman; Conservative prime minister (1957–63)

MacMillan *n* **1** **James** (**Loy**) born 1959, Scottish composer and conductor; his works include two symphonies, the orchestral work *Confession of Isobel Gowdie* (1990), and the opera *Ines de Castro* (1996) **2** Sir **Kenneth** 1929–92, British ballet dancer and choreographer; director (1970–77) and principal choreographer (1977–92) of the Royal Ballet

McMillan (mək'mɪlən) *n* **Edwin M**(**attison**) 1907–91, US physicist; Nobel prize for chemistry 1951 (with Glenn Seaborg) for the discovery of transuranic elements

Mcmurdo Sound (mək'mɜːdəʊ) *n* an inlet of the Ross Sea in Antarctica, north of Victoria Land

McNaughten Rules *or* **McNaghten Rules** (mək'nɔːtᵊn) *pl n* (in English law) a set of rules established by the case of Regina v. McNaughten (1843) by which legal proof of criminal insanity depends on the accused being shown to be incapable of understanding what he has done

MacNeice (mək'niːs) *n* **Louis** 1907–63, British poet, born in Northern Ireland. His works include *Autumn Journal* (1939) and *Solstices* (1961) and a translation of *Agamemnon* (1936)

Macon ('meɪkən) *n* a city in the US, in central Georgia, on the Ocmulgee River. Pop: 97 255 (2000)

Mâcon (*French* makɔ̃) *n* **1** a city in E central France, in the Saône valley: a centre of the wine-producing region of lower Burgundy. Pop: 39 700 (1995 est) **2** a red or white wine from the Mâcon area, heavier than the other burgundies

Maconchy (mə'kɒŋkɪ) *n* Dame **Elizabeth,** married name *Elizabeth LeFanu*. 1907–94, British composer of Irish parentage; noted esp for her chamber music, which includes 13 string quartets and *Romanza* (1980) for viola and ensemble

McPartlin (mək'pɑːtlɪn) *n* **Antony** born 1975, British television presenter, who appears with Declan Donnelly as Ant and Dec

Macpherson (mək'fɜːsᵊn) *n* **James** 1736–96, Scottish poet and translator. He published supposed translations of the legendary Gaelic poet Ossian, in reality largely his own work

McPherson (mɑc'fɜːsən) *n* **Conor** born 1972, Irish playwright and theatre director; his plays include *The Weir* (1997) and *Port Authority* (2001)

Macquarie (mə'kwɒrɪ) *n* **Lachlan** 1762–1824, Australian colonial administrator; Governor of New South Wales (1809–21), noted for his reformist policies towards ex-convicts and for his record in public works such as road-building in the colony

McQueen (mə'kwiːn) *n* **1 Alexander** born 1969, British fashion designer and master tailor **2 Steve** 1930–80, US film actor, noted for his portrayal of tough characters

macramé (mə'krɑːmɪ) *n* a type of ornamental work made by knotting and weaving coarse thread [c19 via F & It. from Turkish *makrama* towel, from Ar. *migramah* striped cloth]

Macready (mə'kriːdɪ) *n* **William Charles** 1793–1873, English actor and theatre manager

macro ('mækrəʊ) *n, pl* **macros 1** *photog* a camera lens used for close-up photography. Also called: **macro lens 2** *computing* a single computer instruction that initiates a set of instructions. Also called: **macro instruction** [c20 from Gk *makros* large]

macro- *or before a vowel* **macr-** *combining form* **1** large, long, or great in size or duration: *macroscopic* **2** *pathol* indicating abnormal enlargement or overdevelopment: *macrocephaly* [from Gk *makros* large]

macrobiotics (ˌmækrəʊbaɪ'ɒtɪks) *n (functioning as sing)* a dietary system which advocates whole grains and vegetables grown without chemical additives [c20 from MACRO- + Gk *biotos* life + -ICS] > ˌ**macrobi'otic** *adj*

macrocarpa (ˌmækrəʊ'kɑːpə) *n* a large Californian coniferous tree, used in New Zealand and elsewhere to form shelter belts on farms and for rough timber [c19 from NL, from MACRO- + Gk *karpos* fruit]

macrocephaly (ˌmækrəʊ'sɛfəlɪ) *n* the condition of having an abnormally large head or skull > **macrocephalic** (ˌmækrəʊsɪ'fælɪk) *or* ˌ**macro'cephalous** *adj*

macroclimate ('mækrəʊˌklaɪmɪt) *n* the predominant climate over a large area

macrocosm ('mækrəˌkɒzəm) *n* a complex structure, such as the universe or society, regarded as an entirety ▷ Cf **microcosm** [c16 via F & L from Gk *makros kosmos* great world] > ˌ**macro'cosmic** *adj* > ˌ**macro'cosmically** *adv*

macroeconomics (ˌmækrəʊˌiːkə'nɒmɪks, -ˌɛk-) *n (functioning as sing)* the branch of economics concerned with aggregates, such as national income, consumption, and investment > ˌ**macroˌeco'nomic** *adj*
▷ www.elsevier.com/homepage/sae/econworld/econbase/jmacro/frame.htm
▷ www.stern.nyu.edu/globalmacro

macromolecule (ˌmækrəʊ'mɒlɪˌkjuːl) *n* any very large molecule, such as a protein or synthetic polymer

macron ('mækrɒn) *n* a diacritical mark (¯) placed over a letter to represent a long vowel [c19 from Gk *makron* something long, from *makros* long]

macropod ('mækrəʊˌpɒd) *n* any member of a family of marsupials consisting of the kangaroos and related animals

macroscopic (ˌmækrəʊ'skɒpɪk) *adj* **1** large enough to be visible to the naked eye **2** comprehensive; concerned with large units [c19 see MACRO-, -SCOPIC] > ˌ**macro'scopically** *adv*

macula ('mækjʊlə) *or* **macule** ('mækjuːl) *n, pl* **maculae** (-jʊˌliː) *or* **macules** *anat* **1** a small spot or area of distinct colour, esp the macula lutea **2** any small discoloured spot or blemish on the skin, such as a freckle [c14 from L] > '**macular** *adj* > ˌ**macu'lation** *n*

macula lutea ('luːtɪə) *n, pl* **maculae luteae** ('luːtɪˌiː) a small yellowish oval-shaped spot on the retina of the eye, where vision is especially sharp [NL, lit.: yellow spot]

macular degeneration *n* pathological changes in the macula lutea, resulting in loss of central vision: a common cause of blindness in the elderly

mad (mæd) *adj* **madder, maddest 1** mentally deranged; insane **2** senseless; foolish **3** (often foll by *at*) *inf* angry; resentful **4** (foll by *about, on,* or *over;* often *postpositive*) wildly enthusiastic (about) or fond (of) **5** extremely excited or confused; frantic: *a mad rush* **6** temporarily overpowered by violent reactions, emotions, etc: *mad with grief* **7** (of animals) **7a** unusually ferocious: *a mad buffalo* **7b** afflicted with rabies **8 like mad** *inf* with great energy, enthusiasm, or haste ▷ *vb* **mads, madding, madded 9** *US or arch* to make or become mad; act or cause to act as if mad [OE *gemǣded*, p.p. of *gemǣdan* to render insane]

Madag. *abbrev for* Madagascar

Madagascar (ˌmædə'gæskə) *n* an island republic in the Indian Ocean, off the E coast of Africa: made a French protectorate in 1895; became autonomous in 1958 and fully independent in 1960; contains unique flora and fauna. Languages: Malagasy and French. Religions: animist and Christian. Currency: franc. Capital: Antananarivo. Pop: 15 983 000 (2001 est). Area: 587 041 sq km (266 657 sq miles). Official name (since 1975): **Democratic Republic of Madagascar** Former name (1958–75): **Malagasy Republic** > ˌ**Mada'gascan** *n, adj*
▷ www.embassy.org/madagascar
▷ www.madagascar-guide.com

madam ('mædəm) *n, pl* **madams** *or* (for sense 1) **mesdames 1** a polite term of address for a woman, esp one of relatively high social status **2** a woman who runs a brothel **3** *Brit inf* a precocious or pompous little girl [c13 from OF *ma dame* my lady]

madame ('mædəm) *n, pl* **mesdames** a married Frenchwoman: used as a title equivalent to *Mrs*, and sometimes extended to older unmarried women to show respect [c17 from F; see MADAM]

madcap ('mædˌkæp) *adj* **1** impulsive, reckless, or lively ▷ *n* **2** an impulsive, reckless, or lively person

mad cow disease *n* an informal name for **BSE**

madden ('mædᵊn) *vb* to make or become mad or angry > '**maddening** *adj* > '**maddeningly** *adv*

madder ('mædə) *n* **1** a plant having small yellow flowers and a red fleshy root **2** this root **3** a dark reddish-purple dye formerly obtained from this root **4** a red lake obtained from alizarin and an inorganic base; used as a pigment in inks and paints [OE *mædere*]

madding ('mædɪŋ) *adj arch* **1** acting or behaving as if mad: *the madding crowd* **2** making mad; maddening > '**maddingly** *adv*

made (meɪd) *vb* **1** the past tense and past participle of **make** ▷ *adj* **2** artificially produced **3** (*in combination*) produced or shaped as specified: *handmade* **4 get** *or* **have it made** *inf* to be assured of success

Madeira (mə'dɪərə; *Portuguese* mə'ðirə) *n* **1** a group of volcanic islands in the N Atlantic, west of Morocco: constitutes the Portuguese administrative district of Funchal; consists of the chief island, Madeira, Pôrto Santo, and the uninhabited Deserta and Selvagen Islands; gained partial autonomy in 1976. Capital: Funchal. Pop: 242 603 (2001). Area: 797 sq km (311 sq miles) **2** a river in W Brazil, flowing northeast to the Amazon below Manaus. Length: 3241 km (2013 miles) **3** a rich strong fortified white wine made on Madeira

madeleine ('mædəlɪn, -ˌleɪn) *n* a small fancy sponge cake [c19 ? after *Madeleine* Paulmier, F pastry cook]

mademoiselle (ˌmædmwə'zɛl) *n, pl* **mesdemoiselles 1** a young unmarried French girl or woman: used as a title equivalent to *Miss* **2** a French teacher or governess [c15 F, from *ma* my + *demoiselle* DAMSEL]

made-up *adj* **1** invented; fictional **2** wearing make-up **3** put together **4** (of a road) surfaced with tarmac, concrete, etc

madhouse ('mæd,haʊs) *n inf* **1** a mental hospital or asylum **2** a state of uproar or confusion

Madhya Bharat ('mʌdjə 'bɑːrət) *n* a former state of central India: part of Madhya Pradesh since 1956

Madhya Pradesh ('mʌdjə prɑː'dɛʃ) *n* a state of central India, situated on the Deccan Plateau: rich in mineral resources, with several industrial cities: formerly the largest Indian state, it lost much of the SE to the new state of Chhattisgarh in 2000. Capital: Bhopal. Pop: 60 385 118 (2001). Area: 308 332 sq km (119 016 sq miles)

Madiba (mə'diːbə) *n S African* a title of respect for Nelson Mandela, deriving from his Xhosa clan name

Madison[1] ('mædɪsᵊn) *n* a city in the US, in S central Wisconsin, on an isthmus between Lakes Mendota and Monona: the state capital. Pop: 208 054 (2000)

Madison[2] ('mædɪsᵊn) *n* **James** 1751–1836, US statesman; 4th president of the US (1809–17) He helped to draft the US Constitution and Bill of Rights. His presidency was dominated by the War of 1812

Madison Avenue *n* a street in New York City: a centre of American advertising and public-relations firms and a symbol of their attitudes and methods

madly ('mædlɪ) *adv* **1** in an insane or foolish manner **2** with great speed and energy **3** *inf* extremely or excessively: *I love you madly*

madman ('mædmən) *or (fem)* **madwoman** *n, pl* **madmen** *or* **madwomen** a person who is insane

madness ('mædnɪs) *n* **1** insanity; lunacy **2** extreme anger, excitement, or foolishness **3** a nontechnical word for **rabies**

Madonna[1] (mə'dɒnə) *n* **1** *chiefly RC Church* a designation of the Virgin Mary **2** (*sometimes not cap*) a picture or statue of the Virgin Mary [c16 It. from *ma* my + *donna* lady]

Madonna[2] (mə'dɒnə) *n* full name *Madonna Louise Veronica Ciccone*. born 1958, US rock singer and film actress. Her records include "Like a Virgin" (1985), "Like a Prayer" (1989), *Ray of Light* (1998), and *Music* (2000). Her films include *Desperately Seeking Susan* (1985), and *Evita* (1996)

Madonna lily *n* a perennial widely cultivated Mediterranean lily plant with white trumpet-shaped flowers

madras ('mædrəs, mə'dræs) *n* **1** a strong fine cotton or silk fabric, usually with a woven stripe **2** a medium-hot curry: *chicken madras* [from MADRAS]

Madras (mə'drɑːs, -'dræs) *n* **1** a port in SE India, capital of Tamil Nadu, on the Bay of Bengal: founded in 1639 by the English East India Company as **Fort St George;** traditional burial place of St Thomas; university (1857). Pop (city): 3 841 396 (1991), with a conurbation of 5 421 985 (1991). Official name: **Chennai** **2** the former name (until 1968) for the state of **Tamil Nadu**

madrasah, madrasa (mə'dræsə, 'mɑːdræsə), *or* **medrese** (mə'drɛseɪ) *n Islam* an educational institution, particularly for Islamic religious instruction [from Arabic, literally: place of learning]

Madre de Dios (*Spanish* 'maðre ðe 'ðios) *n* a river in NE South America, rising in SE Peru and flowing northeast to the Beni River in N Bolivia. Length: about 965 km (600 miles)

madrepore (,mædrɪ'pɔː) *n* any coral of the genus *Madrepora*, many of which occur in tropical seas and form large coral reefs [c18 via F from It. *madrepora* mother-stone] > ,**madre'poral, madreporic** (,mædrɪ'pɒrɪk), *or* ,**madre'porian** *adj*

Madrid (mə'drɪd) *n* the capital of Spain, situated centrally in New Castile: the highest European capital, at an altitude of about 700 m (2300 ft); a Moorish fortress in the 10th century, captured by Castile in 1083 and made capital of Spain in 1561 (replacing **Valladolid**); university (1836). Pop: 2 881 506 (1998 est)
▷ www.madridtourism.org
▷ www.europeanrailguide.com/destinationguides/madrid

madrigal ('mædrɪgᵊl) *n* **1** *music* a type of 16th- or 17th-century part song for unaccompanied voices, with an amatory or pastoral text **2** a short love poem [c16 from It., from Med. L *mātricāle* primitive, apparently from L *mātrīcālis*, from *matrīx* womb] > '**madrigal,esque** *adj* > **madrigalian** (,mædrɪ'gælɪən, -'geɪ-) *adj* > '**madrigalist** *n*

Madura (mə'dʊərə) *n* an island in Indonesia, off the NE coast of Java: extensive forests and saline springs. Capital: Pamekasan. Area: 5472 sq km (2113 sq miles) > **Madurese** (,mædjʊə'riːz) *adj, n*

Madurai ('mædjʊ,raɪ) *n* a city in S India, in S Tamil Nadu: centre of Dravidian culture for over 2000 years; cotton industry. Pop: 940 989 (1991). Former name: **Madura**

Maeander (miː'ændə) *n* ancient name of the river **Menderes** (sense 1) Also spelt: **Meander**

Maebashi ('mɑːɛ'bɑːʃiː) *n* a city in central Japan, on central Honshu: centre of sericulture and silk-spinning; university (1949). Pop: 284 780 (1995)

Maecenas (miː'siːnæs) *n* **1** **Gaius** ('gaɪəs) ?70–8 BC, Roman statesman; adviser to Augustus and patron of Horace and Virgil **2** a wealthy patron of the arts

maelstrom ('meɪlstrəʊm) *n* **1** a large powerful whirlpool **2** any turbulent confusion [c17 from obs. Du. *maelstroom*, from *malen* to whirl round + *stroom* STREAM]

Maelstrom ('meɪlstrəʊm) *n* a strong tidal current in a restricted channel in the Lofoten Islands off the NW coast of Norway

maenad ('miːnæd) *n* **1** *classical history* a woman participant in the orgiastic rites of Dionysus, Greek god of wine **2** a frenzied woman [c16 from L *Maenas*, from Gk *mainas* madwoman] > **mae'nadic** *adj*

maestoso (maɪ'stəʊsəʊ) *music* ▷ *adj, adv* **1** to be performed majestically ▷ *n, pl* **maestosos** **2** a piece or passage directed to be played in this way [c18 It.: majestic, from L *māiestās* MAJESTY]

Maestricht ('mɑːstrɪxt; *Dutch* maː'strɪxt) *n* an obsolete spelling of **Maastricht**

maestro ('maɪstrəʊ) *n, pl* **maestri** (-trɪ) *or* **maestros** **1** a distinguished music teacher, conductor, or musician **2** any master of an art: often used as a term of address [c18 It.: master]

Maeterlinck ('meɪtə,lɪŋk; *French* mɛtɛrlɛ̃k) *n* Comte **Maurice** (mɔris) 1862–1949, Belgian poet and dramatist, noted particularly for his symbolist plays, such as *Pelléas et Mélisande* (1892), which served as the basis for an opera by Debussy, and *L'Oiseau bleu* (1909). Nobel prize for literature 1911

mae west (meɪ) *n sl* an inflatable life jacket, esp as issued to the US armed forces [c20 after *Mae* WEST (1892–1980), US actress, renowned for her large bust]

Maewo (mɑː'eɪwəʊ) *n* an almost uninhabited island in Vanuatu. Also called: **Aurora**

MAF (mæf) *n* (in New Zealand) *acronym for* Ministry of Agriculture and Forestry

Mafeking ('mæfɪ,kɪŋ) *n* the former name (until 1980) of **Mafikeng**

Mafia ('mæfɪə) *n* **1** **the** an international secret criminal organization founded in Sicily, and carried to the US by Italian immigrants **2** any group considered to resemble the Mafia [c19 from Sicilian dialect of It., lit.: hostility to the law, ?from Ar. *mahyah* bragging]

Mafikeng ('mæfɪ,kɛŋ) *n* a town in N South Africa: besieged by the Boers for 217 days (1899–1900) during the second Boer War: administrative headquarters of the British protectorate of Bechuanaland until 1965, although outside its borders. Pop: 7000 (latest est). Former name (until 1980): **Mafeking**

mafioso (ˌmæfɪˈəʊsəʊ) *n, pl* **mafiosos** *or* **mafiosi** (-sɪ) a person belonging to the Mafia

mag. *abbrev for:* **1** magazine **2** magnitude

magainin (məˈgeɪnɪn) *n* any of a series of related substances with antibacterial properties, derived from the skins of frogs [c20 from Heb. *magain* a shield]

Magallanes (*Spanish* maɣaˈʎanes) *n* the former name of **Punta Arenas**

magazine (ˌmægəˈziːn) *n* **1** a periodical paperback publication containing articles, fiction, photographs, etc **2** a metal case holding several cartridges used in some firearms; it is removed and replaced when empty **3** a building or compartment for storing weapons, explosives, military provisions, etc **4** a stock of ammunition **5** *photog* another name for **cartridge** (sense 3) **6** a rack for automatically feeding slides through a projector **7** a TV or radio programme made up of a series of short nonfiction items [c16 via F *magasin* from It. *magazzino*, from Ar. *makhāzin*, pl. of *makhzan* storehouse, from *khazana* to store away]

magdalen (ˈmægdəlɪn) *or* **magdalene** (ˈmægdəˌliːn) *n* **1** *literary* a reformed prostitute **2** *rare* a reformatory for prostitutes [from Mary MAGDALENE]

Magdalena (ˌmægdəˈleɪnə, -ˈliː-; *Spanish* maɣðaˈlena) *n* a river in SW Colombia, rising on the E slopes of the Andes and flowing north to the Caribbean near Barranquilla. Length: 1540 km (956 miles)

Magdalena Bay *n* an inlet of the Pacific on the coast of NW Mexico, in Lower California

Magdalene (ˈmægdəˌliːn, ˌmægdəˈliːnɪ) *n* See **Mary Magdalene**

Magdalenian (ˌmægdəˈliːnɪən) *adj* **1** of or relating to the latest Palaeolithic culture in Europe, which ended about 10 000 years ago ▷ *n* **2 the** the Magdalenian culture [c19 from F *magdalénien*, after *La Madeleine*, village in Dordogne, France, near which artefacts of the culture were found]

Magdeburg (ˈmægdəˌbɜːg; *German* ˈmakdəbʊrk) *n* an industrial city and port in central Germany, on the River Elbe, capital of Saxony-Anhalt: a leading member of the Hanseatic League, whose local laws, the **Magdeburg Laws** were adopted by many European cities. Pop: 238 000 (1999 est)

Magellan[1] (məˈgɛlən) *n* **Strait of** a strait between the mainland of S South America and Tierra del Fuego, linking the S Pacific with the S Atlantic. Length: 600 km (370 miles). Width: up to 32 km (20 miles)

Magellan[2] (məˈgɛlən) *n* **Ferdinand** Portuguese name *Fernão de Magalhães*. ?1480–1521, Portuguese navigator in the service of Spain. He commanded an expedition of five ships that set out to sail to the East Indies via the West. He discovered the Strait of Magellan (1520), crossed the Pacific, and reached the Philippines (1521), where he was killed by natives. One of his ships reached Spain (1522) and was therefore the first to circumnavigate the world

Magellanic cloud (ˌmægɪˈlænɪk) *n* either of two small irregular galaxies near the S celestial pole. Distances: 163 000 light years (Large Magellanic Cloud), 196 000 light years (Small Magellanic Cloud)

magenta (məˈdʒɛntə) *n* **1a** a deep purplish red **1b** (*as adj*): *a magenta filter* **2** another name for **fuchsin** [c19 after *Magenta*, Italy, alluding to the blood shed in a battle there (1859)]

Maggiore (ˌmædʒɪˈɔːrɪ; *Italian* madˈdʒore) *n* **Lake** a lake in N Italy and S Switzerland, in the S Lepontine Alps

maggot (ˈmægət) *n* **1** the limbless larva of dipterous insects, esp the housefly and blowfly **2** *rare* a fancy or whim [c14 from earlier *mathek*; rel. to ON *mathkr* worm, OE *matha*, OHG *mado* grub]

maggoty (ˈmægətɪ) *adj* **1** of, like, or ridden with maggots **2** *Austral sl* angry

Magherafelt (ˈmæhərəˌfɛlt) *n* a district of N Northern Ireland, in Co Londonderry. Pop: 39 780 (2001). Area: 572 sq km (221 sq miles)

Maghreb *or* **Maghrib** (ˈmʌgrəb) *n* NW Africa, including Morocco, Algeria, Tunisia, and sometimes Libya [from Arabic, literally: the West] > **ˈMaghrebi** *or* **ˈMaghribi** *adj, n*

magi (ˈmeɪdʒaɪ) *pl n*, *sing* **magus** (ˈmeɪgəs) **1** See **magus 2 the three Magi** the wise men from the East who came to do homage to the infant Jesus (Matthew 2:1–12) [see MAGUS] > **magian** (ˈmeɪdʒɪən) *adj*

magic (ˈmædʒɪk) *n* **1** the art that, by use of spells, supposedly invokes supernatural powers to influence events; sorcery **2** the practice of this art **3** the practice of illusory tricks to entertain; conjuring **4** any mysterious or extraordinary quality or power **5 like magic** very quickly ▷ *adj* also: **magical 6** of or relating to magic **7** possessing or considered to possess mysterious powers **8** unaccountably enchanting **9** *inf* wonderful; marvellous ▷ *vb* **magics, magicking, magicked** (*tr*) **10** to transform or produce by or as if by magic **11** (foll by *away*) to cause to disappear as if by magic [c14 via OF *magique*, from Gk *magikē* witchcraft, from *magos* MAGUS] > **ˈmagically** *adv*

▷ www.themagiccircle.co.uk
▷ http://magic.rufy.com
▷ www.magictricks.com

magic bullet *n inf* any therapeutic agent, esp one in the early stages of development, reputed to be very effective in treating a condition, such as a malignant tumour, by specifically targeting the diseased tissue

magic eye *n* a miniature cathode-ray tube in some radio receivers, on the screen of which a pattern is displayed to assist tuning. Also called: **electric eye**

magician (məˈdʒɪʃən) *n* **1** another term for **conjuror 2** a person who practises magic **3** a person with extraordinary skill, influence, etc

magic lantern *n* an early type of slide projector

magic mushroom *n inf* any of various types of fungi that contain a hallucinogenic substance

magic realism *or* **magical realism** *n* a style of painting or writing that depicts images or scenes of surreal fantasy in a representational or realistic way > **magic realist** *or* **magical realist** *n*

magic square *n* a square array of rows of integers arranged so that the sum of the integers is the same when taken vertically, horizontally, or diagonally

Maginot line (ˈmæʒɪˌnəʊ) *n* **1** a line of fortifications built by France to defend its border with Germany prior to World War II; it proved ineffective **2** any line of defence in which blind confidence is placed [after André *Maginot* (1877–1932), F minister of war when the fortifications were begun in 1929]

magisterial (ˌmædʒɪˈstɪərɪəl) *adj* **1** commanding; authoritative **2** domineering; dictatorial **3** of or relating to a teacher or person of similar status **4** of or relating to a magistrate [c17 from LL *magisteriālis*, from *magister* master] > ˌ**magisˈterially** *adv*

magistracy (ˈmædʒɪstrəsɪ) *or* **magistrature** (ˈmædʒɪstrəˌtjʊə) *n, pl* **magistracies** *or* **magistratures 1** the office or function of a magistrate **2** magistrates collectively **3** the district under the jurisdiction of a magistrate

magistral (məˈdʒɪstrəl) *adj* **1** *pharmacol, obs* made up according to a special prescription **2** of a master; masterly [c16 from L *magistrālis*, from *magister* master] > **magistrality** (ˌmædʒɪˈstrælɪtɪ) *n*

magistrate (ˈmædʒɪˌstreɪt, -strɪt) *n* **1** a public officer concerned with the administration of law **2** another name for **justice of the peace** [c17 from L *magistrātus*, from *magister* master] > **ˈmagisˌtrateship** *n*

magistrates' court *n* (in England) a court held before two or more justices of the peace or a stipendiary magistrate to deal with minor crimes, certain civil actions, and preliminary hearings

Maglemosian *or* **Maglemosean** (ˌmæɡləˈməʊzɪən) *n* 1 the first Mesolithic culture of N Europe, dating from 8000 BC to about 5000 BC ▷ *adj* 2 designating or relating to this culture [c20 after the site at *Maglemose*, Denmark, where the culture was first classified]

magma (ˈmæɡmə) *n, pl* **magmas** *or* **magmata** (-mətə) 1 a paste or suspension consisting of a finely divided solid dispersed in a liquid 2 hot molten rock within the earth's crust which sometimes finds its way to the surface where it solidifies to form igneous rock [c15 from L: dregs (of an ointment), from Gk: salve made by kneading, from *massein* to knead] > **magmatic** (mæɡˈmætɪk) *adj*

Magna Carta *or* **Magna Charta** (ˈmæɡnə ˈkɑːtə) *n English history* the charter granted by King John at Runnymede in 1215, recognizing the rights and privileges of the barons, church, and freemen [Med. L: great charter]
▷ www.bl.uk/collections/treasures/magna.html

Magna Graecia (ˈmæɡnə ˈɡriːʃɪə) *n* (in the ancient world) S Italy, where numerous colonies were founded by Greek cities [Latin: Great Greece]

magnanimity (ˌmæɡnəˈnɪmɪtɪ) *n, pl* **magnanimities** generosity [c14 via OF from L *magnanimitās*, from *magnus* great + *animus* soul]

magnanimous (mæɡˈnænɪməs) *adj* generous and noble [c16 from L *magnanimus* great-souled] > **magˈnanimously** *adv*

magnate (ˈmæɡneɪt, -nɪt) *n* 1 a person of power and rank, esp in industry 2 *history* a great nobleman [c15 back formation from earlier *magnates*, from LL: great men, from L *magnus* great] > **ˈmagnateˌship** *n*

magnesia (mæɡˈniːʃə) *n* another name for **magnesium oxide** [c14 via Med. L from Gk *Magnēsia*, of *Magnēs*, ancient mineral-rich region] > **magˈnesian** *or* **magnesic** (mæɡˈniːsɪk) *adj*

magnesium (mæɡˈniːzɪəm) *n* a light silvery-white metallic element of the alkaline earth series that burns with an intense white flame: used in light structural alloys, flashbulbs, flares, and fireworks. Symbol: Mg; atomic no.: 12; atomic wt.: 24.305 [c19 NL, from MAGNESIA]

magnesium oxide *n* a white tasteless substance used as an antacid and laxative and in refractory materials. Formula: MgO. Also called: **magnesia**

magnet (ˈmæɡnɪt) *n* 1 a body that can attract certain substances, such as iron or steel, as a result of a magnetic field; a piece of ferromagnetic substance. See also **electromagnet** 2 a person or thing that exerts a great attraction [c15 via L from Gk *magnēs*, shortened from *ho Magnēs lithos* the Magnesian stone. See MAGNESIA]

magnetar (ˈmæɡnɪtɑː) *n* a type of neutron star that has a very intense magnetic field, over 1000 times greater than that of a pulsar [c20 from MAGNET(IC) (ST)AR, on the model of QUASAR]

magnetic (mæɡˈnɛtɪk) *adj* 1 of, producing, or operated by means of magnetism 2 of or concerned with a magnet 3 of or concerned with the magnetism of the earth: *the magnetic equator* 4 capable of being magnetized 5 exerting a powerful attraction: *a magnetic personality* > **magˈnetically** *adv*

magnetic constant *n* the magnetic permeability of free space; it has the value $4\pi \times 10^{-7}$ H m^{-1}

magnetic declination *n* the angle that a compass needle makes with the direction of the geographical north pole at any given point on the earth's surface

magnetic dip *or* **inclination** *n* another name for **dip** (sense 24)

magnetic dipole moment *n* a measure of the magnetic strength of a magnet or current-carrying coil, expressed as the torque produced when the magnet or coil is set with its axis perpendicular to unit magnetic field

magnetic disk *n* another name for **disk** (sense 2)

magnetic equator *n* an imaginary line on the earth's surface, near the equator, at all points on which there is no magnetic dip

magnetic field *n* a field of force surrounding a permanent magnet or a moving charged particle, in which another permanent magnet or moving charge experiences a force

magnetic flux *n* a measure of the strength of a magnetic field over a given area, equal to the product of the area and the magnetic flux density through it. Symbol: ϕ

magnetic mine *n* a mine designed to explode when a magnetic field such as that generated by the metal of a ship's hull is detected

magnetic needle *n* a slender magnetized rod used in certain instruments, such as the magnetic compass, for indicating the direction of a magnetic field

magnetic north *n* the direction in which a compass needle points, at an angle (the declination) from the direction of true (geographic) north

magnetic pick-up *n* a type of record-player pick-up in which the stylus moves an iron core in a coil, causing a changing magnetic field that produces the current

magnetic pole *n* 1 either of two regions in a magnet where the magnetic induction is concentrated 2 either of two variable points on the earth's surface towards which a magnetic needle points, where the lines of force of the earth's magnetic field are vertical

magnetic resonance *n* the response by atoms, molecules, or nuclei subjected to a magnetic field to radio waves or other forms of energy: used in medicine for scanning. See MAGNETIC RESONANCE IMAGING; MAGNETIC RESONANCE ANGIOGRAPHY

magnetic resonance angiography *n* a form of magnetic resonance imaging in which either the injection of a magnetic resonance contrast agent or the movement of the blood provides information of value in diagnosis. Abbrev: **MRA**

magnetic resonance imaging *n* a noninvasive medical diagnostic technique in which the absorption and transmission of high-frequency radio waves are analysed as they irradiate the hydrogen atoms in water molecules and other tissue components placed in a strong magnetic field. This computerized analysis provides a powerful aid to the diagnosis and treatment planning of many diseases, including cancer. Abbrev: **MRI**

magnetic storm *n* a sudden severe disturbance of the earth's magnetic field, caused by emission of charged particles from the sun

magnetic stripe *n* (across the back of various types of bank card, credit card, etc) a dark stripe of magnetic material consisting of several tracks onto which information may be coded and which may be read or written to electronically

magnetic tape *n* a long narrow plastic or metal strip coated or impregnated with iron oxide, chrome dioxide, etc, used to record sound or video signals or to store information in computing

magnetism (ˈmæɡnɪˌtɪzəm) *n* 1 the property of attraction displayed by magnets 2 any of a class of phenomena in which a field of force is caused by a moving electric charge 3 the branch of physics concerned with magnetic phenomena 4 powerful attraction

magnetite (ˈmæɡnɪˌtaɪt) *n* a black magnetizable mineral that is an important source of iron

magnetize *or* **magnetise** (ˈmæɡnɪˌtaɪz) *vb* **magnetizes, magnetizing, magnetized** *or* **magnetises, magnetising, magnetised** (*tr*) 1 to make (a substance or object) magnetic 2 to attract strongly > **ˈmagnetˌizable** *or* **ˈmagnetˌisable** *adj* > **ˌmagnetiˈzation** *or* **ˌmagnetiˈsation**

Mm

n > 'magnet,izer *or* 'magnet,iser *n*

magneto (mæg'ni:təʊ) *n, pl* **magnetos** a small electric generator in which the magnetic field is produced by a permanent magnet, esp one for providing the spark in an internal-combustion engine [c19 short for *magnetoelectric generator*]

magneto- *combining form* indicating magnetism or magnetic properties: *magnetosphere*

magnetoelectricity (mæg,ni:təʊɪlɛk'trɪsɪtɪ) *n* electricity produced by the action of magnetic fields > **mag,netoe'lectric** *or* **mag,netoe'lectrical** *adj*

magnetometer (,mægnɪ'tɒmɪtə) *n* any instrument for measuring the intensity or direction of a magnetic field, esp the earth's field > **,magne'tometry** *n*

magnetomotive (mæg,ni:təʊ'məʊtɪv) *adj* causing a magnetic flux

magnetosphere (mæg'ni:təʊ,sfɪə) *n* the region surrounding a planet, such as the earth, in which the behaviour of charged particles is controlled by the planet's magnetic field

magnetron ('mægnɪ,trɒn) *n* a two-electrode electronic valve used with an applied magnetic field to generate high-power microwave oscillations, esp for use in radar [c20 from MAGNET + ELECTRON]

magnet school *n* a school that attracts pupils from outside its immediate vicinity, either because of its high educational standards or because of its concentration on some specialist area

Magnificat (mæg'nɪfɪ,kæt) *n Christianity* the hymn of the Virgin Mary (Luke 1:46-55), used as a canticle [from the opening phrase, *Magnificat anima mea Dominum* (my soul doth magnify the Lord)]

magnification (,mægnɪfɪ'keɪʃən) *n* **1** the act of magnifying or the state of being magnified **2** the degree to which something is magnified **3** a magnified copy, photograph, drawing, etc, of something **4** a measure of the ability of a lens or other optical instrument to magnify

magnificence (mæg'nɪfɪsəns) *n* the quality of being magnificent [c14 via F from L *magnificentia*]

magnificent (mæg'nɪfɪsᵊnt) *adj* **1** splendid or impressive in appearance **2** superb or very fine **3** (esp of ideas) noble or elevated [c16 from L *magnificentior*, irregular comp. of *magnificus* great in deeds, from *magnus* great + *facere* to do] > **mag'nificently** *adv*

magnifico (mæg'nɪfɪkəʊ) *n, pl* **magnificoes** a magnate; grandee [c16 It. from L *magnificus*; see MAGNIFICENT]

magnify ('mægnɪ,faɪ) *vb* **magnifies, magnifying, magnified 1** to increase, cause to increase, or be increased in apparent size, as through the action of a lens, microscope, etc **2** to exaggerate or become exaggerated in importance: *don't magnify your troubles* **3** (*tr*) *arch* to glorify [c14 via OF from L *magnificāre* to praise] > **'magni,fiable** *adj*

magnifying glass *or* **magnifier** *n* a convex lens used to produce an enlarged image of an object

magniloquent (mæg'nɪləkwənt) *adj* (of speech) lofty in style; grandiloquent [c17 from L *magnus* great + *loquī* to speak] > **mag'niloquence** *n* > **mag'niloquently** *adv*

Magnitogorsk (*Russian* məgnita'gɔrsk) *n* a city in central Russia, on the Ural River: founded in 1930 to exploit local magnetite ores; site of one of the world's largest, but outdated, metallurgical plants. Pop: 428 100 (1999 est)

magnitude ('mægnɪ,tju:d) *n* **1** relative importance or significance: *a problem of the first magnitude* **2** relative size or extent **3** *maths* a number assigned to a quantity as a basis of comparison for the measurement of similar quantities **4** Also called: **apparent magnitude** *astron* the apparent brightness of a celestial body expressed on a numerical scale on which bright stars have a low value **5** Also called: **earthquake magnitude** *geol* a measure of the size of an earthquake based on the quantity of energy released [c14 from L *magnitūdō* size, from *magnus* great]

magnolia (mæg'nəʊlɪə) *n* **1** any tree or shrub of the genus *Magnolia* of Asia and North America: cultivated for their white, pink, purple, or yellow showy flowers **2** the flower of any of these plants **3a** a very pale pinkish-white colour **3b** (*as adj*): *magnolia walls* [c18 NL, after Pierre *Magnol* (1638–1715), F botanist]

magnox ('mægnɒks) *n* an alloy consisting mostly of magnesium with small amounts of aluminium, used in fuel elements of nuclear reactors [c20 from *mag(nesium) n(o) ox(idation)*]

magnox reactor *n* a nuclear reactor using carbon dioxide as the coolant, graphite as the moderator, and uranium cased in magnox as the fuel

magnum ('mægnəm) *n, pl* **magnums** a wine bottle holding the equivalent of two normal bottles (approximately 52 fluid ounces) [c18 from L: a big thing, from *magnus* large]

magnum opus *n* a great work of art or literature, esp the greatest single work of an artist [L]

Magog ('meɪgɒg) *n* See **Gog and Magog**

magpie ('mæg,paɪ) *n* **1** any of various birds having a black-and-white plumage, long tail, and a chattering call **2** any of various similar birds of Australia **3** *Brit* a person who hoards small objects **4** a person who chatters **5a** the outermost ring but one on a target **5b** a shot that hits this ring [c17 from *Mag*, dim. of *Margaret*, used to signify a chatterbox + PIE[2]]

Magritte (*French* magrit) *n* **René** (rəne) 1898–1967, Belgian surrealist painter. By juxtaposing incongruous objects, depicted with meticulous realism, his works create a bizarre and disturbing impression

maguey ('mægweɪ) *n* **1** any of various tropical American agave plants, esp one that yields a fibre or is used in making an alcoholic beverage **2** the fibre from any of these plants, used esp for rope [c16 Sp., of Amerind origin]

magus ('meɪgəs) *n, pl* **magi 1** a Zoroastrian priest **2** an astrologer, sorcerer, or magician of ancient times [c14 from L, from Gk *magos*, from OPersian *magus* magician]

Magus ('meɪgəs) *n* **Simon** *New Testament* a sorcerer who tried to buy spiritual powers from the apostles (Acts 8:9-24)

Magyar ('mægjɑ:) *n* **1** (*pl* **Magyars**) a member of the predominant ethnic group of Hungary **2** the Hungarian language ▷ *adj* **3** of or relating to the Magyars or their language **4** *sewing* of or relating to a style of sleeve cut in one piece with the bodice

Magyarország ('mɔdjɔrorsa:g) *n* the Hungarian name for **Hungary**

Mahabharata (,mɑ:hə'bɑ:rətə), **Mahabharatam,** *or* **Mahabharatum** (,mɑ:hə'bɑ:rətəm) *n* an epic Sanskrit poem of India of which the *Bhagavad-Gita* forms a part [Sansk., from *mahā* great + *bhārata* story]

▷ http://web.utk.edu/~jftzgrld/MBhHome.html

▷ http://larryavisbrown.homestead.com/files/xeno.mahabsynop.htm

Mahajanga (,mæhə'dʒæŋgə) *n* a port in NW Madagascar, on Bombetoka Bay. Pop: 100 807 (1993). Former name: **Majunga**

Mahalla el Kubra (mə'hɑ:lə ɛl 'ku:brə) *n* a city in N Egypt, on the Nile delta: one of the largest diversified textile centres in Egypt. Pop: 395 402 (1996)

Mahanadi (mə'hɑ:nədɪ) *n* a river in E India, rising in Chhattisgarh and flowing north, then south and east to the Bay of Bengal. Length: 885 km (550 miles)

maharajah *or* **maharaja** (,mɑ:hə'rɑ:dʒə) *n* any of various Indian princes, esp any of the rulers of the former native states [c17 Hindi, from *mahā* great + RAJAH]

maharani *or* **maharanee** (,mɑ:hə'rɑ:ni:) *n* **1** the wife of a maharajah **2** a woman holding the rank of

maharajah [c19 from Hindi, from *mahā* great + RANI]
Maharashtra (ˌmɑːhəˈræʃtrə) *n* a state of W central India, formed in 1960 from the Marathi-speaking S and E parts of former Bombay state: lies mainly on the Deccan plateau; mainly agricultural. Capital: Bombay. Pop: 96 752 247 (1994 est). Area: 307 690 sq km (118 800 sq miles)
maharishi (ˌmɑːhəˈriːʃɪ, məˈhɑːriːʃɪ) *n Hinduism* a Hindu teacher of religious and mystical knowledge [from Hindi, from *mahā* great + *rishi* sage]
mahatma (məˈhɑːtmə) *n (sometimes cap)* **1** *Hinduism* a Brahman sage **2** *theosophy* an adept or sage [c19 from Sansk. *mahātman*, from *mahā* great + *ātman* soul]
Mahayana (ˌmɑːhəˈjɑːnə) *n* **a** a liberal Buddhist school of Tibet, China, and Japan, whose adherents seek enlightenment for all sentient beings **b** *(as modifier)*: *Mahayana Buddhism* [from Sansk., from *mahā* great + *yāna* vehicle]
Mahdi (ˈmɑːdɪ) *n* **1** the title assumed by *Mohammed Ahmed*. ?1843–85, Sudanese military leader, who led a revolt against Egypt (1881) and captured Khartoum (1885) **2** *Islam* any of a number of Muslim messiahs expected to forcibly convert all mankind to Islam [Arabic *mahdīy* one who is guided, from *madā* to guide aright]
Mahé (mɑːˈheɪ) *n* an island in the Indian Ocean, the chief island of the Seychelles. Capital: Victoria. Pop: 67 338 (1997). Area: 147 sq km (57 sq miles)
Mahfouz *or* **Mahfuz** (mɑːˈfuːz) *n* **Naguib** (nɑːˈgiːb) born 1911, Egyptian novelist and writer, author of the trilogy of novels *Bain al-Kasrain* (1945–57). His novel *Children of Gebelawi* (1959) was banned by the Muslim authorities in Egypt. Nobel prize for literature 1988
mah jong *or* **mah-jongg** (ˌmɑːˈdʒɒŋ) *n* a game of Chinese origin, usually played by four people, using tiles bearing various designs [from Chinese, lit.: sparrows]
Mahler (ˈmɑːlə) *n* **Gustav** (ˈgʊstaf) 1860–1911, Austrian composer and conductor, whose music links the romantic tradition of the 19th century with the music of the 20th century. His works include nine complete symphonies for large orchestras, the symphonic song cycle *Das Lied von der Erde* (1908), and the song cycle *Kindertotenlieder* (1902)
mahlstick (ˈmɔːlˌstɪk) *n* a variant spelling of **maulstick**
mahogany (məˈhɒgənɪ) *n, pl* **mahoganies** **1** any of various tropical American trees valued for their hard reddish-brown wood **2** any of several trees with similar wood, such as African mahogany and Philippine mahogany **3a** the wood of any of these trees **3b** *(as modifier)*: *a mahogany table* **4a** a reddish-brown colour **4b** *(as adj)*: *mahogany skin* [c17 from ?]
Mahomet (məˈhɒmɪt) *n* a variant of **Mohammed**
Mahometan (məˈhɒmɪtᵊn) *n, adj* a former word for **Muslim**
mahonia (məˈhəʊnɪə) *n* any evergreen shrub of the Asian and American genus *Mahonia*: cultivated for their ornamental spiny divided leaves and clusters of small yellow flowers [c19 NL, after Bernard *McMahon* (died 1816), American botanist]
Mahound (məˈhaʊnd, -ˈhuːnd) *n* an archaic name for **Mohammed** [c16 from Old French *Mahun*]
mahout (məˈhaʊt) *n* (in India and the East Indies) an elephant driver or keeper [c17 Hindi *mahāut*, from Sansk. *mahāmātra* of great measure, orig. a title]
Mähren (ˈmɛːrən) *n* the German name for **Moravia**
mahseer (ˈmɑːsɪə) *n* any of various large freshwater Indian cyprinid fishes [from Hindi]
Mahy (ˈmɑːhɪ) *n* **Margaret** born 1936, New Zealand writer for children. Her books include *A Lion in the Meadow* (1969), *The Changeover* (1984), and *Alchemy* (2002)
Maia (ˈmaɪə) *n Greek myth* the eldest of the seven Pleiades, mother by Zeus of Hermes
maid (meɪd) *n* **1** *arch or literary* a young unmarried girl; maiden **2a** a female servant **2b** *(in combination)*: *a housemaid* **3** a spinster [c12 form of MAIDEN]
maiden (ˈmeɪdᵊn) *n* **1** *arch or literary* **1a** a young unmarried girl, esp a virgin **1b** *(as modifier)*: *a maiden blush* **2** *horse racing* **2a** a horse that has never won a race **2b** *(as modifier)*: *a maiden race* **3** *cricket* See **maiden over** **4** *(modifier)* of or relating to an older unmarried woman: *a maiden aunt* **5** *(modifier)* of or involving an initial experience or attempt: *a maiden voyage* **6** *(modifier)* (of a person or thing) untried; unused **7** *(modifier)* (of a place) never trodden, penetrated, or captured [OE *mægden*] > ˈ**maidenish** *adj* > ˈ**maidenˌlike** *adj*
maidenhair fern *or* **maidenhair** (ˈmeɪdᵊnˌhɛə) *n* any of various ferns having delicate fan-shaped fronds with small pale green leaflets [c15 from the hairlike appearance of its fronds]
maidenhair tree *n* another name for **ginkgo**
maidenhead (ˈmeɪdᵊnˌhɛd) *n* **1** a nontechnical word for the **hymen** **2** virginity; maidenhood [c13 from *maiden* + *-hed*, var. of -HOOD]
Maidenhead (ˈmeɪdᵊnˌhɛd) *n* a town in S England, in Windsor and Maidenhead unitary authority, Berkshire, on the River Thames. Pop: 59 605 (1991)
maidenhood (ˈmeɪdᵊnˌhʊd) *n* **1** the time during which a woman is a maiden or virgin **2** the condition of being a maiden or virgin
maidenly (ˈmeɪdᵊnlɪ) *adj* of or befitting a maiden > ˈ**maidenliness** *n*
maiden name *n* a woman's surname before marriage
maiden over *n cricket* an over in which no runs are scored
maid of honour *n* **1** *US & Canad* the principal unmarried attendant of a bride **2** *Brit* a small tart with an almond-flavoured filling **3** an unmarried lady attending a queen or princess
Maid of Orléans *n* **the** another name for **Joan of Arc**
maidservant (ˈmeɪdˌsɜːvənt) *n* a female servant
Maidstone (ˈmeɪdstən, -ˌstəʊn) *n* a town in SE England, administrative centre of Kent, on the River Medway. Pop: 90 878 (1991)
Maiduguri (ˌmaɪdʊˈguːrɪ) *n* a city in NE Nigeria, capital of Bornu State; agricultural trade centre. Pop: 320 000 (1996 est). Also called: **Yerwa-Maiduguri**
maihem (ˈmeɪhɛm) *n* a variant spelling of **mayhem**
Maikop (*Russian* majˈkɔp) *n* a city in SW Russia, capital of the Adygei Republic: extensive oilfields to the southwest; mineral springs. Pop: 167 000 (1999 est)
mail[1] (meɪl) *n* **1** Also called (esp Brit): **post** letters, packages, etc, that are transported and delivered by the post office **2** the postal system **3** a single collection or delivery of mail **4** a train, ship, or aircraft that carries mail **5** short for **electronic mail** **6** *(modifier)* of, involving, or used to convey mail: *a mail train* ▷ *vb (tr)* **7** *chiefly US & Canad* to send by mail **8** to contact (a person) by electronic mail **9** to send (a message, document, etc) by electronic mail [c13 from OF *male* bag, prob. from OHG *malha* wallet] > ˈ**mailable** *adj*
mail[2] (meɪl) *n* **1** a type of flexible armour consisting of riveted metal rings or links **2** the hard protective shell of such animals as the turtle and lobster ▷ *vb* **3** *(tr)* to clothe or arm with mail [c14 from OF *maille* mesh, from L *macula* spot]
mailbag (ˈmeɪlˌbæg) *or* **mailsack** *n* a large bag for transporting or delivering mail
mailbox (ˈmeɪlˌbɒks) *n* **1** another name (esp US and Canad) for **letter box** **2** (on a computer) **2a** the directory in which e-mail messages are stored **2b** the icon that can be clicked to provide access to e-mails
Mailer (ˈmeɪlə) *n* **Norman** born 1923, US author. His works, which are frequently critical of modern American society, include the war novel *The Naked and the Dead* (1948), *An American Dream* (1965), his account of the 1967 peace march on Washington *The Armies of the*

Night (1968), *The Executioner's Song* (1979), and *Barbary Shore* (1998)
mailing list *n* a register of names and addresses to which advertising matter, etc, is sent by post or electronic mail
Maillol (*French* majɔl) *n* **Aristide** (aristid) 1861–1944, French sculptor, esp of monumental female nudes
maillot (mæ'jəʊ) *n* **1** tights worn for ballet, gymnastics, etc **2** a woman's swimsuit **3** a jersey [from F]
mailman ('meɪl,mæn) *n, pl* **mailmen** *chiefly US & Canad* another name for **postman**
mail merging *n computing* a software facility that can produce a large number of personalized letters by combining a file containing a list of names and addresses with one containing a single standard document
mail order *n* **1** an order for merchandise sent by post **2a** a system of buying and selling merchandise through the post **2b** (*as modifier*): *a mail-order firm*
mailshot ('meɪl,ʃɒt) *n* a circular, leaflet, or other advertising material sent by post, or the posting of such material to a large group of people at one time
maim (meɪm) *vb* (*tr*) **1** to mutilate, cripple, or disable a part of the body of (a person or animal) **2** to make defective [c14 from OF *mahaignier* to wound, prob. of Gmc origin]
mai mai (maɪ maɪ) *n* NZ a duck shooter's shelter; hide [probably from Australian Aboriginal *mia-mia* shelter]
Maimonides (maɪ'mɒnɪ,di:z) *n* also called Rabbi *Moses ben Maimon*. 1135–1204, Jewish philosopher, physician, and jurist, born in Spain. He codified Jewish law in *Mishneh Torah* (1180)
main[1] (meɪn) *adj* (*prenominal*) **1** chief or principal **2** sheer or utmost (esp in **by main force**) **3** *naut* of, relating to, or denoting any gear, such as a stay or sail, belonging to the mainmast ▷ *n* **4** a principal pipe, conduit, duct, or line in a system used to distribute water, electricity, etc **5** (*pl*) **5a** the main distribution network for water, gas, or electricity **5b** (*as modifier*): *mains voltage* **6** the chief or most important part or consideration **7** great strength or force (now esp in **might and main**) **8** *literary* the open ocean **9** *arch* short for **Spanish Main** **10** *arch* short for **mainland** **11** **in** (*or* **for**) **the main** on the whole; for the most part [c13 from OE *mægen* strength]
main[2] (meɪn) *n* **1** a throw of the dice in dice games **2** a cockfighting contest **3** a match in archery, boxing, etc [c16 from ?]
Main (meɪn; *German* main) *n* a river in central and W Germany, flowing west through Würzburg and Frankfurt to the Rhine. Length: about 515 km (320 miles)
mainbrace ('meɪn,breɪs) *n naut* **1** a brace attached to the main yard **2** **splice the mainbrace** See **splice**
main clause *n grammar* a clause that can stand alone as a sentence
Maine (meɪn) *n* a state of the northeastern US, on the Atlantic: chiefly hilly, with many lakes, rivers, and forests. Capital: Augusta. Pop: 1 274 923 (2000). Area: 86 156 sq km (33 265 sq miles). Abbreviation: **Me** or (with zip code) **ME**
Maine-et-Loire (*French* mɛnelwar) *n* a department of W France, in Pays de la Loire region. Capital: Angers. Pop: 732 942 (1999). Area: 7218 sq km (2815 sq miles)
mainframe ('meɪn,freɪm) *computing* ▷ *adj* **1** denoting a high-speed general-purpose computer, usually with a large store capacity ▷ *n* **2** such a computer **3** the central processing unit of a computer
mainland ('meɪnlənd) *n* the main part of a landmass as opposed to an island or peninsula > **'mainlander** *n*
Mainland ('meɪnlənd) *n* **1** an island off N Scotland: the largest of the Shetland Islands. Chief town: Lerwick. Pop: 17 596 (1991). Area: about 583 sq km (225 sq miles) **2** Also called: **Pomona** an island off N Scotland: the largest of the Orkney Islands. Chief town: Kirkwall. Pop: 15 128 (1991). Area: 492 sq km (190 sq miles) **3** **the Mainland** NZ a South Islanders' name for **South Island**
main line *n* **1** *railways* **1a** the trunk route between two points, usually fed by branch lines **1b** (*as modifier*): *a main-line station* **2** *US* a main road ▷ *vb* **mainline, mainlines, mainlining, mainlined** **3** (*intr*) *sl* to inject a drug into a vein ▷ *adj* **mainline** **4** having an important position > **'main,liner** *n*
mainly ('meɪnlɪ) *adv* for the most part; to the greatest extent; principally
main market *n* the market for trading in the listed securities of companies on the London stock exchange ▷ Cf **Third Market, Unlisted Securities Market**
mainmast ('meɪn,mɑ:st) *n naut* the chief mast of a sailing vessel with two or more masts
mainsail ('meɪn,seɪl; *naut* 'meɪnsᵊl) *n naut* the largest and lowermost sail on the mainmast
mainsheet ('meɪn,ʃi:t) *n naut* the line used to control the angle of the mainsail to the wind
mainspring ('meɪn,sprɪŋ) *n* **1** the principal spring of a mechanism, esp in a watch or clock **2** the chief cause or motive of something
mainstay ('meɪn,steɪ) *n* **1** *naut* the forestay that braces the mainmast **2** a chief support
mainstream ('meɪn,stri:m) *n* **1a** the main current (of a river, cultural trend, etc) **1b** (*as modifier*): *mainstream politics* ▷ *adj* **2** of or relating to the style of jazz that lies between the traditional and the modern
mainstreeting ('meɪn,stri:tɪŋ) *n Canad* the practice of a politician walking about the streets of a town or city to gain votes and greet supporters
maintain (meɪn'teɪn) *vb* (*tr*) **1** to continue or retain; keep in existence **2** to keep in proper or good condition **3** to enable (a person) to support a style of living: *the money maintained us for a month* **4** (*takes a clause as object*) to state or assert **5** to defend against contradiction; uphold: *she maintained her innocence* **6** to defend against physical attack [c13 from OF *maintenir*, ult. from L *manū tenēre* to hold in the hand] > **main'tainable** *adj* > **main'tainer** *n*
maintenance ('meɪntɪnəns) *n* **1** the act of maintaining or the state of being maintained **2** a means of support; livelihood **3** (*modifier*) of or relating to the maintaining of buildings, machinery, etc: *maintenance man* **4** *law* the interference in a legal action by a person having no interest in it, as by providing funds to continue the action **5** *law* a provision ordered to be made by way of periodical payments or a lump sum, as for a spouse after a divorce [c14 from OF; see MAINTAIN]
Maintenon (*French* mɛ̃tnɔ̃) *n* **Marquise de,** title of *Françoise d'Aubigné*. 1635–1719, the mistress and, from about 1685, second wife of Louis XIV
maintop ('meɪn,tɒp) *n* a top or platform at the head of the mainmast
main-topmast *n naut* the mast immediately above the mainmast
maintopsail (,meɪn'tɒpsᵊl) *n naut* a topsail on the mainmast
main yard *n naut* a yard for a square mainsail
Mainz (*German* maints) *n* a port in W Germany, capital of the Rhineland-Palatinate, at the confluence of the Main and Rhine: an archbishopric from about 780 until 1801; important in the 15th century for the development of printing (by Johann Gutenberg). Pop: 185 600 (1999 est). French name: **Mayence**
maiolica (mə'jɒlɪkə) *n* a variant of **majolica**
maisonette *or* **maisonnette** (,meɪzə'nɛt) *n* self-contained living accommodation often occupying two floors of a larger house and having its own outside entrance [c19 from F, dim. of *maison* house]
mai tai ('maɪ ,taɪ) *n* a mixed drink consisting of rum, Curaçao, fruit juice, and grenadine [c20 from ?]
Maitland[1] ('meɪtlənd) *n* a town in SE Australia, in E

New South Wales: industrial centre of an agricultural region. Pop: 38 865 (latest est)
Maitland[2] (ˈmeɪtlənd) *n* **Frederic William** 1850–1906, English legal historian
maître d'hôtel (ˌmɛtrə dəʊˈtɛl) *n, pl* **maîtres d'hôtel** **1** a head waiter or steward **2** the manager or owner of a hotel [c16 from F: master of (the) hotel]
maize (meɪz) *n* **1** Also called: **sweet corn, Indian corn** **1a** a tall annual grass cultivated for its yellow edible grains, which develop on a spike **1b** the grain of this plant, used for food, for fodder, and as a source of oil **2a** a yellow colour **2b** (*as adj*): *a maize gown* [c16 from Sp. *maíz*, from Taino *mahiz*]
Maj. *abbrev for* Major
majestic (məˈdʒɛstɪk) *adj* having or displaying majesty or great dignity; grand; lofty > **maˈjestically** *adv*
majesty (ˈmædʒɪstɪ) *n* **1** great dignity of bearing; loftiness; grandeur **2** supreme power or authority [c13 from OF, from L *mājestās*; rel. to L *major*, comp. of *magnus* great]
Majesty (ˈmædʒɪstɪ) *n, pl* **Majesties** (preceded by *Your, His, Her,* or *Their*) a title used to address or refer to a sovereign or the wife or widow of a sovereign
majolica (məˈdʒɒlɪkə, məˈjɒl-) *or* **maiolica** *n* a type of porous pottery glazed with bright metallic oxides. It was originally imported into Italy via Majorca and was extensively made in Renaissance Italy [c16 from It., from LL *Mājorica* Majorca]
major (ˈmeɪdʒə) *n* **1** *mil* an officer immediately junior to a lieutenant colonel **2** a person who is superior in a group or class **3** a large or important company: *the oil majors* **4** (often preceded by *the*) *music* a major key, chord, mode, or scale **5** *US, Canad, Austral, & NZ* **5a** the principal field of study of a student **5b** a student who is studying a particular subject as his or her principal field: *a sociology major* **6** a person who has reached the age of legal majority **7** a principal or important record company, film company, etc **8** *logic* a major term or premise ▷ *adj* **9** larger in extent, number, etc **10** of greater importance or priority **11** very serious or significant **12** main, chief, or principal **13** of, involving, or making up a majority **14** *music* **14a** (of a scale or mode) having notes separated by a whole tone, except for the third and fourth degrees, and seventh and eighth degrees, which are separated by a semitone **14b** relating to or employing notes from the major scale: *a major key* **14c** (*postpositive*) denoting a specified key or scale as being major: *C major* **14d** denoting a chord or triad having a major third above the root **14e** (in jazz) denoting a major chord with a major seventh added above the root **15** *logic* constituting the major term or major premise of a syllogism **16** *chiefly US, Canad, Austral, & NZ* of or relating to a student's principal field of study at a university, etc **17** *Brit* the elder: used after a schoolboy's surname if he has one or more younger brothers in the same school: *Price major* **18** of full legal age ▷ *vb* **19** (*intr; usually foll by in*) *US, Canad, Austral, & NZ*. to do one's principal study (in a particular subject): *to major in English literature* **20** (*intr; usually foll by on*) to take or deal with as the main area of interest: *the book majors on peasant dishes* [c15 (adj): from L, comp. of *magnus* great; c17 (n, in military sense): from F, short for SERGEANT MAJOR] > ˈ**majorship** *n*
Major (ˈmeɪdʒə) *n* **John** born 1943, British Conservative politician: Chancellor of the Exchequer (1989–90); prime minister (1990–97)
Majorca (məˈjɔːkə, -ˈdʒɔː-) *n* an island in the W Mediterranean: the largest of the Balearic Islands; tourism. Capital: Palma. Pop: 605 510 (latest est). Area: 3639 sq km (1465 sq miles). Spanish name: **Mallorca**
major-domo (-ˈdəʊməʊ) *n, pl* **major-domos** **1** the chief steward or butler of a great household **2** *facetious* a steward or butler [c16 from Sp. *mayordomo*, from Med. L *mājor domūs* head of the household]
majorette (ˌmeɪdʒəˈrɛt) *n* **1** one of a group of girls who practise formation marching and baton twirling **2** See **drum majorette**
major general *n mil* an officer immediately junior to a lieutenant general > ˌ**major-ˈgeneralship** *or* **major-ˈgeneralcy** *n*
majority (məˈdʒɒrɪtɪ) *n, pl* **majorities** **1** the greater number or part of something **2** (in an election) the number of votes or seats by which the strongest party or candidate beats the combined opposition or the runner-up **3** the largest party or group that votes together in a legislative or deliberative assembly **4** the time of reaching or state of having reached full legal age **5** the rank, office, or commission of major **6** *euphemistic* the dead (esp in **join the majority, go** *or* **pass over to the majority**) **7** (*modifier*) of, involving, or being a majority: *a majority decision* **8** **in the majority** forming or part of the greater number of something [c16 from Med. L *mājoritās*, from MAJOR (adj)]

USAGE *The majority of* can only refer to a number of things or people. When talking about an amount, *most of* should be used: *most of* (not *the majority of*) *the harvest was saved*

major league *n US & Canad* a league of highest classification in baseball, football, hockey, etc
majorly (ˈmeɪdʒəlɪ) *adv sl, chiefly US & Canad* very; extremely: *it was majorly important for us to do that*
major orders *pl n RC Church* the three higher degrees of holy orders: bishop, priest, and deacon
major premise *n logic* the premise of a syllogism containing the predicate of its conclusion
major term *n logic* the predicate of the conclusion of a syllogism
Majunga (*French* maʒỹga) *n* the former name of **Mahajanga**
majuscule (ˈmædʒəˌskjuːl) *n* **1** a large letter, either capital or uncial, used in printing or writing ▷ *adj* **2** relating to, printed, or written in such letters ▷ Cf. **minuscule** [c18 via F from L *mājusculus*, dim. of *mājor* bigger] > **majuscular** (məˈdʒʌskjʊlə) *adj*
Makalu (ˈmʌkəˌluː) *n* a massif in NE Nepal, on the border with Tibet in the Himalayas
Makarios III (məˈkɑːrɪˌɒs) *n* original name *Mikhail Christodoulou Mouskos*. 1913–77, Cypriot archbishop, patriarch, and statesman; first president of the republic of Cyprus (1960–74; 1974–77)
Makasar, Makassar, *or* **Macassar** (məˈkæsə, -ˈkɑː-) *n* another name for **Ujung Pandang**
make (meɪk) *vb* **makes, making, made** (*mainly tr*) **1** to bring into being by shaping, changing, or combining materials, ideas, etc; form or fashion **2** to draw up, establish, or form: *to make one's will* **3** to cause to exist, bring about, or produce: *don't make a noise* **4** to cause, compel, or induce: *please make him go away* **5** to appoint or assign: *they made him chairman* **6** to constitute: *one swallow doesn't make a summer* **7** (*also intr*) to come or cause to come into a specified state or condition: *to make merry* **8** (*copula*) to be or become through development: *he will make a good teacher* **9** to cause or ensure the success of: *your news has made my day* **10** to amount to: *twelve inches make a foot* **11** to serve as or be suitable for: *that piece of cloth will make a coat* **12** to prepare or put into a fit condition for use: *to make a bed* **13** to be the essential element in or part of: *charm makes a good salesman* **14** to carry out, effect, or do **15** (*intr; foll by to, as if to,* or *as though to*) to act with the intention or with a show of doing something: *he made as if to hit her* **16** to use for a specified purpose: *I will make this town my base* **17** to deliver or pronounce: *to make a speech* **18** to give information or an opinion: *what time do you make it?* **19** to cause to seem or represent as being **20** to earn, acquire, or win for oneself: *to make friends* **21** to engage in: *to make war* **22** to traverse or cover (distance) by travelling: *we can*

Mm

make a hundred miles by nightfall **23** to arrive in time for: *he didn't make the first act of the play* **24** *cards* **24a** to win a trick with (a specified card) **24b** to shuffle (the cards) **24c** *bridge* to fulfil (a contract) by winning the necessary number of tricks **25** *cricket* to score (runs) **26** *electronics* to close (a circuit) permitting a flow of current **27** (*intr*) to increase in depth: *the water in the hold was making a foot a minute* **28** *inf* to gain a place or position on or in: *to make the headlines* **29** *inf, chiefly US* to achieve the rank of **30** *sl* to seduce **31** **make a book** to take bets on a race or another contest **32** **make a day, night,** etc, **of it** to cause an activity to last a day, night, etc **33** **make do** See **do**[1] (sense 32) **34** **make eyes at** to flirt with or ogle **35** **make it** **35a** *inf* to be successful in doing something **35b** (foll by *with*) *sl* to have sexual intercourse **36** **make like** *sl, chiefly US & Canad* **36a** to imitate **36b** to pretend ▷ *n* **37** brand, type, or style **38** the manner or way in which something is made **39** disposition or character; make-up **40** the act or process of making **41** the amount or number made **42** *cards* a player's turn to shuffle **43** **on the make** *sl* **43a** out for profit or conquest **43b** in search of a sexual partner ▷ See also **make away, make for,** etc [OE *macian*] > **'makable** *adj*

make away *vb* (*intr, adv*) **1** to depart in haste **2** **make away with** **2a** to steal or abduct **2b** to kill, destroy, or get rid of

Makeba (mə'keɪbə) *n* **Miriam** born 1932, South African singer and political activist; banned from South Africa from 1960 to 1990

make believe *vb* **makes believe, making believe, made believe** **1** to pretend or enact a fantasy ▷ *n* **make-believe** **2a** a fantasy or pretence **2b** (*as modifier*): *a make-believe world*

Makedhonia (ˌmakɛðɔ'nia) *n* transliteration of the Modern Greek name for **Macedonia** (sense 2)

make for *vb* (*intr, prep*) **1** to head towards **2** to prepare to attack **3** to help bring about

make of *vb* (*tr, prep*) **1** to interpret as the meaning of **2** to produce or construct from: *houses made of brick* **3** **make little, much,** etc, **of** **3a** to gain little, much, etc, benefit from **3b** to attribute little, much, etc, significance to

make off *vb* **1** (*intr, adv*) to go or run away in haste **2** **make off with** to steal or abduct

make out *vb* (*adv*) **1** (*tr*) to discern or perceive **2** (*tr*) to understand or comprehend **3** (*tr*) to write out: *he made out a cheque* **4** (*tr*) to attempt to establish or prove: *he made me out to be a liar* **5** (*intr*) to pretend: *he made out that he could cook* **6** (*intr*) to manage or fare

make over *vb* (*tr, adv*) **1** to transfer the title or possession of (property, etc) **2** to renovate or remodel: *she made over the dress to fit her sister* ▷ *n* **makeover** **3** a complete remodelling **4** a series of alterations, including beauty treatments and new clothes, intended to make a significant improvement to a person's appearance

maker ('meɪkə) *n* **1** a person or company who makes something; fabricator **2** a person who executes a legal document, esp one who signs a promissory note

Maker ('meɪkə) *n* **1** a title given to God (as Creator) **2** (**go to**) **meet one's Maker** to die

makeshift ('meɪkˌʃɪft) *adj* **1** serving as a temporary or expedient means ▷ *n* **2** something serving in this capacity

make-up *n* **1** cosmetics, such as powder, lipstick, etc, applied to the face **2a** the cosmetics, false hair, etc, used by an actor to adapt his appearance **2b** the art or result of applying such cosmetics **3** the manner of arrangement of the parts or qualities of someone or something **4** the arrangement of type matter and illustrations on a page or in a book **5** mental or physical constitution ▷ *vb* **make up** (*adv*) **6** (*tr*) to form or constitute: *these arguments make up the case for the defence* **7** (*tr*) to devise, construct, or compose, sometimes with the intent to deceive: *to make up an excuse* **8** (*tr*) to supply what is lacking or deficient in; complete: *these extra people will make up our total* **9** (*tr*) to put in order, arrange, or prepare: *to make up a bed* **10** (*intr*; foll by *for*) to compensate or atone (for) **11** to settle (differences) amicably (often in **make it up**) **12** to apply cosmetics to (the face) to enhance one's appearance or for a theatrical role **13** to assemble (type and illustrations) into (columns or pages) **14** (*tr*) to surface (a road) with tarmac, concrete, etc **15** **make up to** *inf* **15a** to make friendly overtures to **15b** to flirt with

makeweight ('meɪkˌweɪt) *n* **1** something put on a scale to make up a required weight **2** an unimportant person or thing added to make up a lack

Makeyevka (*Russian* ma'kjejɪfkə) *n* a city in the SE Ukraine: coal-mining centre. Pop: 394 800 (1998 est)

Makhachkala (*Russian* məxətʃka'la) *n* a port in SW Russia, capital of the Dagestan Republic, on the Caspian Sea: fishing fleet; oil refining. Pop: 334 900 (1999 est). Former name (until 1921): **Petrovsk**

making ('meɪkɪŋ) *n* **1a** the act of a person or thing that makes or the process of being made **1b** (*in combination*): *watchmaking* **2** **be the making of** to cause the success of **3** **in the making** in the process of becoming or being made **4** something made or the quantity of something made at one time

makings ('meɪkɪŋz) *pl n* **1** potentials, qualities, or materials: *he had the makings of a leader* **2** Also called: **rollings** *sl* the tobacco and cigarette paper used for rolling a cigarette **3** profits; earnings

Makkah *or* **Makah** ('mækə, -kɑː) *n* transliteration of the Arabic name for **Mecca**

mako[1] ('mɑːkəʊ) *n, pl* **makos** a blue-pointer game shark [from Maori]

mako[2] ('mɑːkəʊ) *n, pl* **makos** a small evergreen New Zealand tree [from Maori]

Makurdi (mə'kɜːdɪ) *n* a port in E central Nigeria, capital of Benue State on the Benue River: agricultural trade centre. Pop: 123 100 (1996 est)

Mal. *abbrev for:* **1** *Bible* Malachi **2** Malay(an)

mal- *combining form* bad or badly; wrong or wrongly; imperfect or defective: *maladjusted; malfunction* [OF, from L *malus* bad, *male* badly]

Malabar Coast *or* **Malabar** ('mæləˌbɑː) *n* a region along the SW coast of India, extending from Goa to Cape Comorin: includes most of Kerala state

Malabo (mə'lɑːbəʊ) *n* the capital and chief port of Equatorial Guinea, on the island of Bioko in the Gulf of Guinea. Pop: 58 040 (1991 est). Former name (until 1973): **Santa Isabel**

malabsorption (mæləb'sɔːpʃən) *n* a failure of absorption, esp by the small intestine in coeliac disease, cystic fibrosis, etc

malacca *or* **malacca cane** (mə'lækə) *n* **1** the stem of the rattan palm **2** a walking stick made from this stem

Malacca (mə'lækə) *n* a state of SW Peninsular Malaysia: rubber plantations. Capital: Malacca. Pop: 602 867 (2000). Area: 1650 sq km (637 sq miles)

Malachi ('mæləˌkaɪ) *n Old Testament* **1** a Hebrew prophet of the 5th century BC **2** the book containing his oracles. Douay spelling: **Malachias** (ˌmælə'kaɪəs)

malachite ('mæləˌkaɪt) *n* a green mineral consisting of hydrated basic copper carbonate: a source of copper, also used for making ornaments [C16 via OF from L *molochītēs*, from Gk *molokhitis* mallow-green stone, from *molokhē* mallow]

maladjustment (ˌmælə'dʒʌstmənt) *n* **1** *psychol* a failure to meet the demands of society, such as coping with problems and social relationships **2** faulty or bad adjustment > ˌ**malad'justed** *adj*

maladminister (ˌmæləd'mɪnɪstə) *vb* (*tr*) to administer badly, inefficiently, or dishonestly

maladministration (ˌmælədˌmɪnɪ'streɪʃən) *n* bad, inefficient, or dishonest management of the affairs of an organization, such as a business or institution

maladroit (ˌmæləˈdrɔɪt) *adj* **1** clumsy; not dexterous **2** tactless and insensitive [c17 from F, from *mal* badly + ADROIT] > ˌ**malaˈdroitly** *adv* > ˌ**malaˈdroitness** *n*

malady (ˈmælədɪ) *n, pl* **maladies** **1** any disease or illness **2** any unhealthy, morbid, or desperate condition [c13 from OF, from Vulgar L *male habitus* (unattested) in poor condition, from L *male* badly + *habitus*, from *habēre* to have]

Málaga (ˈmæləgə; *Spanish* ˈmalaɣa) *n* **1** a port and resort in S Spain, in Andalusia on the Mediterranean. Pop: 528 079 (1998 est) **2** a sweet fortified dessert wine from Málaga

Malagasy (ˌmæləˈgæsɪ) *n* **1** (*pl* **Malagasy** *or* **Malagasies**) a native or inhabitant of Madagascar **2** the official language of Madagascar ▷ *adj* **3** of or relating to Madagascar, its people, or their language

Malagasy Republic *n* the former name (1958–75) of **Madagascar**

malaise (mæˈleɪz) *n* **1** a feeling of unease or depression **2** a mild sickness, not symptomatic of any disease or ailment **3** a complex of problems affecting a country, economy, etc: *Bulgaria's economic malaise* [c18 from OF, from *mal* bad + *aise* EASE]

Malamud (ˈmæləməd, -mʊd) *n* **Bernard** 1914–86, US novelist and short-story writer. His works include *The Fixer* (1966) and *Dubin's Lives* (1979)

malamute *or* **malemute** (ˈmæləˌmuːt) *n* an Alaskan dog of the spitz type [from the name of an Inuit tribe]

Malang (ˈmælæŋ) *n* a city in S Indonesia, on E Java: commercial centre. Pop: 763 400 (1995 est)

malapropism (ˈmæləprɒpˌɪzəm) *n* **1** the unintentional misuse of a word by confusion with one of similar sound, esp when creating a ridiculous effect, as in *under the affluence of alcohol* **2** the habit of misusing words in this manner [c18 after Mrs *Malaprop* in Sheridan's play *The Rivals* (1775), a character who misused words, from MALAPROPOS]

malapropos (ˌmælæprəˈpəʊ) *adj* **1** inappropriate or misapplied ▷ *adv* **2** in an inappropriate way or manner ▷ *n* **3** something inopportune or inappropriate [c17 from F *mal à propos* not to the purpose]

Mälar (ˈmeɪlə) *n* **Lake** a lake in S Sweden, extending 121 km (75 miles) west from Stockholm, where it joins with an inlet of the Baltic Sea (the **Saltsjön**). Area: 1140 sq km (440 sq miles) Swedish name: **Mälaren** (ˈmelaren)

malaria (məˈlɛərɪə) *n* an infectious disease characterized by recurring attacks of chills and fever, caused by the bite of an anopheles mosquito infected with any of certain protozoans [c18 from It. *mala aria* bad air, from the belief that the disease was caused by the unwholesome air in swampy districts] > **maˈlarial, maˈlarian,** *or* **maˈlarious** *adj*

malarkey *or* **malarky** (məˈlɑːkɪ) *n sl* nonsense; rubbish [c20 from ?]

Malatesta (*Italian* malaˈtɛsta) *n* an Italian family that ruled Rimini from the 13th to the 16th century

Malathion (ˌmæləˈθaɪɒn) *n trademark* an insecticide consisting of an organic phosphate [c20 from (*diethyl*) MAL(EATE) + THIO- + -ON]

Malatya (ˌmɑːlɑːˈtjɑː) *n* a city in E central Turkey: nearby is the ruined Roman and medieval city of Melitene (Old Malatya). Pop: 400 248 (1997)

Malawi (məˈlɑːwɪ) *n* **1** a republic in E central Africa: established as a British protectorate in 1891; became independent in 1964 and a republic, within the Commonwealth, in 1966; lies along the Great Rift Valley, with Lake Nyasa (Malawi) along the E border, the Nyika Plateau in the northwest, and the Shiré Highlands in the southeast. Official language: Chichewa; English and various other Bantu languages are also widely spoken. Religion: Christian majority, Muslim, and animist minorities. Currency: kwacha. Capital: Lilongwe. Pop: 10 491 000 (2001 est). Area: 118 484 sq km (45 747 sq miles). Former name: **Nyasaland** **2** **Lake** the Malawi name for (Lake) **Nyasa**
▷ www.maform.malawi.net
▷ www.tourismmalawi.com

Malay (məˈleɪ) *n* **1** a member of a people living chiefly in Malaysia and Indonesia **2** the language of this people ▷ *adj* **3** of or relating to the Malays or their language

Malaya (məˈleɪə) *n* **1** **States of the Federation of** part of Malaysia, in the S Malay Peninsula, constituting Peninsular Malaysia: consists of the former Federated Malay States, the former Unfederated Malay States, and the former Straits Settlements. Capital: Kuala Lumpur. Pop: 16 567 142 (2000). Area: 131 587 sq km (50 806 sq miles) **2** **Federation of** a federation of the nine Malay States of the Malay Peninsula and two of the Straits Settlements (Malacca and Penang): formed in 1948: became part of the British Commonwealth in 1957 and joined Malaysia in 1963 > **Maˈlayan** *adj, n*

Malayalam *or* **Malayalaam** (ˌmælɪˈɑːləm) *n* a language of SW India

Malay Archipelago *n* a group of islands in the Indian and Pacific Oceans, between SE Asia and Australia: the largest group of islands in the world; includes over 3000 Indonesian islands, about 7000 islands of the Philippines, and, sometimes, New Guinea

Malayo-Polynesian *n* **1** Also called: **Austronesian** a family of languages extending from Madagascar to the central Pacific ▷ *adj* **2** of or relating to this family of languages

Malay Peninsula *n* a peninsula of SE Asia, extending south from the Isthmus of Kra in Thailand to Cape Tanjong Piai in Malaysia: consists of SW Thailand and the states of Malaya (Peninsular Malaysia). Ancient name: **Chersonesus Aurea** (ˌkɜːsəˈniːsəs ˈɔːrɪə)

Malaysia (məˈleɪzɪə) *n* a federation in SE Asia (within the Commonwealth), consisting of **Peninsular Malaysia** on the Malay Peninsula, and **East Malaysia** (Sabah and Sarawak), occupying the N part of the island of Borneo: formed in 1963 as a federation of Malaya, Sarawak, Sabah, and Singapore (the latter seceded in 1965); densely forested and mostly mountainous. Official language: Malay; English and various Chinese and Indian minority languages are also spoken. Official religion: Muslim. Currency: ringgit. Capital: Putrajaya (the transfer of government from Kuala Lumpur is scheduled for completion by 2005). Pop: 22 602 000 (2001 est). Area: 333 403 sq km (128 727 sq miles) > **Maˈlaysian** *adj, n*
▷ http://mcsl.mampu.gov.my
▷ http://tourism.gov.my
▷ www.visitmalaysia.com

Malay States *pl n* the former states of the Malay Peninsula that, together with Penang and Malacca, formed the Union of Malaya (1946) and the Federation of Malaya (1948). Perak, Selangor, Negri Sembilan, and Pahang were established as the **Federated Malay States** by the British in 1895 and Perlis, Kedah, Kelantan, and Trengannu as the **Unfederated Malay States** in 1909 (joined by Johore in 1914)

Malcolm III *n* died 1093, king of Scotland (1057–93). He became king after Macbeth

Malcolm X (ɛks) *n* original name *Malcolm Little*. 1925–65, US Black civil-rights leader: assassinated

malcontent (ˈmælkənˌtɛnt) *adj* **1** disgusted or discontented ▷ *n* **2** a person who is malcontent [c16 from OF]

mal de mer *French* (mal də mɛr) *n* seasickness

Maldives (ˈmɔːldaɪvz) *pl n* **Republic of** a republic occupying an archipelago of 1087 coral islands in the Indian Ocean, southwest of Sri Lanka: came under British protection in 1887; became independent in 1965 and a republic in 1968; a member of the

Mm

Commonwealth. Official language: Divehi. Official religion: (Sunni) Muslim. Currency: rufiyaa. Capital: Malé. Pop: 275 000 (2001 est). Area: 298 sq km (115 sq miles). Also called: **Maldive Islands** > **Maldivian** (mɔːlˈdɪvɪən) *or* **Maldivan** (ˈmɔːldaɪvᵊn, -dɪ-) *adj, n*
▷ www.visitmaldives.com
▷ www.maldive.com

Maldon (ˈmɔːldən) *n* a market town in SE England, in Essex; scene of a battle (991) between the East Saxons and the victorious Danes, celebrated in *The Battle of Maldon*, an Old English poem. Pop: 15 841 (1991)

male (meɪl) *adj* **1** of, relating to, or designating the sex producing gametes (spermatozoa) that can fertilize female gametes (ova) **2** of, relating to, or characteristic of a man **3** for or composed of men or boys: *a male choir* **4** (of gametes) capable of fertilizing an egg cell **5** (of reproductive organs) capable of producing male gametes **6** (of flowers) bearing stamens but lacking a functional pistil **7** *electronics, engineering* having a projecting part or parts that fit into a female counterpart: *a male plug* ▷ *n* **8** a male person, animal, or plant [c14 via OF from L *masculus* MASCULINE] > ˈ**maleness** *n*

Malé (ˈmɑːleɪ) *n* the capital of the Republic of Maldives, on Malé Island in the centre of the island group. Pop: 62 973 (1995 est)
▷ www.visitmaldives.com/thecapital/index.html

maleate (ˈmælɪˌeɪt) *n* any salt or ester of maleic acid [c19 from MALE(IC) ACID + -ATE[1]]

Malebranche (*French* malbrɑ̃ʃ) *n* **Nicolas** (nikɔla) 1638–1715, French philosopher. Originally a follower of Descartes, he developed the philosophy of occasionalism, esp in *De la recherche de la vérité* (1674)

male chauvinism *n* the belief, held or alleged to be held by certain men, that men are superior to women > **male chauvinist** *n, adj*

malediction (ˌmælɪˈdɪkʃən) *n* **1** the utterance of a curse against someone or something **2** a slanderous accusation or comment [c15 from L *maledictiō* a reviling, from *male* ill + *dīcere* to speak] > ˌ**maleˈdictive** *or* ˌ**maleˈdictory** *adj*

malefactor (ˈmælɪˌfæktə) *n* a criminal; wrongdoer [c15 via OF from L, from *malefacere* to do evil] > ˈ**maleˌfaction** *n*

maleficent (məˈlɛfɪsənt) *adj* causing evil or mischief; harmful or baleful [c17 from L, from *maleficus* wicked, from *malum* evil] > **maˈlefic** *adj* > **maˈleficence** *n*

maleic acid (məˈleɪɪk) *n* a colourless soluble crystalline substance used to synthesize other compounds, such as polyester resins. Formula: HOOCCH:CHCOOH. Systematic name: **cis-butenedioic acid** [c19 from F *maléique*, altered form of *malique*; see MALIC ACID]

male menopause *n* a period in a man's later middle age in which he may experience an identity crisis as he feels age overtake his sexual powers

Malenkov (*Russian* məlɪnˈkɔf) *n* **Georgi Maksimilianovich** (gɪˈɔrgij ˌməksjimɪlˈjanəvjɪtʃ) 1902–88, Soviet politician; prime minister (1953–55). He was removed from the party presidium (1957) for plotting against Khrushchev; expelled from the Communist Party (1961)

Malevich (*Russian* ˈmalɪvitʃ) *n* **Kasimir** (kəziˈmir) 1878–1935, Russian painter. He founded the abstract art movement known as Suprematism

malevolent (məˈlɛvələnt) *adj* wishing or appearing to wish evil to others; malicious [c16 from L *malevolens*, from *male* ill + *volens*, present participle of *velle* to wish] > **maˈlevolence** *n* > **maˈlevolently** *adv*

malfeasance (mælˈfiːzᵊns) *n law* the doing of a wrongful or illegal act, esp by a public official ▷ Cf **misfeasance, nonfeasance** [c17 from OF *mal faisant*, from *mal* evil + *faisant*, from *faire* to do, from L *facere*] > **malˈfeasant** *n, adj*

malformation (ˌmælfɔːˈmeɪʃən) *n* **1** the condition of being faulty or abnormal in form or shape **2** *pathol* a deformity, esp when congenital > **malˈformed** *adj*

malfunction (mælˈfʌŋkʃən) *vb* **1** (*intr*) to function imperfectly or fail to function ▷ *n* **2** failure to function or defective functioning

Malherbe (*French* malɛrb) *n* **François de** (frɑ̃swa də) 1555–1628, French poet and critic. He advocated the classical ideals of clarity and concision of meaning

Mali (ˈmɑːlɪ) *n* a landlocked republic in West Africa: conquered by the French by 1898 and incorporated (as French Sudan) into French West Africa; became independent in 1960; settled chiefly in the basins of the Rivers Senegal and Niger in the south. Official language: French. Religion: Muslim majority, also animist. Currency: franc. Capital: Bamako. Pop: 11 009 000 (2001 est). Area: 1 248 574 sq km (482 077 sq miles). Former name (1898–1959): **French Sudan**

malic acid (ˈmælɪk, ˈmeɪ-) *n* a colourless crystalline compound occurring in apples and other fruits [c18 *malic*, via F *malique* from L *mālum* apple]

malice (ˈmælɪs) *n* **1** the desire to do harm or mischief **2** evil intent **3** *law* the state of mind with which an act is committed and from which the intent to do wrong may be inferred [c13 via OF from L *malitia*, from *malus* evil]

malice aforethought *n law* **1** the predetermination to do an unlawful act, esp to kill or seriously injure **2** the intent with which an unlawful killing is effected, which must be proved for the crime to constitute murder

malicious (məˈlɪʃəs) *adj* **1** characterized by malice **2** motivated by wrongful, vicious, or mischievous purposes > **maˈliciously** *adv* > **maˈliciousness** *n*

malign (məˈlaɪn) *adj* **1** evil in influence, intention, or effect ▷ *vb* **2** (*tr*) to slander or defame [c14 via OF from L *malīgnus* spiteful, from *malus* evil] > **maˈligner** *n* > **maˈlignly** *adv*

malignancy (məˈlɪgnənsɪ) *n, pl* **malignancies 1** the state or quality of being malignant **2** *pathol* a cancerous growth

malignant (məˈlɪgnənt) *adj* **1** having or showing desire to harm others **2** tending to cause great harm; injurious **3** *pathol* (of a tumour) uncontrollable or resistant to therapy [c16 from LL *malīgnāre* to behave spitefully, from L *malīgnus* MALIGN] > **maˈlignantly** *adv*

malignity (məˈlɪgnɪtɪ) *n, pl* **malignities 1** the condition or quality of being malign or deadly **2** (*often pl*) a malign or malicious act or feeling

malines (məˈliːn) *n* **1** a type of silk net used in dressmaking **2** another name for **Mechlin lace** [c19 from F *Malines* (Mechelen), where this lace was traditionally made]

Malines (malin) *n* the French name for **Mechelen**

malinger (məˈlɪŋgə) *vb* (*intr*) to pretend or exaggerate illness, esp to avoid work [c19 from F *malingre* sickly, ?from *mal* badly + OF *haingre* feeble] > **maˈlingerer** *n*

Malinowski (ˌmælɪˈnɒfskɪ) *n* **Bronislaw Kasper** (brɔˈnislaf ˈkaspɛr) 1884–1942, Polish anthropologist in England and the US, who researched into the sexual behaviour of primitive people in New Guinea and Melanesia

Maliseet (ˈmæləˈsiːt) *n* a member of a Native Canadian people of New Brunswick and E Quebec **2** the Algonquian language of this people [from Micmac *malisiit*, one speaking an incomprehensible language]

mall (mɔːl, mæl) *n* **1** a shaded avenue, esp one open to the public **2** short for **shopping mall** [c17 after *the Mall*, in St James's Park, London]

mallard (ˈmælɑːd) *n, pl* **mallard** *or* **mallards** a duck common over most of the N hemisphere, the male of which has a dark green head and reddish-brown breast: the ancestor of all domestic breeds of duck [c14 from OF *mallart*, ?from *maslart* (unattested); see MALE, -ARD]

Mallarmé (*French* malarme) *n* **Stéphane** (stefan) 1842–98, French symbolist poet, noted for his free verse, in which he chooses words for their evocative qualities; his works include *L'Après-midi d'un Faune* (1876), *Vers et Prose* (1893), and *Divagations* (1897)

Malle (*French* mal) *n* **Louis** 1932–95, French film director: his films include *Le Feu follet* (1963), *Au revoir les enfants* (1987), and *Vanya on 42nd Street* (1994)

malleable ('mælɪəbᵊl) *adj* **1** (esp of metal) able to be worked, hammered, or shaped under pressure or blows without breaking **2** able to be influenced; pliable or tractable [c14 via OF from Med. L *malleābilis*, from L *malleus* hammer] > ˌ**mallea'bility** *or* (*less commonly*) '**malleableness** *n* > '**malleably** *adv*

mallee ('mæli:) *n* **1** any of several low shrubby eucalyptus trees in desert regions of Australia **2** (usually preceded by *the*) *Austral inf* another name for the **bush** (sense 4) [c19 Abor.]

Mallee ('mæli:) *n* a region in NW Victoria, Australia

mallee fowl *n* an Australian megapode

malleolus (mə'li:ələs) *n, pl* **malleoli** (-ˌlaɪ) either of two rounded bony projections, one on each side of the ankle [c17 dim. of L *malleus* hammer]

mallet ('mælɪt) *n* **1** a tool resembling a hammer but having a large head of wood, copper, lead, leather, etc, used for driving chisels, beating sheet metal, etc **2** a long stick with a head like a hammer used to strike the ball in croquet or polo [c15 from OF *maillet* wooden hammer, dim. of *mail* MAUL (n)]

malleus ('mælɪəs) *n, pl* **mallei** (-lɪˌaɪ) the outermost and largest of the three small bones in the middle ear of mammals. See also **incus, stapes** [c17 from L: hammer]

mallie ('mɔ:lɪ) *n inf, chiefly US* a teenage girl who spends most of her spare time loitering in shopping malls

Mallorca (ma'ʎɔrka) *n* the Spanish name for **Majorca**

mallow ('mæləʊ) *n* **1** any of several malvaceous plants of Europe, having purple, pink, or white flowers **2** any of various related plants, such as the marsh mallow [OE *mealuwe*, from L *malva*]

malm (mɑ:m) *n* **1** a soft greyish limestone that crumbles easily **2** a chalky soil formed from this **3** an artificial mixture of clay and chalk used to make bricks [OE *mealm-* (in compound words)]

Malmédy (*French* malmedi) *n* See **Eupen and Malmédy**

Malmö ('mælməʊ; *Swedish* 'malmø:) *n* a port in S Sweden, on the Sound: part of Denmark until 1658; industrial centre. Pop: 257 574 (2000 est)

malmsey ('mɑ:mzɪ) *n* a sweet Madeira wine [c15 from Med. L *Malmasia*, corruption of Gk *Monembasia*, Gk port from which the wine was shipped]

malnutrition (ˌmælnju:'trɪʃən) *n* lack of adequate nutrition resulting from insufficient food, unbalanced diet, or defective assimilation

malodorous (mæl'əʊdərəs) *adj* having a bad smell

Malory ('mælərɪ) *n* Sir **Thomas** 15th-century English author of *Le Morte d'Arthur* (?1470), a prose collection of Arthurian legends, translated from the French

Malouf ('mɑ:lu:f) *n* **David** born 1934, Australian novelist, short-story writer, and poet. His novels include *An Imaginary Life* (1978), *Remembering Babylon* (1993), and *The Conversations at Curlow Creek* (1996)

Malpighi (*Italian* mal'pi:gi) *n* **Marcello** (mar'tʃɛllo) 1628–94, Italian physiologist. A pioneer in microscopic anatomy, he identified the capillary system (1661)

malpractice (mæl'præktɪs) *n* **1** immoral, illegal, or unethical professional conduct or neglect of professional duty **2** any instance of improper professional conduct

Malraux (*French* malro) *n* **André** (ɑ̃dre) 1901–76, French writer and statesman. His novels include *La Condition humaine* (1933) on the Kuomintang revolution (1927–28) and *L'Espoir* (1937) on the Spanish Civil War, in both of which events he took part. He also wrote on art, notably in *Les Voix du silence* (1951)

malt (mɔ:lt) *n* **1** cereal grain, such as barley, that is kiln-dried after it has germinated by soaking in water **2** See **malt liquor, malt whisky** ▷ *vb* **3** to make into or become malt **4** to make (something, esp liquor) with malt [OE *mealt*] > '**malty** *adj*

Malta ('mɔ:ltə) *n* a republic occupying the islands of Malta, Gozo, and Comino, in the Mediterranean south of Sicily: governed by the Knights Hospitallers from 1530 until Napoleon's conquest in 1798; French driven out, with British help, 1800; became British dependency 1814; suffered severely in World War II; became independent in 1964 and a republic in 1974; joined the EU in 2004; a member of the Commonwealth. Official languages: Maltese and English. Official religion: Roman Catholic. Currency: Maltese lira. Capital: Valletta. Pop: 381 000 (2001 est). Area: 316 sq km (122 sq miles)
▷ www.malta.co.uk/malta/geninfo.htm
▷ www.visitmalta.com

malted milk *n* **1** a soluble powder made from dehydrated milk and malted cereals **2** a drink made from this powder

Maltese (mɔ:l'ti:z) *adj* **1** of or relating to Malta, its inhabitants, or their language ▷ *n* **2** (*pl* **Maltese**) a native or inhabitant of Malta or a descendant of one **3** the official language of Malta, a form of Arabic with borrowings from Italian, etc

Maltese cross *n* a cross with triangular arms that taper towards the centre, sometimes having indented outer sides

malt extract *n* a sticky substance obtained from an infusion of malt

Malthus ('mælθəs) *n* **Thomas Robert** 1766–1834, English economist. He propounded his population theory in *An Essay on the Principle of Population* (1798)

Malthusian (mæl'θju:zɪən) *adj* **1** of or relating to the theory of Malthus stating that increases in population tend to exceed increases in the means of subsistence and that therefore sexual restraint should be exercised ▷ *n* **2** a supporter of this theory > **Mal'thusianism** *n*

Mm

malting ('mɔ:ltɪŋ) *n* a building in which malt is made or stored. Also called: **malt house**

malt liquor *n* any alcoholic drink brewed from malt

maltose ('mɔ:ltəʊz) *n* a sugar formed by the enzymic hydrolysis of starch [c19 from MALT + -OSE²]

maltreat (mæl'tri:t) *vb* (*tr*) to treat badly, cruelly, or inconsiderately [c18 from F *maltraiter*] > **mal'treater** *n* > **mal'treatment** *n*

maltster ('mɔ:ltstə) *n* a person who makes or deals in malt

malt whisky *n* whisky made from malted barley

Maluku (mɑ:'lu:ku:) *n* the Indonesian name for the **Moluccas**

malvaceous (mæl'veɪʃəs) *adj* of, relating to, or belonging to a family of plants that includes mallow, cotton, okra, althaea, and abutilon [c17 from L *malvāceus*, from *malva* MALLOW]

Malvern ('mɔ:lvən) *n* a town and resort in W England, in S Worcestershire on the E slopes of the **Malvern Hills**: annual dramatic festival; mineral springs. Pop: 31 537 (1991)

malversation (ˌmælvɜ:'seɪʃən) *n rare* professional or public misconduct [c16 from F, from *malverser* to behave badly, from L *male versārī*]

Malvinas (*Spanish* mal'βinas) *pl n* **Islas** ('izlas) the Argentine name for the **Falkland Islands**

mam (mæm) *n inf or dialect* another word for **mother**

mama *or esp US* **mamma** (mə'mɑ:) *n old-fashioned* an informal word for **mother**¹ [c16 reduplication of childish syllable *ma*]

mamba ('mæmbə) *n* any of various partly arboreal tropical African venomous snakes, esp the **green** and **black mambas** [from Zulu *im-amba*]

mambo ('mæmbəʊ) *n, pl* **mambos** **1** a modern Latin

American dance, resembling the rumba ▷ *vb* **2** (*intr*) to perform this dance [American Sp., prob. from Haitian Creole: voodoo priestess]

Mameluke *or* **Mamaluke** (ˈmæmɪˌluːk) *n* **1** a member of a military class, originally of Turkish slaves, ruling in Egypt from about 1250 to 1517 and remaining powerful until 1811 **2** (in Muslim countries) a slave [c16 via F, ult. from Ar. *mamlūk* slave, from *malaka* to possess]

Mamet (ˈmæmɪt) *n* **David** born 1947, US dramatist and film director. His plays include *Sexual Perversity in Chicago* (1974), *American Buffalo* (1976), *Glengarry Glen Ross* (1983), and *Oleanna* (1992); films include *House of Games* (1987) and *The Spanish Prisoner* (1998)

mamilla *or US* **mammilla** (mæˈmɪlə) *n, pl* **mamillae** (-liː) *or US* **mammillae** **1** a nipple or teat **2** any nipple-shaped prominence [c17 from L, dim. of *mamma* breast] > **ˈmamillary** *or US* **ˈmammillary** *adj*

mamma (ˈmæmə) *n, pl* **mammae** (-miː) the milk-secreting organ of female mammals: the breast in women, the udder in cows, sheep, etc [c17 from L: breast] > **ˈmammary** *adj*

mammal (ˈmæməl) *n* any animal of the *Mammalia*, a large class of warm-blooded vertebrates having mammary glands in the female [c19 via NL from L *mamma* breast] > **mammalian** (mæˈmeɪlɪən) *adj, n*

mammary gland *n* any of the milk-producing glands in mammals

mammogram (ˈmæməʊˌgræm) *n* an X-ray photograph of the breast

mammography (mæˈmɒgrəfɪ) *n* examination of the breasts by X-ray, esp to detect early signs of cancer

mammon (ˈmæmən) *n* riches or wealth regarded as a source of evil and corruption [c14 via LL from New Testament Gk *mammōnas*, from Aramaic *māmōnā* wealth] > **ˈmammonish** *adj* > **ˈmammonism** *n* > **ˈmammonist** *or* **ˈmammonite** *n*

Mammon (ˈmæmən) *n* *Bible* the personification of riches and greed in the form of a false god

mammoth (ˈmæməθ) *n* **1** any large extinct elephant of the Pleistocene epoch, such as the **woolly mammoth**, having a hairy coat and long curved tusks ▷ *adj* **2** of gigantic size or importance [c18 from Russian *mamot*, from Tartar *mamont*, ?from *mamma* earth, because of a belief that the animal made burrows]

mammy *or* **mammie** (ˈmæmɪ) *n, pl* **mammies** **1** a child's word for **mother**[1] (senses 1–3) **2** *chiefly southern US* a Black woman employed as a nurse or servant to a White family

Mamoré (*Spanish* mamoˈre) *n* a river in central Bolivia, flowing north to the Beni River to form the Madeira River. Length: about 1500 km (930 miles)

man (mæn) *n, pl* **men** **1** an adult male human being, as distinguished from a woman **2** (*modifier*) male; masculine: *a man child* **3** a human being, considered as representative of mankind **4** human beings collectively; mankind **5** Also called: **modern man** **5a** a member of any of the living races of *Homo sapiens*, characterized by erect bipedal posture, a highly developed brain, and powers of articulate speech, abstract reasoning, and imagination **5b** any extinct member of the species *Homo sapiens*, such as Cro-Magnon man **6** a member of any of the extinct species of the genus *Homo*, such as Java man **7** an adult male human being with qualities associated with the male, such as courage or virility: *be a man* **8** manly qualities or virtues: *the man in him was outraged* **9a** a subordinate, servant, or employee **9b** (*in combination*): *the man-days required to complete a job* **10** (*usually pl*) a member of the armed forces who does not hold commissioned, warrant, or noncommissioned rank (as in **officers and men**) **11** a member of a group, team, etc **12** a husband, boyfriend, etc **13** an expression used parenthetically to indicate an informal relationship between speaker and hearer **14** a movable piece in various games, such as draughts **15** a vassal of a feudal lord **16** *S African sl* any person: used as a term of address **17** **as one man** with unanimous action or response **18** **be one's own man** to be independent or free **19** **he's your man** he's the person needed **20** **man and boy** from childhood **21** **sort out** *or* **separate the men from the boys** to separate the experienced from the inexperienced **22** **to a man** without exception ▷ *interj* **23** *inf* an exclamation or expletive, often indicating surprise or pleasure ▷ *vb* **mans, manning, manned** (*tr*) **24** to provide with sufficient men for operation, defence, etc **25** to take one's place at or near in readiness for action [OE *mann*]

Man (mæn) *n* **Isle of** an island in the British Isles, in the Irish Sea between Cumbria and Northern Ireland: a Crown possession with its own parliament, the Court of Tynwald; a dependency of Norway until 1266, when it came under Scottish rule; its own language, Manx became extinct in the 19th century but has been revived. Capital: Douglas. Pop: 73 500 (2001 est). Area: 588 sq km (227 sq miles)

-man *n combining form* indicating a person who has a role, works in a place, or operates equipment as specified: *salesman; barman; cameraman.*

> **USAGE** The use of words ending in *-man* is avoided as implying a male in job advertisements, where sexual discrimination is illegal, and in many other contexts where a term that is not gender-specific is available, such as *salesperson*, *barperson*, *camera operator*. See also at **chairman**

mana (ˈmɑːnə) *n* *anthropol* **1** (in Polynesia, Melanesia, etc) a concept of a life force associated with high social status and ritual power **2** any power achieved by ritual means; prestige; authority [of Polynesian origin]

man about town *n* a fashionable sophisticate, esp one in a big city

manacle (ˈmænəkᵊl) *n* **1** (*usually pl*) a shackle, handcuff, or fetter, used to secure the hands of a prisoner, convict, etc ▷ *vb* **manacles, manacling, manacled** (*tr*) **2** to put manacles on **3** to confine or constrain [c14 via OF from L *manicula*, dim. of *manus* hand]

Manado (məˈnɑːdəʊ) *n* a variant of **Menado**

manage (ˈmænɪdʒ) *vb* **manages, managing, managed** (*mainly tr*) **1** (*also intr*) to be in charge (of); administer: *to manage a shop* **2** to succeed in being able (to do something); contrive **3** to have room, time, etc, for: *can you manage dinner tomorrow?* **4** to exercise control or domination over **5** (*intr*) to contrive to carry on despite difficulties, esp financial ones **6** to wield or handle (a weapon) [c16 from It. *maneggiare* to train (esp horses), ult. from L *manus* hand]

manageable (ˈmænɪdʒəbᵊl) *adj* able to be managed or controlled > **ˌmanageaˈbility** *or* **ˈmanageableness** *n* > **ˈmanageably** *adv*

managed currency *n* a currency subject to governmental control with respect to the amount in circulation and rate of exchange

managed fund *n* an investment managed by an insurance company to provide low-risk investments for the small investor

management (ˈmænɪdʒmənt) *n* **1** the members of the executive or administration of an organization or business **2** managers or employers collectively **3** the technique, practice, or science of managing or controlling **4** the skilful or resourceful use of materials, time, etc **5** the specific treatment of a disease, etc

management buyout *n* the purchase of a company by its managers, usually with outside backing from a bank or other institution

management company *n* a company that manages a unit trust

manager (ˈmænɪdʒə) *n* **1** a person who directs or manages an organization, industry, shop, etc **2** a person who controls the business affairs of an actor, entertainer, etc **3** a person who controls the training of a sportsman or team **4** a person who has a talent for managing efficiently **5** (in Britain) a member of either House of Parliament appointed to arrange a matter in which both Houses are concerned **6** *computing* a computer program that organizes a resource, such as a set of files or a database > ˈ**managership** *n*

manageress (ˌmænɪdʒəˈrɛs) *n* a woman who is in charge of a shop, department, etc

managerial (ˌmænɪˈdʒɪərɪəl) *adj* of or relating to a manager or management > ˌ**manaˈgerially** *adv*

managing (ˈmænɪdʒɪŋ) *adj* having administrative control or authority: *a managing director*

Managua (məˈnægwə; *Spanish* maˈnaɣwa) *n* **1** the capital of Nicaragua, on the S shore of Lake Managua: chosen as capital in 1857. Pop (urban area): 1 195 000 (1995 est) **2 Lake** a lake in W Nicaragua: drains into Lake Nicaragua by the Tipitapa River. Length: 61 km (38 miles). Width: about 26 km (16 miles)

▷ www.edicioneslupita.com/paseo/managuai.html

Manama (məˈnɑːmə) *n* the capital of Bahrain, at the N end of Bahrain Island: transit port. Pop: 162 000 (1999 est)

▷ www.bahraintourism.com/manama_map

mana motuhake (ˈmɑːnə məʊtuːˈhɑːkɪ) *n* NZ independence or autonomy [Maori]

mañana *Spanish* (məˈnjɑːnə) *n, adv* **a** tomorrow **b** some other and later time

Manassas (məˈnæsəs) *n* a town in NE Virginia, west of Alexandria: site of the victory of Confederate forces in the Battles of Bull Run, or First and Second Manassas (1861; 1862), during the American Civil War. Pop: 27 957 (1990)

Manasseh (məˈnæsɪ) *n Old Testament* **1** the elder son of Joseph (Genesis 41:51) **2** the Israelite tribe descended from him **3** the territory of this tribe, in the upper Jordan valley. Douay spelling: **Manases** (məˈnæsiːz)

man-at-arms *n, pl* **men-at-arms** a soldier, esp a heavily armed mounted soldier in medieval times

manatee (ˌmænəˈtiː) *n* a sirenian mammal occurring in tropical coastal waters of America, the Caribbean, and Africa, having a prehensile upper lip and a broad flattened tail [c16 via Sp. from Carib *Manattouī*]

Manaus (*Portuguese* məˈnaus) *n* a port in N Brazil, capital of Amazonas state, on the Rio Negro 19 km (12 miles) above its confluence with the Amazon: chief commercial centre of the Amazon basin. Pop conurbation: 1 394 724 (2000)

Manche (*French* mɑ̃ʃ) *n* **1** a department of NW France, in Basse-Normandie region. Capital: St Lô. Pop: 481 471 (1999). Area: 6412 sq km (2501 sq miles) **2 La** the French name for the **English Channel**

manchester (ˈmæntʃɪstə) *n Austral & NZ* **1** goods, such as sheets and pillowcases, which are, or were originally, made of cotton **2 manchester department** a section of a store which sells such goods [from MANCHESTER, England]

Manchester (ˈmæntʃɪstə) *n* **1** a city in NW England, in Manchester unitary authority, Greater Manchester: linked to the Mersey estuary by the **Manchester Ship Canal**: commercial, industrial, and cultural centre; formerly the centre of the cotton and textile trades; two universities. Pop: 402 889 (1991) Latin name: **Man'cunium** **2** a unitary authority in NW England, in Greater Manchester. Pop: 392 819 (2001). Area: 116 sq km (45 sq miles)

manchineel (ˌmæntʃɪˈniːl) *n* a tropical American tree having fruit and milky highly caustic poisonous sap, which causes skin blisters [c17 via F from Sp. MANZANILLA]

Manchu (mænˈtʃuː) *n* **1** (*pl* **Manchus** *or* **Manchu**) a member of a Mongoloid people of Manchuria, a region of NE China, who conquered China in the 17th century, establishing a dynasty that lasted until 1912 **2** the language of this people ▷ *adj* **3** Also: **Ching** of or relating to the dynasty of the Manchus [from Manchu, lit.: pure]

Manchukuo *or* **Manchoukuo** (ˈmænˈtʃuːˈkwəʊ) *n* a former state of E Asia (1932–45), consisting of the three provinces of old Manchuria and Jehol

Manchuria (mænˈtʃʊərɪə) *n* a region of NE China, historically the home of the Manchus, rulers of China from 1644 to 1912: includes part of the Inner Mongolian AR and the provinces of Heilongjiang, Jilin, and Liaoning. Area: about 1 300 000 sq km (502 000 sq miles) > **Manˈchurian** *adj, n*

manciple (ˈmænsɪpᵊl) *n* a steward who buys provisions, esp in an Inn of Court [c13 via OF from L *mancipium* purchase, from *manceps* purchaser, from *manus* hand + *capere* to take]

Mancunian (mæŋˈkjuːnɪən) *n* **1** a native or inhabitant of Manchester ▷ *adj* **2** of or relating to Manchester [from Med. L *Mancunium* Manchester]

-mancy *n combining form* indicating divination of a particular kind: *chiromancy* [from OF *-mancie*, from L *-mantia*, from Gk *manteia* soothsaying] > **-mantic** *adj combining form*

mandala (ˈmændələ, mænˈdɑːlə) *n Hindu & Buddhist art* any of various designs symbolizing the universe, usually circular [Sansk.: circle]

Mandalay (ˌmændəˈleɪ) *n* a city in central Myanmar, on the Irrawaddy River: the second largest city in the country and former capital of Burma and of Upper Burma; Buddhist religious centre. Pop: 677 000 (1995 est)

mandamus (mænˈdeɪməs) *n, pl* **mandamuses** *law* (formerly) a writ from (now an order of) a superior court commanding an inferior tribunal, public official, etc, to carry out a public duty [c16 L, lit.: we command, from *mandāre*]

Mm

mandarin (ˈmændərɪn) *n* **1** (in the Chinese Empire) a member of a senior grade of the bureaucracy **2** a high-ranking official whose powers are extensive and thought to be outside political control **3** a person of standing and influence, as in literary or intellectual circles, esp one regarded as conservative or reactionary **4a** a small citrus tree cultivated for its edible fruit **4b** the fruit, resembling the tangerine [c16 from Port. via Malay from Sansk. *mantrin* counsellor, from *mantra* counsel] > ˈ**mandarinate** *n*

Mandarin Chinese *or* **Mandarin** *n* the official language of China since 1917

Mandarin collar *n* a high stiff round collar

mandarin duck *n* an Asian duck, the male of which has a distinctive brightly coloured and patterned plumage and crest

mandate *n* (ˈmændeɪt, -dɪt) **1** an official or authoritative instruction or command **2** *politics* the support or commission given to a government and its policies or an elected representative and his or her policies through an electoral victory **3** (*often cap*) Also called: **mandated territory** (formerly) any of the territories under the trusteeship of the League of Nations administered by one of its member states **4a** *Roman law* a contract by which one person commissions another to act for him or her gratuitously **4b** *contract law* a contract under which a party entrusted with goods undertakes to perform gratuitously some service in respect of such goods **4c** *Scots law* a contract by which a person is engaged to act in the management of the affairs of another ▷ *vb* (ˈmændeɪt), **mandates, mandating, mandated** (*tr*) **5** to assign (territory) to a nation under a mandate **6** to delegate authority to [c16 from L *mandātum* something commanded, from *mandāre* to

command, ?from *manus* hand + *dāre* to give]
> **'mandator** *n*

mandatory ('mændətərɪ, -trɪ) *adj* **1** having the nature or powers of a mandate **2** obligatory; compulsory **3** (of a state) having received a mandate over some territory ▷ *n, pl* **mandatories** *also* **mandatary 4** a person or state holding a mandate > **'mandatorily** *adv*

Mandela (mæn'dɛlə) *n* **1 Nelson** (**Rolihlahla**) born 1918, Black South African statesman: president of South Africa (1994–99). Jailed in 1962 for 5 years and, in 1964, for life, he was released in 1990 after a long international campaign; deputy president of the African National Congress (1990–91) and president (1991–97); elected president of South Africa in 1994; Nobel peace prize jointly with F. W. de Klerk in 1993

Mandelson ('mændəlsən) *n* **Peter** (**Benjamin**) born 1953, British Labour politician; secretary of state for Northern Ireland (1999–2001)

Mandelstam *or* **Mandelshtam** ('mændəlʃtɑːm) *n* **1 Nadezhda** (**Yakovlevna**) (næ'dɛʃdə), born *Nadezhda Khazina*. 1899–1980, Soviet writer, wife of Osip Mandelstam: noted for her memoirs *Hope against Hope* (1971) and *Hope Abandoned* (1973) describing life in Stalin's Russia **2 Osip** (**Emilyevich**) ('ɒsiːp) 1891–?1938, Soviet poet and writer, born in Warsaw; he was persecuted by Stalin and died in a labour camp. His works include *Tristia* (1922), *Poems* (1928), and the autobiographical *Journey to Armenia* (1933)

Mandeville ('mændəvɪl) *n* **1 Bernard de** ?1670–1733, English author, born in Holland, noted for his satire *The Fable of the Bees* (1723) **2** Sir **John** 14th century, English author of *The Travels of Sir John Mandeville*. The book claims to be an account of the author's journeys in the East but is largely a compilation from other works

mandible ('mændɪbəl) *n* **1** the lower jawbone in vertebrates **2** either of a pair of mouthparts in insects and other arthropods that are usually used for biting and crushing food **3** *ornithol* either part of the bill, esp the lower part [C16 via OF from LL *mandibula* jaw, from *mandere* to chew] > **mandibular** (mæn'dɪbjʊlə) *adj* > **mandibulate** (mæn'dɪbjʊlɪt, -ˌleɪt) *n, adj*

mandolin *or* **mandoline** (ˌmændə'lɪn) *n* a plucked stringed instrument having four pairs of strings stretched over a small light body with a fretted fingerboard: usually played with a plectrum [C18 via F from It. *mandolino*, dim. of *mandora* lute, ult. from Gk *pandoura* musical instrument with three strings]
> **ˌmando'linist** *n*

mandrake ('mændreɪk) *or* **mandragora** (mæn'drægərə) *n* **1** a Eurasian plant with purplish flowers and a forked root. It was formerly thought to have magic powers and a narcotic was prepared from its root **2** another name for the **May apple** [C14 prob. via MDu. from L *mandragoras*, from Gk. The form *mandrake* was prob. adopted through folk etymology, because of the allegedly human appearance of the root and because *drake* (dragon) suggested magical powers]

mandrel *or* **mandril** ('mændrəl) *n* **1** a spindle on which a workpiece is supported during machining operations **2** a shaft or arbor on which a machining tool is mounted [C16 ? rel. to F *mandrin* lathe]

mandrill ('mændrɪl) *n* an Old World monkey of W Africa. It has a short tail and brown hair, and the ridged muzzle, nose, and hindquarters are red and blue [C18 from MAN + DRILL[4]]

mane (meɪn) *n* **1** the long coarse hair that grows from the crest of the neck in such mammals as the lion and horse **2** long thick human hair [OE *manu*] > **maned** *adj*

manège *or* **manege** (mæ'neɪʒ) *n* **1** the art of training horses and riders **2** a riding school [C17 via F from It. *maneggio*, from *maneggiare* to MANAGE]
▷ www.horsesport.org

manes ('mɑːneɪz) *pl n* (*sometimes cap*) (in Roman legend) **1** the spirits of the dead, often revered as minor deities **2** (*functioning as sing*) the shade of a dead person [C14 from L, prob.: the good ones, from OL *mānus* good]

Manes ('meɪniːz) *n* See **Mani**

Manet (*French* manɛ) *n* **Édouard** (edwar) 1832–83, French painter. His painting *Le Déjeuner sur l'herbe* (1863), which was condemned by the Parisian establishment, was acclaimed by the impressionists, whom he decisively influenced

maneuver (mə'nuːvə) *n, vb* the usual US spelling of **manoeuvre**

man Friday *n* **1** a loyal male servant or assistant **2** Also: **girl Friday, person Friday** any factotum, esp in an office [after the native in Daniel Defoe's novel *Robinson Crusoe* (1719)]

manful ('mænfʊl) *adj* resolute, strong; manly
> **'manfully** *adv* > **'manfulness** *n*

mangabey ('mæŋgəˌbeɪ) *n* any of several large agile arboreal Old World monkeys of central Africa, having long limbs and tail [C18 after a region in Madagascar]

Mangalore (ˌmæŋgə'lɔː) *n* a port in S India, in Karnataka on the Malabar Coast. Pop: 273 304 (1991)

manganese ('mæŋgəˌniːz) *n* a brittle greyish-white metallic element: used in making steel and other alloys. Symbol: Mn; atomic no.: 25; atomic wt.: 54.938 [C17 via F from It., prob. altered form of Med. L MAGNESIA]

mange (meɪndʒ) *n* an infectious disorder mainly affecting domestic animals, characterized by itching and loss of hair: caused by parasitic mites [C14 from OF *mangeue* itch, from *mangier* to eat]

mangelwurzel ('mæŋgəlˌwɜːzəl) *or* **mangoldwurzel** ('mæŋgəʊldˌwɜːzəl) *n* a Eurasian variety of beet, cultivated as a cattle food, having a large yellowish root [C18 from G *Mangoldwurzel*, from *Mangold* beet + *Wurzel* root]

manger ('meɪndʒə) *n* a trough or box in a stable, barn, etc, from which horses or cattle feed [C14 from OF *maingeure* food trough, from *mangier* to eat, ult. from L *mandūcāre* to chew]

mangetout (ˌmɒnʒ'tuː) *n* a variety of garden pea in which the pod is also edible. Also called: **sugar pea** [C20 from F lit.: eat all]

mangey ('meɪndʒɪ) *adj* **mangier, mangiest** a variant spelling of **mangy**

mangle[1] ('mæŋgəl) *vb* **mangles, mangling, mangled** (*tr*) **1** to mutilate, disfigure, or destroy by cutting, crushing, or tearing **2** to ruin, spoil, or mar [C14 from Norman F *mangler*, prob. from OF *mahaignier* to maim] > **'mangled** *adj* > **'mangler** *n*

mangle[2] ('mæŋgəl) *n* **1** Also called: **wringer** a machine for pressing or drying textiles, clothes, etc, consisting of two heavy rollers between which the cloth is passed ▷ *vb* **mangles, mangling, mangled** (*tr*) **2** to press or dry in a mangle [C18 from Du. *mangel*, ult. from LL *manganum*. See MANGONEL]

mango ('mæŋgəʊ) *n, pl* **mangoes** *or* **mangos 1** a tropical Asian evergreen tree, cultivated in the tropics for its fruit **2** the ovoid edible fruit of this tree, having a smooth rind and sweet juicy flesh [C16 via Port. from Malay *mangā*, from Tamil *mānkāy*, from *mān* mango tree + *kāy* fruit]

mangonel ('mæŋgəˌnɛl) *n history* a war engine for hurling stones [C13 via OF from Med. L *manganellus*, ult. from Gk *manganon*]

mangrove ('mæŋgrəʊv, 'mæn-) *n* any of various tropical evergreen trees or shrubs, having stiltlike intertwining aerial roots and growing below the highest tide levels in estuaries and along coasts, forming dense thickets [C17 *mangrow* (changed through infl. of *grove*), from Port. *mangue*, ult. from Taino]

mangulate ('mæŋgjʊˌleɪt) *vb* (*tr*) *Austral sl* to bend or twist out of shape; mangle

mangy *or* **mangey** ('meɪndʒɪ) *adj* **mangier, mangiest**

1 having or caused by mange **2** scruffy or shabby
> 'mangily *adv* > 'manginess *n*
manhandle ('mænˌhændᵊl, ˌmæn'hændᵊl) *vb* **manhandles, manhandling, manhandled** (*tr*) **1** to handle or push (someone) about roughly **2** to move or do by manpower rather than by machinery
Manhattan (mæn'hætᵊn, mən-) *n* **1** an island at the N end of New York Bay, between the Hudson, East, and Harlem Rivers: administratively (with adjacent islets) a borough of New York City; a major financial, commercial, and cultural centre. Pop: 1 487 536 (1990). Area: 47 sq km (22 sq miles) **2** a mixed drink consisting of four parts whisky, one part vermouth, and a dash of bitters
Manhire ('mænhɪə) *n* **Bill** born 1946, New Zealand poet and writer. His poetry collections include *How to Take Off Your Clothes at the Picnic* (1977), *Zoetropes* (1984), and *Sunshine* (1996)
manhole ('mænˌhəʊl) *n* **1** Also called: **inspection chamber** a shaft with a removable cover that leads down to a sewer or drain **2** a hole, usually with a detachable cover, through which a man can enter a boiler, tank, etc
manhood ('mænhʊd) *n* **1** the state or quality of being a man or being manly **2** men collectively **3** the state of being human
man-hour *n* a unit of work in industry, equal to the work done by one man in one hour
manhunt ('mænˌhʌnt) *n* an organized search, usually by police, for a wanted man or fugitive
Mani ('mɑːnɪ) *n* ?216–?276 AD, Persian prophet who founded Manichaeism. Also called: **Manes, Manichaeus**
mania ('meɪnɪə) *n* **1** a mental disorder characterized by great excitement and occasionally violent behaviour **2** obsessional enthusiasm or partiality [C14 via LL from Gk: madness]
-mania *n combining form* indicating extreme desire or pleasure of a specified kind or an abnormal excitement aroused by something: *kleptomania; nymphomania; pyromania* [from MANIA] > **-maniac** *n and adj combining form*
maniac ('meɪnɪˌæk) *n* **1** a wild disorderly person **2** a person who has a great craving or enthusiasm for something **3** *psychiatry, obs* a person afflicted with mania [C17 from LL *maniacus* belonging to madness, from Gk]
maniacal (mə'naɪəkᵊl) *or* **maniac** *adj* **1** affected with or characteristic of mania **2** characteristic of or befitting a maniac: *maniacal laughter* > **ma'niacally** *adv*
manic ('mænɪk) *adj* **1** characterizing, denoting, or affected by mania ▷ *n* **2** a person afflicted with mania [C19 from Gk, from MANIA]
manic-depressive *psychiatry* ▷ *adj* **1** denoting a mental disorder characterized by an alternation between extreme euphoria and deep depression ▷ *n* **2** a person afflicted with this disorder
Manichaeism *or* **Manicheism** ('mænɪkiːˌɪzəm) *n* the system of religious doctrines taught by the Persian prophet Mani about the 3rd century AD. It was based on a supposed primordial conflict between light and darkness or goodness and evil [C14 from LL *Manichaeus*, from LGk *Manikhaios* of Mani] > ˌ**Mani'chaean** *or* ˌ**Mani'chean** *adj, n* > '**Manichee** *n*
Manichaeus *or* **Manicheus** (ˌmænɪ'kiːəs) *n* See **Mani**
manicure ('mænɪˌkjʊə) *n* **1** care of the hands and fingernails, involving shaping the nails, removing cuticles, etc **2** Also called: **manicurist** a person who gives manicures, esp as a profession ▷ *vb* **manicures, manicuring, manicured** **3** to care for (the hands and fingernails) in this way [C19 from F, from L *manus* hand + *cūra* care]
manifest ('mænɪˌfɛst) *adj* **1** easily noticed or perceived; obvious **2** *psychoanal* of or relating to the ostensible elements of a dream: *manifest content* ▷ Cf **latent** (sense 5) ▷ *vb* **3** (*tr*) to show plainly; reveal or display **4** (*tr*) to prove beyond doubt **5** (*intr*) (of a disembodied spirit) to appear in visible form ▷ *n* **6** a customs document containing particulars of a ship, its cargo, and its destination **7a** a list of cargo, passengers, etc, on an aeroplane **7b** a list of railway trucks or their cargo [C14 from L *manifestus* plain, lit.: struck with the hand]
> '**maniˌfestable** *adj* > '**maniˌfestly** *adv*
manifestation (ˌmænɪfɛ'steɪʃən) *n* **1** the act of demonstrating; display **2** the state of being manifested **3** an indication or sign **4** a public demonstration of feeling **5** the materialization of a disembodied spirit
> ˌ**mani'festative** *adj*
manifesto (ˌmænɪ'fɛstəʊ) *n, pl* **manifestos** *or* **manifestoes** a public declaration of intent, policy, aims, etc, as issued by a political party, government, or movement [C17 from It., from *manifestare* to MANIFEST]
manifold ('mænɪˌfəʊld) *adj formal* **1** of several different kinds; multiple **2** having many different forms, features, or elements ▷ *n* **3** something having many varied parts, forms, or features **4** a chamber or pipe with a number of inlets or outlets used to collect or distribute a fluid. In an internal-combustion engine the **inlet manifold** carries the vaporized fuel from the carburettor to the inlet ports and the **exhaust manifold** carries the exhaust gases away ▷ *vb* (*tr*) **5** to duplicate (a page, book, etc) **6** to make manifold; multiply [OE *manigfeald*. See MANY, -FOLD] > '**maniˌfoldly** *adv*
> '**maniˌfoldness** *n*
manikin *or* **mannikin** ('mænɪkɪn) *n* **1** a little man; dwarf or child **2** an anatomical model of the body or a part of the body, esp for use in medical or art instruction **3** a variant of **mannequin** [C17 from Du. *manneken*, dim. of MAN]
Manila (mə'nɪlə) *n* **1** the chief port of the Philippines, on S Luzon on Manila Bay: capital of the republic until 1948 and from 1976; seat of the Far Eastern University and the University of Santo Tomas (1611). Pop: 1 581 082 (2000), with a conurbation of 9 932 560 (2000) **2** a type of cigar made in this city **3** (*often not capital*) short for **Manila hemp, Manila paper**
▷ www.tourism.gov.ph/top_25/manilam.htm
Manila Bay *n* an almost landlocked inlet of the South China Sea in the Philippines, in W Luzon: mostly forms Manila harbour. Area: 1994 sq km (770 sq miles)
Manila hemp *or* **Manilla hemp** *n* a fibre obtained from the abaca plant, used for rope, paper, etc
Manila paper *or* **Manilla paper** *n* a strong usually brown paper made from Manila hemp or similar fibres
manilla (mə'nɪlə) *n* an early form of currency in W Africa in the pattern of a small bracelet [from Sp.: bracelet, dim. of *mano* hand, from L *manus*]
man in the street *n* the typical or ordinary person
manioc ('mænɪˌɒk) *or* **manioca** (ˌmænɪ'əʊkə) *n* another name for **cassava** (sense 1) [C16 from Tupi *mandioca*]
manipulate (mə'nɪpjʊˌleɪt) *vb* **manipulates, manipulating, manipulated** **1** (*tr*) to handle or use, esp with some skill **2** to control or influence (something or someone) cleverly, deviously, or skilfully **3** to falsify (a bill, accounts, etc) for one's own advantage **4** (in physiotherapy) to examine or treat manually, as in loosening a joint [C19 back formation from *manipulation*, from L *manipulus* handful] > **manipulability** (məˌnɪpjʊlə'bɪlɪtɪ) *n* > **ma'nipuˌlatable** *or* **ma'nipulable** *adj* > **maˌnipu'lation** *n* > **ma'nipulative** *adj*
> **ma'nipuˌlator** *n* > **ma'nipulatory** *adj*
Manipur (ˌmʌnɪ'pʊə) *n* a state in NE India: largely densely forested mountains. Capital: Imphal. Pop: 2 388 634 (2001). Area: 22 327 sq km (8621 sq miles)
Manisa ('mɑːnɪˌsɑː) *n* a city in W Turkey: the Byzantine seat of government (1204–1313). Pop: 201 340 (1997)
Manitoba (ˌmænɪ'təʊbə) *n* **1** a province of W Canada: consists of prairie in the southwest, with extensive forests in the north and tundra near Hudson Bay in the

northeast. Capital: Winnipeg. Pop: 1 150 200 (2001 est). Area: 650 090 sq km (251 000 sq miles). Abbreviation: **MB 2 Lake** a lake in W Canada, in S Manitoba: fed by the outflow from Lake Winnipegosis; drains into Lake Winnipeg. Area: 4706 sq km (1817 sq miles) > ˌ**Mani'toban** *n, adj*
▷ www.gov.mb.ca
▷ www.travelmanitoba.com

Manitoba maple *n* a Canadian fast-growing variety of maple

manitou, manitu ('mænɪˌtuː), *or* **manito** ('mænɪˌtəʊ) *n, pl* **manitous, manitus, manitos** *or* **manitou, manitu, manito** (among the Algonquian Indians) a deified spirit or force [c17 of Amerind origin]

Manitoulin Island (ˌmænɪ'tuːlɪn) *n* an island in N Lake Huron in Ontario: the largest freshwater island in the world. Length: 129 km (80 miles). Width: up to 48 km (30 miles)

Manizales (ˌmænɪ'zɑːlɛs; *Spanish* mani'θales) *n* a city in W Colombia, in the Cordillera Central of the Andes at an altitude of 2100 m (7000 ft): commercial centre of a rich coffee-growing area. Pop: 337 580 (1999 est)

man jack *n inf* a single individual (in **every man jack, no man jack**)

mankind (ˌmæn'kaɪnd) *n* **1** human beings collectively; humanity **2** men collectively, as opposed to womankind.

> **USAGE** Some people object to the use of *mankind* to refer to all human beings and prefer the term *humankind*

Manley ('mænlɪ) *n* **Michael Norman** 1924–97, Jamaican statesman; prime minister of Jamaica (1972–80; 1989–92)

manlike ('mænˌlaɪk) *adj* resembling or befitting a man

manly ('mænlɪ) *adj* **manlier, manliest 1** possessing qualities, such as vigour or courage, generally regarded as appropriate to or typical of a man; masculine **2** characteristic of or befitting a man > '**manliness** *n*

man-made *adj* made by man; artificial

Mann (*German* man) *n* **1 Heinrich** ('hainrɪç) 1871–1950, German novelist: works include *Professor Unrat* (1905), which was filmed as *The Blue Angel* (1928), and *Man of Straw* (1918) **2** his brother, **Thomas** ('toːmas) 1875–1955, German novelist, in the US after 1937. His works deal mainly with the problem of the artist in bourgeois society and include the short story *Death in Venice* (1913) and the novels *Buddenbrooks* (1900), *The Magic Mountain* (1924), and *Doctor Faustus* (1947): Nobel prize for literature 1929

manna ('mænə) *n* **1** *Old Testament* the miraculous food which sustained the Israelites in the wilderness (Exodus 16:14–36) **2** any spiritual or divine nourishment **3** a windfall (esp in **manna from heaven**) **4** a sweet substance obtained from various plants, esp from the **manna** or **flowering ash** of S Europe, used as a mild laxative [OE via LL from Gk, from Heb. *mān*]

Mannar (mə'nɑː) *n* **Gulf of** the part of the Indian Ocean between SE India and the island of Sri Lanka: pearl fishing

manned (mænd) *adj* **1** supplied or equipped with men, esp soldiers **2** (of spacecraft, etc) having a human crew

mannequin ('mænɪkɪn) *n* **1** a woman who wears the clothes displayed at a fashion show; model **2** a life-size dummy of the human body used to fit or display clothes [c18 via F from Du. *manneken* MANIKIN]

manner ('mænə) *n* **1** a way of doing or being **2** a person's bearing and behaviour **3** the style or customary way of doing or accomplishing something **4** type or kind **5** mannered style, as in art; mannerism **6 in a manner of speaking** in a way; so to speak **7 to the manner born** naturally fitted to a specified role or activity. See also **manners** [c12 via Norman F from OF *maniere*, from Vulgar L *manuāria* (unattested) a way of handling something, noun use of L *manuārius* belonging to the hand, from *manus* hand]

mannered ('mænəd) *adj* **1** having idiosyncrasies or mannerisms; affected **2** (*in combination*) having manners as specified: *ill-mannered*

Mannerheim ('mænəˌheɪm) *n* Baron **Carl Gustaf Emil** 1867–1951, Finnish soldier and statesman; president of Finland (1944–46)

mannerism ('mænəˌrɪzəm) *n* **1** a distinctive and individual gesture or trait **2** (*often cap*) a principally Italian movement in art and architecture between the High Renaissance and Baroque periods (1520–1600), using distortion and exaggeration of human proportions, perspective, etc **3** adherence to a distinctive or affected manner, esp in art or literature > '**mannerist** *n, adj* > ˌ**manner'istic** *adj* > ˌ**manner'istically** *adv*
▷ www.artcyclopedia.com/history/mannerism.html
▷ www.artlex.com/ArtLex/m/mannerism.html
▷ www.tigtail.org/TVM/M_View/X1/c.Mannerism

mannerless ('mænəlɪs) *adj* having bad manners; boorish > '**mannerlessness** *n*

mannerly ('mænəlɪ) *adj* **1** well-mannered; polite ▷ *adv* **2** *now rare* with good manners; politely > '**mannerliness** *n*

manners ('mænəz) *pl n* **1** social conduct **2** a socially acceptable way of behaving

Mannheim ('mænhaɪm; *German* 'manhaim) *n* a city in SW Germany, in Baden-Württemberg at the confluence of the Rhine and Neckar: one of Europe's largest inland harbours; a cultural and musical centre. Pop: 308 400 (1999 est)

mannikin ('mænɪkɪn) *n* a variant spelling of **manikin**

Manning ('mænɪŋ) *n* **1 Henry Edward** 1808–92, British churchman. Originally an Anglican, he was converted to Roman Catholicism (1851) and made archbishop of Westminster (1865) and cardinal (1875) **2 Olivia** 1908–80, British novelist and short-story writer, best known for her novel sequence *Fortunes of War*, comprising the *Balkan Trilogy* (1960–65) and the *Levant Trilogy* (1977–80)

mannish ('mænɪʃ) *adj* **1** (of a woman) displaying qualities regarded as typical of a man **2** of or resembling a man > '**mannishly** *adv* > '**mannishness** *n*

manoeuvre *or US* **maneuver** (mə'nuːvə) *n* **1** a contrived, complicated, and possibly deceptive plan or action **2** a movement or action requiring dexterity and skill **3a** a tactic or movement of a military or naval unit **3b** (*pl*) tactical exercises, usually on a large scale **4** a planned movement of an aircraft in flight **5** any change from the straight steady course of a ship ▷ *vb* **manoeuvres, manoeuvring, manoeuvred** *or US* **manoeuvers, manoeuvering, manoeuvered 6** (*tr*) to contrive or accomplish with skill or cunning **7** (*intr*) to manipulate situations, etc, in order to gain some end **8** (*intr*) to perform a manoeuvre or manoeuvres **9** to move or deploy or be moved or deployed, as military units, etc [c15 from F, from Med. L *manuopera* manual work, from L *manū operāre* to work with the hand] > **ma'noeuvrable** *or US* **ma'neuverable** *adj* > **maˌnoeuvra'bility** *or US* **maˌneuvera'bility** *n* > **ma'noeuvrer** *or US* **ma'neuverer** *n* > **ma'noeuvring** *or US* **ma'neuvering** *n*

man of God *n* **1** a saint or prophet **2** a clergyman

man of straw *n* **1** a man who cannot be relied upon to honour his financial commitments, esp because of his limited resources **2** any weak or vulnerable man

man-of-war *or* **man o' war** *n, pl* **men-of-war** *or* **men o' war 1** a warship **2** See **Portuguese man-of-war**

man-of-war bird *or* **man-o'-war bird** *n* another name for **frigate bird**

Manolete (*Spanish* mano'lete) *n* original name *Manuel Rodriguez y Sánchez*. 1917–47, Spanish bullfighter

manometer (mə'nɒmɪtə) *n* an instrument for comparing pressures [c18 from F *manomètre*, from Gk *manos* sparse + *metron* measure] > **manometric**

(ˌmænəʊˈmɛtrɪk) *or* ˌ**manoˈmetrical** *adj*

manor (ˈmænə) *n* **1** (in medieval Europe) the manor house of a lord and the lands attached to it **2** a manor house **3** a landed estate **4** *Brit sl* a geographical area of operation, esp of a local police force [C13 from OF *manoir* dwelling, from *maneir* to dwell, from L *manēre* to remain] > **manorial** (məˈnɔːrɪəl) *adj*

manor house *n* (esp formerly) the house of the lord of a manor

manpower (ˈmænˌpaʊə) *n* **1** power supplied by men **2** a unit of power based on the rate at which a man can work; roughly 75 watts **3** the number of people needed or available for a job

manqué *French* (ˈmɒŋkeɪ) *adj (postpositive)* unfulfilled; potential; would-be: *the manager is an actor manqué* [C19 lit.: having missed]

Manresa (*Spanish* manˈrɛsa) *n* a city in NE Spain: contains a cave used as the spiritual retreat of St Ignatius Loyola. Pop: 65 610 (latest est)

mansard (ˈmænsɑːd, -səd) *n* a roof having two slopes on both sides and both ends, the lower slopes being steeper than the upper. Also called: **mansard roof** [C18 from F *mansarde*, after François MANSART]

Mansart (*French* mɑ̃sar) *n* **1 François** (frɑ̃swa) 1598–1666, French architect, who established the classical style in French architecture **2** his great-nephew, **Jules Hardouin** (ʒyl ardwɛ̃) 1646–1708, French architect and town planner, who completed the Palace of Versailles

manse (mæns) *n* (in certain religious denominations) the house provided for a minister [C15 from Med. L *mansus* dwelling, from pp of L *manēre* to stay]

manservant (ˈmænˌsɜːvənt) *n, pl* **menservants** a male servant, esp a valet

Mansfield[1] (ˈmænsˌfiːld) *n* a town in central England, in W Nottinghamshire: former coal-mining and cotton-textiles industries. Pop: 71 858 (1991)

Mansfield[2] (ˈmænsˌfiːld) *n* **Katherine,** real name *Kathleen Mansfield Beauchamp*. 1888–1923, British writer, born in New Zealand, noted for her short stories, such as those in *Bliss* (1920) and *The Garden Party* (1922)

Mansholt (*Dutch* ˈmɑnshɔlt) *n* **Sicco Leendert** (ˈsɪko ˈleːndərt) 1908–95, Dutch economist and politician; vice president (1958–72) and president (1972–73) of the European Economic Community Commission. He was the author of the Mansholt Plan for the agricultural organization of the European Economic Community

mansion (ˈmænʃən) *n* **1** Also called: **mansion house** a large and imposing house **2** a less common word for **manor house** **3** (*pl*) *Brit* a block of flats [C14 via OF from L *mansio* a remaining, from *mansus*; see MANSE]

Mansion House *n* **the 1** the residence of the Lord Mayor of London **2** the residence of the Lord Mayor of Dublin

man-sized *adj* **1** of a size appropriate for or convenient for a man **2** *inf* big; large

manslaughter (ˈmænˌslɔːtə) *n* **1** *law* the unlawful killing of one human being by another without malice aforethought ▷ Cf **murder** **2** (loosely) the killing of a human being

Mansûra (mænˈsʊərə) *n* See **El Mansûra**

manta (ˈmæntə) *n* **1** Also called: **manta ray, devilfish, devil ray** any large ray (fish), having very wide winglike pectoral fins and feeding on plankton **2** a rough cotton cloth made in Spain and Spanish America **3** a piece of this used as a blanket or shawl [Sp.: cloak, from Vulgar L; see MANTLE]

manteau (ˈmæntəʊ) *n, pl* **manteaus** (-təʊz) *or* **manteaux** (-təʊ) a cloak or mantle [C17 via F from L *mantellum* MANTLE]

Mantegna (*Italian* manˈteɲɲa) *n* **Andrea** (anˈdrɛːa) 1431–1506, Italian painter and engraver, noted esp for his frescoes, such as those in the Ducal Palace, Mantua

mantel (ˈmæntᵊl) *n* **1** a wooden, stone, or iron frame around the opening of a fireplace, together with its decorative facing **2** Also called: **mantel shelf** a shelf above this frame [C15 from F, var. of MANTLE]

mantelet (ˈmæntᵊˌlɛt) *or* **mantlet** *n* **1** a woman's short mantle, worn in the mid-19th century **2** a portable bulletproof screen or shelter [C14 from OF, dim. of *mantel* MANTLE]

mantelpiece (ˈmæntᵊlˌpiːs) *n* **1** Also called: **mantel shelf, chimneypiece** a shelf above a fireplace often forming part of the mantel **2** another word for **mantel** (sense 1)

mantic (ˈmæntɪk) *adj* **1** of or relating to divination and prophecy **2** having divining or prophetic powers [C19 from Gk *mantikos* prophetic, from *mantis* seer] > ˈ**mantically** *adv*

-mantic *adj combining form* forming adjectives from nouns ending in **-mancy**

mantilla (mænˈtɪlə) *n* a woman's lace or silk scarf covering the shoulders and head, worn esp in Spain [C18 Sp., dim. of *manta* cloak]

Mantinea *or* **Mantineia** (ˌmæntɪˈneɪə) *n* (in ancient Greece) a city in E Arcadia; site of several battles

mantis (ˈmæntɪs) *n, pl* **mantises** *or* **mantes** (-tiːz) any carnivorous typically green insect of warm and tropical regions, having a long body and large eyes and resting with the first pair of legs raised as if in prayer. Also called: **praying mantis** [C17 NL, from Gk: prophet, alluding to its praying posture]

mantissa (mænˈtɪsə) *n* the fractional part of a common logarithm representing the digits of the associated number but not its magnitude: *the mantissa of 2.4771 is .4771* [C17 from L: something added]

mantle (ˈmæntᵊl) *n* **1** *arch* a loose wrap or cloak **2** such a garment regarded as a symbol of someone's power or authority **3** anything that covers completely or envelops **4** a small dome-shaped or cylindrical mesh, used to increase illumination in a gas or oil lamp by becoming incandescent **5** *zool* a protective layer of epidermis in molluscs and brachiopods that secretes a substance forming the shell **6** *ornithol* the feathers of the folded wings and back, esp when of a different colour from the remaining feathers **7** *geol* the part of the earth between the crust and the core **8** a less common spelling of **mantel** ▷ *vb* **mantles, mantling, mantled** **9** (*tr*) to envelop or supply with a mantle **10** (*tr*) to spread over or become spread over **11** (*intr*) to blush; flush [C13 via OF from L *mantellum*, dim. of *mantum* cloak]

mantle rock *n* the loose rock material, including glacial drift, soils, etc, that covers the bedrock and forms the land surface

Mantova (ˈmantova) *n* the Italian name for **Mantua**

mantra (ˈmæntrə, ˈmʌn-) *n* **1** *Hinduism* any of those parts of the Vedic literature which consist of the metrical psalms of praise **2** *Hinduism, Buddhism* any sacred word or syllable used as an object of concentration [C19 from Sansk., lit.: speech, instrument of thought, from *man* to think]

mantua (ˈmæntjʊə) *n* a woman's loose gown of the 17th and 18th centuries [C17 changed from MANTEAU, through the infl. of MANTUA]

Mantua (ˈmæntjʊə) *n* a city in N Italy, in E Lombardy, surrounded by lakes: birthplace of Virgil. Pop: 54 808 (1990). Italian name: **Mantova**

manual (ˈmænjʊəl) *adj* **1** of or relating to a hand or hands **2** operated or done by hand **3** physical, as opposed to mental or mechanical: *manual labour* **4** by human labour rather than automatic or computer-aided means ▷ *n* **5** a book, esp of instructions or information **6** *music* one of the keyboards played by hand on an organ **7** *mil* the prescribed drill with small arms [C15 via OF from L *manuālis*, from *manus* hand] > ˈ**manually** *adv*

manufactory (ˌmænjʊˈfæktərɪ, -trɪ) *n, pl* **manufactories** an obsolete word for **factory** [C17 from obs. *manufact*; see MANUFACTURE]

Mm

manufacture (ˌmænjʊˈfæktʃə) *vb* **manufactures, manufacturing, manufactured 1** to process or make (a product) from a raw material, esp as a large-scale operation using machinery **2** (*tr*) to invent or concoct ▷ *n* **3** the production of goods, esp by industrial processes **4** a manufactured product **5** the creation or production of anything [C16 from obs. *manufact* handmade, from LL *manūfactus*, from L *manus* hand + *facere* to make] > ˌ**manuˈfacturing** *n, adj*

manufacturer (ˌmænjʊˈfæktʃərə) *n* a person or business concern that manufactures goods or owns a factory

manuhiri (ˌmɑːnuːˈhiːrɪ) *n NZ* **1** a visitor to a Maori marae **2** a Maori term for a non-Maori person, seen as a guest in the country [Maori]

manuka (ˈmɑːnʊkə) *n* a New Zealand tree with strong elastic wood and aromatic leaves. Also called: **tea tree** [from Maori]

Manukau (ˈmɑːnʊˌkaʊ) *n* a city in New Zealand, on **Manukau Harbour** (an inlet of the Tasman Sea) near Auckland on NW North Island. Pop: 281 800 (1999 est)

manumission (ˌmænjʊˈmɪʃən) *n* the act of freeing or the state of being freed from slavery, servitude, etc

manumit (ˌmænjʊˈmɪt) *vb* **manumits, manumitting, manumitted** (*tr*) to free from slavery, servitude, etc; emancipate [C15 from L *manūmittere* to release, from *manū* from one's hand + *ēmittere* to send away]

manure (məˈnjʊə) *n* **1** animal excreta, usually with straw, etc, used to fertilize land **2** *chiefly Brit* any material, esp chemical fertilizer, used to fertilize land ▷ *vb* **manures, manuring, manured 3** (*tr*) to spread manure upon (fields or soil) [C14 from Med. L *manuopera* manual work; see MANOEUVRE] > **maˈnurer** *n*

manus (ˈmeɪnəs) *n, pl* **manus 1** *anat* the wrist and hand **2** the corresponding part in other vertebrates [C19 L: hand]

Manu Samoa (ˈmænʊ) *n* the international Rugby Union football team of Western Samoa

manuscript (ˈmænjʊˌskrɪpt) *n* **1** a book or other document written by hand **2** the original handwritten or typed version of a book, article, etc, as submitted by an author for publication **3** handwriting, as opposed to printing [C16 from Med. L *manūscriptus*, from L *manus* hand + *scribere* to write]

Manutius (məˈnjuːʃɪəs) *n* See **Aldus Manutius**

Manx (mæŋks) *adj* **1** of or relating to the Isle of Man (an island in the Irish Sea), its inhabitants, their language, or their dialect of English ▷ *n* **2** an almost extinct language of the Isle of Man, closely related to Scottish Gaelic **3 the Manx** (*functioning as pl*) the people of the Isle of Man [C16 earlier *Maniske*, of Scand. origin, from *Mana* Isle of Man + *-iske* -ISH]

Manx cat *n* a short-haired tailless variety of cat, believed to originate on the Isle of Man

Manxman (ˈmæŋksmən) *or* (*fem*) **Manxwoman** (ˈmæŋksˌwʊmən) *n, pl* **Manxmen** *or* **Manxwomen** a native or inhabitant of the Isle of Man

many (ˈmɛnɪ) *determiner* **1** (sometimes preceded by *a great* or *a good*) **1a** a large number of: *many times* **1b** (*as pronoun; functioning as plural*): *many are seated already* **2** (foll by *a*, *an*, or *another*, and a sing noun) each of a considerable number of: *many a man* **3** (preceded by *as*, *too*, *that*, etc) **3a** a great number of: *as many apples as you like* **3b** (*as pronoun; functioning as plural*): *I have as many as you* ▷ *n* **4 the many** the majority of mankind, esp the common people [OE *manig*]

many-sided *adj* having many sides, aspects, etc > ˌ**many-ˈsidedness** *n*

many-valued logic *n* any of various logics in which the truth-values that a proposition may have are not restricted to truth and falsity

manzanilla (ˌmænzəˈnɪlə) *n* a very dry pale sherry [C19 from Sp.: camomile (referring to its bouquet)]

Manzoni (*Italian* manˈdzoːni) *n* **Alessandro** (alesˈsandro) 1785–1873, Italian romantic novelist and poet, famous for his historical novel *I Promessi sposi* (1825–27)

Maoism (ˈmaʊɪzəm) *n* **1** Marxism-Leninism as interpreted by Mao Tse-tung: distinguished by its theory of guerrilla warfare and its emphasis on the revolutionary potential of the peasantry **2** adherence to or reverence for Mao Tse-tung and his teachings > **ˈMaoist** *n, adj*

Maori (ˈmaʊrɪ) *n* **1** (*pl* **Maoris** *or* **Maori**) a member of the people of Polynesian origin living in New Zealand and the Cook Islands since before the arrival of European settlers **2** the language of this people, belonging to the Malayo-Polynesian family ▷ *adj* **3** of or relating to this people or their language

Maori bread *n NZ* bread made with fermented potato yeast

Maoriland (ˈmaʊrɪˌlænd) *n* an obsolete name for **New Zealand** > **ˈMaoriˌlander** *n*

Mao Tse-tung (ˈmaʊ tseɪˈtʊŋ) *or* **Mao Ze Dong** *n* 1893–1976, Chinese Marxist theoretician and statesman. The son of a peasant farmer, he helped to found the Chinese Communist Party (1921) and established a soviet republic in SE China (1931–34). He led the retreat of Communist forces to NW China known as the Long March (1935–36), emerging as leader of the party. In opposing the Japanese in World War II, he united with the Kuomintang regime, which he then defeated in the ensuing civil war. He founded the People's Republic of China (1949) of which he was chairman until 1959. As party chairman until his death, he instigated the Cultural Revolution in 1966

map (mæp) *n* **1** a diagrammatic representation of the earth's surface or part of it, showing the geographical distributions, positions, etc, of features such as roads, towns, relief, rainfall, etc **2** a diagrammatic representation of the stars or of the surface of a celestial body **3** a maplike drawing of anything **4** *maths* another name for **function** (sense 5) **5** a slang word for **face** (sense 1) **6 off the map** no longer important; out of existence (esp in **wipe off the map**) **7 put on the map** to make (a town, company, etc) well-known ▷ *vb* **maps, mapping, mapped 8** (*tr*) to make a map of **9** (*tr*) *maths* to represent or transform (a function, figure, set, etc): *the results were mapped onto a graph* ▷ See also **map out 10** (*intr*) **map onto** to fit in with or correspond to [C16 from Med. L *mappa* (*mundi*) map (of the world), from L *mappa* cloth]

Map (mæp) *or* **Mapes** (mæps, ˈmeɪpiːz) *n* **Walter** ?1140–?1209, Welsh ecclesiastic and satirical writer. His chief work is the miscellany *De Nugis curialium*

maple (ˈmeɪpᵊl) *n* **1** any tree or shrub of a N temperate genus, having winged seeds borne in pairs and lobed leaves **2** the hard wood of any of these trees, used for furniture and flooring **3** the flavour of the sap of the sugar maple ▷ See also **sugar maple** [C14 from OE *mapel-*, as in *mapeltrēow* maple tree]

maple leaf *n* the leaf of the maple tree, the national emblem of Canada

maple sugar *n US & Canad* sugar made from the sap of the sugar maple

maple syrup *n chiefly US & Canad* a very sweet syrup made from the sap of the sugar maple

map out *vb* (*tr, adv*) to plan or design

mapping (ˈmæpɪŋ) *n maths* another name for **function** (sense 5)

map projection *n* a means of representing or a representation of a globe or celestial sphere or part of it on a flat map

Maputo (məˈpuːtəʊ) *n* the capital and chief port of Mozambique, in the south on Delagoa Bay: became capital in 1907; the nearest port to the Rand gold-mining and industrial region of South Africa. Pop: 989 386 (1997). Former name (until 1975): **Lourenço Marques**

▹ www.mozambique.mz/turismo/emaputo.htm
▹ www.go2africa.com/mozambique/maputo/maputo

maquette (mæ'kɛt) *n* a sculptor's small preliminary model or sketch [c20 from F, from It. *macchietta* a little sketch, from *macchiare*, from L *macula* blemish]

maquis (mɑː'kiː) *n, pl* **maquis** (-'kiː) **1** shrubby, mostly evergreen, vegetation found in coastal regions of the Mediterranean **2** (*often cap*) **2a** the French underground movement that fought against the German occupying forces in World War II **2b** a member of this movement [c20 from F, from It. *macchia* thicket, from L *macula* spot]

mar (mɑː) *vb* **mars, marring, marred** (*tr*) to cause harm to; spoil or impair [OE *merran*] > **'marrer** *n*

Mar. *abbrev for* March

marabou ('mærəˌbuː) *n* **1** a large black-and-white African carrion-eating stork **2** a down feather of this bird, used to trim garments [c19 from F, from Ar. *murābit* MARABOUT: the stork is considered a holy bird in Islam]

marabout ('mærəˌbuː) *n* **1** a Muslim holy man or hermit of North Africa **2** a shrine of the grave of a marabout [c17 via F & Port. *marabuto*, from Ar. *murābit*]

maraca (mə'rækə) *n* a percussion instrument, usually one of a pair, consisting of a gourd or plastic shell filled with dried seeds, pebbles, etc [c20 Brazilian Port., of Amerind origin]

Maracaibo (ˌmærə'kaɪbəʊ; *Spanish* mara'kaiβo) *n* **1** a port in NW Venezuela, on the channel from Lake Maracaibo to the Gulf of Venezuela: the second largest city in the country; University of Zulia (1891); major oil centre. Pop: 1 764 038 (2000 est) **2 Lake** a lake in NW Venezuela, linked with the Gulf of Venezuela by a dredged channel: centre of the Venezuelan and South American oil industry. Area: about 13 000 sq km (500 sq miles)

Maracanda (ˌmærə'kændə) *n* the ancient name for **Samarkand**

Maracay (*Spanish* mara'kai) *n* a city in N central Venezuela: developed greatly as the headquarters of Juan Vicente Gómez during his dictatorship; textile industries. Pop: 459 007 (2000 est)

Maradona (ˌmærə'dɒnə) *n* **Diego Armando** (dɪ'eɪgəʊ) born 1960, Argentinian footballer

marae (mə'raɪ) *n* **1** NZ the enclosed space in front of a Maori meeting house **2** NZ a Maori meeting house, with its courtyard and associated buildings **3** (in Polynesia) an open-air place of worship [from Maori]

Marajó (*Portuguese* mara'ʒɔ) *n* an island in N Brazil, at the mouth of the Amazon. Area: 38 610 sq km (15 444 sq miles)

Maranhão (*Portuguese* marə'ɲə̃u) *n* a state of NE Brazil, on the Atlantic: forested and humid in the northwest, with high plateaus in the east and south. Capital: São Luís. Pop: 5 638 381 (2000). Area: 328 666 sq km (128 179 sq miles)

Marañón (*Spanish* mara'ɲɔn) *n* a river in NE Peru, rising in the Andes and flowing northwest into the Ucayali River, forming the Amazon. Length: about 1450 km (900 miles)

maranta (mɑː'ræntə) *n* any of various tropical monocotyledons with ornamental leaves [c19 after B. *Maranta* 16th-century Venetian botanist]

Maraş (mæ'ræʃ) *n* a town in S Turkey: noted formerly for the manufacture of weapons but now for carpets and embroidery. Pop: 303 594 (1997)

marasca (mə'ræskə) *n* a European cherry tree with red acid-tasting fruit [c19 from It., var. of *amarasca*, ult. from L *amārus* bitter]

maraschino (ˌmærə'skiːnəʊ, -'ʃiːnəʊ) *n* a liqueur made from marasca cherries, having a taste like bitter almonds [c18 from It.; see MARASCA]

maraschino cherry *n* a cherry preserved in maraschino or an imitation of this liqueur

marasmus (mə'ræzməs) *n pathol* general emaciation, esp of infants, thought to be associated with severe malnutrition or impaired utilization of nutrients [c17 from NL, from Gk *marasmos*, from *marainein* to waste] > **ma'rasmic** *adj*

Marat (*French* mara) *n* **Jean Paul** (ʒɑ̃ pɔl) 1743–93, French revolutionary leader and journalist. He founded the radical newspaper *L'Ami du peuple* and was elected to the National Convention (1792). He was instrumental in overthrowing the Girondists (1793); he was stabbed to death in his bath by Charlotte Corday

marathon ('mærəθən) *n* **1** a race on foot of 26 miles 385 yards (42.195 kilometres) **2a** any long or arduous task, etc **2b** (*as modifier*): *a marathon effort* [referring to the feat of the messenger who ran more than 20 miles from Marathon to Athens to bring the news of victory in 490 BC]

Marathon ('mærəθən) *n* a plain in Attica northeast of Athens: site of a victory of the Athenians and Plataeans over the Persians (490 BC)

marathoner ('mærəθənə) *n* a person who runs in a marathon

marathon group *n* (in psychotherapy) an encounter group that lasts for many hours or days

maraud (mə'rɔːd) *vb* to wander or raid in search of plunder [c18 from F *marauder* to prowl, from *maraud* vagabond] > **ma'rauder** *n*

marauding (mə'rɔːdɪŋ) *adj* wandering or raiding in search of plunder or victims

Marbella (mɑː'bɜlə) *n* a coastal resort in S Spain, on the Costa del Sol. Pop: 100 000 (2004 est)

marble ('mɑːbᵊl) *n* **1a** a hard crystalline metamorphic rock resulting from the recrystallization of a limestone **1b** (*as modifier*): *a marble bust* **2** a block or work of art of marble **3** a small round glass or stone ball used in playing marbles ▹ *vb* **marbles, marbling, marbled 4** (*tr*) to mottle with variegated streaks in imitation of marble [c12 via OF from L *marmor*, from Gk *marmaros*, rel. to Gk *marmairein* to gleam] > **'marbled** *adj*

Mm

marbles ('mɑːbᵊlz) *n* **1** (*functioning as sing*) a game in which marbles are rolled at one another, similar to bowls **2** (*functioning as pl*) *inf* wits: *to lose one's marbles*

marbling ('mɑːblɪŋ) *n* **1** a mottled effect or pattern resembling marble **2** such an effect obtained by transferring floating colours from a gum solution **3** the streaks of fat in lean meat

Marburg ('mɑːˌbɜːg; *German* 'maːrbʊrk) *n* **1** a city in W central Germany, in Hesse: famous for the religious debate between Luther and Zwingli in 1529; Europe's first Protestant university (1527). Pop: 75 400 (1995 est) **2** the German name for **Maribor**

Marburg disease *n* a severe, sometimes fatal, viral disease of vervet (green) monkeys, which may be transmitted to humans. Also called: **green monkey disease** [c20 after MARBURG, in which the first human cases were recorded]

marc (mɑːk) *n* **1** the remains of grapes or other fruit that have been pressed for wine-making **2** a brandy distilled from these [c17 from F, from OF *marchier* to trample (grapes)]

Marc (*German* mark) *n* **Franz** (frants) 1880–1916, German expressionist painter; cofounder with Kandinsky of the *Blaue Reiter* group (1911). He is noted for his symbolic compositions of animals

marcasite ('mɑːkəˌsaɪt) *n* **1** a metallic pale yellow mineral consisting of iron sulphide in crystalline form used in jewellery **2** a cut and polished form of steel or any white metal used for making jewellery [c15 from Med. L *marcasīta*, from Ar. *marqashītā*, ?from Persian]

marcato (mɑː'kɑːtəʊ) *adj, adv music* with each note heavily accented [from It.: marked]

Marceau (*French* marso) *n* **Marcel** (marsɛl) born 1923, French mime artist

Marcellus (mɑː'sɛləs) *n* **Marcus Claudius** ('mɑːkəs 'klɔːdɪəs) ?268–208 BC, Roman general and consul, who captured Syracuse (212) in the Second Punic War

march¹ (mɑːtʃ) *vb* **1** (*intr*) to walk or proceed with stately or regular steps, usually in a procession or military formation **2** (*tr*) to make (a person or group) proceed **3** (*tr*) to traverse or cover by marching ▷ *n* **4** the act or an instance of marching **5** a regular stride **6** a long or exhausting walk **7** advance; progression (of time, etc) **8** a distance or route covered by marching **9** a piece of music, as for a march **10** **steal a march on** to gain an advantage over, esp by a secret enterprise or trick [c16 from OF *marchier* to tread, prob. of Gmc origin] > **'marcher** *n*

march² (mɑːtʃ) *n* **1** a frontier, border, or boundary or the land lying along it, often of disputed ownership ▷ *vb* **2** (*intr; often foll by upon or with*) to share a common border (with) [c13 from OF *marche*, of Gmc origin]

March¹ (mɑːtʃ) *n* the third month of the year, consisting of 31 days [from OF, from L *Martius* (month) of Mars]

March² (març) *n* the German name for the **Morava** (sense 1)

Marche (*French* marʃ) *n* a former province of central France

Marches ('mɑːtʃɪz) *n* **the 1** the border area between England and Wales or Scotland, both characterized by continual feuding (13th–16th centuries) **2** a region of central Italy. Capital: Ancona. Pop: 1 460 989 (2000 est). Area: 9692 sq km (3780 sq miles). Italian name: **Le Marche** (le 'marke) **3** any of various other border regions

March hare *n* a hare during its breeding season in March, noted for its wild and excitable behaviour (esp in **mad as a March hare**)

marching girl *n* (*often plural*) *Austral and NZ* one of a team of girls dressed in fancy uniform who perform marching formations

marching orders *pl n* **1** military orders, esp to infantry, giving instructions about a march, its destination, etc **2** *inf* any dismissal, esp notice of dismissal from employment

marchioness ('mɑːʃənɪs, ˌmɑːʃə'nɛs) *n* **1** the wife or widow of a marquis **2** a woman who holds the rank of marquis [c16 from Med. L *marchionissa*, fem. of *marchiō* MARQUIS]

marchpane ('mɑːtʃˌpeɪn) *n* an archaic word for **marzipan** [c15 from F]

Marciano (ˌmɑːsɪ'ænəʊ, -'ɑːnəʊ) *n* **Rocky** original name *Rocco Francis Marchegiano*. 1923–69, US heavyweight boxer; world heavyweight champion, 1952–56

Marconi (mɑː'kəʊnɪ) *n* **Guglielmo** (guʎ'ʎɛlmo) 1874–1937, Italian physicist, who developed radiotelegraphy and succeeded in transmitting signals across the Atlantic (1901): Nobel prize for physics 1909

Marco Polo ('mɑːkəʊ 'pəʊləʊ) *n* See (Marco) **Polo**

Marcos ('mɑːkɒs) *n* **Ferdinand** (**Edralin**) 1917–89, Filipino statesman; president of the Philippines from 1965; deposed and exiled in 1986

Marcus Aurelius Antoninus ('mɑːkəs ɔː'riːlɪəs ˌæntə'naɪnəs) *n* original name *Marcus Annius Verus*. 121–180 AD, Roman emperor (161–180) noted particularly for his *Meditations*, propounding his stoic view of life

Marcuse (mɑː'kuːzə) *n* **Herbert** 1898–1979, US philosopher, born in Germany. In his later works he analysed the situation of man under monopoly capitalism and the dehumanizing effects of modern technology. His works include *Eros and Civilization* (1958) and *One Dimensional Man* (1964)

Mar del Plata (*Spanish* 'mar ðel 'plata) *n* a city and resort in E Argentina, on the Atlantic: fishing port. Pop: 579 483 (1999 est)

Mardi Gras ('mɑːdɪ 'grɑː) *n* the festival of Shrove Tuesday, celebrated in some cities with great revelry [F: fat Tuesday]

Marduk ('mɑːdʊk) *n* the chief god of the Babylonian pantheon

mare¹ (mɛə) *n* the adult female of a horse or zebra [c12 from OE, of Gmc origin]

mare² ('mɑːreɪ, -rɪ) *n, pl* **maria 1** (*cap when part of a name*) any of a large number of huge dry plains on the surface of the moon, visible as dark markings and once thought to be seas **2** a similar area on the surface of Mars [from L: sea]

Marengo (mə'rɛŋgəʊ; *Italian* ma'reŋgo) *n* a village in NW Italy: site of a major battle in which Napoleon decisively defeated the Austrians (1800)

Marenzio (*Italian* ma'rɛntsjo) *n* **Luca** ('luːka) 1553–99, Italian composer of madrigals

mare's-nest ('mɛəzˌnɛst) *n* **1** a discovery imagined to be important but proving worthless **2** a disordered situation

mare's-tail ('mɛəzˌteɪl) *n* **1** a wisp of trailing cirrus cloud, often indicating high winds in the upper atmosphere **2** an erect pond plant with minute flowers and crowded whorls of narrow leaves

Margaret ('mɑːgrət) *n* **1** called the *Maid of Norway*. ?1282–90, queen of Scotland (1286–90); daughter of Eric II of Norway. Her death while sailing to England to marry the future Edward II led Edward I to declare dominion over Scotland **2** 1353–1412, queen of Sweden (1388–1412) and regent of Norway and Denmark (1380–1412), who united the three countries under her rule

Margaret of Anjou *n* 1430–82, queen of England. She married the mentally unstable Henry VI of England in 1445 to confirm the truce with France during the Hundred Years' War. She became a leader of the Lancastrians in the Wars of the Roses and was defeated at Tewkesbury (1471) by Edward IV

Margaret of Navarre *n* Also called: **Margaret of Angoulême** 1492–1549, queen of Navarre (1544–49) by marriage to Henry II of Navarre; sister of Francis I of France. She was a poet, a patron of humanism, and author of the *Heptaméron* (1558)

Margaret of Scotland *n* **Saint** 1045–93, queen consort of Malcolm III of Scotland. Her piety and benefactions to the church led to her canonization (1250) Feast days: June 10, Nov. 16

Margaret of Valois *n* 1553–1615, daughter of Henry II of France and Catherine de' Medici; queen of Navarre (1572) by marriage to Henry of Navarre. The marriage was dissolved (1599) after his accession as Henry IV of France: noted for her *Mémoires*

margaric (mɑː'gærɪk) *or* **margaritic** *adj* of or resembling pearl [c19 from Gk *margaron* pearl]

margarine (ˌmɑːdʒə'riːn, ˌmɑːgə-) *n* a substitute for butter, prepared from vegetable and animal fats with added small amounts of milk, salt, vitamins, colouring matter, etc [c19 from MARGARIC]

Margarita (ˌmɑːgə'riːtə) *n* an island in the Caribbean, off the NE coast of Venezuela: pearl fishing. Capital: La Asunción

Margate ('mɑːgeɪt) *n* a town and resort in SE England, in E Kent on the Isle of Thanet. Pop: 56 734 (1991)

marge¹ (mɑːdʒ) *n Brit inf* short for **margarine**

marge² (mɑːdʒ) *n arch* a margin [c16 from F]

margin ('mɑːdʒɪn) *n* **1** an edge or rim, and the area immediately adjacent to it; border **2** the blank space surrounding the text on a page **3** a vertical line on a page, esp on the left-hand-side, delineating this space **4** an additional amount or one beyond the minimum necessary: *a margin of error* **5** *chiefly Austral* a payment made in addition to a basic wage, esp for special skill or responsibility **6** a bound or limit **7** the amount by which one thing differs from another **8** *commerce* the profit on a transaction **9** *econ* the minimum return below which an enterprise becomes unprofitable **10** *finance* collateral deposited by a client with a broker as security ▷ Also (archaic): **margent** ('mɑːdʒənt) ▷ *vb* (*tr*) **11** to provide with a margin; border **12** *finance* to

deposit a margin upon [c14 from L *margō* border]
marginal (ˈmɑːdʒɪnᵊl) *adj* **1** of, in, on, or constituting a margin **2** close to a limit, esp a lower limit: *marginal legal ability* **3** not considered central or important; insignificant **4** *econ* relating to goods or services produced and sold at the margin of profitability: *marginal cost* **5** *politics, chiefly Brit & NZ* of or designating a constituency in which elections tend to be won by small margins: *a marginal seat* **6** designating agricultural land on the margin of cultivated zones ▷ *n* **7** *politics, chiefly Brit & NZ* a marginal constituency > **marginality** (ˌmɑːdʒɪˈnælɪtɪ) *n* > ˈ**marginally** *adv*
marginalia (ˌmɑːdʒɪˈneɪlɪə) *pl n* notes in the margin of a book, manuscript, or letter [c19 NL, noun (neuter pl) from *marginālis* marginal]
marginate (ˈmɑːdʒɪˌneɪt) *vb* **marginates, marginating, marginated** **1** (*tr*) to provide with a margin or margins ▷ *adj* **2** *biol* having a margin of a distinct colour or form [c18 from L *margināre*] > ˌ**marginˈation** *n*
Margolis (ˈmɑːɡəlɪs) *n* **Donald** born 1955, US playwright; plays include *The Loman Family Picnic* (1989) and the Pulitzer Prize-winning *Dinner with Friends* (1999)
margrave (ˈmɑːˌɡreɪv) *n* a German nobleman ranking above a count. Margraves were originally counts appointed to govern frontier provinces, but all eventually became princes of the Holy Roman Empire [c16 from MDu. *markgrave*, lit.: count of the MARCH[2]] > **margravate** (ˈmɑːɡrəvɪt) *n*
margravine (ˈmɑːɡrəˌviːn) *n* **1** the wife or widow of a margrave **2** a woman who holds the rank of margrave [c17 from MDu., fem of MARGRAVE]
marguerite (ˌmɑːɡəˈriːt) *n* **1** a cultivated garden plant whose flower heads have white or pale yellow rays around a yellow disc **2** any of various related plants with daisy-like flowers [c19 from F: daisy, pearl, from L, from Gk, from *margaron*]
maria (ˈmɑːrɪə) *n* the plural of **mare[2]**
mariachi (ˌmɑːrɪˈɑːtʃɪ) *n* a small ensemble of street musicians in Mexico [c20 from Mexican Sp.]
Maria de' Medici (*Italian* maˈriːa de ˈmɛːditʃi) *n* French name *Marie de Médicis*. 1573–1642, queen of France (1600–10) by marriage to Henry IV of France; daughter of Francesco, grand duke of Tuscany. She became regent for her son (later Louis XIII) but continued to wield power after he came of age (1614). She was finally exiled from France in 1631 after plotting to undermine Richelieu's influence at court
Mariana Islands (ˌmærɪˈɑːnə) *pl n* a chain of volcanic and coral islands in the W Pacific, east of the Philippines and north of New Guinea: divided politically into Guam (a US unincorporated territory) and the islands north of Guam constituting the Commonwealth of the Northern Mariana Islands (a US commonwealth territory). Pop: (Guam) 158 000 (2001 est); (Northern Marianas) 73 400 (2001 est). Area: 958 sq km (370 sq miles). Former name (1521–1668): **Ladrone Islands**
Marianao (*Spanish* marjaˈnao) *n* a city in NW Cuba, adjacent to W Havana city: the chief Cuban military base. Pop: 133 015 (latest est)
Mariánské Lázně (*Czech* ˈmarjanskɛː ˈlaːznjɛ) *n* a town in the W Czech Republic: a fashionable spa in the 18th and 19th centuries. Pop: 15 380 (1991). German name: **Marienbad**
Maria Theresa (məˈriːə təˈreɪzə) *n* 1717–80, archduchess of Austria and queen of Hungary and Bohemia (1740–80); the daughter and heiress of Emperor Charles VI of Austria; the wife of Emperor Francis I; the mother of Emperor Joseph II. In the War of the Austrian Succession (1740–48) she was confirmed in all her possessions except Silesia, which she attempted unsuccessfully to regain in the Seven Years' War (1756–63)
Maribor (ˈmærɪbɔː) *n* an industrial city in N Slovenia on the Drava River: a flourishing Hapsburg trading centre in the 13th century; resort. Pop: 134 289 (1996 est). German name: **Marburg**
Marie Antoinette (*French* mari ɑ̃twanɛt) *n* 1755–93, queen of France (1774–93) by marriage to Louis XVI of France. Her opposition to reform during the Revolution contributed to the overthrow of the monarchy; guillotined
Marie Byrd Land (ˈmɑːrɪ ˈbɜːd) *n* the former name of **Byrd Land**
Marie Galante (*French* mari galɑ̃t) *n* an island in the E Caribbean southeast of Guadeloupe, of which it is a dependency. Chief town: Grand Bourg. Pop: 13 463 (1990). Area: 155 sq km (60 sq miles)
Mariehamn (mariəˈhamn) *n* a city in SW Finland, chief port of the Åland Islands. Pop: 10 260 (1990). Finnish name: **Maarianhamina**
Marie Louise (*French* mari lwiz) *n* 1791–1847, empress of France (1811–15) as the second wife of Napoleon I; daughter of Francis I of Austria. On Napoleon's abdication (1815) she became Duchess of Parma
Mari El Republic (ˈmɑːrɪ) *n* a constituent republic of W central Russia, in the middle Volga basin. Capital: Yoshkar-Ola. Pop: 766 000 (1996 est). Area: 23 200 sq km (8955 sq miles)
Marienbad (ˈmærɪənˌbæd; *German* maˈriːənbaːt) *n* the German name for **Mariánské Lázně**
marigold (ˈmærɪˌɡəʊld) *n* **1** any of various tropical American plants cultivated for their yellow or orange flower heads and strongly scented foliage **2** any of various similar or related plants, such as the marsh marigold [c14 from *Mary* (the Virgin) + GOLD]
marijuana *or* **marihuana** (ˌmærɪˈhwɑːnə) *n* **1** the dried leaves and flowers of the hemp plant, used for its euphoric effects, esp in cigarettes. See also **cannabis** **2** another name for **hemp** (the plant) [c19 from Mexican Sp.]
marimba (məˈrɪmbə) *n* a Latin American percussion instrument consisting of a set of hardwood plates placed over tuned metal resonators, played with two soft-headed sticks in each hand [c18 of West African origin]
Marin (ˈmɑːrɪn) *n* **John** 1870–1953, US painter, noted esp for his watercolour landscapes and seascapes
marina (məˈriːnə) *n* an elaborate docking facility for yachts and other pleasure boats [c19 via It. & Sp. from L: MARINE]
marinade *n* (ˌmærɪˈneɪd) **1** a spiced liquid mixture of oil, wine, vinegar, etc, in which meat or fish is soaked before cooking **2** meat or fish soaked in this ▷ *vb* (ˈmærɪˌneɪd), **marinades, marinading, marinaded** **3** a variant of **marinate** [c17 from F, from Sp., from *marinar* to MARINATE]
marinate (ˈmærɪˌneɪt) *vb* **marinates, marinating, marinated** to soak in marinade [c17 prob. from It. *marinato*, from *marinare* to pickle, ult. from L *marīnus* MARINE] > ˌ**mariˈnation** *n*
Marinduque (ˌmɑːrɪnˈduːkeɪ) *n* an island of the central Philippines, east of Mindoro: forms, with offshore islets, a province of the Philippines. Capital: Boac. Pop: 173 715 (latest est). Area: 960 sq km (370 sq miles)
marine (məˈriːn) *adj* (*usually prenominal*) **1** of, found in, or relating to the sea **2** of or relating to shipping, navigation, etc **3** of or relating to a body of seagoing troops: *marine corps* **4** of or relating to a government department concerned with maritime affairs **5** used or adapted for use at sea ▷ *n* **6** shipping and navigation in general **7** (*cap when part of a name*) a member of a marine corps or similar body **8** a picture of a ship, seascape, etc **9** **tell it to the marines** *inf* an expression of disbelief [c15 from OF *marin*, from L *marīnus*, from *mare* sea]
mariner (ˈmærɪnə) *n* a formal or literary word for

Mm

seaman [c13 from Anglo-F, ult. from L *marīnus* MARINE]
Marinetti (*Italian* mari'netti) *n* **Filippo Tommaso** (fi'lippo tom'ma:zo) 1876–1944, Italian poet; founder of futurism (1909)
Mariolatry (ˌmɛərɪ'ɒlətrɪ) *n derog* devotion to the Virgin Mary, considered as excessive > ˌ**Mari'olater** *n* > ˌ**Mari'olatrous** *adj*
marionette (ˌmærɪə'nɛt) *n* a puppet or doll whose jointed limbs are moved by strings [c17 from F, from *Marion*, dim. of *Marie* Mary + -ETTE]
Marist ('mɛərɪst) *n RC Church* a member of the Society of Mary, a religious congregation founded in 1824 [c19 from F *Mariste*, from *Marie* Mary (the Virgin)]
Maritain (*French* maritɛ̃) *n* **Jacques** (ʒak) 1882–1973, French neo-Thomist Roman Catholic philosopher
marital ('mærɪtᵊl) *adj* **1** of or relating to marriage **2** of or relating to a husband [c17 from L *marītālis*, from *marītus* married (adj), husband (n)] > '**maritally** *adv*
maritime ('mærɪˌtaɪm) *adj* **1** of or relating to navigation, shipping, etc **2** of, relating to, near, or living near the sea **3** (of a climate) having small temperature differences between summer and winter [c16 from L *maritimus*, from *mare* sea]
Maritime Alps *pl n* a range of the W Alps in SE France and NW Italy. Highest peak: Argentera, 3297 m (10 817 ft)
Maritime Command *n Canad* the naval branch of the Canadian armed forces
Maritime Provinces *or* **Maritimes** *pl n* **the** another name for the **Atlantic Provinces** but often excluding Newfoundland
Maritimer ('mærɪˌtaɪmə) *n* a native or inhabitant of the Maritime Provinces of Canada
Maritsa (*Bulgarian* ma'ritsa) *n* a river in S Europe, rising in S Bulgaria and flowing east into Turkey, then south from Edirne as part of the border between Turkey and Greece to the Aegean. Length: 483 km (300 miles). Turkish name: **Meriç** Greek name: **Évros**
Mariupol (*Russian* məri'upəlj) *n* a port in SE Ukraine, on an estuary leading to the Sea of Azov. Pop: 504 400 (1998 est). Former name (1948–91): **Zhdanov**
Marius ('mɛərɪəs, 'mærɪəs) *n* **Gaius** ('gaɪəs) ?155–86 BC, Roman general and consul. He defeated Jugurtha, the Cimbri, and the Teutons (107–101), but his rivalry with Sulla caused civil war (88). He was exiled but returned (87) and took Rome
Marivaux (*French* marivo) *n* **Pierre Carlet de Chamblain de** (pjɛr karlɛ də ʃɑ̃blɛ̃ də) 1688–1763, French dramatist and novelist, noted particularly for his comedies, such as *Le jeu de l'amour et du hasard* (1730) and *La Vie de Marianne* (1731–41)
marjoram ('mɑːdʒərəm) *n* **1** Also called: **sweet marjoram** an aromatic Mediterranean plant with sweet-scented leaves, used for seasoning food and in salads **2** Also called: **wild marjoram, pot marjoram, origan** a similar and related European plant. See also **oregano** [c14 via OF *majorane*, from Med. L *marjorana*]
mark¹ (mɑːk) *n* **1** a visible impression, stain, etc, on a surface, such as a spot or scratch **2** a sign, symbol, or other indication that distinguishes something **3** a cross or other symbol made instead of a signature **4** a written or printed sign or symbol, as for punctuation **5** a letter, number, or percentage used to grade academic work **6** a thing that indicates position or directs; marker **7** a desired or recognized standard: *up to the mark* **8** an indication of some quality, feature, or prowess **9** quality or importance: *a person of little mark* **10** a target or goal **11** impression or influence **12** one of the temperature settings on a gas oven: *gas mark 5* **13** *sl* a suitable victim, esp for swindling **14** (*often cap*) (in trade names) a model, brand, or type **15** *naut* one of the intervals distinctively marked on a sounding lead **16** *rugby* an action in which a player within his or her own 22 m line catches a forward kick by an opponent and shouts "mark", which entitles him or her to a free kick **17** *Australian rules football* **17a** a catch of the ball from a kick of at least 10 yards, after which a free kick is taken **17b** the spot where this occurs **18** (in medieval England and Germany) a piece of land held in common by the free men of a community **19** **the mark** *boxing* the middle of the stomach **20** **make one's mark** to succeed or achieve recognition **21** **on your mark** *or* **marks** a command given to runners in a race to prepare themselves at the starting line ▹ *vb* **22** to make or receive (a visible impression, trace, or stain) on (a surface) **23** (*tr*) to characterize or distinguish **24** (often foll by *off* or *out*) to set boundaries or limits (on) **25** (*tr*) to select, designate, or doom by or as if by a mark: *a marked man* **26** (*tr*) to put identifying or designating labels, stamps, etc, on, esp to indicate price **27** (*tr*) to pay heed or attention to: *mark my words* **28** to observe; notice **29** to grade or evaluate (scholastic work) **30** *football, etc* to stay close to (an opponent) to hamper his or her play **31** to keep (score) in some games **32** **mark time** **32a** to move the feet alternately as in marching but without advancing **32b** to act in a mechanical and routine way **32c** to halt progress temporarily ▹ See also **markdown, mark-up** [OE *mearc* mark] > '**marker** *n*
mark² (mɑːk) *n* **1** See **Deutschmark, markka, Reichsmark, Ostmark** **2** a former monetary unit and coin in England and Scotland worth two thirds of a pound sterling **3** a silver coin of Germany until 1924 [OE *marc* unit of weight of precious metal, ?from the marks on metal bars; apparently of Gmc origin and rel. to MARK¹]
Mark (mɑːk) *n New Testament* **1** one of the four Evangelists. Feast day: April 25 **2** the second Gospel, traditionally ascribed to him
Mark Antony *n* See (Mark) **Antony**
markdown ('mɑːkˌdaʊn) *n* **1** a price reduction ▹ *vb* **mark down** **2** (*tr, adv*) to reduce in price
marked (mɑːkt) *adj* **1** obvious, evident, or noticeable **2** singled out, esp as the target of attack: *a marked man* **3** *linguistics* distinguished by a specific feature, as in phonology. For example, of the two phonemes /t/ and /d/, the /d/ is marked because it exhibits the feature of voice > **markedly** ('mɑːkɪdlɪ) *adv* > '**markedness** *n*
market ('mɑːkɪt) *n* **1a** an event or occasion, usually held at regular intervals, at which people meet to buy and sell merchandise **1b** (*as modifier*): *market day* **2** a place at which a market is held **3** a shop that sells a particular merchandise: *an antique market* **4** the trading or selling opportunities provided by a particular group of people: *the foreign market* **5** demand for a particular product or commodity **6** See **stock market** **7** See **market price, market value** **8** **be in the market for** to wish to buy or acquire **9** **on the market** available for purchase **10** **seller's** (*or* **buyer's**) **market** a market characterized by excess demand (or supply) and thus favourable to sellers (or buyers) **11** **the market** business or trade in a commodity as specified: *the sugar market* ▹ *vb* **markets, marketing, marketed** **12** (*tr*) to offer or produce for sale **13** (*intr*) to buy or deal in a market [c12 from L *mercātus*, from *mercārī* to trade, from *merx* merchandise] > '**marketable** *adj* > '**marketer** *n*
marketeer (ˌmɑːkɪ'tɪə) *n* **1** *Brit* (formerly) a supporter of the Common Market and of Britain's membership of it; a Europhile **2** a person employed in marketing
market forces *pl n* the effect of supply and demand on trading within a free market
market garden *n chiefly Brit* an establishment where fruit and vegetables are grown for sale > **market gardener** *n* > **market gardening** *n*
▹ http://attra.ncat.org/attra-pub/marketgardening.html
▹ www.cityfarmer.org
▹ www.marketgardening.com

marketing ('mɑːkɪtɪŋ) *n* the provision of goods or services to meet consumer needs
market maker *n* a dealer in securities on the London stock exchange, who buys and sells as a principal and since 1986 can also deal directly with the public
marketplace ('mɑːkɪtˌpleɪs) *n* **1** a place where a public market is held **2** any centre where ideas, etc, are exchanged **3** the commercial world of buying and selling
market price *n* the prevailing price, as determined by supply and demand, at which goods, services, etc, may be bought or sold
market-test *vb* (*tr*) to put (a section of a public-sector enterprise) out to tender, often as a prelude to full-scale privatization
market town *n chiefly Brit* a town that holds a market, esp an agricultural centre
market value *n* the amount obtainable on the open market for the sale of property, financial assets, or goods and services
Markham ('mɑːkəm) *n* **Mount** a mountain in Antarctica, in Victoria Land. Height: 4350 m (14 272 ft)
markhor ('mɑːkɔː) *or* **markhoor** ('mɑːkʊə) *n, pl* **markhors, markhor** *or* **markhoors, markhoor** a large wild Himalayan goat with large spiralled horns [C19 from Persian, lit.: snake-eater]
Markiewicz (mɑː'kjeɪvɪtʃ) *n* **Constance,** Countess, original name *Constance Gore-Booth.* 1868–1927, Irish nationalist, married to a Polish count. She fought in the Easter Rising (1916) and was sentenced to death but reprieved. The first woman elected to the British parliament (1918), she refused to take her seat
marking ('mɑːkɪŋ) *n* **1** a mark or series of marks **2** the arrangement of colours on an animal, plant, etc **3** assessment and correction of pupils' or students' written work by teachers
markka ('mɑːkɑː, -kə) *n, pl* **markkaa** (-kɑː) the former standard monetary unit of Finland; replaced by the euro in 2002 [Finnish; see MARK²]
Markova (mɑː'kəʊvə) *n* Dame **Alicia** real name *Lilian Alicia Marks.* born 1910, English ballerina
marksman ('mɑːksmən) *n, pl* **marksmen** **1** a person skilled in shooting **2** a serviceman selected for his skill in shooting > **'marksmanship** *n* > **'marks,woman** *fem n*
mark-up *n* **1** an amount added to the cost of a commodity to provide the seller with a profit **2a** an increase in the price of a commodity **2b** the amount of this ▷ *vb* **mark up** (*tr, adv*) **3** to add a percentage for profit, etc, to the cost of (a commodity) **4** to increase the price of
marl (mɑːl) *n* **1** a fine-grained sedimentary rock consisting of clay minerals, calcium carbonate, and silt: used as a fertilizer ▷ *vb* **2** (*tr*) to fertilize (land) with marl [C14 via OF, from LL *margila,* dim. of L *marga*] > **'marly** *adj*
Marlborough¹ ('mɑːlbərə, -brə, 'mɔːl-) *n* a town in S England, in Wiltshire: besieged and captured by Royalists in the Civil War (1642); site of Marlborough College, a public school founded in 1843. Pop: 6429 (1991)
Marlborough² ('mɑːlbərə, -brə, 'mɔːl-) *n* **1st Duke of** title of *John Churchill.* 1650–1722, English general; commander of British forces in the War of the Spanish Succession (1701- 14), in which he won victories at Blenheim (1704), Ramillies (1706), Oudenaarde (1708), and Malplaquet (1709)
▷ www.marlborough.govt.nz
▷ www.marlborough.co.nz
Marley ('mɑːlɪ) *n* **Bob,** full name *Robert Nesta Marley.* 1945–81, Jamaican reggae singer, guitarist, and songwriter. With his group, the Wailers, his albums included *Burnin'* (1973), *Natty Dread* (1975), *Rastaman Vibration* (1976), and *Exodus* (1977)
marlin ('mɑːlɪn) *n, pl* **marlin** *or* **marlins** any of several large food and game fishes of warm and tropical seas, having a very long upper jaw [C20 from MARLINESPIKE, from shape of the beak]
marline *or* **marlin** ('mɑːlɪn) *n naut* a light rope, usually tarred, made of two strands laid left-handed [C15 from Du. *marlijn,* from *marren* to tie + *lijn* line]
marlinespike *or* **marlinspike** ('mɑːlɪnˌspaɪk) *n naut* a pointed metal tool used in separating strands of rope, etc
marlite ('mɑːlaɪt) *or* **marlstone** ('mɑːlˌstəʊn) *n* a type of marl that is resistant to the decomposing action of air
Marlowe ('mɑːləʊ) *n* **Christopher** 1564–93, English dramatist and poet, who established blank verse as a creative form of dramatic expression. His plays include *Tamburlaine the Great* (1590), *Edward II* (?1592), and *Dr Faustus* (1604). He was stabbed to death in a tavern brawl
marmalade ('mɑːməˌleɪd) *n* a preserve made by boiling the pulp and rind of citrus fruits, esp oranges, with sugar [C16 via F from Port. *marmelada,* from *marmelo* quince, from L, from Gk *melimēlon,* from *meli* honey + *mēlon* apple]
Marmara *or* **Marmora** ('mɑːmərə) *n* **Sea of** a deep inland sea in NW Turkey, linked with the Black Sea by the Bosporus and with the Aegean by the Dardanelles: separates Turkey in Europe from Turkey in Asia. Area: 11 471 sq km (4429 sq miles). Ancient name: **Propontis**
marmite ('mɑːmaɪt) *n* a large cooking pot [from F: pot]
Marmite ('mɑːmaɪt) *n trademark* a yeast and vegetable extract used as a spread, flavouring, etc
Marmolada (*Italian* marmo'laːda) *n* a mountain in NE Italy: highest peak in the Dolomites. Height: 3342 m (10 965 ft)
marmoreal (mɑː'mɔːrɪəl) *adj* of, relating to, or resembling marble [C18 from L *marmoreus,* from *marmor* marble]
marmoset ('mɑːməˌzɛt) *n* **1** any of various small South American monkeys having long hairy tails **2** **pygmy marmoset** a related form: the smallest monkey, inhabiting tropical forests of the Amazon [C14 from OF *marmouset* grotesque figure, from ?]
marmot ('mɑːmət) *n* **1** any of various burrowing rodents of Europe, Asia, and North America. They are heavily built and have coarse fur **2** **prairie marmot** another name for **prairie dog** [C17 from F *marmotte,* ? ult. from L *mūr-* (stem of *mūs*) mouse + *montis* of the mountain]
Marne (*French* marn) *n* **1** a department of NE France, in Champagne-Ardenne region. Capital: Châlons-sur-Marne. Pop: 565 229 (1999). Area: 8205 sq km (3200 sq miles) **2** a river in NE France, rising on the plateau of Langres and flowing north, then west to the River Seine, north of Paris: linked by canal with the Rivers Saône, Rhine, and Aisne; scene of two unsuccessful German offensives (1914, 1918) during World War I. Length: 525 km (326 miles)
Maroc (marɔk) *n* the French name for **Morocco**
marocain ('mærəˌkeɪn) *n* **1** a fabric of ribbed crepe **2** a garment made from this fabric [C20 from F *maroquin* Moroccan]
maroon¹ (mə'ruːn) *vb* (*tr*) **1** to abandon ashore, esp on an island **2** to isolate without resources ▷ *n* **3** a descendant of a group of runaway slaves living in the remoter areas of the Caribbean or Guyana [C17 (applied to fugitive slaves): from American Sp. *cimarrón* wild, lit.: dwelling on peaks, from Sp. *cima* summit]
maroon² (mə'ruːn) *n* **1a** a dark red to purplish-red colour **1b** (*as adj*): *a maroon carpet* **2** an exploding firework, esp one used as a warning signal [C18 from F, lit.: chestnut]
Maros ('mɔrɔʃ) *n* the Hungarian name for the **Mureş**
Marprelate ('mɑːprɛlɪt) *n* **Martin,** the pen name of the anonymous author or authors of a series of satirical Puritan tracts (1588–89), attacking the bishops of the Church of England

Mm

Marq. *abbrev for:* **1** Marquess **2** Marquis

Marquand (mɑːˈkwɒnd) *n* **J(ohn) P(hillips)** 1893–1960, US novelist, noted for his stories featuring the Japanese detective Mr Moto and for his satirical comedies of New England life, such as *The Late George Apley* (1937)

marque (mɑːk) *n* **1** a brand of product, esp of a car **2** See **letter of marque** [from F, from *marquer* to MARK[1]]

marquee (mɑːˈkiː) *n* **1** a large tent used for entertainment, exhibition, etc **2** Also called: **marquise** *chiefly US & Canad* a canopy over the entrance to a theatre, hotel, etc [C17 (orig. an officer's tent): invented sing form of MARQUISE, erroneously taken to be pl]

Marquesas Islands (mɑːˈkeɪsæs) *pl n* a group of volcanic islands in the S Pacific, in French Polynesia. Pop: 8064 (1996). Area: 1287 sq km (497 sq miles). French name: **Îles Marquises** (il markiz)

marquess (ˈmɑːkwɪs) *n* **1** (in the British Isles) a nobleman ranking between a duke and an earl **2** See **marquis**

marquetry *or* **marqueterie** (ˈmɑːkɪtrɪ) *n, pl* **marquetries** *or* **marqueteries** a pattern of inlaid veneers of wood, brass, ivory, etc, used chiefly as ornamentation in furniture [C16 from OF, from *marqueter* to inlay, from *marque* MARK[1]]

▷ www.marquetry.org

Marquette (mɑːˈkɛt) *n* **Jacques** (ʒak), known as *Père Marquette.* 1637–75, French Jesuit missionary and explorer, with Louis Jolliet, of the Mississippi river

Márquez (ˈmɑːkɛz) *n* **Gabriel García** See (Gabriel) **García Márquez**

marquis (ˈmɑːkwɪs, mɑːˈkiː) *n, pl* **marquises** *or* **marquis** (in various countries) a nobleman ranking above a count, corresponding to a British marquess. The title of marquis is often used in place of that of marquess [C14 from OF *marchis*, lit.: count of the march, from *marche* MARCH[2]]

Marquis (ˈmɑːkwɪs) *n* **Don(ald Robert Perry)** 1878–1937, US humorist; author of *archy and mehitabel* (1927)

marquise (mɑːˈkiːz) *n* **1** (in various countries) another word for **marchioness** **2a** a gemstone, esp a diamond, cut in a pointed oval shape and usually faceted **2b** a piece of jewellery, esp a ring, set with such a stone or with an oval cluster of stones **3** another name for **marquee** (sense 2) [C18 from F, fem of MARQUIS]

marquisette (ˌmɑːkɪˈzɛt, -kwɪ-) *n* a leno-weave fabric of cotton, silk, etc [C20 from F, dim. of MARQUISE]

Marrakech *or* **Marrakesh** (məˈrækɛʃ, ˌmærəˈkɛʃ) *n* a city in W central Morocco: several times capital of Morocco; tourist centre. Pop: 621 914 (1994)

marram grass (ˈmærəm) *n* any of several grasses that grow on sandy shores: often planted to stabilize sand dunes [C17 *marram*, from ON *marálmr*, from *marr* sea + *hálmr* HAULM]

marri (ˈmærɪ) *n* a species of eucalyptus of Western Australia, widely cultivated for its coloured flowers [C19 from Abor.]

marriage (ˈmærɪdʒ) *n* **1** the state or relationship of being husband and wife **2a** the legal union or contract made by a man and woman to live as husband and wife **2b** (*as modifier*): *marriage certificate* **3** the ceremony formalizing this union; wedding **4** a close or intimate union, relationship, etc [C13 from OF; see MARRY[1], -AGE]

marriageable (ˈmærɪdʒəbᵊl) *adj* (esp of women) suitable for marriage, usually with reference to age
> ˌ**marriagea**ˈ**bility** *n*

marriage guidance *n* advice given to couples who have problems in their married life

married (ˈmærɪd) *adj* **1** having a husband or wife **2** joined in marriage **3** of or involving marriage or married persons **4** closely or intimately united ▷ *n* **5** (*usually plural*) a married person (esp in **young marrieds**)

Marriner (ˈmærɪnə) *n* Sir **Neville** born 1924, British conductor and violinist; founder (1956) and director of the Academy of St Martin in the Fields, which specializes in baroque music

marrons glacés *French* (marɔ̃ glase) *pl n* chestnuts cooked in syrup and glazed

marrow (ˈmærəʊ) *n* **1** the fatty network of connective tissue that fills the cavities of bones **2** the vital part; essence **3** *Brit* short for **vegetable marrow** [OE *mærg*]
> ˈ**marrowy** *adj*

marrowbone (ˈmærəʊˌbəʊn) *n* **a** a bone containing edible marrow **b** (*as modifier*): *marrowbone jelly*

marrowfat (ˈmærəʊˌfæt) *or* **marrow pea** *n* **1** any of several varieties of pea plant that have large seeds **2** the seed of such a plant

marry[1] (ˈmærɪ) *vb* **marries, marrying, married** **1** to take (someone as one's husband or wife) in marriage **2** (*tr*) to join or give in marriage **3** to unite closely or intimately **4** (*tr; sometimes foll by up*) to fit together or align (two things); join **5** (*tr*) *naut* to match up (the strands of ropes) before splicing [C13 from OF *marier*, from L *marītāre*, from *marītus* married (man), ?from *mās* male]

marry[2] (ˈmærɪ) *interj arch* an exclamation of surprise, anger, etc [C14 euphemistic for the Virgin *Mary*]

Marryat (ˈmærɪət) *n* **Frederick,** known as *Captain Marryat.* 1792–1848, English novelist and naval officer; author of novels of sea life, such as *Mr Midshipman Easy* (1836), and children's stories, such as *The Children of the New Forest* (1847)

marry off *vb* (*tr, adv*) to find a husband or wife for (a person, esp one's son or daughter)

Mars[1] (mɑːz) *n* the Roman god of war

Mars[2] (mɑːz) *n* the fourth planet from the sun

▷ http://mars.jpl.nasa.gov

▷ www.solarviews.com/eng/mars.htm

Marsala (mɑːˈsɑːlə) *n* **1** a port in W Sicily: landing place of Garibaldi at the start of his Sicilian campaign (1860). Pop: 80 760 (1990) **2** (*sometimes not capital*) a dark sweet dessert wine made in Sicily

Marsalis (mɑːˈsɑːlɪs) *n* **Wynton** born 1962, US jazz and classical trumpeter

Marseillaise (ˌmɑːseɪˈjeɪz, -səˈleɪz) *n* **the** the French national anthem [C18 from F (*chanson*) *marseillaise* song of Marseilles (first sung in Paris by the battalion of Marseilles)]

marseille (mɑːˈseɪl) *or* **marseilles** (mɑːˈseɪlz) *n* a strong cotton fabric with a raised pattern, used for bedspreads, etc [C18 from *Marseille quilting*, made in Marseilles]

Marseille (*French* marsɛj) *n* a port in SE France, on the Gulf of Lions: second largest city in the country and a major port; founded in about 600 BC by Greeks from Phocaea; oil refining. Pop: 797 486 (1999). Ancient name: **Massilia** English name: **Marseilles** (mɑːˈseɪ, -ˈseɪlz)

marsh (mɑːʃ) *n* low poorly drained land that is sometimes flooded and often lies at the edge of lakes, etc Cf. **swamp** (sense 1) [OE *merisc*]

Marsh (mɑːʃ) *n* **1** Dame **(Edith) Ngaio** (ˈnaɪəʊ) 1899–1981, New Zealand crime writer, living in Britain (from 1928). Her many detective novels include *Final Curtain* (1947) and *Last Ditch* (1977) **2** **Rodney (William)** born 1947, Australian cricketer. He finished his career with a world record of 355 Test match dismissals

marshal (ˈmɑːʃəl) *n* **1** (in some armies and air forces) an officer of the highest rank **2** (in England) an officer who accompanies a judge on circuit and performs secretarial duties **3** (in the US) **3a** a Federal court officer assigned to a judicial district whose functions are similar to those of a sheriff **3b** (in some states) the chief police or fire officer **4** an officer who organizes or conducts ceremonies, parades, etc **5** Also called: **knight marshal** (formerly in England) an officer of the royal family or court, esp one in charge of protocol ▷ *vb* **marshals, marshalling, marshalled** *or US* **marshals, marshaling, marshaled** (*tr*) **6** to arrange in order: *to marshal the facts* **7** to assemble and organize (troops, vehicles, etc) prior to onward movement **8** to guide or lead, esp in a ceremonious way **9** to combine (coats of arms) on one shield [c13 from OF *mareschal*; rel. to OHG *marahscalc*, from *marah* horse + *scalc* servant] > '**marshalcy** *or* '**marshalship** *n*

Marshall ('mɑːʃəl) *n* **1** 1842–1924, English economist, author of *Principles of Economics* (1890) **2 George Catlett** 1880–1959, US general and statesman. He was chief of staff of the US army (1939–45) and, as secretary of state (1947–49), he proposed the Marshall Plan (1947), later called the European Recovery Programme: Nobel peace prize 1953 **3 John** 1755–1835, US jurist and statesman. As chief justice of the Supreme Court (1801–35), he established the principles of US constitutional law **4** Sir **John Ross** 1912–88, New Zealand politician; prime minister (1972)

marshalling yard *n railways* a place or depot where railway wagons are shunted and made up into trains

Marshall Islands ('mɑːʃəl) *pl n* a republic, consisting of a group of 34 coral islands in the W central Pacific: administratively part of the Trust Territory of the Pacific Islands (1947–87); status of free association with the US from 1986; consists of two parallel chains, Ralik and Ratak. Official languages: Marshallese and English. Religion: Roman Catholic majority. Currency: US dollar. Capital: Majuro. Pop: 52 300 (2001). Area: (land) 181 sq km (70 sq miles); (lagoon) 11 655 sq km (4500 sq miles)

▹ www.visitmarshallislands.com

Marshal of the Royal Air Force *n* a rank in the Royal Air Force comparable to that of a field marshal in the army

marsh fever *n* another name for **malaria**

marsh gas *n* a hydrocarbon gas largely composed of methane formed when organic material decays in the absence of air

marshmallow (ˌmɑːʃ'mæləʊ) *n* **1** a spongy sweet containing gum arabic or gelatine, sugar, etc **2** a sweetened paste or confection made from the root of the marsh mallow

marsh mallow *n* a malvaceous plant that grows in salt marshes and has pale pink flowers. The roots yield a mucilage formerly used to make marshmallows

marsh marigold *n* a yellow-flowered plant that grows in swampy places

marshy ('mɑːʃɪ) *adj* **marshier, marshiest** of, involving, or like a marsh > '**marshiness** *n*

Marsilius of Padua (mɑː'sɪlɪəs) *n* Italian name *Marsiglio dei Mainardini*. ?1290–?1343, Italian political philosopher, best known as the author of the *Defensor pacis* (1324), which upheld the power of the temporal ruler over that of the church

Marston ('mɑːstən) *n* **John** ?1576–1634, English dramatist and satirist. His works include the revenge tragedies *Antonio and Mellida* (1602) and *Antonio's Revenge* (1602) and the satirical comedy *The Malcontent* (1604)

Marston Moor *n* a flat low-lying area in NE England, west of York: scene of a battle (1644) in which the Parliamentarians defeated the Royalists

marsupial (mɑː'sjuːpɪəl, -'suː-) *n* **1** any mammal of an order in which the young are born in an immature state and continue development in the marsupium. The order occurs mainly in Australia and South and Central America and includes the opossums and kangaroos ▹ *adj* **2** of, relating to, or belonging to marsupials **3** of or relating to a marsupium [c17 see MARSUPIUM]

marsupium (mɑː'sjuːpɪəm, -'suː-) *n, pl* **marsupia** (-pɪə) an external pouch in most female marsupials within which the newly born offspring complete their development [c17 NL, from L: purse, from Gk, dim. of *marsipos*]

mart (mɑːt) *n* a market or trading centre [c15 from MDu.: MARKET]

Martaban (ˌmɑːtɑː'bɑːn) *n* **Gulf of** an inlet of the Bay of Bengal in Myanmar

martagon *or* **martagon lily** ('mɑːtəgən) *n* a Eurasian lily plant cultivated for its mottled purplish-red flowers [c15 from F, from Turkish *martagān* a type of turban]

Martel (mɑː'tɛl) *n* See **Charles Martel**

Martello tower (mɑː'tɛləʊ) *n* a small circular tower for coastal defence [c18 after Cape *Mortella* in Corsica, where the British navy captured a tower of this type in 1794]

marten ('mɑːtɪn) *n, pl* **martens** *or* **marten** **1** any of several agile arboreal mammals of Europe, Asia, and North America, having bushy tails and golden-brown to blackish fur. See also **pine marten** **2** the highly valued fur of these animals ▹ See also **sable** (sense 1) [c15 from MDu. *martren*, from OF (*peau*) *martrine* skin of a marten, from *martre*, prob. of Gmc origin]

Martha ('mɑːθə) *n* **Saint** *New Testament* a sister of Mary and Lazarus, who lived at Bethany and ministered to Jesus (Luke 10:38–42). Feast day: July 29 or June 4

martial ('mɑːʃəl) *adj* of, relating to, or characteristic of war, soldiers, or the military life [c14 from L *martiālis* of MARS[1]] > '**martialism** *n* > '**martialist** *n* > '**martially** *adv*

Martial ('mɑːʃəl) *n* full name *Marcus Valerius Martialis*. ?40–?104 AD, Latin epigrammatist and poet, born in Spain

martial art *n* any of various philosophies of self-defence and techniques of single combat, such as judo or karate, originating in the Far East

▹ www.martialinfo.com

▹ http://martialarts.about.com

martial law *n* rule of law maintained by the military in the absence of civil law

Martian ('mɑːʃən) *adj* **1** of, occurring on, or relating to the planet Mars ▹ *n* **2** an inhabitant of Mars, esp in science fiction

martin ('mɑːtɪn) *n* any of various birds of the swallow family, having a square or slightly forked tail. See also **house martin** [c15 ?from St MARTIN, because the birds were believed to migrate at the time of Martinmas]

Martin ('mɑːtɪn) *n* **1 Archer John Porter** 1910–2002, British biochemist; Nobel prize for chemistry 1952 (with Richard Synge; 1914–94) for developing paper chromatography (1944). He subsequently developed gas chromatography (1953) **2 Chris** born 1977, British rock musician, lead singer of Coldplay. He is married to the US actress Gwyneth Paltrow **3** (*French* martɛ̃) **Frank** 1890–1974, Swiss composer. He used a modified form of the twelve-note technique in some of his works, which include *Petite Symphonie Concertante* (1946) and the oratorio *Golgotha* (1949) **4** Sir **George** (**Henry**) born 1926, British record producer and arranger, noted for his work with the Beatles **5 John** 1789–1854, British painter, noted for his visionary landscapes and large-scale works with biblical subjects **6 Michael** (**John**) born 1945, Scottish Labour politician; speaker of the House of Commons from 2000 **7 Paul** (**Edgar Philippe**) born 1938, Canadian Liberal politician; prime minister of Canada from 2003 **8 Saint** called *Saint Martin of Tours*. ?316–?397 AD, bishop of Tours (?371–?397); a patron saint of France. He furthered monasticism in Gaul. Feast day: Nov 11 or 12 **9 Steve**(**n**) born 1945, US film actor and comedian; his films include *The Jerk* (1979), *Roxanne* (1987), and *Bowfinger* (1999)

Martin du Gard (*French* martɛ̃ dy gar) *n* **Roger** (rɔʒe) 1881–1958, French novelist, noted for his series of novels, *Les Thibault* (1922–40): Nobel prize for literature 1937

martinet (ˌmɑːtɪ'nɛt) *n* a person who maintains strict discipline, esp in a military force [c17 from F, from General *Martinet*, drillmaster under Louis XIV]

martingale ('mɑːtɪnˌgeɪl) *n* **1** a strap from the reins to the girth of a horse, preventing it from carrying its head too high **2** any gambling system in which the stakes are raised, usually doubled, after each loss **3** Also called: **martingale boom** *naut* a chain or cable running from a jib boom to the stern or stem [c16 from F, from ?]

martini (mɑːˈtiːnɪ) *n* **1** (*often cap*) *trademark* an Italian vermouth **2** a cocktail of gin and vermouth [c19 (sense 2): ?from the name of the inventor]

Martini (*Italian* marˈtiːni) *n* **Simone** (siˈmoːne) ?1284–1344, Sienese painter

Martinique (ˌmɑːtɪˈniːk) *n* an island in the E Caribbean, in the Windward Islands of the Lesser Antilles: administratively an overseas region of France. Capital: Fort-de-France. Pop: 388 000 (2001 est). Area: 1090 sq km (420 sq miles) > ˌ**Martiˈnican** *n, adj*

Martinmas (ˈmɑːtɪnməs) *n* the feast of St Martin on Nov. 11; a quarter day in Scotland

Martinů (ˈmɑːtɪˌnuː; *Czech* ˈmartjinuː) *n* **Bohuslav** (ˈbɔhuslaf) 1890–1959, Czech composer

martyr (ˈmɑːtə) *n* **1** a person who suffers death rather than renounce his or her religious beliefs **2** a person who suffers greatly or dies for a cause, belief, etc **3** a person who suffers from poor health, misfortune, etc: *a martyr to rheumatism* ▷ *vb also* ˈ**martyrize** *or* **martyrise** (*tr*) **4** to kill as a martyr **5** to make a martyr of [OE *martir*, from Church L *martyr*, from LGk *martur-*, *martus* witness] > ˈ**martyrdom** *n* > ˌ**martyriˈzation** *or* ˌ**martyriˈsation** *n*

martyrology (ˌmɑːtəˈrɒlədʒɪ) *n, pl* **martyrologies** **1** an official list of martyrs **2** *Christianity* the study of the lives of the martyrs **3** a historical account of the lives of martyrs > ˌ**martyrˈologist** *n*

marvel (ˈmɑːvᵊl) *vb* **marvels, marvelling, marvelled** *or US* **marvels, marveling, marveled** **1** (when *intr*, often foll by *at* or *about*; when *tr*, *takes a clause as object*) to be filled with surprise or wonder ▷ *n* **2** something that causes wonder **3** *arch* astonishment [c13 from OF *merveille*, from LL *mīrābilia*, from L *mīrābilis* from *mīrārī* to wonder at]

Marvell (ˈmɑːvᵊl) *n* **Andrew** 1621–78, English poet and satirist. He is noted for his lyrical poems and verse and prose satires attacking the government after the Restoration

marvellous *or US* **marvelous** (ˈmɑːvᵊləs) *adj* **1** causing great wonder, surprise, etc; extraordinary **2** improbable or incredible **3** excellent; splendid > ˈ**marvellously** *or US* ˈ**marvelously** *adv* > ˈ**marvellousness** *or US* ˈ**marvelousness** *n*

marvel-of-Peru *n, pl* **marvels-of-Peru** another name for **four-o'clock** (the plant) [c16 first found in Peru]

Marx (mɑːks) *n* **Karl** (karl) 1818–83, German founder of modern communism, in England from 1849. With Engels, he wrote *The Communist Manifesto* (1848). He developed his theories of the class struggle and the economics of capitalism in *Das Kapital* (1867; 1885; 1895). He was one of the founders of the International Workingmen's Association (First International) (1864)

Marx Brothers (mɑːks) *n* **the** a US family of film comedians, esp **Arthur Marx,** known as *Harpo* (1888–1964), **Herbert Marx,** known as *Zeppo* (1901–79), **Julius Marx,** known as *Groucho* (1890–1977), and **Leonard Marx** known as *Chico* (1886–1961). Their films include *Animal Crackers* (1930), *Monkey Business* (1931), *Horsefeathers* (1932), *Duck Soup* (1933), and *A Day at the Races* (1937)

Marxism (ˈmɑːksɪzəm) *n* the economic and political theory originated by Karl Marx and Friedrich Engels, holding that human institutions are economically determined, the class struggle is the agency of historical change, and communism will ultimately replace capitalism > ˈ**Marxist** *n, adj*

Marxism-Leninism *n* the modification of Marxism by Lenin stressing that imperialism is the highest form of capitalism > ˈ**Marxist-ˈLeninist** *n, adj*

Mary (ˈmɛərɪ) *n* **1** *New Testament* **1a** **Saint** Also called: the **Virgin Mary** the mother of Jesus, believed to have conceived and borne him while still a virgin; she was married to Joseph (Matthew 1:18–25). Major feast days: Feb 2, Mar 25, May 31, Aug 15, Sept 8 **1b** the sister of Martha and Lazarus (Luke 10:38–42; John 11:1–2) **2** original name *Princess Mary of Teck*. 1867–1953, queen of Great Britain and Northern Ireland (1910–36) by marriage to George V **3** (*pl* **Maries**) *Austral derog sl* an Aboriginal woman or girl

Mary I *n* family name *Tudor*, known as *Bloody Mary*. 1516–58, queen of England (1553–58). The daughter of Henry VIII and Catherine of Aragon, she married Philip II of Spain in 1554. She restored Roman Catholicism to England and about 300 Protestants were burnt at the stake as heretics

Mary II *n* 1662–94, queen of England, Scotland, and Ireland (1689–94), ruling jointly with her husband William III. They were offered the crown by parliament, which objected to the arbitrary rule of her father James II

Maryland (ˈmɛərɪˌlænd, ˈmɛrɪlənd) *n* a state of the eastern US, on the Atlantic: divided into two unequal parts by Chesapeake Bay: mostly low-lying, with the Alleghenies in the northwest. Capital: Annapolis. Pop: 5 296 486 (2000 est). Area: 31 864 sq km (12 303 sq miles). Abbreviations: **Md** or (with zip code) **MD**

Mary Magdalene *n New Testament* **Saint** a woman of **Magdala** (ˈmægdələ) in Galilee whom Jesus cured of evil spirits (Luke 8:2) and who is often identified with the sinful woman of Luke 7:36–50. In Christian tradition she is usually taken to have been a prostitute. See **magdalen** Feast day: July 22

Mary, Queen of Scots *n* family name *Stuart*. 1542–87, queen of Scotland (1542–67); daughter of James V of Scotland and Mary of Guise. She was married to Francis II of France (1558–60), her cousin Lord Darnley (1565–67), and the Earl of Bothwell (1567–71), who was commonly regarded as Darnley's murderer. She was forced to abdicate in favour of her son (later James VI of Scotland) and fled to England. Imprisoned by Elizabeth I until 1587, she was beheaded for plotting against the English crown

marzipan (ˈmɑːzɪˌpæn) *n* **1** a paste made from ground almonds, sugar, and egg whites, used to coat fruit cakes or moulded into sweets **2** (*modifier*) *inf* of or relating to the stratum of middle managers in a financial institution or other business: *marzipan layer job losses* [c19 via G from It. *marzapane*]

-mas *n combining form* indicating a Christian festival: *Christmas; Michaelmas* [from Mass]

Masaccio (*Italian* maˈzattʃo) *n* original name *Tommaso Guidi*. 1401–28, Florentine painter. He was the first to apply to painting the laws of perspective discovered by Brunelleschi. His chief work is the frescoes in the Brancacci chapel in the church of Sta Maria del Carmine, Florence

Masada (məˈsɑːdə) *n* an ancient mountaintop fortress in Israel, 400 m (1300 ft) above the W shore of the Dead Sea: the last Jewish stronghold during a revolt in Judaea (66–73 AD). Besieged by the Romans for a year, almost all of the inhabitants killed themselves rather than surrender. The site is an Israeli national monument

Masai (ˈmɑːsaɪ, mɑːˈsaɪ) *n* **1** (*pl* **Masais** *or* **Masai**) a member of a Nilotic people, formerly noted as warriors, living chiefly in Kenya and Tanzania **2** the language of this people

masala (mɑːˈsɑːlə) *n* a mixture of spices ground into a paste, used in Indian cookery [from Urdu *masalah*, from Ar. *masalih* ingredients]

Masan (ˈmɑːˌsɑːn) *n* a port in SE South Korea, on an inlet of the Korea Strait: first opened to foreign trade in 1899. Pop: 441 358 (1995)

Masaryk (ˈmæsərɪk; *Czech* ˈmasarik) *n* **1** **Jan** (jan) 1886–1948, Czech statesman; foreign minister (1941–48). He died in mysterious circumstances after the Communists took control of the government **2** his father, **Tomáš Garrigue** (ˈtɔmaːʃ ˈgarik) 1850–1937, Czech philosopher and statesman; a founder of

Czechoslovakia (1918) and its first president (1918–35)
Masbate (mæs'bɑːtɪ) *n* **1** an island in the central Philippines, between Negros and SE Luzon: agricultural, with resources of gold, copper, and manganese. Pop: 599 355 (1990). Area: 4045 sq km (1562 sq miles) **2** the capital of this island, a port in the northeast. Pop: 52 944 (1980)
masc. *abbrev for* masculine
Mascagni (*Italian* mas'kaɲɲi) *n* **Pietro** ('pjɛːtro) 1863–1945, Italian composer of operas, including *Cavalleria rusticana* (1890)
mascara (mæ'skɑːrə) *n* a cosmetic for darkening the eyelashes [c20 from Sp.: mask]
Mascarene Islands (ˌmæskə'riːn) *pl n* a group of volcanic islands in the W Indian Ocean, east of Madagascar: consists of the islands of Réunion, Mauritius, and Rodrigues. French name: **Îles Mascareignes**
mascarpone (ˌmæskə'pəʊnɪ) *n* an Italian soft cream cheese [from It. from dialect *mascherpa* ricotta]
mascon ('mæskɒn) *n* any of several lunar regions of high gravity [c20 from MAS(S) + CON(CENTRATION)]
mascot ('mæskət) *n* a person, animal, or thing considered to bring good luck [c19 from F *mascotte*, from Provençal *mascotto* charm, from *masco* witch]
masculine ('mæskjʊlɪn) *adj* **1** possessing qualities or characteristics considered typical of or appropriate to a man; manly **2** unwomanly **3** *grammar* denoting a gender of nouns that includes all kinds of referents as well as some male animate referents **4** *prosody* denoting an ending consisting of a single stressed syllable **5** *prosody* denoting a rhyme between pairs of single final stressed syllables [c14 via F from L *masculīnus*, from *masculus* male, from *mās* a male] > **'masculinely** *adv* > **ˌmascu'linity** *n*
masculinize *or* **masculinise** ('mæskjʊlɪnˌaɪz) *vb* **masculinizes, masculinizing, masculinized** *or* **masculinises, masculinising, masculinised** to make or become masculine, esp to cause (a woman) to show male secondary characteristics as a result of taking steroids > **ˌmasculini'zation** *or* **ˌmasculini'sation** *n*
Masefield ('meɪsˌfiːld) *n* **John** 1878–1967, English poet, novelist, and critic; poet laureate (1930–67)
maser ('meɪzə) *n* a device for amplifying microwaves, working on the same principle as a laser [c20 *m(icrowave) a(mplification by) s(timulated) e(mission of) r(adiation)*]
Maseru (mə'sɛəruː) *n* the capital of Lesotho, in the northwest near the W border with South Africa; established as capital of Basutoland in 1869. Pop: 160 100 (1996 est)
▷ www.gozafrica.com/Lesotho/Lesotho/Maseru
mash (mæʃ) *n* **1** a soft pulpy mass or consistency **2** *agriculture* a feed of bran, meal, or malt mixed with water and fed to horses, cattle, or poultry **3** (esp in brewing) a mixture of mashed malt grains and hot water, from which malt is extracted **4** *Brit inf* mashed potatoes ▷ *vb* (*tr*) **5** to beat or crush into a mash **6** to steep (malt grains) in hot water in order to extract malt **7** *Scot & N English dialect* to brew (tea) [OE *mǣsc-* (in compound words)] > **mashed** *adj* > **'masher** *n*
Masharbrum *or* **Masherbrum** ('mʌʃəˌbrʊm) *n* a mountain in N India, in N Kashmir in the Karakoram Range of the Himalayas. Height: 7822 m (25 660 ft)
Mashhad (mæʃ'hæd) *or* **Meshed** *n* a city in NE Iran: the holy city of Shi'ite Muslims; carpet manufacturing. Pop: 1 887 405 (1996)
mashie *or* **mashy** ('mæʃɪ) *n, pl* **mashies** *golf* (formerly) an iron for lofting shots, usually No 5 [c19 ?from F *massue* club, ult. from L *mateola* mallet]
mashup ('mæʃʌp) *n* a piece of recorded or live music in which a producer or DJ blends together two or more tracks, often of contrasting genres [c20 from MASH blend + UP]
Masinissa *or* **Massinissa** (ˌmæsɪ'nɪsə) *n* ?238–?149 BC, king of Numidia (?210–149), who fought as an ally of Rome against Carthage in the Second Punic War
mask (mɑːsk) *n* **1** any covering for the whole or a part of the face worn for amusement, protection, disguise, etc **2** a fact, action, etc, that conceals something **3** another name for **masquerade** **4** a likeness of a face or head, either sculpted or moulded, such as a death mask **5** an image of a face worn by an actor, esp in classical drama, in order to symbolize a character **6** a variant spelling of **masque** **7** *surgery* a sterile gauze covering for the nose and mouth worn to minimize the spread of germs **8** *sport* a protective covering for the face worn for fencing, ice hockey, etc **9** a carving in the form of a face or head, used as an ornament **10** a device placed over the nose and mouth to facilitate or prevent inhalation of a gas **11** *photog* a shield of paper, paint, etc, placed over an area of unexposed photographic surface to stop light falling on it **12** the face or head of an animal, such as a fox **13** *rare* a person wearing a mask ▷ *vb* **14** to cover with or put on a mask **15** (*tr*) to conceal; disguise: *to mask an odour* **16** (*tr*) to cover; protect **17** (*tr*) *photog* to shield a particular area of (an unexposed photographic surface) to prevent or reduce the action of light there [c16 from It. *maschera*, ult. from Ar. *maskharah* clown, from *sakhira* mockery] > **masked** *adj* > **'masker**
masked ball *n* a ball at which masks are worn
masking tape *n* an adhesive tape used to protect surfaces surrounding an area to be painted
maskinonge ('mæskəˌnɒndʒ) *n* another name for **muskellunge**
masochism ('mæsəˌkɪzəm) *n* **1** *psychiatry* an abnormal condition in which pleasure, esp sexual pleasure, is derived from pain or from humiliation, domination, etc, by another person **2** a tendency to take pleasure from one's own suffering ▷ Cf **sadism** [c19 after Leopold von Sacher *Masoch* (1836–95), Austrian novelist, who described it] > **'masochist** *n, adj* > **ˌmaso'chistic** *adj* > **ˌmaso'chistically** *adv*
mason ('meɪsᵊn) *n* **1** a person skilled in building with stone **2** a person who dresses stone ▷ *vb* **3** (*tr*) to construct or strengthen with masonry [c13 from OF *masson*, of Frankish origin; ? rel. to OE *macian* to make]
Mason ('meɪsᵊn) *n* short for **Freemason**
Mason-Dixon Line (-'dɪksən) *n* in the US, the state boundary between Maryland and Pennsylvania: surveyed between 1763 and 1767 by Charles Mason and Jeremiah Dixon; popularly regarded as the dividing line between North and South
masonic (mə'sɒnɪk) *adj* **1** (*often cap*) of or relating to Freemasons or Freemasonry **2** of or relating to masons or masonry > **ma'sonically** *adv*
Masonite ('meɪsənaɪt) *n Austral trademark* a kind of dark brown hardboard
masonry ('meɪsənrɪ) *n, pl* **masonries** **1** the craft of a mason **2** work that is built by a mason; stonework or brickwork **3** (*often cap*) short for **Freemasonry**
Masqat ('mʌskət, -kæt) *n* a transliteration of the Arabic name for **Muscat**
masque *or* **mask** (mɑːsk) *n* **1** a dramatic entertainment of the 16th to 17th centuries, consisting of pantomime, dancing, dialogue, and song **2** the words and music for this **3** short for **masquerade** [c16 var. of MASK]
masquerade (ˌmæskə'reɪd) *n* **1** a party or other gathering at which the guests wear masks and costumes **2** the disguise worn at such a function **3** a pretence or disguise ▷ *vb* **masquerades, masquerading, masqueraded** (*intr*) **4** to participate in a masquerade; disguise oneself **5** to dissemble [c16 from Sp. *mascarada*, from *mascara* MASK] > **ˌmasquer'ader** *n*
mass (mæs) *n* **1** a large coherent body of matter without a definite shape **2** a collection of the component parts of something **3** a large amount or number, as of people

Mm

4 the main part or majority **5 in the mass** in the main; collectively 6 the size of a body; bulk 7 *physics* a physical quantity expressing the amount of matter in a body. It is a measure of a body's resistance to changes in velocity (**inertial mass**) and also of the force experienced in a gravitational field (**gravitational mass**) 8 (in painting, drawing, etc) an area of unified colour, shade, or intensity, usually denoting a solid form or plane ▷ (*modifier*) 9 done or occurring on a large scale: *mass hysteria* 10 consisting of a mass or large number, esp of people: *a mass meeting* ▷ *vb* 11 to form (people or things) or (of people or things) to join together into a mass ▷ See also **masses** [C14 from OF *masse*, from L *massa* that which forms a lump, from Gk *maza* barley cake]

Mass (mæs, mɑːs) *n* 1 (in the Roman Catholic Church and certain Protestant Churches) the celebration of the Eucharist. See also **High Mass, Low Mass** 2 a musical setting of those parts of the Eucharistic service sung by choir or congregation [OE *mæsse*, from Church L *missa*, ult. from L *mittere* to send away; ?from the concluding dismissal in the Roman Mass, *Ite, missa est* Go, it is the dismissal]

Mass. *abbrev for* Massachusetts

Massa (*Italian* 'massa) *n* a town in W Italy, in NW Tuscany. Pop: 67 780 (1990)

Massachusetts (ˌmæsəˈtʃuːsɪts) *n* a state of the northeastern US, on the Atlantic: a centre of resistance to English colonial policy during the War of American Independence; consists of a coastal plain rising to mountains in the west. Capital: Boston. Pop: 6 349 097 (2000 est). Area: 20 269 sq km (7826 sq miles). Abbreviations: **Mass** or (with zip code) **MA**

Massachusetts Bay *n* an inlet of the Atlantic on the E coast of Massachusetts

massacre ('mæsəkə) *n* 1 the wanton or savage killing of large numbers of people, as in battle 2 *inf* an overwhelming defeat, as in a game ▷ *vb* **massacres, massacring, massacred** (*tr*) 3 to kill indiscriminately or in large numbers 4 *inf* to defeat overwhelmingly [C16 from OF]

mass affluent *pl n* the large number of individuals with liquid assets of around £250,000

massage ('mæsɑːʒ, -sɑːdʒ) *n* 1 the act of kneading, rubbing, etc, parts of the body to promote circulation, suppleness, or relaxation ▷ *vb* **massages, massaging, massaged** (*tr*) 2 to give a massage to 3 to treat (stiffness, etc) by a massage 4 to manipulate (statistics, etc) to produce a desired result; doctor **5 massage (someone's) ego** to boost (someone's) sense of self-esteem by flattery [C19 from F, from *masser* to rub]

massasauga (ˌmæsəˈsɔːgə) *n* a North American venomous snake that has a horny rattle at the end of the tail [C19 after the *Missisauga* River, Ontario, Canada, where it was first found]

Massasoit ('mæsəˌsɔɪt) *n* died 1661, Wampanoag Indian chief, who negotiated peace with the Pilgrim Fathers (1621)

Massawa *or* **Massaua** (məˈsɑːwə) *n* a port in E central Eritrea, on the Red Sea: capital of Eritrea during Italian occupation, from 1885 until 1900. Pop: 40 000 (1992)

mass defect *n physics* the amount by which the mass of a particular nucleus is less than the total mass of its constituent particles

massé *or* **massé shot** ('mæsɪ) *n billiards* a stroke made by hitting the cue ball off centre with the cue held nearly vertically, esp so as to make the ball move in a curve [C19 from F, from *masser*, from *masse* sledgehammer, from OF *mace* MACE[1]]

Masséna (*French* masena) *n* **André** (ɑ̃dre), Prince d'Essling. 1758–1817, French marshal under Napoleon I: victories at Saorgio (1794), Loano (1795), Rivoli (1797), Zürich (1799), and Caldiero (1805): defeated by Wellington in the Peninsular War (1810–11)

Massenet ('mæsəˌneɪ; *French* masnɛ) *n* **Jules Émile Frédéric** (ʒyl emil frederik) 1842–1912, French composer of operas, including *Manon* (1884), *Werther* (1892), and *Thaïs* (1894)

masses ('mæsɪz) *pl n* 1 (preceded by *the*) the body of common people 2 (often foll by *of*) *inf, chiefly Brit* great numbers or quantities: *masses of food*

masseur (mæˈsɜː) *or* (*fem*) **masseuse** (mæˈsɜːz) *n* a person who gives massages, esp as a profession [C19 from F *masser* to MASSAGE]

Massey ('mæsɪ) *n* 1 1896–1983, Canadian actor and film star. His films include *The Scarlet Pimpernel* (1934) and *East of Eden* (1955). He also appeared in the television series *Dr Kildare* (1961–65) 2 **Vincent** 1887–1967, Canadian statesman: first Canadian governor general of Canada (1952–59) 3 **William Ferguson** 1856–1925, New Zealand statesman, born in Ireland: prime minister of New Zealand (1912–25)

massif ('mæsiːf) *n* a mass of rock or a series of connected masses forming a mountain range [C19 from F, noun use of *massif* MASSIVE]

Massif Central (*French* masif sɑ̃tral) *n* a mountainous plateau region of S central France, occupying about one sixth of the country: contains several extinct volcanic cones, notably Puy de Dôme, 1465 m (4806 ft). Highest point: Puy de Sancy, 1886 m (6188 ft). Area: about 85 000 sq km (33 000 sq miles)

Massine (mɑːˈsiːn) *n* **Léonide** (leɔnid) 1896–1979, US ballet dancer and choreographer, born in Russia

Massinger ('mæsɪndʒə) *n* **Philip** 1583–?1640, English dramatist, noted esp for his comedy *A New Way to Pay Old Debts* (1633)

Massinissa (ˌmæsɪˈnɪsə) *n* a variant spelling of **Masinissa**

massive ('mæsɪv) *adj* 1 (of objects) large in mass; bulky, heavy, and usually solid 2 impressive or imposing 3 relatively intensive or large; considerable: *a massive dose* 4 *geol* **4a** (of igneous rocks) having no stratification, cleavage, etc; homogeneous **4b** (of sedimentary rocks) arranged in thick poorly defined strata 5 *mineralogy* without obvious crystalline structure [C15 from F *massif*, from *masse* MASS] > **'massively** *adv* > **'massiveness** *n*

mass-market *adj* of, for, or appealing to a large number of people; popular: *mass-market paperbacks*

mass media *pl n* the means of communication that reach large numbers of people, such as television, newspapers, magazines, and radio

mass noun *n* a noun that refers to an extended substance rather than to each of a set of objects, eg, *water* as opposed to *lake*. In English when used indefinitely they are characteristically preceded by *some* rather than *a* or *an*; they do not have normal plural forms ▷ Cf **count noun**

mass number *n* the total number of neutrons and protons in the nucleus of a particular atom

mass observation *n* (*sometimes cap*) *chiefly Brit* the study of the social habits of people through observation, interviews, etc

mass-produce *vb* **mass-produces, mass-producing, mass-produced** (*tr*) to manufacture (goods) to a standardized pattern on a large scale by means of extensive mechanization and division of labour > ˌ**mass-proˈduced** *adj* > ˌ**mass-proˈducer** *n* > **mass production** *n*

mass spectrometer *or* **spectroscope** *n* an instrument in which ions, produced from a sample, are separated by electric or magnetic fields according to their ratios of charge to mass. A record is produced (**mass spectrum**) of the types of ion present and their amounts

mast[1] (mɑːst) *n* 1 *naut* any vertical spar for supporting sails, rigging, flags, etc, above the deck of a vessel 2 any sturdy upright pole used as a support **3 before the mast**

naut as an apprentice seaman ▷ *vb* **4** *(tr) naut* to equip with a mast or masts [OE *mæst;* rel. to MDu. *mast* & L *mālus* pole]

mast² (mɑːst) *n* the fruit of forest trees, such as beech, oak, etc, used as food for pigs [OE *mæst;* rel. to OHG *mast* food]

mastaba *or* **mastabah** (ˈmæstəbə) *n* a mudbrick superstructure above tombs in ancient Egypt [from Ar.: bench]

mast cell *n* any of a number of cells in connective tissue that release heparin, histamine, and serotonin during inflammation and allergic reactions

mastectomy (mæˈstɛktəmɪ) *n, pl* **mastectomies** the surgical removal of a breast

master (ˈmɑːstə) *n* **1** the man in authority, such as the head of a household, the employer of servants, or the owner of slaves or animals **2a** a person with exceptional skill at a certain thing **2b** *(as modifier): a master thief* **3** *(often cap)* a great artist, esp an anonymous but influential one **4a** a person who has complete control of a situation, etc **4b** an abstract thing regarded as having power or influence: *they regarded fate as the master of their lives* **5a** a workman or craftsman fully qualified to practise his trade and to train others **5b** *(as modifier): master carpenter* **6a** an original copy, stencil, tape, etc, from which duplicates are made **6b** *(as modifier): master copy* **7** a player of a game, esp chess or bridge, who has won a specified number of tournament games **8** the principal of some colleges **9** a highly regarded teacher or leader **10** a graduate holding a master's degree **11** the chief executive officer aboard a merchant ship **12** a person presiding over a function, organization, or institution **13** *chiefly Brit* a male teacher **14** an officer of the Supreme Court of Judicature subordinate to a judge **15** the superior person or side in a contest **16** *(often cap)* the heir apparent of a Scottish viscount or baron ▷ *(modifier)* **17** overall or controlling: *master plan* **18** designating a device or mechanism that controls others: *master switch* **19** main; principal: *master bedroom* ▷ *vb (tr)* **20** to become thoroughly proficient in **21** to overcome; defeat **22** to rule or control as master [OE *magister* teacher, from L]

Master (ˈmɑːstə) *n* **1** a title of address for a boy **2** a term of address, esp as used by disciples addressing or referring to a religious teacher **3** an archaic equivalent of **Mr**

master aircrew *n* a warrant rank in the Royal Air Force, equal to but before a warrant officer

master-at-arms *n, pl* **masters-at-arms** the senior rating in a naval unit responsible for discipline and police duties

master builder *n* **1** a person skilled in the design and construction of buildings, esp before the foundation of the profession of architecture **2** a self-employed builder who employs labour

masterclass (ˈmɑːstəˌklɑːs) *n* a session of tuition by an expert, esp a musician, for exceptional students, usually given in public or on television

masterful (ˈmɑːstəfʊl) *adj* **1** having or showing mastery **2** fond of playing the master; imperious > ˈ**masterfully** *adv* > ˈ**masterfulness** *n*

> **USAGE** In current usage there is a lot of overlap between the meanings of *masterful* and *masterly*. According to some, the first should only be used where there is a connotation of power and domination, the second where the connotations are of great skill. Nevertheless, as the Bank of English shows, the majority of uses of *masterful* these days relate to the second meaning, as in *musically, it was a masterful display of the folk singer's art*. Anyone wishing to observe the distinction would use only *masterly* in the context just given, and *masterful* in contexts such as: *...his need to be masterful with women was extreme; Alec was so masterful that he surprised himself*

master key *n* a key that opens all the locks of a set. Also called: **passkey**

masterly (ˈmɑːstəlɪ) *adj* of the skill befitting a master > ˈ**masterliness** *n*

master mason *n* **1** see **master** (sense 5a) **2** a Freemason who has reached the rank of third degree

mastermind (ˈmɑːstəˌmaɪnd) *vb* **1** *(tr)* to plan and direct (a complex undertaking) ▷ *n* **2** a person of great intelligence or executive talent, esp one who directs an undertaking

Master of Arts *n* a degree, usually postgraduate and in a nonscientific subject, or the holder of this degree. Abbrev: **MA**

master of ceremonies *n* a person who presides over a public ceremony, formal dinner, or entertainment, introducing the events, performers, etc

Master of Science *n* a postgraduate degree, usually in science, or the holder of this degree. Abbrev: **MSc**

Master of the Rolls *n* (in England) a judge of the court of appeal: the senior civil judge in the country and the Keeper of the Records at the Public Record Office

masterpiece (ˈmɑːstəˌpiːs) *or (less commonly)* **masterwork** (ˈmɑːstəˌwɜːk) *n* **1** an outstanding work or performance **2** the most outstanding piece of work of a creative artist, craftsman, etc [C17 cf. Du. *meesterstuk*, G *Meisterstück*, a sample of work submitted to a guild by a craftsman in order to qualify for the rank of master]

masterplan (ˈmɑːstəˌplæn) *n* a comprehensive, often long-term, strategy

masterstroke (ˈmɑːstəˌstrəʊk) *n* an outstanding piece of strategy, skill, talent, etc

mastery (ˈmɑːstərɪ) *n, pl* **masteries** **1** full command or understanding of a subject **2** outstanding skill; expertise **3** the power of command; control **4** victory or superiority

masthead (ˈmɑːstˌhɛd) *n* **1** *naut* the head of a mast **2** the name of a newspaper or periodical, its proprietors, staff, etc, printed at the top of the front page ▷ *vb (tr)* **3** to send (a sailor) to the masthead as a punishment **4** to raise (a sail) to the masthead

mastic (ˈmæstɪk) *n* **1** an aromatic resin obtained from the mastic tree and used as an astringent and to make varnishes and lacquers **2** **mastic tree** a small Mediterranean evergreen tree that yields the resin mastic **3** any of several putty-like substances used as a filler, adhesive, or seal in wood, plaster, or masonry **4** a liquor flavoured with mastic gum [C14 via OF from LL *mastichum*, from L from Gk *mastikhē* resin used as chewing gum]

masticate (ˈmæstɪˌkeɪt) *vb* **masticates, masticating, masticated** **1** to chew (food) **2** to reduce (materials such as rubber) to a pulp by crushing, grinding, or kneading [C17 from LL *masticāre*, from Gk *mastikhan* to grind the teeth] > ˌ**mastiˈcation** *n* > ˈ**mastiˌcator** *n*

masticatory (ˈmæstɪkətərɪ, -trɪ) *adj* **1** of, relating to, or adapted to chewing ▷ *n, pl* **masticatories** **2** *obs* a medicinal substance chewed to increase the secretion of saliva

mastiff (ˈmæstɪf) *n* a breed of large powerful short-haired dog, usually fawn or brindled [C14 from OF, ult. from L *mansuētus* tame]

mastitis (mæˈstaɪtɪs) *n* inflammation of a breast or an udder

masto- *or before a vowel* **mast-** *combining form* indicating the breast, mammary glands, or something resembling a breast or nipple: *mastodon; mastoid* [from Gk *mastos* breast]

mastodon (ˈmæstəˌdɒn) *n* an extinct elephant-like mammal common in Pliocene times [C19 from NL, lit.:

breast-tooth, referring to the nipple-shaped projections on the teeth]

mastoid ('mæstɔɪd) *adj* **1** shaped like a nipple or breast **2** designating or relating to a nipple-like process of the temporal bone behind the ear ▷ *n* **3** the mastoid process **4** *inf* mastoiditis

mastoiditis (ˌmæstɔɪ'daɪtɪs) *n* inflammation of the mastoid process

masturbate ('mæstəˌbeɪt) *vb* **masturbates, masturbating, masturbated** to stimulate the genital organs of (oneself or another) to achieve sexual pleasure [C19 from L *masturbārī*, from ?; formerly thought to be derived from *manus* hand + *stuprāre* to defile] > **ˌmastur'bation** *n* > **'masturˌbator** *n* > **masturbatory** ('mæstəˌbeɪtərɪ) *adj*

Masuria (mə'sjʊərɪə) *n* a region of NE Poland: until 1945 part of East Prussia: includes the **Masurian Lakes,** scene of Russian defeats by the Germans (1914, 1915) during World War I > **Ma'surian** *adj, n*

mat[1] (mæt) *n* **1** a thick flat piece of fabric used as a floor covering, a place to wipe one's shoes, etc **2** a smaller pad of material used to protect a surface from the heat, scratches, etc, of an object placed upon it **3** a large piece of thick padded material put on the floor as a surface for wrestling, judo, etc **4** any surface or mass that is densely interwoven or tangled: *a mat of weeds* ▷ *vb* **mats, matting, matted 5** to tangle or weave or become tangled or woven into a dense mass **6** (*tr*) to cover with a mat or mats [OE *matte*]

mat[2] (mæt) *n* **1** a border of cardboard, cloth, etc, placed around a picture as a frame or between picture and frame ▷ *adj* **2** having a dull, lustreless, or roughened surface ▷ *vb* **mats, matting, matted** (*tr*) **3** to furnish (a picture) with a mat **4** to give (a surface) a mat finish ▷ Also (for senses 2 & 4): **matt** [C17 from F, lit.: dead]

mat[3] (mæt) *n printing, inf* short for **matrix** (senses 4 and 5)

mat. *abbrev for* matinée

Matabeleland (ˌmætə'biːlɪˌlænd, -'bɛlɪ-) *n* a region of W Zimbabwe, between the Rivers Limpopo and Zambezi, comprises three provinces, Matabeleland North, Matabeleland South, and Bulawayo: rich gold deposits. Chief town: Bulawayo. Area: 181 605 sq km (70 118 sq miles)

Matadi (mə'tɑːdɪ) *n* the chief port of the Democratic Republic of Congo (formerly Zaïre), in the west at the mouth of the River Congo. Pop: 172 730 (1994 est)

matador ('mætədɔː) *n* **1** the principal bullfighter who kills the bull **2** (in some card games) one of the highest cards **3** a game played with dominoes in which the dots on adjacent halves must total seven [C17 from Sp., from *matar* to kill]

matagouri (ˌmætə'guːrɪ) *n* a New Zealand thorny bush which forms thickets in open country. Also called: **wild Irishman** [from Maori *tumatakuru*]

Mata Hari ('mɑːtə 'hɑːrɪ) *n* real name *Gertrud Margarete Zelle*. 1876–1917, Dutch dancer in France, who was executed as a German spy in World War I

matai ('mɑːtaɪ) *n* a New Zealand tree, the black pine, the wood of which is used as building timber. Also called: **black pine** [from Maori]

Matamoros (ˌmætə'mɔːrəs; *Spanish* mata'morɔs) *n* a port in NE Mexico, on the Río Grande: scene of bitter fighting during the US-Mexican War; centre of a cotton-growing area. Pop: 370 000 (2000 est)

Matanzas (mə'tænzəs; *Spanish* ma'tanθas) *n* a port in W central Cuba: founded in 1693 and developed into the second city of Cuba in the mid-19th century; exports chiefly sugar. Pop: 123 843 (1994 est)

Matapan ('mætəˌpæn, ˌmætə'pæn) *n* **Cape** a cape in S Greece, at the S central tip of the Peloponnese: the southern point of the mainland of Greece. Modern Greek name: **Taínaron**

match[1] (mætʃ) *n* **1** a formal game or sports event in which people, teams, etc, compete **2** a person or thing able to provide competition for another: *she's met her match* **3** a person or thing that resembles, harmonizes with, or is equivalent to another in a specified respect **4** a person or thing that is an exact copy or equal of another **5a** a partnership between a man and a woman, as in marriage **5b** an arrangement for such a partnership **6** a person regarded as a possible partner, as in marriage ▷ *vb* (*mainly tr*) **7** to fit (parts) together **8** (*also intr; sometimes foll by up*) to resemble, harmonize with, or equal (one another or something else) **9** (sometimes foll by *with* or *against*) to compare in order to determine which is the superior **10** (often foll by *to* or *with*) to adapt so as to correspond with: *to match hope with reality* **11** (often foll by *with* or *against*) to arrange a competition between **12** to find a match for **13** *electronics* to connect (two circuits) so that their impedances are equal, to produce a maximum transfer of energy [OE *gemæcca* spouse] > **'matchable** *adj* > **'matching** *adj*

match[2] (mætʃ) *n* **1** a thin strip of wood or cardboard tipped with a chemical that ignites by friction on a rough surface or a surface coated with a suitable chemical (see **safety match**) **2** a length of cord or wick impregnated with a chemical so that it burns slowly. It is used to fire cannons, explosives, etc [C14 from OF *meiche*, ?from L *myxa* wick, from Gk *muxa* lamp nozzle]

matchboard ('mætʃˌbɔːd) *n* a long flimsy board tongued and grooved for lining work

matchbox ('mætʃˌbɒks) *n* a small box for holding matches

match-fit *adj sport* in good physical condition for competing in a match

matchless ('mætʃlɪs) *adj* unequalled; incomparable; peerless > **'matchlessly** *adv*

matchlock ('mætʃˌlɒk) *n* **1** an obsolete type of gunlock igniting the powder by means of a slow match **2** a gun having such a lock

matchmaker ('mætʃˌmeɪkə) *n* **1** a person who brings together suitable partners for marriage **2** a person who arranges competitive matches > **'matchˌmaking** *n, adj*

match play *n golf* scoring according to the number of holes won and lost ▷ Cf **Stableford, stroke play** > **match player** *n*

match point *n* **1** *tennis, squash, etc* the final point needed to win a match **2** *bridge* the unit used for scoring in tournaments

matchstick ('mætʃˌstɪk) *n* **1** the wooden part of a match ▷ *adj* **2** made with or as if with matchsticks **3** (esp of drawn figures) thin and straight: *matchstick men* **4** made (or as if made) with matchsticks

matchwood ('mætʃˌwʊd) *n* **1** wood suitable for making matches **2** splinters or fragments

mate[1] (meɪt) *n* **1** the sexual partner of an animal **2** a marriage partner **3a** *inf, chiefly Brit, Austral & NZ* a friend, usually of the same sex: often used to any male in direct address **3b** (*in combination*) an associate, colleague, fellow sharer, etc: *a classmate* **4** one of a pair of matching items **5** *naut* **5a** short for **first mate 5b** any officer below the master on a commercial ship **6** (in some trades) an assistant: *a plumber's mate* ▷ *vb* **mates, mating, mated 7** to pair (a male and female animal) or (of animals) to pair for reproduction **8** to marry or join in marriage **9** (*tr*) to join as a pair [C14 from MLow G; rel. to OE *gemetta* table-guest, from *mete* MEAT]

mate[2] (meɪt) *n, vb* **mates, mating, mated** *chess* See **checkmate**

maté *or* **mate** ('mɑːteɪ) *n* **1** an evergreen tree cultivated in South America for its leaves, which contain caffeine **2** a stimulating milky beverage made from the dried leaves of this tree ▷ Also called: **Paraguay tea, yerba, yerba maté** [C18 from American Sp. (orig. referring to the vessel in which the drink was brewed), from Quechua *máti* gourd]

matelot, matlo, *or* **matlow** (ˈmætləʊ) *n sl, chiefly Brit* a sailor [c20 from F]

mater (ˈmeɪtə) *n Brit sl* a word for **mother**[1]: often used facetiously [c16 from L]

material (məˈtɪərɪəl) *n* **1** the substance of which a thing is made or composed; component or constituent matter **2** facts, notes, etc, that a finished work may be based on or derived from **3** cloth or fabric **4** a person who has qualities suitable for a given occupation, training, etc: *that boy is university material* ▷ *adj* **5** of, relating to, or composed of physical substance: *material possessions* **6** of, relating to, or affecting economic or physical wellbeing: *material ease* **7** of or concerned with physical rather than spiritual interests **8** of great import or consequence: *material benefit* **9** (often foll by *to*) relevant **10** *philosophy* of or relating to matter as opposed to form ▷ See also **materials** [c14 via F from LL *māteriālis*, from L *māteria* MATTER] > **maˌteriˈality** *n*

material implication *n logic* a form of implication in which the proposition "if A then B" is true except when A is true and B is false

materialism (məˈtɪərɪəˌlɪzəm) *n* **1** interest in and desire for money, possessions, etc, rather than spiritual or ethical values **2** *philosophy* the doctrine that matter is the only reality and that the mind, the emotions, etc, are merely functions of it ▷ Cf **idealism, dualism** **3** *ethics* the rejection of any religious or supernatural account of things > **maˈterialist** *n* > **maˌterialˈistic** *adj* > **maˌterialˈistically** *adv*

materialize *or* **materialise** (məˈtɪərɪəˌlaɪz) *vb* **materializes, materializing, materialized** *or* **materialises, materialising, materialised** **1** (*intr*) to become fact; actually happen **2** to invest or become invested with a physical shape or form **3** to cause (a spirit, as of a dead person) to appear in material form or (of a spirit) to appear in such form **4** (*intr*) to take shape; become tangible > **maˌterialiˈzation** *or* **maˌterialiˈsation** *n* > **maˈterialˌizer** *or* **maˈterialˌiser** *n*

materially (məˈtɪərɪəlɪ) *adv* **1** to a significant extent; considerably **2** with respect to material objects **3** *philosophy* with respect to substance as distinct from form

materials (məˈtɪərɪəlz) *pl n* the equipment necessary for a particular activity

materia medica (məˈtɪərɪə ˈmɛdɪkə) *n* **1** the branch of medical science concerned with the study of drugs used in the treatment of disease **2** the drugs used in the treatment of disease [c17 from Med. L: medical matter]

materiel *or* **matériel** (məˌtɪərɪˈɛl) *n* the materials and equipment of an organization, esp of a military force [c19 from F: MATERIAL]

maternal (məˈtɜːnᵊl) *adj* **1** of, relating to, or characteristic of a mother **2** related through the mother's side of the family: *his maternal uncle* [c15 from Med. L *māternālis*, from L *māternus*, from *māter* mother] > **maˈternalism** *n* > **maˌternalˈistic** *adj* > **maˈternally** *adv*

maternity (məˈtɜːnɪtɪ) *n* **1** motherhood **2** the characteristics associated with motherhood; motherliness **3** (*modifier*) relating to pregnant women or women at the time of childbirth: *a maternity ward*

mateship (ˈmeɪtʃɪp) *n Austral* friendly egalitarian comradeship

mate's rates *pl n NZ inf* discounted or preferential rates of payment offered to a friend or colleague: *he got the job done cheaply by a plumber friend at mate's rates*

matey *or* **maty** (ˈmeɪtɪ) *Brit inf* ▷ *adj* **1** friendly or intimate ▷ *n* **2** friend or fellow: usually used in direct address > **ˈmateyness** *or* **ˈmatiness** *n*

math (mæθ) *n US & Canad inf* short for **mathematics** Brit equivalent: **maths**

mathematical (ˌmæθəˈmætɪkᵊl) *or* **mathematic** *adj* **1** of, used in, or relating to mathematics **2** characterized by or using the precision of mathematics **3** using, determined by, or in accordance with the principles of mathematics > **ˌmatheˈmatically** *adv*

mathematical logic *n* symbolic logic, esp when concerned with the foundations of mathematics

mathematician (ˌmæθəməˈtɪʃən) *n* an expert or specialist in mathematics

mathematics (ˌmæθəˈmætɪks) *n* **1** (*functioning as sing*) a group of related sciences, including algebra, geometry, and calculus, concerned with the study of number, quantity, shape, and space and their interrelationships by using a specialized notation **2** (*functioning as sing or pl*) mathematical operations and processes involved in the solution of a problem or study of some scientific field [c14 *mathematik* (n), via L from Gk (adj), from *mathēma* a science; rel. to *manthanein* to learn]

▷ www.martindalecenter.com/GradMath.html
▷ www.math.psu.edu/MathLists/Contents.html
▷ http://carbon.cudenver.edu/~hgreenbe/glossary/index.php

maths (mæθs) *n* (*functioning as sing*) *Brit inf* short for **mathematics** US and Canad equivalent: **math**

Mathura (ˈmʌtʊərə, mʌˈθʊərə) *n* a city in N India, in W Uttar Pradesh on the Jumna River: a place of Hindu pilgrimage, revered as the birthplace of Krishna. Pop: 226 691 (1991). Former name: **Muttra** (məˈtɪldə)

Matilda[1] (məˈtɪldə) *n Austral inf* **1** a bushman's swag **2** **waltz Matilda** to travel as a bushman carrying one's swag [c20 from the Christian name]

Matilda[2] (məˈtɪldə) *n* known as *the Empress Maud*. 1102–67, only daughter of Henry I of England and wife of Geoffrey of Anjou. After her father's death (1135) she unsuccessfully waged a civil war with Stephen for the English throne; her son succeeded as Henry II

matin, mattin (ˈmætɪn), *or* **matinal** *adj* of or relating to matins [c14 see MATINS]

matinée (ˈmætɪˌneɪ) *n* a daytime, esp afternoon, performance of a play, concert, etc [c19 from F; see MATINS]

matinée coat *or* **jacket** *n* a short coat for a baby

matins *or* **mattins** (ˈmætɪnz) *n* (*functioning as sing or pl*) **1a** *chiefly RC Church* the first of the seven canonical hours of prayer **1b** the service of morning prayer in the Church of England **2** *literary* a morning song, esp of birds [c13 from OF, ult. from L *mātūtīnus* of the morning, from *Mātūta* goddess of dawn]

Matisse (*French* matis) *n* **Henri** (ɑ̃ri) 1869–1954, French painter and sculptor; leader of Fauvism

matlo *or* **matlow** (ˈmætləʊ) *n* variant spellings of **matelot**

Matlock (ˈmætˌlɒk) *n* a town in England, on the River Derwent, administrative centre of Derbyshire: mineral springs. Pop: 14 680 (1991)

Mato Grosso (ˈmætəʊ ˈgrɒsəʊ; *Portuguese* ˈmatu ˈgrosu) *n* **1** a high plateau of SW Brazil: forms the watershed separating the Amazon and Plata river systems **2** a state of W central Brazil: mostly on the Mato Grosso Plateau, with the Amazon basin to the north; valuable mineral resources. Capital: Cuiabá. Pop: 2 498 150 (2000). Area: 881 001 sq km (340 083 sq miles)

Mato Grosso do Sul (ˈduː sul) *n* a state of W central Brazil: formed in 1979 from part of Mato Grosso state. Capital: Campo Grande. Pop: 2 075 275 (2000). Area: 350 548 sq km (135 318 sq miles)

Matopo Hills (məˈtəʊpə) *or* **Matopos** *pl n* the granite hills south of Bulawayo, Zimbabwe, where Cecil Rhodes chose to be buried

Matozinhos (*Portuguese* mətuˈziɲuʃ) *n* a port in N Portugal, on the estuary of the Leça River north of Oporto: fishing industry. Pop: 26 500 (latest est)

matrass (ˈmætrəs) *n chem, obs* a long-necked glass flask, used for distilling, dissolving substances, etc [c17 from F, ? rel. to L *mētīri* to measure]

Mm

matri- *combining form* mother or motherhood: *matriarchy* [from L *māter* mother]

matriarch ('meɪtrɪˌɑːk) *n* **1** a woman who dominates an organization, community, etc **2** the female head of a tribe or family **3** a very old or venerable woman [C17 from MATRI- + -ARCH, by false analogy with PATRIARCH] > **'matriˌarchal** *or* **'matriˌarchic** *adj*

matriarchy ('meɪtrɪˌɑːkɪ) *n, pl* **matriarchies 1** a form of social organization in which a female is head of the family or society, and descent and kinship are traced through the female line **2** any society dominated by women

matric (mə'trɪk) *n Brit* short for **matriculation** (see **matriculate**)

matrices ('meɪtrɪˌsiːz, 'mæ-) *n* a plural of **matrix**

matricide ('mætrɪˌsaɪd, 'meɪ-) *n* **1** the act of killing one's own mother **2** a person who kills his or her mother [C16 from L *mātrīcīdium* (the act), *mātrīcīda* (the agent). See MATRI-, -CIDE] > **ˌmatri'cidal** *adj*

matriculate (mə'trɪkjʊˌleɪt) *vb* **matriculates, matriculating, matriculated 1** to enrol or be enrolled in an institution, esp a college or university **2** (*intr*) to attain the academic standard required for a course at such an institution [C16 from Med. L *mātrīculāre* to register, from *mātrīcula*, dim. of *matrix* list] > **maˌtricu'lation** *n*

matrilineal (ˌmætrɪ'lɪnɪəl, ˌmeɪ-) *adj* relating to descent or kinship through the female line

matrimony ('mætrɪmənɪ) *n, pl* **matrimonies 1** the state or condition of being married **2** the ceremony of marriage **3a** a card game in which the king and queen together are a winning combination **3b** such a combination [C14 via Norman F from L *mātrimōnium* wedlock, from *māter* mother] > **ˌmatri'monial** *adj*

matrix ('meɪtrɪks, 'mæ-) *n, pl* **matrices** *or* **matrixes 1** a substance, situation, or environment in which something has its origin, takes form, or is enclosed **2** the intercellular substance of bone, cartilage, connective tissue, etc **3** the rock in which fossils, pebbles, etc, are embedded **4** *printing* **4a** a metal mould for casting type **4b** a papier-mâché or plastic mould impressed from the forme and used for stereotyping **5** a mould used in the production of gramophone records **6** a bed of perforated material placed beneath a workpiece in a press or stamping machine against which the punch operates **7** *maths* a rectangular array of elements set out in rows and columns, used to facilitate the solution of problems, such as transformation of coordinates **8** *obs* the womb [C16 from L: womb, female animal used for breeding, from *māter* mother]

matrix printer *n computing* another name for **dot-matrix printer**

matron ('meɪtrən) *n* **1** a married woman regarded as staid or dignified **2** a woman in charge of the domestic or medical arrangements in an institution **3** *US* a wardress in a prison **4** *Brit* the former name for the administrative head of the nursing staff in a hospital. Official name: **nursing officer** [C14 via OF from L *mātrōna*, from *māter* mother] > **'matronal** *or* **'matronly** *adj* > **'matronˌhood** *or* **'matronship** *n*

matron of honour *n, pl* **matrons of honour** a married woman serving as chief attendant to a bride

Matsu *or* **Mazu** (mæt'suː) *n* an island group in Formosa Strait, off the SE coast of mainland China: belongs to Taiwan. Pop: 3145 (1990 est). Area: 44 sq km (17 sq miles)

Matsuo Basho ('mætzuːəʊ bɑː'ʃɔː) *n* See **Basho**

Matsuyama (ˌmætsʊ'jɑːmə) *n* a port in SW Japan, on NW Shikoku: textile and chemical industries; Ehime University (1949). Pop: 460 870 (1995)

matt *or* **matte** (mæt) *adj, vb* **matts, matting, matted** *or* **mattes, matting, matted** variant spellings of **mat²** (senses 2 & 4)

Matt. *Bible abbrev for:* Matthew

mattamore ('mætəˌmɔː) *n* a subterranean storehouse or dwelling [C17 from F, from Ar. *matmurā*, from *tamara* to store, bury]

matted ('mætɪd) *adj* **1** tangled into a thick mass **2** covered with or formed of matting

matter ('mætə) *n* **1** that which makes up something, esp a physical object; material **2** substance that occupies space and has mass, as distinguished from substance that is mental, spiritual, etc **3** substance of a specified type: *vegetable matter* **4** (sometimes foll by *of* or *for*) thing; affair; concern; question: *a matter of taste* **5** a quantity or amount: *a matter of a few pence* **6** the content of written or verbal material as distinct from its style or form **7** (*used with a negative*) importance; consequence **8** *philosophy* (in the writings of Aristotle and the Scholastics) that which is itself formless but can receive form and become substance **9** *philosophy* (in the Cartesian tradition) one of two basic modes of existence, the other being mind **10** *printing* **10a** type set up **10b** copy to be set in type **11** a secretion or discharge, such as pus **12** *law* **12a** something to be proved **12b** statements or allegations to be considered by a court **13 for that matter** as regards that **14 no matter 14a** regardless of; irrespective of: *no matter what the excuse, you must not be late* **14b** (*sentence substitute*) it is unimportant **15 the matter** wrong; the trouble: *there's nothing the matter* ▷ *vb* (*intr*) **16** to be of consequence or importance **17** to form and discharge pus [C13 (n), C16 (vb): from L *māteria* cause, substance, esp wood, or a substance that produces something else]

Matterhorn ('mætəˌhɔːn) *n* a mountain on the border between Italy and Switzerland, in the Pennine Alps. Height: 4477 m (14 688 ft). French name: **Mont Cervin** Italian name: **Monte Cervino** ('monte tʃer'viːno)

matter of course *n* **1** an event or result that is natural or inevitable ▷ *adj* **matter-of-course 2** (*usually postpositive*) occurring as a matter of course **3** accepting things as inevitable or natural: *a matter-of-course attitude*

matter of fact *n* **1** a fact that is undeniably true **2** *law* a statement of facts the truth of which the court must determine on the basis of the evidence before it **3 as a matter of fact** actually; in fact ▷ *adj* **matter-of-fact 4** unimaginative or emotionless: *he gave a matter-of-fact account of the murder*

Matthew ('mæθjuː) *n New Testament* **1** Also called: **Levi** a tax collector of Capernaum called by Christ to be one of the 12 apostles (Matthew 9:9–13; 10:3). Feast day: Sept. 12 or Nov. 16 **2** the first Gospel, traditionally ascribed to him

Matthew Paris *n* See (Matthew) **Paris²** (sense 2)

Matthews ('mæθjuːz) *n* Sir **Stanley** 1915–2002, English footballer

Matthias (mə'θaɪəs) *n New Testament* the disciple chosen by lot to replace Judas as one of the 12 apostles (Acts 1:15–26)

Matthias I Corvinus (kɔː'vaɪnəs) *n* ?1440–90, king of Hungary (1458–90): built up the most powerful kingdom in Central Europe. A patron of Renaissance art, he founded the Corvina library, one of the finest in Europe. Hungarian name: **Mátyás Hollós** ('maːtjaːʃ 'holoʃ)

matting¹ ('mætɪŋ) *n* **1** a coarsely woven fabric, usually made of a natural fibre such as straw or hemp and used as a floor covering, packing material, etc **2** the act or process of making mats **3** material for mats

matting² ('mætɪŋ) *n* **1** another word for **mat²** (sense 1) **2** the process of producing a mat finish

mattins ('mætɪnz) *n* a variant spelling of **matins**

mattock ('mætək) *n* a type of large pick that has one end of its blade shaped like an adze, used for loosening soil, cutting roots, etc [OE *mattuc*, from ?; rel. to L *mateola* club, mallet]

mattress ('mætrɪs) *n* **1** a large flat pad with a strong cover, filled with straw, foam rubber, etc, and often incorporating coiled springs, used as a bed or as part of a bed **2** a woven mat of brushwood, poles, etc, used to protect an embankment, dyke, etc, from scour **3** a concrete or steel raft or slab used as a foundation or footing [c13 via OF from It. *materasso*, from Ar. *almatrah* place where something is thrown]

maturate ('mætjʊˌreɪt, 'mætʃʊ-) *vb* **maturates, maturating, matured 1** to mature or bring to maturity **2** a less common word for **suppurate** > **maturative** (məˈtjʊərətɪv, məˈtʃʊə-) *adj*

maturation (ˌmætjʊˈreɪʃən, ˌmætʃʊ-) *n* **1** the process of maturing or ripening **2** *zool* the development of ova and spermatozoa from precursor cells in the ovary and testis, involving meiosis **3** a less common word for **suppuration**

mature (məˈtjʊə, -ˈtʃʊə) *adj* **1** relatively advanced physically, mentally, etc; grown-up **2** (of plans, theories, etc) fully considered; perfected **3** due or payable: *a mature debenture* **4** *biol* **4a** fully developed or differentiated: *a mature cell* **4b** fully grown; adult: *a mature animal* **5** (of fruit, wine, cheese, etc) ripe or fully aged ▷ *vb* **matures, maturing, matured 6** to make or become mature **7** (*intr*) (of notes, bonds, etc) to become due for payment or repayment [c15 from L *mātūrus* early, developed] > **maˈturely** *adv* > **maˈtureness** *n*

mature student *n* a student at a college or university who has passed the usual age for formal education

maturity (məˈtjʊərɪtɪ, -ˈtʃʊə-) *n* **1** the state or quality of being mature; full development **2** *finance* **2a** the date upon which a bond, note, etc, becomes due for repayment **2b** the state of a bill, note, etc, when due

matutinal (ˌmætjʊˈtaɪnᵊl) *adj* of, occurring in, or during the morning [c17 from LL *mātūtīnālis*, from L, from *Mātūta* goddess of the dawn]

matzo, matzoh ('mætsəʊ) *or* **matza, matzah** ('mætsə) *n, pl* **matzos, matzohs, matzas, matzahs,** *or* **matzoth** (*Hebrew* maˈtsɔt) a large very thin biscuit of unleavened bread, traditionally eaten during Passover [from Heb. *matsāh*]

Maubeuge (*French* mobøʒ) *n* an industrial town in N France, near the border with Belgium. Pop: 35 225 (1990)

maudlin ('mɔːdlɪn) *adj* foolishly tearful or sentimental, as when drunk [c17 from ME *Maudelen* Mary Magdalene, typically portrayed as a tearful penitent]

mauger ('mɔːgə) *adj Caribbean* (of persons or animals) thin or lean [from Du. *mager* thin, MEAGRE]

Maugham ('mɔːm) *n* **W(illiam) Somerset** 1874–1965, English writer. His works include the novels *Of Human Bondage* (1915) and *Cakes and Ale* (1930), short stories, and comedies

maugre *or* **mauger** ('mɔːgə) *prep obs* in spite of [c13 (meaning: ill will): from OF *maugre*, lit.: bad pleasure]

Maui ('maʊɪ) *n* a volcanic island in S central Hawaii: the second largest of the Hawaiian Islands. Pop: 91 361 (1990). Area: 1885 sq km (728 sq miles)

maul (mɔːl) *vb* (*tr*) **1** to handle clumsily; paw **2** to batter or lacerate ▷ *n* **3** a heavy two-handed hammer **4** *rugby* a loose scrum [c13 from OF *mail*, from L *malleus* hammer] > **ˈmauler** *n*

maulstick *or* **mahlstick** ('mɔːlˌstɪk) *n* a long stick used by artists to steady the hand holding the brush [c17 partial translation of Du. *maalstok*, from obs. *malen* to paint + *stok* STICK[1]]

Mauna Kea ('maʊnaː 'keɪɑː) *n* an extinct volcano in Hawaii, on N central Hawaii Island: the highest island mountain in the world. Height: 4206 m (13 799 ft)

Mauna Loa ('maʊnaː 'ləʊɑː) *n* an active volcano in Hawaii, on S central Hawaii Island. Height: 4171 m (13 684 ft)

maunder ('mɔːndə) *vb* (*intr*) to move, talk, or act aimlessly or idly [c17 ?from obs. *maunder* to beg, from L *mendīcāre*]

maundy ('mɔːndɪ) *n, pl* **maundies** *Christianity* the ceremonial washing of the feet of poor persons in commemoration of Jesus' washing of his disciples' feet [c13 from OF *mandé* something commanded, from L, ult. from Christ's words: *Mandātum novum dō vōbīs* A new commandment give I unto you]

Maundy money *n* specially minted coins distributed by the British sovereign on the Thursday before Easter (**Maundy Thursday**)

Maupassant (*French* mopɑsɑ̃) *n* (**Henri René Albert**) **Guy de** (gi də) 1850–93, French writer, noted esp for his short stories, such as *Boule de suif* (1880), *La Maison Tellier* (1881), and *Mademoiselle Fifi* (1883). His novels include *Bel Ami* (1885) and *Pierre et Jean* (1888)

Maupertuis (*French* mopɛrtɥi) *n* **Pierre Louis Moreau de** (pjɛr lwi mɔro də) 1698–1759, French mathematician, who originated the principle of least action (or Maupertuis principle)

Mauretania (ˌmɒrɪˈteɪnɪə) *n* an ancient region of N Africa, corresponding approximately to the N parts of modern Algeria and Morocco > **ˌMaureˈtanian** *adj, n*

Mauriac (*French* mɔrjak) *n* **François** (frɑ̃swa) 1885–1970, French novelist, noted esp for his psychological studies of the conflict between religious belief and human desire. His works include *Le désert de l'amour* (1925), *Thérèse Desqueyroux* (1927), and *Le nœud de vipères* (1932): Nobel prize for literature 1952

Maurice ('mɒrɪs) *n* **1** 1521–53, duke of Saxony (1541–53) and elector of Saxony (1547–53). He was instrumental in gaining recognition of Protestantism in Germany **2** known as *Maurice of Nassau*. 1567–1625, prince of Orange and count of Nassau; the son of William the Silent, after whose death he led the United Provinces of the Netherlands in their struggle for independence from Spain (achieved by 1609) **3** **Frederick Denison** 1805–72, English Anglican theologian and pioneer of Christian socialism

Mauritania (ˌmɒrɪˈteɪnɪə) *n* a republic in NW Africa, on the Atlantic: established as a French protectorate in 1903 and a colony in 1920; gained independence in 1960; lies in the Sahara; contains rich resources of iron ore. Official language: Arabic; Fulani, Soninke, Wolof, and French are also spoken. Official religion: Muslim. Currency: ouguiya. Capital: Nouakchott. Pop: 2 591 000 (2001 est). Area: 1 030 700 sq km (398 000 sq miles). Official name: > **ˌMauriˈtanian** *adj, n* **Islamic Republic of Mauritania**

▷ www.mauritania.mr
▷ www.ambarim-dc.org

Mm

Mauritius (məˈrɪʃəs) *n* an island and state in the Indian Ocean, east of Madagascar: originally uninhabited, it was settled by the Dutch (1638–1710) then abandoned; taken by the French in 1715 and the British in 1810; became an independent member of the Commonwealth in 1968. It is economically dependent on sugar. Official language: English; a French creole is widely spoken. Religion: Hindu majority, large Christian minority. Currency: rupee. Capital: Port Louis. Pop: 1 195 000 (2001 est). Area: 1865 sq km (720 sq miles). Former name (1715–1810): **Île-de-France** > **Mauˈritian** *adj, n*

▷ http://ncb.intnet.mu/govt/house.htm
▷ www.mauritius.net

Maurois (*French* mɔrwa) *n* **André** (ɑ̃dre), pen name of *Émile Herzog*. 1885–1967, French writer, best known for his biographies, such as those of Shelley, Byron, and Proust

Maury ('mɔːrɪ) *n* **Matthew Fontaine** 1806–73, US pioneer hydrographer and oceanographer

mausoleum (ˌmɔːsəˈlɪəm) *n, pl* **mausoleums** *or* **mausolea** (-ˈlɪə) a large stately tomb [c16 via L from Gk *mausōleion*, the tomb of *Mausolus*, king of Caria; built at Halicarnassus in the 4th cent. BC]

mauve (məʊv) *n* **1a** any of various pale to moderate pinkish-purple or bluish-purple colours **1b** (*as adj*): *a* *mauve flower* **2** a reddish-purple aniline dye [c19 from F, from L *malva* MALLOW]

maven *or* **mavin** ('meɪvən) *n US* an expert or connoisseur [c20 from Yiddish, from Heb. *mevin* understanding]

maverick ('mævərɪk) *n* **1** (in the US and Canada) an unbranded animal, esp a stray calf **2a** a person of independent or unorthodox views **2b** *(as modifier): a maverick politician* [c19 after Samuel A. *Maverick* (1803–70), Texas rancher, who did not brand his cattle]

mavis ('meɪvɪs) *n* a popular name for the **song thrush** [c14 from OF *mauvis* thrush; from ?]

maw (mɔː) *n* **1** the mouth, throat, crop, or stomach of an animal, esp of a voracious animal **2** *inf* the mouth or stomach of a greedy person [OE *maga*]

mawkish ('mɔːkɪʃ) *adj* **1** falsely sentimental, esp in a weak or maudlin way **2** nauseating or insipid [c17 from obs. *mawk* MAGGOT + -ISH] > **'mawkishly** *adv* > **'mawkishness** *n*

Mawson ('mɔːsən) *n* Sir **Douglas** 1882–1958, Australian Antarctic explorer, born in England

max (mæks) *n inf* **1** the most significant, highest, furthest, or greatest thing **2 to the max** to the ultimate extent

max. *abbrev for* maximum

maxi ('mæksɪ) *adj* **1a** (of a garment) reaching the ankle **1b** *(as n): she wore a maxi* **1c** *(in combination): a maxidress* **2** large or considerable [c20 from MAXIMUM]

maxilla (mæk'sɪlə) *n, pl* **maxillae** (-liː) **1** the upper jawbone in vertebrates **2** any member of one or two pairs of mouthparts in insects and other arthropods [c17 NL, from L: jaw] > **max'illary** *adj*

maxim ('mæksɪm) *n* a brief expression of a general truth, principle, or rule of conduct [c15 via F from Med. L, from *maxima*, in the phrase *maxima prōpositio* basic axiom (lit.: greatest proposition)]

Maxim ('mæksɪm) *n* Sir **Hiram Stevens** 1840–1916, British inventor of the first automatic machine gun (1884), born in the US

maxima ('mæksɪmə) *n* a plural of **maximum**

maximal ('mæksɪməl) *adj* of, relating to, or achieving a maximum; being the greatest or best possible > **'maximally** *adv*

Maximilian (ˌmæksɪ'mɪlɪən) *n* full name *Ferdinand Maximilian Joseph*. 1832–67, archduke of Austria and emperor of Mexico (1864–67). After the French had partially conquered Mexico, he was offered the throne but was defeated and shot by the Mexicans under Juárez

Maximilian I *n* 1459–1519, king of Germany (1486–1519) and Holy Roman Emperor (1493–1519)

maximin ('mæksɪˌmɪn) *n* **1** *maths* the highest of a set of minimum values **2** (in game theory, etc) the procedure of choosing the strategy that most benefits the least advantaged member of a group ▷ Cf **minimax** [c20 from MAXI(MUM) + MIN(IMUM)]

maximize *or* **maximise** ('mæksɪˌmaɪz) *vb* **maximizes, maximizing, maximized** *or* **maximises, maximising, maximised** *(tr)* to make as high or great as possible; increase to a maximum > **ˌmaximi'zation** *or* **ˌmaximi'sation** *n* > **'maxiˌmizer** *or* **'maxiˌmiser** *n*

maximum ('mæksɪməm) *n, pl* **maximums** *or* **maxima** **1** the greatest possible amount, degree, etc **2** the highest value of a variable quantity ▷ *adj* **3** of, being, or showing a maximum or maximums ▷ Abbrev: **max** [c18 from L: greatest (neuter form used as noun), from *magnus* great]

Max Müller (*German* maks 'mylər) *n* See (Friedrich Max) **Müller**

maxwell ('mækswəl) *n* the cgs unit of magnetic flux equal to the flux through one square centimetre normal to a field of one gauss. It is equivalent to 10^{-8} weber. Symbol: Mx [c20 after J. C. MAXWELL]

Maxwell ('mækswəl) *n* **1 James Clerk** 1831–79, Scottish physicist. He made major contributions to the electromagnetic theory, developing the equations (**Maxwell equations**) upon which classical theory is based. He also contributed to the kinetic theory of gases, and colour vision **2** (**Ian**) **Robert**, original name *Robert Hoch*. 1923–91, British publisher, born in Slovakia: founder (1949) of Pergamon Press; chairman of Mirror Group Newspapers Ltd. (1984–91); theft from his employees' pension funds and other frauds discovered after his death led to the collapse of his business

may[1] (meɪ) *vb past* **might** (takes an infinitive without *to* or an implied infinitive) used as an auxiliary: **1** to indicate that permission is requested by or granted to someone: *he may go* **2** (often foll by *well*) to indicate possibility: *the rope may break* **3** to indicate ability or capacity, esp in questions: *may I help you?* **4** to express a strong wish: *long may she reign* **5** to indicate result or purpose: used only in clauses introduced by *that* or *so that: he writes so that the average reader may understand* **6** another word for **might**[1] **7** to express courtesy in a question: *whose child may this little girl be?* **8 be that as it may** in spite of that: a sentence connector conceding the possible truth of a previous statement and introducing an adversative clause: *be that as it may, I still think he should come* **9 come what may** whatever happens **10 that's as may be** (foll by a clause introduced by *but*) that may be so [OE *mæg*, from *magan*]

may[2] *or* **may tree** (meɪ) *n* a Brit name for **hawthorn** [c17 from MAY]

May[1] (meɪ) *n* the fifth month of the year, consisting of 31 days [from OF, from L *Maius* (month) of *Maia*, Roman goddess]

May[2] (meɪ) *n* Sir **Robert McCredie** born 1936, Australian biologist and ecologist

Maya[1] ('maɪə) *n* **1** (*pl* **Maya** *or* **Mayas**) Also called: **Mayan** a member of an American Indian people of Yucatán, Belize, and N Guatemala, once having an advanced civilization **2** the language of this people

▷ www.indians.org/welker/mayamenu.htm

▷ www.wsu.edu:8080/~ dee/CIVAMRCA/MAYAS.HTM

Maya[2] ('maɪə, 'mɑːjə, 'mɑːjɑː) *n* the Hindu goddess of illusion, the personification of the idea that the material world is illusory > **'Mayan** *adj*

Mayagüez (*Spanish* maja'ɣweθ) *n* a port in W Puerto Rico; needlework industry. Pop: 100 937 (1996 est)

Mayakovski *or* **Mayakovsky** (*Russian* məjɪ'kɔfskij) *n* **Vladimir Vladimirovich** (vla'dimir vla'dimirəvitʃ) 1893–1930, Russian Futurist poet and dramatist. His poems include *150 000 000* (1921) and *At the Top of my Voice* (1930); his plays include *Vladimir Mayakovsky *Z— a Tragedy* (1913) and *The Bedbug* (1929)

May apple *n* **1** an American plant with edible yellowish egg-shaped fruit **2** the fruit

maybe ('meɪˌbiː) *adv* **1** perhaps ▷ *sentence substitute* **2** possibly; neither yes nor no

May beetle *or* **bug** *n* another name for **cockchafer**

Mayday ('meɪˌdeɪ) *n* the international radiotelephone distress signal [c20 phonetic spelling of F *m'aidez* help me]

May Day *n* the first day of May, traditionally a celebration of the coming of spring: in some countries now observed as a holiday in honour of workers

Mayence (majɑ̃s) *n* the French name for **Mainz**

Mayenne (*French* majɛn) *n* a department of NW France, in Pays de la Loire region. Capital: Laval. Pop: 285 338 (1999). Area: 5212 sq km (2033 sq miles)

Mayer *n* **1** (*German* 'maiər) **Julius Robert von** ('juːlius'roːbɛrt fɔn) 1814–78, German physicist whose research in thermodynamics (1842) contributed to the discovery of the law of conservation of energy **2** ('meɪə) **Louis B(urt)** 1885–1957, US film producer, born in Russia; founder and first head (1924–48) of the Metro-Goldwyn-Mayer (MGM) film company

mayest ('meɪɪst) *vb* a variant of **mayst**

Mayfair ('meɪˌfɛə) *n* a fashionable district of west central London

mayflower ('meɪˌflaʊə) *n* **1** any of various plants that bloom in May **2** *Brit* another name for **hawthorn, cowslip,** or **marsh marigold**

Mayflower ('meɪˌflaʊə) *n* **the** the ship in which the Pilgrim Fathers sailed from Plymouth to America in 1620

mayfly ('meɪˌflaɪ) *n, pl* **mayflies** any of an order of short-lived insects having large transparent wings

mayhap ('meɪˌhæp) *adv* an archaic word for **perhaps** [c16 shortened from *it may hap*]

mayhem *or* **maihem** ('meɪhɛm) *n* **1** *law* the wilful and unlawful infliction of injury upon a person, esp (formerly) the injuring or removing of a limb rendering him less capable of defending himself against attack **2** any violent destruction or confusion [c15 from Anglo-F *mahem* injury, of Gmc origin]

Mayhew ('meɪhjuː) *n* **Henry** 1812–87, British social commentator, journalist, and writer; a founder of *Punch* (1841): best known for *London Labour and the London Poor* (1851–62)

Maying ('meɪɪŋ) *n* the celebration of May Day

mayn't ('meɪənt, meɪnt) *contraction of* may not

Mayo[1] ('meɪəʊ) *n* a county of NW Republic of Ireland, in NW Connacht province, on the Atlantic: has many offshore islands and several large lakes. County town: Castlebar. Pop: 111 524 (1996). Area: 5397 sq km (2084 sq miles)

Mayo[2] ('meɪəʊ) *n* a family of US medical practitioners. They pioneered group practice and established (1903) the **Mayo Clinic** in Rochester, Minnesota. Foremost among them were **William Worrall Mayo** (1819–1911), his sons **William James Mayo** (1861–1939) and **Charles Horace Mayo** (1865–1939), and Charles's son, **Charles William Mayo** (1898–1968)

Mayon (mɑː'jɔːn) *n* a volcano in the Philippines, on SE Luzon: Height: 2421 m (7943 ft)

mayonnaise (ˌmeɪə'neɪz) *n* a thick creamy sauce made from egg yolks, oil, and vinegar or lemon juice [c19 from F, ? from *mahonnais* of Mahón, a port in Minorca]

mayor (mɛə) *n* the civic head of a municipal corporation in many countries. Scot equivalent: **provost** [c13 from OF *maire*, from L *maior* greater] > '**mayoral** *adj* > '**mayorship** *n*

mayoralty ('mɛərəltɪ) *n, pl* **mayoralties** the office or term of office of a mayor [c14 from OF *mairalté*]

mayoress ('mɛərɪs) *n* **1** *chiefly Brit* the wife of a mayor **2** a female mayor

Mayotte (*French* majɔt) *n* an island in the Indian Ocean, northwest of Madagascar; administered by France. Pop (including Pamanzi): 159 000 (2001 est). Area: 374 sq km (146 sq miles)

maypole ('meɪˌpəʊl) *n* a tall pole around which people dance during May-Day celebrations

May queen *n* a girl chosen, esp for her beauty, to preside over May-Day celebrations

mayst (meɪst) *or* **mayest** *vb arch* (used with *thou* or its relative equivalent) a singular form of the present tense of **may**[1]

mayweed ('meɪˌwiːd) *n* **1** Also called: **dog fennel, stinking mayweed** a widespread Eurasian weedy plant having evil-smelling leaves and daisy-like flower heads **2 scentless mayweed** a similar and related plant, with scentless leaves [c16 changed from OE *mægtha* mayweed + WEED]

Mazar-e-Sharif *or* **Mazar-i-Sharif** ('mæzaː iː ʒə'riːf) *n* a city in N Afghanistan, reputed burial place of the caliph Ali; trading, agricultural, and military centre. Pop: 127 800 (1993 est)

Mazarin ('mæzərɪn; *French* mazarɛ̃) *n* **Jules** (ʒyl), original name *Giulio Mazarini*. 1602–61, French cardinal and statesman, born in Italy. He succeeded Richelieu (1642) as chief minister to Louis XIII and under the regency of Anne of Austria (1643–61). Despite the disturbances of the Fronde (1648–53), he strengthened the power of France in Europe

Mazatlán (*Spanish* maθa'tlan) *n* a port in W Mexico, in S Sinaloa on the Pacific: situated opposite the tip of the peninsula of Lower California, for which it is the chief link with the mainland. Pop: 325 000 (2000 est)

maze (meɪz) *n* **1** a complex network of paths or passages, esp one with high hedges in a garden, designed to puzzle those walking through it **2** a similar system represented diagrammatically as a pattern of lines **3** any confusing network of streets, paths, etc **4** a state of confusion ▷ *vb* **mazes, mazing, mazed 5** an archaic or dialect word for **amaze** [c13 see AMAZE] > '**mazement** *n* > '**mazy** *adj*

Mazu ('mæ'zuː) *n* the Pinyin transliteration of the Chinese name for **Matsu**

mazurka *or* **mazourka** (mə'zɜːkə) *n* **1** a Polish national dance in triple time **2** a piece of music composed for this dance [c19 from Polish: (dance) of *Mazury* (Mazovia) province in Poland]

Mazzini (*Italian* mat'tsiːni) *n* **Giuseppe** (dʒu'zɛppe) 1805–72, Italian nationalist. In 1831, in exile, he established the Young Italy association in Marseille, which sought to unite Italy as a republic. In 1849 he was one of the triumvirate that ruled the short-lived Roman republic

Mb *computing abbrev for:* megabyte

MB *abbrev for* Bachelor of Medicine

MBA *abbrev for* Master of Business Administration

Mbabane (ᵊmbɑː'bɑːnɪ) *n* the capital of Swaziland, in the northwest: administrative and financial centre, with a large iron mine nearby. Pop: 60 000 (1998 est) ▷ www.mbabane.org.sz

mbaqanga (ᵊmbɑː'kæŋgə) *n* a style of Black popular music of urban South Africa [c20 ? from Zulu *umbaqanga* mixture]

MBE *abbrev for* Member of the Order of the British Empire (a Brit title)

Mbeki (ᵊm'bɛkɪ) *n* **Thabo (Mvuyelwa)** ('tɑːbəʊ) born 1942, South African politician: a member of the African National Congress (ANC); president of South Africa from 1999; deputy president of South Africa (1994–99)

mbira (ᵊm'biːrə) *n* an African musical instrument consisting of tuned metal strips attached to a resonating box, which are plucked with the thumbs. Also called: **thumb piano** [Bantu]

MBO *abbrev for* management buyout

Mbujimayi (ᵊm'buːdʒɪˌmaɪiː) *n* a city in S Democratic Republic of Congo (formerly Zaïre): diamond mining. Pop: 806 475 (1994 est)

MC *abbrev for:* **1** Master of Ceremonies **2** (in the US) Member of Congress **3** (in Britain) Military Cross

Mc- *prefix* a variant of **Mac-** For entries beginning with this prefix, see under **Mac-**

MCC (in Britain) *abbrev for* Marylebone Cricket Club ▷ www.lords.org/mcc

MCG (in Australia) *abbrev for* Melbourne Cricket Ground

MCh *abbrev for* Master of Surgery [L *Magister Chirurgiae*]

MCP *inf abbrev for:* male chauvinist pig

Md *the chemical symbol for* mendelevium

MD *abbrev for:* **1** Doctor of Medicine [from L *Medicinae Doctor*] **2** Managing Director **3** mentally deficient **4** (in Canada) municipal district

Md. *abbrev for* Maryland

MDF *abbrev for* medium density fibreboard: a material made of compressed wood fibres used as a substitute for wood, esp in interior decoration

MDMA *abbrev for* 3,4-methylenedioxymethamphetamine. See **ecstasy** (sense 4)

MDS See **MMDS**

MDT (in the US and Canada) *abbrev for* Mountain Daylight Time

me[1] (miː; *unstressed* mɪ) *pron (objective)* 1 refers to the speaker or writer: *that shocks me* ▷ *n* 2 *inf* the personality of the speaker or writer or something that expresses it: *the real me* [OE *mē* (dative)]

> **USAGE** It was formerly regarded as correct to use *I*, *he*, *she*, etc, rather than *me*, *him*, *her*, after the verb *to be*, as in: *it is I who told him*. Since both I and *me* can sound strange in a sentence like this, it is better to use a different construction altogether: *I am the one who told him*. The use of a possessive before an *-ing* form of a verb was formerly thought to be preferable to using *me*, etc, but now both forms are acceptable: *he didn't like my/me having a job of my own*

me[2] (miː) *n* a variant spelling of **mi** (sense 2)

ME *abbrev for*: 1 Marine Engineer 2 Mechanical Engineer 3 Methodist Episcopal 4 Middle English 5 Mining Engineer 6 (in titles) Most Excellent 7 myalgic encephalopathy

Me. *abbrev for* Maine

mea culpa *Latin* (ˈmeɪɑː ˈkʊlpɑː) an acknowledgment of guilt [lit.: my fault]

mead[1] (miːd) *n* an alcoholic drink made by fermenting a solution of honey, often with spices added [OE *meodu*]

mead[2] (miːd) *n* an archaic or poetic word for **meadow** [OE *mæd*]

Mead[1] (miːd) *n* **Lake** a reservoir in NW Arizona and SE Nevada, formed by the Hoover Dam across the Colorado River: one of the largest man-made lakes in the world. Area: 588 sq km (227 sq miles)

Mead[2] (miːd) *n* **Margaret** 1901–78, US anthropologist. Her works include *Coming of Age in Samoa* (1928) and *Male and Female* (1949)

Meade (miːd) *n* **George Gordon** 1815–72, Union general in the American Civil War. He commanded the Army of the Potomac, defeating the Confederates at Gettysburg (1863)

meadow (ˈmɛdəʊ) *n* 1 an area of grassland, often used for hay or for grazing of animals 2 a low-lying piece of grassland, often boggy and near a river [OE *mædwe*, from *mǣd* MEAD[2]] > ˈ**meadowy** *adj*

meadow grass *n* a perennial grass that grows in meadows and similar places in N temperate regions

meadow saffron *n* another name for **autumn crocus**

meadowsweet (ˈmɛdəʊˌswiːt) *n* 1 a Eurasian plant with dense heads of small fragrant cream-coloured flowers 2 any of several related North American plants. See also **spiraea**

meagre *or US* **meager** (ˈmiːɡə) *adj* 1 deficient in amount, quality, or extent 2 thin or emaciated 3 lacking in richness or strength [C14 from OF *maigre*, from L *macer* lean, poor] > ˈ**meagrely** *adv* > ˈ**meagreness** *n*

meal[1] (miːl) *n* 1a any of the regular occasions, such as breakfast, lunch, dinner, etc, when food is served and eaten 1b (*in combination*): *mealtime* 2 the food served and eaten 3 **make a meal of** *inf* to perform (a task) with unnecessarily great effort [OE *mǣl* measure, set time, meal]

meal[2] (miːl) *n* 1 the edible part of a grain or pulse (excluding wheat) ground to a coarse powder 2 *Scot* oatmeal 3 *chiefly US* maize flour [OE *melu*]

mealie *or* **mielie** (ˈmiːlɪ) *n (often pl)* a S African word for **maize** [C19 from Afrik. *milie*, from Port. *milho*, from L *milium* millet]

mealie-meal *n S African* meal made from finely ground maize

meals-on-wheels *n (functioning as sing)* a service taking hot meals to the elderly, infirm, etc, in their own homes

meal ticket *n sl* a person, situation, etc, providing a source of livelihood or income [from orig. US sense of ticket entitling holder to a meal]

mealworm (ˈmiːlˌwɜːm) *n* the larva of various beetles feeding on stored foods, esp meal and flour

mealy (ˈmiːlɪ) *adj* **mealier, mealiest** 1 resembling meal; powdery 2 containing or consisting of meal or grain 3 sprinkled or covered with meal or similar granules 4 (esp of horses) spotted; mottled 5 pale in complexion 6 short for **mealy-mouthed** > ˈ**mealiness** *n*

mealy bug *n* any of various plant-eating insects coated with a powdery waxy secretion: some species are pests of citrus fruits and greenhouse plants

mealy-mouthed *adj* hesitant or afraid to speak plainly; not outspoken [C16 from MEALY (in the sense: soft, soft-spoken)]

mean[1] (miːn) *vb* **means, meaning, meant** (*mainly tr*) 1 (*may take a clause as object or an infinitive*) to intend to convey or express 2 (*may take a clause as object or an infinitive*) to intend: *she didn't mean to hurt it* 3 (*may take a clause as object*) to say or do in all seriousness: *the boss means what he says* 4 (*often passive*; often foll by *for*) to destine or design (for a certain person or purpose): *she was meant for greater things* 5 (*may take a clause as object*) to denote or connote; signify; represent 6 (*may take a clause as object*) to produce; cause: *the weather will mean long traffic delays* 7 (*may take a clause as object*) to foretell; portend: *those dark clouds mean rain* 8 to have the importance of: *money means nothing to him* 9 (*intr*) to have the intention of behaving or acting (esp in **mean well** *or* **mean ill**) [OE *mænan*]

> **USAGE** In standard British English *mean* should not be followed by *for* when expressing intention: *I didn't mean this to happen* (not *I didn't mean for this to happen*)

mean[2] (miːn) *adj* 1 *chiefly Brit* miserly, ungenerous, or petty 2 despicable, ignoble, or callous: *a mean action* 3 poor or shabby: *a mean abode* 4 *inf, chiefly US & Canad* bad-tempered; vicious 5 *inf* ashamed: *he felt mean about not letting the children stay out late* 6 *sl* excellent; skilful: *he plays a mean trombone* 7 **no mean** 7a of high quality: *no mean performer* 7b difficult: *no mean feat* [C12 from OE *gemǣne* common] > ˈ**meanly** *adv* > ˈ**meanness** *n*

mean[3] (miːn) *n* 1 the middle point, state, or course between limits or extremes 2 moderation 3 *maths* 3a the second and third terms of a proportion, as *b* and *c* in $a/b = c/d$ 3b another name for **average** (sense 2) 4 *statistics* a statistic obtained by multiplying each possible value of a variable by its probability and then taking the sum or integral over the range of the variable ▷ *adj* 5 intermediate or medium in size, quantity, etc 6 occurring halfway between extremes or limits; average [C14 via Anglo-Norman from OF *moien*, from LL *mediānus* MEDIAN]

meander (mɪˈændə) *vb (intr)* 1 to follow a winding course 2 to wander without definite aim or direction ▷ *n* 3 (*often pl*) a curve or bend, as in a river 4 (*often pl*) a winding course or movement 5 an ornamental pattern, esp as used in ancient Greek architecture [C16 from L *maeander*, from Gk *Maiandros* the River Maeander; see MENDERES (sense 1)] > **meˈandering** *adj*

Meander (miːˈændə) *n* a variant spelling of **Maeander**

mean deviation *n statistics* 1 the difference between an observed value of a variable and its mean 2 Also called: **mean deviation from the mean** (*or* **median**), **average deviation** a measure of dispersion derived by computing the mean of the absolute values of the differences between observed values of a variable and the variable's mean

meanie *or* **meany** (ˈmiːnɪ) *n inf* 1 *chiefly Brit* a miserly or stingy person 2 *chiefly US* a nasty ill-tempered person

meaning (ˈmiːnɪŋ) *n* 1 the sense or significance of a word, sentence, symbol, etc; import 2 the purpose behind speech, action, etc 3 the inner, symbolic, or true interpretation, value, or message 4 valid content; efficacy ▷ *adj* 5 expressive of some sense, intention, criticism, etc: *a meaning look* ▹ See also **well-meaning**

meaningful ('miːnɪŋfʊl) *adj* **1** having great meaning or validity **2** eloquent; expressive: *a meaningful silence* > '**meaningfully** *adv* > '**meaningfulness** *n*

meaningless ('miːnɪŋlɪs) *adj* futile or empty of meaning > '**meaninglessly** *adv* > '**meaninglessness** *n*

mean lethal dose *n* another term for **median lethal dose**

mean life *n physics* the average time of existence of an unstable or reactive entity, such as a nucleus, elementary particle, etc

means (miːnz) *n* **1** (*functioning as sing or pl*) the medium, method, or instrument used to obtain a result or achieve an end: *a means of communication* **2** (*functioning as pl*) resources or income **3** (*functioning as pl*) considerable wealth or income: *a man of means* **4 by all means** without hesitation or doubt; certainly **5 by means of** with the use or help of **6 by no manner of means** definitely not **7 by no** (*or* **not by any**) **means** on no account; in no way

means test *n* the checking of a person's income to determine whether he or she qualifies for financial or social aid from a government

mean sun *n* an imaginary sun moving along the celestial equator at a constant speed and completing its annual course in the same time as the sun takes to move round the ecliptic at a varying speed. It is used in the measurement of mean solar time

meant (mɛnt) *vb* the past tense and past participle of **mean**[1]

meantime ('miːnˌtaɪm) *or* **meanwhile** ('miːnˌwaɪl) *n* **1** the intervening time or period (esp in **in the meantime**) ▹ *adv* **2** during the intervening time or period **3** at the same time, esp in another place

mean time *or* **mean solar time** *n* the times, at a particular place, measured in terms of the passage of the mean sun, giving 24-hour days (mean solar days) throughout a year

meany ('miːnɪ) *n, pl* **meanies** a variant of **meanie**

Mearns (mɛənz) *n* **the** another name for **Kincardineshire**

measles ('miːzəlz) *n* (*functioning as sing*) **1** a highly contagious viral disease common in children, characterized by fever, profuse nasal discharge of mucus, conjunctivitis, and a rash of small red spots. See also **German measles** **2** a disease of cattle, sheep, and pigs, caused by infestation with tapeworm larvae [C14 from MLow G *masele* spot on the skin; infl. by ME *mesel* leper, from L *misellus*, dim. of *miser* wretched]

measly ('miːzlɪ) *adj* **measlier, measliest** **1** *inf* meagre in quality or quantity **2** (of meat) infested with tapeworm larvae **3** having or relating to measles [C17 see MEASLES]

measurable ('mɛʒərəbᵊl) *adj* able to be measured; perceptible or significant > '**measurably** *adv*

measure ('mɛʒə) *n* **1** the extent, quantity, amount, or degree of something, as determined by measurement or calculation **2** a device for measuring distance, volume, etc, such as a graduated scale or container **3** a system of measurement: *metric measure* **4** a standard used in a system of measurements **5** a specific or standard amount of something: *a measure of grain; full measure* **6** a basis or standard for comparison **7** reasonable or permissible limit or bounds: *within measure* **8** degree or extent (often in **in some measure, in a measure,** etc): *a measure of freedom* **9** (*often pl*) a particular action intended to achieve an effect **10** a legislative bill, act, or resolution **11** *music* another word for **bar**[1] (sense 15) **12** *prosody* poetic rhythm or cadence; metre **13** a metrical foot **14** *poetic* a melody or tune **15** the act of measuring; measurement **16** *arch* a dance **17** *printing* the width of a page or column of type **18 for good measure** as an extra precaution or beyond requirements **19 made to measure** (of clothes) made to fit an individual purchaser ▹ *vb* **measures, measuring, measured** **20** (*tr; often foll by up*) to determine the size, amount, etc, of by measurement **21** (*intr*) to make a measurement **22** (*tr*) to estimate or determine **23** (*tr*) to function as a measurement of: *the ohm measures electrical resistance* **24** (*tr*) to bring into competition or conflict with: *he measured his strength against that of his opponent* **25** (*intr*) to be as specified in extent, amount, etc: *the room measures six feet* **26** (*tr*) to travel or move over as if measuring ▹ See also **measure up** [C13 from OF, from L *mēnsūra*, from *mēnsus*, pp of *mētīrī* to measure]

measured ('mɛʒəd) *adj* **1** determined by measurement **2** slow or stately **3** carefully considered; deliberate > '**measuredly** *adv*

measureless ('mɛʒəlɪs) *adj* limitless, vast, or infinite > '**measurelessly** *adv*

measurement ('mɛʒəmənt) *n* **1** the act or process of measuring **2** an amount, extent, or size determined by measuring **3** a system of measures based on a particular standard

measures ('mɛʒəz) *pl n* rock strata that are characterized by a particular type of sediment or deposit: *coal measures*

measure up *vb* **1** (*adv*) to determine the size of (something) by measurement **2 measure up to** to fulfil (expectations, standards, etc)

measuring jug *n* a graduated jug used in cooking to measure ingredients

measuring worm *n* the larva of a geometrid moth: it moves in a series of loops. Also called: **inchworm**

meat (miːt) *n* **1** the flesh of mammals used as food **2** anything edible, esp flesh with the texture of meat: *crab meat* **3** food, as opposed to drink **4** the essence or gist **5** an archaic word for **meal**[1] (senses 1 and 2) **6 meat and drink** a source of pleasure [OE *mete*] > '**meatless** *adj*

▹ www.meatuk.com

▹ www.recipesource.com

meatball ('miːtˌbɔːl) *n* **1** minced beef, shaped into a ball before cooking **2** *US & Canad sl* a stupid or boring person

Meath (miːð, miːθ) *n* a county of E Republic of Ireland, in Leinster province on the Irish Sea: formerly a kingdom much larger than the present county; livestock farming. County town: Trim. Pop: 109 732 (1996). Area: 2338 sq km (903 sq miles)

meatspace ('miːtˌspeɪs) *n sl* the real physical world, as contrasted with the world of cyberspace

meatus (mɪ'eɪtəs) *n, pl* **meatuses** *or* **meatus** *anat* a natural opening or channel, such as the canal leading from the outer ear to the eardrum [C17 from L: passage, from *meāre* to pass]

meaty ('miːtɪ) *adj* **meatier, meatiest** **1** of, relating to, or full of meat **2** heavily built; fleshy or brawny **3** full of import or interest: *a meaty discussion* > '**meatily** *adv* > '**meatiness** *n*

mebi- ('mɛbɪ) *prefix computing* denoting 2^{20}: *mebibyte*. Symbol: Mi [C20 from ME(GA-) + BI(NARY)]

MEC (in South Africa) *abbrev for:* Member of the Executive Council

Mecca *or* **Mekka** ('mɛkə) *n* **1** a city in W Saudi Arabia, joint capital (with Riyadh) of Saudi Arabia: birthplace of Mohammed; the holiest city of Islam, containing the Kaaba. Pop: 965 697 (1992). Arabic name: **Makkah** **2** (*sometimes not capital*) a place that attracts many visitors: *Athens is a Mecca for tourists*

Meccano (mɪ'kɑːnəʊ) *n trademark* a construction set of miniature metal parts from which mechanical models can be made

mechanic (mɪ'kænɪk) *n* a person skilled in maintaining or operating machinery, motors, etc [C14 from L *mēchanicus*, from Gk, from *mēkhanē* MACHINE]

mechanical (mɪ'kænɪkᵊl) *adj* **1** made, performed, or operated by or as if by a machine or machinery **2** concerned with machines or machinery **3** relating to or controlled or operated by physical forces **4** of or concerned with mechanics **5** (of a gesture, etc)

Mm

automatic; lacking thought, feeling, etc **6** *philosophy* accounting for phenomena by physically determining forces > **me'chanicalism** *n* > **me'chanically** *adv* > **me'chanicalness** *n*

mechanical advantage *n* the ratio of the working force exerted by a mechanism to the applied effort

mechanical drawing *n* a drawing to scale of a machine, machine component, architectural plan, etc, from which dimensions can be taken

mechanical engineering *n* the branch of engineering concerned with the design, construction, and operation of machines

▹ www.memagazine.org

mechanical equivalent of heat *n physics* a factor for converting units of energy into heat units

mechanician (ˌmɛkəˈnɪʃən) *or* **mechanist** *n* a person skilled in making machinery and tools; technician

mechanics (mɪˈkænɪks) *n* **1** (*functioning as sing*) the branch of science, divided into statics, dynamics, and kinematics, concerned with the equilibrium or motion of bodies in a particular frame of reference **2** (*functioning as sing*) the science of designing, constructing, and operating machines **3** the working parts of a machine **4** the technical aspects of something

mechanism (ˈmɛkəˌnɪzəm) *n* **1** a system or structure of moving parts that performs some function, esp in a machine **2** something resembling a machine in the arrangement and working of its parts **3** any mechanical device or part of such a device **4** a process or technique: *the mechanism of novel writing* **5** *philosophy* the doctrine that human action can be explained in purely physical terms **6** *psychoanal* **6a** the ways in which psychological forces interact and operate **6b** a structure having an influence on the behaviour of a person, such as a defence mechanism

mechanistic (ˌmɛkəˈnɪstɪk) *adj* **1** *philosophy* of or relating to the theory of mechanism **2** *maths* of or relating to mechanics > **ˈmechanist** *n* > **ˌmechaˈnistically** *adv*

mechanize *or* **mechanise** (ˈmɛkəˌnaɪz) *vb* **mechanizes, mechanizing, mechanized** *or* **mechanises, mechanising, mechanised** (*tr*) **1** to equip (a factory, industry, etc) with machinery **2** to make mechanical, automatic, or monotonous **3** to equip (an army, etc) with motorized or armoured vehicles > **ˌmechaniˈzation** *or* **ˌmechaniˈsation** *n* > **ˈmechaˌnizer** *or* **ˈmechaˌniser** *n*

mechanoreceptor (ˌmɛkənəʊrɪˈsɛptə) *n physiol* a sensory receptor, as in the skin, that is sensitive to a mechanical stimulus, such as pressure

mechanotherapy (ˌmɛkənəʊˈθɛrəpɪ) *n* the treatment of disorders or injuries by means of mechanical devices, esp devices that provide exercise for bodily parts

Mechelen (ˈmɛxələn) *n* a city in N Belgium, in Antwerp province: capital of the Netherlands from 1507 to 1530; formerly famous for lace-making; now has an important vegetable market. Pop: 75 718 (1995 est). French name: **Malines** English name: **Mechlin**

Mechlin (ˈmɛklɪn) *n* the English name for **Mechelen**

Mechlin lace *n* bobbin lace made at Mechelin, characterized by patterns outlined by a heavier flat thread. Also called: **malines**

Mecklenburg (ˈmɛklənˌbɜːg; *German* ˈmeːklənbʊrk) *n* a historic region and former state of NE Germany, along the Baltic coast; now part of Mecklenburg-West Pomerania: formerly (1949–90) in East Germany

Mecklenburg-West Pomerania (ˌpɒməˈreɪnɪə) *n* a state of NE Germany, along the Baltic coast: consists of the former state of Mecklenburg and those parts of W Pomerania not incorporated into Poland after World War II: part of East Germany until 1990. Pop: 1 789 300 (2000 est)

meconium (mɪˈkəʊnɪəm) *n* the mucoid material that forms the first faeces of a newborn infant [C17 from NL, from L: poppy juice, from Gk, from *mēkōn* poppy]

meconopsis (ˌmiːkənˈɒpsɪs) *n* any of various mainly Asiatic poppies [C19 from Gk *mēkōn* poppy + -OPSIS]

Med (mɛd) *n inf* the Mediterranean region

MEd *abbrev for* Master of Education

med. *abbrev for*: **1** medical **2** medicine **3** medium

médaillons *French* (mɛdaɪˈjɔ̃) *pl n cookery* small round pieces of meat, fish, vegetables, etc. Also called: **medallions**

medal (ˈmɛdᵊl) *n* a small flat piece of metal bearing an inscription or image, given as an award or commemoration of some outstanding event, etc [C16 from F *médaille*, prob. from It. *medaglia*, ult. from L *metallum* METAL]

▹ www.medals.org.uk

▹ www.omsa.org

medallion (mɪˈdæljən) *n* **1** a large medal **2** an oval or circular decorative device resembling a medal, usually bearing a portrait or relief moulding, used in architecture and textile design [C17 from F, from It., from *medaglia* MEDAL]

medallist *or US* **medalist** (ˈmɛdᵊlɪst) *n* **1** a designer, maker, or collector of medals **2** *chiefly sport* a recipient of a medal or medals

medal play *n golf* another name for **stroke play**

Medan (ˈmɛdɑːn) *n* a city in Indonesia, in NE Sumatra: seat of the University of North Sumatra (1952) and the Indonesian Islam University (1952). Pop: 1 909 700 (1995 est)

Medawar (ˈmɛdəwə) *n* Sir **Peter Brian** 1915–87, English zoologist, who shared the Nobel prize for physiology or medicine (1960) with Sir Macfarlane Burnet for work on immunology

meddle (ˈmɛdᵊl) *vb* **meddles, meddling, meddled** (*intr*) **1** (usually foll by *with*) to interfere officiously or annoyingly **2** (usually foll by *in*) to involve oneself unwarrantedly [C14 from OF *medler*, ult. from L *miscēre* to mix] > **ˈmeddler** *n* > **ˈmeddling** *adj*

meddlesome (ˈmɛdᵊlsəm) *adj* intrusive or meddling > **ˈmeddlesomely** *adv* > **ˈmeddlesomeness** *n*

Mede (miːd) *n* a member of an Indo-European people who established an empire in SW Asia in the 7th and 6th centuries BC > **ˈMedian** *n, adj*

Medea (mɪˈdɪə) *n Greek myth* a princess of Colchis, who assisted Jason in obtaining the Golden Fleece from her father

Medellín (*Spanish* meðeˈʎin) *n* a city in W Colombia, at an altitude of 1554 m (5100 ft): the second largest city in the country, with three universities; important coffee centre, with large textile mills; dominated by drug cartels in recent years. Pop: 1 861 265 (1999 est)

media (ˈmiːdɪə) *n* **1** a plural of **medium** **2a** the means of communication that reach large numbers of people, such as television, newspapers, and radio **2b** (*as modifier*): *media hype.*

> USAGE When *media* refers to the mass media, it is sometimes treated as a singular, as in: *the media has shown great interest in these events.* Many people think this use is incorrect and that *media* should always be treated as a plural form: *the media have shown great interest in these events*

Media (ˈmiːdɪə) *n* an ancient country of SW Asia, south of the Caspian Sea: inhabited by the Medes; overthrew the Assyrian Empire in 612 BC in alliance with Babylonia; conquered by Cyrus the Great in 550 BC; corresponds to present-day NW Iran

mediaeval (ˌmɛdɪˈiːvᵊl) *adj* a variant spelling of **medieval**

media event *n* an event that is staged for or exploited by the mass media

medial (ˈmiːdɪəl) *adj* **1** of or situated in the middle **2** ordinary or average in size **3** *maths* relating to an average 4 another word for **median** (senses 1, 2) [C16 from LL *mediālis*, from *medius* middle] > '**medially** *adv*

median ('miːdɪən) *adj* 1 of, relating to, situated in, or directed towards the middle 2 *statistics* of or relating to the median ▷ *n* 3 a middle point, plane, or part 4 *geom* 4a a straight line joining one vertex of a triangle to the midpoint of the opposite side 4b a straight line joining the midpoints of the nonparallel sides of a trapezium 5 *statistics* the middle value in a frequency distribution, below and above which lie values with equal total frequencies 6 *statistics* the middle number or average of the two middle numbers in an ordered sequence of numbers [C16 from L *mediānus*, from *medius* middle] > '**medianly** *adv*

median lethal dose *or* **mean lethal dose** *n* 1 the amount of a drug or other substance that, when administered to a group of experimental animals, will kill 50 per cent of the group in a specified time 2 the amount of ionizing radiation that will kill 50 per cent of a population in a specified time ▷ Abbrev: LD_{50}

mediant ('miːdɪənt) *n music* a the third degree of a major or minor scale b (*as modifier*): *a mediant chord* [C18 from It. *mediante*, from LL *mediāre* to be in the middle]

mediastinum (ˌmiːdɪə'staɪnəm) *n, pl* **mediastina** (-nə) *Anat* 1 a membrane between two parts of an organ or cavity such as the pleural tissue between the two lungs 2 the part of the thoracic cavity that lies between the lungs, containing the heart, trachea, etc [C16 from Medical L, neuter of Med. L *mediastīnus* median, from L: low grade of servant, from *medius* mean] > ˌ**medias'tinal** *adj*

mediate *vb* ('miːdɪˌeɪt), **mediates, mediating, mediated** 1 (*intr; usually foll by between or in*) to intervene (between parties or in a dispute) in order to bring about agreement 2 to bring about (an agreement) between parties in a dispute 3 to resolve (differences) by mediation 4 (*intr*) to be in an intermediate position 5 (*tr*) to serve as a medium for causing (a result) or transferring (objects, information, etc) ▷ *adj* ('miːdɪɪt) 6 occurring as a result of or dependent upon mediation [C16 from LL *mediāre* to be in the middle] > '**mediately** *adv* > '**mediˌator** *n*

mediation (ˌmiːdɪ'eɪʃən) *n* the act of mediating; intercession between people, states, etc in an attempt to reconcile disputed matters

Medibank ('mɛdɪbæŋk) *n* (in Australia), a government-run health insurance scheme

medic[1] ('mɛdɪk) *n inf* a doctor, medical orderly, or medical student [C17 from MEDICAL]

medic[2] ('mɛdɪk) *n* the usual US spelling of **medick**

medicable ('mɛdɪkəbᵊl) *adj* potentially able to be treated or cured medically

medical ('mɛdɪkᵊl) *adj* 1 of or relating to the science of medicine or to the treatment of patients by drugs, etc, as opposed to surgery ▷ *n* 2 *inf* a medical examination [C17 from Med. L *medicālis*, from L *medicus* physician, surgeon, from *medērī* to heal] > '**medically** *adv*

medical certificate *n* 1 a document stating the result of a satisfactory medical examination 2 a doctor's certificate giving evidence of a person's unfitness for work

medical jurisprudence *n* another name for **forensic medicine**

medicament (mɪ'dɪkəmənt, 'mɛdɪ-) *n* a medicine or remedy in a specified formulation [C16 via F from L *medicāmentum*, from *medicāre* to cure]

medicate ('mɛdɪˌkeɪt) *vb* **medicates, medicating, medicated** (*tr*) 1 to cover or impregnate (a wound, etc) with an ointment, etc 2 to treat (a patient) with a medicine 3 to add a medication to (a bandage, shampoo, etc) [C17 from L *medicāre* to heal] > '**medicative** *adj*

medication (ˌmɛdɪ'keɪʃən) *n* 1 treatment with drugs or remedies 2 a drug or remedy

Medici ('mɛdɪtʃɪ, mə'diːtʃɪ; *Italian* 'mɛːditʃi) *n* 1 an Italian family of bankers, merchants, and rulers of Florence and Tuscany, prominent in Italian political and cultural history in the 15th, 16th, and 17th centuries, including 2 **Catherine de'** (ka'triːn de) See **Catherine de' Medici** 3 **Cosimo I** ('kɔːzimo), known as *Cosimo the Great*. 1519–74, duke of Florence and first grand duke of Tuscany (1569–74) 4 **Cosimo de'**, known as *Cosimo the Elder*. 1389–1464, Italian banker, statesman, and patron of arts, who established the political power of the family in Florence (1434) 5 **Giovanni de'**, (dʒo'vanni de) See **Leo X** 6 **Giulio de'** ('dʒuːljo de) See **Clement VII** 7 **Lorenzo de'** (lo'rɛntso de), known as *Lorenzo the Magnificent*. 1449–92, Italian statesman, poet, and scholar; ruler of Florence (1469–92) and first patron of Michelangelo 8 **Maria de'** (ma'riːa de) See **Maria de' Medici** ▷ French name **Médicis** (medisis)

medicinal (mɛ'dɪsɪnᵊl) *adj* 1 relating to or having therapeutic properties ▷ *n* 2 a medicinal substance > **me'dicinally** *adv*

medicine ('mɛdɪsɪn, 'mɛdsɪn) *n* 1 any drug or remedy for use in treating, preventing, or alleviating the symptoms of disease 2 the science of preventing, diagnosing, alleviating, or curing disease 3 any nonsurgical branch of medical science 4 the practice or profession of medicine 5 something regarded by primitive people as having magical or remedial properties 6 **a taste** (*or* **dose**) **of one's own medicine** an unpleasant experience in retaliation for a similar unkind or aggressive act 7 **take one's medicine** to accept a deserved punishment [C13 via OF from L *medicīna* (*ars*) (art) of healing, from *medicus* doctor, from *medērī* to heal]

▷ www.medhelp.org
▷ www.medbioworld.com/home/lists/med-db.html
▷ www.ipl.org/div/subject/browse/hea00.00.00/

medicine ball *n* a heavy ball used for physical training

medicine man *n* (among certain peoples, esp North American Indians) a person believed to have supernatural powers of healing; a magician or sorcerer

medick *or US* **medic** ('mɛdɪk) *n* any of various small plants having yellow or purple flowers and trifoliate leaves [C15 from L *mēdica*, from Gk *mēdikē* (*poa*) Median (grass), a type of clover]

medico ('mɛdɪˌkəʊ) *n, pl* **medicos** *inf* a doctor or medical student [C17 via It. from L *medicus*]

medieval *or* **mediaeval** (ˌmɛdɪ'iːvᵊl) *adj* 1 of, relating to, or in the style of the Middle Ages 2 *inf* old-fashioned; primitive [C19 from NL *medium aevum* the middle age]

Medieval Greek *n* the Greek language from the 7th century AD to shortly after the sacking of Constantinople in 1204. Also called: **Middle Greek, Byzantine Greek**

medievalism *or* **mediaevalism** (ˌmɛdɪ'iːvəˌlɪzəm) *n* 1 the beliefs, life, or style of the Middle Ages or devotion to those 2 a belief, custom, or point of style copied or surviving from the Middle Ages

medievalist *or* **mediaevalist** (ˌmɛdɪ'iːvəlɪst) *n* a student or devotee of the Middle Ages

Medieval Latin *n* the Latin language as used throughout Europe in the Middle Ages

Medina (mɛ'diːnə) *n* a city in W Saudi Arabia: the second most holy city of Islam (after Mecca), with the tomb of Mohammed; university (1960). Pop: 608 295 (1992). Arabic name: **Al Madinah** Ancient Arabic name: **Yathrib**

mediocre (ˌmiːdɪ'əʊkə) *adj often derog* average or ordinary in quality [C16 via F from L *mediocris* moderate, lit.: halfway up the mountain, from *medius* middle + *ocris* stony mountain]

mediocrity (ˌmiːdɪ'ɒkrɪtɪ, ˌmɛd-) *n, pl* **mediocrities** 1 the state or quality of being mediocre 2 a mediocre person or thing

meditate ('mɛdɪˌteɪt) *vb* **meditates, meditating**

Mm

meditated 1 (*intr;* foll by *on* or *upon*) to think about something deeply 2 (*intr*) to reflect deeply on spiritual matters, esp as a religious act 3 (*tr*) to plan, consider, or think of doing (something) [c16 from L *meditārī* to reflect upon] > **'meditative** *adj* > **'meditatively** *adv* > **'medi,tator** *n*

meditation (,mɛdɪ'teɪʃən) *n* 1 the act of meditating; reflection 2 contemplation of spiritual matters, esp as a religious practice

Mediterranean (,mɛdɪtə'reɪnɪən) *n* 1 short for the **Mediterranean Sea** 2 a native or inhabitant of a Mediterranean country. *adj* 3 of, relating to, situated or dwelling on or near the Mediterranean Sea 4 denoting a postulated subdivision of the Caucasoid race, characterized by slender build and dark complexion 5 *meteorol* (of a climate) characterized by hot summers and relatively warm winters when most of the annual rainfall occurs 6 (*often not cap*) *obs* situated in the middle of a landmass; inland [c16 from Latin *mediterrāneus*, from *medius* middle + *-terrāneus*, from *terra* land, earth]

Mediterranean Sea *n* a large inland sea between S Europe, N Africa, and SW Asia: linked with the Atlantic by the Strait of Gibraltar, with the Red Sea by the Suez Canal, and with the Black Sea by the Dardanelles, Sea of Marmara, and Bosporus; many ancient civilizations developed around its shores. Greatest depth: 4770 m (15 900 ft). Length: (west to east) over 3700 km (2300 miles). Greatest width: about 1368 km (850 miles). Area: (excluding the Black Sea) 2 512 300 sq km (970 000 sq miles). Ancient name: **Mare Internum**

medium ('mi:dɪəm) *adj* 1 midway between extremes; average ▷ *n, pl* **media** *or* **mediums** 2 an intermediate or middle state, degree, or condition; mean: *the happy medium* 3 an intervening substance or agency for transmitting or producing an effect; vehicle 4 a means or agency for communicating or diffusing information, news, etc, to the public 5 a person supposedly used as a spiritual intermediary between the dead and the living 6 the substance in which specimens of animals and plants are preserved or displayed 7 *biol* Also called: **culture medium** a nutritive substance in which cultures of bacteria or fungi are grown 8 the substance or surroundings in which an organism naturally lives or grows 9 *art* 9a the category of a work of art, as determined by its materials and methods of production 9b the materials used in a work of art 10 any solvent in which pigments are mixed and thinned [c16 from L: neuter sing of *medius* middle]

USAGE See at **media**

medium-dated *adj* (of a gilt-edged security) having between five and fifteen years to run before redemption ▷ Cf **long-dated, short-dated**

medium frequency *n* a radio-frequency band or radio frequency lying between 3000 and 300 kilohertz. Abbrev: **MF**

medium wave *n* **a** a radio wave with a wavelength between 100 and 1000 metres **b** (*as modifier*): *a medium-wave broadcast*

medlar ('mɛdlə) *n* 1 a small Eurasian tree 2 its fruit, which resembles the crab apple and is not edible until it has begun to decay [c14 from OF *medlier*, from L *mespilum* medlar fruit, from Gk *mespilon*]

medley ('mɛdlɪ) *n* 1 a mixture of various types or elements 2 a musical composition consisting of various tunes arranged as a continuous whole 3a *swimming* a race in which a different stroke is used for each length: *an individual medley* 3b *athletics* a relay race in which each leg has a different distance 3c (*as modifier*): *a medley relay* [c14 from OF *medlee*, from *medler* to mix, quarrel]

Médoc (meɪ'dɒk, 'mɛdɒk; *French* medɔk) *n* 1 a district of SW France, on the left bank of the Gironde estuary: famous vineyards 2 a fine red wine from this district

medulla (mɪ'dʌlə) *n, pl* **medullas** *or* **medullae** (-li:) 1 *anat* 1a the innermost part of an organ or structure 1b short for **medulla oblongata** 2 *bot* another name for **pith** (sense 4) [c17 from L: marrow, prob. from *medius* middle] > **me'dullary** *or* **me'dullar** *adj*

medulla oblongata (,ɒblɒŋ'gɑ:tə) *n, pl* **medulla oblongatas** *or* **medullae oblongatae** (mɪ'dʌli: ,ɒblɒŋ'gɑ:ti:) the lower stalklike section of the brain, continuous with the spinal cord, containing control centres for the heart and lungs [c17 NL: oblong-shaped medulla]

medusa (mɪ'dju:zə) *n, pl* **medusas** *or* **medusae** (-zi:) another name for **jellyfish** (sense 1) [c18 from the likeness of its tentacles to the snaky locks of MEDUSA] > **me'dusoid** *adj, n*

Medusa (mɪ'dju:zə) *n Greek myth* a mortal woman who was transformed by Athena into one of the three Gorgons. She became so hideous that those who looked at her were turned to stone. Perseus eventually slew her. See also **Pegasus** > **Me'dusan** *adj*

Medway ('mɛd,weɪ) *n* 1 a river in SE England, flowing through Kent and the **Medway towns** (Rochester, Chatham, and Gillingham) to the Thames estuary. Length: 110 km (70 miles) 2 a unitary authority in SE England, in Kent. Pop: 249 502 (2001). Area: 204 sq km (79 sq miles)

meed (mi:d) *n arch* a recompense; reward [OE: wages]

meek (mi:k) *adj* 1 patient, long-suffering, or submissive; humble 2 spineless or spiritless; compliant [c12 rel. to ON *mjūkr* amenable] > **'meekly** *adv* > **'meekness** *n*

meerkat ('mɪə,kæt) *n* any of several South African mongooses, esp the slender-tailed meerkat or suricate, which has a lemur-like face and four-toed feet [c19 from Du.: sea-cat]

meerschaum ('mɪəʃəm) *n* 1 a white, yellowish, or pink compact earthy mineral consisting of hydrated magnesium silicate: used to make tobacco pipes and as a building stone 2 a tobacco pipe having a bowl made of this mineral [c18 from G *Meerschaum* lit.: sea foam]

Meerut ('mɪərət) *n* an industrial city in N India, in W Uttar Pradesh: founded as a military base by the British in 1806 and scene of the first uprising (1857) of the Indian Mutiny. Pop: 753 778 (1991)

meet[1] (mi:t) *vb* **meets, meeting, met** 1 (sometimes foll by *up* or (US) *with*) to come together (with), either by design or by accident; encounter 2 to come into or be in conjunction or contact with (something or each other) 3 (*tr*) to come to or be at the place of arrival of: *to meet a train* 4 to make the acquaintance of or be introduced to (someone or each other) 5 to gather in the company of (someone or each other) 6 to come into the presence of (someone or each other) as opponents 7 (*tr*) to cope with effectively; satisfy: *to meet someone's demands* 8 (*tr*) to be apparent to (esp in **meet the eye**) 9 (*tr*) to return or counter: *to meet a blow with another* 10 to agree with (someone or each other): *we met him on the price he suggested* 11 (*tr;* sometimes foll by *with*) to experience; suffer: *he met his death in a road accident* 12 (*intr*) to occur together: *courage and kindliness met in him* ▷ *n* 13 **meet and greet** (of a celebrity, politician, etc) to have a session of being introduced to and questioned by members of the public or journalists 14 the assembly of hounds, huntsmen, etc, prior to a hunt 15 a meeting, esp a sports meeting [OE *mētan*] > **'meeter** *n*

meet[2] (mi:t) *adj arch* proper, fitting, or correct [c13 from var. of OE *gemǣte*] > **'meetly** *adv*

meeting ('mi:tɪŋ) *n* 1 an act of coming together; encounter 2 an assembly or gathering 3 a conjunction or union 4 a sporting competition, as of athletes, or of horse racing

meeting house *n* the place in which certain religious groups, esp Quakers, hold their meetings for worship

mefloquine ('mɛfləʊ,kwi:n) *n* a synthetic drug

administered orally to prevent or treat malaria [c20]
mega ('mɛgə) *adj sl* extremely good, great, or successful [c20 prob. independent use of MEGA-]
mega- *prefix* **1** denoting 10^6: *megawatt* **2** Also: **mebi-** *computing* denoting 2^{20} (1 048 576): *megabyte* **3** large or great: *megalith* ▷ Symbol (for senses 1, 2): M [from Gk *megas* huge, powerful]

USAGE See at **kilo-**

megabit ('mɛgə,bɪt) *n computing* **1** one million bits **2** 2^{20} bits
megabuck ('mɛgə,bʌk) *n US & Canad sl* a million dollars
megacephaly (,mɛgə'sɛfəlɪ) *or* **megalocephaly** *n* the condition of having an unusually large head or cranial capacity > **megacephalic** (,mɛgəsɪ'fælɪk), **,mega'cephalous, ,megaloce'phalic,** *or* **,megalo'cephalous** *adj*
megacity ('mɛgə,sɪtɪ) *n, pl* **megacities** a city with over 10 million inhabitants
megacycle ('mɛgə,saɪkᵊl) *n* a former unit of frequency equal to one million cycles per second; megahertz
megadeath ('mɛgə,dɛθ) *n* the death of a million people, esp in a nuclear war or attack
Megaera (mɪ'dʒɪərə) *n Greek myth* one of the three Furies; the others are Alecto and Tisiphone
megafauna ('mɛgə,fɔːnə) *n* the component of the fauna of a region or period that comprises the larger terrestrial animals
megaflop ('mɛgə,flɒp) *n computing* a measure of processing speed, consisting of a million floating-point operations a second [c20 from MEGA- + *flo(ating) p(oint)*]
megahertz ('mɛgə,hɜːts) *n, pl* **megahertz** one million hertz. Former name: **megacycle**
megalith ('mɛgəlɪθ) *n* a stone of great size, esp one forming part of a prehistoric monument > **,mega'lithic** *adj*
megalo- *or before a vowel* **megal-** *combining form* indicating greatness or abnormal size: *megalopolis* [from Gk *megas* great]
megalomania (,mɛgələʊ'meɪnɪə) *n* **1** a mental illness characterized by delusions of grandeur, power, wealth, etc **2** *inf* a lust or craving for power > **,megalo'maniac** *adj, n* > **megalomaniacal** (,mɛgələʊmə'naɪəkᵊl) *adj*
megalopolis (,mɛgə'lɒpəlɪs) *n* an urban complex, usually comprising several large towns [c20 MEGALO- + Gk *polis* city] > **megalopolitan** (,mɛgələ'pɒlɪtᵊn) *adj, n*
megalosaur ('mɛgələʊ,sɔː) *n* any very large Jurassic or Cretaceous bipedal carnivorous dinosaur [c19 from NL *megalosaurus*, from MEGALO- + Gk *sauros* lizard]
megaphone ('mɛgə,fəʊn) *n* a funnel-shaped instrument used to amplify the voice. See also **loud-hailer** > **megaphonic** (,mɛgə'fɒnɪk) *adj*
megapixel ('mɛgə,pɪksᵊl) *n computing* one million pixels: a term used to describe the degree of resolution supplied by digital cameras, scanners, etc
megapode ('mɛgə,pəʊd) *n* any of various ground-living gallinaceous birds of Australia, New Guinea, and adjacent islands. Their eggs incubate in mounds of sand, rotting vegetation, etc, by natural heat
Megara ('mɛgərə) *n* a town in E central Greece: an ancient trading city, founding many colonies in the 7th and 8th centuries BC. Pop: 26 562 (1991 est)
megathere ('mɛgə,θɪə) *n* any of various gigantic extinct American sloths, common in late Cenozoic times [c19 from NL *megathērium*, from MEGA- + *-there*, from Gk *thērion* wild beast]
megaton ('mɛgə,tʌn) *n* **1** one million tons **2** an explosive power, esp of a nuclear weapon, equal to the power of one million tons of TNT
Me generation *n* **the** the generation, originally in the 1970s, characterized by self-absorption; in the 1980s, characterized by material greed
Megger ('mɛgə) *n trademark* an instrument that generates a high voltage in order to measure the electrical resistance of insulation, etc
Meghalaya (,meɪgə'leɪə) *n* a state of NE India, created in 1969 from part of Assam. Capital: Shillong. Pop: 2 306 069 (2001). Area: 22 429 sq km (7800 sq miles)
Megiddo (mə'gɪdəʊ) *n* an ancient town in N Palestine, strategically located on a route linking Egypt to Mesopotamia: site of many battles, including an important Egyptian victory over rebel chieftains in 1469 or 1468 BC. See also **Armageddon**
megilp *or* **magilp** (mə'gɪlp) *n* an oil-painting medium of linseed oil mixed with mastic varnish or turpentine [c18 from ?]
megohm ('mɛg,əʊm) *n* one million ohms
megrim ('miːgrɪm) *n arch* **1** a caprice **2** a migraine **3** (*pl*) *Rare.* a fit of depression **4** (*pl*) a disease of horses and cattle; staggers [c14 see MIGRAINE]
Mehemet Ali (mɪ'hɛmɪt 'ɑːlɪ) *or* **Mohammed Ali** *n* 1769–1849, Albanian commander in the service of Turkey. He was made viceroy of Egypt (1805) and its hereditary ruler (1841), founding a dynasty that ruled until 1952
mehndi ('mendiː) *n* (esp in India) the practice of painting designs on the hands, feet, etc using henna [c20 from Hindi]
Mehta ('meɪtə) *n* **Zubin** ('zuːbɪn) born 1936, Indian conductor; musical director of the Israel Philharmonic orchestra from 1969
meibomian gland (maɪ'bəʊmɪən) *n* any of the small sebaceous glands in the eyelid, beneath the conjunctiva [c19 after H. *Meibom* (1638–1700), G anatomist]
meiosis (maɪ'əʊsɪs) *n, pl* **meioses** (-,siːz) **1** a type of cell division in which a nucleus divides into four daughter nuclei, each containing half the chromosome number of the parent nucleus **2** *rhetoric* another word for **litotes** [c16 via NL from Gk, from *meioun* to diminish, from *meiōn* less] > **meiotic** (maɪ'ɒtɪk) *adj* > **mei'otically** *adv*
Meir (meɪ'ɪə) *n* **Golda** ('gəʊldə) 1898–1978, Israeli stateswoman, born in Russia; prime minister (1969–74)
Meissen (*German* 'maisən) *n* a town in E Germany, in Saxony, in Dresden district on the River Elbe: famous for its porcelain (Dresden china), first made here in 1710. Pop: 38 100 (latest est)
-meister ('maɪstə) *n combining form* a person who excels at a particular activity: *spinmeister*; *horror-meister* [c20 from G *Meister* master]
Meistersinger ('maɪstə,sɪŋə) *n, pl* **Meistersinger** *or* **Meistersingers** a member of one of the German guilds organized to compose and perform poetry and music, esp in the 15th and 16th centuries [c19 from G *Meistersinger* master singer]
Meitner (*German* 'maitnər) *n* **Lise** ('liːzə) 1878–1968, Austrian nuclear physicist. With Hahn, she discovered protactinium (1918), and they demonstrated with F. Strassmann the fission of uranium
meitnerium (,maɪt'nɛərɪəm) *n* a synthetic element produced in small quantities by high-energy ion bombardment. Symbol: Mt; atomic no.: 109 [c20 from Lise MEITNER]
Méjico ('mɛxiko) *n* the Spanish name for **Mexico**
Mekka ('mɛkə) *n* a variant spelling of **Mecca**
Meknès (mɛk'nɛs) *n* a city in N central Morocco, in the Middle Atlas Mountains: noted for the making of carpets. Pop: 188 224 (1994)
Mekong (,miː'kɒŋ) *n* a river in SE Asia, rising in SW China in Qinghai province: flows southeast forming the border between Laos and Myanmar, and part of the border between Laos and Thailand, then continues south across Cambodia and Vietnam to the South China Sea by an extensive delta, one of the greatest rice-growing areas in Asia. Length: about 4025 km (2500 miles)
melaleuca (,mɛlə'luːkə) *n* any shrub or tree of the

mostly Australian genus *Melaleuca*, found in sandy or swampy regions [c19 NL from Gk *melas* black + *leukos* white, from its black trunk and white branches]

melamine ('mɛləˌmiːn) *n* **1** a colourless crystalline compound used in making synthetic resins. Formula: $C_3N_6H_6$ **2** a resin produced from melamine (**melamine resin**) or a material made from this resin [c19 from G *Melamin*, from *Melam* distillate of ammonium thiocyanate, with *-am* representing *ammonia*]

melancholia (ˌmɛlənˈkəʊlɪə) *n* a former name for **depression** (sense 3) > ˌ**melanˈcholiˌac** *adj, n*

melancholy ('mɛlənkəlɪ) *n, pl* **melancholies** **1** a tendency to gloominess or depression **2** a sad thoughtful state of mind **3** *arch* **3a** a gloomy character **3b** one of the four bodily humours; black bile ▷ *adj* **4** characterized by, causing, or expressing sadness, dejection, etc [c14 via OF from LL *melancholia*, from Gk, from *melas* black + *kholē* bile] > '**melanˌcholic** *adj, n*

Melanchthon (məˈlæŋkθən; *German* meˈlançtɔn) *n* **Philipp** ('fiːlɪp) original surname *Schwarzerd*. 1497–1560, German Protestant reformer. His *Loci Communes* (1521) was the first systematic presentation of Protestant theology and in the Augsburg Confession (1530) he stated the faith of the Lutheran churches. He also reformed the German educational system

Melanesia (ˌmɛləˈniːzɪə) *n* one of the three divisions of islands in the Pacific (the others being Micronesia and Polynesia); the SW division of Oceania: includes Fiji, New Caledonia, Vanuatu, the Bismarck Archipelago, and the Louisiade, Solomon, Santa Cruz, and Loyalty Islands, which all lie northeast of Australia [c19 from Greek *melas* black + *nēsos* island; with reference to the dark skins of the inhabitants; on the model of *Polynesia*]

Melanesian (ˌmɛləˈniːʒən, -ʒɪən) *adj* **1** of or relating to Melanesia, its people, or their languages ▷ *n* **2** a native or inhabitant of Melanesia: generally Negroid with frizzy hair and small stature **3** a group or branch of languages spoken in Melanesia

melange *or* **mélange** (meɪˈlɑːnʒ) *n* a mixture; confusion [c17 from F *mêler* to mix]

melanin ('mɛlənɪn) *n* any of a group of black or dark brown pigments present in the hair, skin, and eyes of man and animals: produced in excess in certain skin diseases and in melanomas

melanism ('mɛləˌnɪzəm) *n* **1** the condition in man and animals of having dark-coloured or black skin, feathers, etc **2** another name for **melanosis** > ˌ**melaˈnistic** *adj*

melano- *or before a vowel* **melan-** *combining form* black or dark: *melanin; melanism; melanoma* [from Gk *melas* black]

melanoma (ˌmɛləˈnəʊmə) *n, pl* **melanomas** *or* **melanomata** (-mətə) *pathol* a malignant tumour composed of melanin-containing cells, occurring esp in the skin, often as a result of excessive exposure to sunlight

melanosis (ˌmɛləˈnəʊsɪs) *or* **melanism** ('mɛləˌnɪzəm) *n pathol* a skin condition characterized by excessive deposits of melanin > **melanotic** (ˌmɛləˈnɒtɪk) *adj*

Melba ('mɛlbə) *n* **1** Dame **Nellie**, stage name of *Helen Porter Mitchell*. 1861–1931, Australian operatic soprano **2** **do a Melba** *Austral sl* to make repeated farewell appearances

Melba toast *n* very thin crisp toast [c20 after Dame Nellie MELBA]

Melbourne[1] ('mɛlbən) *n* a port in SE Australia, capital of Victoria, on Port Phillip Bay: the second largest city in the country; settled in 1835 and developed rapidly with the discovery of rich goldfields in 1851; three universities. Pop: 2 865 329 (1998 est) > **Melburnian** (mɛlˈbɜːnɪən) *n, adj*

Melbourne[2] ('mɛlbən) *n* **William Lamb**, 2nd Viscount. 1779–1848; Whig prime minister (1834; 1835–41) He was the chief political adviser to the young Queen Victoria

Melbourne Cup *n* an annual horse race, the most famous in Australia, run in Melbourne, since 1861

Melchior ('mɛlkɪˌɔː) *n* **1** (in Christian tradition) one of the Magi, the others being Balthazar and Caspar **2** **Lauritz** ('laʊrɪts) 1890–1973, US operatic tenor, born in Denmark

Melchizedek (mɛlˈkɪzəˌdɛk) *n Old Testament* the priest-king of Salem who blessed Abraham (Genesis 14:18-19) and was taken as a prototype of Christ's priesthood (Hebrews 7). Douay spelling: **Melchisedech**

meld[1] (mɛld) *vb* to blend or become blended; combine [c20 blend of MELT + WELD[1]]

meld[2] (mɛld) *vb* **1** (in some card games) to declare or lay down (cards), which then score points ▷ *n* **2** the act of melding **3** a set of cards for melding [c19 from G *melden* to announce]

Meleager (ˌmɛlɪˈeɪgə) *n Greek myth* one of the Argonauts, slayer of the Calydonian boar

melee *or* **mêlée** ('mɛleɪ) *n* a noisy riotous fight or brawl [c17 from F *mêlée*, from *mêler* to mix]

Méliès (*French* meljɛs) *n* **Georges** (ʒɔrʒ) 1861–1938, French pioneer film director

Melilla (*French* melija) *n* the chief town of a Spanish enclave in Morocco, on the Mediterranean coast: founded by the Phoenicians; exports iron ore. Pop: 59 576 (1996 est)

meliorate ('miːlɪəˌreɪt) *vb* **meliorates, meliorating, meliorated** a variant of **ameliorate** > ˌ**melioˈration** *n* > **meliorative** ('miːlɪərətɪv) *adj, n*

melisma (mɪˈlɪzmə) *n, pl* **melismata** (-mətə) *or* **melismas** *music* an expressive vocal phrase or passage consisting of several notes sung to one syllable [c19 from Gk: melody]

Melitopol (*Russian* mɪliˈtɔpəlj) *n* a city in the SE Ukraine. Pop: 171 000 (1998 est)

Melk (mɛlk) *n* a town in N Austria, on the River Danube: noted for its baroque Benedictine abbey. Pop: 5163 (1991)

melliferous (mɪˈlɪfərəs) *or* **mellific** (mɪˈlɪfɪk) *adj* forming or producing honey [c17 from L *mellifer*, from *mel* honey + *ferre* to bear]

mellifluous (mɪˈlɪflʊəs) *or* **mellifluent** *adj* (of sounds or utterances) smooth or honeyed; sweet [c15 from LL *mellifluus*, from L *mel* honey + *fluere* to flow] > **melˈlifluously** *adv* > **melˈlifluousness** *or* **melˈlifluence** *n*

mellow ('mɛləʊ) *adj* **1** (esp of fruits) full-flavoured; sweet; ripe **2** (esp of wines) well-matured **3** (esp of colours or sounds) soft or rich **4** kind-hearted, esp through maturity or old age **5** genial, as through the effects of alcohol **6** (of soil) soft and loamy ▷ *vb* **7** to make or become mellow **8** (foll by *out*) to become calm and relaxed or (esp of a drug) to have a calming and relaxing effect on (someone) [c15 ?from OE *meru* soft (as through ripeness)] > '**mellowness** *n*

melodeon *or* **melodion** (mɪˈləʊdɪən) *n music* **1** a type of small accordion **2** a type of keyboard instrument similar to the harmonium [c19 from G, from *Melodie* melody]

melodic (mɪˈlɒdɪk) *adj* **1** of or relating to melody **2** of or relating to a part in a piece of music **3** melodious > **meˈlodically** *adv*

melodic minor scale *n music* a minor scale modified from the natural by the sharpening of the sixth and seventh when taken in ascending order and the restoration of their original pitches when taken in descending order

melodious (mɪˈləʊdɪəs) *adj* **1** having a tune that is pleasant to the ear **2** of or relating to melody; melodic > **meˈlodiously** *adv* > **meˈlodiousness** *n*

melodist ('mɛlədɪst) *n* **1** a composer of melodies **2** a singer

melodize *or* **melodise** ('mɛləˌdaɪz) *vb* **melodizes, melodizing, melodized** *or* **melodises, melodising, melodised** **1** (*tr*) to provide with a melody **2** (*tr*) to make melodious **3** (*intr*) to sing or play melodies > '**meloˌdizer** *or* '**meloˌdiser** *n*

melodrama ('mɛlə,drɑ:mə) *n* **1** a play, film, etc, characterized by extravagant action and emotion **2** (formerly) a romantic drama characterized by sensational incident, music, and song **3** overdramatic emotion or behaviour [c19 from F *mélodrame*, from Gk *melos* song + *drame* DRAMA] > **melodramatist** (,mɛlə'dræmətɪst) *n* > **melodramatic** (,mɛlədrə'mætɪk) *adj* > ,**melodra'matics** *pl n* > ,**melodra'matically** *adv*

melody ('mɛlədɪ) *n, pl* **melodies** **1** *music* **1a** a succession of notes forming a distinctive sequence; tune **1b** the horizontally represented aspect of the structure of a piece of music ▷ Cf **harmony** (sense 4b) **2** sounds that are pleasant because of tone or arrangement, esp words of poetry [c13 from OF, from LL *melōdia*, from Gk *melōidia*, from *melos* song + *aoidein* to sing]

melon ('mɛlən) *n* **1** any of several varieties of trailing plants (see **muskmelon, watermelon**), cultivated for their edible fruit **2** the fruit of any of these plants, which has a hard rind and juicy flesh [c14 via OF from LL *mēlo*, form of *mēlopepō*, from Gk, from *mēlon* apple + *pepōn* gourd]

Melos ('mi:lɒs) *n* an island in the SW Aegean Sea, in the Cyclades: of volcanic origin, with hot springs; centre of early Aegean civilization, where the Venus de Milo was found. Pop: 5000 (latest est). Area: 132 sq km (51 sq miles). Modern Greek name: **Mílos**

Melpomene (mɛl'pɒmɪnɪ) *n Greek myth* the Muse of tragedy

melt (mɛlt) *vb* **melts, melting, melted; melted** *or* **molten** **1** to liquefy (a solid) or (of a solid) to become liquefied, as a result of the action of heat **2** to become or make liquid; dissolve **3** (often foll by *away*) to disappear; fade **4** (foll by *down*) to melt (metal scrap) for reuse **5** (often foll by *into*) to blend or cause to blend gradually **6** to make or become emotional or sentimental; soften ▷ *n* **7** the act or process of melting **8** something melted or an amount melted [OE *meltan* to digest] > '**meltable** *adj* > '**melter** *n* > '**meltingly** *adv*

meltdown ('mɛlt,daʊn) *n* **1** (in a nuclear reactor) the melting of the fuel rods as a result of a defect in the cooling system, with the possible escape of radiation **2** *inf* a sudden disastrous failure with potential for widespread harm, as a stock-exchange crash **3** *inf* the process or state of irreversible breakdown or decline: *the community is slowly going into meltdown*

melting point *n* the temperature at which a solid turns into a liquid

melting pot *n* **1** a pot in which metals or other substances are melted, esp in order to mix them **2** an area in which many races, ideas, etc, are mixed

melton ('mɛltən) *n* a heavy smooth woollen fabric with a short nap. Also called: **melton cloth** [c19 from MELTON MOWBRAY, a former centre for making this]

Melton Mowbray ('mɛltən 'məʊbrɪ) *n* a town in central England, in Leicestershire: pork pies and Stilton cheese. Pop: 24 348 (1991)

meltwater ('mɛlt,wɔ:tə) *n* melted snow or ice

Melville ('mɛlvɪl) *n* **Herman** 1819–91, US novelist and short-story writer. Among his works, *Moby Dick* (1851) and *Billy Budd* (written 1891, published 1924) are outstanding

Melville Island ('mɛlvɪl) *n* **1** a Canadian island in the Arctic Ocean, north of Victoria Island: in the Northwest Territories and Nunavut. Area: 41 865 sq km (16 164 sq miles) **2** an island in the Arafura Sea, off the N central coast of Australia, separated from the mainland by Clarence Strait. Area: 6216 sq km (2400 sq miles)

Melville Peninsula *n* a peninsula of N Canada, in Nunavut, between the Gulf of Boothia and Foxe Basin

member ('mɛmbə) *n* **1** a person who belongs to a club, political party, etc **2** any individual plant or animal in a taxonomic group **3** any part of an animal body, such as a limb **4** any part of a plant, such as a petal, root, etc **5** *maths, logic* any individual object belonging to a set or logical class **6** a component part of a building or construction [c13 from L *membrum* limb, part] > '**memberless** *adj*

Member ('mɛmbə) *n* (*sometimes not cap*) **1** short for **Member of Parliament** **2** short for **Member of Congress** **3** a member of some other legislative body

Member of Congress *n* a member of the US Congress, esp of the House of Representatives

Member of Parliament *n* a member of the House of Commons or similar legislative body, as in many Commonwealth countries

membership ('mɛmbəʃɪp) *n* **1** the members of an organization collectively **2** the state of being a member

membrane ('mɛmbreɪn) *n* **1** any thin pliable sheet of material **2** a pliable sheetlike usually fibrous tissue that covers, lines, or connects plant and animal organs or cells [c16 from L *membrāna* skin covering a part of the body, from *membrum* MEMBER] > **membranous** ('mɛmbrənəs) *or* **membraneous** (mɛm'breɪnɪəs) *adj*

meme (mi:m) *n* an idea or element of social behaviour passed on through generations in a culture, esp by imitation [c20 possibly from MIMIC, on the model of GENE]

Memel ('me:məl) *n* **1** the German name for **Klaipeda** **2** the lower course of the Neman River

memento (mɪ'mɛntəʊ) *n, pl* **mementos** *or* **mementoes** something that reminds one of past events; a souvenir [c15 from L, imperative of *meminisse* to remember]

memento mori ('mɔ:ri:) *n, pl* **memento mori** an object, such as a skull, intended to remind people of death [c16 L: remember you must die]

Memling ('mɛmlɪŋ) *or* **Memlinc** ('mɛmlɪŋk) *n* **Hans** (hɑns) ?1430–94, Flemish painter of religious works and portraits

Memnon ('mɛmnɒn) *n* **1** *Greek myth* a king of Ethiopia, son of Eos: slain by Achilles in the Trojan War **2** a colossal statue of Amenhotep III at Thebes in ancient Egypt, which emitted a sound thought by the Greeks to be the voice of Memnon > **Memnonian** (mɛm'nəʊnɪən) *adj*

memo ('mɛməʊ, 'mi:məʊ) *n, pl* **memos** short for **memorandum**

memoir ('mɛmwɑ:) *n* **1** a biography or historical account, esp one based on personal knowledge **2** an essay, as on a specialized topic [c16 from F, from L *memoria* MEMORY] > '**memoirist** *n*

memoirs ('mɛmwɑ:z) *pl n* **1** a collection of reminiscences about a period, series of events, etc, written from personal experience or special sources **2** an autobiographical record **3** a record, as of transactions of a society, etc

memorabilia (,mɛmərə'bɪlɪə) *pl n*, *sing* **memorabile** (-'ræbɪlɪ) **1** memorable events or things **2** objects connected with famous people or events [c17 from L, from *memorābilis* MEMORABLE]

memorable ('mɛmərəbᵊl) *adj* worth remembering or easily remembered [c15 from L *memorābilis*, from *memorāre* to recall, from *memor* mindful] > ,**memora'bility** *n* > '**memorably** *adv*

memorandum (,mɛmə'rændəm) *n, pl* **memorandums** *or* **memoranda** (-də) **1** a written statement, record, or communication **2** a note of things to be remembered **3** an informal diplomatic communication **4** *law* a short written summary of the terms of a transaction ▷ Often (esp for senses 1, 2) shortened to **memo** [c15 from L: (something) to be remembered]

memorial (mɪ'mɔ:rɪəl) *adj* **1** serving to preserve the memory of the dead or a past event **2** of or involving memory ▷ *n* **3** something serving as a remembrance **4** a written statement of facts submitted to a government, authority, etc, in conjunction with a petition **5** an informal diplomatic paper [c14 from LL

Mm

memoriāle a reminder, neuter of *memoriālis*] > **me'morially** *adv*

memorialize *or* **memorialise** (mɪ'mɔːrɪə,laɪz) *vb* **memorializes, memorializing, memorialized** *or* **memorialises, memorialising, memorialised** (*tr*) **1** to honour or commemorate **2** to present or address a memorial to

memorize *or* **memorise** ('mɛmə,raɪz) *vb* **memorizes, memorizing, memorized** *or* **memorises, memorising, memorised** (*tr*) to commit to memory; learn so as to remember

memory ('mɛmərɪ) *n, pl* **memories 1a** the ability of the mind to store and recall past sensations, thoughts, knowledge, etc: *he can do it from memory* **1b** the part of the brain that appears to have this function **2** the sum of everything retained by the mind **3** a particular recollection of an event, person, etc **4** the time over which recollection extends: *within his memory* **5** commemoration or remembrance: *in memory of our leader* **6** the state of being remembered, as after death **7** a part of a computer in which information is stored for immediate use by the central processing unit ▷ Cf **RAM¹** [C14 from OF *memorie*, from L *memoria*, from *memor* mindful]

Memphis ('mɛmfɪs) *n* **1** a port in SW Tennessee, on the Mississippi River: the largest city in the state; a major cotton and timber market; Memphis State University (1909). Pop: 650 100 (2000 est) **2** a ruined city in N Egypt, the ancient centre of Lower Egypt, on the Nile: administrative and artistic centre, sacred to the worship of Ptah > **'Memphian** *adj, n*

Memphremagog (,mɛmfriː'meɪgɒg) *n* **Lake** a lake on the border between the US and Canada, in N Vermont and S Quebec. Length: about 43 km (27 miles). Width: up to 6 km (4 miles)

memsahib ('mɛm,sɑːɪb, -hɪb) *n* (formerly, in India) a term of respect used for a European married woman [C19 from MA'AM + SAHIB]

men (mɛn) *n* the plural of **man**

menace ('mɛnɪs) *vb* **menaces, menacing, menaced 1** to threaten with violence, danger, etc ▷ *n* **2** *literary* a threat **3** something menacing; a source of danger **4** *inf* a nuisance [C13 ult. rel. to L *minax* threatening, from *mināri* to threaten] > **'menacer** *n* > **'menacing** *adj* > **'menacingly** *adv*

menad ('miːnæd) *n* a variant spelling of **maenad**

Menado (mɛ'nɑːdəʊ) *or* **Manado** *n* a port in NE Indonesia, on NE Sulawesi: founded by the Dutch in 1657. Pop: 398 900 (1995 est)

ménage (meɪ'nɑːʒ) *n* the persons of a household [C17 from F, from Vulgar L (unattested) *mansiōnāticum* household]

ménage à trois *French* (menaʒ a trwɑ) *n, pl* ***ménages à trois*** (menaʒ a trwɑ). a sexual arrangement involving a married couple and the lover of one of them [lit.: household of three]

menagerie (mɪ'nædʒərɪ) *n* **1** a collection of wild animals kept for exhibition **2** the place where such animals are housed [C18 from F: household management, which formerly included care of domestic animals]

Menai Strait ('mɛnaɪ) *n* a channel of the Irish Sea between the island of Anglesey and the mainland of NW Wales: famous suspension bridge (1819–26) designed by Thomas Telford and tubular bridge (1846–50) by Robert Stephenson. Length: 24 km (15 miles). Width: up to 3 km (2 miles)

Menander (mə'nændə) *n* **1** ?160 BC–?120 BC, Greek king of the Punjab. A Buddhist convert, he reigned over much of NW India **2** ?342–?292 BC, Greek comic dramatist. The *Dyskolos* is his only complete extant comedy but others survive in adaptations by Terence and Plautus

Mencius ('mɛnʃɪəs, -ʃəs) *n* Chinese name *Mengzi* or *Meng-tze*. ?372–?289 BC, Chinese philosopher, who propounded the ethical system of Confucius

Mencken ('mɛŋkən) *n* **H**(**enry**) **L**(**ouis**) 1880–1956, US journalist and literary critic, noted for *The American Language* (1919): editor of the *Smart Set* and the *American Mercury*, which he founded (1924)

mend (mɛnd) *vb* **1** (*tr*) to repair (something broken or unserviceable) **2** to improve or undergo improvement; reform (often in **mend one's ways**) **3** (*intr*) to heal or recover **4** (*intr*) (of conditions) to improve; become better ▷ *n* **5** the act of repairing **6** a mended area, esp on a garment **7** **on the mend** becoming better, esp in health [C12 from AMEND] > **'mendable** *adj* > **'mender** *n*

mendacity (mɛn'dæsɪtɪ) *n, pl* **mendacities 1** the tendency to be untruthful **2** a falsehood [C17 from LL *mendācitās*, from L *mendāx* untruthful] > **mendacious** (mɛn'deɪʃəs) *adj* > **men'daciously** *adv*

Mendel ('mɛndᵊl) *n* **Gregor Johann** ('greːgɔr jo'han) 1822–84, Austrian monk and botanist; founder of the science of genetics. He developed his theory of organic inheritance from his experiments on the hybridization of green peas. His findings were published (1865) but remained unrecognized until 1900. See **Mendel's laws**

mendelevium (,mɛndɪ'liːvɪəm) *n* a transuranic element artificially produced by bombardment of einsteinium. Symbol: Md; atomic no.: 101; half-life of most stable isotope, ^{258}Md: 60 days (approx.) [C20 after D. I. MENDELEYEV]

Mendeleyev *or* **Mendeleev** (*Russian* mɪndɪ'ljejɪf) *n* **Dmitri Ivanovich** ('dmitrij i'vanəvitʃ) 1834–1907, Russian chemist. He devised the original periodic table of the elements (1869)

Mendelian (mɛn'diːlɪən) *adj* of or relating to Mendel's laws

Mendel's laws *pl n* the principles of heredity proposed by Gregor Mendel. The **Law of Segregation** states that each hereditary character is determined by a pair of units in the reproductive cells: the pairs separate during meiosis so that each gamete carries only one unit of each pair. The **Law of Independent Assortment** states that the separation of the units of each pair is not influenced by that of any other pair

Mendelssohn ('mɛndᵊlsən; *German* 'mɛndəlzoːn) *n* **1** **Felix** ('feːlɪks), full name *Jacob Ludwig Felix Mendelssohn-Bartholdy*. 1809–47, German romantic composer. His works include the overtures *A Midsummer Night's Dream* (1826) and *Fingal's Cave* (1832), five symphonies, the oratorio *Elijah* (1846), piano pieces, and songs. He was instrumental in the revival of the music of J. S. Bach in the 19th century **2** his grandfather, **Moses** ('moːzəs) 1729–86, German Jewish philosopher. His best-known work is *Jerusalem* (1783), in which he defends Judaism and appeals for religious toleration

Menderes (,mɛndɛ'rɛs) *n* **1** a river in SW Turkey flowing southwest, then west to the Aegean. Length: about 386 km (240 miles). Ancient name: **Maeander** **2** a river in NW Turkey flowing west and northwest to the Dardanelles. Length: 104 km (65 miles). Ancient name: **Scamander**

Mendes ('mɛndɛz) *n* **Sam**(**uel**) (**Alexander**) born 1965, British theatre and film director, who made his name as artistic director of the Donmar Warehouse, London (1992–2002) before directing the films *American Beauty* (1999) and *The Road to Perdition* (2002). He is married to the actress Kate Winslet

Mendès-France (*French* mɛ̃dɛsfrɑ̃s) *n* **Pierre** (pjɛr) 1907–82, French statesman; prime minister (1954–55). He concluded the war in Indochina and granted independence to Tunisia

mendicant ('mɛndɪkənt) *adj* **1** begging **2** (of a member of a religious order) dependent on alms for sustenance ▷ *n* **3** a mendicant friar **4** a less common word for **beggar** [C16 from L *mendīcāre*, from *mendīcus* beggar, from *mendus* flaw] > '**mendicancy** *or* **mendicity** (mɛn'dɪsɪtɪ) *n*

Mendips ('mɛndɪps) *pl n* a range of limestone hills in SW England, in N Somerset: includes the Cheddar Gorge and numerous caves. Highest point: 325 m (1068 ft). Also called: **Mendip Hills**

Mendoza[1] (mɛn'dəʊzə; *Spanish* men'doθa) *n* a city in W central Argentina, in the foothills of the Sierra de los Paramillos: largely destroyed by an earthquake in 1861; commercial centre of an intensively cultivated irrigated region; University of Cuyo (1939). Pop: 119 681 (1999 est)

Mendoza[2] (*Spanish* men'doθa) *n* **Pedro de** ('peðro de) died 1537, Spanish soldier and explorer; founder of Buenos Aires (1536)

meneer (mə'nɪə) *n* a S African title of address equivalent to *sir* when used alone or *Mr* when placed before a name [Afrik.]

Menelaus (ˌmɛnɪ'leɪəs) *n Greek myth* a king of Sparta and the brother of Agamemnon. He was the husband of Helen, whose abduction led to the Trojan War

Menelik II ('mɛnɪlɪk) *n* 1844–1913, emperor of Abyssinia (1889–1910). He defeated the Italians at Aduwa (1896), maintaining the independence of Abyssinia in an era of European expansion in Africa

Menes ('mi:ni:z) *n* the first king of the first dynasty of Egypt (?3100 BC). He is said to have united Upper and Lower Egypt and founded Memphis

menfolk ('mɛnˌfəʊk) *pl n* men collectively, esp the men of a particular family

Mengelberg ('mɛŋgᵊlˌbɜ:g; *Dutch* 'mɛŋəlbɛrx) *n* (**Josef**) **Willem** ('wɪləm) 1871–1951, Dutch orchestral conductor, noted for his performances of the music of Mahler

Mengistu Haile Mariam (mɛŋ'gɪstu: 'haɪlɪ 'mɑ:rɪəm) *n* born 1937, Ethiopian soldier and statesman; head of state from 1977 until 1991 when rebels seized power and he fled into exile

Mengzi *or* **Meng-tze** ('mɛŋ'tseɪ) *n* the Chinese name for **Mencius**

menhaden (mɛn'heɪdᵊn) *n, pl* **menhaden** a marine North American fish: source of fishmeal, fertilizer, and oil [c18 from Algonquian; prob. rel. to another Amerind word, *munnawhatteaúg* fertilizer]

menhir ('mɛnhɪə) *n* a single standing stone, dating from prehistoric times [c19 from Breton *men* stone + *hir* long]

menial ('mi:nɪəl) *adj* **1** consisting of or occupied with work requiring little skill, esp domestic duties **2** of, involving, or befitting servants **3** servile ▷ *n* **4** a domestic servant **5** a servile person [c14 from Anglo-Norman *meignial*, from OF *meinie* household]

Meninga (mɪn'ɪŋgə) *n* **Mal** born 1960, Australian rugby league player

meninges (mɪ'nɪndʒi:z) *pl n* , *sing* **meninx** ('mi:nɪŋks) the three membranes (**dura mater, arachnoid, pia mater**) that envelop the brain and spinal cord [c17 from Gk, pl of *meninx* membrane] > **meningeal** (mɪ'nɪndʒɪəl) *adj*

meningitis (ˌmɛnɪn'dʒaɪtɪs) *n* inflammation of the membranes that surround the brain or spinal cord, caused by infection > **meningitic** (ˌmɛnɪn'dʒɪtɪk) *adj*

meningococcus (mɛˌnɪŋgəʊ'kɒkəs) *n, pl* **meningococci** (-'kɒkaɪ, 'kɒki:) the bacterium that causes cerebrospinal meningitis > **meˌningo'coccal** *adj*

meniscus (mɪ'nɪskəs) *n, pl* **menisci** (-'nɪsaɪ) *or* **meniscuses** **1** the curved upper surface of a liquid standing in a tube, produced by the surface tension **2** a crescent-shaped lens; a concavo-convex or convexo-concave lens [c17 from NL, from Gk *mēniskos* crescent, dim. of *mēnē* moon] > **me'niscoid** *adj*

Mennonite ('mɛnəˌnaɪt) *n* a member of a Protestant sect that rejects infant baptism and Church organization, and in most cases refuses military service, public office, and the taking of oaths [c16 from G *Mennonit*, after *Menno* Simons (1496–1561), Frisian religious leader] > '**Mennonitism** *n*

meno ('mɛnəʊ) *adv music* to be played less quickly, less softly, etc [from It., from L *minus* less]

meno- *combining form* menstruation [from Gk *mēn* month]

Menon ('mɛnən) *n* **Vengalil Krishnan Krishna** ('vɛŋgəlɪl 'kri:ʃnən 'kri:ʃnə) 1897–1974, Indian diplomat and politician, who was a close associate of Nehru and played a key role in the Indian nationalist movement

menopause ('mɛnəʊˌpɔ:z) *n* the period during which a woman's menstrual cycle ceases, normally at an age of 45 to 50 [c19 from F, from Gk *mēn* month + *pausis* halt] > ˌ**meno'pausal** *addition*

menopolis (mɛ'nɒpəlɪs) *n* an area or city with a high proportion of single men [c21 from MEN + (METR)OPOLIS]

menorah (mɪ'nɔ:rə) *n Judaism* **1** a seven-branched candelabrum used in the Temple and now an emblem of Judaism and the badge of the state of Israel **2** a similar lamp lit during the Chanukah festival [from Heb.: candlestick]

Menorca (me'nɔrka) *n* the Spanish name for **Minorca** (sense 1)

menorrhagia (ˌmɛnɔ:'reɪdʒɪə) *n* excessive bleeding during menstruation

menorrhoea (ˌmɛnə'rɪə) *n* normal bleeding in menstruation

Menotti (mə'nɒtɪ; *Italian* me'nɔtti) *n* **Gian Carlo** (dʒan 'karlo) born 1911, Italian composer, in the US from 1928. His works include the operas *The Medium* (1946), *The Consul* (1950), *Amahl and the Night Visitors* (1951), and *Giorno di Nozze* (1988)

menses ('mɛnsi:z) *n* (*functioning as sing or pl*) **1** another name for **menstruation** **2** the period of time during which one menstruation occurs **3** the matter discharged during menstruation [c16 from L, pl of *mensis* month]

Menshevik ('mɛnʃɪvɪk) *or* **Menshevist** *n* a member of the moderate wing of the Russian Social Democratic Party ▷ Cf **Bolshevik** [c20 from Russian, lit.: minority, from *menshe* less, from *malo* few] > '**Msheˌvism** *n*

menstruate ('mɛnstrʊˌeɪt) *vb* **menstruates, menstruating, menstruated** (*intr*) to undergo menstruation [c17 from L *menstruāre*, from *mensis* month]

menstruation (ˌmɛnstrʊ'eɪʃən) *n* the approximately monthly discharge of blood and cellular debris from the uterus by nonpregnant women from puberty to the menopause > '**menstrual** *or* '**menstruous** *adj*

menstruum ('mɛnstrʊəm) *n, pl* **menstruums** *or* **menstrua** (-strʊə) *obs* a solvent, esp one used in the preparation of a drug [c17 (meaning: solvent), c14 (menstrual discharge): from Med. L, from L *mēnstruus* monthly, from *mēnsis* month; from alchemical comparison between a base metal being transmuted into gold and the supposed action of the menses]

mensurable ('mɛnsjʊrəbᵊl, -ʃə-) *adj* a less common word for **measurable** [c17 from LL *mēnsūrābilis*, from *mēnsūra* MEASURE] > ˌ**mensura'bility** *n*

mensural ('mɛnʃərəl) *adj* **1** of or involving measure **2** *music* of or relating to music in which notes have fixed values [c17 from LL *mēnsūrālis*, from *mēnsūra* MEASURE]

mensuration (ˌmɛnʃə'reɪʃən) *n* **1** the study of the measurement of geometric magnitudes such as length **2** the act or process of measuring > **mensurative** ('mɛnʃərətɪv) *adj*

-ment *suffix forming nouns, esp from verbs* **1** indicating state, condition, or quality: *enjoyment* **2** indicating the result or product of an action: *embankment* **3** indicating process or action: *management* [from F, from L *-mentum*]

mental ('mɛntᵊl) *adj* **1** of or involving the mind **2** occurring only in the mind: *mental arithmetic* **3** affected by mental illness: *a mental patient* **4** concerned with mental illness: *a mental hospital* **5** *sl* insane [c15 from LL *mentālis*, from L *mēns* mind] > '**mentally** *adv*

mental deficiency *n psychiatry* a less common term for **mental retardation**

Mm

mental handicap *n* any intellectual disability resulting from injury to the brain or from abnormal neurological development > **mentally handicapped** *adj*
mental healing *n* the healing of a disorder by mental concentration or suggestion
mental illness *n* any of various disorders in which a person's thoughts, emotions, or behaviour are so abnormal as to cause suffering to himself, herself, or other people
mentalism ('mɛntᵊˌlɪzəm) *n philosophy* the doctrine that mind is the fundamental reality and that objects of knowledge exist only as aspects of the subject's consciousness > ˌ**mental'istic** *adj*
mentality (mɛn'tælɪtɪ) *n, pl* **mentalities** **1** the state or quality of mental or intellectual ability **2** a way of thinking; mental inclination or character
mental lexicon *n* the store of words in a person's mind
mental reservation *n* a tacit withholding of full assent or an unexpressed qualification made when taking an oath, making a statement, etc
mental retardation *n psychiatry* the condition of having a low intelligence quotient (below 70)
menthol ('mɛnθɒl) *n* an organic compound found in peppermint oil and used as an antiseptic, in inhalants, and as an analgesic. Formula: $C_{10}H_{19}OH$ [C19 from G, from L *mentha* MINT[1]]
mentholated ('mɛnθəˌleɪtɪd) *adj* containing, treated with, or impregnated with menthol
mention ('mɛnʃən) *vb* (*tr*) **1** to refer to or speak about briefly or incidentally **2** to acknowledge or honour **3 not to mention (something)** to say nothing of (something too obvious to mention) ▷ *n* **4** a recognition or acknowledgment **5** a slight reference or allusion **6** the act of mentioning [C14 via OF from L *mentiō* a calling to mind, from *mēns* mind] > '**mentionable** *adj*
Menton (mɛn'təʊn; *French* mɑ̃tɔ̃) *n* a town and resort in SE France, on the Mediterranean: belonged to Monaco from the 14th century until 1848, then an independent republic until purchased by France in 1860. Pop: 25 500 (latest est)
mentor ('mɛntɔː) *n* a wise or trusted adviser or guide [C18 from MENTOR]
Mentor ('mɛntɔː) *n* the friend whom Odysseus put in charge of his household when he left for Troy. He was the adviser of the young Telemachus
mentoring ('mɛntərɪŋ) *n* (in business) the practice of assigning a junior member of staff to the care of a more experienced person who assists him in his career
menu ('mɛnjuː) *n* **1** a list of dishes served at a meal or that can be ordered in a restaurant **2** a list of options displayed on a visual display unit from which the operator selects an action to be carried out [C19 from F *menu* small, detailed (list), from L *minūtus* MINUTE[2]]
menuetto (mɛnjʊ'ɛtəʊ) *n, pl* **menuettos** *music* another term for **minuet** [from It.]
Menuhin ('mɛnjʊɪn) *n* **Yehudi** (jɛ'huːdɪ), Baron. 1916–99, British violinist, born in the US
Menzies ('mɛnzɪz) *n* Sir **Robert Gordon** 1894–1978, Australian statesman; prime minister (1939–41; 1949–66)
meow, miaou, miaow (mɪ'aʊ, mjaʊ), *or* **miaul** (mɪ'aʊl, mjaʊl) *vb* **1** (*intr*) (of a cat) to make a characteristic crying sound ▷ *interj* **2** an imitation of this sound
MEP (in Britain) *abbrev for* Member of the European Parliament
mepacrine ('mɛpəkrɪn) *n Brit* a drug formerly widely used to treat malaria [C20 from ME(THYL) + PA(LUDISM + A)CR(ID)INE]
meperidine (mə'pɛrɪˌdiːn, -dɪn) *n* the US name for **pethidine** [C20 from METHYL + PIPERIDINE]
Mephistopheles (ˌmɛfɪ'stɒfɪˌliːz) *or* **Mephisto** (mə'fɪstəʊ) *n* a devil in medieval mythology and the one to whom Faust sold his soul in German legend > **Mephistophelean** *or* **Mephistophelian** (ˌmɛfɪstə'fiːlɪən) *adj*
mephitic (mɪ'fɪtɪk) *or* **mephitical** *adj* **1** poisonous; foul **2** foul-smelling; putrid [C17 from LL *mephīticus* pestilential]
meprobamate (mə'prəʊbəˌmeɪt, ˌmɛprəʊ'bæmeɪt) *n* a white bitter powder used as a hypnotic [C20 from ME(THYL) + PRO(PYL + *car*)*bamate* a salt or ester of an amide of carbonic acid]
-mer *suffix forming nouns chem* denoting a substance of a particular class: *monomer; polymer* [from Gk *meros* part]
Merano (mə'rɑːnəʊ; *Italian* me'raːno) *n* a town and resort in NE Italy, in the foothills of the central Alps: capital of the Tyrol (12th–15th century); under Austrian rule until 1919. Pop: 33 638 (1993 est). German name: **Meran** (me'raːn)
Merca ('mɛəkə) *n* a port in S Somalia on the Indian Ocean. Pop: 100 000 (latest est)
mercantile ('mɜːkənˌtaɪl) *adj* **1** of, relating to, or characteristic of trade or traders; commercial **2** of or relating to mercantilism [C17 from F, from It., from *mercante* MERCHANT]
mercantilism ('mɜːkəntɪˌlɪzəm) *n econ* a theory prevalent in Europe during the 17th and 18th centuries asserting that the wealth of a nation depends on possession of precious metals and therefore that a government must maximize foreign trade surplus and foster national commercial interests, a merchant marine, the establishment of colonies, etc > '**mercantilist** *n, adj*
mercaptan (mɜː'kæptæn) *n* another name (not in technical use) for **thiol** [C19 from G, from Med. L *mercurium captans*, lit.: seizing quicksilver]
Mercator (mɜː'keɪtə) *n* **Gerardus** (dʒə'rɑːdəs) Latinized name of *Gerhard Kremer*. 1512–94, Flemish cartographer and mathematician
Mercator projection *n* a conformal map projection on which parallels and meridians form a rectangular grid, scale being exaggerated with increasing distance from the equator. Also called: **Mercator's projection** [C17 after G. MERCATOR]
mercenary ('mɜːsɪnərɪ, -sɪnrɪ) *adj* **1** influenced by greed or desire for gain **2** of or relating to a mercenary or mercenaries ▷ *n, pl* **mercenaries** **3** a man hired to fight for a foreign army, etc **4** *rare* any person who works solely for pay [C16 from L *mercēnārius*, from *mercēs* wages]
mercer ('mɜːsə) *n Brit* a dealer in textile fabrics and fine cloth [C13 from OF *mercier* dealer, from Vulgar L, from L *merx* wares] > '**mercery** *n*
mercerize *or* **mercerise** ('mɜːsəˌraɪz) *vb* **mercerizes, mercerizing, mercerized** *or* **mercerises, mercerising, mercerised** (*tr*) to treat (cotton yarn) with an alkali to increase its strength and reception to dye and impart a lustrous silky appearance [C19 after John *Mercer* (1791–1866), E maker of textiles]
merchandise *n* ('mɜːtʃənˌdaɪs, -ˌdaɪz) **1** commercial goods; commodities ▷ *vb* ('mɜːtʃənˌdaɪz), **merchandises, merchandising, merchandised** **2** to engage in the commercial purchase and sale of (goods or services); trade [C13 from OF; see MERCHANT]
merchandising ('mɜːtʃənˌdaɪzɪŋ) *n* **1** the selection and display of goods in a retail outlet **2** commercial goods, esp ones issued to exploit the popularity of a pop group, sporting event, etc
merchant ('mɜːtʃənt) *n* **1** a person engaged in the purchase and sale of commodities for profit; trader **2** *chiefly Scot, US, & Canad* a person engaged in retail trade **3** (esp in historical contexts) any trader **4** *derog* a person dealing or involved in something undesirable: *a gossip merchant* **5** (*modifier*) **5a** of the merchant navy: *a merchant sailor* **5b** of or concerned with trade: *a merchant ship* ▷ *vb* **6** (*tr*) to conduct trade in; deal in [C13 from OF, prob.

from Vulgar L, from L *mercārī* to trade, from *merx* wares]

Merchant ('mɜːtʃənt) *n* **Ismail** ('ɪzmeɪəl) born 1936, Indian film producer, noted for his collaboration with James Ivory on such films as *Shakespeare Wallah* (1965), *The Europeans* (1979), *A Room with a View* (1986), *The Remains of the Day* (1993), and *The Golden Bowl* (2000)

merchantable ('mɜːtʃəntəbᵊl) *adj* suitable for trading

merchant bank *n Brit* a financial institution engaged primarily in accepting foreign bills, advising companies on flotations and takeovers, underwriting new issues, hire-purchase finance, making long-term loans to companies, and managing investment portfolios, funds, and trusts > **merchant banker** *n*

merchantman ('mɜːtʃəntmən) *n, pl* **merchantmen** a merchant ship

merchant navy *or* **marine** *n* the ships or crew engaged in a nation's commercial shipping

▷ www.mna.org.uk

Mercia ('mɜːʃɪə) *n* a kingdom and earldom of central and S England during the Anglo-Saxon period that reached its height under King Offa (757–96)

Mercian ('mɜːʃɪən) *adj* **1** of or relating to Mercia, or its dialect ▷ *n* **2** the dialect of Old and Middle English spoken in Mercia **3** a native or inhabitant of Mercia

merciful ('mɜːsɪfʊl) *adj* showing or giving mercy; compassionate > **'mercifully** *adv* > **'mercifulness** *n*

merciless ('mɜːsɪlɪs) *adj* without mercy; pitiless, cruel, or heartless > **'mercilessly** *adv* > **'mercilessness** *n*

Merckx ('mɛrks) *n* **Eddy** born 1945, Belgian professional cyclist: five times winner of the Tour de France, including four consecutive victories (1969–72)

Mercouri (mɜː'kuːrɪ) *n* **Melina** (mə'liːnə) 1925–94, Greek actress and politician: her films include *Never on Sunday* (1960); minister of culture (1981–85 and 1993–94)

mercurial (mɜː'kjʊərɪəl) *adj* **1** of, like, containing, or relating to mercury **2** volatile; lively: *a mercurial temperament* **3** (*sometimes cap*) of, like, or relating to the god or the planet Mercury ▷ *n* **4** *med* any salt of mercury for use as a medicine [c14 from L *mercuriālis*] > **mer,curi'ality** *n* > **mer'curially** *adv*

mercuric (mɜː'kjʊərɪk) *adj* of or containing mercury in the divalent state; denoting a mercury(II) compound

mercuric chloride *n* a white poisonous crystalline substance used as a pesticide, antiseptic, and preservative for wood. Formula: $HgCl_2$. Systematic name: **mercury(II) chloride**

Mercurochrome (mə'kjʊərə,krəʊm) *n trademark* a solution of a crystalline compound, used as topical antibacterial agent

mercurous ('mɜːkjʊrəs) *adj* of or containing mercury in the monovalent state; denoting a mercury(I) compound

mercury ('mɜːkjʊrɪ) *n, pl* **mercuries** **1** Also called: **quicksilver** a heavy silvery-white toxic liquid metallic element: used in thermometers, barometers, mercury-vapour lamps, and dental amalgams. Symbol: Hg; atomic no.: 80; atomic wt.: 200.59 **2** any plant of the genus *Mercurialis* **3** *arch* a messenger or courier [c14 from L *Mercurius*, messenger of Jupiter, god of commerce; rel. to *merx* merchandise]

Mercury¹ ('mɜːkjʊrɪ) *n Roman myth* the messenger of the gods

Mercury² ('mɜːkjʊrɪ) *n* the second smallest planet and the nearest to the sun

▷ http://nssdc.gsfc.nasa.gov/planetary/planets

▷ http://solarsystem.nasa.gov/features/planets

▷ www.solarviews.com/eng/mercury.htm

mercury-vapour lamp *n* a lamp in which an electric discharge through mercury vapour is used to produce a greenish-blue light

mercy ('mɜːsɪ) *n, pl* **mercies** **1** compassionate treatment of or attitude towards an offender, adversary, etc, who is in one's power or care; clemency; pity **2** the power to show mercy **3** a relieving or welcome occurrence or state of affairs **4** **at the mercy of** in the power of [c12 from OF, from L *mercēs* recompense, from *merx* goods]

mercy flight *n* an aircraft flight to bring a seriously ill or injured person to hospital from an isolated community

mercy killing *n* another term for **euthanasia**

mere¹ (mɪə) *adj* being nothing more than something specified: *a mere child* [c15 from L *merus* pure] > **'merely** *adv*

mere² (mɪə) *n* **1** *dialect or arch* a lake or marsh **2** *obs* the sea or an inlet of it [OE *mere* sea, lake]

mere³ ('mɛrɪ) *n* a short flat Maori striking weapon [from Maori]

-mere *n combining form* indicating a part or division [from Gk *meros* part] > **meric** *adj combining form*

Meredith ('mɛrɪdɪθ) *n* **George** 1828–1909, English novelist and poet. His works, notable for their social satire and analysis of character, include the novels *Beauchamp's Career* (1876) and *The Egoist* (1879) and the long tragic poem *Modern Love* (1862)

meretricious (,mɛrɪ'trɪʃəs) *adj* **1** superficially or garishly attractive **2** insincere **3** *arch* of, like, or relating to a prostitute [c17 from L *merētrīcius*, from *merētrix* prostitute, from *merēre* to earn money] > **,mere'triciously** *adv* > **,mere'triciousness** *n*

merganser (mɜː'gænsə) *n, pl* **mergansers** *or* **merganser** any of several typically crested large marine diving ducks, having a long slender hooked bill with serrated edges [c18 from NL, from L *mergus* waterfowl, from *mergere* to plunge + *anser* goose]

merge (mɜːdʒ) *vb* **merges, merging, merged** **1** to meet and join or cause to meet and join **2** to blend or cause to blend; fuse [c17 from L *mergere* to plunge] > **'mergence** *n*

merger ('mɜːdʒə) *n* **1** *commerce* the combination of two or more companies **2** *law* the absorption of an estate, interest, offence, etc, into a greater one **3** the act of merging or the state of being merged

Mergui Archipelago (mɜː'gwiː) *n* a group of over 200 islands in the Andaman Sea, off the Tenasserim coast of S Myanmar: mountainous and forested

Meriç (mə'riːtʃ) *n* the Turkish name for the **Maritsa**

Mérida (*Spanish* 'meriða) *n* **1** a city in SE Mexico, capital of Yucatán state: founded in 1542 on the site of the ancient Mayan city of T'ho; centre of the henequen industry; university. Pop: 660 848 (2000) **2** a city in W Venezuela: founded in 1558 by Spanish conquistadores; University of Los Andes (1785). Pop: 230 101 (2000 est) **3** a market town in W Spain, in Estremadura, on the Guadiana River: founded in 25 BC; became the capital of Lusitania and one of the chief cities of Iberia. Pop: 49 830 (1991). Latin name: **Augusta Emerita**

meridian (mə'rɪdɪən) *n* **1a** one of the imaginary lines joining the north and south poles at right angles to the equator, designated by degrees of longitude from 0° at Greenwich to 180° **1b** the great circle running through both poles **2** *astron* the great circle on the celestial sphere passing through the north and south celestial poles and the zenith and nadir of the observer **3** the peak; zenith: *the meridian of his achievements* **4** (in acupuncture, etc) any of the channels through which vital energy is believed to circulate round the body **5** *obs* noon ▷ *adj* **6** along or relating to a meridian **7** of or happening at noon **8** relating to the peak of something [c14 from L *merīdiānus* of midday, from *merīdiēs* midday, from *medius* MID¹ + *diēs* day]

meridional (mə'rɪdɪənᵊl) *adj* **1** along, relating to, or resembling a meridian **2** characteristic of or located in the south, esp of Europe ▷ *n* **3** an inhabitant of the south, esp of France [c14 from LL *merīdiōnālis* southern; see MERIDIAN]

Mérimée (*French* merime) *n* **Prosper** (prɔspɛr) 1803–70, French novelist, dramatist, and short-story writer, noted particularly for his short novels *Colomba* (1840) and *Carmen* (1845), on which Bizet's opera was based

meringue (mə'ræŋ) *n* **1** stiffly beaten egg whites mixed with sugar and baked **2** a small cake or shell of this mixture, often filled with cream [c18 from F, from ?]

merino (məˈriːnəʊ) *n, pl* **merinos** **1** a breed of sheep originating in Spain, bred for their fleece **2** the long fine wool of this sheep **3** the yarn made from this wool ▷ *adj* **4** made from merino wool [c18 from Sp., from ?]

Merionethshire (ˌmɛrɪˈɒnɪθʃɪə, -ʃə) *n* (until 1974) a county of N Wales, now part of Gwynedd

meristem (ˈmɛrɪˌstɛm) *n* a plant tissue responsible for growth, whose cells divide and differentiate to form the tissues and organs of the plant [c19 from Gk *meristos* divided, from *merizein*, from *meris* portion] > **meristematic** (ˌmɛrɪstɪˈmætɪk) *adj*

merit (ˈmɛrɪt) *n* **1** worth or superior quality; excellence **2** (*often pl*) a deserving or commendable quality or act **3** *Christianity* spiritual credit granted or received for good works **4** the fact or state of deserving; desert ▷ *vb* **merits, meriting, merited** **5** (*tr*) to be worthy of; deserve [c13 via OF from L *meritum* reward, from *merēre* to deserve] > **ˈmerited** *adj* > **ˈmeritless** *adj*

meritocracy (ˌmɛrɪˈtɒkrəsɪ) *n, pl* **meritocracies** **1** rule by persons chosen for their superior talents or intellect **2** the persons constituting such a group **3** a social system formed on such a basis > **meritocratic** (ˌmɛrɪtəˈkrætɪk) *adj*

meritorious (ˌmɛrɪˈtɔːrɪəs) *adj* praiseworthy; showing merit [c15 from L *meritōrius* earning money] > ˌ**meriˈtoriously** *adv* > ˌ**meriˈtoriousness** *n*

merits (ˈmɛrɪts) *pl n* **1** the actual and intrinsic rights and wrongs of an issue, esp in a law case **2 on its (his, her,** etc) **merits** on the intrinsic qualities or virtues

merle *or* **merl** (mɜːl) *n Scot* another name for the (European) **blackbird** [c15 via OF from L *merula*]

merlin (ˈmɜːlɪn) *n* a small falcon that has a dark plumage with a black-barred tail [c14 from OF *esmerillon*, from *esmeril*, of Gmc origin]

Merlin (ˈmɜːlɪn) *n* (in Arthurian legend) a wizard and counsellor to King Arthur eternally imprisoned in a tree by a woman to whom he revealed his secret craft

Merlot (ˈmɜːləʊ) *n* (*sometimes not cap*) **1** a black grape grown in France, Hungary, Bulgaria, etc, used, often in a blend, for making wine **2** any of various wines made from this grape [from *merlot*, lit.: young blackbird, dim. of *merle* MERLE, prob. alluding to the colour of the grape]

mermaid (ˈmɜːˌmeɪd) *n* an imaginary sea creature fabled to have a woman's head and upper body and a fish's tail [c14 from MERE[2] + MAID]

merman (ˈmɜːˌmæn) *n, pl* **mermen** a male counterpart of the mermaid [c17 see MERMAID]

Meroë (ˈmɛrəʊˌiː) *n* an ancient city in N Sudan, on the Nile; capital of a kingdom that flourished from about 700 BC to about 350 AD

-merous *adj combining form* (in biology) having a certain number or kind of parts [from Gk *meros* part]

Merovingian (ˌmɛrəʊˈvɪndʒɪən) *adj* **1** of or relating to a Frankish dynasty which ruled Gaul and W Germany from about 500 to 751 AD ▷ *n* **2** a member of this dynasty [c17 from F, from Med. L *Merovingi* offspring of *Merovaeus*, L form of *Merowig*, traditional founder of the line]

merriment (ˈmɛrɪmənt) *n* gaiety, fun, or mirth

merry (ˈmɛrɪ) *adj* **merrier, merriest** **1** cheerful; jolly **2** very funny; hilarious **3** *Brit inf* slightly drunk **4 make merry** to revel; be festive **5 play merry hell with** *inf* to disturb greatly; disrupt [OE *merige* agreeable] > **ˈmerrily** *adv* > **ˈmerriness** *n*

merry-andrew (-ˈændruː) *n* a joker, clown, or buffoon [c17 from ?]

merry-go-round *n* **1** another name for **roundabout** (sense 1) **2** a whirl of activity

merrymaking (ˈmɛrɪˌmeɪkɪŋ) *n* fun, revelry, or festivity > **ˈmerryˌmaker** *n*

merrythought (ˈmɛrɪˌθɔːt) *n Brit* a less common word for **wishbone**

Merse (mɜːs; *Scot* mɛrs) *n* **the** a fertile lowland area of SE Scotland, in Scottish Borders, north of the Tweed

Merseburg (*German* ˈmɛrzəbʊrk) *n* a city in E Germany, on the Saale River, in Saxony-Anhalt: residence of the dukes of Saxe-Merseburg (1656–1738); chemical industry. Pop: 46 250 (latest est)

Mersey (ˈmɜːzɪ) *n* a river in W England, rising in N Derbyshire and flowing northwest and west to the Irish Sea through a large estuary on which is situated the port of Liverpool. Length: about 112 km (70 miles)

Merseyside (ˈmɜːzɪˌsaɪd) *n* a metropolitan county of NW England, administered since 1986 by the unitary authorities of Sefton, Liverpool, St Helens, Knowsley, and Wirral. Area: 652 sq km (252 sq miles)

Mersin (mɛəˈsiːn) *n* a port in S Turkey, on the Mediterranean: oil refinery. Pop: 501 398 (1997). Also called: **Içel**

Merthyr Tydfil (ˈmɜːθə ˈtɪdvɪl) *n* **1** a town in SE Wales, in Merthyr Tydfil county borough: formerly an important centre for the mining industry. Pop: 39 482 (1991) **2** a county borough in SE Wales, created from part of N Mid Glamorgan in 1996. Pop: 55 983 (2001). Area: 111 sq km (43 sq miles)

Merton[1] (ˈmɜːtᵊn) *n* a borough in SW Greater London. Pop: 187 908 (2001). Area: 38 sq km (15 sq miles)

Merton[2] (ˈmɜːtᵊn) *n* **Thomas (Feverel)** 1915–68, US writer, monk, and mystic; noted esp for his autobiography *The Seven Storey Mountain* (1948)

mesa (ˈmeɪsə) *n* a flat tableland with steep edges, common in the southwestern US [from Sp.: table]

mésalliance (mɛˈzælɪəns) *n* a marriage with a person of lower social status [c18 from F: MISALLIANCE]

Mesa Verde (ˈmeɪsə ˈvɜːd) *n* a high plateau in SW Colorado: remains of numerous prehistoric cliff dwellings, inhabited by the Pueblo Indians

mescal (mɛˈskæl) *n* **1** Also called: **peyote** a spineless globe-shaped cactus of Mexico and the southwestern US. Its button-like tubercles (**mescal buttons**) are chewed by certain Indian tribes for their hallucinogenic effects **2** a colourless alcoholic spirit distilled from the fermented juice of certain agave plants [c19 from American Sp., from Nahuatl *mexcalli* the liquor, from *metl* MAGUEY + *ixcalli* stew]

mescaline *or* **mescalin** (ˈmɛskəˌliːn, -lɪn) *n* a hallucinogenic drug derived from mescal buttons. Formula: $C_{11}H_{17}NO_3$

mesdames (ˈmeɪˌdæm) *n* the plural of **madame** and **madam** (sense 1)

mesdemoiselles (ˌmeɪdmwəˈzɛl) *n* the plural of **mademoiselle**

meseems (mɪˈsiːmz) *vb* (*tr; takes a clause as object*) *arch* it seems to me

mesembryanthemum (mɪzˌɛmbrɪˈænθɪməm) *n* any of a genus of plants with succulent leaves and bright flowers with rayed petals which typically open at midday [c18 NL, from Gk *mesēmbria* noon + *anthemon* flower]

mesencephalon (ˌmɛsɛnˈsɛfəˌlɒn) *n* the part of the brain that develops from the middle portion of the embryonic neural tube. Nontechnical name: **midbrain**

mesentery (ˈmɛsəntərɪ, ˈmɛz-) *n, pl* **mesenteries** the double layer of peritoneum that is attached to the back wall of the abdominal cavity and supports most of the small intestine [c16 from NL *mesenterium*, *from* MESO- + Gk *enteron* intestine] > ˌ**mesenˈteric** *adj* > **mesenteritis** (mɛsˌɛntəˈraɪtɪs) *n*

mesh (mɛʃ) *n* **1** a network; net **2** an open space between the strands of a network **3** (*often pl*) the strands surrounding these spaces **4** anything that ensnares, or holds like a net **5** the engagement of teeth on interacting gearwheels: *the gears are in mesh* ▷ *vb* **6** to entangle or become entangled **7** (of gear teeth) to engage or cause to engage **8** (*intr; often foll by with*) to coordinate (with) **9** to work or cause to work in harmony [c16 prob. from Du. *maesche*]

Meshach ('mi:ʃæk) *n Old Testament* one of Daniel's three companions who, together with Shadrach and Abednego, was miraculously saved from destruction in Nebuchadnezzar's fiery furnace (Daniel 3:12-30)

Meshed (mɛ'ʃɛd) *n* a variant of **Mashhad**

mesial ('mi:zɪəl) *adj anat* another word for **medial** (sense 1) [c19 from MESO- + -IAL]

mesmerism ('mɛzmə,rɪzəm) *n psychol* **1** a hypnotic state induced by the operator's imposition of his or her will on that of the patient **2** an early doctrine concerning this [c19 after F. A. *Mesmer* (1734–1815), Austrian physician] > **mesmeric** (mɛz'mɛrɪk) *adj* > **'mesmerist** *n*

mesmerize *or* **mesmerise** ('mɛzmə,raɪz) *vb* **mesmerizes, mesmerizing, mesmerized** *or* **mesmerises, mesmerising, mesmerised** (*tr*) **1** to hold (someone) as if spellbound **2** a former word for **hypnotize** > **,mesmeri'zation** *or* **,mesmeri'sation** *n* > **'mesmer,izer** *or* **'mesmer,iser** *n*

mesne (mi:n) *adj law* **1** intermediate or intervening: *a mesne assignment of property* **2 mesne profits** rents or profits accruing during the rightful owner's exclusion from his land [c15 from legal F *meien* in the middle]

meso- *or before a vowel* **mes-** *combining form* middle or intermediate: *mesomorph* [from Gk *misos* middle]

mesoblast ('mɛsəʊ,blæst) *n* another name for **mesoderm** > **,meso'blastic** *adj*

mesocarp ('mɛsəʊ,kɑ:p) *n* the middle layer of the pericarp of a fruit, such as the flesh of a peach

mesocephalic (,mɛsəʊsɪ'fælɪk) *anat* ▷ *adj* **1** having a medium-sized head ▷ *n* **2** an individual with such a head > **mesocephaly** (,mɛsəʊ'sɛfəlɪ) *n*

mesoderm ('mɛsəʊ,dɜ:m) *n* the middle germ layer of an animal embryo, giving rise to muscle, blood, bone, connective tissue, etc > **,meso'dermal** *or* **,meso'dermic** *adj*

Mesolithic (,mɛsəʊ'lɪθɪk) *n* **1** the period between the Palaeolithic and the Neolithic, in Europe from about 12 000 to 3000 BC ▷ *adj* **2** of or relating to the Mesolithic

Mesolonghi (,mɛsə'lɔ:ŋgɪ) *n* a variant of **Missolonghi**

Mesolóngion (,mɛsə'lɒŋgɪ,ɒn) *n* transliteration of the Modern Greek name for **Missolonghi**

mesomorph ('mɛsəʊ,mɔ:f) *n* a type of person having a muscular body build with a relatively prominent underlying bone structure

mesomorphic (,mɛsəʊ'mɔ:fɪk) *adj* **1** *chem* existing in or concerned with an intermediate state of matter between a true liquid and a true solid **2** relating to or being a mesomorph ▷ Also: **mesomorphous** > **,meso'morphism** *n*

meson ('mi:zɒn) *n* any of a group of elementary particles that has a rest mass between those of an electron and a proton, and an integral spin [c20 from MESO- + -ON] > **me'sonic** *or* **'mesic** *adj*

mesophyte ('mɛsəʊ,faɪt) *n* any plant that grows in surroundings receiving an average supply of water

Mesopotamia (,mɛsəpə'teɪmɪə) *n* a region of SW Asia between the lower and middle reaches of the Tigris and Euphrates rivers: site of several ancient civilizations [Latin from Greek *mesopotamia* (*khora*) (the land) between rivers] > **,Mesopo'tamian** *n, adj*
▷ www.mesopotamia.co.uk/menu.html
▷ www.fordham.edu/halsall/ancient/asbook03.html

mesosphere ('mɛsəʊ,sfɪə) *n* the atmospheric layer lying between the stratosphere and the thermosphere

Mesozoic (,mɛsəʊ'zəʊɪk) *adj* **1** of, denoting, or relating to an era of geological time that began 250 million years ago and lasted about 185 million years ▷ *n* **2 the** the Mesozoic era

mesquite *or* **mesquit** (mɛ'ski:t, 'mɛski:t) *n* any of various small trees, esp a tropical American variety, whose sugary pods (**mesquite beans**) are used as animal fodder [c19 from Mexican Sp., from Nahautl *mizquitl*]

mess (mɛs) *n* **1** a state of confusion or untidiness, esp if dirty or unpleasant **2** a chaotic or troublesome state of affairs; muddle **3** *inf* a dirty or untidy person or thing **4** *arch* a portion of food, esp soft or semiliquid food **5** a place where service personnel eat or take recreation **6** a group of people, usually servicemen, who eat together **7** the meal so taken ▷ *vb* **8** (*tr; often foll by up*) to muddle or dirty **9** (*intr*) to make a mess **10** (*intr; often foll by with*) to interfere; meddle **11** (*intr; often foll by with or together*) *Mil.* to group together, esp for eating [c13 from OF *mes* dish of food, from LL *missus* course (at table), from L *mittere* to send forth]

mess about *or* **around** *vb* (*adv*) **1** (*intr*) to occupy oneself trivially; potter **2** (when *intr*, often foll by *with*) to interfere or meddle (with) **3** (*intr; sometimes foll by with*) *chiefly US* to engage in adultery

message ('mɛsɪdʒ) *n* **1** a communication, usually brief, from one person or group to another **2** an implicit meaning, as in a work of art **3** a formal communiqué **4** an inspired communication of a prophet or religious leader **5** a mission; errand **6 get the message** *inf* to understand ▷ *vb* **messages, messaging, messaged 7** (*tr*) to send as a message [c13 from OF, from Vulgar L *missāticum* (unattested) something sent, from L *missus*, p.p. of *mittere*]

Messager (*French* mɛsaʒe) *n* **André** (**Charles Prosper**) (ɑ̃dre) 1853–1929, French composer and conductor

messages ('mɛsɪdʒɪz) *pl n Scot & NE English dialect* household shopping

message stick *n* a stick bearing carved symbols, carried by a native Australian as identification

messaging ('mɛsidʒɪŋ) *n* the sending and processing of a message by any form of electronic communication

Messalina (,mɛsə'li:nə) *n* **Valeria** (və'lɪərɪə) died 48 AD, wife of the Roman emperor Claudius, notorious for her debauchery and cruelty

Messene (mɛ'si:nɪ) *n* an ancient Greek city in the SW Peloponnese: founded in 369 BC as the capital of Messenia

messenger ('mɛsɪndʒə) *n* **1** a person who takes messages from one person or group to another **2** a person who runs errands **3** a carrier of official dispatches; courier [c13 from OF *messagier*, from MESSAGE]

messenger RNA *n biochem* a form of RNA, transcribed from a single strand of DNA, that carries genetic information required for protein synthesis from DNA to the ribosomes. Shortened to **mRNA**

Messenia (mə'si:nɪə) *n* the southwestern area of the Peloponnese in S Greece

Messerschmitt (*German* 'mɛsərʃmɪt) *n* **Willy** ('vɪli) 1898–1978, German aeronautical engineer. His military planes figured prominently in World War II, including the Me-262, the first jet fighter

mess hall *n* a military dining room

Messiaen (*French* mɛsjɑ̃) *n* **Olivier** (ɔlivje) 1908–92, French composer and organist. His music is distinguished by its rhythmic intricacy; he was influenced by Hindu and Greek rhythms and bird song

Messiah (mɪ'saɪə) *n* **1** *Judaism* the awaited king of the Jews, to be sent by God to free them **2** Jesus Christ, when regarded in this role **3** an exceptional or hoped-for liberator of a country or people [c14 from OF *Messie*, ult. from Heb. *māshīah* anointed] > **Mes'siahship** *n* > **Messianic** *or* **messianic** (,mɛsɪ'ænɪk) *adj*

Messier catalogue ('mɛsɪ,eɪ) *n astron* a catalogue of 103 nonstellar objects, such as nebulae and galaxies, prepared in 1781–86. An object is referred to by its number in this catalogue, for example the Andromeda Galaxy is referred to as *M31* [c18 after Charles *Messier* (1730–1817), F astronomer]

messieurs ('mɛsəz) *n* the plural of **monsieur**

Messina (mɛ'si:nə) *n* a port in NE Sicily, on the **Strait of**

Messina: colonized by Greeks around 730 BC; under Spanish rule (1282–1676 and 1678–1713); university (1549). Pop: 259 156 (2000 est)

mess jacket *n* a waist-length jacket, worn by officers in the mess for formal dinners

mess kit *n mil* 1 *Brit* formal evening wear for officers 2 Also called: **mess gear** eating utensils used esp in the field

messmate ('mɛs,meɪt) *n* a person with whom one shares meals in a mess, esp in the army

Messrs ('mɛsəz) *n* the plural of **Mr** [C18 abbrev from F *messieurs*, pl. of MONSIEUR]

messy ('mɛsɪ) *adj* **messier, messiest** dirty, confused, or untidy > **'messily** *adv* > **'messiness** *n*

mestizo (mɛ'sti:zəʊ, mɪ-) *n, pl* **mestizos** *or* **mestizoes** a person of mixed parentage, esp the offspring of a Spanish American and an American Indian [C16 from Sp., ult. from L *miscēre* to mix] > **mestiza** (mɛ'sti:zə) *fem n*

mestranol ('mɛstrə,nɒl, -,nəʊl) *n* a synthetic oestrogen used in combination with progestogen as an oral contraceptive [C20 from M(ETHYL) + (O)ESTR(OGEN) + (*pregn*)*an*(*e*) + -OL]

Meštrović (*Serbo-Croat* 'mɛʃtrɔvitʃ) *n* **Ivan** ('ivan) 1883–1962, US sculptor, born in Austria: his works include portraits of Sir Thomas Beecham and Pope Pius XI

met (mɛt) *vb* the past tense and past participle of **meet**[1]

met. *abbrev for:* 1 meteorological 2 meteorology

meta- *or sometimes before a vowel* **met-** *prefix* 1 indicating change or alternation: *metabolism; metamorphosis* 2 (of an academic discipline) concerned with the concepts and results of that discipline: *metamathematics* 3 occurring or situated behind or after: *metaphysics* 4 (*often in italics*) denoting that an organic compound contains a benzene ring with substituents in the 1,3-positions: *meta*-cresol. Abbrev: *m-* 5 denoting an isomer, polymer, or compound related to a specified compound: *metaldehyde* 6 denoting an oxyacid that is the least hydrated form of the anhydride or a salt of such an acid: *metaphosphoric acid* [from Gk (prep)]

metabolism (mɪ'tæbə,lɪzəm) *n* 1 the sum total of the chemical processes that occur in living organisms, resulting in growth, production of energy, elimination of waste, etc 2 the sum total of the chemical processes affecting a particular substance in the body: *carbohydrate metabolism* [C19 from Gk *metabolē* change, from *metaballein*, from META- + *ballein* to throw] > **metabolic** (,mɛtə'bɒlɪk) *adj* > **,meta'bolically** *adv*

metabolize *or* **metabolise** (mɪ'tæbə,laɪz) *vb* **metabolizes, metabolizing, metabolized** *or* **metabolises, metabolising, metabolised** to bring about or subject to metabolism

metacarpal (,mɛtə'kɑ:pəl) *anat* ▷ *adj* 1 of or relating to the metacarpus ▷ *n* 2 a metacarpal bone

metacarpus (,mɛtə'kɑ:pəs) *n, pl* **metacarpi** (-paɪ) 1 the skeleton of the hand between the wrist and the fingers, consisting of five long bones 2 the corresponding bones in other vertebrates

metacentre *or US* **metacenter** ('mɛtə,sɛntə) *n* the intersection of a vertical line through the centre of buoyancy of a floating body at equilibrium with a vertical line through the centre of buoyancy when the body is tilted > **,meta'centric** *adj*

metacomputer (,mɛtəkəm'pju:tə) *n* an interconnected and balanced set of computers that operate as a single unit > **,metacom'puting** *n*

meta-data *pl n computing.* information that is held as a description of stored data

metage ('mi:tɪdʒ) *n* 1 the official measuring of weight or contents 2 a charge for this [C16 from METE[1]]

metal ('mɛtəl) *n* **1a** any of a number of chemical elements, such as iron or copper, that are often lustrous ductile solids, have basic oxides, form positive ions, and are good conductors of heat and electricity **1b** an alloy, such as brass or steel, containing one or more of these elements 2 the substance of glass in a molten state or as the finished product 3 short for **road metal** 4 *inf* short for **heavy metal** 5 *heraldry* gold or silver 6 the basic quality of a person or thing; stuff 7 (*pl*) the rails of a railway ▷ *adj* 8 made of metal ▷ *vb* **metals, metalling, metalled** *or US* **metals, metaling, metaled** (*tr*) 9 to fit or cover with metal 10 to make or mend (a road) with road metal [C13 from L *metallum* mine, product of a mine, from Gk *metallon*] > **'metalled** *adj*

> USAGE *Metal* is sometimes mistakenly used instead of *mettle*: *this is a real test of the club's mettle* (not *metal*)

metal. *or* **metall.** *abbrev for:* 1 metallurgical 2 metallurgy

metalanguage ('mɛtə,læŋgwɪdʒ) *n* a language or system of symbols used to discuss another language or system ▷ Cf **object language**

metal detector *n* a device that gives an audible or visual signal when its search head comes close to a metallic object embedded in food, buried in the ground, etc

metallic (mɪ'tælɪk) *adj* 1 of, concerned with, or consisting of metal or a metal 2 suggestive of a metal: *a metallic click; metallic lustre* 3 *chem* (of a metal element) existing in the free state rather than in combination: *metallic copper*

metallic soap *n* any one of a number of salts or esters containing a metal, such as aluminium, calcium, magnesium, iron, and zinc. They are used as bases for ointments, fungicides, fireproofing and waterproofing agents, and dryers for paints and varnishes

metalliferous (,mɛtə'lɪfərəs) *adj* containing a high concentration of metallic elements [C17 from L *metallifer* yielding metal, from *metallum* metal + *ferre* to bear]

metallize, metallise, *or US* **metalize** ('mɛtə,laɪz) *vb* **metallizes, metallizing, metallized; metallises, metallising, metallised** *or US* **metalizes, metalizing, metalized** (*tr*) to make metallic or to coat or treat with metal > **,metalli'zation, metalli'sation,** *or US* **,metali'zation** *n*

metallography (,mɛtə'lɒgrəfɪ) *n* the branch of metallurgy concerned with the composition and structure of metals and alloys > **metallographic** (mɪ,tælə'græfɪk) *adj*

metalloid ('mɛtə,lɔɪd) *n* 1 a nonmetallic element, such as arsenic or silicon, that has some of the properties of a metal ▷ *adj also* **,metal'loidal** 2 of or being a metalloid 3 resembling a metal

metallurgy (mɛ'tælədʒɪ) *n* the scientific study of the extraction, refining, alloying, and fabrication of metals and of their structure and properties > **metallurgic** (,mɛtə'lɜ:dʒɪk) *or* **,metal'lurgical** *adj* > **metallurgist** (mɛ'tælədʒɪst, 'mɛtə,lɜ:dʒɪst) *n*

▷ www.psigate.ac.uk/newsite/materials-gateway.html

metal road *n Austral & NZ* an unsealed road covered in gravel or shingle

metal tape *n* a magnetic recording tape coated with pure iron: it gives enhanced recording quality

metalwork ('mɛtəl,wɜ:k) *n* 1 the craft of working in metal 2 work in metal or articles made from metal

metalworking ('mɛtəl,wɜ:kɪŋ) *n* the processing of metal to change its shape, size, etc > **'metal,worker** *n*

metamere ('mɛtə,mɪə) *n* one of the similar body segments into which earthworms, crayfish, and similar animals are divided longitudinally > **metameral** (mɪ'tæmərəl) *adj*

metamerism (mɪ'tæmə,rɪzəm) *n* 1 Also called: (**metameric**) **segmentation** the division of an animal into metameres 2 *chem* a type of isomerism in which molecular structures differ by the attachment of different groups to the same atom > **metameric** (,mɛtə'mɛrɪk) *adj*

metamict ('mɛtəˌmɪkt) *adj* of or denoting the amorphous state of a substance that has lost its crystalline structure as a result of the radioactivity of uranium or thorium within it > ˌ**metaˌmictiˈzation** *or* ˌ**metaˌmictiˈsation** *n*

metamorphic (ˌmɛtəˈmɔːfɪk) *or* **metamorphous** *adj* **1** relating to or resulting from metamorphosis or metamorphism **2** (of rocks) altered considerably from their original structure and mineralogy by pressure and heat

metamorphism (ˌmɛtəˈmɔːfɪzəm) *n* **1** the process by which metamorphic rocks are formed **2** a variant of **metamorphosis**

metamorphose (ˌmɛtəˈmɔːfəʊz) *vb* **metamorphoses, metamorphosing, metamorphosed** to undergo or cause to undergo metamorphosis or metamorphism

metamorphosis (ˌmɛtəˈmɔːfəsɪs) *n, pl* **metamorphoses** (-ˌsiːz) **1** a complete change of physical form or substance **2** a complete change of character, appearance, etc **3** a person or thing that has undergone metamorphosis **4** *zool* the rapid transformation of a larva into an adult that occurs in certain animals, for example the stage between chrysalis and butterfly [c16 via L from Gk: transformation, from META- + *morphē* form]

metaphor ('mɛtəfə, -ˌfɔː) *n* a figure of speech in which a word or phrase is applied to an object or action that it does not literally denote in order to imply a resemblance, for example *he is a lion in battle* ▷ Cf **simile** [c16 from L, from Gk *metaphora*, from *metapherein* to transfer, from META- + *pherein* to bear] > **metaphoric** (ˌmɛtəˈfɒrɪk) *or* ˌ**metaˈphorical** *adj* > ˌ**metaˈphorically** *adv*

metaphrase ('mɛtəˌfreɪz) *n* **1** a literal translation ▷ *vb* **metaphrases, metaphrasing, metaphrased** (*tr*) **2** to alter or manipulate the wording of **3** to translate literally [c17 from Gk *metaphrazein* to translate]

metaphrast ('mɛtəˌfræst) *n* a person who metaphrases, esp one who changes the form of a text, as by rendering verse into prose [c17 from Med. Gk *metaphrastēs* translator] > ˌ**metaˈphrastic** *or* ˌ**metaˈphrastical** *adj* > ˌ**metaˈphrastically** *adv*

metaphysic (ˌmɛtəˈfɪzɪk) *n* the system of first principles and assumptions underlying an inquiry or philosophical theory

metaphysical (ˌmɛtəˈfɪzɪkᵊl) *adj* **1** of or relating to metaphysics **2** (of a statement or theory) having an empirical form but in fact immune from empirical testing **3** (popularly) abstract, abstruse, or unduly theoretical **4** incorporeal; supernatural > ˌ**metaˈphysically** *adv*

Metaphysical (ˌmɛtəˈfɪzɪkᵊl) *adj* **1** denoting or relating to certain 17th-century poets who combined intense feeling with elaborate imagery ▷ *n* **2** a poet of this group

metaphysics (ˌmɛtəˈfɪzɪks) *n* (*functioning as sing*) **1** the branch of philosophy that deals with first principles, esp of being and knowing **2** the philosophical study of the nature of reality **3** (popularly) abstract or subtle discussion or reasoning [c16 from Med. L, from Gk *ta meta ta phusika* the things after the physics, from the arrangement of subjects treated in the works of Aristotle] > **metaphysician** (ˌmɛtəfɪˈzɪʃən) *or* **metaphysicist** (ˌmɛtəˈfɪzɪsɪst) *n*

▷ www.foolquest.com/metaphysics_for_dummies.htm
▷ http://pespmc1.vub.ac.be/METAPHI.html
▷ www.qozi.com/philosophy/metaphysics.html

metapsychology (ˌmɛtəsaɪˈkɒlədʒɪ) *n* *psychol* **1** the study of philosophical questions, such as the relation between mind and body, that go beyond the laws of experimental psychology **2** any attempt to state the general laws of psychology **3** another word for **parapsychology** > **metapsychological** (ˌmɛtəˌsaɪkəˈlɒdʒɪkᵊl) *adj*

metastable (ˌmɛtəˈsteɪbᵊl) *adj* *Physics.* (of a body or system) having a state of apparent equilibrium although capable of changing to a more stable state > ˌ**metastaˈbility** *n*

metastasis (mɪˈtæstəsɪs) *n, pl* **metastases** (-ˌsiːz) *pathol* the spreading of a disease organism, esp cancer cells, from one part of the body to another [c16 via L from Gk: transition] > **metastatic** (ˌmɛtəˈstætɪk) *adj* > ˌ**metaˈstatically** *adv*

metastasize *or* **metastasise** (mɪˈtæstəˌsaɪz) *vb* **metastasizes, metastasizing, metastasized** *or* **metastasises, metastasising, metastasised** (*intr*) *pathol* (esp of cancer cells) to spread to a new site in the body via blood or lymph vessels

metatarsal (ˌmɛtəˈtɑːsᵊl) *anat* ▷ *adj* **1** of or relating to the metatarsus ▷ *n* **2** any bone of the metatarsus

metatarsus (ˌmɛtəˈtɑːsəs) *n, pl* **metatarsi** (-saɪ) **1** the skeleton of the human foot between the toes and the tarsus, consisting of five long bones **2** the corresponding skeletal part in other vertebrates

metathesis (mɪˈtæθəsɪs) *n, pl* **metatheses** (-ˌsiːz) the transposition of two sounds or letters in a word [c16 from LL, from Gk, from *metatithenai* to transpose] > **metathetic** (ˌmɛtəˈθɛtɪk) *or* ˌ**metaˈthetical** *adj*

metazoan (ˌmɛtəˈzəʊən) *n* **1** any multicellular animal: includes all animals except sponges ▷ *adj also* **metazoic** **2** of or relating to the metazoans [c19 from NL *Metazoa*; see META-, -ZOA]

Metchnikoff (*French* mɛtʃnikɔf; *Russian* ˈmjetʃnikəf) *n* **Élie** (eli) 1845–1916, Russian bacteriologist in France. He formulated the theory of phagocytosis and shared the Nobel prize for physiology or medicine 1908

mete[1] (miːt) *vb* **metes, meting, meted** (*tr*) **1** (usually foll by *out*) *Formal.* to distribute or allot (something, often unpleasant) **2** *poetic, dialect* to measure [OE *metan*]

mete[2] (miːt) *n* *rare* a mark, limit, or boundary (esp in **metes and bounds**) [c15 from OF, from L *mēta* goal, turning post (in race)]

Mm

metempsychosis (ˌmɛtəmsaɪˈkəʊsɪs) *n, pl* **metempsychoses** (-siːz) the migration of a soul from one body to another [c16 via LL from Gk, from *metempsukhousthai*, from META- + *-em-* in + *psukhē* soul] > ˌ**metempsyˈchosist** *n*

meteor (ˈmiːtɪə) *n* **1** a very small meteoroid that has entered the earth's atmosphere **2** Also called: **shooting star, falling star** the bright streak of light appearing in the sky due to the incandescence of such a body heated by friction at its surface [c15 from Med. L *meteōrum*, from Gk *meteōron*, from *meteōros* lofty, from *meta-* (intensifier) + *aeirein* to raise]

meteoric (ˌmiːtɪˈɒrɪk) *adj* **1** of, formed by, or relating to meteors **2** like a meteor in brilliance, speed, or transience **3** *rare* of weather; meteorological > ˌ**meteˈorically** *adv*

meteorism (ˈmiːtɪəˌrɪzəm) *n* *med* another name for **tympanites**

meteorite (ˈmiːtɪəˌraɪt) *n* a rocklike object consisting of the remains of a meteoroid that has fallen on earth > **meteoritic** (ˌmiːtɪəˈrɪtɪk) *adj*

meteoroid (ˈmiːtɪəˌrɔɪd) *n* any of the small celestial bodies that are thought to orbit the sun. When they enter the earth's atmosphere, they become visible as meteors > ˌ**meteorˈoidal** *adj*

meteorol. *or* **meteor.** *abbrev for:* **1** meteorological **2** meteorology

meteorology (ˌmiːtɪəˈrɒlədʒɪ) *n* the study of the earth's atmosphere, esp of weather-forming processes and weather forecasting [c17 from Gk; see METEOR, -LOGY] > **meteorological** (ˌmiːtɪərəˈlɒdʒɪkᵊl) *or* ˌ**meteoroˈlogic** *adj* > ˌ**meteoroˈlogically** *adv* > ˌ**meteorˈologist** *n*

▷ http://sciencepolicy.colorado.edu/socasp/toc_img.html
▷ http://personal.cmich.edu/~francım/homepage.htm

▹ www.wmo.ch
▹ www.worldweather.org

meteor shower *n* a transient rain of meteors occurring at regular intervals and coming from a particular region in the sky

meter[1] ('mi:tə) *n* **1** any device that measures and records a quantity, such as of gas, current, voltage, etc, that has passed through it during a specified period **2** See **parking meter** ▹ *vb* (*tr*) **3** to measure (a rate of flow) with a meter [C19 see METE[1]]

meter[2] ('mi:tə) *n* the US spelling of **metre**[1]

meter[3] ('mi:tə) *n* the US spelling of **metre**[2]

-meter *n combining form* **1** indicating an instrument for measuring: *barometer* **2** *prosody* indicating a verse having a specified number of feet: *pentameter* [from Gk *metron* measure]

Meth. *abbrev for* Methodist

meth- *combining form* indicating a chemical compound derived from methane or containing methyl groups: *methacrylic acid*

methacrylic acid (ˌmɛθə'krɪlɪk) *n* a colourless crystalline water-soluble substance used in the manufacture of acrylic resins

methadone ('mɛθəˌdəʊn) *or* **methadon** ('mɛθəˌdɒn) *n* a narcotic analgesic drug similar to morphine, used to treat opiate addiction [C20 from (*di*)*meth*(*yl*) + A(MINO) + *d*(*iphenyl*) + -ONE]

methamphetamine (ˌmɛθæm'fɛtəmi:n, -mɪn) *n* a variety of amphetamine used for its stimulant action [C20 from METH- + AMPHETAMINE]

methanal ('mɛθəˌnæl) *n* the systematic name for **formaldehyde**

methane ('mi:θeɪn) *n* a colourless odourless flammable gas, the main constituent of natural gas: used as a fuel. Formula: CH_4

methane series *n* another name for **alkane series**

methanoic acid ('mɛθəˌnəʊɪk) *n* the systematic name for **formic acid**

methanol ('mɛθəˌnɒl) *n* a colourless volatile poisonous liquid compound used as a solvent and fuel. Formula: CH_3OH. Also called: **methyl alcohol, wood alcohol** [C20 from METHANE + -OL[1]]

methinks (mɪ'θɪŋks) *vb past* **methought** (*tr; takes a clause as object*) *arch* or *hum* it seems to me: *methinks a pint would help the situation*

metho ('mɛθəʊ) *n Austral inf* **1** another name for **methylated spirits** **2** (*pl* **methos**) a drinker of methylated spirits

method ('mɛθəd) *n* **1** a way of proceeding or doing something, esp a systematic or regular one **2** orderliness of thought, action, etc **3** (*often pl*) the techniques or arrangement of work for a particular field or subject [C16 via F from L, from Gk *methodos*, lit.: a going after, from *meta-* after + *hodos* way]

Method ('mɛθəd) *n* (*sometimes not cap*) **a** a technique of acting in which the actor bases his role on the inner motivation of the character played **b** (*as modifier*): *a Method actor*

▹ www.vtheatre.net/acting/method.html
▹ www.theatrelinks.com
▹ www.theatrgroup.com/Method

methodical (mɪ'θɒdɪk[ə]l) *or* (*less commonly*) **methodic** *adj* characterized by method or orderliness; systematic > **me'thodically** *adv*

Methodism ('mɛθəˌdɪzəm) *n* the system and practices of the Methodist Church

Methodist ('mɛθədɪst) *n* **1** a member of any of the Nonconformist denominations that derive from the system of faith and practice initiated by John Wesley and his followers ▹ *adj also* ˌ**Method'istic** *or* ˌ**Method'istical** **2** of or relating to Methodism or the Church embodying it (the **Methodist Church**)

▹ http://www.methodist.org.uk/
▹ http://www.methodist.co.za/
▹ http://www.methodist.org.nz/

Methodius (mɛ'θəʊdɪəs) *n* **Saint,** with his younger brother Saint Cyril called *the Apostles of the Slavs*. 815–885 AD, Greek Christian theologian sent as a missionary to the Moravians. Feast day: Feb 14 or May 11

methodize *or* **methodise** ('mɛθəˌdaɪz) *vb* **methodizes, methodizing, methodized** *or* **methodises, methodising, methodised** (*tr*) to organize according to a method; systematize > '**methodˌizer** *or* '**methodˌiser** *n*

methodology (ˌmɛθə'dɒlədʒɪ) *n, pl* **methodologies** **1** the system of methods and principles used in a particular discipline **2** the branch of philosophy concerned with the science of method > **methodological** (ˌmɛθədə'lɒdʒɪk[ə]l) *adj* > ˌ**methodo'logically** *adv* > ˌ**method'ologist** *n*

methought (mɪ'θɔ:t) *vb arch* the past tense of **methinks**

meths (mɛθs) *n chiefly Brit, Austral, & NZ* an informal name for **methylated spirits**

Methuselah (mɪ'θju:zələ) *n Old Testament* a patriarch reputed to have lived 969 years (Genesis 5:21–27), regarded as epitomizing longevity. Douay spelling: **Mathusala**

methyl ('mi:θaɪl, 'mɛθɪl) *n* **1** (*modifier*) of, consisting of, or containing the monovalent group of atoms CH_3 **2** a compound in which methyl groups are bound directly to a metal atom [C19 from F *méthyle*, back formation from METHYLENE] > **methylic** (mə'θɪlɪk) *adj*

methyl acetate *n* a colourless volatile flammable liquid ester used as a solvent, esp in paint removers. Formula: CH_3COOCH_3. Systematic name: **methyl ethanoate**

methyl alcohol *n* another name for **methanol**

methylate ('mɛθɪˌleɪt) *vb* **methylates, methylating, methylated** (*tr*) to mix with methanol

methylated spirits *n* (*functioning as sing or pl*) alcohol that has been denatured by the addition of methanol and pyridine and a violet dye. Also: **methylated spirit**

methyl chloride *n* a colourless gas with an ether-like odour, used as a refrigerant and anaesthetic. Formula: CH_3Cl. Systematic name: **chloromethane**

methylene ('mɛθɪˌli:n) *n* (*modifier*) of, consisting of, or containing the divalent group of atoms $=CH_2$: *a methylene group or radical* [C19 from F *méthylène*, from Gk *methu* wine + *hulē* wood + -ENE: orig. referring to a substance distilled from wood]

methylene dichloride *n* the traditional name for **dichloromethane**

methylphenol (ˌmi:θaɪl'fi:nɒl) *n* the systematic name for **cresol**

meticulous (mɪ'tɪkjʊləs) *adj* very precise about details; painstaking [C16 (meaning: timid): from L *meticulōsus* fearful, from *metus* fear] > **me'ticulously** *adv* > **me'ticulousness** *n*

métier ('mɛtɪeɪ) *n* **1** a profession or trade **2** a person's strong point or speciality [C18 from F, ult. from L *ministerium* service]

me-time *n* the time a person has to himself or herself, in which to do something for his or her own enjoyment

Métis (mɛ'ti:s) *n, pl* **Métis** (-'ti:s, -'ti:z) a person of mixed parentage, esp the offspring of a French Canadian and a North American Indian [C19 from F, from Vulgar L *mixtīcius* (unattested) of mixed race] > **Métisse** (mɛ'ti:s) *fem n*

metol ('mi:tɒl) *n* a colourless soluble organic substance used, in the form of its sulphate, as a photographic developer [C20 from G, arbitrary coinage]

Metonic cycle (mɪ'tɒnɪk) *n* a cycle of 235 synodic months after which the phases of the moon recur on the same day of the month [C17 after *Meton*, 5th-cent. BC Athenian astronomer]

metonymy (mɪ'tɒnɪmɪ) *n, pl* **metonymies** the substitution of a word referring to an attribute for the thing that is meant, eg *the crown*, used to refer to a monarch ▹ Cf **synecdoche** [C16 from LL, from Gk, from

meta- (indicating change) + *onoma* name] > **metonymical** (ˌmɛtəˈnɪmɪkᵊl) *or* **ˌmetoˈnymic** *adj*
metope (ˈmɛtəʊp, ˈmɛtəpɪ) *n archit* a square space between triglyphs in a Doric frieze [C16 via L from Gk, from *meta* between + *opē* one of the holes for the beam-ends]
metre[1] *or US* **meter** (ˈmiːtə) *n* **1** a metric unit of length equal to approximately 1.094 yards **2** the basic SI unit of length; the length of the path travelled by light in free space during a time interval of 1/299 792 458 of a second. Symbol: m [C18 from F; see METRE[2]]
metre[2] *or US* **meter** (ˈmiːtə) *n* **1** *prosody* the rhythmic arrangement of syllables in verse, usually according to the number and kind of feet in a line **2** *music* another word (esp US) for **time** (sense 22) [C14 from L *metrum*, from Gk *metron* measure]
metre-kilogram-second *n* See **mks units**
metric (ˈmɛtrɪk) *adj* of or relating to the metre or metric system
metrical (ˈmɛtrɪkᵊl) *or* **metric** *adj* **1** of or relating to measurement **2** of or in poetic metre > **ˈmetrically** *adv*
metricate (ˈmɛtrɪˌkeɪt) *vb* **metricates, metricating, metricated** to convert (a measuring system, instrument, etc) from nonmetric to metric units > **ˌmetriˈcation** *n*
metric system *n* any decimal system of units based on the metre. For scientific purposes SI units are used

Metric Prefixes

Metric prefixes and their numerical equivalents stated in the US system of nomenclature for large numbers

yotta-	(Y-)	10^{24}	1 septillion
zetta-	(Z-)	10^{21}	1 sextillion
exa-	(E-)	10^{18}	1 quintillion
peta-	(P-)	10^{15}	1 quadrillion
tera-	(T-)	10^{12}	1 trillion
giga-	(G-)	10^{9}	1 billion
mega-	(M-)	10^{6}	1 million
***myria-**	(my-)	10^{4}	10 thousand
kilo-	(k-)	10^{3}	1 thousand
hecto-	(h-)	10^{2}	1 hundred
****deca-**	(da-)	10	1 ten
deci-	(d-)	10^{-1}	1 tenth
centi-	(c-)	10^{-2}	1 hundredth
milli-	(m-)	10^{-3}	1 thousandth
micro-	(mu-)	10^{-6}	1 millionth
nano-	(n-)	10^{-9}	1 billionth
pico-	(p-)	10^{-12}	1 trillionth
femto-	(f-)	10^{-15}	1 quadrillionth
atto-	(a-)	10^{-18}	1 quintillionth
zepto-	(z-)	10^{-21}	1 sextillionth
yocto-	(y-)	10^{-24}	1 septillionth

NOTES
*The prefix myria- is now considered obsolete. It is not approved for use with SI units.
**The SI Brochure spelling is *deca-* but the US National Institute of Standards and technology recommends *deka-*

▷ www.bipm.fr/en/si

metric ton *n* another name for **tonne**
metro (ˈmɛtrəʊ) *or* **métro** *French.* (metro) *n, pl* **metros** an underground, or largely underground, railway system in certain cities, such as that in Paris [C20 from F, *chemin de fer métropolitain* metropolitan railway]
Metro (ˈmɛtrəʊ) *n Canad* a metropolitan city administration, esp Metropolitan Toronto
metronome (ˈmɛtrəˌnəʊm) *n* a device which indicates the tempo of music by producing a clicking sound from a pendulum with an adjustable period of swing [C19 from Gk *metron* measure + *nomos* law] > **metronomic** (ˌmɛtrəˈnɒmɪk) *adj*
metronymic (ˌmɛtrəʊˈnɪmɪk) *adj* **1** (of a name) derived from the name of the mother or other female ancestor ▷ *n* **2** a metronymic name [C19 from Gk *mētronumikos*, from *mētēr* mother + *onoma* name]
metropolis (mɪˈtrɒpəlɪs) *n, pl* **metropolises 1** the main city, esp of a country or region **2** a centre of activity **3** the chief see in an ecclesiastical province [C16 from LL from Gk, from *mētēr* mother + *polis* city]
metropolitan (ˌmɛtrəˈpɒlɪtən) *adj* **1** of or characteristic of a metropolis **2** constituting a city and its suburbs **3** of, relating to, or designating an ecclesiastical metropolis **4** of or belonging to the home territories of a country, as opposed to overseas territories: *metropolitan France* ▷ *n* **5a** *Eastern Churches.* the head of an ecclesiastical province, ranking between archbishop and patriarch **5b** *Church of England* an archbishop **5c** *RC Church* an archbishop or bishop having authority over the dioceses in his province > **ˌmetroˈpolitanism** *n*
metropolitan county *n* (in England) any of the six conurbations established as units in the new local government system in 1974; the metropolitan county councils were abolished in 1986
metropolitan district *n* (in England since 1974) any of the districts that make up the metropolitan counties of England: since 1986 they have functioned as unitary authorities
Metropolitan Museum of Art *n* the principal museum in New York City: founded in 1870 and housed in its present premises in Central Park since 1880
▷ www.metmuseum.org
metrorrhagia (ˌmiːtrɔːˈreɪdʒɪə, ˌmɛt-) *n* abnormal bleeding from the uterus [C19 NL, from Gk *mētra* womb + *-rrhagia* a breaking forth]
metrosexual (ˌmɛtrəʊˈsɛksjʊəl) *adj inf* of or relating to a heterosexual man who spends a lot of time and money on his appearance and likes to shop
-metry *n combining form* indicating the process or science of measuring: *geometry* [from OF *-metrie*, from L, ult. from Gk *metron* measure] > **-metric** *adj combining form*
Metternich (*German* ˈmɛtərnɪç) *n* **Klemens** (ˈkleːməns) 1773–1859, Austrian statesman. He became foreign minister (1809) and made a significant contribution to the Congress of Vienna (1815). From 1821 to 1848 he was both foreign minister and chancellor of Austria and is noted for his defence of autocracy in Europe
mettle (ˈmɛtᵊl) *n* **1** courage; spirit **2** character **3 on one's mettle** roused to making one's best efforts [C16 orig. var. of METAL]
USAGE See at **metal**
mettled (ˈmɛtᵊld) *or* **mettlesome** (ˈmɛtᵊlsəm) *adj* courageous, spirited, or valiant
Metz (mɛts; *French* mɛs) *n* a city in NE France on the River Moselle: a free imperial city in the 13th century; annexed by France in 1552; part of Germany (1871–1918); centre of iron-mining in Lorraine. Pop: 123 776 (1999)
Meung (*French* mỹ) *n* See **Jean de Meung**
Meurthe-et-Moselle (*French* mœrtemozɛl) *n* a department of NE France, in Lorraine. Capital: Nancy. Pop: 713 779 (1999). Area: 5280 sq km (2059 sq miles)
Meuse (mɜːz; *French* møz) *n* **1** a department of N France, in Lorraine region: heavy fighting occurred here in World War I. Capital: Bar-le-Duc. Pop: 192 198 (1999). Area: 6241 sq km (2434 sq miles) **2** a river in W Europe, rising in NE France and flowing north across E Belgium and the S Netherlands to join the Waal River before

entering the North Sea. Length: 926 km (575 miles). Dutch name: **Maas**

MeV *symbol for* million electronvolts (10^6 electronvolts)

mevrou (mə'frəʊ) *n* a S African title of address equivalent to *Mrs* when placed before a surname or *madam* when used alone [Afrik.]

mew[1] (mjuː) *vb* **1** (*intr*) (esp of a cat) to make a characteristic high-pitched cry ▷ *n* **2** such a sound [C14 imit.]

mew[2] (mjuː) *n* any seagull, esp the common gull [OE *mǣw*]

mew[3] (mjuː) *n* **1** a room or cage for hawks, esp while moulting ▷ *vb* (*tr*) **2** (often foll by *up*) to confine (hawks or falcons) in a shelter, cage, etc **3** to confine; conceal [C14 from OF *mue*, from *muer* to moult, from L *mūtāre* to change]

Mewar (mɛ'wɑː) *n* another name for **Udaipur** (sense 1)

mewl (mjuːl) *vb* **1** (*intr*) (esp of a baby) to cry weakly; whimper ▷ *n* **2** such a cry [C17 imit.]

mews (mjuːz) *n* (*functioning as sing or pl*) *chiefly Brit* **1** a yard or street lined by buildings originally used as stables but now often converted into dwellings **2** the buildings around a mews [C14 pl of MEW[3], orig. referring to royal stables built on the site of hawks' mews at Charing Cross in London]

Mex. *abbrev for:* **1** Mexican **2** Mexico

Mexicali (ˌmɛksɪ'kɑːlɪ; *Spanish* mexi'kali) *n* a city in NW Mexico, capital of Baja California Norte state, on the border with the US adjoining Calexico, California: centre of a rich irrigated agricultural region. Pop: 550 000 (2000 est)

Mexican wave *n* the rippling effect produced when the spectators in successive sections of a sports stadium stand up while raising their arms and then sit down [C20 first seen at the World Cup in Mexico in 1986]

Mexico ('mɛksɪˌkəʊ) *n* **1** a republic in North America, on the Gulf of Mexico and the Pacific: early Mexican history includes the Maya, Toltec, and Aztec civilizations; conquered by the Spanish between 1519 and 1525 and achieved independence in 1821; lost Texas to the US in 1836 and California and New Mexico in 1848. It is generally mountainous with three ranges of the Sierra Madre (east, west, and south) and a large central plateau. Official language: Spanish. Religion: Roman Catholic majority. Currency: peso. Capital: Mexico City. Pop: 99 969 000 (2001 est). Area: 1 967 183 sq km (761 530 sq miles). Official name: **United Mexican States** Spanish name: **Méjico** **2** a state of Mexico, on the central plateau surrounding Mexico City, which is not administratively part of the state. Capital: Toluca. Pop: 11 704 934 (1995 est). Area: 21 460 sq km (8287 sq miles) **3 Gulf of** an arm of the Atlantic, bordered by the US, Cuba, and Mexico: linked with the Atlantic by the Straits of Florida and with the Caribbean by the Yucatán Channel. Area: about 1 600 000 sq km (618 000 sq miles) > **Mexican** ('mɛksɪkən) *adj, n*
▷ www.presidencia.gob.mx
▷ www.visitmexico.com
▷ www.travelguidemexico.com

Mexico City *n* the capital of Mexico, on the central plateau at an altitude of 2240 m (7350 ft): founded as the Aztec capital (Tenochtitlán) in about 1300; conquered and rebuilt by the Spanish in 1521; forms, with its suburbs, the federal district of Mexico; the largest industrial complex in the country. Pop: 8 591 309 (2000 est)
▷ www.mexicocity.gob.mx

Meyerbeer (*German* 'maiərbeːr) *n* **Giacomo** ('dʒaːkomo), real name *Jakob Liebmann Beer*. 1791–1864, German composer, esp of operas, such as *Robert le diable* (1831) and *Les Huguenots* (1836)

Meyerhof (*German* 'maiərhoːf) *n* **Otto** (**Fritz**) ('ɔto) 1884–1951, German physiologist, noted for his work on the metabolism of muscles. He shared the Nobel prize for physiology or medicine 1922

Meyerhold ('maɪəhəʊlt) *n* **Vsevolod Emilievich,** original name *Karl Theodor Kasimir*. 1874–*c* 1940, Russian theatre director, noted for his experimental nonrealistic productions. He was arrested in 1939 and died in custody

MEZ *abbrev for* Central European Time [from G *Mitteleuropäische Zeit*]

mezcal (mɛ'skæl) *n* a variant spelling of **mescal**

mezcaline ('mɛskəˌliːn) *n* a variant spelling of **mescaline**

Mézières (*French* mezjɛr) *n* a town in NE France, on the River Meuse opposite Charleville. See **Charleville-Mézières**

mezuzah (mə'zʊzə) *n, pl* **mezuzahs** *or* **mezuzoth** (*Hebrew* məzu'zɔt) *Judaism* **1** a piece of parchment inscribed with biblical passages and fixed to the doorpost of a Jewish house **2** a metal case for such a parchment, sometimes worn as an ornament [from Heb., lit.: doorpost]

mezzanine ('mɛzəˌniːn, 'mɛtsəˌniːn) *n* **1** Also called: **mezzanine floor** an intermediate storey, esp a low one between the ground and first floor of a building **2** *theatre, US & Canad* the first balcony **3** *theatre, Brit* a room or floor beneath the stage ▷ *adj* **4** often shortened to **mezz** of or relating to an intermediate stage in a financial process: *mezzanine funding* [C18 from F, from It., dim. of *mezzano* middle, from L *mediānus* MEDIAN]

mezzo ('mɛtsəʊ) *adv music* moderately; quite: *mezzo piano* [C19 from It., lit.: half, from L *medius* middle]

mezzo-soprano *n, pl* **mezzo-sopranos** **1** a female voice intermediate between a soprano and contralto **2** a singer with such a voice

mezzotint ('mɛtsəʊˌtɪnt) *n* **1** a method of engraving a copper plate by scraping and burnishing the roughened surface **2** a print made from a plate so treated ▷ *vb* **3** (*tr*) to engrave (a copper plate) in this fashion [C18 from It. *mezzotinto* half tint]

mf *music symbol for:* mezzo forte [It.: moderately loud]

MF *abbrev for:* **1** *radio* medium frequency **2** Middle French

MFAT ('ɛmfæt) *n* (in New Zealand) *acronym for* Ministry of Foreign Affairs and Trade

mfd *abbrev for* manufactured

mfg *abbrev for* manufacturing

MFH *hunting abbrev for:* Master of Foxhounds

mfr *abbrev for:* **1** manufacture **2** manufacturer

mg *symbol for* milligram

Mg *the chemical symbol for* magnesium

Mgr *abbrev for:* **1** manager **2** Monseigneur **3** Monsignor

MHA (in Australia) *abbrev for* Member of the House of Assembly

MHG *abbrev for* Middle High German

mho (məʊ) *n, pl* **mhos** the former name for **siemens** [C19 formed by reversing the letters of OHM (first used by Lord Kelvin)]

MHR (in the US and Australia) *abbrev for* Member of the House of Representatives

MHz *symbol for* megahertz

mi (miː) *n music* **1** the syllable used in the fixed system of solmization for the note E **2** Also: **me** (in tonic sol-fa) the third degree of any major scale; a mediant [C14 see GAMUT]

MI *abbrev for:* **1** Michigan **2** Military Intelligence

mi. *abbrev for* mile

MI5 *abbrev for* Military Intelligence, section five; a former official and current popular name for the counterintelligence agency of the British Government

MI6 *abbrev for* Military Intelligence, section six; a former official and current popular name for the intelligence and espionage agency of the British Government

Miami (maɪ'æmɪ) *n* a city and resort in SE Florida, on Biscayne Bay: developed chiefly after 1896, esp with the Florida land boom of the 1920s; centre of an extensive tourist area. Pop: 362 470 (2000)

Miami Beach *n* a resort in SE Florida, on an island

separated from Miami by Biscayne Bay. Pop: 87 933 (2000)

Miandad (mɪˈændæd) *n* **Javed** (ˈdʒævɪd) born 1957, Pakistani cricketer, a famous batsman; played for Pakistan 1976–94; national team coach 1999–2001

miaou *or* **miaow** (mɪˈaʊ, mjaʊ) *vb, interj* variant spellings of **meow**

miasma (mɪˈæzmə) *n, pl* **miasmata** (-mətə) *or* **miasmas** 1 an unwholesome or foreboding atmosphere 2 pollution in the atmosphere, esp noxious vapours from decomposing organic matter [C17 NL, from Gk: defilement, from *miainein* to defile] > **miˈasmal** *or* **miasmatic** (ˌmi:əzˈmætɪk) *adj*

Mic. *Bible abbrev for:* Micah

mica (ˈmaɪkə) *n* any of a group of minerals consisting of hydrous silicates of aluminium, potassium, etc, in monoclinic crystalline form, occurring in igneous and metamorphic rock. Because of their resistance to electricity and heat they are used as dielectrics, in heating elements, etc [C18 from L: crumb] > **micaceous** (maɪˈkeɪʃəs) *adj*

Micah (ˈmaɪkə) *n Old Testament* 1 a Hebrew prophet of the late 8th century BC 2 the book containing his prophecies. Douay spelling: **Micheas** (maɪˈki:əs)

mice (maɪs) *n* the plural of **mouse**

micelle, micell (mɪˈsɛl) *or* **micella** (mɪˈsɛlə) *n chem* **a** a charged aggregate of molecules of colloidal size in a solution **b** any molecular aggregate of colloidal size [C19 from NL *micella*, dim. of L *mīca* crumb]

Mich. *abbrev for:* 1 Michaelmas 2 Michigan

Michael (ˈmaɪkᵊl) *n* 1 1596–1645, tsar of Russia (1613–45); founder of the Romanov dynasty 2 **Saint** *Bible* one of the archangels. Feast day: Sept 29 or Nov 8

Michaelmas (ˈmɪkᵊlməs) *n* Sept 29, the feast of St Michael the archangel; in England, Ireland, and Wales, one of the four quarter days

Michaelmas daisy *n Brit* any of various composite plants that have small autumn-blooming purple, pink, or white flowers

Michaelmas term *n* the autumn term at Oxford and Cambridge Universities, the Inns of Court, and some other educational establishments

Michelangelo (ˌmaɪkᵊlˈændʒɪˌləʊ) *n* full name *Michelangelo Buonarroti*. 1475–1564, Florentine sculptor, painter, architect, and poet; one of the outstanding figures of the Renaissance. Among his creations are the sculptures of *David* (1504) and of *Moses* which was commissioned for the tomb of Julius II, for whom he also painted the ceiling of the Sistine Chapel (1508–12). *The Last Judgment* (1533–41), also in the Sistine, includes a torturous vision of Hell and a disguised self-portrait. His other works include the design of the Laurentian Library (1523–29) and of the dome of St Peter's, Rome

Michelet (*French* miʃəle) *n* **Jules** (ʒyl) 1798–1874, French historian, noted esp for his *Histoire de France* (17 vols, 1833–67)

Michelin (*French* miʃəlɛ̃) *n* **André** (ɑ̃dre) 1853–1931, French industrialist; founder, with his brother **Édouard Michelin** (1859–1940), of the Michelin Tyre Company (1888): the first to use demountable pneumatic tyres on motor vehicles

Michelozzo (*Italian* mikeˈlɔttso) *n* full name *Michelozzo di Bartolommeo*. 1396–1472, Italian architect and sculptor. His most important design was the Palazzo Riccardo for the Medici family in Florence (1444–59)

Michelson (ˈmaɪkᵊlsᵊn) *n* **Albert Abraham** 1852–1931, US physicist, born in Germany: noted for his part in the Michelson-Morley experiment: Nobel prize for physics 1907

Michigan (ˈmɪʃɪgən) *n* 1 a state of the N central US, occupying two peninsulas between Lakes Superior, Huron, Michigan, and Erie: generally low-lying. Capital: Lansing. Pop: 9 938 444 (2000). Area: 147 156 sq km (56 817 sq miles). Abbreviations: **Mich** or (with zip code) **MI** 2 **Lake** a lake in the N central US between Wisconsin and Michigan: the third largest of the five Great Lakes and the only one wholly in the US; linked with Lake Huron by the Straits of Mackinac. Area: 58 000 sq km (22 400 sq miles) > **Michigander** (ˌmɪʃɪˈgændə) *n* > **ˈMichiganˌite** *adj, n*

Michoacán (*Spanish* mitʃoaˈkan) *n* a state of SW Mexico, on the Pacific: rich mineral resources. Capital: Morelia. Pop: 3 979 177 (2000). Area: 59 864 sq km (23 114 sq miles)

Mick (mɪk) *n* (*sometimes not cap*) 1 Also: **Mickey** *derog* a slang name for an **Irishman** or a **Roman Catholic** 2 *Austral* the tails side of a coin [C19 from nickname for *Michael*]

mickey[1] *or* **micky** (ˈmɪkɪ) *n inf* **take the mickey** (**out of**) to tease [C20 from ?]

mickey[2] (ˈmɪkɪ) *n Canad* a liquor bottle of 0.375 litre capacity, flat on one side and curved on the other to fit into a pocket [C20 from ?

Mickey Finn *n sl* **a** a drink containing a drug to make the drinker unconscious **b** the drug itself ▷ Often shortened to **Mickey** [C20 from ?]

Mickiewicz (*Polish* mitsˈkjɛvitʃ) *n* **Adam** (ˈadam) 1798–1855, Polish poet, whose epic *Thaddeus* (1834) is regarded as a masterpiece of Polish literature

mickle (ˈmɪkᵊl) *or* **muckle** (ˈmʌkᵊl) *arch or Scot & N English dialect* ▷ *adj* 1 great or abundant ▷ *adv* 2 much; greatly ▷ *n* 3 a great amount, esp in the proverb, *many a little makes a mickle* 4 *Scot* a small amount, esp in the proverb *mony a mickle makes a muckle* [C13 *mikel*, from ON *mikell*, replacing OE *micel* MUCH]

micro (ˈmaɪkrəʊ) *adj* 1 very small ▷ *n, pl* **micros** 2 short for **microcomputer, microprocessor, microwave oven**

micro- *or* **micr-** *combining form* 1 small or minute: *microdot* 2 involving the use of a microscope: *microscopy* 3 indicating a method or instrument for dealing with small quantities: *micrometer* 4 (in pathology) indicating abnormal smallness or underdevelopment: *microcephaly* 5 denoting 10^{-6}: *microsecond*. Symbol: μ [from Gk *mikros* small]

microbe (ˈmaɪkrəʊb) *n* any microscopic organism, esp a disease-causing bacterium [C19 from F, from MICRO- + Gk *bios* life] > **miˈcrobial** *or* **miˈcrobic** *adj*

microbiology (ˌmaɪkrəʊbaɪˈɒlədʒɪ) *n* the branch of biology involving the study of microorganisms > **microbiological** (ˌmaɪkrəʊˌbaɪəˈlɒdʒɪkᵊl) *or* **ˌmicroˌbioˈlogic** *adj* > **ˌmicroˌbioˈlogically** *adv* > **ˌmicrobiˈologist** *n*

▷ www.microbiol.org/vl_micro
▷ www.microbes.inf
▷ www.virology.net

microbrewery (ˈmaɪkrəʊˌbrʊərɪ) *n, pl* **microbreweries** a small, usually independent brewery that produces limited quantities of specialized beers, often sold for consumption on the premises

microcephaly (ˌmaɪkrəʊˈsɛfəlɪ) *n* the condition of having an abnormally small head or cranial capacity > **microcephalic** (ˌmaɪkrəʊsɪˈfælɪk) *adj, n* > **ˌmicroˈcephalous** *adj*

microchemistry (ˌmaɪkrəʊˈkɛmɪstrɪ) *n* chemical experimentation with minute quantities of material > **ˌmicroˈchemical** *adj*

microchip (ˈmaɪkrəʊˌtʃɪp) *n* another word for **chip** (sense 7)

microcircuit (ˈmaɪkrəʊˌsɜ:kɪt) *n* a miniature electronic circuit, esp one in which a number of permanently connected components are contained in one small chip of semiconducting material. See **integrated circuit** > **ˌmicroˈcircuitry** *n*

microclimate (ˈmaɪkrəʊˌklaɪmɪt) *n ecology* the atmospheric conditions affecting an individual or a small group of organisms, esp when they differ from the climate of the rest of the community

Mm

> **microclimatic** (ˌmaɪkrəʊklaɪˈmætɪk) *adj* > ˌ**microˌclimaˈtology** *n*

microcomputer (ˌmaɪkrəʊkəmˈpjuːtə) *n* a computer in which the central processing unit is contained in one or more silicon chips

microcosm (ˈmaɪkrəʊˌkɒzəm) *or* **microcosmos** (ˌmaɪkrəʊˈkɒzmɒs) *n* **1** a miniature representation of something **2** man regarded as epitomizing the universe ▷ Cf. **macrocosm** [c15 via Med. L from Gk *mikros kosmos* little world] > ˌ**microˈcosmic** *or* ˌ**microˈcosmical** *adj*

micro-credit *n* the practice of lending small amounts of money on minimal security, esp to help small businesses and communities in the developing world

microdot (ˈmaɪkrəʊˌdɒt) *n* **1** a greatly reduced photographic copy (about the size of a pinhead) of a document, etc, used esp in espionage **2** a tiny tablet containing LSD

microeconomics (ˌmaɪkrəʊˌiːkəˈnɒmɪks, -ˌɛkə-) *n (functioning as sing)* the branch of economics concerned with particular commodities, firms, or individuals and the economic relationships between them > ˌ**microˌecoˈnomic** *adj*

▷ www.helsinki.fi/WebEc/webecd.html

microelectronics (ˌmaɪkrəʊɪlɛkˈtrɒnɪks) *n (functioning as sing)* the branch of electronics concerned with microcircuits

microfibre (ˈmaɪkrəʊˌfaɪbə) *n* a very fine synthetic fibre used for textiles

microfiche (ˈmaɪkrəʊˌfiːʃ) *n* a sheet of film, usually the size of a filing card, on which books, newspapers, documents, etc, can be recorded in miniaturized form [c20 from F, from MICRO- + *fiche* small card]

microfilm (ˈmaɪkrəʊˌfɪlm) *n* **1** a strip of film on which books, documents, etc, can be recorded in miniaturized form ▷ *vb* **2** to photograph (a page, document, etc) on microfilm

microgravity (ˈmaɪkrəʊˌɡrævɪtɪ) *n* gravitational effects operating, or apparently operating, in a localized region, as in a spacecraft under conditions of weightlessness

microhabitat (ˌmaɪkrəʊˈhæbɪtæt) *n ecology* the smallest part of the environment that supports a distinct flora and fauna, such as a fallen log in a forest

microlight *or* **microlite** (ˈmaɪkrəʊˌlaɪt) *n* a small private aircraft carrying no more than two people, with a wing area not less than 10 square metres: used in pleasure flying and racing

microlith (ˈmaɪkrəʊˌlɪθ) *n archaeol* a small Mesolithic flint tool which formed part of a hafted tool > ˌ**microˈlithic** *adj*

micrometer (maɪˈkrɒmɪtə) *n* **1** any of various instruments or devices for the accurate measurement of distances or angles **2** Also called: **micrometer gauge, micrometer calliper** a type of gauge for the accurate measurement of small distances, thicknesses, etc The gap between its measuring faces is adjusted by a fine screw (**micrometer screw**) > **micrometric** (ˌmaɪkrəʊˈmɛtrɪk) *or* ˌ**microˈmetrical** *adj* > **miˈcrometry** *n*

microminiaturization *or* **microminiaturisation** (ˌmaɪkrəʊˌmɪnɪtʃəraɪˈzeɪʃən) *n* the production and application of very small components and the circuits and equipment in which they are used

micron (ˈmaɪkrɒn) *n, pl* **microns** *or* **micra** (-krə) a unit of length equal to 10^{-6} metre. It is being replaced by the micrometre, the equivalent SI unit [c19 NL, from Gk *mikros* small]

Micronesia (ˌmaɪkrəʊˈniːzɪə) *n* **1** one of the three divisions of islands in the Pacific (the others being Melanesia and Polynesia); the NW division of Oceania: includes the Mariana, Caroline, Marshall, and Kiribati island groups, and Nauru Island **2 Federated States of** an island group in the W Pacific, formerly within the United States Trust Territory of the Pacific Islands: comprises the islands of Truk, Yap, Ponape, and Kosrae: formed in 1979 when the islands became self-governing: status of free association with the US from 1982. Languages: English and Micronesian languages. Religion: Christian majority. Currency: US dollar. Capital: Palikir. Pop: 118 000 (2001 est) [c19 from MICRO- + Greek *nēsos* island; so called from the small size of many of the islands; on the model of *Polynesia*]

▷ www.fsmgov.org

▷ http://visit-fsm.org/

Micronesian (ˌmaɪkrəʊˈniːʒən, -ʒɪən) *adj* **1** of or relating to Micronesia, its inhabitants, or their languages ▷ *n* **2** a native or inhabitant of Micronesia or a descendant of one **3** a group of languages spoken in Micronesia

microorganism (ˌmaɪkrəʊˈɔːɡəˌnɪzəm) *n* any organism, such as a bacterium, of microscopic size

micropayment (ˈmaɪkrəʊˌpeɪmənt) *n* a system whereby a user pays a small fee to access a specific area of a website

microphone (ˈmaɪkrəˌfəʊn) *n* a device used in sound-reproduction systems for converting sound into electrical energy > **microphonic** (ˌmaɪkrəˈfɒnɪk) *adj*

microprint (ˈmaɪkrəʊˌprɪnt) *n* a greatly reduced photographic copy of print, read by a magnifying device. It is used in order to reduce the size of large books, etc

microprocessor (ˌmaɪkrəʊˈprəʊsɛsə) *n computing* a single integrated circuit performing the basic functions of the central processing unit in a small computer

micro-scooter *n* a foldable lightweight aluminium foot-propelled scooter, used by both adults and children

microscope (ˈmaɪkrəˌskəʊp) *n* **1** an optical instrument that uses a lens or combination of lenses to produce a magnified image of a small, close object **2** any instrument, such as the electron microscope, for producing a magnified visual image of a small object

microscopic (ˌmaɪkrəˈskɒpɪk) *or (less commonly)* **microscopical** *adj* **1** not large enough to be seen with the naked eye but visible under a microscope **2** very small; minute **3** of, concerned with, or using a microscope > ˌ**microˈscopically** *adv*

microscopy (maɪˈkrɒskəpɪ) *n* **1** the study, design, and manufacture of microscopes **2** investigation by use of a microscope > **microscopist** (maɪˈkrɒskəpɪst) *n*

microsecond (ˈmaɪkrəʊˌsɛkənd) *n* one millionth of a second

microsite (ˈmaɪkrəʊˌsaɪt) *n* a website that is intended for a specific limited purpose and is often temporary

microstructure (ˈmaɪkrəʊˌstrʌktʃə) *n* structure on a microscopic scale, esp the structure of an alloy as observed by etching, polishing, and observation under a microscope

microsurgery (ˌmaɪkrəʊˈsɜːdʒərɪ) *n* intricate surgery performed on cells, tissues, etc, using a specially designed operating microscope and miniature precision instruments

microswitch (ˈmaɪkrəʊˌswɪtʃ) *n electrical engineering* a switch that operates by small movements of a lever

microtome (ˈmaɪkrəʊˌtəʊm) *n* an instrument used for cutting thin sections for microscopical examination > **microtomy** (maɪˈkrɒtəmɪ) *n*

microwave (ˈmaɪkrəʊˌweɪv) *n* **1a** electromagnetic radiation in the wavelength range 0.3 to 0.001 metres: used in radar, cooking, etc **1b** *(as modifier): microwave oven* **2** short for **microwave oven** ▷ *vb* **microwaves, microwaving, microwaved** *(tr)* **3** to cook in a microwave oven

microwave background *n* a background of microwave electromagnetic radiation discovered in space in 1965, believed to have emanated from the big bang with which the universe began

microwave detector *n* NZ a device for recording the speed of a motorist

microwave oven *n* an oven in which food is cooked by microwaves. Often shortened to **micro, microwave**

microwave spectroscopy *n* a type of spectroscopy in which information is obtained on the structure and chemical bonding of molecules and crystals by measurements of the wavelengths of microwaves emitted or absorbed by the sample > **microwave spectroscope** *n*

micturate (ˈmɪktjʊˌreɪt) *vb* **micturates, micturating, micturated** (*intr*) a less common word for **urinate** [C19 from L *micturīre* to desire to urinate, from *mingere* to urinate] > **micturition** (ˌmɪktjʊˈrɪʃən) *n*

mid[1] (mɪd) *adj* **1** *phonetics* of, relating to, or denoting a vowel whose articulation lies approximately halfway between high and low, such as *e* in English *bet* ▷ *n* **2** an archaic word for **middle** [C12 *midre* (inflected form of *midd*, unattested)]

mid[2] *or* **ˈmid** (mɪd) *prep* a poetic word for **amid**

mid- *combining form* indicating a middle part, point, time, or position: *midday; mid-April; mid-Victorian* [OE; see MIDDLE, MID[1]]

midair (ˌmɪdˈɛə) *n* **a** some point above ground level, in the air **b** (*as modifier*): *a midair collision of aircraft*

Midas (ˈmaɪdəs) *n* **1** *Greek legend* a king of Phrygia given the power by Dionysus of turning everything he touched to gold **2** **the Midas touch** ability to make money

mid-Atlantic *adj* characterized by a blend of British and American styles, elements, etc: *a mid-Atlantic accent*

midbrain (ˈmɪdˌbreɪn) *n* the nontechnical name for **mesencephalon**

midday (ˈmɪdˈdeɪ) *n* **a** the middle of the day; noon **b** (*as modifier*): *a midday meal*

Middelburg (ˈmɪdəlˌbɜːg; *Dutch* ˈmɪdəlbyrx) *n* a city in the SW Netherlands, capital of Zeeland province, on Walcheren Island: an important trading centre in the Middle Ages and member of the Hanseatic League; 12th-century abbey; market town. Pop: 40 118 (1994)

middelmannetjie (ˌmɪdəlˈmænɪkɪ) *n S African* a continuous hump between wheel ruts on a dirt road [Afrik.]

middelskot (ˈmɪdəlˌskɒt) *n* (in South Africa) an intermediate payment to a farmers' cooperative for a crop or wool clip [from Afrik. *middel* middle + *skot* payment]

midden (ˈmɪdən) *n* **1a** *arch or dialect* a dunghill or pile of refuse **1b** *dialect* a dustbin **2** See **kitchen midden** [C14 from ON]

middle (ˈmɪdəl) *adj* **1** equally distant from the ends or periphery of something; central **2** intermediate in status, situation, etc **3** located between the early and late parts of a series, time sequence, etc **4** not extreme, esp in size; medium **5** (esp in Greek and Sanskrit grammar) denoting a voice of verbs expressing reciprocal or reflexive action **6** (*usually cap*) (of a language) intermediate between the earliest and the modern forms ▷ *n* **7** an area or point equal in distance from the ends or periphery or in time between the early and late parts **8** an intermediate part or section, such as the waist **9** *grammar* the middle voice **10** *logic* See **middle term** **11** *cricket* a position on the batting crease in alignment with the middle stumps on which a batsman may take guard ▷ *vb* **middles, middling, middled** (*tr*) **12** to place in the middle **13** *naut* to fold in two **14** *cricket* to hit (the ball) with the middle of the bat [OE *middel*]

middle age *n* the period of life between youth and old age, usually (in man) considered to occur approximately between the ages of 40 and 60 > ˌ**middle-ˈaged** *adj*

Middle Ages *n* **the** *European history* **1** (broadly) the period from the deposition of the last W Roman emperor in 476 AD to the Italian Renaissance (or the fall of Constantinople in 1453) **2** (narrowly) the period from about 1000 AD to the 15th century ▷ Cf **Dark Ages**
▷ www.mnsu.edu/emuseum/history/middleages
▷ http://radiantworks.com/middleages

Middle America *n* **1** the territories between the US and South America: Mexico, Central America, Panama, and the Greater and Lesser Antilles **2** the US middle class, esp those groups that are politically conservative > **Middle American** *adj, n*

middle-and-leg *n cricket* a position on the batting crease in alignment with the space between the middle and leg stumps on which a batsman may take guard

middle-and-off *n cricket* a position on the batting crease in alignment with the space between the middle and off stumps on which a batsman may take guard

Middle Atlantic States *or* **Middle States** *pl n* the states of New York, Pennsylvania, and New Jersey

middlebrow (ˈmɪdəlˌbraʊ) *disparaging* ▷ *n* **1** a person with conventional tastes and limited cultural appreciation ▷ *adj also* **middlebrowed** **2** of or appealing to middlebrows

middle C *n music* the note written on the first ledger line below the treble staff or the first ledger line above the bass staff

middle class *n* **1** Also called: **bourgeoisie** a social stratum between the lower and upper classes. It consists of businessmen, professional people, etc, along with their families, and is marked by bourgeois values ▷ *adj* **middle-class** **2** of, relating to, or characteristic of the middle class

Middle Congo *n* one of the four territories of former French Equatorial Africa, in W central Africa: became an autonomous member of the French Community, as the Republic of the Congo, in 1958

middle ear *n* the sound-conducting part of the ear, containing the malleus, incus, and stapes

Middle East *n* **1** (loosely) the area around the E Mediterranean, esp Israel and the Arab countries from Turkey to North Africa and eastwards to Iran **2** (formerly) the area extending from the Tigris and Euphrates to Myanmar > **Middle Eastern** *adj*

Middle England *n* a characterization of a predominantly middle-class, middle-income section of British society living mainly in suburban and rural England

Middle English *n* the English language from about 1100 to about 1450

middle game *n chess* the central phase between the opening and the endgame

Middle High German *n* High German from about 1200 to about 1500

Middle Low German *n* Low German from about 1200 to about 1500

middleman (ˈmɪdəlˌmæn) *n, pl* **middlemen** **1** a trader engaged in the distribution of goods from producer to consumer **2** an intermediary

middlemost (ˈmɪdəlˌməʊst) *adj* another word for **midmost**

middle name *n* **1** a name between a person's first name and surname **2** a characteristic quality for which a person is known: *caution is my middle name*

middle-of-the-road *adj* **1** not extreme, esp in political views; moderate **2** of, denoting, or relating to popular music having a wide general appeal

middle passage *n* **the** *history* the journey across the Atlantic Ocean from W Africa to the Caribbean: the longest part of the journey of the slave ships

Middlesbrough (ˈmɪdəlzbrə) *n* **1** an industrial town in NE England, in Middlesbrough unitary authority, North Yorkshire: on the Tees estuary; university (1992). Pop: 145 800 (1994 est) **2** a unitary authority in NE England, in North Yorkshire: formerly (1974–96) part of Cleveland county. Pop: 134 847 (2001). Area: 54 sq km (21 sq miles)

middle school *n* (in England and Wales) a school for children aged between 8 or 9 and 12 or 13

Middlesex ('mɪdᵊl,sɛks) *n* a former county of SE England: became mostly part of N and W Greater London in 1965. Abbreviation: **Middx**

Middle States *pl n* another name for the **Middle Atlantic States**

middle term *n logic* the term that appears in both minor and major premises but not in the conclusion of a syllogism

Middleton[1] ('mɪdᵊltən) *n* a town in NW England, in Oldham unitary authority, Greater Manchester. Pop: 45 621 (1991)

Middleton[2] ('mɪdᵊltən) *n* **Thomas** ?1570–1627, English dramatist. His plays include the tragedies *Women beware Women* (1621) and, in collaboration with William Rowley (?1585–?1642), *The Changeling* (1622) and the political satire *A Game at Chess* (1624)

middle watch *n naut* the watch between midnight and 4 am

middleweight ('mɪdᵊl,weɪt) *n* **1a** a professional boxer weighing 154–160 pounds (70–72.5 kg) **1b** an amateur boxer weighing 71–75 kg (157–165 pounds) **2a** a professional wrestler weighing 166–176 pounds (76–80 kg) **2b** an amateur wrestler weighing 75–82 kg (162–180 pounds)

Middle West *n* another name for the **Midwest** > **Middle Western** *adj* > **Middle Westerner** *n*

middle youth *n* the period of life between about 30 and 50

middling ('mɪdlɪŋ) *adj* **1** mediocre in quality, size, etc; neither good nor bad, esp in health (often in **fair to middling**) ▷ *adv* **2** *inf* moderately: *middling well* [C15 (N English & Scot): from MID[1] + -LING[2]] > '**middlingly** *adv*

Middx. *abbrev for* Middlesex

middy ('mɪdɪ) *n, pl* **middies** **1** *inf* short for **midshipman** **2** *Austral* **2a** a glass of middling size, used for beer **2b** the measure of beer it contains

Mideast (,mɪd'i:st) *n chiefly US* another name for **Middle East**

midfield (,mɪd'fi:ld) *n soccer* **a** the general area between the two opposing defences **b** (*as modifier*): *a midfield player*

mid-flight *adj, adv* **1** during a flight; whilst airborne: *a mid-flight celebration; doors opening mid-flight* ▷ *n* **2 in mid-flight** during a flight; whilst airborne

Midgard ('mɪdgɑ:d), **Midgarth** ('mɪdgɑ:ð), *or* **Mithgarthr** ('mɪðgɑ:ðə) *n Norse myth* the dwelling place of mankind, formed from the body of the giant Ymir and linked by the bridge Bifrost to Asgard, home of the gods [C19 from Old Norse *mithgarthr*; see MID[1], YARD[2]]

midge (mɪdʒ) *n* **1** a mosquito-like dipterous insect of the family *Chironomidae*, occurring in dancing swarms, esp near water **2** a small or diminutive person or animal [OE *mycge*] > '**midgy** *adj*

midget ('mɪdʒɪt) *n* **1** a dwarf whose skeleton and features are of normal proportions **2a** something small of its kind **2b** (*as modifier*): *a midget car* [C19 from MIDGE + -ET]

Mid Glamorgan *n* a former county of S Wales, formed in 1974 from parts of Breconshire, Glamorgan, and Monmouthshire: replaced in 1996 by the county boroughs of Bridgend, Rhondda Cynon Taff, Merthyr Tydfil, and part of Caerphilly

midgut ('mɪd,gʌt) *n* **1** the middle part of the digestive tract of vertebrates, including the small intestine **2** the middle part of the digestive tract of arthropods

mid-heavyweight *n* **a** a professional wrestler weighing 199–209 pounds (91–95 kg) **b** an amateur wrestler weighing 91–100 kg (199–220 pounds)

midi ('mɪdɪ) *adj* (formerly) **a** (of a skirt, coat, etc) reaching to below the knee or midcalf **b** (*as n*): *she wore her new midi* [C20 from MID-, on the model of MINI]

Midi (*French* midi) *n* **1** the south of France **2 Canal du** a canal in S France, extending from the River Garonne at Toulouse to the Mediterranean at Sète and providing a link between the Mediterranean and Atlantic coasts: built between 1666 and 1681. Length: 181 km (150 miles)

MIDI ('mɪdɪ) *n* (*modifier*) a generally accepted specification for the external control of electronic musical instruments: *a MIDI synthesizer; a MIDI system* [C20 from *m(usical) i(nstrument) d(igital) i(nterface)*]

midi- *combining form* of medium or middle size, length, etc: *midibus; midi system*

Midian ('mɪdɪən) *n Old Testament* **1** a son of Abraham (Genesis 25:1–2) **2** a nomadic nation claiming descent from him > '**Midian,ite** *n, adj* > '**Midian,itish** *adj*

midinette (,mɪdɪ'nɛt) *n* a Parisian seamstress or salesgirl in a clothes shop [C20 from F, from *midi* noon + *dinette* light meal; the girls had time for only a snack at midday]

Midi-Pyrénées (*French* midipirene) *n* a region of SW France: consists of N slopes of the Pyrenees in the south, a fertile lowland area in the west crossed by the River Garonne, and the edge of the Massif Central in the north and east

midiron ('mɪd,aɪən) *n golf* a club, usually a No 5, 6, or 7 iron, used for medium-length approach shots

midi system *n* a complete set of hi-fi sound equipment designed as a single unit that is more compact than the standard equipment

midland ('mɪdlənd) *n* **a** the central or inland part of a country **b** (*as modifier*): *a midland region*

Midlands ('mɪdləndz) *n* (*functioning as plural or singular*) **the** the central counties of England, including Warwickshire, Northamptonshire, Leicestershire, Nottinghamshire, Derbyshire, Staffordshire, the former West Midlands metropolitan county, and Worcestershire: characterized by manufacturing industries > '**Midlander** *n*

midlife crisis *n* a crisis that may be experienced in middle age involving frustration, panic, and feelings of pointlessness, sometimes resulting in radical and often ill-advised changes of lifestyle

Midlothian (mɪd'ləʊðɪən) *n* a council area of SE central Scotland: the historical county of Midlothian (including Edinburgh) became part of Lothian region in 1975; separate unitary authorities were created for Midlothian and City of Edinburgh in 1996; mainly agricultural. Administrative centre: Dalkeith. Pop: 80 941 (2001). Area: 356 sq km (137 sq miles)

midmost ('mɪd,məʊst) *adj, adv* in the middle or midst

midnight ('mɪd,naɪt) *n* **1a** the middle of the night; 12 o'clock at night **1b** (*as modifier*): *the midnight hour* **2 burn the midnight oil** to work or study late into the night

midnight sun *n* the sun visible at midnight during the summer inside the Arctic and Antarctic circles

mid-off *n cricket* the fielding position on the off side closest to the bowler

mid-on *n cricket* the fielding position on the on side closest to the bowler

midpoint ('mɪd,pɔɪnt) *n* **1** the point on a line that is at an equal distance from either end **2** a point in time halfway between the beginning and end of an event

midrib ('mɪd,rɪb) *n* the main vein of a leaf, running down the centre of the blade

midriff ('mɪdrɪf) *n* **1a** the middle part of the human body, esp between waist and bust **1b** (*as modifier*): *midriff bulge* **2** *anat* another name for the **diaphragm** (sense 1) **3** the part of a woman's garment covering the midriff [OE *midhrif*, from MID[1] + *hrif* belly]

midship ('mɪd,ʃɪp) *naut* ▷ *adj* **1** in, of, or relating to the middle of a vessel ▷ *n* **2** the middle of a vessel

midshipman ('mɪd,ʃɪpmən) *n, pl* **midshipmen** a probationary rank held by young naval officers under training, or an officer holding such a rank

midships ('mɪd,ʃɪps) *adv, adj naut* See **amidships**

midst[1] (mɪdst) *n* **1** **in our midst** among us **2** **in the midst of** surrounded or enveloped by; at a point during [C14 back formation from *amiddes* AMID]
midst[2] (mɪdst) *prep Poetic.* See **amid**
midsummer (ˈmɪdˈsʌmə) *n* **1a** the middle or height of the summer **1b** (*as modifier*): *a midsummer carnival* **2** another name for **summer solstice**
Midsummer's Day *or* **Midsummer Day** *n* June 24, the feast of St John the Baptist; in England, Ireland, and Wales, one of the four quarter days. See also **summer solstice**
midterm (ˈmɪdˈtɜːm) *n* **1a** the middle of a term in a school, university, etc **1b** (*as modifier*): *midterm exam* **2** *US politics* **2a** the middle of a term of office, esp of a presidential term, when congressional and local elections are held **2b** (*as modifier*): *midterm elections* **3a** the middle of the gestation period **3b** (*as modifier*): *midterm pregnancy*. See **term** (sense 6)
mid-Victorian *adj* **1** *Brit history* of or relating to the middle period of the reign of Queen Victoria (1837–1901) ▷ *n* **2** a person of the mid-Victorian era
midway *adj* (ˈmɪdˌweɪ) **1** in or at the middle of the distance; halfway ▷ *adv* (ˌmɪdˈweɪ) **2** to the middle of the distance ▷ *n* (ˌmɪdˈweɪ) **3** *obs* a middle place, way, etc
Midway Islands *pl n* an atoll in the central Pacific, about 2100 km (1300 miles) northwest of Honolulu: annexed by the US in 1867: scene of a decisive battle (June, 1942), in which the US combined fleets destroyed Japan's carrier fleet. Pop: 450 (1995 est). Area: 5 sq km (2 sq miles)
midweek (ˈmɪdˈwiːk) *n* **a** the middle of the week **b** (*as modifier*): *a midweek holiday*
Midwest (ˈmɪdˈwɛst) *or* **Middle West** *n* the N central part of the US; the region consisting of the states from Ohio westwards that border on the Great Lakes, often extended to include the upper Mississippi and Missouri valleys > ˈ**Midˈwestern** *adj* > ˈ**Midˈwesterner** *n*
mid-wicket *n cricket* the fielding position on the on side, midway between square leg and mid-on
midwife (ˈmɪdˌwaɪf) *n, pl* **midwives** (-ˌwaɪvz) a person qualified to deliver babies and to care for women before, during, and after childbirth [C14 from OE *mid* with + *wif* woman]
midwifery (ˈmɪdˌwɪfərɪ) *n* the training, art, or practice of a midwife; obstetrics
midwinter (ˈmɪdˈwɪntə) *n* **1a** the middle or depth of the winter **1b** (*as modifier*): *a midwinter festival* **2** another name for **winter solstice**
midyear (ˈmɪdˈjɪə) *n* the middle of the year
mien (miːn) *n literary* a person's manner, bearing, or appearance [C16 prob. var. of obs. *demean* appearance; rel. to F *mine* aspect]
Mieres (*Spanish* ˈmjeres) *n* a city in N Spain, south of Oviedo: steel and chemical industries; iron and coal mines. Pop: 26 500 (latest est)
Mies van der Rohe (ˈmiːz væn də ˈrəʊə) *n* **Ludwig** 1886–1969, US architect, born in Germany. He directed the Bauhaus (1929–33) and developed a functional style, characterized by geometrical design. His works include the Seagram building, New York (1958)
mifepristone (mɪˈfɛprɪˌstəʊn) *n* an antiprogestogenic steroid, used in the medical termination of pregnancy
miff (mɪf) *inf* ▷ *vb* **1** to take offence or to offend ▷ *n* **2** a petulant mood **3** a petty quarrel [C17 ? an imitative expression of bad temper] > ˈ**miffy** *adj*
MIG (mɪg) *n acronym for* minimum income guarantee: a minimum assured weekly income in retirement
might[1] (maɪt) *vb* (takes an implied infinitive or an infinitive without *to*) used as an auxiliary: **1** making the past tense or subjunctive mood of **may**[1]: *he might have come* **2** (often foll by *well*) expressing possibility: *he might well come*. In this sense *might* looks to the future and functions as a weak form of *may*. See **may**[1] (sense 2) [OE *miht*]
might[2] (maɪt) *n* **1** power, force, or vigour, esp of a great or supreme kind **2** physical strength **3** (**with**) **might and main** See **main**[1] (sense 7) [OE *miht*]
mighty (ˈmaɪtɪ) *adj* **mightier, mightiest** **1a** having or indicating might; powerful or strong **1b** (*as collective n; preceded by the*): *the mighty* **2** very large; vast **3** very great in extent, importance, etc ▷ *adv* **4** *inf, chiefly US & Canad* (intensifier): *mighty tired* > ˈ**mightily** *adv* > ˈ**mightiness** *n*
mignon (ˈmɪnjɒn) *adj* small and pretty; dainty [C16 from F, from OF *mignot* dainty] > **mignonne** (ˈmɪnjɒn) *fem n*
mignonette (ˌmɪnjəˈnɛt) *n* **1** any of various mainly Mediterranean plants, such as **garden mignonette**, that have spikes of small greenish-white flowers **2** a type of fine pillow lace **3a** a greyish-green colour **3b** (*as adj*): *mignonette ribbons* [C18 from F, dim. of MIGNON]
migraine (ˈmiːgreɪn, ˈmaɪ-) *n* a throbbing headache usually affecting only one side of the head and commonly accompanied by nausea and visual disturbances [C18 (earlier form, C14 *mygrame* MEGRIM): from F, from LL *hēmicrānia* pain in half of the head, from Gk, from HEMI- + *kranion* CRANIUM] > ˈ**migrainous** *adj*
migrant (ˈmaɪgrənt) *n* **1** a person or animal that moves from one region, place, or country to another **2** an itinerant agricultural worker ▷ *adj* **3** moving from one region, place, or country to another; migratory
migrate (maɪˈgreɪt) *vb* **migrates, migrating, migrated** (*intr*) **1** to go from one place to settle in another, esp in a foreign country **2** (of birds, fishes, etc) to journey between different areas at specific times of the year [C17 from L *migrāre* to change one's abode] > **miˈgrator** *n*
migration (maɪˈgreɪʃən) *n* **1** the act or an instance of migrating **2** a group of people, birds, etc, migrating in a body **3** *chem* a movement of atoms, ions, or molecules, such as the motion of ions in solution under the influence of electric fields > **miˈgrational** *adj*
migratory (ˈmaɪgrətərɪ, -trɪ) *adj* **1** of or characterized by migration **2** nomadic; itinerant
mihi (ˈmiːhɪ) *n NZ* a Maori ceremonial greeting [Maori]
mihrab (ˈmiːræb, -rəb) *n Islam* the niche in a mosque showing the direction of Mecca [from Ar.]
mikado (mɪˈkɑːdəʊ) *n, pl* **mikados** (*often cap*) *arch* the Japanese emperor [C18 from Japanese, from *mi-* honourable + *kado* gate]
mike (maɪk) *n inf* short for **microphone**
Míkonos (*Greek* ˈmikonos) *n* transliteration of the modern Greek name for **Mykonos**
mil (mɪl) *n* **1** a unit of length equal to one thousandth of an inch **2** a unit of angular measure, used in gunnery, equal to one six-thousand-four-hundredth of a circumference **3** *photog* short for millimetre: *35-mil film* [C18 from L *millēsimus* thousandth]
mil. *abbrev for*: **1** military **2** militia
milady *or* **miladi** (mɪˈleɪdɪ) *n, pl* **miladies** (formerly) a continental title used for an English gentlewoman
Milan (mɪˈlæn) *n* a city in N Italy, in central Lombardy: Italy's second largest city and chief financial and industrial centre; a centre of the Renaissance under the Visconti and Sforza families. Pop: 1 300 977 (2000 est). Italian name: **Milano** (miˈlaːno) > ˌ**Milaˈnese** *adj, n*
milatainment (ˌmɪləˈteɪnmənt) *n* entertainment programmes about the military, often with a documentary or factual element [C21 from MIL(ITARY) + (ENTER)TAINMENT]
Milazzo (*Italian* miˈlattso) *n* a port in NE Sicily: founded in the 8th century BC; scene of a battle (1860), in which Garibaldi defeated the Bourbon forces. Pop: 32 000 (latest est). Ancient name: **Mylae** (ˈmaɪˌliː)
milch (mɪltʃ) *n* **1** (*modifier*) (esp of cattle) yielding milk **2** **milch cow** *inf* a source of easy income, esp a person [C13 from OE *-milce* (in compounds); rel. to OE *melcan* to milk]
mild (maɪld) *adj* **1** (of a taste, sensation, etc) not powerful or strong; bland **2** gentle or temperate in character, climate, behaviour, etc **3** not extreme;

Mm

moderate **4** feeble; unassertive ▷ *n* **5** *Brit* draught beer, of darker colour than bitter and flavoured with fewer hops [OE *milde*] > **'mildly** *adv* > **'mildness** *n*

mildew ('mɪl,djuː) *n* **1** any of various diseases of plants that affect mainly the leaves and are caused by parasitic fungi **2** any fungus causing this **3** another name for **mould²** ▷ *vb* **4** to affect or become affected with mildew [OE *mildēaw*, from *mil-* honey + *dēaw* DEW] > **'mil,dewy** *adj*

mild steel *n* any of a class of strong tough steels that contain a low quantity of carbon

mile (maɪl) *n* **1** Also called: **statute mile** a unit of length used in the UK, the US, and certain other countries, equal to 1760 yards. 1 mile is equivalent to 1.60934 kilometres **2** See **nautical mile** **3** the Roman mile, equivalent to 1620 yards **4** (*often pl*) *inf* a great distance; great deal: *he missed by a mile* **5** a race extending over a mile ▷ *adv* **6** **miles** (intensifier): *that's miles better* [OE *mīl*, from L *mīlia (passuum)* a thousand (paces)]

mileage *or* **milage** ('maɪlɪdʒ) *n* **1** a distance expressed in miles **2** the total number of miles that a motor vehicle has travelled **3** allowance for travelling expenses, esp as a fixed rate per mile **4** the number of miles a motor vehicle will travel on one gallon of fuel **5** *inf* use, benefit, or service provided by something **6** *inf* grounds, substance, or weight: *some mileage in their arguments*

mileometer *or* **milometer** (maɪ'lɒmɪtə) *n* a device that records the number of miles that a bicycle or motor vehicle has travelled

milepost ('maɪl,pəʊst) *n* **1** *horse racing* a marking post on a racecourse a mile before the finishing line **2** *chiefly US & Canad* a signpost that shows the distance in miles to or from a place

miler ('maɪlə) *n* an athlete, horse, etc, that runs or specializes in races of one mile

Miles (maɪlz) *n* **Bernard,** Baron Miles of Blackfriars. 1907–91, British actor and theatre manager. He founded the Mermaid Theatre in London, and was known as a character actor

milestone ('maɪl,stəʊn) *n* **1** a stone pillar that shows the distance in miles to or from a place **2** a significant event in life, history, etc

Miletus (mɪ'liːtəs) *n* an ancient city on the W coast of Asia Minor: a major Ionian centre of trade and learning in the ancient world > **Mi'lesian** *adj, n*

milfoil ('mɪl,fɔɪl) *n* **1** another name for **yarrow** **2** See **water milfoil** [C13 from OF, from L *milifolium*, from *mille* thousand + *folium* leaf]

Milford Haven ('mɪlfəd) *n* a port in SW Wales, in Pembrokeshire on **Milford Haven** (a large inlet of St George's Channel): major oil port. Pop: 13 194 (1991)

Milhaud (*French* mijo) *n* **Darius** (darjys) 1892–1974, French composer; member of Les Six. A notable exponent of polytonality, his large output includes operas, symphonies, ballets, string quartets, and songs

miliaria (,mɪlɪ'ɛərɪə) *n* an acute itching eruption of the skin, caused by blockage of the sweat glands [C19 from NL, from L *miliārius* MILIARY]

miliary ('mɪljərɪ) *adj* **1** resembling or relating to millet seeds **2** (of a disease or skin eruption) characterized by small lesions resembling millet seeds: *miliary fever* [C17 from L *miliārius*, from *milium* MILLET]

milieu ('miːljɜː; *French* miljø) *n, pl* **milieux** (-ljɜː, -ljɜːz; *French* -ljø) *or* **milieus** (miljø) surroundings, location, or setting [C19 from F, from *mi-* MID¹ + *lieu* place]

militant ('mɪlɪtənt) *adj* **1** aggressive or vigorous, esp in the support of a cause **2** warring; engaged in warfare ▷ *n* **3** a militant person [C15 from L *mīlitāre* to be a soldier, from *mīles* soldier] > **'militancy** *n* > **'militantly** *adv*

militarism ('mɪlɪtə,rɪzəm) *n* **1** military spirit; pursuit of military ideals **2** domination by the military, esp on a political level **3** a policy of maintaining a strong military organization in aggressive preparedness for war > **'militarist** *n*

militarize *or* **militarise** ('mɪlɪtə,raɪz) *vb* **militarizes, militarizing, militarized** *or* **militarises, militarising, militarised** (*tr*) **1** to convert to military use **2** to imbue with militarism > **,militari'zation** *or* **,militari'sation** *n*

military ('mɪlɪtərɪ, -trɪ) *adj* **1** of or relating to the armed forces, warlike matters, etc **2** of or characteristic of soldiers ▷ *n, pl* **militaries** *or* **military** **3** (preceded by *the*) the armed services, esp the army [C16 via F from L *mīlitāris*, from *mīles* soldier] > **mili'tarily** *adv*

military police *n* a corps within an army that performs police and disciplinary duties > **military policeman** *n*

militate ('mɪlɪ,teɪt) *vb* **militates, militating, militated** (*intr; usually foll by against* or *for*) (of facts, etc) to have influence or effect: *the evidence militated against his release* [C17 from L *mīlitātus*, from *mīlitāre* to be a soldier]

USAGE See at **mitigate**

militia (mɪ'lɪʃə) *n* **1** a body of citizen (as opposed to professional) soldiers **2** an organization containing men enlisted for service in emergency only [C16 from L: soldiery, from *mīles* soldier] > **mi'litiaman** *n*

milk (mɪlk) *n* **1a** a whitish fluid secreted by the mammary glands of mature female mammals and used for feeding their young until weaned **1b** the milk of cows, goats, etc, used by man as a food or in the production of butter, cheese, etc **2** any similar fluid in plants, such as the juice of a coconut **3** a milklike pharmaceutical preparation, such as milk of magnesia **4** **cry over spilt milk** to lament something that cannot be altered ▷ *vb* **5** to draw milk from the udder of (an animal) **6** (*intr*) (of animals) to yield milk **7** (*tr*) to draw off or tap in small quantities: *to milk the petty cash* **8** (*tr*) to extract as much money, help, etc, as possible from: *to milk a situation of its news value* **9** (*tr*) to extract venom, sap, etc, from [OE *milc*] > **'milker** *n*

milk-and-water *adj* (**milk and water** *when postpositive*). weak, feeble, or insipid

milk bar *n* **1** a snack bar at which milk drinks and light refreshments are served **2** (in Australia) a shop selling, in addition to milk, basic provisions and other items

milk chocolate *n* chocolate that has been made with milk, having a creamy taste

milk float *n Brit* a small motor vehicle used to deliver milk to houses

milk leg *n* inflammation and thrombosis of the femoral vein following childbirth, characterized by painful swelling of the leg

milkmaid ('mɪlk,meɪd) *n* a girl or woman who milks cows

milkman ('mɪlkmən) *n, pl* **milkmen** a man who delivers or sells milk

milk of magnesia *n* a suspension of magnesium hydroxide in water, used as an antacid and laxative

milk pudding *n chiefly Brit* a pudding made by boiling or baking milk with a grain, esp rice

milk round *n Brit* **1** a route along which a milkman regularly delivers milk **2** a regular series of visits, esp as made by recruitment officers from industry to universities

milk run *n aeronautics, inf* a routine and uneventful flight [C20 from a milkman's safe and regular routine]

milk shake *n* a cold frothy drink made of milk, flavouring, and sometimes ice cream, whisked or beaten together

milksop ('mɪlk,sɒp) *n* a feeble or ineffectual man or youth

milk sugar *n* another name for **lactose**

milk tooth *n* any of the first teeth to erupt; a deciduous tooth. Also called: **baby tooth**

milkwort ('mɪlk,wɜːt) *n* any of several plants having small blue, pink, or white flowers. They were formerly believed to increase milk production in cows

milky ('mɪlkɪ) *adj* **milkier, milkiest** **1** resembling milk, esp in colour or cloudiness **2** of or containing milk

3 spiritless or spineless > **'milkily** *adv* > **'milkiness** *n*

Milky Way *n* **the** the diffuse band of light stretching across the night sky that consists of millions of faint stars, nebulae, etc, and forms part of the Galaxy [c14 translation of L *via lactea*]

mill (mɪl) *n* **1** a building in which grain is crushed and ground to make flour **2** a building fitted with machinery for processing materials, manufacturing goods, etc; factory **3** a machine that processes materials, manufactures goods, etc, by performing a continuous or repetitive operation, such as a machine to grind flour, pulverize solids, or press fruit **4** a machine that tools or polishes metal **5** a small machine for grinding solids: *a pepper mill* **6** a system, institution, etc, that influences people or things in the manner of a factory: *the educational mill* **7** an unpleasant experience; ordeal (esp in **go** *or* **be put through the mill**) **8** a fist fight ▷ *vb* **9** (*tr*) to grind, press, or pulverize in or as if in a mill **10** (*tr*) to process or produce in or with a mill **11** to cut or roll (metal) with or as if with a milling machine **12** (*tr*) to groove or flute the edge of (a coin) **13** (*intr; often foll by about or around*) to move about in a confused manner **14** *arch sl* to fight, esp with the fists [OE *mylen* from LL *molīna* a mill, from L *mola* mill, from *molere* to grind] > **'millable** *adj* > **milled** *adj*

Mill (mɪl) *n* **1 James** 1773–1836, Scottish philosopher, historian, and economist. He expounded Bentham's utilitarian philosophy in *Elements of Political Economy* (1821) and *Analysis of the Phenomena of the Human Mind* (1829) and also wrote a *History of British India* (1817–18) **2** his son, **John Stuart** 1806–73, English philosopher and economist. He modified Bentham's utilitarian philosophy in *Utilitarianism* (1861) and in his treatise *On Liberty* (1859) he defended the rights and freedom of the individual. Other works include *A System of Logic* (1843) and *Principles of Political Economy* (1848)

Millais ('mɪleɪ) *n* Sir **John Everett** 1829–96, English painter, who was a founder of the Pre-Raphaelite Brotherhood. His works include *The Order of Release* (1853) and *The Blind Girl* (1856)

Millay (mɪ'leɪ) *n* **Edna St Vincent** 1892–1950, US poet, noted esp for her sonnets; her collections include *The Buck in the Snow* (1928) and *Fatal Interview* (1931)

millboard ('mɪl,bɔːd) *n* strong pasteboard, used esp in book covers [c18 from *milled board*]

milldam ('mɪl,dæm) *n* a dam built in a stream to raise the water level sufficiently for it to turn a millwheel

millefeuille *French* (milfœj) *n Brit* a small iced cake made of puff pastry filled with jam and cream [lit.: thousand leaves]

millefleurs ('miːl,flɜː) *n* (*functioning as sing*) a design of stylized floral patterns, used in textiles, paperweights, etc [F: thousand flowers]

millenarian (,mɪlɪ'nɛərɪən) *adj* **1** of or relating to a thousand or to a thousand years **2** of or relating to the millennium or millenarianism ▷ *n* **3** an adherent of millenarianism

millenarianism (,mɪlɪ'nɛərɪə,nɪzəm) *n* **1** *Christianity* the belief in a future millennium during which Christ will reign on earth: based on Revelation 20:1–5 **2** any belief in a future period of ideal peace and happiness

millenary (mɪ'lɛnərɪ) *n, pl* **millenaries 1** a sum or aggregate of one thousand **2** another word for a **millennium** ▷ *adj, n* **3** another word for **millenarian** [c16 from LL *millēnārius* containing a thousand, from L *mille* thousand]

millennium (mɪ'lɛnɪəm) *n, pl* **millennia** (-nɪə) *or* **millenniums 1 the** *Christianity* the period of a thousand years of Christ's awaited reign upon earth **2** a period or cycle of one thousand years **3** a time of peace and happiness, esp in the distant future [c17 from NL, from L *mille* thousand + *annus* year] > **mil'lennial** *adj* > **mil'lennialist** *n*

millennium bug *n computing* any software problem arising from the change in date at the start of the 21st century

millepede ('mɪlɪ,piːd) *or* **milleped** *n* variants of **millipede**

millepore ('mɪlɪ,pɔː) *n* any of a genus of tropical colonial coral-like hydrozoans, having a calcareous skeleton [c18 from NL, from L *mille* thousand + *porus* hole]

miller ('mɪlə) *n* **1** a person who keeps, operates, or works in a mill, esp a corn mill **2** another name for **milling machine 3** a person who operates a milling machine

Miller ('mɪlə) *n* **1 Arthur** born 1915, US dramatist. His plays include *Death of a Salesman* (1949), *The Crucible* (1953), *A View from the Bridge* (1955), and *Mr Peters' Connections* (1998) **2 (Alton) Glenn** 1904–44, US composer, trombonist, and band leader. His popular compositions include "Moonlight Serenade". During World War II he was leader of the US Air Force band in Europe. He disappeared without trace on a flight between England and France **3 Henry (Valentine)** 1891–1980, US novelist, author of *Tropic of Cancer* (1934) and *Tropic of Capricorn* (1938) **4 Hugh** 1802–56, Scottish geologist and writer **5** Sir **Jonathan (Wolfe)** born 1934, British doctor, actor, and theatre director. His productions include Shakespeare, Ibsen, and Chekhov as well as numerous operas. He has also presented many television medical programmes

miller's thumb *n* any of several small freshwater European fishes having a flattened body [c15 from the alleged likeness of the fish's head to a thumb]

millesimal (mɪ'lɛsɪməl) *adj* **1a** denoting a thousandth **1b** (*as n*): *a millesimal* **2** of, consisting of, or relating to a thousandth [c18 from L *millēsimus*]

millet ('mɪlɪt) *n* **1** a cereal grass cultivated for grain and animal fodder **2a** an Indian annual grass cultivated for grain and forage, having pale round shiny seeds **2b** the seed of this plant **3** any of various similar or related grasses [c14 via OF from L *milium*]

Millet (*French* milɛ) *n* **Jean François** (ʒɑ̃ frɑ̃swa) 1814–75, French painter of the Barbizon school, noted for his studies of peasants at work

Mm

milli- *prefix* denoting 10^{-3}: *millimetre*. Symbol: m [from F, from L *mille* thousand]

milliard ('mɪlɪ,ɑːd, 'mɪljɑːd) *n Brit* (no longer in technical use) a thousand million. US & Canad equivalent: **billion** [c19 from F]

millibar ('mɪlɪ,bɑː) *n* a cgs unit of atmospheric pressure equal to 10^{-3} bar, 100 newtons per square metre or 0.7500617 millimetre of mercury

Milligan ('mɪlɪgən) *n* **Spike,** real name *Terence Alan Milligan*. born 1918, Irish radio, stage, and film comedian and author, born in India. He appeared in *The Goon Show* (with Peter Sellers and Harry Secombe; BBC Radio, 1952–60) and his films include *Adolf Hitler, My Part in his Downfall* (1972) from his own book: honorary knighthood 2000

milligram *or* **milligramme** ('mɪlɪ,græm) *n* one thousandth of a gram [c19 from F]

Millikan ('mɪlɪkən) *n* **Robert Andrews** 1868–1953, US physicist. He measured the charge of an electron (1910), verified Einstein's equation for the photoelectric effect (1916), and studied cosmic rays; Nobel prize for physics 1923

millilitre *or US* **milliliter** ('mɪlɪ,liːtə) *n* one thousandth of a litre

millimetre *or US* **millimeter** ('mɪlɪ,miːtə) *n* one thousandth of a metre

millimicron ('mɪlɪ,maɪkrɒn) *n obs* one thousand-millionth of a metre; nanometre

milliner ('mɪlɪnə) *n* a person who makes or sells women's hats [c16 orig. *Milaner*, a native of *Milan*, at that time famous for its fancy goods]

millinery ('mɪlɪnərɪ, -ɪnrɪ) *n* **1** hats, trimmings, etc, sold by a milliner **2** the business or shop of a milliner

▷ www.thehatsite.com
▷ www.hatsuk.com

milling ('mɪlɪŋ) *n* **1** the act or process of grinding, pressing, or crushing in a mill **2** the grooves or fluting on the edge of a coin, etc

milling machine *n* a machine tool in which a horizontal arbor or vertical spindle rotates a cutting tool above a horizontal table

million ('mɪljən) *n, pl* **millions** *or* **million 1** the cardinal number that is the product of 1000 multiplied by 1000 **2** a numeral, 1 000 000, 10^6, $\bar{M}$, etc, representing this number **3** *(often pl) inf* an extremely large but unspecified number or amount: *I have millions of things to do* ▷ *determiner* **4** (preceded by *a* or by a numeral) **4a** amounting to a million: *a million light years* **4b** *(as pron): I can see a million* [c17 via OF from early It. *millione*, from *mille* thousand, from L]

millionaire (ˌmɪljə'nɛə) *n* a person whose assets are worth at least a million of the standard monetary units of his or her country > ˌ**million'airess** *fem n*

millionth ('mɪljənθ) *n* **1a** one of 1 000 000 equal parts of something **1b** *(as modifier): a millionth part* **2** one of 1 000 000 equal divisions of a scientific quantity **3** the fraction one divided by 1 000 000 ▷ *adj* **4** *(usually prenominal)* **4a** being the ordinal number of 1 000 000 in numbering or counting order, etc **4b** *(as n): the millionth to be manufactured*

millipede, millepede ('mɪlɪˌpiːd), *or* **milleped** ('mɪlɪˌpɛd) *n* any of various terrestrial herbivorous arthropods, having a cylindrical segmented body, each segment of which bears two pairs of legs [c17 from L, from *mille* thousand + *pēs* foot]

millisecond ('mɪlɪˌsɛkənd) *n* one thousandth of a second

millpond ('mɪlˌpɒnd) *n* **1** a pool formed by damming a stream to provide water to turn a mill-wheel **2** any expanse of calm water

millrace ('mɪlˌreɪs) *or* **millrun** *n* **1** the current of water that turns a millwheel **2** the channel for this water

Mills (mɪlz) *n* **1 Hayley** born 1946, British actress. Her films include *Pollyanna* (1960) and *The Parent Trap* (1961) **2** her father, Sir **John** born 1908, British actor. His films include *This Happy Breed* (1944), *Great Expectations* (1946), and *Ryan's Daughter* (1971)

Mills bomb (mɪlz) *n* a type of high-explosive hand grenade [c20 after Sir William *Mills* (1856–1932), Brit inventor]

millstone ('mɪlˌstəʊn) *n* **1** one of a pair of heavy flat disc-shaped stones that are rotated one against the other to grind grain **2** a heavy burden, such as a responsibility or obligation

millstream ('mɪlˌstriːm) *n* a stream of water used to turn a millwheel

millwheel ('mɪlˌwiːl) *n* a wheel, esp a waterwheel, that drives a mill

millwork ('mɪlˌwɜːk) *n* work done in a mill

millwright ('mɪlˌraɪt) *n* a person who designs, builds, or repairs grain mills or mill machinery

Milne (mɪln) *n* **A(lan) A(lexander)** 1882–1956, English writer, noted for his books and verse for children, including *When We Were Very Young* (1924) and *Winnie the Pooh* (1926)

milometer (maɪ'lɒmɪtə) *n* a variant spelling of **mileometer**

milord (mɪ'lɔːd) *n* (formerly) a continental title used for an English gentleman [c19 via F from E *my lord*]

Mílos ('milɔs) *n* transliteration of the Modern Greek name for **Melos**

Milošević (miːlɒsɛˌvɪtʃ) *n* **Slobodan** ('slɒbədæn) born 1941, Serbian politician, president of Serbia (1989–97) and of the Federal Republic of Yugoslavia (1997–2000). He supported ethnic cleansing in Bosnia-Herzegovina (1992–95) and Kosovo (1998–99). He was ousted in 2000 and brought to trial (2001) for war crimes

Miłosz ('miːlɒʃ; *Polish* 'miwɔʃ) *n* **Czesław** ('tʃɛslɔː; 'tʃɛswaf) born 1911, Polish poet and writer; author of *The Captive Mind* (1953). Nobel prize for literature 1980

milt (mɪlt) *n* **1** the testis of a fish **2** the spermatozoa and seminal fluid produced by a fish **3** *rare* the spleen, esp of fowls and pigs ▷ *vb* **4** to fertilize (fish roe) with milt, esp artificially [OE *milte* spleen; in the sense: fish sperm, prob. from MDu. *milte*] > '**milter** *n*

Miltiades (mɪl'taɪəˌdiːz) *n* ?540–?489 BC, Athenian general, who defeated the Persians at Marathon (490)

Milton ('mɪltən) *n* **John** 1608–74, English poet. His early works, notably *L'Allegro* and *Il Penseroso* (1632), the masque *Comus* (1634), and the elegy *Lycidas* (1637), show the influence of his Christian humanist education and his love of Italian Renaissance poetry. A staunch Parliamentarian and opponent of episcopacy, he published many pamphlets during the Civil War period, including *Areopagitica* (1644), which advocated freedom of the press. His greatest works were the epic poems *Paradise Lost* (1667; 1674), and *Paradise Regained* (1671) and the verse drama *Samson Agonistes* (1671)

Milton Keynes ('mɪltən 'kiːnz) *n* **1** a new town in central England, in Milton Keynes unitary authority, N Buckinghamshire: founded in 1967: electronics, clothing, machinery; seat of the Open University. Pop: 207 063 (2001) **2** a unitary authority in central England, in Buckinghamshire. Pop: 188 400 (1994 est). Area: 310 sq km (119 sq miles)

Milwaukee (mɪl'wɔːkiː) *n* a port in SE Wisconsin, on Lake Michigan: the largest city in the state; established as a trading post in the 18th century; an important industrial centre. Pop: 596 974 (2000) > **Mil'waukeean** *adj, n*

mim (mɪm) *adj dialect* prim, modest, or demure [c17 ? imit. of lip-pursing]

mime (maɪm) *n* **1** the theatrical technique of expressing an idea or mood or portraying a character entirely by gesture and bodily movement without the use of words **2** Also called: **mime artist** a performer specializing in this **3** a dramatic presentation using such a technique **4** (in the classical theatre) **4a** a comic performance with exaggerated gesture and physical action **4b** an actor in such a performance ▷ *vb* **mimes, miming, mimed 5** to express (an idea, etc) in actions or gestures without speech **6** (of singers or musicians) to perform as if singing a song or playing a piece of music that is actually prerecorded [OE *mīma*, from L *mīmus* mimic actor, from Gk *mimos* imitator] > '**mimer** *n*

MIME *computing abbrev for* multipurpose Internet mail extensions

Mimeograph ('mɪmɪəˌgrɑːf) *n* **1** *trademark* an office machine for printing multiple copies of text or line drawings from a stencil **2** a copy produced by this ▷ *vb* **3** to print copies from (a prepared stencil) using this machine

mimesis (mɪ'miːsɪs) *n* **1** *art, literature* the imitative representation of nature or human behaviour **2** *biol* another name for **mimicry** (sense 2) **3** *rhetoric* representation of another person's alleged words in a speech [c16 from Gk, from *mimeisthai* to imitate]

mimetic (mɪ'mɛtɪk) *adj* **1** of, resembling, or relating to mimesis or imitation, as in art, etc **2** *biol* of or exhibiting mimicry > **mi'metically** *adv*

mimic ('mɪmɪk) *vb* **mimics, mimicking, mimicked** *(tr)* **1** to imitate (a person, a manner, etc), esp for satirical effect; ape **2** to take on the appearance of: *certain flies mimic wasps* **3** to copy closely or in a servile manner ▷ *n* **4** a person or an animal, such as a parrot, that is clever at mimicking **5** an animal that displays mimicry ▷ *adj* **6** of, relating to, or using mimicry **7** simulated, make-believe, or mock [c16 from L *mīmicus*, from Gk *mimikos*, from *mimos* MIME] > '**mimicker** *n*

mimicry ('mɪmɪkrɪ) *n, pl* **mimicries 1** the act or art of copying or imitating closely; mimicking **2** the resemblance shown by one animal species to another, which protects it from predators

MIMinE *abbrev for* Member of the Institute of Mining Engineers

Mimir (ˈmiːmɪə) *n Norse myth* a giant who guarded the well of wisdom near the roots of Yggdrasil

mimosa (mɪˈməʊsə, -zə) *n* any of various tropical shrubs or trees having ball-like clusters of yellow or pink flowers and leaves that are often sensitive to touch or light. See also **sensitive plant** [c18 from NL, prob. from L *mīmus* MIME, because the plant's sensitivity to touch imitates the similar reaction of animals]

mimulus (ˈmɪmjʊləs) *n* any of a genus of flowering plants of temperate regions. See **monkey flower** [c19 Med. L, from L *mimus* MIME, alluding to masklike flowers]

min. *abbrev for:* **1** minimum **2** minute *or* minutes

Min. *abbrev for:* **1** Minister **2** Ministry

Mina Hassan Tani (ˈmiːnə hɑːˈsɑːn ˈtɑːnɪ) *n* a port in NW Morocco, on the Sebou River 16 km (10 miles) from the Atlantic. Pop: 234 000 (1993 est). Also called: **Kénitra** Former name (1932–56): **Port Lyautey**

minaret (ˌmɪnəˈrɛt, ˈmɪnəˌrɛt) *n* a slender tower of a mosque having one or more balconies [c17 from F, from Turkish, from Ar. *manārat* lamp, from *nār* fire] > **ˌminaˈreted** *adj*

Minas Basin (ˈmaɪnəs) *n* a bay in E Canada, in central Nova Scotia: the NE arm of the Bay of Fundy, with which it is linked by **Minas Channel**

Minas Gerais (*Portuguese* ˈminaʒ ʒəˈraiʒ) *n* an inland state of E Brazil: situated on the high plateau of the Brazilian Highlands; large reserves of iron ore and manganese. Capital: Belo Horizonte. Pop: 17 835 488 (2000). Area: 587 172 sq km (226 707 sq miles)

minatory (ˈmɪnətərɪ, -trɪ) *or* **minatorial** *adj* threatening or menacing [c16 from LL *minātōrius*, from L *minārī* to threaten]

mince (mɪns) *vb* **minces, mincing, minced** **1** (*tr*) to chop, grind, or cut into very small pieces **2** (*tr*) to soften or moderate: *I didn't mince my words* **3** (*intr*) to walk or speak in an affected dainty manner ▷ *n* **4** *chiefly Brit* minced meat [c14 from OF *mincier*, ult. from LL *minūtia*; see MINUTIAE] > **ˈmincer** *n*

mincemeat (ˈmɪnsˌmiːt) *n* **1** a mixture of dried fruit, spices, etc, used esp for filling pies **2** **make mincemeat of** *inf* to defeat completely

mince pie *n* a small round pastry tart filled with mincemeat

Minch (mɪntʃ) *n* **the** a channel of the Atlantic divided into the **North Minch** between the mainland of Scotland and the Isle of Lewis, and the **Little Minch** between the Isle of Skye and Harris and North Uist

mincing (ˈmɪnsɪŋ) *adj* (of a person) affectedly elegant in gait, manner, or speech > **ˈmincingly** *adv*

mind (maɪnd) *n* **1** the human faculty to which are ascribed thought, feelings, intention, etc **2** intelligence or the intellect, esp as opposed to feelings or wishes **3** recollection or remembrance: *it comes to mind* **4** the faculty of original or creative thought; imagination: *it's all in the mind* **5** a person considered as an intellectual being: *great minds* **6** condition, state, or manner of feeling or thought: *his state of mind* **7** an inclination, desire, or purpose: *I have a mind to go* **8** attention or thoughts: *keep your mind on your work* **9** a sound mental state; sanity (esp in **out of one's mind**) **10** (in Cartesian philosophy) one of two basic modes of existence, the other being matter **11** **blow someone's mind** *sl* **11a** (of a drug) to alter someone's mental state **11b** to astound or surprise someone **12** **change one's mind** to alter one's decision or opinion **13** **in** *or* **of two minds** undecided; wavering **14** **give (someone) a piece of one's mind** to criticize or censure (someone) frankly or vehemently **15** **make up one's mind** to decide (something or to do something) **16** **on one's mind** in one's thoughts ▷ *vb* **17** (when *tr*, *may take a clause as object*) to take offence at: *do you mind if I smoke?* **18** to pay attention to (something); heed; notice: *to mind one's own business* **19** (*tr; takes a clause as object*) to make certain; ensure: *mind you tell her* **20** (*tr*) to take care of; have charge of: *to mind the shop* **21** (when *tr*, *may take a clause as object*) to be cautious or careful about (something): *mind how you go* **22** (*tr*) to obey (someone or something); heed: *mind your father!* **23** to be concerned (about); be troubled (about): *never mind about your hat* **24** (*tr; passive; takes an infinitive*) to be intending or inclined (to do something): *clearly he was not minded to finish the story* **25** **mind you** an expression qualifying a previous statement: *Dogs are nice. Mind you, I don't like all dogs* ▷ Related adj: **mental** ▷ See also **mind out** [OE *gemynd* mind]

Mindanao (ˌmɪndəˈnaʊ) *n* the second largest island of the Philippines, in the S part of the archipelago: mountainous and volcanic. Chief towns: Davao, Zamboanga. Pop: 14 298 000 (1990 est). Area: (including offshore islands) 94 631 sq km (36 537 sq miles)

mind-bending *adj inf* **1** Also: **mind-blowing** altering one's state of consciousness, esp as a result of taking drugs **2** reaching the limit of credibility: *they offered a mind-bending salary* ▷ *n* **3** the process of brainwashing

mind-boggling *adj inf* astonishing; bewildering

minded (ˈmaɪndɪd) *adj* **1** having a mind, inclination, intention, etc, as specified: *politically minded* **2** (*in combination*): *money-minded*

minder (ˈmaɪndə) *n* **1** someone who looks after someone or something **2** short for **childminder** **3** *sl* an aide to someone in public life who keeps control of press and public relations **4** *sl* someone acting as a bodyguard or assistant, esp in the criminal underworld

mindfuck (ˈmaɪndˌfʌk) *n taboo sl* the deliberate infliction of psychological damage

mindful (ˈmaɪndfʊl) *adj* (usually *postpositive* and foll by *of*) keeping aware; heedful: *mindful of your duty* > **ˈmindfully** *adv* > **ˈmindfulness** *n*

mind games *pl n* actions or statements intended to undermine or mislead someone else, often to gain advantage for oneself: *she started playing mind games with me*

mindless (ˈmaɪndlɪs) *adj* **1** stupid or careless **2** requiring little or no intellectual effort > **ˈmindlessly** *adv* > **ˈmindlessness** *n*

mind-numbing *adj* extremely boring and uninspiring > **ˈmind-ˌnumbingly** *adv*

Mindoro (mɪnˈdɔːrəʊ) *n* a mountainous island in the central Philippines, south of Luzon. Pop: 912 000 (1995 est). Area: 9736 sq km (3759 sq miles)

mind out *vb* (*intr, adv*) *Brit* to be careful or pay attention

mind-reader *n* a person seemingly able to discern the thoughts of another > **ˈmind-ˌreading** *n*

mind-set *n* the ideas and attitudes with which a person approaches a situation, esp when these are seen as being difficult to alter

mind's eye *n* the visual memory or the imagination

Mindszenty (ˈmɪndsɛntɪ) *n* **Joseph** 1892–1975, Hungarian cardinal. He was sentenced to life imprisonment on a charge of treason (1949) but released during the 1956 Revolution

mine[1] (maɪn) *pron* **1** something or someone belonging to or associated with me: *mine is best* **2** **of mine** belonging to or associated with me ▷ *determiner* **3** (*preceding a vowel*) an archaic word for **my**: *mine eyes; mine host* [OE *mīn*]

mine[2] (maɪn) *n* **1** a system of excavations made for the extraction of minerals, esp coal, ores, or precious stones **2** any deposit of ore or minerals **3** a lucrative source or abundant supply: *a mine of information* **4** a device containing explosive designed to destroy ships, vehicles, or personnel, usually laid beneath the ground or in water **5** a tunnel dug to undermine a fortification,

Mm

etc ▷ *vb* **mines, mining, mined 6** to dig into (the earth) for (minerals) **7** to make (a hole, tunnel, etc) by digging or boring **8** to place explosive mines in position below the surface of (the sea or land) **9** to undermine (a fortification, etc) by digging mines **10** another word for **undermine** [c13 from OF, prob. of Celtic origin]

mine detector *n* an instrument designed to detect explosive mines > **mine detection** *n*

mine dump *n S African* a large mound of residue esp from gold-mining operations

minefield ('maɪn,fiːld) *n* **1** an area of ground or water containing explosive mines **2** a subject, situation, etc, beset with hidden problems

minelayer ('maɪn,leɪə) *n* a warship or aircraft designed for the carrying and laying of mines

miner ('maɪnə) *n* **1** a person who works in a mine **2** any of various insects or insect larvae that bore into and feed on plant tissues. See also **leaf miner 3** *Austral* any of several honeyeaters of the genus *Manorina*, esp *M melanocephala*, of scrub regions

mineral ('mɪnərəl, 'mɪnrəl) *n* **1** any of a class of naturally occurring solid inorganic substances with a characteristic crystalline form and a homogeneous chemical composition **2** any inorganic matter **3** any substance obtained by mining, esp a metal ore **4** (*often pl*) *Brit* short for **mineral water 5** *Brit* a soft drink containing carbonated water and flavourings ▷ *adj* **6** of, relating to, containing, or resembling minerals [c15 from Med. L *minerāle* (n), from *minerālis* (adj); rel. to *minera* mine, ore, from ?]

▷ www.psigate.ac.uk/newsite/earth-gateway.html
▷ http://un2sg4.unige.ch/athena/mineral/mineral.html
▷ www.minerals.net/glossary/glossary.htm
▷ http://homepage.boku.ac.at/h9440283/eetymol.htm

mineral. *abbrev for* mineralogy *or* mineralogical

mineralize *or* **mineralise** ('mɪnərə,laɪz) *vb* **mineralizes, mineralizing, mineralized** *or* **mineralises, mineralising, mineralised** (*tr*) **1a** to impregnate (organic matter, water, etc) with a mineral substance **1b** to convert (such matter) into a mineral; petrify **2** (of gases, vapours, etc, in magma) to transform (a metal) into an ore > **,minerali'zation** *or* **,minerali'sation** *n* > **'mineral,izer** *or* **'mineral,iser** *n*

mineralogy (,mɪnə'rælədʒɪ) *n* the branch of geology concerned with the study of minerals > **mineralogical** (,mɪnərə'lɒdʒɪkəl) *or* **,minera'logic** *adj* > **,miner'alogist** *n*

mineral oil *n Brit* any oil of mineral origin, esp petroleum

mineral water *n* water containing dissolved mineral salts or gases, usually having medicinal properties

mineral wool *n* a fibrous material made by blowing steam or air through molten slag and used for packing and insulation

miner's right *n Austral* a licence to prospect for and mine gold, etc

Minerva (mɪ'nɜːvə) *n* the Roman goddess of wisdom. Greek counterpart: **Athena**

minestrone (,mɪnɪ'strəʊnɪ) *n* a soup made from a variety of vegetables and pasta [from It., from *minestrare* to serve]

minesweeper ('maɪn,swiːpə) *n* a naval vessel equipped to clear mines > **'mine,sweeping** *n*

Ming (mɪŋ) *n* **1** the imperial dynasty of China from 1368 to 1644 ▷ *adj* **2** of or relating to Chinese porcelain from the Ming dynasty

minging ('mɪŋɪŋ) *adj Brit inf* **1** ugly, disgusting, or malodorous **2** extremely poor in quality [c20 originally Scottish, of obscure origin]

mingle ('mɪŋgəl) *vb* **mingles, mingling, mingled 1** to mix or cause to mix **2** (*intr; often foll by with*) to come into close association [c15 from OE *mengan* to mix] > **'mingler** *n*

Mingus ('mɪŋgəs) *n* **Charles**, known as *Charlie Mingus*. 1922–79, US jazz double bassist, composer, and band leader

mingy ('mɪndʒɪ) *adj* **mingier, mingiest** *Brit inf* miserly, stingy, or niggardly [c20 prob. a blend of MEAN[2] + STINGY[1]]

Minho ('miɲu) *n* the Portuguese name for the **Miño**

mini ('mɪnɪ) *adj* **1** (of a woman's dress, skirt, etc) very short; thigh-length **2** (*prenominal*) small; miniature ▷ *n, pl* **minis 3** something very small of its kind, esp a small car or a miniskirt

mini- *combining form* smaller or shorter than the standard size: *minibus; miniskirt* [c20 from MINIATURE & MINIMUM]

miniature ('mɪnɪtʃə) *n* **1** a model, copy, or representation on a very small scale **2** anything that is very small of its kind **3** a very small painting, esp a portrait **4** an illuminated decoration in a manuscript **5 in miniature** on a small scale ▷ *adj* **6** greatly reduced in size, etc **7** on a small scale; minute [c16 from It., from Med. L, from *miniāre* to paint red (in illuminating manuscripts), from *minium* red lead] > **'miniaturist** *n*

miniaturize *or* **miniaturise** ('mɪnɪtʃə,raɪz) *vb* **miniaturizes, miniaturizing, miniaturized** *or* **miniaturises, miniaturising, miniaturised** (*tr*) to make or construct (something, esp electronic equipment) on a very small scale; reduce in size > **,miniaturi'zation** *or* **,miniaturi'sation** *n*

minibar ('mɪnɪ,bɑː) *n* a selection of drinks and confectionery provided in a hotel room and charged to the guest's bill if used

minibus ('mɪnɪ,bʌs) *n* a small bus able to carry approximately ten passengers

minicab ('mɪnɪ,kæb) *n Brit* a small saloon car used as a taxi

minicomputer (,mɪnɪkəm'pjuːtə) *n* a small comparatively cheap digital computer

minidisc ('mɪnɪ,dɪsk) *n* a small recordable disc similar to a compact disc, used mainly for sound recording

minidish ('mɪnɪ,dɪʃ) *n* a small parabolic aerial for reception or transmission to a communications satellite

minim ('mɪnɪm) *n* **1** a unit of fluid measure equal to one sixtieth of a drachm. It is approximately equal to one drop. Symbol: **M 2** *music* a note having the time value of half a semibreve **3** a small or insignificant thing **4** a downward stroke in calligraphy [c15 (*music*): from L *minimus* smallest]

minimal art *n* abstract painting or sculpture in which expressiveness and illusion are minimized by the use of simple geometric shapes, flat colour, and arrangements of ordinary objects > **minimal artist** *n*

▷ www.artlex.com/ArtLex/m/minimalism.html
▷ www.artcyclopedia.com/history/minimalism.html

minimalism ('mɪnɪmə,lɪzəm) *n* **1** another name for **minimal art 2** a type of music based on simple elements and avoiding elaboration or embellishment **3** design or style in which the simplest and fewest elements are used to create the maximum effect > **'minimalist** *adj, n*

▷ www.nortexinfo.net/McDaniel/minimalist_music.htm
▷ www.sbgmusic.com/html/teacher/reference/styles/minimal.html

minimax ('mɪnɪ,mæks) *n* **1** *maths* the lowest of a set of maximum values **2** (in game theory, etc) the procedure of choosing the strategy that least benefits the most advantaged member of a group ▷ Cf **maximin** [c20 from MINI(MUM) + MAX(IMUM)]

Mini-Me ('mɪnɪ,miː) *n inf* **1** a person who resembles a smaller or younger version of another person **2** a person who adopts the opinions or mannerisms of a more powerful or senior person in order to win favour, achieve promotion, etc [c20 after a character in the 1999 film *Austin Powers: The Spy who Shagged Me*]

minimize *or* **minimise** ('mɪnɪ,maɪz) *vb* **minimizes,**

minimizing, minimized *or* **minimises, minimising, minimised** *(tr)* **1** to reduce to or estimate at the least possible degree or amount **2** to rank or treat at less than the true worth; belittle > ˌ**minimiˈzation** *or* ˌ**minimiˈsation** *n* > ˈ**miniˌmizer** *or* ˈ**miniˌmiser** *n*

minimum (ˈmɪnɪməm) *n, pl* **minimums** *or* **minima** (-mə) **1** the least possible amount, degree, or quantity **2** the least amount recorded, allowed, or reached **3** *(modifier)* being the least possible, recorded, allowed, etc: *minimum age* ▷ *adj* **4** of or relating to a minimum or minimums [c17 from L: smallest thing, from *minimus* least] > ˈ**minimal** *adj* > ˈ**minimally** *adv*

minimum lending rate *n* (in Britain) the minimum rate at which the Bank of England would lend to discount houses between 1971 and 1981, after which it was replaced by the less formal base rate

minimum wage *n* the lowest wage that an employer is permitted to pay by law or union contract

mining (ˈmaɪnɪŋ) *n* **1** the act, process, or industry of extracting coal, ores, etc, from the earth **2** *mil* the process of laying mines
▷ http://dir.yahoo.com/Science/Engineering/Mining

minion (ˈmɪnjən) *n* **1** a favourite or dependant, esp a servile or fawning one **2** a servile agent [c16 from F *mignon*, from OF *mignot*, of Gaulish origin]

minipill (ˈmɪnɪˌpɪl) *n* a low-dose oral contraceptive containing progesterone only

miniseries (ˈmɪnɪˌsɪəriːz) *n, pl* **miniseries** a television programme in several parts that is shown on consecutive days for a short period

miniskirt (ˈmɪnɪˌskɜːt) *n* a very short skirt, originally in the 1960s, one at least four inches above the knee. Often shortened to **mini**

minister (ˈmɪnɪstə) *n* **1** (esp in Presbyterian and some Nonconformist Churches) a member of the clergy **2** a head of a government department **3** any diplomatic agent accredited to a foreign government or head of state **4** Also called: **minister plenipotentiary** another term for **envoy**[1] (sense 1) **5** Also called: **minister resident** a diplomat ranking after an envoy **6** a person who attends to the needs of others, esp in religious matters **7** a person who acts as the agent or servant of a person or thing ▷ *vb* **8** *(intr; often foll by to)* to attend to the needs (of); take care (of) **9** *(tr) arch* to provide; supply [c13 via OF from L: servant; rel. to *minus* less]

ministerial (ˌmɪnɪˈstɪərɪəl) *adj* **1** of or relating to a minister of religion or his or her office **2** of or relating to a government minister or ministry **3** *(often cap)* of or supporting the ministry against the opposition **4** *law* relating to or possessing delegated executive authority **5** acting as an agent or cause; instrumental > ˌ**minisˈterially** *adv*

minister of state *n* **1** (in the British Parliament) a minister, usually below cabinet rank, appointed to assist a senior minister **2** any government minister

Minister of the Crown *n Brit* any Government minister of cabinet rank

minister plenipotentiary *n, pl* **ministers plenipotentiary** another term for **envoy**[1] (sense 1)

ministrant (ˈmɪnɪstrənt) *adj* **1** ministering or serving as a minister ▷ *n* **2** a person who ministers [c17 from L *ministrans*, from *ministrāre* to wait upon]

ministration (ˌmɪnɪˈstreɪʃən) *n* **1** the act or an instance of serving or giving aid **2** the act or an instance of ministering religiously [c14 from L *ministrātiō*, from *ministrāre* to wait upon] > **ministrative** (ˈmɪnɪstrətɪv) *adj*

ministry (ˈmɪnɪstrɪ) *n, pl* **ministries** **1a** the profession or duties of a minister of religion **1b** the performance of these duties **2** ministers of religion or government ministers considered collectively **3** the tenure of a minister **4a** a government department headed by a minister **4b** the buildings of such a department [c14 from L *ministerium* service; see MINISTER]

miniver (ˈmɪnɪvə) *n* white fur, used in ceremonial costumes [c13 from OF *menu vair*, from *menu* small + *vair* variegated fur]

mink (mɪŋk) *n, pl* **mink** *or* **minks** **1** any of several mammals of Europe, Asia, and North America, having slightly webbed feet **2** their highly valued fur, esp that of the American mink **3** a garment made of this, esp a woman's coat or stole [c15 from ON]

Minkowski (mɪŋˈkɒfskɪ) *n* **Hermann** (ˈhɜːmən) 1864–1909, German mathematician, born in Russia. His concept of a four-dimensional space-time continuum (1907) proved crucial for the general theory of relativity developed by Einstein

Minn. *abbrev for* Minnesota

Minna (ˈmɪnə) *n* a city in W central Nigeria, capital of Niger state. Pop: 136 900 (1996 est)

Minneapolis (ˌmɪnɪˈæpəlɪs) *n* a city in SE Minnesota, on the Mississippi River adjacent to St Paul: the largest city in the state; important centre for the grain trade. Pop: 382 618 (2000 est)

minneola (ˌmɪnɪˈəʊlə) *n* a juicy citrus fruit that is a cross between a tangerine and a grapefruit [c20 ?from *Mineola*, Texas]

minnesinger (ˈmɪnɪˌsɪŋə) *n* one of the German lyric poets and musicians of the 12th to 14th centuries [c19 from G *Minnesinger* love-singer]

Minnesota (ˌmɪnɪˈsəʊtə) *n* **1** a state of the N central US: chief US producer of iron ore. Capital: St Paul. Pop: 4 919 479 (2000). Area: 218 600 sq km (84 402 sq miles). Abbreviations: **Minn** or (with zip code) **MN** **2** a river in S Minnesota, flowing southeast and northeast to the Mississippi River near St Paul. Length: 534 km (332 miles) > ˌ**Minneˈsotan** *adj, n*

minnow (ˈmɪnəʊ) *n, pl* **minnows** *or* **minnow** **1** a small slender European freshwater cyprinid fish **2** a small or insignificant person [c15 rel. to OE *myne* minnow]

Miño (*Spanish* ˈmiɲo) *n* a river in SW Europe, rising in NW Spain and flowing southwest (as part of the border between Spain and Portugal) to the Atlantic. Length: 338 km (210 miles). Portuguese name: **Minho**

Minoan (mɪˈnəʊən) *adj* **1** of or denoting the Bronze Age culture of Crete from about 3000 BC to about 1100 BC ▷ *n* **2** a Cretan belonging to the Minoan culture [c19 after MINOS from the excavations at his supposed palace at Knossos]
▷ www.historywiz.com/minoans-mm.htm
▷ www.dragonridge.com/greece/minoam.htm

Minogue (mɪˈnəʊg) *n* **Kylie** (ˈkaɪlɪ) born 1968, Australian singer and actress: appeared in the television series *Neighbours* from 1986; records include "I Should Be So Lucky" (1988), *Kylie Minogue* (1994), and *Fever* (2001)

minor (ˈmaɪnə) *adj* **1** lesser or secondary in amount, importance, etc **2** of or relating to the minority **3** below the age of legal majority **4** *music* **4a** (of a scale) having a semitone between the second and third and fifth and sixth degrees (**natural minor**) **4b** (of a key) based on the minor scale **4c** *(postpositive)* denoting a specified key based on the minor scale: *C minor* **4d** (of an interval) reduced by a semitone from the major **4e** (of a chord, esp a triad) having a minor third above the root. **f** (esp in jazz) of or relating to a chord built upon a minor triad and containing a minor seventh: *a minor ninth* **5** *logic* (of a term or premise) having less generality or scope than another term or proposition **6** *US education* of or relating to an additional secondary subject taken by a student **7** *(immediately postpositive) Brit* the younger or junior: sometimes used after the surname of a schoolboy if he has an older brother in the same school ▷ *n* **8** a person or thing that is lesser or secondary **9** a person below the age of legal majority **10** *US & Canad education* a subsidiary subject **11** *music* a minor key, chord, mode, or scale **12** *logic* a minor term or premise ▷ *vb* **13** *(intr; usually foll*

Mm

by *in*) *US education.* to take a minor [c13 from L: less, smaller]

minor axis *n* the shorter or shortest axis of an ellipse or ellipsoid

Minorca (mɪˈnɔːkə) *n* **1** an island in the W Mediterranean, northeast of Majorca: the second largest of the Balearic Islands. Chief town: Mahón. Pop: 55 500 (latest est). Area: 702 sq km (271 sq miles). Spanish name: **Menorca** **2** a breed of light domestic fowl with glossy white, black, or blue plumage > **Miˈnorcan** *adj, n*

minority (maɪˈnɒrɪtɪ, mɪ-) *n, pl* **minorities** **1** the smaller of two parts, factions, or groups **2** a group that is different racially, politically, etc, from a larger group of which it is a part **3a** the state of being a minor **3b** the period during which a person is below legal age **4** (*modifier*) relating to or being a minority: *a minority opinion* [c16 from Med. L *minōritās*, from L MINOR]

minor league *n US & Canad* any professional league in baseball other than a major league

minor orders *pl n RC Church* the four lower degrees of holy orders, namely porter, exorcist, lector, and acolyte

minor premise *n logic* the premise of a syllogism containing the subject of its conclusion

minor term *n logic* the subject of the conclusion of a syllogism

Minos (ˈmaɪnɒs) *n Greek myth* a king of Crete for whom Daedalus built the Labyrinth to contain the Minotaur

Minotaur (ˈmaɪnətɔː) *n Greek myth* a monster with the head of a bull and the body of a man. It was kept in the Labyrinth in Crete, feeding on human flesh, until destroyed by Theseus [c14 via L from Gk *Minōtauros*, from MINOS + *tauros* bull]

Minsk (mɪnsk) *n* the capital of Belarus: an industrial city and educational and cultural centre, with a university (1921). Pop: 1 717 000 (1998 est)
▹ www.belarustourist.minsk.by/english/city

minster (ˈmɪnstə) *n Brit* any of certain cathedrals and large churches, usually originally connected to a monastery [OE *mynster*, prob. from Vulgar L *monisterium* (unattested), var. of Church L *monastērium* MONASTERY]

minstrel (ˈmɪnstrəl) *n* **1** a medieval musician who performed songs or recited poetry with instrumental accompaniment **2** a performer in a minstrel show **3** *arch or poetic* any poet, musician, or singer [c13 from OF *menestral*, from LL *ministeriālis* an official, from L MINISTER]

minstrel show *n* a theatrical entertainment consisting of songs, dances, etc, performed by actors wearing black face make-up

minstrelsy (ˈmɪnstrəlsɪ) *n, pl* **minstrelsies** **1** the art of a minstrel **2** the poems, music, or songs of a minstrel **3** a troupe of minstrels

mint[1] (mɪnt) *n* **1** any N temperate plant of a genus having aromatic leaves. The leaves of some species are used for seasoning and flavouring. See also **peppermint, spearmint** **2** a sweet flavoured with mint [OE *minte*, from L *mentha*, from Gk *minthē*] > **ˈminty** *adj*

mint[2] (mɪnt) *n* **1** a place where money is coined by governmental authority **2** a very large amount of money ▹ *adj* **3** (of coins, postage stamps, etc) in perfect condition as issued **4** **in mint condition** in perfect condition; as if new ▹ *vb* **5** to make (coins) by stamping metal **6** (*tr*) to invent (esp phrases or words) [OE *mynet* coin, from L *monēta* money, mint, from the temple of Juno *Monēta*, used as a mint in ancient Rome] > **ˈminter** *n*

mintage (ˈmɪntɪdʒ) *n* **1** the process of minting **2** the money minted **3** a fee paid for minting a coin **4** an official impression stamped on a coin

minted (ˈmɪntɪd) *adj Brit sl* wealthy

mint julep *n chiefly US* a long drink consisting of bourbon whiskey, crushed ice, sugar, and sprigs of mint

minuend (ˈmɪnjʊˌɛnd) *n* the number from which another number, the **subtrahend,** is to be subtracted [c18 from L *minuendus* (*numerus*) (the number) to be diminished]

minuet (ˌmɪnjʊˈɛt) *n* **1** a stately court dance of the 17th and 18th centuries in triple time **2** a piece of music composed for or in the rhythm of this dance [c17 from F *menuet* dainty, from *menu* small]

minus (ˈmaɪnəs) *prep* **1** reduced by the subtraction of: *four minus two* (written 4 – 2) **2** *inf* deprived of; lacking: *minus the trimmings* ▹ *adj* **3a** indicating or involving subtraction: *a minus sign* **3b** Also: **negative** having a value or designating a quantity less than zero: *a minus number* **4** involving a disadvantage, harm, etc: *a minus factor* **5** (*postpositive*) *Education.* slightly below the standard of a particular grade: *a B minus* **6** denoting a negative electric charge ▹ *n* **7** short for **minus sign** **8** a negative quantity **9** a disadvantage, loss, or deficit **10** *inf* something detrimental or negative ▹ Mathematical symbol: – [c15 from L, neuter of MINOR]

minuscule (ˈmɪnəˌskjuːl) *n* **1** a lower-case letter **2** writing using such letters **3** a small cursive 7th-century style of lettering ▹ *adj* **4** relating to, printed in, or written in small letters ▹ Cf **majuscule** **5** very small **6** (of letters) lower-case [c18 from F, from L (*littera*) *minuscula* very small (letter), dim. of MINOR] > **minuscular** (mɪˈnʌskjʊlə) *adj*

minus sign *n* the symbol –, indicating subtraction or a negative quantity

minute[1] (ˈmɪnɪt) *n* **1** a period of time equal to 60 seconds; one sixtieth of an hour **2** Also called: **minute of arc** a unit of angular measure equal to one sixtieth of a degree. Symbol: ′ **3** any very short period of time; moment **4** a short note or memorandum **5** the distance that can be travelled in a minute: *it's only two minutes away* **6** **up to the minute** (**up-to-the-minute** *when prenominal*). the very latest or newest ▹ *vb* **minutes, minuting, minuted** (*tr*) **7** to record in minutes: *to minute a meeting* **8** to time in terms of minutes ▹ See also **minutes** [c14 from OF, from Med. L *minūta*, n. use of L *minūtus* MINUTE[2]] > **minutely** (ˈmɪnɪtlɪ) *adv*

minute[2] (maɪˈnjuːt) *adj* **1** very small; diminutive; tiny **2** unimportant; petty **3** precise or detailed [c15 from L *minūtus*, p.p. of *minuere* to diminish] > **miˈnuteness** *n* > **miˈnutely** *adv*

minute gun (ˈmɪnɪt) *n* a gun fired at one-minute intervals as a sign of distress or mourning

minute hand (ˈmɪnɪt) *n* the pointer on a timepiece that indicates minutes

Minuteman (ˈmɪnɪtˌmæn) *n, pl* **Minutemen** **1** (*sometimes not cap*) (in the War of American Independence) a colonial militiaman who promised to be ready to fight at one minute's notice **2** a US three-stage intercontinental ballistic missile

minutes (ˈmɪnɪts) *pl n* an official record of the proceedings of a meeting, conference, etc

minute steak (ˈmɪnɪt) *n* a small piece of steak that can be cooked quickly

minutiae (mɪˈnjuːʃɪˌiː) *pl n, sing* **minutia** (-ʃɪə) small, precise, or trifling details [c18 pl of LL *minūtia* smallness, from L *minūtus* MINUTE[2]]

minx (mɪŋks) *n* a bold, flirtatious, or scheming woman [c16 from ?]

Minya (ˈmɪnjə) *n* See **El Minya**

Miocene (ˈmaɪəˌsiːn) *adj* **1** of or denoting the fourth epoch of the Tertiary period, which lasted for 19 million years ▹ *n* **2** **the** this epoch or rock series [c19 Gk *meiōn* less + -CENE]

miosis *or* **myosis** (maɪˈəʊsɪs) *n, pl* **mioses** (-siːz) *or* **myoses** **1** excessive contraction of the pupil of the eye **2** a variant spelling of **meiosis** (sense 1) [c20 from Gk *muein* to shut the eyes + -OSIS] > **miotic** *or* **myotic** (maɪˈɒtɪk) *adj, n*

MIP *abbrev for:* **1** monthly investment plan **2** maximum investment plan: an endowment assurance policy designed to produce maximum profits

Miquelon ('mi:kə,lɒn; *French* miklɔ̃) *n* a group of islands in the French territory of **Saint Pierre and Miquelon**

Mir (mɪə) *n* the Russian (formerly Soviet) orbiting space station launched in 1986: it is scheduled to be destroyed in 2001 [Russian]

Mirabeau (*French* mirabo) *n* **Comte de,** title of *Honoré-Gabriel Riqueti*. 1749–91, French Revolutionary politician

mirabelle (,mɪrə'bɛl) *n* **1** a small sweet yellow-orange variety of greengage **2** a liqueur produced from this [c18 from F]

miracle ('mɪrəkᵊl) *n* **1** an event contrary to the laws of nature and attributed to a supernatural cause **2** any amazing or wonderful event **3** a marvellous example of something: *a miracle of engineering* **4** short for **miracle play** **5** (*modifier*) being or seeming a miracle: *a miracle cure* [c12 from L *mīrāculum*, from *mīrārī* to wonder at]

miracle play *n* a medieval play based on a biblical story or the life of a saint ▷ Cf **mystery play**

miraculous (mɪ'rækjʊləs) *adj* **1** of, like, or caused by a miracle; marvellous **2** surprising **3** having the power to work miracles > **mi'raculously** *adv* > **mi'raculousness** *n*

Miraflores (,mɪrə'flɔ:rəs; *Spanish* mira'flores) *n* **Lake** an artificial lake in Panama, in the S Canal Zone of the Panama Canal

mirage (mɪ'rɑ:ʒ) *n* **1** an image of a distant object or sheet of water, often inverted or distorted, caused by atmospheric refraction by hot air **2** something illusory [c19 from F, from (*se*) *mirer* to be reflected]

mire ('maɪə) *n* **1** a boggy or marshy area **2** mud, muck, or dirt ▷ *vb* **mires, miring, mired** **3** to sink or cause to sink in a mire **4** (*tr*) to make dirty or muddy **5** (*tr*) to involve, esp in difficulties [c14 from ON *mýrr*]

mirepoix (mɪə'pwɑ:) *n* a mixture of sautéed root vegetables used as a base for braising meat or for various sauces [F, prob. after Duke of *Mirepoix*, 18th-cent. F general]

Miriam ('mɪrɪəm) *n* *Old Testament* the sister of Moses and Aaron. (Numbers 12:1–15). Douay name: **Mary**

mirk (mɜ:k) *n* a variant spelling of **murk** > **'mirky** *adj* > **'mirkily** *adv* > **'mirkiness** *n*

Miró (*Spanish* mi'ro) *n* **Joan** (xwan) 1893–1983, Spanish surrealist painter

mirror ('mɪrə) *n* **1** a surface, such as polished metal or glass coated with a metal film, that reflects an image of an object placed in front of it **2** such a reflecting surface mounted in a frame **3** any reflecting surface **4** a thing that reflects or depicts something else ▷ *vb* **5** (*tr*) to reflect, represent, or depict faithfully: *he mirrors his teacher's ideals* [c13 from OF from *mirer* to look at, from L *mīrārī* to wonder at]

mirror ball *n* a large revolving ball covered with small pieces of mirror glass so that it reflects light in changing patterns: used in discos and ballrooms

mirror carp *n* a variety of carp with a smooth shiny body surface

mirror image *n* **1** an image as observed in a mirror **2** an object that corresponds to another but has left and right reversed as if seen in a mirror

mirror writing *n* backward writing that forms a mirror image of normal writing

mirth (mɜ:θ) *n* laughter, gaiety, or merriment [OE *myrgth*] > **'mirthful** *adj* > **'mirthfulness** *n* > **'mirthless** *adj* > **'mirthlessness** *n*

MIRV (mɜ:v) *n acronym for* multiple independently targeted re-entry vehicle: a missile that has several warheads, each one being directed to a different enemy target

mis- *prefix* **1** wrong or bad; wrongly or badly: *misunderstanding; misfortune; mistreat; mislead* **2** lack of; not: *mistrust* [OE *mis(se)*-]

misadventure (,mɪsəd'vɛntʃə) *n* **1** an unlucky event; misfortune **2** *law* accidental death not due to crime or negligence

misalliance (,mɪsə'laɪəns) *n* an unsuitable alliance or marriage > **,misal'ly** *vb*

misanthrope ('mɪzən,θrəʊp) *or* **misanthropist** (mɪ'zænθrəpɪst) *n* a person who dislikes or distrusts other people or mankind in general [c17 from Gk *mīsanthrōpos*, from *misos* hatred + *anthrōpos* man] > **misanthropic** (,mɪzən'θrɒpɪk) *or* **,misan'thropical** *adj* > **misanthropy** (mɪ'zænθrəpɪ) *n*

misapply (,mɪsə'plaɪ) *vb* **misapplies, misapplying, misapplied** (*tr*) **1** to apply wrongly or badly **2** another word for **misappropriate** > **misapplication** (,mɪsæplɪ'keɪʃən) *n*

misapprehend (,mɪsæprɪ'hɛnd) *vb* (*tr*) to misunderstand > **,misappre'hensive** *adj* > **,misappre'hensiveness** *n*

misapprehension (,mɪsæprɪ'hɛnʃən) *n* a failure to understand fully; misconception: *the misapprehension that acting was easy*

misappropriate (,mɪsə'prəʊprɪ,eɪt) *vb* **misappropriates, misappropriating, misappropriated** (*tr*) to appropriate for a wrong or dishonest use; embezzle or steal > **,misap,propri'ation** *n*

misbecome (,mɪsbɪ'kʌm) *vb* **misbecomes, misbecoming, misbecame, misbecome** (*tr*) to be unbecoming to or unsuitable for

misbegotten (,mɪsbɪ'gɒtᵊn) *adj* **1** unlawfully obtained **2** badly conceived, planned, or designed **3** *literary and dialect* illegitimate; bastard

misbehave (,mɪsbɪ'heɪv) *vb* **misbehaves, misbehaving, misbehaved** to behave (oneself) badly > **,misbe'haver** *n* > **misbehaviour** *or US* **misbehavior** (,mɪsbɪ'heɪvjə) *n*

misbelief (,mɪsbɪ'li:f) *n* a false or unorthodox belief > **,misbe'liever** *n*

misc. *abbrev for* miscellaneous

miscalculate (,mɪs'kælkjʊ,leɪt) *vb* **miscalculates, miscalculating, miscalculated** (*tr*) to calculate wrongly > **,miscalcu'lation** *n*

miscall (,mɪs'kɔ:l) *vb* (*tr*) **1** to call by the wrong name **2** *dialect* to abuse or malign > **,mis'caller** *n*

miscarriage (mɪs'kærɪdʒ) *n* **1** (*also* 'mɪskær-) spontaneous expulsion of a fetus from the womb, esp prior to the 20th week of pregnancy **2** an act of mismanagement or failure: *a miscarriage of justice* **3** *Brit* the failure of freight to reach its destination

miscarry (mɪs'kærɪ) *vb* **miscarries, miscarrying, miscarried** (*intr*) **1** to expel a fetus prematurely from the womb; abort **2** to fail **3** *Brit* (of freight, mail, etc) to fail to reach a destination

miscast (,mɪs'kɑ:st) *vb* **miscasts, miscasting, miscast** (*tr*) **1** to cast badly **2** (*often passive*) **2a** to cast (a role) in (a play, film, etc) inappropriately: *Falstaff was miscast* **2b** to assign an inappropriate role to: *he was miscast as Othello*

miscegenation (,mɪsɪdʒɪ'neɪʃən) *n* interbreeding of races, esp where differences of pigmentation are involved [c19 from L *miscēre* to mingle + *genus* race]

miscellanea (,mɪsə'leɪnɪə) *pl n* a collection of miscellaneous items, esp literary works [c16 from L: neuter pl of *miscellāneus* MISCELLANEOUS]

miscellaneous (,mɪsə'leɪnɪəs) *adj* **1** composed of or containing a variety of things; mixed **2** having varied capabilities, sides, etc [c17 from L *miscellāneus*, from *miscellus* mixed, from *miscēre* to mix] > **,miscel'laneously** *adv* > **,miscel'laneousness** *n*

miscellany (mɪ'sɛlənɪ; *US* 'mɪsə,leɪnɪ) *n, pl* **miscellanies** **1** a mixed assortment of items **2** (*sometimes pl*) a miscellaneous collection of items, esp essays, poems, etc [c16 from F *miscellanées* (pl) MISCELLANEA] > **miscellanist** (mɪ'sɛlənɪst) *n*

mischance (mɪs'tʃɑ:ns) *n* **1** bad luck **2** a stroke of bad luck

mischief ('mɪstʃɪf) *n* **1** wayward but not malicious behaviour, usually of children, that causes trouble,

Mm

irritation, etc **2** a playful inclination to behave in this way or to tease or disturb **3** injury or harm caused by a person or thing **4** a person, esp a child, who is mischievous **5** a source of trouble, difficulty, etc [C13 from OF *meschief*, from *meschever* to meet with calamity; from *mes-* MIS- + *chever*, from *chef* end]

mischievous ('mɪstʃɪvəs) *adj* **1** inclined to acts of mischief **2** teasing; slightly malicious **3** causing or intended to cause harm > '**mischievously** *adv* > '**mischievousness** *n*

miscible ('mɪsɪbᵊl) *adj* capable of mixing: *miscible with water* [C16 from Med. L *miscibilis*, from L *miscēre* to mix] > ˌ**misci'bility** *n*

misconceive (ˌmɪskən'siːv) *vb* **misconceives, misconceiving, misconceived** to have the wrong idea; fail to understand > ˌ**miscon'ceiver** *n*

misconception (ˌmɪskən'sɛpʃən) *n* a false or mistaken view, opinion, or attitude

misconduct *n* (mɪs'kɒndʌkt) **1** behaviour, such as adultery or professional negligence, that is regarded as immoral or unethical ▷ *vb* (ˌmɪskən'dʌkt) (*tr*) **2** to conduct (oneself) in such a way **3** to manage (something) badly

misconstrue (ˌmɪskən'struː) *vb* **misconstrues, misconstruing, misconstrued** (*tr*) to interpret mistakenly > ˌ**miscon'struction** *n*

miscreant ('mɪskrɪənt) *n* **1** a wrongdoer or villain **2** *arch* an unbeliever or heretic ▷ *adj* **3** evil or villainous **4** *arch* unbelieving or heretical [C14 from OF *mescreant* unbelieving, from *mes-* MIS- + *creant*, ult. from L *credere* to believe]

miscue (ˌmɪs'kjuː) *n* **1** *billiards, etc* a faulty stroke in which the cue tip slips off the cue ball or misses it **2** *inf* a blunder or mistake ▷ *vb* **miscues, miscuing, miscued** (*intr*) **3** *billiards* to make a miscue **4** *theatre* to fail to answer one's cue

miscue analysis *n Brit education* analysis of the errors a pupil makes while reading

misdate (mɪs'deɪt) *vb* **misdates, misdating, misdated** (*tr*) to date (a letter, event, etc) wrongly

misdeal (ˌmɪs'diːl) *vb* **misdeals, misdealing, misdealt** **1** (*intr*) to deal out cards incorrectly ▷ *n* **2** a faulty deal > ˌ**mis'dealer** *n*

misdeed (ˌmɪs'diːd) *n* an evil or illegal action

misdemean (ˌmɪsdɪ'miːn) *vb* a rare word for **misbehave**

misdemeanour *or US* **misdemeanor** (ˌmɪsdɪ'miːnə) *n* **1** *criminal law* (formerly) an offence generally less heinous than a felony **2** any minor offence or transgression

misdirect (ˌmɪsdɪ'rɛkt) *vb* (*tr*) **1** to give (a person) wrong directions or instructions **2** to address (a letter, parcel, etc) wrongly > ˌ**misdi'rection** *n*

misdoubt (mɪs'daʊt) *vb* an archaic word for **doubt** or **suspect**

mise en scène *French* (miz ɑ̃ sɛn) *n* **1a** the arrangement of properties, scenery, etc, in a play **1b** the objects so arranged; stage setting **2** the environment of an event

Miseno (*Italian* mi'zɛːno) *n* a cape in SW Italy, on the N shore of the Bay of Naples: remains of the town of **Misenum**, a naval base constructed by Agrippa in 31 BC

miser ('maɪzə) *n* **1** a person who hoards money or possessions, often living miserably **2** a selfish person [C16 from L: wretched]

miserable ('mɪzərəbᵊl) *adj* **1** unhappy or depressed; wretched **2** causing misery, discomfort, etc: *a miserable life* **3** contemptible: *a miserable villain* **4** sordid or squalid: *miserable living conditions* **5** mean; stingy [C16 from OF, from L *miserābilis*, from *miserārī* to pity, from *miser* wretched] > '**miserableness** *n* > '**miserably** *adv*

misère (mɪ'zɛə) *n* **1** a call in solo whist, etc declaring a hand that will win no tricks **2** a hand that will win no tricks [C19 from F: misery]

Miserere (ˌmɪzə'rɛərɪ, -'rɪərɪ) *n* the 51st psalm, the Latin version of which begins "Miserere mei, Deus" ("Have mercy on me, O God")

misericord *or* **misericorde** (mɪ'zɛrɪˌkɔːd) *n* **1** a ledge projecting from the underside of the hinged seat of a choir stall in a church, on which the occupant can support himself while standing **2** *Christianity* **2a** a relaxation of certain monastic rules for infirm or aged monks or nuns **2b** a monastery or room where this can be enjoyed **3** a medieval dagger used to give the death stroke to a wounded foe [C14 from OF, from L *misericordia* compassion, from *miserēre* to pity + *cor* heart]

miserly ('maɪzəlɪ) *adj* of or resembling a miser; avaricious > '**miserliness** *n*

misery ('mɪzərɪ) *n, pl* **miseries** **1** intense unhappiness, suffering, etc **2** a cause of such unhappiness, etc **3** squalid or poverty-stricken conditions **4** *Brit inf* a person who is habitually depressed: *he is such a misery* [C14 via Anglo-Norman from L *miseria*, from *miser* wretched]

misfeasance (mɪs'fiːzəns) *n law* the improper performance of an act that is lawful in itself ▷ Cf **malfeasance, nonfeasance** [C16 from OF *mesfaisance*, from *mesfaire* to perform misdeeds]

misfile (ˌmɪs'faɪl) *vb* **misfiles, misfiling, misfiled** to file (papers, records, etc) wrongly

misfire (ˌmɪs'faɪə) *vb* **misfires, misfiring, misfired** (*intr*) **1** (of a firearm or its projectile) to fail to fire or explode as expected **2** (of a motor engine or vehicle, etc) to fail to fire at the appropriate time **3** to fail to operate or occur as intended ▷ *n* **4** the act or an instance of misfiring

misfit *n* ('mɪsˌfɪt) **1** a person not suited to a particular social environment **2** something that does not fit or fits badly ▷ *vb* (ˌmɪs'fɪt), **misfits, misfitting, misfitted** (*intr*) **3** to fail to fit or be fitted

misfortune (mɪs'fɔːtʃən) *n* **1** evil fortune; bad luck **2** an unfortunate or disastrous event

misgive (mɪs'gɪv) *vb* **misgives, misgiving, misgave, misgiven** to make or be apprehensive or suspicious

misgiving (mɪs'gɪvɪŋ) *n* (*often pl*) a feeling of uncertainty, apprehension, or doubt

misguide (ˌmɪs'gaɪd) *vb* **misguides, misguiding, misguided** (*tr*) to guide or direct wrongly or badly

misguided (ˌmɪs'gaɪdɪd) *adj* foolish or unreasonable, esp in action or behaviour > ˌ**mis'guidedly** *adv*

mishandle (ˌmɪs'hændᵊl) *vb* **mishandles, mishandling, mishandled** (*tr*) to handle or treat badly or inefficiently

mishap ('mɪshæp) *n* **1** an unfortunate accident **2** bad luck

Mishima ('mɪʃɪmə) *n* **Yukio** ('juːkɪəʊ) 1925–70, Japanese novelist and short-story writer, whose works reflect a preoccupation with homosexuality and death. He committed harakiri in protest at the decline of traditional Japanese values

mishit *sport* ▷ *n* ('mɪsˌhɪt) **1** a faulty shot or stroke ▷ *vb* (ˌmɪs'hɪt), **mishits, mishitting, mishit** **2** to hit (a ball) with a faulty stroke

mishmash ('mɪʃˌmæʃ) *n* a confused collection or mixture [C15 reduplication of MASH]

Mishna ('mɪʃnə) *n, pl* **Mishnayoth** (mɪʃ'nɑːjəʊt) *Judaism.* a compilation of precepts collected in the late second century AD. It forms the earlier part of the Talmud [C17 from Heb., from *shānāh* to repeat] > **Mishnaic** (mɪʃ'neɪɪk) *or* '**Mishnic** *adj*

misinform (ˌmɪsɪn'fɔːm) *vb* (*tr*) to give incorrect information to > **misinformation** (ˌmɪsɪnfə'meɪʃən) *n*

misinterpret (ˌmɪsɪn'tɜːprɪt) *vb* (*tr*) to interpret badly, misleadingly, or incorrectly > ˌ**misinˌterpre'tation** *n*

misjudge (mɪs'dʒʌdʒ) *vb* **misjudges, misjudging, misjudged** to judge (a person or persons) wrongly or unfairly > **mis'judger** *n* > **mis'judgment** *or* **mis'judgement** *n*

Miskolc (*Hungarian* 'miʃkolts) *n* a city in NE Hungary: the second most important industrial centre in Hungary; iron and steel industries. Pop: 172 357 (2000 est)

mislay (mɪsˈleɪ) *vb* **mislays, mislaying, mislaid** (*tr*) **1** to lose (something) temporarily, esp by forgetting where it is **2** to lay (something) badly

mislead (mɪsˈliːd) *vb* **misleads, misleading, misled** (*tr*) **1** to give false or confusing information to **2** to lead or guide in the wrong direction > **misˈleader** *n* > **misˈleading** *adj*

mismarriage (mɪsˈmærɪdʒ) *n* a marriage to an unsuitable partner

mismatch (ˌmɪsˈmætʃ) *vb* **1** to match badly, esp in marriage ▷ *n* **2** a bad match

misname (mɪsˈneɪm) *vb* **misnames, misnaming, misnamed** (*tr*) to call by a wrong or inappropriate name

misnomer (ˌmɪsˈnəʊmə) *n* **1** an incorrect or unsuitable name for a person or thing **2** the act of referring to a person by the wrong name [C15 via Anglo-Norman from OF *mesnommer* to misname, from L *nōmināre* to call by name]

miso- *or before a vowel* **mis-** *combining form* indicating hatred: *misogyny* [from Gk *misos* hatred]

misogamy (mɪˈsɒɡəmɪ, maɪ-) *n* hatred of marriage > **miˈsogamist** *n*

misogyny (mɪˈsɒdʒɪnɪ, maɪ-) *n* hatred of women [C17 from Gk, from MISO- + *gunē* woman] > **miˈsogynist** *n* > **miˈsogynous** *or* **miˌsogyˈnistic** *adj*

misplace (ˌmɪsˈpleɪs) *vb* **misplaces, misplacing, misplaced** (*tr*) **1** to put (something) in the wrong place, esp to lose (something) temporarily by forgetting where it was placed **2** (*often passive*) to bestow (trust, affection, etc) unadvisedly > ˌ**misˈplacement** *n*

misplaced modifier *n grammar* a participle intended to modify a noun but having the wrong grammatical relationship to it, for example *having left* in the sentence *Having left Europe for good, Peter's future seemed bleak*

misplay (ˌmɪsˈpleɪ) *vb* **1** (*tr*) to play badly or wrongly in games or sports ▷ *n* **2** a wrong or unskilful play

misprint *n* (ˈmɪsˌprɪnt) **1** an error in printing, made through damaged type, careless reading, etc ▷ *vb* (ˌmɪsˈprɪnt) **2** (*tr*) to print (a letter) incorrectly

misprision[1] (mɪsˈprɪʒən) *n* **a** a failure to inform the authorities of the commission of an act of treason **b** the deliberate concealment of the commission of a felony [C15 via Anglo-F from OF *mesprision* error, from *mesprendre* to mistake, from *mes-* MIS- + *prendre* to take]

misprision[2] (mɪsˈprɪʒən) *n arch* **1** contempt **2** failure to appreciate the value of something [C16 from MISPRIZE]

misprize *or* **misprise** (mɪsˈpraɪz) *vb* **misprizes, misprizing, misprized** *or* **misprises, misprising, misprised** to fail to appreciate the value of; disparage [C15 from OF *mesprisier*, from *mes-* MIS- + *prisier* to PRIZE[2]]

mispronounce (ˌmɪsprəˈnaʊns) *vb* **mispronounces, mispronouncing, mispronounced** to pronounce (a word) wrongly > **mispronunciation** (ˌmɪsprəˌnʌnsɪˈeɪʃən) *n*

misproportion (ˌmɪsprəˈpɔːʃən) *n* a lack of due proportion

misquote (ˌmɪsˈkwəʊt) *vb* **misquotes, misquoting, misquoted** to quote (a text, speech, etc) inaccurately > ˌ**misquoˈtation** *n*

misread (ˌmɪsˈriːd) *vb* **misreads, misreading, misread** (-ˈrɛd) (*tr*) **1** to read incorrectly **2** to misinterpret

misrepresent (ˌmɪsrɛprɪˈzɛnt) *vb* (*tr*) to represent wrongly or inaccurately > ˌ**misrepresenˈtation** *n* > ˌ**misrepreˈsentative** *adj*

misrule (ˌmɪsˈruːl) *vb* **misrules, misruling, misruled** **1** (*tr*) to govern inefficiently or without justice ▷ *n* **2** inefficient or unjust government **3** disorder

miss[1] (mɪs) *vb* **1** to fail to reach, hit, meet, find, or attain (some aim, target, etc) **2** (*tr*) to fail to attend or be present for: *to miss an appointment* **3** (*tr*) to fail to see, hear, understand, or perceive **4** (*tr*) to lose, overlook, or fail to take advantage of: *to miss an opportunity* **5** (*tr*) to leave out; omit: *to miss an entry in a list* **6** (*tr*) to discover or regret the loss or absence of: *she missed him* **7** (*tr*) to escape or avoid (something, esp a danger), usually narrowly: *he missed death by inches* ▷ *n* **8** a failure to reach, hit, etc **9** **give (something) a miss** *inf* to avoid (something): *give the pudding a miss* ▷ See also **miss out** [OE *missan* (meaning: to fail to hit)]

miss[2] (mɪs) *n inf* an unmarried woman or girl [C17 from MISTRESS]

Miss (mɪs) *n* a title of an unmarried woman or girl, usually used before the surname or sometimes alone in direct address [C17 shortened from MISTRESS]

Miss. *abbrev for* Mississippi

missal (ˈmɪsəl) *n RC Church* a book containing the prayers, rites, etc, of the Masses for a complete year [C14 from Church L *missale* (n), from *missālis* concerning the MASS]

mis-sell *vb* **mis-sells, mis-selling, mis-sold** to sell (a financial product) that is inappropriate for the needs of the customer

misshape *vb* (ˌmɪsˈʃeɪp), **misshapes, misshaping, misshaped; misshaped** *or* **misshapen** **1** (*tr*) to shape badly; deform ▷ *n* (ˈmɪsˌʃeɪp) **2** something that is badly shaped

misshapen (ˌmɪsˈʃeɪpən) *adj* badly shaped; deformed > ˌ**misˈshapenness** *n*

missile (ˈmɪsaɪl) *n* **1** any object or weapon that is thrown at a target or shot from an engine, gun, etc **2** a rocket-propelled weapon that flies either in a fixed trajectory (**ballistic missile**) or in a trajectory controlled during flight (**guided missile**) [C17 from L *missilis*, from *mittere* to send]
▷ http://jmr.janes.com
▷ www.fas.org/man/dod-101/sys/missile

missilery *or* **missilry** (ˈmɪsaɪlrɪ) *n* **1** missiles collectively **2** the design, operation, or study of missiles

missing (ˈmɪsɪŋ) *adj* **1** not present; absent or lost **2** not able to be traced and not known to be dead: *nine men were missing after the attack* **3** **go missing** to become lost or disappear

missing link *n* **1** (*sometimes cap*; usually preceded by *the*) a hypothetical extinct animal, formerly thought to be intermediate between the anthropoid apes and man **2** any missing section or part in a series

mission (ˈmɪʃən) *n* **1** a specific task or duty assigned to a person or group of people **2** a person's vocation (often in **mission in life**) **3** a group of persons representing or working for a particular country, business, etc, in a foreign country **4** a special embassy sent to a foreign country for a specific purpose **5a** a group of people sent by a religious body, esp a Christian church, to a foreign country to do religious and social work **5b** the campaign undertaken by such a group **6a** a building in which missionary work is performed **6b** the area assigned to a particular missionary **7** the dispatch of aircraft or spacecraft to achieve a particular task **8** a charitable centre that offers shelter or aid to the destitute or underprivileged **9** (*modifier*) of or relating to an ecclesiastical mission: *a mission station* ▷ *vb* **10** (*tr*) to direct a mission to or establish a mission in (a given region) [C16 from L *missiō*, from *mittere* to send]

missionary (ˈmɪʃənərɪ) *n, pl* **missionaries** **1** a member of a religious mission ▷ *adj* **2** of or relating to missionaries: *missionary work* **3** resulting from a desire to convert people to one's own beliefs: *missionary zeal*

missionary position *n inf* a position for sexual intercourse in which the man lies on top of the woman and they are face to face [C20 from the belief that missionaries advocated this as the proper position to primitive peoples among whom it was unknown]

Missionary Ridge *n* a ridge in NW Georgia and SE Tennessee: site of a battle (1863) during the Civil War: Northern victory leading to the campaign in Georgia

mission creep *n* the tendency for a task, esp a military operation, to become unintentionally wider in scope than its initial objectives

mission statement *n* an official statement of the aims and objectives of a business or other organization

Mississauga (ˌmɪsəˈsɔːɡə) *n* a town in SE Ontario: a SW suburb of Toronto. Pop: 463 388 (1991)

Mississippi (ˌmɪsɪˈsɪpɪ) *n* **1** a state of the southeastern US, on the Gulf of Mexico: consists of a largely forested undulating plain, with swampy regions in the northwest and on the coast, the Mississippi River forming the W border; cotton, rice, and oil. Capital: Jackson. Pop: 2 844 658 (2000). Area: 122 496 sq km (47 296 sq miles). Abbreviations: **Miss** or (with zip code) **MS** **2** a river in the central US, rising in NW Minnesota and flowing generally south to the Gulf of Mexico through several mouths, known as the Passes: the second longest river in North America (after its tributary, the Missouri), with the third largest drainage basin in the world (after the Amazon and the Congo). Length: 3780 km (2348 miles)

Mississippian (ˌmɪsɪˈsɪpɪən) *adj* **1** of or relating to the state of Mississippi, or the Mississippi river **2** (in North America) of or denoting the lower of two subdivisions of the Carboniferous period (see also **Pennsylvanian** (sense 2)), which lasted for 30 million years ▷ *n* **3** an inhabitant or native of the state of Mississippi **4** **the** the Mississippian period or rock system

missive (ˈmɪsɪv) *n* **1** a formal or official letter **2** a formal word for **letter** [c15 from Med. L *missivus*, from *mittere* to send]

Missolonghi (ˌmɪsəˈlɒŋɡɪ) *or* **Mesolonghi** *n* a town in W Greece, near the Gulf of Patras: famous for its defence against the Turks in 1822–23 and 1825–26 and for its association with Lord Byron, who died here in 1824. Pop: 11 275 (latest est). Modern Greek name: **Mesolóngion**

Missouri (mɪˈzʊərɪ) *n* **1** a state of the central US: consists of rolling prairies in the north, the Ozark Mountains in the south, and part of the Mississippi flood plain in the southeast, with the Mississippi forming the E border; chief US producer of lead and barytes. Capital: Jefferson City. Pop: 5 595 211 (2000). Area: 178 699 sq km (68 995 sq miles). Abbreviations: **Mo** or (with zip code) **MO** **2** a river in the W and central US, rising in SW Montana: flows north, east, and southeast to join the Mississippi above St Louis; the longest river in North America; chief tributary of the Mississippi. Length: 3970 km (2466 miles) > **Misˈsourian** *n, adj*

miss out *vb (adv)* **1** *(tr)* to leave out; overlook **2** *(intr; often foll by on)* to fail to experience: *you missed out on the celebrations*

misspell (ˌmɪsˈspɛl) *vb* **misspells, misspelling, misspelt** *or* **misspelled** to spell (a word or words) wrongly

misspelling (ˌmɪsˈspɛlɪŋ) *n* a wrong spelling

misspend (ˌmɪsˈspɛnd) *vb* **misspends, misspending, misspent** to spend thoughtlessly or wastefully

misstep (ˌmɪsˈstɛp) *n* **1** a false step **2** an error

missus *or* **missis** (ˈmɪsɪz, -ɪs) *n* **1** (usually preceded by *the*) *inf* one's wife or the wife of the person addressed or referred to **2** an informal term of address for a woman [c19 spoken version of MISTRESS]

missy (ˈmɪsɪ) *n, pl* **missies** *inf* an affectionate or disparaging form of address to a young girl

mist (mɪst) *n* **1** a thin fog resulting from condensation in the air near the earth's surface **2** *meteorol* such an atmospheric condition with a horizontal visibility of 1–2 kilometres **3** a fine spray of liquid, such as that produced by an aerosol container **4** condensed water vapour on a surface **5** something that causes haziness or lack of clarity, such as a film of tears ▷ *vb* **6** to cover or be covered with or as if with mist [OE]

mistake (mɪˈsteɪk) *n* **1** an error or blunder in action, opinion, or judgment **2** a misconception or misunderstanding ▷ *vb* **mistakes, mistaking, mistook, mistaken** **3** *(tr)* to misunderstand; misinterpret: *she mistook his meaning* **4** *(tr; foll by for)* to take (for), interpret (as), or confuse (with): *she mistook his directness for honesty* **5** *(tr)* to choose badly or incorrectly: *he mistook his path* **6** *(intr)* to make a mistake [c13 (meaning: to do wrong, err): from ON *mistaka* to take erroneously] > **misˈtakable** *adj*

mistaken (mɪˈsteɪkən) *adj* **1** *(usually predicative)* wrong in opinion, judgment, etc: *a mistaken viewpoint* **2** arising from error in opinion, judgment, etc > **misˈtakenly** *adv* > **misˈtakenness** *n*

Mistassini (ˌmɪstəˈsiːnɪ) *n* **Lake** a lake in E Canada, in N Quebec: the largest lake in the province; drains through the Rupert River into James Bay. Area: 2175 sq km (840 sq miles). Length: about 160 km (100 miles)

mister (ˈmɪstə) *(sometimes cap)* ▷ *n* **1** an informal form of address for a man **2** *mil* the official form of address for subordinate or senior warrant officers **3** *naval* the official form of address for all officers in a merchant ship, other than the captain **4** *Brit* the form of address for a surgeon **5** the form of address for officials holding certain positions: *mister chairman* ▷ *vb* **6** *(tr) inf* to call (someone) mister [c16 var. of MASTER]

Mister (ˈmɪstə) *n* the full form of **Mr**

misterioso (mɪˌstɛrɪˈəʊsəʊ) *adv music* in a mysterious manner; mysteriously [It.]

Misti (*Spanish* ˈmisti) *n* See **El Misti**

mistigris (ˈmɪstɪɡriː) *n* **1** the joker or a blank card used as a wild card in a variety of draw poker **2** the game [c19 from F: jack of clubs, game in which this card was wild]

mistime (ˌmɪsˈtaɪm) *vb* **mistimes, mistiming, mistimed** *(tr)* to time (an action, utterance, etc) wrongly

mistle thrush *or* **missel thrush** (ˈmɪsᵊl) *n* a large European thrush with a brown back and spotted breast, noted for feeding on mistletoe berries [c18 from OE *mistel* MISTLETOE]

mistletoe (ˈmɪsᵊlˌtəʊ) *n* **1** a Eurasian evergreen shrub with waxy white berries: grows as a partial parasite on various trees: used as a Christmas decoration **2** any of several similar and related American plants [OE *misteltān*, from *mistel* mistletoe + *tān* twig; rel. to ON *mistilteinn*]

mistook (mɪˈstʊk) *vb* the past tense of **mistake**

mistral (ˈmɪstrəl, mɪˈstrɑːl) *n* a strong cold dry wind that blows through the Rhône valley and S France to the Mediterranean coast, mainly in the winter [c17 via F from Provençal, from L *magistrālis* MAGISTRAL]

Mistral *n* **1** (*French* mistral) **Frédéric** (frederik) 1830–1914, French Provençal poet, who led a movement to revive Provençal language and literature: shared the Nobel prize for literature 1904 **2** (*Spanish* misˈtral) **Gabriela** (ɡaˈβrjela), pen name of *Lucila Godoy de Alcayaga*. 1889–1957, Chilean poet, educationalist, and diplomatist. Her poetry includes the collection *Desolación* (1922): Nobel prize for literature 1945

mistreat (ˌmɪsˈtriːt) *vb (tr)* to treat badly > ˌ**misˈtreatment** *n*

mistress (ˈmɪstrɪs) *n* **1** a woman who has a continuing extramarital sexual relationship with a man, esp a married man **2** a woman in a position of authority, ownership, or control **3** a woman having control over something specified: *mistress of her own destiny* **4** *chiefly Brit* short for **schoolmistress** **5** an archaic or dialect word for **sweetheart** [c14 from OF; see MASTER, -ESS]

Mistress (ˈmɪstrɪs) *n* an archaic or dialect title equivalent to **Mrs**

Mistress of the Robes *n* (in Britain) a lady of high rank in charge of the Queen's wardrobe

mistrial (mɪsˈtraɪəl) *n* **1** a trial made void because of some error **2** *US* an inconclusive trial, as when a jury cannot agree on a verdict

mistrust (ˌmɪsˈtrʌst) *vb* **1** to have doubts or suspicions about (someone or something) ▷ *n* **2** distrust > ˌ**misˈtrustful** *adj* > ˌ**misˈtrustfully** *adv* > ˌ**misˈtrustfulness** *n*

misty ('mɪstɪ) *adj* **mistier, mistiest** 1 consisting of or resembling mist 2 obscured as by mist 3 indistinct; blurred > '**mistily** *adv* > '**mistiness** *n*

misunderstand (ˌmɪsʌndə'stænd) *vb* **misunderstands, misunderstanding, misunderstood** to fail to understand properly

misunderstanding (ˌmɪsʌndə'stændɪŋ) *n* 1 a failure to understand properly 2 a disagreement

misunderstood (ˌmɪsʌndə'stʊd) *adj* not properly or sympathetically understood: *a misunderstood adolescent*

misuse *n* (ˌmɪs'juːs) *also* **misusage** 1 erroneous, improper, or unorthodox use: *misuse of words* 2 cruel or inhumane treatment ▷ *vb* (ˌmɪs'juːz) **misuses, misusing, misused** (*tr*) 3 to use wrongly 4 to treat badly or harshly > ˌ**mis'user** *n*

Mitchell ('mɪtʃəl) *n* 1 **Joni,** original name *Roberta Joan Anderson.* born 1943, Canadian folk-rock singer and songwriter. Her albums include *Blue* (1971), *Court and Spark* (1974), *Mingus* (1979), *Turbulent Indigo* (1994), and *Travelogue* (2002) 2 **Margaret** 1900–49, US novelist; author of *Gone with the Wind* (1936) 3 **Reginald Joseph** 1895–1937, British aeronautical engineer; designer of the Spitfire fighter 4 Sir **Thomas Livingstone,** known as *Major Mitchell.* 1792–1855, Australian explorer born in Scotland

Mitchum ('mɪtʃəm) *n* **Robert** 1917–97, US film actor. His many films include *Night of the Hunter* (1955) and *Farewell my Lovely* (1975)

mite[1] (maɪt) *n* any of numerous small terrestrial or aquatic free-living or parasitic arachnids [OE *mīte*]

mite[2] (maɪt) *n* 1 a very small particle, creature, or object 2 a very small contribution or sum of money. See also **widow's mite** 3 a former Flemish coin of small value 4 **a mite** *inf* somewhat: *he's a mite foolish* [c14 from MLow G, MDu. *mīte*]

Mithgarthr ('mɪðˌgɑːðə) *n* a variant of **Midgard**

Mithraism ('mɪθreɪˌɪzəm) *or* **Mithraicism** (mɪθ'reɪɪˌsɪzəm) *n* the ancient religion of Mithras > **Mithraic** (mɪθ'reɪɪk) *adj* > '**Mithraist** *n, adj*

Mithras ('mɪθræs) *or* **Mithra** ('mɪθrə) *n Persian myth* the god of light, identified with the sun, who slew a primordial bull and fertilized the world with its blood

Mithridates VI *or* **Mithradates VI** (ˌmɪθrɪ'deɪtiːz) *n* called *the Great.* ?132–63 BC, king of Pontus (?120–63). He waged three wars against Rome (88–84; 83–81; 74–64) and was finally defeated by Pompey: committed suicide

mithridatism ('mɪθrɪdeɪˌtɪzəm) *n* immunity to large doses of poison by prior ingestion of gradually increased doses > **mithridatic** (ˌmɪθrɪ'dætɪk, -'deɪ-) *adj*

mitigate ('mɪtɪˌgeɪt) *vb* **mitigates, mitigating, mitigated** to make or become less severe or harsh; moderate [c15 from L *mītigāre,* from *mītis* mild + *agere* to make] > '**mitigable** *adj* > ˌ**miti'gation** *n* > '**mitiˌgative** *or* '**mitiˌgatory** *adj* > '**mitiˌgator** *n*

USAGE *Mitigate* is sometimes wrongly used where *militate* is meant: *his behaviour militates* (not *mitigates*) *against his chances of promotion*

Mitilíni (miti'lini) *n* transliteration of the Modern Greek name for **Mytilene** (sense 1)

mitochondrion (ˌmaɪtəʊ'kɒndrɪən) *n, pl* **mitochondria** (-drɪə) a small spherical or rodlike body, in the cytoplasm of most cells: contains enzymes responsible for energy production [c19 NL, from Gk *mitos* thread + *khondrion* small grain]

mitosis (maɪ'təʊsɪs, mɪ-) *n* a method of cell division, in which the nucleus divides into daughter nuclei, each containing the same number of chromosomes as the parent nucleus [c19 from NL, from Gk *mitos* thread] > **mitotic** (maɪ'tɒtɪk, mɪ-) *adj*

mitral ('maɪtrəl) *adj* 1 of or like a mitre 2 *anat* of or relating to the mitral valve

mitral valve *n* the valve between the left atrium and the left ventricle of the heart

mitre *or US* **miter** ('maɪtə) *n* 1 *Christianity* the liturgical headdress of a bishop or abbot, consisting of a tall pointed cleft cap with two bands hanging down at the back 2 Also called: **mitre joint** a corner joint formed by cutting bevels of equal angles at the ends of each piece of material 3 a bevelled surface of a mitre joint ▷ *vb* **mitres, mitring, mitred** *or US* **miters, mitering, mitered** (*tr*) 4 to make a mitre joint between (two pieces of material) 5 to confer a mitre upon: *a mitred abbot* [c14 from OF, from L *mitra,* from Gk: turban]

mitre box *n* an open-ended box with sides slotted to guide a saw in cutting mitre joints

mitt (mɪt) *n* 1 any of various glovelike hand coverings, such as one that does not cover the fingers 2 short for **mitten** (sense 1) 3 *baseball* a large round thickly padded leather mitten worn by the catcher 4 (*often pl*) a slang word for **hand** 5 *sl* a boxing glove [c18 from MITTEN]

Mittelland Canal (*German* 'mɪtəllant) *n* a canal in Germany, linking the Rivers Rhine and Elbe. Length: 325 km (202 miles)

mitten ('mɪtᵊn) *n* 1 a glove having one section for the thumb and a single section for the other fingers. Sometimes shortened to **mitt** 2 *sl* a boxing glove [c14 from OF *mitaine,* from ?]

Mitterrand (*French* mitɛrɑ̃) *n* **François Maurice Marie** (frɑ̃swa mɔris mari) 1916–96, French statesman; first secretary of the socialist party (1971–95); president (1981–95)

mittimus ('mɪtɪməs) *n, pl* **mittimuses** *law* a warrant of commitment to prison or a command to a jailer to hold someone in prison [c15 from L: we send, the first word of such a command]

mix (mɪks) *vb* 1 (*tr*) to combine or blend (ingredients, liquids, objects, etc) together into one mass 2 (*intr*) to become or have the capacity to become combined, joined, etc: *some chemicals do not mix* 3 (*tr*) to form (something) by combining constituents: *to mix cement* 4 (*tr; often foll by in or into*) to add as an additional element (to a mass or compound): *to mix flour into a batter* 5 (*tr*) to do at the same time: *to mix study and pleasure* 6 (*tr*) to consume (different alcoholic drinks) in close succession 7 to come or cause to come into association socially: *Pauline mixed well* 8 (*intr; often foll by with*) to go together; complement 9 (*tr*) to crossbreed (differing strains of plants or breeds of livestock), esp more or less at random 10 *music* to balance and adjust (individual performers' parts) to make an overall sound by electronic means 11 **mix it** *inf* to cause mischief or trouble, often for a person named: *she tried to mix it for John* ▷ *n* 12 the act or an instance of mixing 13 the result of mixing; mixture 14 a mixture of ingredients, esp one commercially prepared for making a cake, bread, etc 15 *inf* a state of confusion 16 *music* the sound produced by mixing ▷ See also **mix-up** [c15 back formation from *mixt* mixed, via OF from L *mixtus,* from *miscēre* to mix] > '**mixable** *adj*

mixed (mɪkst) *adj* 1 formed or blended together by mixing 2 composed of different elements, races, sexes, etc: *a mixed school* 3 consisting of conflicting elements, thoughts, attitudes, etc: *mixed feelings* 4 *maths* (of a number) consisting of the sum of an integer and a fraction or a decimal fraction, as 5½ or 17.43 > **mixedness** ('mɪksɪdnɪs) *n*

mixed bag *n inf* something composed of diverse elements, characteristics, people, etc

mixed blessing *n* an event, situation, etc, having both advantages and disadvantages

mixed doubles *pl n tennis* a doubles game with a man and a woman as partners on each side

mixed economy *n* an economic system in which the public and private sectors coexist

mixed farming *n* combined arable and livestock farming (on **mixed farms**)

Mm

mixed marriage *n* a marriage between persons of different races or religions
mixed metaphor *n* a combination of incongruous metaphors, as *when the Nazi jackboots sing their swan song*
mixed-up *adj* in a state of mental confusion
mixer ('mɪksə) *n* 1 a person or thing that mixes 2 *inf* 2a a person considered in relation to his or her ability to mix socially 2b a person who creates trouble for others 3 a kitchen appliance, usually electrical, used for mixing foods, etc 4 a drink such as ginger ale, fruit juice, etc, used in preparing cocktails 5 *electronics* a device in which two or more input signals are combined to give a single output signal
mixer tap *n* a tap in which hot and cold water supplies have a joint outlet but are controlled separately
mixture ('mɪkstʃə) *n* 1 the act of mixing or state of being mixed 2 something mixed; a result of mixing 3 *chem* a substance consisting of two or more substances mixed together without any chemical bonding between them 4 *pharmacol* a liquid medicine in which an insoluble compound is suspended in the liquid 5 *music* an organ stop that controls several ranks of pipes 6 the mixture of petrol vapour and air in an internal-combustion engine [c16 from L *mixtūra*, from *mixtus*, pp of *miscere* to mix]
mix-up *n* 1 a confused condition or situation 2 *inf* a fight ▷ *vb* **mix up** (*tr, adv*) 3 to make into a mixture 4 to confuse or confound: *Tom mixes John up with Bill* 5 (*often passive*) to put (someone) into a state of confusion: *I'm all mixed up* 6 (foll by *in* or *with*; *usually passive*) to involve (in an activity or group, esp one that is illegal): *mixed up in the drugs racket*
Mizoguchi (ˌmiːtsə'guːtʃɪ) *n* **Kenji** ('kɛndʒɪ) 1898–1956, Japanese film director. His films include *A Paper Doll's Whisper of Spring* (1925), *Woman of Osaka* (1940), and *Ugetsu Monogatari* (1952)
Mizoram (mɪ'zɔːrəm) *n* a state (since 1986) in NE India, created in 1972 from the former Mizo Hills District of Assam. Capital: Aijal. Pop: 891 058 (2001). Area: about 21 081 sq km (8140 sq miles)
mizzen *or* **mizen** ('mɪzᵊn) *naut* ▷ *n* 1 a sail set on a mizzenmast 2 short for **mizzenmast** ▷ *adj* 3 of or relating to a mizzenmast: *a mizzen staysail* [c15 from F *misaine*, from It. *mezzana*, *mezzano* middle]
mizzenmast *or* **mizenmast** ('mɪzᵊnməst) *n naut* (on a vessel with three or more masts) the third mast from the bow
mizzle[1] ('mɪzᵊl) *vb* **mizzles, mizzling, mizzled,** *n* a dialect word for **drizzle** [c15 ?from Low G *miseln* to drizzle] > **'mizzly** *adj*
mizzle[2] ('mɪzᵊl) *vb* **mizzles, mizzling, mizzled** (*intr*) *Brit sl* to decamp [c18 from ?]
mk *currency symbol for:* 1 mark 2 markka
mks units *pl n* a metric system of units based on the metre, kilogram, and second as the units of length, mass, and time; it forms the basis of the SI units
mkt *abbrev for* market
ml *symbol for:* 1 mile 2 millilitre
ML *abbrev for* Medieval Latin
MLA *abbrev for:* 1 Member of the Legislative Assembly (of Northern Ireland) 2 Modern Language Association (of America)
Mladic (mə'ladɪtʃ) *n* **Ratko** ('ratko) born 1943, Bosnian military figure, commander of the Bosnian Serb forces during the civil war of 1992–95; indicted by the UN for war crimes, including the massacre of 6000 Bosnian Muslims at Srebrenica (1995)
MLC (in Australia and India) *abbrev for* Member of the Legislative Council
MLitt *abbrev for* Master of Letters [L *Magister Litterarum*]
Mlle *or* **Mlle.** *pl* **Mlles** *or* **Mlles** the French equivalent of **Miss** [from F *Mademoiselle*]
MLR *abbrev for* minimum lending rate
mm *symbol for* millimetre
MM 1 the French equivalent of **Messrs** [from F *Messieurs*] 2 *abbrev for* Military Medal
MMDS *abbrev for* multipoint microwave distribution system: a radio alternative to cable television. Sometimes shortened to **MDS**
Mme *pl* **Mmes** the French equivalent of **Mrs** [from F *Madame, Mesdames*]
MMP *abbrev for* mixed member proportional: a system of proportional representation, used in Germany and New Zealand
MMR *n* a combined vaccine against measles, mumps, and rubella, given to very young children
MMS *abbrev for* multimedia messaging service: a method of transmitting graphics, video or sound files and short text messages over wireless networks, esp on mobile phones
MMus *abbrev for* Master of Music
Mn *the chemical symbol for* manganese
MN *abbrev for:* 1 (in Britain) Merchant Navy 2 Minnesota
MNA (in Canada) *abbrev for* Member of the National Assembly (of Quebec)
mnemonic (nɪ'mɒnɪk) *adj* 1 aiding or meant to aid one's memory 2 of or relating to memory or mnemonics ▷ *n* 3 something, such as a verse, to assist memory [c18 from Gk *mnēmonikos*, from *mnēmōn* mindful, from *mnasthai* to remember] > **mne'monically** *adv*
mnemonics (nɪ'mɒnɪks) *n* (*usually functioning as sing*) 1 the art or practice of improving or of aiding the memory 2 a system of rules to aid the memory
Mnemosyne (niː'mɒzɪˌniː, -'mɒs-) *n Greek myth* the goddess of memory and mother by Zeus of the Muses
mo (məʊ) *n inf* 1 *chiefly Brit* short for **moment** (sense 1) (esp in **half a mo**) 2 *Austral* short for **moustache** (sense 1)
Mo *the chemical symbol for* molybdenum
MO *abbrev for:* 1 Missouri 2 Medical Officer 3 modus operandi
Mo. *abbrev for* Missouri
m.o. *or* **MO** *abbrev for:* 1 mail order 2 money order
-mo *suffix forming nouns* (in bookbinding) indicating book size by specifying the number of leaves formed by folding one sheet of paper: *16mo* or *sixteenmo* [abstracted from DUODECIMO]
moa ('məʊə) *n* any of various recently extinct large flightless birds of New Zealand (see **ratite**) [c19 from Maori]
Moab ('məʊæb) *n Old Testament* an ancient kingdom east of the Dead Sea, in what is now the SW part of Jordan: flourished mainly from the 9th to the 6th centuries BC > **Moabite** ('məʊəˌbaɪt) *adj, n*
moa hunter *n NZ obs* an anthropologists' term for an early Maori
moan (məʊn) *n* 1 a low prolonged mournful sound expressive of suffering or pleading 2 any similar mournful sound, esp that made by the wind 3 *inf* a grumble or complaint ▷ *vb* 4 to utter (words, etc) in a low mournful manner 5 (*intr*) to make a sound like a moan 6 (*usually intr*) *inf* to grumble or complain [c13 rel. to OE *mǣnan* to grieve over] > **'moaner** *n* > **'moanful** *adj* > **'moaning** *n, adj*
moat (məʊt) *n* 1 a wide water-filled ditch surrounding a fortified place, such as a castle ▷ *vb* 2 (*tr*) to surround with or as if with a moat [c14 from OF *motte* mound]
mob (mɒb) *n* 1a a riotous or disorderly crowd of people; rabble 1b (*as modifier*): *mob law* 2 *often derog* a group or class of people, animals, or things 3 *often derog* the masses 4 *sl* a gang of criminals 5 *Austral & NZ* a large number of anything 6 *Austral & NZ* a flock or herd of animals 7 **mobs of** *Austral & NZ inf* lots of ▷ *vb* **mobs, mobbing, mobbed** (*tr*) 8 to attack in a group resembling a mob 9 (of a group of animals of a prey species) to harass (a predator) 10 to surround, esp in order to acclaim 11 to crowd into (a building, etc) [c17 shortened from L *mōbile*

vulgus the fickle populace. See MOBLIE]
MOB *abbrev for* mobile phone
mobcap ('mɒb,kæp) *n* a woman's large cotton cap with a pouched crown, worn esp during the 18th century [C18 from obs. *mob* woman, esp loose-living, + CAP]
mobe (məʊb) *n inf* a mobile phone
mobie ('məʊbɪ) *n inf* a mobile phone
mobile ('məʊbaɪl) *adj* **1** having freedom of movement; movable **2** changing quickly in expression: *a mobile face* **3** *sociol* (of individuals or social groups) moving within and between classes, occupations, and localities **4** (of military forces) able to move freely and quickly **5** (*postpositive*) *inf* having transport available: *are you mobile?* ▷ *n* **6a** a sculpture suspended in midair with delicately balanced parts that are set in motion by air currents **6b** (*as modifier*): *mobile sculpture* **7** short for **mobile phone** [C15 via OF from L *mōbilis*, from *movēre* to move] > **mobility** (məʊ'bɪlɪtɪ) *n*
-mobile (məʊ,bi:l) *suffix forming nouns* indicating a vehicle designed for a particular person or purpose: *Popemobile*
Mobile ('məʊbi:l, məʊ'bi:l) *n* a port in SW Alabama, on **Mobile Bay** (an inlet of the Gulf of Mexico): the state's only port and its first permanent settlement, made by French colonists in 1711. Pop: 198 915 (2000)
Mobile Command *n Canad* the Canadian army and other land forces
mobile home *n* living quarters mounted on wheels and capable of being towed by a motor vehicle
mobile phone *n* a portable telephone that works by means of a cellular radio system
mobilize *or* **mobilise** ('məʊbɪ,laɪz) *vb* **mobilizes, mobilizing, mobilized** *or* **mobilises, mobilising, mobilised** **1** to prepare for war or another emergency by organizing (national resources, the armed services, etc) **2** (*tr*) to organize for a purpose **3** (*tr*) to put into motion or use > **'mobi,lizable** *or* **'mobi,lisable** *adj* > **,mobili'zation** *or* **,mobili'sation** *n*
Möbius strip ('mɜ:bɪəs) *n maths* a one-sided continuous surface, formed by twisting a long narrow rectangular strip of material through 180° and joining the ends [C19 after August *Möbius* (1790–1868), G mathematician]
moblog ('mɒblɒg) *n* a chronicle, which may be shared with others, of someone's thoughts and experiences recorded in the form of mobile phone calls, text messages, and photographs [C21 MOB(ILE) + LOG[1]]
mobocracy (mɒ'bɒkrəsɪ) *n, pl* **mobocracies** **1** rule or domination by a mob **2** the mob that rules
mobster ('mɒbstə) *n* a US slang word for **gangster**
Mobutu[1] (mə'bu:tu:) *n* the former name (until 1997) of **Lake Albert**
Mobutu[2] (mə'bu:tu:) *n* **Sese Seko** ('sɛsɛ 'sɛkəʊ), original name *Joseph*. 1930–97, Zaïrese statesman; president of Zaïre (now the Democratic Republic of Congo) (1970–97); accused of corruption and overthrown by rebels in 1997; died in exile
Moçambique (musəm'bikə) *n* the Portuguese name for **Mozambique**
moccasin ('mɒkəsɪn) *n* **1** a shoe of soft leather, esp deerskin, worn by North American Indians **2** any soft shoe resembling this **3** short for **water moccasin** [C17 of Amerind origin]
moccasin flower *n* any of several North American orchids with a pink solitary flower. See also **lady's-slipper, cypripedium**
mocha ('mɒkə) *n* **1** a dark brown coffee originally imported from the port of Mocha in Arabia **2** a flavouring made from coffee and chocolate **3** a soft glove leather, made from goatskin or sheepskin **4a** a dark brown colour **4b** (*as adj*): *mocha shoes*
Mocha *or* **Mokha** ('mɒkə) *n* a port in Yemen, on the Red Sea; in North Yemen until 1990: formerly important for the export of Arabian coffee. Pop: about 2000 (1990 est)
mock (mɒk) *vb* **1** (when *intr*, often foll by *at*) to behave with scorn or contempt (towards); show ridicule (for) **2** (*tr*) to imitate, esp in fun; mimic **3** (*tr*) to deceive, disappoint, or delude **4** (*tr*) to defy or frustrate ▷ *n* **5** the act of mocking **6** a person or thing mocked **7** a counterfeit; imitation **8** (*often pl*) *inf* (in England and Wales) school examinations taken as practice before public exams ▷ *adj* (*prenominal*) **9** sham or counterfeit **10** serving as an imitation or substitute, esp for practice purposes: *a mock battle* ▷ See also **mock-up** [C15 from OF *mocquer*] > **'mocker** *n* > **'mocking** *n, adj* > **'mockingly** *adv*
mockers ('mɒkəz) *pl n inf* **put the mockers on** to ruin the chances of success of [C20 ?from MOCK]
mockery ('mɒkərɪ) *n, pl* **mockeries** **1** ridicule, contempt, or derision **2** a derisive action or comment **3** an imitation or pretence, esp a derisive one **4** a person or thing that is mocked **5** a person, thing, or action that is inadequate
mock-heroic *adj* **1** (of a literary work, esp a poem) imitating the style of heroic poetry in order to satirize an unheroic subject ▷ *n* **2** burlesque imitation of the heroic style
mockingbird ('mɒkɪŋ,bɜ:d) *n* any of various American songbirds, noted for their ability to mimic the song of other birds
mock orange *n* **1** Also called: **syringa, philadelphus** a shrub with white fragrant flowers resembling those of the orange **2** an Australian shrub with white flowers and dark shiny leaves
mock turtle soup *n* an imitation turtle soup made from a calf's head
mock-up *n* **1** a working full-scale model of a machine, apparatus, etc, for testing, research, etc **2** a layout of printed matter ▷ *vb* **mock up** **3** (*tr, adv*) to build or make a mock-up of
mod[1] (mɒd) *n Brit* **a** a member of a group of teenagers, originally in the mid-1960s, noted for their clothes-consciousness **b** a member of a revived group of this type in the late 1970s and early 1980s [C20 from MODERNIST]
mod[2] (mɒd) *n* an annual Highland Gaelic meeting with musical and literary competitions [C19 from Gaelic *mōd* assembly, from ON]
MOD (in Britain) *abbrev for* Ministry of Defence
mod. *abbrev for:* **1** moderate **2** moderato **3** modern
modal ('məʊdᵊl) *adj* **1** of or relating to mode or manner **2** *grammar* (of a verb form or auxiliary verb) expressing a distinction of mood, such as that between possibility and actuality **3** qualifying, or expressing a qualification of, the truth of some statement **4** *metaphysics* of or relating to the form of a thing as opposed to its attributes, substance, etc **5** *music* of or relating to a mode **6** of or relating to a statistical mode > **mo'dality** *n* > **'modally** *adv*
modal logic *n* **1** the logical study of such philosophical concepts as necessity, possibility, contingency, etc **2** the logical study of concepts whose formal properties resemble certain moral, epistemological, and psychological concepts
mod cons *pl n inf* modern conveniences; the usual installations of a modern house, such as hot water, heating, etc
mode (məʊd) *n* **1** a manner or way of doing, acting, or existing **2** the current fashion or style **3** *music* **3a** any of the various scales of notes within one octave, esp any of the twelve natural diatonic scales taken in ascending order used in plainsong, folk song, and art music until 1600 **3b** (in the music of classical Greece) any of the descending diatonic scales from which the liturgical modes evolved **3c** either of the two main scale systems in music since 1600: *major mode; minor mode* **4** *logic, linguistics* another name for **mood**[2] **5** *philosophy* a complex combination of ideas which is not simply the sum of its component ideas **6** that one of a range of values that

Mm

has the highest frequency as determined statistically [c14 from L *modus* manner]

model ('mɒdᵊl) *n* **1a** a representation, usually on a smaller scale, of a device, structure, etc **1b** (*as modifier*): *a model train* **2a** a standard to be imitated **2b** (*as modifier*): *a model wife* **3** a representative form, style, or pattern **4** a person who poses for a sculptor, painter, or photographer **5** a person who wears clothes to display them to prospective buyers; mannequin **6** a preparatory sculpture in clay, wax, etc, from which the finished work is copied **7** a design or style of a particular product ▷ *vb* **models, modelling, modelled** *or US* **models, modeling, modeled** **8** to make a model of (something or someone) **9** to form in clay, wax, etc; mould **10** to display (clothing and accessories) as a mannequin **11** to plan or create according to a model or models [c16 from OF *modelle*, from It., from L *modulus*, dim. of *modus* MODE] > **'modeller** *or US* **'modeler** *n*
▷ www.modelmaking.co.uk
▷ www.ukmodelrailways.freeserve.co.uk

modelling *or US* **modeling** ('mɒdᵊlɪŋ) *n* **1** the act or an instance of making a model **2** the practice or occupation of a person who models clothes **3** a technique in psychotherapy in which the therapist encourages the patient to model his behaviour on his own

modem ('məʊdɛm) *n computing* a device for connecting two computers by a telephone line, consisting of a modulator that converts computer signals into audio signals and a corresponding demodulator [c20 from *mo(dulator) dem(odulator)*]

Modena (*Italian* 'mɔːdena) *n* **1** a city in N Italy, in Emilia-Romagna: ruled by the Este family (18th–19th century); university (1678). Pop: 176 022 (2000 est). Ancient name: **Mutina** **2** (*sometimes not capital*) a popular variety of domestic fancy pigeon originating in Modena

moderate *adj* ('mɒdərɪt) **1** not extreme or excessive **2** not violent; mild or temperate **3** of average quality or extent: *moderate success* ▷ *n* ('mɒdərɪt) **4** a person who holds moderate views, esp in politics ▷ *vb* ('mɒdəˌreɪt) **moderates, moderating, moderated** **5** to become or cause to become less extreme or violent **6** (when *intr*, often foll by *over*) to preside over a meeting, discussion, etc **7** *physics* to slow down (neutrons), esp by using a moderator [c14 from L *moderātus*, from *moderārī* to restrain]

moderate breeze *n* a wind of force 4 on the Beaufort scale, reaching speeds of 13 to 18 mph

moderation (ˌmɒdə'reɪʃən) *n* **1** the state or an instance of being moderate **2** the act of moderating **3** **in moderation** within moderate or reasonable limits

moderato (ˌmɒdə'rɑːtəʊ) *adv music* **1** at a moderate tempo **2** a direction indicating that the tempo specified is to be used with restraint: *allegro moderato* [It.]

moderator ('mɒdəˌreɪtə) *n* **1** a person or thing that moderates **2** *Presbyterian Church* a minister appointed to preside over a Church court, synod, or general assembly **3** a presiding officer at a public or legislative assembly **4** a material, such as heavy water, used for slowing down neutrons in nuclear reactors **5** an examiner at Oxford or Cambridge Universities in first public examinations **6** (in Britain and New Zealand) one who is responsible for consistency of standards in the grading of some public examinations > **'moderˌatorship** *n*

modern ('mɒdən) *adj* **1** of, involving, or befitting the present or a recent time; contemporary **2** of, relating to, or characteristic of contemporary styles or schools of art, literature, music, etc, esp those of an experimental kind **3** belonging or relating to the period in history from the end of the Middle Ages to the present ▷ *n* **4** a contemporary person [c16 from OF, from LL *modernus*, from *modō* (adv) just recently, from *modus* MODE] > **mo'dernity** *or* **'modernness** *n*

modern apprenticeship *n* an arrangement that allows a school-leaver to gain vocational qualifications while being trained in a job

Modern English *n* the English language since about 1450

Modern Hebrew *n* the official language of Israel; a revived form of ancient Hebrew

modernism ('mɒdəˌnɪzəm) *n* **1** modern tendencies, thoughts, etc, or the support of these **2** something typical of contemporary life or thought **3** a 20th-century divergence in the arts from previous traditions, esp in architecture. See **International Style** **4** (*cap*) *RC Church.* the movement at the end of the 19th and beginning of the 20th centuries that sought to adapt doctrine to modern thought > **'modernist** *n, adj* > **ˌmodern'istic** *adj* > **ˌmodern'istically** *adv*
▷ www.artsmia.org/modernism
▷ www.bc.edu/bc_org/avp/cas/fnart/HP/20th_mod.html

modernize *or* **modernise** ('mɒdəˌnaɪz) *vb* **modernizes, modernizing, modernized** *or* **modernises, modernising, modernised** **1** (*tr*) to make modern in appearance or style **2** (*intr*) to adopt modern ways, ideas, etc > **ˌmoderni'zation** *or* **ˌmoderni'sation** *n* > **'modernˌizer** *or* **'modernˌiser** *n*

modern pentathlon *n* an athletic contest consisting of five different events: horse riding with jumps, fencing with electric épée, freestyle swimming, pistol shooting, and cross-country running

modest ('mɒdɪst) *adj* **1** having or expressing a humble opinion of oneself or one's accomplishments or abilities **2** reserved or shy **3** not ostentatious or pretentious **4** not extreme or excessive **5** decorous or decent [c16 via OF from L *modestus* moderate, from *modus* MODE] > **'modestly** *adv*

modesty ('mɒdɪstɪ) *n, pl* **modesties** the quality or condition of being modest

modicum ('mɒdɪkəm) *n* a small amount or portion [c15 from L: a little way, from *modicus* moderate]

modification (ˌmɒdɪfɪ'keɪʃən) *n* **1** the act of modifying or the condition of being modified **2** something modified **3** a small change or adjustment **4** *grammar* the relation between a modifier and the word or phrase that it modifies > **'modifiˌcatory** *or* **'modifiˌcative** *adj*

modifier ('mɒdɪˌfaɪə) *n* **1** Also called: **qualifier** *grammar* a word or phrase that qualifies the sense of another word; for example, the noun *alarm* is a modifier of *clock* in *alarm clock* and the phrase *every day* is an adverbial modifier of *walks* in *he walks every day* **2** a person or thing that modifies

modify ('mɒdɪˌfaɪ) *vb* **modifies, modifying, modified** (*mainly tr*) **1** to change the structure, character, intent, etc, of **2** to make less extreme or uncompromising **3** *grammar* (of a word or phrase) to bear the relation of modifier to (another word or phrase) **4** *linguistics* to change (a vowel) by umlaut **5** (*intr*) to be or become modified [c14 from OF *modifier*, from L *modificāre* to limit, from *modus* measure + *facere* to make] > **'modiˌfiable** *adj*

Modigliani (*Italian* modiʎ'ʎaːni) *n* **Amedeo** (ame'dɛːo) 1884–1920, Italian painter and sculptor, noted esp for the elongated forms of his portraits

modish ('məʊdɪʃ) *adj* in the current fashion or style > **'modishly** *adv* > **'modishness** *n*

modiste (məʊ'diːst) *n* a fashionable dressmaker or milliner [c19 from F, from *mode* fashion]

Modred ('məʊdrɪd) *or* **Mordred** *n* (in Arthurian legend) a knight of the Round Table who rebelled against and killed his uncle King Arthur

modular ('mɒdjʊlə) *adj* of, consisting of, or resembling a module or modulus

modulate ('mɒdjʊˌleɪt) *vb* **modulates, modulating, modulated** **1** (*tr*) to change the tone, pitch, or volume of

2 (*tr*) to adjust or regulate the degree of 3 *music* 3a to change or cause to change from one key to another 3b (often foll by *to*) to make or become in tune (with a pitch, key, etc) 4 *physics, electronics* to superimpose the amplitude, frequency, phase, etc, of a wave or signal onto another wave or signal or onto an electron beam [c16 from L *modulātus* in due measure, melodious, from *modulārī*, from *modus* measure] > ˌ**moduˈlation** *n* > ˈ**moduˌlator** *n*

module (ˈmɒdjuːl) *n* 1 a standard unit of measure, esp one used to coordinate the dimensions of buildings and components 2 a standard self-contained unit or item, such as an assembly of electronic components, or a standardized piece of furniture, that can be used in combination with other units 3 *astronautics* any of several self-contained separable units making up a spacecraft or launch vehicle, each of which has one or more specified tasks 4 *education* a short course of study that together with other such courses counts towards a qualification [c16 from L *modulus*, dim. of *modus* MODE]

modulus (ˈmɒdjʊləs) *n, pl* **moduli** (-ˌlaɪ) 1 *physics* a coefficient expressing a specified property of a specified substance. See **modulus of elasticity** 2 *maths* another name for the **absolute value** of a complex number 3 *maths* the number by which a logarithm to one base is multiplied to give the corresponding logarithm to another base 4 *maths* an integer that can be divided exactly into the difference between two other integers: *7 is a modulus of 25 and 11* [c16 from L, dim. of *modus* measure]

modulus of elasticity *n* the ratio of the stress applied to a body or substance to the resulting strain within the elastic limit. Also called: **elastic modulus**

modus operandi (ˈməʊdəs ˌɒpəˈrændiː, -ˈrændaɪ) *n, pl* **modi operandi** (ˈməʊdiː ˌɒpəˈrændiː, ˈməʊdaɪ ˌɒpəˈrændaɪ) procedure; method of operating [c17 from L]

modus vivendi (ˈməʊdəs vɪˈvɛndiː, -ˈvɛndaɪ) *n, pl* **modi vivendi** (ˈməʊdiː vɪˈvɛndiː, ˈməʊdaɪ vɪˈvɛndaɪ) a working arrangement between conflicting interests; practical compromise [c19 from L: way of living]

moer (muːr) *n S African taboo sl* a despicable person [Afrik.]

Moers (*German* møːrs) *n* a city in W Germany, in North Rhine-Westphalia: coalmining centre. Pop 106 704 (1999 est)

mog (mɒg) *or* **moggy** *n, pl* **mogs** *or* **moggies** *Brit* a slang name for **cat**[1] [c20 dialect, orig. a pet name for a cow]

Mogadishu (ˌmɒgəˈdɪʃuː) *or* **Mogadiscio** (ˌmɒgəˈdɪʃɪˌəʊ, -ˈdɪʃəʊ) *n* the capital and chief port of Somalia, on the Indian Ocean: founded by Arabs around the 10th century; taken by the Sultan of Zanzibar in 1871 and sold to Italy in 1905. Pop: 1 162 000 (1999 est)

Mogadon (ˈmɒgəˌdɒn) *n trademark* a minor tranquillizer used to treat insomnia

Mogador (ˌmɒgəˈdɔː; *French* mɔgadɔr) *n* the former name (until 1956) of **Essaouira**

Mogilev (*Russian* məgiˈljɔf) *or* **Mohilev** *n* an industrial city in E Belarus on the Dnieper River: passed to Russia in 1772 after Polish rule. Pop: 369 000 (1998 est)

mogul (ˈməʊgʌl, məʊˈgʌl) *n* an important or powerful person [c18 from MOGUL]

Mogul (ˈməʊgʌl, məʊˈgʌl) *n* 1 a member of the Muslim dynasty of Indian emperors established in 1526 2 a Muslim Indian, Mongol, or Mongolian ▷ *adj* 3 of or relating to the Moguls or their empire [c16 from Persian *mughul* Mongolian]

▷ www.wikipedia.org/wiki/Mogul_Empire

▷ www.nationmaster.com/encyclopedia/Mogul-Empire

mogul skiing *n* an event in which skiers descend a slope covered in mounds of snow, making two jumps during their descent [c20 *mogul* ? from G dialect *Mugl* hillock or hummock]

mohair (ˈməʊˌhɛə) *n* 1 Also called: **angora** the long soft silky hair of the Angora goat 2a a fabric made from the yarn of this hair and cotton or wool 2b (*as modifier*): *a mohair suit* [c16 (infl. by *hair*), ult. from Ar. *mukhayyar*, lit.: choice]

Moham. *abbrev for* Mohammedan

Mohammed (məʊˈhæmɪd) *or* **Muhammad** *n* ?570–632 AD, the prophet believed by Muslims to be the channel for the final unfolding of God's revelation to mankind: popularly regarded as the founder of Islam. He began to teach in Mecca in 610 but persecution forced him to flee with his followers to Medina in 622. After several battles, he conquered Mecca (630), establishing the principles of Islam (embodied in the Koran) over all Arabia. Other names: **Mahomet,** (archaic) **Mahound**

Mohammed II *n* ?1430–81, Ottoman sultan of Turkey (1451–81) He captured Constantinople (1453) and conquered large areas of the Balkans

Mohammed Ahmed (məʊˈhæmɪd ˈɑːmɛd) *n* the original name of the **Mahdi**

Mohammed Ali *n* 1 See **Mehemet Ali** 2 See **Muhammad Ali**

Mohammedan (məʊˈhæmɪdᵊn) *n, adj* another word (not in Muslim use) for **Muslim**

Mohammedanism (məʊˈhæmɪdᵊˌnɪzəm) *n* another word (not in Muslim use) for **Islam**

Mohammed Reza Pahlavi (məʊˈhæmɪd ˈriːzə ˈpɑːləvɪ) *n* See **Pahlavi**[1]

Mohave Desert *n* another name for **Mojave Desert**

Mohawk[1] (ˈməʊhɔːk) *n* 1 (*pl* **Mohawks** *or* **Mohawk**) a member of a North American Indian people formerly living along the Mohawk River 2 the Iroquoian language of this people

Mohawk[2] (ˈməʊhɔːk) *n* a river in E central New York State, flowing south and east to the Hudson River at Cohoes: the largest tributary of the Hudson. Length: 238 km (148 miles)

Mohenjo-Daro (məˈhɛndʒəʊˈdɑːrəʊ) *n* an excavated city in SE Pakistan, southwest of Sukkur near the River Indus: flourished during the third millennium BC

mohican (məʊˈhiːkən) *n* a punk hairstyle in which the head is shaved at the sides and the remaining strip of hair is worn stiffly erect and sometimes brightly coloured

Moholy-Nagy (məˈhəʊlɪˈnɒdʒ) *n* **Laszlo** (ˈlæzləʊ) *or* **Ladislaus** (ˈlɑːdɪsˌlaʊs) 1895–1946, US painter and teacher, born in Hungary. He worked at the Bauhaus (1923–29)

moidore (ˈmɔɪdɔː) *n* a former Portuguese gold coin [c18 from Port. *moeda de ouro* money of gold]

moiety (ˈmɔɪɪtɪ) *n, pl* **moieties** one of two parts or divisions of something: *the sugar moiety of a molecule* [c15 from OF *moitié*, from L *mediētās* middle, from *medius*]

moil (mɔɪl) *arch or dialect* ▷ *vb* 1 to moisten or soil or become moist, soiled, etc 2 (*intr*) to toil or drudge (esp in **toil and moil**) ▷ *n* 3 toil; drudgery 4 confusion [c14 (to moisten; later: to work hard in unpleasantly wet conditions) from OF *moillier*, ult. from L *mollis* soft]

Moirai (ˈmɔɪriː) *pl n, sing* **Moira** (ˈmɔɪrə), **the** the Greek goddesses of fate. Roman counterparts: the **Parcae.** See **Fates**

moire (mwɑː) *n* a fabric, usually silk, having a watered effect [c17 from F, earlier *mouaire*, from MOHAIR]

moiré (ˈmwɑːreɪ) *adj* 1 having a watered or wavelike pattern ▷ *n* 2 such a pattern, impressed on fabrics by means of engraved rollers 3 any fabric having such a pattern; moire 4 Also: **moiré pattern** a pattern seen when two geometrical patterns, such as grids, are visually superimposed [c17 from F, from *moire* MOHAIR]

Moism (ˈməʊˌɪzəm) *n* the religious and ethical teaching of Mo-Zi (?470–?391 BC), Chinese philosopher, and his followers, emphasizing universal love, ascetic self-discipline, and obedience to the will of Heaven

moist (mɔɪst) *adj* 1 slightly damp or wet 2 saturated

Mm

with or suggestive of moisture [c14 from OF, ult. rel. to L *mūcidus* musty] > **'moistly** *adv* > **'moistness** *n*
moisten ('mɔɪsᵊn) *vb* to make or become moist
moisture ('mɔɪstʃə) *n* water or other liquid diffused as vapour or condensed on or in objects
moisturize *or* **moisturise** ('mɔɪstʃəˌraɪz) *vb* **moisturizes, moisturizing, moisturized** *or* **moisturises, moisturising, moisturised** (*tr*) to add moisture to (the air, the skin, etc) > **'moisturˌizer** *or* **'moisturˌiser** *n*
Mojave Desert *or* **Mohave Desert** *n* a desert in S California, south of the Sierra Nevada: part of the Great Basin. Area: 38 850 sq km (15 000 sq miles)
mojo ('məʊdʒəʊ) *n, pl* **mojos** *or* **mojoes** *US sl* **1** an amulet, charm, or magic spell **2** the art of casting magic spells [c20 of W African origin]
moke (məʊk) *n Brit sl* a donkey [c19 from ?]
Mokha ('məʊkə, 'mɒk-) *n* a variant of **Mocha**
mokopuna (ˌməʊkəʊ'pu:nə) *n NZ* a grandchild or young person [Maori]
Mokpo (ˌməʊk'pəʊ) *n* a port in SW South Korea, on the Yellow Sea. Pop: 247 524 (1995)
mol *chem symbol for* mole³
mol. *abbrev for:* **1** molecular **2** molecule
molal ('məʊləl) *adj chem* of or consisting of a solution containing one mole of solute per thousand grams of solvent [c20 from MOLE³ + -AL¹]
molar¹ ('məʊlə) *n* **1** any of the 12 grinding teeth in man **2** a corresponding tooth in other mammals ▷ *adj* **3** of or relating to any of these teeth **4** used for or capable of grinding [c16 from L *molāris*, from *mola* millstone]
molar² ('məʊlə) *adj* **1** (of a physical quantity) per unit amount of substance: *molar volume* **2** (not recommended in technical usage) (of a solution) containing one mole of solute per litre of solution [c19 from L *mōlēs* a mass]
molasses (mə'læsɪz) *n* (*functioning as sing*) **1** the thick brown uncrystallized bitter syrup obtained from sugar during refining **2** the US and Canad name for **treacle** (sense 1) [c16 from Port. *melaço*, from LL *mellāceum* must, from L *mel* honey]
mold (məʊld) *n, vb* the US spelling of **mould**
Moldau ('mɔldau) *n* **1** the German name for **Moldavia** **2** the German name for the **Vltava**
Moldavia (mɒl'deɪvɪə) *n* **1** another name for **Moldova** **2** a former principality of E Europe, consisting of the basins of the Rivers Prut and Dniester: the E part (Bessarabia) became Moldova; the W part remains a province of Romania. Romanian name: **Moldova** (mol'dova) German name: **Moldau** > **Mol'davian** *adj, n*
moldboard ('məʊldˌbɔ:d) *n* the US spelling of **mouldboard**
molder ('məʊldə) *vb* the US spelling of **moulder**
molding ('məʊldɪŋ) *n* the US spelling of **moulding**
Moldova (mɒl'dəʊvə) *n* a republic in SE Europe: comprising the E part of the former principality of Moldavia, the E part of which (Bessarabia) was ceded to the Soviet Union in 1940 and formed the Moldavian Soviet Socialist Republic until it gained independence in 1991; an agricultural region with many vineyards. Official language: Romanian. Religion: nonreligious and Christian. Currency: leu. Capital: Kishinev. Pop: 4 431 000 (2001 est). Area: 33 670 sq km (13 000 sq miles). Also called: **Moldavia** (mɒl'deɪvɪə) > **Mol'dovan** *adj, n*
▷ www.turism.md
▷ www.moldova.org
▷ www.moldova.4pla.net
moldy ('məʊldɪ) *adj* the US spelling of **mouldy**
mole¹ (məʊl) *n pathol* a nontechnical name for **naevus** [OE *māl*]
mole² (məʊl) *n* **1** any small burrowing mammal of a family of Europe, Asia, and North and Central America. They have velvety, typically dark fur and forearms specialized for digging **2** *inf* a spy who has infiltrated an organization and become a trusted member of it [c14 from MDu. *mol*, of Gmc origin]
mole³ (məʊl) *n* the basic SI unit of amount of substance; the amount that contains as many elementary entities as there are atoms in 0.012 kilogram of carbon-12. The entity may be an atom, a molecule, an ion, a radical, etc Symbol: mol. See **gram molecule** [c20 from G *Mol*, short for *Molekül* MOLECULE]
mole⁴ (məʊl) *n* **1** a breakwater **2** a harbour protected by a breakwater [c16 from F *môle*, from L *mōlēs* mass]
Molech ('məʊlɛk) *n Old Testament* a variant of **Moloch**
molecular (məʊ'lɛkjʊlə, mə-) *adj* of or relating to molecules > **mo'lecularly** *adv*
molecular biology *n* the study of biological phenomena at the molecular level
molecular formula *n* a chemical formula indicating the numbers and types of atoms in a molecule: *H_2SO_4 is the molecular formula of sulphuric acid*
molecular genetics *n* (*functioning as sing*) the study of the molecular constitution of genes and chromosomes
molecular weight *n* the former name for **relative molecular mass**
molecule ('mɒlɪˌkju:l) *n* **1** the simplest unit of a chemical compound that can exist, consisting of two or more atoms held together by chemical bonds **2** a very small particle [c18 via F from NL *mōlēcula*, dim. of L *mōlēs* mass]
molehill ('məʊlˌhɪl) *n* **1** the small mound of earth thrown up by a burrowing mole **2** **make a mountain out of a molehill** to exaggerate an unimportant matter out of all proportion
moleskin ('məʊlˌskɪn) *n* **1** the dark grey dense velvety pelt of a mole, used as a fur **2** a hard-wearing cotton fabric of twill weave **3** (*modifier*): *a moleskin waistcoat*
molest (mə'lɛst) *vb* (*tr*) **1** to disturb or annoy by malevolent interference **2** to accost or attack, esp with the intention of assaulting sexually [c14 from L *molestāre* to annoy, from *molestus* troublesome, from *mōlēs* mass] > **molestation** (ˌməʊlɛ'steɪʃən) *n* > **mo'lester** *n*
Molière (*French* mɔljɛr) *n* real name *Jean-Baptiste Poquelin*. 1622–73, French dramatist, regarded as the greatest French writer of comedy. His works include *Tartuffe* (1664), *Le Misanthrope* (1666), *L'Avare* (1668), *Le Bourgeois gentilhomme* (1670), and *Le Malade imaginaire* (1673)
Molise (*Italian* mo'li:ze) *n* a region of S central Italy, the second smallest of the regions: separated from **Abruzzi e Molise** in 1965. Capital: Campobasso. Pop: 327 987 (2000 est). Area: 4438 sq km (1731 sq miles)
moll (mɒl) *n sl* **1** the female accomplice of a gangster **2** a prostitute [c17 from *Moll*, familiar form of *Mary*]
mollify ('mɒlɪˌfaɪ) *vb* **mollifies, mollifying, mollified** (*tr*) **1** to pacify; soothe **2** to lessen the harshness or severity of [c15 from OF *mollifier*, via LL, from L *mollis* soft + *facere* to make] > **'molliˌfiable** *adj* > **ˌmollifi'cation** *n* > **'molliˌfier** *n*
mollusc *or US* **mollusk** ('mɒləsk) *n* any of various invertebrates having a soft unsegmented body and often a shell, secreted by a fold of skin (the mantle). The group includes the gastropods (snails, slugs, etc), bivalves (clams, mussels, etc), and cephalopods (squid, octopuses, etc) [c18 via NL from L *molluscus*, from *mollis* soft] > **molluscan** *or US* **molluskan** (mɒ'lʌskən) *adj, n* > **mollusc-like** *or US* **mollusk-like** *adj*
molly¹ ('mɒlɪ) *n, pl* **mollies** any of various brightly coloured tropical or subtropical American freshwater fishes [c19 from NL *Mollienisia*, from Comte F. N. *Mollien* (1758–1850), F statesman]
molly² ('mɒlɪ) *n, pl* **mollies** *Irish inf* an effeminate, weak, or cowardly boy or man [c18 perhaps from *Molly*, pet name for *Mary*]
mollycoddle ('mɒlɪˌkɒdᵊl) *vb* **mollycoddles, mollycoddling, mollycoddled** **1** (*tr*) to treat with indulgent care; pamper ▷ *n* **2** a pampered person [c19 from MOLLY² + CODDLE]

Molnár (*Hungarian* 'molna:r) *n* **Ferenc** ('fɛrɛnts) 1878–1952, Hungarian dramatist and novelist. His plays include *Liliom* (1909)
Moloch ('məʊlɒk) *or* **Molech** ('məʊlɛk) *n* *Old Testament* a Semitic deity to whom parents sacrificed their children
Molokai (ˌməʊləʊ'kɑ:ɪ) *n* an island in central Hawaii. Pop: 6717 (1990). Area: 676 sq km (261 sq miles)
Molopo (mə'ləʊpəʊ) *n* a seasonal river rising in N South Africa and flowing west and southwest to the Orange river. Length: about 1000 km (600 miles)
Molotov[1] ('mɒləˌtɒf; *Russian* 'mɔlətəf) *n* the former name (1940–62) for **Perm**
Molotov[2] ('mɒləˌtɒf; *Russian* 'mɔlətəf) *n* **Vyacheslav Mikhailovich** (vɪtʃɪ'slaf mi'xajləvitʃ), original surname *Skriabin*. 1890–1986, Soviet statesman. As commissar and later minister for foreign affairs (1939–49; 1953–56) he negotiated the nonaggression pact with Nazi Germany and attended the founding conference of the United Nations and the Potsdam conference (1945)
Molotov cocktail *n* an elementary incendiary weapon, usually a bottle of petrol with a short delay fuse or wick; petrol bomb [c20 after V. M. MOLOTOV]
molt (məʊlt) *vb, n* the usual US spelling of **moult** > **'molter** *n*
molten ('məʊltən) *adj* **1** liquefied; melted **2** made by having been melted: *molten casts* ▷ *vb* **3** the past participle of **melt**
Moltke (*German* 'mɔltkə) *n* **1** Count **Helmuth Johannes Ludwig von** ('hɛlmu:t jo'hanəs 'lu:tvɪç fɔn) 1848–1916, German general; chief of the German general staff (1906–14) **2** his uncle Count **Helmuth Karl Bernhard von** ('hɛlmu:t karl 'bɛrnhart fɔn) 1800–91, German field marshal; chief of the Prussian general staff (1858–88)
molto ('mɒltəʊ) *adv music* very: *allegro molto; molto adagio* [from It., from L *multum* (adv) much]
Moluccas (məʊ'lʌkəz, mə-) *or* **Molucca Islands** *pl n* a group of islands in the Malay Archipelago, between Sulawesi (Celebes) and New Guinea. Capital: Amboina. Pop: 2 223 000 (1999 est). Area: about 74 505 sq km (28 766 sq miles). Indonesian name: **Maluku** Former name: **Spice Islands**
mol. wt. *abbrev for* molecular weight
moly ('məʊlɪ) *n, pl* **molies** **1** *Greek myth* a magic herb given by Hermes to Odysseus to nullify the spells of Circe **2** a variety of wild garlic of S Europe having yellow flowers [c16 from L *mōly*, from Gk *mōlu*]
molybdenite (mɒ'lɪbdɪˌnaɪt) *n* a soft grey mineral consisting of molybdenum sulphide in hexagonal crystalline form with rhenium as an impurity. Formula: MoS_2
molybdenum (mɒ'lɪbdɪnəm) *n* a very hard silvery-white metallic element occurring principally in molybdenite: used in alloys, esp to harden and strengthen steels. Symbol: Mo; atomic no.: 42; atomic wt.: 95.94 [c19 from NL, from L *molybdaena* galena, from Gk, from *molubdos* lead]
mom (mɒm) *n chiefly US & Canad* an informal word for **mother**[1]
Mombasa (mɒm'bæsə) *n* a port in S Kenya, on a coral island in a bay of the Indian Ocean: the chief port for Kenya, Uganda, and NE Tanzania; became British in 1887, capital of the East African Protectorate until 1907. Pop: 461 753 (1999)
moment ('məʊmənt) *n* **1** a short indefinite period of time **2** a specific instant or point in time: *at that moment the phone rang* **3** **the moment** the present point of time: *at the moment it's fine* **4** import, significance, or value: *a man of moment* **5** *physics* **5a** a tendency to produce motion, esp rotation about a point or axis **5b** the product of a physical quantity, such as force or mass, and its distance from a fixed reference point. See also **moment of inertia** [c14 from OF, from L *mōmentum*, from *movēre* to move]
momentarily ('məʊməntərɪlɪ, -trɪlɪ, ˌməʊmən'tærɪlɪ) *adv* **1** for an instant; temporarily **2** from moment to moment; every instant **3** *US & Canad* very soon ▷ Also (for senses 1, 2): **momently**
momentary ('məʊməntərɪ, -trɪ) *adj* **1** lasting for only a moment; temporary **2** *rare* occurring or present at each moment > **'momentariness** *n*
moment of inertia *n* the tendency of a body to resist angular acceleration, expressed as the sum of the products of the mass of each particle in the body and the square of its perpendicular distance from the axis of rotation
moment of truth *n* **1** a moment when a person or thing is put to the test **2** the point in a bullfight when the matador is about to kill the bull
momentous (məʊ'mɛntəs) *adj* of great significance > **mo'mentously** *adv* > **mo'mentousness** *n*
momentum (məʊ'mɛntəm) *n, pl* **momenta** (-tə) *or* **momentums** **1** *physics* the product of a body's mass and its velocity **2** the impetus of a body resulting from its motion **3** driving power or strength [c17 from L: movement; see MOMENT]
momma ('mɒmə) *n chiefly US* **1** an informal or childish word for **mother**[1] **2** *inf* a buxom and voluptuous woman
Mommsen (*German* 'mɔmzən) *n* **Theodor** ('te:odo:r) 1817–1903, German historian, noted esp for *The History of Rome* (1854–56): Nobel prize for literature 1902
Momus ('məʊməs) *n, pl* **Momuses** *or* **Momi** (-maɪ) **1** *Greek myth* the god of blame and mockery **2** a cavilling critic
Mon. *abbrev for* Monday
mon- *combining form* a variant of **mono-** before a vowel
Monaco ('mɒnəˌkəʊ, mə'nɑ:kəʊ; *French* mɔnako) *n* a principality in SW Europe, on the Mediterranean and forming an enclave in SE France: the second smallest sovereign state in the world (after the Vatican); consists of **Monaco-Ville** (the capital) on a rocky headland, **La Condamine** (a business area and port), **Monte Carlo** (the resort centre), and **Fontvieille** a light industrial area. Language: French. Religion: Roman Catholic. Currency: euro. Pop: 31 800 (2001 est). Area: 189 hectares (476 acres). Related adj: **Monegasque** > **Monacan** ('mɒnəkən, mə'nɑ:-) *n, adj*
▷ http://monaco.gouv.mc/PortGb
▷ www.visitmonaco.com
▷ www.monaco-congres.com

Mm

monad ('mɒnæd, 'məʊ-) *n* **1** (*pl* **monads** *or* **monades** (-əˌdi:z)) *philosophy* any fundamental singular metaphysical entity, esp if autonomous **2** a single-celled organism **3** an atom, ion, or radical with a valency of one ▷ Also (for senses 1, 2): **monas** [c17 from LL *monas*, from Gk: unit, from *monos* alone] > **monadic** (mɒ'nædɪk) *adj*
monadelphous (ˌmɒnə'dɛlfəs) *adj* **1** (of stamens) having united filaments forming a tube around the style **2** (of flowers) having monadelphous stamens [c19 from MONO- + Gk *adelphos* brother]
monadnock (mə'nædnɒk) *n* a residual hill of hard rock in an otherwise eroded area [c19 after Mount *Monadnock*, New Hampshire, US]
Monaghan ('mɒnəhən) *n* **1** a county of NE Republic of Ireland, in Ulster province: many small lakes. County town: Monaghan. Pop: 51 313 (1996). Area: 1292 sq km (499 sq miles) **2** a town in NE Republic of Ireland, county town of Co Monaghan. Pop 6200 (1995 est)
monandrous (mɒ'nændrəs) *adj* **1** having only one male sexual partner over a period of time **2** (of plants) having flowers with only one stamen **3** (of flowers) having only one stamen [c19 from MONO- + -ANDROUS] > **mo'nandry** *n*
Mona Passage ('maʊnə) *n* a strait between Puerto Rico and the Dominican Republic, linking the Atlantic with the Caribbean
monarch ('mɒnək) *n* **1** a sovereign head of state, esp a king, queen, or emperor, who rules usually by

hereditary right **2** a supremely powerful or pre-eminent person or thing **3** Also called: **milkweed** a large migratory orange-and-black butterfly that feeds on the milkweed plant [c15 from LL *monarcha*, from Gk; see MONO-, -ARCH] > **monarchal** (mɒˈnɑːkᵊl) *or* **moˈnarchial** *adj* > **moˈnarchical** *or* **moˈnarchic** *adj* > **ˈmonarchism** *n* > **ˈmonarchist** *n, adj* > **ˌmonarˈchistic** *adj*

monarchy (ˈmɒnəkɪ) *n, pl* **monarchies** **1** a form of government in which supreme authority is vested in a single and usually hereditary figure, such as a king **2** a country reigned over by a monarch

monarda (mɒˈnɑːdə) *n* any of various mintlike North American plants [c19 from NL, after N. *Monardés* (1493–1588), Sp. botanist]

monastery (ˈmɒnəstərɪ) *n, pl* **monasteries** the residence of a religious community, esp of monks, living in seclusion from secular society and bound by religious vows [c15 from Church L *monastērium*, ult. from Gk *monazein* to live alone, from *monos* alone] > **monasterial** (ˌmɒnəˈstɪərɪəl) *adj*

monastic (məˈnæstɪk) *adj* **1** of or relating to monasteries or monks, nuns, etc **2** resembling this sort of life ▷ *n* **3** a person committed to this way of life, esp a monk

monasticism (məˈnæstɪˌsɪzəm) *n* the monastic system, movement, or way of life

monatomic (ˌmɒnəˈtɒmɪk) *or* **monoatomic** (ˌmɒnəʊəˈtɒmɪk) *adj chem* **1** (of an element) having or consisting of single atoms **2** (of a compound or molecule) having only one atom or group that can be replaced in a chemical reaction **3** a less common word for **monovalent**

monaural (mɒˈnɔːrəl) *adj* **1** relating to, having, or hearing with only one ear **2** another word for **monophonic** > **monˈaurally** *adv*

monazite (ˈmɒnəˌzaɪt) *n* a yellow to reddish-brown mineral consisting of a phosphate of thorium, cerium, and lanthanum in monoclinic crystalline form [c19 from G, from Gk *monazein* to live alone, so called because of its rarity]

Mönchengladbach (*German* mœnçənˈglatbax) *n* a city in W Germany, in W North Rhine-Westphalia: headquarters of NATO forces in N central Europe; textile industry. Pop: 264 100 (1999 est). Former name: **München-Gladbach**

Monck (mʌŋk) *n* **George** 1st Duke of Albemarle. 1608–70, English general. In the Civil War he was a Royalist until captured (1644) and persuaded to support the Commonwealth. After Cromwell's death he was instrumental in the restoration of Charles II (1660)

Moncton (ˈmɒŋktən) *n* a city in E Canada, in SE New Brunswick. Pop: 80 744 (1991)

Monday (ˈmʌndɪ) *n* the second day of the week; first day of the working week [OE *mōnandæg* moon's day, translation of LL *lūnae diēs*]

Mondrian (*Dutch* ˈmɔndriːaːn) *n* **Piet** (piːt) 1872–1944, Dutch painter, noted esp as an exponent of the abstract art movement De Stijl

monecious (mɒˈniːʃəs) *adj* a variant spelling of **monoecious**

Monel metal *or* **Monell metal** (mɒˈnɛl) *n trademark* any of various silvery corrosion-resistant alloys [c20 after A. *Monell* (died 1921), president of the International Nickel Co., New York, which introduced the alloys]

Monet (*French* mɔnɛ) *n* **Claude** (klod) 1840–1926, French landscape painter; the leading exponent of impressionism. His interest in the effect of light on colour led him to paint series of pictures of the same subject at different times of day. These include *Haystacks* (1889–93), *Rouen Cathedral* (1892–94), the *Thames* (1899–1904), and *Water Lilies* (1899–1906)

monetarism (ˈmʌnɪtəˌrɪzəm) *n* **1** the theory that inflation is caused by an excess quantity of money in an economy **2** an economic policy based on this theory and on a belief in the efficiency of free market forces > **ˈmonetarist** *n, adj*

▷ www.econlib.org/library/Enc/Monetarism.html

monetary (ˈmʌnɪtərɪ, -trɪ) *adj* **1** of or relating to money or currency **2** of or relating to monetarism [c19 from LL *monētārius*, from L *monēta* MONEY] > **ˈmonetarily** *adv*

monetize *or* **monetise** (ˈmʌnɪˌtaɪz) *vb* **monetizes, monetizing, monetized** *or* **monetises, monetising, monetised** (*tr*) **1** to establish as legal tender **2** to give a legal value to (a coin) > **ˌmonetiˈzation** *or* **ˌmonetiˈsation** *n*

money (ˈmʌnɪ) *n* **1** a medium of exchange that functions as legal tender **2** the official currency, in the form of banknotes, coins, etc, issued by a government or other authority **3** a particular denomination or form of currency: *silver money* **4** (*law or arch plural* **moneys** *or* **monies**) a pecuniary sum or income **5** an unspecified amount of paper currency or coins: *money to lend* **6** **for one's money** in one's opinion **7** **in the money** *inf* well-off; rich **8** **one's money's worth** full value for the money one has paid for something **9** **put money on** to place a bet on ▷ Related adj: **pecuniary** [c13 from OF *moneie*, from L *monēta*; see MINT[2]]

moneybags (ˈmʌnɪˌbægz) *n* (*functioning as sing*) *inf* a very rich person

moneychanger (ˈmʌnɪˌtʃeɪndʒə) *n* **1** a person engaged in the business of exchanging currencies or money **2** *chiefly US* a machine for dispensing coins

moneyed *or* **monied** (ˈmʌnɪd) *adj* **1** having a great deal of money; rich **2** arising from or characterized by money

money-grubbing *adj inf* seeking greedily to obtain money > **ˈmoney-ˌgrubber** *n*

moneylender (ˈmʌnɪˌlɛndə) *n* a person who lends money at interest as a living > **ˈmoneyˌlending** *adj, n*

moneymaker (ˈmʌnɪˌmeɪkə) *n* **1** a person who is intent on accumulating money **2** a person or thing that is or might be profitable > **ˈmoneyˌmaking** *adj, n*

money of account *n* another name (esp US and Canad) for **unit of account**

money purchase *n* relating to a pension scheme in which both employer and employee make contributions to a fund that is used to buy an annuity on retirement. The amount paid as a pension depends on the size of the fund

money-spinner *n inf* an enterprise, idea, person, or thing that is a source of wealth

money supply *n* the total amount of money in a country's economy at a given time, which can be calculated in various ways

monger (ˈmʌŋgə) *n* **1** (*in combination except in archaic use*) a trader or dealer: *ironmonger* **2** (*in combination*) a promoter of something: *warmonger* [OE *mangere*, ult. from L *mangō* dealer] > **ˈmongering** *n, adj*

mongol (ˈmɒŋgᵊl) *n* (not in technical use) a person affected by Down's syndrome.

> USAGE This term is nowadays considered offensive and should be replaced by reference to Down's syndrome

Mongol (ˈmɒŋgɒl, -gᵊl) *n* another word for **Mongolian**

Mongolia (mɒŋˈgəʊlɪə) *n* **1** a republic in E central Asia: made a Chinese province in 1691; became autonomous in 1911 and a republic in 1924; multiparty democracy introduced in 1990. It consists chiefly of a high plateau, with the Gobi Desert in the south, a large lake district in the northwest, and the Altai and Khangai Mountains in the west. Official language: Khalkha. Religion: nonreligious majority. Currency: tugrik. Capital: Ulan Bator. Pop: 2 435 000 (2001 est). Area: 1 565 000 sq km (604 095 sq miles). Former names: **Outer Mongolia** (until 1924), **Mongolian People's Republic** (1924–92) **2** a vast region of central Asia, inhabited chiefly by Mongols: now divided into the republic of Mongolia,

the Inner Mongolian Autonomous Region of China, and the Tuva Republic of S Russia; at its height during the 13th century under Genghis Khan
▷ www.pmis.gov.mn/indexeng.php
▷ www.mongoliatourism.gov.mn
▷ www.asianinfo.org

mongolian (mɒŋˈɡəʊlɪən) *adj* (not in technical use) of, relating to, or affected by Down's syndrome

Mongolian (mɒŋˈɡəʊlɪən) *adj* **1** of or relating to Mongolia, its people, or their language ▷ *n* **2** a native or inhabitant of Mongolia **3** the language of Mongolia

Mongolic (mɒŋˈɡɒlɪk) *n* **1** a branch or subfamily of the Altaic family of languages, including Mongolian and Kalmuck **2** another word for **Mongoloid**

mongolism (ˈmɒŋɡəˌlɪzəm) *n pathol* a former name (not in technical use) for **Down's syndrome** [c20 the condition produces facial features similar to those of the Mongoloid peoples]

mongoloid (ˈmɒŋɡəˌlɔɪd) *adj* (not in technical use) **1** relating to or characterized by Down's syndrome ▷ *n* **2** a person affected by Down's syndrome

Mongoloid (ˈmɒŋɡəˌlɔɪd) *adj* **1** of or relating to a major racial group of mankind, characterized by yellowish complexion, straight black hair, slanting eyes, short nose, and scanty facial hair, including most of the peoples of Asia, the Inuit, and the North American Indians ▷ *n* **2** a member of this group

mongoose (ˈmɒŋˌɡuːs) *n, pl* **mongooses** any of various small predatory mammals occurring in Africa and from S Europe to SE Asia, typically having a long tail and brindled coat [c17 from Marathi (a language of India) *mangūs*]

mongrel (ˈmʌŋɡrəl) *n* **1** a plant or animal, esp a dog, of mixed or unknown breeding **2** *derog* a person of mixed race ▷ *adj* **3** of mixed origin, breeding, character, etc [c15 from obs. *mong* mixture] > **ˈmongrelism** *n* > **ˈmongreˌlize** *or* **ˈmongreˌlise** *vb* > **ˌmongreliˈzation** *or* **ˌmongreliˈsation** *n* > **ˈmongrelly** *adj*

'mongst (mʌŋst) *prep Poetic.* short for **amongst**

monied (ˈmʌnɪd) *adj* a less common spelling of **moneyed**

monies (ˈmʌnɪz) *n law, arch* a plural of **money**

moniker *or* **monicker** (ˈmɒnɪkə) *n sl* a person's name or nickname [c19 from Shelta *munnik*, altered from Irish Gaelic *ainm* name]

monism (ˈmɒnɪzəm) *n* **1** *philosophy* the doctrine that reality consists of only one basic substance or element, such as mind or matter ▷ Cf **dualism** (sense 2), **pluralism** (sense 4) **2** the attempt to explain anything in terms of one principle only > **ˈmonist** *n, adj* > **moˈnistic** *adj*

monition (məʊˈnɪʃən) *n* **1** a warning or caution; admonition **2** *Christianity* a formal notice from a bishop or ecclesiastical court requiring a person to refrain from committing a specific offence [c14 via OF from L *monitiō*, from *monēre* to warn]

monitor (ˈmɒnɪtə) *n* **1** a person or piece of equipment that warns, checks, controls, or keeps a continuous record of something **2** *education* **2a** a senior pupil with various supervisory duties, etc **2b** a pupil assisting a teacher in classroom organization, etc **3** a television set used to display certain kinds of information in a television studio, airport, etc **4a** a loudspeaker used in a recording studio to determine quality or balance **4b** a loudspeaker used on stage to enable musicians to hear themselves **5** any of various large predatory lizards inhabiting warm regions of Africa, Asia, and Australia **6** (formerly) a small heavily armoured warship used for coastal assault ▷ *vb* **7** to act as a monitor of **8** (*tr*) to observe or record (the activity or performance of) (an engine or other device) **9** (*tr*) to check (the technical quality of) (a radio or television broadcast) [c16 from L, from *monēre* to advise] > **monitorial** (ˌmɒnɪˈtɔːrɪəl) *adj* > **ˈmonitorship** *n* > **ˈmonitress** *fem n*

monitory (ˈmɒnɪtərɪ, -trɪ) *adj also* **monitorial** **1** warning or admonishing ▷ *n, pl* **monitories** **2** *rare* a letter containing a monition

monk (mʌŋk) *n* a male member of a religious community bound by vows of poverty, chastity, and obedience. Related adj: **monastic** [OE *munuc*, from LL *monachus*, from LGk: solitary (man), from Gk *monos* alone] > **ˈmonkish** *adj*

Monk (mʌŋk) *n* **1** **Thelonious (Sphere)** (θəˈləʊnɪəs) 1920–82, US jazz pianist and composer **2** a variant spelling of (George) **Monck**

monkey (ˈmʌŋkɪ) *n* **1** any of numerous long-tailed primates excluding lemurs, tarsiers, etc: see **Old World monkey, New World monkey** **2** any primate except man **3** a naughty or mischievous person, esp a child **4** the head of a pile-driver (**monkey engine**) or of some similar mechanical device **5** *US & Canad sl* an addict's dependence on a drug (esp in **have a monkey on one's back**) **6** *sl* a butt of derision; someone made to look a fool (esp in **make a monkey of**) **7** *sl* (esp in bookmaking) £500 **8** *US & Canad sl* $500 ▷ *vb* **9** (*intr*; usually foll by *around*, *with*, etc) to meddle, fool, or tinker **10** (*tr*) *rare* to imitate; ape [c16 ?from Low G; cf. MLow G *Moneke*, name of the ape's son in the tale of Reynard the Fox]

monkey business *n inf* mischievous, suspect, or dishonest behaviour or acts

monkey flower *n* any of various plants of the genus *Mimulus*, cultivated for their yellow or red flowers

monkey jacket *n* a short close-fitting jacket, esp a waist-length jacket similar to a mess jacket

monkey nut *n Brit* another name for a **peanut**

monkey puzzle *n* a South American coniferous tree having branches shaped like a candelabrum and stiff sharp leaves. Also called: **Chile pine**

monkey's wedding *n S African inf* a combination of rain and sunshine [from ?]

monkey tricks *or US* **monkey shines** *pl n inf* mischievous behaviour or acts

monkey wrench *n* a wrench with adjustable jaws

monkfish (ˈmʌŋkˌfɪʃ) *n, pl* **monkfish** *or* **monkfishes** **1** any of various angler fishes **2** another name for **angelfish** (sense 3)

monk's cloth *n* a heavy cotton fabric of basket weave, used mainly for bedspreads

monkshood (ˈmʌŋkshʊd) *n* any of several poisonous N temperate plants that have hooded blue-purple flowers

Monmouth¹ (ˈmɒnməθ) *n* a market town in E Wales, in Monmouthshire: Norman castle, where Henry V was born in 1387. Pop: 7246 (1991)

Monmouth² (ˈmɒnməθ) *n* **James Scott,** Duke of Monmouth. 1649–85, the illegitimate son of Charles II of England, he led a rebellion against James II in support of his own claim to the Crown; captured and beheaded

Monmouthshire (ˈmɒnməθʃɪə, -ʃə) *n* a county of E Wales: administratively part of England for three centuries (until 1830); mainly absorbed into the county of Gwent in 1974; reinstated with reduced boundaries in 1996: chiefly agricultural, with the Black Mountains in the N. Administrative centre: Cwmbran. Pop: 84 879 (2001). Area: 851 sq km (329 sq miles)

Monnet (*French* mɔnɛ) *n* **Jean** (ʒɑ̃) 1888–1979, French economist and public servant, regarded as founding father of the European Economic Community. He was first president (1952–55) of the European Coal and Steel Community

mono (ˈmɒnəʊ) *adj* **1** short for **monophonic** ▷ *n* **2** monophonic sound

mono- *or before a vowel* **mon-** *combining form* **1** one; single: *monorail* **2** indicating that a chemical compound contains a single specified atom or group: *monoxide* [from Gk *monos*]

monoacid (ˌmɒnəʊˈæsɪd), **monacid, monoacidic** (ˌmɒnəʊəˈsɪdɪk), *or* **monacidic** *adj chem* (of a base) capable of reacting with only one molecule of a

Mm

monobasic acid; having only one hydroxide ion per molecule

monobasic (ˌmɒnəʊˈbeɪsɪk) *adj chem* (of an acid, such as hydrogen chloride) having only one replaceable hydrogen atom per molecule

monocarpic (ˌmɒnəʊˈkɑːpɪk) *or* **monocarpous** *adj* another word for **semelparous**

monochromatic (ˌmɒnəʊkrəʊˈmætɪk) *or* **monochroic** (ˌmɒnəʊˈkrəʊɪk) *adj* (of light or other electromagnetic radiation) having only one wavelength

monochromator (ˌmɒnəʊˈkrəʊmˌeɪtə) *n physics* a device that isolates a single wavelength of radiation

monochrome (ˈmɒnəˌkrəʊm) *n* **1** a black-and-white photograph or transparency **2** *photog* black-and-white **3a** a painting, drawing, etc, done in a range of tones of a single colour **3b** the technique or art of this **4** (*modifier*) executed in or resembling monochrome: *a monochrome print* ▷ *adj* **5** devoid of any distinctive or stimulating characteristics ▷ Also called (for senses 3, 4): **monotint** [C17 via Med. L from Gk *monokhrōmos* of one colour] > ˌ**monoˈchromic** *adj* > ˈ**monoˌchromist** *n*

monocle (ˈmɒnəkᵊl) *n* a lens for correcting defective vision of one eye, held in position by the facial muscles [C19 from F, from LL, from MONO- + *oculus* eye] > ˈ**monocled** *adj*

monocline (ˈmɒnəʊˌklaɪn) *n* a fold in stratified rocks in which the strata are inclined in the same direction from the horizontal [C19 from MONO- + Gk *klīnein* to lean] > ˌ**monoˈclinal** *adj, n*

monoclinic (ˌmɒnəʊˈklɪnɪk) *adj crystallog* relating to or belonging to the crystal system characterized by three unequal axes, one pair of which are not at right angles to each other [C19 from MONO- + Gk *klīnein* to lean]

monoclinous (ˌmɒnəʊˈklaɪnəs, ˈmɒnəʊˌklaɪnəs) *adj* (of flowering plants) having the male and female reproductive organs on the same flower ▷ Cf **diclinous** [C19 from MONO- + Gk *klīnē* bed] > ˈ**monoˌclinism** *n*

monoclonal antibody (ˌmɒnəʊˈkləʊnᵊl) *n* an antibody, produced by a single clone of cells grown in culture, that is both pure and specific and capable of proliferating indefinitely: used in diagnosis, therapy, and biotechnology

monocoque (ˈmɒnəˌkɒk) *n* **1** a type of aircraft fuselage, car body, etc, in which all or most of the loads are taken by the skin **2** a type of racing-car, racing-cycle, or powerboat design with no separate chassis and body ▷ *adj* **3** of or relating to the design characteristic of a monocoque [C20 from French, from MONO- + *coque* shell]

monocotyledon (ˌmɒnəʊˌkɒtɪˈliːdᵊn) *n* any of various flowering plants having a single embryonic seed leaf, leaves with parallel veins, and flowers with parts in threes: includes grasses, lilies, palms, and orchids ▷ Cf **dicotyledon** > ˌ**monoˌcotyˈledonous** *adj*

monocracy (mɒˈnɒkrəsɪ) *n, pl* **monocracies** government by one person > **monocrat** (ˈmɒnəˌkræt) *n* > ˌ**monoˈcratic** *adj*

monocular (mɒˈnɒkjʊlə) *adj* having or intended for the use of only one eye [C17 from LL *monoculus* one-eyed] > **moˈnocularly** *adv*

monoculture (ˈmɒnəʊˌkʌltʃə) *n* the continuous growing of one type of crop

monocycle (ˈmɒnəˌsaɪkᵊl) *n* another name for **unicycle**

monocyte (ˈmɒnəʊˌsaɪt) *n* the largest type of white blood cell that acts as part of the immune system by engulfing particles, such as invading microorganisms

monody (ˈmɒnədɪ) *n, pl* **monodies** **1** (in Greek tragedy) an ode sung by a single actor **2** any poem of lament for someone's death **3** *music* a style of composition consisting of a single vocal part, usually with accompaniment [C17 via LL from Gk *monōidia*, from MONO- + *aeidein* to sing] > **monodic** (mɒˈnɒdɪk) *adj* > ˈ**monodist** *n*

monoecious (mɒˈniːʃəs) *adj* **1** (of some flowering plants) having the male and female reproductive organs in separate flowers on the same plant **2** (of some animals and lower plants) hermaphrodite [C18 from NL *monoecia*, from MONO- + Gk *oikos* house]

monofilament (ˌmɒnəˈfɪləmənt) *or* **monofil** (ˈmɒnəfɪl) *n* synthetic thread or yarn composed of a single strand rather than twisted fibres

monogamy (mɒˈnɒgəmɪ) *n* **1** the state or practice of having only one husband or wife over a period of time **2** *zool* the practice of having only one mate [C17 via F from LL *monogamia*, from Gk; see MONO- + -GAMY] > **moˈnogamist** *n* > **moˈnogamous** *adj*

monogenesis (ˌmɒnəʊˈdʒɛnɪsɪs) *or* **monogeny** (mɒˈnɒdʒɪnɪ) *n* **1** the hypothetical descent of all organisms from a single cell **2** asexual reproduction in animals **3** the direct development of an ovum into an organism resembling the adult **4** the hypothetical descent of all human beings from a single pair of ancestors

monogram (ˈmɒnəˌgræm) *n* a design of one or more letters, esp initials, on clothing, stationery, etc [C17 from LL *monogramma*, from Gk; see MONO-, -GRAM] > **monogrammatic** (ˌmɒnəgrəˈmætɪk) *adj*

monograph (ˈmɒnəˌgrɑːf) *n* **1** a paper, book, or other work concerned with a single subject or aspect of a subject ▷ *vb* **monographs, monographing, monographed** (*tr*) **2** to write a monograph on > **monographer** (mɒˈnɒgrəfə) *or* **moˈnographist** *n* > ˌ**monoˈgraphic** *adj*

monogyny (mɒˈnɒdʒɪnɪ) *n* the custom of having only one female sexual partner over a period of time > **moˈnogynous** *adj*

monohull (ˈmɒnəʊˌhʌl) *n* a single-hulled sailing vessel

monokini (ˈmɒnəʊˌkiːnɪ) *n* a woman's one-piece bathing garment usually equivalent to the bottom half of a bikini [C20 from MONO- + BIKINI (as if *bikini* were from BI-)]

monolayer (ˈmɒnəʊˌleɪə) *n* a single layer of atoms or molecules adsorbed on a surface. Also called: **molecular film**

monolingual (ˌmɒnəʊˈlɪŋgwəl) *adj* knowing or expressed in only one language

monolith (ˈmɒnəlɪθ) *n* **1** a large block of stone or anything that resembles one in appearance, intractability, etc **2** a statue, obelisk, column, etc, cut from one block of stone **3** a large hollow foundation piece sunk as a caisson and filled with concrete [C19 via F from Gk *monolithos* made from a single stone] > ˌ**monoˈlithic** *adj*

monologue (ˈmɒnəˌlɒg) *n* **1** a long speech made by one actor in a play, film, etc, esp when alone **2** a dramatic piece for a single performer **3** any long speech by one person, esp when interfering with conversation [C17 via F from Gk *monologos* speaking alone] > **monologic** (ˌmɒnəˈlɒdʒɪk) *or* ˌ**monoˈlogical** *adj* > **monologist** (ˈmɒnəˌlɒgɪst) *n* > **monologize** *or* **monologise** (mɒˈnɒlədʒaɪz) *vb*

USAGE See at **soliloquy**

monomania (ˌmɒnəʊˈmeɪnɪə) *n* an excessive mental preoccupation with one thing, idea, etc > ˌ**monoˈmaniˌac** *n, adj* > **monomaniacal** (ˌmɒnəʊməˈnaɪəkᵊl) *adj*

monomark (ˈmɒnəmɑːk) *n Brit* a series of letters or figures to identify goods, personal articles, etc

monomer (ˈmɒnəmə) *n chem* a compound whose molecules can join together to form a polymer > **monomeric** (ˌmɒnəˈmɛrɪk) *adj*

monometallism (ˌmɒnəʊˈmɛtᵊˌlɪzəm) *n* **1** the use of one metal, esp gold or silver, as the sole standard of value and currency **2** the economic policies supporting a monometallic standard > **monometallic** (ˌmɒnəʊmɪˈtælɪk) *adj* > ˌ**monoˈmetallist** *n*

monomial (mɒˈnəʊmɪəl) *n* **1** *maths* an expression

consisting of a single term, such as *5ax* ▷ *adj* **2** consisting of a single algebraic term [c18 MONO- + (BIN)OMIAL]

monomorphic (ˌmɒnəʊˈmɔːfɪk) *or* **monomorphous** *adj* **1** (of an individual organism) showing little or no change in structure during the entire life history **2** (of a species) existing or having parts that exist in only one form **3** (of a chemical compound) having only one crystalline form

Monongahela (məˌnɒŋɡəˈhiːlə) *n* a river in the northeastern US, flowing generally north to the Allegheny River at Pittsburgh, Pennsylvania, forming the Ohio River. Length: 206 km (128 miles)

mononucleosis (ˌmɒnəʊˌnjuːklɪˈəʊsɪs) *n* **1** *pathol* the presence of a large number of monocytes in the blood **2** See **infectious mononucleosis**

monophonic (ˌmɒnəʊˈfɒnɪk) *adj* **1** Also: **monaural** (of a system of broadcasting, recording, or reproducing sound) using only one channel between source and loudspeaker. Sometimes shortened to **mono** Cf. **stereophonic** **2** *music* of or relating to a style of musical composition consisting of a single melodic line

monophthong (ˈmɒnəfˌθɒŋ) *n* a simple or pure vowel [c17 from Gk *monophthongos*, from MONO- + *thongos* sound]

Monophysite (mɒˈnɒfɪˌsaɪt) *n* *Christianity* a person who holds that there is only one nature in the person of Christ, which is primarily divine with human attributes [c17 via Church L from LGk, from MONO- + *phusis* nature] > **Monophysitic** (ˌmɒnəʊfɪˈsɪtɪk) *adj*

monoplane (ˈmɒnəʊˌpleɪn) *n* an aeroplane with only one pair of wings ▷ Cf **biplane**

monopole (ˈmɒnəˌpəʊl) *n* *physics* **1** an electric charge or magnetic pole considered in isolation **2** Also called: **magnetic monopole** a hypothetical elementary particle postulated in certain theories of particle physics to exist as an isolated north or south magnetic pole

monopolize *or* **monopolise** (məˈnɒpəˌlaɪz) *vb* **monopolizes, monopolizing, monopolized** *or* **monopolises, monopolising, monopolised** (*tr*) **1** to have, control, or make use of fully, excluding others **2** to obtain, maintain, or exploit a monopoly of (a market, commodity, etc) > **moˌnopoliˈzation** *or* **moˌnopoliˈsation** *n* > **moˈnopoˌlizer** *or* **moˈnopoˌliser** *n*

monopoly (məˈnɒpəlɪ) *n, pl* **monopolies** **1** exclusive control of the market supply of a product or service **2a** an enterprise exercising this control **2b** the product or service so controlled **3** *law* the exclusive right granted to a person, company, etc, by the state to purchase, manufacture, use, or sell some commodity or to trade in a specified area **4** exclusive control, possession, or use of something [c16 from LL, from Gk *monopōlion*, from MONO- + *pōlein* to sell] > **moˈnopolist** *n* > **moˌnopoˈlistic** *adj*

Monopoly (məˈnɒpəlɪ) *n* *trademark* a board game for two to six players who throw dice to advance their tokens, the object being to acquire the property on which their tokens land

▷ www.hasbro.com/monopoly

monorail (ˈmɒnəʊˌreɪl) *n* a single-rail railway, often elevated and with suspended cars

▷ http://faculty.washington.edu/~jbs/itrans/itrans2.htm

monorchid (ˈmɒnɔːkɪd) *adj* **1** having only one testicle ▷ *n* **2** an animal or person with only one testicle

monosaccharide (ˌmɒnəʊˈsækəˌraɪd) *n* a simple sugar, such as glucose or fructose, that does not hydrolyse to yield other sugars

monosaturated (ˌmɒnəʊˈsætʃəˌreɪtɪd) *adj* of or relating to fats that are liquid at room temperature and derive mostly from foods such as olives, avocados, and nuts

monoski (ˈmɒnəʊˌskiː) *n* a wide ski on which the skier stands with both feet > **ˈmonoˌskier** *n* > **ˈmonoˌskiing** *n*

monosodium glutamate (ˌmɒnəʊˈsəʊdɪəm ˈɡluːtəˌmeɪt) *n* a white crystalline substance that has little flavour itself but enhances protein flavours: used as a food additive

monospaced type (ˈmɒnəʊˌspeɪst) *n* *computing* a typeface in which the width of all letters, including the space around them, is the same

monostable (ˌmɒnəʊˈsteɪbᵊl) *adj* *physics* (of an electronic circuit) having only one stable state but able to pass into a second state in response to an input pulse

monosyllabic (ˌmɒnəsɪˈlæbɪk) *adj* **1** (of a word) containing only one syllable **2** characterized by monosyllables; curt > **ˌmonosylˈlabically** *adv*

monosyllable (ˈmɒnəˌsɪləbᵊl) *n* a word of one syllable, esp one used as a sentence

monoterpene (ˈmɒnəˌtɜːpiːn) *n* *chem* an isoprene unit, C_5H_8, forming a terpene

monotheism (ˈmɒnəʊθɪˌɪzəm) *n* the belief or doctrine that there is only one God > **ˈmonoˌtheist** *n, adj* > **ˌmonotheˈistic** *adj* > **ˌmonotheˈistically** *adv*

monotint (ˈmɒnəˌtɪnt) *n* another word for **monochrome** (senses 3, 4)

monotone (ˈmɒnəˌtəʊn) *n* **1** a single unvaried pitch level in speech, sound, etc **2** utterance, etc, without change of pitch **3** lack of variety in style, expression, etc ▷ *adj* **4** unvarying

monotonous (məˈnɒtənəs) *adj* **1** tedious, esp because of repetition **2** in unvarying tone > **moˈnotonously** *adv* > **moˈnotonousness** *n*

monotony (məˈnɒtənɪ) *n, pl* **monotonies** **1** wearisome routine; dullness **2** lack of variety in pitch or cadence

monotreme (ˈmɒnəʊˌtriːm) *n* any mammal of a primitive order of Australia and New Guinea, having a single opening (cloaca) for the passage of eggs or sperm, faeces, and urine. The group contains only the echidnas and the platypus [c19 via NL from MONO- + Gk *trēma* hole] > **monotrematous** (ˌmɒnəʊˈtriːmətəs) *adj*

monotype (ˈmɒnəˌtaɪp) *n* **1** a single print made from a metal or glass plate on which a picture has been painted **2** *biol* a monotypic genus or species

Monotype (ˈmɒnəˌtaɪp) *n* **1** *trademark* any of various typesetting systems, esp originally one in which each character was cast individually from hot metal **2** type produced by such a system

monotypic (ˌmɒnəʊˈtɪpɪk) *adj* **1** (of a genus or species) consisting of only one type of animal or plant **2** of or relating to a monotype

monounsaturated (ˌmɒnəʊʌnˈsætʃəˌreɪtɪd) *adj* of or relating to a class of vegetable oils, such as olive oil, the molecules of which have long chains of carbon atoms containing only one double bond. See also **polyunsaturated**

monovalent (ˌmɒnəʊˈveɪlənt) *adj* *chem* **a** having a valency of one **b** having only one valency ▷ Also: **univalent** > **ˌmonoˈvalence** *or* **ˌmonoˈvalency** *n*

monoxide (mɒˈnɒksaɪd) *n* an oxide that contains one oxygen atom per molecule

Monroe (mənˈrəʊ) *n* **1 James** 1758–1831, US statesman; fifth president of the US (1817–25) He promulgated the Monroe Doctrine (1823) **2 Marilyn,** real name *Norma Jean Baker* or *Mortenson*. 1926–62, US film actress. Her films include *Niagara* (1952), *Gentlemen Prefer Blondes* (1953), and *Some Like It Hot* (1959)

Monrovia (mɒnˈrəʊvɪə) *n* the capital and chief port of Liberia, on the Atlantic: founded in 1822 as a home for freed American slaves; University of Liberia (1862). Pop: 479 000 (1999 est)

Mons (*French* mɔ̃s) *n* a town in SW Belgium, capital of Hainaut province: scene of the first battle (1914) of the British Expeditionary Force during World War I. Pop: 92 666 (1995 est). Flemish name: **Bergen**

Monseigneur *French* (mɔ̃sɛɲœr) *n, pl* ***Messeigneurs*** (mesɛɲœr). a title given to French bishops, prelates, and princes [lit.: my lord]

Mm

monsieur (məs'jɜː) *n, pl* **messieurs** a French title of address equivalent to *sir* when used alone or *Mr* before a name [lit.: my lord]

Monsignor (mɒn'siːnjə) *n, pl* **Monsignors** *or* **Monsignori** (*Italian* monsiɲ'ɲoːri) *RC Church.* an ecclesiastical title attached to certain offices [c17 from It., from F MONSEIGNEUR]

monsoon (mɒn'suːn) *n* **1** a seasonal wind of S Asia from the southwest in summer and from the northeast in winter **2** the rainy season when the SW monsoon blows, from about April to October **3** any wind that changes direction with the seasons [c16 from obs. Du. *monssoen,* from Port., from Ar. *mawsim* season] > **mon'soonal** *adj*

mons pubis ('mɒnz 'pjuːbɪs) *n, pl* **montes pubis** ('mɒntiːz) the fatty flesh in human males over the junction of the pubic bones ▷ Cf **mons veneris** [c17 NL: hill of the pubes]

monster ('mɒnstə) *n* **1** an imaginary beast, usually made up of various animal or human parts **2** a person, animal, or plant with a marked deformity **3** a cruel, wicked, or inhuman person **4a** a very large person, animal, or thing **4b** (*as modifier*): *a monster cake* [c13 from OF *monstre,* from L *monstrum* portent, from *monēre* to warn]

monstera (mɒn'stɪərə) *n* any of various tropical evergreen climbing plants [from ?]

monstrance ('mɒnstrəns) *n RC Church* a receptacle in which the consecrated Host is exposed for adoration [c16 from Med. L *mōnstrantia,* from L *mōnstrāre* to show]

monstrosity (mɒn'strɒsɪtɪ) *n, pl* **monstrosities 1** an outrageous or ugly person or thing; monster **2** the state or quality of being monstrous

monstrous ('mɒnstrəs) *adj* **1** abnormal, hideous, or unnatural in size, character, etc **2** (of plants and animals) abnormal in structure **3** outrageous, atrocious, or shocking **4** huge **5** of, relating to, or resembling a monster > **'monstrously** *adv* > **'monstrousness** *n*

mons veneris ('mɒnz 'vɛnərɪs) *n, pl* **montes veneris** ('mɒntiːz) the fatty flesh in human females over the junction of the pubic bones ▷ Cf **mons pubis** [c17 NL: hill of Venus]

Mont. *abbrev for* Montana

montage (mɒn'tɑːʒ) *n* **1** the art or process of composing pictures of miscellaneous elements, such as other pictures or photographs **2** such a composition **3** a method of film editing by juxtaposition or partial superimposition of several shots to form a single image **4** a film sequence of this kind [c20 from F, from *monter* to MOUNT[1]]

Montagnais (ˌmɒntən'jeɪ) *n* **1** a member of an Innu people living in Labrador and eastern Quebec **2** the Algonquian language of this people [c18 from F: of the mountain, from *montagne* MOUNTAIN]

Montagu ('mɒntəˌgjuː) *n* **1 Charles** See (Earl of) **Halifax 2** Lady **Mary Wortley** 1689–1762, English writer, noted for her *Letters from the East* (1763)

Montaigne (*French* mɔ̃tɛɲ) *n* **Michel Eyquem de** (miʃɛl ikɛm də) 1533–92, French writer. His life's work, the *Essays* (begun in 1571), established the essay as a literary genre and record the evolution of his moral ideas

Montale (*Italian* mon'taːle) *n* **Eugenio** (eu'dʒɛːnjo) 1896–1981, Italian poet: Nobel prize for literature 1975

Montana[1] (mɒn'tænə) *n* a state of the western US: consists of the Great Plains in the east and the Rocky Mountains in the west. Capital: Helena. Pop: 902 195 (2000 est). Area: 377 070 sq km (145 587 sq miles). Abbreviations: **Mont** or (with zip code) **MT** > **Mon'tanan** *adj, n*

Montana[2] (mɒn'tænə) *n* **Joe** born 1958, American football quarterback

montane ('mɒnteɪn) *adj* of or inhabiting mountainous regions [c19 from L *montānus,* from *mons* MOUNTAIN]

Montauban (*French* mɔ̃tobɑ̃) *n* a city in SW France: a stronghold in the 16th and 17th centuries, taken by Richelieu in 1629. Pop: 53 280 (1990)

Montbéliard (*French* mɔ̃beljar) *n* an industrial town in E France: former capital of the duchy of Burgundy Pop: 30 639 (1990)

Mont Blanc (*French* mɔ̃ blɑ̃) *n* a massif in SW Europe, mainly between France and Italy: the highest mountain in the Alps; beneath it is **Mont Blanc Tunnel,** 12 km (7.5 miles) long. Highest peak (in France): 4807 m (15 771 ft). Italian name: **Monte Bianco** ('monte 'bjaŋko)

montbretia (mɒn'briːʃə) *n* a widely cultivated plant of an African genus related to the iris with ornamental orange or yellow flowers [c19 NL, after A. F. E. Coquebert de *Montbret* (1780–1801), F botanist]

Montcalm (mɒnt'kɑːm; *French* mɔ̃kalm) *n* **Louis Joseph** (lwi ʒozɛf), Marquis de Montcalm de Saint-Véran. 1712–59, French general in Canada (1756); killed in Quebec by British forces under General Wolfe

Mont Cenis (*French* mɔ̃səni) *n* See (Mont) **Cenis**

Mont Cervin (mɔ̃ sɛrvɛ̃) *n* the French name for the **Matterhorn**

monte ('mɒntɪ) *n* a gambling card game of Spanish origin [c19 from Sp.: mountain, hence pile of cards]

Monte Carlo ('mɒntɪ 'kɑːləʊ; *French* mɔ̃te karlo) *n* a town and resort forming part of the principality of Monaco, on the Riviera: famous casino and the destination of an annual car rally (the **Monte Carlo Rally**). Pop: 12 000 (latest est)

Monte Cassino ('mɒntɪ kə'siːnəʊ; *Italian* 'monte kas'siːno) *n* a hill above Cassino in central Italy: site of Benedictine monastery (530 AD); in 1944 mistaken for German observation post and destroyed by the Allies

Monte Corno (*Italian* 'monte 'korno) *n* See (Monte) **Corno**

Montego Bay (mɒn'tiːgəʊ) *n* a port and resort in NW Jamaica: the second largest town on the island Pop: 83 446 (1991)

Montenegro (ˌmɒntɪ'niːgrəʊ) *n* a constituent republic of the Union of Serbia and Montenegro, bordering on the Adriatic: declared a kingdom in 1910 and united with Serbia, Croatia, and other territories in 1918 to form Yugoslavia; remained united with Serbia as the Federal Republic of Yugoslavia when the other Yugoslav constituent republics became independent in 1991–92; Union of Serbia and Montenegro formed in 2002. Capital: Podgorica. Pop: 631 164 (1997 est). Area: 13 812 sq km (5387 sq miles) > ˌ**Monte'negrin** *adj, n*

Monterey (ˌmɒntə'reɪ) *n* a city in W California: capital of Spain's Pacific empire from 1774 to 1825; taken by the US (1846). Pop: 31 954 (1990)

Monterrey (ˌmɒntə'reɪ; *Spanish* monte'rrei) *n* a city in NE Mexico, capital of Nuevo Léon state: the third largest city in Mexico; a major industrial centre, esp for metals. Pop: 1 108 400 (2000 est)

Montespan (*French* mɔ̃tɛspɑ̃) *n* **Marquise de,** title of *Françoise Athénaïs de Rochechouart.* 1641–1707, French noblewoman; mistress of Louis XIV of France

Montesquieu (*French* mɔ̃tɛskjø) *n* **Baron de la Brède et de** (barɔ̃ də la brɛd e də), title of *Charles Louis de Secondat.* 1689–1755, French political philosopher. His chief works are the satirical *Lettres persanes* (1721) and *L'Esprit des lois* (1748), a comparative analysis of various forms of government, which had a profound influence on political thought in Europe and the US

Montessori (ˌmɒntɪ'sɔːrɪ; *Italian* montes'sɔːri) *n* **Maria** (ma'riːa) 1870–1952, Italian educational reformer, who evolved the Montessori method of teaching children

Monteux (*French* mɔ̃tø) *n* **Pierre** (pjɛr) 1875–1964, US conductor, born in France

Monteverdi (ˌmɒntɪ'vɛədɪ) *n* **Claudio** ('klaʊdɪˌəʊ) ?1567–1643, Italian composer, noted esp for his innovations in opera and for his expressive use of dissonance. His operas include *Orfeo* (1607) and

L'Incoronazione di Poppea (1642) and he also wrote many motets and madrigals

Montevideo (ˌmɒntɪvɪˈdeɪəʊ; *Spanish* mɔnteβiˈðeo) *n* the capital and chief port of Uruguay, in the south on the Río de la Plata estuary: the largest city in the country: University of the Republic (1849); resort. Pop: 1 378 707 (1996)
▷ www.visit-uruguay.com/montevideo.htm

Montezuma II (ˌmɒntɪˈzuːmə) *n* 1466–1520, Aztec emperor of Mexico (?1502–20). He was overthrown and killed by the Spanish conquistador Cortés

Montfort (ˈmɒntfət) *n* **Simon de,** Earl of Leicester. ?1208–65, English soldier, born in Normandy. He led the baronial rebellion against Henry III and ruled England from 1264 to 1265; he was killed at Evesham

Montgolfier (*French* mɔ̃gɔlfje) *n* **Jacques Étienne** (ʒak etjɛn), 1745–99, and his brother **Joseph Michel** (ʒozɛf miʃɛl), 1740–1810, French inventors, who built (1782) and ascended in (1783) the first practical hot-air balloon

Montgomery[1] (məntˈgʌmərɪ) *n* a city in central Alabama, on the Alabama River: state capital; capital of the Confederacy (1861). Pop: 201 568 (2000)

Montgomery[2] (məntˈgʌmərɪ) *n* **Bernard Law,** 1st Viscount Montgomery of Alamein, nicknamed *Monty.* 1887–1976, British field marshal. As commander of the 8th Army in North Africa, he launched the offensive, beginning with the victory at El Alamein (1942), that drove Rommel's forces back to Tunis. He also commanded the ground forces in the invasion of Normandy (1944) and accepted Germany's surrender at Lüneburg Heath (May 7, 1945)

Montgomeryshire (məntˈgʌmərɪʃɪə, -ʃə) *n* (until 1974) a county of central Wales, now part of Powys

month (mʌnθ) *n* **1** one of the twelve divisions (**calendar months**) of the calendar year **2** a period of time extending from one date to a corresponding date in the next calendar month **3** a period of four weeks or of 30 days **4** the period of time (**solar month**) taken by the moon to return to the same longitude after one complete revolution around the earth; 27.321 58 days (approximately 27 days, 7 hours, 43 minutes, 4.5 seconds) **5** the period of time (**sidereal month**) taken by the moon to make one complete revolution around the earth, measured between two successive conjunctions with a particular star; 27.321 66 days (approximately 27 days, 7 hours, 43 minutes, 11 seconds) **6** Also called: **lunation** the period of time (**lunar** or **synodic month**) taken by the moon to make one complete revolution around the earth, measured between two successive new moons; 29.530 59 days (approximately 29 days, 12 hours, 44 minutes, 3 seconds) [OE *mōnath*]

Montherlant (*French* mɔ̃tɛrlɑ̃) *n* **Henri** (**Millon**) **de** (ɑ̃ri də) 1896–1972, French novelist and dramatist: his novels include *Les Jeunes Filles* (1935–39) and *Le Chaos et la nuit* (1963)

monthly (ˈmʌnθlɪ) *adj* **1** occurring, done, appearing, payable, etc, once every month **2** lasting or valid for a month ▷ *adv* **3** once a month ▷ *n, pl* **monthlies 4** a book, periodical, magazine, etc, published once a month **5** *inf* a menstrual period

Montluçon (*French* mɔ̃lysɔ̃) *n* an industrial city in central France, on the Cher River. Pop: 56 435 (latest est)

Montmartre (*French* mɔ̃martrə) *n* a district of N Paris, on a hill above the Seine: the highest point in the city; famous for its associations with many artists

Montparnasse (*French* mɔ̃parnas) *n* a district of S Paris, on the left bank of the Seine: noted for its cafés, frequented by artists, writers, and students

Montpelier (mɒntˈpiːljə) *n* a city in N central Vermont, on the Winooski River: the state capital Pop: 8254 (1990)

Montpellier (*French* mɔ̃pɛlje) *n* a city in S France, the chief town of Languedoc: its university was founded by Pope Nicholas IV in 1289; wine trade. Pop: 225 392 (1999)

Montreal (ˌmɒntrɪˈɔːl) *n* a city and major port in central Canada, in S Quebec on **Montreal Island** at the junction of the Ottawa and St Lawrence Rivers. Pop: 1 016 376 (1996), with a conurbation of 3 127 242 (1991). French name: **Montréal** (mɔ̃real)

Montreuil (*French* mɔ̃trœj) *n* an E suburb of Paris: formerly famous for peaches, but now increasingly industrialized. Pop: 94 754 (1990)

Montreux (*French* mɔ̃trø) *n* a town and resort in W Switzerland, in Vaud canton on Lake Geneva annual television festival. Pop: 19 850 (1990)

Montrose (mɒnˈtrəʊz) *n* **James Graham,** 1st Marquess and 5th Earl of Montrose. 1612–50, Scottish general, noted for his victories in Scotland for Charles I in the Civil War. He was later captured and hanged

Mont-Saint-Michel (*French* mɔ̃sɛ̃miʃɛl) *n* a rocky islet off the coast of NW France, accessible at low tide by a causeway, in the **Bay of St Michel** (an inlet of the Gulf of St Malo): Benedictine abbey (966), used as a prison from the Revolution until 1863; reoccupied by Benedictine monks since 1966. Area: 1 hectare (3 acres)

Montserrat *n* **1** (ˌmɒntsəˈræt) a volcanic island in the Caribbean, in the Leeward Islands: a UK Overseas Territory: much of the island rendered uninhabitable by volcanic eruptions in 1997. Capital: Plymouth. Pop: 4 500 (1998 est). Area: 103 sq km (40 sq miles) **2** (*Spanish* mɔnsɛˈrrat) a mountain in NE Spain, northwest of Barcelona: famous Benedictine monastery. Height: 1235 m (4054 ft). Ancient name: **Mons Serratus** (mɒnz səˈrætəs)

monument (ˈmɒnjʊmənt) *n* **1** an obelisk, statue, building, etc, erected in commemoration of a person or event **2** a notable building or site, esp one preserved as public property **3** a tomb or tombstone **4** a literary or artistic work regarded as commemorative of its creator or a particular period **5** *US* a boundary marker **6** an exceptional example: *his lecture was a monument of tedium* [C13 from L *monumentum*, from *monēre* to remind]

Monument (ˈmɒnjʊmənt) *n* **the** a tall columnar building designed (1671) by Sir Christopher Wren to commemorate the Fire of London (1666), which destroyed a large part of the medieval city

monumental (ˌmɒnjʊˈmɛntᵊl) *adj* **1** like a monument, esp in large size, endurance, or importance **2** of, relating to, or being a monument **3** *inf* (intensifier): *monumental stupidity* > ˌ**monuˈmentally** *adv*

Monza (*Italian* ˈmontsa) *n* a city in N Italy, northeast of Milan: the ancient capital of Lombardy; scene of the assassination of King Umberto I in 1900; motor-racing circuit. Pop: 119 516 (2000 est)

moo (muː) *vb* **1** (*intr*) (of a cow, bull, etc) to make a characteristic deep long sound; low ▷ *interj* **2** an instance or imitation of this sound

mooch (muːtʃ) *vb sl* **1** (*intr; often with* around) to loiter or walk aimlessly **2** (*intr*) to lurk; skulk **3** (*tr*) to cadge **4** (*tr*) *chiefly US & Canad* to steal [C17 ?from OF *muchier* to skulk] > ˈ**moocher** *n*

mood[1] (muːd) *n* **1** a temporary state of mind or temper: *a cheerful mood* **2** a sullen or gloomy state of mind, esp when temporary: *she's in a mood* **3** a prevailing atmosphere or feeling **4 in the mood** in a favourable state of mind [OE *mōd* mind, feeling]

mood[2] (muːd) *n* **1** *grammar* a category of the verb or verbal inflections that expresses semantic and grammatical differences, including such forms as the indicative, subjunctive, and imperative **2** *logic* one of the possible arrangements of the syllogism, classified by whether the component propositions are universal or particular and affirmative or negative ▷ Also called: **mode** [C16 from MOOD[1], infl. in meaning by MODE]

moody (ˈmuːdɪ) *adj* **moodier, moodiest 1** sullen, sulky, or gloomy **2** temperamental or changeable > ˈ**moodily** *adv* > ˈ**moodiness** *n*

Mm

Moody (ˈmuːdɪ) *n* **Dwight Lyman** 1837–99, US evangelist and hymnodist, noted for his revivalist campaigns in Britain and the US with I. D. Sankey
Moog (muːg, məʊg) *n music, trademark* a type of synthesizer [c20 after Robert *Moog* (born 1934), US engineer]
mooi (mɔɪ) *adj S African sl* pleasing; nice [from Afrik.]
mooli (ˈmuːlɪ) *n* a type of large white radish [E African native name]
moolvie *or* **moolvi** (ˈmuːlviː) *n* (esp in India) a Muslim doctor of the law, teacher, or learned man: also used as a title of respect [c17 from Urdu, from Ar. *mawlawīy*; cf. MULLAH]
Moomba (ˈmuːmbə) *n* an annual carnival that takes place in Melbourne, Australia, in March [from Abor. *moom* buttocks, anus; *moomba* orig. thought to be Abor. word meaning "Let's get together and have fun"]
moon (muːn) *n* **1** the natural satellite of the earth **2** the face of the moon as it is seen during its revolution around the earth, esp at one of its phases: *new moon; full moon* **3** any natural satellite of a planet **4** moonlight **5** something resembling a moon **6** a month, esp a lunar one **7** **over the moon** *inf* extremely happy; ecstatic ▷ *vb* **8** (when *tr*, often foll by *away*; when *intr*, often foll by *around*) to be idle in a listless way, as if in love, or to idle (time) away **9** (*intr*) *sl* to expose one's buttocks to passers-by [OE *mōna*] > ˈ**moonless** *adj*
Moon (muːn) *n* **William** 1818–94, British inventor of the Moon writing system in 1847, who, himself blind, taught blind children in Brighton and printed mainly religious works from stereotyped plates of his own designing
moonbeam (ˈmuːnˌbiːm) *n* a ray of moonlight
mooncalf (ˈmuːnˌkɑːf) *n, pl* **mooncalves** (-ˌkɑːvz) **1** a born fool; dolt **2** a person who idles time away
moon-faced *adj* having a round face
moonlight (ˈmuːnˌlaɪt) *n* **1** light from the sun received on earth after reflection by the moon **2** (*modifier*) illuminated by the moon: *a moonlight walk* ▷ *vb* **moonlights, moonlighting, moonlighted** **3** (*intr*) *inf* to work at a secondary job, esp at night and illegally > ˈ**moonˌlighter** *n*
moonlight flit *n Brit inf* a hurried departure at night, esp from rented accommodation to avoid payments of rent owed. Often shortened to **moonlight**
moonlit (ˈmuːnlɪt) *adj* illuminated by the moon
moonquake (ˈmuːnˌkweɪk) *n* a light tremor of the moon, detected on the moon's surface
moonscape (ˈmuːnˌskeɪp) *n* the general surface of the moon or a representation of it
moonshine (ˈmuːnˌʃaɪn) *n* **1** another word for **moonlight** (sense 1) **2** *US & Canad* illegally distilled or smuggled whisky **3** foolish talk or thought
moonshot (ˈmuːnˌʃɒt) *n* the launching of a spacecraft, rocket, etc, to the moon
moonstone (ˈmuːnˌstəʊn) *n* a gem variety of orthoclase or albite that is white and translucent
moonstruck (ˈmuːnˌstrʌk) *or* **moonstricken** (ˈmuːnˌstrɪkən) *adj* deranged or mad
moony (ˈmuːnɪ) *adj* **moonier, mooniest** **1** *inf* dreamy or listless **2** of or like the moon
moor[1] (mʊə, mɔː) *n* a tract of unenclosed ground, usually covered with heather, coarse grass, bracken, and moss [OE *mōr*]
moor[2] (mʊə, mɔː) *vb* **1** to secure (a ship, boat, etc) with cables or ropes **2** (of a ship, boat, etc) to be secured in this way **3** (not in technical usage) a less common word for **anchor** (senses 7 and 8) [c15 of Gmc origin; rel. to OE *mǣrelsrāp* rope for mooring] > **moorage** (ˈmʊərɪdʒ) *n*
Moor (mʊə, mɔː) *n* a member of a Muslim people of North Africa, of mixed Arab and Berber descent [c14 via OF from L *Maurus*, from Gk *Mauros*, ?from Berber] > ˈ**Moorish** *adj*
▷ www.vivagranada.com/alhambra
▷ www.spanish-fiestas.com/andalucia/history-moorish-spain.htm
moorcock (ˈmʊəˌkɒk, ˈmɔː-) *n* the male of the red grouse
Moore (mʊə, mɔː) *n* **1** **Bobby** full name *Robert Frederick Moore*. 1941–93, British footballer captain of the England team that won the World Cup in 1966 **2** **Dudley** (**Stuart John**) 1935–2002, British actor, comedian, and musician noted for his comedy partnership (1960–73) with Peter Cook and such films as *10* (1979) and *Arthur* (1981) **3** **George** 1852–1933, Irish novelist. His works include *Esther Waters* (1894) and *The Brook Kerith* (1916) **4** **G**(**eorge**) **E**(**dward**) 1873–1958, British philosopher, noted esp for his *Principia Ethica* (1903) **5** **Gerald** 1899–1987, British pianist, noted as an accompanist esp to lieder singers **6** **Henry** 1898–1986, British sculptor. His works are characterized by monumental organic forms and include the *Madonna and Child* (1943) at St Matthew's Church, Northampton **7** Sir **John** 1761–1809, British general; commander of the British army (1808–09) in the Peninsular War: killed at Corunna **8** **Marianne** (**Craig**) 1887–1972, US poet: her works include *Observations* (1924) and *Selected Poems* (1935) **9** **Thomas** 1779–1852, Irish poet, best known for *Irish Melodies* (1807–34)
moorhen (ˈmʊəˌhɛn, ˈmɔː-) *n* **1** a bird of the rail family, inhabiting ponds, lakes, etc, having a black plumage, red bill, and a red shield above the bill **2** the female of the red grouse
mooring (ˈmʊərɪŋ, ˈmɔː-) *n* **1** a place for mooring a vessel **2** a permanent anchor with a floating buoy, to which vessels can moor
moorings (ˈmʊərɪŋz, ˈmɔː-) *pl n* **1** *naut* the ropes, anchors, etc, used in mooring a vessel **2** (*sometimes sing*) something that provides security or stability
Moorish idol *n* a tropical marine spiny-finned fish that is common around coral reefs. It has a deeply compressed body with yellow and black stripes
moorland (ˈmʊələnd) *n Brit* an area of moor
moose (muːs) *n, pl* **moose** a large North American deer having large flattened palmate antlers: also occurs in Europe and Asia where it is called an elk [c17 of Amerind origin]
Moose Jaw *n* a city in W Canada, in S Saskatchewan. Pop: 33 593 (1991)
moose milk *n Canad* a mixed alcoholic drink made with ingredients such as milk and eggs and usually rum
moose pasture *n Canad inf* land considered to be worthless, esp when lacking in extractable mineral deposits
moot (muːt) *adj* **1** subject or open to debate: *a moot point* ▷ *vb* **2** (*tr*) to suggest or bring up for debate **3** (*intr*) to plead or argue hypothetical cases, as an academic exercise or as training for law students ▷ *n* **4** a discussion or debate of a hypothetical case or point, held as an academic activity **5** (in Anglo-Saxon England) an assembly dealing with local legal and administrative affairs [OE *gemōt*]
USAGE See at **mute**
moot court *n* a mock court trying hypothetical legal cases
mop (mɒp) *n* **1** an implement with a wooden handle and a head made of twists of cotton or a piece of synthetic sponge, used for polishing or washing floors, or washing dishes **2** something resembling this, such as a tangle of hair ▷ *vb* **mops, mopping, mopped** (*tr*) **3** (often foll by *up*) to clean or soak up as with a mop ▷ See also **mop up** [c15 *mappe*, ult. from L *mappa* napkin]
mopani *or* **mopane** (mɒˈpɑːnɪ) *n* **1** a leguminous tree, native to southern Africa, that is highly resistant to drought and produces very hard wood **2** Also called: **mopani worm** an edible caterpillar that feeds on mopani leaves [c19 from Bantu]
mope (məʊp) *vb* **mopes, moping, moped** (*intr*) **1** to be

gloomy or apathetic **2** to move or act in an aimless way ▷ *n* **3** a gloomy person [c16 ?from obs. *mope* fool & rel. to *mop* grimace] > **'moper** *n* > **'mopy** *adj*

moped ('məʊpɛd) *n* a light motorcycle not over 50cc [c20 from MOTOR + PEDAL[1]]

mopes (məʊps) *pl n* **the** low spirits

mopoke ('məʊˌpəʊk) *n* **1** a small spotted owl of Australia and New Zealand. In Australia the tawny frogmouth is often wrongly identified as the mopoke **2** *Austral & NZ sl* a slow or lugubrious person ▷ Also called: **morepork** [c19 imit. of the bird's cry]

moppet ('mɒpɪt) *n* a less common word for **poppet** (sense 1) [c17 from obs. *mop* rag doll; from ?]

mop up *vb (tr, adv)* **1** to clean with a mop **2** *inf* to complete (a task, etc) **3** *mil* to clear (remaining enemy forces) after a battle, as by killing, taking prisoner, etc

moquette (mɒ'kɛt) *n* a thick velvety fabric used for carpets, upholstery, etc [c18 from F; from ?]

MOR *abbrev for* middle-of-the-road: used esp in radio programming

Mor. *abbrev for* Morocco

mora *or* **morra** ('mɔːrə) *n* a guessing game played with the fingers, esp in Italy and China [c18 from It. *mora*]

Moradabad (ˌmɔːrədə'bæd) *n* a city in N India, in N Uttar Pradesh. Pop: 429 214 (1991)

moraine (mɒ'reɪn) *n* a mass of debris, carried by glaciers and forming ridges and mounds when deposited [c18 from F, from Savoy dialect *morena*, from ?] > **mo'rainal** *or* **mo'rainic** *adj*

moral ('mɒrəl) *adj* **1** concerned with or relating to human behaviour, esp the distinction between good and bad or right and wrong behaviour: *moral sense* **2** adhering to conventionally accepted standards of conduct **3** based on a sense of right and wrong according to conscience: *moral courage; moral law* **4** having psychological rather than tangible effects: *moral support* **5** having the effects but not the appearance of (victory or defeat): *a moral victory* **6** having a strong probability: *a moral certainty* ▷ *n* **7** the lesson to be obtained from a fable or event **8** a concise truth; maxim **9** *(pl)* principles of behaviour in accordance with standards of right and wrong **10** *Austral sl* a certainty: *a moral to win* [c14 from L *mōrālis* relating to morals or customs, from *mōs* custom] > **'morally** *adv*

morale (mɒ'rɑːl) *n* the degree of mental or moral confidence of a person or group [c18 morals, from F, n use of MORAL (adj)]

moralist ('mɒrəlɪst) *n* **1** a person who seeks to regulate the morals of others **2** a person who lives in accordance with moral principles > ˌ**moral'istic** *adj* > ˌ**moral'istically** *adv*

morality (mə'rælɪtɪ) *n, pl* **moralities** **1** the quality of being moral **2** conformity, or degree of conformity, to conventional standards of moral conduct **3** a system of moral principles **4** an instruction or lesson in morals **5** short for **morality play**

morality play *n* a type of drama between the 14th and 16th centuries concerned with the conflict between personified virtues and vices

moralize *or* **moralise** ('mɒrəˌlaɪz) *vb* **moralizes, moralizing, moralized** *or* **moralises, moralising, moralised** **1** *(intr)* to make moral pronouncements **2** *(tr)* to interpret or explain in a moral sense **3** *(tr)* to improve the morals of > ˌ**morali'zation** *or* ˌ**morali'sation** *n* > **'moralˌizer** *or* **'moralˌiser** *n*

moral majority *n* a presumed majority of people believed to be in favour of a stricter code of public morals [c20 after *Moral Majority*, a right-wing US religious organization, based on SILENT MAJORITY]

moral philosophy *n* the branch of philosophy dealing with ethics

Moral Rearmament *n* a worldwide movement for moral and spiritual renewal founded by Frank Buchman in 1938. Also called: **Buchmanism** Former name: **Oxford Group**

moral theology *n* the branch of theology dealing with ethics

Morar ('mɔːrə) *n* **Loch** a lake in W Scotland, in the SW Highlands: the deepest in Scotland Length: 18 km (11 miles). Depth: 296 m (987 ft)

morass (mə'ræs) *n* **1** a tract of swampy low-lying land **2** a disordered or muddled situation or circumstance, esp one that impedes progress [c17 from Du. *moeras*, ult. from OF *marais* MARSH]

moratorium (ˌmɒrə'tɔːrɪəm) *n, pl* **moratoria** (-rɪə) *or* **moratoriums** **1** a legally authorized postponement of the fulfilment of an obligation **2** an agreed suspension of activity [c19 NL, from LL *morātōrius* dilatory, from *mora* delay]

Morava (mə'rɑːvə) *n* **1** a river in central Europe, rising in the Sudeten Mountains, in the Czech Republic, and flowing south through Slovakia to the Danube: forms part of the border between the Czech Republic, Slovakia, and Austria. Length: 370 km (230 miles). German name: **March** **2** a river in E Serbia and Montenegro, formed by the confluence of the Southern Morava and the Western Morava near Stalac: flows north to the Danube. Length: 209 km (130 miles) **3** ('mɔrava) the Czech name for **Moravia**

Moravia[1] (mə'reɪvɪə, mɒ-) *n* a region of the Czech Republic around the Morava River, bounded by the Bohemian-Moravian Highlands, the Sudeten Mountains, and the W Carpathians: became a separate Austrian crownland in 1848; part of Czechoslovakia 1918–92; valuable mineral resources. Czech name: **Morava** German name: **Mähren**

Moravia[2] (*Italian* mo'raːvja) *n* **Alberto** (al'bɛrto), pen name of *Alberto Pincherle*. 1907–90, Italian novelist and short-story writer: his works include *The Time of Indifference* (1929), *The Woman of Rome* (1949), *The Lie* (1966), and *Erotic Tales* (1985)

Moravian (mə'reɪvɪən, mɒ-) *adj* **1** of or relating to Moravia, its people, or their dialect of Czech **2** of or relating to the Moravian Church ▷ *n* **3** the Moravian dialect **4** a native or inhabitant of Moravia **5** a member of the Moravian Church > **Mo'ravianism** *n*

moray (mɒ'reɪ) *n, pl* **morays** a voracious marine coastal eel marked with brilliant colours [c17 from Port. *moréia*, from L *mūrēna*, from Gk *muraina*]

Moray[1] ('mʌrɪ) *n* a council area and historical county of NE Scotland: part of Grampian region from 1975 to 1996: mainly hilly, with the Cairngorm mountains in the S. Administrative centre: Elgin. Pop: 86 940 (2001). Area: 2238 sq km (874 sq miles). Former name: **Elgin**

Moray[2] *or* **Murray** ('mʌrɪ) *n* **1st Earl of**, title of *James Stuart*. ?1531–70, regent of Scotland (1567–70) following the abdication of Mary, Queen of Scots, his half-sister. He defeated Mary and Bothwell at Langside (1568); assassinated by a follower of Mary

Moray Firth *n* an inlet of the North Sea on the NE coast of Scotland. Length: about 56 km (35 miles)

Morayshire ('mʌrɪˌʃɪə, -ʃə) *n* a historic county of NE Scotland. Former name: **Elgin**

morbid ('mɔːbɪd) *adj* **1** having an unusual interest in death or unpleasant events **2** gruesome **3** relating to or characterized by disease [c17 from L *morbidus* sickly, from *morbus* illness] > **mor'bidity** *n* > **'morbidly** *adv* > **'morbidness** *n*

morbid anatomy *n* the branch of medical science concerned with the study of the structure of diseased organs and tissues

morbific (mɔː'bɪfɪk) *adj* causing disease

Morbihan (*French* mɔrbiɑ̃) *n* a department of NW France, in S Brittany. Capital: Vannes. Pop: 643 873 (1999). Area: 7092 sq km (2766 sq miles)

mordant ('mɔːdᵊnt) *adj* **1** sarcastic or caustic **2** having the properties of a mordant **3** pungent ▷ *n* **4** a substance used before the application of a dye, possessing the ability to fix colours **5** an acid or other corrosive fluid used to etch lines on a printing plate [c15 from OF: biting, from *mordre* to bite, from L *mordēre*] > **'mordancy** *n* > **'mordantly** *adv*

Mordecai (ˌmɔːdəˈkaɪ, ˈmɔːdəˌkaɪ) *n Old Testament* the cousin of Esther who averted a threatened massacre of the Jews (Esther 2–9)

mordent (ˈmɔːdᵊnt) *n music* a melodic ornament consisting of the rapid alternation of a note with a note one degree lower than it [c19 from G, from It. *mordente*, from *mordere* to bite]

Mordred (ˈmɔːdrɪd) *n* a variant of **Modred**

Mordvinian Republic (mɔːˈdvɪnɪən) *n* a constituent republic of W central Russia, in the middle Volga basin. Capital: Saransk. Pop: 929 000 (2000 est). Area: 26 200 sq km (10 110 sq miles). Also called: **Mordovian Republic** (mɔːˈdəʊvɪən), **Mordovia**

more (mɔː) *determiner* **1a** the comparative of **much** or **many**: *more joy than you know; more sausages* **1b** (*as pron; functioning as sing or pl*): *he has more than she has; even more are dying* **2a** additional; further: *no more bananas* **2b** (*as pron; functioning as sing or pl*): *I can't take any more; more than expected* **3 more of** to a greater extent or degree: *we see more of Sue; more of a nuisance* ▷ *adv* **4** used to form the comparative of some adjectives and adverbs: *a more believable story; more quickly* **5** the comparative of **much**: *people listen to the radio more now* **6 more or less 6a** as an estimate; approximately **6b** to an unspecified extent or degree: *the party was ruined, more or less* [OE *māra*]

USAGE See at **most**

More (mɔː) *n* **1 Hannah** 1745–1833, English writer, noted for her religious tracts, esp *The Shepherd of Salisbury Plain* **2** Sir **Thomas** 1478–1535, English statesman, humanist, and Roman Catholic Saint; Lord Chancellor to Henry VIII (1529–32) His opposition to the annulment of Henry's marriage to Catherine of Aragon and his refusal to recognize the Act of Supremacy resulted in his execution on a charge of treason. In *Utopia* (1516) he set forth his concept of the ideal state. Feast day: June 22 or July 6

Morea (mɔːˈrɪə) *n* the medieval name for the **Peloponnese**

Moreau (*French* mɔro) *n* **1 Gustave** (gystav) 1826–98, French symbolist painter **2 Jean Victor** (ʒɑ̃ viktɔr) 1763–1813, French general in the Revolutionary and Napoleonic Wars **3 Jeanne** (ʒan) born 1928, French stage and film actress. Her films include *Jules et Jim* (1961), *Diary of a Chambermaid* (1964), and *The Proprietor* (1996)

Morecambe (ˈmɔːkəm) *n* a port and resort in NW England, in NW Lancashire on **Morecambe Bay** (an inlet of the Irish Sea) Pop (with Heysham): 46 657 (1991)

Morecambe and Wise (ˈmɔːkəm; waɪz) *n* a team of British comedians, **Eric Morecambe**, real name *John Eric Bartholomew*, 1926–84, and **Ernie Wise**, real name *Ernest Wiseman*, 1925–99

moreish *or* **morish** (ˈmɔːrɪʃ) *adj inf* (of food) causing a desire for more

morel (mɒˈrɛl) *n* an edible fungus in which the mushroom has a pitted cap [c17 from F *morille*, prob. of Gmc origin]

Morelia (*Spanish* moˈrelia) *n* a city in central Mexico, capital of Michoacán state: a cultural centre during colonial times; two universities. Pop: 549 404 (2000 est). Former name (until 1828): **Valladolid**

morello (məˈrɛləʊ) *n, pl* **morellos** a variety of small very dark sour cherry [c17 ?from Med. L *amārellum*, dim. of L *amārus* bitter, but also infl. by It. *morello* blackish]

Morelos (*Spanish* moˈrelɔs) *n* an inland state of S central Mexico, on the S slope of the great plateau. Capital: Cuernavaca. Pop: 1 552 878 (2000 est). Area: 4988 sq km (1926 sq miles)

morendo (mɒrˈɛndəʊ) *adv music* gradually dying away [It.: dying]

moreover (mɔːˈrəʊvə) *sentence connector.* in addition to what has already been said

morepork (ˈmɔːˌpɔːk) *n* another name, esp in New Zealand, for **mopoke**

mores (ˈmɔːreɪz) *pl n* the customs and conventions embodying the fundamental values of a group or society [c20 from L, pl of *mōs* custom]

Morgan (ˈmɔːgən) *n* **1 Edwin** (**George**) born 1920, Scottish poet, noted esp for his collection *The Second Life* (1968) and his many concrete and visual poems **2** Sir **Henry** 1635–88, Welsh buccaneer, who raided Spanish colonies in the West Indies for the English **3 John Pierpont** 1837–1913, US financier, philanthropist, and art collector **4** (**Hywel**) **Rhodri** (ˈrɒdrɪ) born 1939, Welsh Labour politician; first secretary of Wales from 2000 **5 Thomas Hunt** 1866–1945, US biologist. He formulated the chromosome theory of heredity. Nobel prize for physiology or medicine 1933

morganatic (ˌmɔːgəˈnætɪk) *adj* of or designating a marriage between a person of high rank and a person of low rank, by which the latter is not elevated to the higher rank and any issue have no rights to the succession of the higher party's titles, property, etc [c18 from Med. L *mātrimōnium ad morganāticum* marriage based on the morning-gift (a token present after consummation representing the husband's only liability); *morganātica*, ult. from OHG *morgan* morning] > **ˌmorgaˈnatically** *adv*

Morgan le Fay (ˈmɔːgən lə ˈfeɪ) *or* **Morgain le Fay** (ˈmɔːgaɪn, -gən) *n* a wicked sorceress of Arthurian legend, the half-sister of King Arthur

morgen (ˈmɔːgən) *n* **1** a South African unit of area, equal to about two acres or 0.8 hectare **2** a unit of area, formerly used in Prussia and Scandinavia, equal to about two thirds of an acre [c17 from Du.: morning, a morning's ploughing]

morgue (mɔːg) *n* **1** another word for **mortuary** **2** *inf* a room or file containing clippings, etc, used for reference in a newspaper [c19 from F *le Morgue*, a Paris mortuary]

moribund (ˈmɒrɪˌbʌnd) *adj* **1** near death **2** without force or vitality [c18 from L, from *morī* to die] > **ˌmoriˈbundity** *n* > **ˈmoriˌbundly** *adv*

Mörike (*German* ˈmøːrɪkə) *n* **Eduard** (ˈeːduart) 1804–75, German poet, noted for his lyrics, such as *On a Winter's Morning before Sunrise* and *At Midnight*

Morisco (məˈrɪskəʊ) *or* **Moresco** (məˈrɛskəʊ) *n, pl* **Moriscos** *or* **Moriscoes** **1** a Spanish Moor **2** a morris dance ▷ *adj* **3** another word for **Moorish**; see **Moor** [c16 from Sp., from *Moro* MOOR]

morish (ˈmɔːrɪʃ) *adj* a variant spelling of **moreish**

Morisot (*French* morizo) *n* **Berthe** (bɛrtə) 1841–95, French impressionist painter; noted for her studies of women and children

Morley[1] (ˈmɔːlɪ) *n* an industrial town in N England, in Leeds unitary authority, West Yorkshire. Pop: 47 579 (1991)

Morley[2] (ˈmɔːlɪ) *n* **1 Edward Williams** 1838–1923, US chemist who collaborated with A. A. Michelson in the Michelson-Morley experiment **2 John,** Viscount Morley of Blackburn. 1838–1923, British Liberal statesman and writer; secretary of state for India (1905–10) **3 Robert** 1908–92, British actor. His many films include *Major Barbara* (1940), *Oscar Wilde* (1960), and *The Blue Bird* (1976) **4 Thomas** ?1557–?1603, English composer and organist, noted for his madrigals and his textbook on music, *A Plaine and Easie Introduction to Practicall Musicke* (1597)

Mormon (ˈmɔːmən) *n* **1** a member of the Church of Jesus Christ of Latter-day Saints, founded in 1830 in New York by Joseph Smith **2** a prophet whose supposed revelations were recorded by Joseph Smith in the Book of Mormon ▷ *adj* **3** of or relating to the Mormons, their

Church, or their beliefs > '**Mormonism** *n*
▷ http://www.mormon.org/

morn (mɔːn) *n* a poetic word for **morning** [OE *morgen*]

mornay ('mɔːneɪ) *adj* (*often immediately postpositive*) denoting a cheese sauce: *eggs mornay* [? after Philippe de MORNAY]

Mornay (*French* mɔrnɛ) *n* **Philippe de** (filip də), Seigneur du Plessis-Marly. 1549–1623, French Huguenot leader. Also called: **Duplessis-Mornay**

morning ('mɔːnɪŋ) *n* **1** the first part of the day, ending at noon **2** sunrise; daybreak; dawn **3** the beginning or early period **4** **the morning after** *inf* the aftereffects of excess, esp a hangover **5** (*modifier*) of, used in, or occurring in the morning: *morning coffee* [C13 *morwening*, from MORN, on the model of EVENING]

morning-after pill *n* an oral contraceptive effective if taken within 72 hours after unprotected intercourse

morning dress *n* formal day dress for men, comprising a cutaway frock coat (**morning coat**), usually with grey trousers and top hat

morning-glory *n, pl* **morning-glories** any of various mainly tropical plants of the convolvulus family, with trumpet-shaped blue, pink, or white flowers, which close in late afternoon

mornings ('mɔːnɪŋz) *adv inf* in the morning, esp regularly, or during every morning

morning sickness *n* nausea occurring shortly after rising: a symptom of pregnancy

morning star *n* a planet, usually Venus, seen just before sunrise. Also called: **daystar**

Moro[1] ('mɔːrəʊ) *n* **1** (*pl* **Moros** *or* **Moro**) a member of a group of predominantly Muslim peoples of the S Philippines **2** the language of these peoples [C19 via Sp. from L *Maurus* MOOR]

Moro[2] (*Italian* 'mɔːro) *n* **Aldo** ('aldo) 1916–78, Italian Christian Democrat statesman; prime minister of Italy (1963–68; 1974–76) and minister of foreign affairs (1965–66; 1969–72; 1973–74). He negotiated the entry of the Italian Communist Party into coalition government before being kidnapped by the Red Brigades in 1978 and murdered

morocco (mə'rɒkəʊ) *n* a fine soft leather made from goatskins, used for bookbinding, shoes, etc [C17 after MOROCCO, where it was orig. made]

Morocco (mə'rɒkəʊ) *n* a kingdom in NW Africa, on the Mediterranean and the Atlantic: conquered by the Arabs in about 683, who introduced Islam; at its height under Berber dynasties (11th–13th centuries); became a French protectorate in 1912 and gained independence in 1956. It is mostly mountainous, with the Atlas Mountains in the centre and the Rif range along the Mediterranean coast, with the Sahara in the south and southeast; an important exporter of phosphates. Official language: Arabic; Berber and French are also widely spoken. Official religion: (Sunni) Muslim. Currency: dirham. Capital: Rabat. Pop: 29 237 000 (2001 est). Area: 458 730 sq km (177 117 sq miles). French name: **Maroc** > **Moroccan** (mə'rɒkən) *adj, n*
▷ www.mincom.gov.ma
▷ www.iexplore.com/dmap/Morocco/Where+to+Go

moron ('mɔːrɒn) *n* **1** a foolish or stupid person **2** a person having an intelligence quotient of between 50 and 70 [C20 from Gk *mōros* foolish] > **moronic** (mə'rɒnɪk) *adj* > **mo'ronically** *adv* > '**moronism** *or* **mo'ronity** *n*

Moroni (mə'rəʊnɪ; *French* mɔrɔni) *n* the capital of Comoros, on the island of Njazídja (Grande Comore). Pop 30 000 (1991)

morose (mə'rəʊs) *adj* ill-tempered or gloomy [C16 from L *mōrōsus* peevish, from *mōs* custom, will] > **mo'rosely** *adv* > **mo'roseness** *n*

-morph *n combining form* indicating shape, form, or structure of a specified kind: *ectomorph* [from Gk *-morphos*, from *morphē* shape] > **-morphic** *or* **-morphous** *adj combining form* > **-morphy** *n combining form*

morpheme ('mɔːfiːm) *n linguistics* a speech element having a meaning or grammatical function that cannot be subdivided into further such elements [C20 from F, from Gk *morphē* form, on the model of PHONEME] > **mor'phemic** *adj* > **mor'phemically** *adv*

Morpheus ('mɔːfɪəs, -fjuːs) *n Greek myth* the god of sleep and dreams > '**Morphean** *adj*

morphine ('mɔːfiːn) *or* **morphia** ('mɔːfɪə) *n* an alkaloid extracted from opium: used in medicine as an analgesic and sedative [C19 from F, from MORPHEUS]

morphing ('mɔːfɪŋ) *n* a computer technique used for graphics and in films, in which one image is gradually transformed into another [C20 from METAMORPHOSIS]

morphogenesis (ˌmɔːfəʊ'dʒɛnɪsɪs) *n* **1** the development of form in an organism during its growth **2** the evolutionary development of form in an organism or part of an organism > **morphogenetic** (ˌmɔːfəʊdʒɪ'nɛtɪk) *adj*

morphology (mɔː'fɒlədʒɪ) *n* **1** the branch of biology concerned with the form and structure of organisms **2** the form and structure of words in a language **3** the form and structure of anything > **morphologic** (ˌmɔːfə'lɒdʒɪk) *or* ˌ**morpho'logical** *adj* > ˌ**morpho'logically** *adv* > **mor'phologist** *n*

Morphy ('mɔːfɪ) *n* **Paul** 1837–84, US chess player, widely considered to have been the world's greatest player

Morris ('mɒrɪs) *n* **William** 1834–96, English poet, designer, craftsman, and socialist writer. He founded the Kelmscott Press (1890)

Morris chair *n* an armchair with an adjustable back [C19 after William MORRIS]

morris dance *n* any of various old English folk dances usually performed by men (**morris men**) adorned with bells and often representing characters from folk tales. Often shortened to **morris** [C15 *moreys daunce* Moorish dance] > **morris dancing** *n*
▷ www.streetswing.com/histmain/z3moris.htm
▷ http://web.syr.edu/~rsholmes/morris/rich

Mm

Morrison ('mɒrɪsᵊn) *n* **1** **Herbert Stanley,** Baron Morrison of Lambeth. 1888–1965, British Labour statesman, Home Secretary and Minister for Home Security in Churchill's War Cabinet (1942–45) **2** **Jim,** full name *James Douglas Morrison*. 1943–71, US rock singer and songwriter, lead vocalist with the Doors **3** **Toni,** full name *Chloe Anthony Morrison*. born 1931, US novelist, whose works include *Sula* (1974), *Song of Solomon* (1977), *Beloved* (1987), *Jazz* (1992), and *Paradise* (1998): awarded the Nobel Prize for literature in 1993 **4** **Van,** full name *George Ivan Morrison*. born 1945, Northern Irish rock singer and songwriter. His albums include *Astral Weeks* (1968), *Moondance* (1970), *Avalon Sunset* (1989), and *Days Like These* (1995)

morro ('mɒrəʊ) *n, pl* **morros** (-rəʊz) a rounded hill or promontory [from Sp.]

morrow ('mɒrəʊ) *n* (usually preceded by *the*) *arch or poetic* **1** the next day **2** the period following a specified event **3** the morning [C13 *morwe*, from OE *morgen* morning]

Mors (mɔːz) *n* the Roman god of death. Greek counterpart: **Thanatos**

Morse (mɔːs) *n* **Samuel Finley Breese** ('fɪnlɪ briːz) 1791–1872, US inventor and painter. He invented the first electric telegraph and the Morse code

Morse code *n* a telegraph code formerly used internationally for transmitting messages. Letters, numbers, etc, are represented by groups of shorter dots and longer dashes, or by groups of the corresponding sounds

morsel ('mɔːsᵊl) *n* **1** a small slice or mouthful of food **2** a small piece; bit **3** *Irish inf* a term of endearment for a child [C13 from OF, from *mors* a bite, from L *morsus*, from *mordēre* to bite]

mortal ('mɔːtᵊl) *adj* **1** (of living beings, esp human beings) subject to death **2** of or involving life or the world **3** ending in or causing death; fatal: *a mortal blow* **4** deadly or unrelenting: *a mortal enemy* **5** of or like the fear of death: *mortal terror* **6** great or very intense: *mortal pain* **7** conceivable or possible: *there was no mortal reason to go* **8** *sl* long and tedious: *for three mortal hours* ▷ *n* **9** a mortal being **10** *inf* a person: *a mean mortal* [c14 from L *mortālis*, from *mors* death] > '**mortally** *adv*

mortality (mɔː'tælɪtɪ) *n, pl* **mortalities** **1** the condition of being mortal **2** great loss of life, as in war or disaster **3** the number of deaths in a given period **4** mankind; humanity

mortal sin *n Christianity* a sin regarded as involving total loss of grace

mortar ('mɔːtə) *n* **1** a mixture of cement or lime or both with sand and water, used as a bond between bricks or stones or as a covering on a wall **2** a cannon having a short barrel and relatively wide bore that fires low-velocity shells in high trajectories **3** a vessel, usually bowl-shaped, in which substances are pulverized with a pestle ▷ *vb (tr)* **4** to join (bricks or stones) or cover (a wall) with mortar **5** to fire on with mortars [c13 from L *mortārium* basin in which mortar is mixed; in some senses, via OF *mortier* substance mixed inside such a vessel]

mortarboard ('mɔːtə,bɔːd) *n* **1** a black tasselled academic cap with a flat square top **2** a small square board with a handle on the underside for carrying mortar

mortgage ('mɔːgɪdʒ) *n* **1** an agreement under which a person borrows money to buy property, esp a house, and the lender may take possession of the property if the borrower fails to repay the money **2** the deed affecting such an agreement **3** the loan obtained under such an agreement: *a mortgage of £48,000* **4** a regular payment of money borrowed under such an agreement: *a mortgage of £347 per month* ▷ *vb* **mortgages, mortgaging, mortgaged** *(tr)* **4** to convey (property) by mortgage **5** *inf* to pledge [c14 from OF, lit.: dead pledge] > '**mortgageable** *adj*

mortgagee (,mɔːgɪ'dʒiː) *n law* the party to a mortgage who makes the loan

mortgagor (,mɔːgɪ'dʒɔː) *or* **mortgager** *n property law* a person who borrows money by mortgaging his or her property to the lender as security

mortician (mɔː'tɪʃən) *n chiefly US* another word for **undertaker** [c19 from MORTUARY + *-ician*, as in *physician*]

mortification (,mɔːtɪfɪ'keɪʃən) *n* **1** a feeling of humiliation **2** something causing this **3** *Christianity* the practice of mortifying the senses **4** another word for **gangrene**

mortify ('mɔːtɪ,faɪ) *vb* **mortifies, mortifying, mortified** **1** *(tr)* to humiliate or cause to feel shame **2** *(tr) Christianity* to subdue and bring under control by self-denial, disciplinary exercises, etc **3** *(intr)* to undergo tissue death or become gangrenous [c14 via OF from Church L *mortificāre* to put to death, from L *mors* death + *facere* to do] > '**morti,fier** *n* > '**morti,fying** *adj*

Mortimer ('mɔːtɪmə) *n* **1** Sir **John** (**Clifford**) born 1923, British barrister, playwright, and novelist, best known for the television series featuring the barrister Horace Rumpole. His novels include *Paradise Postponed* (1985) and *The Sound of Trumpets* (1998) **2** **Roger de,** 8th Baron of Wigmore and 1st Earl of March. 1287–1330, lover of Isabella, the wife of Edward II of England: they invaded England in 1326 and compelled the king to abdicate in favour of his son, Edward III; executed

mortise *or* **mortice** ('mɔːtɪs) *n* **1** a slot or recess cut into a piece of wood, stone, etc, to receive a matching projection (tenon) of another piece, or a mortise lock ▷ *vb* **mortises, mortising, mortised** *or* **mortices, morticing, morticed** *(tr)* **2** to cut a slot or recess in (a piece of wood, stone, etc) **3** to join (two pieces of wood, stone, etc) by means of a mortise and tenon [c14 from OF *mortoise*, ?from Ar. *murtazza* fastened in position]

mortise lock *n* a lock set into a mortise in a door so that the mechanism of the lock is enclosed by the door

mortmain ('mɔːt,meɪn) *n law* the state or condition of lands, buildings, etc, held inalienably, as by an ecclesiastical or other corporation [c15 from OF *mortemain*, from Med. L *mortua manus* dead hand, inalienable ownership]

Morton ('mɔːtᵊn) *n* **1** **4th Earl of,** title of *James Douglas*. 1516–81, regent of Scotland (1572–78) for the young James VI. He was implicated in the murders of Rizzio (1566) and Darnley (1567) and played a leading role in ousting Mary, Queen of Scots; executed **2** **Jelly Roll,** real name *Ferdinand Joseph La Menthe Morton*. 1885–1941, US jazz pianist, singer, and songwriter; one of the creators of New Orleans jazz

mortuary ('mɔːtʃʊərɪ) *n, pl* **mortuaries** **1** Also called: **morgue** a building where dead bodies are kept before cremation or burial ▷ *adj* **2** of or relating to death or burial [c14 (as n, a funeral gift to a parish priest): via Med. L *mortuārium* (n) from L *mortuārius* of the dead]

morwong ('mɔː,wɒŋ) *n* a food fish of Australasian coastal waters [from Abor.]

moryah (mɒr'jæ) *interj Irish.* an exclamation of annoyance, disbelief, etc [from Irish Gaelic *Mar dhea* forsooth]

mosaic (mə'zeɪɪk) *n* **1** a design or decoration made up of small pieces of coloured glass, stone, etc **2** the process of making a mosaic **3a** a mottled yellowing that occurs in the leaves of plants affected with any of various virus diseases **3b** Also called: **mosaic disease** any of the diseases, such as **tobacco mosaic,** that produce this discoloration **4** a light-sensitive surface on a television camera tube, consisting of a large number of granules of photoemissive material [c16 via F & It. from Med. L, from LGk: mosaic work, from Gk: of the Muses, from *mousa* MUSE] > **mosaicist** (mə'zeɪɪsɪst) *n*

Mosaic (məʊ'zeɪɪk) *adj* of or relating to Moses or the laws and traditions ascribed to him

Mosaic law *n Bible* the laws ascribed to Moses and contained in the Pentateuch

moschatel (,mɒskə'tɛl) *n* a small N temperate plant with greenish-white musk-scented flowers. Also called: **townhall clock, five-faced bishop** [c18 via F from It. *moscatella*, dim. of *moscato* MUSK]

Moscow ('mɒskəʊ) *n* the capital of Russia and of the Moscow Autonomous Region, on the Moskva River: dates from the 11th century; capital of the grand duchy of Russia from 1547 to 1712; capital of the Soviet Union 1918–91; centres on the medieval Kremlin; chief political, cultural, and industrial centre of Russia, with two universities. Pop: 8 389 700 (1999 est). Russian name: **Moskva** Related noun: **Muscovite**

▷ www.intourist.com/ENG/MOSCOW/info.shtml

▷ www.all-moscow.ru

Moseley ('məʊzlɪ) *n* **Henry Gwyn-Jeffreys** 1887–1915, English physicist. He showed that the wavelengths of X-rays emitted from the elements are related to their atomic numbers

Moselle (məʊ'zɛl) *n* **1** a department of NE France, in Lorraine region. Capital: Metz. Pop 1 023 447 (1999). Area: 6253 sq km (2439 sq miles) **2** a river in W Europe, rising in NE France and flowing northwest, forming part of the border between Luxembourg and Germany, then northeast to the Rhine: many vineyards along its lower course. Length: 547 km (340 miles). German name: **Mosel** ('moːzᵊl) **3** *(sometimes not capital)* a German white wine from the Moselle valley

Moses ('məʊzɪz) *n* **1** *Old Testament* the Hebrew prophet who led the Israelites out of Egypt to the Promised Land and gave them divinely revealed laws **2** **Ed** born 1956, US hurdler; winner of the 400 m hurdles in the 1976 and 1984 Olympic Games **3** **Grandma,** real name *Anna Mary*

Robertson Moses. 1860–1961, US painter of primitives, who began to paint at the age of 75

mosey ('məʊzɪ) *vb (intr) inf* (often foll by *along* or *on*) to amble [c19 from ?]

mosh (mɒʃ) *n* **1** a type of dance, performed to loud rock music, in which people throw themselves about in a frantic and violent manner ▹ *vb* **2** *(intr)* to dance in this manner [c20 of uncertain origin]

mosher ('mɒʃə) *n* **1** someone who moshes **2** (in Britain) a young person who typically enjoys rock music and skateboarding

Moshesh (mɒ'ʃɛʃ) *or* **Moshoeshoe** (mɒ'ʃuʃu) *n* died 1870, African chief, who founded the Basotho nation, now Lesotho

Moskva (*Russian* mas'kva) *n* **1** transliteration of the Russian name for **Moscow** **2** a river in W central Russia, rising in the Smolensk-Moscow upland, and flowing southeast through Moscow to the Oka River: linked with the River Volga by the Moscow Canal. Length: about 500 km (310 miles)

Moslem ('mɒzləm) *n, pl* **Moslems** *or* **Moslem** *adj* a variant of **Muslim** > **Moslemic** (mɒz'lɛmɪk) *adj* > **'Moslemism** *n*

Mosley ('məʊzlɪ) *n* Sir **Oswald Ernald** 1896–1980, British politician; founder of the British Union of Fascists (1932)

mosque (mɒsk) *n* a Muslim place of worship [c14 earlier *mosquee*, from OF via It. *moschea*, ult. from Ar. *masjid* temple]

mosquito (mə'ski:təʊ) *n, pl* **mosquitoes** *or* **mosquitos** any dipterous insect of the family Culicidae: the females have a long proboscis adapted for piercing the skin of man and animals to suck blood. See also **aedes, anopheles, culex** [c16 from Sp., dim. of *mosca* fly, from L *musca*]

mosquito net *or* **netting** *n* a fine curtain or net to keep mosquitoes out

moss (mɒs) *n* **1** any of a class of plants, typically growing in dense mats on trees, rocks, moist ground, etc **2** a clump or growth of any of these plants **3** any of various similar but unrelated plants, such as Spanish moss and reindeer moss **4** *Scot & N English* a peat bog or marsh [OE *mos* swamp] > **'moss,like** *adj* > **'mossy** *adj* > **'mossiness** *n*

Moss (mɒs) *n* **Kate** born 1974, British supermodel

moss agate *n* a variety of chalcedony with dark greenish mossy markings

mossie ('mɒsɪ) *n* another name for the **Cape sparrow** [Afrik.]

mosso ('mɒsəʊ) *adv music* to be performed with rapidity [It., pp of *muovere* to MOVE]

moss rose *n* a variety of rose that has a mossy stem and calyx and fragrant pink flowers

moss stitch *n* a knitting stitch made up of alternate plain and purl stitches

mosstrooper ('mɒs,tru:pə) *n* a raider in the Borders of England and Scotland in the mid-17th century [c17 *moss*, in dialect sense: bog]

most (məʊst) *determiner* **1a** a great majority of; nearly all: *most people like eggs* **1b** *(as pron; functioning as sing or pl)*: *most of them don't know; most of it is finished* **2 the most 2a** the superlative of **many** and **much**: *you have the most money; the most apples* **2b** *(as pron)*: *the most he can afford is two pounds* **3 at (the) most** at the maximum: *that girl is four at the most* **4 make the most of** to use to the best advantage: *she makes the most of her accent* ▹ *adv* **5 the most** used to form the superlative of some adjectives and adverbs: *he suffered the most terribly of all* **6** the superlative of **much**: *people welcome a drink most after work* **7** (intensifier): *a most absurd story* [OE *māst* or *mǣst*, whence ME *moste*, *mēst*]

> USAGE *More* and *most* should be distinguished when used in comparisons. *More* applies to cases involving two people, objects, etc, *most* to cases involving three or more: *John is the more intelligent of the two; he is the most intelligent of the students*

-most *suffix forming the superlative degree of some adjectives and adverbs: hindmost; uppermost* [OE *-mǣst*, *-mest*, orig. a sup. suffix, later mistakenly taken as from *mǣst* (adv) most]

Mostaganem (mə,stægə'nɛm) *n* a port in NW Algeria, on the Mediterranean Sea: exports wine, fruit, and vegetables. Pop: 124 399 (1998)

mostly ('məʊstlɪ) *adv* **1** almost entirely; chiefly **2** on many or most occasions; usually

Most Reverend *n* (in Britain) a courtesy title applied to Anglican and Roman Catholic archbishops

Mosul ('məʊsᵊl) *n* a city in N Iraq, on the River Tigris opposite the ruins of Nineveh: an important commercial centre with nearby Ayn Zalah oilfield; university. Pop: 664 220 (latest est)

mot (məʊ) *n* short for **bon mot** [c16 via F from Vulgar L *mottum* (unattested) utterance, from L *muttum*, from *muttīre* to mutter]

MOT *abbrev for:* **1** (in New Zealand and formerly in Britain) Ministry of Transport (*in Britain*, now Department of Transport) **2** *Brit* MOT test: a compulsory annual test for road vehicles over a certain age, which require a valid **MOT certificate**

mote (məʊt) *n* a tiny speck [OE *mot*]

motel (məʊ'tɛl) *n* a roadside hotel for motorists [c20 from *motor* + *hotel*]

motet (məʊ'tɛt) *n* a polyphonic choral composition used as an anthem in the Roman Catholic service [c14 from OF, dim. of *mot* word; see MOT]

moth (mɒθ) *n* any of numerous insects that typically have stout bodies with antennae of various shapes (but not clubbed), including large brightly coloured species, such as hawk moths, and small inconspicuous types, such as the clothes moths ▹ Cf **butterfly** (sense 1) [OE *moththe*]

mothball ('mɒθ,bɔ:l) *n* **1** a small ball of camphor or naphthalene used to repel clothes moths in stored clothing, etc **2 put in mothballs** to postpone work on (a project, activity, etc) ▹ *vb (tr)* **3** to prepare (a ship) for a long period of storage by sealing with plastic **4** to take (a factory, etc) out of operation but maintain it for future use **5** to postpone work on (a project, activity, etc)

moth-eaten *adj* **1** decayed, decrepit, or outdated **2** eaten away by or as if by moths

mother[1] ('mʌðə) *n* **1a** a female who has given birth to offspring **1b** *(as modifier)*: *a mother bird* **2** *(often cap, esp as a term of address)* a person's own mother **3** a female substituting in the function of a mother **4** *(often cap) chiefly arch* a term of address for an old woman **5a** motherly qualities, such as maternal affection: *it appealed to the mother in her* **5b** *(as modifier)*: *mother love* **5c** *(in combination)*: *mothercraft* **6a** a female or thing that creates, nurtures, protects, etc, something **6b** *(as modifier)*: *mother church; mother earth* **7** a title given to certain members of female religious orders **8** *(modifier)* native or innate: *mother wit* **9 the mother of all…** *inf* the greatest example of its kind: *the mother of all parties* ▹ *vb (tr)* **10** to give birth to or produce **11** to nurture, protect, etc as a mother [OE *mōdor*] > **'motherless** *adj*

mother[2] ('mʌðə) *n* a stringy slime containing various bacteria that forms on the surface of liquids undergoing fermentation. Also called: **mother of vinegar** [c16 ?from MOTHER[1], but cf. Sp. *madre* scum, Du. *modder* dregs, MLow G *modder* decaying object, *mudde* sludge]

Mother Carey's chicken ('kɛərɪz) *n* another name for **stormy petrel** [from ?]

mother country *n* **1** the original country of colonists or settlers **2** a person's native country

Mother Goose *n* the imaginary author of a collection of nursery rhymes [c18 translated from F *Contes de ma mère l'Oye* (1697), a collection of tales by Charles PERRAULT]

motherhood ('mʌðə,hʊd) *n* **1** the state of being a mother **2** the qualities characteristic of a mother

Mm

Mothering Sunday ('mʌðərɪŋ) *n* another name for **Mother's Day** (sense 1)
mother-in-law *n, pl* **mothers-in-law** the mother of one's wife or husband
motherland ('mʌðə,lænd) *n* a person's native country
mother lode *n mining* the principal lode in a system
motherly ('mʌðəlɪ) *adj* of or resembling a mother, esp in warmth or protectiveness > '**motherliness** *n*
mother-of-pearl *n* a hard iridescent substance that forms the inner layer of the shells of certain molluscs, such as the oyster. It is used to make buttons, etc. Also called: **nacre**
mother-out-law *n inf* the mother of one's ex-husband or ex-wife
Mother's Day *n* **1** Also called: **Mothering Sunday** *Brit* the fourth Sunday in Lent, when mothers traditionally receive presents from their children **2** *US & Canad* the second Sunday in May, observed as a day in honour of mothers
mother ship *n* a ship providing facilities and supplies for a number of small vessels
mother superior *n, pl* **mother superiors** *or* **mothers superior** the head of a community of nuns
mother tongue *n* **1** the language first learned by a child **2** a language from which another has evolved
Motherwell ('mʌðəwəl) *n* a town in S central Scotland, the administrative centre of North Lanarkshire on the River Clyde: industrial centre. Pop: 30 717 (1991)
mother wit *n* native practical intelligence; common sense
mothproof ('mɒθ,pru:f) *adj* **1** (esp of clothes) chemically treated so as to repel clothes moths ▷ *vb* **2** (*tr*) to make (clothes, etc) mothproof
mothy ('mɒθɪ) *adj* **mothier, mothiest 1** moth-eaten **2** containing moths; full of moths
motif (məʊ'ti:f) *n* **1** a distinctive idea, esp a theme elaborated on in a piece of music, literature, etc **2** Also called: **motive** a recurring shape in a design **3** a single decoration, such as a symbol or name on a jumper, sweatshirt, etc [C19 from F; see MOTIVE]
motile ('məʊtaɪl) *adj* capable of moving spontaneously and independently [C19 from L *mōtus* moved, from *movēre* to move] > **motility** (məʊ'tɪlɪtɪ) *n*
motion ('məʊʃən) *n* **1** the process of continual change in the physical position of an object; movement **2** a movement or action, esp of part of the human body; a gesture **3a** the capacity for movement **3b** a manner of movement, esp walking; gait **4** a mental impulse **5** a formal proposal to be discussed and voted on in a debate, meeting, etc **6** *law* an application made to a judge or court for an order or ruling necessary to the conduct of legal proceedings. **7** *Brit* **7a** the evacuation of the bowels **7b** excrement **8a** part of a moving mechanism **8b** the action of such a part **9 go through the motions 9a** to act or perform the task (of doing something) mechanically or without sincerity **9b** to mimic the action (of something) by gesture **10 in motion** operational or functioning (often in **set in motion, set the wheels in motion**) ▷ *vb* **11** (when *tr, may take a clause as object or an infinitive*) to signal or direct (a person) by a movement or gesture [C15 from L *mōtiō* a moving, from *movēre* to move] > '**motionless** *adj*
Motion ('məʊʃən) *n* **Andrew** born 1952, British poet and biographer; his collections include *Pleasure Steamers* (1978) and *Public Property* (2002): poet laureate from 1999
motion picture *n* a US and Canad term for **film** (sense 1)
motivate ('məʊtɪ,veɪt) *vb* **motivates, motivating, motivated** (*tr*) to give incentive to > ,**moti'vation** *n* > '**moti,vator** *n*
motivational research (,məʊtɪ'veɪʃənᵊl) *n* the application of psychology to the study of consumer behaviour, esp the planning of advertising and sales campaigns. Also called: **motivation research**
motive ('məʊtɪv) *n* **1** the reason for a certain course of action, whether conscious or unconscious **2** a variant of **motif** (sense 2) ▷ *adj* **3** of or causing motion: *a motive force* **4** of or acting as a motive; motivating ▷ *vb* **motives, motiving, motived** (*tr*) **5** to motivate [C14 from OF *motif*, from LL *mōtīvus* (adj) moving, from L *mōtus*, pp of *movēre* to move] > '**motiveless** *adj*
motive power *n* **1** any source of energy used to produce motion **2** the means of supplying power to an engine, vehicle, etc
mot juste *French* (mo ʒyst) *n, pl* ***mots justes*** (mo ʒyst). the appropriate word or expression
motley ('mɒtlɪ) *adj* **1** made up of elements of varying type, quality, etc **2** multicoloured ▷ *n* **3** a motley collection **4** the particoloured attire of a jester [C14 ?from *mot* speck]
moto ('məʊtəʊ) *n music* movement [It.]
motocross ('məʊtəʊ,krɒs) *n* **1** cross-country motorcycle racing across rough ground **2** another name for **rallycross** [C20 from MOTO(R) + CROSS(-COUNTRY)]
motor ('məʊtə) *n* **1a** the engine, esp an internal-combustion engine, of a vehicle **1b** (*as modifier*): *a motor scooter* **2** Also called: **electric motor** a machine that converts electrical energy into mechanical energy **3** any device that converts another form of energy into mechanical energy to produce motion **4a** *chiefly Brit* a car **4b** (*as modifier*): *motor spares* ▷ *adj* **5** producing or causing motion **6** *physiol* **6a** of or relating to nerves or neurons that carry impulses that cause muscles to contract **6b** of or relating to movement or to muscles that induce movement ▷ *vb* **7** (*intr*) to travel by car **8** (*tr*) *Brit* to transport by car **9** (*intr*) *inf* to move fast; make good progress [C16 from L *mōtor* a mover, from *movēre* to move]
▷ www.formula1.com
▷ www.fia.com
▷ www.imca.com
motorbicycle ('məʊtə,baɪsɪkᵊl) *n* **1** a motorcycle **2** a moped
motorbike ('məʊtə,baɪk) *n* a less formal name for **motorcycle**
motorboat ('məʊtə,bəʊt) *n* any boat powered by a motor
motorbus ('məʊtə,bʌs) *n* a bus driven by an internal-combustion engine
motorcade ('məʊtə,keɪd) *n* a parade of cars [C20 from MOTOR + CAVALCADE]
motorcar ('məʊtə,kɑ:) *n* **1** a more formal word for **car** **2** a self-propelled electric railway car
motorcycle ('məʊtə,saɪkᵊl) *n* **1** Also called: **motorbike** a two-wheeled vehicle that is driven by a petrol engine ▷ *vb* **motorcycles, motorcycling, motorcycled** (*intr*) **2** to ride on a motorcycle > '**motor,cyclist** *n*
▷ www.bmrc.co.uk
▷ www.fim.ch
▷ http://motorcycles.about.com/
▷ www.crmc.co.uk/links.htm
motor home *n* a motorized vehicle similar to a large van with living quarters in the back
motorist ('məʊtərɪst) *n* a driver of a car
motorize *or* **motorise** ('məʊtə,raɪz) *vb* **motorizes, motorizing, motorized** *or* **motorises, motorising, motorised** (*tr*) **1** to equip with a motor **2** to provide (military units) with motor vehicles > ,**motori'zation** *or* ,**motori'sation** *n*
motorman ('məʊtəmən) *n, pl* **motormen 1** the driver of an electric train **2** the operator of a motor
motormouth ('məʊtə,maʊθ) *n sl* a garrulous person
motor scooter *n* a light motorcycle with small wheels and an enclosed engine. Often shortened to **scooter**
motor vehicle *n* a road vehicle driven esp by an internal-combustion engine
motorway ('məʊtə,weɪ) *n Brit, Austral, & NZ* a main road for fast-moving traffic, having separate carriageways for vehicles travelling in opposite directions

Motown ('məʊˌtaʊn) *n trademark* music combining rhythm and blues and pop, or gospel rhythms and modern ballad harmony [C20 from *Motown Records* of Detroit, from *Mo(tor) Town*, nickname for Detroit, centre of the US car industry]
▹ www.motown.com

motte (mɒt) *n history* a mound on which a castle was erected [C14 see MOAT]

MOT test *n* (in Britain) See **MOT** (sense 2)

mottle ('mɒtᵊl) *vb* **mottles, mottling, mottled** **1** (*tr*) to colour with streaks or blotches of different shades ▹ *n* **2** a mottled appearance, as of the surface of marble [C17 back formation from MOTLEY]

mottled ('mɒtᵊld) *adj* coloured with streaks or blotches of different shades

motto ('mɒtəʊ) *n, pl* **mottoes** *or* **mottos** **1** a short saying expressing the guiding maxim or ideal of a family, organization, etc, esp when part of a coat of arms **2** a verse or maxim contained in a paper cracker **3** a quotation prefacing a book or chapter of a book [C16 via It. from L *muttum* utterance]

moue *French* (mu) *n* a pouting look

moufflon ('mu:flɒn) *n* a wild short-fleeced mountain sheep of Corsica and Sardinia [C18 via F from Romance *mufrone*, from LL *mufrō*]

mouillé ('mwi:eɪ) *adj phonetics* palatalized, as in the sounds represented by Spanish *ll* or *ñ*, (pronounced as (ʎ) and (ɲ)), or French *ll* (representing a (j) sound) [C19 from F, pp of *mouiller* to moisten, from L *mollis* soft]

moujik ('mu:ʒɪk) *n* a variant spelling of **muzhik**

mould[1] *or US* **mold** (məʊld) *n* **1** a shaped cavity used to give a definite form to fluid or plastic material **2** a frame on which something may be constructed **3** something shaped in or made on a mould **4** a shape, form, design, or pattern **5** a specific nature, character, or type ▹ *vb* (*tr*) **6** to make in a mould **7** to shape or form, as by using a mould **8** to influence or direct: *to mould opinion* **9** to cling to **10** *metallurgy* to make (a material) into a mould used in casting [C13 (n): from OF *modle*, from L *modulus* a small measure] > '**mouldable** *or US* '**moldable** *adj* > '**moulder** *or US* '**molder** *n*

mould[2] *or US* **mold** (məʊld) *n* **1** a coating or discoloration caused by various fungi that develop in a damp atmosphere on the surface of food, fabrics, etc **2** any of the fungi that cause this growth ▹ *vb* **3** to become or cause to become covered with this growth ▹ Also called: **mildew** [C15 dialect (N English) *mowlde* mouldy, from p.p. of *moulen* to become mouldy, prob. from ON]

mould[3] *or US* **mold** (məʊld) *n* loose soil, esp when rich in organic matter [OE *molde*]

mouldboard *or US* **moldboard** ('məʊldˌbɔ:d) *n* the curved blade of a plough, which turns over the furrow

moulder *or US* **molder** ('məʊldə) *vb* (often foll by *away*) to crumble or cause to crumble, as through decay [C16 verbal use of MOULD[3]]

moulding *or US* **molding** ('məʊldɪŋ) *n* **1** *archit* **1a** a shaped outline, esp one used on cornices, etc **1b** a shaped strip made of wood, stone, etc **2** something moulded

mouldy *or US* **moldy** ('məʊldɪ) *adj* **mouldier, mouldiest** *or US* **moldier, moldiest** **1** covered with mould **2** stale or musty, esp from age or lack of use **3** *sl* boring; dull > '**mouldiness** *or US* '**moldiness** *n*

Moulin (*French* mulɛ̃) *n* **Jean** (ʒɑ̃) 1899–1943, French lawyer and Resistance hero; Chairman of the National Council of the Resistance (1943): tortured to death by the Nazis

Moulins (*French* mulɛ̃) *n* a market town in central France, on the Allier River. Pop: 23 350 (1990)

Moulmein (maʊl'meɪn) *n* a port in S Myanmar, near the mouth of the Salween River: exports teak and rice. Pop: 307 600 (1993 est)

moult *or US* **molt** (məʊlt) *vb* **1** (of birds, mammals, arthropods, etc) to shed (feathers, hair, or cuticle) in order that new growth can take place ▹ *n* **2** the periodic process of moulting [C14 *mouten*, from OE *mūtian*, as in *bimūtian* to exchange for, from L *mūtāre* to change] > '**moulter** *or US* '**molter** *n*

mound (maʊnd) *n* **1** a raised mass of earth, debris, etc **2** any heap or pile: *a mound of washing* **3** a small natural hill **4** an artificial ridge of earth, stone, etc, as used for defence ▹ *vb* **5** (often foll by *up*) to gather into a mound; heap **6** (*tr*) to cover or surround with a mound: *to mound a grave* [C16 earthwork, ?from OE *mund* hand, hence defence]

Mound Builder *n* a member of a group of prehistoric inhabitants of the Mississippi region of the US, who built altar mounds, barrows, etc

mound-builder *n* another name for **megapode**

mount[1] (maʊnt) *vb* **1** to go up (a hill, stairs, etc); climb **2** to get up on (a horse, a platform, etc) **3** (*intr*; often foll by *up*) to increase; accumulate: *excitement mounted* **4** (*tr*) to fix onto a backing, setting, or support: *to mount a photograph; to mount a slide* **5** (*tr*) to provide with a horse for riding, or to place on a horse **6** (of male animals) to climb onto (a female animal) for copulation **7** (*tr*) to prepare (a play, etc) for production **8** (*tr*) to plan and organize (a campaign, etc) **9** (*tr*) to prepare (a skeleton, etc) for exhibition as a specimen **10** (*tr*) to place or carry (weapons) in such a position that they can be fired **11 mount guard** See **guard** ▹ *n* **12** a backing, setting, or support onto which something is fixed **13** the act or manner of mounting **14** a horse for riding **15** a slide used in microscopy [C16 from OF *munter*, from Vulgar L *montāre* (unattested) from L *mons* MOUNT[2]] > '**mountable** *adj* > '**mounter** *n*

mount[2] (maʊnt) *n* a mountain or hill: used in literature and (when cap) in proper names: *Mount Everest* [OE *munt*, from L *mons* mountain, but infl. in ME by OF *mont*]

mountain ('maʊntɪn) *n* **1a** a natural upward projection of the earth's surface, higher and steeper than a hill **1b** (*as modifier*): *mountain scenery* **1c** (*in combination*): *a mountaintop* **2** a huge heap or mass: *a mountain of papers* **3** anything of great quantity or size **4** a surplus of a commodity, esp in the European Union: *a butter mountain* [C13 from OF *montaigne*, ult. from L *montānus*, from *mons* mountain]

mountain ash *n* **1** any of various trees, such as the European mountain ash or rowan, having clusters of small white flowers and bright red berries **2** any of several Australian eucalyptus trees, such as *Eucalyptus regnans*

mountain avens *n* See **avens** (sense 2)

mountain bike *n* a type of sturdy bicycle with at least 16 gears, straight handlebars, and heavy-duty tyres
▹ www.imba.com

mountain cat *n* any of various wild feline mammals, such as the bobcat, lynx, or puma

mountaineer (ˌmaʊntɪ'nɪə) *n* **1** a person who climbs mountains **2** a person living in a mountainous area ▹ *vb* **3** (*intr*) to climb mountains > ˌ**mountain'eering** *n*
▹ www.thebmc.co.uk
▹ www.uiaa.ch

mountain goat *n* any wild goat inhabiting mountainous regions

mountain laurel *n* any of various ericaceous shrubs or trees of E North America having leathery poisonous leaves and clusters of pink or white flowers. Also called: **calico bush**

mountain lion *n* another name for **puma**

mountainous ('maʊntɪnəs) *adj* **1** of or relating to mountains: *a mountainous region* **2** like a mountain, esp in size or impressiveness

mountain sickness *n* nausea, headache, and shortness

Mm

of breath caused by climbing to high altitudes. Also called: **altitude sickness**

Mountbatten (maʊntˈbætᵊn) *n* **Louis (Francis Albert Victor Nicholas)**, 1st Earl Mountbatten of Burma 1900–79, British naval commander; great-grandson of Queen Victoria. During World War II he was supreme allied commander in SE Asia (1943–46) He was the last viceroy of India (1947) and governor general (1947–48); killed by an IRA bomb

Mount Desert Island *n* an island off the coast of Maine: lakes and granite peaks. Area: 279 sq km (108 sq miles)

mountebank (ˈmaʊntɪˌbæŋk) *n* **1** (formerly) a person who sold quack medicines in public places **2** a charlatan; fake ▷ *vb* **3** (*intr*) to play the mountebank [C16 from It. *montambanco* a climber on a bench, from *montare* to MOUNT[1] + *banco* BENCH] > ˌ**mounteˈbankery** *n*

mounted (ˈmaʊntɪd) *adj* **1** riding horses: *mounted police* **2** provided with a support, backing, etc

Mountie *or* **Mounty** (ˈmaʊntɪ) *n, pl* **Mounties** *inf* a member of the Royal Canadian Mounted Police [from MOUNTED]

mounting (ˈmaʊntɪŋ) *n* another word for **mount**[1] (sense 12)

mounting-block *n* a block of stone formerly used to aid a person when mounting a horse

Mount Isa (ˈaɪzə) *n* a city in NE Australia in NW Queensland: mining of copper and other minerals. Pop: 24 104 (1988 est)

Mount McKinley National Park (məˈkɪnlɪ) *n* a national park in S central Alaska: contains part of the Alaska Range Area: 7847 sq km (3030 sq miles)

Mount Rainier National Park (ˈraɪnɪə, reɪˈnɪə, rə-) *n* a national park in W Washington, in the Cascade Range. Area: 976 sq km (377 sq miles)

mourn (mɔːn) *vb* **1** to feel or express sadness for the death or loss of (someone or something) **2** (*intr*) to observe the customs of mourning, as by wearing black [OE *murnan*] > ˈ**mourner** *n*

mournful (ˈmɔːnfʊl) *adj* **1** evoking grief; sorrowful **2** gloomy; sad > ˈ**mournfully** *adv* > ˈ**mournfulness** *n*

mourning (ˈmɔːnɪŋ) *n* **1** the act or feelings of one who mourns; grief **2** the conventional symbols of grief, such as the wearing of black **3** the period of time during which a death is officially mourned ▷ *adj* **4** of or relating to mourning > ˈ**mourningly** *adv*

mourning band *n* a piece of black material, esp an armband, worn to indicate that the wearer is in mourning

mourning dove *n* a brown North American dove with a plaintive song

mouse *n* (maʊs), *pl* **mice** (maɪs) **1** any of numerous small long-tailed rodents that are similar to but smaller than rats. See also **fieldmouse, harvest mouse, house mouse** **2** any of various related rodents, such as the jumping mouse **3** a quiet, timid, or cowardly person **4** *computing* a hand-held device used to control cursor movements and computing functions without keying **5** *sl* a black eye ▷ *vb* (maʊz), **mouses, mousing, moused** **6** to stalk and catch (mice, etc) **7** (*intr*) to go about stealthily [OE *mūs*] > ˈ**mouseˌlike** *adj*

mousemat (ˈmaʊsˌmæt) *n* a piece of material on which a computer mouse is moved

mouseover (ˈmaʊsˌəʊvə) *n computing* (on the page of a website) an item, esp a graphic, that changes or pops up when the pointer of a mouse moves over it

mouser (ˈmaʊzə, ˈmaʊsə) *n* a cat or other animal that is used to catch mice

mousetrap (ˈmaʊsˌtræp) *n* **1** any trap for catching mice, esp one with a spring-loaded metal bar that is released by the taking of the bait **2** *Brit inf* cheese of indifferent quality

moussaka *or* **mousaka** (mʊˈsɑːkə) *n* a dish originating in the Balkan States, consisting of meat, aubergines, and tomatoes, topped with cheese sauce [C20 from Mod. Gk]

mousse (muːs) *n* **1** a light creamy dessert made with eggs, cream, fruit, etc, set with gelatine **2** a similar dish made from fish or meat **3** short for **styling mousse** [C19 from F: froth]

mousseline (*French* muslin) *n* **1** a fine fabric made of rayon or silk **2** a type of fine glass [C17 F: MUSLIN]

Moussorgsky (mʊˈsɔːgskɪ; *Russian* ˈmusərkskij) *n* a variant spelling of (Modest Petrovich) **Mussorgsky**

moustache *or US* **mustache** (məˈstɑːʃ) *n* **1** the unshaved growth of hair on the upper lip **2** a similar growth of hair or bristles (in animals) **3** a mark like a moustache [C16 via F from It. *mostaccio*, ult. from Doric Gk *mustax* upper lip] > **mousˈtached** *or US* **musˈtached** *adj*

moustache cup *n* a cup with a partial cover to protect a drinker's moustache

Mousterian (muːˈstɪərɪən) *n* **1** a culture characterized by flint flake tools and associated with Neanderthal man, dating from before 70 000–32 000 BC ▷ *adj* **2** of or relating to this culture [C20 from F *moustérien*, from archaeological finds of the same period in the cave of *Le Moustier*, Dordogne, France]

mousy *or* **mousey** (ˈmaʊsɪ) *adj* **mousier, mousiest** **1** resembling a mouse, esp in hair colour **2** shy or ineffectual **3** infested with mice > ˈ**mousily** *adv* > ˈ**mousiness** *n*

mouth *n* (maʊθ), *pl* **mouths** (maʊðz) **1** the opening through which many animals take in food and issue vocal sounds **2** the system of organs surrounding this opening, including the lips, tongue, teeth, etc **3** the visible part of the lips on the face **4** a person regarded as a consumer of food: *four mouths to feed* **5** a particular manner of speaking: *a foul mouth* **6** *inf* boastful, rude, or excessive talk: *he is all mouth* **7** the point where a river issues into a sea or lake **8** the opening of a container, such as a jar **9** the opening of a cave, tunnel, volcano, etc **10** that part of the inner lip of a horse on which the bit acts **11** a pout; grimace **12** **down in** *or* **at the mouth** in low spirits ▷ *vb* (maʊð) **13** to speak or say (something) insincerely, esp in public **14** (*tr*) to form (words) with movements of the lips but without speaking **15** (*tr*) to take (something) into the mouth or to move (something) around inside the mouth **16** (*intr*; usually foll by *at*) to make a grimace [OE *mūth*]

mouthful (ˈmaʊθˌfʊl) *n, pl* **mouthfuls** **1** as much as is held in the mouth at one time **2** a small quantity, as of food **3** a long word or phrase that is difficult to say **4** *Brit inf* an abusive response

mouth off *vb* (*intr, adv*) *Brit inf* to give an opinion or speak emotionally, often without much care or consideration

mouth organ *n* another name for **harmonica**

mouthpart (ˈmaʊθˌpɑːt) *n* any of the paired appendages in arthropods that surround the mouth and are specialized for feeding

mouthpiece (ˈmaʊθˌpiːs) *n* **1** the part of a wind instrument into which the player blows **2** the part of a telephone receiver into which a person speaks **3** the part of a container forming its mouth **4** a person who acts as a spokesman, as for an organization **5** a publication expressing the official views of an organization

mouthwash (ˈmaʊθˌwɒʃ) *n* a medicated solution for gargling and cleansing the mouth

mouthy (ˈmaʊðɪ) *adj* **mouthier, mouthiest** bombastic; excessively talkative

mouton (ˈmuːtɒn) *n* sheepskin processed to resemble the fur of another animal, esp beaver or seal [from F: sheep]

movable *or* **moveable** (ˈmuːvəbᵊl) *adj* **1** able to be moved; not fixed **2** (esp of Easter) varying in date from year to year **3** (usually spelt **moveable**) *law* denoting or relating to personal property as opposed to realty ▷ *n*

4 (*often pl*) a movable article, esp a piece of furniture > ˌ**mova'bility** *or* '**movableness** *n* > '**movably** *adv*

move (muːv) *vb* **moves, moving, moved** 1 to go or take from one place to another; change in position 2 (*usually intr*) to change (one's dwelling, place of business, etc) 3 to be or cause to be in motion; stir 4 (*intr*) (of machines, etc) to work or operate 5 (*tr*) to cause (to do something); prompt 6 (*intr*) to begin to act: *move soon or we'll lose the order* 7 (*intr*) to associate oneself with a specified social circle: *to move in exalted spheres* 8 (*intr*) to make progress 9 (*tr*) to arouse affection, pity, or compassion in; touch 10 (in board games) to change the position of (a piece) or (of a piece) to change position 11 (*intr*) (of merchandise) to be disposed of by being bought 12 (when *tr*, *often takes a clause as object*; when *intr*, often foll by *for*) to suggest (a proposal) formally, as in debating or parliamentary procedure 13 (*intr*; usually foll by *on* or *along*) to go away or to another place; leave 14 to cause (the bowels) to evacuate or (of the bowels) to be evacuated ▷ *n* 15 the act of moving; movement 16 one of a sequence of actions, usually part of a plan; manoeuvre 17 the act of moving one's residence, place of business, etc 18 (in board games) 18a a player's turn to move his or her piece 18b a manoeuvre of a piece 19 **get a move on** *inf* 19a to get started 19b to hurry up 20 **on the move** 20a travelling from place to place 20b advancing; succeeding 20c very active; busy [c13 from Anglo-F *mover*, from L *movēre*]

move in *vb* (*mainly adverb*) 1 (*also prep*) Also (when *preposition*): **move into** to occupy or take possession of (a new residence, place of business, etc) 2 (*intr*; often foll by *on*) *inf* to creep close (to), as in preparing to capture 3 (*intr*; often foll by *on*) *inf* to try to gain power or influence (over)

movement ('muːvmənt) *n* 1a the act, process, or result of moving 1b an instance of moving 2 the manner of moving 3a a group of people with a common ideology 3b the organized action of such a group 4 a trend or tendency 5 the driving and regulating mechanism of a watch or clock 6 (*often pl*) a person's location and activities during a specific time 7a the evacuation of the bowels 7b the matter evacuated 8 *music* a principal self-contained section of a symphony, sonata, etc 9 tempo or pace, as in music or literature 10 *fine arts* the appearance of motion in painting, sculpture, etc 11 *prosody* the rhythmic structure of verse 12 a positional change by one or a number of military units 13 a change in the market price of a security or commodity

mover ('muːvə) *n* 1 *inf* a person, business, idea, etc, that is advancing or progressing 2 a person or thing that moves 3 a person who moves a proposal, as in a debate 4 *US & Canad* a removal firm or a person who works for one

movers and shakers *pl n inf* the people with power and influence in a particular field of activity [c20 ? from the line "We are the movers and shakers of the world for ever" in 'Ode' by Arthur O'Shaughnessy (1844–81), Brit poet]

movie ('muːvɪ) *n* **a** an informal word for **film** (sense 1) **b** (*as modifier*): *movie ticket*

moving ('muːvɪŋ) *adj* 1 arousing or touching the emotions 2 changing or capable of changing position 3 causing motion > '**movingly** *adv*

moving staircase *or* **stairway** *n* less common terms for **escalator** (sense 1)

mow (məʊ) *vb* **mows, mowing, mowed; mowed** *or* **mown** 1 to cut down (grass, crops, etc), with a hand implement or machine 2 (*tr*) to cut the growing vegetation of (a field, lawn, etc) [OE *māwan*] > '**mower** *n*

mow down *vb* (*tr, adv*) to kill in large numbers, esp by gunfire

mown (məʊn) *vb* the past participle of **mow**

Moya ('mɔɪjə) *n* **(John) Hidalgo** 1920–94, British architect: in partnership with Philip Powell, his designs include Skylon, Festival of Britain (1950), Wolfson College, Oxford (1974), and the Queen Elizabeth Conference Centre, Westminster (1986)

Moyle (mɔɪl) *n* a district of NE Northern Ireland, in Co Antrim. Pop: 15 933 (2001) Area: 494 sq km (191 sq miles)

Mozambique (ˌməʊzəm'biːk) *n* a republic in SE Africa: colonized by the Portuguese from 1505 onwards and a slave-trade centre until 1878; made an overseas province of Portugal in 1951; became an independent republic in 1975; became a member of the Commonwealth in 1995. Official language: Portuguese. Religion: animist majority. Currency: metical. Capital: Maputo. Pop: 19 371 000 (2001 est). Area: 812 379 sq km (313 661 sq miles). Portuguese name: **Moçambique** Also called (until 1975): **Portuguese East Africa**
▷ www.mozambique.mz

Mozambique Channel *n* a strait between Mozambique and Madagascar. Length: about 1600 km (1000 miles). Width: 400 km (250 miles)

Mozart ('məʊtsɑːt) *n* **Wolfgang Amadeus** ('vɔlfgaŋ ama'deːʊs) 1756–91, Austrian composer. A child prodigy and prolific genius, his works include operas, such as *The Marriage of Figaro* (1786), *Don Giovanni* (1787), and *The Magic Flute* (1791), symphonies, concertos for piano, violin, clarinet, and French horn, string quartets and quintets, sonatas, songs, and Masses, such as the unfinished *Requiem* (1791)

mozzarella (ˌmɒtsə'rɛlə) *n* a moist white curd cheese originally made in Italy from buffalo milk [from It., dim. of *mozza* a type of cheese, from *mozzare* to cut off]

mp 1 *abbrev. for* melting point ▷ 2 *music symbol for* mezzo piano [It.: moderately soft]

MP *abbrev for*: 1 (in Britain, Canada, etc) Member of Parliament 2 (in Britain) Metropolitan Police 3 Military Police 4 Mounted Police

MP3 ('ɛm'piː'θriː) *n computing* **a** a format used for the digital compression of audio files without loss of sound quality, used extensively on the World Wide Web **b** an audio file held in this format [c20 from MP(EG, *Audio Layer-*)3]

MPEG ('ɛmpɛg) *n computing* **a** a standard compressed file format used for audio and video files **b** a file in this format **c** (*as modifier*): *an MPEG video* [c20 technique devised by the *M(otion) P(icture) E(xperts) G(roup)*]

mpg *abbrev for* miles per gallon

mph *abbrev for* miles per hour

MPhil *or* **MPh** *abbrev for* Master of Philosophy

MPP (in Canada) *abbrev for* Member of Provincial Parliament

Mpumalanga (ᵊm'pʌmɑːˌlɑːŋgə) *n* a province of E South Africa. Capital: Nelspruit. Pop: 3 007 100 (1995 est). Area: 78 370 sq km (30 259 sq miles)
▷ http://mpulanga.mpu.gov.za
▷ www.mpulanga.com

MPV *abbrev for* multipurpose vehicle

Mr ('mɪstə) *n, pl* **Messrs** a title used before a man's name or before some office that he holds: *Mr Jones; Mr President* [c17 abbrev of MISTER]

MR *abbrev for*: 1 (in Britain) Master of the Rolls 2 motivation(al) research

MRA *abbrev for*: 1 magnetic resonance angiography 2 Moral Rearmament

MRC (in Britain) *abbrev for* Medical Research Council

MRI *abbrev for* magnetic resonance imaging

mRNA *abbrev for* messenger RNA

MRP *abbrev for* manufacturers' recommended price

Mrs ('mɪsɪz) *n, pl* **Mrs** *or* **Mesdames** a title used before the name or names of a married woman [c17 orig. abbrev of MISTRESS]

MRSA *abbrev for* methicillin-resistant *Staphylococcus aureus*: a bacterium that enters the skin through open wounds to cause septicaemia and is extremely resistant to most

Mm

antibiotics. It has been responsible for outbreaks of untreatable infections among patients in hospitals

Ms (mɪz, məz) *n* a title substituted for **Mrs** or **Miss** to avoid making a distinction between married and unmarried women

MS *abbrev for:* **1** Master of Surgery **2** (on gravestones, etc) memoriae sacrum [L: sacred to the memory of] **3** multiple sclerosis

MS. *or* **ms.** *pl* **MSS** *or* **mss** *abbrev for* manuscript

MSc *abbrev for* Master of Science

MSD (in New Zealand) *abbrev for* Ministry of Social Development

MS-DOS (ɛm'ɛs'dɒs) *n trademark, computers* a type of disk operating system [c20 from *M(icro)s(oft)*, the company that developed it, + DOS]

MSG *abbrev for* monosodium glutamate

Msgr *abbrev for* Monsignor

MSP *abbrev for* Member of the Scottish Parliament

MST *abbrev for* Mountain Standard Time

Mt *or* **mt** *abbrev for:* **1** mount: *Mt Everest* **2** Also: **mtn** mountain

MT *abbrev for* Montana

MTech *abbrev for* Master of Technology

mtg *abbrev for:* **1** meeting **2** Also: **mtge** mortgage

MTV *abbrev for* music television: a US music channel that operates 24 hours a day

mu (mju:) *n* the 12th letter in the Greek alphabet (Μ, μ)

Mubarak (mʊ'bɑ:rək) *n* (**Muhammad**) **Hosni** ('hʊsnɪ) born 1928, Egyptian statesman; president of Egypt from 1981

much (mʌtʃ) *determiner* **1a** (*usually used with a negative*) a great quantity or degree of: *there isn't much honey left* **1b** (*as pron*): *much has been learned from this* **2** **a bit much** *inf* rather excessive **3** **make much of** **3a** (*used with a negative*) to make sense of: *he couldn't make much of her babble* **3b** to give importance to: *she made much of this fact* **3c** to pay flattering attention to: *the reporters made much of the film star* **4** **not much of** not to any appreciable degree or extent: *he's not much of an actor really* **5** **not up to much** *inf* of a low standard: *this beer is not up to much* ▷ *adv* **6** considerably: *they're much better now* **7** practically; nearly (esp in **much the same**) **8** (*usually used with a negative*) often; a great deal: *it doesn't happen much in this country* **9** (**as**) **much as** even though; although: *much as I'd like to, I can't come* ▷ See also **more, most** [OE *mycel*]

muchness ('mʌtʃnɪs) *n* **1** *arch or inf* magnitude **2** **much of a muchness** *Brit* very similar

mucilage ('mju:sɪlɪdʒ) *n* **1** a sticky preparation, such as gum or glue, used as an adhesive **2** a complex glutinous carbohydrate secreted by certain plants [c14 via OF from LL *mūcilāgo* mouldy juice, from L, from *mucēre* to be mouldy] > **mucilaginous** (ˌmju:sɪ'lædʒɪnəs) *adj*

muck (mʌk) *n* **1** farmyard dung or decaying vegetable matter **2** an organic soil rich in humus and used as a fertilizer **3** dirt or filth **4** *sl, chiefly Brit* rubbish **5** **make a muck of** *sl, chiefly Brit* to ruin or spoil ▷ *vb* (*tr*) **6** to spread manure upon (fields, etc) **7** to soil or pollute **8** (usually foll by *up*) *Brit sl* to ruin or spoil **9** (often foll by *out*) to clear muck from [c13 prob. from ON] > '**mucky** *adj*

muck about *vb Brit sl* **1** (*intr*) to waste time; misbehave **2** (when *intr*, foll by *with*) to interfere (with), annoy, or waste the time (of)

mucker ('mʌkə) *n Brit sl* **a** a friend; mate **b** a coarse person > '**muckerish** *adj*

muck in *vb* (*intr, adv*) *Brit sl* to share duties, work, etc (with other people)

muckrake ('mʌkˌreɪk) *vb* **muckrakes, muckraking, muckraked** (*intr*) to seek out and expose scandal, esp concerning public figures > '**muckˌraker** *n* > '**muckˌraking** *n*

mucksweat ('mʌkˌswɛt) *n Brit inf* profuse sweat or a state of profuse sweating

mucous ('mju:kəs) *adj* of, resembling, or secreting mucus [c17 from L *mūcōsus* slimy, from MUCUS] > **mucosity** (mju:'kɒsɪtɪ) *n*

> **USAGE** The noun *mucus* is often misspelt *mucous*. *Mucous* can only be correctly used as an adjective

mucous membrane *n* a mucus-secreting membrane that lines body cavities or passages that are open to the external environment

mucus ('mju:kəs) *n* the slimy protective secretion of the mucous membranes [c17 from L: nasal secretions; cf. *mungere* to blow the nose]

> **USAGE** See at **mucous**

mud (mʌd) *n* **1** a fine-grained soft wet deposit that occurs on the ground after rain, at the bottom of ponds, etc **2** *inf* slander or defamation **3** **clear as mud** *inf* not at all clear **4** **here's mud in your eye** *inf* a humorous drinking toast **5** (**someone's**) **name is mud** *inf* (someone) is disgraced **6** **throw** (*or* **sling**) **mud at** *inf* to slander; vilify ▷ *vb* **muds, mudding, mudded** **7** (*tr*) to soil or cover with mud [c14 prob. from MLow G *mudde*]

mud bath *n* **1** a medicinal bath in heated mud **2** a dirty or muddy occasion, state, etc

mudbrick ('mʌdˌbrɪk) *n* a brick made with mud

mud crab *n* a large edible crab, *Scylla serrata*, of Australian mangrove regions

muddle ('mʌdᵊl) *vb* **muddles, muddling, muddled** (*tr*) **1** (often foll by *up*) to mix up (objects, items, etc) **2** to confuse **3** *US* to mix or stir (alcoholic drinks, etc) ▷ *n* **4** a state of physical or mental confusion [c16 ?from MDu. *moddelen* to make muddy] > '**muddled** *adj* > '**muddler** *n* > '**muddling** *adj, n*

muddleheaded (ˌmʌdᵊl'hɛdɪd) *adj* mentally confused or vague > ˌ**muddle'headedness** *n*

muddle through *vb* (*intr, adv*) *chiefly Brit* to succeed in spite of lack of organization

muddy ('mʌdɪ) *adj* **muddier, muddiest** **1** covered or filled with mud **2** not clear or bright: *muddy colours* **3** cloudy: *a muddy liquid* **4** (esp of thoughts) confused or vague ▷ *vb* **muddies, muddying, muddied** **5** to become or cause to become muddy > '**muddily** *adv* > '**muddiness** *n*

mudfish ('mʌdˌfɪʃ) *n, pl* **mudfish** *or* **mudfishes** any of various fishes, such as the bowfin, that live at the muddy bottoms of rivers, lakes, etc

mud flat *n* a tract of low muddy land that is covered at high tide and exposed at low tide

mudflow ('mʌdˌfləʊ) *n geol* a flow of soil or fine-grained sediment mixed with water down a steep unstable slope

mudguard ('mʌdˌgɑ:d) *n* a curved part of a motorcycle, bicycle, etc, attached above the wheels to reduce the amount of water or mud thrown up by them. US and Canad name: **fender**

mud hen *n* any of various birds that frequent marshes, esp the coots, rails, etc

mudlark ('mʌdˌlɑ:k) *n* **1** (formerly) a person who made a living by picking up odds and ends in the mud of tidal rivers **2** *sl, now rare* a street urchin **3** *Austral sl* a racehorse that runs well on a wet or muddy course

mud map *n Austral* **1** a rough map drawn on the ground with a stick **2** any rough sketch map

mudpack ('mʌdˌpæk) *n* a cosmetic astringent paste containing fuller's earth

mud puppy *n* an aquatic North American salamander having persistent larval features

mudskipper ('mʌdˌskɪpə) *n* any of various gobies that occur in tropical coastal regions of Africa and Asia and can move on land by means of their strong pectoral fins

mudslinging ('mʌdˌslɪŋɪŋ) *n* casting malicious slurs on an opponent, esp in politics > '**mudˌslinger** *n*

mudstone ('mʌdˌstəʊn) *n* a dark grey clay rock similar to shale

mud turtle *n* any of various small turtles that inhabit muddy rivers in North and Central America

muesli ('mju:zlɪ) *n* a mixture of rolled oats, nuts, fruit, etc, usually eaten with milk [Swiss G, from G *Mus* mush, purée + *-li*, dim. suffix]

muesli bar *n* a snack made of compressed muesli ingredients

muezzin (mu:'ɛzɪn) *n Islam* the official of a mosque who calls the faithful to prayer from the minaret [c16 from Ar. *mu'adhdhin*]

muff[1] (mʌf) *n* an open-ended cylinder of fur or cloth into which the hands are placed for warmth [c16 prob. from Du. *mof*, ult. from F *mouffle* MUFFLE[1]]

muff[2] (mʌf) *vb* **1** to perform (an action) awkwardly **2** (*tr*) to bungle (a shot, catch, etc) ▷ *n* **3** any unskilful play, esp a dropped catch **4** any bungled action **5** a bungler [c19 from ?]

muffin ('mʌfɪn) *n* **1** *Brit* a thick round baked yeast roll, usually toasted and served with butter **2** *US & Canad* a small cup-shaped sweet bread roll, usually eaten hot with butter [c18 ?from Low G *muffen* cakes]

muffle[1] ('mʌf°l) *vb* **muffles, muffling, muffled** (*mainly tr*) **1** (*also intr; often foll by up*) to wrap up (the head) in a scarf, cloak, etc, esp for warmth **2** (*also intr*) to deaden (a sound or noise), esp by wrapping **3** to prevent (the expression of something) by (someone) ▷ *n* **4** something that muffles **5** a kiln with an inner chamber for firing porcelain, enamel, etc [c15 prob. from OF; cf. OF *moufle* mitten, *emmouflé* wrapped up]

muffle[2] ('mʌf°l) *n* the fleshy hairless part of the upper lip and nose in ruminants and some rodents [c17 from F *mufle*, from ?]

muffler ('mʌflə) *n* **1** a thick scarf, collar, etc **2** the US and Canad name for **silencer** (sense 1)

mufti ('mʌftɪ) *n* civilian dress, esp as worn by a person who normally wears a military uniform [c19 ?from MUFTI]

Mufti ('mʌftɪ) *n, pl* **Muftis** a Muslim legal expert and adviser on the law of the Koran [c16 from Ar. *muftī*, from *aftā* to give a (legal) decision]

Mufulira (ˌmu:fu:'lɪərə) *n* a mining town in the Copper Belt of Zambia. Pop: 152 944 (1990)

mug[1] (mʌg) *n* **1** a drinking vessel with a handle, usually cylindrical and made of earthenware **2** Also called: **mugful** the quantity held by a mug or its contents [c16 prob. of Scand. origin]

mug[2] (mʌg) *n* **1** *sl* a person's face or mouth: *get your ugly mug out of here!* **2** *Brit sl* a gullible person, esp one who is swindled easily **3 a mug's game** a worthless activity ▷ *vb* **mugs, mugging, mugged 4** (*tr*) *inf* to attack or rob (someone) violently [c18 ?from MUG[1], since drinking vessels were sometimes modelled into the likeness of a face] > **'mugger** *n*

Mugabe (mʊ'gɑ:bɪ) *n* **Robert** born 1925, Zimbabwean politician; leader of one wing of the Patriotic Front against the government of Ian Smith of Rhodesia, and of the Zanu party; prime minister (1980–87); president from 1988

muggins ('mʌgɪnz) *n* (*functioning as sing*) **1** *Brit sl* **1a** a simpleton **1b** a title used humorously to refer to oneself as a dupe or victim **2** a card game [c19 prob. from the surname *Muggins*]

muggy ('mʌgɪ) *adj* **muggier, muggiest** (of weather, air, etc) unpleasantly warm and humid [c18 dialect *mug* drizzle, prob. of Scand. origin] > **'mugginess** *n*

Mughal ('mu:gɑ:l) *n* a variant spelling of **Mogul**

mug shot *n inf* a photograph of a person's face, esp one resembling a police-file picture

mug up *vb* (*adv*) *Brit sl* to study (a subject) hard, esp for an exam [c19 from ?]

Muhammad (mʊ'hæməd) *n* a variant of **Mohammed**

Muhammad Ali, Muhammed Ali, or **Mohammed Ali** ('ɑ:lɪ, ɑ:'li:, 'ælɪ) *n* original name *Cassius (Marcellus) Clay*. born 1942, US boxer, who was world heavyweight champion three times (1964–67; 1974–78; 1978)

Muhammadan or **Muhammedan** (mʊ'hæməd°n) *n, adj* another word (not in Muslim use) for **Muslim**

Mühlhausen (my:l'hauzən) *n* the German name for **Mulhouse**

Muir (mjʊə) *n* **Edwin** 1887–1959, Scottish poet, novelist, and critic

Muir Glacier (mjʊə) *n* a glacier in SE Alaska, in the St Elias Mountains, flowing southeast from Mount Fairweather. Area: about 900 sq km (350 sq miles)

mujaheddin or **mujahedeen** (ˌmu:dʒəhə'di:n) *pl n* (preceded by *the*; *sometimes cap*) (in Afghanistan and Iran) fundamentalist Muslim guerrillas. In Afghanistan in 1992 the mujaheddin overthrew the government but were unable to agree on a new constitution and were themselves overthrown by the Taliban militia in 1996 [c20 from Ar. *mujāhidīn* fighters, ult. from JIHAD]

Mukden ('mʊkdən) *n* a former name of **Shenyang**

mukluk ('mʌklʌk) *n* a soft boot, usually of sealskin, worn by Inuit [from Inuktitut *muklok* large seal]

muktuk ('mʌktʌk) *n Canad* the thin outer skin of the beluga, used as food [from Inuktitut]

mulatto (mju:'lætəʊ) *n, pl* **mulattos** or **mulattoes 1** a person having one Black and one White parent ▷ *adj* **2** of a light brown colour; tawny [c16 from Sp. *mulato* young mule, var. of *mulo* MULE[1]]

mulberry ('mʌlbərɪ, -brɪ) *n, pl* **mulberries 1** a tree having edible blackberry-like fruit, such as the white mulberry, the leaves of which are used to feed silkworms **2** the fruit of any of these trees **3** any of several similar or related trees **4a** a dark purple colour **4b** (*as adj*): *a mulberry dress* [c14 from L *mōrum*, from Gk *moron*; rel. to OE *mōrberie*]

mulch (mʌltʃ) *n* **1** half-rotten vegetable matter, peat, etc, used to prevent soil erosion or enrich the soil ▷ *vb* **2** (*tr*) to cover (the surface of land) with mulch [c17 from obs. *mulch* soft; rel. to OE *mylisc* mellow]

Mulciber ('mʌlsɪbə) *n* another name for **Vulcan**

mulct (mʌlkt) *vb* (*tr*) **1** to cheat or defraud **2** to fine (a person) ▷ *n* **3** a fine or penalty [c15 via F from L *multa* a fine]

Muldoon (mʌl'du:n) *n* Sir **Robert David** 1921–92, New Zealand statesman; prime minister of New Zealand (1975–84)

mule[1] (mju:l) *n* **1** the sterile offspring of a male donkey and a female horse, used as a beast of burden **2** any hybrid animal: *a mule canary* **3** Also called: **spinning mule** a machine that spins cotton into yarn and winds the yarn on spindles **4** *inf* an obstinate or stubborn person [c13 from OF *mul*, from L *mūlus* ass, mule]

mule[2] (mju:l) *n* a backless shoe or slipper [c16 from OF from L *mulleus* a magistrate's shoe]

muleta (mju:'lɛtə) *n* the small cape attached to a stick used by the matador during a bullfight [Sp.: small mule, crutch, from *mula* MULE[1]]

muleteer (ˌmju:lɪ'tɪə) *n* a person who drives mules

mulga ('mʌlgə) *n Austral* **1** any of various Australian acacia shrubs **2** scrub comprised of a dense growth of acacia **3** *inf* the outback; bush [from Abor.]

Mulhacén (*Spanish* mula'θen) *n* a mountain in S Spain, in the Sierra Nevada: the highest peak in Spain Height: 3478 m (11 410 ft)

Mülheim an der Ruhr (*German* 'my:lhaim an der 'ru:r) or **Mülheim** *n* an industrial city in W Germany, in North Rhine-Westphalia on the River Ruhr: river port. Pop: 174 300 (1999 est)

Mulhouse (*French* myluz) *n* a city in E France, on the Rhône-Rhine canal: under German rule (1871–1918); textiles. Pop: 110 359 (1999). German name: **Mühlhausen**

muliebrity (ˌmju:lɪ'ɛbrɪtɪ) *n* **1** the condition of being a woman **2** femininity [c16 via LL from L *muliēbris* womanly, from *mulier* woman]

mulish ('mju:lɪʃ) *adj* stubborn; obstinate > **'mulishly** *adv* > **'mulishness** *n*

mull[1] (mʌl) *vb (tr)* (often foll by *over*) to study or ponder [c19 prob. from MUDDLE]

mull[2] (mʌl) *vb (tr)* to heat (wine, ale, etc) with sugar and spices [c17 from ?] > **mulled** *adj*

mull[3] (mʌl) *n* a light muslin fabric of soft texture [c18 earlier *mulmull*, from Hindi *malmal*]

mull[4] (mʌl) *n Scot* a promontory [c14 rel. to Gaelic *maol*, Icelandic *múli*]

Mull (mʌl) *n* a mountainous island off the west coast of Scotland, in the Inner Hebrides, separated from the mainland by the **Sound of Mull**. Chief town: Tobermory. Pop: 2605 (latest est) Area: 909 sq km (351 sq miles)

mullah *or* **mulla** (ˈmʌlə, ˈmʊlə) *n* (formerly) a Muslim scholar, teacher, or religious leader: also used as a title of respect [c17 from Turkish *molla*, Persian & Hindi *mulla*, from Ar. *mawlā* master]

mullein (ˈmʌlɪn) *n* any of various European herbaceous plants such as the common mullein or Aaron's rod, typically having tall spikes of yellow flowers and broad hairy leaves [c15 from OF *moleine*, prob. from OF *mol* soft, from L *mollis*]

muller (ˈmʌlə) *n* a flat heavy implement of stone or iron used to grind material against a slab of stone, etc [c15 prob. from *mullen* to grind to powder]

Muller (ˈmʌlə) *n* **Hermann Joseph** 1890–1967, US geneticist, noted for his work on the transmutation of genes by X-rays: Nobel prize for physiology or medicine 1946

Müller (*German* ˈmylər) *n* **1 Friedrich Max** (ˈfriːdrɪç maks) 1823–1900, British Sanskrit scholar born in Germany **2 Johann** (joˈhan) See **Regiomontanus** **3 Johannes Peter** (joˈhanəs ˈpeːtər) 1801–58, German physiologist, anatomist, and experimental psychologist **4 Paul Hermann** (paul ˈhɛrman) 1899–1965, Swiss chemist. He synthesized DDT (1939) and discovered its use as an insecticide: Nobel prize for physiology or medicine 1948

mullet[1] (ˈmʌlɪt) *n* any of various teleost food fishes such as the grey mullet or red mullet [c15 via OF from L *mullus*, from Gk *mullos*]

mullet[2] (ˈmʌlɪt) *n* a hairstyle in which the hair is short at the top and long at the back [c20 origin unknown]

Mulligan (ˈmʌlɪɡən) *n* **Gerry**, full name *Gerald Joseph Mulligan*. 1927–96, US jazz saxophonist, who pioneered the cool jazz style of the 1950s

mulligatawny (ˌmʌlɪɡəˈtɔːnɪ) *n* a curry-flavoured soup of Anglo-Indian origin, made with meat stock [c18 from Tamil *milakutanni*, from *milaku* pepper + *tanni* water]

Mulliken (ˈmʌlɪkən) *n* **Robert Sanderson** 1896–1986, US physicist and chemist, who won the Nobel prize for chemistry (1966) for his work on bonding and the electronic structure of molecules

Mullingar (ˌmʌlɪnˈɡɑː) *n* a town in N central Republic of Ireland, the county town of Co Westmeath; site of cathedral; cattle raised. Pop: 11 800 (1995 est)

mullion (ˈmʌlɪən) *n* **1** a vertical member between the casements or panes of a window ▷ *vb* **2** *(tr)* to furnish (a window, screen, etc) with mullions [c16 var. of ME *munial*, from OF *moinel*, from ?]

mullock (ˈmʌlək) *n Austral* **1** waste material from a mine **2 poke mullock at** *inf* to ridicule [c14 rel. to OE *myl* dust, ON *mylja* to crush]

mulloway (ˈmʌləˌweɪ) *n* a large Australian marine food fish [c19 from ?]

Mulroney (mʌlˈrəʊnɪ) *n* (**Martin**) **Brian** born 1939, Canadian statesman; Conservative prime minister (1984–93)

Multan (ˌmʊlˈtɑːn) *n* a city in central Pakistan, near the Chenab River. Pop: 1 182 441 (1998 est)

multangular (mʌlˈtæŋɡjʊlə) *or* **multiangular** *adj* having many angles

multi- *combining form* **1** many or much: *multimillion* **2** more than one: *multistorey* [from L *multus* much, many]

multicultural (ˌmʌltɪˈkʌltʃərəl) *adj* consisting of, relating to, or designed for the cultures of several different races > ˌ**multiˈculturalˌism** *n*

multifactorial (ˌmʌltɪfækˈtɔːrɪəl) *adj* having many separate factors, causes, components, etc: *multifactorial disease; multifactorial inheritance*

multifarious (ˌmʌltɪˈfɛərɪəs) *adj* having many parts of great variety [c16 from LL *multifārius* manifold, from L *multifāriam* on many sides] > ˌ**multiˈfariously** *adv* > ˌ**multiˈfariousness** *n*

multiflora rose (ˌmʌltɪˈflɔːrə) *n* an Asian climbing shrubby rose having clusters of small fragrant flowers

multiform (ˈmʌltɪˌfɔːm) *adj* having many forms

multigym (ˈmʌltɪˌdʒɪm) *n* an exercise apparatus incorporating a variety of weights, used for toning the muscles

multilateral (ˌmʌltɪˈlætərəl, -ˈlætrəl) *adj* **1** of or involving more than two nations or parties: *a multilateral pact* **2** having many sides > ˌ**multiˈlaterally** *adv*

multilingual (ˌmʌltɪˈlɪŋɡwəl) *adj* **1** able to speak more than two languages **2** written or expressed in more than two languages

multimedia (ˌmʌltɪˈmiːdɪə) *adj* **1** of or relating to the combined use of such media as television, slides, etc **2** *computing* of or relating to any of various systems that can manipulate data in a variety of forms, such as sound, graphics, or text

multimillionaire (ˌmʌltɪˌmɪljəˈnɛə) *n* a person with a fortune of several million pounds, dollars, etc

multinational (ˌmʌltɪˈnæʃənᵊl) *adj* **1** (of a large business company) operating in several countries ▷ *n* **2** such a company

multipack (ˈmʌltɪˌpæk) *n* a form of packaging of foodstuffs, etc, that contains several units and is offered at a price below that of the equivalent number of units

multiparous (mʌlˈtɪpərəs) *adj* (of certain species of mammal) producing many offspring at one birth [c17 from NL *multiparus*]

multipartite (ˌmʌltɪˈpɑːtaɪt) *adj* **1** divided into many parts or sections **2** *government* a less common word for **multilateral**

multiparty (ˌmʌltɪˈpɑːtɪ) *adj* of or relating to a state, political system, etc, in which more than one political party is permitted: *multiparty democracy*

multiple (ˈmʌltɪpᵊl) *adj* **1** having or involving more than one part, individual, etc **2** *electronics, US & Canad* (of a circuit) having a number of conductors in parallel ▷ *n* **3** the product of a given number or polynomial and any other one: *6 is a multiple of 2* **4** short for **multiple store** [c17 via F from LL *multiplus*, from L MULTIPLEX] > ˈ**multiply** *adv*

multiple-choice *adj* having a number of possible given answers out of which the correct one must be chosen

multiple personality *n psychiatry* a mental disorder in which an individual's personality appears to have become separated into two or more distinct personalities. Nontechnical name: **split personality**

multiple sclerosis *n* a chronic progressive disease of the central nervous system, resulting in speech and visual disorders, tremor, muscular incoordination, partial paralysis, etc

multiple store *n* one of several retail enterprises under the same ownership and management. Also called: **multiple shop**

multiplex (ˈmʌltɪˌplɛks) *n* **1** *telecomm* **1a** the use of a common communications channel for sending two or more messages or signals **1b** *(as modifier)*: *a multiplex transmitter* **2a** a purpose-built complex containing a number of cinemas and usually a restaurant or bar **2b** *(as modifier)*: *a multiplex cinema* ▷ *adj* **3** a less common word for **multiple** ▷ *vb* **4** to send (messages or signals) or (of messages and signals) to be sent by multiplex [c16 from L: having many folds, from MULTI- + *plicāre* to fold]

multiplexer *or* **multiplexor** (ˈmʌltɪˌplɛksə) *n computing* a device that enables the simultaneous transmission of several messages or signals over one communications channel

multiplicand (ˌmʌltɪplɪˈkænd) *n* a number to be multiplied by another number, the **multiplier** [c16 from L *multiplicandus*, gerund of *multiplicāre* to MULTIPLY]

multiplication (ˌmʌltɪplɪˈkeɪʃən) *n* **1** a mathematical operation, the inverse of division, in which the product of two or more numbers or quantities is calculated. Usually written *a* × *b*, *a.b*, *ab* **2** the act of multiplying or state of being multiplied **3** the act or process in animals, plants, or people, of reproducing or breeding

multiplication sign *n* the symbol ×, placed between numbers to be multiplied

multiplication table *n* one of a group of tables giving the results of multiplying two numbers together

multiplicity (ˌmʌltɪˈplɪsɪtɪ) *n, pl* **multiplicities** **1** a large number or great variety **2** the state of being multiple

multiplier (ˈmʌltɪˌplaɪə) *n* **1** a person or thing that multiplies **2** the number by which another number, the **multiplicand,** is multiplied **3** *physics* any instrument, such as a photomultiplier, for increasing an effect **4** *econ* the ratio of the total change in income (resulting from successive rounds of spending) to an initial autonomous change in expenditure

multiply (ˈmʌltɪˌplaɪ) *vb* **multiplies, multiplying, multiplied** **1** to increase or cause to increase in number, quantity, or degree **2** (*tr*) to combine (two numbers or quantities) by multiplication **3** (*intr*) to increase in number by reproduction [c13 from OF *multiplier*, from L *multiplicāre* to multiply, from *multus* much, many + *plicāre* to fold] > **ˈmultiˌpliable** *or* **multiplicable** (ˈmʌltɪˌplɪkəbᵊl) *adj*

multiprocessor (ˌmʌltɪˈprəʊsɛsə) *n computing* a number of central processing units linked together to enable parallel processing to take place

multipurpose vehicle *n* a large car, similar to a van, designed to carry up to eight passengers. Abbrev: **MPV**

multiskilling (ˈmʌltɪˌskɪlɪŋ) *n* the practice of training employees to do a number of different tasks

multistage (ˈmʌltɪˌsteɪdʒ) *adj* **1** (of a rocket or missile) having several stages, each of which can be jettisoned after it has burnt out **2** (of a turbine, compressor, or supercharger) having more than one rotor **3** (of any process or device) having more than one stage

multistorey (ˌmʌltɪˈstɔːrɪ) *adj* **1** (of a building) having many storeys ▷ *n* **2** a multistorey car park

multitasking (ˌmʌltɪˈtɑːskɪŋ) *n* **1** *computing* the execution of various diverse tasks simultaneously **2** the carrying out of two or more tasks at the same time by one person

multitrack (ˈmʌltɪˌtræk) *adj* (in sound recording) using tape containing two or more tracks, usually four to twenty-four

multitude (ˈmʌltɪˌtjuːd) *n* **1** a large gathering of people **2** **the** the common people **3** a large number **4** the state or quality of being numerous [c14 via OF from L *multitūdō*]

multitudinous (ˌmʌltɪˈtjuːdɪnəs) *adj* **1** very numerous **2** *rare* great in extent, variety, etc **3** *poetic* crowded > **ˌmultiˈtudinously** *adv* > **ˌmultiˈtudinousness** *n*

multi-user *adj* (of a computer) capable of being used by several people at once

multivalent (ˌmʌltɪˈveɪlənt) *adj* another word for **polyvalent** > **ˌmultiˈvalency** *n*

multiverse (ˈmʌltɪˌvɜːs) *n astron* the aggregate of all existing matter, of which the universe is but a tiny fragment

mum¹ (mʌm) *n chiefly Brit* an informal word for **mother** [c19 a child's word]

mum² (mʌm) *adj* **1** keeping information, etc, to oneself; silent ▷ *n* **2** **mum's the word** (*interj*) silence or secrecy is to be observed [c14 suggestive of closed lips]

mum³ (mʌm) *vb* **mums, mumming, mummed** (*intr*) to act in a mummer's play [c16 verbal use of MUM²]

Mumbai (mʊmˈbaɪ) *n* the Hindi name for **Bombay**

mumble (ˈmʌmbᵊl) *vb* **mumbles, mumbling, mumbled** **1** to utter indistinctly, as with the mouth partly closed **2** *rare* to chew (food) ineffectually ▷ *n* **3** an indistinct or low utterance or sound [c14 *momelen*, from MUM²] > **ˈmumbler** *n* > **ˈmumbling** *adj* > **ˈmumblingly** *adv*

mumbo jumbo (ˈmʌmbəʊ) *n, pl* **mumbo jumbos** **1** foolish religious reverence, ritual, or incantation **2** meaningless or unnecessarily complicated language **3** an object of superstitious awe or reverence [c18 prob. from W African *mama dyumbo*, name of a tribal god]

mu meson (mjuː) *n* a former name for **muon**

Mumford (ˈmʌmfəd) *n* **Lewis** 1895–1990, US sociologist, whose works are chiefly concerned with the relationship between man and his environment. They include *The City in History* (1962) and *Roots of Contemporary Architecture* (1972)

mummer (ˈmʌmə) *n* **1** one of a group of masked performers in a folk play or mime **2** *humorous or derog* an actor [c15 from OF *momeur*, from *momer* to mime]

Mummerset (ˈmʌməsɪt, -ˌsɛt) *n* an imitation West Country accent used in drama [c20 from MUMMER + (SOMER)SET]

mummery (ˈmʌmərɪ) *n, pl* **mummeries** **1** a performance by mummers **2** hypocritical or ostentatious ceremony

mummify (ˈmʌmɪˌfaɪ) *vb* **mummifies, mummifying, mummified** **1** (*tr*) to preserve (a body) as a mummy **2** (*intr*) to dry up; shrivel > **ˌmummifiˈcation** *n*

mummy¹ (ˈmʌmɪ) *n, pl* **mummies** **1** an embalmed or preserved body, esp as prepared for burial in ancient Egypt **2** a mass of pulp **3** a dark brown pigment [c14 from OF *momie*, from Med. L, from Ar.: asphalt, from Persian *mūm* wax]

mummy² (ˈmʌmɪ) *n, pl* **mummies** *chiefly Brit* a child's word for **mother¹** (senses 1–3) [c19 var. of MUM¹]

mumps (mʌmps) *n* (*functioning as sing or pl*) **1** an acute contagious viral disease of the parotid salivary glands, characterized by swelling of the affected parts, fever, and pain beneath the ear **2** sulks [c16 from *mump* to grimace] > **ˈmumpish** *adj*

Mm

mumsy (ˈmʌmzɪ) *adj* **mumsier, mumsiest** homely or drab > **ˈmumsiness** *n*

munch (mʌntʃ) *vb* to chew (food) steadily, esp with a crunching noise [c14 *monche*, imit.]

Munch (mʊŋk) *n* **Edvard** (ˈɛdvard) 1863–1944, Norwegian painter and engraver, whose works, often on the theme of death, include *The Scream* (1893); a major influence on the expressionists, esp on *die Brücke*

München (ˈmynçən) *n* the German name for **Munich**

München-Gladbach (mynçənˈglatbax) *n* the former name of **Mönchengladbach**

mundane (mʌnˈdeɪn, ˈmʌndeɪn) *adj* **1** everyday, ordinary, or banal **2** relating to the world or worldly matters [c15 from F *mondain*, via LL, from L *mundus* world] > **munˈdanely** *adv* > **munˈdaneness** *n*

mung bean (mʌŋ) *n* **1** an E Asian bean plant grown for forage and as the source of bean sprouts for cookery **2** the seed of this plant [c20 from *mung*, changed from *mungo*, from Tamil *mūngu*, from Sansk. *mudga*]

Munich (ˈmjuːnɪk) *n* a city in SW Germany, capital of the state of Bavaria, on the Isar River: became capital of Bavaria in 1508; headquarters of the Nazi movement in the 1920s; a major financial, commercial, and manufacturing centre. Pop: 1 193 600 (1999 est). German name: **München**

municipal (mjuːˈnɪsɪpᵊl) *adj* of or relating to a town, city, or borough or its local government [c16 from L *mūnicipium* a free town, from *mūniceps* citizen, from *mūnia* responsibilities + *capere* to take] > **muˈnicipally** *adv*

municipality (mjuːˌnɪsɪˈpælɪtɪ) *n, pl* **municipalities** **1** a city, town, or district enjoying local self-government **2** the governing body of such a unit

municipalize *or* **municipalise** (mjuːˈnɪsɪpəˌlaɪz) *vb* **municipalizes, municipalizing, municipalized** *or* **municipalises, municipalising, municipalised** (*tr*) **1** to bring under municipal ownership or control **2** to make a municipality of > **muˌnicipaliˈzation** *or* **muˌnicipaliˈsation** *n*

munificent (mjuːˈnɪfɪsənt) *adj* **1** (of a person) generous; bountiful **2** (of a gift) liberal [c16 back formation from L *mūnificentia* liberality, from *mūnificus*, from *mūnus* gift + *facere* to make] > **muˈnificence** *n* > **muˈnificently** *adv*

muniments (ˈmjuːnɪmənts) *pl n law* the title deeds and other documentary evidence relating to the title to land [c15 via OF from L *munire* to defend]

munition (mjuːˈnɪʃən) *vb* (*tr*) to supply with munitions [c16 via F from L *mūnītiō* fortification, from *mūnīre* to fortify]

munitions (mjuːˈnɪʃənz) *pl n* (*sometimes sing*) military equipment and stores, esp ammunition

Munro[1] (mʌnˈrəʊ) *n, pl* **Munros** *mountaineering* any separate mountain peak over 3000 feet high: originally used of Scotland only but now sometimes extended to other parts of the British Isles [c20 after Hugh Thomas *Munro* (1856–1919), who listed these in 1891]

Munro[2] (mʌnˈrəʊ) *n* **1 Alice,** original name *Alice Laidlaw*. born 1931, Canadian short-story writer; her books include *Lives of Girls and Women* (1971), *The Moons of Jupiter* (1982), and *The Love of a Good Woman* (1999) **2 H(ector) H(ugh)**, pen name Saki. 1870–1916, Scottish author, born in Burma (now Myanmar), noted for his collections of satirical short stories, such as *Reginald* (1904) and *Beasts and Superbeasts* (1914)

Munster (ˈmʌnstə) *n* a province of SW Republic of Ireland: the largest of the four provinces and historically a kingdom; consists of the counties of Clare, Cork, Kerry, Limerick, Tipperary, and Waterford. Capital: Cork. Pop: 1 033 903 (1996). Area: 24 125 sq km (9315 sq miles)

Münster (*German* ˈmynstər) *n* a city in NW Germany, in North Rhine-Westphalia on the Dortmund-Ems Canal: one of the treaties comprising the Peace of Westphalia (1648) was signed here; became capital of Prussian Westphalia in 1815. Pop: 264 700 (1999 est)

munted (ˈmʌntɪd) *adj NZ sl* **1** (of an object) destroyed or ruined **2** (of a person) abnormal or peculiar [c20 from ?]

muntjac *or* **muntjak** (ˈmʌntˌdʒæk) *n* any small Asian deer typically having a chestnut-brown coat and small antlers [c18 prob. from Javanese *mindjangan* deer]

Müntzer (ˈmʊntzə; *German* ˈmyntzər) *n* **Thomas** c. 1490–1525, German radical religious and political reformer; executed for organizing the Peasants' War (1524–25)

muon (ˈmjuːɒn) *n* a positive or negative elementary particle with a mass 207 times that of an electron. It was originally called the **mu meson** [c20 short for MU MESON] > **muˈonic** *adj*

muppet (ˈmʌpɪt) *n sl* a stupid person [c20 from the name for the puppets used in the television programme *The Muppet Show*]

mural (ˈmjʊərəl) *n* **1** a large painting on a wall ▷ *adj* **2** of or relating to a wall [c15 from L *mūrālis*, from *mūrus* wall] > **ˈmuralist** *n*

Muralitharan (ˌmɜːrəˈlɪθərən) *n* **Muttiah** (məˈtaɪə) born 1972, Sri Lankan cricketer, a famous spin bowler; has played for Sri Lanka since 1992

Murasaki Shikibu (ˌmʊərɑːˈsɑːkiː ˈʃiːkiːˌbuː) *n* 11th-century Japanese court lady, author of *The Tale of Genji*, perhaps the world's first novel

Murat (*French* myra) *n* **Joachim** (ʒɔaʃɛ̃) 1767-1815, French marshal, during the Napoleonic Wars; king of Naples (1808–15)

Murchison (ˈmɜːtʃɪsᵊn) *n* Sir **Roderick Impey** 1792–1871, Scottish geologist: played a major role in establishing parts of the geological time scale, esp the Silurian, Permian, and Devonian periods

Murcia (*Spanish* ˈmurθja) *n* **1** a region and ancient kingdom of SE Spain, on the Mediterranean: taken by the Moors in the 8th century; an independent Muslim kingdom in the 11th and 12th centuries **2** a city in SE Spain, capital of Murcia province: trading centre for a rich agricultural region; silk industry; university (1915). Pop: 34 904 (1995 est)

murder (ˈmɜːdə) *n* **1** the unlawful premeditated killing of one human being by another ▷ Cf **manslaughter** **2** *inf* something dangerous, difficult, or unpleasant: *driving around London is murder* **3 cry blue murder** *inf* to make an outcry **4 get away with murder** *inf* to escape censure; do as one pleases ▷ *vb* (*mainly tr*) **5** (*also intr*) to kill (someone) unlawfully with premeditation or during the commission of a crime **6** to kill brutally **7** *inf* to destroy; ruin **8** *inf* to defeat completely; beat decisively: *the home team murdered their opponents* [OE *morthor*] > **ˈmurderer** *n* > **ˈmurderess** *fem n*

murderous (ˈmɜːdərəs) *adj* **1** intending, capable of, or guilty of murder **2** *inf* very dangerous or difficult: *a murderous road* > **ˈmurderously** *adv* > **ˈmurderousness** *n*

Murdoch (ˈmɜːdɒk) *n* **1** Dame **(Jean) Iris** 1919–99, British writer. Her books include *The Bell* (1958), *A Severed Head* (1961), *The Sea, The Sea* (1978), which won the Booker Prize, *The Philosopher's Pupil* (1983), and *Existentialists and Mystics* (1997) **2 (Keith) Rupert** born 1931, US publisher and media entrepreneur, born in Australia; chairman of News International Ltd. (including Times Newspapers Ltd), 20th Century-Fox, and HarperCollins

Mureş (ˈmʊərɛʃ) *n* a river in SE central Europe, rising in central Romania in the Carpathian Mountains and flowing west to the Tisza River at Szeged, Hungary. Length: 885 km (550 miles). Hungarian name: **Maros**

murex (ˈmjʊərɛks) *n, pl* **murices** (ˈmjʊərɪˌsiːz) any of a genus of spiny-shelled marine gastropods: formerly used as a source of the dye Tyrian purple [c16 from L *mūrex* purple fish]

muriatic acid (ˌmjʊərɪˈætɪk) *n* a former name for **hydrochloric acid** [c17 from L *muriāticus* pickled, from *muria* brine]

Murillo (mjʊəˈrɪləʊ; *Spanish* muˈriʎo) *n* **Bartolomé Esteban** (bartoloˈme esˈteβan) 1618–82, Spanish painter, esp of religious subjects and beggar children

murk *or* **mirk** (mɜːk) *n* **1** gloomy darkness ▷ *adj* **2** an archaic variant of **murky** [c13 prob. from ON *myrkr* darkness]

murky *or* **mirky** (ˈmɜːkɪ) *adj* **murkier, murkiest** *or* **mirkier, mirkiest** **1** gloomy or dark **2** cloudy or impenetrable, as with smoke or fog **3** *inf* obscure and suspicious; shady: *she had a murky past* > **ˈmurkily** *or* **ˈmirkily** *adv* > **ˈmurkiness** *or* **ˈmirkiness** *n*

Murman Coast (ˈmʊəmən) *or* **Murmansk Coast** *n* a coastal region of NW Russia, in the north of the Kola Peninsula within the Arctic Circle, but ice-free

Murmansk (*Russian* ˈmurmənsk) *n* a port in NW Russia, on the Kola Inlet of the Barents Sea: founded in 1915; the world's largest town north of the Arctic Circle, with a large fishing fleet. Pop: 382 700 (1999 est)

murmur (ˈmɜːmə) *n* **1** a continuous low indistinct sound, as of distant voices **2** an indistinct utterance: *a murmur of satisfaction* **3** a complaint; grumble: *he made no murmur at my suggestion* **4** *med* any abnormal blowing sound heard usually over the chest (**heart murmur**) ▷ *vb* **murmurs, murmuring, murmured** **5** to utter (something) in a murmur **6** (*intr*) to complain [c14 as n, from L *murmur*; vb. via OF *murmurer* from L *murmurāre* to rumble] > **ˈmurmurer** *n* > **ˈmurmuring** *n, adj* > **ˈmurmuringly** *adv* > **ˈmurmurous** *adj*

murphy (ˈmɜːfɪ) *n, pl* **murphies** a dialect or informal word for **potato** [c19 from the common Irish surname *Murphy*]

Murphy *n* **Eddie,** full name *Edward Regan Murphy*. born 1951, US film actor and comedian. His films include *48*

Hours (1982), *Beverly Hills Cop* (1984), *Coming to America* (1988), and *Dr Dolittle* (1998)

Murphy-O'Connor ('mɜːfɪəʊ'kɒnə) *n* **Cormac** born 1932, British cardinal, Archbishop of Westminster from 2000

murrain ('mʌrɪn) *n* **1** *arch* any plaguelike disease in cattle **2** *arch* a plague [c14 from OF *morine*, from *morir* to die, from L *morī*]

Murray[1] ('mʌrɪ) *n* a river in SE Australia, rising in New South Wales and flowing northwest into SE South Australia, then south into the sea at Encounter Bay: the main river of Australia, important for irrigation and power. Length: 2590 km (1609 miles)

Murray[2] ('mʌrɪ) *n* **1 1st Earl of** See (1st Earl of) **Moray** **2** Sir (**George**) **Gilbert** (**Aimé**) 1866–1957, British classical scholar, born in Australia: noted for his verse translations of Greek dramatists, esp Euripides **3** Sir **James Augustus Henry** 1837–1915, Scottish lexicographer; one of the original editors (1879–1915) of what became the *Oxford English Dictionary* **4 Les,** full name *Leslie Allan Murray*. born 1938, Australian poet; his collections include *The Weatherboard Cathedral* (1969), *The Daylight Moon* (1987), and *Subhuman Redneck Poems* (1996) **5 Murray of Epping Forest,** Baron, title of *Lionel Murray*, known as *Len*. born 1922, British trades union leader; general secretary of the Trades Union Congress (1973–84)

Murray cod *n* a large Australian freshwater fish, *Maccullochella peeli*, chiefly of the Murray and Darling rivers [after MURRAY River]

Murrumbidgee (ˌmʌrəm'bɪdʒɪ) *n* a river in SE Australia, rising in S New South Wales and flowing north and west to the Murray River: important for irrigation. Length: 1690 km (1050 miles)

murther ('mɜːðə) *n, vb* an archaic word for **murder** > '**murtherer** *n*

mus. *abbrev for:* **1** museum **2** music

MusB *or* **MusBac** *abbrev for* Bachelor of Music

muscadine ('mʌskədɪn, -ˌdaɪn) *n* **1** a woody climbing plant of the southeastern US **2** the musk-scented purple grape produced by this plant: used to make wine [c16 from MUSCATEL]

muscae volitantes ('mʌsiː vɒlɪ'tæntiːz) *pl n pathol* moving black specks or threads seen before the eyes, caused by opaque fragments floating in the vitreous humour or a defect in the lens [c18 NL: flying flies]

muscat ('mʌskət, -kæt) *n* **1** any of various grapevines that produce sweet white grapes used for making wine or raisins **2** another name for **muscatel** (sense 1) [c16 via OF from Provençal, from *musc* MUSK]

Muscat ('mʌskət, -kæt) *n* the capital of the Sultanate of Oman, a port on the Gulf of Oman: a Portuguese port from the early 16th century; controlled by Persia (1650–1741). Pop: 51 969 (1993). Arabic name: **Masqat**
▷ www.omanet.com

Muscat and Oman *n* the former name (until 1970) of (the Sultanate of) **Oman**

muscatel (ˌmʌskə'tɛl) *or* **muscadel** *n* **1** Also called: **muscat** a rich sweet wine made from muscat grapes **2** the grape or raisin from a muscat vine [c14 from OF *muscadel*, from OProvençal, from *moscadel*, from *muscat* musky]

muscle ('mʌsᵊl) *n* **1** a tissue composed of bundles of elongated cells capable of contraction and relaxation to produce movement in an organ or part **2** an organ composed of muscle tissue **3** strength or force ▷ *vb* **muscles, muscling, muscled** **4** (*intr; often foll by in, on, etc*) *inf* to force one's way (in) [c16 from Medical L *musculus* little mouse, from the imagined resemblance of some muscles to mice] > '**muscly** *adj*

muscle-bound *adj* **1** having overdeveloped and inelastic muscles **2** lacking flexibility

muscleman ('mʌsᵊlˌmæn) *n, pl* **musclemen** **1** a man with highly developed muscles **2** a henchman employed by a gangster to intimidate or use violence upon victims: *a well-known Mafia muscleman*

Muscovite ('mʌskəˌvaɪt) *n* **1** a native or inhabitant of Moscow ▷ *adj* **2** an archaic word for **Russian**

Muscovy ('mʌskəvɪ) *n* **1** a Russian principality (13th to 16th centuries), of which Moscow was the capital **2** an archaic name for **Russia** and **Moscow**

Muscovy duck *or* **musk duck** *n* a large crested widely domesticated South American duck, having a greenish-black plumage with white markings and a large red caruncle on the bill [c17 orig. *musk duck*, a name later mistakenly associated with MUSCOVY]

muscular ('mʌskjʊlə) *adj* **1** having well-developed muscles; brawny **2** of, relating to, or consisting of muscle [c17 from NL *muscularis*, from *musculus* MUSCLE] > **muscularity** (ˌmʌskjʊ'lærɪtɪ) *n* > '**muscularly** *adv*

muscular dystrophy *n* a genetic disease characterized by progressive deterioration and wasting of muscle fibres

musculature ('mʌskjʊlətʃə) *n* **1** the arrangement of muscles in an organ or part **2** the total muscular system of an organism

MusD *or* **MusDoc** *abbrev for* Doctor of Music

muse[1] (mjuːz) *vb* **muses, musing, mused** **1** (*when intr, often foll by on or about*) to reflect (about) or ponder (on), usually in silence **2** (*intr*) to gaze thoughtfully ▷ *n* **3** a state of abstraction [c14 from OF *muser*, ?from *mus* snout, from Med. L *mūsus*]

muse[2] (mjuːz) *n* a goddess or woman who inspires a poet or other creative artist [c14 from OF, from L *Mūsa*, from Gk *Mousa* a Muse]

Muse (mjuːz) *n Greek myth* any of nine sister goddesses, each of whom was regarded as the protectress of a different art or science

musette (mjuː'zɛt) *n* **1** a type of bagpipe popular in France during the 17th and 18th centuries **2** a dance, originally accompanied by a musette [c14 from OF, dim. of *muse* bagpipe]

museum (mjuː'zɪəm) *n* a building where objects of historical, artistic, or scientific interest are exhibited and preserved [c17 via L from Gk *Mouseion* home of the Muses, from *Mousa* MUSE]

museum piece *n* **1** an object of sufficient age or interest to be kept in a museum **2** *inf* a person or thing regarded as antiquated

mush[1] (mʌʃ) *n* **1** a soft pulpy mass or consistency **2** *US* a thick porridge made from corn meal **3** *inf* cloying sentimentality ▷ *vb* **4** (*tr*) to reduce (a substance) to a soft pulpy mass [c17 from obs. *moose* porridge; prob. rel. to MASH]

mush[2] (mʌʃ) *Canad* ▷ *interj* **1** an order to dogs in a sled team to start up or go faster ▷ *vb* **2** to travel by or drive a dogsled ▷ *n* **3** a journey with a dogsled [c19 ?from imperative of F *marcher* to advance]

Musharraf (mə'ʃærəf) *n* **Pervez** ('pɛrveɪz) born 1943, Pakistani general and politician; became military leader of Pakistan following a coup in 2001; president from 2002

mushroom ('mʌʃruːm, -rʊm) *n* **1a** the fleshy spore-producing body of any of various fungi, typically consisting of a cap at the end of a stem. Some species, such as the field mushroom, are edible ▷ Cf **toadstool** **1b** (*as modifier*): *mushroom soup* **2a** something resembling a mushroom in shape or rapid growth **2b** (*as modifier*): *mushroom expansion* ▷ *vb* (*intr*) **3** to grow rapidly: *demand mushroomed overnight* **4** to assume a mushroom-like shape [c15 from OF *mousseron*, from LL *mussiriō*, from ?]

mushroom cloud *n* the large mushroom-shaped cloud produced by a nuclear explosion

mushy ('mʌʃɪ) *adj* **mushier, mushiest** **1** soft and pulpy **2** *inf* excessively sentimental or emotional > '**mushily** *adv* > '**mushiness** *n*

music ('mjuːzɪk) *n* **1** an art form consisting of sequences of sounds in time, esp tones of definite pitch organized melodically, harmonically and rhythmically **2** the sounds so produced, esp by singing or musical instruments **3** written or printed music, such as a score or set of parts **4** any sequence of sounds perceived as pleasing or harmonious **5** **face the music** *inf* to confront the consequences of one's actions [C13 via OF from L *mūsica*, from Gk *mousikē* (*tekhnē*) (art) belonging to the Muses, from *Mousa* MUSE]

▹ www.allmusic.com
▹ www.musicsearch.com
▹ www.dotmusic.com
▹ www.music.ucc.ie/wrrm
▹ www.classical.net
▹ www.essentialsofmusic.com/glossary/n.html
▹ www.nme.com

MUSICAL EXPRESSIONS AND TEMPO INSTRUCTIONS

accelerando with increasing speed
adagio slowly
agitato in an agitated manner
allegretto fairly quickly or briskly
allegro quickly, in a brisk, lively manner
amoroso lovingly
andante at a moderately slow tempo
andantino slightly faster than andante
animato in a lively manner
appassionato impassioned
assai (in combination) very
calando with gradually decreasing tone and speed
cantabile in a singing style
con (in combination) with
con affeto with tender emotion
con amore lovingly
con anima with spirit
con brio vigorously
con fuoco with fire
con moto quickly
crescendo gradual increase in loudness
diminuendo gradual decrease in loudness
dolce gently and sweetly
doloroso in a sorrowful manner
energico energetically
espressivo expressively
forte loud or loudly
fortissimo very loud
furioso in a frantically rushing manner
giocoso merry
grave solemn and slow
grazioso graceful
lacrimoso sad and mournful
largo slowly and broadly
larghetto slowly and broadly, but less so than largo
legato smoothly and connectedly
leggiero light
lento slowly
maestoso majestically
marziale martial
mezzo (in combination) moderately
moderato at a moderate tempo
molto (in combination) very
non troppo *or* non tanto (in combination) not too much
pianissimo very quietly
piano softly
più (in combination) more
pizzicato (in music for stringed instruments) to be plucked with the finger
poco *or* un poco (in combination) a little
pomposo in a pompous manner
presto very fast
prestissimo faster than presto
quasi (in combination) almost, as if
rallentando becoming slower
rubato with a flexible tempo
scherzando in jocular style
sciolto free and easy
semplice simple and unforced
sforzando with strong initial attack
smorzando dying away
sospirando 'sighing', plaintive
sostenuto in a smooth and sustained manner
sotto voce extremely quiet
staccato (of notes) short, clipped, and separate
strascinando stretched out
strepitoso noisy
stringendo with increasing speed
tanto (in combination) too much
tardo slow
troppo (in combination) too much
vivace in a brisk lively manner
volante 'flying', fast and light

musical (ˈmjuːzɪkᵊl) *adj* **1** of, relating to, or used in music **2** harmonious; melodious: *musical laughter* **3** talented in or fond of music **4** involving or set to music ▹ *n* **5** Also called: **musical comedy** a light romantic play or film having dialogue interspersed with songs and dances > ˌ**musiˈcality** *n* > ˈ**musically** *adv*
▹ www.musicals101.com

musical box *or* **music box** *n* a mechanical instrument that plays tunes by means of pins on a revolving cylinder striking the tuned teeth of a comblike metal plate, contained in a box

musical chairs *n* (*functioning as sing*) **1** a party game in which players walk around chairs while music is played, there being one more player than chairs. Whenever the music stops, the player who fails to find a chair is eliminated **2** any situation involving several people in a series of interrelated changes

music centre *n* a single hi-fi unit containing a turntable, amplifier, radio, cassette player, and compact disc player

music drama *n* **1** an opera in which the musical and dramatic elements are of equal importance and strongly interfused **2** the genre of such operas [C19 from G *Musikdrama*, coined by Wagner to describe his later operas]
▹ http://users.belgacom.net/wagnerlibrary/articles
▹ www.trell.org/wagner

music hall *n chiefly Brit* **1** a variety entertainment consisting of songs, comic turns, etc. US and Canad name: **vaudeville** **2** a theatre at which such entertainments are staged
▹ www.rfwilmut.clara.net
▹ www.theatrelinks.com

musician (mjuːˈzɪʃən) *n* a person who plays or composes music, esp as a profession > **muˈsicianly** *adj* > **muˈsicianship** *n*

musicology (ˌmjuːzɪˈkɒlədʒɪ) *n* the scholarly study of music > **musicological** (ˌmjuːzɪkəˈlɒdʒɪkᵊl) *adj* > ˌ**musiˈcologist** *n*
▹ www.societymusictheory.org/mto
▹ www.music.ucc.ie/wrrm

music paper *n* paper ruled or printed with a stave for writing music

Musil (*German* ˈmuːzɪl) *n* **Robert** (ˈroːbɛrt) 1880–1942, Austrian novelist, whose novel *The Man Without Qualities* (1930–42) is an ironic examination of contemporary ills

musique concrète *French* (myzik kɔ̃krɛt) *n* another term for **concrete music**

Range of some musical instruments

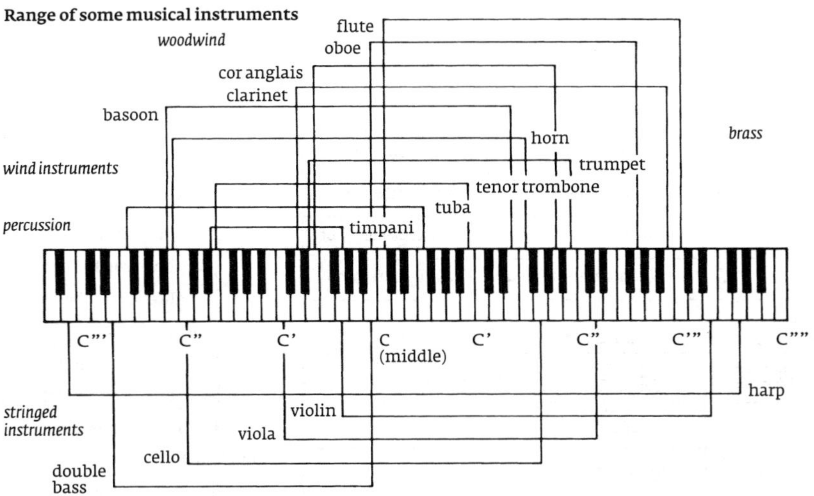

Keys and key signatures

Major key	*Relative minor key*	*Key signature (sharp keys)*	*Key signature (flat keys)*
C	A		
G	E		
D	B		
A	F♯		
E	C♯		
B = C♭	G♯		
F♯ = G♭	E♭		
C♯ = D♭	B♭		
A♭	F		
E♭	C		
B♭	G		
F	D		

Notes and rests

Note	Rest	British	American
		breve	double-whole note
		semibreve	whole note
		minim	half note
	or	crotchet	quarter note
		quaver	eighth note
		semiquaver	sixteenth note
		demisemiquaver	thirty-second note
		hemidemisemiquaver	sixty-fourth note

Clefs

Fixed note	Position of middle C	Clef
		G *or* treble clef
		F *or* bass clef
		C (soprano) clef
		C (alto) clef
		C (tenor) clef

Accidentals

♯	sharp; raising note one semitone
𝄪	double sharp; raising note one tone
♭	flat; lowering note one semitone
♭♭	double flat; lowering note one tone
♮	natural; restoring note to normal pitch after sharp or flat

Ornaments and decorations

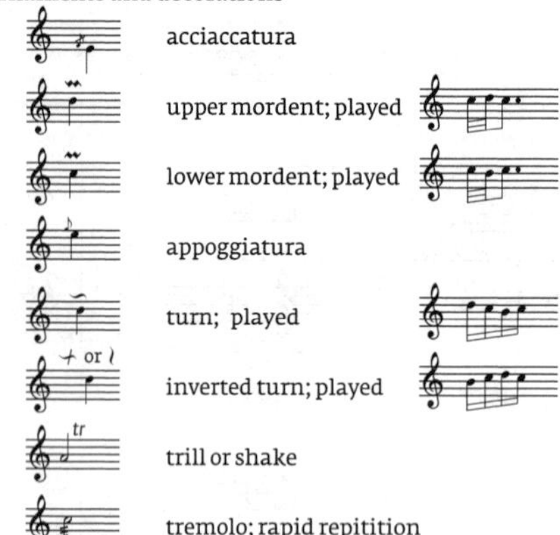

Staccato marks and signs of accentuation

or *mezzo-staccato*: shorten note by about ¼

staccato: shorten note by about ½

staccatissimo: shorten note by about ¾

detached: accented

attack

Time signatures

Simple duple

$\frac{2}{2}$ *or* ¢ two minim beats

$\frac{2}{4}$ two crotchet beats

$\frac{2}{8}$ two quaver beats

Compound duple

$\frac{6}{4}$ two dotted minim beats

$\frac{6}{8}$ two dotted crotchet beats

$\frac{6}{16}$ two dotted quaver beats

Simple triple

$\frac{3}{2}$ three miinim beats

$\frac{3}{4}$ three crotchet beats

$\frac{3}{8}$ three quaver beats

Compound triple

$\frac{9}{4}$ three dotted minim beats

$\frac{9}{8}$ three dotted crotchet beats

$\frac{9}{16}$ three dotted quaver beats

Simple quadruple

$\frac{4}{2}$ four minim beats

$\frac{4}{4}$ *or* **C** four crotchet beats

$\frac{4}{8}$ four quaver beats

Compound quadruple

$\frac{12}{4}$ four dotted minim beats

$\frac{12}{8}$ four dotted crotchet beats

$\frac{12}{16}$ four dotted quaver beats

Irregular rhythms

2 duplet or couplet

3 triplet

4 quadruplet

5 quintruplet

Dynamics

crescendo

diminuendo

Curved lines

tie or bind; two notes played as one

slur or legato; play smoothly (in one bow on stringed instrument)

Other

repeat preceding section

end of section or piece

pause

8[e] play an octave above notes written

musk (mʌsk) *n* **1** a strong-smelling glandular secretion of the male musk deer, used in perfumery **2** a similar substance produced by certain other animals, such as the civet and otter, or manufactured synthetically **3** a North American plant which has yellow flowers and was formerly cultivated for its musky scent **4** the smell of musk or a similar heady smell **5** (*modifier*) containing or resembling musk: *musk oil* [c14 from LL *muscus*, from Gk, from Persian, prob. from Sansk. *mushká* scrotum (from the appearance of the musk deer's musk bag), dim. of *mūsh* MOUSE]
musk deer *n* a small central Asian mountain deer. The male secretes musk
musk duck *n* **1** another name for **Muscovy duck 2** a duck inhabiting swamps, lakes, and streams in Australia. The male emits a musky odour
muskeg ('mʌsˌkɛg) *n chiefly Canad* **1** undrained boggy land **2** a bog or swamp of this nature [c19 of Amerind origin: grassy swamp]
muskellunge ('mʌskəˌlʌndʒ) *or* **maskinonge** ('mæskɪˌnɒndʒ) *n, pl* **muskellunges** *or* **muskellunge, maskinonges** *or* **maskinonge** a large North American freshwater game fish, related to the pike. Often shortened (informally) to **musky** or **muskie** [c18 *maskinunga*, of Amerind origin]
musket ('mʌskɪt) *n* a long-barrelled muzzle-loading shoulder gun used between the 16th and 18th centuries by infantry soldiers [c16 from F *mousquet*, from It. *moschetto* arrow, earlier: sparrow hawk, from *moscha* a fly, from L *musca*]
musketeer (ˌmʌskɪ'tɪə) *n* (formerly) a soldier armed with a musket
musketry ('mʌskɪtrɪ) *n* **1** muskets or musketeers collectively **2** the technique of using small arms
muskmelon ('mʌskˌmɛlən) *n* **1** any of several varieties of the melon, such as the cantaloupe and honeydew **2** the fruit of any of these melons, having ribbed or warty rind and sweet yellow, white, orange, or green flesh with a musky aroma
musk ox *n* a large bovid mammal, which has a dark shaggy coat, short legs, and widely spaced downward-curving horns, and emits a musky smell: now confined to the tundras of Canada and Greenland
muskrat ('mʌskˌræt) *n, pl* **muskrats** *or* **muskrat 1** a North American beaver-like amphibious rodent, closely related to but larger than the voles **2** the brown fur of this animal ▷ Also called: **musquash**
musk rose *n* a Mediterranean rose, cultivated for its white musk-scented flowers
musky ('mʌskɪ) *adj* **muskier, muskiest** resembling the smell of musk; having a heady or pungent sweet aroma > '**muskiness** *n*
Muslim ('mʊzlɪm, 'mʌz-) *or* **Moslem** *n, pl* **Muslims** *or* **Muslim, Moslems** *or* **Moslem 1** a follower of the religion of Islam ▷ *adj* **2** of or relating to Islam, its doctrines, culture, etc ▷ Also (but not in Muslim use): **Mohammedan, Muhammadan** [c17 from Ar., lit.: one who surrenders] > '**Muslimism** *or* '**Moslemism** *n*

MUSLIM CALENDAR

Muharram *or* **Moharram**
Safar *or* **Saphar**
Rabia I
Rabia II
Jumada I
Jumada II
Rajab
Shaban *or* **Shaaban**
Ramadan, Rhamadhan, *or* **Ramazan**
Shawwal
Dhu'l-Qa'dah
Dhu'l-Hijjah

muslin ('mʌzlɪn) *n* a fine plain-weave cotton fabric [c17 from F *mousseline*, from It., from Ar. *mawṣilīy* of Mosul (Iraq), where it was first produced]
muso ('mjuːzəʊ) *n, pl* **musos** *sl* **1** *Brit derog* a musician, esp a pop musician, regarded as being overconcerned with technique rather than musical content or expression **2** *Austral* any musician, esp a professional one
musquash ('mʌskwɒʃ) *n* another name for **muskrat,** esp the fur [c17 of Amerind origin]
muss (mʌs) *US & Canad inf* ▷ *vb* **1** (*tr*; often foll by *up*) to make untidy; rumple: *Foley had mussed up his hair* ▷ *n* **2** a state of disorder; muddle [c19 prob. a blend of MESS + FUSS] > '**mussy** *adj*
mussel ('mʌsᵊl) *n* **1** any of various marine bivalves, esp the edible mussel, having a dark slightly elongated shell and living attached to rocks, etc **2** any of various freshwater bivalves, attached to rocks, sand, etc, having a flattened oval shell (a source of mother-of-pearl) [OE *muscle*, from Vulgar L *muscula* (unattested), from L *musculus*, dim. of *mūs* mouse]
musselcracker ('mʌsᵊlˌkrækə) *n S African* a large variety of sea bream that feeds on shellfish and is a popular food and game fish
Musset (*French* mysɛ) *n* **Alfred de** (alfrɛd də) 1810–57, French romantic poet and dramatist: his works include the play *Lorenzaccio* (1834) and the lyrics *Les Nuits* (1835–37), tracing his love affair with George Sand
Mussolini (ˌmʊsə'liːnɪ; *Italian* musso'liːni) *n* **Benito** (be'niːto) known as *il Duce*. 1883–1945, Italian Fascist dictator. After the Fascist march on Rome, he was appointed prime minister by King Victor Emmanuel III (1922) and assumed dictatorial powers. He annexed Abyssinia and allied Italy with Germany (1936), entering World War II in 1940. He was forced to resign following the Allied invasion of Sicily (1943) and was eventually shot by Italian partisans
Mussorgsky *or* **Moussorgsky** (mʊ'sɔːgskɪ; *Russian* 'musərkskij) *n* **Modest Petrovich** (ma'dɛst pɪ'trɔvitʃ) 1839–81, Russian composer. He translated inflections of speech into melody in such works as the song cycle *Songs and Dances of Death* (1875–77) and the opera *Boris Godunov* (1874). His other works include *Pictures at an Exhibition* (1874) for piano
Mussulman ('mʌsᵊlmən) *n, pl* **Mussulmans** an archaic word for **Muslim** [c16 from Persian *Musulmān* (pl) from Ar. *Muslimūn*, pl. of MUSLIM]
must[1] (mʌst; *unstressed* məst, məs) *vb* (takes an infinitive without *to* or an implied infinitive) used as an auxiliary: **1** to express obligation or compulsion: *you must pay your dues*. In this sense, *must* does not form a negative. If used with a negative infinitive it indicates obligatory prohibition **2** to indicate necessity: *I must go to the bank tomorrow* **3** to indicate the probable correctness of a statement: *he must be there by now* **4** to indicate inevitability: *all good things must come to an end* **5** to express resolution: **5a** on the part of the speaker: *I must finish this* **5b** on the part of another or others: *let him get drunk if he must* **6** (used emphatically) to express conviction or certainty on the part of the speaker: *you must be joking* **7** (foll by *away*) used with an implied verb of motion to express compelling haste: *I must away* ▷ *n* **8** an essential or necessary thing: *strong shoes are a must for hill walking* [OE *mōste*, pt of *mōtan* to be allowed, be obliged to]
must[2] (mʌst) *n* the pressed juice of grapes or other fruit ready for fermentation [OE, from L *mustum* new wine, from *mustus* newborn]
must[3] (mʌst) *n* mustiness or mould [c17 back formation from MUSTY]

must- *combining form* indicating that something is highly recommended or desirable: *a must-see film; this season's must-haves*

mustache (mə'stɑːʃ) *n* the US spelling of **moustache**

mustachio (mə'stɑːʃɪˌəʊ) *n, pl* **mustachios** *(often pl) Often humorous.* a moustache, esp when bushy or elaborately shaped [c16 from Sp. *mostacho* & It. *mostaccio*]

mustachioed (mə'stɑːʃɪˌəʊd) *adj Often humorous.* having a moustache, esp when bushy or elaborately shaped

Mustafa Kemal ('mʊstəfə kə'mɑːl) *n* See (Kemal) **Atatürk**

mustang ('mʌstæŋ) *n* a small breed of horse, often wild or half wild, found in the southwestern US [c19 from Mexican Sp. *mestengo*, from *mesta* a group of stray animals]

mustard ('mʌstəd) *n* **1** any of several Eurasian plants, esp black mustard and white mustard, having yellow or white flowers and slender pods and cultivated for their pungent seeds **2** a paste made from the powdered seeds of any of these plants and used as a condiment **3a** a brownish-yellow colour **3b** *(as adj)*: *a mustard carpet* **4** *sl, chiefly US* zest or enthusiasm [c13 from OF *moustarde*, from L *mustum* MUST², since the original was made by adding must]

mustard and cress *n* seedlings of white mustard and garden cress, used in salads, etc

mustard gas *n* an oily liquid vesicant compound used in chemical warfare. Its vapour causes blindness and burns

mustard plaster *n med* a mixture of powdered black mustard seeds applied to the skin for its counterirritant effects

musteline ('mʌstɪˌlaɪn, -lɪn) *adj* of or belonging to a family of typically predatory mammals, including weasels, ferrets, badgers, skunks, and otters [c17 from L *mustēlīnus*, from *mustēla* weasel]

muster ('mʌstə) *vb* **1** to call together (numbers of men) for duty, inspection, etc, or (of men) to assemble in this way **2** **muster in** *or* **out** *US* to enlist into or discharge from military service **3** *(tr; sometimes foll by up)* to summon or gather: *to muster one's arguments; to muster up courage* **4** *(tr) Austral & NZ* to round up (stock) ▷ *n* **5** an assembly of military personnel for duty, etc **6** a collection, assembly, or gathering **7** *Austral & NZ* the act of rounding up stock **8** **pass muster** to be acceptable [c14 from OF *moustrer*, from L *monstrāre* to show, from *monstrum* portent]

musth *or* **must** (mʌst) *n* (often preceded by *in*) a state of frenzied sexual excitement in the males of certain large mammals, esp elephants [c19 from Urdu *mast*, from Persian: drunk]

must-have *n* **1** an essential possession: *the mobile phone is now a must-have for children* ▷ *adj* **2** essential: *a must-have fashion accessory*

musty ('mʌstɪ) *adj* **mustier, mustiest** **1** smelling or tasting old, stale, or mouldy **2** old-fashioned, dull, or hackneyed: *musty ideas* [c16 ? var. of obs. *moisty*] > '**mustily** *adv* > '**mustiness** *n*

mutable ('mjuːtəbᵊl) *adj* able to or tending to change [c14 from L *mūtābilis* fickle, from *mūtāre* to change] > ˌ**muta'bility** *or (less commonly)* '**mutableness** *n* > '**mutably** *adv*

mutagen ('mjuːtədʒən) *n* a substance that can induce genetic mutation [c20 from MUTATION + -GEN] > **mutagenic** (ˌmjuːtə'dʒɛnɪk) *adj*

mutagenesis (ˌmjuːtə'dʒɛnɪsɪs) *n genetics* the generation, usually intentional, of mutations [c20 from MUTA(TION) + -GENESIS]

mutant ('mjuːtᵊnt) *n* **1** Also called: **mutation** an animal, organism, or gene that has undergone mutation ▷ *adj* **2** of, undergoing, or resulting from mutation [c20 from L *mutāre* to change]

Mutare (muː'tɑːrɪ) *n* a city in E Zimbabwe, near the Mozambique border: rail and trade centre in a mining and tobacco-growing region. Pop: 165 000 (1998 est). Former name (until 1982): **Umtali**

mutate (mjuː'teɪt) *vb* **mutates, mutating, mutated** to undergo or cause to undergo mutation [c19 from L *mūtātus*, pp of *mūtāre* to change]

mutation (mjuː'teɪʃən) *n* **1** the act or process of mutating; change; alteration **2** a change or alteration **3** a change in the chromosomes or genes of a cell which may affect the structure and development of the resultant offspring **4** another word for **mutant** (sense 1) **5** a physical characteristic of an individual resulting from this type of chromosomal change **6** *phonetics* **6a** (in Germanic languages) another name for **umlaut** **6b** (in Celtic languages) a phonetic change in certain initial consonants caused by a preceding word > **mu'tational** *adj* > **mu'tationally** *adv*

mutatis mutandis *Latin* (muː'tɑːtɪs muː'tændɪs) the necessary changes having been made

mutch (mʌtʃ) *n* a close-fitting linen cap formerly worn by women and children in Scotland [c15 from MDu. *mutse* cap, from Med. L *almucia* AMICE]

mute (mjuːt) *adj* **1** not giving out sound or speech; silent **2** unable to speak; dumb **3** unspoken or unexpressed **4** *law* (of a person arraigned on indictment) refusing to answer a charge **5** *phonetics* another word for **plosive** **6** (of a letter in a word) silent ▷ *n* **7** a person who is unable to speak **8** *law* a person who refuses to plead **9** any of various devices used to soften the tone of stringed or brass instruments **10** *phonetics* a plosive consonant **11** a silent letter **12** an actor in a dumb show **13** a hired mourner ▷ *vb* **mutes, muting, muted** *(tr)* **14** to reduce the volume of (a musical instrument) by means of a mute, soft pedal, etc **15** to subdue the strength of (a colour, tone, lighting, etc) [c14 *muwet* from OF *mu*, from L *mūtus* silent] > '**mutely** *adv* > '**muteness** *n*

USAGE *Mute* is occasionally wrongly used in the phrase *moot* (not *mute*) *point*

mute swan *n* a Eurasian swan with a pure white plumage and an orange-red bill

muti ('muːtɪ) *n S African inf* medicine, esp herbal [from Zulu *umuthi* tree, medicine]

mutilate ('mjuːtɪˌleɪt) *vb* **mutilates, mutilating, mutilated** *(tr)* **1** to deprive of a limb, essential part, etc; maim **2** to expurgate, damage, etc (a text, book, etc) [c16 from L *mutilāre* to cut off; rel. to *mutilus* maimed] > ˌ**muti'lation** *n* > '**mutiˌlative** *adj* > '**mutiˌlator** *n*

mutineer (ˌmjuːtɪ'nɪə) *n* a person who mutinies

mutinous ('mjuːtɪnəs) *adj* **1** openly rebellious **2** characteristic or indicative of mutiny > '**mutinously** *adv* > '**mutinousness** *n*

mutiny ('mjuːtɪnɪ) *n, pl* **mutinies** **1** open rebellion against constituted authority, esp by seamen or soldiers against their officers ▷ *vb* **mutinies, mutinying, mutinied** **2** *(intr)* to engage in mutiny [c16 from obs. *mutine*, from OF *mutin* rebellious, from *meute* mutiny, ult. from L *movēre* to move]

mutism ('mjuːˌtɪzəm) *n* **1** the state of being mute **2** *psychiatry* **2a** a refusal to speak **2b** the lack of development of speech

mutt (mʌt) *n sl* **1** an inept, ignorant, or stupid person **2** a mongrel dog; cur [c20 from MUTTONHEAD]

mutter ('mʌtə) *vb* **1** to utter (something) in a low and indistinct tone **2** *(intr)* to grumble or complain **3** *(intr)* to make a low continuous murmuring sound ▷ *n* **4** a muttered sound or complaint [c14 *moteren*] > '**muttering** *n, adj*

Mutter ('mʊtə) *n* **Anne-Sophie** born 1963, German violinist

mutton ('mʌtᵊn) *n* **1** the flesh of sheep, esp of mature sheep, used as food **2** **mutton dressed as lamb** an older woman dressed up to look young [c13 *moton* sheep, from OF, from Med. L *multō*, of Celtic origin] > '**muttony** *adj*

mutton bird *n* **1** any of several shearwaters, having a dark plumage with greyish underparts, esp the sooty shearwater (*Puffinus griseus*) of New Zealand, which is collected for food by Maoris. It inhabits the Pacific Ocean and in summer nests in Australia and New Zealand. *Austral* **2** any of various petrols esp the short tailed shearwater, *Puffinus tenuirostris*, which inhabits the Pacific Ocean and in summer nests in S Australia [c19 so named because their cooked flesh is claimed to taste like mutton]

mutton chop *n* a piece of mutton from the loin

muttonchops ('mʌtᵊn,tʃɒps) *pl n* side whiskers trimmed in the shape of chops

muttonhead ('mʌtᵊn,hɛd) *n sl* a stupid or ignorant person; fool > **'mutton,headed** *adj*

Muttra ('mʌtrə) *n* the former name of **Mathura**

mutual ('mju:tʃʊəl) *adj* **1** experienced or expressed by each of two or more people about the other; reciprocal: *mutual distrust* **2** *inf* common to or shared by both: *a mutual friend* **3** denoting an insurance company, etc, in which the policyholders share the profits and expenses and there are no shareholders. See also **mutual insurance** [c15 from OF *mutuel*, from L *mūtuus* reciprocal (orig.: borrowed); rel. to *mūtāre* to change] > **mutuality** (,mju:tʃʊ'ælɪtɪ) *n* > **'mutually** *adv*

USAGE The use of *mutual* to mean 'common to or shared by two or more people' was formerly considered incorrect by some people, on the grounds of its original meaning in Latin, but usage has now made it generally acceptable

mutual induction *n* the production of an electromotive force in a circuit by a current change in a second circuit magnetically linked to the first

mutual insurance *n* a system of insurance by which all policyholders become company members under contract to pay premiums into a common fund out of which claims are paid. See also **mutual** (sense 3)

mutuel ('mju:tʃʊəl) *n* short for **pari-mutuel**

muu-muu ('mu:,mu:) *n* a loose brightly coloured dress worn by women in Hawaii [from Hawaiian]

Muzak ('mju:zæk) *n trademark* recorded light music played in shops, restaurants, factories, etc

muzhik *or* **moujik** ('mu:ʒɪk) *n* a Russian peasant, esp under the tsars [c16 from Russian: peasant]

Muzorewa (,mʊzə'reɪwə) *n* **Abel (Tendekayi)** ('eɪbᵊl) born 1925, Zimbabwean Methodist bishop and politician; president of the African National Council (1971–85). He was one of the negotiators of an internal settlement (1978–79); prime minister of Rhodesia (1979)

muzzle ('mʌzᵊl) *n* **1** the projecting part of the face, usually the jaws and nose, of animals such as the dog and horse **2** a guard or strap fitted over an animal's nose and jaws to prevent it biting or eating **3** the front end of a gun barrel ▷ *vb* **muzzles, muzzling, muzzled** (*tr*) **4** to prevent from being heard or noticed **5** to put a muzzle on (an animal) [c15 *mosel*, from OF *musel*, dim. of *muse* snout, from Med. L *mūsus*, from ?] > **'muzzler** *n*

muzzle-loader *n* a firearm receiving its ammunition through the muzzle > **'muzzle-,loading** *adj*

muzzle velocity *n* the velocity of a projectile as it leaves a firearm's muzzle

muzzy ('mʌzɪ) *adj* **muzzier, muzziest** **1** blurred or hazy **2** confused or befuddled [c18 from ?] > **'muzzily** *adv* > **'muzziness** *n*

MVO (in Britain) *abbrev for* Member of the Royal Victorian Order

MVP (in the US and Australia) *abbrev for* most valuable player: the man or woman judged to be the outstanding player in a sport during a particular season or championship

MW **1** *symbol for* megawatt ▷ **2** *radio abbrev for*: medium wave

Mweru ('mwɛəru:) *n* a lake in central Africa, on the border between Zambia and the Democratic Republic of Congo (formerly Zaïre). Area: 4196 sq km (1620 sq miles)

Mx *physics symbol for*: maxwell

my (maɪ) *determiner* **1** of, belonging to, or associated with the speaker or writer (me): *my own ideas* **2** used in various forms of address: *my lord* ▷ *interj* **3** an exclamation of surprise, awe, etc: *my, how you've grown!* [c12 *mī*, var. of OE *mīn* when preceding a word beginning with a consonant]

USAGE See at **me**

myalgia (maɪ'ældʒɪə) *n* pain in a muscle or a group of muscles [c19 from MYO- + -ALGIA]

myalgic encephalopathy (maɪ'ældʒɪk ɛn,sɛfəl'ɒpfɪ) *n* a condition characterized by painful muscles, extreme fatigue, and general debility, sometimes occuring as a sequel to viral illness. Also called **chronic fatigue syndrome** Formerly called: **myalgic encephalomyelitis** Abbreviation: **ME**

myalism ('maɪə,lɪzəm) *n* a kind of witchcraft practised esp in the Caribbean [c19 from *myal*, prob. West African]

myall ('maɪəl) *n* **1** any of several Australian acacias having hard scented wood **2** a native Australian living independently of society [c19 Abor. name]

Myanmar *or* **Myanma** ('maɪænmɑ:, 'mjænmɑ:) *n* a republic in SE Asia, on the Bay of Bengal and the Andaman Sea: unified from small states in 1752; annexed by Britain (1823–85) and made a province of India in 1886; became independent in 1948. It is generally mountainous, with the basins of the Chindwin and Irrawaddy Rivers in the central part and the Irrawaddy delta in the south. Official language: Burmese. Religion: Buddhist majority. Currency: kyat. Capital: Yangon. Pop: 41 995 000 (2001 est). Area: 676 577 sq km (261 228 sq miles). Official name: **the Union of Myanmar** Former name (until 1989): **Burma**
▷ www.myanmar.com
▷ www.myanmar-tourism.com/about_myanmar.htm

mycelium (maɪ'si:lɪəm) *n, pl* **mycelia** (-lɪə) the vegetative body of fungi: a mass of branching filaments (hyphae) [c19 (lit.: nail of fungus): from MYCO- + Gk *hēlos* nail] > **my'celial** *adj*

Mycenae (maɪ'si:ni:) *n* an ancient Greek city in the NE Peloponnesus on the plain of Argos

Mycenaean (,maɪsɪ'ni:ən) *adj* **1** of or relating to ancient Mycenae, or its inhabitants **2** of or relating to the Aegean civilization of Mycenae (1400 to 1100 BC)
▷ www.archaeonia.com/history/mycenaean.htm

-mycete *n combining form* indicating a member of a class of fungi: *myxomycete* [from NL *-mycetes*, from Gk *mukētes*, pl. of *mukēs* fungus]

myco- *or before a vowel* **myc-** *combining form* indicating fungus: *mycology* [from Gk *mukēs* fungus]

mycology (maɪ'kɒlədʒɪ) *n* the branch of biology concerned with the study of fungi > **mycological** (,maɪkə'lɒdʒɪkᵊl) *or* **,myco'logic** *adj* > **my'cologist** *n*

mycoplasma (,maɪkəʊ'plæzmə) *n* any one of a genus of prokaryotic microorganisms some species of which cause disease (**mycoplasmosis**) in animals and humans

mycorrhiza *or* **mycorhiza** (,maɪkə'raɪzə) *n, pl* **mycorrhizae** (-zi:) *or* **mycorrhizas, mycorhizae** *or* **mycorhizas** an association of a fungus and a plant in which the fungus lives within or on the outside of the plant's roots forming a symbiotic or parasitic relationship [c19 from MYCO- + Gk *rhiza* root] > **,mycor'rhizal** *or* **,myco'rhizal** *adj*

mycosis (maɪ'kəʊsɪs) *n* any infection or disease caused by fungus > **mycotic** (maɪ'kɒtɪk) *adj*

mycotoxin (,maɪkə'tɒksɪn) *n* any of various toxic substances produced by fungi, some of which may affect food > **,mycotox'ology** *n*

mycotrophic (,maɪkəʊ'trɒfɪk) *adj bot* (of a plant) symbiotic with a fungus, esp a mycorrhizal fungus > **mycotrophy** (maɪ'kɒtrəfɪ) *n*

myelin ('maɪɪlɪn) *or* **myeline** ('maɪɪ,liːn) *n* a white tissue forming an insulating sheath (**myelin sheath**) around certain nerve fibres. Damage to the myelin sheath causes neurological disease, as in multiple sclerosis

myelitis (,maɪɪ'laɪtɪs) *n* inflammation of the spinal cord or of the bone marrow

myeloma (,maɪə'ləʊmə) *n, pl* **myelomas** *or* **myelomata** (-mətə) a usually malignant tumour of the bone marrow

Myers ('maɪəz) *n* **L(eopold) H(amilton)** 1881–1944, British novelist, best known for his novel sequence *The Near and the Far* (1929–40)

Mykonos ('mɪkənɒs, -əʊs, 'miːkə-) *n* a Greek island in the S Aegean Sea, one of the Cyclades: a popular tourist resort with many churches. Pop: 5500 (latest est). Greek name: **Míkonos**

My Lai ('maɪ 'laɪ, 'miː) *n* a village in S Vietnam where in 1968 US troops massacred over 400 civilians

mynah *or* **myna** ('maɪnə) *n* any of various tropical Asian starlings, some of which can mimic human speech [c18 from Hindi *mainā*, from Sansk. *madana*]

Mynheer (mə'nɪə) *n* a Dutch title of address equivalent to *Sir* when used alone or to *Mr* before a name [c17 from Du. *mijnheer* my lord]

myo- *or before a vowel* **my-** *combining form* muscle: *myocardium* [from Gk *mus* MUSCLE]

myocardium (,maɪəʊ'kɑːdɪəm) *n, pl* **myocardia** (-dɪə) the muscular tissue of the heart [c19 *myo-* + *cardium*, from Gk *kardia* heart] > ,**myo'cardial** *adj*

myology (maɪ'ɒlədʒɪ) *n* the branch of medical science concerned with muscles

myope ('maɪəʊp) *n* any person afflicted with myopia [c18 via F from Gk *muōps*; see MYOPIA]

myopia (maɪ'əʊpɪə) *n* inability to see distant objects clearly because the images are focused in front of the retina; short-sightedness [c18 via NL from Gk *muōps* short-sighted, from *muein* to close (the eyes), + *ōps* eye] > **myopic** (maɪ'ɒpɪk) *adj* > **my'opically** *adv*

myosin ('maɪəsɪn) *n* the chief protein of muscle [c19 from MYO- + -OSE[2] + -IN]

myosotis (,maɪə'səʊtɪs) *n* any plant of the genus *Myosotis*. See **forget-me-not** [c18 NL from Gk *muosōtis* mouse-ear (referring to its furry leaves), from *mus* mouse + *ous* ear]

myriad ('mɪrɪəd) *adj* **1** innumerable ▷ *n* (*also used in pl*) **2** a large indefinite number **3** *arch* ten thousand [c16 via LL from Gk *murias* ten thousand]

myriapod ('mɪrɪə,pɒd) *n* **1** any of a group of terrestrial arthropods having a long segmented body and many walking limbs, such as the centipedes and millipedes ▷ *adj* **2** of, relating to, or belonging to this group [c19 from NL *Myriapoda*. See MYRIAD, -POD]

Myrmidon ('mɜːmɪ,dɒn, -dᵊn) *n* **1** *Greek myth* one of a race of people who were led against Troy by Achilles **2** (*often not cap*) a follower or henchman

myrobalan (maɪ'rɒbələn, mɪ-) *n* **1** the dried plumlike fruit of various tropical trees used in dyeing, tanning, ink, and medicine **2** a dye extracted from this fruit [c16 via L from Gk *murobalanos*, from *muron* ointment + *balanos* acorn]

Myron ('maɪərən) *n* 5th century BC, Greek sculptor. He worked mainly in bronze and introduced a greater variety of pose into Greek sculpture, as in his *Discobolus*

myrrh (mɜː) *n* **1** any of several trees and shrubs of Africa and S Asia that exude an aromatic resin **2** the resin obtained from such a plant, used in perfume, incense, and medicine [OE *myrre*, via L from Gk *murrha*, ult. from Akkadian *murrū*]

myrtle ('mɜːtᵊl) *n* an evergreen shrub or tree, esp a S European shrub with pink or white flowers and aromatic blue-black berries [c16 from Med. L *myrtilla*, from L *myrtus*, from Gk *murtos*]

myself (maɪ'sɛlf) *pron* **1a** the reflexive form of I or *me* **1b** (intensifier): *I myself know of no answer* **2** (*preceded by a copula*) my usual self: *I'm not myself today* **3** *not standard* used instead of I or *me* in compound noun phrases: *John and myself are voting together*

Mysia ('mɪsɪə) *n* an ancient region in the NW corner of Asia Minor > '**Mysian** *adj, n*

Mysore (maɪ'sɔː) *n* **1** a city in S India, in S Karnataka state: former capital of the state of Mysore; manufacturing and trading centre; university (1916). Pop: 480 692 (1991) **2** the former name (until 1973) of **Karnataka**

mysterious (mɪ'stɪərɪəs) *adj* **1** characterized by or indicative of mystery **2** puzzling, curious > **mys'teriously** *adv* > **mys'teriousness** *n*

mystery[1] ('mɪstərɪ, -trɪ) *n, pl* **mysteries** **1** an unexplained or inexplicable event, phenomenon, etc **2** a person or thing that arouses curiosity or suspense because of an unknown, obscure, or enigmatic quality **3** the state or quality of being obscure, inexplicable, or enigmatic **4** a story, film, etc, which arouses suspense and curiosity because of facts concealed **5** *Christianity* any truth that is divinely revealed but otherwise unknowable **6** *Christianity* a sacramental rite, such as the Eucharist, or (*when pl*) the consecrated elements of the Eucharist **7** (*often pl*) any rites of certain ancient Mediterranean religions **8** short for **mystery play** [c14 via L from Gk *mustērion* secret rites]

mystery[2] ('mɪstərɪ) *n, pl* **mysteries** *arch* **1** a trade, occupation, or craft **2** a guild of craftsmen [c14 from Med. L *mistērium*, from L *ministerium* occupation, from *minister* official]

mystery play *n* (in the Middle Ages) a type of drama based on the life of Christ ▷ Cf **miracle play**

mystery tour *n* an excursion to an unspecified destination

mystic ('mɪstɪk) *n* **1** a person who achieves mystical experience or an apprehension of divine mysteries ▷ *adj* **2** another word for **mystical** [c14 via L from Gk *mustikos*, from *mustēs* mystery initiate; rel. to *muein* to initiate into sacred rites]

mystical ('mɪstɪkᵊl) *adj* **1** relating to or characteristic of mysticism **2** *Christianity* having a divine or sacred significance that surpasses human apprehension **3** having occult or metaphysical significance > '**mystically** *adv*

mysticism ('mɪstɪ,sɪzəm) *n* **1** belief in or experience of a reality surpassing normal human understanding or experience **2** a system of contemplative prayer and spirituality aimed at achieving direct intuitive experience of the divine **3** obscure or confused belief or thought

mystify ('mɪstɪ,faɪ) *vb* **mystifies, mystifying, mystified** (*tr*) **1** to confuse, bewilder, or puzzle **2** to make obscure [c19 from F *mystifier*, from *mystère* MYSTERY[1] or *mystique* MYSTIC] > ,**mystifi'cation** *n* > '**mysti,fying** *adj*

mystique (mɪ'stiːk) *n* an aura of mystery, power, and awe that surrounds a person or thing [c20 from F (adj): MYSTIC]

myth (mɪθ) *n* **1a** a story about superhuman beings of an earlier age, usually of how natural phenomena, social customs, etc, came into existence **1b** another word for **mythology** (senses 1, 3) **2** a person or thing whose existence is fictional or unproven [c19 via LL from Gk *muthos* fable]

myth. *abbrev for:* **1** mythological **2** mythology

mythical ('mɪθɪkᵊl) *or* **mythic** *adj* **1** of or relating to myth **2** imaginary or fictitious > '**mythically** *adv*

mythicize *or* **mythicise** ('mɪθɪ,saɪz) *vb* **mythicizes, mythicizing, mythicized** *or* **mythicises, mythicising, mythicised** (*tr*) to make into or treat as a myth > '**mythicist** *n*

mytho- *combining form* myth: *mythopoeia*

mythologize *or* **mythologise** (mɪˈθɒləˌdʒaɪz) *vb* **mythologizes, mythologizing, mythologized** *or* **mythologises, mythologising, mythologised** **1** to tell, study, or explain (myths) **2** (*intr*) to create or make up myths **3** (*tr*) to convert into a myth > **myˈtholoˌgizer** *or* **myˈtholoˌgiser** *n*

mythology (mɪˈθɒlədʒɪ) *n, pl* **mythologies** **1** a body of myths, esp one associated with a particular culture, person, etc **2** a body of stories about a person, institution, etc **3** myths collectively **4** the study of myths > **mythological** (ˌmɪθəˈlɒdʒɪkᵊl) *adj* > **myˈthologist** *n*

▷ www.ugcs.caltech.edu/~cherryne/mythology.html

▷ http://members.bellatlantic.net/~vze33gpz/myth.html

mythomania (ˌmɪθəʊˈmeɪnɪə) *n psychiatry* the tendency to lie or exaggerate, occurring in some mental disorders > **ˌmythoˈmaniˌac** *n, adj*

mythopoeia (ˌmɪθəʊˈpiːə) *n* the composition or making of myths [C19 from Gk, ult. from *muthos* myth + *poiein* to make] > **ˌmythoˈpoeic** *adj*

mythos (ˈmaɪθɒs, ˈmɪθɒs) *n, pl* **mythoi** (-θɔɪ) **1** the complex of beliefs, values, attitudes, etc, characteristic of a specific group or society: *characters of the Arthurian mythos* **2** another word for **myth** or **mythology**

Mytilene (ˌmɪtɪˈliːnɪ) *n* **1** a port on the Greek island of Lesbos: Roman remains; Byzantine fortress Pop: 25 000 (latest est). Modern Greek name: **Mitilíni** **2** a former name for **Lesbos**

myxo (ˈmɪksəʊ) *n Austral sl* myxomatosis

myxo- *or before a vowel* **myx-** *combining form* mucus or slime: *myxomatosis* [from Gk *muxa*]

myxoedema *or US* **myxedema** (ˌmɪksɪˈdiːmə) *n* a disease resulting from underactivity of the thyroid gland characterized by puffy eyes, face, and hands and mental sluggishness. See also **cretinism**

myxoma (mɪkˈsəʊmə) *n, pl* **myxomas** *or* **myxomata** (-mətə) a tumour composed of mucous connective tissue, usually situated in subcutaneous tissue > **myxomatous** (mɪkˈsɒmətəs) *adj*

myxomatosis (ˌmɪksəməˈtəʊsɪs) *n* an infectious and usually fatal viral disease of rabbits characterized by swelling of the mucous membranes and formation of skin tumours, and transmitted by flea bites

myxomycete (ˌmɪksəʊmaɪˈsiːt) *n* a slime mould, esp a slime mould of the phylum *Myxomycota* (division *Myxomycetes* in traditional classifications)

myxovirus (ˈmɪksəʊˌvaɪrəs) *n* any of a group of viruses that cause influenza, mumps, etc

Nn

n *or* **N** (ɛn) *n, pl* **n's, N's,** *or* **Ns** **1** the 14th letter of the English alphabet **2** a speech sound represented by this letter

n[1] *symbol for:* **1** neutron **2** *optics* index of refraction **3** nano-

n[2] (ɛn) *determiner* an indefinite number (of): *there are n objects in a box*

N *symbol for:* **1** Also: **kt** *chess* knight **2** newton(s) **3** *chem* nitrogen **4** North **5** noun **6** (*in combination*) nuclear: *N-power; N-plant*

n. *abbrev for:* **1** neuter **2** new **3** nominative **4** noun

Na *the chemical symbol for* sodium [L *natrium*]

NA *abbrev for* North America

NAAFI *or* **Naafi** ('næfɪ) *n* **1** *acronym for* Navy, Army, and Air Force Institutes: an organization providing canteens, shops, etc, for British military personnel at home or overseas **2** a canteen, shop, etc, run by this organization

naartjie ('nɑːtʃɪ) *n S African* a tangerine [from Afrik., from Tamil]

nab (næb) *vb* **nabs, nabbing, nabbed** (*tr*) *inf* **1** to arrest (a criminal, etc) **2** to seize suddenly; snatch [c17 ? of Scand. origin]

nabla ('næblə) *n maths* another name for **del** [c19 from Gk: stringed instrument, because it is shaped like a harp]

Nablus ('nɑːbləs) *n* a town in the West Bank: near the site of ancient Shechem. Pop: 100 231 (1997)

nabob ('neɪbɒb) *n* **1** *inf* a rich or important man **2** (formerly) a European who made a fortune in India **3** another name for a **nawab** [c17 from Port. *nababo*, from Hindi *nawwāb*; see NAWAB]

Nabokov (nə'bɒkɒf, 'næbəˌkɒf) *n* **Vladimir Vladimirovich** (vla'dimir vla'dimirəvitʃ) 1899–1977, US novelist, born in Russia. His works include *Lolita* (1955), *Pnin* (1957), *Pale Fire* (1962), and *Ada* (1969)

Naboth ('neɪbɒθ) *n Old Testament* an inhabitant of Jezreel, murdered by King Ahab at the instigation of his wife Jezebel for refusing to sell his vineyard (I Kings 21)

nacelle (nə'sɛl) *n* a streamlined enclosure on an aircraft, not part of the fuselage, to accommodate an engine, passengers, crew, etc [c20 from F: small boat, from LL *nāvicella*, a dim. of L *nāvis* ship]

nacho ('nɑːtʃəʊ) *n, pl* **nachos** a Mexican snack consisting of a piece of tortilla topped with melted cheese

NACODS ('neɪkɒdz) *n* (in Britain) *acronym for* National Association of Colliery Overmen, Deputies, and Shotfirers

nacre ('neɪkə) *n* the technical name for **mother-of-pearl** [c16 via F from OIt. *naccara*, from Ar. *naqqārah* shell, drum] > **'nacred** *adj*

nacreous ('neɪkrɪəs) *adj* relating to, consisting of, or having the lustre of mother-of-pearl

NACRO *or* **Nacro** ('nækrəʊ) *n* (in Britain) *acronym for* National Association for the Care and Resettlement of Offenders

Nader ('neɪdə) *n* **Ralph** born 1934, US lawyer and campaigner for consumer rights: stood as a Green Party candidate for president in 1996 and 2000 and an independent in 2004

nadir ('neɪdɪə, 'næ-) *n* **1** the point on the celestial sphere directly below an observer and diametrically opposite the zenith **2** the lowest point; depths [c14 from OF, from Ar. *nazīr as-samt*, lit.: opposite the zenith]

nadors ('nɑːˌdɔːz) *n S African* a thirst brought on by excessive consumption of alcohol [from Afrik. *na* after + *dors* thirst]

nae (neɪ) *or* **na** (nɑː) a Scot word for **no**[2] or **not**

naevus *or US* **nevus** ('niːvəs) *n, pl* **naevi** *or US* **nevi** (-vaɪ) any pigmented blemish on the skin; birthmark or mole [c19 from L; rel. to *(g)natus* born, produced by nature] > '**naevoid** *or US* '**nevoid** *adj*

naff (næf) *adj Brit sl* inferior; in poor taste [c19 ?from back slang on *fan*, short for FANNY] > '**naffness** *n*

naff off *sentence substitute Brit sl* a forceful expression of dismissal or contempt

NAFTA ('næftə) *n acronym for* North American Free Trade Agreement
▷ www.nafta-customs.org

nag[1] (næg) *vb* **nags, nagging, nagged** 1 to scold or annoy constantly 2 (when *intr*, often foll by *at*) to be a constant source of discomfort or worry (to) ▷ *n* 3 a person, esp a woman, who nags [c19 of Scand. origin] > '**nagger** *n*

nag[2] (næg) *n* 1 *often derog* a horse 2 a small riding horse [c14 of Gmc origin]

Nagaland ('nɑːgəˌlænd) *n* a state of NE India: formed in 1962 from parts of Assam and the North-East Frontier Agency; inhabited chiefly by Naga tribes; consists of almost inaccessible forested hills and mountains (the **Naga Hills**); shifting cultivation predominates. Capital: Kohima. Pop: 1 988 636 (2001) Area: 16 579 sq km (6401 sq miles)

nagana (nəˈgɑːnə) *n* a disease of all domesticated animals of central and southern Africa, transmitted by tsetse flies [from Zulu *u-nakane*]

Nagano (nəˈgɑːnəʊ) *n* a city in central Japan, on central Honshu: Buddhist shrine; two universities. Pop: 358 512 (1995)

Nagasaki (ˌnɑːgəˈsɑːkɪ) *n* a port in SW Japan, on W Kyushu: almost completely destroyed in 1945 by the second atomic bomb dropped on Japan by the US; shipbuilding industry. Pop: 438 724 (1995)

Nagorno-Karabakh Autonomous Region (nəˈgɔːnəʊkərʌˈbɑːk) *n* an administrative division in S Azerbaijan. In 1990–94 Armenian claims to the region led to violent unrest and fighting between national forces. Capital: Stepanakert. Pop: 193 300 (1991 est). Area: 4400 sq km (1700 sq miles)

Nagoya ('nɑːgəʊjə) *n* a city in central Japan, on S Honshu on Ise Bay: a major industrial centre. Pop: 2 152 258 (1995)

Nagpur (nægˈpʊə) *n* a city in central India, in NE Maharashtra state: became capital of the kingdom of Nagpur (1743); capital of the Central Provinces (later Madhya Pradesh) from 1861 to 1956. Pop: 1 624 752 (1991)

Nagy (*Hungarian* nɔdj) *n* **Imre** ('imrɛ) 1896–1958, Hungarian statesman; prime minister (1953–55; 1956). He was removed from office and later executed when Soviet forces suppressed the revolution of 1956; reburied with honours in 1989

Nagyszeben ('nɔdjseːˌbɛn) *n* the Hungarian name for **Sibiu**

Nagyvárad ('nɔdjvaːrɔd) *n* the Hungarian name for **Oradea**

Nah. *Bible abbrev for* Nahum

Naha ('nɑːhə) *n* a port in S Japan, on the SW coast of Okinawa Island: chief city of the Ryukyu Islands. Pop: 301 928 (1995)

NAHT (in Britain) *abbrev for* National Association of Head Teachers

Nahuatl ('nɑːwɑːtᵊl, nɑːˈwɑːtᵊl) *n* 1 (*pl* **Nahuatl** *or* **Nahuatls**) a member of one of a group of Central American and Mexican Indian peoples including the Aztecs 2 the language of these peoples

Nahum ('neɪhəm) *n Old Testament* 1 a Hebrew prophet of the 7th century BC 2 the book containing his oracles

naiad ('naɪæd) *n, pl* **naiads** *or* **naiades** (-əˌdiːz) 1 *Greek myth* a nymph dwelling in a lake, river, or spring 2 the aquatic larva of the dragonfly, mayfly, and related insects 3 Also called: **water nymph** a submerged aquatic plant, having narrow leaves and small flowers [c17 via L from Gk *nāias* water nymph; rel. to *náein* to flow]

naïf (nɑːˈiːf) *adj, n* a less common word for **naive**

nail (neɪl) *n* 1 a fastening device, usually made of metal, having a point at one end and a head at the other 2 anything resembling such a device in function or shape 3 the horny plate covering part of the dorsal surface of the fingers or toes. Related adj: **ungual** 4 the claw of a mammal, bird, or reptile 5 a unit of length, formerly used for measuring cloth, equal to two and a quarter inches 6 **hit the nail on the head** to do or say something correct or telling 7 **on the nail** (of payments) at once ▷ *vb (tr)* 8 to attach with or as if with nails 9 *inf* to arrest, catch, or seize 10 *inf* to hit or bring down, as with a shot 11 *inf* to expose or detect (a lie or liar) 12 to fix (one's eyes, attention, etc) on 13 to stud with nails [OE *nægl*] > '**nailer** *n*

nail-biting *n* 1 the act or habit of biting one's fingernails 2a anxiety or tension 2b (*as modifier*): *nail-biting suspense*

nail bomb *n* an explosive device containing nails, used by terrorists to cause serious injuries in crowded situations

nailbrush ('neɪlˌbrʌʃ) *n* a small stiff-bristled brush for cleaning the fingernails

nailed-on *adj sl* certain, definite; guaranteed to be successful

nailfile ('neɪlˌfaɪl) *n* a small file of metal or of board coated with emery, used to trim the nails

nail polish *or* **varnish** *or esp US* **enamel** *n* a quick-drying cosmetic lacquer applied to colour the nails or make them shiny or esp both

nail set *or* **punch** *n* a punch for driving the head of a nail below or flush with the surrounding surface

nainsook ('neɪnsʊk, 'næn-) *n* a light soft plain-weave cotton fabric [c19 from Hindi, from *nain* eye + *sukh* delight]

Naipaul (naɪˈpɔːl) *n* Sir **V(idiadhar) S(urajprasad)** born 1932, Trinidadian novelist of Indian descent, living in Britain. His works include *A House for Mr Biswas* (1961), *In a Free State* (1971), which won the Booker Prize, *The Enigma of Arrival* (1987), and *Beyond Belief* (1998): Nobel prize for literature 2001

Nn

naira ('naɪrə) *n* the standard monetary unit of Nigeria [c20 altered from *Nigeria*]

Nairnshire ('nɛənˌʃɪə, -ʃə) *n* (until 1975) a county of NE Scotland, now part of Highland

Nairobi (naɪˈrəʊbɪ) *n* the capital of Kenya, in the southwest at an altitude of 1650 m (5500 ft): founded in 1899; became capital in 1905; commercial and industrial centre; the **Nairobi National Park** (a game reserve) is nearby. Pop: 2 143 254 (1999)
▷ www.kenyaweb.com/vnairobi

naive, naïve (nɑːˈiːv, naɪˈiːv), *or* **naïf** *adj* 1 having or expressing innocence and credulity; ingenuous 2 lacking developed powers of reasoning or criticism: *a naive argument* 3 another word for **primitive** (sense 5) ▷ *n* 4 a person who is naive, esp in artistic style. See **primitive** (sense 10) [c17 from F fem of *naïf*, from OF: native, spontaneous, from L *nātīvus* NATIVE] > **na'ively, na'ïvely,** *or* **na'ïfly** *adv* > **na'iveness, na'ïveness,** *or* **na'ïfness** *n*

naivety (naɪˈiːvtɪ), **naiveté,** *or* **naïveté** (ˌnɑːiːvˈteɪ) *n, pl* **naiveties, naivetés,** *or* **naïvetés** 1 the state or quality of being naive 2 a naive act or statement

Najaf ('nædʒæf) *n* a holy city in central Iraq, near the River Euphrates; burial place of the Caliph Ali and a centre of the Shiite faith. Pop: 309 010 (latest est)

naked ('neɪkɪd) *adj* 1 having the body unclothed; undressed 2 having no covering; exposed: *a naked flame* 3 with no qualification or concealment: *the naked facts* 4 unaided by any optical instrument (esp in **the naked eye**) 5 (usually foll by *of*) destitute: *naked of weapons* 6 (of animals) lacking hair, feathers, scales, etc 7 *law* 7a unsupported by authority: *a naked contract* 7b lacking some essential condition to render valid; incomplete [OE *nacod*] > '**nakedly** *adv* > '**nakedness** *n*

naked ladies *n* (*functioning as sing*) another name for **autumn crocus**

naked lady *n* a pink orchid found in Australia and New Zealand

Nakhichevan (*Russian* nəxitʃɪ'vanj) *n* a city in W Azerbaijan, capital of the Nakhichevan Autonomous Republic: an ancient trading town; ceded to Russia in 1828. Pop: 66 800 (1994). Ancient name: **Naxuana** (ˌnæk'swɑːnə)

Nakhichevan Autonomous Republic (nəˌkɪtʃɛ'vɑːn) *n* a region belonging to Azerbaijan, from which it is separated by part of Armenia; annexed by Russia in 1828; unilaterally declared secession from the Soviet Union in 1990. Capital: Nakhichevan. Pop: 315 000 (1994). Area: 5500 sq km (2120 sq miles)

Nakuru (nə'kuːruː) *n* a town in W Kenya, on Lake Nakuru: commercial centre of an agricultural region. Pop: 231 262 (1999)

Nalchik (*Russian* 'naljtʃik) *n* a city in SW Russia, capital of the Kabardino-Balkar Republic, in a valley of the Greater Caucasus: health resort. Pop: 234 700 (1999 est)

naltrexone (næl'trɛksəʊn) *n* a drug that blocks opioid receptors in the brain and is used in treatments for opioid addiction

Nam *or* **'Nam** (næm) *n US inf* short for Vietnam (referring to the Vietnam War)

Namangan (*Russian* nəman'gan) *n* a city in E Uzbekistan. Pop: 291 000 (1998 est)

Namaqualand (nə'mɑːkwəˌlænd) *n* a semiarid coastal region of SW Africa, extending from near Windhoek, Namibia, into W South Africa: divided by the Orange River into **Little Namaqualand** in South Africa, and **Great Namaqualand** in Namibia; rich mineral resources. Area: 47 961 sq km (18 518 sq miles). Also called: **Namaland** ('nɑːməˌlænd)

namby-pamby (ˌnæmbɪ'pæmbɪ) *adj* **1** sentimental or prim in a weak insipid way **2** clinging, feeble, or spineless ▷ *n, pl* **namby-pambies 3** a person who is namby-pamby [C18 a nickname of Ambrose Phillips (died 1749), whose pastoral verse was ridiculed for being insipid]

Nam Co ('nɑːm 'kɔː) *or* **Nam Tso** *n* a salt lake in SW China, in SE Tibet at an altitude of 4629 m (15 186 ft). Area: about 1800 sq km (700 sq miles). Also called: **Tengri Nor**

name (neɪm) *n* **1** a word or term by which a person or thing is commonly and distinctively known **2** mere outward appearance as opposed to fact: *he was ruler in name only* **3** a word or phrase descriptive of character, usually abusive: *to call a person names* **4** reputation, esp, if unspecified, good reputation: *he's made quite a name for himself* **5a** a famous person or thing: *a name in the advertising world* **5b** *chiefly US & Canad* (*as modifier*): *a name product* **6** a member of Lloyd's who provides part of the capital of a syndicate and shares in its profits or losses but does not arrange its business **7 in the name of 7a** for the sake of **7b** by the authority of **8 name of the game 8a** anything that is significant or important **8b** normal conditions, circumstances, etc: *in gambling, losing money's the name of the game* **9 to one's name** belonging to one: *I haven't a penny to my name* ▷ *vb* **names, naming, named** (*tr*) **10** to give a name to **11** to refer to by name; cite: *he named three French poets* **12** to fix or specify: *they have named a date for the meeting* **13** to appoint or nominate: *he was named Journalist of the Year* **14** (*tr*) to ban (an MP) from the House of Commons by mentioning him or her formally by name as being guilty of disorderly conduct **15 name and shame** to reveal the identity of (a person or organization guilty of illegal or unacceptable behaviour) in order to embarrass him or her into not repeating the offence **6 name names** to cite people, esp in order to blame or accuse them **17 name the day** to choose the day for an event, esp one's wedding [OE *nama*, rel. to L *nomen*, Gk *noma*] > '**namable** *or* '**nameable** *adj*

name-calling *n* verbal abuse

namecheck ('neɪmˌtʃɛk) *vb* (*tr*) **1** to mention (someone) specifically by name ▷ *n* **2** a specific mention of someone's name, for example on a radio or television programme

name day *n* **1** *RC Church* the feast day of a saint whose name one bears **2** another name for **ticket day**

name-dropping *n inf* the practice of referring frequently to famous people, esp as though they were intimate friends, in order to impress others > '**name-ˌdropper** *n*

nameless ('neɪmlɪs) *adj* **1** without a name **2** indescribable: *a nameless horror seized him* **3** too unpleasant or disturbing to be mentioned: *nameless atrocities* > '**namelessness** *n*

namely ('neɪmlɪ) *adv* that is to say

Namen ('nɑːmə) *n* the Flemish name for **Namur**

nameplate ('neɪmˌpleɪt) *n* a small panel on or next to the door of a room or building, bearing the occupant's name and profession

namesake ('neɪmˌseɪk) *n* a person or thing named after another, or with the same name as another [C17 prob. describing people connected *for the name's sake*]

nametape ('neɪmˌteɪp) *n* a tape bearing the owner's name and attached to an article

Namhoi ('nɑːm'hɔɪ) *n* another name for **Foshan**

Namibe (næ'miːb) *n* a port in SW Angola: fishing industry. Pop: 77 000 (latest est)

Namibia (nɑː'mɪbɪə, nə-) *n* a country in southern Africa bordering on South Africa: annexed by Germany in 1884 and mandated by the League of Nations to South Africa in 1920. The mandate was terminated by the UN in 1966 but this was ignored by South Africa, as was the 1971 ruling by the International Court of Justice that the territory be surrendered. Independence was achieved in 1990 and Namibia became a member of the Commonwealth; Walvis Bay remained a South African enclave until 1994 when it was returned to Namibia. Official language: English; Afrikaans and German also spoken. Religion: mostly animist, with some Christians. Currency: dollar. Capital: Windhoek. Pop: 1 798 000 (2001 est). Area: 823 328 sq km (317 887 sq miles). Also called: **South West Africa** Former name (1885–1919): **German Southwest Africa** > **Na'mibian** *adj, n*
▷ www.grnnet.gov.na
▷ www.met.gov.na

Namier ('neɪmɪə) *n* Sir **Lewis Bernstein**, original name *Ludwik Bernsztajn vel Niemirowski*. 1888–1960, British historian, born in Poland: noted esp for his studies of 18th-century British politics

Nam Tso ('nɑːm 'tsɔː) *n* a variant transliteration of the Chinese name for **Nam Co**

Namur (næ'mʊə; *French* namyr) *n* **1** a province of S Belgium. Capital: Namur. Pop: 443 903 (2000 est). Area: 3660 sq km (1413 sq miles) **2** a town in S Belgium, capital of Namur province: strategically situated on a promontory between the Sambre and Meuse Rivers, besieged and captured many times. Pop: 105 419 (2000 est). Flemish name: **Namen**

nan (næn), **nana**, *or* **nanna** ('nænə) *n* a child's word for **grandmother**

nana ('nɑːnə) *n* **1** *sl* a fool **2 do one's nana** *Austral sl* to become very angry **3 off one's nana** *Austral sl* mad; insane [C19 prob. from BANANA]

Nanaimo bar (ˌnə'naɪməʊ) *n Canad* a chocolate-coated sweet with a filling made from butter and icing sugar [C20 named after *Nanaimo*, a city on Vancouver Island]

nan bread *or* **naan** (nɑːn) *n* (in Indian cookery) a slightly leavened bread in a large flat leaf shape [from Hindi]

Nanchang *or* **Nan-ch'ang** ('næn'tʃæŋ) *n* a walled city in SE China, capital of Jiangxi province, on the Kan

River: largest city in the Poyang basin. Pop: 1 264 739 (1999 est)

nancy ('nænsɪ) *n, pl* **nancies** an effeminate or homosexual boy or man. Also called: **nance, nancy boy** [c20 from the girl's name *Nancy*]

Nancy ('nænsɪ; *French* nɑ̃si) *n* a city in NE France: became the capital of the dukes of Lorraine in the 12th century, becoming French in 1766; administrative and financial centre. Pop: 103 605 (1999)

Nanda Devi ('nʌndə 'di:vɪ) *n* a mountain in N India, in Uttaranchal in the Himalayas. Height: 7817 m (25 645 ft)

NAND circuit *or* **gate** (nænd) *n electronics* a computer logic circuit having two or more input wires and one output wire that has an output signal if one or more of the input signals are at a low voltage ▷ Cf **OR circuit** [c20 from *not* + AND; see NOT CIRCUIT, AND CIRCUIT]

nandrolone ('nændrə,ləʊn) *n* an anabolic steroid present in the body in small amounts but also produced by metabolism of other steroids, sometimes taken as performance-enhancing drugs by athletes and bodybuilders

Nanga Parbat ('nʌŋgə 'pɑ:bʌt) *n* a mountain in N India, in NW Kashmir in the W Himalayas. Height: 8126 m (26 660 ft)

Nanhai ('nɑ:n'haɪ) *n* the Chinese name for the **South China Sea**

Nanjing ('næn'dʒɪŋ) *or* **Nanking** ('næn'kɪŋ) *n* a port in E central China, capital of Jiangsu province, on the Yangtze River: capital of the Chinese empire and a literary centre from the 14th to 17th centuries; capital of Nationalist China (1928–37); site of a massacre of about 300 000 civilians by the invading Japanese army in 1937; university (1928). Pop: 2 388 915 (1999 est)

nankeen (næŋ'ki:n) *or* **nankin** ('nænkɪn) *n* **1** a hard-wearing buff-coloured cotton fabric **2a** a pale greyish-yellow colour **2b** (*as adj*): *a nankeen carpet* [c18 after *Nanking*, China, where it originated]

Nanning *or* **Nan-ning** ('næn'nɪŋ) *n* a port in S China, capital of Guanxi Zhuang AR, on the Xiang River: rail links with North Vietnam. Pop: 984 061 (1999 est)

nanny ('nænɪ) *n, pl* **nannies** **1** a nurse or nursemaid for children **2a** any person or thing regarded as treating people like children, esp by being overprotective **2b** (*as modifier*): *the nanny state* **3** a child's word for **grandmother** ▷ *vb* **nannies, nannying, nannied** **4** (*intr*) to nurse or look after someone else's children **5** (*tr*) to be overprotective towards [c19 child's name for a nurse]

nannygai ('nænɪ,gaɪ) *n, pl* **nannygais** an edible red Australian sea fish [from Abor.]

nanny goat *n* a female goat

nano- *combining form* denoting 10^{-9}: *nanometre; nanosecond.* Symbol: n [from L *nānus* dwarf, from Gk *nanos*]

nanobe ('naenəʊb) *n* a microbe that measures between 50 and 100 nanometers across and is smaller than the smallest known bacteria

nanophysics ('nænəʊ,fɪzɪks) *n* (*functioning as sing*) the physics of structures and artefacts with dimensions in the nanometre range or of phenomena occurring in nanoseconds

nanotechnology (,nænəʊtɛk'nɒlədʒɪ) *n* a branch of technology dealing with the manufacture of objects with dimensions of less than 100 thousand-millionths of a metre and the manipulation of individual molecules and atoms
▷ www.nano.org.uk/links.htm
▷ www.nano.gov

Nansen ('nænsən) *n* **Fridtjof** ('fridjɔf) 1861–1930, Norwegian arctic explorer, statesman, and scientist. He crossed Greenland (1888–89) and attempted to reach the North Pole (1893–96), attaining a record 86° 14′ N (1895). He was the League of Nations' high commissioner for refugees (1920–22): Nobel peace prize 1922

Nansen bottle *n* an instrument used by oceanographers for obtaining samples of sea water from a desired depth [c19 after F. NANSEN]

Nan Shan ('næn 'ʃæn) *pl n* a mountain range in N central China, mainly in Qinghai province, with peaks over 6000 m (20 000 ft)

Nanterre (*French* nɑ̃tɛr) *n* a town in N France, on the Seine: an industrial suburb of Paris. Pop: 84 565 (1990)

Nantes (*French* nɑ̃t) *n* **1** a port in W France, at the head of the Loire estuary: scene of the signing of the Edict of Nantes and of the Noyades (drownings) during the French Revolution; extensive shipyards, and large metallurgical and food processing industries. Pop: 268 695 (1999) **2** *history* See **Edict of Nantes**

Nantong *or* **Nantung** ('næn'tʌŋ) *n* a city in E China, in Jiangsu province on the Yangtze estuary. Pop: 468 215 (1999 est)

Nantucket (næn'tʌkɪt) *n* an island off SE Massachusetts: formerly a centre of the whaling industry; now a resort. Length: nearly 24 km (15 miles). Width: 5 km (3 miles). Pop: 6012 (1990)

Naoise ('ni:ʃə) *n Irish myth* the husband of Deirdre, killed by his uncle Conchobar. See also **Deirdre**

Naomi ('neɪəmɪ) *n Old Testament* the mother-in-law of Ruth (Ruth 1:2). Douay spelling: **Noemi**

nap[1] (næp) *vb* **naps, napping, napped** (*intr*) **1** to sleep for a short while; doze **2** to be inattentive or off guard (esp in **catch someone napping**) ▷ *n* **3** a short light sleep; doze [OE *hnappian*]

nap[2] (næp) *n* **1a** the raised fibres of velvet or similar cloth **1b** the direction in which these fibres lie **2** any similar downy coating **3** *Austral inf* blankets; bedding ▷ *vb* **naps, napping, napped** **4** (*tr*) to raise the nap of (velvet, etc) by brushing [c15 prob. from MDu. *noppe*]

nap[3] (næp) *n* **1** Also called: **napoleon** a card game similar to whist, usually played for stakes **2** a call in this game, undertaking to win all five tricks **3** *horse racing* a tipster's choice for a certain winner **4** **nap hand** a position in which there is a very good chance of success if a risk is taken ▷ *vb* **naps, napping, napped** (*tr*) **5** *horse racing* to name (a horse) as likely to win a race [c19 from NAPOLEON, the card game]

napalm ('neɪpɑ:m, 'næ-) *n* **1** a thick and highly incendiary liquid, usually consisting of petrol gelled with aluminium soaps, used in flame-throwers, firebombs, etc ▷ *vb* **2** (*tr*) to attack with napalm [c20 from NA(PHTHENE) + *palm(itate)* salt of PALMITIC ACID]

nape (neɪp) *n* the back of the neck [c13 from ?]

napery ('neɪpərɪ) *n Scot & arch* household linen, esp table linen [c14 from OF *naperie*, from *nape* tablecloth, from L *mappa*]

Naphtali ('næftə,laɪ) *n Old Testament* **1** Jacob's sixth son, whose mother was Rachel's handmaid (Genesis 30:7–8) **2** the tribe descended from him **3** the territory of this tribe, between the Sea of Galilee and the mountains of central Galilee. Douay spelling: **Nephtali**

naphtha ('næfθə, 'næp-) *n* a distillation product from coal tar or petroleum: used as a solvent and in petrol [c16 via L from Gk, from Iranian]

naphthalene ('næfθə,li:n, 'næp-) *n* a white crystalline hydrocarbon with a characteristic penetrating odour, used in mothballs and in dyes, explosives, etc Formula: $C_{10}H_8$ [c19 from NAPHTHA + ALCOHOL + -ENE] > **naphthalic** (næf'θælɪk, næp-) *adj*

naphthene ('næfθi:n, 'næp-) *n* any of various cyclic methylene hydrocarbons found in petroleum [c20 from NAPHTHA + -ENE]

naphthol ('næfθɒl, 'næp-) *n* a white crystalline solid having two isomeric forms, used in dyes and as an antioxidant. Formula: $C_{10}H_7OH$ [c19 from NAPHTHA + -OL[1]]

Napier[1] ('neɪpɪə) *n* a port in New Zealand, on E North Island on Hawke Bay: wool trade centre. Pop: 53 500 (1995 est)

Nn

Napier² (ˈneɪpɪə) *n* **1** Sir **Charles James** 1782–1853, British general and colonial administrator: conquered Sind (1843): governor of Sind (1843–47) **2** **John** 1550–1617, Scottish mathematician: invented logarithms and pioneered the decimal notation used today **3** **Robert (Cornelis)**, 1st Baron Napier of Magdala. 1810–90, British field marshal, who commanded in India during the Sikh Wars (1845, 1848–49) and the Indian Mutiny (1857–59). He captured Magdala (1868) while rescuing British diplomats from Ethiopia

Napierian logarithm (nəˈpɪərɪən, neɪ-) *n* another name for **natural logarithm**

Napier's bones *pl n* a set of graduated rods formerly used for multiplication and division [c17 based on a method invented by John NAPIER]

napkin (ˈnæpkɪn) *n* **1** Also called: **table napkin** a usually square piece of cloth or paper used while eating to protect the clothes, wipe the mouth, etc; serviette **2** *rare* a small piece of cloth **3** a more formal name for **nappy¹** **4** a less common term for **sanitary towel** [c15 from OF, from *nape* tablecloth, from L *mappa* cloth]

Naples (ˈneɪpᵊlz) *n* **1** a port in SW Italy, capital of Campania region, on the Bay of Naples: the third largest city in the country; founded by Greeks in the 6th century BC; incorporated into the Kingdom of the Two Sicilies in 1140 and its capital (1282–1503); university (1224). Pop: 1 002 619 (2000 est). Ancient name: **Neapolis** Italian name: **Napoli** Related adj: **Neapolitan** **2** **Bay of** an inlet of the Tyrrhenian Sea in the SW coast of Italy

napoleon (nəˈpəʊlɪən) *n* **1** a former French gold coin worth 20 francs **2** *cards* the full name for **nap³** (sense 1) [c19 from F *napoléon*, after NAPOLEON I]

Napoleon I (nəˈpəʊlɪən) *n* full name *Napoleon Bonaparte*. 1769–1821, Emperor of the French (1804–15). He came to power as the result of a coup in 1799 and established an extensive European empire. A brilliant general, he defeated every European coalition against him until, irreparably weakened by the Peninsular War and the Russian campaign (1812), his armies were defeated at Leipzig (1813). He went into exile but escaped and ruled as emperor during the Hundred Days. He was finally defeated at Waterloo (1815). As an administrator, his achievements were of lasting significance and include the *Code Napoléon*, which remains the basis of French law

Napoleon II *n* Duke of Reichstadt. 1811–32, son of Napoleon Bonaparte and Marie Louise. He was known as the *King of Rome* during the first French empire and was entitled Napoleon II by Bonapartists after Napoleon I's death (1821)

Napoleon III *n* full name *Charles Louis Napoleon Bonaparte*, known as *Louis-Napoleon*. 1808–73, Emperor of the French (1852–70); nephew of Napoleon I. He led two abortive Bonapartist risings (1836; 1840) and was elected president of the Second Republic (1848), establishing the Second Empire in 1852. Originally successful in foreign affairs, he was deposed after the disastrous Franco-Prussian War

Napoleonic (nəˌpəʊlɪˈɒnɪk) *adj* relating to or characteristic of Napoleon I or his era

Napoli (ˈnaːpoli) *n* the Italian name for **Naples**

nappe (næp) *n* **1** a large sheet or mass of rock, commonly a recumbent fold, that has been thrust from its original position by earth movements **2** the sheet of water that flows over a dam or weir **3** *geom* either of the two parts into which a cone is divided by the vertex [c20 from F: tablecloth]

nappy¹ (ˈnæpɪ) *n, pl* **nappies** *Brit* a piece of soft towelling or a disposable material wrapped around a baby in order to absorb its urine or excrement. Also called: **napkin** US and Canad name: **diaper** [c20 changed from NAPKIN]

nappy² (ˈnæpɪ) *adj* **nappier, nappiest** **1** having a nap; downy; fuzzy **2** (of beer) **2a** having a head; frothy **2b** strong or heady

nappy rash *n Brit* (in babies) any irritation to the skin around the genitals, anus, or buttocks, usually caused by contact with urine or excrement. Formal name: **napkin rash** US and Canad name: **diaper rash**

Nara (ˈnɑːrə) *n* a city in central Japan, on S Honshu: the first permanent capital of Japan (710–784). Pop: 359 234 (1995)

Narayan (nəˈraɪjən) *n* **R(asipuram) K(rishnaswamy)** 1906–2001, Indian novelist writing in English. His books include *Swami and Friends* (1938), *The Man-Eater of Malgudi* (1961), *Under the Banyan Tree* (1985), and *Grandmother's Tale* (1993)

Narayanganj (nəˈrɑːjənˌgʌndʒ) *n* a city in central Bangladesh, on the Ganges delta just southeast of Dhaka. Pop: 276 549 (1991)

Narbada (nəˈbʌdə) *n* another name for the **Narmada**

Narbonne (*French* narbɔn) *n* a city in S France: capital of the Roman province of **Gallia Narbonensis;** harbour silted up in the 14th century. Pop: 47 090 (1990)

narc (nɑːk) *n US sl* a narcotics agent

narcissism (ˈnɑːsɪˌsɪzəm) *or* **narcism** (ˈnɑːsɪzəm) *n* **1** an exceptional interest in or admiration for oneself, esp one's physical appearance **2** sexual satisfaction derived from contemplation of one's own physical endowments [c19 after NARCISSUS] > **ˈnarcissist** *n* > **ˌnarcisˈsistic** *adj*

narcissus (nɑːˈsɪsəs) *n, pl* **narcissuses** *or* **narcissi** (-ˈsɪsaɪ) a plant of a Eurasian genus whose yellow, orange, or white flowers have a crown surrounded by spreading segments [c16 via L from Gk *nárkissos*, ?from *narkē* numbness, because of narcotic properties attributed to the plant]

Narcissus (nɑːˈsɪsəs) *n Greek myth* a beautiful youth who fell in love with his reflection in a pool and pined away, becoming the flower that bears his name

narco- *or sometimes before a vowel* **narc-** *combining form* **1** indicating numbness or torpor: *narcolepsy* **2** connected with or derived from illicit drug production: *narcoeconomies* [from Gk *narkē* numbness]

narcoanalysis (ˌnɑːkəʊəˈnælɪsɪs) *n* psychoanalysis of a patient in a trance induced by a narcotic drug

narcolepsy (ˈnɑːkəˌlɛpsɪ) *n pathol* a rare condition characterized by sudden episodes of deep sleep > **ˌnarcoˈleptic** *adj*

narcosis (nɑːˈkəʊsɪs) *n* unconsciousness induced by narcotics or general anaesthetics

narcosynthesis (ˌnɑːkəʊˈsɪnθɪsɪs) *n* a method of treating severe personality disorders by working with the patient while he is under the influence of a barbiturate drug

narcotic (nɑːˈkɒtɪk) *n* **1** any of a group of drugs, such as morphine, heroin, and pethidine, that produce numbness and stupor **2** anything that relieves pain or induces sleep, mental numbness, etc **3** any illegal drug ▷ *adj* **4** of or relating to narcotics or narcotics addicts **5** of or relating to narcosis [c14 via Med. L from Gk *narkōtikós*, from *narkoūn* to numb, from *narkē* numbness] > **narˈcotically** *adv*

narcotism (ˈnɑːkəˌtɪzəm) *n* stupor or addiction induced by narcotic drugs

narcotize *or* **narcotise** (ˈnɑːkəˌtaɪz) *vb* **narcotizes, narcotizing, narcotized** *or* **narcotises, narcotising, narcotised** (*tr*) to place under the influence of a narcotic drug > **ˌnarcotiˈzation** *or* **ˌnarcotiˈsation** *n*

nard (nɑːd) *n* **1** another name for **spikenard** **2** any of several plants whose aromatic roots were formerly used in medicine [c14 via L from Gk *nárdos*, ? ult. from Sansk. *nalada* Indian spikenard]

nardoo (ˈnɑːduː) *n* (in Australia) **1** any of certain cloverlike ferns that grow in swampy areas **2** the spores of such a plant, used as food [c19 from Abor.]

nares (ˈnɛəriːz) *pl n, sing* **naris** (ˈnɛərɪs) *anat* the technical name for the nostrils [c17 from L; rel. to OE *nasu*, L *nāsus* nose] > **ˈnarial** *adj*

narghile, nargile, *or* **nargileh** ('nɑːgɪlɪ, -ˌleɪ) *n* another name for **hookah** [c19 from F *narguilé*, from Persian *nārgīleh* a pipe having a bowl made of coconut shell, from *nārgīl* coconut]

nark (nɑːk) *sl* ▷ *n* **1** *Brit, Austral, & NZ* an informer or spy, esp one working for the police: *copper's nark* **2** *Brit, Austral, & NZ* someone who complains in an irritating or whining manner ▷ *vb* **3** *Brit, Austral, & NZ* to annoy, upset, or irritate **4** *(intr) Brit, Austral, & NZ* to inform or spy, esp for the police **5** *(intr) Brit* to complain irritatingly [c19 prob. from Romany *nāk* nose]

narky ('nɑːkɪ) *adj* **narkier, narkiest** *sl* irritable, complaining, or sarcastic

Narmada (nə'mʌdə) *or* **Narbada** *n* a river in central India, rising in Madhya Pradesh and flowing generally west to the Gulf of Cambay in a wide estuary: the second most sacred river in India. Length: 1290 km (801 miles)

Narraganset (ˌnærə'gænsɪt) *n* **1** (*pl* **Narraganset** *or* **Narragansets**) a member of a North American Indian people formerly living in Rhode Island **2** the language of this people, belonging to the Algonquian family

Narragansett Bay *n* an inlet of the Atlantic in SE Rhode Island: contains several islands, including Rhode Island, Prudence Island, and Conanicut Island

narrate (nə'reɪt) *vb* **narrates, narrating, narrated 1** to tell (a story); relate **2** to speak in accompaniment of (a film, etc) [c17 from L *narrāre* to recount, from *gnārus* knowing] > **nar'ratable** *adj* > **nar'rator** *n*

narration (nə'reɪʃən) *n* **1** the act or process of narrating **2** a narrated account or story

narrative ('nærətɪv) *n* **1** an account or story, as of events, experiences, etc **2** the part of a literary work, etc, that relates events **3** the process or technique of narrating ▷ *adj* **4** telling a story: *a narrative poem* **5** of or relating to narration: *narrative art*

narrator (nə'reɪtə) *n* **1** a person who tells a story or gives an account of something **2** a person who speaks in accompaniment of a film, television programme, etc

narrow ('nærəʊ) *adj* **1** small in breadth, esp in comparison to length **2** limited in range or extent **3** limited in outlook **4** limited in means or resources **5** barely adequate or successful (esp in **a narrow escape**) **6** painstakingly thorough: *a narrow scrutiny* **7** *finance* denoting an assessment of liquidity as including notes and coins in circulation with the public, banks' till money, and banks' balances: *narrow money* ▷ Cf **broad** (sense 12) **8** *phonetics* another word for **tense**[1] (sense 4) ▷ *vb* **9** to make or become narrow **10** (often foll by *down*) to limit or restrict ▷ *n* **11** a narrow place, esp a pass or strait ▷ See also **narrows** [OE *nearu*] > **'narrowly** *adv* > **'narrowness** *n*

narrowband ('nærəʊˌbænd) *n* a limited-capacity transmission channel such as that used for transmitting telephone calls and faxes

narrowboat ('nærəʊˌbəʊt) *n* a long bargelike boat with a beam of 2.1 metres (7 feet), used on canals

narrow gauge *n* **1** a railway track with a smaller distance between the lines than the standard gauge of 56½ inches ▷ *adj* **narrow-gauge 2** of or denoting a railway with a narrow gauge

narrow-minded *adj* having a biased or illiberal viewpoint; bigoted, intolerant, or prejudiced > **ˌnarrow-'mindedness** *n*

narrows ('nærəʊz) *pl n* a narrow part of a strait, river, current, etc

narthex ('nɑːθɛks) *n* **1** a portico at the west end of a church, esp one at right angles to the nave **2** a rectangular entrance hall between the porch and nave of a church [c17 via L from Med. Gk: enclosed porch (earlier: box), from Gk *narthēx* giant fennel, the stems of which were used to make boxes]

Narva (*Russian* 'narvə) *n* a port in Estonia on the Narva River near the Gulf of Finland: developed around a Danish fortress in the 13th century; textile centre. Pop: 77 770 (1995)

Narvik ('nɑːvɪk; *Norwegian* 'narvik) *n* a port in N Norway: scene of two naval battles in 1940; exports iron ore from Kiruna and Gällivare (Sweden). Pop: 18 500 (1990)

narwhal, narwal ('nɑːwəl), *or* **narwhale** ('nɑːˌweɪl) *n* an arctic toothed whale having a black-spotted whitish skin and, in the male, a long spiral tusk [c17 of Scand. origin; cf. Danish, Norwegian *narhval*, from ON *nāhvalr*, from *nār* corpse + *hvalr* whale]

nary ('nɛərɪ) *adv dialect or inf* not; never: *nary a man was left* [c19 var. of *ne'er a* never a]

NASA ('næsə) *n* (in the US) *acronym for* National Aeronautics and Space Administration ▷ www.nasa.gov

nasal ('neɪzᵊl) *adj* **1** of the nose **2** *phonetics* pronounced with the soft palate lowered allowing air to escape via the nasal cavity ▷ *n* **3** a nasal speech sound, such as English *m*, *n*, or *ng* [c17 from F from LL *nāsālis*, from L *nāsus* nose] > **nasality** (neɪ'zælɪtɪ) *n* > **'nasally** *adv*

nasalize *or* **nasalise** ('neɪzᵊˌlaɪz) *vb* **nasalizes, nasalizing, nasalized** *or* **nasalises, nasalising, nasalised** *(tr)* to pronounce nasally > **ˌnasali'zation** *or* **ˌnasali'sation** *n*

nascent ('næsᵊnt, 'neɪ-) *adj* starting to grow or develop; being born [c17 from L *nascēns*, present participle of *nāscī* to be born] > **'nascency** *n*

nascent hydrogen *n chem* hydrogen produced in a reactive form within the reaction mixture

Nasdaq *or* **NASDAQ** ('næzˌdæk) *n acronym for* National Association of Securities Dealers Automated Quotation System: a computerized system for trading in over-the-counter securities. It is the second largest stock market in the United States ▷ www.nasdaq.com

Naseby ('neɪzbɪ) *n* a village in Northamptonshire: site of a major Parliamentarian victory (1645) in the Civil War, when Cromwell routed Prince Rupert's force

Nash (næʃ) *n* **1 John** 1752–1835, English town planner and architect. He designed Regent's Park, Regent Street, and the Marble Arch in London **2 Ogden** 1902–71, US humorous poet **3 Paul** 1889–1946, English painter, noted esp as a war artist in both World Wars and for his landscapes **4 Richard,** known as *Beau Nash*. 1674–1762, English dandy **5** See (Thomas) **Nashe 6** Sir **Walter** 1882–1968, New Zealand Labour statesman, born in England: prime minister of New Zealand (1957–60)

Nashe *or* **Nash** (næʃ) *n* **Thomas** 1567–1601, English pamphleteer, satirist, and novelist, author of the first picaresque novel in English, *The Unfortunate Traveller, or the Life of Jack Wilton* (1594)

Nashville ('næʃvɪl) *n* a city in central Tennessee, the state capital, on the Cumberland River: an industrial and commercial centre, noted for its recording industry. Pop: 545 524 (2000)

Nasik ('nɑːsɪk) *n* a city in W India, in Maharashtra: a centre for Hindu pilgrims. Pop: 656 925 (1991)

Nasiriyah (ˌnæzɪ'riːə) *n* a city in S Iraq, on the River Euphrates; agricultural and trading centre. Pop: 263 937 (latest est)

Naskapi (nə'skæpɪ) *n* a member of an Innu people living in Quebec [from Cree]

naso- *combining form* nose: *nasopharynx* [from L *nāsus* nose]

nasogastric (ˌneɪzəʊ'gæstrɪk) *adj anat* of or relating to the nose and stomach: *a nasogastric tube*

Nassau *n* **1** (*German* 'nasaʊ) a region of W central Germany: formerly a duchy (1816–66), from which a branch of the House of Orange arose (represented by the present rulers of the Netherlands and Luxembourg); annexed to the Prussian province of Hesse-Nassau in 1866; corresponds to present-day W Hesse and NE Rhineland-Palatinate states; formerly (1949–90) part of West Germany **2** ('næsɔː) the capital and chief port of

Nn

the Bahamas, on the NE coast of New Providence Island: resort. Pop: 214 000 (1999 est)
▷ www.bahamas.com/islands/nassau

nassella tussock (nəˈsɛlə) *n* a type of tussock grass, originally of South America, now regarded as a noxious weed in New Zealand

Nassella Tussock Board *n* NZ one of many local statutory organizations set up in different regions of New Zealand to eradicate the invasive nassella tussock weed

Nasser (ˈnɑːsə, ˈnæsə) *n* **Gamal Abdel** (gəˈmɑːl ˈæbdɛl) 1918–70, Egyptian soldier and statesman; president of Egypt (1956–70). He was one of the leaders of the coup that deposed King Farouk (1952) and became premier (1954). His nationalization of the Suez Canal (1956) led to an international crisis, and during his presidency Egypt was twice defeated by Israel (1956; 1967)

nastic movement (ˈnæstɪk) *n* a response of plant parts that is independent of the direction of the external stimulus, such as the opening of buds caused by an alteration in light intensity [C19 *nastic*, from Gk *nastos* close-packed, from *nassein* to press down]

nasturtium (nəˈstɜːʃəm) *n* a plant having round leaves and yellow, red, or orange trumpet-shaped spurred flowers [C17 from L: kind of cress, from *nāsus* nose + *tortus* twisted; because the pungent smell causes one to wrinkle one's nose]

nasty (ˈnɑːstɪ) *adj* **nastier, nastiest 1** unpleasant or repugnant **2** dangerous or painful: *a nasty wound* **3** spiteful or ill-natured **4** obscene or indecent ▷ *n, pl* **nasties 5** an offensive or unpleasant person or thing: *a video nasty* [C14 from ?; prob. rel. to Swedish dialect *nasket* & Du. *nestig* dirty] > **ˈnastily** *adv* > **ˈnastiness** *n*

NAS/UWT (in Britain) *abbrev for* National Association of Schoolmasters/Union of Women Teachers

nat. *abbrev for:* **1** national **2** natural

natal (ˈneɪtᵊl) *adj* of or relating to birth [C14 from L *nātālis* of one's birth, from *nātus*, from *nascī* to be born]

Natal *n* **1** (nəˈtæl) a former province of E South Africa, between the Drakensberg and the Indian Ocean: set up as a republic by the Boers in 1838; became a British colony in 1843; joined South Africa in 1910; replaced by KwaZulu/Natal in 1994. Capital: Pietermaritzburg **2** (*Portuguese* naˈtal) a port in NE Brazil, capital of Rio Grande do Norte state, near the mouth of the Potengi River. Pop (urban area): 709 422 (2000)

natant (ˈneɪtᵊnt) *adj* floating or swimming [C18 from L *natāns*, present participle of *natāre* to swim]

natation (nəˈteɪʃən) *n* a literary word for **swimming** [C16 from L *natātiō* a swimming, from *natāre* to swim]

natatory (nəˈteɪtərɪ) *or* **natatorial** (ˌnætəˈtɔːrɪəl) *adj* of or relating to swimming [C18 from LL *natātōrius*, from L *natāre* to swim]

natch (nætʃ) *sentence substitute inf* short for **naturally**

nates (ˈneɪtiːz) *pl n, sing* **natis** (-tɪs) a technical word for the **buttocks** [C17 from L]

NATFHE (in Britain) *abbrev for* National Association of Teachers in Further and Higher Education

Nathan (ˈneɪθən) *n Old Testament* a prophet at David's court (II Samuel 7:1–17; 12:1–15)

Nathanael (nəˈθænjəl) *n New Testament* a Galilean who is perhaps to be identified with Bartholomew among the apostles (John 1:45–51; 21:1)

natheless (ˈneɪθlɪs) *or* **nathless** (ˈnæθlɪs) *sentence connector arch* nonetheless [OE *nāthylǣs*, from *nā* never + *thȳ* for that + *lǣs* less]

nation (ˈneɪʃən) *n* **1** an aggregation of people or peoples of one or more cultures, races, etc, organized into a single state: *the Australian nation* **2** a community of persons not constituting a state but bound by common descent, language, history, etc: *the French-Canadian nation* [C13 via OF from L *nātiō* birth, tribe, from *nascī* to be born] > **ˈnationˌhood** *n*

national (ˈnæʃənᵊl) *adj* **1** of or relating to a nation as a whole **2** characteristic of a particular nation: *the national dress of Poland* ▷ *n* **3** a citizen or subject **4** a national newspaper > **ˈnationally** *adv*

national anthem *n* a patriotic song adopted by a nation for use on public occasions
▷ www.thenationalanthems.com

national assistance *n* (formerly, in Britain) a weekly allowance paid to individuals of various groups by the state to bring their incomes up to minimum levels established by law. Now replaced by income support

national bank *n* **1** (in the US) a commercial bank incorporated under a Federal charter and legally required to be a member of the Federal Reserve System **2** a bank operated by a government

national call *n Brit* a telephone call made to a number within the country but outside the local area

National Curriculum *n* (in England and Wales) the curriculum of subjects taught in state schools from 1989. The ten foundation subjects are: English, maths, and science (the core subjects); art, design and technology, geography, history, music, physical education, and a foreign language. Pupils are assessed at four stages. Abbrev: **NC**
▷ www.nc.uk.net/index.html

national debt *n* the total outstanding borrowings of a nation's central government

National Economic Development Council *n* a former advisory body on economic policy in Britain, composed of representatives of government, management, and trade unions: abolished in 1992. Abbrevs: **NEDC,** (inf) **Neddy**

National Enterprise Board *n* a public corporation established in 1975 to help the economy of the UK. In 1981 it merged with the National Research and Development Council to form the British Technology Group. Abbrev: **NEB**

National Football *n* (in Australia) another name for **Australian Rules**

National Front *n* an extreme right-wing British political party founded in 1967

National Gallery *n* a major art gallery in London, in Trafalgar Square. Founded in 1824, it contains the largest collection of paintings in Britain
▷ www.nationalgallery.org.uk

national grid *n Brit* **1** a network of high-voltage electric power lines linking major electric power stations **2** the metric coordinate system used in ordnance survey maps

National Guard *n* **1** (*sometimes not cap*) the armed force that was established in France in 1789 and existed intermittently until 1871 **2** (in the US) a state military force that can be called into federal service by the president

National Health Service *n* (in Britain) the system of national medical services since 1948, financed mainly by taxation. Abbrev: **NHS**

national hunt *n Brit* (*often caps*) **a** the racing of horses on racecourses with jumps **b** (*as modifier*): *a National Hunt jockey*

national income *n econ* the total of all incomes accruing over a specified period to residents of a country

national insurance *n* (in Britain) state insurance based on weekly contributions from employees and employers and providing payments to the unemployed, the sick, the retired, etc, as well as medical services

nationalism (ˈnæʃənəˌlɪzəm) *n* **1** a sentiment based on common cultural characteristics that binds a population and often produces a policy of national independence **2** loyalty to one's country; patriotism **3** exaggerated or fanatical devotion to a national community > **ˈnationalist** *n, adj* > **ˌnationalˈistic** *adj*

nationality (ˌnæʃəˈnælɪtɪ) *n, pl* **nationalities 1** the fact of being a citizen of a particular nation **2** a body of people sharing common descent, history, language, etc; a nation **3** a national group: *30 different nationalities are found in this city* **4** national character **5** the fact of being a nation; national status

nationalize *or* **nationalise** (ˈnæʃənəˌlaɪz) *vb* **nationalizes, nationalizing, nationalized** *or* **nationalises, nationalising, nationalised** (*tr*) **1** to put (an industry, resources, etc) under state control **2** to make national in character or status **3** a less common word for **naturalize** > ˌ**nationaliˈzation** *or* ˌ**nationaliˈsation** *n*

national park *n* an area of countryside for public use designated by a national government as being of notable scenic, environmental, or historical importance

National Park *n* a mountainous volcanic region in New Zealand, in the central North Island: ski resort

National Party *n* **1** (in New Zealand) the more conservative of the two main political parties **2** (in Australia) the former name (until 2003) of the **Nationals** **3** (in South Africa) a political party composed mainly of centre-to-right-wing Afrikaners. It ruled from 1948 until 1994, when South Africa's first multiracial elections were won by the African National Congress; renamed the **New National Party** (NNP) in 1999

Nationals (ˈnæʃənəlz) *pl n* **the** (in Australia) a political party drawing its main support from rural areas. Former names: **National Party, National Country Party**

National Savings Bank *n* (in Britain) a government savings bank, run through the Post Office

national service *n* compulsory military service

National Socialism *n German history* the doctrines and practices of the Nazis, involving the supremacy of Hitler as Führer, anti-Semitism, state control of the economy, and national expansion > **National Socialist** *n, adj*

▷ www.phoenixpress.co.uk/articles/institution/national-socialism-pp.asp
▷ www.tiscali.co.uk/reference/encyclopaedia/hutchinson/M0010979.html
▷ http://en.wikipedia.org/wiki/Nazism

national superannuation *n* NZ a government pension given on the attainment of a specified age; old age pension. Often shortened to **national super**

National Tests *pl n* (*sometimes not cap*) *Brit education* externally devised assessments in the core subjects of English, mathematics and science which school students in England and Wales sit at the end of Key Stages 1 to 3. Often referred to as: **SATs**

National Theatre *n* the former name of the **Royal National Theatre**

National Trust *n* **1** (in Britain) an organization concerned with the preservation of historic buildings and areas of the countryside of great beauty **2** (in Australia) a similar organization in each of the states

nation-building *n S African* the advocacy of national solidarity in South Africa in the post-apartheid era

nationwide (ˈneɪʃənˌwaɪd) *adj* covering or available to the whole of a nation; national

native (ˈneɪtɪv) *adj* **1** relating or belonging to a person by virtue of conditions existing at birth: *a native language* **2** natural or innate: *a native strength* **3** born in a specified place: *a native Indian* **4** (when *postpositive*, foll by *to*) originating in: *kangaroos are native to Australia* **5** relating to the indigenous inhabitants of a country: *the native art of the New Guinea Highlands* **6** (of metals) found naturally in the elemental form; not chemically combined as in an ore **7** unadulterated by civilization, artifice, or adornment; natural **8** *arch* related by birth or race **9** **go native** (of a settler) to adopt the lifestyle of the local population, esp when it appears less civilized ▷ *n* **10** (usually foll by *of*) a person born in a particular place: *a native of Geneva* **11** (usually foll by *of*) a species of animal or plant originating in a particular place **12** a member of an indigenous people of a country, esp a non-White people, as opposed to colonial immigrants [C14 from L *nātīvus* innate, natural, from *nascī* to be born] > ˈ**natively** *adv* > ˈ**nativeness** *n*

Native American *n* another name for an **American Indian**

native bear *n* an Australian name for **koala**

native-born *adj* born in the country or area indicated

native cat *n Austral* any of various Australian catlike carnivorous marsupials of the genus *Dasyurus*

native companion *n* another name for **brolga**

native dog *n Austral* a dingo

Native States *pl n* the former 562 semi-independent states of India, ruled by Indians but subject to varying degrees of British authority: merged with provinces by 1948; largest states were Hyderabad, Gwalior, Baroda, Mysore, Cochin, Jammu and Kashmir, Travancore, Sikkim, and Indore. Also called: **Indian States and Agencies**

nativity (nəˈtɪvɪtɪ) *n, pl* **nativities** birth or origin [C14 from LL *nātīvitas* birth; see NATIVE]

Nativity (nəˈtɪvɪtɪ) *n* **1** the birth of Christ **2** the feast of Christmas as a commemoration of this **3a** an artistic representation of the circumstances of the birth of Christ **3b** (*as modifier*): *a Nativity play*

NATO *or* **Nato** (ˈneɪtəʊ) *n acronym for* North Atlantic Treaty Organization: an international organization established (1949) for purposes of collective security

▷ www.nato.int

Nato Alphabet

Alpha
Bravo
Charlie
Delta
Echo
Foxtrot
Golf
Hotel
India
Juliet
Kilo
Lima
Mike
November
Oscar
Papa
Quebec
Romeo
Sierra
Tango
Uniform
Victor
Whiskey
X-Ray
Yankee
Zulu

▷ www.canadiansoldiers.com/phonetics.htm

natron (ˈneɪtrən) *n* a whitish or yellow mineral that consists of hydrated sodium carbonate and occurs in saline deposits and salt lakes [C17 via F & Sp. from Ar. *natrūn*, from Gk *nitron* NITRE]

natter (ˈnætə) *chiefly Brit inf* ▷ *vb* **1** (*intr*) to talk idly and at length; chatter ▷ *n* **2** prolonged idle chatter [C19 from *gnatter* to grumble, imit.]

natterjack (ˈnætəˌdʒæk) *n* a European toad having a greyish-brown body marked with reddish warty processes [C18 from ?]

natty ('nætɪ) *adj* **nattier, nattiest** *inf* smart; spruce; dapper [C18 from obs. *netty*, from *net* NEAT[1]] > **'nattily** *adv* > **'nattiness** *n*

natural ('nætʃrəl) *adj* **1** of, existing in, or produced by nature: *natural science; natural cliffs* **2** in accordance with human nature **3** as is normal or to be expected: *the natural course of events* **4** not acquired; innate: *a natural gift for sport* **5** being so through innate qualities: *a natural leader* **6** not supernatural or strange: *natural phenomena* **7** genuine or spontaneous **8** lifelike: *she looked more natural without make-up* **9** not affected by man; wild: *in the natural state this animal is not ferocious* **10** being or made from organic material; not synthetic: *a natural fibre like cotton* **11** born out of wedlock **12** not adopted but rather related by blood: *her natural parents* **13** *music* **13a** not sharp or flat **13b** (*postpositive*) denoting a note that is neither sharp nor flat **13c** (of a key or scale) containing no sharps or flats **14** based on the principles and findings of human reason rather than on revelation: *natural religion* ▷ *n* **15** *inf* a person or thing regarded as certain to qualify for success, selection, etc: *the horse was a natural for first place* **16** *music* **16a** Also called (US): **cancel** an accidental cancelling a previous sharp or flat. Usual symbol: ♮ **16b** a note affected by this accidental **17** *obs* an imbecile; idiot > **'naturalness** *n*

natural childbirth *n* a method of childbirth characterized by the absence of anaesthetics, in which the expectant mother is given special breathing and relaxing exercises

natural gas *n* a gaseous mixture, consisting mainly of methane, trapped below ground; used extensively as a fuel

natural history *n* **1** the study of animals and plants in the wild state **2** the sum of these phenomena in a given place or at a given time > **natural historian** *n*

natural immunity *n* immunity with which an individual is born, which has a genetic basis

naturalism ('nætʃrəˌlɪzəm) *n* **1** a movement, esp in art and literature, advocating detailed realistic and factual description **2** the belief that all religious truth is based not on revelation but rather on the study of natural causes and processes **3** *philosophy* a scientific account of the world in terms of causes and natural forces **4** action or thought caused by natural instincts

naturalist ('nætʃrəlɪst) *n* **1** a person who is expert in or interested in botany or zoology, esp in the field **2** a person who advocates or practises naturalism

naturalistic (ˌnætʃrə'lɪstɪk) *adj* **1** of or reproducing nature in effect or characteristics **2** of or characteristic of naturalism **3** of naturalists > **ˌnatural'istically** *adv*

naturalize *or* **naturalise** ('nætʃrəˌlaɪz) *vb* **naturalizes, naturalizing, naturalized** *or* **naturalises, naturalising, naturalised** **1** (*tr*) to give citizenship to (a person of foreign birth) **2** to be or cause to be adopted in another place, as a word, custom, etc **3** (*tr*) to introduce (a plant or animal from another region) and cause it to adapt to local conditions **4** (*intr*) (of a plant or animal) to adapt successfully to a foreign environment and spread there **5** (*tr*) to make natural or more lifelike > **ˌnaturali'zation** *or* **ˌnaturali'sation** *n*

natural language *n* a language that has evolved naturally as a means of communication among people, as opposed to an invented language or a code

natural logarithm *n* a logarithm to the base e. Usually written $\log_e$ or ln. Also called: **Napierian logarithm**

naturally ('nætʃrəlɪ) *adv* **1** in a natural way **2** instinctively ▷ *adv, sentence substitute* **3** of course; surely

natural number *n* any of the numbers 0 ,1, 2, 3, 4,... that can be used to count the members of a set; the non-negative integers

natural philosophy *n* physical science, esp physics > **natural philosopher** *n*

natural resources *pl n* naturally occurring materials such as coal, fertile land, etc, that can be used by man

natural science *n* the sciences that are involved in the study of the physical world and its phenomena, including biology, physics, chemistry, and geology

natural selection *n* a process resulting in the survival of those individuals from a population of animals or plants that are best adapted to the prevailing environmental conditions

natural theology *n* the attempt to derive theological truth, and esp the existence of God, from empirical facts by reasoned argument ▷ Cf **revealed religion**

natural wastage *n* the loss of employees, etc, through not replacing those who retire or resign rather than dismissal or redundancy

nature ('neɪtʃə) *n* **1** fundamental qualities; identity or essential character **2** (*often cap*) the whole system of the existence, forces, and events of all physical life that are not controlled by man **3** plant and animal life, as distinct from man **4** a wild primitive state untouched by man **5** natural unspoilt countryside **6** disposition or temperament **7** desires or instincts governing behaviour **8** the normal biological needs of the body **9** sort; character **10 against nature** unnatural or immoral **11 by nature** essentially or innately **12 call of nature** *inf* the need to urinate or defecate **13 from nature** using natural models in drawing, painting, etc **14 in** (*or* **of**) **the nature of** essentially the same as; by way of [C13 via OF from L *nātūra*, from *nātus*, pp of *nascī* to be born]

nature reserve *n* an area of land that is protected and managed in order to preserve its flora and fauna

nature study *n* the study of the natural world, esp animals and plants, by direct observation at an elementary level

nature trail *n* a path through countryside designed and usually signposted to draw attention to natural features of interest

naturism ('neɪtʃəˌrɪzəm) *n* another name for **nudism** > **'naturist** *n, adj*

naturopathy (ˌnætʃə'rɒpæθɪ) *n* the treatment of illness by stimulating natural healing, esp by herbal remedies, manipulation, etc > **'naturoˌpath** *n* > **ˌnaturo'pathic** *adj*

Naucratis ('nɔːkrətɪs) *n* an ancient Greek city in N Egypt, in the Nile delta: founded in the 7th century BC

naught (nɔːt) *n* **1** *arch or literary* nothing; ruin or failure **2** a variant spelling (esp US) of **nought** **3 set at naught** to disregard or scorn; disdain ▷ *adv* **4** *arch or literary* not at all: *it matters naught* ▷ *adj* **5** *obs* worthless, ruined, or wicked [OE *nāwiht*, from *nā* NO[1] + *wiht* thing, person]

naughty ('nɔːtɪ) *adj* **naughtier, naughtiest** **1** (esp of children) mischievous or disobedient **2** mildly indecent; titillating [C14 (orig.: needy, poor): from NAUGHT] > **'naughtily** *adv* > **'naughtiness** *n*

nauplius ('nɔːplɪəs) *n, pl* **nauplii** (-plɪˌaɪ) the larva of many crustaceans, having a rounded unsegmented body with three pairs of limbs [C19 from L: type of shellfish, from Gk *Nauplios*, one of the sons of the Greek god Poseidon]

Nauru (nɑː'uːruː) *n* an island republic in the SW Pacific, west of Kiribati: administered jointly by Australia, New Zealand, and Britain as a UN trust territory before becoming independent in 1968 as a special member of the Commonwealth (not represented at meetings of Commonwealth heads of state). The economy is based on export of phosphates. Languages: Nauruan (a Malayo-Polynesian language) and English. Religion: Christian. Currency: Australian dollar. Pop: 12 100 (2001 est). Area: 2130 hectares (5263 acres). Former name: **Pleasant Island** > **Na'uruan** *adj, n*

nausea ('nɔːzɪə, -sɪə) *n* **1** the sensation that precedes vomiting **2** a feeling of revulsion [C16 via L from Gk: seasickness, from *naus* ship]

nauseate ('nɔːzɪˌeɪt, -sɪ-) *vb* **nauseates, nauseating, nauseated** **1** (*tr*) to arouse feelings of disgust or revulsion in; sicken **2** to feel or cause to feel sick

> **'nause,ating** *adj* > **,nause'atingly** *adv*
nauseous ('nɔːzɪəs, -sɪəs) *adj* **1** causing nausea **2** distasteful; repulsive > **'nauseously** *adv* > **'nauseousness** *n*
Nausicaä (nɔː'sɪkɪə) *n Greek myth* a daughter of Alcinous, king of the Phaeacians, who assisted the shipwrecked Odysseus after discovering him on a beach
nautch *or* **nauch** (nɔːtʃ) *n* an intricate traditional Indian dance performed by professional dancing girls [c18 from Hindi *nāc*, from Sansk., from *nrtyati* he acts or dances]
nautical ('nɔːtɪkᵊl) *adj* of or involving ships, navigation, or seamen [c16 from L *nauticus*, from Gk *nautikos*, from *naus* ship] > **'nautically** *adv*
nautical mile *n* **1** Also called **international nautical mile, air mile** a unit of length, used esp in navigation, equivalent to the average length of a minute of latitude, and corresponding to a latitude of 45°, i.e. 1852 m (6076.12 ft) **2** a former British unit of length equal to 1853.18 m (6080 ft), which was replaced by the international nautical mile in 1970. Former name: **geographical mile** ▷ Cf **sea mile**
nautilus ('nɔːtɪləs) *n, pl* **nautiluses** *or* **nautili** (-,laɪ) **1** any of a genus of cephalopod molluscs, esp the pearly nautilus **2** short for **paper nautilus** [c17 via L from Gk *nautilos* sailor, from *naus* ship]
NAV *abbrev for* net asset value
Navaho *or* **Navajo** ('nævə,həʊ) *n* **1** (*pl* **Navaho, Navahos, Navahoes** *or* **Navajo, Navajos, Navajoes**) a member of a North American Indian people of Arizona, New Mexico, and Utah **2** the language of this people [c18 from Sp. *Navajó* pueblo, from Tena *Navahu* large planted field]
naval ('neɪvᵊl) *adj* **1** of, characteristic of, or having a navy **2** of or relating to ships; nautical [c16 from L *nāvālis*, from *nāvis* ship]
naval architecture *n* the designing of ships > **naval architect** *n*
▷ www.rina.org.uk/
Navaratri (,nævə'rɑːtrɪ) *n* an annual Hindu festival celebrated over nine days in September–October. It commemorates the slaying of demons by Rama and the goddess Durga. Also called: **Durga Puja** [from Sansk. *navaratri* nine nights]
navarin ('nævərɪn) *n* a stew of mutton or lamb with root vegetables [from F]
Navarino (nava'riːno) *n* **1** the Italian name for **Pylos** **2** a sea battle (Oct 20, 1827) in which the defeat of the Turkish-Egyptian fleet by a combined British, French, and Russian fleet decided Greek independence
Navarre (nə'vɑː) *n* a former kingdom of SW Europe: established in the 9th century by the Basques; the parts south of the Pyrenees joined Spain in 1515 and the N parts passed to France in 1589. Capital: Pamplona. Spanish name: **Navarra** (na'βarra)
nave[1] (neɪv) *n* the central space in a church, extending from the narthex to the chancel and often flanked by aisles [c17 via Med. L from L *nāvis* ship, from the similarity of shape]
nave[2] (neɪv) *n* the central block or hub of a wheel [OE *nafu, nafa*]
navel ('neɪvᵊl) *n* **1** the scar in the centre of the abdomen, usually forming a slight depression, where the umbilical cord was attached. Technical name: **umbilicus** Related adj: **umbilical** **2** a central part or point [OE *nafela*]
navel orange *n* a sweet orange that has at its apex a navel-like depression enclosing an underdeveloped secondary fruit
navelwort ('neɪvᵊl,wɜːt) *n* another name for **pennywort** (sense 1)
navicular (nə'vɪkjʊlə) *anat* ▷ *adj* **1** shaped like a boat ▷ *n* **2** a small boat-shaped bone of the wrist or foot [c16 from LL *nāviculāris*, from L *nāvicula*, dim. of *nāvis* ship]
navigable ('nævɪgəbᵊl) *adj* **1** wide, deep, or safe enough to be sailed through: *a navigable channel* **2** capable of being steered: *a navigable raft* > **,naviga'bility** *n* > **'navigably** *adv*
navigate ('nævɪ,geɪt) *vb* **navigates, navigating, navigated** **1** to direct or plot the path or position of (a ship, an aircraft, etc) **2** (*tr*) to travel over, through, or on in a boat, aircraft, etc **3** *inf* to direct (oneself) carefully or safely: *he navigated his way to the bar* **4** (*intr*) (of a passenger in a motor vehicle) to give directions to the driver; point out the route [c16 from L *nāvigāre* to sail, from *nāvis* ship + *agere* to drive]
navigation (,nævɪ'geɪʃən) *n* **1** the skill or process of plotting a route and directing a ship, aircraft, etc, along it **2** the act or practice of navigating: *dredging made navigation of the river possible* > **,navi'gational** *adj*
▷ www.navcen.uscg.gov
▷ www.rin.org.uk
navigator ('nævɪ,geɪtə) *n* **1** a person who performs navigation **2** (esp formerly) a person who explores by ship **3** an instrument for assisting a pilot to navigate an aircraft
Návpaktos (*Greek* 'nafpaktos) *n* the Greek name for **Lepanto**
Navratilova (næ,vrætɪ'ləʊvə) *n* **Martina** born 1956, Czech-born US tennis player: Wimbledon champion 1978, 1979, 1982–87, 1990; world champion 1980 and 1984
navvy ('nævɪ) *n, pl* **navvies** *Brit inf* a labourer on a building site, etc [c19 from *navigator* builder of a *navigation* (in the sense: canal)]
navy ('neɪvɪ) *n, pl* **navies** **1** the warships and auxiliary vessels of a nation or ruler **2** (*often cap*) the branch of a country's armed services comprising such ships, their crews, and all their supporting services **3** short for **navy blue** **4** *arch or literary* a fleet of ships [c14 via OF from Vulgar L *nāvia* (unattested) ship, from L *nāvis* ship]
navy blue *n* **a** a dark greyish-blue colour **b** (*as adj*): *a navy-blue suit* [c19 from the colour of the British naval uniform]
Navy List *n* (in Britain) an official list of all commissioned officers of the Royal Navy
navy yard *n* a naval shipyard, esp in the US
nawab (nə'wɑːb) *n* (formerly) a Muslim ruling prince or powerful landowner in India [c18 from Hindi *nawwāb*, from Ar. *nuwwāb*, pl. of *na'ib* viceroy]
Naxos ('næksɒs) *n* a Greek island in the S Aegean, the largest of the Cyclades: ancient centre of the worship of Dionysius. Pop: 14 000 (latest est). Area: 438 sq km (169 sq miles)
nay (neɪ) *sentence substitute* **1** a word for **no**[1]: archaic or dialectal except in voting by voice ▷ *n* **2** a person who votes in the negative ▷ *adv* **3** (*sentence modifier*) *arch* an emphatic form of **no**[1] [c12 from ON *nei*, from *ne* not + *ei* ever]
Nayarit (*Spanish* naja'rit) *n* a state of W Mexico, on the Pacific: includes the offshore Tres Marías Islands. Capital: Tepic. Pop: 919 739 (2000). Area: 27 621 sq km (10 772 sq miles)
Nazarene (,næzə'riːn) *n* **1** an early name for a **Christian** (Acts 24:5) or (when preceded by *the*) for **Jesus Christ** **2** a member of one of several groups of Jewish-Christians found principally in Syria ▷ *adj* **3** of Nazareth in N Israel, or the Nazarenes
Nazareth ('næzərɪθ) *n* a town in N Israel, in Lower Galilee: the home of Jesus in his youth. Pop: 51 000 (latest est)
Nazarite ('næzə,raɪt) *or* **Nazirite** *n* a religious ascetic of ancient Israel [c16 from L *Nazaraeus*, from Heb. *nāzar* to consecrate + -ITE[1]]
Naze (neɪz) *n* **the** **1** a flat marshy headland in SE England, in Essex on the North Sea coast **2** another name for **Lindesnes**

Nn

Nazi (ˈnɑːtsɪ) *n, pl* **Nazis** 1 a member of the fascist National Socialist German Workers' Party, which seized political control in Germany in 1933 ▷ *adj* 2 characteristic of or relating to the Nazis [c20 from G, phonetic spelling of the first two syllables of *Nationalsozialist* National Socialist] > **Nazism** (ˈnɑːtˌsɪzəm) *or* **Naziism** (ˈnɑːtsɪˌɪzəm) *n*

Nb *the chemical symbol for* niobium

NB *abbrev for* New Brunswick

NB, N.B., nb, *or* **n.b.** *abbrev for* nota bene [L: note well]

NBA *abbrev for:* 1 (in the US) National Basketball Association 2 (the former) Net Book Agreement

NC *or* **N.C.** *abbrev for:* 1 North Carolina 2 *Brit education* National Curriculum

NCC (in Britain) *abbrev for:* 1 *Brit education* National Curriculum Council: a statutory organization responsible for the content of the National Curriculum 2 (the former) Nature Conservancy Council

NCEA (in New Zealand) *abbrev for* National Certificate of Educational Attainment

NCIS (in Britain) *abbrev for* National Criminal Intelligence Service

NCO *abbrev for* noncommissioned officer

NCU (in Britain) *abbrev for* National Communications Union

nd *abbrev for* no date

Nd *the chemical symbol for* neodymium

ND, N.D., *or* **N. Dak.** *abbrev for* North Dakota

Ndjamena *or* **N'djamena** (ᵊndʒɑːˈmeɪnə) *n* the capital of Chad, in the southwest, at the confluence of the Shari and Logone Rivers: trading centre for livestock. Pop: 530 965 (1993). Former name (until 1973): **Fort Lamy**

Ndola (ᵊnˈdəʊlə) *n* a city in N Zambia: copper, cobalt, and sugar refineries. Pop: 376 311 (1990)

N'Dour (ᵊnˈdʊə) *n* **Youssou** (ˈjusu) born 1959, Senegalese singer and musician, whose work has popularized African music in the West; recordings include *Nelson Mandela* (1986), *Eyes Open* (1992), and *Nothing's in Vain* (2002)

NDP *abbrev for:* 1 net domestic product 2 (in Canada) New Democratic Party

NDT (in Canada) *abbrev for* Newfoundland Daylight Time

Ne *the chemical symbol for* neon

NE 1 *symbol for* northeast(ern) 2 *abbrev for* Nebraska 3 Also: **N.E.** *abbrev for* New England

ne- *combining form* a variant of **neo-,** esp before a vowel: *Nearctic*

Neagh (neɪ) *n* **Lough** a lake in Northern Ireland, in SW Co Antrim: the largest lake in the British Isles. Area: 388 sq km (150 sq miles)

Neanderthal man (nɪˈændəˌtɑːl) *n* a type of primitive man occurring throughout much of Europe in late Palaeolithic times. They are not thought to be ancestors of modern humans [c19 from the anthropological findings (1857) in the Neandertal, a valley near Düsseldorf, Germany]

neap (niːp) *adj* 1 of, relating to, or constituting a neap tide ▷ *n* 2 short for **neap tide** [OE, as in *nēpflōd* neap tide, from ?]

Neapolitan (ˌnɪəˈpɒlɪtᵊn) *n* 1 a native or inhabitant of Naples ▷ *adj* 2 of or relating to Naples [c15 from L *Neāpolītānus*, ult. from Gk *Neapolis* new town]

Neapolitan ice cream *n* ice cream with several layers of different colours and flavours

neap tide *n* either of the tides that occur at the first or last quarter of the moon when the tide-generating forces of the sun and moon oppose each other and produce the smallest rise and fall in tidal level ▷ Cf **spring tide** (sense 1)

near (nɪə) *prep* 1 at or to a place or time not far away from; close to ▷ *adv* 2 at or to a place or time not far away; close by 3 short for **nearly** (sense 1): *I was damn near killed* ▷ *adj* 4 (*postpositive*) at or in a place not far away 5 (*prenominal*) only just successful or only just failing: *a near thing* 6 (*postpositive*) not far away in time; imminent: *departure time was near* 7 (*postpositive*) *inf* miserly, mean 8 (*prenominal*) closely connected or intimate: *a near relation* ▷ *vb* 9 to come or draw close (to) ▷ *n* 10 Also called: **nearside** 10a the left side of a horse, vehicle, etc 10b (*as modifier*): *the near foreleg* [OE *nēar* (adv), comp. of *nēah* close] > ˈ**nearness** *n*

nearby *adj* (ˈnɪəˌbaɪ), *adv* (ˌnɪəˈbaɪ) not far away; close at hand

Nearctic (nɪˈɑːktɪk) *adj* of a zoogeographical region consisting of North America, north of the tropic of Cancer, and Greenland

Near East *n* 1 another term for the **Middle East** 2 (formerly) the Balkan States and the area of the Ottoman Empire

near gale *n meteorol* a wind of force seven on the Beaufort scale or from 32–38 mph

nearly (ˈnɪəlɪ) *adv* 1 almost 2 **not nearly** nowhere near: *not nearly enough* 3 closely: *the person most nearly concerned*

near-market *n* (*modifier*) (of scientific research, etc) very close to being commercially exploitable

near miss *n* 1 a bomb, shell, etc, that does not exactly hit the target 2 any attempt or shot that just fails to be successful 3 an incident in which two aircraft, etc, narrowly avoid collision

near point *n optics* the nearest point to the eye at which an object remains in focus

nearside (ˈnɪəˌsaɪd) *n* 1 (usually preceded by *the*) *chiefly Brit* 1a the side of a vehicle, etc, nearer the kerb 1b (*as modifier*): *the nearside door* 2a the left side of an animal, etc 2b (*as modifier*): *the nearside flank*

near-sighted (ˌnɪəˈsaɪtɪd) *adj* relating to or suffering from myopia > ˌ**near-ˈsightedly** *adv*

near thing *n inf* an event or action whose outcome is nearly a failure, success, disaster, etc

neat[1] (niːt) *adj* 1 clean, tidy, and orderly 2 liking or insisting on order and cleanliness 3 smoothly or competently done; efficient: *a neat job* 4 pat or slick: *his excuse was suspiciously neat* 5 (of alcoholic drinks, etc) undiluted 6 (of language) concise and well-phrased 7 *sl, chiefly US & Canad* pleasing; admirable; excellent [c16 from OF *net*, from L *nitidus* clean, from *nitēre* to shine] > ˈ**neatly** *adv* > ˈ**neatness** *n*

neat[2] (niːt) *n, pl* **neat** *arch or dialect* a domestic bovine animal [OE *neat*]

neaten (ˈniːtᵊn) *vb* (*tr*) to make neat; tidy

neath *or* **'neath** (niːθ) *prep arch* short for **beneath**

Neath Port Talbot (ˈniːθ ˈpɔːt ˈtɔːlbət, ˈtæl-) *n* a county borough in S Wales, created from part of West Glamorgan in 1996. Administrative centre: Port Talbot. Pop: 134 471 (2001). Area: 439 sq km (169 sq miles)

neat's-foot oil *n* a yellow oil obtained by boiling the feet and shinbones of cattle

neb (nɛb) *n arch or dialect* 1 the peak of a cap 2 the beak of a bird or the nose or snout of an animal 3 the projecting end of anything [OE *nebb*]

NEB *abbrev for:* 1 New English Bible 2 (the former) National Enterprise Board

Nebo (ˈniːbəʊ) *n* **Mount** a mountain in Jordan, northeast of the Dead Sea: the highest point of a ridge known as Pisgah, from which Moses viewed the Promised Land just before his death (Deuteronomy 34:1). Height: 802 m (2631 ft)

Nebr. *abbrev for* Nebraska

Nebraska (nɪˈbræskə) *n* a state of the western US: consists of an undulating plain. Capital: Lincoln. Pop: 1 711 263 (2000 est). Area: 197 974 sq km (76 483 sq miles). Abbreviations: **Nebr** or (with zip code) **NE** > **Neˈbraskan** *adj, n*

Nebuchadnezzar *or* **Nebuchadrezzar** (ˌnɛbjʊkədˈnɛzə, -ˈdrɛzə) *n Old Testament* a king of Babylon, 605–562 BC, who conquered and destroyed Jerusalem and exiled the Jews to Babylon (II Kings 24–25)

nebula ('nɛbjʊlə) *n, pl* **nebulae** (-ˌliː) *or* **nebulas** 1 *astron* a diffuse cloud of particles and gases visible either as a hazy patch of light (either an **emission** or **reflection nebula**) or an irregular dark region (**dark nebula**) 2 *pathol* opacity of the cornea [C17 from L: mist, cloud] > '**nebular** *adj*

nebular hypothesis *n* the theory that the solar system evolved from nebular matter

nebulize *or* **nebulise** ('nɛbjʊˌlaɪz) *vb* **nebulizes, nebulizing, nebulized** *or* **nebulises, nebulising, nebulised** (*tr*) to convert (a liquid) into a fine mist or spray; atomize > ˌ**nebuli'zation** *or* ˌ**nebuli'sation** *n*

nebulizer *or* **nebuliser** ('nɛbjʊˌlaɪzə) *n* a device for converting a drug in liquid form into a mist or fine spray which is inhaled through a mask to provide medication for the respiratory system. Also called: **inhalator**

nebulosity (ˌnɛbjʊ'lɒsɪtɪ) *n, pl* **nebulosities** 1 the state of being nebulous 2 *astron* a nebula

nebulous ('nɛbjʊləs) *adj* 1 lacking definite form, shape, or content; vague or amorphous: *nebulous reasons* 2 of, characteristic of, or resembling a nebula 3 *rare* misty or hazy > '**nebulousness** *n*

NEC *abbrev for* National Executive Committee

necessaries ('nɛsɪsərɪz) *pl n* (*sometimes sing*) what is needed; essential items: *the necessaries of life*

necessarily ('nɛsɪsərɪlɪ, ˌnɛsɪ'sɛrɪlɪ) *adv* 1 as an inevitable or natural consequence 2 as a certainty: *he won't necessarily come*

necessary ('nɛsɪsərɪ) *adj* 1 needed to achieve a certain desired result; required 2 inevitable: *the necessary consequences of your action* 3 *logic* 3a (of a statement, formula, etc) true under all interpretations 3b (of a proposition) determined to be true by its meaning, so that its denial would be self-contradictory ▷ Cf **sufficient** (sense 2) 4 *rare* compelled, as by necessity or law; not free ▷ *n* 5 (preceded by *the*) *inf* the money required for a particular purpose 6 **do the necessary** *inf* to do something that is necessary in a particular situation ▷ See also **necessaries** [C14 from L *necessārius* indispensable, from *necesse* unavoidable]

necessitarianism (nɪˌsɛsɪ'tɛərɪəˌnɪzəm) *n philosophy* another word for **determinism** > **neˌcessi'tarian** *n, adj*

necessitate (nɪ'sɛsɪˌteɪt) *vb* **necessitates, necessitating, necessitated** (*tr*) 1 to cause as an unavoidable result 2 (*usually passive*) to compel or require (someone to do something)

necessitous (nɪ'sɛsɪtəs) *adj* very needy; destitute; poverty-stricken

necessity (nɪ'sɛsɪtɪ) *n, pl* **necessities** 1 (*sometimes pl*) something needed; prerequisite: *necessities of life* 2 a condition or set of circumstances that inevitably requires a certain result: *it is a matter of necessity to wear formal clothes when meeting the Queen* 3 the state or quality of being obligatory or unavoidable 4 urgent requirement, as in an emergency 5 poverty or want 6 *rare* compulsion through laws of nature; fate 7 *logic* the property of being necessary 8 **of necessity** inevitably

neck (nɛk) *n* 1 the part of an organism connecting the head with the body 2 the part of a garment around the neck 3 something resembling a neck in shape or position: *the neck of a bottle* 4 *anat* a constricted portion of an organ or part 5 a narrow strip of land; peninsula or isthmus 6 a strait or channel 7 the part of a violin, cello, etc, that extends from the body to the tuning pegs and supports the fingerboard 8 a solid block of igneous rock from the interior of an extinct volcano, exposed after erosion of the surrounding rock 9 the length of a horse's head and neck taken as an approximate distance by which one horse beats another in a race: *to win by a neck* 10 *archit* the narrow band at the top of the shaft of a column 11 *inf* impudence or cheek 12 **get it in the neck** *inf* to be reprimanded or punished severely 13 **neck and neck** absolutely level in a race or competition 14 **neck of the woods** *inf* a particular area: *what brings you to this neck of the woods?* 15 **neck or nothing** at any cost 16 **save one's** *or* **someone's neck** *inf* to escape from or help someone else to escape from a difficult or dangerous situation 17 **stick one's neck out** *inf* to risk criticism, ridicule, etc, by speaking one's mind ▷ *vb* 18 (*intr*) *inf* to kiss or fondle someone or one another passionately [OE *hnecca*]

Neckar ('nɛkɑː) *n* a river in SW Germany, rising in the Black Forest and flowing generally north into the Rhine at Mannheim. Length: 394 km (245 miles)

neckband ('nɛkˌbænd) *n* a band around the neck of a garment as finishing, decoration, or a base for a collar

neckcloth ('nɛkˌklɒθ) *n* a large ornamental usually white cravat worn formerly by men

neckerchief ('nɛkətʃɪf, -ˌtʃiːf) *n* a piece of ornamental cloth, often square, worn round the neck [C14 from NECK + KERCHIEF]

necking ('nɛkɪŋ) *n inf* the activity of kissing and embracing lovingly

necklace ('nɛklɪs) *n* 1 a chain, band, or cord, often bearing beads, pearls, jewels, etc, worn around the neck as an ornament, esp by women 2 (in South Africa) 2a a tyre soaked in petrol, placed round a person's neck, and set on fire in order to burn the person to death 2b (*as modifier*): *necklace victims* ▷ *vb* **necklaces, necklacing, necklaced** (*tr*) 3 (in South Africa) to kill (a person) by means of a necklace

neckline ('nɛkˌlaɪn) *n* the shape or position of the upper edge of a dress, blouse, etc

necktie ('nɛkˌtaɪ) *n* the US name for **tie** (sense 10)

neckwear ('nɛkˌwɛə) *n* articles of clothing, such as ties, scarves, etc, worn round the neck

necro- *or before a vowel* **necr-** *combining form* indicating death, a dead body, or dead tissue: *necrosis* [from Gk *nekros* corpse]

Nn

necrobiosis (ˌnɛkrəʊbaɪ'əʊsɪs) *n physiol* the normal degeneration and death of cells

necrolatry (nɛ'krɒlətrɪ) *n* the worship of the dead

necrology (nɛ'krɒlədʒɪ) *n, pl* **necrologies** 1 a list of people recently dead 2 a less common word for **obituary** > **necrological** (ˌnɛkrə'lɒdʒɪkᵊl) *adj*

necromancy ('nɛkrəʊˌmænsɪ) *n* 1 the art of supposedly conjuring up the dead, esp in order to obtain from them knowledge of the future 2 black magic; sorcery [C13 (sense 1) ult. from Gk *nekromanteia*, from *nekros* corpse; (sense 2) from Med. L *nigromantia*, from L *niger* black, which replaced *necro-* through folk etymology] > '**necroˌmancer** *n* > ˌ**necro'mantic** *adj*

necrophilia (ˌnɛkrəʊ'fɪlɪə) *n* sexual attraction for or sexual intercourse with dead bodies. Also called: **necromania, necrophilism** > **necrophile** ('nɛkrəʊˌfaɪl) *n* > ˌ**necro'philic** *adj*

necropolis (nɛ'krɒpəlɪs) *n, pl* **necropolises** *or* **necropoleis** (-ˌleɪs) a burial site or cemetery [C19 from Gk, from *nekros* dead + *polis* city]

necropsy ('nɛkrɒpsɪ) *or* **necroscopy** (nɛ'krɒskəpɪ) *n, pl* **necropsies** *or* **necroscopies** another name for **autopsy** [C19 from Gk *nekros* dead body + *opsis* sight]

necrosis (nɛ'krəʊsɪs) *n* 1 the death of one or more cells in the body, usually within a localized area, as from an interruption of the blood supply 2 death of plant tissue due to disease, frost, etc [C17 NL, from Gk *nekrōsis*, from *nekroun* to kill, from *nekros* corpse] > **necrotic** (nɛ'krɒtɪk) *adj*

nectar ('nɛktə) *n* 1 a sugary fluid produced in the nectaries of plants and collected by bees and other animals 2 *classical myth* the drink of the gods ▷ Cf **ambrosia** (sense 1) 3 any delicious drink [C16 via L from Gk *nektar*] > '**nectarous** *adj*

nectarine ('nɛktərɪn) *n* 1 a variety of peach tree 2 the smooth-skinned fruit of this tree [C17 apparently from NECTAR]

nectary (ˈnɛktərɪ) *n, pl* **nectaries** any of various structures secreting nectar that occur in the flowers, leaves, stipules, etc, of a plant [C18 from NL *nectarium*, from NECTAR]

ned (nɛd) *n Scot sl* a hooligan [from ?]

neddy (ˈnɛdɪ) *n, pl* **neddies** a child's word for a **donkey** [C18 from *Ned*, pet form of *Edward*]

Nederland (ˈneːdərlɑnt) *n* the Dutch name for the **Netherlands**

née *or* **nee** (neɪ) *adj* indicating the maiden name of a married woman: *Mrs Bloggs née Blandish* [C19 from F: pp (fem) of *naître* to be born, from L *nascī*]

need (niːd) *vb* **1** *(tr)* to be in want of: *to need money* **2** *(tr)* to be obliged: *to need to do more work* **3** (takes an infinitive without *to*) used as an auxiliary to express necessity or obligation and does not add *-s* when used with *he, she, it*, and singular nouns: *need he go?* **4** *(intr) arch* to be essential to: *there needs no reason for this* ▷ *n* **5** the fact or an instance of feeling the lack of something: *he has need of a new coat* **6** a requirement: *the need for vengeance* **7** necessity or obligation: *no need to be frightened* **8** distress: *a friend in need* **9** poverty or destitution ▷ See also **needs** [OE *nēad, nied*]

needful (ˈniːdfʊl) *adj* **1** necessary; required **2** *arch* poverty-stricken ▷ *n* **3 the needful** *inf* what is necessary, esp money > ˈ**needfulness** *n*

needle (ˈniːdᵊl) *n* **1** a pointed slender piece of metal with a hole in it through which thread is passed for sewing **2** a somewhat larger rod with a point at one end, used in knitting **3** a similar instrument with a hook at one end for crocheting **4** a small thin pointed device, esp one made of stainless steel, used to transmit the vibrations from a gramophone record to the pick-up ▷ Cf **stylus** (sense 3) **5** *med* the long hollow pointed part of a hypodermic syringe, which is inserted into the body **6** *surgery* a pointed instrument, often curved, for suturing, puncturing, or ligating **7** a long narrow stiff leaf, esp of a conifer in which water loss is greatly reduced: *pine needles* **8** any slender sharp spine **9** a pointer on the scale of a measuring instrument **10** short for **magnetic needle** **11** a sharp pointed instrument used in engraving **12** anything long and pointed, such as an obelisk **13** *inf* **13a** anger or intense rivalry, esp in a sporting encounter **13b** *(as modifier)*: *a needle match* **14 have** *or* **get the needle** *Brit inf* to feel dislike, nervousness, or annoyance: *she got the needle after he had refused her invitation* ▷ *vb* **needles, needling, needled** *(tr)* **15** *inf* to goad or provoke, as by constant criticism **16** to sew, embroider, or prick (fabric) with a needle [OE *nǣdl*]

needlecord (ˈniːdᵊlˌkɔːd) *n* a corduroy fabric with narrow ribs

needlepoint (ˈniːdᵊlˌpɔɪnt) *n* **1** embroidery done on canvas with various stitches so as to resemble tapestry **2** another name for **point lace**

needless (ˈniːdlɪs) *adj* not required; unnecessary > ˈ**needlessly** *adv* > ˈ**needlessness** *n*

needlestick injury (ˈniːdᵊlˌstɪk) *n* an injury caused by accidentally pricking the skin with a hypodermic needle

needle time *n* the limited time allocated by a radio channel to the broadcasting of music from records

needlewoman (ˈniːdᵊlˌwʊmən) *n, pl* **needlewomen** a woman who does needlework; seamstress

needlework (ˈniːdᵊlˌwɜːk) *n* sewing and embroidery

needs (niːdz) *adv* **1** (preceded or foll by *must*) of necessity: *we must needs go* ▷ *pl n* **2** what is required; necessities: *his needs are modest*

needy (ˈniːdɪ) *adj* **needier, neediest a** in need of practical or emotional support; distressed **b** *(as collective n; preceded by the)*: *the needy*

Néel (*French* neel) *n* **Louis** (lwi) 1904–2000, French physicist, noted for his research on magnetism; shared the Nobel prize for physics in 1970

ne'er (nɛə) *adv* a poetic contraction of **never**

ne'er-do-well *n* **1** an improvident, irresponsible, or lazy person ▷ *adj* **2** useless; worthless: *your ne'er-do-well schemes*

nefarious (nɪˈfɛərɪəs) *adj* evil; wicked; sinful [C17 from L *nefārius*, from *nefās* unlawful deed, from *nē* not + *fās* divine law] > **ne'fariously** *adv* > **ne'fariousness** *n*

Nefertiti (ˌnɛfəˈtiːtɪ) *or* **Nofretete** *n* 14th century BC, Egyptian queen; wife of Akhenaton

neg. *abbrev for* negative(ly)

negate (nɪˈgeɪt) *vb* **negates, negating, negated** *(tr)* **1** to nullify; invalidate **2** to contradict [C17 from L *negāre*, from *neg-*, var. of *nec* not + *aio* I say] > **ne'gator** *or* **ne'gater** *n*

negation (nɪˈgeɪʃən) *n* **1** the opposite or absence of something **2** a negative thing or condition **3** the act of negating **4** *logic* a proposition that is the denial of another proposition and is true only if the original proposition is false

negative (ˈnɛgətɪv) *adj* **1** expressing a refusal or denial: *a negative answer* **2** lacking positive qualities, such as enthusiasm or optimism **3** showing opposition or resistance **4** measured in a direction opposite to that regarded as positive **5** *biol* indicating movement or growth away from a stimulus: *negative geotropism* **6** *med* indicating absence of the disease or condition for which a test was made **7** another word for **minus** (senses 3b, 4) **8** *physics* **8a** (of an electric charge) having the same polarity as the charge of an electron **8b** (of a body, system, ion, etc) having a negative electric charge; having an excess of electrons **9** short for **electronegative** **10** of or relating to a photographic negative **11** *logic* (of a categorial proposition) denying the satisfaction by the subject of the predicate, as in *some men are irrational; no pigs have wings* ▷ *n* **12** a statement or act of denial or refusal **13** a negative thing **14** *photog* a piece of photographic film or a plate, previously exposed and developed, showing an image that, in black-and-white photography, has a reversal of tones **15** *physics* a negative object, such as a terminal or a plate in a voltaic cell **16** a sentence or other linguistic element with a negative meaning, as the English word *not* **17** a quantity less than zero **18** *logic* a negative proposition **19 in the negative** indicating denial or refusal ▷ *vb* **negatives, negativing, negatived** *(tr)* **20** to deny; negate **21** to show to be false; disprove **22** to refuse consent to or approval of: *the proposal was negatived* > ˈ**negatively** *adv* > ˈ**negativeness** *or* ˌ**negaˈtivity** *n*

negative equity *n* the state of holding a property the value of which is less than the amount of mortgage still unpaid

negative feedback *n* See **feedback**

negative resistance *n* a characteristic of certain electronic components in which an increase in the applied voltage increases the resistance, producing a proportional decrease in current

negative sign *n* the symbol (–) used to indicate a negative quantity or a subtraction

negativism (ˈnɛgətɪvˌɪzəm) *n* **1** a tendency to be unconstructively critical **2** any sceptical or derisive system of thought > ˈ**negativist** *n, adj*

Negev (ˈnɛgɛv) *or* **Negeb** (ˈnɛgɛb) *n* the S part of Israel, on the Gulf of Aqaba: a triangular-shaped semidesert region, with large areas under irrigation; scene of fighting between Israeli and Egyptian forces in 1948. Chief town: Beersheba. Area: 12 820 sq km (4950 sq miles)

neglect (nɪˈglɛkt) *vb (tr)* **1** to fail to give due care, attention, or time to: *to neglect a child* **2** to fail (to do something) through carelessness: *he neglected to tell her* **3** to disregard ▷ *n* **4** lack of due care or attention;

negligence: *the child starved through neglect* **5** the act or an instance of neglecting or the state of being neglected [c16 from L *neglegere*, from *nec* not + *legere* to select]

neglectful (nɪˈglɛktfʊl) *adj* (when *postpositive*, foll by *of*) careless; heedless

negligee *or* **negligée** (ˈnɛglɪˌʒeɪ) *n* **1** a woman's light dressing gown, esp one that is lace-trimmed **2** a thin and revealing woman's nightdress **3** (formerly) any informal women's attire [c18 from F *négligée*, pp (fem) of *négliger* to NEGLECT]

negligence (ˈnɛglɪdʒəns) *n* **1** the state of being negligent **2** a negligent act **3** *law* a civil wrong whereby the defendant is in breach of a legal duty of care, resulting in injury to the plaintiff

negligent (ˈnɛglɪdʒənt) *adj* **1** lacking attention, care, or concern; neglectful **2** careless or nonchalant > **ˈnegligently** *adv*

negligible (ˈnɛglɪdʒəbᵊl) *adj* so small, unimportant, etc, as to be not worth considering > **ˈnegligibly** *adv*

negotiable (nɪˈgəʊʃəbᵊl) *adj* **1** able to be negotiated **2** (of a bill of exchange, promissory note, etc) legally transferable in title from one party to another > **neˌgotiaˈbility** *n*

negotiable instrument *n* a legal document, such as a cheque or bill of exchange, that is freely negotiable

negotiate (nɪˈgəʊʃɪˌeɪt) *vb* **negotiates, negotiating, negotiated 1** to talk (with others) to achieve (an agreement, etc) **2** (*tr*) to succeed in passing round or over **3** (*tr*) *finance* **3a** to transfer (a negotiable commercial paper) to another in return for value received **3b** to sell (financial assets) **3c** to arrange for (a loan) [c16 from L *negōtiārī* to do business, from *negōtium* business, from *nec* not + *ōtium* leisure] > **neˌgotiˈation** *n* > **neˈgotiˌator** *n*

Negress (ˈniːgrɪs) *n* a female Black person

Negrillo (nɪˈgrɪləʊ) *n, pl* **Negrillos** *or* **Negrilloes** a member of a dwarfish Negroid race of central and southern Africa [c19 from Sp., dim. of *negro* black]

Negri Sembilan (ˈnɛgrɪ sɛmˈbiːlən) *n* a state of S Peninsular Malaysia: mostly mountainous, with large areas under paddy and rubber. Capital: Seremban. Pop: 830 080 (2000). Area: 6643 sq km (2565 sq miles)

Negrito (nɪˈgriːtəʊ) *n, pl* **Negritos** *or* **Negritoes** a member of any of various dwarfish Negroid peoples of SE Asia and Melanesia [c19 from Sp., dim. of *negro* black]

negritude (ˈniːgrɪˌtjuːd, ˈnɛg-) *n* **1** the fact of being a Negro **2** awareness and cultivation of the Negro heritage, values, and culture [c20 from F, from *nègre* NEGRO[1]] (ˈniːgrəʊ) *old-fashioned* ▷ *n, pl* **Negroes 1** a member of any of the dark-skinned indigenous peoples of Africa and their descendants elsewhere ▷ *adj* **2** relating to or characteristic of Negroes [c16 from Sp. or Port.: black, from L *niger*] > **ˈNegroˌism** *n*

Negro[1] (ˈniːgrəʊ) *old-fashioned* ▷ *n, pl* **Negroes 1** a member of any of the dark-skinned indigenous peoples of Africa and their descendants elsewhere ▷ *adj* **2** relating to or characteristic of Negroes [c16 from Sp. or Port.: black, from L *niger*] > **ˈNegroˌism** *n*

Negro[2] (ˈneɪgrəʊ, ˈnɛg-) *n* **Río 1** a river in NW South America, rising in E Colombia (as the Guainía) and flowing east, then south as part of the border between Colombia and Venezuela, entering Brazil and continuing southeast to join the Amazon at Manáus. Length: about 2250 km (1400 miles) **2** a river in S central Argentina, formed by the confluence of the Neuquén and Limay Rivers and flowing east and southeast to the Atlantic. Length: about 1014 km (630 miles) **3** a river in central Uruguay, rising in S Brazil and flowing southwest into the Uruguay River. Length: about 467 km (290 miles)

Negroid (ˈniːgrɔɪd) *adj* **1** denoting, relating to, or belonging to one of the major racial groups of mankind, characterized by brown-black skin, tightly curled hair, a short nose, and full lips ▷ *n* **2** a member of this racial group

Negropont (ˈnɛgrəʊˌpɒnt) *n* **1** the former English name for **Euboea 2** the medieval English name for **Chalcis**

Negros (ˈneɪgrəʊs; *Spanish* ˈneɣrɔs) *n* an island of the central Philippines, one of the Visayan Islands. Capital: Bacolod. Pop: 3 168 000 (1990 est). Area: 12 704 sq km (4904 sq miles)

negus (ˈniːgəs) *n, pl* **neguses** a hot drink of port and lemon juice, usually spiced and sweetened [c18 after Col. Francis *Negus* (died 1732), its E inventor]

Negus (ˈniːgəs) *n, pl* **Neguses** *history* a title of the emperor of Ethiopia [from Amharic: king]

Neh. *Bible abbrev for* Nehemiah

Nehemiah (ˌniːɪˈmaɪə) *n Old Testament* **1** a Jewish official at the court of Artaxerxes, king of Persia, who in 444 BC became a leader in the rebuilding of Jerusalem after the Babylonian captivity **2** the book recounting the acts of Nehemiah

Nehru (ˈnɛəruː) *n* **1 Jawaharlal** (dʒəwəhəˈlɑːl) 1889–1964, Indian statesman and nationalist leader. He spent several periods in prison for his nationalist activities and practised a policy of noncooperation with Britain during World War II. He was the first prime minister of the republic of India (1947–64) **2** his father, **Motilal** (məʊtɪˈlɑːl), known as *Pandit Nehru*. 1861–1931, Indian nationalist, lawyer, and journalist; first president of the reconstructed Indian National Congress

neigh (neɪ) *n* **1** the high-pitched cry of a horse ▷ *vb* **2** to make a neigh or a sound like a neigh [OE *hnǣgan*]

neighbour *or US* **neighbor** (ˈneɪbə) *n* **1** a person who lives near or next to another **2a** a person or thing near or next to another **2b** (*as modifier*): *neighbour states* ▷ *vb* **3** (when *intr*, often foll by *on*) to be or live close to [OE *nēahbūr*, from *nēah* NIGH + *būr*, *gebūr* dweller; see BOOR] > **ˈneighbouring** *or US* **ˈneighboring** *adj*

neighbourhood *or US* **neighborhood** (ˈneɪbəˌhʊd) *n* **1** the immediate environment; surroundings **2** a district where people live **3** the people in a particular area **4** *maths* the set of all points whose distance from a given point is less than a specified value **5** (*modifier*) living or situated in and serving the needs of a local area: *a neighbourhood community worker* **6 in the neighbourhood of** approximately

neighbourhood watch *n* a scheme in which members of a community agree to take joint responsibility for keeping a watch on each other's property, as a way of preventing crime

neighbourly *or US* **neighborly** (ˈneɪbəlɪ) *adj* kind, friendly, or sociable, as befits a neighbour > **ˈneighbourliness** *or US* **ˈneighborliness** *n*

Neill (niːl) *n* **A(lexander) S(utherland)** 1883–1973, Scottish educationalist and writer, who put his progressive educational theories into practice at Summerhill school (founded 1921)

Neisse (ˈnaɪsə) *n* **1** Also called: **Glatzer Neisse** (ˈglɑːtsə) Polish name: **Nysa** a river in SW Poland, rising on the northern Czech border, and flowing northeast to join the Oder near Brzeg. Length: about 193 km (120 miles) **2** Also called: **Lusatian Neisse** a river in E Europe, rising near Liberec in the Czech Republic and flowing north to join the Oder: forms part of the German-Polish border. Length: 225 km (140 miles)

neither (ˈnaɪðə, ˈniːðə) *determiner* **1a** not one nor the other (of two) **1b** (*as pronoun*): *neither can win* ▷ *conj* **2** (*coordinating*) **2a** (used preceding alternatives joined by *nor*) not: *neither John nor Mary nor Joe went* **2b** another word for **nor** (sense 2) ▷ *adv* (*sentence modifier*) **3** *not standard* another word for **either** (sense 4) [c13 (lit.: *ne either* not either): changed from OE *nāwther*, from *nāhwæther*, from *nā* not + *hwæther* which of two]

USAGE A verb following a compound subject that uses *neither...(nor)* should be in

Nn

the singular if both subjects are in the singular: *neither Jack nor John has done the work*

Nejd (nɛʒd, neɪd) *n* a region of central Saudi Arabia: formerly an independent sultanate of Arabia; united with Hejaz to form the kingdom of Saudi Arabia (1932)

nekton ('nɛktɒn) *n* the population of free-swimming animals that inhabits the middle depths of a sea or lake [c19 via G from Gk *nēkton* a swimming thing, from *nēkhein* to swim]

nelly ('nɛlɪ) *n* **not on your nelly** (*sentence substitute*) *Brit sl* certainly not

nelson ('nɛlsən) *n* any wrestling hold in which a wrestler places an arm or arms under the opponent's arm or arms from behind and exerts pressure with the palms of the hands on the back of the opponent's neck [c19 from a proper name]

Nelson[1] ('nɛlsən) *n* **1** a town in NW England, in E Lancashire: textile industry. Pop: 29 120 (1991) **2** a port in New Zealand, on N South Island on Tasman Bay. Pop: 51 200 (1995 est) **3 River** a river in central Canada, in N central Manitoba, flowing from Lake Winnipeg northeast to Hudson Bay. Length: about 650 km (400 miles)
▷ www.ncc.govt.nz
▷ www.nelsonnz.com

Nelson[2] ('nɛlsən) *n* **1 Horatio, Viscount Nelson.** 1758–1805, British naval commander during the Revolutionary and Napoleonic Wars. He became rear admiral in 1797 after the battle of Cape St Vincent and in 1798 almost destroyed the French fleet at the battle of the Nile. He was killed at Trafalgar (1805) after defeating Villeneuve's fleet **2 Willie** born 1933, US country singer and songwriter

Nelspruit ('nɛls,prɔɪt) *n* a city in NE South Africa, the capital of Mpumalanga province on the Crocodile River: trading and agricultural centre, esp for fruit, with a growing tourist trade. Pop: 94 714 (1996), with a metropolitan area 202 000 (2000)

Neman *or* **Nyeman** (*Russian* 'njɛmən) *n* a river in NE Europe, rising in Belarus and flowing northwest through Lithuania to the Baltic. Length: 937 km (582 miles). Polish name: **Niemen**

nematic (nɪ'mætɪk) *adj chem* (of a substance) existing in or having a mesomorphic state in which a linear orientation of the molecules causes anisotropic properties [c20 NEMAT(O)- (referring to the threadlike chains of molecules in liquid) + -IC]

nemato- *or before a vowel* **nemat-** *combining form* indicating a threadlike form: *nematocyst* [from Gk *nēma* thread]

nematocyst ('nɛmətə,sɪst, nɪ'mætə-) *n* a structure in coelenterates, such as jellyfish, consisting of a capsule containing a hollow coiled thread that can sting or paralyse

nematode ('nɛmə,təʊd) *n* any of a class of unsegmented worms having a tough outer cuticle, including the hookworm and filaria. Also called: **nematode worm, roundworm**

Nembutal ('nɛmbjʊ,tɑːl) *n* a trademark for **pentobarbital sodium**

Nemea (nɪ'miːə) *n* (in ancient Greece) a valley in N Argolis in the NE Peloponnese; site of the **Nemean Games**, a Panhellenic festival and athletic competition held every other year > **Ne'mean** *adj*

Nemean lion *n Greek myth* an enormous lion that was strangled by Hercules as his first labour

nemertean (nɪ'mɜːtɪən) *or* **nemertine** ('nɛmə,taɪn) *n* **1** any of a class of soft flattened ribbon-like marine worms having an eversible threadlike proboscis ▷ *adj* **2** of or belonging to the *Nemertea* [c19 via NL from Gk *Nēmertēs* a NEREID]

nemesia (nɪ'miːʒə) *n* any plant of a southern African genus cultivated for their brightly coloured flowers [c19 NL, from Gk *nemesion*, name of a plant resembling this]

Nemesis ('nɛmɪsɪs) *n* **1** *Greek myth* the goddess of retribution and vengeance **2** (*pl* **Nemeses** (-,siːz)). (*sometimes not cap*) any agency of retribution and vengeance [c16 via L from Gk: righteous wrath, from *nemein* to distribute what is due]

nemophila (nɛ'mɒfɪlə) *n* an annual trailing plant with blue flowers [from Gk *nemos* grove + *philos* loving]

neo- *or sometimes before a vowel* **ne-** *combining form* **1** (*sometimes cap*) new, recent, or a modern form: *neoclassicism; neocolonialism* **2** (*usually cap*) the most recent subdivision of a geological period: *Neogene* [from Gk *neos* new]

neoclassical (,niːəʊ'klæsɪkᵊl) *or* **neoclassic** *adj* **1** of, relating to, or in the style of neoclassicism in art, architecture, etc **2** of, relating to, or in the style of neoclassicism in music

neoclassicism (,niːəʊ'klæsɪ,sɪzəm) *n* **1** a late 18th- and early 19th-century style in architecture and art, based on classical models **2** *music* a movement of the 1920s that sought to avoid the emotionalism of late romantic music
▷ www.comcen.com.au/ ▷ carowley/neoclass.htm
▷ www.hypermusic.ca/hist/twentieth3.html

neocolonialism (,niːəʊkə'ləʊnɪə,lɪzəm) *n* (in the modern world) political control by an outside power of a country that is in theory independent, esp through the domination of its economy > **,neoco'lonial** *adj* > **,neoco'lonialist** *n, adj*

neo-conservatism *n* (in the US) a right-wing tendency that originated amongst supporters of the political left and has become characterized by its support of hawkish foreign policies > **,neo-con'servative** *adj, n*

Neo-Darwinism (,niːəʊ'dɑːwɪn,ɪzəm) *n* the modern version of the Darwin theory of evolution, which incorporates the principles of genetics to explain how inheritable variations can arise by mutation

neodymium (,niːəʊ'dɪmɪəm) *n* a toxic silvery-white metallic element of the lanthanide series. Symbol: Nd; atomic no.: 60; atomic wt.: 144.24 [c19 NL; see NEO- + DIDYMIUM]

neogothic (,niːəʊ'gɒθɪk) *n* another name for **Gothic Revival**

Neolithic (,niːə'lɪθɪk) *n* **1** the cultural period that was characterized by primitive farming and the use of polished stone and flint tools and weapons ▷ *adj* **2** relating to this period

neologism (nɪ'ɒlə,dʒɪzəm) *or* **neology** *n, pl* **neologisms** *or* **neologies** **1** a newly coined word, or a phrase or familiar word used in a new sense **2** the practice of using or introducing neologisms [c18 via F from NEO- + *-logism*, from Gk *logos* word] > **ne'ologist** *n*

neologize *or* **neologise** (nɪ'ɒlə,dʒaɪz) *vb* **neologizes, neologizing, neologized** *or* **neologises, neologising, neologised** (*intr*) to invent or use neologisms

neomycin (,niːəʊ'maɪsɪn) *n* an antibiotic obtained from the bacterium *Streptomyces fradiae*, administered in the treatment of skin and eye infections [c20 from NEO- + Gk *mukēs* fungus + -IN]

neon ('niːɒn) *n* **1** a colourless odourless rare gaseous element occurring in trace amounts in the atmosphere: used in illuminated signs and lights. Symbol: Ne; atomic no.: 10; atomic wt.: 20.179 **2** (*modifier*) of or illuminated by neon: *neon sign* [c19 via NL from Gk *neon* new]

neonatal (,niːəʊ'neɪtᵊl) *adj* occurring in or relating to the first few weeks of life in human babies > **'neo,nate** *n*

neon light *n* a glass bulb or tube containing neon at low pressure that gives a pink or red glow when a voltage is applied

neophyte ('niːəʊ,faɪt) *n* **1** a person newly converted to a religious faith **2** a novice in a religious order **3** a beginner [c16 via Church L from New Testament Gk *neophutos* recently planted, from *neos* new + *phuton* a plant]

neoplasm ('niːəʊˌplæzəm) *n pathol* any abnormal new growth of tissue; tumour

Neo-Platonism (ˌniːəʊ'pleɪtəˌnɪzəm) *n* a philosophical system which was developed in the 3rd century AD as a synthesis of Platonic, Pythagorean, and Aristotelian elements > **Neo-Platonic** (ˌniːəʊplə'tɒnɪk) *adj* > ˌ**Neo-'Platonist** *n, adj*

neoprene ('niːəʊˌpriːn) *n* a synthetic rubber obtained by the polymerization of chloroprene, a colourless liquid derivative of butadiene, resistant to oil and ageing and used in waterproof products [c20 from NEO- + PR(OPYL) + -ENE]

Neoptolemus (ˌniːɒp'tɒləməs) *n Greek myth* a son of Achilles and slayer of King Priam of Troy. Also called: **Pyrrhus**

neoteny (nɪ'ɒtənɪ) *n* the persistence of larval or fetal features in the adult form of an animal [c19 from NL *neotenia*, from Gk NEO- + *teinein* to stretch]

neoteric (ˌniːəʊ'tɛrɪk) *rare* ▷ *adj* **1** belonging to a new fashion or trend; modern ▷ *n* **2** a new writer or philosopher [c16 via LL from Gk *neōterikos* young, fresh, from *neoteros* younger, more recent, from *neos* new, recent]

Nepal (nɪ'pɔːl) *n* a kingdom in S Asia: the world's only Hindu kingdom; united in 1768 by the Gurkhas; consists of swampy jungle in the south and great massifs, valleys, and gorges of the Himalayas over the rest of the country, with many peaks over 8000 m (26 000 ft) (notably Everest and Kangchenjunga). A multiparty democracy was instituted in 1990. Official language: Nepali. Official religion: Hinduism; Mahayana Buddhist minority. Currency: rupee. Capital: Katmandu. Pop: 25 284 000 (2001 est). Area: 147 181 sq km (56 815 sq miles) > **Nepalese** (ˌnɛpə'liːz) *adj, n*
▷ www.nepalhomepage.com
▷ www.welcomenepal.com

Nepali (nɪ'pɔːlɪ) *n* **1** the official language of Nepal, also spoken in Sikkim and parts of India **2** (*pl* **Nepali** *or* **Nepalis**) a native or inhabitant of Nepal; a Nepalese ▷ *adj* **3** of or relating to Nepal, its inhabitants, or their language; Nepalese

nepenthe (nɪ'pɛnθɪ) *or* **nepenthes** (nɪ'pɛnθiːz) *n* a drug that ancient writers referred to as a means of forgetting grief or trouble [c16 via L from Gk *nēpenthes* sedative made from a herb, from *nē-* not + *penthos* grief]

nepeta ('nɛpɛtə, nə'pɛtə) *n* any of a genus of plants found in N temperate regions. It includes catmint [from L]

nephew ('nɛvjuː, 'nɛf-) *n* a son of one's sister or brother [c13 from OF *neveu*, from L *nepōs*]

nephology (nɪ'fɒlədʒɪ) *n* the study of clouds [c19 from Gk *nephos* cloud + -LOGY]

nephridium (nɪ'frɪdɪəm) *n, pl* **nephridia** (-ɪə) a simple excretory organ of many invertebrates, consisting of a tube through which waste products pass to the exterior [c19 NL: little kidney]

nephrite ('nɛfraɪt) *n* a tough fibrous mineral: a variety of jade. Also called: **kidney stone** [c18 via G from Gk *nephros* kidney; it was thought to help in kidney disorders]

nephritic (nɪ'frɪtɪk) *adj* **1** of or relating to the kidneys **2** relating to or affected with nephritis

nephritis (nɪ'fraɪtɪs) *n* inflammation of a kidney

nephro- *or before a vowel* **nephr-** *combining form* kidney or kidneys: *nephritis* [from Gk *nephros*]

nephrology (nɪ'frɒlədʒɪ) *n* the branch of medicine concerned with diseases of the kidney > **ne'phrologist** *n*

nephron ('nɛfrɒn) *n* one of the units of the kidney that secretes urine, via ducts, into the ureter

nephroscope ('nɛfrəˌskəʊp) *n* a tubular medical instrument inserted through an incision in the skin to enable examination of a kidney > **ne'phroscopy**

ne plus ultra *Latin* ('neɪ 'plʊs 'ʊltrɑː) *n* the extreme or perfect point or state [lit.: not more beyond (that is, go no further), allegedly a warning to sailors inscribed on the Pillars of Hercules at Gibraltar]

nepotism ('nɛpəˌtɪzəm) *n* favouritism shown to relatives or close friends by those with power [c17 from It. *nepotismo*, from *nepote* NEPHEW, from the former papal practice of granting favours to nephews or other relatives] > **'nepotist** *n*

Neptune[1] ('nɛptjuːn) *n* the Roman god of the sea. Greek counterpart: **Poseidon**

Neptune[2] ('nɛptjuːn) *n* the eighth planet from the sun, having 11 satellites, including Triton and Nereid
▷ http://solarsystem.nasa.gov/features/planets
▷ www.solarviews.com/eng/neptune.htm

neptunium (nɛp'tjuːnɪəm) *n* a silvery metallic element synthesized in the production of plutonium and occurring in trace amounts in uranium ores. Symbol: Np; atomic no.: 93; half-life of most stable isotope, ^{237}Np: 2.14×10^6 years [c20 from NEPTUNE[2], the planet beyond Uranus, because neptunium is beyond uranium in the periodic table]

NERC *abbrev for* Natural Environment Research Council
▷ www.nerc.ac.uk

nerd *or* **nurd** (nɜːd) *n sl* **1** a boring or unpopular person, esp one obsessed with something specified: *a computer nerd* **2** a stupid and feeble person [c20 from ?] > **'nerdish** *or* **'nurdish** *adj* > **'nerdy** *or* **'nurdy** *adj*

Nereid ('nɪərɪɪd) *n, pl* **Nereides** (nə'riːədiːz) *Greek myth* any of 50 sea nymphs who were the daughters of the sea god Nereus [c17 via L from Gk]

Nereus ('nɪərɪˌuːs) *n Greek myth* a sea god who lived in the depths of the sea with his wife Doris and their daughters the Nereides

Neri ('nɪərɪ) *n* **Saint Philip** Italian name *Filippo de' Neri*. 1515–95, Italian priest; founder of the Congregation of the Oratory (1564). Feast day: May 26

nerine (nɪ'raɪnɪ; *S African* nə'riːn) *n* any of a genus of bulbous plants native to South Africa and grown elsewhere as greenhouse plants for their pink, red, or orange flowers: includes the Guernsey lily [after the water nymph *Nerine* in Roman myth]

Nernst (*German* nɛrnst) *n* **Walther Hermann** ('valtər 'hɛrman) 1864–1941, German physical chemist who formulated the third law of thermodynamics: Nobel prize for chemistry 1920

Nero ('nɪərəʊ) *n* full name *Nero Claudius Caesar Drusus Germanicus*; original name *Lucius Domitius Ahenobarbus*. 37–68 AD, Roman emperor (54–68). He became notorious for his despotism and cruelty, and was alleged to have started the fire (64) that destroyed a large part of Rome

neroli oil *or* **neroli** ('nɪərəlɪ) *n* a brown oil distilled from the flowers of various orange trees: used in perfumery [c17 after Anne Marie de la Tremoïlle of *Neroli*, French-born It. princess believed to have discovered it]

Neruda (*Spanish* ne'ruða) *n* **Pablo** ('paβlo), real name *Neftalí Ricardo Reyes*. 1904–73, Chilean poet. His works include *Veinte poemas de amor y una canción desesperada* (1924) and *Canto general* (1950), an epic history of the Americas: Nobel prize for literature 1971

Nerva ('nɜːvə) *n* full name *Marcus Cocceius Nerva*. ?30–98 AD, Roman emperor (96–98), who introduced some degree of freedom after the repressive reign of Domitian. He adopted Trajan as his son and successor

Nerval (*French* nɛrval) *n* **Gérard de** (ʒerar də), real name *Gérard Labrunie*. 1808–55, French poet, noted esp for the sonnets of mysticism, myth, and private passion in *Les Chimères* (1854)

nervate ('nɜːveɪt) *adj* (of leaves) having veins

nervation (nɜː'veɪʃən) *or* **nervature** ('nɜːvətʃə) *n* a less common word for **venation**

nerve (nɜːv) *n* **1** any of the cordlike bundles of fibres that conduct impulses between the brain or spinal cord and another part of the body **2** bravery or steadfastness **3 lose one's nerve** to become timid, esp failing to perform some audacious act **4** *inf* effrontery; impudence **5** muscle or sinew (often in **strain every nerve**) **6** a vein in a leaf or an insect's wing ▷ *vb* **nerves, nerving, nerved** (*tr*) **7** to give courage to (oneself); steel (oneself) **8** to provide with nerve or nerves ▷ See also **nerves** [c16 from L *nervus*; rel. to Gk *neuron*]

nerve block *n* induction of anaesthesia in a specific part of the body by injecting a local anaesthetic close to the sensory nerves that supply it

nerve cell *n* another name for **neurone**

nerve centre *n* **1** a group of nerve cells associated with a specific function **2** a principal source of control over any complex activity

nerve fibre *n* a threadlike extension of a nerve cell; axon

nerve gas *n* any of various poisonous gases that have a paralysing effect on the central nervous system that can be fatal

nerve impulse *n* the electrical wave transmitted along a nerve fibre, usually following stimulation of the nerve-cell body

nerveless (ˈnɜːvlɪs) *adj* **1** calm and collected **2** listless or feeble > ˈ**nervelessly** *adv*

nerve-racking *or* **nerve-wracking** *adj* very distressing, exhausting, or harrowing

nerves (nɜːvz) *pl n Inf* **1** the imagined source of emotional control: *my nerves won't stand it* **2** anxiety, tension, or imbalance: *she's all nerves* **3 get on one's nerves** to irritate or upset one

nervine (ˈnɜːviːn) *adj* **1** having a soothing effect upon the nerves ▷ *n* **2** *obsolete* a nervine agent [c17 from NL *nervīnus*, from L *nervus* NERVE]

nervous (ˈnɜːvəs) *adj* **1** very excitable or sensitive; highly strung **2** (often foll by *of*) apprehensive or worried **3** of or containing nerves: *nervous tissue* **4** affecting the nerves or nervous tissue: *a nervous disease* **5** *arch* vigorous or forceful > ˈ**nervously** *adv* > ˈ**nervousness** *n*

nervous breakdown *n* any mental illness not primarily of organic origin, in which the patient ceases to function properly, often accompanied by severely impaired concentration, anxiety, insomnia, and lack of self-esteem

nervous system *n* the sensory and control apparatus of animals, consisting of a network of neurones

nervure (ˈnɜːvjʊə) *n* **1** *entomol* any of the chitinous rods that form the framework of an insect's wing; vein **2** *bot* any of the veins of a leaf [c19 from F; see NERVE, -URE]

nervy (ˈnɜːvɪ) *adj* **nervier, nerviest 1** *Brit inf* tense or apprehensive **2** having or needing bravery or endurance **3** *US & Canad inf* brash or cheeky **4** *arch* muscular; sinewy

nescience (ˈnɛsɪəns) *n* a formal or literary word for **ignorance** [c17 from LL *nescientia*, from L *nescīre* to be ignorant of, from *ne* not + *scīre* to know] > ˈ**nescient** *adj*

ness (nɛs) *n arch* a promontory or headland [OE *næs* headland]

Ness (nɛs) *n* **Loch** a lake in NW Scotland, in the Great Glen: said to be inhabited by a legendary aquatic monster. Length: 36 km (22.5 miles). Depth: 229 m (754 ft)

-ness *suffix forming nouns chiefly from adjectives and participles* indicating state, condition, or quality: *greatness; selfishness* [OE *-nes*, of Gmc origin]

Nessus (ˈnɛsəs) *n Greek myth* a centaur that killed Hercules. A garment dipped in its blood fatally poisoned Hercules, who had been given it by Deianira who thought it was a love charm

nest (nɛst) *n* **1** a place or structure in which birds, fishes, etc, lay eggs or give birth to young **2** a number of animals of the same species occupying a common habitat: *an ants' nest* **3** a place fostering something undesirable: *a nest of thievery* **4** a cosy or secluded place **5** a set of things, usually of graduated sizes, designed to fit together: *a nest of tables* ▷ *vb* **6** (*intr*) to make or inhabit a nest **7** (*intr*) to hunt for birds' nests **8** (*tr*) to place in a nest **9** *computing* to position (data) within other data at different ranks or levels so that the different levels of data can be used or accessed recursively [OE]

nest egg *n* **1** a fund of money kept in reserve; savings **2** a natural or artificial egg left in a nest to induce hens to lay their eggs in it

nestle (ˈnɛsᵊl) *vb* **nestles, nestling, nestled 1** (*intr*; often foll by *up* or *down*) to snuggle, settle, or cuddle closely **2** (*intr*) to be in a sheltered position; lie snugly **3** (*tr*) to shelter or place snugly or partly concealed, as in a nest [OE *nestlian*]

nestling (ˈnɛstlɪŋ, ˈnɛslɪŋ) *n* **a** a young bird not yet fledged **b** (*as modifier*): *a nestling thrush* [c14 from NEST + -LING[1]]

Nestor (ˈnɛstɔː) *n Greek myth* the oldest and wisest of the Greeks in the Trojan War

Nestorius (nɛˈstɔːrɪəs) *n* died ?451 AD, Syrian churchman; patriarch of Constantinople (428–431); deposed for heresy by the Council of Ephesus

net[1] (nɛt) *n* **1** an openwork fabric of string, wire, etc; mesh **2** a device made of net, used to protect or enclose things or to trap animals **3** a thin light mesh fabric used for curtains, etc **4** a plan, strategy, etc, intended to trap or ensnare: *the murderer slipped through the police net* **5** *tennis, badminton, etc* **5a** a strip of net that divides the playing area into two equal parts **5b** a shot that hits the net **6** the goal in soccer, hockey, etc **7** (*often pl*) *Cricket* **7a** a pitch surrounded by netting, used for practice **7b** a practice session in a net **8** *inf* short for **Internet** **9** another word for **network** (sense 2) ▷ *vb* **nets, netting, netted 10** (*tr*) to ensnare **11** (*tr*) to shelter or surround with a net **12** (*intr*) *tennis, badminton, etc* to hit a shot into the net **13** to make a net out of (rope, string, etc) [OE *net*; rel. to Gothic *nati*, Du. *net*]

net[2] *or* **nett** (nɛt) *adj* **1** remaining after all deductions, as for taxes, expenses, losses, etc: *net profit* ▷ Cf **gross** (sense 2) **2** (of weight) after deducting tare **3** final; conclusive (esp in **net result**) ▷ *n* **4** net income, profits, weight, etc ▷ *vb* **nets, netting, netted 5** (*tr*) to yield or earn as clear profit [c14 clean, neat, from F *net* NEAT[1]]

Netaji (ˈneɪtɑːdʒɪ) *n* the title for (Subhash Chandra) **Bose** [Hindi, from *neta* leader + -JI]

Netanyahu (ˌnɛtᵊnˈjɑːhuː) *n* **Benjamin** (ˈbɪnjæˌmiːn) born 1949, Israeli politician: leader of the Likud party (1993–99); prime minister (1996–99)

net asset value *n* the total value of the assets of an organization less its liabilities and capital charges. Abbrev: **NAV**

netball (ˈnɛtˌbɔːl) *n* a game for two teams of seven players (usually women) played on a hard court. Points are scored by shooting the ball through a net hanging from a ring at the top of a pole

▷ www.netball.org

Net Book Agreement *n* a former (until 1995) agreement between UK publishers and booksellers that prohibited booksellers from reducing the price of books. Abbrev: **NBA**

net domestic product *n econ* the gross domestic product minus an allowance for the depreciation of capital goods. Abbrev: **NDP**

Neth. *abbrev for* Netherlands

nether (ˈnɛðə) *adj* below, beneath, or underground: *nether regions* [OE *niothera*, *nithera*, lit.: further down, from *nither* down]

Netherlands (ˈnɛðələndz) *n* (*functioning as singular or plural*) **the 1** Also called: **Holland** a kingdom in NW Europe, on the North Sea: declared independence from Spain in 1581 as the United Provinces; became a major maritime

and commercial power in the 17th century, gaining many overseas possessions; a member of the European Union. It is mostly flat and low-lying, with about 40 per cent of the land being below sea level, much of it on polders protected by dykes. Official language: Dutch. Religion: Christian majority, Protestant and Roman Catholic, large nonreligious minority. Currency: euro. Capital: Amsterdam, with the seat of government at The Hague. Pop: 15 968 000 (2001 est). Area: 41 526 sq km (16 033 sq miles). Dutch name: **Nederland** 2 the kingdom of the Netherlands together with the Flemish-speaking part of Belgium, esp as ruled by Spain and Austria before 1581; the Low Countries > **Netherlander** ('nɛðəˌlændə) *n*
▷ www.overheid.nl/guest
▷ www.nbt.nl

Netherlands Antilles *pl n* **the** the two groups of islands in the Caribbean, in the Lesser Antilles: overseas division of the Netherlands, consisting of the S group of Curaçao, Aruba, and Bonaire, and the N group of Saint Eustatius, Saba, and the S part of Saint Martin; economy based on refining oil from Venezuela. Capital: Willemstad (on Curaçao). Pop: 205 000 (2001 est). Area: 996 sq km (390 sq miles). Former names: **Curaçao** (until 1949), **Dutch West Indies, Netherlands West Indies**

Netherlands East Indies *pl n* **the** a former name (1798–1945) for **Indonesia**

Netherlands Guiana *n* a former name for **Surinam**

Netherlands West Indies *pl n* **the** a former name for the **Netherlands Antilles**

nethermost ('nɛðəˌməʊst) *adj* **the** farthest down; lowest

netherworld ('nɛðəˌwɜːld) *n* 1 the world after death; the underworld 2 hell 3 a criminal underworld ▷ Also called (for senses 1, 2): **nether regions**

netiquette ('nɛtɪˌkɛt) *n* the informal code of behaviour on the Internet [C20 from NET(WORK) + (ET)IQUETTE]

netizen ('nɛtɪzᵊn) *n inf* a person who regularly uses the Internet [C20 from (INTER)NET + (CIT)IZEN]

net national product *n* gross national product minus an allowance for the depreciation of capital goods. Abbrev: **NNP**

net present value *n accounting* an assessment of the long-term profitability of a project made by adding together all the revenue it can be expected to achieve over its whole life and deducting all the costs involved. Abbrev: **NPV**

net profit *n* gross profit minus all operating costs not included in the calculation of gross profit, esp wages, overheads, and depreciation

net realizable value *n* the net value of an asset if it were to be sold. Abbrev: **NRV**

net statutory income *n* (in Britain) the total taxable income of a person for the tax assessment year, after the deduction of personal allowances

netsuke ('nɛtsʊkɪ) *n* (in Japan) a carved toggle, esp of wood or ivory, originally used to tether a medicine box, purse, etc, worn dangling from the waist [C19 from Japanese]

nett (nɛt) *adj, n, vb* a variant spelling of **net²**

netting ('nɛtɪŋ) *n* any netted fabric or structure

nettle ('nɛtᵊl) *n* 1 a plant having serrated leaves with stinging hairs and greenish flowers 2 any of various other plants with stinging hairs or spines 3 any of various plants that resemble nettles, such as the dead-nettle 4 **grasp the nettle** to attempt something with boldness and courage ▷ *vb* **nettles, nettling, nettled** (*tr*) 5 to bother; irritate 6 to sting as a nettle does [OE *netele*]

nettle rash *n* a nontechnical name for **urticaria**

network ('nɛtˌwɜːk) *n* 1 an interconnected group or system: *a network of shops* 2 a system of intersecting lines, roads, veins, etc 3 another name for **net¹** (sense 1) or **netting** 4 *radio & TV* a group of broadcasting stations that all transmit the same programme simultaneously 5 *computing* a system of interconnected computer systems, terminals, and other equipment 6 *electronics* a system of interconnected components or circuits ▷ *vb* 7 *radio & TV* to broadcast over a network 8 (of computers, terminals, etc) to connect or be connected 9 (*intr*) to form business contacts through informal social meetings

Neubrandenburg (*German* nɔyˈbrandənbʊrk) *n* a city in NE Germany, in Mecklenburg-West Pomerania: 14th-century city walls. Pop: 87 880 (1991)

Neuchâtel (*French* nøʃatɛl) *n* 1 a canton in the Jura Mountains of W Switzerland. Capital: Neuchâtel. Pop: 165 600 (2000 est). Area: 798 sq km (308 sq miles) 2 a town in W Switzerland, capital of Neuchâtel canton, on Lake Neuchâtel: until 1848 the seat of the last hereditary rulers in Switzerland. Pop: 32 509 (1990) 3 **Lake** a lake in W Switzerland: the largest lake wholly in Switzerland. Area: 216 sq km (83 sq miles) ▷ German name (for senses 1, 2) **Neuenburg** ('nɔyənbʊrk)

Neuilly-sur-Seine (*French* nœjisyrsɛn) *n* a town in N France, on the Seine: a suburb of NW Paris. Pop: 61 768 (1990)

Neumann *n* 1 (*German* 'nɔyman) **Johann Balthasar** (jo'han 'baltazar) 1687–1753, German rococo architect. His masterpiece is the church of Vierzehnheiligen in Bavaria 2 ('njuːmən) See (John) **von Neumann**

neume *or* **neum** (njuːm) *n music* one of a series of notational symbols used before the 14th century [C15 from Med. L *neuma* group of notes sung on one breath, from Gk *pneuma* breath]

Neumünster (*German* nɔyˈmynstər) *n* a town in N Germany, in Schleswig-Holstein: manufacturing of textiles and machinery. Pop: 81 175 (1991)

neural ('njʊərəl) *adj* of or relating to a nerve or the nervous system > **'neurally** *adv*

neural chip *n* another name for **neurochip**

neural computer *n* another name for **neurocomputer**

neuralgia (njʊˈrældʒə) *n* severe spasmodic pain caused by damage to or malfunctioning of a nerve and often following the course of the nerve > **neu'ralgic** *adj*

neural tube *n* the embryonic brain and spinal cord in mammals. Incomplete development results in **neural-tube defects,** such as spina bifida, in a newborn baby

neurasthenia (ˌnjʊərəsˈθiːnɪə) *n* (no longer in technical use) a neurosis characterized by extreme lassitude and inability to cope with any but the most trivial tasks

neuritis (njʊˈraɪtɪs) *n* inflammation of a nerve or nerves, often accompanied by pain and loss of function in the affected part > **neuritic** (njʊˈrɪtɪk) *adj*

neuro- *or before a vowel* **neur-** *combining form* indicating a nerve or the nervous system: *neurology* [from Gk *neuron* nerve; rel. to L *nervus*]

neurobiology (ˌnjʊərəʊbaɪˈɒlədʒɪ) *n* the study of the anatomy, physiology, and biochemistry of the nervous system > ˌ**neurobi'ologist** *n*

neurochip ('njʊərəʊˌtʃɪp) *n computing* a semiconductor chip designed for use in an electronic neural network. Also called: **neural chip**

neurocomputer ('njʊərəʊkəmˌpjuːtə) *n* a type of computer designed to mimic the action of the human brain by use of an electronic neural network. Also called: **neural computer**

neuroendocrine (ˌnjʊərəʊˈɛndəʊˌkraɪn) *adj* of, relating to, or denoting the dual control of certain body functions by both nervous and hormonal stimulation: *neuroendocrine system*

neuroglia (njʊˈrɒglɪə) *n* another name for **glia**

neurohormone ('njʊərəʊˌhɔːməʊn) *n* a hormone, such as noradrenaline, that is produced by specialized nervous tissue rather than by endocrine glands

neurolemma (ˌnjʊərəʊˈlɛmə) *n* the thin membrane that

Nn

forms a sheath around nerve fibres [C19 NL, from NEURO- + Gk *eilēma* covering]

neurology (njʊˈrɒlədʒɪ) *n* the study of the anatomy, physiology, and diseases of the nervous system > **neurological** (ˌnʊərəˈlɒdʒɪkᵊl) *adj*

neuromuscular (ˌnjʊərəʊˈmʌskjʊlə) *adj* of, relating to, or affecting nerves and muscles

neurone (ˈnjʊərəʊn) *or* **neuron** (ˈnjʊərɒn) *n* a cell specialized to conduct nerve impulses: consists of a cell body, axon, and dendrites. Also called: **nerve cell** > **neuˈronal** *adj* > **neuronic** (njʊˈrɒnɪk) *adj*

neuropathology (ˌnjʊərəʊpəˈθɒlədʒɪ) *n* the study of diseases of the nervous system

neuropathy (njʊˈrɒpəθɪ) *n* any disease of the nervous system > **neuropathic** (ˌnjʊərəʊˈpæθɪk) *adj* > **ˌneuroˈpathically** *adv*

neurophysiology (ˌnjʊərəʊˌfɪzɪˈɒlədʒɪ) *n* the study of the functions of the nervous system > **neurophysiological** (ˌnjʊərəʊˌfɪzɪəˈlɒdʒɪkᵊl) *adj*

neuropterous (njʊˈrɒptərəs) *or* **neuropteran** *adj* of or belonging to an order of insects having two pairs of large much-veined wings and biting mouthparts [C18 from NL *Neuroptera*, from NEURO- + Gk *pteron* wing]

neuroscience (ˈnjʊərəʊˌsaɪəns) *n* the study of the anatomy, physiology, biochemistry, and pharmacology of the nervous system > **ˈneuroˌscientist** *n*

neurosis (njʊˈrəʊsɪs) *n, pl* **neuroses** (-siːz) a relatively mild mental disorder, characterized by hysteria, anxiety, depression, or obsessive behaviour

neurosurgery (ˈnjʊərəʊˌsɜːdʒərɪ) *n* the branch of surgery concerned with the nervous system > **ˌneuroˈsurgical** *adj*

neurotic (njʊˈrɒtɪk) *adj* **1** of or afflicted by neurosis ▷ *n* **2** a person who is afflicted with a neurosis or who tends to be emotionally unstable > **neuˈrotically** *adv* > **neuˈrotiˌcism** *n*

neurotomy (njʊˈrɒtəmɪ) *n, pl* **neurotomies** the surgical cutting of a nerve

neurotransmitter (ˌnjʊərəʊtrænzˈmɪtə) *n* a chemical by which a nerve cell communicates with another nerve cell or with a muscle

Neusatz (ˈnɔyzats) *n* the German name for **Novi Sad**

Neuss (*German* nɔys) *n* an industrial city in W Germany, in North Rhine-Westphalia west of Düsseldorf: founded as a Roman fortress in the 1st century AD. Pop: 149 206 (1999 est). Latin name: **Novaesium**

Neustria (ˈnjuːstrɪə) *n* the western part of the kingdom of the Merovingian Franks formed in 561 AD in what is now N France > **ˈNeustrian** *adj*

neuter (ˈnjuːtə) *adj* **1** *grammar* **1a** denoting or belonging to a gender of nouns which do not specify the sex of their referents **1b** (*as n*): *German "Mädchen" (meaning "girl") is a neuter* **2** (of animals and plants) having nonfunctional, underdeveloped, or absent reproductive organs **3** giving no indication of sex ▷ *n* **4** a sexually underdeveloped female insect, such as a worker bee **5** a castrated animal ▷ *vb* **6** (*tr*) to castrate or spay (an animal) [C14 from L, from *ne* not + *uter* either (of two)]

neutral (ˈnjuːtrəl) *adj* **1** not siding with any party to a war or dispute **2** of or belonging to a neutral party, country, etc **3** of no distinctive quality or type **4** (of a colour) **4a** having no hue; achromatic **4b** dull, but harmonizing with most other colours **5** a less common term for **neuter** (sense 2) **6** *chem* neither acidic nor alkaline **7** *physics* having zero charge or potential **8** *phonetics* (of a vowel) articulated with the tongue relaxed in mid-central position: *"about" begins with a neutral vowel* ▷ *n* **9** a neutral person, nation, etc **10** a citizen of a neutral state **11** the position of the controls of a gearbox that leaves the transmission disengaged [C16 from L *neutrālis*; see NEUTER] > **ˈneutrally** *adv*

neutralism (ˈnjuːtrəˌlɪzəm) *n* (in international affairs) the policy or practice of noninvolvement or nonalignment with power blocs > **ˈneutralist** *n*

neutrality (njuːˈtrælɪtɪ) *n* **1** the state of being neutral **2** the condition of being chemically or electrically neutral

neutralize *or* **neutralise** (ˈnjuːtrəˌlaɪz) *vb* **neutralizes, neutralizing, neutralized** *or* **neutralises, neutralising, neutralised** (*mainly tr*) **1** (*also intr*) to render or become neutral by counteracting, mixing, etc **2** (*also intr*) to make or become electrically or chemically neutral **3** to exclude (a country) from warfare or alliances by international agreement: *the great powers neutralized Belgium in the 19th century* > **ˌneutraliˈzation** *or* **ˌneutraliˈsation** *n* > **ˈneutralˌizer** *or* **ˈneutralˌiser** *n*

neutretto (njuːˈtrɛtəʊ) *n, pl* **neutrettos** *physics* **1** the neutrino associated with the muon **2** (formerly) any of various hypothetical neutral particles [C20 from NEUTR(INO) + diminutive suffix *-etto*]

neutrino (njuːˈtriːnəʊ) *n, pl* **neutrinos** *physics* a stable elementary particle with zero rest mass and spin ½ that travels at the speed of light [C20 from It., dim. of *neutrone* NEUTRON]

neutron (ˈnjuːtrɒn) *n* *physics* a neutral elementary particle with approximately the same mass as a proton. In the nucleus of an atom it is stable but when free it decays [C20 from NEUTRAL, on the model of ELECTRON]

neutron bomb *n* a type of nuclear weapon designed to cause little blast or long-lived radioactive contamination. The neutrons destroy all life in the target area. Technical name: **enhanced radiation weapon**

neutron gun *n* *physics* a device used for producing a beam of fast neutrons

neutron number *n* the number of neutrons in the nucleus of an atom. Symbol: N

neutron star *n* a star, composed solely of neutrons, that has collapsed under its own gravity

Nev. *abbrev for* Nevada

Neva (ˈniːvə; *Russian* nɪˈva) *n* a river in NW Russia, flowing west to the Gulf of Finland by the delta on which Saint Petersburg stands. Length: 74 km (46 miles)

Nevada (nɪˈvɑːdə) *n* a state of the western US: lies almost wholly within the Great Basin, a vast desert plateau; noted for production of gold and copper. Capital: Carson City. Pop: 1 998 257 (2000). Area: 284 612 sq km (109 889 sq miles). Abbreviations: **Nev** or (with zip code) **NV**

névé (ˈnɛveɪ) *n* a mass of porous ice, formed from snow, that has not yet become frozen into glacier ice [C19 from Swiss F *névé* glacier, from LL *nivātus* snow-cooled, from *nix* snow]

never (ˈnɛvə) *adv, sentence substitute* **1** at no time; not ever **2** certainly not; by no means; in no case ▷ *sentence substitute* **3** Also: **well I never!** surely not! [OE *nǣfre*, from *ne* not + *æfre* EVER]

USAGE In informal speech and writing, *never* can be used for emphasis instead of *not* with the simple past tenses of certain verbs (*I never said that; I never realized how clever he was*), but this usage should be avoided in careful writing

nevermore (ˌnɛvəˈmɔː) *adv literary* never again

never-never *inf* ▷ *n* **1** *Brit* the hire-purchase system of buying **2** *Austral* remote desert country ▷ *adj* **3** imaginary; idyllic (esp in **never-never land**)

Nevers (*French* nəvɛr) *n* a city in central France: capital of the former duchy of Nivernais; engineering industry. Pop: 43 890 (1990)

nevertheless (ˌnɛvəðəˈlɛs) *sentence connector* in spite of that; however; yet

Nevis *n* **1** (ˈniːvɪs, ˈnɛvɪs) an island in the Caribbean, part of St Kitts-Nevis; the volcanic cone of **Nevis Peak,** which rises to 1002 m (3287 ft), lies in the centre of the island. Capital: Charlestown. Pop: 8010 (1995 est). Area: 129 sq km (50 sq miles) **2** ('nɛvɪs) See **Ben Nevis**

Nevski ('nɛfskɪ; *Russian* 'njɛfskij) *n* See **Alexander Nevski**

new (njuː) *adj* **1a** recently made or brought into being **1b** (*as collective n; preceded by the*): *the new* **2** of a kind never before existing; novel: *a new concept in marketing* **3** recently discovered: *a new comet* **4** markedly different from what was before: *the new liberalism* **5** (often foll by *to* or *at*) recently introduced (to); inexperienced (in) or unaccustomed (to): *new to this neighbourhood* **6** (*cap in names or titles*) more or most recent of things with the same name: *the New Testament* **7** (*prenominal*) fresh; additional: *send some new troops* **8** (often foll by *to*) unknown: *this is new to me* **9** (of a cycle) beginning or occurring again: *a new year* **10** (*prenominal*) (of crops) harvested early **11** changed, esp for the better: *she returned a new woman* **12** up-to-date; fashionable **13 the new** (to be) set to replace the current vogue: *comedy is the new rock 'n' roll* ▷ *adv* (*usually in combination*) **14** recently, freshly: *new-laid eggs* **15** anew; again ▷ See also **news** [OE *nīowe*] > **'newness** *n*

New Age *n* **1a** a philosophy, originating in the late 1980s, characterized by a belief in alternative medicine, astrology, spiritualism, etc **1b** (*as modifier*): *New Age therapies* **2** short for **New Age music**
▷ www.xs4all.nl/~wichm/newage3.html

New Age music *or* **New Age** *n* a type of gentle melodic popular music originating in the US in the late 1980s, which takes in elements of jazz, folk, and classical music and is played largely on synthesizers and acoustic instruments
▷ www.newagemusic.com
▷ www.allmusic.com

New Amsterdam *n* the Dutch settlement established on Manhattan (1624–26); capital of New Netherlands; captured by the English and renamed New York in 1664

Newark ('njuːək) *n* **1** a town in N central England, in Nottinghamshire. Pop: 35 129 (1991). Official name: **Newark-on-Trent** **2** a port in NE New Jersey, just west of New York City, on Newark Bay and the Passaic River: the largest city in the state; founded in 1666 by Puritans from Connecticut; industrial and commercial centre. Pop: 273 546 (2000)

New Australia *n* the colony on socialist principles founded by William Lane in Paraguay in 1893

New Australian *n* an Australian name for a recent immigrant, esp one from Europe

New Bedford *n* a port and resort in SE Massachusetts, near Buzzards Bay: settled by Plymouth colonists in 1652; a leading whaling port (18th–19th centuries). Pop: 93 768 (2000)

newbie ('njuːbɪ) *n sl* a newcomer, esp in computing or on the Internet [C20 ? from *new boy*]

newborn ('njuːˌbɔːn) *adj* **1** recently or just born **2** (of hope, faith, etc) reborn

New Britain *n* an island in the S Pacific, northeast of New Guinea: the largest island of the Bismarck Archipelago; part of Papua New Guinea; mountainous, with several active volcanoes. Capital: Rabaul. Pop: 435 307 (1999 est). Area: 36 519 sq km (14 100 sq miles)

New Brunswick *n* a province of SE Canada on the Gulf of St Lawrence and the Bay of Fundy: extensively forested. Capital: Fredericton. Pop: 757 100 (2001 est). Area: 72 092 sq km (27 835 sq miles). Abbreviation: **NB** > **New Brunswicker** ('brʌnzwɪkə) *n*
▷ www.gnb.ca
▷ www.tourismenouveau-brunswick.ca/Cultures/en-CA/welcome.htm

new brutalism *n* another name for **brutalism**

Newbury ('njuːbərɪ) *n* a market town in West Berkshire unitary authority, S England: scene of a Parliamentarian victory (1643) and a Royalist victory (1644) during the Civil War; telecommunications, racecourse. Pop: 33 273 (1991)

New Caledonia *n* an island in the SW Pacific, east of Australia: forms, with its dependencies, an overseas territory of France; discovered by Captain Cook in 1774; rich mineral resources. Capital: Nouméa. Pop: 216 000 (2001 est). Area: 19 103 sq km (7374 miles). French name: **Nouvelle-Calédonie**

New Canadian *n Canad* a recent immigrant to Canada

New Castile *n* a region and former province of central Spain. Chief town: Toledo

Newcastle[1] ('njuːˌkɑːsᵊl) *n* a port in SE Australia, in E New South Wales near the mouth of the Hunter River: important industrial centre, with extensive steel, metalworking, engineering, shipbuilding, and chemical industries. It suffered Australia's first fatal earthquake in 1989. Pop: 139 171 (1998 est)

Newcastle[2] ('njuːˌkɑːsᵊl) *n* **Duke of,** the title of *Thomas Pelham Holles*. 1693–1768, English Whig prime minister (1754–56; 1757–62): brother of Henry Pelham

Newcastle-under-Lyme *n* a town in W central England, in Staffordshire. Pop: 73 731 (1991). Often shortened to **Newcastle**

Newcastle upon Tyne *n* **1** a port in NE England in Newcastle upon Tyne unitary authority, Tyne and Wear, near the mouth of the River Tyne opposite Gateshead: Roman remains; engineering industries, including ship repairs; two universities (1937, 1992). Pop: 189 150 (1991). Often shortened to **Newcastle** **2** a unitary authority in NE England, in Tyne and Wear. Pop: 259 573 (2001). Area: 112 sq km (43 sq miles)

new chum *n* **1** *Austral* a novice in any activity **2** *Austral & NZ inf* (formerly) a recent British immigrant

Newcombe ('njuːkəm) *n* **John** (**David**) born 1944, Australian tennis player; winner of seven Grand Slam singles titles (1967–74)

Newcomen ('njuːˌkʌmən) *n* **Thomas** 1663–1729, English engineer who invented a steam engine, which James Watt later modified and developed

newcomer ('njuːˌkʌmə) *n* a person who has recently arrived or started to participate in something

New Country *n* a style of country music that emerged in the late 1980s characterized by a more contemporary sound and down-to-earth rather than sentimental lyrics

New Delhi *n* See **Delhi**

new economy *n* the postindustrial world economy based on Internet trading and advanced technology

newel ('njuːəl) *n* **1** the central pillar of a winding staircase, esp one that is made of stone **2** Also called: **newel post** the post at the top or bottom of a flight of stairs that supports the handrail [C14 from OF *nouel* knob, from Med. L *nōdellus*, dim. of *nōdus* NODE]

New England *n* **1** the NE part of the US, consisting of the states of Maine, New Hampshire, Vermont, Massachusetts, Rhode Island, and Connecticut: settled originally chiefly by Puritans in the mid 17th century **2** a region in SE Australia, in the northern tablelands of New South Wales > **New Englander** ('ɪŋgləndə) *n*

New England Range *n* a mountain range in SE Australia, in NE New South Wales: part of the Great Dividing Range. Highest peak: Ben Lomond, 1520 m (4986 ft)

New English Bible *n* a new translation of the Bible made between 1962 and 1970

newfangled ('njuː'fæŋgᵊld) *adj* newly come into existence or fashion, esp excessively modern [C14 *newefangel* liking new things, from *new* + *-fangel*, from OE *fōn* to take]

New Forest *n* a region of woodland and heath in S England, in SW Hampshire: a hunting ground of the West Saxon kings; tourist area, noted for its ponies. Area: 336 sq km (130 sq miles)

new-found *adj* newly or recently discovered: *new-found confidence*

Nn

Newfoundland ('nju:fəndlənd, -fənlənd, -ˌlænd, nju:'faʊndlənd) *n* **1** an island of E Canada, separated from the mainland by the Strait of Belle Isle: with the Coast of Labrador forms the province of Newfoundland; consists of a rugged plateau with the Long Range Mountains in the west. Area: 110 681 sq km (42 734 sq miles) **2** a province of E Canada, consisting of the island of Newfoundland and the Coast of Labrador. Capital: St John's. Pop: 533 800 (2001 est). Area: 404 519 sq km (156 185 sq miles). Abbreviations: **Nfld, NF 3** a very large heavy breed of dog similar to a Saint Bernard with a flat coarse usually black coat > **New'foundlander** *n*

▷ www.gov.nf.ca

▷ www.gov.nf.ca/tourism

Newfoundland Standard Time *n* one of the standard times used in Canada, three and a half hours behind Greenwich Mean Time

New France *n* the former French colonies and possessions in North America, most of which were lost to England and Spain by 1763: often restricted to the French possessions in Canada

Newgate ('nju:gɪt, -ˌgeɪt) *n* a famous London prison, in use from the Middle Ages: demolished in 1902

New Georgia *n* **1** a group of islands in the SW Pacific, in the Solomon Islands **2** the largest island in this group. Area: about 1300 sq km (500 sq miles)

New Granada *n* **1** a former Spanish presidency and later viceroyalty in South America. At its greatest extent it consisted of present-day Panama, Colombia, Venezuela, and Ecuador **2** the name of Colombia when it formed, with Panama, part of Great Colombia (1819–30)

New Guinea *n* **1** an island in the W Pacific, north of Australia: divided politically into Irian Jaya (a province of Indonesia) in the west and Papua New Guinea in the east. There is a central chain of mountains and a lowland area of swamps in the south and along the Sepik River in the north. Area: 775 213 sq km (299 310 sq miles) **2 Trust Territory of** (until 1975) an administrative division of the former Territory of Papua and New Guinea, consisting of the NE part of the island of New Guinea together with the Bismarck Archipelago; now part of Papua New Guinea

Newham ('nju:əm) *n* a borough of E Greater London, on the River Thames: established in 1965. Pop: 243 737 (2001). Area: 36 sq km (14 sq miles)

New Hampshire *n* a state of the northeastern US: generally hilly. Capital: Concord. Pop: 1 235 786 (2000 est). Area: 23 379 sq km (9027 sq miles). Abbreviations: **N.H.** or (with zip code) **NH**

New Harmony *n* a village in SW Indiana, on the Wabash River: scene of two experimental cooperative communities, the first founded in 1815 by George Rapp, a German religious leader, and the second by Robert Owen in 1825

Newhaven ('nju:ˌheɪvᵊn) *n* a ferry port and resort on the S coast of England, in East Sussex. Pop: 11 208 (1991)

New Haven *n* an industrial city and port in S Connecticut, on Long Island Sound: settled in 1638 by English Puritans, who established it as a colony in 1643; seat of Yale University (1701). Pop: 123 626 (2000 est)

New Hebrides *pl n* the former name (until 1980) of **Vanuatu**

Ne Win ('neɪ 'wɪn) *n* **U** (u:) 1911–2002, Burmese statesman and general; prime minister (1958–60), head of the military government (1962–74), and president (1974–81)

New Ireland *n* an island in the S Pacific, in the Bismarck Archipelago, separated from New Britain by St George's Channel: part of Papua New Guinea. Chief town and port: Kavieng. Pop: 87 194 (1990.). Area (including adjacent islands): 9850 sq km (3800 sq miles)

newish ('nju:ɪʃ) *adj* fairly new

new issue *n stock exchange* an issue of shares that is being offered to the public for the first time

New Jersey *n* a state of the eastern US, on the Atlantic and Delaware Bay: mostly low-lying, with a heavy industrial area in the northeast and many coastal resorts. Capital: Trenton. Pop: 8 414 350 (2000). Area: 19 479 sq km (7521 sq miles). Abbreviations: **N.J.** or (with zip code) **NJ**

New Jerusalem *n Christianity* heaven

New Journalism *n* a style of journalism using techniques borrowed from fiction to portray a situation or event as vividly as possible

Newlands ('nju:ləndz) *n* **John Alexander** 1838–98, British chemist: classified the elements in order of their atomic weight, noticing similarities in every eighth and thus discovering his law of octaves

New Latin *n* the form of Latin used since the Renaissance, esp for scientific nomenclature

New Look *n* **the** a fashion in women's clothes introduced in 1947, characterized by long full skirts

newly ('nju:lɪ) *adv* **1** recently **2** again; anew: *newly raised hopes* **3** in a new manner; differently: *a newly arranged hairdo*

newlywed ('nju:lɪˌwɛd) *n* (*often pl*) a recently married person

Newman ('nju:mən) *n* **1 Barnet** 1905–70, US painter, a founder of Abstract Expressionism: his paintings include the series *Stations of the Cross* (1965–66) **2 John Henry** 1801–90, British theologian and writer. Originally an Anglican minister, he was a prominent figure in the Oxford Movement. He became a Roman Catholic (1845) and a priest (1847) and was made a cardinal (1879). His writings include the spiritual autobiography, *Apologia pro vita sua* (1864), a treatise on the nature of belief, *The Grammar of Assent* (1870), and hymns **3 Paul** born 1925, US film actor and director, who appeared in such films as *Hud* (1963), *Butch Cassidy and the Sundance Kid* (1969), *The Sting* (1973), *The Verdict* (1982), *The Color of Money* (1986), *Nobody's Fool* (1994), and *Road to Perdition* (2002)

New Man *n* **the** a type of modern man who allows the caring side of his nature to show by being supportive and by sharing child care and housework

Newmarket ('nju:ˌmɑ:kɪt) *n* a town in SE England, in W Suffolk: a famous horse-racing centre since the reign of James I. Pop: 18 430 (1991)

new maths *n* (*functioning as singular*) *Brit* an approach to mathematics in which the basic principles of set theory are introduced at an elementary level

new media *n* **a** the Internet and other postindustrial forms of telecommunication **b** (*as modifier*): *the new-media industry*. Compare **old media**

New Mexico *n* a state of the southwestern US: has high semiarid plateaus and mountains, crossed by the Rio Grande and the Pecos River; large Spanish-American and Indian populations; contains over two-thirds of US uranium reserves. Capital: Santa Fé. Pop: 1 819 046 (2000). Area: 314 451 sq km (121 412 sq miles). Abbreviations: **N Mex, N.M.** or (with zip code) **NM** > **New Mexican** *adj, n*

new moon *n* the moon when it appears as a narrow waxing crescent

New National Party *n see* **National Party** (sense 3)

New Netherland ('nɛðələnd) *n* a Dutch North American colony of the early 17th century, centred on the Hudson valley. Captured by the English in 1664, it was divided into New York and New Jersey

New Orleans ('ɔ:li:ənz, -lənz, ɔ:'li:nz) *n* a port in SE Louisiana, on the Mississippi River about 172 km (107 miles) from the sea: the largest city in the state and the second most important port in the US; founded by the French in 1718; belonged to Spain (1763–1803). It is largely below sea level, built around the Vieux Carré (French quarter); famous for its annual Mardi Gras festival and for its part in the history of jazz; a major commercial, industrial, and transportation centre. Pop: 484 674 (2000)

New Plymouth *n* a port in New Zealand, on W North Island: founded in 1841. Pop: 49 800 (1995 est)

Newport (ˈnjuːˌpɔːt) *n* **1** a city and port in SE Wales, in Newport county borough on the River Usk: electronics. Pop: 129 900 (1991) **2** a county borough in SE Wales, created from part of Gwent in 1996. Pop: 137 017 (2001). Area: 190 sq km (73 sq miles) **3** a port in SE Rhode Island: founded in 1639, it became one of the richest towns of colonial America; centre of a large number of US naval establishments. Pop: 28 227 (1990) **4** a town in S England, administrative centre of the Isle of Wight. Pop: 20 574 (1991)

Newport News *n (functioning as singular)* a port in SE Virginia, at the mouth of the James River: an industrial centre, with one of the world's largest shipyards. Pop: 180 150 (1996 est)

New Providence *n* an island in the Atlantic, in the Bahamas. Chief town: Nassau. Pop: 172 196 (1990). Area: 150 sq km (58 sq miles)

New Quebec *n* a region of E Canada, formerly the Ungava district of Northwest Territories (1895–1912), extending from the line of the Eastmain and Hamilton Rivers north between Hudson Bay and Labrador: absorbed by Quebec in 1912: contains extensive iron deposits. Area: about 777 000 sq km (300 000 sq miles)

New Romney *n* a market town in SE England, in Kent on Romney Marsh: of early importance as one of the Cinque Ports, but is now over 1.6 km (1 mile) inland. Pop: 4565 (latest est). Former name (until 1563): **Romney**

Newry (ˈnjʊərɪ) *n* a city and port in Northern Ireland, in Newry and Mourne district, Co Down: close to the border with the Republic of Ireland, it has been the scene of sectarian violence in recent years. Pop: 22 975 (1991)

Newry and Mourne (ˈmɔːn) *n* a district of SE Northern Ireland, in Co. Down. Pop: 87 058 (2001). Area: 909 sq km (351 sq miles)

news (njuːz) *n (functioning as sing)* **1** important or interesting recent happenings **2** information about such events, as in the mass media **3** **the news** a presentation, such as a radio broadcast, of information of this type **4** interesting or important information not previously known **5** a person, fashion, etc, widely reported in the mass media: *she is news in the film world* [c15 from ME *newes*, pl. of *newe* new (adj), a model of OF *noveles* or Med. L *nova* new things] > ˈ**newsless** *adj*

news agency *n* an organization that collects news reports for newspapers, etc. Also called: **press agency**

newsagent (ˈnjuːzˌeɪdʒənt) *or US* **newsdealer** *n* a shopkeeper who sells newspapers, stationery, etc

newscast (ˈnjuːzˌkɑːst) *n* a radio or television broadcast of the news [c20 from NEWS + (BROAD)CAST] > ˈ**newsˌcaster** *n*

news conference *n* another term for **press conference**

newsflash (ˈnjuːzˌflæʃ) *n* a brief item of important news, often interrupting a radio or television programme

newsgroup (ˈnjuːzˌgruːp) *n computing* a forum where subscribers exchange information about a specific subject by electronic mail

New Siberian Islands *pl n* an archipelago in the Arctic Ocean, off the N mainland of Russia, in the Sakha Republic. Area: about 37 555 sq km (14 500 sq miles)

newsletter (ˈnjuːzˌlɛtə) *n* **1** Also called: **news-sheet** a printed periodical bulletin circulated to members of a group **2** *history* a written or printed account of the news

newsmonger (ˈnjuːzˌmʌŋgə) *n old-fashioned* a gossip

New South *n Austral inf* short for **New South Wales**

New South Wales *n* a state of SE Australia: originally contained over half the continent, but was reduced by the formation of other states (1825–1911); consists of a narrow coastal plain, separated from extensive inland plains by the Great Dividing Range; the most populous state; mineral resources. Capital: Sydney. Pop: 6 441 680 (1999 est). Area: 801 428 sq km (309 433 sq miles)
▷ www.nsw.gov.au
▷ www.tourism.nsw.gov.au

New Spain *n* a Spanish viceroyalty of the 16th to 19th centuries, composed of Mexico, Central America north of Panama, the Spanish West Indies, the southwestern US, and the Philippines

newspaper (ˈnjuːzˌpeɪpə) *n* a weekly or daily publication consisting of folded sheets and containing articles on the news, features, reviews, and advertisements. Often shortened to **paper**

newspaperman (ˈnjuːzˌpeɪpəˌmæn) *n, pl* **newspapermen** **1** a person who works for a newspaper as a reporter or editor **2** the owner or proprietor of a newspaper **3** a person who sells newspapers in the street

newspeak (ˈnjuːˌspiːk) *n* the language of bureaucrats and politicians, regarded as deliberately ambiguous and misleading [c20 from *1984*, a novel by George Orwell]

newsprint (ˈnjuːzˌprɪnt) *n* an inexpensive wood-pulp paper used for newspapers

newsreader (ˈnjuːzˌriːdə) *n* a news announcer on radio or television

newsreel (ˈnjuːzˌriːl) *n* a short film with a commentary presenting current events

newsroom (ˈnjuːzˌruːm, -ˌrʊm) *n* a room in a newspaper office, television station, etc, where news is received and prepared for publication or broadcasting

newsstand (ˈnjuːzˌstænd) *n* a portable stand or stall from which newspapers are sold

New Style *n* the present method of reckoning dates using the Gregorian calendar

news vendor *n* a person who sells newspapers

newsworthy (ˈnjuːzˌwɜːðɪ) *adj* sufficiently interesting to be reported in a news bulletin, etc

newsy (ˈnjuːzɪ) *adj* **newsier, newsiest** full of news, esp gossipy or personal news

newt (njuːt) *n* any of various small semiaquatic amphibians having a long slender body and tail and short feeble legs [c15 from *a newt*, a mistaken division of *an ewt*; *ewt*, from OE *eveta* EFT]

New Testament *n* a collection of writings composed soon after Christ's death and added to the Jewish writings of the Old Testament to make up the Christian Bible

newton (ˈnjuːtᵊn) *n* the derived SI unit of force that imparts an acceleration of 1 metre per second per second to a mass of 1 kilogram. Symbol: N [c20 after Sir Isaac NEWTON]

Newton (ˈnjuːtᵊn) *n* **1** **Bert**, full name *Albert Watson Newton*. born 1938, Australian television presenter, host of *Good Morning Australia* since 1993 **2** Sir **Isaac** 1642–1727, English mathematician, physicist, astronomer, and philosopher, noted particularly for his law of gravitation, his three laws of motion, his theory that light is composed of corpuscles, and his development of calculus independently of Leibniz. His works include *Principia Mathematica* (1687) and *Opticks* (1704)

Newtonian telescope *n* a type of astronomical reflecting telescope in which light is reflected from a large concave mirror onto a plane mirror, and through a hole in the side of the body of the telescope to form an image

Newton's law of gravitation *n* the principle that two particles attract each other with forces directly proportional to the product of their masses divided by the square of the distance between them

Newton's laws of motion *pl n* three laws of mechanics describing the motion of a body. **The first law** states that a body remains at rest or in uniform motion unless acted upon by a force. **The second law** states that a

Nn

body's rate of change of momentum is proportional to the force causing it. **The third law** states that when a force acts on a body an equal and opposite force acts simultaneously on another body

Newtown ('njuːtaʊn) *n* a new town in central Wales, in Powys. Pop: 10 548 (1991)

new town *n* (in Britain) a town planned as a complete unit and built with government sponsorship, esp to accommodate overspill population

Newtownabbey (ˌnjuːtᵊn'æbɪ) *n* **1** a town in Northern Ireland, in Newtownabbey district, Co Antrim on Belfast Lough: the third largest town in Northern Ireland, formed in 1958 by the amalgamation of seven villages; light industrial centre, esp for textiles. Pop: 57 103 (1991) **2** a district of E Northern Ireland, in Co Antrim. Pop: 79 995 (2001). Area: 151 sq km (58 sq miles)

Newtown St Boswells ('njuːtaʊn sənt 'bɒzwəlz) *n* a village in SE Scotland, administrative centre of Scottish Borders: agricultural centre. Pop: 1108 (1991)

new-variant Creutzfeldt-Jakob disease *or* **variant Creutzfeldt-Jakob disease** *n* a form of Creutzfeldt-Jakob disease thought to be transmitted by eating beef or beef products infected with BSE. Often shortened to **new-variant** (*or* **variant**) **CJD** Abbrevs: **nvCJD, vCJD**

new wave *n* a movement in art, politics, etc, that consciously breaks with traditional ideas, esp **the New Wave,** a movement in the French cinema of the 1960s, characterized by a fluid use of the camera
▷ www.nyfavideo.com

New Windsor *n* the official name of **Windsor**[1] (sense 1)

New World *n* **the** the Americas; the western hemisphere

New World monkey *n* any of a family of monkeys of Central and South America, many of which are arboreal and have a prehensile tail

New Year *n* the first day or days of the year in various calendars, usually a holiday

New Year's Day *n* January 1, celebrated as a holiday in many countries. Often shortened to (US and Canad inf) **New Year's**

New Year's Eve *n* the evening of Dec 31. See also **Hogmanay**

New York *n* **1** Also called: **New York City** a city in SE New York State, at the mouth of the Hudson River: the largest city and chief port of the US; settled by the Dutch as New Amsterdam in 1624 and captured by the British in 1664, when it was named New York; consists of five boroughs (Manhattan, the Bronx, Queens, Brooklyn, and Richmond) and many islands, with its commercial and financial centre in Manhattan; the country's leading commercial and industrial city. Pop: 8 008 278 (2000). Abbrevs: **N.Y.C., NYC** **2** a state of the northeastern US: consists chiefly of a plateau with the Finger Lakes in the centre, the Adirondack Mountains in the northeast, the Catskill Mountains in the southeast, and Niagara Falls in the west. Capital: Albany. Pop: 18 976 457 (2000). Area: 123 882 sq km (47 831 sq miles). Abbrevs: **N.Y.** or (with zip code) **NY** > **New Yorker** *n*

New York Bay *n* an inlet of the Atlantic at the mouth of the Hudson River: forms the harbour of the port of New York

New York State Barge Canal *n* a system of inland waterways in New York State, connecting the Hudson River with Lakes Erie and Ontario and, via Lake Champlain, with the St Lawrence. Length: 845 km (525 miles)

New Zealand ('ziːlənd) *n* an independent dominion within the Commonwealth, occupying two main islands (the North Island and the South Island), Stewart Island, the Chatham Islands, and a number of minor islands in the SE Pacific: original Maori inhabitants ceded sovereignty to the British government in 1840; became a dominion in 1907; a major world exporter of dairy products, wool, and meat. Official languages: English and Maori. Religion: Christian majority, nonreligious and Maori minorities. Currency: New Zealand dollar. Capital: Wellington. Pop: 3 861 000 (2001 est). Area: 270 534 sq km (104 454 sq miles) > **New Zealander** ('ziːləndə) *n*
▷ www.govt.nz/en/aboutnz
▷ www.purenz.com
▷ www.newzealandnz.co.nz

Nexø (*Danish* 'nɛgsøː) *n* **Martin Andersen** ('marten) 1869–1954, Danish novelist. His chief works are the novels *Pelle the Conqueror* (1906–10), which deals with the labour movement, and *Ditte, Daughter of Man* (1917–21)

next (nɛkst) *adj* **1** immediately following: *the next patient to be examined* **2** immediately adjoining: *the next room* **3** closest to in degree: *the next-best thing* **4** **the next (Sunday) but one** the (Sunday) after the next ▷ *adv* **5** at a time immediately to follow: *the patient to be examined next* **6** **next to 6a** adjacent to: *the house next to ours* **6b** following in degree: *next to your mother, who do you love most?* **6c** almost: *next to impossible* ▷ *prep* **7** *arch* next to [OE *nēhst*, sup. of *nēah* NIGH]

next door *adj* (**next-door** *when prenominal*), *adv* at or to the adjacent house, flat, etc

next of kin *n* a person's closest relative

nexus ('nɛksəs) *n, pl* **nexus** **1** a means of connection; link; bond **2** a connected group or series [C17 from L, from *nectere* to bind]

Ney (neɪ; *French* nɛ) *n* **Michel** (miʃɛl), Duc d'Elchingen. 1769–1815, French marshal, who earned the epithet *Bravest of the Brave* at the battle of Borodino (1812) in the Napoleonic Wars. He rallied to Napoleon on his return from Elba and was executed for treason (1815)

Nez Percé ('nɛz 'pɜːs) *n* **1** (*pl* **Nez Percés** ('pɜːsɪz) *or* **Nez Percé**) a member of a North American Indian people of the Pacific coast **2** the language of this people [F, lit.: pierced nose]

NF (in Britain) *abbrev for* National Front

NFB (in Canada) *abbrev for* National Film Board

NFU (in Britain) *abbrev for* National Farmers' Union

NG *abbrev for:* **1** (in the US) National Guard **2** New Guinea **3** Also: **ng** no good

ngaio ('naɪəʊ) *n, pl* **ngaios** a small evergreen New Zealand tree [from Maori]

Ngaliema Mountain (ᵊŋgɑː'ljeɪmə) *n* the Congolese name for (Mount) **Stanley**

ngati ('nɑːtiː) *n, pl* **ngati** NZ a tribe or clan [from Maori]

Nguyen Kao Ky (ᵊŋ'guːjɛn 'kaʊ 'kiː) *n* See (Nguyen Kao) **Ky**

Nha Trang ('njɑː 'træŋ) *n* a port in SE Vietnam, on the South China Sea: nearby temples of the Cham civilization; fishing industry. Pop: 221 331 (1992 est)

NHI (in Britain) *abbrev for* National Health Insurance

NHL (in Canada) *abbrev for* National Hockey League

NHS (in Britain) *abbrev for* National Health Service

Ni *the chemical symbol for* nickel

NI *abbrev for:* **1** (in Britain) National Insurance **2** Northern Ireland **3** (in New Zealand) North Island

niacin ('naɪəsɪn) *n* another name for **nicotinic acid** [C20 from NI(COTINIC) AC(ID) + -IN]

Niagara (naɪ'ægrə, -'ægərə) *n* **1** a river in NE North America, on the border between W New York State and Ontario, Canada, flowing from Lake Erie to Lake Ontario. Length: 45 km (28 miles) **2** a torrent

Niagara Falls *n* **1** (*functioning as plural*) the falls of the Niagara River, on the border between the US and Canada: divided by Goat Island into the American Falls, 50 m (167 ft) high, and the Horseshoe or Canadian Falls, 47 m (158 ft) high **2** (*functioning as singular*) a city in W New York State, situated at the falls of the Niagara River. Pop: 61 840 (1990) **3** (*functioning as singular*) a city in S Canada, in SE Ontario on the Niagara River just below the falls: linked to the city of Niagara Falls in the US by three bridges. Pop: 76 917 (1996)

Niamey (njɑː'meɪ) *n* the capital of Niger, in the southwest on the River Niger: became capital in 1926; airport and land route centre. Pop: 495 000 (1995 est)

nib (nɪb) *n* **1** the writing point of a pen, esp an insertable tapered metal part **2** a point, tip, or beak **3** (*pl*) crushed cocoa beans ▷ *vb* **nibs, nibbing, nibbed** (*tr*) **4** to provide with a nib **5** to sharpen the nib of [C16 (in the sense: beak): from ?]

nibble ('nɪbᵊl) *vb* **nibbles, nibbling, nibbled** (when *intr*, often foll by *at*) **1** (esp of animals) to take small repeated bites (of) **2** to take dainty or tentative bites: *to nibble at a cake* **3** to bite (at) gently ▷ *n* **4** a small mouthful **5** an instance of nibbling **6** (*pl*) *inf* small items of food, esp savouries, usually served with drinks [C15 rel. to Low G *nibbelen*] > '**nibbler** *n*

Nibelung ('niːbəˌlʊŋ) *n, pl* **Nibelungs** *or* **Nibelungen** (-ˌlʊŋən) *German myth* **1** any of the race of dwarfs who possessed a treasure hoard subsequently stolen by Siegfried **2** one of Siegfried's companions or followers **3** (in the *Nibelungenlied*) a member of the family of Gunther, king of Burgundy

niblick ('nɪblɪk) *n golf* (formerly) a club giving a great deal of lift [C19 from ?]

nibs (nɪbz) *n* (*functioning as sing*) **his nibs** *sl* a mock title used of someone in authority [C19 from ?]

NIC *abbrev for* newly industrialized country

nicad ('naɪˌkæd) *n* a rechargeable dry-cell battery with a nickel anode and a cadmium cathode [C20 NI(CKEL) + CAD(MIUM)]

Nicaea (naɪ'siːə) *n* an ancient city in NW Asia Minor, in Bithynia: site of the **first council of Nicaea** (325 AD), which composed the Nicene Creed. Modern Turkish name: **Iznik** > **Nicene** ('naɪsiːn) *or* **Ni'caean** *adj*

NICAM ('naɪkæm) *n acronym for* near-instantaneous companded audio multiplex: a technique for coding audio signals into digital form

Nicaragua (ˌnɪkə'rægjʊə, -gwə; *Spanish* nika'raɣwa) *n* **1** a republic in Central America, on the Caribbean and the Pacific: colonized by the Spanish from the 1520s; gained independence in 1821 and was annexed by Mexico, becoming a republic in 1838. Official language: Spanish. Religion: Roman Catholic majority. Currency: córdoba. Capital: Managua. Pop: 4 918 000 (2001 est). Area: 131 812 sq km (50 893 sq miles) **2 Lake** a lake in SW Nicaragua, separated from the Pacific by an isthmus 19 km (12 miles) wide: the largest lake in Central America. Area: 8264 sq km (3191 sq miles) > ˌ**Nica'raguan** *adj, n*

▷ www.intur.gob.ni

▷ www.nicaragua.com

nice (naɪs) *adj* **1** pleasant: *a nice day* **2** kind or friendly: *a nice gesture of help* **3** good or satisfactory: *they made a nice job of it* **4** subtle or discriminating: *a nice point in the argument* **5** precise; skilful: *a nice fit* **6** *now rare* fastidious; respectable: *he was not too nice about his methods* **7** *obs* **7a** foolish or ignorant **7b** delicate **7c** shy; modest **7d** wanton [C13 (orig.: foolish): from OF *nice* simple, silly, from L *nescius*, from *nescīre* to be ignorant] > '**nicely** *adv* > '**niceness** *n* > '**nicish** *adj*

Nice (*French* nis) *n* a city in SE France, on the Mediterranean: a leading resort of the French Riviera; founded by Phocaeans from Marseille in about the 3rd century BC. Pop: 342 738 (1999)

NICE (naɪs) *n, acronym for* National Institute for Clinical Excellence

▷ www.nice.org.uk

nice-looking *adj inf* attractive in appearance; pretty or handsome

nicety ('naɪsɪtɪ) *n, pl* **niceties 1** a subtle point: *a nicety of etiquette* **2** (*usually pl*) a refinement or delicacy: *the niceties of first-class travel* **3** subtlety, delicacy, or precision **4 to a nicety** with precision

nicey-nicey (ˌnaɪsɪ'naɪsɪ) *adj, adv inf* trying to be pleasant, but in a way that suggests artifice or exaggeration; ingratiating(ly)

niche (nɪtʃ, niːʃ) *n* **1** a recess in a wall, esp one that contains a statue, etc **2** a position particularly suitable for the person occupying it: *he found his niche in politics* **3** (*modifier*) relating to or aimed at a small specialized group or market: *shampoo shops and other niche retailing ventures* **4** *ecology* the role of a plant or animal within its community and habitat, which determines its activities, relationships with other organisms, etc ▷ *vb* **niches, niching, niched 5** (*tr*) to place (a statue) in a niche; ensconce (oneself) [C17 from F, from OF *nichier* to nest, from Vulgar L *nīdicāre* (unattested), from L *nīdus* NEST]

niche market *n* a demand for a very specialized product or commodity

Nicholas ('nɪkələs) *n* **Saint** 4th-century AD bishop of Myra, in Asia Minor; patron saint of Russia and of children, sailors, merchants, and pawnbrokers. Feast day: Dec 6. See also **Santa Claus**

Nicholas I *n* **1 Saint**, called *the Great*. died 867 AD, Italian ecclesiastic; pope (858–867). He championed papal supremacy. Feast day: Nov 13 **2** 1796–1855, tsar of Russia (1825–55) He gained notoriety for his autocracy and his emphasis on military discipline and bureaucracy

Nicholas II *n* 1868–1918, tsar of Russia (1894–1917). After the disastrous Russo-Japanese War (1904–05), he was forced to summon a representative assembly, but his continued autocracy and incompetence precipitated the Russian Revolution (1917): he abdicated and was shot

Nicholas V *n* original name *Tommaso Parentucelli*. 1397–1455, Italian ecclesiastic; pope (1447–55). He helped to found the Vatican Library

Nicholas of Cusa ('kjuːzə) *n* 1401–64, German cardinal, philosopher, and mathematician: anticipated Copernicus in asserting that the earth revolves around the sun

Nn

Nicholson ('nɪkəlsən) *n* **1 Ben** 1894–1982, English painter, noted esp for his abstract geometrical works **2 Jack** born 1937, US film actor. His films include *Easy Rider* (1969), *One Flew Over the Cuckoo's Nest* (1974), *Terms of Endearment* (1983), *Batman* (1989), *As Good As It Gets* (1998), and *About Schmidt* (2002) **3 John** 1821–57, British general and administrator, born in Ireland: deputy commissioner in the Punjab (1851–56), where he became the object of hero-worship among the natives and kept the Punjab loyal during the Indian Mutiny: played a major role in the capture of Delhi

Nichrome ('naɪˌkrəʊm) *n trademark* any of various alloys containing nickel, iron, and chromium, used in electrical heating elements, furnaces, etc

Nicias ('nɪsɪəs) *n* died 414 BC, Athenian statesman and general. He ended the first part of the Peloponnesian War by making peace with Sparta (421)

nick (nɪk) *n* **1** a small notch or indentation **2** *Brit sl* a prison or police station **3 in good nick** *inf* in good condition **4 in the nick of time** just in time ▷ *vb* **5** (*tr*) to chip or cut **6** *sl, chiefly Brit* **6a** to steal **6b** to arrest **7** (*intr*; often foll by *off*) *inf* to depart rapidly **8 nick (someone) for** *US & Canad sl* to defraud (someone) to the extent of **9** to divide and reset (the tail muscles of a horse) to give the tail a high carriage **10** (*tr*) to guess, catch, etc, exactly [C15 ? changed from C14 *nocke* NOCK]

nickel ('nɪkᵊl) *n* **1** a malleable silvery-white metallic element that is corrosion-resistant: used in alloys, in electroplating, and as a catalyst in organic synthesis. Symbol: Ni; atomic no.: 28; atomic wt.: 58.71 **2** a US or Canadian coin worth five cents ▷ *vb* **nickels, nickelling, nickelled** *or US* **nickels, nickeling, nickeled 3** (*tr*) to plate with nickel [C18 from G *Kupfernickel* niccolite, lit.: copper demon; it was mistakenly thought to contain copper]

nickelodeon (ˌnɪkə'ləʊdɪən) *n US* **1** an early form of jukebox **2** (formerly) a Pianola, esp one operated by inserting a five-cent piece [c20 from NICKEL + (MEL)ODEON]

nickel plate *n* a thin layer of nickel deposited on a surface, usually by electrolysis

nickel silver *n* any of various white alloys containing copper, zinc, and nickel: used in making tableware, etc. Also called: **German silver**

nickel steel *n engineering* steel containing between 0.5 and 6.0 per cent nickel to increase its strength

nicker[1] (ˈnɪkə) *vb* (*intr*) **1** (of a horse) to neigh softly **2** to snigger [c18 ?from NEIGH]

nicker[2] (ˈnɪkə) *n, pl* **nicker** *Brit sl* a pound sterling [c20 from ?]

Nicklaus (ˈnɪklaʊs) *n* **Jack** born 1940, US professional golfer: won the British Open Championship (1966; 1970; 1978) and the US Open Championship (1962; 1967; 1972; 1980)

nick-nack (ˈnɪkˌnæk) *n* a variant spelling of **knick-knack**

nickname (ˈnɪkˌneɪm) *n* **1** a familiar, pet, or derisory name given to a person, animal, or place **2** a shortened or familiar form of a person's name: *Joe is a nickname for Joseph* ▷ *vb* **nicknames, nicknaming, nicknamed 3** (*tr*) to call by a nickname [c15 *a nekename*, mistaken division of *an ekename* an additional name]

Nicobar Islands (ˈnɪkəˌbɑː) *pl n* a group of 19 islands in the Indian Ocean, south of the Andaman Islands, with which they form a territory of India. Area: 1645 sq km (635 sq miles)

Nicodemus (ˌnɪkəˈdiːməs) *n New Testament* a Pharisee and a member of the Sanhedrin, who supported Jesus against the other Pharisees (John 8:50–52)

Nicolai (*German* nikoˈlaɪ) *n* **Carl Otto Ehrenfried** (karl ˈɔto ˈeːrənfriːt) 1810–49, German composer: noted for his opera *The Merry Wives of Windsor* (1849)

Nicol prism (ˈnɪkᵊl) *n* two prisms of Iceland spar or calcite cut at specified angles and cemented together, to produce plane-polarized light [c19 after William *Nicol* (?1768–1851), Scot physicist, its inventor]

Nicosia (ˌnɪkəˈsiːə, -ˈsɪə) *n* the capital of Cyprus, in the central part on the Pedieos River: capital since the 10th century. Pop (Greek and Turkish): 230 935 (1998 est). Greek name: **Levkosia** *or* **Leukosia** Turkish name: **Lefkoşa**

▷ www.kypros.org/Cyprus/nicosia.html

nicotiana (nɪˌkəʊʃɪˈɑːnə) *n* a plant of an American and Australian genus, having white, yellow, or purple fragrant flowers. Also called: **tobacco plant** [c16 see NICOTINE]

nicotinamide (ˌnɪkəˈtɪnəˌmaɪd) *n* the amide of nicotinic acid: a component of the vitamin B complex. Formula: $C_6H_6ON_2$

nicotine (ˈnɪkəˌtiːn) *n* a colourless oily acrid toxic liquid that turns yellowish-brown in air and light: the principal alkaloid in tobacco [c19 from F, from NL *herba nicotiana* Nicot's plant, after J. *Nicot* (1530–1600), F diplomat who introduced tobacco into France] > **ˈnicoˌtined** *adj* > **nicotinic** (ˌnɪkəˈtɪnɪk) *adj*

nicotinic acid *n* a vitamin of the B complex that occurs in milk, liver, yeast, etc. Lack of it in the diet leads to the disease pellagra

nicotinism (ˈnɪkətiːˌnɪzəm) *n pathol* a toxic condition of the body caused by nicotine

Nictheroy (*Portuguese* niteˈrɔi) *n* another name for **Niterói**

nictitate (ˈnɪktɪˌteɪt) *or* **nictate** (ˈnɪkteɪt) *vb* **nictitates, nictitating, nictitated** *or* **nictates, nictating, nictated** a technical word for **blink** [c19 from Med. L *nictitāre* to wink repeatedly, from L *nictāre* to blink] > **ˌnictiˈtation** *or* **nicˈtation** *n*

nictitating membrane *n* (in reptiles, birds, and some mammals) a thin fold of skin beneath the eyelid that can be drawn across the eye

Nidaros (*Norwegian* ˈniːdaroːs) *n* the former name (1930–31) of **Trondheim**

NIDDM *abbrev for* noninsulin-dependent diabetes mellitus; a form of diabetes in which insulin production is inadequate or the body becomes resistant to insulin

nidicolous (nɪˈdɪkələs) *adj* (of young birds) remaining in the nest some time after hatching [c19 from L *nīdus* nest + *colere* to inhabit]

nidifugous (nɪˈdɪfjʊgəs) *adj* (of young birds) leaving the nest very soon after hatching [c19 from L *nīdus* nest + *fugere* to flee]

nidify (ˈnɪdɪˌfaɪ) *or* **nidificate** (ˈnɪdɪfɪˌkeɪt) *vb* **nidifies, nidifying, nidified** *or* **nidificates, nidificating, nidificated** (*intr*) (of birds) to make or build a nest [c17 from L *nīdificāre*, from *nīdus* a nest + *facere* to make] > **ˌnidifiˈcation** *n*

niece (niːs) *n* a daughter of one's sister or brother [c13 from OF: niece, granddaughter, ult. from L *neptis* granddaughter]

Niederösterreich (ˈniːdərøːstəraɪç) *n* the German name for **Lower Austria**

Niedersachsen (ˈniːdərzaksən) *n* the German name for **Lower Saxony**

niello (nɪˈɛləʊ) *n, pl* **nielli** (-lɪ) *or* **niellos 1** a black compound of sulphur and silver, lead, or copper used to incise a design on a metal surface **2** this process **3** an object decorated with niello [c19 from It. from L *nigellus* blackish, from *niger* black]

Nielsen (ˈniːlsən; *Danish* ˈnelsən) *n* **Carl** (**August**) (karl) 1865–1931, Danish composer. His works include six symphonies and the opera *Masquerade* (1906)

Niemen (ˈnjɛmɛn) *n* the Polish name for the **Neman**

Niemeyer (ˈniːˌmaɪə) *n* **Oscar** born 1907, Brazilian architect. His work includes many buildings in Brasília, esp the president's palace (1959) and the cathedral (1964)

Niemöller (*German* ˈniːmœlər) *n* **Martin** (ˈmartiːn) 1892–1984, German Protestant theologian, who was imprisoned (1938–45) for his opposition to Hitler

Niepce (*French* njeps) *n* **Joseph-Nicéphore** (ʒozɛfnisefor) 1765–1833, French inventor. He produced the first photographic image (1816) and the first permanent camera photograph (1826)

Nietzsche (ˈniːtʃə) *n* **Friedrich Wilhelm** (ˈfriːdrɪç ˈvɪlhɛlm) 1844–1900, German philosopher, poet, and critic, noted esp for his concept of the superman and his rejection of traditional Christian values. His chief works are *The Birth of Tragedy* (1872), *Thus Spake Zarathustra* (1883–91), and *Beyond Good and Evil* (1886)

Nièvre (*French* njɛvrə) *n* a department of central France, in Burgundy region. Capital: Nevers. Pop: 225 198 (1999). Area: 6888 sq km (2686 sq miles)

niff (nɪf) *Brit sl* ▷ *n* **1** a bad smell ▷ *vb* (*intr*) **2** to stink [c20 ?from SNIFF] > **ˈniffy** *adj*

Niflheim (ˈnɪvᵊlˌheɪm) *n Norse myth* the abode of the dead [ON, lit.: mist home]

nifty (ˈnɪftɪ) *adj* **niftier, niftiest** *inf* **1** pleasing, apt, or stylish **2** quick; agile [c19 from ?] > **ˈniftily** *adv* > **ˈniftiness** *n*

nigella (naɪˈdʒɛlə) *n* another name for **love-in-a-mist**

Niger *n* **1** (niːˈʒɛə, ˈnaɪdʒə) a landlocked republic in West Africa: important since earliest times for its trans-Saharan trade routes; made a French colony in 1922 and became fully independent in 1960; exports peanuts and livestock. Official language: French. Religion: Muslim majority. Currency: franc. Capital: Niamey. Pop: 10 355 000 (2001 est). Area: 1 267 000 sq km (489 000 sq miles) **2** (ˈnaɪdʒə) a river in West Africa, rising in S Guinea and flowing in a great northward curve through Mali, then southwest through Niger and Nigeria to the Gulf of Guinea: the third longest river in Africa, with the largest delta, covering an area of 36 260 sq km (14 000 sq miles). Length: 4184 km (2600 miles)

3 ('naɪdʒə) a state of W central Nigeria, formed in 1976 from part of North-Western State. Capital: Minna. Pop: 2 775 526 (1995 est). Area: 76 363 sq km (29 476 sq miles)

Nigeria (naɪ'dʒɪərɪə) *n* a republic in West Africa, on the Gulf of Guinea: Lagos annexed by the British in 1861; protectorates of Northern and Southern Nigeria formed in 1900 and united as a colony in 1914; gained independence as a member of the Commonwealth in 1960 (membership suspended from 1995 to 1999 following human rights violations); Eastern Region seceded as the Republic of Biafra for the duration of the severe civil war (1967–70); ruled by military governments from 1966. It consists of a belt of tropical rainforest in the south, with semidesert in the extreme north and highlands in the east; the main export is petroleum. Official language: English; Hausa, Ibo, and Yoruba are the chief regional languages. Religion: animist, Muslim, and Christian. Currency: naira. Capital: Abuja. Pop: 126 636 000 (2001 est). Area: 923 773 sq km (356 669 sq miles) > **Ni'gerian** *adj, n*
▷ www.nigeria.gov.ng
▷ www.nigeriatourism.net

niggard ('nɪgəd) *n* **1** a stingy person ▷ *adj* **2** *arch* miserly [c14 ?from ON]

niggardly ('nɪgədlɪ) *adj* **1** stingy **2** meagre: *a niggardly salary* ▷ *adv* **3** stingily; grudgingly > **'niggardliness** *n*

nigger ('nɪgə) *n derog* **1** another name for a Negro **2** a member of any dark-skinned race **3 nigger in the woodpile** a hidden cause of trouble [c18 from c16 dialect *neeger*, from F *nègre*, from Sp. NEGRO[1]]

niggle ('nɪgᵊl) *vb* **niggles, niggling, niggled 1** (*intr*) to find fault continually **2** (*intr*) to be preoccupied with details; fuss **3** (*tr*) to irritate; worry ▷ *n* **4** a trivial objection or complaint **5** a slight feeling as of misgiving, uncertainty, etc [c16 from Scand.] > **'niggler** *n* > **'niggly** *adj*

niggling ('nɪglɪŋ) *adj* **1** petty **2** fussy **3** irritating **4** requiring painstaking work **5** persistently troubling

nigh (naɪ) *adj, adv, prep* an archaic, poetic, or dialect word for **near** [OE *nēah, nēh*]

night (naɪt) *n* **1** the period of darkness that occurs each 24 hours, as distinct from day **2** (*modifier*) of, occurring, working, etc, at night: *a night nurse* **3** this period considered as a unit: *four nights later they left* **4** the period between sunset and retiring to bed; evening **5** the time between bedtime and morning **6** the weather at night: *a clear night* **7** the activity or experience of a person during a night **8** (*sometimes cap*) any evening designated for a special observance or function **9** nightfall or dusk **10** a state or period of gloom, ignorance, etc **11 make a night of it** to celebrate for most of the night ▷ Related adj: **nocturnal** ▷ See also **nights** [OE *niht*]

night blindness *n pathol* a nontechnical term for **nyctalopia** > **'night-ˌblind** *adj*

nightcap ('naɪtˌkæp) *n* **1** a bedtime drink **2** a soft cap formerly worn in bed

nightclothes ('naɪtˌkləʊðz) *pl n* clothes worn in bed

nightclub ('naɪtˌklʌb) *n* a place of entertainment open in the evening until the early hours of the morning, offering drink and dancing, and occasionally, food and a floorshow

nightdress ('naɪtˌdrɛs) *n Brit* a loose dress worn in bed by women. Also called: **nightgown, nightie**

nightfall ('naɪtˌfɔːl) *n* the approach of darkness; dusk

night fighter *n* an interceptor aircraft used for operations at night

nightgown ('naɪtˌgaʊn) *n* **1** another name for nightdress **2** a man's nightshirt

nighthawk ('naɪtˌhɔːk) *n* **1** any of various nocturnal American birds **2** *inf* another name for **night owl**

nightie *or* **nighty** ('naɪtɪ) *n, pl* **nighties** *inf* short for nightdress

nightingale ('naɪtɪŋˌgeɪl) *n* a brownish European songbird with a broad reddish-brown tail: well known for its musical song, usually heard at night [OE *nihtegale*, from NIGHT + *galan* to sing]

Nightingale ('naɪtɪŋˌgeɪl) *n* **Florence**, known as *the Lady with the Lamp*. 1820–1910, English nurse, famous for her work during the Crimean War. She helped to raise the status and quality of the nursing profession and founded a training school for nurses in London (1860)

nightjar ('naɪtˌdʒɑː) *n* any of a family of nocturnal birds which have large eyes and feed on insects [c17 NIGHT + JAR[2], so called from its discordant cry]

night latch *n* a door lock operated by means of a knob on the inside and a key on the outside

nightlife ('naɪtˌlaɪf) *n* social life or entertainment taking place at night

night-light *n* a dim light burning at night, esp for children

nightlong ('naɪtˌlɒŋ) *adj, adv* throughout the night

nightly ('naɪtlɪ) *adj* **1** happening or relating to each night **2** happening at night ▷ *adv* **3** at night or each night

nightmare ('naɪtˌmɛə) *n* **1** a terrifying or deeply distressing dream **2a** an event or condition resembling a terrifying dream **2b** (*as modifier*): *a nightmare drive* **3** a thing that is feared **4** (formerly) an evil spirit supposed to suffocate sleeping people [c13 (meaning: incubus; c16 bad dream): from NIGHT + OE *mare, mære* evil spirit, from Gmc] > **'nightˌmarish** *adj*

night owl *or* **nighthawk** *n inf* a person who is or prefers to be up and about late at night

nights (naɪts) *adv inf* at night, esp regularly: *he works nights*

night safe *n* a safe built into the outside wall of a bank, in which customers can deposit money at times when the bank is closed

night school *n* an educational institution that holds classes in the evening

nightshade ('naɪtˌʃeɪd) *n* any of various solanaceous plants, such as deadly nightshade and black nightshade [OE *nihtscada*, apparently NIGHT + SHADE, referring to the poisonous or soporific qualities of these plants]

night shift *n* **1** a group of workers who work a shift during the night **2** the period worked

nightshirt ('naɪtˌʃɜːt) *n* a loose knee-length or longer shirtlike garment worn in bed

nightspot ('naɪtˌspɒt) *n* an informal word for **nightclub**

night-time *n* the time from sunset to sunrise; night as distinct from day

night watch *n* **1** a watch or guard kept at night, esp for security **2** the period of time the watch is kept **3** a night watchman

night watchman *n* **1** Also called: **night watch** a person who keeps guard at night on a factory, public building, etc **2** *cricket* a batsman sent in to bat to play out time when a wicket has fallen near the end of a day's play

nightwear ('naɪtˌwɛə) *n* apparel worn in bed or before retiring to bed; pyjamas, etc

nigrescent (naɪ'grɛsᵊnt) *adj* blackish; dark [c18 from L *nigrescere* to grow black, from *niger* black] > **ni'grescence** *n*

nihilism ('naɪɪˌlɪzəm) *n* **1** a complete denial of all established authority and institutions **2** *philosophy* an extreme form of scepticism that systematically rejects all values, belief in existence, etc **3** a revolutionary doctrine of destruction for its own sake **4** the practice of terrorism [c19 from L *nihil* nothing] > **'nihilist** *n, adj* > **ˌnihil'istic** *adj* > **nihility** (naɪ'hɪlɪtɪ) *n*

nihil obstat ('naɪhɪl 'ɒbstæt) the phrase used by a Roman Catholic censor to declare publication inoffensive to faith or morals [L, lit.: nothing hinders]

Nihon ('niː'hɒn) *n* transliteration of a Japanese name for **Japan**

Niigata ('niːɪˌgɑːtə) *n* a port in central Japan, on NW

Nn

Honshu at the mouth of the Shinano River: the chief port on the Sea of Japan. Pop: 494 785 (1995)

Nijinsky (nɪˈdʒɪnskɪ) *n* **Waslaw** *or* **Vaslaw** (vatsˈlaf) 1890–1950, Russian ballet dancer and choreographer, who was associated with Diaghilev. His creations include settings of Stravinsky's *The Rite of Spring*

Nijmegen (ˈnaɪˌmeɪɡən; *Dutch* ˈnɛimeːxə) *n* an industrial town in the E Netherlands, in Gelderland province on the Waal River: the oldest town in the country; scene of the signing (1678) of the peace treaty between Louis XIV, the Netherlands, Spain, and the Holy Roman Empire. Pop: 151 864 (1999 est). Latin name: **Noviomagus** German name: **Nimwegen**

-nik *suffix forming nouns* denoting a person associated with a specified state or quality: *beatnik* [c20 from Russian *-nik*, as in SPUTNIK, and infl. by Yiddish *-nik* (agent suffix)]

Nikaria (nɪˈkɛərɪə, naɪ-) *n* another name for **Icaria**

Nike (ˈnaɪkiː) *n Greek myth* the winged goddess of victory. Roman counterpart: **Victoria** [from Gk: victory]

Nikkei Stock Average (ˈnɪkeɪ) *n* an index of share prices based on an average of 225 equities quoted on the Tokyo Stock Exchange [c20 from *Nik(on) Kei(zai Shimbun)*, a Japanese newspaper group]

Nikko (ˈniːkəʊ) *n* a town in central Japan, on NE Honshu: a major pilgrimage centre, with a 4th-century Shinto shrine, a Buddhist temple (767), and the shrines of the Tokugawa shoguns. Pop: 20 128 (1990)

Nikolainkaupunki (*Finnish* ˌnikəlaɪnˈkaʊpʊŋki) *n* the former name of **Vaasa**

Nikolayev (*Russian* nikaˈlajɪf) *n* a city in the S Ukraine on the Southern Bug about 64 km (40 miles) from the Black Sea: founded as a naval base in 1788; one of the leading Black Sea ports. Pop: 517 900 (1998 est). Former name: **Vernoleninsk**

nil (nɪl) *n* nothing: used esp in the scoring of certain games [c19 from L]

Nile (naɪl) *n* a river in Africa, rising in S central Burundi in its remotest headstream, the **Luvironza**: flows into Lake Victoria and leaves the lake as the **Victoria Nile**, flowing to Lake Albert, which is drained by the **Albert Nile**, becoming the White Nile on the border between Uganda and the Sudan; joined by its chief tributary, the **Blue Nile** (which rises near Lake Tana, Ethiopia) at Khartoum, and flows north to its delta on the Mediterranean; the longest river in the world. Length: (from the source of the Luvironza to the Mediterranean) 6741 km (4187 miles)

Nile green *n* **a** a pale bluish-green colour **b** (*as adj*): *a Nile-green dress*

nilgai (ˈnɪlɡaɪ) *or* **nilghau** (ˈnɪlɡɔː) *n, pl* **nilgai, nilgais** *or* **nilghau, nilghaus** a large Indian antelope, the male of which has small horns [c19 from Hindi *nīlgāw*, from Sansk. *nīla* blue + *go* bull]

Nilgiri Hills (ˈnɪlɡɪrɪ) *or* **Nilgiris** *pl n* a plateau in S India, in Tamil Nadu. Average height: 2000 m (6500 ft), reaching 2635 m (8647 ft) in Doda Betta

Nilotic (naɪˈlɒtɪk) *adj* **1** of the Nile **2** of or belonging to a Negroid pastoral people inhabiting the S Sudan, parts of Kenya and Uganda, and neighbouring countries **3** relating to the group of languages spoken by the Nilotic peoples [c17 via L from Gk *Neilotikós*, from *Neilos* the NILE]

Nilsson (*Swedish* ˈnilsɔn) *n* **Birgit** (ˈbirɡit) born 1918, Swedish operatic soprano

nimble (ˈnɪmbᵊl) *adj* **1** agile, quick, and neat in movement **2** alert; acute [OE *nǣmel* quick to grasp, & *numol* quick at seizing, both from *niman* to take] > **ˈnimbleness** *n* > **ˈnimbly** *adv*

nimbostratus (ˌnɪmbəʊˈstreɪtəs, -ˈstrɑːtəs) *n, pl* **nimbostrati** (-taɪ) a dark rain-bearing stratus cloud

nimbus (ˈnɪmbəs) *n, pl* **nimbi** (-baɪ) *or* **nimbuses 1a** a dark grey rain-bearing cloud **1b** (*in combination*): *cumulonimbus clouds* **2a** an emanation of light surrounding a saint or deity **2b** a representation of this emanation **3** a surrounding aura [c17 from L: cloud]

NIMBY (ˈnɪmbɪ) *n acronym for* not in my back yard: a person who objects to the occurrence of something if it will affect him or her or take place in his or her locality

Nîmes (*French* nim) *n* a city in S France: Roman remains including an amphitheatre and the Pont du Gard aqueduct. Pop: 133 424 (1999)

Nimrod (ˈnɪmrɒd) *n* **1** a hunter famous for his prowess (Genesis 10:8–9) **2** a person dedicated to or skilled in hunting

Nimrud (nɪmˈruːd) *n* an ancient city in Assyria, near the present-day city of Mosul (Iraq): founded in about 1250 BC and destroyed by the Medes in 612 BC; excavated by Sir Austen Henry Layard

Nimwegen (ˈnɪmveːɡən) *n* the German name for **Nijmegen**

nincompoop (ˈnɪnkəmˌpuːp, ˈnɪŋ-) *n* a stupid person; fool; idiot [c17 from ?]

nine (naɪn) *n* **1** the cardinal number that is the sum of one and eight **2** a numeral, 9, IX, etc, representing this number **3** something representing, represented by, or consisting of nine units, such as a playing card with nine symbols on it **4** Also: **nine o'clock** nine hours after noon or midnight: *the play starts at nine* **5 dressed** (**up**) **to the nines** *inf* elaborately dressed **6 999** (in Britain) the telephone number of the emergency services **7 nine to five** normal office hours: *a nine-to-five job* ▷ *determiner* **8a** amounting to nine: *nine days* **8b** (*as pronoun*): *nine are ready* [OE *nigon*]

nine-days wonder *n* something that arouses great interest but only for a short period

nine-eleven, 9-11, *or* **9/11** *n* the eleventh of September 2001, the day on which the twin towers of the World Trade Center in New York were flown into and destroyed by aeroplanes hijacked by Islamic fundamentalists [c21 from the US custom of expressing dates in figures, the day of the month after the number of the month]

ninefold (ˈnaɪnˌfəʊld) *adj* **1** equal to or having nine times as many or as much **2** composed of nine parts ▷ *adv* **3** by nine times as much

ninepins (ˈnaɪnˌpɪnz) *n* **1** (*functioning as sing*) another name for **skittles 2** (*sing*) a pin used in this game

nineteen (ˈnaɪnˈtiːn) *n* **1** the cardinal number that is the sum of ten and nine **2** a numeral, 19, XIX, etc, representing this number **3** something represented by, representing, or consisting of 19 units **4 talk nineteen to the dozen** to talk incessantly ▷ *determiner* **5a** amounting to nineteen: *nineteen pictures* **5b** (*as pronoun*): *only nineteen voted* [OE *nigontīne*]

nineteenth (ˌnaɪnˈtiːnθ) *adj* **1** (*usually prenominal*) **1a** coming after the eighteenth in numbering, position, etc; being the ordinal number of *nineteen*. Often written: 19th **1b** (*as n*): *the nineteenth was rainy* ▷ *n* **2a** one of 19 equal parts of something **2b** (*as modifier*): *a nineteenth part* **3** the fraction equal to one divided by 19 ($^1/_{19}$)

nineteenth hole *n golf, sl* the bar in a golf clubhouse [c20 from its being the next objective after a standard 18-hole round]

ninetieth (ˈnaɪntɪɪθ) *adj* **1** (*usually prenominal*) **1a** being the ordinal number of *ninety* in numbering, position, etc Often written: 90th **1b** (*as n*): *ninetieth in succession* ▷ *n* **2a** one of 90 equal parts of something **2b** (*as modifier*): *a ninetieth part* **3** the fraction one divided by 90 ($^1/_{90}$)

ninety (ˈnaɪntɪ) *n, pl* **nineties 1** the cardinal number that is the product of ten and nine **2** a numeral, 90, XC, etc, representing this number **3** something represented by, representing, or consisting of 90 units ▷ *determiner* **4a** amounting to ninety: *ninety times* **4b** (*as pronoun*): *at least ninety are missing* [OE *nigontig*] > **ˈninetieth** *adj, n*

Nineveh (ˈnɪnɪvə) *n* the ancient capital of Assyria, on the River Tigris opposite the present-day city of Mosul (N Iraq): at its height in the 8th and 7th centuries BC; destroyed in 612 BC by the Medes and Babylonians > **'Ninevite** *n*

Ningbo *or* **Ningpo** ('nɪŋ'pəʊ) *n* a port in E China, in NE Zhejiang, on the Yung River, about 20 km (12 miles) from its mouth at Hangzhou Bay: one of the first sites of European settlement in China. Pop: 1 704 819 (1999 est)

Ningsia *or* **Ninghsia** ('nɪŋ'ʃjɑː) *n* **1** a former province of NW China: mostly included in the Inner Mongolian AR in 1956, with the smaller part constituted as the Ningxia Hui AR in 1958 **2** the former name of **Yinchuan**

Ningxia Hui Autonomous Region ('nɪŋ'ʃjɑː 'huːɪ) *n* an administrative division of NW China, south of the Inner Mongolian AR. Capital: Yinchuan. Pop: 5 620 000 (2000 est). Area: 66 400 sq km (25 896 sq miles)

Ninian ('nɪnjən) *n* **Saint** ?360–?432 AD, the first known apostle of Scotland; built a stone church (*candida casa*) at Whithorn on his native Solway; preached to the Picts. Feast day: Sept 16

ninja ('nɪndʒə) *n, pl* **ninja** *or* **ninjas** (*sometimes cap*) a person skilled in **ninjutsu,** a Japanese martial art characterized by stealthy movement and camouflage [Japanese]

ninny ('nɪnɪ) *n, pl* **ninnies** a dull-witted person [c16 ?from *an innocent* simpleton]

ninth (naɪnθ) *adj* **1** (*usually prenominal*) **1a** coming after the eighth in order, position, etc; being the ordinal number of *nine.* Often written: 9th **1b** (*as n*): *the person ninth in line to the throne* ▷ *n* **2a** one of nine equal parts **2b** (*as modifier*): *a ninth part* **3** the fraction one divided by nine ($^1/_9$) **4** *music* an interval of one octave plus a second ▷ *adv* **5** Also: **ninthly** after the eighth person, position, event, etc [OE *nigotha*]

Ninus ('naɪnəs) *n* a king of Assyria and the legendary founder of Nineveh, husband of Semiramis

Niobe ('naɪəbɪ) *n Greek myth* a daughter of Tantalus, whose children were slain after she boasted of them: although turned into stone, she continued to weep

niobium (naɪ'əʊbɪəm) *n* a ductile white superconductive metallic element that occurs principally in the black mineral columbite and tantalite. Symbol: Nb; atomic no.: 41; atomic wt.: 92.906. Former name: **columbium** [c19 from NL, from NIOBE; because it occurred in TANTALITE]

nip[1] (nɪp) *vb* **nips, nipping, nipped** (*mainly tr*) **1** to compress, as between a finger and the thumb; pinch **2** (often foll by *off*) to remove by clipping, biting, etc **3** (when *intr*, often foll by *at*) to give a small sharp bite (to): *the dog nipped at his heels* **4** (esp of the cold) to affect with a stinging sensation **5** to harm through cold: *the frost nipped the young plants* **6** to check or destroy the growth of (esp in **nip in the bud**) **7** (*intr;* foll by *along, up, out,* etc) *Brit inf* to hurry; dart **8** *sl, chiefly US & Canad* to snatch ▷ *n* **9** a pinch, snip, etc **10** severe frost or cold: *the first nip of winter* **11 put the nips in** *Austral & NZ sl* to exert pressure on someone, esp in order to extort money **12** *arch* a taunting remark **13 nip and tuck** *US & Canad* neck and neck [c14 from ON]

nip[2] (nɪp) *n* **1** a small drink of spirits; dram ▷ *vb* **nips, nipping, nipped 2** to drink spirits, esp habitually in small amounts [c18 from *nipperkin* a vessel holding a half-pint or less, from ?]

Nipigon ('nɪpəgɒn) *n* **Lake** a lake in central Canada, in NW Ontario, draining into Lake Superior via the **Nipigon River** Area: 4843 sq km (1870 sq miles)

Nipissing ('nɪpɪsɪŋ) *n* **Lake** a lake in central Canada, in E Ontario between the Ottawa River and Georgian Bay. Area: 855 sq km (330 sq miles)

nipper ('nɪpə) *n* **1** a person or thing that nips **2** the large pincer-like claw of a lobster, crab, etc **3** *inf, chiefly Brit & Austral* a small child **4** *Austral* a type of small prawn used as bait

nippers ('nɪpəz) *pl n* an instrument or tool, such as a pair of pliers, for snipping or squeezing

nipple ('nɪpᵊl) *n* **1** the small conical projection in the centre of each breast, which in women contains the outlet of the milk ducts **2** something resembling a nipple in shape or function **3** Also called: **grease nipple** a small drilled bush, usually screwed into a bearing, through which grease is introduced [c16 from earlier *neble, nible,* ?from NEB, NIB]

Nippon ('nɪpɒn) *n* transliteration of a Japanese name for **Japan** > **Nipponese** (ˌnɪpə'niːz) *adj, n*

Nippur (nɪ'pʊə) *n* an ancient Sumerian and Babylonian city, the excavated site of which is in SE Iraq: an important religious centre, abandoned in the 12th or 13th century

nippy ('nɪpɪ) *adj* **nippier, nippiest 1** (of weather) frosty or chilly **2** *Brit inf* **2a** quick; nimble; active **2b** (of a motor vehicle) small and relatively powerful **3** (of dogs) inclined to bite > **'nippily** *adv*

Nirenberg ('naɪrənbɜːg) *n* **Marshall Warren** born 1927, US biochemist; shared the Nobel prize for physiology or medicine (1968) for his role in deciphering the genetic code

NIREX ('naɪrɛks) *n acronym for* Nuclear Industry Radioactive Waste Executive
▷ www.nirex.co.uk

nirvana (nɪə'vɑːnə, nɜː-) *n Buddhism & Hinduism* final release from the cycle of reincarnation attained by extinction of all desires and individual existence, culminating (in Buddhism) in absolute blessedness, or (in Hinduism) in absorption into Brahman [c19 from Sansk.: extinction, from *nir-* out + *vāti* it blows]

Niš *or* **Nish** (niːʃ) *n* an industrial town in E Serbia and Montenegro, in SE Serbia: situated on routes between central Europe and the Aegean. Pop: 182 583 (2000)

Nisei ('niːseɪ) *n* a native-born citizen of the United States or Canada whose parents were Japanese immigrants [Japanese, lit.: second generation]

Nishapur (ˌniːʃɑː'pʊə) *n* a town in NE Iran, at an altitude of 1195 m (3920 ft): birthplace and burial place of Omar Khayyám. Pop: 135 681 (1991)

Nishinomiya (ˌniːʃɪ'nɒmɪjə) *n* an industrial city in central Japan, on S Honshu, northwest of Osaka. Pop: 390 388 (1995)

nisi ('naɪsaɪ) *adj* (*postpositive*) *law* (of a court order) coming into effect on a specified date unless cause is shown why it should not: *a decree nisi* [c19 from: unless, if not]

Nissen hut ('nɪsᵊn) *n* a military shelter of semicircular cross section, made of corrugated steel sheet [c20 after Lt Col. Peter *Nissen* (1871–1930), British mining engineer, its inventor]

nit[1] (nɪt) *n* **1** the egg of a louse, esp adhering to human hair **2** the larva of a louse [OE *hnitu*]

nit[2] (nɪt) *n* a unit of luminance equal to 1 candela per square metre [c20 from L *nitor* brightness]

nit[3] (nɪt) *n inf, chiefly Brit* short for **nitwit**

nit[4] (nɪt) *n* a unit of information equal to 1.44 bits. Also called: **nepit** [c20 from N(*apierian dig*)*it*]

nit[5] (nɪt) *n* **keep nit** *Austral inf* to keep watch, esp during illegal activity [c19 from *nix!* a shout of warning]

Niterói (*Portuguese* nite'rɔi) *n* a port in SE Brazil, on Guanabara Bay opposite Rio de Janeiro: contains Brazil's chief shipyards. Pop: 458 465 (2000). Also called: **Nictheroy**

nit-picking *inf* ▷ *n* **1** a concern with insignificant details, esp with the intention of finding fault ▷ *adj* **2** showing such a concern; fussy [c20 from NIT[1] + PICK[1]] > **'nit-ˌpicker** *n*

nitrate ('naɪtreɪt) *n* **1** any salt or ester of nitric acid **2** a fertilizer containing nitrate salts ▷ *vb* **nitrates, nitrating, nitrated 3** (*tr*) to treat with nitric acid or a nitrate **4** to convert or be converted into a nitrate > **ni'tration** *n*

nitre *or US* **niter** ('naɪtə) *n* another name for **potassium**

Nn

nitrate or **sodium nitrate** [C14 via OF from L *nitrum*, prob. from Gk *nitron*]

nitric ('naɪtrɪk) *adj* of or containing nitrogen

nitric acid *n* a colourless corrosive liquid important in the manufacture of fertilizers, explosives, and many other chemicals. Formula: HNO_3. Former name: **aqua fortis**

nitric oxide *n* a colourless reactive gas. Formula: NO. Systematic name: **nitrogen monoxide**

nitride ('naɪtraɪd) *n* a compound of nitrogen with a more electropositive element

nitrification (ˌnaɪtrɪfɪ'keɪʃən) *n* **1** the oxidation of the ammonium compounds in dead organic material into nitrites and nitrates by soil nitrobacteria, making nitrogen available to plants **2** the addition of a nitro group to an organic compound

nitrify ('naɪtrɪˌfaɪ) *vb* **nitrifies, nitrifying, nitrified** (*tr*) **1** to treat or cause to react with nitrogen **2** to treat (soil) with nitrates **3** (of nitrobacteria) to convert (ammonium compounds) into nitrates by oxidation

nitrite ('naɪtraɪt) *n* any salt or ester of nitrous acid

nitro- *or before a vowel* **nitr-** *combining form* **1** indicating that a chemical compound contains a nitro group, $-NO_2$: *nitrobenzene* **2** indicating that a chemical compound is a nitrate ester: *nitrocellulose* [from Gk *nitron* NATRON]

nitrobacteria (ˌnaɪtrəʊbæk'tɪərɪə) *pl n, sing* **nitrobacterium** (-'tɪərɪəm) soil bacteria that are involved in nitrification

nitrobenzene (ˌnaɪtrəʊ'bɛnziːn) *n* a yellow oily liquid compound, used as a solvent and in the manufacture of aniline. Formula: $C_6H_5NO_2$

nitrocellulose (ˌnaɪtrəʊ'sɛljʊˌləʊs) *n* another name (not in chemical usage) for **cellulose nitrate**

nitrogen ('naɪtrədʒən) *n* a colourless odourless relatively unreactive gaseous element that forms 78 per cent of the air and is an essential constituent of proteins and nucleic acids. Symbol: N; atomic no.: 7; atomic wt.: 14.0067

nitrogen cycle *n* the natural circulation of nitrogen by living organisms. Nitrates in the soil, derived from dead organic matter by bacterial action, are absorbed and synthesized into complex organic compounds by plants and reduced to nitrates again when the plants and the animals feeding on them die and decay

nitrogen dioxide *n* a red-brown poisonous gas that is an intermediate in the manufacture of nitric acid, a nitrating agent, and an oxidizer for rocket fuels. Formula: NO_2

nitrogen fixation *n* **1** the conversion of atmospheric nitrogen into nitrogen compounds by certain bacteria in the root nodules of legumes **2** a process in which atmospheric nitrogen is converted into a nitrogen compound, used esp for fertilizer

nitrogenize *or* **nitrogenise** (naɪ'trɒdʒɪˌnaɪz) *vb* **nitrogenizes, nitrogenizing, nitrogenized** *or* **nitrogenises, nitrogenising, nitrogenised** to combine or treat with nitrogen or a nitrogen compound > **niˌtrogeni'zation** *or* **niˌtrogeni'sation** *n*

nitrogen monoxide *n* the systematic name for **nitric oxide**

nitrogen mustard *n* any of a class of organic compounds resembling mustard gas in their molecular structure: important in the treatment of cancer

nitrogenous (naɪ'trɒdʒɪnəs) *adj* containing nitrogen or a nitrogen compound

nitroglycerine (ˌnaɪtrəʊ'glɪsəˌriːn) *or* **nitroglycerin** (ˌnaɪtrəʊ'glɪsərɪn) *n* a pale yellow viscous explosive liquid made from glycerol and nitric and sulphuric acids. Formula: $CH_2NO_3CHNO_3CH_2NO_3$. Also called: **trinitroglycerine**

nitromethane (ˌnaɪtrəʊ'miːθeɪn) *n* an oily colourless liquid obtained from methane and used as a solvent and rocket fuel

nitrous ('naɪtrəs) *adj* of, derived from, or containing nitrogen, esp in a low valency state [C17 from L *nitrōsus* full of natron]

nitrous acid *n* a weak monobasic acid known only in solution and in the form of nitrite salts. Formula: HNO_2. Systematic name: **dioxonitric(III) acid**

nitrous oxide *n* a colourless gas with a sweet smell: used as an anaesthetic in dentistry. Formula: N_2O. Also called: **laughing gas.** Systematic name: **dinitrogen oxide**

nitty ('nɪtɪ) *adj* **nittier, nittiest** infested with nits

nitty-gritty ('nɪtɪ'grɪtɪ) *n* **the** *inf* the basic facts of a matter, situation, etc; the core [C20 ? rhyming compound from GRIT]

nitwit ('nɪtˌwɪt) *n inf* a foolish or dull person [C20 ?from NIT[1] + WIT[1]]

Niue ('njuːeɪ) *n* an island in the S Pacific, between Tonga and the Cook Islands: annexed by New Zealand (1901); achieved full internal self-government in 1974. Chief town and port: Alofi. Pop: 1977 (1993 est). Area: 260 sq km (100 sq miles). Also called: **Savage Island** > **Niuean** (njuː'ɪən) *n, adj*

Niven ('nɪvᵊn) *n* **David** 1909–83, British film actor and author. His films include *The Prisoner of Zenda* (1937), *Around the World in 80 Days* (1956), *Casino Royale* (1967), and *Paper Tiger* (1975). He wrote the autobiographical *The Moon's a Balloon* (1972) and *Bring on the Empty Horses* (1975)

Nivernais (*French* nivɛrnɛ) *n* a former province of central France, around Nevers

nix[1] (nɪks) *inf* ▷ *sentence substitute* **1** another word for **no**[1] ▷ *n* **2** a refusal **3** nothing [C18 from G, inf. form of *nichts* nothing]

nix[2] (nɪks) *or* (*fem*) **nixie** ('nɪksɪ) *n Germanic myth* a water sprite, usually unfriendly to humans [C19 from G *Nixe*, from OHG *nihhus*]

Nixon ('nɪksən) *n* **Richard M(ilhous)** 1913–94, US Republican politician; 37th president from 1969 until he resigned over the Watergate scandal in 1974

Nizam (nɪ'zɑːm) *n* the title of the ruler of Hyderabad, India, from 1724 to 1948

Nizhni Novgorod (*Russian* 'niʒnij 'nɔvgərət) *n* a city and port in central Russia, at the confluence of the Volga and Oka Rivers: situated on the Volga route from the Baltic to central Asia; birthplace of Maxim Gorki. Pop: 1 364 900 (1999 est). Former name (1932–91): **Gorki**

Nizhni Tagil (*Russian* 'niʒnij ta'gil) *n* a city in central Russia, on the E slopes of the Ural Mountains: a major metallurgical centre. Pop: 395 800 (1999 est)

NJ *or* **N.J.** *abbrev for* New Jersey

Njord (njɔːd) *or* **Njorth** (njɔːθ) *n Norse myth* the god of the sea, fishing, and prosperity

Nkomo (ᵊŋ'kəʊməʊ) *n* **Joshua** 1917–99, Zimbabwean politician; coleader, with Robert Mugabe, of the Patriotic Front (1976–80) against the government of Ian Smith in Rhodesia; minister (1980–82; 1988–99) and vice-president (1990–96)

nkosi (ᵊŋ'kɔːsɪ) *n S African* a term of address to a superior; master [Nguni *inkosi* chief, lord]

Nkosi Sikele' iAfrica (ŋ'kosɪ ˌsɪkɛ'lɛlɪ ˌɑfrɪ'kɑ) *n* the unofficial anthem of the Black people of South Africa, officially recognized as a national anthem (along with 'Die Stem') in 1991 [from Xhosa, Lord Bless Africa]

Nkrumah (ᵊŋ'kruːmə) *n* **Kwame** ('kwɑːmɪ) 1909–72, Ghanaian statesman, prime minister (1957–60) and president (1960–66). He led demands for self-government in the 1950s, achieving Ghanaian independence in 1957. He was overthrown by a military coup (1966)

NM *or* **N. Mex.** *abbrev for* New Mexico

NMR *abbrev for* nuclear magnetic resonance

NNE *symbol for* north-northeast

NNP *abbrev for*: **1** net national product **2** (in South Africa) New National Party

NNW *symbol for* north-northwest

no[1] (nəʊ) *sentence substitute* **1** used to express denial, disagreement, refusal, etc ▷ *n, pl* **noes** *or* **nos 2** an answer or vote of *no* **3 not take no for an answer** to continue in a course of action, etc, despite refusals **4** (*often pl*) a person who votes in the negative **5 the noes have it** there is a majority of votes in the negative [OE *nā*, from *ne* not, no + *ā* ever]

no[2] (nəʊ) *determiner* **1** not any, not a, or not one: *there's no money left; no card in the file* **2** not at all: *she's no youngster* **3** (foll by comparative adjectives and adverbs) not: *no less than forty; no taller than a child* [OE *nā*, from *nān* NONE]

No[1] *or* **Noh** (nəʊ) *n, pl* **No** *or* **Noh** the stylized classic drama of Japan, developed in the 15th century or earlier, using music, dancing, and themes from religious stories or myths [from Japanese *nō* talent, from Chinese *neng*]

▷ www.jinjapan.org/access/noh

▷ www.iijnet.or.jp/NOH-KYOGEN/english/english.html

No[2] *the chemical symbol for* nobelium

No[3] (nəʊ) *n* **Lake** a lake in the S central Sudan, where the Bahr el Jebel (White Nile) is joined by the Bahr el Ghazal. Area: about 103 sq km (40 sq miles)

no' (no, nəʊ) *adv Scot* not

No. *abbrev for:* **1** north(ern) **2** Also: **no** (*pl* **Nos** *or* **nos.**) number [from L *numero* the ablative of *numerus* number]

n.o. *cricket abbrev for* not out

no-account *adj* **1** worthless; good-for-nothing ▷ *n* **2** a worthless person

Noah (ˈnəʊə) *n Old Testament* a Hebrew patriarch, who saved himself, his family, and specimens of every animal and bird from the Flood by building a ship (**Noah's Ark**) in which they all survived (Genesis 6–8)

nob[1] (nɒb) *n cribbage* **1** the jack of the suit turned up **2 one for his nob** the call made with this jack, scoring one point [c19 from ?]

nob[2] (nɒb) *n sl, chiefly Brit* a person of wealth or social distinction [c19 from ?]

no-ball *n* **1** *cricket* an illegal ball, as for overstepping the crease, for which the batting side scores a run, and from which the batsman can only be out by being run out **2** *rounders* an illegal ball, esp one bowled too high or too low ▷ *interj* **3** *cricket, rounders* a call by the umpire indicating a no-ball ▷ *vb* (*tr*) **4** *cricket* (of an umpire) **4a** to declare (a bowler) to have bowled a no-ball **4b** to declare (a delivery) to be a no-ball

nobble (ˈnɒbəl) *vb* **nobbles, nobbling, nobbled** (*tr*) *Brit sl* **1** to disable (a racehorse), esp with drugs **2** to win over or outwit (a person) by underhand means **3** to suborn (a person, esp a juror) by threats, bribery, etc **4** to steal **5** to grab **6** to kidnap [c19 from *nobbler*, from a false division of *an hobbler* (one who hobbles horses) as *a nobbler*]

Nobel (nəʊˈbɛl) *n* **Alfred Bernhard** (ˈalfreːd ˈbæːrnhard) 1833–96, Swedish chemist and philanthropist, noted for his invention of dynamite (1866) and his bequest founding the Nobel prizes

nobelium (nəʊˈbiːlɪəm) *n* a transuranic element produced artificially from curium. Symbol: No; atomic no.: 102; half-life of most stable isotope, ^{255}No: 180 seconds (approx) [c20 NL, after *Nobel* Institute, Stockholm, where it was discovered]

Nobel prize *n* a prize for outstanding contributions to chemistry, physics, physiology or medicine, literature, economics, and peace that may be awarded annually; established 1901 [c20 after Alfred NOBEL]

▷ www.nobel.se

▷ www.improb.com/ig/ig-top.html

nobility (nəʊˈbɪlɪtɪ) *n, pl* **nobilities 1** a privileged class whose titles are conferred by descent or royal decree **2** the quality of being good; dignity: *nobility of mind* **3** (in the British Isles) the class of people holding the title of dukes, marquesses, earls, viscounts, or barons and their feminine equivalents; peerage

nobilmente (ˌnəʊbɪlˈmɛnteɪ) *adj, adv music* to be performed in a noble manner [It.]

noble (ˈnəʊbəl) *adj* **1** of or relating to a hereditary class with special status, often derived from a feudal period **2** of or characterized by high moral qualities; magnanimous: *a noble deed* **3** having dignity or eminence; illustrious **4** imposing; magnificent: *a noble avenue of trees* **5** superior; excellent: *a noble strain of horses* **6** *chem* **6a** (of certain elements) chemically unreactive **6b** (of certain metals, esp copper, silver, and gold) resisting oxidation ▷ *n* **7** a person belonging to a privileged class whose status is usually indicated by a title **8** (in the British Isles) a person holding the title of duke, marquess, earl, viscount, or baron, or a feminine equivalent **9** a former British gold coin having the value of one third of a pound [c13 via OF from L *nōbilis*, orig., capable of being known, hence well-known, from *noscere* to know] > **ˈnobleness** *n* > **ˈnobly** *adv*

nobleman (ˈnəʊbəlmən) *or* (*fem*) **noblewoman** *n, pl* **noblemen** *or* **noblewomen** a person of noble rank, title, or status; peer; aristocrat

noble savage *n* (in romanticism) an idealized view of primitive man

noblesse oblige (nəʊˈblɛs əʊˈbliːʒ) *n often ironic* the supposed obligation of nobility to be honourable and generous [F, lit.: nobility obliges]

nobody (ˈnəʊbədɪ) *pron* **1** no person; no-one ▷ *n, pl* **nobodies 2** an insignificant person.

USAGE See at **everyone**

nock (nɒk) *n* **1** a notch on an arrow that fits on the bowstring **2** either of the grooves at each end of a bow that hold the bowstring ▷ *vb* (*tr*) **3** to fit (an arrow) on a bowstring [c14 rel. to Swedish *nock* tip]

no-claims bonus *n* a reduction on an insurance premium, esp one covering a motor vehicle, if no claims have been made within a specified period. Also called: **no-claim bonus**

Nn

noctambulism (nɒkˈtæmbjʊˌlɪzəm) *or* **noctambulation** *n* another word for **somnambulism** [c19 from L *nox* night + *ambulāre* to walk]

noctilucent (ˌnɒktɪˈluːsənt) *adj* shining at night, usually of very thin high altitude clouds observable in the summer twilight sky [from L, from *nox* night + *lūcēre* to shine]

noctuid (ˈnɒktjʊɪd) *n* any of a large family of nocturnal moths that includes the underwings [c19 via NL from L *noctua* night owl, from *nox* night]

noctule (ˈnɒktjuːl) *n* any of several large Old World insectivorous bats [c18 prob. from LL *noctula* small owl, from L *noctua* night owl]

nocturnal (nɒkˈtɜːnəl) *adj* **1** of, used during, occurring in, or relating to the night **2** (of animals) active at night **3** (of plants) having flowers that open at night and close by day [c15 from LL *nocturnālis*, from L *nox* night] > **ˌnocturˈnality** *n* > **nocˈturnally** *adv*

nocturne (ˈnɒktɜːn) *n* **1** a short, dreamy, and melodic piece of music, esp one for the piano **2** a painting of a night scene

nod (nɒd) *vb* **nods, nodding, nodded 1** to lower and raise (the head) briefly, as to indicate agreement, etc **2** (*tr*) to express by nodding: *she nodded approval* **3** (*intr*) (of flowers, trees, etc) to sway or bend forwards and back **4** (*intr*) to let the head fall forwards through drowsiness; be almost asleep **5** (*intr*) to be momentarily careless: *even Homer sometimes nods* **6 nodding acquaintance** a slight, casual, or superficial knowledge (of a subject or person) ▷ *n* **7** a quick down-and-up movement of the head, as in assent, command, etc **8 on the nod** *inf* agreed, as in committee, without formal procedure **9** See **land of Nod** ▷ See also **nod off** [c14 *nodde*, from ?] > **ˈnodding** *adj, n*

noddle[1] (ˈnɒdəl) *n inf, chiefly Brit* the head or brains: *use your noddle!* [c15 from ?]

noddle[2] (ˈnɒdəl) *vb* **noddles, noddling, noddled** *inf, chiefly*

Brit to nod (the head), as through drowsiness [C18 from NOD]

noddy[1] ('nɒdɪ) *n, pl* **noddies** **1** any of several tropical terns, typically having a dark plumage **2** a fool or dunce [C16 ? n use of obs. *noddy* foolish, drowsy, ?from NOD (vb); the bird is so called because it allows itself to be caught by hand]

noddy[2] ('nɒdɪ) *n, pl* **noddies** (*usually pl*) *television* film footage of an interviewer's reactions to comments made by an interviewee, used in editing the interview after it has been recorded [C20 from NOD]

node (nəʊd) *n* **1** a knot, swelling, or knob **2** the point on a plant stem from which the leaves or lateral branches grow **3** *physics* a point at which the amplitude of one of the two kinds of displacement in a standing wave has zero or minimum value **4** Also called: **crunode** *maths* a point at which two branches of a curve intersect **5** *maths, linguistics* one of the objects of which a graph or a tree consists **6** *astron* either of the two points at which the orbit of a body intersects the plane of the ecliptic **7** *anat* any natural bulge or swelling, such as those along the course of a lymphatic vessel (**lymph node**) **8** *computing* an interconnection point on a computer network [C16 from L *nōdus* knot] > '**nodal** *adj*

nod off *vb (intr, adv) inf* to fall asleep

nodule ('nɒdjuːl) *n* **1** a small knot, lump, or node **2** any of the knoblike outgrowths on the roots of clover and other legumes that contain bacteria involved in nitrogen fixation **3** a small rounded lump of rock or mineral substance, esp in a matrix of different rock material [C17 from L *nōdulus*, from *nōdus* knot] > '**nodular,** '**nodulose,** *or* '**nodulous** *adj*

Noel *or* **Noël** (nəʊ'ɛl) *n* (in carols, etc) another word for **Christmas** [C19 from F, from L *nātālis* a birthday]

noetic (nəʊ'ɛtɪk) *adj* of or relating to the mind [C17 from Gk *noētikos*, from *noein* to think]

Nofretete (ˌnɒfrɛ'tiːtɪ) *n* a variant of **Nefertiti**

nog *or* **nogg** (nɒg) *n* **1** Also called: **flip** a drink, esp an alcoholic one, containing beaten egg **2** *East Anglian dialect* strong local beer [C17 (orig.: a strong beer): from ?]

noggin ('nɒgɪn) *n* **1** a small quantity of spirits **2** a small mug **3** *inf* the head [C17 from ?]

no-go area *n* a district in a town that is barricaded off, usually by a paramilitary organization, which the police, army, etc, can only enter by force

Noh (nəʊ) *n* a variant spelling of **No**[1]

noir (nwɑː) *adj* (of a film) showing characteristics of a *film noir*, in plot or style [C20 from French, lit.: black]

noise (nɔɪz) *n* **1** a sound, esp one that is loud or disturbing **2** loud shouting; clamour; din **3** any undesired electrical disturbance in a circuit, etc **4** undesired or irrelevant elements in a visual image: *removing noise from pictures* **5** (*pl*) conventional comments or sounds conveying a reaction: *sympathetic noises* **6** **make a noise** to talk a great deal or complain (about) ▷ *vb* **noises, noising, noised** **7** (*tr; usually foll by abroad or about*) to spread (news, gossip, etc) [C13 from OF, from L: NAUSEA]

noiseless ('nɔɪzlɪs) *adj* making little or no sound > '**noiselessly** *adv* > '**noiselessness** *n*

noise pollution *n* annoying or harmful noise in an environment

noisette (nwɑː'zɛt) *adj* **1** flavoured with hazelnuts **2** nutbrown, as butter browned over heat ▷ *n* **3** a small round or oval piece of meat **4** a hazelnut chocolate [from F: hazelnut]

noisome ('nɔɪsəm) *adj* **1** (esp of smells) offensive **2** harmful or noxious [C14 from obs. *noy*, var. of ANNOY + -SOME[1]] > '**noisomeness** *n*

noisy ('nɔɪzɪ) *adj* **noisier, noisiest** **1** making a loud or constant noise **2** full of or characterized by noise > '**noisily** *adv* > '**noisiness** *n*

Nolan ('nəʊlən) *n* **1** **Michael Patrick,** Baron. born 1928, British judge; chairman of the Committee on Standards in Public Life (1994–97) **2** **Sir Sidney** 1917–92, Australian painter, whose works explore themes in Australian folklore

nolens volens *Latin* ('nəʊlɛnz 'vəʊlɛnz) *adv* whether willing or unwilling

nolle prosequi ('nɒlɪ 'prɒsɪˌkwaɪ) *n law* an entry made on the court record when the plaintiff or prosecutor undertakes not to continue the action or prosecution [L: do not pursue]

nomad ('nəʊmæd) *n* **1** a member of a people or tribe who move from place to place to find pasture and food **2** a wanderer [C16 via F from L *nomas* wandering shepherd, from Gk] > **no'madic** *adj* > '**nomadism** *n*

no-man's-land *n* **1** land between boundaries, esp an unoccupied zone between opposing forces **2** an unowned or unclaimed piece of land **3** an ambiguous area of activity

nom de guerre ('nɒm də 'gɛə) *n, pl* **noms de guerre** ('nɒm də 'gɛə) an assumed name [F, lit.: war name]

nom de plume ('nɒm də 'pluːm) *n, pl* **noms de plume** ('nɒm də 'pluːm) another term for **pen name** [F]

nomenclature (nəʊ'mɛnklətʃə; *US* 'nəʊmənˌkleɪtʃər) *n* the terminology used in a particular science, art, activity, etc [C17 from L *nōmenclātūra* list of names]

nominal ('nɒmɪnᵊl) *adj* **1** in name only; theoretical: *the nominal leader* **2** minimal in comparison with real worth; token: *a nominal fee* **3** of, constituting, or giving a name **4** *grammar* of or relating to a noun or noun phrase ▷ *n* **5** *grammar* a noun, noun phrase, or syntactically similar structure [C15 from L *nōminālis*, from *nōmen* name] > '**nominally** *adv*

nominalism ('nɒmɪnᵊˌlɪzəm) *n* the philosophical theory that the variety of objects to which a single general name, such as *dog*, applies have nothing in common other than that name > '**nominalist** *n*

nominal value *n* another name for **par value**

nominate ('nɒmɪˌneɪt) *vb* **nominates, nominating, nominated** (*mainly tr*) **1** to propose as a candidate, esp for an elective office **2** to appoint to an office or position **3** to name (someone) to act on one's behalf, esp to conceal one's identity **4** (*intr*) *Austral* to stand as a candidate in an election [C16 from L *nōmināre* to call by name, from *nōmen* name] > ˌ**nomi'nation** *n* > '**nomiˌnator** *n*

nominative ('nɒmɪnətɪv) *adj* **1** *grammar* denoting a case of nouns and pronouns in inflected languages that is used esp to identify the subject of a finite verb **2** appointed rather than elected to a position, office, etc ▷ *n* **3** *grammar* **3a** the nominative case **3b** a word or speech element in the nominative case [C14 from L *nōminātīvus* belonging to naming, from *nōmen* name] > **nominatival** (ˌnɒmɪnə'taɪvᵊl) *adj*

nominee (ˌnɒmɪ'niː) *n* **1** a person who is nominated to an office or as a candidate **2a** a person or organization named to act on behalf of someone else, esp to conceal the identity of the nominator **2b** (*as modifier*): *nominee shareholder* [C17 from NOMINATE + -EE]

nomogram ('nɒməˌgræm, 'nəʊmə-) *or* **nomograph** *n* an arrangement of two linear or logarithmic scales such that an intersecting straight line enables intermediate values or values on a third scale to be read off [C20 from Gk *nomos* law + -GRAM]

-nomy *n combining form* indicating a science or the laws governing a certain field of knowledge: *agronomy; economy* [from Gk *-nomia* law] > **-nomic** *adj combining form*

non- *prefix* **1** indicating negation: *nonexistent* **2** indicating refusal or failure: *noncooperation* **3** indicating exclusion from a specified class: *nonfiction* **4** indicating lack or absence: *nonobjective; nonevent* [from L *nōn* not]

nonaddictive (ˌnɒnə'dɪktɪv) *adj* (of a drug, etc) not causing addiction

nonage ('nəʊnɪdʒ) *n* **1** *law* the state of being under any of various ages at which a person may legally enter into certain transactions, such as marrying, etc **2** any period of immaturity

nonagenarian (ˌnəʊnədʒɪˈnɛərɪən) *n* **1** a person who is from 90 to 99 years old ▷ *adj* **2** of, relating to, or denoting a nonagenarian [C19 from L *nōnāgēnārius*, from *nōnāginta* ninety]

nonaggression (ˌnɒnəˈgrɛʃən) *n* **a** restraint of aggression, esp between states **b** (*as modifier*): *a nonaggression pact*

nonagon (ˈnɒnəˌgɒn) *n* a polygon having nine sides > **nonagonal** (nɒnˈægənᵊl) *adj*

nonalcoholic (ˌnɒnˌælkəˈhɒlɪk) *adj* (of a drink, etc) not containing alcohol

nonaligned (ˌnɒnəˈlaɪnd) *adj* (of states, etc) not part of a major alliance or power bloc > ˌ**nonaˈlignment** *n*

non-A, non-B hepatitis *n* the former name for **hepatitis C**

nonce (nɒns) *n* the present time or occasion (now only in **for the nonce**) [C12 from *for the nonce*, a mistaken division of *for then anes*, from *then* dative singular of *the* + *anes* ONCE]

nonce word *n* a word coined for a single occasion

nonchalant (ˈnɒnʃələnt) *adj* casually unconcerned or indifferent; uninvolved [C18 from F, from *nonchaloir* to lack warmth, from NON- + *chaloir* from L *calēre* to be warm] > ˈ**nonchalance** *n*

non-com (ˈnɒnˌkɒm) *n* short for **noncommissioned officer**

noncombatant (nɒnˈkɒmbətənt) *n* **1** a civilian in time of war **2** a member of the armed forces whose duties do not include fighting, such as a chaplain or surgeon

noncommissioned officer (ˌnɒnkəˈmɪʃənd) *n* (in the armed forces) a person, such as a sergeant or corporal, who is appointed from the ranks as a subordinate officer

noncommittal (ˌnɒnkəˈmɪtᵊl) *adj* not involving or revealing commitment to any particular opinion or action

non compos mentis *Latin* (ˈnɒn ˈkɒmpəs ˈmɛntɪs) *adj* mentally incapable of managing one's own affairs; of unsound mind [L: not in control of one's mind]

nonconformist (ˌnɒnkənˈfɔːmɪst) *n* **1** a person who does not conform to generally accepted patterns of behaviour or thought ▷ *adj* **2** of or characterized by behaviour that does not conform to accepted patterns > ˌ**nonconˈformity** *or* ˌ**nonconˈformism** *n*

Nonconformist (ˌnɒnkənˈfɔːmɪst) *n* **1** a member of a Protestant denomination that dissents from an Established Church, esp the Church of England ▷ *adj* **2** of, relating to, or denoting Nonconformists > ˌ**Nonconˈformity** *or* ˌ**Nonconˈformism** *n*

noncontributory (ˌnɒnkənˈtrɪbjʊtərɪ) *adj* **1** denoting an insurance or pension scheme for employees, the premiums of which are paid by the employer **2** (of a state benefit) not dependent on national insurance contributions

nondenominational (ˌnɒndɪˌnɒmɪˈneɪʃənᵊl) *adj* not restricted with regard to religious denomination

nondescript (ˈnɒndɪˌskrɪpt) *adj* **1** having no outstanding features ▷ *n* **2** a nondescript person or thing [C17 from NON- + L *dēscriptus*, pp of *dēscribere* to copy]

nondomiciled (nɒnˈdɒmɪˌsaɪld) *adj* of, relating to, or denoting a person who is not domiciled in his or her country of origin

none[1] (nʌn) *pron* **1** not any of a particular class: *none of my letters has arrived* **2** no-one; nobody: *there was none to tell the tale* **3** not any (of): *none of it looks edible* **4** **none other** no other person: *none other than the Queen herself* **5** **none the** (*foll by a comparative adj*) in no degree: *she was none the worse for her ordeal* **6** **none too** not very: *he was none too pleased* [OE *nān*, lit.: not one]

none[2] (nəʊn) *n* another word for **nones**

nonentity (nɒnˈɛntɪtɪ) *n, pl* **nonentities** **1** an insignificant person or thing **2** a nonexistent thing **3** the state of not existing; nonexistence

nones (nəʊnz) *n* (*functioning as sing or pl*) **1** (in the Roman calendar) the ninth day before the ides of each month: the seventh day of March, May, July, and October, and the fifth of each other month **2** *chiefly RC Church* the fifth of the seven canonical hours of the divine office, originally fixed at the ninth hour of the day, about 3 pm [OE *nōn*, from L *nōna hora* ninth hour, from *nōnus* ninth]

nonesuch *or* **nonsuch** (ˈnʌnˌsʌtʃ) *n* *arch* a matchless person or thing; nonpareil

nonet (nəʊˈnɛt) *n* **1** a piece of music for nine instruments or voices **2** a group of nine singers or instrumentalists

nonetheless (ˌnʌnðəˈlɛs) *sentence connector.* despite that; however; nevertheless

non-Euclidean geometry *n* the branch of modern geometry in which certain axioms of Euclidean geometry are denied

nonevent (ˌnɒnɪˈvɛnt) *n* a disappointing or insignificant occurrence, esp one predicted to be important

nonexecutive director (ˌnɒnɪgˈzɛkjʊtɪv) *n* a director of a commercial company who is not a full-time employee of the company

nonexistent (ˌnɒnɪgˈzɪstənt) *adj* **1** not having being or reality **2** not present under specified conditions or in a specified place > **nonexˈistence** *n*

nonfeasance (nɒnˈfiːzᵊns) *n* *law* a failure to act when under an obligation to do so ▷ Cf **malfeasance, misfeasance** [C16 from NON- + *feasance* (obs.) doing, from F *faisance*, from *faire* to do, L *facere*]

nonferrous (nɒnˈfɛrəs) *adj* **1** denoting any metal other than iron **2** not containing iron

nonflammable (nɒnˈflæməbᵊl) *adj* incapable of burning or not easily set on fire

nonfunctional (ˌnɒnˈfʌŋkʃənᵊl) *adj* not having a function

nong (nɒŋ) *n* *Austral sl* a stupid or incompetent person [C19 ?from obs. E dialect *nigmenog* silly fellow, from ?]

non-Hodgkin's lymphoma *n* any form of lymphoma other than Hodgkin's disease

nonillion (nəʊˈnɪljən) *n* **1** (in Britain, France, and Germany) the number represented as one followed by 54 zeros (10^{54}) **2** (in the US and Canada) the number represented as one followed by 30 zeros (10^{30}). Brit word: **quintillion** [C17 from F, from L *nōnus* ninth, on the model of MILLION]

nonintervention (ˌnɒnɪntəˈvɛnʃən) *n* refusal to intervene, esp the abstention by a state from intervening in the affairs of other states or in its own internal disputes

noninvasive (ˌnɒnɪnˈveɪsɪv) *adj* (of medical treatment) not involving the making of a relatively large incision in the body or the insertion of instruments, etc, into the patient

nonjudgmental (ˌnɒndʒʌdʒˈmɛntᵊl) *adj* avoiding moral judgments, esp relating to the conduct of others

nonjuror (nɒnˈdʒʊərə) *n* a person who refuses to take an oath, as of allegiance

Nonjuror (nɒnˈdʒʊərə) *n* any of a group of clergy in England and Scotland who declined to take the oath of allegiance to William and Mary in 1689

nonlinear (ˌnɒnˈlɪnɪə) *adj* not linear, esp with regard to dimension

nonmetal (nɒnˈmɛtᵊl) *n* any of a number of chemical elements that have acidic oxides and are poor conductors of heat and electricity

nonmetallic (ˌnɒnmɪˈtælɪk) *adj* **1** not of metal **2** of, concerned with, or being a nonmetal

nonmoral (nɒnˈmɒrəl) *adj* not involving morality or

ethics; neither moral nor immoral

Nono (*Italian* 'nɔ:no) *n* **Luigi** (lu'i:dʒi) 1924–90, Italian composer of 12-tone music

nonobjective (ˌnɒnəb'dʒɛktɪv) *adj* of or designating an art movement in which things are depicted in an abstract or purely formalized way

no-nonsense (ˌnəʊ'nɒnsəns) *adj* sensible, practical, and straightforward: *a severe no-nonsense look*

nonpareil ('nɒnpərəl, ˌnɒnpə'reɪl) *n* a person or thing that is unsurpassed; peerless example [c15 from F, from NON- + *pareil* similar]

nonpersistent (ˌnɒnpə'sɪstənt) *adj* (of pesticides) breaking down rapidly after application; not persisting in the environment

non-person *n* a person regarded as nonexistent or unimportant; a nonentity

nonplus (nɒn'plʌs) *vb* **nonplusses, nonplussing, nonplussed** *or US* **nonpluses, nonplusing, nonplused** 1 (*tr*) to put at a loss; confound ▷ *n, pl* **nonpluses** 2 a state of utter perplexity prohibiting action or speech [c16 from L *nōn plūs* no further]

nonprofessional (ˌnɒnprə'fɛʃənᵊl) *adj* 1 not professional in status ▷ *n* 2 a person who is not a professional

non-profit-making *adj* not yielding a profit, esp because organized or established for some other reason: *a non-profit-making organization*

nonproliferation (ˌnɒnprəˌlɪfər'eɪʃən) *n* **a** limitation of the production or spread of something, esp nuclear or chemical weapons **b** (*as modifier*): *a nonproliferation treaty*

non-pros (ˌnɒn'prɒs) *n* 1 short for **non prosequitur** ▷ *vb* **non-prosses, non-prossing, non-prossed** 2 (*tr*) to enter a judgment of non prosequitur against (a plaintiff)

non prosequitur ('nɒn prəʊ'sɛkwɪtə) *n law* (formerly) a judgment in favour of a defendant when the plaintiff failed to take the necessary steps in an action within the time allowed [L, lit.: he does not prosecute]

nonracial (ˌnɒn'reɪʃəl) *adj* not involving race or racial factors

nonrepresentational (ˌnɒnrɛprɪzɛn'teɪʃənᵊl) *adj art* another word for **abstract**

nonresident (nɒn'rɛzɪdənt) *n* 1 a person who is not residing in the place implied or specified 2 a British person employed abroad for a minimum of one year, who is exempt from UK income tax provided that he or she does not spend more than 90 days in the UK during that tax year ▷ *adj* 3 not residing in the place specified > **non'residence** *or* **non'residency** *n* > **ˌnonresi'dential** *adj*

nonresistant (ˌnɒnrɪ'zɪstənt) *adj* 1 incapable of resisting something, such as a disease; susceptible 2 *history* (esp in 17th-century England) practising passive obedience to royal authority even when its commands were unjust

nonrestrictive (ˌnɒnrɪ'strɪktɪv) *adj* 1 not limiting 2 *grammar* denoting a relative clause that is not restrictive ▷ Cf **restrictive** (sense 2)

non-secure *adj computing* of or relating to a channel of communication, esp on the Internet, that is not restricted to authorized users and is not therefore guaranteed to be private and confidential

nonsense ('nɒnsəns) *n* 1 something that has or makes no sense; unintelligible language; drivel 2 conduct or action that is absurd 3 foolish behaviour: *she'll stand no nonsense* 4 things of little or no value; trash ▷ *interj* 5 an exclamation of disagreement > **nonsensical** (nɒn'sɛnsɪkᵊl) *adj* > **non'sensically** *adv* > **non'sensicalness** *or* **nonˌsensi'cality** *n*

nonsense verse *n* verse in which the sense is nonexistent or absurd

non sequitur ('nɒn 'sɛkwɪtə) *n* 1 a statement having little or no relevance to what preceded it 2 *logic* a conclusion that does not follow from the premises [L, lit.: it does not follow]

nonsmoker (nɒn'sməʊkə) *n* 1 a person who does not smoke 2 a train compartment in which smoking is forbidden > **non'smoking** *adj*

nonspecific urethritis *n* inflammation of the urethra as a result of a sexually transmitted infection that cannot be traced to a specific cause. Abbrev: **NSU**

nonstandard (nɒn'stændəd) *adj* 1 denoting or characterized by idiom, vocabulary, etc, that is not regarded as correct and acceptable by educated native speakers of a language; not standard 2 deviating from a given standard

nonstarter (nɒn'stɑ:tə) *n* 1 a horse that fails to run in a race for which it has been entered 2 a person or thing that has little chance of success

nonstick ('nɒn'stɪk) *adj* (of saucepans, etc) coated with a substance that prevents food sticking to them

nonstop ('nɒn'stɒp) *adj, adv* done without pause or interruption: *a nonstop flight*

nonsuch ('nʌnˌsʌtʃ) *n* a variant spelling of **nonesuch**

nonsuit (nɒn'su:t) *law* ▷ *n* 1 an order of a judge dismissing a suit when the plaintiff fails to show he or she has a good cause of action or fails to produce any evidence ▷ *vb* 2 (*tr*) to order the dismissal of the suit of (a person)

nontechnical (ˌnɒn'tɛknɪkᵊl) *adj* 1 not technical in nature 2 (of a person) not having technical knowledge or aptitude

non troppo ('nɒn 'trɒpəʊ) *adv music* (preceded by a direction, esp a tempo marking) not to be observed too strictly (esp in **allegro ma non troppo, adagio ma non troppo**) [It.]

non-U (nɒn'ju:) *adj Brit inf* (esp of language) not characteristic of or used by the upper class

nonunion (nɒn'ju:njən) *adj* 1 not belonging or related to a trade union: *nonunion workers* 2 not favouring or employing union labour: *a nonunion shop* 3 not produced by union labour

nonvoter (nɒn'vəʊtə) *n* 1 a person who does not vote 2 a person not eligible to vote

nonvoting (nɒn'vəʊtɪŋ) *adj* 1 of or relating to a nonvoter 2 *finance* (of shares, etc) not entitling the holder to vote at company meetings

noodle[1] ('nu:dᵊl) *n* (*often pl*) pasta in the form of ribbons or fine strands [c18 from G *Nudel* from ?]

noodle[2] ('nu:dᵊl) *n* 1 *US & Canad sl* the head 2 a simpleton [c18 ? a blend of NODDLE[1] & NOODLE[1]]

noodling ('nu:dlɪŋ) *n sl* aimless musical improvisation

nook (nʊk) *n* 1 a corner or narrow recess 2 a secluded or sheltered place [c13 from ?]

nooky *or* **nookie** ('nʊkɪ) *n sl* lovemaking

noon (nu:n) *n* **1a** the middle of the day; 12 o'clock **1b** (*as modifier*): *the noon sun* 2 *poetic* the most important part; culmination [OE *nōn*, from L *nōna* (*hōra*) ninth hour (orig. 3 pm, the ninth hour from sunrise)]

noonday ('nu:nˌdeɪ) *n* the middle of the day; noon

no-one *or* **no one** *pron* no person; nobody.

USAGE See at **everyone**

noontime ('nu:nˌtaɪm) *or* **noontide** *n* the middle of the day; noon

Noordbrabant (no:rd'bra:bɑnt) *n* the Dutch name for **North Brabant**

Noordholland (no:rt'hɔlɑnt) *n* the Dutch name for **North Holland**

noose (nu:s) *n* 1 a loop in the end of a rope, such as a lasso or hangman's halter, usually tied with a slipknot 2 something that restrains or traps 3 **put one's head in a noose** to bring about one's own downfall ▷ *vb* **nooses, noosing, noosed** (*tr*) 4 to secure as in a noose 5 to make a noose of or in [c15 ?from Provençal *nous*, from L *nōdus* NODE]

no-par *adj* (of securities) without a par value

nor (nɔ:; *unstressed* nə) *conj* (*coordinating*) 1 (used to join alternatives, the first of which is preceded by *neither*) and not: *neither measles nor mumps* **2** (foll by a verb) (and) not...either: *they weren't talented — nor were they particularly funny* **3** *poetic* neither: *nor wind nor rain* [c13 contraction of OE *nōther*, from *nāhwæther* NEITHER]

noradrenaline (ˌnɔːrəˈdrɛnəlɪn, -ˌliːn) *or* **noradrenalin** *n* a hormone secreted by the adrenal medulla, increasing blood pressure and heart rate. US name: **norepinephrine**

NOR circuit *or* **gate** (nɔː) *n computing* a logic circuit having two or more input wires and one output wire that has a high-voltage output signal only if all input signals are at a low voltage ▷ Cf **AND circuit** [c20 from NOR; the action performed is similar to the operation of the conjunction *nor* in logic]

Nord (*French* nɔr) *n* a department of N France, in Nord-Pas-de-Calais region. Capital: Lille. Pop: 2 555 020 (1999). Area: 5774 sq km (2252 sq miles)

Nordenskjöld (*Swedish* ˈnuːrdənʃœld) *n* Baron **Nils Adolf Erik** (nils ˈɑːdɔlf ˈeːrik) 1832–1901, Swedish Arctic explorer and geologist, born in Finland. He was the first to navigate the Northeast Passage (1878–79)

Nordenskjöld Sea (*Swedish* ˈnuːrdənʃœld) *n* the former name of the **Laptev Sea** [named after Nils Adolf Erik *Nordenskjöld* (1832–1901), Swedish Arctic explorer and geologist]

nordic (ˈnɔːdɪk) *adj skiing* of competitions in cross-country racing and ski-jumping ▷ Cf **alpine** (sense 4)

Nordic (ˈnɔːdɪk) *adj* of or belonging to a subdivision of the Caucasoid race typified by the tall blond blue-eyed long-headed inhabitants of Scandinavia [c19 from F *nordique*, from *nord* NORTH]

Nordkyn Cape (*Norwegian* ˈnuːrçyːn) *n* a cape in N Norway: the northernmost point of the European mainland

Nord-Pas-de-Calais (*French* nɔrpɑdəkalɛ) *n* a region of N France, on the Straits of Dover (the **Pas de Calais**): coal-mining, textile, and metallurgical industries

Nordrhein-Westfalen (ˈnɔrtrainvɛstˈfaːlən) *n* the German name for **North Rhine-Westphalia**

norepinephrine (ˌnɔːrɛpɪˈnɛfrɪn, -riːn) *n* the US name for **noradrenaline**

Norfolk (ˈnɔːfək) *n* **1** a county of E England, on the North Sea and the Wash: low-lying, with large areas of fens in the west and the Broads in the east; rich agriculturally. Administrative centre: Norwich. Pop: 796 733 (2001). Area: 5368 sq km (2072 sq miles) **2** a port in SE Virginia, on the Elizabeth River and Hampton Roads: headquarters of the US Atlantic fleet; shipbuilding. Pop: 234 403 (2000)

Norfolk Island *n* an island in the S Pacific, between New Caledonia and N New Zealand: an Australian external territory; discovered by Captain Cook in 1774; a penal settlement in early years. Pop: 2665 (1993). Area: 36 sq km (14 sq miles)

Norfolk jacket *n* a man's single-breasted belted jacket with one or two chest pockets and a box pleat down the back [c19 worn in NORFOLK for duck shooting]

Norge (ˈnɔrgə) *n* the Norwegian name for **Norway**

noria (ˈnɔːrɪə) *n* a water wheel with buckets attached to its rim for raising water from a stream into irrigation canals, etc [c18 via Sp. from Ar. *nā'ūra*, from *na'ara* to creak]

Noricum (ˈnɒrɪkəm) *n* an Alpine kingdom of the Celts, south of the Danube: comprises present-day central Austria and parts of Bavaria; a Roman province from about 16 BC

nork (nɔːk) *n* (*usually pl*) *Austral sl* a female breast [c20 from ?]

norm (nɔːm) *n* **1** an average level of achievement or performance, as of a group **2** a standard of achievement or behaviour that is required, desired, or designated as normal [c19 from L *norma* carpenter's square]

normal (ˈnɔːməl) *adj* **1** usual; regular; common; typical: *the normal level* **2** constituting a standard: *if we take this as normal* **3** *psychol* **3a** being within certain limits of intelligence, ability, etc **3b** conforming to the conventions of one's group **4** (of laboratory animals) maintained in a natural state for purposes of comparison with animals treated with drugs, etc **5** *chem* (of a solution) containing a number of grams equal to the equivalent weight of the solute in each litre of solvent **6** *geom* another word for **perpendicular** (sense 1) ▷ *n* **7** the usual, average, or typical state, degree, form, etc **8** anything that is normal **9** *geom* a perpendicular line or plane [c16 from L *normālis* conforming to the carpenter's square, from *norma* NORM] > **normality** (nɔːˈmælɪtɪ) *or esp US* ˈ**normalcy** *n*

normal curve *n statistics* a symmetrical bell-shaped curve representing the probability density function of a normal distribution

normal distribution *n statistics* a continuous distribution of a random variable with its mean, median, and mode equal

normalize *or* **normalise** (ˈnɔːməˌlaɪz) *vb* **normalizes, normalizing, normalized** *or* **normalises, normalising, normalised** (*tr*) **1** to bring or make into the normal state **2** to bring into conformity with a standard **3** to heat (steel) above a critical temperature and allow it to cool in air to relieve internal stresses; anneal > ˌ**normaliˈzation** *or* ˌ**normaliˈsation** *n*

normally (ˈnɔːməlɪ) *adv* **1** as a rule; usually; ordinarily **2** in a normal manner

normal time *n sport* the standard length of time allowed for a match before any extra time, such as injury time, is added

Norman[1] (ˈnɔːmən) *n* **1** (in the Middle Ages) a member of the people of Normandy in N France, descended from the 10th-century Scandinavian conquerors of the country and the native French **2** a native or inhabitant of Normandy **3** another name for **Norman French** ▷ *adj* **4** of or characteristic of the Normans, esp the Norman kings of England and the Norman people living in England, or their dialect of French **5** of or characteristic of Normandy **6** denoting or having the style of Romanesque architecture used in Britain from the Norman Conquest until the 12th century, characterized by the rounded arch, massive masonry walls, etc

▷ www.bbc.co.uk/history/war/normans/index.shtml
▷ www.spartacus.schoolnet.co.uk/Normans.htm

Norman[2] (ˈnɔːmən) *n* **1 Greg** born 1955, Australian golfer **2 Jessye** (ˈdʒɛsɪ) born 1945, US soprano

Norman Conquest *n* the invasion and settlement of England by the Normans, following the Battle of Hastings (1066)

Normandy (ˈnɔːməndɪ) *n* a former province of N France, on the English Channel: settled by Vikings under Rollo in the 10th century; scene of the Allied landings in 1944. Chief town: Rouen. French name: **Normandie** (nɔrmɑ̃di)

Norman French *n* the medieval Norman and English dialect of Old French

normative (ˈnɔːmətɪv) *adj* **1** implying, creating, or prescribing a norm or standard, as in language: *normative grammar* **2** expressing value judgments as contrasted with stating facts

Norn[1] (nɔːn) *n Norse myth* any of the three virgin goddesses of fate [c18 ON]

Norn[2] (nɔːn) *n* the medieval Norse language of the Orkneys, Shetlands, and parts of N Scotland [c17 from ON *norr*]*na* Norwegian, from *northr* north]

Norodom Sihanouk (ˌnɒrəˈdɒm ˈsiːənʊk) *n* See (Norodom) **Sihanouk**

Norrington (ˈnɒrɪŋtən) *n* Sir **Roger** (**Arthur Carver**) born 1934, British conductor; noted for period performances of early music

Nn

Norrköping (*Swedish* 'nɔrcøːpiŋ) *n* a port in SE Sweden, near the Baltic. Pop: 122 212 (2000 est)

Norse (nɔːs) *adj* **1** of ancient and medieval Scandinavia or its inhabitants **2** of or characteristic of Norway ▷ *n* **3a** the N group of Germanic languages, spoken in Scandinavia **3b** any one of these languages, esp in their ancient or medieval forms **4 the Norse** (*functioning as pl*) **4a** the Norwegians **4b** the Vikings

Norseman ('nɔːsmən) *n, pl* **Norsemen** another name for a **Viking**

north (nɔːθ) *n* **1** one of the four cardinal points of the compass, at 0° or 360°, that is 90° from east and west and 180° from south **2** the direction along a meridian towards the North Pole **3** the direction in which a compass needle points; magnetic north **4 the north** (*often cap*) any area lying in or towards the north **5** (*usually cap*) *Cards.* the player or position at the table corresponding to north on the compass ▷ *adj* **6** in, towards, or facing the north **7** (esp of the wind) from the north ▷ *adv* **8** in, to, or towards the north [OE] (nɔːθ) *n* **the 1** the northern area of England, generally regarded as reaching the southern boundaries of Yorkshire, Derbyshire, and Cheshire **2** (in the US) the states north of the Mason-Dixon Line that were known as the Free States during the Civil War **3** the northern part of North America, esp Alaska, the Yukon, Nunavut, and the Northwest Territories **4** the countries of the world that are economically and technically advanced ▷ *adj* **5** of or denoting the northern part of a specified country, area, etc

North[1] (nɔːθ) *n* **the 1** the northern area of England, generally regarded as reaching the southern boundaries of Yorkshire, Derbyshire, and Cheshire **2** (in the US) the states north of the Mason-Dixon Line that were known as the Free States during the Civil War **3** the northern part of North America, esp Alaska, the Yukon, Nunavut, and the Northwest Territories **4** the countries of the world that are economically and technically advanced ▷ *adj* **5** of or denoting the northern part of a specified country, area, etc

North[2] (nɔːθ) *n* **1 Frederick,** 2nd Earl of Guildford, called *Lord North.* 1732–92, British statesman; prime minister (1770–82), dominated by George III. He was held responsible for the loss of the American colonies **2 Sir Thomas** ?1535–?1601, English translator of Plutarch's *Lives* (1579), which was the chief source of Shakespeare's Roman plays

North Africa *n* the part of Africa between the Mediterranean and the Sahara: consists chiefly of Morocco, Algeria, Tunisia, Libya, and N Egypt > **North African** *adj, n*

Northallerton (nɔː'θælətᵊn) *n* a market town in N England, administrative centre of North Yorkshire. Pop: 13 774 (1991)

North America *n* the third largest continent, linked with South America by the Isthmus of Panama and bordering on the Arctic Ocean, the N Pacific, the N Atlantic, the Gulf of Mexico, and the Caribbean. It consists generally of a great mountain system (the Western Cordillera) extending along the entire W coast, actively volcanic in the extreme north and south, with the Great Plains to the east and the Appalachians still further east, separated from the Canadian Shield by an arc of large lakes (Great Bear, Great Slave, Winnipeg, Superior, Michigan, Huron, Erie, Ontario); reaches its greatest height of 6194 m (20 320 ft) in Mount McKinley, Alaska, and its lowest point of 85 m (280 ft) below sea level in Death Valley, California, and ranges from snowfields, tundra, and taiga in the north to deserts in the southwest and tropical forests in the extreme south. Pop: 421 006 000 (1996 est). Area: over 24 000 000 sq km (9 500 000 sq miles) > **North American** *adj, n*

North American Free Trade Agreement *n* an international trade agreement between the United States, Canada, and Mexico. Abbreviation: **NAFTA**

Northampton (nɔː'θæmptən, nɔːθ'hæmp-) *n* **1** a town in central England, administrative centre of Northamptonshire, on the River Nene: footwear and engineering industries. Pop: 179 596 (1991) **2** short for **Northamptonshire**

Northamptonshire (nɔː'θæmptənʃɪə, -ʃə, nɔːθ'hæmp-) *n* a county of central England: agriculture, food processing, engineering, and footwear industries. Administrative centre: Northampton. Pop: 629 676 (2001). Area: 2367 sq km (914 sq miles). Abbreviation: **Northants**

Northants (nɔː'θænts) *abbrev for* Northamptonshire

North Atlantic Drift *or* **Current** *n* the warm ocean current flowing northeast, under the influence of prevailing winds, from the Gulf of Mexico towards NW Europe and warming its climate. Also called: **Gulf Stream**

North Atlantic Treaty Organization *n* See **Nato**

North Ayrshire ('ɛəʃɪə, -ʃə) *n* a council area of W central Scotland, on the Firth of Clyde: comprises the N part of the historical county of Ayrshire, including the Isle of Arran; formerly part of Strathclyde Region (1975–96): chiefly agricultural, with fishing and tourism. Administrative centre: Irvine. Pop: 135 817 (2001). Area: 884 sq km (341 sq miles)

North Borneo *n* the former name (until 1963) of **Sabah**

northbound ('nɔːθˌbaʊnd) *adj* going or leading towards the north

North Brabant *n* a province of the S Netherlands: formed part of the medieval duchy of Brabant. Capital: 's Hertogenbosch. Pop: 2 356 000 (2000 est). Area: 4965 sq km (1917 sq miles). Dutch name: **Noordbrabant**

north by east *n* one point on the compass east of north

north by west *n* one point on the compass west of north

North Cape *n* **1** a cape on N Magerøy Island, in the Arctic Ocean off the N coast of Norway **2** a cape on N North Island, New Zealand

North Carolina *n* a state of the southeastern US, on the Atlantic: consists of a coastal plain rising to the Piedmont Plateau and the Appalachian Mountains in the west. Capital: Raleigh. Pop: 8 049 313 (2000). Area: 126 387 sq km (48 798 sq miles). Abbreviations: **N.C.** or (with zip code) **NC** > **North Carolinian** *adj, n*

North Channel *n* a strait between NE Ireland and SW Scotland, linking the North Atlantic with the Irish Sea

Northcliffe ('nɔːθklɪf) *n* **Viscount** title of *Alfred Charles William Harmsworth.* 1865–1922, British newspaper proprietor. With his brother, 1st Viscount Rothermere, he built up a vast chain of newspapers. He founded the *Daily Mail* (1896), the *Daily Mirror* (1903), and acquired *The Times* (1908)

North Country *n* (usually preceded by *the*) **1** another name for **North**[1] (sense 1) **2** another name for **North**[1] (sense 3)

Northd *abbrev for* Northumberland

North Dakota *n* a state of the western US: mostly undulating prairies and plains, rising from the Red River valley in the east to the Missouri plateau in the west, with the infertile Bad Lands in the extreme west. Capital: Bismarck. Pop: 642 200 (2000). Area: 183 019 sq km (70 664 sq miles). Abbreviations: **N.Dak, N.D.**, or (with zip code) **ND** > **North Dakotan** *adj, n*

North Down *n* a district of E Northern Ireland, in Co. Down. Pop: 76 323 (1991). Area: 82 sq km (32 sq miles)

northeast (ˌnɔːθ'iːst; *naut* ˌnɔːr'iːst) *n* **1** the point of the compass or direction midway between north and east **2** (*often cap; usually preceded by the*) any area lying in or towards this direction ▷ *adj also* **northeastern** **3** (*sometimes cap*) of or denoting the northeastern part of a specified country, area, etc: *northeast Lincolnshire* **4** in, towards, or facing the northeast **5** (esp of the wind) from the northeast ▷ *adv* **6** in, to, or towards the northeast > ˌ**north'easternmost** *adj*

Northeast (ˌnɔːθ'iːst) *n* (usually preceded by *the*) the northeastern part of England, esp Northumberland, Durham, and the Tyneside area

northeast by east *n* one point on the compass east of northeast

northeast by north *n* one point on the compass north of northeast

northeaster (ˌnɔːθ'iːstə; *naut* ˌnɔːr'iːstə) *n* a strong wind or storm from the northeast

northeasterly (ˌnɔːθ'iːstəlɪ; *naut* ˌnɔːr'iːstəlɪ) *adj, adv* **1** in, towards, or (esp of a wind) from the northeast ▷ *n, pl* **northeasterlies 2** a wind or storm from the northeast

North East Frontier Agency *n* the former name (until 1972) of **Arunachal Pradesh**

North East Lincolnshire *n* a unitary authority in NE England, in Lincolnshire: formerly (1974–96) part of the county of Humberside. Pop: 157 983 (2001). Area: 192 sq km (74 sq miles)

Northeast Passage *n* a shipping route along the Arctic coasts of Europe and Asia, between the Atlantic and Pacific: first navigated by Nordenskjöld (1878–79)

northeastward (ˌnɔːθ'iːstwəd; *naut* ˌnɔːr'iːstwəd) *adj* **1** towards or (esp of a wind) from the northeast ▷ *n* **2** a direction towards or area in the northeast > ˌ**north'eastwardly** *adj, adv*

norther ('nɔːðə) *n chiefly southern US* a wind or storm from the north

northerly ('nɔːðəlɪ) *adj* **1** of or situated in the north ▷ *adv, adj* **2** towards the north **3** from the north: *a northerly wind* ▷ *n, pl* **northerlies 4** a wind from the north > '**northerliness** *n*

northern ('nɔːðən) *adj* **1** in or towards the north **2** (esp of winds) proceeding from the north **3** (*sometimes cap*) of or characteristic of the north or North

Northern Cape *n* the largest but least populated province in South Africa, in the NW part of the country; created in 1994 from part of Cape Province: agriculture, mining (esp diamonds). Capital: Kimberley. Pop: 875 222 (1999 est). Area: 139 703 sq km (361 830 sq miles)
▷ www.northern-cape.gov.za
▷ www.northerncape.org.za

Northern Dvina *n* See **Dvina** (sense 1)

Northerner ('nɔːðənə) *n* (*sometimes not cap*) a native or inhabitant of the north of any specified region, esp England, the US, or the far north of Canada

northern hemisphere *n* (*often caps.*) that half of the globe lying north of the equator

Northern Ireland *n* that part of the United Kingdom occupying the NE part of Ireland: separated from the rest of Ireland, which became independent in law in 1920; it remained part of the United Kingdom, with a separate Parliament (Stormont), inaugurated in 1921, and limited self-government: scene of severe conflict between Catholics and Protestants, including terrorist bombing from 1969: direct administration from Westminster from 1972: assembly and power-sharing executive established in 1998–99 following the Good Friday Agreement of 1998. Capital: Belfast. Pop: 1 685 267 (2001). Area: 14 121 sq km (5452 sq miles)
▷ www.nio.gov.uk
▷ www.discovernorthernireland.com

Northern Isles *pl n* the Orkneys and Shetland

northern lights *pl n* another name for **aurora borealis**

northernmost ('nɔːðənˌməʊst) *adj* situated or occurring farthest north

Northern Province *n* the former name for **Limpopo** (sense 1)

Northern Rhodesia *n* the former name (until 1964) of **Zambia**

Northern Territories *pl n* a former British protectorate in W Africa, established in 1897; attached to the Gold Coast in 1901; now constitutes the Northern Region of Ghana (since 1957)

Northern Territory *n* an administrative division of N central Australia, on the Timor and Arafura Seas: includes Ashmore and Cartier Islands; the Arunta Desert lies in the east, the Macdonnell Ranges in the south, and Arnhem Land in the north (containing Australia's largest Aboriginal reservation). Capital: Darwin. Pop: 192 880 (1999 est). Area: 1 347 525 sq km (520 280 sq miles)
▷ www.nt.gov.au
▷ www.nttc.com.au

North Holland *n* a province of the NW Netherlands, on the peninsula between the North Sea and IJsselmeer: includes the West Frisian Island of Texel. Capital: Haarlem. Pop: 2 518 400 (2000 est). Area: 2663 sq km (1029 sq miles). Dutch name: **Noordholland**

northing ('nɔːθɪŋ, -ðɪŋ) *n* **1** *navigation* movement or distance covered in a northerly direction, esp as expressed in the resulting difference in latitude **2** *astron* a north or positive declination

North Island *n* the northernmost of the two main islands of New Zealand. Pop: 2 849 724 (2001). Area: 114 729 sq km (44 297 sq miles)

North Korea *n* a republic in NE Asia, on the Sea of Japan and the Yellow Sea: established in 1948 as a people's republic; mostly rugged and mountainous, with fertile lowlands in the west. Language: Korean. Currency: won. Capital: Pyongyang. Pop: 21 968 000 (2001 est). Area: 122 313 sq km (47 225 sq miles). Official name: **Democratic People's Republic of Korea** Korean name: **Chosŏn** > **North Korean** *adj, n*
▷ www.korea-dpr.com

North Lanarkshire ('lænəkʃɪə, -ʃə) *n* a council area of central Scotland: consists mainly of the NE part of the historical county of Lanarkshire; formerly (1974–96) part of Strathclyde Region: engineering and metalworking industries. Administrative centre: Motherwell. Pop: 321 067 (2001). Area: 1771 sq km (684 sq miles)

Northland ('nɔːθlənd) *n* **1** the peninsula containing Norway and Sweden **2** (in Canada) the far north > '**Northlander** *n*
▷ www.nrc.govt.nz
▷ www.northland-nz.worldweb.com

North Lincolnshire *n* a unitary authority of NE England, in Lincolnshire: formerly (1975–96) part of the county of Humberside. Pop: 152 839 (2001). Area: 1497 sq km (578 sq miles)

Northman ('nɔːθmən) *n, pl* **Northmen** another name for a **Viking**

north-northeast *n* **1** the point on the compass or the direction midway between north and northeast ▷ *adj, adv* **2** in, from, or towards this direction

north-northwest *n* **1** the point on the compass or the direction midway between northwest and north ▷ *adj, adv* **2** in, from, or towards this direction

North Ossetian Republic (ə'siːʃən) *n* a constituent republic of S Russia, on the N slopes of the central Caucasus Mountains. Capital: Vladikavkaz. Pop: 674 000 (2000 est). Area: about 8000 sq km (3088 sq miles). Also called: **North Ossetia, Alania**

North Pole *n* **1** the northernmost point on the earth's axis, at a latitude of 90°N **2** Also called: **north celestial pole** *astron* the point of intersection of the earth's extended axis and the northern half of the celestial sphere **3** (*usually not cap*) the pole of a freely suspended magnet, which is attracted to the earth's magnetic North Pole

North Rhine-Westphalia *n* a state of W Germany: formed in 1946 by the amalgamation of the Prussian province of Westphalia with the N part of the Prussian Rhine province and later with the state of Lippe; part of

Nn

West Germany until 1990: highly industrialized. Capital: Düsseldorf. Pop: 17 999 000 (2000 est). Area: 34 039 sq km (13 142 sq miles). German name: **Nordrhein-Westfalen**

North Riding *n* (until 1974) an administrative division of Yorkshire, now constituting most of North Yorkshire

North Saskatchewan *n* a river in W Canada, rising in W Alberta and flowing northeast, east, and southeast to join the South Saskatchewan River and form the Saskatchewan River. Length: 1223 km (760 miles)

North Sea *n* an arm of the Atlantic between Great Britain and the N European mainland. Area: about 569 800 sq km (220 000 sq miles). Former name: **German Ocean**

North-Sea gas *n* (in Britain) natural gas obtained from deposits below the North Sea

North Somerset *n* a unitary authority of SW England, in Somerset: formerly (1974–96) part of the county of Avon. Pop: 188 556 (2001). Area: 375 sq km (145 sq miles)

North Star *n* **the** another name for **Polaris**

North Tyneside ('taɪnsaɪd) *n* a unitary authority of NE England, in Tyne and Wear. Pop: 191 663 (2001). Area: 84 sq km (32 sq miles)

Northumberland[1] (nɔː'θʌmbələnd) *n* the northernmost county of England, on the North Sea: hilly in the north (the Cheviots) and west (the Pennines), with many Roman remains, notably Hadrian's Wall; shipbuilding, coal mining. Administrative centre: Morpeth. Pop: 307 186 (2001). Area: 5032 sq km (1943 sq miles). Abbreviation: **Northd**

Northumberland[2] (nɔː'θʌmbələnd) *n* **1st Duke of,** title of *John Dudley*. 1502–53, English statesman and soldier, who governed England (1549–53) during the minority of Edward VI. His attempt (1553) to gain the throne for his daughter-in-law, Lady Jane Grey, led to his execution

Northumbria (nɔː'θʌmbrɪə) *n* **1** (in Anglo-Saxon Britain) a region that stretched from the Humber to the Firth of Forth: formed in the 7th century AD, it became an important intellectual centre; a separate kingdom until 876 AD **2** an area of NE England roughly corresponding to the Anglo-Saxon region of Northumbria > **Nor'thumbrian** *adj*

North Vietnam *n* a region of N Vietnam, on the Gulf of Tonkin: an independent Communist state from 1954 until 1976. Area: 164 061 sq km (63 344 sq miles)

northward ('nɔːθwəd; *naut* 'nɔːðəd) *adj* **1** moving, facing, or situated towards the north ▷ *n* **2** the northward part, direction, etc; the north ▷ *adv also* **northwards** **3** towards the north

northwest (ˌnɔːθ'wɛst; *naut* ˌnɔː'wɛst) *n* **1** the point of the compass or direction midway between north and west **2** (*often cap;* usually preceded by *the*) any area lying in or towards this direction ▷ *adj also* **northwestern** **3** (*sometimes cap*) of or denoting the northwestern part of a specified country, area, etc: *northwest Greenland* ▷ *adj, adv* **4** in, to, or towards the northwest > ˌ**north'westernmost** *adj*

Northwest (ˌnɔːθ'wɛst) *n* (usually preceded by *the*) the northwestern part of England, esp Merseyside, Greater Manchester, Lancashire, and the Lake District

North West *n* a province of South Africa incorporating part of the former Transvaal. Capital: Mafikeng. Pop: 3 354 825 (1996). Area: 116 320 sq km (44 911 sq miles)
▷ www.nwpg.gov.za
▷ www.tourismnorthwest.co.za

northwest by north *n* one point on the compass north of northwest

northwest by west *n* one point on the compass south of northwest

northwester (ˌnɔːθ'wɛstə; *naut* ˌnɔː'wɛstə) *n* a strong wind or storm from the northwest

northwesterly (ˌnɔːθ'wɛstəlɪ; *naut* ˌnɔː'wɛstəlɪ) *adj, adv* **1** in, towards, or (esp of a wind) from the northwest ▷ *n, pl* **northwesterlies** **2** a wind or storm from the northwest

North-West Frontier Province *n* a province in N Pakistan between Afghanistan and Jammu and Kashmir: part of British India from 1901 until 1947; of strategic importance, esp for the Khyber Pass. Capital: Peshawar. Pop: 17 555 000 (1998 est). Area: 74 522 sq km (28 773 sq miles)

Northwest Passage *n* the passage by sea from the Atlantic to the Pacific along the N coast of America: attempted for over 300 years by Europeans seeking a short route to the Far East, before being successfully navigated by Amundsen (1903–06)

Northwest Territories *pl n* a territory of NW Canada including part of Victoria Island and several other islands of the Arctic; comprised over a third of Canada's total area until Nunavut became a separate territory in 1999: rich mineral resources. Pop: 41 800 (1999 est). Area: 2 082 910 sq km (804 003 sq miles). Abbreviation: **NWT**
▷ www.gov.nt.com
▷ www.nwttravel.nt.ca

Northwest Territory *n* See **Old Northwest**

northwestward (ˌnɔːθ'wɛstwəd; *naut* ˌnɔː'wɛstwəd) *adj* **1** towards or (esp of a wind) from the northwest ▷ *n* **2** a direction towards or area in the northwest > ˌ**north'westwardly** *adj, adv*

Northwich ('nɔːθwɪtʃ) *n* a town in NW England, in Cheshire. Pop: 34 520 (1991)

North Yemen *n* a former republic in SW Arabia, on the Red Sea; now part of Yemen: declared a republic in 1962: united with South Yemen in 1990. Official name: **Yemen Arab Republic** See also **Yemen, South Yemen**

North Yorkshire *n* a county in N England, formed in 1974 from most of the North Riding of Yorkshire and parts of the East and West Ridings: the geographical and ceremonial county includes the unitary authorities of Middlesbrough, Redcar, and Cleveland, and part of Stockton-on-Tees (all within Cleveland until 1996), and York (created in 1997). Administrative centre: Northallerton. Pop (excluding unitary authorities): 569 660 (2001). Area (excluding unitary authorities): 8037 sq km (3102 sq miles)

Norton ('nɔːtᵊn) *n* **Graham**, real name *Graham Walker*. born 1963, Irish comedian noted for his camp humour

Norw. *abbrev for:* **1** Norway **2** Norwegian

Norway ('nɔːˌweɪ) *n* a kingdom in NW Europe, occupying the W part of the Scandinavian peninsula: first united in the Viking age (800–1050); under the rule of Denmark (1523–1814) and Sweden (1814–1905); became an independent monarchy in 1905. Its coastline is deeply indented by fjords and fringed with islands, rising inland to plateaus and mountains. Norway has a large fishing fleet and its merchant navy is among the world's largest. Official language: Norwegian. Official religion: Evangelical Lutheran. Currency: krone. Capital: Oslo. Pop: 4 516 000 (2001 est). Area: 323 878 sq km (125 050 sq miles). Norwegian name: **Norge**
▷ www.odin.dep.no/smk/engelsk/regjeringen/index-b-n-a.html
▷ www.visitnorway.com

Norway lobster *n* a European lobster fished for food

Norway maple *n* a large Eurasian maple tree

Norway spruce *n* a European spruce tree having drooping branches and dark green needle-like leaves

Norwegian (nɔː'wiːdʒən) *adj* **1** of or characteristic of Norway, its language, or its people ▷ *n* **2** any of the various North Germanic languages of Norway **3** a native or inhabitant of Norway

Norwegian Sea *n* part of the Arctic Ocean between Greenland and Norway

Norwich ('nɒrɪdʒ) *n* a city in E England, administrative centre of Norfolk: cathedral (founded 1096); University of East Anglia (1963); traditionally a centre of the footwear industry, now has engineering, financial services. Pop: 171 304 (1991)

Nos. *or* **nos.** *abbrev for* numbers

nose (nəʊz) *n* **1** the organ of smell and entrance to the respiratory tract, consisting of a prominent structure divided into two hair-lined air passages. Related adj: **nasal 2** the sense of smell itself: in animals, the ability to follow trails by scent (esp in **a good nose**) **3** the scent, aroma, bouquet of something, esp wine **4** instinctive skill in discovering things (sometimes in **follow one's nose**): *he had a nose for good news stories* **5** any part resembling a nose in form or function, such as a nozzle or spout **6** the forward part of a vehicle, aircraft, etc **7** narrow margin of victory (in (**win**) **by a nose**) **8 cut off one's nose to spite one's face** to carry out a vengeful action that hurts oneself more than another **9 get up** (**someone's**) **nose** *inf* to annoy or irritate (someone) **10 keep one's nose clean** to stay out of trouble **11 lead by the nose** to make (someone) do unquestioningly all one wishes; dominate **12 look down one's nose at** *inf* to be disdainful of **13 nose to tail** (of vehicles) moving or standing very close behind one another **14 on the nose** *sl* **14a** (in horse-race betting) to win only: *I bet twenty pounds on the nose on that horse* **14b** *chiefly US & Canad* precisely; exactly **14c** *Austral* bad or bad-smelling **15 pay through the nose** *inf* to pay an exorbitant price **16 put someone's nose out of joint** *inf* to thwart or offend someone **17 rub someone's nose in it** *inf* to remind someone unkindly of a failing or error **18 turn up one's nose** (**at**) *inf* to behave disdainfully (towards) **19 with one's nose in the air** haughtily ▷ *vb* **noses, nosing, nosed 20** (*tr*) (esp of horses, dogs, etc) to rub, touch, or sniff with the nose; nuzzle **21** to smell or sniff (wine, etc) **22** (*intr*; usually foll by *after* or *for*) to search (for) by or as if by scent **23** to move or cause to move forwards slowly and carefully: *we nosed the car into the garage* **24** (*intr*; foll by *into, around, about*, etc) to pry or snoop (into) or meddle (in) [OE *nosu*] > '**noseless** *adj* > '**nose,like** *adj*

nosebag ('nəʊz,bæg) *n* a bag, fastened around the head of a horse and covering the nose, in which feed is placed

noseband ('nəʊz,bænd) *n* the detachable part of a horse's bridle that goes around the nose

nosebleed ('nəʊz,bli:d) *n* bleeding from the nose as the result of injury, etc

nose cone *n* the conical forward section of a missile, spacecraft, etc, designed to withstand high temperatures, esp during re-entry into the earth's atmosphere

nose dive *n* **1** a sudden plunge with the nose or front pointing downwards, esp of an aircraft **2** *inf* a sudden drop or sharp decline: *prices took a nose dive* ▷ *vb* **nose-dive, nose-dives, nose-diving, nose-dived** (*intr*) **3** to perform a nose dive

nose flute *n* (esp in the South Sea Islands) a type of flute blown through the nose

nosegay ('nəʊz,geɪ) *n* a small bunch of flowers; posy [C15 from NOSE + *gay* (arch) toy]

nose job *n sl* a surgical remodelling of the nose for cosmetic reasons

nosepiece ('nəʊz,pi:s) *n* **1** a piece of armour to protect the nose **2** the connecting part of a pair of spectacles that rests on the nose; bridge **3** the part of a microscope to which one or more objective lenses are attached **4** a less common word for **noseband**

nose rag *n sl* a handkerchief

nose ring *n* a ring fixed through the nose, as for leading a bull

nose wheel *n* a wheel fitted to the forward end of a vehicle, esp the landing wheel under the nose of an aircraft

nosey ('nəʊzɪ) *adj* a variant spelling of **nosy**

nosh (nɒʃ) *sl* ▷ *n* **1** food or a meal ▷ *vb* **2** to eat [C20 from Yiddish; cf. G *naschen* to nibble]

no-show *n* a person who fails to take up a reserved seat, place, etc, without having cancelled it

nosh-up *n Brit sl* a large and satisfying meal

no-side *n rugby* the end of a match, signalled by the referee's whistle

nosocomial (,nɒsə'kəʊmɪəl) *adj* of or denoting an infection that originates in a hospital [C19 from Gk *nosokomos* one that tends the sick, from *nosos* disease + *komein* to tend]

nosology (nɒ'sɒlədʒɪ) *n* the branch of medicine concerned with the classification of diseases [C18 from Gk *nosos* disease] > **nosological** (,nɒsə'lɒdʒɪkᵊl) *adj*

nostalgia (nɒ'stældʒə, -dʒɪə) *n* **1** a yearning for past circumstances, events, etc **2** the evocation of this emotion, as in a book, film, etc **3** homesickness [C18 NL, from Gk *nostos* a return home + -ALGIA] > **nos'talgic** *adj* > **nos'talgically** *adv*

nostoc ('nɒstɒk) *n* a gelatinous cyanobacterium occurring in moist places [C17 NL, coined by Paracelsus (1493–1541), Swiss physician]

Nostradamus (,nɒstrə'dɑ:məs) *n* Latinized name of *Michel de Notredame*. 1503–66, French physician and astrologer; author of a book of prophecies in rhymed quatrains, *Centuries* (1555)

nostril ('nɒstrɪl) *n* either of the two external openings of the nose. See **nares** [OE *nosthyrl*, from *nosu* NOSE + *thyrel* hole]

nostro account ('nɒstrəʊ) *n* a bank account conducted by a British bank with a foreign bank, usually in the foreign currency ▷ Cf **vostro account**

nostrum ('nɒstrəm) *n* **1** a patent or quack medicine **2** a favourite remedy [C17 from L: our own (make), from *noster* our]

nosy *or* **nosey** ('nəʊzɪ) *adj* **nosier, nosiest** *inf* prying or inquisitive > '**nosily** *adv* > '**nosiness** *n*

nosy parker *n inf* a prying person [C20 arbitrary use of surname *Parker*]

Nn

not (nɒt) *adv* **1a** used to negate the sentence, phrase, or word that it modifies: *I will not stand for it* **1b** (*in combination*): *they cannot go* **2 not that** (*conj*) Also (arch): **not but what** which is not to say or suppose that: *I expect to lose the game — not that I mind* ▷ *sentence substitute* **3** used to indicate denial or refusal: *certainly not* [C14 *not*, var. of *nought* nothing, from OE *nāwiht*, from *nā* no + *wiht* creature, thing]

nota bene *Latin* ('nəʊtə 'bi:nɪ) note well; take note. Abbrevs.: **NB, N.B., nb, n.b.**

notability (,nəʊtə'bɪlɪtɪ) *n, pl* **notabilities 1** the quality of being notable **2** a distinguished person

notable ('nəʊtəbᵊl) *adj* **1** worthy of being noted or remembered; remarkable; distinguished ▷ *n* **2** a notable person [C14 via OF from L *notābilis*, from *notāre* to NOTE] > '**notably** *adv*

notarize *or* **notarise** ('nəʊtə,raɪz) *vb* **notarizes, notarizing, notarized** *or* **notarises, notarising, notarised** (*tr*) US to attest to (a document, etc), as a notary

notary ('nəʊtərɪ) *n, pl* **notaries 1** a notary public **2** (formerly) a clerk licensed to prepare legal documents **3** *arch* a clerk or secretary [C14 from L *notārius* clerk, from *nota* a mark, note] > **notarial** (nəʊ'tɛərɪəl) *adj* > '**notaryship** *n*

notary public *n, pl* **notaries public** a public official, usually a solicitor, who is legally authorized to administer oaths, attest and certify certain documents, etc

notation (nəʊ'teɪʃən) *n* **1** any series of signs or symbols used to represent quantities or elements in a specialized system, such as music or mathematics **2** the act or process of notating **3** a note or record [C16 from L *notātiō*, from *notāre* to NOTE] > **no'tational** *adj*

notch (nɒtʃ) *n* **1** a V-shaped cut or indentation; nick **2** a nick made in a tally stick **3** *US & Canad* a narrow gorge **4** *inf* a step or level (esp in **a notch above**) ▷ *vb* (*tr*) **5** to cut or make a notch in **6** to record with or as if with a notch **7** (usually foll by *up*) *inf* to score or achieve: *the team notched up its fourth win* [C16 from incorrect division of *an otch* (as *a notch*), from OF *oche* notch, from L *obsecāre*, from *secāre* to cut]

NOT circuit *or* **gate** (nɒt) *n computing* a logic circuit that has a high-voltage output signal if the input signal is low, and vice versa: used extensively in computing. Also called: **inverter, negator** [C20 the action performed on electrical signals is similar to the operation of *not* in logical constructions]

note (nəʊt) *n* **1** a brief record in writing, esp a jotting for future reference **2** a brief informal letter **3** a formal written communication, esp from one government to another **4** a short written statement giving any kind of information **5** a critical comment, explanatory statement, or reference in a book **6** short for **banknote** **7** a characteristic atmosphere: *a note of sarcasm* **8** a distinctive vocal sound, as of a species of bird or animal **9** any of a series of graphic signs representing the pitch and duration of a musical sound **10** Also called (esp US and Canad): **tone** a musical sound of definite fundamental frequency or pitch **11** a key on a piano, organ, etc **12** a sound used as a signal or warning: *the note to retreat was sounded* **13** short for **promissory note** **14** *arch or poetic* a melody **15 of note 15a** distinguished or famous **15b** important: *nothing of note* **16 strike the right** (*or* **a false**) **note** to behave appropriately (or inappropriately) **17 take note** (often foll by *of*) to pay attention (to) ▷ *vb* **notes, noting, noted** (*tr; may take a clause as object*) **18** to notice; perceive **19** to pay close attention to: *they noted every movement* **20** to make a written note of: *she noted the date in her diary* **21** to remark upon: *I note that you do not wear shoes* **22** to write down (music, a melody, etc) in notes **23** to take (an unpaid or dishonoured bill of exchange) to a notary public to re-present the bill and if it is still unaccepted or unpaid to note the circumstances in a register. See **protest** (sense 9) **24** a less common word for **annotate** [C13 via OF from L *nota* sign] > **'noteless** *adj*

notebook ('nəʊt,bʊk) *n* a book for recording notes or memoranda

notebook computer *n* a portable computer smaller than a laptop model, often approximately the size of a sheet of A4 paper

notecase ('nəʊt,keɪs) *n* a less common word for **wallet** (sense 1)

noted ('nəʊtɪd) *adj* **1** celebrated; famous **2** of special significance; noticeable > **'notedly** *adv*

notelet ('nəʊtlɪt) *n* a folded card with a printed design on the front, for writing a short letter

notepaper ('nəʊt,peɪpə) *n* paper for writing letters; writing paper

noteworthy ('nəʊt,wɜːðɪ) *adj* worthy of notice; notable > **'note,worthiness** *n*

nothing ('nʌθɪŋ) *pron* **1** (*indefinite*) no thing; not anything: *I can give you nothing* **2** no part or share: *to have nothing to do with this crime* **3** a matter of no importance: *it doesn't matter, it's nothing* **4** indicating the absence of anything perceptible; nothingness **5** indicating the absence of meaning, value, worth, etc: *to amount to nothing* **6** zero quantity; nought **7 be nothing to 7a** not to concern or be significant to (someone) **7b** to be not nearly as good, etc, as **8 have** *or* **be nothing to do with** to have no connection with **9 nothing but** not something other than; only **10 nothing doing** *inf* an expression of dismissal, refusal, etc **11 nothing if not** at the very least; certainly **12 nothing less than** *or* **nothing short of** downright; truly **13 there's nothing to it** it is very simple, easy, etc **14 think nothing of 14a** to regard as easy or natural **14b** to have no compunction about **14c** to have a very low opinion of ▷ *adv* **15** in no way; not at all: *he looked nothing like his brother* ▷ *n* **16** *inf* a person or thing of no importance or significance **17 sweet nothings** words of endearment or affection [OE *nāthing*, *nān thing*, from *nān* NONE[1] + THING]

nothingness ('nʌθɪŋnɪs) *n* **1** the state of being nothing; nonexistence **2** absence of consciousness or life **3** complete insignificance **4** something that is worthless

notice ('nəʊtɪs) *n* **1** observation; attention: *to escape notice* **2 take notice** to pay attention **3 take no notice of** to ignore or disregard **4** a warning; announcement **5** a displayed placard or announcement giving information **6** advance notification of intention to end an arrangement, contract, etc, as of employment (esp in **give notice**) **7 at short notice** with notification only a little in advance **8** *chiefly Brit* dismissal from employment **9** favourable, interested, or polite attention: *she was beneath his notice* **10** a theatrical or literary review: *the play received very good notices* ▷ *vb* **notices, noticing, noticed 11** to become aware (of); perceive; note **12** (*tr*) to point out or remark upon **13** (*tr*) to pay polite or interested attention to **14** (*tr*) to acknowledge (an acquaintance, etc) [C15 via OF from L *notitia* fame, from *nōtus* known]

noticeable ('nəʊtɪsəb^{ə}l) *adj* easily seen or detected; perceptible > **'noticeably** *adv*

notice board *n* a board on which notices, advertisements, bulletins, etc, are displayed. US and Canad name: **bulletin board**

notifiable ('nəʊtɪ,faɪəb^{ə}l) *adj* **1** denoting certain infectious diseases of humans, such as tuberculosis, outbreaks of which must be reported to the public health authorities **2** denoting certain infectious diseases of animals, such as BSE and rabies, outbreaks of which must be reported to the appropriate veterinary authority

notification (,nəʊtɪfɪ'keɪʃən) *n* **1** the act of notifying **2** a formal announcement **3** something that notifies; a notice

notify ('nəʊtɪ,faɪ) *vb* **notifies, notifying, notified** (*tr*) **1** to tell **2** *chiefly Brit* to make known; announce [C14 from OF *notifier*, from L *notificāre*, from *nōtus* known + *facere* to make] > **'noti,fier** *n*

notion ('nəʊʃən) *n* **1** a vague idea; impression **2** an idea, concept, or opinion **3** an inclination or whim ▷ See also **notions** [C16 from L *nōtiō* a becoming acquainted (with), examination (of), from *noscere* to know]

notional ('nəʊʃən^{ə}l) *adj* **1** expressing or consisting of ideas **2** not evident in reality; hypothetical or imaginary: *a notional tax credit* **3** characteristic of a notion, esp in being speculative or abstract **4** *grammar* **4a** (of a word) having lexical meaning **4b** another word for **semantic** > **'notionally** *adv*

notions ('nəʊʃənz) *pl n chiefly US & Canad* pins, cotton, ribbon, etc, used for sewing; haberdashery

notochord ('nəʊtə,kɔːd) *n* a fibrous longitudinal rod in all embryo and some adult chordate animals, immediately above the gut, that supports the body [C19 from Gk *nōton* the back + CHORD[1]]

notorious (nəʊ'tɔːrɪəs) *adj* **1** well-known for some bad or unfavourable quality, deed, etc; infamous **2** *rare* generally known or widely acknowledged [C16 from Med. L *notōrius* well-known, from *nōtus* known] > **notoriety** (,nəʊtə'raɪɪtɪ) *n* > **no'toriously** *adv*

notornis (nəʊ'tɔːnɪs) *n* a rare flightless rail of New Zealand [C19 NL, from Gk *notos* south + *ornis* bird]

not proven ('prəʊv^{ə}n) *adj* (*postpositive*) a third verdict available to Scottish courts, returned when there is insufficient evidence against the accused to convict

Notre Dame ('nəʊtrə 'dɑːm, 'nɒtrə; *French* nɔtrə dam) *n* the early Gothic cathedral of Paris, on the Île de la Cité: built between 1163 and 1257

no-trump *cards* ▷ *n also* **no-trumps 1** a bid or contract to play without trumps ▷ *adj also* **no-trumper 2** (of a hand) suitable for playing without trumps

Nottingham ('nɒtɪŋəm) *n* **1** a city in N central England, administrative centre of Nottinghamshire, on the River Trent: scene of the outbreak of the Civil War (1642); famous for its associations with the Robin Hood legend; two universities. Pop: 283 800 (1995 est) **2** a unitary authority in N central England, in Nottinghamshire. Pop: 266 995 (2001). Area: 78 sq km (30 sq miles)

Nottinghamshire ('nɒtɪŋəmʃɪə, -ʃə) *n* an inland county of central England: generally low-lying, with part of the S Pennines and the remnant of Sherwood Forest in the east. Nottingham became an independent unitary authority in 1998. Administrative centre: Nottingham. Pop (excluding Nottingham): 748 503 (2001). Area (excluding Nottingham): 2086 sq km (805 sq miles). Abbreviation: **Notts**

Nottm *abbrev for* Nottingham

Notts (nɒts) *abbrev for* Nottinghamshire

Notus ('nəʊtəs) *n classical myth* a personification of the south or southwest wind

notwithstanding (ˌnɒtwɪθ'stændɪŋ) *prep* **1** (*often immediately postpositive*) in spite of; despite ▷ *conj* **2** (*subordinating*) although ▷ *sentence connector* **3** nevertheless

Nouakchott (*French* nwakʃɔt) *n* the capital of Mauritania, near the Atlantic coast: replaced St Louis as capital in 1957; situated on important caravan routes. Pop (urban area): 881 000 (1999 est)
▷ http://lexicorient.com/mauritania/nouakch.htm

nougat ('nu:gɑ:) *n* a hard chewy pink or white sweet containing chopped nuts, cherries, etc [c19 via F from Provençal *nogat*, from *noga* nut, from L *nux* nut]

nought (nɔ:t) *n also* **naught, ought, aught 1** another name for **zero**: used esp in numbering ▷ *n, adj, adv* **2** a variant spelling of **naught** [OE *nōwiht*, from *ne* not, no + *ōwiht* something]

noughties ('nɔ:tɪz) *pl n inf* the years from 2000 to 2009

noughts and crosses *n* (*functioning as sing*) a game in which two players, one using a nought, "O", the other a cross, "X", alternately mark squares formed by two pairs of crossed lines, the winner being the first to get three of his symbols in a row. US and Canad term: **tick-tack-toe,** (US) **crisscross**

Nouméa (nu:'meɪə; *French* numea) *n* the capital and chief port of the French Overseas Territory of New Caledonia. Pop: 76 293 (1996)

noun (naʊn) *n* **a** a word or group of words that refers to a person, place, or thing **b** (*as modifier*): *a noun phrase*. Abbrev: **N, n** Related adj: **nominal** [c14 via Anglo-F from L *nōmen* NAME] > '**nounal** *adj*

nourish ('nʌrɪʃ) *vb* (*tr*) **1** to provide with the materials necessary for life and growth **2** to encourage (an idea, etc); foster: *to nourish resentment* [c14 from OF *norir*, from L *nūtrīre* to feed] > '**nourisher** *n* > '**nourishing** *adj*

nourishment ('nʌrɪʃmənt) *n* **1** the act or state of nourishing **2** a substance that nourishes; food

nous (naʊs) *n* **1** *metaphysics* mind or reason, esp regarded as the principle governing all things **2** *Brit sl* common sense [c17 from Gk: mind]

nouveau *or before a plural noun* **nouveaux** ('nu:vəʊ) *adj* (*prenominal*) *Facetious or derog.* having recently become the thing specified: *a nouveau hippy* [c20 F, lit.: new; on the model of NOUVEAU RICHE]

nouveau riche (ri:ʃ) *n, pl* **nouveaux riches** (ri:ʃ) (often preceded by *the*) a person who has acquired wealth recently and is regarded as vulgarly ostentatious or lacking in social graces [c19 from F lit.: new rich]

Nouvelle-Calédonie (*French* nuvɛlkaledɔni) *n* the French name for **New Caledonia**

nouvelle cuisine ('nu:vɛl kwi:'zi:n; *French* nuvɛl kɥizin) *n* a style of cooking based on presenting small attractively arranged helpings of lightly cooked fresh ingredients [c20 F, lit.: new cookery]

Nov. *abbrev for* November

nova ('nəʊvə) *n, pl* **novae** (-vi:) *or* **novas** a variable star that undergoes a cataclysmic eruption, observed as a sudden large increase in brightness with a subsequent decline over months or years; it is a close binary system with one component a white dwarf [c19 NL *nova (stella)* new (star), from L *novus* new]

Novalis (*German* no'va:lɪs) *n* real name *Friedrich von Hardenberg*. 1772–1801, German romantic poet. His works include the mystical *Hymnen an die Nacht* (1797; published 1800) and *Geistliche Lieder* (1799)

Nova Lisboa (*Portuguese* 'nɔvə liʒ'βoə) *n* the former name (1928–73) of **Huambo**

Novara (*Italian* no'va:ra) *n* a city in NW Italy, in NE Piedmont: scene of the Austrian defeat of the Piedmontese in 1849. Pop: 102 037 (2000 est)

Nova Scotia ('nəʊvə 'skəʊʃə) *n* **1** a peninsula in E Canada, between the Gulf of St Lawrence and the Bay of Fundy **2** a province of E Canada, consisting of the Nova Scotia peninsula and Cape Breton Island: first settled by the French as Acadia. Capital: Halifax. Pop: 942 700 (2001 est). Area: 52 841 sq km (20 402 sq miles). Abbreviation: **NS** > ˌ**Nova** '**Scotian** *n, adj*
▷ www.gov.ns.ca
▷ www.gov.ns.ca/tourism.htm

Nova Scotia duck tolling retriever *n* a Canadian variety of retriever

Novaya Zemlya (*Russian* 'nɔvəjə zɪm'lja) *n* an archipelago in the Arctic Ocean, off the NE coast of Russia: consists of two large islands and many islets. Area: about 81 279 sq km (31 382 sq miles)

novel[1] ('nɒvᵊl) *n* **1** an extended fictional work in prose dealing with character, action, thought, etc, esp in the form of a story **2 the novel** the literary genre represented by novels [c15 from OF *novelle*, from L *novella (narrātiō)* new (story); see NOVEL[2]]

novel[2] ('nɒvᵊl) *adj* of a kind not seen before; fresh; new; original [c15 from L *novellus*, dim. of *novus* new]

novelette (ˌnɒvə'lɛt) *n* **1** an extended prose narrative or short novel **2** a novel that is regarded as slight, trivial, or sentimental **3** a short piece of lyrical music, esp for piano

novelettish (ˌnɒvə'lɛtɪʃ) *adj* characteristic of a novelette; trite or sentimental

novelist ('nɒvəlɪst) *n* a writer of novels

novelistic (ˌnɒvə'lɪstɪk) *adj* of or characteristic of novels, esp in style or method of treatment

novella (nəʊ'vɛlə) *n, pl* **novellas** *or* **novelle** (-leɪ) **1** a short narrative tale, esp one having a satirical point, such as those in Boccaccio's *Decameron* **2** a short novel [c20 from It.; see NOVEL[1]]

Novello (nə'vɛləʊ) *n* **Ivor,** real name *Ivor Novello Davies*. 1893–1951, Welsh actor, composer, songwriter, and dramatist

novelty ('nɒvᵊltɪ) *n, pl* **novelties 1a** the quality of being new and interesting **1b** (*as modifier*): *novelty value* **2** a new or unusual experience **3** (*often pl*) a small usually cheap new ornament or trinket [c14 from OF *novelté*; see NOVEL[2]]

November (nəʊ'vɛmbə) *n* the eleventh month of the year, consisting of 30 days [c13 via OF from L: ninth month (the Roman year orig. began in March), from *novem* nine]

novena (nəʊ'vi:nə) *n, pl* **novenas** *or* **novenae** (-ni:) RC *Church*. a devotion consisting of prayers or services on nine consecutive days [c19 from Med. L, from L *novem* nine]

Novgorod (*Russian* 'nɔvgərət) *n* a city in NW Russia, on the Volkhov River; became a principality in 862 under Rurik, an event regarded as the founding of the Russian state; a major trading centre in the Middle Ages; destroyed by Ivan the Terrible in 1570. Pop: 231 700 (1999 est)

Nn

novice ('nɒvɪs) *n* **1a** a person who is new to or inexperienced in a certain task, situation, etc; beginner; tyro **1b** (*as modifier*): *novice driver* **2** a probationer in a religious order **3** a racehorse that has not won a specified number of races [C14 via OF from L *novīcius*, from *novus* new]

Novi Sad (*Serbo-Croat* 'nɔvi: 'sa:d) *n* a port in NE Serbia and Montenegro, in Serbia, on the River Danube: founded in 1690 as the seat of the Serbian patriarch; university (1960). Pop: 179 626 (1991). German name: **Neusatz**

novitiate *or* **noviciate** (nəʊ'vɪʃɪɪt, -,eɪt) *n* **1** the state of being a novice, esp in a religious order, or the period for which this lasts **2** the part of a religious house where the novices live [C17 from F *noviciat*, from L *novīcius* NOVICE]

Novocaine ('nəʊvə,keɪn) *n* a trademark for **procaine hydrochloride** See **procaine**

Novokuznetsk (*Russian* nɔvəkuz'njɛtsk) *n* a city in S central Russia: iron and steel works. Pop: 562 800 (1999 est). Former name (1932–61): **Stalinsk**

Novosibirsk (*Russian* nəvəsi'birsk) *n* a city in W central Russia, on the River Ob: the largest town in Siberia; developed with the coming of the Trans-Siberian railway in 1893; important industrial centre. Pop: 1 402 400 (1999 est)

now (naʊ) *adv* **1** at or for the present time **2** immediately **3** in these times; nowadays **4** given the present circumstances: *now we'll have to stay to the end* **5** (preceded by *just*) very recently: *he left just now* **6** (often preceded by *just*) very soon: *he is leaving just now* **7** (**every**) **now and again** *or* **then** occasionally; on and off **8** **now now!** an exclamation used to rebuke or pacify someone ▷ *conj* **9** (*subordinating*; often foll by *that*) seeing that: *now you're in charge, things will be better* ▷ *sentence connector* **10a** used as a hesitation word: *now, I can't really say* **10b** used for emphasis: *now listen to this* **10c** used at the end of a command: *run along, now* ▷ *n* **11** the present time: *now is the time to go* ▷ *adj* **12** *inf* of the moment; fashionable: *the now look* [OE *nū*]

nowadays ('naʊə,deɪz) *adv* in these times [C14 from NOW + *adays* from OE *a* on + *daeges* genitive of DAY]

noway ('nəʊ,weɪ) *adv* **1** not at all ▷ *sentence substitute* **no way** **2** used to make an emphatic refusal, denial, etc

Nowel *or* **Nowell** (nəʊ'ɛl) *n* archaic spellings of **Noel**

nowhere ('nəʊwɛə) *adv* **1** in, at, or to no place; not anywhere **2** **get nowhere** (**fast**) *inf* to fail completely to make any progress **3** **nowhere near** far from; not nearly ▷ *n* **4** a nonexistent or insignificant place **5** **middle of nowhere** a completely isolated place

no-win *adj* offering no possibility of a favourable outcome (esp in **a no-win situation**)

nowise ('nəʊ,waɪz) *adv* in no manner; not at all

nowt (naʊt) *n* *N English* a dialect word for **nothing** [from NAUGHT]

Nox (nɒks) *n* the Roman goddess of the night. Greek counterpart: **Nyx**

noxious ('nɒkʃəs) *adj* poisonous or harmful [C17 from L *noxius* harmful, from *noxa* injury] > '**noxiously** *adv* > '**noxiousness** *n*

Noyon (*French* nwajɔ̃) *n* a town in N France: scene of the coronations of Charlemagne (768) and Hugh Capet (987); birthplace of John Calvin. Pop: 14 426 (1990)

nozzle ('nɒzᵊl) *n* a projecting pipe or spout from which fluid is discharged [C17 *nosle*, *nosel*, dim. of NOSE]

Np *the chemical symbol for* neptunium

NP *or* **np.** *abbrev for* Notary Public

NPA *abbrev for* Newspaper Publishers' Association
▷ www.adassoc.org.uk/members/npa.html

NPD *commerce abbrev for* new product development

NPL *abbrev for* National Physical Laboratory

NPV *abbrev for*: **1** net present value **2** no par value

NRC (in Canada) *abbrev for* National Research Council

NRL (in Australia) *abbrev for*: **1** National Roads and Motorists Association **2** National Rugby League

NRMA (in Australia) *abbrev for* National Roads and Motorists Association

NRN *text messaging abbrev for* no reply necessary

NRT *abbrev for* nicotine replacement therapy: a type of treatment designed to help people give up smoking in which gradually decreasing doses of nicotine are administered through patches on the skin etc to avoid the effects of sudden withdrawal from the drug

NRV *abbrev for* net realizable value

NS *abbrev for*: **1** New Style (method of reckoning dates) **2** Nova Scotia **3** Nuclear Ship

NSAID *abbrev for* nonsteroidal anti-inflammatory drug: any of a class of drugs, including aspirin and ibuprofen, used for treating rheumatic diseases

NSB (in Britain) *abbrev for* National Savings Bank

NSG *Brit education abbrev for* nonstatutory guidelines: practical nonmandatory advice and information on the implementation of the National Curriculum

NSPCC (in Britain) *abbrev for* National Society for the Prevention of Cruelty to Children

NST (in Canada) abbrev for Newfoundland Standard Time

NSU *abbrev for* nonspecific urethritis

NSW *abbrev for* New South Wales

NT *abbrev for*: **1** (in Britain) National Trust **2** New Testament **3** Northern Territory (of Australia) **4** Nunavut **5** no-trump

-n't *contraction of* not: used as an enclitic after *be* and *have* when they function as main verbs and after auxiliary verbs or verbs operating syntactically as auxiliaries: *can't; don't; isn't*

nth (ɛnθ) *adj* **1** *maths* of or representing an unspecified ordinal number, usually the greatest in a series: *the nth power* **2** *inf* being the last or most extreme of a long series: *for the nth time* **3** **to the nth degree** *inf* to the utmost extreme

NTO (in Britain) *abbrev for* National Training Organization

NTP *abbrev for* normal temperature and pressure. Also: **STP**

nt. wt. *or* **nt wt** *abbrev for* net weight

n-type *adj* **1** (of a semiconductor) having more conduction electrons than mobile holes **2** associated with or resulting from the movement of electrons in a semiconductor

nu (nju:) *n* the 13th letter in the Greek alphabet (Ν, ν), a consonant [from Gk, of Semitic origin]

Nu (nju:) *n* **U** (u:), original name *Thakin Nu*. 1907–95, Burmese statesman and writer; prime minister (1948–56, 1957–58, 1960–62). He attempted to establish parliamentary democracy, but was ousted (1962) by Ne Win

nuance (nju:'ɑ:ns, 'nju:ɑ:ns) *n* a subtle difference in colour, meaning, tone, etc [C18 from F, from *nuer* to show light and shade, ult. from L *nūbēs* a cloud]

nub (nʌb) *n* **1** a small lump or protuberance **2** a small piece or chunk **3** the point or gist: *the nub of a story* [C16 var. of *knub*, from MLow G *knubbe* KNOB] > '**nubbly** *or* '**nubby** *adj*

nubble ('nʌbᵊl) *n* a small lump [C19 dim. of NUB]

Nubia ('nju:bɪə) *n* an ancient region of NE Africa, on the Nile, extending from Aswan to Khartoum

Nubian ('nju:bɪən) *n* **1** a native or inhabitant of Nubia **2** the language spoken by the people of Nubia ▷ *adj* **3** of or relating to Nubia **4** *inf* of or relating to Black culture

Nubian Desert *n* a desert in the NE Sudan, between the Nile valley and the Red Sea: mainly a sandstone plateau

nubile ('nju:baɪl) *adj* (of a girl) **1** ready or suitable for marriage by virtue of age or maturity **2** sexually attractive [C17 from L *nūbilis*, from *nūbere* to marry] > **nubility** (nju:'bɪlɪtɪ) *n*

Nubuck ('nju:ˌbʌk) *n* leather that has been rubbed on the flesh side of the skin to give it a fine velvet-like finish

nucha ('nju:kə) *n, pl* **nuchae** (-ki:) *Zool., anat.* the back or nape of the neck [C14 from Med. L, from Ar.: spinal marrow] > '**nuchal** *adj*

nuclear ('nju:klɪə) *adj* **1** of or involving the nucleus of an atom: *nuclear fission* **2** *biol* of, relating to, or contained within the nucleus of a cell: *a nuclear membrane* **3** of, forming, or resembling any other kind of nucleus **4** of or operated by energy from fission or fusion of atomic nuclei: *a nuclear weapon* **5** involving or possessing nuclear weapons: *nuclear war*

nuclear bomb *n* a bomb whose force is due to uncontrolled nuclear fusion or nuclear fission
▹ http://science.howstuffworks.com/nuclear-bomb.htm

nuclear chemistry *n* the branch of chemistry concerned with nuclear reactions

nuclear energy *n* energy released during a nuclear reaction as a result of fission or fusion. Also called: **atomic energy**

nuclear family *n sociol, anthropol* a primary social unit consisting of parents and their offspring

nuclear fission *n* the splitting of an atomic nucleus into approximately equal parts, either spontaneously or as a result of the impact of a particle usually with an associated release of energy. Sometimes shortened to **fission**

nuclear fuel *n* a fuel that provides nuclear energy, used in nuclear submarines, etc

nuclear fusion *n* a reaction in which two nuclei combine to form a nucleus with the release of energy. Sometimes shortened to **fusion**

nuclear magnetic resonance *n* a technique for determining the magnetic moments of nuclei by subjecting a substance to high-frequency radiation and a large magnetic field. It is used for determining structure, esp in body scanning. Abbrev: **NMR**

nuclear medicine *n* the branch of medicine concerned with the use of radionuclides in the diagnosis and treatment of disease

nuclear physics *n (functioning as sing)* the branch of physics concerned with the structure and behaviour of the nucleus and the particles of which it consists
▹ http://ie.lbl.gov/education/glossary/glossaryf.htm
▹ www.atomicarchive.com
▹ www.visionlearning.com/library/module_viewer.php?mid=59
▹ www.iaea.org/inis/ws/

nuclear power *n* power, esp electrical or motive, produced by a nuclear reactor. Also called: **atomic power**

nuclear reaction *n* a process in which the structure and energy content of an atomic nucleus is changed by interaction with another nucleus or particle

nuclear reactor *n* a device in which a nuclear reaction is maintained and controlled for the production of nuclear energy. Sometimes shortened to **reactor**

nuclear waste *n* another name for **radioactive waste**

nuclear winter *n* a period of low temperatures and little light that has been suggested would occur after a nuclear war

nuclease ('nju:klɪˌeɪz) *n* any of a group of enzymes that hydrolyse nucleic acids to simple nucleotides

nucleate *adj* ('nju:klɪɪt, -ˌeɪt) **1** having a nucleus ▹ *vb* ('nju:klɪˌeɪt), **nucleates, nucleating, nucleated** *(intr)* **2** to form a nucleus

nuclei ('nju:klɪˌaɪ) *n* a plural of **nucleus**

nucleic acid (nju:'kli:ɪk, -'kleɪ-) *n biochem* any of a group of complex compounds with a high molecular weight that are vital constituents of all living cells. See also **RNA, DNA**

nucleo- *or before a vowel* **nucle-** *combining form* **1** nucleus or nuclear **2** nucleic acid [from Latin *nucleus* kernel, from *nux* nut]

nucleolus (ˌnju:klɪ'əʊləs) *n, pl* **nucleoli** (-laɪ) a small rounded body within a resting cell nucleus that contains RNA and proteins and is involved in the production of ribosomes. Also called: **nucleole** [C19 from L, dim. of NUCLEUS] > ˌ**nucle'olar** *adj*

nucleon ('nju:klɪˌɒn) *n* a proton or neutron, esp one present in an atomic nucleus

nucleonics (ˌnju:klɪ'ɒnɪks) *n (functioning as sing)* the branch of physics concerned with the applications of nuclear energy > ˌ**nucle'onic** *adj* > ˌ**nucle'onically** *adv*

nucleon number *n* the number of nucleons in an atomic nucleus; mass number

nucleophile ('nju:klɪəˌfaɪl) *n* a molecule or ion that can donate electrons > **nucleophilic** (ˌnju:klɪə'fɪlɪk) *adj*

nucleoside ('nju:klɪəˌsaɪd) *n biochem* a compound containing a purine or pyrimidine base linked to a sugar (usually ribose or deoxyribose)

nucleotide ('nju:klɪəˌtaɪd) *n biochem* a compound consisting of a nucleoside linked to phosphoric acid

nucleus ('nju:klɪəs) *n, pl* **nuclei** *or* **nucleuses** **1** a central or fundamental thing around which others are grouped; core **2** a centre of growth or development; basis: *the nucleus of an idea* **3** *biol* (in the cells of eukaryotes) a large compartment, bounded by a double membrane, that contains the chromosomes and associated molecules and controls the characteristics and growth of the cell **4** *astron* the central portion in the head of a comet, consisting of small solid particles of ice and frozen gases **5** *physics* the positively charged dense region at the centre of an atom, composed of protons and neutrons, about which electrons orbit **6** *chem* a fundamental group of atoms in a molecule serving as the base structure for related compounds [C18 from L: kernel, from *nux* nut]

nuclide ('nju:klaɪd) *n* a species of atom characterized by its atomic number and its mass number [C20 from NUCLEO- + *-ide*, from Gk *eidos* shape]

nude (nju:d) *adj* **1** completely undressed **2** having no covering; bare; exposed **3** *law* **3a** lacking some essential legal requirement **3b** (of a contract, etc) made without consideration and void unless under seal ▹ *n* **4** the state of being naked (esp in **in the nude**) **5** a naked figure, esp in painting, sculpture, etc [C16 from L *nūdus*] > '**nudely** *adv*

nudge (nʌdʒ) *vb* **nudges, nudging, nudged** *(tr)* **1** to push (someone) gently, esp with the elbow, to get attention; jog **2** to push slowly or lightly: *as I drove out, I just nudged the gatepost* **3** to give (someone) a gentle reminder ▹ *n* **4** a gentle poke or push **5** a gentle reminder [C17 ?from Scand.] > '**nudger** *n*

nudibranch ('nju:dɪˌbræŋk) *n* a marine gastropod of an order characterized by a shell-less, often beautifully coloured, body bearing external gills. Also called: **sea slug** [C19 from L *nudus* naked + *branche*, from L *branchia* gills]

nudism ('nju:dɪzəm) *n* the practice of nudity, esp for reasons of health, etc > '**nudist** *n, adj*

nudity ('nju:dɪtɪ) *n, pl* **nudities** the state or fact of being nude; nakedness

Nuevo Laredo (*Spanish* 'nweβo la'reðo) *n* a city and port of entry in NE Mexico, in Tamaulipas state on the Rio Grande opposite Laredo, Texas: oil industries. Pop: 309 000 (2000 est)

Nuevo León ('nweɪvəʊ leɪ'əʊn, nu:'eɪ-; *Spanish* 'nweβo le'ɔn) *n* a state of NE Mexico: the first centre of heavy industry in Latin America. Capital: Monterrey. Pop: 3 826 240 (2000). Area: 64 555 sq km (24 925 sq miles)

Nuffield ('nʌfi:ld) *n* **William Richard Morris,** 1st Viscount Nuffield. 1877–1963, English motorcar manufacturer and philanthropist. He endowed Nuffield College at

Nn

Oxford (1937) and the Nuffield Foundation (1943), a charitable trust for the furtherance of medicine and education

nugatory ('nju:gətərɪ, -trɪ) *adj* **1** of little value; trifling **2** not valid: *a nugatory law* [c17 from L *nūgātōrius*, from *nūgārī* to jest, from *nūgae* trifles]

nugget ('nʌgɪt) *n* **1** a small piece or lump, esp of gold in its natural state **2** something small but valuable or excellent [c19 from ?]

Nugget ('nʌgɪt) *NZ* ▷ *n* **1** *trademark* shoe polish ▷ *vb* **2** *inf* to shine (shoes)

nuggety ('nʌgɪtɪ) *adj* **1** of or resembling a nugget **2** *Austral & NZ inf* (of a person) thickset; stocky

nuisance ('nju:səns) *n* **1a** a person or thing that causes annoyance or bother **1b** (*as modifier*): *nuisance calls* **2** *law* something unauthorized that is obnoxious or injurious to the community at large or to an individual, esp in relation to his ownership of property **3 nuisance value** the usefulness of a person's or thing's capacity to cause difficulties or irritation [c15 via OF from *nuire* to injure, from L *nocēre*]

NUJ (in Britain) *abbrev for* National Union of Journalists

Nu Jiang ('nu: 'dʒjæŋ) *n* the Chinese name for the **Salween**

nuke (nju:k) *sl, chiefly US* ▷ *vb* **nukes, nuking, nuked** (*tr*) **1** to attack or destroy with nuclear weapons ▷ *n* **2** a nuclear bomb

Nuku'alofa (ˌnu:ku:ə'lɔ:fə) *n* the capital of Tonga, a port on the N coast of Tongatapu Island. Pop: 37 000 (1999 est)

Nukus (*Russian* nu'kus) *n* a city in Uzbekistan, capital of the Kara-Kalpak Autonomous Republic, on the Amu Darya River. Pop: 185 000 (1998 est)

null (nʌl) *adj* **1** without legal force; invalid (esp in **null and void**) **2** without value or consequence; useless **3** lacking distinction; characterless **4** nonexistent; amounting to nothing **5** *maths* **5a** quantitatively zero **5b** relating to zero **5c** (of a set) having no members **6** *physics* involving measurement in which conditions are adjusted so that an instrument has a zero reading, as with a Wheatstone bridge [c16 from L *nullus* none, from *ne* not + *ullus* any]

nullah ('nʌlɑ:) *n* a stream or drain [c18 from Hindi *nālā*]

Nullarbor Plain ('nʌləˌbɔ:) *n* a vast low plateau of S Australia: extends north from the Great Australian Bight to the Great Victoria Desert; has no surface water or trees. Area: 260 000 sq km (100 000 sq miles)

null hypothesis *n statistics* the residual hypothesis if the alternative hypothesis tested against it fails to achieve a predetermined significance level

nullify ('nʌlɪˌfaɪ) *vb* **nullifies, nullifying, nullified** (*tr*) **1** to render legally void or of no effect **2** to render ineffective or useless; cancel out [c16 from LL *nullificāre* to despise, from L *nullus* of no account + *facere* to make] > **ˌnullifi'cation** *n*

nullity ('nʌlɪtɪ) *n, pl* **nullities 1** the state of being null **2** a null or legally invalid act or instrument **3** something null, ineffective, characterless, etc [c16 from Med. L *nullitās*, from L *nullus* no, not any]

NUM (in Britain and South Africa) *abbrev for* National Union of Mineworkers

Num. *Bible abbrev for* Numbers

Numantia (nju:'mæntɪə) *n* an ancient city in N Spain: a centre of Celtic resistance to Rome in N Spain: captured by Scipio the Younger in 133 B.C > **Nu'mantian** *adj, n*

Numa Pompilius ('nju:mə pɒm'pɪlɪəs) *n* the legendary second king of Rome (?715–?673 BC), said to have instituted religious rites

numb (nʌm) *adj* **1** deprived of feeling through cold, shock, etc **2** unable to move; paralysed ▷ *vb* **3** (*tr*) to make numb; deaden, shock, or paralyse [c15 *nomen*, lit.: taken (with paralysis), from OE *niman* to take] > **'numbly** *adv* > **'numbness** *n*

numbat ('nʌmˌbæt) *n* a small Australian marsupial having a long snout and tongue and strong claws for hunting and feeding on termites [c20 from Abor.]

number ('nʌmbə) *n* **1** a concept of quantity that is or can be derived from a single unit, the sum of a collection of units, or zero. Every number occupies a unique position in a sequence, enabling it to be used in counting. See also **cardinal number, ordinal number 2** the symbol used to represent a number; numeral **3** a numeral or string of numerals used to identify a person or thing: *a telephone number* **4** the person or thing so identified or designated: *she was number seven in the race* **5** sum or quantity: *a large number of people* **6** one of a series, as of a magazine; issue **7a** a self-contained piece of pop or jazz music **7b** a self-contained part of an opera or other musical score **8** a group of people, esp an exclusive group: *he was not one of our number* **9** *sl* a person, esp a sexually attractive girl: *who's that nice little number?* **10** *inf* an admired article: *that little number is by Dior* **11** a grammatical category for the variation in form of nouns, pronouns, and any words agreeing with them, depending on how many persons or things are referred to **12 any number of** several or many **13 by numbers** *mil* (of a drill procedure, etc) performed step by step, each move being made on the call of a number **14 get** *or* **have someone's number** *inf* to discover a person's true character or intentions **15 one's number is up** *Brit inf* one is finished; one is ruined or about to die **16 without** *or* **beyond number** innumerable ▷ *vb* (*mainly tr*) **17** to assign a number to **18** to add up to; total **19** (*also intr*) to list (items) one by one; enumerate **20** (*also intr*) to put or be put into a group, category, etc: *they were numbered among the worst hit* **21** to limit the number of: *his days were numbered* [c13 from OF *nombre*, from L *numerus*]

number crunching *n computing* the large-scale processing of numerical data

numbered account *n banking* an account identified only by a number, esp one in a Swiss bank that could contain funds illegally obtained

numberless ('nʌmbəlɪs) *adj* **1** too many to be counted; countless **2** not containing or consisting of numbers > **'numberlessly** *adv*

number one *n* **1** the first in a series or sequence **2** an informal phrase for **oneself, myself,** etc: *to look after number one* **3** *inf* the most important person; chief: *he's number one in the organization* **4** *inf* the bestselling pop record in any one week ▷ *adj* **5** first in importance, urgency, quality, etc: *number one priority*

numberplate ('nʌmbəˌpleɪt) *n* a plate mounted on the front and back of a motor vehicle bearing the registration number. Usual US term: **license plate,** (Canad) **licence plate**

numbers game *or* **racket** *n US* an illegal lottery in which money is wagered on a certain combination of digits appearing at the beginning of a series of numbers published in a newspaper, as in share prices or sports results. Often shortened to **numbers**

Number Ten *n* 10 Downing Street, the British prime minister's official London residence

number theory *n* the study of integers, their properties, and the relationship between integers

numbfish ('nʌmˌfɪʃ) *n, pl* **numbfish** *or* **numbfishes** any of several electric rays [c18 so called because it numbs its victims]

numbles ('nʌmbᵊlz) *pl n arch* the heart, lungs, liver, etc, of a deer or other animal [c14 from OF *nombles*, pl. of *nomble* thigh muscle of a deer, changed from L *lumbulus*, dim. of *lumbus* loin]

numbskull *or* **numskull** ('nʌmˌskʌl) *n* a stupid person; dolt; blockhead

numen ('nju:mɛn) *n, pl* **numina** (-mɪnə) **1** (esp in ancient Roman religion) a deity or spirit presiding over a thing or place **2** a guiding principle, force, or spirit [c17 from

Large Numbers

n =	10^{3}	US NAME	EUROPEAN NAME	SI PREFIX	GREEK-BASED NAME
3	10^{9}	billion	milliard	giga-	gillion
4	10^{12}	trillion	billion	tera-	tetrillion
5	10^{15}	quadrillion	billiard	peta-	pentillion
6	10^{18}	quintillion	trillion	exa-	hexillion
7	10^{21}	sextillion	trilliard	zetta-	heptillion
8	10^{24}	septillion	quadrillion	yotta-	oktillion
9	10^{27}	octillion	quadrilliard		ennillion
10	10^{30}	nonillion	quintillion		dekillion
11	10^{33}	decillion	quintilliard		hendekillion
12	10^{36}	undecillion	sextillion		dodekillion
13	10^{39}	duodecillion	sextilliard		trisdekillion
14	10^{42}	tredecillion	septillion		tetradekillion
15	10^{45}	quattuordecillion	septilliard		pentadekillion
16	10^{48}	quindecillion	octillion		hexadekillion
17	10^{51}	sexdecillion	octilliard		heptadekillion
18	10^{54}	septendecillion	nonillion		oktadekillion
19	10^{57}	nonilliard	nonilliard		enneadekillion
20	10^{60}	novemdecillion	decillion		icosillion
21	10^{63}	vigintillion	decilliard		icosihenillion
22	10^{66}	unvigintillion	undecillion		icosidillion
23	10^{69}	duovigintillion	undecilliard		icositrillion
24	10^{72}	trevigintillion	duodecillion		icositetrillion
25	10^{75}	quattuorvigintillion	duodecilliard		icosipentillion
26	10^{78}	quinvigintillion	tredecillion		icosihexillion
27	10^{81}	sexvigintillion	tredecilliard		icosiheptillion
28	10^{84}	septenvigintillion	quattuordecillion		icosioktillion
29	10^{87}	octovigintillion	quattuordecilliard		icosiennillion
30	10^{90}	novemvigintillion	quindecillion		triacontillion
31	10^{93}	trigintillion	quindecilliard		triacontahenillion
32	10^{96}	untrigintillion	sexdecillion		triacontadillion
33	10^{99}	duotrigintillion	sexdecilliard		triacontratrillion

▹ http://mathworld.wolfram.com/LargeNumber.html
▹ www.unc.edu/~rowlett/units/large.html

L: a nod (indicating a command), divine power]

numerable ('nju:mərəbᵊl) *adj* able to be numbered or counted > '**numerably** *adv*

numeracy ('nju:mərəsɪ) *n* the ability to use numbers, esp in arithmetical operations

numeral ('nju:mərəl) *n* **1** a symbol or group of symbols used to express a number: for example, *6 (Arabic)*, *VI (Roman)*, *110 (binary)* ▹ *adj* **2** of, consisting of, or denoting a number [C16 from LL *numerālis* belonging to number, from L *numerus*]

numerate *adj* ('nju:mərɪt) **1** able to use numbers, esp in arithmetical operations ▹ *vb* ('nju:mə,reɪt), **numerates, numerating, numerated** (*tr*) **2** to read (a numerical expression) **3** a less common word for **enumerate** [C18 (vb): from L *numerus* number + -ATE¹, by analogy with *literate*]

numeration (,nju:mə'reɪʃən) *n* **1** the writing, reading, or naming of numbers **2** a system of numbering > '**numerative** *adj*

numerator ('nju:mə,reɪtə) *n* **1** *maths* the dividend of a fraction: the numerator of ⅞ is 7 ▹ Cf **denominator** **2** a person or thing that numbers; enumerator

numerical (nju:'mɛrɪkᵊl) *or* **numeric** *adj* **1** of, relating to, or denoting a number or numbers **2** measured or expressed in numbers: *numerical value* > **nu'merically** *adv*

numerology (,nju:mə'rɒlədʒɪ) *n* the study of numbers, such as the figures in a birth date, and of their supposed influence on human affairs > **numerological** (,nju:mərə'lɒdʒɪkᵊl) *adj*

numerous ('nju:mərəs) *adj* **1** being many **2** consisting of many parts: *a numerous collection* > '**numerously** *adv* > '**numerousness** *n*

Numidia (nju:'mɪdɪə) *n* an ancient country of N Africa, corresponding roughly to present-day Algeria: flourished until its invasion by Vandals in 429; chief towns were Cirta and Hippo Regius > **Nu'midian** *n, adj*

numinous ('nju:mɪnəs) *adj* **1** denoting, being, or relating to a numen; divine **2** arousing spiritual or religious emotions **3** mysterious or awe-inspiring [C17 from L *numin-*, NUMEN + -OUS]

numismatics (,nju:mɪz'mætɪks) *n* (*functioning as sing*) the study or collection of coins, medals, etc. Also called: ,**numisma'tology** [C18 from F *numismatique*, from L *nomisma*, from Gk: piece of currency, from *nomizein* to have in use, from *nōmos* use] > ,**numis'matic** *adj* > ,**numis'matically** *adv*
▹ www.numis.org

nummulite ('nʌmjʊ,laɪt) *n* any of a family of large fossil protozoans common in Tertiary times [C19 from NL, from L *nummulus*, from *nummus* coin]

numpty ('nʌmptɪ) *n, pl* **numpties** *Scot inf* a foolish or ignorant person

numskull ('nʌm,skʌl) *n* a variant spelling of **numbskull**

nun (nʌn) *n* a female member of a religious order; sister [OE *nunne*, from Church L *nonna*, from LL: form of address used for an elderly woman] > '**nunhood** *n* > '**nunlike** *adj*

Nunavut ('nu:nəvu:t) *n* a territory of NW Canada, formed in 1999 from part of the Northwest Territories as a semiautonomous region for the Inuit; includes Baffin Island and Ellesmere Island. Capital: Iqaluit. Pop: 26 745 (2001). Area: 2 093 190 sq km (808 185 sq miles)
▹ www.gov.nu.ca
▹ www.nunavuttourism.com

nun buoy *n naut* a buoy, conical at the top, marking the right side of a channel leading into a harbour: green in British waters but red in US waters [C18 from obs. *nun* child's spinning top + BUOY]

Nunc Dimittis ('nʌŋk dɪ'mɪtɪs, 'nʊŋk) *n* **1** the Latin name for the Canticle of Simeon (Luke 2:29–32) **2** a musical setting of this [from the opening words (Vulgate): now let depart]

nunciature ('nʌnsɪətʃə) *n* the office or term of office of a nuncio [C17 from It. *nunziatura;* see NUNCIO]

nuncio ('nʌnʃɪˌəʊ, -sɪ-) *n, pl* **nuncios** *RC Church* a diplomatic representative of the Holy See [C16 via It. from L *nuntius* messenger]

Nuneaton (nʌn'iːtᵊn) *n* a town in central England, in Warwickshire. Pop: 66 715 (1991)

Nunn (nʌn) *n* Sir **Trevor** (**Robert**) born 1940, British theatre director; artistic director (1968–86) and chief executive (1968–86) of the Royal Shakespeare Company; artistic director of the Royal National Theatre (1997–2003). His productions include *Nicholas Nickleby* (1980), *Cats* (1981), and *Les Misérables* (1985)

nunnery ('nʌnərɪ) *n, pl* **nunneries** the convent or religious house of a community of nuns

nuptial ('nʌpʃəl, -tʃəl) *adj* **1** relating to marriage; conjugal: *nuptial vows* **2** *zool* of or relating to mating: *the nuptial flight of a queen bee* [C15 from L *nuptiālis*, from *nuptiae* marriage, from *nubere* to marry] > '**nuptially** *adv*

nuptials ('nʌpʃəlz, -tʃəlz) *pl n* (*sometimes sing*) a marriage ceremony; wedding

nurd (nɜːd) *n* a variant spelling of **nerd**

Nuremberg ('njʊərəmˌbɜːg) *n* a city in S Germany, in N Bavaria: scene of annual Nazi rallies (1933–38), the anti-Semitic Nuremberg decrees (1935), and the trials of Nazi leaders for their war crimes (1945–46); important metalworking and electrical industries. Pop: 486 400 (1999 est). German name: **Nürnberg**

Nureyev ('njʊərɪɛf, njʊ'reɪ-) *n* **Rudolf** 1938–93, Austrian ballet dancer, born in the Soviet Union: he lived in England (1961–83) and France (1983–89). He became an Austrian citizen in 1982

Nuristan (ˌnʊərɪ'stɑːn) *n* a region of E Afghanistan: consists mainly of high mountains (including part of the Hindu Kush), steep narrow valleys, and forests. Area: about 13 000 sq km (5000 sq miles). Former name: **Kafiristan**

Nürnberg ('nyrnbɛrk) *n* the German name for **Nuremberg**

nurse (nɜːs) *n* **1** a person, often a woman, who is trained to tend the sick and infirm, assist doctors, etc **2** short for **nursemaid** **3** a woman employed to breast-feed another woman's child; wet nurse **4** a worker in a colony of social insects that takes care of the larvae ▷ *vb* **nurses, nursing, nursed** (*mainly tr*) **5** (*also intr*) to tend (the sick) **6** (*also intr*) to feed (a baby) at the breast **7** to try to cure (an ailment) **8** to clasp fondly: *she nursed the child in her arms* **9** to look after (a child) as one's employment **10** to harbour; preserve: *to nurse a grudge* **11** to give special attention to, esp in order to promote goodwill: *to nurse a difficult constituency* **12** *billiards* to keep (the balls) together for a series of cannons [C16 from earlier *norice*, OF *nourice*, from LL *nūtrīcia*, from L *nūtrīcius* nourishing, from *nūtrīre* to nourish]

nursemaid ('nɜːsˌmeɪd) *or* **nurserymaid** *n* a woman employed to look after someone else's children. Often shortened to **nurse**

nurse practitioner *n* a nurse who has specialized advanced skills in diagnosis, psychosocial assessment, and patient management, and is permitted to prescribe certain drugs

nursery ('nɜːsrɪ) *n, pl* **nurseries** **1** a room in a house set apart for children **2** a place where plants, young trees, etc, are grown commercially **3** an establishment providing daycare for babies and young children; crèche **4** anywhere serving to foster or nourish new ideas, etc **5** Also called: **nursery cannon** *billiards* **5a** a series of cannons with the three balls adjacent to a cushion, esp near a corner pocket **5b** a cannon in such a series

nurseryman ('nɜːsrɪmən) *n, pl* **nurserymen** a person who owns or works in a nursery in which plants are grown

nursery rhyme *n* a short traditional verse or song for children, such as *Little Jack Horner*

nursery school *n* a school for young children, usually from three to five years old

nursery slopes *pl n* gentle slopes used by beginners in skiing

nursery stakes *pl n* a race for two-year-old horses

nurse shark *n* any of various sharks having an external groove on each side of the head between the mouth and nostril [C15 *nusse fisshe* (later infl. in spelling by NURSE), ?from a division of obs. *an huss* shark, dogfish (from ?) as *a nuss*]

nursing ('nɜːsɪŋ) *n* **a** the practice or profession of caring for the sick and injured **b** (*as modifier*): *a nursing home*

nursing home *n* a private hospital or residence for aged or infirm persons

nursing officer *n* (in Britain) the official name for **matron** (sense 4)

nursling *or* **nurseling** ('nɜːslɪŋ) *n* a child or young animal that is being suckled, nursed, or fostered

nurture ('nɜːtʃə) *n* **1** the act or process of promoting the development, etc, of a child **2** something that nourishes ▷ *vb* **nurtures, nurturing, nurtured** (*tr*) **3** to feed or support **4** to educate or train [C14 from OF *norriture*, from L *nūtrīre* to nourish] > '**nurtural** *adj* > '**nurturer** *n*

NUS (in Britain) *abbrev for* National Union of Students

Nusa Tenggara ('nuːsə tɛŋ'gɑːrə) *n* an island chain east of Java, mostly in Indonesia: the main islands are Bali, Lombok, Sumbawa, Sumba, Flores, Alor, and Timor. Pop: 7 237 600 (1995 est). Area: 73 144 sq km (28 241 sq miles). Former name: **Lesser Sunda Islands**

nut (nʌt) *n* **1** a dry one-seeded indehiscent fruit that usually possesses a woody wall **2** (*not in technical use*) any similar fruit, such as the walnut, having a hard shell and an edible kernel **3** the edible kernel of such a fruit **4** *sl* an eccentric or mad person **5** *sl* the head **6** **do one's nut** *Brit sl* to be extremely angry **7** **off one's nut** *sl* mad or foolish **8** a person or thing that presents difficulties (esp in **a tough nut to crack**) **9** a small square hexagonal block, usually metal, with a threaded hole through the middle for screwing on the end of a bolt **10** Also called (US and Canad): **frog** *music* **10a** the ridge at the upper end of the fingerboard of a violin, cello, etc, over which the strings pass to the tuning pegs **10b** the end of a violin bow that is held by the player **11** a small usually gingery biscuit **12** *Brit* a small piece of coal ▷ *vb* **nuts, nutting, nutted** **13** (*intr*) to gather nuts ▷ See also **nuts** [OE *hnutu*]

▷ www.treenuts.org
▷ www.users.globalnet.co.uk/~aair/nuts.htm
▷ www.cooks.com

NUT (in Britain) *abbrev for* National Union of Teachers

nutant ('njuːtᵊnt) *adj bot* having the apex hanging down [C18 from L *nūtāre* to nod]

nutation (njuː'teɪʃən) *n* **1** *astron* a periodic variation in the precession of the earth's axis causing the earth's poles to oscillate about their mean position **2** the spiral growth of a shoot or similar plant organ, caused by variation in the growth rate in different parts. Also called: **circumnutation** **3** the act of nodding [C17 from L *nūtātiō*, from *nūtāre* to nod]

nutbrown ('nʌt'braʊn) *adj* reddish-brown

nutcase ('nʌtˌkeɪs) *n sl* an insane or very foolish person

nutcracker ('nʌtˌkrækə) *n* **1** (*often pl*) a device for cracking the shells of nuts **2** either an Old World bird or a North American bird (**Clark's nutcracker**) having

speckled plumage and feeding on nuts, seeds, etc
nutgall ('nʌt,gɔːl) *n* a nut-shaped gall caused by gall wasps on the oak and other trees
nuthatch ('nʌt,hætʃ) *n* a songbird having strong feet and bill, and feeding on insects, seeds, and nuts [C14 *notehache*, from *note* nut + *hache* hatchet, from its habit of splitting nuts]
nuthouse ('nʌt,haʊs) *n sl* a mental hospital
nutmeg ('nʌt,mɛg) *n* **1** an East Indian evergreen tree cultivated in the tropics for its hard aromatic seed. See also **mace²** **2** the seed of this tree, used as a spice ▷ *vb* **nutmegs, nutmegging, nutmegged** (*tr*) **3** *Brit sport inf* to kick or hit the ball between the legs of (an opposing player) [C13 from OF *nois muguede*, from OProvençal *noz muscada* musk-scented nut, from L *nux* NUT + *muscus* MUSK]
nutraceutical (,njuːtrə'sjuːtɪkᵊl) *n* another name for **functional food**
nutria ('njuːtrɪə) *n* another name for **coypu**, esp the fur [C19 from Sp., var. of *lutria*, ult. from L *lūtra* otter]
nutrient ('njuːtrɪənt) *n* **1** any of the mineral substances that are absorbed by the roots of plants **2** any substance that nourishes an organism ▷ *adj* **3** providing or contributing to nourishment [C17 from L *nūtrīre* to nourish]
nutriment ('njuːtrɪmənt) *n* any material providing nourishment [C16 from L *nūtrīmentum*, from *nūtrīre* to nourish] > **nutrimental** (,njuːtrɪ'mɛntᵊl) *adj*
nutrition (njuː'trɪʃən) *n* **1** a process in animals and plants involving the intake and assimilation of nutrient materials **2** the act or process of nourishing **3** the study of nutrition, esp in humans [C16 from LL *nūtrītiō*, from *nūtrīre* to nourish] > **nu'tritional** *adj* > **nu'tritionist** *n*
▷ www.crnusa.org
nutritious (njuː'trɪʃəs) *adj* nourishing [C17 from L *nūtrīcius*, from *nūtrix* NURSE] > **nu'tritiously** *adv* > **nu'tritiousness** *n*
nutritive ('njuːtrɪtɪv) *adj* **1** providing nourishment **2** of, concerning, or promoting nutrition ▷ *n* **3** a nutritious food
nuts (nʌts) *adj* **1** a slang word for **insane** **2** (foll by *about* or *on*) *sl* extremely fond (of) or enthusiastic (about) ▷ *interj* **3** *sl* an expression of contempt, refusal, or defiance
nuts and bolts *pl n inf* the essential or practical details
nutshell ('nʌt,ʃɛl) *n* **1** the shell around the kernel of a nut **2** **in a nutshell** in essence; briefly
nutter ('nʌtə) *n Brit sl* a mad or eccentric person
nutty ('nʌtɪ) *adj* **nuttier, nuttiest** **1** containing nuts **2** resembling nuts **3** a slang word for **insane** **4** (foll by *over* or *about*) *inf* extremely enthusiastic (about) > **'nuttiness** *n*
Nuuk (nuːk) *n* the capital of Greenland, in the southwest: the oldest Danish settlement in Greenland, founded in 1721. Pop: 13 838 (2000 est). Former name (until 1979): **Godthaab**
Nuxalk (nuː'xɒlk) *n* a member of a Salishan Native Canadian people of British Columbia. Formerly called: **Bella Coola** [from Salish]
nux vomica ('nʌks 'vɒmɪkə) *n* **1** an Indian tree with orange-red berries containing poisonous seeds **2** any of the seeds of this tree, which contain strychnine and other poisonous alkaloids **3** a medicine manufactured from the seeds of this tree, formerly used as a heart stimulant [C16 from Med. L: vomiting nut]
nuzzle ('nʌzᵊl) *vb* **nuzzles, nuzzling, nuzzled** **1** to push or rub gently with the nose or snout **2** (*intr*) to nestle; lie close **3** (*tr*) to dig out with the snout [C15 *nosele*, from NOSE (n)]
NV *abbrev for* Nevada
nvCJD *abbrev for* new-variant Creutzfeldt-Jakob disease
NVQ *abbrev for* National Vocational Qualification
NW *symbol for* northwest(ern)
NWMP (in Canada) *abbrev for* North West Mounted Police
NWT *abbrev for* Northwest Territories (of Canada)
NY *or* **N.Y.** *abbrev for* New York (city or state)
nyala ('njɑːlə) *n, pl* **nyala** *or* **nyalas** **1** a spiral-horned southern African antelope with a fringe of white hairs along the length of the back and neck **2** **mountain nyala** a similar Ethiopian animal lacking the white crest [from Zulu]
Nyasa *or* **Nyassa** (nɪ'æsə, naɪ'æsə) *n* **Lake** a lake in central Africa at the S end of the Great Rift Valley: the third largest lake in Africa, drained by the Shiré River into the Zambezi. Area: about 28 500 sq km (11 000 sq miles). Malawi name: **Lake Malawi**
Nyasaland (nɪ'æsə,lænd, naɪ'æsə-) *n* the former name (until 1964) of **Malawi**
NYC *abbrev for* New York City
nyctalopia (,nɪktə'ləʊpɪə) *n* inability to see normally in dim light. Nontechnical name: **night blindness** [C17 via LL from Gk *nuktálōps*, from *nux* night + *alaos* blind + *ōps* eye]
nyctitropism (nɪk'tɪtrə,pɪzəm) *n* a tendency of some plant parts to assume positions at night that are different from their daytime positions [C19 *nyct-*, from Gk *nukt-*, *nux* night + -TROPISM]
nye (naɪ) *n* a flock of pheasants. Also called: **nide, eye** [C15 from OF *ni*, from L *nīdus* nest]
Nyeman (*Russian* 'njɛmən) *n* a variant spelling of **Neman**
Nyerere (njə'rɛrɪ, nɪ-) *n* **Julius Kambarage** (kæm'baːraːgə) 1922–99, Tanzanian statesman; president (1964–85). He became prime minister of Tanganyika in 1961 and president in 1962, negotiating the union of Tanganyika and Zanzibar to form Tanzania (1964)
Nyíregyháza (*Hungarian* 'njiːrɛtjhaːzɔ) *n* a market town in NE Hungary. Pop: 112 419 (2000 est)
Nykøbing (*Danish* 'nykøːbeŋ) *n* a port in Denmark, on the W coast of Falster Island. Pop: 64 428 (latest est)
nylon ('naɪlɒn) *n* **1** a class of synthetic polyamide materials of which monofilaments are used for bristles, etc, and fibres can be spun into yarn **2** yarn or cloth made of nylon, used for clothing, stockings, etc [C20 orig. a trademark]
NYLON ('naɪlɒn) *n inf* a high-earning business executive who enjoys a transatlantic lifestyle, living part of the year in New York City and part in London [C20 from *N(ew) Y(ork)* + *Lon(don)*]
nylons ('naɪlɒnz) *pl n* stockings made of nylon
Nyman ('naɪmən) *n* **Michael** born 1944, British composer; works include the opera *The Man Who Mistook His Wife For a Hat* (1986) and scores for films, including *The Piano* (1992) and several films by Peter Greenaway
nymph (nɪmf) *n* **1** *myth* a spirit of nature envisaged as a beautiful maiden **2** *chiefly poetic* a beautiful young woman **3** the larva of insects such as the dragonfly. It resembles the adult, apart from having underdeveloped wings, and develops without a pupal stage [C14 via OF from L, from Gk *numphē*] > **'nymphal** *or* **nymphean** ('nɪmfɪən) *adj* > **'nymphlike** *adj*
nympha ('nɪmfə) *n, pl* **nymphae** (-fiː) *anat* either one of the labia minora [C17 from L: bride]
nymphet ('nɪmfɪt) *n* a young girl who is sexually precocious and desirable [C17 (meaning: a young nymph): dim. of NYMPH]
nympho ('nɪmfəʊ) *n, pl* **nymphos** *inf* short for **nymphomaniac**
nympholepsy ('nɪmfə,lɛpsɪ) *n, pl* **nympholepsies** a state of violent emotion, esp when associated with a desire for something that one cannot have [C18 from Gk *numpholēptos* caught by nymphs, from *numphē* nymph + *lambanein* to seize] > **'nympho,lept** *n* > **,nympho'leptic** *adj*
nymphomania (,nɪmfə'meɪnɪə) *n* a neurotic compulsion in women to have sexual intercourse with

Nn

many men without being able to have lasting relationships with them [C18 NL, from Gk *numphē* nymph + -MANIA] > ˌ**nympho'maniac** *n, adj* >ˌnymphoma'niacal *adj*

Nysa ('nɪsə) *n* the Polish name for the **Neisse** (sense 1)

NYSE *abbrev for* New York Stock Exchange

nystagmus (nɪ'stægməs) *n* involuntary movement of the eye comprising a smooth drift followed by a flick back [C19 NL, from Gk *nustagmos*] > **nys'tagmic** *adj*

Nyx (nɪks) *n Greek myth* the goddess of the night, daughter of Chaos. Roman counterpart: **Nox**

NZ *or* **N. Zeal.** *abbrev for* New Zealand

NZEF (in New Zealand) *abbrev for* New Zealand Expeditionary Force, the New Zealand army that served in 1914–18. **2NZEF** refers to the Second New Zealand Expeditionary Force, in World War II.

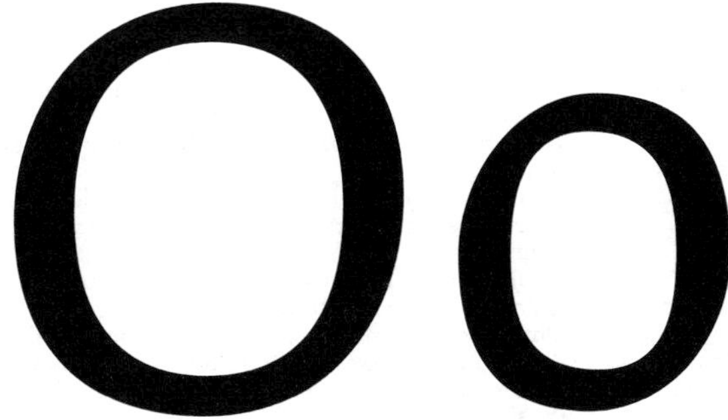

o *or* **O** (əʊ) *n, pl* **o's, O's,** *or* **Os** **1** the 15th letter and fourth vowel of the English alphabet **2** any of several speech sounds represented by this letter, as in *code, pot, cow,* or *form* **3** another name for **nought**

O¹ *symbol for:* **1** *chem* oxygen **2** a human blood type of the ABO group **3** Old

O² (əʊ) *interj* **1** a variant of **oh** **2** an exclamation introducing an invocation, entreaty, wish, etc: *O God! O for the wings of a dove!*

o' (ə) *prep inf or arch* shortened form of **of:** *a cup o' tea*

O'- *prefix* (in surnames of Irish Gaelic origin) descendant of: *O'Corrigan* [from Irish Gaelic *ó, ua* descendant]

-o *suffix forming nouns* indicating a diminutive or slang abbreviation: *wino*

oaf (əʊf) *n* a stupid or loutish person [C17 var. of OE *ælf* ELF] > **'oafish** *adj* > **'oafishness** *n*

Oahu (əʊ'ɑːhuː) *n* an island in central Hawaii: the third largest of the Hawaiian Islands. Chief town: Honolulu. Pop: 836 231 (1990). Area: 1574 sq km (608 sq miles)

oak (əʊk) *n* **1** any deciduous or evergreen tree or shrub having acorns as fruits and lobed leaves **2a** the wood of any of these trees, used esp as building timber and for making furniture **2b** (*as modifier*): *an oak table* **3** any of various trees that resemble the oak, such as the poison oak **4** the leaves of an oak tree, worn as a garland [OE *āc*]

oak apple *or* **gall** *n* any of various brownish round galls on oak trees, containing the larvae of certain wasps

oaked (əʊkt) *adj* relating to wine which is stored for a time in oak barrels prior to bottling

oaken ('əʊkən) *adj* made of the wood of the oak

Oakham ('əʊkəm) *n* a market town in E central England, the administrative centre of Rutland. Pop: 8691 (1991)

Oakland ('əʊklənd) *n* a port and industrial centre in W California, on San Francisco Bay; damaged by earthquake in 1989. Pop: 399 484 (2000)

Oakley ('əʊklɪ) *n* **Annie,** real name *Phoebe Anne Oakley Mozee.* 1860–1926, US markswoman

Oaks (əʊks) *n* (*functioning as sing*) **the** a horse race for fillies held annually at Epsom since 1779: one of the classics of English flat racing [named after an estate near Epsom]

oakum ('əʊkəm) *n* loose fibre obtained by unravelling old rope, used esp for caulking seams in wooden ships [OE *ācuma,* var. of *ācumba,* lit.: off-combings, from *ā-* off + *-cumba,* from *cemban* to COMB]

Oakville ('əʊkvɪl) *n* a city in SE Canada, in SE Ontario on Lake Ontario southwest of Toronto: motor-vehicle industry. Pop: 128 405 (1996)

O & M *abbrev for* organization and method (in studies of working methods)

OAP (in Britain) *abbrev for* old age pension *or* pensioner

oar (ɔː) *n* **1** a long shaft of wood for propelling a boat by rowing, having a broad blade that is dipped into and pulled against the water **2** short for **oarsman** **3** **stick** *or* **put one's oar in** to interfere or interrupt ▷ *vb* **4** to row or propel with or as if with oars [OE *ār,* of Gmc origin] > **'oarless** *adj* > **'oar,like** *adj*

oarfish ('ɔː,fɪʃ) *n, pl* **oarfish** *or* **oarfishes** a very long ribbonfish with long slender ventral fins [C19 referring to the flattened oarlike body]

oarlock ('ɔː,lɒk) *n* the usual US and Canad word for **rowlock**

oarsman ('ɔːzmən) *n, pl* **oarsmen** a man who rows, esp one who rows in a racing boat > **'oarsmanship** *n*

OAS *abbrev for:* **1** Organization of American States **2** Organisation de l'Armée Secrète; an organization which opposed Algerian independence by acts of terrorism

▷ www.oas.org

oasis (əʊ'eɪsɪs) *n, pl* **oases** (-iːz) **1** a fertile patch in a desert occurring where the water table approaches or reaches the ground surface **2** a place of peace, safety, or happiness [c17 via L from Gk, prob. from Egyptian]

oast (əʊst) *n chiefly Brit* **1** a kiln for drying hops **2** Also called: **oast house** a building containing such kilns, usually having a conical or pyramidal roof [OE *āst*]

oat (əʊt) *n* **1** an erect annual grass grown in temperate regions for its edible seed **2** (*usually pl*) the seeds or fruits of this grass **3** any of various other grasses such as the wild oat **4** *poetic* a flute made from an oat straw **5** **feel one's oats** *US & Canad inf* **5a** to feel exuberant **5b** to feel self-important **6** **sow one's (wild) oats** to indulge in adventure or promiscuity during youth [OE *āte*, from ?]

oatcake ('əʊt,keɪk) *n* a crisp brittle unleavened biscuit made of oatmeal

oaten ('əʊtᵊn) *adj* made of oats or oat straw

Oates (əʊts) *n* **1** Captain **Lawrence Edward Grace** 1880–1912, English explorer. He died on Scott's second Antarctic expedition **2** **Titus** ('taɪtəs) 1649–1705, English conspirator. He fabricated the Popish Plot (1678), a supposed Catholic conspiracy to kill Charles II, burn London, and massacre Protestants. His perjury caused the execution of many innocent Catholics

oath (əʊθ) *n, pl* **oaths** (əʊðz) **1** a solemn pronouncement to affirm the truth of a statement or to pledge a person to some course of action **2** the form of such a pronouncement **3** an irreverent or blasphemous expression, esp one involving the name of a deity; curse **4** **my oath** *Austral sl* certainly; yes indeed **5** **on, upon,** *or* **under oath** **5a** under the obligation of an oath **5b** *law* having sworn to tell the truth, usually with one's hand on the Bible **6** **take an oath** to declare formally with a pledge, esp before giving evidence [OE *āth*]

oatmeal ('əʊt,miːl) *n* **1** meal ground from oats, used for making porridge, oatcakes, etc **2a** a greyish-yellow colour **2b** (*as adj*): *an oatmeal coat*

OAU *abbrev for* Organization of African Unity; superseded by the African Union in 2001

▷ www.africa-union.org

Oaxaca (wə'hɑːkə; *Spanish* oa'xaka) *n* **1** a state of S Mexico, on the Pacific: includes most of the Isthmus of Tehuantepec; inhabited chiefly by Indians. Capital: Oaxaca de Juárez. Pop: 3 432 180 (2000). Area: 95 363 sq km (36 820 sq miles) **2** a city in S Mexico, capital of Oaxaca state: founded in 1486 by the Aztecs and conquered by Spain in 1521. Pop: 252 586 (2000 est). Official name: **Oaxaca de Juárez** (de 'xwarɛθ)

Ob (*Russian* ɔpj) *n* a river in N central Russia, formed at Bisk by the confluence of the Biya and Katun Rivers and flowing generally north to the **Gulf of Ob** (an inlet of the Arctic Ocean): one of the largest rivers in the world, with a drainage basin of about 2 930 000 sq km (1 131 000 sq miles). Length: 3682 km (2287 miles)

OB *Brit abbrev for:* **1** Old Boy **2** outside broadcast

ob. *abbrev for:* **1** (on tombstones, etc) obiit [L: he (or she) died] **2** obiter [L: incidentally; in passing] **3** oboe

ob- *prefix* inverse or inversely: *obovate* [from OF, from L *ob*. In compound words from L, *ob-* (and *oc-*, *of-*, *op-*) indicates: to, towards (*object*); against (*oppose*); away from (*obsolete*); before (*obstetric*); and is used as an intensifier (*oblong*)]

Obad. *Bible abbrev for* Obadiah

Obadiah (,əʊbə'daɪə) *n Old Testament* **1** a Hebrew prophet **2** the book containing his oracles, chiefly directed against Edom ▷ Douay spelling: **Abdias** (æb'daɪəs)

Oban ('əʊbᵊn) *n* a small port and resort in W Scotland, in Argyll and Bute on the Firth of Lorne. Pop: 8203 (1991)

Obasanjo (,ɒbə'sændʒeʊ) *n* **Olusegun** (,ɒlʊ'seɪgən) born 1937, Nigerian politician and general; head of the military government (1976–79); president from 1999

obbligato *or* **obligato** (,ɒblɪ'gɑːtəʊ) *Music* ▷ *adj* **1** not to be omitted in performance ▷ *n, pl* **obbligatos, obbligati** (-tiː) *or* **obligatos, obligati** (-tiː) **2** an essential part in a score: *with oboe obbligato* [c18 from It., from *obbligare* to OBLIGE]

obconic (ɒb'kɒnɪk) *or* **obconical** *adj bot* (of a fruit) shaped like a cone and attached at the pointed end

obcordate (ɒb'kɔːdeɪt) *adj bot* heart-shaped and attached at the pointed end: *obcordate leaves*

obdurate ('ɒbdjʊrɪt) *adj* **1** not easily moved by feelings or supplication; hardhearted **2** impervious to persuasion [c15 from L *obdūrāre* to make hard, from *ob-* (intensive) + *dūrus* hard] > **'obduracy** *or* **'obdurateness** *n* > **'obdurately** *adv*

OBE *abbrev for* Officer of the Order of the British Empire (a Brit title)

obeah ('əʊbɪə) *n* **1** a kind of witchcraft practised by some West Indians **2** a charm used in this [of W African origin]

obedience (ə'biːdɪəns) *n* **1** the condition or quality of being obedient **2** the act or an instance of obeying; dutiful or submissive behaviour **3** the authority vested in a Church or similar body **4** the collective group of persons submitting to this authority

obedient (ə'biːdɪənt) *adj* obeying or willing to obey [c13 from OF, from L *oboediens*, present participle of *oboedīre* to OBEY] > **o'bediently** *adv*

obeisance (əʊ'beɪsəns) *n* **1** an attitude of deference or homage **2** a gesture expressing obeisance [c14 from OF *obéissant*, present participle of *obéir* to OBEY] > **o'beisant** *adj*

obelisk ('ɒbɪlɪsk) *n* **1** a stone pillar having a square or rectangular cross section and sides that taper towards a pyramidal top **2** *printing* another name for **dagger** (sense 2) [c16 via L from Gk *obeliskos* a little spit, from *obelos* spit] > **,obe'liscal** *adj* > **,obe'liskoid** *adj*

obelus ('ɒbɪləs) *n, pl* **obeli** (-laɪ) **1** a mark (— or ÷) used in ancient documents to indicate spurious words or passages **2** another name for **dagger** (sense 2) [c14 via LL from Gk *obelos* spit]

Oberammergau (*German* oːbər'amərgau) *n* a village in S Germany, in Bavaria in the foothills of the Alps: famous for its Passion Play, performed by the villagers every ten years (except during the World Wars) since 1634, in thanksgiving for the end of the Black Death. Pop: 4740 (latest est)

Oberhausen (*German* 'oːbərhauzən) *n* an industrial city in W Germany, in North Rhine-Westphalia on the Rhine-Herne Canal: site of the first ironworks in the Ruhr. Pop: 222 300 (1999 est)

Oberland ('əʊbə,lænd) *n* the lower parts of the Bernese Alps in central Switzerland, mostly in S Bern canton

Oberon ('əʊbə,rɒn) *n* (in medieval folklore) the king of the fairies, husband of Titania

Oberösterreich ('oːbər,øːstəraiç) *n* the German name for **Upper Austria**

obese (əʊ'biːs) *adj* excessively fat or fleshy; corpulent [c17 from L *obēsus*, from *ob-* (intensive) + *edere* to eat] > **o'besity** *or* **o'beseness** *n*

obey (ə'beɪ) *vb* **1** to carry out (instructions or orders); comply with (demands) **2** to behave or act in accordance with (one's feelings, whims, etc) [c13 from OF *obéir*, from L *oboedīre*, from *ob-* towards + *audīre* to hear] > **o'beyer** *n*

obfuscate ('ɒbfʌs,keɪt) *vb* **obfuscates, obfuscating, obfuscated** (*tr*) **1** to obscure or darken **2** to perplex or bewilder [c16 from L *ob-* (intensive) + *fuscāre* to blacken, from *fuscus* dark] > **,obfus'cation** *n* > **'obfus,catory** *adj*

obi ('əʊbɪ) *n, pl* **obis** *or* **obi** a broad sash tied in a large flat bow at the back, worn as part of the Japanese national costume [c19 from Japanese]

obit ('ɒbɪt, 'əʊbɪt) *n inf* **1** short for **obituary** **2** a memorial service

obiter dictum ('ɒbɪtə 'dɪktəm, 'əʊ-) *n, pl* **obiter dicta** ('dɪktə) **1** *law* an observation by a judge on some point of law not directly in issue in the case before him **2** any comment or remark made in passing [L: something said in passing]

obituary (əˈbɪtjʊərɪ) *n, pl* **obituaries** a published announcement of a death, often accompanied by a short biography of the dead person [c18 from Med. L *obituārius*, from L *obīre* to fall] > **oˈbituarist** *n*

obj. *abbrev for:* **1** objection **2** *grammar* object(ive)

object[1] (ˈɒbdʒɪkt) *n* **1** a tangible and visible thing **2** a person or thing seen as a focus for feelings, thought, etc **3** an aim or objective **4** *inf* a ridiculous or pitiable person, spectacle, etc **5** *philosophy* that towards which cognition is directed as contrasted with the thinking subject **6** *grammar* a noun, pronoun, or noun phrase whose referent is the recipient of the action of a verb. See also **direct object, indirect object** **7** *grammar* a noun, pronoun, or noun phrase that is governed by a preposition **8** *computing* a self-contained identifiable component of a software system or design **9** **no object** not a hindrance or obstacle: *money is no object* [c14 from LL *objectus* something thrown before (the mind), from L *obicere;* see OBJECT[2]]

object[2] (əbˈdʒɛkt) *vb* **1** (*tr; takes a clause as object*) to state as an objection **2** (*intr; often foll by to*) to raise or state an objection (to); present an argument (against) [c15 from L *obicere*, from *ob-* against + *jacere* to throw] > **obˈjector** *n*

object glass *n optics* another name for **objective** (sense 10)

objectify (əbˈdʒɛktɪˌfaɪ) *vb* **objectifies, objectifying, objectified** (*tr*) to represent concretely; present as an object > **obˌjectifiˈcation** *n*

objection (əbˈdʒɛkʃən) *n* **1** an expression or feeling of opposition or dislike **2** a cause for such an expression or feeling **3** the act of objecting

objectionable (əbˈdʒɛkʃənəbᵊl) *adj* unpleasant, offensive, or repugnant > **obˌjectionaˈbility** *or* **obˈjectionableness** *n* > **obˈjectionably** *adv*

objective (əbˈdʒɛktɪv) *adj* **1** existing independently of perception or an individual's conceptions **2** undistorted by emotion or personal bias **3** of or relating to actual and external phenomena as opposed to thoughts, feelings, etc **4** *med* (of disease symptoms) perceptible to persons other than the individual affected **5** *grammar* denoting a case of nouns and pronouns, esp in languages having only two cases, that is used to identify the direct object of a finite verb or preposition. See also **accusative** **6** of or relating to a goal or aim ▷ *n* **7** the object of one's endeavours; goal; aim **8** an actual phenomenon; reality **9** *grammar* the objective case **10** Also called: **object glass** *optics* the lens or combination of lenses nearest to the object in an optical instrument ▷ Abbreviation: **obj** ▷ Cf **subjective** > **objectival** (ˌɒbdʒɛkˈtaɪvəl) *adj* > **obˈjectively** *adv* > **ˌobjecˈtivity** *or* (*less commonly*) **obˈjectiveness** *n*

objectivism (əbˈdʒɛktɪˌvɪzəm) *n* **1** the tendency to stress what is objective **2** the philosophical doctrine that reality is objective, and that sense data correspond with it > **obˈjectivist** *n, adj* > **obˌjectivˈistic** *adj*

object language *n* a language described by another language ▷ Cf **metalanguage**

object lesson *n* a convincing demonstration of some principle or ideal

object linking and embedding *n* See **OLE**

object program *n* a computer program translated from the equivalent source program into machine language by the compiler or assembler

object relations theory *n* a form of psychoanalytic theory postulating that people relate to others in order to develop themselves

objet d'art *French* (ɔbʒɛ dar) *n, pl* ***objets d'art*** (ɔbʒɛ dar). a small object considered to be of artistic worth [lit.: object of art]

objurgate (ˈɒbdʒəˌgeɪt) *vb* **objurgates, objurgating, objurgated** (*tr*) to scold or reprimand [c17 from L *objurgāre*, from *ob-* against + *jurgāre* to scold] > **ˌobjurˈgation** *n* > **ˈobjurˌgator** *n* > **objurgatory** (ɒbˈdʒɜːgətərɪ, -trɪ) *adj*

oblate[1] (ˈɒbleɪt) *adj* having an equatorial diameter of greater length than the polar diameter: *the earth is an oblate sphere* ▷ Cf **prolate** [c18 from NL *oblātus* lengthened, from L *ob-* towards + *lātus*, p.p. of *ferre* to bring]

oblate[2] (ˈɒbleɪt) *n* a person dedicated to a monastic or religious life [c19 from F *oblat*, from Med. L *oblātus*, from L *offerre* to OFFER]

oblation (ɒˈbleɪʃən) *n* **1** *Christianity* the offering of the Eucharist to God **2** any offering made for religious or charitable purposes [c15 from Church L *oblātiō;* see OBLATE[2]] > **oblatory** (ˈɒblətərɪ, -trɪ) *or* **obˈlational** *adj*

obligate (ˈɒblɪˌgeɪt) *vb* **obligates, obligating, obligated** **1** to compel, constrain, or oblige morally or legally **2** (in the US) to bind (property, funds, etc) as security ▷ *adj* **3** compelled, bound, or restricted **4** *biol* able to exist under only one set of environmental conditions [c16 from L *obligāre* to OBLIGE] > **ˈobligable** *adj* > **obˈligative** *adj* > **ˈobliˌgator** *n*

obligation (ˌɒblɪˈgeɪʃən) *n* **1** a moral or legal requirement; duty **2** the act of obligating or the state of being obligated **3** *law* **3a** a written contract containing a penalty **3b** an instrument acknowledging indebtedness to secure the repayment of money borrowed **4** a person or thing to which one is bound morally or legally **5** a service or favour for which one is indebted

obligato (ˌɒblɪˈgɑːtəʊ) *adj, n music* a variant spelling of **obbligato**

obligatory (ɒˈblɪgətərɪ, -trɪ) *adj* **1** required to be done, obtained, possessed, etc **2** of the nature of or constituting an obligation > **obˈligatorily** *adv*

oblige (əˈblaɪdʒ) *vb* **obliges, obliging, obliged** **1** (*tr; often passive*) to bind or constrain (someone to do something) by legal, moral, or physical means **2** (*tr; usually passive*) to make indebted or grateful (to someone) by doing a favour **3** to do a service or favour to (someone): *she obliged the guests with a song* [c13 from OF *obliger*, from L *obligāre*, from *ob-* towards + *ligāre* to bind] > **oˈbliger** *n*

obligee (ˌɒblɪˈdʒiː) *n* a person in whose favour an obligation, contract, or bond is created; creditor

obliging (əˈblaɪdʒɪŋ) *adj* ready to do favours; agreeable; kindly > **oˈbligingly** *adv* > **oˈbligingness** *n*

obligor (ˌɒblɪˈgɔː) *n* a person who binds himself or herself by contract to perform some obligation; debtor

oblique (əˈbliːk) *adj* **1** at an angle; slanting; sloping **2** *geom* **2a** (of lines, planes, etc) neither perpendicular nor parallel to one another or to another line, plane, etc **2b** not related to or containing a right angle **3** indirect or evasive **4** *grammar* denoting any case of nouns, pronouns, etc, other than the nominative and vocative **5** *biol* having asymmetrical sides or planes: *an oblique leaf* ▷ *n* **6** something oblique, esp a line **7** another name for **solidus** (sense 1) ▷ *vb* **obliques, obliquing, obliqued** (*intr*) **8** to take or have an oblique direction **9** (of a military formation) to move forward at an angle [c15 from OF, from L *oblīquus*, from ?] > **oˈbliquely** *adv* > **oˈbliqueness** *n* > **obliquity** (əˈblɪkwɪtɪ) *n*

oblique angle *n* an angle that is not a right angle or any multiple of a right angle

obliterate (əˈblɪtəˌreɪt) *vb* **obliterates, obliterating, obliterated** (*tr*) to destroy every trace of; wipe out completely [c16 from L *oblitterāre* to erase, from *ob-* out + *littera* letter] > **oˌbliteˈration** *n* > **oˈbliterative** *adj* > **oˈbliterˌator** *n*

oblivion (əˈblɪvɪən) *n* **1** the condition of being forgotten or disregarded **2** *law* amnesty; pardon [c14 via OF from L *oblīviō* forgetfulness, from *oblīviscī* to forget]

oblivious (əˈblɪvɪəs) *adj* (foll by *of* or *to*) unaware or forgetful > **obˈliviously** *adv* > **obˈliviousness** *n*

Oo

USAGE It was formerly considered incorrect to use *oblivious* to mean *unaware*, but this use is now acceptable. When employed with this meaning, it is followed either by *to* or *of*, *to* being much the commoner

oblong ('ɒbˌlɒŋ) *adj* **1** having an elongated, esp rectangular, shape ▷ *n* **2** a figure or object having this shape [C15 from L *oblongus*, from *ob-* (intensive) + *longus* LONG[1]]

obloquy ('ɒbləkwɪ) *n, pl* **obloquies 1** defamatory or censorious statements, esp when directed against one person **2** disgrace brought about by public abuse [C15 from L *obloquium* contradiction, from *ob-* against + *loquī* to speak]

obnoxious (əb'nɒkʃəs) *adj* **1** extremely unpleasant **2** *obs* exposed to harm, injury, etc [C16 from L *obnoxius*, from *ob-* to + *noxa* injury, from *nocēre* to harm] > **ob'noxiously** *adv* > **ob'noxiousness** *n*

oboe ('əʊbəʊ) *n* **1** a woodwind instrument consisting of a conical tube fitted with a mouthpiece having a double reed. It has a penetrating nasal tone **2** a person who plays this instrument in an orchestra ▷ arch form: **hautboy** [C18 via It. *oboe*, phonetic approximation to F *haut bois*, lit.: high wood (referring to its pitch)] > **'oboist** *n*

oboe d'amore (dɑː'mɔːreɪ) *n* a type of oboe pitched a minor third lower than the oboe itself: used chiefly in baroque music

Obote (ɒ'bəʊteɪ, -tɪ) *n* **(Apollo) Milton** born 1924, Ugandan politician; prime minister of Uganda (1962–66) and president (1966–71; 1980–85). He was deposed by Amin in 1971 and remained in exile until 1980; deposed again in 1985 by the Acholi army

O'Brien (ə'braɪən) *n* **1 Conor Cruise** born 1917, Irish diplomat and writer. As an Irish Labour MP he served in the coalition government of 1973–77, becoming a senator (1977–79). He edited the *Observer* (1978–81) **2 Flann,** real name *Brian O'Nolan*. 1911–66, Irish novelist and journalist. His novels include *At Swim-Two-Birds* (1939) and the posthumously published *The Third Policeman* (1967). As Myles na Gopaleen he wrote a satirical column for the *Irish Times*

obs. *abbrev for:* **1** observation **2** obsolete

obscene (əb'siːn) *adj* **1** offensive or outrageous to accepted standards of decency or modesty **2** *law* (of publications, etc) having a tendency to deprave or corrupt **3** disgusting; repellent [C16 from L *obscēnus* inauspicious] > **ob'scenely** *adv*

obscenity (əb'sɛnɪtɪ) *n, pl* **obscenities 1** the state or quality of being obscene **2** an obscene act, statement, word, etc

obscurant (əb'skjʊərənt) *n* an opposer of reform and enlightenment > **obscurantism** (ˌɒbskjʊə'rænˌtɪzəm) *n* > **ˌobscu'rantist** *n, adj*

obscure (əb'skjʊə) *adj* **1** unclear **2** indistinct, vague, or indefinite **3** inconspicuous or unimportant **4** hidden, secret, or remote **5** (of a vowel) reduced to a neutral vowel (ə) **6** gloomy, dark, clouded, or dim ▷ *vb* **obscures, obscuring, obscured** (*tr*) **7** to make unclear, vague, or hidden **8** to cover or cloud over **9** *phonetics* to pronounce (a vowel) so that it becomes a neutral sound represented by (ə) [C14 via OF from L *obscūrus* dark] > **obscuration** (ˌɒbskjʊ'reɪʃən) *n* > **ob'scurely** *adv* > **ob'scureness** *n*

obscurity (əb'skjʊərɪtɪ) *n, pl* **obscurities 1** the state or quality of being obscure **2** an obscure person or thing

obsequies ('ɒbsɪkwɪz) *pl n, sing* **obsequy** funeral rites [C14 via Anglo-Norman from Med. L *obsequiae* (infl. by L *exsequiae*), from *obsequium* compliance]

obsequious (əb'siːkwɪəs) *adj* **1** obedient or attentive in an ingratiating or servile manner **2** *now rare* submissive or compliant [C15 from L *obsequiōsus* compliant, from *obsequi* to follow] > **ob'sequiously** *adv* > **ob'sequiousness** *n*

observance (əb'zɜːvəns) *n* **1** recognition of or compliance with a law, custom, practice, etc **2** a ritual, ceremony, or practice, esp of a religion **3** observation or attention **4** the degree of strictness of a religious order in following its rule **5** *arch* respectful or deferential attention

observant (əb'zɜːvənt) *adj* **1** paying close attention to detail; watchful or heedful **2** adhering strictly to rituals, ceremonies, laws, etc > **ob'servantly** *adv*

observation (ˌɒbzə'veɪʃən) *n* **1** the act of observing or the state of being observed **2** a comment or remark **3** detailed examination of phenomena prior to analysis, diagnosis, or interpretation: *the patient was under observation* **4** the facts learned from observing **5** *navigation* **5a** a sight taken with an instrument to determine the position of an observer relative to that of a given heavenly body **5b** the data so taken > **ˌobser'vational** *adj* > **ˌobser'vationally** *adv*

observatory (əb'zɜːvətərɪ, -trɪ) *n, pl* **observatories 1** an institution or building specially designed and equipped for observing meteorological and astronomical phenomena **2** any building or structure providing an extensive view of its surroundings

observe (əb'zɜːv) *vb* **observes, observing, observed 1** (*tr; may take a clause as object*) to see; perceive; notice: *we have observed that you steal* **2** (when *tr, may take a clause as object*) to watch (something) carefully; pay attention to (something) **3** to make observations of (something), esp scientific ones **4** (when *intr*, usually foll by *on* or *upon;* when *tr, may take a clause as object*) to make a comment or remark: *the speaker observed that times had changed* **5** (*tr*) to abide by, keep, or follow (a custom, tradition, etc) [C14 via OF from L *observāre*, from *ob-* to + *servāre* to watch] > **ob'servable** *adj* > **ob'server** *n*

obsess (əb'sɛs) *vb* **1** (*tr;* when passive, foll by *with* or *by*) to preoccupy completely; haunt **2** (*intr*, usually foll by *on* or *over*) to brood in an obsessional way [C16 from L *obsessus* besieged, p.p. of *obsidēre*, from *ob-* in front of + *sedēre* to sit]

obsession (əb'sɛʃən) *n* **1** *psychiatry* a persistent idea or impulse, often associated with anxiety and mental illness **2** a persistent preoccupation, idea, or feeling **3** the act of obsessing or the state of being obsessed > **ob'sessional** *adj* > **ob'sessionally** *adv*

obsessive (əb'sɛsɪv) *adj* **1** *psychiatry* motivated by a persistent overriding idea or impulse, often associated with anxiety and mental illness **2** continually preoccupied with a particular activity, person, or thing ▷ *n* **3** *psychiatry* a person subject to obsession **4** a person who is continually preoccupied with a particular activity, person, or thing > **ob'sessively** *adv* > **ob'sessiveness** *n*

obsidian (ɒb'sɪdɪən) *n* a dark volcanic glass formed by very rapid solidification of lava. Also called: **Iceland agate** [C17 from L *obsidiānus*, erroneous transcription of *obsiānus* (*lapis*) (stone of) *Obsius*, (in Pliny) the discoverer of a stone resembling obsidian]

obsolesce (ˌɒbsə'lɛs) *vb* **obsolesces, obsolescing, obsolesced** (*intr*) to become obsolete

obsolescent (ˌɒbsə'lɛsᵊnt) *adj* becoming obsolete or out of date [C18 from L *obsolescere;* see OBSOLETE] > **ˌobso'lescence** *n*

obsolete ('ɒbsəˌliːt, ˌɒbsə'liːt) *adj* **1** out of use or practice; not current **2** out of date; unfashionable or outmoded **3** *biol* (of parts, organs, etc) vestigial; rudimentary [C16 from L *obsolētus* worn out, p.p. of *obsolēre* (unattested), from *ob-* opposite to + *solēre* to be used] > **'obsoˌletely** *adv* > **'obsoˌleteness** *n*

obstacle ('ɒbstəkᵊl) *n* **1** a person or thing that opposes or hinders something **2** *Brit* a fence or hedge used in showjumping [C14 via OF from L *obstāculum*, from *obstāre*, from *ob-* against + *stāre* to stand]

obstacle race *n* a race in which competitors have to negotiate various obstacles

obstetric (ɒb'stɛtrɪk) *or* **obstetrical** *adj* of or relating to childbirth or obstetrics [c18 via NL from L *obstetrīcius*, from *obstetrix* a midwife, lit.: woman who stands opposite, from *obstāre* to stand in front of; see OBSTACLE] > **ob'stetrically** *adv*

obstetrician (ˌɒbstɪ'trɪʃən) *n* a physician who specializes in obstetrics

obstetrics (ɒb'stɛtrɪks) *n* (*functioning as sing*) the branch of medicine concerned with childbirth and the treatment of women before and after childbirth

obstinacy ('ɒbstɪnəsɪ) *n, pl* **obstinacies** 1 the state or quality of being obstinate 2 an obstinate act, attitude, etc

obstinate ('ɒbstɪnɪt) *adj* 1 adhering fixedly to a particular opinion, attitude, course of action, etc: *an obstinate faith in human nature* 2 self-willed or headstrong 3 difficult to subdue or alleviate; persistent: *an obstinate fever* [c14 from L *obstinātus*, p.p. of *obstināre* to persist in, from *ob-* (intensive) + *stin-*, var. of *stare* to stand] > **'obstinately** *adv*

obstreperous (əb'strɛpərəs) *adj* noisy or rough, esp in resisting restraint or control [c16 from L, from *obstrepere*, from *ob-* against + *strepere* to roar] > **ob'streperously** *adv* > **ob'streperousness** *n*

obstruct (əb'strʌkt) *vb* (*tr*) 1 to block (a road, passageway, etc) with an obstacle 2 to make (progress or activity) difficult 3 to impede or block a clear view of [c17 L *obstructus* built against, p.p. of *obstruere*, from *ob-* against + *struere* to build] > **ob'structive** *adj, n* > **ob'structively** *adv* > **ob'structiveness** *n* > **ob'structor** *n*

obstruction (əb'strʌkʃən) *n* 1 a person or thing that obstructs 2 the act or an instance of obstructing 3 delay of business, esp in a legislature by means of procedural devices 4 *sport* the act of unfairly impeding an opposing player > **ob'structional** *adj*

obstructionist (əb'strʌkʃənɪst) *n* a person who deliberately obstructs business, etc, esp in a legislature > **ob'structionism** *n*

obtain (əb'teɪn) *vb* 1 (*tr*) to gain possession of; acquire; get 2 (*intr*) to be customary, valid, or accepted: *a new law obtains in this case* [c15 via OF from L *obtinēre* to take hold of] > **ob'tainable** *adj* > **obˌtaina'bility** *n* > **ob'tainer** *n* > **ob'tainment** *n*

obtrude (əb'tru:d) *vb* **obtrudes, obtruding, obtruded** 1 to push (oneself, one's opinions, etc) on others in an unwelcome way 2 (*tr*) to push out or forward [c16 from L *obtrūdere*, from *ob-* against + *trūdere* to push forward] > **ob'truder** *n* > **obtrusion** (əb'tru:ʒən) *n*

obtrusive (əb'tru:sɪv) *adj* 1 obtruding or tending to obtrude 2 sticking out; protruding; noticeable > **ob'trusively** *adv* > **ob'trusiveness** *n*

obtuse (əb'tju:s) *adj* 1 mentally slow or emotionally insensitive 2 *maths* (of an angle) lying between 90° and 180° 3 not sharp or pointed 4 indistinctly felt, heard, etc; dull: *obtuse pain* 5 (of a leaf or similar flat part) having a rounded or blunt tip [c16 from L *obtūsus* dulled, p.p. of *obtundere* to beat down] > **ob'tusely** *adv* > **ob'tuseness** *n*

obverse ('ɒbvɜ:s) *adj* 1 facing or turned towards the observer 2 forming or serving as a counterpart 3 (of leaves) narrower at the base than at the top ▷ *n* 4 a counterpart or complement 5 *logic* a proposition derived from another by replacing the original predicate by its negation and changing the proposition from affirmative to negative or vice versa, as *no sum is correct* from *every sum is incorrect* 6 the side of a coin that bears the main design or device [c17 from L *obversus* turned towards, p.p. of *obvertere*] > **ob'versely** *adv*

obvert (ɒb'vɜ:t) *vb* (*tr*) 1 *logic* to deduce the obverse of (a proposition) 2 *rare* to turn so as to show the main or other side [c17 from L *obvertere* to turn towards] > **ob'version** *n*

obviate ('ɒbvɪˌeɪt) *vb* **obviates, obviating, obviated** (*tr*) to avoid or prevent (a need or difficulty) [c16 from LL *obviātus* prevented, p.p. of *obviāre*; see OBVIOUS] > **ˌobvi'ation** *n*

obvious ('ɒbvɪəs) *adj* 1 easy to see or understand; evident 2 exhibiting motives, feelings, intentions, etc, clearly or without subtlety 3 naive or unsubtle: *the play was rather obvious* [c16 from L *obvius*, from *obviam* in the way] > **'obviousness** *n*

obviously ('ɒbvɪəslɪ) *adv* 1 in a way that is easy to see or understand; evidently 2 without subtlety 3 (*sentence modifier*) it is obvious that; clearly: *obviously not everyone wants a bank account*

OC *abbrev for* Officer Commanding

o/c *abbrev for* overcharge

O Canada *n* the Canadian national anthem.

ocarina (ˌɒkə'ri:nə) *n* an egg-shaped wind instrument with a protruding mouthpiece and six to eight finger holes, producing an almost pure tone [c19 from It.: little goose, from *oca* goose, ult. from L *avis* bird]

O'Casey (əʊ'keɪsɪ) *n* **Sean** (ʃɔ:n) 1880–1964, Irish dramatist. His plays include *Juno and the Paycock* (1924) and *The Plough and the Stars* (1926), which are realistic pictures of Dublin slum life

Occam ('ɒkəm) *n* a variant spelling of (William of) **Ockham**

Occam's razor *n* a variant spelling of **Ockham's razor**

occasion (ə'keɪʒən) *n* 1 (sometimes foll by *of*) the time of a particular happening or event 2 (sometimes foll by *for*) a reason or cause (to do or be something); grounds: *there was no occasion to complain* 3 an opportunity (to do something); chance 4 a special event, time, or celebration: *the party was quite an occasion* 5 **on occasion** every so often 6 **rise to the occasion** to have the courage, wit, etc, to meet the special demands of a situation 7 **take occasion** to avail oneself of an opportunity (to do something) ▷ *vb* 8 (*tr*) to bring about, esp incidentally or by chance [c14 from L *occāsiō* a falling down, from *occidere* to fall]

occasional (ə'keɪʒənᵊl) *adj* 1 taking place from time to time; not frequent or regular 2 of, for, or happening on special occasions 3 serving as an occasion (for something)

occasionally (ə'keɪʒənəlɪ) *adv* from time to time

occasional table *n* a small table with no regular use

occident ('ɒksɪdənt) *n* a literary or formal word for **west** ▷ Cf **orient** [c14 via OF from L *occidere* to fall (with reference to the setting sun)]

Occident ('ɒksɪdənt) *n* (usually preceded by *the*) 1 the countries of Europe and America 2 the western hemisphere > **ˌOcci'dental** *adj, n*

occidental (ˌɒksɪ'dɛntᵊl) *adj* a literary or formal word for **western**

occipital (ɒk'sɪpɪtᵊl) *adj* 1 of or relating to the back of the head or skull ▷ *n* 2 short for **occipital bone** [See OCCIPUT]

occipital bone *n* the bone that forms the back part of the skull and part of its base

occipital lobe *n* the posterior portion of each cerebral hemisphere, concerned with the interpretation of visual sensory impulses

occiput ('ɒksɪˌpʌt) *n, pl* **occiputs** *or* **occipita** (ɒk'sɪpɪtə) the back part of the head or skull [c14 from L, from *ob-* at the back of + *caput* head]

occlude (ə'klu:d) *vb* **occludes, occluding, occluded** 1 (*tr*) to block or stop up (a passage or opening); obstruct 2 (*tr*) to prevent the passage of 3 (*tr*) *chem* (of a solid) to incorporate (a substance) by absorption or adsorption 4 *meteorol* to form or cause to form an occluded front 5 *dentistry* to produce or cause to produce occlusion, as in chewing [c16 from L *occlūdere*, from *ob-* (intensive) + *claudere* to close] > **oc'cludent** *adj*

occluded front *n meteorol* the line or plane occurring where the cold front of a depression has overtaken the warm front, raising the warm sector from ground level. Also called: **occlusion**

Oo

occlusion (ə'klu:ʒən) *n* **1** the act of occluding or the state of being occluded **2** *meteorol* another term for **occluded front** **3** *dentistry* the normal position of the teeth when the jaws are closed > **oc'clusive** *adj*

occult *adj* (ɒ'kʌlt, 'ɒkʌlt) **1a** of or characteristic of mystical or supernatural phenomena or influences **1b** (*as noun*): *the occult* **2** beyond ordinary human understanding **3** secret or esoteric ▷ *vb* (ɒ'kʌlt) **4** *astron* (of a celestial body) to hide (another celestial body) from view by occultation or (of a celestial body) to become hidden by occultation **5** to hide or become hidden or shut off from view **6** (*intr*) (of lights, esp in lighthouses) to shut off at regular intervals [C16 from L *occultus*, p.p. of *occulere*, from *ob-* over, up + *-culere*, rel. to *celāre* to conceal] > **'occul,tism** *n* > **'occultist** *n* > **oc'cultness** *n*

occultation (,ɒkʌl'teɪʃən) *n* the temporary disappearance of one celestial body as it moves out of sight behind another body

occupancy ('ɒkjʊpənsɪ) *n, pl* **occupancies** **1** the act of occupying; possession of a property **2** *law* the possession and use of property by or without agreement and without any claim to ownership **3** *law* the act of taking possession of unowned property, esp land, with the intent of thus acquiring ownership **4** the condition or fact of being an occupant, esp a tenant **5** the period of time during which one is an occupant, esp of property

occupant ('ɒkjʊpənt) *n* **1** a person, thing, etc, holding a position or place **2** *law* a person who has possession of something, esp an estate, house, etc; tenant **3** *law* a person who acquires by occupancy the title to something previously without an owner

occupation (,ɒkjʊ'peɪʃən) *n* **1** a person's regular work or profession; job **2** any activity on which time is spent by a person **3** the act of occupying or the state of being occupied **4** the control of a country by a foreign military power **5** the period of time that a nation, place, or position is occupied **6** (*modifier*) for the use of the occupier of a particular property: *occupation road* > **,occu'pational** *adj*

occupational psychology *n* the scientific study of mental or emotional problems associated with the working environment

occupational therapy *n med* treatment of people with physical, emotional, or social problems, using purposeful activity to help them overcome or learn to deal with their problems

occupation groupings *pl n* a system of classifying people according to occupation, based originally on information obtained by government census and subsequently developed by market research. The classifications are used by the advertising industry to identify potential markets. The groups are **A, B, C1, C2, D,** and **E**

occupier ('ɒkjʊ,paɪə) *n* **1** *Brit* a person who is in possession or occupation of a house or land **2** a person or thing that occupies

occupy ('ɒkjʊ,paɪ) *vb* **occupies, occupying, occupied** (*tr*) **1** to live or be established in (a house, flat, office, etc) **2** (*often passive*) to keep (a person) busy or engrossed **3** (*often passive*) to take up (time or space) **4** to take and hold possession of, esp as a demonstration: *students occupied the college buildings* **5** to fill or hold (a position or rank) [C14 from OF *occuper*, from L *occupāre* to seize hold of]

occur (ə'kɜ:) *vb* **occurs, occurring, occurred** (*intr*) **1** to happen; take place; come about **2** to be found or be present; exist **3** (foll by *to*) to be realized or thought of (by); suggest itself (to) [C16 from L *occurrere* to run up to]

> **USAGE** It is usually regarded as incorrect to talk of prearranged events *occurring* or *happening*: *the wedding took place* (not *occurred* or *happened*) *in the afternoon*

occurrence (ə'kʌrəns) *n* **1** something that occurs; a happening; event **2** the act or an instance of occurring: *a crime of frequent occurrence* > **oc'current** *adj*

ocean ('əʊʃən) *n* **1** a very large stretch of sea, esp one of the five oceans of the world, the Atlantic, Pacific, Indian, Arctic, and Antarctic **2** the body of salt water covering approximately 70 per cent of the earth's surface **3** a huge quantity or expanse: *an ocean of replies* **4** *literary* the sea [C13 via OF from L *ōceanus*, from OCEANUS]

oceanarium (,əʊʃə'nɛərɪəm) *n, pl* **oceanariums** *or* **oceanaria** (-ɪə) a large saltwater aquarium for marine life

ocean-going *adj* (of a ship, boat, etc) suited for travel on the open ocean

Oceania (,əʊʃɪ'ɑ:nɪə) *n* the islands of the central and S Pacific, including Melanesia, Micronesia, and Polynesia: sometimes also including Australasia and the Malay Archipelago > **,Oce'anian** *adj, n*

oceanic (,əʊʃɪ'ænɪk) *adj* **1** of or relating to the ocean **2** living in the depths of the ocean beyond the continental shelf at a depth exceeding 200 metres: *oceanic fauna* **3** huge or overwhelming

Oceanid (əʊ'sɪənɪd) *n, pl* **Oceanids** *or* **Oceanides** (,əʊsɪ'ænɪ,di:z) *Greek myth.* an ocean nymph

oceanography (,əʊʃə'nɒgrəfɪ, ,əʊʃɪə-) *n* the branch of science dealing with the physical, chemical, geological, and biological features of the oceans > **,ocean'ographer** *n* > **oceanographic** (,əʊʃənə'græfɪk, ,əʊʃɪə-) *or* **,oceano'graphical** *adj*

oceanology (,əʊʃə'nɒlədʒɪ, ,əʊʃɪə-) *n* the study of the sea, esp of its economic geography

Oceanus (əʊ'sɪənəs) *n Greek myth* a Titan, divinity of the stream believed to flow around the earth

ocellus (ɒ'sɛləs) *n, pl* **ocelli** (-laɪ) **1** the simple eye of insects and some other invertebrates, consisting basically of light-sensitive cells **2** any eyelike marking in animals, such as the eyespot on the tail feather of a peacock [C19 via NL from L: small eye, from *oculus* eye] > **o'cellar** *adj* > **ocellate** ('ɒsɪ,leɪt) *or* **'ocel,lated** *adj* > **,ocel'lation** *n*

ocelot ('ɒsɪ,lɒt, 'əʊ-) *n* a feline mammal inhabiting Central and South America and having a dark-spotted buff-brown coat [C18 via F from Nahuatl *ocelotl* jaguar]

och (ɒx) *interj Scot & Irish.* an expression of surprise, contempt, disagreement, etc

oche ('ɒkɪ) *n darts* the mark or ridge on the floor behind which a player must stand to throw [from ?]

ochlocracy (ɒk'lɒkrəsɪ) *n, pl* **ochlocracies** rule by the mob; mobocracy [C16 via F, from Gk *okhlokratia*, from *okhlos* mob + *kratos* power] > **ochlocrat** ('ɒklə,kræt) *n* > **,ochlo'cratic** *adj*

ochone (ɒ'xəʊn) *interj Scot & Irish* an expression of sorrow or regret [from Gaelic *ochóin*]

ochre *or US* **ocher** ('əʊkə) *n* **1** any of various natural earths containing ferric oxide, silica, and alumina: used as yellow or red pigments **2a** a moderate yellow-orange to orange colour **2b** (*as adj*): *an ochre dress* ▷ *vb* **ochres, ochring, ochred** *or US* **ochers, ochering, ochered** **3** (*tr*) to colour with ochre [C15 from OF *ocre*, from L *ōchra*, from Gk *ōkhros* pale yellow] > **ochreous** ('əʊkrɪəs, 'əʊkərəs), **ochrous** ('əʊkrəs), **ochry** ('əʊkərɪ, 'əʊkrɪ) *or US* **'ocherous, 'ochery** *adj*

-ock *suffix forming nouns* indicating smallness: *hillock* [OE *-oc, -uc*]

ocker ('ɒkə) *Austral sl* ▷ *n* **1** (*often cap*) an uncultivated or boorish Australian ▷ *adj* **2** typical of such a person [C20 after an Australian TV character]

Ockham *or* **Occam** ('ɒkəm) *n* **William of** died ?1349, English nominalist philosopher, who contested the temporal power of the papacy and ended the conflict between nominalism and realism. See **Ockham's razor**

Ockham's razor *or* **Occam's razor** *n* a maxim, attributed to William of Ockham, stating that in explaining something assumptions must not be needlessly multiplied. Also called: **the principle of economy**

o'clock (ə'klɒk) *adv* **1** used after a number from one to twelve to indicate the hour of the day or night **2** used after a number to indicate direction or position relative to the observer, twelve o'clock being directly ahead and other positions being obtained by comparisons with a clock face [c18 abbrev for *of the clock*]

O'Connell (əʊ'kɒnᵊl) *n* **Daniel** 1775–1847, Irish nationalist leader and orator, whose election to the British House of Commons (1828) forced the acceptance of Catholic emancipation (1829)

OCR *abbrev for* optical character reader *or* recognition

oct. *abbrev for* octavo

Oct. *abbrev for* October

oct- *combining form* a variant of **octo-** before a vowel

octa- *combining form* a variant of **octo-**

octad ('ɒktæd) *n* **1** a group or series of eight **2** *chem* an element with a valency of eight [c19 from Gk *oktās*, from *oktō* eight] > **oc'tadic** *adj*

octagon ('ɒktəgən) *n* a polygon having eight sides [c17 via L from Gk *oktagōnos* having eight angles] > **octagonal** (ɒk'tægənᵊl) *adj*

octahedron (ˌɒktə'hi:drən) *n, pl* **octahedrons** *or* **octahedra** (-drə) a solid figure having eight plane faces

octal notation *or* **octal** ('ɒktəl) *n computing* a number system having a base 8, one octal digit being equivalent to a group of three bits

octane ('ɒkteɪn) *n* a liquid hydrocarbon found in petroleum. Formula: C_8H_{18}

octane number *or* **rating** *n* a measure of the antiknock quality of a petrol expressed as a percentage

octant ('ɒktənt) *n* **1** *maths* **1a** any of the eight parts into which the three planes containing the Cartesian coordinate axes divide space **1b** an eighth part of a circle **2** *astron* the position of a celestial body when it is at an angular distance of 45° from another body **3** an instrument used for measuring angles, similar to a sextant but having a graduated arc of 45° [c17 from L *octans* half quadrant, from *octo* eight]

octavalent (ˌɒktə'veɪlənt) *adj chem* having a valency of eight

octave ('ɒktɪv) *n* **1a** the interval between two musical notes one of which has twice the pitch of the other and lies eight notes away from it counting inclusively along the diatonic scale **1b** one of these two notes, esp the one of higher pitch **1c** *(as modifier): an octave leap* **2** *prosody* a rhythmic group of eight lines of verse **3** ('ɒkteɪv) **3a** a feast day and the seven days following **3b** the final day of this period **4** the eighth of eight basic positions in fencing **5** any set or series of eight ▷ *adj* **6** consisting of eight parts [c14 (orig.: eighth day) via OF from Med. L *octāva diēs* eighth day (after a festival), from L *octo* eight]

Octavian (ɒk'teɪvɪən) *n* the name of **Augustus** before he became emperor (27 BC)

octavo (ɒk'teɪvəʊ) *n, pl* **octavos** **1** a book size resulting from folding a sheet of paper of a specified size to form eight leaves: *demi-octavo*. Often written: **8vo, 8°** **2** a book of this size [c16 from NL *in octavo* in an eighth (of a sheet)]

octennial (ɒk'tɛnɪəl) *adj* **1** occurring every eight years **2** lasting for eight years [c17 from L *octennium*, from *octo* eight + *annus* year] > **oc'tennially** *adv*

octet (ɒk'tɛt) *n* **1** any group of eight, esp singers or musicians **2** a piece of music composed for such a group **3** *prosody* another word for **octave** (sense 2) **4** *chem* a stable group of eight electrons ▷ Also (for senses 1, 2, 3): **octette** [c19 from L *octo* eight, on the model of DUET]

octillion (ɒk'tɪljən) *n* **1** (in Britain and Germany) the number represented as one followed by 48 zeros (10^{48}) **2** (in the US, Canada, and France) the number represented as one followed by 27 zeros (10^{27}) [c17 from F, on the model of MILLION] > **oc'tillionth** *adj, n*

octo-, octa-, *or before a vowel* **oct-** *combining form* eight: *octosyllabic; octagon* [from L *octo*, Gk *okto*]

October (ɒk'təʊbə) *n* the tenth month of the year, consisting of 31 days [OE, from L, from *octo* eight, since it was orig. the eighth month in Roman reckoning]

Octobrist (ɒk'təʊbrɪst) *n* a member of a Russian political party favouring the constitutional reforms granted in a manifesto issued by Nicholas II in Oct. 1905

octocentenary (ˌɒktəʊsɛn'ti:nərɪ) *n, pl* **octocentenaries** an 800th anniversary

octogenarian (ˌɒktəʊdʒɪ'nɛərɪən) *n* **1** a person who is from 80 to 89 years old ▷ *adj* **2** of or relating to an octogenarian [c19 from L *octōgēnārius* containing eighty, from *octōgēnī* eighty each]

octopus ('ɒktəpəs) *n, pl* **octopuses** **1** a cephalopod mollusc having a soft oval body with eight long suckered tentacles and occurring at the sea bottom **2** a powerful influential organization, etc, with far-reaching effects, esp harmful ones [c18 via NL from Gk *oktōpous* having eight feet]

octoroon *or* **octaroon** (ˌɒktə'ru:n) *n* a person having one quadroon and one White parent and therefore having one-eighth Black blood ▷ Cf **quadroon** [c19 OCTO- + *-roon* as in QUADROON]

octosyllable ('ɒktəˌsɪləbᵊl) *n* **1** a line of verse composed of eight syllables **2** a word of eight syllables > **octosyllabic** (ˌɒktəʊsɪ'læbɪk) *adj*

octroi ('ɒktrwɑ:) *n* **1** (in some European countries, esp France) a duty on goods brought into certain towns **2** the place where it is collected **3** the officers responsible for its collection [c17 from F *octroyer* to concede, from Med. L *auctorizāre* to AUTHORIZE]

octuple ('ɒktjʊpᵊl) *n* **1** a quantity or number eight times as great as another ▷ *adj* **2** eight times as much or as many **3** consisting of eight parts ▷ *vb* **octuples, octupling, octupled** **4** *(tr)* to multiply by eight [c17 from L *octuplus*, from *octo* eight + *-plus* as in *duplus* double]

Oo

ocular ('ɒkjʊlə) *adj* **1** of or relating to the eye ▷ *n* **2** another name for **eyepiece** [c16 from L *oculāris* from *oculus* eye] > **'ocularly** *adv*

ocularist ('ɒkjʊlərɪst) *n* a person who makes artificial eyes

oculate ('ɒkjʊlɪt) *adj zool* **1** having eyes **2** relating to or resembling eyes: *oculate markings*

oculist ('ɒkjʊlɪst) *n med* a former term for **ophthalmologist** [c17 via F from L *oculus* eye]

od (ɒd, əʊd), **odyl,** *or* **odyle** ('ɒdɪl) *n arch* a hypothetical force formerly thought to be responsible for many natural phenomena, such as magnetism, light, and hypnotism [c19 coined by Baron Karl von Reichenbach (1788–1869), G scientist] > **'odic** *adj*

OD[1] (ˌəʊ'di:) *inf* ▷ *n* **1** an overdose of a drug ▷ *vb* **OD's, OD'ing, OD'd** *(intr)* **2** to take an overdose of a drug [c20 from *o(ver)d(ose)*]

OD[2] *abbrev for:* **1** Officer of the Day **2** Also: **o.d.** *mil* olive drab **3** Also: **O/D** *banking* **3a** on demand **3b** overdrawn **4** ordnance datum **5** outside diameter

odalisque *or* **odalisk** ('əʊdəlɪsk) *n* a female slave or concubine [c17 via F, changed from Turkish *ōdalik*, from *ōdah* room + *-lik*, n. suffix]

odd (ɒd) *adj* **1** unusual or peculiar in appearance, character, etc **2** occasional, incidental, or random: *odd jobs* **3** leftover or additional: *odd bits of wool* **4a** not divisible by two **4b** represented or indicated by a number that is not divisible by two: *graphs are on odd pages* ▷ Cf **even**[1] (sense 7) **5** being part of a matched pair or set when the other or others are missing: *an odd sock* **6** *(in combination)* used to designate an indefinite quantity more than the quantity specified in round numbers: *fifty-odd pounds* **7a** out-of-the-way or secluded: *odd corners* **7b** appearing not to correspond or match **8** **odd man out** a person or thing excluded from others forming a group, unit, etc ▷ *n* **9** *golf* **9a** one stroke more than the score of one's opponent **9b** a handicap of one stroke **10** a thing or person that is odd in sequence or number ▷ See also **odds** [from ON *oddi* triangle, point] > **'oddly** *adv* > **'oddness** *n*

oddball ('ɒd,bɔːl) *inf* ▷ *n* **1** Also: **odd bod, odd fish** a strange or eccentric person or thing ▷ *adj* **2** strange or peculiar

Oddfellow ('ɒd,fɛləʊ) *n* a member of a secret benevolent and fraternal association founded in England in the 18th century

oddity ('ɒdɪtɪ) *n, pl* **oddities 1** an odd person or thing **2** an odd quality or characteristic **3** the condition of being odd

odd-jobman *or* **odd-jobber** *n* a person who does casual work, esp domestic repairs

oddment ('ɒdmənt) *n* **1** (*often pl*) an odd piece or thing; leftover **2** *printing* **2a** pages that do not make a complete signature **2b** any individual part of a book excluding the main text

odd pricing *n* pricing goods in such a way as to imply that a bargain is being offered, as £5.99 instead of £6

odds (ɒdz) *pl n* **1** (foll by *on* or *against*) the probability, expressed as a ratio, that a certain event will take place: *the odds against the outsider are a hundred to one* **2** the amount, expressed as a ratio, by which the wager of one better is greater than that of another: *he was offering odds of five to one* **3** the likelihood that a certain state of affairs will be so: *the odds are that he is drunk* **4** an equalizing allowance, esp one given to a weaker side in a contest **5** the advantage that one contender is judged to have over another **6** *Brit* a significant difference (esp in **it makes no odds**) **7 at odds** on bad terms **8 give** *or* **lay odds** to offer a bet with favourable odds **9 over the odds 9a** more than is expected, necessary, etc **9b** unfair or excessive **10 take odds** to accept a bet with favourable odds **11 what's the odds?** *Brit inf* what does it matter?

odds and ends *pl n* miscellaneous items or articles

odds-on *adj* **1** (of a horse, etc) rated at even money or less to win **2** regarded as more or most likely to win, succeed, happen, etc

ode (əʊd) *n* **1** a lyric poem, typically addressed to a particular subject, with lines of varying lengths and complex rhythms **2** (formerly) a poem meant to be sung [C16 via F from LL *ōda*, from Gk *ōidē*, from *aeidein* to sing]

-ode[1] *n combining form* denoting resemblance: *nematode* [from Gk *-ōdēs*, from *eidos* shape]

-ode[2] *n combining form* denoting a path or way: *electrode* [from Gk *-odos*, from *hodos* a way]

Odense (*Danish* 'oːðənsə) *n* a port in S Denmark, on Funen Island: cathedral founded by King Canute in the 11th century. Pop: 189 912 (2000 est)

Oder ('əʊdə) *n* a river in central Europe, rising in the NE Czech Republic and flowing north and west, forming part of the border between Germany and Poland, to the Baltic. Length: 913 km (567 miles). Czech and Polish name: **Odra**

Oder-Neisse Line ('əʊdə'naɪsə) *n* the present-day boundary between Germany and Poland along the Rivers Oder and Neisse. Established in 1945, it originally separated the Soviet Zone of Germany from the regions under Polish administration

Odessa (əʊ'dɛsə; *Russian* a'djɛsə) *n* a port in the S Ukraine on the Black Sea: the chief Russian grain port in the 19th century; university (1865); industrial centre and important naval base. Pop: 1 027 400 (1998 est)

odeum ('əʊdɪəm) *n, pl* **odea** ('əʊdɪə) (esp in ancient Greece and Rome) a building for musical performances. Also called: **odeon** [C17 from L, from Gk *ōideion*, from *ōidē* ODE]

Odin ('əʊdɪn) *or* **Othin** *n Norse myth* the supreme creator; the divinity of wisdom, culture, war, and the dead. Germanic counterpart: **Wotan, Woden**

odious ('əʊdɪəs) *adj* very unpleasant; offensive; repugnant [C17 from L; see ODIUM] > **'odiousness** *n*

odium ('əʊdɪəm) *n* **1** the dislike accorded to a hated person or thing **2** hatred; repugnance [C17 from L; rel. to *ōdī* I hate, Gk *odussasthai* to be angry]

Odoacer (,ɒdə'eɪsə) *or* **Odovacar** (,əʊdə'vɑːkə) *n* ?434–493 AD, barbarian ruler of Italy (476–493); assassinated by Theodoric

odometer (ɒ'dɒmɪtə, əʊ-) *n* the usual US and Canad name for **mileometer** [C18 *hodometer*, from Gk *hodos* way + -METER] > **o'dometry** *n*

-odont *adj and n combining form* -toothed: *acrodont* [from Gk *odōn* tooth]

odonto- *or before a vowel* **odont-** *combining form* indicating a tooth or teeth: *odontology* [from Gk *odōn* tooth]

odontoglossum (ɒ,dɒntə'glɒsəm) *n* a tropical American epiphytic orchid having clusters of brightly coloured flowers

odontology (,ɒdɒn'tɒlədʒɪ) *n* the branch of science concerned with the anatomy, development, and diseases of teeth > **odontological** (ɒ,dɒntə'lɒdʒɪkᵊl) *adj* > **,odon'tologist** *n*

odoriferous (,əʊdə'rɪfərəs) *adj* having or emitting an odour, esp a fragrant one > **,odor'iferously** *adv* > **,odor'iferousness** *n*

odoriphore (əʊ'dɒrɪ,fɔː) *n chem* the group of atoms in an odorous molecule responsible for its odour

odorous ('əʊdərəs) *adj* having or emitting a characteristic smell or odour > **'odorously** *adv* > **'odorousness** *n*

odour *or US* **odor** ('əʊdə) *n* **1** the property of a substance that gives it a characteristic scent or smell **2** a pervasive quality about something: *an odour of dishonesty* **3** repute or regard (in **in good odour, in bad odour**) **4** *arch* a sweet-smelling fragrance [C13 from OF *odur*, from L *odor*] > **'odourless** *or US* **'odorless** *adj*

Odovacar (,əʊdə'vɑːkə) *n* a variant of **Odoacer**

Odra ('ɔdra) *n* the Czech and Polish name for the **Oder**

Odysseus (ə'diːsɪəs) *n Greek myth* one of the foremost of the Greek heroes at the siege of Troy, noted for his courage and ingenuity. His return to his kingdom of Ithaca was fraught with adventures in which he lost all his companions. Roman name: **Ulysses**

Odyssey ('ɒdɪsɪ) *n* **1** a Greek epic poem, attributed to Homer, describing the ten-year homeward wanderings of Odysseus after the fall of Troy **2** (*often not cap*) any long eventful journey > **Odyssean** (,ɒdɪ'siːən) *adj*

Oe *symbol for* oersted

OE *abbrev for* Old English (language)

Ōe ('aʊi) *n* **Kenzaburo** (kɛnzə'bʊrəʊ) born 1932, Japanese novelist and writer; his books include *The Catch* (1958), *A Personal Matter* (1964), and *Silent Cry* (1989): Nobel prize for literature 1994

OECD *abbrev for* Organization for Economic Cooperation and Development
▷ www.oecd.org

OECS *abbrev for* Organization of Eastern Caribbean States

OED *abbrev for* Oxford English Dictionary

oedema *or US* **edema** (ɪ'diːmə) *n, pl* **oedemata** *or US* **edemata** (-mətə) **1** *pathol* an excessive accumulation of serous fluid in the intercellular spaces of tissue **2** *bot* an abnormal swelling in a plant caused by parenchyma or an accumulation of water in the tissues [C16 via NL from Gk *oidēma*, from *oidein* to swell] > **oedematous** (ɪ'dɛmətəs), **oe'dema,tose** *or US* **e'dematous, e'dema,tose** *adj*

Oedipus ('iːdɪpəs) *n Greek myth* the son of Laius and Jocasta. He killed his father, unaware of his identity, and unwittingly married his mother. When the truth was revealed, he put out his eyes and Jocasta killed herself

Oedipus complex *n psychoanal* the repressed sexual feeling of a child, esp a male child, for its parent of the opposite sex combined with a rivalry with the parent of the same sex > **'oedipal** *or* **,oedi'pean** *adj*

OEEC *abbrev for* Organization for European Economic Cooperation. It was superseded by the OECD in 1961

Oehlenschläger *or* **Öhlenschläger** (*Danish* 'øːlənslɛːgər) *n* **Adam Gottlob** ('adam 'gɔtlɔp) 1779–1850, Danish romantic poet and dramatist

OEM *abbrev for* original equipment manufacturer: a computer company whose products are made by combining basic parts supplied by others to meet a customer's needs

oenology *or* **enology** (iː'nɒlədʒɪ) *n* the study of wine [C19 from Gk *oinos* wine + -LOGY] > **oenological** *or* **enological** (,iːnə'lɒdʒɪkᵊl) *adj* > **oe'nologist** *or* **e'nologist** *n*

Oenone (iː'nəʊnɪ) *n Greek myth* a nymph of Mount Ida, whose lover Paris left her for Helen

oenothera (iː'nɒθərə) *n* any of various hardy biennial or herbaceous perennial plants having yellow flowers. Also called: **evening primrose** [from Gk *oinothēras*, ?from *onothēras* a plant whose roots smell of wine]

o'er (ɔː, əʊə) *prep, adv* a poetic contraction of **over**

oersted ('ɜːstɛd) *n* the cgs unit of magnetic field strength; the field strength that would cause a unit magnetic pole to experience a force of 1 dyne in free space. It is equivalent to 79.58 amperes per metre. Symbol Oe [C20 after H. C. *Oersted* (1777–1851), Danish physicist who discovered electromagnetism]

oesophagus *or US* **esophagus** (iː'sɒfəgəs) *n, pl* **oesophagi** *or US* **esophagi** (-,gaɪ) the part of the alimentary canal between the pharynx and the stomach; gullet [C16 via NL from Gk *oisophagos*, from *oisein*, future infinitive of *pherein* to carry + *-phagos*, from *phagein* to eat] > **oesophageal** *or US* **esophageal** (iː,sɒfə'dʒiːəl) *adj*

oestradiol (,iːstrə'daɪɒl, ,ɛstrə-) *or US* **estradiol** *n* the most potent oestrogenic hormone secreted by the mammalian ovary: synthesized and used to treat oestrogen deficiency and cancer of the breast [C20 from NL, from OESTRIN + DI-[1] + -OL[1]]

oestrin ('iːstrɪn) *n* an obsolete term for **oestrogen** [C20 from OESTR(US) + -IN]

oestrogen ('iːstrədʒən, 'ɛstrə-) *or US* **estrogen** *n* any of several hormones that induce oestrus, stimulate changes in the female reproductive organs, and promote development of female secondary sexual characteristics [C20 from OESTRUS + -GEN] > **oestrogenic** (,iːstrə'dʒɛnɪk, ,ɛstrə-) *or US* **estrogenic** (,ɛstrə'dʒɛnɪk, ,iːstrə-) *adj* > **,oestro'genically** *or US* **,estro'genically** *adv*

oestrous cycle ('iːstrəs) *n* a hormonally controlled cycle of activity of the reproductive organs in many female mammals

oestrus ('iːstrəs, 'ɛstrəs) *or US* **estrus, estrum** ('ɛstrəm, 'iːstrəm) *n* a regularly occurring period of sexual receptivity in most female mammals, except humans, during which ovulation occurs and copulation can take place; heat [C17 from L *oestrus* gadfly, hence frenzy, from Gk *oistros*] > **'oestrous, 'oestral** *or US* **'estrous, 'estral** *adj*

oeuvre *French* (œvrə) *n* **1** a work of art, literature, music, etc **2** the total output of a writer, painter, etc [ult. from L *opera*, pl. of *opus* work]

of (ɒv; *unstressed* əv) *prep* **1** used with a verbal noun or gerund to link it with a following noun that is either the subject or the object of the verb embedded in the gerund: *the breathing of a fine swimmer* (subject); *the breathing of clean air* (object) **2** used to indicate possession, origin, or association: *the house of my sister; to die of hunger* **3** used after words or phrases expressing quantities: *a pint of milk* **4** constituted by, containing, or characterized by: *a family of idiots; a rod of iron; a man of some depth* **5** used to indicate separation, as in time or space: *within a mile of the town; within ten minutes of the beginning of the concert* **6** used to mark apposition: *the city of Naples; a speech on the subject of archaeology* **7** about; concerning: *speak to me of love* **8** used in passive constructions to indicate the agent: *he was beloved of all* **9** *inf* used to indicate a day or part of a period of time when some activity habitually occurs: *I go to the pub of an evening* **10** *US* before the hour of: *a quarter of nine* [OE (as prep & adv); rel. to L *ab*]

USAGE See at **off**

OF *abbrev for* Old French (language)

Ofcom ('ɒfkɒm) *n* (in Britain) *acronym for* Office of Communications: a government body regulating the telecommunications industries; a super-regulator merging the Radio Authority, Independent Television Commission, and Oftel

off (ɒf) *prep* **1** used to indicate actions in which contact is absent, as between an object and a surface: *to lift a cup off the table* **2** used to indicate the removal of something that is appended to or in association with something else: *to take the tax off potatoes* **3** out of alignment with: *we are off course* **4** situated near to or leading away from: *just off the High Street* **5** not inclined towards: *I've gone off you* ▷ *adv* **6** (*particle*) so as to be deactivated or disengaged: *turn off the radio* **7** (*particle*) **7a** so as to get rid of: *sleep off a hangover* **7b** so as to be removed from, esp as a reduction: *he took ten per cent off* **8** spent away from work or other duties: *take the afternoon off* **9a** on a trip, journey, or race: I *saw her off at the station* **9b** (*particle*) so as to be completely absent, used up, or exhausted: *this stuff kills off all vermin* **10** out from the shore or land: *the ship stood off* **11a** out of contact; at a distance: *the ship was 10 miles off* **11b** out of the present location: *the girl ran off* **12** away in the future: *August is less than a week off* **13** (*particle*) so as to be no longer taking place: *the match has been rained off* **14** (*particle*) removed from contact with something, as clothing from the body: *the girl took all her clothes off* **15** offstage: *noises off* **16** **off and on** intermittently; from time to time: *he comes here off and on* **17** **off with** (*interj*) a command or an exhortation to remove or cut off (something specified): *off with his head; off with that coat* ▷ *adj* **18** not on; no longer operative: *the off position on the dial* **19** (*postpositive*) not taking place; cancelled or postponed: *the meeting is off* **20** in a specified condition regarding money, provisions, etc: *well off; how are you off for bread?* **21** unsatisfactory or disappointing: *his performance was rather off; an off year for good tennis* **22** (*postpositive*) in a condition as specified: *I'd be better off without this job* **23** (*postpositive*) no longer on the menu: *haddock is off* **24** (*postpositive*) (of food or drink) having gone bad, sour, etc: *this milk is off* ▷ *n* **25** *cricket* **25a** the part of the field on that side of the pitch to which the batsman presents his bat when taking strike **25b** (*in combination*) a fielding position in this part of the field: *mid-off* **25c** (*as modifier*): *the off stump* [orig. var. of OF; fully distinguished from it in the 17th cent.]

USAGE In standard English, *off* is not followed by *of*: *he stepped off* (not *off of*) *the platform*. The use of *off* after verbs such as *borrow, buy, get*, as in *I got this chair off an antique dealer*, is acceptable in conversation, but should be replaced in formal writing by *from*

Offa ('ɒfə) *n* died 796 AD, king of Mercia (757–796), who constructed an earthwork (**Offa's Dyke**) between Wales and Mercia

offal ('ɒfᵊl) *n* **1** the edible internal parts of an animal, such as the heart, liver, and tongue **2** dead or decomposing organic matter **3** refuse; rubbish [C14 from OFF + FALL, referring to parts fallen or cut off]

Offaly ('ɒfəlɪ) *n* an inland county of E central Republic of Ireland, in Leinster province: formerly an ancient kingdom, which also included parts of Tipperary, Leix, and Kildare. County town: Tullamore. Pop: 59 117 (1996). Area: 2000 sq km (770 sq miles)

off-balance-sheet reserve *n accounting* a sum of money or an asset that should appear on a company's balance but does not; hidden reserve

offbeat ('ɒf,bi:t) *n* **1** *music* any of the normally unaccented beats in a bar, such as the second and fourth beats in a bar of four-four time ▷ *adj* **2a** unusual, unconventional, or eccentric **2b** (*as noun*): *he liked the offbeat in fashion*

off break *n cricket* a bowled ball that spins from off to leg on pitching

off-Broadway *adj* **1** designating the kind of experimental, low-budget, or noncommercial productions associated with theatre outside the Broadway area in New York **2** (of theatres) not located on Broadway

off colour *adj* (**off-colour** *when prenominal*) **1** *chiefly Brit* slightly ill; unwell **2** indecent or indelicate; risqué

offcut ('ɒf,kʌt) *n* a piece of paper, wood, fabric, etc, remaining after the main pieces have been cut; remnant

Offenbach[1] (*German* 'ɔfənbax) *n* a city in central Germany, on the River Main in Hesse opposite Frankfurt am Main: leather-goods industry. Pop: 116 400 (1999 est)

Offenbach[2] ('ɒfən,bɑ:k; *French* ɔfɛnbak) *n* **Jacques** (ʒak) 1819–80, German-born French composer of many operettas, including *Orpheus in the Underworld* (1858), and of the opera *The Tales of Hoffmann* (1881)

offence *or US* **offense** (ə'fɛns) *n* **1** a violation or breach of a law, rule, etc **2** any public wrong or crime **3** annoyance, displeasure, or resentment **4 give offence** (**to**) to cause annoyance or displeasure (to) **5 take offence** to feel injured, humiliated, or offended **6** a source of annoyance, displeasure, or anger **7** attack; assault **8** *arch* injury or harm

offend (ə'fɛnd) *vb* **1** to hurt the feelings, sense of dignity, etc, of (a person, etc) **2** (*tr*) to be disagreeable to; disgust: *the smell offended him* **3** (*intr except in archaic uses*) to break (a law) [C14 via OF *offendre* to strike against, from L *offendere*] > **of'fender** *n* > **of'fending** *adj*

offensive (ə'fɛnsɪv) *adj* **1** unpleasant or disgusting, as to the senses **2** causing anger or annoyance; insulting **3** for the purpose of attack rather than defence ▷ *n* **4** (usually preceded by *the*) an attitude or position of aggression **5** an assault, attack, or military initiative, esp a strategic one > **of'fensively** *adv* > **of'fensiveness** *n*

offer ('ɒfə) *vb* **1** to present (something, someone, oneself, etc) for acceptance or rejection **2** (*tr*) to present as part of a requirement: *she offered English as a second subject* **3** (*tr*) to provide or make accessible: *this stream offers the best fishing* **4** (*intr*) to present itself: *if an opportunity should offer* **5** (*tr*) to show or express willingness or the intention (to do something) **6** (*tr*) to put forward (a proposal, opinion, etc) for consideration **7** (*tr*) to present for sale **8** (*tr*) to propose as payment; bid or tender **9** (when *tr*, often foll by *up*) to present (a prayer, sacrifice, etc) as or during an act of worship **10** (*tr*) to show readiness for: *to offer battle* **11** (*intr*) *arch* to make a proposal of marriage ▷ *n* **12** something, such as a proposal or bid, that is offered **13** the act of offering or the condition of being offered **14** a proposal of marriage **15 on offer** for sale at a reduced price [OE, from L *offerre* to present, from *ob-* to + *ferre* to bring]

offer document *n* a document sent by a person or firm making a takeover bid to the shareholders of the target company, giving details of the offer that has been made and, usually, reasons for accepting it

offering ('ɒfərɪŋ) *n* **1** something that is offered **2** a contribution to the funds of a religious organization **3** a sacrifice, as of an animal, to a deity

offertory ('ɒfətərɪ) *n, pl* **offertories** *Christianity* **1** the oblation of the bread and wine at the Eucharist **2** the offerings of the worshippers at this service **3** the prayers said or sung while the worshippers' offerings are being brought to the altar during the **offertory procession** [C14 from Church L *offertōrium* place appointed for offerings, from L *offerre* to OFFER]

offhand (,ɒf'hænd) *adj also* **offhanded,** *adv* **1** without care, thought, attention, or consideration; sometimes, brusque or ungracious: *an offhand manner* **2** without preparation or warning; impromptu > ,**off'handedly** *adv* > ,**off'handedness** *n*

Offiah (ɒ'faɪə) *n* **Martin** born 1965, British Rugby League football player

office ('ɒfɪs) *n* **1a** a room or rooms in which business, professional duties, clerical work, etc, are carried out **1b** (*as modifier*): *office furniture; an office boy* **2** (*often pl*) the building or buildings in which the work of an organization, such as a business, is carried out **3** a commercial or professional business: *the architect's office approved the plans* **4** the group of persons working in an office: *it was a happy office until she came* **5** (*cap when part of a name*) a department of the national government: *the Home Office* **6** (*cap when part of a name*) **6a** a governmental agency, esp of the Federal government in the US **6b** a subdivision of such an agency: *Office of Science and Technology* **7a** a position of trust, responsibility, or duty, esp in a government or organization: *to seek office* **7b** (*in combination*): *an office-holder* **8** duty or function: *the office of an administrator* **9** (*often pl*) a minor task or service: *domestic offices* **10** (*often pl*) an action performed for another, usually a beneficial action: *through his good offices* **11** a place where tickets, information, etc, can be obtained: *a ticket office* **12** *Christianity* **12a** (*often pl*) a ceremony or service, prescribed by ecclesiastical authorities, esp one for the dead **12b** *RC Church* the official daily service **12c** short for **divine office** **13** (*pl*) the parts of a house or estate where work is done, goods are stored, etc **14** (*usually pl*) *Brit, euphemistic.* a lavatory (esp in **usual offices**) **15 in** (*or* **out of**) **office** (of a government) in (*or* out of) power **16 the office** a hint or signal [C13 via OF from L *officium* service, duty, from *opus* work, service + *facere* to do]

office block *n* a large building designed to provide office accommodation

office boy *n* a male office junior

office junior *n* a young person, esp a school-leaver, employed in an office for running errands and doing other minor jobs

officer ('ɒfɪsə) *n* **1** a person in the armed services who holds a position of responsibility, authority, and duty **2** See **police officer** **3** (on a non-naval ship) any person, including the captain and mate, who holds a position of authority and responsibility: *radio officer; engineer officer* **4** a person appointed or elected to a position of responsibility or authority in a government, society, etc **5** a government official: *a customs officer* **6** (in the Order of the British Empire) a member of the grade below commander ▷ *vb* (*tr*) **7** to furnish with officers **8** to act as an officer over (some section, group, organization, etc)

officer of the day *n* a military officer whose duty is to take charge of the security of the unit or camp for a day. Also called: **orderly officer**

official (ə'fɪʃəl) *adj* **1** of or relating to an office, its administration, or its duration **2** sanctioned by, recognized by, or derived from authority: *an official statement* **3** having a formal ceremonial character: *an official dinner* ▷ *n* **4** a person who holds a position in an organization, government department, etc, esp a subordinate position

officialdom (ə'fɪʃəldəm) *n* **1** the outlook or behaviour of officials, esp those rigidly adhering to regulations; bureaucracy **2** officials or bureaucrats collectively

officialese (ə,fɪʃə'li:z) *n* language characteristic of official documents, esp when verbose or pedantic

officially (ə'fɪʃəlɪ) *adv* **1** in a formal or authoritative manner: *the Queen officially opened the dome* **2** in a way that is formally acknowledged but is not necessarily the case: *officially on the dole but actually holding a job*

Official Receiver *n* an officer appointed by the Department of Trade and Industry to receive the income and manage the estate of a bankrupt. See also **receiver** (sense 2)

officiant (əˈfɪʃɪənt) *n* a person who presides and officiates at a religious ceremony

officiate (əˈfɪʃɪˌeɪt) *vb* **officiates, officiating, officiated** (*intr*) **1** to hold the position, responsibility, or function of an official **2** to conduct a religious or other ceremony [c17 from Med. L *officiāre*, from L *officium*; see OFFICE] > **ofˌficiˈation** *n* > **ofˈficiˌator** *n*

officious (əˈfɪʃəs) *adj* **1** unnecessarily or obtrusively ready to offer advice or services **2** *diplomacy* informal or unofficial [c16 from L *officiōsus* kindly, from *officium* service; see OFFICE] > **ofˈficiously** *adv* > **ofˈficiousness** *n*

offing (ˈɒfɪŋ) *n* **1** the part of the sea that can be seen from the shore **2 in the offing** likely to occur soon

offish (ˈɒfɪʃ) *adj inf* aloof or distant in manner > **ˈoffishly** *adv* > **ˈoffishness** *n*

off key *adj* (**off-key** *when prenominal*), *adv* **1** *music* **1a** not in the correct key **1b** out of tune **2** out of keeping; discordant

off-licence *n Brit* **1** a shop or a counter in a pub or hotel where alcoholic drinks are sold for consumption elsewhere. US & Canad equivalents: **package store, liquor store 2** a licence permitting such sales

off limits *adj* (**off-limits** *when prenominal*) **1** *US, chiefly mil* not to be entered; out of bounds ▷ *adv* **2** in or into an area forbidden by regulations

off line *adj* (**off-line** *when prenominal*) **1** of or concerned with a part of a computer system not connected to the central processing unit but controlled by a computer storage device **2** disconnected from a computer; switched off ▷ *adv* **3** while not connected to a computer or the Internet ▷ Cf **on line**

off-load *vb* (*tr*) to get rid of (something unpleasant), as by delegation to another

off message *adj* (**off-message** *when prenominal*) not adhering to or reflecting the official line of a political party, government, or other organization

off-peak *adj* of or relating to services as used outside periods of intensive use

off-piste *adj* of or relating to skiing on virgin snow off the regular runs

off plan *adj* (**off-plan** *when prenominal*) (of a new building) considered with reference to its plans, before it has been built

off-putting *adj Brit inf* arousing reluctance or aversion

off-ramp *n* a ramp that leads away from the specified part of a road system: *the Govan Road off-ramp from the tunnel*

off-road *adj* **1** denoting the use of a vehicle away from public roads, esp on rough terrain: *off-road motorcycling* **2** (of a vehicle) designed or built for off-road use

off-roader *n* a motor vehicle designed for use away from public roads, esp on rough terrain

off-sales *pl n Brit* sales of alcoholic drink for consumption off the premises by a pub or an off-licence attached to a pub

off season *adj* (**off-season** *when prenominal*) **1** denoting or occurring during a period of little activity in a trade or business ▷ *n* **2** such a period ▷ *adv* **3** in an off-season period

offset *n* (ˈɒfˌsɛt) **1** something that counterbalances or compensates for something else **2a** a printing method in which the impression is made onto an intermediate surface, such as a rubber blanket, which transfers it to the paper **2b** (*modifier*) relating to, involving, or printed by offset: *offset letterpress* **3** another name for **set-off 4** *bot* a short runner in certain plants that produces roots and shoots at the tip **5** a ridge projecting from a range of hills or mountains **6** a narrow horizontal or sloping surface formed where a wall is reduced in thickness towards the top **7** *surveying* a measurement of distance to a point at right angles to a survey line ▷ *vb* (ˌɒfˈsɛt), **offsets, offsetting, offset 8** (*tr*) to counterbalance or compensate for **9** (*tr*) to print (text, etc) using the offset process **10** (*tr*) to construct an offset in (a wall) **11** (*intr*) to project or develop as an offset

offshoot (ˈɒfˌʃuːt) *n* **1** a shoot or branch growing from the main stem of a plant **2** something that develops or derives from a principal source or origin

offshore (ˌɒfˈʃɔː) *adj, adv* **1** from, away from, or at some distance from the shore **2** NZ overseas; abroad ▷ *adj* **2** sited or conducted at sea: *offshore industries* **3** based or operating abroad: *offshore banking; offshore fund*

offside *adj, adv* (ˌɒfˈsaɪd) **1** *sport* (in football, etc) in a position illegally ahead of the ball when it is played ▷ Cf **onside** ▷ *n* (ˈɒfˌsaɪd) **2** (usually preceded by *the*) *chiefly Brit* **2a** the side of a vehicle, etc, nearest the centre of the road **2b** (*as modifier*): *the offside passenger door*

off-sider (ˌɒfˈsaɪdə) *n Austral & NZ* a partner or assistant

offspring (ˈɒfˌsprɪŋ) *n* **1** the immediate descendant or descendants of a person, animal, etc; progeny **2** a product, outcome, or result

offstage (ˈɒfˈsteɪdʒ) *adj, adv* out of the view of the audience; off the stage

off-the-peg *adj* (of clothing) ready to wear; not produced especially for the person buying

off the shelf *adv* **1** from stock and readily available: *you can have this model off the shelf* ▷ *adj* (**off-the-shelf** *when prenominal*) **2** of or relating to a product that is readily available: *an off-the-shelf model* **3** of or denoting a company that has been registered with the Registrar of Companies for the sole purpose of being sold

off-the-wall *adj* (**off the wall** *when postpositive*) *sl* new or unexpected in an unconventional or eccentric way [c20 ?from the use of the phrase in handball and squash to describe a shot that is unexpected]

off-white *n* **1** a colour consisting of white with a tinge of grey or yellow ▷ *adj* **2** of such a colour: *an off-white coat*

Oo

Ofgem (ˈɒfˌdʒɛm) *n* (in Britain) *acronym for* Office of Gas and Electricity Markets: a government body formed in 1999 by the merger of the separate regulatory bodies for gas and electricity; its functions are to promote competition and protect consumers' interests

Ofili (ɒˈfiːlɪ) *n* **Chris**(**topher**) born 1968, British painter, noted esp for his brightly coloured collages using elephant dung: Turner Prize 1998

OFS *abbrev for* (Orange) Free State

oft (ɒft) *adv* short for **often** (archaic or poetic except in combinations such as **oft-repeated** and **oft-recurring**) [OE *oft*; rel. to OHG *ofto*]

OFT (in Britain) *abbrev for* Office of Fair Trading

often (ˈɒfᵊn) *adv* **1** frequently or repeatedly; much of the time. Arch equivalents: **ˈoftenˌtimes, ˈoftˌtimes 2 as often as not** quite frequently **3 every so often** at intervals **4 more often than not** in more than half the instances ▷ *adj* **5** *arch* repeated; frequent [c14 var. of OFT before vowels and *h*]

Ogaden (ˌɒgəˈdɛn) *n* **the** a region of SE Ethiopia, bordering on Somalia: consists of a desert plateau, inhabited by Somali nomads; a secessionist movement, supported by Somalia, has existed within the region since the early 1960s and led to bitter fighting between Ethiopia and Somalia (1977–78)

Ogasawara Gunto (ˌɒgəsəˈwɑːrə ˈgʌntəʊ) *n* transliteration of the Japanese name for the **Bonin Islands**

Ogbomosho (ˌɒgbəˈməʊʃəʊ) *n* a city in SW Nigeria: the third largest town in Nigeria; trading centre for an agricultural region. Pop: 730 000 (1996 est)

Ogden (ˈɒgdən) *n* **C**(**harles**) **K**(**ay**) 1889–1957, English linguist, who, with I A Richards, devised Basic English

ogee (ˈəʊdʒiː) *n archit* **1** Also called: **talon** a moulding having a cross section in the form of a letter S **2** short for **ogee arch** [c15 prob. var. of OGIVE]

ogee arch *n archit* a pointed arch having an S-shaped curve on both sides. Sometimes shortened to **ogee**

Ogen melon ('əʊgɛn) *n* a variety of small melon with sweet pale orange flesh [c20 after a kibbutz in Israel where it was first developed]

ogham *or* **ogam** ('ɒgəm) *n* an ancient alphabetical writing system used by the Celts in Britain, consisting of straight lines drawn or carved perpendicular to or at an angle to another long straight line [c17 from OIrish *ogom*, from ?, but associated with the name *Ogma*, legendary inventor of this alphabet]

ogive ('əʊdʒaɪv, əʊ'dʒaɪv) *n* **1** a diagonal rib or groin of a Gothic vault **2** another name for **lancet arch** [c17 from OF, from ?] > **o'gival** *adj*

ogle ('əʊgᵊl) *vb* **ogles, ogling, ogled 1** to look at (someone) amorously or lustfully **2** (*tr*) to stare or gape at ▷ *n* **3** a flirtatious or lewd look [c17 prob. from Low G *oegeln*, from *oegen* to look at] > **'ogler** *n*

Oglethorpe ('əʊgᵊl,θɔːp) *n* **James Edward** 1696–1785, English general and colonial administrator; founder of the colony of Georgia (1733)

Ogooué *or* **Ogowe** (ɒ'gəʊweɪ) *n* a river in W central Africa, rising in SW Congo-Brazzaville and flowing generally northwest and north through Gabon to the Atlantic. Length: about 970 km (683 miles)

Ogopogo (,əʊgəʊ'pəʊgəʊ) *n* an aquatic monster said to live in Okanagan Lake in British Columbia, Canada [apparently an arbitrary coinage]

O grade *n* (formerly, in Scotland) **1a** the basic level of the Scottish Certificate of Education, now replaced by **Standard Grade 1b** (*as modifier*): *O-grade history* **2** a pass in a subject at O grade: *she has ten O grades*

ogre ('əʊgə) *n* **1** (in folklore) a giant, usually given to eating human flesh **2** any monstrous or cruel person [c18 from F, ?from L *Orcus*, god of the infernal regions] > **'ogreish** *adj* > **'ogress** *fem n*

Ogun (əʊ'gʊn) *n* a state of SW Nigeria, formed in 1976 from part of Western State. Capital: Abeokuta. Pop: 2 614 747 (1995 est). Area: 16 762 sq km (6472 sq miles)

oh (əʊ) *interj* an exclamation expressive of surprise, pain, pleasure, etc

OH *abbrev for* Ohio

OHG *abbrev for* Old High German

O'Higgins (əʊ'hɪgɪnz; *Spanish* o'iɣins) *n* **1 Ambrosio** (æm'brəʊzɪ,əʊ) ?1720–1801, Irish soldier, who became viceroy of Chile (1789–96) and of Peru (1796–1801) **2** his son, **Bernardo** (bɛr'narðo) 1778–1842, Chilean revolutionary. He was one of the leaders in the struggle for independence from Spain and was Chile's first president (1817–23)

Ohio (əʊ'haɪəʊ) *n* **1** a state of the central US, in the Midwest on Lake Erie: consists of prairies in the W and the Allegheny plateau in the E, the Ohio River forming the S and most of the E borders. Capital: Columbus. Pop: 11 353 140 (2000). Area: 107 044 sq km (41 330 sq miles). Abbreviation and zip code: **OH 2** a river in the eastern US, formed by the confluence of the Allegheny and Monongahela Rivers at Pittsburgh: flows generally W and SW to join the Mississippi at Cairo, Illinois, as its chief E tributary. Length: 1570 km (975 miles)

Öhlenschläger (*Danish* 'øːlənslɛːɣər) *n* a variant spelling of **Oehlenschläger**

ohm (əʊm) *n* the derived SI unit of electrical resistance; the resistance between two points on a conductor when a constant potential difference of 1 volt between them produces a current of 1 ampere. Symbol: Ω [c19 after Georg Simon OHM] > **'ohmage** *n*

Ohm (əʊm) *n* **Georg Simon** ('geːɔrk 'ziːmɔn) 1787–1854, German physicist, who formulated the law named after him

ohmmeter ('əʊm,miːtə) *n* an instrument for measuring electrical resistance. See **ohm**

OHMS (in Britain and the Commonwealth) *abbrev for* On Her (*or* His) Majesty's Service

Ohm's law *n* the principle that the electric current passing through a conductor is directly proportional to the potential difference across it. The constant of proportionality is the resistance of the conductor

oho (əʊ'həʊ) *interj* an exclamation expressing surprise, exultation, or derision

-oic *suffix forming adjectives* indicating that a chemical compound is a carboxylic acid: *ethanoic acid*

-oid *suffix forming adjectives and associated nouns* indicating likeness, resemblance, or similarity: *anthropoid* [from Gk *-oeidēs* resembling, from *eidos* form]

-oidea *suffix forming plural proper nouns* forming the names of zoological classes or superfamilies: *Canoidea* [from NL, from L *-oīdēs* -OID]

oil (ɔɪl) *n* **1** any of a number of viscous liquids with a smooth sticky feel. They are usually flammable, insoluble in water, soluble in organic solvents, and are obtained from plants and animals, from mineral deposits, and by synthesis. See also **essential oil 2a** another name for **petroleum 2b** (*as modifier*): *an oil engine; an oil rig* **3a** any of a number of substances usually derived from petroleum and used for lubrication **3b** (*in combination*): *an oilcan* **3c** (*as modifier*): *an oil pump* **4** Also called: **fuel oil** a petroleum product used as a fuel in domestic heating, marine engines, etc **5** *Brit* **5a** paraffin, esp when used as a domestic fuel **5b** (*as modifier*): *an oil lamp* **6** any substance of a consistency resembling that of oil: *oil of vitriol* **7** the solvent, usually linseed oil, with which pigments are mixed to make artists' paints **8a** (*often pl*) oil colour or paint **8b** (*as modifier*): *an oil painting* **9** an oil painting **10** *Austral & NZ sl* facts or news: *he gave me the dinkum oil* **11 strike oil 11a** to discover petroleum while drilling for it **11b** *inf* to become very rich or successful ▷ *vb* (*tr*) **12** to lubricate, smear, polish, etc, with oil or an oily substance **13 oil one's tongue** *inf* to speak flatteringly or glibly **14 oil someone's palm** *inf* to bribe someone **15 oil the wheels** to make things run smoothly [c12 from OF *oile*, from L *oleum* (olive) oil, from *olea* olive tree, from Gk *elaia* OLIVE] > **'oiler** *n* > **'oil-,like** *adj*

oil cake *n* stock feed consisting of compressed cubes made from the residue of the crushed seeds of oil-bearing crops such as linseed

oilcan ('ɔɪl,kæn) *n* a container with a long nozzle for applying lubricating oil to machinery

oilcloth ('ɔɪl,klɒθ) *n* **1** waterproof material made by treating one side of a cotton fabric with a drying oil or a synthetic resin **2** another name for **linoleum**

oil drum *n* a metal drum used to contain or transport oil

oilfield ('ɔɪl,fiːld) *n* an area containing reserves of petroleum, esp one that is already being exploited

oilfired ('ɔɪl,faɪəd) *adj* (of central heating, etc) using oil as fuel

oilgas ('ɔɪl,gæs) *n* a gaseous mixture of hydrocarbons used as a fuel, obtained by the destructive distillation of mineral oils

oilman ('ɔɪlmən) *n, pl* **oilmen 1** a person who owns or operates oil wells **2** a person who sells oil

oil minister *n* a government official in charge of or representing the interests of an oil-producing country

oil of cloves *n* another name for **clove oil**

oil of vitriol *n* another name for **sulphuric acid**

oil paint *n* paint made of pigment ground in oil, usually linseed oil

oil painting *n* **1** a picture painted with oil paints **2** the art or process of painting with oil paints **3 he's** *or* **she's no oil painting** *inf* he *or* she is not good-looking

oil palm *n* a tropical African palm tree, the fruits of which yield palm oil

oil rig *n* See **rig** (sense 6)

Oil Rivers *pl n* the delta of the Niger River in S Nigeria
oil sand *n* a sandstone impregnated with hydrocarbons, esp such deposits in Alberta, Canada
oil-seed rape *n* another name for **rape**[2]
oil shale *n* a carbonaceous rock from which oil can be extracted
oilskin ('ɔɪlˌskɪn) *n* **1a** a cotton fabric treated with oil and pigment to make it waterproof **1b** (*as modifier*): *an oilskin hat* **2** (*often pl*) a protective outer garment of this fabric
oil slick *n* a mass of floating oil covering an area of water
oilstone ('ɔɪlˌstəʊn) *n* a stone with a fine grain lubricated with oil and used for sharpening cutting tools. See also **whetstone**
oil well *n* a boring into the earth or sea bed for the extraction of petroleum
oily ('ɔɪlɪ) *adj* **oilier, oiliest 1** soaked in or smeared with oil or grease **2** consisting of, containing, or resembling oil **3** flatteringly servile or obsequious > **'oilily** *adv* > **'oiliness** *n*
oink (ɔɪŋk) *interj* an imitation or representation of the grunt of a pig
ointment ('ɔɪntmənt) *n* **1** a fatty or oily medicated formulation applied to the skin to heal or protect **2** a similar substance used as a cosmetic [c14 from OF *oignement*, from L *unguentum* UNGUENT]
Oireachtas ('ɛrəkθəs) *n* the parliament of the Republic of Ireland [Irish Gaelic: assembly, from OIrish *airech* nobleman]
Oise (*French* waz) *n* **1** a department of N France, in Picardy region. Capital: Beauvais. Pop: 766 441 (1999). Area: 5887 sq km (2296 sq miles) **2** a river in N France, rising in Belgium, in the Ardennes, and flowing southwest to join the Seine at Conflans. Length: 302 km (188 miles)
Oistrakh ('ɔɪstrɑːk; *Russian* 'ɔjstrəx) *n* **1 David** (da'vit) 1908–74, Russian violinist **2** his son, **Igor** ('igərj) born 1931, Russian violinist
Oita ('ɔɪtə) *n* an industrial city in SW Japan, on NE Kyushu: dominated most of Kyushu in the 16th century. Pop: 426 981 (1995)
Ojibwa (əʊ'dʒɪbwə) *n* **1** (*pl* **Ojibwas** *or* **Ojibwa**) a member of a North American Indian people living west of Lake Superior **2** the language of this people
OK *abbrev for* Oklahoma
O.K. (ˌəʊ'keɪ) *inf* ▷ *sentence substitute* **1** an expression of approval or agreement ▷ *adj* (*usually postpositive*), *adv* **2** in good or satisfactory condition **3** permissible: *is it O.K. if I bring a friend?* **4** satisfactory without being exceptional: *the party was O.K* ▷ *vb* **O.K.s, O.K.ing** (ˌəʊ'keɪɪŋ), **O.K.ed** (ˌəʊ'keɪd) **5** (*tr*) to approve or endorse ▷ *n, pl* **O.K.s** **6** approval or agreement ▷ Also: **okay** [c19 ?from *o(ll) k(orrect)*, jocular alteration of *all correct*]
Okanagan (ˌəʊkə'nɑːgən) *n* **1** Also (US): **Okanogan** a river in North America that flows south from Okanagan Lake in Canada into the Columbia River in NE Washington, US Length: about 483 km (300 miles) **2** Also: **Okanogan, Okinagan** a member of a North American Indian people living in the Okanagan River valley in British Columbia and Washington **3** Also: **Okanogan, Okinagan** the language of this people, belonging to the Salish family
Okanagan Lake *n* a lake in SW Canada, in S British Columbia: drained by the Okanagan River into the Columbia River. Length: about 111 km (69 miles). Width: from 3.2–6.4 km (2–4 miles)
okapi (əʊ'kɑːpɪ) *n, pl* **okapis** *or* **okapi** a ruminant mammal of the forests of central Africa, having a reddish-brown coat with horizontal white stripes on the legs, and small horns [c20 from a Central African word]
Okavango (ˌəʊkə'vɑːŋgəʊ) *n* a river in SW central Africa, rising in central Angola and flowing southeast, then east as part of the border between Angola and Namibia, then southeast across the Caprivi Strip into Botswana to form a great marsh known as the **Okavango Basin** Length: about 1600 km (1000 miles)
okay (ˌəʊ'keɪ) *sentence substitute, adj, adv, vb, n* a variant spelling of **O.K.**
Okayama (ˌɒkə'jɑːmə) *n* a city in SW Japan, on W Honshu on the Inland Sea. Pop: 616 056 (1995)
oke (əʊk) *n S African* an informal word for **man** [from Afrik.]
Okeechobee (ˌəʊkɪ'tʃəʊbɪ) *n* **Lake** a lake in S Florida, in the Everglades: second largest freshwater lake wholly within the US Area: 1813 sq km (700 sq miles)
O'Keeffe (əʊ'kiːf) *n* **Georgia** 1887–1986, US painter, best known for her semiabstract still lifes, esp of flowers: married the photographer Alfred Stieglitz
Okefenokee Swamp (ˌəʊkɪfɪ'nəʊkɪ) *n* a swamp in the US, in SE Georgia and N Florida: protected flora and fauna. Area: 1554 sq km (600 sq miles)
Okhotsk ('əʊkɒtsk; *Russian* a'xɔtsk) *n* **Sea of** part of the NW Pacific, surrounded by the Kamchatka Peninsula, the Kurile Islands, Sakhalin Island, and the E coast of Siberia. Area: 1 589 840 sq km (613 838 sq miles)
Okinawa (ˌəʊkɪ'nɑːwə) *n* a coral island of SW Japan, the largest of the Ryukyu Islands in the N Pacific: scene of heavy fighting in World War II; administered by the US (1945–72); agricultural. Chief town: Naha City. Pop: 1 273 508 (1995). Area: 1176 sq km (454 sq miles)
Okla. *abbrev for* Oklahoma
Oklahoma (ˌəʊklə'həʊmə) *n* a state in the S central US: consists of plains in the west, rising to mountains in the southwest and east; important for oil. Capital: Oklahoma City. Pop: 3 450 654 (2000). Area: 181 185 sq km (69 956 sq miles). Abbreviations: **Okla.** or (with zip code) **OK** > ˌ**Okla'homan** *adj, n*
Oklahoma City *n* a city in central Oklahoma: the state capital and a major agricultural and industrial centre. Pop: 506 132 (2000)
okra ('əʊkrə) *n* **1** an annual plant of the Old World tropics, with yellow-and-red flowers and edible oblong green pods **2** the pod of this plant, eaten in soups, stews, etc See also **gumbo** (sense 1) [c18 of West African origin]
-ol[1] *suffix forming nouns* denoting a chemical compound containing a hydroxyl group, esp alcohols and phenols: *ethanol; quinol* [from ALCOHOL]
-ol[2] *n combining form* (not used systematically) a variant of **-ole**[1]
Olaf I ('əʊləf) *or* **Olav I** ('əʊləv) *n* known as *Olaf Tryggvesson*. ?965–?1000 AD, king of Norway (995–?1000). He began the conversion of Norway to Christianity
Olaf II *or* **Olav II** *n* **Saint** 995–1030 AD, king of Norway (1015–28), who worked to complete the conversion of Norway to Christianity; deposed by Canute; patron saint of Norway. Feast day: July 29
Olaf V *or* **Olav V** *n* 1903–91, king of Norway 1957–91; son of Haakon VII
Öland (*Swedish* 'øːland) *n* an island in the Baltic Sea, separated from the mainland of SE Sweden by Kalmar Sound: the second largest Swedish island. Chief town: Borgholm. Pop: 24 100 (latest est). Area: 1347 sq km (520 sq miles)
old (əʊld) *adj* **1** having lived or existed for a relatively long time: *an old man; an old tradition; an old house* **2a** of or relating to advanced years or a long life: *old age* **2b** (*as collective noun*; preceded by *the*): *the old* **2c old and young** people of all ages **3** decrepit or senile **4** worn with age or use: *old clothes; an old car* **5a** (*postpositive*) having lived or existed for a specified period: *a child who is six years old* **5b** (*in combination*): *a six-year-old child* **5c** (*as noun in combination*): *a six-year-old* **6** (*cap when part of a name or title*) earlier or earliest of two or more things with the same name: *the old edition; the Old Testament* **7** (*cap when part of a name*) designating the form of a language in which the earliest known records are written: *Old English*

Oo

8 (*prenominal*) familiar through long acquaintance or repetition: *an old friend; an old excuse* 9 practised; hardened: *old in cunning* 10 (*prenominal*; often preceded by *good*) cherished; dear: used as a term of affection or familiarity: *good old George* 11 *inf* (with any of several nouns) used as a familiar form of address to a person: *old thing; old bean; old stick* 12 skilled through long experience (esp in **an old hand**) 13 out of date; unfashionable 14 remote or distant in origin or time of origin: *an old culture* 15 (*prenominal*) former; previous: *my old house was small* 16a (*prenominal*) established for a relatively long time: *an old member* 16b (*in combination*): *old-established* 17 sensible, wise, or mature: *old beyond one's years* 18 (intensifier) (esp in **a high old time, any old thing, any old how,** etc) 19 **good old days** an earlier period of time regarded as better than the present 20 **little old** *inf* indicating affection, esp humorous affection 21 **the old one** (*or* **gentleman**) *inf* a jocular name for **Satan** ▷ *n* 22 an earlier or past time: *in days of old* [OE *eald*] > **'oldish** *adj* > **'oldness** *n*

old age pension *n* a former name for **retirement pension** > **old age pensioner** *n*

Old Bailey ('beɪlɪ) *n* the Central Criminal Court of England

Old Bill (bɪl) *n* (*functioning as pl*; preceded by *the*) *Brit sl* policemen collectively [c20 ?from the World War I cartoon of a soldier with a drooping moustache]

old boy *n* 1 (*sometimes caps*) *Brit & Canad* a male ex-pupil of a school 2 *inf, chiefly Brit* 2a a familiar name used to refer to a man 2b an old man

old boy network *n Brit & Canad inf* the appointment to power of former pupils of the same small group of public schools or universities

Old Castile *n* a region of N Spain, on the Bay of Biscay: formerly a province. Spanish name: **Castilla la Vieja**

Oldcastle ('əʊldˌkɑːsᵊl) *n* Sir **John,** Baron Cobham. ?1378–1417, Lollard leader. In 1411 he led an English army in France but in 1413 he was condemned as a heretic and later hanged and burnt. He is thought to have been a model for Shakespeare's character Falstaff in *Henry IV*

Old Contemptibles *pl n* the British expeditionary force to France in 1914 [from the Kaiser's alleged reference to them as a "contemptible little army"]

old country *n* the country of origin of an immigrant or an immigrant's ancestors

Old Dart *n* **the** *Austral sl* Britain, esp England [c19 from ?]

Old Delhi *n* See **Delhi**

olden ('əʊldᵊn) *adj* an archaic or poetic word for **old** (often in **in olden days** and **in olden times**)

Oldenbarneveldt (ˌɒldən'bɑːnəˌvɛlt) *n* **Johan van** 1547–1619, Dutch statesman, regarded as a founder of Dutch independence; the leading figure (from 1586) in the United Provinces of the Netherlands: executed by Maurice of Nassau

Oldenburg[1] ('əʊldᵊnˌbɜːg; *German* 'ɔldənbʊrk) *n* 1 a city in NW Germany, in Lower Saxony: former capital of Oldenburg state. Pop: 154 100 (1999 est) 2 a former state of NW Germany: became part of Lower Saxony in 1946

Oldenburg[2] ('əʊldᵊnˌbɜːg) *n* **Claes** (klɔːs) born 1929, US pop sculptor and artist, born in Sweden

Old English *n* 1 Also called: **Anglo-Saxon** the English language from the time of the earliest Saxon settlements in the fifth century AD to about 1100. Abbreviation: **OE** 2 *printing* a Gothic typeface commonly used in England up to the 18th century

Old English sheepdog *n* a breed of large bobtailed sheepdog with a profuse shaggy coat

older ('əʊldə) *adj* 1 the comparative of **old** 2 Also (of people): **elder** of greater age

old-fashioned *adj* 1 belonging to, characteristic of, or favoured by former times; outdated: *old-fashioned ideas* 2 favouring or adopting the dress, manners, fashions, etc, of a former time 3 *Scot & N English dialect* old for one's age: *an old-fashioned child* ▷ *n* 4 a cocktail containing spirit, bitters, fruit, etc

Old French *n* the French language in its earliest forms, from about the 9th century up to about 1400. Abbreviation: **OF**

old girl *n* 1 (*sometimes caps*) *Brit & Canad* a female ex-pupil of a school 2 *inf, chiefly Brit* 2a a familiar name used to refer to a woman 2b an old woman

Old Glory *n* a nickname for the flag of the United States of America

old gold *n* **a** a dark yellow colour, sometimes with a brownish tinge **b** (*as adj*): *an old-gold carpet*

old guard *n* 1 a group that works for a long-established or old-fashioned cause or principle 2 the conservative element in a political party or other group [c19 after Napoleon's imperial guard]

Oldham ('əʊldəm) *n* 1 a town in NW England, in Oldham unitary authority, Greater Manchester. Pop: 103 931 (1991) 2 a unitary authority in NW England, in Greater Manchester. Pop: 217 393 (2001). Area: 141 sq km (54 sq miles)

old hat *adj* (*postpositive*) old-fashioned or trite

Old High German *n* a group of West Germanic dialects that eventually developed into modern German; High German up to about 1200. Abbreviation: **OHG**

oldie ('əʊldɪ) *n inf* 1 an old joke, song, film, person, etc 2 *Austral* a parent: *children and their oldies*

Old Irish *n* the Celtic language of Ireland up to about 900 AD

old lady *n* an informal term for **mother** or **wife**

Old Latin *n* the Latin language before the classical period, up to about 100 BC

Old Low German *n* the Saxon and Low Franconian dialects of German up to about 1200; the old form of modern Low German and Dutch. Abbreviation: **OLG**

old maid *n* 1 a woman regarded as unlikely ever to marry; spinster 2 *inf* a prim, fastidious, or excessively cautious person 3 a card game in which players try to avoid holding the unpaired card at the end of the game > **ˌold-'maidish** *adj*

old man *n* 1 an informal term for **father** or **husband** 2 (*sometimes caps*) *inf* a man in command, such as an employer, foreman, or captain of a ship 3 *sometimes facetious* an affectionate term used in addressing a man 4 Also called: **southernwood** an aromatic shrubby wormwood of S Europe, having drooping yellow flowers 5 *Christianity* the unregenerate aspect of human nature

old man's beard *n* any of various plants having a white feathery appearance, esp traveller's joy and Spanish moss

old master *n* 1 one of the great European painters of the period 1500 to 1800 2 a painting by one of these

old moon *n* a phase of the moon lying between last quarter and new moon, when it appears as a waning crescent

Old Nick *n inf* a jocular name for **Satan**

Old Norse *n* the language or group of dialects of medieval Scandinavia and Iceland from about 700 to about 1350. Abbreviation: **ON**

Old Northwest *n* (in the early US) the land between the Great Lakes, the Mississippi, and the Ohio River. Awarded to the US in 1783, it was organized into the **Northwest Territory** in 1787 and now forms the states of Ohio, Indiana, Illinois, Wisconsin, Michigan, and part of Minnesota

Old Pretender *n* See (James Francis Edward) **Stuart**

Old Prussian *n* the former language of the non-German Prussians, belonging to the Baltic branch of the Indo-European family: extinct by 1700

old rose *n* **a** a greyish-pink colour **b** (*as adj*): *old-rose gloves*

Old Saxon *n* the Saxon dialect of Low German up to about 1200, from which modern Low German is derived. Abbreviation: **OS**

old school *n* **1** *chiefly Brit* one's former school **2** a group of people favouring traditional ideas or conservative practices
old school tie *n* **1** *Brit* a distinctive tie that indicates which school the wearer attended **2** the attitudes, loyalties, values, etc, associated with British public schools
Old South *n* the American South before the Civil War
oldster ('əʊldstə) *n inf* an older person
old style *n printing* a type style reviving the characteristics of **old face,** a type style that originated in the 18th century and was characterized by having little contrast between thick and thin strokes
Old Style *n* the former method of reckoning dates using the Julian calendar ▷ Cf **New Style**
Old Testament *n* the collection of books comprising the sacred Scriptures of the Hebrews; the first part of the Christian Bible
old-time *adj (prenominal)* of or relating to a former time; old-fashioned: *old-time dancing*
old-timer *n* **1** a person who has been in a certain place, occupation, etc, for a long time **2** *US* an old man
Olduvai Gorge ('ɒldʊ,vaɪ) *n* a gorge in N Tanzania, north of the Ngorongoro Crater: fossil evidence of early man and other closely related species, together with artefacts
old wives' tale *n* a belief, usually superstitious or erroneous, passed on by word of mouth as a piece of traditional wisdom
old woman *n* **1** an informal term for **mother** or **wife** **2** a timid, fussy, or cautious person > ˌ**old-'womanish** *adj*
Old World *n* that part of the world that was known before the discovery of the Americas; the eastern hemisphere
old-world *adj* of or characteristic of former times, esp, in Europe, quaint or traditional
Old World monkey *n* any monkey such as a macaque, baboon, or mandrill, which has nostrils that are close together and a nonprehensile tail
OLE *computing abbrev for* object linking and embedding: a system for linking and embedding data, images, and programs from different sources
-ole[1] *or* **-ol** *n combining form* **1** denoting an organic unsaturated compound containing a 5-membered ring: *thiazole* **2** denoting an aromatic organic ether: *anisole* [from L *oleum* oil, from Gk *elaion,* from *elaia* olive]
-ole[2] *suffix of nouns* indicating something small: *arteriole* [from L *-olus,* dim. suffix]
oleaceous (ˌəʊlɪ'eɪʃəs) *adj* of, relating to, or belonging to a family of trees and shrubs which includes the ash, jasmine, privet, lilac, and olive [C19 via NL from L *olea* OLIVE; see also OIL]
oleaginous (ˌəʊlɪ'ædʒɪnəs) *adj* **1** resembling or having the properties of oil **2** containing or producing oil [C17 from L *oleāginus,* from *olea* OLIVE; see also OIL]
oleander (ˌəʊlɪ'ændə) *n* a poisonous evergreen Mediterranean shrub or tree with fragrant white, pink, or purple flowers. Also called: **rosebay** [C16 from Med. L, var. of *arodandrum,* ?from L RHODODENDRON]
olearia (ˌɒlɪ'ɛərɪə) *n Austral* another name for **daisy bush**
oleate ('əʊlɪˌeɪt) *n* any salt or ester of oleic acid
OLED *abbrev for* organic light-emitting diode
oleic acid (əʊ'liːɪk) *n* a colourless oily liquid unsaturated acid occurring, as the glyceride, in almost all natural fats; used in making soaps, ointments, cosmetics, and lubricating oils. Formula: $CH_3(CH_2)_7CH{:}CH(CH_2)_7COOH$. Systematic name: ***cis*-9-octadecenoic acid** [C19 *oleic,* from L *oleum* oil + -IC]
olein ('əʊlɪɪn) *n* another name for **triolein** [C19 from F *oléine,* from L *oleum* oil + -IN]
oleo- *combining form* oil: *oleomargarine; oleoresin* [from L *oleum* OIL]
oleomargarine (ˌəʊlɪəʊˌmɑːdʒə'riːn) *or* **oleomargarin** (ˌəʊlɪəʊ'mɑːdʒərɪn) *n* another name (esp US) for **margarine**
oleoresin (ˌəʊlɪəʊ'rɛzɪn) *n* **1** a semisolid mixture of a resin and essential oil, obtained from certain plants **2** *pharmacol* a liquid preparation of resins and oils, obtained by extraction from plants > ˌ**oleo'resinous** *adj*
oleum ('əʊlɪəm) *n, pl* **olea** ('əʊlɪə) *or* **oleums** another name for **fuming sulphuric acid** [from L: oil, referring to its oily consistency]
O level *n Brit* **1a** the former basic (ordinary) level of the General Certificate of Education **1b** *(as modifier): O-level maths* **2** a pass in a particular subject at O level: *he has eight O levels*
olfaction (ɒl'fækʃən) *n* **1** the sense of smell **2** the act or function of smelling
olfactory (ɒl'fæktərɪ, -trɪ) *adj* **1** of or relating to the sense of smell ▷ *n, pl* **olfactories** **2** *(usually pl)* an organ or nerve concerned with the sense of smell [C17 from L *olfactus,* p.p. of *olfacere,* from *olere* to smell + *facere* to make]
OLG *abbrev for* Old Low German
oligarch ('ɒlɪˌgɑːk) *n* a member of an oligarchy
oligarchy ('ɒlɪˌgɑːkɪ) *n, pl* **oligarchies** **1** government by a small group of people **2** a state or organization so governed **3** a small body of individuals ruling such a state **4** *chiefly US* a small clique of private citizens who exert a strong influence on government [C16 via Med. L from Gk *oligarkhia,* from *oligos* few + -ARCHY] > ˌ**oli'garchic** *or* ˌ**oli'garchical** *adj*
oligo- *or before a vowel* **olig-** *combining form* indicating a few or little: *oligopoly* [from Gk *oligos* little, few]
Oligocene ('ɒlɪgəʊˌsiːn, ɒ'lɪg-) *adj* **1** of, denoting, or formed in the third epoch of the Tertiary period, which lasted for 10 million years ▷ *n* **2** **the** the Oligocene epoch or rock series [C19 OLIGO- + -CENE]
oligochaete ('ɒlɪgəʊˌkiːt) *n* **1** any freshwater or terrestrial annelid worm having bristles borne singly along the length of the body: includes the earthworms ▷ *adj* **2** of or relating to this type of worm [C19 from NL from OLIGO- + Gk *khaitē* long hair]
oligopoly (ˌɒlɪ'gɒpəlɪ) *n, pl* **oligopolies** *econ* a market situation in which control over the supply of a commodity is held by a small number of producers [C20 from OLIGO- + Gk *pōlein* to sell] > ˌ**oliˌgopo'listic** *adj*
oligospermia (ˌɒlɪgəʊ'spɜːmɪə) *n* the condition of having less than the normal number of spermatozoa in the semen: a cause of infertility in men
oligotrophic (ˌɒlɪgəʊ'trɒfɪk) *adj* (of lakes and similar habitats) poor in nutrients and plant life and rich in oxygen [C20 from OLIGO- + Gk *trophein* to nourish + -IC] > **oligotrophy** (ˌɒlɪ'gɒtrəfɪ) *n*
Ólimbos ('ɔlimbɔs) *n* transliteration of the Modern Greek name for (Mount) **Olympus** (sense 1)
olio ('əʊlɪˌəʊ) *n, pl* **olios** **1** a dish of many different ingredients **2** a miscellany or potpourri [C17 from Sp. *olla* stew, from L: jar]
Oliphant ('ɒlɪfənt) *n* Sir **Mark Laurence Elwin** 1901–2000, British nuclear physicist, born in Australia
olivaceous (ˌɒlɪ'veɪʃəs) *adj* of an olive colour
olive ('ɒlɪv) *n* **1** an evergreen oleaceous tree of the Mediterranean region having white fragrant flowers and edible fruits that are black when ripe **2** the fruit of this plant, eaten as a relish and used as a source of olive oil **3** the wood of the olive tree, used for ornamental work **4a** a yellow-green colour like that of an unripe olive **4b** *(as adj): an olive coat* ▷ *adj* **5** of, relating to, or made of the olive tree, its wood, or its fruit [C13 via OF from L *oliva,* rel. to Gk *elaia* olive tree]
olive branch *n* **1** a branch of an olive tree used to symbolize peace **2** any offering of peace or conciliation
olive crown *n* (esp in ancient Greece and Rome) a garland of olive leaves awarded as a token of victory
olive drab *n US* **1a** a dull but fairly strong greyish-olive colour **1b** *(as adj): an olive-drab jacket* **2** cloth or clothes in

Oo

this colour, esp the uniform of the US Army

olive green *n* **a** a colour that is greener, stronger, and brighter than olive; deep yellowish-green **b** (*as adj*): *an olive-green coat*

olive oil *n* a yellow to yellowish-green oil pressed from ripe olive fruits and used in cooking, medicines, etc
▷ www.internationaloliveoil.org

Oliver ('ɒlɪvə) *n* **1** one of Charlemagne's 12 paladins. See also **Roland** **2** **Isaac** ?1556–1617, English portrait miniaturist, born in France: he studied under Hilliard and worked at James I's court **3** **Jamie** (**Trevor**) born 1975, British chef and presenter of television cookery programmes **4** **Joseph,** known as *King Oliver*. 1885–1938, US pioneer jazz cornetist

Olives ('ɒlɪvz) *n* **Mount of** a hill to the east of Jerusalem: in New Testament times the village Bethany (Mark 11:11) was on its eastern slope and Gethsemane on its western one

Olivier (ə'lɪvɪˌeɪ) *n* **Laurence** (**Kerr**), Baron Olivier of Brighton. 1907–89, English stage, film, and television actor and director: director of the National Theatre Company (1961–73): films include the Shakespeare adaptations *Henry V* (1944), *Hamlet* (1948), and *Richard III* (1956)

olivine ('ɒlɪˌviːn, ˌɒlɪ'viːn) *n* any of a group of hard glassy olive-green minerals consisting of magnesium iron silicate in crystalline form. Also called: **chrysolite** [c18 from G, after its colour]

olla ('ɒlə) *n* **1** a cooking pot **2** short for **olla podrida** [Sp., from L *olla*, var. of *aulla* pot]

olla podrida ('ɒlə pɒ'driːdə) *n* **1** a Spanish dish, consisting of a stew with beans, sausages, etc **2** an assortment; miscellany [Sp., lit.: rotten pot]

Olmec ('ɒlmɛk) *n, pl* **Olmecs** *or* **Olmec** **1** a member of an ancient Central American Indian people who inhabited the S Gulf Coast of Mexico ▷ *adj* **2** of or relating to this people
▷ www.beautyworlds.com/olmecs.htm
▷ www.bbc.co.uk/dna/h2g2/A414109

Olmütz ('ɔlmyts) *n* the German name for **Olomouc**

ology ('ɒlədʒɪ) *n, pl* **ologies** *inf* a science or other branch of knowledge [c19 abstracted from words such as *theology, biology*, etc; see -LOGY]

-ology *n combining form* See **-logy**

Olomouc (*Czech* 'ɔlɔmɔuts) *n* a city in the Czech Republic, in North Moravia on the Morava River: capital of Moravia until 1640; university (1576). Pop: 103 015 (2000 est). German name: **Olmütz**

oloroso (ˌɒlə'rəʊsəʊ) *n, pl* **olorosos** a full-bodied golden-coloured sweet sherry [from Sp.: fragrant]

Olsen ('olsᵊn) *n* **Mary-Kate** and **Ashley** ('æʃlɪ) born 1986, US twin juvenile act who became famous sharing a role in the sitcom *Full House* (1987–95); now known for their videos, CDs, and numerous branded products

Olsztyn (*Polish* 'ɔlʃtin) *n* a town in NE Poland: founded in 1334 by the Teutonic Knights; communications centre. Pop: 170 904 (1999 est)

Olympia (ə'lɪmpɪə) *n* **1** a plain in Greece, in the NW Peloponnese: in ancient times a major sanctuary of Zeus and site of the original Olympic Games **2** a port in W Washington, the state capital, on Puget Sound. Pop: 33 840 (1990)

Olympiad (ə'lɪmpɪˌæd) *n* **1** a staging of the modern Olympic Games **2** the four-year period between consecutive celebrations of the Olympic Games; a unit of ancient Greek chronology dating back to 776 BC **3** an international contest in chess, bridge, etc

Olympian (ə'lɪmpɪən) *adj* **1** of or relating to Mount Olympus or to the classical Greek gods **2** majestic or godlike in manner or bearing **3** of or relating to ancient Olympia, a plain in Greece, or its inhabitants ▷ *n* **4** a god of Mount Olympus **5** an inhabitant of ancient Olympia **6** *chiefly US* a competitor in the Olympic Games

Olympic (ə'lɪmpɪk) *adj* **1** of or relating to the Olympic Games **2** of or relating to ancient Olympia

Olympic Games *n* (*functioning as sing or pl*) **1** the greatest Panhellenic festival, held every fourth year in honour of Zeus at ancient Olympia, consisting of games and festivities **2** Also called: **the Olympics** the modern revival of these games, consisting of international athletic and sporting contests held every four years in a selected country
▷ www.olympics.org

Olympic Mountains *pl n* a mountain range in NW Washington: part of the Coast Range. Highest peak: Mount Olympus, 2427 m (7965 ft)

Olympic Peninsula *n* a large peninsula of W Washington

Olympus (əʊ'lɪmpəs) *n* **1** **Mount** a mountain in NE Greece: the highest mountain in Greece, believed in Greek mythology to be the dwelling place of the greater gods. Height: 2911 m (9550 ft). Modern Greek name: **Ólimbos** **2** **Mount** a mountain in NW Washington: highest peak of the Olympic Mountains. Height: 2427 m (7965 ft) **3** a poetic word for **heaven**

Olynthus (əʊ'lɪnθəs) *n* an ancient city in N Greece: the centre of Chalcidice

OM *abbrev for* Order of Merit (a Brit title)

-oma *n combining form* indicating a tumour: *carcinoma* [from Gk *-ōma*]

Omagh (əʊ'mɑː, 'əʊmə) *n* **1** a market town in Northern Ireland. Pop: 17 280 (1991) **2** a district of W Northern Ireland, in Co Tyrone. Pop: 47 952 (2001). Area: 1130 sq km (436 sq miles)

Omaha ('əʊməˌhɑː) *n* a city in E Nebraska, on the Missouri River opposite Council Bluffs, Iowa: the largest city in the state; the country's largest livestock market and meat-packing centre. Pop: 390 007 (2000)

Oman (əʊ'mɑːn) *n* a sultanate in SE Arabia, on the **Gulf of Oman** and the Arabian Sea: the most powerful state in Arabia in the 19th century, ruling Zanzibar, much of the Persian coast, and part of Pakistan. Official language: Arabic. Official religion: Muslim. Currency: rial. Capital: Muscat. Pop: 2 497 000 (2001 est). Area: about 306 000 sq km (118 150 sq miles). Former name (until 1970): **Muscat and Oman** > **O'mani** *adj, n*
▷ www.omanet.com
▷ www.omantourism.gov.om

Omar ('əʊmɑː) *or* **Umar** *n* died 644 AD, the second caliph of Islam (634–44). During his reign Islamic armies conquered Syria and Mesopotamia: murdered

Omar Khayyám ('əʊmɑː kaɪ'ɑːm) *n* ?1050–?1123, Persian poet, mathematician, and astronomer, noted for the *Rubáiyát*, a collection of quatrains, popularized in the West by Edward Fitzgerald's version (1859)

omasum (əʊ'meɪsəm) *n, pl* **omasa** (-sə) another name for **psalterium** [c18 from L: bullock's tripe]

Omayyad *or* **Ommiad** (əʊ'maɪæd) *n pl* **-yads, -yades** (-əˌdiːz) *or* **-ads, -ades** (-əˌdiːz) **1** a caliph of the dynasty ruling (661–750 AD) from its capital at Damascus **2** an emir (756–929 AD) or caliph (929–1031 AD) of the Omayyad dynasty in Spain

ombre *or US* **omber** ('ɒmbə) *n* an 18th-century card game [c17 from Sp. *hombre* man, referring to the player who attempts to win the stakes]

ombudsman ('ɒmbʊdzmən) *n, pl* **ombudsmen** an official who investigates citizens' complaints against the government or its servants. Also called (*Brit*): **Parliamentary Commissioner** See also **Financial Ombudsman** [c20 from Swedish: commissioner]

Omdurman (ˌɒmdɜː'mɑːn) *n* a city in the central Sudan, on the White Nile, opposite Khartoum: the largest town in the Sudan; scene of the **Battle of Omdurman** (1898), in which the Mahdi's successor was defeated by Lord Kitchener's forces. Pop: 1 267 077 (1993)

-ome *n combining form* denoting a mass or part of a

specified kind: *rhizome; trichonie* [var. of -OMA]

omega ('əʊmɪgə) *n* **1** the 24th and last letter of the Greek alphabet (Ω, ω) **2** the ending or last of a series [c16 from Gk *ō mega* big o]

omega minus *n* an unstable negatively charged elementary particle, classified as a baryon, that has a mass 3276 times that of the electron

omega-3 *n* a type of unsaturated fatty acid present in some foodstuffs, esp fish oils, the consumption of which may reduce the risk of heart disease

omega-3 fatty acid *n* an unsaturated fatty acid that occurs naturally in fish oil and is valuable in reducing blood-cholesterol levels

omelette *or esp US* **omelet** ('ɒmlɪt) *n* a savoury or sweet dish of beaten eggs cooked in fat [c17 from F *omelette*, changed from *alumette*, from *alumelle* sword blade, changed by mistaken division from *la lemelle*, from L (see LAMELLA); apparently from the flat shape of the omelette]

omen ('əʊmən) *n* **1** a phenomenon or occurrence regarded as a sign of future happiness or disaster **2** prophetic significance ▷ *vb* **3** (*tr*) to portend [c16 from L]

omentum (əʊ'mɛntəm) *n, pl* **omenta** (-tə) *anat* a double fold of peritoneum connecting the stomach with other abdominal organs [c16 from L: membrane, esp a caul, from ?]

omertà *Italian* (omer'ta) *n* a conspiracy of silence

omicron (əʊ'maɪkrɒn, 'ɒmɪkrɒn) *n* the 15th letter in the Greek alphabet (Ο, ο) [from Gk *ō mikron* small o]

ominous ('ɒmɪnəs) *adj* **1** foreboding evil **2** serving as or having significance as an omen [c16 from L *ōminōsus*, from OMEN] > **'ominously** *adv* > **'ominousness** *n*

omission (əʊ'mɪʃən) *n* **1** something that has been omitted or neglected **2** the act of omitting or the state of having been omitted [c14 from L *omissiō*, from *omittere* to OMIT] > **o'missive** *adj*

omit (əʊ'mɪt) *vb* **omits, omitting, omitted** (*tr*) **1** to neglect to do or include **2** to fail (to do something) [c15 from L *omittere*, from *ob-* away + *mittere* to send] > **omissible** (əʊ'mɪsɪbᵊl) *adj* > **o'mitter** *n*

omni- *combining form* all or everywhere: *omnipresent* [from L *omnis* all]

omnibus ('ɒmnɪˌbʌs, -bəs) *n, pl* **omnibuses** **1** a formal word for **bus** (sense 1) **2** Also called: **omnibus volume** a collection of works by one author or several works on a similar topic, reprinted in one volume **3** Also called: **omnibus edition** a television or radio programme consisting of two or more episodes of a serial broadcast earlier in the week ▷ *adj* **4** (*prenominal*) of, dealing with, or providing for many different things or cases [c19 from L, lit.: for all, dative pl of *omnis* all]

omnicompetent (ˌɒmnɪ'kɒmpɪtənt) *adj* able to judge or deal with all matters > **ˌomni'competence** *n*

omnidirectional (ˌɒmnɪdɪ'rɛkʃənᵊl, -daɪ-) *adj* (of an antenna) capable of transmitting and receiving radio signals equally in any direction of the horizontal plane

omnifarious (ˌɒmnɪ'fɛərɪəs) *adj* of many or all varieties or forms [c17 from LL *omnifārius*, from L *omnis* all + *-farius* doing] > **ˌomni'fariously** *adv* > **ˌomni'fariousness** *n*

omnific (ɒm'nɪfɪk) *or* **omnificent** (ɒm'nɪfɪsənt) *adj rare* creating all things [c17 via Med. L from L *omni-* + *-ficus*, from *facere* to do] > **om'nificence** *n*

omnipotent (ɒm'nɪpətənt) *adj* **1** having very great or unlimited power ▷ *n* **2 the Omnipotent** an epithet for God [c14 via OF from L *omnipotens* all-powerful, from OMNI- + *potens*, from *posse* to be able] > **om'nipotence** *n* > **om'nipotently** *adv*

omnipresent (ˌɒmnɪ'prɛzᵊnt) *adj* (esp of a deity) present in all places at the same time > **ˌomni'presence** *n*

omniscient (ɒm'nɪsɪənt) *adj* **1** having infinite knowledge or understanding **2** having very great or seemingly unlimited knowledge [c17 from Med. L *omnisciens*, from L OMNI- + *scīre* to know] > **om'niscience** *n* > **om'nisciently** *adv*

omnium-gatherum ('ɒmnɪəm'gæðərəm) *n often facetious* a miscellaneous collection [c16 from L *omnium* of all, + Latinized form of E *gather*]

omnivorous (ɒm'nɪvərəs) *adj* **1** eating any type of food indiscriminately **2** taking in or assimilating everything, esp with the mind [c17 from L *omnivorus* all-devouring, from OMNI- + *vorāre* to eat greedily] > **'omniˌvore** *n* > **om'nivorously** *adv* > **om'nivorousness** *n*

omov ('əʊmɒv) *n acronym for* one member one vote

Omphale ('ɒmfəˌliː) *n Greek myth* a queen of Lydia, whom Hercules was required to serve as a slave to atone for the murder of Iphitus

omphalos ('ɒmfəˌlɒs) *n* **1** (in antiquity) a sacred conical object, esp a stone. The famous omphalos at Delphi was assumed to mark the centre of the earth **2** the central point **3** *literary* another word for **navel** [Gk: navel]

Omsk (ɒmsk) *n* a city in W central Russia, at the confluence of the Irtysh and Om Rivers: a major industrial centre, with pipelines from the second Baku oilfield. Pop: 1 157 600 (1999 est)

Omuta ('əʊmuːˌtɑː) *n* a city in SW Japan, on W Kyushu on Ariake Bay: former coal-mining centre; chemical industries and manufacturing. Pop: 146 691 (1996)

on (ɒn) *prep* **1** in contact or connection with the surface of; at the upper surface of: *an apple on the ground; a mark on the tablecloth* **2** attached to: *a puppet on a string* **3** carried with: *I've no money on me* **4** in the immediate vicinity of; close to or along the side of: *a house on the sea* **5** within the time limits of (a day or date): *he arrived on Thursday* **6** being performed upon or relayed through the medium of: *what's on television?* **7** at the occasion of: *on his retirement* **8** used to indicate support, subsistence, contingency, etc: *he lives on bread* **9a** regularly taking (a drug): *she's on the pill* **9b** addicted to: *he's on heroin* **10** by means of (something considered as a mode of transport) (esp in **on foot, on horseback,** etc) **11** in the process or course of: *on a journey; on strike* **12** concerned with or relating to: *a programme on archaeology* **13** used to indicate the basis or grounds, as of a statement or action: *I have it on good authority* **14** against: used to indicate opposition: *they marched on the city at dawn* **15** used to indicate a meeting or encounter: *he crept up on her* **16** (used with an adj preceded by *the*) indicating the manner or way in which an action is carried out: *on the sly; on the cheap* **17** staked or wagered as a bet upon: *ten pounds on that horse* **18** *inf* charged to: *the drinks are on me* ▷ *adv* (*often used as a particle*) **19** in the position or state required for the commencement or sustained continuation, as of a mechanical operation: *the radio's been on all night* **20** attached to, surrounding, or placed in contact with something: *the child had nothing on* **21** arranged: *we've nothing on for tonight* **22** in a manner indicating continuity, persistence, etc: *don't keep on about it; the play went on all afternoon* **23** in a direction towards something, esp forward: *we drove on towards London; march on!* **24 on and off** intermittently; from time to time **25 on and on** without ceasing; continually ▷ *adj* **26** functioning; operating: *put the switch into the on position* **27** (*postpositive*) *inf* performing, as on stage, etc: *I'm on in five minutes* **28** definitely taking place: *the match is on for Friday* **29** tolerable or practicable, acceptable, etc: *your plan just isn't on* **30** *cricket* (of a bowler) bowling **31 on at** *inf* nagging: *she was always on at her husband* ▷ *n* **32** *cricket* **32a** (*modifier*) relating to or denoting the leg side of a cricket field or pitch: *an on drive* **32b** (*in combination*) used to designate certain fielding positions on the leg side: *mid-on* [OE *an, on*]

On (ɒn) *n* the ancient Egyptian and biblical name for **Heliopolis**

ON *abbrev for:* **1** Old Norse **2** Ontario

-on *suffix forming nouns* **1** indicating a chemical substance:

interferon **2** (in physics) indicating an elementary particle or quantum: *electron; photon* **3** (in chemistry) indicating an inert gas: *neon; radon* **4** (in biochemistry) a molecular unit: *codon; operon* [from ION]

onager ('ɒnədʒə) *n, pl* **onagri** (-ˌgraɪ) *or* **onagers** **1** a Persian variety of the wild ass **2** an ancient war engine for hurling stones, etc [C14 from LL: military engine for stone throwing, from L: wild ass, from Gk *onagros*, from *onos* ass + *agros* field]

onanism ('əʊnəˌnɪzəm) *n* **1** the withdrawal of the penis from the vagina before ejaculation **2** masturbation [C18 after *Onan*, son of Judah; see Genesis 38:9] > **'onanist** *n, adj* > **ˌonan'istic** *adj*

Onassis (əʊ'næsɪs) *n* **Aristotle (Socrates)** 1906–75, Argentinian (formerly Greek) shipowner, born in Turkey. In 1968 he married **Jacqueline** (1929–94), the widow of US President John F. Kennedy

once (wʌns) *adv* **1** one time; on one occasion or in one case **2** at some past time: *I could speak French once* **3** by one step or degree (of relationship): *a cousin once removed* **4** (*in conditional clauses, negatives, etc*) ever; at all: *if you once forget it* **5** multiplied by one **6** **once and away** **6a** conclusively **6b** occasionally **7** **once and for all** conclusively; for the last time **8** **once in a while** occasionally; now and then **9** **once or twice** *or* **once and again** a few times **10** **once upon a time** used to begin fairy tales and children's stories ▷ *conj* **11** (*subordinating*) as soon as; if ever: *once you begin, you'll enjoy it* ▷ *n* **12** one occasion or case: *you may do it, this once* **13** **all at once** **13a** suddenly **13b** simultaneously **14** **at once** **14a** immediately **14b** simultaneously **15** **for once** this time, if (or but) at no other time [C12 *ones, anes*, adverbial genitive of *on, an* ONE]

once-over *n inf* **1** a quick examination or appraisal **2** a quick but comprehensive piece of work **3** a violent beating or thrashing (esp in **give (a person** or **thing) the** (or **a**) **once-over**)

oncer ('wʌnsə) *n* **1** *Brit sl* (formerly) a one-pound note **2** *Austral sl* a person elected to Parliament who can only expect to serve one term **3** *Austral & NZ* something that happens only once [C20 from ONCE]

oncogene ('ɒŋkəʊˌdʒiːn) *n* any of several genes, present in all cells, that when abnormally activated can cause cancer [C20 from Gk *onkos* mass, tumour + GENE] > **oncogenic** (ˌɒŋkəʊ'dʒɛnɪk) *adj*

oncoming ('ɒnˌkʌmɪŋ) *adj* **1** coming nearer in space or time; approaching ▷ *n* **2** the approach or onset: *the oncoming of winter*

oncost ('ɒnˌkɒst) *n Brit* **1** another word for **overhead** (sense 5) **2** (*sometimes pl*) another word for **overheads**

Ondaatje (ɒn'dɑːtʃe) *n* **Michael** born 1943, Sri Lankan-born Canadian writer: his works include the poetry collection *There's a Trick with a Knife I'm Learning to Do* (1979), the Booker-prizewinning novel *The English Patient* (1992, filmed 1997), and *Anil's Ghost* (2000)

on dit *Fr* (ɔ̃ di) *n, pl* **on dits** (ɔ̃ di). a rumour; piece of gossip [lit.: it is said, they say]

Ondo ('ɒndəʊ) *n* a state of SW Nigeria, on the Bight of Benin: formed in 1976 from part of Western State. Capital: Akure. Pop: 4 343 230 (1995 est). Area: 20 959 sq km (8092 sq miles)

one (wʌn) *determiner* **1a** single; lone; not two or more **1b** (*as pron*): *one is enough for now; one at a time* **1c** (*in combination*): *one-eyed* **2a** distinct from all others; only; unique: *one girl in a million* **2b** (*as pron*): *one of a kind* **3a** a specified (person, item, etc) as distinct from another or others of its kind: *raise one hand and then the other* **3b** (*as pron*): *which one is correct?* **4** a certain, indefinite, or unspecified (time); some: *one day you'll be sorry* **5** *inf* an emphatic word for **a** or **an**[1]: *it was one hell of a fight* **6** a certain (person): *one Miss Jones was named* **7** **(all) in one** combined; united **8** **all one** **8a** all the same **8b** of no consequence: *it's all one to me* **9** **at one** (often foll by *with*) in a state of agreement or harmony **10** **be made one** to become married **11** **many a one** many people **12** **neither one thing nor the other** indefinite, undecided, or mixed **13** **never a one** none **14** **one and all** everyone, without exception **15** **one by one** one at a time; individually **16** **one or two** a few **17** **one way and another** on balance **18** **one with another** on average ▷ *pron* **19** an indefinite person regarded as typical of every person: *one can't say any more than that* **20** any indefinite person: used as the subject of a sentence to form an alternative grammatical construction to that of the passive voice: *one can catch fine trout in this stream* **21** *arch* an unspecified person: *one came to him* ▷ *n* **22** the smallest natural number and the first cardinal number; unity **23** a numeral (1, I, i, etc) representing this number **24** *inf* a joke or story (esp in **the one about**) **25** something representing, represented by, or consisting of one unit **26** Also: **one o'clock** one hour after noon or midnight **27** a blow or setback (esp in **one in the eye for**) **28** **the Evil one** Satan **29** **the Holy One** *or* **the One above** God ▷ Related prefixes: **mono-**, **uni-** [OE *ān*]

-one *suffix forming nouns* indicating that a chemical compound is a ketone: *acetone* [arbitrarily from Gk *-ōnē*, fem. patronymic suffix, but ? infl. by *-one* in OZONE]

one another *pron* the reflexive form of plural pronouns when the action, attribution, etc, is reciprocal: *they kissed one another; knowing one another.* Also: **each other**

one-armed bandit *n inf* a fruit machine operated by pulling down a lever at one side

Onega (*Russian* a'njɛgə) *n* a lake in NW Russia, mostly in the Karelian Republic: the second largest lake in Europe. Area: 9891 sq km (3819 sq miles)

one-horse *adj* **1** drawn by or using one horse **2** (*prenominal*) *inf* small or obscure: *a one-horse town*

Oneida (əʊ'naɪdə) *n pl* **-das** *or* **-da** **1** **Lake** a lake in central New York State: part of the New York State Barge Canal system. Length: about 35 km (22 miles). Greatest width: 9 km (6 miles) **2** (preceded by *the; functioning as plural*) a North American Indian people formerly living east of Lake Ontario; one of the Iroquois peoples **3** a member of this people **4** the language of this people, belonging to the Iroquoian family [from Iroquois *onēyóte'*, literally: standing stone]

O'Neill (əʊ'niːl) *n* **Eugene (Gladstone)** 1888–1953, US dramatist. His works, which are notable for their emotional power and psychological analysis, include *Desire under the Elms* (1924), *Strange Interlude* (1928), *Mourning becomes Elektra* (1931), *Long Day's Journey into Night* (1941), and *The Iceman Cometh* (1946): Nobel prize for literature 1936

one-liner *n inf* a short joke or witty remark

one-man *adj* consisting of or done by or for one man: *a one-man band; a one-man show*

oneness ('wʌnnɪs) *n* **1** the state or quality of being one; singleness **2** the state of being united; agreement **3** uniqueness **4** sameness

one-night stand *n* **1** a performance given only once at any one place **2** *inf* a sexual encounter lasting only one evening or night

one-off *n Brit* **a** something that is carried out or made only once **b** (*as modifier*): *a one-off job*

one-on-one *adj* another term for **one-to-one** (sense 2)

one-parent family *n* another name for **single-parent family**

one-piece *adj* **1** (of a garment, esp a bathing costume) consisting of one piece ▷ *n* **2** a garment, esp a bathing costume, consisting of one piece

onerous ('ɒnərəs, 'əʊ-) *adj* **1** laborious or oppressive **2** *law* (of a contract, etc) having or involving burdens or obligations [C14 from L *onerōsus* burdensome, from *onus* load] > **'onerously** *adv* > **'onerousness** *n*

oneself (wʌn'sɛlf) *pron* **1a** the reflexive form of **one** (sense 19) **1b** (intensifier): *one doesn't do that oneself* **2** (*preceded by a copula*) one's normal or usual self: *one doesn't feel oneself after such an experience*

one-sided *adj* 1 considering or favouring only one side of a matter, problem, etc 2 having all the advantage on one side: *a one-sided boxing match* 3 larger or more developed on one side 4 having, existing on, or occurring on one side only > ˌ**one-ˈsidedly** *adv* > ˌ**one-ˈsidedness** *n*

one-size-fits-all *adj* relating to policies or approaches that are standard and not tailored to individual needs

one-step *n* an early 20th-century ballroom dance with long quick steps, the precursor of the foxtrot

one-stop *adj* having or providing a range of related services or goods in one place: *a one-stop shop*

One Thousand Guineas *n* See **Thousand Guineas**

one-time *adj* (*prenominal*) at some time in the past; former

one-to-one *adj* 1 (of two or more things) corresponding exactly 2 denoting a relationship or encounter in which someone is involved with only one other person: *one-to-one tuition* 3 *maths* involving the pairing of each member of one set with only one member of another set, without remainder

one-track *adj* 1 *inf* obsessed with one idea, subject, etc 2 having or consisting of a single track

one-trick pony *n inf chiefly US* a person or thing considered as being limited to only one single talent, capability, quality, etc

one-up *adj inf* having an advantage or lead over someone or something > ˌ**one-ˈupmanship** *n*

one-way *adj* 1 moving or allowing travel in one direction only: *one-way traffic; a one-way bus ticket* 2 entailing no reciprocal obligation, action, etc: *a one-way agreement*

ongoing (ˈɒnˌɡəʊɪŋ) *adj* 1 actually in progress: *ongoing projects* 2 continually moving forward; developing 3 remaining in existence; continuing

onion (ˈʌnjən) *n* 1 an alliaceous plant having greenish-white flowers: cultivated for its rounded edible bulb 2 the bulb of this plant, consisting of concentric layers of white succulent leaf bases with a pungent odour and taste 3 **know one's onions** *Brit sl* to be fully acquainted with a subject [c14 via Anglo-Norman from OF *oignon*, from L *unio* onion] > ˈ**oniony** *adj*

onionskin (ˈʌnjənˌskɪn) *n* a glazed translucent paper

Onitsha (əˈnɪtʃə) *n* a port in S Nigeria, in Anambra State on the Niger River: industrial centre. Pop: 371 900 (1996 est)

on line *or* **online** *adj* (**on-line** *or* **online** *when prenominal*) 1 of or concerned with a peripheral device that is directly connected to and controlled by the central processing unit of a computer 2 of or relating to the Internet: *online shopping* 3 occurring as part of, or involving, a continuous sequence of operations, such as a production line. ▷ *adv* 4 while connected to a computer or the Internet ▷ Cf **off line**

onlooker (ˈɒnˌlʊkə) *n* a person who observes without taking part > ˈ**onˌlooking** *adj*

only (ˈəʊnlɪ) *adj* (*prenominal*) 1 **the** being single or very few in number: *the only men left in town were too old to bear arms* 2 (of a child) having no siblings 3 unique by virtue of being superior to anything else; peerless 4 **one and only** 4a (*adj*) incomparable; unique 4b (*as n*) the object of all one's love: *you are my one and only* ▷ *adv* 5 without anyone or anything else being included; alone: *you have one choice only; only a genius can do that* 6 merely or just: *it's only Henry* 7 no more or no greater than: *we met only an hour ago* 8 used in conditional clauses introduced by *if* to emphasize the impossibility of the condition ever being fulfilled: *if I had only known, this would never have happened* 9 not earlier than; not...until: *I only found out yesterday* 10 **if only** *or* **if...only** an expression used to introduce a wish, esp one felt to be unrealizable 11 **only if** never...except when 12 **only too** 12a (intensifier): *he was only too pleased to help* 12b most regrettably (esp in **only too true**) ▷ *sentence connector* 13 but; however: used to introduce an exception or condition: *you may play outside: only don't go into the street* [OE *ānlīc*, from *ān* ONE + *-līc* -LY[1]]

> USAGE In informal English, *only* is often used as a sentence connector: *I would have phoned you, only I didn't know your number*. This use should be avoided in formal writing: *I would have phoned you, but I didn't know your number*

on message *adj* (**on-message** *when prenominal*) adhering to or reflecting the official line of a political party, government, or other organization

o.n.o. *abbrev for* or near(est) offer

onomastics (ˌɒnəˈmæstɪks) *n* (*functioning as sing*) the study of proper names, esp of their origins [from Gk *onomastikos*, from *onomazein* to name, from *onoma* NAME]

onomatopoeia (ˌɒnəˌmætəˈpiːə) *n* 1 the formation of words whose sound is imitative of the sound of the noise or action designated, such as *hiss* 2 the use of such words for poetic or rhetorical effect [c16 via LL from Gk *onoma* name + *poiein* to make] > ˌ**onoˌmatoˈpoeic** *or* **onomatopoetic** (ˌɒnəˌmætəpəʊˈɛtɪk) *adj* > ˌ**onoˌmatoˈpoeically** *or* ˌ**onoˌmatopoˈetically** *adv*

Onondaga (ˌɒnənˈdɑːɡə) *n* 1 **Lake** a salt lake in central New York State. Area: about 13 sq km (5 sq miles) 2 (*pl* **-gas** *or* **-ga**) a member of a North American Indian Iroquois people formerly living between Lake Champlain and the St Lawrence River 3 the language of this people, belonging to the Iroquoian family [from Iroquois *onōtáge'*, literally: on the top of the hill (the name of their principal village)]

on-ramp *n* 1 a ramp that provides access to the specified part of a road system: *an interstate highway on-ramp* 2 a method of accessing a service or facility: *an important on-ramp to the online world*

onrush (ˈɒnˌrʌʃ) *n* a forceful forward rush or flow

ONS (in Britain) *abbrev for* Office for National Statistics

onset (ˈɒnˌsɛt) *n* 1 an attack; assault 2 a start; beginning

onshore (ˈɒnˈʃɔː) *adj, adv* 1 towards the land: *an onshore gale* 2 on land; not at sea

onside (ˌɒnˈsaɪd) *adj, adv* 1 *football, etc* (of a player) in a legal position, as when behind the ball or with a required number of opponents between oneself and the opposing team's goal line ▷ Cf **offside** 2 taking one's part or side; working towards the same goal: *the government may be onside; every effort to bring them onside*

onslaught (ˈɒnˌslɔːt) *n* a violent attack [c17 from MDu. *aenslag*, from *aan* ON + *slag* a blow]

Ont. *abbrev for* Ontario

Ontario (ɒnˈtɛərɪəʊ) *n* 1 a province of central Canada: lies mostly on the Canadian Shield and contains the fertile plain of the lower Great Lakes and the St Lawrence River, one of the world's leading industrial areas; the second largest and the most populous province. Capital: Toronto. Pop: 11 874 400 (2001 est). Area: 891 198 sq km (344 092 sq miles). Abbreviations: **Ont** *or* **ON** 2 **Lake** a lake between the US and Canada, bordering on New York State and Ontario province: the smallest of the Great Lakes; linked with Lake Erie by the Niagara River and Welland Canal; drained by the St Lawrence. Area: 19 684 sq km (7600 sq miles) > **On'tarian** *or* **Ontarioan** (ɒnˈtɛərɪˌəʊən) *n, adj*

▷ www.gov.on.ca

▷ www.tourism.gov.on.ca/english

onto *or* **on to** (ˈɒntʊ; *unstressed* ˈɒntə) *prep* 1 to a position that is on: *step onto the train* 2 having become aware of (something illicit or secret): *the police are onto us* 3 into contact with: *get onto the factory*.

> USAGE *Onto* is now generally accepted as a word in its own right. *On to* is still used, however, where *on* is considered to be part of the verb: *he moved on to a different town* as contrasted with *he jumped onto the stage*

Oo

onto- *combining form* existence or being: *ontogeny; ontology* [from LGk, from *ōn* (stem *ont-*) being, present participle of *einai* to be]

ontogeny (ɒn'tɒdʒənɪ) *or* **ontogenesis** (ˌɒntə'dʒɛnɪsɪs) *n* the entire sequence of events involved in the development of an individual organism ▷ Cf **phylogeny** > **ontogenic** (ˌɒntə'dʒɛnɪk) *or* **ontogenetic** (ˌɒntədʒɪ'nɛtɪk) *adj* > ˌ**onto'genically** *or* ˌ**ontoge'netically** *adv*

ontology (ɒn'tɒlədʒɪ) *n* **1** *philosophy* the branch of metaphysics that deals with the nature of being **2** *logic* the set of entities presupposed by a theory > ˌ**onto'logical** *adj* > ˌ**onto'logically** *adv*

onus ('əʊnəs) *n, pl* **onuses** a responsibility, task, or burden [C17 L: burden]

onward ('ɒnwəd) *adj* **1** directed or moving forwards, onwards, etc ▷ *adv* **2** a variant of **onwards**

onwards ('ɒnwədz) *or* **onward** *adv* at or towards a point or position ahead, in advance, etc

onychophoran (ˌɒnɪ'kɒfərən) *n* a wormlike invertebrate having a segmented body and short unjointed limbs, and breathing by means of tracheae [from NL *Onychophora*, from Gk *onukh-* claw + -PHORE]

-onym *n combining form* indicating a name or word: *pseudonym* [from Gk *-onumon*, from var. of *onoma* name]

onyx ('ɒnɪks) *n* **1** a variety of chalcedony with alternating black-and-white parallel bands, used as a gemstone **2** a variety of calcite used as an ornamental stone; onyx marble [C13 from L, from Gk: fingernail (so called from its veined appearance)]

ONZ *abbrev for* Order of New Zealand

oo- *or* **oö-** *combining form* egg or ovum: *oosperm* [from Gk *ōion* EGG[1]]

oocyte ('əʊəˌsaɪt) *n* an immature female germ cell that gives rise to an ovum after two meiotic divisions

oodles ('uːdəlz) *pl n inf* great quantities: *oodles of money* [C20 from ?]

oogamy (əʊ'ɒgəmɪ) *n* sexual reproduction involving a small motile male gamete and a large much less motile female gamete > **o'ogamous** *adj*

Ookpik ('uːkpɪk) *n Canad trademark* a sealskin doll resembling an owl, first made in 1963 by an Inuit and used abroad as a symbol of Canadian handicrafts [from Inuktitut *ukpik* a snowy owl]

oolite ('əʊəˌlaɪt) *n* any sedimentary rock, esp limestone, consisting of tiny spherical concentric grains within a fine matrix [C18 from F, from NL *oolitēs*, lit.: egg stone; prob. a translation of G *Rogenstein* roe stone] > **oolitic** (ˌəʊə'lɪtɪk) *adj*

oolith ('əʊəˌlɪθ) *n* any of the tiny spherical grains of sedimentary rock of which oolite is composed

oology (əʊ'ɒlədʒɪ) *n* the branch of ornithology concerned with the study of birds' eggs > **oological** (ˌəʊə'lɒdʒɪkəl) *adj* > **o'ologist** *n*

oolong ('uːˌlɒŋ) *n* a kind of dark tea, grown in China, that is partly fermented before being dried [C19 from Chinese *wu lung*, from *wu* black + *lung* dragon]

oom ('uːəm) *n S African* a title of respect used to address an elderly man [Afrik., lit.: uncle]

oomiak *or* **oomiac** ('uːmɪˌæk) *n* a variant of **umiak**

oompah ('uːmˌpɑː) *n* a representation of the sound made by a deep brass instrument, esp in military band music

oomph (ʊmf) *n inf* **1** enthusiasm, vigour, or energy **2** sex appeal [C20 from ?]

oops (ʊps, uːps) *interj* an exclamation of surprise or of apology as when someone drops something or makes a mistake

Oostende (oːst'ɛndə) *n* the Flemish name for **Ostend**

ooze[1] (uːz) *vb* **oozes, oozing, oozed 1** (*intr*) to flow or leak out slowly, as through small holes **2** to emit (moisture, etc) **3** (*tr*) to overflow with: *to ooze charm* **4** (*intr*; often foll by *away*) to disappear or escape gradually ▷ *n* **5** a slow flowing or leaking **6** an infusion of vegetable matter, such as oak bark, used in tanning [OE *wōs* juice]

ooze[2] (uːz) *n* **1** a soft thin mud found at the bottom of lakes and rivers **2** a fine-grained marine deposit consisting of the hard parts of planktonic organisms **3** muddy ground, esp of bogs [OE *wāse* mud]

oozy[1] ('uːzɪ) *adj* **oozier, ooziest** moist or dripping

oozy[2] ('uːzɪ) *adj* **oozier, ooziest** of, resembling, or containing mud; slimy > **'oozily** *adv* > **'ooziness** *n*

OP *abbrev for:* **1** Ordo Praedicatorum (the Dominicans) [L: Order of Preachers] **2** organophosphate

op. *abbrev for:* **1** operation **2** operator **3** opus

o.p. *or* **O.P.** *abbrev for* out of print

opacity (əʊ'pæsɪtɪ) *n, pl* **opacities 1** the state or quality of being opaque **2** the degree to which something is opaque **3** an opaque object or substance **4** obscurity of meaning; unintelligibility

opah ('əʊpə) *n* a large soft-finned deep-sea teleost fish having a deep, brilliantly coloured body. Also called: **moonfish, kingfish** [C18 of West African origin]

opal ('əʊpəl) *n* an amorphous form of hydrated silicon dioxide that can be of almost any colour. It is used as a gemstone [C16 from L *opalus*, from Gk *opallios*, from Sansk. *upala* precious stone] > **'opal-ˌlike** *adj*

opalescent (ˌəʊpə'lɛsənt) *adj* having or emitting an iridescence like that of an opal > ˌ**opa'lesce** *vb* > ˌ**opal'escence** *n*

opal glass *n* glass that is opalescent or white, made by the addition of fluorides

opaline ('əʊpəˌlaɪn) *adj* **1** opalescent ▷ *n* **2** an opaque or semiopaque whitish glass

opaque (əʊ'peɪk) *adj* **1** not transmitting light; not transparent or translucent **2** not reflecting light; lacking lustre or shine; dull **3** hard to understand; unintelligible **4** unintelligent; dense ▷ *n* **5** *photog* an opaque pigment used to block out areas on a negative ▷ *vb* **opaques, opaquing, opaqued** (*tr*) **6** to make opaque **7** *photog* to block out areas on (a negative), using an opaque [C15 from L *opācus* shady] > **o'paquely** *adv* > **o'paqueness** *n*

op art (ɒp) *n* a style of abstract art chiefly concerned with the exploitation of optical effects such as the illusion of movement [C20 *op*, short for *optical*]
▷ www.artcyclopedia.com/history/optical.html
▷ www.artlex.com/ArtLex/o/opart.html

op. cit. (in textual annotations) *abbrev for* opere citato [L: in the work cited]

ope (əʊp) *vb* **opes, oping, oped,** *adj* an archaic or poetic word for **open**

OPEC ('əʊpɛk) *n acronym for* Organization of Petroleum-Exporting Countries
▷ www.opec.org

op-ed ('ɒpˌɛd) *n* **a** a page of a newspaper where varying opinions are expressed by columnists, commentators, etc **b** (*as modifier*): *an op-ed column in the New York Times* [C20 from *op(posite) ed(itorial page)*]

open ('əʊpən) *adj* **1** not closed or barred **2** affording free passage, access, view, etc; not blocked or obstructed **3** not sealed, fastened, or wrapped **4** having the interior part accessible: *an open drawer* **5** extended, expanded, or unfolded: *an open flower* **6** ready for business **7** able to be obtained; available: *the position is no longer open* **8** unobstructed by buildings, trees, etc: *open countryside* **9** free to all to join, enter, use, visit, etc: *an open competition* **10** unengaged or unoccupied: *the doctor has an hour open for you to call* **11** See **open season 12** not decided or finalized: *an open question* **13** ready to entertain new ideas; not biased or prejudiced **14** unreserved or candid **15** liberal or generous: *an open hand* **16** extended or eager to receive (esp in **with open arms**) **17** exposed to view; blatant: *open disregard of the law* **18** liable or susceptible: *you will leave yourself open to attack* **19** (of climate or seasons) free from frost; mild **20** free from navigational hazards, such as ice, sunken ships, etc **21** having large or numerous spacing or apertures: *open ranks* **22** full of small openings or gaps; porous: *an open texture* **23** *music* **23a** (of a string) not stopped with the finger **23b** (of a pipe, such as an organ pipe) not closed at either end **23c** (of a note) played on such a string or pipe **24** *commerce* **24a** in operation; active: *an open account* **24b** unrestricted; unlimited: *open credit; open insurance cover* **25** See **open cheque** **26** (of a return ticket) not specifying a date for travel **27** *sport* (of a goal, court, etc) unguarded or relatively unprotected **28** (of a wound) exposed to the air **29** (esp of the large intestine) free from obstruction **30** undefended and of no military significance: *an open city* **31** *phonetics* **31a** denoting a vowel pronounced with the lips relatively wide apart **31b** denoting a syllable that does not end in a consonant, as in *pa* **32** *maths* (of a set) containing points whose neighbourhood consists of other points of the same set **33** *computing* designed to an internationally agreed standard in order to allow communication between computers, irrespective of size, manufacturer, etc ▷ *vb* **34** to move from a closed or fastened position: *to open a window* **35** (when *intr*, foll by *on* or *onto*) to render, be, or become accessible or unobstructed: *to open a road; to open a parcel* **36** (*intr*) to come into or appear in view: *the lake opened before us* **37** to extend or unfold or cause to extend or unfold: *to open a newspaper* **38** to disclose or uncover or be disclosed or uncovered: *to open one's heart* **39** to cause (the mind) to become receptive or (of the mind) to become receptive **40** to operate or cause to operate: *to open a shop* **41** (when *intr*, sometimes foll by *out*) to make or become less compact or dense in structure: *to open ranks* **42** to set or be set in action; start: *to open the batting* **43** (*tr*) to arrange for (a bank account, etc), usually by making an initial deposit **44** to turn to a specified point in (a book, etc): *open at page one* **45** *law* to make the opening statement in (a case before a court of law) **46** (*intr*) *cards* to bet, bid, or lead first on a hand ▷ *n* **47** (often preceded by *the*) any wide or unobstructed space or expanse, esp of land or water **48** See **open air** **49** *sport* a competition which anyone may enter **50** **bring** (*or* **come**) **into the open** to make (*or* become) evident or public ▷ See also **open up** [OE] > **'openable** *adj* > **'opener** *n* > **'openly** *adv* > **'openness** *n*

open air *n* **a** the place or space where the air is unenclosed; the outdoors **b** (*as modifier*): *an open-air concert*

open-and-shut *adj* easily decided or solved; obvious: *an open-and-shut case*

opencast mining ('əʊpᵊnˌkɑːst) *n Brit* mining by excavating from the surface. Also called: (esp US) **strip mining,** (Austral and NZ) **open cut mining** [c18 from OPEN + arch. *cast* ditch, cutting]

open chain *n* a chain of atoms in a molecule that is not joined at its ends into the form of a ring

open cheque *n* an uncrossed cheque that can be cashed at the drawee bank

open circuit *n* an incomplete electrical circuit in which no current flows

Open College *n* **the** (in Britain) a college of art founded in 1987 for mature students studying foundation courses in arts and crafts by television programmes, written material, and tutorials

open day *n* an occasion on which an institution, such as a school, is open for inspection by the public

open door *n* **1** a policy or practice by which a nation grants opportunities for trade to all other nations equally **2** free and unrestricted admission ▷ *adj* **open-door** **3** open to all; accessible

open-ended *adj* **1** without definite limits, as of duration or amount: *an open-ended contract* **2** denoting a question, esp one on a questionnaire, that cannot be answered "yes", "no", or "don't know"

open-eyed *adj* **1** with the eyes wide open, as in amazement **2** watchful; alert

open-faced *adj* **1** having an ingenuous expression **2** (of a watch) having no lid or cover other than the glass

open-handed *adj* generous > ˌ**open-'handedly** *adv* > ˌ**open-'handedness** *n*

open-hearted *adj* **1** kindly and warm **2** disclosing intentions and thoughts clearly; candid > ˌ**open-'heartedness** *n*

open-hearth furnace *n* (esp formerly) a steel-making reverbatory furnace in which pig iron and scrap are contained in a shallow hearth and heated by producer gas

open-heart surgery *n* surgical repair of the heart during which the blood circulation is often maintained mechanically

open house *n* **1** a US and Canad name for **at-home** **2** **keep open house** to be always ready to receive guests

opening ('əʊpənɪŋ) *n* **1** the act of making or becoming open **2** a vacant or unobstructed space, esp one that will serve as a passageway; gap **3** *chiefly US* a tract in a forest in which trees are scattered or absent **4** the first part or stage of something **5a** the first performance of something, esp a theatrical production **5b** (*as modifier*): *the opening night* **6** a specific or formal sequence of moves at the start of any of certain games, esp chess or draughts **7** an opportunity or chance **8** *law* the preliminary statement made by counsel to the court or jury

opening batsman *n cricket* one of the two batsmen beginning an innings

opening time *n Brit* the time at which public houses can legally start selling alcoholic drinks

open-jaw *n* **a** a ticket that allows a traveller to arrive in one place and depart from another **b** (*as modifier*): *an open-jaw itinerary*

open learning *n* a system of further education on a flexible part-time basis

open letter *n* a letter, esp one of protest, addressed to a person but also made public, as through the press

Oo

open market *n* **a** a market in which prices are determined by supply and demand, there are no barriers to entry, and trading is not restricted to a specific area **b** (*as modifier*): *open-market value*

open marriage *n* a marriage in which the partners agree to pursue separate social and sexual lives

open-minded *adj* having a mind receptive to new ideas, arguments, etc; unprejudiced > ˌ**open-'mindedness** *n*

open-mouthed *adj* **1** having an open mouth, esp in surprise **2** greedy or ravenous **3** clamorous or vociferous

open-plan *adj* having no or few dividing walls between areas: *an open-plan office floor*

open position *n commerce* a situation in which a dealer in commodities, securities, or currencies has either unsold stock or uncovered sales

open prison *n* a penal establishment in which the prisoners are trusted to serve their sentences and so do not need to be locked up

open punctuation *n* punctuation which has relatively few semicolons, commas, etc ▷ Cf **close punctuation**

open question *n* **1** a matter which is undecided **2** a question that cannot be answered with "yes" or "no" but requires a developed answer

open-reel *adj* another term for **reel-to-reel**

open season *n* a specified period of time in the year when it is legal to hunt or kill game or fish protected at other times by law

open secret *n* something that is supposed to be secret but is widely known

open sesame *n* a very successful means of achieving a result [from the magical words used in the *Arabian Nights' Entertainments* to open the robbers' den]

open shop *n* an establishment in which persons are employed irrespective of their membership or nonmembership of a trade union

open slather *n* See **slather**

open source *n computing* **a** software in which the source code is freely available to the general public for use or modification **b** (*as modifier*): *open-source operating systems*

open system *n computing* an operating system that is not specific to a particular supplier, but conforms to more widely compatible standards

Open University *n* **the** (in Britain) a university founded in 1969 for mature students studying by television and radio lectures, correspondence courses, local counselling, and summer schools

open up *vb* (*adv*) **1** (*intr*) to start firing a gun or guns **2** (*intr*) to speak freely or without restraint **3** (*intr*) *inf* (of a motor vehicle) to accelerate **4** (*tr*) to render accessible: *the motorway opened up the remoter areas* **5** (*intr*) to make or become more exciting or lively: *the game opened up after half-time*

open verdict *n* a finding by a coroner's jury of death without stating the cause

openwork ('əʊpᵊn,wɜːk) *n* ornamental work, as of metal or embroidery, having a pattern of openings or holes

opera[1] ('ɒpərə, 'ɒprə) *n* **1** an extended dramatic work in which music constitutes a dominating feature **2** the branch of music or drama represented by such works **3** the score, libretto, etc, of an opera **4** a theatre where opera is performed [C17 via It. from L: work, a work, pl of *opus* work]

▹ www.aria-database.com/index2.html
▹ www.theoperacritic.com
▹ www.teatroallascala.org
▹ http://classicalmus.hispeed.com/operalinks.html

opera[2] ('ɒpərə) *n* a plural of **opus**

operable ('ɒpərəbᵊl, 'ɒprə-) *adj* **1** capable of being treated by a surgical operation **2** capable of being operated **3** capable of being put into practice > ˌ**opera'bility** *n* > '**operably** *adv*

opéra bouffe ('ɒpərə 'buːf) *n, pl* **opéras bouffes** ('ɒpərə 'buːf) a type of light or satirical opera common in France during the 19th century [F: comic opera]

opera buffa ('buːfə) *n, pl* **opera buffas** comic opera, esp that originating in Italy during the 18th century [It.: comic opera]

opéra comique (kɒ'miːk) *n, pl* **opéras comiques** ('ɒpərə kɒ'miːk) a type of opera current in France during the 19th century and characterized by spoken dialogue [F: comic opera: it originated in satirical parodies of grand opera]

opera glasses *pl n* small low-powered binoculars used by audiences in theatres, etc

opera hat *n* a collapsible top hat operated by a spring

opera house *n* a theatre designed for opera

operand ('ɒpə,rænd) *n* a quantity or function upon which a mathematical or logical operation is performed [C19 from L *operandum* (something) to be worked upon, from *operārī* to work]

operant ('ɒpərənt) *adj* **1** producing effects; operating ▹ *n* **2** a person or thing that operates **3** *psychol* any response by an organism that is not directly caused by stimulus

opera seria ('sɪərɪə) *n, pl* **opera serias** a type of opera current in 18th-century Italy based on a serious plot, esp a mythological tale [It.: serious opera]

operate ('ɒpə,reɪt) *vb* **operates, operating, operated 1** to function or cause to function **2** (*tr*) to control the functioning of **3** to manage, direct, run, or pursue (a business, system, etc) **4** (*intr*) to perform a surgical operation (upon a person or animal) **5** (*intr*) to produce a desired effect **6** (*tr; usually foll by on*) to treat or process in a particular or specific way **7** (*intr*) to conduct military or naval operations **8** (*intr*) to deal in securities on a stock exchange [C17 from L *operārī* to work]

operatic (ˌɒpə'rætɪk) *adj* **1** of or relating to opera **2** histrionic or exaggerated > ˌ**oper'atically** *adv*

operating budget *n accounting* a forecast of the sales revenue, production costs, overheads, cash flow, etc, of an organization, used to monitor its trading activities, usually for one year

operating cycle *n* the time taken by a firm to convert its raw materials into finished goods and thereafter sell them and collect payment

operating system *n* the set of software controlling a computer

operating theatre *n* a room in which surgical operations are performed

operation (ˌɒpə'reɪʃən) *n* **1** the act, process, or manner of operating **2** the state of being in effect, in action, or operative (esp in **in** *or* **into operation**) **3** a process, method, or series of acts, esp of a practical or mechanical nature **4** *surgery* any manipulation of the body or one of its organs or parts to repair damage, arrest the progress of a disease, remove foreign matter, etc **5a** a military or naval action, such as a campaign, manoeuvre, etc **5b** (*cap and prenominal when part of a name*): *Operation Crossbow* **6** *maths* any procedure, such as addition, in which one or more numbers or quantities are operated upon according to specific rules **7** a commercial or financial transaction

operational (ˌɒpə'reɪʃənᵊl) *adj* **1** of or relating to an operation **2** in working order and ready for use **3** *mil* capable of, needed in, or actually involved in operations > ˌ**oper'ationally** *adv*

operationalism (ˌɒpə'reɪʃənə,lɪzəm) *or* **operationism** (ˌɒpə'reɪʃə,nɪzəm) *n philosophy* the theory that scientific terms are defined by the experimental operations which determine their applicability > ˌ**oper,ational'istic** *adj*

operations research *n* the analysis of problems in business and industry involving quantitative techniques. Also called: **operational research**

operative ('ɒpərətɪv) *adj* **1** in force, effect, or operation **2** exerting force or influence **3** producing a desired effect; significant: *the operative word* **4** of or relating to a surgical procedure ▹ *n* **5** a worker, esp one with a special skill **6** *US* a private detective **7** *chiefly US & Canad* a spy > '**operatively** *adv* > '**operativeness** *or* ˌ**opera'tivity** *n*

operator ('ɒpə,reɪtə) *n* **1** a person who operates a machine, instrument, etc, esp a telephone switchboard **2** a person who owns or operates an industrial or commercial establishment **3** a speculator, esp one who operates on currency or stock markets **4** *inf* a person who manipulates affairs and other people **5** *maths* any symbol, term, letter, etc, used to indicate or express a specific operation or process, such as ∫ (the integral operator)

operculum (əʊ'pɜːkjʊləm) *n, pl* **opercula** (-lə) *or* **operculums 1** *zool* **1a** the hard bony flap covering the gill slits in fishes **1b** the bony plate in certain gastropods covering the opening of the shell when the body is withdrawn **2** *biol & bot* any other covering or lid in various organisms [C18 via NL from L: lid, from *operīre* to cover] > **o'percular** *or* **operculate** (əʊ'pɜːkjʊlɪt, -ˌleɪt) *adj*

operetta (ˌɒpə'rɛtə) *n* a type of comic or light-hearted opera [C18 from It.: a small OPERA[1]] > ˌ**oper'ettist** *n*

▹ www.operetta.org

ophicleide ('ɒfɪ,klaɪd) *n music* an obsolete keyed wind instrument of bass pitch [C19 from F *ophicléide*, from Gk *ophis* snake + *kleis* key]

ophidian (əʊ'fɪdɪən) *adj* **1** snakelike **2** of, relating to, or belonging to the suborder of reptiles that comprises the snakes ▹ *n* **3** any reptile of this suborder; a snake [C19 from NL *Ophidia*, name of suborder, from Gk *ophidion*, from *ophis* snake]

Ophir ('əʊfə) *n Bible* a region, probably situated on the SW coast of Arabia on the Red Sea, renowned, esp in

King Solomon's reign, for its gold and precious stones (I Kings 9:28; 10:10)

ophthalmia (ɒf'θælmɪə) *n* inflammation of the eye, often including the conjunctiva [C16 via LL from Gk, from *ophthalmos* eye; see OPTIC]

ophthalmic (ɒf'θælmɪk) *adj* of or relating to the eye

ophthalmic optician *n* See **optician**

ophthalmo- *or before a vowel* **ophthalm-** *combining form* indicating the eye or the eyeball [from Gk *ophthalmos* EYE]

ophthalmology (ˌɒfθæl'mɒlədʒɪ) *n* the branch of medicine concerned with the eye and its diseases > **ophthalmological** (ɒfˌθælmə'lɒdʒɪkᵊl) *adj* > ˌ**ophthal'mologist** *n*

ophthalmoscope (ɒf'θælməˌskəʊp) *n* an instrument for examining the interior of the eye > **ophthalmoscopic** (ɒfˌθælmə'skɒpɪk) *adj*

-opia *n combining form* indicating a visual defect or condition: *myopia* [from Gk, from *ōps* eye] > **-opic** *adj combining form*

opiate *n* ('əʊpɪɪt) **1** any of various narcotic drugs, such as morphine and heroin, that act on opioid receptors **2** any other narcotic or sedative drug **3** something that soothes, deadens, or induces sleep ▷ *adj* ('əʊpɪɪt) **4** containing or consisting of opium **5** inducing relaxation; soporific ▷ *vb* ('əʊpɪˌeɪt), **opiates, opiating, opiated** (*tr*) *rare* **6** to treat with an opiate **7** to dull or deaden [C16 from Med. L *opiātus*, from L *opium* OPIUM]

opine (əʊ'paɪn) *vb* **opines, opining, opined** (when *tr*, *usually takes a clause as object*) to hold or express an opinion: *he opined that it was a mistake* [C16 from L *opīnārī*]

opinion (ə'pɪnjən) *n* **1** judgment or belief not founded on certainty or proof **2** the prevailing or popular feeling or view: *public opinion* **3** evaluation, impression, or estimation of the value or worth of a person or thing **4** an evaluation or judgment given by an expert: *a medical opinion* **5** the advice given by counsel on a case submitted to him or her for his or her view on the legal points involved **6 a matter of opinion** a point open to question **7 be of the opinion (that)** to believe (that) [C13 via OF from L *opīniō* belief, from *opīnārī* to think]

opinionated (ə'pɪnjəˌneɪtɪd) *adj* holding obstinately and unreasonably to one's own opinions; dogmatic > **o'pinionˌatedly** *adv* > **o'pinionˌatedness** *n*

opinionative (ə'pɪnjənətɪv) *adj rare* **1** of or relating to opinion **2** another word for **opinionated** > **o'pinionatively** *adv* > **o'pinionativeness** *n*

opinion poll *n* another term for a **poll** (sense 3)

opioid ('əʊpɪˌɔɪd) *n* any of a group of substances that resemble morphine in their physiological or pharmacological effects, esp in their pain-relieving properties

opium ('əʊpɪəm) *n* **1** the dried juice extracted from the seed capsules of the opium poppy: used in medicine as an analgesic **2** something having a tranquillizing or stupefying effect [C14 from L: poppy juice, from Gk *opion*, dim. of *opos*, juice of a plant]

opium poppy *n* a poppy of SW Asia, with greyish-green leaves and typically white or reddish flowers: widely cultivated as a source of opium

Oporto (ə'pɔːtəʊ) *n* a port in NW Portugal, near the mouth of the Douro River: the second largest city in Portugal, famous for port wine (begun in 1678). Pop: 262 928 (2001). Portuguese name: **Pôrto**

opossum (ə'pɒsəm) *n, pl* **opossums** *or* **opossum** **1** a thick-furred marsupial, esp the **common opossum** of North and South America, having an elongated snout and a hairless prehensile tail **2** *Austral & NZ* any of various similar animals, esp a phalanger ▷ Often shortened to **possum** [C17 from Algonquian *aposoum*]

Oppenheimer ('ɒpənˌhaɪmə) *n* **J(ulius) Robert** 1904–67, US nuclear physicist. He was director of the Los Alamos laboratory (1943–45), which produced the first atomic bomb. He opposed the development of the hydrogen bomb (1949) and in 1953 was alleged to be a security risk. He was later exonerated

opponent (ə'pəʊnənt) *n* **1** a person who opposes another in a contest, battle, etc **2** *anat* an opponent muscle ▷ *adj* **3** opposite, as in position **4** *anat* (of a muscle) bringing two parts into opposition **5** opposing; contrary [C16 from L *oppōnere* to oppose] > **op'ponency** *n*

opportune ('ɒpəˌtjuːn) *adj* **1** occurring at a time that is suitable or advantageous **2** fit or suitable for a particular purpose or occurrence [C15 via OF from L *opportūnus*, from *ob-* to + *portus* harbour (orig.: coming to the harbour, obtaining timely protection)] > **'opporˌtunely** *adv* > **'opporˌtuneness** *n*

opportunist (ˌɒpə'tjuːnɪst) *n* **1** a person who adapts his or her actions, responses, etc, to take advantage of opportunities, circumstances, etc ▷ *adj* **2** taking advantage of opportunities and circumstances in this way > ˌ**oppor'tunism** *n*

opportunistic (ˌɒpətjʊ'nɪstɪk) *adj* **1** of or characterized by opportunism **2** *med* (of an infection) caused by any microorganism that is harmless to a healthy person but debilitates a person whose immune system has been weakened

opportunity (ˌɒpə'tjuːnɪtɪ) *n, pl* **opportunities** **1** a favourable, appropriate, or advantageous combination of circumstances **2** a chance or prospect

opportunity shop *n Austral & NZ* a shop selling used goods for charitable funds. Often shortened to **op shop**

opposable (ə'pəʊzəbᵊl) *adj* **1** capable of being opposed **2** Also: **apposable** (of the thumb of primates, esp man) capable of being moved into a position facing the other digits so as to be able to touch the ends of each **3** capable of being placed opposite something else > **opˌposa'bility** *n* > **op'posably** *adv*

oppose (ə'pəʊz) *vb* **opposes, opposing, opposed** **1** (*tr*) to fight against, counter, or resist strongly **2** (*tr*) to be hostile or antagonistic to; be against **3** (*tr*) to place or set in opposition; contrast or counterbalance **4** (*tr*) to place opposite or facing **5** (*intr*) to be or act in opposition [C14 via OF from L *oppōnere*, from *ob-* against + *pōnere* to place] > **op'poser** *n* > **op'posing** *adj* > **oppositive** (ə'pɒzɪtɪv) *adj*

Oo

opposite ('ɒpəzɪt, -sɪt) *adj* **1** situated or being on the other side or at each side of something between **2** facing or going in contrary directions: *opposite ways* **3** diametrically different in character, tendency, belief, etc **4** *bot* **4a** (of leaves) arranged in pairs on either side of the stem **4b** (of parts of a flower) arranged opposite the middle of another part **5** *maths* (of a side in a triangle) facing a specified angle. Abbreviation: **opp** ▷ *n* **6** a person or thing that is opposite; antithesis ▷ *prep* **7** Also: **opposite to** facing; corresponding to (something on the other side of a division) **8** as a co-star with: *she played opposite Olivier* ▷ *adv* **9** on opposite sides: *she lives opposite* > **'oppositely** *adv* > **'oppositeness** *n*

opposite number *n* a person holding an equivalent and corresponding position on another side or situation

opposition (ˌɒpə'zɪʃən) *n* **1** the act of opposing or the state of being opposed **2** hostility, unfriendliness, or antagonism **3** a person or group antagonistic or opposite in aims to another **4a** (usually preceded by *the*) a political party or group opposed to the ruling party or government **4b** (*cap as part of a name, esp in Britain and Commonwealth countries*): *Her Majesty's Loyal Opposition* **4c in opposition** (of a political party) opposing the government **5** a position facing or opposite another **6** something that acts as an obstacle to some course or progress **7** *astron* the position of an outer planet or the moon when it is in line with the earth as seen from the sun and is approximately at its nearest to the earth **8** *astrol* an exact aspect of 180° between two planets, etc, an orb of 8° being allowed **9** *logic* the relation between propositions having the same subject and predicate but differing in quality, quantity, or both, as with *all men are wicked; no men are wicked; some men are not wicked* > ˌ**oppo'sitional** *adj* > ˌ**oppo'sitionist** *n* > ˌ**oppo'sitionless** *adj*

oppress (ə'prɛs) *vb* (*tr*) 1 to subjugate by cruelty, force, etc 2 to afflict or torment 3 to lie heavy on (the mind, etc) [C14 via OF from Med. L *oppressāre*, from L *opprimere*, from *ob-* against + *premere* to press] > **op'pressing** *adj* > **op'pressor** *n*

oppression (ə'prɛʃən) *n* 1 the act of subjugating by cruelty, force, etc or the state of being subjugated in this way 2 the condition of being afflicted or tormented 3 the condition of having something lying heavily on one's mind, imagination, etc

oppressive (ə'prɛsɪv) *adj* 1 cruel, harsh, or tyrannical 2 heavy, constricting, or depressing > **op'pressively** *adv* > **op'pressiveness** *n*

opprobrious (ə'prəʊbrɪəs) *adj* 1 expressing scorn, disgrace, or contempt 2 shameful or infamous > **op'probriously** *adv* > **op'probriousness** *n*

opprobrium (ə'prəʊbrɪəm) *n* 1 the state of being abused or scornfully criticized 2 reproach or censure 3 a cause of disgrace or ignominy [C17 from L *ob-* against + *probrum* a shameful act]

oppugn (ə'pjuːn) *vb* (*tr*) to call into question; dispute [C15 from L *oppugnāre*, from *ob-* against + *pugnāre* to fight, from *pugnus* clenched fist] > **op'pugner** *n*

OPRA ('əʊprə) *n* (in Britain) *acronym for* Occupational Pensions Regulatory Authority

Ops (ɒps) *n* the Roman goddess of abundance and fertility, wife of Saturn. Greek counterpart: **Rhea**

op-shop *n Austral and NZ inf* short for **opportunity shop**

opsin ('ɒpsɪn) *n* the protein that together with retinene makes up the purple visual pigment rhodopsin [C20 back formation from RHODOPSIN]

-opsis *n combining form* indicating a specified appearance or resemblance: *meconopsis* [from Gk *opsis* sight]

opsonin ('ɒpsənɪn) *n* a constituent of blood serum that renders bacteria more susceptible to ingestion by phagocytes [C20 from Gk *opsōnion* victuals] > **opsonic** (ɒp'sɒnɪk) *adj*

opt (ɒpt) *vb* (when *intr*, foll by *for*) to show preference (for) or choose (to do something). See also **opt in**, **opt out** [C19 from F *opter*, from L *optāre* to choose]

optative ('ɒptətɪv) *adj* 1 indicating or expressing choice or wish 2 *grammar* denoting a mood of verbs in Greek and Sanskrit expressing a wish ▷ *n* 3 *grammar* 3a the optative mood 3b a verb in this mood [C16 via F *optatif*, from LL *optātīvus*, from L *optāre* to desire]

optic ('ɒptɪk) *adj* 1 of or relating to the eye or vision 2 a less common word for **optical** ▷ *n* 3 an informal word for **eye**[1] 4 *Brit, trademark* a device attached to an inverted bottle for dispensing measured quantities of liquid [C16 from Med. L *opticus*, from Gk *optikos*, from *optos* visible; rel. to *ōps* eye]

optical ('ɒptɪkᵊl) *adj* 1 of, relating to, producing, or involving light 2 of or relating to the eye or to the sense of sight; optic 3 (esp of a lens) aiding vision or correcting a visual disorder > **'optically** *adv*

optical activity *n* the ability of substances that are optical isomers to rotate the plane of polarization of a transmitted beam of plane-polarized light

optical character reader *n* a computer peripheral device enabling letters, numbers, or other characters usually printed on paper to be optically scanned and input to a storage device, such as magnetic tape. The device uses the process of **optical character recognition** Abbreviation (for both *reader* and *recognition*): **OCR**

optical crown *n* an optical glass of low dispersion and relatively low refractive index

optical disc *n computing* an inflexible disc on which information is stored in digital form by laser technology. Also called: **video disc**

optical fibre *n* a communications cable consisting of a thin glass fibre in a protective sheath. Light transmitted along the fibre may be modulated with vision, sound, or data signals. See also **fibre optics**

optical flint *n* an optical glass of high dispersion and high refractive index containing lead oxide, used in the manufacture of lenses, artificial gems, and cut glass

optical glass *n* any of several types of clear homogeneous glass of known refractive index used in the construction of lenses, etc

optical isomerism *n* isomerism of chemical compounds in which the two isomers differ only in that their molecules are mirror images of each other > **optical isomer** *n*

optical mouse *n computing* a type of computer mouse that uses light-emitting and -sensing devices to detect where it is

optical scanner *n* a computer peripheral device enabling printed material, including characters and diagrams, to be scanned and converted into a form that can be stored in a computer. See also **optical character reader**

optician (ɒp'tɪʃən) *n* a general name used to refer to: **a** an **ophthalmic optician** one qualified to examine the eyes and prescribe and supply spectacles and contact lenses **b** a **dispensing optician** one who supplies and fits spectacle frames and lenses, but is not qualified to prescribe lenses

optics ('ɒptɪks) *n* (*functioning as sing*) the branch of science concerned with vision and the generation, nature, propagation, and behaviour of electromagnetic light

optimal ('ɒptɪməl) *adj* another word for **optimum** (sense 2)

optimism ('ɒptɪˌmɪzəm) *n* 1 the tendency to expect the best in all things 2 hopefulness; confidence 3 the doctrine of the ultimate triumph of good over evil 4 the philosophical doctrine that this is the best of all possible worlds ▷ Cf **pessimism** [C18 from F *optimisme*, from L *optimus* best, sup. of *bonus* good] > **'optimist** *n* > ˌ**opti'mistic** *adj* > ˌ**opti'mistically** *adv*

optimize *or* **optimise** ('ɒptɪˌmaɪz) *vb* **optimizes, optimizing, optimized** *or* **optimises, optimising, optimised** 1 (*tr*) to take full advantage of 2 (*tr*) to plan or carry out (an economic activity) with maximum efficiency 3 (*intr*) to be optimistic 4 (*tr*) to write or modify (a computer program) to achieve maximum efficiency > ˌ**optimi'zation** *or* ˌ**optimi'sation** *n*

optimum ('ɒptɪməm) *n, pl* **optima** (-mə) *or* **optimums** 1 a condition, degree, amount, or compromise that produces the best possible result ▷ *adj* 2 most favourable or advantageous; best: *optimum conditions* [C19 from L: the best (thing), from *optimus* best; see OPTIMISM]

optimum population *n econ* a population that is sufficiently large to provide an adequate workforce with minimal unemployment

opt in *vb* (*intr, adv*) to choose to be involved in or part of a scheme, etc

option ('ɒpʃən) *n* 1 the act or an instance of choosing or deciding 2 the power or liberty to choose 3 an exclusive opportunity, usually for a limited period, to buy something at a future date: *a six-month option on the Canadian rights to this book* 4 *commerce* the right to buy (**call option**) or sell (**put option**) a fixed quantity of a commodity, security, foreign exchange, etc, at a fixed price at a specified date in the future. See also **traded option** 5 something chosen; choice 6 **keep** (*or* **leave**) **one's options open** not to commit oneself 7 **soft option** an easy alternative ▷ *vb* 8 (*tr*) to obtain or grant an option on: *the BBC have optioned her latest novel* [C17 from L *optiō* free choice, from *optāre* to choose]

optional ('ɒpʃənᵊl) *adj* possible but not compulsory; left to personal choice > **'optionally** *adv*

option money *n commerce* the price paid for buying an option

optometrist (ɒp'tɒmɪtrɪst) *n* a person who is qualified to examine the eyes and prescribe and supply spectacles and contact lenses. Also called (esp Brit): **ophthalmic optician**

optometry (ɒp'tɒmɪtrɪ) *n* the science or practice of testing visual acuity and prescribing corrective lenses > **optometric** (ˌɒptə'mɛtrɪk) *adj*

optophone ('ɒptəˌfəʊn) *n* a device for blind people that converts printed words into sounds

opt out *vb* **1** (*intr, adv; often foll by of*) to choose not to be involved (in) or part (of) ▷ *n* **opt-out 2** the act of opting out, esp of a local-authority administration: *opt-outs by hospitals and schools*

opulent ('ɒpjʊlənt) *adj* **1** having or indicating wealth **2** abundant or plentiful [c17 from L *opulens*, from *opēs* (pl) wealth] > '**opulence** *or (less commonly)* '**opulency** *n* > '**opulently** *adv*

opuntia (ɒ'pʌnʃɪə) *n* a cactus, esp the prickly pear, having fleshy branched stems and green, red, or yellow flowers [c17 NL, from L *Opuntia (herba)* the Opuntian (plant), from *Opus*, ancient town of Locris, Greece]

opus ('əʊpəs) *n, pl* **opuses** *or* **opera 1** an artistic composition, esp a musical work **2** (*often cap*) (usually followed by a number) a musical composition by a particular composer, generally catalogued in order of publication: *Beethoven's opus 61*. Abbreviation: **op** [c18 from L: a work]

Opus Dei ('əʊpəs 'deiː) *n* **1** another name for **divine office 2** an international Roman Catholic organization founded in Spain in 1928 by Josemaria Escrivá de Balaguer (1902–75), to spread Christian principles

or[1] (ɔː; *unstressed* ə) *conj (coordinating)* **1** used to join alternatives **2** used to join rephrasings of the same thing: *twelve, or a dozen* **3** used to join two alternatives when the first is preceded by *either* or *whether*: *either yes or no* **4** **one or two, four or five,** etc a few **5** a poetic word for **either** or **whether,** as the first element in correlatives, with *or* also preceding the second alternative [c13 contraction of *other*, changed (through infl. of EITHER) from OE *oththe*]

or[2] (ɔː) *adj (usually postpositive) Heraldry.* of the metal gold [c16 via F from L *aurum* gold]

OR *abbrev for:* **1** operational research **2** Oregon **3** *mil* other ranks

-or[1] *suffix forming nouns from verbs* a person or thing that does what is expressed by the verb: *actor; conductor; generator; sailor* [via OF *-eur, -eor*, from L *-or* or *-ātor*]

-or[2] *suffix forming nouns* **1** indicating state, condition, or activity: *terror; error* **2** the US spelling of **-our**

ora ('ɔːrə) *n* the plural of **os**[2]

orache *or esp US* **orach** ('ɒrɪtʃ) *n* any of several herbaceous plants or small shrubs of the goosefoot family, esp **garden orache,** which is cultivated as a vegetable. They have typically greyish-green lobed leaves and inconspicuous flowers [c15 from OF *arache*, from L *atriplex*, from Gk *atraphaxus*, from ?]

oracle ('ɒrək[ə]l) *n* **1** a prophecy revealed through the medium of a priest or priestess at the shrine of a god **2** a shrine at which an oracular god is consulted **3** an agency through which a prophecy is transmitted **4** any person or thing believed to indicate future action with infallible authority [c14 via OF from L *ōrāculum*, from *ōrāre* to request]

Oracle ('ɒrək[ə]l) *n trademark* the Teletext system operated by ITV. See **Teletext** [c20 acronym of *o(ptional) r(eception of) a(nnouncements by) c(oded) l(ine) e(lectronics)*]

oracular (ɒ'rækjʊlə) *adj* **1** of or relating to an oracle **2** wise and prophetic **3** mysterious or ambiguous > **o'racularly** *adv*

oracy ('ɔːrəsɪ) *n* the capacity to express oneself in and understand speech: *oracy evolved from gesticulation* [c20 from L *or-, os* mouth, by analogy with *literacy*]

Oradea (*Romanian* o'radea) *n* an industrial city in NW Romania, in Transylvania: ceded by Hungary (1919). Pop: 223 288 (1997 est). German name: **Grosswardein** Hungarian name: **Nagyvárad**

oral ('ɔːrəl, 'ɒrəl) *adj* **1** spoken or verbal **2** relating to, affecting, or for use in the mouth: *an oral thermometer* **3** denoting a drug to be taken by mouth: *an oral contraceptive* **4** of, relating to, or using spoken words **5** *psychoanal* relating to a stage of psychosexual development during which the child's interest is concentrated on the mouth ▷ *n* **6** an examination in which the questions and answers are spoken rather than written [c17 from LL *orālis*, from L *ōs* face] > '**orally** *adv*

oral history *n* the memories of living people about events or social conditions in their earlier lives taped and preserved as historical evidence

oral hygiene *n* the maintenance of healthy teeth and gums by brushing, etc. Also called: **dental hygiene**

oral society *n* a society that has not developed literacy

Oran (ə'ræn, ə'rɑːn; *French* ɔrɑ̃) *n* a port in NW Algeria: the second largest city in the country; scene of the destruction by the British of most of the French fleet in the harbour in 1940 to prevent its capture by the Germans. Pop: 692 516 (1998)

orange ('ɒrɪndʒ) *n* **1** any of several citrus trees, esp **sweet orange** and the Seville orange, cultivated in warm regions for their round edible fruit **2a** the fruit of any of these trees, having a yellowish-red bitter rind and segmented juicy flesh **2b** (*as modifier*): *orange peel* **3** the hard wood of any of these trees **4** any of a group of colours, such as that of the skin of an orange, that lie between red and yellow in the visible spectrum **5** a dye or pigment producing these colours **6** orange cloth or clothing: *dressed in orange* **7** any of several trees or herbaceous plants that resemble the orange, such as mock orange ▷ *adj* **8** of the colour orange [c14 via OF *auranja*, from Ar. *nāranj*, from Persian, from Sansk. *nāranga*]

Orange[1] *n* **1** ('ɒrɪndʒ) a river in S Africa, rising in NE Lesotho and flowing generally west across the South African plateau to the Atlantic: the longest river in South Africa. Length: 2093 km (1300 miles) **2** (*French* ɔrɑ̃ʒ) a town in SE France: a small principality in the Middle Ages, the descendants of which formed the House of Orange. Pop: 28 136 (1990). Ancient name: **Arausio** (ə'raʊsɪəʊ)

Orange[2] ('ɒrɪndʒ) *n* **1** a princely family of Europe. Its possessions, originally centred in S France, passed in 1544 to the count of Nassau, who became William I of Orange and helped to found the United Provinces of the Netherlands. Since 1815 it has been the name of the reigning house of the Netherlands. It was the ruling house of Great Britain and Ireland under William III and Mary (1689–94) and under William III as sole monarch (1694–1702) **2** (*modifier*) of or relating to the Orangemen **3** (*modifier*) of or relating to the royal dynasty of Orange

orangeade (ˌɒrɪndʒ'eɪd) *n* an effervescent or still orange-flavoured drink

orange blossom *n* the flowers of the orange tree, traditionally worn by brides

Orange Free State *n* a former province of central South Africa, between the Orange and Vaal rivers: settled by Boers in 1836 after the Great Trek; annexed by Britain in 1848; became a province of South Africa in 1910; replaced in 1994 by the new province of Free State; economy based on agriculture and mineral resources (esp gold and uranium). Capital: Bloemfontein

Orangeman ('ɒrɪndʒmən) *n, pl* **Orangemen** a member of a society founded in Ireland (1795) to uphold Protestantism [c18 after William, prince of *Orange*, later William III]

Orangeman's Day *n* the 12th of July, celebrated by Protestants in Northern Ireland and elsewhere, to commemorate the anniversary of the Battle of the Boyne (1690)

orange pekoe *n* a superior grade of black tea growing in India and Sri Lanka

orange roughy ('rʌfɪ) *n, pl* **roughies** a marine food fish of S Pacific waters

orangery ('ɒrɪndʒərɪ, -dʒrɪ) *n, pl* **orangeries** a building, such as a greenhouse, in which orange trees are grown

orange stick *n* a small stick used to clean the fingernails and cuticles

orangewood ('ɒrɪndʒ,wʊd) *n* **a** the hard fine-grained yellowish wood of the orange tree **b** (*as modifier*): *an orangewood table*

orang-utan (ɔː,ræŋuː'tæn, ˌɔːræŋ'uːtæn) *or* **orang-utang** (ɔː,ræŋuː'tæŋ, ˌɔːræŋ'uːtæŋ) *n* a large anthropoid ape of the forests of Sumatra and Borneo, with shaggy reddish-brown hair and strong arms. Sometimes shortened to **orang** [C17 from Malay *orang hutan*, from *ōrang* man + *hūtan* forest]

orate (ɔː'reɪt) *vb* **orates, orating, orated** (*intr*) **1** to make or give an oration **2** to speak pompously and lengthily

oration (ɔː'reɪʃən) *n* **1** a formal public declaration or speech **2** any rhetorical, lengthy, or pompous speech [C14 from L *ōrātiō* speech, harangue, from *ōrāre* to plead, pray]

orator ('ɒrətə) *n* **1** a public speaker, esp one versed in rhetoric **2** a person given to lengthy or pompous speeches **3** *obs* the plaintiff in a cause of action in chancery

oratorio (ˌɒrə'tɔːrɪəʊ) *n, pl* **oratorios** a dramatic but unstaged musical composition for soloists, chorus, and orchestra, based on a religious theme [C18 from It., lit.: ORATORY², referring to the Church of the Oratory at Rome where musical services were held]

oratory¹ ('ɒrətərɪ, -trɪ) *n* **1** the art of public speaking **2** rhetorical skill or style [C16 from L (*ars*) *ōrātōria* (the art of) public speaking] > ˌ**ora'torical** *adj* > ˌ**ora'torically** *adv*

oratory² ('ɒrətərɪ, -trɪ) *n, pl* **oratories** a small room or secluded place, set apart for private prayer [C14 from Anglo-Norman, from Church L *ōrātōrium* place of prayer, from *ōrāre* to plead, pray]

orb (ɔːb) *n* **1** (in regalia) an ornamental sphere surmounted by a cross **2** a sphere; globe **3** *poetic* another word for **eye¹** (sense 1) **4** *Obs or poetic* **4a** a celestial body, esp the earth or sun **4b** the orbit of a celestial body ▷ *vb* **5** to make or become circular or spherical **6** (*tr*) an archaic word for **encircle** [C16 from L *orbis* circle, disc]

orbicular (ɔː'bɪkjʊlə), **orbiculate,** *or* **orbiculated** *adj* **1** circular or spherical **2** (of a leaf or similar flat part) circular or nearly circular > **orbicularity** (ɔː,bɪkjʊ'lærɪtɪ) *n* > **or'bicularly** *adv*

orbit ('ɔːbɪt) *n* **1** *astron* the curved path followed by a planet, satellite, etc, in its motion around another celestial body **2** a range or field of action or influence; sphere **3** the bony cavity containing the eyeball; eye socket **4** *zool* **4a** the skin surrounding the eye of a bird **4b** the hollow in which lies the eye or eyestalk of an insect **5** *physics* the path of an electron around the nucleus of an atom **6** **go into orbit** *inf* to reach an extreme and often uncontrolled state: *when he realized the price he nearly went into orbit* ▷ *vb* **7** to move around (a body) in a curved path **8** (*tr*) to send (a satellite, spacecraft, etc) into orbit **9** (*intr*) to move in or as if in an orbit [C16 from L *orbita* course, from *orbis* circle]

orbital ('ɔːbɪtəl) *adj* **1** of or denoting an orbit **2** (of a motorway or major road) circling a large city ▷ *n* **3** the region around an atomic nucleus, or around two nuclei in a molecule, within which an electron moves **4** an orbital road > **'orbitally** *adv*

orbital velocity *n* the velocity required by a spacecraft to enter and maintain a given orbit

orc (ɔːk) *n* **1** any of various whales, such as the killer and grampus **2** a mythical monster [C16 via L *orca*, ?from Gk *orux* whale]

Orcadian (ɔː'keɪdɪən) *n* **1** a native or inhabitant of the Orkneys ▷ *adj* **2** of or relating to the Orkneys [from L *Orcades* the Orkney Islands]

Orcagna (*Italian* or'kaɲa) *n* **Andrea** (an'drɛːa), original name *Andrea di Cione*. ?1308–68, Florentine painter, sculptor, and architect

orchard ('ɔːtʃəd) *n* **1** an area of land devoted to the cultivation of fruit trees **2** a collection of fruit trees especially cultivated [OE *orceard, ortigeard*, from *ort-*, from L *hortus* garden + *geard* YARD²]

orchestra ('ɔːkɪstrə) *n* **1** a large group of musicians, esp one whose members play a variety of different instruments **2** a group of musicians, each playing the same type of instrument **3** Also called: **orchestra pit** the space reserved for musicians in a theatre, immediately in front of or under the stage **4** *chiefly US & Canad* the stalls in a theatre **5** (in ancient Greek theatre) the semicircular space in front of the stage [C17 via L from Gk: the space in the theatre for the chorus, from *orkheisthai* to dance] > **orchestral** (ɔː'kɛstrəl) *adj* > **or'chestrally** *adv*

orchestrate ('ɔːkɪ,streɪt) *vb* **orchestrates, orchestrating, orchestrated** (*tr*) **1** to score or arrange (a piece of music) for orchestra **2** to arrange, organize, or build up for special or maximum effect > ˌ**orches'tration** *n* > **'orches,trator** *n*

orchid ('ɔːkɪd) *n* a terrestrial or epiphytic plant, often having flowers of unusual shapes and beautiful colours, usually with one petal larger than the other two. The flowers are specialized for pollination by certain insects [C19 from NL *Orchideae*; see ORCHIS]

orchidectomy (ˌɔːkɪ'dɛktəmɪ) *n, pl* **orchidectomies** the surgical removal of one or both testes [C19 from Gk *orkhis* testicle + -ECTOMY]

orchil ('ɔːkɪl, -tʃɪl) *or* **archil** *n* **1** a purplish dye obtained by treating various lichens with aqueous ammonia **2** the lichens yielding this dye [C15 from OF *orcheil*, from ?]

orchis ('ɔːkɪs) *n* **1** a N temperate terrestrial orchid having fleshy tubers and spikes of typically pink flowers **2** any of various temperate or tropical orchids such as the fringed orchis [C16 via L from Gk *orkhis* testicle; so called from the shape of its roots]

OR circuit *or* **gate** (ɔː) *n computing* a logic circuit having two or more input wires and one output wire that gives a high-voltage output signal if one or more input signals are at a high voltage: used extensively as a basic circuit in computing [C20 from its similarity to the function of *or* in logical constructions]

Orcus ('ɔːkəs) *n* another name for **Dis** (sense 1)

Orczy ('ɔːtsɪ) *n* Baroness **Emmuska** ('ɛmʊʃkə) 1865–1947, British novelist, born in Hungary; author of *The Scarlet Pimpernel* (1905)

Ord (ɔːd) *n* a river in NE Western Australia, rising on the Kimberley Plateau and flowing generally north to the Timor Sea: subject of a major irrigation scheme. Length: about 500 km (300 miles)

ordain (ɔː'deɪn) *vb* (*tr*) **1** to consecrate (someone) as a priest; confer holy orders upon **2** (*may take a clause as object*) to decree, appoint, or predestine irrevocably **3** (*may take a clause as object*) to order, establish, or enact with authority [C13 from Anglo-Norman *ordeiner*, from LL *ordināre*, from L *ordo* ORDER] > **or'dainer** *n* > **or'dainment** *n*

ordeal (ɔː'diːl) *n* **1** a severe or trying experience **2** *history* a method of trial in which the innocence of an accused person was determined by subjecting him to physical danger, esp by fire or water [OE *ordāl, ordēl* verdict]

order ('ɔːdə) *n* **1** a state in which all components or elements are arranged logically, comprehensibly, or naturally **2** an arrangement or disposition of things in succession; sequence: *alphabetical order* **3** an established or customary method or state, esp of society **4** a peaceful or harmonious condition of society: *order reigned in the streets* **5** (*often pl*) a class, rank, or hierarchy: *the lower orders* **6** *biol* any of the taxonomic groups into which a class is divided and which contains one or more families **7** an instruction that must be obeyed; command **8a** a commission or instruction to produce or supply something in return for payment **8b** the commodity produced or supplied **8c** (*as modifier*): *order form* **9** a procedure followed by an assembly, meeting, etc **10** (*cap when part of a name*) a body of people united in a particular aim or purpose **11** (*usually cap*) Also called: **religious order** a group of persons who bind themselves by vows in order to devote themselves to the pursuit of religious aims **12** (*often pl*) another name for **holy orders, major orders,** or **minor orders** **13** *history* a society of knights constituted as a fraternity, such as the Knights Templars **14a** a group of people holding a specific honour for service or merit, conferred on them by a sovereign or state **14b** the insignia of such a group **15a** any of the five major classical styles of architecture classified by the style of columns and entablatures used **15b** any style of architecture **16** *Christianity* **16a** the sacrament by which bishops, priests, etc, have their offices conferred upon them **16b** any of the degrees into which the ministry is divided **16c** the office of an ordained Christian minister **17** *maths* **17a** the number of times a function must be differentiated to obtain a given derivative **17b** the order of the highest derivative in a differential equation **17c** the number of rows or columns in a determinant or square matrix **17d** the number of members of a finite group **18** *mil* (often preceded by *the*) the dress, equipment, or formation directed for a particular purpose or undertaking: *battle order* **19** **a tall order** something difficult, demanding, or exacting **20** **in order** **20a** in sequence **20b** properly arranged **20c** appropriate or fitting **21** **in order that** (*conj*) with the purpose that; so that **22** **in order to** (*prep*; foll by an infinitive) so that it is possible to: *to eat in order to live* **23** **keep order** to maintain or enforce order **24** **of** *or* **in the order of** having an approximately specified size or quantity **25** **on order** having been ordered but not having been delivered **26** **out of order** **26a** not in sequence **26b** not working **26c** not following the rules or customary procedure **27** **to order** **27a** according to a buyer's specifications **27b** on request or demand ▷ *vb* **28** (*tr*) to give a command to (a person or animal to do or be something) **29** to request (something) to be supplied or made, esp in return for payment **30** (*tr*) to instruct or command to move, go, etc (to a specified place): *they ordered her into the house* **31** (*tr; may take a clause as object*) to authorize; prescribe: *the doctor ordered a strict diet* **32** (*tr*) to arrange, regulate, or dispose (articles, etc) in their proper places **33** (*tr*) (of fate) to will; ordain ▷ *interj* **34** an exclamation demanding that orderly behaviour be restored [c13 from OF *ordre*, from L *ordō*] > **'orderer** *n*

order-driven *adj* denoting an electronic market system, esp for stock exchanges, in which prices are determined by the publication of orders to buy or sell ▷ Cf **quote-driven**

order in council *n* (in Britain and Canada) a decree of the Cabinet, usually made under the authority of a statute: in theory a decree of the sovereign and Privy Council

orderly ('ɔːdəlɪ) *adj* **1** in order, properly arranged, or tidy **2** obeying or appreciating method, system, and arrangement **3** *mil* of or relating to orders: *an orderly book* ▷ *n, pl* **orderlies** **4** *med* a male hospital attendant **5** *mil* a junior rank detailed to carry orders or perform minor tasks for a more senior officer > **'orderliness** *n*

orderly room *n mil* a room in the barracks of a battalion or company used for general administrative purposes

Order of Australia *n* an order awarded to Australians for outstanding achievement or for service to Australia or to humanity at large; established in 1975

Order of Canada *n* an order awarded to Canadians for outstanding achievement

order of magnitude *n* a numerical value expressed to the nearest power of ten

Order of Merit *n Brit* an order conferred on civilians and servicemen for eminence in any field

order of the day *n* **1** the general directive of a commander in chief or the specific instructions of a commanding officer **2** *inf* the prescribed or only thing offered or available **3** (in Parliament) any item of public business ordered to be considered on a specific day **4** an agenda or programme

Order of the Garter *n* See **Garter**

order paper *n* a list indicating the order in which business is to be conducted, esp in Parliament

ordinal ('ɔːdɪnᵊl) *adj* **1** denoting a certain position in a sequence of numbers **2** of, relating to, or characteristic of an order in biological classification ▷ *n* **3** short for **ordinal number** **4** a book containing the forms of services for the ordination of ministers **5** *RC Church* a service book

ordinal number *n* a number denoting relative position in a sequence, such as *first, second, third*. Sometimes shortened to **ordinal**

ordinance ('ɔːdɪnəns) *n* an authoritative regulation, decree, law, or practice [c14 from OF *ordenance*, from L *ordināre* to set in order]

ordinarily ('ɔːdᵊnrɪlɪ) *adv* in ordinary, normal, or usual practice; usually; normally

ordinary ('ɔːdᵊnrɪ) *adj* **1** of common or established type or occurrence **2** familiar, everyday, or unexceptional **3** uninteresting or commonplace **4** having regular or ex officio jurisdiction: *an ordinary judge* **5** *maths* (of a differential equation) containing two variables only and derivatives of one of the variables with respect to the other ▷ *n, pl* **ordinaries** **6** a common or average situation, amount, or degree (esp in **out of the ordinary**) **7** a normal or commonplace person or thing **8** *civil law* a judge who exercises jurisdiction in his or her own right **9** (*usually cap*) an ecclesiastic, esp a bishop, holding an office to which certain jurisdictional powers are attached **10** *RC Church* **10a** the parts of the Mass that do not vary from day to day **10b** a prescribed form of divine service, esp the Mass **11** the US name for **penny-farthing** **12** *heraldry* any of several conventional figures, such as the bend, and the cross, commonly charged upon shields **13** *history* a clergyman who visited condemned prisoners **14** *Brit obs* **14a** a meal provided regularly at a fixed price **14b** the inn, etc, providing such meals **15** **in ordinary** *Brit* (used esp in titles) in regular service or attendance: *physician in ordinary to the sovereign* [c16 (adj) & c13 (some n senses): ult. from L *ordinārius* orderly, from *ordō* order]

Ordinary level *n* a formal name for **O level**

ordinary rating *n* a rank in the Royal Navy comparable to that of a private in the army

ordinary seaman *n* a seaman of the lowest rank, being insufficiently experienced to be an able-bodied seaman

ordinary shares *pl n Brit* shares representing part of the capital issued by a company, entitling their holders to a share in the profits and the net assets. US equivalent: **common stock** ▷ Cf **preference shares**

ordinate ('ɔːdɪnɪt) *n* the vertical or *y*-coordinate of a point in a two-dimensional system of Cartesian coordinates ▷ Cf **abscissa** [c16 from NL (*linea*) *ordināte* (*applicāta*) (line applied) in an orderly manner, from *ordināre* to arrange in order]

ordination (ˌɔːdɪ'neɪʃən) *n* **1a** the act of conferring holy orders **1b** the reception of holy orders **2** the condition of being ordained or regulated **3** an arrangement or order

ordnance ('ɔːdnəns) *n* **1** cannon or artillery **2** military

Oo

supplies; munitions **3** **the** a department of an army or government dealing with military supplies [C14 var. of ORDINANCE]

ordnance datum *n* mean sea level calculated from observation taken at Newlyn, Cornwall, and used as the official basis for height calculation on British maps. Abbreviation: **OD**

Ordnance Survey *n* the official map-making body of the British or Irish government

Ordovician (ˌɔːdəʊˈvɪʃɪən) *adj* **1** of, denoting, or formed in the second period of the Palaeozoic era, between the Cambrian and Silurian periods, which lasted for 45 million years ▷ *n* **2** **the** the Ordovician period or rock system [C19 from L *Ordovices*, ancient Celtic tribe in N Wales]

ordure (ˈɔːdjʊə) *n* excrement; dung [C14 via OF, from *ord* dirty, from L *horridus* shaggy]

Ordzhonikidze *or* **Orjonikidze** (*Russian* ardʒəniˈkidzɪ) *n* the former name (until 1991) of **Vladikavkaz**

ore (ɔː) *n* any naturally occurring mineral or aggregate of minerals from which economically important constituents, esp metals, can be extracted [OE *ār*, *ōra*]

öre (ˈøːrə) *n, pl* **öre** a Scandinavian monetary unit worth one hundredth of a Swedish krona and (**øre**) one hundredth of a Danish and Norwegian krone

oread (ˈɔːrɪˌæd) *n Greek myth* a mountain nymph [C16 via L from Gk *Oreias*, from *oros* mountain]

Örebro (*Swedish* œːrəˈbruː) *n* a town in S Sweden: one of Sweden's oldest towns; scene of the election of Jean Bernadotte as heir to the throne in 1810. Pop: 123 503 (2000 est)

Oreg. *abbrev for* Oregon

oregano (ˌɒrɪˈɡɑːnəʊ) *n* **1** a Mediterranean variety of wild marjoram (*Origanum vulgare*), with pungent leaves **2** the dried powdered leaves of this plant, used to season food [C18 American Sp., from Sp., from L *orīganum*, from Gk *origanon* an aromatic herb, ? marjoram]

Oregon (ˈɒrɪɡən) *n* a state of the northwestern US, on the Pacific: consists of the Coast and Cascade Ranges in the west and a plateau in the east; important timber production. Capital: Salem. Pop: 3 421 399 (2000). Area: 251 418 sq km (97 073 sq miles). Abbreviations: **Oreg.** or (with zip code) **OR**

Oregon trail *n* an early pioneering route across the central US, from Independence, W Missouri, to the Columbia River country of N Oregon: used chiefly between 1804 and 1860. Length: about 3220 km (2000 miles)

Orel (*Russian* aˈrjɔl) *n* a city in W Russia; founded in 1564 but damaged during World War II. Pop: 346 500 (1999 est)

Ore Mountains (ɔː) *pl n* another name for the **Erzgebirge**

Orenburg (ˈɒrənˌbɜːɡ; *Russian* arɪnˈburk) *n* a city in W Russia, on the Ural River. Pop: 526 800 (1999 est). Former name (1938–57): **Chkalov**

Orense (*Spanish* oˈrense) *n* a city in NW Spain, in Galicia on the Miño River: warm springs. Pop: 107 965 (1998 est)

Orestes (ɒˈrɛstiːz) *n Greek myth* the son of Agamemnon and Clytemnestra, who killed his mother and her lover Aegisthus in revenge for their murder of his father

Øresund (œːrəˈsʊnd) *n* the Swedish and Danish name for the **Sound**

orfe (ɔːf) *n* a small slender European cyprinoid fish, occurring in two colour varieties, namely the **silver orfe** and the **golden orfe**, popular aquarium fishes [C17 from G; rel. to L *orphus*, Gk *orphos* the sea perch]

Orff (ɔːf) *n* **Carl** (karl) 1895–1982, German composer. His works include the secular oratorio *Carmina Burana* (1937) and the opera *Antigone* (1949)

org *an Internet domain name for* an organization, usually a nonprofit-making organization

organ (ˈɔːɡən) *n* **1a** Also called: **pipe organ** a large complex musical keyboard instrument in which sound is produced by means of a number of pipes arranged in sets or stops, supplied with air from a bellows **1b** (*as modifier*): *organ stop; organ loft* **2** any instrument, such as a harmonium, in which sound is produced in this way **3** a fully differentiated structural and functional unit, such as a kidney or a root, in an animal or plant **4** an agency or medium of communication, esp a periodical issued by a specialist group or party **5** an instrument with which something is done or accomplished **6** a euphemistic word for **penis** [C13 from OF *organe*, from L *organum* implement, from Gk *organon* tool]

organdie *or esp US* **organdy** (ˈɔːɡəndɪ) *n, pl* **organdies** a fine and slightly stiff cotton fabric used for dresses, etc [C19 from F *organdi*, from ?]

organelle (ˌɔːɡəˈnɛl) *n* a structural and functional unit in a cell or unicellular organism [C20 from NL *organella*, from L *organum*; see ORGAN]

organ-grinder *n* a street musician playing a hand organ for money

organic (ɔːˈɡænɪk) *adj* **1** of, relating to, or derived from living plants and animals **2** of or relating to animal or plant constituents or products having a carbon basis **3** of or relating to one or more organs of an animal or plant **4** of, relating to, or belonging to the class of chemical compounds that are formed from carbon: *an organic compound* **5** constitutional in the structure of something; fundamental; integral **6** of or characterized by the coordination of integral parts; organized **7** of or relating to the essential constitutional laws regulating the government of a state: *organic law* **8** of, relating to, or grown with the use of fertilizers or pesticides deriving from animal or vegetable matter, rather than from chemicals ▷ *n* **9** any substance, such as a fertilizer or pesticide, that is derived from animal or vegetable matter rather than from chemicals > **orˈganically** *adv*

organic chemistry *n* the branch of chemistry concerned with the compounds of carbon

organic light-emitting diode *n* a cell that emits light when voltage is applied: used as a display device replacing LCD technology in hand-held devices such as mobile phones because it is brighter, thinner, faster, and cheaper. Abbreviation: **OLED**

organism (ˈɔːɡəˌnɪzəm) *n* **1** any living biological entity, such as an animal, plant, fungus, or bacterium **2** anything resembling a living creature in structure, behaviour, etc > ˌ**organˈismal** *or* ˌ**organˈismic** *adj* > ˌ**organˈismally** *adv*

organist (ˈɔːɡənɪst) *n* a person who plays the organ

organization *or* **organisation** (ˌɔːɡənaɪˈzeɪʃən) *n* **1** the act of organizing or the state of being organized **2** an organized structure or whole **3** a business or administrative concern united and constructed for a particular end **4** a body of administrative officials, as of a government department, etc **5** order, tidiness, or system; method > ˌ**organiˈzational** *or* ˌ**organiˈsational** *adj*

organizational psychology *n* the study of the structure of an organization and of the ways in which the people in it interact, usually undertaken in order to improve the organization

organize *or* **organise** (ˈɔːɡəˌnaɪz) *vb* **organizes, organizing, organized** *or* **organises, organising, organised** **1** to form (parts or elements of something) into a structured whole; coordinate **2** (*tr*) to arrange methodically or in order **3** (*tr*) to provide with an organic structure **4** (*tr*) to enlist (the workers) of (a factory, etc) in a trade union **5** (*intr*) to join or form an organization or trade union **6** (*tr*) *inf* to put (oneself) in an alert and responsible frame of mind [C15 from Med. L *organizare*, from L *organum* ORGAN] > ˈ**organˌizer** *or* ˈ**organˌiser** *n*

organometallic (ɔːˌɡænəʊmɪˈtælɪk) *adj* of, concerned with, or being an organic compound with one or more metal atoms in its molecules

organon ('ɔːgəˌnɒn) *or* **organum** *n, pl* **organa** (-nə), **organons** *or* **organa, organums** 1 *epistemology* a system of logical or scientific rules, esp that of Aristotle 2 *arch* a sense organ, regarded as an instrument for acquiring knowledge [C16 from Gk: implement; see ORGAN]

organophosphate (ɔːˌgænəʊ'fɒsfeɪt) *n* any of a group of organic compounds containing phosphorus and used as a pesticide

organotin (ɔːˌgænəʊ'tɪn) *adj* 1 of, concerned with, or being an organic compound with one or more tin atoms in its molecules ▷ *n* 2 such a compound used as a pesticide, formerly believed to decompose safely, now found to be toxic in the food chain

organza (ɔː'gænzə) *n* a thin stiff fabric of silk, cotton, nylon, rayon, etc [C20 from ?]

orgasm ('ɔːgæzəm) *n* 1 the most intense point during sexual excitement 2 *rare* intense or violent excitement [C17 from NL *orgasmus*, from Gk *orgasmos*, from *organ* to mature, swell] > **or'gasmic** *or* **or'gastic** *adj*

orgeat ('ɔːʒɑː) *n* a drink made from barley or almonds, and orangeflower water [C18 via F, from *orge* barley, from L *hordeum*]

orgy ('ɔːdʒɪ) *n, pl* **orgies** 1 a wild gathering marked by promiscuous sexual activity, excessive drinking, etc 2 an act of immoderate or frenzied indulgence 3 (*often pl*) secret religious rites of Dionysus, Bacchus, etc, marked by drinking, dancing, and songs [C16 from F *orgies*, from L *orgia*, from Gk: nocturnal festival] > ˌ**orgi'astic** *adj*

oribi ('ɒrɪbɪ) *n, pl* **oribi** *or* **oribis** a small African antelope of the grasslands and bush south of the Sahara, with fawn-coloured coat and, in the male, ridged spikelike horns [C18 from Afrik., prob. from Khoikhoi *arab*]

oriel window ('ɔːrɪəl) *n* a bay window, esp one that is supported by one or more brackets or corbels. Sometimes shortened to **oriel** [C14 from OF *oriol* gallery, ?from Med. L *auleolum* niche]

orient *n* ('ɔːrɪənt) 1 *poetic* another word for **east** Cf. **occident** 2 *arch* the eastern sky or the dawn 3a the iridescent lustre of a pearl 3b (*as modifier*): *orient pearls* 4 a pearl of high quality ▷ *adj* ('ɔːrɪənt) 5 *now chiefly poetic* oriental 6 *arch* (of the sun, stars, etc) rising ▷ *vb* ('ɔːrɪˌɛnt) 7 to adjust or align (oneself or something else) according to surroundings or circumstances 8 (*tr*) to position or set (a map, etc) with reference to the compass or other specific directions 9 (*tr*) to build (a church) with the chancel end facing in an easterly direction [C18 via F from L *oriēns* rising (sun), from *orīrī* to rise]

Orient ('ɔːrɪənt) *n* (usually preceded by *the*) 1 the countries east of the Mediterranean 2 the eastern hemisphere

oriental (ˌɔːrɪ'ɛntᵊl) *adj* another word for **eastern**

Oriental (ˌɔːrɪ'ɛntᵊl) *adj* 1 (*sometimes not cap*) of or relating to the Orient 2 of or denoting a region consisting of southeastern Asia from India to Borneo, Java, and the Philippines ▷ *n* 3 (*sometimes not cap*) an inhabitant, esp a native, of the Orient

Orientalism (ˌɔːrɪ'ɛntəˌlɪzəm) *n* 1 knowledge of or devotion to the Orient 2 an Oriental quality, style, or trait > ˌ**Ori'entalist** *n* > ˌ**Oriˌental'istic** *adj*

orientate ('ɔːrɪɛnˌteɪt) *vb* **orientates, orientating, orientated** another word for **orient** (senses 7, 8, 9)

orientation (ˌɔːrɪɛn'teɪʃən) *n* 1 the act or process of orienting or the state of being oriented 2 positioning with relation to the compass or other specific directions 3 the adjustment or alignment of oneself or one's ideas to surroundings or circumstances 4 Also called: **orientation course** *chiefly US & Canad* 4a a course, lecture, etc, introducing a new situation or environment 4b (*as modifier*): *an orientation talk* 5 *psychol* the knowledge of one's own temporal, social, and practical circumstances 6 basic beliefs or preferences 7 the siting of a church on an east-west axis > ˌ**orien'tational** *adj*

-oriented *suffix forming adjectives* geared or directed towards: *sports-oriented*

orienteer (ˌɔːrɪən'tɪə) *vb* (*intr*) 1 to take part in orienteering ▷ *n* 2 a person who takes part in orienteering

orienteering (ˌɔːrɪɛn'tɪərɪŋ) *n* a sport in which contestants race on foot over a course consisting of checkpoints found with the aid of a map and a compass [C20 from Swedish *orientering*]

▷ www.orienteering.org

orifice ('ɒrɪfɪs) *n chiefly technical* an opening or mouth into a cavity; vent; aperture [C16 via F from LL *ōrificium*, from L *ōs* mouth + *facere* to make]

oriflamme ('ɒrɪˌflæm) *n* a scarlet flag adopted as the national banner of France in the Middle Ages [C15 via OF, from L *aurum* gold + *flamma* flame]

orig. *abbrev for:* 1 origin 2 original(ly)

origami (ˌɒrɪ'gɑːmɪ) *n* the art or process, originally Japanese, of paper folding [from Japanese, from *ori* a fold + *kami* paper]

▷ www.origami.com
▷ www.paperfolding.com
▷ www.origami-usa.org

origan ('ɒrɪgən) *n* another name for **marjoram** (sense 2) [C16 from L *orīganum*, from Gk *origanon* an aromatic herb]

origanum (ˌɒrɪ'gɑːnəm) *n* See **oregano**

Origen ('ɒrɪˌdʒɛn) *n* ?185–?254 AD, Christian theologian, born in Alexandria. His writings include *Hexapla*, a synopsis of the Old Testament, *Contra Celsum*, a defence of Christianity, and *De Principiis*, a statement of Christian theology

origin ('ɒrɪdʒɪn) *n* 1 a primary source; derivation 2 the beginning of something; first part 3 (*often pl*) ancestry or parentage; birth; extraction 4 *anat* 4a the end of a muscle, opposite its point of insertion 4b the beginning of a nerve or blood vessel or the site where it first starts to branch out 5 *maths* 5a the point of intersection of coordinate axes or planes 5b the point whose coordinates are all zero 6 *commerce* the country from which a commodity or product originates: *shipment from origin* [C16 from F *origine*, from L *orīgō* beginning, from *orīrī* to spring from]

original (ə'rɪdʒɪnᵊl) *adj* 1 of or relating to an origin or beginning 2 fresh and unusual; novel 3 able to think of or carry out new ideas or concepts 4 being that from which a copy, translation, etc, is made ▷ *n* 5 the first and genuine form of something, from which others are derived 6 a person or thing used as a model in art or literature 7 a person whose way of thinking is unusual or creative 8 the first form or occurrence of something

originality (əˌrɪdʒɪ'nælɪtɪ) *n, pl* **originalities** 1 the quality or condition of being original 2 the ability to create or innovate

originally (ə'rɪdʒɪnəlɪ) *adv* 1 in the first place 2 in an original way 3 with reference to the origin or beginning

original sin *n* a state of sin held to be innate in mankind as the descendants of Adam

originate (ə'rɪdʒɪˌneɪt) *vb* **originates, originating, originated** 1 to come or bring into being 2 (*intr*) *US & Canad* (of a bus, train, etc) to begin its journey at a specified point > **oˌrigi'nation** *n* > **o'rigiˌnator** *n*

O-ring *n* a rubber ring used in machinery as a seal against oil, air, etc

Orinoco (ˌɒrɪ'nəʊkəʊ) *n* a river in N South America, rising in S Venezuela and flowing west, then north as part of the border between Colombia and Venezuela, then east to the Atlantic by a great delta: the third largest river system in South America, draining an area of 945 000 sq km (365 000 sq miles); reaches a width of 22 km (14 miles) during the rainy season. Length: about 2575 km (1600 miles)

Oo

oriole ('ɔːrɪˌəʊl) *n* **1** a tropical Old World songbird, such as the **golden oriole**, having a long pointed bill and a mostly yellow-and-black plumage **2** an American songbird, esp the Baltimore oriole, with a typical male plumage of black with either orange or yellow [c18 from Med. L *oryolus*, from L *aureolus*, dim. of *aureus*, from *aurum* gold]

Orion[1] (ə'raɪən) *n Greek myth* a Boeotian giant famed as a great hunter, who figures in several tales

Orion[2] (ə'raɪən) *n* a conspicuous constellation containing two first-magnitude stars (Betelgeuse and Rigel) and a distant bright emission nebula (the **Orion Nebula**)

orison ('ɒrɪzᵊn) *n literary* another word for **prayer**[1] (senses 1 and 2) [c12 from OF *oreison*, from LL *ōrātiō*, from L: speech, from *ōrāre* to speak]

Orissa (ɒ'rɪsə) *n* a state of E India, on the Bay of Bengal: part of the province of Bihar and Orissa (1912–36); enlarged by the addition of 25 native states in 1949. Capital: Bhubaneswar. Pop: 36 706 920 (2001). Area: 155 707 sq km (60 119 sq miles)

Oriya (ɒ'riːə) *n* **1** (*pl* **Oriya**) a member of a people of India living chiefly in Orissa **2** the state language of Orissa, belonging to the Indo-European family

Orizaba (ˌɔːrɪ'zɑːbə; *Spanish* ori'θaβa) *n* **1** a city and resort in SE Mexico, in Veracruz state. Pop: 118 400 (2000 est) **2 Pico de** the Spanish name for **Citlaltépetl**

Orjonikidze (*Russian* ardʒəni'kidzɪ) *n* a variant spelling of **Ordzhonikidze**

Orkneys ('ɔːknɪz), **Orkney Islands** *pl n or* **Orkney** ('ɔːknɪ) *n* a group of over 70 islands off the N coast of Scotland, separated from the mainland by the Pentland Firth: constitutes an island authority of Scotland; low-lying and treeless; prehistoric remains. Administrative centre: Kirkwall. Pop: 19 245 (2001). Area: 974 sq km (376 sq miles). Related word: **Orcadian** > **'Orkneyman** *or fem* **'Orkneyˌwoman** *n*

Orlando (ɔː'lændəʊ) *n* a city in the US, in Florida: site of Walt Disney World. Pop: 185 951 (2000)

Orléans[1] (ɔː'lɪənz; *French* ɔrleɑ̃) *n* a city in N central France, on the River Loire: famous for its deliverance by Joan of Arc from the long English siege in 1429; university (1305); an important rail and road junction. Pop: 112 833 (1999)

Orléans[2] (*French* ɔrleɑ̃) *n* **1 Charles** (ʃarl), Duc d'Orléans. 1394–1465, French poet; noted for the poems written during his imprisonment in England; father of Louis XII **2 Louis Philippe Joseph** (lwi filip ʒozɛf), Duc d'Orléans, known as *Philippe Égalité* (after 1792). 1747–93, French nobleman, who supported the French Revolution and voted for the death of his cousin, Louis XVI, but was executed after his son, the future king Louis-Philippe, defected to the Austrians

Orlon ('ɔːlɒn) *n trademark* a crease-resistant acrylic fibre or fabric used for clothing, etc

orlop *or* **orlop deck** ('ɔːlɒp) *n naut* (in a vessel with four or more decks) the lowest deck [c15 from Du. *overloopen* to spill]

Orly ('ɔːliː; *French* ɔrli) *n* a suburb of SE Paris, France, with an international airport

Ormandy ('ɔːməndɪ) *n* **Eugene** 1899–1985, US conductor, born in Hungary

Ormazd ('ɔːməzd) *n Zoroastrianism* the creative deity, embodiment of good and opponent of Ahriman. Also called: **Ahura Mazda** [from Persian]

ormer ('ɔːmə) *n* **1** Also called: **sea-ear** an edible marine gastropod mollusc that has an ear-shaped shell perforated with holes and occurs near the Channel Islands **2** any other abalone [c17 from F, apparently from L *auris* ear + *mare* sea]

ormolu ('ɔːməˌluː) *n* **1a** a gold-coloured alloy of copper, tin, or zinc used to decorate furniture, etc **1b** (*as modifier*): *an ormolu candlestick* **2** gold prepared to be used for gilding [c18 from F *or moulu* ground gold]

Ormuz ('ɔːmʌz) *n* a variant spelling of **Hormuz**

ornament *n* ('ɔːnəmənt) **1** anything that enhances the appearance of a person or thing **2** decorations collectively: *she was totally without ornament* **3** a small decorative object **4** something regarded as a source of pride or beauty **5** *music* any of several decorations, such as the trill, etc ▷ *vb* ('ɔːnəˌmɛnt) (*tr*) **6** to decorate with or as if with ornaments **7** to serve as an ornament to [c14 from L *ornāmentum*, from *ornāre* to adorn] > **ˌornamen'tation** *n*

ornamental (ˌɔːnə'mɛntᵊl) *adj* **1** of value as an ornament; decorative **2** (of a plant) used to decorate houses, gardens, etc ▷ *n* **3** a plant cultivated for show or decoration > **ˌorna'mentally** *adv*

ornate (ɔː'neɪt) *adj* **1** heavily or elaborately decorated **2** (of style in writing, etc) over-embellished; flowery [c15 from L *ornāre* to decorate] > **or'nately** *adv* > **or'nateness** *n*

Orne (*French* ɔrn) *n* a department of NW France, in Basse-Normandie. Capital: Alençon. Pop: 292 337 (1999). Area: 6144 sq km (2396 sq miles)

ornery ('ɔːnərɪ) *adj US & Canad dialect or inf* **1** stubborn or vile-tempered **2** low; treacherous: *an ornery trick* **3** ordinary [c19 alteration of ORDINARY] > **'orneriness** *n*

ornitho- *or before a vowel* **ornith-** *combining form* bird or birds [from Gk *ornis*, *ornith-* bird]

ornithology (ˌɔːnɪ'θɒlədʒɪ) *n* the study of birds > **ornithological** (ˌɔːnɪθə'lɒdʒɪkᵊl) *adj* > **ˌornitho'logically** *adv* > **ˌorni'thologist** *n*

ornithorhynchus (ˌɔːnɪθəʊ'rɪŋkəs) *n* the technical name for **duck-billed platypus** [c19 NL, from ORNITHO- + Gk *rhunkhos* bill]

oro-[1] *combining form* mountain: *orogeny* [from Gk *oros*]

oro-[2] *combining form* oral; mouth: *oromaxillary* [from L, from *ōs*]

orogeny (ɒ'rɒdʒɪnɪ) *or* **orogenesis** (ˌɒrəʊ'dʒɛnɪsɪs) *n* the formation of mountain ranges > **orogenic** (ˌɒrəʊ'dʒɛnɪk) *or* **orogenetic** (ˌɒrəʊdʒɪ'nɛtɪk) *adj*

Orontes (ɒ'rɒntiːz) *n* a river in SW Asia, rising in Lebanon and flowing north through Syria into Turkey, where it turns west to the Mediterranean. Length: 571 km (355 miles). Arabic name: **'Asi**

orotund ('ɒrəʊˌtʌnd) *adj* **1** (of the voice) resonant; booming **2** (of speech or writing) bombastic; pompous [c18 from L *ore rotundo* with rounded mouth]

Orozco (*Spanish* o'rɔθko) *n* **José Clemente** (xo'se kle'mente) 1883–1949, Mexican painter, noted for his monumental humanistic murals

orphan ('ɔːfən) *n* **1a** a child, one or both of whose parents are dead **1b** (*as modifier*): *an orphan child* ▷ *vb* **2** (*tr*) to deprive of one or both parents [c15 from LL *orphanus*, from Gk *orphanos*]

orphanage ('ɔːfənɪdʒ) *n* **1** an institution for orphans and abandoned children **2** the state of being an orphan

Orphean ('ɔːfɪən) *adj* **1** of or relating to Orpheus **2** melodious or enchanting

Orpheus ('ɔːfɪəs, -fjuːs) *n Greek myth* a poet and lyre-player credited with the authorship of the poems forming the basis of Orphism. He married Eurydice and sought her in Hades after her death. He failed to win her back and was killed by a band of bacchantes

Orphic ('ɔːfɪk) *adj* **1** of or relating to Orpheus or Orphism **2** (*sometimes not cap*) mystical or occult > **'Orphically** *adv*

Orphism ('ɔːfɪzəm) *n* a mystery religion of ancient Greece, widespread from the 6th century BC > **Or'phistic** *adj*

orpine ('ɔːpaɪn) *or* **orpin** ('ɔːpɪn) *n* a succulent perennial N temperate plant with toothed leaves and heads of small purplish-white flowers [c14 from OF, apparently from *orpiment*, a yellow mineral (? referring to the yellow flowers of a related species)]

Orpington ('ɔːpɪŋtən) *n* a district of SE London, part of the Greater London borough of Bromley from 1965

Orr (ɔː) *n* **Robert Gordon**, known as *Bobby*, born 1948, Canadian ice-hockey player

orrery ('ɒrərɪ) *n, pl* **orreries** a mechanical model of the solar system in which the planets can be moved at the correct relative velocities around the sun [C18 orig. made for Charles Boyle, Earl of *Orrery*]

orris[1] *or* **orrice** ('ɒrɪs) *n* **1** any of various irises that have fragrant rhizomes **2** Also: **orrisroot** the rhizome of such a plant, prepared and used as perfume [C16 var. of IRIS]

orris[2] ('ɒrɪs) *n* a kind of lace made of gold or silver, used esp in the 18th century [from Old French *orfreis*, from L *auriphrygium* Phrygian gold]

Orsini (*Italian* or'siːni) *n* an Italian aristocratic family that was prominent in Rome from the 12th to the 18th century

Orsk (*Russian* ɔrsk) *n* a city in W Russia, on the Ural River: a major railway and industrial centre, with an oil refinery linked by pipeline with the Emba field (on the Caspian). Pop: 274 400 (1995 est)

Ortegal (*Spanish* ɔrte'ɣal) *n* **Cape** a cape in NW Spain, projecting into the Bay of Biscay

Ortega y Gasset (*Spanish* ɔr'teɣa i ga'sɛt) *n* **José** (xo'se) 1883–1955, Spanish essayist and philosopher. His best-known work is *The Revolt of the Masses* (1930)

orthicon ('ɔːθɪˌkɒn) *n* a television camera tube in which an optical image produces a corresponding electrical charge pattern on a mosaic surface that is scanned from behind by an electron beam. The resulting discharge of the mosaic provides the output signal current. See also **image orthicon** [C20 from ORTHO- + ICON(OSCOPE)]

ortho- *or before a vowel* **orth-** *combining form* **1** straight or upright: *orthorhombic* **2** perpendicular or at right angles: *orthogonal* **3** correct or right: *orthodontics* **4** (*often in italics*) denoting an organic compound containing a benzene ring with substituents attached to adjacent carbon atoms (the 1,2- positions) **5** denoting an oxyacid regarded as the highest hydrated form of the anhydride or a salt of such an acid: *orthophosphoric acid* **6** denoting a diatomic substance in which the spins of the two atoms are parallel: *orthohydrogen* [from Gk *orthos* straight, upright]

orthochromatic (ˌɔːθəʊkrəʊ'mætɪk) *adj photog* of or relating to an emulsion giving a rendering of relative light intensities of different colours that corresponds approximately to the colour sensitivity of the eye, esp one that is insensitive to red light. Sometimes shortened to **ortho** > **orthochromatism** (ˌɔːθəʊ'krəʊməˌtɪzəm) *n*

orthoclase ('ɔːθəʊˌkleɪs, -ˌkleɪz) *n* a white or coloured feldspar mineral consisting of an aluminium silicate of potassium in monoclinic crystalline form

orthodontics (ˌɔːθəʊ'dɒntɪks) *or* **orthodontia** (ˌɔːθəʊ'dɒntɪə) *n* (*functioning as sing*) the branch of dentistry concerned with preventing or correcting irregularities of the teeth > ˌ**ortho'dontic** *adj* > ˌ**ortho'dontist** *n*

orthodox ('ɔːθəˌdɒks) *adj* **1** conforming with established standards, as in religion, behaviour, or attitudes **2** conforming to the Christian faith as established by the early Church [C16 via Church L from Gk *orthodoxos*, from *orthos* correct + *doxa* belief] > '**orthoˌdoxy** *n*

Orthodox ('ɔːθəˌdɒks) *adj* **1** of or relating to the Orthodox Church of the East **2** (*sometimes not cap*) of or relating to Orthodox Judaism

Orthodox Church *n* **1** the collective body of those Eastern Churches that were separated from the western Church in the 11th century and are in communion with the Greek patriarch of Constantinople **2** any of these Churches

Orthodox Judaism *n* a form of Judaism characterized by traditional interpretation and strict observance of the Mosaic Law

orthoepy ('ɔːθəʊˌɛpɪ) *n* the study of correct or standard pronunciation [C17 from Gk *orthoepeia*, from ORTHO- straight + *epos* word] > **orthoepic** (ˌɔːθəʊ'ɛpɪk) *adj* > ˌ**ortho'epically** *adv*

orthogenesis (ˌɔːθəʊ'dʒɛnɪsɪs) *n* **1** *biol* **1a** evolution of a group of organisms predetermined to occur in a particular direction **1b** the theory that proposes such a development **2** the theory that there is a series of stages through which all cultures pass in the same order > **orthogenetic** (ˌɔːθəʊdʒɪ'nɛtɪk) *adj* > ˌ**orthoge'netically** *adv*

orthogonal (ɔː'θɒgənᵊl) *adj* relating to, consisting of, or involving right angles; perpendicular > **or'thogonally** *adv*

orthographic (ˌɔːθə'græfɪk) *or* **orthographical** *adj* of or relating to spelling > ˌ**ortho'graphically** *adv*

orthography (ɔː'θɒgrəfɪ) *n, pl* **orthographies** **1** a writing system **2a** spelling considered to be correct **2b** the principles underlying spelling **3** the study of spelling > **or'thographer** *or* **or'thographist** *n*

orthopaedics *or US* **orthopedics** (ˌɔːθəʊ'piːdɪks) *n* (*functioning as sing*) **1** the branch of surgery concerned with correcting deformities or disorders of the bones and joints **2** **dental orthopaedics** another name for **orthodontics** > ˌ**ortho'paedic** *or US* ˌ**ortho'pedic** *adj* > ˌ**ortho'paedist** *or US* ˌ**ortho'pedist** *n*

orthopteran (ɔː'θɒptərən) *n, pl* **orthoptera** (-tərə) **1** Also: **orthopteron** (*pl* **orthoptera**) any orthopterous insect ▷ *adj* **2** another word for **orthopterous**

orthopterous (ɔː'θɒptərəs) *adj* of, relating to, or belonging to a large order of insects, including crickets, locusts, and grasshoppers, having leathery forewings and membranous hind wings

orthoptic (ɔː'θɒptɪk) *adj* relating to normal binocular vision

orthoptics (ɔː'θɒptɪks) *n* (*functioning as sing*) the science or practice of correcting defective vision, as by exercises to strengthen weak eye muscles > **or'thoptist** *n*

orthorhombic (ˌɔːθəʊ'rɒmbɪk) *adj crystallog* relating to the crystal system characterized by three mutually perpendicular unequal axes

Ortles (*Italian* 'ɔrtles) *pl n* a range of the Alps in N Italy. Highest peak: 3899 m (12 792 ft). Also called: **Ortler** ('ɔːtlə)

ortolan ('ɔːtələn) *n* **1** a brownish Old World bunting regarded as a delicacy **2** any of various other small birds eaten as delicacies, esp the bobolink [C17 via F from L *hortulānus*, from *hortulus*, dim. of *hortus* garden]

Orton ('ɔːtᵊn) *n* **Joe** (**Kingsley**) 1933–67, British dramatist, noted for his black comedies: these include *Entertaining Mr Sloane* (1964), *Loot* (1966), and *What the Butler Saw* (1969)

Oruro (*Spanish* o'ruro) *n* a city in W Bolivia: a former silver-mining centre; university (1892); tin, copper, and tungsten. Pop: 232 311 (2000 est)

Orvieto (*Italian* or'vjɛːto) *n* **1** a market town in central Italy, in Umbria: Etruscan remains. Pop: 21 575 (1990). Latin name: **Urbs Vetus** ('ʊəbz 'viːtəs) **2** a light white wine from this region

Orwell ('ɔːwəl, -wɛl) *n* **George**, real name *Eric Arthur Blair*. 1903–50, English novelist and essayist, born in India. He is notable for his social criticism, as in *The Road to Wigan Pier* (1932); his account of his experiences of the Spanish Civil War *Homage to Catalonia* (1938); and his satirical novels *Animal Farm* (1945), an allegory on the Russian Revolution, and *1984* (1949), in which he depicts an authoritarian state of the future

-ory[1] *suffix forming nouns* **1** indicating a place for: *observatory* **2** something having a specified use: *directory* [via OF *-orie*, from L *-ōrium*, *-ōria*]

-ory[2] *suffix forming adjectives* of or relating to; characterized by; having the effect of: *contributory* [via OF *-orie*, from L *-ōrius*]

oryx ('ɒrɪks) *n, pl* **oryxes** *or* **oryx** any large African

Oo

antelope of the genus *Oryx*, typically having long straight nearly upright horns [c14 via L from Gk *orux* stonemason's axe, used also of the pointed horns of an antelope]

os[1] (ɒs) *n, pl* **ossa** ('ɒsə) *anat* the technical name for **bone** [c16 from L: bone]

os[2] (ɒs) *n, pl* **ora** *anat, zool* a mouth or mouthlike part or opening [c18 from L]

Os *the chemical symbol for* osmium

OS *abbrev for:* **1** Old Saxon (language) **2** Old Style **3** Ordinary Seaman **4** (in Britain) Ordnance Survey **5** outsize

Osage orange (əʊ'seɪdʒ) *n* **1** a North American thorny tree, grown for hedges and ornament **2** the warty orange-like fruit of this plant [from *Osage* Amerind tribe]

Osaka (əʊ'sɑːkə) *n* a port in S Japan, on S Honshu on **Osaka Bay** (an inlet of the Pacific): the third largest city in Japan (the chief commercial city during feudal times); university (1931); an industrial and commercial centre. Pop: 2 602 352 (1995)

Osborne ('ɒzbən, -ˌbɔːn) *n* **John (James)** 1929–94, British dramatist. His plays include *Look Back in Anger* (1956), containing the prototype of the angry young man, Jimmy Porter, *The Entertainer* (1957), and *Inadmissible Evidence* (1964)

Oscar ('ɒskə) *n* any of several small gold statuettes awarded annually in the US for outstanding achievements in films. Official name: **Academy Award** [c20 said to have been named after a remark made by a secretary that it reminded her of her uncle Oscar]

▷ www.oscars.org
▷ www.oscar.com
▷ www.howstuffworks.com/oscar.htm

Oscar II *n* 1829–1907, king of Sweden (1872–1907) and of Norway (1872–1905)

oscillate ('ɒsɪˌleɪt) *vb* **oscillates, oscillating, oscillated** **1** (*intr*) to move or swing from side to side regularly **2** (*intr*) to waver between opinions, courses of action, etc **3** *physics* to undergo or produce or cause to undergo or produce oscillation [c18 from L *oscillāre* to swing]

oscillating universe theory *n* the theory that the universe is oscillating between periods of expansion and contraction

oscillation (ˌɒsɪ'leɪʃən) *n* **1** *statistics, physics* **1a** regular fluctuation in value, position, or state about a mean value, such as the variation in an alternating current **1b** a single cycle of such a fluctuation **2** the act or process of oscillating > **oscillatory** ('ɒsɪlətərɪ, -trɪ) *adj*

oscillator ('ɒsɪˌleɪtə) *n* **1** a circuit or instrument for producing an alternating current or voltage of a required frequency **2** any instrument for producing oscillations **3** a person or thing that oscillates

oscillogram (ɒ'sɪləˌgræm) *n* the recording obtained from an oscillograph or the trace on an oscilloscope screen

oscillograph (ɒ'sɪləˌgrɑːf) *n* a device for producing a graphical record of the variation of an oscillating quantity, such as an electric current > **oscillographic** (ɒˌsɪlə'græfɪk) *adj* > **oscillography** (ˌɒsɪ'lɒgrəfɪ) *n*

oscilloscope (ɒ'sɪləˌskəʊp) *n* an instrument for producing a representation of a rapidly changing quantity on the screen of a cathode-ray tube

oscine ('ɒsaɪn, 'ɒsɪn) *adj* of, relating to, or belonging to the suborder of passerine birds that includes most of the songbirds [c17 via NL from L *oscen* singing bird]

oscitancy ('ɒsɪtənsɪ) *or* **oscitance** *n, pl* **oscitancies** *or* **oscitances** **1** the state of being drowsy, lazy, or inattentive **2** the act of yawning ▷ Also called: **oscitation** [c17 from L *oscitāre* to yawn] > **'oscitant** *adj*

oscular ('ɒskjʊlə) *adj* **1** *zool* of or relating to a mouthlike aperture, esp of a sponge **2** of or relating to the mouth or to kissing

osculate ('ɒskjʊˌleɪt) *vb* **osculates, osculating, osculated** **1** *usually humorous* to kiss **2** (*intr*) (of an organism) to be intermediate between two taxonomic groups **3** *geom* to touch in osculation [c17 from L *ōsculārī* to kiss]

osculation (ˌɒskjʊ'leɪʃən) *n* **1** *maths* Also called: **tacnode** a point at which two branches of a curve have a common tangent, each branch extending in both directions of the tangent **2** *rare* the act of kissing > **osculatory** ('ɒskjʊlətərɪ, -trɪ) *adj*

-ose[1] *suffix forming adjectives* possessing; resembling: *grandiose* [from L *-ōsus*; see -OUS]

-ose[2] *suffix forming nouns* **1** indicating a carbohydrate, esp a sugar: *lactose* **2** indicating a decomposition product of protein: *albumose* [from GLUCOSE]

Oshawa ('ɒʃəwə) *n* a city in central Canada, in SE Ontario on Lake Ontario: motor-vehicle industry. Pop: 134 364 (1996)

Oshogbo (ə'ʃɒgbəʊ) *n* a city in SW Nigeria: trade centre. Pop: 476 800 (1996 est)

osier ('əʊzɪə) *n* **1** any of various willow trees, whose flexible branches or twigs are used for making baskets, etc **2** a twig or branch from such a tree **3** any of several North American dogwoods, esp the red osier [c14 from OF, prob. from Med. L *ausēria*, ? of Gaulish origin]

Osijek (*Serbo-Croat* 'ɔsijɛk) *n* a town in NE Croatia on the Drava River: under Turkish rule from 1526 to 1687. Pop: 129 792 (1991). Ancient name: **Mursa** ('mʊəsə)

Osiris (əʊ'saɪrɪs) *n* an ancient Egyptian god, ruler of the underworld and judge of the dead > **O'sirian** *adj*

-osis *suffix forming nouns* **1** indicating a process or state: *metamorphosis* **2** indicating a disease: *tuberculosis* ▷ Cf **-iasis** **3** indicating the formation or development of something: *fibrosis* [from Gk, suffix used to form nouns from verbs with infinitives in *-oein* or *-oun*]

Oslo ('ɒzləʊ; *Norwegian* 'uslu) *n* the capital and chief port of Norway, in the southeast at the head of **Oslo Fjord** (an inlet of the Skagerrak): founded in about 1050; university (1811); a major commercial and industrial centre, producing about a quarter of Norway's total output. Pop: 507 467 (2000 est). Former names: **Christiania** (1624–1877), **Kristiania** (1877–1924)

▷ www.a-zoftourism.com/Shopping-in-Oslo.htm

Osman I ('ɒzmən, ɒz'mɑːn) *or* **Othman I** *n* 1259–1326, Turkish sultan; founder of the Ottoman Empire

Osmanli (ɒz'mænlɪ) *adj* **1** of or relating to the Ottoman Empire ▷ *n* **2** (formerly) a subject of the Ottoman Empire [c19 from Turkish, from OSMAN I]

osmiridium (ˌɒzmɪ'rɪdɪəm) *n* a very hard corrosion-resistant white or grey natural alloy of osmium and iridium: used in pen nibs, etc [c19 from OSM(IUM) + IRIDIUM]

osmium ('ɒzmɪəm) *n* a very hard brittle bluish-white metal, the heaviest known element, occurring with platinum and alloyed with iridium in osmiridium. Symbol: Os; atomic no.: 76; atomic wt.: 190.2 [c19 from Gk *osmē* smell, from its penetrating odour]

osmoregulation (ˌɒzməʊˌrɛgjʊ'leɪʃən) *n zool* the adjustment of the osmotic pressure of a cell or organism in relation to the surrounding fluid

osmose ('ɒzməʊs, -məʊz, 'ɒs-) *vb* **osmoses, osmosing, osmosed** to undergo or cause to undergo osmosis [c19 (n): abstracted from the earlier terms *endosmose* and *exosmose*; rel. to Gk *ōsmos* push]

osmosis (ɒz'məʊsɪs, ɒs-) *n* **1** the tendency of the solvent of a less concentrated solution of dissolved molecules to pass through a semipermeable membrane into a more concentrated solution until both solutions are of the same concentration **2** diffusion through any membrane or porous barrier, as in dialysis **3** gradual or unconscious assimilation or adoption, as of ideas [c19 Latinized form from OSMOSE, from Gk *ōsmos* push] > **osmotic** (ɒz'mɒtɪk, ɒs-) *adj* > **os'motically** *adv*

osmotic pressure *n* the pressure necessary to prevent

osmosis into a given solution when the solution is separated from the pure solvent by a semipermeable membrane

osmunda (ɒzˈmʌndə) *or* **osmund** (ˈɒzmənd) *n* any of a genus of ferns having large spreading fronds [c13 from OF *osmonde*, from ?]

Osnabrück (*German* ɔsnaˈbryk) *n* an industrial city in NW Germany, in Lower Saxony: a member of the Hanseatic League in the Middle Ages; one of the treaties comprising the Peace of Westphalia (1648) was signed here. Pop: 164 900 (1999 est)

osprey (ˈɒsprɪ, -preɪ) *n* **1** a large broad-winged fish-eating diurnal bird of prey, with a dark back and whitish head and underparts. Often called (US and Canad): **fish hawk** **2** any of the feathers of various other birds, used esp as trimming for hats [c15 from OF *ospres*, apparently from L *ossifraga*, lit.: bone-breaker, from *os* bone + *frangere* to break]

Ossa (ˈɒsə) *n* a mountain in NE Greece, in E Thessaly: famous in mythology for the attempt of the twin giants, Otus and Ephialtes, to reach heaven by piling Ossa on Olympus and Pelion on Ossa. Height: 1978 m (6489 ft)

ossein (ˈɒsɪɪn) *n* a protein that forms the organic matrix of bone [c19 from L *osseus* bony, from *os* bone]

osseous (ˈɒsɪəs) *adj* consisting of or containing bone, bony [c17 from L *osseus*, from *os* bone] > **ˈosseously** *adv*

Ossetia (ɒˈsiːʃə) *n* a region of central Asia, in the Caucasus: consists administratively of the North Ossetian Republic in Russia and the South Ossetian Autonomous Region in Georgia > **Osˈsetic** *or* **Osˈsetian** *adj*

Ossian (ˈɒsɪən) *n* a legendary Irish hero and bard of the 3rd century AD. See also (James) **Macpherson**

Ossietzky (ˌɒsɪˈɛtskɪ) *n* **Carl von** (karl fɔn) 1889–1938, German pacifist leader. He was imprisoned for revealing Germany's secret rearmament (1931–32) and again under Hitler (1933–36): Nobel peace prize 1935

ossify (ˈɒsɪˌfaɪ) *vb* **ossifies, ossifying, ossified** **1** to convert or be converted into bone **2** (*intr*) (of habits, attitudes, etc) to become inflexible [c18 from F *ossifier*, from L *os* bone + *facere* to make] > **ˌossifiˈcation** *n* > **ˈossiˌfier** *n*

ossuary (ˈɒsjʊərɪ) *n, pl* **ossuaries** any container for the burial of human bones, such as an urn or vault [c17 from LL *ossuārium*, from L *os* bone]

osteal (ˈɒstɪəl) *adj* **1** of or relating to bone or to the skeleton **2** composed of bone; osseous [c19 from Gk *osteon* bone]

osteitis (ˌɒstɪˈaɪtɪs) *n* inflammation of a bone > **osteitic** (ˌɒstɪˈɪtɪk) *adj*

Ostend (ɒsˈtɛnd) *n* a port and resort in NW Belgium, in West Flanders on the North Sea. Pop: 68 858 (1995 est). French name: **Ostende** (ɔstɑ̃d) Flemish name: **Oostende**

ostensible (ɒˈstɛnsɪbᵊl) *adj* **1** apparent; seeming **2** pretended [c18 via F from Med. L *ostensibilis*, from L *ostendere* to show, from *ob-* before + *tendere* to extend] > **osˌtensiˈbility** *n* > **osˈtensibly** *adv*

ostensive (ɒˈstɛnsɪv) *adj* **1** manifestly demonstrative **2** (of a definition) giving examples of objects to which a word or phrase is properly applied **3** a less common word for **ostensible** [c17 from LL *ostentīvus*, from L *ostendere* to show; see OSTENSIBLE] > **osˈtensively** *adv*

ostentation (ˌɒstɛnˈteɪʃən) *n* pretentious, showy, or vulgar display > **ˌostenˈtatious** *adj* > **ˌostenˈtatiously** *adv* > **ˌostenˈtatiousness** *n*

osteo- *or before a vowel* **oste-** *combining form* indicating bone or bones [from Gk *osteon*]

osteoarthritis (ˌɒstɪəʊɑːˈθraɪtɪs) *n* chronic inflammation of the joints, esp those that bear weight, with pain and stiffness > **osteoarthritic** (ˌɒstɪəʊɑːˈθrɪtɪk) *adj, n*

osteology (ˌɒstɪˈɒlədʒɪ) *n* the study of the structure and function of bones > **osteological** (ˌɒstɪəˈlɒdʒɪkᵊl) *adj* > **ˌosteoˈlogically** *adv* > **ˌosteˈologist** *n*

osteoma (ˌɒstɪˈəʊmə) *n, pl* **osteomata** (-mətə) *or* **osteomas** a benign tumour composed of bone or bonelike tissue

osteomalacia (ˌɒstɪəʊməˈleɪʃɪə) *n* a disease characterized by softening of the bones, resulting from a deficiency of vitamin D and of calcium and phosphorus [c19 from NL, from OSTEO- + Gk *malakia* softness] > **ˌosteomaˈlacial** *or* **osteomalacic** (ˌɒstɪəʊməˈlæsɪk) *adj*

osteomyelitis (ˌɒstɪəʊˌmaɪɪˈlaɪtɪs) *n* inflammation of bone marrow, caused by infection

osteopathy (ˌɒstɪˈɒpəθɪ) *n* a system of healing based on the manipulation of bones or other parts of the body > **ˈosteoˌpath** *n* > **osteopathic** (ˌɒstɪəˈpæθɪk) *adj* > **ˌosteoˈpathically** *adv*

osteoplasty (ˈɒstɪəˌplæstɪ) *n, pl* **osteoplasties** the branch of surgery concerned with bone repair or bone grafting

osteoporosis (ˌɒstɪəʊpɔːˈrəʊsɪs) *n* porosity and brittleness of the bones caused by loss of calcium from the bone matrix [c19 from OSTEO- + PORE² + -OSIS] > **osteoporotic** (ˌɒstɪəʊpɔːˈrɒtɪk) *adj*

Österreich (ˈøːstəraiç) *n* the German name for **Austria**

Ostia (ˈɒstɪə) *n* an ancient town in W central Italy, originally at the mouth of the Tiber but now about 6 km (4 miles) inland: served as the port of ancient Rome; harbours built by Claudius and Trajan; ruins excavated since 1854

ostinato (ˌɒstɪˈnɑːtəʊ) *n, pl* **ostinatos** **a** a continuously reiterated musical phrase **b** (*as modifier*): *an ostinato passage* [It.: from L *obstinātus* OBSTINATE]

ostler *or* **hostler** (ˈɒslə) *n arch* a stableman, esp one at an inn [c15 var. of *hostler*, from HOSTEL]

Ostmark (ˈɒstmɑːk; *German* ˈɔstmark) *n* (formerly) the standard monetary unit of East Germany, divided into 100 pfennigs [G, lit.: east mark]

Ostpreussen (ˈɔstprɔysən) *n* the German name for **East Prussia**

ostracize *or* **ostracise** (ˈɒstrəˌsaɪz) *vb* **ostracizes, ostracizing, ostracized** *or* **ostracises, ostracising, ostracised** (*tr*) **1** to exclude or banish (a person) from a particular group, society, etc **2** (in ancient Greece) to punish by temporary exile [c17 from Gk *ostrakizein* to select someone for banishment by voting on potsherds, from *ostrakon* potsherd] > **ˈostracism** *n* > **ˈostraˌcizable** *or* **ˈostraˌcisable** *adj* > **ˈostraˌcizer** *or* **ˈostraˌciser** *n*

Ostrava (*Czech* ˈɔstrava) *n* an industrial city in the E Czech Republic, on the River Oder: the chief coal-mining area in the Czech Republic, in Upper Silesia. Pop: 321 263 (2000 est)

ostrich (ˈɒstrɪtʃ) *n, pl* **ostriches** *or* **ostrich** **1** a fast-running flightless African bird that is the largest living bird with stout two-toed feet and dark feathers, except on the naked head, neck, and legs **2** **American ostrich** another name for **rhea** **3** a person who refuses to recognize the truth, reality, etc [c13 from OF *ostrice*, from L *avis* bird + LL *struthio* ostrich, from Gk *strouthion*]

Ostwald (*German* ˈɔstvalt) *n* **Wilhelm** (ˈvɪlhɛlm) 1853–1932, German chemist, noted for his pioneering work in catalysis. He also invented a process for making nitric acid from ammonia and developed a new theory of colour: Nobel prize for chemistry 1909

Osun (əʊˈsʌn) *n* a state of SW Nigeria. Capital: Oshogbo. Pop: 2 463 185 (1995 est). Area 9251 sq km (3570 sq miles)

Oswald (ˈɒzwəld) *n* **1** **Lee Harvey** 1939–63, presumed assassin (1963) of US president John F. Kennedy; murdered by Jack Ruby two days later **2** **Saint** ?605–41 AD, king of Northumbria (634–41); with St Aidan he restored Christianity to the region. He was killed in battle by Penda of Mercia. Feast day: Aug 5

Oświęcim (*Polish* ɔʃˈfjɛntʃim) *n* the Polish name for **Auschwitz**

Oo

OT *abbrev for:* **1** occupational therapy **2** Old Testament **3** overtime

Otago (ɒ'tɑ:gəʊ) *n* a council region of New Zealand, formerly a province, founded by Scottish settlers in the south of South Island. The University of Otago (1869) in Dunedin is the oldest university in New Zealand. Chief town: Dunedin. Pop: 192 936 (2001)
▷ www.orc.govt.nz
▷ www.tco.org.nz

otalgia (əʊ'tældʒɪə, -dʒə) *n* the technical name for **earache**

OTC (in Britain) *abbrev for:* **1** Officers' Training Corps **2** over-the-counter

OTE *abbrev for* on target earnings: referring to the salary a salesperson should be able to achieve

other ('ʌðə) *determiner* **1a** (when used before a singular noun, usually preceded by *the*) the remaining (one or ones in a group of which one or some have been specified): *I'll read the other sections of the paper later* **1b** **the other** (*as pron; functioning as sing*): *one walks while the other rides* **2** (a) different (one or ones from that or those already specified or understood): *no other man but you* **3** additional; further: *there are no other possibilities* **4** (preceded by *every*) alternate; two: *it buzzes every other minute* **5** **other than 5a** apart from; besides: *a lady other than his wife* **5b** different from: *he couldn't be other than what he is.* Archaic form: **other from** **6** **no other** *arch* nothing else: *I can do no other* **7** **or other** (preceded by a phrase or word with *some*) used to add vagueness to the preceding pronoun, noun, or noun phrase: *he's somewhere or other* **8** **other things being equal** conditions being the same or unchanged **9** **the other day, night,** etc a few days, nights, etc, ago **10** **the other thing** an unexpressed alternative ▷ *pron* **11** another: *show me one other* **12** (*pl*) additional or further ones **13** (*pl*) other people or things **14** **the others** the remaining ones (of a group) ▷ *adv* **15** (usually used with a negative and foll by *than*) otherwise; differently: *they couldn't behave other than they do* [OE *ōther*] > **'otherness** *n*

other-directed *adj* guided by values derived from external influences

other ranks *pl n* (*rarely sing*) *chiefly Brit* (in the armed forces) all those who do not hold a commissioned rank

otherwise ('ʌðə,waɪz) *sentence connector* **1** or else; if not, then: *go home — otherwise your mother will worry* ▷ *adv* **2** differently: *I wouldn't have thought otherwise* **3** in other respects: *an otherwise hopeless situation* ▷ *adj* **4** (*predicative*) of an unexpected nature; different: *the facts are otherwise* ▷ *pron* **5** something different in outcome: *success or otherwise* [c14 from OE *on ōthre wīsan* in other manner]

other world *n* the spirit world or afterlife

otherworldly (,ʌðə'wɜ:ldlɪ) *adj* **1** of or relating to the spiritual or imaginative world **2** impractical or unworldly > **,other'worldliness** *n*

Othin ('əʊðɪn) *n* a variant of **Odin**

Othman ('ɒθmən, ɒθ'mɑ:n) *adj, n* a variant of **Ottoman**

Othman I *n* a variant of **Osman I**

Otho I ('əʊθəʊ) *n* a variant of **Otto I**

otic ('əʊtɪk, 'ɒtɪk) *adj* of or relating to the ear [c17 from Gk *ōtikos*, from *ous* ear]

-otic *suffix forming adjectives* **1** relating to or affected by: *sclerotic* **2** causing: *narcotic* [from Gk *-ōtikos*]

otiose ('əʊtɪ,əʊs, -,əʊz) *adj* **1** serving no useful purpose: *otiose language* **2** *rare* indolent; lazy [c18 from L *ōtiōsus* leisured, from *ōtium* leisure] > **otiosity** (,əʊtɪ'ɒsɪtɪ) *or* **'oti,oseness** *n*

otitis (əʊ'taɪtɪs) *n* inflammation of the ear

oto- *or before a vowel* **ot-** *combining form* indicating the ear [from Gk *ous, ōt-* ear]

otolaryngology (,əʊtəʊ,lærɪŋ'gɒlədʒɪ) *n* another name for **otorhinolaryngology** > **otolaryngological** (,əʊtəʊlə,rɪŋgə'lɒdʒɪkᵊl) *adj* > **,oto,laryn'gologist** *n*

otolith ('əʊtəʊ,lɪθ) *n* any of the granules of calcium carbonate in the inner ear of vertebrates. Movement of otoliths, caused by a change in the animal's position, stimulates sensory hair cells, which convey information to the brain > **,oto'lithic** *adj*

otology (əʊ'tɒlədʒɪ) *n* the branch of medicine concerned with the ear > **otological** (,əʊtə'lɒdʒɪkᵊl) *adj* > **o'tologist** *n*

O'Toole (əʊ'tu:l) *n* (**Seamus** ('ʃeɪməs)) **Peter** born 1932, British actor, born in Ireland. His films include *Lawrence of Arabia* (1962), *The Lion in Winter* (1968), *High Spirits* (1988), and *Fairytale* (1998); stage appearances include *Jeffrey Bernard is Unwell* (1989)

otorhinolaryngology (,əʊtəʊ,raɪnəʊ,lærɪŋ'gɒlədʒɪ) *n* the branch of medicine concerned with the ear, nose, and throat. Sometimes called **otolaryngology**

otorrhoea (,əʊtə'rɪə) *n pathol* a discharge from the ears

otoscope ('əʊtəʊ,skəʊp) *n* a medical instrument for examining the external ear > **otoscopic** (,əʊtəʊ'skɒpɪk) *adj*

Otranto (*Italian* 'ɔ:tranto) *n* a small port in SE Italy, in Apulia on the **Strait of Otranto**: the most easterly town in Italy; dates back to Greek times and was an important Roman port; its ruined castle was the setting of Horace Walpole's *Castle of Otranto*. Pop: 5075 (latest est)

OTT *sl abbrev for* over the top: see **top¹** (sense 16b)

ottava rima (əʊ'tɑ:və 'ri:mə) *n prosody* a stanza form consisting of eight iambic pentameter lines, rhyming a b a b a b c c [It.: eighth rhyme]

Ottawa ('ɒtəwə) *n* **1** the capital of Canada, in E Ontario on the Ottawa River: name changed from Bytown to Ottawa in 1854. Pop: 323 340 (1996) **2** a river in central Canada, rising in W Quebec and flowing west, then southeast to join the St Lawrence River as its chief tributary at Montreal; forms the border between Quebec and Ontario for most of its length. Length: 1120 km (696 miles)
▷ www.city.ottawa.on.ca

otter ('ɒtə) *n, pl* **otters** *or* **otter** **1** a freshwater carnivorous mammal, esp the **Eurasian otter**, typically having smooth fur, a streamlined body, and webbed feet **2** the fur of this animal **3** Also called: **otterboard** a type of fishing tackle consisting of a weighted board to which hooked and baited lines are attached ▷ *v* **4** to fish using an otter [OE *otor*]

Otterburn ('ɒtə,bɜ:n) *n* a village in NE England, in central Northumberland: scene of a battle (1388) in which the Scots, led by the earl of Douglas, defeated the English, led by Hotspur

otter hound *n* a large rough-coated dog of a breed formerly used for otter hunting

Otto (*German* 'ɔto) *n* **Rudolf** ('ru:dɔlf) 1869–1937, German theologian: his best-known work is *The Idea of the Holy* (1923)

Otto I ('ɒtəʊ) *or* **Otho I** *n* called *the Great*. 912–73 AD, king of Germany (936–73); Holy Roman Emperor (962–73)

ottoman ('ɒtəmən) *n, pl* **ottomans** **1a** a low padded seat, usually armless, sometimes in the form of a chest **1b** a cushioned footstool **2** a corded fabric [c17 from F *ottomane*, fem. of OTTOMAN]

Ottoman ('ɒtəmən) *or* **Othman** ('ɒθmən) *adj* **1** *history* of or relating to the Ottomans or the Ottoman Empire **2** denoting or relating to the Turkish language ▷ *n, pl* **Ottomans** *or* **Othmans** **3** a member of a Turkish people who invaded the Near East in the late 13th century [c17 from F, via Med. L, from Ar. *Othmānī* Turkish, from Turkish *Othman* OSMAN I]

Ottoman Empire *n* the former Turkish empire in Europe, Asia, and Africa, which lasted from the late 13th century until the end of World War I
▷ www.wsu.edu:8080/~dee/OTTOMAN/CONTENTS.HTM
▷ http://campus.northpark.edu/history/WebChron/MiddleEast/Ottoman.html

Otway ('ɒtweɪ) *n* **Thomas** 1652–85, English dramatist, noted for *The Orphan* (1680) and *Venice Preserv'd* (1682)
ou (əʊ) *n S African sl* a man, bloke, or chap [from Afrik., ?from Du.]
OU *abbrev for:* **1** the Open University **2** Oxford University
Ouachita *or* **Washita** ('wɒʃɪ,tɔː) *n* a river in the S central US, rising in the **Ouachita Mountains** and flowing east, south, and southeast into the Red River in E Louisiana. Length: 974 km (605 miles)
Ouagadougou (,wɑːgə'duːguː) *n* the capital of Burkina-Faso, on the central plateau: terminus of the railway from Abidjan (Côte d'Ivoire). Pop: 690 000 (1993 est)
ouananiche (,wɑːnə'niːʃ) *n* a landlocked variety of the Atlantic salmon found in lakes in SE Canada [from Canad F, of Amerind origin, from *wananish*, dim. of *wanans* salmon]
oubaas ('əʊ,bɑːs) *n S African* a man in authority [from Afrik., from Du. *oud* old + *baas* boss]
Oubangui (uː'bɑːŋgiː) *n* the French name for **Ubangi**
oubliette (,uːblɪ'ɛt) *n* a dungeon, the only entrance to which is through the top [c19 from F, from *oublier* to forget]
ouch (aʊtʃ) *interj* an exclamation of sharp sudden pain
Oudh (aʊd) *n* **1** a region of N India, in central Uttar Pradesh: annexed by Britain in 1856 and a centre of the Indian Mutiny (1857–58); joined with Agra in 1877, becoming the United Provinces of Agra and Oudh in 1902, which were renamed Uttar Pradesh in 1950 **2** another name for **Ayodha**
Ouessant (wɛsɑ̃) *n* the French name for **Ushant**
ought[1] (ɔːt) *vb* (*foll by to; takes an infinitive or implied infinitive*) used as an auxiliary: **1** to indicate duty or obligation: *you ought to pay* **2** to express prudent expediency: *you ought to be more careful with your money* **3** (usually with reference to future time) to express probability or expectation: *you ought to finish this by Friday* **4** to express a desire or wish on the part of the speaker: *you ought to come next week* [OE *āhte*, p.t. of *āgan* to OWE]

> USAGE In correct English, *ought* is not used with *did* or *had*. *I ought not to do it*, not *I didn't ought to do it*; *I ought not to have done it*, not *I hadn't ought to have done it*

ought[2] (ɔːt) *pron, adv* a variant spelling of **aught**
ought[3] (ɔːt) *n* a less common word for **nought** (zero) [c19 mistaken division of *a nought* as *an ought*; see NOUGHT]
Ouija board ('wiːdʒə) *n trademark* a board on which are marked the letters of the alphabet. Answers to questions are spelt out by a pointer and are supposedly formed by spirits [c19 from F *oui* yes + G *ja* yes]
Oujda (uːdʒ'dɑː) *n* a city in NE Morocco, near the border with Algeria: frontier post. Pop: 146 142 (1994)
Oulu ('ɔulu) *n* an industrial city and port in W Finland, on the Gulf of Bothnia: university (1959). Pop: 117 670 (2000 est). Swedish name: **Uleåborg**
ouma ('əʊmɑː) *n S African* **1** grandmother, esp in titular use with her surname **2** *sl* any elderly woman [from Afrik., from Du. *oma* grandmother]
ounce[1] (aʊns) *n* **1** a unit of weight equal to one sixteenth of a pound (avoirdupois). Abbreviation: **oz** **2** a unit of weight equal to one twelfth of a Troy or Apothecaries' pound; 1 ounce is equal to 480 grains **3** short for **fluid ounce** **4** a small portion or amount [c14 from OF *unce*, from L *uncia* a twelfth]
ounce[2] (aʊns) *n* another name for **snow leopard** [c18 from OF *once*, by mistaken division of *lonce* as if *l'once*, from L LYNX]
oupa ('əʊpɑː) *n S African* **1** grandfather, esp in titular use with surname **2** *sl* any elderly man [Afrik.]
our ('aʊə) *determiner* **1** of, belonging to, or associated in some way with us: *our best vodka; our parents are good to us* **2** belonging to or associated with all people or people in general: *our nearest planet is Venus* **3** a formal word for *my* used by editors or other writers, and monarchs [OE *ūre* (genitive pl), from US]
-our *suffix forming nouns* indicating state, condition, or activity: *behaviour; labour* [in OF *-eur*, from L *-or*, n. suffix]
Our Father *n* another name for the **Lord's Prayer,** taken from its opening words
ours ('aʊəz) *pron* **1** something or someone belonging to or associated with us: *ours have blue tags* **2** **of ours** belonging to or associated with us
ourself (aʊə'sɛlf) *pron arch* a variant of **myself,** formerly used by monarchs or editors
ourselves (aʊə'sɛlvz) *pron* **1a** the reflexive form of *we* or *us* **1b** (intensifier): *we ourselves will finish it* **2** (*preceded by a copula*) our usual selves: *we are ourselves when we're together* **3** *not standard* used instead of *we* or *us* in compound noun phrases: *other people and ourselves*
-ous *suffix forming adjectives* **1** having or full of: *dangerous; spacious* **2** (in chemistry) indicating that an element is chemically combined in the lower of two possible valency states: *ferrous* ▷ Cf **-ic** (sense 2) [from OF, from L *-ōsus* or *-us*, Gk *-os*, adj. suffixes]
Ouse (uːz) *n* **1** Also called: **Great Ouse** a river in E England, rising in Northamptonshire and flowing northeast to the Wash near King's Lynn; for the last 56 km (35 miles) follows mainly artificial channels. Length: 257 km (160 miles) **2** a river in NE England, in Yorkshire, formed by the confluence of the Swale and Ure Rivers: flows southeast to the Humber. Length: 92 km (57 miles) **3** a river in S England, rising in Sussex and flowing south to the English Channel. Length: 48 km (30 miles)
ousel ('uːzᵊl) *n* a variant spelling of **ouzel**
oust (aʊst) *vb* (*tr*) **1** to force out of a position or place; supplant or expel **2** *property law* to deprive (a person) of the possession of land, etc [c16 from Anglo-Norman *ouster*, from L *obstāre* to withstand]
ouster ('aʊstə) *n property law* the act of dispossessing of freehold property; eviction

Oo

out (aʊt) *adv* (*when predicative, can in some senses be regarded as adj*) **1** (*often used as a particle*) at or to a point beyond the limits of some location; outside: *get out at once* **2** (*particle*) used to indicate exhaustion or extinction: *the sugar's run out; put the light out* **3** not in a particular place, esp, not at home **4** public; revealed: *the secret is out* **5** on sale or on view to the public: *the book is being brought out next May* **6** (of the sun, stars, etc) visible **7** in flower: *the roses are out now* **8** not in fashion, favour, or current usage **9** not or not any longer worth considering: *that plan is out* **10** not allowed: *smoking on duty is out* **11** (of a fire or light) no longer burning or providing illumination **12** not working: *the radio's out* **13** Also: **out on strike** on strike **14** (of a jury) withdrawn to consider a verdict in private **15** (*particle*) out of consciousness: *she passed out* **16** (*particle*) used to indicate a burst of activity as indicated by the verb: *fever broke out* **17** (*particle*) used to indicate obliteration of an object: *the graffiti was painted out* **18** (*particle*) used to indicate an approximate drawing or description: *chalk out* **19** at or to the fullest length or extent: *spread out* **20** loudly; clearly: *calling out* **21** desirous of or intent on (something or doing something): *I'm out for as much money as I can get* **22** (*particle*) used to indicate a goal or object achieved at the end of the action specified by the verb: *he worked it out* **23** (*preceded by a superlative*) existing: *the friendliest dog out* **24** an expression in signalling, radio, etc, to indicate the end of a transmission **25** used up; exhausted: *our supplies are completely out* **26** worn into holes: *out at the elbows* **27** inaccurate, deficient, or discrepant: *out by six pence* **28** not in office or authority **29** completed or concluded, as of time: *before the year is out* **30** *obs* (of a young woman) in or into society: *Lucinda had a large party when she came out* **31** *sport* denoting the state in which a player is caused to discontinue active participation, esp in some specified role **32** **out of** **32a** at or to a point outside: *out of his reach* **32b** away from; not in: *stepping out of line; out of focus* **32c** because of; motivated by: *out of jealousy* **32d** from (a material or source): *made out of plastic* **32e** not or no longer having any of (a substance, material, etc): *we're out of sugar.* **f** no longer in a specified state or condition: *out of work; out of practice.* **g** (of a horse) born of ▹ *adj* **33** directed or indicating direction outwards: *the out tray* **34** (of an island) remote from the mainland **35** *inf* not concealing one's homosexuality ▹ *prep* **36** *nonstandard or US* out of; out through: *he ran out the door* ▹ *interj* **37a** an exclamation of dismissal, reproach, etc **37b** (in wireless telegraphy) an expression used to signal that the speaker is signing off **38** **out with it** a command to make something known immediately, without missing any details ▹ *n* **39** *chiefly US* a method of escape from a place, difficult situation, etc **40** *baseball* an instance of causing a batter to be out by fielding ▹ *vb* **41** (*tr*) to put or throw out **42** (*intr*) to be made known or effective despite efforts to the contrary (esp in **the truth will out**) **43** (*tr*) *inf* (of homosexuals) to expose (a public figure) as being a fellow homosexual **44** *inf* to expose something secret, embarrassing, or unknown about (a person): *he was eventually outed as a talented goal scorer* [OE ūt]

USAGE The use of *out* as a preposition, though common in American English, is regarded as incorrect in British English: *he climbed out of* (not *out*) *a window; he went out through the door*

out- *prefix* **1** excelling or surpassing in a particular action: *outlast; outlive* **2** indicating an external location or situation away from the centre: *outpost; outpatient* **3** indicating emergence, an issuing forth, etc: *outcrop; outgrowth* **4** indicating the result of an action: *outcome*

outage ('aʊtɪdʒ) *n* **1** a quantity of goods missing or lost after storage or shipment **2** a period of power failure, machine stoppage, etc

out and away *adv* by far

out-and-out *adj* (*prenominal*) thoroughgoing; complete

outback ('aʊt,bæk) *n* **a** the remote bush country of Australia **b** (*as modifier*): *outback life*

outbalance (,aʊt'bæləns) *vb* **outbalances, outbalancing, outbalanced** another word for **outweigh**

outboard ('aʊt,bɔːd) *adj* **1** (of a boat's engine) portable, with its own propeller, and designed to be attached externally to the stern **2** in a position away from, or further away from, the centre line of a vessel or aircraft, esp outside the hull or fuselage ▹ *adv* **3** away from the centre line of a vessel or aircraft, esp outside the hull or fuselage ▹ *n* **4** an outboard motor

outbound ('aʊt,baʊnd) *adj* going out; outward bound

outbrave (,aʊt'breɪv) *vb* **outbraves, outbraving, outbraved** (*tr*) **1** to surpass in bravery **2** to confront defiantly

outbreak ('aʊt,breɪk) *n* a sudden, violent, or spontaneous occurrence, esp of disease or strife

outbuilding ('aʊt,bɪldɪŋ) *n* a building separate from a main building; outhouse

outburst ('aʊt,bɜːst) *n* **1** a sudden and violent expression of emotion **2** an explosion or eruption

outcast ('aʊt,kɑːst) *n* **1** a person who is rejected or excluded from a social group **2** a vagabond or wanderer **3** anything thrown out or rejected ▹ *adj* **4** rejected, abandoned, or discarded; cast out

outcaste ('aʊt,kɑːst) *n* **1** a person who has been expelled from a caste **2** a person having no caste ▹ *vb* **outcastes, outcasting, outcasted** **3** (*tr*) to cause (someone) to lose his or her caste

outclass (,aʊt'klɑːs) *vb* (*tr*) **1** to surpass in class, quality, etc **2** to defeat easily

outcome ('aʊt,kʌm) *n* something that follows from an action or situation; result; consequence

outcrop *n* ('aʊt,krɒp) **1** part of a rock formation or mineral vein that appears at the surface of the earth **2** an emergence; appearance ▹ *vb* (,aʊt'krɒp), **outcrops, outcropping, outcropped** **3** (*intr*) (of rock strata, mineral veins, etc) to protrude through the surface of the earth

outcry *n* ('aʊt,kraɪ), *pl* **outcries** **1** a widespread or vehement protest **2** clamour; uproar **3** *commerce* a method of trading in which dealers shout out bids and offers at a prearranged meeting: *sale by open outcry* ▹ *vb* (,aʊt'kraɪ), **outcries, outcrying, outcried** (*tr*) **4** to cry louder or make more noise than (someone or something)

outdated (,aʊt'deɪtɪd) *adj* old-fashioned or obsolete

outdo (,aʊt'duː) *vb* **outdoes, outdoing, outdid, outdone** (*tr*) to surpass or exceed in performance

outdoor ('aʊt'dɔː) *adj* (*prenominal*) taking place, existing, or intended for use in the open air: *outdoor games; outdoor clothes.* Also: **out-of-door**

outdoors (,aʊt'dɔːz) *adv* **1** Also: **out-of-doors** in the open air; outside ▹ *n* **2** the world outside or far away from human habitation

outer ('aʊtə) *adj* (*prenominal*) **1** being or located on the outside; external **2** further from the middle or central part ▹ *n* **3** *archery* **3a** the white outermost ring on a target **3b** a shot that hits this ring **4** *Austral & NZ* the unsheltered part of the spectator area at a sports ground **5** **on the outer** *Austral & NZ* excluded or neglected

outer bar *n* (in England) a collective name for junior barristers who plead from outside the bar of the court

outercourse ('aʊtə,kɔːs) *n* sexual acts not involving penetration [C20 OUTER + INTERCOURSE]

Outer Hebrides *pl n* See **Hebrides**

Outer Mongolia *n* the former name (until 1924) of the republic of **Mongolia**

outermost ('aʊtə,məʊst) *adj* furthest from the centre or middle; outmost

outer space *n* any region of space beyond the atmosphere of the earth

outfall ('aʊt,fɔːl) *n* the end of a river, sewer, drain, etc, from which it discharges

outfield ('aʊt,fiːld) *n* **1** *cricket* the area of the field relatively far from the pitch; the deep ▹ Cf **infield** (sense 1) **2** *baseball* **2a** the area of the playing field beyond the lines connecting first, second, and third bases **2b** the positions of the left fielder, centre fielder, and right fielder taken collectively **3** *agriculture* farmland most distant from the farmstead > **'out,fielder** *n*

outfit ('aʊt,fɪt) *n* **1** a set of articles or equipment for a particular task, etc **2** a set of clothes, esp a carefully selected one **3** *inf* any group or association regarded as a cohesive unit, such as a military company, etc ▹ *vb* **outfits, outfitting, outfitted** **4** to furnish or be furnished with an outfit, equipment, etc > **'out,fitter** *n*

outflank (,aʊt'flæŋk) *vb* (*tr*) **1** to go around the flank of (an opposing army, etc) **2** to get the better of

outflow ('aʊt,fləʊ) *n* **1** anything that flows out, such as liquid, money, etc **2** the amount that flows out **3** the act or process of flowing out

outfox (,aʊt'fɒks) *vb* (*tr*) to surpass in guile or cunning

outgeneral (,aʊt'dʒɛnərəl) *vb* **outgenerals, outgeneralling, outgeneralled** *or US* **outgenerals, outgeneraling, outgeneraled** (*tr*) to surpass in generalship

outgo *vb* (,aʊt'gəʊ), **outgoes, outgoing, outwent, outgone** **1** (*tr*) to exceed or outstrip ▹ *n* ('aʊt,gəʊ) **2** cost; outgoings; outlay **3** something that goes out; outflow

outgoing ('aʊt,gəʊɪŋ) *adj* **1** departing; leaving **2** retiring from office **3** friendly and sociable ▹ *n* **4** the act of going out

outgoings ('aʊt,gəʊɪŋz) *pl n* expenditure

outgrow (,aʊt'grəʊ) *vb* **outgrows, outgrowing, outgrew, outgrown** (*tr*) **1** to grow too large for (clothes, shoes, etc) **2** to lose (a habit, idea, reputation, etc) in the course of development or time **3** to grow larger or faster than

outgrowth ('aʊt,grəʊθ) *n* **1** a thing growing out of a main body **2** a development, result, or consequence **3** the act of growing out

outgun (,aʊt'gʌn) *vb* **outguns, outgunning, outgunned** (*tr*) **1** to surpass in fire power **2** to surpass in shooting **3** *inf* to surpass or excel

outhouse ('aʊt,haʊs) *n* a building near to, but separate from, a main building; outbuilding

outing ('aʊtɪŋ) *n* **1** a short outward and return journey; trip; excursion **2** *inf* the naming by homosexuals of other prominent homosexuals, often against their will

outjockey (,aʊt'dʒɒkɪ) *vb* (*tr*) to outwit by deception

outlandish (aʊt'lændɪʃ) *adj* **1** grotesquely unconventional in appearance, habits, etc **2** *arch* foreign > **out'landishly** *adv* > **out'landishness** *n*

outlast (,aʊt'lɑːst) *vb* (*tr*) to last longer than

outlaw ('aʊt,lɔː) *n* **1** (formerly) a person excluded from the law and deprived of its protection **2** any fugitive from the law, esp a habitual transgressor ▷ *vb* (*tr*) **3** to put (a person) outside the law and deprive of its protection **4** to ban > **'out,lawry** *n*

outlay *n* ('aʊt,leɪ) **1** an expenditure of money, effort, etc ▷ *vb* (,aʊt'leɪ), **outlays, outlaying, outlaid** **2** (*tr*) to spend (money, etc)

outlet ('aʊtlɛt, -lɪt) *n* **1** an opening or vent permitting escape or release **2a** a market for a product or service **2b** a commercial establishment retailing the goods of a particular producer or wholesaler **3** a channel that drains a body of water **4** a point in a wiring system from which current can be taken to supply electrical devices

outlier ('aʊt,laɪə) *n* **1** an outcrop of rocks that is entirely surrounded by older rocks **2** a person, thing, or part situated away from a main or related body **3** a person who lives away from his or her place of work, duty, etc

outline ('aʊt,laɪn) *n* **1** a preliminary or schematic plan, draft, etc **2** (*usually pl*) the important features of a theory, work, etc **3** the line by which an object or figure is or appears to be bounded **4a** a drawing or manner of drawing consisting only of external lines **4b** (*as modifier*): *an outline map* ▷ *vb* **outlines, outlining, outlined** (*tr*) **5** to draw or display the outline of **6** to give the main features or general idea of

outline font *n computing* a font format that makes use of fillable geometric outlines of letters and symbols, allowing fonts to be scaled up or down while still retaining their intended shape. Also: **vector font** ▷ Cf **bitmap font**

outlive (,aʊt'lɪv) *vb* **outlives, outliving, outlived** (*tr*) **1** to live longer than (someone) **2** to live beyond (a date or period): *he outlived the century* **3** to live through (an experience)

outlook ('aʊt,lʊk) *n* **1** a mental attitude or point of view **2** the probable or expected condition or outcome of something: *the weather outlook* **3** the view from a place **4** view or prospect **5** the act or state of looking out

outlying ('aʊt,laɪɪŋ) *adj* distant or remote from the main body or centre, as of a town or region

outmanoeuvre *or US* **outmaneuver** (,aʊtmə'nuːvə) *vb* **outmanoeuvres, outmanoeuvring, outmanoeuvred** *or US* **outmaneuvers, outmaneuvering, outmaneuvered** (*tr*) to secure a strategic advantage over by skilful manoeuvre

outmoded (,aʊt'məʊdɪd) *adj* no longer fashionable or widely accepted > **,out'modedly** *adv* > **,out'modedness** *n*

outmost ('aʊt,məʊst) *adj* another word for **outermost**

out of bounds *adj* (*postpositive*), *adv* **1** (often foll by *to*) not to be entered (by); barred (to) **2** outside specified or prescribed limits

out of date *adj* (**out-of-date** *when prenominal*), *adv* no longer valid, current, or fashionable; outmoded

out-of-door *adj* (*prenominal*) another term for **outdoor**

out-of-doors *adv, adj* (*postpositive*) in the open air; outside. Also: **outdoors**

out of pocket *adj* (**out-of-pocket** *when prenominal*) **1** (*postpositive*) having lost money, as in a commercial enterprise **2** without money to spend **3** (*prenominal*) (of expenses) unbudgeted and paid for in cash

out of the way *adj* (**out-of-the-way** *when prenominal*) **1** distant from more populous areas **2** uncommon or unusual

outpace (,aʊt'peɪs) *vb* **outpaces, outpacing, outpaced** (*tr*) **1** to go faster than (someone) **2** to surpass or outdo (something or someone) in growth, development. etc

outpatient ('aʊt,peɪʃənt) *n* a nonresident hospital patient ▷ Cf **inpatient**

outperform (,aʊtpə'fɔːm) *vb* (*tr*) to outdo or surpass in a specified field or activity

outplacement ('aʊt,pleɪsmənt) *n* a service that offers counselling and careers advice, esp to redundant executives, which is paid for by their previous employer

outpoint (,aʊt'pɔɪnt) *vb* (*tr*) to score more points than

outport ('aʊt,pɔːt) *n* **1** *chiefly Brit* a subsidiary port built in deeper water than the original port **2** *Canad* a small fishing village of Newfoundland

outpost ('aʊt,pəʊst) *n* **1** *mil* **1a** a position stationed at a distance from the area occupied by a major formation **1b** the troops assigned to such a position **2** an outlying settlement or position

outpour *n* ('aʊt,pɔː) **1** the act of flowing or pouring out **2** something that pours out ▷ *vb* (,aʊt'pɔː) **3** to pour or cause to pour out freely or rapidly

outpouring ('aʊt,pɔːrɪŋ) *n* **1** a passionate or exaggerated outburst; effusion **2** another word for **outpour** (senses 1, 2)

output ('aʊt,pʊt) *n* **1** the act of production or manufacture **2** the amount produced, as in a given period: *a weekly output* **3** the material produced, manufactured, etc **4** *electronics* **4a** the power, voltage, or current delivered by a circuit or component **4b** the point at which the signal is delivered **5** the power, energy, or work produced by an engine or a system **6** *computing* **6a** the information produced by a computer **6b** the operations and devices involved in producing this information **7** (*modifier*) of or relating to electronic or computer output: *output signal* ▷ *vb* **outputs, outputting, outputted** *or* **output** **8** (*tr*) *computing* to cause (data) to be emitted as output

outrage ('aʊt,reɪdʒ) *n* **1** a wantonly vicious or cruel act **2** a gross violation of decency, morality, honour, etc **3** profound indignation, anger, or hurt, caused by such an act ▷ *vb* **outrages, outraging, outraged** (*tr*) **4** to cause profound indignation, anger, or resentment in **5** to offend grossly **6** to commit an act of wanton viciousness, cruelty, or indecency on **7** a euphemistic word for **rape**[1] [C13 (meaning: excess): via F from *outré* beyond, from L *ultrā*]

outrageous (aʊt'reɪdʒəs) *adj* **1** being or having the nature of an outrage **2** grossly offensive to decency, authority, etc **3** violent or unrestrained in behaviour or temperament **4** extravagant or immoderate > **out'rageously** *adv* > **out'rageousness** *n*

outrank (,aʊt'ræŋk) *vb* (*tr*) **1** to be of higher rank than **2** to take priority over

outré ('uːtreɪ) *adj* deviating from what is usual or proper [C18 from F, p.p. of *outrer* to pass beyond]

outride (,aʊt'raɪd) *vb* **outrides, outriding, outrode, outridden** (*tr*) **1** to outdo by riding faster, farther, or better than **2** (of a vessel) to ride out (a storm)

outrider ('aʊt,raɪdə) *n* **1** a person who goes in advance to investigate, discover a way, etc; scout **2** a person who rides in front of or beside a carriage, esp as an attendant or guard **3** *US* a mounted herdsman

outrigger ('aʊt,rɪgə) *n* **1** a framework for supporting a pontoon outside and parallel to the hull of a boat to provide stability **2** a boat equipped with such a framework, esp one of the canoes of the South Pacific

3 any projecting framework attached to a boat, aircraft, building, etc, to act as a support 4 *rowing* another name for **rigger** (sense 2) [C18 from OUT- + RIG + -ER[1]]

outright *adj* ('aʊtˌraɪt). (*prenominal*) 1 without qualifications or limitations: *outright ownership* 2 complete; total 3 straightforward; direct ▷ *adv* (ˌaʊt'raɪt) 4 without restrictions 5 without reservation or concealment: *ask outright* 6 instantly: *he was killed outright*

outrush ('aʊtˌrʌʃ) *n* a flowing or rushing out

outset ('aʊtˌsɛt) *n* a start; beginning (esp in **from** (*or* **at**) **the outset**)

outside *prep* (ˌaʊt'saɪd) 1 (sometimes foll by *of*) on or to the exterior of: *outside the house* 2 beyond the limits of 3 apart from; other than: *no-one knows outside you* ▷ *adj* ('aʊtˌsaɪd) 4 (*prenominal*) situated on the exterior: *an outside lavatory* 5 remote; unlikely 6 not a member of 7 the greatest possible or probable (prices, odds, etc) 8 (of a road lane, esp in a dual carriageway or motorway) situated nearer or nearest to the central reservation, for use by faster or overtaking vehicles ▷ *adv* (ˌaʊt'saɪd) 9 outside a specified thing or place; out of doors 10 *sl* not in prison ▷ *n* ('aʊt'saɪd) 11 the external side or surface 12 the external appearance or aspect 13 (of a pavement, etc) the side nearest the road or away from a wall 14 *sport* an outside player, as in football 15 (*pl*) the outer sheets of a ream of paper 16 *Canad* (in the north) the settled parts of Canada 17 **at the outside** *inf* at the most or at the greatest extent: *two days at the outside.*

> **USAGE** The use of *outside of* and *inside of*, although fairly common, is generally thought to be incorrect or nonstandard: *She waits outside* (not *outside of*) *the school*

outside broadcast *n radio, television* a broadcast not made from a studio

outside director *n* a director of a company who is not employed by that company but is often employed by a holding or associated company

outsider (ˌaʊt'saɪdə) *n* 1 a person or thing excluded from or not a member of a set, group, etc 2 a contestant, esp a horse, thought unlikely to win in a race 3 *Canad* a person who does not live in the Arctic regions

outsize ('aʊtˌsaɪz) *adj* 1 Also: **outsized** very large or larger than normal ▷ *n* 2 something outsize, such as a garment or person 3 (*modifier*) relating to or dealing in outsize clothes: *an outsize shop*

outskirts ('aʊtˌskɜːts) *pl n* (*sometimes sing*) outlying or bordering areas, districts, etc, as of a city

outsmart (ˌaʊt'smɑːt) *vb* (*tr*) *inf* to get the better of; outwit

outspan *S African* ▷ *n* ('aʊtˌspæn) 1 an area on a farm kept available for travellers to rest and refresh animals, etc 2 the act of unharnessing or unyoking ▷ *vb* (ˌaʊt'spæn), **outspans, outspanning, outspanned** 3 (*tr*) to unharness or unyoke (animals) 4 (*intr*) to relax [C19 partial translation of Afrik. *uitspan*, from *uit* out + *spannen* to stretch]

outspoken (ˌaʊt'spəʊkən) *adj* 1 candid or bold in speech 2 said or expressed with candour or boldness

outspread *vb* (ˌaʊt'sprɛd), **outspreads, outspreading, outspread** 1 to spread out ▷ *adj* ('aʊt'sprɛd) 2 spread or stretched out 3 scattered or diffused widely ▷ *n* ('aʊtˌsprɛd) 4 a spreading out

outstanding (ˌaʊt'stændɪŋ) *adj* 1 superior; excellent 2 prominent, remarkable, or striking 3 unsettled, unpaid, or unresolved 4 (of shares, bonds, etc) issued and sold 5 projecting or jutting upwards or outwards > ˌ**out'standingly** *adv*

outstare (ˌaʊt'stɛə) *vb* **outstares, outstaring, outstared** (*tr*) 1 to outdo in staring 2 to disconcert by staring

outstation ('aʊtˌsteɪʃən) *n* a station or post at a distance from the base station or in a remote region

outstay (ˌaʊt'steɪ) *vb* (*tr*) 1 to stay longer than 2 to stay beyond (a limit) 3 **outstay one's welcome** See **overstay** (sense 2)

outstretch (ˌaʊt'strɛtʃ) *vb* (*tr*) 1 to extend or expand; stretch out 2 to stretch or extend beyond

outstrip (ˌaʊt'strɪp) *vb* **outstrips, outstripping, outstripped** (*tr*) 1 to surpass in a sphere of activity, competition, etc 2 to be or grow greater than 3 to go faster than and leave behind

outtake ('aʊtˌteɪk) *n* an unreleased take from a recording session, film, or television programme

out there *adj Slang* (**out-there** *when prenominal*). unconventional or eccentric: *he blends sublime pop moments with some real out-there stuff*

out-tray *n* (in an office, etc) a tray for outgoing correspondence, documents, etc

outturn ('aʊtˌtɜːn) *n* another word for **output** (sense 2)

outvote (ˌaʊt'vəʊt) *vb* **outvotes, outvoting, outvoted** (*tr*) to defeat by a majority of votes

outward ('aʊtwəd) *adj* 1 of or relating to what is apparent or superficial 2 of or relating to the outside of the body 3 belonging or relating to the external, as opposed to the mental, spiritual, or inherent 4 of, relating to, or directed towards the outside or exterior 5 **the outward man** 5a *theol* the body as opposed to the soul 5b *facetious* clothing ▷ *adv* 6 (of a ship) away from port 7 a variant of **outwards** ▷ *n* 8 the outward part; exterior > '**outwardness** *n*

Outward Bound movement *n trademark* (in Britain) a scheme to provide adventure training for young people

outwardly ('aʊtwədlɪ) *adv* 1 in outward appearance 2 with reference to the outside or outer surface; externally

outwards ('aʊtwədz) *or* **outward** *adv* towards the outside; out

outwear (ˌaʊt'wɛə) *vb* **outwears, outwearing, outwore, outworn** (*tr*) 1 to use up or destroy by wearing 2 to last or wear longer than 3 to outlive, outgrow, or develop beyond 4 to deplete or exhaust in strength, determination, etc

outweigh (ˌaʊt'weɪ) *vb* (*tr*) 1 to prevail over; overcome 2 to be more important or significant than 3 to be heavier than

outwit (ˌaʊt'wɪt) *vb* **outwits, outwitting, outwitted** (*tr*) to get the better of by cunning or ingenuity

outwith (ˌaʊt'wɪθ) *prep Scot* outside; beyond

outwork *n* ('aʊtˌwɜːk) 1 (*often pl*) defences which lie outside main defensive works 2 work done away from the factory, etc, by which it has been commissioned ▷ *vb* (ˌaʊt'wɜːk) (*tr*) 3 to work better, harder, etc, than 4 to work out to completion > '**outˌworker** *n*

ouzel *or* **ousel** ('uːzᵊl) *n* 1 short for **water ouzel.** See **dipper** (sense 2) 2 an archaic name for the (European) **blackbird** [OE *ōsle*]

ouzo ('uːzəʊ) *n, pl* **ouzos** a strong aniseed-flavoured spirit from Greece [Mod. Gk *ouzon*, from ?]

ova ('əʊvə) *n* the plural of **ovum**

oval ('əʊvᵊl) *adj* 1 having the shape of an ellipse or ellipsoid ▷ *n* 2 anything that is oval in shape, such as a sports ground 3 *Austral* 3a an Australian Rules ground 3b any sports field [C16 from Med. L *ōvālis*, from L *ōvum* egg] > '**ovally** *adv* > '**ovalness** *or* **ovality** (əʊ'vælɪtɪ) *n*

Oval ('əʊvᵊl) *n* **the** a cricket ground in south London, in the borough of Lambeth

ovariectomy (əʊˌvɛərɪ'ɛktəmɪ) *n, pl* **ovariectomies** *surgery* surgical removal of an ovary or ovarian tumour

ovary ('əʊvərɪ) *n, pl* **ovaries** 1 either of the two female reproductive organs, which produce ova and secrete oestrogen hormones 2 the corresponding organ in vertebrate and invertebrate animals 3 *bot* the hollow basal region of a carpel containing one or more ovules [C17 from NL *ōvārium*, from L *ōvum* egg] > **ovarian** (əʊ'vɛərɪən) *adj*

ovate ('əʊveɪt) *adj* **1** shaped like an egg **2** (esp of a leaf) shaped like the longitudinal section of an egg, with the broader end at the base [c18 from L *ōvātus* egg-shaped] > **'ovately** *adv*

ovation (əʊ'veɪʃən) *n* **1** an enthusiastic reception, esp one of prolonged applause **2** a victory procession less glorious than a triumph awarded to a Roman general [c16 from L *ovātiō* rejoicing, from *ovāre* to exult] > **o'vational** *adj*

oven ('ʌvᵊn) *n* **1** an enclosed heated compartment or receptacle for baking or roasting food **2** a similar device, usually lined with a refractory material, used for drying substances, firing ceramics, heat-treating, etc ▷ *vb* **3** (*tr*) to cook in an oven [OE *ofen*] > **'oven-ˌlike** *adj*

ovenable ('ʌvᵊnəbᵊl) *adj* suitable for cooking in or using in an oven

ovenbird ('ʌvᵊnˌbɜːd) *n* **1** any of numerous small brownish South American passerine birds that build oven-shaped clay nests **2** a common North American warbler that has an olive-brown striped plumage with an orange crown and builds a cup-shaped nest on the ground

oven-ready *adj* (of various foods) bought already prepared so that they are ready to be cooked in the oven

ovenware ('ʌvᵊnˌwɛə) *n* heat-resistant dishes in which food can be both cooked and served

over ('əʊvə) *prep* **1** directly above; on the top of; via the top or upper surface of: *over one's head* **2** on or to the other side of: *over the river* **3** during; through or throughout (a period of time) **4** in or throughout all parts of: *to travel over England* **5** throughout the whole extent of: *over the racecourse* **6** above; in preference to **7** by the agency of (an instrument of telecommunication): *over the radio* **8** more than: *over a century ago* **9** on the subject of; about: *an argument over nothing* **10** while occupied in: *discussing business over golf* **11** having recovered from the effects of **12 over and above** added to; in addition to ▷ *adv* **13** in a state, condition, situation, or position that is placed or put over something: *to climb over* **14** (*particle*) so as to cause to fall: *knocking over a policeman* **15** at or to a point across intervening space, water, etc **16** throughout a whole area: *the world over* **17** (*particle*) from beginning to end, usually cursorily: *to read a document over* **18** throughout a period of time: *stay over for this week* **19** (esp in signalling and radio) it is now your turn to speak, act, etc **20** more than is expected or usual: *not over well* **21 over again** once more **22 over against 22a** opposite to **22b** contrasting with **23 over and over** (often foll by *again*) repeatedly ▷ *adj* **24** (*postpositive*) finished; no longer in progress ▷ *adv, adj* **25** remaining; surplus (often in **left over**) ▷ *n* **26** *cricket* **26a** a series of six balls bowled by a bowler from the same end of the pitch **26b** the play during this [OE *ofer*]

over- *prefix* **1** excessive or excessively; beyond an agreed or desirable limit: *overcharge; overdue* **2** indicating superior rank: *overseer* **3** indicating location or movement above: *overhang* **4** indicating movement downwards: *overthrow*

overage (ˌəʊvər'eɪdʒ) *adj* beyond a specified age

overall *adj* ('əʊvərˌɔːl) (*prenominal*) **1** from one end to the other **2** including or covering everything: *the overall cost* ▷ *adv* (ˌəʊvər'ɔːl) **3** in general; on the whole ▷ *n* ('əʊvərˌɔːl) **4** *Brit* a protective work garment usually worn over ordinary clothes **5** (*pl*) hard-wearing work trousers with a bib and shoulder straps or jacket attached

overarch (ˌəʊvər'ɑːtʃ) *vb* (*tr*) to form an arch over

overarching (ˌəʊvər'ɑːtʃɪŋ) *adj* overall; all-encompassing: *an overarching concept*

overarm ('əʊvərˌɑːm) *adj* **1** *sport, esp cricket* bowled, thrown, or performed with the arm raised above the shoulder ▷ *adv* **2** with the arm raised above the shoulder

overawe (ˌəʊvər'ɔː) *vb* **overawes, overawing, overawed** (*tr*) to subdue, restrain, or overcome by affecting with a feeling of awe

overbalance *vb* (ˌəʊvə'bæləns), **overbalances, overbalancing, overbalanced 1** to lose or cause to lose balance **2** (*tr*) another word for **outweigh** ▷ *n* ('əʊvəˌbæləns) **3** excess of weight, value, etc

overbear (ˌəʊvə'bɛə) *vb* **overbears, overbearing, overbore, overborne 1** (*tr*) to dominate or overcome **2** (*tr*) to press or bear down with weight or physical force **3** to produce (fruit, etc) excessively

overbearing (ˌəʊvə'bɛərɪŋ) *adj* **1** domineering or dictatorial in manner or action **2** of particular or overriding importance or significance > **ˌover'bearingly** *adv*

overblown (ˌəʊvə'bləʊn) *adj* **1** overdone or excessive **2** bombastic; turgid: *overblown prose* **3** (of flowers) past the stage of full bloom

overboard ('əʊvəˌbɔːd) *adv* **1** from on board a vessel into the water **2 go overboard** *inf* **2a** to be extremely enthusiastic **2b** to go to extremes **3 throw overboard** to reject or abandon

overbook (ˌəʊvə'bʊk) *vb* (*tr, also absol*) to make more reservations than there are places, tickets, hotel rooms, etc, available

overbuild (ˌəʊvə'bɪld) *vb* **overbuilds, overbuilding, overbuilt** (*tr*) **1** to build over or on top of **2** to erect too many buildings in (an area) **3** to build too large or elaborately

overburden *vb* (ˌəʊvə'bɜːdᵊn) **1** (*tr*) to load with excessive weight, work, etc ▷ *n* ('əʊvəˌbɜːdᵊn) **2** an excessive burden or load **3** *geol* the sedimentary rock material that covers coal seams, mineral veins, etc > **ˌover'burdensome** *adj*

overcast *adj* ('əʊvəˌkɑːst) **1** covered over or obscured, esp by clouds **2** *meteorol* (of the sky) cloud-covered **3** gloomy or melancholy **4** sewn over by overcasting ▷ *vb* (ˌəʊvə'kɑːst), **overcasts, overcasting, overcast 5** to sew (an edge, as of a hem) with long stitches passing successively over the edge ▷ *n* ('əʊvəˌkɑːst) **6** *meteorol* the state of the sky when it is cloud-covered

Oo

overcharge *vb* (ˌəʊvə'tʃɑːdʒ), **overcharges, overcharging, overcharged 1** to charge too much **2** (*tr*) to fill or load beyond capacity **3** *literary* another word for **exaggerate** ▷ *n* ('əʊvəˌtʃɑːdʒ) **4** an excessive price or charge **5** an excessive load

overcloud (ˌəʊvə'klaʊd) *vb* **1** to make or become covered with clouds **2** to make or become dark or dim

overcoat ('əʊvəˌkəʊt) *n* a warm heavy coat worn over the outer clothes in cold weather

overcome (ˌəʊvə'kʌm) *vb* **overcomes, overcoming, overcame, overcome 1** (*tr*) to get the better of in a conflict **2** (*tr; often passive*) to render incapable or powerless by laughter, sorrow, exhaustion, etc **3** (*tr*) to surmount (obstacles, objections, etc) **4** (*intr*) to be victorious

overcrop (ˌəʊvə'krɒp) *vb* **overcrops, overcropping, overcropped** (*tr*) to exhaust (land) by excessive cultivation

overdo (ˌəʊvə'duː) *vb* **overdoes, overdoing, overdid, overdone** (*tr*) **1** to take or carry too far; do to excess **2** to exaggerate, overelaborate, or overplay **3** to cook or bake too long **4 overdo it** *or* **things** to overtax one's strength, capacity, etc

overdose *n* ('əʊvəˌdəʊs) **1** (esp of drugs) an excessive dose ▷ *vb* (ˌəʊvə'dəʊs), **overdoses, overdosing, overdosed 2** to take an excessive dose or give an excessive dose to > **ˌover'dosage** *n*

overdraft ('əʊvəˌdrɑːft) *n* **1** a deficit in a bank or building-society cheque account caused by withdrawing more money than is credited to it **2** the amount of this deficit

overdraw (ˌəʊvə'drɔː) *vb* **overdraws, overdrawing,**

overdrew, overdrawn **1** to draw on (a bank account) in excess of the credit balance **2** *(tr)* to exaggerate in describing or telling

overdress *vb* (ˌəʊvəˈdrɛs) **1** to dress (oneself or another) too elaborately or finely ▷ *n* (ˈəʊvəˌdrɛs) **2** a dress that may be worn over a jumper, blouse, etc

overdrive *n* (ˈəʊvəˌdraɪv) **1** a very high gear in a motor vehicle used at high speeds to reduce wear ▷ *vb* (ˌəʊvəˈdraɪv), **overdrives, overdriving, overdrove, overdriven** **2** *(tr)* to drive too hard or too far; overwork or overuse

overdub (in multitrack recording) ▷ *vb* (ˌəʊvəˈdʌb), **overdubs, overdubbing, overdubbed** **1** to add (new sound) on a spare track or tracks ▷ *n* (ˈəʊvəˌdʌb) **2** the blending of various layers of sound in one recording by this method

overdue (ˌəʊvəˈdjuː) *adj* past the time specified, required, or preferred for arrival, occurrence, payment, etc

overegg (ˌəʊvərˈɛg) *vb (tr)* to exaggerate (a feature of something) to the point of unreasonableness (esp in the phrase **overegg the pudding**)

overestimate *vb* (ˌəʊvərˈɛstɪˌmeɪt), **overestimates, overestimating, overestimated** **1** *(tr)* to estimate too highly ▷ *n* (ˌəʊvərˈɛstɪmɪt) **2** an estimate that is too high > ˌ**overˌestiˈmation** *n*

overexpose (ˌəʊvərɪksˈpəʊz) *vb* **overexposes, overexposing, overexposed** *(tr)* **1** to expose too much or for too long **2** *photog* to expose (a film, etc) for too long or with too bright a light > ˌ**overexˈposure** *n*

overflow *vb* (ˌəʊvəˈfləʊ), **overflows, overflowing, overflowed** *or (formerly)* **overflown** **1** to flow or run over (a limit, brim, etc) **2** to fill or be filled beyond capacity so as to spill or run over **3** *(intr; usually foll by with)* to be filled with happiness, tears, etc **4** *(tr)* to spread or cover over; flood or inundate ▷ *n* (ˈəʊvəˌfləʊ) **5** overflowing matter, esp liquid **6** any outlet that enables surplus liquid to be discharged or drained off **7** the amount by which a limit, capacity, etc, is exceeded

overfold (ˈəʊvəˌfəʊld) *n geol* a fold in the form of an anticline in which one or both limbs have been inclined more than 90° from their original orientation

overfunding (ˈəʊvəˌfʌndɪŋ) *n* (in Britain) a government policy in which it sells more of its securities than would be required to finance public spending, with the object of absorbing surplus funds to curb inflation

overgrow (ˌəʊvəˈgrəʊ) *vb* **overgrows, overgrowing, overgrew, overgrown** **1** *(tr)* to grow over or across (an area, path, etc) **2** *(tr)* to choke or supplant by a stronger growth **3** *(tr)* to grow too large for **4** *(intr)* to grow beyond normal size > ˈ**overˌgrowth** *n*

overhand (ˈəʊvəˌhænd) *adj* **1** thrown or performed with the hand raised above the shoulder **2** sewn with thread passing over two edges in one direction ▷ *adv* **3** with the hand above the shoulder; overarm **4** with shallow stitches passing over two edges ▷ *vb* **5** to sew (two edges) overhand

overhang *vb* (ˌəʊvəˈhæŋ), **overhangs, overhanging, overhung** **1** to project or extend beyond (a surface, building, etc) **2** *(tr)* to hang or be suspended over **3** *(tr)* to menace, threaten, or dominate ▷ *n* (ˈəʊvəˌhæŋ) **4** a formation, object, etc, that extends beyond or hangs over something, such as an outcrop of rock overhanging a mountain face **5** the amount or extent of projection

overhaul *vb* (ˌəʊvəˈhɔːl) *(tr)* **1** to examine carefully for faults, necessary repairs, etc **2** to make repairs or adjustments to (a car, machine, etc) **3** to overtake ▷ *n* (ˈəʊvəˌhɔːl) **4** a thorough examination and repair

overhead *adj* (ˈəʊvəˌhɛd) **1** situated or operating above head height or some other reference level **2** *(prenominal)* inclusive: *the overhead price included meals* ▷ *adv* (ˌəʊvəˈhɛd) **3** over or above head height, esp in the sky ▷ *n* (ˈəʊvəˌhɛd) **4a** a stroke in racket games played from above head height **4b** *(as modifier): an overhead smash* **5** *(modifier)* of, concerned with, or resulting from overheads: *overhead costs*

overhead camshaft *n* a type of camshaft situated above the cylinder head in an internal-combustion engine

overhead projector *n* a projector that throws an enlarged image of a transparency onto a surface above and behind the person using it

overheads (ˈəʊvəˌhɛdz) *pl n* business expenses, such as rent, that are not directly attributable to any department or product and can therefore be assigned only arbitrarily

overhead-valve engine *n* a type of internal-combustion engine in which the inlet and exhaust valves are in the cylinder head above the pistons. US name: **valve-in-head engine**

overhear (ˌəʊvəˈhɪə) *vb* **overhears, overhearing, overheard** *(tr)* to hear (a person, remark, etc) without the knowledge of the speaker

overheat (ˌəʊvəˈhiːt) *vb* **1** to make or become excessively hot **2** *(tr; often passive)* to make very agitated, irritated, etc **3** *(intr)* (of an economy) to tend towards inflation, often as a result of excessive growth in demand **4** *(tr)* to cause (an economy) to tend towards inflation ▷ *n* **5** the condition of being overheated

Overijssel (*Dutch* oːvərˈɛisəl) *n* a province of the E Netherlands: generally low-lying. Capital: Zwolle. Pop: 1 077 600 (2000 est). Area: 3929 sq km (1517 sq miles)

overjoy (ˌəʊvəˈdʒɔɪ) *vb (tr)* to give great delight to

overjoyed (ˌəʊvəˈdʒɔɪd) *adj* delighted; excessively happy

overkill (ˈəʊvəˌkɪl) *n* **1** the capability to deploy more weapons, esp nuclear weapons, than is necessary to ensure military advantage **2** any capacity or treatment that is greater than that required or appropriate

overland (ˈəʊvəˌlænd) *adj (prenominal), adv* **1** over or across land ▷ *vb* **2** *Austral* (formerly) to drive (cattle or sheep) overland > ˈ**overˌlander** *n*

overlap *vb* (ˌəʊvəˈlæp), **overlaps, overlapping, overlapped** **1** (of two things) to extend or lie partly over (each other) **2** to cover and extend beyond (something) **3** *(intr)* to coincide partly in time, subject, etc ▷ *n* (ˈəʊvəˌlæp) **4** a part that overlaps or is overlapped **5** the amount, length, etc, overlapping **6** *geol* the horizontal extension of the lower beds in a series of rock strata beyond the upper beds

overlay *vb* (ˌəʊvəˈleɪ), **overlays, overlaying, overlaid** *(tr)* **1** to lay or place over or upon (something else) **2** (often foll by *with*) to cover, overspread, or conceal (with) **3** (foll by *with*) to cover (a surface) with an applied decoration: *ebony overlaid with silver* **4** to achieve the correct printing pressure all over (a forme or plate) by adding to the appropriate areas of the packing ▷ *n* (ˈəʊvəˌleɪ) **5** something that is laid over something else; covering **6** an applied decoration or layer, as of gold leaf **7** a transparent sheet giving extra details to a map or diagram over which it is designed to be placed **8** *printing* material, such as paper, used to overlay a forme or plate

overleaf (ˌəʊvəˈliːf) *adv* on the other side of the page

overlie (ˌəʊvəˈlaɪ) *vb* **overlies, overlying, overlay, overlain** *(tr)* **1** to lie or rest upon ▷ Cf **overlay** **2** to kill (a baby or newborn animal) by lying upon it

overlong (ˌəʊvəˈlɒŋ) *adj, adv* too or excessively long

overlook *vb* (ˌəʊvəˈlʊk). *(tr)* **1** to fail to notice or take into account **2** to disregard deliberately or indulgently **3** to afford a view of from above: *the house overlooks the bay* **4** to rise above **5** to look at carefully **6** to cast the evil eye upon (someone) ▷ *n* (ˈəʊvəˌlʊk) *US* **7** a high place affording a view **8** an act of overlooking

overlord (ˈəʊvəˌlɔːd) *n* a supreme lord or master > ˈ**overˌlordship** *n*

overly (ˈəʊvəlɪ) *adv* too; excessively

overman *vb* (ˌəʊvəˈmæn), **overmans, overmanning, overmanned** **1** *(tr)* to supply with an excessive number of men ▷ *n* (ˈəʊvəˌmæn), *pl* **overmen** 2 a man who oversees others 3 a superman

overmaster (ˌəʊvəˈmɑːstə) *vb* (*tr*) to overpower

overmatch *chiefly US* ▷ *vb* (ˌəʊvəˈmætʃ) (*tr*) 1 to be more than a match for 2 to match with a superior opponent ▷ *n* (ˈəʊvəˌmætʃ) 3 a person superior in ability 4 a match in which one contestant is superior

overmuch (ˌəʊvəˈmʌtʃ) *adv, adj* 1 too much; very much ▷ *n* 2 an excessive amount

overnice (ˌəʊvəˈnaɪs) *adj* too fastidious, precise, etc

overnight *adv* (ˌəʊvəˈnaɪt) 1 for the duration of the night 2 in or as if in the course of one night; suddenly: *the situation changed overnight* ▷ *adj* (ˈəʊvəˌnaɪt) (*usually prenominal*) 3 done in, occurring in, or lasting the night: *an overnight stop* 4 staying for one night 5 for use during a single night 6 occurring in or as if in the course of one night; sudden: *an overnight victory*

overpass *n* (ˈəʊvəˌpɑːs) 1 another name for **flyover** (sense 1) ▷ *vb* (ˌəʊvəˈpɑːs) (*tr*) *now rare* 2 to pass over, through, or across 3 to exceed 4 to ignore

overplay (ˌəʊvəˈpleɪ) *vb* 1 (*tr*) to exaggerate the importance of 2 to act or behave in an exaggerated manner 3 **overplay one's hand** to overestimate the worth or strength of one's position

overpower (ˌəʊvəˈpaʊə) *vb* (*tr*) 1 to conquer or subdue by superior force 2 to have such a strong effect on as to make helpless or ineffective 3 to supply with more power than necessary > ˌ**over**ˈ**powering** *adj*

overprice (ˌəʊvəˈpraɪs) *vb* **overprices, overpricing, overpriced** (*tr*) to ask too high a price for

overprint *vb* (ˌəʊvəˈprɪnt) 1 (*tr*) to print (additional matter or another colour) on a sheet of paper ▷ *n* (ˈəʊvəˌprɪnt) 2 additional matter or another colour printed onto a previously printed sheet 3 additional matter applied to a finished postage stamp by printing, stamping, etc

overqualified (ˌəʊvəˈkwɒlɪfaɪd) *adj* having more managerial experience or academic qualifications than required for a particular job

overrate (ˌəʊvəˈreɪt) *vb* **overrates, overrating, overrated** (*tr*) to assess too highly

overreach (ˌəʊvəˈriːtʃ) *vb* 1 (*tr*) to defeat or thwart (oneself) by attempting to do or gain too much 2 (*tr*) to aim for but miss by going too far 3 to get the better of (a person) by trickery 4 (*tr*) to reach beyond or over 5 (*intr*) to reach or go too far 6 (*intr*) (of a horse) to strike the back of a forefoot with the edge of the opposite hind foot

overreact (ˌəʊvərɪˈækt) *vb* (*intr*) to react excessively to something > ˌ**overre**ˈ**action** *n*

override *vb* (ˌəʊvəˈraɪd), **overrides, overriding, overrode, overridden** (*tr*) 1 to set aside or disregard with superior authority or power 2 to supersede or annul 3 to dominate or vanquish by or as if by trampling down 4 to take manual control of (a system that is usually under automatic control) 5 to extend or pass over, esp to overlap 6 to ride (a horse, etc) too hard 7 to ride over ▷ *n* (ˈəʊvəˌraɪd) 8 a device that can override an automatic control

overrider (ˈəʊvəˌraɪdə) *n* either of two attachments fitted to the bumper of a motor vehicle to prevent it interlocking with that of another vehicle

overriding (ˌəʊvəˈraɪdɪŋ) *adj* taking precedence

overrule (ˌəʊvəˈruːl) *vb* **overrules, overruling, overruled** (*tr*) 1 to disallow the arguments of (a person) by the use of authority 2 to rule or decide against (an argument, decision, etc) 3 to prevail over, dominate, or influence 4 to exercise rule over

overrun *vb* (ˌəʊvəˈrʌn), **overruns, overrunning, overran, overrun** 1 (*tr*) to swarm or spread over rapidly 2 to run over (something); overflow 3 to extend or run beyond a limit 4 (*intr*) (of an engine) to run with a closed throttle at a speed dictated by that of the vehicle it drives 5 (*tr*) to print (a book, journal, etc) in a greater quantity than ordered 6 (*tr*) *printing* to transfer (set type) from one column, line, or page, to another 7 (*tr*) *arch* to run faster than ▷ *n* (ˈəʊvəˌrʌn) 8 the act or an instance of overrunning 9 the amount or extent of overrunning 10 the number of copies of a publication in excess of the quantity ordered

overseas *adv* (ˌəʊvəˈsiːz) 1 beyond the sea; abroad ▷ *adj* (ˈəʊvəˈsiːz) 2 of, to, in, from, or situated in countries beyond the sea 3 Also: **oversea** of or relating to passage over the sea ▷ *n* (ˌəʊvəˈsiːz) 4 (*functioning as sing*) *inf* a foreign country or foreign countries collectively

overseas territory *n* See **United Kingdom overseas territory**

oversee (ˌəʊvəˈsiː) *vb* **oversees, overseeing, oversaw, overseen** (*tr*) 1 to watch over and direct; supervise 2 to watch secretly or accidentally 3 *arch* to scrutinize; inspect

overseer (ˈəʊvəˌsiːə) *n* 1 a person who oversees others, esp workmen 2 *Brit history* a minor official of a parish attached to the poorhouse

oversell (ˌəʊvəˈsɛl) *vb* **oversells, overselling, oversold** 1 (*tr*) to sell more of (a commodity, etc) than can be supplied 2 to use excessively aggressive methods in selling (commodities) 3 (*tr*) to exaggerate the merits of

overset (ˌəʊvəˈsɛt) *vb* **oversets, oversetting, overset** (*tr*) 1 to disturb or upset 2 *printing* to set (type or copy) in excess of the space available

oversew (ˈəʊvəˌsəʊ, ˌəʊvəˈsəʊ) *vb* **oversews, oversewing, oversewed; oversewn** *or* **oversewed** to sew (two edges) with close stitches that pass over them both

oversexed (ˌəʊvəˈsɛkst) *adj* having an excessive preoccupation with sexual activity

overshadow (ˌəʊvəˈʃædəʊ) *vb* (*tr*) 1 to render insignificant or less important in comparison 2 to cast a shadow or gloom over

overshoe (ˈəʊvəˌʃuː) *n* a protective shoe worn over an ordinary shoe

overshoot *vb* (ˌəʊvəˈʃuːt), **overshoots, overshooting, overshot** 1 to shoot or go beyond (a mark or target) 2 (of an aircraft) to fly or taxi too far along a runway 3 (*tr*) to pass swiftly over or down over, as water over a wheel ▷ *n* (ˈəʊvəˌʃuːt) 4 an act or instance of overshooting 5 the extent of such overshooting: *an overshoot of ten feet*

overshot (ˈəʊvəˌʃɒt) *adj* 1 having or designating an upper jaw that projects beyond the lower jaw 2 (of a water wheel) driven by a flow of water that passes over the wheel

oversight (ˈəʊvəˌsaɪt) *n* 1 an omission or mistake, esp one made through failure to notice something 2 supervision

oversize *adj* (ˌəʊvəˈsaɪz) 1 Also: **oversized** larger than the usual size ▷ *n* (ˈəʊvəˌsaɪz) 2 a size larger than the usual or proper size 3 something that is oversize

overskirt (ˈəʊvəˌskɜːt) *n* an outer skirt, esp one that reveals a decorative underskirt

overspend *vb* (ˌəʊvəˈspɛnd), **overspends, overspending, overspent** 1 to spend in excess of (one's desires or what one can afford or is allocated) 2 (*tr; usually passive*) to wear out; exhaust ▷ *n* (ˈəʊvəˌspɛnd) 3 the amount by which someone or something is overspent

overspill *n* (ˈəʊvəˌspɪl) 1a something that spills over or is in excess 1b (*as modifier*): *overspill population* ▷ *vb* (ˌəʊvəˈspɪl), **overspills, overspilling, overspilt** *or* **overspilled** 2 (*intr*) to overflow

overspread (ˌəʊvəˈsprɛd) *vb* (*tr*) **overspreads, overspreading, overspread** to extend or spread over

overstate (ˌəʊvəˈsteɪt) *vb* **overstates, overstating, overstated** (*tr*) to state too strongly; exaggerate or overemphasize > ˌ**over**ˈ**statement** *n*

overstay (ˌəʊvəˈsteɪ) *vb* (*tr*) 1 to stay beyond the time, limit, or duration of 2 **overstay** *or* **outstay one's**

Oo

welcome to stay (at a party, etc), longer than pleases the host or hostess
overstayer ('əʊvə,steɪə) *n* a person who remains illegally in a country after the period of the permitted visit has expired
overstep (,əʊvə'stɛp) *vb* **oversteps, overstepping, overstepped** (*tr*) to go beyond (a certain or proper limit)
overstrung (,əʊvə'strʌŋ) *adj* **1** too highly strung; tense **2** (of a piano) having two sets of strings crossing each other at an oblique angle
overstuff (,əʊvə'stʌf) *vb* (*tr*) **1** to force too much into **2** to cover (furniture, etc) entirely with upholstery
oversubscribe (,əʊvəsəb'skraɪb) *vb* (*tr; often passive*) to subscribe or apply for in excess of available supply > ,**oversub'scription** *n*
overt ('əʊvɜːt, əʊ'vɜːt) *adj* **1** open to view; observable **2** *law* open; deliberate [C14 via OF, from *ovrir* to open, from L *aperīre*] > '**overtly** *adv*
overtake (,əʊvə'teɪk) *vb* **overtakes, overtaking, overtook, overtaken 1** *chiefly Brit* to move past (another vehicle or person) travelling in the same direction **2** (*tr*) to pass or do better than, after catching up with **3** (*tr*) to come upon suddenly or unexpectedly: *night overtook him* **4** (*tr*) to catch up with; draw level with
overtax (,əʊvə'tæks) *vb* (*tr*) **1** to tax too heavily **2** to impose too great a strain on
over-the-counter *adj* **1a** (of securities) not listed or quoted on a stock exchange **1b** (of a security market) dealing in such securities **1c** (of security transactions) conducted through a broker's office directly between purchaser and seller and not on a stock exchange **2** (of a medicinal drug) able to be sold without prescription ▷ Cf **POM** ▷ Abbreviation: **OTC**
overthrow *vb* (,əʊvə'θrəʊ), **overthrows, overthrowing, overthrew, overthrown 1** (*tr*) to effect the downfall or destruction of (a ruler, institution, etc), esp by force **2** (*tr*) to throw or turn over **3** to throw (something, esp a ball) too far ▷ *n* ('əʊvə,θrəʊ) **4** downfall; destruction **5** *cricket* **5a** a ball thrown back too far by a fielder **5b** a run scored because of this
overthrust ('əʊvə,θrʌst) *n geol* a reverse fault in which the rocks on the upper surface of a fault plane have moved over the rocks on the lower surface
overtime *n* ('əʊvə,taɪm) **1a** work at a regular job done in addition to regular working hours **1b** (*as modifier*): *overtime pay* **2** the rate of pay established for such work **3** time in excess of a set period **4** *sport, US & Canad* extra time ▷ *adv* ('əʊvə,taɪm) **5** beyond the regular or stipulated time ▷ *vb* (,əʊvə'taɪm), **overtimes, overtiming, overtimed 6** (*tr*) to exceed the required time for (a photographic exposure, etc)
overtone ('əʊvə,təʊn) *n* **1** (*often pl*) additional meaning or nuance: *overtones of despair* **2** *music, acoustics* any of the tones, with the exception of the fundamental, that constitute a musical sound and contribute to its quality
overture ('əʊvə,tjʊə) *n* **1** *music* **1a** a piece of orchestral music that is played at the beginning of an opera or oratorio, often containing the main musical themes of the work **1b** a one-movement orchestral piece, usually having a descriptive or evocative title **2** (*often pl*) a proposal, act, or gesture initiating a relationship, negotiation, etc **3** something that introduces what follows ▷ *vb* **overtures, overturing, overtured** (*tr*) **4** to make or present an overture to **5** to introduce with an overture [C14 via OF from LL *apertūra* opening, from L *aperīre* to open]
overturn *vb* (,əʊvə'tɜːn) **1** to turn or cause to turn from an upright or normal position **2** (*tr*) to overthrow or destroy **3** (*tr*) to invalidate; reverse ▷ *n* ('əʊvə,tɜːn) **4** the act of overturning or the state of being overturned
overuse *vb* (,əʊvə'juːz), **overuses, overusing, overused 1** (*tr*) to use excessively ▷ *n* (,əʊvə'juːs) **2** excessive use
overview ('əʊvə,vjuː) *n* a general survey
overweening (,əʊvə'wiːnɪŋ) *adj* **1** (of a person) excessively arrogant or presumptuous **2** (of opinions, appetites, etc) excessive; immoderate [C14 from OVER + *weening* from OE *wēnan* WEEN] > ,**over'weeningness** *n*
overweight *adj* (,əʊvə'weɪt) **1** weighing more than is usual, allowed, or healthy ▷ *n* ('əʊvə,weɪt) **2** extra or excess weight ▷ *vb* (,əʊvə'weɪt) (*tr*) **3** to give too much emphasis or consideration to **4** to add too much weight to **5** to weigh down
overwhelm (,əʊvə'wɛlm) *vb* (*tr*) **1** to overpower the thoughts, emotions, or senses of **2** to overcome with irresistible force **3** to cover over or bury completely **4** to weigh or rest upon overpoweringly
overwhelming (,əʊvə'wɛlmɪŋ) *adj* overpowering in effect, force, or number > ,**over'whelmingly** *adv*
overwind (,əʊvə'waɪnd) *vb* **overwinds, overwinding, overwound** (*tr*) to wind (a watch, etc) beyond the proper limit
overwork *vb* (,əʊvə'wɜːk) (*mainly tr*) **1** (*also intr*) to work too hard or too long **2** to use too much: *to overwork an excuse* **3** to decorate the surface of ▷ *n* ('əʊvə,wɜːk) **4** excessive or excessively tiring work
overwrite (,əʊvə'raɪt) *vb* **overwrites, overwriting, overwrote, overwritten 1** to write (something) in an excessively ornate style **2** to write too much about (someone or something) **3** to write on top of (other writing) **4** to record on a storage medium, such as a magnetic disk, thus destroying what was originally recorded there
overwrought (,əʊvə'rɔːt) *adj* **1** full of nervous tension; agitated **2** too elaborate; fussy: *an overwrought style* **3** (*often postpositive* and foll by *with*) with the surface decorated or adorned
ovi- *or* **ovo-** *combining form* egg or ovum: *oviform; ovoviviparous* [from L *ōvum*]
Ovid ('ɒvɪd) *n* Latin name *Publius Ovidius Naso* 43 BC–?17 AD, Roman poet. His verse includes poems on love, *Ars Amatoria*, on myths, *Metamorphoses*, and on exile, *Tristia*
oviduct ('ɒvɪ,dʌkt, 'əʊ-) *n* the tube through which ova are conveyed from an ovary. Also called (in mammals): **Fallopian tube** > **oviducal** (,ɒvɪ'djuːkᵊl, ,əʊ-) *or* ,**ovi'ductal** *adj*
Oviedo (*Spanish* o'βjeðo) *n* a city in NW Spain: capital of Asturias from 810 until 1002; centre of a coal- and iron-mining area. Pop: 199 549 (1998 est)
oviform ('əʊvɪ,fɔːm) *adj biol* shaped like an egg
ovine ('əʊvaɪn) *adj* of, relating to, or resembling a sheep [C19 from LL *ovīnus*, from L *ovis* sheep]
oviparous (əʊ'vɪpərəs) *adj* (of fishes, reptiles, birds, etc) producing eggs that hatch outside the body of the mother ▷ Cf **ovoviviparous, viviparous** (sense 1) > **oviparity** (,əʊvɪ'pærɪtɪ) *n* > **o'viparously** *adv*
ovipositor (,əʊvɪ'pɒzɪtə) *n* **1** the egg-laying organ of most female insects, consisting of a pair of specialized appendages at the end of the abdomen **2** a similar organ in certain female fishes, formed by an extension of the edges of the genital opening [C19 from OVI- + L *positor*, from *ponere* to place] > ,**ovi'posit** *vb* (*intr*)
ovoid ('əʊvɔɪd) *adj* **1** egg-shaped ▷ *n* **2** something that is ovoid
ovoviviparous (,əʊvəʊvaɪ'vɪpərəs) *adj* (of certain reptiles, fishes, etc) producing eggs that hatch within the body of the mother ▷ Cf **oviparous, viviparous** (sense 1) > **ovoviviparity** (,əʊvəʊ,vaɪvɪ'pærɪtɪ) *n*
ovulate ('ɒvjʊ,leɪt) *vb* **ovulates, ovulating, ovulated** (*intr*) to produce or discharge eggs from an ovary [C19 from OVULE] > ,**ovu'lation** *n*
ovulation method *n* another name for **Billings method**
ovule ('ɒvjuːl) *n* **1** a small body in seed-bearing plants that contains the egg cell and develops into the seed after fertilization **2** *zool* an immature ovum [C19 via F from Med. L *ōvulum* a little egg, from L *ōvum* egg] > '**ovular** *adj*

ovum ('əʊvəm) *n, pl* **ova** an unfertilized female gamete; egg cell [from L: egg]

ow (aʊ) *interj* an exclamation of pain

owe (əʊ) *vb* **owes, owing, owed** (*mainly tr*) **1** to be under an obligation to pay (someone) to the amount of **2** (*intr*) to be in debt: *he still owes for his house* **3** (often foll by *to*) to have as a result (of) **4** to feel the need or obligation to do, give, etc **5** to hold or maintain in the mind or heart (esp in **owe a grudge**) [OE *āgan* to have (c12 to have to)]

Owen ('əʊɪn) *n* **1 Michael** (**James**) born 1979, British footballer; plays for Liverpool and England (from 1997) **2** Sir **Richard** 1804–92, English comparative anatomist and palaeontologist **3 Robert** 1771–1858, Welsh industrialist and social reformer. He formed a model industrial community at New Lanark, Scotland, and pioneered cooperative societies. His books include *New View of Society* (1813) **4 Wilfred** 1893–1918, English poet of World War I, who was killed in action

Owen gun *n* a type of simple recoil-operated sub-machine-gun first used by Australian forces in World War II [after E. E. *Owen* (1915–49), its Austral inventor]

Owens ('əʊɪnz) *n* **Jesse,** real name *John Cleveland Owens.* 1913–80, US Black athlete: won four gold medals at the Berlin Olympics (1936)

Owen Stanley Range *n* a mountain range in SE New Guinea. Highest peak: Mount Victoria, 4073 m (13 363 ft)

Owerri (ə'wɛrɪ) *n* a market town in S Nigeria, capital of Imo state. Pop: 35 010 (latest est)

owing ('əʊɪŋ) *adj* **1** (*postpositive*) owed; due **2 owing to** because of or on account of

owl (aʊl) *n* **1** a nocturnal bird of prey having large front-facing eyes, a small hooked bill, soft feathers, and a short neck **2** any of various breeds of owl-like fancy domestic pigeon **3** a person who looks or behaves like an owl, esp in having a solemn manner [OE *ūle*] > **'owlish** *adj* > **'owl-,like** *adj*

owlet ('aʊlɪt) *n* a young or nestling owl

own (əʊn) *determiner* (*preceded by a possessive*) **1a** (intensifier): *John's own idea* **1b** (*as pron*): *I'll use my own* **2** on behalf of oneself or in relation to oneself: *he is his own worst enemy* **3 come into one's own 3a** to become fulfilled: *she really came into her own when she got divorced* **3b** to receive what is due to one **4 hold one's own** to maintain one's situation or position, esp in spite of opposition or difficulty **5 on one's own 5a** without help **5b** by oneself; alone ▷ *vb* **6** (*tr*) to have as one's possession **7** (when *intr,* often foll by *up, to,* or *up to*) to confess or admit; acknowledge **8** (*tr; takes a clause as object*) *now rare* to concede: *I own that you are right* [OE *āgen,* orig. p.p. of *āgan* to have. See OWE]

own brand *n* a product which displays the name of the retailer rather than the producer

owner ('əʊnə) *n* a person who owns; legal possessor

owner-occupier *n* someone who has bought or is buying the house in which he or she lives

ownership ('əʊnəʃɪp) *n* **1** the state or fact of being an owner **2** legal right of possession; proprietorship

own goal *n* **1** *soccer* a goal scored by a player accidentally playing the ball into his or her own team's net **2** *inf* any action that results in disadvantage to the person who took it or to his or her associates

ox (ɒks) *n, pl* **oxen 1** an adult castrated male of any domesticated species of cattle used for draught work and meat **2** any bovine mammal, esp any of the domestic cattle [OE *oxa*]

oxalic acid (ɒk'sælɪk) *n* a colourless poisonous crystalline acid found in many plants: used as a bleach and a cleansing agent for metals. Formula: $(COOH)_2$. Recommended name: **ethanedioic acid** [c18 from F *oxalique,* from L *oxalis* garden sorrel; see OXALIS]

oxalis ('ɒksəlɪs, ɒk'sælɪs) *n* a plant having clover-like leaves which contain oxalic acid and white, pink, red, or yellow flowers. See also **wood sorrel** [c18 via L from Gk: sorrel, sour wine, from *oxus* acid, sharp]

oxblood ('ɒks,blʌd) *or* **oxblood red** *adj* of a dark reddish-brown colour

oxbow ('ɒks,bəʊ) *n* **1** a U-shaped piece of wood fitted under and around the neck of a harnessed ox and attached to the yoke **2** Also called: **oxbow lake** a small curved lake lying on the flood plain of a river and constituting the remnant of a former meander

Oxbridge ('ɒks,brɪdʒ) *n* **a** the British universities of Oxford and Cambridge, esp considered as ancient and prestigious academic institutions, bastions of privilege and superiority, etc **b** (*as modifier*): *Oxbridge graduates*

oxen ('ɒksən) *n* the plural of **ox**

oxeye ('ɒks,aɪ) *n* **1** a Eurasian composite plant having daisy-like flower heads with yellow rays and dark centres **2** any of various North American plants having daisy-like flowers **3 oxeye daisy** a type of hardy perennial chrysanthemum

ox-eyed *adj* having large round eyes, like those of an ox

Oxfam ('ɒks,fæm) *n acronym for* Oxford Committee for Famine Relief

Oxford[1] ('ɒksfəd) *n* **1** a city in S England, administrative centre of Oxfordshire, at the confluence of the Rivers Thames and Cherwell: Royalist headquarters during the Civil War; seat of Oxford University, consisting of 40 separate colleges, the oldest being University College (1249), and Oxford Brookes University (1993); motor-vehicle industry. Pop: 118 795 (1991). Related word: **Oxonian 2** Also called: **Oxford Down** a breed of sheep with middle-length wool and a dark brown face and legs **3** a type of stout laced shoe with a low heel **4** a lightweight fabric of plain or twill weave used esp for men's shirts

Oxford[2] ('ɒksfəd) *n* **1st Earl of** title of (Robert) **Harley**

Oxford bags *pl n* trousers with very wide baggy legs

Oxford blue *n* **1a** a dark blue colour **1b** (*as adj*): *an Oxford-blue scarf* **2** a person who has been awarded a blue from Oxford University

Oxford Movement *n* a movement within the Church of England that began at Oxford in 1833. It affirmed the continuity of the Church with early Christianity and strove to restore the High-Church ideals of the 17th century. Also called: **Tractarianism**

Oxfordshire ('ɒksfəd,ʃɪə, -ʃə) *n* an inland county of S central England: situated mostly in the basin of the Upper Thames, with the Cotswolds in the west and the Chilterns in the southeast. Administrative centre: Oxford. Pop: 605 492 (2001). Area: 2608 sq km (1007 sq miles). Abbreviation: **Oxon**

oxidant ('ɒksɪdənt) *n* a substance that acts or is used as an oxidizing agent. Also called (esp in rocketry): **oxidizer**

oxidation (,ɒksɪ'deɪʃən) *n* **a** the act or process of oxidizing **b** (*as modifier*): *an oxidation state* > **'oxi,date** *vb* > **,oxi'dational** *adj* > **'oxi,dative** *adj*

oxidation-reduction *n* **a** a reversible chemical process usually involving the transfer of electrons, in which one reaction is an oxidation and the reverse reaction is a reduction **b** (*as modifier*): *an oxidation-reduction reaction* ▷ Also: **redox**

oxide ('ɒksaɪd) *n* **1** any compound of oxygen with another element **2** any organic compound in which an oxygen atom is bound to two alkyl groups; an ether [c18 from F, from *ox(ygène)* + *(ac)ide*]

oxidize *or* **oxidise** ('ɒksɪ,daɪz) *vb* **oxidizes, oxidizing, oxidized** *or* **oxidises, oxidising, oxidised 1** to undergo or cause to undergo a chemical reaction with oxygen, as in formation of an oxide **2** to form or cause to form a layer of metal oxide, as in rusting **3** to lose or cause to lose hydrogen atoms **4** to undergo or cause to undergo a decrease in the number of electrons > **,oxidi'zation** *or* **,oxidi'sation** *n*

oxidizing agent *n chem* a substance that oxidizes

Oo

another substance, being itself reduced in the process
oxlip (ˈɒksˌlɪp) *n* **1** a Eurasian woodland plant, with small drooping pale yellow flowers **2** Also called: **false oxlip** a similar and related plant that is a natural hybrid between the cowslip and primrose [OE *oxanslyppe*, lit.: ox's slippery dropping; see SLIP[3]]
oxo acid (ˈɒksəʊ) *n* another name for **oxyacid**
Oxon *abbrev for* Oxfordshire [from L *Oxonia*]
Oxon. *abbrev for* (in degree titles, etc) of Oxford [from L *Oxoniensis*]
Oxonian (ɒkˈsəʊnɪən) *adj* **1** of or relating to Oxford or Oxford University ▷ *n* **2** a member of Oxford University **3** an inhabitant or native of Oxford
oxpecker (ˈɒksˌpɛkə) *n* either of two African starlings, having flattened bills with which they obtain food from the hides of cattle. Also called: **tick-bird**
oxtail (ˈɒksˌteɪl) *n* the skinned tail of an ox, used esp in soups and stews
oxter (ˈəʊkstə) *n Scot, Irish, & N English dialect* the armpit [C16 from OE *oxta*]
oxtongue (ˈɒksˌtʌŋ) *n* **1** any of various Eurasian composite plants having oblong bristly leaves and clusters of dandelion-like flowers **2** any of various other plants having bristly tongue-shaped leaves **3** the tongue of an ox, braised or boiled as food
Oxus (ˈɒksəs) *n* the ancient name for the **Amu Darya**
oxy-[1] *combining form* denoting something sharp; acute: *oxytone* [from Gk, from *oxus*]
oxy-[2] *combining form* containing or using oxygen: *oxyacetylene*
oxyacetylene (ˌɒksɪəˈsɛtɪˌliːn) *n* **a** a mixture of oxygen and acetylene; used in torches for cutting or welding metals at high temperatures **b** (*as modifier*): *an oxyacetylene burner*
oxyacid (ˌɒksɪˈæsɪd) *n* any acid that contains oxygen with the acidic hydrogen atoms bound to oxygen atoms. Also called: **oxo acid**
oxygen (ˈɒksɪdʒən) *n* **a** a colourless odourless highly reactive gaseous element: the most abundant element in the earth's crust. Symbol: O; atomic no.: 8; atomic wt.: 15.9994 **b** (*as modifier*): *an oxygen mask* > **oxygenic** (ˌɒksɪˈdʒɛnɪk) *or* **oxygenous** (ɒkˈsɪdʒɪnəs) *adj*
oxygenate (ˈɒksɪdʒɪˌneɪt) *or* **oxygenize, oxygenise** *vb* **oxygenates, oxygenating, oxygenated** *or* **oxygenizes, oxygenizing, oxygenized; oxygenises, oxygenising, oxygenised** to enrich or be enriched with oxygen: *to oxygenate blood* > **ˌoxygenˈation** *n* > **ˈoxygenˌizer** *or* **ˈoxygenˌiser** *n*
oxygen tent *n med* a transparent enclosure covering a bedridden patient, into which oxygen is released to help maintain respiration
oxyhaemoglobin (ˌɒksɪˌhiːməʊˈgləʊbɪn) *n biochem* the bright red product formed when oxygen from the lungs combines with haemoglobin in the blood
oxyhydrogen (ˌɒksɪˈhaɪdrɪdʒən) *n* **a** a mixture of hydrogen and oxygen used to provide an intense flame for welding **b** (*as modifier*): *an oxyhydrogen blowpipe*
oxymoron (ˌɒksɪˈmɔːrɒn) *n, pl* **oxymora** (-ˈmɔːrə) *Rhetoric.* an epigrammatic effect, by which contradictory terms are used in conjunction: *living death* [C17 via NL from Gk *oxumōron*, from *oxus* sharp + *mōros* stupid]
oxytetracycline (ˌɒksɪˌtɛtrəˈsaɪklɪn) *n* a broad-spectrum antibiotic obtained from *Streptomyces rimosus*
oyer and terminer (ˈɔɪə; ˈtɜːmɪnə) *n* **1** *English law* (formerly) a commission issued to judges to try cases on assize **2** the court in which such a hearing was held [C15 from Anglo-Norman, from *oyer* to hear + *terminer* to judge]
oyez *or* **oyes** (əʊˈjɛs, -ˈjɛz) *sentence substitute* **1** a cry, usually uttered three times, by a public crier or court official for silence and attention before making a proclamation ▷ *n* **2** such a cry [C15 via Anglo-Norman from OF *oiez!* hear!]
-oyl *suffix of nouns* (in chemistry) indicating an acyl group or radical: *ethanoyl, methanoyl* [C20 from O(XYGEN) + -YL]
Oyo (ˈəʊjəʊ) *n* a state of SW Nigeria, formed in 1976 from part of Western State. Capital: Ibadan. Pop: 3 900 803 (1995 est). Area: 28 454 sq km (10 986 sq miles)
oyster (ˈɔɪstə) *n* **1a** an edible marine bivalve mollusc having a rough irregularly shaped shell and occurring on the sea bed, mostly in coastal waters **1b** (*as modifier*): *oyster farm; oyster knife* **2** any of various similar and related molluscs, such as the pearl oyster and the saddle oyster **3** the oyster-shaped piece of dark meat in the hollow of the pelvic bone of a fowl **4** something from which advantage, delight, profit, etc, may be derived: *the world is his oyster* **5** *inf* a very uncommunicative person ▷ *vb* **6** (*intr*) to dredge for, gather, or raise oysters [C14 *oistre*, from OF *uistre*, from L *ostrea*, from Gk *ostreon*; rel. to Gk *osteon* bone, *ostrakon* shell]
oyster bed *n* a place, esp on the sea bed, where oysters breed and grow naturally or are cultivated for food or pearls. Also called: **oyster bank, oyster park**
oystercatcher (ˈɔɪstəˌkætʃə) *n* a shore bird having a black or black-and-white plumage and a long stout laterally compressed red bill
oyster crab *n* any of several small soft-bodied crabs that live as commensals in the mantles of oysters
oyster plant *n* **1** another name for **salsify** (sense 1) **2** Also called: **sea lungwort** a prostrate coastal plant with clusters of blue flowers
oz *or* **oz.** *abbrev for* ounce [from It. *onza*]
Oz (ɒz) *n Austral sl* Australia
Özal (əʊˈzɑːl) *n* **Turgut** (ˈtɜːgʊt) 1927–93, Turkish statesman: prime minister of Turkey (1983–89); president (1989–93)
Ozalid (ˈɒzəlɪd) *n* **1** *trademark* a method of duplicating type matter, illustrations, etc, when printed on translucent paper **2** a reproduction produced by this method
Ozark Plateau (ˈəʊzɑːk) *n or* **Ozark Mountains** *or* **Ozarks** *pl n* an eroded plateau in S Missouri, N Arkansas, and NE Oklahoma. Area: about 130 000 sq km (50 000 sq miles)
ozocerite *or* **ozokerite** (əʊˈzəʊkəˌraɪt) *n* a brown or greyish wax that occurs associated with petroleum and is used for making candles and waxed paper [C19 from G *Ozokerit*, from Gk *ozein* to smell + *kēros* beeswax]
ozone (ˈəʊzəʊn, əʊˈzəʊn) *n* **1** a colourless gas with a chlorine-like odour, formed by an electric discharge in oxygen: a strong oxidizing agent, used in bleaching, sterilizing water, purifying air, etc Formula: O_3. Technical name: **trioxygen** **2** *inf* clean bracing air, as found at the seaside [C19 from G *Ozon*, from Gk: smell] > **ozonic** (əʊˈzɒnɪk) *or* **ˈozonous** *adj*
ozone-friendly *adj* not harmful to the ozone layer; using substances that do not produce gases harmful to the ozone layer: *an ozone-friendly refrigerator*
ozone layer *n* the region of the stratosphere with the highest concentration of ozone molecules, which by absorbing high-energy solar ultraviolet radiation protects organisms on earth. Also called: **ozonosphere**
ozonize *or* **ozonise** (ˈəʊzəʊˌnaɪz) *vb* **ozonizes, ozonizing, ozonized** *or* **ozonises, ozonising, ozonised** (*tr*) **1** to convert (oxygen) into ozone **2** to treat (a substance) with ozone > **ˌozoniˈzation** *or* **ˌozoniˈsation** *n* > **ˈozoˌnizer** *or* **ˈozoˌniser** *n*
ozonosphere (əʊˈzəʊnəˌsfɪə, -ˈzɒnə-) *n* another name for **ozone layer**

Pp

p *or* **P** (piː) *n, pl* **p's, P's,** *or* **Ps 1** the 16th letter of the English alphabet **2** a speech sound represented by this letter **3 mind one's p's and q's** to be careful to behave correctly and use polite or suitable language

p *symbol for:* **1** (in Britain) penny *or* pence **2** *music* piano: an instruction to play quietly **3** *physics* pico- **4** *physics* **4a** momentum **4b** proton **4c** pressure

P *symbol for:* **1** *chem* phosphorus **2** *physics* **2a** parity **2b** poise **2c** power **2d** pressure **3** (on road signs) parking **4** *chess* pawn **5** *currency* **5a** (the former) peseta **5b** peso **6** (of a medicine or drug) used to label medicines that can be obtained without a prescription, but only at a shop at which there is a pharmacist

p. *abbrev for:* **1** (*pl* **pp.**) page **2** part **3** participle **4** past **5** per **6** post [L: after] **7** pro [L: in favour of; for]

p- *prefix* short for **para-**[1] (sense 6)

P45 *n* (in Britain) **1** a severance form issued by the Inland Revenue via an employer to a person leaving employment **2 get one's P45** *inf* to be dismissed from one's employment

pa[1] (pɑː) *n* an informal word for **father**

pa[2] or **pah** (pɑː) *n* NZ **1** a Maori village or settlement **2** *history* a Maori defensive position and settlement on a hilltop

Pa 1 *the chemical symbol for* protactinium **2** *symbol for* pascal

PA *abbrev for:* **1** personal assistant **2** *mil* Post Adjutant **3** power of attorney **4** press agent **5** Press Association **6** private account **7** public-address system **8** publicity agent **9** Publishers Association **10** purchasing agent **11** *insurance* particular average

▷ www.pa.press.net

▷ www.publishers.org.uk

Pa. *abbrev for* Pennsylvania

p.a. *abbrev for* per annum [L: yearly]

Pablum (ˈpɑːbləm) *n trademark* a cereal food for infants, developed in Canada

Pabst (*German* paːpst) *n* **G**(**eorge**) **W**(**ilhelm**) 1885–1967, German film director, whose films include *Joyless Street* (1925), *Pandora's Box* (1929), and *The Last Act* (1954)

pabulum (ˈpæbjʊləm) *n rare* **1** food **2** food for thought, esp when bland or dull [c17 from L, from *pascere* to feed]

PABX (in Britain) *abbrev for* private automatic branch exchange. See also **PBX**

Pac. *abbrev for* Pacific

PAC *abbrev for* Pan-Africanist Congress

paca (ˈpɑːkə, ˈpækə) *n* a large burrowing rodent of Central and South America, having white-spotted brown fur [c17 from Sp., from Amerind]

pace[1] (peɪs) *n* **1a** a single step in walking **1b** the distance covered by a step **2** a measure of length equal to the average length of a stride, approximately 3 feet **3** speed of movement, esp of walking or running **4** rate or style of proceeding at some activity: *to live at a fast pace* **5** manner or action of stepping, walking, etc; gait **6** any of the manners in which a horse or other quadruped walks or runs **7** a manner of moving, sometimes developed in the horse, in which the two legs on the same side are moved at the same time **8 keep pace with** to proceed at the same speed as **9 put** (**someone**) **through his** *or* **her paces** to test the ability of (someone) **10 set the pace** to determine the rate at which a group runs or walks or proceeds at some other activity ▷ *vb* **paces, pacing, paced 11** (*tr*) to set or determine the pace for, as in a race **12** (often foll by *about, up and down,* etc) to walk with regular slow or fast paces, as in boredom, agitation, etc: *to pace the room* **13** (*tr;* often foll by *out*) to measure by paces: *to pace out the distance* **14** (*intr*) to walk with slow regular strides **15** (*intr*) (of a horse) to move at the pace (the specially developed gait) [c13 via OF from L *passūs* step, from *pandere* to extend (the legs as in walking)]

pace[2] (ˈpeɪsɪ; *Latin* ˈpɑːkɛ) *prep* with due deference to: used to acknowledge politely someone who disagrees [c19 from L, from *pāx* peace]

PACE (peɪs) *n* (in England and Wales) *acronym for* Police and Criminal Evidence Act

pace bowler *n cricket* a bowler who characteristically delivers the ball rapidly

pacemaker (ˈpeɪsˌmeɪkə) *n* **1** a person, horse, vehicle, etc, used in a race or speed trial to set the pace **2** a person, organization, etc, regarded as being the leader in a particular activity **3** Also called: **cardiac pacemaker** a small area of specialized tissue within the wall of the heart whose spontaneous electrical activity initiates and controls the heartbeat **4** Also called: **artificial pacemaker** an electronic device to assume the functions of the natural cardiac pacemaker

pacer (ˈpeɪsə) *n* **1** a horse trained to move at a special gait **2** another word for **pacemaker** (sense 1)

pacesetter (ˈpeɪsˌsɛtə) *n* another word for **pacemaker** (senses 1, 2)

paceway (ˈpeɪsˌweɪ) *n Austral* a racecourse for trotting and pacing

Pachelbel (*German* ˈpakəlbɛl) *n* **Johann** (ˈjohan) 1653–1706, German organist and composer, noted esp for his popular *Canon in D Major*

pachinko (pəˈtʃɪŋkəʊ) *n* a Japanese game similar to pinball [c20 possibly from Japanese *pachin*, imitative of the sound of a ball being fired by a trigger]

pachisi (pəˈtʃiːzɪ) *n* an Indian game somewhat resembling backgammon, played on a cruciform board using six cowries as dice [c18 from Hindi, from *pacīs* twenty-five (the highest throw)]

Pachuca (*Spanish* paˈtʃuka) *n* a city in central Mexico, capital of Hidalgo state, in the Sierra Madre Oriental: silver mines; university (1961). Pop: 231 089 (2000 est)

pachyderm (ˈpækɪˌdɜːm) *n* any very large thick-skinned mammal, such as an elephant, rhinoceros, or hippopotamus [c19 from F *pachyderme*, from Gk *pakhudermos*, from *pakhus* thick + *derma* skin] > ˌ**pachyˈdermatous** *adj*

pacific (pəˈsɪfɪk) *adj* **1** tending or conducive to peace; conciliatory **2** not aggressive **3** free from conflict; peaceful [c16 from OF, from L *pācificus*, from *pāx* peace + *facere* to make] > **paˈcifically** *adv*

Pacific (pəˈsɪfɪk) *n* **1** the short for **Pacific Ocean** ▷ *adj* **2** of or relating to the Pacific Ocean or its islands

Pacific Islands *pl n* a former Trust Territory; an island group in the W Pacific Ocean, mandated to Japan after World War I and assigned to the US by the United Nations in 1947: comprised 2141 islands (96 inhabited) of the Caroline, Marshall, and Mariana groups (excluding Guam). In 1978 the Northern Marianas became a commonwealth in union with the US. The three remaining entities consisting of the Marshall Islands, the Republic of Belau (formerly Palau), and the Federated States of Micronesia became self-governing during the period 1979–80. In 1982 they signed agreements of free association with the US. Administrative centre: Saipan (Mariana Islands). Land area: about 1800 sq km (700 sq miles), scattered over about 7 500 000 sq km (3 000 000 sq miles) of ocean

Pacific Northwest *n* the region of North America lying north of the Columbia River and west of the Rockies

Pacific Ocean *n* the world's largest and deepest ocean, lying between Asia and Australia and North and South America: almost landlocked in the north, linked with the Arctic Ocean only by the Bering Strait, and extending to Antarctica in the south; has exceptionally deep trenches, and a large number of volcanic and coral islands. Area: about 165 760 000 sq km (64 000 000 sq miles). Average depth: 4215 m (14 050 ft). Greatest depth: Challenger Deep (in the Marianas Trench), 11 033 m (37 073 ft). Greatest width: (between Panama and Mindanao, Philippines) 17 066 km (10 600 miles)

Pacific rim *n* the regions, countries, etc that lie on the western shores of the Pacific Ocean, esp in the context of their developing manufacturing capacity and consumer markets

Pacific Rose *n* a large variety of eating apple from New Zealand, with sweet flesh

pacifier (ˈpæsɪˌfaɪə) *n* **1** a person or thing that pacifies **2** *US & Canad* a baby's dummy or teething ring

pacifism (ˈpæsɪˌfɪzəm) *n* **1** the belief that violence of any kind is unjustifiable and that one should not participate in war, etc **2** the belief that international disputes can be settled by arbitration rather than war > ˈ**pacifist** *n, adj*

pacify (ˈpæsɪˌfaɪ) *vb* **pacifies, pacifying, pacified** (*tr*) **1** to calm the anger or agitation of; mollify **2** to restore to peace or order [c15 from OF *pacifier*; see PACIFIC] > ˈ**paciˌfiable** *adj* > **pacification** (ˌpæsɪfɪˈkeɪʃən) *n*

Pacino (pəˈtʃiːnəʊ) *n* **Al**, full name *Alfredo James Pacino*. born 1940, US film actor; his films include *The Godfather* (1972), *Dog Day Afternoon* (1975), *Scent of a Woman* (1992), for which he won an Oscar, and *Insomnia* (2002)

pack[1] (pæk) *n* **1a** a bundle or load, esp one carried on the back **1b** (*as modifier*): *a pack animal* **2** a collected amount of anything **3** a complete set of similar things, esp a set of 52 playing cards **4** a group of animals of the same kind, esp hunting animals: *a pack of hounds* **5** any group or band that associates together, esp for criminal purposes **6** any group or set regarded dismissively: *a pack of fools; a pack of lies* **7** *rugby* the forwards of a team **8** the basic organizational unit of Cub Scouts and Brownie Guides **9** *US & Canad* same as **packet** (sense 1) **10** short for **pack ice** **11** the quantity of something, such as food, packaged for preservation **12** *med* a sheet or blanket, either damp or dry, for wrapping about the body, esp for its soothing effect **13** another name for **rucksack** *or* **backpack** **14** Also called: **face pack** a cream treatment that cleanses and tones the skin **15** a parachute folded and ready for use **16** **go to the pack** *Austral & NZ inf* to fall into a worse state or condition **17** *computing* another name for **deck** (sense 4) ▷ *vb* **18** to place or arrange (articles) in (a container), such as clothes in a suitcase **19** (*tr*) to roll up into a bundle **20** (when *passive*, often foll by *out*) to press tightly together; cram: *the audience packed into the foyer; the hall was packed out* **21** to form (snow, ice, etc) into a hard compact mass or (of snow, etc) to become compacted **22** (*tr*) to press in or cover tightly **23** (*tr*) to load (a horse, donkey, etc) with a burden **24** (often foll by *off* or *away*) to send away or go away, esp hastily **25** (*tr*) to seal (a joint) by inserting a layer of compressible material between the faces **26** (*tr*) *med* to treat with a pack **27** (*tr*) *sl* to be capable of inflicting (a blow, etc): *he packs a mean punch* **28** (*tr*) *US inf* to carry or wear habitually: *he packs a gun* **29** (*tr*; often foll by *in, into, to*, etc) *US, Canad, & NZ* to carry (goods, etc), esp on the back **30** **send packing** *inf* to dismiss peremptorily ▷ See also **pack in, pack up** [c13 from ?] > ˈ**packable** *adj*

pack[2] (pæk) *vb* (*tr*) to fill (a legislative body, committee, etc) with one's own supporters: *to pack a jury* [c16 ? changed from PACT]

package (ˈpækɪdʒ) *n* **1** any wrapped or boxed object or group of objects **2a** a proposition, offer, or thing for sale in which separate items are offered together as a unit **2b** (*as modifier*): *a package holiday; a package deal* **3** the act or process of packing or packaging **4** *computing* a set of programs designed for a specific type of problem **5** the usual US and Canad word for **packet** (sense 1) ▷ *vb* **packages, packaging, packaged** (*tr*) **6** to wrap in or put into a package **7** to design and produce a package for (retail goods) **8** to group (separate items) together as a single unit **9** to compile (complete books) for a publisher to market > '**packager** *n*

package store *n US & Canad* another name for **liquor store**

packaging ('pækɪdʒɪŋ) *n* **1** the box or wrapping in which a product is offered for sale **2** the presentation of a person, product, etc, to the public in a way designed to build up a favourable image

pack drill *n* a military punishment of marching about carrying a full pack of equipment

packer ('pækə) *n* **1** a person or company whose business is to pack goods, esp food: *a meat packer* **2** a person or machine that packs

packet ('pækɪt) *n* **1** a small or medium-sized container of cardboard, paper, etc, often together with its contents: *a packet of biscuits*. Usual US and Canad word: **package, pack 2** a small package; parcel **3** Also called: **packet boat** a boat that transports mail, passengers, goods, etc, on a fixed short route **4** *sl* a large sum of money: *to cost a packet* **5** *computing* a unit into which a larger piece of data is broken down for more efficient transmission ▷ *vb* **6** (*tr*) to wrap up in a packet or as a packet [c16 from OF *pacquet*, from *pacquer* to pack, from ODu. *pak* a pack]

packhorse ('pæk,hɔːs) *n* a horse used to transport goods, equipment, etc

pack ice *n* a large area of floating ice, consisting of pieces that have become massed together

pack in *vb* (*tr, adv*) *Brit & NZ inf* to stop doing (something) (esp in **pack it in**)

packing ('pækɪŋ) *n* **1a** material used to cushion packed goods **1b** (*as modifier*): *a packing needle* **2** the packaging of foodstuffs **3** any substance or material used to make joints watertight or gastight

pack rat *n* a rat of W North America, having a long tail that is furry in some species

packsaddle ('pæk,sædᵊl) *n* a saddle hung with packs, equipment, etc, used on a pack animal

packthread ('pæk,θrɛd) *n* a strong twine for sewing or tying up packages

pack up *vb* (*adv*) **1** to put (things) away in a proper or suitable place **2** *inf* to give up (an attempt) or stop doing (something) **3** (*intr*) (of an engine, etc) to fail to operate; break down

pact (pækt) *n* an agreement or compact between two or more parties, nations, etc [c15 from OF *pacte*, from L *pactum*, from *pacīscī* to agree]

pad[1] (pæd) *n* **1** a thick piece of soft material used to make something comfortable, give it shape, or protect it **2** Also called: **stamp pad, ink pad** a block of firm absorbent material soaked with ink for transferring to a rubber stamp **3** Also called: **notepad, writing pad** a number of sheets of paper fastened together along one edge **4** a flat piece of stiff material used to back a piece of blotting paper **5a** the fleshy cushion-like underpart of the foot of a cat, dog, etc **5b** any of the parts constituting such a structure **6** any of various level surfaces or flat-topped structures, such as a launch pad **7** the large flat floating leaf of the water lily **8** *sl* a person's residence ▷ *vb* **pads, padding, padded** (*tr*) **9** to line, stuff, or fill out with soft material, esp in order to protect or shape **10** (often foll by *out*) to inflate with irrelevant or false information: *to pad out a story* [c16 from ?]

pad[2] (pæd) *vb* **pads, padding, padded 1** (*intr;* often foll by *along, up*, etc) to walk with a soft or muffled tread **2** (when *intr*, often foll by *around*) to travel (a route, etc) on foot, esp at a slow pace; tramp: *to pad around the country* ▷ *n* **3** a dull soft sound, esp of footsteps [c16 ?from MDu. *paden*, from *pad* PATH]

Padang ('pɑːdɑːŋ) *n* a port in W Indonesia, in W Sumatra at the foot of the **Padang Highlands** on the Indian Ocean. Pop: 721 500 (1995 est)

padded cell *n* a room, esp one in a mental hospital, with padded surfaces in which violent inmates are placed

padding ('pædɪŋ) *n* **1** any soft material used to pad clothes, etc **2** superfluous material put into a speech or written work to pad it out; waffle **3** inflated or false entries in a financial account, esp an expense account

paddle[1] ('pædᵊl) *n* **1** a short light oar with a flat blade at one or both ends, used without a rowlock **2** Also called: **float** a blade of a water wheel or paddle wheel **3** a period of paddling: *to go for a paddle upstream* **4a** a paddle wheel used to propel a boat **4b** (*as modifier*): *a paddle steamer* **5** any of various instruments shaped like a paddle and used for beating, mixing, etc **6** a table-tennis bat **7** the flattened limb of a seal, turtle, etc, specialized for swimming ▷ *vb* **paddles, paddling, paddled 8** to propel (a canoe, etc) with a paddle **9 paddle one's own canoe 9a** to be self-sufficient **9b** to mind one's own business **10** (*tr*) to stir or mix with or as if with a paddle **11** to row (a boat) steadily, but not at full pressure **12** (*intr*) to swim with short rapid strokes, like a dog **13** (*tr*) *US & Canad inf* to spank [c15 from ?] > '**paddler** *n*

paddle[2] ('pædᵊl) *vb* **paddles, paddling, paddled** (*mainly intr*) **1** to walk or play barefoot in shallow water, mud, etc **2** to dabble the fingers, hands, or feet in water **3** to walk unsteadily, like a baby **4** (*tr*) *arch* to fondle with the fingers ▷ *n* **5** the act of paddling in water [c16 from ?] > '**paddler** *n*

paddle wheel *n* a large wheel fitted with paddles, turned by an engine to propel a vessel

paddock ('pædək) *n* **1** a small enclosed field, often for grazing or training horses **2** (in horse racing) the enclosure in which horses are paraded and mounted before a race **3** *Austral & NZ* any area of fenced land [c17 var. of dialect *parrock*, from OE *pearruc* enclosure, of Gmc origin. See PARK]

paddy[1] ('pædɪ) *n, pl* **paddies 1** Also called: **paddy field** a field planted with rice **2** rice as a growing crop or when harvested but not yet milled [from Malay *pādī*]

Pp

paddy[2] ('pædɪ) *n, pl* **paddies** *Brit inf* a fit of temper [c19 from *Paddy* inf. name for an Irishman]

pademelon *or* **paddymelon** ('pædɪ,mɛlən) *n* a small wallaby of coastal scrubby regions of Australia [c19 of Abor. origin]

Paderborn (*German* paːdər'bɔrn) *n* a market town in NW Germany, in North Rhine-Westphalia: scene of the meeting between Charlemagne and Pope Leo III (799 AD) that led to the foundation of the Holy Roman Empire. Pop: 131 851 (1999 est)

Paderewski (*Polish* padɛ'rɛfski) *n* **Ignace Jan** (iɲas jan) 1860–1941, Polish pianist, composer, and statesman; prime minister (1919)

padkos ('pæt,kɒs) *pl, n S African* snacks and provisions for a journey [Afrik., lit.: road food]

padlock ('pæd,lɒk) *n* **1** a detachable lock having a hinged or sliding shackle, which can be used to secure a door, lid, etc, by passing the shackle through rings or staples ▷ *vb* **2** (*tr*) to fasten as with a padlock [c15 *pad*, from ?]

Padova ('paːdova) *n* the Italian name for **Padua**

padre ('pɑːdrɪ) *n inf* (*sometimes cap*) **1** father: used to address or refer to a priest **2** a chaplain to the armed forces [via Sp. or It. from L *pater* father]

padsaw ('pæd,sɔː) *n* a small narrow saw used for cutting curves [c19 from PAD[1] (in the sense: a handle that can be fitted to various tools) + SAW[1]]

Padua ('pædʒʊə, 'pædjʊə) *n* a city in NE Italy, in Veneto: important in Roman and Renaissance times; university (1222); botanical garden (1545). Pop: 211 391 (2000 est). Latin name: **Patavium** (pə'teɪvɪəm) Italian name: **Padova**

Padus ('peɪdəs) *n* the Latin name for the **Po**[2]

paean *or US* (*sometimes*) **pean** ('piːən) *n* **1** a hymn sung in ancient Greece in thanksgiving to a deity **2** any song of praise **3** enthusiastic praise: *the film received a paean from the critics* [C16 via L from Gk *paiān* hymn to Apollo, from his title *Paiān*, the physician of the gods]

paediatrician *or esp US* **pediatrician** (ˌpiːdɪəˈtrɪʃən) *n* a medical practitioner who specializes in paediatrics

paediatrics *or esp US* **pediatrics** (ˌpiːdɪˈætrɪks) *n (functioning as sing)* the branch of medical science concerned with children and their diseases > ˌ**paediˈatric** *or esp US* ˌ**pediˈatric** *adj*

paedo-, *before a vowel* **paed-,** *or esp US* **pedo-, ped-** *combining form* indicating a child or children: *paedophilia* [from Gk *pais, paid-* child]

paedomorphosis (ˌpiːdəˈmɔːfəsɪs) *n* the resemblance of adult animals to the young of their ancestors

paedophilia *or esp US* **pedophilia** (ˌpiːdəʊˈfɪlɪə) *n* the condition of being sexually attracted to children > **paedophile** *or esp US* **pedophile** (ˈpiːdəʊˌfaɪl) *or* ˌ**paedoˈphiliˌac** *or esp US* ˌ**pedoˈphiliˌac** *n, adj*

paella (paɪˈɛlə) *n, pl* **paellas** (-ləz) **1** a Spanish dish made from rice, shellfish, chicken, and vegetables **2** the pan in which a paella is cooked [from Catalan, from OF *paelle*, from L *patella* small pan]

paeony (ˈpiːənɪ) *n, pl* **paeonies** a variant spelling of **peony**

Paestum (ˈpɛstəm) *n* an ancient Greek colony on the coast of Lucania in S Italy

PAGAD *abbrev for S African* People Against Gangsterism and Drugs, a popular organization formed in the Western Cape around 1995

pagan (ˈpeɪgən) *n* **1** a member of a group professing any religion other than Christianity, Judaism, or Islam **2** a person without any religion; heathen ▷ *adj* **3** of or relating to pagans **4** heathen; irreligious [C14 from Church L *pāgānus* civilian (hence, not a soldier of Christ), from L: villager, from *pāgus* village] > ˈ**pagandom** *n* > ˈ**paganish** *adj* > ˈ**paganism** *n*
▷ www.paganfed.demon.co.uk/
▷ www.pagansunite.com/

Paganini (*Italian* pagaˈniːni) *n* **Niccolò** (nikkoˈlɔ) 1782–1840, Italian violinist and composer

paganize *or* **paganise** (ˈpeɪgəˌnaɪz) *vb* **paganizes, paganizing, paganized** *or* **paganises, paganising, paganised** to become pagan or convert to paganism

page[1] (peɪdʒ) *n* **1** one side of one of the leaves of a book, newspaper, etc, or the written or printed matter it bears **2** such a leaf considered as a unit **3** an episode, phase, or period: *a glorious page in the revolution* **4** a screenful of information from a website, teletext service, etc, displayed on a television monitor or visual display unit ▷ *vb* **pages, paging, paged 5** another word for **paginate** [C15 via OF from L *pāgina*]

page[2] (peɪdʒ) *n* **1** a boy employed to run errands, carry messages, etc, for the guests in a hotel, club, etc **2** a youth in attendance at official functions or ceremonies, esp weddings **3** *medieval history* **3a** a boy in training for knighthood in personal attendance on a knight **3b** a youth in the personal service of a person of rank ▷ *vb* **pages, paging, paged** *(tr)* **4** to call out the name of (a person), esp by a loudspeaker system, so as to give him a message **5** to call (a person) by an electronic device, such as a bleeper **6** to act as a page to or attend as a page [C13 via OF from It. *paggio*, prob. from Gk *paidion* boy, from *pais* child]

Page (peɪdʒ) *n* Sir **Frederick Handley** 1885–1962, English pioneer in the design and manufacture of aircraft

pageant (ˈpædʒənt) *n* **1** an elaborate colourful display portraying scenes from history, etc **2** any magnificent or showy display, procession, etc [C14 from Med. L *pāgina* scene of a play, from L: PAGE[1]]

pageantry (ˈpædʒəntrɪ) *n, pl* **pageantries 1** spectacular display or ceremony **2** *arch* pageants collectively

pageboy (ˈpeɪdʒˌbɔɪ) *n* **1** a smooth medium-length hairstyle with the ends of the hair curled under **2** a less common word for **page**[2]

pager (ˈpeɪdʒə) *n* an electronic device, capable of receiving short messages, used by people who need to be contacted urgently

page-three *n modifier Brit* denoting a scantily dressed attractive girl, as photographed on page three of some tabloid newspapers

page-turner *n* a very exciting or interesting book [C20 from the notion that a reader cannot stop turning the pages]

pageview (ˈpeɪdʒˌvjuː) *n computing* an electronic page of information displayed in response to a user's request, such as one page of a website

paginate (ˈpædʒɪˌneɪt) *vb* **paginates, paginating, paginated** *(tr)* to number the pages of (a book, manuscript, etc) in sequence ▷ Cf **foliate** > ˌ**pagiˈnation** *n*

Paglia (ˈpæglɪə) *n* **Camille** born 1947, US writer and academic, noted for provocative cultural studies such as *Sexual Personae* (1990) and *Vamps and Tramps* (1995)

Pagnol (*French* panjol) *n* **Marcel** (**Paul**) (marsɛl) 1895–1974, French dramatist, film director, and novelist, noted for his depiction of Provençal life in such films as *Manon des Sources* (1952; remade 1986)

pagoda (pəˈgəʊdə) *n* an Indian or Far Eastern temple, esp a tower, usually pyramidal and having many storeys [C17 from Port. *pagode*, ult. from Sansk. *bhagavatī* divine]

pagoda tree *n* a Chinese leguminous tree with ornamental white flowers

Pago Pago (ˈpɑːŋgəʊ ˈpɑːŋgəʊ) *n* a port in American Samoa, on SE Tutuila Island. Pop: 4000 (1990). Former name: **Pango Pango**

Pahang (pəˈhʌŋ) *n* a state of Peninsular Malaysia, on the South China Sea: the largest Malayan state; mountainous and heavily forested. Capital: Kuantan. Pop: 1 231 176 (2000). Area: 35 964 sq km (13 886 sq miles)

Pahlavi (ˈpɑːləvɪ) *n* **1 Mohammed Reza** (ˈriːzə) 1919–80, shah of Iran (1941–79); forced into exile (1979) during civil unrest following which an Islamic republic was established led by the Ayatollah Khomeini **2** his father, **Reza** 1877–1944, shah of Iran (1925–41) Originally an army officer, he gained power by a coup d'état (1921) and was chosen shah by the National Assembly. He reorganized the army and did much to modernize Iran

Pahsien (ˈpɑːˈʃjɛn) *n* another name for **Chongqing**

paid (peɪd) *vb* **1** the past tense and past participle of **pay**[1] **2 put paid to** *chiefly Brit & NZ* to end or destroy: *breaking his leg put paid to his hopes of running in the Olympics*

paid-up *adj* **1** having paid the required fee to be a member of an organization, etc **2** denoting a security in which all the instalments have been paid; fully paid: *a paid-up share* **3** denoting all the money that a company has received from its shareholders: *the paid-up capital* **4** denoting an endowment assurance policy on which the payment of premiums has stopped and the surrender value has been used to purchase a new single-premium policy

Paignton (ˈpeɪntən) *n* a town and resort in SW England, in Devon: administratively part of Torbay since 1968

pail (peɪl) *n* **1** a bucket, esp one made of wood or metal **2** Also called: **pailful** the quantity that fills a pail [OE *pægel*]

paillasse (ˈpælɪˌæs, ˌpælɪˈæs) *n* a variant spelling (esp US) of **palliasse**

pain (peɪn) *n* **1** the sensation of acute physical hurt or discomfort caused by injury, illness, etc **2** emotional suffering or mental distress **3 on pain of** subject to the penalty of **4** Also called: **pain in the neck** *inf* a person or thing that is a nuisance ▷ *vb (tr)* **5** to cause (a person) hurt, grief, anxiety, etc **6** *inf* to annoy; irritate ▷ See also **pains** [C13 from OF *peine*, from L *poena* punishment, grief, from Gk *poinē* penalty] > ˈ**painless** *adj*

▷ www.painconsultant.com
▷ www.theacpa.org

Paine (peɪn) *n* **Thomas** 1737–1809, American political pamphleteer, born in England. His works include the pamphlets *Common Sense* (1776) and *Crisis* (1776–83), supporting the American colonists' fight for independence; *The Rights of Man* (1791–92), a justification of the French Revolution; and *The Age of Reason* (1794–96), a defence of deism

pained (peɪnd) *adj* having or expressing pain or distress, esp mental or emotional distress

painful (ˈpeɪnfʊl) *adj* **1** causing pain; distressing: *a painful duty* **2** affected with pain **3** tedious or difficult **4** *inf* extremely bad > **ˈpainfully** *adv* > **ˈpainfulness** *n*

painkiller (ˈpeɪn,kɪlə) *n* **1** an analgesic drug or agent **2** anything that relieves pain

pains (peɪnz) *pl n* **1** care or trouble (esp in **take pains, be at pains to**) **2** painful sensations experienced during contractions in childbirth; labour pains

painstaking (ˈpeɪnz,teɪkɪŋ) *adj* extremely careful, esp as to fine detail > **ˈpains,takingly** *adv* > **ˈpains,takingness** *n*

paint (peɪnt) *n* **1** a substance used for decorating or protecting a surface, esp a mixture consisting of a solid pigment suspended in a liquid that dries to form a hard coating **2** a dry film of paint on a surface **3** *inf* face make-up, such as rouge **4** short for **greasepaint** ▷ *vb* **5** to make (a picture) of (a figure, landscape, etc) with paint applied to a surface such as canvas **6** to coat (a surface, etc) with paint, as in decorating **7** (*tr*) to apply (liquid, etc) onto (a surface): *she painted the cut with antiseptic* **8** (*tr*) to apply make-up onto (the face, lips, etc) **9** (*tr*) to describe vividly in words **10 paint the town red** *inf* to celebrate uninhibitedly [c13 from OF *peint* painted, from *peindre* to paint, from L *pingere* to paint] > **ˈpainty** *adj*

paintball game (ˈpeɪnt,bɔːl) *n* a game in which teams of players simulate a military skirmish, shooting each other with paint pellets that explode on impact

▷ www.angelfire.com/wi2/ipa

paintbox (ˈpeɪnt,bɒks) *n* a box containing a tray of dry watercolour paints

paintbrush (ˈpeɪnt,brʌʃ) *n* a brush used to apply paint

Painted Desert *n* a section of the high plateau country of N central Arizona, along the N side of the Little Colorado River Valley: brilliant-coloured rocks; occupied largely by Navaho and Hopi Indians. Area: about 20 000 sq km (7500 sq miles)

painted lady *n* a migratory butterfly with pale brownish-red mottled wings

painter[1] (ˈpeɪntə) *n* **1** a person who paints surfaces as a trade **2** an artist who paints pictures > **ˈpainterly** *adj*

painter[2] (ˈpeɪntə) *n* a line attached to the bow of a boat for tying it up [c15 prob. from OF *penteur* strong rope]

painting (ˈpeɪntɪŋ) *n* **1** the art of applying paints to canvas, etc **2** a picture made in this way **3** the act of applying paint to a surface

paint stripper *or* **remover** *n* a liquid, often caustic, used to remove paint from a surface

paintwork (ˈpeɪnt,wɜːk) *n* a surface, such as wood or a car body, that is painted

pair (pɛə) *n, pl* **pairs** *or (functioning as sing or pl)* **pair 1** two identical or similar things matched for use together: *a pair of socks* **2** two persons, animals, things, etc, used or grouped together: *a pair of horses; a pair of scoundrels* **3** an object considered to be two identical or similar things joined together: *a pair of trousers* **4** two people joined in love or marriage **5** a male and a female animal of the same species kept for breeding purposes **6** *parliament* **6a** two opposed members who both agree not to vote on a specified motion **6b** the agreement so made **7** two playing cards of the same rank or denomination **8** one member of a matching pair: *I can't find the pair to this glove* ▷ *vb* **9** (often foll by *off*) to arrange or fall into groups of twos **10** to group or be grouped in matching pairs **11** to join or be joined in marriage; mate or couple **12** (when *tr, usually passive*) *parliament* to form or cause to form a pair [c13 from OF *paire*, from L *paria* equal (things), from *pār* equal]

> **USAGE** Like other collective nouns, *pair* takes a singular or a plural verb according to whether it is seen as a unit or as a collection of two things: *the pair are said to dislike each other; a pair of good shoes is essential*

paisley (ˈpeɪzlɪ) *n* **1** a pattern of small curving shapes with intricate detailing **2** a soft fine wool fabric traditionally printed with this pattern **3** a shawl made of this fabric, popular in the late 19th century **4** (*modifier*) of or decorated with this pattern: *a paisley scarf* [c19 after PAISLEY[1]]

▷ www.paisley.org/paisley1/history/pattern.php

Paisley[1] (ˈpeɪzlɪ) *n* an industrial town in SW Scotland, the administrative centre of Renfrewshire: one of the world's chief centres for the manufacture of thread, linen, and gauze in the 19th century. Pop: 75 526 (1991)

Paisley[2] (ˈpeɪzlɪ) *n* **1 Bob** 1919–96, English footballer and manager **2** Rev **Ian** (**Richard Kyle**) born 1926, Northern Ireland politician and Presbyterian minister; cofounder (1972) and leader of the Ulster Democratic Unionist Party

pajamas (pəˈdʒɑːməz) *pl n* the US spelling of **pyjamas**

Pakeha (ˈpɑːkɪ,hɑː) *n* NZ a European, as distinct from a Maori: *Maori and Pakeha* [from Maori]

Paki (ˈpækɪ) *Brit sl, offens* ▷ *n, pl* **Pakis 1** a Pakistani or person of Pakistani descent ▷ *adj* **2** Pakistani or of Pakistani descent

Pakistan (,pɑːkɪˈstɑːn) *n* **1** a republic in S Asia, on the Arabian Sea: the Union of Pakistan, formed in 1947, comprised West and East Pakistan; East Pakistan gained independence as Bangladesh in 1971 and West Pakistan became Pakistan; a member of the Commonwealth from 1947, it withdrew from 1972 until 1989; contains the fertile plains of the Indus valley rising to mountains in the north and west. Official language: Urdu. Official religion: Muslim. Currency: rupee. Capital: Islamabad. Pop: 144 617 000 (2001 est). Area: 801 508 sq km (309 463 sq miles) **2** a former republic in S Asia consisting of the provinces of West Pakistan and East Pakistan (now Bangladesh), 1500 km (900 miles) apart: formed in 1947 from the predominantly Muslim parts of India > **,Pakiˈstani** *n, adj*

▷ www.pak.org
▷ www.tourism.gov.pk
▷ www.islamabad.net/offsites.htm

pakora (pəˈkɔːrə) *n* an Indian dish consisting of pieces of vegetable, chicken, etc, dipped in spiced batter and deep-fried [c20 from Hindi]

pal (pæl) *inf* ▷ *n* **1** a close friend; comrade ▷ *vb* **pals, palling, palled 2** (*intr;* usually foll by *with*) to associate as friends [c17 from E Gypsy: brother, ult. from Sansk. *bhrātar* BROTHER]

PAL (pæl) *n acronym for* phase alternation line: a colour-television broadcasting system used generally in Europe

Pal. *abbrev for* Palestine

palace (ˈpælɪs) *n* (*cap when part of a name*) **1** the official residence of a reigning monarch **2** the official residence of various high-ranking people, as of an archbishop **3** a large and richly furnished building resembling a royal palace [c13 from OF *palais*, from L *Palātium* PALATINE]

Palacio Valdés (*Spanish* paˈlaθjo balˈdes) *n* **Armando** (arˈmando) 1853–1938, Spanish novelist and critic

paladin (ˈpælədɪn) *n* **1** one of the legendary twelve peers of Charlemagne's court **2** a knightly champion [c16 via F from It. *paladino*, from L *palātīnus* imperial official]

palaeo-, *before a vowel* **palae-** *or esp US* **paleo-, pale-** *combining form* old, ancient, or prehistoric: *palaeography;*

palaeoclimatology [from Gk *palaios* old]

palaeobotany *or US* **paleobotany** (ˌpælɪəʊˈbɒtənɪ) *n* the study of fossil plants > **ˌpalaeoˈbotanist** *or US* **ˌpaleoˈbotanist** *n*

Palaeocene *or US* **Paleocene** (ˈpælɪəʊˌsiːn) *adj* **1** of, denoting, or formed in the first epoch of the Tertiary period ▷ *n* **2** the the Palaeocene epoch or rock series [C19 from F, from *paléo* PALAEO- + Gk *kainos* new]

palaeoclimatology *or US* **paleoclimatology** (ˌpælɪəʊˌklaɪməˈtɒlədʒɪ) *n* the study of climates of the geological past > **ˌpalaeoˌclimaˈtologist** *or US* **ˌpaleoˌclimaˈtologist** *n*

palaeoecology *or US* **paleoecology** (ˌpælɪəʊɪˈkɒlədʒɪ) *n* the study of fossil animals and plants in order to deduce their ecology and the environmental conditions in which they lived > **ˌpalaeoˌecoˈlogical** *or US* **ˌpaleoˌecoˈlogical** *adj* > **ˌpalaeoeˈcologist** *or US* **ˌpaleoeˈcologist** *n*

palaeography *or US* **paleography** (ˌpælɪˈɒgrəfɪ) *n* **1** the study of the handwritings of the past, and often the manuscripts, etc, so that they may be dated, read, etc **2** a handwriting of the past > **ˌpalaeˈographer** *or US* **ˌpaleˈographer** *n* > **palaeographic** (ˌpælɪəʊˈgræfɪk), **ˌpalaeoˈgraphical** *or US* **ˌpaleoˈgraphic, ˌpaleoˈgraphical** *adj*

Palaeolithic *or US* **Paleolithic** (ˌpælɪəʊˈlɪθɪk) *n* **1** the period of the emergence of primitive man and the manufacture of unpolished chipped stone tools, about 2.5 million to 3 million years ago ▷ *adj* **2** (*sometimes not cap*) of or relating to this period

palaeomagnetism *or US* **paleomagnetism** (ˌpælɪəʊˈmægnɪtɪzəm) *n* the study of the fossil magnetism in rocks, used to determine the past configuration of the earth's constituents

palaeontology *or US* **paleontology** (ˌpælɪɒnˈtɒlədʒɪ) *n* the study of fossils to determine the structure and evolution of extinct animals and plants and the age and conditions of deposition of the rock strata in which they are found [C19 from PALAEO- + ONTO- + -LOGY] > **palaeontological** *or US* **paleontological** (ˌpælɪˌɒntəˈlɒdʒɪkᵊl) *adj* > **ˌpalaeonˈtologist** *or US* **ˌpaleonˈtologist** *n*

▷ www.ucmp.berkeley.edu/index.html
▷ www.dinosauria.com

Palaeozoic (ˌpælɪəʊˈzəʊɪk) *adj* **1** of, denoting, or relating to an era of geological time that began 600 million years ago with the Cambrian period and lasted about 375 million years until the end of the Permian period ▷ *n* **2** the the Palaeozoic era [C19 from PALAEO- + Gk *zōē* life + -IC]

Palagi (pɑːˈlʌŋiː) *n, pl* **Palagis** NZ a Samoan word for a European

palanquin *or* **palankeen** (ˌpælənˈkiːn) *n* a covered litter, formerly used in the Orient, carried on the shoulders of four men [C16 from Port. *palanquim*, from Prakrit *pallanka*, from Sansk. *paryanka* couch]

palatable (ˈpælətəbᵊl) *adj* **1** pleasant to taste **2** acceptable or satisfactory > **ˌpalataˈbility** *or* **ˈpalatableness** *n* > **ˈpalatably** *adv*

palatal (ˈpælətᵊl) *adj* **1** Also: **palatine** of or relating to the palate **2** *phonetics* of, relating to, or denoting a speech sound articulated with the blade of the tongue touching the hard palate ▷ *n* **3** Also called: **palatine** the bony plate that forms the palate **4** *phonetics* a palatal speech sound, such as (j) > **ˈpalatally** *adv*

palatalize *or* **palatalise** (ˈpælətəˌlaɪz) *vb* **palatalizes, palatalizing, palatalized** *or* **palatalises, palatalising, palatalised** (*tr*) to pronounce (a speech sound) with the blade of the tongue touching the palate > **ˌpalataliˈzation** *or* **ˌpalataliˈsation** *n*

palate (ˈpælɪt) *n* **1** the roof of the mouth, separating the oral and nasal cavities. See **hard palate, soft palate** **2** the sense of taste: *she had no palate for the wine* **3** relish or enjoyment [C14 from L *palātum*, ? of Etruscan origin]

USAGE See at **palette**

palatial (pəˈleɪʃəl) *adj* of, resembling, or suitable for a palace; sumptuous > **paˈlatially** *adv*

palatinate (pəˈlætɪnɪt) *n* a territory ruled by a palatine prince or noble or count palatine

Palatinate (pəˈlætɪnɪt) *n* **1** the either of two territories in SW Germany, once ruled by the counts palatine. **Upper Palatinate** is now in Bavaria; **Lower** or **Rhine Palatinate** is now in Rhineland-Palatinate, Baden-Württemberg, and Hesse. German name: **Pfalz** **2** a native or inhabitant of the Palatinate > **ˈPalaˌtine** *adj, n*

palatine[1] (ˈpæləˌtaɪn) *adj* **1** (of an individual) possessing royal prerogatives in a territory **2** of or relating to a count palatine, county palatine, palatinate, or palatine **3** of or relating to a palace ▷ *n* **4** *Feudal history* the lord of a palatinate **5** any of various important officials at the late Roman, Merovingian, or Carolingian courts [C15 via F from L *palātīnus* belonging to the palace, from *palātium*; see PALACE]

palatine[2] (ˈpæləˌtaɪn) *adj* **1** of the palate ▷ *n* **2** either of two bones forming the hard palate [C17 from F *palatin*, from L *palātum* palate]

Palatine (ˈpæləˌtaɪn) *n* **1** one of the Seven Hills of Rome: traditionally the site of the first settlement of Rome ▷ *adj* **2** of, relating to, or designating this hill

Palau Islands (pɑːˈlaʊ) *pl n* a former name (until 1981) of the (Republic of) **Belau**

palaver (pəˈlɑːvə) *n* **1** tedious or time-consuming business, esp when of a formal nature: *all the palaver of filling in forms* **2** confused talk and activity; hubbub **3** (often used humorously) a conference **4** *now rare* talk intended to flatter or persuade ▷ *vb* **5** (*intr*) (often used humorously) to have a conference **6** (*intr*) to talk confusedly **7** (*tr*) to flatter or cajole [C18 from Port. *palavra* talk, from L *parabola* PARABLE]

Palawan (*Spanish* paˈlavan) *n* an island of the SW Philippines between the South China Sea and the Sulu Sea: the westernmost island in the country; mountainous and forested. Capital: Puerto Princesa. Pop: 311 550 (latest est). Area: 11 785 sq km (4550 sq miles)

palazzo pants (pəˈlætsəʊ) *pl n* women's trousers with very wide legs [C20 *palazzo* from It., lit.: PALACE]

pale[1] (peɪl) *adj* **1** lacking brightness or colour: *pale morning light* **2** (of a colour) whitish **3** dim or wan: *the pale stars* **4** feeble: *a pale imitation* ▷ *vb* **pales, paling, paled** **5** to make or become pale or paler; blanch **6** (*intr; often foll by before*) to lose superiority (in comparison to): *her beauty paled before that of her hostess* [C13 from OF *palle*, from L *pallidus*, from *pallēre* to look wan] > **ˈpalely** *adv* > **ˈpaleness** *n* > **ˈpalish** *adj*

pale[2] (peɪl) *n* **1** a wooden post or strip used as an upright member in a fence **2** an enclosing barrier, esp a fence made of pales **3** an area enclosed by a pale **4** *heraldry* a vertical stripe, usually in the centre of a shield **5** **beyond the pale** outside the limits of social convention [C14 from OF *pal*, from L *pālus* stake]

paleface (ˈpeɪlˌfeɪs) *n* a derogatory term for a White person, said to have been used by North American Indians

Palembang (pɑːˈlɛmbɑːŋ) *n* a port in W Indonesia, in S Sumatra; oil refineries; university (1955). Pop: 1 352 300 (1995 est)

Palencia (*Spanish* paˈlenθia) *n* a city in N central Spain: earliest university in Spain (1208); seat of Castilian kings (12th–13th centuries); communications centre. Pop: 77 752 (1991)

Palenque (*Spanish* paˈleŋke) *n* the site of an ancient Mayan city in S Mexico famous for its architectural ruins

paleo- *or before a vowel* **pale-** *combining form* variants (esp US) of **palaeo-**

Palermo (pəˈlɛəməʊ, -ˈlɜː-; *Italian* paˈlɛrmo) *n* the capital of Sicily, on the NW coast: founded by the Phoenicians in the 8th century BC. Pop: 683 794 (2000 est)

Palestine (ˈpælɪˌstaɪn) *n* **1** Also called: **the Holy Land, Canaan** the area between the Jordan River and the Mediterranean Sea in which most of the biblical narrative is located **2** the province of the Roman Empire in this region **3** the former British mandatory territory created by the League of Nations in 1922 (but effective from 1920), and including all of the present territories of Israel and Jordan between whom it was partitioned by the UN in 1948

Palestine Liberation Organization *n* an organization founded in 1964 with the aim of creating a state for Palestinian Arabs. In 1993 it signed a peace agreement with Israel, which granted Palestinian autonomy in the Gaza Strip and parts of the West Bank. Abbrev: **PLO**

Palestinian (ˌpælɪˈstɪnɪən) *adj* **1** of or relating to Palestine, its native Arab population, or their descendants ▷ *n* **2** a Palestinian Arab, esp one now living in the Palestinian Administered Territories, Israel, Jordan, Lebanon, or as a refugee from Israeli-occupied territory

Palestinian Administered Territories *n* the Gaza Strip and parts of the West Bank in Israel: these areas were granted autonomous status under the control of the Palestinian National Authority following the 1993 peace agreement between Israel and the Palestine Liberation Organization. Also called: **Palestinian Autonomous Areas**

Palestinian National Authority *n* the authority formed in 1994 to govern the Palestinian Administered Territories. Abbrev: **PNA**

Palestrina (ˌpælɛˈstriːnə) *n* **Giovanni Pierluigi da** (dʒoˈvanni pierˈluiːdʒi da) ?1525–94, Italian composer and master of counterpoint. His works, nearly all for unaccompanied choir and religious in nature, include the *Missa Papae Marcelli* (1555)

palette (ˈpælɪt) *n* **1** Also: **pallet** a flat piece of wood, plastic, etc, used by artists as a surface on which to mix their paints **2** the range of colours characteristic of a particular artist, painting, or school of painting: *a restricted palette* **3** the available range of colours or patterns that can be displayed by a computer on a visual display unit [C17 from F, dim. of *pale* shovel, from L *pala* spade]

> USAGE This word is occasionally used when *palate* is meant: *I have a sweet palate* (not *palette*)

palette *or* **pallet knife** *n* a spatula with a thin flexible blade used in painting and cookery

Paley (ˈpeɪlɪ) *n* **William** 1743–1805, English theologian and utilitarian philosopher. His chief works are *The Principles of Moral and Political Philosophy* (1785), *Horae Paulinae* (1790), *A View of the Evidences of Christianity* (1794), and *Natural Theology* (1802)

palfrey (ˈpɔːlfrɪ) *n arch* a light saddle horse, esp ridden by women [C12 from OF *palefrei*, from Med. L, from LL *paraverēdus*, from Gk *para* beside + L *verēdus* light fleet horse, of Celtic origin]

Pali (ˈpɑːlɪ) *n* an ancient language of India derived from Sanskrit; the language of the Buddhist scriptures [C19 from Sansk. *pāli-bhāsa*, from *pāli* canon + *bhāsa* language, of Dravidian origin]

palimony (ˈpælɪmənɪ) *n US* alimony awarded to a nonmarried partner after the break-up of a long-term relationship [C20 from PAL + ALIMONY]

palimpsest (ˈpælɪmpˌsɛst) *n* **1** a manuscript on which two or more texts have been written, each one being erased to make room for the next ▷ *adj* **2** (of a text) written on a palimpsest **3** (of a document, etc) used as a palimpsest [C17 from L *palimpsestus*, from Gk *palimpsēstos*, from *palin* again + *psēstos* rubbed smooth]

palindrome (ˈpælɪnˌdrəʊm) *n* a word or phrase the letters of which, when taken in reverse order, read the same: *able was I ere I saw Elba* [C17 from Gk *palindromos* running back again] > **palindromic** (ˌpælɪnˈdrɒmɪk) *adj*

paling (ˈpeɪlɪŋ) *n* **1** a fence made of pales **2** pales collectively **3** a single pale **4** the act of erecting pales

palisade (ˌpælɪˈseɪd) *n* **1** a strong fence made of stakes driven into the ground, esp for defence **2** one of the stakes used in such a fence ▷ *vb* **palisades, palisading, palisaded 3** (*tr*) to enclose with a palisade [C17 via F from OProvençal *palissada*, ult. from L *pālus* stake]

Palk Strait (pɔːk, pɔːlk) *n* a channel between SE India and N Ceylon. Width: about 64 km (40 miles)

pall[1] (pɔːl) *n* **1** a cloth covering, usually black, spread over a coffin or tomb **2** a coffin, esp during the funeral ceremony **3** a dark heavy covering; shroud: *the clouds formed a pall over the sky* **4** a depressing or oppressive atmosphere: *her bereavement cast a pall on the party* **5** *heraldry* a Y-shaped bearing **6** *Christianity* a small square linen cloth with which the chalice is covered at the Eucharist ▷ *vb* **7** (*tr*) to cover or depress with a pall [OE *pæll*, from L *pallium* cloak]

pall[2] (pɔːl) *vb* **1** (*intr*; often foll by *on*) to become boring, insipid, or tiresome (to): *history classes palled on me* **2** to cloy or satiate, or become cloyed or satiated [C14 var. of APPAL]

Palladian (pəˈleɪdɪən) *adj* denoting, relating to, or having the style of architecture created by Andrea Palladio [C18 after Andrea PALLADIO] > **Palˈladianˌism** *n*
▷ www.britainexpress.com/architecture

Palladio (*Italian* palˈlaːdio) *n* **Andrea** (anˈdrɛːa) 1508–80, Italian architect who revived and developed classical architecture, esp the ancient Roman ideals of symmetrical planning and harmonic proportions. His treatise *Four Books on Architecture* (1570) and his designs for villas and palaces profoundly influenced 18th-century domestic architecture in England and the US

Pp

palladium[1] (pəˈleɪdɪəm) *n* a ductile malleable silvery-white element of the platinum metal group: used as a catalyst and, alloyed with gold, in jewellery, etc Symbol: Pd; atomic no.: 46; atomic wt.: 106.4 [C19 after the asteroid *Pallas*, at the time (1803) a recent discovery]

palladium[2] (pəˈleɪdɪəm) *n* something believed to ensure protection; safeguard [C17 after the *Palladium*, a statue of Pallas Athena, Gk goddess of wisdom]

Pallas Athena *or* **Pallas** *n* another name for **Athena**

pallbearer (ˈpɔːlˌbɛərə) *n* a person who carries or escorts the coffin at a funeral

pallet[1] (ˈpælɪt) *n* a straw-filled mattress or bed [C14 from Anglo-Norman *paillet*, from OF *paille* straw, from L *palea* straw]

pallet[2] (ˈpælɪt) *n* **1** an instrument with a handle and a flat, sometimes flexible, blade used by potters for shaping **2** a portable platform for storing and moving goods **3** *horology* the locking lever that engages and disengages to give impulses to the balance **4** a variant spelling of **palette** (sense 1) **5** *music* a flap valve that opens to allow air from the wind chest to enter an organ pipe, causing it to sound [C16 from OF *palette* a little shovel, from L *pala* spade]

palletize *or* **palletise** (ˈpælətaɪz) *vb* **palletizes, palletizing, palletized** *or* **palletises, palletising, palletised** (*tr*) to store or transport (goods) on pallets > **ˌpalletiˈzation** *or* **ˌpalletiˈsation** *n*

palliasse *or esp US* **paillasse** (ˈpælɪˌæs, ˌpælɪˈæs) *n* a straw-filled mattress; pallet [C18 from F *paillasse*, from It. *pagliaccio*, ult. from L *palea* PALLET[1]]

palliate (ˈpælɪˌeɪt) *vb* **palliates, palliating, palliated** (*tr*) **1** to lessen the severity of (pain, disease, etc) without curing; alleviate **2** to cause (an offence, etc) to seem less serious; extenuate [C16 from LL *palliāre* to cover up, from

L *pallium* a cloak] > ˌ**palli'ation** *n*
palliative ('pælɪətɪv) *adj* **1** relieving without curing ▷ *n* **2** something that palliates, such as a sedative drug > '**palliatively** *adv*
pallid ('pælɪd) *adj* lacking colour, brightness, or vigour: *a pallid complexion; a pallid performance* [C17 from L *pallidus*, from *pallēre* to be PALE[1]] > '**pallidly** *adv* > '**pallidness** *or* **pal'lidity** *n*
Pall Mall ('pæl 'mæl) *n* a street in London, noted for its many clubs
pall-mall ('pæl'mæl) *n obs* **1** a game in which a ball is driven by a mallet along an alley and through an iron ring **2** the alley itself [C17 from obs. F, from It. *pallamaglio*, from *palla* ball + *maglio* mallet]
pallor ('pælə) *n* a pale condition, esp when unnatural: *fear gave his face a deathly pallor* [C17 from L: whiteness (of the skin), from *pallēre* to be PALE[1]]
pally ('pælɪ) *adj* **pallier, palliest** *inf* on friendly terms
palm[1] (pɑːm) *n* **1** the inner part of the hand from the wrist to the base of the fingers **2** a linear measure based on the breadth or length of a hand, equal to three to four inches (7.5 to 10 centimetres) or seven to ten inches (17.5 to 25 centimetres) respectively **3** the part of a glove that covers the palm **4a** one side of the blade of an oar **4b** the face of the fluke of an anchor **5** a flattened part of the antlers of certain deer **6 in the palm of one's hand** at one's mercy or command ▷ *vb (tr)* **7** to conceal in or about the hand, as in sleight-of-hand tricks, etc ▷ See also **palm off** [C14 *paume*, via OF from L *palma*] > **palmar** ('pælmə) *adj*
palm[2] (pɑːm) *n* **1** any treelike plant of a tropical and subtropical family usually having a straight unbranched trunk crowned with large pinnate or palmate leaves **2** a leaf or branch of any of these trees, a symbol of victory, success, etc **3** merit or victory [OE, from L *palma*, from the likeness of its spreading fronds to a hand; see PALM[1]] > **palmaceous** (pæl'meɪʃəs) *adj*
Palma[1] (*Spanish* 'palma) *n* the capital of the Balearic Islands, on the SW coast of Majorca: a tourist centre. Pop: 296 754 (1991). Official name: **Palma de Mallorca**
Palma[2] (*Italian* 'palma) *n* **Jacopo** (ja'kopo), known as *Palma Vecchio*, original name *Jacopo Negretti*. ?1480–1528, Venetian painter, noted esp for his portraits of women
palmate ('pælmeɪt, -mɪt) *or* **palmated** *adj* **1** shaped like an open hand: *palmate antlers* **2** *bot* having more than three lobes that spread out from a common point: *palmate leaves* **3** (of most water birds) having three toes connected by a web
Palm Beach *n* a town in SE Florida, on an island between Lake Worth (a lagoon) and the Atlantic: major resort and tourist centre. Pop: 9814 (1990)
Palme (*Swedish* 'palmə) *n* **(Sven) Olof (Joachim)** ('uːlof) 1927–86, Swedish Social Democratic statesman; prime minister (1969–76, 1982–86); assassinated
palmer ('pɑːmə) *n* (in medieval Europe) **1** a pilgrim bearing a palm branch as a sign of his visit to the Holy Land **2** any pilgrim [C13 from OF *palmier*, from Med. L, from L *palma* PALM[2]]
Palmer ('pɑːmə) *n* **1 Arnold** born 1929, US professional golfer: won the US Open Championship (1960) and the British Open Championship (1961; 1962) **2 Samuel** 1805–81, English painter of visionary landscapes, influenced by William Blake
Palmer Archipelago *n* a group of islands between South America and Antarctica: part of the British colony of Falkland Islands and Dependencies. Former name: **Antarctic Archipelago**
Palmer Land *n* the S part of the Antarctic Peninsula
Palmer Peninsula *n* the former name (until 1964) for the **Antarctic Peninsula**
Palmerston[1] ('pɑːməstən) *n* the former name (1869–1911) of **Darwin**[1]
Palmerston[2] ('pɑːməstən) *n* **Henry John Temple,** 3rd Viscount Palmerston. 1784–1865, British statesman; foreign secretary (1830–34; 1835–41; 1846–51); prime minister (1855–58; 1859–65). His talent was for foreign affairs, in which he earned a reputation as a British nationalist and for high-handedness and gunboat diplomacy
Palmerston North *n* a city in New Zealand, in the S North Island on the Manawatu River. Pop (urban area): 76 300 (1995 est)
Palmer-Tomkinson ('pɑːmə'tɒmkɪnsᵊn) *n* **Tara** born 1971, British socialite, television personality, and journalist
palmetto (pæl'mɛtəʊ) *n, pl* **palmettos** *or* **palmettoes** any of several small chiefly tropical palms with fan-shaped leaves [C16 from Sp. *palmito* a little PALM[2]]
Palmira (*Spanish* pal'mira) *n* a city in W Colombia: agricultural trading centre. Pop: 226 500 (1999 est)
palmistry ('pɑːmɪstrɪ) *n* the process or art of telling fortunes, etc, by the configuration of lines and bumps on a person's hand. Also called: **chiromancy** [C15 *pawmestry*, from *paume* PALM[1]; the second element is unexplained] > '**palmist** *n*
palmitic acid (pæl'mɪtɪk) *n* a white crystalline solid that is a saturated fatty acid: used in the manufacture of soap and candles. Formula: $C_{15}H_{31}COOH$. Systematic name: **hexadecanoic acid** [C19 from F]
palm off *vb (tr, adv; often foll by on)* **1** to offer, sell, or spend fraudulently: *to palm off a counterfeit coin* **2** to divert in order to be rid of: *I palmed the unwelcome visitor off on John*
palm oil *n* an oil obtained from the fruit of certain palms, used as an edible fat and in soap, etc
Palm Springs *n* a city in the US, in California: a popular tourist resort. Pop: 40 181 (1990)
Palm Sunday *n* the Sunday before Easter commemorating Christ's triumphal entry into Jerusalem
palmtop computer ('pɑːmˌtɒp) *n* a computer that is small enough to be held in the hand; a hand-held computer. Often shortened to **palmtop** ▷ Cf **laptop computer**
palmy ('pɑːmɪ) *adj* **palmier, palmiest 1** prosperous, flourishing, or luxurious: *a palmy life* **2** covered with, relating to, or resembling palms
palmyra (pæl'maɪrə) *n* a tall tropical Asian palm with large fan-shaped leaves used for thatching and weaving [C17 from Port. *palmeira* palm tree; ? infl. by PALMYRA, in Syria]
Palmyra (pæl'maɪrə) *n* **1** an ancient city in central Syria: said to have been built by Solomon. Biblical name: **Tadmor 2** an island in the central Pacific, in the Line Islands: under US administration
Palo Alto *n* **1** ('pæləʊ 'æltəʊ) a city in W California, southeast of San Francisco: founded in 1891 as the seat of Stanford University. Pop: 55 900 (1990) **2** (*Spanish* 'palo 'alto) a battlefield in E Mexico, northwest of Monterrey, where the first battle (1846) of the Mexican War took place, in which the Mexicans under General Mariano Arista were defeated by the Americans under General Zachary Taylor
palo cortado ('pæləʊ kɔː'tɑːdəʊ) *n* a rich dry sherry [from Sp., lit.: crossed stick (referring to the classification system in which butts of palo cortado are marked with a vertical line and one or more horizontal lines)]
Palomar ('pæləˌmɑː) *n* **Mount** a mountain in S California, northeast of San Diego: site of **Mount Palomar Observatory,** which has a large (200-inch) reflecting telescope. Height: 1871 m (6140 ft)
palomino (ˌpælə'miːnəʊ) *n, pl* **palominos** a golden horse with a white mane and tail [American Sp., from Sp.: dovelike, from L, from *palumbēs* ring dove]
Palos (*Spanish* 'palɔs) *n* a village and former port in SW

Spain: starting point of Columbus' voyage of discovery to America (1492)

palp (pælp) *or* **palpus** ('pælpəs) *n, pl* **palps** *or* **palpi** ('pælpaɪ) either of a pair of sensory appendages that arise from the mouthparts of crustaceans and insects [c19 from F, from L *palpus* a touching]

palpable ('pælpəbᵊl) *adj* **1** (*usually prenominal*) easily perceived by the senses or the mind; obvious: *a palpable lie* **2** capable of being touched; tangible [c14 from LL *palpābilis* that may be touched, from L *palpāre* to touch] > ˌ**palpa'bility** *n* > '**palpably** *adv*

palpate ('pælpeɪt) *vb* **palpates, palpating, palpated** (*tr*) *med* to examine (an area of the body) by the sense of touch [c19 from L *palpāre* to stroke] > **pal'pation** *n*

palpebral ('pælpɪbrəl) *adj* of or relating to the eyelid [c19 from LL, from L *palpebra* eyelid]

palpitate ('pælpɪˌteɪt) *vb* **palpitates, palpitating, palpitated** (*intr*) **1** (of the heart) to beat with abnormal rapidity **2** to flutter or tremble [c17 from L *palpitāre* to throb, from *palpāre* to stroke] > '**palpitant** *adj* > ˌ**palpi'tation** *n*

palsy ('pɔːlzɪ) *pathol* ▷ *n, pl* **palsies 1** paralysis, esp of a specified type: *cerebral palsy* ▷ *vb* **palsies, palsying, palsied** (*tr*) **2** to paralyse [c13 *palesi*, from OF *paralisie*, from L PARALYSIS] > '**palsied** *adj*

palter ('pɔːltə) *vb* (*intr*) **1** to act or talk insincerely **2** to haggle [c16 from ?]

Paltrow ('pɒltrəʊ) *n* **Gwyneth** (**Kate**) born 1973, US film actress; her films include *Emma* (1996), *Sliding Doors* (1998), *Shakespeare in Love* (1998), and *Sylvia* (2003)

paltry ('pɔːltrɪ) *adj* **paltrier, paltriest 1** insignificant; meagre **2** worthless or petty [c16 from Low Gmc *palter*, *paltrig* ragged] > '**paltrily** *adv* > '**paltriness** *n*

paludal (pə'ljuːdᵊl) *adj rare* **1** of or relating to marshes **2** malarial [c19 from L *palus* marsh]

paludism ('pæljʊˌdɪzəm) *n* a less common word for **malaria** [c19 from L *palus* marsh]

palynology (ˌpælɪ'nɒlədʒɪ) *n* the study of living and fossil pollen grains and plant spores [c20 from Gk *palunein* to scatter + -LOGY] > **palynological** (ˌpælɪnə'lɒdʒɪkᵊl) *adj* > ˌ**paly'nologist** *n*

Pamirs (pə'mɪəz) *pl n* **the** a mountainous area of central Asia, mainly in Tajikistan and partly in Kyrgyzstan, extending into China and Afghanistan: consists of a complex of high ranges, from which the Tian Shan projects to the north, the Kunlun and Karakoram to the east, and the Hindu Kush to the west; Kommunizma Peak is situated in the Tajik Pamirs. Highest peak: Kongur Shan, 7719 m (25 326 ft). Also called: **Pamir**

Pamlico Sound ('pæmlɪkəʊ) *n* an inlet of the Atlantic between the E coast of North Carolina and its chain of offshore islands. Length: 130 km (80 miles)

pampas ('pæmpəz) *n* (*functioning as sing or more often pl*) **a** the extensive grassy plains of temperate South America, esp in Argentina **b** (*as modifier*): *pampas dwellers* [c18 from American Sp. *pampa* (sing), from Amerind *bamba* plain] > **pampean** ('pæmpɪən, pæm'piːən) *adj*

pampas grass ('pæmpəs, -pəz) *n* any of various large South American grasses, widely cultivated for their large feathery silver-coloured flower branches

Pampeluna (ˌpæmpə'luːnə) *n* the former name of **Pamplona**

pamper ('pæmpə) *vb* (*tr*) **1** to treat with affectionate and usually excessive indulgence; coddle; spoil **2** *arch* to feed to excess [c14 of Gmc origin] > '**pamperer** *n*

pamphlet ('pæmflɪt) *n* **1** a brief publication generally having a paper cover; booklet **2** a brief treatise, often on a subject of current interest, in pamphlet form [c14 *pamflet*, from Med. L *Pamphilus* title of a 12th-century amatory poem from Gk *Pamphilos* proper name]

pamphleteer (ˌpæmflɪ'tɪə) *n* **1** a person who writes or issues pamphlets ▷ *vb* **2** (*intr*) to write or issue pamphlets

Pamphylia (pæm'fɪlɪə) *n* an area on the S coast of ancient Asia Minor

Pamplona (pæm'pləʊnə; *Spanish* pam'plona) *n* a city in N Spain in the foothills of the Pyrenees: capital of the kingdom of Navarre from the 11th century until 1841. Pop: 171 150 (1998 est). Former name: **Pampeluna**

pan[1] (pæn) *n* **1a** a wide metal vessel used in cooking **1b** (*in combination*): *saucepan* **2** Also called: **panful** the amount such a vessel will hold **3** any of various similar vessels used in industry, etc **4** a dish used esp by gold prospectors for separating gold from gravel by washing and agitating **5** either of the two dishlike receptacles on a balance **6** Also called: **lavatory pan** *Brit* the bowl of a lavatory **7a** a natural or artificial depression in the ground where salt can be obtained by the evaporation of brine **7b** a natural depression containing water or mud **8** See **hardpan, brainpan 9** a small cavity containing priming powder in the locks of old guns **10** a hard substratum of soil ▷ *vb* **pans, panning, panned 11** (when *tr*, often foll by *off* or *out*) to wash (gravel) in a pan to separate particles of (valuable minerals) from it **12** (*intr; often foll by out*) (of gravel, etc) to yield valuable minerals by this process **13** (*tr*) *inf* to criticize harshly: *the critics panned his new play* ▷ See also **pan out** [OE *panne*]

pan[2] (pæn) *vb* **pans, panning, panned 1** to move (a film camera) or (of a film camera) to be moved so as to follow a moving object or obtain a panoramic effect ▷ *n* **2** the act of panning [c20 shortened from PANORAMIC]

Pan (pæn) *n Greek myth* the god of fields, woods, shepherds, and flocks, represented as a man with a goat's legs, horns, and ears. Related adjs: **Pandean, Panic**

Pan. *abbrev for* Panama

pan- *combining form* **1** all or every: *panchromatic* **2** including or relating to all parts or members: *Pan-American; pantheistic* [from Gk *pan*, neuter of *pas* all]

Pp

panacea (ˌpænə'sɪə) *n* a remedy for all diseases or ills [c16 via L from Gk *panakeia*, from *pan* all + *akēs* remedy] > ˌ**pana'cean** *adj*

panache (pə'næʃ, -'nɑːʃ) *n* **1** a dashing manner; swagger: *he rides with panache* **2** a plume on a helmet [c16 via F from OIt. *pennacchio*, from LL *pinnāculum* feather, from L *pinna* feather]

panada (pə'nɑːdə) *n* a mixture of flour, water, etc, or of breadcrumbs soaked in milk, used as a thickening [c16 from Sp., from *pan* bread, from L *pānis*]

Pan-Africanist Congress *n* a South African political party, founded as a liberation movement in 1959. Abbrev: **PAC**

Panaji (pɑː'nɑːdʒiː) *n* a variant of **Panjim**

Panama (ˌpænə'mɑː, 'pænəˌmɑː) *n* **1** a republic in Central America, occupying the Isthmus of Panama: gained independence from Spain in 1821 and joined Greater Colombia; became independent in 1903, with the immediate area around the canal forming the Canal Zone under US jurisdiction; Panama assumed sovereignty over the Canal Zone in 1979 and full control in 1999. Official language: Spanish; English is also widely spoken. Religion: Roman Catholic majority. Currency: balboa. Capital: Panama City. Pop: 2 903 000 (2001 est). Area: 75 650 sq km (29 201 sq miles) **2 Isthmus of** an isthmus linking North and South America, between the Pacific and the Caribbean. Length: 676 km (420 miles). Width (at its narrowest point): 50 km (31 miles). Former name: (Isthmus of) Darien **3 Gulf of** a wide inlet of the Pacific in Panama > **Panamanian** (ˌpænə'meɪnɪən) *adj, n*

▷ www.visitpanama.com

Panama Canal *n* a canal across the Isthmus of Panama, linking the Atlantic and Pacific Oceans: extends from Colón on the Caribbean Sea southeast to Balboa on the

Gulf of Panama; built by the US (1904–14), after an unsuccessful previous attempt (1880–89) by the French under de Lesseps. Length: 64 km (40 miles)

Panama Canal Zone *n* See **Canal Zone**

Panama City *n* the capital of Panama, near the Pacific entrance of the Panama Canal: developed rapidly with the building of the Panama Canal; seat of the University of Panama (1935). Pop: 415 964 (2000)

Panama hat *n* (*sometimes not cap*) a hat made of the plaited leaves of a palmlike plant of Central and South America. Often shortened to **panama** or **Panama**

Pan-American *adj* of, relating to, or concerning North, South, and Central America collectively or the advocacy of political or economic unity among American countries > **'Pan-A'merican,ism** *n*

panatella (ˌpænəˈtɛlə) *n* a long slender cigar [American Sp. *panetela* long slim biscuit, from It. *panatella* small loaf, from *pane* bread, from L *pānis*]

Panay (pɑːˈnaɪ) *n* an island in the central Philippines, the westernmost of the Visayan Islands. Pop: 2 595 315 (latest est). Area: 12 300 sq km (4750 sq miles)

pancake (ˈpænˌkeɪk) *n* **1** a thin flat cake made from batter and fried on both sides **2** a stick or flat cake of compressed make-up **3** Also called: **pancake landing** an aircraft landing made by levelling out a few feet from the ground and then dropping onto it ▷ *vb* **pancakes, pancaking, pancaked 4** to cause (an aircraft) to make a pancake landing or (of an aircraft) to make a pancake landing

Pancake Day *n* another name for **Shrove Tuesday** See **Shrovetide**

panchromatic (ˌpænkrəʊˈmætɪk) *adj photog* (of an emulsion or film) made sensitive to all colours > **panchromatism** (pænˈkrəʊməˌtɪzəm) *n*

pancosmism (pænˈkɒzˌmɪzəm) *n* the philosophical doctrine that the material universe is all that exists

pancreas (ˈpæŋkrɪəs) *n* a large elongated glandular organ, situated behind the stomach, that secretes insulin and pancreatic juice [C16 via NL from Gk *pankreas*, from PAN- + *kreas* flesh] > **pancreatic** (ˌpæŋkrɪˈætɪk) *adj*

pancreatic juice *n* the clear alkaline secretion of the pancreas that is released into the duodenum and contains digestive enzymes

pancreatin (ˈpæŋkrɪətɪn) *n* the powdered extract of the pancreas of certain animals, used in medicine as an aid to digestion by virtue of the enzymes it contains

panda (ˈpændə) *n* **1** Also called: **giant panda** a large black-and-white herbivorous bearlike mammal, related to the raccoons and inhabiting the high mountain bamboo forests of China **2 lesser** *or* **red panda** a closely related smaller animal resembling a raccoon, of the mountain forests of S Asia, having a reddish-brown coat and ringed tail [C19 via F from a native Nepalese word]

panda car *n Brit* a police patrol car [C20 so called because its blue-and-white markings resemble the black-and-white markings of the giant panda]

pandanus (pænˈdeɪnəs) *n, pl* **pandanuses** any of various Old World tropical palmlike plants having leaves and roots yielding a fibre used for making mats, etc [C19 via NL from Malay *pandan*]

Pandarus (ˈpændərəs) *n* **1** *Greek myth* the leader of the Lycians, allies of the Trojans in their war with the Greeks. He broke the truce by shooting Menelaus with an arrow and was killed in the ensuing battle by Diomedes **2** (in medieval legend) the procurer of Cressida on behalf of Troilus

Pandean (pænˈdiːən) *adj* of or relating to the god Pan

pandect (ˈpændɛkt) *n* **1** a treatise covering all aspects of a particular subject **2** (*often pl*) the complete body of laws of a country; legal code, esp the digest of Roman civil law made in the 6th century by order of Justinian [C16 via LL from Gk *pandektēs* containing everything, from PAN- + *dektēs* receiver]

pandemic (pænˈdɛmɪk) *adj* **1** (of a disease) affecting persons over a wide geographical area; extensively epidemic ▷ *n* **2** a pandemic disease [C17 from LL *pandēmus*, from Gk *pandēmos* general, from PAN- + *demos* the people]

pandemonium (ˌpændɪˈməʊnɪəm) *n* **1** wild confusion; uproar **2** a place of uproar and chaos [C17 coined by Milton for the capital of hell in *Paradise Lost*, from PAN- + Gk *daimōn* DEMON]

pander (ˈpændə) *vb* **1** (*intr; foll by to*) to give gratification (to weaknesses or desires) **2** (*arch* when tr) to act as a go-between in a sexual intrigue (for) ▷ *n Also:* **panderer 3** a person who caters for vulgar desires **4** a person who procures a sexual partner for another; pimp [C16 (n) from *Pandare* Pandarus, in legend, the procurer of Cressida for Troilus]

pandit (ˈpʌndɪt; *spelling pron* ˈpændɪt) *n Hinduism* a variant of **pundit** (sense 3)

P&L *abbrev for* profit and loss

P&O *abbrev for* the Peninsular and Oriental Steam Navigation Company

Pandora (pænˈdɔːrə) *or* **Pandore** (pænˈdɔː, ˈpændɔː) *n Greek myth* the first woman, made out of earth as the gods' revenge on man for obtaining fire from Prometheus. Given a box (**Pandora's box**) that she was forbidden to open, she disobeyed out of curiosity and released from it all the ills that beset man, leaving only hope within [from Gk, lit.: all-gifted]

p&p *Brit abbrev for* postage and packing

pane (peɪn) *n* **1** a sheet of glass in a window or door **2** a panel of a window, door, wall, etc **3** a flat section or face, as of a cut diamond [C13 from OF *pan* portion, from L *pannus* rag]

paneer (pəˈnɪə) *n* a soft white cheese, used in Indian cookery [C20 from Hindi *panīr* cheese]

panegyric (ˌpænɪˈdʒɪrɪk) *n* a formal public commendation; eulogy [C17 via F & L from Gk, from *panēguris* public gathering] > **ˌpaneˈgyrical** *adj* > **ˌpaneˈgyrically** *adv* > **ˌpaneˈgyrist** *n* > **panegyrize** *or* **panegyrise** (ˈpænɪdʒɪˌraɪz) *vb*

panel (ˈpænᵊl) *n* **1** a flat section of a wall, door, etc **2** any distinct section of something formed from a sheet of material, esp of a car body **3** a piece of material inserted in a skirt, etc **4a** a group of persons selected to act as a team in a quiz, to discuss a topic before an audience, etc **4b** (*as modifier*): *a panel game* **5** *law* **5a** a list of persons summoned for jury service **5b** the persons on a jury **6** *Scots law* a person accused of a crime **7a** a thin board used as a surface or backing for an oil painting **7b** a painting done on such a surface **8** any picture with a length much greater than its breadth **9** See **instrument panel 10** *Brit* (formerly) **10a** a list of patients insured under the National Health Insurance Scheme **10b** a list of medical practitioners available for consultation by these patients ▷ *vb* **panels, panelling, panelled** *or US* **panels, paneling, paneled** (*tr*) **11** to furnish or decorate with panels **12** *law* **12a** to empanel (a jury) **12b** (in Scotland) to bring (a person) to trial; indict [C13 from OF: portion, from *pan* piece of cloth, from L *pannus*]

panel beater *n* a person who beats out the bodywork of motor vehicles, etc

panelling *or US* **paneling** (ˈpænᵊlɪŋ) *n* **1** panels collectively, as on a wall or ceiling **2** material used for making panels

panellist *or US* **panelist** (ˈpænᵊlɪst) *n* a member of a panel, esp on radio or television

panel pin *n* a slender nail with a narrow head

panel saw *n* a saw with a long narrow blade for cutting thin wood

panel van *n Austral & NZ* a small van

Pan-European *adj* of or relating to all European

countries or the advocacy of political or economic unity among European countries

pang (pæŋ) *n* a sudden brief sharp feeling, as of loneliness, physical pain, or hunger [c16 var. of earlier *prange*, of Gmc origin]

panga ('pæŋgə) *n* a broad heavy knife of E Africa [from a native E African word]

Pang-fou ('pæŋ'fu:) *n* a variant transliteration of the Chinese name for **Bengbu**

pangolin (pæŋ'gəʊlɪn) *n* a mammal of tropical Africa, S Asia, and Indonesia, having a scaly body and a long snout for feeding on ants and termites. Also called: **scaly anteater** [c18 from Malay *peng-gōling*, from *gōling* to roll over; from its ability to roll into a ball]

Pango Pango ('pɑ:ŋgəʊ 'pɑ:ŋgəʊ) *n* the former name of **Pago Pago**

panhandle[1] ('pæn,hændəl) *n* (*sometimes cap*) (in the US) a narrow strip of land that projects from one state into another

panhandle[2] ('pæn,hændəl) *vb* **panhandles, panhandling, panhandled** *US inf* to beg from (passers-by) [c19 prob. a back formation from *panhandler* a person who begs with a pan] > **'pan,handler** *n*

Panhellenic (,pænhɛ'lɛnɪk) *adj* of or relating to all the Greeks or all Greece

panic ('pænɪk) *n* **1** a sudden overwhelming feeling of terror or anxiety, esp one affecting a whole group of people **2** (*modifier*) of or resulting from such terror: *panic measures* **3** (*modifier*) for use in an emergency: *panic stations; panic button* ▷ *vb* **panics, panicking, panicked 4** to feel or cause to feel panic [c17 from F *panique*, from NL, from Gk *panikos* emanating from PAN, considered as the source of irrational fear] > **'panicky** *adj*

Panic ('pænɪk) *adj* of or relating to the god Pan

panic attack *n* an episode of acute and disabling anxiety associated with such physical symptoms as hyperventilation and sweating

panic button *n* a button or switch that operates a safety device or alarm, for use in an emergency

panic disorder *n psychiatry* a condition in which a person experiences recurrent panic attacks

panic grass *n* any of various grasses, such as millet, grown in warm and tropical regions for fodder and grain [c15 *panic*, from L *pānicum*, prob. a back formation from *pānicula* PANICLE]

panicle ('pænɪkəl) *n* a compound raceme, as in the oat [c16 from L *pānicula* tuft, dim. of *panus* thread, ult. from Gk *penos* web] > **'panicled** *adj* > **paniculate** (pə'nɪkjʊ,leɪt, -lɪt) *adj*

panic room *n* a secure room with a separate telephone line within a house, to which a person can flee if someone breaks in

panic-stricken *or* **panic-struck** *adj* affected by panic

panist ('pænɪst) *n Caribbean* a player in a steel band, esp one with considerable skill and experience

panjandrum (pæn'dʒændrəm) *n* a pompous self-important official or person of rank [c18 after a character in a nonsense work (1755) by S. Foote, E playwright]

Panjim ('pɑ:n,ʒɪm) *or* **Panaji** *n* the capital of the Indian union territory of Goa, Daman, and Diu: a port on the Arabian Sea on the coast of Goa. Pop: 85 515 (1991)

Pankhurst ('pæŋkhɜ:st) *n* **1** Dame **Christabel** 1880–1958, English suffragette **2** her mother, **Emmeline** 1858–1928, English suffragette leader, who founded the militant Women's Social and Political Union (1903) **3** **Sylvia,** daughter of Emmeline Pankhurst. 1882–1960, English suffragette and pacifist

pan loaf *n Scot* a loaf of bread with a light crust all the way round. Often shortened to **pan**

Panmunjom ('pɑ:n'mʊn'dʒɒm) *n* a village in the demilitarized zone of Korea: site of truce talks leading to the end of the Korean War (1950–53)

pannage ('pænɪdʒ) *n arch* **1** the right to pasture pigs in a forest **2** payment for this **3** acorns, beech mast, etc, on which pigs feed [c13 from OF *pasnage*, ult. from L *pastion-*, *pastiō* feeding, from *pascere* to feed]

pannier ('pænɪə) *n* **1** a large basket, esp one of a pair slung over a beast of burden **2** one of a pair of bags slung either side of the back wheel of a motorcycle, etc **3** (esp in the 18th century) **3a** a hooped framework to distend a woman's skirt **3b** one of two puffed-out loops of material worn drawn back onto the hips [c13 from OF *panier*, from L *pānārium* basket for bread, from *pānis* bread]

pannikin ('pænɪkɪn) *n chiefly Brit* a small metal cup or pan [c19 from PAN[1] + -KIN]

pannikin boss *n Austral sl* a minor overseer

Pannonia (pə'nəʊnɪə) *n* a region of the ancient world south and west of the Danube: made a Roman province in 6 AD

panoply ('pænəplɪ) *n, pl* **panoplies 1** a complete or magnificent array **2** the entire equipment of a warrior [c17 via F from Gk, from PAN- + *hopla* armour] > **'panoplied** *adj*

panoptic (pæn'ɒptɪk) *adj* taking in all parts, aspects, etc, in a single view; all-embracing [c19 from Gk *panoptēs* seeing everything]

panorama (,pænə'rɑ:mə) *n* **1** an extensive unbroken view in all directions **2** a wide or comprehensive survey of a subject **3** a large extended picture of a scene, unrolled before spectators a part at a time so as to appear continuous **4** another name for **cyclorama** [c18 from PAN- + Gk *horāma* view] > **panoramic** (,pænə'ræmɪk) *adj* > **,pano'ramically** *adv*

pan out *vb* (*intr, adv*) *inf* to work out; result

panpipes ('pæn,paɪps) *pl n* (*often sing; often cap*) a number of reeds or whistles of graduated lengths bound together to form a musical wind instrument. Also called: **pipes of Pan, syrinx**

pansy ('pænzɪ) *n, pl* **pansies 1** a garden plant having flowers with rounded velvety petals, white, yellow, or purple in colour. See also **wild pansy 2** *sl* an effeminate or homosexual man or boy [c15 from OF *pensée* thought, from *penser* to think, from L *pensāre*]

pant (pænt) *vb* **1** to breathe with noisy deep gasps, as when out of breath from exertion **2** to say (something) while breathing thus **3** (*intr; often foll by for*) to have a frantic desire (for) **4** (*intr*) to throb rapidly ▷ *n* **5** the act or an instance of panting **6** a short deep gasping noise [c15 from OF *pantaisier*, from Gk *phantasioun* to have visions, from *phantasia* FANTASY]

pantalets *or* **pantalettes** (,pæntə'lɛts) *pl n* **1** long drawers extending below the skirts: worn during the 19th century **2** ruffles for the ends of such drawers [c19 dim. of PANTALOONS]

pantaloon (,pæntə'lu:n) *n* **1** (in pantomime) an absurd old man, the butt of the clown's tricks **2** (*usually cap*) (in commedia dell'arte) a lecherous old merchant dressed in pantaloons [c16 from F *Pantalon*, from It. *Pantalone*, prob. from *San Pantaleone*, a fourth-century Venetian saint]

pantaloons (,pæntə'lu:nz) *pl n* **1** *history* **1a** men's tight-fitting trousers fastened below the calf or under the shoe **1b** children's trousers resembling these **2** *inf* any trousers, esp baggy ones

pantechnicon (pæn'tɛknɪkən) *n Brit* **1** a large van, esp one used for furniture removals **2** a warehouse where furniture is stored [c19 from PAN- + Gk *tekhnikon* relating to the arts, from *tekhnē* art; orig. a London bazaar, later used as a furniture warehouse]

Pantelleria (*Italian* pantelle'ri:a) *n* an Italian island in the Mediterranean, between Sicily and Tunisia: of volcanic origin; used by the Romans as a place of banishment. Pop: 7316 (1991 est). Area: 83 sq km (32 sq miles). Ancient name: **Cossyra** (kə'saɪrə)

pantheism ('pænθɪ,ɪzəm) *n* **1** the doctrine that regards

Pp

God as identical with the material universe or the forces of nature **2** readiness to worship all gods > **'pantheist** *n* > **,panthe'istic** *or* **,panthe'istical** *adj* > **,panthe'istically** *adv*

pantheon ('pænθɪən) *n* **1** (esp in ancient Greece or Rome) a temple to all the gods **2** all the gods of a religion **3** a building commemorating a nation's dead heroes [C14 via L from Gk *Pantheion*, from PAN- + *-theios* divine, from *theos* god]

Pantheon (pæn'θiːən, 'pænθɪən) *n* a circular temple in Rome dedicated to all the gods, built by Agrippa in 27 BC, rebuilt by Hadrian 120–24 AD, and used since 609 AD as a Christian church

panther ('pænθə) *n, pl* **panthers** *or* **panther 1** another name for **leopard** (sense 1), esp the black variety (**black panther**) **2** *US & Canad* any of various related animals, esp the puma [C14 from OF *pantère*, from L *panthēra*, from Gk *panthēr*]

panties ('pæntɪz) *pl n* a pair of women's or children's underpants

pantihose ('pæntɪ,həʊz) *pl n* See **panty hose**

pantile ('pæn,taɪl) *n* a roofing tile, with an S-shaped cross section, so that the downward curve of one tile overlaps the upward curve of the next [C17 from PAN[1] + TILE]

pantisocracy (,pæntɪ'sɒkrəsɪ) *n, pl* **pantisocracies** a community, social group, etc, in which all have rule and everyone is equal [C18 (coined by Robert SOUTHEY) from Gk, from PANTO- + *isos* equal + -CRACY]

panto ('pæntəʊ) *n, pl* **pantos** *Brit inf* short for **pantomime** (sense 1)

panto- *or before a vowel* **pant-** *combining form* all: *pantisocracy; pantograph; pantomime* [from Gk *pant-, pas*]

pantograph ('pæntə,grɑːf) *n* **1** an instrument consisting of pivoted levers for copying drawings, maps, etc, to any scale **2** a sliding type of current collector, esp a diamond-shaped frame mounted on a train roof in contact with an overhead wire **3** a device used to suspend a studio lamp so that its height can be adjusted > **pantographic** (,pæntə'græfɪk) *adj*

pantomime ('pæntə,maɪm) *n* **1** (in Britain) a kind of play performed at Christmas time characterized by farce, music, lavish sets, stock roles, and topical jokes **2** a theatrical entertainment in which words are replaced by gestures and bodily actions **3** action without words as a means of expression **4** *inf, chiefly Brit* a confused or farcical situation ▷ *vb* **pantomimes, pantomiming, pantomimed 5** another word for **mime** [C17 via L from Gk *pantomīmos*] > **pantomimic** (,pæntə'mɪmɪk) *adj* > **pantomimist** ('pæntə,maɪmɪst) *n*

pantothenic acid (,pæntə'θɛnɪk) *n* an oily acid that is a vitamin of the B complex: occurs in animal and vegetable foods [C20 from Gk *pantothen* from every side]

pantry ('pæntrɪ) *n, pl* **pantries** a small room in which provisions, cooking utensils, etc, are kept; larder [C13 via Anglo-Norman from OF *paneterie* store for bread, ult. from L *pānis* bread]

pants (pænts) *pl n* **1** *Brit* an undergarment covering the body from the waist to the thighs or knees **2** the usual US and Canad name for **trousers 3** *sl* rubbish; nonsense **4 bore, scare,** etc, **the pants off** *inf* to bore, scare, etc, extremely ▷ *adj* **5** *sl* bad; inferior: *a pants film* ▷ *interj* **6** *sl* an exclamation expressing disgust or disapproval [C19 shortened from *pantaloons*]

panty girdle ('pæntɪ) *n* a foundation garment with a crotch, often of lighter material than a girdle

panty hose *pl n* the US name for **tights** (sense 1). Also (Canad and NZ) **pantyhose,** (Austral) **pantihose**

Panufnik (pæ'nuːfnɪk) *n* Sir **Andrzej** (ændreɪ) 1914–91, British composer and conductor, born in Poland. His works include nine symphonies, the cantata *Winter Solstice* (1972), Polish folk-song settings, and ballet music

panyard (,pæn'jɑːd) *n* *Caribbean* an enclosed area in which a steel band practises

panzer ('pænzə; *German* 'pantsər) *n* **1** (*modifier*) of or relating to the fast mechanized armoured units employed by the German army in World War II: *a panzer attack* **2** a vehicle belonging to a panzer unit, esp a tank **3** (*pl*) armoured troops [C20 from G, from MHG, from OF *panciere* coat of mail, from L *pantex* PAUNCH]

Pão de Açúcar (pə̃un di a'sukar) *n* the Portuguese name for the **Sugar Loaf Mountain**

Paolozzi (paʊ'lɒtsɪ) *n* Sir **Eduardo** (**Luigi**) born 1924, British sculptor and designer, noted esp for his semiabstract metal figures

Paoting *or* **Pao-ting** ('paʊ'tɪŋ) *n* a variant transliteration of the Chinese name for **Baoding**

Paotow ('paʊ'taʊ) *n* a variant transliteration of the Chinese name for **Baotou**

pap[1] (pæp) *n* **1** any soft or semiliquid food, esp for babies or invalids; mash **2** worthless or oversimplified ideas, etc; drivel **3** *S African* maize porridge [C15 from MLow G *pappe*, via Med. L from L *pappāre* to eat]

pap[2] (pæp) *n* **1** *arch or Scot & N English dialect* a nipple or teat **2** something resembling a breast, such as one of a pair of rounded hilltops [C12 from ON, imit. of a sucking sound]

pap[3] (pæp) *vb* **paps, papping, papped** (*tr*) (of the paparazzi) to follow and photograph (a famous person) [C20 from PAPARAZZO]

papa (pə'pɑː) *n* *old-fashioned* an informal word for **father** [C17 from F, a children's word for father]

papacy ('peɪpəsɪ) *n, pl* **papacies 1** the office or term of office of a pope **2** the system of government in the Roman Catholic Church that has the pope as its head [C14 from Med. L *pāpātia*, from *pāpa* POPE]

▷ www.wayoflife.org/papacy

papain (pə'peɪɪn, -'paɪɪn) *n* an enzyme occurring in the unripe fruit of the papaya tree: used as a meat tenderizer and in medicine as an aid to protein digestion [C19 from PAPAYA]

papal ('peɪpᵊl) *adj* of or relating to the pope or the papacy > **'papally** *adv*

Papal States *pl n* the temporal domain of the popes in central Italy from 756 AD until the unification of Italy in 1870. Also called: **States of the Church**

Papandreou (,pæpən'dreɪuː; *Greek* papan'ðreu) *n* **Andreas** (**George**) (an'dreas) 1919–96, Greek economist and socialist politician; prime minister (1981–89; 1993–96)

paparazzo (,pæpə'rætsəʊ) *n, pl* **paparazzi** (-'rætsiː) a freelance photographer who specializes in candid camera shots of famous people [C20 from It.]

papaver (pæ'pɑːvə) *n* any of a genus of hardy annual or perennial plants with showy flowers; poppy [L: poppy]

papaveraceous (pə,peɪvə'reɪʃəs) *adj* of or relating to a family of plants having large showy flowers and a cylindrical seed capsule with pores beneath the lid: includes the poppies and greater celandine [C19 from NL, from L *papāver* poppy]

papaverine (pə'peɪvə,riːn, -rɪn) *n* a white crystalline alkaloid found in opium and used to treat coronary spasms and some colic [C19 from L *papāver* poppy]

papaw (pə'pɔː) *or* **pawpaw** ('pɔːpɔː) *n* **1** another name for **papaya** (sense 2). Also called: **custard apple 2** a bush or small tree of Central North America, having small fleshy edible fruit **3** the fruit of this tree [C16 from Sp. PAPAYA]

papaya (pə'paɪə) *n* **1** a Caribbean evergreen tree with a crown of large dissected leaves and large green hanging fruit **2** the fruit of this tree, having a yellow sweet edible pulp and small black seeds ▷ Also called: **papaw, pawpaw** [C15 *papaye*, from Sp. *papaya*, of Amerind origin]

Papeete (,pɑːpɪ'iːtɪ) *n* the capital of French Polynesia, on the NW coast of Tahiti: one of the largest towns in the S Pacific. Pop: 25 353 (1996), with a conurbation of 121 000 (1996 est)

Papen (*German* 'pa:pən) *n* **Franz von** (frants fɔn) 1879–1969, German statesman; chancellor (1932) and vice chancellor (1933–34) under Hitler, whom he was instrumental in bringing to power

paper ('peɪpə) *n* **1** a substance made from cellulose fibres derived from rags, wood, etc, and formed into flat thin sheets suitable for writing on, decorating walls, wrapping, etc **2** a single piece of such material, esp if written or printed on **3** (*usually pl*) documents for establishing the identity of the bearer **4** (*pl*) Also called: **ship's papers** official documents relating to a ship **5** (*pl*) collected diaries, letters, etc **6** See **newspaper, wallpaper 7** *government* See **white paper, green paper 8** a lecture or treatise on a specific subject **9** a short essay **10a** a set of examination questions **10b** the student's answers **11** *commerce* See **commercial paper 12** *theatre sl* a free ticket **13 on paper** in theory, as opposed to fact ▷ *adj* **14** made of paper: *paper cups do not last long* **15** thin like paper: *paper walls* **16** (*prenominal*) existing only as recorded on paper but not yet in practice: *paper expenditure* **17** taking place in writing: *paper battles* ▷ *vb* **18** to cover (walls) with wallpaper **19** (*tr*) to cover or furnish with paper **20** (*tr*) *theatre sl* to fill (a performance, etc) by giving away free tickets (esp in **paper the house**) ▷ See also **paper over** [C14 from L PAPYRUS] > **'paperer** *n* > **'papery** *adj*

paperback ('peɪpəˌbæk) *n* **1** a book or edition with covers made of flexible card, sold relatively cheaply ▷ Cf **hardback** ▷ *adj also* **paperbound soft-cover 2** of or denoting a paperback or publication of paperbacks ▷ *vb* (*tr*) **3** to publish in paperback > **'paperˌbacker** *n*

paperbark ('peɪpəˌbɑ:k) *n* **1** any of several Australian myrtaceous trees of the genus *Melaleuca*, esp *M. quinquenervia*, of swampy regions, having spear-shaped leaves and papery bark that can be peeled off in thin layers **2** the papery bark of any of these trees

paperboy ('peɪpəˌbɔɪ) *n* a boy employed to deliver newspapers, etc > **'paperˌgirl** *fem n*

paper chase *n* a former type of cross-country run in which a runner laid a trail of paper for others to follow

paperclip ('peɪpəˌklɪp) *n* a clip for holding sheets of paper together, esp one of bent wire

paper-cutter *n* a machine for cutting paper, usually a blade mounted over a table

paperhanger ('peɪpəˌhæŋə) *n* a person who hangs wallpaper as an occupation

paperknife ('peɪpəˌnaɪf) *n, pl* **paperknives** a knife with a comparatively blunt blade for opening sealed envelopes, etc

paper money *n* paper currency issued by the government or the central bank as legal tender and which circulates as a substitute for specie

paper mulberry *n* a small E Asian tree, the inner bark of which was formerly used for making paper in Japan. See also **tapa**

paper nautilus *n* a cephalopod mollusc of warm and tropical seas, having a papery external spiral shell. Also called: **argonaut**

paper over *vb* (*tr, adv*) to conceal (something controversial or unpleasant) (esp in **paper over the cracks**)

paper tape *n* a strip of paper for recording information in the form of rows of either six or eight holes, some or all of which are punched to produce a combination used as a discrete code symbol, formerly used in computers, telex machines, etc. US equivalent: **perforated tape**

paper tiger *n* a nation, institution, etc, that appears powerful but is in fact weak or insignificant [C20 translation of a Chinese phrase first applied to the US]

paperweight ('peɪpəˌweɪt) *n* a small heavy object to prevent loose papers from scattering

paperwork ('peɪpəˌwɜ:k) *n* clerical work, such as the writing of reports or letters

Paphian ('peɪfɪən) *adj* **1** of or relating to Paphos **2** of or relating to Aphrodite **3** *literary* of sexual love

Paphlagonia (ˌpæfləˈgəʊnɪə) *n* an ancient country and Roman province in N Asia Minor, on the Black Sea

Paphos[1] ('peɪfɒs) *n* a village in SW Cyprus, near the sites of two ancient cities: famous as the centre of Aphrodite worship and traditionally the place at which she landed after her birth among the waves. Pop: 32 575 (1992 est)

Paphos[2] ('peɪfɒs) *or* **Paphus** ('peɪfəs) *n* *Greek myth* the son of Pygmalion and Galatea, who succeeded his father on the throne of Cyprus

papier-mâché (ˌpæpjeɪˈmæʃeɪ) *n* **1** a hard strong substance made of paper pulp or layers of paper mixed with paste, size, etc, and moulded when moist ▷ *adj* **2** made of papier-mâché [C18 from F, lit.: chewed paper]

papilla (pəˈpɪlə) *n, pl* **papillae** (-li:) **1** the small projection of tissue at the base of a hair, tooth, or feather **2** any similar protuberance [C18 from L: nipple] > **pa'pillary** *or* **'papillate** *adj*

papilloma (ˌpæpɪˈləʊmə) *n, pl* **papillomata** (-mətə) *or* **papillomas** *pathol* a benign tumour forming a rounded mass [C19 from PAPILLA + -OMA]

papillon ('pæpɪˌlɒn) *n* a breed of toy dog with large ears [F: butterfly, from L *pāpiliō*]

papillote ('pæpɪˌləʊt) *n* **1** a paper frill around cutlets, etc **2 en papillote** (*French* ɑ̃ papijɔt) (of food) cooked in oiled greaseproof paper or foil: *Dover sole en papillote* [C18 from F PAPILLON]

papist ('peɪpɪst) *n, adj* (*often cap*) *usually disparaging* another term for **Roman Catholic** [C16 from F *papiste*, from Church L *pāpa* POPE] > **pa'pistical** *or* **pa'pistic** *adj* > **'papistry** *n*

papoose (pəˈpu:s) *n* **1** an American Indian baby **2** a pouchlike bag used for carrying a baby, worn on the back [C17 from Algonquian *papoos*]

pappus ('pæpəs) *n, pl* **pappi** ('pæpaɪ) a ring of fine feathery hairs surrounding the fruit in composite plants, such as the thistle [C18 via NL from Gk *pappos* old man, old man's beard, hence: pappus, down] > **'pappose** *or* **'pappous** *adj*

paprika ('pæprɪkə, pæˈpri:-) *n* **1** a mild powdered seasoning made from a sweet variety of red pepper **2** the fruit or plant from which this seasoning is obtained [C19 via Hungarian from Serbian, from *papar* PEPPER]

Pap test *or* **smear** (pæp) *n* *med* **1** another name for **cervical smear 2** a similar test for precancerous cells in organs other than the cervix ▷ Also called: **Papanicolaou smear** [C20 after George *Papanicolaou* (1883–1962), US anatomist, who devised it]

Papua ('pæpjʊə) *n* **1 Territory of** a former territory of Australia, consisting of SE New Guinea and adjacent islands: now part of Papua New Guinea. Former name (1888–1906): **British New Guinea 2 Gulf of** an inlet of the Coral Sea in the SE coast of New Guinea > **'Papuan** *adj, n*

Papua New Guinea *n* a country in the SW Pacific; consists of the E half of New Guinea, the Bismarck Archipelago, the W Solomon Islands, Trobriand Islands, D'Entrecasteaux Islands, Woodlark Island, and the Louisiade Archipelago; administered by Australia from 1949 until 1975, when it became an independent member of the Commonwealth. Official language: English; Tok Pisin (English Creole) and Motu are widely spoken. Religion: Christian majority. Currency: kina. Capital: Port Moresby. Pop: 5 287 000 (2001 est). Area: 461 693 sq km (178 260 sq miles)
▷ www.pngonline.gov.pg

papule ('pæpju:l) *or* **papula** ('pæpjʊlə) *n, pl* **papules** *or* **papulae** (-jʊˌli:) *pathol* a small solid usually round elevation of the skin [C19 from L *papula* pustule] > **'papular** *adj*

papyrology (ˌpæpɪˈrɒlədʒɪ) *n* the study of ancient papyri > **ˌpapy'rologist** *n*

Pp

papyrus (pəˈpaɪrəs) *n, pl* **papyri** (-raɪ) *or* **papyruses** 1 a tall aquatic plant of S Europe and N and central Africa 2 a kind of paper made from the stem pith of this plant, used by the ancient Egyptians, Greeks, and Romans 3 an ancient document written on this paper [C14 via L from Gk *papūros* reed used in making paper]

par (pɑː) *n* 1 an accepted standard, such as an average (esp in **up to par**) 2 a state of equality (esp in **on a par with**) 3 *finance* the established value of the unit of one national currency in terms of the unit of another 4 *commerce* 4a See **par value** 4b equality between the current market value of a share, bond, etc, and its face value, indicated by **at par**; **above** (*or* **below**) **par** indicates that the market value is above (or below) face value 5 *golf* a standard score for a hole or course that a good player should make: *par for the course was 72* ▷ *adj* 6 average or normal 7 (*usually prenominal*) of or relating to par: *par value* [C17 from L *pār* equal]

par. *abbrev for:* 1 paragraph 2 parenthesis 3 parish

Par. *abbrev for* Paraguay

para (ˈpærə) *n inf* 1a a soldier in an airborne unit 1b an airborne unit 2 a paragraph

para-[1] *or before a vowel* **par-** *prefix* 1 beside; near: *parameter* 2 beyond: *parapsychology* 3 resembling: *paratyphoid fever* 4 defective; abnormal: *paranoia* 5 (*usually in italics*) denoting that an organic compound contains a benzene ring with substituents attached to atoms that are directly opposite (the 1,4- positions): *paracresol* 6 denoting an isomer, polymer, or compound related to a specified compound: *paraldehyde* 7 denoting the form of a diatomic substance in which the spins of the two constituent atoms are antiparallel: *parahydrogen* [from Gk *para* (prep) alongside, beyond]

para-[2] *combining form* indicating an object that acts as a protection against something: *parachute; parasol* [via F from It. *para-*, from *parare* to defend, ult. from L *parāre* to prepare]

Pará (*Portuguese* paˈra) *n* 1 a state of N Brazil, on the Atlantic: mostly dense tropical rainforest. Capital: Belém. Pop: 6 188 685 (2000). Area: 1 248 042 sq km (474 896 sq miles) 2 another name for **Belém** 3 an estuary in N Brazil into which flow the Tocantins River and a branch of the Amazon. Length: about 320 km (200 miles)

para-aminobenzoic acid (əˌmaɪnəʊbɛnˈzəʊɪk, -ˌmiː-) *n biochem* an acid present in yeast and liver: used in the manufacture of dyes and pharmaceuticals

parabasis (pəˈræbəsɪs) *n, pl* **parabases** (-ˌsiːz) (in classical Greek comedy) an address by the chorus [C19 from Gk, from *parabanein* to step forward]

parabiosis (ˌpærəbaɪˈəʊsɪs) *n* 1 the natural union of two individuals, such as Siamese twins 2 a similar union induced for experimental or therapeutic purposes [C20 from PARA-[1] + Gk *biōsis* manner of life, from *bios* life] > **parabiotic** (ˌpærəbaɪˈɒtɪk) *adj*

parable (ˈpærəbᵊl) *n* 1 a short story that uses familiar events to illustrate a religious or ethical point 2 any of the stories of this kind told by Jesus Christ [C14 from OF *parabole*, from L *parabola* comparison, from Gk *parabolē* analogy, from *paraballein* to throw alongside]

parabola (pəˈræbələ) *n* a conic section formed by the intersection of a cone by a plane parallel to its side [C16 via NL from Gk *parabolē* a setting alongside; see PARABLE]

parabolic[1] (ˌpærəˈbɒlɪk) *adj* 1 of, relating to, or shaped like a parabola 2 shaped like a paraboloid: *a parabolic mirror*

parabolic[2] (ˌpærəˈbɒlɪk) *or* **parabolical** *adj* of or like a parable > ˌ**paraˈbolically** *adv*

parabolic aerial *n* a formal name for **dish aerial**

paraboloid (pəˈræbəˌlɔɪd) *n* a geometric surface whose sections parallel to two coordinate planes are parabolic and whose sections parallel to the third plane are either elliptical or hyperbolic > **paˌraboˈloidal** *adj*

Paracelsus (ˌpærəˈsɛlsəs) *n* **Philippus Aureolus** (ˈfɪlɪpəs ˌɔːrɪˈəʊləs), real name *Theophrastus Bombastus von Hohenheim*. 1493–1541, Swiss physician and alchemist, who pioneered the use of specific treatment, based on observation and experience, to remedy particular diseases

paracetamol (ˌpærəˈsiːtəˌmɒl, -ˈsɛtə-) *n* a mild analgesic and antipyretic drug [C20 from *para-acetamidophenol*]

parachronism (pəˈrækrəˌnɪzəm) *n* an error in dating, esp by giving too late a date [C17 from PARA-[1] + *-chronism*, as in ANACHRONISM]

parachute (ˈpærəˌʃuːt) *n* 1 a device used to retard the fall of a person or package from an aircraft, consisting of a large fabric canopy connected to a harness ▷ *vb* **parachutes, parachuting, parachuted** 2 (of troops, supplies, etc) to land or cause to land by parachute from an aircraft [C18 from F, from PARA-[2] + *chute* fall] > ˈ**paraˌchutist** *n*

Paraclete (ˈpærəˌkliːt) *n Christianity* the Holy Ghost as comforter or advocate [C15 via OF from Church L *Paraclētus*, from LGk *Paraklētos* advocate, from Gk *parakalein* to summon help]

parade (pəˈreɪd) *n* 1 an ordered, esp ceremonial, march or procession, as of troops being reviewed 2 Also called: **parade ground** a place where military formations regularly assemble 3 a visible show or display: *to make a parade of one's grief* 4 a public promenade or street of shops 5 a successive display of things or people 6 **on parade** 6a on display 6b showing oneself off ▷ *vb* **parades, parading, paraded** 7 (when *intr*, often foll by *through* or *along*) to walk or march, esp in a procession 8 (*tr*) to exhibit or flaunt: *he was parading his medals* 9 (*tr*) to cause to assemble in formation, as for a military parade 10 (*intr*) to walk about in a public place [C17 from F: a making ready, a boasting display] > **paˈrader** *n*

paradiddle (ˈpærəˌdɪdᵊl) *n* a group of four drumbeats played with alternate sticks in the pattern right-left-right-right or left-right-left-left [C20 imit.]

paradigm (ˈpærəˌdaɪm) *n* 1 the set of all the inflected forms of a word 2 a pattern or model 3 (in the philosophy of science) a general conception of the nature of scientific endeavour within which a given enquiry is undertaken [C15 via F & L from Gk *paradeigma* pattern, from *paradeiknunai* to compare] > **paradigmatic** (ˌpærədɪɡˈmætɪk) *adj*

paradigm shift *n* a radical change in underlying beliefs or theory [C20 coined by T.S. Kuhn (1922–96), US philosopher of science]

paradisal (ˌpærəˈdaɪsᵊl), **paradisiacal** (ˌpærədɪˈsaɪəkᵊl), *or* **paradisiac** (ˌpærəˈdɪsɪˌæk) *adj* of, relating to, or resembling paradise

paradise (ˈpærəˌdaɪs) *n* 1 heaven as the ultimate abode or state of the righteous 2 *Islam* the sensual garden of delights that the Koran promises the faithful after death 3 Also called: **limbo** (according to some theologians) the intermediate abode or state of the just prior to the Resurrection of Jesus 4 the Garden of Eden 5 any place or condition that fulfils all one's desires or aspirations 6 a park in which foreign animals are kept [OE, from Church L *paradīsus*, from Gk *paradeisos* garden, of Persian origin]

paradise duck *n* a New Zealand duck with bright plumage

paradox (ˈpærəˌdɒks) *n* 1 a seemingly absurd or self-contradictory statement that is or may be true: *religious truths are often expressed in paradox* 2 a self-contradictory proposition, such as *I always tell lies* 3 a person or thing exhibiting apparently contradictory characteristics 4 an opinion that conflicts with common belief [C16 from LL *paradoxum*, from Gk *paradoxos* opposed to existing notions] > ˌ**paraˈdoxical** *adj* > ˌ**paraˈdoxically** *adv*

paradoxical sleep *n physiol* sleep that appears deep but is characterized by a brain wave pattern similar to that of wakefulness, rapid eye movements, and heavier breathing

paraffin ('pærəfɪn) *n* **1** Also called: **paraffin oil**, (esp US, Canad, Austral, & NZ) **kerosene** a liquid mixture consisting mainly of alkane hydrocarbons, used as an aircraft fuel, in domestic heaters, and as a solvent **2** another name for **alkane** **3** See **paraffin wax** **4** See **liquid paraffin** ▷ *vb* (*tr*) **5** to treat with paraffin [c19 from G, from L *parum* too little + *affinis* adjacent; so called from its chemical inertia]

paraffin wax *n* a white insoluble odourless waxlike solid consisting mainly of alkane hydrocarbons, used in candles, waterproof paper, and as a sealant. Also called: **paraffin**

paragliding ('pærəˌglaɪdɪŋ) *n* the sport of cross-country gliding using a specially designed parachute shaped like flexible wings. The parachutist glides from an aeroplane to a predetermined landing area
▷ www.fai.org/paragliding

paragon ('pærəgən) *n* a model of excellence; pattern: *a paragon of virtue* [c16 via F from OIt. *paragone* comparison, from Med. Gk *parakonē*, from PARA-[1] + *akonē* whetstone]

paragraph ('pærəˌgrɑːf) *n* **1** (in a piece of writing) one of a series of subsections each usually devoted to one idea and each marked by the beginning of a new line, indention, etc **2** *printing* the character ¶, used to indicate the beginning of a new paragraph **3** a short article, etc, in a newspaper ▷ *vb* (*tr*) **4** to form into paragraphs **5** to express or report in a paragraph [c16 from Med. L *paragraphus*, from Gk *paragraphos* line drawing attention to part of a text, from *paragraphein* to write beside] > **paragraphic** (ˌpærə'græfɪk) *adj*

paragraphia (ˌpærə'grɑːfɪə) *n psychiatry* the habitual writing of a different word or letter from the one intended, often the result of a mental disorder [c20 from NL; see PARA-[1], -GRAPH]

Paraguay ('pærəˌgwaɪ) *n* **1** an inland republic in South America: colonized by the Spanish from 1537, gaining independence in 1811; lost 142 500 sq km (55 000 sq miles) of territory and over half its population after its defeat in the war against Argentina, Brazil, and Uruguay (1865–70). It is divided by the Paraguay River into a sparsely inhabited semiarid region (Chaco) in the west, and a central region of wooded hills, tropical forests, and rich grasslands, rising to the Paraná plateau in the east. Official languages: Spanish and Guarani. Religion: Roman Catholic majority. Currency: guarani. Capital: Asunción. Pop: 5 636 000 (2001 est). Area: 406 750 sq km (157 047 sq miles) **2** a river in South America flowing south through Brazil and Paraguay to the Paraná River. Length: about 2400 km (1500 miles) > ˌ**Para'guayan** *adj, n*
▷ www.presidencia.gov.py/Presidencia/default.htm
▷ www.paraguay-tourism.com

Paraguay tea *n* another name for **maté**

parahydrogen (ˌpærə'haɪdrədʒən) *n chem* the form of molecular hydrogen in which the nuclei of the two atoms in each molecule spin in opposite directions

Paraíba (*Portuguese* para'iba) *n* **1** a state of NE Brazil, on the Atlantic: consists of a coastal strip, with hills and plains inland; irrigated agriculture. Capital: João Pessoa. Pop: 3 436 718 (2000). Area: 56 371 sq km (21 765 sq miles) **2** Also called: **Paraíba do Sul** ('duː sul) a river in SE Brazil, flowing southwest and then northeast to the Atlantic near Campos. Length: 1060 km (660 miles) **3** Also called: **Paraíba do Norte** ('duː 'nɔrtə) a river in NE Brazil, in Paraíba state, flowing northeast and east to the Atlantic. Length: 386 km (240 miles) **4** the former name (until 1930) of **João Pessoa**

parakeet *or* **parrakeet** ('pærəˌkiːt) *n* any of numerous small long-tailed parrots [c16 from Sp. *periquito* & OF *paroquet* parrot, from ?]

paraldehyde (pə'rældɪˌhaɪd) *n* a colourless liquid that is a cyclic trimer of acetaldehyde: used as a hypnotic

paralipsis (ˌpaerə'lɪpsɪs) *or* **paraleipsis** (ˌpærə'laɪpsɪs) *n, pl* **paralipses** *or* **paraleipses** (-siːz) a rhetorical device in which an idea is emphasized by the pretence that it is too obvious to discuss, as in *there are many practical drawbacks, not to mention the cost* [c16 via LL from Gk: neglect, from *paraleipein* to leave aside]

parallax ('pærəˌlæks) *n* **1** an apparent change in the position of an object resulting from a change in position of the observer **2** *astron* the angle subtended at a celestial body, esp a star, by the radius of the earth's orbit [c17 via F from NL *parallaxis*, from Gk: change, from *parallassein* to change] > **parallactic** (ˌpærə'læktɪk) *adj*

parallel ('pærəˌlɛl) *adj* (when *postpositive*, usually foll by *to*) **1** separated by an equal distance at every point; never touching or intersecting: *parallel walls* **2** corresponding; similar: *parallel situations* **3** *music* Also: **consecutive** (of two or more parts or melodies) moving in similar motion but keeping the same interval apart throughout: *parallel fifths* **4** *grammar* denoting syntactic constructions in which the constituents of one construction correspond to those of the other **5** *computing* operating on several items of information, instructions, etc, simultaneously ▷ *n* **6** *maths* one of a set of parallel lines, planes, etc **7** an exact likeness **8** a comparison **9** Also called: **parallel of latitude** any of the imaginary lines around the earth parallel to the equator, designated by degrees of latitude **10** *electronics* **10a** an arrangement of two or more electrical components connected between two points in a circuit so that the same voltage is applied to each (esp in **in parallel**) ▷ Cf **series** (sense 6) **10b** (*as modifier*): *a parallel circuit* **11** *printing* the character (‖) used as a reference mark ▷ *vb* **parallels, paralleling, paralleled** (*tr*) **12** to make parallel **13** to supply a parallel to **14** to be a parallel to or correspond with: *your experience parallels mine* [c16 via F & L from Gk *parallēlos* alongside one another, from PARA-[1] + *allēlos* one another]

parallel bars *pl n gymnastics* a pair of wooden bars on uprights used for various exercises

parallelepiped (ˌpærəˌlɛlɪ'paɪpɛd) *or* **parallelepipedon** (ˌpærəˌlɛlɪ'paɪpɪdən) *n* a geometric solid whose six faces are parallelograms [c16 from Gk, from *parallēlos* PARALLEL + *epipedon* plane surface, from EPI- + *pedon* ground]

parallel importing *n* the importing of certain goods, esp pharmaceutical drugs, by dealers who undersell local manufacturers

paralleling ('pærəˌlɛlɪŋ) *n* a form of trading in which companies buy highly priced goods in a market in which the prices are low in order to be able to sell them in a market in which the prices are higher

parallelism ('pærəˌlɛlɪzəm) *n* **1** the state of being parallel **2** *grammar* the repetition of a syntactic construction in successive sentences for rhetorical effect **3** *philosophy* the doctrine that mental and physical processes are regularly correlated but are not casually connected, so that, for example, pain always accompanies, but is not caused by, a pinprick

parallelogram (ˌpærə'lɛləˌgræm) *n* a quadrilateral whose opposite sides are parallel and equal in length [c16 via F from LL, from Gk *parallēlogrammon*, from *parallēlos* PARALLEL + *grammē* line]

parallelogram rule *n maths, physics* a rule for finding the resultant of two vectors by constructing a parallelogram with two adjacent sides representing the magnitudes and directions of the vectors, the diagonal through the point of intersection of the vectors representing their resultant

parallel port *n computing* (on a computer) a socket that can be used for connecting devices that send and receive data at more than one bit at a time; often used for connecting printers

parallel processing *n* the performance by a computer system of two or more simultaneous operations

parallel ruler *n engineering* a drawing instrument in which two parallel edges are connected so that they remain parallel, although the distance between them can be varied

paralogism (pəˈræləˌdʒɪzəm) *n* **1** *logic, psychol* an argument that is unintentionally invalid ▷ Cf **sophism** **2** any invalid argument or conclusion [C16 via LL from Gk *paralogismos*, from *paralogizesthai* to argue fallaciously, from PARA-[1] + *-logizesthai*, ult. from *logos* word] > **paˈralogist** *n*

Paralympian (ˌpærəˈlɪmpɪən) *n* a competitor in the Paralympics

Paralympics (ˌpærəˈlɪmpɪks) *n* **the** (*functioning as sing or pl*) a sporting event, modelled on the Olympic Games, held solely for disabled competitors. Also called: **the Parallel Olympics** [C20 from PARALLEL + OLYMPICS]
▷ www.paralympics.org

paralyse *or US* **paralyze** (ˈpærəˌlaɪz) *vb* **paralyses, paralysing, paralysed** *or US* **paralyzes, paralyzing, paralyzed** (*tr*) **1** *pathol* to affect with paralysis **2** *med* to render (a part of the body) insensitive to pain, touch, etc **3** to make immobile; transfix [C19 from F *paralyser*, from *paralysie* PARALYSIS] > ˌ**paralyˈsation** *or US* ˌ**paralyˈzation** *n* > ˈ**paraˌlyser** *or US* ˈ**paraˌlyzer** *n*

paralysis (pəˈrælɪsɪs) *n, pl* **paralyses** (-ˌsiːz) **1** *pathol* **1a** impairment or loss of voluntary muscle function or of sensation (**sensory paralysis**) in a part or area of the body **1b** a disease characterized by such impairment or loss; palsy **2** cessation or impairment of activity: *paralysis of industry by strikes* [C16 via L from Gk *paralusis*; see PARA-[1], -LYSIS]

paralytic (ˌpærəˈlɪtɪk) *adj* **1** of, relating to, or of the nature of paralysis **2** afflicted with or subject to paralysis **3** *Brit inf* very drunk ▷ *n* **4** a person afflicted with paralysis

paramagnetism (ˌpærəˈmægnɪˌtɪzəm) *n physics* a weakly magnetic condition of substances with a relative permeability just greater than unity: used in some special low temperature techniques > **paramagnetic** (ˌpærəmægˈnɛtɪk) *adj*

Paramaribo (ˌpærəˈmærɪˌbəʊ; *Dutch* paːraːˈmaːriːboː) *n* the capital and chief port of Surinam, 27 km (17 miles) from the Atlantic on the Surinam River: the only large town in the country. Pop: 233 000 (1999 est)
▷ www.sr.net/srnet/InfoSurinam/paramaribo.html

paramatta *or* **parramatta** (ˌpærəˈmætə) *n* a lightweight twill-weave dress fabric of wool with silk or cotton, now used esp for rubber-proofed garments [C19 after *Parramatta*, New South Wales, Australia, where orig. produced]

paramecium (ˌpærəˈmiːsɪəm) *n, pl* **paramecia** (-sɪə) any of a genus of freshwater protozoa having an oval body covered with cilia and a ventral groove for feeding [C18 NL, from Gk *paramēkēs* elongated, from PARA-[1] + *mēkos* length]

paramedic (ˌpærəˈmɛdɪk) *n* **1** a person, such as a laboratory technician, who supplements the work of the medical profession **2** a member of an ambulance crew trained in a number of life-saving skills, including infusion and cardiac care > ˌ**paraˈmedical** *adj*

parameter (pəˈræmɪtə) *n* **1** an arbitrary constant that determines the specific form of a mathematical expression, such as a and b in $y = ax^2 + b$ **2** a characteristic constant of a statistical population, such as its variance or mean **3** *inf* any constant or limiting factor: *a designer must work within the parameters of budget and practicality* [C17 from NL; see PARA-[1], -METER] > **parametric** (ˌpærəˈmɛtrɪk) *adj*

parametric amplifier *n* a type of high-frequency amplifier in which energy is transferred to the input signal through a circuit with a varying reactance

paramilitary (ˌpærəˈmɪlɪtərɪ, -trɪ) *adj* **1** denoting or relating to a group of personnel with military structure functioning either as a civil force or in support of military forces **2** denoting or relating to a force with military structure conducting armed operations against a ruling power

paramount (ˈpærəˌmaʊnt) *adj* of the greatest importance or significance [C16 via Anglo-Norman from OF *paramont*, from *par* by + *-amont* above, from L *ad montem* to the mountain] > ˈ**paraˌmountcy** *n* > ˈ**paraˌmountly** *adv*

paramour (ˈpærəˌmʊə) *n* **1** *now usually derog* a lover, esp adulterous **2** an archaic word for **beloved** [C13 from OF, lit.: through love]

Paraná *n* **1** (paraˈna) a state of S Brazil, on the Atlantic: consists of a coastal plain and a large rolling plateau with extensive forests. Capital: Curitiba. Pop: 9 558 126 (2000). Area: 199 555 sq km (77 048 sq miles) **2** (paraˈna) a city in E Argentina, on the Paraná River opposite Santa Fe: capital of Argentina (1853–1862). Pop: 256 602 (1999 est) **3** (*Portuguese* paraˈna; *Spanish* paraˈna) a river in central South America, formed in S Brazil by the confluence of the Rio Grande and the Paranaíba River and flowing generally south to the Atlantic through the Río de la Plata estuary. Length: 2900 km (1800 miles)

parang (ˈpɑːræŋ) *n* a Malay short stout straight-edged knife used in Borneo [C19 from Malay]

paranoia (ˌpærəˈnɔɪə) *n* **1** a mental disorder characterized by any of several types of delusions, as of grandeur or persecution **2** *inf* intense fear or suspicion, esp when unfounded [C19 via NL from Gk: frenzy, from *paranoos* distraught, from PARA-[1] + *noos* mind] > ˈ**paraˌnoid, paranoiac** (ˌpærəˈnɔɪɪk) *or* **paranoic** (ˌpærəˈnəʊɪk) *adj, n*

paranormal (ˌpærəˈnɔːməl) *adj* **1** beyond normal explanation ▷ *n* **2** **the** paranormal happenings generally
▷ www.paraseek.com/
▷ http://paranormal.com/

parapente (ˈpærəˌpɒnt) *n* **1** another name for **paraskiing** **2** the form of parachute used in this sport [C20 from PARA(CHUTE) + F *pente* slope]

parapet (ˈpærəpɪt, -ˌpɛt) *n* **1** a low wall or railing along the edge of a balcony, roof, etc **2** *mil* a rampart, mound of sandbags, etc, in front of a trench giving protection from fire [C16 from It. *parapetto*, lit.: chest-high wall, from L *pectus* breast]

paraph (ˈpærəf) *n* a flourish after a signature, originally to prevent forgery [C14 via F from Med. L *paraphus*, var. of *paragraphus* PARAGRAPH]

paraphernalia (ˌpærəfəˈneɪlɪə) *pl n* (*sometimes functioning as sing*) **1** miscellaneous articles or equipment **2** *law* (formerly) articles of personal property given to a married woman by her husband and regarded in law as her possessions [C17 via Med. L from L *parapherna* personal property of a married woman, apart from her dowry, from Gk, from PARA-[1] + *phernē* dowry, from *pherein* to carry]

paraphrase (ˈpærəˌfreɪz) *n* **1** an expression of a statement or text in other words ▷ *vb* **paraphrases, paraphrasing, paraphrased** **2** to put into other words; restate [C16 via F from L *paraphrasis*, from Gk, from *paraphrazein* to recount] > **paraphrastic** (ˌpærəˈfræstɪk) *adj*

paraplegia (ˌpærəˈpliːdʒə) *n pathol* paralysis of the lower half of the body, usually as the result of disease or injury of the spine [C17 via NL from Gk: a blow on one side, from PARA-[1] + *plēssein* to strike] > ˌ**paraˈplegic** *adj, n*

parapraxis (ˌpærəˈpræksɪs) *n, pl* **parapraxes** (-ˈpræksiːz) *psychoanal* a minor error in action, such as a slip of the tongue [C20 from PARA-[1] + Gk *praxis* a deed]

parapsychology (ˌpærəsaɪˈkɒlədʒɪ) *n* the study of mental phenomena, such as telepathy, which are beyond the scope of normal physical explanation > ˌ**parapsyˈchologist** *n*

▹ www.parapsychology.org/
▹ www.psiresearch.org/para1.html

Paraquat ('pærəˌkwɒt) *n trademark* a yellow extremely poisonous weedkiller

parascending ('pærəˌsɛndɪŋ) *n* a sport in which a parachutist, starting from ground level, is towed by a vehicle until he is airborne and then descends in the normal way

paraselene (ˌpærəsɪ'li:nɪ) *n, pl* **paraselenae** (-ni:) a bright image of the moon on a lunar halo. Also called: **mock moon** [c17 NL, from PARA-[1] + Gk *selēnē* moon]

parasite ('pærəˌsaɪt) *n* **1** an animal or plant that lives in or on another (the host) from which it obtains nourishment **2** a person who habitually lives at the expense of others; sponger [c16 via L from Gk *parasitos* one who lives at another's expense, from PARA-[1] + *sitos* grain] > **parasitic** (ˌpærə'sɪtɪk) *or* **ˌpara'sitical** *adj* > **ˌpara'sitically** *adv* > **'parasiˌtism** *n*

parasitize *or* **parasitise** ('pærəsɪˌtaɪz) *vb* **parasitizes, parasitizing, parasitized** *or* **parasitises, parasitising, parasitised** (*tr*) **1** to infest with parasites **2** to live on (another organism) as a parasite > **ˌparasiti'zation** *or* **ˌparasiti'sation** *n*

parasitoid ('pærəsɪˌtɔɪd) *n zool* an animal, esp an insect, that is parasitic as a larva but becomes free-living when adult

parasitology (ˌpærəsaɪ'tɒlədʒɪ) *n* the branch of biology that is concerned with the study of parasites > **ˌparasit'ologist** *n*

paraskiing ('pærəˌski:ɪŋ) *n* the sport of jumping off high mountains wearing skis and a light parachute composed of inflatable fabric tubes that form a semirigid wing. Also called: **parapente**

parasol ('pærəˌsɒl) *n* an umbrella used for protection against the sun; sunshade [c17 via F from It. *parasole*, from PARA-[2] + *sole* sun, from L *sōl*]

parasuicide (ˌpærə'su:ɪˌsaɪd) *n* an attempt to inflict an injury on oneself, not motivated by a desire to die

parasympathetic (ˌpærəˌsɪmpə'θɛtɪk) *adj anat, physiol* of or relating to the division of the autonomic nervous system that acts by slowing the heartbeat, constricting the bronchi of the lungs, stimulating the smooth muscles of the digestive tract, etc ▹ Cf **sympathetic** (sense 4)

parasynthesis (ˌpærə'sɪnθɪsɪs) *n* formation of words by compounding a phrase and adding an affix, as *light-headed*, *light* + *head* with the affix *-ed* > **parasynthetic** (ˌpærəsɪn'θɛtɪk) *adj*

parataxis (ˌpærə'tæksɪs) *n* the juxtaposition of clauses without the use of a conjunction, as *None of my friends stayed—they all left early* [c19 NL from Gk, from *paratassein*, lit.: to arrange side by side] > **paratactic** (ˌpærə'tæktɪk) *adj*

parathion (ˌpærə'θaɪɒn) *n* a toxic oil used as an insecticide [from PARA-[1] + Gk *theion* sulphur]

parathyroid gland (ˌpærə'θaɪrɔɪd) *n* any one of the small egg-shaped endocrine glands situated near or embedded within the thyroid gland

paratroops ('pærəˌtru:ps) *pl n* troops trained and equipped to be dropped by parachute into a battle area. Also called: **paratroopers**

paratyphoid fever (ˌpærə'taɪfɔɪd) *n* a disease resembling but less severe than typhoid fever, caused by bacteria of the genus *Salmonella*

paravane ('pærəˌveɪn) *n* a torpedo-shaped device towed from the bow of a vessel so that the cables will cut the anchors of any moored mines [c20 from PARA-[2] + VANE]

par avion *French* (par avjɔ̃) *adv* by aeroplane: used in labelling mail sent by air

parazoan (ˌpærə'zəʊən) *n, pl* **parazoa** (-'zəʊə) any multicellular invertebrate of a division of the animal kingdom, the sponges [c19 from *parazoa*, on the model of *protozoa* & *metazoa*, from PARA-[1] + Gk *zōon* animal]

parboil ('pɑ:ˌbɔɪl) *vb* (*tr*) **1** to boil until partially cooked **2** to subject to uncomfortable heat [c15 from OF *parboillir*, from LL *perbullīre* to boil thoroughly (see PER-, BOIL[1]); modern meaning due to confusion of *par-* with *part*]

parbuckle ('pɑ:ˌbʌkᵊl) *n* **1** a rope sling for lifting or lowering a heavy cylindrical object, such as a cask ▹ *vb* **parbuckles, parbuckling, parbuckled 2** (*tr*) to raise or lower (an object) with such a sling [c17 *parbunkel*: from ?]

Parcae ('pɑ:si:) *pl n, sing* **Parca** ('pɑ:kə) **the** the Roman goddesses of fate. Greek counterparts: The **Moirai**

parcel ('pɑ:sᵊl) *n* **1** something wrapped up; package **2** a group of people or things having some common characteristic **3** a quantity of some commodity offered for sale; lot **4** a distinct portion of land ▹ *vb* **parcels, parcelling, parcelled** *or US* **parcels, parceling, parceled** (*tr*) **5** (often foll by *up*) to make a parcel of; wrap up **6** (often foll by *out*) to divide (up) into portions [c14 from OF *parcelle*, from L *particula* PARTICLE]

parch (pɑ:tʃ) *vb* **1** to deprive or be deprived of water; dry up: *the sun parches the fields* **2** (*tr; usually passive*) to make very thirsty **3** (*tr*) to roast (corn, etc) lightly [c14 from ?]

Parcheesi (pɑ:'tʃi:zɪ) *n trademark* a board game derived from the ancient game of pachisi

parchment ('pɑ:tʃmənt) *n* **1** the skin of certain animals, such as sheep, treated to form a durable material, as for manuscripts **2** a manuscript, etc, made of this material **3** a type of stiff yellowish paper resembling parchment [c13 from OF *parchemin*, via L from Gk *pergamēnē*, from *Pergamēnos* of Pergamum (where parchment was made); OF *parchemin* was infl. by *parche* leather, from L *Parthica* (*pellis*) Parthian (leather)]

pard (pɑ:d) *n arch* a leopard or panther [c13 via OF from L *pardus*, from Gk *pardos*]

pardon ('pɑ:dᵊn) *vb* (*tr*) **1** to excuse or forgive (a person) for (an offence, mistake, etc): *to pardon someone; to pardon a fault* ▹ *n* **2** forgiveness **3a** release from punishment for an offence **3b** the warrant granting such release **4** a Roman Catholic indulgence ▹ *sentence substitute* **5** Also: **pardon me, I beg your pardon 5a** sorry; excuse me **5b** what did you say? [c13 from OF, from Med. L *perdōnum*, from *perdōnāre* to forgive freely, from L *per* (intensive) + *dōnāre* to grant] > **'pardonable** *adj* > **'pardonably** *adv*

Pp

pardoner ('pɑ:dᵊnə) *n* (before the Reformation) a person licensed to sell ecclesiastical indulgences

Pardubice (*Czech* 'pardubitsɛ) *n* a city in the central Czech Republic, on the Elbe River: 13th-century cathedral; oil refinery. Pop: 163 000 (1993)

pare (pɛə) *vb* **pares, paring, pared** (*tr*) **1** to peel (the outer layer) from (something) **2** to cut the edges from (the nails) **3** to decrease bit by bit [c13 from OF *parer* to adorn, from L *parāre* to make ready] > **'parer** *n*

Paré (*French* pare) *n* **Ambroise** (ɑ̃brwaz) 1510–90, French surgeon. He reintroduced ligature of arteries following amputation instead of cauterization

paregoric (ˌpærə'gɒrɪk) *n* a medicine consisting of opium, benzoic acid, and camphor, formerly widely used to relieve diarrhoea and coughing [c17 (meaning: relieving pain): via LL from Gk *parēgoros* relating to soothing speech, from PARA-[1] (beside) + *agora* assembly]

pareira (pə'rɛərə) *n* the root of a South American climbing plant, used as a diuretic, tonic, and as a source of curare [c18 from Port. *pareira brava*, lit.: wild vine]

parenchyma (pə'rɛŋkɪmə) *n* **1** a soft plant tissue consisting of simple thin-walled cells: constitutes the greater part of fruits, stems, roots, etc **2** animal tissue that constitutes the essential part of an organ as distinct from the blood vessels, connective tissue, etc [c17 via NL from Gk *parenkhuma* something poured in beside, from PARA-[1] + *enkhuma* infusion] > **parenchymatous** (ˌpærɛŋ'kɪmətəs) *adj*

parent ('pɛərənt) *n* **1** a father or mother **2** a person acting as a father or mother; guardian **3** *rare* an ancestor **4** a source or cause **5** an organism or organization that has produced one or more organisms similar to itself **6** *physics, chem* a precursor, such as a nucleus or compound, of a derived entity [C15 via OF from L *parens* parent, from *parere* to bring forth] > **pa'rental** *adj* > **'parenthood** *n*

parentage ('pɛərəntɪdʒ) *n* **1** ancestry **2** derivation from a particular origin **3** the state or condition of being a parent

parent company *n* a company that owns a number of subsidiary companies

parenteral (pæ'rɛntərəl) *adj med* **1** (esp of the route by which a drug is administered) by means other than through the digestive tract, esp by injection **2** designating a drug to be injected [C20 from PARA-[1] + ENTERO- + -AL[1]]

parenthesis (pə'rɛnθɪsɪs) *n, pl* **parentheses** (-ˌsiːz) **1** a phrase, often explanatory or qualifying, inserted into a passage with which it is not grammatically connected, and marked off by brackets, dashes, etc **2** Also called: **bracket** either of a pair of characters, ( ), used to enclose such a phrase or as a sign of aggregation in mathematical or logical expressions **3** an interlude; interval **4** **in parenthesis** inserted as a parenthesis [C16 via LL from Gk: something placed in besides, from *parentithenai*, from PARA-[1] + EN-[2] + *tithenai* to put] > **parenthetic** (ˌpærən'θɛtɪk) *or* **ˌparen'thetical** *adj* > **ˌparen'thetically** *adv*

parenthesize *or* **parenthesise** (pə'rɛnθɪˌsaɪz) *vb* **parenthesizes, parenthesizing, parenthesized** *or* **parenthesises, parenthesising, parenthesised** *(tr)* **1** to place in parentheses **2** to insert as a parenthesis **3** to intersperse (a speech, writing, etc) with parentheses

parenting ('pɛərəntɪŋ) *n* all the skills and experience of bringing up children

parent teacher association *n* a social group of the parents of children at a school and their teachers formed in order to foster better understanding between them and to organize fund-raising activities on behalf of the school

parergon (pə'rɛəgɒn) *n, pl* **parerga** (-gə) work that is not one's main employment [C17 from L, from Gk, from PARA-[1] + *ergon* work]

paresis (pə'riːsɪs, 'pærɪsɪs) *n, pl* **pareses** (-ˌsiːz) *pathol* incomplete or slight paralysis of motor functions [C17 via NL from Gk: a relaxation, from *parienai* to let go] > **paretic** (pə'rɛtɪk) *adj*

Pareto (*Italian* pa'rɛːto) *n* **1** **Vilfredo** (vil'freːdo) 1848–1923, Italian sociologist and economist. He anticipated Fascist principles of government in his *Mind and Society* (1916) **2** *(modifier)* denoting a law, mathematical formula, etc, originally used by Pareto to express the frequency distribution of incomes in a society

par excellence *French* (par ɛksɛlɑ̃s; *English* pɑːr 'ɛksələns) *adv* to a degree of excellence; beyond comparison [lit.: by (way of) excellence]

parfait (pɑː'feɪ) *n* a rich frozen dessert made from eggs and cream, fruit, etc [from F: PERFECT]

parget ('pɑːdʒɪt) *n* **1** Also called: **pargeting** **1a** plaster, mortar, etc, used to line chimney flues or cover walls **1b** plasterwork that has incised ornamental patterns ▷ *vb (tr)* **2** to cover or decorate with parget [C14 from OF *pargeter* to throw over, from *par* PER- + *geter* to throw]

parhelic circle *n meteorol* a luminous band at the same altitude as the sun, parallel to the horizon, caused by reflection of the sun's rays by ice crystals in the atmosphere

parhelion (pɑː'hiːlɪən) *n, pl* **parhelia** (-lɪə) one of several bright spots on the parhelic circle or solar halo, caused by the diffraction of light by ice crystals in the atmosphere. Also called: **mock sun** [C17 via L from Gk *parēlion*, from PARA-[1] (beside) + *hēlios* sun] > **par'helic** *or* **parheliacal** (ˌpɑːhɪ'laɪəkᵊl) *adj*

pariah (pə'raɪə, 'pærɪə) *n* **1** a social outcast **2** (formerly) a member of a low caste in South India [C17 from Tamil *paraiyan* drummer, from *parai* drum: members were drummers at festivals]

pariah dog *n* another term for **pye-dog**

Paricutín (*Spanish* pariku'tin) *n* a volcano in W central Mexico, in Michoacán state, formed in 1943 after a week of earth tremors; grew to a height of 2500 m (8200 ft) in a year and buried the village of Paricutín

parietal (pə'raɪɪtᵊl) *adj* **1** *anat, biol* of or forming the walls of a bodily cavity: *the parietal bones of the skull* **2** of or relating to the side of the skull **3** (of plant ovaries) having ovules attached to the walls **4** *US* living or having authority within a college ▷ *n* **5** a parietal bone [C16 from LL *parietālis*, from L *pariēs* wall]

parietal lobe *n* the portion of each cerebral hemisphere concerned with the perception of sensations of touch, temperature, and taste and with muscular movements

pari-mutuel (ˌpærɪ'mjuːtʃʊəl) *n, pl* **pari-mutuels** *or* **paris-mutuels** (ˌpærɪ'mjuːtʃʊəlz) a system of betting in which those who have bet on the winners of a race share in the total amount wagered less a percentage for the management [C19 from F, lit.: mutual wager]

paring ('pɛərɪŋ) *n (often pl)* something pared or cut off

pari passu *Latin* (ˌpærɪ 'pæsuː, 'pɑːrɪ) *adv usually legal* with equal speed or progress

Paris[1] ('pærɪs; *French* pari) *n* **1** the capital of France, in the north on the River Seine: constitutes a department; dates from the 3rd century BC, becoming capital of France in 987; centre of the French Revolution; centres around its original site on an island in the Seine, the **Île de la Cité**, containing Notre Dame; university (1150). Pop: 2 123 261 (1999). Ancient name: **Lutetia** **2** **Treaty of Paris** **2a** a treaty of 1783 between the US, Britain, France, and Spain, ending the War of American Independence **2b** a treaty of 1763 signed by Britain, France, and Spain that ended their involvement in the Seven Years' War **2c** a treaty of 1898 between Spain and the US bringing to an end the Spanish-American War [via F and OF, from LL (*Lūtētia*) *Parisiōrum* (marshes) of the *Parisii*, a tribe of Celtic Gaul] > **Parisian** (pə'rɪzɪən) *n, adj*
▷ www.paris.org

Paris[2] ('pærɪs) *n* **1** *Greek myth* a prince of Troy, whose abduction of Helen from her husband Menelaus started the Trojan War **2** **Matthew** ?1200–59, English chronicler, whose principal work is the *Chronica Majora*

Paris Club *n* a group of the richest members of the International Monetary Fund, which meets informally in Paris

Paris Commune *n French history* the council established in Paris in the spring of 1871 in opposition to the National Assembly and esp to the peace negotiated with Prussia following the Franco-Prussian War
▷ www.wikipedia.org/wiki/Paris_commune
▷ www.library.northwestern.edu/spec/siege

Paris green *n* an emerald-green poisonous substance used as a pigment and insecticide

parish ('pærɪʃ) *n* **1** a subdivision of a diocese, having its own church and a clergyman **2** the churchgoers of such a subdivision **3** (in England and, formerly, Wales) the smallest unit of local government **4** (in Louisiana) a county **5** (in Quebec and New Brunswick, Canada) a subdivision of a county **6** the people living in a parish **7** **on the parish** *history* receiving parochial relief [C13 from OF *paroisse*, from Church L, from LGk, from *paroikos* Christian, sojourner, from Gk: neighbour, from PARA-[1] (beside) + *oikos* house]

parish clerk *n* a person designated to assist in various church duties

parish council *n* (in England and, formerly, Wales) the administrative body of a parish. See **parish** (sense 3)

parishioner (pəˈrɪʃənə) *n* a member of a particular parish

parish pump *adj* of only local interest; parochial

parish register *n* a book in which the births, baptisms, marriages, and deaths in a parish are recorded

parity (ˈpærɪtɪ) *n, pl* **parities** **1** equality of rank, pay, etc **2** close or exact analogy or equivalence **3** *finance* the amount of a foreign currency equivalent to a specific sum of domestic currency **4** equality between prices of commodities or securities in two separate markets **5** *physics* **5a** a property of a physical system characterized by the behaviour of the sign of its wave function when reflected in space. The wave function either remains unchanged (**even parity**) or changes in sign (**odd parity**) **5b** a quantum number describing this property, equal to +1 for even parity systems and −1 for odd parity systems. Symbol: P **6** *maths* a relationship between two integers. If both are odd or both even they have the same parity; if one is odd and one even they have different parity [c16 from LL *pāritās*; see PAR]

parity check *n* a check made of computer data to ensure that the total number of bits of value 1 (or 0) in each unit of information remains odd or even after transfer between a peripheral device and the memory or vice versa

park (pɑːk) *n* **1** a large area of land preserved in a natural state for recreational use by the public **2** a piece of open land for public recreation in a town **3** a large area of land forming a private estate **4** an area designed to accommodate a number of related enterprises: *a business park* **5** *US & Canad* a playing field or sports stadium **6 the park** *Brit inf* a soccer pitch **7** a gear selector position on the automatic transmission of a motor vehicle that acts as a parking brake **8** the area in which the equipment and supplies of a military formation are assembled ▷ *vb* **9** to stop and leave (a vehicle) temporarily **10** to manoeuvre (a motor vehicle) into a space for it to be left: *try to park without hitting the kerb* **11** *stock exchange* to register (securities) in the name of another or of nominees in order to conceal their real ownership **12** (*tr*) *inf* to leave or put somewhere: *park yourself in front of the fire* **13** (*intr*) *mil* to arrange equipment in a park **14** (*tr*) to enclose in or as a park [c13 from OF *parc*, from Med. L *parricus* enclosure, from Gmc]

Park (pɑːk) *n* **1 Mungo** (ˈmʌŋgəʊ) 1771–1806, Scottish explorer. He led two expeditions (1795–97; 1805–06) to trace the course of the Niger in Africa. He was drowned during the second expedition **2 Nick**, full name *Nicholas Wulstan Park*. born 1958, British animator and film director; his films include *A Grand Day Out* (1992), which introduced the characters Wallace and Gromit, and the feature-length *Chicken Run* (2000) **3 Chung Hee** (ˈtʃʊŋ ˈhiː) 1917–79, South Korean politician; president of the Republic of Korea (1963–79); assassinated

parka (ˈpɑːkə) *n* a warm weatherproof coat with a hood, originally worn by the Inuit [c19 from Aleutian: skin]

parkade (ˈpɑːkeɪd) *n Canad* a building used as a car park [c20 from PARK + (ARC)ADE]

Parker (ˈpɑːkə) *n* **1 Alan (William)** born 1944, British film director and screenwriter; his films include *Midnight Express* (1978), *Mississippi Burning* (1988), *The Commitments* (1991), and *Angela's Ashes* (2000); chairman of the British Film Institute (1998–99) and of the Film Council from 1999 **2 Charlie** nickname *Bird* or *Yardbird*. 1920–55, US jazz alto saxophonist and composer; the leading exponent of early bop **3 Dorothy (Rothschild)** 1893–1967, US writer, noted esp for the ironical humour of her short stories **4 Matthew** 1504–75, English prelate. As archbishop of Canterbury (1559–75), he supervised Elizabeth I's religious settlement

Parker Bowles (ˈpɑːkə bəulz) *n* **Camilla** (née *Shand*) born 1947, British mistress of Prince Charles. Her marriage to the cavalry officer Andrew Parker Bowles was dissolved in 1995

Parkes (pɑːks) *n* Sir **Henry** 1815–96, Australian journalist and politician born in England, five times premier of New South Wales, advocate of free trade and Federation, and a founder of the public education system

parkette (ˌpɑːkˈɛt) *n Canad* a small public park

parkin (ˈpɑːkɪn) *n* (in Britain and New Zealand) moist spicy ginger cake usually containing oatmeal [c19 from ?]

parking lot *n* the US and Canad term for **car park**

parking meter *n* a timing device, usually coin-operated, that indicates how long a vehicle may be left parked

parking orbit *n* an orbit around the earth or moon in which a spacecraft can be placed temporarily in order to prepare for the next step in its programme

parking ticket *n* a summons served for a parking offence

Parkinson's disease (ˈpɑːkɪnsənz) *n* a progressive chronic disorder of the central nervous system characterized by impaired muscular coordination and tremor. Often shortened to **Parkinson's** Also called: **Parkinsonism** [c19 after James *Parkinson* (1755–1824), Brit surgeon, who first described it]

Parkinson's law *n* the notion, expressed facetiously as a law of economics, that work expands to fill the time available for its completion [c20 after C. N. *Parkinson* (1909–93), Brit historian and writer, who formulated it]

park keeper *n* (in Britain) an official who patrols and supervises a public park

parkland (ˈpɑːkˌlænd) *n* grassland with scattered trees

parky (ˈpɑːkɪ) *adj* **parkier, parkiest** (*usually postpositive*) *Brit inf* (of the weather) chilly; cold [c19 ?from PERKY]

parlance (ˈpɑːləns) *n* a particular manner of speaking, esp when specialized; idiom: *political parlance* [c16 from OF, from *parler* to talk, via Med. L from LL *parabola* speech]

parlando (pɑːˈlændəʊ) *adj, adv music* to be performed as though speaking [It.: speaking]

parley (ˈpɑːlɪ) *n* **1** a discussion, esp between enemies under a truce to decide terms of surrender, etc ▷ *vb* **2** (*intr*) to discuss, esp with an enemy [c16 from F, from *parler* to talk, from Med. L *parabolāre*, from LL *parabola* speech]

parliament (ˈpɑːləmənt) *n* **1** an assembly of the representatives of a political nation or people, often the supreme legislative authority **2** any legislative or deliberative assembly, conference, etc [c13 from Anglo-L *parliamentum*, from OF *parlement*, from *parler* to speak; see PARLEY]

▷ www.ipu.org/english/parlweb.htm

Parliament (ˈpɑːləmənt) *n* **1** the highest legislative authority in Britain, consisting of the House of Commons, which exercises effective power, the House of Lords, and the sovereign **2** a similar legislature in another country or state **3** any of the assemblies of such a body created by a general election and royal summons and dissolved before the next election

parliamentarian (ˌpɑːləmɛnˈtɛərɪən) *n* **1** an expert in parliamentary procedures ▷ *adj* **2** of or relating to a parliament

parliamentary (ˌpɑːləˈmɛntərɪ) *adj* (*sometimes cap*) **1** of or proceeding from a parliament or Parliament: *a parliamentary decree* **2** conforming to the procedures of a parliament or Parliament: *parliamentary conduct* **3** having a parliament or Parliament

Parliamentary Commissioner *or in full* **Parliamentary Commissioner for Administration** *n* (in Britain) the official name for **ombudsman** (sense 2)

parliamentary private secretary *n* (in Britain) a backbencher in Parliament who assists a minister. Abbrev: **PPS**

Pp

parliamentary secretary *n* a member of Parliament appointed to assist a minister of the Crown with his departmental responsibilities

parlour *or US* **parlor** ('pɑːlə) *n* 1 *old-fashioned* a living room, esp one kept tidy for the reception of visitors 2 a small room for guests away from the public rooms in an inn, club, etc 3 *chiefly US, Canad, & NZ* a room or shop equipped as a place of business: *a billiard parlor; a beauty parlour* 4 a building equipped for the milking of cows [C13 from Anglo-Norman *parlur*, from OF *parleur* room in convent for receiving guests, from *parler* to speak; see PARLEY]

parlous ('pɑːləs) *arch or humorous* ▷ *adj* 1 dangerous or difficult 2 cunning ▷ *adv* 3 extremely [C14 *perlous*, var. of PERILOUS] > '**parlously** *adv*

Parma *n* 1 (*Italian* 'parma) a city in N Italy, in Emilia-Romagna: capital of the duchy of Parma and Piacenza from 1545 until it became part of Italy in 1860; important food industry (esp Parmesan cheese). Pop: 168 717 (2000 est) 2 ('pɑːmə) a city in NE Ohio, south of Cleveland. Pop: 85 006 (1996 est) > **Parmesan** (ˌpɑːmɪ'zæn, 'pɑːmɪˌzæn) *adj, n*

Parmenides (pɑː'mɛnɪˌdiːz) *n* 5th century BC, Greek Eleatic philosopher, born in Italy. He held that the universe is single and unchanging and denied the existence of change and motion. His doctrines are expounded in his poem *On Nature*, of which only fragments are extant

Parmesan cheese *n* a hard dry cheese used grated, esp on pasta dishes and soups

Parmigianino (*Italian* parmidʒa'nino) *n* real name *Girolamo Francesco Maria Mazzola*. 1503–40, Italian painter, one of the originators of mannerism. Also called: **Parmigiano** (parmi'dʒano)

Parnaíba *or* **Parnahiba** (*Portuguese* parna'iba) *n* a river in NE Brazil, rising in the Serra das Mangabeiras and flowing generally northeast, to the Atlantic. Length: about 1450 km (900 miles)

Parnassus (pɑː'næsəs) *n* 1 **Mount** a mountain in central Greece, in NW Boeotia: in ancient times sacred to Dionysus, Apollo, and the Muses, with the Castalian Spring and Delphi on its slopes. Height: 2457 m (8061 ft). Modern Greek names: **Parnassós** (ˌparna'sɔs), **Liákoura** 2a the world of poetry 2b a centre of poetic or other creative activity 3 a collection of verse or belles-lettres > **Par'nassian** *adj*

Parnell ('pɑːnᵊl, pɑː'nɛl) *n* **Charles Stewart** 1846–91, Irish nationalist, who led the Irish Home Rule movement in Parliament (1880–90) with a calculated policy of obstruction. Although Gladstone was converted to Home Rule (1886), Parnell's career was ruined by the scandal over his adultery with Mrs O'Shea

parochial (pə'rəʊkɪəl) *adj* 1 narrow in outlook or scope; provincial 2 of or relating to a parish [C14 via OF from Church L *parochiālis*; see PARISH] > **pa'rochialˌism** *n* > **pa'rochially** *adv*

parody ('pærədɪ) *n, pl* **parodies** 1 a musical, literary, or other composition that mimics the style of another composer, author, etc, in a humorous or satirical way 2 something so badly done as to seem an intentional mockery; travesty ▷ *vb* **parodies, parodying, parodied** 3 (*tr*) to make a parody of [C16 via L from Gk *paroidiā* satirical poem, from PARA-[1] + *ōidē* song] > **parodic** (pə'rɒdɪk) *or* **pa'rodical** *adj* > '**parodist** *n*

parol ('pærəl, pə'rəʊl) *law* ▷ *n* 1 an oral statement; word of mouth (now only in **by parol**) ▷ *adj* 2a (of a contract, lease, etc) made orally or in writing but not under seal 2b expressed or given by word of mouth: *parol evidence* [C15 from OF *parole* speech; see PAROLE]

parole (pə'rəʊl) *n* 1a the freeing of a prisoner before his or her sentence has expired, on the condition that he or she is of good behaviour 1b the duration of such conditional release 2 a promise given by a prisoner, as to be of good behaviour if granted liberty or partial liberty 3 *linguistics* language as manifested in the individual speech acts of particular speakers 4 **on parole** conditionally released from detention ▷ *vb* **paroles, paroling, paroled** (*tr*) 5 to place (a person) on parole [C17 from OF, from *parole d'honneur* word of honour; *parole* from LL *parabola* speech] > **parolee** (pəˌrəʊ'liː) *n*

paronomasia (ˌpærənəʊ'meɪzɪə) *n rhetoric* a play on words, esp a pun [C16 via L from Gk, from *paronomazein* to make a change in naming, from PARA-[1] (besides) + *onomazein* to name, from *onoma* a name]

Páros ('pærɒs) *n* a Greek island in the S Aegean Sea, in the Cyclades: site of the discovery (1627) of the Parian Chronicle, a marble tablet outlining Greek history from before 1000 BC to about 354 BC (now at Oxford University). Pop: 8000 (latest est). Area: 166 sq km (64 sq miles) > '**Parian** *adj, n*

parotid (pə'rɒtɪd) *adj* 1 relating to or situated near the parotid gland ▷ *n* 2 See **parotid gland** [C17 via F, via L from Gk *parōtis*, from PARA-[1] (near) + *-ōtis*, from *ous* ear]

parotid gland *n* a large salivary gland, in man situated in front of and below each ear

parotitis (ˌpærə'taɪtɪs) *n* inflammation of the parotid gland. See also **mumps**

-parous *adj combining form* giving birth to: *oviparous* [from L *-parus*, from *parere* to bring forth]

paroxysm ('pærəkˌsɪzəm) *n* 1 an uncontrollable outburst: *a paroxysm of giggling* 2 *pathol* 2a a sudden attack or recurrence of a disease 2b any fit or convulsion [C17 via F from Med. L *paroxysmus* annoyance, from Gk, from *paroxunein* to goad, from PARA-[1] (intensifier) + *oxunein* to sharpen, from *oxus* sharp] > ˌ**parox'ysmal** *adj*

parquet ('pɑːkeɪ, -kɪ) *n* 1 a floor covering of pieces of hardwood fitted in a decorative pattern; parquetry 2 Also called: **parquet floor** a floor so covered 3 *US* the stalls of a theatre ▷ *vb* (*tr*) 4 to cover a floor with parquet [C19 from OF: small enclosure, from *parc* enclosure; see PARK]

parquetry ('pɑːkɪtrɪ) *n* a geometric pattern of inlaid pieces of wood, esp as used to cover a floor

parr (pɑː) *n, pl* **parrs** *or* **parr** a salmon up to two years of age [C18 from ?]

Parr (pɑː) *n* **Catherine** 1512–48, sixth wife of Henry VIII of England

parrakeet ('pærəˌkiːt) *n* a variant spelling of **parakeet**

parramatta (ˌpærə'mætə) *n* a variant spelling of paramatta

parricide ('pærɪˌsaɪd) *n* 1 the act of killing either of one's parents 2 a person who kills his or her parent [C16 from L *parricīdium* murder of a parent or relative, & from *parricīda* one who murders a relative, from *parri-* (rel. to Gk *pēos* kinsman) + -CIDE] > ˌ**parri'cidal** *adj*

parrot ('pærət) *n* 1 any of several related tropical and subtropical birds having a short hooked bill, bright plumage, and an ability to mimic sounds 2 a person who repeats or imitates the words or actions of another 3 **sick as a parrot** *usually facetious* extremely disappointed ▷ *vb* **parrots, parroting, parroted** 4 (*tr*) to repeat or imitate without understanding [C16 prob. from F *paroquet*, from ?]

parrot-fashion *adv inf* without regard for meaning; by rote: *she learned it parrot-fashion*

parrot fever *or* **disease** *n* another name for **psittacosis**

parrotfish ('pærətˌfɪʃ) *n, pl* **parrotfish** *or* **parrotfishes** a brightly coloured tropical marine percoid fish having parrot-like jaws

parry ('pærɪ) *vb* **parries, parrying, parried** 1 to ward off (an attack, etc) by blocking or deflecting, as in fencing 2 (*tr*) to evade (questions, etc), esp adroitly ▷ *n, pl* **parries** 3 an act of parrying 4 a skilful evasion, as of a question [C17 from F *parer* to ward off, from L *parāre* to prepare]

Parry ('pærɪ) *n* 1 Sir (**Charles**) **Hubert** (**Hastings**) 1848–1918, English composer, noted esp for his choral works **2** Sir **William Edward** 1790–1855, English arctic explorer, who searched for the Northwest Passage (1819–25) and attempted to reach the North Pole (1827)

parse (pɑːz) *vb* **parses, parsing, parsed** *grammar* to assign constituent structure to (a sentence or the words in a sentence) [C16 from L *pars* (*ōrātionis*) part (of speech)]

parsec (ˈpɑːˌsɛk) *n* a unit of astronomical distance equivalent to 3.0857×10^{16} metres or 3.262 light years [C20 from PARALLAX + SECOND²]

Parsee *or* **Parsi** (ˌpɑːˈsiː, ˈpɑːˌsiː) *n* an adherent of a Zoroastrian religion, the practitioners of which were driven out of Persia by the Muslims in the eighth century AD. It is now found chiefly in western India [C17 from Persian *Pārsī* a Persian, from OPersian *Pārsa* PERSIA] > **ˈParseeˌism** *or* **ˈParsiˌism** *n*

parser (ˈpɑːzə) *n computing* a program that interprets ordinary language typed into a computer by recognizing key words or analysing sentence structure and then translating it into the appropriate machine language

Parsifal *or* **Parzival** (ˈpɑːsɪfᵊl, -ˌfɑːl) *n German myth* the hero of a medieval cycle of legends about the Holy Grail. English equivalent: **Percival**

parsimony (ˈpɑːsɪmənɪ) *n* extreme care in spending; niggardliness [C15 from L *parcimōnia*, from *parcere* to spare] > **parsimonious** (ˌpɑːsɪˈməʊnɪəs) *adj* > **ˌparsiˈmoniously** *adv*

parsley (ˈpɑːslɪ) *n* **1** a S European umbelliferous plant, widely cultivated for its curled aromatic leaves, which are used in cooking **2** any of various similar and related plants, such as fool's-parsley and cow parsley [C14 *persely*, from OE *petersilie* + OF *persil*, *peresil*, both ult. from L *petroselīnum* rock parsley, from Gk, from *petra* rock + *selinon* parsley]

parsnip (ˈpɑːsnɪp) *n* **1** an umbelliferous plant cultivated for its long whitish root **2** the root of this plant, eaten as a vegetable [C14 from OF *pasnaie*, from L *pastināca*, from *pastināre* to dig, from *pastinum* two-pronged tool for digging]

parson (ˈpɑːsᵊn) *n* **1** a parish priest in the Church of England **2** any clergyman [C13 from Med. L *persōna* parish priest, from L: personage; see PERSON]

parsonage (ˈpɑːsᵊnɪdʒ) *n* the residence of a parson, as provided by the parish

parson bird *n* another name for **tui**

Parsons (ˈpɑːsənz) *n* **1** Sir **Charles Algernon.** 1854–1931, English engineer, who developed the steam turbine **2** **Gram,** real name *Cecil Connor.* 1946–73 US country-rock singer and songwriter; founder of the Flying Burrito Brothers (1968–70), he later released the solo albums *G.P.* (1973) and *Grievous Angel* (1974) **3** **Talcott** 1902–79, US sociologist, author of *The Structure of Social Action* (1937) and *The Social System* (1951)

parson's nose *n* the fatty extreme end portion of the tail of a fowl when cooked

part (pɑːt) *n* **1** a piece or portion of a whole **2** an integral constituent of something: *dancing is part of what we teach* **3** an amount less than the whole; bit: *they only recovered part of the money* **4** one of several equal divisions: *mix two parts flour to one part water* **5** an actor's role in a play **6** a person's proper role or duty: *everyone must do his part* **7** (*often pl*) region; area: *you're well known in these parts* **8** *anat* any portion of a larger structure **9** a component that can be replaced in a machine, etc **10** the US, Canad, and Austral word for **parting** (sense 1) **11** *music* one of a number of separate melodic lines which is assigned to one or more instrumentalists or singers **12** **for one's part** as far as one is concerned **13** **for the most part** generally **14** **in part** to some degree; partly **15** **of many parts** having many different abilities **16** **on the part of** on behalf of **17** **part and parcel** an essential ingredient **18** **play a part 18a** to pretend to be what one is not **18b** to have something to do with; be instrumental **19** **take in good part** to respond to (teasing, etc) with good humour **20** **take part in** to participate in **21** **take someone's part** to support one person in an argument, etc ▷ *vb* **22** to divide or separate from one another; take or come apart: *to part the curtains; the seams parted when I washed the dress* **23** to go away or cause to go away from one another: *the couple parted amicably* **24** (*intr;* foll by *from*) to leave; say goodbye to **25** (*intr;* foll by *with*) to relinquish, esp reluctantly: *I couldn't part with my teddy bear* **26** (*tr;* foll by *from*) to cause to relinquish, esp reluctantly: *he's not easily parted from his cash* **27** (*intr*) to split; separate: *the path parts here* **28** (*tr*) to arrange (the hair) in such a way that a line of scalp is left showing **29** (*intr*) *euphemistic* to die **30** (*intr*) *arch* to depart ▷ *adv* **31** to some extent; partly ▷ See also **parts** [C13 via OF from L *partīre* to divide, from *pars* a part]

part. *abbrev for:* **1** participle **2** particular

partake (pɑːˈteɪk) *vb* **partakes, partaking, partook, partaken** (*mainly intr*) **1** (foll by *in*) to have a share; participate **2** (foll by *of*) to take or receive a portion, esp of food or drink **3** (foll by *of*) to suggest or have some of the quality (of): *music partaking of sadness* [C16 back formation from *partaker*, earlier *part taker*, based on L *particeps* participant] > **parˈtaker** *n*

> USAGE *Partake of* is sometimes inappropriately used as if it were a synonym of *eat* or *drink*. Strictly speaking, you can only *partake of* food or drink which is available for several people to share

parterre (pɑːˈtɛə) *n* **1** a formally patterned flower garden **2** the pit of a theatre [C17 from F, from *par* along + *terre* ground]

parthenogenesis (ˌpɑːθɪnəʊˈdʒɛnɪsɪs) *n* a type of reproduction, occurring in some insects and flowers, in which the unfertilized ovum develops directly into a new individual [C19 from Gk *parthenos* virgin + *genesis* birth] > **parthenogenetic** (ˌpɑːθɪˌnəʊdʒɪˈnɛtɪk) *adj*

Parthenon (ˈpɑːθəˌnɒn, -nən) *n* the temple on the Acropolis in Athens built in the 5th century BC and regarded as the finest example of the Greek Doric order

Parthenopaeus (ˌpɑːθənəʊˈpiːəs) *n Greek myth* one of the Seven against Thebes, son of Atalanta

Parthenope (pɑːˈθɛnəpɪ) *n Greek myth* a siren, who drowned herself when Odysseus evaded the lure of the sirens' singing. Her body was said to have been cast ashore at what became Naples

Parthia (ˈpɑːθɪə) *n* a country in ancient Asia, southeast of the Caspian Sea, that expanded into a great empire dominating SW Asia in the 2nd century BC. It was destroyed by the Sassanids in the 3rd century AD > **ˈParthian** *n, adj*

Parthian shot *n* a hostile remark or gesture delivered while departing [alluding to the custom of Parthian archers who shot their arrows backwards while retreating]

partial (ˈpɑːʃəl) *adj* **1** relating to only a part; not general or complete: *a partial eclipse* **2** biased: *a partial judge* **3** (*postpositive;* foll by *to*) having a particular liking (for) **4** *maths* designating or relating to an operation in which only one of a set of independent variables is considered at a time ▷ *n* **5** Also called: **partial tone** *music, acoustics* any of the component tones of a single musical sound **6** *maths* a partial derivative [C15 from OF *parcial*, from LL *partiālis* incomplete, from L *pars* part] > **ˈpartially** *adv* > **ˈpartialness** *n*

> USAGE See at **partly**

partial derivative *n* the derivative of a function of two or more variables with respect to one of the variables, the other or others being considered constant. Written $\partial f/\partial x$

partiality (ˌpɑːʃɪˈælɪtɪ) *n, pl* **partialities** **1** favourable prejudice or bias **2** (usually foll by *for*) liking or fondness

Pp

3 the state or condition of being partial

partible ('pɑːtəbᵊl) *adj* (esp of property or an inheritance) divisible; separable [c16 from LL *partibilis*, from *part-*, *pars* part]

participate (pɑː'tɪsɪˌpeɪt) *vb* **participates, participating, participated** (*intr*; often foll by *in*) to take part, be or become actively involved, or share (in) [c16 from L *participāre*, from *pars* part + *capere* to take] > **par'ticipant** *adj, n* > **parˌtici'pation** *n* > **par'ticiˌpator** *n* > **par'ticipatory** *adj*

participle ('pɑːtɪsɪpᵊl) *n* a nonfinite form of verbs, in English and other languages, used adjectivally and in the formation of certain compound tenses. See also **present participle, past participle** [c14 via OF from L *participium*, from *particeps*, from *pars* part + *capere* to take] > **participial** (ˌpɑːtɪ'sɪpɪəl) *adj* > ˌ**parti'cipially** *adv*

particle ('pɑːtɪkᵊl) *n* **1** an extremely small piece of matter; speck **2** a very tiny amount; iota: *it doesn't make a particle of difference* **3** a function word, esp (in certain languages) a word belonging to an uninflected class having grammatical function: *"up" is sometimes regarded as an adverbial particle* **4** a common affix, such as *re-*, *un-*, or *-ness* **5** *physics* a body with finite mass that can be treated as having negligible size, and internal structure **6** See **elementary particle** [c14 from L *particula* a small part, from *pars* part]

particle accelerator *n* a machine for accelerating charged elementary particles to very high energies, used in nuclear physics

particle physics *n* the study of fundamental particles and their properties. Also called: **high-energy physics**

parti-coloured ('pɑːtɪˌkʌləd) *adj* having different colours in different parts; variegated [c16 *parti*, from (obs.) *party* of more than one colour, from OF: striped, from L *partīre* to divide]

particular (pə'tɪkjʊlə) *adj* **1** (*prenominal*) of or belonging to a single or specific person, thing, category, etc; specific; special: *the particular demands of the job* **2** (*prenominal*) exceptional or marked: *a matter of particular importance* **3** (*prenominal*) relating to or providing specific details or circumstances: *a particular account* **4** exacting or difficult to please, esp in details; fussy **5** (of the solution of a differential equation) obtained by giving specific values to the arbitrary constants in a general equation **6** *logic* (of a proposition) affirming or denying something about only some members of a class of objects, as in *some men are not wicked* ▷ Cf **universal** (sense 9) ▷ *n* **7** a separate distinct item that helps to form a generalization: opposed to *general* **8** (*often pl*) an item of information; detail: *complete in every particular* **9** **in particular** especially or exactly [c14 from OF *particuler*, from LL *particulāris* concerning a part, from L *particula* PARTICLE]

particular average *n* *insurance* partial damage to or loss of a ship or its cargo affecting only the shipowner or one cargo owner. Abbrev: **PA** ▷ Cf **general average**

particularism (pə'tɪkjʊləˌrɪzəm) *n* **1** exclusive attachment to the interests of one group, class, sect, etc **2** the principle of permitting each state in a federation the right to further its own interests **3** *Christian theol* the doctrine that divine grace is restricted to the elect > **par'ticularist** *n, adj*

particularity (pəˌtɪkjʊ'lærɪtɪ) *n, pl* **particularities** **1** (*often pl*) a specific circumstance: *the particularities of the affair* **2** great attentiveness to detail; fastidiousness **3** the quality of being precise: *a description of great particularity* **4** the state or quality of being particular as opposed to general; individuality

particularize *or* **particularise** (pə'tɪkjʊləˌraɪz) *vb* **particularizes, particularizing, particularized** *or* **particularises, particularising, particularised** **1** to treat in detail; give details (about) **2** (*intr*) to go into detail > **parˌticulari'zation** *or* **parˌticulari'sation** *n*

particularly (pə'tɪkjʊləlɪ) *adv* **1** very much; exceptionally: *I wasn't particularly successful* **2** in particular; specifically: *pensioners, particularly the less well-off*

particulate (pɑː'tɪkjʊlɪt, -ˌleɪt) *n* **1** a substance consisting of separate particles ▷ *adj* **2** of or made up of separate particles

parting ('pɑːtɪŋ) *n* **1** *Brit* the line of scalp showing when sections of hair are combed in opposite directions. US, Canad, and Austral equivalent: **part** **2** the act of separating or the state of being separated **3a** a departure or leave-taking, esp one causing a final separation **3b** (*as modifier*): *a parting embrace* **4** a place or line of separation or division **5** a euphemism for **death** ▷ *adj* (*prenominal*) **6** *literary* departing: *the parting day* **7** serving to divide or separate

partisan *or* **partizan** (ˌpɑːtɪ'zæn, 'pɑːtɪˌzæn) *n* **1** an adherent or devotee of a cause, party, etc **2** a member of an armed resistance group within occupied territory ▷ *adj* **3** of, relating to, or characteristic of a partisan **4** excessively devoted to one party, faction, etc; one-sided [c16 via F from OIt. *partigiano*, from *parte* faction, from L *pars* part] > ˌ**parti'sanship** *or* ˌ**parti'zanship** *n*

partita (pɑː'tiːtə) *n, pl* **partite** (-teɪ) *or* **partitas** *music* a type of suite [It.: divided (piece), from L *partīre* to divide]

partite ('pɑːtaɪt) *adj* **1** (*in combination*) composed of or divided into a specified number of parts: *bipartite* **2** (esp of plant leaves) divided almost to the base to form two or more parts [c16 from L *partīre* to divide]

partition (pɑː'tɪʃən) *n* **1** a division into parts; separation **2** something that separates, such as a large screen dividing a room in two **3** a part or share **4** *property law* a division of property, esp realty, among joint owners ▷ *vb* (*tr*) **5** (often foll by *off*) to separate or apportion into sections: *to partition a room off with a large screen* **6** *property law* to divide (property, esp realty) among joint owners [c15 via OF from L *partītiō*, from *partīre* to divide] > **par'titioner** *or* **par'titionist** *n*

partitive ('pɑːtɪtɪv) *adj* **1** *grammar* indicating that a noun involved in a construction refers only to a part of what it otherwise refers to. The phrase *some of the butter* is a partitive construction **2** serving to separate or divide into parts ▷ *n* **3** *grammar* a partitive linguistic element or feature [c16 from Med. L *partītīvus* serving to divide, from L *partīre* to divide] > **'partitively** *adv*

partly ('pɑːtlɪ) *adv* not completely.

> USAGE *Partly* and *partially* are to some extent interchangeable, but *partly* should be used when referring to a part or parts of something: *the building is partly* (not *partially*) *of stone*, while *partially* is preferred for the meaning *to some extent*: *his mother is partially* (not *partly*) *sighted*

partner ('pɑːtnə) *n* **1** an ally or companion: *a partner in crime* **2** a member of a partnership **3** one of a pair of dancers or players on the same side in a game: *my bridge partner* **4** either member of a couple in a relationship ▷ *vb* **5** to be or cause to be a partner (of) [c14 var. (infl. by PART) of *parcener* one who shares equally with another, from OF *parçonier*, ult. from L *partīre* to divide]

partnership ('pɑːtnəʃɪp) *n* **1a** a contractual relationship between two or more persons carrying on a joint business venture **1b** the deed creating such a relationship **1c** the persons associated in such a relationship **2** the state or condition of being a partner

part of speech *n* a class of words sharing important syntactic or semantic features; a group of words in a language that may occur in similar positions or fulfil similar functions in a sentence. The chief parts of speech in English are noun, pronoun, adjective, determiner, adverb, verb, preposition, conjunction, and interjection

parton ('pɑːˌtɒn) *n* *physics* a hypothetical elementary particle postulated as a constituent of neutrons and protons [from PART + -ON]

Parton ('pɑːtən) *n* **Dolly** born 1946, US country and pop singer and songwriter

partook (pɑː'tʊk) *vb* the past tense of **partake**

partridge ('pɑːtrɪdʒ) *n, pl* **partridges** *or* **partridge** any of various small Old World game birds of the pheasant family, esp the common or European partridge [c13 from OF *perdriz*, from L *perdix*, from Gk]

parts (pɑːts) *pl n* **1** personal abilities or talents: *a man of many parts* **2** short for **private parts**

Parts of Holland *n* See **Holland**[1] (sense 3)

Parts of Kesteven *n* See (Parts of) **Kesteven**

Parts of Lindsey *n* See (Parts of) **Lindsey**

part song *n* **1** a song composed in harmonized parts **2** (*in more technical usage*) a piece of homophonic choral music in which the topmost part carries the melody

part-time *adj* **1** occupying less than the full time normally associated with an activity: *a part-time job* ▷ *adv* **part time** **2** on a part-time basis: *he works part time* ▷ Cf. **full-time** > ˌ**part-'timer** *n*

parturient (pɑː'tjʊərɪənt) *adj* **1** of or relating to childbirth **2** giving birth **3** producing a new idea, etc [c16 via L *parturīre*, from *parere* to bring forth] > **par'turiency** *n*

parturition (ˌpɑːtjʊ'rɪʃən) *n* the act or process of giving birth [c17 from LL *parturītiō*, from *parturīre* to be in labour]

part work *n Brit* a series of magazines issued weekly or monthly, which are designed to be bound together to form a complete book

party ('pɑːtɪ) *n, pl* **parties** **1a** a social gathering for pleasure, often held as a celebration **1b** (*as modifier*): *party spirit* **1c** (*in combination*): *partygoer* **2** a group of people associated in some activity: *a rescue party* **3a** (*often cap*) a group of people organized together to further a common political aim, etc **3b** (*as modifier*): *party politics* **4** a person, esp one entering into a contract **5** the person or persons taking part in legal proceedings: *a party to the action* **6** *inf, humorous* a person ▷ *vb* **parties, partying, partied** (*intr*) **7** *inf* to celebrate; revel ▷ *adj* **8** *heraldry* (of a shield) divided vertically into two colours, metals, or furs [c13 from OF *partie* part, from L *partīre* to divide; see PART]

party line *n* **1** a telephone line serving two or more subscribers **2** the policies of a political party, etc

party list *n* (*modifier*) of or relating to a system of voting in which people vote for a party rather than for a candidate. Parties are assigned the number of seats that reflects their share of the vote. See **proportional representation**

party pooper ('puːpə) *n inf* a person whose behaviour or personality spoils other people's enjoyment [c20 orig. US]

party popper *n* a small plastic cylinder that, when a string is pulled, makes a small bang and fires thin paper streamers into the air

party wall *n property law* a wall separating two properties or pieces of land and over which each of the adjoining owners has certain rights

par value *n* the value imprinted on the face of a share certificate or bond and used to assess dividend, capital ownership, or interest

parvenu *or* (*fem*) **parvenue** ('pɑːvəˌnjuː) *n* **1** a person who, having risen socially or economically, is considered to be an upstart ▷ *adj* **2** of or characteristic of a parvenu [c19 from F, from *parvenir* to attain, from L *pervenīre*, from *per* through + *venīre* to come]

parvovirus ('pɑːvəʊˌvaɪrəs) *n* any of a group of viruses characterized by their very small size, each of which is specific to a particular species, as for example canine parvovirus [c20 NL, from L *parvus* little + VIRUS]

Parzival (*German* 'partsifal) *n* a variant of **Parsifal**

pas (pɑː) *n, pl* **pas** a dance step or movement, esp in ballet [c18 from F, lit.: step]

Pasadena (ˌpæsə'diːnə) *n* a city in SW California, east of Los Angeles. Pop: 133 936 (2000)

Pasargadae (pæ'sɑːgəˌdiː) *n* an ancient city in Persia, northeast of Persepolis in present-day Iran: built by Cyrus the Great

Pasay ('pɑːsaɪ) *n* a city in the Philippines, on central Luzon just south of Manila, on Manila Bay. Pop: 354 908 (2000). Also called: **Rizal**

pascal ('pæskᵊl) *n* the derived SI unit of pressure; the pressure exerted on an area of 1 square metre by a force of 1 newton; equivalent to 10 dynes per square centimetre or 1.45×10^{-4} pound per square inch. Symbol: Pa [c20 after B. PASCAL]

Pascal (*French* paskal) *n* **Blaise** (blɛz) 1623–62, French philosopher, mathematician, and physicist. As a scientist, he made important contributions to hydraulics and the study of atmospheric pressure and, with Fermat, developed the theory of probability. His chief philosophical works are *Lettres provinciales* (1656–57), written in defence of Jansenism and against the Jesuits, and *Pensées* (1670), fragments of a Christian apologia

PASCAL ('pæsˌkæl) *n* a high-level computer-programming language developed as a teaching language

Pascal's triangle *n* a triangle consisting of rows of numbers; the apex is 1 and each row starts and ends with 1, other numbers being obtained by adding together the two numbers on either side in the row above: used to calculate probabilities [c17 after B. PASCAL]

paschal ('pæskᵊl) *adj* **1** of or relating to **Passover** (sense 1) **2** of or relating to **Easter** [c15 from OF *pascal*, via Church L from Heb. *pesakh* Passover]

Paschal Lamb *n* **1** (*sometimes not caps*) *Old Testament* the lamb killed and eaten on the first day of the Passover **2** Christ regarded as this sacrifice

pas de basque (ˌpɑː də 'bɑː) *n, pl* **pas de basque** a dance step performed usually on the spot and used esp in reels and jigs [from F, lit.: Basque step]

Pas-de-Calais (*French* pɑdkalɛ) *n* a department of N France, in Nord-Pas-de-Calais region, on the Straits of Dover (the **Pas de Calais**): the part of France closest to the British Isles. Capital: Arras. Pop: 1 441 568 (1999) Area: 6752 sq km (2633 sq miles)

pas de deux (*French* pɑddø) *n, pl* **pas de deux** *ballet* a sequence for two dancers [F: step for two]

pash (pæʃ) *n sl* infatuation [c20 from PASSION]

pasha *or* **pacha** ('pɑːʃə, 'pæʃə) *n* (formerly) a high official of the Ottoman Empire or the modern Egyptian kingdom: placed after a name when used as a title [c17 from Turkish *paşa*]

pashm ('pæʃəm) *n* the underfur of various Tibetan animals, esp goats, used for Cashmere shawls [from Persian, lit.: wool]

pashmina (pæʃ'miːnə) *n* a scarf or shawl made of pashm [from Persian *pashmina*; see PASHM]

Pashto, Pushto ('pʌʃtəʊ), *or* **Pushtu** *n* **1** a language of Afghanistan and NW Pakistan **2** (*pl* **Pashto** *or* **Pashtos, Pushto** *or* **Pushtos, Pushtu** *or* **Pushtus**) a speaker of the Pashto language; a Pathan ▷ *adj* **3** denoting or relating to this language or a speaker of it

Pasionaria (*Spanish* pasjo'narja) *n* **La** (la), real name *Dolores Ibarruri* 1895–1989, Spanish Communist leader, who lived in exile in the Soviet Union (1939–75)

Pasiphaë (pə'sɪfɪiː) *n Greek myth* the wife of Minos and mother (by a bull) of the Minotaur

Pasmore ('pæsˌmɔː) *n* **Victor** 1908–98, British artist. Originally a figurative painter, he devoted himself to abstract paintings and reliefs after 1947

paso doble ('pæsəʊ 'dəʊbleɪ) *n, pl* **paso dobles** *or* **pasos dobles** **1** a modern ballroom dance in fast duple time **2** a piece of music composed for or in the rhythm of this dance [Sp.: double step]

Pasolini (*Italian* pazoˈlini) *n* **Pier Paolo** (pjɛr ˈpaːolo) 1922–75, Italian film director. His films include *The Gospel according to St. Matthew* (1964), *Oedipus Rex* (1967), *Theorem* (1968), *Pigsty* (1969), and *Decameron* (1970)

pas op (ˈpɑːs ˌɒp) *interj S African* beware [Afrik.]

pasqueflower (ˈpɑːskˌflaʊə) *n* **1** a purple-flowered herbaceous plant of N and Central Europe and W Asia **2** any of several related North American plants [C16 from F *passefleur*, from *passer* to excel + *fleur* flower; changed to *pasqueflower* Easter flower, because it blooms at Easter]

pasquinade (ˌpæskwɪˈneɪd) *n* an abusive lampoon or satire, esp one posted in a public place [C17 from It. *Pasquino* name given to an ancient Roman statue disinterred in 1501, which was annually posted with satirical verses]

pass (pɑːs) *vb* **1** to go onwards or move by or past (a person, thing, etc) **2** to run, extend, or lead through, over, or across (a place): *the route passes through the city* **3** to go through or cause to go through (an obstacle or barrier): *to pass a needle through cloth* **4** to move or cause to move onwards or over: *he passed his hand over her face* **5** *(tr)* to go beyond or exceed: *this victory passes all expectation* **6** to gain or cause to gain an adequate mark or grade in (an examination, course, etc) **7** (often foll by *away* or *by*) to elapse or allow to elapse: *we passed the time talking* **8** *(intr)* to take place or happen: *what passed at the meeting?* **9** to speak or exchange or be spoken or exchanged: *angry words passed between them* **10** to spread or cause to spread: *we passed the news round the class* **11** to transfer or exchange or be transferred or exchanged: *the bomb passed from hand to hand* **12** *(intr)* to undergo change or transition: *to pass from joy to despair* **13** (when *tr*, often foll by *down*) to transfer or be transferred by inheritance: *the house passed to the younger son* **14** to agree to or be agreed to by a legislative body, etc: *the assembly passed 10 resolutions* **15** *(tr)* (of a legislative measure) to undergo (a procedural stage) and be agreed: *the bill passed the committee stage* **16** (when *tr*, often foll by *on* or *upon*) to pronounce (judgment, findings, etc): *the court passed sentence* **17** to go or allow to go without comment or censure: *the insult passed unnoticed; I'll let that remark pass* **18** *(intr)* to opt not to exercise a right, as by not answering a question or not making a bid or a play in card games **19** to discharge (urine, etc) from the body **20** *(intr)* to come to an end or disappear: *his anger soon passed* **21** *(intr;* usually foll by *for* or *as)* to be likely to be mistaken for (someone or something else): *you could easily pass for your sister* **22** *(intr;* foll by *away, on,* or *over) Euphemistic.* to die **23** *sport* to hit, kick, or throw (the ball, etc) to another player **24 bring to pass** *arch* to cause to happen **25 come to pass** *arch* to happen ▷ *n* **26** the act of passing **27** a route through a range of mountains where there is a gap between peaks **28** a permit, licence, or authorization to do something without restriction **29a** a document allowing entry to and exit from a military installation **29b** a document authorizing leave of absence **30** *Brit* **30a** the passing of a college or university examination to a satisfactory standard but not as high as honours **30b** *(as modifier)*: *a pass degree* **31** a dive, sweep, or bombing or landing run by an aircraft **32** a motion of the hand or of a wand as part of a conjuring trick **33** *inf* an attempt to invite sexual intimacy (esp in **make a pass at**) **34** a state of affairs, esp a bad one (esp in **a pretty pass**) **35** *sport* the transfer of a ball, etc, from one player to another **36** *fencing* a thrust or lunge **37** *bridge, etc* the act of passing (making no bid) ▷ *sentence substitute* **38** *bridge, etc* a call indicating that a player has no bid to make ▷ See also **pass off, pass out, pass over,** etc [C13 from OF *passer* to pass, surpass, from L *passūs* step]

USAGE The past participle of *pass* is sometimes wrongly spelt *past*: *the time for recriminations has passed* (not *past*)

pass. *abbrev for* passive

passable (ˈpɑːsəbᵊl) *adj* **1** adequate, fair, or acceptable **2** (of an obstacle) capable of being crossed **3** (of currency) valid for circulation **4** (of a proposed law) able to be enacted > ˈ**passableness** *n* > ˈ**passably** *adv*

passacaglia (ˌpæsəˈkɑːljə) *n* **1** an old Spanish dance in slow triple time **2** a slow instrumental piece characterized by a series of variations on a particular theme played over a repeated bass part [C17 earlier *passacalle*, from Sp. *pasacalle* street dance, from *paso* step + *calle* street]

passage (ˈpæsɪdʒ) *n* **1** a channel, opening, etc, through or by which a person or thing may pass **2** *music* a section or division of a piece, movement, etc **3** a way, as in a hall or lobby **4** a section of a written work, speech, etc **5** a journey, esp by ship **6** the act or process of passing from one place, condition, etc, to another: *passage of a gas through a liquid* **7** the permission, right, or freedom to pass: *to be denied passage through a country* **8** the enactment of a law by a legislative body **9** *rare* an exchange, as of blows, words, etc [C13 from OF from *passer* to PASS]

passageway (ˈpæsɪdʒˌweɪ) *n* a way, esp one in or between buildings; passage

Passamaquoddy Bay (ˌpæsəməˈkwɒdɪ) *n* an inlet of the Bay of Fundy between New Brunswick (Canada) and Maine (US) at the mouth of the St Croix River

pass band *n* the band of frequencies that is transmitted with maximum efficiency through a circuit, filter, etc

passbook (ˈpɑːsˌbʊk) *n* **1** a book for keeping a record of withdrawals from and payments into a building society **2** another name for **bankbook** **3** *S African* an official document to identify the bearer, his race, residence, and employment

Passchendaele (ˈpæʃənˌdeɪl) *n* a village in NW Belgium, in West Flanders province: the scene of heavy fighting during the third battle of Ypres in World War I during which 245 000 British troops were lost

passé (ˈpɑːseɪ, ˈpæseɪ) *adj* **1** out-of-date: *passé ideas* **2** past the prime; faded: *a passé society beauty* [C18 from F, p.p. of *passer* to PASS]

passenger (ˈpæsɪndʒə) *n* **1a** a person travelling in a car, train, boat, etc, driven by another person **1b** *(as modifier)*: *a passenger seat* **2** *chiefly Brit* a member of a group or team who is not participating fully in the work [C14 from OF *passager* passing, from PASSAGE]

passenger pigeon *n* a gregarious North American pigeon, now extinct

passe-partout (ˌpæspɑːˈtuː) *n* **1** a mounting for a picture in which strips of gummed paper bind together the glass, picture, and backing **2** the gummed paper used for this **3** a mat on which a photograph, etc, is mounted **4** something that secures entry everywhere, esp a master key [C17 from F, lit.: pass everywhere]

passepied (pɑːsˈpjeɪ) *n, pl* **passepieds** (-ˈpjeɪ) **1** a lively minuet in triple time, popular in the 17th century **2** a piece of music composed for or in the rhythm of this dance [C17 from F: pass foot]

passer-by *n, pl* **passers-by** a person who is passing or going by, esp on foot

passerine (ˈpæsəˌraɪn, -ˌriːn) *adj* **1** of, relating to, or belonging to an order of birds characterized by the perching habit: includes the larks, finches, starlings, etc ▷ *n* **2** any bird belonging to this order [C18 from L *passer* sparrow]

passim *Latin* (ˈpæsɪm) *adv* here and there; throughout: used to indicate that what is referred to occurs frequently in the work cited

passing (ˈpɑːsɪŋ) *adj* **1** transitory or momentary: *a passing fancy* **2** cursory or casual in action or manner: *a passing reference* ▷ *adv, adj* **3** *arch* to an extreme degree: *the events were passing strange* ▷ *n* **4** a place where or means by which one may pass, cross, ford, etc **5** a euphemistic word for **death** **6 in passing** by the way; incidentally

passing bell *n* a bell rung to announce a death or a funeral. Also called: **death knell**

passing note *or US* **passing tone** *n* a nonharmonic note through which a melody passes from one harmonic note to the next

passion ('pæʃən) *n* **1** ardent love or affection **2** intense sexual love **3** a strong affection or enthusiasm for an object, concept, etc: *a passion for poetry* **4** any strongly felt emotion, such as love, hate, envy, etc **5** an outburst of anger: *he flew into a passion* **6** the object of an intense desire, ardent affection, or enthusiasm **7** an outburst expressing intense emotion: *he burst into a passion of sobs* **8** the sufferings and death of a Christian martyr [c12 via F from Church L *passiō* suffering, from L *patī* to suffer] > '**passional** *adj* > '**passionless** *adj*

Passion ('pæʃən) *n* **1** the sufferings of Christ from the Last Supper to his death on the cross **2** any of the four Gospel accounts of this **3** a musical setting of this: *the St Matthew Passion*

passionate ('pæʃənɪt) *adj* **1** manifesting or exhibiting intense sexual feeling or desire **2** capable of, revealing, or characterized by intense emotion **3** easily roused to anger; quick-tempered > '**passionately** *adv*

passionflower ('pæʃən,flaʊə) *n* any plant of a tropical American genus cultivated for their red, yellow, greenish, or purple showy flowers: some species have edible fruit [c17 from alleged resemblance betweeen parts of the flower and the instruments of the Crucifixion]

passion fruit *n* the edible fruit of any of various passionflowers, esp granadilla

Passion play *n* a play depicting the Passion of Christ

passive ('pæsɪv) *adj* **1** not active or not participating perceptibly in an activity, organization, etc **2** unresisting and receptive to external forces; submissive **3** affected or acted upon by an external object or force **4** *grammar* denoting a voice of verbs in sentences in which the grammatical subject is the recipient of the action described by the verb, as *was broken* in the sentence *The glass was broken by a boy* **5** *chem* (of a substance, esp a metal) apparently chemically unreactive **6** *electronics, telecomm* **6a** capable only of attenuating a signal: *a passive network* **6b** not capable of amplifying a signal or controlling a function: *a passive communications satellite* **7** *finance* (of a bond, share, debt, etc) yielding no interest ▷ *n* **8** *grammar* **8a** the passive voice **8b** a passive verb [c14 from L *passīvus* susceptible of suffering, from *patī* to undergo] > '**passively** *adv* > **pas'sivity** *or* '**passiveness** *n*

passive-aggressive *adj psychoanal* of or relating to a personality that harbours aggressive emotions while behaving in a calm or detached manner

passive euthanasia *n* a form of euthanasia in which medical treatment that will keep a dying patient alive for a time is withdrawn

passive resistance *n* resistance to a government, law, etc, without violence, as by fasting, demonstrating, or refusing to cooperate

passive smoking *n* the inhalation of smoke from other people's cigarettes by a nonsmoker

passkey ('pɑːs,kiː) *n* **1** any of various keys, esp a latchkey **2** another term for **master key** or **skeleton key**

pass law *n* (formerly, in South Africa) a law restricting the movement of Black Africans

pass off *vb* (*adv*) **1** to be or cause to be accepted in a false character: *he passed the fake diamonds off as real* **2** (*intr*) to come to a gradual end; disappear: *eventually the pain passed off* **3** (*intr*) to take place: *the meeting passed off without disturbance* **4** (*tr*) to set aside or disregard: *I managed to pass off his insult*

pass out *vb* (*adv*) **1** (*intr*) *inf* to become unconscious; faint **2** (*intr*) *Brit* (esp of an officer cadet) to qualify for a military commission, etc **3** (*tr*) to distribute

pass over *vb* **1** (*tr, adv*) to take no notice of; disregard: *they passed me over in the last round of promotions* **2** (*intr, prep*) to disregard (something bad or embarrassing)

Passover ('pɑːs,əʊvə) *n* **1** an eight-day Jewish festival celebrated in commemoration of the passing over or sparing of the Israelites in Egypt (Exodus 12) **2** another term for the **Paschal Lamb** [c16 from *pass over*, translation of Heb. *pesah*, from *pāsah* to pass over]

passport ('pɑːspɔːt) *n* **1** an official document issued by a government, identifying an individual, granting him or her permission to travel abroad, and requesting the protection of other governments for him or her **2** a quality, asset, etc, that gains a person admission or acceptance [c15 from F *passeport*, from *passer* to PASS + PORT[1]]

pass up *vb* (*tr, adv*) *inf* to let go by; ignore: *I won't pass up this opportunity*

password ('pɑːs,wɜːd) *n* **1** a secret word, phrase, etc, that ensures admission by proving identity, membership, etc **2** an action, quality, etc, that gains admission or acceptance **3** *computing* a sequence of characters used to gain access to a computer system

past (pɑːst) *adj* **1** completed, finished, and no longer in existence: *past happiness* **2** denoting or belonging to the time that has elapsed at the present moment: *the past history of the world* **3** denoting a specific unit of time that immediately precedes the present one: *the past month* **4** (*prenominal*) denoting a person who has held an office or position; former: *a past president* **5** *grammar* denoting any of various tenses of verbs that are used in describing actions, events, or states that have been begun or completed at the time of utterance ▷ *n* **6** **the past** the period of time that has elapsed: *forget the past* **7** the history, experience, or background of a nation, person, etc **8** an earlier period of someone's life, esp one regarded as disreputable **9** *grammar* **9a** a past tense **9b** a verb in a past tense ▷ *adv* **10** at a time before the present; ago: *three years past* **11** on or onwards: *I greeted him but he just walked past* ▷ *prep* **12** beyond in time: *it's past midnight* **13** beyond in place or position: *the library is past the church* **14** moving beyond: *he walked past me* **15** beyond or above the reach, limit, or scope of: *his foolishness is past comprehension* **16** **past it** *inf* unable to perform the tasks one could do when one was younger **17** **not put it past someone** to consider someone capable of (the action specified) [c14 from *passed*, pp of PASS]

USAGE The past participle of *pass* is sometimes wrongly spelt *past*: *the time for recrimination has passed* (not *past*)

pasta ('pæstə) *n* any of several variously shaped edible preparations made from a flour and water dough, such as spaghetti [It., from LL: PASTE]

▷ www.ilovepasta.org
▷ www.e-rcps.com/pasta/home.shtml
▷ www.pastrywiz.com/archive/category/pasta.htm

paste (peɪst) *n* **1** a mixture of a soft or malleable consistency, such as toothpaste **2** an adhesive made from water and flour or starch, used for joining pieces of paper, etc **3** a preparation of food, such as meat, that has been pounded to a creamy mass, for spreading on bread, etc **4** any of various sweet doughy confections: *almond paste* **5** dough, esp for making pastry **6a** a hard shiny glass used for making imitation gems **6b** an imitation gem made of this glass **7** the combined ingredients of porcelain. See also **hard paste, soft paste** ▷ *vb* **pastes, pasting, pasted** (*tr*) **8** (often foll by *on* or *onto*) to attach as by using paste: *he pasted posters onto the wall* **9** (usually foll by *with*) to cover (a surface) with paper, etc: *he pasted the wall with posters* **10** *sl* to thrash or beat; defeat [c14 via OF from LL *pasta* dough, from Gk *pastē* barley porridge, from *passein* to sprinkle]

pasteboard ('peɪst,bɔːd) *n* **1** a stiff board formed from

Pp

layers of paper or pulp pasted together ▷ *adj* **2** flimsy or fake

pastel (ˈpæstᵊl, pæˈstɛl) *n* **1a** a substance made of ground pigment bound with gum **1b** a crayon of this **1c** a drawing done in such crayons **2** the medium or technique of pastel drawing **3** a pale delicate colour ▷ *adj* **4** (of a colour) pale; delicate: *pastel blue* [C17 via F from It. *pastello*, from LL *pastellus* woad, dim. of *pasta* PASTE] > ˈ**pastelist** *or* ˈ**pastellist** *n*

pastern (ˈpæstən) *n* the part of a horse's foot between the fetlock and the hoof [C14 from OF *pasturon*, from *pasture* a hobble, from L *pāstōrius* of a shepherd, from PASTOR]

Pasternak (ˈpæstəˌnæk; *Russian* pəstɪrˈnak) *n* **Boris Leonidovich** (baˈris lɪaˈnidəvitʃ) 1890–1960, Russian lyric poet, novelist, and translator, noted particularly for his novel of the Russian Revolution, *Dr. Zhivago* (1957). He was awarded the Nobel prize for literature in 1958, but was forced to decline it

paste-up *n printing* a sheet of paper or board on which are pasted artwork, proofs, etc, for photographing prior to making a plate

Pasteur (*French* pastœr) *n* **Louis** (lwi) 1822–95, French chemist and bacteriologist. His discovery that the fermentation of milk and alcohol was caused by microorganisms resulted in the process of pasteurization. He also devised methods of immunization against anthrax and rabies and pioneered stereochemistry

pasteurism (ˈpæstəˌrɪzəm, -stjə-, ˈpɑː-) *n med* a method of securing immunity from rabies or of treating patients with other viral infections by the serial injection of progressively more virulent suspensions of the causative virus. Also called: **Pasteur treatment**

pasteurization *or* **pasteurisation** (ˌpæstəraɪˈzeɪʃən, -stjə-, ˌpɑː-) *n* the process of heating beverages, such as milk, beer, wine, or cider, or solid foods, such as cheese or crab meat, to destroy harmful microorganisms

pasteurize *or* **pasteurise** (ˈpæstəˌraɪz, -stjə-, ˈpɑː-) *vb* **pasteurizes, pasteurizing, pasteurized** *or* **pasteurises, pasteurising, pasteurised** (*tr*) to subject (milk, beer, etc) to pasteurization > ˈ**pasteurˌizer** *or* ˈ**pasteurˌiser** *n*

pastiche (pæˈstiːʃ) *or* **pasticcio** (pæˈstɪtʃəʊ) *n, pl* **pastiches** *or* **pasticcios** **1** a work of art that mixes styles, materials, etc **2** a work of art that imitates the style of another artist or period [C19 F *pastiche*, It. *pasticcio*, lit.: piecrust (hence, something blended) from LL *pasta* PASTE]

pastille *or* **pastil** (ˈpæstɪl) *n* **1** a small flavoured or medicated lozenge **2** an aromatic substance burnt to fumigate the air [C17 via F from L *pastillus* small loaf, from *pānis* bread]

pastime (ˈpɑːsˌtaɪm) *n* an activity or entertainment which makes time pass pleasantly

past master *n* **1** a person with talent for, or experience in, a particular activity **2** a person who has held the office of master in a guild, etc

Pasto (*Spanish* ˈpasto) *n* a city in SE Colombia, at an altitude of 2590 m (8500 ft). Pop: 332 396 (1999 est)

pastor (ˈpɑːstə) *n* **1** a clergyman or priest in charge of a congregation **2** a person who exercises spiritual guidance over a number of people **3** a S Asian starling having a black head and wings and a pale pink body [C14 from L: shepherd, from *pascere* to feed] > ˈ**pastorship** *n*

pastoral (ˈpɑːstərəl) *adj* **1** of, characterized by, or depicting rural life, scenery, etc **2** (of a literary work) dealing with an idealized form of rural existence **3** (of land) used for pasture **4** of or relating to a member of the clergy in charge of a congregation or his or her duties as such **5** of or relating to shepherds, their work, etc **6** of or relating to a teacher's responsibility for the personal, as distinct from the educational, development of pupils ▷ *n* **7** a literary work or picture portraying rural life, esp in an idealizing way **8** *music* a variant spelling of **pastorale** **9a** a letter from a member of the clergy to the people under his or her charge **9b** the letter of a bishop to the clergy or people of his or her diocese **9c** Also called: **pastoral staff** the crosier carried by a bishop [C15 from L, from PASTOR] > ˈ**pastoralism** *n* > ˈ**pastorally** *adv*

pastorale (ˌpæstəˈrɑːl) *n, pl* **pastorales** *music* **1** a composition evocative of rural life, sometimes with a droning accompaniment **2** a musical play based on a rustic story [C18 It., from L: PASTORAL]

pastoralist (ˈpɑːstərəlɪst) *n Austral* a grazier raising sheep, cattle, etc, on a large scale

pastorate (ˈpɑːstərɪt) *n* **1** the office or term of office of a pastor **2** a body of pastors

pastourelle (ˌpɑːstuːˈrɛl) *n music* **1** a pastoral piece of music **2** one of the figures in a quadrille [C19 from F: little shepherdess]

past participle *n* a participial form of verbs used to modify a noun that is logically the object of a verb, also used in certain compound tenses and passive forms of the verb

past perfect *grammar* ▷ *adj* **1** denoting a tense of verbs used in relating past events where the action had already occurred at the time of the action of a main verb that is itself in a past tense. In English this is a compound tense formed with *had* plus the past participle ▷ *n* **2a** the past perfect tense **2b** a verb in this tense

pastrami (pəˈstrɑːmɪ) *n* highly seasoned smoked beef [from Yiddish, from Romanian *pastramă*, from *păstra* to preserve]

pastry (ˈpeɪstrɪ) *n, pl* **pastries** **1** a dough of flour, water, and fat **2** baked foods, such as tarts, made with this dough **3** an individual cake or pastry pie [C16 from PASTE]

▷ www.cooksrecipes.com/pies/pie-crust-recipes.html
▷ www.pastrychef.info
▷ www.basic-recipes.com/r/pas

pasturage (ˈpɑːstʃərɪdʒ) *n* **1** the business of grazing cattle **2** another word for **pasture**

pasture (ˈpɑːstʃə) *n* **1** land covered with grass or herbage and grazed by or suitable for grazing by livestock **2** the grass or herbage growing on it ▷ *vb* **pastures, pasturing, pastured** **3** (*tr*) to cause (livestock) to graze or (of livestock) to graze (a pasture) [C13 via OF from LL *pāstūra*, from *pascere* to feed]

pasty[1] (ˈpeɪstɪ) *adj* **pastier, pastiest** **1** of or like the colour, texture, etc, of paste **2** (esp of the complexion) pale or unhealthy-looking > ˈ**pastily** *adv* > ˈ**pastiness** *n*

pasty[2] (ˈpæstɪ) *n, pl* **pasties** a round of pastry folded over a filling of meat, vegetables, etc [C13 from OF *pastée*, from LL *pasta* dough]

PA system *n* See **public-address system**

pat[1] (pæt) *vb* **pats, patting, patted** **1** to hit (something) lightly with the palm of the hand or some other flat surface: *to pat a ball* **2** to slap (a person or animal) gently, esp on the back, as an expression of affection, congratulation, etc **3** (*tr*) to shape, smooth, etc, with a flat instrument or the palm **4** (*intr*) to walk or run with light footsteps **5** **pat (someone) on the back** *inf* to congratulate ▷ *n* **6** a light blow with something flat **7** a gentle slap **8** a small mass of something: *a pat of butter* **9** the sound of patting **10** **pat on the back** *inf* a gesture or word indicating approval [C14 ? imit.]

pat[2] (pæt) *adv* **1** Also: **off pat** exactly or fluently memorized: *he recited it pat* **2** opportunely or aptly **3** **stand pat** **3a** *chiefly US & Canad* to refuse to abandon a belief, decision, etc **3b** (in poker, etc) to play without adding new cards to the hand dealt ▷ *adj* **4** exactly right; apt: *a pat reply* **5** too exactly fitting; glib: *a pat answer to a difficult problem* **6** exactly right: *a pat hand in poker* [C17 ? adv use ("with a light stroke") of PAT[1]]

pat[3] (pæt) *n* **on one's pat** *Austral inf* alone [c20 rhyming slang, from Pat Malone]

patagium (pəˈteɪdʒɪəm) *n, pl* **patagia** (-dʒɪə) **1** a web of skin in bats and gliding mammals that functions as a wing **2** a membranous fold of skin connecting a bird's wing to the shoulder [c19 NL, from L, from Gk *patageion* gold border on a tunic]

Patagonia (ˌpætəˈgəʊnɪə) *n* **1** the southernmost region of South America, in Argentina and Chile extending from the Andes to the Atlantic. Area: about 777 000 sq km (300 000 sq miles) **2** an arid tableland in the southernmost part of Argentina, rising towards the Andes in the west > ˌ**Pataˈgonian** *adj*

patch (pætʃ) *n* **1** a piece of material used to mend a garment, etc, or to make patchwork, a sewn-on pocket, etc **2a** a small plot of land **2b** its produce: *a patch of cabbages* **3** *med* **3a** a protective covering for an injured eye **3b** any protective dressing **4** an imitation beauty spot made of black silk, etc, worn esp in the 18th century **5** an identifying piece of fabric worn on the shoulder of a uniform **6** a small contrasting section: *a patch of cloud in the blue sky* **7** a scrap; remnant **8** **a bad patch** a difficult or troubled time **9** **not a patch on** not nearly as good as ▷ *vb (tr)* **10** to mend or supply (a garment, etc) with a patch or patches **11** to put together or produce with patches **12** (of material) to serve as a patch to **13** (often foll by *up*) to mend hurriedly or in a makeshift way **14** (often foll by *up*) to make (up) or settle (a quarrel, etc) **15** to connect (electric circuits) together temporarily by means of a patch board [c16 *pacche*, ?from F *pieche* PIECE] > ˈ**patcher** *n*

patch board *or* **panel** *n* a device with a large number of sockets into which electrical plugs can be inserted to form many different temporary circuits: used in telephone exchanges, computer systems, etc. Also called: **plugboard**

patchouli *or* **patchouly** (ˈpætʃʊlɪ, pəˈtʃuːlɪ) *n, pl* **patchoulis** *or* **patchoulies** **1** any of several Asiatic trees, the leaves of which yield a heavy fragrant oil **2** the perfume made from this oil [c19 from Tamil *paccilai*, from *paccu* green + *ilai* leaf]

patch pocket *n* a pocket on the outside of a garment

patch test *n med* a test to detect an allergic reaction by applying small amounts of a suspected substance to the skin

patchwork (ˈpætʃˌwɜːk) *n* **1** needlework done by sewing pieces of different materials together **2** something made up of various parts

patchy (ˈpætʃɪ) *adj* **patchier, patchiest** **1** irregular in quality, occurrence, intensity, etc: *a patchy essay* **2** having or forming patches > ˈ**patchily** *adv* > ˈ**patchiness** *n*

pate (peɪt) *n* the head, esp with reference to baldness or (in facetious use) intelligence [c14 from ?]

pâté (ˈpæteɪ) *n* **1** a spread of finely minced liver, poultry, etc, served usually as an hors d'oeuvre **2** a savoury pie [c18 from F: PASTE]

pâté de foie gras (pɑte də fwa grɑ) *n, pl* **pâtés de foie gras** (pɑte) a smooth rich paste made from the liver of a specially fattened goose [F: pâté of fat liver]

patella (pəˈtɛlə) *n, pl* **patellae** (-liː) *anat* a small flat triangular bone in front of and protecting the knee joint. Nontechnical name: **kneecap** [c17 from L, from *patina* shallow pan] > **paˈtellar** *adj*

paten (ˈpætᵊn) *n* a plate, usually made of silver or gold, esp for the bread in the Eucharist [c13 from OF *patene*, from Med. L, from L *patina* pan]

patency (ˈpeɪtᵊnsɪ) *n* the condition of being obvious

patent (ˈpeɪtᵊnt, ˈpætᵊnt) *n* **1a** a government grant to an inventor assuring him or her the sole right to make, use, and sell his or her invention for a limited period **1b** a document conveying such a grant **2** an invention, privilege, etc, protected by a patent **3a** an official document granting a right **3b** any right granted by such a document ▷ *adj* **4** open or available for inspection (esp in **letters patent, patent writ**) **5** (ˈpeɪtᵊnt) obvious: *their scorn was patent to everyone* **6** concerning protection, appointment, etc, of or by a patent or patents **7** proprietary **8** (esp of a bodily passage or duct) being open or unobstructed ▷ *vb (tr)* **9** to obtain a patent for **10** to grant by a patent [c14 via OF from L *patēre* to lie open; n use, short for *letters patent*, from Med. L *litterae patentes* letters lying open (to public inspection)] > ˈ**patentable** *adj* > ˌ**patenˈtee** *n* > ˌ**patenˈtor** *n*

> **USAGE** The pronunciation ˈpætnt is heard in *letters patent* and *Patent Office* and is the usual US pronunciation for all senses. In Britain, although ˈpætnt is sometimes heard for senses 1–4 and 6–10, ˈpeɪtnt is commoner

patent leather (ˈpeɪtᵊnt) *n* leather processed with lacquer to give a hard glossy surface

patently (ˈpeɪtᵊntlɪ) *adv* obviously

patent medicine (ˈpeɪtᵊnt) *n* a medicine with a patent, available without a prescription

Patent Office (ˈpætᵊnt) *n* a government department that issues patents

Patent Rolls (ˈpætᵊnt) *pl n* (in Britain) the register of patents issued

pater (ˈpeɪtə) *n Brit sl* another word for **father**: now chiefly used facetiously [from L]

Pater (ˈpeɪtə) *n* **Walter (Horatio)** 1839–94, English essayist and critic, noted for his prose style and his advocation of the "love of art for its own sake". His works include the philosophical romance *Marius the Epicurean* (1885), *Studies in the History of the Renaissance* (1873), and *Imaginary Portraits* (1887)

paterfamilias (ˌpeɪtəfəˈmɪlɪˌæs) *n, pl* **patresfamilias** (ˌpɑːtreɪzfəˈmɪlɪˌæs) the male head of a household [L: father of the family]

Pp

paternal (pəˈtɜːnᵊl) *adj* **1** relating to or characteristic of a father; fatherly **2** (*prenominal*) related through the father: *his paternal grandfather* **3** inherited or derived from the male parent [c17 from LL *paternālis*, from L *pater* father] > **paˈternally** *adv*

paternalism (pəˈtɜːnəˌlɪzəm) *n* the attitude or policy of a government or other authority that manages the affairs of a country, company, etc, in the manner of a father, esp in usurping individual responsibility > **paˈternalist** *n, adj* > **paˌternalˈistic** *adj* > **paˌternalˈistically** *adv*

paternity (pəˈtɜːnɪtɪ) *n* **1a** the fact or state of being a father **1b** (*as modifier*): *a paternity suit; paternity leave* **2** descent or derivation from a father **3** authorship or origin [c15 from LL *paternitās*, from L *pater* father]

paternoster (ˌpætəˈnɒstə) *n* **1** *RC Church* the beads at the ends of each decade of the rosary at which the Paternoster is recited **2** a type of fishing tackle in which short lines and hooks are attached at intervals to the main line **3** a type of lift in which platforms are attached to continuous chains: passengers enter while it is moving [L, lit.: our father (from the opening of the Lord's Prayer)]

Paternoster (ˌpætəˈnɒstə) *n (sometimes not cap) RC Church* **1** the Lord's Prayer, esp in Latin **2** the recital of this as an act of devotion

Paterson[1] (ˈpætəsᵊn) *n* a city in NE New Jersey: settled by the Dutch in the late 17th century. Pop: 149 222 (1999)

Paterson[2] (ˈpætəsᵊn) *n* **1** **Andrew Barton**, known as *Banjo Paterson*. 1864–1941, Australian poet. His works include "Waltzing Matilda" and "The Man from Snowy River" **2** **William** 1658–1719, Scottish merchant and banker: founded the Bank of England (1694)

Paterson's curse *n* an Australian name for **viper's bugloss**

path (pɑːθ) *n, pl* **paths** (pɑːðz) **1** a road or way, esp a narrow trodden track **2** a surfaced walk, as through a garden **3** the course or direction in which something moves: *the path of a whirlwind* **4** a course of conduct: *the path of virtue* **5** *computing* the directions for reaching a particular file or directory, as traced hierarchically through each of the parent directories, usually from the root [OE *pæth*] > **'pathless** *adj*

path. *abbrev for:* **1** pathological **2** pathology

-path *n combining form* **1** denoting a person suffering from a specified disease or disorder: *neuropath* **2** denoting a practitioner of a particular method of treatment: *osteopath* [back formation from -PATHY]

Pathan (pə'tɑːn) *n* a member of the Pashto-speaking people of Afghanistan, NW Pakistan, and elsewhere [C17 from Hindi]

pathetic (pə'θɛtɪk) *adj* **1** evoking or expressing pity, sympathy, etc **2** distressingly inadequate: *the old man sat huddled before a pathetic fire* **3** *Brit sl* ludicrously or contemptibly uninteresting or worthless **4** *obs* of or affecting the feelings [C16 from F *pathétique*, via LL from Gk *pathetikos* sensitive, from *pathos* suffering] > **pa'thetically** *adv*

pathetic fallacy *n* (in literature) the presentation of inanimate objects in nature as possessing human feelings

pathfinder ('pɑːθˌfaɪndə) *n* **1** a person who makes or finds a way, esp through unexplored areas or fields of knowledge **2** an aircraft or parachutist that indicates a target area by dropping flares, etc **3** a radar device used for navigation or homing onto a target

pathfinder prospectus *n* a prospectus regarding the flotation of a new company that contains only sufficient details to test the market reaction

pathname ('pɑːθˌneɪm) *n computing* the name of a file or directory together with its position in relation to other directories traced back in a line to the root; the names of the file and each of the parent directories are separated from one another by slashes

patho- *or before a vowel* **path-** *combining form* disease: *pathology* [from Gk *pathos* suffering]

pathogen ('pæθəˌdʒɛn) *n* any agent that can cause disease > **ˌpatho'genic** *adj*

pathogenesis (ˌpæθə'dʒɛnɪsɪs) *or* **pathogeny** (pə'θɒdʒɪnɪ) *n* the development of a disease > **pathogenetic** (ˌpæθədʒɪ'nɛtɪk) *adj*

pathological (ˌpæθə'lɒdʒɪkᵊl) *or (less commonly)* **pathologic** *adj* **1** of or relating to pathology **2** relating to, involving, or caused by disease **3** *inf* compulsively motivated: *a pathological liar* > **ˌpatho'logically** *adv*

pathologize *or* **pathologise** (pə'θɒlədgaɪz) *vb (tr)* to represent (something) as a disease: *this pathologizing of parenthood*

pathology (pə'θɒlədʒɪ) *n, pl* **pathologies 1** the branch of medicine concerned with the cause, origin, and nature of disease, including the changes occurring as a result of disease **2** the manifestations of disease, esp changes occurring in tissues or organs > **pa'thologist** *n*

▷ www.medbioworld.com/home/lists/diseases.html
▷ www.cdc.gov/health

pathos ('peɪθɒs) *n* **1** the quality or power, esp in literature or speech, of arousing feelings of pity, sorrow, etc **2** a feeling of sympathy or pity [C17 from Gk: suffering]

pathway ('pɑːθˌweɪ) *n* **1** a path **2** *biochem* a chain of reactions associated with a particular metabolic process

-pathy *n combining form* **1** indicating feeling or perception: *telepathy* **2** indicating disease: *psychopathy* **3** indicating a method of treating disease: *osteopathy* [from Gk *patheia* suffering; see PATHOS] > **-pathic** *adj combining form*

Patiala (ˌpʌtɪ'ɑːlə) *n* a city in N India, in E Punjab: seat of the Punjabi University (1962). Pop: 238 368 (1991)

patience ('peɪʃəns) *n* **1** tolerant and even-tempered perseverance **2** the capacity for calmly enduring pain, trying situations, etc **3** *chiefly Brit* any of various card games for one player only. US word: **solitaire** [C13 via OF from L *patientia* endurance, from *patī* to suffer]

patient ('peɪʃənt) *adj* **1** enduring trying circumstances with even temper **2** tolerant; understanding **3** capable of accepting delay with equanimity **4** persevering or diligent: *a patient worker* ▷ *n* **5** a person who is receiving medical care [C14 see PATIENCE] > **'patiently** *adv*

patina[1] ('pætɪnə) *n, pl* **patinas 1** a film formed on the surface of a metal, esp the green oxidation of bronze or copper **2** any fine layer on a surface: *a patina of frost* **3** the sheen on a surface caused by much handling [C18 from It.: coating, from L: PATINA[2]]

patina[2] ('pætɪnə) *n, pl* **patinae** (-ˌniː) a broad shallow dish used in ancient Rome [from L, from Gk *patanē* platter]

patio ('pætɪˌəʊ) *n, pl* **patios 1** an open inner courtyard, esp one in a Spanish or Spanish-American house **2** an area adjoining a house, esp one that is paved [C19 from Sp.: courtyard]

patisserie (pə'tiːsərɪ) *n* **1** a shop where fancy pastries are sold **2** such pastries [C18 F, from *pâtissier* pastry cook, ult. from LL *pasta* PASTE]

Patmore ('pætmɔː) *n* **Coventry** (**Kersey Dighton**) 1823–96, English poet. His works, celebrating both conjugal and divine love, include *The Angel in the House* (1854–62) and *The Unknown Eros* (1877)

Patmos ('pætmɒs) *n* a Greek island in the Aegean, in the NW Dodecanese: St John's place of exile (about 95 AD), where he wrote the Apocalypse. Pop: 2650 (1995 est). Area: 34 sq km (13 sq miles)

Patna ('pætnə) *n* a city in NE India, capital of Bihar state, on the River Ganges: founded in the 5th century BC; university (1917); centre of a rice-growing region. Pop: 917 243 (1991)

Patna rice *n* a variety of long-grain rice, used for savoury dishes

patois ('pætwɑː) *n, pl* **patois** ('pætwɑːz) **1** a regional dialect of a language, usually considered substandard **2** the jargon of a particular group [C17 from OF: rustic speech, ?from *patoier* to handle awkwardly, from *patte* paw]

Paton ('peɪtᵊn) *n* **Alan** (**Stewart**) 1903–88, South African writer, noted esp for his novel dealing with racism and apartheid in South Africa, *Cry, the Beloved Country* (1965)

pat. pend. *abbrev for* patent pending

Patras (pə'træs, 'pætrəs) *n* a port in W Greece, in the NW Peloponnese on the **Gulf of Patras** (an inlet of the Ionian Sea): one of the richest cities in Greece until the 3rd century BC; under Turkish rule from 1458 to 1687 and from 1715 until the War of Greek Independence, which began here in 1821. Pop: 155 180 (1991). Modern Greek name: **Pátrai** ('patrɛ)

patri- *combining form* father: *patricide; patriarch* [from L *pater*, Gk *patēr* father]

patrial ('peɪtrɪəl) *n* (in Britain, formerly) a person having by statute the right of abode in the United Kingdom [C20 from L *patria* native land]

patriarch ('peɪtrɪˌɑːk) *n* **1** the male head of a tribe or family **2** a very old or venerable man **3** *Bible* **3a** any of a number of persons regarded as the fathers of the human race **3b** any of the three ancestors of the Hebrew people: Abraham, Isaac, or Jacob **3c** any of Jacob's twelve sons, regarded as the ancestors of the twelve tribes of Israel **4** *early Christian Church* the bishop of one of several principal sees, esp those of Rome, Antioch, and Alexandria **5** *Eastern Orthodox Church* the bishops of the four ancient principal sees of Constantinople, Antioch, Alexandria, and Jerusalem, and also of Russia, Romania, and Serbia **6** *RC Church* **6a** a title given to the pope **6b** a title given to a number of bishops, esp of the Uniat Churches, indicating their rank as immediately below that of the pope **7** the oldest or most venerable member of a group, community, etc **8** a person regarded as the founder of a community, tradition, etc [C12 via OF from Church L *patriarcha*] > ˌ**patri'archal** *adj*

patriarchate ('peɪtrɪˌɑːkɪt) *n* the office, jurisdiction, province, or residence of a patriarch

patriarchy ('peɪtrɪˌɑːkɪ) *n, pl* **patriarchies** **1** a form of social organization in which a male is the head of the family and descent, kinship, and title are traced through the male line **2** any society governed by such a system

patriate ('pætrɪˌeɪt, 'peɪtrɪˌeɪt) *vb (tr)* to bring under the authority of an autonomous country, for example as in the transfer of the Canadian constitution from UK to Canadian responsibility > ˌ**patri'ation** *n*

patrician (pə'trɪʃən) *n* **1** a member of the hereditary aristocracy of ancient Rome **2** (in medieval Europe) a member of the upper class in numerous Italian republics and German free cities **3** an aristocrat **4** a person of refined conduct, tastes, etc ▹ *adj* **5** (esp in ancient Rome) of, relating to, or composed of patricians **6** aristocratic [C15 from OF *patricien*, from L *patricius* noble, from *pater* father]

patricide ('pætrɪˌsaɪd) *n* **1** the act of killing one's father **2** a person who kills his or her father > ˌ**patri'cidal** *adj*

Patrick ('pætrɪk) *n* **Saint** 5th century AD, Christian missionary in Ireland, probably born in Britain; patron saint of Ireland. Feast day: March 17

patrilineal (ˌpætrɪ'lɪnɪəl) *adj* tracing descent, kinship, or title through the male line

patrimony ('pætrɪmənɪ) *n, pl* **patrimonies** **1** an inheritance from one's father or other ancestor **2** the endowment of a church [C14 *patrimoyne*, from OF, from L *patrimonium* paternal inheritance] > **patrimonial** (ˌpætrɪ'məʊnɪəl) *adj*

patriot ('peɪtrɪət, 'pæt-) *n* a person who vigorously supports his or her country and its way of life [C16 via F from LL *patriōta*, from Gk *patriotēs*, from *patris* native land; rel. to Gk *patēr* father; cf. L *pater* father, *patria* fatherland] > **patriotic** (ˌpætrɪ'ɒtɪk) *adj* > ˌ**patri'otically** *adv*

Patriot ('peɪtrɪət) *n* a US surface-to-air missile system with multiple launch stations and the capability to track multiple targets by radar

patriotism ('pætrɪəˌtɪzəm) *n* devotion to one's own country and concern for its defence

patristic (pə'trɪstɪk) *or* **patristical** *adj* of or relating to the Fathers of the Church, their writings, or the study of these > **pa'tristics** *n (functioning as sing)*

Patroclus (pə'trɒkləs) *n Greek myth* a friend of Achilles, killed in the Trojan War by Hector. His death made Achilles return to the fight after his quarrel with Agamemnon

patrol (pə'trəʊl) *n* **1** the action of going round a town, etc, at regular intervals for purposes of security or observation **2** a person or group that carries out such an action **3** a military detachment with the mission of security or combat with enemy forces **4** a division of a troop of Scouts or Guides ▹ *vb* **patrols, patrolling, patrolled** **5** to engage in a patrol of (a place) [C17 from F *patrouiller*, from *patouiller* to flounder in mud, from *patte* paw] > **pa'troller** *n*

patrol car *n* a police car used for patrolling streets and motorways

patrology (pə'trɒlədʒɪ) *n* **1** the study of the writings of the Fathers of the Church **2** a collection of such writings [C17 from Gk *patr-*, *patēr* father + -LOGY] > **pa'trologist** *n*

patrol wagon *n* the usual US and Austral name for **Black Maria**

patron[1] ('peɪtrən) *n* **1** a person who sponsors or aids artists, charities, etc; protector or benefactor **2** a customer of a shop, hotel, etc, esp a regular one **3** See **patron saint** [C14 via OF from L *patrōnus* protector, from *pater* father] > '**patroness** *fem n*

patron[2] (patrɔ̃) *n* the owner of a restaurant, hotel, etc, esp of a French one [F]

patronage ('pætrənɪdʒ) *n* **1a** the support given or custom brought by a patron **1b** the position of a patron **2** (in politics) **2a** the practice of making appointments to office, granting contracts, etc **2b** the favours, etc, so distributed **3a** a condescending manner **3b** any kindness done in a condescending way

patronize *or* **patronise** ('pætrəˌnaɪz) *vb* **patronizes, patronizing, patronized** *or* **patronises, patronising, patronised** **1** to behave or treat in a condescending way **2** *(tr)* to act as a patron by sponsoring or bringing trade to > '**patronˌizer** *or* '**patronˌiser** *n* > '**patronˌizing** *or* '**patronˌising** *adj* > '**patronˌizingly** *or* '**patronˌisingly** *adv*

patron saint *n* a saint regarded as the particular guardian of a country, person, etc

patronymic (ˌpætrə'nɪmɪk) *adj* **1** (of a name) derived from the name of its bearer's father or ancestor ▹ *n* **2** a patronymic name [C17 via LL from Gk *patronumikos*, from *patēr* father + *onoma* NAME]

patroon (pə'truːn) *n US* a Dutch land holder in New Netherland and New York with manorial rights in the colonial era [C18 from Du.: PATRON[1]]

patsy ('pætsɪ) *n, pl* **patsies** *sl, chiefly US & Canad* **1** a person who is easily cheated, victimized, etc **2** a scapegoat [C20 from ?]

patten ('pætᵊn) *n* a wooden clog or sandal on a raised wooden platform or metal ring [C14 from OF *patin*, prob. from *patte* paw]

patter[1] ('pætə) *vb* **1** *(intr)* to walk or move with quick soft steps **2** to strike with or make a quick succession of light tapping sounds ▹ *n* **3** a quick succession of light tapping sounds, as of feet: *the patter of mice* [C17 from PAT[1]]

patter[2] ('pætə) *n* **1** the glib rapid speech of comedians, etc **2** quick idle talk; chatter **3** the jargon of a particular group, etc; lingo ▹ *vb* **4** *(intr)* to speak glibly and rapidly **5** to repeat (prayers, etc) in a mechanical or perfunctory manner [C14 from L *pater* in *Pater Noster* Our Father]

Pp

pattern ('pætᵊn) *n* **1** an arrangement of repeated or corresponding parts, decorative motifs, etc **2** a decorative design: *a paisley pattern* **3** a style: *various patterns of cutlery* **4** a plan or diagram used as a guide in making something: *a paper pattern for a dress* **5** a standard way of moving, acting, etc: *traffic patterns* **6** a model worthy of imitation: *a pattern of kindness* **7** a representative sample **8** a wooden or metal shape or model used in a foundry to make a mould ▹ *vb (tr)* **9** (often foll by *after* or *on*) to model **10** to arrange as or decorate with a pattern [C14 *patron*, from Med. L *patrōnus* example, from L: PATRON[1]]

Patti ('pætɪ) *n* **Adelina** (ade'liːna) 1843–1919, Italian operatic coloratura soprano, born in Spain

Patton ('pætᵊn) *n* **George Smith** 1885–1945, US general, who successfully developed tank warfare as an extension of cavalry tactics in World War II: captured Palermo, Sicily (1942) and much of France (1944)

patty ('pætɪ) *n, pl* **patties** **1** a small cake of minced food **2** a small pie [C18 from F PÂTÉ]

patu ('pɑːtuː) *n, pl* **patus** *NZ* a short Maori club, now ceremonial only [from Maori]

patulous ('pætjʊləs) *adj bot* spreading widely or expanded: *patulous branches* [C17 from L *patulus* open, from *patēre* to lie open]

Pau (*French* po) *n* a city in SW France: residence of the French kings of Navarre; tourist centre for the Pyrenees. Pop: 82 157 (1990)

paua ('pɑːʊɑ) *n* an edible abalone of New Zealand, having an iridescent shell used for jewellery, etc [from Maori]

paucity ('pɔːsɪtɪ) *n* **1** insufficiency; dearth **2** smallness of number; fewness [C15 from L *paucitās* scarcity, from *paucus* few]

Paul (pɔːl) *n* **1 Saint** Also called: **Paul the Apostle, Saul of Tarsus** original name *Saul*. died ?67 AD, one of the first Christian missionaries to the Gentiles, who died a martyr in Rome. Until his revelatory conversion he had assisted in persecuting the Christians. He wrote many of the Epistles in the New Testament. Feast day: June 29. Related adj: **Pauline 2 Jean** See **Jean Paul 3 Les**, real name *Lester Polfuss*. born 1915, US guitarist: creator of the solid-body electric guitar and pioneer in multitrack recording

Paul III *n* original name *Alessandro Farnese*. 1468–1549, Italian ecclesiastic; pope (1534–49). He excommunicated Henry VIII of England (1538) and inaugurated the Counter-Reformation by approving the establishment of the Jesuits (1540), instituting the Inquisition in Italy, and convening the Council of Trent (1545)

Paul VI *n* original name *Giovanni Battista Montini*. 1897–1978, Italian ecclesiastic; pope (1963–1978)

Pauli ('pɔːlɪ, 'paʊlɪ) *n* **Wolfgang** ('vɒlf,gæŋ) 1900–58, US physicist, born in Austria. He formulated the exclusion principle (1924) and postulated the existence of the neutrino (1931), later confirmed by Fermi: Nobel prize for physics 1945

Pauli exclusion principle *n physics* the principle that two identical fermions cannot occupy the same quantum state in a body, such as an atom; sometimes shortened to **exclusion principle**

Pauline ('pɔːlaɪn) *adj* relating to Saint Paul or his doctrines

Pauling ('pɔːlɪŋ) *n* **Linus Carl** ('laɪnəs) 1901–94, US chemist, noted particularly for his work on the nature of the chemical bond and his opposition to nuclear tests: Nobel prize for chemistry 1954; Nobel peace prize 1962

Paulinus (pɔː'laɪnəs) *n* **Saint** died 644 AD, Roman missionary to England; first bishop of York and archbishop of Rochester. Feast day: Oct 10

Paul Jones *n* an old-time dance in which partners are exchanged [C19 after John Paul JONES]

paulownia (pɔː'ləʊnɪə) *n* a tree of a Japanese genus, esp one having large heart-shaped leaves and clusters of purplish or white flowers [C19 NL, after Anna *Paulovna*, daughter of Paul I of Russia]

Paumotu Archipelago (paʊ'məʊtuː) *n* another name for the **Tuamotu Archipelago**

paunch (pɔːntʃ) *n* **1** the belly or abdomen, esp when protruding **2** another name for **rumen** ▷ *vb (tr)* **3** to stab in the stomach; disembowel [C14 from Anglo-Norman *paunche*, from OF *pance*, from L *panticēs* (pl) bowels] > '**paunchy** *adj* > '**paunchiness** *n*

pauper ('pɔːpə) *n* **1** a person who is extremely poor **2** (formerly) a person supported by public charity [C16 from L: poor] > '**pauper,ism** *n*

pauperize *or* **pauperise** ('pɔːpə,raɪz) *vb* **pauperizes, pauperizing, pauperized** *or* **pauperises, pauperising, pauperised** *(tr)* to make a pauper of; impoverish

Pausanias (pɔː'seɪnɪəs) *n* 2nd century AD, Greek geographer and historian. His *Description of Greece* gives a valuable account of the topography of ancient Greece

pause (pɔːz) *vb* **pauses, pausing, paused** *(intr)* **1** to cease an action temporarily **2** to hesitate; delay: *she replied without pausing* ▷ *n* **3** a temporary stop or rest, esp in speech or action; short break **4** *prosody* another word for **caesura 5** Also called: **fermata** *music* a continuation of a note or rest beyond its normal length. Usual symbol: 𝄐 **6 give pause to** to cause to hesitate [C15 from L *pausa* pause, from Gk *pausis*, from *pauein* to halt]

pav (pæv) *n Austral & NZ inf* short for **pavlova**

pavane *or* **pavan** (pə'vɑːn, 'pævən) *n* **1** a slow and stately dance of the 16th and 17th centuries **2** a piece of music composed for or in the rhythm of this dance [C16 *pavan*, via F from Sp. *pavana*, from OIt. *padovana* Paduan (dance), from *Padova* Padua]

Pavarotti (*Italian* pava'rɔtti) *n* **Luciano** born 1935, Italian operatic tenor, specializing in works by Verdi and Puccini

pave (peɪv) *vb* **paves, paving, paved** *(tr)* **1** to cover (a road, etc) with a firm surface suitable for travel, as with paving stones or concrete **2** to serve as the material for a pavement or other hard layer: *bricks paved the causeway* **3** (often foll by *with*) to cover with a hard layer (of): *shelves paved with marble* **4** to prepare or make easier (esp in **pave the way**) [C14 from OF *paver*, from L *pavīre* to ram down] > '**paver** *n*

pavement ('peɪvmənt) *n* **1** a hard-surfaced path for pedestrians alongside and a little higher than a road. US and Canad word: **sidewalk 2** the material used in paving [C13 from L *pavīmentum* hard floor, from *pavīre* to beat hard]

Pavese (*Italian* pa've:se) *n* **Cesare** ('tʃe:zare) 1908–50, Italian writer and translator. His works include collections of poems, such as *Verrà la morte e avrà i tuoi occhi* (1953), short stories, such as the collection *Notte di festa* (1953), and the novel *La Luna e i falò* (1950)

Pavia ('pɑːvɪə) *n* a town in N Italy, in Lombardy: noted for its Roman and medieval remains, including the tomb of St Augustine. Pop: 80 650 (1990). Latin name: **Ticinum**

pavilion (pə'vɪljən) *n* **1** *Brit* a building at a sports ground, esp a cricket pitch, in which players change, etc **2** a summerhouse or other decorative shelter **3** a building or temporary structure, esp one that is open and ornamental, for housing exhibitions, etc **4** a large ornate tent, esp one with a peaked top, as used by medieval armies **5** one of a set of buildings that together form a hospital or other large institution ▷ *vb (tr) literary* **6** to place as in a pavilion: *pavilioned in splendour* **7** to provide with a pavilion or pavilions [C13 from OF *pavillon* canopied structure, from L *pāpiliō* butterfly, tent]

paving ('peɪvɪŋ) *n* **1** a paved surface; pavement **2** material used for a pavement

Pavlodar (*Russian* pəvla'dar) *n* a port in NE Kazakhstan on the Irtysh River: major industrial centre with an oil refinery. Pop: 300 500 (1999)

Pavlov ('pævlɒv; *Russian* 'pavləf) *n* **Ivan Petrovich** (i'van pɪ'trɔvitʃ) 1849–1936, Russian physiologist. His study of conditioned reflexes in dogs influenced behaviourism. He also made important contributions to the study of digestion: Nobel prize for physiology or medicine 1904

pavlova (pæv'ləʊvə) *n* a meringue cake topped with whipped cream and fruit [C20 after Anna PAVLOVA]

Pavlova (pæv'ləʊvə; *Russian* 'pavləvə) *n* **Anna** ('annə) 1885–1931, Russian ballerina

paw (pɔː) *n* **1** any of the feet of a four-legged mammal, bearing claws or nails **2** *inf* a hand, esp one that is large, clumsy, etc ▷ *vb* **3** to scrape or contaminate with the paws or feet **4** *(tr) inf* to touch or caress in a clumsy, rough, or overfamiliar manner [C13 via OF from Gmc]

pawky ('pɔːkɪ) *adj* **pawkier, pawkiest** *dialect or Scot* having a dry wit [C17 from Scot *pawk* trick, from ?] > '**pawkily** *adv* > '**pawkiness** *n*

pawl (pɔːl) *n* a pivoted lever shaped to engage with a ratchet to prevent motion in a particular direction [C17 ?from Du. *pal* pawl]

pawn[1] (pɔːn) *vb (tr)* **1** to deposit (an article) as security for the repayment of a loan, esp from a pawnbroker: *to pawn jewellery* **2** to stake: *to pawn one's honour* ▷ *n* **3** an article deposited as security **4** the condition of being so deposited (esp in **in pawn**) **5** a person or thing that is held as a security **6** the act of pawning [C15 from OF *pan* security, from L *pannus* cloth, apparently because

clothing was often left as a surety] > '**pawnage** *n*
pawn² (pɔːn) *n* **1** a chess man of the lowest theoretical value **2** a person, group, etc, manipulated by another [C14 from Anglo-Norman *poun*, from OF, from Med. L *pedō* infantryman, from L *pēs* foot]
pawnbroker ('pɔːnˌbrəʊkə) *n* a dealer licensed to lend money at a specified rate of interest on the security of movable personal property, which can be sold if the loan is not repaid within a specified period > '**pawnˌbroking** *n*
pawnshop ('pɔːnˌʃɒp) *n* the premises of a pawnbroker
pawn ticket *n* a receipt for goods pawned
pawpaw ('pɔːˌpɔː) *n* another name for **papaw** or **papaya**
pax (pæks) *n* **1** *chiefly RC Church* **1a** the kiss of peace **1b** a small metal or ivory plate, formerly used to convey the kiss of peace from the celebrant at Mass to those attending it ▷ *interj* **2** *Brit school sl* a call signalling an end to hostilities or claiming immunity from the rules of a game [L: peace]
Pax (pæks) *n* the Roman goddess of peace. Greek counterpart: **Irene** [L: peace]
PAX (in Britain) *abbrev for* private automatic exchange
Paxman ('pæksmən) *n* **Jeremy** (**Dickson**) born 1950, British journalist, broadcaster, and author, noted esp for his political interviews
Paxton ('pækstən) *n* Sir **Joseph** 1801–65, English architect, who designed Crystal Palace (1851), the first large structure of prefabricated glass and iron parts
pay¹ (peɪ) *vb* **pays, paying, paid** **1** to discharge (a debt, obligation, etc) by giving or doing something: *he paid his creditors* **2** (when *intr*, often foll by *for*) to give (money, etc) to (a person) in return for goods or services: *they pay their workers well; they pay by the hour* **3** to give or afford (a person, etc) a profit or benefit: *it pays one to be honest* **4** (*tr*) to give or bestow (a compliment, regards, attention, etc) **5** (*tr*) to make (a visit or call) **6** (*intr*; often foll by *for*) to give compensation or make amends **7** (*tr*) to yield a return of: *the shares pay 15 per cent* **8** *Austral inf* to acknowledge or accept (something) as true, just, etc **9** **pay one's way** **9a** to contribute one's share of expenses **9b** to remain solvent without outside help ▷ *n* **10a** money given in return for work or services; a salary or wage **10b** (*as modifier*): *a pay slip; a pay claim* **11** paid employment (esp in **in the pay of**) **12** (*modifier*) requiring the insertion of money before or during use: *a pay phone* **13** (*modifier*) rich enough in minerals to be profitably worked: *pay gravel* ▷ See also **pay back, pay for,** etc [C12 from OF *payer*, from L *pācāre* to appease (a creditor), from *pāx* peace] > '**payer** *n*
pay² (peɪ) *vb* **pays, paying, payed** (*tr*) *naut* to caulk (the seams of a wooden vessel) with pitch or tar [C17 from OF *peier*, from L *picāre*, from *pix* pitch]
payable ('peɪəbᵊl) *adj* **1** (often foll by *on*) to be paid: *payable on the third of each month* **2** that is capable of being paid **3** capable of being profitable **4** (of a debt, etc) imposing an obligation on the debtor to pay, esp at once
pay-and-display *adj* denoting a car-parking system in which a motorist buys a permit to park for a specified period, usually from a coin-operated machine, and displays the permit on or near the windscreen of his or her car so that it can be seen by a parking attendant
pay back *vb* (*tr, adv*) **1** to retaliate against: *to pay someone back for an insult* **2** to give or do (something equivalent) in return for a favour, insult, etc **3** to repay (a loan, etc) ▷ *n* **payback** **4a** the return on an investment **4b** Also called: **payback period.** the time taken for a project to cover its outlay **5a** something done in order to gain revenge **5b** (*as modifier*): *payback killings*
pay bed *n* an informal name for **private pay bed**
payday ('peɪˌdeɪ) *n* the day on which wages or salaries are paid
pay dirt *n chiefly US* **1** soil, gravel, ore, etc that contains sufficient minerals to make it worthwhile mining **2** **hit** (*or* **strike**) **pay dirt** *inf* to become wealthy, successful, etc
PAYE (in Britain and New Zealand) *abbrev for* pay as you earn; a system by which income tax levied on wage and salary earners is paid by employers directly to the government
payee (peɪ'iː) *n* the person to whom a cheque, money order, etc, is made out
pay for *vb* (*prep*) **1** to make payment for **2** (*intr*) to suffer or be punished, as for a mistake, wrong decision, etc
paying guest *n* a euphemism for **lodger**
payload ('peɪˌləʊd) *n* **1** that part of a cargo earning revenue **2a** the passengers, cargo, or bombs carried by an aircraft **2b** the equipment carried by a rocket, satellite, or spacecraft **3** the explosive power of a warhead, bomb, etc, carried by a missile or aircraft
paymaster ('peɪˌmɑːstə) *n* an official of a government, business, etc, responsible for the payment of wages and salaries
payment ('peɪmənt) *n* **1** the act of paying **2** a sum of money paid **3** something given in return; punishment or reward
paynim ('peɪnɪm) *n arch* **1** a heathen or pagan **2** a Muslim [C13 from OF *paienime*, from LL *pāgānismus* paganism, from *pāgānus* PAGAN]
pay off *vb* **1** (*tr, adv*) to pay all that is due in wages, etc, and discharge from employment **2** (*tr, adv*) to pay the complete amount of (a debt, bill, etc) **3** (*intr, adv*) to turn out to be profitable, effective, etc: *the gamble paid off* **4** (*tr, adv* or *intr, prep*) to take revenge on (a person) or for (a wrong done): *to pay someone off for an insult* **5** (*tr, adv*) *inf* to give a bribe to ▷ *n* **payoff** **6** the final settlement, esp in retribution **7** *inf* the climax, consequence, or outcome of events, a story, etc **8** the final payment of a debt, salary, etc **9** the time of such a payment **10** *inf* a bribe
payola (peɪ'əʊlə) *n inf* **1** a bribe given to secure special treatment, esp to a disc jockey to promote a commercial product **2** the practice of paying or receiving such bribes [C20 from PAY¹ + *-ola*, as in PIANOLA]
pay out *vb* (*adv*) **1** to distribute (money, etc); disburse **2** (*tr*) to release (a rope) gradually, hand over hand ▷ *n* **payout** **3** a sum of money paid out
pay-per-view *n* **a** a system of television broadcasting by which subscribers pay for each programme they wish to receive **b** (*as modifier*): *a pay-per-view channel*
payphone ('peɪˌfəʊn) *n* a public telephone operated by coins or a phonecard
payroll ('peɪˌrəʊl) *n* **1** a list of employees, specifying the salary or wage of each **2a** the total of these amounts or the actual money equivalent **2b** (*as modifier*): *a payroll tax*
Paysandú (*Spanish* paisan'du) *n* a port in W Uruguay, on the Uruguay River: the third largest city in the country. Pop: 75 200 (latest est)
Pays de la Loire (*French* pei də la lwar) *n* a region of W France, on the Bay of Biscay: generally low-lying, drained by the River Loire and its tributaries; agricultural
payt *abbrev for* payment
pay up *vb* (*adv*) to pay (money) promptly, in full, or on demand
Paz (*Spanish* pas) *n* **Octavio** (ɔk'taβjo) 1914–98, Mexican poet and essayist. His poems include the cycle *Piedra de Sol* (1957) and *Blanco* (1967). Nobel prize for literature 1990
Pb *the chemical symbol for* lead [from NL *plumbum*]
PB *athletics abbrev for* personal best
PBS *US abbrev for* Public Broadcasting Service
PBX (in Britain) *abbrev for* private branch exchange; a telephone system that handles the internal and external calls of a building, firm, etc
pc *abbrev for:* **1** per cent **2** postcard **3** *obsolete* (in prescriptions) post cibum [L: after meals]
PC *abbrev for:* **1** personal computer **2** Parish Council(lor) **3** (in Britain and Canada) Police Constable **4** politically

Pp

correct **5** (in Britain and Canada) Privy Council(lor) **6** (in Canada) Progressive Conservative

PCB *abbrev for* polychlorinated biphenyl; any of a group of compounds in which chlorine atoms replace the hydrogen atoms in biphenyl: used in electrical insulators and in the manufacture of plastics; a toxic pollutant

PCC (in Britain) *abbrev for* Press Complaints Commission ▷ www.pcc.org.uk/index2.html

PCP *n trademark* phenylcyclohexylpiperidine (phencyclidine); a depressant drug used illegally as a hallucinogen

PCR *abbrev for* polymerase chain reaction: a technique for rapidly producing many copies of a fragment of DNA for diagnostic or research purposes

PCV (in Britain) *abbrev for* passenger carrying vehicle

pd *abbrev for:* **1** paid **2** Also: **PD** per diem **3** potential difference

Pd *the chemical symbol for* palladium

PDA *abbrev for* personal digital assistant

PDF *computing abbrev for* portable document format: a format in which documents may be viewed

PDR *abbrev for* price-dividend ratio

P-D ratio *n* short for **price-dividend ratio**

PDSA (in Britain) *abbrev for* People's Dispensary for Sick Animals

PDT (in the US and Canada) *abbrev for* Pacific Daylight Time

PE *abbrev for:* **1** physical education **2** potential energy **3** Presiding Elder **4** Also: **p.e.** printer's error **5** *statistics* probable error **6** Protestant Episcopal

pea (pi:) *n* **1** an annual climbing plant with small white flowers and long green pods containing edible green seeds: cultivated in temperate regions **2** the seed of this plant, eaten as a vegetable **3** any of several other leguminous plants, such as the sweet pea [C17 from PEASE (incorrectly assumed to be a pl)]

Peabody (ˈpi:ˌbɒdɪ) *n* **George** 1795–1869, US merchant, banker, and philanthropist in the US and England

peace (pi:s) *n* **1a** the state existing during the absence of war **1b** (*as modifier*): *peace negotiations* **2** (*often cap*) a treaty marking the end of a war **3** a state of harmony between people or groups **4** law and order within a state: *a breach of the peace* **5** absence of mental anxiety (often in **peace of mind**) **6** a state of stillness, silence, or serenity **7 at peace 7a** in a state of harmony or friendship **7b** in a state of serenity **7c** dead: *the old lady is at peace now* **8 hold** *or* **keep one's peace** to keep silent **9 keep the peace** to maintain law and order ▷ *vb* **peaces, peacing, peaced 10** (*intr*) *Obs except as an imperative* to be or become silent or still ▷ *modifier* **11** denoting a person or thing symbolizing support for international peace: *peace women* [C12 from OF *pais*, from L *pāx*]

peaceable (ˈpi:səbᵊl) *adj* **1** inclined towards peace **2** tranquil; calm > ˈ**peaceableness** *n* > ˈ**peaceably** *adv*

Peace Corps *n* an agency of the US government that sends volunteers to developing countries to work on educational projects, etc

peace dividend *n* additional money available to a government from cuts in defence expenditure because of the end of a period of hostilities

peaceful (ˈpi:sfʊl) *adj* **1** not in a state of war or disagreement **2** calm; tranquil **3** not involving violence: *peaceful picketing* **4** of, relating to, or in accord with a time of peace **5** inclined towards peace > ˈ**peacefully** *adv* > ˈ**peacefulness** *n*

peacekeeping (ˈpi:sˌki:pɪŋ) *n* **a** the maintenance of peace, esp the prevention of further fighting between hostile forces **b** (*as modifier*): *a UN peacekeeping force*

peacemaker (ˈpi:sˌmeɪkə) *n* a person who establishes peace, esp between others > ˈ**peaceˌmaking** *n*

peace offering *n* **1** something given to an adversary in the hope of procuring or maintaining peace **2** *judaism* a sacrificial meal shared between the offerer and Jehovah

peace pipe *n* a long decorated pipe smoked by North American Indians, esp as a token of peace. Also called: **calumet**

Peace River *n* a river in W Canada, rising in British Columbia as the Finlay River and flowing northeast into the Slave River. Length: 1715 km (1065 miles)

peace sign *n* a gesture made with the palm of the hand outwards and the index and middle fingers raised in a V

peacetime (ˈpi:sˌtaɪm) *n* **a** a period without war; time of peace **b** (*as modifier*): *a peacetime agreement*

peach[1] (pi:tʃ) *n* **1** a small tree with pink flowers and rounded edible fruit: cultivated in temperate regions **2** the soft juicy fruit of this tree, which has a downy reddish-yellow skin, yellowish-orange sweet flesh, and a single stone **3a** a pinkish-yellow to orange colour **3b** (*as adj*): *a peach dress* **4** *inf* a person or thing that is especially pleasing [C14 *peche*, from OF, from Med. L *persica*, from L *Persicum mālum* Persian apple]

peach[2] (pi:tʃ) *vb* (*intr*) *sl* to inform against an accomplice [C15 var. of earlier *apeche*, from F, from LL *impedicāre* to entangle; see IMPEACH]

peach brandy *n* (esp in S Africa) a coarse brandy made from fermented peaches

peach Melba *n* a dessert made of halved peaches, vanilla ice cream, and raspberries [C20 after Dame Nellie MELBA]

peachy (ˈpi:tʃɪ) *adj* **peachier, peachiest 1** of or like a peach, esp in colour or texture **2** *inf* excellent; fine > ˈ**peachiness** *n*

peacock (ˈpi:ˌkɒk) *n, pl* **peacocks** *or* **peacock 1** a male peafowl, having a crested head and a very large fanlike tail marked with blue and green eyelike spots **2** another name for **peafowl 3** a vain strutting person ▷ *vb* **4** to display (oneself) proudly [C14 *pecok*, *pe-* from OE *pāwa* (from L *pāvō* peacock) + COCK[1]] > ˈ**peaˌcockish** *adj* > ˈ**peaˌhen** *fem n*

Peacock (ˈpi:ˌkɒk) *n* **Thomas Love** 1785–1866, English novelist and poet, noted for his satirical romances, including *Headlong Hall* (1816) and *Nightmare Abbey* (1818)

peacock blue *n* **a** a greenish-blue colour **b** (*as adj*): *a peacock-blue car*

peafowl (ˈpi:ˌfaʊl) *n, pl* **peafowls** *or* **peafowl** either of two large pheasants of India and Ceylon and of SE Asia. The males (see **peacock** (sense 1)) have a characteristic bright plumage

pea green *n* **a** a yellowish-green colour **b** (*as adj*): *a pea-green teapot*

pea jacket *or* **peacoat** (ˈpi:ˌkəʊt) *n* a sailor's short heavy woollen overcoat [C18 from Du. *pijjekker*, from *pij* coat of coarse cloth + *jekker* jacket]

peak[1] (pi:k) *n* **1** a pointed end, edge, or projection: *the peak of a roof* **2** the pointed summit of a mountain **3** a mountain with a pointed summit **4** the point of greatest development, strength, etc: *the peak of his career* **5a** a sharp increase followed by a sharp decrease: *a voltage peak* **5b** the maximum value of this quantity **5c** (*as modifier*): *peak voltage* **6** Also called: **visor** a projecting piece on the front of some caps **7** *naut* **7a** the extreme forward (**forepeak**) or aft (**afterpeak**) part of the hull **7b** (of a fore-and-aft quadrilateral sail) the after uppermost corner **7c** the after end of a gaff ▷ *vb* **8** to form or reach or cause to form or reach a peak **9** (*tr*) *naut* to set (a gaff) or tilt (oars) vertically ▷ *adj* **10** of or relating to a period of greatest use or demand: *peak viewing hours* [C16 ?from PIKE[2], infl. by BEAK[1]]

peak[2] (pi:k) *vb* (*intr*) to become wan, emaciated, or sickly [C16 from ?] > ˈ**peaky** *or* ˈ**peakish** *adj*

Peak District *n* a region of N central England, mainly in N Derbyshire at the S end of the Pennines: consists of moors in the north and a central limestone plateau; many caves. Highest point: 727 m (2088 ft)

Peake (pi:k) *n* **Mervyn** 1911–68, English novelist, poet, and illustrator. In his trilogy *Gormenghast* (1946–59), he creates, with vivid imagination, a grotesque Gothic world

peaked (piːkt) *adj* having a peak; pointed

peak load *n* the maximum load on an electrical power-supply system

peal (piːl) *n* **1** a loud prolonged usually reverberating sound, as of bells, thunder, or laughter **2** *bell-ringing* a series of changes rung in accordance with specific rules **3** (*not in technical usage*) the set of bells in a belfry ▷ *vb* **4** (*intr*) to sound with a peal or peals **5** (*tr*) to give forth loudly and sonorously **6** (*tr*) to ring (bells) in peals [C14 *pele*, var. of *apele* APPEAL]

peanut (ˈpiːˌnʌt) *n* **a** a leguminous plant widely cultivated for its edible seeds **b** the edible nutlike seed of this plant, used for food and as a source of oil. Also called: **groundnut, monkey nut** ▷ See also **peanuts**

peanut butter *n* a brownish oily paste made from peanuts

peanuts (ˈpiːˌnʌts) *n sl* a trifling amount of money

pear (pɛə) *n* **1** a widely cultivated tree, having white flowers and edible fruits **2** the sweet gritty-textured juicy fruit of this tree, which has a globular base and tapers towards the apex **3** the wood of this tree, used for making furniture **4 go pear-shaped** *inf* to go wrong: *the plan started to go pear-shaped* [OE *pere*, ult. from L *pirum*]

Pearce (pɪəs) *n* **Guy** born 1967, Australian film actor, born in Britain; he became famous in the TV soap opera *Neighbours* (1986–90) and went on to star in *Priscilla, Queen of the Desert* (1994), *Memento* (2000), and *Till Human Voices Wake Us* (2002)

pearl¹ (pɜːl) *n* **1** a hard smooth lustrous typically rounded structure occurring on the inner surface of the shell of a clam or oyster around an invading particle such as a sand grain; much valued as a gem **2** any artificial gem resembling this **3** See **mother-of-pearl** **4** a person or thing that is like a pearl, esp in beauty or value **5** a pale greyish-white colour, often with a bluish tinge ▷ *adj* **6** of, made of, or set with pearl or mother-of-pearl **7** having the shape or colour of a pearl ▷ *vb* **8** (*tr*) to set with or as if with pearls **9** to shape into or assume a pearl-like form or colour **10** (*intr*) to dive or search for pearls [C14 from OF, from Vulgar L *pernula* (unattested), from L *perna* sea mussel]

pearl² (pɜːl) *n, vb* a variant spelling of **purl¹** (senses 2, 3, 5)

pearl ash *n* the granular crystalline form of potassium carbonate

pearl barley *n* barley ground into small round grains, used esp in soups and stews

Pearl Harbor *n* an almost landlocked inlet of the Pacific on the S coast of the island of Oahu, Hawaii: site of a US naval base attacked by the Japanese in 1941, resulting in the US entry into World War II

▷ www.history.navy.mil/faqs/faq66-1.htm

▷ www.ibiscom.com/pearl.htm

Pearl River *n* **1** a river in central Mississippi, flowing southwest and south to the Gulf of Mexico. Length: 789 km (490 miles) **2** the English name for the **Zhu Jiang**

pearly (ˈpɜːlɪ) *adj* **pearlier, pearliest** **1** resembling a pearl, esp in lustre **2** decorated with pearls or mother-of-pearl ▷ *n, pl* **pearlies** *Brit* **3** a London costermonger or his wife who wear on ceremonial occasions a traditional dress of dark clothes covered with pearl buttons **4** (*pl*) the clothes or the buttons themselves > ˈ**pearliness** *n*

Pearly Gates *pl n inf* the entrance to heaven

pearly king *or* (*fem*) **pearly queen** *n* the London costermonger whose ceremonial clothes display the most lavish collection of pearl buttons

pearly nautilus *n* any of several cephalopod molluscs of warm and tropical seas, having a partitioned pale pearly external shell with brown stripes. Also called: **chambered nautilus**

pearmain (ˈpɛəˌmeɪn) *n* any of several varieties of apple having a red skin [C15 from OF *permain* a type of pear, ?from L *Parmēnsis* of Parma]

Pears (pɪəz) *n* Sir **Peter** 1910–86, British tenor, associated esp with the works of Benjamin Britten

Pearse (pɪəs) *n* **Patrick** (**Henry**), Irish name *Pádraic*. 1879–1916, Irish nationalist, who planned and led the Easter Rising (1916): executed by the British

Pearson (ˈpɪəsən) *n* **1 Karl** 1857–1936, British mathematician, noted for his work in statistics, esp as applied to biological problems **2 Lester B**(**owles**) 1897–1972, Canadian Liberal statesman; prime minister (1963–68): Nobel peace prize 1957 for helping to resolve the Suez crisis (1956)

peart (pɪət) *adj dialect* lively; spirited; brisk [C15 var. of PERT] > ˈ**peartly** *adv*

Peary (ˈpɪərɪ) *n* **Robert Edwin** 1856–1920, US arctic explorer, generally regarded as the first man to reach the North Pole (1909)

peasant (ˈpɛzᵊnt) *n* **1** a member of a class of low social status that depends on either cottage industry or agricultural labour as a means of subsistence **2** *inf* a person who lives in the country; rustic **3** *inf* an uncouth or uncultured person [C15 from Anglo-F, from OF *païsant*, from *païs* country, from L *pāgus* rural area]

peasantry (ˈpɛzᵊntrɪ) *n* peasants as a class

pease (piːz) *n, pl* **pease** *arch or dialect* another word for **pea** [OE *peose*, via LL from L *pisa* peas, pl of *pisum*, from Gk *pison*]

peasecod *or* **peascod** (ˈpiːzˌkɒd) *n arch* the pod of a pea plant [C14 from PEASE + COD²]

pease pudding *n* (esp in Britain) a dish of split peas that have been soaked and boiled

peashooter (ˈpiːˌʃuːtə) *n* a tube through which dried peas are blown, used as a toy weapon

peasouper (ˌpiːˈsuːpə) *n* **1** *inf, chiefly Brit* dense dirty yellowish fog **2** *Canad* a disparaging name for a **French Canadian**

peat (piːt) *n* **a** a compact brownish deposit of partially decomposed vegetable matter saturated with water: found in uplands and bogs and used as a fuel (when dried) and as a fertilizer **b** (*as modifier*): *peat bog* [C14 from Anglo-L *peta*, ?from Celtic] > ˈ**peaty** *adj*

peat moss *n* any of various mosses, esp sphagnum, that grow in wet places and decay to form peat. See also **sphagnum**

pebble (ˈpɛbᵊl) *n* **1** a small smooth rounded stone, esp one worn by the action of water **2a** a transparent colourless variety of rock crystal, used for making certain lenses **2b** such a lens **3** (*modifier*) *inf* (of a lens or of spectacles) thick, with a high degree of magnification or distortion **4a** a grainy irregular surface, esp on leather **4b** leather having such a surface ▷ *vb* **pebbles, pebbling, pebbled** (*tr*) **5** to cover with pebbles **6** to impart a grainy surface to (leather) [OE *papolstān*, from *papol-* (? imit.) + *stān* stone] > ˈ**pebbly** *adj*

pebble dash *n Brit* a finish for external walls consisting of small stones embedded in plaster

pebi- (ˈpɛbɪ) *prefix computing* denoting 2^{50}: *pebibyte* [C20 from PE(TA-) + BI(NARY)]

USAGE See at **kilo-**

pec (pɛk) *n* (*usually pl*) *inf* short for **pectoral muscle**

pecan (pɪˈkæn, ˈpiːkən) *n* **1** a hickory tree of the southern US having deeply furrowed bark and edible nuts **2** the smooth oval nut of this tree, which has a sweet oily kernel [C18 from Algonquian *paccan*]

peccable (ˈpɛkəbᵊl) *adj* liable to sin [C17 via F from Med. L *peccābilis*, from L *peccāre* to sin]

peccadillo (ˌpɛkəˈdɪləʊ) *n, pl* **peccadilloes** *or* **peccadillos** a petty sin or fault [C16 from Sp., from *pecado* sin, from L *peccātum*, from *peccāre* to transgress]

peccant (ˈpɛkənt) *adj rare* **1** guilty of an offence; corrupt **2** violating or disregarding a rule; faulty **3** producing

Pp

disease; morbid [c17 from L *peccans*, from *peccāre* to sin] > **'peccancy** *n*

peccary ('pɛkərɪ) *n, pl* **peccaries** *or* **peccary** either of two piglike mammals of forests of southern North America, Central and South America [c17 from Carib]

Pechora (*Russian* pɪ'tʃɔrə) *n* a river in N Russia, rising in the Ural Mountains and flowing north in a great arc to the **Pechora Sea** (the SE part of the Barents Sea) Length: 1814 km (1127 miles)

peck[1] (pɛk) *n* **1** a unit of dry measure equal to 8 quarts or one quarter of a bushel **2** a container used for measuring this quantity **3** a large quantity or number [c13 from Anglo-Norman, from ?]

peck[2] (pɛk) *vb* **1** (when *intr*, sometimes foll by *at*) to strike with the beak or with a pointed instrument **2** (*tr*; sometimes foll by *out*) to dig (a hole, etc) by pecking **3** (*tr*) (of birds) to pick up (corn, worms, etc) by pecking **4** (*intr*; often foll by *at*) to nibble or pick (at one's food) **5** *inf* to kiss (a person) quickly and lightly **6** (*intr*; foll by *at*) to nag ▷ *n* **7** a quick light blow, esp from a bird's beak **8** a mark made by such a blow **9** *inf* a quick light kiss [c14 from ?]

Peck (pɛk) *n* **Gregory** (1916–2003)., US film actor; his films include *Keys of the Kingdom* (1944), *The Gunfighter* (1950), *The Big Country* (1958), *To Kill a Mockingbird* (1963), *The Omen* (1976), and *Other People's Money* (1991)

pecker ('pɛkə) *n Brit sl* spirits (esp in **keep one's pecker up**)

pecking order *n* **1** Also called: **peck order** a natural hierarchy in a group of gregarious birds, such as domestic fowl **2** any hierarchical order, as among people in a particular group

Peckinpah ('pɛkɪn,pɑː) *n* **Sam(uel David)** 1926–84, US film director, esp of Westerns, such as *The Wild Bunch* (1969). Among his other films are *Straw Dogs* (1971), *Bring me the Head of Alfredo Garcia* (1974), and *Cross of Iron* (1977)

peckish ('pɛkɪʃ) *adj inf, chiefly Brit* feeling slightly hungry [c18 from PECK[2]]

Pecos ('peɪkəs; *Spanish* 'pekɔs) *n* a river in the southwestern US, rising in N central New Mexico and flowing southeast to the Rio Grande. Length: about 1180 km (735 miles)

Pécs (*Hungarian* peːtʃ) *n* an industrial city in SW Hungary: university (1367). Pop: 157 332 (2000 est)

pecten ('pɛktɪn) *n, pl* **pectens** *or* **pectines** (-tɪ,niːz) **1** a comblike structure in the eye of birds and reptiles, consisting of a network of blood vessels projecting inwards from the retina **2** any other comblike part or organ [c18 from L: a comb, from *pectere* to comb]

pectin ('pɛktɪn) *n biochem* any of the acidic polysaccharides that occur in ripe fruit and vegetables: used in the manufacture of jams because of their ability to solidify to a gel [c19 from Gk *pēktos* congealed, from *pegnuein* to set] > **'pectic** *or* **'pectinous** *adj*

pectoral ('pɛktərəl) *adj* **1** of or relating to the chest, breast, or thorax: *pectoral fins* **2** worn on the breast or chest: *a pectoral medallion* ▷ *n* **3** a pectoral organ or part, esp a muscle or fin **4** a medicine for disorders of the chest or lungs **5** anything worn on the chest or breast for decoration or protection [c15 from L *pectorālis*, from *pectus* breast] > **'pectorally** *adv*

pectoral fin *n* either of a pair of fins, situated just behind the head in fishes, that help to control the direction of movement during locomotion

pectoral muscle *n* either of two large chest muscles (**pectoralis major** and **pectoralis minor**), that assist in movements of the shoulder and upper arm

peculate ('pɛkjʊ,leɪt) *vb* **peculates, peculating, peculated** to appropriate or embezzle (public money, etc) [c18 from L *pecūlārī*, from *pecūlium* private property (orig., cattle); see PECULIAR] > **,pecu'lation** *n* > **'pecu,lator** *n*

peculiar (pɪ'kjuːlɪə) *adj* **1** strange or unusual; odd: *a peculiar idea* **2** distinct from others; special **3** (*postpositive*; foll by *to*) belonging characteristically or exclusively (to): *peculiar to North America* [c15 from L *pecūliāris* concerning private property, from *pecūlium*, lit.: property in cattle, from *pecus* cattle] > **pe'culiarly** *adv*

peculiarity (pɪ,kjuːlɪ'ærɪtɪ) *n, pl* **peculiarities** **1** a strange or unusual habit or characteristic **2** a distinguishing trait, etc, that is characteristic of a particular person; idiosyncrasy **3** the state or quality of being peculiar

pecuniary (pɪ'kjuːnɪərɪ) *adj* **1** of or relating to money **2** *law* (of an offence) involving a monetary penalty [c16 from L *pecūniāris*, from *pecūnia* money] > **pe'cuniarily** *adv*

pecuniary advantage *n law* financial advantage that is dishonestly obtained by deception and that constitutes a criminal offence

-ped *or* **-pede** *n combining form* foot or feet: *quadruped; centipede* [from L *pēs*, *ped-* foot]

pedagogue *or US* (*sometimes*) **pedagog** ('pɛdə,gɒg) *n* **1** a teacher or educator **2** a pedantic or dogmatic teacher [c14 from L *paedagōgus*, from Gk *paidagōgos* slave who looked after his master's son, from *pais* boy + *agōgos* leader] > **,peda'gogic** *or* **,peda'gogical** *adj* > **,peda'gogically** *adv*

pedagogy ('pɛdə,gɒgɪ, -,gɒdʒɪ, -,gəʊdʒɪ) *n* the principles, practice, or profession of teaching

pedal[1] ('pɛdᵊl) *n* **1a** any foot-operated lever, esp one of the two levers that drive the chainwheel of a bicycle, the foot brake, clutch control, or accelerator of a car, one of the levers on an organ controlling deep bass notes, or one of the levers on a piano used to mute or sustain tone **1b** (*as modifier*): *a pedal cycle* ▷ *vb* **pedals, pedalling, pedalled** *or US* **pedals, pedaling, pedaled** **2** to propel (a bicycle, etc) by operating the pedals **3** (*intr*) to operate the pedals of an organ, piano, etc **4** to work (pedals of any kind) [c17 from L *pedālis*; see PEDAL[2]]

pedal[2] ('piːdᵊl) *adj* of or relating to the foot or feet [c17 from L *pedālis*, from *pēs* foot]

pedal point ('pɛdᵊl) *n music* a sustained bass note, over which the other parts move bringing changing harmonies. Often shortened to **pedal**

pedal steel guitar ('pɛdᵊl) *n* a floor-mounted multineck steel guitar with each set of strings tuned to a different open chord and foot pedals to raise or lower the pitch

pedant ('pɛdᵊnt) *n* **1** a person who relies too much on academic learning or who is concerned chiefly with insignificant detail **2** *arch* a schoolmaster or teacher [c16 via OF from It. *pedante* teacher] > **pedantic** (pɪ'dæntɪk) *adj* > **pe'dantically** *adv*

pedantry ('pɛdᵊntrɪ) *n, pl* **pedantries** the habit or an instance of being a pedant, esp in the display of useless knowledge or minute observance of petty rules or details

pedate ('pɛdeɪt) *adj* **1** (of a plant leaf) divided into several lobes **2** *zool* having or resembling a foot: *a pedate appendage* [c18 from L *pedātus* equipped with feet, from *pēs* foot]

peddle ('pɛdᵊl) *vb* **peddles, peddling, peddled** **1** to go from place to place selling (goods, esp small articles) **2** (*tr*) to sell (illegal drugs, esp narcotics) **3** (*tr*) to advocate (ideas, etc) persistently: *to peddle a new philosophy* [c16 back formation from PEDLAR]

peddler ('pɛdlə) *n* **1** a person who sells illegal drugs, esp narcotics **2** the usual US spelling of **pedlar**

pederasty *or* **paederasty** ('pɛdə,ræstɪ) *n* homosexual relations between men and boys [c17 from NL *paederastia*, from Gk, from *pais* boy + *erastēs* lover, from *eran* to love] > **'peder,ast** *or* **'paeder,ast** *n* > **,peder'astic** *or* **,paeder'astic** *adj*

pedestal ('pɛdɪstᵊl) *n* **1** a base that supports a column, statue, etc **2** a position of eminence or supposed superiority (esp in **place, put,** *or* **set on a pedestal**) [c16 from F *piédestal*, from OIt. *piedestallo*, from *pie* foot + *di* of + *stallo* a stall]

pedestrian (pɪˈdɛstrɪən) *n* **1a** a person travelling on foot; walker **1b** (*as modifier*): *a pedestrian precinct* ▷ *adj* **2** dull; commonplace: *a pedestrian style of writing* [C18 from L *pedester*, from *pēs* foot]

pedestrian crossing *n Brit* a path across a road marked as a crossing for pedestrians

pedestrianize *or* **pedestrianise** (pɪˈdɛstrɪəˌnaɪz) *vb* **pedestrianizes, pedestrianizing, pedestrianized** *or* **pedestrianises, pedestrianising, pedestrianised** (*tr*) to convert (a street, etc) into an area for the use of pedestrians only > **peˌdestrianiˈzation** *or* **peˌdestrianiˈsation** *n*

pedi- *combining form* indicating the foot: *pedicure* [from L *pēs, ped-* foot]

pedicab (ˈpɛdɪˌkæb) *n* a pedal-operated tricycle, available for hire, with an attached seat for one or two passengers

pedicel (ˈpɛdɪˌsɛl) *n* **1** the stalk bearing a single flower of an inflorescence **2** Also called: **peduncle** *biol* any short stalk bearing an organ or organism ▷ Also called: **pedicle** [C17 from NL *pedicellus*, from L *pedīculus*, from *pēs* foot] > **pedicellate** (pɪˈdɪsɪˌleɪt) *adj*

pediculosis (pɪˌdɪkjʊˈləʊsɪs) *n pathol* the state of being infested with lice [C19 via NL from L *pedīculus* louse] > **pediculous** (pɪˈdɪkjʊləs) *adj*

pedicure (ˈpɛdɪˌkjʊə) *n* treatment of the feet, either by a medical expert or a cosmetician [C19 via F from L *pēs* foot + *curāre* to care for]

pedigree (ˈpɛdɪˌgriː) *n* **1a** the line of descent of a purebred animal **1b** (*as modifier*): *a pedigree bull* **2** a document recording this **3** a genealogical table, esp one indicating pure ancestry [C15 from OF *pie de grue* crane's foot, alluding to the spreading lines used in a genealogical chart] > **ˈpediˌgreed** *adj*

pediment (ˈpɛdɪmənt) *n* a low-pitched gable, esp one that is triangular as used in classical architecture [C16 from obs. *periment*, ? workman's corruption of PYRAMID] > **ˌpediˈmental** *adj*

pedipalp (ˈpɛdɪˌpælp) *n* either member of the second pair of head appendages of arachnids: specialized for feeding, locomotion, etc [C19 from NL *pedipalpi*, from L *pēs* foot + *palpus* palp]

pedlar *or esp US* **peddler** (ˈpɛdlə) *n* a person who peddles; hawker [C14 changed from *peder*, from *ped, pedde* basket, from ?]

pedo- *or before a vowel* **ped-** a variant (esp US) of **paedo-**

pedology (pɪˈdɒlədʒɪ) *n* the study of soils [C20 from Gk *pedon* ground, earth + -OLOGY]

pedometer (pɪˈdɒmɪtə) *n* a device that records the number of steps taken in walking and hence the distance travelled

peduncle (pɪˈdʌŋkᵊl) *n* **1** the stalk of a plant bearing an inflorescence or solitary flower **2** *anat, pathol* any stalklike structure **3** *biol* another name for **pedicel** (sense 2) [C18 from NL *pedunculus*, from L *pedīculus* little foot] > **peduncular** (pɪˈdʌŋkjʊlə) *or* **pedunculate** (pɪˈdʌŋkjʊlɪt, -ˌleɪt) *adj*

pee (piː) *inf* ▷ *vb* **pees, peeing, peed 1** (*intr*) to urinate ▷ *n* **2** urine **3** the act of urinating [C18 euphemistic for PISS, based on the initial letter]

Peebles (ˈpiːbᵊlz) *n* a town in SE Scotland, in Scottish Borders. Pop: 7065 (1991)

Peeblesshire (ˈpiːbᵊlzˌʃɪə, -ʃə) *n* (until 1975) a county of SE Scotland, now part of Scottish Borders. Also called: **Tweeddale**

peek (piːk) *vb* **1** (*intr*) to glance quickly or furtively ▷ *n* **2** such a glance [C14 *pike*, rel. to M Du *kiken* to peek]

peekaboo (ˈpiːkəˌbuː) *n* **1** a game for young children, in which one person hides his or her face and suddenly reveals it and cries "peekaboo" ▷ *adj* **2** (of a garment) made of fabric that is sheer or patterned with small holes [C16 from PEEK + BOO]

peel[1] (piːl) *vb* **1** (*tr*) to remove (the skin, rind, etc) of (a fruit, egg, etc) **2** (*intr*) (of paint, etc) to be removed from a surface, esp by weathering **3** (*intr*) (of a surface) to lose its outer covering of paint, etc, esp by weathering **4** (*intr*) (of a person or part of the body) to shed skin in flakes or (of skin) to be shed in flakes, esp as a result of sunburn ▷ *n* **5** the skin or rind of a fruit, etc ▷ See also **peel off** [OE *pilian* to strip off the outer layer, from L *pilāre* to make bald, from *pilus* a hair] > **ˈpeeler** *n*

peel[2] (piːl) *n* a long-handled shovel used by bakers for moving bread in an oven [C14 *pele*, from OF, from L *pāla* spade, from *pangere* to drive in]

peel[3] (piːl) *n Brit* a fortified tower of the 16th century on the borders of Scotland [C14 (fence made of stakes): from OF *piel* stake, from L *pālus*]

Peel (piːl) *n* **1 John,** real name *John Robert Parker Ravenscroft*. born 1939, British broadcaster; has presented his Radio 1 music programme since 1967 and Radio 4's *Home Truths* since 1998 **2** Sir **Robert** 1788–1850, British statesman; Conservative prime minister (1834–35; 1841–46) As Home Secretary (1828–30) he founded the Metropolitan Police and in his second ministry carried through a series of free-trade budgets culminating in the repeal of the Corn Laws (1846), which split the Tory party

Peele (piːl) *n* **George** ?1556–?96, English dramatist and poet. His works include the pastoral drama *The Arraignment of Paris* (1584) and the comedy *The Old Wives' Tale* (1595)

peeler (ˈpiːlə) *n Irish & obs Brit sl* another word for **policeman** [C19 from the founder of the police force, Sir Robert PEEL]

peeling (ˈpiːlɪŋ) *n* a strip of skin, rind, bark, etc, that has been peeled off: *a potato peeling*

peel off *vb* (*adv*) **1** to remove or be removed by peeling **2** (*intr*) *sl* to undress **3** (*intr*) (of an aircraft) to turn away as by banking, and leave a formation

peen (piːn) *n* **1** the end of a hammer head opposite the striking face, often rounded or wedge-shaped ▷ *vb* **2** (*tr*) to strike with the peen of a hammer or a stream of metal shot [C17 var. of *pane*, ?from F *panne*, ult. from L *pinna* point]

Peenemünde (ˌpiːnəˈmʊndə) *n* a village in N Germany, in Mecklenburg-West Pomerania on the Baltic coast: site of a German rocket-development centre in World War II

peep[1] (piːp) *vb* (*intr*) **1** to look furtively or secretly, as through a small aperture or from a hidden place **2** to appear partially or briefly: *the sun peeped through the clouds* ▷ *n* **3** a quick or furtive look **4** the first appearance: *the peep of dawn* [C15 var. of PEEK]

peep[2] (piːp) *vb* (*intr*) **1** (esp of young birds) to utter shrill small noises **2** to speak in a weak voice ▷ *n* **3** a peeping sound [C15 imit.]

peeper (ˈpiːpə) *n* **1** a person who peeps **2** (*often pl*) a slang word for **eye[1]** (sense 1)

peephole (ˈpiːpˌhəʊl) *n* a small aperture, as in a door for observing callers before opening

Peeping Tom *n* a man who furtively observes women undressing; voyeur [C19 after the tailor who, according to legend, peeped at Lady Godiva when she rode naked through Coventry]

peepshow (ˈpiːpˌʃəʊ) *n* **1** Also called: **raree show** a box with a peephole through which a series of pictures can be seen **2** a booth from which a viewer can see a live nude model for a fee

peepul (ˈpiːpᵊl) *or* **pipal** *n* an Indian tree resembling the banyan: regarded as sacred by Buddhists. Also called: **bo tree** [C18 from Hindi *pīpal*, from Sansk. *pippala*]

peer[1] (pɪə) *n* **1** a member of a nobility; nobleman **2** a person who holds any of the five grades of the British nobility: duke, marquess, earl, viscount, and baron. See also **life peer 3** a person who is an equal in social standing, rank, age, etc: *to be tried by one's peers* [C14 (in sense 3): from OF *per*, from L *pār* equal]

Pp

peer² (pɪə) *vb (intr)* **1** to look intently with or as if with difficulty: *to peer into the distance* **2** to appear partially or dimly: *the sun peered through the fog* [c16 from Flemish *pieren* to look with narrowed eyes]

peerage ('pɪərɪdʒ) *n* **1** the whole body of peers; aristocracy **2** the position, rank, or title of a peer **3** (esp in the British Isles) a book listing the peers and giving their genealogy

peeress ('pɪərɪs) *n* **1** the wife or widow of a peer **2** a woman holding the rank of a peer in her own right

peer group *n* a social group composed of individuals of approximately the same age

peerless ('pɪəlɪs) *adj* having no equals; matchless

peer-to-peer *adj* (of a computer network) designed so that computers can send information directly to one another without passing through a centralized server. Abbreviation: **P2P**

peeve (piːv) *inf* ▷ *vb* **peeves, peeving, peeved** **1** *(tr)* to irritate; vex; annoy ▷ *n* **2** something that irritates; vexation [c20 back formation from PEEVISH] > **peeved** *adj*

peevish ('piːvɪʃ) *adj* fretful or irritable [c14 from ?] > **'peevishly** *adv* > **'peevishness** *n*

peewee ('piːwiː) *n* **1** a small black-and-white Australian bird with long thin legs **2** *Canad* a small person or thing **3** *Canad* (in sports) a player aged 12 or 13 [imit.]

peewit *or* **pewit** ('piːwɪt) *n* another name for **lapwing** [c16 imit. of its call]

peg (pɛg) *n* **1** a small cylindrical pin or dowel used to join two parts together **2** a pin pushed or driven into a surface: used to mark scores, define limits, support coats, etc **3** any of several pins on a violin, etc, which can be turned so as to tune strings wound around them **4** Also called: **clothes peg** *Brit, Austral, & NZ* a split or hinged pin for fastening wet clothes to a line to dry. US and Canad equivalent: **clothespin** **5** *Brit* a small drink of wine or spirits **6** an opportunity or pretext for doing something: *a peg on which to hang a theory* **7** *inf* a level of self-esteem, importance, etc (esp in **bring** *or* **take down a peg**) **8** *inf* See **peg leg** **9** **off the peg** *chiefly Brit* (of clothes) ready-to-wear, as opposed to tailor-made ▷ *vb* **pegs, pegging, pegged** **10** *(tr)* to knock or insert a peg into **11** *(tr)* to secure with pegs: *to peg a tent* **12** *(tr)* to mark (a score) with pegs, as in some card games **13** *(tr) inf* to throw (stones, etc) at a target **14** *(intr; foll by away, along, etc) chiefly Brit* to work steadily: *he pegged away at his job for years* **15** *(tr)* to stabilize (the price of a commodity, an exchange rate, etc) [c15 from Low Gmc *pegge*]

Pegasus ('pɛgəsəs) *n Greek myth* an immortal winged horse, which sprang from the blood of the slain Medusa and enabled Bellerophon to achieve many great deeds as his rider

pegboard ('pɛg,bɔːd) *n* **1** a board having a pattern of holes into which small pegs can be fitted, used for playing certain games or keeping a score **2** another name for **solitaire** (sense 1) **3** hardboard perforated by a pattern of holes in which articles may be hung, as for display

peg leg *n inf* **1** an artificial leg, esp one made of wood **2** a person with an artificial leg

pegmatite ('pɛgmə,taɪt) *n* any of a class of exceptionally coarse-grained intrusive igneous rocks consisting chiefly of quartz and feldspar [c19 from Gk *pegma* something joined together]

peg out *vb (adv)* **1** *(intr) inf* to collapse or die **2** *(intr) cribbage* to score the point that wins the game **3** *(tr)* to mark or secure with pegs: *to peg out one's claims to a piece of land*

peg top *n* a child's spinning top, usually made of wood with a metal centre pin

peg-top *adj* (of skirts, trousers, etc) wide at the hips then tapering off towards the ankle

Pegu (pɛ'guː) *n* a city in S Myanmar: capital of a united Burma (16th century). Pop: 190 900 (1993 est)

Péguy (*French* pegi) *n* **Charles** (ʃarl) 1873–1914, French poet and essayist, whose works include *Le Mystère de la charité de Jeanne d'Arc* (1910); founder of the journal *Cahiers de la quinzaine* (1900–14): killed in World War I

Pei (peɪ) *n* **I(eoh) M(ing)** born 1917, US architect, born in China. His buildings include the E wing of the National Museum of Art, Washington DC (1978), a glass and steel pyramid at the Louvre, Paris (1989), and the Rock and Roll Hall of Fame, Cleveland, USA. (1995)

PEI *abbrev for* Prince Edward Island

peignoir ('peɪnwɑː) *n* a woman's dressing gown [c19 from F, from *peigner* to comb, since the garment was worn while the hair was combed]

Peipus ('paɪpəs) *n* a lake in W Russia, on the boundary with Estonia: drains into the Gulf of Finland. Area: 3512 sq km (1356 sq miles). Russian name: **Chudskoye Ozero**

Peiraeus (paɪ'riːəs, pɪ'reɪ-) *n* a variant spelling of **Piraeus**

Peirce (pɪəs) *n* **Charles Sanders** 1839–1914, US logician, philosopher, and mathematician; pioneer of pragmatism

pejoration (,piːdʒə'reɪʃən) *n* **1** semantic change whereby a word acquires unfavourable connotations **2** the process of worsening

pejorative (pɪ'dʒɒrətɪv, 'piːdʒər-) *adj* **1** (of words, expressions, etc) having an unpleasant or disparaging connotation ▷ *n* **2** a pejorative word, etc [c19 from F *péjoratif*, from LL *pējōrātus*, p.p. of *pējōrāre* to make worse, from L *pēior* worse] > **pe'joratively** *adv*

pekan ('pɛkən) *n* another name for **fisher** (the animal) [c18 from Canad F *pékan*, from Amerind]

peke (piːk) *n inf* a Pekingese dog

Peking ('piː'kɪŋ) *n* the former English name of **Beijing**

Pekingese (,piːkɪŋ'iːz) *or* **Pekinese** (,piːkə'niːz) *n* **1** *(pl* **Pekingese** *or* **Pekinese**) a small breed of pet dog with a profuse straight coat, curled plumed tail, and short wrinkled muzzle **2** the dialect of Mandarin Chinese spoken in Beijing (formerly Peking) **3** *(pl* **Pekingese** *or* **Pekinese**) a native or inhabitant of Beijing (formerly Peking) ▷ *adj* **4** of Beijing (formerly Peking) or its inhabitants

Peking man (piː'kɪŋ) *n* an early type of man, of the Lower Palaeolithic age, remains of which were found in a cave near Beijing (formerly Peking)

pekoe ('piːkəʊ) *n* a high-quality tea made from the downy tips of the young buds of the tea plant [c18 from Chinese *peh ho*, from *peh* white + *ho* down]

pelage ('pɛlɪdʒ) *n* the coat of a mammal, consisting of hair, wool, fur, etc [c19 via F from OF *pel* animal's coat, from L *pilus* hair]

Pelagian Islands (pɛ'leɪdʒɪən) *pl n* a group of Italian islands (Lampedusa, Linosa, and Lampione) in the Mediterranean, between Tunisia and Malta. Pop: 4500 (latest est). Area: about 27 sq km (11 sq miles). Italian name: **Isole Pelagie** ('iːzole pe'ladʒe)

Pelagianism (pɛ'leɪdʒɪə,nɪzəm) *n Christianity* a heretical doctrine, first formulated by Pelagius, that rejected the concept of original sin > **Pe'lagian** *n, adj*

pelagic (pɛ'lædʒɪk) *adj* **1** of or relating to the open sea: *pelagic whaling* **2** (of marine life) occurring in the upper waters of open sea [c17 from L *pelagicus*, from *pelagus*, from Gk *pelagos* sea]

Pelagius (pɛ'leɪdʒɪəs) *n* ?360–?420 AD, British monk, who originated the body of doctrines known as Pelagianism and was condemned for heresy (417)

pelargonium (,pɛlə'gəʊnɪəm) *n* any plant of a chiefly southern African genus having circular or lobed leaves and red, pink, or white aromatic flowers: includes many cultivated geraniums [c19 via NL from Gk *pelargos* stork, on the model of GERANIUM; from the likeness of the seed vessels to a stork's bill]

Pelé ('pɛleɪ) *n* real name *Edson Arantes do Nascimento*. born 1940, Brazilian footballer. He was awarded an honorary knighthood in 1997

Pelée (pə'leɪ) *n* **Mount** a volcano in the Caribbean, in N

Martinique: erupted in 1902, killing every person but one in the town of Saint Pierre. Height: 1463 m (4800 ft)

Peleus ('pɛlɪəs, 'piːlɪəs) *n Greek myth* a king of the Myrmidons; father of Achilles

Pelew Islands (piː'luː) *pl n* a former name of (the Republic of) **Belau**

pelf (pɛlf) *n contemptuous* money or wealth; lucre [c14 from OF *pelfre* booty]

pelham ('pɛləm) *n* a horse's bit for a double bridle, less severe than a curb but more severe than a snaffle [prob. from the name *Pelham*]

Pelham ('pɛləm) *n* **Henry** 1696–1754, British statesman: prime minister (1743–54); brother of Thomas Pelham Holles, 1st Duke of Newcastle

Pelham Holles ('pɛləm 'hɒlɪs) *n* **Thomas** See (1st Duke of) **Newcastle**

Pelias ('piːlɪˌæs) *n Greek myth* a son of Poseidon and Tyro. He feared his nephew Jason and sent him to recover the Golden Fleece, hoping he would not return

pelican ('pɛlɪkən) *n* any aquatic bird of a tropical and warm water family. They have a long straight flattened bill, with a distensible pouch for engulfing fish [OE *pellican*, from LL *pelicānus*, from Gk *pelekān*]

pelican crossing *n* a type of road crossing with a pedestrian-operated traffic-light system [c20 from *pe(destrian) li(ght) con(trolled) crossing*, with *-con* adapted to *-can* of *pelican*]

Pelion ('piːlɪən) *n* a mountain in NE Greece, in E Thessaly. In Greek mythology it was the home of the centaurs. Height: 1548 m (5079 ft). Modern Greek name: **Pílion**

pelisse (pɛ'liːs) *n* **1** a fur-trimmed cloak **2** a loose coat, usually fur-trimmed, worn esp by women in the early 19th century [c18 via OF from Med. L *pellicia* cloak, from L *pellis* skin]

Pella ('pɛlə) *n* an ancient city in N Greece: the capital of Macedonia under Philip II

pellagra (pə'leɪgrə, -'læ-) *n pathol* a disease caused by a dietary deficiency of nicotinic acid, characterized by scaling of the skin, inflammation of the mouth, diarrhoea, mental impairment, etc [c19 via It. from *pelle* skin + *-agra*, from Gk *agra* paroxysm] > **pel'lagrous** *adj*

pellet ('pɛlɪt) *n* **1** a small round ball, esp of compressed matter **2a** an imitation bullet used in toy guns **2b** a piece of small shot **3** a stone ball formerly used in a catapult **4** *ornithol* a mass of undigested food that is regurgitated by birds of prey **5** a small pill ▷ *vb (tr)* **6** to strike with pellets **7** to make or form into pellets [c14 from OF *pelote*, from Vulgar L *pilota* (unattested), from L *pila* ball]

Pelletier (*French* pɛltje) *n* **Pierre Joseph** (pjɛr ʒozɛf) 1788–1842, French chemist, who isolated quinine, chlorophyll, and other chemical substances

pellitory ('pɛlɪtərɪ, -trɪ) *n, pl* **pellitories** **1** any of various plants of a S and W European genus, esp wall pellitory, that grow in crevices and have long narrow leaves and small pink flowers **2** **pellitory of Spain** a small Mediterranean plant, the root of which contains an oil formerly used to relieve toothache [c16 *peletre*, from OF *piretre*, from L, from Gk *purethron*, from *pur* fire, from the hot pungent taste of the root]

pell-mell ('pɛl'mɛl) *adv* **1** in a confused headlong rush: *the hounds ran pell-mell into the yard* **2** in a disorderly manner: *the things were piled pell-mell in the room* ▷ *adj* **3** disordered; tumultuous: *a pell-mell rush for the exit* ▷ *n* **4** disorder; confusion [c16 from OF *pesle-mesle*, jingle based on *mesler* to MEDDLE]

pellucid (pɛ'luːsɪd) *adj* **1** transparent or translucent **2** extremely clear in style and meaning [c17 from L *pellūcidus*, var. of *perlūcidus*, from *perlūcēre* to shine through] > ˌ**pellu'cidity** *or* **pel'lucidness** *n* > **pel'lucidly** *adv*

pelmet ('pɛlmɪt) *n* an ornamental drapery or board fixed above a window to conceal the curtain rail [c19 prob. from F *palmette* palm-leaf decoration on cornice moulding]

Peloponnese (ˌpɛləpə'niːs) *n* **the** the S peninsula of Greece, joined to central Greece by the Isthmus of Corinth: chief cities in ancient times were Sparta and Corinth, now Patras. Pop: 632 955 (2001). Area: 21 439 sq km (8361 sq miles). Medieval name: **Morea** Modern Greek name: **Peloponnesos** Also called: **Peloponnesus** > **Peloponnesian** (ˌpɛləpə'niːʃən) *adj*

Pelops ('piːlɒps) *n Greek myth* the son of Tantalus, who as a child was killed by his father and served up as a meal for the gods

pelota (pə'lɒtə) *n* any of various games played in Spain, Spanish America, SW France, etc, by two players who use a basket strapped to their wrists or a wooden racket to propel a ball against a specially marked wall [c19 from Sp.: ball, from OF *pelote*; see PELLET]

▷ www.fipv.com

Pelotas (*Portuguese* pe'lɔtas) *n* a port in S Brazil, in Rio Grande do Sul on the Canal de São Gonçalo. Pop: 300 952 (2000 est)

peloton ('pɛləˌtɒn) *n* the main field of riders in a cycling race [c20 F, lit.: pack]

pelt[1] (pɛlt) *vb* **1** *(tr)* to throw (missiles, etc) at (a person, etc) **2** *(tr)* to hurl (insults, etc) at (a person, etc) **3** *(intr;* foll by *along*, etc) to hurry **4** *(intr)* to rain heavily ▷ *n* **5** a blow **6** speed (esp in **at full pelt**) [c15 from ?]

pelt[2] (pɛlt) *n* **1** the skin of a fur-bearing animal, esp when it has been removed from the carcass **2** the hide of an animal, stripped of hair [c15 ? back formation from PELTRY]

peltate ('pɛlteɪt) *adj* (of leaves) having the stalk attached to the centre of the lower surface [c18 from L *peltātus* equipped with a *pelta* small shield]

peltry ('pɛltrɪ) *n, pl* **peltries** the pelts of animals collectively [c15 from OF *peleterie* collection of pelts, from L *pilus* hair]

pelvic fin *n* either of a pair of fins attached to the pelvic girdle of fishes that help to control the direction of movement during locomotion

pelvic inflammatory disease *n* inflammation of a woman's womb, Fallopian tubes, or ovaries as a result of infection. Abbrev: **PID**

pelvimetry (pɛl'vɪmɪtrɪ) *n obstetrics* measurement of the dimensions of the female pelvis

pelvis ('pɛlvɪs) *n, pl* **pelvises** *or* **pelves** (-viːz) **1** the large funnel-shaped structure at the lower end of the trunk of most vertebrates **2** Also called: **pelvic girdle** the bones that form this structure **3** any anatomical cavity or structure shaped like a funnel or cup [c17 from L: basin] > '**pelvic** *adj*

Pemba ('pɛmbə) *n* an island in the Indian Ocean, off the E coast of Africa north of Zanzibar: part of Tanzania; produces most of the world's cloves. Chief town: Chake Chake. Pop: 322 466 (1995 est). Area: 984 sq km (380 sq miles)

Pembroke ('pɛmbrʊk) *n* **1** a town in SW Wales, in Pembrokeshire on Milford Haven: 11th-century castle where Henry VII was born. Pop (with Pembroke Dock): 15 424 (1991) **2** the smaller variety of corgi, usually having a short tail

Pembrokeshire ('pɛmbrʊkˌʃɪə, -ʃə) *n* a county of SW Wales, on the Irish Sea and the Bristol Channel: formerly (1974–96) part of Dyfed: a hilly peninsula with a deeply indented coast: tourism, agriculture, oil refining. Administrative centre: Haverfordwest. Pop: 112 901 (2001). Area: 1589 sq km (614 sq miles)

pemmican *or* **pemican** ('pɛmɪkən) *n* a small pressed cake of shredded dried meat, pounded into paste, used originally by Native Americans and now chiefly for emergency rations [c19 from Amerind *pimikân*, from *pimii* grease]

pemphigus ('pɛmfɪgəs, pɛm'faɪ-) *n pathol* any of a group

Pp

of blistering skin diseases [C18 via NL from Gk *pemphix* bubble]

pen[1] (pɛn) *n* **1** an implement for writing or drawing using ink, formerly consisting of a sharpened and split quill, and now of a metal nib attached to a holder. See also **ballpoint, fountain pen** **2** the writing end of such an implement; nib **3** style of writing **4** **the pen** writing as an occupation ▷ *vb* **pens, penning, penned** **5** (*tr*) to write or compose [OE *pinne*, from LL *penna* (quill) pen, from L: feather]

pen[2] (pɛn) *n* **1** an enclosure in which domestic animals are kept **2** any place of confinement **3** a dock for servicing submarines, esp having a bombproof roof ▷ *vb* **pens, penning, penned** *or* **pent** **4** (*tr*) to enclose in a pen [OE *penn*]

pen[3] (pɛn) *n US & Canad inf* short for **penitentiary** (sense 1)

pen[4] (pɛn) *n* a female swan [C16 from ?]

PEN (pɛn) *n acronym for* International Association of Poets, Playwrights, Editors, Essayists, and Novelists ▷ www.pencanada.ca/framesetñetscape.htm

Pen. *abbrev for* Peninsula

penal (ˈpiːnᵊl) *adj* **1** of, relating to, constituting, or prescribing punishment **2** used or designated as a place of punishment: *a penal institution* [C15 from LL *poenālis* concerning punishment, from L *poena* penalty] > **ˈpenally** *adv*

penal code *n* the codified body of the laws that relate to crime and its punishment

penalize *or* **penalise** (ˈpiːnəˌlaɪz) *vb* **penalizes, penalizing, penalized** *or* **penalises, penalising, penalised** (*tr*) **1** to impose a penalty on (someone), as for breaking a law or rule **2** to inflict a disadvantage on **3** *sport* to award a free stroke, point, or penalty against (a player or team) **4** to declare (an act) legally punishable > **ˌpenaliˈzation** *or* **ˌpenaliˈsation** *n*

penalty (ˈpɛnᵊltɪ) *n, pl* **penalties** **1** a legal or official punishment, such as a term of imprisonment **2** some other form of punishment, such as a fine or forfeit for not fulfilling a contract **3** loss, suffering, or other misfortune occurring as a result of one's own action, error, etc **4** *sport, games, etc* a handicap awarded against a player or team for illegal play, such as a free shot at goal by the opposing team [C16 from Med. L *poenālitās* penalty; see PENAL]

penalty area *n* another name for **penalty box** (sense 1)

penalty box *n* **1** *soccer* a rectangular area in front of the goal, within which a penalty is awarded for a serious foul by the defending team **2** *ice hockey* a bench for players serving time penalties

penalty corner *n hockey* a free hit from the goal line taken by the attacking side. Also called: **short corner**

penalty point *n* **1** *Brit* an endorsement on a driving licence due to a motoring offence: *he also got eight penalty points on his licence* **2** a point awarded against a sports team or competitor for an infringement of the rules

penalty rates *pl n Austral & NZ* rates of pay for employees working outside normal hours

penalty shoot-out *n* **1** *soccer* a method of deciding the winner of a drawn match, in which players from each team attempt to score with a penalty kick **2** a similar method of resolving a tie in hockey, ice hockey, polo, etc

penance (ˈpɛnəns) *n* **1** voluntary self-punishment to atone for a sin, crime, etc **2** a feeling of regret for one's wrongdoings **3** *Christianity* a punishment usually consisting of prayer, fasting, etc, imposed by church authority as a condition of absolution **4** *RC Church* a sacrament in which repentant sinners are absolved on condition of confession of their sins to a priest and of performing a penance ▷ *vb* **penances, penancing, penanced** **5** (*tr*) (of ecclesiastical authorities) to impose a penance upon (a sinner) [C13 via OF from L *paenitentia* repentance]

Penang (pɪˈnæŋ) *n* **1** a state of Peninsular Malaysia: consists of the island of Penang and the province Wellesley on the mainland, which first united administratively in 1798 as a British colony. Capital: George Town. Pop: 1 225 501 (2000). Area: 1031 sq km (398 sq miles). Also called: **Pulau Pinang** **2** a forested island off the NW coast of Malaya, in the Strait of Malacca. Area: 293 sq km (113 sq miles). Former name (until about 1867): **Prince of Wales Island** **3** another name for **George Town**

penates (pəˈnɑːtiːz) *pl n* See **lares and penates**

pence (pɛns) *n* a plural of **penny**

> USAGE Since the decimalization of British currency and the introduction of the abbreviation *p*, as in *10p, 85p*, etc, the abbreviation has tended to replace *pence* in speech. To talk about only one unit *a penny* is still more common than *a p*, and the use of *a pence* should be avoided

penchant (ˈpɒŋʃɒn) *n* strong inclination or liking; bent or taste [C17 from F, from *pencher* to incline, from L *pendēre* to be suspended]

Penchi (ˈpɛnˈtʃiː) *n* a variant transliteration of the Chinese name for **Benxi**

pencil (ˈpɛnsᵊl) *n* **1** a thin cylindrical instrument used for writing, drawing, etc, consisting of a rod of graphite or other marking substance usually encased in wood and sharpened **2** something similar in shape or function: *a styptic pencil* **3** a narrow set of lines or rays, such as light rays, diverging from or converging to a point **4** *rare* an artist's individual style **5** a type of artist's brush ▷ *vb* **pencils, pencilling, pencilled** *or US* **pencils, penciling, penciled** (*tr*) **6** to draw, colour, or write with a pencil **7** to mark with a pencil [C14 from OF *pincel*, from L *pēnicillus* painter's brush, from *pēniculus* a little tail] > **ˈpenciller** *or US* **ˈpenciler** *n*

pend (pɛnd) *vb* (*intr*) to await judgment or settlement [C15 from L *pendēre* to hang]

pendant (ˈpɛndənt) *n* **1a** an ornament that hangs from a piece of jewellery **1b** a necklace with such an ornament **2** a hanging light, esp a chandelier **3** a carved ornament that is suspended from a ceiling or roof ▷ *adj* **4** a variant spelling of **pendent** [C14 from OF, from *pendre* to hang, from L *pendēre* to hang down]

pendent (ˈpɛndənt) *adj* **1** dangling **2** jutting **3** (of a grammatical construction) incomplete **4** a less common word for **pending** ▷ *n* **5** a variant spelling of **pendant** [C15 from OF *pendant*, from *pendre* to hang; see PENDANT] > **ˈpendency** *n*

pendentive (pɛnˈdɛntɪv) *n* any of four triangular sections of vaulting with concave sides, positioned at a corner of a rectangular space to support a dome [C18 from F *pendentif*, from L *pendens* hanging, from *pendere* to hang]

Penderecki (*Polish* pɛndɛˈrɛtski) *n* **Krzystof** (ˈkʃiʃtɔf) born 1933, Polish composer, noted for his highly individual orchestration. His works include *Threnody for the Victims of Hiroshima* for strings (1960), *Stabat Mater* (1962), *Polish Requiem* (1983–84), and the opera *Ubu Rex* (1991)

pending (ˈpɛndɪŋ) *prep* **1** while waiting for ▷ *adj* (*postpositive*) **2** not yet decided, confirmed, or finished **3** imminent: *these developments have been pending for some time*

pendragon (pɛnˈdræɡən) *n* a supreme war chief or leader of the ancient Britons [Welsh, lit.: head dragon]

pen drive *n computing* another name for **key drive**

pendulous (ˈpɛndjʊləs) *adj* hanging downwards, esp so as to swing from side to side [C17 from L *pendulus*, from *pendēre* to hang down] > **ˈpendulously** *adv* > **ˈpendulousness** *n*

pendulum (ˈpɛndjʊləm) *n* **1** a body mounted so that it can swing freely under the influence of gravity **2** such a device used to regulate a clock mechanism **3** something that changes fairly regularly: *the pendulum of public opinion*

[c17 from L *pendulus* PENDULOUS]

Penelope (pəˈnɛləpɪ) *n Greek myth* the wife of Odysseus, who remained true to him during his long absence despite the importunities of many suitors

peneplain *or* **peneplane** (ˈpiːnɪˌpleɪn) *n* a relatively flat land surface produced by erosion [c19 from L *paene* almost + PLAIN[1]]

penetrant (ˈpɛnɪtrənt) *adj* **1** sharp; penetrating ▷ *n* **2** *chem* a substance that lowers the surface tension of a liquid and thus causes it to penetrate or be absorbed more easily **3** a person or thing that penetrates

penetrate (ˈpɛnɪˌtreɪt) *vb* **penetrates, penetrating, penetrated 1** to find or force a way into or through (something); pierce; enter **2** to diffuse through (a substance, etc); permeate **3** (*tr*) to see through: *their eyes could not penetrate the fog* **4** (*tr*) (of a man) to insert the penis into the vagina of (a woman) **5** (*tr*) to grasp the meaning of (a principle, etc) **6** (*intr*) to be understood: *his face lit up as the new idea penetrated* [c16 from L *penetrāre*] > **ˈpenetrable** *adj* > **ˌpenetraˈbility** *n* > **ˈpeneˌtrator** *n*

penetrating (ˈpɛnɪˌtreɪtɪŋ) *adj* tending to or able to penetrate: *a penetrating mind; a penetrating voice* > **ˈpeneˌtratingly** *adv*

penetration (ˌpɛnɪˈtreɪʃən) *n* **1** the act or an instance of penetrating **2** the ability or power to penetrate **3** keen insight or perception **4** *mil* an offensive manoeuvre that breaks through an enemy's defensive position **5** Also called: **market penetration** the proportion of the total number of potential purchasers of a product or service who either are aware of its existence or actually buy it

Peneus (pɪˈniːəs) *n* the ancient name for the **Salambria**

pen friend *n* a person with whom one exchanges letters, often a person in another country whom one has not met. Also called: **pen pal**

Penghu *or* **P'eng-hu** (ˈpɛŋˈhuː) *n* transliteration of the Chinese name for the **Pescadores**

Pengpu (ˈpɛŋˈpuː) *n* a variant transliteration of the Chinese name for **Bengbu**

penguin (ˈpɛŋgwɪn) *n* a flightless marine bird of cool southern, esp Antarctic, regions: they have wings modified as flippers, webbed feet, and feathers lacking barbs [c16 ?from Welsh *pen gwyn*, from *pen* head + *gwyn* white]

penicillin (ˌpɛnɪˈsɪlɪn) *n* any of a group of antibiotics with powerful action against bacteria: originally obtained from the fungus *Penicillium* [c20 from PENICILLIUM]

penicillium (ˌpɛnɪˈsɪlɪəm) *n, pl* **penicilliums** *or* **penicillia** (-ˈsɪlɪə) any saprotrophic fungus of the genus *Penicillium*, which commonly grow as a green or blue mould on stale food [c19 NL, from L *pēnicillus* tuft of hairs; from the appearance of the sporangia of this fungus]

penillion *or* **pennillion** (pɪˈnɪlɪən) *pl n, sing* **penill** (pɪˈnɪl) the Welsh art or practice of singing poetry in counterpoint to a traditional melody played on the harp [from Welsh: verses]

peninsula (pɪˈnɪnsjʊlə) *n* a narrow strip of land projecting into a sea or lake from the mainland [c16 from L, lit.: almost an island, from *paene* almost + *insula* island] > **penˈinsular** *adj*

> **USAGE** The noun *peninsula* is sometimes confused with the adjective *peninsular*: *the Iberian peninsula* (not *peninsular*)

Peninsula *n* **the** short for the **Iberian Peninsula**

penis (ˈpiːnɪs) *n, pl* **penises** *or* **penes** (-niːz) the male organ of copulation in higher vertebrates, also used for urine excretion in many mammals [c17 from L: penis] > **penile** (ˈpiːnaɪl) *adj*

penitent (ˈpɛnɪtənt) *adj* **1** feeling regret for one's sins; repentant ▷ *n* **2** a person who is penitent **3** *Christianity* **3a** a person who repents his or her sins and seeks forgiveness for them **3b** *RC Church* a person who confesses his or her sins and submits to a penance [c14 from Church L *paenitēns* regretting, from *paenitēre* to repent, from ?] > **ˈpenitence** *n* > **ˈpenitently** *adv*

penitential (ˌpɛnɪˈtɛnʃəl) *adj* **1** of, showing, or constituting penance ▷ *n* **2** *chiefly RC Church* a book or compilation of instructions for confessors **3** a less common word for **penitent** (senses 2, 3) > **ˌpeniˈtentially** *adv*

penitentiary (ˌpɛnɪˈtɛnʃərɪ) *n, pl* **penitentiaries 1** (in the US and Canada) a state or federal prison. Also (US and Canad inf): **pen 2** *RC Church* **2a** a cardinal who presides over a tribunal that decides all matters affecting the sacrament of penance **2b** this tribunal itself ▷ *adj* **3** another word for **penitential** (sense 1) **4** *US & Canad* (of an offence) punishable by imprisonment in a penitentiary [c15 (meaning also: an officer dealing with penances): from Med. L *poenitēntiārius*, from L *paenitēns* PENITENT]

Penki (ˈpɛnˈtʃiː) *n* a variant transliteration of the Chinese name for **Benxi**

penknife (ˈpɛnˌnaɪf) *n, pl* **penknives** a small knife with one or more blades that fold into the handle; pocketknife

penman (ˈpɛnmən) *n, pl* **penmen 1** a person skilled in handwriting **2** a person who writes by hand in a specified way: *a bad penman* **3** an author **4** *rare* a scribe

penmanship (ˈpɛnmənʃɪp) *n* style or technique of writing by hand

Penn (pɛn) *n* **1 Irving** born 1917, US photographer, noted for his portraits and his innovations in colour photography **2 William** 1644–1718, English Quaker and founder of Pennsylvania

Penn. *abbrev for* Pennsylvania

penna (ˈpɛnə) *n, pl* **pennae** (-niː) *ornithol* any large feather that has a vane and forms part of the main plumage of a bird [L: feather]

pen name *n* an author's pseudonym. Also called: **nom de plume**

pennant (ˈpɛnənt) *n* **1** a type of pennon, esp one flown from vessels as identification or for signalling **2** *chiefly US, Canad, & Austral* **2a** a flag serving as an emblem of championship in certain sports **2b** (*as modifier*): *pennant cricket* [c17 prob. a blend of PENDANT & PENNON]

pennate (ˈpɛneɪt) *adj biol* **1** having feathers, wings, or winglike structures **2** another word for **pinnate** [c19 from L *pennātus*, from *penna* wing]

Penney (ˈpɛnɪ) *n* **William George,** Baron Penney of East Hendred. 1909–91, British mathematician. He worked on the first atomic bomb and became chairman of the UK Atomic Energy Authority (1964–67)

penni (ˈpɛnɪ) *n, pl* **penniä** (-nɪə) *or* **pennis** a former Finnish monetary unit worth one hundredth of a markka [Finnish, from Low G *pennig* PENNY]

penniless (ˈpɛnɪlɪs) *adj* very poor; almost totally without money > **ˈpennilessly** *adv* > **ˈpennilessness** *n*

Pennine Alps (ˈpɛnaɪn) *pl n* a range of the Alps between Switzerland and Italy. Highest peak: Monte Rosa, 4634 m (15 204 ft)

Pennines (ˈpɛnaɪnz) *pl n* a system of hills in England, extending from the Cheviot Hills in the north to the River Trent in the south: forms the watershed for the main rivers of N England. Highest peak: Cross Fell, 893 m (2930 ft). Also called: **the Pennine Chain**

Pennine Way *n* a long-distance footpath extending from Edale, Derbyshire, for 402 km (250 miles) to Kirk Yetholm, Scottish Borders

pennon (ˈpɛnən) *n* **1** a long flag, often tapering and divided at the end, originally a knight's personal flag **2** a small tapering or triangular flag borne on a ship or boat **3** a poetic word for **wing** [c14 via OF ult. from L *penna* feather]

Pennsylvania (ˌpɛnsɪlˈveɪnɪə) *n* a state of the northeastern US: almost wholly in the Appalachians, with the Allegheny Plateau to the west and a plain in

Pp

the southeast; the second most important US state for manufacturing. Capital: Harrisburg. Pop: 12 281 054 (2000). Area: 116 462 sq km (44 956 sq miles). Abbreviations: **Pa, Penn, Penna** or (with zip code) **PA**

Pennsylvania Dutch *n* **1** a dialect of German spoken in E Pennsylvania **2** (preceded by *the; functioning as pl*) a group of German-speaking people in E Pennsylvania, descended from 18th-century settlers from SW Germany and Switzerland

Pennsylvanian (ˌpɛnsɪlˈveɪnɪən) *adj* **1** of the state of Pennsylvania **2** (in North America) of, denoting, or formed in the upper of two divisions of the Carboniferous period ▷ *n* **3** an inhabitant or native of the state of Pennsylvania **4** (preceded by *the*) the Pennsylvanian period or rock system

penny (ˈpɛnɪ) *n, pl* **pennies** *or* **pence** (pɛns) **1** Also called: **new penny** *Brit* a bronze coin having a value equal to one hundredth of a pound. Abbrev: **p** **2** *Brit* (before 1971) a bronze or copper coin having a value equal to one twelfth of a shilling. Abbrev: **2d** **3** a former monetary unit of the Republic of Ireland worth one hundredth of a pound **4** (*pl* **pennies**) *US & Canad* a cent **5** a coin of similar value, as used in several other countries **6** (*used with a negative*) *inf, chiefly Brit* the least amount of money: *I don't have a penny* **7** **a pretty penny** *inf* a considerable sum of money **8** **spend a penny** *Brit inf* to urinate **9** **the penny dropped** *inf, chiefly Brit* the explanation of something was finally realized [OE *penig, pening*]

USAGE See at **pence**

penny arcade *n chiefly US* a public place with various coin-operated machines for entertainment

Penny Black *n* the first adhesive postage stamp, issued in Britain in 1840

penny-dreadful *n, pl* **penny-dreadfuls** *Brit inf* a cheap, often lurid book or magazine

penny-farthing *n Brit* an early type of bicycle with a large front wheel and a small rear wheel, the pedals being on the front wheel

penny-pinching *adj* **1** excessively careful with money; miserly ▷ *n* **2** miserliness > **ˈpenny-ˌpincher** *n*

pennyroyal (ˌpɛnɪˈrɔɪəl) *n* **1** a Eurasian plant with hairy leaves and small mauve flowers, yielding an aromatic oil used in medicine **2** a similar and related plant of E North America [c16 var. of Anglo-Norman *puliol real*, from OF *pouliol* (from L *pūleium* pennyroyal) + *real* ROYAL]

penny shares *pl n Stock Exchange* securities with a low market price, esp less than 20p, enabling small investors to purchase a large number for a relatively small outlay

pennyweight (ˈpɛnɪˌweɪt) *n* a unit of weight equal to 24 grains or one twentieth of an ounce (Troy)

penny whistle *n* a type of flageolet with six finger holes, esp a cheap metal one. Also called: **tin whistle**

penny-wise *adj* **1** greatly concerned with saving small sums of money **2** **penny-wise and pound-foolish** careful about trifles but wasteful in large ventures

pennywort (ˈpɛnɪˌwɜːt) *n* **1** a Eurasian rock plant with whitish-green tubular flowers and rounded leaves **2** a marsh plant of Europe and North Africa, having circular leaves and greenish-pink flowers **3** any of various other plants with rounded penny-like leaves

pennyworth (ˈpɛnɪˌwɜːθ) *n* **1** the amount that can be bought for a penny **2** a small amount: *he hasn't got a pennyworth of sense*

penology (piːˈnɒlədʒɪ) *n* **1** the branch of the social sciences concerned with the punishment of crime **2** the science of prison management [c19 from Gk *poinē* punishment] > **penological** (ˌpiːnəˈlɒdʒɪkᵊl) *adj* > **peˈnologist** *n*

pen pal *n* another name for **pen friend**

penpusher (ˈpɛnˌpʊʃə) *n* a person who writes a lot, esp a clerk involved with boring paperwork > **ˈpenˌpushing** *adj, n*

Penrith (pɛnˈrɪθ) *n* a market town in NW England, in Cumbria. Pop: 12 049 (1991)

Penrose (ˈpɛnrəʊz) *n* Sir **Roger** born 1931, British mathematician and theoretical physicist, noted for his investigation of black holes

pension¹ (ˈpɛnʃən) *n* **1** a regular payment made by the state to people over a certain age to enable them to subsist without having to work **2** a regular payment made by an employer to former employees after they retire **3** a regular payment made to a retired person as the result of his or her contributions to a personal pension scheme **4** any regular payment made on charitable grounds, by way of patronage, or in recognition of merit, service, etc: *a pension paid to a disabled soldier* ▷ *vb* **5** to grant a pension to [c14 via Old French from Latin *pēnsiō* a payment, from *pendere* to pay] > **ˈpensioner** *n* > **ˈpensionable** *adj* > **ˈpensionless** *adj*

pension² *French* (pɑ̃sjɔ̃) *n* (in France and some other countries) a relatively cheap boarding house [c17 from F; extended meaning of *pension* grant; see PENSION¹]

pensioneer trustee (ˌpɛnʃəˈnɪə) *n* (in Britain) a person authorized by the Inland Revenue to oversee the management of a pension fund

pension off *vb* (*tr, adv*) **1** to cause to retire from a job and pay a pension to **2** to discard, because of age: *to pension off submarines*

pensive (ˈpɛnsɪv) *adj* **1** deeply or seriously thoughtful, often with a tinge of sadness **2** expressing or suggesting pensiveness [c14 from OF *pensif*, from *penser* to think, from L *pensāre* to consider] > **ˈpensively** *adv* > **ˈpensiveness** *n*

penstemon (pɛnˈstiːmən) *n* a variant (esp US) of **pentstemon**

penstock (ˈpɛnˌstɒk) *n* **1** a conduit that supplies water to a hydroelectric power plant **2** a channel bringing water from the head gates to a water wheel **3** a sluice for controlling water flow [c17 from PEN² + STOCK]

pent (pɛnt) *vb* a past tense and past participle of **pen²** (sense 4)

penta- *or before a vowel* **pent-** *combining form* five: *pentagon; pentode* [from Gk *pente*]

pentacle (ˈpɛntəkᵊl) *n* another name for **pentagram** [c16 from It. *pentacolo* something having five corners]

pentad (ˈpɛntæd) *n* **1** a group or series of five **2** the number or sum of five **3** a period of five years **4** *chem* a pentavalent element, atom, or radical **5** *meteorol* a period of five days [c17 from Gk *pentas* group of five]

pentadactyl (ˌpɛntəˈdæktɪl) *adj* (of the limbs of amphibians, reptiles, birds, and mammals) having a hand or foot bearing five digits

pentagon (ˈpɛntəˌgɒn) *n* a polygon having five sides > **pentagonal** (pɛnˈtægənᵊl) *adj*

Pentagon (ˈpɛntəˌgɒn) *n* **1** the five-sided building in Arlington, Virginia, that houses the headquarters of the US Department of Defense **2** the military leadership of the US

pentagram (ˈpɛntəˌgræm) *n* **1** a star-shaped figure with five points **2** such a figure used by the Pythagoreans, black magicians, etc ▷ Also called: **pentacle, pentangle**

pentahedron (ˌpɛntəˈhiːdrən) *n, pl* **pentahedrons** *or* **pentahedra** (-drə) a solid figure having five plane faces > **ˌpentaˈhedral** *adj*

pentamerous (pɛnˈtæmərəs) *adj* consisting of five parts, esp (of flowers) having the petals, sepals, and other parts arranged in groups of five

pentameter (pɛnˈtæmɪtə) *n* **1** a verse line consisting of five metrical feet **2** (in classical prosody) a verse line consisting of two dactyls, one stressed syllable, two dactyls, and a final stressed syllable ▷ *adj* **3** designating a verse line consisting of five metrical feet

pentamidine (pɛnˈtæmɪˌdiːn, -dɪn) *n* a drug used to treat protozoal infections, esp pneumonia caused by *Pneumocystis carinii* in patients with **AIDS**

pentane ('pɛnteɪn) *n* an alkane hydrocarbon having three isomers, esp the isomer with a straight chain of carbon atoms (*n*-pentane) which is a colourless flammable liquid used as a solvent

pentangle ('pɛn,tæŋgᵊl) *n* another name for **pentagram**

pentanoic acid (,pɛntə'nəʊɪk) *n* a colourless liquid carboxylic acid used in making perfumes, flavourings, and pharmaceuticals. Formula: $CH_3(CH_2)_3COOH$. Former name: **valeric acid**

Pentateuch ('pɛntə,tju:k) *n* the first five books of the Old Testament [C16 from Church L *pentateuchus*, from Gk PENTA- + *teukhos* tool (in LGk: scroll)] > ,**Penta'teuchal** *adj*

pentathlon (pɛn'tæθlən) *n* an athletic contest consisting of five different events [C18 from Gk *pentathlon*, from PENTA- + *athlon* contest]

pentatomic (,pɛntə'tɒmɪk) *adj chem* having five atoms in the molecule

pentatonic scale (,pɛntə'tɒnɪk) *n music* any of several scales consisting of five notes

pentavalent (,pɛntə'veɪlənt) *adj chem* having a valency of five. Also: **quinquevalent**

pentazocine (pɛn'tæzəʊ,si:n) *n* a powerful synthetic drug used in medical practice as a narcotic analgesic

Pentecost ('pɛntɪ,kɒst) *n* **1** a Christian festival occurring on Whit Sunday commemorating the descent of the Holy Ghost on the apostles **2** *Judaism* the harvest festival, celebrated on the fiftieth day after the second day of Passover. Hebrew name: **Shavuot** [OE, from Church L, from Gk *pentēkostē* fiftieth]

Pentecostal (,pɛntɪ'kɒstᵊl) *adj* **1** (*usually prenominal*) of or relating to any of various Christian groups that emphasize the charismatic aspects of Christianity and adopt a fundamental attitude to the Bible **2** of or relating to Pentecost or the influence of the Holy Spirit ▷ *n* **3** a member of a Pentecostal Church > ,**Pente'costalist** *n, adj*
▷ http://pentecostalevangel.ag.org/
▷ http://www.oru.edu/university/library/holyspirit/pentorg1.html
▷ http://www.upci.org/
▷ http://www.paoc.org/
▷ http://www.iphc.org/
▷ http://www.pentecostalworldconf.org/
▷ http://www.wikipedia.org/wiki/Pentecostal

Pentelikon (pɛn'tɛlɪkɒn) *n* a mountain in SE Greece, near Athens: famous for its white marble, worked regularly from the 6th century BC, from which the chief buildings and sculptures in Athens are made. Height: 1109 m (3638 ft). Latin name: **Pentelicus**

Penthesileia *or* **Penthesilea** (,pɛnθəsɪ'leɪə) *n Greek myth* the daughter of Ares and queen of the Amazons, whom she led to the aid of Troy. She was slain by Achilles

Pentheus ('pɛnθɪəs) *n Greek myth* the grandson of Cadmus and his successor as king of Thebes, who resisted the introduction of the cult of Dionysus. In revenge the god drove him mad and he was torn to pieces by a group of bacchantes, one of whom was his mother

penthouse ('pɛnt,haʊs) *n* **1** a flat or maisonette built onto the top floor or roof of a block of flats **2** a construction on the roof of a building, esp one used to house machinery, etc **3** a shed built against a building, esp one that has a sloping roof [C14 *pentis* (later *penthouse*), from OF *apentis*, from LL *appendicium* appendage, from L *appendere* to hang from; see APPEND]

Pentland Firth ('pɛntlənd) *n* a channel between the mainland of N Scotland and the Orkney Islands: notorious for rough seas. Length: 32 km (20 miles). Width: up to 13 km (8 miles)

pentobarbital sodium (,pɛntə'bɑ:bɪ,tæʊn) *n* a barbiturate drug used in medicine as a sedative and hypnotic

pentode ('pɛntəʊd) *n* **1** an electronic valve having five electrodes: a cathode, anode, and three grids **2** (*modifier*) (of a transistor) having three terminals at the base or gate [C20 from PENTA- + Gk *hodos* way]

Pentothal sodium ('pɛntə,θæl) *n* a trademark for **thiopental sodium**

pentstemon (pɛnt'sti:mən) *or esp US* **penstemon** *n* any plant of a North American genus having white, pink, red, blue, or purple flowers with five stamens, one of which is sterile [C18 NL, from PENTA- + Gk *stēmōn* thread (here: stamen)]

pent-up *adj* not released; repressed: *pent-up emotions*

pentyl acetate ('pɛntaɪl, -tɪl) *n* a colourless combustible liquid used as a solvent for paints, in the extraction of penicillin, in photographic film, and as a flavouring. Formula: $C_2H_5OOCCH_3$. Also called: **amyl acetate**

penult ('pɛnʌlt, pɪ'nʌlt) *n* the last syllable but one in a word [C16 L *paenultima syllaba*, from *paene ultima* almost the last]

penultimate (pɪ'nʌltɪmɪt) *adj* **1** next to the last ▷ *n* **2** anything next to last, esp a penult

penumbra (pɪ'nʌmbrə) *n, pl* **penumbrae** (-bri:) *or* **penumbras 1** a fringe region of half shadow resulting from the partial obstruction of light by an opaque object **2** *astron* the lighter and outer region of a sunspot **3** *painting* the area in which light and shade blend [C17 via NL from L *paene* almost + *umbra* shadow] > **pe'numbral** *adj*

penurious (pɪ'njʊərɪəs) *adj* **1** niggardly with money **2** lacking money or means **3** scanty > **pe'nuriously** *adv* > **pe'nuriousness** *n*

penury ('pɛnjʊrɪ) *n* **1** extreme poverty **2** extreme scarcity [C15 from L *pēnūria* dearth, from ?]

Penza (*Russian* 'pjɛnzə) *n* a city in W Russia: manufacturing centre. Pop: 533 300 (1999 est)

Penzance (pɛn'zæns) *n* a town in SW England, in SW Cornwall: the westernmost town in England; resort and fishing port. Pop: 19 709 (1991)

Penzias ('pɛntsɪəs, 'pɛnz-) *n* **Arno Allan** born 1933, US astrophysicist, who shared the Nobel prize for physics (1978) with Robert W. Wilson for their discovery of cosmic microwave background radiation

peon[1] ('pi:ən, 'pi:ɒn) *n* **1** a Spanish-American farm labourer or unskilled worker **2** (formerly, in Spanish America) a debtor compelled to work off his or her debts **3** any very poor person [C19 from Sp. *peón* peasant, from Med. L *pedō* man who goes on foot, from L *pēs* foot] > **'peonage** *n*

peon[2] (pju:n, 'pi:ən, 'pi:ɒn) *n* (in India, Sri Lanka, etc, esp formerly) **1** a messenger or attendant, esp in an office **2** a native policeman **3** a foot soldier [C17 from Port. *peão* orderly; see PEON[1]]

peony *or* **paeony** ('pi:ənɪ) *n, pl* **peonies** *or* **paeonies 1** any of a genus of shrubs and plants of Eurasia and North America, having large pink, red, white, or yellow flowers **2** the flower of any of these plants [OE *peonie*, from L *paeōnia*, from Gk *paiōnia*; rel. to *paiōnios* healing, from *paiōn* physician]

people ('pi:pᵊl) *n* (*usually functioning as pl*) **1** persons collectively or in general **2** a group of persons considered together: *blind people* **3** (*pl* **peoples**) the persons living in a country and sharing the same nationality: *the French people* **4** one's family: *he took her home to meet his people* **5** persons loyal to someone powerful: *the king's people accompanied him in exile* **6** **the people 6a** the mass of persons without special distinction, privileges, etc **6b** the body of persons in a country, etc, esp those entitled to vote ▷ *vb* **peoples, peopling, peopled 7** (*tr*) to provide with or as if with people or inhabitants [C13 from OF *pople*, from L *populus*]

people carrier *n* another name for **multipurpose vehicle**

people mover *n* **1** any of various automated forms of transport for large numbers of passengers over short distances, such as a moving pavement, driverless cars,

Pp

etc **2** another name for **multipurpose vehicle**

people's democracy *n* (in Communist ideology) a country or government in transition from bourgeois democracy to socialism

people's front *n* a less common term for **popular front**

Peoria (piːˈɔːrɪə) *n* a port in N central Illinois, on the Illinois River. Pop: 112 936 (2000)

pep (pɛp) *n* **1** high spirits, energy, or vitality ▷ *vb* **peps, pepping, pepped 2** (*tr*; usually foll by *up*) to liven by imbuing with new vigour [C20 short for PEPPER]

PEP (pɛp) *n* **1** *acronym for* personal equity plan: a method of saving in the UK with certain tax advantages, in which investments up to a fixed annual value could be purchased; replaced by ISAs in 1999 **2** *abbrev for* political and economic planning

peperomia (ˌpɛpərˈəʊmɪə) *n* any of a genus of tropical plants cultivated for their ornamental foliage [C19 NL from Gk *peperi* pepper + *omoros* similar]

Pepin the Short (ˈpɛpɪn) *n* died 768 AD, king of the Franks (751–768); son of Charles Martel and father of Charlemagne. He deposed the Merovingian king (751) and founded the Carolingian dynasty

peplum (ˈpɛpləm) *n, pl* **peplums** *or* **pepla** (-lə) a flared ruffle attached to the waist of a jacket, bodice, etc [C17 from L: full upper garment, from Gk *peplos* shawl]

pepo (ˈpiːpəʊ) *n, pl* **pepos** the fruit of any of various plants, such as the melon, cucumber, and pumpkin, having a firm rind, fleshy watery pulp, and numerous seeds [C19 from L: pumpkin, from Gk *pepōn* edible gourd, from *peptein* to ripen]

pepper (ˈpɛpə) *n* **1** a woody climbing plant, *Piper nigrum*, of the East Indies, having small black berry-like fruits **2** the dried fruit of this plant, which is ground to produce a sharp hot condiment. See also **black pepper, white pepper 3** any of various other plants of the genus *Piper* **4** Also called: **capsicum** any of various tropical plants, the fruits of which are used as a vegetable and a condiment. See also **sweet pepper, red pepper, cayenne pepper 5** the fruit of any of these capsicums, which has a mild or pungent taste **6** the condiment made from the fruits of any of these plants ▷ *vb* (*tr*) **7** to season with pepper **8** to sprinkle liberally; dot: *his prose was peppered with alliteration* **9** to pelt with small missiles [OE *piper*, from L, from Gk *peperi*]

pepper-and-salt *adj* **1** (of cloth, etc) marked with a fine mixture of black and white **2** (of hair) streaked with grey

peppercorn (ˈpɛpəˌkɔːn) *n* **1** the small dried berry of the pepper plant **2** something trifling

peppercorn rent *n* a rent that is very low or nominal

pepper mill *n* a small hand mill used to grind peppercorns

peppermint (ˈpɛpəˌmɪnt) *n* **1** a temperate mint plant with purple or white flowers and downy leaves, which yield a pungent oil **2** the oil from this plant, which is used as a flavouring **3** a sweet flavoured with peppermint

pepperoni (ˌpɛpəˈrəʊnɪ) *n* a highly seasoned dry sausage of pork and beef spiced with pepper, used esp on pizza [C20 from It. *peperoni*, pl of *peperone* cayenne pepper]

pepper pot *n* **1** a small container with perforations in the top for sprinkling pepper **2** a West Indian stew of meat, etc, highly seasoned with an extract of bitter cassava

pepper tree *n* any of several evergreen trees of a chiefly South American genus having yellowish-white flowers and bright red ornamental fruits

peppery (ˈpɛpərɪ) *adj* **1** flavoured with or tasting of pepper **2** quick-tempered; irritable **3** full of bite and sharpness: *a peppery speech* > **ˈpepperiness** *n*

pep pill *n inf* a tablet containing a stimulant drug

peppy (ˈpɛpɪ) *adj* **peppier, peppiest** *inf* full of vitality; bouncy or energetic > **ˈpeppily** *adv* > **ˈpeppiness** *n*

pepsin (ˈpɛpsɪn) *n* an enzyme produced in the stomach, which, when activated by acid, splits proteins into peptones [C19 via G from Gk *pepsis*, from *peptein* to digest]

pep talk *n inf* an enthusiastic talk designed to increase confidence, production, cooperation, etc

peptic (ˈpɛptɪk) *adj* **1** of, relating to, or promoting digestion **2** of, relating to, or caused by pepsin or the action of the digestive juices [C17 from Gk *peptikos* capable of digesting, from *peptein* to digest]

peptic ulcer *n pathol* an ulcer of the mucous membrane lining those parts of the alimentary tract exposed to digestive juices. It can occur in the oesophagus, the stomach, the duodenum, the jejunum, or in the ileum

peptide (ˈpɛptaɪd) *n* any of a group of compounds consisting of two or more amino acids linked by chemical bonding between their respective carboxyl and amino groups

peptide bond *n biochem* a chemical amide linkage, -NH-CO-, formed by the condensation of the amino group of one amino acid with the carboxyl group of another

peptone (ˈpɛptəʊn) *n biochem* any of a group of compounds that form an intermediary group in the digestion of proteins to amino acids [C19 from G *Pepton*, from Gk *pepton* something digested, from *peptein* to digest] > **peptonic** (pɛpˈtɒnɪk) *adj*

Pepys (piːps) *n* **Samuel** 1633–1703, English diarist and naval administrator. His diary, which covers the period 1660–69, is a vivid account of London life through such disasters as the Great Plague, the Fire of London, and the intrusion of the Dutch fleet up the Thames

per (pɜː; *unstressed* pə) *determiner* **1** for every: *three pence per pound* ▷ *prep* **2** (esp in some Latin phrases) by; through **3 as per** according to: *as per specifications* **4 as per usual** *inf* as usual [C15 from L: by, for each]

per- *prefix* **1** through: *pervade* **2** throughout: *perennial* **3** away, beyond: *perfidy* **4** (*intensifier*): *perfervid* **5** indicating that a chemical compound contains a high proportion of a specified element: *peroxide* **6** indicating that a chemical element is in a higher than usual state of oxidation: *permanganate* [from L *per* through]

Pera (ˈpɪərə) *n* the former name of **Beyoğ lu**

peracid (pɜːrˈæsɪd) *n* an acid, such as perchloric acid ($HClO_4$), in which the element forming the acid radical exhibits its highest valency

peradventure (pərədˈvɛntʃə, ˌpɜːr-) *arch* ▷ *adv* **1** by chance; perhaps ▷ *n* **2** chance or doubt [C13 from OF *par aventure* by chance]

Peraea *or* **Perea** (pəˈriːə) *n* a region of ancient Palestine, east of the River Jordan and the Dead Sea

Perak (ˈpɛərə, ˈpɪərə, pɪˈræk) *n* a state of NW Peninsular Malaysia, on the Strait of Malacca: tin mining. Capital: Ipoh. Pop: 2 030 382 (2000). Area: 20 680 sq km (8030 sq miles)

perambulate (pəˈræmbjʊˌleɪt) *vb* **perambulates, perambulating, perambulated 1** to walk about (a place) **2** (*tr*) to walk round in order to inspect [C16 from L *perambulāre* to traverse, from *per-* through + *ambulāre* to walk] > **perˌambuˈlation** *n* > **perambulatory** (pəˈræmbjʊlətərɪ, -trɪ) *adj*

perambulator (pəˈræmbjʊˌleɪtə) *n* a formal word for **pram**[1]

per annum (pər ˈænəm) *adv* every year or by the year [L]

P-E ratio *abbrev for* price-earnings ratio

percale (pəˈkeɪl, -ˈkɑːl) *n* a close-textured woven cotton fabric, used esp for sheets [C17 via F from Persian *pargālah* piece of cloth]

per capita (pə ˈkæpɪtə) *adj, adv* of or for each person [L, lit.: according to heads]

perceive (pəˈsiːv) *vb* **perceives, perceiving, perceived 1** to become aware of (something) through the senses; recognize or observe **2** (*tr; may take a clause as object*) to come to comprehend; grasp [C13 from OF *perçoivre*, from L *percipere* to seize entirely] > **per'ceivable** *adj* > **per'ceivably** *adv*

per cent (pə 'sɛnt) *adv* 1 Also: **per centum** in or for every hundred. Symbol: % ▷ *n Also:* **percent** 2 a percentage or proportion 3 (*often pl*) securities yielding a rate of interest as specified: *he bought three percents* [c16 from Med. L *per centum* out of every hundred]

percentage (pə'sɛntɪdʒ) *n* 1 proportion or rate per hundred parts 2 *commerce* the interest, tax, commission, or allowance on a hundred items 3 any proportion in relation to the whole 4 *inf* profit or advantage

percentile (pə'sɛntaɪl) *n* one of 99 actual or notional values of a variable dividing its distribution into 100 groups with equal frequencies. Also called: **centile**

percept ('pɜːsɛpt) *n* 1 a concept that depends on recognition by the senses, such as sight, of some external object or phenomenon 2 an object or phenomenon that is perceived [c19 from L *perceptum*, from *percipere* to PERCEIVE]

perceptible (pə'sɛptəbᵊl) *adj* able to be perceived; noticeable or recognizable > **per,cepti'bility** *n* > **per'ceptibly** *adv*

perception (pə'sɛpʃən) *n* 1 the act or the effect of perceiving 2 insight or intuition gained by perceiving 3 the ability or capacity to perceive 4 way of perceiving; view 5 the process by which an organism detects and interprets the external world by means of the sensory receptors [c15 from L *perceptiō* comprehension; see PERCEIVE] > **per'ceptional** *adj* > **perceptual** (pə'sɛptjʊəl) *adj*

perceptive (pə'sɛptɪv) *adj* 1 quick at perceiving; observant 2 perceptual 3 able to perceive > **per'ceptively** *adv* > **per'ceptiveness** *or* **,percep'tivity** *n*

Perceval ('pɜːsɪvᵊl) *n* **Spencer** 1762–1812, British statesman; prime minister (1809–12); assassinated

perch¹ (pɜːtʃ) *n* 1 a pole, branch, or other resting place above ground on which a bird roosts 2 a similar resting place for a person or thing 3 another name for **rod** (sense 7) ▷ *vb* 4 (usually foll by *on*) to alight, rest, or cause to rest on or as if on a perch: *the bird perched on the branch; the cap was perched on his head* [c13 *perche* stake, from OF, from L *pertica* long staff]

perch² (pɜːtʃ) *n, pl* **perch** *or* **perches** 1 any of a family of freshwater spiny-finned teleost fishes of Europe and North America: valued as food and game fishes 2 any of various similar or related fishes [c13 from OF *perche*, from L *perca*, from Gk *perkē*]

perchance (pə'tʃɑːns) *adv arch or poetic* 1 perhaps; possibly 2 by chance; accidentally [c14 from Anglo-F *par chance*]

Percheron ('pɜːʃə,rɒn) *n* a compact heavy breed of carthorse [c19 from F, from *le Perche*, region of NW France, where the breed originated]

perchloric acid (pə'klɔːrɪk) *n* a colourless syrupy oxyacid of chlorine containing a greater proportion of oxygen than chloric acid. It is a powerful oxidizing agent. Formula: $HClO_4$. Systematic name: **chloric(VII) acid**

percipient (pə'sɪpɪənt) *adj* 1 able to perceive 2 perceptive ▷ *n* 3 a person who perceives [c17 from L *percipiens* observing, from *percipere* to grasp] > **per'cipience** *n* > **per'cipiently** *adv*

Percival *or* **Perceval** ('pɜːsɪvᵊl) *n* (in Arthurian legend) a knight in King Arthur's court. German equivalent: **Parzival**

percolate *vb* ('pɜːkə,leɪt), **percolates, percolating, percolated** 1 to cause (a liquid) to pass through a fine mesh, porous substance, etc, or (of a liquid) to pass through a fine mesh, etc; trickle: *rain percolated through the roof* 2 to permeate; penetrate gradually: *water percolated the road* 3 to make (coffee) or (of coffee) to be made in a percolator ▷ *n* ('pɜːkəlɪt, -,leɪt) 4 a product of percolation [c17 from L *percolāre*, from PER- + *cōlāre* to strain, from *cōlum* a strainer; see COLANDER] > **percolable** ('pɜːkələbᵊl) *adj* > **,perco'lation** *n*

percolator ('pɜːkə,leɪtə) *n* a kind of coffeepot in which boiling water is forced up through a tube and filters down through the coffee grounds into a container

per contra ('pɜː 'kɒntrə) *adv* on the contrary [from L]

percuss (pə'kʌs) *vb (tr)* 1 to strike sharply or suddenly 2 *med* to tap on (a body surface) with the fingertips or a special hammer to aid diagnosis [c16 from L *percutere*, from *per-* through + *quatere* to shake] > **per'cussor** *n*

percussion (pə'kʌʃən) *n* 1 the act, an instance, or an effect of percussing 2 *music* the family of instruments in which sound arises from the striking of materials with sticks or hammers 3 *music* instruments of this family constituting a section of an orchestra, etc 4 *med* the act of percussing a body surface 5 the act of exploding a percussion cap [c16 from L *percussiō*, from *percutere* to hit; see PERCUSS] > **per'cussive** *adj* > **per'cussively** *adv* > **per'cussiveness** *n*

percussion cap *n* a detonator consisting of a paper or thin metal cap containing material that explodes when struck

percussion instrument *n* any of various musical instruments that produce a sound when their resonating surfaces are struck directly, as with a stick or mallet, or by leverage action

percussionist (pə'kʌʃənɪst) *n music* a person who plays any of several percussion instruments

percutaneous (,pɜːkjʊ'teɪnɪəs) *adj med* effected through the skin, as in the absorption of an ointment

Percy ('pɜːsɪ) *n* 1 Sir **Henry,** known as *Harry Hotspur*. 1364–1403, English rebel, who was killed leading an army against Henry IV 2 **Thomas** 1729–1811, English bishop and antiquary. His *Reliques of Ancient English Poetry* (1765) stimulated the interest of Romantic writers in old English and Scottish ballads

Perdido (*Spanish* pɛr'ðiðo) *n* **Monte** ('mɔnte) a mountain in NE Spain, in the central Pyrenees. Height: 3352 m (10 997 ft). French name: (Mont) Perdu

per diem ('pɜː 'daɪɛm, 'diːɛm) *adv* 1 every day or by the day ▷ *n* 2 an allowance for daily expenses [from L]

perdition (pə'dɪʃən) *n* 1 *Christianity* 1a final and irrevocable spiritual ruin 1b this state as one that the wicked are said to be destined to endure forever 2 another word for **hell** 3 *arch* utter ruin or destruction [c14 from LL *perditiō* ruin, from L *perdere* to lose, from PER- (away) + *dāre* to give]

Perdu (pɛrdy) *n* **Mont** the French name for (Monte) **Perdido**

perdurable (pə'djʊərəbᵊl) *adj rare* extremely durable [c13 from LL *perdūrābilis*, from L *per-* (intensive) + *dūrābilis* long-lasting, from *dūrus* hard]

père *French* (pɛr; *English* pɛə) *n* an addition to a French surname to specify the father rather than the son of the same name: *Dumas père*

Perea (pə'riːə) *n* a variant spelling of **Peraea**

Père David's deer *n* a large grey deer, surviving only in captivity [c20 after Father A. *David* (died 1900), F missionary]

peregrinate ('pɛrɪgrɪ,neɪt) *vb* **peregrinates, peregrinating, peregrinated** 1 (*intr*) to travel or wander about from place to place; voyage 2 (*tr*) to travel through (a place) [c16 from L, from *peregrīnārī* to travel; see PEREGRINE] > **,peregri'nation** *n* > **'peregri,nator** *n*

peregrine ('pɛrɪgrɪn) *adj arch* 1 coming from abroad 2 travelling [c14 from L *peregrīnus* foreign, from *pereger* being abroad, from *per* through + *ager* land (that is, beyond one's own land)]

peregrine falcon *n* a falcon occurring in most parts of the world, having a dark plumage on the back and wings and lighter underparts

Pereira (*Spanish* pe'reira) *n* a town in W central Colombia: cattle trading and coffee processing. Pop: 381 275 (1999 est)

Pp

Perelman ('pɛrəlmən, 'pɜːl-) *n* **S(idney) J(oseph)** 1904–79, US humorous writer. After scriptwriting for the Marx Brothers, he published many collections of articles, including *Crazy Like a Fox* (1944) and *Eastward, Hi!* (1977)

peremptory (pə'rɛmptərɪ) *adj* **1** urgent or commanding: *a peremptory ring on the bell* **2** not able to be remitted or debated; decisive **3** dogmatic **4** *law* **4a** admitting of no denial or contradiction; precluding debate **4b** obligatory rather than permissive [c16 from Anglo-Norman *peremptorie*, from L *peremptōrius* decisive, from *perimere* to take away completely] > **per'emptorily** *adv* > **per'emptoriness** *n*

perennial (pə'rɛnɪəl) *adj* **1** lasting throughout the year or through many years **2** everlasting; perpetual ▷ *n* **3** a woody or herbaceous plant that can continue its growth for at least two years [c17 from L *perennis* continual, from *per* through + *annus* year] > **per'ennially** *adv*

Peres ('pɛrɛs) *n* **Shimon** (ʃiː'məʊn) born 1923, Israeli statesman, born in Poland: prime minister (1984–86; 1995–96); Nobel peace prize 1994 jointly with Yasser Arafat and Yitzhak Rabin

perestroika (ˌpɛrə'strɔɪkə) *n* the policy of reconstructing the economy, etc, of the former Soviet Union under the leadership of Mikhail Gorbachov [c20 Russian, lit.: reconstruction]

Pérez Galdós ('pɛrɛs gɑːl'dəʊs) *n* **Benito** 1843–1920, Spanish novelist. His works include the *Episodios nacionales* (1873–1912), a series of historical novels, and *Fortunata y Jacinta* (1886–87)

perfect *adj* ('pɜːfɪkt) **1** having all essential elements **2** unblemished; faultless: *a perfect gemstone* **3** correct or precise: *perfect timing* **4** utter or absolute: *a perfect stranger* **5** excellent in all respects: *a perfect day* **6** *maths* exactly divisible into equal integral or polynomial roots: *36 is a perfect square* **7** *bot* **7a** (of flowers) having functional stamens and pistils **7b** (of plants) having all parts present **8** *grammar* denoting a tense of verbs used in describing an action that has been completed. In English this is formed with *have* or *has* plus the past participle **9** *music* **9a** of or relating to the intervals of the unison, fourth, fifth, and octave **9b** (of a cadence) ending on the tonic chord, giving a feeling of conclusion. Also: **final** ▷ *n* ('pɜːfɪkt) **10** *grammar* **10a** the perfect tense **10b** a verb in this tense ▷ *vb* (pə'fɛkt) (*tr*) **11** to make perfect; improve to one's satisfaction: *he is in Paris to perfect his French* **12** to make fully accomplished [c13 from L *perfectus*, from *perficere* to perform, from *per-* through + *facere* to do]

> USAGE For most of its meanings, the adjective *perfect* describes an absolute state, i.e. one that cannot be qualified; thus something is either *perfect* or *not perfect*, and cannot be *more perfect* or *less perfect*. However when *perfect* means 'excellent in all respects', *more* and *most* are quite acceptable: *the next day the weather was even more perfect*

perfect gas *n* another name for **ideal gas**

perfectible (pə'fɛktəbᵊl) *adj* capable of becoming or being made perfect > **perˌfecti'bility** *n*

perfection (pə'fɛkʃən) *n* **1** the act of perfecting or the state or quality of being perfect **2** the highest degree of a quality, etc **3** an embodiment of perfection [c13 from L *perfectiō* a completing, from *perficere* to finish]

perfectionism (pə'fɛkʃəˌnɪzəm) *n* **1** *philosophy* the doctrine that man can attain perfection in this life **2** the demand for the highest standard of excellence > **per'fectionist** *n, adj*

perfective (pə'fɛktɪv) *adj* **1** tending to perfect **2** *grammar* denoting an aspect of verbs used to express that the action or event described by the verb is or was completed: *I lived in London for ten years* is perfective; *I have lived in London for ten years* is imperfective, since the implication is that I still live in London

perfectly ('pɜːfɪktlɪ) *adv* **1** completely, utterly, or absolutely **2** in a perfect way

perfect number *n* an integer, such as 28, that is equal to the sum of all its possible factors, excluding itself

perfect participle *n* another name for **past participle**

perfect pitch *n* another name (not in technical usage) for **absolute pitch** (sense 1)

perfervid (pɜː'fɜːvɪd) *adj literary* extremely ardent or zealous [c19 from NL *perfervidus*]

perfidious (pə'fɪdɪəs) *adj* guilty, treacherous, or faithless; deceitful [c18 from L, from *perfidus* faithless] > **per'fidiously** *adv* > **per'fidiousness** *n* > **'perfidy** *n*

perfoliate (pə'fəʊlɪɪt, -ˌeɪt) *adj* (of a leaf) having a base that completely encloses the stem, so that the stem appears to pass through it [c17 from NL *perfoliātus*, from L *per-* through + *folium* leaf] > **perˌfoli'ation** *n*

perforate *vb* ('pɜːfəˌreɪt), **perforates, perforating, perforated 1** to make a hole or holes in (something) **2** (*tr*) to punch rows of holes between (stamps, etc) for ease of separation ▷ *adj* ('pɜːfərɪt) **3** *biol* pierced by small holes: *perforate shells* **4** *philately* another word for **perforated** [c16 from L *perforāre*, from *per-* through + *forāre* to pierce] > **'perforable** *adj* > **'perfoˌrator** *n*

perforated ('pɜːfəˌreɪtɪd) *adj* **1** pierced with holes **2** (esp of stamps) having perforations

perforation (ˌpɜːfə'reɪʃən) *n* **1** the act of perforating or the state of being perforated **2** a hole or holes made in something **3a** a method of making individual stamps, etc easily separable by punching holes along their margins **3b** the holes punched in this way. Abbrev: **perf**

perforce (pə'fɔːs) *adv* by necessity; unavoidably [c14 from OF *par force*]

perform (pə'fɔːm) *vb* **1** to carry out (an action) **2** (*tr*) to fulfil: *to perform someone's request* **3** to present or enact (a play, concert, etc): *the group performed Hamlet* [c14 from Anglo-Norman *perfourmer* (infl. by *forme* FORM), from OF *parfournir*, from *par-* PER- + *fournir* to provide] > **per'formable** *adj* > **per'former** *n*

performance (pə'fɔːməns) *n* **1** the act, process, or art of performing **2** an artistic or dramatic production: *last night's performance was terrible* **3** manner or quality of functioning: *a machine's performance* **4** *inf* mode of conduct or behaviour, esp when distasteful: *what did you mean by that performance at the restaurant?* **5** *inf* any tiresome procedure: *the performance of preparing to go out in the snow*

performance art *n* a theatrical presentation that incorporates various art forms, such as dance, sculpture, etc

performance indicator *n* a quantitative or qualitative measurement, or any other criterion, by which the performance, efficiency, achievement, etc of a person or organization can be assessed, often by comparison with an agreed standard or target

performative (pə'fɔːmətɪv) *adj linguistics, philosophy* **1a** denoting an utterance that itself constitutes the act described by the verb. For example, the sentence *I confess that I was there* is itself a confession **1b** (*as n*): *that sentence is a performative* **2a** denoting a verb that may be used as the main verb in such an utterance **2b** (*as n*): *"promise" is a performative*

performing arts *pl n* the arts, such as a music and drama, that require a public performance

perfume *n* ('pɜːfjuːm) **1** a mixture of alcohol and fragrant essential oils extracted from flowers, etc, or made synthetically **2** a scent or odour, esp a fragrant one ▷ *vb* (pə'fjuːm), **perfumes, perfuming, perfumed 3** (*tr*) to impart a perfume to [c16 from F *parfum*, prob. from OProvençal *perfum*, from *perfumar* to make scented, from *per* through (from L) + *fumar* to smoke, from L *fumāre* to smoke]

▷ www.osmoz.com
▷ www.fragrancehistory.org

perfumer (pəˈfjuːmə) *or* **perfumier** (pəˈfjuːmjeɪ) *n* a person who makes or sells perfume

perfumery (pəˈfjuːmərɪ) *n, pl* **perfumeries** **1** a place where perfumes are sold **2** a factory where perfumes are made **3** the process of making perfumes **4** perfumes in general

perfunctory (pəˈfʌŋktərɪ) *adj* **1** done superficially, only as a matter of routine **2** dull or indifferent [C16 from LL *perfunctōrius* negligent, from *perfunctus* dispatched, from *perfungī* to fulfil] > **perˈfunctorily** *adv* > **perˈfunctoriness** *n*

perfuse (pəˈfjuːz) *vb* **perfuses, perfusing, perfused** (*tr*) **1** to suffuse or permeate (a liquid, colour, etc) through or over (something) **2** *surgery* to pass (a fluid) through (tissue) [C16 from L *perfūsus* wetted, from *perfundere* to pour over] > **perˈfused** *adj*

perfusionist (pəˈfjuːʒənɪst) *n surgery* the person in a surgical team who is responsible for the perfusion of blood through the patient's lung tissue to ensure adequate exchange of oxygen and carbon dioxide

Pergamum (ˈpɜːgəməm) *n* an ancient city in NW Asia Minor, in Mysia: capital of a major Hellenistic monarchy of the same name that later became a Roman province

pergola (ˈpɜːgələ) *n* a horizontal trellis or framework, supported on posts, that carries climbing plants [C17 via It. from L *pergula* projection from a roof, from *pergere* to go forward]

Pergolesi (*Italian* pergoˈleːsi) *n* **Giovanni Battista** (dʒoˈvanni batˈtista) 1710–36, Italian composer: his works include the operetta *La Serva padrona* (1733) and the *Stabat Mater* (1736) for women's voices

perhaps (pəˈhæps; *inf* præps) *adv* **1a** possibly; maybe **1b** (*as sentence modifier*): *he'll arrive tomorrow, perhaps* ▷ *sentence substitute* **2** it may happen, be so, etc; maybe [C16 *perhappes*, from *per* by + *happes* chance]

peri (ˈpɪərɪ) *n, pl* **peris** **1** (in Persian folklore) one of a race of beautiful supernatural beings **2** any beautiful fairy-like creature [C18 from Persian: fairy, from Avestan *pairikā* witch]

peri- *prefix* **1** enclosing, encircling, or around: *pericardium; pericarp* **2** near or adjacent: *perihelion* [from Gk *peri* around]

perianth (ˈpɛrɪˌænθ) *n* the outer part of a flower, consisting of the calyx and corolla [C18 from F *périanthe*, from NL, from PERI- + Gk *anthos* flower]

periapt (ˈpɛrɪˌæpt) *n rare* a charm or amulet [C16 via F from Gk *periapton*, from PERI- + *haptos* clasped, from *haptein* to fasten]

pericarditis (ˌpɛrɪkɑːˈdaɪtɪs) *n* inflammation of the pericardium

pericardium (ˌpɛrɪˈkɑːdɪəm) *n, pl* **pericardia** (-dɪə) the membranous sac enclosing the heart [C16 via NL from Gk *perikardion*, from PERI- + *kardia* heart] > ˌ**periˈcardial** *or* ˌ**periˈcardiˌac** *adj*

pericarp (ˈpɛrɪˌkɑːp) *n* the part of a fruit enclosing the seeds that develops from the wall of the ovary [C18 via F from NL *pericarpium*] > ˌ**periˈcarpial** *adj*

perichondrium (ˌpɛrɪˈkɒndrɪəm) *n, pl* **perichondria** (-drɪə) the fibrous membrane that covers the cartilage [C18 NL, from PERI- + Gk *chondros* cartilage]

periclase (ˈpɛrɪˌkleɪs) *n* a mineral consisting of magnesium oxide [C19 from NL *periclasia*, from Gk *peri* very + *klasis* a breaking, referring to its perfect cleavage]

Pericles (ˈpɛrɪˌkliːz) *n* ?495–429 BC, Athenian statesman and leader of the popular party, who contributed greatly to Athens' political and cultural supremacy in Greece. In power from about 460 BC, he was responsible for the construction of the Parthenon. He conducted the Peloponnesian War (431–404 BC) successfully until his death

pericline (ˈpɛrɪˌklaɪn) *n* **1** a white translucent variety of albite in the form of elongated crystals **2** Also called: **dome** a dome-shaped formation of stratified rock with its slopes following the direction of folding [C19 from Gk *periklinēs* sloping on all sides] > ˌ**periˈclinal** *adj*

pericranium (ˌpɛrɪˈkreɪnɪəm) *n, pl* **pericrania** (-nɪə) the fibrous membrane covering the external surface of the skull [C16 NL, from Gk *perikranion*]

peridot (ˈpɛrɪˌdɒt) *n* a pale green transparent variety of the olivine chrysolite, used as a gemstone [C14 from OF *peritot*, from ?]

perigee (ˈpɛrɪˌdʒiː) *n* the point in its orbit around the earth when the moon or a satellite is nearest the earth [C16 via F from Gk *perigeion*, from PERI- + *gea* earth] > ˌ**periˈgean** *adj*

periglacial (ˌpɛrɪˈgleɪʃəl) *adj* relating to a region bordering a glacier: *periglacial climate*

Périgueux (ˌpɛrɪˈgɜː; *French* perigø) *n* a town in SW France, capital of the Dordogne: noted for its Roman remains, medieval cathedral, and pâté de foie gras. Pop: 32 850 (1990)

perihelion (ˌpɛrɪˈhiːlɪən) *n, pl* **perihelia** (-lɪə) the point in its orbit when a planet or comet is nearest the sun [C17 from NL *perihēlium*, from PERI- + Gk *hēlios* sun]

peril (ˈpɛrɪl) *n* exposure to risk or harm; danger or jeopardy [C13 via OF from L *perīculum*]

perilous (ˈpɛrɪləs) *adj* very hazardous or dangerous: *a perilous journey* > ˈ**perilously** *adv* > ˈ**perilousness** *n*

perilune (ˈpɛrɪˌluːn) *n* the point in a lunar orbit when a spacecraft is nearest the moon [C20 from PERI- + *-lune*, from L *lūna* moon]

perimeter (pəˈrɪmɪtə) *n* **1** *maths* **1a** the curve or line enclosing a plane area **1b** the length of this curve or line **2a** any boundary around something **2b** (*as modifier*): *a perimeter fence* **3** a medical instrument for measuring the field of vision [C16 from F *périmètre*, from L *perimetros*] > **perimetric** (ˌpɛrɪˈmɛtrɪk) *adj*

perinatal (ˌpɛrɪˈneɪtᵊl) *adj* of or occurring in the period from about three months before to one month after birth

perineum (ˌpɛrɪˈniːəm) *n, pl* **perinea** (-ˈniːə) **1** the region of the body between the anus and the genital organs **2** the surface of the human trunk between the thighs [C17 from NL, from Gk *perinaion*, from PERI- + *inein* to empty] > ˌ**periˈneal** *adj*

Pp

period (ˈpɪərɪəd) *n* **1** a portion of time of indefinable length: *he spent a period away from home* **2a** a portion of time specified in some way: *Picasso's blue period* **2b** (*as modifier*): *period costume* **3** a nontechnical name for an occurence of menstruation **4** *geol* a unit of geological time during which a system of rocks is formed: *the Jurassic period* **5** a division of time, esp of the academic day **6** *physics, maths* the time taken to complete one cycle of a regularly recurring phenomenon; the reciprocal of frequency. Symbol: T **7** *astron* **7a** the time required by a body to make one complete rotation on its axis **7b** the time interval between two successive maxima or minima of light variation of a variable star **8** *chem* one of the horizontal rows of elements in the periodic table. Each period starts with an alkali metal and ends with a rare gas **9** another term (esp US and Canad) for **full stop** **10** a complete sentence, esp one with several clauses **11** a completion or end [C14 *peryod*, from L *periodus*, from Gk *periodos* circuit, from PERI- + *hodos* way]

period drama *n* a drama set in a particular historical period

periodic (ˌpɪərɪˈɒdɪk) *adj* **1** happening or recurring at intervals; intermittent **2** of, relating to, or resembling a period **3** having or occurring in a series of repeated periods or cycles > ˌ**periˈodically** *adv* > **periodicity** (ˌpɪərɪəˈdɪsɪtɪ) *n*

periodical (ˌpɪərɪˈɒdɪkᵊl) *n* **1** a publication issued at regular intervals, usually monthly or weekly ▷ *adj* **2** of or relating to such publications **3** published at regular intervals **4** periodic or occasional

periodic function *n maths* a function whose value is repeated at constant intervals

THE PERIODIC TABLE OF THE ELEMENTS

Group

	1	2	3	4	5	6	7	8	9	10	11	12	13	14	15	16	17	18
1	1 H																	2 He
2	3 Li	4 Be											5 B	6 C	7 N	8 O	9 F	10 Ne
3	11 Na	12 Mg											13 Al	14 Si	15 P	16 S	17 Cl	18 Ar
4	19 K	20 Ca	21 Sc	22 Ti	23 V	24 Cr	25 Mn	26 Fe	27 Co	28 Ni	29 Cu	30 Zn	31 Ga	32 Ge	33 As	34 Se	35 Br	36 Kr
5	37 Rb	38 Sr	39 Y	40 Zr	41 Nb	42 Mo	43 Tc	44 Ru	45 Rh	46 Pd	47 Ag	48 Cd	49 In	50 Sn	51 Sb	52 Te	53 I	54 Xe
6	55 Cs	56 Ba	57–71 La–Lu	72 Hf	73 Ta	74 W	75 Re	76 Os	77 Ir	78 Pt	79 Au	80 Hg	81 Tl	82 Pb	83 Bi	84 Po	85 At	86 Rn
7	87 Fr	88 Ra	89–103 Ac–Lr	104 Rf	105 Db	106 Sg	107 Bh	108 Hs	109 Mt	110 Uun	111 Uuu	112 Uub	113 Uut	114 Uuq	115 Uup	116 Uuh	117 Uus	118 Uuo

6	Lanthanoids	57 La	58 Ce	59 Pr	60 Nd	61 Pm	62 Sm	63 Eu	64 Gd	65 Tb	66 Dy	67 Ho	68 Er	69 Tm	70 Yb	71 Lu
7	Actinoids	89 Ac	90 Th	91 Pa	92 U	93 Np	94 Pu	95 Am	96 Cm	97 Bk	98 Cf	99 Es	100 Fm	101 Md	102 No	103 Lr

periodic law *n* the principle that the chemical properties of the elements are periodic functions of their atomic weights or, more accurately, of their atomic numbers

periodic sentence *n rhetoric* a sentence in which the completion of the main clause is left to the end, thus creating an effect of suspense

periodic table *n* a table of the elements, arranged in order of increasing atomic number, based on the periodic law

▷ www.psigate.ac.uk/newsite/reference/periodic-table.html

▷ www.colorado.edu/physics/2000/applets/a2.html

periodontal (ˌpɛrɪəˈdɒntᵊl) *adj* of, denoting, or affecting the gums and other tissues surrounding the teeth: *periodontal disease*

periodontics (ˌpɛrɪəˈdɒntɪks) *n* (*functioning as sing*) the branch of dentistry concerned with diseases affecting the tissues and structures that surround teeth. Also called: **periodontology** [C19 from PERI- + *-odontics*, from Gk *odōn* tooth] > ˌ**perioˈdontical** *adj*

periosteum (ˌpɛrɪˈɒstɪəm) *n, pl* **periostea** (-tɪə) a thick fibrous two-layered membrane covering the surface of bones [C16 NL, from Gk *periosteon*, from PERI- + *osteon* bone] > ˌ**periˈosteal** *adj*

peripatetic (ˌpɛrɪpəˈtɛtɪk) *adj* **1** itinerant **2** *Brit* employed in two or more educational establishments and travelling from one to another: *a peripatetic football coach* ▷ *n* **3** a peripatetic person [C16 from L *peripatēticus*, from Gk, from *peripatein* to pace to and fro] > ˌ**peripaˈtetically** *adv*

Peripatetic (ˌpɛrɪpəˈtɛtɪk) *adj* **1** of or relating to the teachings of Aristotle, who used to teach philosophy while walking about the Lyceum in ancient Athens ▷ *n* **2** a student of Aristotelianism

peripeteia (ˌpɛrɪpɪˈtaɪə, -ˈtɪə) *n* (esp in drama) an abrupt turn of events or reversal of circumstances [C16 from Gk, from PERI- + *piptein* to fall (to change suddenly, lit.: to fall around)]

peripheral (pəˈrɪfərəl) *adj* **1** not relating to the most important part of something; incidental **2** of or relating to a periphery **3** *anat* of, relating to, or situated near the surface of the body: *a peripheral nerve* > **peˈripherally** *adv*

peripheral device *or* **unit** *n computing* any device, such as a disk, printer, modem, or screen, concerned with input/output, storage, etc. Often shortened to **peripheral**

periphery (pəˈrɪfərɪ) *n, pl* **peripheries** **1** the outermost boundary of an area **2** the outside surface of something [C16 from LL *peripherīa*, from Gk, from PERI- + *pherein* to bear]

periphrasis (pəˈrɪfrəsɪs) *n, pl* **periphrases** (-rəˌsiːz) **1** a roundabout way of expressing something; circumlocution **2** an expression of this kind [C16 via L from Gk, from PERI- + *phrazein* to declare]

periphrastic (ˌpɛrɪˈfræstɪk) *adj* **1** employing or involving periphrasis **2** expressed in two or more words rather than by an inflected form of one: used esp of a tense of a verb where the alternative word is an auxiliary verb, as in *he does go* > ˌ**periˈphrastically** *adv*

perisarc (ˈpɛrɪˌsɑːk) *n* the outer chitinous layer secreted by colonial hydrozoan coelenterates [C19 from PERI- + *-sarc*, from Gk *sarx* flesh]

periscope (ˈpɛrɪˌskəʊp) *n* any of a number of optical instruments that enable the user to view objects that are not in the direct line of vision, such as one in a submarine for looking above the surface of the water. They have a system of mirrors or prisms to reflect the light [C19 from Gk *periskopein* to look around] > **periscopic** (ˌpɛrɪˈskɒpɪk) *adj*

perish (ˈpɛrɪʃ) *vb* **1** (*intr*) to be destroyed or die, esp in an untimely way **2** (*tr* sometimes foll by *with* or *from*) to cause to suffer: *we were perished with cold* **3** to rot or cause to rot: *leather perishes if exposed to bad weather* ▷ *n* **4 do a perish** *Austral inf* to die or come near to dying of thirst or starvation [C13 from OF *périr*, from L *perīre* to pass away entirely]

perishable ('pɛrɪʃəbᵊl) *adj* **1** liable to rot ▷ *n* **2** (*often pl*) a perishable article, esp food > ˌ**perishaˈbility** *or* ˈ**perishableness** *n*

perishing ('pɛrɪʃɪŋ) *adj* **1** *inf* (of weather, etc) extremely cold **2** *sl* (intensifier qualifying something undesirable): *it's a perishing nuisance!* > ˈ**perishingly** *adv*

perisperm ('pɛrɪˌspɜːm) *n* the nutritive tissue surrounding the embryo in certain seeds

perissodactyl (pəˌrɪsəʊ'dæktɪl) *n* **1** any of an order of placental mammals having hooves with an odd number of toes: includes horses, tapirs, and rhinoceroses ▷ *adj* **2** of, relating to, or belonging to this order [C19 from NL *perissodactylus*, from Gk *perissos* uneven + *daktulos* digit]

peristalsis (ˌpɛrɪ'stælsɪs) *n, pl* **peristalses** (-siːz) *physiol* the succession of waves of involuntary muscular contraction of various bodily tubes, esp of the alimentary tract, where it effects transport of food and waste products [C19 from NL, from PERI- + Gk *stalsis* compression, from *stellein* to press together] > ˌ**periˈstaltic** *adj*

peristome ('pɛrɪˌstəʊm) *n* **1** a fringe of pointed teeth surrounding the opening of a moss capsule **2** any of various parts surrounding the mouth of invertebrates, such as echinoderms and earthworms, and of protozoans [C18 from NL *peristoma*, from PERI- + Gk *stoma* mouth]

peristyle ('pɛrɪˌstaɪl) *n* **1** a colonnade round a court or building **2** an area surrounded by a colonnade [C17 via F from L *peristȳlum*, from Gk *peristulon*, from PERI- + *stulos* column]

peritoneal dialysis a technique of dialysis used when haemodialysis is inappropriate; it makes use of the peritoneum as an autogenous semipermeable membrane

peritoneum (ˌpɛrɪtə'niːəm) *n, pl* **peritonea** (-'niːə) *or* **peritoneums** a serous sac that lines the walls of the abdominal cavity and covers the viscera [C16 via LL from Gk *peritonaion*, from *peritonos* stretched around] > ˌ**peritoˈneal** *adj*

peritonitis (ˌpɛrɪtə'naɪtɪs) *n* inflammation of the peritoneum

periwig ('pɛrɪˌwɪg) *n* a wig, such as a peruke [C16 *perwyke*, changed from F *perruque* wig, PERUKE]

periwinkle[1] ('pɛrɪˌwɪŋkᵊl) *n* any of various edible marine gastropods having a spirally coiled shell. Often shortened to **winkle** [C16 from ?]

periwinkle[2] ('pɛrɪˌwɪŋkᵊl) *n* any of several Eurasian evergreen plants having trailing stems and blue flowers [C14 *pervenke*, from OE *perwince*, from LL *pervinca*]

perjure ('pɜːdʒə) *vb* **perjures, perjuring, perjured** (*tr*) *criminal law* to render (oneself) guilty of perjury [C15 from OF *parjurer*, from L *perjūrāre*, from PER- + *jūrāre* to make an oath, from *jūs* law] > ˈ**perjurer** *n*

perjured ('pɜːdʒəd) *adj criminal law* **1a** having sworn falsely **1b** having committed perjury **2** involving or characterized by perjury: *perjured evidence*

perjury ('pɜːdʒərɪ) *n, pl* **perjuries** *criminal law* the offence committed by a witness in judicial proceedings who, having been lawfully sworn, wilfully gives false evidence [C14 from Anglo-F *parjurie*, from L *perjūrium* a false oath; see PERJURE] > **perjurious** (pɜː'dʒʊərɪəs) *adj*

perk[1] (pɜːk) *adj* **1** pert; brisk; lively ▷ *vb* **2** See **perk up** [C16 see PERK UP]

perk[2] (pɜːk) *vb inf* short for **percolate** (sense 3)

perk[3] (pɜːk) *n Brit inf* short for **perquisite**

perk up *vb* (*adv*) **1** to make or become more cheerful, hopeful, or lively **2** to rise or cause to rise briskly: *the dog's ears perked up* **3** (*tr*) to make smarter in appearance: *she perked up her outfit with a bright scarf* [C14 *perk*, ?from Norman F *perquer*; see PERCH[1]]

perky ('pɜːkɪ) *adj* **perkier, perkiest 1** jaunty; lively **2** confident; spirited > ˈ**perkily** *adv* > ˈ**perkiness** *n*

Perl (pɜːl) *n* a computer language that is used for text manipulation, esp on the World Wide Web [C20 *p(ractical) e(xtraction and) r(eport) l(anguage)*]

perlemoen ('pɛələˌmʊn) *n S African* another name for **abalone** [from Afrik., from Du. *paarlemoer* mother of pearl]

Perlis ('pɛəlɪs, 'pɜː-) *n* a state of NW Peninsular Malaysia, on the Andaman Sea: a dependency of Thailand until 1909. Capital: Kangar. Pop: 198 335 (2000). Area: 803 sq km (310 sq miles)

perlite ('pɜːlaɪt) *n* a variety of obsidian consisting of masses of globules [C19 from F, from *perle* PEARL[1]]

Perlman ('pɜːlmən) *n* **Itzhak** ('ɪtzæk) born 1945, Israeli violinist; polio victim

perm[1] (pɜːm) *n* **1** a hairstyle produced by treatment with heat, chemicals, etc which gives long-lasting waves or curls. Also called (esp formerly): **permanent wave** ▷ *vb* **2** (*tr*) to give a perm to (hair)

perm[2] (pɜːm) *vb, n inf* short for **permutate, permutation** (sense 4)

Perm (*Russian* pjermj) *n* a port in W Russia, on the Kama River: oil refinery; university (1916). Pop: 1 017 100 (1999 est). Former name (1940–62): **Molotov**

perma- *prefix inf* indicating a fixed state: *a perma-tan*; *perma-grin*

permafrost ('pɜːməˌfrɒst) *n* ground that is permanently frozen [C20 from PERMA(NENT) + FROST]

permalloy (pɜːm'ælɔɪ) *n* any of various alloys containing iron and nickel and sometimes smaller amounts of chromium and molybdenum

permanence ('pɜːmənəns) *n* the state or quality of being permanent

permanency ('pɜːmənənsɪ) *n, pl* **permanencies 1** a person or thing that is permanent **2** another word for **permanence**

permanent ('pɜːmənənt) *adj* **1** existing or intended to exist for an indefinite period: *a permanent structure* **2** not expected to change; not temporary: *a permanent condition* [C15 from L *permanens* continuing, from *permanēre* to stay to the end] > ˈ**permanently** *adv*

permanent health insurance *n* a form of insurance that provides up to 75 per cent of a person's salary, until retirement, in case of prolonged illness or disability

permanent magnet *n* a magnet, often of steel, that retains its magnetization after the magnetic field producing it has been removed

permanent press *n* a chemical treatment for clothing that makes the fabric crease-resistant and sometimes provides a garment with a permanent crease or pleats

permanent resident *n Canad* an immigrant who has been given official residential status, often prior to being granted citizenship

permanent wave *n* another name (esp formerly) for **perm**[1] (sense 1)

permanent way *n chiefly Brit* the track of a railway, including the sleepers, rails, etc

permanganate (pə'mæŋgəˌneɪt, -nɪt) *n* a salt of permanganic acid

permanganic acid (ˌpɜːmæn'gænɪk) *n* a monobasic acid known only in solution and in the form of permanganate salts. Formula: $HMnO_4$. Systematic name: **manganic(VII) acid**

permeability (ˌpɜːmɪə'bɪlɪtɪ) *n* **1** the state or quality of being permeable **2** a measure of the ability of a medium to modify a magnetic field, expressed as the ratio of the magnetic flux density in the medium to the field strength; measured in henries per metre. Symbol: μ

permeable ('pɜːmɪəbᵊl) *adj* capable of being permeated, esp by liquids [C15 from LL *permeābilis*, from L *permeāre* to pervade; see PERMEATE] > 'permeably *adv*

permeance ('pɜːmɪəns) *n* **1** the act of permeating **2** the reciprocal of the reluctance of a magnetic circuit > **'permeant** *adj, n*

permeate ('pɜːmɪˌeɪt) *vb* **permeates, permeating, permeated 1** to penetrate or pervade (a substance, area, etc): *a lovely smell permeated the room* **2** to pass through or cause to pass through by osmosis or diffusion: *to permeate a membrane* [c17 from L *permeāre*, from *per-* through + *meāre* to pass] > **ˌperme'ation** *n* > **'permeative** *adj*

Permian ('pɜːmɪən) *adj* **1** of, denoting, or formed in the last period of the Palaeozoic era, between the Carboniferous and Triassic periods, which lasted for 60 million years ▷ *n* **2 the** the Permian period or rock system [c19 after PERM]

permissible (pə'mɪsəbᵊl) *adj* permitted; allowable > **perˌmissi'bility** *n* > **per'missibly** *adv*

permission (pə'mɪʃən) *n* authorization to do something

permissive (pə'mɪsɪv) *adj* **1** tolerant; lenient: *permissive parents* **2** indulgent in matters of sex: *a permissive society* **3** granting permission > **per'missively** *adv* > **per'missiveness** *n*

permit *vb* (pə'mɪt), **permits, permitting, permitted 1** (*tr*) to grant permission to do something: *you are permitted to smoke* **2** (*tr*) to consent to or tolerate: *she will not permit him to come* **3** (when *intr*, often foll by *of*; when *tr*, often foll by an infinitive) to allow the possibility (of): *the passage permits of two interpretations; his work permits him to relax nowadays* ▷ *n* ('pɜːmɪt) **4** an official document granting authorization; licence **5** permission [c15 from L *permittere*, from *per-* through + *mittere* to send] > **per'mitter** *n*

permittivity (ˌpɜːmɪ'tɪvɪtɪ) *n, pl* **permittivities** a measure of the ability of a substance to transmit an electric field

permutate ('pɜːmjʊˌteɪt) *vb* **permutates, permutating, permutated** to alter the sequence or arrangement (of): *endlessly permutating three basic designs*

permutation (ˌpɜːmjʊ'teɪʃən) *n* **1** *maths* **1a** an ordered arrangement of the numbers, terms, etc, of a set into specified groups: *the permutations of a, b, and c, taken two at a time, are ab, ba, ac, ca, bc, cb* **1b** a group formed in this way **2** a combination of items, etc, made by reordering **3** an alteration; transformation **4** a fixed combination for selections of results on football pools. Usually shortened to **perm** [c14 from L *permūtātiō*, from *permūtāre* to change thoroughly] > **ˌpermu'tational** *adj*

permute (pə'mjuːt) *vb* **permutes, permuting, permuted** (*tr*) **1** to change the sequence of **2** *maths* to subject to permutation [c14 from L *permūtāre*, from PER- + *mūtāre* to change]

Pernambuco (ˌpɜːnəm'bjuːkəʊ; *Portuguese* pernəm'buku) *n* **1** a state of NE Brazil, on the Atlantic: consists of a humid coastal plain rising to a high inland plateau. Capital: Recife. Pop: 7 910 992 (2001 est). Area: 98 280 sq km (37 946 sq miles) **2** the former name of **Recife**

pernicious (pə'nɪʃəs) *adj* **1** wicked or malicious: *pernicious lies* **2** causing grave harm; deadly [c16 from L *perniciōsus*, from *perniciēs* ruin, from PER- (intensive) + *nex* death] > **per'niciously** *adv* > **per'niciousness** *n*

pernicious anaemia *n* a form of anaemia characterized by lesions of the spinal cord, weakness, sore tongue, diarrhoea, etc: associated with inadequate absorption of vitamin B_{12}

pernickety (pə'nɪkɪtɪ) *adj inf* **1** excessively precise; fussy **2** (of a task) requiring close attention [c19 orig. Scot from ?]

Pernik (*Bulgarian* 'pɛrnik) *n* an industrial town in W Bulgaria, on the Struma River. Pop: 99 643 (1990). Former name (1949–62): **Dimitrovo**

Perón (*Spanish* pe'rɔn) *n* **1 Juan Domingo** (xwan do'mɪngo) 1895–1974, Argentine soldier and statesman; dictator (1946–55). He was deposed in 1955, remaining in exile until 1973, when he was elected president (1973–74) **2 (María) Eva (Duarte) de Perón** ('eβa), known as *Evita*. Second wife of Juan Domingo Perón. 1919–52, Argentine film actress: active in politics and social welfare (1946–52)

peroneal (ˌpɛrə'niːəl) *adj anat* of or relating to the fibula [c19 from NL *peronē*, from Gk: fibula]

perorate ('pɛrəˌreɪt) *vb* **perorates, perorating, perorated** (*intr*) **1** to speak at length, esp in a formal manner **2** to conclude a speech or sum up

peroration (ˌpɛrə'reɪʃən) *n* the conclusion of a speech or discourse, in which points made previously are summed up [c15 from L *perōrātiō*, from PER- (thoroughly) + *ōrāre* to speak]

perovskite (pɛ'rɒvskaɪt) *n* a yellow, brown, or greyish-black mineral [c19 after *Perovski*, Russian mineralogist]

peroxide (pə'rɒksaɪd) *n* **1** short for **hydrogen peroxide**, esp when used for bleaching hair **2** any of a class of metallic oxides, such as sodium peroxide, Na_2O_2 **3** (*not in technical usage*) any of certain dioxides, such as manganese(VI) oxide, MnO_2, that resemble peroxides in their formula **4** any of a class of organic compounds whose molecules contain two oxygen atoms bound together **5** (*modifier*) of, relating to, bleached with, or resembling peroxide: *a peroxide blonde* ▷ *vb* **peroxides, peroxiding, peroxided 6** (*tr*) to bleach (the hair) with peroxide

perpendicular (ˌpɜːpən'dɪkjʊlə) *adj* **1** at right angles to a horizontal plane **2** denoting, relating to, or having the style of Gothic architecture used in England during the 14th and 15th centuries, characterized by tracery having vertical lines **3** upright; vertical ▷ *n* **4** *geom* a line or plane perpendicular to another **5** any instrument used for indicating the vertical line through a given point [c14 from L *perpendiculāris*, from *perpendiculum* a plumb line, from *per-* through + *pendēre* to hang] > **perpendicularity** (ˌpɜːpənˌdɪkjʊ'lærɪtɪ) *n* > **ˌperpen'dicularly** *adv*

▷ www.britainexpress.com/architecture

perpetrate ('pɜːpɪˌtreɪt) *vb* **perpetrates, perpetrating, perpetrated** (*tr*) to perform or be responsible for (a deception, crime, etc) [c16 from L *perpetrāre*, from *per-* (thoroughly) + *patrāre* to perform] > **ˌperpe'tration** *n* > **'perpeˌtrator** *n*

USAGE *Perpetrate* and *perpetuate* are sometimes confused: *he must answer for the crimes he has perpetrated* (not *perpetuated*); *the book helped to perpetuate* (not *perpetrate*) *some of the myths surrounding his early life*

perpetual (pə'pɛtjʊəl) *adj* **1** (*usually prenominal*) eternal; permanent **2** (*usually prenominal*) seemingly ceaseless because often repeated: *your perpetual complaints* [c14 via OF from L *perpetuālis* universal, from *perpes* continuous, from *per-* (thoroughly) + *petere* to go towards] > **per'petually** *adv*

perpetual debenture *n* a bond or debenture that can either never be redeemed or cannot be redeemed on demand

perpetual motion *n* motion of a hypothetical mechanism that continues indefinitely without any external source of energy. It is impossible in practice because of friction

perpetuate (pə'pɛtjʊˌeɪt) *vb* **perpetuates, perpetuating, perpetuated** (*tr*) to cause to continue: *to perpetuate misconceptions* [c16 from L *perpetuāre* to continue without interruption, from *perpetuus* PERPETUAL] > **perˌpetu'ation** *n*

USAGE See at **perpetrate**

perpetuity (ˌpɜːpɪ'tjuːɪtɪ) *n, pl* **perpetuities 1** eternity **2** the state of being perpetual **3** *property law* a limitation preventing the absolute disposal of an estate for longer than the period allowed by law **4** an annuity that is payable indefinitely **5 in perpetuity** forever [c15 from OF *perpetuite*, from L *perpetuitās* continuity; see PERPETUAL]

Perpignan (*French* pɛrpiɲɑ̃) *n* a town in S France: historic capital of Roussillon. Pop: 105 115 (1999)

perplex (pəˈplɛks) *vb* (*tr*) **1** to puzzle; bewilder; confuse **2** to complicate: *to perplex an issue* [c15 from obs. *perplex* (adj) intricate, from L *perplexus* entangled, from *per-* (thoroughly) + *plectere* to entwine] > **perplexedly** (pəˈplɛksɪdlɪ, -ˈplɛkstlɪ) *adv* > **perˈplexingly** *adv*

perplexity (pəˈplɛksɪtɪ) *n, pl* **perplexities 1** the state of being perplexed **2** the state of being intricate or complicated **3** something that perplexes

per pro (ˈpɜː ˈprəʊ) *prep* by delegation to: through the agency of: used when signing documents on behalf of someone else [L: abbrev of *per prōcūrātiōnem*]

USAGE See at **pp**

perquisite (ˈpɜːkwɪzɪt) *n* **1** an incidental benefit gained from a certain type of employment, such as the use of a company car **2** a customary benefit received in addition to a regular income **3** a customary tip **4** something expected or regarded as an exclusive right ▷ Often shortened (informal) to **perk** [c15 from Med. L *perquīsītum*, from L *perquīrere* to seek earnestly for something]

Perrault (*French* pɛro) *n* **Charles** (ʃarl) 1628–1703, French author, noted for his *Contes de ma mère l'oye* (1697), which contains the fairy tales *Little Red Riding Hood*, *Cinderella*, and *The Sleeping Beauty*

Perrier water *or* **Perrier** (ˈpɛrɪeɪ) *n trademark* a sparkling mineral water from the south of France [c20 after a spring, *Source Perrier*, at Vergèze, France]

Perrin (*French* pɛrɛ̃) *n* **Jean Baptiste** (ʒɑ̃ batist) 1870–1942, French physicist. His researches on the distribution and diffusion of particles in colloids (1911) gave evidence for the physical reality of molecules, confirmed the explanation of Brownian movement in terms of kinetic theory, and determined the magnitude of the Avogadro constant. He also studied cathode rays: Nobel prize for physics 1926

perron (ˈpɛrən) *n* an external flight of steps, esp one at the front entrance of a building [c14 from OF, from *pierre* stone, from L *petra*]

perry (ˈpɛrɪ) *n, pl* **perries** an alcoholic drink made of pears, similar in taste to cider [c14 *pereye*, from OF *peré*, ult. from L *pirum* pear]

Perry (ˈpɛrɪ) *n* **1 Fred(erick John)** 1909–95, English tennis and table-tennis player; world singles table-tennis champion (1929); Wimbledon singles champion (1934–36) **2 Grayson** born 1960, British potter. A transvestite, he won the Turner Prize (2003) **3 Matthew Calbraith** 1794–1858, US naval officer, who led a naval expedition to Japan that obtained a treaty (1854) opening up Japan to western trade **4** his brother, **Oliver Hazard** 1785–1819, US naval officer. His defeat of a British squadron on Lake Erie (1813) was the turning point in the War of 1812, leading to the recapture of Detroit

perse (pɜːs) *n* **a** a dark greyish-blue colour **b** (*as adj*): *perse cloth* [c14 from OF, from Med. L *persus*, ? changed from L *Persicus* Persian]

per se (ˈpɜː ˈseɪ) *adv* by or in itself; intrinsically [L]

Perse (pɜːs; *French* pɛrs) *n* **Saint-John** (ˈsɪndʒən), real name *Alexis Saint-Léger* 1887–1975, French poet, born in Guadeloupe. His works include *Anabase* (1922) and *Chronique* (1960). Nobel prize for literature 1960

persecute (ˈpɜːsɪˌkjuːt) *vb* **persecutes, persecuting, persecuted** (*tr*) **1** to oppress, harass, or maltreat, esp because of race, religion, etc **2** to bother persistently [c15 from OF, from *persecuteur*, from LL *persecūtor* pursuer, from L *persequī* to take vengeance upon] > **ˈperseˌcutive** *adj* > **ˈperseˌcutor** *n*

persecution (ˌpɜːsɪˈkjuːʃən) *n* the act of persecuting or the state of being persecuted

persecution complex *n psychol* an acute irrational fear that other people are plotting one's downfall

Persephone (pəˈsɛfənɪ) *n Greek myth* a daughter of Zeus and Demeter, abducted by Hades and made his wife and queen of the underworld, but allowed part of each year to leave it. Roman counterpart: **Proserpina**

Persepolis (pəˈsɛpəlɪs) *n* the capital of ancient Persia in the Persian Empire and under the Seleucids: founded by Darius; sacked by Alexander the Great in 330 BC

Perseus (ˈpɜːsɪəs) *n Greek myth* a son of Zeus and Danaë, who with Athena's help slew the Gorgon Medusa and rescued Andromeda from a sea monster

perseverance (ˌpɜːsɪˈvɪərəns) *n* **1** continued steady belief or efforts; persistence **2** *Christian theol* continuance in a state of grace

perseveration (pɜːˌsɛvəˈreɪʃən) *n psychol* the tendency for an impression, idea, or feeling to dissipate only slowly and to recur during subsequent experiences

persevere (ˌpɜːsɪˈvɪə) *vb* **perseveres, persevering, persevered** (*intr*; often foll by *in*) to show perseverance [c14 from OF *perseverer*, from L, from *perseverus* very strict; see SEVERE]

Pershing (ˈpɜːʃɪŋ) *n* **John Joseph**, nickname *Black Jack*. 1860–1948, US general. He was commander in chief of the American Expeditionary Force in Europe (1917–19)

Persia (ˈpɜːʃə) *n* **1** the former name (until 1935) of **Iran** **2** another name for **Persian Empire**

Persian (ˈpɜːʃən) *adj* **1** of or relating to ancient Persia or modern Iran, their inhabitants, or their languages ▷ *n* **2** a native, citizen, or inhabitant of modern Iran; an Iranian **3** the language of Iran or Persia in any of its ancient or modern forms

Persian carpet *or* **rug** *n* a carpet or rug made in Persia or the Near East by knotting silk or wool yarn by hand onto a woven backing in rich colours and flowing or geometric designs

Persian cat *n* a long-haired variety of domestic cat

Persian Empire *n* the S Asian empire established by Cyrus the Great in the 6th century BC and overthrown by Alexander the Great in the 4th century BC. At its height it extended from India to Europe

▷ www.wikipedia.org/wiki/PersianEmpire

▷ http://ancienthistory.about.com/cs/persianempin

Persian Gulf *n* a shallow arm of the Arabian Sea between SW Iran and Arabia: linked with the Arabian Sea by the Strait of Hormuz and the Gulf of Oman; important for the oilfields on its shores. Area: 233 000 sq km (90 000 sq miles)

Persian lamb *n* **1** a black loosely curled fur from the karakul lamb **2** a karakul lamb

persiennes (ˌpɜːsɪˈɛnz) *pl n* outside window shutters having louvres [c19 from F, from *persien* Persian]

persiflage (ˈpɜːsɪˌflɑːʒ) *n* light frivolous conversation, style, or treatment; friendly teasing [c18 via F from *persifler* to tease, from *per-* (intensive) + *siffler* to whistle, from L *sībilāre* to whistle]

persimmon (pɜːˈsɪmən) *n* **1** any of several tropical trees, typically having hard wood and large orange-red fruit **2** Also called: **sharon fruit** the sweet fruit of any of these trees, which is edible when completely ripe [c17 from Amerind]

Persis (ˈpɜːsɪs) *n* an ancient region of SW Iran: homeland of the Achaemenid dynasty

persist (pəˈsɪst) *vb* (*intr*) **1** (often foll by *in*) to continue steadfastly or obstinately despite opposition **2** to continue without interruption: *the rain persisted throughout the night* [c16 from L *persistere*, from *per-* (intensive) + *sistere* to stand steadfast] > **perˈsister** *n*

persistence (pəˈsɪstəns) *or* **persistency** *n* **1** the quality of persisting; tenacity **2** the act of persisting; continued effort or existence

persistent (pəˈsɪstənt) *adj* **1** showing persistence **2** incessantly repeated; unrelenting: *your persistent questioning* **3** (of plant parts) remaining attached to the plant after the normal time of withering **4** *zool* (of parts

Pp

normally present only in young stages) present in the adult **5** (of a chemical, esp when used as a insecticide) slow to break down > **per'sistently** *adv*

persistent organic pollutant *n* a toxin resulting from a manufacturing process, which remains in the environment for many years. Abbreviation: **POP**

persistent vegetative state *n med* an irreversible condition, resulting from brain damage, characterized by lack of consciousness, thought, and feeling, although reflex activities (such as breathing) continue. Abbrev: **PVS**

person ('pɜːsᵊn) *n, pl* **persons** **1** an individual human being **2** the body of a human being: *guns hidden on his person* **3** a grammatical category into which pronouns and forms of verbs are subdivided depending on whether they refer to the speaker, the person addressed, or some other individual, thing, etc **4** a human being or a corporation recognized in law as having certain rights and obligations **5** **in person** actually present: *the author will be there in person* [C13 from OF *persone*, from L *persōna* mask, ?from Etruscan *phersu* mask]

-person *n combining form* sometimes used instead of *-man* and *-woman* or *-lady*: *chairperson*.

USAGE See at **-man**

persona (pɜː'səʊnə) *n, pl* **personae** (-niː) **1** (*often pl*) a character in a play, novel, etc **2** (in Jungian psychology) the mechanism that conceals a person's true thoughts and feelings, esp in adaptation to the outside world [L: mask]

personable ('pɜːsənəbᵊl) *adj* pleasant in appearance and personality > **'personableness** *n* > **'personably** *adv*

personage ('pɜːsənɪdʒ) *n* **1** an important or distinguished person **2** another word for **person** (sense 1) **3** *rare* a figure in literature, history, etc

persona grata *Latin* (pɜː'səʊnə 'grɑːtə) *n, pl* ***personae gratae*** (pɜː'səʊniː 'grɑːtiː) an acceptable person, esp a diplomat

personal ('pɜːsənᵊl) *adj* **1** of or relating to the private aspects of a person's life: *personal letters* **2** (*prenominal*) of or relating to a person's body, its care, or its appearance: *personal hygiene* **3** belonging to or intended for a particular person and no-one else: *for your personal use* **4** (*prenominal*) undertaken by an individual: *a personal appearance by a celebrity* **5** referring to or involving a person's individual personality, intimate affairs, etc, esp in an offensive way: *personal remarks; don't be so personal* **6** having the attributes of an individual conscious being: *a personal God* **7** of, relating to, or denoting grammatical person **8** *law* of or relating to movable property, as money, etc

personal care *n* help given to elderly or infirm people with essential everyday activities such as washing, dressing, and meals

personal column *n* a newspaper column containing personal messages and advertisements

personal computer *n* a small inexpensive computer used in word processing, computer games, etc

personal digital assistant *n* a palmtop computer for storing information. Abbreviation: **PDA**

personal equity plan *n* the full name for **PEP**

personality (ˌpɜːsə'nælɪtɪ) *n, pl* **personalities** **1** *psychol* the sum total of all the behavioural and mental characteristics by means of which an individual is recognized as being unique **2** the distinctive character of a person that makes him or her socially attractive: *a salesman needs a lot of personality* **3** a well-known person in a certain field, such as entertainment **4** a remarkable person **5** (*often pl*) a personal remark

personalize *or* **personalise** ('pɜːsənəˌlaɪz) *vb* **personalizes, personalizing, personalized** *or* **personalises, personalising, personalised** (*tr*) **1** to endow with personal or individual qualities **2** to mark (stationery, clothing, etc) with a person's initials, name, etc **3** to take (a remark, etc) personally **4** another word for **personify** > **ˌpersonali'zation** *or* **ˌpersonali'sation** *n*

personally ('pɜːsənəlɪ) *adv* **1** without the help or intervention of others: *I'll attend to it personally* **2** (*sentence modifier*) in one's own opinion or as regards oneself: *personally, I hate onions* **3** as if referring to oneself: *to take the insults personally* **4** as a person: *we like him personally, but professionally he's incompetent*

personal organizer *n* **1** a diary that stores personal records, appointments, notes, etc **2** a pocket-sized electronic device that performs the same functions

personal pronoun *n* a pronoun having a definite person or thing as an antecedent and functioning grammatically in the same way as the noun that it replaces. The personal pronouns include *I, you, he, she, it, we,* and *they*

personal property *n law* movable property, such as furniture or money. Also called: **personalty** ▷ Cf **real property**

personal shopper *n* a person employed, esp by a shop, to accompany and advise customers on shopping trips or to select items for them

personal stereo *n* a small audio cassette player worn attached to a belt and used with lightweight headphones

personal stylist *n* a person employed by a rich or famous client to offer advice on clothes, hairstyles, and other aspects of personal appearance

persona non grata *Latin* (pɜː'səʊnə nɒn 'grɑːtə) *n, pl* ***personae non gratae*** (pɜː'səʊniː nɒn 'grɑːtiː) **1** an unacceptable or unwelcome person **2** a diplomat who is not acceptable to the government to whom he or she is accredited

personate ('pɜːsəˌneɪt) *vb* **personates, personating, personated** (*tr*) **1** to act the part of (a character in a play); portray **2** *criminal law* to assume the identity of (another person) with intent to deceive > **ˌperson'ation** *n* > **'personative** *adj* > **'personˌator** *n*

personhood ('pɜːsənˌhʊd) *n chiefly US* the condition of being a person who is an individual with inalienable rights, esp under the 14th Amendment of the Constitution of the United States

personification (pɜːˌsɒnɪfɪ'keɪʃən) *n* **1** the attribution of human characteristics to things, abstract ideas, etc **2** the representation of an abstract quality or idea in the form of a person, creature, etc, as in art and literature **3** a person or thing that personifies **4** a person or thing regarded as an embodiment of a quality: *he is the personification of optimism*

personify (pɜː'sɒnɪˌfaɪ) *vb* **personifies, personifying, personified** (*tr*) **1** to attribute human characteristics to (a thing or abstraction) **2** to represent (an abstract quality) in human or animal form **3** (of a person or thing) to represent (an abstract quality), as in art **4** to be the embodiment of > **per'soniˌfier** *n*

personned *adj* another word for **manned**

personnel (ˌpɜːsə'nɛl) *n* **1** the people employed in an organization or for a service **2** Also called: **human resources** **2a** the department that interviews, appoints, or keeps records of employees **2b** (*as modifier*): *a personnel officer* [C19 from F, ult. from LL *persōnālis* personal (adj); see PERSON]

perspective (pə'spɛktɪv) *n* **1** a way of regarding situations, facts, etc, and judging their relative importance **2** the proper or accurate point of view or the ability to see it; objectivity: *try to get some perspective on your troubles* **3** a view over some distance in space or time; prospect **4** the theory or art of suggesting three dimensions on a two-dimensional surface, in order to recreate the appearance and spatial relationships that objects or a scene in recession present to the eye **5** the appearance of objects, buildings, etc, relative to each other, as determined by their distance from the viewer, or the effects of this distance on their appearance [C14 from Med. L *perspectīva ars* the science of optics, from L *perspicere* to inspect carefully] > **per'spectively** *adv*

Perspex ('pɜːspɛks) *n trademark* any of various clear acrylic resins used as a glass substitute

perspicacious (ˌpɜːspɪ'keɪʃəs) *adj* acutely perceptive or discerning [C17 from L *perspicax*, from *perspicere* to look at closely] > **ˌperspi'caciously** *adv* > **perspicacity** (ˌpɜːspɪ'kæsɪtɪ) *or* **ˌperspi'caciousness** *n*

perspicuous (pə'spɪkjʊəs) *adj* (of speech or writing) easily understood; lucid [C15 from L *perspicuus* transparent, from *perspicere* to explore thoroughly] > **per'spicuously** *adv* > **per'spicuousness** *or* **perspicuity** (ˌpɜːspɪ'kjuːɪtɪ) *n*

perspiration (ˌpɜːspə'reɪʃən) *n* **1** the act of insensibly eliminating fluid through the pores of the skin **2** the sensible elimination of fluid through the pores of the skin, which is visible as droplets **3** the salty fluid secreted by the pores of the skin; sweat > **perspiratory** (pə'spaɪərətərɪ) *adj*

perspire (pə'spaɪə) *vb* **perspires, perspiring, perspired** to secrete or exude (perspiration) through the pores of the skin [C17 from L *perspīrāre* to blow, from *per-* (through) + *spīrāre* to breathe] > **per'spiringly** *adv*

persuade (pə'sweɪd) *vb* **persuades, persuading, persuaded** (*tr; may take a clause as object or an infinitive*) **1** to induce, urge, or prevail upon successfully: *he finally persuaded them to buy it* **2** to cause to believe; convince: *even with the evidence, the police were not persuaded* [C16 from L *persuādēre*, from *per-* (intensive) + *suādēre* to urge, advise] > **per'suadable** *or* **per'suasible** *adj* > **perˌsuada'bility** *or* **perˌsuasi'bility** *n* > **per'suader** *n*

persuasion (pə'sweɪʒən) *n* **1** the act of persuading or of trying to persuade **2** the power to persuade **3** a strong belief **4** an established creed or belief, esp a religious one **5** a sect, party, or faction [C14 from L *persuāsiō*]

persuasive (pə'sweɪsɪv) *adj* having the power or tending to persuade: *a persuasive salesman* > **per'suasively** *adv* > **per'suasiveness** *n*

pert (pɜːt) *adj* **1** saucy, impudent, or forward **2** jaunty: *a pert little hat* **3** *obs* clever or brisk [C13 var. of earlier *apert*, from L *apertus* open, from *aperīre* to open] > **'pertly** *adv* > **'pertness** *n*

pertain (pə'teɪn) *vb* (*intr;* often foll by *to*) **1** to have reference or relevance: *issues pertaining to women* **2** to be appropriate: *the product pertains to real user needs* **3** to belong (to) or be a part (of) [C14 from L *pertinēre*, from *per-* (intensive) + *tenēre* to hold]

Perth (pɜːθ) *n* **1** a city in central Scotland, in Perth and Kinross on the River Tay: capital of Scotland from the 12th century until the assassination of James I there in 1437. Pop: 41 453 (1991) **2** a city in SW Australia, capital of Western Australia, on the Swan River: major industrial centre; University of Western Australia (1911). Pop: 1 262 600 (1995 est)

Perth and Kinross (kɪn'rɒs) *n* a council area of N central Scotland, corresponding mainly to the historical counties of Perthshire and Kinross-shire: part of Tayside Region from 1975 until 1996: chiefly mountainous, with agriculture, tourism, and forestry. Administrative centre: Perth. Pop: 134 949 (2001). Area: 5321 sq km (2019 sq miles)

Perthshire ('pɜːθʃɪə, -ʃə) *n* (until 1975) a county of central Scotland, now part of Perth and Kinross council area

pertinacious (ˌpɜːtɪ'neɪʃəs) *adj* **1** doggedly resolute in purpose or belief; unyielding **2** stubbornly persistent [C17 from L *pertināx*, from *per-* (intensive) + *tenāx* clinging, from *tenēre* to hold] > **ˌperti'naciously** *adv* > **pertinacity** (ˌpɜːtɪ'næsɪtɪ) *or* **ˌperti'naciousness** *n*

pertinent ('pɜːtɪnənt) *adj* relating to the matter at hand; relevant [C14 from L *pertinēns*, from *pertinēre* to PERTAIN] > **'pertinence** *or* **'pertinency** *n* > **'pertinently** *adv*

perturb (pə'tɜːb) *vb* (*tr; often passive*) **1** to disturb the composure of; trouble **2** to throw into disorder **3** *physics, astron* to cause (a planet, electron, etc) to undergo a perturbation [C14 from OF *pertourber*, from L *perturbāre* to confuse, from *per-* (intensive) + *turbāre* to agitate] > **per'turbable** *adj* > **per'turbing** *adj*

perturbation (ˌpɜːtə'beɪʃən) *n* **1** the act of perturbing or the state of being perturbed **2** a cause of disturbance **3** *physics* a secondary influence on a system that modifies simple behaviour, such as the effect of the other electrons on one electron in an atom **4** *astron* a small continuous deviation in the orbit of a planet or comet, due to the attraction of neighbouring planets

pertussis (pə'tʌsɪs) *n* the technical name for **whooping cough** [C18 NL, from L *per-* (intensive) + *tussis* cough] > **per'tussal** *adj*

Peru (pə'ruː) *n* a republic in W South America, on the Pacific: the centre of the great Inca Empire when conquered by the Spanish in 1532; gained independence in 1824 by defeating Spanish forces with armies led by San Martín and Bolívar; consists of a coastal desert, rising to the Andes; an important exporter of minerals and a major fishing nation. Official languages: Spanish, Quechua, and Aymara. Official religion: Roman Catholic. Currency: nuevo sol. Capital: Lima. Pop: 26 090 000 (2001 est). Area: 1 285 215 sq km (496 222 sq miles) > **Peruvian** (pə'ruːvɪən) *adj, n*
▹ www.peru.org.pe/defaulteng.htm
▹ www.peruonline.net

Peru Current *n* a cold ocean current flowing northwards off the Pacific coast of South America. Also called: **Humboldt Current**

Perugia (pə'ruːdʒə; *Italian* pe'ruːdʒa) *n* **1** a city in central Italy, in Umbria: centre of the Umbrian school of painting (15th century); university (1308); Etruscan and Roman remains. Pop: 156 673 (2000 est). Ancient name: **Perusia** **2** **Lake** another name for (Lake) **Trasimene**

Perugino (*Italian* peru'dʒino) *n* **Il** (il), real name *Pietro Vannucci*. 1446–1523, Italian painter; master of Raphael. His works include the fresco *Christ giving the Keys to Peter* in the Sistine Chapel, Rome

Pp

peruke (pə'ruːk) *n* a wig for men in the 17th and 18th centuries. Also called: **periwig** [C16 from F *perruque*, from It. *perrucca* wig, from ?]

peruse (pə'ruːz) *vb* **peruses, perusing, perused** (*tr*) **1** to read or examine with care; study **2** to browse or read in a leisurely way [C15 (meaning: to use up): from PER- (intensive) + USE] > **pe'rusal** *n* > **pe'ruser** *n*

Perutz (pə'rʊts) *n* **Max Ferdinand** 1914–2002, British biochemist, born in Austria. With J. C. Kendrew, he worked on the structure of haemoglobin and shared the Nobel prize for chemistry 1962

Peruzzi (*Italian* pe'ruttsi) *n* **Baldassare Tommaso** (baldas'saːre tom'maːzo) 1481–1536, Italian architect and painter of the High Renaissance. The design of the Palazzo Massimo, Rome, is attributed to him

perv (pɜːv) *sl* ▹ *n* **1** a pervert **2** *Austral* a lascivious look ▹ *vb* Also: **perve** (*intr*) **3** *Austral* to behave like a voyeur

pervade (pɜː'veɪd) *vb* **pervades, pervading, pervaded** (*tr*) to spread through or throughout, esp subtly or gradually; permeate [C17 from L *pervādere*, from *per-* through + *vādere* to go] > **pervasion** (pɜː'veɪʒən) *n*

pervasive (pɜː'veɪsɪv) *adj* pervading or tending to pervade [C18 from L *pervāsus* p.p. of *pervādere* to PERVADE] > **per'vasively** *adv* > **per'vasiveness** *n*

perverse (pə'vɜːs) *adj* **1** deliberately deviating from what is regarded as normal, good, or proper **2** persistently holding to what is wrong **3** wayward or contrary; obstinate [C14 from OF *pervers*, from L *perversus* turned the wrong way] > **per'versely** *adv* > **per'verseness** *or* **per'versity** *n*

perversion (pə'vɜːʃən) *n* **1** any abnormal means of obtaining sexual satisfaction **2** the act of perverting or the state of being perverted **3** a perverted form or usage

pervert *vb* (pə'vɜːt) (*tr*) **1** to use wrongly or badly **2** to interpret wrongly or badly; distort **3** to lead into deviant or perverted beliefs or behaviour; corrupt **4** to debase ▷ *n* ('pɜːvɜːt) **5** a person who practises sexual perversion [c14 from OF *pervertir*, from L *pervertere* to turn the wrong way] > **per'verted** *adj* > **per'verter** *n* > **per'vertible** *adj* > **per'versive** *adj*

pervious ('pɜːvɪəs) *adj* **1** able to be penetrated; permeable **2** receptive to new ideas, etc; open-minded [c17 from L *pervius*, from *per-* (through) + *via* a way] > **'perviously** *adv* > **'perviousness** *n*

pes (peɪz, piːz) *n, pl* **pedes** ('pɛdiːz) the technical name for the human **foot** [c19 NL: foot]

Pesaro (*Italian* 'peːzaro) *n* a port and resort in E central Italy, in the Marches on the Adriatic. Pop: 90 340 (1990). Ancient name: **Pisaurum** (pɪ'saʊrəm)

Pescadores (ˌpɛskə'dɔːrɪz) *pl n* a group of 64 islands in Formosa Strait, separated from Taiwan (to which it belongs) by the **Pescadores Channel** Pop: 90 719 (2001 est). Area: 127 sq km (49 sq miles). Chinese names: **Penghu, P'eng-hu**

Pescara (*Italian* pes'kaːra) *n* a city and resort in E central Italy, on the Adriatic. Pop: 115 698 (2000 est)

peseta (pə'seɪtə; *Spanish* pe'seta) *n* the former standard monetary unit of Spain and Andorra, divided into 100 céntimos; replaced by the euro in 2002 [c19 from Sp., dim. of PESO]

Peshawar (pə'ʃɔːə) *n* a city in N Pakistan, at the E end of the Khyber Pass: one of the oldest cities in Pakistan and capital of the ancient kingdom of Gandhara; university (1950). Pop: 988 055 (1998)

pesky ('pɛskɪ) *adj* **peskier, peskiest** *US & Canad inf* troublesome [c19 prob. changed from *pesty*; see PEST] > **'peskily** *adv* > **'peskiness** *n*

peso ('peɪsəʊ; *Spanish* 'peso) *n, pl* **pesos** (-səʊz; *Spanish* -sos) the standard monetary unit of Argentina, Chile, Colombia, Cuba, the Dominican Republic, Guinea-Bissau, Mexico, the Philippines, and Uruguay [c16 from Sp.: weight, from L *pēnsum* something weighed out, from *pendere* to weigh]

pessary ('pɛsərɪ) *n, pl* **pessaries** *med* **1** a device for inserting into the vagina, either as a support for the uterus or (**diaphragm pessary**) to deliver a drug, such as a contraceptive **2** a vaginal suppository [c14 from LL *pessārium*, from L *pessum*, from Gk *pessos* plug]

pessimism ('pɛsɪˌmɪzəm) *n* **1** the tendency to expect the worst in all things **2** the doctrine of the ultimate triumph of evil over good **3** the doctrine that this world is corrupt and that man's sojourn in it is a preparation for some other existence [c18 from L *pessimus* worst, sup. of *malus* bad] > **'pessimist** *n* > **ˌpessi'mistic** *adj* > **ˌpessi'mistically** *adv*

Pessoa (pɛ'səʊə) *n* **Fernando** 1888–1935, Portuguese poet, who ascribed much of his work to three imaginary poets, Alvaro de Campos, Alberto Caeiro, and Ricardo Reis

pest (pɛst) *n* **1** a person or thing that annoys, esp by imposing itself when it is not wanted; nuisance **2** any organism that damages crops, or injures or irritates livestock or man **3** *rare* an epidemic disease [c16 from L *pestis* plague, from ?]

Pestalozzi (ˌpɛstə'lɒtsɪ) *n* **Johann Heinrich** (jo'han 'hainrɪç) 1746–1827, Swiss educational reformer. His emphasis on learning by observation exerted a wide influence on elementary education

pester ('pɛstə) *vb* (*tr*) to annoy or nag continually [c16 from OF *empestrer* to hobble (a horse), from Vulgar L *impāstōriāre* (unattested) to use a hobble, ult. from L *pastor* herdsman]

pesticide ('pɛstɪˌsaɪd) *n* a chemical used for killing pests, esp insects > **ˌpesti'cidal** *adj*

pestiferous (pɛ'stɪfərəs) *adj* **1** *inf* troublesome; irritating **2** breeding, carrying, or spreading infectious disease **3** corrupting; pernicious [c16 from L *pestifer*, from *pestis* contagion + *ferre* to bring]

pestilence ('pɛstɪləns) *n* **1a** any epidemic of a deadly infectious disease, such as the plague **1b** such a disease **2** an evil influence

pestilent ('pɛstɪlənt) *adj* **1** annoying; irritating **2** highly destructive morally or physically; pernicious **3** likely to cause epidemic or infectious disease [c15 from L *pestilens* unwholesome, from *pestis* plague] > **'pestilently** *adv* > **pestilential** (ˌpɛstɪ'lɛnʃəl) *adj* > **ˌpesti'lentially** *adv*

pestle ('pɛsᵊl) *n* **1** a club-shaped instrument for mixing or grinding substances in a mortar **2** a tool for pounding or stamping ▷ *vb* **pestles, pestling, pestled** **3** to pound (a substance or object) with or as if with a pestle [c14 from OF *pestel*, from L *pistillum*]

pesto ('pɛstəʊ) *n* a sauce for pasta, consisting of basil leaves, nuts, garlic, oil, and Parmesan cheese, all crushed together [It., shortened form of *pestato*, p.p. of *pestare* to pound, crush]

pet¹ (pɛt) *n* **1** a tame animal kept for companionship, amusement, etc **2** a person who is fondly indulged; favourite: *teacher's pet* ▷ *adj* **3** kept as a pet: *a pet dog* **4** of or for pet animals: *pet food* **5** particularly cherished: *a pet hatred* **6** familiar or affectionate: *a pet name* ▷ *vb* **pets, petting, petted** **7** (*tr*) to treat (a person, animal, etc) as a pet; pamper **8** (*tr*) to pat or fondle (an animal, child, etc) **9** (*intr*) *inf* (of two people) to caress each other in an erotic manner [c16 from ?] > **'petter** *n*

pet² (pɛt) *n* a fit of sulkiness, esp at what is felt to be a slight; pique [c16 from ?]

PET (pɛt) *n acronym for* positron emission tomography

Pet. *Bible abbrev for* Peter

peta- *prefix* **1** denoting 10^{15}: *petametres* **2** Also: **pebi-** *computing* denoting 10^{50}: *petabyte*. ▷ Symbol: P [c20 so named because it is the SI prefix after TERA-; on the model of PENTA-, the prefix after TETRA-]

USAGE See at **kilo-**

petabyte ('pɛtəˌbaɪt) *n computing* one million gigabytes

Pétain (*French* petɛ̃) *n* **Henri Philippe Omer** (ɑ̃ri filip ɔmɛr) 1856–1951, French marshal, noted for his victory at Verdun (1916) in World War I and his leadership of the pro-Nazi government of unoccupied France at Vichy (1940–44); imprisoned for treason (1945)

petal ('pɛtᵊl) *n* any of the separate parts of the corolla of a flower: often brightly coloured [c18 from NL *petalum*, from Gk *petalon* leaf] > **'petaline** *adj* > **'petalled** *adj* > **'petal-ˌlike** *adj*

-petal *adj combining form* seeking: *centripetal* [from NL *-petus*, from L *petere* to seek]

petard (pɪ'tɑːd) *n* **1** (formerly) a device containing explosives used to breach a wall, doors, etc **2** **hoist with one's own petard** being the victim of one's own schemes, etc [c16 from F: firework, from *péter* to break wind, from L *pēdere*]

petaurist (pət'ɒrɪst) *n* another name for **flying phalanger** [c19 from L, from Gk *petauristēs* performer on the springboard]

petcock ('pɛtˌkɒk) *n* a small valve for checking the water content of a steam boiler or draining waste from the cylinder of a steam engine [c19 from PET¹ or ? F *pet*, from *péter* to break wind + COCK¹]

petechia (pɪ'tiːkɪə) *n, pl* **petechiae** (-kɪˌiː) a minute discoloured spot on the surface of the skin [c18 via NL from It. *petecchia* freckle, from ?] > **pe'techial** *adj*

peter¹ ('piːtə) *vb* (*intr*; foll by *out* or *away*) to fall (off) in volume, intensity, etc, and finally cease [c19 from ?]

peter² ('piːtə) *n sl* **1** a safe, till, or cashbox **2** a prison cell [c17 (meaning a case) from the name *Peter*]

Peter ('piːtə) *n New Testament* **Saint** Also called: **Simon Peter** died ?67 AD, a fisherman of Bethsaida, who became leader of the apostles and is regarded by Roman Catholics as the first pope; probably martyred at Rome

Peter I *n* known as *Peter the Great*. 1672–1725, tsar of Russia

(1682–1725), who assumed sole power in 1689. He introduced many reforms in government, technology, and the western European ideas. He also acquired new territories for Russia in the Baltic and founded the new capital of St Petersburg (1703)

Peter III *n* 1728–62, grandson of Peter I and tsar of Russia (1762): deposed in a coup d'état led by his wife (later Catherine II); assassinated

Peterborough ('pi:təbərə, -brə) *n* **1** a city in central England, in Peterborough unitary authority, N Cambridgeshire on the River Nene: industrial centre; under development as a new town since 1968. Pop: 134 788 (1991 est) **2** a unitary authority in central England, in Cambridgeshire. Pop: 156 060 (2001). Area: 402 sq km (155 sq miles) **3 Soke of** a former administrative unit of E central England, generally considered part of Northamptonshire or Huntingdonshire: absorbed into Cambridgeshire in 1974 **4** a city in SE Canada, in SE Ontario: manufacturing centre. Pop: 68 371 (1991) **5** a traditional type of wooden canoe formerly made in Peterborough, SE Ontario

Peterlee ('pi:tə,li:) *n* a new town in Co Durham, founded in 1948. Pop: 23 500 (1990)

peterman ('pi:təmən) *n, pl* **petermen** *sl* a burglar skilled in safe-breaking [c19 from PETER²]

Petermann Peak ('pi:təmən) *n* a mountain in E Greenland. Height: 2932 m (9645 ft)

Peter Pan *n* a youthful, boyish, or immature man [c20 after the main character in *Peter Pan* (1904), a play by J. M. BARRIE]

Peter Principle *n* **the** the theory, usually taken facetiously, that all members in a hierarchy rise to their own level of incompetence [c20 from the book *The Peter Principle* (1969) by Dr Lawrence J. *Peter* and Raymond Hull]

Petersburg ('pi:təz,bɜ:g) *n* a city in SE Virginia, on the Appomattox River: scene of prolonged fighting (1864–65) during the final months of the American Civil War. Pop: 38 386 (1990)

petersham ('pi:təʃəm) *n* **1** a thick corded ribbon used to stiffen belts, etc **2** a heavy woollen fabric used for coats, etc **3** a kind of overcoat made of such fabric [c19 after Viscount *Petersham* (died 1851), E army officer]

Peterson ('pi:təsᵊn) *n* **Oscar** (**Emmanuel**) born 1925, Canadian jazz pianist and singer, who led his own trio from the early 1950s

Peter's pence *or* **Peter pence** *n* **1** an annual tax, originally of one penny, formerly levied for the maintenance of the Papal See: abolished by Henry VIII in 1534 **2** a voluntary contribution made by Roman Catholics in many countries for the same purpose [c13 referring to St PETER, considered as the first pope]

Peters' projection *n* a form of modified Mercator's map projection that gives prominence to Third World countries [c20 after Arno *Peters*, G historian]

Peter the Hermit *n* ?1050–1115, French monk and preacher of the First Crusade

pethidine ('pɛθɪ,di:n) *n* a white crystalline water-soluble drug used as an analgesic [c20 ? a blend of PIPERIDINE + ETHYL]

petiole ('pɛtɪ,əʊl) *n* **1** the stalk by which a leaf is attached to the plant **2** *zool* a slender stalk or stem, as between the thorax and abdomen of ants [c18 via F from L *petiolus* little foot, from *pēs* foot] > **petiolate** ('pɛtɪə,leɪt) *adj*

petit ('pɛtɪ) *adj* (*prenominal*) *chiefly law* of lesser importance; small [c14 from OF: little, from ?]

Petit (*French* pəti) *n* **Roland** (rɔlɑ̃) born 1924, French ballet dancer and choreographer. His innovative ballets include *Carmen* (1949), *Kraanerg* (1969), and *The Blue Angel* (1985); he also choreographed films, such as *Anything Goes* (1956) and *Black Tights* (1960)

petit bourgeois ('bʊəʒwɑ:) *n, pl* **petits bourgeois** ('bʊəʒwɑ:z) **1** Also called: **petite bourgeoisie, petty bourgeoisie** the section of the middle class with the lowest social status, as shopkeepers, lower clerical staff, etc **2** a member of this stratum ▷ *adj* **3** of, relating to, or characteristic of the petit bourgeois, esp indicating a sense of self-righteousness and conformity to established standards of behaviour

petite (pə'ti:t) *adj* (of a woman) small, delicate, and dainty [c18 from F, fem of *petit* small]

petit four (fɔ:) *n, pl* **petits fours** (fɔ:z) any of various very small fancy cakes and biscuits [F, lit.: little oven]

petition (pɪ'tɪʃən) *n* **1** a written document signed by a large number of people demanding some form of action from a government or other authority **2** any formal request to a higher authority; entreaty **3** *law* a formal application in writing made to a court asking for some specific judicial action: *a petition for divorce* **4** the action of petitioning ▷ *vb* **5** (*tr*) to address or present a petition to (a person in authority, government, etc): *to petition Parliament* **6** (*intr*; foll by *for*) to seek by petition [c14 from L *petītiō*, from *petere* to seek] > **pe'titionary** *adj*

petitioner (pɪ'tɪʃənə) *n* **1** a person who presents a petition **2** *chiefly Brit* the plaintiff in a divorce suit

petitio principii (pɪ'tɪʃɪ,əʊ prɪn'kɪpɪ,aɪ) *n logic* a form of fallacious reasoning in which the conclusion has been assumed in the premises; begging the question [c16 L, translation of Gk *to en arkhei aiteisthai* an assumption at the beginning]

petit jury *n* a jury of 12 persons empanelled to determine the facts of a case and decide the issue pursuant to the direction of the court on points of law. Also called: **petty jury** > **petit juror** *n*

petit larceny *n* (formerly, in England) the stealing of property valued at 12 pence or under. Abolished 1827. Also called: **petty larceny**

petit mal (mæl) *n* a mild form of epilepsy characterized by periods of impairment or loss of consciousness for up to 30 seconds ▷ Cf **grand mal** [c19 F: little illness]

petit point ('pɛtɪ 'pɔɪnt; *French* pəti pwɛ̃) *n* **1** a small diagonal needlepoint stitch used for fine detail **2** work done with such stitches [F: small point]

Petöfi (*Hungarian* 'pɛtø:fi) *n* **Sándor** ('ʃa:ndor) 1823–49, Hungarian lyric poet and patriot

Petra ('pɛtrə, 'pi:trə) *n* an ancient city in the south of present-day Jordan; capital of the Nabataean kingdom

Petrarch ('pɛtrɑ:k) *n* Italian name *Francesco Petrarca*. 1304–74, Italian lyric poet and scholar, who greatly influenced the values of the Renaissance. His collection of poems *Canzoniere*, inspired by his ideal love for Laura, was written in the Tuscan dialect. He also wrote much in Latin, esp the epic poem *Africa* (1341) and the *Secretum* (1342), a spiritual self-analysis

Petrarchan sonnet *n* a sonnet form associated with the poet Petrarch, having an octave rhyming a b b a a b b a and a sestet rhyming either c d e c d e or c d c d c d

petrel ('pɛtrəl) *n* any of a family of oceanic birds having a hooked bill and tubular nostrils: includes albatrosses, storm petrels, and shearwaters [c17 var. of earlier *pitteral*, associated by folk etymology with St *Peter*, because the bird appears to walk on water]

Petri dish ('pɛtrɪ) *n* a shallow dish, often with a cover, used in laboratories, esp for producing cultures of microorganisms [c19 after J. R. *Petri* (1852–1921), G bacteriologist]

Petrie ('pɛtrɪ) *n* Sir (**William Matthew**) **Flinders** 1853–1942, British Egyptologist and archaeologist

petrifaction (,pɛtrɪ'fækʃən) *or* **petrification** (,pɛtrɪfɪ'keɪʃən) *n* **1** the act or process of forming petrified organic material **2** the state of being petrified

Petrified Forest *n* a national park in E Arizona, containing petrified coniferous trees about 170 000 000 years old

Pp

petrify ('pɛtrɪˌfaɪ) *vb* **petrifies, petrifying, petrified** **1** (*tr; often passive*) to convert (organic material) into a fossilized form by impregnation with dissolved minerals so that the original appearance is preserved **2** to make or become dull, unresponsive, etc; deaden **3** (*tr; often passive*) to stun or daze with horror, fear, etc [C16 from F *pétrifier*, ult. from Gk *petra* stone] > **'petriˌfier** *n*

petro- *or before a vowel* **petr-** *combining form* **1** indicating stone or rock: *petrology* **2** indicating petroleum, its products, etc: *petrochemical* **3** of or relating to the production, export, or sale of petroleum: *petrostate* [from Gk *petra* rock or *petros* stone]

petrochemical (ˌpɛtrəʊ'kɛmɪkᵊl) *n* **1** any substance, such as acetone or ethanol, obtained from petroleum ▷ *adj* **2** of, concerned with, or obtained from petrochemicals or related to petrochemistry > **ˌpetro'chemistry** *n*

petrodollar ('pɛtrəʊˌdɒlə) *n* money earned by a country by the exporting of petroleum

petroglyph ('pɛtrəˌglɪf) *n* a drawing or carving on rock, esp a prehistoric one [C19 via F from Gk *petra* stone + *gluphē* carving]

Petrograd ('pɛtrəʊˌgræd; *Russian* pɪtra'grat) *n* a former name (1914–24) of **Saint Petersburg**

petrography (pɛ'trɒgrəfɪ) *n* the branch of petrology concerned with the description and classification of rocks > **pe'trographer** *n* > **petrographic** (ˌpɛtrə'græfɪk) *or* **ˌpetro'graphical** *adj*

petrol ('pɛtrəl) *n* any one of various volatile flammable liquid mixtures of hydrocarbons, obtained from petroleum and used as a solvent and a fuel for internal-combustion engines. US and Canad name: **gasoline** [C16 via F from Med. L PETROLEUM]

petrolatum (ˌpɛtrə'leɪtəm) *n* a translucent gelatinous substance obtained from petroleum; used as a lubricant and in medicine as an ointment base. Also called: **petroleum jelly**

petrol bomb *n* **1** a device filled with petrol that bursts into flames on impact ▷ *vb* **petrol-bomb** (*tr*) **2** to attack with petrol bombs

petrol engine *n* an internal-combustion engine that uses petrol as fuel

petroleum (pə'trəʊlɪəm) *n* a dark-coloured thick flammable crude oil occurring in sedimentary rocks, consisting mainly of hydrocarbons. Fractional distillation separates the crude oil into petrol, paraffin, diesel oil, lubricating oil, etc Fuel oil, paraffin wax, asphalt, and carbon black are extracted from the residue [C16 from Med. L, from L *petra* stone + *oleum* oil]

petroleum jelly *n* another name for **petrolatum**

petrology (pɛ'trɒlədʒɪ) *n, pl* **petrologies** the study of the composition, origin, structure, and formation of rocks > **petrological** (ˌpɛtrə'lɒdʒɪkᵊl) *adj* > **pe'trologist** *n*

petrol station *n Brit* another term for **filling station**

Petronius (pɪ'trəʊnɪəs) *n* **Gaius** ('gaɪəs), known as *Petronius Arbiter*. died 66 AD, Roman satirist, supposed author of the *Satyricon*, a picaresque account of the licentiousness of contemporary society

Petropavlovsk (*Russian* pɪtra'pavləfsk) *n* a city in N Kazakhstan on the Ishim River. Pop: 203 500 (1999)

Petrópolis (*Portuguese* pe'trɔpulis) *n* a city in SE Brazil, north of Rio de Janeiro: resort. Pop (urban area): 270 489 (2000)

petrous ('pɛtrəs, 'piː-) *adj anat* denoting the dense part of the temporal bone that surrounds the inner ear [C16 from L *petrōsus* full of rocks] > **petrosal** (pɛ'trəʊsᵊl) *adj*

Petrovsk (*Russian* pɪ'trɔfsk) *n* the former name (until 1921) of **Makhachkala**

Petrozavodsk (*Russian* pɪtrəza'vɔtsk) *n* a city in NW Russia, capital of the Karelian Autonomous Republic, on Lake Onega: developed around ironworks established by Peter the Great in 1703; university (1940). Pop: 282 500 (1999 est)

Petsamo (*Finnish* 'pɛtsɑmɔ) *n* a former territory of N Finland ceded by the Soviet Union to Finland in 1920 and taken back in 1940; now in NW Russia

petticoat ('pɛtɪˌkəʊt) *n* **1** a woman's underskirt **2** *inf* **2a** a humorous or mildly disparaging name for a woman **2b** (*as modifier*): *petticoat politics* [C15 see PETTY, COAT]

pettifogger ('pɛtɪˌfɒgə) *n* **1** a lawyer who conducts unimportant cases, esp one who resorts to trickery **2** any person who quibbles [C16 from PETTY + *fogger*, from ?, perhaps from *Fugger*, a family (C15–16) of G financiers] > **'pettiˌfoggery** *n*

pettifogging ('pɛtɪˌfɒgɪŋ) *adj* **1** petty: *pettifogging details* **2** mean; quibbling: *pettifogging lawyers*

pettish ('pɛtɪʃ) *adj* peevish; petulant [C16 from PET²] > **'pettishly** *adv* > **'pettishness** *n*

petty ('pɛtɪ) *adj* **pettier, pettiest** **1** trivial; trifling: *petty details* **2** narrow-minded, mean: *petty spite* **3** minor or subordinate in rank: *petty officialdom* **4** *law* a variant of **petit** [C14 from OF PETIT] > **'pettily** *adv* > **'pettiness** *n*

petty cash *n* a small cash fund for minor incidental expenses

petty jury *n* a variant of **petit jury**

petty larceny *n* a variant of **petit larceny**

petty officer *n* a noncommissioned officer in a naval service comparable in rank to a sergeant in an army or marine corps

petty sessions *n* (*functioning as sing or pl*) another term for **magistrates' court**

petulant ('pɛtjʊlənt) *adj* irritable, impatient, or sullen in a peevish or capricious way [C16 via OF from L *petulāns* bold, from *petulāre* (unattested) to attack playfully, from *petere* to assail] > **'petulance** *or* **'petulancy** *n* > **'petulantly** *adv*

petunia (pɪ'tjuːnɪə) *n* any plant of a tropical American genus cultivated for their colourful funnel-shaped flowers [C19 via NL from obs. F *petun* variety of tobacco, from Tupi *petyn*]

petuntse (pɪ'tʌntsɪ, -'tʊn-) *n* a fusible mineral used in hard-paste porcelain [C18 from Chinese, from *pe* white + *tun* heap + *tzu* offspring]

Pevsner ('pɛvznə) *n* **1** **Antoine** (ɑ̃twan) 1886–1962, French constructivist sculptor and painter, born in Russia; brother of Naum Gabo **2** Sir **Nikolaus** ('nɪkəlaʊs) 1902–83, British architectural historian, born in Germany: his series *Buildings of England* (1951–74) describes every structure of account in the country

pew (pjuː) *n* **1** (in a church) **1a** one of several long benchlike seats with backs, used by the congregation **1b** an enclosed compartment reserved for the use of a family or other small group **2** *Brit inf* a seat (esp in **take a pew**) [C14 *pywe*, from OF, from L *podium* a balcony, from Gk *podion* supporting structure, from *pous* foot]

pewit *or* **peewit** ('piːwɪt) *n* other names for **lapwing** [C13 imit. of the bird's cry]

pewter ('pjuːtə) *n* **1a** any of various alloys containing tin, lead, and sometimes copper and antimony **1b** (*as modifier*): *pewter ware; a pewter tankard* **2** plate or kitchen utensils made from pewter [C14 from OF *peaultre*, from ?] > **'pewterer** *n*

peyote (peɪ'əʊtɪ, pɪ-) *n* another name for **mescal** (the plant) [Mexican Sp., from Nahuatl *peyotl*]

pF *abbrev for* picofarad

pf. *abbrev for:* **1** perfect **2** Also: **pfg** pfennig **3** preferred

Pfalz (pfalts) *n* the German name for the **Palatinate**

pfennig ('fɛnɪg; *German* 'pfɛnɪç) *n, pl* **pfennigs** *or* **pfennige** (*German* -nɪgə) a former German monetary unit worth one hundredth of a Deutschmark [G: PENNY]

PFI (in Britain) *abbrev for* Private Finance Initiative

Pforzheim (*German* 'pfɔrtshaim) *n* a city in SW Germany, in W Baden-Württemberg: centre of the German watch and jewellery industry. Pop: 117 500 (1999 est)

PG *symbol for* a film certified for viewing by anyone, but

which contains scenes that may be unsuitable for children, for whom parental guidance is necessary [c20 from abbrev of *parental guidance*]
pg. *abbrev for* page
Pg. *abbrev for:* **1** Portugal **2** Portuguese
PGR *abbrev for* psychogalvanic response
pH *n* potential of hydrogen; a measure of the acidity or alkalinity of a solution. Pure water has a pH of 7, acid solutions have a pH less than 7, and alkaline solutions a pH greater than 7
phacelia (fæ'siːlɪə) *n* any of a genus of N American plants having clusters of blue flowers [NL from Gk *phakelos* a cluster]
Phaeacian (fiː'eɪʃən) *n Greek myth* one of a race of people inhabiting the island of Scheria visited by Odysseus on his way home from the Trojan War
Phaedra ('fiːdrə) *n Greek myth* the wife of Theseus, who falsely accused her stepson Hippolytus of raping her because he spurned her amorous advances
Phaedrus ('fiːdrəs) *n* ?15 BC–?50 AD, Roman author of five books of Latin verse fables, based chiefly on Aesop
Phaëthon ('feɪəθən) *n Greek myth* the son of Helios (the sun god) who borrowed his father's chariot and nearly set the earth on fire by approaching too close to it. Zeus averted the catastrophe by striking him down with a thunderbolt
phaeton ('feɪtᵊn) *n* a light four-wheeled horse-drawn carriage with or without a top [c18 from PHAËTHON]
-phage *n combining form* indicating something that eats or consumes something specified: *bacteriophage* [from Gk *-phagos;* see PHAGO-] > **-phagous** *adj combining form*
phage (feɪdʒ) *n* short for **bacteriophage**
phago- *or before a vowel* **phag-** *combining form* eating, consuming, or destroying: *phagocyte* [from Gk *phagein* to consume]
phagocyte ('fægəˌsaɪt) *n* a cell or protozoan that engulfs particles, such as microorganisms > **phagocytic** (ˌfægə'sɪtɪk) *adj*
phagocytosis (ˌfægəsaɪ'təʊsɪs) *n* the process by which a cell, such as a white blood cell, ingests microorganisms, other cells, etc
-phagy *or* **-phagia** *n combining form* indicating an eating or devouring: *anthropophagy* [from Gk *-phagia;* see PHAGO-]
phalange ('fælændʒ) *n, pl* **phalanges** (fæ'lændʒiːz) *anat* another name for **phalanx** (sense 4) [c16 via F, ult. from Gk PHALANX]
phalangeal (fə'lændʒɪəl) *adj anat* of or relating to a phalanx or phalanges
phalanger (fə'lændʒə) *n* any of various Australasian arboreal marsupials having dense fur and a long tail. Also called (Austral and NZ): **possum** See also **flying phalanger** [c18 via NL from Gk *phalaggion* spider's web, referring to its webbed hind toes]
phalanx ('fælæŋks) *n, pl* **phalanxes** *or* **phalanges** (fæ'lændʒiːz) **1** an ancient Greek and Macedonian battle formation of hoplites presenting long spears from behind a wall of overlapping shields **2** any closely ranked unit or mass of people: *the police formed a phalanx to protect the embassy* **3** a number of people united for a common purpose **4** *anat* any of the bones of the fingers or toes **5** *bot* a bundle of stamens [c16 via L from Gk: infantry formation in close ranks, bone of finger or toe]
phalarope ('fæləˌrəʊp) *n* any of a family of aquatic shore birds of northern oceans and lakes, having a long slender bill and lobed toes [c18 via F from NL *Phalaropus,* from Gk *phalaris* coot + *pous* foot]
phallic ('fælɪk) *adj* **1** of, relating to, or resembling a phallus: *a phallic symbol* **2** *psychoanal* relating to a stage of psychosexual development during which a male child's interest is concentrated on the genital organs **3** of or relating to phallicism
phallicism ('fælɪˌsɪzəm) *or* **phallism** *n* the worship or veneration of the phallus
phallus ('fæləs) *n, pl* **phalluses** *or* **phalli** (-laɪ) **1** another word for **penis** **2** an image of the male sexual organ, esp as a symbol of reproductive power [c17 via LL from Gk *phallos*]
-phane *n combining form* indicating something resembling a specified substance: *cellophane* [from Gk *phainein* to shine, appear]
phanerogam ('fænərəʊˌgæm) *n* any plant of a former major division which included all seed-bearing plants; a former name for **spermatophyte** [c19 from NL *phanerogamus,* from Gk *phaneros* visible + *gamos* marriage] > ˌ**phanero'gamic** *or* **phanerogamous** (ˌfænə'rɒgəməs) *adj*
phantasm ('fæntæzəm) *n* **1** a phantom **2** an illusory perception of an object, person, etc [c13 from OF *fantasme,* from L *phantasma,* from Gk] > **phan'tasmal** *or* **phan'tasmic** *adj*
phantasmagoria (ˌfæntæzmə'gɔːrɪə) *or* **phantasmagory** (fæn'tæzməgərɪ) *n* **1** *psychol* a shifting medley of real or imagined figures, as in a dream **2** *films* a sequence of pictures made to vary in size rapidly **3** a shifting scene composed of different elements [c19 prob. from F, from PHANTASM + *-agorie,* ?from Gk *ageirein* to gather together] > **phantasmagoric** (ˌfæntæzmə'gɒrɪk) *or* ˌ**phantasma'gorical** *adj*
phantasy ('fæntəsɪ) *n, pl* **phantasies** an archaic spelling of **fantasy**
phantom ('fæntəm) *n* **1a** an apparition or spectre **1b** (*as modifier*): *a phantom army marching through the sky* **2** the visible representation of something abstract, esp as in a dream or hallucination: *phantoms of evil haunted his sleep* **3** something apparently unpleasant or horrific that has no material form [c13 from OF *fantosme,* from L *phantasma*]
phantom limb *n* the illusion that a limb still exists following its amputation, sometimes with the sensation of pain (**phantom limb pain**)
phantom pregnancy *n* the occurrence of signs of pregnancy, such as enlarged abdomen and absence of menstruation, when no embryo is present, due to hormonal imbalance. Also called: **false pregnancy**
-phany *n combining form* indicating a manifestation: *theophany* [from Gk *-phania,* from *phainein* to show] > **-phanous** *adj combining form*
phar., Phar., pharm., *or* **Pharm.** *abbrev for:* **1** pharmaceutical **2** pharmacist **3** pharmacopoeia **4** pharmacy
Pharaoh ('fɛərəʊ) *n* the title of the ancient Egyptian kings [OE *Pharaon,* via L, Gk, & Heb., ult. from Egyptian *pr-'o* great house] > **Pharaonic** (fɛə'rɒnɪk) *adj*
Pharisaic (ˌfærɪ'seɪɪk) *or* **Pharisaical** *adj* **1** *Judaism* of, relating to, or characteristic of the Pharisees or Pharisaism **2** (*often not cap*) righteously hypocritical > ˌ**Phari'saically** *adv*
Pharisaism ('færɪseɪˌɪzəm) *or* **Phariseeism** ('færɪsiːˌɪzəm) *n* **1** *Judaism* the tenets and customs of the Pharisees **2** (*often not cap*) observance of the external forms of religion without genuine belief; hypocrisy
Pharisee ('færɪˌsiː) *n* **1** a member of an ancient Jewish sect teaching strict observance of Jewish traditions **2** (*often not cap*) a self-righteous or hypocritical person [OE *Farīsēus,* ult. from Aramaic *perīshāiyā,* pl. of *perīsh* separated]
pharma ('fɑːmə) *n* pharmaceutical companies when considered together as an industry
pharmaceutical (ˌfɑːmə'sjuːtɪkᵊl) *or* (*less commonly*) **pharmaceutic** *adj* of or relating to drugs or pharmacy: *the pharmaceutical industry* [c17 from LL *pharmaceuticus,* from Gk *pharmakeus* purveyor of drugs; see PHARMACY] > ˌ**pharma'ceutically** *adv*
pharmaceutics (ˌfɑːmə'sjuːtɪks) *n* **1** (*functioning as sing*) another term for **pharmacy** (sense 1) **2** (*functioning as pl*) pharmaceutical remedies

Pp

pharmacist ('fɑːməsɪst) *n* a person qualified to prepare and dispense drugs

pharmaco- *combining form* indicating drugs: *pharmacology* [from Gk *pharmakon* drug]

pharmacognosy (ˌfɑːməˈkɒgnəsɪ) *n* the study of crude drugs of plant and animal origin [C19 from PHARMACO- + *gnosy*, from Gk *gnosis* knowledge] > ˌ**pharmaˈcognosist** *n*

pharmacology (ˌfɑːməˈkɒlədʒɪ) *n* the science or study of drugs, including their characteristics, action, and uses > **pharmacological** (ˌfɑːməkəˈlɒdʒɪkᵊl) *adj* > ˌ**pharmacoˈlogically** *adv* > ˌ**pharmaˈcologist** *n*
▷ www.pharmacy.org
▷ www.pharmweb.net
▷ www.medbioworld.com/home/lists/medications.html

pharmacopoeia *or US (sometimes)* **pharmacopeia** (ˌfɑːməkəˈpiːə) *n* an authoritative book containing a list of medicinal drugs with their uses, preparation, dosages, formulas, etc [C17 via NL from Gk *pharmakopoiia* art of preparing drugs, from PHARMACO- + *-poiia*, from *poiein* to make] > ˌ**pharmacoˈpoeial** *adj*

pharmacy ('fɑːməsɪ) *n, pl* **pharmacies** **1** Also: **pharmaceutics** the practice or art of preparing and dispensing drugs **2** a dispensary [C14 from Med. L *pharmacia*, from Gk *pharmakeia* making of drugs, from *pharmakon* drug]

pharming ('fɑːmɪŋ) *n* the practice of rearing or growing genetically-modified animals or plants in order to develop pharmaceutical products [C20 blend of PHARMACEUTICAL + FARMING]

pharos ('fɛərɒs) *n* any marine lighthouse or beacon [C16 after a large Hellenistic lighthouse on an island off Alexandria in Egypt]

Pharsalus (fɑːˈseɪləs) *n* an ancient town in Thessaly in N Greece. Several major battles were fought nearby, including Caesar's victory over Pompey (48 BC)

pharyngeal (ˌfærɪnˈdʒiːəl) *or* **pharyngal** (fəˈrɪŋgᵊl) *adj* **1** of, relating to, or situated in or near the pharynx **2** *phonetics* pronounced with an articulation in or constriction of the pharynx [C19 from NL *pharyngeus*; see PHARYNX]

pharyngitis (ˌfærɪnˈdʒaɪtɪs) *n* inflammation of the pharynx

pharynx ('færɪŋks) *n, pl* **pharynges** (fæˈrɪndʒiːz) *or* **pharynxes** the part of the alimentary canal between the mouth and the oesophagus [C17 via NL from Gk *pharunx* throat]

phascogale ('fæskəgeɪl, ˌfæsˈkaːgəli) *n Austral* another name for **tuan²**

phase (feɪz) *n* **1** any distinct or characteristic period or stage in a sequence of events: *there were two phases to the resolution* **2** *astron* one of the recurring shapes of the portion of the moon or an inferior planet illuminated by the sun **3** *physics* the fraction of a cycle of a periodic quantity that has been completed at a specific reference time, expressed as an angle **4** *physics* a particular stage in a periodic process or phenomenon **5** **in phase** (of two waveforms) reaching corresponding phases at the same time **6** **out of phase** (of two waveforms) not in phase **7** *chem* a distinct state of matter characterized by homogeneous composition and properties and the possession of a clearly defined boundary **8** *zool* a variation in the normal form of an animal, esp a colour variation, brought about by seasonal or geographical change ▷ *vb* **phases, phasing, phased** (*tr*) **9** (*often passive*) to execute, arrange, or introduce gradually or in stages: *the withdrawal was phased over several months* **10** (sometimes foll by *with*) to cause (a part, process, etc) to function or coincide with (another part, etc): *he tried to phase the intake and output of the machine; he phased the intake with the output* **11** *chiefly US* to arrange (processes, goods, etc) to be supplied or executed when required [C19 from NL *phases*, pl. of *phasis*, from Gk: aspect] > '**phasic** *adj*

phase in *vb* (*tr, adv*) to introduce in a gradual or cautious manner: *the legislation was phased in over two years*

phase modulation *n* a type of modulation in which the phase of a radio carrier wave is varied by an amount proportional to the instantaneous amplitude of the modulating signal

phase out *vb* (*tr, adv*) **1** to discontinue or withdraw gradually ▷ *n* **phase-out** **2** *chiefly US* the action or an instance of phasing out: *a phase-out of conventional forces*

phase rule *n* the principle that in any system in equilibrium the number of degrees of freedom is equal to the number of components less the number of phases plus two

-phasia *n combining form* indicating speech disorder of a specified kind: *aphasia* [from Gk, from *phanai* to speak] > **-phasic** *adj and n combining form*

phat (fæt) *adj sl* terrific; superb [C20 from Black slang, a corruption of FAT]

phatic ('fætɪk) *adj* (of speech) used to establish social contact and to express sociability rather than specific meaning [C20 from Gk *phat(os)* spoken + -IC]

PhD *abbrev for* Doctor of Philosophy. Also: **DPhil**

pheasant ('fɛzᵊnt) *n* **1** any of various long-tailed gallinaceous birds, having a brightly-coloured plumage in the male: native to Asia but introduced elsewhere **2** any of various other related birds, including the quails and partridges **3** *US & Canad* any of several other gallinaceous birds, esp the ruffed grouse [C13 from OF *fesan*, from L *phāsiānus*, from Gk *phasianos ornis* Phasian bird, after the River *Phasis*, in Colchis]

Phebe ('fiːbɪ) *n* a variant spelling of **Phoebe**

Pheidippides *or* **Philippides** (faɪˈdɪpɪˌdiːz) *n* 5th century BC. Athenian athlete, who ran to Sparta to seek help against the Persians before the Battle of Marathon (490 BC)

phellem ('fɛləm) *n bot* the technical name for **cork** (sense 4) [C20 from Gk *phellos* cork + PHLOEM]

phenacetin (fɪˈnæsɪtɪn) *n* a white crystalline solid formerly used in medicine to relieve pain and fever. Also called: **acetophenetidin** [C19 from PHENO- + ACETYL + -IN]

phenix ('fiːnɪks) *n* a US spelling of **phoenix**

pheno- *or before a vowel* **phen-** *combining form* **1** showing or manifesting: *phenotype* **2** indicating that a molecule contains benzene rings: *phenobarbitone* [from Gk *phaino-* shining, from *phainein* to show; its use in a chemical sense is exemplified in *phenol*, so called because orig. prepared from illuminating gas]

phenobarbital (ˌfiːnəʊˈbɑːbɪˌtəʊn) *or* **phenobarbital** (ˌfiːnəʊˈbɑːbɪtᵊl) *n* a white crystalline derivative of barbituric acid used as a sedative for treating insomnia and as an anticonvulsant in epilepsy

phenocryst ('fiːnəˌkrɪst, 'fɛn-) *n* any of several large crystals in igneous rocks such as porphyry [C19 from PHENO- (shining) + CRYSTAL]

phenol ('fiːnɒl) *n* **1** Also called: **carbolic acid** a white crystalline derivative of benzene, used as an antiseptic and disinfectant and in the manufacture of resins, explosives, and pharmaceuticals. Formula: C_6H_5OH **2** *chem* any of a class of organic compounds whose molecules contain one or more hydroxyl groups bound directly to a carbon atom in an aromatic ring > **pheˈnolic** *adj*

phenolic resin *n* any one of a class of resins derived from phenol, used in paints, adhesives, and as thermosetting plastics

phenology (fɪˈnɒlədʒɪ) *n* the study of recurring phenomena, such as animal migration, esp as influenced by climatic conditions [C19 from PHENO(MENON) + -LOGY] > **phenological** (ˌfiːnəˈlɒdʒɪkᵊl) *adj* > **pheˈnologist** *n*

phenolphthalein (ˌfiːnɒlˈθeɪliːn, -lɪɪn, -ˈθæl-) *n* a colourless crystalline compound used in medicine as a laxative and in chemistry as an indicator [from PHENO-

+ *phthal-*, short form of NAPHTHALENE + -IN]

phenomena (fɪˈnɒmɪnə) *n* a plural of **phenomenon**

phenomenal (fɪˈnɒmɪnᵊl) *adj* **1** of or relating to a phenomenon **2** extraordinary; outstanding; remarkable: *a phenomenal achievement* **3** *philosophy* known or perceived by the senses rather than the mind > **pheˈnomenally** *adv*

phenomenalism (fɪˈnɒmɪnəˌlɪzəm) *n philosophy* the doctrine that statements about physical objects and the external world can be analysed in terms of possible or actual experiences, and that entities, such as physical objects, are only mental constructions out of phenomenal appearances > **pheˈnomenalist** *n, adj*

phenomenology (fɪˌnɒmɪˈnɒlədʒɪ) *n philosophy* **1** the movement that concentrates on the detailed description of conscious experience **2** the science of phenomena as opposed to the science of being > **phenomenological** (fɪˌnɒmɪnəˈlɒdʒɪkᵊl) *adj*

phenomenon (fɪˈnɒmɪnən) *n, pl* **phenomena** (-ɪnə) *or* **phenomenons** **1** anything that can be perceived as an occurrence or fact by the senses **2** any remarkable occurrence or person **3** *philosophy* **3a** the object of perception, experience, etc **3b** (in the writings of Kant) a thing as it appears, as distinguished from its real nature as a thing-in-itself [c16 via LL from Gk *phainomenon*, from *phainesthai* to appear, from *phainein* to show]

USAGE Although *phenomena* is often treated as a singular, correct usage is to employ *phenomenon* with a singular construction and *phenomena* with a plural: *that is an interesting phenomenon* (not *phenomena*); *several new phenomena were recorded in his notes*

phenotype (ˈfiːnəʊˌtaɪp) *n* the physical and biochemical characteristics of an organism as determined by the interaction of its genetic constitution and the environment > **phenotypic** (ˌfiːnəʊˈtɪpɪk) *or* **ˌphenoˈtypical** *adj* > **ˌphenoˈtypically** *adv*

phenyl (ˈfiːnaɪl, ˈfɛnɪl) *n* (*modifier*) of, containing, or consisting of the monovalent group C_6H_5, derived from benzene: *a phenyl group*

phenylalanine (ˌfiːnaɪlˈæləˌniːn) *n* an essential amino acid; a component of proteins

phenylbutazone (ˌfiːnaɪlˈbjuːtəˌzəʊn) *n* an anti-inflammatory drug used in the treatment of rheumatic diseases; it has been largely superseded by other NSAIDS [c20 from *(dioxodi)phenylbut(ylpyr)azo(lidi)ne*]

phenylethylamine (ˌfiːnaɪlˌɛθɪlˈæmɪn) *n* a chemical produced by the body that has an antidepressant effect

phenylketonuria (ˌfiːnaɪlˌkiːtəˈnjʊərɪə) *n* a congenital metabolic disorder characterized by the abnormal accumulation of phenylalanine in the body fluids, resulting in mental deficiency [c20 NL; see PHENYL, KETONE, -URIA]

pheromone (ˈfɛrəˌməʊn) *n* a chemical substance, secreted externally by certain animals, such as insects, affecting the behaviour of other animals of the same species [c20 *phero-*, from Gk *pherein* to bear + (HOR)MONE]

phew (fjuː) *interj* an exclamation of relief, surprise, disbelief, weariness, etc

phi (faɪ) *n, pl* **phis** the 21st letter in the Greek alphabet, Φ, ϕ

phial (ˈfaɪəl) *n* a small bottle for liquids, etc; vial [c14 from OF *fiole*, from L *phiola* saucer, from Gk *phialē* wide shallow vessel]

Phi Beta Kappa (ˈfaɪ ˈbeɪtə ˈkæpə, ˈbiːtə) *n* (in the US) **1** a national honorary society, founded in 1776, membership of which is based on high academic ability **2** a member of this society [from the initials of the Gk motto *philosophia biou kubernētēs* philosophy the guide of life]

Phidias (ˈfɪdɪˌæs) *n* 5th century BC, Greek sculptor, regarded as one of the greatest of sculptors. He executed the sculptures of the Parthenon and the colossal statue of Zeus at Olympia, one of the Seven Wonders of the World: neither survives in the original

Phidippides (faɪˈdɪpɪˌdiːz) *n* a variant spelling of **Pheidippides**

phil. *abbrev for:* **1** philharmonic **2** philosophy

Phil. *abbrev for:* **1** Philadelphia **2** *Bible* Philippians **3** Philippines **4** Philharmonic

Philadelphia (ˌfɪləˈdɛlfɪə) *n* a city and port in SE Pennsylvania, at the confluence of the Delaware and Schuylkill Rivers: the fourth largest city in the US; founded by Quakers in 1682; cultural and financial centre of the American colonies and the federal capital (1790–1800); scene of the Continental Congresses (1774–83) and the signing of the Declaration of Independence (1776). Pop: 1 517 550 (2000)

philadelphus (ˌfɪləˈdɛlfəs) *n* any of a N temperate genus of shrubs cultivated for their strongly scented showy flowers. See also **mock orange** (sense 1) [c19 NL, from Gk *philadelphon* mock orange, lit.: loving one's brother]

Philae (ˈfaɪliː) *n* an island in Upper Egypt, in the Nile north of the Aswan Dam: of religious importance in ancient times; almost submerged since the raising of the level of the dam

philander (fɪˈlændə) *vb* (*intr*; *often foll by* with) (of a man) to flirt with women [c17 from Gk *philandros* fond of men, used as a name for a lover in literary works] > **phiˈlanderer** *n*

philanthropic (ˌfɪlənˈθrɒpɪk) *or* **philanthropical** *adj* showing concern for humanity, esp by performing charitable actions, donating money, etc > **ˌphilanˈthropically** *adv*

philanthropy (fɪˈlænθrəpɪ) *n, pl* **philanthropies** **1** the practice of performing charitable or benevolent actions **2** love of mankind in general [c17 from LL *philanthrōpia*, from Gk: love of mankind, from *philos* loving + *anthrōpos* man] > **phiˈlanthropist** *or* **philanthrope** (ˈfɪlənˌθrəʊp) *n*

philately (fɪˈlætəlɪ) *n* the collection and study of postage stamps [c19 from F *philatélie*, from PHILO- + Gk *ateleia* exemption from charges (here referring to stamps)] > **philatelic** (ˌfɪləˈtɛlɪk) *adj* > **ˌphilaˈtelically** *adv* > **phiˈlatelist** *n*

▷ www.philately.com

Philby (ˈfɪlbɪ) *n* **1** **Harold Adrian Russell,** known as *Kim.* 1912–88, English double agent; defected to the Soviet Union (1963) **2** his father, **H(arry) Saint John** (**Bridger**) 1885–1960, British explorer, civil servant, and Arabist

-phile *or* **-phil** *n combining form* indicating a person or thing having a fondness for something specified: *bibliophile* [from Gk *philos* loving]

Philem. *Bible abbrev for* Philemon

Philemon¹ (faɪˈliːmɒn) *n New Testament* **1** a Christian of Colossae whose escaped slave came to meet Paul **2** the book (in full **The Epistle of Paul the Apostle to Philemon**), asking Philemon to forgive the slave for escaping

Philemon² (faɪˈliːmɒn) *n Greek myth* a poor Phrygian, who with his wife Baucis offered hospitality to the disguised Zeus and Hermes

philharmonic (ˌfɪlhɑːˈmɒnɪk, ˌfɪlə-) *adj* **1** fond of music **2** (*cap when part of a name*) denoting an orchestra, choir, society, etc, devoted to music ▷ *n* **3** (*cap when part of a name*) a specific philharmonic choir, orchestra, or society [c18 from F *philharmonique*, from It. *filarmonico* music-loving]

philhellene (fɪlˈhɛliːn) *n* **1** a lover of Greece and Greek culture **2** *European history* a supporter of the cause of Greek national independence > **philhellenic** (ˌfɪlhɛˈliːnɪk) *adj*

-philia *n combining form* **1** indicating a tendency towards: *haemophilia* **2** indicating an abnormal liking for: *necrophilia* [from Gk *philos* loving] > **-philiac** *n combining form* > **-philous** *or* **-philic** *adj combining form*

Pp

philibeg ('fɪlɪˌbɛg) *n* a variant spelling of **filibeg**

Philip ('fɪlɪp) *n* **1** *New Testament* **1a** an apostle from Bethsaida (John 1:43–51; 6:5–7; 12:21; 14:8) **1b** Also called: **Philip the Evangelist** one of the seven deacons appointed by the early Church **1c** Also called: **Philip the Tetrarch** one of the sons of Herod the Great, who was ruler of part of former Judaea (4 BC–34 AD) (Luke 3:1) **2** **King,** American Indian name *Metacomet*. died 1676, American Indian chief, the son of Massasoit. He waged King Philip's War against the colonists of New England (1675–76) and was killed in battle **3** **Prince** See (Duke of) **Edinburgh**

Philip II *n* **1** 382–336 BC, king of Macedonia (359–336); the father of Alexander the Great **2** known as *Philip Augustus*. 1165–1223, Capetian king of France (1180–1223); set out on the Third Crusade with Richard I of England (1190) **3** 1527–98, king of Spain (1556–98) and, as Philip I, king of Portugal (1580–98); the husband of Mary I of England (1554–58). He championed the Counter-Reformation, sending the Armada against England (1588)

Philip IV *n* known as *Philip the Fair*. 1268–1314, king of France (1285–1314): he challenged the power of the papacy, obtaining the elevation of Clement V as pope residing at Avignon (the beginning of the Babylonian captivity of the papacy)

Philip V *n* 1683–1746, king of Spain (1700–46) and founder of the Bourbon dynasty in Spain. His accession began the War of Spanish Succession (1701–13)

Philip VI *n* 1293–1350, first Valois king of France (1328–50). Edward III of England claimed his throne, which with other disputes led to the beginning of the Hundred Years' War (1337)

Philippeville ('fɪlɪpˌvɪl) *n* the former name of **Skikda**

Philippi (fɪ'lɪpaɪ, 'fɪlɪ-) *n* an ancient city in NE Macedonia: scene of the victory of Antony and Octavian over Brutus and Cassius (42 BC) > **Phi'lippian** *adj*

philippic (fɪ'lɪpɪk) *n* a bitter or impassioned speech of denunciation; invective [C16 after the orations of Demosthenes, against PHILIP of Macedon]

Philippine ('fɪlɪˌpiːn) *n, adj* another word for **Filipino**

Philippines ('fɪlɪˌpiːnz, ˌfɪlɪ'piːnz) *n* (*functioning as singular*) **Republic of the** a republic in SE Asia, occupying an archipelago of about 7100 islands (including Luzon, Mindanao, Samar, and Negros): became a Spanish colony in 1571 but ceded to the US in 1898 after the Spanish-American War; gained independence in 1946. The islands are generally mountainous and volcanic. Official languages: Filipino, based on Tagalog, and English. Religion: Roman Catholic majority. Currency: peso. Capital: Manila. Pop: 78 609 000 (2001 est). Area: 300 076 sq km (115 860 sq miles). Related word: **Filipino**
▷ www.gov.ph
▷ www.tourism.gov.ph

Philippine Sea *n* part of the NW Pacific Ocean, east and north of the Philippines

Philippopolis (ˌfɪlɪ'pɒpəlɪs) *n* transliteration of the Greek name for **Plovdiv**

Philip the Good *n* 1396–1467, duke of Burgundy (1419–67), under whose rule Burgundy was one of the most powerful states in Europe

Philistia (fɪ'lɪstɪə) *n* an ancient country on the coast of SW Palestine > **Phi'listian** *adj*

Philistine ('fɪlɪˌstaɪn) *n* **1** a person who is hostile towards culture, the arts, etc; a smug boorish person **2** a member of the non-Semitic people who inhabited ancient Philistia ▷ *adj* **3** (*sometimes not cap*) boorishly uncultured **4** of or relating to the ancient Philistines > **Philistinism** ('fɪlɪstɪˌnɪzəm) *n*

Phillip ('fɪlɪp) *n* **Arthur** 1738–1814, English naval commander; captain general of the First Fleet, which carried convicts from Portsmouth to Sydney Cove, Australia, where he founded New South Wales

phillumenist (fɪ'ljuːmənɪst, -'luː-) *n* a person who collects matchbox labels [C20 from PHILO- + L *lumen* light + -IST]

philo- *or before a vowel* **phil-** *combining form* indicating a love of: *philology; philanthropic* [from Gk *philos* loving]

Philoctetes (ˌfɪlɒk'tiːtiːz, fɪ'lɒktɪˌtiːz) *n* *Greek myth* a hero of the Trojan War, in which he killed Paris with the bow and poisoned arrows given to him by Hercules

philodendron (ˌfɪlə'dɛndrən) *n, pl* **philodendrons** *or* **philodendra** (-drə) an evergreen climbing plant of a tropical American genus: cultivated as a house plant [C19 NL from Gk: lover of trees]

philogyny (fɪ'lɒdʒɪnɪ) *n* *rare* fondness for women [C17 from Gk *philogunia*, from PHILO- + *gunē* woman] > **phi'logynist** *n*

Philo Judaeus ('faɪləʊ dʒuː'diːəs) *n* ?20 BC–?50 AD, Jewish philosopher, born in Alexandria. He sought to reconcile Judaism with Greek philosophy

philology (fɪ'lɒlədʒɪ) *n* **1** comparative and historical linguistics **2** the scientific analysis of written records and literary texts **3** (no longer in scholarly use) the study of literature [C17 from L *philologia*, from Gk: love of language] > **philological** (ˌfɪlə'lɒdʒɪkᵊl) *adj* > **ˌphilo'logically** *adv* > **phi'lologist** *or* (*less commonly*) **phi'lologer** *n*
▷ www.britac.ac.uk/portal/

philomel ('fɪləˌmɛl) *or* **philomela** (ˌfɪləʊ'miːlə) *n* poetic names for a **nightingale** [C14 *philomene*, via Med. L from L *philomēla*, from Gk]

Philomela (ˌfɪləʊ'miːlə) *n* *Greek myth* an Athenian princess, who was raped and had her tongue cut out by her brother-in-law Tereus, and subsequently was transformed into a nightingale. See **Procne**

philoprogenitive (ˌfɪləʊprəʊ'dʒɛnɪtɪv) *adj* *rare* **1** fond of children **2** producing many offspring

philos. *abbrev for:* **1** philosopher **2** philosophical

philosopher (fɪ'lɒsəfə) *n* **1** a student, teacher, or devotee of philosophy **2** a person of philosophical temperament, esp one who is patient, wise, and stoical **3** (formerly) an alchemist or devotee of occult science

philosopher's stone *n* a stone or substance thought by alchemists to be capable of transmuting base metals into gold

philosophical (ˌfɪlə'sɒfɪkᵊl) *or* **philosophic** *adj* **1** of or relating to philosophy or philosophers **2** reasonable, wise, or learned **3** calm and stoical, esp in the face of difficulties or disappointments > **ˌphilo'sophically** *adv*

philosophical analysis *n* a philosophical method in which language and experience are analysed in an attempt to provide new insights into various philosophical problems

philosophize *or* **philosophise** (fɪ'lɒsəˌfaɪz) *vb* **philosophizes, philosophizing, philosophized** *or* **philosophises, philosophising, philosophised** **1** (*intr*) to make philosophical pronouncements and speculations **2** (*tr*) to explain philosophically > **phi'losoˌphizer** *or* **phi'losoˌphiser** *n*

philosophy (fɪ'lɒsəfɪ) *n, pl* **philosophies** **1** the academic discipline concerned with making explicit the nature and significance of ordinary and scientific beliefs and investigating the intelligibility of concepts by means of rational argument concerning their presuppositions, implications, and interrelationships **2** the particular doctrines relating to these issues of a specific individual or school: *the philosophy of Descartes* **3** the basic principles of a discipline: *the philosophy of law* **4** any system of belief, values, or tenets **5** a personal outlook or viewpoint **6** serenity of temper [C13 from OF *filosofie*, from L *philosophia*, from Gk, from *philosophos* lover of wisdom]
▷ http://users.ox.ac.uk/~worc0337/philindex.html
▷ www.philosophypages.com
▷ www.utm.edu/research/iep/
▷ http://n-e-x-u-s.com/philosophy/

-philous *or* **-philic** *adj combining form* indicating love of or fondness for: *heliophilous* [from L *-philus*, from Gk *-philos*]

philtre *or US* **philter** ('fɪltə) *n* a drink supposed to arouse desire [c16 from L *philtrum*, from Gk *philtron* love potion, from *philos* loving]

phimosis (faɪ'məʊsɪs) *n* abnormal tightness of the foreskin, preventing its being retracted [c17 via NL from Gk: a muzzling]

phiz (fɪz) *n sl, chiefly Brit* the face or a facial expression. Also called: **phizog** (fɪ'zɒg) [c17 colloquial shortening of PHYSIOGNOMY]

Phiz (fɪz) *n* real name *Hablot Knight Browne.* 1815–82, English painter, noted for his illustrations for Dickens' novels

phlebitis (flɪ'baɪtɪs) *n* inflammation of a vein [c19 via NL from Gk] > **phlebitic** (flɪ'bɪtɪk) *adj*

phlebo- *or before a vowel* **phleb-** *combining form* indicating a vein: *phlebotomy* [from Gk *phleps, phleb-* vein]

phlebotomy (flɪ'bɒtəmɪ) *n, pl* **phlebotomies** surgical incision into a vein [c14 from OF *flebothomie*, from LL *phlebotomia*, from Gk]

Phlegethon ('flɛgɪ,θɒn) *n Greek myth* a river of fire in Hades [c14 from Gk, lit.: blazing, from *phlegethein* to flame, blaze]

phlegm (flɛm) *n* **1** the viscid mucus secreted by the walls of the respiratory tract **2** *arch* one of the four bodily humours **3** apathy; stolidity **4** imperturbability; coolness [c14 from OF *fleume*, from LL *phlegma*, from Gk: inflammation, from *phlegein* to burn] > **'phlegmy** *adj*

phlegmatic (flɛg'mætɪk) *or* **phlegmatical** *adj* **1** having a stolid or unemotional disposition **2** not easily excited > **phleg'matically** *adv*

phloem ('fləʊɛm) *n* tissue in higher plants that conducts synthesized food substances to all parts of the plant [c19 via G from Gk *phloos* bark]

phlogiston (flɒ'dʒɪstɒn, -tən) *n chem* a hypothetical substance formerly thought to be present in all combustible materials [c18 via NL from Gk, from *phlogizein* to set alight]

phlox (flɒks) *n, pl* **phlox** *or* **phloxes** any of a chiefly North American genus of plants cultivated for their clusters of white, red, or purple flowers [c18 via L from Gk: a plant of glowing colour, lit.: flame]

phlyctena (flɪk'ti:nə) *n, pl* **phlyctenae** (-ni:) *pathol* a small blister, vesicle, or pustule [c17 via NL from Gk *phluktaina*, from *phluzein* to swell]

Phnom Penh *or* **Pnom Penh** (,nɒm 'pɛn) *n* the capital of Cambodia, a port in the south at the confluence of the Mekong and Tonle Sap Rivers: capital of the country since 1865; university (1960). Pop: 938 000 (1999 est)

-phobe *n combining form* indicating one that fears or hates: *xenophobe* [from Gk *-phobos* fearing] > **-phobic** *adj combining form*

phobia ('fəʊbɪə) *n psychiatry* an abnormal intense and irrational fear of a given situation, organism, or object [c19 from Gk *phobos* fear] > **'phobic** *adj, n*

-phobia *n combining form* indicating an extreme abnormal fear of or aversion to: *acrophobia; claustrophobia* [via L from Gk, from *phobos* fear] > **-phobic** *adj combining form*

Phocaea (fəʊ'si:ə) *n* an ancient port in Asia Minor, the northernmost of Ionian cities on the W coast of Asia Minor: an important maritime state (about 1000–600 BC)

Phocis ('fəʊsɪs) *n* an ancient district of central Greece, on the Gulf of Corinth: site of the Delphic oracle

phocomelia (,fəʊkəʊ'mi:lɪə) *n* a congenital deformity characterized esp by short stubby hands or feet attached close to the body [c19 via NL from Gk *phōkē* a seal + *melos* a limb]

phoebe ('fi:bɪ) *n* any of several greyish-brown North American flycatchers [c19 imit.]

Phoebe *or* **Phebe** ('fi:bɪ) *n* **1** *classical myth* a Titaness, who later became identified with Artemis (Diana) as goddess of the moon **2** *poetic* a personification of the moon

Phoebus ('fi:bəs) *n* **1** Also called: **Phoebus Apollo** *Greek myth* Apollo as the sun god **2** *poetic* a personification of the sun [c14 via L from Gk *Phoibos* bright; related to *phaos* light]

Phoenicia (fə'nɪʃɪə, -'ni:-) *n* an ancient maritime country extending from the Mediterranean Sea to the Lebanon Mountains, now occupied by the coastal regions of Lebanon and parts of Syria and Israel: consisted of a group of city-states, at their height between about 1200 and 1000 BC, that were leading traders of the ancient world

Phoenician (fə'nɪʃən, -'ni:ʃɪən) *n* **1** a member of an ancient Semitic people of NW Syria **2** the extinct language of this people ▷ *adj* **3** of Phoenicia, the Phoenicians, or their language

▷ www.fordham.edu/halsall/ancient/430phoenicia.html

phoenix *or US* **phenix** ('fi:nɪks) *n* **1** a legendary Arabian bird said to set fire to itself and rise anew from the ashes every 500 years **2** a person or thing of surpassing beauty or quality [OE *fenix*, via L from Gk *phoinix*]

Phoenix ('fi:nɪks) *n* a city in central Arizona, capital city of the state, on the Salt River. Pop: 1 321 045 (1996 est)

Phoenix Islands *pl n* a group of eight coral islands in the central Pacific: administratively part of Kiribati. Area: 28 sq km (11 sq miles)

Phomvihane ('pɒmvɪhɑ:n) *n* **Kaysone** ('kaɪsɒn) 1920–92, Laotian Communist statesman; prime minister of Laos (1975–91); president (1991–92)

phon (fɒn) *n* a unit of loudness that measures the intensity of a sound by the number of decibels it is above a reference tone [c20 via G from Gk *phōnē* sound]

phonate (fəʊ'neɪt) *vb* **phonates, phonating, phonated** (*intr*) to articulate speech sounds, esp voiced speech sounds [c19 from Gk *phōnē* voice] > **pho'nation** *n*

phone[1] (fəʊn) *n, vb* **phones, phoning, phoned** short for **telephone**

phone[2] (fəʊn) *n phonetics* a single speech sound [c19 from Gk *phōnē* sound, voice]

-phone *combining form* **1** (*forming nouns*) indicating a device giving off sound: *telephone* **2** (*forming nouns and adjectives*) (a person) speaking a particular language: *Francophone* [from Gk *phōnē* voice, sound] > **-phonic** *adj combining form*

phonecard ('fəʊn,kɑ:d) *n* a card used instead of coins to operate certain public telephones

phone-in *n* **a** a radio or television programme in which listeners' or viewers' questions, comments, etc, are telephoned to the studio and broadcast live as part of a discussion **b** (*as modifier*): *a phone-in programme*

phoneme ('fəʊni:m) *n linguistics* one of the set of speech sounds in any given language that serve to distinguish one word from another [c20 via F from Gk *phōnēma* sound, speech] > **phonemic** (fə'ni:mɪk) *adj*

phonemics (fə'ni:mɪks) *n* (*functioning as sing*) that aspect of linguistics concerned with the classification and analysis of the phonemes of a language > **pho'nemicist** *n*

phonetic (fə'nɛtɪk) *adj* **1** of or relating to phonetics **2** denoting any perceptible distinction between one speech sound and another **3** conforming to pronunciation: *phonetic spelling* [c19 from NL *phōnēticus*, from Gk, from *phōnein* to make sounds, speak] > **pho'netically** *adv*

phonetics (fə'nɛtɪks) *n* (*functioning as sing*) the science concerned with the study of speech processes, including the production, perception, and analysis of speech sounds > **phonetician** (,fəʊnɪ'tɪʃən) *or* **phonetist** ('fəʊnɪtɪst) *n*

▷ www2.arts.gla.ac.uk/IPA/ipa.html

▷ http://faculty.washington.edu/dillon/PhonResources

phoney *or esp US* **phony** ('fəʊnɪ) *inf* ▷ *adj* **phonier, phoniest** **1** not genuine; fake **2** (of a person) insincere or pretentious ▷ *n, pl* **phoneys** *or esp US* **phonies** **3** an

Pp

insincere or pretentious person **4** something that is not genuine; a fake [c20 from ?] > **'phoneyness** *or esp US* **'phoniness** *n*

phonics ('fɒnɪks) *n (functioning as sing)* **1** an obsolete name for **acoustics** (sense 1) **2** a method of teaching people to read by training them to associate letters with their phonetic values > **'phonic** *adj* > **'phonically** *adv*

phono- *or before a vowel* **phon-** *combining form* indicating a sound or voice: *phonograph; phonology* [from Gk *phōnē* sound, voice]

phonogram ('fəʊnəˌɡræm) *n* any written symbol standing for a sound, syllable, morpheme, or word > **ˌphono'gramic** *or* **ˌphono'grammic** *adj*

phonograph ('fəʊnəˌɡrɑːf) *n* **1** an early form of gramophone capable of recording and reproducing sound on wax cylinders **2** another US and Canad word for **gramophone** or **record player**

phonographic (ˌfəʊnə'ɡræfɪk) *adj* **1** of or relating to phonography **2** of or relating to the recording of music

phonography (fəʊ'nɒɡrəfɪ) *n* **1** a writing system that represents sounds by individual symbols **2** the employment of such a writing system.

phonology (fə'nɒlədʒɪ) *n, pl* **phonologies** **1** the study of the sound system of a language or of languages in general **2** such a sound system > **phonological** (ˌfəʊnə'lɒdʒɪkᵊl, ˌfɒn-) *adj* > **ˌphono'logically** *adv* > **pho'nologist** *n*

phonon ('fəʊnɒn) *n physics* a quantum of vibrational energy in the acoustic vibrations of a crystal lattice [c20 from PHONO- + -ON]

-phony *n combining form* indicating a specified type of sound: *cacophony; euphony* [from Gk *-phōnia*, from *phōnē* sound] > **-phonic** *adj combining form*

phooey ('fuːɪ) *interj inf* an exclamation of scorn, contempt, etc [c20 prob. var. of PHEW]

-phore *n combining form* indicating one that bears or produces: *semaphore* [from NL *-phorus*, from Gk *-phoros* bearing, from *pherein* to bear] > **-phorous** *adj combining form*

-phoresis *n combining form* indicating a transmission: *electrophoresis* [from Gk *phorēsis* being carried, from *pherein* to bear]

phormium ('fɔːmɪəm) *n* any of a genus of plants of the lily family with tough leathery evergreen leaves. Also called: **New Zealand flax, flax lily** [c19 NL from Gk *phormos* basket]

phosgene ('fɒzdʒiːn) *n* a colourless poisonous gas: used in chemical warfare and in the manufacture of pesticides, dyes, and polyurethane resins [c19 from Gk *phōs* light + *-gene*, var. of -GEN]

phosphate ('fɒsfeɪt) *n* **1** any salt or ester of any phosphoric acid **2** *(often pl)* any of several chemical fertilizers containing phosphorous compounds [c18 from F *phosphat*; see PHOSPHORUS, -ATE[1]] > **phosphatic** (fɒs'fætɪk) *adj*

phosphatide ('fɒsfəˌtaɪd) *n* another name for **phospholipid**

phosphatidylcholine (ˌfɒsfæˌtaɪdaɪl'kəʊliːn) *n* the systematic name for **lecithin**

phosphene ('fɒsfiːn) *n* the sensation of light caused by pressure on the eyelid of a closed eye [c19 from Gk *phōs* light + *phainein* to show] > **phos'phenic** *adj*

phosphide ('fɒsfaɪd) *n* any compound of phosphorus with another element, esp a more electropositive element

phosphine ('fɒsfiːn) *n* a colourless flammable gas that is slightly soluble in water and has a strong fishy odour: used as a pesticide. Formula: PH_3

phosphite ('fɒsfaɪt) *n* any salt or ester of phosphorous acid

phospho- *or before a vowel* **phosph-** *combining form* containing phosphorus: *phosphoric* [from F, from *phosphore* PHOSPHORUS]

phospholipid (ˌfɒsfə'lɪpɪd) *n* any of a group of fatty compounds: important constituents of all membranes. Also called: **phosphatide**

phosphonic acid (fɒs'fɒnɪk) *n* the systematic name for **phosphorous acid**

phosphor ('fɒsfə) *n* a substance capable of emitting light when irradiated with particles of electromagnetic radiation [c17 from F, ult. from Gk *phōsphoros* PHOSPHORUS]

phosphorate ('fɒsfəˌreɪt) *vb* **phosphorates, phosphorating, phosphorated** to treat or combine with phosphorus

phosphor bronze *n* any of various hard corrosion-resistant alloys containing phosphorus: used in gears, bearings, cylinder casings, etc

phosphoresce (ˌfɒsfə'rɛs) *vb* **phosphoresces, phosphorescing, phosphoresced** *(intr)* to exhibit phosphorescence

phosphorescence (ˌfɒsfə'rɛsəns) *n* **1** *physics* a fluorescence that persists after the bombarding radiation producing it has stopped **2** the light emitted in phosphorescence **3** the emission of light in which insufficient heat is evolved to cause fluorescence ▷ Cf **fluorescence** > **ˌphospho'rescent** *adj*

phosphoric (fɒs'fɒrɪk) *adj* of or containing phosphorus in the pentavalent state

phosphoric acid *n* **1** a colourless solid tribasic acid used in the manufacture of fertilizers and soap. Formula: H_3PO_4. Systematic name: **phosphoric(V) acid** Also called: **orthophosphoric acid** **2** any oxyacid of phosphorus produced by reaction between phosphorus pentoxide and water

phosphorous ('fɒsfərəs) *adj* of or containing phosphorus in the trivalent state

phosphorous acid *n* **1** a white or yellowish hygroscopic crystalline dibasic acid. Formula: H_3PO_3. Systematic name: **phosphonic acid** Also called: **orthophosphorous acid** **2** any oxyacid of phosphorus containing less oxygen than the corresponding phosphoric acid

phosphorus ('fɒsfərəs) *n* **1** an allotropic nonmetallic element occurring in phosphates and living matter. Ordinary phosphorus is a toxic flammable phosphorescent white solid; the red form is less reactive and nontoxic: used in matches, pesticides, and alloys. The radioisotope **phosphorus-32 (radiophosphorus)**, with a half-life of 14.3 days, is used in radiotherapy and as a tracer. Symbol: P; atomic no.: 15; atomic wt.: 30.974 **2** a less common name for a **phosphor** [c17 via L from Gk *phōsphoros* light-bringing, from *phōs* light + *pherein* to bring]

Phosphorus ('fɒsfərəs) *n* a morning star, esp Venus

phossy jaw ('fɒsɪ) *n* a gangrenous condition of the lower jawbone caused by prolonged exposure to phosphorus fumes [c19 *phossy*, colloquial shortening of PHOSPHORUS]

phot (fɒt, fəʊt) *n* a unit of illumination equal to one lumen per square centimetre. 1 phot is equal to 10 000 lux [c20 from Gk *phōs* light]

photic ('fəʊtɪk) *adj* **1** of or concerned with light **2** designating the zone of the sea where photosynthesis takes place

photo ('fəʊtəʊ) *n, pl* **photos** short for **photograph**

photo- *combining form* **1** of, relating to, or produced by light: *photosynthesis* **2** indicating a photographic process: *photolithography* [from Gk *phōs, phōt-* light]

photo call *n* a time arranged for photographers, esp press photographers, to take pictures of a celebrity

photocell ('fəʊtəʊˌsɛl) *n* a device in which the photoelectric or photovoltaic effect or photoconductivity is used to produce a current or voltage when exposed to light or other electromagnetic radiation. They are used in exposure meters, burglar alarms, etc. Also called: **photoelectric cell, electric eye**

photochemistry (ˌfəʊtəʊ'kɛmɪstrɪ) *n* the branch of

chemistry concerned with the chemical effects of light and other electromagnetic radiations > **photochemical** (ˌfəʊtəʊˈkɛmɪkᵊl) *adj*

photochromic (ˌfəʊtəʊˈkrəʊmɪk) *adj* (of glass) changing colour with the intensity of incident light, used, for example, in sunglasses that darken as the sunlight becomes brighter

photocomposition (ˌfəʊtəʊˌkɒmpəˈzɪʃən) *n* another name (esp US and Canad) for **filmsetting**

photoconductivity (ˌfəʊtəʊˌkɒndʌkˈtɪvɪtɪ) *n* the change in the electrical conductivity of certain substances, such as selenium, as a result of the absorption of electromagnetic radiation > **photoconductive** (ˌfəʊtəʊkənˈdʌktɪv) *adj* > **ˌphotoconˈductor** *n*

photocopier (ˈfəʊtəʊˌkɒpɪə) *n* an instrument using light-sensitive photographic materials to reproduce written, printed, or graphic work

photocopy (ˈfəʊtəʊˌkɒpɪ) *n, pl* **photocopies** **1** a photographic reproduction of written, printed, or graphic work ▷ *vb* **photocopies, photocopying, photocopied** **2** to reproduce (written, printed, or graphic work) on photographic material

photodegradable (ˌfəʊtəʊdɪˈgreɪdəbᵊl) *adj* (of plastic) capable of being decomposed by prolonged exposure to light

photoelectric (ˌfəʊtəʊɪˈlɛktrɪk) *adj* of or concerned with electric or electronic effects caused by light or other electromagnetic radiation > **photoelectricity** (ˌfəʊtəʊɪlɛkˈtrɪsɪtɪ) *n*

photoelectric cell *n* another name for **photocell**

photoelectric effect *n* **1** the ejection of electrons from a solid by an incident beam of sufficiently energetic electromagnetic radiation **2** any phenomenon involving electric current and electromagnetic radiation, such as photoemission

photoelectron (ˌfəʊtəʊɪˈlɛktrɒn) *n* an electron ejected from an atom, molecule, or solid by an incident photon

photoemission (ˌfəʊtəʊɪˈmɪʃən) *n* the emission of electrons due to the impact of electromagnetic radiation

photoengraving (ˌfəʊtəʊɪnˈgreɪvɪŋ) *n* **1** a photomechanical process for producing letterpress printing plates **2** a plate made by this process **3** a print made from such a plate > **ˌphotoenˈgrave** *vb (tr)*

photo finish *n* **1** a finish of a race in which contestants are so close that a photograph is needed to decide the result **2** any race or competition in which the winners are separated by a very small margin

Photofit (ˈfəʊtəʊˌfɪt) *n trademark* **a** a method of combining photographs of facial features, hair, etc, into a composite picture of a face: formerly used by the police to trace suspects, criminals, etc **b** *(as modifier): a Photofit picture*

photoflash (ˈfəʊtəʊˌflæʃ) *n* another name for **flashbulb**

photoflood (ˈfəʊtəʊˌflʌd) *n* a highly incandescent tungsten lamp used for indoor photography, television, etc

photog. *abbrev for:* **1** photograph **2** photographer **3** photographic **4** photography

photogenic (ˌfəʊtəˈdʒɛnɪk) *adj* **1** (esp of a person) having a general facial appearance that looks attractive in photographs **2** *biol* producing or emitting light > **ˌphotoˈgenically** *adv*

photogram (ˈfəʊtəˌgræm) *n* **1** a picture, usually abstract, produced on a photographic material without the use of a camera **2** *obs* a photograph

photogrammetry (ˌfəʊtəʊˈgræmɪtrɪ) *n* the process of making measurements from photographs, used esp in the construction of maps from aerial photographs

photograph (ˈfəʊtəˌgrɑːf) *n* **1** an image of an object, person, scene, etc, in the form of a print or slide recorded by a camera. Often shortened to **photo** ▷ *vb* **2** to take a photograph of (an object, person, scene, etc)

photographic (ˌfəʊtəˈgræfɪk) *adj* **1** of or relating to photography **2** like a photograph in accuracy or detail **3** (of a person's memory) able to retain facts, appearances, etc, in precise detail > **ˌphotoˈgraphically** *adv*

photography (fəˈtɒgrəfɪ) *n* **1** the process of recording images on sensitized material by the action of light, X-rays, etc **2** the art, practice, or occupation of taking photographs > **phoˈtographer** *n*

▷ www.photolinks.net

▷ www.nyip.com

photogravure (ˌfəʊtəʊgrəˈvjʊə) *n* **1** any of various methods in which an intaglio plate for printing is produced by the use of photography **2** matter printed from such a plate [C19 from PHOTO- + F *gravure* engraving]

photojournalism (ˌfəʊtəʊˈdʒɜːnᵊˌlɪzəm) *n* journalism in which photographs are the predominant feature > **ˌphotoˈjournalist** *n*

▷ www.reportage.com

photokinesis (ˌfəʊtəʊkɪˈniːsɪs, -kaɪ-) *n biol* the movement of an organism in response to the stimulus of light

photolithography (ˌfəʊtəʊlɪˈθɒgrəfɪ) *n* **1** a lithographic printing process using photographically made plates. Often shortened to **photolitho** **2** *electronics* a process used in the manufacture of semiconductor devices and printed circuits in which a particular pattern is transferred from a photograph onto a substrate > **ˌphotoliˈthographer** *n*

photoluminescence (ˌfəʊtəʊˌluːmɪˈnɛsəns) *n* luminescence resulting from the absorption of light or infrared or ultraviolet radiation

photolysis (fəʊˈtɒlɪsɪs) *n* chemical decomposition caused by light or other electromagnetic radiation > **photolytic** (ˌfəʊtəʊˈlɪtɪk) *adj*

photomechanical (ˌfəʊtəʊmɪˈkænɪkᵊl) *adj* of or relating to any of various methods by which printing plates are made using photography > **ˌphotomeˈchanically** *adv*

photometer (fəʊˈtɒmɪtə) *n* an instrument used in photometry, usually one that compares the illumination produced by a particular light source with that produced by a standard source

photometry (fəʊˈtɒmɪtrɪ) *n* **1** the measurement of the intensity of light **2** the branch of physics concerned with such measurements > **phoˈtometrist** *n*

photomicrograph (ˌfəʊtəʊˈmaɪkrəˌgrɑːf) *n* a photograph of a microscope image > **photomicrography** (ˌfəʊtəʊmaɪˈkrɒgrəfɪ) *n*

photomontage (ˌfəʊtəʊmɒnˈtɑːʒ) *n* **1** the technique of producing a composite picture by combining several photographs **2** the composite picture so produced

photomultiplier (ˌfəʊtəʊˈmʌltɪˌplaɪə) *n* a device sensitive to electromagnetic radiation which produces a detectable pulse of current

photon (ˈfəʊtɒn) *n* a quantum of electromagnetic radiation with energy equal to the product of the frequency of the radiation and the Planck constant

photo-offset *n printing* an offset process in which the plates are produced photomechanically

photo opportunity *n* an opportunity, either preplanned or accidental, for the press to photograph a politician, celebrity, or event

photoperiodism (ˌfəʊtəʊˈpɪərɪəˌdɪzəm) *n* the response of plants and animals by behaviour, growth, etc, to the period of daylight in every 24 hours (**photoperiod**)

photophobia (ˌfəʊtəʊˈfəʊbɪə) *n* **1** *pathol* abnormal sensitivity of the eyes to light **2** *psychiatry* abnormal fear of sunlight or well-lit places > **ˌphotoˈphobic** *adj*

photopolymer (ˌfəʊtəʊˈpɒlɪmə) *n* a polymeric material that is sensitive to light: used in printing plates, microfilms, etc

Pp

photoreceptor (ˌfəʊtəʊrɪˈsɛptə) *n zool, physiol* a light-sensitive cell or organ that conveys impulses through the sensory neuron connected to it

photo refractive keratomy *n* laser eye surgery that involves scraping away the protective cells of the cornea before reshaping its surface to improve vision. Abbrev: **PRK**

photosensitive (ˌfəʊtəʊˈsɛnsɪtɪv) *adj* sensitive to electromagnetic radiation, esp light > ˌ**photoˌsensiˈtivity** *n* > ˌ**photoˈsensiˌtize** *or* ˌ**photoˈsensiˌtise** *vb (tr)*

photoset (ˈfəʊtəʊˌsɛt) *vb* **photosets, photosetting, photoset** another word for **filmset** > ˈ**photoˌsetter** *n*

photoshoot (ˈfəʊtəʊʃuːt) *n* a session in which a photographer takes pictures of someone for publication

photosphere (ˈfəʊtəʊˌsfɪə) *n* the visible surface of the sun > **photospheric** (ˌfəʊtəʊˈsfɛrɪk) *adj*

photostat (ˈfəʊtəʊˌstæt) *n* **1** a machine or process used to make photographic copies of written, printed, or graphic matter **2** any copy made by such a machine ▷ *vb* **photostats, photostatting** *or* **photostating, photostatted** *or* **photostated 3** to make a photostat copy (of)

photosynthesis (ˌfəʊtəʊˈsɪnθɪsɪs) *n* (in plants) the synthesis of organic compounds from carbon dioxide and water using light energy absorbed by chlorophyll > ˌ**photoˈsynthesize** *or* ˌ**photoˈsynthesise** *vb* > **photosynthetic** (ˌfəʊtəʊsɪnˈθɛtɪk) *adj* > ˌ**photosynˈthetically** *adv*

phototaxis (ˌfəʊtəʊˈtæksɪs) *n* the movement of an entire organism in response to light

phototropism (ˌfəʊtəʊˈtrəʊpɪzəm) *n* the growth response of plant parts to the stimulus of light, producing a bending towards the light source > ˌ**photoˈtropic** *adj*

photovoltaic effect (ˌfəʊtəʊvɒlˈteɪɪk) *n* the effect when electromagnetic radiation falls on a thin film of one solid deposited on the surface of a dissimilar solid producing a difference in potential between the two materials

phrasal verb *n* a phrase that consists of a verb plus an adverbial or prepositional particle, esp one the meaning of which cannot be deduced from the constituents: *"take in" meaning "deceive" is a phrasal verb*

phrase (freɪz) *n* **1** a group of words forming a syntactic constituent of a sentence ▷ Cf **clause** (sense 1) **2** an idiomatic or original expression **3** manner or style of speech or expression **4** *music* a small group of notes forming a coherent unit of melody ▷ *vb* **phrases, phrasing, phrased** *(tr)* **5** *music* to divide (a melodic line, part, etc) into musical phrases, esp in performance **6** to express orally or in a phrase [C16 from L *phrasis*, from Gk: speech, from *phrazein* to tell] > ˈ**phrasal** *adj*

phrase book *n* a book containing frequently used expressions and their equivalents in a foreign language, esp for the use of tourists

phrase marker *n linguistics* a representation, esp a tree diagram, of the constituent structure of a sentence

phraseogram (ˈfreɪzɪəˌɡræm) *n* a symbol representing a phrase, as in shorthand

phraseology (ˌfreɪzɪˈɒlədʒɪ) *n, pl* **phraseologies 1** the manner in which words or phrases are used **2** a set of phrases used by a particular group of people > **phraseological** (ˌfreɪzɪəˈlɒdʒɪkᵊl) *adj*

phrasing (ˈfreɪzɪŋ) *n* **1** the way in which something is expressed, esp in writing; wording **2** *music* the division of a melodic line, part, etc, into musical phrases

phreaking (ˈfriːkɪŋ) *n* the act of gaining unauthorized access to telecommunication systems, esp to obtain free calls [C20 blend of FREAKING + PHONE]

phrenetic (frɪˈnɛtɪk) *adj* an obsolete spelling of **frenetic** > **phreˈnetically** *adv*

phrenic (ˈfrɛnɪk) *adj* **1a** of or relating to the diaphragm **1b** *(as n): the phrenic* **2** *obs* of or relating to the mind [C18 from NL *phrenicus*, from Gk *phrēn* mind, diaphragm]

phrenology (frɪˈnɒlədʒɪ) *n* (formerly) the branch of science concerned with the supposed determination of the strength of the faculties by the shape and size of the skull overlying the parts of the brain thought to be responsible for them > **phrenological** (ˌfrɛnəˈlɒdʒɪkᵊl) *adj* > **phreˈnologist** *n*

Phrixus (ˈfrɪksəs) *n Greek myth* the son of Athamas and Nephele who escaped the wrath of his father's mistress, Ino, by flying to Colchis on a winged ram with a golden fleece. See also **Helle, Golden Fleece**

Phrygia (ˈfrɪdʒɪə) *n* an ancient country of W central Asia Minor

Phrygian (ˈfrɪdʒɪən) *adj* **1** of or relating to ancient Phrygia, its inhabitants, or their extinct language **2** *music* of or relating to an authentic mode represented by the natural diatonic scale from E to E ▷ *n* **3** a native or inhabitant of ancient Phrygia **4** an ancient language of Phrygia

Phrygian cap *n* a conical cap of soft material worn during ancient times, that became a symbol of liberty during the French Revolution

Phryne (ˈfraɪnɪ) *n* real name *Muesarete*. 4th century BC, Greek courtesan; lover of Praxiteles and model for Apelles' painting *Aphrodite Rising from the Waves*

phthalate (ˈθæleɪt, ˈfθæl-) *n* a salt or ester of phthalic acid. Esters are commonly used as plasticizers in PVC; when ingested they can cause kidney and liver damage

phthalic acid (ˈθælɪk, ˈfθæl-) *n* a white crystalline carboxylic acid made from naphthalene and used in the synthesis of dyes and perfumes and the manufacture of plastics [C19 *phthalic* from (NA)PHTHAL(ENE) + -IC]

phthisis (ˈθaɪsɪs, ˈfθaɪ-, ˈtaɪ-) *n* any disease that causes wasting of the body, esp pulmonary tuberculosis [C16 via L from Gk, from *phthinein* to waste away]

Phuket (ˌpuːˈkɛt) *n* **1** an island and province of S Thailand, in the Andaman Sea: mainly flat. Area: 534 sq km (206 sq miles) **2** the chief town of the island of Phuket; a popular tourist resort

phut (fʌt) *inf* ▷ *n* **1** a representation of a muffled explosive sound ▷ *adv* **2 go phut** to break down or collapse [C19 imit.]

phycomycete (ˌfaɪkəʊˈmaɪsiːt) *n* any of a primitive group of fungi formerly included in the class *Phycomycetes*, but now classified in different phyla: includes certain mildews and moulds [from Gk *phukos* seaweed + -MYCETE]

Phyfe *or* **Fife** (faɪf) *n* **Duncan** ?1768–1854, US cabinet-maker, born in Scotland

phyla (ˈfaɪlə) *n* the plural of **phylum**

phylactery (fɪˈlæktərɪ) *n, pl* **phylacteries 1** *Judaism* either of the pair of blackened square cases containing parchments inscribed with biblical passages, bound by leather thongs to the head and left arm, and worn by Jewish men during weekday morning prayers **2** a reminder **3** *arch* an amulet or charm [C14 from LL *phylactērium*, from Gk *phulaktērion* outpost, from *phulax* a guard]

phyletic (faɪˈlɛtɪk) *adj* of or relating to the evolution of a species or group of organisms [C19 from Gk *phuletikos* tribal]

-phyll *or* **-phyl** *n combining form* leaf: *chlorophyll* [from Gk *phullon*]

phyllo- *or before a vowel* **phyll-** *combining form* leaf: *phyllopod* [from Gk *phullon* leaf]

phyllode (ˈfɪləʊd) *n* a flattened leafstalk that resembles and functions as a leaf [C19 from NL *phyllodium*, from Gk *phullōdēs* leaflike]

phylloquinone (ˌfɪləʊkwɪˈnəʊn) *n* a viscous fat-soluble liquid occurring in plants: essential for the production of prothrombin, required in blood clotting. Also called: **vitamin** $\mathbf{K_1}$

phyllotaxis (ˌfɪlə'tæksɪs) *or* **phyllotaxy** *n, pl* **phyllotaxes** (-'tæksiːz) *or* **phyllotaxies** 1 the arrangement of the leaves on a stem 2 the study of this arrangement > ˌ**phyllo'tactic** *adj*

-phyllous *adj combining form* having leaves of a specified number or type: *monophyllous* [from Gk *-phullos* of a leaf]

phylloxera (ˌfɪlɒk'sɪərə, fɪ'lɒksərə) *n, pl* **phylloxerae** (-riː) *or* **phylloxeras** any of a genus of homopterous insects, such as vine phylloxera, typically feeding on plant juices [c19 NL, from PHYLLO- + Gk *xēros* dry]

phylo- *or before a vowel* **phyl-** *combining form* tribe; race; phylum: *phylogeny* [from Gk *phulon* race]

phylogeny (faɪ'lɒdʒɪnɪ) *or* **phylogenesis** (ˌfaɪləʊ'dʒɛnɪsɪs) *n, pl* **phylogenies** *or* **phylogeneses** (-'dʒɛnɪˌsiːz) *biol* the sequence of events involved in the evolution of a species, genus, etc ▷ Cf **ontogeny** [c19 from PHYLO- + -GENY] > **phylogenic** (ˌfaɪləʊ'dʒɛnɪk) *or* **phylogenetic** (ˌfaɪləʊdʒɪ'nɛtɪk) *adj*

phylum ('faɪləm) *n, pl* **phyla** 1 a major taxonomic division of living organisms that contain one or more classes 2 a group of related language families or linguistic stocks [c19 NL, from Gk *phulon* race]

phys. *abbrev for:* 1 physical 2 physician 3 physics 4 physiological 5 physiology

physalis (faɪ'seɪlɪs) *n* any of a genus of plants producing inflated orange seed vessels. See **Chinese lantern** [NL from Gk *physallis* bladder]

physic ('fɪzɪk) *n* 1 *rare* a medicine, esp a cathartic 2 *arch* the art or skill of healing ▷ *vb* **physics, physicking, physicked** 3 (*tr*) *arch* to treat (a patient) with medicine [c13 from OF *fisique*, via L, from Gk *phusikē*, from *phusis* nature]

physical ('fɪzɪkᵊl) *adj* 1 of or relating to the body, as distinguished from the mind or spirit 2 of, relating to, or resembling material things or nature: *the physical universe* 3 involving or requiring bodily contact: *rugby is a physical sport* 4 of or concerned with matter and energy 5 of or relating to physics 6 perceptible to the senses; apparent: *a physical manifestation* ▷ See also **physicals** > '**physically** *adv*

physical anthropology *n* the branch of anthropology dealing with the genetic aspect of human development and its physical variations

physical chemistry *n* the branch of chemistry concerned with the way in which the physical properties of substances depend on their chemical structure, properties, and reactions

physical education *n* training and practice in sports, gymnastics, etc. Abbrev: **PE**

physical geography *n* the branch of geography that deals with the natural features of the earth's surface

physical jerks *pl n Brit inf* See **jerk**[1] (sense 6)

physicals ('fɪzɪkᵊlz) *pl n commerce* commodities that can be purchased and used, as opposed to those bought and sold in a futures market. Also called: **actuals**

physical science *n* any of the sciences concerned with nonliving matter, such as physics, chemistry, astronomy, and geology

physical therapy *n chiefly US* another term for **physiotherapy**

physician (fɪ'zɪʃən) *n* 1 a person legally qualified to practise medicine, esp other than surgery; doctor of medicine 2 *arch* any person who treats diseases; healer [c13 from OF *fisicien*, from *fisique* PHYSIC]

physicist ('fɪzɪsɪst) *n* a person versed in or studying physics

physics ('fɪzɪks) *n (functioning as sing)* 1 the branch of science concerned with the properties of matter and energy and the relationships between them. It is based on mathematics and traditionally includes mechanics, optics, electricity and magnetism, acoustics, and heat. Modern physics, based on quantum theory, includes atomic, nuclear, particle, and solid-state studies 2 physical properties of behaviour: *the physics of the electron* 3 *arch* natural science [c16 from L *physica*, translation of Gk *ta phusika* natural things, from *phusis* nature]

▷ www.physlink.com
▷ www.physicsweb.org
▷ www.vlib.org/Physics.html

physio ('fɪzɪəʊ) *n inf* 1 short for **physiotherapy** 2 (*pl* **physios**) short for **physiotherapist**

physio- *or before a vowel* **phys-** *combining form* 1 of or relating to nature or natural functions: *physiology* 2 physical: *physiotherapy* [from Gk *phusio*, ult. from *phuein* to make grow]

physiocrat ('fɪzɪəʊˌkræt) *n* a believer in the 18th-century French economic theory that the inherent natural order governing society was based on land and its natural products as the only true form of wealth [c18 from F *physiocrate*; see PHYSIO-, -CRAT] > **physiocracy** (ˌfɪzɪ'ɒkrəsɪ) *n*

physiognomy (ˌfɪzɪ'ɒnəmɪ) *n* 1 a person's features considered as an indication of personality 2 the art or practice of judging character from facial features 3 the outward appearance of something [c14 from OF *phisonomie*, via Med. L, from LGk *phusiognōmia*, from *phusis* nature + *gnōmōn* judge] > **physiognomic** (ˌfɪzɪə'nɒmɪk) *or* ˌ**physiog'nomical** *adj* > ˌ**physiog'nomically** *adv* > ˌ**physi'ognomist** *n*

physiography (ˌfɪzɪ'ɒgrəfɪ) *n* another name for **geomorphology** or **physical geography** > ˌ**physi'ographer** *n* > **physiographic** (ˌfɪzɪə'græfɪk) *or* ˌ**physio'graphical** *adj*

physiol. *abbrev for:* 1 physiological 2 physiology

physiology (ˌfɪzɪ'ɒlədʒɪ) *n* 1 the branch of science concerned with the functioning of organisms 2 the processes and functions of all or part of an organism [c16 from L *physiologia*, from Gk] > ˌ**physi'ologist** *n* > **physiological** (ˌfɪzɪə'lɒdʒɪkᵊl) *adj* > ˌ**physio'logically** *adv*

▷ www.physoc.org/links/

physiotherapy (ˌfɪzɪəʊ'θɛrəpɪ) *n* the treatment of disease, injury, etc, by physical means, such as massage or exercises, rather than by drugs > ˌ**physio'therapist** *n*

physique (fɪ'ziːk) *n* the general appearance of the body with regard to size, shape, muscular development, etc [c19 via F from *physique* (adj) natural, from L *physicus* physical]

-phyte *n combining form* indicating a plant of a specified type or habitat: *lithophyte* [from Gk *phuton* plant] > **-phytic** *adj combining form*

phyto- *or before a vowel* **phyt-** *combining form* indicating a plant or vegetation: *phytogenesis* [from Gk *phuton* plant, from *phuein* to make grow]

phytochemical (ˌfaɪtəʊ'kɛmɪkᵊl) *adj* 1 of or relating to the chemical composition or processes of plants ▷ *n* 2 a chemical produced by a plant

phytochemistry (ˌfaɪtəʊ'kɛmɪstrɪ) *n* the branch of chemistry concerned with plants, their chemical composition and processes > ˌ**phyto'chemist** *n*

phytochrome ('faɪtəʊˌkrəʊm) *n bot* a blue-green pigment, present in most plants, that mediates many light-dependent processes, including photoperiodism and the greening of leaves

phytogenesis (ˌfaɪtəʊ'dʒɛnɪsɪs) *or* **phytogeny** (faɪ'tɒdʒənɪ) *n* the branch of botany concerned with the origin and evolution of plants

phyton ('faɪtɒn) *n* a unit of plant structure, usually considered as the smallest part of the plant that is capable of growth when detached from the parent plant [c20 from Gk; see -PHYTE]

phytopathology (ˌfaɪtəʊpə'θɒlədʒɪ) *n* the branch of botany concerned with diseases of plants

phytoplankton (ˌfaɪtə'plæŋktən) *n* the photosynthesizing organisms in plankton, mainly

Pp

unicellular algae and cyanobacteria
phytotherapy (ˌfaɪtəʊˈθɛrəpɪ) *n* the use of plants and plant products for medicinal purposes
phytotoxin (ˌfaɪtəˈtɒksɪn) *n* a toxin, such as strychnine, that is produced by a plant > ˌ**phytoˈtoxic** *adj*
pi[1] (paɪ) *n, pl* **pis** **1** the 16th letter in the Greek alphabet (Π, π) **2** *maths* a transcendental number, fundamental to mathematics, that is the ratio of the circumference of a circle to its diameter. Approximate value: 3.141 592... ; symbol: π [C18 (mathematical use): representing the first letter of Gk *periphereia* PERIPHERY]
pi[2] *or* **pie** (paɪ) *n, pl* **pies** **1** a jumbled pile of printer's type **2** a jumbled mixture ▷ *vb* **pies, piing, pied** *or* **pies, pieing, pied** (*tr*) **3** to spill and mix (set type) indiscriminately **4** to mix up [C17 from ?]
pi[3] (paɪ) *adj Brit sl* short for **pious** (sense 3)
PI *abbrev for:* **1** Phillipine Islands **2** private investigator
Piacenza (*Italian* pjaˈtʃɛntsa) *n* a town in N Italy, in Emilia-Romagna on the River Po. Pop: 101 692 (1994 est). Latin name: **Placentia** (pləˈsɛntʃɪə)
piacevole (piːætʃˈeɪvəʊleɪ) *adv music* in an agreeable, pleasant manner [It.]
piacular (paɪˈækjʊlə) *adj* **1** making expiation **2** requiring expiation [C17 from L *piāculum* propitiatory sacrifice, from *piāre* to appease]
Piaf (*French* pjaf) *n* **Edith** (edit), real name *Edith Giovanna Gassion*, known as *the Little Sparrow*, 1915–63, French singer
piaffe (pɪˈæf) *n dressage* a slow trot done on the spot [C18 from F, from *piaffer* to strut]
Piaget (*French* pjaʒɛ) *n* **Jean** (ʒɑ̃) 1896–1980, Swiss psychologist, noted for his work on the development of the cognitive functions in children
pia mater (ˈpaɪə ˈmeɪtə) *n* the innermost of the three membranes (see **meninges**) that cover the brain and spinal cord [C16 from Med. L, lit.: pious mother]
pianism (ˈpiːəˌnɪzəm) *n* technique, skill, or artistry in playing the piano > ˌ**piaˈnistic** *adj*
pianissimo (pɪəˈnɪsɪˌməʊ) *adj, adv music* to be performed very quietly. Symbol: *pp* [C18 from It., sup. of *piano* soft]
pianist (ˈpɪənɪst) *n* a person who plays the piano
piano[1] (pɪˈænəʊ) *n, pl* **pianos** a musical stringed instrument played by depressing keys that cause hammers to strike the strings and produce audible vibrations [C19 short for PIANOFORTE]
piano[2] (ˈpjɑːnəʊ) *adj, adv music* to be performed softly [C17 from It., from L *plānus* flat]
Piano (*Italian* pjˈano) *n* **Renzo** born 1937, Italian architect; buildings include the Pompidou Centre, Paris (1977; with Richard Rogers) and the Potsdamer Platz redevelopment, Berlin (1998)
piano accordion (pɪˈænəʊ) *n* an accordion in which the right hand plays a piano-like keyboard. See **accordion** > **piano accordionist** *n*
pianoforte (pɪˌænəʊˈfɔːtɪ) *n* the full name for **piano**[1] [C18 from It., orig. (*gravecembalo col*) *piano e forte* (harpsichord with) soft & loud; see PIANO[2], FORTE[2]]
Pianola (pɪəˈnəʊlə) *n trademark* a type of mechanical piano in which the keys are depressed by air pressure, this air flow being regulated by perforations in a paper roll
piano roll (pɪˈænəʊ) *n* a perforated roll of paper for a Pianola
piastre *or* **piaster** (pɪˈæstə) *n* **1** (formerly) the standard monetary unit of South Vietnam **2a** a fractional monetary unit of Egypt, Lebanon, and Syria worth one hundredth of a pound: formerly also used in the Sudan **2b** Also called: **kurus** a Turkish monetary unit worth one hundredth of a lira **2c** a Libyan monetary unit worth one hundredth of a dinar [C17 from F *piastre*, from It. *piastra d'argento* silver plate]
Piauí (*Portuguese* pjaˈui) *n* a state of NE Brazil, on the Atlantic: rises to a semiarid plateau, with the more humid Paranaíba valley in the west. Capital: Teresina. Pop: 2 840 969 (2000). Area: 250 934 sq km (96 886 sq miles)
Piave (*Italian* ˈpjaːve) *n* a river in NE Italy, rising near the border with Austria and flowing south and southeast to the Adriatic: the main line of Italian defence during World War I. Length: 220 km (137 miles)
piazza (pɪˈætsə; *Italian* ˈpjattsa) *n* **1** a large open square in an Italian town **2** *chiefly Brit* a covered passageway or gallery [C16 from It.: marketplace, from L *platēa* courtyard, from Gk *plateia*; see PLACE]
pibroch (ˈpiːbrɒk; *Gaelic* ˈpiːbrɒx) *n* a form of music for Scottish bagpipes, consisting of a theme and variations [C18 from Gaelic *piobaireachd*, from *piobair* piper]
pic (pɪk) *n, pl* **pics** *or* **pix** *inf* a photograph or illustration [C20 shortened from PICTURE]
pica[1] (ˈpaɪkə) *n* **1** another word for **em** **2** (formerly) a size of printer's type equal to 12 point **3** a typewriter type size having 10 characters to the inch [C15 from Anglo-L *pīca* list of ecclesiastical regulations, apparently from L *pīca* magpie, with reference to its habit of collecting things; the connection between the orig. sense & the typography meanings is obscure]
pica[2] (ˈpaɪkə) *n pathol* an abnormal craving to ingest substances such as clay, dirt, or hair [C16 from Medical L, from L: magpie, an allusion to its omnivorous feeding habits]
Picabia (pɪˈkɑːbɪə; *French* pikabja) *n* **Francis** 1879–1953, French painter, designer, and writer, associated with the cubist, Dadaist, and surrealist movements
picador (ˈpɪkəˌdɔː) *n bullfighting* a horseman who pricks the bull with a lance to weaken it [C18 from Sp., lit.: pricker, from *picar* to prick]
Picard (*French* pikar) *n* **Jean** (ʒɑ̃) 1620–82, French astronomer. He was the first to make a precise measurement of a longitude line, enabling him to estimate the earth's radius
Picardy (ˈpɪkədɪ) *n* a region of N France: mostly low-lying; scene of heavy fighting in World War I. French name: **Picardie** (pikardi)
picaresque (ˌpɪkəˈrɛsk) *adj* of or relating to a type of fiction in which the hero, a rogue, goes through a series of episodic adventures [C19 via F from Sp. *picaresco*, from *pícaro* a rogue]
picaroon (ˌpɪkəˈruːn) *n arch* an adventurer or rogue [C17 from Sp. *picarón*, from *pícaro*]
Picasso (pɪˈkæsəʊ) *n* **Pablo** (ˈpæbləʊ) 1881–1973, Spanish painter and sculptor, resident in France: a highly influential figure in 20th-century art and a founder, with Braque, of cubism. A prolific artist, his works include *The Dwarf Dancer* (1901), belonging to his blue period; the first cubist painting *Les Demoiselles d'Avignon* (1907); *Three Dancers* (1925), which appeared in the first surrealist exhibition; and *Guernica* (1937), inspired by an event in the Spanish Civil War
picayune (ˌpɪkəˈjuːn) *adj Also:* **picayunish** *US & Canad inf* **1** of small value or importance **2** mean; petty ▷ *n* **3** any coin of little value, esp a five-cent piece **4** an unimportant person or thing [C19 from F *picaillon* coin from Piedmont, from Provençal *picaioun*, from ?]
Piccadilly (ˌpɪkəˈdɪlɪ) *n* one of the main streets of London, running from Piccadilly Circus to Hyde Park Corner
piccalilli (ˈpɪkəˌlɪlɪ) *n* a pickle of mixed vegetables in a mustard sauce [C18 *piccalillo*, ? based on PICKLE]
piccanin (ˈpɪkəˌnɪn) *n S African offens* a Black African child [var. of PICCANINNY]
piccaninny *or esp US* **pickaninny** (ˌpɪkəˈnɪnɪ) *n, pl* **piccaninnies** *or esp US* **pickaninnies** *offens* a small Black child [C17 ?from Port. *pequenino* tiny one, from *pequeno* small]
Piccard (*French* pikar) *n* **1** **Auguste** (ogyst) 1884–1962, Swiss physicist, whose study of cosmic rays led to his pioneer balloon ascents in the stratosphere (1931–32)

2 his twin brother, **Jean Félix** (ʒɑ̃ feliks) 1884–1963, US chemist and aeronautical engineer, born in Switzerland, noted for his balloon ascent into the stratosphere (1934)

piccolo (ˈpɪkəˌləʊ) *n, pl* **piccolos** a woodwind instrument an octave higher than the flute [c19 from It.: small]

pick[1] (pɪk) *vb* **1** to choose (something) deliberately or carefully, as from a number; select **2** to pluck or gather (fruit, berries, or crops) from (a tree, bush, field, etc) **3** (*tr*) to remove loose particles from (the teeth, the nose, etc) **4** (esp of birds) to nibble or gather (corn, etc) **5** (when *intr*, foll by *at*) to nibble (at) fussily or without appetite **6** to separate (strands, fibres, etc), as in weaving **7** (*tr*) to provoke (an argument, fight, etc) deliberately **8** (*tr*) to steal (money or valuables) from (a person's pocket) **9** (*tr*) to open (a lock) with an instrument other than a key **10** to pluck the strings of (a guitar, banjo, etc) **11** (*tr*) to make (one's way) carefully on foot: *they picked their way through the rubble* **12 pick and choose** to select fastidiously, fussily, etc **13 pick someone's brains** to obtain information or ideas from someone ▹ *n* **14** freedom or right of selection (esp in **take one's pick**) **15** a person, thing, etc, that is chosen first or preferred: *the pick of the bunch* **16** the act of picking **17** the amount of a crop picked at one period or from one area ▹ See also **pick at, pick off,** etc [c15 from earlier *piken* to pick, infl. by F *piquer* to pierce] > ˈ**picker** *n*

pick[2] (pɪk) *n* **1** a tool with a handle carrying a long steel head curved and tapering to a point at one or both ends, used for loosening soil, breaking rocks, etc **2** any of various tools used for picking, such as an ice pick or toothpick **3** a plectrum ▹ *vb* (*tr*) **4 to pierce, dig, or break up (a hard surface) with a pick 5** to form (a hole, etc) in this way [c14 ? a var. of PIKE[2]]

pickaback (ˈpɪkəˌbæk) *n, adv* another word for **piggyback**

pick at *vb* (*intr, prep*) to make criticisms of in a niggling or petty manner

pickaxe *or US* **pickax** (ˈpɪkˌæks) *n* **1** a large pick or mattock ▹ *vb* **pickaxes, pickaxing, pickaxed 2** to use a pickaxe on (earth, rocks, etc) [c15 from earlier *pikois* (but infl. also by AXE), from OF, from *pic* PICK[2]]

pickerel (ˈpɪkərəl, ˈpɪkrəl) *n, pl* **pickerel** *or* **pickerels 1** a small pike **2** any of several North American freshwater game fishes of the pike family [c14 dim. of PIKE[1]]

Pickering (ˈpɪkərɪŋ) *n* **1 Edward Charles** 1846–1919, US astronomer, who invented the meridian photometer **2** his brother, **William Henry** 1858–1938, US astronomer, who discovered Phoebe, the ninth satellite of Saturn, and predicted (1919) the existence and position of Pluto

picket (ˈpɪkɪt) *n* **1** a pointed stake that is driven into the ground to support a fence, etc **2** an individual or group standing outside an establishment to make a protest, to dissuade or prevent employees or clients from entering, etc **3** a small detachment of troops positioned to give early warning of attack ▹ *vb* **4** to post or serve as pickets at (a factory, embassy, etc) **5** to guard (a main body or place) by using or acting as a picket **6** (*tr*) to fasten (a horse or other animal) to a picket **7** (*tr*) to fence (an area, etc) with pickets [c18 from F *piquet*, from OF *piquer* to prick; see PIKE[2]] > ˈ**picketer** *n*

picket fence *n* a fence consisting of pickets driven into the ground

picket line *n* a line of people acting as pickets

Pickford (ˈpɪkfəd) *n* **Mary,** real name *Gladys Mary Smith.* 1893–1979, US actress in silent films, born in Canada

pickings (ˈpɪkɪŋz) *pl n* (*sometimes sing*) money, profits, etc, acquired easily; spoils

pickle (ˈpɪkᵊl) *n* **1** (*often pl*) vegetables, such as onions, etc, preserved in vinegar, brine, etc **2** any food preserved in this way **3** a liquid or marinade, such as spiced vinegar, for preserving vegetables, meat, fish, etc **4** *chiefly US & Canad* a cucumber that has been preserved and flavoured in a pickling solution, as brine or vinegar **5** *inf* an awkward or difficult situation: *to be in a pickle* **6** *Brit inf* a mischievous child ▹ *vb* **pickles, pickling, pickled** (*tr*) **7** to preserve in a pickling liquid **8** to immerse (a metallic object) in a liquid, such as an acid, to remove surface scale [c14 ?from MDu. *pekel*] > ˈ**pickler** *n*

pickled (ˈpɪkᵊld) *adj* **1** preserved in a pickling liquid **2** *inf* intoxicated; drunk

picklock (ˈpɪkˌlɒk) *n* **1** a person who picks locks **2** an instrument for picking locks

pick-me-up *n inf* a tonic or restorative, esp a special drink taken as a stimulant

pick off *vb* (*tr, adv*) to aim at and shoot one by one

pick on *vb* (*intr, prep*) to select for something unpleasant, esp in order to bully or blame

pick out *vb* (*tr, adv*) **1** to select for use or special consideration, etc, as from a group **2** to distinguish (an object from its surroundings), as in painting: *she picked out the woodwork in white* **3** to recognize (a person or thing): *we picked out his face among the crowd* **4** to distinguish (sense or meaning) as from a mass of detail or complication **5** to play (a tune) tentatively, as by ear

pickpocket (ˈpɪkˌpɒkɪt) *n* a person who steals from the pockets of others in public places

pick-up *n* **1** Also called: **pick-up truck** a small truck with an open body used for light deliveries **2** *inf, chiefly US* an ability to accelerate rapidly: *this car has good pick-up* **3** *inf* a casual acquaintance, usually one made with sexual intentions **4** *inf* **4a** a stop to collect passengers, goods, etc **4b** the people or things collected **5** *inf* an improvement **6** *sl* a pick-me-up **7** the light balanced arm of a record player that carries the wires from the cartridge to the preamplifier **8** an electromagnetic transducer that converts vibrations into electric signals **9** another name for **cartridge** (sense 2) ▹ *adj* **10** *US & Canad* organized or assembled hastily and without planning: *a pick-up game* ▹ *vb* **pick up** (*adv*) **11** (*tr*) to gather up in the hand or hands **12** (*reflexive*) to raise (oneself) after a fall or setback **13** (*tr*) to obtain casually, incidentally, etc **14** (*intr*) to improve in health, condition, activity, etc: *the market began to pick up* **15** (*tr*) to learn gradually or as one goes along **16** to resume; return to **17** (*tr*) to accept the responsibility for paying (a bill) **18** (*tr*) to collect or give a lift to (passengers, goods, etc) **19** (*tr*) *inf* to become acquainted with, esp with a view to having sexual relations **20** (*tr*) *inf* to arrest **21** to increase (speed) **22** (*tr*) to receive (electrical signals, a radio signal, sounds, etc)

Pickwickian (pɪkˈwɪkɪən) *adj* **1** of, relating to, or resembling Mr Pickwick in Charles Dickens' *The Pickwick Papers*, esp in being naive or benevolent **2** (of the use or meaning of a word) odd or unusual

picky (ˈpɪkɪ) *adj* **pickier, pickiest** *inf* fussy; finicky > ˈ**pickily** *adv* > ˈ**pickiness** *n*

picnic (ˈpɪknɪk) *n* **1** a trip or excursion on which people bring food to be eaten in the open air **2a** any informal meal eaten outside **2b** (*as modifier*): *a picnic lunch* **3** *inf* an easy or agreeable task ▹ *vb* **picnics, picnicking, picnicked 4** (*intr*) to eat or take part in a picnic [c18 from F *piquenique*, from ?] > ˈ**picnicker** *n*

picnic races *pl n Austral* horse races for amateur riders held in rural areas

pico- *prefix* denoting 10^{-12}: *picofarad*. Symbol: p [from Sp. *pico* small quantity, odd number, peak]

Pico de Aneto (*Spanish* ˈpiko de aˈneto) *n* See **Aneto**

Pico della Mirandola (*Italian* ˈpiːko ˌdɛlla miˈrandola) *n* Count **Giovanni** (dʒoˈvanni) 1463–94, Italian Platonist philosopher. His attempt to reconcile the ideas of classical, Christian, and Arabic writers in a collection of 900 theses, prefaced by his *Oration on the Dignity of Man* (1486), was condemned by the pope

Pico de Teide (*Spanish* ˈpiko de ˈteiðe) *n* See **Teide**

picot (ˈpiːkəʊ) *n* any of a pattern of small loops, as on lace [c19 from F: small point, from *pic* point]

Pp

picotee (ˌpɪkəˈtiː) *n* a type of carnation having pale petals edged with a darker colour [C18 from F *picoté* marked with points, from *picot* PICOT]

picric acid (ˈpɪkrɪk) *n* a toxic sparingly soluble crystalline yellow acid used as a dye, antiseptic, and explosive. Formula: $C_6H_3(NO_2)_3$. Systematic name: **2,4,6-trinitrophenol** [C19 from Gk *pikros* bitter + -IC]

Pict (pɪkt) *n* a member of any of the peoples who lived in N Britain in the first to the fourth centuries AD [OE *Peohtas;* later forms from LL *Pictī* painted men, from *pingere* to paint] > ˈ**Pictish** *adj*

pictograph (ˈpɪktəˌgrɑːf) *n* **1** a picture or symbol standing for a word or group of words, as in written Chinese **2** a chart on which symbols are used to represent values ▷ Also called: **pictogram** [C19 from L *pictus*, from *pingere* to paint] > **pictographic** (ˌpɪktəˈgræfɪk) *adj* > **pictography** (pɪkˈtɒgrəfɪ) *n*

pictorial (pɪkˈtɔːrɪəl) *adj* **1** relating to, consisting of, or expressed by pictures **2** (of language, style, etc) suggesting a picture; vivid; graphic ▷ *n* **3** a magazine, newspaper, etc, containing many pictures [C17 from LL *pictōrius*, from L *pictor* painter, from *pingere* to paint] > **picˈtorially** *adv*

picture (ˈpɪktʃə) *n* **1a** a visual representation of something, such as a person or scene, produced on a surface, as in a photograph, painting, etc **1b** (*as modifier*): *picture gallery; picture postcard* **2** a mental image: *a clear picture of events* **3** a verbal description, esp one that is vivid **4** a situation considered as an observable scene: *the political picture* **5** a person or thing resembling another: *he was the picture of his father* **6** a person, scene, etc, typifying a particular state: *the picture of despair* **7** the image on a television screen **8** a motion picture; film **9 the pictures** *chiefly Brit & NZ* a cinema or film show **10** another name for **tableau vivant** **11 in the picture** informed about a situation ▷ *vb* **pictures, picturing, pictured** (*tr*) **12** to visualize or imagine **13** to describe or depict, esp vividly **14** (*often passive*) to put in a picture or make a picture of: *they were pictured sitting on the rocks* [C15 from L *pictūra* painting, from *pingere* to paint]

picture card *n* another name for **court card**

picture hat *n* a hat with a very wide brim

picture messaging *n* **1** the practice of sending and receiving photographs by mobile phone **2** the practice of communicating by mobile phone using graphics or pictures rather than text

picture moulding *n* **1** the edge around a framed picture **2** Also called: **picture rail** the moulding or rail near the top of a wall from which pictures are hung

picture palace *or* **house** *n Brit, old-fashioned* another name for **cinema**

picture phone *n* a mobile phone that can take, send, and receive photographs

picturesque (ˌpɪktʃəˈrɛsk) *adj* **1** visually pleasing, esp in being striking or quaint: *a picturesque view* **2** (of language) graphic; vivid [C18 from F *pittoresque* (but also infl. by PICTURE), from It., from *pittore* painter, from L *pictor*] > ˌ**picturˈesquely** *adv* > ˌ**picturˈesqueness** *n*

picture tube *n* another name for **television tube**

picture window *n* a large window having a single pane of glass, usually facing a view

picture writing *n* **1** any writing system that uses pictographs **2** a system of artistic expression and communication using pictures

PID *abbrev for* pelvic inflammatory disease

piddle (ˈpɪdᵊl) *vb* **piddles, piddling, piddled** **1** (*intr*) *inf* to urinate **2** (when *tr*, often foll by *away*) to spend (one's time) aimlessly; fritter [C16 from ?] > ˈ**piddler** *n*

piddling (ˈpɪdlɪŋ) *adj inf* petty; trifling; trivial

piddock (ˈpɪdək) *n* a marine bivalve boring into rock, clay, or wood by means of sawlike shell valves [C19 from ?]

pidgin (ˈpɪdʒɪn) *n* a language made up of elements of two or more other languages and used for contacts, esp trading contacts, between the speakers of other languages [C19 ?from Chinese pronunciation of E *business*]

pidgin English *n* a pidgin in which one of the languages involved is English

pie[1] (paɪ) *n* **1** a baked sweet or savoury filling in a pastry-lined dish, often covered with a pastry crust **2 pie in the sky** illusory hope or promise of some future good [C14 from ?]

pie[2] (paɪ) *n* an archaic or dialect name for **magpie** [C13 via OF from L *pīca* magpie]

pie[3] (paɪ) *n, vb* **pies, pieing, pied** *printing* a variant spelling of **pi**[2]

piebald (ˈpaɪˌbɔːld) *adj* **1** marked in two colours, esp black and white ▷ *n* **2** a black-and-white horse [C16 PIE[2] + BALD; see also PIED]

pie cart *n* NZ a mobile van selling warmed-up food and drinks

piece (piːs) *n* **1** an amount or portion forming a separate mass or structure; bit: *a piece of wood* **2** a small part, item, or amount forming part of a whole, esp when broken off or separated: *a piece of bread* **3** a length by which a commodity is sold, esp cloth, wallpaper, etc **4** an instance or occurrence: *a piece of luck* **5** an example or specimen of a style or type: *a beautiful piece of Dresden* **6** *inf* an opinion or point of view: *to state one's piece* **7** a literary, musical, or artistic composition **8** a coin: *a fifty-pence piece* **9** a small object used in playing certain games: *chess pieces* **10** a firearm or cannon **11** any chessman other than a pawn **12** *Brit dialect* a packed lunch taken to work **13** NZ fragments of fleece wool **14 go to pieces** **14a** (of a person) to lose control of oneself; have a breakdown **14b** (of a building, organization, etc) to disintegrate **15 nasty piece of work** *Brit inf* a cruel or mean person **16 of a piece** of the same kind; alike ▷ *vb* **pieces, piecing, pieced** (*tr*) **17** (often foll by *together*) to fit or assemble piece by piece **18** (often foll by *up*) to patch or make up (a garment, etc) by adding pieces [C13 *pece*, from OF, of Gaulish origin]

pièce de résistance *French* (pjɛs də rezistɑ̃s) *n* **1** the principal or most outstanding item in a series **2** the main dish of a meal [lit.: piece of resistance]

piece goods *pl n* goods, esp fabrics, made in standard widths and lengths

piecemeal (ˈpiːsˌmiːl) *adv* **1** by degrees; bit by bit; gradually **2** in or into pieces ▷ *adj* **3** fragmentary or unsystematic: *a piecemeal approach* [C13 *pecemele*, from PIECE + *-mele*, from OE *mælum* quantity taken at one time]

piece of eight *n, pl* **pieces of eight** a former Spanish coin worth eight reals; peso

piecework (ˈpiːsˌwɜːk) *n* work paid for according to the quantity produced

pie chart *n* a circular graph divided into sectors proportional to the magnitudes of the quantities represented

piecrust table (ˈpaɪˌkrʌst) *n* a round table, edged with moulding suggestive of a pie crust

pied (paɪd) *adj* having markings of two or more colours [C14 from PIE[2]; an allusion to the magpie's colouring]

pied-à-terre (ˌpjeɪtɑːˈtɛə) *n, pl* **pieds-à-terre** (ˌpjeɪtɑːˈtɛə) a flat or other lodging for occasional use [from F, lit.: foot on (the) ground]

piedmont (ˈpiːdmɒnt) *adj* (*prenominal*) (of glaciers, plains, etc) formed or situated at the foot of a mountain [via F from It. *piémonte*, from *pié*, var. of *piede* foot + *mont* mountain]

Piedmont (ˈpiːdmɒnt) *n* **1** a region of NW Italy: consists of the upper Po Valley; mainly agricultural. Chief town: Turin. Pop: 4 287 465 (2000 est). Area: 25 399 sq km (9807 sq miles). Italian name: **Piemonte** **2** a low plateau of the eastern US, between the coastal plain and the Appalachian Mountains

Pied Piper *n* **1** Also called: **the Pied Piper of Hamelin** (in German legend) a piper who rid the town of Hamelin of rats by luring them away with his music and then, when he was not paid for his services, lured away its children **2** (*sometimes not caps*) a person who entices others to follow him or her

pied wagtail *n* a British songbird with a black throat and back, long black tail, and white underparts and face

pie-eyed *adj sl* drunk

Piemonte (*Italian* pje'monte) *n* the Italian name for **Piedmont** (sense 1)

Pienaar (pɪə'nɑː) *n* **(Jacobus) Francois** born 1967, South African Rugby Union footballer; captain of the South African team that won the Rugby World Cup in 1995

pier (pɪə) *n* **1** a structure with a deck that is built out over water, and used as a landing place, promenade, etc **2** a pillar that bears heavy loads **3** the part of a wall between two adjacent openings **4** another name for **buttress** (sense 1) [c12 *per*, from Anglo-L *pera* pier supporting a bridge]

pierce (pɪəs) *vb* **pierces, piercing, pierced** (*mainly tr*) **1** to form or cut (a hole) in (something) as with a sharp instrument **2** to thrust into sharply or violently: *the thorn pierced his heel* **3** to force (a way, route, etc) through (something) **4** (of light, etc) to shine through or penetrate (darkness) **5** (*also intr*) to discover or realize (something) suddenly or (of an idea, etc) to become suddenly apparent **6** (of sounds or cries) to sound sharply through (the silence, etc) **7** to move or affect deeply or sharply: *the cold pierced their bones* **8** (*intr*) to penetrate: *piercing cold* [c13 *percen*, from OF *percer*, ult. from L *pertundere*, from *per* through + *tundere* to strike] > **'piercing** *adj* > **'piercingly** *adv*

Pierce (pɪəs) *n* **Franklin** 1804–69, US statesman; 14th president of the US (1853–57)

piercing ('pɪəsɪŋ) *adj* **1** (of a sound) sharp and shrill **2** (of eyes or a look) intense and penetrating **3** (of an emotion) strong and deeply affecting **4** (of cold or wind) intense or biting ▷ *n* **5** the art or practice of piercing body parts for the insertion of jewellery **6** an instance of the piercing of a body part > **'piercingly** *adv*

pier glass *n* a tall narrow mirror, designed to hang on the wall between windows

Pieria (paɪ'ɪərɪə) *n* a region of ancient Macedonia, west of the Gulf of Salonika: site of the Pierian Spring

Pierian Spring (paɪ'ɪərɪən) *n* a sacred fountain in Pieria, in Greece, fabled to inspire those who drank from it

Pierides (paɪ'ɪərɪˌdiːz) *pl n Greek myth* **1** another name for the Muses (see **Muse**) **2** nine maidens of Thessaly, who were defeated in a singing contest by the Muses and turned into magpies for their effrontery

pieris ('paɪrɪs) *n* an evergreen shrub with white flowers like lily of the valley in spring, grown for the bright red colour of its young foliage [c19 from L, from Gk *Pīeris*, a Muse]

Piero della Francesca (*Italian* 'pjɛːro ˌdɛlla fran'tʃeska) *n* ?1420–92, Italian painter, noted particularly for his frescoes of the *Legend of the True Cross* in San Francesco, Arezzo

Piero di Cosimo (*Italian* 'pjɛːro di 'kɔːzimo) *n* 1462–1521, Italian painter, noted for his mythological works

Pierre (pɪə) *n* a city in central South Dakota, capital of the state, on the Missouri River. Pop: 12 906 (1990)

Pierrot ('pɪərəʊ; *French* pjɛro) *n* **1** a male character from French pantomime with a whitened face, white costume, and pointed hat **2** (*usually not cap*) a clown so made up

pier table *n* a side table designed to stand against a wall between windows

pietà (pɪɛ'tɑː) *n* a sculpture, painting, or drawing of the dead Christ, supported by the Virgin Mary [It.: pity, from L *pietās* PIETY]

Pietermaritzburg (ˌpiːtə'mærɪtsˌbɜːg) *n* a city in E South Africa, the capital of KwaZulu/Natal: founded in 1839 by the Boers: gateway to Natal's mountain resorts. Pop: 378 126 (1996)

Pietersburg ('piːtəzˌbɜːg) *n* the former name of **Polokwane**

pietism ('paɪɪˌtɪzəm) *n* exaggerated or affected piety > **'pietist** *n* > ˌ**pie'tistic** *or* ˌ**pie'tistical** *adj*

piet-my-vrou ('pɪtˌmeɪ'frəʊ) *n S African* a red-breasted cuckoo [imit.]

Pietro da Cortona (*Italian* 'pjɛːtro da kor'toːna) *n* real name *Pietro Berrettini*. 1596–1669, Italian baroque painter and architect

piety ('paɪɪtɪ) *n, pl* **pieties 1** dutiful devotion to God and observance of religious principles **2** the quality of being pious **3** a pious action, saying, etc **4** *now rare* devotion and obedience to parents or superiors [c13 *piete*, from OF, from L *pietās* piety, dutifulness, from *pius* pious]

piezoelectric effect (paɪˌiːzəʊɪ'lɛktrɪk) *or* **piezoelectricity** (paɪˌiːzəʊɪlɛk'trɪsɪtɪ) *n physics* **a** the production of electricity or electric polarity by applying a mechanical stress to certain crystals **b** the converse effect in which stress is produced in a crystal as a result of an applied potential difference [c19 from Gk *piezein* to press] > **piˌezoe'lectrically** *adv*

piffle ('pɪfᵊl) *inf* ▷ *n* **1** nonsense ▷ *vb* **piffles, piffling, piffled 2** (*intr*) to talk or behave feebly [c19 from ?]

piffling ('pɪflɪŋ) *adj inf* worthless; trivial

pig (pɪg) *n* **1** any artiodactyl mammal of an African and Eurasian family, esp the domestic pig, typically having a long head with a movable snout and a thick bristle-covered skin. Related adj: **porcine 2** *inf* a dirty, greedy, or bad-mannered person **3** the meat of swine; pork **4** *derog* a slang word for **policeman 5a** a mass of metal cast into a simple shape **5b** the mould used **6** *Brit inf* something that is difficult or unpleasant **7 a pig in a poke** something bought or received without prior sight or knowledge **8 make a pig of oneself** *inf* to overindulge oneself ▷ *vb* **pigs, pigging, pigged 9** (*intr*) (of a sow) to give birth **10** (*intr*) Also: **pig it** *inf* to live in squalor **11** (*tr*) *inf* to devour (food) greedily [c13 *pigge*, from ?]

pigeon[1] ('pɪdʒɪn) *n* **1** any of numerous related birds having a heavy body, small head, short legs, and long pointed wings **2** *sl* a victim or dupe [c14 from OF *pijon* young dove, from LL *pīpiō* young bird, from *pīpīre* to chirp]

pigeon[2] ('pɪdʒɪn) *n Brit inf* concern or responsibility (often in **it's his, her, etc, pigeon**) [c19 altered from PIDGIN]

pigeon breast *n* a deformity of the chest characterized by an abnormal protrusion of the breastbone, caused by rickets

pigeonhole ('pɪdʒɪnˌhəʊl) *n* **1** a small compartment for papers, letters, etc, as in a bureau **2** a hole or recess in a dovecote for pigeons to nest in ▷ *vb* **pigeonholes, pigeonholing, pigeonholed** (*tr*) **3** to put aside or defer **4** to classify or categorize

pigeon-toed *adj* having the toes turned inwards

pigface ('pɪgˌfeɪs) *n Austral* a creeping succulent plant having bright-coloured flowers and red fruits and often grown for ornament

piggery ('pɪgərɪ) *n, pl* **piggeries 1** a place where pigs are kept **2** great greediness

piggish ('pɪgɪʃ) *adj* **1** like a pig, esp in appetite or manners **2** *inf, chiefly Brit* obstinate or mean > **'piggishly** *adv* > **'piggishness** *n*

Piggott ('pɪgət) *n* **Lester (Keith)** born 1935, English flat-racing jockey: he won the Derby nine times

piggy ('pɪgɪ) *n, pl* **piggies 1** a child's word for a **pig 2** a child's word for a **toe** ▷ *adj* **piggier, piggiest 3** another word for **piggish**

piggyback ('pɪgɪˌbæk) *or* **pickaback** *n* **1** a ride on the back and shoulders of another person **2** a system whereby a vehicle, aircraft, etc, is transported for part of

Pp

its journey on another vehicle ▷ *adv* **3** on the back and shoulders of another person **4** on or as an addition ▷ *adj* **5** of or for a piggyback: *a piggyback ride; piggyback lorry trains* **6** of or relating to a type of heart transplant in which the transplanted heart functions in conjunction with the patient's own heart

piggy bank *n* a child's coin bank shaped like a pig with a slot for coins

pig-headed *adj* stupidly stubborn > ˌ**pig-ˈheadedly** *adv* > ˌ**pig-ˈheadedness** *n*

pig iron *n* crude iron produced in a blast furnace and poured into moulds

Pig Island *n NZ inf* New Zealand

piglet (ˈpɪglɪt) *n* a young pig

pigmeat (ˈpɪgˌmiːt) *n* a less common name for pork, ham, or bacon

pigment (ˈpɪgmənt) *n* **1** a substance occurring in plant or animal tissue and producing a characteristic colour **2** any substance used to impart colour **3** a powder that is mixed with a liquid to give a paint, ink, etc [C14 from L *pigmentum*, from *pingere* to paint] > ˈ**pigmentary** *adj*

pigmentation (ˌpɪgmənˈteɪʃən) *n* **1** coloration in plants, animals, or man caused by the presence of pigments **2** the deposition of pigment in animals, plants, or man

Pigmy (ˈpɪgmɪ) *n, pl* **Pigmies** a variant spelling of **Pygmy**

pignut (ˈpɪgˌnʌt) *n* **1** Also called: **hognut 1a** the bitter nut of any of several North American hickory trees **1b** any of the trees bearing such a nut **2** another name for **earthnut**

pig-root *vb (intr) Austral & NZ sl* (of a horse) to buck slightly

pigs (pɪgz) *interj Austral sl* an expression of derision or disagreement. Also: **pig's arse, pig's bum**

Pigs (pɪgz) *n* **Bay of** See **Bay of Pigs**

pigskin (ˈpɪgˌskɪn) *n* **1** the skin of the domestic pig **2** leather made of this skin **3** *US & Canad inf* a football ▷ *adj* **4** made of pigskin

pigsticking (ˈpɪgˌstɪkɪŋ) *n* the sport of hunting wild boar > ˈ**pigˌsticker** *n*

pigsty (ˈpɪgˌstaɪ) *or US & Canad* **pigpen** *n, pl* **pigsties** *or US & Canad* **pigpens 1** a pen for pigs; sty **2** *Brit* an untidy place

pigswill (ˈpɪgˌswɪl) *n* waste food or other edible matter fed to pigs. Also called: **pig's wash**

pigtail (ˈpɪgˌteɪl) *n* **1** a plait of hair or one of two plaits on either side of the face **2** a twisted roll of tobacco

pika (ˈpaɪkə) *n* a burrowing mammal of mountainous regions of North America and Asia, having short rounded ears, a rounded body, and rudimentary tail [C19 from E Siberian *piika*]

pikau (ˈpiːkaʊ) *n NZ* a pack, knapsack, or rucksack [Maori]

pike[1] (paɪk) *n, pl* **pike** *or* **pikes 1** any of several large predatory freshwater teleost fishes having a broad flat snout, strong teeth, and an elongated body covered with small scales **2** any of various similar fishes [C14 short for *pikefish*, from OE *pīc* point, with reference to the shape of its jaw]

pike[2] (paɪk) *n* **1** a medieval weapon consisting of a metal spearhead joined to a long pole **2** a point or spike ▷ *vb* **pikes, piking, piked 3** *(tr)* to pierce using a pike [OE *pīc* point, from ?] > ˈ**pikeman** *n*

pike[3] (paɪk) *n* short for **turnpike** (sense 1)

pike[4] (paɪk) *n Northern English dialect* a pointed or conical hill [OE *pīc*]

pike[5] (paɪk) *or* **piked** (paɪkt) *adj* (of the body position of a diver) bent at the hips but with the legs straight

pike[6] (paɪk) *vb* **pikes, piking, piked** *(intr;* foll by *out) Austral sl* to shirk [from PIKER]

pikelet (ˈpaɪklɪt) *n NZ* a small thick pancake [C18 from Welsh *bara pyglyd* pitchy bread]

pikeperch (ˈpaɪkˌpɜːtʃ) *n, pl* **pikeperch** *or* **pikeperches** any of various pikelike freshwater teleost fishes of the perch family of Europe

piker (ˈpaɪkə) *n US, Austral, & NZ sl* **1** a person who will not accept a challenge; shirker **2** a mean person [C19 from *Pike* county, Missouri, US]

Pikes Peak *n* a mountain in central Colorado, in the Rockies. Height: 4300 m (14 109 ft)

pikestaff (ˈpaɪkˌstɑːf) *n* the wooden handle of a pike

pilaster (pɪˈlæstə) *n* a shallow rectangular column attached to the face of a wall [C16 from F *pilastre*, from L *pīla* pillar] > **piˈlastered** *adj*

Pilate (ˈpaɪlət) *n* **Pontius** (ˈpɒnʃəs, ˈpɒntɪəs) Roman procurator of Judaea (?26–?36 AD), who ordered the crucifixion of Jesus, allegedly against his better judgment

Pilatus (*German* piˈlaːtʊs) *n* a mountain in central Switzerland, in Unterwalden canton: derives its name from the legend that the body of Pontius Pilate lay in a former lake on the mountain. Height: 2122 m (6962 ft)

pilau (pɪˈlaʊ), **pilaf, pilaff** (ˈpɪlæf), *or* **pilaw** (pɪˈlɔː) *n* a dish originating from the East, consisting of rice flavoured with spices and cooked in stock, to which meat, poultry, or fish may be added [C17 from Turkish *pilāw*, from Persian]

pilchard (ˈpɪltʃəd) *n* **1** a European food fish, *Sardina* (or *Clupea*) *pilchardus*, with a rounded body covered with large scales: family *Clupeidae* (herrings) **2** a related fish, *Sardinops neopilchardus*, of S Australian waters [C16 *pylcher*, of obscure origin]

Pilcomayo (*Spanish* pilkoˈmajo) *n* a river in S central South America, rising in W central Bolivia and flowing southeast, forming the border between Argentina and Paraguay, to the Paraguay River at Asunción. Length: about 1600 km (1000 miles)

pile[1] (paɪl) *n* **1** a collection of objects laid on top of one another; heap; mound **2** *inf* a large amount of money (esp in **make a pile**) **3** *(often pl) inf* a large amount: *a pile of work* **4** a less common word for **pyre 5** a large building or group of buildings **6** *physics* a structure of uranium and a moderator used for producing atomic energy; nuclear reactor ▷ *vb* **piles, piling, piled 7** (often foll by *up*) to collect or be collected into or as if into a pile: *snow piled up in the drive* **8** *(intr;* foll by *in, into, off, out,* etc) to move in a group, esp in a hurried or disorganized manner: *to pile off the bus* **9 pile it on** *inf* to exaggerate ▷ See also **pile up** [C15 via OF from L *pīla* stone pier]

pile[2] (paɪl) *n* **1** a long column of timber, concrete, or steel, driven into the ground as a foundation for a structure ▷ *vb* **piles, piling, piled** *(tr)* **2** to drive (piles) into the ground **3** to support (a structure) with piles [OE *pīl*, from L *pīlum*]

pile[3] (paɪl) *n* **1** the yarns in a fabric that stand up or out from the weave, as in carpeting, velvet, etc **2** soft fine hair, fur, wool, etc [C15 from Anglo-Norman *pyle*, from L *pilus* hair]

pileate (ˈpaɪlɪɪt, -ˌeɪt, ˈpɪl-) *or* **pileated** (ˈpaɪlɪˌeɪtɪd, ˈpɪl-) *adj* **1** (of birds) having a crest **2** *bot* having a pileus [C18 from L *pīleātus* wearing a felt cap, from PILEUS]

pile-driver *n* a machine that drives piles into the ground

pileous (ˈpaɪlɪəs, ˈpɪl-) *adj biol* **1** hairy **2** of or relating to hair [C19 ult. from L *pilus* a hair]

piles (paɪlz) *pl n* a nontechnical name for **haemorrhoids** [C15 from L *pilae* balls (referring to the external piles)]

pileum (ˈpaɪlɪəm, ˈpɪl-) *n, pl* **pilea** (-lɪə) the top of a bird's head from the base of the bill to the occiput [C19 NL, from L PILEUS]

pile up *vb (adv)* **1** to gather or be gathered in a pile **2** *inf* to crash or cause to crash ▷ *n* **pile-up 3** *inf* a multiple collision of vehicles

pileus (ˈpaɪlɪəs) *n, pl* **pilei** (-lɪˌaɪ) the upper cap-shaped part of a mushroom [C18 (botanical use): NL, from L: felt cap]

pilewort (ˈpaɪlˌwɜːt) *n* any of several plants, such as lesser celandine, thought to be effective in treating piles

pilfer (ˈpɪlfə) *vb* to steal (minor items), esp in small quantities [c14 *pylfre* (n) from OF *pelfre* booty] > '**pilferage** *n* > '**pilferer** *n*

pilgrim ('pɪlgrɪm) *n* **1** a person who undertakes a journey to a sacred place **2** any wayfarer [c12 from Provençal *pelegrin*, from L *peregrīnus* foreign, from *per* through + *ager* land]

pilgrimage ('pɪlgrɪmɪdʒ) *n* **1** a journey to a shrine or other sacred place **2** a journey or long search made for exalted or sentimental reasons ▷ *vb* **pilgrimages, pilgrimaging, pilgrimaged 3** (*intr*) to make a pilgrimage

Pilgrim Fathers *or* **Pilgrims** *pl n* **the** the English Puritans who sailed on the Mayflower to New England, where they founded Plymouth Colony in SE Massachusetts (1620)
▷ www.usahistory.info/New-England/Pilgrims.html
▷ www.mayflowersteps.co.uk

piliferous (paɪ'lɪfərəs) *adj* (esp of plants) bearing or ending in a hair or hairs [c19 from L *pilus* hair + -FEROUS] > '**pili,form** *adj*

piling ('paɪlɪŋ) *n* **1** the act of driving piles **2** a number of piles **3** a structure formed of piles

Pílion ('piljɔn) *n* transliteration of the Modern Greek name for **Pelion**

pill¹ (pɪl) *n* **1** a small spherical or ovoid mass of a medicinal substance, intended to be swallowed whole **2 the pill** (*sometimes cap*) *inf* an oral contraceptive **3** something unpleasant that must be endured (esp in **bitter pill to swallow**) **4** *sl* a ball or disc **5** *sl* an unpleasant or boring person ▷ *vb* **6** (*tr*) to give pills to [c15 from MFlemish *pille*, from L *pilula* a little ball, from *pila* ball]

pill² (pɪl) *vb* **1** *arch or dialect* to peel or skin (something) **2** *arch* to pillage or plunder (a place, etc) [OE *pilian*, from L *pilāre* to strip]

pillage ('pɪlɪdʒ) *vb* **pillages, pillaging, pillaged 1** to rob (a town, village, etc) of (booty or spoils) ▷ *n* **2** the act of pillaging **3** something obtained by pillaging; booty [c14 via OF from *piller* to despoil, prob. from *peille* rag, from L *pīleus* felt cap] > '**pillager** *n*

pillar ('pɪlə) *n* **1** an upright structure of stone, brick, metal, etc that supports a superstructure **2** something resembling this in shape or function: *a pillar of smoke* **3** a prominent supporter: *a pillar of the Church* **4 from pillar to post** from one place to another [c13 from OF *pilier*, from L *pīla*]

pillar box *n* (in Britain) a red pillar-shaped public letter box situated on a pavement

Pillars of Hercules *pl n* the two promontories at the E end of the Strait of Gibraltar: the Rock of Gibraltar on the European side and the Jebel Musa on the African side; according to legend, formed by Hercules

pillbox ('pɪl,bɒks) *n* **1** a box for pills **2** a small enclosed fortified emplacement, made of reinforced concrete **3** a small round hat

pillion ('pɪljən) *n* **1** a seat or place behind the rider of a motorcycle, scooter, horse, etc ▷ *adv* **2** on a pillion: *to ride pillion* [c16 from Gaelic; cf. Scot *pillean*, Irish *pillīn* couch]

pilliwinks ('pɪlɪ,wɪŋks) *pl n* a medieval instrument of torture for the fingers [c14 from ?]

pillock ('pɪlək) *n Brit sl* a stupid or annoying person [c14 from Scand. dialect *pillicock* penis]

pillory ('pɪlərɪ) *n, pl* **pillories 1** a wooden framework into which offenders were formerly locked by the neck and wrists and exposed to public abuse and ridicule **2** exposure to public scorn or abuse ▷ *vb* **pillories, pillorying, pilloried** (*tr*) **3** to expose to public scorn or ridicule **4** to punish by putting in a pillory [c13 from Anglo-L *pillorium*, from OF *pilori*, from ?]

pillow ('pɪləʊ) *n* **1** a cloth case stuffed with feathers, foam rubber, etc, used to support the head, esp during sleep **2** Also called: **cushion** a padded cushion or board on which pillow lace is made **3** anything like a pillow in shape or function ▷ *vb* (*tr*) **4** to rest (one's head) on or as if on a pillow **5** to serve as a pillow for [OE *pylwe*, from L *pulvīnus* cushion]

pillowcase ('pɪləʊ,keɪs) *or* **pillowslip** ('pɪləʊ,slɪp) *n* a removable washable cover of cotton, linen, nylon, etc, for a pillow

pillow fight *n* a mock fight in which participants thump each other with pillows

pillow lace *n* lace made by winding thread around bobbins on a padded cushion or board ▷ Cf **point lace**

pillow talk *n* confidential talk between sexual partners in bed

Pílos ('pilɔs) *n* transliteration of the Modern Greek name for **Pylos**

pilose ('paɪləʊz) *adj biol* covered with fine soft hairs: *pilose leaves* [c18 from L *pilōsus*, from *pilus* hair] > **pilosity** (paɪ'lɒsɪtɪ) *n*

pilot ('paɪlət) *n* **1** a person who is qualified to operate an aircraft or spacecraft in flight **2a** a person who is qualified to steer or guide a ship into or out of a port, river mouth, etc **2b** (*as modifier*): *a pilot ship* **3** a person who steers a ship **4** a person who acts as a leader or guide **5** *machinery* a guide used to assist in joining two mating parts together **6** an experimental programme on radio or television **7** (*modifier*) serving as a test or trial: *a pilot project* **8** (*modifier*) serving as a guide: *a pilot beacon* ▷ *vb* (*tr*) **9** to act as pilot of **10** to control the course of **11** to guide or lead (a project, people, etc) [c16 from F *pilote*, from Med. L *pilotus*, ult. from Gk *pēdon* oar]

pilotage ('paɪlətɪdʒ) *n* **1** the act of piloting an aircraft or ship **2** a pilot's fee

pilot balloon *n* a meteorological balloon used to observe air currents

pilot fish *n* a small fish of tropical and subtropical seas, marked with dark vertical bands: often accompanies sharks

pilot house *n naut* an enclosed structure on the bridge of a vessel from which it can be navigated; a wheelhouse

pilot lamp *n* a small light in an electric circuit or device that lights when the current is on

pilot light *n* **1** a small auxiliary flame that ignites the main burner of a gas appliance **2** a small electric light used as an indicator

pilot officer *n* the most junior commissioned rank in the British Royal Air Force and in certain other air forces

pilot study *n* a small-scale experiment undertaken to decide whether and how to launch a full-scale project

Pils (pɪlz, pɪls) *n* a type of lager-like beer [c20 abbrev of PILSNER]

Pilsen ('pɪlzən) *n* the German name for **Plzeň**

Pilsner ('pɪlznə) *or* **Pilsener** *n* a type of pale beer with a strong flavour of hops [after PILSEN, where it was orig. brewed]

Pilsudski (*Polish* piw'sutski) *n* **Józef** ('juzɛf) 1867–1935, Polish nationalist leader and statesman; president (1918–21) and premier (1926–28; 1930)

pilule ('pɪlju:l) *n* a small pill [c16 via F from L *pilula* little ball, from *pila* ball] > '**pilular** *adj*

pimento (pɪ'mɛntəʊ) *n, pl* **pimentos** another name for **allspice** or **pimiento** [c17 from Sp. *pimiento* pepper plant, from Med. L *pigmenta* spiced drink, from L *pigmentum* PIGMENT]

pi meson *n* another name for **pion**

pimiento (pɪ'mjɛntəʊ, -'mɛn-) *n, pl* **pimientos** a Spanish pepper with a red fruit used as a vegetable. Also called: **pimento** [var. of PIMENTO]

pimp¹ (pɪmp) *n* **1** a man who solicits for a prostitute or brothel **2** a man who procures sexual gratification for another; procurer; pander ▷ *vb* **3** (*intr*) to act as a pimp [c17 from ?]

pimp² (pɪmp) *sl, chiefly Austral & NZ* ▷ *n* **1** a spy or informer ▷ *vb* **2** (*intr*; often foll by *on*) to inform (on) [from ?]

pimpernel ('pɪmpə,nɛl, -nᵊl) *n* any of several plants,

Pp

such as the scarlet pimpernel, typically having small star-shaped flowers [c15 from OF *pimpernelle*, ult. from L *piper* PEPPER]

pimple (ˈpɪmpᵊl) *n* a small round usually inflamed swelling of the skin [c14 rel. to OE *pipilian* to break out in spots] > ˈ**pimpled** *adj* > ˈ**pimply** *adj* > ˈ**pimpliness** *n*

pin (pɪn) *n* **1** a short stiff straight piece of wire pointed at one end and either rounded or having a flattened head at the other: used mainly for fastening pieces of cloth, paper, etc **2** short for **cotter pin, hairpin, panel pin, rolling pin,** or **safety pin** **3** an ornamental brooch, esp a narrow one **4** a badge worn fastened to the clothing by a pin **5** something of little or no importance (esp in **not care** *or* **give a pin (for)**) **6** a peg or dowel **7** anything resembling a pin in shape, function, etc **8** (in various bowling games) a usually club-shaped wooden object set up in groups as a target **9** Also called: **safety pin** a clip on a hand grenade that prevents its detonation until removed or released **10** *naut* **10a** See **belaying pin** **10b** the sliding closure for a shackle **11** *music* a metal tuning peg on a piano **12** *surgery* a metal rod, esp of stainless steel, for holding together adjacent ends of fractured bones during healing **13** *chess* a position in which a piece is pinned against a more valuable piece or the king **14** *golf* the flagpole marking the hole on a green **15** (*usually pl*) *inf* a leg ▷ *vb* **pins, pinning, pinned** (*tr*) **16** to attach, hold, or fasten with or as if with a pin or pins **17** to transfix with a pin, spear, etc **18** (foll by *on*) *inf* to place (the blame for something): *he pinned the charge on his accomplice* **19** *chess* to cause (an enemy piece) to be effectively immobilized since moving it would reveal a check or expose a more valuable piece to capture ▷ See also **pin down** [OE *pinn*]

PIN (pɪn) *n acronym for* personal identification number: a number used by a holder of a cash card or credit card used in EFTPOS

pinaceous (paɪˈneɪʃəs) *adj* of, relating to, or belonging to a family of conifers with needle-like leaves: includes pine, spruce, fir, larch, and cedar [c19 via NL from L *pīnus* a pine]

pinafore (ˈpɪnəˌfɔː) *n* **1** *chiefly Brit* an apron, esp one with a bib **2** Also called: **pinafore dress** a dress with a sleeveless bodice or bib top, worn over a jumper or blouse [c18 from PIN + AFORE]

Pinar del Río (*Spanish* piˈnar ðɛl ˈrrio) *n* a city in W Cuba: tobacco industry. Pop: 128 570 (1994 est)

pinaster (paɪˈnæstə) *n* a Mediterranean pine tree with paired needles and prickly cones. Also called: **maritime** (*or* **cluster**) **pinaster** [c16 from L: wild pine, from *pīnus* pine]

pinball (ˈpɪnˌbɔːl) *n* **a** a game in which the player shoots a small ball through several hazards on a table, electrically operated machine, etc **b** (*as modifier*): *a pinball machine*

pince-nez (ˈpænsˌneɪ, ˈpɪns-; *French* pɛ̃sne) *n, pl* **pince-nez** eyeglasses that are held in place only by means of a clip over the bridge of the nose [c19 F, lit.: pinch-nose]

pincers (ˈpɪnsəz) *pl n* **1** Also called: **pair of pincers** a gripping tool consisting of two hinged arms with handles at one end and, at the other, curved bevelled jaws that close on the workpiece **2** the pair or pairs of jointed grasping appendages in lobsters and certain other arthropods [c14 from OF *pinceour*, from OF *pincier* to pinch]

pinch (pɪntʃ) *vb* **1** to press (something, esp flesh) tightly between two surfaces, esp between a finger and thumb **2** to confine, squeeze, or painfully press (toes, fingers, etc) because of lack of space: *these shoes pinch* **3** (*tr*) to cause stinging pain to: *the cold pinched his face* **4** (*tr*) to make thin or drawn-looking, as from grief, lack of food, etc **5** (usually foll by *on*) to provide (oneself or another person) with meagre allowances, amounts, etc **6** **pinch pennies** to live frugally because of meanness or to economize **7** (usually foll by *off, out,* or *back*) to remove the tips of (buds, shoots, etc) to correct or encourage growth **8** (*tr*) *inf* to steal or take without asking **9** (*tr*) *inf* to arrest ▷ *n* **10** a squeeze or sustained nip **11** the quantity of a substance, such as salt, that can be taken between a thumb and finger **12** a very small quantity **13** (usually preceded by *the*) sharp, painful, or extreme stress, need, etc: *feeling the pinch of poverty* **14** *sl* a robbery **15** *sl* a police raid or arrest **16** **at a pinch** if absolutely necessary [c16 prob. from OF *pinchier* (unattested)]

pinchbeck (ˈpɪntʃˌbɛk) *n* **1** an alloy of copper and zinc, used as imitation gold **2** a spurious or cheap imitation ▷ *adj* **3** made of pinchbeck **4** sham or cheap [c18 (the alloy), c19 (something spurious): after C. *Pinchbeck* (?1670–1732), E watchmaker who invented it]

pinchpenny (ˈpɪntʃˌpɛnɪ) *adj* **1** niggardly; miserly ▷ *n, pl* **pinchpennies** **2** a miserly person

Pinckney (ˈpɪŋknɪ) *n* **1** **Charles** 1757–1824, US statesman, who was a leading member of the convention that framed the US Constitution (1787) **2** his cousin, **Charles Cotesworth** 1746–1825, US soldier, statesman, and diplomat, who also served at the Constitutional Convention **3** his brother, **Thomas** 1750–1828, US soldier and politician. He was US minister to Britain (1792–96) and special envoy to Spain (1795–96)

Pincus (ˈpɪŋkəs) *n* **Gregory Goodwin** 1903–67, US physiologist, whose work on steroid hormones led to the development of the first contraceptive pill

pincushion (ˈpɪnˌkʊʃən) *n* a small well-padded cushion in which pins are stuck ready for use

Pindar (ˈpɪndə) *n* ?518–?438 BC, Greek lyric poet, noted for his *Epinikia*, odes commemorating victories in the Greek games

pin down *vb* (*tr, adv*) **1** to force (someone) to make a decision or carry out a promise **2** to define clearly: *he had a vague suspicion that he couldn't quite pin down* **3** to confine to a place

Pindus (ˈpɪndəs) *n* a mountain range in central Greece between Epirus and Thessaly. Highest peak: Mount Smólikas, 2633 m (8639 ft). Modern Greek name: **Píndhos** (ˈpinðɔs)

pine[1] (paɪn) *n* **1** any of a genus of evergreen resinous coniferous trees of the N hemisphere, with long needle-shaped leaves (**pine needles**) and brown cones **2** the wood of any of these trees [OE *pīn*, from L *pīnus* pine]

pine[2] (paɪn) *vb* **pines, pining, pined** **1** (*intr;* often foll by *for* or an infinitive) to feel great longing or desire; yearn **2** (*intr;* often foll by *away*) to become ill or thin through worry, longing, etc [OE *pīnian* to torture, from *pīn* pain, from Med. L *pēna*, from L *poena* PAIN]

Pine (paɪn) *n* **Courtney** born 1964, British jazz saxophonist

pineal eye (ˈpɪnɪəl) *n* an outgrowth of the pineal gland that forms an eyelike structure on the top of the head in certain cold-blooded vertebrates [c19 from F, from L *pīnea* pine cone]

pineal gland *or* **body** *n* a pea-sized organ situated at the base of the brain that secretes a hormone, melatonin, into the bloodstream. Technical names: **epiphysis, epiphysis cerebri**

pineapple (ˈpaɪnˌæpᵊl) *n* **1** a tropical American plant cultivated for its large fleshy edible fruit **2** the fruit of this plant, consisting of an inflorescence clustered around a fleshy axis and surmounted by a tuft of leaves **3** *mil sl* a hand grenade [c14 *pinappel* pine cone; c17 applied to the fruit because of its appearance]

pine cone *n* the seed-producing structure of a pine tree. See **cone** (sense 3a)

pine marten *n* a marten of N European and Asian coniferous woods, having dark brown fur with a creamy-yellow patch on the throat

pinene (ˈpaɪniːn) *n* either of two isomeric terpenes,

found in many essential oils and constituting the main part of oil of turpentine [c20 from PINE[1] + -ENE]

pine nut *or* **kernel** *n* the edible seed of certain pine trees

Pinero (pɪˈnɪərəʊ) *n* Sir **Arthur Wing** 1855–1934, English dramatist. His works include the farce *Dandy Dick* (1887) and the problem play *The Second Mrs Tanqueray* (1893)

Pines (paɪnz) *n* **Isle of** the former name of the (Isle of) **Youth**

pine tar *n* a brown or black semisolid, produced by the destructive distillation of pine wood, used in roofing compositions, paints, medicines, etc

pinfeather (ˈpɪnˌfɛðə) *n ornithol* a feather emerging from the skin and still enclosed in its horny sheath

pinfold (ˈpɪnˌfəʊld) *n* **1** a pound for stray cattle ▷ *vb* **2** (*tr*) to gather or confine in or as if in a pinfold [OE *pundfald*]

ping (pɪŋ) *n* **1** a short high-pitched resonant sound, as of a bullet striking metal or a sonar echo **2** *computing* a system for testing whether Internet systems are responding and how long in milliseconds it takes them to respond ▷ *vb* **3** (*intr*) to make a pinging noise **4** *computing* to send a text message to (a computer or server) in order to check whether it is responding or how long it takes to respond [c19 imit.]

pinger (ˈpɪŋə) *n* a device that makes a pinging sound, esp one that can be preset to ring at a particular time

Ping-Pong (ˈpɪŋˌpɒŋ) *n trademark* another name for **table tennis** Also: **ping pong**

pinhead (ˈpɪnˌhɛd) *n* **1** the head of a pin **2** something very small **3** *inf* a stupid person > ˈ**pinˌheaded** *adj* > ˈ**pinˌheadedness** *n*

pinhole (ˈpɪnˌhəʊl) *n* a small hole made with or as if with a pin

pinion[1] (ˈpɪnjən) *n* **1** *chiefly poetic* a bird's wing **2** the part of a bird's wing including the flight feathers ▷ *vb* (*tr*) **3** to hold or bind (the arms) of (a person) so as to restrain or immobilize him **4** to confine or shackle **5** to make (a bird) incapable of flight by removing the flight feathers [c15 from OF *pignon* wing, from L *pinna* wing]

pinion[2] (ˈpɪnjən) *n* a cogwheel that engages with a larger wheel or rack [c17 from F *pignon* cogwheel, from OF *peigne* comb, from L *pecten*]

Piniós (piˈnjɔs) *n* transliteration of the Modern Greek name for the **Salambria**

pink[1] (pɪŋk) *n* **1** a pale reddish colour **2** pink cloth or clothing: *dressed in pink* **3** any of various Old World plants, such as the garden pink, cultivated for their fragrant flowers. See also **carnation** (sense 1) **4** the flower of any of these plants **5** the highest or best degree, condition, etc (esp in **in the pink**) **6a** a huntsman's scarlet coat **6b** a huntsman who wears a scarlet coat ▷ *adj* **7** of the colour pink **8** *Brit inf* left-wing **9** *inf* of or relating to homosexuals or homosexuality: *the pink vote* **10** (of a huntsman's coat) scarlet or red ▷ *vb* **11** (*intr*) another word for **knock** (sense 7) [c16 (the flower), c18 (the colour): ? short for PINKEYE] > ˈ**pinkish** *or* ˈ**pinky** *adj* > ˈ**pinkness** *n*

pink[2] (pɪŋk) *vb* (*tr*) **1** to prick lightly with a sword, etc **2** to decorate (leather, etc) with a perforated or punched pattern **3** to cut with pinking shears [c14 ? of Low G origin]

pink[3] (pɪŋk) *n* a sailing vessel with a narrow overhanging transom [c15 from MDu. *pinke*, from ?]

Pinkerton (ˈpɪŋkətən) *n* **Allan** 1819–84, US private detective, born in Scotland. He founded the first detective agency in the US (1850) and organized an intelligence system for the Federal States of America (1861)

pinkeye (ˈpɪŋkˌaɪ) *n* **1** Also called: **acute conjunctivitis** an acute contagious inflammation of the conjunctiva of the eye, characterized by redness, discharge, etc **2** Also called: **infectious keratitis** a similar condition affecting the cornea of horses and cattle [c16 partial translation of obs. Du. *pinck oogen* small eyes]

Pink Floyd (pɪŋk flɔɪd) *n* British rock group, formed in 1966: originally comprised Syd Barrett (born 1946), Roger Waters (born 1944), Rick Wright (born 1945), and Nick Mason (born 1945); Barrett was replaced by Dave Gilmour (born 1944) in 1968 and Waters left in 1986. Recordings include *The Piper at the Gates of Dawn* (1967), *Dark Side of the Moon* (1973), *Wish You Were Here* (1975), and *The Division Bell* (1994)

pinkie *or* **pinky** (ˈpɪŋkɪ) *n, pl* **pinkies** *Scot, US, & Canad* the little finger [c19 from Du. *pinkje*]

pinking shears *pl n* scissors with a serrated edge on one or both blades, producing a wavy edge to material cut, thus preventing fraying

pink salmon *n* **1** any salmon having pale pink flesh **2** the flesh of such a fish

pin money *n* **1** an allowance by a husband to his wife for personal expenditure **2** money saved or earned for incidental expenses

pinna (ˈpɪnə) *n, pl* **pinnae** (-niː) *or* **pinnas** **1** any leaflet of a pinnate compound leaf **2** *zool* a feather, wing, fin, etc **3** another name for **auricle** (sense 2) [c18 via NL from L: wing]

pinnace (ˈpɪnɪs, -əs) *n* any of various kinds of ship's tender [c16 from F *pinace*, ?from OSp. *pinaza*, lit.: something made of pine, ult. from L *pīnus* pine]

pinnacle (ˈpɪnəkᵊl) *n* **1** the highest point, esp of fame, success, etc **2** a towering peak, as of a mountain **3** a slender upright structure in the form of a spire on the top of a buttress, gable, or tower ▷ *vb* **pinnacles, pinnacling, pinnacled** (*tr*) **4** to set as on a pinnacle **5** to furnish with a pinnacle or pinnacles **6** to crown with a pinnacle [c14 via OF from LL *pinnāculum* a peak, from L *pinna* wing]

pinnate (ˈpɪneɪt, ˈpɪnɪt) *adj* **1** like a feather in appearance **2** (of compound leaves) having the leaflets growing opposite each other in pairs on either side of the stem [c18 from L *pinnātus*, from *pinna* feather] > ˈ**pinnately** *adv* > **pinˈnation** *n*

Pp

pinniped (ˈpɪnɪˌpɛd) *adj* **1** of, relating to, or belonging to an order of aquatic placental mammals having a streamlined body and limbs specialized as flippers: includes seals, sea lions, and the walrus ▷ *n* **2** any pinniped animal [c19 from NL *pinnipēs*, from L *pinna* fin + *pēs* foot]

pinnule (ˈpɪnjuːl) *n* **1** any of the lobes of a leaflet of a pinnate compound leaf, which is itself pinnately divided **2** *zool* any feather-like part, such as any of the arms of a sea lily [c16 from L *pinnula*, dim. of *pinna* feather] > ˈ**pinnular** *adj*

pinny (ˈpɪnɪ) *n, pl* **pinnies** a child's or informal name for **pinafore** (sense 1)

Pinochet (Ugarte) (ˈpiːnəʃeɪ) *n* **Augusto** (auˈɣusto) born 1915, Chilean general and statesman; president of Chile (1974–90) following his overthrow of Allende (1973): charged (2001) with murder and kidnapping but found unfit to stand trial

pinochle *or* **pinocle** (ˈpiːnʌkᵊl) *n* **1** a card game for two to four players similar to bezique **2** the combination of queen of spades and jack of diamonds in this game [c19 from ?]

Pinotage (ˈpɪnətɑːʒ) *n* **1** a red grape variety of South Africa **2** any of the red wines made from this grape

Pinot Grigio (ˈpiːnəʊ ˈgriːdʒəʊ) *n* **1** a variety of grape, grown in Italy for wine-making **2** any of the white Italian wines made from this grape [Italian *grigio* grey]

Pinot Noir (piːˈnəʊ nwɑː) *n* **1** a variety of black grape, grown esp for wine-making **2** any of the red wines made from this grape [F]

pinpoint (ˈpɪnˌpɔɪnt) *vb* (*tr*) **1** to locate or identify exactly: *to pinpoint a problem; to pinpoint a place on a map* ▷ *n* **2** an insignificant or trifling thing **3** the point of a pin **4** (*modifier*) exact: *a pinpoint aim*

pinprick (ˈpɪnˌprɪk) *n* **1** a slight puncture made by or as if by a pin **2** a small irritation ▷ *vb* **3** (*tr*) to puncture with or as if with a pin

pins and needles *n* (*functioning as sing*) *inf* **1** a tingling sensation in the fingers, toes, legs, etc, caused by the return of normal blood circulation after its temporary impairment **2 on pins and needles** in a state of anxious suspense

Pinsk (*Russian* pinsk) *n* a city in SW Belarus: capital of a principality (13th–14th centuries). Pop: 132 000 (1998 est)

pinstripe ('pɪn,straɪp) *n* (in textiles) a very narrow stripe in fabric or the fabric itself

pint (paɪnt) *n* **1** a unit of liquid measure of capacity equal to one eighth of a gallon. 1 Brit pint is equal to 0.568 litre, 1 US pint to 0.473 litre **2** a unit of dry measure of capacity equal to one half of a quart. 1 US dry pint is equal to one sixty-fourth of a US bushel or 0.5506 litre **3** a measure having such a capacity **4** *Brit inf* **4a** a pint of beer **4b** a drink of beer: *he's gone out for a pint* [C14 from OF *pinte*, from ?; ?from Med. L *pincta* marks used in measuring liquids, ult. from L *pingere* to paint]

pinta ('paɪntə) *n inf* a pint of milk [C20 phonetic rendering of *pint of*]

pintail ('pɪn,teɪl) *n, pl* **pintails** *or* **pintail** a greyish-brown duck with a pointed tail

Pinter ('pɪntə) *n* **Harold** born 1930, English dramatist. His plays, such as *The Caretaker* (1959), *The Homecoming* (1964), *No Man's Land* (1974), *Moonlight* (1993), and *Celebration* (2000), are noted for their equivocal and halting dialogue

pintle ('pɪntᵊl) *n* **1** a pin or bolt forming the pivot of a hinge **2** the link bolt, hook, or pin on a vehicle's towing bracket **3** the needle or plunger of the injection valve of an oil engine [OE *pintel* penis]

pinto ('pɪntəʊ) *US & Canad* ▷ *adj* **1** marked with patches of white; piebald ▷ *n, pl* **pintos 2** a pinto horse [C19 from American Sp. (orig.: painted, spotted), ult. from L *pingere* to paint]

pint-size *or* **pint-sized** *adj inf* very small

pin tuck *n* a narrow, ornamental fold, esp used on shirt fronts and dress bodices

Pinturicchio (*Italian* pintu'rikkjo) *or* **Pintoricchio** (*Italian* pinto'rikkjo) *n* real name *Bernardino di Betto*. ?1454–1513, Italian painter of the Umbrian school

pin-up *n* **1** *inf* **1a** a picture of a sexually attractive person, esp when partially or totally undressed **1b** (*as modifier*): *a pin-up magazine* **2** *sl* a person who has appeared in such a picture **3** a photograph of a famous personality

pinus radiata ('paɪnəs ,reɪdɪ'ɑːtə) *n* a pine tree grown in New Zealand and Australia to produce building timber

pinwheel ('pɪn,wiːl) *n* another name for a **Catherine wheel** (sense 1)

pinworm ('pɪn,wɜːm) *n* a parasitic nematode worm, infecting the colon, rectum, and anus of humans. Also called: **threadworm**

piny ('paɪnɪ) *adj* **pinier, piniest** of, resembling, or covered with pine trees

Pinyin ('pɪn'jɪn) *n* a system of spelling used to transliterate Chinese characters into the Roman alphabet

Pinzón (*Spanish* pin'θon) *n* **1 Martín Alonzo** (mar'tin a'lɔnθo) ?1440–93, Spanish navigator, who commanded the *Pinta* on Columbus' first expedition (1492–93), which he abandoned in a vain attempt to be the first to arrive back in Spain **2** his brother, **Vicente Yáñez** (bi'θente 'jaɲɛθ) ?1460–?1524, Spanish navigator, who commanded the *Niña* on Columbus' first expedition (1492–93)

pion ('paɪɒn) *or* **pi meson** *n physics* a meson having a positive or negative charge and a rest mass 273 times that of the electron, or no charge and a rest mass 264 times that of the electron [C20 from Gk letter PI + -ON]

pioneer (,paɪə'nɪə) *n* **1a** a colonist, explorer, or settler of a new land, region, etc **1b** (*as modifier*): *a pioneer wagon* **2** an innovator or developer of something new **3** *mil* a member of an infantry group that digs entrenchments, makes roads, etc ▷ *vb* **4** to be a pioneer (in or of) **5** (*tr*) to initiate, prepare, or open up: *to pioneer a medical programme in the Sudan* [C16 from OF *paonier* infantryman, from *paon* PAWN²]

pious ('paɪəs) *adj* **1** having or expressing reverence for a god or gods; religious; devout **2** marked by reverence **3** marked by false reverence; sanctimonious **4** sacred; not secular [C17 from L *pius*] > **'piously** *adv* > **'piousness** *n*

pip¹ (pɪp) *n* **1** the seed of a fleshy fruit, such as an apple or pear **2** any of the segments marking the surface of a pineapple [C18 short for PIPPIN]

pip² (pɪp) *n* **1** a short high-pitched sound, a sequence of which can act as a time signal, esp on radio **2** a radar blip **3a** a device, such as a spade, diamond, heart, or club on a playing card **3b** any of the spots on dice or dominoes **4** *inf* the emblem worn on the shoulder by junior officers in the British Army, indicating their rank ▷ *vb* **pips, pipping, pipped 5** (of a young bird) **5a** (*intr*) to chirp; peep **5b** to pierce (the shell of its egg) while hatching **6** (*intr*) to make a short high-pitched sound [C16 (in the sense: spot); C17 (vb); C20 (in the sense: short high-pitched sound): ? imit.]

pip³ (pɪp) *n* **1** a contagious disease of poultry characterized by the secretion of thick mucus in the mouth and throat **2** *facetious sl* a minor human ailment **3** *Brit sl* a bad temper or depression (esp in **give (someone) the pip**) ▷ *vb* **pips, pipping, pipped 4** *Brit sl* to cause to be annoyed or depressed [C15 from MDu. *pippe*, ult. from L *pituita* phlegm]

pip⁴ (pɪp) *vb* **pips, pipping, pipped** (*tr*) *Brit sl* **1** to wound, esp with a gun **2** to defeat (a person), esp when his or her success seems certain (often in **pip at the post**) **3** to blackball or ostracize [C19 (orig. in the sense: to blackball): prob. from PIP²]

pipal ('piːpᵊl) *n* a variant of **peepul**

pipe¹ (paɪp) *n* **1** a long tube of metal, plastic, etc, used to convey water, oil, gas, etc **2** a long tube or case **3** an object made in various shapes and sizes, consisting of a small bowl with an attached tubular stem, in which tobacco or other substances are smoked **4** Also called: **pipeful** the amount of tobacco that fills the bowl of a pipe **5 put that in your pipe and smoke it** *inf* accept that fact if you can **6** *zool, bot* any of various hollow organs, such as the respiratory passage of certain animals **7a** any musical instrument whose sound production results from the vibration of an air column in a simple tube **7b** any of the tubular devices on an organ **8 the pipes** See **bagpipes 9** a shrill voice or sound, as of a bird **10a** a boatswain's pipe **10b** the sound it makes **11** (*pl*) *inf* the respiratory tract or vocal cords **12** *metallurgy* a conical hole in the head of an ingot **13** a cylindrical vein of rich ore **14** Also called: **volcanic pipe** a vertical cylindrical passage in a volcano through which molten lava is forced during eruption ▷ *vb* **pipes, piping, piped 15** to play (music) on a pipe **16** (*tr*) to summon or lead by a pipe: *to pipe the dancers* **17** to utter (something) shrilly **18a** to signal orders to (the crew) by a boatswain's pipe **18b** (*tr*) to signal the arrival or departure of: *to pipe the admiral aboard* **19** (*tr*) to convey (water, gas, etc) by a pipe or pipes **20** (*tr*) to provide with pipes **21** (*tr*) to trim (an article, esp of clothing) with piping **22** to force cream or icing, etc, through a shaped nozzle to decorate food ▷ See also **pipe down, pipe up** [OE *pīpe* (n), *pīpian* (vb), ult. from L *pīpāre* to chirp]

pipe² (paɪp) *n* **1** a large cask for wine, oil, etc **2** a measure of capacity for wine equal to four barrels or 105 Brit gallons **3** a cask holding this quantity with its contents [C14 via OF (in the sense: tube), ult. from L *pīpāre* to chirp]

pipe bomb *n* a small explosive device hidden in a pipe or drain, detonated by means of a timer

pipeclay ('paɪp,kleɪ) *n* **1** a fine white pure clay, used in the manufacture of tobacco pipes and pottery and for whitening leather and similar materials ▷ *vb* **2** (*tr*) to whiten with pipeclay

pipe cleaner *n* a short length of thin wires twisted so as to hold tiny tufts of yarn: used to clean the stem of a tobacco pipe

piped music *n* light popular music prerecorded and played through amplifiers in a shop, restaurant, factory, etc, as background music

pipe down *vb* (*intr, adv*) *inf* to stop talking, making noise, etc

pipe dream *n* a fanciful or impossible plan or hope [alluding to dreams produced by smoking an opium pipe]

pipefish ('paɪp,fɪʃ) *n, pl* **pipefish** *or* **pipefishes** any of various teleost fishes having a long tubelike snout and an elongated body covered with bony plates. Also called: **needlefish**

pipefitting ('paɪp,fɪtɪŋ) *n* **a** the act or process of bending and joining pipes **b** the branch of plumbing involving this > '**pipe,fitter** *n*

pipeline ('paɪp,laɪn) *n* **1** a long pipe used to transport oil, natural gas, etc **2** a medium of communication, esp a private one **3** **in the pipeline** in the process of being completed, delivered, or produced ▷ *vb* **pipelines, pipelining, pipelined** (*tr*) **4** to convey by pipeline **5** to supply with a pipeline

pipe major *n* the noncommissioned officer responsible for the training of a pipe band

pipe organ *n* another name for **organ** (the musical instrument)

piper ('paɪpə) *n* **1** a person who plays a pipe or bagpipes **2** **pay the piper and call the tune** to bear the cost of an undertaking and control it

Piper ('paɪpə) *n* **John** 1903–92, British artist. An official war artist in World War II, he is known esp for his watercolours of bombed churches and his stained glass in Coventry Cathedral

piperidine (pɪ'pɛrɪ,di:n) *n* a liquid compound with a peppery ammoniacal odour: used in making rubbers and curing epoxy resins

piperine ('pɪpə,raɪn) *n* an alkaloid that is the active ingredient of pepper, used as a flavouring and as an insecticide [c19 from L *piper* PEPPER]

piperonal ('pɪpərəʊ,næl) *n* a white fragrant aldehyde used in flavourings, perfumery, and suntan lotions

pipette (pɪ'pɛt) *n* a calibrated glass tube drawn to a fine bore at one end, filled by sucking liquid into the bulb, and used to transfer or measure known volumes of liquid [c19 via F: little pipe]

pipe up *vb* (*intr, adv*) **1** to commence singing or playing a musical instrument: *the band piped up* **2** to speak up, esp in a shrill voice

pipi ('pɪpi:) *n, pl* **pipi** *or* **pipis** **1** an edible shellfish of New Zealand **2** an Australian mollusc of sandy beaches, widely used as bait [from Maori]

piping ('paɪpɪŋ) *n* **1** pipes collectively, as in the plumbing of a house **2** a cord of icing, whipped cream, etc, often used to decorate desserts and cakes **3** a thin strip of covered cord or material, used to edge hems, etc **4** the sound of a pipe or bagpipes **5** the art or technique of playing a pipe or bagpipes **6** a shrill voice or sound, esp a whistling sound ▷ *adj* **7** making a shrill sound **8** **piping hot** extremely hot

pipistrelle (,pɪpɪ'strɛl) *n* any of a genus of numerous small brownish insectivorous bats, occurring in most parts of the world [c18 via F from It. *pipistrello*, from L *vespertīliō* a bat, from *vesper* evening, because of its nocturnal habits]

pipit ('pɪpɪt) *n* any of various songbirds, esp the **meadow pipit**, having brownish speckled plumage and a long tail [c18 prob. imit.]

pipkin ('pɪpkɪn) *n* a small earthenware vessel [c16 ? dim. of PIPE²; see -KIN]

pippin ('pɪpɪn) *n* any of several varieties of eating apple [c13 from OF *pepin*, from ?]

pipsissewa (pɪp'sɪsəwə) *n* any of several ericaceous plants of an Asian and American genus, having jagged evergreen leaves and white or pinkish flowers. Also called: **wintergreen** [c19 from Algonquian *pipisisikweu*, lit.: it breaks it into pieces, so called because believed to be efficacious in treating bladder stones]

pipsqueak ('pɪp,skwi:k) *n inf* a person or thing that is insignificant or contemptible

piquant ('pi:kənt, -kɑ:nt) *adj* **1** having an agreeably pungent or tart taste **2** lively or stimulating to the mind [c16 from F (lit.: prickling), from *piquer* to prick, goad] > '**piquancy** *n* > '**piquantly** *adv*

pique (pi:k) *n* **1** a feeling of resentment or irritation, as from having one's pride wounded ▷ *vb* **piques, piquing, piqued** (*tr*) **2** to cause to feel resentment or irritation **3** to excite or arouse **4** (foll by *on* or *upon*) to pride or congratulate (oneself) [c16 from F, from *piquer* to prick]

piqué ('pi:keɪ) *n* a close-textured fabric of cotton, silk, or spun rayon woven with lengthwise ribs [c19 from F *piqué* pricked, from *piquer* to prick]

piquet (pɪ'kɛt, -'keɪ) *n* a card game for two people played with a reduced pack [c17 from F, from ?]

piracy ('paɪrəsɪ) *n, pl* **piracies** **1** *Brit* robbery on the seas **2** a felony, such as robbery or hijacking, committed aboard a ship or aircraft **3** the unauthorized use or appropriation of patented or copyrighted material, ideas, etc [c16 from Anglo-L *pirātia*, from LGk *peirāteia*; see PIRATE]

Piraeus *or* **Peiraeus** (paɪ'ri:əs, pɪ'reɪ-) *n* a port in SE Greece, adjoining Athens: the country's chief port; founded in the 5th century BC as the port of Athens. Pop: 169 622 (1991). Modern Greek name: **Piraiévs** (,pirɛ'ɛfs)

Pirandello (*Italian* piran'dɛllo) *n* **Luigi** (lu'i:dʒi) 1867–1936, Italian short-story writer, novelist, and dramatist. His plays include *Right you are (If you think so)* (1917), *Six Characters in Search of an Author* (1921), and *Henry IV* (1922): Nobel prize for literature 1934

Piranesi (*Italian* pira'ne:si) *n* **Giambattista** (dʒambat'tista) 1720–78, Italian etcher and architect: etchings include *Imaginary Prisons* and *Views of Rome*

piranha *or* **piraña** (pɪ'rɑ:njə) *n* any of various small freshwater voracious fishes of tropical America, having strong jaws and sharp teeth [c19 via Port. from Tupi: fish with teeth, from *pirá* fish + *sainha* tooth]

pirate ('paɪrɪt) *n* **1** a person who commits piracy **2a** a vessel used by pirates **2b** (*as modifier*): *a pirate ship* **3** a person who illicitly uses or appropriates someone else's literary, artistic, or other work **4a** a person or group of people who broadcast illegally **4b** (*as modifier*): *a pirate radio station* ▷ *vb* **pirates, pirating, pirated** **5** (*tr*) to use, appropriate, or reproduce (artistic work, ideas, etc) illicitly [c15 from L *pīrāta*, from Gk *peirātēs* one who attacks, from *peira* an attack] > **pi'ratical** *or* **piratic** (paɪ'rætɪk) *adj* > **pi'ratically** *adv*

piri-piri (,pɪrɪ'pɪrɪ) *n* a hot sauce, of Portuguese colonial origin, made from red chilli peppers [from a Bantu language: literally, pepper]

Pirithoüs (paɪ'rɪθəʊəs) *n Greek myth* a prince of the Lapiths, who accomplished many great deeds with his friend Theseus

pirogue (pɪ'rəʊg) *or* **piragua** (pɪ'rɑ:gwə, -'ræg-) *n* any of various kinds of dugout canoes [c17 via F from Sp., of Amerind origin]

pirouette (,pɪrʊ'ɛt) *n* **1** a body spin, esp in dancing, on the toes or the ball of the foot ▷ *vb* **pirouettes, pirouetting, pirouetted** **2** (*intr*) to perform a pirouette [c18 from F, from OF *pirouet* spinning top]

Pisa ('pi:zə; *Italian* 'pi:sa) *n* a city in Tuscany, NW Italy, near the mouth of the River Arno: flourishing maritime

Pp

republic (11th–12th centuries), contains a university (1343), a cathedral (1063), and the Leaning Tower (begun in 1174 and about 5 m (17 ft) from perpendicular); tourism. Pop: 93 133 (1998)

Pisanello (*Italian* pisa'nɛllo) *n* **Antonio** (an'tɔ:njo) ?1395–?1455, Italian painter and medallist; a major exponent of the International Gothic style. He is best known for his portrait medals and drawings of animals

Pisano (*Italian* pi'sa:no) *n* **1 Andrea** (an'drea), real name *Andrea de Pontedera*. ?1290–1348, Italian sculptor and architect, noted for his bronze reliefs on the door of the baptistry in Florence **2 Giovanni** (dʒo'vanni) ?1250–?1320, Italian sculptor, who successfully integrated classical and Gothic elements in his sculptures, esp in his pulpit in St Andrea, Pistoia **3** his father, **Nicola** (ni'kɔ:la) ?1220–?84, Italian sculptor, who pioneered the classical style and is often regarded as a precursor of the Italian Renaissance: noted esp for his pulpit in the baptistry of Pisa Cathedral

piscatorial (ˌpɪskə'tɔ:rɪəl) *or* **piscatory** ('pɪskətərɪ, -trɪ) *adj* **1** of or relating to fish, fishing, or fishermen **2** devoted to fishing [C19 from L *piscātōrius*, from *piscātor* fisherman] > ˌ**pisca'torially** *adv*

Pisces ('paɪsi:z, 'pɪ-) *n*, *Latin genitive* **Piscium** ('paɪsɪəm) **1** *astron* a faint extensive zodiacal constellation lying between Aquarius and Aries on the ecliptic **2** *astrol* Also called: the **Fishes** the twelfth sign of the zodiac. The sun is in this sign between about Feb 19 and March 20 **3a** a taxonomic group that comprises all fishes. See **fish** (sense 1) **3b** a taxonomic group that comprises the bony fishes only. See **teleost** [C14 L: the fish (pl)]

pisci- *combining form* fish: *pisciculture* [from L *piscis*]

pisciculture ('pɪsɪˌkʌltʃə) *n* the rearing and breeding of fish under controlled conditions > ˌ**pisci'cultural** *adj* > ˌ**pisci'culturist** *n, adj*

piscina (pɪ'si:nə) *n, pl* **piscinae** (-ni:) *or* **piscinas** *RC Church* a stone basin, with a drain, in a church or sacristy where water used at Mass is poured away [C16 from L: fish pond, from *piscis* a fish]

piscine ('pɪsaɪn) *adj* of, relating to, or resembling a fish

piscivorous (pɪ'sɪvərəs) *adj* feeding on fish

Pisgah ('pɪzgə) *n* **Mount** *Old Testament* the mountain slopes to the northeast of the Dead Sea, from one of which, Mount Nebo, Moses viewed Canaan

pish (pʃ, pɪʃ) *interj* **1** an exclamation of impatience or contempt ▷ *vb* **2** to make this exclamation at (someone or something)

Pishpek (pɪʃ'pɛk) *n* a variant transliteration of the Kyrgyz name for **Bishkek**

pisiform ('pɪsɪˌfɔ:m) *adj* **1** *zool, bot* resembling a pea ▷ *n* **2** a small pealike bone on the ulnar side of the carpus [C18 via NL from L *pīsum* pea + *forma* shape]

Pisistratus (paɪ'sɪstrətəs) *n* ?600–527 BC, tyrant of Athens: he established himself in firm control of the city following his defeat of his aristocratic rivals at Pallene (546)

pismire ('pɪsˌmaɪə) *n* an archaic or dialect word for an **ant** [C14 (lit.: urinating ant, from the odour of formic acid): from PISS + obs. *mire* ant, from ON]

piss (pɪs) *sl* ▷ *vb* **1** (*intr*) to urinate **2** (*tr*) to discharge as or in one's urine: *to piss blood* ▷ *n* **3** an act of urinating **4** urine **5 take the piss** to tease or make fun of someone or something [C13 from OF *pisser*, prob. imit.]

Pissarro (pɪ'sɑ:rəʊ; *French* pisaro) *n* **Camille** (kamij) 1830–1903, French impressionist painter, esp of landscapes

piss artist *n sl* **1** a boastful or incompetent person **2** a person who drinks heavily and gets drunk frequently

pissed (pɪst) *adj* **1** *Brit, Austral, and NZ sl* intoxicated; drunk **2** *US sl* annoyed, irritated, or disappointed

piss off *vb (adv) sl* **1** (*tr; often passive*) to annoy, irritate, or disappoint **2** (*intr*) *chiefly Brit* to go away; depart: often used to dismiss a person

piss-poor *adj sl* of a contemptibly low standard or quality; pathetic

piss-up *n sl* a party involving a lot of drinking

pistachio (pɪ'stɑ:ʃɪˌəʊ) *n, pl* **pistachios 1** a tree of the Mediterranean region and W Asia, with small hard-shelled nuts **2** Also called: **pistachio nut** the nut of this tree, having an edible green kernel **3** the sweet flavour of the pistachio nut, used in ice creams, etc ▷ *adj* **4** of a yellowish-green colour [C16 via It. & L from Gk *pistakion* pistachio nut, from *pistakē* pistachio tree, from Persian *pistah*]

piste (pi:st) *n* a slope or course for skiing [C18 via OF from OIt. *pista*, from *pistare* to tread down]

pistil ('pɪstɪl) *n* the female reproductive part of a flower, consisting of one or more separate or fused carpels [C18 from L *pistillum* pestle]

pistillate ('pɪstɪlɪt, -ˌleɪt) *adj* (of plants) **1** having pistils but no anthers **2** having or producing pistils

Pistoia (*Italian* pis'tɔ:ja) *n* a city in N Italy, in N Tuscany: scene of the defeat and death of Catiline in 62 BC. Pop: 89 972 (1990)

pistol ('pɪstᵊl) *n* **1** a short-barrelled handgun **2 hold a pistol to a person's head** to threaten a person in order to force him or her to do what one wants ▷ *vb* **pistols, pistolling, pistolled** *or US* **pistols, pistoling, pistoled 3** (*tr*) to shoot with a pistol [C16 from F *pistole*, from G, from Czech *pišt'ala* pistol, pipe]

pistole (pɪs'təʊl) *n* any of various gold coins of varying value, formerly used in Europe [C16 from OF, shortened from *pistolet*, lit.: little PISTOL]

pistol grip *n* **a** a handle shaped like the butt of a pistol **b** (*as modifier*): *a pistol-grip camera*

pistol-whip *vb* **pistol-whips, pistol-whipping, pistol-whipped** (*tr*) *US* to beat or strike with a pistol barrel

piston ('pɪstən) *n* a disc or cylindrical part that slides to and fro in a hollow cylinder. In an internal-combustion engine it is attached by a pivoted connecting rod to a crankshaft or flywheel, thus converting reciprocating motion into rotation [C18 via F from OIt. *pistone*, from *pistare* to grind, from L *pinsere* to beat]

piston ring *n* a split ring that fits into a groove on the rim of a piston to provide a spring-loaded seal against the cylinder wall

piston rod *n* **1** the rod that connects the piston of a reciprocating steam engine to the crosshead **2** a less common name for a **connecting rod**

pit[1] (pɪt) *n* **1** a large, usually deep opening in the ground **2a** a mine or excavation, esp for coal **2b** the shaft in a mine **2c** (*as modifier*): *pit pony; pit prop* **3** a concealed danger or difficulty **4 the pit** hell **5** Also called: **orchestra pit** the area that is occupied by the orchestra in a theatre, located in front of the stage **6** an enclosure for fighting animals or birds **7** *anat* **7a** a small natural depression on the surface of a body, organ, or part **7b** the floor of any natural bodily cavity: *the pit of the stomach* **8** *pathol* a small indented scar at the site of a former pustule; pockmark **9** a working area at the side of a motor-racing track for servicing or refuelling vehicles **10** a section on the floor of a commodity exchange devoted to a special line of trading **11** the ground floor of the auditorium of a theatre **12** another word for **pitfall** (sense 2) ▷ *vb* **pits, pitting, pitted 13** (*tr; often foll by against*) to match in opposition, esp as antagonists **14** to mark or become marked with pits **15** (*tr*) to place or bury in a pit [OE *pytt*, from L *puteus*]

pit[2] (pɪt) *chiefly US & Canad* ▷ *n* **1** the stone of a cherry, etc ▷ *vb* **pits, pitting, pitted** (*tr*) **2** to extract the stone from (a fruit) [C19 from Du.: kernel]

pitapat ('pɪtəˌpæt) *adv* **1** with quick light taps ▷ *vb* **pitapats, pitapatting, pitapatted 2** (*intr*) to make quick light taps ▷ *n* **3** such taps [C16 imit.]

pit bull terrier *n* a dog resembling the Staffordshire bull terrier but somewhat larger: originally developed for dogfighting. It is regarded as dangerous

Pitcairn Island (pɪtˈkɛən, ˈpɪtkɛən) *n* an island in the S Pacific: forms with other islands a UK Overseas Territory; uninhabited until the landing in 1790 of the mutineers of HMS *Bounty* and their Tahitian companions. Pop: 54 (1999 est). Area: 4.6 sq km (1.75 sq miles)

pitch[1] (pɪtʃ) *vb* **1** to hurl or throw (something); cast; fling **2** (*usually tr*) to set up (a camp, tent, etc) **3** (*tr*) to aim or fix (something) at a particular level, position, style, etc: *if you advertise privately you may pitch the price too low* **4** (*tr*) to aim to sell (a product) to a specified market or on a specified basis **5** (*intr*) to slope downwards **6** (*intr*) to fall forwards or downwards **7** (*intr*) (of a vessel) to dip and raise its bow and stern alternately **8** *cricket* to bowl (a ball) so that it bounces on a certain part of the wicket, or (of a ball) to bounce on a certain part of the wicket **9** (*intr*) (of a missile, aircraft, etc) to deviate from a stable flight attitude by movement of the longitudinal axis about the lateral axis **10** (*tr*) (in golf, etc) to hit (a ball) steeply into the air **11** (*tr*) *music* **11a** to sing or play accurately (a note, interval, etc) **11b** (*usually passive*) (of a wind instrument) to specify or indicate its basic key or harmonic series by its size, manufacture, etc **12** *baseball, softball* **12a** (*tr*) to throw (a ball) to a batter **12b** (*intr*) to act as a pitcher in a game ▷ *n* **13** the degree of elevation or depression **14a** the angle of descent of a downward slope **14b** such a slope **15** the extreme height or depth **16** *mountaineering* a section of a route between two belay points **17** the degree of slope of a roof **18** the distance between corresponding points on adjacent members of a body of regular form, esp the distance between teeth on a gearwheel or between threads on a screw thread **19** the pitching motion of a ship, missile, etc **20** *music* **20a** the height or depth of a note as determined by its frequency relative to that of other notes: *high pitch; low pitch* **20b** an absolute frequency assigned to a specific note, fixing the relative frequencies of all other notes **21** *cricket* the rectangular area between the stumps, 22 yards long and 10 feet wide; the wicket **22** the act or manner of pitching a ball, as in cricket, etc **23** *chiefly Brit* a vendor's station, esp on a pavement **24** *sl* a persuasive sales talk, esp one routinely repeated **25** *chiefly Brit* (in many sports) the field of play **26** *golf* Also called: **pitch shot** an approach shot in which the ball is struck in a high arc **27** **queer someone's pitch** *Brit inf* to upset someone's plans ▷ See also **pitch in, pitch into** [c13 *picchen*]

pitch[2] (pɪtʃ) *n* **1** any of various heavy dark viscid substances obtained as a residue from the distillation of tars **2** any of various similar substances, such as asphalt, occurring as natural deposits **3** crude turpentine obtained as sap from pine trees ▷ *vb* **4** (*tr*) to apply pitch to (something) [OE *pic*, from L *pix*]

pitch-black *adj* **1** extremely dark; unlit: *the room was pitch-black* **2** of a deep black colour

pitchblende (ˈpɪtʃˌblɛnd) *n* a blackish mineral that occurs in veins, frequently associated with silver: the principal source of uranium and radium [c18 partial translation of G *Pechblende*, from *Pech* PITCH[2] (from its black colour) + BLENDE]

pitch-dark *adj* extremely or completely dark

pitched battle *n* **1** a battle ensuing from the deliberate choice of time and place **2** any fierce encounter, esp one with large numbers

pitcher[1] (ˈpɪtʃə) *n* a large jug, usually rounded with a narrow neck and often of earthenware, used mainly for holding water [c13 from OF *pichier*, from Med. L *picārium*, var. of *bicārium* BEAKER]

pitcher[2] (ˈpɪtʃə) *n baseball* the player on the fielding team who throws the ball to the batter

pitcher plant *n* any of various insectivorous plants, having leaves modified to form pitcher-like organs that attract and trap insects, which are then digested

pitchfork (ˈpɪtʃˌfɔːk) *n* **1** a long-handled fork with two or three long curved tines for tossing hay ▷ *vb* (*tr*) **2** to use a pitchfork on (something) **3** to thrust (someone) unwillingly into a position

pitch in *vb* (*intr, adv*) **1** to cooperate or contribute **2** to begin energetically

pitch into *vb* (*intr, prep*) *inf* **1** to assail physically or verbally **2** to get on with doing (something)

pitch pine *n* **1** any of various coniferous trees of North America: valued as a source of turpentine and pitch **2** the wood of any of these trees

pitch pipe *n* a small pipe that sounds a note or notes of standard frequency. It is used for establishing the correct starting note for unaccompanied singing

pitchy (ˈpɪtʃɪ) *adj* **pitchier, pitchiest** **1** full of or covered with pitch **2** resembling pitch > ˈ**pitchiness** *n*

piteous (ˈpɪtɪəs) *adj* exciting or deserving pity > ˈ**piteously** *adv* > ˈ**piteousness** *n*

pitfall (ˈpɪtˌfɔːl) *n* **1** an unsuspected difficulty or danger **2** a trap in the form of a concealed pit, designed to catch men or wild animals [OE *pytt* PIT[1] + *fealle* trap]

pith (pɪθ) *n* **1** the soft fibrous tissue lining the inside of the rind in fruits such as the orange **2** the essential or important part, point, etc **3** weight; substance **4** *bot* the central core of unspecialized cells surrounded by conducting tissue in stems **5** the soft central part of a bone, feather, etc ▷ *vb* (*tr*) **6** to kill (animals) by severing the spinal cord **7** to remove the pith from (a plant) [OE *pitha*]

pithead (ˈpɪtˌhɛd) *n* the top of a mine shaft and the buildings, hoisting gear, etc, around it

pithecanthropus (ˌpɪθɪkænˈθrəʊpəs) *n, pl* **pithecanthropi** (-ˌpaɪ) any primitive apelike man of the former genus *Pithecanthropus*, now included in the genus *Homo*. See **Java man** [c19 NL, from Gk *pithēkos* ape + *anthrōpos* man]

Pp

pith helmet *n* a lightweight hat made of the pith of the sola, an E Indian swamp plant, that protects the wearer from the sun. Also called: **topee, topi**

pithos (ˈpɪθɒs, ˈpaɪ-) *n, pl* **pithoi** (-θɔɪ) a large ceramic container for oil or grain [from Gk]

pithy (ˈpɪθɪ) *adj* **pithier, pithiest** **1** terse and full of meaning or substance **2** of, resembling, or full of pith > ˈ**pithily** *adv* > ˈ**pithiness** *n*

pitiable (ˈpɪtɪəbᵊl) *adj* exciting or deserving pity or contempt > ˈ**pitiableness** *n* > ˈ**pitiably** *adv*

pitiful (ˈpɪtɪfʊl) *adj* **1** arousing or deserving pity **2** arousing or deserving contempt **3** *arch* full of pity or compassion > ˈ**pitifully** *adv* > ˈ**pitifulness** *n*

pitiless (ˈpɪtɪlɪs) *adj* having or showing little or no pity or mercy > ˈ**pitilessly** *adv* > ˈ**pitilessness** *n*

pitman (ˈpɪtmən) *n, pl* **pitmen** *chiefly Scot & N English* a person who works in a pit, esp a coal miner

Pitman (ˈpɪtmən) *n* Sir **Isaac** 1813–97, English inventor of a system of phonetic shorthand (1837)

piton (ˈpiːtɒn) *n mountaineering* a metal spike that may be driven into a crevice and used to secure a rope, etc [c20 from F: ringbolt]

pits (pɪts) *pl n* **the** *sl* the worst possible person, place, or thing [c20 from ? *armpits*]

pit stop *n* **1** *motor racing* a brief stop made at a pit by a racing car for repairs, refuelling, etc **2** *inf* any stop made during a car journey for refreshment, rest, or refuelling

Pitt (pɪt) *n* **1** **William**, known as *Pitt the Elder*, 1st Earl of Chatham. 1708–78, British statesman. He was first minister (1756–57; 1757–61; 1766–68) and achieved British victory in the Seven Years' War (1756–63) **2** his son **William**, known as *Pitt the Younger*. 1759–1806, British statesman. As prime minister (1783–1801; 1804–06), he carried through important fiscal and tariff reforms. From 1793, his attention was focused on the wars with revolutionary and Napoleonic France

pitta bread *or* **pitta** ('pɪtə) *n* a flat rounded slightly leavened bread, originally from the Middle East [from Mod. Gk: a cake]

pittance ('pɪtᵊns) *n* a small amount or portion, esp a meagre allowance of money [c16 from OF *pietance* ration, ult. from L *pietās* duty]

pitter-patter ('pɪtə,pætə) *n* **1** the sound of light rapid taps or pats, as of raindrops ▷ *vb* **2** (*intr*) to make such a sound ▷ *adv* **3** with such a sound

Pittsburgh ('pɪtsbɜːg) *n* a port in SW Pennsylvania, at the confluence of the Allegheny and Monongahela Rivers, which form the Ohio River: settled around Fort Pitt in 1758; developed rapidly with the discovery of iron deposits and one of the world's richest coalfields; the largest river port in the US and an important industrial centre, formerly with large steel mills. Pop: 334 563 (2000)

pituitary (pɪ'tjuːɪtərɪ) *n, pl* **pituitaries 1** See **pituitary gland** ▷ *adj* **2** of or relating to the pituitary gland [c17 from LL *pītuītārius* slimy, from *pītuīta* phlegm]

pituitary gland *or* **body** *n* the master endocrine gland, attached by a stalk to the base of the brain. Its two lobes secrete hormones affecting skeletal growth, development of the sex glands, and the functioning of the other endocrine glands

pit viper *n* any venomous snake of a New World family, having a heat-sensitive organ in a pit on each side of the head: includes the rattlesnakes

pity ('pɪtɪ) *n, pl* **pities 1** sympathy or sorrow felt for the sufferings of another **2 have** (*or* **take**) **pity on** to have sympathy or show mercy for **3** something that causes regret **4** an unfortunate chance: *what a pity you can't come* ▷ *vb* **pities, pitying, pitied** (*tr*) **5** to feel pity for [c13 from OF *pité*, from L *pietās* duty] > **'pitying** *adj* > **'pityingly** *adv*

pityriasis (,pɪtə'raɪəsɪs) *n* any of a group of skin diseases characterized by the shedding of dry flakes of skin [c17 via NL from Gk *pituriasis* scurfiness, from *pituron* bran]

più (pjuː) *adv* (*in combination*) *music* more (quickly, etc): *più allegro* [It., from L *plus* more]

piupiu ('piːuː,piːuː) *n* a skirt made from leaves of the New Zealand flax, worn by Maoris on ceremonial occasions [from Maori]

Piura (*Spanish* 'pjura) *n* a city in NW Peru: the oldest colonial city in Peru, founded by Pizarro in 1532; commercial centre of an agricultural district. Pop: 308 155 (1998 est)

Pius II ('paɪəs) *n* pen name *Aeneas Silvius*, original name *Enea Silvio de' Piccolomini*. 1405–64, Italian ecclesiastic, humanist, poet, and historian; pope (1458–64)

Pius IV *n* original name *Giovanni Angelo de' Medici*. 1499–1565, pope (1559–65). He reconvened the Council of Trent (1562), confirming its final decrees

Pius V *n* **Saint** original name *Michele Ghislieri*. 1504–72, Italian ecclesiastic; pope (1566–72). He attempted to enforce the reforms decreed by the Council of Trent, excommunicated Elizabeth I of England (1570), and organized the alliance that defeated the Turks at Lepanto (1571). Feast day: 30 April

Pius VII *n* original name *Luigi Barnaba Chiaramonti*. 1740–1823, Italian ecclesiastic; pope (1800–23). He concluded a concordat with Napoleon (1801) and consecrated him as emperor of France (1804), but resisted his annexation of the Papal States (1809)

Pius IX *n* original name *Giovanni Maria Mastai-Ferretti*. 1792–1878, Italian ecclesiastic; pope (1846–78). He refused to recognize the incorporation of Rome and the Papal States in the kingdom of Italy, confining himself to the Vatican after 1870. He decreed the dogma of the Immaculate Conception (1854) and convened the Vatican Council, which laid down the doctrine of papal infallibility (1870)

Pius X *n* **Saint** original name *Giuseppe Sarto*. 1835–1914, Italian ecclesiastic; pope (1903–14). He condemned Modernism (1907) and initiated a new codification of canon law. Feast day: Aug. 21

Pius XI *n* original name *Achille Ratti*. 1857–1939, Italian ecclesiastic; pope (1922–39). He signed the Lateran Treaty (1929), by which the Vatican City was recognized as an independent state. His encyclicals condemned Nazism and Communism

Pius XII *n* original name *Eugenio Pacelli*. 1876–1958, Italian ecclesiastic; pope (1939–58): his attitude towards Nazi German anti-Semitism has been a matter of controversy

pivot ('pɪvət) *n* **1** a short shaft or pin supporting something that turns; fulcrum **2** the end of a shaft or arbor that terminates in a bearing **3** a person or thing upon which progress, success, etc, depends **4** the person or position from which a military formation takes its reference when altering position, etc ▷ *vb* **5** (*tr*) to mount on or provide with a pivot or pivots **6** (*intr*) to turn on or as if on a pivot [c17 from OF]

pivotal ('pɪvətᵊl) *adj* **1** of, involving, or acting as a pivot **2** of crucial importance

pix[1] (pɪks) *n* a plural of **pic**

pix[2] (pɪks) *n* a less common spelling of **pyx**

pixel ('pɪksɛl) *n* any of a number of very small picture elements that make up a picture, as on a visual display unit [c20 from *pix* pictures + *el*(*ement*)]

pixie *or* **pixy** ('pɪksɪ) *n, pl* **pixies** (in folklore) a fairy or elf [c17 from ?]

pixilated *or* **pixillated** ('pɪksɪ,leɪtɪd) *adj chiefly US* **1** eccentric or whimsical **2** *sl* drunk [c20 from PIXIE + *-lated*, as in *stimulated*, *titillated*, etc]

Pizarro (pɪ'zɑːrəʊ; *Spanish* pi'θarrɔ) *n* **Francisco** (fran'θisko) ?1475–1541, Spanish conqueror of Peru. He landed in Peru (1532), murdered the Inca King Atahualpa (1533), and founded Lima as the new capital of Peru (1535). He was murdered by his own followers

pizza ('piːtsə) *n* a dish of Italian origin consisting of a baked disc of dough covered with cheese and tomatoes, plus ham, mushrooms, etc [c20 from It., ?from Vulgar L *picea* (unattested), ? rel. to Mod. Gk *pitta* cake]

pizzazz *or* **pizazz** (pə'zæz) *n inf* an attractive combination of energy and style; sparkle. Also: **bezazz** [c20 ?]

pizzeria (,piːtsə'riːə) *n* a place where pizzas are made, sold, or eaten

pizzicato (,pɪtsɪ'kɑːtəʊ) *music* ▷ *adj, adv* **1** (in music for the violin family) to be plucked with the finger ▷ *n* **2** this style or technique of playing [c19 from It.: pinched, from *pizzicare* to twist]

pizzle ('pɪzᵊl) *n arch or dialect* the penis of an animal, esp a bull [c16 of Gmc origin]

pk *pl* **pks** *abbrev for*: **1** pack **2** park **3** peak

pkg. *pl* **pkgs** *abbrev for* package

pl *abbrev for*: **1** place **2** plate **3** plural

Pl. (in street names) *abbrev for* Place

PLA *abbrev for* Port of London Authority

plaas (plɑːs) *n S African* a farm [from Afrik., from Du.]

placable ('plækəbᵊl) *adj* easily placated or appeased [c15 via OF from L *plācābilis*, from *plācāre* to appease] > **,placa'bility** *n*

placard ('plækɑːd) *n* **1** a notice for public display; poster **2** a small plaque or card ▷ *vb* (*tr*) **3** to post placards on or in **4** to advertise by placards **5** to display as a placard [c15 from OF *plaquart*, from *plaquier* to plate, lay flat; see PLAQUE]

placate (plə'keɪt) *vb* **placates, placating, placated** (*tr*) to pacify or appease [c17 from L *plācāre*] > **pla'cation** *n* > **pla'catory** *adj*

place (pleɪs) *n* **1** a particular point or part of space or of a surface, esp that occupied by a person or thing **2** a geographical point, such as a town, city, etc **3** a position or rank in a sequence or order **4** an open square lined with houses in a city or town **5** space or room **6** a house or living quarters **7** a country house with grounds **8** any building or area set aside for a specific purpose **9** a passage in a book, play, film, etc: *to lose one's place* **10** proper, right, or customary surroundings (esp in **out of place, in place**) **11** right, prerogative, or duty: *it is your place to give a speech* **12** appointment, position, or job: *a place at college* **13** position, condition, or state: *if I were in your place* **14a** a space or seat, as at a dining table **14b** (*as modifier*): *place mat* **15** *maths* the relative position of a digit in a number **16** any of the best times in a race **17** *horse racing* **17a** *Brit, Austral, & NZ* the first, second, or third position at the finish **17b** *US & Canad* the first or usually the second position at the finish **17c** (*as modifier*): *a place bet* **18 all over the place** in disorder or disarray **19 give place (to)** to make room (for) or be superseded (by) **20 go places** *inf* **20a** to travel **20b** to become successful **21 in place of 21a** instead of; in lieu of: *go in place of my sister* **21b** in exchange for: *he gave her it in place of her ring* **22 know one's place** to be aware of one's inferior position **23 put someone in his** (*or* **her**) **place** to humble someone who is arrogant, conceited, forward, etc **24 take one's place** to take up one's usual or specified position **25 take place** to happen or occur **26 take the place of** to be a substitute for ▷ *vb* **places, placing, placed** (*mainly tr*) **27** to put or set in a particular or appropriate place **28** to find or indicate the place of **29** to identify or classify by linking with an appropriate context: *to place a face* **30** to regard or view as being: *to place prosperity above sincerity* **31** to make (an order, bet, etc) **32** to find a home or job for (someone) **33** to appoint to an office or position **34** (often foll by *with*) to put under the care (of) **35** to direct or aim carefully **36** (*passive*) *Brit* to cause (a racehorse, greyhound, athlete, etc) to arrive in first, second, third, or sometimes fourth place **37** (*intr*) *US & Canad* (of a racehorse, greyhound, etc) to finish among the first three in a contest, esp in second position **38** to invest (funds) **39** (*tr*) to insert (an advertisement) in a newspaper, journal, etc [c13 via OF from L *platēa* courtyard, from Gk *plateia*, from *platus* broad]

placebo (plə'si:bəʊ) *n, pl* **placebos** *or* **placeboes 1** *med* an inactive substance administered to a patient usually to compare its effects with those of a real drug but sometimes for the psychological benefit to the patient through his believing he is receiving treatment **2** something said or done to please or humour another **3** *RC Church* a traditional name for the vespers of the office for the dead [c13 (in the ecclesiastical sense): from L *Placebo Domino* I shall please the Lord; c19 (in the medical sense)]

placebo effect *n med* a positive therapeutic effect claimed by a patient after receiving a placebo believed by him to be an active drug

place card *n* a card placed on a dinner table before a seat, indicating who is to sit there

place kick *football, etc* ▷ *n* **1** a kick in which the ball is placed in position before it is kicked ▷ *vb* **place-kick 2** to kick (a ball) in this way

placement ('pleɪsmənt) *n* **1** the act of placing or the state of being placed **2** arrangement or position **3** the process of finding employment

placenta (plə'sɛntə) *n, pl* **placentas** *or* **placentae** (-ti:) **1** the vascular organ formed in the uterus of most mammals during pregnancy, consisting of both maternal and embryonic tissues and providing oxygen and nutrients for the fetus **2** *bot* the part of the ovary of flowering plants to which the ovules are attached [c17 via L from Gk *plakoeis* flat cake, from *plax* flat] > **pla'cental** *adj*

placer ('plæsə) *n* **a** surface sediment containing particles of gold or some other valuable mineral **b** (*in combination*): *placer-mining* [c19 from American Sp.: deposit, from Sp. *plaza* PLACE]

place setting *n* the cutlery, crockery, and glassware laid for one person at a dining table

placet ('pleɪsɛt) *n* a vote or expression of assent by saying *placet* [c16 from L, lit.: it pleases]

placid ('plæsɪd) *adj* having a calm appearance or nature [c17 from L *placidus* peaceful] > **placidity** (plə'sɪdɪtɪ) *or* **'placidness** *n* > **'placidly** *adv*

placing ('pleɪsɪŋ) *n stock exchange* a method of issuing securities to the public using an intermediary, such as a stockbroking firm

placket ('plækɪt) *n dressmaking* **1** a piece of cloth sewn in under a closure with buttons, zips, etc **2** the closure itself [c16 ?from MDu. *plackaet* breastplate, from Med. L *placca* metal plate]

placoid ('plækɔɪd) *adj* **1** platelike or flattened **2** (of the scales of sharks) toothlike; composed of dentine with an enamel tip and basal pulp cavity [c19 from Gk *plac-*, *plax* flat]

plafond (plə'fɒn; *French* plafɔ̃) *n* a ceiling, esp one having ornamentation [c17 from F, from *plat* flat + *fond* bottom, from L *fundus*]

plagal ('pleɪgᵊl) *adj* **1** (of a cadence) progressing from the subdominant to the tonic chord, as in the *Amen* of a hymn **2** (of a mode) commencing upon the dominant of an authentic mode, but sharing the same final as the authentic mode ▷ Cf **authentic** (sense 5) [c16 from Med. L *plagālis*, from *plaga*, ?from Gk *plagos* side]

plage (plɑ:ʒ) *n astron* a bright patch in the sun's chromosphere [F, lit.: beach]

plagiarism ('pleɪdʒə,rɪzəm) *n* **1** the act of plagiarizing **2** something plagiarized [c17 from L *plagiārus* plunderer, from *plagium* kidnapping] > **'plagiarist** *n* > **,plagia'ristic** *adj*

plagiarize *or* **plagiarise** ('pleɪdʒə,raɪz) *vb* **plagiarizes, plagiarizing, plagiarized** *or* **plagiarises, plagiarising, plagiarised** to appropriate (ideas, passages, etc) from (another work or author) > **'plagia,rizer** *or* **'plagia,riser** *n*

Pp

plagioclase ('pleɪdʒɪəʊ,kleɪz) *n* a series of feldspar minerals consisting of a mixture of sodium and calcium aluminium silicates in triclinic crystalline form [c19 from Gk, from *plagos* side + -CLASE] > **plagioclastic** (,pleɪdʒɪəʊ'klæstɪk) *adj*

plague (pleɪg) *n* **1** any widespread and usually highly contagious disease with a high fatality rate **2** an infectious disease of rodents, esp rats, transmitted to man by the bite of the rat flea **3** See **bubonic plague** **4** something that afflicts or harasses **5** *inf* an annoyance or nuisance **6** a pestilence, affliction, or calamity on a large scale, esp when regarded as sent by God ▷ *vb* **plagues, plaguing, plagued** (*tr*) **7** to afflict or harass **8** to bring down a plague upon **9** *inf* to annoy [c14 from LL *plāga* pestilence, from L: a blow]

plaguy *or* **plaguey** ('pleɪgɪ) *arch, inf* ▷ *adj* **1** disagreeable or vexing ▷ *adv* **2** disagreeably or annoyingly > **'plaguily** *adv*

plaice (pleɪs) *n, pl* **plaice** *or* **plaices 1** a European flatfish having an oval brown body marked with red or orange spots and valued as a food fish **2** *US & Canad* any of various other related fishes [c13 from OF *plaïz*, from LL *platessa* flatfish, from Gk *platus* flat]

plaid (plæd, pleɪd) *n* **1** a long piece of cloth of a tartan pattern, worn over the shoulder as part of Highland costume **2a** a crisscross weave or cloth **2b** (*as modifier*): *a plaid scarf* [c16 from Scot Gaelic *plaide*, from ?]
▷ www.tartans.scotland.net

Plaid Cymru (,plaɪd 'kʌmrɪ) *n* the Welsh nationalist party. Official name: **Plaid Cymru, the Party of Wales** [Welsh]

plain[1] (pleɪn) *adj* **1** flat or smooth; level **2** not complicated; clear: *the plain truth* **3** not difficult; simple or easy: *a plain task* **4** honest or straightforward **5** lowly, esp in social rank or education **6** without adornment or show: *a plain coat* **7** (of fabric) without pattern or of simple untwilled weave **8** not attractive **9** not mixed; simple: *plain vodka* **10** (of knitting) done in plain stitch ▷ *n* **11** a level or almost level tract of country **12** a simple stitch in knitting made by passing the wool round the front of the needle ▷ *adv* **13** (intensifier): *just plain tired* [C13 from OF: simple, from L *plānus* level, clear] > **'plainly** *adv* > **'plainness** *n*

plain² (pleɪn) *vb* a dialect or poetic word for **complain** [C14 *pleignen*, from OF *plaindre* to lament, from L *plangere* to beat]

plainchant ('pleɪn,tʃɑːnt) *n* another name for **plainsong** [C18 from F, for Med. L *cantus plānus*]

plain chocolate *n* chocolate with a slightly bitter flavour and dark colour

plain clothes *pl n* **a** ordinary clothes, as distinguished from uniform, as worn by a police detective on duty **b** (*as modifier*): *a plain-clothes policeman*

plain flour *n* flour to which no raising agent has been added

plain sailing *n* **1** *inf* smooth or easy progress **2** *naut* sailing in a body of water that is unobstructed

plainsman ('pleɪnzmən) *n, pl* **plainsmen** a person who lives in a plains region, esp in the Great Plains of North America

Plains of Abraham *n* (*functioning as singular*) a field in E Canada between Quebec City and the St Lawrence River: site of an important British victory (1759) in the Seven Years' War, which cost the French their possession of Canada

plainsong ('pleɪn,sɒŋ) *n* the style of unison unaccompanied vocal music used in the medieval Church, esp in Gregorian chant [C16 translation of Med. L *cantus plānus*]
▷ www.1upinfo.com/encyclopedia/P/plainson.html

plain-spoken *adj* candid; frank; blunt

plaint (pleɪnt) *n* **1** *arch* a complaint or lamentation **2** *law* a statement in writing of grounds of complaint made to a court of law [C13 from OF *plainte*, from L *planctus* lamentation, from *plangere* to beat]

plaintiff ('pleɪntɪf) *n* a person who brings a civil action in a court of law [C14 from legal F *plaintif*, from OF *plaintif* (adj) complaining, from *plainte* PLAINT]

plaintive ('pleɪntɪv) *adj* expressing melancholy; mournful [C14 from OF *plaintif* grieving, from PLAINT] > **'plaintively** *adv* > **'plaintiveness** *n*

plait (plæt) *n* **1** a length of hair, etc, that has been plaited **2** a rare spelling of **pleat** ▷ *vb* **3** (*tr*) to intertwine (strands or strips) in a pattern [C15 *pleyt*, from OF *pleit*, from L *plicāre* to fold]

plan (plæn) *n* **1** a detailed scheme, method, etc, for attaining an objective **2** (*sometimes pl*) a proposed, usually tentative idea for doing something **3** a drawing to scale of a horizontal section through a building taken at a given level **4** an outline, sketch, etc ▷ *vb* **plans, planning, planned 5** to form a plan (for) or make plans (for) **6** (*tr*) to make a plan of (a building) **7** (*tr; takes a clause as object or an infinitive*) to have in mind as a purpose; intend [C18 via F from L *plānus* flat]

planar ('pleɪnə) *adj* **1** of or relating to a plane **2** lying in one plane; flat [C19 from LL *plānāris* on level ground, from L *plānus* flat]

planarian (plə'nɛərɪən) *n* any of various free-living mostly aquatic flatworms, having a three-branched intestine [C19 from NL *Plānāria* type genus, from LL *plānārius* flat; see PLANE¹]

planar process *n* a method of producing diffused junctions in semiconductor devices. A pattern of holes is etched into an oxide layer formed on a silicon substrate, into which impurities are diffused through the holes

planchet ('plɑːntʃɪt) *n* a piece of metal ready to be stamped as a coin, medal, etc; flan [C17 from F: little board, from *planche* PLANK]

planchette (plɑːn'ʃɛt) *n* a heart-shaped board on wheels, on which messages are written under supposed spirit guidance [C19 from F: little board, from *planche* PLANK]

Planck (plæŋk; *German* plaŋk) *n* **Max (Karl Ernst Ludwig)** (maks) 1858–1947, German physicist who first formulated the quantum theory (1900): Nobel prize for physics 1918

Planck constant *or* **Planck's constant** *n* a fundamental constant equal to the energy of any quantum of radiation divided by its frequency

plane¹ (pleɪn) *n* **1** *maths* a flat surface in which a straight line joining any two of its points lies entirely on that surface **2** a level surface **3** a level of existence, attainment, etc **4a** short for **aeroplane 4b** a wing or supporting surface of an aircraft ▷ *adj* **5** level or flat **6** *maths* lying entirely in one plane ▷ *vb* **planes, planing, planed** (*intr*) **7** to glide **8** (of a boat) to rise partly and skim over the water when moving at a certain speed [C17 from L *plānum* level surface]
▷ www.planespotting.com

plane² (pleɪn) *n* **1** a tool with a steel blade set obliquely in a wooden or iron body, for smoothing timber surfaces, cutting grooves, etc **2** a flat tool, usually metal, for smoothing the surface of clay or plaster in a mould ▷ *vb* **planes, planing, planed** (*tr*) **3** to smooth or cut (timber, etc) using a plane **4** (often foll by *off*) to remove using a plane [C14 via OF from LL *plāna* plane, from *plānāre* to level]

plane³ (pleɪn) *n* See **plane tree**

plane geometry *n* the study of the properties of plane curves, figures, etc

plane polarization *n* a type of polarization in which waves of light or other radiation are restricted to vibration in a single plane

planet ('plænɪt) *n* **1** Also called: **major planet** any of the nine celestial bodies, Mercury, Venus, Earth, Mars, Jupiter, Saturn, Uranus, Neptune, or Pluto, that revolve around the sun in elliptical orbits **2** any celestial body revolving around a star **3** *astrol* any of the planets of the solar system, excluding the earth but including the sun and moon, each thought to rule one or sometimes two signs of the zodiac [C12 via OF from LL *planēta*, from Gk *planētēs* wanderer, from *planaein* to wander]

plane table *n* a surveying instrument consisting of a drawing board mounted on adjustable legs

planetarium (,plænɪ'tɛərɪəm) *n, pl* **planetariums** *or* **planetaria** (-ɪə) **1** an instrument for simulating the apparent motions of the sun, moon, and planets by projecting images of these bodies onto a domed ceiling **2** a building in which such an instrument is housed **3** a model of the solar system

planetary ('plænɪtərɪ, -trɪ) *adj* **1** of a planet **2** mundane; terrestrial **3** wandering or erratic **4** *astrol* under the influence of one of the planets **5** (of a gear) having an axis that rotates around that of another gear

planetesimal hypothesis (,plænɪ'tɛsɪməl) *n* the discredited theory that the close passage of a star to the sun caused many small bodies (**planetesimals**) to be drawn from the sun, eventually coalescing to form the planets [C20 *planetesimal*, from PLANET + INFINITESIMAL]

planetoid ('plænɪ,tɔɪd) *n* another name for **asteroid** (sense 1) > **,plane'toidal** *adj*

plane tree *or* **plane** *n* a tree with ball-shaped heads of fruit and leaves with pointed lobes [C14 *plane*, from OF, from L *platanus*, from Gk, from *platos* wide, referring to the leaves]

planet Zog (zɒg) *n Brit inf* a place or situation that is far removed from reality or what is happening: *those of you who've been on planet Zog for the last ten years*

plangent ('plændʒənt) *adj* **1** having a loud deep sound **2** resonant and mournful [C19 from L *plangere* to beat (esp the breast, in grief)]

planimeter (plæˈnɪmɪtə) *n* a mechanical instrument for measuring the area of an irregular plane figure, such as the area under a curve, by moving a point attached to an arm > **plaˈnimetry** *n*

planish (ˈplænɪʃ) *vb (tr)* to give a final finish to (metal, etc) by hammering or rolling [C16 from OF *planir* to smooth out, from L *plānus* flat]

planisphere (ˈplænɪˌsfɪə) *n* a projection or representation of all or part of a sphere on a plane surface [C14 from Med. L *plānisphaerium*, from L *plānus* flat + Gk *sphaira* globe]

plank (plæŋk) *n* **1** a stout length of sawn timber **2** something that supports or sustains **3** one of the policies in a political party's programme **4** *Brit sl* a stupid person; idiot **5** **walk the plank** to be forced by pirates, etc, to walk to one's death off the end of a plank jutting out from the side of a ship ▷ *vb* **6** *(tr)* to cover or provide with planks [C13 from OF *planke*, from LL *planca* board, from *plancus* flat-footed]

planking (ˈplæŋkɪŋ) *n* a number of planks

plankton (ˈplæŋktən) *n* the organisms inhabiting the surface layer of a sea or lake, consisting of small drifting plants and animals [C19 via G from Gk *planktos* wandering, from *plazesthai* to roam]

planned economy *n* another name for **command economy**

planned obsolescence *n* the policy of deliberately limiting the life of a product in order to encourage the purchaser to replace it. Also called: **built-in obsolescence**

planner (ˈplænə) *n* **1** a person who makes plans, esp for the development of a town, building, etc **2** a chart for recording future appointments, tasks, goals, etc

planning permission *n* (in Britain) formal permission granted by a local authority for the development or changed use of land or buildings

plano- *or sometimes before a vowel* **plan-** *combining form* indicating flatness or planeness: *plano-concave* [from L *plānus* flat]

plano-concave (ˌpleɪnəʊˈkɒnkeɪv) *adj* (of a lens) having one side concave and the other plane

plano-convex (ˌpleɪnəʊˈkɒnvɛks) *adj* (of a lens) having one side convex and the other plane

plant¹ (plɑːnt) *n* **1** any living organism that typically synthesizes its food from inorganic substances, lacks specialized sense organs, and has no powers of locomotion. Plants do not include algae and fungi **2** such an organism that is smaller than a shrub or tree; a herb **3** a cutting, seedling, or similar structure, esp when ready for transplantation **4** *inf* a thing positioned secretly for discovery by another, esp in order to incriminate an innocent person **5** *inf* a person, placed in an audience, whose rehearsed responses, etc, seem spontaneous to the rest of the audience **6** *inf* a person placed secretly in a group or organization to obtain information, etc ▷ *vb (tr)* **7** (often foll by *out*) to set (seeds, crops, etc) into (ground) to grow **8** to place firmly in position **9** to establish; found **10** (foll by *with*) to stock or furnish **11** to implant in the mind **12** *sl* to deliver (a blow) **13** *inf* to position or hide, esp in order to deceive or observe **14** *inf* to hide or secrete, esp for some illegal purpose or in order to incriminate someone [OE, from *planta* a shoot] > **ˈplantable** *adj*

▷ www.garden.org
▷ http://hortiplex.gardenweb.com/plants/nph-ind.cgi
▷ www.lonker.net/gardening
▷ www.plantfinder.co.nz
▷ www.rhs.org.uk
▷ www.plantzafrica.com
▷ http://home.vicnet.net.au/~iffa/welcome.htm
▷ www.ipni.org/index.html
▷ www.pk.uni-bonn.de/ppigb/ppigb.htm
▷ www.botany.com/

plant² (plɑːnt) *n* **1** the land, buildings, and equipment used in carrying on an industry or business **2** a factory or workshop **3** mobile mechanical equipment for construction, road-making, etc [C20 special use of PLANT¹]

Plantagenet (plænˈtædʒɪnɪt) *n* a line of English kings, ruling from the ascent of Henry II (1154) to the death of Richard III (1485) [C12 from Old French, literally: sprig of broom, with reference to the crest of the Angevin kings, from Latin *planta* sprig + *genista* broom]

▷ www.royal.gov.uk/output/Page58.asp
▷ www.wikipedia.org/wiki/Plantagenet

plantain¹ (ˈplæntɪn) *n* any of various N temperate plants, esp the great plantain, which has a rosette of broad leaves and a slender spike of small greenish flowers. See also **ribwort** [C14 *plauntein*, from OF, from L *plantāgō*, from *planta* sole of the foot]

plantain² (ˈplæntɪn) *n* a large tropical plant with a green-skinned banana-like fruit which is eaten as a staple food in many tropical regions [C16 Sp. *platano* plantain, PLANE TREE]

plantain lily *n* any of several Asian plants of the genus *Hosta*, having broad ribbed leaves

plantar (ˈplæntə) *adj* of or on the sole of the foot [C18 from L *plantāris*, from *planta* sole of the foot]

plantation (plænˈteɪʃən) *n* **1** an estate, esp in tropical countries, where cash crops such as rubber, oil palm, etc, are grown on a large scale: *banana plantations* **2** a group of cultivated trees or plants **3** (formerly) a colony or group of settlers

planter (ˈplɑːntə) *n* **1** the owner or manager of a plantation **2** a machine designed for rapid and efficient planting of seeds **3** a colonizer or settler **4** a decorative pot for house plants

plantigrade (ˈplæntɪˌgreɪd) *adj* **1** walking with the entire sole of the foot touching the ground, as man and bears ▷ *n* **2** a plantigrade animal [C19 via F from NL *plantigradus*, from L *planta* sole of the foot + *gradus* a step]

plant louse *n* another name for an **aphid**

plaque (plæk, plɑːk) *n* **1** an ornamental or commemorative inscribed tablet **2** a small flat brooch or badge **3** *pathol* any small abnormal patch on or within the body **4** short for **dental plaque** [C19 from F, from *plaquier* to plate, from MDu. *placken* to beat into a thin plate]

plash (plæʃ) *vb, n* a less common word for **splash** [OE *plæsc*, prob. imit.] > **ˈplashy** *adj*

-plasia *or* **-plasy** *n combining form* indicating growth, development, or change [from NL, from Gk *plasis* a moulding, from *plassein* to mould]

plasm (ˈplæzəm) *n* **1** protoplasm of a specified type: *germ plasm* **2** a variant of **plasma**

-plasm *n combining form* (in biology) indicating the material forming cells: *protoplasm; cytoplasm* [from Gk *plasma* something moulded; see PLASMA] > **-plasmic** *adj combining form*

plasma (ˈplæzmə) *or* **plasm** *n* **1** the clear yellowish fluid portion of blood or lymph in which the red blood cells, white blood cells, and platelets are suspended **2** Also called: **blood plasma** a sterilized preparation of such fluid, taken from the blood, for use in transfusions **3** a former name for **protoplasm** or **cytoplasm** **4** *physics* a hot ionized gas containing positive ions and electrons **5** a green variety of chalcedony [C18 from LL: something moulded, from Gk, from *plassein* to mould] > **plasmatic** (plæzˈmætɪk) *or* **ˈplasmic** *adj*

plasma torch *n* an electrical device for converting a gas into a plasma, used for melting metal, etc

plasmid (ˈplæzmɪd) *n* a small circle of bacterial DNA that is independent of the main bacterial chromosome. Plasmids often contain genes for drug resistances and can be transmitted between bacteria of the same and

Pp

different species: used in genetic engineering [C20 from PLASM + -ID[1]]

plasmodium (plæz'məʊdɪəm) *n, pl* **plasmodia** (-dɪə) **1** an amoeboid mass of protoplasm, containing many nuclei: a stage in the life cycle of certain organisms **2** a parasitic protozoan which causes malaria [C19 NL; see PLASMA, -ODE[1]] > **plas'modial** *adj*

plasmolysis (plæz'mɒlɪsɪs) *n* the shrinkage of protoplasm away from cell walls that occurs as a result of excessive water loss, esp in plant cells

Plassey ('plæsɪ) *n* a village in NE India, in W Bengal: scene of Clive's victory (1757) over Siraj-ud-daula, which established British supremacy over India

-plast *n combining form* indicating a living cell or particle of living matter: *protoplast* [from Gk *plastos* formed, from *plassein* to form]

plaster ('plɑːstə) *n* **1** a mixture of lime, sand, and water that is applied to a wall or ceiling as a soft paste that hardens when dry **2** *Brit, Austral, & NZ* an adhesive strip of material for dressing a cut, wound, etc **3** short for **mustard plaster** or **plaster of Paris** ▷ *vb* **4** to coat (a wall, ceiling, etc) with plaster **5** (*tr*) to apply like plaster **6** (*tr*) to cause to lie flat or to adhere **7** (*tr*) to apply a plaster cast to **8** (*tr*) *sl* to strike with great force [OE, from Med. L *plastrum* medicinal salve, building plaster, via L from Gk *emplastron* curative dressing] > **'plasterer** *n*

plasterboard ('plɑːstəˌbɔːd) *n* a thin rigid board, in the form of a layer of plaster compressed between two layers of fibreboard, used to form or cover walls, etc

plastered ('plɑːstəd) *adj sl* intoxicated; drunk

plaster of Paris *n* **1** a white powder that sets to a hard solid when mixed with water, used for making sculptures and casts, as an additive for lime plasters, and for making casts for setting broken limbs **2** the hard plaster produced when this powder is mixed with water [C15 from Med. L *plastrum parisiense*, orig. made from the gypsum of *Paris*]

plastic ('plæstɪk) *n* **1** any one of a large number of synthetic materials that have a polymeric structure and can be moulded when soft and then set. Plastics are used in the manufacture of many articles and in coatings, artificial fibres, etc ▷ *adj* **2** made of plastic **3** easily influenced; impressionable **4** capable of being moulded or formed **5a** of moulding or modelling: *the plastic arts* **5b** produced or apparently produced by moulding: *the plastic draperies of Giotto's figures* **6** having the power to form or influence: *the plastic forces of the imagination* **7** *biol* able to change, develop, or grow: *plastic tissues* **8** *sl* superficially attractive yet unoriginal or artificial: *plastic food* [C17 from L *plasticus* relating to moulding, from Gk *plastikos*, from *plassein* to form] > **'plastically** *adv* > **plasticity** (plæ'stɪsɪtɪ) *n*

-plastic *adj combining form* growing or forming [from Gk *plastikos*; see PLASTIC]

plastic bomb *n* a bomb consisting of plastic explosive fitted around a detonator

plastic bullet *n* a bullet consisting of a cylinder of plastic about four inches long, generally causing less severe injuries than an ordinary bullet, and used esp for riot control. Also called: **baton round**

plastic explosive *n* an adhesive jelly-like explosive substance

Plasticine ('plæstɪˌsiːn) *n trademark* a soft coloured material used, esp by children, for modelling

plasticize *or* **plasticise** ('plæstɪˌsaɪz) *vb* **plasticizes, plasticizing, plasticized** *or* **plasticises, plasticising, plasticised** to make or become plastic, as by the addition of a plasticizer > **ˌplastici'zation** *or* **ˌplastici'sation** *n*

plasticizer *or* **plasticiser** ('plæstɪˌsaɪzə) *n* any of a number of substances added to materials. Their uses include softening and improving the flexibility of plastics and preventing dried paint coatings from becoming too brittle

plastic money *n* credit cards as opposed to cash

plastic surgery *n* the branch of surgery concerned with therapeutic or cosmetic repair or re-formation of missing, injured, or malformed tissues or parts > **plastic surgeon** *n*

plastid ('plæstɪd) *n* any of various small particles in the cells of plants and some animals which contain starch, oil, protein, etc [C19 via G from Gk *plastēs* sculptor, from *plassein* to form]

plastron ('plæstrən) *n* the bony plate forming the ventral part of the shell of a tortoise or turtle [C16 via F from It. *piastrone*, from *piastra* breastplate, from L *emplastrum* PLASTER] > **'plastral** *adj*

-plasty *n combining form* indicating plastic surgery: *rhinoplasty* [from Gk *-plastia*; see -PLAST]

plat[1] (plæt) *n* a small area of ground; plot [C16 (also in ME place names): orig. a var. of PLOT[2]]

plat[2] (plæt) *vb* **plats, platting, platted,** *n* a dialect variant spelling of **plait** [C16]

Plata (*Spanish* 'plata) *n* **Río de la** ('rio de la) an estuary on the SE coast of South America, between Argentina and Uruguay, formed by the Uruguay and Paraná Rivers. Length: 275 km (171 miles). Width: (at its mouth) 225 km (140 miles). Also called: **La Plata** English name: (River) Plate

Plataea (plə'tiːə) *n* an ancient city in S Boeotia, traditionally an ally of Athens: scene of the defeat of a great Persian army by the Greeks in 479 BC

platan ('plætᵊn) *n* another name for **plane tree** [C14 see PLANE TREE]

plat du jour ('plɑː də 'ʒʊə; *French* pla dy zur) *n, pl* **plats du jour** ('plɑːz də 'ʒʊə; *French* pla dy zur) the specially prepared or recommended dish of the day on a restaurant's menu [F, lit.: dish of the day]

plate (pleɪt) *n* **1a** a shallow usually circular dish made of porcelain, earthenware, glass, etc, on which food is served **1b** (*as modifier*): *a plate rack* **2a** Also called: **plateful** the contents of a plate **2b** *Austral & NZ* a plate of cakes, sandwiches, etc, brought by a guest to a party: *everyone was asked to bring a plate* **3** an entire course of a meal: *a cold plate* **4** any shallow receptacle, esp for receiving a collection in church **5** flat metal of uniform thickness obtained by rolling, usually having a thickness greater than about three millimetres **6** a thin coating of metal usually on another metal, as produced by electrodeposition **7** metal or metalware that has been coated in this way: *Sheffield plate* **8** dishes, cutlery, etc, made of gold or silver **9** a sheet of metal, plastic, rubber, etc, having a printing surface produced by a process such as stereotyping **10** a print taken from such a sheet or from a woodcut **11** a thin flat sheet of a substance, such as metal or glass **12** a small piece of metal, plastic, etc, designed to bear an inscription and to be fixed to another surface **13** armour made of overlapping or articulated pieces of thin metal **14** *photog* a sheet of glass, or sometimes metal, coated with photographic emulsion on which an image can be formed by exposure to light **15** a device for straightening teeth **16** an informal word for **denture** (sense 1) **17** *anat* any flat platelike structure **18a** a cup awarded to the winner of a sporting contest, esp a horse race **18b** a race or contest for such a prize **19** any of the rigid layers of the earth's lithosphere **20** *electronics, chiefly US* the anode in an electronic valve **21** a horizontal timber joist that supports rafters **22** a light horseshoe for flat racing **23** *RC Church* Also called: **Communion plate** a flat plate held under the chin of a communicant in order to catch any fragments of the consecrated Host **24** **on a plate** acquired without trouble: *he was handed the job on a plate* **25** **on one's plate** waiting to be done or dealt with ▷ *vb* **plates, plating, plated** (*tr*) **26** to coat (a surface, usually metal) with a thin layer of other metal by electrolysis, etc **27** to cover with metal plates, as for protection **28** *printing* to make a stereotype or electrotype from (type or another plate) **29** to form (metal) into plate, esp by rolling [c13 from OF: thin metal sheet, something flat, from Vulgar L *plattus* (unattested)]

Plate (pleɪt) *n* **River** the English name for the (Río de la) **Plata**

plateau (ˈplætəʊ) *n, pl* **plateaus** *or* **plateaux** (-əʊz) **1** a wide mainly level area of elevated land **2** a relatively long period of stability; levelling off: *the rising prices reached a plateau* ▷ *vb (intr)* **3** to remain at a stable level for a relatively long period [c18 from F, from OF *platel* something flat, from *plat* flat]

Plateau (ˈplætəʊ) *n* a state of central Nigeria, formed in 1976 from part of Benue-Plateau State: tin mining. Capital: Jos. Pop (including Nassarawa state): 3 671 498 (1995 est). Area (including Nassarawa state): 58 030 sq km (22 405 sq miles)

plated (ˈpleɪtɪd) *adj* **a** coated with a layer of metal **b** (*in combination*): *gold-plated*

plate glass *n* glass formed into a sheet by rolling, used for windows, etc

platelayer (ˈpleɪtˌleɪə) *n Brit* a workman who lays and maintains railway track. US equivalent: **trackman**

platelet (ˈpleɪtlɪt) *n* a minute cell occurring in the blood of vertebrates and involved in the clotting of the blood [c19 a small PLATE]

platen (ˈplætᵊn) *n* **1** a flat plate in a printing press that presses the paper against the type **2** the roller on a typewriter, against which the keys strike [c15 from OF *platine*, from *plat* flat]

plater (ˈpleɪtə) *n* **1** a person or thing that plates **2** *horse racing* a mediocre horse entered chiefly for minor races

plate tectonics *n (functioning as sing) geol* the study of the earth's crust and mantle with reference to the theory that the lithosphere is divided into rigid blocks (plates) that float on semifluid rock and are thus able to interact with each other at their boundaries

plate up *vb (adv)* to put food on a plate, ready for serving

platform (ˈplætfɔːm) *n* **1** a raised floor or other horizontal surface **2** a raised area at a railway station, from which passengers have access to the trains **3** See **drilling platform** **4** the declared principles, aims, etc, of a political party, etc **5a** the thick raised sole of some shoes **5b** (*as modifier*): *platform shoes* **6** a vehicle or level place on which weapons are mounted and fired **7** a specific type of computer hardware or computer operating system [c16 from F *plateforme*, from *plat* flat + *forme* layout]

platform ticket *n* a ticket for admission to railway platforms but not for travel

Plath (plæθ) *n* **Sylvia** 1932–63, US poet living in England. She wrote two volumes of verse, *The Colossus* (1960) and *Ariel* (1965), and a novel, *The Bell Jar* (1963): she was married to Ted Hughes

plating (ˈpleɪtɪŋ) *n* **1** a coating or layer of material, esp metal **2** a layer or covering of metal plates

Platini (*French* platini) *n* **Michel** born 1955, French football player and sports administrator

platiniridium (ˌplætɪnɪˈrɪdɪəm) *n* any alloy of platinum and iridium

platinize *or* **platinise** (ˈplætɪˌnaɪz) *vb* **platinizes, platinizing, platinized** *or* **platinises, platinising, platinised** (*tr*) to coat with platinum > **ˌplatiniˈzation** *or* **ˌplatiniˈsation** *n*

platinum (ˈplætɪnəm) *n* a ductile malleable silvery-white metallic element, very resistant to heat and chemicals: used in jewellery, laboratory apparatus, electrical contacts, dentistry, electroplating, and as a catalyst. Symbol: Pt; atomic no.: 78; atomic wt.: 195.08 [c19 NL, from Sp. *platina* silvery element, from *plata* silver, from Provençal: silver plate + the suffix *-um*]

platinum black *n chem* a black powder consisting of very finely divided platinum metal

platinum-blond *or (fem)* **platinum-blonde** *adj* **1** (of hair) of a pale silver-blond colour **2a** having hair of this colour **2b** (*as n*): *she was a platinum blonde*

platinum disc *n* **1** (in Britain) an LP record certified to have sold 300 000 copies or a single certified to have sold 600 000 copies **2** (in the US) an LP record or single certified to have sold one million copies

platinum metal *n* any of the group of precious metallic elements consisting of ruthenium, rhodium, palladium, osmium, iridium, and platinum

platitude (ˈplætɪˌtjuːd) *n* **1** a trite, dull, or obvious remark **2** staleness or insipidity of thought or language; triteness [c19 from F, lit.: flatness, from *plat* flat] > **ˌplatiˈtudinous** *adj*

platitudinize *or* **platitudinise** (ˌplætɪˈtjuːdɪˌnaɪz) *vb* **platitudinizes, platitudinizing, platitudinized** *or* **platitudinises, platitudinising, platitudinised** (*intr*) to speak or write in platitudes

Plato (ˈpleɪtəʊ) *n* ?427–?347 BC, Greek philosopher: with his teacher Socrates and his pupil Aristotle, he is regarded as the initiator of western philosophy. His influential theory of ideas, which makes a distinction between objects of sense perception and the universal ideas or forms of which they are an expression, is formulated in such dialogues as *Phaedo*, *Symposium*, and *The Republic*. Other works include *The Apology* and *Laws*

Platonic (pləˈtɒnɪk) *adj* **1** of or relating to Plato or his teachings **2** (*often not cap*) free from physical desire: *Platonic love* > **Plaˈtonically** *adv*

Platonic solid *n* any of the five possible regular polyhedrons: cube, tetrahedron, octahedron, icosahedron, and dodecahedron

Platonism (ˈpleɪtəˌnɪzəm) *n* the teachings of Plato and his followers; esp the philosophical theory that the meanings of general words are real entities (Forms) and that particular objects have properties in common by virtue of their relationship with these Forms > **ˈPlatonist** *n*

platoon (pləˈtuːn) *n* **1** *mil* a subunit of a company, usually comprising three sections of ten to twelve men **2** a group of people sharing a common activity, etc [c17 from F *peloton* little ball, group of men, from *pelote* ball; see PELLET]

Plattdeutsch (*German* ˈplatdɔytʃ) *n* another name for **Low German** [lit.: flat German]

Platte (plæt) *n* a river system of the central US, formed by the confluence of the **North Platte** and **South Platte** at North Platte, Nebraska: flows generally east to the Missouri River. Length: 499 km (310 miles)

platteland (ˈplatəˌlant) *n* **the** (in South Africa) the country districts or rural areas [c20 from Afrik., from Du. *plat* flat + *land* country]

platter (ˈplætə) *n* **1** a large shallow usually oval dish or plate **2** a course of a meal, usually consisting of several different foods served on the same plate: *a seafood platter* [c14 from Anglo-Norman *plater*, from *plat* dish, from OF *plat* flat; see PLATE]

platy- *combining form* indicating something flat, as **platyhelminth**, the flatworm [from Gk *platus* flat]

platypus (ˈplætɪpəs) *n, pl* **platypuses** See **duck-billed platypus** [c18 NL, from PLATY- + *-pus*, from Gk *pous* foot]

platyrrhine (ˈplætɪˌraɪn) *or* **platyrrhinian** (ˌplætɪˈrɪnɪən) *adj* **1** (esp of New World monkeys) having widely separated nostrils opening to the side of the face **2** (of a human) having an unusually short wide nose [c19 from NL *platyrrhinus*, from PLATY- + *-rrhinus*, from Gk *rhis* nose]

plaudit (ˈplɔːdɪt) *n (usually pl)* **1** an expression of enthusiastic approval **2** a round of applause [c17 from earlier *plauditē*, from L: applaud!, from *plaudere* to APPLAUD]

Plauen (*German* ˈplauən) *n* a city in E central Germany, in Saxony: textile centre. Pop: 70 860 (1991)

plausible ('plɔːzɪbᵊl) *adj* **1** apparently reasonable, valid, truthful, etc: *a plausible excuse* **2** apparently trustworthy or believable: *a plausible speaker* [c16 from L *plausibilis* worthy of applause, from *plaudere* to APPLAUD] > ˌ**plausiˈbility** *or* ˈ**plausibleness** *n* > ˈ**plausibly** *adv*

Plautus ('plɔːtəs) *n* **Titus Maccius** ('taɪtəs 'mæksɪəs) ?254–?184 BC, Roman comic dramatist. His 21 extant works, adapted from Greek plays, esp those by Menander, include *Menaechmi* (the basis of Shakespeare's *The Comedy of Errors*), *Miles Gloriosus*, *Rudens*, and *Captivi*

play (pleɪ) *vb* **1** to occupy oneself in (a sport or diversion) **2** (*tr*) to contend against (an opponent) in a sport or game: *Ed played Tony at chess and lost* **3** to fulfil or cause to fulfil (a particular role) in a team game: *he plays in the defence* **4** (*intr*; often foll by *about* or *around*) to behave carelessly, esp in a way that is unconsciously cruel or hurtful: *to play about with a young girl's affections* **5** (when *intr*, often foll by *at*) to perform or act the part (of) in or as in a dramatic production **6** to perform (a dramatic production) **7a** to have the ability to perform on (a musical instrument): *David plays the harp* **7b** to perform as specified: *he plays out of tune* **8** (*tr*) **8a** to reproduce (a piece of music, note, etc) on an instrument **8b** to perform works by: *to play Brahms* **9** to discharge or cause to discharge: *he played the water from the hose onto the garden* **10** to cause (a radio, etc) to emit sound **11** to move freely, quickly, or irregularly: *lights played on the scenery* **12** (*tr*) *stock exchange* to speculate or operate aggressively for gain in (a market) **13** (*tr*) *angling* to attempt to tire (a hooked fish) by alternately letting out and reeling in line **14** to put (a card, counter, piece, etc) into play **15** to gamble **16** **play fair** (*or* **false**) (often foll by *with*) to prove oneself fair (*or* unfair) in one's dealings **17** **play for time** to delay the outcome of some activity so as to gain time to one's own advantage **18** **play into the hands of** to act directly to the advantage of (an opponent) ▷ *n* **19** a dramatic composition written for performance by actors on a stage, etc; drama **20** the performance of a dramatic composition **21a** games, exercise, or other activity undertaken for pleasure, esp by children **21b** (*in combination*): *playroom* **22** conduct: *fair play* **23** the playing of a game or the period during which a game is in progress: *rain stopped play* **24** *US* a manoeuvre in a game: *a brilliant play* **25** the situation of a ball, etc, that is within the defined area and being played according to the rules (in **in play, out of play**) **26** gambling **27** activity or operation: *the play of the imagination* **28** freedom of movement: *too much play in the rope* **29** light, free, or rapidly shifting motion: *the play of light on the water* **30** fun, jest, or joking: *I only did it in play* **31** **call into play** to bring into operation **32** **make a play for** *inf* to make an obvious attempt to gain ▷ See also **play along, playback,** etc [OE *plega* (n), *plegan* (vb)] > ˈ**playable** *adj*

play-act *vb* **1** (*intr*) to pretend or make believe **2** (*intr*) to behave in an overdramatic or affected manner **3** to act in or as in (a play) > ˈ**play-ˌacting** *n* > ˈ**play-ˌactor** *n*

play along *vb* (*adv*) **1** (*intr*; usually foll by *with*) to cooperate (with), esp as a temporary measure **2** (*tr*) to manipulate as if in a game, esp for one's own advantage: *he played the widow along until she gave him her money*

playback ('pleɪˌbæk) *n* **1** the act or process of reproducing a recording, esp on magnetic tape **2** the part of a tape recorder serving to reproduce or used for reproducing recorded material ▷ *vb* **play back** (*adv*) **3** to reproduce (recorded material) on (a magnetic tape) by means of a tape recorder

playbill ('pleɪˌbɪl) *n* **1** a poster or bill advertising a play **2** the programme of a play

playboy ('pleɪˌbɔɪ) *n* a man, esp one of private means, who devotes himself to the pleasures of nightclubs, female company, etc

play-centre *n* the NZ name for **playgroup**

play down *vb* (*tr, adv*) to make little or light of; minimize the importance of

player ('pleɪə) *n* **1** a person who participates in or is skilled at some game or sport **2** a person who plays a game or sport professionally **3** a person who plays a musical instrument **4** an actor **5** *inf* a participant, esp a powerful one, in a particular field of activity: *a leading city player*

Player ('pleɪə) *n* **Gary** ('gærɪ) born 1935, South African professional golfer: won the British Open Championship (1959; 1968; 1974) and the US Open Championship (1965)

player piano *n* a mechanical piano; Pianola

playful ('pleɪfʊl) *adj* **1** full of high spirits and fun: *a playful kitten* **2** good-natured and humorous: *a playful remark* > ˈ**playfully** *adv*

playgoer ('pleɪˌgəʊə) *n* a person who goes to theatre performances, esp frequently

playground ('pleɪˌgraʊnd) *n* **1** an outdoor area for children's play, esp one having swings, slides, etc, or adjoining a school **2** a place popular as a sports or holiday resort

playgroup ('pleɪˌgruːp) *n* a regular meeting of small children for supervised creative play

playhouse ('pleɪˌhaʊs) *n* **1** a theatre **2** *US* a small house for children to play in

playing card *n* one of a pack of 52 rectangular pieces of stiff card, used for playing a wide variety of games, each card having one or more symbols of the same kind on the face, but an identical design on the reverse

playing field *n chiefly Brit* a field or open space used for sport

playlet ('pleɪlɪt) *n* a short play

playlist ('pleɪˌlɪst) *n* **1** a list of records chosen for playing, as on a radio station **2** a list of tracks to be played in a particular order on a CD player ▷ *vb* **3** (*tr*) to put (a song or record) on a playlist

play-lunch *n NZ* a schoolchild's mid-morning snack

playmaker ('pleɪˌmeɪkə) *n sport* a player whose role is to create scoring opportunities for his or her team-mates

playmate ('pleɪˌmeɪt) *or* **playfellow** *n* a friend or partner in play or recreation

play off *vb* (*adv*) **1** (*tr*; usually foll by *against*) to manipulate as if in playing a game: *to play one person off against another* **2** (*intr*) to take part in a play-off ▷ *n* **play-off** **3** *sport* an extra contest to decide the winner when competitors are tied **4** *chiefly US & Canad* a contest or series of games to determine a championship

play on *vb* (*intr*) **1** (*adv*) to continue to play **2** (*prep*) Also: **play upon** to exploit or impose upon (the feelings or weakness of another)

play on words *n* another term for **pun**¹

playpen ('pleɪˌpɛn) *n* a small enclosure, usually portable, in which a young child can be left to play in safety

playschool ('pleɪˌskuːl) *n* an informal nursery group for preschool children

play-the-ball *n rugby league* a method for bringing the ball back into play after a tackle, in which the tackled player is allowed to stand up and kick or heel the ball behind him or her to a team-mate

plaything ('pleɪˌθɪŋ) *n* **1** a toy **2** a person regarded or treated as a toy

playtime ('pleɪˌtaɪm) *n* a time for play or recreation, esp the school break

play up *vb* (*adv*) **1** (*tr*) to highlight: *to play up one's best features* **2** *Brit inf* to behave irritatingly (towards) **3** (*intr*) *Brit inf* (of a machine, etc) to function erratically: *the car is playing up again* **4** to hurt; give (one) trouble: *my back's playing up again* **5** **play up to** **5a** to support (another actor) in a performance **5b** to try to gain favour with by flattery

playwright ('pleɪˌraɪt) *n* a person who writes plays
plaza ('plɑːzə) *n* **1** an open space or square, esp in Spain **2** *chiefly US & Canad* a modern complex of shops, buildings, and parking areas [C17 from Sp., from L *platēa* courtyard; see PLACE]
plc *or* **PLC** *abbrev for* public limited company
plea (pliː) *n* **1** an earnest entreaty or request **2a** *law* something alleged by or on behalf of a party to legal proceedings in support of his claim or defence **2b** *criminal law* the answer made by an accused to the charge: *a plea of guilty* **2c** (in Scotland and formerly in England) a suit or action at law **3** an excuse, justification, or pretext: *he gave the plea of a previous engagement* [C13 from Anglo-Norman *plai*, from OF *plaid* lawsuit, from Med. L *placitum* court order (lit.: what is pleasing), from L *placēre* to please]
plea bargaining *n* an agreement between the prosecution and defence, sometimes including the judge, in which the accused agrees to plead guilty to a lesser charge in return for more serious charges being dropped
plead (pliːd) *vb* **pleads, pleading; pleaded, plead** (plɛd), *or esp Scot & US* **pled 1** (when *intr*, often foll by *with*) to appeal earnestly or humbly (to) **2** (*tr; may take a clause as object*) to give as an excuse: *to plead ignorance* **3** *law* to declare oneself to be (guilty or not guilty) in answer to the charge **4** *law* to advocate (a case) in a court of law **5** (*intr*) *law* **5a** to file pleadings **5b** to address a court as an advocate [C13 from OF *plaidier*, from Med. L *placitāre* to have a lawsuit, from L *placēre* to please] > '**pleadable** *adj* > '**pleader** *n*
pleadings ('pliːdɪŋz) *pl n law* the formal written statements presented alternately by the plaintiff and defendant in a lawsuit
pleasance ('plɛzəns) *n* **1** a secluded part of a garden laid out with trees, walks, etc **2** *arch* enjoyment or pleasure [C14 *plesaunce*, from OF *plaisance*, ult. from *plaisir* to PLEASE]
pleasant ('plɛzᵊnt) *adj* **1** giving or affording pleasure; enjoyable **2** having pleasing or agreeable manners, appearance, habits, etc **3** *obs* merry and lively [C14 from OF *plaisant*, from *plaisir* to PLEASE] > '**pleasantly** *adv*
Pleasant Island *n* the former name of **Nauru**
pleasantry ('plɛzᵊntrɪ) *n, pl* **pleasantries 1** (*often pl*) an agreeable or amusing remark, etc, often one made in order to be polite: *they exchanged pleasantries* **2** an agreeably humorous manner or style [C17 from F *plaisanterie*, from *plaisant* PLEASANT]
please (pliːz) *vb* **pleases, pleasing, pleased 1** to give satisfaction, pleasure, or contentment to (a person) **2** to be the will of or have the will (to): *if it pleases you; the court pleases* **3 if you please** if you will or wish, sometimes used in ironic exclamation **4 pleased with** happy because of **5 please oneself** to do as one likes ▷ *adv* **6** (*sentence modifier*) used in making polite requests, pleading, etc **7 yes please** a polite formula for accepting an offer, invitation, etc [C14 *plese*, from OF *plaisir*, from L *placēre*] > **pleased** *adj* > **pleasedly** ('pliːzɪdlɪ) *adv*
Pleasence ('plɛzəns) *n* **Donald** 1919–95, British actor. His films include *Dr Crippen* (1962) and *Cul de Sac* (1966)
pleasing ('pliːzɪŋ) *adj* giving pleasure; likable or gratifying > '**pleasingly** *adv*
pleasurable ('plɛʒərəbᵊl) *adj* enjoyable, agreeable, or gratifying > '**pleasurably** *adv*
pleasure ('plɛʒə) *n* **1** an agreeable or enjoyable sensation or emotion: *the pleasure of hearing good music* **2** something that gives enjoyment: *his garden was his only pleasure* **3a** amusement, recreation, or enjoyment **3b** (*as modifier*): *a pleasure ground* **4** *euphemistic* sexual gratification: *he took his pleasure of her* **5** a person's preference ▷ *vb* **pleasures, pleasuring, pleasured 6** (when *intr*, often foll by *in*) to give pleasure to or take pleasure (in) [C14 *plesir*, from OF]
pleat (pliːt) *n* **1** any of various types of fold formed by doubling back fabric, etc, and pressing, stitching, or steaming into place ▷ *vb* **2** (*tr*) to arrange (material, part of a garment, etc) in pleats [C16 var. of PLAIT]
pleb (plɛb) *n* **1** short for **plebeian 2** *Brit inf, often derog* a common vulgar person
plebeian (plə'biːən) *adj* **1** of or characteristic of the common people, esp those of ancient Rome **2** lacking refinement; philistine or vulgar: *plebeian tastes* ▷ *n* **3** one of the common people, esp one of the Roman plebs **4** a person who is coarse, vulgar, etc [C16 from L *plēbēius* of the people, from *plēbs* the common people of ancient Rome] > **ple'beian,ism** *n*
plebiscite ('plɛbɪˌsaɪt, -sɪt) *n* **1** a direct vote by the electorate of a state, region, etc, on some question, usually of national importance **2** any expression of public opinion on some matter ▷ See also **referendum** [C16 from OF *plébiscite*, from L *plēbiscītum* decree of the people, from *plēbs* the populace + *scīscere* to decree, from *scīre* to know] > **plebiscitary** (plə'bɪsɪtərɪ, -trɪ) *adj*
plectrum ('plɛktrəm) *n, pl* **-trums** *or* **-tra** (-trə) any implement for plucking a string, such as a small piece of plastic, wood, etc, used to strum a guitar [C17 from L, from Gk *plektron*, from *plessein* to strike]
pled (plɛd) *vb US or (esp in legal usage) Scot* a past tense and past participle of **plead**
pledge (plɛdʒ) *n* **1** a formal or solemn promise or agreement **2a** collateral for the payment of a debt or the performance of an obligation **2b** the condition of being collateral (esp in **in pledge**) **3** a token: *the gift is a pledge of their sincerity* **4** an assurance of support or goodwill, conveyed by drinking a toast: *we drank a pledge to their success* **5** a person who binds himself or herself, as by becoming bail or surety for another **6 take** *or* **sign the pledge** to make a vow to abstain from alcoholic drink ▷ *vb* **pledges, pledging, pledged 7** to promise formally or solemnly **8** (*tr*) to bind by or as if by a pledge: *they were pledged to secrecy* **9** to give or offer (one's word, freedom, property, etc) as a guarantee, as for the repayment of a loan **10** to drink a toast to (a person, cause, etc) [C14 from OF *plege*, from LL *plebium* security, from *plebīre* to pledge, of Gmc origin] > '**pledgable** *adj* > '**pledger** *or* '**pledgor** *n*
pledgee (plɛdʒ'iː) *n* **1** a person to whom a pledge is given **2** a person to whom property is delivered as a pledge
pledget ('plɛdʒɪt) *n* a small flattened pad of wool, cotton, etc, esp for use as a pressure bandage to be applied to wounds [C16 from ?]
-plegia *n combining form* indicating a specified type of paralysis: *paraplegia* [from Gk, from *plēgē* stroke, from *plēssein* to strike] > **-plegic** *adj and n combining form*
pleiad ('plaɪəd) *n* a brilliant or talented group, esp one with seven members [C16 orig. F *Pléiade*, name given by Ronsard to himself and six other poets, ult. after the PLEIADES]
Pleiades ('plaɪəˌdiːz) *pl n Greek myth* the seven daughters of Atlas, placed as stars in the sky either to save them from the pursuit of Orion or, in another account, after they had killed themselves for grief over the death of their half-sisters the Hyades
Pleiocene ('plaɪəʊˌsiːn) *adj, n* a variant spelling of **Pliocene**
Pleistocene ('plaɪstəˌsiːn) *adj* **1** of, denoting, or formed in the first epoch of the Quaternary period. It was characterized by extensive glaciations of the N hemisphere and the evolutionary development of man ▷ *n* **2 the** the Pleistocene epoch or rock series [C19 from Gk *pleistos* most + *kainos* recent]
plenary ('pliːnərɪ, 'plɛn-) *adj* **1** full, unqualified, or complete: *plenary powers; plenary indulgence* **2** (of assemblies, councils, etc) attended by all the members [C15 from LL *plēnārius*, from L *plēnus* full] > '**plenarily** *adv*
plenipotentiary (ˌplɛnɪpə'tɛnʃərɪ) *adj* **1** (esp of a diplomatic envoy) invested with or possessing full

Pp

authority **2** conferring full authority **3** (of power or authority) full; absolute ▷ *n, pl* **plenipotentiaries** **4** a person invested with full authority to transact business, esp a diplomat authorized to represent a country. See also **envoy**[1] (sense 1) [C17 from Med. L *plēnipotentiārius*, from L *plēnus* full + *potentia* POWER]

plenitude (ˈplɛnɪˌtjuːd) *n* **1** abundance **2** the condition of being full or complete [C15 via OF from L *plēnitūdō*, from *plēnus* full]

plenteous (ˈplɛntɪəs) *adj* **1** ample; abundant: *a plenteous supply of food* **2** producing or yielding abundantly: *a plenteous grape harvest* [C13 *plenteus*, from OF, from *plentif*, from *plenté* PLENTY] > **ˈplenteously** *adv* > **ˈplenteousness** *n*

plentiful (ˈplɛntɪfʊl) *adj* **1** ample; abundant **2** having or yielding an abundance: *a plentiful year* > **ˈplentifully** *adv* > **ˈplentifulness** *n*

plenty (ˈplɛntɪ) *n, pl* **plenties** **1** (often foll by *of*) a great number, amount, or quantity; lots: *plenty of time; there are plenty of cars on display here* **2** ample supplies or resources: *the age of plenty* **3** **in plenty** existing in abundance: *food in plenty* ▷ *determiner* **4a** very many; ample: *plenty of people believe in ghosts* **4b** *(as pron): that's plenty, thanks* ▷ *adv* **5** *inf* fully or abundantly: *the coat was plenty big enough* [C13 from OF *plenté*, from LL *plēnitās* fullness, from L *plēnus* full]

Plenty (ˈplɛntɪ) *n* **Bay of** a large bay of the Pacific on the NE coast of the North Island, New Zealand

plenum (ˈpliːnəm) *n, pl* **plenums** *or* **plena** (-nə) **1** an enclosure containing gas at a higher pressure than the surrounding environment **2** a fully attended meeting **3** (esp in the philosophy of the Stoics) space regarded as filled with matter [C17 from L: space filled with matter, from *plēnus* full]

pleochroism (plɪˈɒkrəʊˌɪzəm) *n* a property of certain crystals of absorbing light waves selectively and therefore of showing different colours when looked at from different directions [C19 from Gk *pleiōn* more, from *polus* many + *-chroism* from *khrōs* skin colour] > **pleochroic** (ˌpliːəˈkrəʊɪk) *adj*

pleomorphism (ˌpliːəˈmɔːfɪzəm) *or* **pleomorphy** (ˈpliːəˌmɔːfɪ) *n* **1** the occurrence of more than one different form in the life cycle of a plant or animal **2** another word for **polymorphism** (sense 2) > **ˌpleoˈmorphic** *adj*

pleonasm (ˈpliːəˌnæzəm) *n rhetoric* **1** the use of more words than necessary or an instance of this, such as *a tiny little child* **2** a word or phrase that is superfluous [C16 from L *pleonasmus*, from Gk *pleonasmos* excess, from *pleonazein* to be redundant] > **ˌpleoˈnastic** *adj*

plesiosaur (ˈpliːsɪəˌsɔː) *n* any of various marine reptiles of Jurassic and Cretaceous times, having a long neck, short tail, and paddle-like limbs [C19 from NL *plēsiosaurus*, from Gk *plēsios* near + *sauros* a lizard]

plethora (ˈplɛθərə) *n* **1** superfluity or excess; overabundance **2** *pathol, obs* a condition caused by dilation of superficial blood vessels, characterized esp by a reddish face [C16 via Med. L from Gk *plēthōrē* fullness, from *plēthein* to grow full] > **plethoric** (plɛˈθɒrɪk) *adj*

pleura (ˈplʊərə) *n, pl* **pleurae** (ˈplʊəriː) the thin transparent membrane enveloping the lungs and lining the walls of the thoracic cavity [C17 via Med. L from Gk: side, rib] > **ˈpleural** *adj*

pleurisy (ˈplʊərɪsɪ) *n* inflammation of the pleura, characterized by pain that is aggravated by deep breathing or coughing [C14 from OF *pleurisie*, from LL, from Gk *pleuritis*, from *pleura* side] > **pleuritic** (plʊˈrɪtɪk) *adj, n*

pleuro- *or before a vowel* **pleur-** *combining form* **1** of or relating to the side **2** indicating the pleura [from Gk *pleura* side]

pleuropneumonia (ˌplʊərəʊnjuːˈməʊnɪə) *n* the combined disorder of pleurisy and pneumonia

Pleven (*Bulgarian* ˈplɛvɛn) *or* **Plevna** (*Bulgarian* ˈplɛvna) *n* a town in N Bulgaria: taken by Russia from the Turks in 1877 after a siege of 143 days. Pop: 121 952 (1999 est)

Plexiglas (ˈplɛksɪˌglɑːs) *n US trademark* a transparent plastic, polymethylmethacrylate, used for combs, plastic sheeting, etc

plexor (ˈplɛksə) *or* **plessor** *n med* a small hammer with a rubber head for use in percussion of the chest and testing reflexes [C19 from Gk *plēxis* a stroke, from *plēssein* to strike]

plexus (ˈplɛksəs) *n, pl* **plexuses** *or* **plexus** **1** any complex network of nerves, blood vessels, or lymphatic vessels **2** an intricate network or arrangement [C17 NL, from L *plectere* to braid]

pliable (ˈplaɪəbᵊl) *adj* easily moulded, bent, influenced, or altered > **ˌpliaˈbility** *or* **ˈpliableness** *n* > **ˈpliably** *adv*

pliant (ˈplaɪənt) *adj* **1** easily bent; supple: *a pliant young tree* **2** adaptable; yielding readily to influence; compliant [C14 from OF, from *plier* to fold; see PLY[2]] > **ˈpliancy** *n* > **ˈpliantly** *adv*

plicate (ˈplaɪkeɪt) *or* **plicated** *adj* having or arranged in parallel folds or ridges; pleated: *a plicate leaf; plicate rock strata* [C18 from L *plicātus* folded, from *plicāre* to fold] > **pliˈcation** *n*

plié (ˈpliːeɪ) *n* a classic ballet practice posture with back erect and knees bent [F: bent]

plier (ˈplaɪə) *n* a person who plies a trade

pliers (ˈplaɪəz) *pl n* a gripping tool consisting of two hinged arms usually with serrated jaws [C16 from PLY[1]]

plight[1] (plaɪt) *n* a condition of extreme hardship, danger, etc [C14 *plit*, from OF *pleit* fold; prob. infl. by OE *pliht* PLIGHT[2]]

plight[2] (plaɪt) *vb (tr)* **1** to promise formally or pledge (allegiance, support, etc) **2** **plight one's troth** to make a promise, esp of marriage ▷ *n* **3** *arch or dialect* a solemn promise, esp of engagement; pledge [OE *pliht* peril] > **ˈplighter** *n*

plimsoll *or* **plimsole** (ˈplɪmsəl) *n Brit* a light rubber-soled canvas shoe worn for various sports. Also called: **gym shoe, sandshoe** [C20 from the resemblance of the sole to a Plimsoll line]

Plimsoll line (ˈplɪmsəl) *n* another name for **load line** [C19 after Samuel *Plimsoll* (1824–98), Brit politician who advocated its adoption]

plinth (plɪnθ) *n* **1** the rectangular slab or block that forms the lowest part of the base of a column, statue, pedestal, or pier **2** Also called: **plinth course** the lowest part of the wall of a building, esp one that is formed of a course of stone or brick **3** a flat block on either side of a doorframe, where the architrave meets the skirting [C17 from L *plinthus*, from Gk *plinthos* brick]

Pliny (ˈplɪnɪ) *n* **1** known as *Pliny the Elder*. Latin name *Gaius Plinius Secundus*. 23–79 AD, Roman writer, the author of the encyclopedic *Natural History* (77) **2** his nephew, known as *Pliny the Younger*. Latin name *Gaius Plinius Caecilius Secundus*. ?62–?113 AD, Roman writer and administrator, noted for his letters

Pliocene *or* **Pleiocene** (ˈplaɪəʊˌsiːn) *adj* **1** of, denoting, or formed in the last epoch of the Tertiary period, which lasted for 3 million years, during which many modern mammals appeared ▷ *n* **2** **the** the Pliocene epoch or rock series [C19 from Gk *pleiōn* more, from *polus* many + *-cene* from *kainos* recent]

plissé (ˈpliːseɪ, ˈplɪs-) *n* **1** fabric with a wrinkled finish, achieved by treatment involving caustic soda: *cotton plissé* **2** such a finish on a fabric [F: pleated]

PLO *abbrev for* Palestine Liberation Organization

Płock (plɒk) *n* a town in central Poland, on the River Vistula: several Polish kings are buried in the cathedral: oil refining, petrochemical works. Pop: 131 011 (1999 est)

plod (plɒd) *vb* **plods, plodding, plodded** **1** to make (one's way) or walk along (a path, etc) with heavy usually slow steps **2** *(intr)* to work slowly and perseveringly ▷ *n* **3** the act of plodding **4** *Brit* a slang word for **policeman** [C16 imit.] > 'plodder *n* > 'plodding *adj* > 'ploddingly *adv*

Ploeşti (*Romanian* plo'jeʃtj) *n* a city in SE central Romania: centre of the Romanian petroleum industry. Pop: 253 414 (1997 est)

-ploid *adj and n combining form* indicating a specific multiple of a single set of chromosomes: *diploid* [from Gk *-pl(oos)* -fold + -OID] > **-ploidy** *n combining form*

plonk[1] (plɒŋk) *vb* **1** (often foll by *down*) to drop or be dropped heavily: *he plonked the money on the table* ▷ *n* **2** the act or sound of plonking [var. of PLUNK]

plonk[2] (plɒŋk) *n inf* alcoholic drink, usually wine, esp of inferior quality [c20 ?from F *blanc* white, as in *vin blanc* white wine]

plonker ('plɒŋkə) *n sl* a stupid person [c20 from PLONK[1]]

plop (plɒp) *n* **1** the characteristic sound made by an object dropping into water without a splash ▷ *vb* **plops, plopping, plopped** **2** to fall or cause to fall with the sound of a plop: *the stone plopped into the water* ▷ *interj* **3** an exclamation imitative of this sound: *to go plop* [c19 imit.]

plosion ('pləʊʒən) *n phonetics* the sound of an abrupt break or closure, esp the audible release of a stop. Also called: **explosion**

plosive ('pləʊsɪv) *phonetics* ▷ *adj* **1** accompanied by plosion ▷ *n* **2** a plosive consonant; stop [c20 from F, from *explosif* EXPLOSIVE]

plot[1] (plɒt) *n* **1** a secret plan to achieve some purpose, esp one that is illegal or underhand **2** the story or plan of a play, novel, etc **3** *mil* a graphic representation of an individual or tactical setting that pinpoints an artillery target **4** *chiefly US* a diagram or plan **5** **lose the plot** *inf* to lose one's ability or judgment in a given situation ▷ *vb* **plots, plotting, plotted** **6** to plan secretly (something illegal, revolutionary, etc); conspire **7** (*tr*) to mark (a course, as of a ship or aircraft) on a map **8** (*tr*) to make a plan or map of **9a** to locate and mark (points) on a graph by means of coordinates **9b** to draw (a curve) through these points **10** (*tr*) to construct the plot of (a literary work, etc) [c16 from PLOT[2], infl. by obs. *complot* conspiracy, from OF, from ?] > 'plotter *n*

plot[2] (plɒt) *n* a small piece of land: *a vegetable plot* [OE]

Plotinus (plɒ'taɪnəs) *n* ?205–?270 AD, Roman Neo-Platonist philosopher, born in Egypt

plough *or esp US* **plow** (plaʊ) *n* **1** an agricultural implement with sharp blades for cutting or turning over the earth **2** any of various similar implements, such as a device for clearing snow **3** ploughed land **4** **put one's hand to the plough** to begin or undertake a task ▷ *vb* **5** to till (the soil, etc) with a plough **6** to make (furrows or grooves) in (something) with or as if with a plough **7** (when *intr*, usually foll by *through*) to move (through something) in the manner of a plough **8** (*intr*; foll by *through*) to work at slowly or perseveringly **9** (*intr*; foll by *into* or *through*) (of a vehicle) to run uncontrollably into something in its path **10** (*intr*) *Brit sl* to fail an examination [OE *plōg* plough land] > 'plougher *or esp US* 'plower *n*

Plough (plaʊ) *n* **the** the group of the seven brightest stars in the constellation Ursa Major. Also called: **Charles's Wain** Usual US name: the **Big Dipper**

plough back *vb* (*tr, adv*) to reinvest (the profits of a business) in the same business

ploughman *or esp US* **plowman** ('plaʊmən) *n, pl* **ploughmen** *or esp US* **plowmen** a man who ploughs, esp using horses

ploughman's lunch *n* a snack lunch, served esp in a pub, consisting of bread and cheese with pickle

ploughshare *or esp US* **plowshare** ('plaʊʃɛə) *n* the horizontal pointed cutting blade of a mouldboard plough

Plovdiv (*Bulgarian* 'plɔvdif) *n* a city in S Bulgaria on the Maritsa River: the second largest town in Bulgaria; conquered by Philip II of Macedonia in 341 BC; capital of Roman Thracia; commercial centre of a rich agricultural region. Pop: 342 584 (1999 est). Greek name: **Philippopolis**

plover ('plʌvə) *n* **1** any of a family of shore birds, typically having a round head, straight bill, and large pointed wings **2** **green plover** another name for **lapwing** [c14 from OF *plovier* rainbird, from L *pluvia* rain]

plow (plaʊ) *n, vb* the usual US spelling of **plough**

ploy (plɔɪ) *n* **1** a manoeuvre or tactic in a game, conversation, etc **2** any business, job, hobby, etc, with which one is occupied: *angling is his latest ploy* **3** *chiefly Brit* a frolic, escapade, or practical joke [c18 orig. Scot & N English, obs. n sense of EMPLOY meaning an occupation]

PLP (in Britain) *abbrev for* Parliamentary Labour Party

PLR *abbrev for* Public Lending Right

PLU *text messaging abbrev for* people like us

pluck (plʌk) *vb* **1** (*tr*) to pull off (feathers, fruit, etc) from (a fowl, tree, etc) **2** (when *intr*, foll by *at*) to pull or tug **3** (*tr*; foll by *off, away*, etc) *arch* to pull (something) forcibly or violently (from something or someone) **4** (*tr*) to sound (the strings) of (a musical instrument) with the fingers, a plectrum, etc **5** (*tr*) *sl* to fleece or swindle ▷ *n* **6** courage, usually in the face of difficulties or hardship **7** a sudden pull or tug **8** the heart, liver, and lungs, esp of an animal used for food [OE *pluccian, plyccan*] > 'plucker *n*

pluck up *vb* (*tr, adv*) **1** to pull out; uproot **2** to muster (courage, one's spirits, etc)

plucky ('plʌkɪ) *adj* **pluckier, pluckiest** having or showing courage in the face of difficulties, danger, etc > 'pluckily *adv* > 'pluckiness *n*

plug (plʌg) *n* **1** a piece of wood, cork, or other material, used to stop up holes or waste pipes or as a wedge for taking a screw or nail **2** a device having one or more pins to which an electric cable is attached: used to make an electrical connection when inserted into a socket **3** Also called: **volcanic plug** a mass of solidified magma filling the neck of an extinct volcano **4** See **sparking plug** **5a** a cake of pressed or twisted tobacco, esp for chewing **5b** a small piece of such a cake **6** *inf* a favourable mention of a product, show, etc, as on television ▷ *vb* **plugs, plugging, plugged** **7** (*tr*) to stop up or secure (a hole, gap, etc) with or as if with a plug **8** (*tr*) to insert or use (something) as a plug: *to plug a finger into one's ear* **9** (*tr*) *inf* to make favourable and often-repeated mentions of (a song, product, show, etc), as on television **10** (*tr*) *sl* to shoot: *he plugged six rabbits* **11** (*tr*) *sl* to punch **12** (*intr*; foll by *along, away*, etc) *inf* to work steadily or persistently [c17 from MDu. *plugge*] > 'plugger *n*

Pp

plug-and-play *adj computing* capable of detecting the addition of a new input or output device and automatically activating the appropriate control software

plugged in *adj sl* up to date; abreast of the times

plugged-in *adj sl* up-to-date; abreast of the times

plughole ('plʌg,həʊl) *n* a hole in a sink, etc, through which waste water drains and which can be closed with a plug

plug in *vb* (*tr, adv*) **1** to connect (an electrical appliance, etc) with a power source by means of an electrical plug ▷ *n* **plug-in** **2a** a device that can be connected by means of a plug **2b** (*as modifier*): *a plug-in heater* **3** *computing* **3a** a module or piece of software that can be added to a system to provide extra functions or features, esp software that enhances the capabilities of a web browser **3b** (*as modifier*): *plug-in memory cards*

plug'n'play *or* **plug and play** *n computing* a feature of hardware that means that plug'n'play-compatible computers automatically detect and configure hardware devices without the need for intervention. Abbrev: **PnP**

plug-ugly *adj* **1** *inf* extremely ugly ▷ *n, pl* **plug-uglies** **2** *US sl* a city tough; ruffian [c19 from ?]

plum (plʌm) *n* **1** a small rosaceous tree with an edible oval fruit that is purple, yellow, or green and contains an oval stone **2** the fruit of this tree **3** a raisin, as used in a cake or pudding **4a** a dark reddish-purple colour **4b** (*as adj*): *a plum carpet* **5** *inf* **5a** something of a superior or desirable kind, such as a financial bonus **5b** (*as modifier*): *a plum job* [OE *plūme*]

plumage ('plu:mɪdʒ) *n* the layer of feathers covering the body of a bird [C15 from OF, from *plume* feather, from L *plūma* down]

plumate ('plu:meɪt, -mɪt) *or* **plumose** *adj zool, bot* **1** of or possessing feathers or plumes **2** covered with small hairs: *a plumate seed* [C19 from L *plumātus* covered with feathers; see PLUME]

plumb (plʌm) *n* **1** a weight, usually of lead, suspended at the end of a line and used to determine water depth or verticality **2** the perpendicular position of a freely suspended plumb line (esp in **out of plumb, off plumb**) ▷ *adv Also:* **plum 3** in a vertical or perpendicular line or direction **4** *inf, chiefly US* (intensifier): *plumb stupid* **5** *inf* exactly; precisely ▷ *vb* **6** (*tr; often foll by up*) to test the alignment of or adjust to the vertical with a plumb line **7** (*tr*) to experience (the worst extremes of): *to plumb the depths of despair* **8** (*tr*) to understand or master (something obscure): *to plumb a mystery* **9** to connect or join (a device such as a tap) to a water pipe or drainage system [C13 from OF *plomb* (unattested) lead line, from *plon* lead, from L *plumbum*] > '**plumbable** *adj*

plumbago (plʌm'beɪgəʊ) *n, pl* **plumbagos 1** a plant of warm regions, having clusters of blue, white, or red flowers **2** another name for **graphite** [C17 from L: lead ore, translation of Gk *polubdaina*, from *polubdos* lead]

plumber ('plʌmə) *n* a person who installs and repairs pipes, fixtures, etc, for water, drainage, and gas [C14 from OF *plommier* worker in lead, from LL *plumbārius*, from L *plumbum* lead]

plumbing ('plʌmɪŋ) *n* **1** the trade or work of a plumber **2** the pipes, fixtures, etc, used in a water, drainage, or gas installation **3** the act or procedure of using a plumb

plumbism ('plʌm,bɪzəm) *n* chronic lead poisoning [C19 from L *plumbum* lead]

plumb line *n* a string with a metal weight, or **plumb bob,** at one end that, when suspended, points directly towards the earth's centre of gravity and so is used to determine verticality, depth, etc

plumb rule *n* a plumb line attached to a narrow board, used by builders, surveyors, etc

plume (plu:m) *n* **1** a feather, esp one that is large or ornamental **2** a feather or cluster of feathers worn esp formerly as a badge or ornament in a headband, hat, etc **3** *biol* any feathery part **4** something that resembles a plume: *a plume of smoke* **5** a token or decoration of honour; prize ▷ *vb* **plumes, pluming, plumed** (*tr*) **6** to adorn with feathers or plumes **7** (of a bird) to clean or preen (itself or its feathers) **8** (foll by *on* or *upon*) to pride or congratulate (oneself) [C14 from OF, from L *plūma* downy feather]

plummet ('plʌmɪt) *vb* **plummets, plummeting, plummeted 1** (*intr*) to drop down; plunge ▷ *n* **2** the weight on a plumb line; plumb bob **3** a lead plumb used by anglers [C14 from OF *plommet* ball of lead, from *plomb* lead, from L *plumbum*]

plummy ('plʌmɪ) *adj* **plummier, plummiest 1** of, full of, or resembling plums **2** *Brit inf* (of speech) deep, refined, and somewhat drawling **3** *Brit inf* choice; desirable

plumose ('plu:məʊs, -məʊz) *adj* another word for **plumate** [C17 from L *plūmōsus* feathery]

plump[1] (plʌmp) *adj* **1** well filled out or rounded; chubby: *a plump turkey* **2** bulging; full: *a plump wallet* ▷ *vb* **3** (often foll by *up* or *out*) to make or become plump: *to plump up a pillow* [C15 (meaning: dull, rude), C16 (in current senses): ?from MDu. *plomp* blunt] > '**plumply** *adv* > '**plumpness** *n*

plump[2] (plʌmp) *vb* **1** (often foll by *down, into*, etc) to drop or fall suddenly and heavily **2** (*intr; foll by for*) to give support (to) or make a choice (of) one out of a group or number ▷ *n* **3** a heavy abrupt fall or the sound of this ▷ *adv* **4** suddenly or heavily **5** straight down; directly: *the helicopter landed plump in the middle of the field* ▷ *adj, adv* **6** in a blunt, direct, or decisive manner [C14 prob. imit.]

plum pudding *n Brit* a boiled or steamed pudding made with flour, suet, sugar, and dried fruit

plumule ('plu:mju:l) *n* **1** the embryonic shoot of seed-bearing plants **2** a down feather of young birds [C18 from LL *plūmula* a little feather]

plumy ('plu:mɪ) *adj* **plumier, plumiest 1** plumelike; feathery **2** covered with or adorned with feathers

plunder ('plʌndə) *vb* **1** to steal (valuables, goods, sacred items, etc) from (a town, church, etc) by force, esp in time of war; loot **2** (*tr*) to rob or steal (choice or desirable things) from (a place): *to plunder an orchard* ▷ *n* **3** anything taken by plundering; booty **4** the act of plundering; pillage [C17 prob. from Du. *plunderen* (orig.: to plunder household goods)] > '**plunderer** *n*

plunge (plʌndʒ) *vb* **plunges, plunging, plunged 1** (usually foll by *into*) to thrust or throw (something, oneself, etc): *they plunged into the sea* **2** to throw or be thrown into a certain condition: *the room was plunged into darkness* **3** (usually foll by *into*) to involve or become involved deeply (in) **4** (*intr*) to move or dash violently or with great speed or impetuosity **5** (*intr*) to descend very suddenly or steeply: *the ship plunged in heavy seas; a plunging neckline* **6** (*intr*) *inf* to speculate or gamble recklessly, for high stakes, etc ▷ *n* **7** a leap or dive **8** *inf* a swim; dip **9** a pitching or tossing motion **10 take the plunge** *inf* to resolve to do something dangerous or irrevocable [C14 from OF *plongier*, from Vulgar L *plumbicāre* (unattested) to sound with a plummet, from L *plumbum* lead]

plunger ('plʌndʒə) *n* **1** a rubber suction cup used to clear blocked drains, etc **2** a device or part of a machine that has a plunging or thrusting motion; piston **3** *inf* a reckless gambler

plunk (plʌŋk) *vb* **1** to pluck (the strings) of (a banjo, etc) or (of such an instrument) to give forth a sound when plucked **2** (often foll by *down*) to drop or be dropped, esp heavily or suddenly ▷ *n* **3** the act or sound of plunking [C20 imit.]

Plunket *or* **Plunkett** ('plʌŋkət) *n* **Saint Oliver** 1629–81, Irish Roman Catholic churchman and martyr; wrongly executed as a supposed conspirator in the Popish Plot (1678) Feast day: July 11

pluperfect (plu:'pɜ:fɪkt) *adj, n grammar* another term for **past perfect** [C16 from L *plūs quam perfectum* more than perfect]

plural ('plʊərəl) *adj* **1** containing, involving, or composed of more than one **2** denoting a word indicating that more than one referent is being referred to or described ▷ *n* **3** *grammar* **3a** the plural number **3b** a plural form [C14 from OF *plurel*, from LL *plūrālis* concerning many, from L *plūs* more] > '**plurally** *adv*

pluralism ('plʊərə,lɪzəm) *n* **1** the holding by a single person of more than one ecclesiastical benefice or office; plurality **2** *sociol* a theory of society as several autonomous but interdependent groups **3** the existence in a society of groups having distinctive ethnic origin, cultural forms, religions, etc **4** *philosophy* **4a** the metaphysical doctrine that reality consists of more than two basic types of substance ▷ Cf **monism** (sense 1), **dualism** (sense 2) **4b** the metaphysical doctrine that reality consists of independent entities rather than one unchanging whole > '**pluralist** *n, adj* > ,**plural'istic** *adj*

plurality (plʊə'rælɪtɪ) *n, pl* **pluralities 1** the state of being plural **2** *maths* a number greater than one **3** the US term for **relative majority 4** a large number **5** the greater number; majority **6** another word for **pluralism** (sense 1)

pluralize *or* **pluralise** ('plʊərəˌlaɪz) *vb* **pluralizes, pluralizing, pluralized** *or* **pluralises, pluralising, pluralised** **1** (*intr*) to hold more than one ecclesiastical benefice or office at the same time **2** to make or become plural

pluri- *combining form* denoting several [from L *plur-*, *plus* more, *plures* several]

pluripotent (ˌplʊrɪ'pəʊtᵊnt) *adj biol* capable of differentiating into different types of body cell

plus (plʌs) *prep* **1** increased by the addition of: *four plus two* **2** with or with the addition of: *a good job, plus a new car* ▷ *adj* **3** (*prenominal*) indicating or involving addition: *a plus sign* **4** another word for **positive** (senses 7, 8) **5** on the positive part of a scale or coordinate axis: *a value of +x* **6** indicating the positive side of an electrical circuit **7** involving advantage: *a plus factor* **8** (*postpositive*) *inf* having a value above that which is stated: *she had charm plus* **9** (*postpositive*) slightly above a specified standard: *he received a B+ grade for his essay* ▷ *n* **10** short for **plus sign** **11** a positive quantity **12** *inf* something positive or to the good **13** a gain, surplus, or advantage ▷ Mathematical symbol: + [C17 from L: more]

USAGE *Plus*, *together with*, and *along with* do not create compound subjects in the way that *and* does: the number of the verb depends on that of the subject to which *plus*, *together with*, or *along with* is added: *this task, plus all the others, was* (not *were*) *undertaken by the government; the doctor, together with the nurses, was* (not *were*) *waiting for the patient*

plus fours *pl n* men's baggy knickerbockers reaching below the knee, now only worn for golf, etc [C20 because made with four inches of material to hang over at the knee]

plush (plʌʃ) *n* **1** a fabric with a cut pile that is longer and softer than velvet ▷ *adj* **2** Also: **plushy** *inf* lavishly appointed; rich; costly [C16 from F *pluche*, from OF *peluchier* to pluck, ult. from L *pilus* a hair] > '**plushly** *adv*

plus sign *n* the symbol +, indicating addition or positive quantity

plus size *n* **a** a clothing size designed for people who are above the average size **b** (*as modifier*): *plus-size underwear*

Plutarch ('pluːtɑːk) *n* ?46–?120 AD, Greek biographer and philosopher, noted for his *Parallel Lives* of distinguished Greeks and Romans

Pluto[1] ('pluːtəʊ) *n classical myth* the god of the underworld; Hades > **Plu'tonian** *adj*

Pluto[2] ('pluːtəʊ) *n* the smallest planet and the farthest known from the sun [L, from Gk *Ploutōn*, lit.: the rich one]
▷ www.solarsystem.nasa.gov/features/planets
▷ www.solarviews.com/eng/pluto.htm

plutocracy (pluː'tɒkrəsɪ) *n*, *pl* **plutocracies** **1** the rule of society by the wealthy **2** a state or government characterized by the rule of the wealthy **3** a class that exercises power by virtue of its wealth [C17 from Gk *ploutokratia*, from *ploutos* wealth + *-kratia* rule] > **plutocratic** (ˌpluːtə'krætɪk) *adj* > ˌ**pluto'cratically** *adv*

plutocrat ('pluːtəˌkræt) *n* a member of a plutocracy

pluton ('pluːtɒn) *n* any mass of igneous rock that has solidified below the surface of the earth [C20 back formation from PLUTONIC]

plutonic (pluː'tɒnɪk) *adj* (of igneous rocks) derived from magma that has cooled and solidified below the surface of the earth [C20 after PLUTO[1]]

plutonium (pluː'təʊnɪəm) *n* a highly toxic metallic transuranic element. It occurs in trace amounts in uranium ores and is produced in a nuclear reactor by neutron bombardment of uranium-238. The most stable isotope, **plutonium-239**, readily undergoes fission and is used as a reactor fuel. Symbol: Pu; atomic no.: 94; half-life of ^{239}Pu: 24 360 years [C20 after PLUTO[2] because Pluto lies beyond Neptune and plutonium was discovered soon after NEPTUNIUM]

Plutus ('pluːtʊs) *n* the Greek god of wealth [from Gk *ploutos* wealth]

pluvial ('pluːvɪəl) *adj* **1** of, characterized by, or due to the action of rain; rainy ▷ *n* **2** *geol* a climate characterized by persistent rainfall [C17 from L *pluviālis* rainy, from *pluvia* rain]

pluviometer (ˌpluːvɪ'ɒmɪtə) *n* an obsolete word for **rain gauge** > **pluviometric** (ˌpluːvɪə'mɛtrɪk) *adj* > ˌ**pluvio'metrically** *adv*

ply[1] (plaɪ) *vb* **plies, plying, plied** (*mainly tr*) **1** to carry on, pursue, or work at (a job, trade, etc) **2** to manipulate or wield (a tool, etc) **3** to sell (goods, wares, etc), esp at a regular place **4** (usually foll by *with*) to provide (with) or subject (to) repeatedly or persistently: *he plied us with drink; he plied the speaker with questions* **5** (*intr*) to work steadily or diligently **6** (*also intr*) (esp of a ship, etc) to travel regularly along (a route) or in (an area): *to ply the trade routes* [C14 *plye*, short for *aplye* to APPLY]

ply[2] (plaɪ) *n*, *pl* **plies** **1a** a layer, fold, or thickness, as of yarn **1b** (*in combination*): *four-ply* **2** a thin sheet of wood glued to other similar sheets to form plywood **3** one of the strands twisted together to make rope, yarn, etc [C15 from OF *pli* fold, from *plier* to fold, from L *plicāre*]

Plymouth ('plɪməθ) *n* **1** a port in SW England, in Plymouth unitary authority, SW Devon, on **Plymouth Sound** (an inlet of the English Channel): Britain's chief port in Elizabethan times; the last port visited by the Pilgrim Fathers in the *Mayflower* before sailing to America; naval base; university (1992). Pop: 245 991 (1991) **2** a unitary authority in SW England, in Devon. Pop: 240 718 (2001). Area: 76 sq km (30 sq miles) **3** a city in SE Massachusetts, on **Plymouth Bay**: the first permanent European settlement in New England; founded by the Pilgrim Fathers. Pop: 45 608 (1990)

Plymouth Brethren *pl n* a religious sect founded about 1827, strongly Puritanical in outlook and having no organized ministry
▷ www.brethrenonline.org/
▷ http://withchrist.org/MJS/pbs.htm

plywood ('plaɪˌwʊd) *n* a structural board consisting of thin layers of wood glued together under pressure, with the grain of one layer at right angles to the grain of the adjoining layer

Plzeň (*Czech* 'plzɛnj) *n* an industrial city in the Czech Republic. Pop: 167 534 (2000 est). German name: **Pilsen**

pm *abbrev for* premium

Pm *the chemical symbol for* promethium

PM *abbrev for:* **1** Past Master (of a fraternity) **2** Paymaster **3** Postmaster **4** Prime Minister **5** *mil* Provost Marshal

p.m., P.M., pm, *or* **PM** *abbrev for:* **1** (indicating the time from midday to midnight) post meridiem [L: after noon] **2** postmortem (examination)

PMG *abbrev for:* **1** Paymaster General **2** Postmaster General

PMS *abbrev for* premenstrual syndrome

PMT *abbrev for* premenstrual tension

PNdB *abbrev for* perceived noise decibel

pneumatic (njʊ'mætɪk) *adj* **1** of or concerned with air, gases, or wind **2** (of a machine or device) operated by compressed air or by a vacuum **3** containing compressed air: *a pneumatic tyre* **4** (of the bones of birds) containing air spaces which reduce their weight as an adaptation to flying ▷ *n* **5** a pneumatic tyre [C17 from LL *pneumaticus* of air or wind, from Gk, from *pneuma* breath, wind] > **pneu'matically** *adv*

pneumatics (njʊ'mætɪks) *n* (*functioning as sing*) the branch of physics concerned with the mechanical properties of gases, esp air

pneumatology (ˌnjuːmə'tɒlədʒɪ) *n* **1** the branch of theology concerned with the Holy Ghost and other spiritual beings **2** an obsolete name for **psychology** (the science)

Pp

pneumatophore (njuːˈmætəʊˌfɔː) *n* **1** a specialized root of certain swamp plants, such as the mangrove, that branches upwards, rising above ground, and undergoes gaseous exchange with the atmosphere **2** a polyp such as the Portuguese man-of-war, that is specialized as a float

pneumococcus (ˌnjuːməʊˈkɒkəs) *n, pl* **pneumococci** (-ˈkɒksaɪ, -ˈkɒkiː) a bacterium that causes pneumonia

pneumoconiosis (ˌnjuːməʊˌkəʊnɪˈəʊsɪs) *or* **pneumonoconiosis** (ˌnjuːmənəʊˌkəʊnɪˈəʊsɪs) *n* any disease of the lungs or bronchi caused by the inhalation of metallic or mineral particles [c19 shortened from *pneumonoconiosis*, from Gk *pneumōn* lung + *-coniosis*, from *konis* dust]

pneumoencephalogram (ˌnjuːməʊɛnˈsɛfələˌɡræm) *n* See **encephalogram**

pneumogastric (ˌnjuːməʊˈɡæstrɪk) *adj anat* **1** of or relating to the lungs and stomach **2** a former term for **vagus**

pneumonectomy (ˌnjuːməʊˈnɛktəmɪ) *or* **pneumectomy** *n, pl* **pneumonectomies** *or* **pneumectomies** the surgical removal of a lung or part of a lung [c20 from Gk *pneumōn* lung + -ECTOMY]

pneumonia (njuːˈməʊnɪə) *n* inflammation of one or both lungs, in which the air sacs (alveoli) become filled with liquid [c17 NL from Gk from *pneumōn* lung]
> **pneumonic** (njuːˈmɒnɪk) *adj*

pneumothorax (ˌnjuːməʊˈθɔːræks) *n* the abnormal presence of air between the lung and the wall of the chest (pleural cavity), resulting in collapse of the lung

PNI *abbrev for* psychoneuroimmunology

p-n junction *n electronics* a boundary between a p-type and n-type semiconductor that functions as a rectifier and is used in diodes and junction transistors

Pnom Penh (ˈnɒm ˈpɛn) *n* a variant spelling of **Phnom Penh**

PnP *computing abbrev for* plug'n'play

po (pəʊ) *n, pl* **pos** *Brit* an informal word for **chamber pot** [c19 from POT[1]]

Po[1] *the chemical symbol for* polonium

Po[2] (pəʊ) *n* a river in N Italy, rising in the Cottian Alps and flowing northeast to Turin, then east to the Adriatic: the longest river in Italy. Length: 652 km (405 miles). Latin name: **Padus**

PO *abbrev for:* **1** Personnel Officer **2** petty officer **3** Pilot Officer **4** Also: **p.o.** postal order **5** Post Office

poach[1] (pəʊtʃ) *vb* **1** to catch (game, fish, etc) illegally by trespassing on private property **2** to encroach on or usurp (another person's rights, duties, etc) or steal (an idea, employee, etc) **3** *tennis, badminton, etc* to take or play (shots that should belong to one's partner) **4** to break up (land) into wet muddy patches, as by riding over it [c17 from OF *pocher*, of Gmc origin] > **ˈpoacher** *n*

poach[2] (pəʊtʃ) *vb* to simmer (eggs, fish, etc) very gently in water, milk, stock, etc [c15 from OF *pochier* to enclose in a bag (as the yolks are enclosed by the whites)]
> **ˈpoacher** *n*

Pocahontas (ˌpɒkəˈhɒntəs) *n* original name *Matoaka;* married name *Rebecca Rolfe*. ?1595–1617, American Indian, who allegedly saved the colonist Captain John Smith from being killed

pochard (ˈpəʊtʃəd) *n, pl* **pochards** *or* **pochard** any of various diving ducks, esp a European variety, the male of which has a grey-and-black body and a reddish head [c16 from ?]

pock (pɒk) *n* **1** any pustule resulting from an eruptive disease, esp from smallpox **2** another word for **pockmark** (sense 1) [OE *pocc*] > **ˈpocky** *adj*

pocket (ˈpɒkɪt) *n* **1** a small bag or pouch in a garment for carrying small articles, money, etc **2** any bag or pouch or anything resembling this **3** *S African* a bag or sack of vegetables or fruit **4** a cavity in the earth, etc, such as one containing ore **5** a small enclosed or isolated area: *a pocket of resistance* **6** any of the six holes with pouches or nets let into the corners and sides of a billiard table **7** **in one's pocket** under one's control **8** **in** *or* **out of pocket** having made a profit or loss **9** **line one's pockets** to make money, esp by dishonesty when in a position of trust **10** *(modifier)* small: *a pocket edition* ▷ *vb* **pockets, pocketing, pocketed** *(tr)* **11** to put into one's pocket **12** to take surreptitiously or unlawfully; steal **13** *(usually passive)* to confine in or as if in a pocket **14** to conceal or keep back: *he pocketed his pride and asked for help* **15** *billiards, etc* to drive (a ball) into a pocket [c15 from Anglo-Norman *poket* a little bag, from *poque* bag, from MDu. *poke* bag]
> **ˈpocketless** *adj*

pocket battleship *n* a small heavily armed battle cruiser specially built to conform with treaty limitations on tonnage and armament

pocket billiards *n (functioning as sing)* any game played on a table in which the object is to pocket the balls, esp snooker or pool

pocketbook (ˈpɒkɪtˌbʊk) *n* **1** *chiefly US* a small bag or case for money, papers, etc **2** a pocket-sized notebook

pocket borough *n* (before the Reform Act of 1832) an English borough constituency controlled by one person or family who owned the land

pocket drive *or* **keyring drive** *n computing* a small portable memory device that can be plugged into the USB port of many different types of computer

pocketful (ˈpɒkɪtfʊl) *n, pl* **pocketfuls** as much as a pocket will hold

pocketknife (ˈpɒkɪtˌnaɪf) *n, pl* **pocketknives** a small knife with one or more blades that fold into the handle; penknife

pocket money *n* **1** *Brit* a small weekly sum of money given to children by parents as an allowance **2** money for day-to-day spending, incidental expenses, etc

pockmark (ˈpɒkˌmɑːk) *n* **1** Also called: **pock** a pitted scar left on the skin after the healing of a smallpox or similar pustule **2** any pitting of a surface that resembles such scars ▷ *vb* **3** *(tr)* to scar or pit with pockmarks

poco (ˈpəʊkəʊ; *Italian* ˈpɔːko) *or* **un poco** *adj, adv (in combination) music* a little; to a small degree [from It.: little, from L *paucus* few]

poco a poco *adv (in combination) music* little by little: *poco a poco rall* [It.]

pod (pɒd) *n* **1a** the fruit of any leguminous plant, consisting of a long two-valved case that contains seeds **1b** the seedcase as distinct from the seeds **2** any similar fruit **3** a streamlined structure attached to an aircraft and used to house a jet engine, fuel tank, armament, etc ▷ *vb* **pods, podding, podded** **4** *(tr)* to remove the pod from [c17 ? back formation from earlier *podware* bagged vegetables]

-pod *or* **-pode** *n combining form* indicating a certain type or number of feet: *arthropod; tripod* [from Gk *-podos* footed, from *pous* foot]

podagra (pəˈdæɡrə) *n* gout of the foot or big toe [c15 via L from Gk, from *pous* foot + *agra* a trap]

poddy (ˈpɒdɪ) *n, pl* **poddies** *Austral* a handfed calf or lamb [?from *poddy* (adj) fat]

Podgorica *or* **Podgoritsa** (*Russian* ˈpɔdɡɔˌriːtsa) *n* a city in Serbia and Montenegro, the capital of Montenegro: under Turkish rule (1474–1878). Pop: 130 875 (2000 est). Former name (1946–92): **Titograd**

podgy (ˈpɒdʒɪ) *adj* **podgier, podgiest** **1** short and fat; chubby **2** (of the face, arms, etc) unpleasantly chubby and pasty-looking [c19 from *podge* a short plump person]
> **ˈpodgily** *adv* > **ˈpodginess** *n*

podium (ˈpəʊdɪəm) *n, pl* **podiums** *or* **podia** (-dɪə) **1** a small raised platform used by lecturers, conductors, etc **2** a plinth that supports a colonnade or wall **3** a low wall surrounding the arena of an ancient amphitheatre **4** *zool* any footlike organ, such as the tube foot of a starfish [c18 from L: platform, from Gk *podion* little foot, from *pous* foot]

-podium *n combining form* a part resembling a foot: *pseudopodium* [from NL: footlike; see PODIUM]

Podolsk (*Russian* pa'dɔljsk) *n* an industrial city in W Russia, near Moscow. Pop: 195 900 (1999 est)

podophyllin (ˌpɒdəʊ'fɪlɪn) *n* a bitter yellow resin obtained from the dried underground stems of the May apple and mandrake: used to treat warts and formerly as a cathartic [c19 from NL *Podophyllum*, genus of herbs, from *podo-*, from Gk *pous* foot + *phullon* leaf]

-podous *adj combining form* having feet of a certain kind or number: *cephalopodous*

pod person *n, pl* **pod people** *inf* a person who behaves in a strange esp mechanical way, as if not fully human [c20 from the science-fiction film *Invasion of the Body Snatchers* (1956; remade 1978) in which individual humans are replaced by alien replicas grown in giant pods]

podzol ('pɒdzɒl) *or* **podsol** ('pɒdsɒl) *n* a type of soil characteristic of coniferous forest regions having a greyish-white colour in its upper layers from which certain minerals have leached [c20 from Russian: ash ground]

Poe (pəʊ) *n* **Edgar Allan** 1809–49, US short-story writer, poet, and critic. Most of his short stories, such as *The Fall of the House of Usher* (1839) and the *Tales of the Grotesque and Arabesque* (1840), are about death, decay, and madness. *The Murders in the Rue Morgue* (1841) is regarded as the first modern detective story

poem ('pəʊɪm) *n* **1** a composition in verse, usually characterized by words chosen for their sound and suggestive power as well as for their sense, and using such techniques as metre, rhyme, and alliteration **2** a literary composition that is not in verse but exhibits the intensity of imagination and language common to it: *a prose poem* **3** anything resembling a poem in beauty, effect, etc [c16 from L *poēma*, from Gk, var. of *poiēma* something created, from *poiein* to make]

poep (pʊp) *n S African sl* **1** an emission of intestinal gas from the anus **2** a mean or despicable person [Afrik.]

poesy ('pəʊɪzɪ) *n, pl* **poesies 1** an archaic word for **poetry 2** *poetic* the art of writing poetry [c14 via OF from L *poēsis*, from Gk, from *poiēsis* poetic art, from *poiein* to make]

poet ('pəʊɪt) *or (sometimes when fem)* **poetess** *n* **1** a person who writes poetry **2** a person with great imagination and creativity [c13 from L *poēta*, from Gk *poiētēs* maker, poet]

poetaster (ˌpəʊɪ'tæstə, -'teɪ-) *n* a writer of inferior verse [c16 from Med. L; see POET, -ASTER]

poetic (pəʊ'ɛtɪk) *or* **poetical** *adj* **1** of poetry **2** characteristic of poetry, as in being elevated, sublime, etc **3** characteristic of a poet **4** recounted in verse > **po'etically** *adv*

poeticize, poeticise (pəʊ'ɛtɪˌsaɪz) *or* **poetize, poetise** ('pəʊɪˌtaɪz) *vb* **poeticizes, poeticizing, poeticized; poeticises, poeticising, poeticised** *or* **poetizes, poetizing, poetized; poetises, poetising, poetised 1** *(tr)* to put into poetry or make poetic **2** *(intr)* to speak or write poetically

poetic justice *n* fitting retribution

poetic licence *n* justifiable departure from conventional rules of form, fact, etc, as in poetry

poetics (pəʊ'ɛtɪks) *n (usually functioning as sing)* **1** the principles and forms of poetry or the study of these **2** a treatise on poetry

poet laureate *n, pl* **poets laureate** *Brit* the poet appointed as court poet of Britain and given a post in the Royal Household

poetry ('pəʊɪtrɪ) *n* **1** literature in metrical form; verse **2** the art or craft of writing verse **3** poetic qualities, spirit, or feeling in anything **4** anything resembling poetry in rhythm, beauty, etc [c14 from Med. L *poētria*, from L *poēta* POET]

▷ www.bartleby.com/verse

▷ www.bbc.co.uk/bbcfour/audiointerviews/professions

po-faced *adj* **1** wearing a disapproving stern expression **2** narrow-minded; strait-laced [c20 from PO + POKER-FACED]

pogey *or* **pogy** ('pəʊgɪ) *n, pl* **pogeys** *or* **pogies** *Canad sl* **1** financial or other relief given to the unemployed by the government **2** unemployment insurance **3a** the office distributing relief to the unemployed **3b** *(as modifier)*: *pogey clothes*

pogo stick ('pəʊgəʊ) *n* a stout pole with a handle at the top, steps for the feet and a spring at the bottom, so that the user can spring up, down, and along on it [c20 from ?]

pogrom ('pɒgrəm) *n* an organized persecution or extermination of an ethnic group, esp of Jews [c20 via Yiddish from Russian: destruction, from *po-* like + *grom* thunder]

Pohai (ˌpəʊ'haɪ) *n* a variant transliteration of the Chinese name for **Bohai**

pohutukawa (pəˌhu:tu:'kɑ:wə) *n* a New Zealand tree which grows on the coast and produces red flowers in the summer. Also called: **Christmas tree**

poi (pɔɪ) *n NZ* a ball of woven New Zealand flax swung rhythmically by Maori women while performing poi dances

poi dance *n NZ* a women's formation dance that involves singing and manipulating a poi

-poiesis *n combining form* indicating the act of making or producing something specified: *haematopoieses; lymphopoiesis* [from Gk, from *poiēsis* a making; see POESY] > **-poietic** *adj combining form*

poignant ('pɔɪnjənt, -nənt) *adj* **1** sharply distressing or painful to the feelings **2** to the point; cutting or piercing: *poignant wit* **3** keen or pertinent in mental appeal: *a poignant subject* **4** pungent in smell [c14 from OF, from L *pungens* pricking, from *pungere* to sting] > **'poignancy** *or* **'poignance** *n* > **'poignantly** *adv*

Pp

poikilothermic (ˌpɔɪkɪləʊ'θɜ:mɪk) *or* **poikilothermal** (ˌpɔɪkɪləʊ'θɜ:məl) *adj* (of all animals except birds and mammals) having a body temperature that varies with the temperature of the surroundings [c19 from Gk *poikilos* various + THERMAL] > ˌ**poikilo'thermy** *n*

Poincaré (*French* pwɛ̃kare) *n* **1 Jules Henri** (ʒyl ɑ̃ri) 1854–1912, French mathematician, physicist, and philosopher. He made important contributions to the theory of functions and to astronomy and electromagnetic theory **2** his cousin, **Raymond** (rɛmɔ̃) 1860–1934, French statesman; premier of France (1912–13; 1922–24; 1926–29); president (1913–20)

poinciana (ˌpɔɪnsɪ'ɑ:nə) *n* a tree of a tropical genus having large orange or red flowers [c17 NL, after M. de *Poinci*, 17th-cent. governor of the French Antilles]

poind (pɪnd) *vb (tr) Scots law* **1** to take (property of a debtor, etc) in execution of distress; distrain **2** to impound (stray cattle, etc) [c15 from Scot, var. of OE *pyndan* to impound]

poinsettia (pɔɪn'sɛtɪə) *n* a shrub of Mexico and Central America, widely cultivated for its showy scarlet bracts, which resemble petals [c19 NL, after J. P. *Poinsett* (1799–1851), US Minister to Mexico]

point (pɔɪnt) *n* **1** a dot or tiny mark **2** a location, spot, or position **3** any dot used in writing or printing, such as a decimal point or a full stop **4** the sharp tapered end of a pin, knife, etc **5** *maths* **5a** a geometric element having no dimensions whose position is located by means of its coordinates **5b** a location: *point of inflection* **6** a small promontory **7** a specific condition or degree **8** a moment: *at that point he left the room* **9** a reason, aim, etc: *the point of this exercise is to train new teachers* **10** an essential element in an argument: *I take your point* **11** a suggestion or tip **12** a detail or item **13** a characteristic, physical attribute, etc: *he has his good points* **14** a distinctive characteristic or quality of an animal, esp one used as a standard in judging livestock **15** (*often pl*) any of the extremities, such as the tail, ears, or feet, of a domestic animal **16** (*often pl*) *ballet* the tip of the toes **17** a single unit for measuring or counting, as in the scoring of a game **18** *printing* a unit of measurement equal to one twelfth of a pica. There are approximately 72 points to the inch **19** *finance* a unit of value used to quote security and commodity prices and their fluctuations **20** *navigation* **20a** one of the 32 marks on the compass indicating direction **20b** the angle of 11°15′ between two adjacent marks **21** *cricket* a fielding position at right angles to the batsman on the off side and relatively near the pitch **22** either of the two electrical contacts that make or break the current flow in the distributor of an internal-combustion engine **23** *Brit, Austral, & NZ* (*often pl*) a junction of railway tracks in which a pair of rails can be moved so that a train can be directed onto either of two lines. US and Canad equivalent: **switch 24** (*often pl*) a piece of ribbon, cord, etc, with metal tags at the end: used during the 16th and 17th centuries to fasten clothing **25** *Brit* short for **power point 26** the position of the body of a pointer or setter when it discovers game **27** *boxing* a mark awarded for a scoring blow, knockdown, etc **28** any diacritic used in a writing system, esp in a phonetic transcription, to indicate modifications of vowels or consonants **29** *jewellery* a unit of weight equal to 0.01 carat **30** the act of pointing **31 beside the point** irrelevant **32 case in point** a specific or relevant instance **33 make a point of 33a** to make (something) one's regular habit **33b** to do (something) because one thinks it important **34 not to put too fine a point on it** to speak plainly and bluntly **35 on** (*or* **at**) **the point of** at the moment immediately before: *on the point of leaving the room* **36 score points off** to gain an advantage at someone else's expense **37 to the point** relevant **38 up to a point** not completely ▷ *vb* **39** (usually foll by *at* or *to*) to indicate the location or direction of by or as by extending (a finger or other pointed object) towards it: *he pointed to the front door; don't point that gun at me* **40** (*intr*; usually foll by *at* or *to*) to indicate or identify a specific person or thing among several: *all evidence pointed to Donald as the murderer* **41** (*tr*) to direct or face in a specific direction: *point me in the right direction* **42** (*tr*) to sharpen or taper **43** (*intr*) (of gun dogs) to indicate the place where game is lying by standing rigidly with the muzzle turned in its direction **44** (*tr*) to finish or repair the joints of (brickwork, masonry, etc) with mortar or cement **45** (*tr*) *music* to mark (a psalm text) with vertical lines to indicate the points at which the music changes during chanting **46** (*tr*) *phonetics* to provide (a letter or letters) with diacritics **47** (*tr*) to provide (a Hebrew or similar text) with vowel points ▷ See also **point off, point out, point up** [C13 from OF: spot, from L *punctum* a point, from *pungere* to pierce]

point after *n American football* a score given for a successful kick between the goalposts and above the crossbar, following a touchdown

point-and-click *adj computing* of or relating to the way a computer mouse can be used to select and operate functions from a computer screen: *a bright and cheerful point-and-click interface*

point-blank *adj* **1a** aimed or fired at a target so close that it is unnecessary to make allowance for the drop in the course of the projectile **1b** permitting such aim or fire without loss of accuracy: *at point-blank range* **2** aimed or fired at nearly zero range **3** plain or blunt: *a point-blank question* ▷ *adv* **4** directly or straight **5** plainly or bluntly [C16 from POINT + BLANK (in the sense: centre spot of an archery target)]

Point de Galle (pɔɪnt də 'gɑːlə) *n* a former name of **Galle**

point duty *n* **1** the stationing of a policeman or traffic warden at a road junction to control and direct traffic **2** the position at the head of a military control, regarded as being the most dangerous

pointe (pɔɪnt) *n ballet* the tip of the toe (esp in **on pointes**) [from F: point]

Pointe-à-Pitre (*French* pwɛ̃tapitrə) *n* the chief port of Guadeloupe, on SW Grande Terre Island in the Caribbean. Pop: 26 029 (1990)

pointed ('pɔɪntɪd) *adj* **1** having a point **2** cutting or incisive: *a pointed wit* **3** obviously directed at a particular person or aspect: *pointed criticism* **4** emphasized or made conspicuous: *pointed ignorance* **5** (of an arch or style of architecture) Gothic **6** *music* (of a psalm text) marked to show changes in chanting **7** (of Hebrew text) with vowel points marked > **'pointedly** *adv*

Pointe-Noire (*French* pwɛ̃tnwar) *n* a port in S Congo-Brazzaville, on the Atlantic: the country's chief port and former capital (1950–58). Pop: 576 206 (1995 est)

pointer ('pɔɪntə) *n* **1** a person or thing that points **2** an indicator on a measuring instrument **3** a long rod or cane used by a lecturer to point to parts of a map, blackboard, etc **4** one of a breed of large smooth-coated gun dogs, usually white with black, liver, or lemon markings **5** a helpful piece of information

pointillism ('pwæntɪˌlɪzəm) *n* the technique of painting elaborated from impressionism, in which dots of unmixed colour are juxtaposed on a white ground so that from a distance they fuse in the viewer's eye into appropriate intermediate tones [C19 from F, from *pointiller* to mark with tiny dots, from *pointille* little point, from It., from *punto* POINT] > **'pointillist** *n, adj*
▷ www.artcyclopedia.com/history/pointillism.html

pointing ('pɔɪntɪŋ) *n* the act or process of repairing or finishing joints in brickwork, masonry, etc, with mortar

point lace *n* lace made by a needle with buttonhole stitch on a paper pattern. Also called: **needlepoint** ▷ Cf **pillow lace**

pointless ('pɔɪntlɪs) *adj* **1** without a point **2** without meaning, relevance, or force **3** *sport* without a point scored > **'pointlessly** *adv*

point off *vb* (*tr, adv*) to mark off from the right-hand side (a number of decimal places) in a whole number to create a mixed decimal: *point off three decimal places in 12345 and you get 12.345*

point of honour *n, pl* **points of honour** a circumstance, event, etc, that involves the defence of one's principles, social honour, etc

point of no return *n* **1** a point at which an irreversible commitment must be made to an action, progression, etc **2** a point in a journey at which, if one continues, supplies will be insufficient for a return to the starting place

point of order *n, pl* **points of order** a question raised in a meeting as to whether the rules governing procedures are being breached

point of sale *n* (in retail distribution) **a** the place at which a sale is made. Abbrev: **POS b** (*as modifier*): *a point-of-sale display*

point of view *n, pl* **points of view 1** a position from which someone or something is observed **2** a mental viewpoint or attitude

point out *vb* (*tr, adv*) to indicate or specify

pointsman ('pɔɪntsˌmæn, -mən) *n, pl* **pointsmen 1** a person who operates railway points **2** a policeman or traffic warden on point duty

point source *n optics* a source of light or other radiation that can be considered to have negligible dimensions

points system *n Brit* a system used to assess applicants' eligibility for local authority housing, based on (points awarded for) such factors as the length of time the applicant has lived in the area, how many children are in the family, etc

point-to-point *n Brit* a steeplechase organized by a

recognized hunt or other body, usually restricted to amateurs riding horses that have been regularly used in hunting

point up *vb (tr, adv)* to emphasize, esp by identifying: *he pointed up the difficulties*

poise[1] (pɔɪz) *n* **1** composure or dignity of manner **2** physical balance **3** equilibrium; stability **4** the position of hovering ▷ *vb* **poises, poising, poised 5** to be or cause to be balanced or suspended **6** *(tr)* to hold, as in readiness: *to poise a lance* [c16 from OF *pois* weight, from L *pēnsum*, from *pendere* to weigh]

poise[2] (pwɑːz, pɔɪz) *n* the cgs unit of viscosity; the viscosity of a fluid in which a tangential force of 1 dyne per square centimetre maintains a difference in velocity of 1 centimetre per second between two parallel planes 1 centimetre apart. Symbol: P [c20 after Jean Louis Marie *Poiseuille* (1799–1869), F physician]

poised (pɔɪzd) *adj* **1** self-possessed; dignified **2** balanced and prepared for action

poison (ˈpɔɪzᵊn) *n* **1** any substance that can impair function or otherwise injure the body **2** something that destroys, corrupts, etc **3** a substance that retards a chemical reaction or the activity of a catalyst **4** a substance that absorbs neutrons in a nuclear reactor and thus slows down the reaction ▷ *vb (tr)* **5** to give poison to (a person or animal), esp with intent to kill **6** to add poison to **7** to taint or infect with or as if with poison **8** (foll by *against*) to turn (a person's mind) against: *he poisoned her mind against me* **9** to retard or stop (a chemical or nuclear reaction) by the action of a poison [c13 from OF *puison* potion, from L *pōtiō* a drink, esp a poisonous one, from *pōtāre* to drink] > ˈ**poisoner** *n*

poison ivy *n* any of several North American shrubs or climbing plants that cause an itching rash on contact

poisonous (ˈpɔɪzənəs) *adj* **1** having the effects or qualities of a poison **2** capable of killing or inflicting injury **3** corruptive or malicious > ˈ**poisonously** *adv* > ˈ**poisonousness** *n*

poison-pen letter *n* a letter written in malice, usually anonymously, and intended to abuse, frighten, or insult the recipient

poison pill *n finance* a tactic used by a company fearing an unwelcome takeover bid, in which the value of the company is automatically reduced, as by the sale of an issue of shares having an option unfavourable to the bidders, if the bid is successful

poison sumach *n* a swamp shrub of the southeastern US that causes an itching rash on contact with the skin

Poisson distribution (ˈpwɑːsᵊn) *n statistics* a distribution that represents the number of events occurring randomly in a fixed time at an average rate λ [c19 after S. D. *Poisson* (1781–1840), F mathematician]

Poitiers (*French* pwatje) *n* a city in S central France: capital of the former province of Poitou until 1790; scene of the battle (1356) in which the English under the Black Prince defeated the French; university (1432). Pop: 78 894 (1990)

Poitou (*French* pwatu) *n* a former province of W central France, on the Atlantic. Chief town: Poitiers

Poitou-Charentes (*French* pwatuʃarɑ̃t) *n* a region of W central France, on the Bay of Biscay: mainly low-lying

poke[1] (pəʊk) *vb* **pokes, poking, poked 1** *(tr)* to jab or prod, as with the elbow, a stick, etc **2** *(tr)* to make (a hole) by or as by poking **3** (when *intr*, often foll by *at*) to thrust (at) **4** *(tr) inf* to hit with the fist; punch **5** (usually foll by *in, through*, etc) to protrude or cause to protrude: *don't poke your arm out of the window* **6** *(tr)* to stir (a fire, etc) by poking **7** *(intr)* to meddle or intrude **8** (*intr*; often foll by *about* or *around*) to search or pry **9 poke one's nose into** to interfere with or meddle in ▷ *n* **10** a jab or prod **11** *inf* a blow with one's fist; punch [c14 from Low G & MDu. *poken* to prod]

poke[2] (pəʊk) *n* **1** *dialect* a pocket or bag **2 a pig in a poke** See **pig** [c13 from OF *poque*, of Gmc origin]

poke[3] (pəʊk) *n* **1** Also called: **poke bonnet** a bonnet with a brim that projects at the front, popular in the 18th and 19th centuries **2** the brim itself [c18 from POKE[1] (in the sense: to project)]

poker[1] (ˈpəʊkə) *n* a metal rod, usually with a handle, for stirring a fire

poker[2] (ˈpəʊkə) *n* a card game of bluff and skill in which bets are made on the hands dealt, the highest-ranking hand winning the pool [c19 prob. from F *poque* similar card game]

▷ www.pokerfederation.com

poker face *n inf* a face without expression, as that of a poker player attempting to conceal the value of his cards > ˈ**poker-**ˌ**faced** *adj*

poker machine *n Austral & NZ* a fruit machine

pokerwork (ˈpəʊkəˌwɜːk) *n* the art of producing pictures or designs on wood by charring it with a heated tool

pokeweed (ˈpəʊkˌwiːd), **pokeberry**, *or* **pokeroot** *n* a tall North American plant that has a poisonous purple root used medicinally [c18 *poke*, from Algonquian *puccoon* plant used in dyeing, from *pak* blood]

pokie (ˈpəʊkɪ) *n Austral inf* short for **poker machine**

poky *or* **pokey** (ˈpəʊkɪ) *adj* **pokier, pokiest 1** (esp of rooms) small and cramped **2** *inf, chiefly US* without speed or energy; slow [c19 from POKE[1] (in sl. sense: to confine)] > ˈ**pokily** *adv* > ˈ**pokiness** *n*

Pol. *abbrev for:* **1** Poland **2** Polish

Pola (ˈpɔːla) *n* the Italian name for **Pula**

Poland (ˈpəʊlənd) *n* a republic in central Europe, on the Baltic: first united in the 10th century; dissolved after the third partition effected by Austria, Russia, and Prussia in 1795; re-established independence in 1918; invaded by Germany in 1939; ruled by a Communist government from 1947 to 1989, when a multiparty system was introduced; joined the EU in 2004. It consists chiefly of a low undulating plain in the north, rising to a low plateau in the south, with the Sudeten and Carpathian Mountains along the S border. Official language: Polish. Religion: Roman Catholic majority. Currency: zloty. Capital: Warsaw. Pop: 38 647 000 (2001 est). Area: 311 730 sq km (120 359 sq miles). Polish name: **Polska**

▷ www.poland.pl

▷ www.nto-poland.gov.pl/wydÝwlnd.asp

Polanski (pəˈlænskɪ) *n* **Roman** born 1933, Polish film director with a taste for the macabre, as in *Repulsion* (1965) and *Rosemary's Baby* (1968): later films include *Tess* (1980), *Death and the Maiden* (1995), and *The Pianist* (2002)

polar (ˈpəʊlə) *adj* **1** at, near, or relating to either of the earth's poles or the area inside the Arctic or Antarctic Circles: *polar regions* **2** having or relating to a pole or poles **3** pivotal or guiding in the manner of the Pole Star **4** directly opposite, as in tendency or character **5** *chem* (of a molecule) having an uneven distribution of electrons and thus a permanent dipole moment: *water has polar molecules*

polar bear *n* a white carnivorous bear of coastal regions of the North Pole

polar circle *n* a term for either the **Arctic Circle** or **Antarctic Circle**

polar coordinates *pl n* a pair of coordinates for locating a point in a plane by means of the length of a radius vector, *r*, which pivots about the origin to establish the angle, θ, that the position of the point makes with a fixed line. Usually written (r, θ)

polar distance *n* the angular distance of a star, planet, etc, from the celestial pole; the complement of the declination

polar front *n meteorol* a front dividing cold polar air from warmer temperate or tropical air

Polari (pəˈlɑːrɪ) *n* an English slang derived from the Lingua Franca of Mediterranean ports; brought to

Pp

England by sailors from the 16th century onwards [C19 from It. *parlare* to speak]
polarimeter (ˌpəʊləˈrɪmɪtə) *n* an instrument for measuring the polarization of light > **polarimetric** (ˌpəʊlərɪˈmɛtrɪk) *adj*
Polaris (pəˈlɑːrɪs) *n* **1** Also called: the **Pole Star**, the **North Star** the brightest star in the constellation Ursa Minor, situated slightly less than 1° from the north celestial pole **2** a type of US two-stage intermediate-range ballistic missile, usually fired by a submerged submarine [from Med. L *stella polāris* polar star]
polariscope (pəʊˈlærɪˌskəʊp) *n* an instrument for detecting polarized light or for observing objects under polarized light, esp for detecting strain in transparent materials
polarity (pəʊˈlærɪtɪ) *n, pl* **polarities 1** the condition of having poles **2** the condition of a body or system in which it has opposing physical properties, esp magnetic poles or electric charge **3** the particular state of a part that has polarity: *an electrode with positive polarity* **4** the state of having or expressing two directly opposite tendencies, opinions, etc
polarization *or* **polarisation** (ˌpəʊləraɪˈzeɪʃən) *n* **1** the condition of having or giving polarity **2** *physics* the phenomenon in which waves of light or other radiation are restricted to certain directions of vibration
polarize *or* **polarise** (ˈpəʊləˌraɪz) *vb* **polarizes, polarizing, polarized** *or* **polarises, polarising, polarised 1** to acquire or cause to acquire polarity or polarization **2** (*tr*) to cause (people) to adopt extreme opposing positions: *to polarize opinion* > **ˈpolarˌizer** *or* **ˈpolarˌiser** *n*
polar lights *pl n* the aurora borealis in the N hemisphere or the aurora australis in the S hemisphere
polarography (ˌpəʊləˈrɒgrəfɪ) *n* a technique for analysing and studying ions in solution by using an electrolytic cell with a very small cathode and obtaining a graph (**polarogram**) of the current against the potential to determine the concentration and nature of the ions
Polaroid (ˈpəʊləˌrɔɪd) *n trademark* **1** a type of plastic sheet that can polarize a transmitted beam of normal light because it is composed of long parallel molecules. It only transmits plane-polarized light if these molecules are parallel to the plane of polarization **2 Polaroid Land Camera** any of several types of camera yielding a finished print by means of a special developing and processing technique that occurs inside the camera and takes only a few seconds **3** (*pl*) sunglasses with lenses made from Polaroid plastic
polder (ˈpəʊldə, ˈpɒl-) *n* a stretch of land reclaimed from the sea or a lake, esp in the Netherlands [C17 from MDu. *polre*]
pole¹ (pəʊl) *n* **1** a long slender usually round piece of wood, metal, or other material **2** the piece of timber on each side of which a pair of carriage horses are hitched **3** another name for **rod** (sense 7) **4 up the pole** *Brit, Austral, & NZ inf* **4a** slightly mad **4b** mistaken; on the wrong track ▷ *vb* **poles, poling, poled 5** (*tr*) to strike or push with a pole **6** (*tr*) **6a** to set out (an area of land or garden) with poles **6b** to support (a crop, such as hops) on poles **7** to punt (a boat) [OE *pāl*, from L *pālus* a stake]
pole² (pəʊl) *n* **1** either of the two antipodal points where the earth's axis of rotation meets the earth's surface. See also **North Pole, South Pole 2** *physics* **2a** either of the two regions at the extremities of a magnet to which the lines of force converge **2b** either of two points at which there are opposite electric charges, as at the terminals of a battery **3** *biol* either end of the axis of a cell, spore, ovum, or similar body **4** either of two mutually exclusive or opposite actions, opinions, etc **5 poles apart** (*or* **asunder**) having widely divergent opinions, tastes, etc [C14 from L *polus* end of an axis, from Gk *polos* pivot]
Pole¹ (pəʊl) *n* a native, inhabitant, or citizen of Poland or a speaker of Polish
Pole² (pəʊl) *n* **Reginald** 1500–58, English cardinal; last Roman Catholic archbishop of Canterbury (1556–58)
poleaxe *or US* **poleax** (ˈpəʊlˌæks) *n* **1** another term for a battle-axe or a butcher's axe ▷ *vb* **poleaxes, poleaxing, poleaxed 2** (*tr*) to hit or fell with or as if with a poleaxe [C14 *pollax* battle-axe, from POLL + AXE]
polecat (ˈpəʊlˌkæt) *n, pl* **polecats** *or* **polecat 1** a dark brown musteline mammal of Europe, Asia, and N Africa, that is closely related to but larger than the weasel and gives off an unpleasant smell **2** *US* a nontechnical name for **skunk** (sense 1) [C14 *polcat*, ?from OF *pol* cock, from L *pullus*, + CAT; from its preying on poultry]
polemic (pəˈlɛmɪk) *adj Also* **polemical 1** of or involving dispute or controversy ▷ *n* **2** an argument or controversy, esp over a doctrine, belief, etc **3** a person engaged in such controversy [C17 from Med. L *polemicus*, from Gk *polemikos* relating to war, from *polemos* war] > **poˈlemically** *adv* > **polemicist** (pəˈlɛmɪsɪst) *n*
polemics (pəˈlɛmɪks) *n* (*functioning as sing*) the art or practice of dispute or argument, as in attacking or defending a doctrine or belief
pole position *n* **1** (in motor racing) the starting position on the inside of the front row, generally considered the best one **2** an advantageous starting position
pole star *n* a guiding principle, rule, etc
Pole Star *n* **the** the star closest to the N celestial pole at any particular time. At present this is Polaris, but it will eventually be replaced owing to precession of the earth's axis
pole vault *n* **1 the** a field event in which competitors attempt to clear a high bar with the aid of an extremely flexible long pole ▷ *vb* **pole-vault 2** (*intr*) to perform a pole vault or compete in the pole vault > **ˈpole-ˌvaulter** *n*
poley (ˈpəʊlɪ) *adj Austral* (of cattle) hornless or polled
Poliakoff (ˌpɒlɪˈɑːkɒf) *n* **Stephen** born 1952, British playwright and film director; work includes the stage plays *Breaking the Silence* (1984) and *Blinded by the Sun* (1996) and the television serial *The Lost Prince* (2003)
police (pəˈliːs) *n* **1** (often preceded by *the*) the organized civil force of a state, concerned with maintenance of law and order **2** (*functioning as pl*) the members of such a force collectively **3** any organized body with a similar function: *security police* ▷ *vb* **polices, policing, policed** (*tr*) **4** to regulate, control, or keep in order by means of a police or similar force **5** to observe or record the activity or enforcement of: *a committee was set up to police the new agreement on picketing* [C16 via F from L *polītīa* administration; see POLITY]
▷ www.police.uk
▷ www.ipa-iac.org/index2.htm
police dog *n* a dog, often an Alsatian, trained to help the police, as in tracking
policeman (pəˈliːsmən) *or* (*fem*) **policewoman** *n, pl* **policemen** *or* **policewomen** a member of a police force, esp one holding the rank of constable
police officer *n* a member of a police force, esp a constable; policeman
police procedural *n* a novel, film, or television drama that deals realistically with police work
police state *n* a state or country in which a repressive government maintains control through the police
police station *n* the office or headquarters of the police force of a district
policing (pəˈliːsɪŋ) *n* the policies, techniques, and practice of a police force in keeping order, preventing crime, etc
policy¹ (ˈpɒlɪsɪ) *n, pl* **policies 1** a plan of action adopted or pursued by an individual, government, party, business, etc **2** wisdom, shrewdness, or sagacity **3** (*often pl*) *Scot* the improved grounds surrounding a country house [C14

from OF *policie*, from L *polītīa* administration, POLITY]

policy[2] ('pɒlɪsɪ) *n, pl* **policies** a document containing a contract of insurance [c16 from OF *police* certificate, from OIt. from L *apodixis* proof, from Gk *apodeixis*]
> **'policy,holder** *n*

Polignac (*French* pɔliɲak) *n* **Prince de,** title of *Auguste Jules Armand Marie de Polignac.* 1780–1847, French statesman; prime minister (1829–30) to Charles X: his extreme royalist and ultramontane policies provoked the 1830 revolution

polio ('pəʊlɪəʊ) *n* short for **poliomyelitis**

poliomyelitis (ˌpəʊlɪəʊˌmaɪə'laɪtɪs) *n* an acute infectious viral disease, esp affecting children. In its paralytic form the brain and spinal cord are involved, causing paralysis and wasting of muscle. Also called: **infantile paralysis** [c19 NL, from Gk *polios* grey + *muelos* marrow]

polish ('pɒlɪʃ) *vb* **1** to make or become smooth and shiny by rubbing, esp with wax or an abrasive **2** (*tr*) to make perfect or complete **3** to make or become elegant or refined ▷ *n* **4** a finish or gloss **5** the act of polishing **6** a substance used to produce a shiny, often protective surface **7** elegance or refinement, esp in style, manner, etc [c13 *polis*, from OF *polir*, from L *polīre* to polish]
> **'polisher** *n*

Polish ('pəʊlɪʃ) *adj* **1** of, relating to, or characteristic of Poland, its people, or their language ▷ *n* **2** the official language of Poland

Polish Corridor *n* the strip of land through E Pomerania providing Poland with access to the sea (1919–39), given to her in 1919 in the Treaty of Versailles, and separating East Prussia from the rest of Germany. It is now part of Poland

polished ('pɒlɪʃt) *adj* **1** accomplished: *a polished actor* **2** impeccably or professionally done: *a polished performance* **3** (of rice) milled to remove the outer husk

polish off *vb* (*tr, adv*) *inf* **1** to finish or process completely **2** to dispose of or kill

polish up *vb* (*adv*) **1** to make or become smooth and shiny by polishing **2** (when *intr*, foll by *on*) to study or practise until adept (at): *he's polishing up on his German*

Politburo ('pɒlɪtˌbjʊərəʊ) *n* **1** the executive and policy-making committee of a Communist Party **2** the supreme policy-making authority in most Communist countries [c20 from Russian: contraction of *Politicheskoe Buro* political bureau]

polite (pə'laɪt) *adj* **1** showing a great regard for others, as in manners, etc; courteous **2** cultivated or refined: *polite society* **3** elegant or polished: *polite letters* [c15 from L *polītus* polished] > **po'litely** *adv* > **po'liteness** *n*

politesse (ˌpɒlɪ'tɛs) *n* formal or genteel politeness [c18 via F from It. *politezza*, ult. from L *polīre* to polish]

Politian (pəʊ'lɪʃən, pɒ-) *n* Italian name *Angelo Polliziano;* original name *Angelo Ambrogini.* 1454–94, Florentine humanist and poet

politic ('pɒlɪtɪk) *adj* **1** artful or shrewd; ingenious **2** crafty or unscrupulous; cunning **3** wise or prudent, esp in statesmanship: *a politic choice* **4** an archaic word for **political** ▷ See also **body politic** [c15 from OF *politique*, from L *polīticus* concerning civil administration, from Gk, from *politēs* citizen, from *polis* city] > **'politicly** *adv*

political (pə'lɪtɪk^{ə}l) *adj* **1** of or relating to the state, government, public administration, etc **2a** of or relating to government policy-making as distinguished from administration or law **2b** of or relating to the civil aspects of government as distinguished from the military **3** of, dealing with, or relating to politics: *a political person* **4** of or relating to the parties and the partisan aspects of politics **5** organized with respect to government: *a political unit* > **po'litically** *adv*
▷ www.lib.umich.edu/govdocs/polisci.html
▷ www.political-theory.org/
▷ www.psr.keele.ac.uk/theory.htm
▷ www.psr.keele.ac.uk/thought.htm

political economy *n* the former name for **economics** (sense 1)

politically correct *adj* demonstrating progressive ideals, esp by avoiding vocabulary that is considered offensive, discriminatory, or judgmental, esp concerning race, gender, and sexuality. Abbrev: **PC**
> **political correctness** *n*

political prisoner *n* a person imprisoned for holding or expressing particular political beliefs

political science *n* the study of the state, government, and politics: one of the social sciences > **political scientist** *n*
▷ www.bubl.ac.uk/link/p/politicalscience.htm
▷ www.sosig.ac.uk/politics
▷ www.apsanet.org/PS/
▷ www.britac.ac.uk/portal/bysection.asp?section=S5

politician (ˌpɒlɪ'tɪʃən) *n* **1** a person actively engaged in politics, esp a full-time professional member of a deliberative assembly **2** a person who is experienced or skilled in government or administration; statesman **3** *disparaging, chiefly US* a person who engages in politics out of a wish for personal gain

politicize *or* **politicise** (pə'lɪtɪˌsaɪz) *vb* **politicizes, politicizing, politicized** *or* **politicises, politicising, politicised 1** (*tr*) to render political in tone, interest, or awareness **2** (*intr*) to participate in political discussion or activity > **poˌliticiˈzation** *or* **poˌliticiˈsation** *n*

politicking ('pɒlɪtɪkɪŋ) *n* political activity, esp seeking votes

politico (pə'lɪtɪˌkəʊ) *n, pl* **politicos** *chiefly US* an informal word for a **politician** (senses 1, 3) [c17 from It. or Sp.]

politics ('pɒlɪtɪks) *n* **1** (*functioning as sing*) the art and science of directing and administrating states and other political units; government **2** (*functioning as sing*) the complex or aggregate of relationships of people in society, esp those relationships involving authority or power **3** (*functioning as pl*) political activities or affairs: *party politics* **4** (*functioning as sing*) the business or profession of politics **5** (*functioning as sing or pl*) any activity concerned with the acquisition of power, etc: *company politics are frequently vicious* **6** manoeuvres or factors leading up to or influencing (something): *the politics of the decision* **7** (*functioning as pl*) opinions, sympathies, etc, with respect to politics: *his conservative politics*

Pp

polity ('pɒlɪtɪ) *n, pl* **polities 1** a form of government or organization of a society, etc; constitution **2** a politically organized society, etc **3** the management of public affairs **4** political organization [c16 from L *polītīa*, from Gk *politeia* citizenship, civil administration, from *politēs* citizen, from *polis* city]

Polk (pəʊk) *n* **James Knox** 1795–1849, US statesman; 11th president of the US (1845–49) During his administration, Texas and territory now included in New Mexico, Colorado, Utah, Nevada, Arizona, Oregon, and California were added to the Union

polka ('pɒlkə) *n* **1** a 19th-century Bohemian dance with three steps and a hop, in fast duple time **2** a piece of music composed for or in the rhythm of this dance ▷ *vb* **polkas, polkaing, polkaed 3** (*intr*) to dance a polka [c19 via F from Czech *pulka* half-step]

polka dot *n* one of a pattern of small circular regularly spaced spots on a fabric

poll (pəʊl) *n* **1** the casting, recording, or counting of votes in an election; a voting **2** the result of such a voting: *a heavy poll* **3** Also called: **opinion poll 3a** a canvassing of a representative sample of people on some question in order to determine the general opinion **3b** the results of such a canvassing **4** any counting or enumeration, esp for taxation or voting purposes **5** the back part of the head of an animal ▷ *vb* (*mainly tr*) **6** to receive (a vote or quantity of votes): *he* *polled 10 000 votes* **7** to receive, take, or record the votes of: *he polled the whole town* **8** to canvass (a person, group, area, etc) as part of a survey of opinion **9** (*sometimes intr*) to cast (a vote) in an election **10** to clip or shear **11** to remove or cut short the horns of (cattle) [c13 (in the sense: a human head) & c17 (in the sense: votes): from MLow G *polle* hair of the head, head, top of a tree]

pollack *or* **pollock** ('pɒlək) *n, pl* **pollacks, pollack** *or* **pollocks, pollock** a gadoid food fish that has a projecting lower jaw and occurs in northern seas [c17 from earlier Scot *podlok*, from ?]

Pollaiuolo (*Italian* pollaj'wɔ:lo) *n* **1 Antonio** (an'tɔ:njo), ?1432–98, Florentine painter, sculptor, goldsmith, and engraver: his paintings include the *Martyrdom of St Sebastian* **2** his brother **Piero** ('pjɛ:ro) ?1443–96, Florentine painter and sculptor

pollan ('pɒlən) *n* any of several varieties of whitefish that occur in lakes in Northern Ireland [c18 prob. from Irish *poll* lake]

pollard ('pɒləd) *n* **1** an animal, such as a sheep or deer, that has either shed its horns or antlers or has had them removed **2** a tree that has had its branches cut back to encourage a more bushy growth ▹ *vb* **3** (*tr*) to convert into a pollard; poll [c16 hornless animal; see POLL]

pollen ('pɒlən) *n* a substance produced by the anthers of seed-bearing plants, consisting of numerous fine grains containing the male gametes [c16 from L: powder] > **pollinic** (pə'lɪnɪk) *adj*

Pollen ('pɒlən) *n* **Daniel** 1813–96, New Zealand statesman, born in Ireland: prime minister of New Zealand (1876)

pollen analysis *n* another name for **palynology**

pollen count *n* a measure of the pollen present in the air over a 24-hour period, often published to enable sufferers from hay fever to predict the severity of their attacks

pollex ('pɒlɛks) *n, pl* **pollices** (-lɪˌsi:z) the first digit of the forelimb of amphibians, reptiles, birds, and mammals, such as the thumb of man [c19 from L: thumb, big toe] > **pollical** ('pɒlɪkᵊl) *adj*

pollinate ('pɒlɪˌneɪt) *vb* **pollinates, pollinating, pollinated** (*tr*) to transfer pollen from the anthers to the stigma of (a flower) > **ˌpolli'nation** *n* > **'polliˌnator** *n*

polling booth *n* a semienclosed space in which a voter stands to mark a ballot paper during an election

polling station *n* a building, such as a school, designated as the place to which voters go during an election in order to cast their votes

polliwog *or* **pollywog** ('pɒlɪˌwɒg) *n dialect, US, & Canad* a tadpole [c15 *polwygle*]

Pollock ('pɒlək) *n* **1** Sir **Frederick** 1845–1937, English legal scholar: with Maitland, he wrote *History of English Law before the Time of Edward I* (1895) **2 Jackson** 1912–56, US abstract expressionist painter; chief exponent of action painting in the US

pollster ('pəʊlstə) *n* a person who conducts opinion polls

poll tax *n* **1** a tax levied per head of adult population **2** an informal name for the former **community charge**

pollutant (pə'lu:tᵊnt) *n* a substance that pollutes, esp a chemical produced as a waste product of an industrial process

pollute (pə'lu:t) *vb* **pollutes, polluting, polluted** (*tr*) **1** to contaminate, as with poisonous or harmful substances **2** to make morally corrupt **3** to desecrate [c14 *polute*, from L *polluere* to defile] > **pol'luter** *n*

pollution (pə'lu:ʃən) *n* **1** the act of polluting or the state of being polluted **2** harmful or poisonous substances introduced into an environment

Pollux ('pɒləks) *n classical myth* See **Castor and Pollux**

Pollyanna (ˌpɒlɪ'ænə) *n* a person who is optimistic [c20 after the chief character in *Pollyanna* (1913), a novel by Eleanor Porter (1868–1920), US writer]

polo ('pəʊləʊ) *n* **1** a game similar to hockey played on horseback using long-handled mallets (**polo sticks**) and a wooden ball **2** short for **water polo** **3** Also called: **polo neck** **3a** a collar on a garment, worn rolled over to fit closely round the neck **3b** a garment, esp a sweater, with such a collar [c19 from Balti (dialect of Kashmir): ball, from Tibetan *pulu*]
▹ www.fippolo.com

Polo ('pəʊləʊ) *n* **Marco** ('mɑ:kəʊ) 1254–1324, Venetian merchant, famous for his account of his travels in Asia. After travelling overland to China (1271–75), he spent 17 years serving Kublai Khan before returning to Venice by sea (1292–95)

Polokwane (ˌpɒlə'kwɑ:nɪ) *n* a town in NE South Africa, the capital of Limpopo province: commercial and agricultural centre. Pop: 91 407 (1996), with a metropolitan area of 153 000 (2000). Former name **Pietersburg**.

polonaise (ˌpɒlə'neɪz) *n* **1** a ceremonial marchlike dance in three-four time from Poland **2** a piece of music composed for or in the rhythm of this dance **3** a woman's costume with a tight bodice and an overskirt drawn back to show a decorative underskirt [c18 from F *danse polonaise* Polish dance]

polonium (pə'ləʊnɪəm) *n* a very rare radioactive element that occurs in trace amounts in uranium ores. Symbol: Po; atomic no.: 84; half-life of most stable isotope, ^{209}Po: 103 years [c19 NL, from Med. L *Polōnia* Poland; in honour of the nationality of its discoverer, Marie Curie]

polony (pə'ləʊnɪ) *n, pl* **polonies** *Brit* another name for **bologna sausage**

polo shirt *n* a knitted cotton short-sleeved shirt with a collar and three-button opening at the neck

Pol Pot ('pɒl 'pɒt) *n* original name *Kompong Thom*. 1925–98, Cambodian Communist statesman; prime minister of Kampuchea (1976; 1977–79); his policies led to the deaths of thousands in labour camps before he was overthrown by Vietnamese forces; in 1997 his former supporters in the Khmer Rouge captured him and claimed to have tried and sentenced him to life imprisonment

Polska ('pɔlska) *n* the Polish name for **Poland**

Poltava (*Russian* pal'tavə) *n* a city in the E Ukraine: scene of the victory (1709) of the Russians under Peter the Great over the Swedes under Charles XII; centre of an agricultural region. Pop: 317 300 (1998 est)

poltergeist ('pɒltəˌgaɪst) *n* a spirit believed to manifest its presence by noises and acts of mischief, such as throwing furniture about [c19 from G, from *poltern* to be noisy + *Geist* GHOST]

poltroon (pɒl'tru:n) *n* an abject or contemptible coward [c16 from OF *poultron*, from OIt. *poltrone* lazy good-for-nothing, apparently from *poltrīre* to lie indolently in bed]

poly ('pɒlɪ) *n, pl* **polys** **1** *inf* short for **polytechnic** **2** *inf* short for polyester

poly- *combining form* **1** more than one; many or much: *polyhedron* **2** having an excessive or abnormal number or amount: *polyphagia* [from Gk *polus* much, many]

polyamide (ˌpɒlɪ'æmaɪd, -mɪd) *n* any of a class of synthetic polymeric materials, including nylon

polyandry ('pɒlɪˌændrɪ) *n* **1** the practice or condition of being married to more than one husband at the same time **2** the practice in animals of a female mating with more than one male during one breeding season **3** the condition in flowers of having a large indefinite number of stamens [c18 from Gk *poluandria*, from POLY- + -*andria* from *anēr* man] > **ˌpoly'androus** *adj*

polyanthus (ˌpɒlɪ'ænθəs) *n, pl* **polyanthuses** any of several hybrid garden primroses with brightly coloured flowers [c18 NL, from Gk: having many flowers]

polyatomic (ˌpɒlɪə'tɒmɪk) *adj* (of a molecule)

containing more than two atoms

poly bag ('pɒlɪ) *n Brit inf* a polythene bag, esp one used to store or protect food or household articles

polybasic (ˌpɒlɪ'beɪsɪk) *adj* (of an acid) having two or more replaceable hydrogen atoms per molecule

Polybius (pəʊ'lɪbɪəs) *n* ?205–?123 BC, Greek historian. Under the patronage of Scipio the Younger, he wrote in 40 books a history of Rome from 264 BC to 146 BC

polycarboxylate (ˌpɒlɪkɑː'bɒksɪˌleɪt) *n* a salt or ester of a polycarboxylic acid. Polycarboxylate esters are used in certain detergents

polycarboxylic acid (ˌpɒlɪˌkɑːbɒk'sɪlɪk) *n* a type of carboxylic acid containing two or more carboxyl groups

Polycarp ('pɒlɪˌkɑːp) *n* **Saint** ?69–?155 AD, Christian martyr and bishop of Smyrna, noted for his letter to the church at Philippi. Feast day: Feb 23

polycarpic (ˌpɒlɪ'kɑːpɪk) *or* **polycarpous** *adj* (of a plant) able to produce flowers and fruit several times in successive years or seasons > **'polyˌcarpy** *n*

polycentrism (ˌpɒlɪ'sɛntrɪzəm) *n* (formerly) the fact or advocacy of the existence of more than one predominant ideological or political centre in a political system, alliance, etc, in the Communist world

polychaete ('pɒlɪˌkiːt) *n* **1** a marine annelid worm having a distinct head and paired fleshy appendages (parapodia) that bear bristles and are used in swimming ▷ *adj* **2** Also: **polychaetous** of or denoting such a creature [c19 from NL, from Gk *polukhaitēs* having much hair]

polychromatic (ˌpɒlɪkrəʊ'mætɪk), **polychromic** (ˌpɒlɪ'krəʊmɪk), *or* **polychromous** *adj* **1** having various or changing colours **2** (of light or other radiation) containing radiation with more than one wavelength > **polychromatism** (ˌpɒlɪ'krəʊməˌtɪzəm) *n*

polyclinic (ˌpɒlɪ'klɪnɪk) *n* a hospital or clinic able to treat a wide variety of diseases

Polyclitus, **Polycleitus** (ˌpɒlɪ'klaɪtəs), *or* **Polycletus** (ˌpɒlɪ'kliːtəs) *n* 5th-century BC Greek sculptor, noted particularly for his idealized bronze sculptures of the male nude, such as the *Doryphoros*

polycotton ('pɒlɪkɒtᵊn) *n* a fabric made from a mixture of polyester and cotton

polycotyledon (ˌpɒlɪˌkɒtɪ'liːdᵊn) *n* any of various plants, esp gymnosperms, that have or appear to have more than two cotyledons > **ˌpolyˌcoty'ledonous** *adj*

Polycrates (pə'lɪkrəˌtiːz) *n* died ?522 BC, Greek tyrant of Samos, who was crucified by a Persian satrap

polycyclic (ˌpɒlɪ'saɪklɪk) *adj* **1** (of a molecule or compound) having molecules that contain two or more closed rings of atoms **2** *biol* having two or more rings or whorls: *polycyclic shells* ▷ *n* **3** a polycyclic compound

polycystic (ˌpɒlɪ'sɪstɪk) *adj med* containing many cysts: *a polycystic ovary*

polycystic ovary syndrome *n* a hormonal disorder in which the Graafian follicles in the ovary fail to develop completely so that they are unable to ovulate, remaining as multiple cysts that distend the ovary. The result is infertility, obesity, and hirsutism. Abbreviation: **POS**

polydactyl (ˌpɒlɪ'dæktɪl) *adj* **1** Also: **polydactylous** (of man and other vertebrates) having more than the normal number of digits ▷ *n* **2** a human or other vertebrate having more than the normal number of digits

Polydeuces (ˌpɒlɪ'djuːsiːz) *n* the Greek name of **Pollux** See **Castor and Pollux**

polyester (ˌpɒlɪ'ɛstə) *n* any of a large class of synthetic materials that are polymers containing recurring -COO- groups: used as plastics, textile fibres, and adhesives

polyethene (ˌpɒlɪ'ɛθiːn) *n* the systematic name for **polythene**

polyethylene (ˌpɒlɪ'ɛθɪˌliːn) *n* another name for **polythene**

polygamy (pə'lɪgəmɪ) *n* **1** the practice of having more than one wife or husband at the same time **2** the condition of having male, female, and hermaphrodite flowers on the same plant or on separate plants of the same species **3** the practice in male animals of having more than one mate during one breeding season [c16 via F from Gk *polugamia*] > **po'lygamist** *n* > **po'lygamous** *adj* > **po'lygamously** *adv*

polygene ('pɒlɪˌdʒiːn) *n* any of a group of genes that each produce a small quantitative effect on a particular characteristic, such as height

polygenesis (ˌpɒlɪ'dʒɛnɪsɪs) *n* **1** *biol* evolution of organisms from different ancestral groups **2** the hypothetical descent of different races from different ultimate ancestors > **polygenetic** (ˌpɒlɪdʒɪ'nɛtɪk) *adj*

polygenic (ˌpɒli'dʒɛnik) *adj* of, relating to, or controlled by polygenes: *polygenic inheritance*

polyglot ('pɒlɪˌglɒt) *adj* **1** having a command of many languages **2** written in or containing many languages ▷ *n* **3** a person with a command of many languages **4** a book, esp a Bible, containing several versions of the same text written in various languages **5** a mixture of languages [c17 from Gk *poluglōttos*, lit.: many-tongued]

Polygnotus (ˌpɒlɪg'nəʊtəs) *n* 5th century BC, Greek painter: associated with Cimon in rebuilding Athens

polygon ('pɒlɪˌgɒn) *n* a closed plane figure bounded by three or more straight sides that meet in pairs in the same number of vertices and do not intersect other than at these vertices. Specific polygons are named according to the number of sides, such as triangle, pentagon, etc [c16 via L from Gk *polugōnon* figure with many angles] > **polygonal** (pə'lɪgənᵊl) *adj* > **po'lygonally** *adv*

polygonum (pə'lɪgənəm) *n* a plant having stems with knotlike joints and spikes of small white, green, or pink flowers [c18 NL, from Gk *polugonon* knotgrass, from *polu-* POLY- + *-gonon*, from *gonu* knee]

polygraph ('pɒlɪˌgrɑːf) *n* **1** an instrument for the simultaneous recording of several involuntary physiological activities, including pulse rate and sweating, used esp as a would-be lie detector **2** a device for producing copies of written matter [c18 from Gk *polugraphos* writing copiously]

polygyny (pə'lɪdʒɪnɪ) *n* **1** the practice or condition of being married to more than one wife at the same time **2** the practice in animals of a male mating with more than one female during one breeding season **3** the condition in flowers of having many carpels [c18 from POLY- + *-gyny*, from Gk *gunē* a woman] > **po'lygynous** *adj*

polyhedron (ˌpɒlɪ'hiːdrən) *n, pl* **polyhedrons** *or* **polyhedra** (-drə) a solid figure consisting of four or more plane faces (all polygons), pairs of which meet along an edge, three or more edges meeting at a vertex. Specific polyhedrons are named according to the number of faces, such as tetrahedron, icosahedron, etc [c16 from Gk *poluedron*, from POLY- + *hedron* side] > **ˌpoly'hedral** *adj*

Polyhymnia (ˌpɒlɪ'hɪmnɪə) *n Greek myth* the Muse of singing, mime, and sacred dance [L, from Gk *Polumnia* full of songs]

polymath ('pɒlɪˌmæθ) *n* a person of great and varied learning [c17 from Gk *polumathēs* having much knowledge] > **polymathy** (pə'lɪməθɪ) *n*

polymer ('pɒlɪmə) *n* a naturally occurring or synthetic compound, such as starch or Perspex, that has large molecules made up of many relatively simple repeated units > **polymerism** (pə'lɪməˌrɪzəm, 'pɒlɪmə-) *n*

polymerase ('pɒlɪməˌreɪs, -ˌreɪz) *n* any enzyme that catalyses the synthesis of a polymer, esp the synthesis of DNA or RNA

polymeric (ˌpɒlɪ'mɛrɪk) *adj* of, concerned with, or being a polymer: *a polymeric compound* [c19 from Gk *polumerēs* having many parts]

polymerization *or* **polymerisation** (pəˌlɪməraɪ'zeɪʃən, ˌpɒlɪməraɪ-) *n* the act or process of forming a polymer or

Pp

copolymer, esp a chemical reaction in which a polymer is formed

polymerize *or* **polymerise** ('pɒlɪmə,raɪz, pə'lɪmə-) *vb* **polymerizes, polymerizing, polymerized** *or* **polymerises, polymerising, polymerised** to react or cause to react to form a polymer

polymerous (pə'lɪmərəs) *adj biol* having or being composed of many parts

polymorph ('pɒlɪ,mɔːf) *n* a species of animal or plant, or a crystalline form of a chemical compound, that exhibits polymorphism [c19 from Gk *polumorphos* having many forms]

polymorphic function *n computing* a function in a computer program that can deal with a number of different types of data

polymorphism (,pɒlɪ'mɔːfɪzəm) *n* **1** the occurrence of more than one form of individual in a single species within an interbreeding population **2** the existence or formation of different types of crystal of the same chemical compound

polymorphous (,pɒlɪ'mɔːfəs) *or* **polymorphic** *adj* **1** having, taking, or passing through many different forms or stages **2** exhibiting or undergoing polymorphism

Polynesia (,pɒlɪ'niːʒə, -ʒɪə) *n* one of the three divisions of islands in the Pacific, the others being Melanesia and Micronesia: includes Samoa, Society, Marquesas, Mangareva, Tuamotu, Cook, and Tubuai Islands, and Tonga [c18 via French from POLY- + Greek *nēsos* island]

Polynesian (,pɒlɪ'niːʒən, -ʒɪən) *adj* **1** of or relating to Polynesia, its people, or any of their languages ▷ *n* **2** a member of the people that inhabit Polynesia, generally of Caucasoid features with light skin and wavy hair **3** a branch of the Malayo-Polynesian family of languages, including Maori and Hawaiian

polyneuritis (,pɒlɪnjʊ'raɪtɪs) *n* inflammation of many nerves at the same time

Polynices (,pɒlɪ'naɪsiːz) *n Greek myth* a son of Oedipus and Jocasta, for whom the Seven Against Thebes sought to regain Thebes. He and his brother Eteocles killed each other in single combat before its walls

polynomial (,pɒlɪ'nəʊmɪəl) *adj* **1** of, consisting of, or referring to two or more names or terms ▷ *n* **2a** a mathematical expression consisting of a sum of terms each of which is the product of a constant and one or more variables raised to a positive or zero integral power **2b** Also called: **multinomial** any mathematical expression consisting of the sum of a number of terms **3** *biol* a taxonomic name consisting of more than two terms, such as *Parus major minor* in which *minor* designates the subspecies

polynucleotide (,pɒlɪ'njuːklɪə,taɪd) *n biochem* a molecular chain of nucleotides chemically bonded by a series of ester linkages between the phosphoryl group of one nucleotide and the hydroxyl group of the sugar in the adjacent nucleotide

polynya ('pɒlən,jɑː) *n* a stretch of open water surrounded by ice, esp near the mouths of large rivers, in arctic seas [c19 from Russian, from *poly* open]

polyp ('pɒlɪp) *n* **1** *zool* one of the two forms of individual that occur in coelenterates. It usually has a hollow cylindrical body with a ring of tentacles around the mouth **2** Also called: **polypus** *pathol* a small growth arising from the surface of a mucous membrane [c16 *polip*, from F *polype* nasal polyp, from L *pōlypus*, from Gk *polupous* having many feet] > **'polypous** *or* **'polypoid** *adj*

polypeptide (,pɒlɪ'pɛptaɪd) *n* any of a group of natural or synthetic polymers made up of amino acids chemically linked together; includes the proteins

polypetalous (,pɒlɪ'pɛtələs) *adj* (of flowers) having distinct or separate petals

polyphagia (,pɒlɪ'feɪdʒə) *n* **1** an abnormal desire to consume excessive amounts of food **2** the habit of certain animals, esp certain insects, of feeding on many different types of food [c17 NL, from Gk, from *poluphagos* eating much] > **polyphagous** (pə'lɪfəgəs) *adj*

polyphase ('pɒlɪ,feɪz) *adj* **1** (of an electrical system, circuit, or device) having or using alternating voltages of the same frequency, the phases of which are cyclically displaced by fractions of a period **2** having more than one phase

Polyphemus (,pɒlɪ'fiːməs) *n Greek myth* a cyclops who imprisoned Odysseus and his companions in his cave. To effect his escape, Odysseus blinded him

polyphone ('pɒlɪ,fəʊn) *n* a letter or character having more than one phonetic value, such as *c* in English

polyphonic (,pɒlɪ'fɒnɪk) *adj* **1** *music* composed of relatively independent parts; contrapuntal **2** many-voiced **3** *phonetics* denoting a polyphone > **,poly'phonically** *adv*

polyphony (pə'lɪfənɪ) *n, pl* **polyphonies 1** polyphonic style of composition or a piece of music utilizing it **2** the use of polyphones in a writing system [c19 from Gk *poluphōnia* diversity of tones] > **po'lyphonous** *adj*

polypill ('pɒlɪ,pɪl) *n* a pill that is designed to combat more than one medical condition

polyploid ('pɒlɪ,plɔɪd) *adj* (of cells, organisms, etc) having more than twice the basic (haploid) number of chromosomes > **,poly'ploidal** *adj* > **'poly,ploidy** *n*

polypod ('pɒlɪ,pɒd) *adj* **1** (esp of insect larvae) having many legs or similar appendages ▷ *n* **2** an animal of this type

polypody ('pɒlɪ,pəʊdɪ) *n, pl* **polypodies** any of various ferns having deeply divided leaves and round naked sporangia [c15 from L *polypodium*, from Gk, from POLY- + *pous* foot]

polypropylene (,pɒlɪ'prəʊpɪ,liːn) *n* any of various tough flexible synthetic thermoplastic materials made by polymerizing propylene. Systematic name: **polypropene** (,pɒlɪ'prəʊpiːn)

polypus ('pɒlɪpəs) *n, pl* **polypi** (-paɪ) *pathol* another word for **polyp** (sense 2) [c16 via L from Gk: POLYP]

polysaccharide (,pɒlɪ'sækə,raɪd, -rɪd) *or* **polysaccharose** (,pɒlɪ'sækə,rəʊz, -,rəʊs) *n* any one of a class of carbohydrates whose molecules contain linked monosaccharide units: includes starch, inulin, and cellulose

polysemy (,pɒlɪ'siːmɪ, pə'lɪsəmɪ) *n* the existence of several meanings in a single word [c20 from NL *polysēmia*, from Gk *polusēmos* having many meanings] > **,poly'semous** *adj*

polysomic (,pɒlɪ'səʊmɪk) *adj* of, relating to, or designating a basically diploid chromosome complement, in which some but not all the chromosomes are represented more than twice

polystyrene (,pɒlɪ'staɪriːn) *n* a synthetic thermoplastic material obtained by polymerizing styrene; used as a white rigid foam (**expanded polystyrene**) for insulating and packing and as a glasslike material in light fittings

polysyllable ('pɒlɪ,sɪləbᵊl) *n* a word consisting of more than two syllables > **polysyllabic** (,pɒlɪsɪ'læbɪk) *adj* > **,polysyl'labically** *adv*

polysyndeton (,pɒlɪ'sɪndɪtən) *n rhetoric* the use of several conjunctions in close succession, esp where some might be omitted, as in *he ran and jumped and laughed for joy* [c16 POLY- + *-syndeton*, from Gk *sundetos* bound together]

polytechnic (,pɒlɪ'tɛknɪk) *n* **1** *Brit* (formerly) a college offering advanced courses in many fields at and below degree standard ▷ *adj* **2** of or relating to technical instruction and training [c19 via F from Gk *polutekhnos* skilled in many arts]

polytetrafluoroethylene (,pɒlɪ,tɛtrə,flʊərəʊ'ɛθɪ,liːn) *n* a white thermoplastic material with a waxy texture, made by polymerizing tetrafluoroethylene. It is used for making gaskets, hoses, insulators, bearings, and for coating metal surfaces. Abbrev: **PTFE** Also called (trademark): **Teflon**

polytheism (ˈpɒlɪθiːˌɪzəm, ˌpɒlɪˈθiːɪzəm) *n* the worship of or belief in more than one god > ˌ**polytheˈistic** *adj* > ˌ**polytheˈistically** *adv*

polythene (ˈpɒlɪˌθiːn) *n* any one of various light thermoplastic materials made from ethylene with properties depending on the molecular weight of the polymer. Systematic name: **polyethene** Also called: **polyethylene**

polytonality (ˌpɒlɪtəʊˈnælɪtɪ) *or* **polytonalism** (ˌpɒlɪˈtəʊnəˌlɪzəm) *n music* the simultaneous use of more than two different keys or tonalities > ˌ**polyˈtonal** *adj* > ˌ**polyˈtonally** *adv*

polytunnel (ˈpɒlɪˌtʌnəl) *n* a large tunnel made of polythene and used as a greenhouse

polyunsaturated (ˌpɒlɪʌnˈsætʃəˌreɪtɪd) *adj* of or relating to a class of animal and vegetable fats, the molecules of which consist of long carbon chains with many double bonds. Polyunsaturated compounds are less likely to be converted into cholesterol in the body. See also **monounsaturated**

polyurethane (ˌpɒlɪˈjʊərəˌθeɪn) *n* a class of synthetic materials commonly used as a foam for insulation and packing

polyvalent (ˌpɒlɪˈveɪlənt, pəˈlɪvələnt) *adj* **1** *chem* having more than one valency **2** (of a vaccine) effective against several strains of the same disease-producing microorganism, antigen, or toxin > ˌ**polyˈvalency** *n*

polyvinyl (ˌpɒlɪˈvaɪnɪl, -ˈvaɪnəl) *n* (*modifier*) designating a plastic or resin formed by polymerization of a vinyl derivative

polyvinyl acetate *n* a colourless odourless tasteless resin used in emulsion paints, adhesives, sealers, a substitute for chicle in chewing gum, and for sealing porous surfaces

polyvinyl chloride *n* the full name of **PVC**

polyvinyl resin *n* any of a class of thermoplastic resins made by polymerizing a vinyl compound. The commonest type is PVC

Polyxena (pɒˈlɪksɪnə) *n Greek myth* a daughter of King Priam of Troy, who was sacrificed on the command of Achilles' ghost

polyzoan (ˌpɒlɪˈzəʊən) *n, adj* another word for **bryozoan** [C19 from NL, *Polyzoa* class name, from POLY- + *-zoan*, from Gk *zoion* an animal]

pom (pɒm) *n Austral & NZ sl* short for **pommy**

POM *abbrev for* prescription only medicine (*or* medication) ▷ Cf **OTC**

pomace (ˈpʌmɪs) *n* **1** the pulpy residue of apples or similar fruit after crushing and pressing, as in cider-making **2** any pulpy substance left after crushing, mashing, etc [C16 from Med. L *pōmācium* cider, from L *pōmum* apple]

pomaceous (pɒˈmeɪʃəs) *adj* of, relating to, or bearing pomes, such as the apple and quince trees [C18 from NL *pōmāceus*, from L *pōmum* apple]

pomade (pəˈmɑːd) *n* **1** a perfumed oil or ointment put on the hair, as to make it smooth and shiny ▷ *vb* **pomades, pomading, pomaded 2** (*tr*) to put pomade on ▷ Also: **pomatum** [C16 from F *pommade*, from It. *pomato* (orig. made partly from apples), from L *pōmum* apple]

pomander (pəʊˈmændə) *n* **1** a mixture of aromatic substances in a sachet or an orange, formerly carried as scent or as a protection against disease **2** a container for such a mixture [C15 from OF *pome d'ambre*, from Med. L *pōmum ambrae* apple of amber]

Pombal (*Portuguese* pomˈbal) *n* **Marquês de** (mərkeʃ ˈdəː) title of *Sebastião José de Carvalho e Mello*. 1699–1782, Portuguese statesman, who dominated Portuguese government from 1750 to 1777 and instituted many administrative and economic reforms

pome (pəʊm) *n* the fleshy fruit of the apple and related plants, consisting of an enlarged receptacle enclosing the ovary and seeds [C15 from OF, from LL *pōma*, pl. of L *pōmum* apple]

pomegranate (ˈpɒmɪˌɡrænɪt, ˈpɒmˌɡrænɪt) *n* **1** an Asian shrub or small tree cultivated in semitropical regions for its edible fruit **2** the many-chambered globular fruit of this tree, which has tough reddish rind, juicy red pulp, and many seeds [C14 from OF *pome grenate*, from L *pōmum* apple + *grenate*, from *grānātus* full of seeds]

pomelo (ˈpɒmɪˌləʊ) *n, pl* **pomelos 1** Also called: **shaddock** the edible yellow fruit, resembling a grapefruit, of a tropical tree widely grown in oriental regions **2** *US* another name for **grapefruit** [C19 from Du. *pompelmoes*]

Pomerania (ˌpɒməˈreɪnɪə) *n* a region of N central Europe, extending along the S coast of the Baltic Sea from Stralsund to the Vistula River: now chiefly in Poland, with a small area in NE Germany. German name: **Pommern** Polish name: **Pomorze**

Pomeranian (ˌpɒməˈreɪnɪən) *adj* **1** of or relating to Pomerania ▷ *n* **2** a breed of toy dog of the spitz type with a long thick straight coat

pomfret (ˈpʌmfrɪt, ˈpɒm-) *or* **pomfret-cake** *n* a small black rounded confection of liquorice. Also called: **Pontefract cake** [C19 from *Pomfret*, earlier form of PONTEFRACT, where orig. made]

pomiculture (ˈpɒmɪˌkʌltʃə) *n* the cultivation of fruit [C19 from L *pōmum* fruit + CULTURE]

pommel (ˈpʌməl, ˈpɒm-) *n* **1** the raised part on the front of a saddle **2** a knob at the top of a sword or similar weapon ▷ *vb* **pommels, pommelling, pommelled** *or US* **pommels, pommeling, pommeled 3** a less common word for **pummel** [C14 from OF *pomel* knob, from Vulgar L *pōmellum* (unattested) little apple, from L *pōmum* apple]

Pommern (ˈpɔmərn) *n* the German name for **Pomerania**

pommy (ˈpɒmɪ) *n, pl* **pommies** (*sometimes cap*) *sl* a mildly offensive word used by Australians and New Zealanders for a British person. Sometimes shortened to **pom** [C20 from ?, ? a blend of IMMIGRANT & POMEGRANATE (alluding to the red cheeks of British immigrants)]

pomology (pɒˈmɒlədʒɪ) *n* the branch of horticulture concerned with the study and cultivation of fruit [C19 from NL *pōmologia*, from L *pōmum* fruit] > **pomological** (ˌpɒməˈlɒdʒɪkəl) *adj*

Pomona[1] (pəˈməʊnə) *n* another name for **Mainland** (in Orkney)

Pomona[2] (pəˈməʊnə) *n* the Roman goddess of fruit trees

Pomorze (pɔˈmɔʒɛ) *n* the Polish name for **Pomerania**

pomp (pɒmp) *n* **1** stately or magnificent display; ceremonial splendour **2** vain display, esp of dignity or importance **3** *obs* a procession or pageant [C14 from OF *pompe*, from L *pompa* procession, from Gk *pompē*]

pompadour (ˈpɒmpəˌdʊə) *n* an early 18th-century hairstyle for women, having the front hair arranged over a pad to give it greater height and bulk [C18 after the Marquise de POMPADOUR, who originated it]

Pompadour (*French* pɔ̃padur) *n* **Marquise de,** title of *Jeanne Antoinette Poisson*. 1721–64, mistress of Louis XV of France (1745–64), whom she greatly influenced

pompano (ˈpɒmpəˌnəʊ) *n, pl* **pompano** *or* **pompanos 1** any of several food fishes of American coastal regions of the Atlantic **2** a spiny-finned food fish of North American coastal regions of the Pacific [C19 from Sp. *pámpano*, from ?]

Pompeii (pɒmˈpeɪiː) *n* an ancient city in Italy, southeast of Naples: buried by an eruption of Vesuvius (79 AD); excavation of the site, which is extremely well preserved, began in 1748 > **Pompeiian** (pɒmˈpeɪən, -ˈpiː-) *adj, n*

Pompey[1] (ˈpɒmpɪ) *n* an informal name for **Portsmouth**

Pompey[2] (ˈpɒmpɪ) *n* called *Pompey the Great*; Latin name

Pp

Gnaeus Pompeius Magnus. 106–48 BC, Roman general and statesman; a member with Caesar and Crassus of the first triumvirate (60). He later quarrelled with Caesar, who defeated him at Pharsalus (48). He fled to Egypt and was murdered

Pompidou (*French* pɔ̃pidu) *n* **Georges** (ʒɔrʒ) 1911–74, French statesman; president of France (1969–74)

pompom (ˈpɒmpɒm) *or* **pompon** *n* **1** a ball of tufted silk, wool, feathers, etc, worn on a hat for decoration **2a** the small globelike flower head of certain varieties of dahlia and chrysanthemum **2b** (*as modifier*): *pompom dahlia* [c18 from F, from OF *pompe* knot of ribbons, from ?]

pom-pom (ˈpɒmpɒm) *n* an automatic rapid-firing small-calibre cannon, esp a type of anti-aircraft cannon used in World War II. Also called: **pompom** [c19 imit.]

pomposo (pɒmˈpəʊsəʊ) *adv music* in a pompous manner [It.]

pompous (ˈpɒmpəs) *adj* **1** exaggeratedly or ostentatiously dignified or self-important **2** ostentatiously lofty in style: *a pompous speech* **3** *rare* characterized by ceremonial pomp or splendour > **pomposity** (pɒmˈpɒsɪtɪ) *or* ˈ**pompousness** *n* > ˈ**pompously** *adv*

'pon (pɒn) *poetic or arch contraction of* upon

ponce (pɒns) *derog sl, chiefly Brit* ▷ *n* **1** a man given to ostentatious or effeminate display **2** another word for **pimp[1]** ▷ *vb* **ponces, poncing, ponced 3** (*intr*; often foll by *around* or *about*) to act like a ponce [c19 from Polari, from Sp. *pu(n)to* male prostitute or F *pront* prostitute] > ˈ**poncy** *or* ˈ**poncey** *adj*

Ponce (*Spanish* ˈponθe) *n* a port in S Puerto Rico, on the Caribbean: the second largest town on the island; settled in the 16th century. Pop: 155 038 (2000)

Ponce de León (ˈpɒns də ˈliːən; *Spanish* ˈponθe ðe leˈɔn) *n* **Juan** (xwan) ?1460–1521, Spanish explorer. He settled (1509) and governed (1510–12) Puerto Rico and discovered (1513) Florida

poncho (ˈpɒntʃəʊ) *n, pl* **ponchos** a cloak of a kind originally worn in South America, made of a rectangular or circular piece of cloth with a hole in the middle for the head [c18 from American Sp., of Amerind origin, from *pantho* woollen material]

pond (pɒnd) *n* a pool of still water, often artificially created [c13 *ponde* enclosure]

ponder (ˈpɒndə) *vb* (when *intr*, sometimes foll by *on* or *over*) to give thorough or deep consideration (to); meditate (upon) [c14 from OF *ponderer*, from L *ponderāre* to weigh, consider, from *pondus* weight] > ˈ**ponderable** *adj*

ponderous (ˈpɒndərəs) *adj* **1** heavy; huge **2** (esp of movement) lacking ease or lightness; lumbering or graceless **3** dull or laborious: *a ponderous oration* [c14 from L *ponderōsus* of great weight, from *pondus* weight] > ˈ**ponderously** *adv* > ˈ**ponderousness** *or* **ponderosity** (ˌpɒndəˈrɒsɪtɪ) *n*

pond hockey *n Canad* ice hockey played on a frozen pond

Pondicherry (ˌpɒndɪˈtʃɛrɪ) *n* **1** a Union Territory of SE India: transferred from French to Indian administration in 1954 and made a Union Territory in 1962. Capital: Pondicherry. Pop: 973 829 (2001 est). Area: 479 sq km (185 sq miles) **2** a port in SE India, capital of the Union Territory of Pondicherry, on the Coromandel Coast. Pop: 203 065 (1991)

pond lily *n* another name for **water lily**

pondok (ˈpɒndɒk) *or* **pondokkie** *n* (in southern Africa) a crudely made house built of tin sheet, reeds, etc [c20 from Malay *pondók* leaf house]

Pondoland (ˈpɒndəʊˌlænd) *n* an area in SE central South Africa: inhabited chiefly by the Pondo people

pond scum *n* a greenish layer floating on the surface of stagnant waters, consisting of algae

pondweed (ˈpɒndˌwiːd) *n* **1** any of various water plants of the genus *Potamogeton*, which grow in ponds and slow streams **2** Also called: **waterweed** *Brit* any of various water plants, such as mare's-tail, that have thin or much-divided leaves

pone[1] (pəʊn, ˈpəʊnɪ) *n cards* the player to the right of the dealer, or the nondealer in two-handed games [c19 from L: put!, that is, play, from *ponere* to put]

pone[2] (pəʊn) *n Southern US* bread made of maize. Also called: **pone bread, corn pone** [c17 of Amerind origin]

pong (pɒŋ) *Brit inf* ▷ *n* **1** a disagreeable or offensive smell; stink ▷ *vb* **2** (*intr*) to stink [c20 ?from Romany *pan* to stink] > ˈ**pongy** *adj*

ponga (ˈpɒŋə) *n* a tall New Zealand tree fern with large feathery leaves. Also called: **silver fern**

pongee (pɒnˈdʒiː, ˈpɒndʒiː) *n* **1** a thin plain-weave silk fabric from China or India, left in its natural colour **2** a cotton or rayon fabric similar to this [c18 from Mandarin Chinese (Peking) *pen-chī* woven at home, from *pen* own + *chi* loom]

pongid (ˈpɒŋɡɪd, ˈpɒndʒɪd) *n* **1** any primate of the family Pongidae, which includes the gibbons and the great apes ▷ *adj* **2** of this family [from NL *Pongo* type genus, from Congolese *mpongo* ape]

pongo (ˈpɒŋɡəʊ) *n, pl* **pongos** an anthropoid ape, esp an orang-utan or (formerly) a gorilla [c17 from Congolese *mpongo*]

poniard (ˈpɒnjəd) *n* **1** a small dagger with a slender blade ▷ *vb* **2** (*tr*) to stab with a poniard [c16 from OF *poignard*, from *poing* fist, from L *pugnus*]

pons Varolii (pɒnz vəˈrəʊlɪˌaɪ) *n, pl* **pontes Varolii** (ˈpɒntiːz) a broad white band of connecting nerve fibres that bridges the hemispheres of the cerebellum in mammals. Sometimes shortened to **pons** [c16 NL, lit.: bridge of Varoli, after Costanzo *Varoli* (?1543–75), It. anatomist]

Ponta Delgada (*Portuguese* ˈpontə ðɛlˈɡaðə) *n* a port in the E Azores, on S São Miguel Island: chief commercial centre of the archipelago. Pop: 22 200 (latest est)

Pontchartrain (ˈpɒntʃəˌtreɪn) *n* **Lake** a shallow lagoon in SE Louisiana, linked with the Gulf of Mexico by a narrow channel, the **Rigolets**: resort and fishing centre. Area: 1620 sq km (625 sq miles)

Pontefract (ˈpɒntɪˌfrækt) *n* an industrial town in N England, in Wakefield unitary authority, West Yorkshire: castle (1069), in which Richard II was imprisoned and murdered (1400). Pop: 28 358 (1991)

Pontevedra (*Spanish* ponteˈβeðra) *n* a port in NW Spain: takes its name from a 12-arched Roman bridge, the Pons Vetus. Pop: 74 850 (1991)

Pontiac (ˈpɒntɪˌæk) *n* died 1769, chief of the Ottawa Indians, who led a rebellion against the British (1763–66)

Pontianak (ˌpɒntɪˈɑːnæk) *n* a port in Indonesia, on W coast of Borneo almost exactly on the equator. Pop: 409 632 (1995 est)

Pontic (ˈpɒntɪk) *adj* denoting or relating to the Black Sea [c15 from L *Ponticus*, from Gk, from *Pontos* PONTUS]

pontifex (ˈpɒntɪˌfɛks) *n, pl* **pontifices** (pɒnˈtɪfɪˌsiːz) (in ancient Rome) any of the senior members of the Pontifical College, presided over by the **Pontifex Maximus** [c16 from L, ?from Etruscan but infl. by folk etymology as if meaning lit.: bridge-maker]

pontiff (ˈpɒntɪf) *n* a former title of the pagan high priest at Rome, later used of popes and occasionally of other bishops, and now confined to the pope [c17 from F *pontife*, from L PONTIFEX]

pontifical (pɒnˈtɪfɪkᵊl) *adj* **1** of, relating to, or characteristic of a pontiff **2** having an excessively authoritative manner; pompous ▷ *n* **3** *RC Church, Church of England* a book containing the prayers and ritual instructions for ceremonies restricted to a bishop > **ponˈtifically** *adv*

pontificals (pɒnˈtɪfɪkᵊlz) *pl n chiefly RC Church* the insignia and special vestments worn by a bishop, esp when celebrating High Mass

pontificate *vb* (pɒnˈtɪfɪˌkeɪt), **pontificates, pontificating, pontificated** (*intr*) **1** to speak or behave in a pompous or dogmatic manner **2** to serve or officiate at a Pontifical Mass ▷ *n* (pɒnˈtɪfɪkɪt) **3** the office or term of office of a pope

Pontine Marshes (ˈpɒntaɪn) *pl n* an area of W Italy, southeast of Rome: formerly malarial swamps, drained in 1932–34 after numerous attempts since 160 BC had failed. Italian name: **Agro Pontino** (ˈɑːgro ponˈtiːno)

Pontius Pilate (ˈpɒnʃəs, ˈpɒntɪəs ˈpaɪlət) *n* See **Pilate**

pontoon¹ (pɒnˈtuːn) *n* **a** a watertight float or vessel used where buoyancy is required in water, as in supporting a bridge, in salvage work, or where a temporary or mobile structure is required in military operations **b** (*as modifier*): *a pontoon bridge* [C17 from F *ponton*, from L *pontō* punt, from *pōns* bridge]

pontoon² (pɒnˈtuːn) *n* a gambling game in which players try to obtain card combinations worth 21 points. Also called: **twenty-one** (esp US), **vingt-et-un** [C20 prob. an alteration of F *vingt-et-un*, lit.: twenty-one]

Pontoppidan (*Danish* pontˈtopidan) *n* **Henrik** 1857–1943, Danish novelist and short-story writer, author of the novel sequences *The Promised Land* (1891–95), *Lykke-Per* (1898–1904), and *The Empire of Death* (1912–16). Nobel prize for literature 1917

Pontormo (*Italian* ponˈtormo) *n* **Jacopo da** (ˈjaːkopo da) original name *Jacopo Carrucci*. 1494–1556, Italian mannerist painter

Pontus (ˈpɒntəs) *n* an ancient region of NE Asia Minor, on the Black Sea: became a kingdom in the 4th century BC; at its height under Mithridates VI (about 115–63 BC), when it controlled all Asia Minor; defeated by the Romans in the mid-1st century BC

Pontus Euxinus (juːkˈsaɪnəs) *n* the Latin name of the **Black Sea**

Pontypool (ˌpɒntɪˈpuːl) *n* an industrial town in E Wales, in Torfaen county borough: famous for lacquered ironware in the 18th century. Pop: 35 564 (1991)

Pontypridd (ˌpɒntɪˈpriːð) *n* an industrial town in S Wales, in Rhondda Cynon Taff county borough. Pop: 28 487 (1991)

pony (ˈpəʊnɪ) *n, pl* **ponies 1** any of various breeds of small horse, usually under 14.2 hands **2** a small drinking glass, esp for liqueurs **3** anything small of its kind **4** *Brit sl* a sum of £25, esp in bookmaking **5** Also called: **trot** *US sl* a translation used by students, often illicitly; crib [C17 from Scot *powney*, ?from obs. F *poulenet* a little colt, from L *pullus* young animal, foal]

ponytail (ˈpəʊnɪˌteɪl) *n* a hairstyle in which the hair is gathered together tightly by a band into a bunch at the back of the head

pony trekking *n* the act of riding ponies cross-country, esp as a pastime

poo (puː) *vb* another spelling of: **pooh**

pooch (puːtʃ) *n chiefly US & Canad* a slang word for **dog** [from ?]

poodle (ˈpuːdᵊl) *n* **1** a breed of dog with curly hair, which is often clipped from ribs to tail **2** a servile person; lackey [C19 from G *Pudel*, short for *Pudelhund*, from *pudeln* to splash + *Hund* dog; formerly trained as water dogs]

poof (pʊf, puːf), **poove** (puːv), *or* **poofter** (ˈpuːftə) *n Brit & Austral derog sl* a male homosexual [C20 from F *pouffe* puff] > ˈ**poofy** *adj*

pooh (puː) *interj* **1** an exclamation of disdain, contempt, or disgust **2** a childish word for **faeces 3** a childish word for **defecate**

Pooh-Bah (ˈpuːˈbɑː) *n* a pompous self-important official holding several offices at once and fulfilling none of them [C19 after the character, the Lord-High-Everything-Else, in *The Mikado* (1885), by Gilbert & Sullivan]

pooh-pooh (ˈpuːˈpuː) *vb* (*tr*) to express disdain or scorn for; dismiss or belittle

pool¹ (puːl) *n* **1** a small body of still water, usually fresh; small pond **2** a small isolated collection of spilt liquid; puddle: *a pool of blood* **3** a deep part of a stream or river where the water runs very slowly **4** an underground accumulation of oil or gas **5** See **swimming pool** [OE *pōl*]

pool² (puːl) *n* **1** any communal combination of resources, funds, etc: *a typing pool* **2** the combined stakes of the betters in many gambling games; kitty **3** *commerce* a group of producers who agree to establish and maintain output levels and high prices, each member of the group being allocated a maximum quota **4** *finance, chiefly US* a joint fund organized by security-holders for speculative or manipulative purposes on financial markets **5** any of various billiard games in which the object is to pot all the balls with the cue ball, esp that played with 15 coloured and numbered balls ▷ *vb* (*tr*) **6** to combine (investments, money, interests, etc) into a common fund, as for a joint enterprise **7** *commerce* to organize a pool of (enterprises) [C17 from F *poule*, lit.: hen used to signify stakes in a card game, from Med. L *pulla* hen, from L *pullus* young animal] ▷ www.wpa-pool.com

Poole (puːl) *n* **1** a port and resort in S England, in Poole unitary authority, Dorset, on **Poole Harbour**; seat of Bournemouth University (1992) Pop: 138 479 (1991) **2** a unitary authority in S England, in Dorset. Pop: 138 299 (2001). Area: 37 sq km (14 sq miles)

Pool Malebo (ˈpuːl məˈliːbəʊ) *n* the Congolese name for **Stanley Pool**

pools (puːlz) *pl n* **the** *Brit* an organized nationwide principally postal gambling pool betting on the result of football matches. Also called: **football pools**

Poona *or* **Pune** (ˈpuːnə) *n* a city in W India, in W Maharashtra: under British rule served as the seasonal capital of the Bombay Presidency. Pop: 1 566 651 (1991)

poontang (ˈpuːntæŋ) *n taboo sl* **1** the female pudenda **2** a woman considered as a sexual object **3** sexual intercourse [possibly from F: *putain* prostitute]

Pp

poop¹ (puːp) *naut* ▷ *n* **1** a raised structure at the stern of a vessel, esp a sailing ship **2** Also called: **poop deck** a raised deck at the stern of a ship ▷ *vb* **3** (*tr*) (of a wave or sea) to break over the stern of (a vessel) **4** (*intr*) (of a vessel) to ship a wave or sea over the stern, esp repeatedly [C15 from OF *pupe*, from L *puppis*]

poop² (puːp) *vb US & Canad sl* **1** (*tr; usually passive*) to cause to become exhausted; tire: *he was pooped after the race* **2** (*intr; usually foll by out*) to give up or fail: *he pooped out of the race* [C14 *poupen* to blow, ? imit.]

poop³ (puːp) *inf* ▷ *vb* (*intr*) **1** to defecate ▷ *n* **2** faeces; excrement [perhaps related to POOP²]

pooper-scooper *n* a device used to remove dogs' excrement from public areas [C20 POOP³ + -ER¹ + SCOOP]

Poopó (*Spanish* pooˈpo) *n* **Lake** a lake in SW Bolivia, at an altitude of 3688 m (12 100 ft): fed by the Desaguadero River. Area: 2540 sq km (980 sq miles)

poor (pʊə, pɔː) *adj* **1** lacking financial or other means of subsistence; needy **2** characterized by or indicating poverty: *the country had a poor economy* **3** scanty or inadequate: *a poor salary* **4** (when *postpositive*, usually foll by *in*) badly supplied (with resources, etc): *a region poor in wild flowers* **5** inferior **6** contemptible or despicable **7** disappointing or disagreeable: *a poor play* **8** (*prenominal*) deserving of pity; unlucky: *poor John is ill again* [C13 from OF *povre*, from L *pauper*] > ˈ**poorness** *n*

poor box *n* a box, esp one in a church, used for the collection of alms or money for the poor

poorhouse (ˈpʊəˌhaʊs, ˈpɔː-) *n* another name for **workhouse** (sense 1)

poor law *n English history* a law providing for the relief or support of the poor from parish funds

poorly (ˈpʊəlɪ, ˈpɔː-) *adv* **1** badly ▷ *adj* **2** (*usually postpositive*) *inf* in poor health; rather ill

poort (pʊət) *n* (in South Africa) a steep narrow

mountain pass, usually following a river or stream [c19 from Afrik., from Du.: gateway]

poor White *n often offens* **a** a poverty-stricken and underprivileged White person, esp in the southern US and South Africa **b** *(as modifier): poor White trash*

pop[1] (pɒp) *vb* **pops, popping, popped 1** to make or cause to make a light sharp explosive sound **2** to burst open with such a sound **3** *(intr; often foll by in, out, etc) inf* to come (to) or go (from) rapidly or suddenly **4** *(intr)* (esp of the eyes) to protrude: *her eyes popped with amazement* **5** to shoot at (a target) with a firearm **6** *(tr)* to place with a sudden movement: *she popped some tablets into her mouth* **7** *(tr) inf* to pawn: *he popped his watch yesterday* **8** *(tr) sl* to take (a drug) in pill form or as an injection **9 pop the question** *inf* to propose marriage ▷ *n* **10** a light sharp explosive sound; crack **11** *inf* a flavoured nonalcoholic carbonated beverage ▷ *adv* **12** with a popping sound ▷ See also **pop off** [c14 imit.]

pop[2] (pɒp) *n* **1a** music of general appeal, esp among young people, that originated as a distinctive genre in the 1950s. It is generally characterized by a heavy rhythmic element and the use of electrical amplification **1b** *(as modifier): a pop group* **2** *inf* a piece of popular or light classical music ▷ *adj* **3** *inf* short for **popular**

▷ www.dotmusic.com
▷ www.musicsearch.com
▷ www.nme.com
▷ www.popmusic.com

pop[3] (pɒp) *n* **1** an informal word for **father 2** *inf* a name used in addressing an old man

POP *abbrev for* Post Office Preferred (size of envelopes, etc)

pop. *abbrev for:* **1** popular(ly) **2** population

pop art *n* a movement in modern art that imitates the methods, styles, and themes of popular culture and mass media, such as comic strips, advertising, and science fiction

▷ www.artchive.com/ftp_site_reg.htm
▷ www.artcyclopedia.com/history/pop.html

popcorn (ˈpɒpˌkɔːn) *n* **1** a variety of maize having hard pointed kernels that puff up and burst when heated **2** the puffed edible kernels of this plant

pope (pəʊp) *n* **1** *(often cap)* the bishop of Rome as head of the Roman Catholic Church **2** *Eastern Orthodox Churches* a title sometimes given to a parish priest or to the Greek Orthodox patriarch of Alexandria [OE *papa*, from Church L: bishop, esp of Rome, from LGk *papas* father-in-God, from Gk *pappas* father] > **ˈpopedom** *n*

Pope (pəʊp) *n* **Alexander** 1688–1744, English poet, regarded as the most brilliant satirist of the Augustan period, esp with his *Imitations of Horace* (1733–38) His technical virtuosity is most evident in *The Rape of the Lock* (1712–14). Other works include *The Dunciad* (1728; 1742), the *Moral Essays* (1731–35), and *An Essay on Man* (1733–34)

popery (ˈpəʊpərɪ) *n* a derogatory name for **Roman Catholicism**

popeyed (ˈpɒpˌaɪd) *adj* **1** having bulging prominent eyes **2** staring in astonishment

popgun (ˈpɒpˌɡʌn) *n* a toy gun that fires a pellet or cork by means of compressed air

popinjay (ˈpɒpɪnˌdʒeɪ) *n* **1** a conceited, foppish, or excessively talkative person **2** an archaic word for **parrot 3** the figure of a parrot used as a target [c13 *papeniai*, from OF *papegay* a parrot, from Sp., from Ar. *babaghā*]

popish (ˈpəʊpɪʃ) *adj derog* belonging to or characteristic of Roman Catholicism

poplar (ˈpɒplə) *n* **1** a tree of N temperate regions, having triangular leaves, flowers borne in catkins, and light soft wood **2** *US* the tulip tree [c14 from OF *poplier*, from L *pōpulus*]

poplin (ˈpɒplɪn) *n* a strong fabric, usually of cotton, in plain weave with fine ribbing [c18 from F *papeline*, ?from *Poperinge*, a centre of textile manufacture in Flanders]

popliteal (pɒpˈlɪtɪəl, ˌpɒplɪˈtiːəl) *adj* of, relating to, or near the part of the leg behind the knee [c18 from NL *popliteus* the muscle behind the knee joint, from L *poples* the ham of the knee]

Popocatépetl (ˌpɒpəˈkætəpɛtᵊl, -ˌkætəˈpɛtᵊl; *Spanish* popokaˈtepɛtl) *n* a volcano in SE central Mexico, southeast of Mexico City. Height: 5452 m (17 887 ft)

pop off *vb (intr, adv) inf* **1** to depart suddenly or unexpectedly **2** to die, esp suddenly

Popov (*Russian* paˈpɔf) *n* **1 Alexander Stepanovich** (alɪkˈsandᵊr stɪˈpanəvitʃ) 1859–1906, Russian physicist, the first to use an aerial in experiments with radio waves **2 Oleg** (**Konstantinovich**) born 1930, Russian clown, a member of the Moscow Circus

poppadom *or* **poppadum** (ˈpɒpədəm) *n* a thin round crisp Indian bread, fried or roasted and served with curry, etc [from Hindi]

popper (ˈpɒpə) *n* **1** a person or thing that pops **2** *Brit* an informal name for **press stud 3** *chiefly US & Canad* a container for cooking popcorn in **4** *sl* an amyl nitrite capsule, crushed and inhaled by drug users

Popper (ˈpɒpə) *n* Sir **Karl** 1902–94, British philosopher, born in Vienna. In *The Logic of Scientific Discovery* (1934), he proposes that knowledge cannot be absolutely confirmed, but rather that science progresses by the experimental refutation of the current theory and its consequent replacement by a new theory, equally provisional but covering more of the known data. *The Open Society and its Enemies* (1945) is a critique of dogmatic political philosophies, such as Marxism. Other works are *The Poverty of Historicism* (1957), *Conjectures and Refutations* (1963), and *Objective Knowledge* (1972)

poppet (ˈpɒpɪt) *n* **1** a term of affection for a small child or sweetheart **2** Also called: **poppet valve** a mushroom-shaped valve that is lifted from its seating by applying an axial force to its stem **3** *naut* a temporary supporting brace for a vessel hauled on land [c14 early var. of PUPPET]

popping crease *n cricket* a line four feet in front of and parallel with the bowling crease, at or behind which the batsman stands [c18 from POP[1] (in the obs. sense: to hit) + CREASE]

popple (ˈpɒpᵊl) *vb* **popples, poppling, poppled** *(intr)* **1** (of boiling water or a choppy sea) to heave or toss; bubble **2** (often foll by *along*) (of a stream or river) to move with an irregular tumbling motion [c14 imit.]

poppy[1] (ˈpɒpɪ) *n, pl* **poppies 1** any of numerous papaveraceous plants having red, orange, or white flowers and a milky sap **2** any of several similar or related plants, such as the California poppy and Welsh poppy **3** *obs* any of the drugs, such as opium, that are obtained from these plants **4a** a strong red to reddish-orange colour **4b** *(as adj): a poppy dress* **5** an artificial red poppy flower worn to mark Remembrance Sunday [OE *popæg*, ult. from L *papāver*]

poppy[2] (ˈpɒpɪ) **poppier, poppiest** of or relating to pop music

poppycock (ˈpɒpɪˌkɒk) *n inf* nonsense [c19 from Du. dialect *pappekak*, lit.: soft excrement]

Poppy Day *n* an informal name for **Remembrance Sunday**

poppyhead (ˈpɒpɪˌhɛd) *n* **1** the hard dry seed-containing capsule of a poppy **2** a carved ornament, esp one used on the top of the end of a pew or bench in Gothic church architecture

poppy seed *n* the small grey seeds of the opium poppy, used esp on loaves

pop socks *pl n* knee-length nylon stockings

popsy (ˈpɒpsɪ) *n, pl* **popsies** *old-fashioned Brit sl* an attractive young woman [c19 dim. from *pop*, shortened from POPPET; orig. a nursery term]

populace (ˈpɒpjʊləs) *n (sometimes functioning as pl)* **1** local inhabitants **2** the common people; masses [C16 via F from It. *popolaccio* the common herd, from *popolo* people, from L *populus*]

popular ('pɒpjʊlə) *adj* **1** widely favoured or admired **2** favoured by an individual or limited group: *I'm not very popular with her* **3** prevailing among the general public; common: *popular discontent* **4** appealing to or comprehensible to the layman: *a popular lecture on physics* ▷ *n* **5** (*usually pl*) a cheap newspaper with a mass circulation [C15 from L *populāris* of the people, democratic] > **popularity** (ˌpɒpjʊ'lærɪtɪ) *n* > **'popularly** *adv*

popular front *n* (*often cap*) any of the left-wing groups or parties that were organized from 1935 onwards to oppose the spread of fascism

popularize or **popularise** ('pɒpjʊləˌraɪz) *vb* **popularizes, popularizing, popularized** or **popularises, popularising, popularised** (*tr*) **1** to make popular **2** to make or cause to become easily understandable or acceptable > **ˌpopulari'zation** or **ˌpopulari'sation** *n* > **'popularˌizer** or **'popularˌiser** *n*

populate ('pɒpjʊˌleɪt) *vb* **populates, populating, populated** (*tr*) **1** (*often passive*) to live in; inhabit **2** to provide a population for; colonize or people [C16 from Med. L *populāre*, from L *populus* people]

population (ˌpɒpjʊ'leɪʃən) *n* **1** (*sometimes functioning as pl*) all the persons inhabiting a specified place **2** the number of such inhabitants **3** (*sometimes functioning as pl*) all the people of a particular class in a specific area: *the Chinese population of San Francisco* **4** the act or process of providing a place with inhabitants; colonization **5** *ecology* a group of individuals of the same species inhabiting a given area **6** *astron* either of two main groups of stars classified according to age and location **7** *statistics* the entire aggregate of individuals or items from which samples are drawn

population explosion *n* a rapid increase in the size of a population caused by such factors as a sudden decline in infant mortality or an increase in life expectancy

population pyramid *n* a pyramid-shaped diagram illustrating the age distribution of a population: the youngest are represented by a rectangle at the base, the oldest by one at the apex

populism ('pɒpjʊˌlɪzəm) or **popularism** *n* the practice, esp by a politician of making a calculated appeal to the interests, tastes, or prejudices of ordinary people

populist ('pɒpjʊˌlɪst) *adj* **1** appealing to the interests or prejudices of ordinary people ▷ *n* **2** a person, esp a politician, who appeals to the interests or prejudices of ordinary people

Populist ('pɒpjʊlɪst) *n* **1** *US history* a member of the People's Party, formed largely by agrarian interests to contest the 1892 presidential election ▷ *adj* **2** of or relating to the People's Party or any individual or movement with similar aims. Also: **Populistic** > **'Popuˌlism** *n*

populous ('pɒpjʊləs) *adj* containing many inhabitants [C15 from LL *populōsus*] > **'populously** *adv* > **'populousness** *n*

pop-up *adj* **1** (of an appliance) characterized by or having a mechanism that pops up: *a pop-up toaster* **2** (of a book) having pages that rise when opened to simulate a three-dimensional form ▷ *vb* **pop up 3** (*intr, adverb*) to appear suddenly from below ▷ *n* **4** *computing* something that appears over or above the open window on a computer screen

porangi ('pɔːræŋɪ) *adj NZ inf* crazy; mad [from Maori]

porbeagle ('pɔːˌbiːgᵊl) *n* any of several voracious sharks of northern seas. Also called: **mackerel shark** [C18 from Cornish *porgh-bugel*, from ?]

porcelain ('pɔːslɪn) *n* **1** a more or less translucent ceramic material, the principal ingredients being kaolin and petuntse (hard paste) or other clays, bone ash, etc **2** an object made of this or such objects collectively **3** (*modifier*) of, relating to, or made from this material: *a porcelain cup* [C16 from F *porcelaine*, from It. *porcellana* cowrie shell, lit.: relating to a sow, from *porcella* little sow, from *porca* sow, from L; see PORK] > **porcellaneous** (ˌpɔːsə'leɪnɪəs) *adj*

▷ www.gotheborg.com

▷ www.porcelainpainters.com

porch (pɔːtʃ) *n* **1** a low structure projecting from the doorway of a house and forming a covered entrance **2** *US & Canad* a veranda [C13 from F *porche*, from L *porticus* portico]

porcine ('pɔːsaɪn) *adj* of or characteristic of pigs [C17 from L *porcīnus*, from *porcus* a pig]

porcupine ('pɔːkjʊˌpaɪn) *n* any of various large rodents that have a body covering of protective spines or quills [C14 *porc despyne* pig with spines, from OF *porc espin*; see PORK, SPINE] > **'porcuˌpinish** *adj* > **'porcuˌpiny** *adj*

porcupine fish *n* any of various fishes of temperate and tropical seas having a body that is covered with sharp spines and can be inflated into a globe. Also called: **globefish**

porcupine grass *n Austral* another name for **spinifex**

porcupine provisions *pl n finance* provisions, such as poison pills or staggered directorships, made in the bylaws of a company to deter takeover bids. Also called: **shark repellents**

pore¹ (pɔː) *vb* **pores, poring, pored** (*intr*) **1** (foll by *over*) to make a close intent examination or study (of): *he pored over the documents for several hours* **2** (foll by *over, on,* or *upon*) to think deeply (about) **3** (foll by *over, on,* or *upon*) *Rare.* to gaze fixedly (upon) [C13 *pouren*]

USAGE See at **pour**

pore² (pɔː) *n* **1** any small opening in the skin or outer surface of an animal **2** *bot* any small aperture, esp that of a stoma, through which water vapour and gases pass **3** any other small hole, such as a space in a rock, etc [C14 from LL *porus*, from Gk *poros* passage, pore]

porgy ('pɔːgɪ) *n, pl* **porgy** or **porgies** any of various perchlike fishes, many of which occur in American Atlantic waters [C18 from Sp. *pargo*, from L *phager*, from Gk *phagros* sea bream]

Pori (*Finnish* 'pɔri) *n* a port in SW Finland, on the Gulf of Bothnia. Pop: 76 561 (1994). Swedish name: **Björneborg**

poriferan (pɔː'rɪfərən) *n* any invertebrate of the phylum *Porifera*, which comprises the sponges [C19 from NL *porifer* bearing pores]

Porirua (ˌpɔːrɪ'ruːə) *n* a city in New Zealand, on the North Island just north of Wellington. Pop: 46 601 (1991)

pork (pɔːk) *n* the flesh of pigs used as food [C13 from OF *porc*, from L *porcus* pig]

porker ('pɔːkə) *n* a pig, esp a young one, fattened to provide meat

pork pie *n* **1** a pie filled with minced seasoned pork **2** See **porky²**

porkpie hat ('pɔːkˌpaɪ) *n* a hat with a round flat crown and a brim that can be turned up or down

porky¹ ('pɔːkɪ) *adj* **porkier, porkiest 1** characteristic of pork **2** *inf* fat; obese

porky² ('pɔːkɪ) *n, pl* **porkies** *Brit sl* a lie. Also called: **pork pie** [from rhyming slang *pork pie* lie]

porn (pɔːn) or **porno** ('pɔːnəʊ) *n, adj inf* short for **pornography** or **pornographic**

pornography (pɔː'nɒgrəfɪ) *n* **1** writings, pictures, films, etc, designed to stimulate sexual excitement **2** the production of such material ▷ Sometimes (informal) shortened to **porn** or **porno** [C19 from Gk *pornographos* writing of harlots] > **por'nographer** *n* > **pornographic** (ˌpɔːnə'græfɪk) *adj* > **ˌporno'graphically** *adv*

poromeric (ˌpɔːrə'mɛrɪk) *adj* **1** (of a plastic) permeable to water vapour ▷ *n* **2** a substance having this characteristic, esp one based on polyurethane and used in place of leather in making shoe uppers [C20 from

Pp

PORO(SITY) + (POLY)MER + -IC]

porous ('pɔːrəs) *adj* **1** permeable to water, air, or other fluids **2** having pores **3** easy to cross or penetrate: *the porous border into Thailand; the most porous defence in the league* [c14 from Med. L *porōsus*, from LL *porus* PORE[2]] > **'porously** *adv* > **porosity** (pɔː'rɒsɪtɪ) *or* **'porousness** *n*

porphyria (pɔː'fɪrɪə) *n* a hereditary disease of body metabolism, producing abdominal pain, mental confusion, etc [c19 from NL, from *porphyrin* a purple substance excreted by patients suffering from this condition, from Gk *porphura* purple]

porphyry ('pɔːfɪrɪ) *n, pl* **porphyries** **1** any igneous rock with large crystals embedded in a finer groundmass of minerals **2** *obs* a reddish-purple rock consisting of large crystals of feldspar in a finer groundmass of feldspar, hornblende, etc [c14 *porfurie*, from LL, from Gk *porphuritēs (lithos)* purple (stone), from *porphuros* purple] > **,porphy'ritic** *adj*

Porphyry ('pɔːfɪrɪ) *n* original name *Malchus*. 232–305 AD, Greek Neo-Platonist philosopher, born in Syria; disciple and biographer of Plotinus

porpoise ('pɔːpəs) *n, pl* **porpoises** *or* **porpoise** any of various small cetacean mammals having a blunt snout and many teeth [c14 from F *pourpois*, from Med. L *porcopiscus*, from L *porcus* pig + *piscis* fish]

porridge ('pɒrɪdʒ) *n* **1** a dish made from oatmeal or another cereal, cooked in water or milk to a thick consistency **2** *sl* a term of imprisonment [c16 var. (infl. by ME *porray* pottage) of POTTAGE]

porringer ('pɒrɪndʒə) *n* a small dish, often with a handle, for soup, porridge, etc [c16 changed from ME *potinger*, *poteger*, from OF, from *potage* soup; see POTTAGE]

Porsena ('pɔːsɪnə) *or* **Porsenna** (pɔː'sɛnə) *n* **Lars** (lɑːz) 6th century BC, a legendary Etruscan king, alleged to have besieged Rome in a vain attempt to reinstate Tarquinius Superbus on the throne

port[1] (pɔːt) *n* **1** a town or place alongside navigable water with facilities for the loading and unloading of ships **2** See **port of entry** [OE, from L *portus*]
▷ www.iaphworldports.org/top.htm

port[2] (pɔːt) *n* **1** Also called (formerly): **larboard** the left side of an aircraft or vessel when facing the nose or bow ▷ Cf **starboard** (sense 1) ▷ *vb* **2** to turn or be turned towards the port [c17 from ?]

port[3] (pɔːt) *n* a sweet fortified dessert wine [c17 after *Oporto*, Portugal, from where it came orig.]

port[4] (pɔːt) *n* **1** *naut* **1a** an opening in the side of a ship, fitted with a watertight door, for access to the holds **1b** See **porthole** (sense 1) **2** a small opening in a wall, armoured vehicle, etc, for firing through **3** an aperture by which fluid enters or leaves the cylinder head of an engine, compressor, etc **4** *electronics* a logic circuit for the input and ouput of data **5** *chiefly Scot* a gate in a town or fortress [OE, from L *porta* gate]

port[5] (pɔːt) *vb (tr) mil* to carry (a rifle, etc) in a position diagonally across the body with the muzzle near the left shoulder [c14 from OF, from *porter* to carry, from L *portāre*]

port[6] (pɔːt) *n Austral* (esp in Queensland) a suitcase or school case [c20 shortened from PORTMANTEAU]

Port. *abbrev for:* **1** Portugal **2** Portuguese

portable ('pɔːtəbᵊl) *adj* **1** able to be carried or moved easily, esp by hand **2** (of computer software, files, etc) able to be transferred from one type of computer system to another ▷ *n* **3** an article designed to be readily carried by hand, such as a television, typewriter, etc [c14 from LL *portābilis*, from L *portāre* to carry] > **,porta'bility** *n* > **'portably** *adv*

Port Adelaide *n* the chief port of South Australia, near Adelaide on St Vincent Gulf. Pop: 39 000 (latest est)

Portadown (,pɔːtə'daʊn) *n* a town in S Northern Ireland, in the district of Armagh. Pop: 21 299 (1991)

portage ('pɔːtɪdʒ) *n* **1** the act of carrying; transport **2** the cost of carrying or transporting **3** the transporting of boats, supplies, etc, overland between navigable waterways **4** the route used for such transport ▷ *vb* **portages, portaging, portaged** **5** to transport (boats, supplies, etc) thus [c15 from F, from OF *porter* to carry]

Portakabin ('pɔːtə,kæbɪn) *n trademark* a portable building quickly set up for use as a temporary office, etc

portal ('pɔːtᵊl) *n* **1** an entrance, gateway, or doorway, esp one that is large and impressive **2** an Internet site providing links to other sites ▷ *adj* **3** *anat* of or relating to a portal vein: *hepatic portal system* [c14 via OF from Med. L *portāle*, from L *porta* gate]

portal vein *n* any vein connecting two capillary networks, esp in the liver

portamento (,pɔːtə'mɛntəʊ) *n, pl* **portamenti** (-tɪ) *music* a smooth slide from one note to another in which intervening notes are not separately discernible [c18 from It.: a carrying, from L *portāre* to carry]

Port Arthur *n* **1** a former penal settlement (1833–70) in Australia, on the S coast of the Tasman Peninsula, Tasmania **2** the former name of **Lüshun**

portative ('pɔːtətɪv) *adj* **1** a less common word for **portable** **2** concerned with the act of carrying [c14 from F, from L *portāre* to carry]

Port-au-Prince ('pɔːtəʊ'prɪns; *French* pɔrtoprɛ̃s) *n* the capital and chief port of Haiti, in the south on the Gulf of Gonaïves: founded in 1749 by the French; university (1944). Pop: 917 112 (1997 est)
▷ www.haiti-reference.com/geographie/villes/pap.html

Port Blair (blɛə) *n* the capital of the Indian Union Territory of the Andaman and Nicobar Islands, a port on the SE coast of South Andaman Island: a former penal colony. Pop: 74 955 (1991)

portcullis (pɔːt'kʌlɪs) *n* an iron or wooden grating suspended vertically in grooves in the gateway of a castle or town and able to be lowered so as to bar the entrance [c14 *port colice*, from OF *porte coleïce* sliding gate, from *porte* door + *coleïce*, from *couler* to slide, from LL *cōlāre* to filter]

Porte (pɔːt) *n* short for Sublime Porte; the court or government of the Ottoman Empire [c17 shortened from F *Sublime Porte* High Gate, rendering the Turkish title *Babi Ali*, the imperial gate, regarded as the seat of government]

porte-cochere (,pɔːtkɒ'ʃɛə) *n* **1** a large covered entrance for vehicles leading into a courtyard **2** a large roof projecting over a drive to shelter travellers entering or leaving vehicles [c17 from F: carriage entrance]

Port Elizabeth *n* a port in S South Africa, on Algoa Bay: motor-vehicle manufacture, fruit canning; resort. Pop (urban area): 749 921 (1996)

portend (pɔː'tɛnd) *vb (tr)* to give warning of; foreshadow [c15 from L *portendere* to indicate]

portent ('pɔːtɛnt) *n* **1** a sign of a future event; omen **2** momentous or ominous significance: *a cry of dire portent* **3** a marvel [c16 from L *portentum* sign, from *portendere* to portend]

portentous (pɔː'tɛntəs) *adj* **1** of momentous or ominous significance **2** miraculous, amazing, or awe-inspiring **3** self-important or pompous

porter[1] ('pɔːtə) *n* **1** a person employed to carry luggage, parcels, supplies, etc, at a railway station or hotel **2** (in hospitals) a person employed to move patients from place to place **3** *US & Canad* a railway employee who waits on passengers, esp in a sleeper [c14 from OF *portour*, from LL *portātōr*, from L *portāre* to carry] > **'porterage** *n*

porter[2] ('pɔːtə) *n* **1** *chiefly Brit* a person in charge of a gate or door; doorman or gatekeeper **2** a person employed as a caretaker and doorkeeper who also answers inquiries **3** a person in charge of the maintenance of a building, esp a block of flats [c13 from OF *portier*, from LL *portārius*, from L *porta* door]

porter[3] (ˈpɔːtə) *n Brit* a dark sweet ale brewed from black malt [c18 from *porter's ale*, apparently because it was a favourite beverage of porters]

Porter (ˈpɔːtə) *n* **1 Cole** 1893–1964, US composer and lyricist of musical comedies. His most popular songs include *Night and Day* and *Let's do It* **2 George,** Baron Porter of Luddenham. 1920–2002, British chemist, who shared a Nobel prize for chemistry in 1967 for his work on flash photolysis **3 Katherine Anne** 1890–1980, US short-story writer and novelist. Her best-known collections of stories are *Flowering Judas* (1930) and *Pale Horse, Pale Rider* (1939) **4 Peter** born 1929, Australian poet, living in Britain **5 Rodney Robert** 1917–85, British biochemist: shared the Nobel prize for physiology or medicine 1972 for determining the structure of an antibody **6 William Sidney** original name of **O Henry**

porterhouse (ˈpɔːtəˌhaʊs) *n* **1** Also called: **porterhouse steak** a thick choice steak of beef cut from the middle ribs or sirloin **2** (formerly) a place in which porter, beer, etc, and sometimes chops and steaks, were served [c19 (sense 1): said to be after a porterhouse in New York]

portfire (ˈpɔːtˌfaɪə) *n* a slow-burning fuse used for firing rockets and fireworks and, in mining, for igniting explosives [c17 from F *porte-feu*, from *porter* to carry + *feu* fire]

portfolio (pɔːtˈfəʊlɪəʊ) *n, pl* **portfolios 1** a flat case, esp of leather, used for carrying maps, drawings, etc **2** the contents of such a case, such as drawings or photographs, that demonstrate recent work **3** such a case used for carrying ministerial or state papers **4** the responsibilities or role of the head of a government department: *the portfolio for foreign affairs* **5 Minister without portfolio** a cabinet minister who is not responsible for any government department **6** the complete investments held by an individual investor or a financial organization [c18 from It. *portafoglio*, from *portāre* to carry + *foglio* leaf, from L *folium*]

portfolio management *n* the service provided by an investment adviser who manages a financial portfolio on behalf of the investor

Port-Gentil (*French* pɔrʒɑ̃ti) *n* the chief port of Gabon, in the west near the mouth of the Ogooué River: oil refinery. Pop: 80 841 (1993)

Port Harcourt (ˈhɑːkət, -kɔːt) *n* a port in S Nigeria, capital of Rivers state on the Niger delta: the nation's second largest port; industrial centre. Pop: 410 000 (1996 est)

porthole (ˈpɔːtˌhəʊl) *n* **1** a small aperture in the side of a vessel to admit light and air, fitted with a watertight cover. Sometimes shortened to **port 2** an opening in a wall or parapet through which a gun can be fired

portico (ˈpɔːtɪkəʊ) *n, pl* **porticoes** *or* **porticos 1** a covered entrance to a building; porch **2** a covered walkway in the form of a roof supported by columns or pillars, esp one built on to the exterior of a building [c17 via It. from L *porticus*]

portière (ˌpɔːtɪˈɛə; *French* pɔrtjɛr) *n* a curtain hung in a doorway [c19 via F from Med. L *portāria*, from L *porta* door] > ˌ**portiˈèred** *adj*

Porţile de Fier (pɔrˈtsiːlɛ dɛ ˈfjɛr) *n* the Romanian name for the **Iron Gate**

portion (ˈpɔːʃən) *n* **1** a part of a whole **2** a part allotted or belonging to a person or group **3** an amount of food served to one person; helping **4** *law* **4a** a share of property, esp one coming to a child from the estate of his parents **4b** a dowry **5** a person's lot or destiny ▷ *vb* (*tr*) **6** to divide up; share out **7** to give a share to (a person) [c13 via OF from L *portiō*] > ˈ**portionless** *adj*

Port Jackson *n* an inlet of the Pacific on the coast of SE Australia, forming a fine natural harbour: site of the city of Sydney, spanned by Sydney Harbour Bridge

Port Jackson willow *or* **wattle** *n* an Australian acacia tree introduced in the 19th century into South Africa, where it is now regarded as a pest

Portland[1] (ˈpɔːtlənd) *n* **1 Isle of** a rugged limestone peninsula in SW England, in Dorset, connected to the mainland by a narrow isthmus and by Chesil Bank: the lighthouse of **Portland Bill** lies at the S tip; famous for the quarrying of **Portland stone,** a fine building material. Pop (town): 12 000 (latest est) **2** an inland port in NW Oregon, on the Willamette River: the largest city in the state; shipbuilding and chemical industries. Pop: 529 121 (2000) **3** a port in SW Maine, on Casco Bay: the largest city in the state; settled by the English in 1632, destroyed successively by French, Indian, and British attacks, and rebuilt; capital of Maine (1820–32). Pop: 64 358 (1990)

Portland[2] (ˈpɔːtlənd) *n* **3rd Duke of** title of *William Henry Cavendish Bentinck*. 1738–1809, British statesman; prime minister (1783; 1807–09); father of Lord William Cavendish Bentinck

Portland cement *n* a cement that hardens under water and is made by heating clay and crushed chalk or limestone [c19 after the Isle of PORTLAND, because its colour resembles that of the stone quarried there]

Portlaoise (ˌpɔːtˈliːʃə) *n* a town in central Republic of Ireland, county town of Laois: site of a top-security prison. Pop: 9500 (1990 est)

Port Louis (ˈluːɪs, ˈluːɪ) *n* the capital and chief port of Mauritius, on the NW coast on the Indian Ocean. Pop: 147 648 (1999 est)
▷ www.mauritius.net/whattovisit/historical.places_main.htm

portly (ˈpɔːtlɪ) *adj* **portlier, portliest 1** stout or corpulent **2** *arch* stately; impressive [c16 from PORT[5] (in the sense: deportment)] > ˈ**portliness** *n*

Port Lyautey (ljəʊˈteɪ) *n* the former name (1932–56) of **Mina Hassan Tani**

portmanteau (pɔːtˈmæntəʊ) *n, pl* **portmanteaus** *or* **portmanteaux** (-təʊz) **1** (formerly) a large travelling case made of stiff leather, esp one hinged at the back so as to open out into two compartments **2** (*modifier*) embodying several uses or qualities: *the heroine is a portmanteau figure of all the virtues* [c16 from F: cloak carrier]

portmanteau word *n* another name for **blend** (sense 7) [c19 from the idea that two meanings are packed into one word]

Port Moresby (ˈmɔːzbɪ) *n* the capital and chief port of Papua New Guinea, on the SE coast on the Gulf of Papua: important Allied base in World War II. Pop (urban area): 298 145 (1999 est)
▷ http://portmoresby.com

Portnet (ˈpɔːtnɛt) *n S African* the South African Port Authority

Port Nicholson *n* **1** the first British settlement in New Zealand, established on Wellington Harbour in 1840: grew into Wellington **2** the former name for Wellington Harbour [c19 named after Capt. John Nicholson, Australian naval officer]

Pôrto (ˈportu) *n* the Portuguese name for **Oporto**

Pôrto Alegre (*Portuguese* ˈportu aˈlɛgri) *n* a port in S Brazil, capital of the Rio Grande do Sul state: the country's chief inland port; the chief commercial centre of S Brazil, with two universities (1936 and 1948). Pop: 1 320 000 (2000), with a conurbation of 3 349 000 (1995)

Portobello (ˌpɔːtəʊˈbɛləʊ) *n* a small port in Panama, on the Caribbean northeast of Colón: the most important port in South America in colonial times; declined with the opening of the Panama Canal. Pop: 3026 (1990 est)

port of call *n* **1** a port where a ship stops **2** any place visited on a traveller's itinerary

port of entry *n law* an airport, harbour, etc, where customs officials are stationed to supervise the entry into and exit from a country of persons and merchandise

Port of Spain *n* the capital and chief port of Trinidad

Pp

and Tobago, on the W coast of Trinidad. Pop: 43 396 (1996 est)
▷ www.discover-tt.com/trinidad/port-of-spain.html

Porto Novo ('pɔːtəʊ 'nəʊvəʊ) *n* the capital of Benin, in the southwest on a coastal lagoon: formerly a centre of Portuguese settlement and the slave trade. Pop: 200 000 (1994 est)
▷ www.porto-novo.org

Porto Rico ('pɔːtə 'riːkəʊ) *n* the former name (until 1932) of **Puerto Rico** > **Porto Rican** *adj, n*

Pôrto Velho (*Portuguese* 'portu 'vɛʎu) *n* a city in W Brazil, capital of the federal territory of Rondônia on the Madeira River. Pop: 273 496 (2000)

Port Phillip Bay *or* **Port Phillip** *n* a bay in SE Australia, which forms the harbour of Melbourne

portrait ('pɔːtrɪt, -treɪt) *n* **1** a painting or other likeness of an individual, esp of the face **2** a verbal description, esp of a person's character ▷ *adj* **3** *printing* (of an illustration in a book, magazine, etc) of greater height than width ▷ Cf **landscape** (sense 5a) [C16 from F, from *portraire* to PORTRAY] > '**portraitist** *n*

portraiture ('pɔːtrɪtʃə) *n* **1** the practice or art of making portraits **2a** a portrait **2b** portraits collectively **3** a verbal description

portray (pɔː'treɪ) *vb* (*tr*) **1** to make a portrait of **2** to depict in words **3** to play the part of (a character) in a play or film [C14 from OF *portraire* to depict, from L *prōtrahere* to drag forth] > **por'trayal** *n* > **por'trayer** *n*

Port Royal *n* **1** a fortified town in SE Jamaica, at the entrance to Kingston harbour: capital of Jamaica in colonial times **2** the former name (until 1710) of **Annapolis Royal** **3** (*French* pɔr rwajal) an educational institution about 27 km (17 miles) west of Paris that flourished from 1638 to 1704, when it was suppressed by papal bull as it had become a centre of Jansenism. Its teachers were noted esp for their work on linguistics: their *Grammaire générale et raisonnée* exercised much influence

Port Said ('saːiːd, saɪd) *n* a port in NE Egypt, at the N end of the Suez Canal: founded in 1859 when the Suez Canal was begun; became the largest coaling station in the world and later an oil-bunkering port; damaged in the Arab-Israeli wars of 1967 and 1973. Pop: 469 533 (1996)

Port-Salut ('pɔː sə'luː; *French* pɔrsaly) *n* a mild semihard whole-milk cheese of a round flat shape. Also called: **Port du Salut** [C19 named after the Trappist monastery at *Port du Salut* in NW France where it was first made]

Portsmouth ('pɔːtsməθ) *n* **1** a port in S England, in Portsmouth unitary authority, Hampshire, on the English Channel: Britain's chief naval base; university (1992). Pop: 174 690 (1991). Informal name: **Pompey** **2** a unitary authority in S England, in Hampshire. Pop: 186 704 (2001). Area: 37 sq km (14 sq miles) **3** a port in SE Virginia, on the Elizabeth River: naval base; shipyards. Pop: 100 565 (2000)

Port Sudan *n* the chief port of the Sudan, in the NE on the Red Sea. Pop: 305 385 (1993)

Port Talbot ('tɔːlbət, 'tæl-) *n* a port in SE Wales, in Neath Port Talbot county borough on Swansea Bay: established as a coal port in the mid-19th century; large steelworks; ore terminal. Pop: 37 647 (1991)

Portugal ('pɔːtjʊgᵊl) *n* a republic in SW Europe, on the Atlantic: became an independent monarchy in 1139 and expelled the Moors in 1249 after more than four centuries of Muslim rule; became a republic in 1910; under the dictatorship of Salazar from 1932 until 1968, when he was succeeded by Dr Caetano, who was overthrown by a junta in 1974; constitutional government restored in 1976. Portugal is a member of the European Union. Official language: Portuguese. Religion: Roman Catholic majority. Currency: euro. Capital: Lisbon. Pop: 10 328 000 (2001 est). Area: 91 831 sq km (35 456 sq miles)
▷ www.portugal.gov.pt
▷ www.portugalinsite.pt

Portuguese (ˌpɔːtjʊ'giːz) *n* **1** the official language of Portugal and Brazil; it belongs to the Romance group of the Indo-European family **2** (*pl* **Portuguese**) a native, citizen, or inhabitant of Portugal ▷ *adj* **3** of Portugal, its inhabitants, or their language

Portuguese East Africa *n* a former name (until 1975) of **Mozambique**

Portuguese Guinea *n* the former name (until 1974) of **Guinea-Bissau** > **Portuguese Guinean** *adj, n*

Portuguese India *n* a former Portuguese overseas province on the W coast of India, consisting of Goa, Daman, and Diu: established between 1505 and 1510; annexed by India in 1961

Portuguese man-of-war *n* any of several large hydrozoans having an aerial float and long stinging tentacles. Sometimes shortened to **man-of-war**

Portuguese Timor *n* a former name for **East Timor**

Portuguese West Africa *n* a former name (until 1975) of **Angola**

portulaca (ˌpɔːtjʊ'lækə, -'leɪkə) *n* any of a genus of plants of tropical and subtropical America, having yellow, pink, or purple showy flowers [C16 from L: PURSLANE]

POS *abbrev for* point of sale

pose[1] (pəʊz) *vb* **poses, posing, posed** **1** to assume or cause to assume a physical attitude, as for a photograph or painting **2** (*intr; often foll by as*) to present oneself (as something one is not) **3** (*intr*) to affect an attitude in order to impress others **4** (*tr*) to put forward or ask: *to pose a question* **5** (*intr*) *sl* to adopt a particular style of appearance and stand or strut around, esp in bars, discotheques, etc, in order to attract attention ▷ *n* **6** a physical attitude, esp one deliberately adopted for an artist or photographer **7** a mode of behaviour that is adopted for effect [C14 from OF *poser* to set in place, from LL *pausāre* to cease, put down (infl. by L *pōnere* to place)]

pose[2] (pəʊz) *vb* **poses, posing, posed** (*tr*) *rare* to puzzle or baffle [C16 from obs. *appose*, from L *appōnere* to put to]

Poseidon (pɒ'saɪdᵊn) *n Greek myth* the god of the sea and of earthquakes; brother of Zeus, Hades, and Hera. He is generally depicted in art wielding a trident. Roman counterpart: **Neptune**

Posen ('poːzən) *n* the German name for **Poznań**

poser[1] ('pəʊzə) *n* **1** a person who poses **2** *inf* a person who likes to be seen in trendsetting clothes in fashionable bars, discos, etc

poser[2] ('pəʊzə) *n* a baffling or insoluble question

poseur (pəʊ'zɜː) *n* a person who strikes an attitude or assumes a pose in order to impress others [C19 from F, from *poser* to POSE[1]]

posh (pɒʃ) *adj inf, chiefly Brit* **1** smart, elegant, or fashionable **2** upper-class or genteel [C19 often said to be an acronym of *port out, starboard home*, the most desirable location for a cabin in British ships sailing to & from the East, being the shaded side; but more likely from obs. sl. *posh* (n) a dandy]

posit ('pɒzɪt) *vb* (*tr*) **1** to assume or put forward as fact or the factual basis for an argument; postulate **2** to put in position [C17 from L *pōnere* to place]

position (pə'zɪʃən) *n* **1** place, situation, or location: *he took up a position to the rear* **2** the appropriate or customary location: *the telescope is in position for use* **3** the manner in which a person or thing is placed; arrangement **4** *mil* an area or point occupied for tactical reasons **5** point of view; stand: *what's your position on this issue?* **6** social status, esp high social standing **7** a post of employment; job **8** the act of positing a fact or viewpoint **9** something posited, such as an idea **10** *sport* the part of a field or playing area where a player is placed or where he generally operates **11** *music* the vertical spacing or layout of the written notes in a chord

12 (in classical prosody) the situation in which a short vowel may be regarded as long, that is, when it occurs before two or more consonants **13** *finance* the market commitment of a dealer in securities, currencies, or commodities: *a short position* **14** **in a position** (foll by an infinitive) able (to) ▷ *vb (tr)* **15** to put in the proper or appropriate place; locate **16** *sport* to place (oneself or another player) in a particular part of the field or playing area **17** to put (someone or something) in a position (esp in relation to others) that confers a strategic advantage: *he's trying to position himself for a leadership bid* **18** *marketing* to promote (a product or service) by tailoring it to the needs of a specific market or by clearly differentiating it from its competitors (eg in terms of price or quality) [C15 from LL *positiō* a positioning, affirmation, from *pōnere* to place] > **po'sitional** *adj*

positional notation *n* the method of denoting numbers by the use of a finite number of digits, each digit having its value multiplied by its place value, as in $936 = (9\times100) + (3\times10) + 6$

position audit *n commerce* a systematic assessment of the current strengths and weaknesses of an organization as a prerequisite for future strategic planning

positive ('pɒzɪtɪv) *adj* **1** expressing certainty or affirmation: *a positive answer* **2** possessing actual or specific qualities; real: *a positive benefit* **3** tending to emphasize what is good or laudable; constructive: *he takes a very positive attitude when correcting pupils' mistakes* **4** tending towards progress or improvement **5** *philosophy* constructive rather than sceptical **6** *(prenominal) inf* (intensifier): *a positive delight* **7** *maths* having a value greater than zero: *a positive number* **8** *maths* **8a** measured in a direction opposite to that regarded as negative **8b** having the same magnitude as but opposite sense to an equivalent negative quantity **9** *grammar* denoting the usual form of an adjective as opposed to its comparative or superlative form **10** *physics* **10a** (of an electric charge) having an opposite polarity to the charge of an electron and the same polarity as the charge of a proton **10b** (of a body, system, ion, etc) having a positive electric charge **11** short for **electropositive** **12** *med* (of the results of an examination or test) indicating the presence of a suspected disorder or organism **13** *econ* of or denoting an analysis that is free of ethical, political, or value judgments ▷ *n* **14** something that is positive **15** *maths* a quantity greater than zero **16** *photog* a print or slide showing a photographic image whose colours or tones correspond to those of the original subject **17** *grammar* the positive degree of an adjective or adverb **18** a positive object, such as a terminal or plate in a voltaic cell [C13 from LL *positīvus*, from *pōnere* to place] > **'positiveness** *or* **,posi'tivity** *n*

positive discrimination *n* the provision of special opportunities for a disadvantaged group

positive feedback *n* See **feedback** (sense 2)

positively ('pɒzɪtɪvlɪ) *adv* **1** in a positive manner **2** (intensifier): *he disliked her; in fact, he positively hated her*

positive vetting *n* the checking of a person's background, to assess his suitability for a position that may involve national security

positivism ('pɒzɪtɪ,vɪzəm) *n* **1** a form of empiricism, esp as established by Auguste Comte, that rejects metaphysics and theology and holds that experimental investigation and observation are the only sources of substantial knowledge. See also **logical positivism** **2** the quality of being definite, certain, etc > **'positivist** *n, adj*

positron ('pɒzɪ,trɒn) *n physics* the antiparticle of the electron, having the same mass but an equal and opposite charge [C20 from *posi(tive + elec)tron*]

positron emission tomography *n* a technique for assessing brain activity and function by recording the emission of positrons from radioactively labelled substances, such as glucose or dopamine

positronium (,pɒzɪ'trəʊnɪəm) *n physics* a short-lived entity consisting of a positron and an electron bound together

posology (pə'sɒlədʒɪ) *n* the branch of medicine concerned with the determination of appropriate doses of drugs or agents [C19 from F *posologie*, from Gk *posos* how much]

poss. *abbrev for:* **1** possession **2** possessive **3** possible **4** possibly

posse ('pɒsɪ) *n* **1** *US* short for **posse comitatus,** the able-bodied men of a district forming a group upon whom the sheriff may call for assistance in maintaining law and order **2** *sl* a Jamaican street gang in the US **3** *inf* a group of friends or associates **4** (in W Canada) a troop of trained horses and riders who perform at stampedes **5** *law* possibility (esp in **in posse**) [C16 from Med. L (n): power, from L (vb): to be able]

posse comitatus (,kɒmɪ'tɑːtəs) *n* the formal legal term for **posse** (sense 1) [Med. L: strength (manpower) of the county]

possess (pə'zɛs) *vb (tr)* **1** to have as one's property; own **2** to have as a quality, characteristic, etc: *to possess good eyesight* **3** to have knowledge of: *to possess a little French* **4** to gain control over or dominate: *whatever possessed you to act so foolishly?* **5** (foll by *of*) to cause to be the owner or possessor: *I am possessed of the necessary information* **6** to have sexual intercourse with **7** *now rare* to maintain (oneself or one's feelings) in a certain state or condition: *possess yourself in patience until I tell you the news* [C15 from OF *possesser*, from L *possidēre*] > **pos'sessor** *n* > **pos'sessory** *adj*

possessed (pə'zɛst) *adj* **1** (foll by *of*) owning or having **2** *(usually postpositive)* under the influence of a powerful force, such as a spirit or strong emotion **3** a less common term for **self-possessed**

possession (pə'zɛʃən) *n* **1** the act of possessing or state of being possessed: *in possession of the crown* **2** anything that is owned or possessed **3** *(pl)* wealth or property **4** the state of being controlled by or as if by evil spirits **5** the occupancy of land, property, etc, whether or not accompanied by ownership: *to take possession of a house* **6** a territory subject to a foreign state: *colonial possessions* **7** *sport* control of the ball, puck, etc, as exercised by a player or team: *he got possession in his own half*

possessive (pə'zɛsɪv) *adj* **1** of or relating to possession **2** having or showing an excessive desire to possess or dominate: *a possessive husband* **3** *grammar* **3a** another word for **genitive** **3b** denoting an inflected form of a noun or pronoun used to convey the idea of possession, association, etc, as *my* or *Harry's* ▷ *n* **4** *grammar* **4a** the possessive case **4b** a word or speech element in the possessive case > **pos'sessively** *adv* > **pos'sessiveness** *n*

posset ('pɒsɪt) *n* a drink of hot milk curdled with ale, beer, etc, flavoured with spices, formerly used as a remedy for colds [C15 *poshoote*, from ?]

possibility (,pɒsɪ'bɪlɪtɪ) *n, pl* **possibilities** **1** the state or condition of being possible **2** anything that is possible **3** a competitor, candidate, etc, who has a moderately good chance of winning, being chosen, etc **4** *(often pl)* a future prospect or potential: *my new house has great possibilities*

possible ('pɒsɪbᵊl) *adj* **1** capable of existing, taking place, or proving true without contravention of any natural law **2** capable of being achieved: *it is not possible to finish in three weeks* **3** having potential: *the idea is a possible money-spinner* **4** feasible but less than probable: *it is possible that man will live on Mars* **5** *logic* (of a statement, formula, etc) capable of being true under some interpretation or in some circumstances ▷ *n* **6** another word for **possibility** (sense 3) [C14 from L *possibilis* that may be, from *posse* to be able]

> **USAGE** Although it is very common to talk about something being *very possible* or *more possible*, these uses are thought by some to be incorrect, since *possible* describes an absolute state, and therefore something can only be *possible* or *not possible*: *it is very likely* (not *very possible*) *that he will resign*; *it has now become easier* (not *more possible*) *to obtain an entry visa*

possibly ('pɒsɪblɪ) *sentence substitute, adv* **1a** perhaps or maybe **1b** (*as sentence modifier*): *possibly he'll come* ▷ *adv* **2** by any chance; at all: *he can't possibly come*

possum ('pɒsəm) *n* **1** an informal name for **opossum** **2** an Australian and New Zealand name for **phalanger** **3 play possum** to pretend to be dead, ignorant, asleep, etc, in order to deceive an opponent **4 stir the possum** *Austral sl* to cause trouble

post[1] (pəʊst) *n* **1** a length of wood, metal, etc, fixed upright to serve as a support, marker, point of attachment, etc **2** *horse racing* **2a** either of two upright poles marking the beginning (**starting post**) and end (**winning post**) of a racecourse **2b** the finish of a horse race ▷ *vb* (*tr*) **3** (sometimes foll by *up*) to fasten or put up (a notice) in a public place **4** to announce by or as if by means of a poster: *to post banns* **5** to publish (a name) on a list **6** to denounce publicly; brand [OE, from L *postis*]

post[2] (pəʊst) *n* **1** a position to which a person is appointed or elected; appointment; job **2** a position to which a person, such as a sentry, is assigned for duty **3** a permanent military establishment **4** *Brit* either of two military bugle calls (**first post** and **last post**) giving notice of the time to retire for the night **5** See **trading post** ▷ *vb* **6** (*tr*) to assign to or station at a particular place or position **7** *chiefly Brit* to transfer to a different unit or ship on taking up a new appointment, etc [C16 from F *poste*, from It. *posto*, ult. from L *pōnere* to place]

post[3] (pəʊst) *n* **1** *chiefly Brit* letters, packages, etc, that are transported and delivered by the Post Office; mail **2** *chiefly Brit* a single collection or delivery of mail **3** *Brit* an official system of mail delivery **4** (formerly) any of a series of stations furnishing relays of men and horses to deliver mail over a fixed route **5** a rider who carried mail between such stations **6** *Brit* a postbox or post office **7** any of various book sizes, esp 5¼ by 8¼ inches (**post octavo**) **8 by return of post** *Brit* by the next mail in the opposite direction ▷ *vb* **9** (*tr*) *chiefly Brit* to send by post. US and Canad word: **mail** **10** (*tr*) *book-keeping* **10a** to enter (an item) in a ledger **10b** (often foll by *up*) to compile or enter all paper items in (a ledger) **11** (*tr*) to inform of the latest news **12** (*intr*) (formerly) to travel with relays of post horses **13** *arch* to travel or dispatch with speed; hasten ▷ *adv* **14** with speed; rapidly **15** (formerly) by means of post horses [C16 via F from It. *poste*, from L *posita* something placed, from *pōnere* to put]

post- *prefix* **1** after in time or sequence; following; subsequent: *postgraduate* **2** behind; posterior to: *postorbital* [from L, from *post* after, behind]

postage ('pəʊstɪdʒ) *n* **a** the charge for delivering a piece of mail **b** (*as modifier*): *postage charges*

postage meter *n chiefly US & Canad* a postal franking machine. Also called: **postal meter**

postage stamp *n* **1** a printed paper label with a gummed back for attaching to mail as an official indication that the required postage has been paid **2** a mark printed on an envelope, etc, serving the same function

postal ('pəʊstᵊl) *adj* of or relating to a Post Office or to the mail-delivery service > **'postally** *adv*

postal code *n* a Canadian term for **postcode**

postal note *n Austral* the usual name for **postal order**

postal order *n* a written order for the payment of a sum of money, to a named payee, obtainable and payable at a post office

postbag ('pəʊst,bæg) *n* **1** *chiefly Brit* another name for **mailbag** **2** the mail received by a magazine, radio programme, public figure, etc

postbox ('pəʊst,bɒks) *n* another name for **letter box** (sense 2)

postcard ('pəʊst,kɑːd) *n* a card, often bearing a photograph, picture, etc, on one side (**picture postcard**), for sending a message by post without an envelope. Also called (US): **postal card**

post chaise *n* a closed four-wheeled horse-drawn coach used as a rapid means for transporting mail and passengers in the 18th and 19th centuries [C18 from POST[3] + CHAISE]

postclassical (pəʊst'klæsɪkᵊl) *adj* (esp of Greek or Roman literature) later than the classical period

postcode ('pəʊst,kəʊd) *n* a code of letters and digits used as part of a postal address to aid the sorting of mail. Also called: **postal code** US name: **zip code**

postcode discrimination *n* discrimination on the basis of the area where someone lives, with relation to employment, credit rating, etc

postcode lottery *n Brit* a situation in which the standard of medical care, education, etc, received by the public varies from area to area, depending on the funding policies of various health boards, local authorities, etc

postcode prescribing *n Brit* the practice of prescribing more or less expensive and effective medical treatments to patients depending on where they live in a country, and which treatments their health board is willing and able to provide

postconsonantal (pəʊst,kɒnsə'næntᵊl) *adj* (of a speech sound) immediately following a consonant

post-consumer *adj* **a** (of a consumer item) having been discarded for disposal or recovery **b** having been recycled

postdate (pəʊst'deɪt) *vb* **postdates, postdating, postdated** (*tr*) **1** to write a future date on (a document, etc), as on a cheque to prevent it being paid until then **2** to assign a date to (an event, period, etc) that is later than its previously assigned date of occurrence **3** to be or occur at a later date than

postdoctoral (pəʊst'dɒktərəl) *adj* of, relating to, or designating studies, research, or professional work above the level of a doctorate

poster ('pəʊstə) *n* **1** a large printed picture, used for decoration **2** a placard or bill posted in a public place as an advertisement **3** a person who posts bills

poster boy *or* (*fem*) **poster girl** *n* **1** a person who appears on a poster **2** a person who typifies or represents a particular characteristic, cause, opinion, etc: *a poster girl for late motherhood* ▷ Also called: **poster child**

poste restante ('pəʊst rɪ'stænt) *n* **1** an address on mail indicating that it should be kept at a specified post office until collected by the addressee **2** the mail-delivery service or post-office department that handles mail having this address ▷ US and Canad equivalent: **general delivery** [F, lit.: mail remaining]

posterior (pɒ'stɪərɪə) *adj* **1** situated at the back of or behind something **2** coming after or following another in a series **3** coming after in time ▷ *n* **4** the buttocks; rump [C16 from L: latter, from *posterus* coming next, from *post* after] > **pos'teriorly** *adv*

posterity (pɒ'stɛrɪtɪ) *n* **1** future or succeeding generations **2** all of one's descendants [C14 from F *postérité*, from L *posteritās*, from *posterus* coming after, from *post* after]

postern ('pɒstən) *n* a back door or gate, esp one that is for private use [C13 from OF *posterne*, from LL *posterula* (*jānua*) a back (entrance), from *posterus* coming behind; see POSTERIOR, POSTERITY]

poster paint *or* **colour** *n* a gum-based opaque watercolour paint used for writing posters, etc

postfeminist (pəʊst'fɛmɪnɪst) *adj* **1** resulting from or including the beliefs and ideas of feminism **2** differing from or showing moderation of these beliefs and ideas ▷ *n* **3** a person who believes in or advocates any of the ideas that have developed from the feminist movement

post-Fordism (pəʊst'fɔːd,ɪzəm) *n* the idea that modern industrial production has moved away from mass production in huge factories, as pioneered by Henry Ford, towards specialized markets based on small flexible manufacturing units > **post-'Fordist** *adj*

▷ www.ecn.org/valkohaalarit/english/tyo4.htm
▷ www2.cddc.vt.edu/digitalfordism/fordismtopost.html

post-free *adv, adj* **1** *Brit* with the postage prepaid; postpaid **2** free of postal charge

postglacial (pəʊst'gleɪsɪəl, -ʃəl) *adj* formed or occurring after a glacial period

postgraduate (pəʊst'grædjʊɪt) *n* **1** a student who has obtained a degree from a university, etc, and is pursuing studies for a more advanced qualification **2** (*modifier*) of or relating to such a student or his or her studies ▷ Also: (US and Canad): **graduate**

posthaste ('pəʊst'heɪst) *adv* **1** with great haste ▷ *n* **2** *arch* great haste

post horn *n* a simple valveless natural horn consisting of a long tube of brass or copper

post horse *n* (formerly) a horse kept at an inn or post house for use by postriders or for hire to travellers

post house *n* (formerly) a house or inn where horses were kept for postriders or for hire to travellers

posthumous ('pɒstjʊməs) *adj* **1** happening or continuing after one's death **2** (of a book, etc) published after the author's death **3** (of a child) born after the father's death [c17 from L *postumus* the last, but modified as though from L *post* after + *humus* earth, that is, after the burial] > **'posthumously** *adv*

posthypnotic suggestion (,pəʊsthɪp'nɒtɪk) *n* a suggestion made to the subject while he is in a hypnotic trance, to be acted upon at some time after emerging from the trance

postiche (pɒ'stiːʃ) *adj* **1** (of architectural ornament) inappropriately applied; sham **2** false or artificial; spurious ▷ *n* **3** another term for **hairpiece** (sense 2) **4** anything that is false; sham or pretence [c19 from F, from It. *apposticcio* (n), from LL *appositīcius* (adj); see APPOSITE]

postilion *or* **postillion** (pɒ'stɪljən) *n* a person who rides the near horse of the leaders in order to guide a team of horses drawing a coach [c16 from F *postillon*, from It. *postiglione*, from *posta* POST³]

postimpressionism (,pəʊstɪm'prɛʃə,nɪzəm) *n* a movement in painting in France at the end of the 19th century which rejected the naturalism and momentary effects of impressionism but adapted its use of pure colour to paint subjects with greater subjective emotion > ,**postim'pressionist** *n, adj*

▷ www.artchive.com/ftp_site_reg.htm
▷ www.artcyclopedia.com/history

post-industrial (,pəʊstɪn'dʌstrɪəl) *adj* denoting work or a society that is no longer based on heavy industry

posting ('pəʊstɪŋ) *n* **1** an appointment to a position or post, usually in another town or country **2** *computing* an electronic message sent to a bulletin board, website, etc, and intended for access by every user

postliminy (pəʊst'lɪmɪnɪ) *or* **postliminium** (,pəʊstlɪ'mɪnɪəm) *n, pl* **postliminies** *or* **postliminia** (-ɪə) *international law* the right by which persons and property seized in war are restored to their former status on recovery [c17 from L *post* behind + *limen, liminis* threshold]

postlude ('pəʊstluːd) *n* *music* a final or concluding piece or movement [c19 from POST- + *-lude*, from L *lūdus* game; cf. PRELUDE]

postman ('pəʊstmən) *or* (*fem*) **postwoman** *n, pl* **postmen** *or* **postwomen** a person who carries and delivers mail as a profession

postman's knock *n* a children's party game in which a kiss is exchanged for a pretend letter

postmark ('pəʊst,mɑːk) *n* **1** any mark stamped on mail by postal officials, usually showing the date and place of posting ▷ *vb* **2** (*tr*) to put such a mark on (mail)

postmaster ('pəʊst,mɑːstə) *n* **1** Also: (*fem*) **postmistress** an official in charge of a local post office **2** the person responsible for managing the electronic mail at a site

postmaster general *n, pl* **postmasters general** the executive head of the postal service in certain countries

postmeridian (,pəʊstmə'rɪdɪən) *adj* after noon; in the afternoon or evening [c17 from L *postmerīdiānus* in the afternoon]

post meridiem ('pəʊst mə'rɪdɪəm) the full form of **p.m.** [c17 L: after noon]

post mill *n* a windmill built around a central post on which the whole mill can be turned so that the sails catch the wind

postmillennialism (,pəʊstmɪ'lɛnɪə,lɪzəm) *n* *Christian theol* the doctrine or belief that the Second Coming of Christ will be preceded by the millennium > ,**postmil'lennialist** *n*

postmodernism (pəʊst'mɒdə,nɪzəm) *n* (in the arts, architecture, etc) a style and school of thought that rejects the dogma and practices of any form of modernism; in architecture it contrasts with international modernism and features elements from several periods, esp the Classical, often with ironic use of decoration > **post'modernist** *n, adj*

▷ www.haberarts.com

postmortem (pəʊst'mɔːtəm) *adj* **1** (*prenominal*) occurring after death ▷ *n* **2** analysis or study of a recent event: *a postmortem on a game of chess* **3** See **postmortem examination** [c18 from L, lit.: after death]

postmortem examination *n* dissection and examination of a dead body to determine the cause of death. Also called: **autopsy, necropsy**

Pp

postnatal (pəʊst'neɪt^{ə}l) *adj* of or relating to the period after childbirth

Postnet ('pəʊstnɛt) *n* *S African* an official postal service in South Africa

post-obit (pəʊst'əʊbɪt, -'ɒbɪt) *chiefly law* ▷ *n* **1** a bond given by a borrower, payable after the death of a specified person, esp one given to a moneylender by an expectant heir promising to repay when his interest falls into possession ▷ *adj* **2** taking effect after death [c18 from L *post obitum* after death]

post office *n* a building or room where postage stamps are sold and other postal business is conducted

Post Office *n* a government department or authority in many countries responsible for postal services and often telecommunications

post office box *n* a private numbered place in a post office, in which letters received are kept until called for

postoperative (pəʊst'ɒpərətɪv) *adj* of or occurring in the period following a surgical operation

post-paid *adv, adj* with the postage prepaid

postpone (pəʊst'pəʊn, pə'spəʊn) *vb* **postpones, postponing, postponed** (*tr*) **1** to put off or delay until a future time **2** to put behind in order of importance; defer [c16 from L *postpōnere* to put after] > **post'ponement** *n*

postpositive (pəʊst'pɒzɪtɪv) *adj* **1** (of an adjective or other modifier) placed after the word modified, either immediately after, as in *two men abreast*, or as part of a complement, as in *those men are bad* ▷ *n* **2** a postpositive modifier

postprandial (pəʊst'prændɪəl) *adj* *usually humorous* after a meal

postrider ('pəʊst,raɪdə) *n* (formerly) a person who delivered post on horseback

postscript ('pəʊsˌskrɪpt, 'pəʊst-) *n* **1** a message added at the end of a letter, after the signature **2** any supplement, as to a document or book [C16 from LL *postscribere* to write after]

poststructuralism (pəʊst'strʌktʃərəˌlɪzəm) *n* an approach to literature that, proceeding from the tenets of structuralism, maintains that, as words have no absolute meaning, any text is open to an unlimited range of interpretations > **post'structuralist** *n, adj*

post-traumatic stress disorder *n* a psychological condition, characterized by anxiety, withdrawal, and a proneness to physical illness, that may follow a traumatic experience

postulant ('pɒstjʊlənt) *n* a person who makes a request or application, esp a candidate for admission to a religious order [C18 from L *postulāns* asking, from *postulāre* to ask]

postulate *vb* ('pɒstjʊˌleɪt), **postulates, postulating, postulated** (*tr; may take a clause as object*) **1** to assume to be true or existent; take for granted **2** to ask, demand, or claim **3** to nominate (a person) to a post or office subject to approval by a higher authority ▷ *n* ('pɒstjʊlɪt) **4** something taken as self-evident or assumed as the basis of an argument **5** a prerequisite **6** a fundamental principle **7** *logic, maths* an unproved statement that should be taken for granted: used as an initial premise in a process of reasoning [C16 from L *postulāre* to ask for] > ˌ**postu'lation** *n*

postulator ('pɒstjʊˌleɪtə) *n RC Church* a person who presents a plea for the beatification or canonization of some deceased person

posture ('pɒstʃə) *n* **1** a position or attitude of the limbs or body **2** a characteristic manner of bearing the body: *good posture* **3** the disposition of the parts of a visible object **4** a mental attitude **5** a state or condition **6** a false or affected attitude; pose ▷ *vb* **postures, posturing, postured 7** to assume or cause to assume a bodily attitude **8** (*intr*) to assume an affected posture; pose [C17 via F from It. *postura*, from L *positūra*, from *pōnere* to place] > '**postural** *adj* > '**posturer** *n*

postviral syndrome (ˌpəʊst'vaɪrəl) *n* another name for **chronic fatigue syndrome**. Abbrev: **PVS**

postwar (pəʊst'wɔː) *adj* happening or existing after a war

posy ('pəʊzɪ) *n, pl* **posies 1** a small bunch of flowers **2** *arch* a brief motto or inscription, esp one on a trinket or a ring [C16 var. of POESY]

pot¹ (pɒt) *n* **1** a container, usually round and deep and often having a handle and lid, used for cooking and other domestic purposes **2** the amount that a pot will hold; potful **3** a large mug or tankard **4** *Austral* any of various measures used for serving beer **5** the money or stakes in the pool in gambling games **6** a wicker trap for catching fish, esp crustaceans: *a lobster pot* **7** *billiards, etc* a shot by which a ball is pocketed **8** a chamber pot, esp a small one designed for a baby or toddler **9** (*often pl*) *inf* a large amount (esp of money) **10** *inf* a prize or trophy **11** *chiefly Brit* short for **chimneypot 12** short for **flowerpot, teapot 13** See **potbelly 14 go to pot** to go to ruin ▷ *vb* **pots, potting, potted** (*mainly tr*) **15** to put or preserve (meat, etc) in a pot **16** to plant (a cutting, seedling, etc) in soil in a flowerpot **17** to cause (a baby or toddler) to use or sit on a pot **18** to shoot (game) for food rather than for sport **19** (*also intr*) to shoot casually or without careful aim **20** (*also intr*) to shape clay as a potter **21** *billiards, etc* to pocket (a ball) **22** *inf* to capture or win [LOE *pott*, from Med. L *pottus* (unattested), ?from L *pōtus* a drink]

pot² (pɒt) *n sl* cannabis used as a drug in any form [C20 ? shortened from Mexican Indian *potiguaya*]

potable ('pəʊtəbᵊl) *adj* drinkable [C16 from LL *pōtābilis* drinkable, from L *pōtāre* to drink] > ˌ**pota'bility** *n*

potae ('pɔtaɪ) *n NZ* a hat [Maori]

potage *French* (pɔtaʒ; *English* pəʊ'tɑːʒ) *n* any thick soup [C16 from OF; see POTTAGE]

potamic (pə'tæmɪk) *adj* of or relating to rivers [C19 from Gk *potamos* river]

potash ('pɒtˌæʃ) *n* **1** another name for **potassium carbonate** or **potassium hydroxide 2** potassium chemically combined in certain compounds: *chloride of potash* [C17 *pot ashes*, translation of obs. Du. *potaschen*; because orig. obtained by evaporating the lye of wood ashes in pots]

potassium (pə'tæsɪəm) *n* a light silvery element of the alkali metal group that is highly reactive and rapidly oxidizes in air. Symbol: K; atomic no.: 19; atomic wt.: 39.098 [C19 NL *potassa* potash] > **po'tassic** *adj*

potassium-argon dating *n* a technique for determining the age of minerals based on the occurrence in natural potassium of a small fixed amount of radioisotope ^{40}K that decays to the stable argon isotope ^{40}Ar with a half-life of 1.28×10^9 years. Measurement of the ratio of these isotopes thus gives the age of the mineral

potassium bromide *n* a white crystalline soluble substance with a bitter saline taste used in making photographic papers and plates and in medicine as a sedative. Formula: KBr

potassium carbonate *n* a white odourless substance used in making glass and soft soap and as an alkaline cleansing agent. Formula: K_2CO_3

potassium chlorate *n* a white crystalline soluble substance used in explosives and as a disinfectant and bleaching agent. Formula: $KClO_3$

potassium cyanide *n* a white poisonous granular soluble solid substance used in photography. Formula: KCN

potassium hydrogen tartrate *n* a white soluble crystalline salt used in baking powders, soldering fluxes, and laxatives. Formula: $KHC_4H_4O_6$. Also called: **cream of tartar**

potassium hydroxide *n* a white deliquescent alkaline solid used in the manufacture of soap, liquid shampoos, and detergents. Formula: KOH

potassium nitrate *n* a colourless or white crystalline compound used in gunpowders, pyrotechnics, fertilizers, and as a preservative for foods (**E 252**). Formula: KNO_3. Also called: **saltpetre, nitre**

potassium permanganate *n* a dark purple poisonous odourless soluble crystalline solid, used as a bleach, disinfectant, and antiseptic. Formula: $KMnO_4$. Systematic name: **potassium manganate(VII)**

potation (pəʊ'teɪʃən) *n* **1** the act of drinking **2** a drink or draught, esp of alcoholic drink [C15 from L *pōtātiō*, from *pōtāre* to drink]

potato (pə'teɪtəʊ) *n, pl* **potatoes 1a** a plant of South America widely cultivated for its edible tubers **1b** the starchy oval tuber of this plant, which has a brown or red skin and is cooked and eaten as a vegetable **2** any of various similar plants, esp the sweet potato [C16 from Sp. *patata* white potato, from Taino *batata* sweet potato]
▷ www.indepthinfo.com/potato
▷ www.potatohelp.com
▷ www.bigspud.com

potato beetle *n* another name for the **Colorado beetle**

potato chip *n* (*usually pl*) **1** another name for **chip** (sense 4) **2** the US, Canad, Austral, and NZ term for **crisp** (sense 10)

potato crisp *n* (*usually pl*) another name for **crisp** (sense 10)

potbelly ('pɒtˌbɛlɪ) *n, pl* **potbellies 1** a protruding or distended belly **2** a person having such a belly > '**potˌbellied** *adj*

potboiler ('pɒtˌbɔɪlə) *n inf* an artistic work of little merit produced quickly to make money

pot-bound *adj* (of a pot plant) having grown to fill all the available root space and therefore lacking room for continued growth

potboy ('pɒt,bɔɪ) *or* **potman** ('pɒtmən) *n, pl* **potboys** *or* **potmen** *chiefly Brit* (esp formerly) a man employed at a public house to serve beer, etc

potch (pɒtʃ) *n chiefly Austral, sl* inferior quality opal [c20 from ?]

poteen (pɒ'ti:n) *or* **poitín** (pɒ'tʃi:n) *n* (in Ireland) illicit spirit, often distilled from potatoes [c19 from Irish *poitín* little pot, from *pota* pot]

Potemkin *or* **Potyomkin** (pɒ'tɛmkɪn; *Russian* pa'tjɔmkin) *n* **Grigori Aleksandrovich** (gri'gɔrij alɪk'sandrəvitʃ) 1739–91, Russian soldier and statesman; lover of Catherine II, whose favourite he remained until his death

potent[1] ('pəʊtᵊnt) *adj* **1** possessing great strength; powerful **2** (of arguments, etc) persuasive or forceful **3** influential or authoritative **4** tending to produce violent physical or chemical effects: *a potent poison* **5** (of a male) capable of having sexual intercourse [c15 from L *potēns* able, from *posse* to be able] > '**potency** *or* '**potence** *n* > '**potently** *adv*

potent[2] ('pəʊtᵊnt) *adj heraldry* (of a cross) having flat bars across the ends of the arms [c17 from obs. *potent* a crutch, from L *potentia* power]

potentate ('pəʊtᵊn,teɪt) *n* a ruler or monarch [c14 from LL *potentātus*, from L: rule, from *potens* powerful, from *posse* to be able]

potential (pə'tɛnʃəl) *adj* **1a** possible but not yet actual **1b** (*prenominal*) capable of being or becoming; latent **2** *grammar* (of a verb) expressing possibility, as English *may* and *might* ▷ *n* **3** latent but unrealized ability: *Jones has great potential as a sales manager* **4** *grammar* a potential verb or verb form **5** short for **electric potential** [c14 from OF *potencial*, from LL *potentiālis*, from L *potentia* power] > **po'tentially** *adv*

potential difference *n* the difference in electric potential between two points in an electric field; the work that has to be done in transferring unit positive charge from one point to the other, measured in volts. Abbrev: **pd**

potential energy *n* the energy of a body or system as a result of its position in an electric, magnetic, or gravitational field. Abbrev: **PE**

potentiality (pə,tɛnʃɪ'ælɪtɪ) *n, pl* **potentialities** **1** latent or inherent capacity for growth, fulfilment, etc **2** a person or thing that possesses this

potentiate (pə'tɛnʃɪ,eɪt) *vb* **potentiates, potentiating, potentiated** (*tr*) **1** to cause to be potent **2** *med* to increase (the individual action or effectiveness) of two drugs by administering them in combination

potentilla (,pəʊtᵊn'tɪlə) *n* any rosaceous plant or shrub of the N temperate genus *Potentilla*, having five-petalled flowers [c16 NL, from Med. L: garden valerian, from L *potēns* powerful]

potentiometer (pə,tɛnʃɪ'ɒmɪtə) *n* **1** an instrument for determining a potential difference of electromotive force **2** a device used in electronic circuits, esp as a volume control. Sometimes shortened to **pot** > **po,tenti'ometry** *n*

potful ('pɒtfʊl) *n* the amount held by a pot

pother ('pɒðə) *n* **1** a commotion, fuss, or disturbance **2** a choking cloud of smoke, dust, etc ▷ *vb* **3** to make or be troubled or upset [c16 from ?]

potherb ('pɒt,hɜ:b) *n* any plant having leaves, flowers, stems, etc, that are used in cooking

pothole ('pɒt,həʊl) *n* **1** *geog* **1a** a deep hole in limestone areas resulting from action by running water **1b** a circular hole in the bed of a river produced by abrasion **2** a deep hole produced in a road surface by wear or weathering

potholing ('pɒt,həʊlɪŋ) *n Brit* a sport in which participants explore underground caves > '**pot,holer** *n* ▷ www.caveinfo.org.uk

pothook ('pɒt,hʊk) *n* **1** a curved or S-shaped hook used for suspending a pot over a fire **2** a long hook used for lifting hot pots, lids, etc **3** an S-shaped mark, often made by children when learning to write

pothouse ('pɒt,haʊs) *n Brit* (formerly) a small tavern or pub

pothunter ('pɒt,hʌntə) *n* **1** a person who hunts for profit without regard to the rules of sport **2** *inf* a person who enters competitions for the sole purpose of winning prizes

potion ('pəʊʃən) *n* a drink, esp of medicine, poison, or some supposedly magic beverage [c13 via OF from L *pōtiō* a drink, esp a poisonous one, from *pōtāre* to drink]

Potiphar ('pɒtɪfə) *n Old Testament* one of Pharaoh's officers, who bought Joseph as a slave (Genesis 37:36)

potlatch ('pɒt,lætʃ) *n anthropol* a competitive ceremonial activity among certain North American Indians, involving a lavish distribution of gifts to emphasize the wealth and status of the chief or clan [c19 of Amerind origin, from *patshatl* a present]

pot luck *n inf* **1** whatever food happens to be available without special preparation **2** whatever is available (esp in **take pot luck**)

pot marigold *n* a Central European and Mediterranean plant grown for its rayed orange-and-yellow showy flowers

Potomac (pə'təʊmək) *n* a river in the E central US, rising in the Appalachian Mountains of West Virginia: flows northeast, then generally southeast to Chesapeake Bay. Length (from the confluence of headstreams): 462 km (287 miles)

potometer (pə'tɒmɪtə) *n* an apparatus that measures the rate of water uptake by a plant or plant part [from L *pōtāre* to drink + -METER]

potoroo (,pɒtə'ru:) *n* another name for **kangaroo rat** [from Abor.]

Potosí (*Spanish* poto'si) *n* a city in S Bolivia, at an altitude of 4066 m (13 340 ft): one of the highest cities in the world; developed with the discovery of local silver in 1545; tin mining; university (1571). Pop: 147 351 (2000 est)

potpourri (,pəʊ'pʊərɪ) *n, pl* **potpourris** **1** a collection of mixed flower petals dried and preserved in a pot to scent the air **2** a collection of unrelated items; miscellany **3** a medley of popular tunes [c18 from F, lit.: rotten pot, translation of Sp. *olla podrida* miscellany]

pot roast *n* meat cooked slowly in a covered pot with very little water

Potsdam ('pɒtsdæm; *German* 'pɔtsdam) *n* a city in Germany, the capital of Brandenburg on the Havel River: residence of Prussian kings and German emperors and scene of the **Potsdam Conference** of 1945, at which the main Allied powers agreed on a plan to occupy Germany at the end of the Second World War. Pop: 129 500 (1999 est)

potsherd ('pɒt,ʃɜ:d) *or* **potshard** ('pɒt,ʃɑ:d) *n* a broken fragment of pottery [c14 from POT[1] + *schoord* piece of broken crockery; see SHARD]

pot shot *n* **1** a chance shot taken casually, hastily, or without careful aim **2** a shot fired to kill game in disregard of the rules of sport **3** a shot fired at quarry within easy range

pot still *n* a type of still in which heat is applied directly to the pot in which the wash is contained: used in distilling whisky

pottage ('pɒtɪdʒ) *n* a thick soup [c13 from OF *potage* contents of a pot, from *pot* POT[1]]

potted ('pɒtɪd) *adj* **1** placed or grown in a pot **2** cooked or preserved in a pot: *potted shrimps* **3** *inf* abridged: *a potted version of a novel*

potter[1] ('pɒtə) *n* a person who makes pottery

potter[2] ('pɒtə) *or esp US & Canad* **putter** *vb* **1** (*intr*; often

Pp

foll by *about* or *around*) to busy oneself in a desultory though agreeable manner **2** (*intr; often foll by along* or *about*) to move with little energy or direction: *to potter about town* **3** (*tr;* usually foll by *away*) to waste (time): *to potter the day away* [C16 (in the sense: to poke repeatedly): from OE *potian* to thrust] > **'potterer** *or esp US* **'putterer** *n*

Potter ('pɒtə) *n* **1** (**Helen**) **Beatrix** 1866–1943, British author and illustrator of children's animal stories, such as *The Tale of Peter Rabbit* (1902) **2 Dennis** (**Christopher George**) 1935–94, British dramatist. His TV plays include *Pennies from Heaven* (1978), *The Singing Detective* (1986), and *Blackeyes* (1989) **3 Paulus** 1625–54, Dutch painter, esp of animals **4 Stephen** 1900–70, British humorist and critic. Among his best-known works are *Gamesmanship* (1947) and *One-Upmanship* (1952), on the art of achieving superiority over others

Potteries ('pɒtərɪz) *pl n* (*sometimes functioning as singular*) **the** a region of W central England, in Staffordshire, in which the china and earthenware industries are concentrated

potter's field *n* **1** *New Testament* the land bought by the Sanhedrin with the money paid for the betrayal of Jesus, to be used as a burial place for strangers (Acts 1:19; Matthew 27:7) **2** *US* a cemetery where the poor or unidentified are buried at the public's expense

potter's wheel *n* a device with a horizontal rotating disc, on which clay is shaped by hand

pottery ('pɒtərɪ) *n, pl* **potteries 1** articles made from earthenware and baked in a kiln **2** a place where such articles are made **3** the craft or business of making such articles [C15 from OF *poterie*, from *potier* potter, from *pot* POT[1]]

▷ www.potterymaking.org/pmionline.html
▷ www.ceramicstoday.com
▷ www.studiopottery.com

potting shed *n* a building in which plants are set in flowerpots and in which empty pots, potting compost, etc, are stored

pottle ('pɒtᵊl) *n* **1** *arch* a liquid measure equal to half a gallon **2** *NZ* a plastic or cardboard container for foods such as yoghurt, fruit salad, or cottage cheese [C14 *potel*, from OF: a small POT[1]]

potto ('pɒtəʊ) *n, pl* **pottos** a short-tailed prosimian primate having vertebral spines protruding through the skin in the neck region. Also called: **kinkajou** [C18 of W African origin]

Pott's disease (pɒts) *n* a disease of the spine, characterized by weakening and gradual disintegration of the vertebrae [C18 after Percivall *Pott* (1714–88), Brit surgeon]

Pott's fracture *n* a fracture of the lower part of the fibula, usually with the dislocation of the ankle [C18 see POTT'S DISEASE]

potty[1] ('pɒtɪ) *adj* **pottier, pottiest** *Brit inf* **1** foolish or slightly crazy **2** trivial or insignificant **3** (foll by *about*) very keen (on) [C19 ?from POT[1]] > **'pottiness** *n*

potty[2] ('pɒtɪ) *n, pl* **potties** a child's word for **chamber pot**

Potyomkin (*Russian* pa'tjɔmkin) *n* a variant spelling of **Potemkin**

pouch (paʊtʃ) *n* **1** a small flexible baglike container: *a tobacco pouch* **2** a saclike structure in any of various animals, such as the cheek fold in rodents **3** *anat* any sac, pocket, or pouchlike cavity **4** a Scot word for **pocket** ▷ *vb* **5** (*tr*) to place in or as if in a pouch **6** to arrange or become arranged in a pouchlike form **7** (*tr*) (of certain birds and fishes) to swallow [C14 from OF *pouche*, from OF *poche* bag] > **'pouchy** *adj*

pouf *or* **pouffe** (pu:f) *n* **1** a large solid cushion used as a seat **2a** a woman's hairstyle, fashionable esp in the 18th century, in which the hair is piled up in rolled puffs **2b** a pad set in the hair to make such puffs **3** (*also* pʊf) *Brit derog sl* less common spellings of **poof** [C19 from F]

poulard *or* **poularde** ('pu:lɑ:d) *n* a hen that has been spayed for fattening ▷ Cf **capon** [C18 from OF *pollarde*, from *polle* hen]

Poulenc (*French* pulɛ̃:k) *n* **Francis** (frɑ̃sis) 1899–1963, French composer; a member of Les Six. His works include the operas *Les Mamelles de Tirésias* (1947) and *Dialogues des Carmélites* (1957), and the ballet *Les Biches* (1924)

poult (pəʊlt) *n* the young of a gallinaceous bird, esp of domestic fowl [C15 var. of *poulet* PULLET]

poulterer ('pəʊltərə) *n Brit* another word for a **poultryman** [C17 from obs. *poulter*, from OF *pouletier*, from *poulet* PULLET]

poultice ('pəʊltɪs) *n med* a local moist and often heated application for the skin used to improve the circulation, treat inflamed areas, etc [C16 from earlier *pultes*, from L *puls* a thick porridge]

poultry ('pəʊltrɪ) *n* domestic fowls collectively [C14 from OF *pouletrie*, from *pouletier* poultry dealer]

poultryman ('pəʊltrɪmən) *or* **poulterer** *n, pl* **poultrymen** *or* **poulterers 1** Also called: **chicken farmer** a person who rears domestic fowls for their eggs or meat **2** a dealer in poultry

pounce[1] (paʊns) *vb* **pounces, pouncing, pounced 1** (*intr;* often foll by *on* or *upon*) to spring or swoop, as in capturing prey ▷ *n* **2** the act of pouncing; a spring or swoop **3** the claw of a bird of prey [C17 apparently from ME *punson* pointed tool] > **'pouncer** *n*

pounce[2] (paʊns) *n* **1** a very fine resinous powder, esp of cuttlefish bone, formerly used to dry ink **2** a fine powder, esp of charcoal, that is tapped through perforations in paper in order to transfer the design to another surface ▷ *vb* **pounces, pouncing, pounced** (*tr*) **3** to dust (paper) with pounce **4** to transfer (a design) by means of pounce [C18 from OF *ponce*, from L *pūmex* pumice]

pouncet box ('paʊnsɪt) *n* a box with a perforated top used for perfume [C16 *pouncet*, ? alteration of *pounced* perforated]

pound[1] (paʊnd) *vb* **1** (when *intr*, often foll by *on* or *at*) to strike heavily and often **2** (*tr*) to beat to a pulp; pulverize **3** (*tr;* foll by *out*) to produce, as by typing heavily **4** to walk or move with heavy steps or thuds **5** (*intr*) to throb heavily ▷ *n* **6** the act of pounding [OE *pūnian*] > **'pounder** *n*

pound[2] (paʊnd) *n* **1** an avoirdupois unit of weight that is divided into 16 ounces and is equal to 0.453 592 kilograms. Abbrev: **lb 2** a troy unit of weight divided into 12 ounces equal to 0.373 242 kilograms **3a** the standard monetary unit of the United Kingdom, the Channel Islands, the Isle of Man, and various UK overseas territories, divided into 100 pence. Official name: **pound sterling 3b** (*as modifier*): *a pound coin* **4** the standard monetary unit of various other countries, including Cyprus, Egypt, Israel, and Syria **5** the former standard monetary unit of the Republic of Ireland, replaced by the euro in 2002 **6** Also called: **pound Scots** a former Scottish monetary unit originally worth an English pound but later declining in value to 1 shilling 8 pence [OE *pund*, from L *pondō*]

pound[3] (paʊnd) *n* **1** an enclosure for keeping officially removed vehicles or distrained goods or animals, esp stray dogs **2** a place where people are confined **3** a trap for animals ▷ *vb* **4** (*tr*) to confine in or as if in a pound; impound, imprison, or restrain [C14 from LOE *pund-*, as in *pundfeald* PINFOLD]

Pound (paʊnd) *n* **Ezra** (**Loomis**) 1885–1972, US poet, translator, and critic, living in Europe. Indicted for treason by the US government (1945) for pro-Fascist broadcasts during World War II, he was committed to a mental hospital until 1958. He was a founder of imagism and championed the early work of such writers as T. S. Eliot, Joyce, and Hemingway. His life work, the *Cantos* (1925–70), is an unfinished sequence of poems, which incorporates mythological and historical materials in several languages as well as political, economic, and autobiographical elements

poundage ('paʊndɪdʒ) *n* **1** a charge of so much per pound of weight **2** a charge of so much per pound sterling **3** a weight expressed in pounds

poundal ('paʊndᵊl) *n* the fps unit of force; the force that imparts an acceleration of 1 foot per second per second to a mass of 1 pound. Abbrev: **pdl** [c19 from POUND[2] + QUINTAL]

pound cost averaging *n stock exchange* a method of accumulating capital by investing a fixed sum in a particular security at regular intervals, in order to achieve an average purchase price below the arithmetic average of the market prices on the purchase dates

-pounder ('paʊndə) *n (in combination)* **1** something weighing a specified number of pounds: *a 200-pounder* **2** something worth a specified number of pounds: *a ten-pounder* **3** a gun that discharges a shell weighing a specified number of pounds: *a two-pounder*

pound sterling *n* See **pound**[2] (sense 3)

pour (pɔː) *vb* **1** to flow or cause to flow in a stream **2** *(tr)* to emit in a profuse way **3** *(intr; often foll by down)* Also: **pour with rain** to rain heavily **4** *(intr)* to move together in large numbers; swarm **5** *(intr)* to serve tea, coffee, etc: *shall I pour?* **6 it never rains but it pours** events, esp unfortunate ones, come in rapid succession **7 pour oil on troubled waters** to calm a quarrel, etc ▷ *n* **8** a pouring, downpour, etc [c13 from ?] > '**pourer** *n*

> USAGE The verbs *pour* and *pore* are sometimes confused: *she poured cream over her strudel; she pored* (not *poured*) *over the manuscript*

pourboire *French* (purbwar) *n* a tip; gratuity [lit.: for drinking]

poussin *French* (pusɛ̃) *n* a young chicken reared for eating

Poussin (*French* pusɛ̃) *n* **Nicolas** (nikɔla) 1594–1665, French painter, regarded as a leader of French classical painting. He is best known for the austere historical and biblical paintings and landscapes of his later years

pout[1] (paʊt) *vb* **1** to thrust out (the lips), as when sullen or (of the lips) to be thrust out **2** *(intr)* to swell out; protrude **3** *(tr)* to utter with a pout ▷ *n* **4** Also: **the pouts** a fit of sullenness **5** the act or state of pouting [c14 from ?] > '**poutingly** *adv*

pout[2] (paʊt) *n, pl* **pout** *or* **pouts** **1** short for **eelpout** **2** Also called: **horned pout** a N American catfish with barbels round the mouth **3** any of various gadoid food fishes [OE *-pūte*, as in *ǣlepūte* eelpout]

pouter ('paʊtə) *n* **1** a person or thing that pouts **2** a breed of domestic pigeon with a large crop capable of being greatly puffed out

poutine (ˌpuːˈtiːn) *n Canad* a dish of cheese curds, French fried potatoes, and sauce [from F]

poverty ('pɒvətɪ) *n* **1** the condition of being without adequate food, money, etc **2** scarcity: *a poverty of wit* **3** a lack of elements conducive to fertility in soil [c12 from OF *poverté*, from L *paupertās* restricted means, from *pauper* poor]

poverty-stricken *adj* suffering from extreme poverty

poverty trap *n* the situation of being unable to raise one's living standard because one is dependent on state benefits which are reduced or withdrawn if one gains any extra income

pow (paʊ) *interj* an exclamation imitative of a collision, explosion, etc

POW *abbrev for* prisoner of war

powan ('paʊən) *n* a freshwater whitefish occurring in some Scottish lakes [c17 Scot var. of POLLAN]

powder ('paʊdə) *n* **1** a substance in the form of tiny loose particles **2** any of various preparations in this form, such as gunpowder, face powder, or soap powder ▷ *vb* **3** to turn into powder; pulverize **4** *(tr)* to cover or sprinkle with or as if with powder [c13 from OF *poldre*, from L *pulvis* dust] > '**powderer** *n* > '**powdery** *adj*

powder blue *n* a dusty pale blue colour

powder burn *n* a superficial burn of the skin caused by a momentary intense explosion

powder flask *n* a small flask or case formerly used to carry gunpowder

powder horn *n* a powder flask consisting of the hollow horn of an animal

powder keg *n* **1** a small barrel to hold gunpowder **2** a potential source of violence, disaster, etc

powder metallurgy *n* the science and technology of producing solid metal components from metal powder by compaction and sintering

powder monkey *n* (formerly) a boy who carried powder from the magazine to the guns on warships

powder puff *n* a soft pad of fluffy material used for applying cosmetic powder to the skin

powder room *n* a ladies' cloakroom

powdery mildew *n* a plant disease characterized by a white powdery growth on stems and leaves, caused by parasitic fungi

Powell ('paʊəl) *n* **1** ('pəʊəl) **Anthony** (**Dymoke** 'dɪmək) 1905–2000, British novelist, best known for his sequence of novels under the general title *A Dance to the Music of Time* (1951–75) **2 Cecil Frank** 1903–69, British physicist, who was awarded the Nobel prize for physics in 1950 for his discovery of the pi-meson **3 Colin** (**Luther**) ('kəʊlɪn) born 1937, US politician and general; Republican secretary of state from 2001 **4 Earl,** known as *Bud Powell*. 1924–1966, US modern-jazz pianist **5** (**John**) **Enoch** 1912–98, British politician. An outspoken opponent of Commonwealth immigration into Britain and of British membership of the Common Market (now the European Union), in 1974 he resigned from the Conservative Party, returning to Parliament as a United Ulster Unionist Council member (1974–87) **6 Michael** 1905–90, British film writer, producer, and director, best known for his collaboration (1942–57) with Emeric Pressburger. Films include *The Life and Death of Colonel Blimp* (1943), *A Matter of Life and Death* (1946), *The Red Shoes* (1948), and *Peeping Tom* (1960)

power ('paʊə) *n* **1** ability to do something **2** *(often pl)* a specific ability, capacity, or faculty **3** political, financial, social, etc, force or influence **4** control or dominion or a position of control, dominion, or authority **5** a state or other political entity with political, industrial, or military strength **6** a person or group that exercises control, influence, or authority: *he's a power in the state* **7** a prerogative, privilege, or liberty **8** legal authority to act for another **9a** a military force **9b** military potential **10** *maths* **10a** the value of a number or quantity raised to some exponent **10b** another name for **exponent** (sense 4) **11** *physics, engineering* a measure of the rate of doing work expressed as the work done per unit time. It is measured in watts, horsepower, etc **12a** the rate at which electrical energy is fed into or taken from a device or system. It is measured in watts **12b** *(as modifier)*: *a power amplifier* **13** the ability to perform work **14a** mechanical energy as opposed to manual labour **14b** *(as modifier)*: *a power tool* **15** a particular form of energy: *nuclear power* **16a** a measure of the ability of a lens or optical system to magnify an object **16b** another word for **magnification** **17** *inf* a large amount: *a power of good* **18 in one's power** *(often foll by an infinitive)* able or allowed (to) **19 in (someone's) power** under the control of (someone) **20 the powers that be** established authority ▷ *vb* **21** *(tr)* to give or provide power to **22** *(tr)* to fit (a machine) with a motor or engine **23** *inf* to move or cause to move by the exercise of physical power [c13 from Anglo-Norman *poer*, from Vulgar L *potēre* (unattested), from L *posse* to be able]

power amplifier *n electronics* an amplifier that is usually

Pp

the final amplification stage in a device and is designed to give the required power output
power-assisted *adj* (of a mechanism) helped by mechanical or hydraulic power: *power-assisted steering; power-assisted brakes*
powerboat ('paʊə,bəʊt) *n* a boat, esp a fast one, propelled by an inboard or outboard motor
powerboating ('paʊə,bəʊtɪŋ) *n* the sport of driving powerboats in racing competitions
power broker *n* a person with power and influence, esp one who operates behind the scenes
power cut *n* a temporary interruption or reduction in the supply of electrical power
power dive *n* **1** a steep dive by an aircraft with its engines at high power ▷ *vb* **power-dive, power-dives, power-diving, power-dived 2** to cause (an aircraft) to perform a power dive or (of an aircraft) to perform a power dive
power dressing *n* a style of dressing in severely tailored suits, adopted by some women executives to project an image of efficiency
powerful ('paʊəfʊl) *adj* **1** having great power **2** extremely effective or efficient: *a powerful drug* ▷ *adv* **3** *dialect* very: *he ran powerful fast* > '**powerfully** *adv* > '**powerfulness** *n*
powerhouse ('paʊə,haʊs) *n* **1** an electrical generating station or plant **2** *inf* a forceful or powerful person or thing
powerless ('paʊəlɪs) *adj* without power or authority > '**powerlessly** *adv* > '**powerlessness** *n*
power lunch *n* a high-powered business meeting conducted over lunch
power of attorney *n* **1** legal authority to act for another person in certain specified matters **2** the document conferring such authority
power pack *n* a device for converting the current from a supply into direct or alternating current at the voltage required by a particular electrical or electronic device
power plant *n* **1** the complex, including machinery, associated equipment, and the structure housing it, that is used in the generation of power, esp electrical power **2** the equipment supplying power to a particular machine
power point *n* an electrical socket mounted on or recessed into a wall
power-sharing *n* a political arrangement in which opposing groups in a society participate in government
power station *n* an electrical generating station
power steering *n* a form of steering used on vehicles, where the torque applied to the steering wheel is augmented by engine power. Also called: **power-assisted steering**
power structure *n* the structure or distribution of power and authority in a community
power walking *n* walking at a brisk pace while pumping the arms as part of an aerobic exercise routine
power yoga *n* a form of yoga involving aerobic exercises and constant strenuous movement
Powhatan (,paʊhə'tæn, paʊ'hætᵊn) *n* American Indian name *Wahunsonacock*. died 1618, American Indian chief of a confederacy of tribes; father of Pocahontas
powhiri (,pəʊ'fi:rɪ) *n* NZ a Maori ceremony of welcome, esp to a marae [Maori]
powwow ('paʊ,waʊ) *n* **1** a talk, conference, or meeting **2** a magical ceremony of certain North American Indians **3** (among certain North American Indians) a medicine man **4** a meeting of North American Indians ▷ *vb* **5** (*intr*) to hold a powwow [c17 of Amerind origin]
Powys¹ ('paʊɪs) *n* a county in E Wales, formed in 1974 from most of Breconshire, Montgomeryshire, and Radnorshire. Administrative centre: Llandrindod Wells. Pop: 126 344 (2001). Area: 5077 sq km (1960 sq miles)
Powys² ('pəʊɪs) *n* **1** **John Cowper** ('ku:pə) 1872–1963, British novelist, essayist, and poet, who spent much of his life in the US His novels include *Wolf Solent* (1929), *A Glastonbury Romance* (1932), and *Owen Glendower* (1940) **2** his brother, **Llewelyn** 1884–1939, British essayist and journalist **3** his brother, **T(heodore) F(rancis)** 1875–1953, British novelist and short-story writer, noted for such religious fables as *Mr Weston's Good Wine* (1927) and *Unclay* (1931)
pox (pɒks) *n* **1** any disease characterized by the formation of pustules on the skin that often leave pockmarks when healed **2** (usually preceded by *the*) an informal name for **syphilis 3 a pox on** (**someone** *or* **something**) (*interj*) *arch* an expression of intense disgust or aversion [c15 changed from *pocks*, pl. of POCK]
Poyang *or* **P'o-yang** ('pɔ:'jæŋ) *n* a lake in E China, in N Jiangxi province, connected by canal with the Yangtze River: the second largest lake in China. Area (at its greatest): 2780 sq km (1073 sq miles)
Poznań (*Polish* 'pɔznajn) *n* a city in W Poland, on the Warta River: the centre of Polish resistance to German rule (1815–1918, 1939–45). Pop: 578 235 (1999 est). German name: **Posen**
Pozsony ('poʒonj) *n* the Hungarian name for **Bratislava**
pozzuolana (,pɒtswə'lɑ:nə) *or* **pozzolana** (,pɒtsə'lɑ:nə) *n* **1** a type of porous volcanic ash used in making hydraulic cements **2** any of various artificial substitutes for this ash used in cements [c18 from It.: of POZZUOLI]
Pozzuoli (*Italian* pot'tswɔ:li) *n* a port in SW Italy, in Campania on the **Gulf of Pozzuoli** (an inlet of the Bay of Naples): in a region of great volcanic activity; founded in the 6th century BC by the Greeks. Pop: 65 025 (1987 est)
pp *abbrev for:* **1** past participle **2** (in formal correspondence) per pro [L: *per procurationem*: by delegation to] ▷ **3** *music symbol for* pianissimo.

> **USAGE** In formal correspondence, when Brenda Smith is signing on behalf of Peter Jones, she should write *Peter Jones pp* (or *per pro*) *Brenda Smith*, not the other way about

pp *or* **PP** *abbrev for:* **1** parcel post **2** post-paid **3** (in prescriptions) post prandium [L: after a meal] **4** prepaid
PP *abbrev for:* **1** Parish Priest **2** past President
P2P *abbrev for* **peer-to-peer**
pp. *abbrev for* pages
ppd *abbrev for:* **1** post-paid **2** prepaid
PPE *abbrev for* philosophy, politics, and economics: a university course
ppm *chem abbrev for* parts per million
PPP *abbrev for* **1** purchasing power parity: a rate of exchange between two currencies that gives them equal purchasing powers in their own economies **2** private–public partnership: on agreement in which a private company commits skills or capital to a public-sector project for a financial return
ppr *or* **p.pr.** *abbrev for* present participle
PPS *abbrev for:* **1** parliamentary private secretary **2** Also: **pps** post postscriptum [L: after postscript; additional postscript]
PQ *abbrev for:* **1** (in Canada) Parti Québécois **2** Province of Quebec
pr *abbrev for:* **1** (*pl* **prs**) pair **2** paper **3** power
Pr *the chemical symbol for* praseodymium
PR *abbrev for:* **1** proportional representation **2** public relations **3** Puerto Rico
pr. *abbrev for:* **1** price **2** pronoun
practicable ('præktɪkəbᵊl) *adj* **1** capable of being done; feasible **2** usable [c17 from F *praticable*, from *pratiquer* to practise; see PRACTICAL] > ,**practica'bility** *or* '**practicableness** *n* > '**practicably** *adv*

> **USAGE** See at **practical**

practical ('præktɪkᵊl) *adj* **1** of or concerned with experience or actual use; not theoretical **2** of or concerned with ordinary affairs, work, etc **3** adapted or adaptable for use **4** of, involving, or trained by practice **5** being such for all general purposes; virtual ▷ *n* **6** an examination or lesson in a practical subject [c17 from earlier *practic*, from F *pratique*, via LL from Gk *praktikos*, from *prassein* to experience] > ˌ**practiˈcality** *or* ˈ**practicalness** *n*

> USAGE A distinction is usually made between *practical* and *practicable*. *Practical* refers to a person, idea, project, etc, as being more concerned with or relevant to practice than theory: *he is a very practical person; the idea had no practical application. Practicable* refers to a project or idea as being capable of being done or put into effect: *the plan was expensive, yet practicable*

practical joke *n* a prank or trick usually intended to make the victim appear foolish > **practical joker** *n*

practically (ˈpræktɪkəlɪ, -klɪ) *adv* **1** virtually; almost: *it rained practically every day* **2** in actuality rather than in theory: *what can we do practically to help?*

practice (ˈpræktɪs) *n* **1** a usual or customary action: *it was his practice to rise at six* **2** repetition of an activity in order to achieve mastery and fluency: *they had one last practice the day before the show* **3** the condition of having mastery of a skill or activity through repetition (esp in **in practice, out of practice**) **4** the exercise of a profession: *he set up practice as a lawyer* **5** the act of doing something: *he put his plans into practice* **6** the established method of conducting proceedings in a court of law ▷ *vb* **practices, practicing, practiced 7** the US spelling of **practise** [c16 from Med. L *practicāre* to practise, from Gk *praktikē* practical work, from *prattein* to do]

practise *or US* **practice** (ˈpræktɪs) *vb* **practises, practising, practised** *or US* **practices, practicing, practiced 1** to do or cause to do repeatedly in order to gain skill **2** (*tr*) to do (something) habitually or frequently: *they practise ritual murder* **3** to observe or pursue (something): *to practise Christianity* **4** to work at (a profession, etc): *he practises medicine* [c15 see PRACTICE]

practised *or US* **practiced** (ˈpræktɪst) *adj* **1** expert; skilled; proficient **2** acquired or perfected by practice

practitioner (prækˈtɪʃənə) *n* **1** a person who practises a profession or art **2** *Christian Science* a person authorized to practise spiritual healing [c16 from *practician*, from OF, from *pratiquer* to PRACTISE]

Prader-Willi syndrome (ˌprɑːdəˈvɪlɪ) *n* a congenital condition characterized by obsessive eating, obesity, mental retardation, and small genitalia [c20 after Andrea *Prader* (b. 1919) and H. *Willi* (b. 1900), Swiss paediatricians]

Prado (ˈprɑːdəʊ) *n* an art gallery in Madrid housing an important collection of Spanish paintings
▷ www.spanisharts.com/prado/prado.htm
▷ www.softdoc.es/madrid_guide/culture/prado.html

prae- *prefix* an archaic variant of **pre-**

praedial *or* **predial** (ˈpriːdɪəl) *adj* **1** of or relating to land, farming, etc **2** attached to or occupying land [c16 from Med. L *praediālis*, from L *praedium* farm, estate]

praesidium (prɪˈsɪdɪəm) *n* a variant of **presidium**

praetor *or esp US* **pretor** (ˈpriːtə, -tɔː) *n* (in ancient Rome) any of several senior magistrates ranking just below the consuls [c15 from L: one who leads the way, prob. from *praeīre*, from *prae-* before + *īre* to go] > **praeˈtorian** *or* **preˈtorian** *adj, n* > ˈ**praetorship** *or* ˈ**pretorship** *n*

Praetorius (*German* preˈtoːrius) *n* **Michael** (ˈmɪçaeːl) 1571–1621, German composer and musicologist, noted esp for his description of contemporary musical practices and instruments, *Syntagma musicum* (1615–19)

pragmatic (prægˈmætɪk) *adj* **1** advocating behaviour dictated more by practical consequences than by theory **2** *philosophy* of pragmatism **3** involving everyday or practical business **4** of or concerned with the affairs of a state or community **5** *rare* meddlesome; officious. Also (for senses 3, 5): **pragmatical** [c17 from LL *prāgmaticus*, from Gk *prāgmatikos* from *pragma* act, from *prattein* to do] > **pragˌmatiˈcality** *n* > **pragˈmatically** *adv*

pragmatic sanction *n* an edict, decree, or ordinance issued with the force of fundamental law by a sovereign

pragmatism (ˈprægməˌtɪzəm) *n* **1** action or policy dictated by consideration of the practical consequences rather than by theory **2** *philosophy* the doctrine that the content of a concept consists only in its practical applicability > ˈ**pragmatist** *n, adj*

Prague (prɑːg) *n* the capital and largest city of the Czech Republic, on the Vltava River: a rich commercial centre during the Middle Ages; site of Charles University (1348) and a technical university (1707); scene of defenestrations (1419 and 1618) that contributed to the outbreak of the Hussite Wars and the Thirty Years' War respectively. Pop: 1 186 855 (2000 est). Czech name: **Praha**
▷ www.pis.cz

Praha (ˈpraha) *n* the Czech name for **Prague**

prairie (ˈprɛərɪ) *n* (*often pl*) a treeless grassy plain of the central US and S Canada [c18 from F, from OF *praierie*, from L *prātum* meadow]

prairie chicken, fowl, grouse, *or* **hen** *n* either of two mottled brown-and-white grouse of North America

prairie crocus *n Canad* a spring flower of the buttercup family

prairie dog *n* any of several rodents that live in large complex burrows in the prairies of North America. Also called: **prairie marmot**

prairie-dogging *n* (in an open-plan office) the practice of looking over the top of one's partition in order to discover the source of or reason for a commotion [c20 after the actions of a PRAIRIE DOG, which stands on its hind legs to get a better view of something]

prairie oyster *n* a drink consisting of raw unbeaten egg, vinegar or Worcester sauce, salt, and pepper: a supposed cure for a hangover

Pp

Prairie Provinces *pl n* the Canadian provinces of Manitoba, Saskatchewan, and Alberta, which lie in the N Great Plains region of North America: the chief wheat and petroleum producing area of Canada

prairie schooner *n chiefly US* a horse-drawn covered wagon used in the 19th century to cross the prairies of North America

prairie wolf *n* another name for **coyote**

praise (preɪz) *n* **1** the act of expressing commendation, admiration, etc **2** the rendering of homage and gratitude to a deity **3 sing someone's praises** to commend someone highly ▷ *vb* **praises, praising, praised** (*tr*) **4** to express commendation, admiration, etc, for **5** to proclaim the glorious attributes of (a deity) with homage and thanksgiving [c13 from OF *preisier*, from LL *pretiāre* to esteem highly, from L *pretium* prize]

praiseworthy (ˈpreɪzˌwɜːðɪ) *adj* deserving of praise; commendable > ˈ**praiseˌworthily** *adv* > ˈ**praiseˌworthiness** *n*

Prakrit (ˈprɑːkrɪt) *n* any of the vernacular Indic languages as distinguished from Sanskrit: spoken from about 300 BC to the Middle Ages [c18 from Sansk. *prākrta* original] > **Praˈkritic** *adj*

praline (ˈprɑːliːn) *n* **1** a confection of nuts with caramelized sugar **2** Also called: **sugared almond** a sweet consisting of an almond encased in sugar [c18 from F, after César de Choiseul, comte de Plessis-*Praslin* (1598–1675), F field marshal whose chef first concocted it]

pralltriller (ˈprɑːlˌtrɪlə) *n* an ornament used in 18th-century music consisting of an inverted mordent with an added initial upper note [G: bouncing trill]

pram[1] (præm) *n Brit* a cotlike four-wheeled carriage for a baby. US term: **baby carriage** [C19 shortened & altered from PERAMBULATOR]

pram² (prɑːm) *n naut* a light tender with a flat bottom and a bow formed from the ends of the side and bottom planks meeting in a small raised transom [C16 from MDu. *prame*]

prance (prɑːns) *vb* **prances, prancing, pranced 1** (*intr*) to swagger or strut **2** (*intr*) to caper, gambol, or dance about **3** (*intr*) (of a horse) to move with high lively springing steps **4** (*tr*) to cause to prance ▷ *n* **5** the act or an instance of prancing [C14 *prauncen*, from ?] > **'prancer** *n* > **'prancing** *adj*

prandial ('prændɪəl) *adj facetious* of or relating to a meal [C19 from L *prandium* meal, luncheon]

prang (præŋ) *chiefly Brit sl* ▷ *n* **1** an accident or crash in an aircraft, car, etc **2** an aircraft bombing raid ▷ *vb* **3** to crash or damage (an aircraft, car, etc) **4** to damage (a town, etc) by bombing [C20 ? imit.]

prank¹ (præŋk) *n* a mischievous trick or joke [C16 from ?] > **'prankish** *adj* > **'prankster** *n*

prank² (præŋk) *vb* **1** (*tr*) to dress or decorate showily or gaudily **2** (*intr*) to make an ostentatious display [C16 from MDu. *pronken*]

prase (preɪz) *n* a light green translucent variety of chalcedony [C14 from F, from L *prasius* a leek-green stone, from Gk *prasios*, from *prason* a leek]

praseodymium (ˌpreɪzɪəʊ'dɪmɪəm) *n* a malleable ductile silvery-white element of the lanthanide series of metals. Symbol: Pr; atomic no.: 59; atomic wt.: 140.91 [C20 NL, from Gk *prasios* of a leek-green colour + DIDYMIUM]

Pratchett ('prætʃɪt) *n* **Terry** born 1948, British novelist. His best-known work is a series of fantasy novels, *Discworld*, which began with *The Colour of Magic* (1983); *Hogfather* (1996) was the 20th novel in this series

prate (preɪt) *vb* **prates, prating, prated 1** (*intr*) to talk idly and at length; chatter **2** (*tr*) to utter in an idle or empty way ▷ *n* **3** idle or trivial talk; chatter [C15 of Gmc origin] > **'prater** *n* > **'prating** *adj*

pratfall ('præt,fɔːl) *n US & Canad sl* a fall upon one's buttocks [C20 from C16 *prat* buttocks (from ?) + FALL]

pratincole ('prætɪŋ,kəʊl, 'preɪ-) *n* any of various swallow-like shore birds of the Old World, having long pointed wings, short legs, and a short bill [C18 from NL *pratincola* field-dwelling, from L *prātum* meadow + *incola* inhabitant]

Prato (*Italian* 'praːto) *n* a walled city in central Italy, in Tuscany: woollen industry. Pop: 172 473 (2000 est). Official name: **Prato in Toscana** (in tos'kaːna)

prattle ('prætᵊl) *vb* **prattles, prattling, prattled 1** (*intr*) to talk in a foolish or childish way; babble **2** (*tr*) to utter in a foolish or childish way ▷ *n* **3** foolish or childish talk [C16 from MLow G *pratelen* to chatter] > **'prattler** *n* > **'prattling** *adj*

prau (praʊ) *n* a variant of **proa**

prawn (prɔːn) *n* **1** any of various small edible marine decapod crustaceans having a slender flattened body with a long tail and two pairs of pincers **2 come the raw prawn with** *Austral inf* to attempt to deceive [C15 from ?]

praxis ('præksɪs) *n, pl* **praxes** ('præksiːz) *or* **praxises 1** the practice of a field of study, as opposed to the theory **2** a practical exercise **3** accepted practice or custom [C16 via Med. L from Gk: deed, action, from *prassein* to do]

Praxiteles (præk'sɪtɪ,liːz) *n* 4th-century BC Greek sculptor: his works include statues of Hermes at Olympia, which survives, and of Aphrodite at Cnidus

pray (preɪ) *vb* **1** (when *intr*, often foll by *for*; when *tr*, *usually takes a clause as object*) to utter prayers (to God or other object of worship) **2** (when *tr*, *usually takes a clause as object or an infinitive*) to beg or implore: *she prayed to be allowed to go* ▷ *sentence substitute* **3** *arch* I beg you; please: *pray, leave us alone* [C13 from OF *preier*, from L *precārī* to implore, from *prex* an entreaty]

prayer¹ (prɛə) *n* **1** a personal communication or petition addressed to a deity, esp in the form of supplication, adoration, praise, contrition, or thanksgiving **2** a similar personal communication that does not involve adoration, addressed to beings closely associated with a deity, such as saints **3** the practice of praying: *prayer is our solution to human problems* **4** (*often pl*) a form of devotion spent mainly or wholly praying: *morning prayers* **5** (*cap when part of a recognized name*) a form of words used in praying: *the Lord's Prayer* **6** an object or benefit prayed for **7** an earnest request or entreaty [C13 *preiere*, from OF, from Med. L, from L *precārius* obtained by begging, from *prex* prayer] > **'prayerful** *adj*

prayer² ('preɪə) *n* a person who prays

prayer book (prɛə) *n* a book containing the prayers used at church services or recommended for private devotions

prayer rug (prɛə) *n* the small carpet on which a Muslim kneels and prostrates himself or herself while saying prayers. Also called: **prayer mat**

prayer wheel (prɛə) *n Buddhism* (esp in Tibet) a wheel or cylinder inscribed with or containing prayers, each revolution of which is counted as an uttered prayer, so that such prayers can be repeated by turning it

praying mantis *or* **mantid** *n* another name for **mantis**

PRB *abbrev for* Pre-Raphaelite Brotherhood

pre- *prefix* before in time, position, etc: *predate; pre-eminent* [from L *prae* before]

preach (priːtʃ) *vb* **1** to make known (religious truth) or give religious or moral instruction or exhortation in (sermons) **2** to advocate (a virtue, action, etc), esp in a moralizing way: *preaching abstinence* [C13 from OF *prechier*, from Church L *praedicāre*, from L: to proclaim in public; see PREDICATE]

preacher ('priːtʃə) *n* a person who preaches, esp a Protestant clergyman

preachify ('priːtʃɪ,faɪ) *vb* **preachifies, preachifying, preachified** (*intr*) *inf* to preach or moralize in a tedious manner > **,preachifi'cation** *n*

preachment ('priːtʃmənt) *n* **1** the act of preaching **2** a tedious or pompous sermon

preachy ('priːtʃɪ) *adj* **preachier, preachiest** *inf* inclined to or marked by preaching

preacquisition profit (ˌpriːækwɪ'zɪʃən) *n* the retained profit of a company earned before a takeover and therefore not eligible for distribution as a dividend to the shareholders of the acquiring company

preamble (priː'æmbᵊl) *n* **1** a preliminary or introductory statement, esp attached to a statute setting forth its purpose **2** a preliminary event, fact, etc [C14 from OF *préambule*, from LL *praeambulum*, from L *prae-* before + *ambulāre* to walk]

preamplifier (priː'æmplɪ,faɪə) *n* an electronic amplifier used to improve the signal-to-noise ratio of an electronic device. It boosts a low-level signal to an intermediate level before it is transmitted to the main amplifier

prebend ('prɛbənd) *n* **1** the stipend assigned by a cathedral or collegiate church to a canon or member of the chapter **2** the land, tithe, or other source of such a stipend **3** a less common word for **prebendary 4** *Church of England* the office of a prebendary [C15 from OF *prébende*, from Med. L *praebenda* stipend, from L *praebēre* to offer, from *prae* forth + *habēre* to have] > **prebendal** (prɪ'bɛndᵊl) *adj*

prebendary ('prɛbəndərɪ, -drɪ) *n, pl* **prebendaries 1** a canon or member of the chapter of a cathedral or collegiate church who holds a prebend **2** *Church of England* an honorary canon with the title of prebendary

Precambrian *or* **Pre-Cambrian** (priː'kæmbrɪən) *adj* **1** of, denoting, or formed in the earliest geological era, which lasted for about 4 000 000 000 years before the Cambrian period ▷ *n* **2 the** the Precambrian era

precancel (priːˈkænsᵊl) *vb* **precancels, precancelling, precancelled** *or US* **precancels, precanceling, precanceled** (*tr*) to cancel (postage stamps) before placing them on mail

precancerous *adj* (esp of cells) displaying characteristics that may develop into cancer

precarious (prɪˈkɛərɪəs) *adj* **1** liable to failure or catastrophe; insecure; perilous **2** *arch* dependent on another's will [C17 from L *precārius* obtained by begging, from *prex* PRAYER[1]] > **preˈcariously** *adv* > **preˈcariousness** *n*

precast (ˈpriːˌkɑːst) *adj* (esp of concrete when employed as a structural element in building) cast in a particular form before being used

precaution (prɪˈkɔːʃən) *n* **1** an action taken to avoid a dangerous or undesirable event **2** caution practised beforehand; circumspection [C17 from F, from LL *praecautiō*, from L, from *prae* before + *cavēre* to beware] > **preˈcautionary** *adj*

precede (prɪˈsiːd) *vb* **precedes, preceding, preceded 1** to go or be before (someone or something) in time, place, rank, etc **2** (*tr*) to preface or introduce [C14 via OF from L *praecēdere* to go before]

precedence (ˈprɛsɪdəns) *or* **precedency** *n* **1** the act of preceding or the condition of being precedent **2** the ceremonial order or priority to be observed on formal occasions: *the officers are seated according to precedence* **3** a right to preferential treatment: *I take precedence over you*

precedent *n* (ˈprɛsɪdənt) **1** *law* a judicial decision that serves as an authority for deciding a later case **2** an example or instance used to justify later similar occurrences ▷ *adj* (prɪˈsiːdᵊnt, ˈprɛsɪdənt) **3** preceding

precedented (ˈprɛsɪˌdɛntɪd) *adj* (of a decision, etc) supported by having a precedent

precedential (ˌprɛsɪˈdɛnʃəl) *adj* **1** of or serving as a precedent **2** having precedence

preceding (prɪˈsiːdɪŋ) *adj* (*prenominal*) going or coming before; former

precentor (prɪˈsɛntə) *n* **1** a cleric who directs the choral services in a cathedral **2** a person who leads a congregation or choir in the sung parts of church services [C17 from LL *praecentor*, from *prae* before + *canere* to sing] > **precentorial** (ˌpriːsɛnˈtɔːrɪəl) *adj* > **preˈcentorˌship** *n*

precept (ˈpriːsɛpt) *n* **1** a rule or principle for action **2** a guide or rule for morals; maxim **3** a direction, esp for a technical operation **4** *law* **4a** a writ or warrant **4b** (in England) an order to collect money under a rate [C14 from L *praeceptum* injunction, from *praecipere* to admonish, from *prae* before + *capere* to take] > **preˈceptive** *adj*

preceptor (prɪˈsɛptə) *n* *rare* a tutor or instructor > **preceptorial** (ˌpriːsɛpˈtɔːrɪəl) *or* **preˈceptoral** *adj* > **preˈceptress** *fem n*

precession (prɪˈsɛʃən) *n* **1** the act of preceding **2** See **precession of the equinoxes 3** the motion of a spinning body, such as a top, gyroscope, or planet, in which it wobbles so that the axis of rotation sweeps out a cone [C16 from LL *praecessiō*, from L *praecādere* to precede] > **preˈcessional** *adj* > **preˈcessionally** *adv*

precession of the equinoxes *n* the slightly earlier occurrence of the equinoxes each year due to the slow continuous westward shift of the equinoctial points along the ecliptic

precinct (ˈpriːsɪŋkt) *n* **1a** an enclosed area or building marked by a fixed boundary such as a wall **1b** such a boundary **2** an area in a town, often closed to traffic, that is designed or reserved for a particular activity: *a shopping precinct* **3** *US* **3a** a district of a city for administrative or police purposes **3b** a polling district [C15 from Med. L *praecinctum* (something) surrounded, from L *praecingere* to gird around]

precincts (ˈpriːsɪŋkts) *pl n* the surrounding region or area

preciosity (ˌprɛʃɪˈɒsɪtɪ) *n, pl* **preciosities** fastidiousness or affectation

precious (ˈprɛʃəs) *adj* **1** beloved; dear; cherished **2** very costly or valuable **3** very fastidious or affected, as in speech, manners, etc **4** *inf* worthless: *you and your precious ideas!* ▷ *adv* **5** *inf* (intensifier): *there's precious little left* [C13 from OF *precios*, from L *pretiōsus* valuable, from *pretium* price] > **ˈpreciously** *adv* > **ˈpreciousness** *n*

precious metal *n* gold, silver, or platinum

precious stone *n* any of certain rare minerals, such as diamond, ruby, or opal, that are highly valued as gemstones

precipice (ˈprɛsɪpɪs) *n* **1** the steep sheer face of a cliff or crag **2** the cliff or crag itself [C16 from L *praecipitium* steep place, from *praeceps* headlong] > **ˈprecipiced** *adj*

precipitant (prɪˈsɪpɪtənt) *adj* **1** hasty or impulsive; rash **2** rushing or falling rapidly or without heed **3** abrupt or sudden ▷ *n* **4** *chem* a substance that causes a precipitate to form > **preˈcipitance** *or* **preˈcipitancy** *n*

precipitate *vb* (prɪˈsɪpɪˌteɪt), **precipitates, precipitating, precipitated 1** (*tr*) to cause to happen too soon; bring on **2** to throw or fall from or as from a height **3** to cause (moisture) to condense and fall as snow, rain, etc, or (of moisture, rain, etc) to condense and fall thus **4** *chem* to undergo or cause to undergo a process in which a dissolved substance separates from solution as a fine suspension of solid particles ▷ *adj* (prɪˈsɪpɪtɪt) **5** rushing ahead **6** done rashly or with undue haste **7** sudden and brief ▷ *n* (prɪˈsɪpɪtɪt) **8** *chem* a precipitated solid [C16 from L *praecipitāre* to throw down headlong, from *praeceps* steep, from *prae* before + *caput* head] > **preˈcipitable** *adj* > **preˌcipitaˈbility** *n* > **preˈcipitately** *adv* > **preˈcipiˌtator** *n*

precipitation (prɪˌsɪpɪˈteɪʃən) *n* **1** *meteorol* **1a** rain, snow, sleet, dew, etc, formed by condensation of water vapour in the atmosphere **1b** the deposition of these on the earth's surface **2** the formation of a chemical precipitate **3** the act of precipitating or the state of being precipitated **4** rash or undue haste

precipitous (prɪˈsɪpɪtəs) *adj* **1** resembling a precipice **2** very steep **3** hasty or precipitate > **preˈcipitously** *adv* > **preˈcipitousness** *n*

USAGE Some people think the use of *precipitous* to mean 'hasty' is incorrect, and that *precipitate* should be used instead

precis *or* **précis** (ˈpreɪsiː) *n, pl* **precis** *or* **précis** (ˈpreɪsiːz) **1** a summary of a text; abstract ▷ *vb* **2** (*tr*) to make a precis of [C18 from F: PRECISE]

precise (prɪˈsaɪs) *adj* **1** strictly correct in amount or value: *a precise sum* **2** particular: *this precise location* **3** using or operating with total accuracy: *precise instruments* **4** strict in observance of rules, standards, etc: *a precise mind* [C16 from F *précis*, from L *praecīdere* to curtail, from *prae* before + *caedere* to cut] > **preˈciseness** *n*

precisely (prɪˈsaɪslɪ) *adv* **1** in a precise manner ▷ *sentence substitute* **2** exactly: used to confirm a statement by someone else

precision (prɪˈsɪʒən) *n* **1** the quality of being precise; accuracy **2** (*modifier*) characterized by a high degree of exactness: *precision grinding* [C17 from L *praecīsiō* a cutting off; see PRECISE] > **preˈcisionism** *n* > **preˈcisionist** *n*

preclassical (prɪˈklæsɪkᵊl) *adj* (of music, literature, etc) before a period regarded as classical

preclude (prɪˈkluːd) *vb* **precludes, precluding, precluded** (*tr*) **1** to exclude or debar **2** to make impossible, esp beforehand [C17 from L *praeclūdere* to shut up, from *prae* before + *claudere* to close] > **preclusion** (prɪˈkluːʒən) *n* > **preclusive** (prɪˈkluːsɪv) *adj*

precocial (prɪˈkəʊʃəl) *adj* **1** denoting birds whose young, after hatching, are covered with down and capable of leaving the nest within a few days ▷ *n* **2** a precocial bird ▷ Cf **altricial**

precocious (prɪˈkəʊʃəs) *adj* **1** ahead in development, such as the mental development of a child **2** *bot*

Pp

flowering or ripening early [c17 from L *praecox*, from *prae* early + *coquere* to ripen] > **pre'cociously** *adv* > **pre'cociousness** *or* **precocity** (prɪ'kɒsɪtɪ) *n*

precognition (ˌpriːkɒg'nɪʃən) *n psychol* the alleged ability to foresee future events [c17 from LL *praecognitiō* foreknowledge, from *praecognoscere* to foresee] > **precognitive** (priː'kɒgnɪtɪv) *adj*

preconceive (ˌpriːkən'siːv) *vb* **preconceives, preconceiving, preconceived** (*tr*) to form an idea of beforehand

preconception (ˌpriːkən'sɛpʃən) *n* **1** an idea or opinion formed beforehand **2** a bias; prejudice

precondition (ˌpriːkən'dɪʃən) *n* **1** a necessary or required condition; prerequisite ▷ *vb* **2** (*tr*) *psychol* to present successively two stimuli to (an organism) without reinforcement so that they become associated; if a response is then conditioned to the second stimulus on its own, the same response will be evoked by the first stimulus

preconize *or* **preconise** ('priːkəˌnaɪz) *vb* **preconizes, preconizing, preconized** *or* **preconises, preconising, preconised** (*tr*) **1** to announce or commend publicly **2** to summon publicly **3** (of the pope) to approve the appointment of (a nominee) to one of the higher dignities in the Roman Catholic Church [c15 from Med. L *praecōnīzāre* to make an announcement, from L *praecō* herald] > **ˌpreconi'zation** *or* **ˌpreconi'sation** *n*

precursor (prɪ'kɜːsə) *n* **1** a person or thing that precedes and announces someone or something to come **2** a predecessor **3** a chemical substance that gives rise to another more important substance [c16 from L *praecursor* one who runs in front, from *praecurrere*, from *prae* in front + *currere* to run]

precursory (prɪ'kɜːsərɪ) *or* **precursive** *adj* **1** serving as a precursor **2** preliminary

pred. *abbrev for* predicate

predacious *or* **predaceous** (prɪ'deɪʃəs) *adj* (of animals) habitually hunting and killing other animals for food [c18 from L *praeda* plunder] > **pre'daciousness, pre'daceousness,** *or* **predacity** (prɪ'dæsɪtɪ) *n*

predate (priː'deɪt) *vb* **predates, predating, predated** (*tr*) **1** to affix a date to (a document, paper, etc) that is earlier than the actual date **2** to assign a date to (an event, period, etc) that is earlier than the actual or previously assigned date of occurrence **3** to be or occur at an earlier date than; precede in time

predation (prɪ'deɪʃən) *n* a relationship between two species of animal in a community, in which one hunts, kills, and eats the other

predator ('prɛdətə) *n* **1** any carnivorous animal **2** a predatory person or thing

predatory ('prɛdətərɪ) *adj* **1** *zool* another word for **predacious** **2** of or characterized by plundering, robbing, etc [c16 from L *praedātōrius* rapacious, from *praedārī* to pillage, from *praeda* booty] > **'predatorily** *adv* > **'predatoriness** *n*

predecease (ˌpriːdɪ'siːs) *vb* **predeceases, predeceasing, predeceased** to die before (some other person)

predecessor ('priːdɪˌsɛsə) *n* **1** a person who precedes another, as in an office **2** something that precedes something else **3** an ancestor [c14 via OF from LL *praedēcessor*, from *prae* before + *dēcēdere* to go away]

predella (prɪ'dɛlə) *n, pl* **predelle** (prɪ'dɛliː) **1** a painting or a series of small paintings in a long strip forming the lower edge of an altarpiece or the face of an altar step **2** a platform in a church upon which the altar stands [c19 from It.: step, prob. from OHG *bret* board]

predestinarian (ˌpriːdɛstɪ'nɛərɪən) *n* **1** a person who believes in divine predestination ▷ *adj* **2** of or relating to predestination or those who believe in it

predestinate *vb* (priː'dɛstɪˌneɪt), **predestinates, predestinating, predestinated** **1** another word for **predestine** ▷ *adj* (priː'dɛstɪnɪt, -ˌneɪt) **2** predestined

predestination (priːˌdɛstɪ'neɪʃən) *n* **1** *Christian theol* **1a** the act of God foreordaining every event from eternity **1b** the doctrine or belief, esp associated with Calvin, that the final salvation of some of mankind is foreordained from eternity by God **2** the act of predestining or the state of being predestined

predestine (priː'dɛstɪn) *or* **predestinate** *vb* **predestines, predestining, predestined** *or* **predestinates, predestinating, predestinated** (*tr*) **1** to determine beforehand **2** *Christian theol* (of God) to decree from eternity (any event, esp the final salvation of individuals) [c14 from L *praedestināre* to resolve beforehand]

predetermine (ˌpriːdɪ'tɜːmɪn) *vb* **predetermines, predetermining, predetermined** (*tr*) **1** to determine beforehand **2** to influence or bias > **ˌprede'terminable** *adj* > **ˌprede'terminate** *adj* > **ˌpredeˌtermi'nation** *n*

predicable ('prɛdɪkəbᵊl) *adj* **1** capable of being predicated or asserted ▷ *n* **2** a quality that can be predicated **3** *logic, obs* any of the five Aristotelian classes of predicates, namely genus, species, difference, property, and relation [c16 from L *praedicābilis*, from *praedicāre* to assert publicly; see PREDICATE] > **ˌpredica'bility** *n*

predicament *n* **1** (prɪ'dɪkəmənt) a perplexing, embarrassing, or difficult situation **2** ('prɛdɪkəmənt) *logic* a logical category [c14 from LL *praedicāmentum* what is predicated, from *praedicāre* to announce; see PREDICATE]

predicant ('prɛdɪkənt) *adj* **1** of or relating to preaching ▷ *n* **2** a member of a religious order founded for preaching, esp a Dominican [c17 from L *praedicāns* preaching, from *praedicāre* to say publicly; see PREDICATE]

predicate *vb* ('prɛdɪˌkeɪt), **predicates, predicating, predicated** (*mainly tr*) **1** (*also intr; when tr, may take a clause as object*) to declare or affirm **2** to imply or connote **3** (foll by *on* or *upon*) *chiefly US* to base (a proposition, argument, etc) **4** *logic* to assert (a property or condition) of the subject of a proposition ▷ *n* ('prɛdɪkɪt) **5** *grammar* the part of a sentence in which something is asserted or denied of the subject of a sentence **6** *logic* a term, property, or condition that is affirmed or denied concerning the subject of a proposition ▷ *adj* ('prɛdɪkɪt) **7** of or relating to something that has been predicated [c16 from L *praedicāre* to assert publicly, from *prae* in front + *dīcere* to say] > **ˌpredi'cation** *n*

predicate calculus *n* the system of symbolic logic concerned not only with relations between propositions as wholes but also with the representation by symbols of individuals and predicates in propositions. See also **propositional calculus**

predicative (prɪ'dɪkətɪv) *adj grammar* relating to or occurring within the predicate of a sentence: *a predicative adjective* ▷ Cf **attributive** > **pre'dicatively** *adv*

predict (prɪ'dɪkt) *vb* (*tr; may take a clause as object*) to state or make a declaration about in advance; foretell [c17 from L *praedīcere* to mention beforehand] > **pre'dictable** *adj* > **preˌdicta'bility** *n* > **pre'dictably** *adv* > **pre'dictive** *adj* > **pre'dictor** *n*

prediction (prɪ'dɪkʃən) *n* **1** the act of predicting **2** something predicted; a forecast

predigest (ˌpriːdaɪ'dʒɛst, -dɪ-) *vb* (*tr*) to treat (food) artificially to aid subsequent digestion in the body > **ˌpredi'gestion** *n*

predikant (ˌprɛdɪ'kænt) *n* a minister in the Dutch Reformed Church, esp in South Africa [from Du., from OF *predicant*, from LL, from *praedicāre* to PREACH]

predilection (ˌpriːdɪ'lɛkʃən) *n* a predisposition, preference, or bias [c18 from F *prédilection*, from Med. L *praedīligere* to prefer, from L *prae* before + *dīligere* to love]

predispose (ˌpriːdɪ'spəʊz) *vb* **predisposes, predisposing, predisposed** (*tr*) (often foll by *to* or *towards*) to incline or make (someone) susceptible to something beforehand

> ˌpredisˈposal *n* > ˌpredispoˈsition *n*

prednisolone (prɛdˈnɪsəˌləʊn) *n* a steroid drug derived from prednisone and having the same uses as cortisone [C20 altered from PREDNISONE]

prednisone (ˈprɛdnɪˌsəʊn) *n* a steroid drug derived from cortisone and having the same uses [C20 perhaps from PRE(GNANT) + -D(IE)N(E) + (CORT)ISONE]

predominant (prɪˈdɒmɪnənt) *adj* **1** superior in power, influence, etc, over others **2** prevailing > **preˈdominance** *n* > **preˈdominantly** *adv*

predominate *vb* (prɪˈdɒmɪˌneɪt), **predominates, predominating, predominated** (*intr*) **1** (often foll by *over*) to have power, influence, or control **2** to prevail or preponderate ▷ *adj* (prɪˈdɒmɪnɪt) **3** another word for **predominant** [C16 from Med. L *praedominārī*, from L *prae* before + *dominārī* to bear rule] > **preˈdominately** *adv* > **preˌdomiˈnation** *n*

pre-eclampsia (ˌpriːɪˈklæmpsɪə) *n* a serious condition that can occur late in pregnancy. If not treated it can lead to eclampsia

pre-embryo (priːˈɛmbrɪˌəʊ) *n, pl* **pre-embryos** the structure formed after fertilization of an ovum but before differentiation of embryonic tissue

pre-eminent (prɪˈɛmɪnənt) *adj* extremely eminent or distinguished; outstanding > **pre-ˈeminence** *n* > **pre-ˈeminently** *adv*

pre-empt (prɪˈɛmpt) *vb* **1** (*tr*) to acquire in advance of or to the exclusion of others; appropriate **2** (*tr*) *chiefly US* to occupy (public land) in order to acquire a prior right to purchase **3** (*intr*) *bridge* to make a high opening bid, often on a weak hand, to shut out opposition bidding > **pre-ˈemptor** *n*

pre-emption (prɪˈɛmpʃən) *n* **1** *law* the purchase of or right to purchase property in preference to others **2** *international law* the right of a government to intercept and seize property of the subjects of another state while in transit, esp in time of war [C16 from Med. L *praeemptiō*, from *praeemere* to buy beforehand]

pre-emptive (prɪˈɛmptɪv) *adj* **1** of, involving, or capable of pre-emption **2** *bridge* (of a high bid) made to shut out opposition bidding **3** *mil* designed to reduce or destroy an enemy's attacking strength before it can use it: *a pre-emptive strike*

preen (priːn) *vb* **1** (of birds) to maintain (feathers) in a healthy condition by arrangement, cleaning, and other contact with the bill **2** to dress or array (oneself) carefully; primp **3** (usually foll by *on*) to pride or congratulate (oneself) [C14 *preinen*, prob. from *prunen*, infl. by *prenen* to prick; suggestive of the pricking movement of the bird's beak] > **ˈpreener** *n*

pre-exist (ˌpriːɪɡˈzɪst) *vb* (*intr*) to exist at an earlier time > **ˌpre-exˈistent** *adj* > **ˌpre-exˈistence** *n*

pref. *abbrev for:* **1** preface **2** preference **3** preferred **4** prefix

prefab (ˈpriːˌfæb) *n* a building that is prefabricated, esp a small house

prefabricate (priːˈfæbrɪˌkeɪt) *vb* **prefabricates, prefabricating, prefabricated** (*tr*) to manufacture sections of (a building) so that they can be easily transported to and rapidly assembled on a building site > **preˌfabriˈcation** *n*

preface (ˈprɛfɪs) *n* **1** a statement written as an introduction to a literary or other work, typically explaining its scope, intention, method, etc; foreword **2** anything introductory ▷ *vb* **prefaces, prefacing, prefaced** (*tr*) **3** to furnish with a preface **4** to serve as a preface to [C14 from Med. L *praefātia*, from L *praefātiō* a saying beforehand, from *praefārī* to utter in advance] > **ˈprefacer** *n*

prefatory (ˈprɛfətərɪ, -trɪ) *or* **prefatorial** (ˌprɛfəˈtɔːrɪəl) *adj* of or serving as a preface; introductory [C17 from L *praefārī* to say in advance]

prefect (ˈpriːfɛkt) *n* **1** (in France, Italy, etc) the chief administrative officer in a department **2** (in France, etc) the head of a police force **3** *Brit, Austral, & NZ* a schoolchild appointed to a position of limited power over his or her fellows **4** (in ancient Rome) any of several magistrates or military commanders **5** *RC Church* one of two senior masters in a Jesuit school or college [C14 from L *praefectus* one put in charge, from *praeficere* to place in authority over, from *prae* before + *facere* to do] > **prefectorial** (ˌpriːfɛkˈtɔːrɪəl) *adj*

prefecture (ˈpriːfɛkˌtjʊə) *n* **1** the office, position, or area of authority of a prefect **2** the official residence of a prefect in France, etc

prefer (prɪˈfɜː) *vb* **prefers, preferring, preferred** **1** (when *tr, may take a clause as object or an infinitive*) to like better or value more highly: *I prefer to stand* **2** *law* (esp of the police) to put (charges) before a court, magistrate, etc, for consideration and judgment **3** (*tr; often passive*) to advance in rank over another or others; promote [C14 from L *praeferre* to carry in front, prefer]

> USAGE Normally, *to* is used after *prefer* and *preferable*, not *than*: *I prefer Brahms to Tchaikovsky; a small income is preferable to no income at all; I prefer snowboarding to skiing.* However, *than* or *rather than* should be used to link infinitives: *people who prefer to do rather than to talk*

preferable (ˈprɛfərəbᵊl) *adj* preferred or more desirable > **ˈpreferably** *adv*

> USAGE Since *preferable* already means 'more desirable' it is better when writing not to say something is *more preferable* or *most preferable*. The generally preferred pronunciation of this word in British English is with the stress on the first syllable, though it is occasionally heard with the second syllable stressed, in line with the verb. See also at **prefer**

Pp

preference (ˈprɛfərəns, ˈprɛfrəns) *n* **1** the act of preferring **2** something or someone preferred **3** *international trade* the granting of favour or precedence to particular foreign countries, as by levying differential tariffs

preference shares *pl n Brit & Austral* fixed-interest shares issued by a company and giving their holders a prior right over ordinary shareholders to payment of dividend and to repayment of capital if the company is liquidated. US and Canad name: **preferred stock** ▷ Cf **ordinary shares, preferred ordinary shares**

preferential (ˌprɛfəˈrɛnʃəl) *adj* **1** showing or resulting from preference **2** giving, receiving, or originating from preference in international trade > ˌ**preferˈentially** *adv*

preferment (prɪˈfɜːmənt) *n* **1** the act of promoting to a higher position, office, etc **2** the state of being preferred for promotion or social advancement **3** the act of preferring

preferred ordinary shares *pl n Brit* shares issued by a company that rank between preference shares and ordinary shares in the payment of dividends ▷ Cf **preference shares, ordinary shares**

prefigure (priːˈfɪɡə) *vb* **prefigures, prefiguring, prefigured** (*tr*) **1** to represent or suggest in advance **2** to imagine beforehand > ˌ**prefiguˈration** *n* > **preˈfigurement** *n*

prefix *n* (ˈpriːfɪks) **1** *grammar* an affix that precedes the stem to which it is attached, as for example *un-* in *unhappy* ▷ Cf **suffix** (sense 1) **2** something coming or placed before ▷ *vb* (priːˈfɪks, ˈpriːfɪks) (*tr*) **3** to put or place before **4** *grammar* to add (a morpheme) as a prefix to the beginning of a word > **prefixion** (priːˈfɪkʃən) *n*

prefrontal (priːˈfrʌntᵊl) *adj* in or relating to the foremost part of the frontal lobe of the brain

preglacial (priːˈɡleɪsɪəl, -ʃəl) *adj* formed or occurring

before a glacial period, esp before the Pleistocene epoch
pregnable ('prɛgnəbᵊl) *adj* capable of being assailed or captured [C15 *prenable*, from OF *prendre* to take, from L *prehendere* to catch]
pregnancy ('prɛgnənsɪ) *n, pl* **pregnancies** **1** the state or condition of being pregnant **2** the period from conception to childbirth
pregnant ('prɛgnənt) *adj* **1** carrying a fetus or fetuses within the womb **2** full of meaning or significance **3** inventive or imaginative **4** prolific or fruitful [C16 from L *praegnāns* with child, from *prae* before + *(g)nascī* to be born] > **'pregnantly** *adv*
prehensile (prɪ'hɛnsaɪl) *adj* adapted for grasping, esp by wrapping around a support: *a prehensile tail* [C18 from F *préhensile*, from L *prehendere* to grasp] > **prehensility** (ˌpriːhɛn'sɪlɪtɪ) *n*
prehension (prɪ'hɛnʃən) *n* **1** the act of grasping **2** apprehension by the mind
prehistoric (ˌpriːhɪ'stɒrɪk) *or* **prehistorical** *adj* of or relating to man's development before the appearance of the written word > **ˌprehis'torically** *adv* > **pre'history** *n*
pre-ignition (ˌpriːɪg'nɪʃən) *n* ignition of all or part of the explosive charge in an internal-combustion engine before the exact instant necessary for correct operation
prejudge (priː'dʒʌdʒ) *vb* **prejudges, prejudging, prejudged** *(tr)* to judge beforehand, esp without sufficient evidence
prejudice ('prɛdʒʊdɪs) *n* **1** an opinion formed beforehand, esp an unfavourable one based on inadequate facts **2** the act or condition of holding such opinions **3** intolerance of or dislike for people of a specific race, religion, etc **4** disadvantage or injury resulting from prejudice **5** **in** *(or* **to)** **the prejudice of** to the detriment of **6** **without prejudice** *law* without dismissing or detracting from an existing right or claim ▷ *vb* **prejudices, prejudicing, prejudiced** *(tr)* **7** to cause to be prejudiced **8** to disadvantage or injure by prejudice [C13 from OF *préjudice*, from L *praejūdicium*, from *prae* before + *jūdicium* sentence, from *jūdex* a judge]
prejudicial (ˌprɛdʒʊ'dɪʃəl) *adj* causing prejudice; damaging > **ˌpreju'dicially** *adv*
prelacy ('prɛləsɪ) *n, pl* **prelacies** **1** Also called: **prelature** **1a** the office or status of a prelate **1b** prelates collectively **2** *often derog* government of the Church by prelates
prelapsarian (ˌpriːlæp'sɛərɪən) *adj* of or relating to the human state before the Fall: *prelapsarian innocence*
prelate ('prɛlɪt) *n* a Church dignitary of high rank, such as a cardinal, bishop, or abbot [C13 from OF *prélat*, from Church L *praelātus*, from L *praeferre* to hold in special esteem] > **prelatic** (prɪ'lætɪk) *or* **pre'latical** *adj*
preliminaries (prɪ'lɪmɪnərɪz) *pl n* the full word for **prelims**
preliminary (prɪ'lɪmɪnərɪ) *adj* **1** *(usually prenominal)* occurring before or in preparation; introductory ▷ *n, pl* **preliminaries** **2** a preliminary event or occurrence **3** an eliminating contest held before the main competition [C17 from NL *praelīmināris*, from L *prae* before + *līmen* threshold] > **pre'liminarily** *adv*
prelims ('priːlɪmz, prɪ'lɪmz) *pl n* **1** Also called: **front matter** the pages of a book, such as the title page and contents, before the main text **2** the first public examinations taken for the bachelor's degree in some universities **3** (in Scotland) the school examinations taken before public examinations [C19 a contraction of PRELIMINARIES]
preloved ('priːˌlʌvd) *adj Austral inf* previously owned or used; second-hand
prelude ('prɛljuːd) *n* **1a** a piece of music that precedes a fugue, or forms the first movement of a suite, or an introduction to an act in an opera, etc **1b** (esp for piano) a self-contained piece of music **2** an introduction or preceding event, occurrence, etc ▷ *vb* **preludes, preluding, preluded** **3** to serve as a prelude to (something) **4** *(tr)* to introduce by a prelude [C16 from Med. L *praelūdium*, from *prae* before + L *lūdere* to play] > **preludial** (prɪ'ljuːdɪəl) *adj*
premarital (priː'mærɪtᵊl) *adj* (esp of sexual relations) occurring before marriage
premature (ˌprɛmə'tjʊə, 'prɛməˌtjʊə) *adj* **1** occurring or existing before the normal or expected time **2** impulsive or hasty: *a premature judgment* **3** (of an infant) born before the end of the full period of gestation [C16 from L *praemātūrus* very early, from *prae* in advance + *mātūrus* ripe] > **ˌprema'turely** *adv*
premedical (priː'mɛdɪkᵊl) *adj* **1** of or relating to a course of study prerequisite for entering medical school **2** of or relating to a person engaged in such a course of study
premedication (ˌpriːmɛdɪ'keɪʃən) *n surgery* any drugs administered to sedate and otherwise prepare a patient for general anaesthesia
premeditate (prɪ'mɛdɪˌteɪt) *vb* **premeditates, premeditating, premeditated** to plan or consider (something, such as a violent crime) beforehand > **pre'mediˌtator** *n*
premeditation (prɪˌmɛdɪ'teɪʃən) *n* **1** *law* prior resolve to do some act or to commit a crime **2** the act of premeditating
premenstrual syndrome *or* **tension** *n* symptoms, esp nervous tension, that may be experienced because of hormonal changes in the days before a menstrual period starts. Abbrevs: **PMS, PMT**
premier ('prɛmjə) *n* **1** another name for **prime minister** **2** any of the heads of government of the Canadian provinces and the Australian states **3** *Austral* a team that wins a premiership ▷ *adj (prenominal)* **4** first in importance, rank, etc **5** first in occurrence; earliest [C15 from OF: first, from L *prīmārius* principal, from *prīmus* first]
premiere ('prɛmɪˌɛə, 'prɛmɪə) *n* **1** the first public performance of a film, play, opera, etc **2** the leading lady in a theatre company ▷ *vb* **premieres, premiering, premiered** **3** *(tr)* to give a premiere of: *the show will be premiered on Broadway* [C19 from F, fem of *premier* first]
premiership ('prɛmjəʃɪp) *n* **1** the office of premier **2a** a championship competition held among a number of sporting clubs **2b** a victory in such a championship
premillennialism (ˌpriːmɪ'lɛnɪəˌlɪzəm) *n* the doctrine or belief that the millennium will be preceded by the Second Coming of Christ > **ˌpremil'lennialist** *n* > **ˌpremille'narian** *n, adj*
Preminger ('prɛmɪndʒə) *n* **Otto (Ludwig)** 1906–86, US film director, born in Austria. His films include *Carmen Jones* (1954) and *Anatomy of a Murder* (1959)
premise *n* ('prɛmɪs) Also **premiss** **1** *logic* a statement that is assumed to be true for the purpose of an argument from which a conclusion is drawn ▷ *vb* (prɪ'maɪz, 'prɛmɪs), **premises, premising, premised** **2** (when *tr, may take a clause as object*) to state or assume (a proposition) as a premise in an argument, etc [C14 from OF *prémisse*, from Med. L *praemissa* sent on before, from L *praemittere* to dispatch in advance]
premises ('prɛmɪsɪz) *pl n* **1** a piece of land together with its buildings, esp considered as a place of business **2** *law* (in a deed, etc) the matters referred to previously; the aforesaid
premium ('priːmɪəm) *n* **1** an amount paid in addition to a standard rate, price, wage, etc; bonus **2** the amount paid or payable, usually in regular instalments, for an insurance policy **3** the amount above nominal or par value at which something sells **4** an offer of something free or at a reduced price as an inducement to buy a commodity or service **5** a prize given to the winner of a competition **6** *US* an amount sometimes charged for a loan of money in addition to the interest **7** great value or regard: *to put a premium on someone's services* **8** **at a**

premium **8a** in great demand, usually because of scarcity **8b** above par [c17 from L *praemium* prize]

Premium Savings Bonds *pl n* (in Britain) bonds issued by the Treasury since 1956 for purchase by the public. No interest is paid but there is a monthly draw for cash prizes of various sums. Also called: **premium bonds**

premolar (pri:ˈməʊlə) *adj* **1** situated before a molar tooth ▷ *n* **2** any one of eight bicuspid teeth in the human adult, two on each side of both jaws between the first molar and the canine

premonition (ˌprɛməˈnɪʃən) *n* **1** an intuition of a future, usually unwelcome, occurrence; foreboding **2** an early warning of a future event [c16 from LL *praemonitiō*, from L *praemonēre* to admonish beforehand, from *prae* before + *monēre* to warn] > **premonitory** (prɪˈmɒnɪtərɪ, -trɪ) *adj*

Premonstratensian (ˌpri:mɒnstrəˈtɛnsɪən) *adj* **1** of or denoting an order of regular canons founded in 1119 at Prémontré, in France ▷ *n* **2** a member of this order

prenatal (pri:ˈneɪtᵊl) *adj* **1** occurring or present before birth; during pregnancy ▷ *n* **2** *inf* a prenatal examination ▷ Also: **antenatal**

prenominal (pri:ˈnɒmɪnᵊl) *adj* placed before a noun, esp (of an adjective or sense of an adjective) used only before a noun

prentice (ˈprɛntɪs) *n* an archaic word for **apprentice**

prenup (ˈpri:ˌnʌp) *n inf* a prenuptial agreement

prenuptial agreement *n* a contract made between a man and woman before they marry, agreeing on the distribution of their assets in the event of divorce

preoccupation (pri:ˌɒkjʊˈpeɪʃən) *n* **1** the state of being preoccupied, esp mentally **2** something that preoccupies the mind

preoccupied (pri:ˈɒkjʊˌpaɪd) *adj* **1** engrossed or absorbed in something, esp one's own thoughts **2** already occupied or used

preoccupy (pri:ˈɒkjʊˌpaɪ) *vb* **preoccupies, preoccupying, preoccupied** (*tr*) **1** to engross the thoughts or mind of **2** to occupy before or in advance of another [c16 from L *praeoccupāre* to capture in advance]

preordain (ˌpri:ɔ:ˈdeɪn) *vb* (*tr*) to ordain, decree, or appoint beforehand

prep (prɛp) *n inf* **1** short for **preparation** (sense 5) or (chiefly US) **preparatory school** ▷ *vb* **preps, prepping, prepped** **2** (*tr*) to prepare (a patient) for a medical operation or procedure

prep. *abbrev for:* **1** preparation **2** preparatory **3** preposition

preparation (ˌprɛpəˈreɪʃən) *n* **1** the act or process of preparing **2** the state of being prepared; readiness **3** (*often pl*) a measure done in order to prepare for something; provision: *to make preparations for something* **4** something that is prepared, esp a medicinal formulation **5** (esp in a boarding school) **5a** homework **5b** the period reserved for this. Usually shortened to **prep** **6** *music* **6a** the anticipation of a dissonance so that the note producing it in one chord is first heard in the preceding chord as a consonance **6b** a note so employed

preparative (prɪˈpærətɪv) *adj* **1** preparatory ▷ *n* **2** something that prepares > **preˈparatively** *adv*

preparatory (prɪˈpærətərɪ, -trɪ) *adj* **1** serving to prepare **2** introductory **3** occupied in preparation **4 preparatory to** before: *a drink preparatory to eating* > **preˈparatorily** *adv*

preparatory school *n* **1** (in Britain) a private school, usually single-sex and for children between the ages of 6 and 13, generally preparing pupils for public school **2** (in the US) a private secondary school preparing pupils for college ▷ Often shortened to **prep school**

prepare (prɪˈpɛə) *vb* **prepares, preparing, prepared** **1** to make ready or suitable in advance for some use, event, etc: *to prepare a meal; to prepare to go* **2** to put together using parts or ingredients; construct **3** (*tr*) to equip or outfit, as for an expedition **4** (*tr*) *music* to soften the impact of (a dissonant note) by the use of preparation **5 be prepared** (*foll by an infinitive*) to be willing and able: *I'm not prepared to reveal these figures* [c15 from L *praeparāre*, from *prae* before + *parāre* to make ready] > **preˈparer** *n*

preparedness (prɪˈpɛərɪdnɪs) *n* the state of being prepared, esp militarily ready for war

prepay (pri:ˈpeɪ) *vb* **prepays, prepaying, prepaid** (*tr*) to pay for in advance > **preˈpayable** *adj*

prepense (prɪˈpɛns) *adj* (*postpositive*) (usually in legal contexts) premeditated (esp in **malice prepense**) [c18 from Anglo-Norman *purpensé*, from OF *purpenser* to consider in advance, from L *pēnsāre* to consider]

preponderance (prɪˈpɒndərəns) *n* the quality of being greater in number, weight, influence, etc: *the preponderance of right-handed people*

preponderant (prɪˈpɒndərənt) *adj* greater in weight, force, influence, etc > **preˈponderantly** *adv*

preponderate (prɪˈpɒndəˌreɪt) *vb* **preponderates, preponderating, preponderated** (*intr*) **1** (often foll by *over*) to be more powerful, important, numerous, etc (than) **2** to be of greater weight than something else [c17 from LL *praeponderāre* to be of greater weight, from *pondus* weight] > **preˌponderˈation** *n*

preposition (ˌprɛpəˈzɪʃən) *n* a word or group of words used before a noun or pronoun to relate it grammatically or semantically to some other constituent of a sentence [c14 from L *praepositiō* a putting before, from *pōnere* to place] > ˌ**prepoˈsitional** *adj* > ˌ**prepoˈsitionally** *adv*

> USAGE The practice of ending a sentence with a preposition (*Venice is a place I should like to go to*) was formerly regarded as incorrect, but is now acceptable and is the preferred form in many contexts

prepossess (ˌpri:pəˈzɛs) *vb* (*tr*) **1** to preoccupy or engross mentally **2** to influence in advance, esp to make a favourable impression on beforehand > ˌ**preposˈsession** *n*

prepossessing (ˌpri:pəˈzɛsɪŋ) *adj* creating a favourable impression; attractive

preposterous (prɪˈpɒstərəs) *adj* contrary to nature, reason, or sense; absurd; ridiculous [c16 from L *praeposterus* reversed, from *prae* in front + *posterus* following] > **preˈposterously** *adv* > **preˈposterousness** *n*

prepotency (prɪˈpəʊtᵊnsɪ) *n* **1** the quality of possessing greater power or influence **2** *genetics* the ability of one parent to transmit more characteristics to its offspring than the other parent **3** *bot* the ability of pollen from one source to bring about fertilization more readily than that from other sources > **preˈpotent** *adj*

preppy (ˈprɛpɪ) *inf* ▷ *adj* **1** of or denoting a style of neat, understated, and often expensive clothes; young but classic ▷ *n, pl* **preppies** **2** a person exhibiting such style [c20 orig. US, from *preppy* a person who attends a PREPARATORY SCHOOL]

prep school *n inf* See **preparatory school**

prepuce (ˈpri:pju:s) *n* **1** the retractable fold of skin covering the tip of the penis. Nontechnical name: **foreskin** **2** a similar fold of skin covering the tip of the clitoris [c14 from L *praepūtium*]

prequel (ˈpri:kwəl) *n* a novel or film dealing with events that happened before events in an earlier novel or film, usually made to exploit the success of the earlier work [c20 from PRE- + (*se*)*quel*]

Pre-Raphaelite (ˌpri:ˈræfəlaɪt) *n* **1** a member of the **Pre-Raphaelite Brotherhood,** an association of painters and writers founded in 1848 to revive the fidelity to nature and the vivid realistic colour considered typical of Italian painting before Raphael ▷ *adj* **2** of, in the manner of, or relating to Pre-Raphaelite painting and painters > ˌ**Pre-ˈRaphaelitˌism** *n*
▷ www.artchive.com/ftp_site_reg.htm

prerequisite (pri:ˈrɛkwɪzɪt) *adj* **1** required as a prior

Pp

condition ▷ *n* **2** something required as a prior condition

prerogative (prɪˈrɒɡətɪv) *n* **1** an exclusive privilege or right exercised by a person or group of people holding a particular office or hereditary rank **2** any privilege or right **3** a power, privilege, or immunity restricted to a sovereign or sovereign government ▷ *adj* **4** having or able to exercise a prerogative [C14 from L *praerogātīva* privilege, earlier: group with the right to vote first, from *prae* before + *rogāre* to ask]

Pres. *abbrev for* President

presage *n* (ˈprɛsɪdʒ) **1** an intimation or warning of something about to happen; portent; omen **2** a sense of what is about to happen; foreboding ▷ *vb* (ˈprɛsɪdʒ, prɪˈseɪdʒ) **presages, presaging, presaged** (*tr*) **3** to have a presentiment of **4** to give a forewarning of; portend [C14 from L *praesāgium*, from *praesāgīre* to perceive beforehand] > **preˈsageful** *adj* > **preˈsager** *n*

presale (ˈpriːˌseɪl) *n* the practice of arranging the sale of a product before it is available > **preˈsell** *vb* (*tr*)

presbyopia (ˌprɛzbɪˈəʊpɪə) *n* a progressively diminishing ability of the eye to focus, noticeable from middle to old age, caused by loss of elasticity of the crystalline lens [C18 NL, from Gk *presbus* old man + *ōps* eye] > **presbyopic** (ˌprɛzbɪˈɒpɪk) *adj*

presbyter (ˈprɛzbɪtə) *n* **1a** an elder of a congregation in the early Christian Church **1b** (in some Churches having episcopal politics) an official who is subordinate to a bishop and has administrative and sacerdotal functions **2** (in some hierarchical Churches) another name for **priest** **3** (in the Presbyterian Church) an elder [C16 from LL, from Gk *presbuteros* an older man, from *presbus* old man] > ˌ**presbyˈterial** *adj*

presbyterian (ˌprɛzbɪˈtɪərɪən) *adj* **1** of or designating Church government by presbyters or lay elders ▷ *n* **2** an upholder of this type of Church government > ˌ**presbyˈterianism** *n*

Presbyterian (ˌprɛzbɪˈtɪərɪən) *adj* **1** of or relating to any of various Protestant Churches governed by presbyters or lay elders and adhering to various modified forms of Calvinism ▷ *n* **2** a member of a Presbyterian Church > ˌ**Presbyˈterianism** *n*
▷ http://www.wikipedia.org/wiki/Presbyterian

presbytery (ˈprɛzbɪtərɪ) *n, pl* **presbyteries** **1** *Presbyterian Church* **1a** a local Church court **1b** the congregations within the jurisdiction of any such court **2** the part of a church east of the choir, in which the main altar is situated; a sanctuary **3** presbyters or elders collectively **4** *RC Church* the residence of a parish priest [C15 from OF *presbiterie*, from Church L, from Gk *presbyterion*; see PRESBYTER]

prescience (ˈprɛsɪəns) *n* knowledge of events before they take place; foreknowledge [C14 from L *praescīre* to foreknow] > ˈ**prescient** *adj*

Prescott (ˈprɛskət) *n* **1** **John Leslie** born 1938, British politician: deputy leader of the Labour Party from 1994; deputy prime minister from 1997: secretary of state for the environment, transport, and the regions (1997–2001); head of the cabinet office (2001–02); minister for local government and the regions (2002–) **2** **William Hickling** (ˈhɪklɪŋ) 1796–1859, US historian, noted for his work on the history of Spain and her colonies

prescribe (prɪˈskraɪb) *vb* **prescribes, prescribing, prescribed** **1** (*tr*) to lay down as a rule or directive **2** *med* to recommend or order the use of (a drug or other remedy) [C16 from L *praescrībere* to write previously] > **preˈscriber** *n*

prescript (ˈpriːskrɪpt) *n* something laid down or prescribed [C16 from L *praescriptum* something written down beforehand, from *praescrībere* to PRESCRIBE]

prescription (prɪˈskrɪpʃən) *n* **1a** written instructions from a physician to a pharmacist stating the form, dosage, strength, etc, of a drug to be issued to a specific patient **1b** the drug or remedy prescribed **2a** written instructions for an optician specifying the lenses needed to correct defects of vision **2b** (*as modifier*): *prescription glasses* **3** the act of prescribing **4** something that is prescribed **5** a long-established custom or a claim based on one **6** *law* **6a** the uninterrupted possession of property over a stated time, after which a right or title is acquired (**positive prescription**) **6b** the barring of adverse claims to property, etc, after a specified time has elapsed, allowing the possessor to acquire title (**negative prescription**) [C14 from legal L *praescriptiō* an order; see PRESCRIBE]

prescriptive (prɪˈskrɪptɪv) *adj* **1** making or giving directions, rules, or injunctions **2** sanctioned by long-standing custom **3** based upon legal prescription: *a prescriptive title* > **preˈscriptively** *adv* > **preˈscriptiveness** *n*

preseason (ˈpriːˌsiːzᵊn) *n* **a** the period immediately before the official season for a particular sport begins **b** (*as modifier*): *a series of preseason friendly matches*

presence (ˈprɛzəns) *n* **1** the state or fact of being present **2** immediate proximity **3** personal appearance or bearing, esp of a dignified nature **4** an imposing or dignified personality **5** an invisible spirit felt to be nearby **6** *electronics* a recording control that boosts mid-range frequencies **7** *obs* assembly or company [C14 via OF from L *praesentia* a being before, from *praeesse* to be before]

presence chamber *n* the room in which a great person, such as a monarch, receives guests, assemblies, etc

presence of mind *n* the ability to remain calm and act constructively during times of crisis

presenile dementia (priːˈsiːnaɪl) *n* a form of dementia, of unknown cause, starting before a person is old

present[1] (ˈprɛzᵊnt) *adj* **1** (*prenominal*) in existence at the time at which something is spoken or written **2** (*postpositive*) being in a specified place, thing, etc: *the murderer is present in this room* **3** (*prenominal*) now being dealt with or under discussion: *the present author* **4** *grammar* denoting a tense of verbs used when the action or event described is occurring at the time of utterance or when the speaker does not wish to make any explicit temporal reference **5** *arch* instant: *present help is at hand* ▷ *n* **6** *grammar* **6a** the present tense **6b** a verb in this tense **7** **at present** now **8** **for the present** for the time being; temporarily **9** **the present** the time being; now ▷ See also **presents** [C13 from L *praesens*, from *praeesse* to be in front of]

present[2] *vb* (prɪˈzɛnt) (*mainly tr*) **1** to introduce (a person) to another, esp to someone of higher rank **2** to introduce to the public: *to present a play* **3** to introduce and compere (a radio or television show) **4** to show; exhibit: *he presented a brave face to the world* **5** to bring or suggest to the mind: *to present a problem* **6** to put forward; submit: *she presented a proposal for a new book* **7** to award: *to present a prize; to present a university with a foundation scholarship* **8** to offer formally: *to present one's compliments* **9** to hand over for action or settlement: *to present a bill* **10** to depict in a particular manner: *the actor presented Hamlet as a very young man* **11** to salute someone with (one's weapon) (usually in **present arms**) **12** to aim (a weapon) **13** to nominate (a clergyman) to a bishop for institution to a benefice in his diocese **14** to lay (a charge, etc) before a court, magistrate, etc, for consideration or trial **15** to bring a formal charge or accusation against (a person); indict **16** (*intr*) *med* to seek treatment for a particular problem: *she presented with postnatal depression* **17** (*intr*) *inf* to produce a specified impression: *she presents well in public* **18** **present oneself** to appear, esp at a specific time and place ▷ *n* (ˈprɛzᵊnt) **19** a gift [C13 from OF *presenter*, from L *praesentāre* to exhibit, from *praesens* PRESENT[1]]

presentable (prɪˈzɛntəbᵊl) *adj* **1** fit to be presented or introduced to other people **2** fit to be displayed or offered > **preˌsentaˈbility** *n* > **preˈsentably** *adv*

presentation (ˌprɛzənˈteɪʃən) *n* **1** the act of presenting or state of being presented **2** the manner of presenting; delivery or overall impression **3** a verbal report, often with illustrative material: *a presentation on the company results* **4a** an offering, as of a gift **4b** (*as modifier*): *a presentation copy of a book* **5** a performance or representation, as of a play **6** the formal introduction of a person, as at court; debut **7** the act or right of nominating a member of the clergy to a benefice > ˌ**presenˈtational** *adj*

presentationism (ˌprɛzənˈteɪʃəˌnɪzəm) *n philosophy* the theory that objects are identical with our perceptions of them ▷ Cf **representationalism** > ˌ**presenˈtationist** *n, adj*

presentative (prɪˈzɛntətɪv) *adj* **1** *philosophy* able to be known or perceived immediately **2** conferring the right of ecclesiastical presentation

present-day *n* (*modifier*) of the modern day; current: *I don't like present-day fashions*

presenteeism (ˌprɛzənˈtiːɪzəm) *n* the practice of working persistently longer hours and taking fewer holidays than the terms of one's employment demands, in the hope that this will be noticed and rewarded by one's superiors [C20 a play on ABSENTEEISM]

presenter (prɪˈzɛntə) *n* **1** a person who presents something or someone **2** *radio, television* a person who introduces a show, links items, etc

presentient (prɪˈsɛnʃənt) *adj* characterized by or experiencing a presentiment [C19 from L *praesentiens*, from *praesentire*, from *prae-* PRE- + *sentire* to feel]

presentiment (prɪˈzɛntɪmənt) *n* a sense of something about to happen; premonition [C18 from obs. F, from *pressentir* to sense beforehand]

presently (ˈprɛzəntlɪ) *adv* **1** in a short while; soon **2** at the moment **3** an archaic word for **immediately**

presentment (prɪˈzɛntmənt) *n* **1** the act of presenting or state of being presented; presentation **2** something presented, such as a picture, play, etc **3** *law* a statement on oath by a jury of something within their own knowledge or observation **4** *commerce* the presenting of a bill of exchange, promissory note, etc

present participle (ˈprɛzᵊnt) *n* a participial form of verbs used adjectivally when the action it describes is contemporaneous with that of the main verb of a sentence and also used in the formation of certain compound tenses. In English this form ends in *-ing*

present perfect (ˈprɛzᵊnt) *adj, n grammar* another term for **perfect** (senses 8, 10)

presents (ˈprɛzənts) *pl n law* used in a deed or document to refer to itself: *know all men by these presents*

preservative (prɪˈzɜːvətɪv) *n* **1** something that preserves, esp a chemical added to foods ▷ *adj* **2** tending or intended to preserve

preserve (prɪˈzɜːv) *vb* **preserves, preserving, preserved** (*mainly tr*) **1** to keep safe from danger or harm; protect **2** to protect from decay or dissolution; maintain: *to preserve old buildings* **3** to maintain possession of; keep up: *to preserve a façade of indifference* **4** to prevent from decomposition or chemical change **5** to prepare (food), as by salting, so that it will resist decomposition **6** to make preserves of (fruit, etc) **7** to rear and protect (game) in restricted places for hunting or fishing **8** (*intr*) to maintain protection for game in preserves ▷ *n* **9** something that preserves or is preserved **10** a special domain: *archaeology is the preserve of specialists* **11** (*usually pl*) fruit, etc, prepared by cooking with sugar **12** areas where game is reared for private hunting or fishing [C14 via OF, from LL *praeservāre*, lit.: to keep safe in advance, from L *prae* before + *servāre* to keep safe] > **preˈservable** *adj* > **preservation** (ˌprɛzəˈveɪʃən) *n* > **preˈserver** *n*

preset *vb* (priːˈsɛt), **presets, presetting, preset** (*tr*) **1** to set (a timing device) so that something begins to operate at the time specified ▷ *n* (ˈpriːsɛt) **2** *electronics* a control, such as a variable resistor, that is not as accessible as the main controls and is used to set initial conditions

preshrunk (priːˈʃrʌŋk) *adj* (of fabrics) having undergone shrinking during manufacture so that further shrinkage will not occur

preside (prɪˈzaɪd) *vb* **presides, presiding, presided** (*intr*) **1** to sit in or hold a position of authority, as over a meeting **2** to exercise authority; control [C17 via F from L *praesidēre* to superintend, from *prae* before + *sedēre* to sit]

presidency (ˈprɛzɪdənsɪ) *n, pl* **presidencies** **1** the office, dignity, or term of a president **2** (*often cap*) the office of president of a republic, esp of the President of the US

president (ˈprɛzɪdənt) *n* **1** (*often cap*) the head of state of a republic, esp of the US **2** (in the US) the chief executive officer of a company, corporation, etc **3** a person who presides over an assembly, meeting, etc **4** the chief executive officer of certain establishments of higher education [C14 via OF from LL *praesidens* ruler; see PRESIDE] > **presidential** (ˌprɛzɪˈdɛnʃəl) *adj* > ˌ**presiˈdentially** *adv* > ˈ**presidentship** *n*

presidium *or* **praesidium** (prɪˈsɪdɪəm) *n* **1** (*often cap*) (in Communist countries) a permanent committee of a larger body, such as a legislature, that acts for it when it is in recess **2** a collective presidency [C20 from Russian *prezidium*, from L *praesidium*, from *praesidēre* to superintend; see PRESIDE]

Presley (ˈprɛzlɪ) *n* **Elvis** (**Aaron** *or* **Aron**) 1935–77, US rock and roll singer. His recordings include "That's all Right (Mama)" (1954), "Heartbreak Hotel" (1956), "Hound Dog" (1956), numbers from the films *Loving You* and *Jailhouse Rock* (both 1957), and "Suspicious Minds" (1970)

press[1] (prɛs) *vb* **1** to apply or exert weight, force, or steady pressure (on): *he pressed the button on the camera* **2** (*tr*) to squeeze or compress so as to alter in shape **3** to apply heat or pressure to (clothing) so as to smooth out creases **4** to make (objects) from soft material by pressing with a mould, etc, esp to make gramophone records from plastic **5** (*tr*) to clasp; embrace **6** (*tr*) to extract or force out (juice) by pressure (from) **7** (*tr*) to force or compel **8** to importune (a person) insistently: *they pressed for an answer* **9** to harass or cause harassment **10** (*tr*) to plead or put forward strongly: *to press a claim* **11** (*intr*) to be urgent **12** (*tr; usually passive*) to have little of: *we're hard pressed for time* **13** (when *intr*, often foll by *on* or *forward*) to hasten or advance or cause to hasten or advance in a forceful manner **14** (*intr*) to crowd; push **15** (*tr*) *arch* to trouble or oppress ▷ *n* **16** any machine that exerts pressure to form, shape, or cut materials or to extract liquids, compress solids, or hold components together while an adhesive joint is formed **17** See **printing press** **18** the art or process of printing **19 to (the) press** to be printed: *when is this book going to press?* **20 the press** **20a** news media collectively, esp newspapers **20b** (*as modifier*): *press relations* **21** the opinions and reviews in the newspapers, etc: *the play received a poor press* **22** the act of pressing or state of being pressed **23** the act of crowding or pushing together **24** a closely packed throng; crowd **25** a cupboard, esp a large one used for storing clothes or linen **26** a wood or metal clamp to prevent tennis rackets, etc, from warping when not in use [C14 *pressen*, from OF *presser*, from L, from *premere* to press]

Pp

press[2] (prɛs) *vb* (*tr*) **1** to recruit (men) by forcible measures for military service **2** to use for a purpose other than intended (esp in **press into service**) ▷ *n* **3** recruitment into military service by forcible measures, as by a press gang [C16 back formation from *prest* to recruit soldiers; also infl. by PRESS[1]]

press agent *n* a person employed to obtain favourable publicity, such as notices in newspapers, for an organization, actor, etc

press box *n* an area reserved for reporters, as in a sports stadium

Pressburg ('prɛsbʊrk) *n* the German name for **Bratislava**
Pressburger ('prɛs,bɜːgə) *n* **Emeric** ('ɛmərɪk) 1902–88, Hungarian film writer and producer, living in Britain: best known for his collaboration (1942–57) with Michael Powell. Films include *The Life and Death of Colonel Blimp* (1943), *I Know Where I'm Going* (1945), and *A Matter of Life and Death* (1946)
press conference *n* an interview for press reporters given by a politician, film star, etc
press fit *n engineering* a type of fit for mating parts, usually tighter than a sliding fit, used when the parts do not have to move relative to each other
press gallery *n* an area for newspaper reporters, esp in a legislative assembly
press gang *n* **1** (formerly) a detachment of men used to press civilians for service in the navy ▷ *vb* **press-gang** (*tr*) **2** to force (a person) to join the navy by a press gang **3** to induce (a person) to perform a duty by forceful persuasion
pressing ('prɛsɪŋ) *adj* **1** demanding immediate attention **2** persistent or importunate ▷ *n* **3** a large specified number of gramophone records produced at one time from a master record **4** *football* the tactic of trying to stay very close to the opposition when they are in possession of the ball > **'pressingly** *adv*
pressman ('prɛsmən, -,mæn) *n, pl* **pressmen 1** a journalist **2** a person who operates a printing press
press of sail *n naut* the most sail a vessel can carry under given conditions. Also called: **press of canvas**
press release *n* an official announcement or account of a news item circulated to the press
pressroom ('prɛs,ruːm, -,rʊm) *n* the room in a printing establishment that houses the printing presses
press stud *n* a fastening device consisting of one part with a projecting knob that snaps into a hole on another like part, used esp on clothing. Canad equivalent: **dome fastener**
press-up *n* an exercise in which the body is alternately raised from and lowered to the floor by the arms only, the trunk being kept straight. Also called (US and Canad): **push-up**
pressure ('prɛʃə) *n* **1** the state of pressing or being pressed **2** the exertion of force by one body on the surface of another **3** a moral force that compels: *to bring pressure to bear* **4** urgent claims or demands: *to work under pressure* **5** a burdensome condition that is hard to bear: *the pressure of grief* **6** the force applied to a unit area of a surface, usually measured in pascals, millibars, torrs, or atmospheres **7** short for **atmospheric pressure** or **blood pressure** ▷ *vb* **pressures, pressuring, pressured** (*tr*) **8** to constrain or compel, as by moral force **9** another word for **pressurize** [c14 from LL *pressūra* a pressing, from L *premere* to press]
pressure cooker *n* a strong hermetically sealed pot in which food may be cooked quickly under pressure at a temperature above the normal boiling point of water > **'pressure-,cook** *vb*
pressure group *n* a group of people who seek to exert pressure on legislators, public opinion, etc, in order to promote their own ideas or welfare
pressure point *n* any of several points on the body above an artery that, when firmly pressed, will control bleeding from the artery at a point farther away from the heart
pressure suit *n* an inflatable suit worn by a person flying at high altitudes or in space, to provide protection from low pressure
pressure ulcer *or* **pressure sore** *n* another term for **bedsore**
pressurize *or* **pressurise** ('prɛʃə,raɪz) *vb* **pressurizes, pressurizing, pressurized** *or* **pressurises, pressurising, pressurised** (*tr*) **1** to increase the pressure in (an enclosure, such as an aircraft cabin) in order to maintain approximately atmospheric pressure when the external pressure is low **2** to increase pressure on (a fluid) **3** to make insistent demands of (someone); coerce > **,pressuri'zation** *or* **,pressuri'sation** *n*
pressurized-water reactor *n* a type of nuclear reactor that uses water under pressure as both coolant and moderator
presswork ('prɛs,wɜːk) *n* the operation of, or matter printed by, a printing press
Prestel ('prɛstɛl) *n trademark* (in Britain) the viewdata service operated by British Telecom
Prester John ('prɛstə) *n* a legendary Christian priest and king, believed in the Middle Ages to have ruled in the Far East, but identified in the 14th century with the king of Ethiopia [c14 *Prestre Johan*, from Med. L *presbyter Iohannes* Priest John]
prestidigitation (,prɛstɪ,dɪdʒɪ'teɪʃən) *n* another name for **sleight of hand** [c19 from F: quick-fingeredness, from L *praestigiae* tricks, prob. infl. by F *preste* nimble, & L *digitus* finger] > **,presti'digi,tator** *n*
prestige (prɛ'stiːʒ) *n* **1** high status or reputation achieved through success, influence, wealth, etc; renown **2a** the power to impress; glamour **2b** (*modifier*): *a prestige car* [c17 via F from L *praestigiae* tricks] > **prestigious** (prɛ'stɪdʒəs) *adj*
prestige pricing *n marketing* the practice of giving a product a high price to convey the idea that it must be of high quality or status
prestissimo (prɛ'stɪsɪ,məʊ) *music* ▷ *adj, adv* **1** to be played as fast as possible ▷ *n, pl* **prestissimos 2** a piece to be played in this way [c18 from It.: very quickly, from *presto* fast]
presto ('prɛstəʊ) *adj, adv* **1** *music* to be played very fast ▷ *adv* **2** immediately (esp in **hey presto**) ▷ *n, pl* **prestos 3** *music* a passage directed to be played very quickly [c16 from It.: fast, from LL *praestus* (adj) ready to hand, L *praestō* (adv) present]
Preston ('prɛstən) *n* a city in NW England, administrative centre of Lancashire, on the River Ribble: developed as a weaving centre (17th–18th centuries); university (1992). Pop: 177 660 (1991)
Prestonpans (,prɛstən'pænz) *n* a small town and resort in SE Scotland, in East Lothian on the Firth of Forth: scene of the battle (1745) in which the Jacobite army of Prince Charles Edward defeated government forces under Sir John Cope. Pop: 7014 (1991)
prestressed concrete (,priː'strɛst) *n* concrete that contains steel wires that are stretched to counteract the stresses that will occur under load
Prestwich ('prɛstwɪtʃ) *n* a town in NW England, in Bury unitary authority, Greater Manchester. Pop: 31 801 (1991)
Prestwick ('prɛstwɪk) *n* a town in SW Scotland, in South Ayrshire on the Firth of Clyde; international airport, golf course: tourism. Pop: 13 705 (1991)
presumably (prɪ'zjuːməblɪ) *adv* (*sentence modifier*) one supposes that: *presumably he won't see you, if you're leaving tomorrow*
presume (prɪ'zjuːm) *vb* **presumes, presuming, presumed 1** (when *tr, often takes a clause as object*) to take (something) for granted; assume **2** (when *tr, often foll by an infinitive*) to dare (to do something): *do you presume to copy my work?* **3** (*intr;* foll by *on* or *upon*) to rely or depend: *don't presume on his agreement* **4** (*intr;* foll by *on* or *upon*) to take advantage (of): *don't presume upon his good nature too far* **5** (*tr*) *law* to take as proved until contrary evidence is produced [c14 via OF from L *praesūmere* to take in advance, from *prae* before + *sūmere* to ASSUME] > **presumedly** (prɪ'zjuːmɪdlɪ) *adv* > **pre'suming** *adj*
presumption (prɪ'zʌmpʃən) *n* **1** the act of presuming **2** bold or insolent behaviour **3** a belief or assumption based on reasonable evidence **4** a basis on which to presume **5** *law* an inference of the truth of a fact from other facts proved [c13 via OF from L *praesumptiō*

anticipation, from *praesūmere* to take beforehand; see PRESUME]

presumptive (prɪ'zʌmptɪv) *adj* 1 based on presumption or probability 2 affording reasonable ground for belief > **pre'sumptively** *adv*

presumptuous (prɪ'zʌmptjʊəs) *adj* characterized by presumption or tending to presume; bold; forward > **pre'sumptuously** *adv* > **pre'sumptuousness** *n*

presuppose (ˌpriːsə'pəʊz) *vb* **presupposes, presupposing, presupposed** (*tr*) 1 to take for granted 2 to require as a necessary prior condition > **presupposition** (ˌpriːsʌpə'zɪʃən) *n*

preteen (priː'tiːn) *n* a boy or girl approaching his or her teens

pretence *or US* **pretense** (prɪ'tɛns) *n* 1 the act of pretending 2 a false display; affectation 3 a claim, esp a false one, to a right, title, or distinction 4 make-believe 5 a pretext

pretend (prɪ'tɛnd) *vb* 1 (when *tr, usually takes a clause as object or an infinitive*) to claim or allege (something untrue) 2 (*tr; may take a clause as object or an infinitive*) to make believe, as in a play: *you pretend to be Ophelia* 3 (*intr;* foll by *to*) to present a claim, esp a dubious one: *to pretend to the throne* 4 (*intr;* foll by *to*) *obs* to aspire as a candidate or suitor (for) ▷ *adj* 5 make-believe; imaginary [C14 from L *praetendere* to stretch forth, feign]

pretender (prɪ'tɛndə) *n* 1 a person who pretends or makes false allegations 2 a person who mounts a claim, as to a throne or title

pretension (prɪ'tɛnʃən) *n* 1 (*often pl*) a false claim, esp to merit, worth, or importance 2 a specious or unfounded allegation; pretext 3 the quality of being pretentious

pretentious (prɪ'tɛnʃəs) *adj* 1 making claim to distinction or importance, esp undeservedly 2 ostentatious > **pre'tentiously** *adv* > **pre'tentiousness** *n*

preterite *or esp US* **preterit** ('prɛtərɪt) *grammar* ▷ *n* 1 a tense of verbs used to relate past action, formed in English by inflection of the verb, as *jumped, swam* 2 a verb in this tense ▷ *adj* 3 denoting this tense [C14 from LL *praeteritum (tempus)* past (time), from L *praeterīre* to go by, from *preter-* beyond + *īre* to go]

preterm (priː'tɜːm) *adj* 1 (of a baby) born prematurely ▷ *adv* 2 prematurely

pretermit (ˌpriːtə'mɪt) *vb* **pretermits, pretermitting, pretermitted** (*tr*) *rare* 1 to disregard 2 to fail to do; neglect; omit [C16 from L *praetermittere* to let pass, from *preter-* beyond + *mittere* to send]

preternatural (ˌpriːtə'nætʃrəl) *adj* 1 beyond what is ordinarily found in nature; abnormal 2 another word for **supernatural** [C16 from Med. L *praeternātūrālis*, from L *praeter natūram* beyond the scope of nature] > ˌ**preter'naturally** *adv*

pretext ('priːtɛkst) *n* 1 a fictitious reason given in order to conceal the real one 2 a pretence [C16 from L *praetextum* disguise, from *praetexere* to weave in front, disguise]

pretor ('priːtə, -tɔː) *n* a variant (esp US) spelling of **praetor**

Pretoria (prɪ'tɔːrɪə) *n* a city in N South Africa, the administrative capital of South Africa; formerly capital of Transvaal province: two universities (1873, 1930); large steelworks. Pop (urban area): 1 104 479 (1996)
▷ www.ccp.co.za
▷ www.visitpretoria.co.za
▷ www.sa-venues.com/gauteng_pretoria.htm

Pretorius (prɪ'tɔːrɪəs) *n* 1 **Andries Wilhelmus Jacobus** ('ɑndriːs wɪl'hɛlmys jaː'koːbys) 1799–1853, a Boer leader in the Great Trek (1838) to escape British sovereignty; he also led an expedition to the Transvaal (1848). The town Pretoria was named after him 2 his son, **Marthinus Wessels** (mar'tiːnys 'wɛsəls) 1819–1901, first president of the South African Republic (1857–71) and of the Orange Free State (1859–63)

prettify ('prɪtɪˌfaɪ) *vb* **prettifies, prettifying, prettified** (*tr*) to make pretty, esp in a trivial fashion; embellish > ˌ**prettifi'cation** *n* > '**prettiˌfier** *n*

pretty ('prɪtɪ) *adj* **prettier, prettiest** 1 pleasing or appealing in a delicate or graceful way 2 dainty, neat, or charming 3 *inf, often ironical* excellent, grand, or fine: *here's a pretty mess!* 4 commendable; good of its kind: *he replied with a pretty wit* 5 *inf* effeminate; foppish 6 *arch or Scot* vigorous or brave 7 **sitting pretty** *inf* well placed or established financially, socially, etc ▷ *n, pl* **pretties** 8 a pretty person or thing ▷ *adv inf* 9 fairly; somewhat 10 very ▷ *vb* **pretties, prettying, prettied** 11 (*tr;* often foll by *up*) to make pretty; adorn [OE *prættig* clever] > '**prettily** *adv* > '**prettiness** *n*

pretty-pretty *adj inf* excessively or ostentatiously pretty: *a pretty-pretty village*

pretzel ('prɛtsəl) *n* a brittle savoury biscuit, in the form of a knot or stick, eaten esp in Germany and the US [C19 from G, from OHG *brezitella*]

Preussen ('prɔysən) *n* the German name for **Prussia**

prevail (prɪ'veɪl) *vb* (*intr*) 1 (often foll by *over* or *against*) to prove superior; gain mastery: *skill will prevail* 2 to be the most important feature; be prevalent 3 to exist widely; be in force 4 (often foll by *on* or *upon*) to succeed in persuading or inducing [C14 from L *praevalēre* to be superior in strength] > **pre'vailer** *n*

prevailing (prɪ'veɪlɪŋ) *adj* 1 generally accepted; widespread: *the prevailing opinion* 2 most frequent; predominant: *the prevailing wind is from the north* > **pre'vailingly** *adv*

prevalent ('prɛvələnt) *adj* 1 widespread or current 2 superior in force or power; predominant > '**prevalence** *n* > '**prevalently** *adv*

prevaricate (prɪ'værɪˌkeɪt) *vb* **prevaricates, prevaricating, prevaricated** (*intr*) to speak or act falsely or evasively with intent to deceive [C16 from L *praevāricārī* to walk crookedly, from *prae* beyond + *vāricare* to straddle the legs] > **preˌvari'cation** *n* > **pre'variˌcator** *n*

Pp

prevent (prɪ'vɛnt) *vb* 1 (*tr*) to keep from happening, esp by taking precautionary action 2 (*tr;* often foll by *from*) to keep (someone from doing something) 3 (*intr*) to interpose or act as a hindrance 4 (*tr*) *arch* to anticipate or precede [C15 from L *praevenīre*, from *prae* before + *venīre* to come] > **pre'ventable** *or* **pre'ventible** *adj* > **pre'ventably** *or* **pre'ventibly** *adv*

prevention (prɪ'vɛnʃən) *n* 1 the act of preventing 2 a hindrance or impediment

preventive (prɪ'vɛntɪv) *adj* 1 tending or intended to prevent or hinder 2 *med* tending to prevent disease; prophylactic 3 (in Britain) of, relating to, or belonging to the customs and excise service or the coastguard ▷ *n* 4 something that serves to prevent or hinder 5 *med* any drug or agent that tends to prevent disease. Also (for senses 1, 2, 4, 5): **preventative** > **pre'ventively** *or* **pre'ventatively** *adv*

> USAGE *Preventive* is generally used in preference to *preventative* in medical contexts and otherwise, and is about twice as common in the Bank of English. Overall, *preventative* is much less frequent in American than in British sources

Prévert (*French* prevɛr) *n* **Jacques** (ʒak) 1900–77, Parisian poet, satirist, and writer of film scripts, noted esp for his song poems. He was a member of the surrealist group from 1925 to 1929

preview ('priːvjuː) *n* 1 an advance view or sight 2 an advance showing before public presentation of a film, art exhibition, etc, usually before an invited audience ▷ *vb* 3 (*tr*) to view in advance

Previn ('prɛvɪn) *n* **André** ('ɒndreɪ) born 1929, US orchestral conductor, born in Germany; living in Britain

previous ('priːvɪəs) *adj* **1** (*prenominal*) existing or coming before something else **2** (*postpositive*) *inf* taking place or done too soon; premature **3 previous to** before [C17 from L *praevius* leading the way, from *prae* before + *via* way] > '**previously** *adv* > '**previousness** *n*

previous question *n* **1** (in the House of Commons) a motion to drop the present topic under debate, put in order to prevent a vote **2** (in the House of Lords and US legislative bodies) a motion to vote on a bill without delay

previse (prɪ'vaɪz) *vb* **previses, prevising, prevised** (*tr*) *rare* **1** to predict or foresee **2** to notify in advance [C16 from L *praevidēre* to foresee]

prevision (prɪ'vɪʒən) *n rare* **1** the act or power of foreseeing; prescience **2** a prophetic vision or prophecy

Prévost d'Exiles (*French* prevo dɛgzil) *n* **Antoine François** (ɑ̃twan frɑ̃swa), known as *Abbé Prévost*. 1697–1763, French novelist, noted for his romance *Manon Lescaut* (1731), which served as the basis for operas by Puccini and Massenet

prey (preɪ) *n* **1** an animal hunted or captured by another for food **2** a person or thing that becomes the victim of a hostile person, influence, etc **3 bird** *or* **beast of prey** a bird or animal that preys on others for food **4** an archaic word for **booty** ▷ *vb* (*intr*; often foll by *on* or *upon*) **5** to hunt food by killing other animals **6** to make a victim (of others), as by profiting at their expense **7** to exert a depressing or obsessive effect (on the mind, spirits, etc) [C13 from OF *preie*, from L *praeda* booty] > '**preyer** *n*

Priam ('praɪəm) *n Greek myth* the last king of Troy, killed at its fall. He was father by Hecuba of Hector, Paris, and Cassandra

priapic (praɪ'æpɪk, -'eɪ-) *or* **priapean** (ˌpraɪə'piːən) *adj* **1** (*sometimes cap*) of or relating to Priapus **2** a less common word for **phallic**

priapism ('praɪəˌpɪzəm) *n pathol* prolonged painful erection of the penis, caused by neurological disorders, etc [C17 from LL *priāpismus*, ult. from Gk Priapus]

Priapus (praɪ'eɪpəs) *n* **1** (in classical antiquity) the god of the male procreative power and of gardens and vineyards **2** (*often not cap*) a representation of the penis

Pribilof Islands ('prɪbɪləf) *pl n* a group of islands in the Bering Sea, off SW Alaska, belonging to the US: the breeding ground of the northern fur seal. Area: about 168 sq km (65 sq miles). Also called: **Fur Seal Islands**

price (praɪs) *n* **1** the sum in money or goods for which anything is or may be bought or sold **2** the cost at which anything is obtained **3** the cost of bribing a person **4** a sum of money offered as a reward for a capture or killing **5** value or worth, esp high worth **6** *gambling* another word for **odds 7 at any price** whatever the price or cost **8 at a price** at a high price **9 what price (something)?** what are the chances of (something) happening now? ▷ *vb* **prices, pricing, priced** (*tr*) **10** to fix the price of **11** to discover the price of **12 price out of the market** to charge so highly for as to prevent the sale, hire, etc, of [C13 *pris*, from OF, from L *pretium*] > '**pricer** *n*

price control *n* the establishment and maintenance of maximum price levels for basic goods and services by a government

price-dividend ratio *n* the ratio of the price of a share on a stock exchange to the dividends per share paid in the previous year, used as a measure of a company's potential as an investment. Abbrevs: **P-D ratio, PDR**

price-earnings ratio *n* the ratio of the price of a share on the stock exchange to the earnings per share, used as a measure of a company's future profitability. Abbrev: **P-E ratio**

price-fixing *n* **1** the setting of prices by agreement among producers and distributors **2** another name for **price control** or **resale price maintenance**

price leadership *n marketing* the setting of the price of a product or service by a dominant firm at a level that competitors can match, in order to avoid a price war

priceless ('praɪslɪs) *adj* **1** of inestimable worth; invaluable **2** *inf* extremely amusing or ridiculous > '**pricelessly** *adv* > '**pricelessness** *n*

price ring *n* a group of traders formed to maintain the prices of their goods

price-sensitive *adj* likely to affect the price of property, esp shares and securities: *price-sensitive information*

pricey *or* **pricy** ('praɪsɪ) *adj* **pricier, priciest** an informal word for **expensive**

prick (prɪk) *vb* (*mainly tr*) **1a** to make (a small hole) in (something) by piercing lightly with a sharp point **1b** to wound in this manner **2** (*intr*) to cause or have a piercing or stinging sensation **3** to cause to feel a sharp emotional pain: *knowledge of such poverty pricked his conscience* **4** to puncture **5** to outline by dots or punctures **6** (*also intr*; usually foll by *up*) to rise or raise erect: *the dog pricked his ears up* **7** (usually foll by *out* or *off*) to transplant (seedlings) into a larger container **8** *arch* to urge on, esp to spur a horse on **9 prick up one's ears** to start to listen attentively; become interested ▷ *n* **10** the act of pricking or the sensation of being pricked **11** a mark made by a sharp point; puncture **12** a sharp emotional pain: *a prick of conscience* **13** a taboo slang word for **penis 14** *sl, derog* an obnoxious or despicable person **15** an instrument or weapon with a sharp point **16** the track of an animal, esp a hare **17 kick against the pricks** to hurt oneself by struggling against something in vain [OE *prica* point, puncture] > '**pricker** *n*

pricket ('prɪkɪt) *n* **1** a male deer in the second year of life having unbranched antlers **2** a sharp metal spike on which to stick a candle [C14 *priket*, from *prik* PRICK]

prickle ('prɪk[ə]l) *n* **1** *bot* a pointed process arising from the outer layer of a stem, leaf, etc, and containing no woody tissue ▷ Cf **thorn 2** a pricking or stinging sensation ▷ *vb* **prickles, prickling, prickled 3** to feel or cause to feel a stinging sensation **4** (*tr*) to prick, as with a thorn [OE *pricel*]

prickly ('prɪklɪ) *adj* **pricklier, prickliest 1** having or covered with prickles **2** stinging **3** irritable **4** full of difficulties: *a prickly problem* > '**prickliness** *n*

prickly heat *n* a nontechnical name for **miliaria**

prickly pear *n* **1** any of various tropical cactuses having flattened or cylindrical spiny joints and oval fruit that is edible in some species **2** the fruit of any of these plants

pride (praɪd) *n* **1** a feeling of honour and self-respect; a sense of personal worth **2** excessive self-esteem; conceit **3** a source of pride **4** satisfaction or pleasure in one's own or another's success, achievements, etc (esp in **take (a) pride in**) **5** the better or superior part of something **6** the most flourishing time **7** a group (of lions) **8** courage; spirit **9** *arch* pomp or splendour **10 pride of place** the most important position ▷ *vb* **prides, priding, prided 11** (*tr*; foll by *on* or *upon*) to take pride in (oneself) for [OE *prȳda*] > '**prideful** *adj* > '**pridefully** *adv*

Pride (praɪd) *n* **Thomas** died 1658, English soldier on the Parliamentary side during the Civil War. He expelled members of the Long Parliament hostile to the army (**Pride's Purge,** 1648) and signed Charles I's death warrant

prie-dieu (priː'djɜː) *n* a piece of furniture consisting of a low surface for kneeling upon and a narrow front surmounted by a rest, for use when praying [C18 from F, from *prier* to pray + *Dieu* God]

prier *or* **pryer** ('praɪə) *n* a person who pries

priest (priːst) *n* **1** a person ordained to act as a mediator between God and man in administering the sacraments, preaching, etc **2** (in episcopal Churches) a minister in the second grade of the hierarchy of holy orders, ranking below a bishop but above a deacon **3** a minister of any religion **4** an official who offers

sacrifice on behalf of the people and performs other religious ceremonies ▷ *vb* **5** (*tr*) to make a priest; ordain [OE *prēost*, apparently from PRESBYTER] > **'priestess** *fem n* > **'priest,hood** *n* > **'priest,like** *adj* > **'priestly** *adj*
priestcraft ('pri:st,krɑ:ft) *n* **1** the art and skills involved in the work of a priest **2** *derog* the influence of priests upon politics
priest-hole *or* **priest's hole** *n* a secret chamber in certain houses in England, built as a hiding place for Roman Catholic priests when they were proscribed in the 16th and 17th centuries
Priestley ('pri:stlɪ) *n* **1** **J(ohn) B(oynton)** 1894–1984, English author. His works include the novels *The Good Companions* (1929) and *Angel Pavement* (1930) and the play *An Inspector Calls* (1946) **2** **Joseph** 1733–1804, English chemist, political theorist, and clergyman, in the US from 1794. He discovered oxygen (1774) independently of Scheele and isolated and described many other gases
prig[1] (prɪg) *n* a person who is smugly self-righteous and narrow-minded [c18 from ?] > **'priggery** *or* **'priggishness** *n* > **'priggish** *adj* > **'priggishly** *adv*
prig[2] (prɪg) *Brit arch sl* ▷ *vb* **prigs, prigging, prigged** **1** another word for **steal** ▷ *n* **2** another word for **thief** [c16 from ?]
Prigogine (*French* prigoʒin) *n* Viscount **Ilya** (ilja) 1917–2003, Belgian chemist, born in Russia: Nobel prize for chemistry 1977 for his work on nonequilibrium thermodynamics
prim (prɪm) *adj* **primmer, primmest** **1** affectedly proper, precise, or formal ▷ *vb* **prims, primming, primmed** **2** (*tr*) to make prim **3** to purse (the mouth) primly or (of the mouth) to be so pursed [c18 from ?] > **'primly** *adv* > **'primness** *n*
prima ballerina ('pri:mə) *n* a leading female ballet dancer [from It., lit.: first ballerina]
primacy ('praɪməsɪ) *n, pl* **primacies** **1** the state of being first in rank, grade, etc **2** *Christianity* the office, rank, or jurisdiction of a primate, senior bishop, or pope
prima donna ('pri:mə 'dɒnə) *n, pl* **prima donnas** **1** a leading female operatic star **2** *inf* a temperamental person [c19 from It.: first lady]
prima facie ('praɪmə 'feɪʃɪ) *adv* at first sight; as it seems at first [c15 from L, from *prīmus* first + *faciēs* FACE]
prima-facie evidence *n law* evidence that is sufficient to establish a fact or to raise a presumption of the truth unless controverted
primal ('praɪməl) *adj* **1** first or original **2** chief or most important [c17 from Med. L *prīmālis*, from L *prīmus* first]
primaquine ('praɪmə,kwi:n) *n* a synthetic drug used in the treatment of malaria [c20 from *prima-*, from L *prīmus* first + QUIN(OLIN)E]
primarily ('praɪmərɪlɪ, praɪ'mærɪlɪ, -'mɛərɪlɪ) *adv* **1** principally; chiefly; mainly **2** at first; originally
primary ('praɪmərɪ) *adj* **1** first in importance, degree, rank, etc **2** first in position or time, as in a series **3** fundamental; basic **4** being the first stage; elementary **5** (*prenominal*) of or relating to the education of children up to the age of 11 **6** (of the flight feathers of a bird's wing) growing from the manus **7a** being the part of an electric circuit, such as a transformer, in which a changing current induces a current in a neighbouring circuit: *a primary coil* **7b** (of a current) flowing in such a circuit **8a** (of a product) consisting of a natural raw material; unmanufactured **8b** (of production or industry) involving the extraction or winning of such products **9** (of Latin, Greek, or Sanskrit tenses) referring to present or future time **10** *geol, obs* relating to the Palaeozoic or earlier eras ▷ *n, pl* **primaries** **11** a person or thing that is first in rank, occurrence, etc **12** (in the US) a preliminary election in which the voters of a state or region choose a party's convention delegates, nominees for office, etc. Full name: **primary election** **13** short for **primary colour** or **primary school** **14** any of the flight feathers growing from the manus of a bird's wing **15** a primary coil, winding, inductance, or current in an electric circuit **16** *astron* a celestial body around which one or more specified secondary bodies orbit: *the sun is the primary of the earth* [c15 from L *prīmārius* principal, from *prīmus* first]
primary accent *or* **stress** *n linguistics* the strongest accent in a word or breath group, as that on the first syllable of *agriculture*
primary cell *n* an electric cell that generates an electromotive force by the direct and usually irreversible conversion of chemical energy into electrical energy. Also called: **voltaic cell**
primary colour *n* **1** any of three colours (usually red, green, and blue) that can be mixed to match any other colour, including white light but excluding black **2** any one of the colours cyan, magenta, or yellow. An equal mixture of the three produces a black pigment **3** any one of the colours red, yellow, green, or blue. All other colours look like a mixture of two or more of these colours
primary school *n* **1** (in England and Wales) a school for children below the age of 11. It is usually divided into an infant and a junior section **2** (in Scotland) a school for children below the age of 12 **3** (in the US and Canad) a school equivalent to the first three or four grades of elementary school
primate[1] ('praɪmeɪt) *n* **1** any placental mammal of the order *Primates*, typically having flexible hands, good eyesight, and, in the higher apes, a highly developed brain: includes lemurs, apes, and man ▷ *adj* **2** of, relating to, or belonging to the order *Primates* [c18 from NL *primates*, pl. of *prīmās* principal, from *prīmus* first] > **primatial** (praɪ'meɪʃəl) *adj*
primate[2] ('praɪmeɪt) *n* **1** another name for an **archbishop** **2** **Primate of all England** the Archbishop of Canterbury **3** **Primate of England** the Archbishop of York [c13 from OF, from L *prīmās* principal, from *prīmus* first]

Pp

prime (praɪm) *adj* **1** (*prenominal*) first in quality or value; first-rate **2** (*prenominal*) fundamental; original **3** (*prenominal*) first in importance; chief **4** *maths* **4a** having no factors except itself or one: *x^2+x+3 is a prime polynomial* **4b** (foll by *to*) having no common factors (with): *20 is prime to 21* **5** *finance* having the best credit rating: *prime investments* ▷ *n* **6** the time when a thing is at its best **7** a period of power, vigour, etc (esp in **the prime of life**) **8** *maths* short for **prime number** **9** *chiefly RC Church* the second of the seven canonical hours of the divine office, originally fixed for the first hour of the day, at sunrise **10** the first of eight basic positions from which a parry or attack can be made in fencing ▷ *vb* **primes, priming, primed** **11** to prepare (something) **12** (*tr*) to apply a primer, such as paint or size, to (a surface) **13** (*tr*) to fill (a pump) with its working fluid before starting, in order to expel air from it before starting **14** **prime the pump** **14a** See **pump priming** **14b** to make an initial input in order to set a process going **15** (*tr*) to increase the quantity of fuel in the float chamber of (a carburettor) in order to facilitate the starting of an engine **16** (*tr*) to insert a primer into (a gun, mine, etc) preparatory to detonation or firing **17** (*tr*) to provide with facts beforehand; brief [(adj) c14 from L *prīmus* first; (n) c13 from L *prīma* (*hora*) the first (hour); (vb) c16 from ?] > **'primeness** *n*
prime cost *n* the portion of the cost of a commodity that varies directly with the amount of it produced, principally comprising materials and labour. Also called: **variable cost**
prime meridian *n* the 0° meridian from which the other meridians are calculated, usually taken to pass through Greenwich
prime minister *n* **1** the head of a parliamentary

government **2** the chief minister of a sovereign or a state

prime mover *n* **1** the original force behind an idea, enterprise, etc **2a** the source of power, such as fuel, wind, electricity, etc, for a machine **2b** the means of extracting power from such a source, such as a steam engine

prime number *n* an integer that cannot be factorized into other integers but is only divisible by itself or 1, such as 2, 3, 5, 7, and 11

primer[1] ('praɪmə) *n* an introductory text, such as a school textbook [C14 via Anglo-Norman, from Med. L *primārius (liber)* a first (book), from L *prīmārius* PRIMARY]

primer[2] ('praɪmə) *n* **1** a person or thing that primes **2** a device, such as a tube containing explosive, for detonating the main charge in a gun, mine, etc **3** a substance, such as paint, applied to a surface as a base, sealer, etc [C15 see PRIME (vb)]

prime rate *n* the lowest commercial interest rate charged by a bank at a particular time

prime time *n* the peak viewing time on television, for which advertising rates are the highest

primeval *or* **primaeval** (praɪ'miːvᵊl) *adj* of or belonging to the first ages of the world [C17 from L *prīmaevus* youthful, from *prīmus* first + *aevum* age] > **pri'mevally** *or* **pri'maevally** *adv*

priming ('praɪmɪŋ) *n* **1** something used to prime **2** a substance used to ignite an explosive charge

primitive ('prɪmɪtɪv) *adj* **1** of or belonging to the beginning; original **2** characteristic of an early state, esp in being crude or uncivilized: *a primitive dwelling* **3** *anthropol* denoting a preliterate and nonindustrial social system **4** *biol* of, relating to, or resembling an early stage in development: *primitive amphibians* **5** showing the characteristics of primitive painters; untrained, childlike, or naive **6** *geol* of or denoting rocks formed in or before the Palaeozoic era **7** denoting a word from which another word is derived, as for example *hope*, from which *hopeless* is derived **8** *Protestant theol* of or associated with a group that breaks away from a sect, denomination, or Church in order to return to what is regarded as the original simplicity of the Gospels ▷ *n* **9** a primitive person or thing **10a** an artist whose work does not conform to traditional standards of Western painting, such as a painter from an African civilization **10b** a painter of the pre-Renaissance era in European painting **10c** a painter of any era whose work appears childlike or untrained ▷ Also called (for a, c): **naive** **11** a work by such an artist **12** a word from which another word is derived **13** *maths* a curve or other form from which another is derived [C14 from L *prīmitīvus* earliest of its kind from *prīmus* first] > **'primitively** *adv* > **'primitiveness** *n*

primitivism ('prɪmɪtɪˌvɪzəm) *n* **1** the condition of being primitive **2** the belief that the value of primitive cultures is superior to that of the modern world > **'primitivist** *n, adj*

primo ('priːməʊ) *n, pl* **primos** *or* **primi** ('priːmiː) *Music* **1** the upper or right-hand part of a piano duet **2** **tempo primo** at the same speed as at the beginning of the piece [It.: first, from L *prīmus*]

Primo de Rivera (*Spanish* 'primo de ri'βera) *n* **1** **José Antonio** (xo'se an'tonjo) 1903–36, Spanish politician; founded Falangism **2** his father, **Miguel** (mi'ɣel) 1870–1930, Spanish general; dictator of Spain (1923–30)

primogenitor (ˌpraɪməʊ'dʒɛnɪtə) *n* **1** a forefather; ancestor **2** an earliest parent or ancestor, as of a race [C17 alteration of PROGENITOR after PRIMOGENITURE]

primogeniture (ˌpraɪməʊ'dʒɛnɪtʃə) *n* **1** the state of being a first-born **2** *law* the right of an eldest son to succeed to the estate of his ancestor to the exclusion of all others [C17 from Med. L *prīmōgenitūra* birth of a first child, from L *prīmō* at first + LL *genitūra* a birth] > **primogenitary** (ˌpraɪməʊ'dʒɛnɪtərɪ, -trɪ) *adj*

primordial (praɪ'mɔːdɪəl) *adj* **1** existing at or from the beginning; primeval **2** constituting an origin; fundamental **3** *biol* relating to an early stage of development [C14 from LL *prīmōrdiālis* original, from L *prīmus* first + *ōrdīrī* to begin] > **pri,mordi'ality** *n* > **pri'mordially** *adv*

primp (prɪmp) *vb* to dress (oneself), esp in fine clothes; prink [C19 prob. from PRIM]

primrose ('prɪmˌrəʊz) *n* **1** any of various temperate plants of the genus *Primula*, esp a European variety which has pale yellow flowers **2** short for **evening primrose** **3** Also called: **primrose yellow** a light yellow, sometimes with a greenish tinge ▷ *adj* **4** of or abounding in primroses **5** of the colour primrose [C15 from OF *primerose*, from Med. L *prīma rosa* first rose]

primrose path *n* (often preceded by *the*) a pleasurable way of life

primula ('prɪmjʊlə) *n* any plant of the N temperate genus *Primula*, having white, yellow, pink, or purple funnel-shaped flowers with five spreading petals: includes the primrose, oxlip, cowslip, and polyanthus [C18 NL, from Med. L *prīmula (vēris)* little first one (of the spring)]

primum mobile *Latin* ('praɪmʊm 'məʊbɪlɪ) *n* **1** a prime mover **2** *astron* the outermost empty sphere in the Ptolemaic system that was thought to revolve around the earth from east to west in 24 hours carrying with it the inner spheres of the planets, sun, moon, and fixed stars [C15 from Med. L: first moving (thing)]

Primus ('praɪməs) *n trademark* a portable paraffin cooking stove, used esp by campers. Also called: **Primus stove**

prince (prɪns) *n* **1** (in Britain) a son of the sovereign or of one of the sovereign's sons **2** a nonreigning male member of a sovereign family **3** the monarch of a small territory that was at some time subordinate to an emperor or king **4** any monarch **5** a nobleman in various countries, such as Italy and Germany **6** an outstanding member of a specified group: *a merchant prince* [C13 via OF from L *princeps* first man, ruler] > **'princedom** *n* > **'prince,like** *adj*

prince consort *n* the husband of a female sovereign, who is himself a prince

Prince Edward Island *n* an island in the Gulf of St Lawrence that constitutes the smallest Canadian province. Capital: Charlottetown. Pop: 138 500 (2001 est). Area: 5656 sq km (2184 sq miles). Abbrevs: **PE, PEI** > **Prince Edward Islander** *n*
▷ www.gov.pe.ca
▷ www.gov.pe.ca/visitorsguide/index.php3

princeling ('prɪnslɪŋ) *n* **1** a young prince **2** Also called: **princelet** the ruler of an insignificant territory

princely ('prɪnslɪ) *adj* **princelier, princeliest** **1** generous or lavish **2** of or characteristic of a prince ▷ *adv* **3** in a princely manner > **'princeliness** *n*

Prince of Darkness *n* another name for **Satan**

Prince of Peace *n Bible* the future Messiah (Isaiah 9:6): held by Christians to be Christ

Prince of Wales[1] *n* the eldest son and heir apparent of the British sovereign

Prince of Wales[2] *n* **Cape** a cape in W Alaska, on the Bering Strait opposite the coast of the extreme northeast of Russia: the westernmost point of North America

Prince of Wales Island *n* **1** an island in N Canada, in Nunavut. Area: about 36 000 sq km (14 000 sq miles) **2** an island in SE Alaska, the largest island in the Alexander Archipelago. Area: about 4000 sq km (1500 sq miles) **3** an island in NE Australia, in N Queensland in the Torres Strait **4** the former name (until about 1867) of the island of **Penang**

prince regent *n* a prince who acts as regent during the minority, disability, or absence of the legal sovereign

Prince Regent *n* George IV as regent of Great Britain and Ireland during the insanity of his father (1811–20)

Prince Rupert ('ru:pət) *n* a port in W Canada, on the coast of British Columbia: one of the W termini of the Canadian National transcontinental railway. Pop: 16 620 (1991)

prince's-feather *n* **1** a garden plant with spikes of bristly brownish-red flowers **2** a tall tropical plant with hanging spikes of pink flowers

princess (prɪn'sɛs) *n* **1** (in Britain) a daughter of the sovereign or of one of the sovereign's sons **2** a nonreigning female member of a sovereign family **3** the wife and consort of a prince **4** *arch* a female sovereign **5** Also: **princess dress** a style of dress having a fitted bodice and A-line skirt without a seam at the waistline

princess royal *n* the eldest daughter of a British or (formerly) a Prussian sovereign

Princeton ('prɪnstən) *n* a town in central New Jersey: settled by Quakers in 1696; an important educational centre, seat of Princeton University (founded at Elizabeth in 1747 and moved here in 1756); scene of the battle (1777) during the War of American Independence in which Washington's troops defeated the British on the university campus. Pop: 12 016 (1990)

principal ('prɪnsɪpᵊl) *adj* (*prenominal*) **1** first in importance, rank, value, etc **2** denoting capital or property as opposed to interest, etc ▷ *n* **3** a person who is first in importance or directs some event, organization, etc **4** *law* **4a** a person who engages another to act as his or her agent **4b** an active participant in a crime **4c** the person primarily liable to fulfil an obligation **5** the head of a school or other educational institution **6** (in Britain) a civil servant of an executive grade who is in charge of a section **7** the leading performer in a play **8** *finance* **8a** capital or property, as contrasted with income **8b** the original amount of a debt on which interest is calculated **9** a main roof truss or rafter **10** *music* either of two types of open diapason organ stops [c13 via OF from L *principālis* chief, from *princeps* chief man] > '**principally** *adv* > '**principalship** *n*

USAGE See at **principle**

principal boy *n* the leading male role in a pantomime, traditionally played by a woman

principality (ˌprɪnsɪ'pælɪtɪ) *n, pl* **principalities** **1** a territory ruled by a prince or from which a prince draws his title **2** the authority of a prince

principal nursing officer *n* a grade of nurse concerned with administration in the British National Health Service

principal parts *pl n grammar* the main inflected forms of a verb, from which all other inflections may be deduced

principate ('prɪnsɪˌpeɪt) *n* **1** a state ruled by a prince **2** a form of rule in the early Roman Empire in which some republican forms survived

Principe ('prɪnsɪpi:; *Portuguese* 'prĩsipə) *n* an island in the Gulf of Guinea, off the W coast of Africa: part of São Tomé e Principe. Area: 150 sq km (58 sq miles)

principle ('prɪnsɪpᵊl) *n* **1** a standard or rule of personal conduct: *he would stoop to anything – he has no principles* **2** a set of such moral rules: *he was a man of principle* **3** a fundamental or general truth **4** the essence of something **5** a source; origin **6** a law concerning a natural phenomenon or the behaviour of a system: *the principle of the conservation of mass* **7** *chem* a constituent of a substance that gives the substance its characteristics **8** **in principle** in theory **9** **on principle** because of or in demonstration of a principle [c14 from L *principium* beginning, basic tenet]

USAGE *Principle* and *principal* are often confused: *the principal* (not *principle*) *reason for his departure; the plan was approved in principle* (not *principal*)

principled ('prɪnsɪpᵊld) *adj* **a** having high moral principles **b** (*in combination*): *high-principled*

prink (prɪŋk) *vb* **1** to dress (oneself, etc) finely; deck out **2** (*intr*) to preen oneself [c16 prob. changed from PRANK² (to adorn)]

print (prɪnt) *vb* **1** to reproduce (text, pictures, etc), esp in large numbers, by applying ink to paper or other material **2** to produce or reproduce (a manuscript, data, etc) in print, as for publication **3** to write (letters, etc) in the style of printed matter **4** to mark or indent (a surface) by pressing (something) onto it **5** to produce a photographic print from (a negative) **6** (*tr*) to fix in the mind or memory **7** (*tr*) to make (a mark) by applying pressure ▷ *n* **8** printed matter such as newsprint **9** a printed publication such as a book **10** **in print** **10a** in printed or published form **10b** (of a book, etc) offered for sale by the publisher **11** **out of print** no longer available from a publisher **12** a design or picture printed from an engraved plate, wood block, or other medium **13** printed text, esp with regard to the typeface: *small print* **14** a positive photographic image produced from a negative image on film **15a** a fabric with a printed design **15b** (*as modifier*): *a print dress* **16a** a mark made by pressing something onto a surface **16b** a stamp, die, etc, that makes such an impression **17** See **fingerprint** ▷ See also **print out** [c13 *priente*, from OF: something printed, from *preindre* to make an impression, from L *premere* to press] > '**printable** *adj*

printed circuit *n* an electronic circuit in which certain components and the connections between them are formed by etching a metallic coating or by electrodeposition on one or both sides of a thin insulating board

printer ('prɪntə) *n* **1** a person or business engaged in printing **2** a machine or device that prints **3** *computing* an output device for printing results on paper

printer's devil *n* an apprentice or errand boy in a printing establishment

printing ('prɪntɪŋ) *n* **1** the business or art of producing printed matter **2** printed text **3** Also called: **impression** all the copies of a book, etc, printed at one time **4** a form of writing in which letters resemble printed letters

▷ www.gain.net
▷ www.bpif.org.uk

printing press *n* any of various machines used for printing

printmaker ('prɪntˌmeɪkə) *n* a person who makes print or prints, esp a craftsman or artist

print out *vb* (*tr, adv*) **1** (of a computer output device) to produce (printed information) ▷ *n* **print-out, printout** **2** such printed information

print shop *n* a place in which printing is carried out

prion ('pri:ɒn) *n* a protein in the brain, an abnormal transmissible form of which is thought to be the transmissable agent responsible for certain spongiform encephalopathies, such as BSE, scrapie, Creutzfeldt-Jakob disease, and kuru [c20 from *pr(oteinaceous) i(nfectious particle)* + -ON]

prior¹ ('praɪə) *adj* **1** (*prenominal*) previous **2** **prior to** before; until [c18 from L: previous]

prior² ('praɪə) *n* **1** the superior of a community in certain religious orders **2** the deputy head of a monastery or abbey, immediately below the abbot [c11 from LL: head, from L (adj): previous, from OL *pri* before] > '**priorate** *n* > '**prioress** *fem n*

Prior ('praɪə) *n* **Matthew** 1664–1721, English poet and diplomat, noted for his epigrammatic occasional verse

priority (praɪ'ɒrɪtɪ) *n, pl* **priorities** **1** the condition of being prior; antecedence; precedence **2** the right of

Pp

precedence over others **3** something given specified attention: *my first priority*

priory ('praɪərɪ) *n, pl* **priories** a religious house governed by a prior, sometimes being subordinate to an abbey [c13 from Med. L *priōria*]

Pripet ('pri:pɪt) *n* a river in E Europe, rising in the NW Ukraine and flowing northeast into Belarus across the **Pripet Marshes** (the largest swamp in Europe), then east into the Dnieper River. Length: about 800 km (500 miles). Russian name: **Pripyat** ('prɪpjətj)

Priscian ('prɪʃɪən) *n* Latin name *Priscianus Caesariensis*. 6th century AD, Latin grammarian

prise *or* **prize** (praɪz) *vb* **prises, prising, prised** *or* **prizes, prizing, prized** (*tr*) **1** to force open by levering **2** to extract or obtain with difficulty: *they had to prise the news out of him* [c17 from OF *prise* a taking, from *prendre* to take, from L *prehendere*; see PRIZE[1]]

prism ('prɪzəm) *n* **1** a transparent polygonal solid, often having triangular ends and rectangular sides, for dispersing light into a spectrum or for reflecting light: used in binoculars, periscopes, etc **2** *maths* a polyhedron having parallel bases and sides that are parallelograms [c16 from Med. L *prisma*, from Gk: something shaped by sawing, from *prizein* to saw]

prismatic (prɪz'mætɪk) *adj* **1** of or produced by a prism **2** exhibiting bright spectral colours: *prismatic light* **3** *crystallog* another word for **orthorhombic** > **pris'matically** *adv*

prison ('prɪz^{ə}n) *n* **1** a public building used to house convicted criminals and accused persons awaiting trial **2** any place of confinement [c12 from OF *prisun*, from L *prēnsiō* a capturing, from *prehendere* to lay hold of]

▷ www.hmprisonservice.gov.uk/link_bottom.asp#Sixth
▷ www.homeoffice.gov.uk/justice/prisons/index.html
▷ www.kcl.ac.uk/depsta/rel/icps/home.html

prisoner ('prɪzənə) *n* **1** a person kept in custody as a punishment for a crime, while awaiting trial, or for some other reason **2** a person confined by any of various restraints: *we are all prisoners of time* **3** **take** (**someone**) **prisoner** to capture and hold (someone) as a prisoner

prisoner of war *n* a person, esp a serviceman, captured by an enemy in time of war. Abbrev: **POW**

prisoner's base *n* a children's game involving two teams, members of which chase and capture each other

prissy ('prɪsɪ) *adj* **prissier, prissiest** fussy and prim, esp in a prudish way [c20 prob. from PRIM + SISSY] > '**prissily** *adv* > '**prissiness** *n*

Priština (*Serbo-Croat* 'pri:ʃtina) *n* a city in S Serbia and Montenegro, the capital of Kosovo: under Turkish control until 1912; severely damaged in the Kosovo conflict of 1999; nearby is the 14th-century Gračanica monastery. Pop: 186 611 (2000 est)

pristine ('prɪstaɪn, -ti:n) *adj* **1** of or involving the earliest period, state, etc; original **2** pure; uncorrupted **3** fresh, clean, and unspoiled: *his pristine new car* [c15 from L *pristinus* primitive]

> USAGE The use of *pristine* to mean 'fresh, clean, and unspoiled' was formerly considered by some people to be incorrect, but is now generally acceptable

Pritchett ('prɪtʃɪt) *n* Sir **V**(**ictor**) **S**(**awdon**) 1900–97, British short-story writer, novelist, essayist, and autobiographer; his works include *Mr Beluncle* (1951) and *A Careless Widow* (1989)

prithee ('prɪðɪ) *interj arch* pray thee; please [c16 shortened from *I pray thee*]

privacy ('praɪvəsɪ, 'prɪvəsɪ) *n* **1** the condition of being private **2** secrecy

private ('praɪvɪt) *adj* **1** not widely or publicly known: *they had private reasons for the decision* **2** confidential; secret: *a private conversation* **3** not for general or public use: *a private bathroom* **4** of or provided by a private individual or organization rather than by the state **5** (*prenominal*) individual; special: *my own private recipe* **6** (*prenominal*) having no public office, rank, etc: *a private man* **7** (*prenominal*) denoting a soldier of the lowest military rank **8** (of a place) retired; not overlooked ▷ *n* **9** a soldier of the lowest rank in many armies and marine corps **10** **in private** in secret [c14 from L *prīvātus* belonging to one individual, withdrawn from public life, from *prīvāre* to deprive] > '**privately** *adv*

private bill *n* a bill presented to Parliament or Congress on behalf of a private individual, corporation, etc

private company *n* a limited company that does not issue shares for public subscription and whose owners do not enjoy an unrestricted right to transfer their shareholdings ▷ Cf **public company**

private detective *n* an individual privately employed to investigate a crime or make other inquiries. Also called: **private investigator**

private enterprise *n* economic activity undertaken by private individuals or organizations under private ownership

privateer (ˌpraɪvə'tɪə) *n* **1** an armed privately owned vessel commissioned for war service by a government **2** Also called: **privateersman** a member of the crew of a privateer **3** a competitor, esp in motor racing, who is privately financed rather than sponsored by a manufacturer ▷ *vb* **4** (*intr*) to serve as a privateer

private eye *n inf* a private detective

Private Finance Initiative *n* (in Britain) a government scheme to encourage private investment in public projects. Abbrev: **PFI**

private health insurance *n* insurance against the need for medical treatment as a private patient

private hotel *n* **1** a hotel in which the proprietor has the right to refuse to accept a person as a guest **2** *Austral & NZ* a hotel not having a licence to sell alcoholic liquor

private income *n* an income from sources other than employment, such as investment. Also called: **private means**

private life *n* the social life or personal relationships of an individual, esp of a celebrity

private member *n* a member of a legislative assembly not having an appointment in the government

private member's bill *n* a parliamentary bill sponsored by a Member of Parliament who is not a government minister

private parts *or* **privates** *pl n* euphemistic terms for genitals

private patient *n Brit* a patient receiving medical treatment not paid for by the National Health Service

private pay bed *n* (in Britain) a hospital bed reserved for private patients who are charged by the health service for use of hospital facilities

private practice *n Brit* medical practice that is not part of the National Health Service

private school *n* a school under the financial and managerial control of a private body, accepting mostly fee-paying pupils

private secretary *n* **1** a secretary entrusted with the personal and confidential matters of a business executive **2** a civil servant who acts as aide to a minister or senior government official

private sector *n* the part of a country's economy that consists of privately owned enterprises

privation (praɪ'veɪʃən) *n* **1** loss or lack of the necessities of life, such as food and shelter **2** hardship resulting from this **3** the state of being deprived [c14 from L *prīvātiō* deprivation]

privative ('prɪvətɪv) *adj* **1** causing privation **2** expressing lack or negation, as for example the English suffix *-less* and prefix *un-* [c16 from L *prīvātīvus* indicating loss] > '**privatively** *adv*

privatize *or* **privatise** ('praɪvɪˌtaɪz) *vb* **privatizes, privatizing, privatized** *or* **privatises, privatising,**

privatised (*tr*) to take into, or return to, private ownership, a company or concern that has previously been owned by the state > ˌ**privatiˈzation** *or* ˌ**privatiˈsation** *n*
privet (ˈprɪvɪt) *n* **a** any of a genus of shrubs, esp one having oval dark green leaves, white flowers, and purplish-black berries **b** (*as modifier*): *a privet hedge* [C16 from ?]
privilege (ˈprɪvɪlɪdʒ) *n* **1** a benefit, immunity, etc, granted under certain conditions **2** the advantages and immunities enjoyed by a small usually powerful group or class, esp to the disadvantage of others: *one of the obstacles to social harmony is privilege* **3** *US stock exchange* a speculative contract permitting its purchaser to make optional purchases or sales of securities at a specified time over a limited period ▷ *vb* **privileges, privileging, privileged** (*tr*) **4** to bestow a privilege or privileges upon **5** (foll by *from*) to free or exempt [C12 from OF *privilège*, from L *prīvilēgium* law relevant to rights of an individual, from *prīvus* an individual + *lēx* law]
privileged (ˈprɪvɪlɪdʒd) *adj* **1** enjoying or granted as a privilege or privileges **2** *law* **2a** not actionable as a libel or slander **2b** (of a communication, document, etc) that a witness cannot be compelled to divulge
privity (ˈprɪvɪtɪ) *n, pl* **privities 1** a legally recognized relationship existing between two parties, such as that between the parties to a contract: *privity of contract* **2** secret knowledge that is shared [C13 from OF *priveté*]
privy (ˈprɪvɪ) *adj* **privier, priviest 1** (*postpositive*; foll by *to*) participating in the knowledge of something secret **2** *arch* secret, hidden, etc ▷ *n, pl* **privies 3** a lavatory, esp an outside one **4** *law* a person in privity with another. See **privity** [C13 from OF *privé* something private, from L *prīvātus* PRIVATE] > ˈ**privily** *adv*
privy council *n* **1** the council of state of a monarch, esp formerly **2** *arch* a secret council
Privy Council *n* **1** the private council of the British sovereign, consisting of all current and former ministers of the Crown and other distinguished subjects, all of whom are appointed for life **2** (in Canada) a ceremonial body of advisers of the governor general, the chief of them being the Federal cabinet ministers > **Privy Counsellor** *n*
privy purse *n* (*often caps*) **1** an allowance voted by Parliament for the private expenses of the monarch **2** an official of the royal household responsible for dealing with the monarch's private expenses. Full name: **Keeper of the Privy Purse**
privy seal *n* (*often caps*) (in Britain) a seal affixed to certain documents issued by royal authority: of less importance than the great seal
Prix Goncourt (*French* pri) *n* an annual prize for a work of French fiction [C20 after the Académie GONCOURT]
prize¹ (praɪz) *n* **1a** a reward or honour for having won a contest, competition, etc **1b** (*as modifier*): *prize jockey; prize essay* **2** something given to the winner of any game of chance, lottery, etc **3** something striven for **4** any valuable property captured in time of war, esp a vessel [C14 from OF *prise* a capture, from L *prehendere* to seize; infl. by ME *prise* reward]
prize² (praɪz) *vb* **prizes, prizing, prized** (*tr*) to esteem greatly; value highly [C15 *prise*, from OF *preisier* to PRAISE]
prize court *n law* a court having jurisdiction to determine how property captured at sea in wartime is to be distributed
prizefight (ˈpraɪzˌfaɪt) *n* a boxing match for a prize or purse > ˈ**prizeˌfighter** *n* > ˈ**prizeˌfighting** *n*
prize ring *n* **1** the enclosed area or ring used by prizefighters **2 the prize ring** the sport of prizefighting
PRK *abbrev for* photo refractive keratomy
pro¹ (prəʊ) *adv* **1** in favour of a motion, issue, course of action, etc ▷ *prep* **2** in favour of ▷ *n, pl* **pros 3** (*usually pl*) an argument or vote in favour of a proposal or motion. See also **pros and cons** [from L *prō* (prep) in favour of]
pro² (prəʊ) *n, pl* **pros,** *adj inf* **1** short for **professional 2** a prostitute [C19]
PRO *abbrev for:* **1** Public Records Office **2** public relations officer
pro-¹ *prefix* **1** in favour of; supporting: *pro-Chinese* **2** acting as a substitute for: *proconsul; pronoun* [from L *prō* (adv & prep). In compound words borrowed from L, *prō-* indicates: forward, out (*project*); away from (*prodigal*); onward (*proceed*); in front of (*provide, protect*); on behalf of (*procure*); substitute for (*pronominal*); and sometimes intensive force (*promiscuous*)]
pro-² *prefix* before in time or position; anterior; forward: *prognathous* [from Gk *pro* (prep) before (in time, position, etc)]
proa (ˈprəʊə) *or* **prau** *n* any of several kinds of canoe-like boats used in the South Pacific, esp one equipped with an outrigger and sails [C16 from Malay *parāhū* a boat]
proactive (prəʊˈæktɪv) *adj* **1** tending to initiate change rather than reacting to events **2** *psychol* of or denoting a mental process that affects a subsequent process [C20 from PRO-² + (RE)ACTIVE]
pro-am (ˈprəʊˈæm) *adj* **1** (of a golf tournament, etc) involving both professional and amateur players ▷ *n* **2** a sporting tournament involving both professional and amateur players
probability (ˌprɒbəˈbɪlɪtɪ) *n, pl* **probabilities 1** the condition of being probable **2** an event or other thing that is probable **3** *statistics* a measure of the degree of confidence one may have in the occurrence of an event, measured on a scale from zero (impossibility) to one (certainty)
probable (ˈprɒbəbᵊl) *adj* **1** likely to be or to happen but not necessarily so **2** most likely: *the probable cause of the accident* ▷ *n* **3** a person who is probably to be chosen for a team, event, etc [C14 via OF from L *probābilis* that may be proved, from *probāre* to prove]
probably (ˈprɒbəblɪ) *adv* **1** (*sentence modifier*) in all likelihood or probability: *I'll probably see you tomorrow* ▷ *sentence substitute* **2** I believe such a thing may be the case
proband (ˈprəʊbænd) *n* another name (esp US) for **propositus** [C20 from L *probandus*, *probāre* to test]
probang (ˈprəʊbæŋ) *n surgery* a long flexible rod, often with a small sponge at one end, for inserting into the oesophagus, as to apply medication [C17 var., apparently by association with PROBE, of *provang*, coined by W. Rumsey (1584–1660), Welsh judge, its inventor; from ?]
probate (ˈprəʊbɪt, -beɪt) *n* **1** the process of officially proving the validity of a will **2** the official certificate stating a will to be genuine and conferring on the executors power to administer the estate **3** (*modifier*) relating to probate: *a probate court* ▷ *vb* **probates, probating, probated 4** (*tr*) *chiefly US* to establish officially the validity of (a will) [C15 from L *probāre* to inspect]
probation (prəˈbeɪʃən) *n* **1** a system of dealing with offenders by placing them under the supervision of a probation officer **2 on probation 2a** under the supervision of a probation officer **2b** undergoing a test period **3** a trial period, as for a teacher > **proˈbational** *or* **proˈbationary** *adj*
probationer (prəˈbeɪʃənə) *n* a person on probation
probation officer *n* an officer of a court who supervises offenders placed on probation and assists and befriends them
probe (prəʊb) *vb* **probes, probing, probed 1** (*tr*) to search into closely **2** to examine (something) with or as if with a probe ▷ *n* **3** something that probes or tests **4** *surgery* a slender instrument for exploring a wound, sinus, etc **5** a thorough inquiry, such as one by a newspaper into corrupt practices **6** *electronics* a lead connecting to or containing a monitoring circuit used for testing

Pp

7 anything which provides or acts as a coupling, esp a flexible tube extended from an aircraft to link it with another so that it can refuel 8 See **space probe** [c16 from Med. L *proba* investigation, from L *probāre* to test] > **'probeable** *adj* > **'prober** *n*

probiotic (ˌprəʊbaɪˈɒtɪk) *n* 1 a harmless bacterium that helps to protect the body from harmful bacteria 2 a substance that encourages the growth of natural healthy bacteria in the gut ▷ *adj* 3 of or relating to probiotics: *probiotic yoghurt* [c20 from PRO-[1] + (ANTI)BIOTIC]

probity (ˈprəʊbɪtɪ) *n* confirmed integrity [c16 from L *probitās* honesty, from *probus* virtuous]

problem (ˈprɒbləm) *n* 1a any thing, matter, person, etc, that is difficult to deal with 1b (*as modifier*): *a problem child* 2 a puzzle, question, etc, set for solution 3 *maths* a statement requiring a solution usually by means of several operations or constructions 4 (*modifier*) designating a literary work that deals with difficult moral questions: *a problem play* [c14 from LL *problēma*, from Gk: something put forward]

problematic (ˌprɒbləˈmætɪk) *or* **problematical** *adj* 1 having the nature of a problem; uncertain; questionable 2 *logic, obs* (of a proposition) asserting that a property may or may not hold > ˌ**problem'atically** *adv*

pro bono publico *Latin* (ˈprəʊ ˈbəʊnəʊ ˈpʊblɪkəʊ) for the public good

proboscidean *or* **proboscidian** (ˌprəʊbɒˈsɪdɪən) *adj* 1 of or belonging to an order of massive herbivorous placental mammals having tusks and a long trunk: contains the elephants ▷ *n* 2 any proboscidean animal

proboscis (prəʊˈbɒsɪs) *n, pl* **proboscises** *or* **proboscides** (prəʊˈbɒsɪˌdiːz) 1 a long flexible prehensile trunk or snout, as of an elephant 2 the elongated mouthpart of certain insects 3 any similar organ 4 *inf, facetious* a person's nose [c17 via L from Gk *proboskis* trunk of an elephant, from *boskein* to feed]

procaine (ˈprəʊkeɪn, prəʊˈkeɪn) *n* a colourless or white crystalline water-soluble substance used, as **procaine hydrochloride**, as a local anaesthetic [c20 from PRO-[1] + (CO)CAINE]

procathedral (ˌprəʊkəˈθiːdrəl) *n* a church serving as a cathedral

procedure (prəˈsiːdʒə) *n* 1 a way of acting or progressing, esp an established method 2 the established form of conducting the business of a legislature, the enforcement of a legal right, etc 3 *computing* another name for **subroutine** > **pro'cedural** *adj* > **pro'cedurally** *adv*

proceed (prəˈsiːd) *vb* (*intr*) 1 (often foll by *to*) to advance or carry on, esp after stopping 2 (often foll by *with*) to continue: *he proceeded with his reading* 3 (often foll by *against*) to institute or carry on a legal action 4 to originate; arise: *evil proceeds from the heart* [c14 from L *prōcēdere* to advance] > **pro'ceeder** *n*

proceeding (prəˈsiːdɪŋ) *n* 1 an act or course of action 2a a legal action 2b any step taken in a legal action 3 (*pl*) the minutes of the meetings of a society, etc 4 (*pl*) legal action; litigation 5 (*pl*) the events of an occasion

proceeds (ˈprəʊsiːdz) *pl n* 1 the profit or return derived from a commercial transaction, investment, etc 2 the result, esp the total sum, accruing from some undertaking

process[1] (ˈprəʊsɛs) *n* 1 a series of actions which produce a change or development: *the process of digestion* 2 a method of doing or producing something 3 progress or course of time 4 **in the process of** during or in the course of 5a a summons commanding a person to appear in court 5b the whole proceedings in an action at law 6 a natural outgrowth or projection of a part or organism 7 (*modifier*) relating to the general preparation of a printing forme or plate by the use, at some stage, of photography ▷ *vb* (*tr*) 8 to subject to a routine procedure; handle 9 to treat or prepare by a special method, esp to treat (food) in order to preserve it: *to process cheese* 10a to institute legal proceedings against 10b to serve a process on 11 *photog* 11a to develop, rinse, fix, wash, and dry (exposed film, etc) 11b to produce final prints or slides from (undeveloped film) 12 *computing* to perform operations on (data) according to programmed instructions in order to obtain the required information [c14 from OF *procès*, from L *prōcessus* an advancing, from *prōcēdere* to proceed]

process[2] (prəˈsɛs) *vb* (*intr*) to proceed in a procession [c19 back formation from PROCESSION]

process industry *n* a manufacturing industry, such as oil refining, which converts bulk raw materials into a workable form

procession (prəˈsɛʃən) *n* 1 the act of proceeding in a regular formation 2 a group of people or things moving forwards in an orderly, regular, or ceremonial manner 3 *Christianity* the emanation of the Holy Spirit ▷ *vb* 4 (*intr*) *rare* to go in procession [c12 via OF from L *prōcessiō* a marching forwards]

processional (prəˈsɛʃənəl) *adj* 1 of or suitable for a procession ▷ *n* 2 *Christianity* 2a a book containing the prayers, hymns, etc, prescribed for processions 2b a hymn, etc, used in a procession

processor (ˈprəʊsɛsə) *n* 1 *computing* another name for **central processing unit** 2 a person or thing that carries out a process

process-server *n* a sheriff's officer who serves legal documents such as writs for appearance in court

procès-verbal *French* (prɔsɛvɛrbal) *n, pl* ***procès-verbaux*** (prɔsɛvɛrbo) a written record of an official proceeding; minutes [c17 from F: see PROCESS, VERBAL]

pro-choice *adj* (of an organization, pressure group, etc) supporting the right of a woman to have an abortion ▷ Cf **pro-life**

prochronism (ˈprəʊkrəˌnɪzəm) *n* an error in dating that places an event earlier than it actually occurred [c17 from PRO-[2] + Gk *khronos* time + -ISM, by analogy with ANACHRONISM]

proclaim (prəˈkleɪm) *vb* (*tr*) 1 (*may take a clause as object*) to announce publicly 2 (*may take a clause as object*) to indicate plainly 3 to praise or extol [c14 from L *prōclāmāre* to shout aloud] > **proclamation** (ˌprɒkləˈmeɪʃən) *n* > **pro'claimer** *n* > **proclamatory** (prəˈklæmətərɪ, -trɪ) *adj*

proclitic (prəʊˈklɪtɪk) *adj* 1a denoting a monosyllabic word or form having no stress and pronounced as a prefix of the following word, as in English *'t* for *it* in *'twas* 1b (in classical Greek) denoting a word that throws its accent onto the following word ▷ *n* 2 a proclitic word or form [c19 from NL *proclīticus*, from Gk *proklinein* to lean forwards; on the model of ENCLITIC]

proclivity (prəˈklɪvɪtɪ) *n, pl* **proclivities** a tendency or inclination [c16 from L *prōclīvitās*, from *prōclīvis* steep, from *clīvus* a slope]

Proclus (ˈprəʊkləs, ˈprɒk-) *n* ?410–485 AD, Greek Neo-Platonist philosopher

Procne (ˈprɒknɪ) *n* *Greek myth* a princess of Athens, who punished her husband for raping her sister Philomela by feeding him the flesh of their son. She was changed at her death into a swallow. See **Philomela**

proconsul (prəʊˈkɒnsəl) *n* 1 a governor of a colony or other dependency 2 (in ancient Rome) the governor of a senatorial province > **proconsular** (prəʊˈkɒnsjʊlə) *adj*

Procopius (prəʊˈkəʊpɪəs) *n* ?490–?562 AD, Byzantine historian, noted for his account of the wars of Justinian I against the Persians, Vandals, and Ostrogoths

procrastinate (prəʊˈkræstɪˌneɪt, prə-) *vb* **procrastinates, procrastinating, procrastinated** (*usually intr*) to put off (an action) until later; delay [c16 from L *prōcrāstināre* to postpone until tomorrow, from PRO-[1] + *crās* tomorrow] > **proˌcrasti'nation** *n* > **pro'crastiˌnator** *n*

procreate (ˈprəʊkrɪˌeɪt) *vb* **procreates, procreating,**

procreate 1 to beget or engender (offspring) 2 (*tr*) to bring into being [C16 from L *prōcreāre*, from PRO-[1] + *creāre* to create] > **'procreant** *or* **'procre,ative** *adj* > **,procre'ation** *n* > **'procre,ator** *n*

Procrustean (prəʊ'krʌstɪən) *adj* tending or designed to produce conformity by violent or ruthless methods

Procrustes (prəʊ'krʌsti:z) *n Greek myth* a robber, who put travellers in his bed, stretching or lopping off their limbs so that they fitted it [C16 from Gk *Prokroustēs* the stretcher, from *prokrouein* to extend by hammering out]

proctology (prɒk'tɒlədʒɪ) *n* the branch of medical science concerned with the rectum [from Gk *prōktos* rectum + -OLOGY]

proctor ('prɒktə) *n* 1 a member of the staff of certain universities having duties including the enforcement of discipline 2 (formerly) an agent, esp one engaged to conduct another's case in a court 3 *Church of England* one of the elected representatives of the clergy in Convocation [C14 syncopated var. of PROCURATOR] > **proctorial** (prɒk'tɔ:rɪəl) *adj*

procumbent (prəʊ'kʌmbənt) *adj* 1 (of stems) trailing loosely along the ground 2 leaning forwards or lying on the face [C17 from L *prōcumbere* to fall forwards]

procurator ('prɒkjʊ,reɪtə) *n* 1 (in ancient Rome) a civil official of the emperor's administration, often employed as the governor of a minor province 2 *rare* a person engaged by another to manage his affairs [C13 from L: a manager, from *prōcūrāre* to attend to] > **procuracy** ('prɒkjʊrəsɪ) *or* **'procu,ratorship** *n* > **procuratorial** (,prɒkjʊrə'tɔ:rɪəl) *adj*

procurator fiscal *n* (in Scotland) a legal officer who performs the functions of public prosecutor and coroner

procure (prə'kjʊə) *vb* **procures, procuring, procured** 1 (*tr*) to obtain or acquire; secure 2 to obtain (women or girls) to act as prostitutes [C13 from L *prōcūrāre* to look after] > **pro'curable** *adj* > **pro'curement, pro'cural,** *or* **procuration** (,prɒkjʊ'reɪʃən) *n*

procurer (prə'kjʊərə) *n* a person who procures, esp one who procures women as prostitutes

prod (prɒd) *vb* **prods, prodding, prodded** 1 to poke or jab with or as if with a pointed object 2 (*tr*) to rouse to action ▷ *n* 3 the act or an instance of prodding 4 a sharp object 5 a stimulus or reminder [C16 from ?] > **'prodder** *n*

prod. *abbrev for:* 1 produce 2 produced 3 product

Prodi ('prəʊdɪ) *n* **Romano** (rə'mɑ:nəʊ) born 1939, Italian politician; prime minister (1996–98); president of the European Commission from 1999

prodigal ('prɒdɪg[ə]l) *adj* 1 recklessly wasteful or extravagant, as in disposing of goods or money 2 lavish: *prodigal of compliments* ▷ *n* 3 a person who spends lavishly or squanders money [C16 from Med. L *prōdigālis* wasteful, from L, from *prōdigere* to squander, from *agere* to drive] > **,prodi'gality** *n* > **'prodigally** *adv*

prodigious (prə'dɪdʒəs) *adj* 1 vast in size, extent, power, etc 2 wonderful or amazing [C16 from L *prōdigiōsus* marvellous, from *prōdigium*; see PRODIGY] > **pro'digiously** *adv* > **pro'digiousness** *n*

prodigy ('prɒdɪdʒɪ) *n, pl* **prodigies** 1 a person, esp a child, of unusual or marvellous talents 2 anything that is a cause of wonder 3 something monstrous or abnormal [C16 from L *prōdigium* an unnatural happening]

prodrug ('prəʊ,drʌg) *n* a compound that is itself biologically inactive but is metabolized in the body to produce an active therapeutic drug

produce *vb* (prə'dju:s), **produces, producing, produced** 1 to bring (something) into existence; yield 2 (*tr*) to make: *she produced a delicious dinner* 3 (*tr*) to give birth to 4 (*tr*) to present to view: *to produce evidence* 5 (*tr*) to bring before the public: *he produced a film last year* 6 (*tr*) to act as producer of 7 (*tr*) *geom* to extend (a line) ▷ *n* ('prɒdju:s) 8 anything produced; a product 9 agricultural products collectively: *farm produce* [C15 from L *prōdūcere* to bring forward] > **pro'ducible** *adj* > **pro,duci'bility** *n*

producer (prə'dju:sə) *n* 1 a person or thing that produces 2 *Brit* a person responsible for the artistic direction of a play 3 *US & Canad* a person who organizes the stage production of a play, including the finance, management, etc 4 the person who takes overall administrative responsibility for a film or television programme ▷ Cf **director** (sense 4) 5 the person who supervises the arrangement, recording, and mixing of a record 6 *econ* a person or business enterprise that generates goods or services for sale ▷ Cf **consumer** (sense 1) 7 *chem* an apparatus or plant for making producer gas

producer gas *n* a mixture of carbon monoxide and nitrogen produced by passing air over hot coke, used mainly as a fuel

product ('prɒdʌkt) *n* 1 something produced by effort, or some mechanical or industrial process 2 the result of some natural process 3 a result or consequence 4 *maths* the result of the multiplication of two or more numbers, quantities, etc [C15 from L *prōductum* (something) produced, from *prōdūcere* to bring forth]

product differentiation *n commerce* the real or illusory distinction between competing products in a market

production (prə'dʌkʃən) *n* 1 the act of producing 2 anything that is produced; a product 3 the amount produced or the rate at which it is produced 4 *econ* the creation or manufacture of goods and services with exchange value 5 any work created as a result of literary or artistic effort 6 the presentation of a play, opera, etc 7 *Brit* the artistic direction of a play 8 (*modifier*) manufactured by mass production: *a production model of a car* > **pro'ductional** *adj*

production line *n* a factory system in which parts or components of the end product are transported by a conveyor through a number of different sites at each of which a manual or machine operation is performed on them

productive (prə'dʌktɪv) *adj* 1 producing or having the power to produce; fertile 2 yielding favourable results 3 *econ* 3a producing goods and services that have exchange value: *productive assets* 3b relating to such production: *the productive processes of an industry* 4 (*postpositive;* foll by *of*) resulting in: *productive of good results* > **pro'ductively** *adv* > **pro'ductiveness** *n*

productivity (,prɒdʌk'tɪvɪtɪ) *n* 1 the output of an industrial concern in relation to the materials, labour, etc, it employs 2 the state of being productive

product liability *n* the liability to the public of a manufacturer or trader for selling a faulty product

product life cycle *n marketing* the four stages (introduction, growth, maturity, and decline) into one of which the sales of a product fall during its market life

product line *n marketing* a group of related products marketed by the same company

product placement *n* the practice of a company paying for its product to be placed in a prominent position in a film or television programme as a form of advertising

proem ('prəʊɛm) *n* an introduction or preface, such as to a work of literature [C14 from L *prooemium* introduction, from Gk *prooimion*, from PRO-[2] + *hoimē* song] > **proemial** (prəʊ'i:mɪəl) *adj*

proenzyme (prəʊ'ɛnzaɪm) *n* the inactive form of an enzyme; zymogen

Prof. *abbrev for* Professor

profane (prə'feɪn) *adj* 1 having or indicating contempt, irreverence, or disrespect for a divinity or something sacred 2 not designed for religious purposes; secular 3 not initiated into the inner mysteries or sacred rites 4 coarse or blasphemous: *profane language* ▷ *vb* **profanes, profaning, profaned** (*tr*) 5 to treat (something sacred) with irreverence 6 to put to an unworthy use [C15 from L *profānus* outside the temple] > **profanation** (,prɒfə'neɪʃən) *n* > **pro'fanely** *adv* > **pro'faneness** *n*

profanity (prəˈfænɪtɪ) *n, pl* **profanities** 1 the state or quality of being profane 2 vulgar or irreverent action, speech, etc

profess (prəˈfɛs) *vb* 1 (*tr*) to affirm or acknowledge: *to profess ignorance; to profess a belief in God* 2 (*tr*) to claim (something), often insincerely or falsely: *to profess to be a skilled driver* 3 to receive or be received into a religious order, as by taking vows [C14 from L *prōfitērī* to confess openly]

professed (prəˈfɛst) *adj* (*prenominal*) 1 avowed or acknowledged 2 alleged or pretended 3 professing to be qualified as: *a professed philosopher* 4 having taken vows of a religious order > **professedly** (prəˈfɛsɪdlɪ) *adv*

profession (prəˈfɛʃən) *n* 1 an occupation requiring special training in the liberal arts or sciences, esp one of the three learned professions, law, theology, or medicine 2 the body of people in such an occupation 3 an avowal; declaration 4 Also called: **profession of faith** a declaration of faith in a religion, esp as made on entering the Church or an order belonging to it [C13 from Med. L *professiō* the taking of vows upon entering a religious order, from L: public acknowledgment; see PROFESS]

professional (prəˈfɛʃənᵊl) *adj* 1 of, suitable for, or engaged in as a profession 2 engaging in an activity as a means of livelihood 3a extremely competent in a job, etc 3b (of a piece of work or anything performed) produced with competence or skill 4 undertaken or performed by people who are paid ▷ *n* 5 a person who belongs to one of the professions 6 a person who engages for his or her livelihood in some activity also pursued by amateurs 7 a person who engages in an activity with great competence 8 an expert player of a game who gives instruction, esp to members of a club by whom he or she is hired > **proˈfessionaˌlism** *n* > **proˈfessionally** *adv*

professional foul *n football* a deliberate foul committed as a last-ditch tactic to prevent an opponent from scoring

professor (prəˈfɛsə) *n* 1 the principal teacher in a field of learning at a university or college; holder of a university chair 2 *chiefly US & Canad* any teacher in a university or college 3 a person who professes his or her opinions, beliefs, etc [C14 from Med. L: one who has made his profession in a religious order, from L: a public teacher; see PROFESS] > **professorial** (ˌprɒfɪˈsɔːrɪəl) *adj* > ˌ**profesˈsorially** *adv* > ˌ**profesˈsoriate** *or* **proˈfessorship** *n*

proffer (ˈprɒfə) *vb* 1 (*tr*) to offer for acceptance ▷ *n* 2 the act of proffering [C13 from OF *proffrir*, from PRO-¹ + *offrir* to offer]

proficient (prəˈfɪʃənt) *adj* 1 having great facility (in an art, occupation, etc); skilled ▷ *n* 2 an expert [C16 from L *prōficere* to make progress] > **proˈficiency** *n* > **proˈficiently** *adv*

profile (ˈprəʊfaɪl) *n* 1 a side view or outline of an object, esp of a human head 2 a short biographical sketch 3 a graph, table, etc, representing the extent to which a person, field, or object exhibits various tested characteristics: *a population profile* 4 a vertical section of soil or rock showing the different layers 5 the outline of the shape of a river valley either from source to mouth (**long profile**) or at right angles to the flow of the river (**cross profile**) ▷ *vb* **profiles, profiling, profiled** 6 (*tr*) to draw, write, or make a profile of [C17 from It. *profilo*, from *profilare* to sketch lightly, from L *fīlum* thread] > ˈ**profiler** *or* **profilist** (ˈprəʊfɪlɪst) *n*

profile component *n Brit education* attainment targets in different subjects brought together for the general assessment of a pupil

profit (ˈprɒfɪt) *n* 1 (*often pl*) excess of revenues over outlays and expenses in a business enterprise 2 the monetary gain derived from a transaction 3 income derived from property or an investment, as contrasted with capital gains 4a *econ* the income accruing to a successful entrepreneur and held to be the motivating factor of a capitalist economy 4b (*as modifier*): *the profit motive* 5 a gain, benefit, or advantage ▷ *vb* 6 to gain or cause to gain profit [C14 from L *prōfectus* advance, from *prōficere* to make progress] > ˈ**profitless** *adj*

profitable (ˈprɒfɪtəbᵊl) *adj* affording gain or profit > ˌ**profitaˈbility** *n* > ˈ**profitably** *adv*

profit and loss *n book-keeping* an account compiled at the end of a financial year showing that year's revenue and expense items and indicating gross and net profit or loss

profit centre *n* a section of a commercial organization which is allocated financial targets in its own right

profiteer (ˌprɒfɪˈtɪə) *n* 1 a person who makes excessive profits, esp by charging exorbitant prices for goods in short supply ▷ *vb* 2 (*intr*) to make excessive profits

profiterole (ˈprɒfɪtəˌrəʊl, prəˈfɪtəˌrəʊl) *n* a small case of choux pastry with a sweet or savoury filling [C16 from F, lit.: a small profit]

profit-sharing *n* a system in which a portion of the net profit of a business is distributed to its employees, usually in proportion to their wages or their length of service

profit taking *n* selling commodities, securities, etc, at a profit after a rise in market values or before an expected fall in values

profit warning *n* a public announcement made by a company to shareholders and others warning that profits for a stated period will be much lower than had been expected

profligate (ˈprɒflɪgɪt) *adj* 1 shamelessly immoral or debauched 2 wildly extravagant or wasteful ▷ *n* 3 a profligate person [C16 from L *prōflīgātus* corrupt, from *prōflīgāre* to overthrow, from PRO-¹ + *flīgere* to beat] > **profligacy** (ˈprɒflɪgəsɪ) *n* > ˈ**profligately** *adv*

pro forma (ˈprəʊ ˈfɔːmə) *adj* 1 prescribing a set form or procedure ▷ *adv* 2 performed in a set manner [L: for form's sake]

profound (prəˈfaʊnd) *adj* 1 penetrating deeply into subjects or ideas: *a profound mind* 2 showing or requiring great knowledge or understanding: *a profound treatise* 3 situated at or extending to a great depth 4 stemming from the depths of one's nature: *profound regret* 5 intense or absolute: *profound silence* 6 thoroughgoing; extensive: *profound changes* ▷ *n* 7 *arch or literary* a great depth; abyss [C14 from OF *profund*, from L *profundus* deep, from *fundus* bottom] > **proˈfoundly** *adv* > **profundity** (prəˈfʌndɪtɪ) *n*

Profumo (prəˈfjuːməʊ) *n* **John (Dennis)** born 1915, British Conservative politician; secretary of state for war (1960–63). He resigned after a scandal that threatened the government of Harold Macmillan

profuse (prəˈfjuːs) *adj* 1 plentiful or abundant: *profuse compliments* 2 (often foll by *in*) free or generous in the giving (of): *profuse in thanks* [C15 from L *profundere* to pour lavishly] > **proˈfusely** *adv* > **proˈfuseness** *or* **proˈfusion** *n*

progenitive (prəʊˈdʒɛnɪtɪv) *adj* capable of bearing offspring > **proˈgenitiveness** *n*

progenitor (prəʊˈdʒɛnɪtə) *n* 1 a direct ancestor 2 an originator or founder [C14 from L: ancestor, from *gignere* to beget]

progeny (ˈprɒdʒɪnɪ) *n, pl* **progenies** 1 the immediate descendant or descendants of a person, animal, etc 2 a result or outcome [C13 from L *prōgeniēs* lineage; see PROGENITOR]

progesterone (prəʊˈdʒɛstəˌrəʊn) *n* a steroid hormone, secreted mainly by the corpus luteum in the ovary, that prepares and maintains the uterus for pregnancy [C20 from PRO-¹ + GE(STATION) + STER(OL) + -ONE]

progestogen (prəʊˈdʒɛstədʒən) *or* **progestin** (prəˈdʒɛstɪn) *n* any of a group of steroid hormones with progesterone-like activity, used in oral contraceptives and in treating gynaecological disorders

prognathous (prɒg'neɪθəs) *or* **prognathic** (prɒg'næθɪk) *adj* having a projecting lower jaw [C19 from PRO-[2] + Gk *gnathos* jaw]

prognosis (prɒg'nəʊsɪs) *n, pl* **prognoses** (prog'nəʊsi:z) **1** *med* a prediction of the course or outcome of a disease **2** any prediction [C17 via L from Gk: knowledge beforehand]

prognostic (prɒg'nɒstɪk) *adj* **1** of or serving as a prognosis **2** predicting ▷ *n* **3** *med* any symptom or sign used in making a prognosis **4** a sign of some future occurrence [C15 from OF *pronostique*, from L *prognōsticum*, from Gk, from *progignōskein* to know in advance]

prognosticate (prɒg'nɒstɪˌkeɪt) *vb* **prognosticates, prognosticating, prognosticated** **1** to foretell (future events); prophesy **2** (*tr*) to foreshadow or portend [C16 from Med. L *prognōsticāre* to predict] > **progˌnosti'cation** *n* > **prog'nosticative** *adj* > **prog'nostiˌcator** *n*

program *or* (*sometimes*) **programme** ('prəʊgræm) *n* **1** a sequence of coded instructions fed into a computer, enabling it to perform specified logical and arithmetical operations on data ▷ *vb* **programs** *or* **programmes, programming, programmed** **2** (*tr*) to feed a program into (a computer) **3** (*tr*) to arrange (data) in a suitable form so that it can be processed by a computer **4** (*intr*) to write a program > **'programmer** *n*

> USAGE The spelling *program* is the generally used US spelling of *programme* in all its senses, and is also the generally preferred spelling when referring to *computer programs*

programmable *or* **programable** (prəʊ'græməbəl) *adj* capable of being programmed for automatic operation or computer processing

programme *or US* **program** ('prəʊgræm) *n* **1** a written or printed list of the events, performers, etc, in a public performance **2** a performance presented at a scheduled time, esp on radio or television **3** a specially arranged selection of things to be done: *what's the programme for this afternoon?* **4** a plan, schedule, or procedure **5** a syllabus or curriculum ▷ *vb* **programmes, programming, programmed** *or US* **programs, programing, programed** **6** to design or schedule (something) as a programme ▷ *n, vb* **7** *computing* a variant spelling of **program** [C17 from LL *programma*, from Gk: written public notice, from PRO-[2] + *graphein* to write] > **ˌprogram'matic** *adj*

programmed learning *n* a teaching method in which the material to be learned is broken down into easily understandable parts on which the pupil is able to test himself or herself

programme music *n* music that is intended to depict or evoke a scene or idea

programme of study *n Brit education* the prescribed syllabus that pupils must be taught at each key stage in the National Curriculum

programming language *n* a simple language system designed to facilitate the writing of computer programs

program statement *n* a single instruction in a computer program

program trading *n* trading on international stock exchanges using a computer program to exploit differences between stock index futures and actual share prices on world equity markets

progress *n* ('prəʊgrɛs) **1** movement forwards, esp towards a place or objective **2** satisfactory development or advance **3** advance towards completion or perfection **4** (*modifier*) of or relating to progress: *a progress report* **5** (formerly) a stately royal journey **6** **in progress** taking place ▷ *vb* (prə'grɛs) **7** (*intr*) to move forwards or onwards **8** (*intr*) to move towards completion or perfection **9** (*tr*) to be responsible for the satisfactory progress of (a project, etc) to completion: *I want you to progress this* [C15 from L *prōgressus*, from *prōgredī* to advance, from *gradī* to step]

progression (prə'grɛʃən) *n* **1** the act of progressing; advancement **2** the act or an instance of moving from one thing in a sequence to the next **3** *maths* a sequence of numbers in which each term differs from the succeeding term by a constant relation. See also **arithmetic progression, geometric progression, harmonic progression** **4** *music* movement from one note or chord to the next > **pro'gressional** *adj*

progressive (prə'grɛsɪv) *adj* **1** of or relating to progress **2** progressing by steps or degrees **3** (*often cap*) favouring or promoting political or social reform: *a progressive policy* **4** denoting an educational system that allows flexibility in learning procedures, based on activities determined by the needs and capacities of the individual child **5** (esp of a disease) advancing in severity, complexity, or extent **6** (of a dance, card game, etc) involving a regular change of partners **7** denoting an aspect of verbs in some languages, including English, used to express continuous activity: *a progressive aspect of the verb "to walk" is "is walking"* ▷ *n* **8** a person who advocates progress, as in education, politics, etc **9a** the progressive aspect of a verb **9b** a verb in this aspect > **pro'gressively** *adv* > **pro'gressiveness** *n* > **pro'gressivism** *n* > **pro'gressivist** *n*

progress payment *n* an instalment of a larger payment made to a contractor for work carried out up to a specified stage of the job

prohibit (prə'hɪbɪt) *vb* (*tr*) **1** to forbid by law or other authority **2** to hinder or prevent [C15 from L *prohibēre* to prevent, from PRO-[1] + *habēre* to hold] > **pro'hibiter** *or* **pro'hibitor** *n*

prohibition (ˌprəʊɪ'bɪʃən) *n* **1** the act of prohibiting or state of being prohibited **2** an order or decree that prohibits **3** (*sometimes cap*) (esp in the US) a policy of legally forbidding the manufacture, sale, or consumption of alcoholic beverages **4** *law* an order of a superior court forbidding an inferior court to determine a matter outside its jurisdiction > **ˌprohi'bitionary** *adj* > **ˌprohi'bitionist** *n*

Prohibition (ˌprəʊɪ'bɪʃən) *n* the period (1920–33) when the manufacture, sale, and transportation of intoxicating liquors was banned in the US > **ˌProhi'bitionist** *n*

prohibitive (prə'hɪbɪtɪv) *or* (*less commonly*) **prohibitory** (prə'hɪbɪtərɪ, -trɪ) *adj* **1** prohibiting or tending to prohibit **2** (esp of prices) tending or designed to discourage sale or purchase > **pro'hibitively** *adv* > **pro'hibitiveness** *n*

project *n* ('prɒdʒɛkt) **1** a proposal, scheme, or design **2a** a task requiring considerable or concerted effort, such as one by students **2b** the subject of such a task ▷ *vb* (prə'dʒɛkt) **3** (*tr*) to propose or plan **4** (*tr*) to throw forwards **5** to jut or cause to jut out **6** (*tr*) to make a prediction based on known data and observations **7** (*tr*) to transport in the imagination: *to project oneself into the future* **8** (*tr*) to cause (an image) to appear on a surface **9** to cause (one's voice) to be heard clearly at a distance **10** *psychol* **10a** (*intr*) (esp of a child) to believe that others share one's subjective mental life **10b** to impute to others (one's hidden desires) **11** (*tr*) *geom* to draw a projection of **12** (*intr*) to communicate effectively, esp to a large gathering [C14 from L *prōicere* to throw down]

projectile (prə'dʒɛktaɪl) *n* **1** an object thrown forwards **2** any self-propelling missile, esp a rocket **3** any object that can be fired from a gun, such as a shell ▷ *adj* **4** designed to be hurled forwards **5** projecting forwards **6** *zool* another word for **protrusile** [C17 from NL *prōjectilis* jutting forwards]

projection (prə'dʒɛkʃən) *n* **1** the act of projecting or the state of being projected **2** a part that juts out **3** See **map projection** **4** the representation of a line, figure, or solid on a given plane as it would be seen from a particular direction or in accordance with an accepted set of rules **5** a scheme or plan **6** a prediction based on known

Pp

evidence and observations **7a** the process of showing film on a screen **7b** the images shown **8** *psychol* **8a** the belief that others share one's subjective mental life **8b** the process of projecting one's own hidden desires and impulses > **pro'jectional** *adj* > **pro'jective** *adj*

projectionist (prəˈdʒɛkʃənɪst) *n* a person responsible for the operation of film projection machines

projective geometry *n* the branch of geometry concerned with the properties of solids that are invariant under projection and section

projector (prəˈdʒɛktə) *n* **1** an optical instrument that projects an enlarged image of individual slides. Full name: **slide projector** **2** an optical instrument in which a film is wound past a lens so that the frames can be viewed as a continuously moving sequence. Full name: **film** *or* **cine projector** **3** a device for projecting a light beam **4** a person who devises projects

prokaryote *or* **procaryote** (prəʊˈkærɪɒt) *n* any organism of the kingdom *Prokaryotae* having cells in which the genetic material is in a single DNA chain, not enclosed in a nucleus ▷ Cf **eukaryote** [from PRO-² + KARYO- + *-ote* as in *zygote*] > **prokaryotic** *or* **procaryotic** (prəʊˌkærɪˈɒtɪk) *adj*

Prokofiev (prəˈkɒfɪˌɛf; *Russian* praˈkɔfjɪf) *n* **Sergei Sergeyevich** (sɪrˈgjej sɪrˈgjejɪvitʃ) 1891–1953, Soviet composer. His compositions include the orchestral fairy tale *Peter and the Wolf* (1936), the opera *The Love for Three Oranges* (1921), and seven symphonies

Prokopyevsk (*Russian* praˈkɔpjɪfsk) *n* a city in S Russia: the chief coal-mining centre of the Kuznetsk Basin. Pop: 240 500 (1999 est)

prolactin (prəʊˈlæktɪn) *n* a gonadotrophic hormone secreted by the anterior lobe of the pituitary gland. In mammals it stimulates the secretion of progesterone by the corpus luteum and initiates and maintains lactation

prolapse (ˈprəʊlæps, prəʊˈlæps) *pathol* ▷ *n* **1** Also: **prolapsus** (prəʊˈlæpsəs) the sinking or falling down of an organ or part, esp the womb ▷ *vb* **prolapses, prolapsing, prolapsed** (*intr*) **2** (of an organ, etc) to sink from its normal position [c17 from L *prōlābi* to slide along]

prolate (ˈprəʊleɪt) *adj* having a polar diameter of greater length than the equatorial diameter ▷ Cf **oblate¹** [c17 from L *prōferre* to enlarge] > **ˈprolately** *adv*

prole (prəʊl) *n, adj derog sl, chiefly Brit* short for **proletarian**

prolegomenon (ˌprəʊlɛˈgɒmɪnən) *n, pl* **prolegomenona** (ˌprəʊlɛˈgɒmɪnə) (*often pl*) a preliminary discussion, esp a formal critical introduction to a lengthy text [c17 from Gk, from *prolegein*, from PRO-² + *legein* to say] > **ˌproleˈgomenal** *adj*

prolepsis (prəʊˈlɛpsɪs) *n, pl* **prolepses** (prəʊˈlɛpsiːz) **1** a rhetorical device by which objections are anticipated and answered in advance **2** use of a word after a verb in anticipation of its becoming applicable through the action of the verb, as *flat* in *hammer it flat* [c16 via LL from Gk: anticipation, from *prolambanein* to anticipate, from PRO-² + *lambanein* to take] > **proˈleptic** *adj*

proletarian (ˌprəʊlɪˈtɛərɪən) *adj* **1** of or belonging to the proletariat ▷ *n* **2** a member of the proletariat [c17 from L *prōlētārius* one whose only contribution to the state was his offspring, from *prōlēs* offspring] > **ˌproleˈtarianism** *n*

proletariat (ˌprəʊlɪˈtɛərɪət) *n* **1** all wage-earners collectively **2** the lower or working class **3** (in Marxist theory) the class of wage-earners, esp industrial workers, in a capitalist society, whose only possession of significant material value is their labour **4** (in ancient Rome) the lowest class of citizens, who had no property [c19 via F from L *prōlētārius* PROLETARIAN]

pro-life *adj* (of an organization, pressure group, etc) supporting the right to life of the unborn; against abortion, experiments on embryos, etc > **ˌpro-ˈlifer** *n*

proliferate (prəˈlɪfəˌreɪt) *vb* **proliferates, proliferating, proliferated** **1** to grow or reproduce (new parts, cells, etc) rapidly **2** to grow or increase rapidly [c19 from Med. L *prōlifer* having offspring, from L *prōlēs* offspring + *ferre* to bear] > **proˌliferˈation** *n* > **proˈliferative** *adj*

prolific (prəˈlɪfɪk) *adj* **1** producing fruit, offspring, etc, in abundance **2** producing constant or successful results **3** (often foll by *in* or *of*) rich or fruitful [c17 from Med. L *prōlificus*, from L *prōlēs* offspring] > **proˈlifically** *adv* > **proˈlificness** *or* **proˈlificacy** *n*

prolix (ˈprəʊlɪks, prəʊˈlɪks) *adj* **1** (of a speech, book, etc) so long as to be boring **2** long-winded [c15 from L *prōlixus* stretched out widely, from *līquī* to flow] > **proˈlixity** *n* > **proˈlixly** *adv*

prolocutor (prəʊˈlɒkjʊtə) *n* a chairman, esp of the lower house of clergy in a convocation of the Anglican Church [c15 from L: advocate, from *loqui* to speak] > **proˈlocutorship** *n*

PROLOG *or* **Prolog** (ˈprəʊlɒg) *n* a computer programming language based on mathematical logic [c20 from *pro(gramming in) log(ic)*]

prologue *or US* (*often*) **prolog** (ˈprəʊlɒg) *n* **1** the prefatory lines introducing a play or speech **2** a preliminary act or event **3** (in early opera) **3a** an introductory scene in which a narrator summarizes the main action of the work **3b** a brief independent play preceding the opera, esp one in honour of a patron ▷ *vb* **prologues, prologuing, prologued** *or US* **prologs, prologing, prologed** **4** (*tr*) to introduce with a prologue [c13 from L *prologus*, from Gk, from PRO-² + *logos* discourse]

prolong (prəˈlɒŋ) *vb* (*tr*) to lengthen; extend [c15 from LL *prōlongāre* to extend, from L PRO-¹ + *longus* long] > **prolongation** (ˌprəʊlɒŋˈgeɪʃən) *n*

prolusion (prəˈluːʒən) *n* **1** a preliminary written exercise **2** an introductory essay [c17 from L *prōlūsiō*, from *prōlūdere* to practise beforehand, from PRO-¹ + *lūdere* to play] > **prolusory** (prəˈluːzərɪ) *adj*

prom (prɒm) *n* **1** *Brit* short for **promenade** (sense 1) or **promenade concert** **2** *US & Canad inf* a formal dance held at a high school or college

PROM (prɒm) *n computing acronym for* programmable read only memory

promenade (ˌprɒməˈnɑːd) *n* **1** *chiefly Brit* a public walk, esp at a seaside resort **2** a leisurely walk, esp one in a public place for pleasure or display **3** a marchlike step in dancing **4** a marching sequence in a square or country dance ▷ *vb* **promenades, promenading, promenaded** **5** to take a promenade in or through (a place) **6** (*intr*) *dancing* to perform a promenade **7** (*tr*) to display or exhibit (someone or oneself) on or as if on a promenade [c16 from F, from *promener* to lead out for a walk, from LL *prōmināre* to drive (cattle) along, from *mināre* to drive, prob. from *minārī* to threaten] > **ˌpromeˈnader** *n*

promenade concert *n* a concert at which some of the audience stand rather than sit

promenade deck *n* an upper covered deck of a passenger ship for the use of the passengers

promethazine (prəʊˈmɛθəˌziːn) *n* an antihistamine drug used to treat allergies and to prevent vomiting [c20 from PRO(PYL) + (*di*)*meth*(*ylamine*) + (*phenothi*)*azine*]

Promethean (prəˈmiːθɪən) *adj* **1** of or relating to Prometheus **2** creative, original, or life-enhancing

Prometheus (prəˈmiːθɪəs) *n Greek myth* a Titan, who stole fire from Olympus to give to mankind and in punishment was chained to a rock, where an eagle tore at his liver until Hercules freed him

promethium (prəˈmiːθɪəm) *n* a radioactive element of the lanthanide series artificially produced by the fission of uranium. Symbol: Pm; atomic no.: 61; half-life of most stable isotope, ^{145}Pm: 17.7 years [c20 NL from PROMETHEUS]

prominence (ˈprɒmɪnəns) *n* **1** the state of being prominent **2** something that is prominent, such as a protuberance 3 relative importance 4 *astron* an eruption of incandescent gas from the sun's surface, visible during a total eclipse

prominent ('prɒmɪnənt) *adj* 1 jutting or projecting outwards 2 standing out from its surroundings; noticeable 3 widely known; eminent [C16 from L *prōminēre* to jut out, from PRO-[1] + *ēminēre* to project] > '**prominently** *adv*

promiscuous (prə'mɪskjʊəs) *adj* 1 indulging in casual and indiscriminate sexual relationships 2 consisting of a number of dissimilar parts or elements mingled indiscriminately 3 indiscriminate in selection 4 casual or heedless [C17 from L *prōmiscuus* indiscriminate, from PRO-[1] + *miscēre* to mix] > **pro'miscuously** *adv* > **promiscuity** (ˌprɒmɪ'skju:ɪtɪ) *or* **pro'miscuousness** *n*

promise ('prɒmɪs) *vb* **promises, promising, promised** 1 (often foll by *to*; when *tr, may take a clause as object or an infinitive*) to give an assurance of (something to someone): *I promise that I will come* 2 (*tr*) to undertake to give (something to someone): *he promised me a car for my birthday* 3 (when *tr, takes an infinitive*) to cause people to expect that one is likely (to be or do something): *she promises to be a fine soprano* 4 (*tr; usually passive*) *obs* to betroth: *I'm promised to Bill* 5 (*tr*) to assure (someone) of the authenticity or inevitability of something: *there'll be trouble, I promise you* ▷ *n* 6 an assurance given by one person to another agreeing or guaranteeing to do or not to do something 7 indication of forthcoming excellence: *a writer showing considerable promise* 8 the thing of which an assurance is given [C14 from L *prōmissum* a promise, from *prōmittere* to send forth] > ˌ**promi'see** *n* > '**promiser** *or* (*Law*) '**promisor** *n*

Promised Land *n* 1 *Old Testament* the land of Canaan, promised by God to Abraham and his descendants as their heritage (Genesis 12:7) 2 *Christianity* heaven 3 any longed-for place where one expects to find greater happiness

promising ('prɒmɪsɪŋ) *adj* showing promise of future success > '**promisingly** *adv*

promissory ('prɒmɪsərɪ) *adj* 1 containing, relating to, or having the nature of a promise 2 *insurance* stipulating how the provisions of an insurance contract will be fulfilled

promissory note *n commerce, chiefly US* a document containing a signed promise to pay a stated sum of money to a specified person at a designated date or on demand. Also called: **note, note of hand**

promo ('prəʊməʊ) **a** *n, pl* **promos** *inf* something used to promote a product, esp a videotape film used to promote a pop record **b** (*as modifier*) *a promo video* [C20 shortened from *promotion*]

promontory ('prɒməntərɪ, -trɪ) *n, pl* **promontories** 1 a high point of land, esp of rocky coast, that juts out into the sea 2 *anat* any of various projecting structures [C16 from L *prōmunturium* headland]

promote (prə'məʊt) *vb* **promotes, promoting, promoted** (*tr*) 1 to encourage the progress or existence of 2 to raise to a higher rank, status, etc 3 to advance (a pupil or student) to a higher course, class, etc 4 to work for: *to promote reform* 5 to encourage the sale of (a product) by advertising or securing financial support [C14 from L *prōmovēre* to push onwards] > **pro'motion** *n* > **pro'motional** *adj*

promoter (prə'məʊtə) *n* 1 a person or thing that promotes 2 a person who helps to organize, develop, or finance an undertaking 3 a person who organizes and finances a sporting event, esp a boxing match

prompt (prɒmpt) *adj* 1 performed or executed without delay 2 quick or ready to act or respond ▷ *adv* 3 *inf* punctually ▷ *vb* 4 (*tr*) to urge (someone to do something) 5 to remind (an actor, singer, etc) of lines forgotten during a performance 6 (*tr*) to refresh the memory of 7 (*tr*) to give rise to by suggestion: *his affairs will prompt discussion* ▷ *n* 8 *commerce* **8a** the time limit allowed for payment of the debt incurred by purchasing on credit **8b** Also called: **prompt note** a memorandum sent to a purchaser to remind him of the time limit and the sum due 9 anything that serves to remind [C15 from L *promptus* evident, from *prōmere* to produce, from *emere* to buy] > '**promptly** *adv* > '**promptness** *n*

prompter ('prɒmptə) *n* 1 a person offstage who reminds the actors of forgotten lines or cues 2 a person, thing, etc, that prompts

promptitude ('prɒmptɪˌtju:d) *n* the quality of being prompt; punctuality

prompt side *n theatre* the side of the stage where the prompter is, usually to the actor's left in Britain and to his right in the United States

promulgate ('prɒməlˌgeɪt) *vb* **promulgates, promulgating, promulgated** (*tr*) 1 to put into effect (a law, decree, etc), esp by formal proclamation 2 to announce officially 3 to make widespread [C16 from L *prōmulgāre* to bring to public knowledge] > ˌ**promul'gation** *n* > '**promulˌgator** *n*

pron. *abbrev for:* 1 pronominal 2 pronoun 3 pronounced 4 pronunciation

pronate (prəʊ'neɪt) *vb* **pronates, pronating, pronated** (*tr*) to turn (the forearm or hand) so that the palmar surface is directed downwards [C19 from LL *prōnāre* to bow] > **pro'nation** *n* > **pro'nator** *n*

prone (prəʊn) *adj* 1 lying flat or face downwards; prostrate 2 sloping or tending downwards 3 having an inclination to do something [C14 from L *prōnus* bent forward, from PRO-[1]] > '**pronely** *adv* > '**proneness** *n*

-prone *adj combining form* liable or disposed to suffer: *accident-prone*

prong (prɒŋ) *n* 1 a sharply pointed end of an instrument, such as on a fork 2 any pointed projecting part ▷ *vb* 3 (*tr*) to prick or spear with or as if with a prong [C15] > **pronged** *adj*

pronghorn ('prɒŋˌhɔ:n) *n* a ruminant mammal inhabiting rocky deserts of North America and having small branched horns. Also called: **American antelope**

pronominal (prəʊ'nɒmɪn(ə)l) *adj* relating to or playing the part of a pronoun [C17 from LL *prōnōminālis*, from *prōnōmen* a PRONOUN] > **pro'nominally** *adv*

pronoun ('prəʊˌnaʊn) *n* one of a class of words that serves to replace a noun or noun phrase that has already been or is about to be mentioned in the sentence or context. Abbrev: **pron** [C16 from L *prōnōmen*, from PRO-[1] + *nōmen* noun]

pronounce (prə'naʊns) *vb* **pronounces, pronouncing, pronounced** 1 to utter or articulate (a sound or sounds) 2 (*tr*) to utter (words) in the correct way 3 (*tr; may take a clause as object*) to proclaim officially: *I now pronounce you man and wife* 4 (when *tr, may take a clause as object*) to declare as one's judgment: *to pronounce the death sentence upon someone* [C14 from L *prōnuntiāre* to announce] > **pro'nounceable** *adj* > **pro'nouncer** *n*

pronounced (prə'naʊnst) *adj* 1 strongly marked or indicated 2 (of a sound) articulated with vibration of the vocal cords; voiced > **pronouncedly** (prə'naʊnsɪdlɪ) *adv*

pronouncement (prə'naʊnsmənt) *n* 1 an official or authoritative announcement 2 the act of declaring or uttering formally

pronto ('prɒntəʊ) *adv inf* at once [C20 from Sp.: quick, from L *promptus* PROMPT]

pronunciation (prəˌnʌnsɪ'eɪʃən) *n* 1 the act, instance, or manner of pronouncing sounds 2 the supposedly correct manner of pronouncing sounds in a given language 3 a phonetic transcription of a word.

> **USAGE** The segment *-un-* in this word should be pronounced as in *unkind*, not as in the verb *pronounce*. Occasionally *pronunciation* is misspelt and an *o* added after the *u*

proof (pru:f) *n* 1 any evidence that establishes or helps

Pp

to establish the truth, validity, quality, etc, of something **2** *law* the whole body of evidence upon which the verdict of a court is based **3** *maths, logic* a sequence of steps or statements that establishes the truth of a proposition **4** the act of testing the truth of something (esp in **put to the proof**) **5** *Scots law* trial before a judge without a jury **6** *printing* a trial impression made from composed type for the correction of errors **7** (in engraving, etc) a print made by an artist for his or her own satisfaction before the plate is handed over to a professional printer **8** *photog* a trial print from a negative **9a** the alcoholic strength of proof spirit **9b** the strength of a liquor as measured on a scale in which the strength of proof spirit is 100 degrees ▷ *adj* **10** (*usually postpositive;* foll by *against*) impervious (to): *the roof is proof against rain* **11** having the alcoholic strength of proof spirit **12** of proved impenetrability: *proof armour* ▷ *vb* **13** (*tr*) to take a proof from (type matter, a plate, etc) **14** to proofread (text) or inspect (a print, etc), as for approval **15** to render (something) proof, esp to waterproof [C13 from OF *preuve* a test, from LL *proba*, from L *probāre* to test]

-proof *adj, vb combining form* (to make) impervious to; secure against (damage by): *waterproof* [from PROOF (adj)]

proofread ('pruːfˌriːd) *vb* **proofreads, proofreading, proofread** (-ˌrɛd) to read (copy or printer's proofs) and mark errors to be corrected > **'proofˌreader** *n*

proof spirit *n* (in Britain) a mixture of alcohol and water or an alcoholic beverage that contains 49.28 per cent of alcohol by weight, 57.1 per cent by volume at 51°F: used until 1980 as a standard of alcoholic liquids

prop[1] (prɒp) *vb* **props, propping, propped** (*tr;* often foll by *up*) **1** to support with a rigid object, such as a stick **2** (usually also foll by *against*) to place or lean **3** to sustain or support ▷ *n* **4** something that gives rigid support, such as a stick **5** short for **clothes prop** **6** a person or thing giving support, as of a moral nature **7** *rugby* either of the forwards at either end of the front row of a scrum [C15 rel. to M Du. *proppe* vine prop]

prop[2] (prɒp) *n* short for **property** (sense 8)

prop[3] (prɒp) *n* an informal word for **propeller**

prop. *abbrev for:* **1** proper(ly) **2** property **3** proposition **4** proprietor

propaedeutic (ˌprəʊpɪ'djuːtɪk) *n* **1** (*often pl*) preparatory instruction basic to further study of an art or science ▷ *adj* **2** Also: **propaedeutical** of, relating to, or providing such instruction [C19 from Gk *propaideuein* to teach in advance, from PRO-[2] + *paideuein* to rear]

propaganda (ˌprɒpə'gændə) *n* **1** the organized dissemination of information, allegations, etc, to assist or damage the cause of a government, movement, etc **2** such information, allegations, etc [C18 from It., use of *propāgandā* in the NL title *Sacra Congregatio de Propaganda Fide* Sacred Congregation for Propagating the Faith] > **ˌpropa'gandism** *n* > **ˌpropa'gandist** *n, adj*

Propaganda (ˌprɒpə'gændə) *n RC Church* a congregation responsible for directing the work of the foreign missions

propagandize *or* **propagandise** (ˌprɒpə'gænˌdaɪz) *vb* **propagandizes, propagandizing, propagandized** *or* **propagandises, propagandising, propagandised** **1** (*tr*) to spread by, or subject to, propaganda **2** (*intr*) to spread or organize propaganda

propagate ('prɒpəˌgeɪt) *vb* **propagates, propagating, propagated** **1** *biol* to reproduce or cause to reproduce; breed **2** (*tr*) *horticulture* to produce (plants) by layering, grafting, cuttings, etc **3** (*tr*) to promulgate **4** *physics* to transmit, esp in the form of a wave: *to propagate sound* **5** (*tr*) to transmit (characteristics) from one generation to the next [C16 from L *propāgāre* to increase (plants) by cuttings, from *propāgēs* a cutting, from *pangere* to fasten] > **ˌpropa'gation** *n* > **ˌpropa'gational** *adj* > **'propagative** *adj* > **'propaˌgator** *n*

propane ('prəʊpeɪn) *n* a flammable gaseous alkane found in petroleum and used as a fuel. Formula: $CH_3CH_2CH_3$ [C19 from PROPIONIC (ACID) + -ANE]

propanoic acid (ˌprəʊpə'nəʊɪk) *n* a colourless liquid carboxylic acid used in inhibiting the growth of moulds in bread. Formula: CH_3CH_2COOH. Former name: **propionic acid** [C20 from PROPANE + -OIC]

pro patria *Latin* ('prəʊ 'pætrɪˌɑː) for one's country

propel (prə'pɛl) *vb* **propels, propelling, propelled** (*tr*) to impel, drive, or cause to move forwards [C15 from L *prōpellere*] > **pro'pellant** *or* **pro'pellent** *n*

propeller (prə'pɛlə) *n* **1** a device having blades radiating from a central hub that is rotated to produce thrust to propel a ship, aircraft, etc **2** a person or thing that propels

propelling pencil *n* a pencil consisting of a metal or plastic case containing a replaceable lead. As the point is worn away the lead can be extended, usually by turning part of the case

propene ('prəʊpiːn) *n* a colourless gaseous alkene obtained by cracking petroleum. Formula: $CH_3CH{:}CH_2$. Also called: **propylene**

propensity (prə'pɛnsɪtɪ) *n, pl* **propensities** **1** a natural tendency **2** *obs* partiality [C16 from L *prōpensus* inclined to, from *prōpendēre* to hang forwards]

proper ('prɒpə) *adj* **1** (*usually prenominal*) appropriate or usual: *in its proper place* **2** suited to a particular purpose: *use the proper knife to cut the bread* **3** correct in behaviour **4** vigorously or excessively moral **5** up to a required or regular standard **6** (*immediately postpositive*) (of an object, quality, etc) referred to so as to exclude anything not directly connected with it: *his claim is connected with the deed proper* **7** (*postpositive;* foll by *to*) belonging to or characteristic of a person or thing **8** (*prenominal*) *Brit inf* (intensifier): *I felt a proper fool* **9** (*usually postpositive*) (of heraldic colours) considered correct for the natural colour of the object depicted: *three martlets proper* **10** *arch* pleasant or good **11** **good and proper** *inf* thoroughly ▷ *n* **12** the parts of the Mass that vary according to the particular day or feast on which the Mass is celebrated [C13 via OF from L *prōprius* special] > **'properly** *adv* > **'properness** *n*

proper fraction *n* a fraction in which the numerator has a lower absolute value than the denominator, as $\frac{1}{2}$ or $x/(3+x^2)$

proper motion *n* the very small continuous change in the direction of motion of a star relative to the sun

proper noun *or* **name** *n* the name of a person, place, or object, as for example *Iceland, Patrick,* or *Uranus* ▷ Cf **common noun**

propertied ('prɒpətɪd) *adj* owning land or property

Propertius (prə'pɜːʃɪəs, -ʃəs) *n* **Sextus** ('sɛkstəs) ?50–?15 BC, Roman elegiac poet

property ('prɒpətɪ) *n, pl* **properties** **1** something of value, either tangible, such as land, or intangible, such as copyrights **2** *law* the right to possess, use, and dispose of anything **3** possessions collectively **4a** land or real estate **4b** (*as modifier*): *property rights* **5** *chiefly Austral* a ranch or station **6** a quality or characteristic attribute, such as the density or strength of a material **7** *logic, obs* Also called: **proprium** ('prəʊpɪəm) an attribute that is not essential to a species but is common and peculiar to it **8** any movable object used on the set of a stage play or film. Usually shortened to **prop** [C13 from OF *propriété*, from L *proprietās* something personal, from *proprius* one's own]

property bond *n* a bond issued by a life-assurance company, the premiums for which are invested in a property-owning fund

property centre *n* a service for buying and selling property, including conveyancing, provided by a group of local solicitors. In full: **solicitors' property centre**

property man *n* a member of the stage crew in charge of the stage properties. Usually shortened to **propman**

prophecy (ˈprɒfɪsɪ) *n, pl* **prophecies** **1a** a message of divine truth revealing God's will **1b** the act of uttering such a message **2** a prediction or guess **3** the charismatic endowment of a prophet [c13 ult. from Gk *prophētēs* PROPHET]

prophesy (ˈprɒfɪˌsaɪ) *vb* **prophesies, prophesying, prophesied** **1** to foretell (something) by or as if by divine inspiration **2** (*intr*) *arch* to give instructions in religious subjects [c14 *prophecien*, from PROPHECY] > **ˈpropheˌsiable** *adj* > **ˈpropheˌsier** *n*

prophet (ˈprɒfɪt) *n* **1** a person who supposedly speaks by divine inspiration, esp one through whom a divinity expresses his will **2** a person who predicts the future: *a prophet of doom* **3** a spokesman for a movement, doctrine, etc [c13 from OF *prophète*, from L, from Gk *prophētēs* one who declares the divine will, from PRO-² + *phanai* to speak] > **ˈprophetess** *fem n*

Prophet (ˈprɒfɪt) *n* **the** **1** the principal designation of Mohammed as the founder of Islam **2** a name for Joseph Smith as the founder of the Mormon Church

prophetic (prəˈfɛtɪk) *adj* **1** of or relating to a prophet or prophecy **2** of the nature of a prophecy; predictive > **proˈphetically** *adv*

prophylactic (ˌprɒfɪˈlæktɪk) *adj* **1** protecting from or preventing disease **2** protective or preventive ▷ *n* **3** a prophylactic drug or device, esp a condom [c16 via F from Gk *prophulaktikos*, from *prophulassein* to guard by taking advance measures, from PRO-² + *phulax* a guard]

prophylaxis (ˌprɒfɪˈlæksɪs) *n* the prevention of disease or control of its possible spread

propinquity (prəˈpɪŋkwɪtɪ) *n* **1** nearness in place or time **2** nearness in relationship [c14 from L *propinquitās*, from *propinquus* near, from *prope* nearby]

propionic acid (ˌprəʊpɪˈɒnɪk) *n* the former name for **propanoic acid** [c19 from Gk *pro-* first + *pionic*, from *piōn* fat, because it is first in order of the fatty acids]

propitiate (prəˈpɪʃɪˌeɪt) *vb* **propitiates, propitiating, propitiated** (*tr*) to appease or make well disposed; conciliate [c17 from L *propitiāre*, from *propitius* gracious] > **proˈpitiable** *adj* > **proˌpitiˈation** *n* > **proˈpitiative** *adj* > **proˈpitiˌator** *n* > **proˈpitiatory** *adj*

propitious (prəˈpɪʃəs) *adj* **1** favourable; auguring well **2** gracious or favourably inclined [c15 from L *propitius* well disposed, from *prope* close to] > **proˈpitiously** *adv* > **proˈpitiousness** *n*

propjet (ˈprɒpˌdʒɛt) *n* another name for **turboprop**

propolis (ˈprɒpəlɪs) *n* a greenish-brown resinous aromatic substance collected by bees from the buds of trees for use in the construction of hives. Also called: **bee glue, hive dross** [c17 via L from Gk: suburb, bee glue, from *pro-* before + *polis* city]

proponent (prəˈpəʊnənt) *n* a person who argues in favour of something or puts forward a proposal, etc [c16 from L *prōpōnere* to PROPOSE]

Propontis (prəˈpɒntɪs) *n* the ancient name for (the Sea of) **Marmara**

proportion (prəˈpɔːʃən) *n* **1** relative magnitude or extent; ratio **2** correct or desirable relationship between parts; symmetry **3** a part considered with respect to the whole **4** (*pl*) dimensions or size: *a building of vast proportions* **5** a share or quota **6** a relationship that maintains a constant ratio between two variable quantities: *prices increase in proportion to manufacturing costs* **7** *maths* a relationship between four numbers or quantities in which the ratio of the first pair equals the ratio of the second pair ▷ *vb* (*tr*) **8** to adjust in relative amount, size, etc **9** to cause to be harmonious in relationship of parts [c14 from L *prōportiō*, from *prō portione*, lit.: for (its, one's) PORTION] > **proˈportionable** *adj* > **proˈportionably** *adv* > **proˈportionment** *n*

proportional (prəˈpɔːʃənᵊl) *adj* **1** of, involving, or being in proportion ▷ *n* **2** *maths* an unknown term in a proportion: *in $a/b = c/x$, x is the fourth proportional* > **proˌportionˈality** *n* > **proˈportionally** *adv*

proportional font *n computing* a font type in which the width of letters and symbols varies depending on the letter or symbol

proportional representation *n* representation of parties in an elective body in proportion to the votes they win. Abbrev: **PR** ▷ Cf **first-past-the-post.** See also **Additional Member System, Alternative Vote, party list, Single Transferable Vote**

proportionate *adj* (prəˈpɔːʃənɪt) **1** being in proper proportion ▷ *vb* (prəˈpɔːʃəˌneɪt), **proportionates, proportionating, proportionated** **2** (*tr*) to make proportionate > **proˈportionately** *adv*

proposal (prəˈpəʊzᵊl) *n* **1** the act of proposing **2** something proposed, as a plan **3** an offer, esp of marriage

propose (prəˈpəʊz) *vb* **proposes, proposing, proposed** **1** (when *tr, may take a clause as object*) to put forward (a plan, etc) for consideration **2** (*tr*) to nominate, as for a position **3** (*tr*) to intend (to do something): *I propose to leave town now* **4** (*tr*) to announce the drinking of (a toast) **5** (*intr; often foll by to*) to make an offer of marriage [c14 from OF *proposer*, from L *prōpōnere* to display, from PRO-¹ + *pōnere* to place] > **proˈposable** *adj* > **proˈposer** *n*

proposition (ˌprɒpəˈzɪʃən) *n* **1** a proposal for consideration **2** *philosophy* the content of a sentence that affirms or denies something and is capable of being true or false **3** *maths* a statement or theorem, usually containing its proof **4** *inf* a person or matter to be dealt with: *he's a difficult proposition* **5** *inf* an invitation to engage in sexual intercourse ▷ *vb* **6** (*tr*) to propose a plan, deal, etc, to, esp to engage in sexual intercourse [c14 *proposicioun*, from L *prōpositiō* a setting forth; see PROPOSE] > **ˌpropoˈsitional** *adj*

propositional calculus *n* the system of symbolic logic concerned only with the relations between propositions as wholes, taking no account of their internal structure ▷ Cf **predicate calculus**

Pp

propositus (prəˈpɒzɪtəs) *or* (*fem*) **proposita** (prəˈpɒzɪtə) *n, pl* **propositi** (-ˌtaɪ) *or* (*fem*) **propositae** (-tiː) *Med.* the first patient to be investigated in a family study, to whom all relationships are referred. Also called (esp US): **proband**

propound (prəˈpaʊnd) *vb* (*tr*) **1** to put forward for consideration **2** *English law* to produce (a will or similar instrument) to the proper court or authority for its validity to be established [c16 *propone*, from L *prōpōnere* to set forth, from PRO-¹ + *pōnere* to place] > **proˈpounder** *n*

propranolol (prəʊˈprænəˌlɒl) *n* a drug used in the treatment of heart disease

proprietary (prəˈpraɪɪtərɪ, -trɪ) *adj* **1** of or belonging to property or proprietors **2** privately owned and controlled **3** *med* denoting a drug manufactured and distributed under a trade name ▷ *n, pl* **proprietaries** **4** *med* a proprietary drug **5** a proprietor or proprietors collectively **6a** right to property **6b** property owned **7** (in Colonial America) an owner of a **proprietary colony,** a colony which was granted by the Crown to a particular person or group [c15 from LL *proprietārius* an owner, from *proprius* one's own] > **proˈprietarily** *adv*

proprietary name *n* a name which is restricted in use by virtue of being a trade name

proprietor (prəˈpraɪətə) *n* **1** an owner of a business **2** a person enjoying exclusive right of ownership to some property > **proprietorial** (prəˌpraɪəˈtɔːrɪəl) *adj* > **proˈprietress** *or* **proˈprietrix** *fem n*

propriety (prəˈpraɪətɪ) *n, pl* **proprieties** **1** the quality or state of being appropriate or fitting **2** conformity to the prevailing standard of behaviour, speech, etc **3** **the proprieties** the standards of behaviour considered correct by polite society [c15 from OF *propriété*, from L *proprietās* a peculiarity, from *proprius* one's own]

proprioceptor (ˌprəʊprɪəˈsɛptə) *n physiol* any receptor, as in the gut, blood vessels, muscles, etc, that supplies information about the state of the body [C20 from *proprio-*, from L *proprius* one's own + RECEPTOR] > ˌ**proprio'ceptive** *adj*

proptosis (prɒp'təʊsɪs) *n, pl* **proptoses** (-siːz) *pathol* the forward displacement of an organ or part, such as the eyeball [C17 via LL from Gk, from *propiptein* to fall forwards]

propulsion (prə'pʌlʃən) *n* **1** the act of propelling or the state of being propelled **2** a propelling force [C15 from L *prōpellere* to propel] > **propulsive** (prə'pʌlsɪv) *or* **pro'pulsory** *adj*

propyl ('prəʊpɪl) *n (modifier)* of or containing the monovalent group of atoms C_3H_7- [C19 from PROP(IONIC ACID) + -YL]

propylaeum (ˌprɒpɪ'liːəm) *or* **propylon** ('prɒpɪˌlɒn) *n, pl* **propylaea** (-'liːə) *or* **propylons, propyla** (-lə) a portico, esp one that forms the entrance to a temple [C18 via L from Gk *propulaion* before the gate, from PRO-[2] + *pulē* gate]

propylene ('prəʊpɪˌliːn) *n* another name for **propene** [C19]

propylene glycol *n* a colourless viscous compound used as an antifreeze and brake fluid. Formula: $CH_3CH(OH)CH_2OH$. Systematic name: **1,2-dihydroxypropane**

pro rata ('prəʊ 'rɑːtə) in proportion [Med. L]

prorate (prəʊ'reɪt, 'prəʊreɪt) *vb* **prorates, prorating, prorated** *chiefly US & Canad* to divide, assess, or distribute proportionately [C19 from PRO RATA] > **pro'ratable** *adj* > **pro'ration** *n*

prorogue (prə'rəʊg) *vb* **prorogues, proroguing, prorogued** to discontinue the meetings of (a legislative body) without dissolving it [C15 from L *prorogāre*, lit.: to ask publicly] > **prorogation** (ˌprəʊrə'geɪʃən) *n*

prosaic (prəʊ'zeɪɪk) *adj* **1** lacking imagination **2** having the characteristics of prose [C16 from LL *prōsaicus*, from L *prōsa* PROSE] > **pro'saically** *adv*

pros and cons *pl n* the various arguments in favour of and against a motion, course of action, etc [C16 from L *prō* for + *con*, from *contrā* against]

proscenium (prə'siːnɪəm) *n, pl* **proscenia** (-nɪə) *or* **prosceniums** **1** the arch or opening separating the stage from the auditorium together with the area immediately in front of the arch **2** (in ancient theatres) the stage itself [C17 via L from Gk *proskēnion*, from *pro-* before + *skēnē* scene]

prosciutto (prəʊ'ʃuːtəʊ; *Italian* pro'ʃutto) *n* cured ham from Italy: usually served as an hors d'oeuvre [It., lit.: dried beforehand]

proscribe (prəʊ'skraɪb) *vb* **proscribes, proscribing, proscribed** *(tr)* **1** to condemn or prohibit **2** to outlaw; banish; exile [C16 from L *prōscrībere* to put up a public notice, from *prō-* in public + *scrībere* to write] > **pro'scriber** *n* > **proscription** (prəʊ'skrɪpʃən) *n*

prose (prəʊz) *n* **1** spoken or written language distinguished from poetry by its lack of a marked metrical structure **2** a passage set for translation into a foreign language **3** commonplace or dull discourse, expression, etc **4** *(modifier)* written in prose **5** *(modifier)* matter-of-fact ▷ *vb* **proses, prosing, prosed** **6** to write (something) in prose **7** *(intr)* to speak or write in a tedious style [C14 via OF from L *prōsa ōrātiō* straightforward speech, from *prorsus* prosaic, from *prōvertere* to turn forwards] > **'proseˌlike** *adj*

prosecute ('prɒsɪˌkjuːt) *vb* **prosecutes, prosecuting, prosecuted** **1** *(tr)* to bring a criminal action against (a person) **2** *(intr)* **2a** to seek redress by legal proceedings **2b** to institute or conduct a prosecution **3** *(tr)* to practise (a profession or trade) **4** *(tr)* to continue to do (a task, etc) [C15 from L *prōsequī* to follow] > **'proseˌcutable** *adj* > **'proseˌcutor** *n*

prosecution (ˌprɒsɪ'kjuːʃən) *n* **1** the act of prosecuting or the state of being prosecuted **2a** the institution and conduct of legal proceedings against a person **2b** the proceedings brought in the name of the Crown to put an accused on trial **3** the lawyers acting for the Crown to put the case against a person **4** the following up or carrying on of something begun

proselyte ('prɒsɪˌlaɪt) *n* **1** a person newly converted to a religious faith, esp a Gentile converted to Judaism ▷ *vb* **proselytes, proselyting, proselyted** **2** a less common word for **proselytize** [C14 from Church L *prosēlytus*, from Gk *prosēlutos* recent arrival, convert, from *proserchesthai* to draw near] > **proselytism** ('prɒsɪlɪˌtɪzəm) *n* > **proselytic** (ˌprɒsɪ'lɪtɪk) *adj*

proselytize *or* **proselytise** ('prɒsɪlɪˌtaɪz) *vb* **proselytizes, proselytizing, proselytized** *or* **proselytises, proselytising, proselytised** to convert (someone) from one religious faith to another > **'proselytˌizer** *or* **'proselytˌiser** *n*

prosencephalon (ˌprɒsɛn'sɛfəlɒn) *n, pl* **prosencephala** (-lə) the part of the brain that develops from the anterior portion of the neural tube. Nontechnical name: **forebrain** [C19 from NL, from Gk *prosō* forward + *enkephalos* brain]

prosenchyma (prɒs'ɛŋkɪmə) *n* a plant tissue consisting of long narrow cells with pointed ends: occurs in conducting tissue [C19 from NL, from Gk *pros-* towards + *enkhuma* infusion]

Proserpina (prəʊ'sɜːpɪnə) *n* the Roman goddess of the underworld. Greek counterpart: **Persephone**

prosimian (prəʊ'sɪmɪən) *n* **1** any of a primitive suborder of primates, including lemurs, lorises, and tarsiers ▷ *adj* **2** of or belonging to this suborder [C19 via NL from L *sīmia* ape]

prosit *German* ('proːzɪt) *sentence substitute* good health! cheers! [G, from L, lit.: may it prove beneficial]

prosody ('prɒsədɪ) *n* **1** the study of poetic metre and of the art of versification **2** a system of versification **3** the patterns of stress and intonation in a language [C15 from L *prosōdia* accent of a syllable, from Gk *prosōidia* song set to music, from *pros* towards + *ōidē*, from *aoidē* song; see ODE] > **prosodic** (prə'sɒdɪk) *adj* > **'prosodist** *n*

prosopopoeia *or* **prosopopeia** (ˌprɒsəpə'piːə) *n* **1** *rhetoric* another word for **personification** **2** a figure of speech that represents an imaginary, absent, or dead person speaking or acting [C16 via L from Gk *prosōpopoiia* dramatization, from *prosōpon* face + *poiein* to make]

prospect *n* ('prɒspɛkt) **1** *(sometimes pl)* a probability of future success **2** a view or scene **3** a mental outlook **4** expectation, or what one expects **5** a prospective buyer, project, etc **6** a survey or observation **7** *mining* **7a** a known or likely deposit of ore **7b** the location of a deposit of ore **7c** the yield of mineral obtained from a sample of ore ▷ *vb* (prə'spɛkt) **8** (when *intr*, often foll by *for*) to explore (a region) for gold or other valuable minerals **9** *(tr)* to work (a mine) to discover its profitability **10** *(intr; often foll by for)* to search (for) [C15 from L *prōspectus* distant view, from *prōspicere* to look into the distance]

prospective (prə'spɛktɪv) *adj* **1** looking towards the future **2** *(prenominal)* expected or likely > **pro'spectively** *adv*

prospector (prə'spɛktə) *n* a person who searches for gold, petroleum, etc

prospectus (prə'spɛktəs) *n, pl* **prospectuses** **1** a formal statement giving details of a forthcoming event, such as the issue of shares **2** a brochure giving details of courses, as at a school

prosper ('prɒspə) *vb (usually intr)* to thrive, succeed, etc, or cause to thrive, etc, in a healthy way [C15 from L *prosperāre* to succeed, from *prosperus* fortunate, from PRO-[1] + *spēs* hope]

prosperity (prɒ'spɛrɪtɪ) *n* the condition of prospering; success or wealth

prosperous ('prɒspərəs) *adj* **1** flourishing; prospering

2 affluent; wealthy > ˈ**prosperously** *adv*

Prost (*French* prɒst) *n* **Alain** (alɛ̃) born 1955, French motor-racing driver: world champion 1985, 1986, 1989, and 1993

prostaglandin (ˌprɒstəˈglændɪn) *n* any of a group of hormone-like compounds found in all mammalian tissues, which stimulate the muscles of the uterus and affect the blood vessels; used to induce abortion or birth [C20 from *prosta(te) gland* + -IN; orig. believed to be secreted by the prostate gland]

prostate (ˈprɒsteɪt) *n* **1** Also called: **prostate gland** a gland in male mammals that surrounds the neck of the bladder and secretes a liquid constituent of the semen ▷ *adj* **2** Also: **prostatic** (prɒˈstætɪk) of the prostate gland ▷ See also **PSA** [C17 via Med. L from Gk *prostatēs* something standing in front (of the bladder), from *pro-* in front + *histanai* to cause to stand]

prosthesis (ˈprɒsθɪsɪs) *n, pl* **prostheses** (-ˌsiːz) **1** *surgery* **1a** the replacement of a missing bodily part with an artificial substitute **1b** an artificial part such as a limb, eye, or tooth **2** *linguistics* another word for **prothesis** [C16 via LL from Gk: an addition, from *prostithenai* to add, from *pros-* towards + *tithenai* to place] > **prosthetic** (prɒsˈθɛtɪk) *adj* > **prosˈthetically** *adv*

prosthetics (prɒsˈθɛtɪks) *n* (*functioning as sing*) the branch of surgery concerned with prosthesis

prostitute (ˈprɒstɪˌtjuːt) *n* **1** a woman who engages in sexual intercourse for money **2** a man who engages in such activity, esp in homosexual practices **3** a person who offers his or her talent for unworthy purposes ▷ *vb* **prostitutes, prostituting, prostituted** (*tr*) **4** to offer (oneself or another) in sexual intercourse for money **5** to offer for unworthy purposes [C16 from L *prōstituere* to expose to prostitution, from *prō-* in public + *statuere* to cause to stand] > ˌ**prostiˈtution** *n* > ˈ**prostiˌtutor** *n*

prostrate *adj* (ˈprɒstreɪt) **1** lying face downwards, as in submission **2** exhausted physically or emotionally **3** helpless or defenceless **4** (of a plant) growing closely along the ground ▷ *vb* (prɒˈstreɪt), **prostrates, prostrating, prostrated** (*tr*) **5** to cast (oneself) down, as in submission **6** to lay or throw down flat **7** to make helpless **8** to make exhausted [C14 from L *prōsternere* to throw to the ground, from *prō-* before + *sternere* to lay low] > **prosˈtration** *n*

USAGE This word is sometimes wrongly used where *prostate* is meant: *prostate* (not *prostrate*) *cancer*

prostyle (ˈprəʊstaɪl) *adj* **1** (of a building) having a row of columns in front, esp as in the portico of a Greek temple ▷ *n* **2** a prostyle building, portico, etc [C17 from L *prostȳlos*, from Gk: with pillars in front, from PRO-[2] + *stulos* pillar]

prosy (ˈprəʊzɪ) *adj* **prosier, prosiest** **1** of the nature of or similar to prose **2** dull, tedious, or long-winded > ˈ**prosily** *adv* > ˈ**prosiness** *n*

Prot. *abbrev for* Protestant

protactinium (ˌprəʊtækˈtɪnɪəm) *n* a toxic radioactive element that occurs in uranium ores and is produced by neutron irradiation of thorium. Symbol: Pa; atomic no.: 91; half-life of most stable isotope, ^{231}Pa: 32 500 years

protagonist (prəʊˈtægənɪst) *n* **1** the principal character in a play, story, etc **2** a supporter, esp when important or respected, of a cause, party, etc [C17 from Gk *prōtagōnistēs*, from *prōtos* first + *agōnistēs* actor] > **proˈtagonism** *n*

Protagoras (prəʊˈtægəˌræs) *n* ?485–?411 BC, Greek philosopher and sophist, famous for his dictum "Man is the measure of all things."

protasis (ˈprɒtəsɪs) *n, pl* **protases** (-siːz) **1** *logic, grammar* the antecedent of a conditional statement, such as *it rains* in *if it rains the game will be cancelled* **2** (in classical drama) the introductory part of a play [C17 via L from Gk: a proposal, from *pro-* before + *teinein* to extend]

protea (ˈprəʊtɪə) *n* a shrub of tropical and southern Africa, having flowers with coloured bracts arranged in showy heads [C20 from NL, from PROTEUS]

protean (prəʊˈtiːən, ˈprəʊtɪən) *adj* readily taking on various shapes or forms; variable [C16 from PROTEUS]

protease (ˈprəʊtɪˌeɪs) *n* any enzyme involved in proteolysis [C20 from PROTEIN + -ASE]

protease inhibitor *n* any one of a class of antiviral drugs that impair the growth and replication of HIV by inhibiting the action of protease produced by the virus: used in the treatment of AIDS

protect (prəˈtɛkt) *vb* (*tr*) **1** to defend from trouble, harm, etc **2** *econ* to assist (domestic industries) by the imposition of protective tariffs on imports **3** *commerce* to provide funds in advance to guarantee payment of (a note, etc) [C16 from L *prōtegere* to cover before]

protectant (prəˈtɛktənt) *n* a chemical substance that affords protection, as against frost, rust, insects, etc

protection (prəˈtɛkʃən) *n* **1** the act of protecting or the condition of being protected **2** something that protects **3a** the imposition of duties on imports, for the protection of domestic industries against overseas competition, etc **3b** Also called: **protectionism** the system or theory of such restrictions **4** *inf* **4a** Also called: **protection money** money demanded by gangsters for freedom from molestation **4b** freedom from molestation purchased in this way > **proˈtectionˌism** *n* > **proˈtectionist** *n, adj*

protective (prəˈtɛktɪv) *adj* **1** giving or capable of giving protection **2** *econ* of or intended for protection of domestic industries ▷ *n* **3** something that protects **4** a condom > **proˈtectively** *adv* > **proˈtectiveness** *n*

protective coloration *n* the coloration of an animal that enables it to blend with its surroundings and therefore escape the attention of predators

protector (prəˈtɛktə) *n* **1** a person or thing that protects **2** *history* a person who exercised royal authority during the minority, absence, or incapacity of the monarch > **proˈtectress** *fem n*

Protector (prəˈtɛktə) *n* short for **Lord Protector,** the title borne by Oliver Cromwell (1653–58) and by Richard Cromwell (1658–59) as heads of state during the period known as the Protectorate

protectorate (prəˈtɛktərɪt) *n* **1a** a territory largely controlled by but not annexed to a stronger state **1b** the relation of a protecting state to its protected territory **2** the office or period of office of a protector

protégé *or* (*fem*) **protégée** (ˈprəʊtɪˌʒeɪ) *n* a person who is protected and aided by the patronage of another [C18 from F *protéger* to PROTECT]

protein (ˈprəʊtiːn) *n* any of a large group of nitrogenous compounds of high molecular weight that are essential constituents of all living organisms [C19 via G from Gk *prōteios* primary, from *protos* first + -IN] > ˌ**proteinˈaceous, proˈteinic,** *or* **proˈteinous** *adj*

pro tempore *Latin* (ˈprəʊ ˈtɛmpərɪ) *adv, adj* for the time being. Often shortened to **pro tem** (ˈprəʊ ˈtɛm)

proteolysis (ˌprəʊtɪˈɒlɪsɪs) *n* the hydrolysis of proteins into simpler compounds by the action of enzymes [C19 from NL, from *proteo-* (from PROTEIN) + -LYSIS] > **proteolytic** (ˌprəʊtɪəˈlɪtɪk) *adj*

proteomics (ˌprəʊtɪˈɒmɪks) *n* (*functioning as singular*) the branch of biochemistry concerned with the structure and analysis of the proteins occurring in living organisms

protest *n* (ˈprəʊtɛst) **1a** public, often organized, manifestation of dissent **1b** (*as modifier*): *a protest march* **2** a formal or solemn objection **3** a formal notarial statement drawn up on behalf of a creditor and declaring that the debtor has dishonoured a bill of exchange, etc **4** the act of protesting ▷ *vb* (prəˈtɛst) **5** (when *intr*, foll by *against, at, about*, etc; when *tr*, *may take a clause as object*) to make a strong objection (to something, esp a supposed injustice or offence)

6 (when *tr, may take a clause as object*) to disagree; object: *"I'm OK" she protested* 7 (when *tr, may take a clause as object*) to assert in a formal or solemn manner 8 (*tr*) *chiefly US* to object forcefully to: *a women's rights group at the University of Kansas is protesting violence against women* 9 (*tr*) to declare formally that (a bill of exchange or promissory note) has been dishonoured [C14 from L *prōtestārī* to make a formal declaration, from *prō-* before + *testārī* to assert] > **pro'testant** *adj, n* > **pro'tester** *or* **pro'testor** *n* > **pro'testingly** *adv*

Protestant ('prɒtɪstənt) *n* **a** an adherent of Protestantism **b** (*as modifier*): *the Protestant Church*

Protestantism ('prɒtɪstən,tɪzəm) *n* the religion of any of the Churches of Western Christendom that are separated from the Roman Catholic Church and adhere substantially to principles established during the Reformation

protestation (,prəʊtɛs'teɪʃən) *n* 1 the act of protesting 2 a strong declaration

Proteus ('prəʊtɪəs) *n Greek myth* a prophetic sea god capable of changing his shape at will

prothalamion (,prəʊθə'leɪmɪən) *or* **prothalamium** *n, pl* **prothalamia** (-mɪə) a song or poem in celebration of a marriage [C16 from Gk *pro-* before + *thalamos* marriage]

prothallus (prəʊ'θæləs) *or* **prothallium** (prəʊ'θælɪəm) *n, pl* **prothalli** (-laɪ) *or* **prothallia** (-lɪə) *Bot.* the small flat green disc of tissue that bears the reproductive organs of ferns, horsetails, and club mosses [C19 from NL, from *pro-* before + Gk *thallus* a young shoot]

prothesis ('prɒθɪsɪs) *n, pl* **protheses** (-si:z) 1 a development of a language by which a syllable is prefixed to a word to facilitate pronunciation: *Latin "scala" gives Spanish "escala" by prothesis* 2 *Eastern Orthodox Church* the solemn preparation of the Eucharistic elements before consecration [C16 via LL from Gk: a setting out in public, from *pro-* forth + *thesis* a placing] > **prothetic** (prə'θɛtɪk) *adj* > **pro'thetically** *adv*

prothrombin (prəʊ'θrɒmbɪn) *n biochemistry* a zymogen found in blood that gives rise to thrombin on activation

protist ('prəʊtɪst) *n* (in some classification systems) any organism belonging to a large group, including bacteria, protozoans, and fungi, regarded as distinct from plants and animals. The group is usually now restricted to protozoans, unicellular algae, and simple fungi ▷ Cf **protoctist** [C19 from NL *Protista* most primitive organisms, from Gk *prōtistos* the very first, from *prōtos* first]

protium ('prəʊtɪəm) *n* the most common isotope of hydrogen, having a mass number of 1 [C20 NL, from PROTO- + -IUM]

proto- *or sometimes before a vowel* **prot-** *combining form* 1 first: *protomartyr* 2 primitive or original: *prototype* 3 first in a series of chemical compounds: *protoxide* [from Gk *prōtos* first, from *pro* before]

protocol ('prəʊtə,kɒl) *n* 1 the formal etiquette and procedure for state and diplomatic ceremonies 2 a record of an agreement, esp in international negotiations, etc 3a an amendment to a treaty or convention 3b an annexe appended to a treaty to deal with subsidiary matters 4 *chiefly US* a record of data or observations on a particular experiment or proceeding 5 *computing* the set form in which data must be presented for handling by a particular computer configuration, esp in the transmission of information between different computer systems [C16 from Med. L *prōtocollum*, from LGk *prōtokollon* sheet glued to the front of a manuscript, from PROTO- + *kolla* glue]

protoctist (prəʊ'tɒktɪst) *n* (in modern biological classifications) any unicellular or simple multicellular organism belonging to the kingdom that includes protozoans, algae, and slime moulds [C19 from NL *protoctista*, ?from Gk *prototokos* first born]

protohuman (,prəʊtəʊ'hju:mən) *n* 1 any of various prehistoric primates that resembled modern man ▷ *adj* 2 of these primates

Proto-Indo-European *n* the prehistoric unrecorded language that was the ancestor of all Indo-European languages

protomartyr (,prəʊtəʊ'mɑ:tə) *n* 1 St Stephen as the first Christian martyr 2 the first martyr to lay down his or her life in any cause

proton ('prəʊtɒn) *n* a stable, positively charged elementary particle, found in atomic nuclei in numbers equal to the atomic number of the element [C20 from Gk *prōtos* first]

protoplasm ('prəʊtə,plæzəm) *n biol* the living contents of a cell differentiated into cytoplasm and nucleoplasm [C19 from NL, from PROTO- + Gk *plasma* form] > **,proto'plasmic**, **,proto'plasmal**, *or* **,protoplas'matic** *adj*

prototype ('prəʊtə,taɪp) *n* 1 one of the first units manufactured of a product, which is tested so that the design can be changed if necessary before the product is manufactured commercially 2 a person or thing that serves as an example of a type 3 *biol* the ancestral or primitive form of a species > **,proto'typal**, **prototypic** (,prəʊtə'tɪpɪk), *or* **,proto'typical** *adj*

protozoan (,prəʊtə'zəʊən) *n, pl* **protozoa** (-'zəʊə) 1 Also **protozoon** any of various minute unicellular organisms formerly regarded as invertebrates of the phylum *Protozoa*, but now usually classified in certain phyla of protoctists. Protozoans include amoebas and foraminifers ▷ *adj* 2 Also: **protozoic** of or belonging to protozoans [C19 via NL from Gk PROTO- + *zoion* animal]

protract (prə'trækt) *vb* (*tr*) 1 to lengthen or extend (a speech, etc) 2 (of a muscle) to draw, thrust, or extend (a part, etc) forwards 3 to plot using a protractor and scale [C16 from L *prōtrahere* to prolong, from PRO-[1] + *trahere* to drag] > **pro'traction** *n*

protracted (prə'træktɪd) *adj* extended or lengthened in time; prolonged: *a protracted court case* > **pro'tractedly** *adv* > **pro'tractedness** *n*

protractile (prə'træktaɪl) *adj* able to be extended: *protractile muscle*

protractor (prə'træktə) *n* 1 an instrument for measuring or drawing angles, usually a flat semicircular transparent plastic sheet graduated in degrees 2 *anat* a former term for **extensor**

protrude (prə'tru:d) *vb* **protrudes, protruding, protruded** 1 to thrust forwards or outwards 2 to project or cause to project [C17 from L, from PRO-[2] + *trudere* to thrust] > **pro'trusion** *n* > **pro'trusive** *adj*

protrusile (prə'tru:saɪl) *adj zool* capable of being thrust forwards: *protrusile jaws*

protuberant (prə'tju:bərənt) *adj* swelling out; bulging [C17 from LL *prōtūberāre* to swell, from PRO-[1] + *tūber* swelling] > **pro'tuberance** *or* **pro'tuberancy** *n* > **pro'tuberantly** *adv*

proud (praʊd) *adj* 1 (foll by *of*, an infinitive, or a clause) pleased or satisfied, as with oneself, one's possessions, achievements, etc 2 feeling honoured or gratified by some distinction 3 having an inordinately high opinion of oneself; haughty 4 characterized by or proceeding from a sense of pride: *a proud moment* 5 having a proper sense of self-respect 6 stately or distinguished 7 bold or fearless 8 (of a surface, edge, etc) projecting or protruding 9 (of animals) restive or excited, often sexually ▷ *adv* 10 **do (someone) proud** 10a to entertain (someone) on a grand scale: *they did us proud at the hotel* 10b to honour (someone): *his honesty did him proud* [LOE *prūd*, from OF *prud*, *prod* brave, from LL *prōde* useful, from L *prōdesse* to be of value] > **'proudly** *adv* > **'proudness** *n*

proud flesh *n* a mass of tissue formed around a healing wound

Proudhon (*French* prudɔ̃) *n* **Pierre Joseph** (pjɛr ʒozɛf) 1809–65, French socialist, whose pamphlet *What is*

Property? (1840) declared that property is theft
Proust (*French* prust) *n* 1 **Joseph Louis** (ʒozɛf lwi) 1754–1826, French chemist, who formulated the law of constant proportions 2 **Marcel** (marsɛl) 1871–1922, French novelist whose long novel *À la recherche du temps perdu* (1913–27) deals with the relationship of the narrator to themes such as art, time, memory, and society
Prov. *abbrev for:* 1 *Bible* Proverbs 2 Province 3 Provost
prove (pruːv) *vb* **proves, proving, proved; proved** *or* **proven** (*mainly tr*) 1 (*may take a clause as object or an infinitive*) to demonstrate the truth or validity of, esp by using an established sequence of procedures 2 to establish the quality of, esp by experiment 3 *law* to establish the genuineness of (a will) 4 to show (oneself) able or courageous 5 (*copula*) to be found (to be): *this has proved useless* 6 (*intr*) (of dough) to rise in a warm place before baking [c12 from OF *prover*, from L *probāre* to test, from *probus* honest] > **'provable** *adj* > **'provably** *adv* > **,prova'bility** *n*
proven ('pruːvᵊn, 'prəʊ-) *vb* 1 a past participle of **prove** 2 See **not proven** ▷ *adj* 3 tried; tested: *a proven method*
provenance ('prɒvɪnəns) *n* a place of origin, as of a work of art [c19 from F, from *provenir*, from L *prōvenīre* to originate, from *venīre* to come]
Provençal (,prɒvɒn'sɑːl; *French* prɔvɑ̃sal) *adj* 1 denoting or characteristic of Provence, its inhabitants, their dialect of French, or their Romance language ▷ *n* 2 a language of Provence, closely related to French and Italian, belonging to the Romance group of the Indo-European family 3 a native or inhabitant of Provence
Provence (*French* prɔvɑ̃s) *n* a former province of SE France, on the Mediterranean, and the River Rhône: forms part of the administrative region of Provence-Alpes-Côte d'Azur
provender ('prɒvɪndə) *n* 1 fodder for livestock 2 food in general [c14 from OF *provendre*, from LL *praebenda* grant, from L *praebēre* to proffer]
proverb ('prɒvɜːb) *n* 1 a short memorable saying embodying some commonplace fact 2 a person or thing exemplary of a characteristic: *Antarctica is a proverb for extreme cold* 3 *Bible* a wise saying providing guidance [c14 via OF from L *prōverbium*, from *verbum* word]
proverbial (prə'vɜːbɪəl) *adj* 1 (*prenominal*) commonly or traditionally referred to as an example of some peculiarity, characteristic, etc 2 of, embodied in, or resembling a proverb > **pro'verbially** *adv*
provide (prə'vaɪd) *vb* **provides, providing, provided** (*mainly tr*) 1 to furnish or supply 2 to afford; yield: *this meeting provides an opportunity to talk* 3 (*intr; often foll by for or against*) to take careful precautions: *he provided against financial ruin by wise investment* 4 (*intr; foll by for*) to supply means of support (to): *he provides for his family* 5 (of a person, law, etc) to state as a condition; stipulate 6 to confer and induct into ecclesiastical offices [c15 from L *prōvidēre* to provide for, from *prō-* beforehand + *vidēre* to see] > **pro'vider** *n*
providence ('prɒvɪdəns) *n* 1a *Christianity* God's foreseeing protection and care of his creatures 1b such protection and care as manifest by some other force 2 a supposed manifestation of such care and guidance 3 the foresight or care exercised by a person in the management of his affairs
Providence[1] ('prɒvɪdəns) *n Christianity* God, esp as showing foreseeing care of his creatures
Providence[2] ('prɒvɪdəns) *n* a port in NE Rhode Island, capital of the state, at the head of Narragansett Bay: founded by Roger Williams in 1636. Pop: 173 618 (2000)
provident ('prɒvɪdənt) *adj* 1 providing for future needs 2 exercising foresight in the management of one's affairs 3 characterized by foresight [c15 from L *prōvidens* foreseeing, from *prōvidēre* to PROVIDE] > **'providently** *adv*
providential (,prɒvɪ'dɛnʃəl) *adj* characteristic of or presumed to proceed from or as if from divine providence > **,provi'dentially** *adv*
provident society *n* a mutual insurance society catering esp for those on a low income, providing sickness, death, and pension benefits
providing (prə'vaɪdɪŋ) *or* **provided** *conj* (*subordinating; sometimes foll by that*) on the condition or understanding (that): *I'll play, providing you pay me*
province ('prɒvɪns) *n* 1 a territory governed as a unit of a country or empire 2 (*pl; usually preceded by the*) those parts of a country lying outside the capital and other large cities and regarded as outside the mainstream of sophisticated culture 3 an area of learning, activity, etc 4 the extent of a person's activities or office 5 an ecclesiastical territory, having an archbishop or metropolitan at its head 6 an administrative and territorial subdivision of a religious order 7 *history* a region of the Roman Empire outside Italy ruled by a governor from Rome [c14 from OF, from L *prōvincia* conquered territory]
Provincetown ('prɒvɪns,taʊn) *n* a village in SE Massachusetts, at the tip of Cape Cod: scene of the first landing place of the Pilgrims (1620) and of the signing of the Mayflower Compact (1620). Pop: 3374 (1990)
provincewide ('prɒvɪns,waɪd) *Canad* ▷ *adj* 1 covering or available to the whole of a province: *a provincewide referendum* ▷ *adv* 2 throughout a province: *an advertising campaign to go provincewide*
provincial (prə'vɪnʃəl) *adj* 1 of or connected with a province 2 characteristic of or connected with the provinces 3 having attitudes and opinions supposedly common to people living in the provinces; unsophisticated; limited 4 NZ denoting a football team representing a province, one of the historical administrative areas of New Zealand ▷ *n* 5 a person lacking the sophistications of city life; rustic or narrow-minded individual 6 a person coming from or resident in a province or the provinces 7 the head of an ecclesiastical province 8 the head of a territorial subdivision of a religious order > **provinciality** (prə,vɪnʃɪ'ælɪtɪ) *n* > **pro'vincially** *adv*
provincialism (prə'vɪnʃə,lɪzəm) *n* 1 narrowness of mind; lack of sophistication 2 a word or attitude characteristic of a provincial 3 attention to the affairs of one's local area rather than the whole nation 4 the state or quality of being provincial
provincial police *n* (in Canada) the police force of a province, esp Ontario or Quebec
provirus ('prəʊ,vaɪrəs) *n* the inactive form of a virus in a host cell
provision (prə'vɪʒən) *n* 1 the act of supplying food, etc 2 something that is supplied 3 preparations (esp in **make provision for**) 4 (*pl*) food and other necessities, as for an expedition 5 a condition or stipulation incorporated in a document; proviso 6 the conferring of and induction into ecclesiastical offices ▷ *vb* 7 (*tr*) to supply with provisions [c14 from L *prōvīsiō* a providing; see PROVIDE] > **pro'visioner** *n*
provisional (prə'vɪʒənᵊl) *adj* subject to later alteration; temporary or conditional: *a provisional decision* > **pro'visionally** *adv*
Provisional (prə'vɪʒənᵊl) *adj* 1 of, designating, or relating to the unofficial factions of the IRA and Sinn Féin that became increasingly dominant following a split in 1969. The Provisional movement remained committed to a policy of terrorism until its ceasefires of the mid-1990s ▷ *n* 2 Also called: **Provo** a member of the Provisional IRA or Sinn Féin ▷ Compare **Official**
proviso (prə'vaɪzəʊ) *n, pl* **provisos** *or* **provisoes** 1 a clause in a document or contract that embodies a condition or stipulation 2 a condition or stipulation [c15 from Med. L *prōvīsō quod* it being provided that, from L *prōvīsus* provided]

Pp

provisory (prəˈvaɪzərɪ) *adj* **1** containing a proviso; conditional **2** provisional **3** making provision > **proˈvisorily** *adv*

Provo (ˈprəʊvəʊ) *n, pl* **Provos** another name for a **Provisional** (sense 2)

provocation (ˌprɒvəˈkeɪʃən) *n* **1** the act of provoking or inciting **2** something that causes indignation, anger, etc

provocative (prəˈvɒkətɪv) *adj* serving or intended to provoke or incite, esp to anger or sexual desire: *a provocative look; a provocative remark* > **proˈvocatively** *adv*

provoke (prəˈvəʊk) *vb* **provokes, provoking, provoked** (*tr*) **1** to anger or infuriate **2** to incite or stimulate **3** to promote (anger, etc) in a person **4** to cause; bring about: *the accident provoked an inquiry* [c15 from L *prōvocāre* to call forth] > **proˈvoking** *adj* > **proˈvokingly** *adv*

provost (ˈprɒvəst) *n* **1** the head of certain university colleges or schools **2** (in Scotland) the chairman and civic head of certain district councils or (formerly) of a burgh council ▷ Cf **convener** (sense 2) **3** *Church of England* the senior dignitary of one of the more recent cathedral foundations **4** *RC Church* **4a** the head of a cathedral chapter **4b** (formerly) the member of a monastic community second in authority under the abbot **5** (in medieval times) an overseer, steward, or bailiff [OE *profost*, from Med. L *prōpositus* placed at the head (of), from L *praepōnere* to place first]

provost marshal (prəˈvəʊ) *n* the officer in charge of military police in a camp or city

prow (praʊ) *n* the bow of a vessel [c16 from OF *proue*, from L *prora*, from Gk *prōra*]

prowess (ˈpraʊɪs) *n* **1** outstanding or superior skill or ability **2** bravery or fearlessness, esp in battle [c13 from OF *proesce*, from *prou* good]

prowl (praʊl) *vb* **1** (when *intr*, often foll by *around* or *about*) to move stealthily around (a place) as if in search of prey or plunder ▷ *n* **2** the act of prowling **3** **on the prowl** **3a** moving around stealthily **3b** pursuing members of the opposite sex [c14 *prollen*, from ?] > **ˈprowler** *n*

prox. *abbrev for* proximo (next month)

proximal (ˈprɒksɪməl) *adj anat* situated close to the centre, median line, or point of attachment or origin > **ˈproximally** *adv*

proximate (ˈprɒksɪmɪt) *adj* **1** next or nearest in space or time **2** very near; close **3** immediately preceding or following in a series **4** a less common word for **approximate** [c16 from LL *proximāre* to draw near, from L *proximus* next, from *prope* near] > **ˈproximately** *adv*

proximity (prɒkˈsɪmɪtɪ) *n* **1** nearness in space or time **2** nearness or closeness in a series [c15 from L *proximitās* closeness; see PROXIMATE]

proximo (ˈprɒksɪməʊ) *adv now rare except when abbreviated in formal correspondence* in or during the next or coming month: *a letter of the seventh proximo*. Abbrev: **prox** ▷ Cf **instant, ultimo** [c19 from L: in or on the next]

proxy (ˈprɒksɪ) *n, pl* **proxies** **1** a person authorized to act on behalf of someone else; agent: *vote by proxy* **2** authority, esp in the form of a document, given to a person to act on behalf of someone else **3** *computing* short for **proxy server** [c15 *prokesye*, from *procuracy*, from L *prōcūrātiō* procuration; see PROCURE]

proxy server *n computing* a computer that acts as an intermediary between a client machine and a server, caching information to save access time

Prozac (ˈprəʊzæk) *n trademark* a drug that prolongs the action of serotonin in the brain; used as an antidepressant

PRP *abbrev for:* **1** performance-related pay **2** profit-related pay

PRT *abbrev for* petroleum revenue tax

prude (pruːd) *n* a person who affects or shows an excessively modest, prim, or proper attitude, esp regarding sex [c18 from F, from *prudefemme*, from OF *prode femme* respectable woman; see PROUD] > **ˈprudery** *n* > **ˈprudish** *adj* > **ˈprudishly** *adv*

prudence (ˈpruːdəns) *n* **1** caution in practical affairs; discretion **2** care taken in the management of one's resources **3** consideration for one's own interests **4** the quality of being prudent

prudent (ˈpruːdᵊnt) *adj* **1** discreet or cautious in managing one's activities; circumspect **2** practical and careful in providing for the future **3** exercising good judgment [c14 from L *prūdēns* far-sighted, from *prōvidens* acting with foresight; see PROVIDENT] > **ˈprudently** *adv*

prudential (pruːˈdɛnʃəl) *adj* **1** characterized by or resulting from prudence **2** exercising sound judgment > **pruˈdentially** *adv*

Prudentius (pruːˈdɛnʃəs) *n* **Aurelius Clemens** (ɔːˈriːlɪəs ˈklɛmɛnz) 348–410 AD, Latin Christian poet, born in Spain. His works include the allegory *Psychomachia*

Prud'hon (*French* prydɔ̃) *n* **Pierre Paul** (pjɛr pɔl) 1758–1823, French painter, noted for the romantic and mysterious aura of his portraits

pruinose (ˈpruːɪˌnəʊs, -ˌnəʊz) *adj bot* coated with a powdery or waxy bloom [c19 from L *pruīnōsus* frost-covered, from *pruīna* hoarfrost]

prune¹ (pruːn) *n* **1** a purplish-black partially dried fruit of any of several varieties of plum tree **2** *sl, chiefly Brit* a dull or foolish person **3** **prunes and prisms** denoting an affected and mincing way of speaking [c14 from OF *prune*, from L *prūnum* plum, from Gk *prounon*]

prune² (pruːn) *vb* **prunes, pruning, pruned** **1** to remove (dead or superfluous twigs, branches, etc) from (a tree, shrub, etc), esp by cutting off **2** to remove (anything undesirable or superfluous) from (a book, etc) [c15 from OF *proignier* to clip, prob. from *provigner* to prune vines, ult. from L *propāgo* a cutting] > **ˈprunable** *adj* > **ˈpruner** *n*

prunella (pruːˈnɛlə) *n* a strong fabric, esp a twill-weave worsted, formerly used for academic gowns and the uppers of some shoes [c17 ?from *prunelle*, a green French liqueur, with reference to the colour of the cloth]

pruning hook *n* a tool with a curved steel blade terminating in a hook, used for pruning

prurient (ˈprʊərɪənt) *adj* **1** unusually or morbidly interested in sexual thoughts or practices **2** exciting lustfulness [c17 from L *prūrīre* to lust after, itch] > **ˈprurience** *n* > **ˈpruriently** *adv*

prurigo (prʊəˈraɪgəʊ) *n* a chronic inflammatory disease of the skin characterized by intense itching [c19 from L: an itch] > **pruriginous** (prʊəˈrɪdʒɪnəs) *adj*

pruritus (prʊəˈraɪtəs) *n pathol* any intense sensation of itching [c17 from L: an itching; see PRURIENT] > **pruritic** (prʊəˈrɪtɪk) *adj*

Prussia (ˈprʌʃə) *n* a former German state in N and central Germany, extending from France and the Low Countries to the Baltic Sea and Poland: developed as the chief military power of the Continent, leading the North German Confederation from 1867–71, when the German Empire was established; dissolved in 1947 and divided between East and West Germany, Poland, and the former Soviet Union. Area: (in 1939) 294 081 sq km (113 545 sq miles). German name: **Preussen**

Prussian (ˈprʌʃən) *adj* **1** of Prussia, or its people, esp of the Junkers and their military tradition ▷ *n* **2** a native or inhabitant of Prussia **3** **Old Prussian** the extinct Baltic language of the non-German inhabitants of Prussia

Prussian blue *n* **1** any of a number of blue pigments containing ferrocyanide or ferricyanide ions **2a** the blue or deep greenish-blue colour of this **2b** (*as adj*): *a Prussian-blue carpet*

prussic acid (ˈprʌsɪk) *n* the extremely poisonous aqueous solution of hydrogen cyanide [c18 from F *acide prussique* Prussian acid, because obtained from Prussian blue]

Prut (*Russian* prut) *n* a river in E Europe, rising in the SW

Ukraine and flowing generally southeast, forming part of the border between Romania and Moldova, to join the River Danube. Length: 853 km (530 miles)

PRW *text messaging abbrev for* parents are watching

pry[1] (praɪ) *vb* **pries, prying, pried** 1 (*intr; often foll by into*) to make an impertinent or uninvited inquiry (about a private matter, topic, etc) ▷ *n, pl* **pries** 2 the act of prying 3 a person who pries [C14 from ?]

pry[2] (praɪ) *vb* **pries, prying, pried** the US and Canad word for **prise** [C14 from ?]

pryer (ˈpraɪə) *n* a variant spelling of **prier**

Prynne (prɪn) *n* **William** 1600–69, English Puritan leader and pamphleteer, whose ears were cut off in punishment for his attacks on Laud

Przemyśl (*Polish* ˈpʃɛmiʃl) *n* a city in SE Poland, near the border with the Ukraine on the San River: a fortress in the early Middle Ages; belonged to Austria (1722–1918). Pop: 67 000 (latest est)

Przewalski's horse (ˌpɜːʒəˈvælskɪz) *n* a wild horse of W Mongolia, having an erect mane and no forelock: extinct in the wild, a few survive in captivity [C19 after the Russian explorer Nikolai *Przewalski* (1839–88), who discovered it]

PS *abbrev for:* 1 Passenger Steamer 2 Police Sergeant 3 Also: **ps** postscript 4 private secretary 5 prompt side

Ps. *or* **Psa.** *Bible abbrev for* Psalm(s)

PSA *abbrev for* prostatic specific antigen: an enzyme secreted by the prostate gland, increased levels of which are found in the blood of patients with cancer of the prostate

psalm (sɑːm) *n* 1 (*often cap*) any of the sacred songs that constitute a book (Psalms) of the Old Testament 2 a musical setting of one of these 3 any sacred song [OE, from LL *psalmus*, from Gk *psalmos* song accompanied on the harp, from *psallein* to play (the harp)] > **psalmic** (ˈsɑːmɪk, ˈsæl-) *adj*

psalmist (ˈsɑːmɪst) *n* the composer of a psalm or psalms, esp (when *cap* and preceded by *the*) David, traditionally regarded as the author of The Book of Psalms

psalmody (ˈsɑːmədɪ, ˈsæl-) *n, pl* **psalmodies** 1 the act of singing psalms or hymns 2 the art of setting psalms to music [C14 via LL from Gk *psalmōidia* singing accompanied by a harp, from *psalmos* (see PSALM) + *ōidē* ODE] > **ˈpsalmodist** *n* > **psalmodic** (sælˈmɒdɪk) *adj*

Psalter (ˈsɔːltə) *n* 1 another name for the Book of Psalms, esp in the version in the Book of Common Prayer 2 a translation, musical, or metrical version of the Psalms 3 a book containing a version of Psalms [OE *psaltere*, from LL *psaltērium*, from Gk *psaltērion* stringed instrument, from *psallein* to play a stringed instrument]

psalterium (sɔːlˈtɪərɪəm) *n, pl* **psalteria** (-ˈtɪərɪə) the third compartment of the stomach of ruminants. Also called: **omasum** [C19 from L *psaltērium* PSALTER; from the similarity of its folds to the pages of a book]

psaltery (ˈsɔːltərɪ) *n, pl* **psalteries** *music* an ancient stringed instrument similar to the lyre, but having a trapezoidal sounding board over which the strings are stretched

p's and q's *pl n* behaviour; manners (esp in **mind one's p's and q's**) [altered from *p(lea)se and (than)k yous*]

PSBR (in Britain) *abbrev for* public sector borrowing requirement; the money required by the public sector of the economy for expenditure on items that are not financed from income

psephology (sɛˈfɒlədʒɪ) *n* the statistical and sociological study of elections [C20 from Gk *psephos* pebble, vote + -LOGY, from the ancient Greeks' custom of voting with pebbles] > **psephological** (ˌsɛfəˈlɒdʒɪkᵊl) *adj* > **ˌpsephoˈlogically** *adv* > **pseˈphologist** *n*

pseud (sjuːd) *n* 1 *inf* a false or pretentious person ▷ *adj* 2 another word for **pseudo**

Pseudepigrapha (ˌsjuːdɪˈpɪɡrəfə) *pl n* various Jewish writings from the first century BC to the first century AD that claim to have been divinely revealed but which have been excluded from the Greek canon of the Old Testament [C17 from Gk *pseudepigraphos* falsely entitled, from PSEUDO- + *epigraphein* to inscribe] > **Pseudepigraphic** (ˌsjuːdɛpɪˈɡræfɪk) *or* **ˌPseudepiˈgraphical** *adj*

pseudo (ˈsjuːdəʊ) *adj inf* not genuine

pseudo- *or sometimes before a vowel* **pseud-** *combining form* 1 false, pretending, or unauthentic: *pseudo-intellectual* 2 having a close resemblance to: *pseudopodium* [from Gk *pseudēs* false, from *pseudein* to lie]

pseudocarp (ˈsjuːdəʊˌkɑːp) *n* a fruit, such as the apple, that includes parts other than the ripened ovary > **ˌpseudoˈcarpous** *adj*

pseudoephedrine (ˌsjuːdəʊˈɛfɪˌdriːn, -drɪn) *n* a drug similar in action to ephedrine, used extensively as a decongestant

pseudomorph (ˈsjuːdəʊˌmɔːf) *n* a mineral that has an uncharacteristic crystalline form as a result of assuming the shape of another mineral that it has replaced > **ˌpseudoˈmorphic** *or* **ˌpseudoˈmorphous** *adj* > **ˌpseudoˈmorphism** *n*

pseudonym (ˈsjuːdəˌnɪm) *n* a fictitious name adopted esp by an author [C19 via F from Gk *pseudōnumon*] > **ˌpseudoˈnymity** *n* > **pseudonymous** (sjuːˈdɒnɪməs) *adj*

pseudopodium (ˌsjuːdəʊˈpəʊdɪəm) *n, pl* **pseudopodia** (-dɪə) a temporary projection from the cell of an amoeboid protozoan, etc, used for feeding and locomotion

pseudovector (ˌsjuːdəʊˈvɛktə) *n maths* a variable quantity, such as angular momentum, that has magnitude and orientation with respect to an axis

psf *abbrev for* pounds per square foot

pshaw (pʃɔː) *interj becoming rare* an exclamation of disgust, impatience, disbelief, etc

psi[1] (psaɪ) *n* 1 the 23rd letter of the Greek alphabet (Ψ, ψ), a composite consonant, transliterated as *ps* 2 paranormal or psychic phenomena collectively

psi[2] *abbrev for* pounds per square inch

psilocybin (ˌsɪləˈsaɪbɪn, ˌsaɪlə-) *n* a crystalline phosphate ester that is the active principle of the hallucinogenic fungus *Psilocybe mexicana*. Formula: $C_{12}H_{17}N_2O_4P$ [C20 from NL *Psilocybe* (from Gk *psilos* bare + *kubē* head) + -IN]

psi particle *n* See **J/psi particle**

psittacine (ˈsɪtəˌsaɪn, -sɪn) *adj* of, relating to, or resembling a parrot [C19 from LL *psittacīnus*, from L *psittacus* a parrot]

psittacosis (ˌsɪtəˈkəʊsɪs) *n* a disease of parrots that can be transmitted to man, in whom it produces pneumonia. Also called: **parrot fever** [C19 from NL, from L *psittacus* a parrot, from Gk *psittakos*; see -OSIS]

Pskov (*Russian* pskɔf) *n* 1 a city in NW Russia, on the Velikaya River: one of the oldest Russian cities, at its height in the 13th and 14th centuries. Pop: 202 900 (1999 est) 2 **Lake** the S part of Lake Peipus in NW Russia, linked to the main part by a channel 24 km (15 miles) long. Area: about 1000 sq km (400 sq miles)

PSNI *abbrev for* Police Service of Northern Ireland, established in 2000

psoas (ˈsəʊəs) *n* either of two muscles of the loins that aid in flexing and rotating the thigh [C17 from NL, from Gk *psoai* (pl)]

psoriasis (səˈraɪəsɪs) *n* a skin disease characterized by the formation of reddish spots and patches covered with silvery scales [C17 via NL from Gk: itching disease, from *psōra* itch] > **psoriatic** (ˌsɔːrɪˈætɪk) *adj*

psst (pst) *interj* an exclamation made to attract someone's attention, esp one made surreptitiously

PST (in the US and Canada) *abbrev for* Pacific Standard Time

PSV (in Britain) *abbrev for* public service vehicle (now called passenger carrying vehicle)

psych *or* **psyche** (saɪk) *vb* **psychs** *or* **psyches, psyching,**

Pp

psyched (*tr*) *inf* to psychoanalyse. See also **psych out, psych up** [C20 shortened from PSYCHOANALYSE]
psyche ('saɪkɪ) *n* the human mind or soul [C17 from L, from Gk *psukhē* breath, soul]
Psyche ('saɪkɪ) *n Greek myth* a beautiful girl loved by Eros (Cupid), who became the personification of the soul
psychedelic (ˌsaɪkɪ'dɛlɪk) *adj* **1** relating to or denoting new or altered perceptions or sensory experiences, as through the use of hallucinogenic drugs **2** denoting any of the drugs, esp LSD, that produce these effects **3** *inf* (of painting, etc) having the vivid colours and complex patterns popularly associated with the visual effects of psychedelic states [C20 from PSYCHE + Gk *delos* visible] > **ˌpsyche'delically** *adv*
psychiatry (saɪ'kaɪətrɪ) *n* the branch of medicine concerned with the diagnosis and treatment of mental disorders > **psychiatric** (ˌsaɪkɪ'ætrɪk) *or* **ˌpsychi'atrical** *adj* > **ˌpsychi'atrically** *adv* > **psy'chiatrist** *n*
▷ www.nmha.org
▷ www.psycline.org/journals/psycline.html
psychic ('saɪkɪk) *adj* **1a** outside the possibilities defined by natural laws, as mental telepathy **1b** (of a person) sensitive to forces not recognized by natural laws **2** mental as opposed to physical ▷ *n* **3** a person who is sensitive to parapsychological forces or influences > **'psychical** *adj* > **'psychically** *adv*
psycho ('saɪkəʊ) *n, pl* **psychos,** *adj* an informal word for **psychopath** or **psychopathic**
psycho- *or sometimes before a vowel* **psych-** *combining form* indicating the mind or psychological or mental processes: *psychology* [from Gk *psukhē* spirit, breath]
psychoactive (ˌsaɪkəʊ'æktɪv) *adj* (of drugs such as LSD and barbiturates) capable of affecting mental activity. Also: **psychotropic**
psychoanalyse *or esp US* **psychoanalyze** (ˌsaɪkəʊ'ænəˌlaɪz) *vb* **psychoanalyses, psychoanalysing, psychoanalysed** *or US* **psychoanalyzes, psychoanalyzing, psychoanalyzed** (*tr*) to examine or treat (a person) by psychoanalysis
psychoanalysis (ˌsaɪkəʊə'nælɪsɪs) *n* a method of studying the mind and treating mental and emotional disorders based on revealing and investigating the role of the unconscious mind > **psychoanalyst** (ˌsaɪkəʊ'ænəlɪst) *n* > **psychoanalytic** (ˌsaɪkəʊˌænə'lɪtɪk) *or* **ˌpsychoˌana'lytical** *adj* > **ˌpsychoˌana'lytically** *adv*
▷ http://aapsa.org/
▷ www.freudfile.org/psychoanalysis
psychobiology (ˌsaɪkəʊbaɪ'ɒlədʒɪ) *n psychol* the attempt to understand the psychology of organisms in terms of their biological functions and structures > **psychobiological** (ˌsaɪkəʊˌbaɪə'lɒdʒɪkᵊl) *adj* > **ˌpsychobi'ologist** *n*
psychochemical (ˌsaɪkəʊ'kɛmɪkᵊl) *n* **1** any of various chemicals whose primary effect is the alteration of the normal state of consciousness ▷ *adj* **2** of such compounds
psychodrama ('saɪkəʊˌdrɑːmə) *n* **1** *psychiatry* a form of group therapy in which individuals act out situations from their past **2** a film, television drama, etc, in which the psychological development of the characters is emphasized
psychodynamics (ˌsaɪkəʊdaɪ'næmɪks) *n* (*functioning as sing*) *psychol* the study of interacting motives and emotions > **ˌpsychody'namic** *adj*
psychogenic (ˌsaɪkəʊ'dʒɛnɪk) *adj psychol* (esp of disorders or symptoms) of mental, rather than organic, origin > **ˌpsycho'genically** *adv*
psychokinesis (ˌsaɪkəʊkɪ'niːsɪs, -kaɪ-) *n* (in parapsychology) alteration of the state of an object supposedly by mental influence alone [C20 from PSYCHO- + Gk *kinēsis* motion]
psycholinguistics (ˌsaɪkəʊlɪŋ'gwɪstɪks) *n* (*functioning as sing*) the psychology of language, including language acquisition by children, language disorders, etc > **ˌpsycho'linguist** *n*
psychological (ˌsaɪkə'lɒdʒɪkᵊl) *adj* **1** of or relating to psychology **2** of or relating to the mind or mental activity **3** having no real or objective basis; arising in the mind: *his backaches are all psychological* **4** affecting the mind > **ˌpsycho'logically** *adv*
psychological moment *n* the most appropriate time for producing a desired effect
psychological operations *pl n* another term for **psychological warfare**
psychological warfare *n* the application of psychology, esp to attempts to influence morale in time of war
psychologize *or US* **psychologise** (saɪ'kɒləˌdʒaɪz) *vb* **psychologizes, psychologizing, psychologized** *or US* **psychologises, psychologising, psychologised** (*intr*) **1** to make interpretations of mental processes **2** to carry out investigation in psychology
psychology (saɪ'kɒlədʒɪ) *n, pl* **psychologies 1** the scientific study of all forms of human and animal behaviour **2** *inf* the mental make-up of an individual that causes that person to think or act in the way he or she does > **psy'chologist** *n*
▷ www.psych.neu.edu/facllinks
▷ www.sosig.ac.uk/psychology
▷ www.clas.ufl.edu/users/gthursby/psi
psychometrics (ˌsaɪkəʊ'mɛtrɪks) *n* (*functioning as sing*) **1** the branch of psychology concerned with the design and use of psychological tests **2** the application of statistical techniques to psychological testing
psychometry (saɪ'kɒmɪtrɪ) *n psychol* **1** measurement and testing of mental states and processes **2** (in parapsychology) the supposed ability to deduce facts about events by touching objects related to them > **psychometric** (ˌsaɪkəʊ'mɛtrɪk) *or* **ˌpsycho'metrical** *adj* > **ˌpsycho'metrically** *adv*
psychomotor (ˌsaɪkəʊ'məʊtə) *adj* of, relating to, or characterizing movements of the body associated with mental activity
psychoneuroimmunology (ˌsaɪkəʊˌnjʊərəʊˌɪmjʊ'nɒlədʒɪ) *n* the study of the psychological factors that affect the immune system. Abbrev: **PNI**
psychoneurosis (ˌsaɪkəʊnjʊ'rəʊsɪs) *n, pl* **psychoneuroses** (-'rəʊsiːz) another word for **neurosis**
psychopath ('saɪkəʊˌpæθ) *n* a person with a personality disorder characterized by a tendency to commit antisocial and sometimes violent acts without feeling guilt > **ˌpsycho'pathic** *adj* > **ˌpsycho'pathically** *adv*
psychopathology (ˌsaɪkəʊpə'θɒlədʒɪ) *n* the scientific study of mental disorders > **psychopathological** (ˌsaɪkəʊˌpæθə'lɒdʒɪkᵊl) *adj*
psychopathy (saɪ'kɒpəθɪ) *n* any mental disorder or disease
psychopharmacology (ˌsaɪkəʊˌfɑːmə'kɒlədʒɪ) *n* the study of drugs that affect the mind
psychophysics (ˌsaɪkəʊ'fɪzɪks) *n* (*functioning as sing*) the branch of psychology concerned with the relationship between physical stimuli and their effects in the mind > **ˌpsycho'physical** *adj*
psychophysiology (ˌsaɪkəʊˌfɪzɪ'ɒlədʒɪ) *n* the branch of psychology concerned with the physiological basis of mental processes > **psychophysiological** (ˌsaɪkəʊˌfɪzɪə'lɒdʒɪkᵊl) *adj*
psychosexual (ˌsaɪkəʊ'sɛksjʊəl) *adj* of or relating to the mental aspects of sex, such as sexual fantasies > **ˌpsycho'sexually** *adv*
psychosis (saɪ'kəʊsɪs) *n, pl* **psychoses** (-'kəʊsiːz) any form of severe mental disorder in which the individual's contact with reality becomes highly distorted [C19 NL, from PSYCHO- + -OSIS]
psychosocial (ˌsaɪkəʊ'səʊʃəl) *adj* of or relating to processes or factors that are both social and

psychological in origin: *acute psychosocial problems*

psychosomatic (ˌsaɪkəʊsəˈmætɪk) *adj* of disorders, such as stomach ulcers, thought to be caused or aggravated by psychological factors such as stress

psychosurgery (ˌsaɪkəʊˈsɜːdʒərɪ) *n* any surgical procedure on the brain, such as a frontal lobotomy, to relieve serious mental disorders > **psychosurgical** (ˌsaɪkəʊˈsɜːdʒɪkᵊl) *adj*

psychotherapy (ˌsaɪkəʊˈθɛrəpɪ) *n* the treatment of nervous disorders by psychological methods > ˌ**psychoˌtheraˈpeutic** *adj* > ˌ**psychoˌtheraˈpeutically** *adv* > ˌ**psychoˈtherapist** *n*

psychotic (saɪˈkɒtɪk) *psychiatry* ▷ *adj* **1** of or characterized by psychosis ▷ *n* **2** a person suffering from psychosis > **psyˈchotically** *adv*

psychotomimetic (saɪˌkɒtəʊmɪˈmɛtɪk) *adj* (of drugs such as LSD and mescaline) capable of inducing psychotic symptoms

psych out *vb (mainly tr, adv) inf* **1** to guess correctly the intentions of (another) **2** to analyse (a problem, etc) psychologically **3** to intimidate or frighten

psychrometer (saɪˈkrɒmɪtə) *n* a type of hygrometer consisting of two thermometers, one of which has a dry bulb and the other a bulb that is kept moist and ventilated

psych up *vb (tr, adv) inf* to get (oneself or another) into a state of psychological readiness for an action, performance, etc

psyops (ˈsaɪˌɒps) *pl n* short for **psychological operations**

pt *abbrev for:* **1** part **2** patient **3** payment **4** point **5** port **6** pro tempore

Pt *abbrev for* (in place names): **1** Point **2** Port ▷ **3** *the chemical symbol for* platinum

PT *abbrev for:* **1** physical therapy **2** physical training **3** postal telegraph

pt. *abbrev for* pint

PTA *abbrev for* Parent Teacher Association

Ptah (ptɑː, tɑː) *n* (in ancient Egypt) a major god worshipped as the creative power, esp at Memphis

ptarmigan (ˈtɑːmɪɡən) *n, pl* **ptarmigans** *or* **ptarmigan** any of several arctic and subarctic grouse, esp one which has a white winter plumage [C16 changed (? infl. by Gk *pteron* wing) from Scot Gaelic *tarmachan*, from ?]

Pte *mil abbrev for* private

pteridology (ˌtɛrɪˈdɒlədʒɪ) *n* the branch of botany concerned with the study of ferns [C19 from *pterido-*, from Gk *pteris* fern + -LOGY] > **pteridological** (ˌtɛrɪdəʊˈlɒdʒɪkᵊl) *adj*

pteridophyte (ˈtɛrɪdəʊˌfaɪt) *n* (in traditional classification) a plant, such as a fern, horsetail, or club moss, reproducing by spores and having vascular tissue, roots, stems, and leaves. In modern classifications these plants are placed in separate phyla [C19 from *pterido-*, from Gk *pteris* fern + -PHYTE]

ptero- *combining form* a wing, or a part resembling a wing: *pterodactyl* [from Gk *pteron*]

pterodactyl (ˌtɛrəˈdæktɪl) *n* an extinct flying reptile having membranous wings supported on an elongated fourth digit

pteropod (ˈtɛrəˌpɒd) *n* a small marine gastropod mollusc in which the foot is expanded into two winglike lobes for swimming. Also called: **sea butterfly**

pterosaur (ˈtɛrəˌsɔː) *n* any of an order of extinct flying reptiles of Jurassic and Cretaceous times: included the pterodactyls

-pterous *or* **-pteran** *adj combining form* indicating a specified number or type of wings: *dipterous* [from Gk *-pteros*, from *pteron* wing]

pterygoid process (ˈtɛrɪˌɡɔɪd) *n anat* either of two long bony plates extending downwards from each side of the sphenoid bone within the skull [C18 *pterygoid*, from Gk *pterugoeidēs*, from *pterux* wing; see -OID]

PTN *abbrev for* public telephone network: the telephone network provided in Britain by British Telecom

PTO *or* **pto** *abbrev for* please turn over

Ptolemaic (ˌtɒlɪˈmeɪɪk) *adj* **1** of or relating to the ancient astronomer Ptolemy or to his conception of the universe **2** of or relating to the Macedonian dynasty that ruled Egypt from the death of Alexander the Great (323 BC) to the death of Cleopatra (30 BC)

Ptolemaic system *n* the theory of planetary motion developed by Ptolemy from the hypotheses of earlier philosophers, stating that the earth lay at the centre of the universe with the sun, the moon, and the known planets revolving around it in complicated orbits. Beyond the largest of these orbits lay a sphere of fixed stars

Ptolemy (ˈtɒlɪmɪ) *n* Latin name *Claudius Ptolemaeus*. 2nd century AD, Greek astronomer, mathematician, and geographer. His *Geography* was the standard geographical textbook until the discoveries of the 15th century. His system of astronomy (see **Ptolemaic system**), as expounded in the *Almagest*, remained undisputed until the Copernican system was evolved

Ptolemy I *n* called *Ptolemy Soter*. ?367–283 BC, king of Egypt (323–285 BC), a general of Alexander the Great, who obtained Egypt on Alexander's death and founded the Ptolemaic dynasty: his capital Alexandria became the centre of Greek culture

Ptolemy II *n* called *Philadelphus*. 309–246 BC, the son of Ptolemy I; king of Egypt (285–246). Under his rule the power, prosperity, and culture of Egypt was at its height

ptomaine *or* **ptomain** (ˈtəʊmeɪn) *n* any of a group of amines formed by decaying organic matter [C19 from It. *ptomaina*, from Gk *ptoma* corpse, from *piptein* to fall]

ptomaine poisoning *n* a popular term for **food poisoning**. Ptomaines were once erroneously thought to be a cause of food poisoning

ptosis (ˈtəʊsɪs) *n, pl* **ptoses** (ˈtəʊsiːz) prolapse or drooping of a part, esp the eyelid [C18 from Gk: a falling] > **ptotic** (ˈtɒtɪk) *adj*

PTSD *abbrev for* **post-traumatic stress disorder**

pty *Austral, NZ, & S African abbrev for* proprietary

ptyalin (ˈtaɪəlɪn) *n biochemistry* an amylase secreted in the saliva of man and other animals [C19 from Gk *ptualon* saliva, from *ptuein* to spit]

p-type *adj* **1** (of a semiconductor) having a density of mobile holes in excess of that of conduction electrons **2** associated with or resulting from the movement of holes in a semiconductor: *p-type conductivity*

Pu *the chemical symbol for* plutonium

pub (pʌb) *n* **1** *chiefly Brit* a building with a bar and one or more public rooms licensed for the sale and consumption of alcoholic drink, often also providing light meals. Formal name: **public house** **2** *Austral & NZ* a hotel ▷ *vb* **pubs, pubbing, pubbed** **3** *(intr) inf* to visit a pub or pubs (esp in **go pubbing**)

pub. *abbrev for:* **1** public **2** publication **3** published **4** publisher **5** publishing

pub-crawl *inf, chiefly Brit* ▷ *n* **1** a drinking tour of a number of pubs or bars ▷ *vb* **2** *(intr)* to make such a tour

puberty (ˈpjuːbətɪ) *n* the period at the beginning of adolescence when the sex glands become functional. Also called: **pubescence** [C14 from L *pūbertās* maturity, from *pūber* adult] > ˈ**pubertal** *adj*

pubes (ˈpjuːbiːz) *n, pl* **pubes** **1** the region above the external genital organs, covered with hair from the time of puberty **2** pubic hair **3** the pubic bones **4** the plural of **pubis** [from L]

pubescent (pjuːˈbɛsᵊnt) *adj* **1** arriving or arrived at puberty **2** (of certain plants and animals or their parts) covered with a layer of fine short hairs or down [C17 from L *pūbēscere* to reach manhood, from *pūber* adult] > **puˈbescence** *n*

pubic (ˈpjuːbɪk) *adj* of or relating to the pubes or pubis: *pubic hair*

pubis ('pju:bɪs) *n, pl* **pubes** one of the three sections of the hipbone that forms part of the pelvis [C16 shortened from NL *os pūbis* bone of the PUBES]

public ('pʌblɪk) *adj* **1** of or concerning the people as a whole **2** open to all: *public gardens* **3** performed or made openly: *public proclamation* **4** (*prenominal*) well-known: *a public figure* **5** (*usually prenominal*) maintained at the expense of, serving, or for the use of a community: *a public library* **6** open, acknowledged, or notorious: *a public scandal* **7 go public** (of a private company) to issue shares for subscription by the public ▷ *n* **8** the community or people in general **9** a section of the community grouped because of a common interest, activity, etc: *the racing public* [C15 from L *pūblicus*, changed from *pōplicus* of the people, from *populus* people]

public-address system *n* a system of microphones, amplifiers, and loudspeakers for increasing the sound level, used in auditoriums, public gatherings, etc. Sometimes shortened to **PA system**

publican ('pʌblɪkən) *n* **1** (in Britain) a person who keeps a public house **2** (in ancient Rome) a public contractor, esp one who farmed the taxes of a province [C12 from OF *publicain*, from L *pūblicānus* tax gatherer, from *pūblicum* state revenues]

publication (ˌpʌblɪ'keɪʃən) *n* **1** the act or process of publishing a printed work **2** any printed work offered for sale or distribution **3** the act or an instance of making information public [C14 via OF from L *pūblicātiō* confiscation of property, from *pūblicāre* to seize for public use]

public bar *n Brit* a bar in a public house usually serving drinks at a cheaper price than in the lounge bar

public company *n* a limited company whose shares may be purchased by the public and traded freely on the open market and whose share capital is not less than a statutory minimum; public limited company ▷ Cf **private company**

public convenience *n* a public lavatory

public corporation *n* (in Britain) an organization established to run a nationalized industry or state-owned enterprise. The chairman and board members are appointed by a government minister, and the government has overall control

public domain *n* **1** the status of a published work upon which the copyright has expired or which has not been subject to copyright **2 in the public domain** generally known or accessible

public enemy *n* a notorious person, such as a criminal, who is regarded as a menace to the public

public goods *pl n* services such as national defence, law enforcement, and road building, that are for the benefit of, and available to, all members of the public

public house *n* **1** *Brit* the formal name for **pub** **2** *US & Canad* an inn, tavern, or small hotel

public-interest group *n* the usual US and Canad name for **pressure group**

publicist ('pʌblɪsɪst) *n* **1** a person who publicizes something, esp a press or publicity agent **2** a journalist **3** *rare* a person learned in public or international law

publicity (pʌ'blɪsɪtɪ) *n* **1a** the technique or process of attracting public attention to people, products, etc, as by the use of the mass media **1b** (*as modifier*): *a publicity agent* **2** public interest aroused by such a technique or process **3** information used to draw public attention to people, products, etc **4** the state of being public [C18 via F from Med. L *pūblicitās*; see PUBLIC]

publicize *or* **publicise** ('pʌblɪˌsaɪz) *vb* **publicizes, publicizing, publicized** *or* **publicises, publicising, publicised** (*tr*) to bring to public notice; advertise

Public Lending Right *n* the right of authors to receive payment when their books are borrowed from public libraries

public-liability insurance *n* (in Britain) a form of insurance that pays compensation to a member of the public suffering injury or damage as a result of the policyholder or his employees failing to take reasonable care

public limited company *n* another name for **public company**. Abbrev: **plc** *or* **PLC**

publicly ('pblɪklɪ) *adv* **1** in a public manner; without concealment; openly **2** in the name or with the consent of the public

public nuisance *n* **1** *law* an illegal act causing harm to members of a community rather than to any individual **2** *inf* a person generally considered objectionable

public opinion *n* the attitude of the public, esp as a factor in determining action, policy, etc

public prosecutor *n law* an official in charge of prosecuting important cases

Public Record Office *n* an institution in which official records are stored and kept available for inspection by the public

public relations *n* (*functioning as sing or pl*) **1a** the practice of creating, promoting, or maintaining goodwill and a favourable image among the public towards an institution, public body, etc **1b** the professional staff employed for this purpose. Abbrev: **PR** **1c** the techniques employed **1d** (*as modifier*): *the public-relations industry* **2** the relationship between an organization and the public

public school *n* **1** (in England and Wales) a private independent fee-paying secondary school **2** in certain Canadian provinces, a public elementary school as distinguished from a separate school **3** (in the US) any school that is part of a free local educational system

public sector *n* the part of an economy which consists of state-owned institutions, including nationalized industries and services provided by local authorities

public servant *n* **1** an elected or appointed holder of a public office **2** the Austral and NZ equivalent of **civil servant**

public service *n* the Austral and NZ equivalent of **civil service**

public-spirited *adj* having or showing active interest in the good of the community

public utility *n* an enterprise concerned with the provision to the public of essentials, such as electricity or water. Also called (in the US): **public-service corporation**

public works *pl n* engineering projects and other constructions, financed and undertaken by a government for the community

publish ('pʌblɪʃ) *vb* **1** to produce and issue (a book, journal, music, electronic material, etc) for distribution **2** (*intr*) to have one's work issued for publication **3** (*tr*) to announce formally or in public **4** (*tr*) to communicate (defamatory matter) to someone other than the person defamed: *to publish a libel* [C14 from OF *puplier*, from L *pūblicāre* to make PUBLIC] > '**publishable** *adj*

publisher ('pʌblɪʃə) *n* **1** a company or person engaged in publishing periodicals, books, music, etc **2** *US & Canad* the proprietor of a newspaper
▷ www.publishers.org
▷ www.lights.com/publisher

Puccini (pʊ'tʃi:nɪ) *n* **Giacomo** ('dʒa:komo) 1858–1924, Italian operatic composer, noted for the dramatic realism of his operas, which include *Manon Lescaut* (1893), *La Bohème* (1896), *Tosca* (1900), and *Madame Butterfly* (1904)

puce (pju:s) *n, adj* (of) a colour varying from deep red to dark purplish brown [C18 shortened from F *couleur puce* flea colour, from L *pūlex* flea]

puck[1] (pʌk) *n* **1** a small disc of hard rubber used in ice hockey **2** a stroke at the ball in hurling **3** *Irish sl* a sharp blow ▷ *vb* (*tr*) **4** to strike (the ball) in hurling **5** *Irish sl* to strike hard; punch [C19 from ?]

puck² (pʌk) *n* a mischievous or evil spirit [OE *pūca*, from ?] > **'puckish** *adj*

pucka ('pʌkə) *adj* a less common spelling of **pukka**

pucker ('pʌkə) *vb* **1** to gather (a soft surface such as the skin) into wrinkles, or (of such a surface) to be so gathered ▷ *n* **2** a wrinkle, crease, or irregular fold [C16 ? rel. to POKE², from the baglike wrinkles]

pudding ('pʊdɪŋ) *n* **1** a sweetened usually cooked dessert made in many forms and of various ingredients **2** a savoury dish, usually consisting partially of pastry or batter: *steak-and-kidney pudding* **3** the dessert course in a meal **4** a sausage-like mass of meat, oatmeal, etc, stuffed into a prepared skin or bag and boiled [C13 *poding*] > **'puddingy** *adj*

pudding stone *n* a conglomerate rock in which there is a difference in colour or composition between the pebbles and the matrix

puddle ('pʌdᵊl) *n* **1** a small pool of water, esp of rain **2** a small pool of any liquid **3** a worked mixture of wet clay and sand that is impervious to water and is used to line a pond or canal ▷ *vb* **puddles, puddling, puddled** (*tr*) **4** to make (clay, etc) into puddle **5** to subject (iron) to puddling [C14 *podel*, dim. of OE *pudd* ditch, from ?] > **'puddler** *n* > **'puddly** *adj*

puddling ('pʌdlɪŋ) *n* a process for converting pig iron into wrought iron by heating it with ferric oxide in a furnace and stirring it to oxidize the carbon

pudency ('pjuːdᵊnsɪ) *n* modesty or prudishness [C17 from LL *pudentia*, from L *pudēre* to feel shame]

pudendum (pjuː'dɛndəm) *n, pl* **pudenda** (-də) (*often pl*) the human external genital organs collectively, esp of a female [C17 from LL, from L *pudenda* the shameful (parts), from *pudēre* to be ashamed] > **pu'dendal** *or* **pudic** ('pjuːdɪk) *adj*

pudgy ('pʌdʒɪ) *adj* **pudgier, pudgiest** a variant spelling (esp US) of **podgy** [C19 from ?] > **'pudgily** *adv* > **'pudginess** *n*

Pudsey ('pʌdzɪ) *n* a town in N England, in Leeds unitary authority, West Yorkshire. Pop: 31 636 (1991)

Puebla (*Spanish* 'pweβla) *n* **1** an inland state of S central Mexico, situated on the Anáhuac Plateau. Capital: Puebla. Pop: 5 070 346 (2000 est). Area: 33 919 sq km (13 096 sq miles) **2** a city in S Mexico, capital of Puebla state: founded in 1532; university (1537). Pop: 1 270 989 (2000 est). Full name: **Puebla de Zaragoza** (de θara'ɣoθa)

pueblo ('pwɛbləʊ; *Spanish* 'pweβlo) *n, pl* **pueblos** ('pwɛbləʊz; *Spanish* 'pweβlos) **1** a communal village, built by certain Indians of the southwestern US and parts of Latin America, consisting of one or more flat-roofed houses **2** (in Spanish America) a village or town [C19 from Sp.: people, from L *populus*]

Pueblo¹ ('pwɛbləʊ) *n, pl* **Pueblo** *or* **Pueblos** a member of any of the North American Indian peoples who live in pueblos

Pueblo² ('pwɛbləʊ) *n* a city in the USA, in Colorado: a centre of the steel industry. Pop: 102 121 (2000)

puerile ('pjʊəraɪl) *adj* **1** exhibiting silliness; immature; trivial **2** of or characteristic of a child [C17 from L *puerīlis* childish, from *puer* a boy] > **'puerilely** *adv* > **puerility** (pjʊə'rɪlɪtɪ) *n*

puerperal (pjuː'ɜːpərəl) *adj* of or occurring during the period following childbirth [C18 from NL *puerperālis*, from L *puerperium* childbirth, ult. from *puer* boy + *parere* to bear]

puerperal fever *n* a serious, formerly widespread, form of blood poisoning caused by infection contracted during childbirth

puerperal psychosis *n* a mental disorder sometimes occurring in women after childbirth, characterized by deep depression

Puerto Rico ('pwɜːtəʊ 'riːkəʊ, 'pwɛə-) *n* an autonomous commonwealth (in association with the US) occupying the smallest and easternmost of the Greater Antilles in the Caribbean: one of the most densely populated areas in the world; ceded by Spain to the US in 1899. Currency: US dollar. Capital: San Juan. Pop: 3 829 000 (2001 est). Area: 9104 sq km (3515 sq miles). Former name (until 1932): **Porto Rico** Abbreviation: **PR** > **Puerto Rican** *adj, n*

puff (pʌf) *n* **1** a short quick gust or emission, as of wind, smoke, etc **2** the amount of wind, smoke, etc, released in a puff **3** the sound made by a puff **4** an instance of inhaling and expelling the breath as in smoking **5** a light aerated pastry usually filled with cream, jam, etc **6** a powder puff **7** exaggerated praise, as of a book, product, etc, esp through an advertisement **8** a piece of clothing fabric gathered up so as to bulge in the centre while being held together at the edges **9** a cylindrical roll of hair pinned in place in a coiffure **10** *US* a quilted bed cover **11** one's breath (esp in **out of puff**) **12** *derog sl* a male homosexual ▷ *vb* **13** to blow or breathe or cause to blow or breathe in short quick draughts **14** (*tr*; often foll by *out*; *usually passive*) to cause to be out of breath **15** to take draws at (a cigarette, etc) **16** (*intr*) to move with or by the emission of puffs: *the steam train puffed up the incline* **17** (often foll by *up*, *out*, etc) to swell, as with air, pride, etc **18** (*tr*) to praise with exaggerated empty words, often in advertising **19** (*tr*) to apply (powder, dust, etc) to (something) [OE *pyffan*] > **'puffy** *adj*

puff adder *n* **1** a large venomous African viper that inflates its body when alarmed **2** another name for **hognose snake**

puffball ('pʌf,bɔːl) *n* **1** any of various fungi having a round fruiting body that discharges a cloud of brown spores when mature **2** short for **puffball skirt**

puffball skirt *n* a skirt or a dress with a skirt that puffs out wide and is nipped into a narrow hem

puffer ('pʌfə) *n* **1** a person or thing that puffs **2** Also called: **blowfish, globefish** a marine fish with an elongated spiny body that can be inflated to form a globe

puffin ('pʌfɪn) *n* any of various northern diving birds, having a black-and-white plumage and a brightly coloured vertically flattened bill [C14 ? of Cornish origin]

puff pastry *or US* **puff paste** *n* a dough used for making a rich flaky pastry

puff-puff *n Brit* a children's name for a steam locomotive or railway train

pug¹ (pʌg) *n* a small compact breed of dog with a smooth coat, lightly curled tail, and a short wrinkled nose [C16 from ?] > **'puggish** *adj*

pug² (pʌg) *vb* **pugs, pugging, pugged** (*tr*) **1** to mix (clay) with water to form a malleable mass or paste, often in a **pug mill** **2** to fill or stop with clay or a similar substance [C19 from ?]

pug³ (pʌg) *n* a slang name for **boxer** (sense 1) [C20 shortened from PUGILIST]

Puget Sound ('pjuːdʒɪt) *n* an inlet of the Pacific in NW Washington. Length: about 130 km (80 miles)

pugging ('pʌgɪŋ) *n* material such as clay, sawdust, etc, inserted between wooden flooring and ceiling to deaden sound. Also called: **pug**

puggree, pugree ('pʌgrɪ) *or* **puggaree, pugaree** ('pʌgərɪ) *n* **1** the usual Indian word for **turban** **2** a scarf, usually pleated, around the crown of some hats, esp sun helmets [C17 from Hindi *pagrī*, from Sansk. *parikara*]

pugilism ('pjuːdʒɪ,lɪzəm) *n* the art, practice, or profession of fighting with the fists; boxing [C18 from L *pugil* a boxer] > **'pugilist** *n* > **,pugi'listic** *adj* > **,pugi'listically** *adv*

Pugin ('pjuːdʒɪn) *n* **Augustus (Welby Northmore)** 1812–52, British architect; a leader of the Gothic Revival. He collaborated with Sir Charles Barry on the Palace of Westminster (begun 1836)

Puglia ('puʎʎa) *n* the Italian name for **Apulia**

pugnacious (pʌg'neɪʃəs) *adj* readily disposed to fight; belligerent [C17 from L *pugnāx*] > **pug'naciously** *adv*

Pp

> **pugnacity** (pʌɡˈnæsɪtɪ) *or* **pugˈnaciousness** *n*
pug nose *n* a short stubby upturned nose [C18 from PUG[1]] > **ˈpug-ˌnosed** *adj*
puisne (ˈpjuːnɪ) *adj* (esp of a subordinate judge) of lower rank [C16 from Anglo-F, from OF *puisné* born later, from L *posteā* afterwards + *nascī* to be born]
puissance (ˈpjuːɪsᵊns, ˈpwiːsɑːns) *n* **1** a competition in showjumping that tests a horse's ability to jump large obstacles **2** *arch or poetic* power [C15 from OF; see PUISSANT]
puissant (ˈpjuːɪsᵊnt) *adj arch or poetic* powerful [C15 from OF, ult. from L *potēns* mighty, from *posse* to have power] > **ˈpuissantly** *adv*
puke (pjuːk) *sl* ▹ *vb* **pukes, puking, puked** **1** to vomit ▹ *n* **2** the act of vomiting **3** the matter vomited [C16 prob. imit.]
pukeko (ˈpʊkəkəʊ) *n, pl* **pukekos** a New Zealand wading bird with bright plumage [from Maori]
pukka *or* **pucka** (ˈpʌkə) *adj Anglo-Indian* properly or perfectly done, constructed, etc; good; genuine [C17 from Hindi *pakkā* firm, from Sansk. *pakva*]
puku (ˈpʊkuː) *n NZ inf* the stomach; belly [Maori]
Pula (*Serbo-Croat* ˈpuːla) *n* a port in NW Croatia at the S tip of the Istrian Peninsula: made a Roman military base in 178 BC; became the main Austro-Hungarian naval station and passed to Italy in 1919, to Yugoslavia in 1947, and is now in independent Croatia. Pop: 62 300 (1991). Latin name: **Pietas Julia** (paɪˈɛɪtæs ˈjuːlɪə) Italian name: **Pola**
Pulau Pinang (ˈpʊlaʊ pɪˈnæŋ) *n* another name for **Penang**
pulchritude (ˈpʌlkrɪˌtjuːd) *n formal or literary* physical beauty [C15 from L *pulchritūdō*, from *pulcher* beautiful] > **ˌpulchriˈtudinous** *adj*
pule (pjuːl) *vb* **pules, puling, puled** (*intr*) to cry plaintively; whimper [C16 ? imit.] > **ˈpuler** *n*
Pulitzer (ˈpʊlɪtsə) *n* **Joseph** 1847–1911, US newspaper publisher, born in Hungary. He established the Pulitzer prizes
Pulitzer prize *n* one of a group of prizes established by Joseph Pulitzer and awarded yearly since 1917 for excellence in American journalism, literature, and music
▹ www.pulitzer.org
pull (pʊl) *vb* (*mainly tr*) **1** (*also intr*) to exert force on (an object) so as to draw it towards the source of the force **2** to remove; extract: *to pull a tooth* **3** to strip of feathers, hair, etc; pluck **4** to draw the entrails from (a fowl) **5** to rend or tear **6** to strain (a muscle or tendon) **7** (usually foll by *off*) *inf* to bring about: *to pull off a million-pound deal* **8** (often foll by *on*) *inf* to draw out (a weapon) for use: *he pulled a knife on his attacker* **9** *inf* to attract: *the pop group pulled a crowd* **10** (*also intr*) *sl* to attract (a sexual partner) **11** (*intr*; usually foll by *on* or *at*) to drink or inhale deeply: *to pull at one's pipe* **12** to make (a grimace): *to pull a face* **13** (*also intr*; foll by *away, out, over*, etc) to move (a vehicle) or (of a vehicle) to be moved in a specified manner **14** (*intr*) to possess or exercise the power to move: *this car doesn't pull well on hills* **15** to withdraw or remove: *the board decided to pull their support* **16** *printing* to take (a proof) from type **17** *golf, baseball, etc* to hit (a ball) so that it veers away from the direction in which the player intended to hit it **18** *cricket* to hit (a ball pitched straight or on the off side) to the leg side **19** *hurling* to strike (a fast-moving ball) in the same direction as it is already moving **20** (*also intr*) to row (a boat) or take a stroke of (an oar) in rowing **21** (of a rider) to restrain (a horse), esp to prevent it from winning a race **22** **pull a fast one** *sl* to play a sly trick **23** **pull apart** *or* **to pieces** to criticize harshly **24** **pull (one's) punches** **24a** *inf* to restrain the force of one's criticisms or actions **24b** *boxing* to restrain the force of one's blows ▹ *n* **25** an act or an instance of pulling or being pulled **26** the force or effort used in pulling: *the pull of the moon affects the tides* **27** the act or an instance of taking in drink or smoke **28** *printing* a proof taken from type: *the first pull was smudged* **29** something used for pulling, such as a handle **30** *inf* special advantage or influence: *his uncle is chairman of the company, so he has quite a lot of pull* **31** *inf* the power to attract attention or support **32** a period of rowing **33** a single stroke of an oar in rowing **34** the act of pulling the ball in golf, cricket, etc **35** the act of reining in a horse ▹ See also **pull down, pull in,** etc [OE *pullian*] > **ˈpuller** *n*
pull down *vb* (*tr, adv*) to destroy or demolish: *the old houses were pulled down*
pullet (ˈpʊlɪt) *n* a young hen of the domestic fowl, less than one year old [C14 from OF *poulet* chicken, from L *pullus* a young animal or bird]
pulley (ˈpʊlɪ) *n* **1** a wheel with a grooved rim in which a rope can run in order to change the direction of a force applied to the rope, etc **2** a number of such wheels pivoted in parallel in a block, used to raise heavy loads **3** a wheel with a flat, convex, or grooved rim mounted on a shaft and driven by or driving a belt passing around it [C14 *poley*, from OF *polie*, from Vulgar L *polidium* (unattested), apparently from LGk *polidion* (unattested) a little pole, from Gk *polos* axis]
pull in *vb* (*adv*) **1** (*intr*; often foll by *to*) to reach a destination: *the train pulled in at the station* **2** (*intr*) Also: **pull over** (of a motor vehicle) **2a** to draw in to the side of the road **2b** to stop (at a café, lay-by, etc) **3** (*tr*) to attract: *his appearance will pull in the crowds* **4** (*tr*) *sl* to arrest **5** (*tr*) to earn or gain (money) ▹ *n* **pull-in** **6** *Brit* a roadside café, esp for lorry drivers
Pullman[1] (ˈpʊlmən) *n, pl* **Pullmans** a luxurious railway coach. Also called: **Pullman car** [C19 after G. M. *Pullman* (1831–97), its US inventor]
Pullman[2] (ˈpʊlmən) *n* **Philip** born 1946, British author. Writing primarily for older children, he is best known for the fantasy trilogy *His Dark Materials* (1997–2000)
pull off *vb* (*tr*) **1** to remove (clothing) forcefully **2** (*adv*) to succeed in performing (a difficult feat)
pull out *vb* (*adv*) **1** (*tr*) to extract **2** (*intr*) to depart: *the train pulled out of the station* **3** *mil* to withdraw or be withdrawn: *the troops were pulled out of the ruined city* **4** (*intr*) (of a motor vehicle) **4a** to draw away from the side of the road **4b** to draw out from behind another vehicle to overtake **5** (*intr*) to abandon a position or situation **6** (foll by *of*) to level out (from a dive) ▹ *n* **pull-out** **7** an extra leaf of a book that folds out **8** a removable section of a magazine, etc
pullover (ˈpʊlˌəʊvə) *n* a garment, esp a sweater, that is pulled on over the head
pull through *vb* to survive or recover or cause to survive or recover, esp after a serious illness or crisis. Also: **pull round**
pull together *vb* **1** (*intr, adv*) to cooperate, or work harmoniously **2** **pull oneself together** *inf* to regain one's self-control or composure
pullulate (ˈpʌljʊˌleɪt) *vb* **pullulates, pullulating, pullulated** (*intr*) **1** (of animals, etc) to breed abundantly **2** (of plants) to sprout, bud, or germinate [C17 from L *pullulāre* to sprout, from *pullulus* a baby animal, from *pullus* young animal] > **ˌpulluˈlation** *n*
pull up *vb* (*adv*) **1** (*tr*) to remove by the roots **2** (often foll by *with* or *on*) to move level (with) or ahead (of), esp in a race **3** to stop: *the car pulled up suddenly* **4** (*tr*) to rebuke ▹ *n* **pull-up** **5** an exercise in which a person hangs by the arms from a bar and pulls to lift his or her body **6** *Brit* a roadside café; pull-in
pulmonary (ˈpʌlmənərɪ, ˈpʊl-) *adj* **1** of or affecting the lungs **2** having lungs or lunglike organs [C18 from L *pulmōnārius*, from *pulmō* a lung]
pulmonary artery *n* either of the two arteries that convey oxygen-depleted blood from the heart to the lungs

pulmonary vein *n* any one of the four veins that convey oxygen-rich blood from the lungs to the heart

pulp (pʌlp) *n* **1** soft or fleshy plant tissue, such as the succulent part of a fleshy fruit **2** a moist mixture of cellulose fibres, as obtained from wood, from which paper is made **3a** a magazine or book containing trite or sensational material, and usually printed on cheap rough paper **3b** (*as modifier*): *a pulp novel* **4** *dentistry* the soft innermost part of a tooth, containing nerves and blood vessels **5** any soft soggy mass **6** *mining* pulverized ore ▷ *vb* **7** to reduce (a material) to pulp or (of a material) to be reduced to pulp **8** (*tr*) to remove the pulp from (fruit, etc) [C16 from L *pulpa*] > ˈ**pulpy** *adj*

pulpit (ˈpʊlpɪt) *n* **1** a raised platform, usually surrounded by a barrier, set up in churches as the appointed place for preaching, etc **2** a medium for expressing an opinion, such as a newspaper column **3** (usually preceded by *the*) **3a** the preaching of the Christian message **3b** the clergy or their influence [C14 from L *pulpitum* a platform]

pulpwood (ˈpʌlpˌwʊd) *n* pine, spruce, or any other soft wood used to make paper

pulque (ˈpʊlkɪ) *n* a light alcoholic drink from Mexico made from the juice of various agave plants [C17 from Mexican Sp., apparently from Nahuatl, from *puliuhqui* decomposed, since it will only keep for a day]

pulsar (ˈpʌlˌsɑː) *n* any of a number of very small stars first discovered in 1967, which rotate fast, emitting regular pulses of polarized radiation [C20 from PULS(ATING ST)AR, on the model of QUASAR]

pulsate (pʌlˈseɪt) *vb* **pulsates, pulsating, pulsated** (*intr*) **1** to expand and contract with a rhythmic beat; throb **2** *physics* to vary in intensity, magnitude, etc **3** to quiver or vibrate [C18 from L *pulsāre* to push] > **pulsative** (ˈpʌlsətɪv) *adj* > **pulˈsation** *n* > **pulˈsator** *n* > **pulsatory** (ˈpʌlsətərɪ, -trɪ) *adj*

pulsatilla (ˌpʌlsəˈtɪlə) *n* any of a genus of plants related to the anemone, with feathery or hairy foliage [C16 from Med. L, from *pulsāta* beaten (by the wind)]

pulsating star *n* a type of variable star, the variation in brightness resulting from expansion and subsequent contraction of the star

pulse[1] (pʌls) *n* **1** *physiol* **1a** the rhythmic contraction and expansion of an artery at each beat of the heart **1b** a single such pulsation **2** *physics, electronics* **2a** a transient sharp change in some quantity normally constant in a system **2b** one of a series of such transient disturbances, usually recurring at regular intervals **3a** a recurrent rhythmic series of beats, vibrations, etc **3b** any single beat, wave, etc, in such a series **4** an inaudible electronic "ping" to operate a slide projector **5** bustle, vitality, or excitement: *the pulse of a city* **6** **keep one's finger on the pulse** to be well informed about current events, opinions, etc ▷ *vb* **pulses, pulsing, pulsed** **7** (*intr*) to beat, throb, or vibrate **8** (*tr*) to provide an electronic pulse to operate (a slide projector) [C14 *pous*, from L *pulsus* a beating, from *pellere* to beat] > ˈ**pulseless** *adj*

pulse[2] (pʌls) *n* **1** the edible seeds of any of several leguminous plants, such as peas, beans, and lentils **2** the plant producing any of these [C13 *pols*, from OF, from L *puls* pottage of pulse]

pulsejet (ˈpʌlsˌdʒɛt) *n* a type of ramjet engine in which air is admitted through movable vanes that are closed by the pressure resulting from each intermittent explosion of the fuel in the combustion chamber, thus causing a pulsating thrust. Also called: **pulsejet engine, pulsojet**

pulse modulation *n electronics* a type of modulation in which a train of pulses is used as the carrier wave, one or more of its parameters, such as amplitude, being modulated or modified in order to carry information

pulsimeter (pʌlˈsɪmɪtə) *n med* an instrument for measuring the rate of the pulse

pulverize *or* **pulverise** (ˈpʌlvəˌraɪz) *vb* **pulverizes, pulverizing, pulverized** *or* **pulverises, pulverising, pulverised** **1** to reduce (a substance) to fine particles, as by grinding, or (of a substance) to be so reduced **2** (*tr*) to destroy completely [C16 from LL *pulverizare*, from L *pulvis* dust] > ˈ**pulverˌizable** *or* ˈ**pulverˌisable** *adj* > ˌ**pulveriˈzation** *or* ˌ**pulveriˈsation** *n* > ˈ**pulverˌizer** *or* ˈ**pulverˌiser** *n*

pulverulent (pʌlˈvɛrʊlənt) *adj* consisting of, covered with, or crumbling to dust or fine particles [C17 from L *pulverulentus*, from *pulvis* dust]

puma (ˈpjuːmə) *n* a large American feline mammal that resembles a lion, having a plain greyish-brown coat and long tail. Also called: **cougar, mountain lion** [C18 via Sp. from Quechua]

pumice (ˈpʌmɪs) *n* **1** Also called: **pumice stone** a light porous volcanic rock used for scouring and, in powdered form, as an abrasive and for polishing ▷ *vb* **pumices, pumicing, pumiced** **2** (*tr*) to rub or polish with pumice [C15 *pomys*, from OF *pomis*, from L *pūmex*] > **pumiceous** (pjuːˈmɪʃəs) *adj*

pummel (ˈpʌməl) *vb* **pummels, pummelling, pummelled** *or US* **pummels, pummeling, pummeled** (*tr*) to strike repeatedly with or as if with the fists. Also (less commonly): **pommel** [C16 see POMMEL]

pump[1] (pʌmp) *n* **1** any device for compressing, driving, raising, or reducing the pressure of a fluid, esp by means of a piston or set of rotating impellers **2** *biol* a mechanism for the active transport of ions, such as protons, calcium ions, and sodium ions, across cell membranes: *a sodium pump* ▷ *vb* **3** (when *tr*, usually foll by *from, out*, etc) to raise or drive (air, liquid, etc, esp into or from something) with a pump **4** (*tr*; usually foll by *in* or *into*) to supply in large amounts: *to pump capital into a project* **5** (*tr*) to deliver (bullets, etc) repeatedly **6** to operate (something, esp a handle) in the manner of a pump or (of something) to work in this way: *to pump the pedals of a bicycle* **7** (*tr*) to obtain (information) from (a person) by persistent questioning **8** (*intr*; usually foll by *from* or *out of*) (of liquids) to flow freely in large spurts: *oil pumped from the fissure* **9** **pump iron** *sl* to exercise with weights; do body-building exercises [C15 from MDu. *pumpe* pipe, prob. from Sp. *bomba*, imit.]

pump[2] (pʌmp) *n* **1** a low-cut low-heeled shoe without fastenings, worn esp for dancing **2** a type of shoe with a rubber sole, used in games such as tennis; plimsoll [C16 from ?]

pumpernickel (ˈpʌmpəˌnɪkəl) *n* a slightly sour black bread, originating in Germany, made of coarse rye flour [C18 from G, from ?]

pumpkin (ˈpʌmpkɪn) *n* **1** any of several creeping plants **2** the large round fruit of any of these plants, which has a thick orange rind, pulpy flesh, and numerous seeds **3** (*often capital*) *chiefly US* a term of endearment [C17 from earlier *pumpion*, from OF, from L *pepo*, from Gk, from *peptein* to ripen]

pump priming *n* **1** the process of introducing fluid into a pump to improve starting and to expel air from it **2** government expenditure designed to stimulate economic activity in stagnant or depressed areas **3** another term for **deficit financing**

pun[1] (pʌn) *n* **1** the use of words to exploit ambiguities and innuendoes for humorous effect; a play on words. An example is: "*Ben Battle was a soldier bold, And used to war's alarms: But a cannonball took off his legs, So he laid down his arms.*" (Thomas Hood) ▷ *vb* **puns, punning, punned** **2** (*intr*) to make puns [C17 ?from It. *puntiglio* wordplay; see PUNCTILIO]

pun[2] (pʌn) *vb* **puns, punning, punned** (*tr*) *Brit* to pack (earth, rubble, etc) by pounding [C16 var. of POUND[1]]

puna *Spanish* (ˈpuna) *n* **1** a high cold dry plateau **2** another name for **mountain sickness** [C17 from

Pp

American Sp., of Amerind origin]
Punakha *or* **Punaka** ('pu:nəkə) *n* a town in W central Bhutan: a former capital of the country
punch[1] (pʌntʃ) *vb* 1 to strike at, esp with a clenched fist 2 *(tr) western US* to herd or drive (cattle), esp for a living 3 *(tr)* to poke with a stick, etc ▷ *n* 4 a blow with the fist 5 *inf* point or vigour: *his arguments lacked punch* [C15 ? var. of *pounce*, from OF *poinçonner* to stamp] > **'puncher** *n*
punch[2] (pʌntʃ) *n* 1 a tool or machine for piercing holes in a material 2 a tool or machine used for stamping a design on something or shaping it by impact 3 the solid die of a punching machine 4 *computing, obs* a device for making holes in a card or paper tape ▷ *vb* 5 *(tr)* to pierce, cut, stamp, shape, or drive with a punch [C14 shortened from *puncheon*, from OF *ponçon*; see PUNCHEON[2]]
punch[3] (pʌntʃ) *n* any mixed drink containing fruit juice and, usually, alcoholic liquor, generally hot and spiced [C17 ?from Hindi *pānch*, from Sansk. *pañca* five; it orig. had five ingredients]
Punch (pʌntʃ) *n* the main character in the traditional children's puppet show **Punch and Judy**
punchbag ('pʌntʃ,bæg) *n* a suspended stuffed bag that is punched for exercise, esp boxing training. Also called (US and Canad): **punching bag**
punchball ('pʌntʃ,bɔ:l) *n* 1 a stuffed or inflated ball, supported by a flexible rod, that is punched for exercise, esp boxing training 2 *US* a game resembling baseball
punchbowl ('pʌntʃ,bəʊl) *n* 1 a large bowl for serving punch, often having small drinking glasses hooked around the rim 2 *Brit* a bowl-shaped depression in the land
punch-drunk *adj* 1 demonstrating or characteristic of the behaviour of a person who has suffered repeated blows to the head, esp a professional boxer 2 dazed; stupefied
punched card *or esp US* **punch card** *n* a card on which data can be coded in the form of punched holes, formerly used in computing
punched tape *or US (sometimes)* **perforated tape** *n* other terms for **paper tape**
puncheon[1] ('pʌntʃən) *n* a large cask of variable capacity, usually between 70 and 120 gallons [C15 *poncion*, from OF *ponchon*, from ?]
puncheon[2] ('pʌntʃən) *n* 1 a short wooden post used as a vertical strut 2 a less common name for **punch**[2] (sense 1) [C14 *ponson*, from OF *ponçon*, from L *punctiō* a puncture, from *pungere* to prick]
Punchinello (,pʌntʃɪ'nɛləʊ) *n, pl* **Punchinellos** *or* **Punchinelloes** 1 a clown from Italian puppet shows, the prototype of Punch 2 *(sometimes not cap)* any grotesque or absurd character [C17 from earlier *Polichinello*, from It. *Polecenella*, from *pulcino* chicken, ult. from L *pullus* young animal]
punch line *n* the culminating part of a joke, funny story, etc, that gives it its point
punch-up *n Brit inf* a fight or brawl
punchy ('pʌntʃɪ) *adj* **punchier, punchiest** 1 an informal word for **punch-drunk** 2 *inf* incisive or forceful > **'punchily** *adv* > **'punchiness** *n*
punctate ('pʌŋkteɪt) *adj* having or marked with minute spots or depressions [C18 from NL *punctātus*, from L *punctum* a point] > **punc'tation** *n*
punctilio (pʌŋk'tɪlɪ,əʊ) *n, pl* **punctilios** 1 strict attention to minute points of etiquette 2 a petty formality or fine point of etiquette [C16 from It. *puntiglio* small point, from L *punctum* point]
punctilious (pʌŋk'tɪlɪəs) *adj* 1 paying scrupulous attention to correctness in etiquette 2 attentive to detail > **punc'tiliously** *adv* > **punc'tiliousness** *n*
punctual ('pʌŋktjʊəl) *adj* 1 arriving or taking place at an arranged time 2 (of a person) having the characteristic of always keeping to arranged times 3 *obs* precise; exact 4 *maths* consisting of or confined to a point [C14 from Med. L *punctuālis* concerning detail, from L *punctum* point] > **,punctu'ality** *n* > **'punctually** *adv*
punctuate ('pʌŋktjʊ,eɪt) *vb* **punctuates, punctuating, punctuated** *(mainly tr)* 1 *(also intr)* to insert punctuation marks into (a written text) 2 to interrupt or insert at frequent intervals: *a meeting punctuated by heckling* 3 to give emphasis to [C17 from Med. L *punctuāre* to prick, from L, from *pungere* to puncture]
punctuation (,pʌŋktjʊ'eɪʃən) *n* 1 the use of symbols not belonging to the alphabet of a writing system to indicate aspects of the intonation and meaning not otherwise conveyed in the written language 2 the symbols used for this purpose
punctuation mark *n* any of the signs used in punctuation, such as a comma
puncture ('pʌŋktʃə) *n* 1 a small hole made by a sharp object 2 a perforation and loss of pressure in a pneumatic tyre 3 the act of puncturing or perforating ▷ *vb* **punctures, puncturing, punctured** 4 *(tr)* to pierce a hole in (something) with a sharp object 5 to cause (something pressurized, esp a tyre) to lose pressure by piercing, or (of a tyre, etc) to collapse in this way 6 *(tr)* to depreciate (a person's self-esteem, pomposity, etc) [C14 from L *punctūra*, from *pungere* to prick]
pundit ('pʌndɪt) *n* 1 an expert 2 (formerly) a learned person 3 Also: **pandit** a Brahman learned in Sanskrit, Hindu religion, philosophy or law [C17 from Hindi *pandit*, from Sansk. *pandita* learned man]
punditry ('pʌndɪtrɪ) *n* the expressing of expert opinions
Pune ('pu:nə) *n* another name for **Poona**
punga ('pʌŋə) *n* a variant spelling of **ponga**
pungent ('pʌndʒənt) *adj* 1 having an acrid smell or sharp bitter flavour 2 (of wit, satire, etc) biting; caustic 3 *biol* ending in a sharp point [C16 from L *pungens* piercing, from *pungere* to prick] > **'pungency** *n* > **'pungently** *adv*
Punic ('pju:nɪk) *adj* 1 of or relating to ancient Carthage or the Carthaginians 2 treacherous; faithless ▷ *n* 3 the language of the Carthaginians; a late form of Phoenician [C15 from L *Pūnicus*, var. of *Poenicus* Carthaginian, from Gk *Phoinix*]
punish ('pʌnɪʃ) *vb* 1 to force (someone) to undergo a penalty for some crime or misdemeanour 2 *(tr)* to inflict punishment for (some crime, etc) 3 *(tr)* to treat harshly, esp as by overexertion: *to punish a horse* 4 *(tr) inf* to consume in large quantities: *to punish the bottle* [C14 *punisse*, from OF *punir*, from L *pūnīre* to punish, from *poena* penalty] > **'punishable** *adj* > **'punisher** *n* > **'punishing** *adj*
punishment ('pʌnɪʃmənt) *n* 1 a penalty for a crime or offence 2 the act of punishing or state of being punished 3 *inf* rough treatment
punitive ('pju:nɪtɪv) *adj* relating to, involving, or with the intention of inflicting punishment: *a punitive expedition* [C17 from Med. L *pūnītīvus* concerning punishment, from L *pūnīre* to punish] > **'punitively** *adv*
Punjab (pʌn'dʒɑ:b, 'pʌndʒɑ:b) *n* 1 (formerly) a province in NW British India: divided between India and Pakistan in 1947 2 a state of NW India: reorganized in 1966 as a Punjabi-speaking state, a large part forming the new state of Haryana; mainly agricultural. Capital: Chandigarh. Pop: 24 289 296 (2001). Area: 50 255 sq km (19 403 sq miles) 3 a province of W Pakistan: created in 1947. Capital: Lahore. Pop: 72 585 000 (1998). Area: 205 344 sq km (127 595 sq miles)
Punjabi (pʌn'dʒɑ:bɪ) *n* 1 *(pl* **Punjabis***)* a member of the chief people of the Punjab 2 the language of the Punjab, belonging to the Indic branch of the Indo-European family ▷ *adj* 3 of the Punjab, its people, or their language
Punjab States *pl n* (formerly) a group of states in NW India, amalgamated in 1956 with Punjab state
punk[1] (pʌŋk) *n* 1 a youth movement of the late 1970s, characterized by anti-Establishment slogans and

outrageous clothes and hairstyles **2** an inferior, rotten, or worthless person or thing **3** worthless articles collectively **4** short for **punk rock** **5** *obs* a young male homosexual; catamite **6** *obs* a prostitute ▷ *adj* **7** rotten or worthless [c16 from ?]

punk² (pʌŋk) *n* dried decayed wood or other substance that smoulders when ignited: used as tinder [c18 from ?]

punka *or* **punkah** ('pʌŋkə) *n* **1** a fan made of a palm leaf or leaves **2** a large fan made of palm leaves, etc, worked mechanically to cool a room [c17 from Hindi *pankhā*, from Sansk. *paksaka* fan, from *paksa* wing]

punk rock *n* a fast abrasive style of rock music of the late 1970s, characterized by aggressive lyrics and performance, usually expressing rage and frustration > **punk rocker** *n*
▷ www.punkrock.org
▷ www.punk77.co.uk

punnet ('pʌnɪt) *n chiefly Brit* a small basket for fruit. [c19 ? dim. of dialect *pun* POUND²]

punster ('pʌnstə) *n* a person who is fond of making puns, esp one who makes a tedious habit of this

punt¹ (pʌnt) *n* **1** an open flat-bottomed boat with square ends, propelled by a pole ▷ *vb* **2** to propel (a boat, esp a punt) by pushing with a pole on the bottom of a river, etc [OE *punt* shallow boat, from L *pontō* punt]

punt² (pʌnt) *n* **1** a kick in certain sports, such as rugby, in which the ball is released and kicked before it hits the ground **2** any long high kick ▷ *vb* **3** to kick (a ball, etc) using a punt [c19 ? var. of dialect *bunt* to push]

punt³ (pʌnt) *chiefly Brit* ▷ *vb* **1** (*intr*) to gamble; bet ▷ *n* **2** a gamble or bet, esp against the bank, as in roulette, or on horses **3** Also called: **punter** a person who bets **4 take a punt at** *Austral & NZ inf* to make an attempt at [c18 from F *ponter* to punt, from *ponte* bet laid against the banker, from Sp. *punto* point, from L *punctum*]

punt⁴ (pʊnt) *n* (formerly) the Irish pound [Irish Gaelic: pound]

Punta Arenas (*Spanish* 'punta a'renas) *n* a port in S Chile, on the Strait of Magellan: the southernmost city in the world. Pop: 120 148 (1999 est). Former name: **Magallanes**

punter¹ ('pʌntə) *n* a person who punts a boat

punter² ('pʌntə) *n* a person who kicks a ball

punter³ ('pʌntə) *n* **1** a person who gambles or bets **2** *sl* any client or customer, esp a prostitute's client **3** *sl* a victim of a con man

puny ('pjuːnɪ) *adj* **punier, puniest** **1** small and weakly **2** paltry; insignificant [c16 from OF *puisne* PUISNE] > '**puniness** *n*

pup (pʌp) *n* **1a** a young dog; puppy **1b** the young of various other animals, such as the seal **2 in pup** (of a bitch) pregnant **3** *inf, chiefly Brit* a conceited young man (esp in **young pup**) **4 sell (someone) a pup** to swindle (someone) by selling him or her something worthless ▷ *vb* **pups, pupping, pupped** **5** (of dogs, seals, etc) to give birth to (young) [c18 back formation from PUPPY]

pupa ('pjuːpə) *n, pl* **pupae** (-piː) *or* **pupas** an insect at the immobile nonfeeding stage of development between larva and adult, when many internal changes occur [c19 via NL, from L: a doll] > '**pupal** *adj*

pupate (pjuː'peɪt) *vb* **pupates, pupating, pupated** (*intr*) (of an insect larva) to develop into a pupa > **pu'pation** *n*

pupil¹ ('pjuːpᵊl) *n* **1** a student who is taught by a teacher **2** *civil & Scots Law* a boy under 14 or a girl under 12 who is in the care of a guardian [c14 from L *pupillus* an orphan, from *pūpus* a child] > '**pupillage** *or US* '**pupilage** *n* > '**pupillary** *or* '**pupilary** *adj*

pupil² ('pjuːpᵊl) *n* the dark circular aperture at the centre of the iris of the eye, through which light enters [c16 from L *pūpilla*, dim. of *pūpa* doll; from the tiny reflections in the eye] > '**pupillary** *or* '**pupilary** *adj*

pupiparous (pjuː'pɪpərəs) *adj* (of certain dipterous flies) producing young that have already reached the pupa stage at the time of hatching [c19 from NL *pupiparus*, from PUPA + *parere* to bring forth]

puppet ('pʌpɪt) *n* **1a** a small doll or figure moved by strings attached to its limbs or by the hand inserted in its cloth body **1b** (*as modifier*): *a puppet theatre* **2a** a person, state, etc, that appears independent but is controlled by another **2b** (*as modifier*): *a puppet government* [c16 *popet*, ?from OF *poupette* little doll, ult. from L *pūpa* doll]

puppeteer (ˌpʌpɪ'tɪə) *n* a person who manipulates puppets

puppetry ('pʌpɪtrɪ) *n* **1** the art of making and manipulating puppets and presenting puppet shows **2** unconvincing or specious presentation
▷ www.sagecraft.com/puppetry
▷ www.cln.org/themes/puppetry.html
▷ www.puppetryindia.org/
▷ http://discover-indo.tierranet.com/wayang.html

puppy ('pʌpɪ) *n, pl* **puppies** **1** a young dog; pup **2** *inf, contemptuous* a brash or conceited young man; pup [c15 *popi*, from OF *popée* doll] > '**puppyhood** *n* > '**puppyish** *adj*

puppy fat *n* fatty tissue that develops in childhood or adolesence and usually disappears with maturity

puppy love *n* another term for **calf love**

Purana (pʊ'rɑːnə) *n* any of a class of Sanskrit writings not included in the Vedas, characteristically recounting the birth and deeds of Hindu gods and the creation of the universe [c17 from Sansk.: ancient, from *purā* formerly]

Purbeck marble *or* **stone** ('pɜːbɛk) *n* a fossil-rich limestone that takes a high polish [c15 after *Purbeck*, Dorset, where quarried]

purblind ('pɜːˌblaɪnd) *adj* **1** partly or nearly blind **2** lacking in insight or understanding; obtuse [c13 see PURE, BLIND]

Purcell ('pɜːsᵊl) *n* **1 Edward Mills** 1912–97, US physicist, noted for his work on the magnetic moments of atomic nuclei: shared the Nobel prize for physics (1952) **2 Henry** ?1659–95, English composer, noted chiefly for his rhythmic and harmonic subtlety in setting words. His works include the opera *Dido and Aeneas* (1689), music for the theatrical pieces *King Arthur* (1691) and *The Fairy Queen* (1692), several choral odes, fantasias, sonatas, and church music

Pp

purchase ('pɜːtʃɪs) *vb* **purchases, purchasing, purchased** (*tr*) **1** to obtain (goods, etc) by payment **2** to obtain by effort, sacrifice, etc: *to purchase one's freedom* **3** to draw or lift (a load) with mechanical apparatus ▷ *n* **4** something that is purchased **5** the act of buying **6** acquisition of an estate by any lawful means other than inheritance **7** the mechanical advantage achieved by a lever **8** a firm foothold, grasp, etc, as for climbing something [c13 from OF *porchacier* to strive to obtain; see CHASE¹] > '**purchasable** *adj* > '**purchaser** *n*

purchase tax *n* (in Britain, formerly) a tax levied on nonessential consumer goods and added to selling prices by retailers

purdah ('pɜːdə) *n* **1** the custom in some Muslim and Hindu communities of keeping women in seclusion, with clothing that conceals them completely when they go out **2** a screen in a Hindu house used to keep the women out of view [c19 from Hindi *parda* veil, from Persian *pardah*]

pure (pjʊə) *adj* **1** not mixed with any extraneous or dissimilar materials, elements, etc **2** free from tainting or polluting matter: *pure water* **3** free from moral taint or defilement: *pure love* **4** (*prenominal*) (intensifier): *a pure coincidence* **5** (of a subject, etc) studied in its theoretical aspects rather than for its practical applications: *pure mathematics* **6** (of a vowel) pronounced with more or less unvarying quality without any glide **7** (of a consonant) not accompanied by another consonant **8** of unmixed descent **9** *genetics, biol* breeding true; homozygous [c13 from OF *pur*, from L *pūrus* unstained] > '**purely** *adv* > '**pureness** *n*

purebred *adj* ('pjʊə'brɛd) **1** denoting a pure strain obtained through many generations of controlled breeding for desirable traits ▷ *n* ('pjʊəˌbrɛd) **2** a purebred animal

purée ('pjʊəreɪ) *n* **1** a smooth thick pulp of sieved fruit, vegetables, meat, or fish ▷ *vb* **purées, puréeing, puréed** **2** (*tr*) to make (cooked foods) into a purée [C19 from F *purer* to PURIFY]

pure laine (pjʊə 'lɛn) *n* (in Quebec) a person belonging to a long-established family of French descent [F, lit: pure wool]

purfle ('pɜːfᵊl) *n* **1** Also: **purfling** a ruffled or curved ornamental band, as on clothing, furniture, etc ▷ *vb* **purfles, purfling, purfled** **2** (*tr*) to decorate with such a band [C14 from OF *purfiler* to decorate with a border, from *fil* thread, from L *filum*]

purgation (pɜː'geɪʃən) *n* the act of purging or state of being purged; purification

purgative ('pɜːgətɪv) *med* ▷ *n* **1** a drug or agent for purging the bowels ▷ *adj* **2** causing evacuation of the bowels > **'purgatively** *adv*

purgatory ('pɜːgətərɪ, -trɪ) *n* **1** *chiefly RC Church* a state or place in which the souls of those who have died in a state of grace are believed to undergo a limited amount of suffering to expiate their venial sins **2** a place or condition of suffering or torment, esp one that is temporary [C13 from OF *purgatoire*, from Med. L *pūrgātōrium*, lit.: place of cleansing, from L *pūrgāre* to purge] > **ˌpurga'torial** *adj*

purge (pɜːdʒ) *vb* **purges, purging, purged** **1** (*tr*) to rid (something) of (impure elements) **2** (*tr*) to rid (a state, political party, etc) of (dissident people) **3** (*tr*) **3a** to empty (the bowels) by evacuation of faeces **3b** to cause (a person) to evacuate his or her bowels **4a** to clear (a person) of a charge **4b** to free (oneself) of guilt, as by atonement **5** (*intr*) to be purified ▷ *n* **6** the act or process of purging **7** the elimination of opponents or dissidents from a state, political party, etc **8** a purgative drug or agent [C14 from OF *purger*, from L *pūrgāre* to purify]

Puri ('pʊəriː, pʊə'riː) *n* a port in E India, in Orissa on the Bay of Bengal: 12th-century temple of Jagannath. Pop: 125 199 (1991)

purificator ('pjʊərɪfɪˌkeɪtə) *n Christianity* a small white linen cloth used to wipe the chalice and paten at the Eucharist

purify ('pjʊərɪˌfaɪ) *vb* **purifies, purifying, purified** **1** to free (something) of contaminating or debasing matter **2** (*tr*) to free (a person, etc) from sin or guilt **3** (*tr*) to make clean, as in a ritual [C14 from OF *purifier*, from LL *pūrificāre* to cleanse, from *pūrus* pure + *facere* to make] > **ˌpurifi'cation** *n* > **purificatory** ('pjʊərɪfɪˌkeɪtərɪ, -trɪ) *adj* > **'puriˌfier** *n*

Purim ('pʊərɪm; *Hebrew* puː'riːm) *n* a Jewish holiday in February or March to commemorate the deliverance of the Jews from the massacre planned by Haman (Esther 9) [Heb. *pūrīm*, pl. of *pūr* lot; from the casting of lots by Haman]

purine ('pjʊəriːn) *or* **purin** ('pjʊərɪn) *n* **1** a colourless crystalline solid that can be prepared from uric acid. Formula: $C_5H_5N_4$ **2** Also called: **purine base** any of a number of nitrogenous bases that are derivatives of purine [C19 from G *Purin*]

puriri (puː'riːriː) *n* a New Zealand tree with hard timber and red berries [from Maori]

purism ('pjʊəˌrɪzəm) *n* insistence on traditional canons of correctness of form or purity of style or content > **'purist** *adj, n* > **pu'ristic** *adj*

puritan ('pjʊərɪtᵊn) *n* **1** a person who adheres to strict moral or religious principles, esp one opposed to luxury and sensual enjoyment ▷ *adj* **2** characteristic of a puritan [C16 from LL *pūritās* purity] > **'puritanˌism** *n*

Puritan ('pjʊərɪtᵊn) (in the late 16th and 17th centuries) ▷ *n* **1** any of the extreme English Protestants who wished to purify the Church of England of most of its ceremony and other aspects that they deemed to be Catholic ▷ *adj* **2** of or relating to the Puritans > **'Puritanˌism** *n*

puritanical (ˌpjʊərɪ'tænɪkᵊl) *adj* **1** *usually disparaging* strict in moral or religious outlook, esp in shunning sensual pleasures **2** (*sometimes cap*) of or relating to a puritan or the Puritans > **ˌpuri'tanically** *adv*

purity ('pjʊərɪtɪ) *n* the state or quality of being pure

purl[1] (pɜːl) *n* **1** a knitting stitch made by doing a plain stitch backwards **2** a decorative border, as of lace **3** gold or silver wire thread ▷ *vb* **4** to knit in purl stitch **5** to edge (something) with a purl ▷ Also (for senses 2, 3, 5): **pearl** [C16 from dialect *pirl* to twist into a cord]

purl[2] (pɜːl) *vb* **1** (*intr*) (of a stream, etc) to flow with a gentle swirling or rippling movement and a murmuring sound ▷ *n* **2** a swirling movement of water; eddy **3** a murmuring sound, as of a shallow stream [C16 rel. to Norwegian *purla* to bubble]

purler[1] ('pɜːlə) *n inf* a headlong or spectacular fall (esp in **come a purler**)

purler[2] ('pɜːlə) *n Austral sl* something outstanding in its class [from ?]

purlieu ('pɜːljuː) *n* **1** *English history* land on the edge of a forest once included within the bounds of the royal forest but later separated although still subject to some of the forest laws **2** (*usually pl*) a neighbouring area; outskirts **3** (*often pl*) a place one frequents; haunt [C15 *purlewe*, from Anglo-F *puralé* a going through (infl. also by OF *lieu* place), from OF *puraler*, from *pur* through + *aler* to go]

purlin *or* **purline** ('pɜːlɪn) *n* a horizontal beam that supports the common rafters of a roof and is carried by the principal rafters or trusses [C15 from ?]

purloin (pɜː'lɔɪn) *vb* to steal [C15 from OF *porloigner* to put at a distance, from *por-* for + *loin* distant, from L *longus* long] > **pur'loiner** *n*

purple ('pɜːpᵊl) *n* **1** a colour between red and blue **2** a dye or pigment producing such a colour **3** cloth of this colour, often used to symbolize royalty or nobility **4** (usually preceded by *the*) high rank; nobility **5a** the official robe of a cardinal **5b** the rank of a cardinal as signified by this ▷ *adj* **6** of the colour purple **7** (of writing) excessively elaborate or full of imagery: *purple prose* [OE, from L *purpura* purple dye, from Gk *porphura* the purple fish (murex)] > **'purpleness** *n* > **'purplish** *or* **'purply** *adj*

purple heart *n* **1** any of several tropical American trees **2** *inf, chiefly Brit* a heart-shaped purple tablet consisting mainly of amphetamine

Purple Heart *n* a decoration awarded to members of the US Armed Forces for a wound received in action

purple patch *n* **1** Also called: **purple passage** a section in a piece of writing characterized by fanciful or ornate language **2** *sl* a period of good fortune

purport *vb* (pɜː'pɔːt) (*tr*) **1** to claim to be (true, official, etc) by manner or appearance, esp falsely **2** (esp of speech or writing) to signify or imply ▷ *n* ('pɜːpɔːt) **3** meaning; significance **4** object; intention [C15 from Anglo-F: contents, from OF *porporter* to convey, from L *portāre*]

purpose ('pɜːpəs) *n* **1** the reason for which anything is done, created, or exists **2** a fixed design or idea that is the object of an action or other effort **3** determination: *a man of purpose* **4** practical advantage or use: *to work to good purpose* **5** that which is relevant (esp in **to** *or* **from the purpose**) **6** *arch* purport **7** **on purpose** intentionally ▷ *vb* **purposes, purposing, purposed** **8** (*tr*) to intend or determine to do (something) [C13 from OF *porpos*, from *porposer* to plan, from L *prōpōnere* to PROPOSE] > **'purposeless** *adj*

purpose-built *adj* made to serve a specific purpose

purposeful ('pɜːpəsfʊl) *adj* **1** having a definite purpose in view **2** determined > '**purposefully** *adv* > '**purposefulness** *n*

> USAGE Someone who is *purposeful* has an aim in mind and is determined to achieve it. Probably because the adjective conveys the idea of having such an aim, the adverb *purposefully* is sometimes wrongly used where *purposely* is meant: *he had purposely* (not *purposefully*) *left the door unlocked*. The use of *purposefully* in the following example is correct: *she rose purposefully from her chair to confront them...*

purposely ('pɜːpəslɪ) *adv* on purpose.

> USAGE See at **purposeful**

purposive ('pɜːpəsɪv) *adj* **1** having or indicating conscious intention **2** serving a purpose; useful > '**purposively** *adv* > '**purposiveness** *n*

purpura ('pɜːpjʊrə) *n* *pathol* any of several blood diseases causing purplish spots on the skin due to subcutaneous bleeding [C18 via L from Gk *porphura* a shellfish yielding purple dye]

purr (pɜː) *vb* **1** (*intr*) (esp of cats) to make a low vibrant sound, usually considered as expressing pleasure, etc **2** (*tr*) to express (pleasure, etc) by this sound or by a sound suggestive of purring ▷ *n* **3** a purring sound [C17 imit.]

purse (pɜːs) *n* **1** a small bag or pouch for carrying money, esp coins **2** *US & Canad* a woman's handbag **3** anything resembling a small bag or pouch in form or function **4** wealth; funds; resources **5** a sum of money that is offered, esp as a prize ▷ *vb* **purses, pursing, pursed 6** (*tr*) to contract (the mouth, lips, etc) into a small rounded shape [OE *purs*, prob. from LL *bursa* bag, ult. from Gk: leather]

purser ('pɜːsə) *n* an officer aboard a ship or aircraft who keeps the accounts and attends to the welfare of the passengers

purse seine *n* a large net that encloses fish and is then closed at the bottom by means of a line resembling the string formerly used to draw shut the neck of a money pouch

purse strings *pl n* control of expenditure (esp in **hold** *or* **control the purse strings**)

purslane ('pɜːslɪn) *n* a plant with fleshy leaves used (esp formerly) in salads and as a potherb [C14 *purcelane*, from OF *porcelaine*, from LL, from L *porcillāca*, var. of *portulāca*]

pursuance (pə'sjuːəns) *n* the carrying out or pursuing of an action, plan, etc

pursuant (pə'sjuːənt) *adj* **1** (*usually postpositive*; often foll by *to*) *chiefly law* in agreement or conformity **2** *arch* pursuing [C17 rel. to ME *poursuivant* following after, from OF; see PURSUE] > **pur'suantly** *adv*

pursue (pə'sjuː) *vb* **pursues, pursuing, pursued** (*mainly tr*) **1** (*also intr*) to follow (a fugitive, etc) in order to capture or overtake **2** to follow closely or accompany: *ill health pursued her* **3** to seek or strive to attain (some desire, etc) **4** to follow the precepts of (a plan, policy, etc) **5** to apply oneself to (studies, interests, etc) **6** to follow persistently or seek to become acquainted with **7** to continue to discuss or argue (a point, subject, etc) [C13 from Anglo-Norman *pursiwer*, from OF *poursivre*, from L *prōsequī* to follow after] > **pur'suer** *n*

pursuit (pə'sjuːt) *n* **1a** the act of pursuing **1b** (*as modifier*): *a pursuit plane* **2** an occupation or pastime **3** (in cycling) a race in which the riders set off at intervals along the track and attempt to overtake each other [C14 from OF *poursieute*, from *poursivre* to PURSUE]

pursuivant ('pɜːsɪvənt) *n* **1** the lowest rank of heraldic officer **2** *history* a state or royal messenger **3** *history* a follower or attendant [C14 from OF, from *poursivre* to PURSUE]

purulent ('pjʊərʊlənt) *adj* of, relating to, or containing pus [C16 from L *pūrulentus*, from *pūs*] > '**purulence** *n*

Purús (*Spanish* (*Portuguese* pu'rus)) *n* a river in NW central South America, rising in SE Peru and flowing northeast to the Amazon. Length: about 3200 km (2000 miles)

purvey (pə'veɪ) *vb* (*tr*) **1** to sell or provide (commodities, esp foodstuffs) on a large scale **2** to publish (lies, scandal, etc) [C13 from OF *porveeir*, from L *prōvidēre* to PROVIDE] > **pur'veyor** *n*

purveyance (pə'veɪəns) *n* **1** *history* the collection or requisition of provisions for a sovereign **2** *rare* the act of purveying

purview ('pɜːvjuː) *n* **1** scope of operation **2** breadth or range of outlook **3** *law* the body of a statute, containing the enacting clauses [C15 from Anglo-Norman *purveu*, from *porveeir* to furnish; see PURVEY]

pus (pʌs) *n* the yellow or greenish fluid product of inflammation [C16 from L *pūs*]

Pusan ('puː'sæn) *n* a port in SE South Korea, on the Korea Strait: the second largest city and chief port of the country; industrial centre; two universities. Pop: 3 813 814 (1995)

Pusey ('pjuːzɪ) *n* **Edward Bouverie** ('buːvərɪ) 1800–82, British ecclesiastic; a leader with Keble and Newman of the Oxford Movement

push (pʊʃ) *vb* **1** (when *tr*, often foll by *off*, *away*, etc) to apply steady force to in order to move **2** to thrust (one's way) through something, such as a crowd **3** (*tr*) to encourage or urge (a person) to some action, decision, etc **4** (when *intr*, often foll by *for*) to be an advocate or promoter (of): *to push for acceptance of one's theories* **5** (*tr*) to use one's influence to help (a person): *to push one's own candidate* **6** to bear upon (oneself or another person) in order to achieve better results, etc **7** *cricket, etc* to hit (a ball) with a stiff pushing stroke **8** (*tr*) *inf* to sell (narcotic drugs) illegally **9** (*intr*; foll by *out*, *into*, etc) to extend: *the cliffs pushed out to the sea* **10 push one's luck** *or* **push it 10a** to take undue risks, esp through overconfidence **10b** (*intr*) to act overconfidently ▷ *n* **11** the act of pushing; thrust **12** a part or device that is pressed to operate some mechanism **13** *inf* drive, energy, etc **14** *inf* a special effort or attempt to advance, as of an army: *to make a push* **15** *Austral sl* a group, gang, or clique **16** *cricket, etc* a stiff pushing stroke **17 at a push** *inf* with difficulty; only just **18 the push** *inf, chiefly Brit* dismissal, esp from employment ▷ See also **push off, push in**, etc [C13 from OF *pousser*, from L *pulsāre*, from *pellere* to drive]

Pp

push-bike *n Brit* an informal name for **bicycle**

push button *n* **1** an electrical switch operated by pressing a button, which closes or opens a circuit ▷ *modifier* **push-button 2a** operated by a push button: *a push-button radio* **2b** initiated as simply as by pressing a button: *push-button warfare*

pushcart ('pʊʃˌkɑːt) *n* another name (esp US and Canad) for **barrow**[1] (sense 3)

pushchair ('pʊʃˌtʃɛə) *n* a usually collapsible chair-shaped carriage for a small child. Also called: **baby buggy, buggy** US and Canad word: **stroller** Austral words: **pusher, stroller**

pushed (pʊʃt) *adj* (often foll by *for*) *inf* short (of) or in need (of time, money, etc)

pusher ('pʊʃə) *n* **1** *inf* a person who sells illegal drugs, esp narcotics such as heroin **2** *inf* an aggressively ambitious person **3** a person or thing that pushes **4** *Austral* the usual name for **pushchair**

push in *vb* (*intr, adv*) to force one's way into a group of people, queue, etc

pushing ('pʊʃɪŋ) *adj* **1** enterprising or aggressively ambitious **2** impertinently self-assertive ▷ *adv* **3** almost or nearly (a certain age, speed, etc): *pushing fifty* > '**pushingly** *adv*

Pushkin[1] ('pʊʃkɪn) *n* a town in NW Russia: site of the imperial summer residence and Catherine the Great's palace. Pop: 97 000 (latest est). Former name: **Tsarskoye Selo** (1708–1937)

Pushkin² (ˈpʊʃkɪn) *n* **Aleksander Sergeyevich** (alɪkˈsandr sɪrˈgjejɪvitʃ) 1799–1837, Russian poet, novelist, and dramatist. His works include the romantic verse tale *The Prisoner of the Caucasus* (1822), the verse novel *Eugene Onegin* (1833), the tragedy *Boris Godunov* (1825), and the novel *The Captain's Daughter* (1836)
push money *n* a cash inducement provided by a manufacturer or distributor for a retailer or his staff, to reward successful selling
push off *vb (adv)* **1** Also: **push out** to move into open water, as by being cast off from a mooring **2** *(intr) inf* to go away; leave
pushover (ˈpʊʃˌəʊvə) *n inf* **1** something that is easily achieved **2** a person, team, etc, that is easily taken advantage of or defeated
push-pull *n (modifier)* using two similar electronic devices made to operate out of phase with each other to produce a signal that replicates the input waveform: *a push-pull amplifier*
push-start *vb (tr)* **1** to start (a motor vehicle) by pushing it while it is in gear, thus turning the engine ▷ *n* **2** this process
push through *vb (tr)* to compel to accept: *the bill was pushed through Parliament*
Pushto (ˈpʌʃtəʊ) *or* **Pushtu** (ˈpʌʃtuː) *n, adj* variant spellings of **Pashto**
push-up *n* the US and Canad term for **press-up**
pushy (ˈpʊʃɪ) *adj* **pushier, pushiest** *inf* **1** offensively assertive **2** aggressively or ruthlessly ambitious > ˈ**pushily** *adv* > ˈ**pushiness** *n*
pusillanimous (ˌpjuːsɪˈlænɪməs) *adj* characterized by a lack of courage or determination [c16 from LL *pusillanimis* from L *pusillus* weak + *animus* courage] > **pusillanimity** (ˌpjuːsɪləˈnɪmɪtɪ) *n* > ˌ**pusilˈlanimously** *adv*
Puskas (ˈpʊskəs) *n* **Ferenc** (ˈfɛrɛnk) born 1927, Hungarian footballer; played for Hungary (1945–56) and Real Madrid (1958–66)
puss (pʊs) *n* **1** an informal name for **cat** **2** *sl* a girl or woman **3** an informal name for a **hare** [c16 rel. to MLow G *pūs*]
pussy¹ (ˈpʊsɪ) *n, pl* **pussies** **1** Also called: **puss, pussycat** an informal name for **cat** **2** a furry catkin **3** *taboo sl* the female pudenda **4** *sl, chiefly US* an ineffectual or timid man [c18 from PUSS]
pussy² (ˈpʌsɪ) *adj* **pussier, pussiest** containing or full of pus
pussycat (ˈpʊsɪˌkæt) *n* **1** an informal or child's name for **cat¹** **2** *Brit inf* an endearing or gentle person
pussyfoot (ˈpʊsɪˌfʊt) *vb (intr) inf* **1** to move about stealthily or warily like a cat **2** to avoid committing oneself
pussy willow (ˈpʊsɪ) *n* a willow tree with silvery silky catkins
pustulant (ˈpʌstjʊlənt) *adj* **1** causing the formation of pustules ▷ *n* **2** an agent causing such formation
pustulate *vb* (ˈpʌstjʊˌleɪt), **pustulates, pustulating, pustulated** **1** to form or cause to form into pustules ▷ *adj* (ˈpʌstjʊlɪt) **2** covered with pustules > ˌ**pustuˈlation** *n*
pustule (ˈpʌstjuːl) *n* **1** a small inflamed elevated area of skin containing pus **2** any spot resembling a pimple [c14 from L *pustula* a blister, var. of *pūsula*] > **pustular** (ˈpʌstjʊlə) *adj*
put (pʊt) *vb* **puts, putting, put** *(mainly tr)* **1** to cause to be (in a position or place): *to put a book on the table* **2** to cause to be (in a state, relation, etc): *to put one's things in order* **3** (foll by *to*) to cause (a person) to experience or suffer: *to put to death* **4** to set or commit (to an action, task, or duty), esp by force: *he put him to work* **5** to render or translate: *to put into English* **6** to set (words) in a musical form (esp in **put to music**) **7** (foll by *at*) to estimate: *he put the distance at fifty miles* **8** (foll by *to*) to utilize: *he put his knowledge to use* **9** (foll by *to*) to couple (a female animal) with a male for breeding: *the farmer put his heifer to the bull* **10** to express: *to put it bluntly* **11** to make (an end or limit): *he put an end to the proceedings* **12** to present for consideration; propose: *he put the question to the committee* **13** to invest (money) in or expend (time, energy, etc) on: *he put five thousand pounds into the project* **14** to impart: *to put zest into a party* **15** to throw or cast **16** **not know where to put oneself** to feel embarrassed **17** **stay put** to remain in one place; keep one's position ▷ *n* **18** a throw, esp in putting the shot **19** Also called: **put option** *stock exchange* an option to sell a stated number of securities at a specified price during a limited period ▷ See also **put about, put across,** etc [c12 *puten* to push]
put about *vb (adv)* **1** *naut* to change course **2** *(tr)* to make widely known: *he put about the news of the air disaster* **3** *(tr; usually passive)* to disconcert or disturb
put across *vb (tr)* **1** *(adv)* to communicate in a comprehensible way: *he couldn't put things across very well* **2** **put one across** *inf* to get (someone) to believe a claim, excuse, etc, by deception: *they put one across their teacher*
put aside *vb (tr, adv)* **1** to move (an object, etc) to one side, esp in rejection **2** to save: *to put money aside for a rainy day* **3** to disregard: *let us put aside our differences*
putative (ˈpjuːtətɪv) *adj (prenominal)* **1** commonly regarded as being: *the putative father* **2** considered to exist or have existed; inferred [c15 from LL *putātīvus* supposed, from L *putāre* to consider] > ˈ**putatively** *adv*
put away *vb (tr, adv)* **1** to return (something) to the proper place **2** to save: *to put away money for the future* **3** to lock up in a prison, mental institution, etc: *they put him away for twenty years* **4** to eat or drink, esp in large amounts
put back *vb (tr, adv)* **1** to return to its former place **2** to move to a later time: *the wedding was put back a fortnight* **3** to impede the progress of: *the strike put back production*
put by *vb (tr, adv)* to set aside for the future; save
put down *vb (tr, adv)* **1** to make a written record of **2** to repress: *to put down a rebellion* **3** to consider: *they put him down for an ignoramus* **4** to attribute: *I put the mistake down to inexperience* **5** to put (an animal) to death, because of old age or illness **6** to table on the agenda: *the MPs put down a motion on the increase in crime* **7** *sl* to reject or humiliate ▷ *n* **put-down** **8** a cruelly crushing remark
put forth *vb (tr, adv) formal* **1** to propose **2** (of a plant) to produce or bear (leaves, etc)
put forward *vb (tr, adv)* **1** to propose; suggest **2** to offer the name of; nominate
put in *vb (adv)* **1** *(intr) naut* to bring a vessel into port **2** (often foll by *for*) to apply (for a job, etc) **3** *(tr)* to submit: *he put in his claims form* **4** to intervene with (a remark) during a conversation **5** *(tr)* to devote (time, effort, etc): *he put in three hours overtime last night* **6** *(tr)* to establish or appoint: *he put in a manager* **7** *(tr) cricket* to cause to bat: *England won the toss and put the visitors in to bat*
Putin (ˈpuːtɪn) *n* **Vladimir** (**Vladimirovich**) born 1952, Russian statesman: prime minister (1999); acting president (1999–2000) following Boris Yeltsin's resignation; president from 2000
Putnam (ˈpʌtnəm) *n* **1** **Israel** 1718–90, American general in the War of Independence **2** his cousin **Rufus** 1738–1824, American soldier in the War of Independence; surveyor general of the US (1796–1803)
put off *vb (tr)* **1** *(adv)* to postpone: *they have put off the dance until tomorrow* **2** *(adv)* to evade (a person) by postponement or delay: *they tried to put him off, but he came anyway* **3** *(adv)* to cause aversion: *he was put off by her appearance* **4** *(prep)* to cause to lose interest in: *the accident put him off driving*
put on *vb (tr, mainly adv)* **1** to clothe oneself in **2** *(usually passive)* to adopt (an attitude or feeling) insincerely: *his misery was just put on* **3** to present (a play, show, etc) **4** to add: *she put on weight* **5** to cause (an electrical device) to function **6** *(also prep)* to wager (money) on a horse race,

game, etc **7** (*also prep*) to impose: *to put a tax on cars* **8** *cricket* to cause (a bowler) to bowl

put out *vb* (*tr, adv*) **1** (*often passive*) **1a** to annoy; anger **1b** to disturb; confuse **2** to extinguish (a fire, light, etc) **3** to poke forward: *to put out one's tongue* **4** to be a source of inconvenience to: *I hope I'm not putting you out* **5** to publish; broadcast: *the authorities put out a leaflet* **6** to render unconscious **7** to dislocate: *he put out his shoulder in the accident* **8** to give out (work to be done) at different premises **9** to lend (money) at interest **10** *cricket, etc* to dismiss (a player or team)

put over *vb* (*tr, adv*) **1** *inf* to communicate (facts, information, etc) **2** *chiefly US* to postpone **3** **put (a fast) one over on** *inf* to get (someone) to believe a claim, excuse, etc, by deception: *he put one over on his boss*

put-put ('pʌt,pʌt) *inf* ▷ *n* **1** a light chugging or popping sound, as made by a petrol engine ▷ *vb* **put-puts, put-putting, put-putted** **2** (*intr*) to make such a sound

putrefy ('pju:trɪ,faɪ) *vb* **putrefies, putrefying, putrefied** (of organic matter) to decompose or rot with an offensive smell [c15 from OF *putrefier* + L *putrefacere*, from *puter* rotten + *facere* to make] > **putrefaction** (,pju:trɪ'fækʃən) *n* > ,**putre'factive** *or* **putrefacient** (,pju:trɪ'feɪʃənt) *adj*

putrescent (pju:'trɛsᵊnt) *adj* **1** becoming putrid; rotting **2** characterized by or undergoing putrefaction [c18 from L *putrescere* to become rotten] > **pu'trescence** *n*

putrid ('pju:trɪd) *adj* **1** (of organic matter) in a state of decomposition: *putrid meat* **2** morally corrupt **3** sickening; foul: *a putrid smell* **4** *inf* deficient in quality or value: *a putrid film* [c16 from L *putridus*, from *putrēre* to be rotten] > **pu'tridity** *or* '**putridness** *n* > '**putridly** *adv*

putsch (pʊtʃ) *n* a violent and sudden uprising; political revolt [c20 from G, from Swiss G: a push, imit.]

putt (pʌt) *golf* ▷ *n* **1** a stroke on the green with a putter to roll the ball into or near the hole ▷ *vb* **2** to strike (the ball) in this way [c16 of Scot origin]

puttee *or* **putty** ('pʌtɪ) *n, pl* **puttees** *or* **putties** (*usually pl*) a strip of cloth worn wound around the leg from the ankle to the knee, esp as part of a military uniform in World War I [c19 from Hindi *paṭṭī*, from Sansk. *paṭṭikā*, from *paṭṭa* cloth]

putter[1] ('pʌtə) *n golf* **1** a club for putting, usually having a solid metal head **2** a golfer who putts: *he is a good putter*

putter[2] ('pʌtə) *vb* the usual US and Canad word for **potter**[2] > '**putterer** *n*

putter[3] ('pʊtə) *n* **1** a person who puts: *the putter of a question* **2** a person who puts the shot

put through *vb* (*tr, mainly adv*) **1** to carry out to a conclusion: *he put through his plan* **2** (*also prep*) to organize the processing of: *she put through his application to join the organization* **3** to connect by telephone **4** to make (a telephone call)

putting green ('pʌtɪŋ) *n* **1** (on a golf course) the area of closely mown grass at the end of a fairway where the hole is **2** an area of smooth grass with several holes for putting games

Puttnam ('pʌtnəm) *n* **David,** Baron. born 1941, British film producer. Films include *Chariots of Fire* (1981), *The Killing Fields* (1984), *Memphis Belle* (1990), and *My Life So Far* (1999)

putto ('pʊtəʊ) *n, pl* **putti** ('pʊti:) a representation of a small boy, a cherub or cupid, esp in baroque painting or sculpture [from It., from L *putus* boy]

putty ('pʌtɪ) *n, pl* **putties** **1** a stiff paste made of whiting and linseed oil that is used to fix glass into frames and to fill cracks in woodwork, etc **2** any substance with a similar function or appearance **3** a mixture of lime and water with sand or plaster of Paris used on plaster as a finishing coat **4** (*as modifier*): *a putty knife* **5** a person who is easily influenced: *he's putty in her hands* **6a** a colour varying from greyish yellow to greyish brown **6b** (*as adj*): *putty wool* ▷ *vb* **putties, puttying, puttied** **7** (*tr*) to fix, fill, or coat with putty [c17 from F *potée* a potful]

Putumayo (*Spanish* putu'majo) *n* a river in NW South America, rising in S Colombia and flowing southeast as most of the border between Colombia and Peru, entering the Amazon in Brazil: scene of the Putumayo rubber scandal (1910–11) during the rubber boom, in which many Indians were enslaved and killed by rubber exploiters. Length: 1578 km (980 miles). Brazilian name: **Içá**

put up *vb* (*adv, mainly tr*) **1** to build; erect: *to put up a statue* **2** to accommodate or be accommodated at: *can you put me up for tonight?* **3** to increase (prices) **4** to submit (a plan, case, etc) **5** to offer: *to put a house up for sale* **6** to give: *to put up a good fight* **7** to provide (money) for: *they put up five thousand for the new project* **8** to preserve or can (jam, etc) **9** to pile up (long hair) on the head in any of several styles **10** (*also intr*) to nominate or be nominated as a candidate: *he put up for president* **11** *arch* to return (a weapon) to its holder: *put up your sword!* **12** **put up to** **12a** to inform or instruct (a person) about (tasks, duties, etc) **12b** to incite to **13** **put up with** *inf* to endure; tolerate ▷ *adj* **put-up** **14** dishonestly or craftily prearranged (esp in **put-up job**)

put upon *vb* (*intr, prep; usually passive*) **1** to presume on (a person's generosity, good nature, etc): *he's always being put upon* **2** to impose hardship on: *he was sorely put upon*

putz (pʌts) *n US sl* a despicable or stupid person [from Yiddish *puts* ornament]

Puvis de Chavannes (*French* pyvis də ʃavan) *n* **Pierre Cécile** (pjɛr sesil) 1824–98, French mural painter

Puy de Dôme (pwi də dom) *n* **1** a department of central France in Auvergne region. Capital: Clermont-Ferrand. Pop: 604 266 (1999). Area: 8016 sq km (3094 sq miles) **2** a mountain in central France, in the Auvergne Mountains: a volcanic plug. Height: 1485 m (4872 ft)

Puy de Sancy (*French* pwi də sɑ̃si) *n* a mountain in S central France: highest peak of the Monts Dore. Height: 1886 m (6188 ft)

Pu-yi ('pu:'ji:) *n* **Henry** 1906–67, last emperor of China as Xuan-Tong (1908–12); emperor of the Japanese puppet state of Manchukuo as Kang-de (1934–45)

puzzle ('pʌzᵊl) *vb* **puzzles, puzzling, puzzled** **1** to perplex or be perplexed **2** (*intr; foll by over*) to ponder about the cause of: *he puzzled over her absence* **3** (*tr; usually foll by out*) to solve by mental effort: *he puzzled out the meaning* ▷ *n* **4** a person or thing that puzzles **5** a problem that cannot be easily solved **6** the state of being puzzled **7** a toy, game, or question presenting a problem that requires skill or ingenuity for its solution [c16 from ?] > '**puzzlement** *n* > '**puzzler** *n* > '**puzzling** *adj* > '**puzzlingly** *adv*

▷ www.puzzles.com

PVC *abbrev for* polyvinyl chloride; a synthetic thermoplastic material made by polymerizing vinyl chloride. The flexible forms are used in insulation, shoes, etc Rigid PVC is used for moulded articles

PVR *abbrev for* personal(ized) video recorder: a device for recording and replaying television programmes, films, etc, that uses a hard disk rather than videocassettes or DVDs and has various computer functions

PVS *abbrev for:* **1** persistent vegetative state **2** postviral syndrome

Pvt. *mil abbrev for* private

PW *abbrev for* policewoman

PWA *abbrev for* person with AIDS

PWR *abbrev for* pressurized-water reactor

pyaemia *or* **pyemia** (paɪ'i:mɪə) *n* blood poisoning characterized by pus-forming microorganisms in the blood [c19 from NL, from Gk *puon* pus + *haima* blood] > **py'aemic** *or* **py'emic** *adj*

Pydna ('pɪdnə) *n* a town in ancient Macedonia: site of a major Roman victory over the Macedonians, resulting in the downfall of their kingdom (168 BC)

pye-dog, pie-dog, *or* **pi-dog** ('paɪ,dɒg) *n* an ownerless half-wild Asian dog [c19 Anglo-Indian, from Hindi *pāhī* outsider]

pyelitis (ˌpaɪəˈlaɪtɪs) *n* inflammation of the pelvis of the kidney [c19 NL, from Gk *puelos* trough] > **pyelitic** (ˌpaɪəˈlɪtɪk) *adj*

Pygmalion (pɪgˈmeɪlɪən) *n Greek myth* a king of Cyprus, who fell in love with the statue of a woman he had sculpted and which his prayers brought to life as Galatea

pygmy *or* **pigmy** (ˈpɪgmɪ) *n, pl* **pygmies** *or* **pigmies** **1** an abnormally undersized person **2** something that is a very small example of its type **3** a person of little importance or significance **4** (*modifier*) very small [c14 *pigmeis* the Pygmies, from L *Pygmaeus* a Pygmy, from Gk *pugmaios* undersized, from *pugmē* fist] > **pygmaean** *or* **pygmean** (pɪgˈmiːən) *adj*

Pygmy *or* **Pigmy** (ˈpɪgmɪ) *n, pl* **Pygmies** *or* **Pigmies** a member of one of the dwarf peoples of Equatorial Africa, noted for their hunting and forest culture

pyinkado (pjɪŋˈkɑːdəʊ) *n, pl* **pyinkados** **1** a leguminous tree, native to India and Myanmar **2** the heavy durable timber of this tree, used for construction [c19 from Burmese]

pyjamas *or US* **pajamas** (pəˈdʒɑːməz) *pl n* **1** loose-fitting nightclothes comprising a jacket or top and trousers **2** full loose-fitting ankle-length trousers worn by either sex in various Eastern countries [c19 from Hindi, from Persian *pai* leg + *jāma* garment]

pyknic (ˈpɪknɪk) *adj* characterized by a broad squat fleshy physique with a large chest and abdomen [c20 from Gk *puknos* thick]

pylon (ˈpaɪlən) *n* **1** a large vertical steel tower-like structure supporting high-tension electrical cables **2** a post or tower for guiding pilots or marking a turning point in a race **3** a streamlined aircraft structure for attaching an engine pod, etc, to the main body of the aircraft **4** a monumental gateway, such as one at the entrance to an ancient Egyptian temple [c19 from Gk *pulōn* a gateway]

pylorus (paɪˈlɔːrəs) *n, pl* **pylori** (paɪˈlɔːraɪ) the small circular opening at the base of the stomach through which partially digested food passes to the duodenum [c17 via LL from Gk *pulōrus* gatekeeper, from *pulē* gate + *ouros* guardian]

Pylos (ˈpaɪlɒs) *n* a port in SW Greece, in the SW Peloponnese; scene of a defeat of the Spartans by the Athenians (425 BC) during the Peloponnesian War and of the Battle of Navarino (see **Navarino**). Italian name: **Navarino** Modern Greek name: **Pílos**

Pym (pɪm) *n* **1** **Barbara** (**Mary Crampton**) 1913–80, British novelist, noted for such comedies of middle-class English life as *Excellent Women* (1952), *A Glass of Blessings* (1958), and *The Sweet Dove Died* (1978) **2** **John** ?1584–1643, leading English parliamentarian during the events leading to the Civil War. He took a prominent part in the impeachment of Buckingham (1626) and of Strafford and Laud (1640)

Pynchon (ˈpɪntʃən) *n* **Thomas** born 1937, US novelist, author of *V* (1963), *The Crying of Lot 49* (1967), *Gravity's Rainbow* (1973), and *Mason and Dixon* (1997)

pyo- *or before a vowel* **py-** *combining form* denoting pus: *pyosis* [from Gk *puon*]

Pyongyang *or* **P'yŏng-yang** (ˈpjɒŋˈjæŋ) *n* the capital of North Korea, in the southwest on the Taedong River: industrial centre; university (1946). Pop: 2 355 000 (latest est)

pyorrhoea *or esp US* **pyorrhea** (ˌpaɪəˈrɪə) *n* inflammation of the gums characterized by the discharge of pus and loosening of the teeth; periodontal disease > ˌ**pyorˈrhoeal**, ˌ**pyorˈrhoeic** *or esp US* ˌ**pyorˈrheal**, ˌ**pyorˈrheic** *adj*

pyracantha (ˌpaɪrəˈkænθə) *n* any of a genus of shrubs with yellow, orange, or scarlet berries, widely cultivated for ornament [c17 from Gk *purakantha*, from PYRO- + *akantha* thorn]

pyramid (ˈpɪrəmɪd) *n* **1** a huge masonry construction that has a square base and, as in the case of the ancient Egyptian royal tombs, four sloping triangular sides **2** an object or structure resembling such a construction **3** *maths* a solid having a polygonal base and triangular sides that meet in a common vertex **4** *crystallog* a crystal form in which three planes intersect all three axes of the crystal **5** *finance* a group of enterprises containing a series of holding companies structured so that the top holding company controls the entire group with a relatively small proportion of the total capital invested **6** (*pl*) a game similar to billiards ▷ *vb* **pyramids, pyramiding, pyramided** **7** to build up or be arranged in the form of a pyramid **8** *finance* to form (companies) into a pyramid [c16 (earlier *pyramis*): from L *pyramis*, from Gk *puramis*, prob. from Egyptian] > **pyramidal** (pɪˈræmɪdᵊl), ˌ**pyraˈmidical**, *or* ˌ**pyraˈmidic** *adj* > **pyˈramidally** *or* ˌ**pyraˈmidically** *adv*

pyramid selling *n* a practice adopted by some manufacturers of advertising for distributors and selling them batches of goods. The first distributors then advertise for more distributors who are sold subdivisions of the original batches at an increased price. This process continues until the final distributors are left with a stock that is unsaleable except at a loss

Pyramus and Thisbe (ˈpɪrəməs; ˈθɪzbɪ) *n* (in Greek legend) two lovers of Babylon: Pyramus, wrongly supposing Thisbe to be dead, killed himself and she, encountering him in his death throes, did the same

pyre (ˈpaɪə) *n* a pile of wood or other combustible material, esp one for cremating a corpse [c17 from L *pyra*, from Gk *pura* hearth, from *pur* fire]

Pyrenees (ˌpɪrəˈniːz) *pl n* a mountain range between France and Spain, extending from the Bay of Biscay to the Mediterranean. Highest peak: Pico de Aneto, 3404 m (11 168 ft) > ˌ**PyreˈNean** *adj*

Pyrénées *or* **Pyrénées-Atlantiques** (*French* pirenezatlɑ̃tik) *n* a department of SW France in Aquitaine region. Capital: Pau. Pop: 600 018 (1999). Area: 7712 sq km (3008 sq miles). Former name: **Basses-Pyrénées**

Pyrénées-Orientales (*French* pirenezɔrjɑ̃tal) *n* a department of S France, in Languedoc-Roussillon region. Capital: Perpignan. Pop: 392 803 (1999). Area: 4144 sq km (1616 sq miles)

pyrethrin (paɪˈriːθrɪn) *n* either of two oily compounds found in pyrethrum and used as insecticides [c19 from PYRETHRUM + -IN]

pyrethrum (paɪˈriːθrəm) *n* **1** any of several cultivated Eurasian chrysanthemums with white, pink, red, or purple flowers **2** any insecticide prepared from the dried flowers of any of these plants [c16 via L from Gk *purethron* feverfew, prob. from *puretos* fever; see PYRETIC]

pyretic (paɪˈrɛtɪk) *adj pathol* of, relating to, or characterized by fever [c18 from NL *pyreticus*, from Gk *puretos* fever, from *pur* fire]

Pyrex (ˈpaɪrɛks) *n trademark* **a** any of a variety of glasses that have low coefficients of expansion, making them suitable for heat-resistant glassware used in cookery and chemical apparatus **b** (*as modifier*): *a Pyrex dish*

pyrexia (paɪˈrɛksɪə) *n* a technical name for **fever** [c18 from NL, from Gk *purexis*, from *puressein* to be feverish, from *pur* fire] > **pyˈrexial** *or* **pyˈrexic** *adj*

pyridine (ˈpɪrɪˌdiːn) *n* a colourless hygroscopic liquid heterocyclic compound with a characteristic odour: used as a solvent and in preparing other organic chemicals. Formula: C_5H_5N [c19 from PYRO- + -ID² + -INE²]

pyridoxine (ˌpɪrɪˈdɒksiːn) *n biochemistry* a derivative of pyridine that is a precursor of the compounds pyridoxal and pyridoxamine. Also called: **vitamin B$_6$**

pyrimidine (paɪˈrɪmɪˌdiːn) *n* **1** a liquid or crystalline organic compound with a penetrating odour. Formula: $C_4H_4N_2$ **2** Also called: **pyrimidine base** any of a number of similar compounds having a basic structure that is derived from pyrimidine, and which are constituents of nucleic acids [C20 var. of PYRIDINE]

pyrite (ˈpaɪraɪt) *n* a yellow mineral consisting of iron sulphide in cubic crystalline form. It occurs in igneous and metamorphic rocks and in veins, associated with various metals, and is used mainly in the manufacture of sulphuric acid and paper. Formula: FeS_2. Also called: **iron pyrites, pyrites** [C16 from L *pyrites* flint, from Gk *puritēs (lithos)* fire(stone), from *pur* fire] > **pyritic** (paɪˈrɪtɪk) *or* **pyˈritous** *adj*

pyrites (paɪˈraɪtiːz; *in combination* ˈpaɪraɪts) *n, pl* **pyrites** **1** another name for **pyrite** **2** any of a number of other disulphides of metals, esp of copper and tin

pyro- *or before a vowel* **pyr-** *combining form* **1** denoting fire or heat: *pyromania; pyrometer* **2** *chem* denoting a new substance obtained by heating another: *pyroboric acid is obtained by heating boric acid* **3** *mineralogy* **3a** having a property that changes upon the application of heat **3b** having a flame-coloured appearance: *pyroxylin* [from Gk *pur* fire]

pyroelectricity (ˌpaɪrəʊɪlɛkˈtrɪsɪtɪ) *n* the development of opposite charges at the ends of the axis of certain crystals as a result of a change in temperature

pyrogallol (ˌpaɪrəʊˈgælɒl) *n* a crystalline soluble phenol with weakly acidic properties: used as a photographic developer and for absorbing oxygen in gas analysis. Formula: $C_6H_3(OH)_3$ [C20 from PYRO- + GALL(IC ACID) + -OL[1]]

pyrogenic (ˌpaɪrəʊˈdʒɛnɪk) *or* **pyrogenous** (paɪˈrɒdʒɪnəs) *adj* **1** produced by or producing heat **2** *pathol* causing or resulting from fever **3** *geol* less common words for **igneous**

pyrography (paɪˈrɒgrəfɪ) *n* another name for **pokerwork**

pyroligneous (ˌpaɪrəʊˈlɪgnɪəs) *or* **pyrolignic** *adj* (of a substance) produced by the action of heat on wood, esp by destructive distillation

pyrolysis (paɪˈrɒlɪsɪs) *n* **1** the application of heat to chemical compounds in order to cause decomposition **2** such chemical decomposition > **pyrolytic** (ˌpaɪrəʊˈlɪtɪk) *adj*

pyromania (ˌpaɪrəʊˈmeɪnɪə) *n psychiatry* the uncontrollable impulse and practice of setting things on fire > ˌ**pyroˈmaniˌac** *n*

pyrometer (paɪˈrɒmɪtə) *n* an instrument for measuring high temperatures, esp by measuring the brightness or total quantity of the radiation produced > **pyrometric** (ˌpaɪrəʊˈmɛtrɪk) *or* ˌ**pyroˈmetrical** *adj* > ˌ**pyroˈmetrically** *adv* > **pyˈrometry** *n*

pyrope (ˈpaɪrəʊp) *n* a deep yellowish-red garnet that consists of magnesium aluminium silicate and is used as a gemstone [C14 (used loosely of a red gem; modern sense C19): from OF *pirope*, from L *pyrōpus* bronze, from Gk *purōpus* fiery-eyed]

pyrophoric (ˌpaɪrəʊˈfɒrɪk) *adj* **1** (of a chemical) igniting spontaneously on contact with air **2** (of an alloy) producing sparks when struck or scraped: *lighter flints are made of pyrophoric alloy* [C19 from NL *pyrophorus*, from Gk *purophoros* fire-bearing, from *pur* fire + *pherein* to bear]

pyrosis (paɪˈrəʊsɪs) *n pathol* a technical name for **heartburn** [C18 from NL, from Gk: a burning, from *puroun* to burn, from *pur* fire]

pyrostat (ˈpaɪrəʊˌstæt) *n* **1** a device that activates an alarm or extinguisher in the event of a fire **2** a thermostat for use at high temperatures > ˌ**pyroˈstatic** *adj*

pyrotechnics (ˌpaɪrəʊˈtɛknɪks) *n* **1** *(functioning as sing)* the art of making fireworks **2** *(functioning as sing or pl)* a firework display **3** *(functioning as sing or pl)* brilliance of display, as in the performance of music > ˌ**pyroˈtechnic** *or* ˌ**pyroˈtechnical** *adj*

pyroxene (paɪˈrɒksiːn) *n* any of a large group of minerals consisting of the silicates of magnesium, iron, and calcium. They occur in basic igneous rocks [C19 PYRO- + *-xene* from Gk *xenos* foreign, because mistakenly thought to have originated elsewhere when found in igneous rocks]

pyroxylin (paɪˈrɒksɪlɪn) *n* a yellow substance obtained by nitrating cellulose with a mixture of nitric and sulphuric acids; guncotton: used to make collodion, plastics, lacquers, and adhesives

pyrrhic (ˈpɪrɪk) *prosody* ▷ *n* **1** a metrical foot of two short or unstressed syllables ▷ *adj* **2** of or composed in pyrrhics [C16 via L, from Gk *purrhikhē*, said to be after its inventor *Purrhikhos*]

Pyrrhic victory *n* a victory in which the victor's losses are as great as those of the defeated. Also called: **Cadmean victory** [after PYRRHUS, who defeated the Romans at Asculum in 279 BC but suffered heavy losses]

Pyrrho (ˈpɪrəʊ) *n* ?365–?275 BC, Greek philosopher; founder of scepticism. He maintained that true wisdom and happiness lie in suspension of judgment, since certain knowledge is impossible to attain

Pyrrhus (ˈpɪrəs) *n* **1** 319–272 BC, king of Epirus (306–272) He invaded Italy but was ultimately defeated by the Romans (275 BC) **2** another name for **Neoptolemus**

pyruvic acid (paɪˈruːvɪk) *n* a liquid formed during the metabolism of proteins and carbohydrates, helping to release energy to the body [C19 from PYRO- + L *ūva* grape]

Pythagoras (paɪˈθægərəs) *n* ?580–?500 BC, Greek philosopher and mathematician. He founded a religious brotherhood, which followed a life of strict asceticism and greatly influenced the development of mathematics and its application to music and astronomy

Pythagoras' theorem *n* the theorem that in a right-angled triangle the square of the length of the hypotenuse equals the sum of the squares of the other two sides

Pythagorean (paɪˌθægəˈriːən) *adj* **1** of or relating to Pythagoras ▷ *n* **2** a follower of Pythagoras

Pytheas (ˈpɪθɪəs) *n* 4th century BC, Greek navigator. He was the first Greek to visit and describe the coasts of Spain, France, and the British Isles and may have reached Iceland

Pythia (ˈpɪθɪə) *n Greek myth* the priestess of Apollo at Delphi, who transmitted the oracles

Pythian (ˈpɪθɪən) *adj* **1** Also: **Pythic** of or relating to Delphi or its oracle ▷ *n* **2** the priestess of Apollo at the oracle of Delphi [C16 via L *Pȳthius* from Gk *Puthios* of Delphi]

python (ˈpaɪθən) *n* any of a family of large nonvenomous snakes of Africa, S Asia, and Australia. They can reach a length of more than 20 feet and kill their prey by constriction [C16 NL, after PYTHON] > **pythonic** (paɪˈθɒnɪk) *adj*

Python (ˈpaɪθən) *n Greek myth* a dragon, killed by Apollo at Delphi

pythoness (ˈpaɪθənɛs) *n* a woman, such as Apollo's priestess at Delphi, believed to be possessed by an oracular spirit [C14 *phitonesse*, ult. from Gk *Puthōn* PYTHON]

pyuria (paɪˈjʊərɪə) *n pathol* any condition characterized by the presence of pus in the urine [C19 from NL, from Gk *puon* pus + *ouron* urine]

pyx (pɪks) *n* **1** Also called: **pyx chest** the chest in which coins from the British mint are placed to be tested for weight, etc **2** *Christianity* any receptacle in which the Eucharistic Host is kept [C14 from L *pyxis* small box, from Gk, from *puxos* box tree]

pyxidium (pɪkˈsɪdɪəm) *or* **pyxis** (ˈpɪksɪs) *n, pl* **pyxidia**

Pp

(pɪk'sɪdɪə) *or* **pyxides** ('pɪksɪˌdi:z) the dry fruit of such plants as the plantain: a capsule whose upper part falls off when mature so that the seeds are released [c19 via NL from Gk *puxidion* a little box, from *puxis* box]

pyxis ('pɪksɪs) *n, pl* **pyxides** ('pɪksɪˌdi:z) **1** a small box used by the ancient Greeks and Romans to hold medicines, etc **2** another name for **pyxidium** [c14 via L from Gk: box]

q *or* **Q** (kjuː) *n, pl* **q's, Q's,** *or* **Qs** **1** the 17th letter of the English alphabet **2** a speech sound represented by this letter

q *symbol for* quintal

Q *symbol for:* **1** *physics* heat **2** *chess* queen **3** question **4** Q factor

q. *abbrev for:* **1** quart **2** quarter **3** quarterly

Q. *abbrev for:* **1** quartermaster **2** (*pl* **Qq., qq.**) Also: **q** quarto **3** Queen **5** question

Qabis (ˈkɑːbɪs) *n* the Arabic name for **Gabès**

Qaboos bin Said (kəˈbuːs bɪn ˈsaɪd) *n* born 1940, sultan of Oman from 1970

Qaddafi (gəˈdɑːfɪ) *n* **Moamar al** (ˈməʊəˌmɑː ˌæl) See (Moamar al) **Gaddafi**

qadi (ˈkɑːdɪ, ˈkeɪdɪ) *n, pl* **qadis** a variant spelling of **cadi**

Qairwan (kaɪəˈwɑːn) *n* a variant of **Kairouan**

QANTAS (ˈkwɒntəs) *n* the national airline of Australia [c20 from *Q(ueensland) a(nd) N(orthern) T(erritory) A(erial) S(ervices Ltd.)*]

Qaraghandy (*Kazakh* kɑrɑɣɑnˈdɪ) *n* a variant transliteration of the Kazakh name for **Karaganda**

QARANC *abbrev for* Queen Alexandra's Royal Army Nursing Corps

Qatar *or* **Katar** (kæˈtɑː) *n* a state in E Arabia, occupying a peninsula in the Persian Gulf: under Persian rule until the 19th century; became a British protectorate in 1916; declared independence in 1971; exports petroleum and natural gas. Official language: Arabic. Official religion: (Sunni) Muslim. Currency: riyal. Capital: Doha. Pop: 596 000 (2001 est). Area: about 11 000 sq km (4250 sq miles) > **Qaˈtari** *or* **Kaˈtari** *adj, n*

▹ www.mofa.gov.qa
▹ www.qatartourism.org
▹ www.qatar-info.com

Qattara Depression (kəˈtɑːrə) *n* an arid basin in the Sahara, in NW Egypt, impassable to vehicles. Area: about 18 000 sq km (7000 sq miles). Lowest point: 133 m (435 ft) below sea level

qawwali (kəˈvɑːlɪ) *n* an Islamic religious song, esp in Asia

QB *abbrev for* Queen's Bench

QC *abbrev for* **1** Queen's Counsel **2** Quebec

QED *abbrev for:* **1** quantum electrodynamics **2** quod erat demonstrandum [L: which was to be shown or proved]

Qeshm (ˈkɛʃəm) *or* **Qishm** *n* **1** the largest island in the Persian Gulf: part of Iran. Area: 1336 sq km (516 sq miles) **2** the chief town of this island

Q factor *n* **1** a measure of the relationship between stored energy and rate of energy dissipation in certain electrical components, devices, etc **2** Also called: **Q value** the heat released in a nuclear reaction ▹ Symbol: Q [c20 short for *quality factor*]

Q fever *n* an acute disease characterized by fever and pneumonia, transmitted to man by a rickettsia [c20 from *q(uery) fever* (the cause being orig. unknown)]

qi (tʃiː) *n* a variant spelling of **chi**[2]

Qingdao (ˈtʃɪŋˈdaʊ), **Tsingtao**, *or* **Chingtao** *n* a port in E China, in E Shandong province on Jiazhou Bay, developed as a naval base and fort in 1891. Shandong university (1926). Pop: 1 702 108 (1999 est)

Qinghai, Tsinghai, *or* **Chinghai** (ˈtʃɪŋˈhaɪ) *n* **1** a province of NW China: consists largely of mountains and high plateaus. Capital: Xining. Pop: 5 180 000 (2000 est). Area: 721 000 sq km (278 400 sq miles) **2** the Pinyin transliteration of the Chinese name for **Koko Nor**

Qiqihar, Chichihaerh, Ch'i-ch'i-haerh, *or* **Tsitsihar** (ˈtʃiːˌtʃiːˈhɑː) *n* a city in NE China, in Heilongjiang province on the Nonni River. Pop: 1 115 766 (1999 est)

Qishm (ˈkɪʃəm) *n* a variant of **Qeshm**

Qld *or* **QLD** *abbrev for* Queensland

QM *abbrev for* Quartermaster
QMG *abbrev for* Quartermaster General
QMV *abbrev for* Qualified Majority Voting
Qom (kɒm), **Qum**, *or* **Kum** *n* a city in NW central Iran: a place of pilgrimage for Shiite Muslims. Pop: 777 677 (1996)
qr. *pl* **qrs** *abbrev for:* **1** quarter **2** quarterly **3** quire
Q-ship *n* a merchant ship with concealed guns, used to decoy enemy ships [C20 from Q short for QUERY]
QSM (in New Zealand) *abbrev for* Queen's Service Medal
QSO *abbrev for:* **1** quasi-stellar object **2** (in New Zealand) Queen's Service Order
qt *pl* **qt** *or* **qts** *abbrev for* quart
q.t. *inf* **1** *abbrev for* quiet **2 on the q.t.** secretly
QTS (in Britain) *abbrev for* Qualified Teacher Status
qua (kweɪ, kwɑː) *prep* in the capacity of; by virtue of being [C17 from L, ablative sing (fem) of *qui* who]
quack[1] (kwæk) *vb (intr)* **1** (of a duck) to utter a harsh guttural sound **2** to make a noise like a duck ▷ *n* **3** the sound made by a duck [C17 imit.]
quack[2] (kwæk) *n* **1a** an unqualified person who claims medical knowledge or other skills **1b** (*as modifier*): *a quack doctor* **2** *Brit, Austral, & NZ inf* a doctor; physician or surgeon ▷ *vb* **3** (*intr*) to act in the manner of a quack [C17 short for QUACKSALVER] > **'quackish** *adj*
quackery ('kwækərɪ) *n, pl* **quackeries** the activities or methods of a quack
quack grass *n* another name for **couch grass**
quacksalver ('kwæk,sælvə) *n* an archaic word for **quack**[2] [C16 from Du., from *quack*, apparently: to hawk + *salf* SALVE]
quad[1] (kwɒd) *n* short for **quadrangle**
quad[2] (kwɒd) *n printing* a block of type metal used for spacing [C19 shortened from QUADRAT]
quad[3] (kwɒd) *n* short for **quadruplet**
quad[4] (kwɒd) *n, adj inf* short for **quadraphonics** *or* **quadraphonic**
quad bike *or* **quad** *n* a vehicle like a motorcycle with four large wheels, designed for agricultural, sporting, and other off-road uses
Quadragesima (,kwɒdrə'dʒɛsɪmə) *n* the first Sunday in Lent. Also called: **Quadragesima Sunday** [C16 from Med. L *quadrāgēsima dies* the fortieth day]
Quadragesimal (,kwɒdrə'dʒɛsɪməl) *adj* of, relating to, or characteristic of Lent
quadrangle ('kwɒd,ræŋgᵊl) *n* **1** *geom* a plane figure consisting of four points connected by four lines **2** a rectangular courtyard, esp one having buildings on all four sides **3** the building surrounding such a courtyard [C15 from LL *quadrangulum* figure having four corners] > **quadrangular** (kwɒ'dræŋgjʊlə) *adj*
quadrant ('kwɒdrənt) *n* **1** *geom* **1a** a quarter of the circumference of a circle **1b** the area enclosed by two perpendicular radii of a circle **1c** any of the four sections into which a plane is divided by two coordinate axes **2** a piece of a mechanism in the form of a quarter circle **3** an instrument formerly used in astronomy and navigation for measuring the altitudes of stars [C14 from L *quadrāns* a quarter] > **quadrantal** (kwɒ'dræntᵊl) *adj*
quadraphonics *or* **quadrophonics** (,kwɒdrə'fɒnɪks) *n (functioning as sing)* a system of sound recording and reproduction that uses four independent loudspeakers to give directional sources of sound > **,quadra'phonic** *or* **,quadro'phonic** *adj*
quadrat ('kwɒdrət) *n* **1** *ecology* an area of vegetation selected at random for study **2** *printing* an archaic name for **quad**[2] [C14 (meaning "a square"): var. of QUADRATE]
quadrate *n* ('kwɒdrɪt, -,dreɪt) **1** a cube, square, or a square or cubelike object **2** one of a pair of bones of the upper jaw of fishes, amphibians, reptiles, and birds ▷ *adj* ('kwɒdrɪt, -,dreɪt) **3** of or relating to this bone **4** square or rectangular ▷ *vb* (kwɒ'dreɪt), **quadrates, quadrating, quadrated 5** (*tr*) to make square or rectangular **6** (often foll by *with*) to conform or cause to conform [C14 from L *quadrāre* to make square]
quadratic (kwɒ'drætɪk) *maths* ▷ *n* **1** Also called: **quadratic equation** an equation containing one or more terms in which the variable is raised to the power of two, but to no higher power ▷ *adj* **2** of or relating to the second power
quadrature ('kwɒdrətʃə) *n* **1** *maths* the process of determining a square having an area equal to that of a given figure or surface **2** the process of making square or dividing into squares **3** *astron* a configuration in which two celestial bodies form an angle of 90° with a third body **4** *electronics* the relationship between two waves that are 90° out of phase
quadrella (kwɒ'drɛlə) *n Austral* a form of betting in which the punter must select the winner of four specified races
quadrennial (kwɒ'drɛnɪəl) *adj* **1** occurring every four years **2** lasting four years ▷ *n* **3** a period of four years > **quad'rennially** *adv*
quadrennium (kwɒ'drɛnɪəm) *n, pl* **quadrenniums** *or* **quadrennia** (-nɪə) a period of four years [C17 from L *quadriennium*, from QUADRI- + *annus* year]
quadri- *or before a vowel* **quadr-** *combining form* four: *quadrilateral* [from L; cf. *quattuor* four]
quadric ('kwɒdrɪk) *maths* ▷ *adj* **1** having or characterized by an equation of the second degree **2** of the second degree ▷ *n* **3** a quadric curve, surface, or function
quadriceps ('kwɒdrɪ,sɛps) *n, pl* **quadricepses** (-,sɛpsɪz) *or* **quadriceps** *anat* a large four-part muscle of the front of the thigh, which extends the leg [C19 NL, from QUADRI- + *-ceps* as in BICEPS]
quadrifid ('kwɒdrɪfɪd) *adj bot* divided into four lobes or other parts: *quadrifid leaves*
quadrilateral (,kwɒdrɪ'lætərəl) *adj* **1** having or formed by four sides ▷ *n* **2** Also called: **tetragon** a polygon having four sides
quadrille[1] (kwɒ'drɪl) *n* **1** a square dance for four couples **2** a piece of music for such a dance [C18 via F from Sp. *cuadrilla*, dim. of *cuadro* square, from L *quadra*]
quadrille[2] (kwɒ'drɪl, kwə-) *n* an old card game for four players [C18 from F, from Sp. *cuartillo*, from *cuarto* fourth, from L *quartus*, infl. by QUADRILLE[1]]
quadrillion (kwɒ'drɪljən) *n, pl* **quadrillions** *or* **quadrillion** **1** (in Britain, France, and Germany) the number represented as one followed by 24 zeros (10^{24}). US and Canad word: **septillion 2** (in the US and Canada) the number represented as one followed by 15 zeros (10^{15}) ▷ *determiner* **3** amounting to this number: *a quadrillion atoms* [C17 from F *quadrillon*, from QUADRI- + *-illion*, on the model of *million*] > **quad'rillionth** *adj*
quadrinomial (,kwɒdrɪ'nəʊmɪəl) *n* an algebraic expression containing four terms
quadriplegia (,kwɒdrɪ'pliːdʒɪə) *n* paralysis of all four limbs. Also called: **tetraplegia** [C20 from QUADRI- + Gk *plēssein* to strike] > **quadriplegic** (,kwɒdrɪ'pliːdʒɪk) *adj*
quadrivalent (,kwɒdrɪ'veɪlənt) *adj chem* another word for **tetravalent** > **,quadri'valency** *or* **,quadri'valence** *n*
quadrivium (kwɒ'drɪvɪəm) *n, pl* **quadrivia** (-ə) (in medieval learning) a course consisting of arithmetic, geometry, astronomy, and music [from Med. L, from L: crossroads, from QUADRI- + *via* way]
quadroon (kwɒ'druːn) *n* a person who is one-quarter Black [C18 from Sp. *cuarterón*, from *cuarto* quarter, from L *quartus*]
quadrumanous (kwɒ'druːmənəs) *adj* (of monkeys and apes) having all four feet specialized for use as hands [C18 from NL *quadrumanus*, from QUADRI- + L *manus* hand]
quadruped ('kwɒdrʊ,pɛd) *n* **1** an animal, esp a mammal, that has all four limbs specialized for walking ▷ *adj* **2** having four feet [C17 from L *quadrupēs*, from *quadru-* (see QUADRI-) + *pēs* foot] > **quadrupedal** (kwɒ'druːpɪdᵊl) *adj*

quadruple ('kwɒdrʊpᵊl, kwɒ'druːpᵊl) *vb* **quadruples, quadrupling, quadrupled 1** to multiply by four or increase fourfold ▷ *adj* **2** four times as much or as many; fourfold **3** consisting of four parts **4** *music* having four beats in each bar ▷ *n* **5** a quantity or number four times as great as another [C16 via OF from L *quadruplus*, from *quadru-* (see QUADRI-) + *-plus* -fold] > '**quadruply** *adv*

quadruplet ('kwɒdrʊplɪt, kwɒ'druːplɪt) *n* **1** one of four offspring born at one birth **2** a group of four similar things **3** *music* a group of four notes to be played in a time value of three

quadruplicate *adj* (kwɒ'druːplɪkɪt) **1** fourfold or quadruple ▷ *vb* (kwɒ'druːplɪˌkeɪt), **quadruplicates, quadruplicating, quadruplicated 2** to multiply or be multiplied by four ▷ *n* (kwɒ'druːplɪkɪt) **3** a group or set of four things [C17 from L *quadruplicāre* to increase fourfold]

quaestor ('kwiːstə) *or US (sometimes)* **questor** ('kwɛstə) *n* any of several magistrates of ancient Rome, usually a financial administrator [C14 from L, from *quaerere* to inquire] > **quaestorial** (kwɛ'stɔːrɪəl) *adj*

quaff (kwɒf) *vb* to drink heartily or in one draught [C16 ? imit.; cf. MLow G *quassen* to eat or drink excessively] > '**quaffer** *n*

quag (kwæg) *n* a quagmire [C16 ? rel. to QUAKE]

quagga ('kwægə) *n, pl* **quaggas** *or* **quagga** a recently extinct member of the horse family of southern Africa: it had zebra-like stripes on the head and shoulders [C18 from obs. Afrik., from Khoikhoi *quăgga*]

quaggy ('kwægɪ) *adj* **quaggier, quaggiest 1** resembling a quagmire; boggy **2** soft or flabby

quagmire ('kwægˌmaɪə) *n* **1** a soft wet area of land that gives way under the feet; bog **2** an awkward, complex, or embarrassing situation [C16 from QUAG + MIRE]

quahog ('kwɑːˌhɒg) *n* an edible clam native to the Atlantic coast of North America, having a large heavy rounded shell [C18 from Amerind, short for *poquauhock*, from *pohkeni* dark + *hogki* shell]

quaich *or* **quaigh** (kweɪx) *n Scot* a small shallow drinking cup, usually with two handles [from Gaelic *cuach* cup]

Quai d'Orsay (*French* ke dɔrsɛ) *n* the quay along the S bank of the Seine, Paris, where the French foreign office is situated

quail[1] (kweɪl) *n, pl* **quails** *or* **quail** any of various small Old World game birds having rounded bodies and small tails [C14 from OF *quaille*, from Med. L *quaccula*, prob. imit.]

quail[2] (kweɪl) *vb* (*intr*) to shrink back with fear; cower [C15 ?from OF *quailler*, from L *coāgulāre* to curdle]

quaint (kweɪnt) *adj* **1** attractively unusual, esp in an old-fashioned style **2** odd or inappropriate [C13 (in the sense: clever): from OF *cointe*, from L *cognitus* known, from *cognoscere* to ascertain] > '**quaintly** *adv* > '**quaintness** *n*

quair (kwɛə) *n Scot* a book [var. of QUIRE[1]]

quake (kweɪk) *vb* **quakes, quaking, quaked** (*intr*) **1** to shake or tremble with or as with fear **2** to convulse or quiver, as from instability ▷ *n* **3** a quaking **4** *inf* an earthquake [OE *cwacian*]

Quaker ('kweɪkə) *n* **1** a member of the Religious Society of Friends, a Christian sect founded by George Fox about 1650. Quakers reject sacraments, ritual, and formal ministry, and have promoted many causes for social reform ▷ *adj* **2** of the Religious Society of Friends or its beliefs or practices [C17 orig. a derog. nickname] > '**Quakeress** *fem n* > '**Quakerish** *adj* > '**Quakerism** *n*
▷ http://www.quaker.org/

quaking ('kweɪkɪŋ) *adj* unstable or unsafe to walk on, as a bog or quicksand

quaking grass *n* any of various grasses having delicate branches that shake in the wind

quaky ('kweɪkɪ) *adj* **quakier, quakiest** inclined to quake; shaky; tremulous > '**quakily** *adv* > '**quakiness** *n*

qualification (ˌkwɒlɪfɪ'keɪʃən) *n* **1** an official record of achievement awarded on the successful completion of a course of training or passing of an examination **2** an ability, quality, or attribute, esp one that fits a person to perform a particular job or task **3** a condition that modifies or limits; restriction **4** a qualifying or being qualified

qualified ('kwɒlɪˌfaɪd) *adj* **1** having the abilities, qualities, attributes, etc, necessary to perform a particular job or task **2** limited, modified, or restricted; not absolute

Qualified Majority Voting *n* a voting system, used by the EU Council of Ministers, by which resolutions concerning certain areas of policy may be passed without unanimity. Abbrev: **QMV**

qualify ('kwɒlɪˌfaɪ) *vb* **qualifies, qualifying, qualified 1** to provide or be provided with the abilities or attributes necessary for a task, office, duty, etc: *his degree qualifies him for the job* **2** (*tr*) to make less strong, harsh, or violent; moderate or restrict **3** (*tr*) to modify or change the strength or flavour of **4** (*tr*) *grammar* another word for **modify 5** (*tr*) to attribute a quality to; characterize **6** (*intr*) to progress to the final stages of a competition, as by winning preliminary contests [C16 from OF *qualifier*, from Med. L *quālificāre* to characterize, from L *quālis* of what kind + *facere* to make] > '**qualiˌfiable** *adj* > '**qualiˌfier** *n*

qualitative ('kwɒlɪtətɪv) *adj* involving or relating to distinctions based on quality or qualities > '**qualitatively** *adv*

qualitative analysis *n* See **analysis** (sense 4)

quality ('kwɒlɪtɪ) *n, pl* **qualities 1** a distinguishing characteristic or attribute **2** the basic character or nature of something **3** a feature of personality **4** degree or standard of excellence, esp a high standard **5** (formerly) high social status or the distinction associated with it **6** musical tone colour; timbre **7** *logic* the characteristic of a proposition that makes it affirmative or negative **8** *phonetics* the distinctive character of a vowel, determined by the configuration of the mouth, tongue, etc **9** (*modifier*) having or showing excellence or superiority: *a quality product* [C13 from OF *qualité*, from L *quālitās* state, from *quālis* of what sort]

quality control *n* control of the quality of a manufactured product, usually by statistical sampling techniques

quality time *n* a short period during the day in which a person gives the whole of his or her attention to some matter other than work, esp family relationships

qualm (kwɑːm) *n* **1** a sudden feeling of sickness or nausea **2** a pang of doubt, esp concerning moral conduct; scruple **3** a sudden sensation of misgiving [OE *cwealm* death or plague] > '**qualmish** *adj*

quandary ('kwɒndrɪ) *n, pl* **quandaries** a difficult situation; predicament [C16 from ?; ? rel. to L *quandō* when]

quandong, quandang ('kwɒnˌdɒŋ), *or* **quantong** ('kwɒnˌtɒŋ) *n* **1** Also called: **native peach 1a** a small Australian tree **1b** the edible fruit or nut of this tree **2** *Austral sl* a sponger or parasite **3 silver quandong 3a** an Australian tree **3b** its timber [from Abor.]

quango ('kwæŋgəʊ) *n, pl* **quangos** a semipublic government-financed administrative body whose members are appointed by the government [C20 *qu(asi-)a(utonomous) n(on) g(overnmental) o(rganization)*]

quangocracy (kwæŋ'gɒkrəsɪ) *n, pl* **quangocracies 1** the control or influence ascribed to quangos **2** quangos collectively

quant[1] (kwɒnt) *n* **1** a long pole for propelling a boat, esp a punt ▷ *vb* **2** to propel (a boat) with a quant [C15 prob. from L *contus* pole, from Gk *kontos*]

quant[2] (kwɒnt) *n inf* a highly paid analyst with a degree

Qq

in a quantitative science, employed by a financial house to predict price movements of securities, commodities, etc [C20 from QUANTITATIVE]

Quant (kwɒnt) *n* **Mary** born 1934, British fashion designer, whose Chelsea Look of miniskirts and geometrically patterned fabrics dominated London fashion in the 1960s

quanta (ˈkwɒntə) *n* the plural of **quantum**

quantic (ˈkwɒntɪk) *n* a homogeneous function of two or more variables in a rational and integral form [C19 from L *quantus* how great]

quantifier (ˈkwɒntɪˌfaɪə) *n* **1** *logic* a symbol indicating the quantity of a term: *the existential quantifier corresponds to the words "there is something, such that"* **2** *grammar* a word or phrase, such as *some, all,* or *no*, expressing quantity

quantify (ˈkwɒntɪˌfaɪ) *vb* **quantifies, quantifying, quantified** (*tr*) **1** to discover or express the quantity of **2** *logic* to specify the quantity of (a term) by using a quantifier, such as *all, some,* or *no* [C19 from Med. L *quantificāre*, from L *quantus* how much + *facere* to make] > **ˈquantifiable** *adj* > **ˌquantifiˈcation** *n*

quantitative (ˈkwɒntɪtətɪv) *or* **quantitive** *adj* **1** involving or relating to considerations of amount or size **2** capable of being measured **3** *prosody* of a metrical system that is based on the length of syllables > **ˈquantitatively** *or* **ˈquantitively** *adv*

quantitative analysis *n* See **analysis** (sense 4)

quantity (ˈkwɒntɪtɪ) *n, pl* **quantities 1a** a specified or definite amount, number, etc **1b** (*as modifier*): *a quantity estimate* **2** the aspect of anything that can be measured, weighed, counted, etc **3 unknown quantity** a person or thing whose action, effort, etc, is unknown or unpredictable: *the redesigned course is an unknown quantity* **4** a large amount **5** *maths* an entity having a magnitude that may be denoted by a numerical expression **6** *physics* a specified magnitude or amount **7** *logic* the characteristic of a proposition that makes it universal or particular **8** *prosody* the relative duration of a syllable or the vowel in it [C14 from OF *quantité*, from L *quantitās* amount, from *quantus* how much]

> **USAGE** The use of a plural noun after *quantity of* as in *a large quantity of bananas* was formerly considered incorrect, but is now acceptable

quantity surveyor *n* a person who estimates the cost of the materials and labour necessary for a construction job

quantize *or* **quantise** (ˈkwɒntaɪz) *vb* **quantizes, quantizing, quantized** *or* **quantises, quantising, quantised** (*tr*) **1** *physics* to restrict (a physical quantity) to one of a set of fixed values **2** *maths* to limit to values that are multiples of a basic unit > **ˌquantiˈzation** *or* **ˌquantiˈsation** *n*

quantum (ˈkwɒntəm) *n, pl* **quanta 1** *physics* **1a** the smallest quantity of some physical property that a system can possess according to the quantum theory **1b** a particle with such a unit of energy **2** amount or quantity, esp a specific amount ▷ *adj* **3** of or designating a major breakthrough or sudden advance: *a quantum leap forward* [C17 from L *quantus* (adj) how much]

quantum electrodynamics *n physics* the study of electromagnetic radiation and its interaction with charged particles in terms of quantum theory. Abbrev: **QED**

quantum mechanics *n* (*functioning as sing*) the branch of mechanics, based on the quantum theory, used for interpreting the behaviour of elementary particles and atoms, which do not obey Newtonian mechanics

quantum meruit *Latin* (ˈmɛruːɪt) as much as he has earned

quantum number *n physics* one of a set of integers or half-integers characterizing the energy states of a particle or system of particles

quantum theory *n* a theory concerning the behaviour of physical systems based on the idea that they can only possess certain properties, such as energy and angular momentum, in discrete amounts (quanta)

quaquaversal (ˌkwɑːkwəˈvɜːsəl) *adj geol* directed outwards in all directions from a common centre [C18 from L *quāquā* in every direction + *versus* towards]

quarantine (ˈkwɒrənˌtiːn) *n* **1** a period of isolation or detention, esp of persons or animals arriving from abroad, to prevent the spread of disease **2** the place where such detention is enforced **3** any period or state of enforced isolation ▷ *vb* **quarantines, quarantining, quarantined 4** (*tr*) to isolate in or as if in quarantine [C17 from It. *quarantina* period of forty days, from *quaranta* forty, from L *quadrāgintā*]

quarantine flag *n naut* the yellow signal flag for the letter Q, flown alone from a vessel to indicate that there is no disease aboard or, with a second signal flag, to indicate that there is disease aboard. Also called: **yellow jack**

quark[1] (kwɑːk) *n physics* any of a set of six elementary particles that, together with their antiparticles, are thought to be fundamental units of all baryons and mesons but unable to exist in isolation [C20 coined by James JOYCE in the novel *Finnegans Wake*, and given special application in physics]

quark[2] (kwɑːk) *n* a type of low-fat soft cheese [from G]

Quarles (kwɔːlz, kwɑːlz) *n* **Francis** 1592–1644, English poet

quarrel[1] (ˈkwɒrəl) *n* **1** an angry disagreement; argument **2** a cause of dispute; grievance ▷ *vb* **quarrels, quarrelling, quarrelled** *or US* **quarrels, quarreling, quarreled** (*intr; often foll by with*) **3** to engage in a disagreement or dispute; argue **4** to find fault; complain [C14 from OF *querele*, from L *querēlla* complaint, from *querī* to complain] > **ˈquarreller** *or US* **ˈquarreler** *n*

quarrel[2] (ˈkwɒrəl) *n* **1** an arrow having a four-edged head, fired from a crossbow **2** a small square or diamond-shaped pane of glass [C13 from OF *quarrel* pane, from Med. L *quadrellus*, dim. of L *quadrus* square]

quarrelsome (ˈkwɒrəlsəm) *adj* inclined to quarrel or disagree; belligerent

quarrian *or* **quarrion** (ˈkwɒrɪən) *n* a cockatiel of inland Australia that feeds on seeds and grasses [C20 prob. from Abor.]

quarry[1] (ˈkwɒrɪ) *n, pl* **quarries 1** an open surface excavation for the extraction of building stone, slate, marble, etc **2** a copious source, esp of information ▷ *vb* **quarries, quarrying, quarried 3** to extract (stone, slate, etc) from or as if from a quarry **4** (*tr*) to excavate a quarry in **5** to obtain (something) diligently and laboriously [C15 from OF *quarriere*, from *quarre* (unattested) square-shaped stone, from L *quadrāre* to make square]

quarry[2] (ˈkwɒrɪ) *n, pl* **quarries 1** an animal, etc, that is hunted, esp by other animals; prey **2** anything pursued [C14 *quirre* entrails offered to the hounds, from OF *cuirée* what is placed on the hide, from *cuir* hide, from L *corium* leather; prob. also infl. by OF *coree* entrails, from L *cor* heart]

quarryman (ˈkwɒrɪmən) *n, pl* **quarrymen** a man who works in or manages a quarry

quarry tile *n* an unglazed floor tile

quart (kwɔːt) *n* **1** a unit of liquid measure equal to a quarter of a gallon or two pints. 1 US quart (0.946 litre) is equal to 0.8326 UK quart. 1 UK quart (1.136 litres) is equal to 1.2009 US quarts **2** a unit of dry measure equal to 2 pints or one eighth of a peck [C14 from OF *quarte*, from L *quartus* fourth]

quartan (ˈkwɔːtᵊn) *adj* (of a fever) occurring every third day [C13 from L *febris quartāna* fever occurring every fourth day, reckoned inclusively]

quarte (kɑːt) *n* the fourth of eight basic positions from which a parry or attack can be made in fencing [C18 F from OF *quarte*, from L *quartus* fourth]

quarter (ˈkwɔːtə) *n* **1** one of four equal parts of an object, quantity, etc **2** the fraction equal to one divided by four (¼) **3** *US, Canad, etc* a 25-cent piece **4** a unit of weight equal to a quarter of a hundredweight. 1 US quarter is equal to 25 pounds; 1 Brit quarter is equal to 28 pounds **5** short for **quarter-hour** **6** a fourth part of a year; three months **7** *astron* **7a** one fourth of the moon's period of revolution around the earth **7b** either of two phases of the moon when half of the lighted surface is visible **8** *inf* a unit of weight equal to a quarter of a pound or 4 ounces **9** *Brit* a unit of capacity for grain, etc, usually equal to 8 UK bushels **10** *sport* one of the four periods into which certain games are divided **11** *naut* the part of a vessel's side towards the stern **12** a region or district of a town or city: *the Spanish quarter* **13** a region, direction, or point of the compass **14** (*sometimes pl*) an unspecified person or group of people: *to get word from the highest quarter* **15** mercy or pity, as shown to a defeated opponent (esp in **ask for** *or* **give quarter**) **16** any of the four limbs, including the adjacent parts, of a quadruped or bird **17** *heraldry* one of four quadrants into which a shield may be divided ▷ *vb* **18** (*tr*) to divide into four equal parts **19** (*tr*) to divide into any number of parts **20** (*tr*) (esp formerly) to dismember (a human body) **21** to billet or be billeted in lodgings, esp (of military personnel) in civilian lodgings **22** (*intr*) (of hounds) to range over an area of ground in search of game or the scent of quarry **23** (*intr*) *naut* (of the wind) to blow onto a vessel's quarter **24** (*tr*) *heraldry* **24a** to divide (a shield) into four separate bearings **24b** to place (one set of arms) in diagonally opposite quarters to another ▷ *adj* **25** being or consisting of one of four equal parts ▷ See also **quarters** [c13 from OF *quartier*, from L *quartārius* a fourth part, from *quartus* fourth]

quarterback (ˈkwɔːtəˌbæk) *n* a player in American football who directs attacking play

quarter-bound *adj* (of a book) having a binding consisting of two types of material, the better type being used on the spine

quarter day *n* any of four days in the year when certain payments become due. In England, Wales, and Northern Ireland these are Lady Day, Midsummer's Day, Michaelmas, and Christmas. In Scotland they are Candlemas, Whit Sunday, Lammas, and Martinmas

quarterdeck (ˈkwɔːtəˌdɛk) *n naut* the after part of the upper deck of a ship, traditionally the deck for official or ceremonial use

quartered (ˈkwɔːtəd) *adj* **1** *heraldry* (of a shield) divided into four sections, each having contrasting arms or having two sets of arms, each repeated in diagonally opposite corners **2** (of a log) sawn into four equal parts along two diameters at right angles to each other

quarterfinal (ˌkwɔːtəˈfaɪnᵊl) *n* the round before the semifinal in a competition

quarter-hour *n* **1** a period of 15 minutes **2** either of the points on a timepiece that mark 15 minutes before or after the hour

quartering (ˈkwɔːtərɪŋ) *n* **1** *mil* the allocation of accommodation to service personnel **2** *heraldry* **2a** the marshalling of several coats of arms on one shield, usually representing intermarriages **2b** any coat of arms marshalled in this way

quarterlife crisis (ˈkwɔːtəˌlaɪf) *n* a crisis that may be experienced in one's twenties, involving anxiety over the direction and quality of one's life

quarterlight (ˈkwɔːtəˌlaɪt) *n Brit* a small pivoted window in the door of a car for ventilation

quarterly (ˈkwɔːtəlɪ) *adj* **1** occurring, done, paid, etc, at intervals of three months **2** of, relating to, or consisting of a quarter ▷ *n, pl* **quarterlies** **3** a periodical issued every three months ▷ *adv* **4** once every three months

quartermaster (ˈkwɔːtəˌmɑːstə) *n* **1** an officer responsible for accommodation, food, and equipment in a military unit **2** a rating in the navy, usually a petty officer, with particular responsibility for navigational duties

quarter-miler *n* an athlete who specializes in running the quarter mile or in running 400-metre races

quartern (ˈkwɔːtən) *n* **1** a fourth part of certain weights or measures **2** Also called: **quartern loaf** *Brit* **2a** a type of loaf 4 inches square **2b** any loaf weighing 1600 g [c13 from OF *quarteron*, from *quart* a quarter]

quarter note *n* the usual US and Canad name for **crotchet** (sense 1)

quarter plate *n* a photographic plate measuring 3¼ × 4¼ inches (8.3 × 10.8 cm)

quarters (ˈkwɔːtəz) *pl n* **1** accommodation, esp as provided for military personnel **2** the stations assigned to crew members of a warship: *general quarters*

quarter sessions *n* (*functioning as sing or pl*) (formerly) any of various courts held four times a year before justices of the peace or a recorder

quarterstaff (ˈkwɔːtəˌstɑːf) *n, pl* **quarterstaves** (-ˌsteɪvz) a stout iron-tipped wooden staff about 6ft long, formerly used as a weapon [c16 from ?]

quarter tone *n music* a quarter of a whole tone

quartet *or* **quartette** (kwɔːˈtɛt) *n* **1** a group of four singers or instrumentalists or a piece of music composed for such a group **2** any group of four [c18 from It. *quartetto*, dim. of *quarto* fourth]

quartic (ˈkwɔːtɪk) *adj, n* another word for **biquadratic** [c19 from L *quartus* fourth]

quartile (ˈkwɔːtaɪl) *n* **1** *statistics* one of three values of a variable dividing its distribution into four groups with equal frequencies ▷ *adj* **2** *statistics* of a quartile **3** *astrol* denoting an aspect of two heavenly bodies when their longitudes differ by 90° [c16 from Med. L *quartīlis*, from L *quartus* fourth]

quarto (ˈkwɔːtəʊ) *n, pl* **quartos** a book size resulting from folding a sheet of paper into four leaves or eight pages [c16 from NL *in quartō* in quarter]

quartz (kwɔːts) *n* a hard glossy mineral consisting of silicon dioxide in crystalline form. It occurs as colourless rock crystal and as several impure coloured varieties including agate, chalcedony, flint, and amethyst. Formula: SiO_2 [c18 from G *Quarz*, of Slavic origin]

quartz clock *or* **watch** *n* a clock or watch that is operated by a vibrating quartz crystal

quartz crystal *n* a thin plate or rod cut from a piece of piezoelectric quartz and ground so that it vibrates at a particular frequency

quartz glass *n* a colourless glass composed of almost pure silica, resistant to very high temperatures

quartz-iodine lamp *or* **quartz lamp** *n* a type of tungsten-halogen lamp containing small amounts of iodine and having a quartz envelope, operating at high temperature and producing an intense light for use in car headlamps, etc

quartzite (ˈkwɔːtsaɪt) *n* **1** a very hard rock consisting of intergrown quartz crystals **2** a sandstone composed of quartz

quasar (ˈkweɪzɑː, -sɑː) *n* any of a class of quasi-stellar objects that emit an immense amount of energy in the form of light, infrared radiation, etc, from a compact source. They are extremely distant and hence the youngest objects observed in the universe, and their energy generation is thought to involve a black hole located in a galaxy [c20 *quasi(i-stell)ar (object)*]

quash (kwɒʃ) *vb* (*tr*) **1** to subdue forcefully and completely **2** to annul or make void (a law, etc) **3** to reject (an indictment, etc) as invalid [c14 from OF *quasser*, from L *quassāre* to shake]

quasi- *combining form* **1** almost but not really; seemingly: *a quasi-religious cult* **2** resembling but not actually being;

Qq

so-called: *a quasi-scholar* [from L, lit.: as if]

Quasimodo (ˌkwɔːzɪˈməʊdəʊ) *n* **1** another name for **Low Sunday** [from the opening words of the Latin introit for that day, *quasimodo geniti infantes* as new-born babies] **2** a character in Victor Hugo's novel *Notre-Dame de Paris* (1831), a grotesque hunch-backed bellringer of the cathedral of Notre Dame **3** (*Italian* kwaˈziːmodo) **Salvatore** (salvaˈtoːre) 1901–68, Italian poet, whose early work expresses symbolist ideas and techniques. His later work is more concerned with political and social issues: Nobel prize for literature 1959

quasi-stellar object (ˈkwɑːzɪ, ˈkweɪsaɪ) *n* a member of any of several classes of astronomical bodies, including **quasars** and **quasi-stellar galaxies**, both of which have exceptionally large red shifts. Abbrev: **QSO**

quassia (ˈkwɒʃə) *n* **1** any of a genus of tropical American trees having bitter bark and wood **2** the wood of this tree or a bitter compound extracted from it, formerly used as a tonic and vermifuge, now used in insecticides [c18 from NL, after Graman *Quassi*, a slave who discovered (1730) the medicinal value of the root]

quatercentenary (ˌkwætəsɛnˈtiːnərɪ) *n, pl* **quatercentenaries** a 400th anniversary [c19 from L *quater* four times + CENTENARY] > ˌ**quatercenˈtennial** (ˌkwætəsɛnˈtɛnɪəl) *adj, n*

quaternary (kwəˈtɜːnərɪ) *adj* **1** consisting of fours or by fours **2** fourth in a series **3** *chem* containing or being an atom bound to four other atoms or groups ▷ *n, pl* **quaternaries 4** the number four or a set of four [c15 from L *quaternārius* each containing four, from *quaternī* by fours, from *quattuor* four]

Quaternary (kwəˈtɜːnərɪ) *adj* **1** of or denoting the most recent period of geological time, which succeeded the Tertiary period nearly two million years ago ▷ *n* **2 the** the Quaternary period or rock system

quaternion (kwəˈtɜːnɪən) *n* **1** *maths* a generalized complex number consisting of four components, $x = x_0 + x_1i + x_2j + x_3k$, where $x, x_0 \ldots x_3$ are real numbers and $i^2 = j^2 = k^2 = -1$, $ij = -ji = k$, etc **2** a set of four [c14 from LL, from L *quaternī* four at a time]

Quathlamba (kwɑːtˈlɑːmbɑː) *n* the Sotho name for the **Drakensberg**

quatrain (ˈkwɒtreɪn) *n* a stanza or poem of four lines [c16 from F, from *quatre* four, from L *quattuor*]

Quatre Bras (*French* katrə bra) *n* a village in Belgium near Brussels; site of a battle in June 1815 where Wellington defeated the French under Marshal Ney, immediately preceding the battle of Waterloo

quatrefoil (ˈkætrəˌfɔɪl) *n* **1** a leaf composed of four leaflets **2** *archit* a carved ornament having four foils arranged about a common centre [c15 from OF, from *quatre* four + *-foil* leaflet]

quattrocento (ˌkwætrəʊˈtʃɛntəʊ) *n* the 15th century, esp in reference to Renaissance Italian art and literature [It., lit.: four hundred (short for fourteen hundred)]

quaver (ˈkweɪvə) *vb* **1** to say or sing (something) with a trembling voice **2** (*intr*) (esp of the voice) to quiver or tremble **3** (*intr*) *rare* to sing or play trills ▷ *n* **4** *music* a note having the time value of an eighth of a semibreve. Usual US and Canad name: **eighth note 5** a tremulous sound or note [c15 (in the sense: to vibrate): from *quaven* to tremble, of Gmc origin] > ˈ**quavering** *adj* > ˈ**quaveringly** *adv*

quay (kiː) *n* a wharf, typically one built parallel to the shoreline [c14 *keye*, from OF *kai*, of Celtic origin]

quayage (ˈkiːɪdʒ) *n* **1** a system of quays **2** a charge for the use of a quay

Quayle (kweɪl) *n* Sir (**John**) **Anthony** 1913–89, British actor and theatrical producer: director (1948–56) of the Shakespeare Memorial Theatre

quayside (ˈkiːˌsaɪd) *n* the edge of a quay along the water

Que. *abbrev for* Quebec

quean (kwiːn) *n* **1** *arch* **1a** a boisterous impudent woman **1b** a prostitute **2** *Scot* an unmarried girl [OE *cwene*]

queasy (ˈkwiːzɪ) *adj* **queasier, queasiest 1** having the feeling that one is about to vomit; nauseous **2** feeling or causing uneasiness [c15 from ?] > ˈ**queasily** *adv* > ˈ**queasiness** *n*

Quebec (kwɪˈbɛk, kə-, kɛ-) *n* **1** a province of E Canada: the largest Canadian province; a French colony from 1608 to 1763, when it passed to Britain; lying mostly on the Canadian Shield, it has vast areas of forest and extensive tundra and is populated mostly in the plain around the St Lawrence River. Capital: Quebec. Pop: 7 410 500 (2001 est). Area: 1 540 680 sq km (594 860 sq miles). Abbreviation: **PQ 2** a port in E Canada, capital of the province of Quebec, situated on the St Lawrence River: founded in 1608 by Champlain; scene of the battle of the Plains of Abraham (1759), by which the British won Canada from the French. Pop: 167 264 (1996) **3** *communications* a code word for the letter *q* > **Queˈbecker** *or* **Queˈbecer** *n*

▷ www.gouv.qc.ca/index_en.html

▷ www.tourisme.gouv.qc.ca/anglais

Québecois (*French* kebɛkwa) *n, pl* **Québecois** (-kwa) a native or inhabitant of the province of Quebec, esp a French-speaking one > **Québecoise** (*French* kebɛkwaz) *fem n*

quebracho (keɪˈbrɑːtʃəʊ) *n, pl* **quebrachos** (-tʃəʊz) **1** either of two South American trees having a tannin-rich hard wood used in tanning and dyeing **2** a South American tree, whose bark yields alkaloids used in medicine and tanning **3** the wood or bark of any of these trees [c19 from American Sp., from *quiebracha*, from *quebrar* to break (from L *crepāre* to rattle) + *hacha* axe (from F)]

Quechua (ˈkɛtʃwə) *n* **1** (*pl* **Quechuas** *or* **Quechua**) a member of any of a group of South American Indian peoples of the Andes, including the Incas **2** the language or family of languages spoken by these peoples > ˈ**Quechuan** *adj, n*

queen (kwiːn) *n* **1** a female sovereign who is the official ruler or head of state **2** the wife of a king **3** a woman or a thing personified as a woman considered the best or most important of her kind: *the queen of ocean liners* **4** *sl* an effeminate male homosexual **5** the only fertile female in a colony of bees, ants, etc **6** an adult female cat **7** a playing card bearing the picture of a queen **8** the most powerful chess piece, able to move in a straight line in any direction or diagonally ▷ *vb* **9** *chess* to promote (a pawn) to a queen when it reaches the eighth rank **10** (*tr*) to crown as queen **11** (*intr*) to reign as queen **12 queen it** (often foll by *over*) *inf* to behave in an overbearing manner [OE *cwēn*]

Queen-Anne *n* **1** a style of furniture popular in England about 1700–20 and in America about 1720–70, characterized by walnut veneer and cabriole legs ▷ *adj* **2** in or of this style **3** of a style of architecture popular in early 18th-century England, characterized by red-brick construction with classical ornamentation

Queen Anne's lace *n* another name for the **cow parsley**

queen bee *n* **1** the fertile female bee in a hive **2** *inf* a woman in a position of dominance over her associates

Queenborough in Sheppey (ˈkwiːnbərə, ˈʃɛpɪ) *n* a town in SE England, in Kent: formed in 1968 by the amalgamation of Queenborough, Sheerness, and Sheppey. Pop: 30 790 (1991)

Queen Charlotte Islands *pl n* a group of about 150 islands off the W coast of Canada: part of British Columbia. Pop: 5316 (1991). Area: 9596 sq km (3705 sq miles)

queen consort *n* the wife of a reigning king

queen dowager *n* the widow of a king

Queen Elizabeth Islands *pl n* a group of islands off the N coast of Canada: the northernmost islands of the Canadian Arctic archipelago, lying N of latitude 74°N;

part of Nunavut. Area: about 390 000 sq km (150 000 sq miles)

queenly ('kwi:nlı) *adj* **queenlier, queenliest** **1** resembling or appropriate to a queen ▷ *adv* **2** in a manner appropriate to a queen

Queen Mab (mæb) *n* (in British folklore) a bewitching fairy who rules over men's dreams

Queen Maud Land (mɔ:d) *n* the large section of Antarctica between Coats Land and Enderby Land: claimed by Norway in 1939

Queen Maud Range *n* a mountain range in Antarctica, in S Ross Dependency, extending for about 800 km (500 miles)

queen mother *n* the widow of a former king who is also the mother of the reigning sovereign

queen olive *n* a variety of olive having large fleshy fruit suitable for pickling

queen post *n* one of a pair of vertical posts that connect the tie beam of a truss to the principal rafters ▷ Cf **king post**

Queens (kwi:nz) *n* a borough of E New York City, on Long Island. Pop: 1 951 598 (1990)

Queen's Award *n* either of two awards instituted by royal warrant (1976) for increased export earnings by a British firm (**Queen's Award for Export Achievement**) or for an advance in technology (**Queen's Award for Technological Achievement**)

Queen's Bench *n* (in England when the sovereign is female) one of the divisions of the High Court of Justice

Queensberry rules ('kwi:nzbərı) *pl n* **1** the code of rules followed in modern boxing **2** *inf* gentlemanly conduct, esp in a dispute [c19 after the ninth Marquess of *Queensberry*, who originated the rules in 1869]

Queen's Counsel *n* (when the sovereign is female) **1** a barrister (in England and Wales) or an advocate (in Scotland) appointed Counsel to the Crown by the sovereign on the recommendation of the Lord Chancellor (in England and Wales) or the Lord President (in Scotland) **2** (in Australia) a similar appointment, usually made on the recommendation of the Chief Justice of each state, through the state governor **3** (in Canada) an honorary title which may be bestowed by the government on lawyers with long experience

Queen's County *n* the former name of **Laois**

Queen's English *n* (when the British sovereign is female) standard Southern British English

queen's evidence *n* *English & Canad law* (when the sovereign is female) evidence given for the Crown against former associates in crime by an accomplice (esp in **turn queen's evidence**) US equivalent: **state's evidence**

Queen's Guide *n* (in Britain and the Commonwealth when the sovereign is female) a Guide who has passed the highest tests of proficiency

queen's highway *n* **1** (in Britain when the sovereign is female) any public road or right of way **2** (in Canada) a main road maintained by the provincial government

queen-size *or* **queen-sized** *adj* (of a bed, etc) larger or longer than normal size but smaller or shorter than king-size

Queensland ('kwi:nz,lænd, -lənd) *n* a state of NE Australia: fringed on the Pacific side by the Great Barrier Reef; the Great Dividing Range lies in the east, separating the coastal lowlands from the dry Great Artesian Basin in the south. Capital: Brisbane. Pop: 3 512 360 (1999 est). Area: 1 727 500 sq km (667 000 sq miles) > '**Queens,lander** *n*

▷ www.qld.gov.au

▷ www.qttc.com.au

Queensland nut *n* another name for **macadamia**

Queen's Scout *n* (in Britain and the Commonwealth when the sovereign is female) a Scout who has passed the highest tests of endurance, resourcefulness, proficiency, and skill. US equivalent: **Eagle Scout**

queer (kwıə) *adj* **1** differing from the normal or usual; odd or strange: *a queer way of talking* **2** dubious; shady **3** faint, giddy, or queasy **4** *inf, derog* homosexual **5** *inf* eccentric or slightly mad **6** *sl* worthless or counterfeit ▷ *n* **7** *inf, derog* a homosexual ▷ *vb (tr) inf* **8** to spoil or thwart (esp in **queer someone's pitch**) **9** to put in a difficult position [c16 ? from G *quer* oblique, ult. from OHG *twërh*] > '**queerly** *adv* > '**queerness** *n*

USAGE Although the term *queer* meaning 'gay' is still considered derogatory when used by non-gays, it is now being used by gay people themselves as a positive term in certain contexts, such as *queer politics*, *queer cinema*. Nevertheless, many gay people would not wish to have the term applied to them, nor would they use it of themselves

queer fish *n* *Brit inf* an odd person

queer street *n* (*sometimes cap*) *inf* a difficult situation, such as debt or bankruptcy (in **in queer street**)

quell (kwɛl) *vb (tr)* **1** to suppress (rebellion, etc); subdue **2** to overcome or allay [OE *cwellan* to kill] > '**queller** *n*

Quelpart ('kwɛl,pɑ:t) *n* another name for **Cheju**

Quemoy (kɛ'mɔı) *n* an island in Formosa Strait, off the SE coast of China: administratively part of Taiwan. Pop (with associated islets): 53 237 (1996 est). Area: 130 sq km (50 sq miles)

quench (kwɛntʃ) *vb (tr)* **1** to satisfy (one's thirst, desires, etc); slake **2** to put out (a fire, etc); extinguish **3** to put down; suppress; subdue **4** to cool (hot metal) by plunging it into cold water [OE *ācwencan* to extinguish] > '**quenchable** *adj* > '**quencher** *n*

Queneau (*French* kəno) *n* **Raymond** (rɛmɔ̃) 1903–76. French writer, influenced in the 1920s by surrealism. His novels include *Zazie dans le métro* (1959)

quenelle (kə'nɛl) *n* a ball of sieved meat or fish [c19 from F, from G *Knödel* dumpling, from OHG *knodo* knot]

Querétaro (*Spanish* ke'retaro) *n* **1** an inland state of central Mexico: economy based on agriculture and mining. Capital: Querétaro. Pop: 1 402 010 (2000). Area: 11 769 sq km (4544 sq miles) **2** a city in central Mexico, capital of Querétaro state: scene of the signing (1848) of the treaty ending the US-Mexican War and of the execution of Emperor Maximilian (1867). Pop: 535 468 (2000 est)

querist ('kwıərıst) *n* a person who makes inquiries or queries; questioner

quern (kwɜ:n) *n* a stone hand mill for grinding corn [OE *cweorn*]

quernstone ('kwɜ:n,stəʊn) *n* **1** another name for **millstone** (sense 1) **2** one of the two stones used in a quern

querulous ('kwɛrʊləs, 'kwɛrjʊ-) *adj* **1** inclined to make whining or peevish complaints **2** characterized by or proceeding from a complaining fretful attitude or disposition [c15 from L *querulus*, from *querī* to complain] > '**querulously** *adv* > '**querulousness** *n*

query ('kwıərı) *n, pl* **queries** **1** a question, esp one expressing doubt **2** a question mark ▷ *vb* **queries, querying, queried** *(tr)* **3** to express uncertainty, doubt, or an objection concerning (something) **4** to express as a query **5** *US* to put a question to (a person); ask [c17 from earlier *quere*, from L *quaerē* ask!, from *quaerere* to seek]

query language *n* *computing* the instructions and procedures used to retrieve information from a database

Quesnay (*French* kɛnɛ) *n* **François** (frɑ̃swa) 1694–1774, French political economist, encyclopedist, and physician. He propounded the theory championed by the physiocrats in his *Tableau économique* (1758)

quest (kwɛst) *n* **1** a looking for or seeking; search **2** (in medieval romance) an expedition by a knight or knights to accomplish a task, such as finding the Holy Grail

3 the object of a search; a goal or target ▷ *vb* (*mainly intr*) 4 (foll by *for* or *after*) to go in search (of) 5 (of dogs, etc) to search for game 6 (*also tr*) *arch* to seek [C14 from OF *queste*, from L *quaesita* sought, from *quaerere* to seek] > '**quester** *n* > '**questing** *adj* > '**questingly** *adv*

question ('kwɛstʃən) *n* 1 a form of words addressed to a person in order to elicit information or evoke a response; interrogative sentence 2 a point at issue: *it's only a question of time until she dies* 3 a difficulty or uncertainty 4a an act of asking 4b an investigation into some problem 5 a motion presented for debate 6 **put the question** to require members of a deliberative assembly to vote on a motion presented 7 *law* a matter submitted to a court or other tribunal 8 **beyond (all) question** beyond (any) dispute or doubt 9 **call in** *or* **into question** 9a to make (something) the subject of disagreement 9b to cast doubt upon the truth, etc, of (something) 10 **in question** under discussion: *this is the man in question* 11 **out of the question** beyond consideration; unthinkable or impossible 12 **put to the question** (formerly) to interrogate by torture ▷ *vb* (*mainly tr*) 13 to put a question or questions to (a person); interrogate 14 to make (something) the subject of dispute 15 to express uncertainty about the truth of (something); doubt [C13 via OF from L *quaestiō*, from *quaerere* to seek] > '**questioner** *n*

questionable ('kwɛstʃənəbᵊl) *adj* 1 (esp of a person's morality or honesty) admitting of some doubt; dubious 2 of disputable value or authority > '**questionableness** *n* > '**questionably** *adv*

questioning ('kwɛstʃənɪŋ) *adj* 1 proceeding from or characterized by a feeling of doubt or uncertainty 2 intellectually inquisitive: *a questioning mind* > '**questioningly** *adv*

questionless ('kwɛstʃənlɪs) *adj* 1 blindly adhering; unquestioning 2 a less common word for **unquestionable** > '**questionlessly** *adv*

question mark *n* 1 the punctuation mark ?, used at the end of questions and in other contexts where doubt or ignorance is implied 2 this mark used for any other purpose, as to draw attention to a possible mistake

question master *n Brit* the chairman of a quiz or panel game

questionnaire (ˌkwɛstʃə'nɛə, ˌkɛs-) *n* a set of questions on a form, submitted to a number of people in order to collect statistical information.

> **USAGE** The most generally heard pronunciation of the first syllable of this word is the naturalized one, *kwess*. The French-sounding pronunciation *kess* is much less common, and may sound affected to certain people

question time *n* (in parliamentary bodies of the British type) the time set aside each day for questions to government ministers

Quetta ('kwɛtə) *n* a city in W central Pakistan, at an altitude of 1650 m (5500 ft): a summer resort, military station, and trading centre. Pop: 560 387 (1998)

quetzal ('kɛtsəl) *n, pl* **quetzals** *or* **quetzales** (-'sɑːlɛs) 1 a crested bird of Central and N South America, which has a brilliant green, red, and white plumage and, in the male, long tail feathers 2 *pl* **quetzales** the standard monetary unit of Guatemala [via American Sp. from Nahuatl *quetzalli* brightly coloured tail feather]

Quetzalcoatl (ˌkɛtsəlkəʊ'ætᵊl) *n* a god of the Aztecs and Toltecs, represented as a feathered serpent

queue (kjuː) *chiefly Brit* ▷ *n* 1 a line of people, vehicles, etc, waiting for something 2 *computing* a list in which entries are deleted from one end and inserted at the other 3 a pigtail ▷ *vb* **queues, queuing** *or* **queueing, queued** 4 (*intr, often foll by up*) to form or remain in a line while waiting 5 (*tr*) *computing* to arrange (a number of programs) in a predetermined order for accessing by a computer ▷ Usual US word (senses 1, 4): **line** [C16 (in the sense: tail); C18 (in the sense: pigtail): via F from L *cauda* tail]

queue-jump *vb* (*intr*) 1 to take a place in a queue ahead of those already queuing; push in 2 to obtain some advantage out of turn or unfairly > '**queue-jumper** *n*

Quezon City ('keɪzɒn) *n* a city in the Philippines, on central Luzon adjoining Manila: capital of the Philippines from 1948 to 1976; seat of the University of the Philippines (1908). Pop: 2 173 831 (2000)

Quezon y Molina ('keɪzɒn iː mɒ'liːnə; *Spanish* ke'θon i mo'lina) *n* **Manuel Luis** (ma'nwɛl lwis) 1878–1944, Philippine statesman: first president of the Philippines (from 1935) and head of the government in exile after the Japanese conquest of the islands in World War II

quibble ('kwɪbᵊl) *vb* **quibbles, quibbling, quibbled** (*intr*) 1 to make trivial objections 2 *arch* to play on words; pun ▷ *n* 3 a trivial objection or equivocation, esp one used to avoid an issue 4 *arch* a pun [C17 prob. from obs. *quib*, ?from L *quibus* (from *quī* who, which), as used in legal documents, with reference to their obscure phraseology] > '**quibbler** *n* > '**quibbling** *adj*

Quiberon (*French* kibrɔ̃) *n* a peninsula of NW France, on the S coast of Brittany: a naval battle was fought off its coast in 1759 during the Seven Years' War, in which the British defeated the French

quiche (kiːʃ) *n* an open savoury tart with an egg custard filling to which bacon, onion, cheese, etc, are added [F, from G *Kuchen* cake]

quick (kwɪk) *adj* 1 performed or occurring during a comparatively short time: *a quick move* 2 lasting a short time; brief 3 accomplishing something in a time that is shorter than normal: *a quick worker* 4 characterized by rapidity of movement; fast 5 immediate or prompt 6 (*postpositive*) eager or ready to perform (an action): *quick to criticize* 7 responsive to stimulation; alert; lively 8 eager or enthusiastic for learning 9 easily excited or aroused 10 nimble in one's movements or actions; deft: *quick fingers* 11 *arch* 11a alive; living 11b (*as n*) living people (esp in **the quick and the dead**) 12 **quick with child** *arch* pregnant ▷ *n* 13 any area of sensitive flesh, esp that under a toenail or fingernail 14 the most important part (of a thing) 15 **cut (someone) to the quick** to hurt (someone's) feelings deeply ▷ *adv inf* 16 in a rapid manner; swiftly 17 soon: *I hope he comes quick* ▷ *sentence substitute* 18 a command to perform an action immediately [OE *cwicu* living] > '**quickly** *adv* > '**quickness** *n*

quick-change artist *n* an actor or entertainer who undertakes several rapid changes of costume during his performance

quicken ('kwɪkən) *vb* 1 to make or become faster; accelerate 2 to impart to or receive vigour, enthusiasm, etc: *science quickens man's imagination* 3 to make or become alive; revive 4a (of an unborn fetus) to begin to show signs of life 4b (of a pregnant woman) to reach the stage of pregnancy at which movements of the fetus can be felt

quick-freeze *vb* **quick-freezes, quick-freezing, quick-froze, quick-frozen** (*tr*) to preserve (food) by subjecting it to rapid refrigeration at temperatures of 0°C or lower

quickie ('kwɪkɪ) *n inf* 1 Also called (esp Brit): **quick one** a speedily consumed alcoholic drink 2a anything made or done rapidly 2b (*as modifier*): *a quickie divorce*

quicklime ('kwɪkˌlaɪm) *n* another name for **calcium oxide**

quick march *n* 1 a march at quick time or the order to proceed at such a pace ▷ *interj* 2 a command to commence such a march

quicksand ('kwɪkˌsænd) *n* a deep mass of loose wet sand that sucks anything on top of it inextricably into it

quickset ('kwɪkˌsɛt) *chiefly Brit* ▷ *n* 1a a plant or cutting, esp of hawthorn, set so as to form a hedge **1b** such plants or cuttings collectively **2** a hedge composed of such plants ▷ *adj* **3** composed of such plants

quicksilver (ˈkwɪkˌsɪlvə) *n* **1** another name for **mercury** (sense 1) ▷ *adj* **2** rapid or unpredictable in movement or change

quickstep (ˈkwɪkˌstɛp) *n* **1** a modern ballroom dance in rapid quadruple time **2** a piece of music composed for or in the rhythm of this dance ▷ *vb* **quicksteps, quickstepping, quickstepped** **3** (*intr*) to perform this dance

quick-tempered *adj* readily roused to anger; irascible

quickthorn (ˈkwɪkˌθɔːn) *n* hawthorn, esp when planted as a hedge [C17 prob. from *quick* in the sense "fast-growing": cf. QUICKSET]

quick time *n mil* the normal marching rate of 120 paces to the minute

quick-witted *adj* having a keenly alert mind, esp as used to avert danger, make effective reply, etc > ˌ**quick-ˈwittedly** *adv* > ˌ**quick-ˈwittedness** *n*

quid¹ (kwɪd) *n* a piece of tobacco, suitable for chewing [OE *cwidu* chewing resin]

quid² (kwɪd) *n, pl* **quid** *Brit sl* **1** a pound (sterling) **2** (**be**) **quids in** (to be) in a very favourable or advantageous position [C17 from ?]

quidditch (ˈkwɪdɪtʃ) an imaginary game in which players fly on broomsticks [C20 coined by the British novelist J.K. Rowling (born 1965) in the novel *Harry Potter and the Philosopher's Stone*]

quiddity (ˈkwɪdɪtɪ) *n, pl* **quiddities** **1** the essential nature of something **2** a petty or trifling distinction; quibble [C16 from Med. L *quidditās*, from L *quid* what]

quidnunc (ˈkwɪdˌnʌŋk) *n* a person eager to learn news and scandal; gossipmonger [C18 from L, lit.: what now]

quid pro quo (ˈkwɪd prəʊ ˈkwəʊ) *n, pl* **quid pro quos** **1** a reciprocal exchange **2** something given in compensation, esp an advantage or object given in exchange for another [C16 from L: something for something]

quiescent (kwɪˈɛsᵊnt) *adj* quiet, inactive, or dormant [C17 from L *quiescere* to rest] > **quiˈescence** *or* **quiˈescency** *n* > **quiˈescently** *adv*

quiet (ˈkwaɪət) *adj* **1** characterized by an absence of noise **2** calm or tranquil: *the sea is quiet tonight* **3** free from activities, distractions, etc; untroubled: *a quiet life* **4** short of work, orders, etc; not busy: *business is quiet today* **5** private; not public; secret: *a quiet word with someone* **6** free from anger, impatience, or other extreme emotion **7** free from pretentiousness; modest or reserved: *quiet humour* **8** *astron* (of the sun) exhibiting a very low number of sunspots, solar flares, etc; inactive ▷ *n* **9** the state of being silent, peaceful, or untroubled **10** **on the quiet** without other people knowing ▷ *vb* **11** a less common word for **quieten** [C14 from L *quiētus*, p.p. of *quiēscere* to rest, from *quiēs* repose] > ˈ**quietness** *n*

quieten (ˈkwaɪətᵊn) *vb chiefly Brit* **1** (often foll by *down*) to make or become calm, silent, etc **2** (*tr*) to allay (fear, doubts, etc)

quietism (ˈkwaɪəˌtɪzəm) *n* **1** a form of religious mysticism originating in Spain in the late 17th century, requiring complete passivity to God's will **2** passivity and calmness of mind towards external events > ˈ**quietist** *n, adj*

quietly (ˈkwaɪətlɪ) *adv* **1** in a quiet manner **2** **just quietly** *Austral* confidentially

quietude (ˈkwaɪəˌtjuːd) *n* the state or condition of being quiet, peaceful, calm, or tranquil

quietus (kwaɪˈiːtəs, -ˈeɪtəs) *n, pl* **quietuses** **1** anything that serves to quash, eliminate, or kill **2** a release from life; death **3** the discharge or settlement of debts, duties, etc [C16 from L *quiētus est*, lit.: he is at rest]

quiff (kwɪf) *n Brit* a tuft of hair brushed up above the forehead [C19 from ?]

quill (kwɪl) *n* **1a** any of the large stiff feathers of the wing or tail of a bird **1b** the long hollow part of a feather; calamus **2** Also called: **quill pen** a feather made into a pen for writing **3** any of the stiff hollow spines of a porcupine or hedgehog **4** a device, formerly made from a crow quill, for plucking a harpsichord string **5** a small roll of bark, esp one of dried cinnamon **6** a bobbin or spindle **7** a fluted fold, as in a ruff ▷ *vb* (*tr*) **8** to wind (thread, etc) onto a spool or bobbin **9** to make or press fluted folds in (a ruff, etc) [C15 (in the sense: hollow reed or pipe): from ?; cf. MLow G *quiele* quill]

▷ www.handcraftersvillage.com/quilling.htm

Quilmes (*Spanish* ˈkilmes) *n* a city in E Argentina: a resort and suburb of Buenos Aires. Pop: 550 069 (1999 est)

quilt (kwɪlt) *n* **1** a cover for a bed, consisting of a soft filling sewn between two layers of material, usually with crisscross seams **2** short for **continental quilt** **3** a bedspread **4** anything resembling a quilt ▷ *vb* (*tr*) **5** to stitch together (two pieces of fabric) with (a thick padding or lining) between them **6** to create (a garment, etc) in this way **7** to pad with material [C13 from OF *coilte* mattress, from L *culcita* stuffed item of bedding] > ˈ**quilted** *adj* > ˈ**quilter** *n*

quilting (ˈkwɪltɪŋ) *n* **1** material for quilts **2** the act of making a quilt **3** quilted work

▷ www.quilts.com

▷ www.pbs.org/americaquilts

Quimper (*French* kɛ̃pɛr) *n* a city in NW France: capital of Finistère department. Pop: 62 540 (1990)

quin (kwɪn) *n Brit* short for **quintuplet** (sense 1) US and Canad word: **quint**

quinary (ˈkwaɪnərɪ) *adj* **1** of or by fives **2** fifth in a series **3** (of a number system) having a base of five [C17 from L *quīnārius* containing five, from *quīnī* five each]

quince (kwɪns) *n* **1** a small widely cultivated Asian tree with edible pear-shaped fruits **2** the fruit of this tree, much used in preserves **3** **Japanese** *or* **flowering quince** another name for **japonica** [C14 *qwince* pl. of *quyn*, from OF *coin*, from L *cotōneum*, from Gk *kudōnion* quince]

quincentenary (ˌkwɪnsɛnˈtiːnərɪ) *n, pl* **quincentenaries** a 500th anniversary [C19 irregularly from L *quinque* five + CENTENARY] > **quincentennial** (ˌkwɪnsɛnˈtɛnɪəl) *adj, n*

quincunx (ˈkwɪnkʌŋks) *n* a group of five objects arranged in the shape of a rectangle with one at each of the four corners and the fifth in the centre [C17 from L: five twelfths, from *quinque* five + *uncia* twelfth; in ancient Rome, this was a coin worth five twelfths of an AS² and marked with five spots] > **quincuncial** (kwɪnˈkʌnʃəl) *adj*

Quine (kwaɪn) *n* **Willard van Orman** 1908–2000, US philosopher. His works include *Word and Object* (1960), *Philosophy of Logic* (1970), *The Roots of Reference* (1973), and *The Logic of Sequences* (1990)

quinella (kwɪˈnɛlə) *n Austral* a form of betting in which the punter must select the first and second place winners, in any order [from American Sp. *quiniela*]

Qui Nhong (ˈkwiː ˈnjɒŋ) *n* a port in SE Vietnam, on the South China Sea. Pop: 163 385 (1992 est)

quinidine (ˈkwɪnɪˌdiːn) *n* a crystalline alkaloid drug used to treat heart arrhythmias

quinine (kwɪˈniːn; *US* ˈkwaɪnaɪn) *n* a bitter crystalline alkaloid extracted from cinchona bark, the salts of which are used as a tonic, analgesic, etc, and in malaria therapy [C19 from Sp. *quina* cinchona bark, from Quechua *kina* bark]

quinoa (ˈkiːnəʊə, kwɪˈnəʊə) *n* a grain high in nutrients traditionally grown as a staple food high in the Andes [Sp.]

quinol (ˈkwɪnɒl) *n* another name for **hydroquinone**

quinoline (ˈkwɪnəˌliːn, -lɪn) *n* an oily colourless insoluble compound synthesized by heating aniline, nitrobenzene, glycerol, and sulphuric acid: used as a food preservative and in the manufacture of dyes and antiseptics. Formula: C_9H_7N

quinquagenarian (ˌkwɪŋkwədʒɪˈnɛərɪən) *n* **1** a person between 50 and 59 years old ▷ *adj* **2** being between 50 and 59 years old **3** of a quinquagenarian [c16 from L *quinquāgēnārius* containing fifty, from *quinquāgēnī* fifty each]
Quinquagesima (ˌkwɪŋkwəˈdʒɛsɪmə) *n* the Sunday preceding Lent. Also called: **Quinquagesima Sunday** [c14 via Med. L from L *quinquāgēsima diēs* fiftieth day]
quinquecentenary (ˌkwɪŋkwɪsɛnˈtiːnərɪ) *n, pl* **quinquecentenaries** another name for **quincentenary**
quinquennial (kwɪnˈkwɛnɪəl) *adj* **1** occurring once every five years or over a period of five years ▷ *n* **2** a fifth anniversary > **quinˈquennially** *adv*
quinquennium (kwɪnˈkwɛnɪəm) *n, pl* **quinquennia** (-nɪə) a period or cycle of five years [c17 from L *quinque* five + *annus* year]
quinquereme (ˌkwɪŋkwɪˈriːm) *n* an ancient Roman galley with five banks of oars [c16 from L *quinquerēmis*, from *quinque-* five + *rēmus* oar]
quinquevalent (ˌkwɪŋkwɪˈveɪlənt) *adj chem* another word for **pentavalent** > **ˌquinqueˈvalency** *or* **ˌquinqueˈvalence** *n*
quinsy (ˈkwɪnzɪ) *n* inflammation of the tonsils and surrounding tissues with the formation of abscesses [c14 via OF & Med. L from Gk *kunankhē*, from *kuōn* dog + *ankhein* to strangle]
quint[1] *n* **1** (kwɪnt) an organ stop sounding a note a fifth higher **2** (kɪnt) *piquet* a sequence of five cards in the same suit [c17 from F *quinte*, from L *quintus* fifth]
quint[2] (kwɪnt) *n* the US and Canad word for **quin**
quintain (ˈkwɪntɪn) *n* (esp in medieval Europe) a post or target set up for tilting exercises for mounted knights or foot soldiers [c14 from OF *quintaine*, from L: street in a Roman camp between the fifth & sixth maniples (the maniple was a unit of 120–200 soldiers in ancient Rome), from *quintus* fifth]
quintal (ˈkwɪntᵊl) *n* **1** a unit of weight equal to (esp in Britain) 112 pounds or (esp in US) 100 pounds **2** a unit of weight equal to 100 kilograms [c15 via OF from Ar. *qinṭār*, possibly from L *centēnārius* consisting of a hundred]
quintan (ˈkwɪntən) *adj* (of a fever) occurring every fourth day [c17 from L *febris quintāna* fever occurring every fifth day, reckoned inclusively]
Quintana Roo (*Spanish* kinˈtana ˈrɔo) *n* a state of SE Mexico, on the E Yucatán Peninsula: hot, humid, forested, and inhabited chiefly by Maya Indians. Capital: Chetumal. Pop: 873 804 (2000). Area: 50 350 sq km (19 463 sq miles)
quinte (kænt) *n* the fifth of eight basic positions from which a parry or attack can be made in fencing [c18 F from L *quintus* fifth]
quintessence (kwɪnˈtɛsəns) *n* **1** the most typical representation of a quality, state, etc **2** an extract of a substance containing its principle in its most concentrated form **3** (in ancient philosophy) ether, the fifth essence or element, which was thought to be the constituent matter of the heavenly bodies and latent in all things [c15 via F from Med. L *quinta essentia* the fifth essence, translation of Gk] > **quintessential** (ˌkwɪntɪˈsɛnʃəl) *adj* > **ˌquintesˈsentially** *adv*
quintet *or* **quintette** (kwɪnˈtɛt) *n* **1** a group of five singers or instrumentalists or a piece of music composed for such a group **2** any group of five [c19 from It. *quintetto*, from *quinto* fifth]
quintillion (kwɪnˈtɪljən) *n, pl* **quintillions** *or* **quintillion** **1** (in Britain, France, and Germany) the number represented as one followed by 30 zeros (10^{30}). US and Canad word: **nonillion** **2** (in the US and Canada) the number represented as one followed by 18 zeros (10^{18}). Brit word: **trillion** [c17 from L *quintus* fifth + *-illion*, as in MILLION] > **quinˈtillionth** *adj*
quintuple (ˈkwɪntjʊpᵊl, kwɪnˈtjuːpᵊl) *vb* **quintuples, quintupling, quintupled** **1** to multiply by five ▷ *adj* **2** five times as much or as many; fivefold **3** consisting of five parts ▷ *n* **4** a quantity or number five times as great as another [c16 from F, from L *quintus*, on the model of QUADRUPLE]
quintuplet (ˈkwɪntjʊplɪt, kwɪnˈtjuːplɪt) *n* **1** one of five offspring born at one birth **2** a group of five similar things **3** *music* a group of five notes to be played in a time value of three or four
quintuplicate *adj* (kwɪnˈtjuːplɪkɪt) **1** fivefold or quintuple ▷ *vb* (kwɪnˈtjuːplɪˌkeɪt), **quintuplicates, quintuplicating, quintuplicated** **2** to multiply or be multiplied by five ▷ *n* (kwɪnˈtjuːplɪkɪt) **3** a group or set of five things
quip (kwɪp) *n* **1** a sarcastic remark **2** a witty saying **3** *arch* another word for **quibble** ▷ *vb* **quips, quipping, quipped** **4** (*intr*) to make a quip [c16 from earlier *quippy*, prob. from L *quippe* indeed, to be sure] > **ˈquipster** *n*
quire (ˈkwaɪə) *n* **1** a set of 24 or 25 sheets of paper **2** four sheets of paper folded to form 16 pages **3** a set of all the sheets in a book [c15 *quayer*, from OF *quaier*, from L *quaternī* four at a time, from *quater* four times]
Quirinal (ˈkwɪrɪnᵊl) *n* one of the seven hills on which ancient Rome was built
Quirinus (kwɪˈraɪnəs) *n Roman myth* a god of war, who came to be identified with the deified Romulus
quirk (kwɜːk) *n* **1** a peculiarity of character; mannerism or foible **2** an unexpected twist or turn: *a quirk of fate* **3** a continuous groove in an architectural moulding **4** a flourish, as in handwriting [c16 from ?] > **ˈquirky** *adj* > **ˈquirkiness** *n*
quirt (kwɜːt) *US & S African* *n* **1** a whip with a leather thong at one end ▷ *vb* (*tr*) **2** to strike with a quirt [c19 from Sp. *cuerda* CORD]
quisling (ˈkwɪzlɪŋ) *n* a traitor who aids an occupying enemy force; collaborator [c20 after Major Vidkun *Quisling* (1887–1945), Norwegian collaborator with the Nazis]
quit (kwɪt) *vb* **quits, quitting, quitted** *or* **quit** **1** (*tr*) to depart from; leave **2** to resign; give up (a job) **3** (*intr*) (of a tenant) to give up occupancy of premises and leave them **4** to desist or cease from (something or doing something) **5** (*tr*) to pay off (a debt) **6** (*tr*) *arch* to conduct or acquit (oneself); comport (oneself) ▷ *adj* **7** (*usually predicative; foll by of*) free (from); released (from) [c13 from OF *quitter*, from L *quiētus* QUIET]
quitch grass (kwɪtʃ) *n* another name for **couch grass** Sometimes shortened to **quitch** [OE *cwice*; ? rel. to *cwicu* living, QUICK (with the implication that the grass cannot be killed)]
quitclaim (ˈkwɪtˌkleɪm) *law* ▷ *n* **1** a renunciation of a claim or right ▷ *vb* **2** (*tr*) to renounce (a claim) [c14 from Anglo-F *quiteclame*, from *quite* QUIT + *clamer* to declare (from L *clamāre* to shout)]
quite (kwaɪt) *adv* **1** completely or absolutely: *you're quite right* **2** (*not used with a negative*) somewhat: *she's quite pretty* **3** in actuality; truly **4** **quite a** *or* **an** (*not used with a negative*) of an exceptional, considerable, or noticeable kind: *quite a girl* **5** **quite something** a remarkable or noteworthy thing or person ▷ *sentence substitute* **6** Also: **quite so** an expression used to indicate agreement [c14 adverbial use of *quite* (adj) QUIT]

USAGE See at **very**

Quito (ˈkiːtəʊ; *Spanish* ˈkito) *n* the capital of Ecuador, in the north at an altitude of 2850 m (9350 ft), just south of the equator: the oldest capital in South America, existing many centuries before the Incan conquest in 1487; a cultural centre since the beginning of Spanish rule (1534); two universities. Pop: 1 487 513 (1997 est) ▷ www.quito.gov.ec
quitrent (ˈkwɪtˌrɛnt) *n* (formerly) a rent payable by a freeholder or copyholder to his lord in lieu of services
quits (kwɪts) *adj* (*postpositive*) *inf* **1** on an equal footing;

even **2 call it quits** to agree to end a dispute, contest, etc, agreeing that honours are even
quittance ('kwɪtᵊns) *n* **1** release from debt or other obligation **2** a receipt or other document certifying this [C13 from OF, from *quitter* to release from obligation; see QUIT]
quitter ('kwɪtə) *n* a person who gives up easily
quiver[1] ('kwɪvə) *vb* **1** *(intr)* to shake with a tremulous movement; tremble ▷ *n* **2** the state, process, or noise of shaking or trembling [C15 from obs. *cwiver* quick, nimble] > **'quivering** *adj* > **'quivery** *adj*
quiver[2] ('kwɪvə) *n* a case for arrows [C13 from OF *cuivre*]
qui vive (ˌkiː 'viːv) *n* **on the qui vive** on the alert; attentive [C18 from F, lit.: long live who?, sentry's challenge (equivalent to "Whose side are you on?")]
Quixote ('kwɪksət; *Spanish* ki'xote) *n* See **Don Quixote**
quixotic (kwɪk'sɒtɪk) *adj* preoccupied with an unrealistically optimistic or chivalrous approach to life; impractically idealistic [C18 after DON QUIXOTE] > **quix'otically** *adv*
quiz (kwɪz) *n, pl* **quizzes 1a** an entertainment in which the knowledge of the players is tested by a series of questions **1b** *(as modifier)*: *a quiz programme* **2** any set of quick questions designed to test knowledge **3** an investigation by close questioning **4** *obs* a practical joke **5** *obs* a puzzling individual **6** *obs* a person who habitually looks quizzically at others ▷ *vb* **quizzes, quizzing, quizzed** *(tr)* **7** to investigate by close questioning; interrogate **8** *US & Canad inf* to test the knowledge of (a student or class) **9** *(tr) obs* to look quizzically at, esp through a small monocle [C18 from ?] > **'quizzer** *n*
quizzical ('kwɪzɪkᵊl) *adj* questioning and mocking or supercilious > **'quizzically** *adv*
Qum (kʊm) *n* a variant of **Qom**
Qumran ('kʊmrɑːn) *n* See **Khirbet Qumran**
Qungur ('kʊngʊə) *n* a variant transliteration of the Chinese name for **Kongur Shan**
quod (kwɒd) *n chiefly Brit* a slang word for **jail** [C18 from ?]
quod erat demonstrandum *Latin* ('kwɒd 'ɛræt ˌdɛmən'strændʊm) (at the conclusion of a proof, esp of a theorem in Euclidean geometry) which was to be proved. Abbrev: **QED**
quodlibet ('kwɒdlɪˌbɛt) *n* **1** a light piece of music **2** a subtle argument, esp one prepared as an exercise on a theological topic [C14 from L, from *quod* what + *libet* pleases, that is, whatever you like]
quoin (kwɔɪn, kɔɪn) *n* **1** an external corner of a wall **2** a stone forming the external corner of a wall **3** another name for **keystone** (sense 1) **4** *printing* a wedge or an expanding device used to lock type up in a chase **5** a wedge used for any of various other purposes [C16 var. of *coin* (in former sense of corner)]
quoit (kɔɪt) *n* a ring of iron, plastic, etc, used in the game of quoits [C15 from ?]
quoits (kɔɪts) *pl n (usually functioning as sing)* a game in which quoits are tossed at a stake in the ground in attempts to encircle it
▷ www.britishsports.com/quoits
quokka ('kwɒkə) *n* a small wallaby of Western Australia, now rare [of Abor. origin]
quoll ('kwɒl) *n Austral* another name for **native cat** [C18 from a native Australian language]
quondam ('kwɒndæm) *adj (prenominal)* of an earlier time; former [C16 from L]
quorate ('kwɔːˌreɪt) *adj Brit* consisting of or being a quorum: *the meeting was quorate*
Quorn (kwɔːn) *n trademark* a vegetable protein developed from a type of fungus and used as a meat substitute
quorum ('kwɔːrəm) *n* a minimum number of members in an assembly, etc, required to be present before any business can be transacted [C15 from L, lit.: of whom, occurring in L commissions in the formula *quorum vos...duos* (etc.) *volumus* of whom we wish that you be...two (etc.)]
quota ('kwəʊtə) *n* **1** the proportional share or part that is due from, due to, or allocated to a person or group **2** a prescribed number or quantity, as of items to be imported or students admitted to a college, etc [C17 from L *quota pars* how big a share?, from *quotus* of what number]
quotable ('kwəʊtəbᵊl) *adj* apt or suitable for quotation > **ˌquota'bility** *n*
quota sampling *n marketing* a method of conducting marketing research in which the sample is selected according to a quota system based on such factors as age, sex, social class, etc
quotation (kwəʊ'teɪʃən) *n* **1** a phrase or passage from a book, speech, etc, remembered and repeated, usually with an acknowledgment of its source **2** the act or habit of quoting **3a** a cost estimate for goods or services given to a prospective client **3b** the current market price of a commodity, security, etc **4** *printing* a quad used to fill up spaces
quotation mark *n* either of the punctuation marks used to begin or end a quotation, respectively " and " or ' and ' Also called: **inverted comma**
quote (kwəʊt) *vb* **quotes, quoting, quoted 1** to recite a quotation **2** *(tr)* to put quotation marks round (a phrase, etc) **3a** to give (a cost estimate for specified goods or services) to a prospective client **3b** to state (the current market price) of (a security or commodity) ▷ *n* **4** an informal word for **quotation 5** *(often pl)* an informal word for **quotation mark** ▷ *interj* **6** an expression used to indicate that the words that follow it form a quotation [C14 from Med. L *quotāre* to assign reference numbers to passages, from L *quot* how many]
quoted company *n* a company whose shares are quoted on a stock exchange
quote-driven *adj* denoting an electronic market system, esp for stock exchanges, in which prices are determined by quotations made by market makers or dealers ▷ Cf **order-driven**
quote-unquote *interj* an expression used before or part before and part after a quotation to identify it as such, and sometimes to dissociate the writer or speaker from it
quoth (kwəʊθ) *vb arch* (used with all pronouns except *thou* and *you*, and with nouns) said [OE *cwæth*, third person sing of *cwethan* to say]
quotha ('kwəʊθə) *interj arch* an expression of mild sarcasm, used in picking up a word or phrase used by someone else [C16 from *quoth a* quoth he]
quotidian (kwəʊ'tɪdɪən) *adj* **1** (esp of fever) recurring daily **2** commonplace ▷ *n* **3** a fever characterized by attacks that recur daily [C14 from L *quotīdiānus*, var. of *cottīdiānus* daily]
quotient ('kwəʊʃənt) *n* **1a** the result of the division of one number or quantity by another **1b** the integral part of the result of division **2** a ratio of two numbers or quantities to be divided [C15 from L *quotiens* how often]
quo vadis ('kwəʊ 'vɑːdɪs) where are you going? [L from the Vulgate version of John 16:5]
quo warranto ('kwəʊ wɒ'ræntəʊ) *n law* a proceeding initiated to determine or (formerly) a writ demanding by what authority a person claims an office, franchise, or privilege [from Med. L: by what warrant]
Qur'an (kʊ'rɑːn, -'ræn) *n* a variant spelling of **Koran**
q.v. (denoting a cross-reference) *abbrev for* quod vide [NL: which (word, item, etc) see]
qwerty *or* **QWERTY keyboard** ('kwɜːtɪ) *n* the standard English language typewriter keyboard layout with the characters q, w, e, r, t, and y at the top left of the keyboard.

Rr

r *or* **R** (ɑː) *n, pl* **r's, R's,** *or* **Rs 1** the 18th letter of the English alphabet **2** a speech sound represented by this letter **3** See **three Rs**

R *symbol for:* **1** *chem* gas constant **2** *chem* radical **3** *currency* **3a** rand **3b** rupee **4** Réaumur (scale) **5** *physics, electronics* resistance **6** roentgen *or* röntgen **7** *chess* rook **8** Royal **9** (in the US and Australia) **9a** restricted exhibition (used to describe a category of film certified as unsuitable for viewing by anyone under the age of 18) **9b** *(as modifier): an R film*

r. *abbrev for:* **1** rare **2** recto **3** Also: r rod (unit of length) **4** ruled **5** *cricket* run(s)

R. *abbrev for:* **1** rabbi **2** rector **3** Regina [L: Queen] **4** Republican **5** Rex [L: King] **6** River **7** Royal

R. *or* **r.** *abbrev for:* **1** radius **2** railway **3** registered (trademark) **4** right **5** river **6** road **7** rouble

Ra[1] *the chemical symbol for* radium

Ra[2] (rɑː) *or* **Re** *n* the ancient Egyptian sun god, depicted as a man with a hawk's head surmounted by a solar disc and serpent

RA *abbrev for:* **1** rear admiral **2** *astron* right ascension **3** (in Britain) Royal Academician *or* Academy **4** (in Britain) Royal Artillery

RAAF *abbrev for* Royal Australian Air Force
▷ www.defence.gov.au/raaf

Rabat (rəˈbɑːt) *n* the capital of Morocco, in the northwest on the Atlantic coast, served by the port of Salé: became a military centre in the 12th century and a Corsair republic in the 17th century. Pop (with Salé): 1 386 000 (1994 est)
▷ www.mincom.gov.ma/english/reg_cit/cities/rabat/rabat.html
▷ www.cyber.net.ma/chadiatours/images/rabat2.htm

Rabaul (rɑːˈbaʊl) *n* a port in Papua New Guinea, on NE New Britain Island, in the Bismarck Archipelago: capital of the Territory of New Guinea until 1941; almost surrounded by volcanoes. Pop: 17 022 (1990)

Rabbath Ammon (ˈræbəθ ˈæmən) *n Old Testament* the ancient royal city of the Ammonites, on the site of modern Amman

rabbet (ˈræbɪt) *or* **rebate** *n* **1** a recess, groove, or step, usually of rectangular section, cut into a piece of timber to receive a mating piece ▷ *vb* **rabbets, rabbeting, rabbeted** *or* **rebates, rebating, rebated** *(tr)* **2** to cut a rabbet in (timber) **3** to join (pieces of timber) using a rabbet [c15 from OF *rabattre* to beat down]

rabbi (ˈræbaɪ) *n, pl* **rabbis 1** the spiritual leader of a Jewish congregation; the chief religious minister of a synagogue **2** a scholar learned in Jewish Law, esp one authorized to teach it [Heb., from *rabh* master + -ī my]

rabbinate (ˈræbɪnɪt) *n* **1** the position, function, or tenure of office of a rabbi **2** rabbis collectively

rabbinic (rəˈbɪnɪk) *or* **rabbinical** (rəˈbɪnɪkᵊl) *adj* of or relating to the rabbis, their teachings, writings, views, language, etc > **rabˈbinically** *adv*

Rabbinic (rəˈbɪnɪk) *n* the form of the Hebrew language used by the rabbis of the Middle Ages

rabbit (ˈræbɪt) *n, pl* **rabbits** *or* **rabbit 1** any of various common gregarious burrowing mammals of Europe and North Africa. They are closely related and similar to hares but are smaller and have shorter ears **2** the fur of such an animal **3** *Brit inf* a poor performer at a game or sport ▷ *vb* **4** *(intr)* to hunt or shoot rabbits **5** *(intr)* (often foll by *on* or *away*) *Brit inf* to talk inconsequentially; chatter [c14 ?from Walloon *robett*, dim. of Flemish *robbe* rabbit, from ?]

rabbit fever *n pathol* another name for **tularaemia**

rabbit punch *n* a short sharp blow to the back of the neck that can cause loss of consciousness or even death. Austral name: **rabbit killer**

rabble (ˈræbᵊl) *n* **1** a disorderly crowd; mob **2 the rabble** *contemptuous* the common people [c14 (in the sense: a pack of animals): from ?]

rabble-rouser *n* a person who manipulates the passions of the mob; demagogue > **ˈrabble-ˌrousing** *adj, n*

Rabelais (ˈræbəˌleɪ; *French* rablɛ) *n* **François** (frɑ̃swa) ?1494–1553, French writer. His written works, esp *Gargantua and Pantagruel* (1534), contain a lively mixture of earthy wit, common sense, and satire

Rabelaisian (ˌræbəˈleɪzɪən, -ʒən) *adj* **1** of, relating to, or resembling the work of Rabelais, esp by broad, often bawdy, humour and sharp satire ▷ *n* **2** a student or admirer of Rabelais > **ˌRabeˈlaisianism** *n*

Rabi (ˈrɑːbɪ) *n* **Isidor Isaac** 1898–1988, US physicist, born in Austria, who devised the atomic and molecular beam resonance method of observing atomic spectra. Nobel prize for physics 1944

rabid (ˈræbɪd, ˈreɪ-) *adj* **1** relating to or having rabies: *a rabid dog* **2** zealous; fanatical; violent; raging: *a rabid anti-semite* [c17 from L *rabidus* frenzied, from *rabere* to be mad] > **rabidity** (rəˈbɪdɪtɪ) *or* **ˈrabidness** *n* > **ˈrabidly** *adv*

rabies (ˈreɪbiːz) *n pathol* an acute infectious viral disease of the nervous system transmitted by the saliva of infected animals, esp dogs [c17 from L: madness, from *rabere* to rave] > **rabic** (ˈræbɪk) *or* **rabietic** (ˌreɪbɪˈɛtɪk) *adj*

Rabin (rəˈbiːn) *n* **Yitzhak** 1922–95, Israeli statesman; prime minister of Israel (1974–77; 1992–95); assassinated

RAC *abbrev for:* **1** Royal Armoured Corps **2** Royal Automobile Club

raccoon *or* **racoon** (rəˈkuːn) *n, pl* **raccoons, raccoon** *or* **racoons, racoon 1** an omnivorous mammal, esp the **North American raccoon**, inhabiting forests of North and Central America. Raccoons have a pointed muzzle, long tail, and greyish-black fur with black bands around the tail and across the face **2** the fur of the raccoon [c17 from Algonquian *ärähkun*, from *ärähkuněm* he scratches with his hands]

race¹ (reɪs) *n* **1** a contest of speed, as in running, etc **2** any competition or rivalry **3** rapid or constant onward movement: *the race of time* **4** a rapid current of water, esp one through a narrow channel that has a tidal range greater at one end than the other **5** a channel of a stream, esp one for conducting water to or from a water wheel for energy: *a mill race* **6a** a channel or groove that contains ball bearings or roller bearings **6b** the inner or outer cylindrical ring in a ball bearing or roller bearing **7** *Austral & NZ* a narrow passage or enclosure in a sheep yard through which sheep pass individually, as to a sheep dip **8** *Austral* a wire tunnel through which footballers pass from the changing room onto a football field **9** *arch* the span or course of life ▷ *vb* **races, racing, raced 10** to engage in a contest of speed with (another) **11** to cause (animals, etc) to engage in a race: *to race pigeons* **12** to move or go as fast as possible **13** to run (an engine, propeller, etc) or (of an engine, propeller, etc) to run at high speed, esp after reduction of the load ▷ See also **races** [c13 from ON *rās* running]

race² (reɪs) *n* **1** a group of people of common ancestry, distinguished from others by physical characteristics, such as hair type, colour of skin, stature, etc **2 the human race** human beings collectively **3** a group of animals or plants having common characteristics that distinguish them from other members of the same species, usually forming a geographically isolated group; subspecies **4** a group of people sharing the same interests, characteristics, etc: *race of authors* [c16 from F, from It. *razza*, from ?]

Race (reɪs) *n* **Cape** a cape at the SE extremity of Newfoundland, Canada

racecard (ˈreɪsˌkɑːd) *n* a card at a race meeting with the races and runners, etc, printed on it

racecourse (ˈreɪsˌkɔːs) *n* a long broad track, over which horses are raced. Also called (esp US and Canad): **racetrack**

racehorse (ˈreɪsˌhɔːs) *n* a horse specially bred for racing

raceme (rəˈsiːm) *n* an inflorescence in which the flowers are borne along the main stem [c18 from L *racēmus* bunch of grapes] > **racemose** (ˈræsɪˌməʊs, -məʊz) *adj*

race meeting *n* a prearranged fixture for racing horses (or greyhounds) over a set course

racemic (rəˈsiːmɪk, -ˈsɛm-) *adj chem* of, or being a mixture of dextrorotatory and laevorotatory isomers in such proportions that the mixture has no optical activity [c19 from RACEME + -IC] > **racemism** (ˈræsɪˌmɪzəm) *n*

racer (ˈreɪsə) *n* **1** a person, animal, or machine that races **2** a turntable used to traverse a heavy gun **3** any of several slender nonvenomous North American snakes, such as the **striped racer**

race relations *n* **1** (*functioning as pl*) the relations between members of two or more human races, esp within a single community **2** (*functioning as sing*) the branch of sociology concerned with such relations

race riot *n* a riot among members of different races in the same community

races (ˈreɪsɪz) *pl n* **the races** a series of contests of speed between horses (or greyhounds) over a set course

racetrack (ˈreɪsˌtræk) *n* **1** a circuit or course, esp an oval one, used for motor racing, etc **2** the usual US and Canad word for **racecourse**

raceway (ˈreɪsˌweɪ) *n* **1** another word for **race¹** (senses 5, 6) **2** *chiefly US* a racetrack

Rachel (ˈreɪtʃəl) *n Old Testament* the second wife of Jacob; mother of Joseph and Benjamin (Genesis 29–35)

rachis *or* **rhachis** (ˈreɪkɪs) *n, pl* **rachises, rhachises** *or* **rachides, rhachides** (ˈrækɪˌdiːz, ˈreɪ-) **1** *bot* the main axis or stem of an inflorescence or compound leaf **2** *ornithol* the shaft of a feather, esp the part that carries the barbs **3** another name for **spinal column** [c17 via NL from Gk *rhakhis* ridge] > **rachial, rhachial** (ˈreɪkɪəl) *or* **rachidial, rhachidial** (rəˈkɪdɪəl) *adj*

Rr

rachitis (rəˈkaɪtɪs) *n pathol* another name for **rickets** > **rachitic** (rəˈkɪtɪk) *adj*

Rachmaninoff *or* **Rachmaninov** (rækˈmænɪˌnɒf; *Russian* raxˈmaninəf) *n* **Sergei Vassilievich** (sɪrˈgjej vaˈsiljɪvɪtʃ) 1873–1943, Russian piano virtuoso and composer

Rachmanism (ˈrækməˌnɪzəm) *n* extortion or exploitation by a landlord of tenants of slum property [c20 after Perec *Rachman* (1920–62), Brit property-owner]

racial (ˈreɪʃəl) *adj* **1** denoting or relating to the division of the human species into races on grounds of physical characteristics **2** characteristic of any such group > **ˈracially** *adv*

Racine (*French* rasin) *n* **Jean Baptiste** (ʒɑ̃ batist) 1639–99, French tragic poet and dramatist. His plays include *Andromaque* (1667), *Bérénice* (1670), and *Phèdre* (1677)

racism (ˈreɪsɪzəm) *or* **racialism** (ˈreɪʃəˌlɪzəm) *n* **1** the belief that races have distinctive cultural characteristics determined by hereditary factors and that this endows some races with an intrinsic superiority **2** abusive or aggressive behaviour towards members of another race on the basis of such a belief > **ˈracist** *or* **ˈracialist** *n, adj*

rack¹ (ræk) *n* **1** a framework for holding, carrying, or displaying a specific load or object **2** a toothed bar designed to engage a pinion to form a mechanism that will adjust the position of something **3** (preceded by *the*) an instrument of torture that stretched the body of the victim **4** a cause or state of mental or bodily stress, suffering, etc (esp in **on the rack**) **5** *US & Canad* (in pool, snooker, etc) **5a** the triangular frame used to arrange the balls for the opening shot **5b** the balls so grouped. Brit equivalent: **frame** ▷ *vb* (*tr*) **6** to torture on the rack **7** to cause great suffering to: *guilt racked his conscience* **8** to strain or shake (something) violently: *the storm racked the town* **9** to place or arrange in or on a rack **10** to move (parts of machinery or a mechanism) using a toothed rack **11** to raise (rents) exorbitantly **12** **rack one's brains** to strain in mental effort [C14 *rekke*, prob. from MDu. *rec* framework] > '**racker** *n*

USAGE See at **wrack**

rack² (ræk) *n* destruction; wreck (obs. except in **go to rack and ruin**) [C16 var. of WRACK¹]

rack³ (ræk) *n* another word for **single-foot** [C16 ? based on ROCK²]

rack⁴ (ræk) *n* **1** a group of broken clouds moving in the wind ▷ *vb* **2** (*intr*) (of clouds) to be blown along by the wind [OE *wrǣc* what is driven]

rack⁵ (ræk) *vb* (*tr*) to clear (wine, beer, etc) as by siphoning it off from the dregs [C15 from OProvençal *arraca*, from *raca* dregs of grapes after pressing]

rack-and-pinion *n* **1** a device for converting rotary into linear motion and vice versa, in which a gearwheel (the pinion) engages with a flat toothed bar (the rack) ▷ *adj* **2** (of a type of steering gear in motor vehicles) having a track rod with a rack along part of its length that engages with a pinion attached to the steering column

racket¹ ('rækɪt) *n* **1** a noisy disturbance or loud commotion; clamour; din **2** an illegal enterprise carried on for profit, such as extortion, fraud, etc **3** *sl* a business or occupation: *what's your racket?* **4** *music* a medieval woodwind instrument of deep bass pitch ▷ *vb* **5** (*intr*; often foll by *about*) *Now rare.* to go about gaily or noisily, in search of pleasure, etc [C16 prob. imit.] > '**rackety** *adj*

racket² *or* **racquet** ('rækɪt) *n* **1** a bat consisting of an open network of strings stretched in an oval frame with a handle, used to strike a tennis ball, etc **2** a snowshoe shaped like a tennis racket ▷ *vb* **3** (*tr*) to strike (a ball, etc) with a racket ▷ See also **rackets** [C16 from F *raquette*, from Ar. *rāhat* palm of the hand]

racketeer (ˌrækɪ'tɪə) *n* **1** a person engaged in illegal enterprises for profit ▷ *vb* **2** (*intr*) to operate an illegal enterprise > ˌ**racket'eering** *n*

racket press *n* a device consisting of a frame closed by a spring mechanism, for keeping taut the strings of a tennis racket, squash racket, etc

rackets ('rækɪts) *n* (*functioning as sing*) **a** a game similar to squash played in a four-walled court by two or four players using rackets and a small hard ball **b** (*as modifier*): *a rackets court*

Rackham ('rækəm) *n* **Arthur** 1867–1939, English artist, noted for his book illustrations, esp of fairy tales

rack off *vb* (*intr, adverb; usually imperative*) *Austral and NZ sl* to go away; depart

rack railway *n* a steep mountain railway having a middle rail fitted with a rack that engages a pinion on the locomotive to provide traction. Also called: **cog railway**

rack-rent *n* **1** a high rent that annually equals the value of the property upon which it is charged **2** any extortionate rent ▷ *vb* **3** to charge an extortionate rent for > '**rack-**ˌ**renter** *n*

rack saw *n building trades* a wide-toothed saw

racon ('reɪkɒn) *n* another name for **radar beacon** [C20 from RA(DAR) + (BEA)CON]

raconteur (ˌrækɒn'tɜː) *n* a person skilled in telling stories [C19 F, from *raconter* to tell]

racoon (rə'kuːn) *n, pl* **racoons** *or* **racoon** a variant spelling of **raccoon**

racquet ('rækɪt) *n* a variant spelling of **racket²**

racy ('reɪsɪ) *adj* **racier, raciest 1** (of a person's manner, literary style, etc) having a distinctively lively and spirited quality **2** having a characteristic or distinctive flavour: *a racy wine* **3** suggestive; slightly indecent; risqué > '**racily** *adv* > '**raciness** *n*

rad¹ (ræd) *n* a former unit of absorbed ionizing radiation dose equivalent to an energy absorption per unit mass of 0.01 joule per kilogram of irradiated material [C20 from RADIATION]

rad² *symbol for* radian

rad. *abbrev for:* **1** radical **2** radius

RADA ('rɑːdə) *n* (in Britain) *acronym for* Royal Academy of Dramatic Art

▷ www.rada.org

radar ('reɪdɑː) *n* **1** a method for detecting the position and velocity of a distant object. A narrow beam of extremely high-frequency radio pulses is transmitted and reflected by the object back to the transmitter. The direction of the reflected beam and the time between transmission and reception of a pulse determine the position of the object **2** the equipment used in such detection [C20 *ra(dio) d(etecting) a(nd) r(anging)*]

radar astronomy *n* the use of radar to map the surfaces of the planets, their satellites, and other bodies

radar beacon *n* a device for transmitting a coded radar signal in response to a signal from an aircraft or ship. The coded signal is then used by the navigator to determine his position. Also called: **racon**

radarscope ('reɪdɑːˌskəʊp) *n* a cathode-ray oscilloscope on which radar signals can be viewed

radar trap *n* a device using radar to detect motorists who exceed the speed limit

Radcliffe ('rædklɪf) *n* **1 Ann** 1764–1823, British novelist, noted for her Gothic romances *The Mysteries of Udolpho* (1794) and *The Italian* (1797) **2 Paula** (**Jane**) born 1973, British athlete, winner of the London Marathon (2002, 2003), and European Record Holder for the 10 000m

raddle ('rædᵊl) *vb* **raddles, raddling, raddled 1** (*tr*) *chiefly Brit* to paint (the face) with rouge ▷ *n, vb* **2** another word for **ruddle** [C16 var. of RUDDLE]

raddled ('rædᵊld) *adj* (esp of a person) unkempt or run-down in appearance

Radetzky (*German* ra'dɛtski) *n* Count **Joseph** ('joːzɛf) 1766–1858, Austrian field marshal: served in the war against Sardinia (1848–9), winning brilliant victories at Custozza (1848) and Novara (1849): governor of Lombardy-Venetia in N Italy (1849-57)

radial ('reɪdɪəl) *adj* **1** (of lines, etc) emanating from a common central point; arranged like the radii of a circle **2** of, like, or relating to a radius or ray **3** short for **radial-ply** **4** *anat* of or relating to the radius or forearm **5** *astron* (of velocity) in a direction along the line of sight of a celestial object and measured by means of the red shift (or blue shift) of the spectral lines of the object ▷ *n* **6** a radial part or section [C16 from Med. L *radiālis*, from RADIUS] > '**radially** *adv*

radial engine *n* an internal-combustion engine having a number of cylinders arranged about a central crankcase

radial-ply *adj* (of a motor tyre) having the fabric cords in the outer casing running radially to enable the sidewalls to be flexible

radial symmetry *n* a type of structure of an organism in which a vertical cut through the axis in any of two or more planes produces two halves that are mirror images of each other ▷ Cf **bilateral symmetry**

radian ('reɪdɪən) *n* an SI unit of plane angle; the angle between two radii of a circle that cut off on the circumference an arc equal in length to the radius. 1 radian is equivalent to 57.296 degrees. Symbol: rad [C19 from RADIUS]

radiance ('reɪdɪəns) *or* **radiancy** *n, pl* **radiances** *or* **radiancies 1** the quality or state of being radiant **2** a measure of the amount of electromagnetic radiation leaving or arriving at a point on a surface

radiant ('reɪdɪənt) *adj* **1** sending out rays of light; bright; shining **2** characterized by health, happiness, etc: *a radiant smile* **3** emitted or propagated by or as radiation; radiated: *radiant heat* **4** sending out heat by radiation: *a radiant heater* **5** *physics* (of a physical quantity in photometry) evaluated by absolute energy measurements: *radiant flux* ▷ *n* **6** a point or object that emits radiation, esp the part of a heater that gives out heat **7** *astron* the point in the sky from which a meteor shower appears to emanate [C15 from L *radiāre* to shine, from *radius* ray of light] > **'radiancy** *n* > **'radiantly** *adv*

radiant energy *n* energy that is emitted or propagated in the form of particles or electromagnetic radiation

radiant heat *n* heat transferred in the form of electromagnetic radiation rather than by conduction or convection; infrared radiation

radiata pine (ˌreɪdɪ'ɑːtə) *n* a pine tree grown in Australia, New Zealand, and elsewhere to produce building timber. Often shortened to **radiata** [from NL]

radiate *vb* ('reɪdɪˌeɪt), **radiates, radiating, radiated** **1** Also: **eradiate** to emit (heat, light, or other forms of radiation) or (of heat, light, etc) to be emitted as radiation **2** (*intr*) (of lines, beams, etc) to spread out from a centre or be arranged in a radial pattern **3** (*tr*) (of a person) to show (happiness, etc) to a great degree ▷ *adj* ('reɪdɪɪt, -ˌeɪt) **4** having rays; radiating **5** (of a capitulum) consisting of ray flowers **6** (of animals) showing radial symmetry [C17 from L *radiāre* to emit rays] > **'radiative** *adj*

radiation (ˌreɪdɪ'eɪʃən) *n* **1** *physics* **1a** the emission or transfer of radiant energy as particles, electromagnetic waves, sound, etc **1b** the particles, etc, emitted, esp the particles and gamma rays emitted in nuclear decay **2** Also called: **radiation therapy** *med* treatment using a radioactive substance **3** the act, state, or process of radiating or being radiated > **ˌradi'ational** *adj*

radiation sickness *n pathol* illness caused by overexposure of the body to ionizing radiations from radioactive material or X-rays

radiator ('reɪdɪˌeɪtə) *n* **1** a device for heating a room, building, etc, consisting of a series of pipes through which hot water or steam passes **2** a device for cooling an internal-combustion engine, consisting of thin-walled tubes through which water passes **3** *electronics* the part of an aerial or transmission line that radiates electromagnetic waves

radical ('rædɪkᵊl) *adj* **1** of, relating to, or characteristic of the basic or inherent constitution of a person or thing; fundamental: *a radical fault* **2** concerned with or tending to concentrate on fundamental aspects of a matter; searching or thoroughgoing: *radical thought* **3** favouring or tending to produce extreme or fundamental changes in political, economic, or social conditions, institutions, etc: *a radical party* **4** *med* (of treatment) aimed at removing the source of a disease: *radical surgery* **5** *sl, chiefly US* very good; excellent **6** of or arising from the root or the base of the stem of a plant: *radical leaves* **7** *maths* of, relating to, or containing roots of numbers or quantities **8** *linguistics* of or relating to the root of a word ▷ *n* **9** a person who favours extreme or fundamental change in existing institutions or in political, social, or economic conditions **10** *maths* a root of a number or quantity, such as $\sqrt[3]{5}$ **11** *chem* **11a** short for **free radical** **11b** another name for **group** (sense 9) **12** *linguistics* another word for **root**[1] (sense 8) [C14 from LL *rādīcālis* having roots, from L *rādix* a root] > **'radicalness** *n*

radicalism ('rædɪkəˌlɪzəm) *n* **1** the principles, desires, or practices of political radicals **2** a radical movement, esp in politics > **ˌradical'istic** *adj* > **ˌradical'istically** *adv*

radically ('rædɪkəlɪ) *adv* thoroughly; completely; fundamentally: *to alter radically*

radical sign *n* the symbol √ placed before a number or quantity to indicate the extraction of a root, esp a square root. The value of a higher root is indicated by a raised digit in front of the symbol, as in $\sqrt[3]{}$

radicand ('rædɪˌkænd, ˌrædɪ'kænd) *n* a number or quantity from which a root is to be extracted, usually preceded by a radical sign: *3 is the radicand of* $\sqrt{3}$ [C20 from L *rādīcandum*, lit.: that which is to be rooted, from *rādīcāre*, from *rādīx* root]

radicchio (ræ'diːkɪəʊ) *n, pl* **radicchios** an Italian variety of chicory, having purple leaves streaked with white that are eaten raw in salads

radices ('reɪdɪˌsiːz) *n* a plural of **radix**

radicle ('rædɪkᵊl) *n* **1** *bot* **1a** the part of the embryo of seed-bearing plants that develops into the main root **1b** a very small root or rootlike part **2** *anat* any bodily structure resembling a rootlet, esp one of the smallest branches of a vein or nerve **3** *chem* a variant spelling of **radical** (sense 11) [C18 from L *rādīcula*, from *rādīx* root]

Radiguet (*French* radigɛ) *n* **Raymond** (rɛmɔ̃) 1903–23, French novelist; the author of *The Devil in the Flesh* (1923) and *Count d'Orgel* (1924)

radii ('reɪdɪˌaɪ) *n* a plural of **radius**

radio ('reɪdɪəʊ) *n, pl* **radios** **1** the use of electromagnetic waves, lying in the radio-frequency range, for broadcasting, two-way communications, etc **2** an electronic device designed to receive, demodulate, and amplify radio signals from sound broadcasting stations, etc **3** the broadcasting, content, etc, of radio programmes: *he thinks radio is poor these days* **4** the occupation or profession concerned with any aspect of the broadcasting of radio programmes **5** short for **radiotelegraph, radiotelegraphy,** or **radiotelephone** **6** (*modifier*) **6a** of, relating to, or sent by radio signals: *a radio station* **6b** of, concerned with, using, or operated by radio frequencies: *radio spectrum* **6c** relating to or produced for radio: *radio drama* ▷ *vb* **radios, radioing, radioed** **7** to transmit (a message, etc) to (a person, etc) by means of radio waves ▷ Also called (esp Brit): **wireless** [C20 short for *radiotelegraphy*]

radio- *combining form* **1** denoting radio, broadcasting, or radio frequency: *radiogram* **2** indicating radioactivity or radiation: *radiocarbon* [from F, from L *radius* ray]
▷ www.ebu.ch
▷ www.nexus.org

Rr

radioactive (ˌreɪdɪəʊ'æktɪv) *adj* exhibiting, using, or concerned with radioactivity > **ˌradio'actively** *adv*

radioactive dating *n* another term for **radiometric dating**

radioactive decay *n* disintegration of a nucleus that occurs spontaneously or as a result of electron capture. Also called: **disintegration**

radioactive series *n physics* a series of nuclides each of which undergoes radioactive decay into the next member of the series, ending with a stable element, usually lead

radioactive tracer *n med* See **tracer** (sense 3)

radioactive waste *n* any waste material containing radionuclides. Also called: **nuclear waste**

radioactivity (ˌreɪdɪəʊæk'tɪvɪtɪ) *n* the spontaneous emission of radiation from atomic nuclei. The radiation can consist of alpha, beta, or gamma radiation

radio astronomy *n* a branch of astronomy in which a radio telescope is used to detect and analyse radio signals received on earth from radio sources in space

radio beacon *n* a fixed radio transmitting station that broadcasts a characteristic signal by means of which a vessel or aircraft can determine its bearing or position

radiobiology (ˌreɪdɪəʊbaɪ'ɒlədʒɪ) *n* the branch of biology concerned with the effects of radiation on living organisms and the study of biological processes using radioactive substances as tracers > **radiobiological** (ˌreɪdɪəʊˌbaɪə'lɒdʒɪkᵊl) *adj* > **ˌradioˌbio'logically** *adv* > **ˌradiobi'ologist** *n*

radiocarbon (ˌreɪdɪəʊ'kɑːbᵊn) *n* a radioactive isotope of carbon, esp carbon-14. See **carbon** (sense 1)

radiocarbon dating *n* See **carbon dating**

radiochemistry (ˌreɪdɪəʊ'kɛmɪstrɪ) *n* the chemistry of radioactive elements and their compounds > **ˌradio'chemical** *adj* > **ˌradio'chemist** *n*

radio compass *n* any navigational device that gives a bearing by determining the direction of incoming radio waves transmitted from a particular radio station or beacon. See also **goniometer** (sense 2)

radio control *n* remote control by means of radio signals from a transmitter > **'radio-con'trolled** *adj*

radioelement (ˌreɪdɪəʊ'ɛlɪmənt) *n* an element that is naturally radioactive

radio frequency *n* **1a** any frequency that lies in the range 10 kilohertz to 300 000 megahertz and can be used for broadcasting. Abbrevs: **rf, RF** **1b** (*as modifier*): *a radio-frequency amplifier* **2** the frequency transmitted by a particular radio station

radio galaxy *n* a galaxy that is a strong emitter of radio waves

radiogram ('reɪdɪəʊˌgræm) *n* **1** *Brit* a unit comprising a radio and record player **2** a message transmitted by radiotelegraphy **3** another name for **radiograph**

radiograph ('reɪdɪəʊˌgrɑːf) *n* an image produced on a specially sensitized photographic film or plate by radiation, usually by X-rays or gamma rays

radiography (ˌreɪdɪ'ɒgrəfɪ) *n* the production of radiographs of opaque objects for use in medicine, surgery, industry, etc > **ˌradi'ographer** *n* > **radiographic** (ˌreɪdɪəʊ'græfɪk) *adj* > **ˌradio'graphically** *adv*

radioimmunoassay ('reɪdɪəʊˌɪmjʊnəʊ'æseɪ) *n* a sensitive immunological assay, making use of antibodies and radioactive labelling, of such things as hormone concentrations in the blood

radioisotope (ˌreɪdɪəʊ'aɪsətəʊp) *n* a radioactive isotope > **radioisotopic** (ˌreɪdɪəʊˌaɪsə'tɒpɪk) *adj*

radiolarian (ˌreɪdɪəʊ'lɛərɪən) *n* any of various marine protozoans typically having a siliceous shell and stiff radiating cytoplasmic projections [C19 from NL *Radiolaria*, from LL *radiolus* little sunbeam, from L *radius* ray]

radiology (ˌreɪdɪ'ɒlədʒɪ) *n* the use of X-rays and radioactive substances in the diagnosis and treatment of disease > **ˌradi'ologist** *n*

radiometer (ˌreɪdɪ'ɒmɪtə) *n* any instrument for the detection or measurement of radiant energy > **radiometric** (ˌreɪdɪəʊ'mɛtrɪk) *adj* > **ˌradi'ometry** *n*

radiometric dating *n* any method of dating material based on the decay of its constituent radioactive atoms, such as potassium-argon dating or rubidium-strontium dating. Also called: **radioactive dating**

radiopager ('reɪdɪəʊˌpeɪdʒə) *n* a small radio receiver fitted with a buzzer to alert a person to telephone their home, office, etc, to receive a message > **'radioˌpaging** *n*

radiopaque (ˌreɪdɪəʊ'peɪk) *or* **radio-opaque** *adj* not permitting X-rays or other radiation to pass through > **radiopacity** (ˌreɪdɪəʊ'pæsɪtɪ) *or* **ˌradio-o'pacity** *n*

radio receiver *n* an apparatus that receives incoming modulated radio waves and converts them into sound

radioscopy (ˌreɪdɪ'ɒskəpɪ) *n* another word for **fluoroscopy** > **radioscopic** (ˌreɪdɪəʊ'skɒpɪk) *adj* > **ˌradio'scopically** *adv*

radiosonde ('reɪdɪəʊˌsɒnd) *n* an airborne instrument to send meteorological information back to earth by radio [C20 RADIO- + F *sonde* sounding line]

radio source *n* a celestial object, such as a supernova remnant or quasar, that is a source of radio waves

radio spectrum *n* the range of electromagnetic frequencies used in radio transmission, between 10 kilohertz and 300 000 megahertz

radiotelegraphy (ˌreɪdɪəʊtɪ'lɛgrəfɪ) *n* a type of telegraphy in which messages (formerly in Morse code) are transmitted by radio waves > **ˌradio'teleˌgraph** *vb, n* > **radiotelegraphic** (ˌreɪdɪəʊˌtɛlɪ'græfɪk) *adj*

radiotelephone (ˌreɪdɪəʊ'tɛlɪˌfəʊn) *n* **1** a device for communications by means of radio waves rather than by transmitting along wires or cables ▷ *vb* **radiotelephones, radiotelephoning, radiotelephoned** **2** to telephone (a person) by radiotelephone > **radiotelephonic** (ˌreɪdɪəʊˌtɛlɪ'fɒnɪk) *adj* > **radiotelephony** (ˌreɪdɪəʊtɪ'lɛfənɪ) *n*

radio telescope *n* an instrument consisting of an antenna or system of antennas connected to one or more radio receivers, used in radio astronomy to detect and analyse radio waves from space

radioteletype (ˌreɪdɪəʊ'tɛlɪˌtaɪp) *n* **1** a teleprinter that transmits or receives information by means of radio waves **2** a network of such devices widely used for communicating news, messages, etc. Abbrevs: **RTT, RTTY**

radiotherapy (ˌreɪdɪəʊ'θɛrəpɪ) *n* the treatment of disease by means of alpha or beta particles emitted from an implanted or ingested radioisotope, or by means of a beam of high-energy radiation ▷ Cf **chemotherapy** > **radiotherapeutic** (ˌreɪdɪəʊˌθɛrə'pjuːtɪk) *adj* > **ˌradio'therapist** *n*

radio wave *n* an electromagnetic wave of radio frequency

radish ('rædɪʃ) *n* **1** any of a genus of plants of Europe and Asia, with petals arranged like a cross, cultivated for their edible roots **2** the root of this plant, which has a pungent taste and is eaten raw in salads [OE *rǣdīc*, from L *rādīx* root]

radium ('reɪdɪəm) *n* **a** a highly radioactive luminescent white element of the alkaline earth group of metals. It occurs in pitchblende and other uranium ores. Symbol: Ra; atomic no.: 88; half-life of most stable isotope, ^{226}Ra: 1620 years **b** (*as modifier*): *radium needle* [C20 from L *radius* ray]

radium therapy *n* treatment of disease, esp cancer, by exposing affected tissues to radiation from radium

radius ('reɪdɪəs) *n, pl* **radii** *or* **radiuses** **1** a straight line joining the centre of a circle or sphere to any point on the circumference or surface **2** the length of this line, usually denoted by the symbol *r* **3** *anat* the outer, slightly shorter of the two bones of the human forearm, extending from the elbow to the wrist **4** a corresponding bone in other vertebrates **5** any of the veins of an insect's wing **6** a group of ray florets, occurring in such plants as the daisy **7a** any radial or radiating part, such as a spoke **7b** (*as modifier*): *a radius arm* **8** a circular area of a size indicated by the length of its radius: *the police stopped every lorry within a radius of four miles* **9** the operational limit of a ship, aircraft, etc [C16 from L: rod, ray, spoke]

radix ('reɪdɪks) *n, pl* **radices** *or* **radixes** **1** *maths* any number that is the base of a number system or of a system of logarithms: *10 is the radix of the decimal system* **2** *biol* the root or point of origin of a part or organ **3** *linguistics* a less common word for **root**[1] (sense 8) [C16 from L *rādīx* root]

radix point *n* a point, such as the decimal point in the decimal system, separating the integral part of a number from the fractional part

Radnorshire ('rædnəʃɪə, -ʃə) *or* **Radnor** *n* (until 1974) a county of E Wales, now part of Powys

Radom (*Polish* 'radɔm) *n* a city in E Poland: under Austria from 1795 to 1815 and Russia from 1815 to 1918. Pop: 232 262 (1999 est)

radome ('reɪdəʊm) *n* a protective housing for a radar antenna made from a material that is transparent to radio waves [C20 RA(DAR) + DOME]

radon ('reɪdɒn) *n* a colourless radioactive element of the rare gas group, the most stable isotope of which, radon-222, is a decay product of radium. Symbol: Rn; atomic no.: 86; half-life of ^{222}Rn: 3.82 days [C20 from RADIUM + -ON]

radula ('rædjʊlə) *n, pl* **radulae** (-ˌliː) a horny tooth-bearing strip on the tongue of molluscs that is used for rasping food [C19 from LL: a scraping iron, from L *rādere* to scrape] > **'radular** *adj*

Raeburn ('reɪ,bɜːn) *n* Sir **Henry** 1756–1823, Scottish portrait painter

RAF (*not standard* ræf) *abbrev for* Royal Air Force

Rafferty ('ræfətɪ) *or* **Rafferty's rules** *pl n Austral & NZ sl* no rules at all [c20 from ?]

raffia *or* **raphia** ('ræfɪə) *n* **1** a palm tree, native to Madagascar, that has large plumelike leaves, the stalks of which yield a useful fibre **2** the fibre obtained from this plant, used for weaving, etc **3** any of several related palms or the fibre obtained from them [c19 from Malagasy]

raffish ('ræfɪʃ) *adj* **1** careless or unconventional in dress, manners, etc; rakish **2** tawdry; flashy; vulgar [c19 from *raff* rubbish, rabble] > **'raffishly** *adv* > **'raffishness** *n*

raffle ('ræfᵊl) *n* **1a** a lottery in which the prizes are goods rather than money **1b** (*as modifier*): *a raffle ticket* ▷ *vb* **raffles, raffling, raffled 2** (*tr*; often foll by *off*) to dispose of (goods) in a raffle [c14 (a dice game): from OF, from ?] > **'raffler** *n*

Raffles ('ræfᵊlz) *n* Sir **Thomas Stamford** 1781–1826, British colonial administrator: founded Singapore (1819) as a station for the British East India Company

rafflesia (ræ'fliːzɪə) *n* any of various tropical Asian parasitic leafless plants, the flowers of which grow up to 45 cm (18 inches) across, smell of putrid meat, and are pollinated by carrion flies [c19 NL, after Sir Stamford RAFFLES, who discovered it]

raft[1] (rɑːft) *n* **1** a buoyant platform of logs, planks, etc, used as a vessel or moored platform **2** a thick slab of reinforced concrete laid over soft ground to provide a foundation for a building ▷ *vb* **3** to convey on or travel by raft, or make a raft from [c15 from ON *raptr* RAFTER]

raft[2] (rɑːft) *n inf* a large collection or amount: *a raft of old notebooks discovered in a cupboard*

rafter ('rɑːftə) *n* any one of a set of parallel sloping beams that form the framework of a roof [OE *ræfter*]

RAFVR *abbrev for* Royal Air Force Volunteer Reserve

rag[1] (ræg) *n* **1a** a small piece of cloth, such as one torn from a discarded garment, or such pieces of cloth collectively **1b** (*as modifier*): *a rag doll* **2** a fragmentary piece of any material; scrap; shred **3** *inf* a newspaper, esp one considered as worthless, sensational, etc **4** *inf* an item of clothing **5** *inf* a handkerchief **6** *Brit sl, esp naval* a flag or ensign **7 from rags to riches** *inf* **7a** from poverty to great wealth **7b** (*as modifier*): *a rags-to-riches tale* [c14 prob. back formation from RAGGED from OE *raggig*]

rag[2] (ræg) *vb* **rags, ragging, ragged** (*tr*) **1** to draw attention facetiously and persistently to the shortcomings of (a person) **2** *Brit* to play rough practical jokes on ▷ *n* **3** *Brit* a boisterous practical joke **4** (in British universities, etc) **4a** a period in which various events are organized to raise money for charity **4b** (*as modifier*): *rag day* [c18 from ?]

rag[3] (ræg) *jazz* ▷ *n* **1** a piece of ragtime music ▷ *vb* **rags, ragging, ragged 2** (*tr*) to compose or perform in ragtime [c20 from RAGTIME]

raga ('rɑːgə) *n* (in Indian music) **1** any of several conventional patterns of melody and rhythm that form the basis for freely interpreted compositions **2** a composition based on one of these patterns [c18 from Sansk. *rāga* tone, colour]

ragamuffin ('rægə,mʌfɪn) *n* **1** a ragged unkempt person, esp a child **2** another name for **ragga** [c14 *Ragamoffyn*, a demon in the poem *Piers Plowman* (1393); prob. based on RAG[1]]

rag-and-bone man *n Brit* a man who buys and sells discarded clothing, etc. US equivalent: **junkman**

ragbag ('ræg,bæg) *n* **1** a bag for storing odd rags **2** a confused assortment; jumble

ragbolt ('ræg,bəʊlt) *n* a bolt that has angled projections on it to prevent it working loose

rage (reɪdʒ) *n* **1** intense anger; fury **2** violent movement or action, esp of the sea, wind, etc **3** great intensity of hunger or other feelings **4** aggressive behaviour associated with a specified environment or activity: *road rage; school rage* **5** a fashion or craze (esp in **all the rage**) **6** *Austral & NZ inf* a dance or party ▷ *vb* **rages, raging, raged** (*intr*) **7** to feel or exhibit intense anger **8** (esp of storms, fires, etc) to move or surge with great violence **9** (esp of a disease) to spread rapidly and uncontrollably **10** *Austral & NZ inf* to have a good time [c13 via OF from L *rabiēs* madness]

ragga ('rægə) *n* a dance-oriented style of reggae. Also called: **ragamuffin** [c20 shortened from RAGAMUFFIN]

▷ www.ragga-jungle.com

ragged ('rægɪd) *adj* **1** (of clothes) worn to rags; tattered **2** (of a person) dressed in tattered clothes **3** having a neglected or unkempt appearance: *ragged weeds* **4** having a rough or uneven surface or edge; jagged **5** uneven or irregular: *a ragged beat; a ragged shout* [c13 prob. from *ragge* RAG[1]] > **'raggedly** *adv* > **'raggedness** *n*

ragged robin *n* a plant related to the carnation family and native to Europe and Asia, that has pink or white flowers with ragged petals. See also **catchfly**

raggedy ('rægɪdɪ) *adj inf, chiefly US & Canad* somewhat ragged; tattered: *a raggedy doll*

ragi, raggee, *or* **raggy** ('rægɪ) *n* a cereal grass, cultivated in Africa and Asia for its edible grain [c18 from Hindi]

raglan ('ræglən) *n* **1** a coat, jumper, etc, with sleeves that continue to the collar instead of having armhole seams ▷ *adj* **2** cut in this design: *a raglan sleeve* [c19 after Lord RAGLAN]

Raglan ('ræglən) *n* **Fitzroy James Henry Somerset**, 1st Baron Raglan. 1788–1855, British field marshal, diplomatist, politician, and protégé of Wellington: commanded British troops (1854–55) in the Crimean War

ragout (ræ'guː) *n* **1** a richly seasoned stew of meat and vegetables ▷ *vb* **ragouts** (-'guːz), **ragouting** (-'guːɪŋ), **ragouted** (-'guːd) **2** (*tr*) to make into a ragout [c17 from F, from *ragoûter* to stimulate the appetite again, from *ra-* RE- + *goûter* from L *gustāre* to taste]

rag-rolling *n* a decorating technique in which paint is applied with a roughly folded cloth in order to create a marbled effect

ragtag ('ræg,tæg) *n derog* the common people; rabble (esp in **ragtag and bobtail**) [c19 from RAG[1] + TAG[1]]

ragtime ('ræg,taɪm) *n* a style of jazz piano music, developed by Scott Joplin around 1900, having a two-four rhythm base and a syncopated melody [c20 prob. from RAGGED + TIME]

▷ www.wikipedia.org/wiki/Ragtime

▷ www.dropbears.com/r/ragtime

▷ www.jazzinamerica.org

rag trade *n inf* the clothing business

Ragusa (*Italian* ra'guːza) *n* **1** an industrial town in SE Sicily. Pop: 68 850 (1990) **2** the Italian name (until 1918) for **Dubrovnik**

ragweed ('ræg,wiːd) *n* a North American plant of the composite family such as the **common ragweed**. Its green tassel-like flowers produce large amounts of pollen, which causes hay fever. Also called: **ambrosia**

ragworm ('ræg,wɜːm) *n* any polychaete worm living chiefly in burrows in sand and having a flattened body with a row of fleshy lateral appendages along each side. US name: **clamworm**

ragwort ('ræg,wɜːt) *n* any of several European plants of the composite family that have yellow daisy-like flowers. See also **groundsel**

rah (rɑː) *interj inf, chiefly US* short for **hurrah**

rahui (,rɑː'huːɪ) *n NZ* a Maori prohibition [Maori]

rai (raɪ) *n* a type of Algerian popular music based on traditional Algerian music influenced by modern Western pop [c20 Ar., lit.: opinion]

raid (reɪd) *n* **1** a sudden surprise attack **2** a surprise visit

Rr

by police searching for criminals or illicit goods: *a fraud-squad raid* ▷ *vb* **3** to make a raid against (a person, thing, etc) **4** to sneak into (a place) in order to take something, steal, etc: *raiding the larder* ▷ See also **bear raid, dawn raid, ram raid** [c15 Scot dialect, from OE *rād* military expedition] > **'raider** *n*

rail[1] (reɪl) *n* **1** a horizontal bar of wood, etc, supported by vertical posts, functioning as a fence, barrier, etc **2** a horizontal bar fixed to a wall on which to hang things: *a picture rail* **3** a horizontal framing member in a door ▷ Cf **stile**[2] **4** short for **railing** **5** one of a pair of parallel bars laid on a track, roadway, etc, that serve as a guide and running surface for the wheels of a train, tramcar, etc **6a** short for **railway** **6b** (*as modifier*): *rail transport* **7** *naut* a trim for finishing the top of a bulwark **8 off the rails** **8a** into or in a state of disorder **8b** eccentric or mad ▷ *vb* (*tr*) **9** to provide with a rail or railings **10** (usually foll by *in* or *off*) to fence (an area) with rails [c13 from OF *raille* rod, from L *rēgula* ruler]

rail[2] (reɪl) *vb* (*intr*; foll by *at* or *against*) to complain bitterly or vehemently [c15 from OF *railler* to mock, from OProvençal *ralhar* to chatter, from LL *ragere* to yell] > **'railer** *n*

rail[3] (reɪl) *n* any of various small cranelike wading marsh birds with short wings and neck, long legs, and dark plumage [c15 from OF *raale*, ?from L *rādere* to scrape]

railcar ('reɪl,kɑː) *n* a passenger-carrying railway vehicle consisting of a single coach with its own power unit

railcard ('reɪl,kɑːd) *n Brit* a card issued to students or senior citizens to entitle them to cheap rail fares

railhead ('reɪl,hɛd) *n* **1** a terminal of a railway **2** the farthest point reached by completed track on an unfinished railway

railing ('reɪlɪŋ) *n* **1** (*often pl*) a fence, balustrade, or barrier that consists of rails supported by posts **2** rails collectively or material for making rails

raillery ('reɪlərɪ) *n, pl* **railleries** **1** light-hearted satire or ridicule; banter **2** a bantering remark [c17 from F, from *railler* to tease; see RAIL[2]]

railroad ('reɪl,rəʊd) *n* **1** the usual US word for **railway** ▷ *vb* **2** (*tr*) *inf* to force (a person) into (an action) with haste or by unfair means

railway ('reɪl,weɪ) *or US* **railroad** *n* **1** a permanent track composed of a line of parallel metal rails fixed to sleepers, for transport of passengers and goods in trains **2** any track for the wheels of a vehicle to run on: *a cable railway* **3** the entire equipment, rolling stock, buildings, property, and system of tracks used in such a transport system **4** the organization responsible for operating a railway network **5** (*modifier*) of, relating to, or used on a railway: *a railway engine*

▷ http://routesinternational.com/rail.htm

▷ http://RAILlinks.com/railfan/pages/

raiment ('reɪmənt) *n arch or poetic* attire; clothing [c15 from *arrayment*, from OF *areement*; see ARRAY]

rain (reɪn) *n* **1a** precipitation from clouds in the form of drops of water, formed by the condensation of water vapour in the atmosphere **1b** a fall of rain; shower **1c** (*in combination*): *a raindrop* **2** a large quantity of anything falling rapidly or in quick succession: *a rain of abuse* **3** **(come) rain or (come) shine** regardless of the weather or circumstances **4 right as rain** *Brit inf* perfectly all right ▷ *vb* **5** (*intr*; with *it* as subject) to be the case that rain is falling **6** (often with *it* as subject) to fall or cause to fall like rain **7** (*tr*) to bestow in large measure: *to rain abuse on someone* **8 rained off** cancelled or postponed on account of rain. US and Canad term: **rained out** ▷ See also **rains** [OE *regn*] > **'rainless** *adj*

rainbird ('reɪn,bɜːd) *n* any of various birds whose cry is supposed to portend rain, such as the green woodpecker in Britain and Burchell's coucal in South Africa

rainbow ('reɪn,bəʊ) *n* **1a** a bow-shaped display in the sky of the colours of the spectrum, caused by the refraction and reflection of the sun's rays through rain **1b** (*as modifier*): *a rainbow pattern* **2** an illusory hope: *to chase rainbows* **3** (*modifier*) of or relating to a political grouping together by several minorities, esp of different races: *the rainbow coalition*

Rainbow Bridge *n* a natural stone bridge over a creek in SE Utah. Height: 94 m (309 ft). Span: 85 m (278 ft)

rainbow lorikeet *n* a small Australasian parrot, *Trichoglossus haematodus*, with brightly-coloured plumage

rainbow nation *n S African* an epithet, alluding to its multiracial population, of **South Africa** [c20 coined by Nelson MANDELA following the end of apartheid]

rainbow trout *n* a freshwater trout of North American origin, marked with many black spots and two longitudinal red stripes

rain check *n US & Canad* **1** a ticket stub for a baseball game that allows readmission on a future date if the event is cancelled because of rain **2** the deferral of acceptance of an offer **3 take a rain check** *inf* to accept or request the postponement of an offer

raincoat ('reɪn,kəʊt) *n* a coat made of a waterproof material

rainfall ('reɪn,fɔːl) *n* **1** precipitation in the form of raindrops **2** *meteorol* the amount of precipitation in a specified place and time

rainforest ('reɪn,fɒrɪst) *n* dense forest found in tropical areas of heavy rainfall

rain gauge *n* an instrument for measuring rainfall or snowfall, consisting of a cylinder covered by a funnel-like lid

Rainier ('reɪnɪə, reɪ'nɪə, rə-) *n* **Mount** a mountain in W Washington State: the highest mountain in the state and in the Cascade Range. Height: 4392 m (14 410 ft)

rainproof ('reɪn,pruːf) *adj* **1** Also: **'rain,tight** (of garments, materials, etc) impermeable to rainwater ▷ *vb* **2** (*tr*) to make rainproof

rains (reɪnz) *pl n* **the rains** the season of heavy rainfall, esp in the tropics

rain shadow *n* the relatively dry area on the leeward side of high ground in the path of rain-bearing winds

rainstorm ('reɪn,stɔːm) *n* a storm with heavy rain

rainwater ('reɪn,wɔːtə) *n* pure water from rain (as distinguished from spring water, tap water, etc, which may contain minerals and impurities)

rainy ('reɪnɪ) *adj* **rainier, rainiest** **1** characterized by a large rainfall: *a rainy climate* **2** wet or showery; bearing rain > **'rainily** *adv* > **'raininess** *n*

rainy day *n* a future time of need, esp financial

Rais (*French* res) *or* **Retz** *n* **Gilles de** (ʒil də) 1404–40, French nobleman who fought with Joan of Arc: marshal of France (1429–40). He was executed for the torture and murder of more than 140 children

raise (reɪz) *vb* **raises, raising, raised** (*mainly tr*) **1** to move or elevate to a higher position or level; lift **2** to set or place in an upright position **3** to construct, build, or erect: *to raise a barn* **4** to increase in amount, size, value, etc: *to raise prices* **5** to increase in degree, strength, intensity, etc: *to raise one's voice* **6** to advance in rank or status; promote **7** to arouse or awaken from sleep or death **8** to stir up or incite; activate: *to raise a mutiny* **9 raise Cain** (*or* **the devil, hell, the roof,** etc) **9a** to create a disturbance, esp by making a great noise **9b** to protest vehemently **10** to give rise to; cause or provoke: *to raise a smile* **11** to put forward for consideration: *to raise a question* **12** to cause to assemble or gather together: *to raise an army* **13** to grow or cause to grow: *to raise a crop* **14** to bring up; rear: *to raise a family* **15** to cause to be heard or known; utter or express: *to raise a shout* **16** to bring to an end; remove: *to raise a siege* **17** to cause (bread, etc) to rise, as by the addition of yeast **18** *poker* to bet more than (the previous player) **19** *bridge* to bid (one's partner's suit) at a higher level **20** *naut* to cause (something) to seem to rise above the horizon by approaching: *we raised land after 20* *days* **21** to establish radio communications with: *we raised Moscow last night* **22** to obtain (money, funds, etc) **23** to bring (a surface, a design, etc) into relief; cause to project **24** to cause (a blister, etc) to form on the skin **25** *maths* to multiply (a number) by itself a specified number of times: *8 is 2 raised to the power 3* **26 raise one's glass (to)** to drink a toast (to) **27 raise one's hat** *old-fashioned* to take one's hat briefly off one's head as a greeting or mark of respect ▷ *n* **28** the act or an instance of raising **29** *chiefly US & Canad* an increase, esp in salary, wages, etc; rise [c12 from ON *reisa*] > **'raisable** *or* **'raiseable** *adj*

raised beach *n* a wave-cut platform raised above the shoreline by a relative fall in the water level

raisin ('reɪzᵊn) *n* a dried grape [c13 from OF: grape, ult. from L *racēmus* cluster of grapes] > **'raisiny** *adj*

raison d'être *French* (rɛzɔ̃ dɛtrə) *n, pl* ***raisons d'être*** (rɛzɔ̃ dɛtrə) reason or justification for existence

raita ('raɪtə) *n* an Indian dish of finely chopped cucumber, peppers, mint, etc, in yogurt, served with curries [c20 from Hindi]

raj (rɑːdʒ) *n* **1** (in India) government; rule **2** (*cap* and preceded by *the*) the British government in India before 1947 [c19 from Hindi, from Sansk., from *rājati* he rules]

rajah *or* **raja** ('rɑːdʒə) *n* **1** (in India, formerly) a ruler: sometimes used as a title preceding a name **2** a Malayan or Javanese prince or chieftain [c16 from Hindi, from Sansk. *rājan* king]

Rajasthan (ˌrɑːdʒə'stɑːn) *n* a state of NW India, bordering on Pakistan: formed in 1958; contains the Thar Desert in the west; now the largest state in India. Capital: Jaipur. Pop: 56 473 122 (2001). Area: 342 239 sq km (132 111 sq miles)

Rajkot ('rɑːdʒkəʊt) *n* a city in W India, in S Gujarat. Pop: 559 407 (1991)

Rajput *or* **Rajpoot** ('rɑːdʒpʊt) *n Hinduism* one of a Hindu military caste claiming descent from the Kshatriya, the original warrior caste [c16 from Hindi, from Sansk. *rājan* king]

Rajputana (ˌrɑːdʒpʊ'tɑːnə) *n* a former group of princely states in NW India: now mostly part of Rajasthan

Rakata (rə'kɑːtə) *n* another name for **Krakatoa**

rake[1] (reɪk) *n* **1** a hand implement consisting of a row of teeth set in a headpiece attached to a long shaft and used for gathering hay, straw, etc, or for smoothing loose earth **2** any of several mechanical farm implements equipped with rows of teeth or rotating wheels mounted with tines and used to gather hay, straw, etc **3** any of various implements similar in shape or function **4** the act of raking ▷ *vb* **rakes, raking, raked** **5** to scrape, gather, or remove (leaves, refuse, etc) with a rake **6** to level or prepare (a surface) with a rake **7** (*tr*; sometimes foll by *out*) to clear (ashes, etc) from (a fire) **8** (*tr*; foll by *up* or *together*) to gather (items or people) with difficulty, as from a scattered area or limited supply **9** (*tr*; often foll by *through, over*, etc) to search or examine carefully **10** (when *intr*, foll by *against, along*, etc) to scrape or graze: *the ship raked the side of the quay* **11** (*tr*) to direct (gunfire) along the length of (a target): *machine-guns raked the column* **12** (*tr*) to sweep (one's eyes) along the length of (something); scan ▷ See also **rake in, rake-off**, etc [OE *raca*] > **'raker** *n*

rake[2] (reɪk) *n* a dissolute man, esp one in fashionable society; roué [c17 short for *rakehell* a dissolute man]

rake[3] (reɪk) *vb* **rakes, raking, raked** (*mainly intr*) **1** to incline from the vertical by a perceptible degree, esp (of a ship's mast) towards the stern **2** (*tr*) to construct with a backward slope ▷ *n* **3** the degree to which an object, such as a ship's mast, inclines from the perpendicular, esp towards the stern **4** *theatre* the slope of a stage from the back towards the footlights **5** the angle between the working face of a cutting tool and a plane perpendicular to the surface of the workpiece [c17 from ?; ? rel. to G *ragen* to project, Swedish *raka*]

rake in *vb* (*tr, adv*) *inf* to acquire (money) in large amounts

rake-off *sl* ▷ *n* **1** a share of profits, esp one that is illegal or given as a bribe ▷ *vb* **rake off** **2** (*tr, adv*) to take or receive (such a share of profits)

rake up *vb* (*tr, adv*) to revive, discover, or bring to light (something forgotten): *to rake up an old quarrel*

raki *or* **rakee** (rɑː'kiː, 'rækɪ) *n* a strong spirit distilled in Turkey from grain, usually flavoured with aniseed or other aromatics [c17 from Turkish *rāqī*]

raking ('reɪkɪŋ) *n rugby* the offence committed when a player deliberately scrapes an opponent's leg, arm, etc with the studs of his or her boots

rakish[1] ('reɪkɪʃ) *adj* dissolute; profligate [c18 from RAKE[2]] > **'rakishly** *adv* > **'rakishness** *n*

rakish[2] ('reɪkɪʃ) *adj* **1** dashing; jaunty: *a hat set at a rakish angle* **2** *naut* (of a ship or boat) having lines suggestive of speed [c19 prob. from RAKE[3]]

rale *or* **râle** (rɑːl) *n med* an abnormal coarse crackling sound heard on auscultation of the chest, usually caused by the accumulation of fluid in the lungs [c19 from F, from *râler* to breathe with a rattling sound]

Raleigh[1] ('rɔːlɪ, 'rɑː-) *n* a city in E central North Carolina, capital of the state. Pop: 276 093 (2000)

Raleigh[2] *or* **Ralegh** ('rɔːlɪ, 'rɑː-) *n* Sir **Walter** ?1552–1618, English courtier, explorer, and writer; favourite of Elizabeth I. After unsuccessful attempts to colonize Virginia (1584–89), he led two expeditions to the Orinoco to search for gold (1595; 1616). He introduced tobacco and potatoes into England, and was imprisoned (1603–16) for conspiracy under James I. He was beheaded in 1618

rallentando (ˌrælɛn'tændəʊ) *adj, adv music* becoming slower. Also: **ritardando** [c19 It., from *rallentare* to slow down]

rally[1] ('rælɪ) *vb* **rallies, rallying, rallied** **1** to bring (a group, unit, etc) into order, as after dispersal, or (of such a group) to reform and come to order **2** (when *intr*, foll by *to*) to organize (supporters, etc) for a common cause or (of such people) to come together for a purpose **3** to summon up (one's strength, spirits, etc) or (of a person's health, strength, or spirits) to revive or recover **4** (*intr*) *stock exchange* to increase sharply after a decline **5** (*intr*) *tennis, squash, etc* to engage in a rally ▷ *n, pl* **rallies** **6** a large gathering of people for a common purpose **7** a marked recovery of strength or spirits, as during illness **8** a return to order after dispersal or rout, as of troops, etc **9** *stock exchange* a sharp increase in price or trading activity after a decline **10** *tennis, squash, etc* an exchange of several shots before one player wins the point **11** a type of motoring competition over public roads [c16 from OF *rallier*, from RE- + *alier* to unite] > **'rallier** *n*

▷ www.worldrally.net
▷ www.ukmotorsport.com

rally[2] ('rælɪ) *vb* **rallies, rallying, rallied** to mock or ridicule (someone) in a good-natured way; chaff; tease [c17 from OF *railler* to tease; see RAIL[2]]

rallycross ('rælɪˌkrɒs) *n* a form of motor sport in which cars race over a one-mile circuit of rough grass with some hard-surfaced sections

rally round *vb* (*intr*) to come to the aid of (someone); offer moral or practical support

ram (ræm) *n* **1** an uncastrated adult male sheep **2** a piston or moving plate, esp one driven hydraulically or pneumatically **3** the falling weight of a pile driver **4** short for **battering ram** **5** a pointed projection in the stem of an ancient warship for puncturing the hull of enemy ships **6** a warship equipped with a ram ▷ *vb* **rams, ramming, rammed** **7** (*tr*; usually foll by *into*) to force or drive, as by heavy blows: *to ram a post into the ground* **8** (of a moving object) to crash with force (against another object) or (of two moving objects) to collide in this way **9** (*tr*; often foll by *in* or *down*) to stuff or cram (something into a hole, etc) **10** (*tr*; foll by *onto, against,* etc) to thrust violently: *he rammed the books onto the desk* 11 (*tr*) to present (an idea, argument, etc) forcefully or aggressively (esp in **ram (something) down someone's throat**) 12 (*tr*) to drive (a charge) into a firearm [OE *ramm*] > **'rammer** *n*

Ram (ræm) *n* **the** the constellation Aries, the first sign of the zodiac

RAM[1] (ræm) *n computing acronym for* random access memory: semiconductor memory in which all storage locations can be rapidly accessed in the same amount of time. It forms the main memory of a computer, used by applications to perform tasks while the device is operating

RAM[2] *abbrev for* Royal Academy of Music
▷ www.ram.ac.uk

Ramadan *or* **Rhamadhan** (ˌræməˈdɑːn) *n* 1 the ninth month of the Muslim year, lasting 30 days, during which strict fasting is observed from sunrise to sunset 2 the fast itself [C16 from Ar., lit.: the hot month, from *ramad* dryness]

Ramakrishna (ˌrɑːməˈkrɪʃnə) *n* **Sri** (sriː) 1834–86, Hindu yogi and religious reformer. He preached the equal value of all religions as different paths to God

Raman effect (ˈrɑːmən) *n* the change in wavelength of light that is scattered by electrons within a material: used in **Raman spectroscopy** for studying molecules [C20 after Sir Chandasekhara *Raman* (1888–1970), Indian physicist]

Ramat Gan (rɑːˈmɑːt ˈgɑːn) *n* a city in Israel, E of Tel Aviv. Pop: 126 900 (1999 est)

Rambert (ˈrɒmbɛə) *n* Dame **Marie** 1888–1982, British ballet dancer and teacher, born in Poland: founded the **Ballet Rambert** (1926)

ramble (ˈræmbᵊl) *vb* **rambles, rambling, rambled** (*intr*) 1 to stroll about freely, as for relaxation, with no particular direction 2 (of paths, streams, etc) to follow a winding course; meander 3 to grow or develop in a random fashion 4 (of speech, writing, etc) to lack organization ▷ *n* 5 a leisurely stroll, esp in the countryside [C17 prob. rel. to MDu. *rammelen* to ROAM (of animals)]

rambler (ˈræmblə) *n* 1 a weak-stemmed plant that straggles over other vegetation 2 a person who rambles, esp one who takes country walks 3 a person who lacks organization in his or her speech or writing

rambling (ˈræmblɪŋ) *adj* 1 straggling or sprawling haphazardly: *a rambling old house* 2 (of speech or writing) diffuse and disconnected 3 (of a plant, esp a rose) climbing and straggling 4 nomadic; wandering

Ramboesque (ˌræmbəʊˈɛsk) *adj* looking or behaving like or characteristic of Rambo, a mindlessly brutal fictional film character > **'Rambo,ism** *n*

Rambouillet[1] (*French* rɑ̃bujɛ) *n* a town in N France, in the Yvelines department: site of the summer residence of French presidents. Pop: 25 300 (1990)

rambunctious (ræmˈbʌŋkʃəs) *adj inf* boisterous; unruly [C19 prob. from Icelandic *ram* (intensifying prefix) + *-bunctious*, from BUMPTIOUS] > **ram'bunctiousness** *n*

rambutan (ræmˈbuːtᵊn) *n* 1 a tree related to the soapberry, native to SE Asia, that has bright red edible fruit covered with hairs 2 the fruit of this tree [C18 from Malay, from *rambut* hair]

RAMC *abbrev for* Royal Army Medical Corps

Rameau (*French* ramo) *n* **Jean Philippe** (ʒɑ̃ filip) 1683–1764, French composer. His works include the opera *Castor et Pollux* (1737), chamber music, harpsichord pieces, church music, and cantatas. His *Traité de l'harmonie* (1722) was of fundamental importance in the development of modern harmony

ramekin *or* **ramequin** (ˈræmɪkɪn) *n* 1 a savoury dish made from a cheese mixture baked in a fireproof container 2 the container itself [C18 F *ramequin*, of Gmc origin]

ramen (ˈrɑːmən) *n* 1 a Japanese dish consisting of a clear broth containing thin white noodles and sometimes vegetables, meat, etc ▷ *pl n* 2 thin white noodles served in such a broth [Japanese, from Chinese *la* to pull + *mian* noodles]

Rameses (ˈræmɪˌsiːz) *n* a variant of **Ramses**

ramification (ˌræmɪfɪˈkeɪʃən) *n* 1 the act or process of ramifying or branching out 2 an offshoot or subdivision 3 a structure of branching parts

ramify (ˈræmɪˌfaɪ) *vb* **ramifies, ramifying, ramified** 1 to divide into branches or branchlike parts 2 (*intr*) to develop complicating consequences [C16 from F *ramifier*, from L *rāmus* branch + *facere* to make]

Ramillies (ˈræmɪliːz; *French* ramiji) *n* a village in central Belgium where the Duke of Marlborough defeated the French in 1706

ramjet *or* **ramjet engine** (ˈræmˌdʒɛt) *n* **a** a type of jet engine in which fuel is burned in a duct using air compressed by the forward speed of the aircraft **b** an aircraft powered by such an engine

ramose (ˈreɪməʊs, ræˈməʊs) *or* **ramous** (ˈreɪməs) *adj* having branches [C17 from L *rāmōsus*, from *rāmus* branch] > **'ramosely** *or* **'ramously** *adv* > **ramosity** (ræˈmɒsɪtɪ) *n*

ramp (ræmp) *n* 1 a sloping floor, path, etc, that joins two surfaces at different levels 2 a place where the level of a road surface changes because of roadworks 3 a movable stairway by which passengers enter and leave an aircraft 4 the act of ramping 5 *Brit sl* a swindle, esp one involving exorbitant prices ▷ *vb* 6 (*intr*) (often foll by *about* or *around*) (esp of animals) to rush around in a wild excited manner 7 (*intr*) to act in a violent or threatening manner (esp in **ramp and rage**) 8 (*tr*) *finance* to buy (a security) in the market with the object of raising its price and enhancing the image of the company behind it for financial gain [C18 (n): from C13 *rampe*, from OF *ramper* to crawl or rear, prob. of Gmc origin]

rampage *vb* (ræmˈpeɪdʒ), **rampages, rampaging, rampaged** 1 (*intr*) to rush about in a violent or agitated fashion ▷ *n* (ˈræmpeɪdʒ, ræmˈpeɪdʒ) 2 angry or destructive behaviour 3 **on the rampage** behaving violently or destructively [C18 from Scot, from ?; ? based on RAMP] > **ram'pageous** *adj* > **ram'pageously** *adv* > **'rampager** *n*

rampant (ˈræmpənt) *adj* 1 unrestrained or violent in behaviour, etc 2 growing or developing unchecked 3 (*postpositive*) *heraldry* (of a beast) standing on the hind legs, the right foreleg raised above the left 4 (of an arch) having one abutment higher than the other [C14 from OF *ramper* to crawl, rear; see RAMP] > **'rampancy** *n* > **'rampantly** *adv*

rampart (ˈræmpɑːt) *n* 1 the surrounding embankment of a fort, often including any walls, parapets, etc, that are built on the bank 2 any defence or bulwark ▷ *vb* 3 (*tr*) to provide with a rampart; fortify [C16 from OF, from RE- + *emparer* to take possession of, from OProvençal *antparar*, from L *ante* before + *parāre* to prepare]

rampike (ˈræmˌpaɪk) *n Canad* a tall tree that has been burned or is bare of branches

rampion (ˈræmpɪən) *n* a plant, native to Europe and Asia, that has clusters of bell-shaped bluish flowers and an edible white tuberous root used in salads [C16 prob. from OF *raiponce*, from OIt. *raponzo*, from *rapa* turnip, from L *rāpum*]

ramp up *vb* (*adv*) 1 to increase or cause to increase 2 to increase the effort involved in a process

Rampur (ˈræmpʊə) *n* a city in N India, in N Uttar Pradesh. Pop: 243 742 (1991)

ram raid *n inf* a raid in which a stolen car is driven through a shop window in order to steal goods from the shop > **ram raiding** *n* > **ram raider** *n*

ramrod ('ræm,rɒd) *n* **1** a rod for cleaning the barrel of a rifle, etc **2** a rod for ramming in the charge of a muzzle-loading firearm

Ramsay ('ræmzɪ) *n* **1 Allan** ?1686–1758, Scottish poet, editor, and bookseller, noted particularly for his pastoral comedy *The Gentle Shepherd* (1725): first person to introduce the circulating library in Scotland **2** his son, **Allan** 1713–84, Scottish portrait painter **3 Gordon** born 1963, British chef and restaurateur; the only British-born chef to achieve a third Michelin star (2001) **4 James Andrew Broun.** See (1st Marquis and 10th Earl of) **Dalhousie** **5** Sir **William** 1852–1916, Scottish chemist. He discovered argon (1894) with Rayleigh, isolated helium (1895), and identified neon, krypton, and xenon: Nobel prize for chemistry 1904

Ramses ('ræmsiːz) *or* **Rameses** *n* any of 12 kings of ancient Egypt, who ruled from ?1315 to ?1090 BC

Ramses II *or* **Rameses II** *n* died ?1225 BC, king of ancient Egypt (?1292–?25). His reign was marked by war with the Hittites and the construction of many colossal monuments, esp the rock temple at Abu Simbel

Ramses III *or* **Rameses III** *n* died ?1167 BC, king of ancient Egypt (?1198–?67). His reign was marked by wars in Libya and Syria

Ramsey ('ræmzɪ) *n* Sir **Alf(red)** (**Ernest**) 1922–99, English footballer and football manager, who played for England 32 times and managed England when they won the World Cup (1966)

Ramsgate ('ræmz,geɪt) *n* a port and resort in SE England, in E Kent on the North Sea coast. Pop: 37 895 (1991)

ramshackle ('ræm,ʃækᵊl) *adj* (esp of buildings) rickety, shaky, or derelict [C17 *ramshackled*, from obs. *ransackle* to RANSACK]

ramsons ('ræmzənz, -sənz) *pl n* (*usually functioning as sing*) **1** a broad-leaved garlic native to Europe and Asia **2** the bulbous root of this plant, eaten as a relish [OE *hramesa*]

ran (ræn) *vb* the past tense of **run**

RAN *abbrev for* Royal Australian Navy
▷ www.navy.gov.au

Rancagua (*Spanish* raŋ'kagwa) *n* a city in central Chile. Pop: 202 067 (1999 est)

ranch (rɑːntʃ) *n* **1** a large tract of land, esp one in North America, together with the necessary personnel, buildings, and equipment, for rearing livestock, esp cattle **2a** any large farm for the rearing of a particular kind of livestock or crop: *a mink ranch* **2b** the buildings, land, etc, connected with it ▷ *vb* **3** (*intr*) to run a ranch **4** (*tr*) to raise (animals) on or as if on a ranch [C19 from Mexican Sp. *rancho* small farm] > '**rancher** *n*

rancherie ('rɑːntʃərɪ) *n* (in British Columbia, Canada) a settlement of North American Indians, esp on a reserve [from Sp. *rancheria*]

Ranchi ('ræntʃɪ) *n* an industrial city in E India, between the coal and iron belts of the Chota Nagpur Plateau; the capital of Jharkand from 2000. Pop: 599 306 (1991)

rancid ('rænsɪd) *adj* **1** (of food) having an unpleasant stale taste or smell as the result of decomposition **2** (of a taste or smell) rank or sour; stale [C17 from L *rancidus*, from *rancēre* to stink] > **rancidity** (ræn'sɪdɪtɪ) *or* '**rancidness** *n*

rancour *or US* **rancor** ('ræŋkə) *n* malicious resentfulness or hostility; spite [C14 from OF, from LL *rancor* rankness] > '**rancorous** *adj* > '**rancorously** *adv*

rand¹ (rænd, rɒnt) *n* the standard monetary unit of South Africa, divided into 100 cents [C20 from Afrik., from WITWATERSRAND, referring to the gold-mining there; rel. to RAND²]

rand² (rænd) *n* **1** *shoemaking* a leather strip put in the heel of a shoe before the lifts are put on **2** *dialect* **2a** a strip or margin; border **2b** a strip of cloth; selvage [OE; rel. to OHG *rant* border, rim of a shield, ON *rönd* shield, rim]

R & B *abbrev for* rhythm and blues

Rand (rænd) *n* **the** short for **Witwatersrand**

R & D *abbrev for* research and development

Randers (*Danish* 'randərs) *n* a port and industrial centre in Denmark, in E Jutland on **Randers Fjord** (an inlet of the Kattegat) Pop: 61 435 (1995)

randlord ('rænd,lɔːd) *n S African* a mining magnate during the 19th-century gold boom in Johannesburg

Randolph ('rændɒlf, -dəlf) *n* **1 Edmund Jennings** 1753–1813, US politician. He was a member of the convention that framed the US constitution (1787), attorney general (1789–94), and secretary of state (1794–95) **2 John**, called *Randolph of Roanoke*. 1773–1833, US politician, noted for his eloquence: in 1820 he opposed the Missouri Compromise that outlawed slavery **3** Sir **Thomas**, 1st Earl of Moray died 1332, Scottish soldier: regent after the death of Robert the Bruce (1329)

random ('rændəm) *adj* **1** lacking any definite plan or prearranged order; haphazard: *a random selection* **2** *statistics* **2a** having a value which cannot be determined but only described in terms of probability: *a random variable* **2b** chosen without regard to any characteristics of the individual members of the population so that each has an equal chance of being selected: *random sampling* ▷ *n* **3 at random** not following any prearranged order [C14 from OF *randon*, from *randir* to gallop, of Gmc origin] > '**randomly** *adv* > '**randomness** *n*

random access *n* another name for **direct access**

randomize *or* **randomise** ('rændə,maɪz) *vb* **randomizes, randomizing, randomized** *or* **randomises, randomising, randomised** (*tr*) to set up (a selection process, sample, etc) in a deliberately random way in order to enhance the statistical validity of any results obtained > ,**randomi'zation** *or* ,**randomi'sation** *n* > '**random,izer** *or* '**random,iser** *n*

random walk theory *n stock exchange* the theory that the future movement of share prices does not reflect past movements and therefore will not follow a discernible pattern

R and R *US mil abbrev for* rest and recreation

randy ('rændɪ) *adj* **randier, randiest** **1** *inf, chiefly Brit* sexually eager or lustful **2** *chiefly Scot* lacking any sense of propriety; reckless ▷ *n, pl* **randies** **3** *chiefly Scot* a rude or reckless person [C17 prob. from obs. *rand* to RANT] > '**randily** *adv* > '**randiness** *n*

ranee ('rɑːnɪ) *n* a variant spelling of **rani**

rang (ræŋ) *vb* the past tense of **ring²**

USAGE See at **ring**

rangatira (,rʌŋgə'tɪərə) *n NZ* a Maori chief of either sex [from Maori]

rangatiratanga (,rʌŋgətɪərə'tʌŋgə) *n NZ* the condition of being a Maori chief; sovereignty [Maori]

range (reɪndʒ) *n* **1** the limits within which a person or thing can function effectively: *the violin has a range of five octaves* **2** the limits within which any fluctuation takes place: *a range of values* **3** the total products of a manufacturer, designer, or stockist: *the new spring range* **4a** the maximum effective distance of a projectile fired from a weapon **4b** the distance between a target and a weapon **5** an area set aside for shooting practice or rocket testing **6** the total distance which a ship, aircraft, or land vehicle is capable of covering without taking on fresh fuel: *the range of this car is about 160 miles* **7** *maths* (of a function or variable) the set of values that a function or variable can take **8** *US & Canad* **8a** an extensive tract of open land on which livestock can graze **8b** (*as modifier*): *range cattle* **9** the geographical region in which a species of plant or animal normally grows or lives **10** a rank, row, or series of items **11** a series or chain of mountains **12** a large stove with burners and one or more ovens, usually heated by solid fuel **13** the act or process of ranging ▷ *vb* **ranges, ranging, ranged** **14** to establish or be situated in a line, row, or series **15** (*tr; often reflexive*, foll by *with*) to put into a specific category; classify: *she ranges herself with the angels* **16** (foll by *on*) to aim or point (a telescope, gun, etc) or (of a gun, telescope, etc) to be pointed or aimed **17** to establish the distance of (a target) from (a weapon) **18** (*intr*) (of a gun or missile) to have a specified range **19** (when *intr*, foll by *over*) to wander about (in) an area; roam (over) **20** (*intr*; foll by *over*) (of an animal or plant) to live or grow in its normal habitat **21** (*tr*) to put (cattle) to graze on a range **22** (*intr*) to fluctuate within specific limits **23** (*intr*) to extend or run in a specific direction **24** (*intr*) *naut* (of a vessel) to swing back and forth while at anchor **25** (*tr*) to make (lines of printers' type) level or even at the margin [C13 from OF: row, from *ranger* to position, from *renc* line]

rangefinder ('reɪndʒ,faɪndə) *n* an instrument for determining the distance of an object from the observer, esp in order to sight a gun or focus a camera

ranger ('reɪndʒə) *n* **1** (*sometimes cap*) an official in charge of a forest, park, nature reserve, etc **2** *orig US* a person employed to patrol a State or national park. Brit equivalent: **warden** **3** *US* one of a body of armed troops employed to police a State or district: *a Texas ranger* **4** (in the US) a commando specially trained in making raids **5** a person who wanders about; a rover

Ranger *or* **Ranger Guide** ('reɪndʒə) *n Brit* a member of the senior branch of the Guides

rangiora (,ræŋgɪ'ɔːrə) *n* a broad-leaved shrub of New Zealand [from Maori]

Rangoon (ræŋ'guːn) *n* the former name (until 1989) of **Yangon**

rangy ('reɪndʒɪ) *adj* **rangier, rangiest** **1** having long slender limbs **2** adapted to wandering or roaming **3** allowing considerable freedom of movement; spacious > **'rangily** *adv* > **'ranginess** *n*

rani *or* **ranee** ('rɑːnɪ) *n* an Indian queen or princess; the wife of a rajah [C17 from Hindi: queen, from Sansk. *rājñī*]

Ranjit Singh ('rʌndʒɪt 'sɪŋ) *n* called *the Lion of the Punjab*. 1780–1839; founder of the Sikh kingdom in the Punjab

rank[1] (ræŋk) *n* **1** a position, esp an official one, within a social organization: *the rank of captain* **2** high social or other standing; status **3** a line or row of people or things **4** the position of an item in any ordering or sequence **5** *Brit* a place where taxis wait to be hired **6** a line of soldiers drawn up abreast of each other **7** any of the eight horizontal rows of squares on a chessboard **8** **close ranks** to maintain discipline or solidarity **9** **pull rank** to get one's own way by virtue of one's superior position or rank **10** **rank and file** **10a** the ordinary soldiers, excluding the officers **10b** the great mass or majority of any group, as opposed to the leadership **10c** (*modifier*): *rank-and-file support* ▷ *vb* **11** (*tr*) to arrange (people or things) in rows or lines; range **12** to accord or be accorded a specific position in an organization or group **13** (*tr*) to array a set of objects as a sequence: *to rank students by their test scores* **14** (*intr*) to be important; rate: *money ranks low in her order of priorities* **15** *chiefly US* to take precedence or surpass in rank [C16 from OF *ranc* row, rank, of Gmc origin]

rank[2] (ræŋk) *adj* **1** showing vigorous and profuse growth: *rank weeds* **2** highly offensive or disagreeable, esp in smell or taste **3** (*prenominal*) complete or absolute; utter: *a rank outsider* **4** coarse or vulgar; gross: *his language was rank* [OE *ranc* straight, noble] > **'rankly** *adv* > **'rankness** *n*

Rank *n* **1** (ræŋk) **J(oseph) Arthur**, 1st Baron 1888–1972, British industrialist and film executive, whose companies dominated the British film industry in the 1940s and 1950s **2** (*German* raŋk) **Otto** ('ɔto) 1884–1939, Austrian psychoanalyst, noted for his theory that the trauma of birth may be reflected in certain forms of mental illness

ranker ('ræŋkə) *n* **1** a soldier in the ranks **2** a commissioned officer who entered service as a noncommissioned recruit

ranking ('ræŋkɪŋ) *adj* **1** *chiefly US & Canad* prominent; high ranking **2** *Caribbean sl* possessed of style; exciting ▷ *n* **3** a position on a scale; rating: *a ranking in a tennis tournament*

rankism ('ræənk,ɪzəm) *n* discrimininination against people on the grounds of rank

rankle ('ræŋkᵊl) *vb* **rankles, rankling, rankled** (*intr*) to cause severe and continuous irritation, anger, or bitterness; fester [C14 *ranclen*, from OF *draoncle* ulcer, from L *dracunculus* dim. of *dracō* serpent]

ransack ('rænsæk) *vb* (*tr*) **1** to search through every part of (a house, box, etc); examine thoroughly **2** to plunder; pillage [C13 from ON *rann* house + *saka* to search] > **'ransacker** *n*

ransom ('rænsəm) *n* **1** the release of captured prisoners, property, etc, on payment of a stipulated price **2** the price demanded or stipulated for such a release **3** **hold to ransom** **3a** to keep (prisoners, etc) in confinement until payment for their release is received **3b** to attempt to force (a person) to comply with one's demands **4** **a king's ransom** a very large amount of money or valuables ▷ *vb* (*tr*) **5** to pay a stipulated price and so obtain the release of (prisoners, property, etc) **6** to set free (prisoners, property, etc) upon receiving the payment demanded **7** to redeem; rescue: *Christ ransomed men from sin* [C14 from OF *ransoun*, from L *redemptiō* a buying back] > **'ransomer** *n*

Ransom ('rænsəm) *n* **John Crowe** 1888–1974, US poet and critic

Ransome ('rænsəm) *n* **Arthur** 1884–1967, English writer, best known for his books for children, including *Swallows and Amazons* (1930) and *Great Northern?* (1947)

rant (rænt) *vb* **1** to utter (something) in loud, violent, or bombastic tones ▷ *n* **2** loud, declamatory, or extravagant speech; bombast [C16 from Du. *ranten* to rave] > **'ranter** *n* > **'ranting** *adj, n* > **'rantingly** *adv*

ranunculaceous (rə,nʌŋkjʊ'leɪʃəs) *adj* of, relating to, or belonging to a N temperate family of flowering plants typically having flowers with five petals and numerous anthers and styles. The family includes the buttercup, clematis, and columbine

ranunculus (rə'nʌŋkjʊləs) *n, pl* **ranunculuses** *or* **ranunculi** (-,laɪ) any of a genus of ranunculaceous plants having finely divided leaves and typically yellow five-petalled flowers. The genus includes buttercup, crowfoot, and spearwort [C16 from L: tadpole, from *rāna* frog]

RAOC *abbrev for* Royal Army Ordnance Corps

rap[1] (ræp) *vb* **raps, rapping, rapped** **1** to strike (a fist, stick, etc) against (something) with a sharp quick blow; knock **2** (*intr*) to make a sharp loud sound, esp by knocking **3** (*tr*) to rebuke or criticize sharply **4** (*tr*; foll by *out*) to put (forth) in sharp rapid speech; utter in an abrupt fashion: *to rap out orders* **5** (*intr*) *sl* to talk, esp volubly **6** (*intr*) to perform a rhythmic monologue with musical backing **7** **rap over the knuckles** to reprimand ▷ *n* **8** a sharp quick blow or the sound produced by such a blow **9** a sharp rebuke or criticism **10** *sl* voluble talk; chatter **11a** a fast, rhythmic monologue over a musical backing **11b** (*as modifier*): *rap music* **12** **beat the rap** *US & Canad sl* to escape punishment or be acquitted of a crime **13** **take the rap** *sl* to suffer the punishment for a crime, whether guilty or not [C14 prob. from ON; cf. Swedish *rappa* to beat]

rap[2] (ræp) *n* (*used with a negative*) the least amount (esp in **not care a rap**) [C18 prob. from *ropaire* counterfeit coin formerly current in Ireland]

rap[3] (ræp) *vb* **raps, rapping, rapped** *n Austral inf* a variant spelling of **wrap** (senses 8, 14)

rapacious (rə'peɪʃəs) *adj* **1** practising pillage or rapine **2** greedy or grasping **3** (of animals, esp birds) subsisting by catching living prey [c17 from L *rapāx*, from *rapere* to seize] > **ra'paciously** *adv* > **rapacity** (rə'pæsɪtɪ) *or* **ra'paciousness** *n*

Rapacki (*Polish* ra'patski) *n* **Adam** ('adam) 1909–70, Polish politician: foreign minister (1956–68): proposed (1957) the denuclearization of Poland, Czechoslovakia, East Germany, and West Germany (the **Rapacki Plan**): rejected by the West because of Soviet predominance in conventional weapons

Rapallo (*Italian* ra'pallo) *n* a port and resort in NW Italy, in Liguria on the **Gulf of Rapallo** (an inlet of the Ligurian Sea): scene of the signing of two treaties after World War I. Pop: 30 000 (1990 est)

Rapa Nui ('rɑːpɑː 'nuːɪ) *n* another name for **Easter Island**

rape[1] (reɪp) *n* **1** the offence of forcing a person, esp a woman, to submit to sexual intercourse against that person's will **2** the act of despoiling a country in warfare **3** any violation or abuse: *the rape of justice* **4** *arch* abduction: *the rape of the Sabine women* ▹ *vb* **rapes, raping, raped** (*mainly tr*) **5** to commit rape upon (a person) **6** *arch* to carry off by force; abduct [c14 from L *rapere* to seize] > **'rapist** *n*

rape[2] (reɪp) *n* a Eurasian plant that is cultivated for its seeds, **rapeseed,** which yield a useful oil, **rape oil,** and as a fodder plant. Also called: **colza, cole** [c14 from L *rāpum* turnip]

rape[3] (reɪp) *n* (*often pl*) the skins and stalks of grapes left after wine-making: used in making vinegar [c17 from F *râpe*, of Gmc origin]

Raphael ('ræfeɪəl) *n* **1** *Bible* one of the archangels; the angel of healing and the guardian of Tobias (Tobit 3:17; 5-12). Feast day: Sept 29 **2** original name *Raffaello Santi* or *Sanzio*. 1483–1520, Italian painter and architect; his paintings include the *Sistine Madonna* (?1513) > ˌ**Raphael'esque** *adj*

raphia ('ræfɪə) *n* a variant spelling of **raffia**

raphide ('reɪfaɪd) *or* **raphis** ('reɪfɪs) *n, pl* **raphides** ('ræfɪˌdiːz) needle-shaped crystals, usually of calcium oxalate, that occur in many plant cells [c18 from F, from Gk *rhaphis* needle]

rapid ('ræpɪd) *adj* **1** (of an action) performed or occurring during a short interval of time; quick **2** acting or moving quickly; fast: *a rapid worker* ▹ See also **rapids** [c17 from L *rapidus* tearing away, from *rapere* to seize] > **'rapidly** *adv* > **rapidity** (rə'pɪdɪtɪ) *or* **'rapidness** *n*

rapid eye movement *n* movement of the eyeballs during paradoxical sleep, while the sleeper is dreaming. Abbrev: **REM**

rapid fire *n* **1** a fast rate of gunfire ▹ *adj* **rapid-fire** **2** firing shots rapidly **3** done, delivered, or occurring in rapid succession

rapids ('ræpɪdz) *pl n* part of a river where the water is very fast and turbulent

rapier ('reɪpɪə) *n* **1** a long narrow two-edged sword with a guarded hilt, used as a thrusting weapon, popular in the 16th and 17th centuries **2** a smaller single-edged 18th-century sword, used principally in France [c16 from OF *espee rapiere*, lit.: rasping sword]

rapine ('ræpaɪn) *n* the seizure of property by force; pillage [c15 from L *rapīna* plundering, from *rapere* to snatch]

rap jumping *n* the sport of descending high buildings, attached to ropes and a pulley

rappee (ræ'piː) *n* a moist English snuff [c18 from F *tabac râpé*, lit.: scraped tobacco]

rappel (ræ'pɛl) *vb* **rappels, rappelling, rappelled,** *n* **1** another word for **abseil** ▹ *n* **2** (formerly) a drumbeat to call soldiers to arms [c19 from F, from *rappeler* to call back, from L *appellāre* to summon]

rappé pie ('ræpeɪ) *or* **rappe** *n Canad* an Acadian dish of grated potatoes and pork or chicken [from Acadian F *tarte râpée* grated pie]

rapport (ræ'pɔː) *n* (often foll by *with*) a sympathetic relationship or understanding. See also **en rapport** [c15 from F, from *rapporter* to bring back, from RE- + *aporter*, from L *apportāre*, from *ad* to + *portāre* to carry]

rapprochement *French* (raprɔʃmɑ̃) *n* a resumption of friendly relations, esp between two countries [c19 lit.: bringing closer]

rapscallion (ræp'skæljən) *n* a disreputable person; rascal or rogue [c17 from earlier *rascallion*; see RASCAL]

rapt[1] (ræpt) *adj* **1** totally absorbed; engrossed; spellbound, esp through or as if through emotion: *rapt with wonder* **2** characterized by or proceeding from rapture: *a rapt smile* [c14 from L *raptus* carried away, from *rapere* to seize] > **'raptly** *adv*

rapt[2] (ræpt) *adj Austral inf* Also: **wrapped** very pleased; delighted

raptor ('ræptə) *n* **1** another name for **bird of prey** **2** *inf* a carnivorous bipedal dinosaur of the late Cretaceous period [c17 from L: plunderer, from *rapere* to take by force]

raptorial (ræp'tɔːrɪəl) *adj zool* **1** (of the feet of birds) adapted for seizing prey **2** of or relating to birds of prey [c19 from L *raptor* robber, from *rapere* to snatch]

rapture ('ræptʃə) *n* **1** the state of mind resulting from feelings of high emotion; joyous ecstasy **2** (*often pl*) an expression of ecstatic joy **3** the act of transporting a person from one sphere of existence to another ▹ *vb* **raptures, rapturing, raptured** **4** (*tr*) *arch or literary* to enrapture [c17 from Med. L *raptūra*, from L *raptus* RAPT[1]] > **'rapturous** *adj*

RAR *abbrev for* Royal Australian Regiment
▹ www.rar.org.au

rara avis ('rɛərə 'eɪvɪs) *n, pl* **rarae aves** ('rɛəriː 'eɪviːz) an unusual, uncommon, or exceptional person or thing [L: rare bird]

rare[1] (rɛə) *adj* **1** not widely known; not frequently used or experienced; uncommon or unusual: *a rare word* **2** not widely distributed; not generally occurring: *a rare herb* **3** (of a gas, esp the atmosphere at high altitudes) having a low density; thin; rarefied **4** uncommonly great; extreme: *kind to a rare degree* **5** exhibiting uncommon excellence: *rare skill* [c14 from L *rārus* sparse] > **'rareness** *n*

Rr

rare[2] (rɛə) *adj* (of meat, esp beef) very lightly cooked [OE *hrēr*; rel. to *hreaw* RAW]

rarebit ('rɛəbɪt) *n* another term for **Welsh rabbit** [c18 by folk etymology from (WELSH) RABBIT; see RARE[2], BIT[1]]

rare earth *n* **1** any oxide of a lanthanide **2** Also called: **rare-earth element** any element of the lanthanide series

raree show ('rɛəriː) *n* **1** a street show or carnival **2** another name for **peepshow** [c17 *raree* from RARE[1]]

rarefaction (ˌrɛərɪ'fækʃən) *or* **rarefication** (ˌrɛərɪfɪ'keɪʃən) *n* the act or process of making less dense or the state of being less dense > ˌ**rare'factive** *adj*

rarefied ('rɛərɪˌfaɪd) *adj* **1** exalted in nature or character; lofty: *a rarefied spiritual existence* **2** current within only a small group **3** thin: *air rarefied at altitude*

rarefy ('rɛərɪˌfaɪ) *vb* **rarefies, rarefying, rarefied** to make or become rarer or less dense; thin out [c14 from OF *raréfier*, from L *rārēfacere*, from *rārus* RARE[1] + *facere* to make] > **'rareˌfiable** *adj* > **'rareˌfier** *n*

rare gas *n* another name for **inert gas**

rarely ('rɛəlɪ) *adv* **1** hardly ever; seldom **2** to an unusual degree; exceptionally **3** *dialect* uncommonly well; excellently: *he did rarely at market yesterday.*

> USAGE Since *rarely* means *hardly ever*, in writing you should not use *rarely ever*, even though it is quite often used in speaking for extra emphasis

raring ('rɛərɪŋ) *adj* ready; willing; enthusiastic (esp in **raring to go**) [c20 from *rare*, var. of REAR[2]]

rarity ('rɛərɪtɪ) *n, pl* **rarities** **1** a rare person or thing, esp something valued because it is uncommon **2** the state of being rare

rark up *vb (tr, adverb) NZ inf* to give (someone) a severe reprimand

Rarotonga (ˌrɛərəˈtɒŋɡə) *n* an island in the S Pacific, in the SW Cook Islands: the chief island of the group. Chief settlement: Avarua. Pop: 9281 (latest est). Area: 67 sq km (26 sq miles)

rasbora (ræzˈbɔːrə) *n* any of the small cyprinid fishes of tropical Asia and East Africa. Many species are brightly coloured and are popular aquarium fishes [from NL, from an East Indian language]

rascal (ˈrɑːskᵊl) *n* **1** a disreputable person; villain **2** a mischievous or impish rogue **3** an affectionate or mildly reproving term, esp for a child: *you little rascal* **4** *obs* a person of lowly birth ▷ *adj* **5** *(prenominal) Obs* **5a** belonging to the rabble **5b** dishonest; knavish [c14 from OF *rascaille* rabble, ?from OF *rasque* mud]

rascality (rɑːˈskælɪtɪ) *n, pl* **rascalities** mischievous or disreputable character or action

rascally (ˈrɑːskəlɪ) *adj* **1** dishonest or mean; base ▷ *adv* **2** in a dishonest or mean fashion

rase (reɪz) *vb* **rases, rasing, rased** a variant spelling of raze

rash[1] (ræʃ) *adj* **1** acting without due thought; impetuous **2** resulting from excessive haste or impetuosity: *a rash word* [c14 from OHG *rasc* hurried, clever] > **ˈrashly** *adv* > **ˈrashness** *n*

rash[2] (ræʃ) *n* **1** *pathol* any skin eruption **2** a series of unpleasant and unexpected occurrences: *a rash of forest fires* [c18 from OF *rasche*, from *raschier* to scratch, from L *rādere* to scrape]

rasher (ˈræʃə) *n* a thin slice of bacon or ham [c16 from ?]

Rashid[1] (ræˈʃiːd) *n* a town in N Egypt, on the Nile delta. Pop: 52 015 (latest est). Former name: **Rosetta**

Rashid[2] (ræˈʃiːd) *n* **Harun al-** See **Harun al-Rashid**

Rasht (ræʃt) *or* **Resht** *n* a city in NW Iran, near the Caspian Sea: agricultural and commercial centre in a rice-growing area. Pop: 417 748 (1996)

Rask (*Danish* rasg) *n* **Rasmus Christian** (ˈrasmus ˈkresdjan) 1787–1832, Danish philologist. He pioneered comparative philology with his work on Old Norse (1818)

Rasmussen (*Danish* ˈrasmusən) *n* **Knud Johan Victor** (knuð joˈhan ˈviktɔr) 1879–1933, Danish arctic explorer and ethnologist. He led several expeditions through the Arctic in support of his theory that the North American Indians were originally migrants from Asia

rasp (rɑːsp) *n* **1** a harsh grating noise **2** a coarse file with rows of raised teeth ▷ *vb* **3** *(tr)* to scrape or rub (something) roughly, esp with a rasp; abrade **4** to utter with or make a harsh grating noise **5** to irritate (one's nerves); grate (upon) [c16 from OF *raspe*, of Gmc origin; cf. OHG *raspōn* to scrape] > **ˈrasper** *n* > **ˈrasping** *adj* > **ˈraspish** *adj*

raspberry (ˈrɑːzbərɪ, -brɪ) *n, pl* **raspberries** **1** a prickly rosaceous shrub of North America and Europe that has pinkish-white flowers and typically red berry-like fruits (drupelets). See also **bramble** **2a** the fruit of any such plant **2b** *(as modifier): raspberry jelly* **3a** a dark purplish-red colour **3b** *(as adj): a raspberry dress* **4** a spluttering noise made with the tongue and lips to express contempt (esp in **blow a raspberry**) [c17 from earlier *raspis* raspberry, from ? + BERRY]

Rasputin (ræˈspjuːtɪn; *Russian* rasˈputin) *n* **Grigori Efimovich** (ɡriˈɡɔrij jɪˈfimәvitʃ) ?1871–1916, Siberian peasant monk, notorious for his debauchery, who wielded great influence over Tsarina Alexandra. He was assassinated by a group of Russian noblemen

Ras Tafari (ræs təˈfɑːrɪ) *n* See **Haile Selassie**

Rastafarian (ˌræstəˈfɛərɪən) *n* **1** a member of an originally Jamaican religion that regards Ras Tafari, the former emperor of Ethiopia, Haile Selassie, as God ▷ *adj* **2** of, characteristic of, or relating to the Rastafarians ▷ Often shortened to **Rasta**
▷ www.rastafarian.net/

raster (ˈræstə) *n* a pattern of horizontal scanning lines, esp those traced by an electron beam on a television screen or those in a digitized bitmap image [c20 via G from L: rake, from *rādere* to scrape]

rat (ræt) *n* **1** any of numerous long-tailed Old World rodents, that are similar to but larger than mice and are now distributed all over the world **2** *inf* a person who deserts his or her friends or associates, esp in time of trouble **3** *inf* a worker who works during a strike; blackleg; scab **4** *inf* a despicable person **5** **have** *or* **be rats** *Austral sl* to be mad or eccentric **6** **smell a rat** to detect something suspicious ▷ *vb* **rats, ratting, ratted** **7** *(intr; usually foll by on)* **7a** to divulge secret information (about); betray the trust (of) **7b** to default (on); abandon **8** to hunt and kill rats [OE *rætt*]

rata (ˈrɑːtə) *n* a New Zealand tree with red flowers [from Maori]

ratable *or* **rateable** (ˈreɪtəbᵊl) *adj* **1** able to be rated or evaluated **2** *Brit* (of property) liable to payment of rates > **ˌrataˈbility** *or* **ˌrateaˈbility** *n* > **ˈratably** *or* **ˈrateably** *adv*

ratable value *n Brit* (formerly) a fixed value assigned to a property by a local authority, on the basis of which variable annual rates are charged

ratafia (ˌrætəˈfɪə) *or* **ratafee** (ˌrætəˈfiː) *n* **1** any liqueur made from fruit or from brandy with added fruit **2** a flavouring essence made from almonds **3** *chiefly Brit* Also called: **ratafia biscuit** a small macaroon flavoured with almonds [c17 from West Indian Creole F]

ratan (ræˈtæn) *n* a variant spelling of **rattan**

rat-arsed *adj Brit sl* drunk

rat-a-tat-tat (ˈrætəˌtætˈtæt) *or* **rat-a-tat** (ˈrætəˈtæt) *n* the sound of knocking on a door

ratatouille (ˌrætəˈtwiː) *n* a vegetable casserole made of tomatoes, aubergines, peppers, etc, fried in oil and stewed slowly [c19 from F, from *touiller* to stir, from L, from *tudes* hammer]

ratbag (ˈrætˌbæɡ) *n sl* an eccentric, stupid, or unreliable person

rat-catcher *n* a person whose job is to destroy or drive away vermin, esp rats

ratchet (ˈrætʃɪt) *n* **1** a device in which a toothed rack or wheel is engaged by a pawl to permit motion in one direction only **2** the toothed rack or wheel forming part of such a device [c17 from F *rochet*, from OF *rocquet* blunt head of a lance, of Gmc origin]

ratchet effect *n econ* an effect that occurs when a price or wage increases as a result of temporary pressure but fails to fall back when the pressure is removed

rate[1] (reɪt) *n* **1** a quantity or amount considered in relation to or measured against another quantity or amount: *a rate of 70 miles an hour* **2a** a price or charge with reference to a standard or scale: *rate of interest* **2b** *(as modifier): a rate card* **3** a charge made per unit for a commodity, service, etc **4** See **rates** **5** the relative speed of progress or change of something variable; pace: *the rate of production has doubled* **6a** relative quality; class or grade **6b** *(in combination): first-rate ideas* **7** **at any rate** in any case; at all events; anyway ▷ *vb* **rates, rating, rated** *(mainly tr)* **8** *(also intr)* to assign or receive a position on a scale of relative values; rank: *he is rated fifth in the world* **9** to estimate the value of; evaluate: *we rate your services highly* **10** to be worthy of; deserve: *this hotel does not rate four stars* **11** to consider; regard: *I rate him among my friends* **12** *Brit* to assess the value of (property) for the purpose of local taxation [c15 from OF, from Med. L *rata*, from L *prō ratā parte* according to a fixed proportion, from *ratus* fixed, from *rērī* to think, decide]

rate[2] (reɪt) *vb* **rates, rating, rated** *(tr)* to scold or criticize severely; rebuke harshly [c14 ? rel. to Swedish *rata* to chide]

rateable ('reɪtəbᵊl) *adj* a variant spelling of **ratable**

rate-cap ('reɪt,kæp) *vb* **rate-caps, rate-capping, rate-capped** (*tr*) (formerly in Britain) to impose on (a local authority) an upper limit on the rate it may levy > **'rate-,capping** *n*

ratel ('reɪtᵊl) *n* **1** a carnivorous mammal related to the badger family, inhabiting wooded regions of Africa and S Asia. It has a massive body, strong claws, and a thick coat that is paler on the back. It feeds on honey and small animals **2** *S African* a six-wheeled armoured vehicle [c18 from Afrik.]

rate of exchange *n* See **exchange rate**

rate of return *n finance* the ratio of the annual income from an investment to the original investment, often expressed as a percentage

ratepayer ('reɪt,peɪə) *n* **1** (in Canada) a person subject to local rates, esp a householder **2** (in Britain) a person subject to local nondomestic rates

rates (reɪts) *pl n* (in Australia, Canada and Britain) a tax levied on property (in Britain on business and other nondomestic property only) by a local authority

Rathenau (*German* 'ra:tənau) *n* **Walther** ('valtər) 1867–1922, German industrialist and statesman: he organized the German war industries during World War I, became minister of reconstruction (1921) and of foreign affairs (1922), and was largely responsible for the treaty of Rapallo with Russia. His assassination by right-wing extremists caused a furore

rather ('rɑ:ðə) *adv* (*in senses 1-4, not used with a negative*) **1** relatively or fairly; somewhat: *it's rather dull* **2** to a significant or noticeable extent; quite: *she's rather pretty* **3** to a limited extent or degree: *I rather thought that was the case* **4** with better or more just cause: *this text is rather to be deleted than rewritten* **5** more readily or willingly; sooner: *I would rather not see you tomorrow* ▷ *sentence connector* **6** on the contrary: *it's not cold. Rather, it's very hot* ▷ *sentence substitute* ('rɑ:'ðɜ:) **7** an expression of strong affirmation: *Is it worth seeing? Rather!* [OE *hrathor* comp. of *hræth* READY, quick]

> USAGE Both *would* and *had* are used with *rather* in sentences such as *I would rather* (or *had rather*) *go to the film than to the play*. *Had rather* is less common and now widely regarded as slightly old-fashioned

ratify ('rætɪ,faɪ) *vb* **ratifies, ratifying, ratified** (*tr*) to give formal approval or consent to [c14 via OF from L *ratus* fixed (see RATE[1]) + *facere* to make] > **'rati,fiable** *adj* > **,ratifi'cation** *n* > **'rati,fier** *n*

rating[1] ('reɪtɪŋ) *n* **1** a classification according to order or grade; ranking **2** an ordinary seaman **3** *sailing* a handicap assigned to a racing boat based on its dimensions, draught, etc **4** the estimated financial or credit standing of a business enterprise or individual **5** *radio, television, etc* a figure based on statistical sampling indicating what proportion of the total audience tune in to a specific programme

rating[2] ('reɪtɪŋ) *n* a sharp scolding or rebuke

ratio ('reɪʃɪəʊ) *n, pl* **ratios 1** a measure of the relative size of two classes expressible as a proportion: *the ratio of boys to girls is 2 to 1* **2** *maths* a quotient of two numbers or quantities. See also **proportion** (sense 6) [c17 from L: a reckoning, from *rērī* to think]

ratiocinate (,rætɪ'ɒsɪ,neɪt) *vb* **ratiocinates, ratiocinating, ratiocinated** (*intr*) to think or argue logically and methodically; reason [c17 from L *ratiōcinārī* to calculate, from *ratiō* REASON] > **,rati,oci'nation** *n* > **,rati'oci,native** *adj* > **,rati'oci,nator** *n*

ration ('ræʃən) *n* **1a** a fixed allowance of food, provisions, etc, esp a statutory one for civilians in time of scarcity or soldiers in time of war **1b** (*as modifier*): *a ration book* **2** a sufficient or adequate amount: *you've had your ration of television for today* ▷ *vb* (*tr*) **3** (often foll by *out*) to distribute (provisions), esp to an army **4** to restrict the distribution or consumption of (a commodity) by (people): *the government has rationed sugar* ▷ See also **rations** [c18 via F from L *ratiō* REASON]

rational ('ræʃənᵊl) *adj* **1** using reason or logic in thinking out a problem **2** in accordance with the principles of logic or reason; reasonable **3** of sound mind; sane: *the patient seemed rational* **4** endowed with the capacity to reason: *rational beings* **5** *maths* **5a** expressible as a ratio of two integers **5b** (of an expression, equation, etc) containing no variable either in irreducible radical form or raised to a fractional power ▷ *n* **6** a rational number [c14 from L *ratiōnālis*, from *ratiō* REASON] > **,ratio'nality** *n* > **'rationally** *adv* > **'rationalness** *n*

rationale (,ræʃə'nɑ:l) *n* a reasoned exposition, esp one defining the fundamental reasons for an action, etc [c17 from NL, from L *ratiōnālis*]

rationalism ('ræʃənə,lɪzəm) *n* **1** reliance on reason rather than intuition to justify one's beliefs or actions **2** *philosophy* the doctrine that knowledge is acquired by reason without regard to experience **3** the belief that knowledge and truth are ascertained by rational thought and not by divine or supernatural revelation > **'rationalist** *n* > **,rational'istic** *adj* > **,rational'istically** *adv*

▷ http://radicalacademy.com/adiphilrationalism.htm

rationalize *or* **rationalise** ('ræʃənə,laɪz) *vb* **rationalizes, rationalizing, rationalized** *or* **rationalises, rationalising, rationalised 1** to justify (one's actions) with plausible reasons, esp after the event **2** to apply logic or reason to (something) **3** (*tr*) to eliminate unnecessary equipment, etc, from (a group of businesses, factory, etc), in order to make it more efficient **4** (*tr*) *maths* to eliminate radicals without changing the value of (an expression) or the roots of (an equation) > **,rationali'zation** *or* **,rationali'sation** *n* > **'rational,izer** *or* **'rational,iser** *n*

rational number *n* any real number of the form *a*/*b*, where *a* and *b* are integers and *b* is not zero, as 7 or 7/3

Rr

rations ('ræʃənz) *pl n* (*sometimes sing*) a fixed daily allowance of food, esp to military personnel or when supplies are limited

Ratisbon ('rætɪz,bɒn) *n* the former English name for **Regensburg**

ratite ('rætaɪt) *adj* **1** (of flightless birds) having a breastbone that lacks a keel for the attachment of flight muscles **2** of or denoting the flightless birds, that have a flat breastbone, feathers lacking vanes, and reduced wings ▷ *n* **3** a bird, such as an ostrich, that belongs to this group; a flightless bird [c19 from L *ratis* raft]

rat kangaroo *n* any of several ratlike kangaroos that occur in Australia and Tasmania

ratline *or* **ratlin** ('rætlɪn) *n naut* any of a series of light lines tied across the shrouds of a sailing vessel for climbing aloft [c15 from ?]

ratoon *or* **rattoon** (ræ'tu:n) *n* **1** a new shoot that grows from near the root of crop plants, esp the sugar cane, after the old growth has been cut back ▷ *vb* **2** to propagate by such a growth [c18 from Sp. *retoño*, from RE- + *otoñar* to sprout in autumn, from *otoño* AUTUMN]

ratpack ('ræt,pæk) *n derog sl* those members of the press who pursue celebrities and give wide, often intrusive, coverage of their private lives: *the royal ratpack*

rat race *n* a continual routine of hectic competitive activity: *working in the City is a real rat race*

rat-run *n* a route through residential side streets taken by drivers who want to avoid congested main areas > **'rat-,runner** *n* > **'rat-,running** *n*

ratsbane ('ræts,beɪn) *n* rat poison, esp arsenic oxide

rat-tail *n* **1a** a horse's tail that has no hairs **1b** a horse having such a tail **2** a style of spoon in which the line of the handle is prolonged in a tapering moulding along the back of the bowl

rattan *or* **ratan** (ræ'tæn) *n* **1** a climbing palm having tough stems used for wickerwork and canes **2** the stems of such a plant collectively **3** a stick made from one of these stems [c17 from Malay *rōtan*]

ratter ('rætə) *n* **1** a dog or cat that catches and kills rats **2** another word for **rat** (sense 3)

Rattigan ('rætɪgən) *n* Sir **Terence Mervyn** 1911–77, English playwright. His plays include *The Winslow Boy* (1946), *Separate Tables* (1954), and *Ross* (1960)

rattle ('ræt^əl) *vb* **rattles, rattling, rattled 1** to make a rapid succession of short sharp sounds, as of loose pellets colliding when shaken in a container **2** to shake with such a sound **3** to send, move, drive, etc, with such a sound: *the car rattled along the country road* **4** (*intr;* foll by *on*) to chatter idly: *he rattled on about his work* **5** (*tr;* foll by *off, out,* etc) to recite perfunctorily or rapidly **6** (*tr*) *inf* to disconcert; make frightened or anxious ▷ *n* **7** a rapid succession of short sharp sounds **8** a baby's toy filled with small pellets that rattle when shaken **9** a series of loosely connected horny segments on the tail of a rattlesnake, vibrated to produce a rattling sound **10** any of various European scrophulariaceous plants having a capsule in which the seeds rattle, such as the **red rattle** and the **yellow rattle 11** idle chatter **12** *med* another name for **rale** [c14 from MDu. *ratelen,* imit.] > **'rattly** *adj*

Rattle ('ræt^əl) *n* Sir **Simon** born 1955, British conductor. Principal conductor (1980–91) and music director (1991–98) of the City of Birmingham Symphony Orchestra; chief conductor of the Berlin Philharmonic Orchestra from 2002

rattler ('rætlə) *n* **1** a person or thing that rattles **2** *inf* a rattlesnake

rattlesnake ('ræt^əl,sneɪk) *n* any of the venomous New World snakes such as the **black** or **timber rattlesnake** belonging to the family of pit vipers. They have a series of loose horny segments on the tail that are vibrated to produce a buzzing or whirring sound

rattletrap ('ræt^əl,træp) *n inf* a broken-down old vehicle, esp an old car

rattling ('rætlɪŋ) *adv inf* (intensifier qualifying something good, fine, etc): *a rattling good lunch*

ratty ('rætɪ) *adj* **rattier, rattiest 1** *Brit & NZ inf* irritable; annoyed **2** *inf* (of the hair) straggly, unkempt, or greasy **3** *US & Canad sl* shabby; dilapidated **4** *Austral sl* mad, eccentric, or odd **5** of, like, or full of rats > **'rattily** *adv* > **'rattiness** *n*

Ratushinskaya (,rætuː'ʃɪnskaɪjɑː) *n* **Irina** (ɪ'riːnə) born 1954, Russian poet and writer, living in Britain: imprisoned (1983–86) in a Soviet labour camp on charges of subversion. Her publications include *Poems* (1984), *Grey is the Colour of Hope* (1988), and *The Odessans* (1992)

raucous ('rɔːkəs) *adj* (of voices, cries, etc) harshly or hoarsely loud [c18 from L *raucus* hoarse] > **'raucously** *adv* > **'raucousness** *n*

raunchy ('rɔːntʃɪ) *adj* **raunchier, raunchiest** *sl* **1** openly sexual; lusty; earthy **2** *chiefly US* slovenly; dirty [c20 from ?] > **'raunchily** *adv* > **'raunchiness** *n*

raupatu (,raʊ'pɑːtuː) *n NZ* the confiscation or seizure of land [Maori]

raupo ('raʊpəʊ) *n, pl* **raupos** a marsh reed common in New Zealand [from Maori]

Rauschenberg ('raʊʃənbɜːg) *n* **Robert** born 1925, US artist; one of the foremost exponents of pop art

rauwolfia (rɔː'wʊlfɪə, raʊ-) *n* **1** a tropical flowering tree or shrub of SE Asia with latex in its stem **2** the powdered root of this plant: a source of various drugs, esp reserpine [c19 NL, after Leonhard *Rauwolf* (died 1596), G botanist]

ravage ('rævɪdʒ) *vb* **ravages, ravaging, ravaged 1** to cause extensive damage to ▷ *n* **2** (*often pl*) destructive action: *the ravages of time* [c17 from F, from OF *ravir* to snatch away, RAVISH] > **'ravager** *n*

rave (reɪv) *vb* **raves, raving, raved 1** to utter (something) in a wild or incoherent manner, as when delirious **2** (*intr*) to speak in an angry uncontrolled manner **3** (*intr*) (of the sea, wind, etc) to rage or roar **4** (*intr;* foll by *over* or *about*) *inf* to write or speak (about) with great enthusiasm **5** (*intr*) *Brit sl* to enjoy oneself wildly or uninhibitedly ▷ *n* **6** *inf* **6a** enthusiastic or extravagant praise **6b** (*as modifier*): *a rave review* **7** *Brit sl* **7a** Also called: **rave-up** a party **7b** a professionally organized party for young people, with electronic dance music, sometimes held in a field or disused building **8** a name given to various types of dance music, such as techno, that feature fast electronic rhythm [c14 *raven,* apparently from OF *resver* to wander]

ravel ('ræv^əl) *vb* **ravels, ravelling, ravelled** *or US* **ravels, raveling, raveled 1** to tangle (threads, fibres, etc) or (of threads, etc) to become entangled **2** (often foll by *out*) to tease or draw out (the fibres of a fabric) or (of a fabric) to fray out in loose ends; unravel **3** (*tr;* usually foll by *out*) to disentangle or resolve: *to ravel out a complicated story* ▷ *n* **4** a tangle or complication [c16 from MDu. *ravelen*] > **'raveller** *n* > **'ravelly** *adj*

Ravel (*French* ravɛl) *n* **Maurice (Joseph)** (mɔris) 1875–1937, French composer, noted for his use of unresolved dissonances and mastery of tone colour. His works include *Gaspard de la Nuit* (1908) and *Le Tombeau de Couperin* (1917) for piano, *Boléro* (1928) for orchestra, and the ballet *Daphnis et Chloé* (1912)

raven[1] ('reɪv^ən) *n* **1** a large passerine bird of the crow family, having a large straight bill, long wedge-shaped tail, and black plumage **2a** a shiny black colour **2b** (*as adj*): *raven hair* [OE *hrǣfn*]

raven[2] ('ræv^ən) *vb* **1** to seize or seek (plunder, prey, etc) **2** to eat (something) voraciously or greedily [c15 from OF *raviner* to attack impetuously; see RAVENOUS]

Raven ('reɪv^ən) *n* a traditional trickster hero among the native peoples of the Canadian Pacific Northwest [from RAVEN]

ravening ('rævənɪŋ) *adj* (of animals) voracious; predatory > **'raveningly** *adv*

Ravenna (rə'vɛnə; *Italian* ra'venna) *n* a city and port in NE Italy, in Emilia-Romagna: capital of the Western Roman Empire from 402 to 476, of the Ostrogoths from 493 to 526, and of the Byzantine exarchate from 584 to 751; famous for its ancient mosaics. Pop: 138 418 (2000 est)

ravenous ('rævənəs) *adj* **1** famished; starving **2** rapacious; voracious [c16 from OF *ravineux,* from L *rapīna* plunder, from *rapere* to seize] > **'ravenously** *adv* > **'ravenousness** *n*

raver ('reɪvə) *n* **1** *Brit sl* a person who leads a wild or uninhibited social life **2** *sl* a person who enjoys rave music, esp one who frequents raves

ravine (rə'viːn) *n* a deep narrow steep-sided valley [c15 from OF: torrent, from L *rapīna* robbery, infl. by L *rapidus* RAPID, both from *rapere* to snatch]

raving ('reɪvɪŋ) *adj* **1a** delirious; frenzied **1b** (*as adv*): *raving mad* **2** *inf* (intensifier): *a raving beauty* ▷ *n* **3** (*usually pl*) frenzied or wildly extravagant talk or utterances > **'ravingly** *adv*

ravioli (,rævɪ'əʊlɪ) *n* small squares of pasta containing a savoury mixture of meat, cheese, etc [c19 It. dialect, lit.: little turnips, from It. *rava* turnip, from L *rāpa*]

ravish ('rævɪʃ) *vb* (*tr*) **1** (*often passive*) to enrapture **2** to rape **3** *arch* to carry off by force [c13 from OF *ravir,* from L *rapere* to seize] > **'ravisher** *n* > **'ravishment** *n*

ravishing ('rævɪʃɪŋ) *adj* delightful; lovely; entrancing > **'ravishingly** *adv*

raw (rɔː) *adj* **1** (of food) not cooked **2** (*prenominal*) in an unfinished, natural, or unrefined state; not treated by manufacturing or other processes: *raw materials* **3** (of the skin, a wound, etc) having the surface exposed or abraded, esp painfully **4** (of an edge of material) unhemmed; liable to fray **5** ignorant, inexperienced, or immature: *a raw recruit* **6** (*prenominal*) not selected or modified: *raw statistics* **7** frank or realistic: *a raw picture of a marriage* **8** (of spirits) undiluted **9** *chiefly US* coarse, vulgar, or obscene **10** (of the weather) harshly cold and damp **11** *inf* unfair; unjust (esp in **a raw deal**) ▷ *n* **12** **in the raw 12a** *inf* without clothes; naked **12b** in a natural or unmodified state **13** **the raw** *Brit inf* a sensitive point: *his criticism touched me on the raw* [OE *hreaw*] > **'rawish** *adj* > **'rawly** *adv* > **'rawness** *n*

Rawalpindi (rɔːl'pɪndɪ) *n* an ancient city in N Pakistan: interim capital of Pakistan (1959–67) during the building of Islamabad. Pop: 1 406 214 (1998)

rawboned ('rɔː'bəʊnd) *adj* having a lean bony physique

rawhide ('rɔːˌhaɪd) *n* **1** untanned hide **2** a whip or rope made of strips cut from such a hide

rawhide hammer *n* a hammer, used to avoid damaging a surface, having a head consisting of a metal tube from each end of which a tight roll of hide protrudes

rawinsonde ('reɪwɪnˌsɒnd) *n* a hydrogen balloon carrying meteorological instruments and a radar target, enabling the velocity of winds in the atmosphere to be measured [c20 blend of *radar* + *wind* + *radiosonde*]

Rawlplug ('rɔːlplʌg) *n* *trademark* a short fibre or plastic tube used to provide a fixing in a wall for a screw

raw material *n* **1** material on which a particular manufacturing process is carried out **2** a person or thing regarded as suitable for some particular purpose: *raw material for the army*

raw silk *n* **1** untreated silk fibres reeled from the cocoon **2** fabric woven from such fibres

Rawsthorne ('rɔːsˌθɔːn) *n* **Alan** 1905–71, English composer, whose works include three symphonies, several concertos, and a set of *Symphonic Studies* (1939)

ray[1] (reɪ) *n* **1** a narrow beam of light; gleam **2** a slight indication: *a ray of solace* **3** *maths* a straight line extending from a point **4** a thin beam of electromagnetic radiation or particles **5** any of the bony or cartilaginous spines of the fin of a fish that form the support for the soft part of the fin **6** any of the arms or branches of a starfish **7** *bot* any strand of tissue that runs radially through the vascular tissue of some higher plants ▷ *vb* **8** (of an object) to emit (light) in rays or (of light) to issue in the form of rays **9** (*intr*) (of lines, etc) to extend in rays or on radiating paths **10** (*tr*) to adorn (an ornament, etc) with rays or radiating lines [c14 from OF *rai*, from L *radius* spoke]

ray[2] (reɪ) *n* any of various marine selachian fishes typically having a flattened body, greatly enlarged winglike pectoral fins, gills on the undersurface of the fins, and a long whiplike tail [c14 from OF *raie*, from L *raia*]

ray[3] (reɪ) *n* *music* (in tonic sol-fa) the second degree of any major scale; supertonic [c18 later variant of *re*; see GAMUT]

Ray[1] (reɪ) *n* **Cape** a promontory in SW Newfoundland, Canada

Ray[2] (reɪ) *n* **1** **John** 1627–1705, English naturalist. He originated natural botanical classification and the division of flowering plants into monocotyledons and dicotyledons **2** **Man**, real name *Emmanuel Rudnitsky*. 1890–1976, US surrealist photographer **3** **Satyajit** ('sætjədʒɪt) 1921–92, Indian film director, noted for his *Apu* trilogy (1955–59)

Raybans ('reɪˌbænz) *pl n trademark* a brand of sunglasses

ray floret *or* **flower** *n* any of the small strap-shaped florets in the flower head of certain composite plants, such as the daisy

ray gun *n* (in science fiction) a gun that emits rays to paralyse, stun, or destroy

Rayleigh ('reɪlɪ) *n* **Lord**, title of *John William Strutt*, 1842–1919, British physicist. He discovered argon (1894) with Ramsay and made important contributions to the theory of sound, the theory of scattering of radiation, etc. Nobel prize for physics 1904

rayless ('reɪlɪs) *adj* **1** dark; gloomy **2** lacking rays: *a rayless flower*

raylet ('reɪlɪt) *n* a small ray

rayon ('reɪɒn) *n* **1** any of a number of textile fibres made from wood pulp or other forms of cellulose **2** any fabric made from such a fibre **3** (*as modifier*): *a rayon shirt* [c20 from F, from OF *rai* RAY[1]]

raze *or* **rase** (reɪz) *vb* **razes, razing, razed** *or* **rases, rasing, rased** (*tr*) **1** to demolish (buildings, etc) completely (esp in **raze to the ground**) **2** to delete; erase **3** *arch* to graze [c16 from OF *raser*, from L *rādere* to scrape] > **'razer** *or* **'raser** *n*

razoo (rɑː'zuː) *n, pl* **razoos** *Austral & NZ inf* an imaginary coin: *not a brass razoo; they took every last razoo* [c20 from ?]

razor ('reɪzə) *n* **1** a sharp implement used esp for shaving the face **2** **on a razor's edge** *or* **razor-edge** in an acute dilemma ▷ *vb* **3** (*tr*) to cut or shave with a razor [c13 from OF *raseor*, from *raser* to shave; see RAZE]

razorback ('reɪzəˌbæk) *n* **1** Also called: **finback** another name for the **common rorqual** (see **rorqual**) **2** a wild pig of the US, having a narrow body, long legs, and a ridged back

razorbill ('reɪzəˌbɪl) *or* **razor-billed auk** *n* a common auk of the North Atlantic, having a thick laterally compressed bill with white markings

razor blade *n* a small rectangular piece of metal sharpened on one or both long edges for use in a razor for shaving

razor-shell *n* any of various sand-burrowing bivalve molluscs which have a long tubular shell. US name: **razor clam**

razor wire *n* strong wire with pieces of sharp metal set across it at close intervals

razz (ræz) *US & Canad sl* ▷ *vb* **1** (*tr*) to make fun of; deride ▷ *n* **2** short for **raspberry** (sense 4)

razzle ('ræz[ə]l) *n* *inf* **on the razzle** out enjoying oneself or celebrating, esp while drinking freely [c20 from RAZZLE-DAZZLE]

razzle-dazzle ('ræz[ə]l'dæz[ə]l) *or* **razzmatazz** ('ræzmə'tæz) *n sl* **1** noisy or showy fuss or activity **2** a spree or frolic [c19 rhyming compound from DAZZLE]

Rb *the chemical symbol for* rubidium

RBT *abbrev for* random breath testing

RC *abbrev for*: **1** Red Cross **2** Roman Catholic

RCA *abbrev for*: **1** (formerly) Radio Corporation of America **2** Royal College of Art
▷ www.rca.ac.uk

RCAF *abbrev for* Royal Canadian Air Force
▷ www.airforce.forces.gc.ca

RC CH *abbrev for* Roman Catholic Church

RCM *abbrev for* Royal College of Music

RCMP *abbrev for* Royal Canadian Mounted Police

RCN *abbrev for*: **1** Royal Canadian Navy **2** Royal College of Nursing
▷ www.navy.forces.ca
▷ www.rcn.org.uk

RCP *abbrev for* Royal College of Physicians
▷ www.rcplondon.ac.uk

RCS *abbrev for*: **1** Royal College of Science **2** Royal College of Surgeons **3** Royal Corps of Signals
▷ www.rcsa.org.uk
▷ www.rcseng.ac.uk
▷ www.rcsed.ac.uk

rd *abbrev for*: **1** road **2** rod (unit of length) **3** round **4** *physics* rutherford

Rd *abbrev for* Road

RDA *abbrev for*: **1** recommended daily (*or* dietary) amount (*or* allowance) **2** (in England) Regional Development Agency

re[1] (reɪ, riː) *n* *music* the syllable used in the fixed system of solmization for the note D [c14 see GAMUT]

Rr

re² (riː) *prep* with reference to [C18 from L *rē*, ablative case of *rēs* thing]

> **USAGE** In contexts such as *re your letter*, *your remarks have been noted* or *he spoke to me re your complaint*, *re* is common in business or official correspondence. In spoken and in general written English *with reference to* is preferable in the former case and *about* or *concerning* in the latter. Even in business correspondence, the use of *re* is often restricted to the letter heading

Re¹ (reɪ) *n* another name for **Ra²**

Re² *the chemical symbol for* rhenium

RE *abbrev for:* **1** Religious Education **2** Royal Engineers

re- *prefix* **1** indicating return to a previous condition, withdrawal, etc: *rebuild; renew* **2** indicating repetition of an action: *remarry* [L]

> **USAGE** Verbs beginning with *re-* indicate repetition or restoration. It is unnecessary to add an adverb such as *back* or *again*: *this must not occur again* (not *recur again*); *we recounted the votes* (not *recounted the votes again*, which implies that the votes were counted three times, not twice)

reach (riːtʃ) *vb* **1** (*tr*) to arrive at or get to (a place, person, etc) in the course of movement or action: *to reach the office* **2** to extend as far as (a point or place): *to reach the ceiling; can you reach?* **3** (*tr*) to come to (a certain condition or situation): *to reach the point of starvation* **4** (*intr*) to extend in influence or operation: *the Roman conquest reached throughout England* **5** (*tr*) *inf* to pass or give (something to a person) with the outstretched hand **6** (*intr; foll by out, for, or after*) to make a movement (towards), as if to grasp or touch **7** (*tr*) to make contact or communication with (someone): *we tried to reach him all day* **8** (*tr*) to strike, esp in fencing or boxing **9** (*tr*) to amount to (a certain sum): *to reach five million* **10** (*intr*) *naut* to sail on a tack with the wind on or near abeam ▷ *n* **11** the act of reaching **12** the extent or distance of reaching: *within reach* **13** the range of influence, power, etc **14** an open stretch of water, esp on a river **15** *naut* the direction or distance sailed by a vessel on one tack **16** *advertising* the proportion of a market that an advertiser hopes to reach at least once in a campaign [OE *rǣcan*] > **'reachable** *adj* > **'reacher** *n*

reach-me-down *n* **1a** (*often pl*) a cheaply ready-made or second-hand garment **1b** (*as modifier*): *reach-me-down finery* **2** (*modifier*) not original; derivative: *reach-me-down ideas*

react (rɪ'ækt) *vb* **1** (*intr; foll by to, upon, etc*) (of a person or thing) to act in response to another person, a stimulus, etc **2** (*intr; foll by against*) to act in an opposing or contrary manner **3** (*intr*) *physics* to exert an equal force in the opposite direction to an acting force **4** *chem* to undergo or cause to undergo a chemical reaction [C17 from LL *reagere*, from RE- + L *agere* to do]

re-act (riː'ækt) *vb* (*tr*) to act or perform again

reactance (rɪ'æktəns) *n* the opposition to the flow of alternating current by the capacitance or inductance of an electrical circuit

reactant (rɪ'æktənt) *n* a substance that participates in a chemical reaction

reaction (rɪ'ækʃən) *n* **1** a response to some foregoing action or stimulus **2** the reciprocal action of two things acting together **3** opposition to change, esp political change, or a desire to return to a former system **4** a response indicating a person's feelings or emotional attitude **5** *med* **5a** any effect produced by the action of a drug **5b** any effect produced by a substance (allergen) to which a person is allergic **6** *chem* a process that involves changes in the structure and energy content of atoms, molecules, or ions **7** the equal and opposite force that acts on a body whenever it exerts a force on another body > **re'actional** *adj*

> **USAGE** *Reaction* is used to refer both to an instant response (*her reaction was one of amazement*) and to a considered response in the form of a statement (*the Minister gave his reaction to the court's decision*). Some people think this second use is incorrect

reactionary (rɪ'ækʃənərɪ, -ʃənrɪ) *or* **reactionist** *adj* **1** of, relating to, or characterized by reaction, esp against radical political or social change ▷ *n, pl* **reactionaries** *or* **reactionists 2** a person opposed to radical change > **re'actionism** *n*

reaction engine *or* **motor** *n* an engine, such as a jet engine, that ejects gas at high velocity and develops its thrust from the ensuing reaction

reaction turbine *n* a turbine in which the working fluid is accelerated by expansion in both the static nozzles and the rotor blades

reactivate (rɪ'æktɪ,veɪt) *vb* **reactivates, reactivating, reactivated** (*tr*) to make (something) active again > **re,acti'vation** *n*

reactive (rɪ'æktɪv) *adj* **1** readily partaking in chemical reactions: *sodium is a reactive metal* **2** of, concerned with, or having a reactance **3** responsive to stimulus **4** (of mental illnesses) precipitated by an external cause > **reactivity** (,riːæk'tɪvɪtɪ) *or* **re'activeness** *n*

reactor (rɪ'æktə) *n* **1** short for **nuclear reactor 2** a vessel in which a chemical reaction occurs **3** a coil of low resistance and high inductance that introduces reactance into a circuit **4** *med* a person sensitive to a particular drug or agent **5** *chem* a substance that takes part in a reaction

read¹ (riːd) *vb* **reads, reading, read** (rɛd) **1** to comprehend the meaning of (something written or printed) by looking at and interpreting the written or printed characters **2** (when *tr*, often foll by *out*) to look at, interpret, and speak aloud (something written or printed) **3** (*tr*) to interpret the significance or meaning of through scrutiny and recognition: *to read a map* **4** (*tr*) to interpret or understand the meaning of (signs, characters, etc) other than by visual means: *to read Braille* **5** (*tr*) to have sufficient knowledge of (a language) to understand the written or printed word **6** (*tr*) to discover or make out the true nature or mood of: *to read someone's mind* **7** to interpret or understand (something read) in a specified way: *I read this speech as satire* **8** (*tr*) to adopt as a reading in a particular passage: *for "boon" read "bone"* **9** (*intr*) to have or contain a certain form or wording: *the sentence reads as follows* **10** to undertake a course of study in (a subject): *to read history* **11** to gain knowledge by reading: *he read about the war* **12** (*tr*) to register, indicate, or show: *the meter reads 100* **13** (*tr*) to put into a specified condition by reading: *to read a child to sleep* **14** (*tr*) to hear and understand, esp when using a two-way radio: *we are reading you loud and clear* **15** *computing* to obtain (data) from a storage device, such as magnetic tape **16 read a lesson** (*or* **lecture**) *inf* to censure or reprimand ▷ *n* **17** matter suitable for reading: *this book is a very good read* **18** the act or a spell of reading ▷ See also **read into, read out,** etc [OE *rǣdan* to advise, explain]

read² (rɛd) *vb* **1** the past tense and past participle of **read¹** ▷ *adj* **2** having knowledge gained from books (esp in **widely read** and **well-read**) **3 take (something) as read** to take (something) for granted as a fact; understand or presume

readable ('riːdəbᵊl) *adj* **1** (of handwriting, etc) able to be read or deciphered; legible **2** (of style of writing) interesting, easy, or pleasant to read > **,reada'bility** *or* **'readableness** *n* > **'readably** *adv*

Reade (riːd) *n* **Charles** 1814–84, English novelist: author of *The Cloister and the Hearth* (1861), a historical romance

reader ('riːdə) *n* **1** a person who reads **2** *chiefly Brit* a member of staff below a professor but above a senior lecturer at a university **3a** a book that is part of a planned series for those learning to read **3b** a standard textbook, esp for foreign-language learning **4** a person who reads aloud in public **5** a person who reads and assesses the merit of manuscripts submitted to a publisher **6** a proofreader **7** short for **lay reader**

readership ('riːdəʃɪp) *n* all the readers collectively of a publication or author: *a readership of five million*

reading ('riːdɪŋ) *n* **1a** the act of a person who reads **1b** (*as modifier*): *a reading room* **2a** ability to read **2b** (*as modifier*): *a child of reading age* **3** any matter that can be read; written or printed text **4** a public recital or rendering of a literary work **5** the form of a particular word or passage in a given text, esp where more than one version exists **6** an interpretation, as of a piece of music, a situation, or something said or written **7** knowledge gained from books: *a person of little reading* **8** a measurement indicated by a gauge, dial, scientific instrument, etc **9** *parliamentary procedure* **9a** the formal recital of the body or title of a bill in a legislative assembly in order to begin one of the stages of its passage **9b** one of the three stages in the passage of a bill through a legislative assembly. See **first reading, second reading, third reading** **10** the formal recital of something written, esp a will

Reading ('rɛdɪŋ) *n* **1** a town in S England, in Reading unitary authority, Berkshire, on the River Thames: university (1892). Pop: 134 600 (1991) **2** a unitary authority in S England, in Berkshire. Pop: 143 124 (2001). Area: 37 sq km (14 sq miles)

reading group *n* a group of people who meet regularly to discuss a book that they have all read

read into (riːd) *vb* (*tr, prep*) to discern in or infer from a statement (meanings not intended by the speaker or writer)

read out (riːd) *vb* (*adv*) **1** (*tr*) to read (something) aloud **2** to retrieve (information) from a computer memory or storage device **3** (*tr*) *US & Canad* to expel (someone) from a political party or other society ▹ *n* **read-out** **4a** the act of retrieving information from a computer memory or storage device **4b** the information retrieved

read up (riːd) *vb* (*adv*; when *intr*, often foll by *on*) to acquire information about (a subject) by reading intensively

read-write head ('riːd'raɪt) *n computing* an electromagnet that can both read and write information on a magnetic tape or disk

ready ('rɛdɪ) *adj* **readier, readiest** **1** in a state of completion or preparedness, as for use or action **2** willing or eager: *ready helpers* **3** prompt or rapid: *a ready response* **4** (*prenominal*) quick in perceiving; intelligent: *a ready mind* **5** (*postpositive*) (foll by *to*) on the point (of) or liable (to): *ready to collapse* **6** (*postpositive*) conveniently near (esp in **ready to hand**) **7** **make** *or* **get ready** to prepare (oneself or something) for use or action ▹ *n* **8** *inf* (*often preceded by* the) short for **ready money** **9** **at** *or* **to the ready** **9a** (of a rifle) in the position adopted prior to aiming and firing **9b** poised for use or action: *with pen at the ready* ▹ *vb* **readies, readying, readied** **10** (*tr*) to put in a state of readiness; prepare [OE (*ge*)*rǣde*] > '**readily** *adv* > '**readiness** *n*

ready-made *adj* **1** made for purchase and immediate use by any customer **2** extremely convenient or ideally suited: *a ready-made solution* **3** unoriginal or conventional: *ready-made phrases* ▹ *n* **4** a ready-made article, esp a garment

ready-mix *n* **1** (*modifier*) consisting of ingredients blended in advance, esp of food that is ready to cook or eat after addition of milk or water: *a ready-mix cake* **2** concrete that is mixed before or during delivery to a building site

ready money *or* **cash** *n* funds for immediate use; cash. Also: **the ready, the readies**

ready reckoner *n* a table of numbers for facilitating simple calculations, esp for working out interest, etc

ready-to-wear *adj* (**ready to wear** *when postpositive*) **1** (of clothes) not tailored for the wearer; of a standard size ▹ *n* **2** an article or suit of such clothes

reafforest (ˌriːə'fɒrɪst) *or* **reforest** *vb* (*tr*) to replant (an area that was formerly forested) > ˌ**reafˌforest'ation** *or* ˌ**reforest'ation** *n*

Reagan ('reɪgən) *n* **Ronald** 1911–2004, US film actor and Republican statesman: Governor of California (1966–74): 40th president of the US (1981–89)

reagent (riː'eɪdʒənt) *n* a substance for use in a chemical reaction, esp for use in chemical synthesis and analysis

real[1] (rɪəl) *adj* **1** existing or occurring in the physical world; not imaginary, fictitious, or theoretical; actual **2** (*prenominal*) true; actual; not false: *the real reason* **3** (*prenominal*) deserving the name; rightly so called: *a real friend* **4** not artificial or simulated; genuine: *real fur* **5** (of food, etc) traditionally made and having a distinct flavour: *real ale*; *real cheese* **6** *philosophy* existent or relating to actual existence (as opposed to nonexistent, potential, contingent, or apparent) **7** (*prenominal*) *econ* (of prices, incomes, etc) considered in terms of purchasing power rather than nominal currency value **8** (*prenominal*) denoting or relating to immovable property such as land and tenements: *real estate* **9** *maths* involving or containing real numbers alone; having no imaginary part **10** *inf* (intensifier): *a real genius* **11** **the real thing** the genuine article, not a substitute ▹ *n* **12** **for real** *sl* not as a test or trial; in earnest **13** **the real** that which exists in fact; reality [C15 from OF *réel*, from LL *reālis*, from L *rēs* thing] > '**realness** *n*

real[2] (reɪ'ɑːl) *n, pl* **reals** *or* **reales** (*Spanish* re'ales) a former small Spanish or Spanish-American silver coin [C17 from Sp., lit.: royal, from L *rēgālis*; see REGAL]

real ale *n* any beer which is allowed to ferment in the barrel and which is pumped up from the keg without using carbon dioxide

real estate *n* another term, chiefly US and Canad, for **real property**

realgar (rɪ'ælgə) *n* a rare orange-red soft mineral consisting of arsenic sulphide in monoclinic crystalline form [C14 via Med. L from Ar. *rahj al-ghar* powder of the mine]

realism ('rɪəˌlɪzəm) *n* **1** awareness or acceptance of the physical universe, events, etc, as they are, as opposed to the abstract or ideal **2** a style of painting and sculpture that seeks to represent the familiar or typical in real life **3** any similar style in other arts, esp literature **4** *philosophy* the thesis that general terms refer to entities that have a real existence separate from the individuals which fall under them **5** *philosophy* the theory that physical objects continue to exist whether they are perceived or not > '**realist** *n*

▹ www.artlex.com/ArtLex/r/realism.html

▹ www.artcyclopedia.com/history/realism.html

realistic (ˌrɪə'lɪstɪk) *adj* **1** showing awareness and acceptance of reality **2** practical or pragmatic rather than ideal or moral **3** (of a book, etc) depicting what is real and actual **4** of or relating to philosophical realism > ˌ**real'istically** *adv*

reality (rɪ'ælɪtɪ) *n, pl* **realities** **1** the state of things as they are or appear to be, rather than as one might wish them to be **2** something that is real **3** the state of being real **4** *philosophy* **4a** that which exists, independent of human awareness **4b** the totality of facts **5** **in reality** actually; in fact

reality check *n* an event or occasion that forces a person to face the truth about a situation

reality principle *n psychoanal* control of behaviour by the ego to meet the conditions imposed by the external world

reality show *n* a television show in which members of the public or celebrities are filmed living their everyday lives or undertaking specific challenges

Rr

reality TV *n* television programmes focusing on members of the public living in conditions created especially by the programme makers
▷ www.orwellproject.com

realize *or* **realise** (ˈrɪəˌlaɪz) *vb* **realizes, realizing, realized** *or* **realises, realising, realised 1** (when *tr, may take a clause as object*) to become conscious or aware of (something) **2** (*tr, often passive*) to bring (a plan, ambition, etc) to fruition **3** (*tr*) to give (a drama or film) the appearance of reality **4** (*tr*) (of goods, property, etc) to sell for or make (a certain sum): *this table realized £800* **5** (*tr*) to convert (property or goods) into cash **6** (*tr*) (of a musicologist or performer) to reconstruct (a composition) from an incomplete set of parts > **ˈrealˌizable** *or* **ˈrealˌisable** *adj* > **ˈrealˌizably** *or* **ˈrealˌisably** *adv* > **ˌrealiˈzation** *or* **ˌrealiˈsation** *n*

real life *n* actual human life, as lived by real people, esp contrasted with the lives of fictional characters: *miracles don't happen in real life*

really (ˈrɪəlɪ) *adv* **1** in reality; in actuality; assuredly: *it's really quite harmless* **2** truly; genuinely: *really beautiful* ▷ *interj* **3** an exclamation of dismay, disapproval, doubt, surprise, etc **4 not really?** an exclamation of surprise or polite doubt.

USAGE See at **very**

realm (rɛlm) *n* **1** a royal domain; kingdom: *peer of the realm* **2** a field of interest, study, etc: *the realm of the occult* [C13 from OF *reialme*, from L *regimen* rule, infl. by OF *reial*, from L *rēgālis* REGAL]

real number *n* any rational or irrational number. See **number**

real presence *n* the doctrine that the body of Christ is actually present in the Eucharist

real property *n property law* immovable property, esp freehold land ▷ Cf **personal property**

real tennis *n* an ancient form of tennis played in a four-walled indoor court
▷ www.real-tennis.com

real-time *adj* denoting or relating to a data-processing system in which a computer is on-line to a source of data and processes the data as it is generated

realtor (ˈrɪəltə, -ˌtɔː) *n* a US word for an **estate agent,** esp an accredited one [C20 from REALTY + -OR[1]]

realty (ˈrɪəltɪ) *n* another term for **real property**

ream¹ (riːm) *n* **1** a number of sheets of paper, formerly 480 sheets (**short ream**), now 500 sheets (**long ream**) or 516 sheets (**printer's ream** or **perfect ream**) One ream is equal to 20 quires **2** (*often pl*) *inf* a large quantity, esp of written matter: *he wrote reams* [C14 from OF, from Sp., from Ar. *rizmah* bale]

ream² (riːm) *vb* (*tr*) **1** to enlarge (a hole) by use of a reamer **2** *US* to extract (juice) from (a citrus fruit) using a reamer [C19 ?from C14 *remen* to open up, from OE *rȳman* to widen]

reamer (ˈriːmə) *n* **1** a steel tool with a cylindrical or tapered shank around which longitudinal teeth are ground, used for smoothing the bores of holes accurately to size **2** *US* a utensil with a conical projection used for extracting juice from citrus fruits

reap (riːp) *vb* **1** to cut or harvest (a crop) from (a field) **2** (*tr*) to gain or get (something) as a reward for or result of some action or enterprise [OE *riopan*] > **ˈreapable** *adj*

reaper (ˈriːpə) *n* **1** a person who reaps or a machine for reaping **2 the grim reaper** death

rear¹ (rɪə) *n* **1** the back or hind part **2** the area or position that lies at the back: *a garden at the rear of the house* **3** the section of a military force farthest from the front **4** an informal word for **buttocks** (see **buttock**) **5 bring up the rear** to be at the back in a procession, race, etc **6 in the rear** at the back **7** (*modifier*) of or in the rear: *the rear side* [C17 prob. from REARWARD or REARGUARD]

rear² (rɪə) *vb* **1** (*tr*) to care for and educate (children) until maturity; raise **2** (*tr*) to breed (animals) or grow (plants) **3** (*tr*) to place or lift (a ladder, etc) upright **4** (*tr*) to erect (a monument, building, etc) **5** (*intr; often foll by up*) (esp of horses) to lift the front legs in the air and stand nearly upright **6** (*intr; often foll by up or over*) (esp of tall buildings) to rise high; tower **7** (*intr*) to start with anger, resentment, etc [OE *rǣran*] > **ˈrearer** *n*

rear admiral *n* an officer holding flag rank in any of certain navies, junior to a vice admiral

rearguard (ˈrɪəˌgɑːd) *n* **1** a detachment detailed to protect the rear of a military formation, esp in retreat **2** an entrenched or conservative element, as in a political party **3** (*modifier*) of, relating to, or characteristic of a rearguard: *a rearguard action* [C15 from OF *rereguarde*, from *rer*, from L *retro* back + *guarde* GUARD]

rear light *or* **lamp** *n* a red light, usually one of a pair, attached to the rear of a motor vehicle. Also called: **tail-light, tail lamp**

rearm (riːˈɑːm) *vb* **1** to arm again **2** (*tr*) to equip (an army, etc) with better weapons > **reˈarmament** *n*

rearmost (ˈrɪəˌməʊst) *adj* nearest the rear; coming last

rear-view mirror *n* a mirror on a motor vehicle enabling the driver to see traffic behind him

rearward (ˈrɪəwəd) *adj, adv* **1** Also (for adv only): **rearwards** towards or in the rear ▷ *n* **2** a position in the rear, esp the rear division of a military formation [C14 (*as n*: the part of an army behind the main body of troops): from Anglo-F *rerewarde*, var. of *reregarde*; see REARGUARD]

Rea Silvia (ˈrɪə ˈsɪlvɪə) *n* a variant spelling of **Rhea Silvia**

reason (ˈriːzᵊn) *n* **1** the faculty of rational argument, deduction, judgment, etc **2** sound mind; sanity **3** a cause or motive, as for a belief, action, etc **4** an argument in favour or a justification for something **5** *philosophy* the intellect regarded as a source of knowledge, as contrasted with experience **6** *logic* a premise of an argument in favour of the given conclusion **7 by reason of** because of **8 in** *or* **within reason** within moderate or justifiable bounds **9 it stands to reason** it is logical or obvious **10 listen to reason** to be persuaded peaceably **11 reasons of State** political justifications for an immoral act ▷ *vb* **12** (when *tr, takes a clause as object*) to think logically or draw (logical conclusions) from facts or premises **13** (*intr; usually foll by with*) to seek to persuade by reasoning **14** (*tr; often foll by out*) to work out or resolve (a problem) by reasoning [C13 from OF *reisun*, from L *ratiō* reckoning, from *rērī* to think] > **ˈreasoner** *n*

USAGE The expression *the reason is because...* should be avoided. Instead one should say either *this is because...* or *the reason is that...*

reasonable (ˈriːzənəbᵊl) *adj* **1** showing reason or sound judgment **2** having the ability to reason **3** having modest or moderate expectations **4** moderate in price **5** fair; average > **ˈreasonably** *adv* > **ˈreasonableness** *n*

reasoned (ˈriːzᵊnd) *adj* well thought-out or well presented: *a reasoned explanation*

reasoning (ˈriːzənɪŋ) *n* **1** the act or process of drawing conclusions from facts, evidence, etc **2** the arguments, proofs, etc, so adduced

reassure (ˌriːəˈʃʊə) *vb* **reassures, reassuring, reassured** (*tr*) **1** to relieve (someone) of anxieties; restore confidence to **2** to insure again > **ˌreasˈsurance** *n* > **ˌreasˈsurer** *n* > **ˌreasˈsuringly** *adv*

Réaumur (ˈreɪəˌmjʊə) *adj* indicating measurement on the Réaumur scale

Réaumur scale *n* a scale of temperature in which the freezing point of water is taken as 0° and the boiling point as 80° [C18 after René de *Réaumur* (1683–1757), F physicist, who introduced it]

reave (riːv) *vb* **reaves, reaving, reaved** *or* **reft** *arch* **1** to carry off (property, prisoners, etc) by force **2** (*tr; foll by of*) to deprive; strip. See **reive** [OE *reāfian*]

rebadge (ˌriːˈbædʒ) *vb* (*tr*) to relaunch (a product) under a new name, brand, or logo

rebarbative (rɪˈbɑːbətɪv) *adj* fearsome; forbidding [c19 from F *rébarbatif*, from OF *rebarber* to repel (an enemy)]

rebate[1] *n* (ˈriːbeɪt) **1** a refund of a fraction of the amount payable; discount ▷ *vb* (rɪˈbeɪt), **rebates, rebating, rebated** (*tr*) **2** to deduct (a part) of a payment from (the total) **3** *arch* to reduce [c15 from OF *rabattre* to beat down, hence reduce, from RE- + *abatre* to put down] > **reˈbatable** *or* **reˈbateable** *adj* > **ˈrebater** *n*

rebate[2] (ˈriːbeɪt, ˈræbɪt) *n, vb* **rebates, rebating, rebated** another word for **rabbet**

rebec *or* **rebeck** (ˈriːbɛk) *n* a medieval stringed instrument resembling the violin but having a lute-shaped body [c16 from OF *rebebe*, from Ar. *rebāb*; ? infl. by OF *bec* beak]

Rebecca (rɪˈbɛkə) *n Old Testament* the sister of Laban, who became the wife of Isaac and the mother of Esau and Jacob (Genesis 24–27). Douay spelling: **Rebekah**

rebel *vb* (rɪˈbɛl), **rebels, rebelling, rebelled** (*intr*; *often foll by* ***against***) **1** to resist or rise up against a government or authority, esp by force of arms **2** to dissent from an accepted moral code or convention of behaviour, etc **3** to show repugnance (towards) ▷ *n* (ˈrɛbᵊl) **4a** a person who rebels **4b** (*as modifier*): *a rebel soldier* **5** a person who dissents from some accepted moral code or convention of behaviour, etc [c13 from OF *rebelle*, from L *rebellis* insurgent, from RE- + *bellum* war]

rebellion (rɪˈbɛljən) *n* **1** organized opposition to a government or other authority **2** dissent from an accepted moral code or convention of behaviour, etc [c14 via OF from L *rebelliō* revolt (of those conquered); see REBEL]

rebellious (rɪˈbɛljəs) *adj* **1** showing a tendency towards rebellion **2** (of a problem, etc) difficult to overcome; refractory > **reˈbelliously** *adv* > **reˈbelliousness** *n*

rebirth (riːˈbɜːθ) *n* **1** a revival or renaissance: *the rebirth of learning* **2** a second or new birth

reboot (riːˈbuːt) *vb* to shut down and then restart (a computer system) or (of a computer system) to shut down and restart

rebore *n* (ˈriːˌbɔː) **1** the process of boring out the cylinders of a worn reciprocating engine and fitting oversize pistons ▷ *vb* (riːˈbɔː), **rebores, reboring, rebored 2** (*tr*) to carry out this process

rebound *vb* (rɪˈbaʊnd) (*intr*) **1** to spring back, as from a sudden impact **2** to misfire, esp so as to hurt the perpetrator ▷ *n* (ˈriːbaʊnd) **3** the act or an instance of rebounding **4 on the rebound 4a** in the act of springing back **4b** *inf* in a state of recovering from rejection, etc: *he married her on the rebound from an unhappy love affair* [c14 from OF *rebondir*, from RE- + *bondir* to BOUND[2]]

rebounder (rɪˈbaʊndə) *n* a type of small trampoline used for aerobic exercising

rebozo (rɪˈbəʊzəʊ) *n, pl* **rebozos** a long wool or linen scarf covering the shoulders and head, worn by Latin American women [c19 from Sp., from *rebozar* to muffle]

rebrand (riːˈbrænd) *vb* to change or update the image of (an organization or product)

rebuff (rɪˈbʌf) *vb* (*tr*) **1** to snub, reject, or refuse (help, sympathy, etc) **2** to beat back (an attack); repel ▷ *n* **3** a blunt refusal or rejection; snub [c16 from OF *rebuffer*, from It., from *ribuffo* a reprimand, from *ri-* RE- + *buffo* puff, gust, apparently imit.]

rebuke (rɪˈbjuːk) *vb* **rebukes, rebuking, rebuked 1** (*tr*) to scold or reprimand (someone) ▷ *n* **2** a reprimand or scolding [c14 from OF *rebuker*, from RE- + *buchier* to hack down, from *busche* log, of Gmc origin] > **reˈbukable** *adj* > **reˈbuker** *n* > **reˈbukingly** *adv*

rebus (ˈriːbəs) *n, pl* **rebuses 1** a puzzle consisting of pictures, symbols, etc, representing syllables and words; the word *hear* might be represented by H and a picture of an ear **2** a heraldic device that is a pictorial representation of the name of the bearer [c17 from F *rébus*, from L *rēbus* by things, from RES]

rebut (rɪˈbʌt) *vb* **rebuts, rebutting, rebutted** (*tr*) to refute or disprove, esp by offering a contrary contention or argument [c13 from OF *reboter*, from RE- + *boter* to thrust, BUTT[3]] > **reˈbuttable** *adj* > **reˈbuttal** *n*

rebutter (rɪˈbʌtə) *n* **1** *law* a defendant's pleading in reply to a plaintiff's surrejoinder **2** a person who rebuts

recalcitrant (rɪˈkælsɪtrənt) *adj* **1** not susceptible to control; refractory ▷ *n* **2** a recalcitrant person [c19 via F from L, from RE- + *calcitrāre* to kick, from *calx* heel] > **reˈcalcitrance** *n*

recalescence (ˌriːkəˈlɛsəns) *n* a sudden spontaneous increase in the temperature of cooling iron [c19 from L *recalēscere* to grow warm again, from RE- + *calēscere*, from *calēre* to be hot] > **ˌrecalˈesce** *vb* (*intr*) > **ˌrecaˈlescent** *adj*

recall (rɪˈkɔːl) *vb* (*tr*) **1** (*may take a clause as object*) to bring back to mind; recollect; remember **2** to order to return **3** to revoke or take back **4** to cause (one's thoughts, attention, etc) to return from a reverie or digression ▷ *n* **5** the act of recalling or state of being recalled **6** revocation or cancellation **7** the ability to remember things; recollection **8** *mil* (formerly) a signal to call back troops, etc **9** US the process by which elected officials may be deprived of office by popular vote > **reˈcallable** *adj*

recant (rɪˈkænt) *vb* to repudiate or withdraw (a former belief or statement), esp formally in public [c16 from L *recantāre*, from RE- + *cantāre* to sing] > **recantation** (ˌriːkænˈteɪʃən) *n* > **reˈcanter** *n*

recap *vb* (ˈriːˌkæp, riːˈkæp), **recaps, recapping, recapped,** *n* (ˈriːˌkæp) *inf* short for **recapitulate** *or* **recapitulation** > **reˈcappable** *adj*

recapitulate (ˌriːkəˈpɪtjʊˌleɪt) *vb* **recapitulates, recapitulating, recapitulated 1** to restate the main points of (an argument, speech, etc) **2** (*tr*) (of an animal) to repeat (stages of its evolutionary development) during the embryonic stages of its life [c16 from LL *recapitulāre*, lit.: to put back under headings; see CAPITULATE] > **ˌrecaˈpitulative** *or* **ˌrecaˈpitulatory** *adj*

recapitulation (ˌriːkəˌpɪtjʊˈleɪʃən) *n* **1** the act of recapitulating, esp summing up, as at the end of a speech **2** Also called: **palingenesis** *biol* the apparent repetition in the embryonic development of an animal of the changes that occurred during its evolutionary history **3** *music* the repeating of earlier themes, esp in the final section of a movement in sonata form

recapture (riːˈkæptʃə) *vb* **recaptures, recapturing, recaptured** (*tr*) **1** to capture or take again **2** to recover, renew, or repeat (a lost or former ability, sensation, etc) ▷ *n* **3** the act of recapturing or fact of being recaptured

recce (ˈrɛkɪ) *n, vb* **recces, recceing, recced** *or* **recceed** a slang word for **reconnaissance** or **reconnoitre**

recd *or* **rec'd** *abbrev for* received

recede (rɪˈsiːd) *vb* **recedes, receding, receded** (*intr*) **1** to withdraw from a point or limit; go back: *the tide receded* **2** to become more distant: *hopes of rescue receded* **3** to slope backwards: *apes have receding foreheads* **4a** (of a man's hair) to cease to grow at the temples and above the forehead **4b** (of a man) to start to go bald in this way **5** to decline in value **6** (*usually foll by* ***from***) to draw back or retreat, as from a promise [c15 from L *recēdere* to go back, from RE- + *cēdere* to yield]

re-cede (riːˈsiːd) *vb* **re-cedes, re-ceding, re-ceded** (*tr*) to restore to a former owner

receipt (rɪˈsiːt) *n* **1** a written acknowledgment by a receiver of money, goods, etc, that payment or delivery has been made **2** the act of receiving or fact of being received **3** (*usually pl*) an amount or article received **4** *obs* another word for **recipe** ▷ *vb* **5** (*tr*) to acknowledge payment of (a bill), as by marking it [c14 from OF *receite*, from Med. L *recepta*, from L *recipere* to RECEIVE]

receivable (rɪˈsiːvəbᵊl) *adj* **1** suitable for or capable of being received, esp as payment or legal tender **2** (of a bill, etc) awaiting payment: *accounts receivable* ▷ *n* **3** (*usually pl*) the part of the assets of a business

Rr

represented by accounts due for payment

receive (rɪˈsiːv) *vb* **receives, receiving, received** *(mainly tr)* 1 to take (something offered) into one's hand or possession 2 to have (an honour, blessing, etc) bestowed 3 to accept delivery or transmission of (a letter, etc) 4 to be informed of (news) 5 to hear and consent to or acknowledge (a confession, etc) 6 (of a container) to take or hold (a substance, commodity, or certain amount) 7 to support or sustain (the weight of something); bear 8 to apprehend or perceive (ideas, etc) 9 to experience, undergo, or meet with: *to receive a crack on the skull* 10 *(also intr)* to be at home to (visitors) 11 to greet or welcome (guests), esp in formal style 12 to admit (a person) to a place, society, condition, etc: *he was received into the priesthood* 13 to accept or acknowledge (a precept or principle) as true or valid 14 to convert (incoming radio signals) into sounds, pictures, etc, by means of a receiver 15 *(also intr) tennis, etc* to play at the other end from the server 16 *(also intr)* to partake of (the Christian Eucharist) 17 *(intr) chiefly Brit* to buy and sell stolen goods [C13 from OF *receivre*, from L *recipere*, from RE- + *capere* to take]

received (rɪˈsiːvd) *adj* generally accepted or believed: *received wisdom*

Received Pronunciation *n* the accent of standard Southern British English. Abbrev: **RP**

receiver (rɪˈsiːvə) *n* 1 a person who receives something; recipient 2 a person appointed by a court to manage property pending the outcome of litigation, during the infancy of the owner, or after the owner has been declared bankrupt or insane 3 *chiefly Brit* a person who receives stolen goods knowing that they have been stolen 4 the equipment in a telephone, radio, or television that receives incoming electrical signals or modulated radio waves and converts them into the original audio or video signals 5 the detachable part of a telephone that is held to the ear 6 *chem* a vessel in which the distillate is collected during distillation 7 *US sport* a player whose function is to receive the ball

receivership (rɪˈsiːvəʃɪp) *n law* 1 the office or function of a receiver 2 the condition of being administered by a receiver

receiving order *n Brit* a court order appointing a receiver to manage the property of a debtor or bankrupt

recension (rɪˈsɛnʃən) *n* 1 a critical revision of a literary work 2 a text revised in this way [C17 from L *recēnsiō*, from *recēnsēre*, from RE- + *cēnsēre* to assess]

recent (ˈriːsᵊnt) *adj* having appeared, happened, or been made not long ago; modern, fresh, or new [C16 from L *recens* fresh; rel. to Gk *kainos* new] > **ˈrecently** *adv* > **ˈrecentness** *or* **ˈrecency** *n*

Recent (ˈriːsᵊnt) *adj, n geol* another word for **Holocene**

receptacle (rɪˈsɛptəkᵊl) *n* 1 an object that holds something; container 2 *bot* 2a the enlarged or modified tip of the flower stalk that bears the parts of the flower 2b the part of lower plants that bears the reproductive organs or spores [C15 from L *receptāculum* store-place, from *receptāre*, from *recipere* to RECEIVE]

reception (rɪˈsɛpʃən) *n* 1 the act of receiving or state of being received 2 the manner in which something, such as a guest or a new idea, is received: *a frosty reception from some of the players* 3 a formal party for guests, such as after a wedding 4 an area in an office, hotel, etc, where visitors or guests are received and appointments or reservations dealt with 5 short for **reception room** 6 the quality or fidelity of a received radio or television broadcast: *the reception was poor* [C14 from L *receptiō*, from *recipere* to RECEIVE]

reception centre *n* a place to which distressed people, such as vagrants, addicts, victims of a disaster, refugees, etc, go pending more permanent arrangements

receptionist (rɪˈsɛpʃənɪst) *n* a person employed in an office, surgery, etc, to receive clients or guests, arrange appointments, etc

reception room *n* 1 a room in a private house suitable for entertaining guests 2 a room in a hotel suitable for receptions, etc

receptive (rɪˈsɛptɪv) *adj* 1 able to apprehend quickly 2 tending to receive new ideas or suggestions favourably 3 able to hold or receive > **reˈceptively** *adv* > **receptivity** (ˌriːsɛpˈtɪvɪtɪ) *or* **reˈceptiveness** *n*

receptor (rɪˈsɛptə) *n* 1 *physiol* a sensory nerve ending that changes specific stimuli into nerve impulses 2 any of various devices that receive information, signals, etc

recess *n* (rɪˈsɛs, ˈriːsɛs) 1 a space, such as a niche or alcove, set back or indented 2 *(often pl)* a secluded or secret place: *recesses of the mind* 3 a cessation of business, such as the closure of Parliament during a vacation 4 *anat* a small cavity or depression in a bodily organ 5 *US & Canad* a break between classes at a school ▷ *vb* (rɪˈsɛs) 6 *(tr)* to place or set (something) in a recess 7 *(tr)* to build a recess in (a wall, etc) [C16 from L *recessus* a retreat, from *recēdere* to RECEDE]

recession¹ (rɪˈsɛʃən) *n* 1 a temporary depression in economic activity or prosperity 2 the withdrawal of the clergy and choir in procession after a church service 3 the act of receding 4 a part of a building, wall, etc, that recedes [C17 from L *recessio*; see RECESS]

recession² (riːˈsɛʃən) *n* the act of restoring possession to a former owner [C19 from RE- + CESSION]

recessional (rɪˈsɛʃənᵊl) *adj* 1 of or relating to recession ▷ *n* 2 a hymn sung as the clergy and choir withdraw after a church service

recessive (rɪˈsɛsɪv) *adj* 1 tending to recede or go back 2 *genetics* 2a (of a gene) capable of producing its characteristic phenotype in the organism only when its allele is identical 2b (of a character) controlled by such a gene ▷ Cf **dominant** (sense 4) 3 *linguistics* (of stress) tending to be placed on or near the initial syllable of a polysyllabic word ▷ *n* 4 *genetics* a recessive gene or character > **reˈcessively** *adv* > **reˈcessiveness** *n*

recharge (ˌriːˈtʃɑːdʒ) *vb* **recharges, recharging, recharged** *(tr)* 1 to cause (an accumulator, capacitor, etc) to take up and store electricity again 2 to revive or renew (one's energies) (esp in **recharge one's batteries**) > **reˈchargeable** *adj*

recherché (rəˈʃɛəʃeɪ) *adj* 1 known only to connoisseurs; choice or rare 2 studiedly refined or elegant [C18 from F: p.p. of *rechercher* to make a thorough search for]

recidivism (rɪˈsɪdɪˌvɪzəm) *n* habitual relapse into crime [C19 from L *recidīvus* falling back, from RE- + *cadere* to fall] > **reˈcidivist** *n, adj* > **reˌcidiˈvistic** *or* **reˈcidivous** *adj*

Recife (rɛˈsiːfə) *n* a port at the easternmost point of Brazil on the Atlantic: capital of Pernambuco state; built partly on an island, with many waterways and bridges. Pop (city): 1 421 947 (2000), with a conurbation of 3 168 000 (1995 est). Former name: **Pernambuco**

recipe (ˈrɛsɪpɪ) *n* 1 a list of ingredients and directions for making something, esp when preparing food 2 *med* (formerly) a medical prescription 3 a method for achieving some desired objective: *a recipe for success* [C14 from L, lit.: take (it)! from *recipere* to take]

recipient (rɪˈsɪpɪənt) *n* 1 a person who or thing that receives ▷ *adj* 2 receptive [C16 via F from L, from *recipere* to RECEIVE] > **reˈcipience** *or* **reˈcipiency** *n*

reciprocal (rɪˈsɪprəkᵊl) *adj* 1 of, relating to, or designating something given by each of two people, countries, etc, to the other; mutual: *reciprocal trade* 2 given or done in return: *a reciprocal favour* 3 (of a pronoun) indicating that action is given and received by each subject; for example, *each other* in *they started to shout at each other* 4 *maths* of or relating to a number or quantity divided into one ▷ *n* 5 something that is reciprocal 6 Also called: **inverse** *maths* a number or quantity that when multiplied by a given number or quantity gives a product of one: *the reciprocal of 2 is 0.5* [c16 from L *reciprocus* alternating] > **re,cipro'cality** *n* > **re'ciprocally** *adv*

reciprocate (rɪ'sɪprə,keɪt) *vb* **reciprocates, reciprocating, reciprocated** 1 to give or feel in return 2 to move or cause to move backwards and forwards 3 (*intr*) to be correspondent or equivalent [c17 from L *reciprocāre*, from *reciprocus* RECIPROCAL] > **re,cipro'cation** *n* > **re'ciprocative** *or* **re'cipro,catory** *adj* > **re'cipro,cator** *n*

reciprocating engine *n* an engine in which one or more pistons move backwards and forwards inside a cylinder or cylinders

reciprocity (,rɛsɪ'prɒsɪtɪ) *n* 1 reciprocal action or relation 2 a mutual exchange of commercial or other privileges [c18 via F from L *reciprocus* RECIPROCAL]

recision (rɪ'sɪʒən) *n* the act of cancelling or rescinding; annulment: *the recision of a treaty* [c17 from L *recīsiō*, from *recīdere* to cut back]

recital (rɪ'saɪtᵊl) *n* 1 a musical performance by a soloist or soloists 2 the act of reciting or repeating something learned or prepared 3 an account, narration, or description 4 (*often pl*) *law* the preliminary statement in a deed showing the reason for its existence and explaining the operative part > **re'citalist** *n*

recitation (,rɛsɪ'teɪʃən) *n* 1a the act of reciting from memory 1b a formal reading of verse before an audience 2 something recited

recitative[1] (,rɛsɪtə'ti:v) *n* a passage in a musical composition, esp the narrative parts in an oratorio, reflecting the natural rhythms of speech [c17 from It. *recitativo*; see RECITE]

recitative[2] (rɪ'saɪtətɪv) *adj* of or relating to recital

recite (rɪ'saɪt) *vb* **recites, reciting, recited** 1 to repeat (a poem, etc) aloud from memory before an audience 2 (*tr*) to give a detailed account of 3 (*tr*) to enumerate (examples, etc) [c15 from L *recitāre* to cite again, from RE- + *citāre* to summon] > **re'citable** *adj* > **re'citer** *n*

reck (rɛk) *vb* *arch* (*used mainly with a negative*) 1 to mind or care about (something): *to reck nought* 2 (*usually impersonal*) to concern or interest (someone) [OE *reccan*]

reckless ('rɛklɪs) *adj* having or showing no regard for danger or consequences: *a reckless driver* [OE *recceleās*; see RECK, -LESS] > **'recklessly** *adv* > **'recklessness** *n*

Recklinghausen (*German* rɛklɪŋ'hauzən) *n* an industrial city in NW Germany, in North Rhine-Westphalia on the N edge of the Ruhr. Pop: 126 241 (1999 est)

reckon ('rɛkən) *vb* 1 to calculate or ascertain by calculating; compute 2 (*tr*) to include; count as part of a set or class 3 (*usually passive*) to consider or regard: *he is reckoned clever* 4 (when *tr*, *takes a clause as object*) to think or suppose; be of the opinion: *I reckon you don't know* 5 (*intr*; foll by *with*) to settle accounts (with) 6 (*intr*; foll by *with* or *without*) to take into account or fail to take into account: *they reckoned without John* 7 (*intr*; foll by *on* or *upon*) to rely or depend: *I reckon on your support* 8 (*tr*) *inf* to have a high opinion of 9 **to be reckoned with** of considerable importance or influence [OE (*ge*)*recenian* recount]

reckoner ('rɛkənə) *n* any of various devices or tables used to facilitate reckoning, esp a ready reckoner

reckoning ('rɛkənɪŋ) *n* 1 the act of counting or calculating 2 settlement of an account or bill 3 a bill or account 4 retribution for one's actions (esp in **day of reckoning**) 5 *navigation* short for **dead reckoning**

reclaim (rɪ'kleɪm) *vb* (*tr*) 1 to claim back: *reclaim baggage* 2 to convert (desert, marsh, etc) into land suitable for growing crops 3 to recover (useful substances) from waste products 4 to convert (someone) from sin, folly, vice, etc ▷ *n* 5 the act of reclaiming or state of being reclaimed [c13 from OF *réclamer*, from L *reclāmāre* to cry out, from RE- + *clāmāre* to shout] > **re'claimable** *adj* > **re'claimant** *or* **re'claimer** *n*

reclamation (,rɛklə'meɪʃən) *n* 1 the conversion of desert, marsh, etc, into land suitable for cultivation 2 the recovery of useful substances from waste products 3 the act of reclaiming or state of being reclaimed

réclame *French* (reklam) *n* 1 public acclaim or attention; publicity 2 the capacity for attracting publicity

reclinate ('rɛklɪ,neɪt) *adj* *bot* naturally curved or bent backwards so that the upper part rests on the ground [c18 from L *reclīnātus* bent back]

recline (rɪ'klaɪn) *vb* **reclines, reclining, reclined** to rest in a leaning position [c15 from OF *recliner*, from L *reclīnāre*, from RE- + *clīnāre* to LEAN[1]] > **re'clinable** *adj* > **reclination** (,rɛklɪ'neɪʃən) *n*

recliner (rɪ'klaɪnə) *n* a person or thing that reclines, esp a type of armchair having a back that can be adjusted to slope at various angles

recluse (rɪ'klu:s) *n* 1 a person who lives in seclusion, esp to devote himself or herself to prayer and religious meditation; a hermit ▷ *adj* 2 solitary; retiring [c13 from OF *reclus*, from LL *reclūdere* to shut away, from L RE- + *claudere* to close] > **reclusion** (rɪ'klu:ʒən) *n* > **re'clusive** *adj*

recognition (,rɛkəg'nɪʃən) *n* 1 the act of recognizing or fact of being recognized 2 acceptance or acknowledgment of a claim, duty, etc 3 a token of thanks 4 formal acknowledgment of a government or of the independence of a country [c15 from L *recognitiō*, from *recognoscere*, from RE- + *cognoscere* to know] > **recognitive** (rɪ'kɒgnɪtɪv) *or* **re'cognitory** *adj*

recognizance *or* **recognisance** (rɪ'kɒgnɪzəns) *n* *law* a a bond entered into before a court or magistrate by which a person binds himself to do a specified act, as to appear in court on a stated day, keep the peace, or pay a debt b a monetary sum pledged to the performance of such an act [c14 from OF *reconoissance*, from *reconoistre* to RECOGNIZE] > **re'cognizant** *or* **re'cognisant** *adj*

recognize *or* **recognise** ('rɛkəg,naɪz) *vb* **recognizes, recognizing, recognized** *or* **recognises, recognising, recognised** (*tr*) 1 to perceive (a person or thing) to be the same as or belong to the same class as something previously seen or known; know again 2 to accept or be aware of (a fact, problem, etc): *to recognize necessity* 3 to give formal acknowledgment of the status or legality of (a government, a representative, etc) 4 *chiefly US & Canad* to grant (a person) the right to speak in a deliberative body 5 to give a token of thanks for (a service rendered, etc) 6 to make formal acknowledgment of (a claim, etc) 7 to show approval or appreciation of (something good) 8 to acknowledge or greet (a person) [c15 from L *recognoscere*, from RE- + *cognoscere* to know] > **'recog,nizable** *or* **'recog,nisable** *adj* > **,recog,niza'bility** *or* **,recog,nisa'bility** *n* > **'recog,nizably** *or* **'recog,nisably** *adv* > **'recog,nizer** *or* **'recog,niser** *n*

Rr

recoil *vb* (rɪ'kɔɪl) (*intr*) 1 to jerk back, as from an impact or violent thrust 2 (often foll by *from*) to draw back in fear, horror, or disgust 3 (foll by *on* or *upon*) to go wrong, esp so as to hurt the perpetrator 4 (of an atom, etc) to change momentum as a result of the emission of a particle ▷ *n* (rɪ'kɔɪl, 'ri:kɔɪl) 5a the backward movement of a gun when fired 5b the distance moved 6 the motion acquired by an atom, etc, as a result of its emission of a particle 7 the act of recoiling [c13 from OF *reculer*, from RE- + *cul* rump, from L *cūlus*] > **re'coiler** *n*

recollect (,rɛkə'lɛkt) *vb* (when *tr*, *often takes a clause as object*) to recall from memory; remember [c16 from L *recolligere*, from RE- + *colligere* to COLLECT] > **,recol'lection** *n* > **,recol'lective** *adj* > **,recol'lectively** *adv*

recombinant (ri:'kɒmbɪnənt) *genetics* ▷ *adj* 1 produced by the combining of genetic material from more than one origin ▷ *n* 2 a chromosome, cell, organism, etc, the genetic makeup of which results from recombination

recombinant DNA *n* DNA molecules that are extracted from different sources and chemically joined together

recombination (,ri:kɒmbɪ'neɪʃən) *n* *genetics* any of several processes by which genetic material of different origins becomes combined

recommend (ˌrɛkəˈmɛnd) *vb (tr)* **1** *(may take a clause as object or an infinitive)* to advise as the best course or choice; counsel **2** to praise or commend: *to recommend a new book* **3** to make attractive or advisable: *the trip has little to recommend it* **4** *arch* to entrust (a person or thing) to someone else's care; commend [C14 via Med. L from L RE- + *commendāre* to COMMEND] > ˌ**recomˈmendable** *adj* > ˌ**recomˈmendatory** *adj* > ˌ**recomˈmender** *n*

recommendation (ˌrɛkəmɛnˈdeɪʃən) *n* **1** the act of recommending **2** something that recommends, esp a letter **3** something that is recommended, such as a course of action

recommit (ˌriːkəˈmɪt) *vb* **recommits, recommitting, recommitted** *(tr)* **1** to send (a bill) back to a committee for further consideration **2** to commit again > ˌ**recomˈmitment** *or* ˌ**recomˈmittal** *n*

recompense (ˈrɛkəmˌpɛns) *vb* **recompenses, recompensing, recompensed** *(tr)* **1** to pay or reward for service, work, etc **2** to compensate for loss, injury, etc ▷ *n* **3** compensation for loss, injury, etc **4** reward, remuneration, or repayment [C15 from OF *recompenser*, from L RE- + *compensāre* to balance in weighing] > ˈ**recomˌpensable** *adj* > ˈ**recomˌpenser** *n*

reconcile (ˈrɛkənˌsaɪl) *vb* **reconciles, reconciling, reconciled** *(tr)* **1** *(often passive;* usually foll by *to)* to make (oneself or another) no longer opposed; cause to acquiesce in something unpleasant: *she reconciled herself to poverty* **2** to become friendly with (someone) after estrangement or to re-establish friendly relations between (two or more people) **3** to settle (a quarrel) **4** to make (two apparently conflicting things) compatible or consistent with each other **5** to reconsecrate (a desecrated church, etc) [C14 from L *reconciliāre*, from RE- + *conciliāre* to make friendly, CONCILIATE] > ˈ**reconˌcilement** *n* > ˈ**reconˌciler** *n* > **reconciliation** (ˌrɛkənˌsɪlɪˈeɪʃən) *n* > **reconciliatory** (ˌrɛkənˈsɪlɪətərɪ, -trɪ) *adj*

recondite (rɪˈkɒndaɪt, ˈrɛkənˌdaɪt) *adj* **1** requiring special knowledge; abstruse **2** dealing with abstruse or profound subjects [C17 from L *reconditus* hidden away, from RE- + *condere* to conceal] > **reˈconditely** *adv* > **reˈconditeness** *n*

recondition (ˌriːkənˈdɪʃən) *vb (tr)* to restore to good condition or working order: *to recondition an engine* > ˌ**reconˈditioned** *adj*

reconnaissance (rɪˈkɒnɪsəns) *n* **1** the act of reconnoitring **2** the process of obtaining information about the position, etc, of an enemy **3** a preliminary inspection of an area of land [C18 from F, from OF *reconoistre* to explore, RECOGNIZE]

reconnoitre *or US* **reconnoiter** (ˌrɛkəˈnɔɪtə) *vb* **reconnoitres, reconnoitring, reconnoitred** *or US* **reconnoiters, reconnoitering, reconnoitered** **1** to survey or inspect (an enemy's position, region of land, etc) ▷ *n* **2** the act or process of reconnoitring; a reconnaissance [C18 from obs. F *reconnoître* to inspect, explore; see RECOGNIZE] > ˌ**reconˈnoitrer** *or US* ˌ**reconˈnoiterer** *n*

reconsider (ˌriːkənˈsɪdə) *vb* to consider (something) again, with a view to changing one's policy or course of action > ˌ**reconˌsiderˈation** *n*

reconstitute (riːˈkɒnstɪˌtjuːt) *vb* **reconstitutes, reconstituting, reconstituted** *(tr)* **1** to restore (food, etc) to its former or natural state, as by the addition of water to a concentrate **2** to reconstruct; form again > **reconstituent** (ˌriːkənˈstɪtjʊənt) *adj, n* > ˌ**reconstiˈtution** *n*

reconstruct (ˌriːkənˈstrʌkt) *vb (tr)* **1** to construct or form again; rebuild **2** to form a picture of (a crime, past event, etc) by piecing together evidence > ˌ**reconˈstructible** *adj* > ˌ**reconˈstruction** *n* > ˌ**reconˈstructive** *or* ˌ**reconˈstructional** *adj* > ˌ**reconˈstructor** *n*

reconvert (ˌriːkənˈvɜːt) *vb (tr)* **1** to change (something) back to a previous state or form **2** to bring (someone) back to his or her former religion > **reconversion** (ˌriːkənˈvɜːʃən) *n*

record *n* (ˈrɛkɔːd) **1** an account in permanent form, esp in writing, preserving knowledge or information **2** a written account of some transaction that serves as legal evidence of the transaction **3** a written official report of the proceedings of a court of justice or legislative body **4** anything serving as evidence or as a memorial: *the First World War is a record of human folly* **5** *(often pl)* information or data on a specific subject collected methodically over a long period: *weather records* **6a** the best or most outstanding amount, rate, height, etc, ever attained, as in some field of sport: *a world record* **6b** *(as modifier)*: *a record time* **7** the sum of one's recognized achievements, career, or performance **8** a list of crimes of which an accused person has previously been convicted **9** **have a record** to be a known criminal **10** Also called: **gramophone record, disc** a thin disc of a plastic material upon which sound has been recorded. Each side has a spiral groove, which undulates in accordance with the frequency and amplitude of the sound **11** the markings made by a recording instrument such as a seismograph **12** *computing* a group of data or piece of information preserved as a unit in machine-readable form **13** **for the record** for the sake of strict factual accuracy **14** **go on record** to state one's views publicly **15** **off the record** confidential or confidentially **16** **on record** **16a** stated in a public document **16b** publicly known **17** **set** *or* **put the record straight** to correct an error ▷ *vb* (rɪˈkɔːd) *(mainly tr)* **18** to set down in some permanent form so as to preserve the true facts of: *to record the minutes of a meeting* **19** to contain or serve to relate (facts, information, etc) **20** to indicate, show, or register: *his face recorded his disappointment* **21** to remain as or afford evidence of: *these ruins record the life of the Romans in Britain* **22** *(also intr)* to make a recording of (music, speech, etc) for reproduction, esp on a record player or tape recorder, or for later broadcasting **23** *(also intr)* (of an instrument) to register or indicate (information) on a scale: *the barometer recorded a low pressure* [C13 from OF *recorder*, from L *recordārī* to remember, from RE- + *cor* heart] > **reˈcordable** *adj*

recorded delivery *n* a Post Office service by which an official record of posting and delivery is obtained for a letter or package

recorder (rɪˈkɔːdə) *n* **1** a person who records, such as an official or historian **2** something that records, esp an apparatus that provides a permanent record of experiments, etc **3** short for **tape recorder** **4** *music* a wind instrument of the flute family, blown through a fipple in the mouth end, having a reedlike quality of tone **5** (in England) a barrister or solicitor of at least ten years' standing appointed to sit as a part-time judge in the crown court > **reˈcordership** *n*

recording (rɪˈkɔːdɪŋ) *n* **1a** the act or process of making a record, esp of sound on a gramophone record or magnetic tape **1b** *(as modifier)*: *recording studio* **2** the record or tape so produced **3** something that has been recorded, esp a radio or television programme

Recording Angel *n* an angel who supposedly keeps a record of every person's good and bad acts

record label *n* a company that produces and sells records, CDs, and recordings

record of achievement *n Brit* a statement of the personal and educational development of each pupil

record player *n* a device for reproducing the sounds stored on a record. A stylus vibrates in accordance with the undulations of the walls of the groove in the record as it rotates

recount (rɪˈkaʊnt) *vb (tr)* to tell the story or details of; narrate [C15 from OF *reconter*, from RE- + *conter* to tell; see COUNT[1]] > **reˈcountal** *n*

re-count *vb* (riːˈkaʊnt) **1** to count (votes, etc) again ▷ *n* (ˈriːˌkaʊnt) **2** a second or further count, esp of votes in a closely contested election

recoup (rɪ'kuːp) *vb* **1** to regain or make good (a financial or other loss) **2** *(tr)* to reimburse or compensate (someone), as for a loss **3** *law* to keep back (something due), having rightful claim to do so ▷ *n* **4** *rare* the act of recouping; recoupment [C15 from OF *recouper* to cut back, from RE- + *couper*, from *coper* to behead] > **re'coupable** *adj* > **re'coupment** *n*

recourse (rɪ'kɔːs) *n* **1** the act of resorting to a person, course of action, etc, in difficulty (esp in **have recourse to**) **2** a person, organization, or course of action that is turned to for help, etc **3** the right to demand payment, esp from the drawer or endorser of a bill of exchange or other negotiable instrument when the person accepting it fails to pay **4** **without recourse** a qualified endorsement on such a negotiable instrument, by which the endorser protects himself from liability to subsequent holders [C14 from OF *recours*, from LL *recursus* a running back, from RE- + L *currere* to run]

recover (rɪ'kʌvə) *vb* **1** *(tr)* to find again or obtain the return of (something lost) **2** to regain (loss of money, time, etc) **3** (of a person) to regain (health, spirits, composure, etc) **4** to regain (a former and better condition): *industry recovered after the war* **5** *law* **5a** *(tr)* to gain (something) by the judgment of a court of law: *to recover damages* **5b** *(intr)* to succeed in a lawsuit **6** *(tr)* to obtain (useful substances) from waste **7** *(intr)* (in fencing, rowing, etc) to make a recovery [C14 from OF *recoverer*, from L *recuperāre* RECUPERATE] > **re'coverable** *adj* > **re,covera'bility** *n* > **re'coverer** *n*

re-cover (riː'kʌvə) *vb (tr)* **1** to cover again **2** to provide (furniture, etc) with a new cover

recovery (rɪ'kʌvərɪ) *n, pl* **recoveries** **1** the act or process of recovering, esp from sickness, a shock, or a setback **2** restoration to a former or better condition **3** the regaining of something lost **4** the extraction of useful substances from waste **5** the retrieval of a space capsule after a spaceflight **6** *law* the obtaining of a right, etc, by the judgment of a court **7** *fencing* a return to the position of guard after making an attack **8** *swimming, rowing, etc* the action of bringing the arm, an oar, etc, forward for another stroke **9** *golf* a stroke played from the rough or a bunker to the fairway or green

recovery stock *n stock exchange* a security that has fallen in price but is believed to have the ability to recover

recreant ('rɛkrɪənt) *arch* ▷ *adj* **1** cowardly; faint-hearted **2** disloyal ▷ *n* **3** a disloyal or cowardly person [C14 from OF, from *recroire* to surrender, from RE- + L *crēdere* to believe] > **'recreance** *or* **'recreancy** *n* > **'recreantly** *adv*

recreate ('rɛkrɪ,eɪt) *vb* **recreates, recreating, recreated** *rare* to amuse (oneself or someone else) [C15 from L *recreāre* to invigorate, renew, from RE- + *creāre* to CREATE] > **'recreative** *adj* > **'recreatively** *adv* > **'recre,ator** *n*

re-create (,riːkrɪ'eɪt) *vb* **re-creates, re-creating, re-created** to create anew; reproduce > **,re-cre'ation** *n* > **,re-cre'ator** *n*

recreation (,rɛkrɪ'eɪʃən) *n* **1** refreshment of health or spirits by relaxation and enjoyment **2** an activity that promotes this **3a** an interval of free time between school lessons **3b** *(as modifier)*: *recreation period*

recreational (,rɛkrɪ'eɪʃənᵊl) *adj* **1** of, relating to, or used for recreation: *recreational facilities* **2** (of a drug) taken for pleasure rather than for medical reasons or because of an addiction

recreational vehicle *n chiefly US* a large vanlike vehicle equipped to be lived in. Abbrev: **RV**

recriminate (rɪ'krɪmɪ,neɪt) *vb* **recriminates, recriminating, recriminated** *(intr)* to return an accusation against someone or engage in mutual accusations [C17 via Med. L, from L *crīminārī* to accuse, from *crīmen* accusation] > **re'criminative** *or* **re'criminatory** *adj* > **re'crimi,nator** *n*

recrimination (rɪ,krɪmɪ'neɪʃən) *n* the act or an instance of recriminating: *post-match recriminations*

recrudesce (,riːkruː'dɛs) *vb* **recrudesces, recrudescing, recrudesced** *(intr)* (of a disease, trouble, etc) to break out or appear again after a period of dormancy [C19 from L *recrūdēscere*, from RE- + *crūdēscere* to grow worse, from *crūdus* bloody, raw] > **,recru'descence** *n*

recruit (rɪ'kruːt) *vb* **1a** to enlist (men) for military service **1b** to raise or strengthen (an army, etc) by enlistment **2** *(tr)* to enrol or obtain (members, support, etc) **3** to furnish or be furnished with a fresh supply; renew **4** *arch* to recover (health, spirits, etc) ▷ *n* **5** a newly joined member of a military service **6** any new member or supporter [C17 from F *recrute* lit.: new growth, from *recroître*, from L, from RE- + *crēscere* to grow] > **re'cruitable** *adj* > **re'cruiter** *n* > **re'cruitment** *n*

recta ('rɛktə) *n* a plural of **rectum**

rectal ('rɛktəl) *adj* of or relating to the rectum > **'rectally** *adv*

rectangle ('rɛk,tæŋgᵊl) *n* a parallelogram having four right angles [C16 from Med. L *rectangulum*, from L *rectus* straight + *angulus* angle]

rectangular (rɛk'tæŋgjʊlə) *adj* **1** shaped like a rectangle **2** having or relating to right angles **3** mutually perpendicular: *rectangular coordinates* **4** having a base or section shaped like a rectangle > **rec,tangu'larity** *n* > **rec'tangularly** *adv*

rectangular coordinates *pl n* the Cartesian coordinates in a system of mutually perpendicular axes

rectangular hyperbola *n* a hyperbola with perpendicular asymptotes

recti ('rɛktaɪ) *n* the plural of **rectus**

recti- *or before a vowel* **rect-** *combining form* straight or right: *rectangle* [from L *rectus*]

rectifier ('rɛktɪ,faɪə) *n* **1** an electronic device that converts an alternating current to a direct current **2** *chem* an apparatus for condensing a hot vapour to a liquid in distillation; condenser **3** a thing or person that rectifies

rectify ('rɛktɪ,faɪ) *vb* **rectifies, rectifying, rectified** *(tr)* **1** to put right; correct; remedy **2** to separate (a substance) from a mixture or refine (a substance) by fractional distillation **3** to convert (alternating current) into direct current **4** *maths* to determine the length of (a curve) [C14 via OF from Med. L *rectificāre*, from L *rectus* straight + *facere* to make] > **'recti,fiable** *adj* > **,rectifi'cation** *n*

rectilinear (,rɛktɪ'lɪnɪə) *or* **rectilineal** *adj* **1** in, moving in, or characterized by a straight line **2** consisting of, bounded by, or formed by a straight line > **,recti'linearly** *or* **,recti'lineally** *adv*

rectitude ('rɛktɪ,tjuːd) *n* **1** moral or religious correctness **2** correctness of judgment [C15 from LL *rectitūdō*, from L *rectus* right, from *regere* to rule]

recto ('rɛktəʊ) *n, pl* **rectos** **1** the front of a sheet of printed paper **2** the right-hand pages of a book ▷ Cf **verso** (sense 1b) [C19 from L *rectō foliō* on the right-hand page]

rectocele ('rɛktəʊ,siːl) *n pathol* a protrusion or herniation of the rectum into the vagina

rector ('rɛktə) *n* **1** *Church of England* a clergyman in charge of a parish in which, as its incumbent, he would formerly have been entitled to the whole of the tithes **2** *RC Church* a cleric in charge of a college, religious house, or congregation **3** *Protestant Episcopal Church* a clergyman in charge of a parish **4** *chiefly Brit* the head of certain schools, colleges, or universities **5** (in Scotland) a high-ranking official in a university **6** (in South Africa) a principal of an Afrikaans university [C14 from L: director, ruler, from *regere* to rule] > **'rectorate** *n* > **rectorial** (rɛk'tɔːrɪəl) *adj* > **'rectorship** *n*

rectory ('rɛktərɪ) *n, pl* **rectories** **1** the official house of a rector **2** *Church of England* the office and benefice of a rector

Rr

rectrix ('rɛktrɪks) *n, pl* **rectrices** ('rɛktrɪ,si:z, rɛk'traɪsi:z) any of the large stiff feathers of a bird's tail, used in controlling the direction of flight [C17 from LL, fem of L *rector* RECTOR] > **rectricial** (rɛk'trɪʃəl) *adj*
rectum ('rɛktəm) *n, pl* **rectums** *or* **recta** the lower part of the alimentary canal, between the sigmoid flexure of the colon and the anus [C16 from NL *rectum intestinum* the straight intestine]
rectus ('rɛktəs) *n, pl* **recti** *anat* a straight muscle [C18 from NL *rectus musculus*]
recumbent (rɪ'kʌmbənt) *adj* **1** lying down; reclining **2** (of an organ) leaning or resting against another organ [C17 from L *recumbere* to lie back, from RE- + *cumbere* to lie] > **re'cumbence** *or* **re'cumbency** *n* > **re'cumbently** *adv*
recumbent bicycle *n* a type of bicycle that is ridden in a reclining position
recuperate (rɪ'ku:pə,reɪt, -'kju:-) *vb* **recuperates, recuperating, recuperated 1** (*intr*) to recover from illness or exhaustion **2** to recover (financial losses, etc) [C16 from L *recuperāre* to recover, from RE- + *capere* to gain] > **re,cuper'ation** *n* > **re'cuperative** *adj*
recur (rɪ'kɜ:) *vb* **recurs, recurring, recurred** (*intr*) **1** to happen again **2** (of a thought, etc) to come back to the mind **3** (of a problem, etc) to come up again **4** *maths* (of a digit or group of digits) to be repeated an infinite number of times at the end of a decimal fraction [C15 from L *recurrere*, from RE- + *currere* to run] > **re'curring** *adj*
recurrent (rɪ'kʌrənt) *adj* **1** tending to happen again or repeatedly **2** *anat* (of certain nerves, etc) turning back, so as to run in the opposite direction > **re'currence** *n* > **re'currently** *adv*
recurrent fever *n* another name for **relapsing fever**
recurring decimal *n* a rational number that contains a pattern of digits repeated indefinitely after the decimal point
recursion (rɪ'kɜ:ʃən) *n* **1** the act or process of returning or running back **2** *maths, logic* the application of a function to its own values to generate an infinite sequence of values [C17 from L *recursio*, from *recurrere* RECUR] > **re'cursive** *adj*
recurve (rɪ'kɜ:v) *vb* **recurves, recurving, recurved** to curve or bend (something) back or down or (of something) to be so curved or bent [C16 from L *recurvāre*, from RE- + *curvāre* to CURVE]
recusant ('rɛkjʊzənt) *n* **1** (in 16th to 18th century England) a Roman Catholic who did not attend the services of the Church of England **2** any person who refuses to submit to authority ▷ *adj* **3** (formerly, of Catholics) refusing to attend services of the Church of England **4** refusing to submit to authority [C16 from L *recūsāns* refusing, from *recūsāre*, from RE- + *causārī* to dispute, from *causa* a CAUSE] > **'recusance** *or* **'recusancy** *n*
recycle (ri:'saɪkᵊl) *vb* **recycles, recycling, recycled** (*tr*) **1** to pass (a substance) through a system again for further treatment or use **2** to reclaim (packaging or products with a limited useful life) for further use: *to recycle water* ▷ *n* **3** the repetition of a fixed sequence of events > **re'cyclable** *or* **re'cycleable** *adj*
red[1] (rɛd) *n* **1** any of a group of colours, such as that of a ripe tomato or fresh blood **2** a pigment or dye of or producing these colours **3** red cloth or clothing: *dressed in red* **4** a red ball in snooker, etc **5** (in roulette) one of two colours on which players may place even bets **6** *inf* red wine: *a bottle of red* **7 in the red** *inf* in debt **8 see red** *inf* to become very angry ▷ *adj* **redder, reddest 9** of the colour red **10** reddish in colour or having parts or marks that are reddish: *red deer* **11** having the face temporarily suffused with blood, being a sign of anger, shame, etc **12** (of the complexion) rosy; florid **13** (of the eyes) bloodshot **14** (of the hands) stained with blood **15** bloody or violent: *red revolution* **16** denoting the highest degree of urgency in an emergency; used by the police and the army and informally (esp in the phrase **red alert**) **17** (of wine) made from black grapes and coloured by their skins ▷ *vb* **reds, redding, redded 18** another word for **redden** [OE *rēad*] > **'reddish** *adj* > **'redness** *n*
red[2] (rɛd) *vb* **reds, redding, red** *or* **redded** (*tr*) a variant spelling of **redd**
Red (rɛd) *inf* ▷ *adj* **1** Communist, Socialist, or Soviet **2** radical, leftist, or revolutionary ▷ *n* **3** a member or supporter of a Communist or Socialist Party or a national of the Soviet Union **4** a radical, leftist, or revolutionary [C19 from the colour chosen to symbolize revolutionary socialism]
redact (rɪ'dækt) *vb* (*tr*) **1** to compose or draft (an edict, proclamation, etc) **2** to put (a literary work, etc) into appropriate form for publication; edit [C15 from L *redigere* to bring back, from *red-* RE- + *agere* to drive] > **re'daction** *n* > **re'dactional** *adj* > **re'dactor** *n*
red admiral *n* a butterfly of temperate Europe and Asia, having black wings with red and white markings. See also **white admiral**
red algae *pl n* the numerous algae which contain a red pigment in addition to chlorophyll. The group includes carrageen and dulse
Red Army Faction *n* another name for **Baader-Meinhof Gang**
redback ('rɛd,bæk) *n Austral* a small, venomous spider, the female of which has a red stripe on its back. Also called: **redback spider**
red bark *n* a kind of cinchona containing a high proportion of alkaloids
red-bellied black snake *n* a highly venomous Australian black snake, *Pseudechis porphyriacus*, with a reddish underside
red biddy *n inf* cheap red wine fortified with methylated spirits
red blood cell *n* another name for **erythrocyte**
red-blooded *adj inf* vigorous; virile > **,red-'bloodedness** *n*
red book *n Brit* (sometimes caps) a government publication bound in red, esp the Treasury's annual forecast of revenue, expenditure, growth, and inflation
redbreast ('rɛd,brɛst) *n* any of various birds having a red breast, esp the Old World robin
redbrick ('rɛd,brɪk) *n* (*modifier*) denoting, relating to, or characteristic of a provincial British university of relatively recent foundation
Redbridge ('rɛd,brɪdʒ) *n* a borough of NE Greater London: includes part of Epping Forest. Pop: 238 628 (2001). Area: 56 sq km (22 sq miles)
redcap ('rɛd,kæp) *n* **1** *Brit inf* a military policeman **2** *US & Canad* a porter at an airport or station
Redcar and Cleveland ('rɛdkɑ:) *n* a unitary authority in NE England, in North Yorkshire: formerly (1975–96) part of Cleveland county. Pop: 139 141 (2001). Area: 240 sq km (93 sq miles)
red card *soccer, etc* ▷ *n* **1** a card of a red colour displayed by a referee to indicate that a player has been sent off ▷ *vb* **red-card 2** (*tr*) to send off (a player)
red carpet *n* **1** a strip of red carpeting laid for important dignitaries to walk on **2a** deferential treatment accorded to a person of importance **2b** (*as modifier*): *a red-carpet reception*
red cedar *n* **1** any of several North American coniferous trees, esp a juniper that has fragrant reddish wood **2** the wood of any of these trees **3** any of several Australian timber trees
red cent *n* (*used with a negative*) *inf, chiefly US* a cent considered as a trivial amount of money (esp in **not have a red cent,** etc)
Red China *n* an unofficial name for (the People's Republic of) **China**
redcoat ('rɛd,kəʊt) *n* **1** (formerly) a British soldier **2** *Canad inf* another name for **Mountie**
red coral *n* any of several corals, the skeletons of which

are pinkish red in colour and used to make ornaments, etc

red corpuscle *n* another name for **erythrocyte**

Red Crescent *n* the emblem of the Red Cross Society in a Muslim country

Red Cross *n* **1** an international humanitarian organization (**Red Cross Society**) formally established by the Geneva Convention of 1864 **2** the emblem of this organization, consisting of a red cross on a white background

redcurrant (ˌrɛdˈkʌrənt) *n* **1** a N temperate shrub having greenish flowers and small edible rounded red berries **2a** the fruit of this shrub **2b** (*as modifier*): *redcurrant jelly*

redd *or* **red** (rɛd) *Scot & N English dialect* ▷ *vb* **redds, redding, redd** *or* **redded 1** (*tr; often foll by up*) to bring order to; tidy (up) ▷ *n* **2** the act or an instance of redding [C15 *redden* to clear, ? a variant of RID] > ˈ**redder** *n*

red deer *n* a large deer formerly widely distributed in the woodlands of Europe and Asia. The coat is reddish brown in summer and the short tail is surrounded by a patch of light-coloured hair

Red Deer *n* **1** a town in S Alberta on the Red Deer River: trade centre for mixed farming, dairying region, and natural gas processing. Pop: 58 134 (1991) **2** a river in W Canada, in SW Alberta, flowing southeast into the South Saskatchewan River. Length: about 620 km (385 miles) **3** a river in W Canada, flowing east through **Red Deer Lake** into Lake Winnipegosis. Length: about 225 km (140 miles)

redden (ˈrɛdᵊn) *vb* **1** to make or become red **2** (*intr*) to flush with embarrassment, anger, etc

Redding (ˈrɛdɪŋ) *n* **Otis** 1941–67, US soul singer and songwriter. His recordings include "Respect" (1965), *Dictionary of Soul* (1966), and "(Sittin' on) The Dock of the Bay" (1968)

Redditch (ˈrɛdɪtʃ) *n* a town in W central England, in N Worcestershire: designated a new town in the mid-1960s; metal-working industries. Pop: 73 372 (1991)

reddle (ˈrɛdᵊl) *n, vb* **reddles, reddling, reddled** a variant spelling of **ruddle**

red duster *n Brit* an informal name for the **Red Ensign**

red dwarf *n* one of a class of stars of relatively small mass and low luminosity

rede (riːd) *arch* ▷ *n* **1** advice or counsel **2** an explanation ▷ *vb* **redes, reding, reded** (*tr*) **3** to advise; counsel **4** to explain [OE *rǣdan* to rule]

red earth *n* a clayey zonal soil of tropical savanna lands, formed by extensive chemical weathering and coloured by iron compounds

redeem (rɪˈdiːm) *vb* (*tr*) **1** to recover possession or ownership of by payment of a price or service; regain **2** to convert (bonds, shares, etc) into cash **3** to pay off (a loan, etc) **4** to recover (something pledged, mortgaged, or pawned) **5** to convert (paper money) into bullion or specie **6** to fulfil (a promise, pledge, etc) **7** to exchange (coupons, etc) for goods **8** to reinstate in someone's estimation or good opinion: *he redeemed himself by his altruistic action* **9** to make amends for **10** to recover from captivity, esp by a money payment **11** *Christianity* (of Christ as Saviour) to free (humanity) from sin by death on the Cross [C15 from OF *redimer*, from L *redimere*, from *red-* RE- + *emere* to buy] > **reˈdeemable** *or* **reˈdemptible** *adj* > **reˈdeemer** *n*

Redeemer (rɪˈdiːmə) *n* **the** Jesus Christ as having brought redemption to mankind

redeeming (rɪˈdiːmɪŋ) *adj* serving to compensate for faults or deficiencies

red emperor *n Austral* a brightly-coloured marine food fish, *Lutjanus sebae*, of the Great Barrier Reef

redemption (rɪˈdɛmpʃən) *n* **1** the act or process of redeeming **2** the state of being redeemed **3** *Christianity* **3a** deliverance from sin through the incarnation, sufferings, and death of Christ **3b** atonement for guilt [C14 via OF from L *redemptiō* a buying back; see REDEEM] > **reˈdemptional, reˈdemptive,** *or* **reˈdemptory** *adj* > **reˈdemptively** *adv*

redemption yield *n stock exchange* the yield produced by a redeemable gilt-edged security taking into account the annual interest it pays and an annualized amount to account for any profit or loss when it is redeemed

Red Ensign *n* the ensign of the British Merchant Navy, having the Union Jack on a red background at the upper corner of the vertical edge alongside the hoist. It was also the national flag of Canada until 1965

redeploy (ˌriːdɪˈplɔɪ) *vb* **1** to assign new positions or tasks to (labour, troops, etc) **2** *S African* to assign (an employee) to a new position after some embarrassment or display of incompetence > ˌ**redeˈployment** *n*

redevelopment area (ˌriːdɪˈvɛləpmənt) *n* an urban area in which all or most of the buildings are demolished and rebuilt

redeye (ˈrɛdˌaɪ) *n* **1** *US sl* inferior whisky **2** another name for **rudd 3** *Canad sl* a drink incorporating beer and tomato juice

red-eye *n inf* **a** an aeroplane flight leaving late at night or arriving early in the morning **b** (*as modifier*): *a red-eye flight*

red-faced *adj* **1** flushed with embarrassment or anger **2** having a florid complexion > **red-facedly** (ˌrɛdˈfeɪsɪdlɪ, -ˈfeɪstlɪ) *adv*

redfin (ˈrɛdˌfɪn) *n* any of various small cyprinid fishes with reddish fins

redfish (ˈrɛdˌfɪʃ) *n, pl* **redfish** *or* **redfishes 1** a male salmon that has recently spawned ▷ Cf **blackfish** (sense 2) **2** *Canad* another name for **kokanee**

red flag *n* **1** a symbol of socialism, communism, or revolution **2** a warning of danger or a signal to stop

Redford (ˈrɛdfəd) *n* **Robert** born 1937, US film actor and director. His films include (as actor) *Barefoot in the Park* (1966), *Butch Cassidy and the Sundance Kid* (1969), *The Sting* (1973), *All the President's Men* (1976), *Up Close and Personal* (1996) and (as director) *Ordinary People* (1980), *A River Runs Through It* (1992), and *The Horse Whisperer* (1998)

red fox *n* the common fox of Europe and N America, which has a reddish-brown coat

red giant *n* a giant star that emits red light

Redgrave (ˈrɛdˌgreɪv) *n* **1** Sir **Michael** 1908–85, British stage and film actor. Among his films are *The Lady Vanishes* (1938), *The Dam Busters* (1955), *The Loneliness of the Long Distance Runner* (1963), and *The Go-Between* (1971) **2** his elder daughter, **Vanessa** born 1937, British stage and film actress, whose roles include performances in the films *Isadora* (1968), *Julia* (1977), *Howards End* (1992), and *Mrs Dalloway* (1998): noted also for her active commitment to left-wing politics **3** Sir **Steve** born 1962, British oarsman; won five gold medals in rowing events at consecutive Olympic Games (1984, 1988, 1992, 1996, 2000)

red grouse *n* a reddish-brown grouse of upland moors of Great Britain

Red Guard *n* a member of a Communist Chinese youth movement that attempted to effect the Cultural Revolution (1966–69)

red-handed *adj* (*postpositive*) in the act of committing a crime or doing something wrong or shameful (esp in **catch red-handed**) [C19 (earlier, C15 *red hand*)]

red hat *n* the broad-brimmed crimson hat given to cardinals as the symbol of their rank

redhead (ˈrɛdˌhɛd) *n* a person with red hair > ˈ**redˌheaded** *adj*

red heat *n* **1** the temperature at which a substance is red-hot **2** the state or condition of being red-hot

red herring *n* **1** anything that diverts attention from a topic or line of inquiry **2** a herring cured by salting and smoking

Rr

red-hot *adj* **1** (esp of metal) heated to the temperature at which it glows red **2** extremely hot **3** keen, excited, or eager **4** furious; violent: *red-hot anger* **5** very recent or topical: *red-hot information* **6** *Austral sl* extreme, unreasonable, or unfair

red-hot poker *n* a liliaceous plant: widely cultivated for its showy spikes of red or yellow flowers

Red Indian *n, adj* another name, now considered offensive, for **American Indian** [see REDSKIN]

redingote ('rɛdɪŋˌɡəʊt) *n* **1** a man's full-skirted outer coat of the 18th and 19th centuries **2** a woman's coat of the 18th century, with an open-fronted skirt, revealing a decorative underskirt **3** a woman's coat with a close-fitting top and a full skirt [C19 from F, from E *riding coat*]

redintegrate (rɛ'dɪntɪˌɡreɪt) *vb* **redintegrates, redintegrating, redintegrated** (*tr*) to make whole or complete again; restore to a perfect state; renew [C15 from L *redintegrāre* to renew, from *red-* RE- + *integer* complete] > **reˌdinte'gration** *n* > **red'integrative** *adj*

redistribution (ˌri:dɪstrɪ'bju:ʃən) *n* **1** the act or an instance of distributing again **2** a revision of the number of seats in the Canadian House of Commons allocated to each province, made every ten years on the basis of a new census

redivivus (ˌrɛdɪ'vaɪvəs) *adj rare* returned to life; revived [C17 from LL, from L *red-* RE- + *vīvus* alive]

red lead (lɛd) *n* a bright-red poisonous insoluble oxide of lead

red-letter day *n* a memorably important or happy occasion: *a red-letter day for Australian cricket* [C18 from the red letters used in ecclesiastical calendars to indicate saints' days and feasts]

red light *n* **1** a signal to stop, esp a red traffic signal **2** a danger signal **3a** a red lamp indicating that a house is a brothel **3b** (*as modifier*): *a red-light district*

redline ('rɛdˌlaɪn) *vb* **redlines, redlining, redlined** (*tr*) (esp of a bank or group of banks) to refuse to consider giving a loan to (a person or country) because of the presumed risks involved

red meat *n* any meat that is dark in colour, esp beef and lamb ▷ Cf **white meat**

Redmond ('rɛdmənd) *n* **John Edward** 1856–1918, Irish politician. He led the Parnellites from 1891 and helped to procure the Home Rule bill of 1912, but was considered too moderate by extreme nationalists

red mullet *n* a food fish of European waters with a pair of long barbels beneath the chin and a reddish coloration. US name: **goatfish**

redneck ('rɛdˌnɛk) *n disparaging* **1** (in the southwestern US) a poor uneducated White farm worker **2** a person or institution that is extremely reactionary ▷ *adj* **3** reactionary and bigoted: *redneck laws*

redo (ri:'du:) *vb* **redoes, redoing, redid, redone** (*tr*) **1** to do over again **2** *inf* to redecorate, esp thoroughly: *we redid the house last summer*

red ochre *n* any of various natural red earths containing ferric oxide: used as pigments

redolent ('rɛdəʊlənt) *adj* **1** having a pleasant smell; fragrant **2** (*postpositive;* foll by *of* or *with*) having the odour or smell (of): *a room redolent of flowers* **3** (*postpositive;* foll by *of* or *with*) reminiscent or suggestive (of): *a picture redolent of the 18th century* [C14 from L *redolens* smelling (of), from *redolēre* to give off an odour, from *red-* RE- + *olēre* to smell] > '**redolence** *or* '**redolency** *n* > '**redolently** *adv*

Redon (*French* rədɔ̃) *n* **Odilon** (ɔdilɔ̃) 1840–1916, French symbolist painter and etcher. He foreshadowed the surrealists in his paintings of fantastic dream images

redouble (rɪ'dʌbᵊl) *vb* **redoubles, redoubling, redoubled** **1** to make or become much greater in intensity, number, etc: *to redouble one's efforts* **2** to send back (sounds) or (of sounds) to be sent back **3** *bridge* to double (an opponent's double) ▷ *n* **4** the act of redoubling

redoubt (rɪ'daʊt) *n* **1** an outwork or fieldwork defending a hilltop, pass, etc **2** a temporary defence work built inside a fortification as a last defensive position [C17 via F from obs. It. *ridotta*, from Med. L *reductus* shelter, from L *redūcere*, from RE- + *dūcere* to lead]

redoubtable (rɪ'daʊtəbᵊl) *adj* **1** to be feared; formidable **2** worthy of respect [C14 from OF, from *redouter* to dread, from RE- + *douter* to be afraid, DOUBT] > **re'doubtableness** *n* > **re'doubtably** *adv*

redound (rɪ'daʊnd) *vb* **1** (*intr;* foll by *to*) to have an advantageous or disadvantageous effect (on): *brave deeds redound to your credit* **2** (*intr;* foll by *on* or *upon*) to recoil or rebound **3** (*tr*) *arch* to reflect; bring: *his actions redound dishonour upon him* [C14 from OF *redonder*, from L *redundāre* to stream over, from *red-* RE- + *undāre* to rise in waves]

redox ('ri:dɒks) *n* (*modifier*) another term for **oxidation-reduction** [C20 from RED(UCTION) + OX(IDATION)]

red pepper *n* **1** any of several varieties of the pepper plant cultivated for their hot pungent red podlike fruits **2** the fruit of any of these plants **3** the ripe red fruit of the sweet pepper **4** another name for **cayenne pepper**

Red Planet *n* **the** an informal name for **Mars**[2]

redpoll ('rɛdˌpɒl) *n* either of two widely distributed types of finches, having a greyish-brown plumage with a red crown and pink breast

red rag *n* a provocation; something that infuriates [so called because red objects supposedly infuriate bulls]

redress (rɪ'drɛs) *vb* (*tr*) **1** to put right (a wrong), esp by compensation; make reparation for **2** to correct or adjust (esp in **redress the balance**) **3** to make compensation to (a person) for a wrong ▷ *n* **4** the act or an instance of setting right a wrong; remedy or cure **5** compensation, amends, or reparation for a wrong, injury, etc [C14 from OF *redrecier* to set up again, from RE- + *drecier* to straighten; see DRESS] > **re'dressable** *or* **re'dressible** *adj* > **re'dresser** *or* **re'dressor** *n*

re-dress (ri:'drɛs) *vb* (*tr*) to dress (something) again

red ribbon *n Canad* an award presented for coming first in a competition

Red River *n* **1** Also called: **Red River of the South** a river in the S central US, flowing east from N Texas through Arkansas into the Mississippi in Louisiana. Length: 1639 km (1018 miles) **2** a river in the northern US, flowing north as the border between North Dakota and Minnesota and into Lake Winnipeg, Canada. Length: 515 km (320 miles) **3** a river in SE Asia, rising in SW China in Yünnan province and flowing southeast across N Vietnam to the Gulf of Tongkin: the chief river of N Vietnam, with an extensive delta. Length: 500 km (310 miles). Vietnamese name: **Song Koi**

Red River cart *n Canad history* a strongly-built, two-wheeled, ox- or horse-drawn cart used in W Canada

red roman *n S African* a marine food fish

red rose *n English history* the emblem of the House of Lancaster

red salmon *n* any salmon having reddish flesh, esp the sockeye salmon

Red Sea *n* a long narrow sea between Arabia and NE Africa, linked with the Mediterranean in the north by the Suez Canal and with the Indian Ocean in the south: occasionally reddish in appearance through algae. Area: 438 000 sq km (169 000 sq miles)

redshank ('rɛdˌʃæŋk) *n* any of various large common European sandpipers, esp the **spotted redshank,** having red legs

red shift *n* a shift in the lines of the spectrum of an astronomical object towards a longer wavelength (the red end of an optical spectrum), relative to the wavelength of these lines in the terrestrial spectrum, usually as a result of the Doppler effect caused by the recession of the object

redskin ('rɛdˌskɪn) *n* an informal name, now considered offensive, for an **American Indian** [so called because one

now extinct tribe painted themselves with red ochre]
red snapper *n* any of various marine percoid food fishes of the snapper family, having a reddish coloration, common in American coastal regions of the Atlantic
red spider *n* short for **red spider mite** (see **spider mite**)
Red Spot *n* See **Great Red Spot**
red squirrel *n* a reddish-brown squirrel, inhabiting woodlands of Europe and parts of Asia
redstart (ˈrɛdˌstɑːt) *n* **1** a European songbird of the thrush family: the male has a black throat, orange-brown tail and breast, and grey back **2** a North American warbler [OE *rēad* red + *steort* tail]
red tape *n* obstructive official routine or procedure; time-consuming bureaucracy [c18 from the red tape used to bind official government documents]
red-top *n* a tabloid newspaper characterized by sensationalism [c20 from the colour of the masthead on these publications]
reduce (rɪˈdjuːs) *vb* **reduces, reducing, reduced** (*mainly tr*) **1** (*also intr*) to make or become smaller in size, number, etc **2** to bring into a certain state, condition, etc: *to reduce a forest to ashes; he was reduced to tears* **3** (*also intr*) to make or become slimmer; lose or cause to lose excess weight **4** to impoverish (esp in **in reduced circumstances**) **5** to bring into a state of submission to one's authority; subjugate: *the whole country was reduced after three months* **6** to bring down the price of (a commodity) **7** to lower the rank or status of; demote: *reduced to the ranks* **8** to set out systematically as an aid to understanding; simplify: *his theories have been reduced in a treatise* **9** *maths* to modify or simplify the form of (an expression or equation), esp by substitution of one term by another **10** *cookery* to make (a sauce, stock, etc) more concentrated by boiling away some of the water in it **11** to thin out (paint) by adding oil, turpentine, etc **12** (*also intr*) *chem* **12a** to undergo or cause to undergo a chemical reaction with hydrogen **12b** to lose or cause to lose oxygen atoms **12c** to undergo or cause to undergo an increase in the number of electrons **13** *photog* to lessen the density of (a negative or print) **14** *surgery* to manipulate or reposition (a broken or displaced bone, organ, or part) back to its normal site [c14 from L *redūcere* to bring back, from RE- + *dūcere* to lead] > **reˈducible** *adj* > **reˌduciˈbility** *n* > **reˈducibly** *adv*
reduced instruction set computer *n computing* a processor that only responds to a limited number of instructions but which, as a result, can perform much more quickly than a more complex processor. Abbrev: **RISC**
reducer (rɪˈdjuːsə) *n* **1** *photog* a chemical solution used to lessen the density of a negative or print by oxidizing some of the blackened silver to soluble silver compounds **2** a pipe fitting connecting two pipes of different diameters **3** a person or thing that reduces
reducing agent *n chem* a substance that reduces another substance in a chemical reaction, being itself oxidized in the process
reducing glass *n* a lens or curved mirror that produces an image smaller than the object observed
reductase (rɪˈdʌkteɪz) *n* any enzyme that catalyses a biochemical reduction reaction [c20 from REDUCTION + -ASE]
reductio ad absurdum (rɪˈdʌktɪəʊ æd æbˈsɜːdəm) *n* **1** a method of disproving a proposition by showing that its inevitable consequences would be absurd **2** a method of indirectly proving a proposition by assuming its negation to be true and showing that this leads to an absurdity **3** application of a principle or proposed principle to an instance in which it is absurd [L, lit.: reduction to the absurd]
reduction (rɪˈdʌkʃən) *n* **1** the act or process or an instance of reducing **2** the state or condition of being reduced **3** the amount by which something is reduced **4** a form of an original resulting from a reducing process, such as a copy on a smaller scale **5** *maths* **5a** the process of converting a fraction into its decimal form **5b** the process of dividing out the common factors in the numerator and denominator of a fraction
> **reˈductive** *adj*
reduction formula *n maths* a formula expressing the values of a trigonometric function of any angle greater than 90° in terms of a function of an acute angle
reductionism (rɪˈdʌkʃəˌnɪzəm) *n* **1** the analysis of complex things, data, etc, into less complex constituents **2** *often disparaging* any theory or method that holds that a complex idea, system, etc, can be completely understood in terms of its simpler parts or components > **reˈductionist** *n, adj* > **reˌductionˈistic** *adj*
redundancy (rɪˈdʌndənsɪ) *n, pl* **redundancies** **1a** the state or condition of being redundant or superfluous, esp superfluous in one's job **1b** (*as modifier*): *a redundancy payment* **2** excessive proliferation or profusion, esp of superfluity
redundant (rɪˈdʌndənt) *adj* **1** surplus to requirements; unnecessary or superfluous **2** verbose or tautological **3** deprived of one's job because it is no longer necessary [c17 from L *redundans* overflowing, from *redundāre* to stream over; see REDOUND] > **reˈdundantly** *adv*
red underwing *n* a large noctuid moth having hind wings coloured red and black
reduplicate *vb* (rɪˈdjuːplɪˌkeɪt), **reduplicates, reduplicating, reduplicated** **1** to make or become double; repeat **2** to repeat (a sound or syllable) in a word or (of a sound or syllable) to be repeated
▷ *adj* (rɪˈdjuːplɪkɪt) **3** doubled or repeated **4** (of petals or sepals) having the margins curving outwards
> **reˌdupliˈcation** *n* > **reˈduplicative** *adj*
red-water *n* a disease of cattle which destroys the red blood cells, characterized by the passage of red or blackish urine. It is transmitted by tick bites
redwing (ˈrɛdˌwɪŋ) *n* a small European thrush having a speckled breast, reddish flanks, and brown back Rr
redwood (ˈrɛdˌwʊd) *n* a giant coniferous tree of coastal regions of California, having reddish fibrous bark and durable timber
reebok (ˈriːbʌk, -bɒk) *n, pl* **reeboks** *or* **reebok** a variant spelling of **rhebuck** *or* **rhebok**
re-echo (riːˈɛkəʊ) *vb* **re-echoes, re-echoing, re-echoed** **1** to echo (a sound that is already an echo); resound **2** (*tr*) to repeat like an echo
reed (riːd) *n* **1** any of various widely distributed tall grasses that grow in swamps and shallow water and have jointed hollow stalks **2** the stalk, or stalks collectively, of any of these plants, esp as used for thatching **3** *music* **3a** a thin piece of cane or metal inserted into the tubes of certain wind instruments, which sets in vibration the air column inside the tube **3b** a wind instrument or organ pipe that sounds by means of a reed **4** one of the several vertical parallel wires on a loom that may be moved upwards to separate the warp threads **5** a small semicircular architectural moulding **6** an archaic word for **arrow** **7** **broken reed** a weak, unreliable, or ineffectual person ▷ *vb* (*tr*) **8** to fashion into or supply with reeds or reeding **9** to thatch using reeds [OE *hreod*]
Reed (riːd) *n* **1** Sir **Carol** 1906–76, English film director. His films include *The Third Man* (1949), *An Outcast of the Islands* (1951), and *Oliver!* (1968), for which he won an Oscar **2** **Lou** born 1942, US rock singer, songwriter, and guitarist: member of the Velvet Underground (1965–70) His albums include *Transformer* (1972), *Street Hassle* (1978), *New York* (1989), *Set the Twilight Reeling* (1996), and *The Raven* (2003) **3** **Walter** 1851–1902, US physician, who proved that yellow fever is transmitted by mosquitoes (1900)
reedbuck (ˈriːdˌbʌk) *n, pl* **reedbucks** *or* **reedbuck** an antelope of Africa south of the Sahara, having a buff-coloured coat and inward-curving horns

reed bunting *n* a common European bunting that has a brown streaked plumage with, in the male, a black head
reed grass *n* a tall perennial grass of rivers and ponds of Europe, Asia, and Canada
reeding ('ri:dɪŋ) *n* **1** a set of small semicircular architectural mouldings **2** the milling on the edges of a coin
reedling ('ri:dlɪŋ) *n* a titlike Eurasian songbird, common in reed beds, which belongs to the family of Old World flycatchers and has a tawny back and tail and, in the male, a grey-and-black head. Also called: **bearded tit**
reed mace *n* a tall reedlike marsh plant, with straplike leaves and flowers in long brown spikes. Also called: (popularly) **bulrush, cat's-tail**
reed organ *n* **1** a wind instrument, such as the harmonium, accordion, or harmonica, in which the sound is produced by reeds, each reed producing one note only **2** a type of pipe organ in which all the pipes are fitted with reeds
reed pipe *n* an organ pipe sounded by a vibrating reed
reed stop *n* an organ stop controlling a rank of reed pipes
reed warbler *n* any of various common Old World warblers that inhabit marshy regions and have a brown plumage
reedy ('ri:dɪ) *adj* **reedier, reediest 1** (of a place) abounding in reeds **2** of or like a reed **3** having a tone like a reed instrument; shrill or piping > **'reedily** *adv* > **'reediness** *n*
reef[1] (ri:f) *n* **1** a ridge of rock, sand, coral, etc, the top of which lies close to the surface of the sea **2** a vein of ore, esp one of gold-bearing quartz **3** (*cap*) **the 3a** the Great Barrier Reef in Australia **3b** the Witwatersrand in South Africa, a gold-bearing ridge [C16 from MDu. *ref*, from ON *rif* RIB[1], REEF[2]]
reef[2] (ri:f) *naut* ▷ *n* **1** the part gathered in when sail area is reduced, as in a high wind ▷ *vb* **2** to reduce the area of (sail) by taking in a reef **3** (*tr*) to shorten or bring inboard (a spar) [C14 from MDu. *rif*; rel. to ON *rif* reef, RIB[1]]
Reef (ri:f) *n* **the 1** another name for the **Great Barrier Reef 2** another name for the **Witwatersrand**
reefer ('ri:fə) *n* **1** *naut* a person who reefs, such as a midshipman **2** another name for **reefing jacket 3** *sl* a hand-rolled cigarette containing cannabis [C19 from REEF[2]; applied to the cigarette from its resemblance to the rolled reef of a sail]
reefing jacket *n* a man's short double-breasted jacket of sturdy wool
reef knot *n* a knot consisting of two overhand knots turned opposite ways. Also called: **square knot**
reef point *n naut* one of several short lengths of line stitched through a sail for tying a reef
reek (ri:k) *vb* **1** (*intr*) to give off or emit a strong unpleasant odour; smell or stink **2** (*intr*; often foll by *of*) to be permeated (by): *the letter reeks of subservience* **3** (*tr*) to treat with smoke; fumigate **4** (*tr*) *chiefly dialect* to give off or emit (smoke, fumes, etc) ▷ *n* **5** a strong offensive smell; stink **6** *chiefly dialect* smoke or steam; vapour [OE *rēocan*] > **'reeky** *adj*
reel[1] (ri:l, rɪəl) *n* **1** any of various cylindrical objects or frames that turn on an axis and onto which film, tape, wire, etc, may be wound. US equivalent: **spool 2** *angling* a device for winding, casting, etc, consisting of a revolving spool with a handle, attached to a fishing rod ▷ *vb* (*tr*) **3** to wind (cotton, thread, etc) onto a reel **4** (foll by *in*, *out*, etc) to wind or draw with a reel: *to reel in a fish* [OE *hrēol*] > **'reelable** *adj* > **'reeler** *n*
reel[2] (ri:l, rɪəl) *vb* (*mainly intr*) **1** to sway, esp under the shock of a blow or through dizziness or drunkenness **2** to whirl about or have the feeling of whirling about: *his brain reeled* ▷ *n* **3** a staggering or swaying motion or sensation [C14 *relen*, prob. from REEL[1]]
reel[3] (ri:l, rɪəl) *n* **1** any of various lively Scottish dances for a fixed number of couples who combine in square and circular formations **2** a piece of music composed for or in the rhythm of this dance [C18 from REEL[2]]
reel-fed *adj printing* involving or printing on a web of paper: *a reel-fed press*
reelman ('ri:lmən, 'rɪəl-) *n*, *pl* **reelmen** *Austral & NZ* (formerly) the member of a beach life-saving team who controlled the reel on which the line was wound
reel off *vb* (*tr*, *adv*) to recite or write fluently and without apparent effort
reel-to-reel *adj* **1** (of magnetic tape) wound from one reel to another in use **2** (of a tape recorder) using magnetic tape wound from one reel to another, as opposed to cassettes
re-entrant (ri:'ɛntrənt) *adj* **1** (of an angle) pointing inwards ▷ *n* **2** an angle or part that points inwards
re-entry (ri:'ɛntrɪ) *n*, *pl* **re-entries 1** the act of retaking possession of land, etc **2** the return of a spacecraft into the earth's atmosphere
re-entry vehicle *n* the portion of a ballistic missile that carries a nuclear warhead and re-enters the earth's atmosphere
reeve[1] (ri:v) *n* **1** *English history* the local representative of the king in a shire until the early 11th century **2** (in medieval England) a manorial steward who supervised the daily affairs of the manor **3** *Canad government* (in some provinces) a president of a local council, esp in a rural area **4** (formerly) a minor local official in England and the US [OE *gerēva*]
reeve[2] (ri:v) *vb* **reeves, reeving, reeved** *or* **rove** (*tr*) *naut* **1** to pass (a rope or cable) through an eye or other narrow opening **2** to fasten by passing through or around something [C17 ?from Du. *rēven* REEF[2]]
reeve[3] (ri:v) *n* the female of the ruff (the bird) [C17 from ?]
re-export *vb* (ˌri:ɪk'spɔ:t, ˌri:'ɛkspɔ:t) **1** to export (imported goods, esp after processing) ▷ *n* (ri:'ɛkspɔ:t) **2** the act of re-exporting **3** a re-exported commodity > ˌ**re-expor'tation** *n* > ˌ**re-ex'porter** *n*
ref (rɛf) *n inf* short for **referee**
ref. *abbrev for*: **1** referee **2** reference
refection (rɪ'fɛkʃən) *n* refreshment with food and drink [C14 from L *refectiō* a restoring, from *reficere*, from RE- + *facere* to make]
refectory (rɪ'fɛktərɪ, -trɪ) *n*, *pl* **refectories** a dining hall in a religious or academic institution [C15 from LL *refectōrium*, from L *refectus* refreshed]
refectory table *n* a long narrow dining table
refer (rɪ'fɜ:) *vb* **refers, referring, referred** (often foll by *to*) **1** (*intr*) to make mention (of) **2** (*tr*) to direct the attention of (someone) for information, facts, etc: *the reader is referred to Chomsky, 1965* **3** (*intr*) to seek information (from): *he referred to his notes* **4** (*intr*) to be relevant (to); pertain or relate (to) **5** (*tr*) to assign or attribute: *Cromwell referred his victories to God* **6** (*tr*) to hand over for consideration, reconsideration, or decision: *to refer a complaint to another department* **7** (*tr*) to hand back to the originator as unacceptable or unusable **8** (*tr*) *Brit* to fail (a student) in an examination **9 refer to drawer** a request by a bank that the payee consult the drawer concerning a cheque payable by that bank **10** (*tr*) to direct (a patient, client, etc) to another doctor, agency, etc [C14 from L *referre*, from RE- + *ferre* to BEAR[1]] > **referable** ('rɛfərəbᵊl) *or* **referrable** (rɪ'fɜ:rəbᵊl) *adj* > **re'ferral** *n* > **re'ferrer** *n*

> USAGE The not uncommon addition of *back* to *refer* is often unnecessary, since this meaning is already contained in the *re-* of *refer*: *this refers to* (not *back to*) *what has already been said*. However, when *refer* is used in the sense of returning a document or question for further consideration to the person from whom it came, it may be appropriate to say *he referred the matter back*

referee (ˌrɛfə'ri:) *n* **1** a person to whom reference is made, esp for an opinion, information, or a decision **2** the umpire or judge in any of various sports, esp football and boxing **3** a person who is willing to testify to the character or capabilities of someone **4** *law* a person appointed by a court to report on a matter ▷ *vb* **referees, refereeing, refereed** **5** to act as a referee (in); preside (over)

reference ('rɛfərəns, 'rɛfrəns) *n* **1** the act or an instance of referring **2** something referred, esp proceedings submitted to a referee in law **3** a direction of the attention to a passage elsewhere or to another book, etc **4** a book or passage referred to **5** a mention or allusion: *this book contains several references to the Civil War* **6** the relation between a word or phrase and the object or idea to which it refers **7a** a source of information or facts **7b** (*as modifier*): *a reference book; a reference library* **8** a written testimonial regarding one's character or capabilities **9** a person referred to for such a testimonial **10a** (foll by *to*) relation or delimitation, esp to or by membership of a specific group: *without reference to sex or age* **10b** (*as modifier*): *a reference group* **11** **terms of reference** the specific limits of responsibility that determine the activities of an investigating body, etc ▷ *vb* **references, referencing, referenced** (*tr*) **12** to furnish or compile a list of references for (a publication, etc) **13** to make a reference to; refer to ▷ *prep* **14** *business jargon* with reference to: *reference your letter of the 9th inst.* Abbrev: **re** > **referential** (ˌrɛfə'rɛnʃəl) *adj*

referendum (ˌrɛfə'rɛndəm) *n, pl* **referendums** *or* **referenda** (-də) **1** submission of an issue of public importance to the direct vote of the electorate **2** a vote on such a measure ▷ See also **plebiscite** [c19 from L: something to be carried back, from *referre* to REFER]

referent ('rɛfərənt) *n* the object or idea to which a word or phrase refers [c19 from L *referens* from *referre* to REFER]

referred pain *n psychol* pain felt at some place other than its actual place of origin

refill *vb* (riː'fɪl) **1** to fill (something) again ▷ *n* ('riːfɪl) **2** a replacement for a consumable substance in a permanent container **3** a second or subsequent filling > **re'fillable** *adj*

refine (rɪ'faɪn) *vb* **refines, refining, refined** **1** to make or become free from impurities or foreign matter; purify **2** (*tr*) to separate (a mixture) into pure constituents, as in an oil refinery **3** to make or become elegant or polished **4** (*intr*; often foll by *on* or *upon*) to enlarge or improve (upon) by making subtle or fine distinctions **5** (*tr*) to make (language) more subtle or polished [c16 from RE- + FINE[1]] > **re'finable** *adj* > **re'finer** *n*

refined (rɪ'faɪnd) *adj* **1** not coarse or vulgar; genteel, elegant, or polite **2** subtle; discriminating **3** freed from impurities; purified

refinement (rɪ'faɪnmənt) *n* **1** the act of refining or the state of being refined **2** a fine or delicate point or distinction; a subtlety **3** fineness or precision of thought, expression, manners, etc **4** an improvement to a piece of equipment, etc

refinery (rɪ'faɪnərɪ) *n, pl* **refineries** a factory for the purification of some crude material, such as sugar, oil, etc

refit *vb* (riː'fɪt), **refits, refitting, refitted** **1** to make or be made ready for use again by repairing, re-equipping, or resupplying ▷ *n* ('riːˌfɪt) **2** a repair or re-equipping, as of a ship, for further use > **re'fitment** *n*

reflate (riː'fleɪt) *vb* **reflates, reflating, reflated** to inflate or be inflated again [c20 back formation from REFLATION]

reflation (riː'fleɪʃən) *n* **1** an increase in economic activity **2** an increase in the supply of money and credit designed to cause such economic activity ▷ Cf **inflation** (sense 2) [c20 from RE- + *-flation*, as in INFLATION]

reflect (rɪ'flɛkt) *vb* **1** to undergo or cause to undergo a process in which light, other electromagnetic radiation, sound, particles, etc, are thrown back after impinging on a surface **2** (of a mirror, etc) to form an image of (something) by reflection **3** (*tr*) to show or express: *his tactics reflect his desire for power* **4** (*tr*) to bring as a consequence: *their success reflected great credit on them* **5** (*intr*; foll by *on* or *upon*) to cause to be regarded in a specified way: *her behaviour reflects well on her* **6** (*intr*; often foll by *on* or *upon*) to cast dishonour or honour, credit or discredit, etc (on) **7** (*intr*; usually foll by *on*) to think, meditate, or ponder [c15 from L *reflectere*, from RE- + *flectere* to bend] > **re'flectingly** *adv*

reflectance (rɪ'flɛktəns) *or* **reflection factor** *n* a measure of the ability of a surface to reflect light or other electromagnetic radiation, equal to the ratio of the reflected flux to the incident flux

reflecting telescope *n* a type of telescope in which the initial image is formed by a concave mirror. Also called: **reflector** ▷ Cf **refracting telescope**

reflection *or* **reflexion** (rɪ'flɛkʃən) *n* **1** the act of reflecting or the state of being reflected **2** something reflected or the image so produced, as by a mirror **3** careful or long consideration or thought **4** attribution of discredit or blame **5** *maths* a transformation in which the direction of one axis is reversed or changes the polarity of one of the variables **6** *anat* the bending back of a structure or part upon itself > **re'flectional** *or* **re'flexional** *adj*

reflection density *n physics* a measure of the extent to which a surface reflects light or other electromagnetic radiation. Symbol: *D*

reflective (rɪ'flɛktɪv) *adj* **1** characterized by quiet thought or contemplation **2** capable of reflecting: *a reflective surface* **3** produced by reflection > **re'flectively** *adv*

reflectivity (ˌriːflɛk'tɪvɪtɪ) *n* **1** *physics* a measure of the ability of a surface to reflect radiation, equal to the reflectance of a layer of material sufficiently thick for the reflectance not to depend on the thickness **2** Also: **reflectiveness** the quality or capability of being reflective

reflector (rɪ'flɛktə) *n* **1** a person or thing that reflects **2** a surface or object that reflects light, sound, heat, etc **3** another name for **reflecting telescope**

reflet (rə'fleɪ) *n* an iridescent glow or lustre, as on ceramic ware [c19 from F: a reflection, from It. *riflesso*, from L *reflexus*, from *reflectere* to reflect]

reflex *n* ('riːflɛks) **1a** an immediate involuntary response, such as coughing, evoked by a given stimulus **1b** (*as modifier*): *a reflex action*. See also **reflex arc** **2a** a mechanical response to a particular situation, involving no conscious decision **2b** (*as modifier*): *a reflex response* **3** a reflection; an image produced by or as if by reflection ▷ *adj* ('riːflɛks) **4** *maths* (of an angle) between 180° and 360° **5** (*prenominal*) turned, reflected, or bent backwards ▷ *vb* (rɪ'flɛks) **6** (*tr*) to bend, turn, or reflect backwards [c16 from L *reflexus* bent back, from *reflectere* to reflect] > **re'flexible** *adj* > **reˌflexi'bility** *n*

reflex arc *n physiol* the neural pathway over which impulses travel to produce a reflex action

reflex camera *n* a camera in which the image is composed and focused on a ground-glass viewfinder screen

reflexion (rɪ'flɛkʃən) *n Brit* a less common spelling of **reflection** > **re'flexional** *adj*

reflexive (rɪ'flɛksɪv) *adj* **1** denoting a class of pronouns that refer back to the subject of a sentence or clause. Thus, in *that man thinks a great deal of himself*, the pronoun *himself* is reflexive **2** denoting a verb used transitively with the reflexive pronoun as its direct object, as in *to dress oneself* **3** *physiol* of or relating to a reflex ▷ *n* **4** a reflexive pronoun or verb > **re'flexively** *adv* > **re'flexiveness** *or* **reflexivity** (ˌriːflɛk'sɪvɪtɪ) *n*

reflexology (ˌriːflɛk'sɒlədʒɪ) *n* a form of therapy in

Rr

alternative medicine in which the soles of the feet are massaged: designed to stimulate the blood supply and nerves and thus relieve tension > ˌ**reflex'ologist** *n*

reflux ('riːflʌks) *vb* **1** *chem* to boil or be boiled in a vessel attached to a condenser, so that the vapour condenses and flows back into the vessel ▷ *n* **2** *chem* **2a** an act of refluxing **2b** (*as modifier*): *a reflux condenser* **3** the act or an instance of flowing back; ebb [C15 from Med. L *refluxus*, from L *refluere* to flow back]

reflux oesophagitis (iːˌsɒfə'dʒaɪtɪs) *n* inflammation of the gullet caused by regurgitation of stomach acids, producing heartburn: may be associated with a hiatus hernia

reform (rɪ'fɔːm) *vb* **1** (*tr*) to improve (an existing institution, law, etc) by alteration or correction of abuses **2** to give up or cause to give up a reprehensible habit or immoral way of life ▷ *n* **3** an improvement or change for the better, esp as a result of correction of legal or political abuses or malpractices **4** a principle, campaign, or measure aimed at achieving such change **5** improvement of morals or behaviour [C14 via OF from L *reformāre* to form again] > **re'formable** *adj* > **re'formative** *adj* > **re'former** *n*

re-form (riː'fɔːm) *vb* to form anew > ˌ**re-for'mation** *n*

reformation (ˌrɛfə'meɪʃən) *n* **1** the act or an instance of reforming or the state of being reformed **2** (*usually cap*) a religious and political movement of 16th-century Europe that began as an attempt to reform the Roman Catholic Church and resulted in the establishment of the Protestant Churches > ˌ**refor'mational** *adj*

▷ http://history.hanover.edu/early/prot.htm
▷ www.wikipedia.org/wiki/Protestant_Reformation
▷ http://reformation.org/
▷ http://lepg.org/religion.htm

reformatory (rɪ'fɔːmətərɪ, -trɪ) *n, pl* **reformatories 1** Also called: **reform school** (formerly) a place of instruction where young offenders were sent for corrective training ▷ *adj* **2** having the purpose or function of reforming

Reformed (rɪ'fɔːmd) *adj* **1** of or designating a Protestant Church, esp the Calvinist **2** of or designating Reform Judaism

reformism (rɪ'fɔːmɪzəm) *n* a doctrine advocating reform, esp political or religious reform rather than abolition > **re'formist** *n, adj*

Reform Judaism *n* a movement in Judaism that does not require strict observance of the law, but adapts to the contemporary world

refract (rɪ'frækt) *vb* **1** to cause to undergo refraction **2** (*tr*) to measure the amount of refraction of (the eye, a lens, etc) [C17 from L *refractus* broken up, from *refringere*, from RE- + *frangere* to break] > **re'fractable** *adj* > **re'fractive** *adj*

refracting telescope *n* a type of telescope in which the image is formed by a set of lenses. Also called: **refractor** ▷ Cf **reflecting telescope**

refraction (rɪ'frækʃən) *n* **1** *physics* the change in direction of a propagating wave, such as light or sound, in passing from one medium to another in which it has a different velocity **2** the amount by which a wave is refracted **3** the ability of the eye to refract light > **re'fractional** *adj*

refractive index *n physics* a measure of the extent to which a medium refracts light; the ratio of the speed of light in free space to that in the medium

refractometer (ˌriːfræk'tɒmɪtə) *n* any instrument for measuring the refractive index > **refractometric** (rɪˌfræktə'mɛtrɪk) *adj* > ˌ**refrac'tometry** *n*

refractor (rɪ'fræktə) *n* **1** an object or material that refracts **2** another name for **refracting telescope**

refractory (rɪ'fræktərɪ) *adj* **1** unmanageable or obstinate **2** *med* not responding to treatment **3** (of a material) able to withstand high temperatures without fusion or decomposition ▷ *n, pl* **refractories 4** a material, such as fire clay, that is able to withstand high temperatures > **re'fractorily** *adv* > **re'fractoriness** *n*

refrain[1] (rɪ'freɪn) *vb* (*intr*; usually foll by *from*) to abstain (from action); forbear [C14 from L *refrēnāre* to check with a bridle, from RE- + *frēnum* a bridle] > **re'frainer** *n* > **re'frainment** *n*

refrain[2] (rɪ'freɪn) *n* **1** a regularly recurring melody, such as the chorus of a song **2** a much repeated saying or idea [C14 via OF, ult. from L *refringere* to break into pieces]

refrangible (rɪ'frændʒɪbᵊl) *adj* capable of being refracted [C17 from L *refringere* to break up, from RE- + *frangere* to break] > **reˌfrangi'bility** *or* **re'frangibleness** *n*

refresh (rɪ'frɛʃ) *vb* **1** (*usually tr or reflexive*) to make or become fresh or vigorous, as through rest, drink, or food; revive or reinvigorate **2** (*tr*) to enliven (something worn or faded), as by adding new decorations **3** to pour cold water over previously blanched and drained food **4** (*tr*) to stimulate (the memory, etc) **5** (*tr*) to replenish, as with new equipment or stores **6** *computing* to display the latest updated version (of a web page or document); reload [C14 from OF *refreschir*; see RE-, FRESH] > **re'fresher** *n* > **re'freshing** *adj*

refresher course *n* a short educational course for people to review their subject and developments in it

refreshment (rɪ'frɛʃmənt) *n* **1** the act of refreshing or the state of being refreshed **2** (*pl*) snacks and drinks served as a light meal

refresh rate *n computing* the frequency at which the image on a monitor is renewed

refrigerant (rɪ'frɪdʒərənt) *n* **1** a fluid capable of changes of phase at low temperatures: used as the working fluid of a refrigerator **2** a cooling substance, such as ice or solid carbon dioxide **3** *med* an agent that provides a sensation of coolness or reduces fever ▷ *adj* **4** causing cooling or freezing

refrigerate (rɪ'frɪdʒəˌreɪt) *vb* **refrigerates, refrigerating, refrigerated** to make or become frozen or cold, esp for preservative purposes; chill or freeze [C16 from L *refrīgerāre* to make cold, from RE- + *frīgus* cold] > **reˌfriger'ation** *n* > **re'frigerative** *adj* > **re'frigeratory** *adj, n*

refrigerator (rɪ'frɪdʒəˌreɪtə) *n* a chamber in which food, drink, etc, are kept cool. Informal name: **fridge**

refringent (rɪ'frɪndʒənt) *adj physics* of, concerned with, or causing refraction; refractive [C18 from L *refringere*; see REFRACT] > **re'fringency** *or* **re'fringence** *n*

reft (rɛft) *vb* a past tense and past participle of **reave**

refuel (riː'fjuːəl) *vb* **refuels, refuelling, refuelled** *or US* **refuels, refueling, refueled** to supply or be supplied with fresh fuel

refuge ('rɛfjuːdʒ) *n* **1** shelter or protection, as from the weather or danger **2** any place, person, action, or thing that offers protection, help, or relief [C14 via OF from L *refugium*, from *refugere*, from RE- + *fugere* to escape]

refugee (ˌrɛfjʊ'dʒiː) *n* **a** a person who has fled from some danger or problem, esp political persecution **b** (*as modifier*): *a refugee camp* > ˌ**refu'geeism** *n*

refugee capital *n finance* money from abroad invested, esp for a short term, in the country offering the highest interest rate

refugium (rɪ'fjuːdʒɪəm) *n, pl* **refugia** (-dʒɪə) a geographical region that has remained unaltered by a climatic change affecting surrounding regions and that therefore forms a haven for relict fauna and flora [C20 L: REFUGE]

refulgent (rɪ'fʌldʒənt) *adj literary* shining, brilliant, or radiant [C16 from L *refulgēre*, from RE- + *fulgēre* to shine] > **re'fulgence** *or* **re'fulgency** *n* > **re'fulgently** *adv*

refund *vb* (rɪ'fʌnd) (*tr*) **1** to give back (money, etc), as when an article purchased is unsatisfactory **2** to reimburse (a person) ▷ *n* ('riːˌfʌnd) **3** return of money to a purchaser or the amount so returned [C14 from L *refundere*, from RE- + *fundere* to pour] > **re'fundable** *adj*

re-fund (riːˈfʌnd) *vb* (*tr*) *finance* to discharge (an old or matured debt) by new borrowing, as by a new bond issue [C20 from RE- + FUND]

refurbish (riːˈfɜːbɪʃ) *vb* (*tr*) to renovate, re-equip, or restore > **reˈfurbishment** *n*

refusal (rɪˈfjuːzᵊl) *n* **1** the act or an instance of refusing **2** the opportunity to reject or accept; option: *you can have first refusal on the house*

refuse[1] (rɪˈfjuːz) *vb* **refuses, refusing, refused 1** (*tr*) to decline to accept (something offered): *to refuse promotion* **2** to decline to give or grant (something) to (a person, etc) **3** (when *tr, takes an infinitive*) to express determination not (to do something); decline: *he refuses to talk about it* **4** (of a horse) to be unwilling to take (a jump) [C14 from OF *refuser*, from L *refundere* to pour back] > **reˈfusable** *adj* > **reˈfuser** *n*

refuse[2] (ˈrɛfjuːs) *n* **a** anything thrown away; waste; rubbish **b** (*as modifier*): *a refuse collection* [C15 from OF *refuser* to REFUSE[1]]

refusenik *or* **refusnik** (rɪˈfjuːznɪk) *n* **1** (formerly) a Jew in the Soviet Union who had been refused permission to emigrate **2** a person who refuses to cooperate with a system or comply with a law because of a moral conviction [C20 from REFUSE[1] + -NIK]

refute (rɪˈfjuːt) *vb* **refutes, refuting, refuted** (*tr*) to prove (a statement, theory, charge, etc) of (a person) to be false or incorrect; disprove [C16 from L *refūtāre* to rebut] > **refutable** (ˈrɛfjʊtəbᵊl, rɪˈfjuː-) *adj* > **ˈrefutably** *adv* > **ˌrefuˈtation** *n* > **reˈfuter** *n*

> USAGE The use of *refute* to mean *deny* as in *I'm not refuting the fact that…* is thought by some people to be incorrect. In careful writing it may be advisable to use *refute* only where there is an element of disproving something through argument and evidence, as in *we haven't got evidence to refute their hypothesis*

regain (rɪˈɡeɪn) *vb* (*tr*) **1** to take or get back; recover **2** to reach again > **reˈgainer** *n*

regal (ˈriːɡᵊl) *adj* of, relating to, or befitting a king or queen; royal [C14 from L *rēgālis*, from *rēx* king] > **reˈgality** *n* > **ˈregally** *adv*

regale (rɪˈɡeɪl) *vb* **regales, regaling, regaled** (*tr*; usually foll by *with*) **1** to give delight or amusement to: *he regaled them with stories* **2** to provide with choice or abundant food or drink ▹ *n* **3** *arch* **3a** a feast **3b** a delicacy of food or drink [C17 from F *régaler*, from *gale* pleasure] > **reˈgalement** *n*

regalia (rɪˈɡeɪlɪə) *n* (*pl, sometimes functioning as sing*) **1** the ceremonial emblems or robes of royalty, high office, an order, etc **2** any splendid or special clothes; finery [C16 from Med. L: royal privileges, from L *rēgālis* REGAL]

regard (rɪˈɡɑːd) *vb* **1** to look closely or attentively at (something or someone); observe steadily **2** (*tr*) to hold (a person or thing) in respect, admiration, or affection: *we regard your work very highly* **3** (*tr*) to look upon or consider in a specified way: *she regarded her brother as her responsibility* **4** (*tr*) to relate to; concern; have a bearing on **5** to take notice of or pay attention to (something); heed: *he has never regarded the conventions* **6 as regards** (*prep*) in respect of; concerning ▹ *n* **7** a gaze; look **8** attention; heed: *he spends without regard to his bank balance* **9** esteem, affection, or respect **10** reference, relation, or connection (esp in **with regard to** *or* **in regard to**) **11** (*pl*) good wishes or greetings (esp in **with kind regards,** used at the close of a letter) **12 in this regard** on this point [C14 from OF *regarder* to look at, care about, from RE- + *garder* to GUARD]

> USAGE In writing, care should be taken to avoid putting *with regards to* instead of *with regard to*. This mistake is common, particularly in speaking, perhaps under the influence of the phrase *as regards*

regardant (rɪˈɡɑːdᵊnt) *adj* (*usually postpositive*) *heraldry* (of a beast) shown looking backwards over its shoulder [C15 from OF; see REGARD]

regardful (rɪˈɡɑːdfʊl) *adj* **1** (often foll by *of*) showing regard (for); heedful (of) **2** showing regard, respect, or consideration > **reˈgardfully** *adv*

regarding (rɪˈɡɑːdɪŋ) *prep* in respect of; on the subject of

regardless (rɪˈɡɑːdlɪs) *adj* **1** (usually foll by *of*) taking no regard or heed; heedless ▹ *adv* **2** in spite of everything; disregarding drawbacks > **reˈgardlessly** *adv* > **reˈgardlessness** *n*

regatta (rɪˈɡætə) *n* an organized series of races of yachts, rowing boats, etc [C17 from obs. It. *rigatta* contest, from ?]

regd *abbrev for* registered

regelation (ˌriːdʒɪˈleɪʃən) *n* the rejoining together of two pieces of ice as a result of melting under pressure at the interface between them and subsequent refreezing > **ˈregeˌlate** *vb*

regency (ˈriːdʒənsɪ) *n, pl* **regencies 1** government by a regent **2** the office of a regent **3** a territory under the jurisdiction of a regent [C15 from Med. L *regentia*, from L *regere* to rule]

Regency (ˈriːdʒənsɪ) *n* (preceded by *the*) **1** (in Britain) the period (1811–20) of the regency of the Prince of Wales (later George IV) **2** (in France) the period (1715-23) of the regency of Philip, Duke of Orleans ▹ *adj* **3** characteristic of or relating to the Regency periods or to the styles of architecture, art, etc, produced in them

regenerate *vb* (rɪˈdʒɛnəˌreɪt), **regenerates, regenerating, regenerated 1** to undergo or cause to undergo moral, spiritual, or physical renewal or invigoration **2** to form or be formed again; come or bring into existence once again **3** to replace (lost or damaged tissues or organs) by new growth, or to cause (such tissues) to be replaced **4** (*tr*) *electronics* to use positive feedback to improve the demodulation and amplification of a signal ▹ *adj* (rɪˈdʒɛnərɪt) **5** morally, spiritually, or physically renewed or reborn > **reˈgeneracy** *n* > **reˌgenerˈation** *n* > **reˈgenerative** *adj* > **reˈgenerˌator** *n*

Regensburg (*German* ˈreːɡənsbʊrk) *n* a city in SE Germany, in Bavaria on the River Danube: a free Imperial city from 1245 and the leading commercial city of S Germany in the 12th and 13th centuries; the Imperial Diet was held in the town hall from 1663 to 1806. Pop: 125 200 (1999 est). Former English name: **Ratisbon**

regent (ˈriːdʒənt) *n* **1** the ruler or administrator of a country during the minority, absence, or incapacity of its monarch **2** *US & Canad* a member of the governing board of certain schools and colleges ▹ *adj* **3** (*usually postpositive*) acting or functioning as a regent: *a queen regent* [C14 from L *regēns*, from *regere* to rule] > **ˈregental** *adj* > **ˈregentship** *n*

regent-bird *n Austral* a bowerbird, the male of which has showy yellow and velvety-black plumage [after the PRINCE REGENT]

regent honeyeater *n* a large brightly-coloured Australian honeyeater

Reger (*German* ˈreːɡər) *n* **Max** (maks) 1873–1916, German composer, noted esp for his organ works

reggae (ˈrɛɡeɪ) *n* a type of West Indian popular music having four beats to the bar, the upbeat being strongly accented [C20 of West Indian origin]
▹ http://niceup.com
▹ www.allmusic.com

Reggio di Calabria (*Italian* ˈreddʒo di kaˈlaːbrja) *n* a port in S Italy, in Calabria on the Strait of Messina: founded about 720 BC by Greek colonists. Pop: 179 617 (2000 est)

Reggio nell'Emilia (*Italian* ˈreddʒo nɛlleˈmiːlja) *n* a city in N central Italy, in Emilia-Romagna: founded in the 2nd century BC by Marcus Aemilius Lepidus; ruled by the Este family in the 15th–18th centuries. Pop: 143 664 (2000 est)

Rr

regicide ('rɛdʒɪˌsaɪd) *n* **1** the killing of a king **2** a person who kills a king [C16 from L *rēx* king + -CIDE] > ˌ**regi'cidal** *adj*

regime *or* **régime** (reɪ'ʒiːm) *n* **1** a system of government or a particular administration: *a fascist regime; Castro's regime* **2** a social system or order **3** another word for **regimen** (sense 1) [C18 from F, from L *regimen* guidance, from *regere* to rule]

regime change *n* the transition from one political regime to another, esp through concerted political or military action

regimen ('rɛdʒɪˌmɛn) *n* **1** Also called: **regime** a systematic course of therapy, often including a recommended diet **2** administration or rule [C14 from L: guidance]

regiment *n* ('rɛdʒɪmənt) **1** a military formation varying in size from a battalion to a number of battalions **2** a large number in regular or organized groups ▷ *vb* ('rɛdʒɪˌmɛnt) (*tr*) **3** to force discipline or order on, esp in a domineering manner **4** to organize into a regiment **5** to form into organized groups [C14 via OF from LL *regimentum* government, from L *regere* to rule] > ˌ**regi'mental** *adj* > ˌ**regi'mentally** *adv* > ˌ**regimen'tation** *n*

regimentals (ˌrɛdʒɪ'mɛntᵊlz) *pl n* **1** the uniform and insignia of a regiment **2** military dress

Regin ('reɪgɪn) *n Norse myth* a dwarf smith, tutor of Sigurd, whom he encouraged to kill Fafnir for the gold he guarded

Regina[1] (rɪ'dʒaɪnə) *n* queen: now used chiefly in documents, inscriptions, etc ▷ Cf **Rex** [L]

Regina[2] (rɪ'dʒaɪnə) *n* a city in W Canada, capital and largest city of Saskatchewan: founded in 1882 as Pile O'Bones. Pop: 180 400 (1996)

Regiomontanus (ˌriːdʒɪəʊmɒn'teɪnəs, -'tɑː-, -'tæn-) *n* original name *Johann Müller.* 1436–76, German mathematician and astronomer, who furthered the development of trigonometry

region ('riːdʒən) *n* **1** any large, indefinite, and continuous part of a surface or space **2** an area considered as a unit for geographical, functional, social, or cultural reasons **3** an administrative division of a country, or a Canadian province **4** a realm or sphere of activity or interest **5** range, area, or scope: *in what region is the price likely to be?* **6** a division or part of the body: *the lumbar region* [C14 from L *regiō*, from *regere* to govern]

regional ('riːdʒənᵊl) *adj* of, characteristic of, or limited to a region > '**regionally** *adv*

regionalism ('riːdʒənəˌlɪzəm) *n* **1** division of a country into administrative regions having partial autonomy **2** loyalty to one's home region; regional patriotism > '**regionalist** *n, adj*

régisseur *French* (reʒisœr) *n* an official in a dance company with varying duties, usually including directing productions [F, from *régir* to manage]

register ('rɛdʒɪstə) *n* **1** an official or formal list recording names, events, or transactions **2** the book in which such a list is written **3** an entry in such a list **4** a recording device that accumulates data, totals sums of money, etc: *a cash register* **5** a movable plate that controls the flow of air into a furnace, chimney, room, etc **6** *music* **6a** the timbre characteristic of a certain manner of voice production **6b** any of the stops on an organ as classified in respect of its tonal quality: *the flute register* **7** *printing* the exact correspondence of lines of type, etc, on the two sides of a printed sheet of paper **8** a form of a language associated with a particular social situation or subject matter **9** the act or an instance of registering ▷ *vb* **10** (*tr*) to enter or cause someone to enter (an event, person's name, ownership, etc) on a register **11** to show or be shown on a scale or other measuring instrument: *the current didn't register on the meter* **12** to show or be shown in a person's face, bearing, etc: *his face registered surprise* **13** (*intr*) *inf* to have an effect; make an impression: *the news of her uncle's death just did not register* **14** to send (a letter, package, etc) by registered post **15** (*tr*) *printing* to adjust (a printing press, forme, etc) to ensure that the printed matter is in register [C14 from Med. L *registrum*, from L *regerere* to transcribe, from RE- + *gerere* to bear] > '**registrable** *adj*

Registered General Nurse *n* (in Britain) a nurse who has completed a three-year training course and has been registered with the United Kingdom Central Council for Nursing, Midwifery, and Health Visiting. Abbrev: **RGN**

registered post *n* **1** a Post Office service by which compensation is paid for loss or damage to mail for which a registration fee has been paid **2** mail sent by this service

Registered Trademark *n* See **trademark** (sense 1)

register office *n Brit* a government office where civil marriages are performed and births, marriages, and deaths are recorded. Often called: **registry office**

register ton *n* the full name for **ton**[1] (sense 6)

registrar (ˌrɛdʒɪ'strɑː, 'rɛdʒɪˌstrɑː) *n* **1** a person who keeps official records **2** an administrative official responsible for student records, enrolment procedure, etc, in a school, college, or university **3** See **specialist registrar** **4** *Austral* the chief medical administrator of a large hospital **5** *chiefly US* a person employed by a company to maintain a register of its security issues > '**regis**ˌ**trarship** *n*

registration (ˌrɛdʒɪ'streɪʃən) *n* **1a** the act of registering or state of being registered **1b** (*as modifier*): *a registration number* **2** an entry in a register **3** a group of people, such as students, who register at a particular time **4** *Austral* **4a** a tax payable by the owner of a motor vehicle **4b** the period paid for

registration document *n Brit* a document giving identification details of a motor vehicle, including its manufacturer, date of registration, and owner's name

registration number *n* a sequence of letters and numbers assigned to a motor vehicle when it is registered, usually indicating the year and place of registration, displayed on numberplates at the front and rear of the vehicle

registration plate *n Austral & NZ* the numberplate of a vehicle

registry ('rɛdʒɪstrɪ) *n, pl* **registries** **1** a place where registers are kept **2** the registration of a ship's country of origin: *a ship of Liberian registry* **3** another word for **registration**

registry office *n Brit* another term for **register office**

Regius professor ('riːdʒɪəs) *n Brit* a person appointed by the Crown to a university chair founded by a royal patron [C17 *regius*, from L: royal, from *rex* king]

reglet ('rɛglɪt) *n* **1** a flat narrow architectural moulding **2** *printing* a strip of oiled wood used for spacing between lines [C16 from OF, lit.: a little rule, from *régle* rule, from L *rēgula*]

regmaker ('rɛxˌmɑːkə) *n S African* a drink to relieve the symptoms of a hangover [from Afrik., right maker]

regnal ('rɛgnəl) *adj* **1** of a sovereign or reign **2** designating a year of a sovereign's reign calculated from the date of accession [C17 from Med. L *rēgnālis*, from L *rēgnum* sovereignty; see REIGN]

regnant ('rɛgnənt) *adj* **1** (*postpositive*) reigning **2** prevalent; current [C17 from L *regnāre* to REIGN] > '**regnancy** *n*

regorge (rɪ'gɔːdʒ) *vb* **regorges, regorging, regorged** **1** (*tr*) to vomit up; disgorge **2** (*intr*) (esp of water) to flow or run back [C17 from F *regorger*; see GORGE]

regress *vb* (rɪ'grɛs) **1** (*intr*) to return or revert, as to a former place, condition, or mode of behaviour **2** (*tr*) *statistics* to measure the extent to which (a dependent variable) is associated with one or more independent variables ▷ *n* ('riːgrɛs) **3** movement in a backward direction; retrogression [C14 from L *regressus*, from *regredī* to go back, from RE- + *gradī* to go] > **re'gressive** *adj* > **re'gressor** *n*

regression (rɪ'grɛʃən) *n* **1** *psychol* the adoption by an adult of behaviour more appropriate to a child **2** *statistics* **2a** the measure of the association between one variable (the dependent variable) and other variables (the independent variables) **2b** (*as modifier*): *regression curve* **3** *geol* the retreat of the sea from the land **4** the act of regressing

regret (rɪ'grɛt) *vb* **regrets, regretting, regretted** (*tr*) **1** (*may take a clause as object or an infinitive*) to feel sorry, repentant, or upset about **2** to bemoan or grieve the death or loss of ▷ *n* **3** a sense of repentance, guilt, or sorrow **4** a sense of loss or grief **5** (*pl*) a polite expression of sadness, esp in a formal refusal of an invitation [C14 from OF *regreter*, from ON] > **re'gretful** *adj* > **re'gretfully** *adv* > **re'gretfulness** *n* > **re'grettable** *adj* > **re'grettably** *adv*

> USAGE *Regretful* and *regretfully* are sometimes wrongly used where *regrettable* and *regrettably* are meant. A simple way of making the distinction is that when you regret something **you** have done, you are *regretful*: *he gave a regretful smile*; *he smiled regretfully*. In contrast, when you are sorry about an occurrence you did not yourself cause, you view the occurrence as *regrettable*: *this is a regrettable* (not *regretful*) *mistake*; *regrettably* (not *regretfully*, i.e. because of circumstances beyond my control) *I shall be unable to attend*

regroup (riː'gruːp) *vb* **1** to reorganize (military forces), esp after an attack or a defeat **2** (*tr*) to rearrange into a new grouping

Regt *abbrev for*: **1** Regent **2** Regiment

regulable ('rɛgjʊləbᵊl) *adj* able to be regulated

regular ('rɛgjʊlə) *adj* **1** normal, customary, or usual **2** according to a uniform principle, arrangement, or order **3** occurring at fixed or prearranged intervals: *a regular call on a customer* **4** following a set rule or normal practice; methodical or orderly **5** symmetrical in appearance or form; even: *regular features* **6** (*prenominal*) organized, elected, conducted, etc, in a proper or officially prescribed manner **7** (*prenominal*) officially qualified or recognized: *he's not a regular doctor* **8** (*prenominal*) (intensifier): *a regular fool* **9** *US & Canad inf* likable, dependable, or nice: *a regular guy* **10** denoting or relating to the personnel or units of the permanent military services: *a regular soldier* **11** (of flowers) having any of their parts, esp petals, alike in size, etc; symmetrical **12** *grammar* following the usual pattern of formation in a language **13** *maths* **13a** (of a polygon) equilateral and equiangular **13b** (of a polyhedron) having identical regular polygons as faces **13c** (of a prism) having regular polygons as bases **13d** (of a pyramid) having a regular polygon as a base and the altitude passing through the centre of the base **14** *bot* (of a flower) having radial symmetry **15** (*postpositive*) subject to the rule of an established religious order or community: *canons regular* ▷ *n* **16** a professional long-term serviceman in a military unit **17** *inf* a person who does something regularly, such as attending a theatre **18** a member of a religious order or congregation, as contrasted with a secular [C14 from OF *reguler*, from L *rēgulāris* of a bar of wood or metal, from *rēgula* ruler, model] > ˌ**regu'larity** *n* > '**regularˌize** *or* '**regularˌise** *vb* > '**regularly** *adv*

regulate ('rɛgjʊˌleɪt) *vb* **regulates, regulating, regulated** (*tr*) **1** to adjust (the amount of heat, sound, etc) as required; control **2** to adjust (an instrument or appliance) so that it operates correctly **3** to bring into conformity with a rule, principle, or usage [C17 from LL *rēgulāre* to control, from L *rēgula* ruler] > '**regulative** *or* '**regulatory** *adj* > '**regulatively** *adv*

regulation (ˌrɛgjʊ'leɪʃən) *n* **1** the act or process of regulating **2** a rule, principle, or condition that governs procedure or behaviour **3** (*modifier*) as required by official rules: *regulation uniform* **4** (*modifier*) normal; usual; conforming to accepted standards: *a regulation haircut*

regulator ('rɛgjʊˌleɪtə) *n* **1** a person or thing that regulates **2** the mechanism by which the speed of a timepiece is regulated **3** any of various mechanisms or devices, such as a governor valve, for controlling fluid flow, pressure, temperature, etc

regulo ('rɛgjʊləʊ) *n* any of a number of temperatures to which a gas oven may be set: *cook at regulo 4* [C20 from *Regulo*, trademark for a type of thermostatic control on gas ovens]

regulus ('rɛgjʊləs) *n, pl* **reguluses** *or* **reguli** (-ˌlaɪ) impure metal forming beneath the slag during the smelting of ores [C16 from L: a petty king, from *rēx* king; formerly used for *antimony*, because it combines readily with gold, the king of metals] > '**reguline** *adj*

Regulus[1] ('rɛgjʊləs) *n* **Marcus Atilius** ('mɑːkəs ə'tɪlɪəs) died ?250 BC, Roman general; consul (267; 256). Captured by the Carthaginians in the First Punic War, he was sent to Rome on parole to deliver the enemy's peace terms, advised the Senate to refuse them, and was tortured to death on his return to Carthage

regurgitate (rɪ'gɜːdʒɪˌteɪt) *vb* **regurgitates, regurgitating, regurgitated** **1** to vomit forth (partially digested food) **2** (of some birds and animals) to bring back to the mouth (undigested or partly digested food to feed the young) **3** (*intr*) to be cast up or out, esp from the mouth **4** (*intr*) *med* (of blood) to flow in a direction opposite to the normal one, esp through a defective heart valve [C17 from Med. L *regurgitāre*, from RE- + *gurgitāre* to flood, from L *gurges* whirlpool] > **re'gurgitant** *n, adj* > **reˌgurgi'tation** *n*

Rr

rehabilitate (ˌriːə'bɪlɪˌteɪt) *vb* **rehabilitates, rehabilitating, rehabilitated** (*tr*) **1** to help (a physically or mentally disabled person or an ex-prisoner) to readapt to society or a new job, as by vocational guidance, retraining, or therapy **2** to restore to a former position or rank **3** to restore the good reputation of [C16 from Med. L *rehabilitāre* to restore, from RE- + L *habilitās* skill] > ˌ**rehaˌbili'tation** *n* > ˌ**reha'bilitative** *adj*

Rehabilitation Department *n* NZ a government department set up after World War II to assist ex-servicemen. Often shortened to **rehab**

rehash *vb* (riː'hæʃ) **1** (*tr*) to rework, reuse, or make over (old or already used material) ▷ *n* ('riːˌhæʃ) **2** something consisting of old, reworked, or reused material [C19 from RE- + HASH[1] (to chop into pieces)]

rehearsal (rɪ'hɜːsᵊl) *n* **1** a session of practising a play, concert, etc, in preparation for public performance **2 in rehearsal** being prepared for public performance

rehearse (rɪ'hɜːs) *vb* **rehearses, rehearsing, rehearsed** **1** to practise (a play, concert, etc), in preparation for public performance **2** (*tr*) to run through; recount; recite: *he rehearsed the grievances of the committee* **3** (*tr*) to train or drill (a person) for public performance [C16 from Anglo-Norman *rehearser*, from OF *rehercier* to harrow a second time, from RE- + *herce* harrow] > **re'hearser** *n*

reheat *vb* (riː'hiːt) **1** to heat or be heated again: *to reheat yesterday's soup* **2** (*tr*) to add fuel to (the exhaust gases of an aircraft jet engine) to produce additional heat and thrust ▷ *n* ('riːˌhiːt), *also* **reheating** **3** a process in which additional fuel is ignited in the exhaust gases of a jet engine to produce additional thrust > **re'heater** *n*

rehoboam (ˌriːə'bəʊəm) *n* a wine bottle holding the equivalent of six normal bottles [after *Rehoboam*, a son of King Solomon, from Heb., lit.: the nation is enlarged]

Reich (raɪk) *n* **1** the Holy Roman Empire (962–1806) (**First Reich**) **2** the Hohenzollern empire in Germany from

1871 to 1918 (**Second Reich**) **3** the Nazi dictatorship (1933–45) in Germany (**Third Reich**) [G: kingdom]

Reichenberg ('raiçənbɛrk) *n* the German name for **Liberec**

Reichsmark ('raɪks,mɑːk) *n, pl* **Reichsmarks** *or* **Reichsmark** the standard monetary unit of Germany between 1924 and 1948

Reichstag ('raɪks,tɑːg) *n* **1** the legislative assembly of Germany (1867–1933) **2** the building in Berlin in which this assembly met

Reid (riːd) *n* **1** Sir **George Houston** 1845–1918, Australian statesman, born in Scotland: premier of New South Wales (1894–99); prime minister of Australia (1904–05) **2 Thomas** 1710–96, Scottish philosopher and founder of what came to be known as the philosophy of common sense

reify ('riːɪ,faɪ) *vb* **reifies, reifying, reified** *(tr)* to consider or make (an abstract idea or concept) real or concrete [C19 from L *rēs* thing] > ,**reifi'cation** *n* > ,**reifi'catory** *adj* > '**rei,fier** *n*

Reigate ('raɪgɪt, -geɪt) *n* a town in S England, in Surrey at the foot of the North Downs. Pop: 47 602 (1991)

reign (reɪn) *n* **1** the period during which a monarch is the official ruler of a country **2** a period during which a person or thing is dominant or powerful: *the reign of violence* ▷ *vb (intr)* **3** to exercise the power and authority of a sovereign **4** to be accorded the rank and title of a sovereign without having ruling authority **5** to predominate; prevail: *darkness reigns* **6** *(usually present participle)* to be the most recent winner of a contest, etc: *the reigning champion* [C13 from OF *reigne*, from L *rēgnum* kingdom, from *rēx* king]

> **USAGE** *Reign* is sometimes wrongly written for *rein* in certain phrases: *he gave full rein* (not *reign*) *to his feelings; it will be necessary to rein in* (not *reign in*) *public spending*

reiki ('reɪkɪ) *n* a form of therapy in which the practitioner is believed to channel energy into the patient in order to encourage healing or restore well-being [Japanese, from *rei* universal + *ki* life force]

reimburse (,riːɪm'bɜːs) *vb* **reimburses, reimbursing, reimbursed** *(tr)* to repay or compensate (someone) for (money already spent, losses, damages, etc) [C17 from RE- + *imburse*, from Med. L *imbursāre* to put in a moneybag, from *bursa* PURSE] > ,**reim'bursable** *adj* > ,**reim'bursement** *n* > ,**reim'burser** *n*

reimport *vb* (,riːɪm'pɔːt, riː'ɪmpɔːt) **1** *(tr)* to import (goods manufactured from exported raw materials) ▷ *n* (riː'ɪmpɔːt) **2** the act of reimporting **3** a reimported commodity > ,**reimpor'tation** *n*

Reims *or* **Rheims** (riːmz; *French* rɛ̃s) *n* a city in NE France: scene of the coronation of most French monarchs. Pop: 187 206 (1999)

rein (reɪn) *n* **1** *(often pl)* one of a pair of long straps, usually connected together and made of leather, used to control a horse **2** a similar device used to control a very young child **3** any form or means of control: *to take up the reins of government* **4** the direction in which a rider turns (in **on a left rein**) **5** something that restrains, controls, or guides **6 give (a) free rein** to allow considerable freedom; remove restraints **7 keep a tight rein on** to control carefully; limit: *we have to keep a tight rein on expenditure* ▷ *vb* **8** *(tr)* to check, restrain, hold back, or halt with or as if with reins **9** to control or guide (a horse) with a rein or reins: *they reined left* ▷ See also **rein in** [C13 from OF *resne*, from L *retinēre* to hold back, from RE- + *tenēre* to hold]

> **USAGE** See at **reign**

reincarnate *vb* (,riːɪn'kɑː,neɪt), **reincarnates, reincarnating, reincarnated** *(tr; often passive)* **1** to cause to undergo reincarnation; be born again ▷ *adj* (,riːɪn'kɑːnɪt) **2** born again in a new body

reincarnation (,riːɪnkɑː'neɪʃən) *n* **1** the belief that on the death of the body the soul transmigrates to or is born again in another body **2** the incarnation or embodiment of a soul in a new body after it has left the old one at physical death **3** embodiment again in a new form, as of a principle or idea > ,**reincar'nationist** *n, adj*

reindeer ('reɪn,dɪə) *n, pl* **reindeer** *or* **reindeers** a large deer, having large branched antlers in the male and female and inhabiting the arctic regions. It also occurs in North America, where it is known as a caribou [C14 from ON *hreindȳri*, from *hreinn* reindeer + *dyr* animal]

Reindeer Lake *n* a lake in W Canada, in Saskatchewan and Manitoba: drains into the Churchill River via the **Reindeer River**. Area: 6390 sq km (2467 sq miles)

reindeer moss *n* any of various lichens which occur in arctic and subarctic regions, providing food for reindeer

reinforce (,riːɪn'fɔːs) *vb* **reinforces, reinforcing, reinforced** *(tr)* **1** to give added strength or support to **2** to give added emphasis to; stress or increase: *his rudeness reinforced my determination* **3** to give added support to (a military force) by providing more men, supplies, etc [C17 from F *renforcer*] > ,**rein'forcement** *n*

reinforced concrete *n* concrete with steel bars, mesh, etc, embedded in it to enable it to withstand tensile and shear stresses

reinforced plastic *n* plastic with fibrous matter, such as carbon fibre, embedded in it to strengthen it

Reinhardt ('raɪn,hɑːt) *n* **1 Django** ('dʒæŋgəʊ), real name *Jean Baptiste Reinhardt*. 1910–53, French jazz guitarist, whose work was greatly influenced by Gypsy music. With Stéphane Grappelli, he led the Quintet of the Hot Club of France between 1934 and 1939 **2 Max**, original name *Max Goldmann*. 1873–1943, Austrian theatre producer and director, in the US after 1933

rein in *vb (adv)* to stop (a horse) by pulling on the reins

reins (reɪnz) *pl n arch* the kidneys or loins [C14 from OF, from L *rēnēs* the kidneys]

reinstate (,riːɪn'steɪt) *vb* **reinstates, reinstating, reinstated** *(tr)* to restore to a former rank or condition > ,**rein'statement** *n* > ,**rein'stator** *n*

reinsurer (,riːɪn'ʃʊərə) *n* an insurance company which will accept business from other insurance companies, thus enabling the risks to be spread > ,**rein'surance** *n*

reinvent (,riːɪn'vɛnt) *vb (tr)* **1** to replace (a product, etc) with an entirely new version **2** to duplicate (something that already exists) in what is therefore a wasted effort (esp in **reinvent the wheel**)

reissue (,riː'ɪʃjuː) *n* **1** a book, record, etc, that is published or released again after being unavailable for a time ▷ *vb* **2** *(tr)* to publish or release (a book, record, etc) again after a period of unavailability

reiterate (riː'ɪtə,reɪt) *vb* **reiterates, reiterating, reiterated** *(tr; may take a clause as object)* to say or do again or repeatedly [C16 from L *reiterāre*, from RE- + *iterāre* to do again, from *iterum* again] > **re,iter'ation** *n* > **re'iterative** *adj* > **re'iteratively** *adv*

Reith (riːθ) *n* **John (Charles Walsham)**, 1st Baron. 1889–1971, British public servant: first general manager (1922–27) and first director general (1927–38) of the BBC

reive (riːv) *vb* **reives, reiving, reived** *(intr) Scot & N English dialect* to go on a plundering raid [var. of REAVE] > '**reiver** *n*

reject *vb* (rɪ'dʒɛkt) *(tr)* **1** to refuse to accept, use, believe, etc **2** to throw out as useless or worthless; discard **3** to rebuff (a person) **4** (of an organism) to fail to accept (a foreign tissue graft or organ transplant) ▷ *n* ('riːdʒɛkt) **5** something rejected as imperfect, unsatisfactory, or useless [C15 from L *rēicere* to throw back, from RE- + *jacere* to hurl] > **re'jecter** *or* **re'jector** *n* > **re'jection** *n* > **re'jective** *adj*

rejig (riː'dʒɪg) *vb* **rejigs, rejigging, rejigged** *(tr)* **1** to re-equip (a factory or plant) **2** *inf* to rearrange, manipulate, etc, sometimes in an unscrupulous way ▷ *n* **3** the act or process of rejigging > **re'jigger** *n*

rejoice (rɪ'dʒɔɪs) *vb* **rejoices, rejoicing, rejoiced** (when *tr, takes a clause as object or an infinitive;* when *intr,* often foll by *in*) to feel or express great joy or happiness [C14 from OF *resjoir,* from RE- + *joir* to be glad, from L *gaudēre* to rejoice] > **re'joicer** *n*
rejoin¹ (riː'dʒɔɪn) *vb* **1** to come again into company with (someone or something) **2** (*tr*) to put or join together again; reunite
rejoin² (rɪ'dʒɔɪn) *vb* (*tr*) **1** to answer or reply **2** *law* to answer (a plaintiff's reply) [C15 from OF *rejoign-,* stem of *rejoindre;* see RE-, JOIN]
rejoinder (rɪ'dʒɔɪndə) *n* **1** a reply or response to a question or remark **2** *law* (in pleading) the answer made by a defendant to the plaintiff's reply [C15 from OF *rejoindre* to REJOIN²]
rejuvenate (rɪ'dʒuːvɪˌneɪt) *vb* **rejuvenates, rejuvenating, rejuvenated** (*tr*) **1** to give new youth, restored vitality, or youthful appearance to **2** (*usually passive*) *geog* to cause (a river) to begin eroding more vigorously to a new lower base level [C19 from RE- + L *juvenis* young] > **reˌjuve'nation** *n* > **re'juveˌnator** *n*
rejuvenesce (rɪˌdʒuːvə'nɛs) *vb* **rejuvenesces, rejuvenescing, rejuvenesced** **1** to make or become youthful or restored to vitality **2** *biol* to convert (cells) or (of cells) to be converted into a more active form > **reˌjuve'nescence** *n* > **reˌjuve'nescent** *adj*
rel. *abbrev for:* **1** relating **2** relative(ly)
relapse (rɪ'læps) *vb* **relapses, relapsing, relapsed** (*intr*) **1** to lapse back into a former state or condition, esp one involving bad habits **2** to become ill again after apparent recovery ▷ *n* **3** the act or an instance of relapsing **4** the return of ill health after an apparent or partial recovery [C16 from L *relabī,* from RE- + *labī* to slip, slide] > **re'lapser** *n*
relapsing fever *n* any of various infectious diseases characterized by recurring fever, caused by the bite of body lice or ticks. Also called: **recurrent fever**
relata (rɪ'leɪtə) *n* the plural of **relatum**
relate (rɪ'leɪt) *vb* **relates, relating, related** **1** (*tr*) to tell or narrate (a story, etc) **2** (often foll by *to*) to establish association (between two or more things) or (of something) to have relation or reference (to something else) **3** (*intr;* often foll by *to*) to form a sympathetic or significant relationship (with other people, things, etc) [C16 from L *relātus* brought back, from *referre,* from RE- + *ferre* to bear] > **re'latable** *adj* > **re'later** *n*
related (rɪ'leɪtɪd) *adj* **1** connected; associated **2** connected by kinship or marriage **3** (in diatonic music) denoting or relating to a key that has notes in common with another key or keys > **re'latedness** *n*
relation (rɪ'leɪʃən) *n* **1** the state or condition of being related or the manner in which things are related **2** connection by blood or marriage; kinship **3** a person who is connected by blood or marriage; relative **4** reference or regard (esp in **in** *or* **with relation to**) **5** the position, association, connection, or status of one person or thing with regard to another **6** the act of relating or narrating **7** an account or narrative **8** *law* the statement of grounds of complaint made by a relator **9** *logic, maths* **9a** an association between ordered pairs of objects, numbers, etc, such as ... is greater than ... **9b** the set of ordered pairs whose members have such an association ▷ See also **relations** [C14 from L *relātiō* a narration, a relation (between philosophical concepts)]
relational (rɪ'leɪʃənᵊl) *adj* **1** *grammar* indicating or expressing syntactic relation, as for example the case endings in Latin **2** having relation or being related **3** *computing* based on data that is interconnected, often in tabular form
relations (rɪ'leɪʃənz) *pl n* **1** social, political, or personal connections or dealings between or among individuals, groups, nations, etc **2** family or relatives **3** *euphemistic* sexual intercourse
relationship (rɪ'leɪʃənʃɪp) *n* **1** the state of being connected or related **2** association by blood or marriage; kinship **3** the mutual dealings, connections, or feelings that exist between two countries, people, etc **4** an emotional or sexual affair or liaison
relative ('rɛlətɪv) *adj* **1** having meaning or significance only in relation to something else; not absolute **2** (*prenominal*) (of a scientific quantity) being measured or stated relative to some other substance or measurement: *relative density* **3** (*prenominal*) comparative or respective: *the relative qualities of speed and accuracy* **4** (*postpositive;* foll by *to*) in proportion (to); corresponding (to): *earnings relative to production* **5** having reference (to); pertinent (to) **6** *grammar* denoting or belonging to a class of words that function as subordinating conjunctions in introducing relative clauses such as *who, which,* and *that* ▷ Cf **demonstrative** **7** *grammar* denoting or relating to a clause (**relative clause**) that modifies a noun or pronoun occurring earlier in the sentence **8** (of a musical key or scale) having the same key signature as another key or scale ▷ *n* **9** a person who is related by blood or marriage; relation **10** a relative pronoun, clause, or grammatical construction [C16 from LL *relātīvus* referring] > **'relativeness** *n*
relative aperture *n photog* the ratio of the equivalent focal length of a lens to the effective aperture of the lens
relative atomic mass *n* the ratio of the average mass per atom of the naturally occurring form of an element to one-twelfth of the mass of an atom of carbon-12. Symbol: A_r. Abbrev: **r.a.m.** Former name: **atomic weight**
relative density *n* the ratio of the density of a substance to the density of a standard substance under specified conditions. For liquids and solids the standard is usually water at 4°C. For gases the standard is air or hydrogen at the same temperature and pressure as the substance. See also **specific gravity, vapour density**
relative frequency *n statistics* the ratio of the actual number of favourable events to the total possible number of events
relative humidity *n* the mass of water vapour present in the air expressed as a percentage of the mass present in an equal volume of saturated air at the same temperature
relatively ('rɛlətɪvlɪ) *adv* in comparison or relation to something else; not absolutely
relative majority *n Brit* the excess of votes or seats won by the winner of an election over the runner-up when no candidate or party has more than 50 per cent ▷ Cf **absolute majority**
relative molecular mass *n* the sum of all the relative atomic masses of the atoms in a molecule; the ratio of the average mass per molecule of a specified isotopic composition of a substance to one-twelfth the mass of an atom of carbon-12. Symbol: M_r. Abbrev: **r.m.m.** Former name: **molecular weight**
relative permeability *n* the ratio of the permeability of a medium to that of free space
relative permittivity *n* the ratio of the permittivity of a substance to that of free space
relativism ('rɛlətɪˌvɪzəm) *n* any theory holding that truth or moral or aesthetic value, etc, is not universal or absolute but may differ between individuals or cultures > **'relativist** *n, adj* > **ˌrelativ'istic** *adj*
relativity (ˌrɛlə'tɪvɪtɪ) *n* **1** either of two theories developed by Albert Einstein, the **special theory of relativity**, which requires that the laws of physics shall be the same as seen by any two different observers in uniform relative motion, and the **general theory of relativity**, which considers observers with relative acceleration and leads to a theory of gravitation **2** the state or quality of being relative
relator (rɪ'leɪtə) *n* **1** a person who relates a story; narrator **2** *English law* a person who gives information

upon which the attorney general brings an action

relatum (rɪˈleɪtəm) *n, pl* **relata** (-tə) *logic* one of the objects between which a relation is said to hold

relaunch *vb* (riːˈlɔːntʃ) (*tr*) **1** to launch again **2** to start, set in motion, or make available again ▷ *n* (ˈriːˌlɔːntʃ) **3** another launching, or something that is relaunched

relax (rɪˈlæks) *vb* **1** to make (muscles, a grip, etc) less tense or rigid or (of muscles, a grip, etc) to become looser or less rigid **2** (*intr*) to take rest, as from work or effort **3** to lessen the force of (effort, concentration) or (of effort) to become diminished **4** to make (rules or discipline) less rigid or strict or (of rules, etc) to diminish in severity **5** (*intr*) (of a person) to become less formal; unbend [C15 from L *relaxāre* to loosen, from RE- + *laxāre*, from *laxus* loose] > **reˈlaxed** *adj* > **relaxedly** (rɪˈlæksɪdlɪ) *adv* > **reˈlaxer** *n*

relaxant (rɪˈlæksᵊnt) *n* **1** *med* a drug or agent that relaxes, esp one that relaxes tense muscles ▷ *adj* **2** of or tending to produce relaxation

relaxation (ˌriːlækˈseɪʃən) *n* **1** rest or refreshment, as after work or effort; recreation **2** a form of rest or recreation: *his relaxation is cricket* **3** a partial lessening of a punishment, duty, etc **4** the act of relaxing or state of being relaxed **5** *physics* the return of a system to equilibrium after a displacement from this state

relaxin (rɪˈlæksɪn) *n* **1** a mammalian polypeptide hormone secreted during pregnancy, which relaxes the pelvic ligaments **2** a preparation of this hormone, used to facilitate childbirth [C20 from RELAX + -IN]

relay *n* (ˈriːleɪ) **1** a person or team of people relieving others, as on a shift **2** a fresh team of horses, etc, posted along a route to relieve others **3** the act of relaying or process of being relayed **4** short for **relay race** **5** an automatic device that controls a valve, switch, etc, by means of an electric motor, solenoid, or pneumatic mechanism **6** *electronics* an electrical device in which a small change in current or voltage controls the switching on or off of circuits **7** *radio* **7a** a combination of a receiver and transmitter designed to receive radio signals and retransmit them **7b** (*as modifier*): *a relay station* ▷ *vb* (rɪˈleɪ) (*tr*) **8** to carry or spread (news or information) by relays **9** to supply or replace with relays **10** to retransmit (a signal) by means of a relay **11** *Brit* to broadcast (a performance) by sending out signals through a transmitting station [C15 *relaien*, from OF *relaier* to leave behind, from RE- + *laier* to leave, ult. from L *laxāre* to loosen]

relay race *n* a race between two or more teams of contestants in which each contestant covers a specified portion of the distance

release (rɪˈliːs) *vb* **releases, releasing, released** (*tr*) **1** to free (a person or animal) from captivity or imprisonment **2** to free (someone) from obligation or duty **3** to free (something) from (one's grip); let fall **4** to issue (a record, film, or book) for sale or circulation **5** to make (news or information) known or allow (news, etc) to be made known **6** *law* to relinquish (a right, claim, or title) in favour of someone else ▷ *n* **7** the act of freeing or state of being freed **8** the act of issuing for sale or publication **9** something issued for sale or public showing, esp a film or a record: *a new release from Bob Dylan* **10** a news item, etc, made available for publication, broadcasting, etc **11** *law* the surrender of a claim, right, title, etc, in favour of someone else **12** a control mechanism for starting or stopping an engine **13** the control mechanism for the shutter in a camera [C13 from OF *relesser*, from L *relaxāre* to slacken] > **reˈleaser** *n*

relegate (ˈrɛlɪˌgeɪt) *vb* **relegates, relegating, relegated** (*tr*) **1** to move to a position of less authority, importance, etc; demote **2** (*usually passive*) *chiefly Brit* to demote (a football team, etc) to a lower division **3** to assign or refer (a matter) to another **4** (foll by *to*) to banish or exile **5** to assign (something) to a particular group or category [C16 from L *relēgāre*, from RE- + *lēgāre* to send] > ˈ**releˌgatable** *adj* > ˌ**releˈgation** *n*

relent (rɪˈlɛnt) *vb* (*intr*) **1** to change one's mind about some decision, esp a harsh one; become more mild or amenable **2** (of the pace or intensity of something) to slacken **3** (of the weather) to become more mild [C14 from RE- + L *lentāre* to bend, from *lentus* flexible]

relentless (rɪˈlɛntlɪs) *adj* **1** (of an enemy, etc) implacable; inflexible; inexorable **2** (of pace or intensity) sustained; unremitting > **reˈlentlessly** *adv* > **reˈlentlessness** *n*

Relenza (rɪˈlɛnzə) *n trademark* a preparation of an antiviral drug, zanamivir, used in the treatment of influenza to reduce the duration and severity of the illness

relevant (ˈrɛlɪvənt) *adj* having direct bearing on the matter in hand; pertinent [C16 from Med. L *relevans*, from L *relevāre*, from RE- + *levāre* to raise, RELIEVE] > ˈ**relevance** *or* ˈ**relevancy** *n* > ˈ**relevantly** *adv*

reliable (rɪˈlaɪəbᵊl) *adj* able to be trusted; dependable > **reˌliaˈbility** *or* **reˈliableness** *n* > **reˈliably** *adv*

reliance (rɪˈlaɪəns) *n* **1** dependence, confidence, or trust **2** something or someone upon which one relies > **reˈliant** *adj* > **reˈliantly** *adv*

relic (ˈrɛlɪk) *n* **1** something that has survived from the past, such as an object or custom **2** something treasured for its past associations; keepsake **3** (*usually pl*) a remaining part or fragment **4** *RC Church, Eastern Church* part of the body of a saint or his belongings, venerated as holy **5** *inf* an old or old-fashioned person or thing **6** (*pl*) *arch* the remains of a dead person; corpse [C13 from OF *relique*, from L *reliquiae* remains, from *relinquere* to leave behind]

relict (ˈrɛlɪkt) *n* **1** *ecology* **1a** a group of animals or plants that exists as a remnant of a formerly widely distributed group **1b** (*as modifier*): *a relict fauna* **2** *geol* a mountain, lake, glacier, etc, that is a remnant of a pre-existing formation after a destructive process has occurred **3** an archaic word for **widow** **4** an archaic word for **relic** [C16 from L *relictus* left behind, from *relinquere* to RELINQUISH]

relief (rɪˈliːf) *n* **1** a feeling of cheerfulness or optimism that follows the removal of anxiety, pain, or distress **2** deliverance from or alleviation of anxiety, pain, etc **3a** help or assistance, as to the poor or needy **3b** (*as modifier*): *relief work* **4** a diversion from monotony **5** a person who replaces another at some task or duty **6** a bus, plane, etc, that carries additional passengers when a scheduled service is full **7** a road (**relief road**) carrying traffic round an urban area; bypass **8a** the act of freeing a beleaguered town, fortress, etc: *the relief of Mafeking* **8b** (*as modifier*): *a relief column* **9** Also called: **relievo, rilievo** *sculpture, archit* **9a** the projection of forms or figures from a flat ground, so that they are partly or wholly free of it **9b** a piece of work of this kind **10** a printing process that employs raised surfaces from which ink is transferred to the paper **11** any vivid effect resulting from contrast: *comic relief* **12** variation in altitude in an area; difference between highest and lowest level **13** *law* redress of a grievance or hardship: *to seek relief through the courts* **14** short for **tax relief** **15** **on relief** *US & Canad* (of people) in receipt of government aid because of personal need [C14 from OF, from *relever*; see RELIEVE]

relief map *n* a map that shows the configuration and height of the land surface, usually by means of contours

relieve (rɪˈliːv) *vb* **relieves, relieving, relieved** (*tr*) **1** to bring alleviation of (pain, distress, etc) to (someone) **2** to bring aid or assistance to (someone in need, etc) **3** to take over the duties or watch of (someone) **4** to bring aid or a relieving force to (a besieged town, etc) **5** to free (someone) from an obligation **6** to make (something) less unpleasant, arduous, or monotonous **7** to bring into relief or prominence, as by contrast

8 (foll by *of*) *inf* to take from: *the thief relieved him of his watch* 9 **relieve oneself** to urinate or defecate [C14 from OF *relever*, from L *relevāre* to lift up, relieve, from RE- + *levāre* to lighten] > **re'lievable** *adj* > **re'liever** *n*

relieved (rɪ'li:vd) *adj (postpositive; often foll by at, about, etc)* experiencing relief, esp from worry or anxiety

religieuse *French* (rəliʒjøz) *n* a nun [C18 fem of RELIGIEUX]

religieux *French* (rəliʒjø) *n, pl* ***religieux*** (-ʒjø) a member of a monastic order or clerical body [C17 from L *religiōsus* religious]

religion (rɪ'lɪdʒən) *n* 1 belief in, worship of, or obedience to a supernatural power or powers considered to be divine or to have control of human destiny 2 any formal or institutionalized expression of such belief: *the Christian religion* 3 the attitude and feeling of one who believes in a transcendent controlling power or powers 4 *chiefly RC Church* the way of life entered upon by monks and nuns: *to enter religion* 5 something of overwhelming importance to a person: *football is his religion* [C12 via OF from L *religiō* fear of the supernatural, piety, prob. from *religāre*, from RE- + *ligāre* to bind]

religionism (rɪ'lɪdʒəˌnɪzəm) *n* extreme religious fervour > **re'ligionist** *n, adj*

religiose (rɪ'lɪdʒɪˌəʊs) *adj* affectedly or extremely pious; sanctimoniously religious > **re'ligiˌosely** *adv* > **religiosity** (rɪˌlɪdʒɪ'ɒsɪtɪ) *n*

religious (rɪ'lɪdʒəs) *adj* 1 of, relating to, or concerned with religion 2a pious; devout; godly 2b *(as collective n; preceded by the)*: *the religious* 3 appropriate to or in accordance with the principles of a religion 4 scrupulous, exact, or conscientious 5 *Christianity* of or relating to a way of life dedicated to religion and defined by a monastic rule ▷ *n* 6 *Christianity* a monk or nun > **re'ligiously** *adv* > **re'ligiousness** *n*

Religious Society of Friends *n* the official name for the Quakers

relinquish (rɪ'lɪŋkwɪʃ) *vb (tr)* 1 to give up (a task, struggle, etc); abandon 2 to surrender or renounce (a claim, right, etc) 3 to release; let go [C15 from F *relinquir*, from L *relinquere*, from RE- + *linquere* to leave] > **re'linquisher** *n* > **re'linquishment** *n*

reliquary ('rɛlɪkwərɪ) *n, pl* **reliquaries** a receptacle or repository for relics, esp relics of saints [C17 from OF *reliquaire*, from *relique* RELIC]

relique (rə'li:k, 'rɛlɪk) *n* an archaic spelling of **relic**

reliquiae (rɪ'lɪkwɪˌi:) *pl n* fossil remains of animals or plants [C19 from L: remains]

relish ('rɛlɪʃ) *vb (tr)* 1 to savour or enjoy (an experience) to the full 2 to anticipate eagerly; look forward to 3 to enjoy the taste or flavour of (food, etc); savour ▷ *n* 4 liking or enjoyment, as of something eaten or experienced (esp in **with relish**) 5 pleasurable anticipation: *he didn't have much relish for the idea* 6 an appetizing or spicy food added to a main dish to enhance its flavour 7 an appetizing taste or flavour 8 a zestful trace or touch: *there was a certain relish in all his writing* [C16 from earlier *reles* aftertaste, from OF, from *relaisser* to leave behind; see RELEASE] > **'relishable** *adj*

relive (ri:'lɪv) *vb* **relives, reliving, relived** *(tr)* to experience (a sensation, event, etc) again, esp in the imagination > **re'livable** *adj*

rellies ('rɛlɪz) *pl n Austral and NZ inf* relatives or relations

relocate (ˌri:ləʊ'keɪt) *vb* **relocates, relocating, relocated** to move or be moved to a new place, esp (of an employee, a business, etc) to a new area or place of employment > **ˌrelo'cation** *n*

reluctance (rɪ'lʌktəns) *or* **reluctancy** *n* 1 lack of eagerness or willingness; disinclination 2 *physics* a measure of the resistance of a closed magnetic circuit to a magnetic flux [C16 from L *reluctārī* to resist, from RE- + *luctārī* to struggle]

reluctant (rɪ'lʌktənt) *adj* not eager; unwilling; disinclined: *a reluctant hero; reluctant to leave* [C17 from L *reluctārī* to resist] > **re'luctantly** *adv*

reluctivity (ˌrɛlʌk'tɪvɪtɪ) *n, pl* **reluctivities** *physics* a specific or relative reluctance of a magnetic material [C19 from obs. *reluct* to struggle + -ivity]

rely (rɪ'laɪ) *vb* **relies, relying, relied** *(intr; foll by on or upon)* 1 to be dependent (on): *he relies on his charm* 2 to have trust or confidence (in): *you can rely on us* [C14 from OF *relier* to fasten together, from L *religāre*, from RE- + *ligāre* to tie]

REM *abbrev for* rapid eye movement

remain (rɪ'meɪn) *vb (mainly intr)* 1 to stay behind or in the same place: *to remain at home* 2 *(copula)* to continue to be: *to remain cheerful* 3 to be left, as after use, the passage of time, etc 4 to be left to be done, said, etc: *it remains to be pointed out* [C14 from OF *remanoir*, from L *remanēre*, from RE- + *manēre* to stay]

remainder (rɪ'meɪndə) *n* 1 a part or portion that is left, as after use, subtraction, expenditure, the passage of time, etc: *the remainder of the milk* 2 *maths* 2a the amount left over when one quantity cannot be exactly divided by another: *for 10 ÷ 3, the remainder is 1* 2b another name for **difference** (sense 7) 3 *property law* a future interest in property; an interest in a particular estate that will pass to one at some future date, as on the death of the current possessor 4 a number of copies of a book left unsold when demand ceases, which are sold at a reduced price ▷ *vb* 5 *(tr)* to sell (copies of a book) as a remainder

remains (rɪ'meɪnz) *pl n* 1 any pieces, fragments, etc, that are left unused or still extant, as after use, consumption, the passage of time: *archaeological remains* 2 the body of a dead person; corpse 3 Also called: **literary remains** the unpublished writings of an author at the time of his or her death

remake *n* ('ri:ˌmeɪk) 1 something that is made again, esp a new version of an old film 2 the act of making again ▷ *vb* (ri:'meɪk), **remakes, remaking, remade** 3 *(tr)* to make again or anew

remand (rɪ'mɑ:nd) *vb (tr)* 1 *law* (of a court or magistrate) to send (a prisoner or accused person) back into custody 2 to send back ▷ *n* 3 the sending of a prisoner or accused person back into custody to await trial 4 the act of remanding or state of being remanded 5 **on remand** in custody or on bail awaiting trial [C15 from Med. L *remandāre* to send back word, from L RE- + *mandāre* to command]

remand centre *n* (in Britain) an institution to which accused persons are sent for detention while awaiting appearance before a court

remanence ('rɛmənəns) *n physics* the ability of a material to retain magnetization after the removal of the magnetizing field [C17 from L *remanēre* to stay behind]

remark (rɪ'mɑ:k) *vb* 1 (when *intr*, often foll by *on* or *upon*; when *tr*, *may take a clause as object*) to pass a casual comment (about); reflect in informal speech or writing 2 *(tr; may take a clause as object)* to perceive; observe; notice ▷ *n* 3 a brief casually expressed thought or opinion 4 notice, comment, or observation: *the event passed without remark* 5 a variant of **remarque** [C17 from OF *remarquer* to observe, from RE- + *marquer* to note, MARK[1]] > **re'marker** *n*

remarkable (rɪ'mɑ:kəb[ə]l) *adj* 1 worthy of note or attention: *a remarkable achievement* 2 unusual, striking, or extraordinary: *a remarkable sight* > **re'markableness** *n* > **re'markably** *adv*

remarque (rɪ'mɑ:k) *n* a mark in the margin of an engraved plate to indicate the stage of production [C19 from F; see REMARK]

Remarque (rɪ'mɑ:k) *n* **Erich Maria** ('e:rɪç ma'ri:a) 1898–1970, US novelist, born in Germany, noted for his novel of World War I, *All Quiet on the Western Front* (1929)

remaster (ri:'mɑ:stə) *vb (tr)* to make a new master audio recording, now usually digital, from (an earlier original recording), in order to produce compact discs or stereo

Rr

records with improved sound reproduction

Rembrandt ('rɛmbrænt) *n* full name *Rembrandt Harmensz* (or *Harmenszoon*) *van Rijn* (or *van Ryn*). 1606–69, Dutch painter, noted for his handling of shade and light, esp in his portraits

REME ('ri:mɪ) *n acronym for* Royal Electrical and Mechanical Engineers

remedial (rɪ'mi:dɪəl) *adj* **1** affording a remedy; curative **2** denoting or relating to special teaching for backward and slow learners: *remedial education* > **re'medially** *adv*

remediation (rɪ,mi:dɪ'eɪʃən) *n* the action of remedying something, esp the reversal or stopping of damage to the environment

remedy ('rɛmɪdɪ) *n, pl* **remedies 1** (usually foll by *for* or *against*) any drug or agent that cures a disease or controls its symptoms **2** (usually foll by *for* or *against*) anything that serves to cure defects, improve conditions, etc: *a remedy for industrial disputes* **3** the legally permitted variation from the standard weight or quality of coins ▷ *vb* (*tr*) **4** to relieve or cure (a disease, etc) by a remedy **5** to put to rights (a fault, error, etc); correct [C13 from Anglo-Norman *remedie*, from L *remedium* a cure, from *remedērī*, from RE- + *medērī* to heal] > **remediable** (rɪ'mi:dɪəbᵊl) *adj* > **re'mediably** *adv* > **'remediless** *adj*

remember (rɪ'mɛmbə) *vb* **1** to become aware of (something forgotten) again; bring back to one's consciousness **2** to retain (an idea, intention, etc) in one's conscious mind: *remember to do one's shopping* **3** (*tr*) to give money, etc, to (someone), as in a will or in tipping **4** (*tr;* foll by *to*) to mention (a person's name) to another person, as by way of greeting: *remember me to your mother* **5** (*tr*) to mention (a person) favourably, as in prayer **6** (*tr*) to commemorate (a person, event, etc): *to remember the dead of the wars* **7 remember oneself** to recover one's good manners after a lapse [C14 from OF *remembrer*, from LL *rememorārī* to recall to mind, from L RE- + *memor* mindful] > **re'memberer** *n*

remembrance (rɪ'mɛmbrəns) *n* **1** the act of remembering or state of being remembered **2** something that is remembered; reminiscence **3** a memento or keepsake **4** the extent in time of one's power of recollection **5** the act of honouring some past event, person, etc

Remembrance Day *n* **1** (in Britain) another name for **Remembrance Sunday 2** (in Canada) a statutory holiday observed on November 11 in memory of the dead of both World Wars

remembrancer (rɪ'mɛmbrənsə) *n* **1** *arch* a reminder, memento, or keepsake **2** (*usually cap*) (in Britain) any of several officials of the Exchequer, esp one (**Queen's** *or* **King's Remembrancer**) whose duties include collecting debts due to the Crown **3** (*usually cap*) an official (**City Remembrancer**) appointed by the Corporation of the City of London to represent its interests to Parliament

Remembrance Sunday *n* (in Britain) the Sunday closest to November 11, on which the dead of both World Wars are commemorated. Also called: **Remembrance Day**

remex ('ri:mɛks) *n, pl* **remiges** ('rɛmɪ,dʒi:z) any of the large flight feathers of a bird's wing [C18 from L: rower, from *rēmus* oar] > **remigial** (rɪ'mɪdʒɪəl) *adj*

remind (rɪ'maɪnd) *vb* (*tr;* usually foll by *of; may take a clause as object or an infinitive*) to cause (a person) to remember (something or to do something); put (a person) in mind (of something): *remind me to phone home; flowers remind me of holidays* > **re'minder** *n*

remindful (rɪ'maɪndfʊl) *adj* **1** serving to remind **2** (*postpositive*) mindful

reminisce (,rɛmɪ'nɪs) *vb* **reminisces, reminiscing, reminisced** (*intr*) to talk or write about old times, past experiences, etc

reminiscence (,rɛmɪ'nɪsəns) *n* **1** the act of recalling or narrating past experiences **2** (*often pl*) some past experience, event, etc, that is recalled **3** an event, phenomenon, or experience that reminds one of something else **4** *philosophy* the doctrine that the mind has seen the universal forms of all things in a previous disembodied existence

reminiscent (,rɛmɪ'nɪsᵊnt) *adj* **1** (*postpositive;* foll by *of*) stimulating memories (of) or comparisons (with) **2** characterized by reminiscence **3** (of a person) given to reminiscing [C18 from L *reminiscī* to call to mind, from RE- + *mēns* mind] > ,**remi'niscently** *adv*

remise (rɪ'maɪz) *vb* **remises, remising, remised 1** (*tr*) *law* to give up or relinquish (a right, claim, etc) **2** (*intr*) *fencing* to make a remise ▷ *n* **3** *fencing* a second thrust made on the same lunge after the first has missed **4** *obs* a coach house [C17 from F *remettre* to put back, from L *remittere*, from RE- + *mittere* to send]

remiss (rɪ'mɪs) *adj* (*postpositive*) **1** lacking in care or attention to duty; negligent **2** lacking in energy [C15 from L *remissus*, from *remittere*, from RE- + *mittere* to send] > **re'missly** *adv* > **re'missness** *n*

remissible (rɪ'mɪsɪbᵊl) *adj* able to be remitted [C16 from L *remissibilis;* see REMIT] > **re,missi'bility** *n*

remission (rɪ'mɪʃən) *or* (*less commonly*) **remittal** (rɪ'mɪtᵊl) *n* **1** the act of remitting or state of being remitted **2** a reduction of the term of a sentence of imprisonment, as for good conduct **3** forgiveness for sin **4** discharge or release from penalty, obligation, etc **5** lessening of intensity; abatement, as in the symptoms of a disease **6** *rare* the act of sending a remittance > **re'missive** *adj* > **re'missively** *adv*

remit *vb* (rɪ'mɪt), **remits, remitting, remitted** (*mainly tr*) **1** (*also intr*) to send (payment, etc), as for goods or service, esp by post **2** *law* (esp of an appeal court) to send back (a case) to an inferior court for further consideration **3** to cancel or refrain from exacting (a penalty or punishment) **4** (*also intr*) to relax (pace, intensity, etc) or (of pace) to slacken or abate **5** to postpone; defer **6** *arch* to pardon or forgive (crime, sins, etc) ▷ *n* ('ri:mɪt, rɪ'mɪt) **7** area of authority (of a committee, etc) **8** *law* the transfer of a case from one court or jurisdiction to another **9** the act of remitting [C14 from L *remittere*, from RE- + *mittere* to send] > **re'mittable** *adj* > **re'mitter** *n*

remittance (rɪ'mɪtəns) *n* **1** payment for goods or services received or as an allowance, esp when sent by post **2** the act of remitting

remittance man *n* a man living abroad on money sent from home, esp in the days of the British Empire

remittent (rɪ'mɪtᵊnt) *adj* (of the symptoms of a disease) characterized by periods of diminished severity > **re'mittence** *n* > **re'mittently** *adv*

remix *vb* (ri:'mɪks) **1** to change the balance and separation of (a recording) ▷ *n* ('ri:,mɪks) **2** a remixed version of a recording

remnant ('rɛmnənt) *n* **1** (*often pl*) a part left over after use, processing, etc **2** a surviving trace or vestige: *a remnant of imperialism* **3** a piece of material from the end of a roll ▷ *adj* **4** remaining; left over [C14 from OF *remenant* remaining, from *remanoir* to REMAIN]

remonetize *or* **remonetise** (ri:'mʌnɪ,taɪz) *vb* **remonetizes, remonetizing, remonetized** *or* **remonetises, remonetising, remonetised** (*tr*) to reinstate as legal tender: *to remonetize silver* > **re,moneti'zation** *or* **re,moneti'sation** *n*

remonstrance (rɪ'mɒnstrəns) *n* **1** the act of remonstrating **2** a protest or reproof, esp a petition protesting against something

remonstrant (rɪ'mɒnstrənt) *n* **1** a person who remonstrates, esp one who signs a remonstrance ▷ *adj* **2** *rare* remonstrating

remonstrate ('rɛmən,streɪt) *vb* **remonstrates, remonstrating, remonstrated** (*intr*) (usually foll by *with, against*, etc) to argue in protest or objection: *to remonstrate with the government* [C16 from Med. L *remonstrāre* to point out (errors, etc), from L RE- + *monstrāre* to show] > ˌ**remonˈstration** *n* > **remonstrative** (rɪˈmɒnstrətɪv) *adj* > ˈ**remonˌstrator** *n*

remontant (rɪˈmɒntənt) *adj* **1** (esp of roses) flowering more than once in a single season ▹ *n* **2** a rose having such a growth [c19 from F: coming up again, from *remonter*]

remora (ˈrɛmərə) *n* a marine spiny-finned fish which has a flattened elongated body and attaches itself to larger fish, rocks, etc, by a sucking disc on the top of the head [c16 from L, from RE- + *mora* delay; from its alleged habit of delaying ships]

remorse (rɪˈmɔːs) *n* **1** a sense of deep regret and guilt for some misdeed **2** compunction; pity; compassion [c14 from Med. L *remorsus* a gnawing, from L *remordēre*, from RE- + *mordēre* to bite] > **reˈmorseful** *adj* > **reˈmorsefully** *adv* > **reˈmorsefulness** *n* > **reˈmorseless** *adj*

remote (rɪˈməʊt) *adj* **1** located far away; distant **2** far from society or civilization; out-of-the-way **3** distant in time **4** distantly related or connected: *a remote cousin* **5** slight or faint (esp in **not the remotest idea**) **6** (of a person's manner) aloof or abstracted **7** operated from a distance; remote-controlled: *a remote monitor* [c15 from L *remōtus* far removed, from *removēre*, from RE- + *movēre* to move] > **reˈmotely** *adv* > **reˈmoteness** *n*

remote access *n computing* access to a computer from a physically separate terminal

remote control *n* control of a system or activity from a distance, usually by radio, ultrasonic, or electrical signals > **reˌmote-conˈtrolled** *adj*

remote sensor *n* any instrument, such as a radar device or camera, that scans the earth or another planet from space in order to collect data about some aspect of it > **remote sensing** *adj, n*

rémoulade (ˌrɛməˈleɪd) *n* a mayonnaise sauce flavoured with herbs, mustard, and capers, served with salads, cold meat, etc [c19 from F, from dialect *ramolas* horseradish, from L *armoracea*]

remould *vb* (ˌriːˈməʊld). (*tr*) **1** to mould again **2** to bond a new tread onto the casing of (a worn pneumatic tyre) ▹ *n* (ˈriːˌməʊld) **3** a tyre made by this process

remount *vb* (riːˈmaʊnt) **1** to get on (a horse, bicycle, etc) again **2** (*tr*) to mount (a picture, jewel, exhibit, etc) again ▹ *n* (ˈriːˌmaʊnt) **3** a fresh horse

removal (rɪˈmuːvᵊl) *n* **1** the act of removing or state of being removed **2a** a change of residence **2b** (*as modifier*): *a removal company* **3** dismissal from office

removalist (rɪˈmuːvəlɪst) *n Austral* a person or company that transports household effects to a new home

remove (rɪˈmuːv) *vb* **removes, removing, removed** (*mainly tr*) **1** to take away and place elsewhere **2** to dismiss (someone) from office **3** to do away with; abolish; get rid of **4** *euphemistic* to assassinate; kill **5** (*intr*) *formal* to change the location of one's home or place of business ▹ *n* **6** the act of removing, esp (formal) a removal of one's residence or place of work **7** the degree of difference: *only one remove from madness* **8** *Brit* (in certain schools) a class or form [c14 from OF *removoir*, from L *removēre*; see MOVE] > **reˈmovable** *adj* > **reˌmovaˈbility** *n* > **reˈmover** *n*

removed (rɪˈmuːvd) *adj* **1** separated by distance or abstract distinction **2** (*postpositive*) separated by a degree of descent or kinship: *the child of a person's first cousin is his first cousin once removed*

Remscheid (*German* ˈrɛmʃait) *n* an industrial city in W Germany, in North Rhine-Westphalia. Pop: 119 500 (1999 est)

remunerate (rɪˈmjuːnəˌreɪt) *vb* **remunerates, remunerating, remunerated** (*tr*) to reward or pay for work, service, etc [c16 from L *remūnerārī* to reward, from RE- + *mūnerāre* to give, from *mūnus* a gift] > **reˈmunerable** *adj* > **reˈmunerative** *adj* > **reˈmuneratively** *adv* > **reˈmunerˌator** *n*

remuneration (rɪˌmjuːnəˈreɪʃən) *n* **1** the act of remunerating **2** pay; recompense

Remus (ˈriːməs) *n Roman myth* the brother of Romulus

renaissance (rəˈneɪsəns, ˈrɛnəˌsɑːns) *or* **renascence** *n* a revival or rebirth, esp of culture and learning [c19 from F, from L RE- + *nascī* to be born]

Renaissance (rəˈneɪsəns, ˈrɛnəˌsɑːns) *n* **1** **the** the great revival of art, literature, and learning in Europe in the 14th, 15th, and 16th centuries **2** the spirit, culture, art, science, and thought of this period ▹ *adj* **3** of, characteristic of, or relating to the Renaissance, its culture, etc

▹ www.learner.org/exhibits/renaissance

▹ www.ibiblio.org/wm/paint/glo/renaissance

renal (ˈriːnᵊl) *adj* of, relating to, resembling, or situated near the kidney [c17 from F, from LL *rēnālis*, from L *rēnēs* kidneys, from ?]

renal pelvis *n* a small funnel-shaped cavity of the kidney into which urine is discharged before passing into the ureter

Renan (*French* ranɑ̃) *n* (**Joseph**) **Ernest** (ernest) 1823–92, French philosopher, theologian, and historian; best known for his *Life of Jesus* (1863), which discounted the supernatural aspects of the Gospels

renascent (rɪˈnæsᵊnt, -ˈneɪ-) *adj* becoming active or vigorous again; reviving: *renascent nationalism* [c18 from L *renascī* to be born again]

rencounter (rɛnˈkaʊntə) *arch* ▹ *n also* **rencontre** (rɛnˈkɒntə) **1** an unexpected meeting **2** a hostile clash, as of two armies, adversaries, etc; skirmish ▹ *vb* **3** to meet (someone) unexpectedly [c16 from F *rencontre*, from *rencontrer*; as ENCOUNTER]

rend (rɛnd) *vb* **rends, rending, rent** **1** to tear with violent force or to be torn in this way; rip **2** (*tr*) to tear or pull (one's clothes, etc), esp as a manifestation of rage or grief **3** (*tr*) (of a noise or cry) to disturb (the silence) with a shrill or piercing tone [OE *rendan*] > ˈ**rendible** *adj*

Rendell (ˈrɛndᵊl, rɛnˈdɛl) *n* **Ruth** (**Barbara**), Baroness born 1930, British crime writer: author of detective novels, such as *Wolf to the Slaughter* (1967), and psychological thrillers, such as *The Lake of Darkness* (1980) and (under the name **Barbara Vine**) *A Fatal Inversion* (1987) and *The Chimney Sweeper's Boy* (1998)

render (ˈrɛndə) *vb* (*tr*) **1** to present or submit (accounts, etc) for payment, etc **2** to give or provide (aid, charity, a service, etc) **3** to show (obedience), as expected **4** to give or exchange, as by way of return or requital: *to render blow for blow* **5** to cause to become: *grief had rendered him simple-minded* **6** to deliver (a verdict or opinion) formally **7** to portray or depict (something), as in painting, music, or acting **8** to translate (something) **9** (sometimes foll by *up*) to yield or give: *the tomb rendered up its secret* **10** (often foll by *back*) to return (something); give back **11** to cover the surface of (brickwork, etc) with a coat of plaster **12** (often foll by *down*) to extract (fat) from (meat) by melting ▹ *n* **13** a first thin coat of plaster applied to a surface **14** one who or that which rends [c14 from OF *rendre*, from L *reddere* to give back (infl. by L *prendere* to grasp), from RE- + *dare* to give] > ˈ**renderable** *adj* > ˈ**renderer** *n* > ˈ**rendering** *n*

rendezvous (ˈrɒndɪˌvuː) *n, pl* **rendezvous** (-ˌvuːz) **1** a meeting or appointment to meet at a specified time and place **2** a place where people meet ▹ *vb* (*intr*) **3** to meet at a specified time or place [c16 from F, from *rendez-vous!* present yourselves! from *se rendre* to present oneself; see RENDER]

rendition (rɛnˈdɪʃən) *n* **1** a performance of a musical composition, dramatic role, etc **2** a translation **3** the act of rendering [c17 from obs. F, from LL *redditiō*; see RENDER]

renegade (ˈrɛnɪˌgeɪd) *n* **1a** a person who deserts his or her cause or faith for another; traitor **1b** (*as modifier*): *a renegade priest* **2** any outlaw or rebel [c16 from Sp. *renegado*,

Rr

ult. from L RE- + *negāre* to deny]

renege *or* **renegue** (rɪˈniːg, -ˈneɪg) *vb* **reneges, reneging, reneged** *or* **renegues, reneguing, renegued** 1 (*intr; often foll by on*) to go back (on one's promise, etc) ▷ *vb, n* 2 *cards* other words for **revoke** [C16 (in the sense: to deny, renounce): from Med. L *renegāre* to renounce] > **reˈneger** *or* **reˈneguer** *n*

renew (rɪˈnjuː) *vb* (*mainly tr*) 1 to take up again 2 (*also intr*) to begin (an activity) again; recommence 3 to restate or reaffirm (a promise, etc) 4 (*also intr*) to make (a lease, etc) valid for a further period 5 to regain or recover (vigour, strength, activity, etc) 6 to restore to a new or fresh condition 7 to replace (an old or worn-out part or piece) 8 to replenish (a supply, etc) > **reˈnewable** *adj* > **reˈnewal** *n* > **reˈnewer** *n*

renewable energy *n* another name for **alternative energy**

renewables *pl n* sources of alternative energy, such as wind and wave power

Renfrew (ˈrɛnfruː) *n* an industrial town in W central Scotland, in Renfrewshire, W of Glasgow. Pop: 20 764 (1991)

Renfrewshire (ˈrɛnfruːʃɪə, -ʃə) *n* 1 a council area of W central Scotland, on the River Clyde W of Glasgow: corresponds to part of the historical county of Renfrewshire; part of Strathclyde region from 1975 to 1996: agricultural and residential, with clothing and manufacturing industries in Paisley. Administrative centre: Paisley. Pop: 172 867 (2001 est). Area: 261 sq km (101 sq miles) 2 a former county of W central Scotland, on the Firth of Clyde: became part of Strathclyde region in 1975; now covered by the council areas of Renfrewshire, East Renfrewshire, and Inverclyde

reni- *combining form* kidney or kidneys: *reniform* [from L *rēnēs*]

Reni (*Italian* ˈrɛːni) *n* **Guido** (ˈgwiːdo) 1575–1642, Italian baroque painter and engraver

reniform (ˈrɛnɪˌfɔːm) *adj* having the shape or profile of a kidney: *a reniform leaf*

renin (ˈriːnɪn) *n* a proteolytic enzyme secreted by the kidneys, which plays an important part in the maintenance of blood pressure [C20 from RENI- + -IN]

Rennes (*French* rɛn) *n* a city in NW France: the ancient capital of Brittany. Pop: 206 229 (1999)

rennet (ˈrɛnɪt) *n* 1 the membrane lining the fourth stomach of a young calf 2 a substance prepared esp from the stomachs of calves and used for curdling milk in making cheese [C15 rel. to OE *gerinnan* to curdle, RUN]

rennin (ˈrɛnɪn) *n* an enzyme that occurs in gastric juice and is an active constituent of rennet. It coagulates milk [C20 from RENNET + -IN]

Reno (ˈriːnəʊ) *n* a city in W Nevada, at the foot of the Sierra Nevada: noted as a divorce, wedding, and gambling centre by reason of its liberal laws. Pop: 180 480 (2000)

Renoir (ˈrɛnwɑː; *French* rənwar) *n* 1 **Jean** (ʒɑ̃) 1894–1979, French film director: his films include *La grande illusion* (1937), *La règle du jeu* (1939), and *Diary of a Chambermaid* (1945) 2 his father, **Pierre Auguste** (pjɛr ogyst) 1841–1919, French painter. One of the initiators of impressionism, he broke away from the movement with his later paintings, esp his many nude studies, which are more formal compositions

renounce (rɪˈnaʊns) *vb* **renounces, renouncing, renounced** 1 (*tr*) to give up formally (a claim or right): *to renounce a title* 2 (*tr*) to repudiate: *to renounce Christianity* 3 (*tr*) to give up (some habit, etc) voluntarily: *to renounce one's old ways* 4 (*intr*) *cards* to fail to follow suit because one has no more cards of the suit led ▷ *n* 5 *cards* a failure to follow suit [C14 from OF *renoncer*, from L *renuntiāre*, from RE- + *nuntiāre* to announce, from *nuntius* messenger] > **reˈnouncement** *n* > **reˈnouncer** *n*

renovate (ˈrɛnəˌveɪt) *vb* **renovates, renovating, renovated** (*tr*) 1 to restore (something) to good condition 2 to revive or refresh (one's spirits, health, etc) [C16 from L *renovāre*, from RE- + *novāre* to make new] > ˌ**renoˈvation** *n* > ˈ**renoˌvative** *adj* > ˈ**renoˌvator** *n*

renown (rɪˈnaʊn) *n* widespread reputation, esp of a good kind; fame [C14 from Anglo-Norman *renoun*, from OF *renom*, from *renomer* to celebrate, from RE- + *nomer* to name, from L *nōmināre*]

renowned (rɪˈnaʊnd) *adj* having a widespread, esp good, reputation; famous

rent[1] (rɛnt) *n* 1 a payment made periodically by a tenant to a landlord or owner for the occupation or use of land, buildings, etc 2 *econ* the return derived from the cultivation of land in excess of production costs 3 **for rent** *chiefly US & Canad* available for use and occupation subject to the payment of rent ▷ *vb* 4 (*tr*) to grant (a person) the right to use one's property in return for periodic payments 5 (*tr*) to occupy or use (property) in return for periodic payments 6 (*intr; often foll by at*) to be let or rented (for a specified rental) [C12 from OF *rente* revenue, from Vulgar L *rendere* (unattested) to yield; see RENDER] > ˈ**rentable** *adj* > ˈ**renter** *n*

rent[2] (rɛnt) *n* 1 a slit or opening made by tearing or rending 2 a breach or division ▷ *vb* 3 the past tense and past participle of **rend**

rent-a- *prefix* 1 denoting a rental service 2 *derog or facetious* denoting a person or group that performs a function as if hired from a rental service: *rent-a-mob*

rental (ˈrɛntᵊl) *n* 1a the amount paid by a tenant as rent 1b an income derived from rents received 2 property available for renting ▷ *adj* 3 of or relating to rent

rent boy *n* a young male prostitute

rent control *n* regulation by law of the rent a landlord can charge for domestic accommodation and of his right to evict tenants

rent-free *adj, adv* without payment of rent

rentier *French* (rɑ̃tje) *n* a person whose income consists primarily of fixed unearned amounts, such as rent or interest [from *rente*; see RENT[1]]

rent-roll *n* 1 a register of lands and buildings owned by a person, company, etc, showing the rent due from each tenant 2 the total income arising from rented property

renunciation (rɪˌnʌnsɪˈeɪʃən) *n* 1 the act or an instance of renouncing 2 a formal declaration renouncing something 3 *stock exchange* the surrender to another of the rights to buy new shares in a rights issue [C14 from L *renunciātiō* a declaration, from *renuntiāre* to report] > **reˈnunciative** *or* **reˈnunciatory** *adj*

reo (ˈriːəʊ) *n* NZ a language [Maori]

rep[1] *or* **repp** (rɛp) *n* a silk, wool, rayon, or cotton fabric with a transversely corded surface [C19 from F *reps*, ?from E *ribs*] > **repped** *adj*

rep[2] (rɛp) *n theatre* short for **repertory company**

rep[3] (rɛp) *n* 1 short for **representative** (sense 2) 2 *NZ inf* a rugby player selected to represent his district

rep[4] (rɛp) *n US inf* short for **reputation**

Rep. *abbrev for:* 1 *US* Representative 2 Republic 3 *US* Republican

repair[1] (rɪˈpɛə) *vb* (*tr*) 1 to restore (something damaged or broken) to good condition or working order 2 to heal (a breach or division) in (something): *to repair a broken marriage* 3 to make amends for (a mistake, injury, etc) ▷ *n* 4 the act, task, or process of repairing 5 a part that has been repaired 6 state or condition: *in good repair* [C14 from OF *reparer*, from L *reparāre*, from RE- + *parāre* to make ready] > **reˈpairable** *adj* > **reˈpairer** *n*

repair[2] (rɪˈpɛə) *vb* (*intr*) 1 (usually foll by *to*) to go (to a place) 2 (usually foll by *to*) to have recourse (to) for help, etc: *to repair to one's lawyer* ▷ *n* 3 a haunt or resort [C14 from OF *repairier*, from LL *repatriāre* to return to one's native land, from L RE- + *patria* fatherland]

repairman (rɪˈpɛəˌmæn) *n, pl* **repairmen** a man whose job it is to repair machines, etc

repand (rɪˈpænd) *adj bot* having a wavy margin: *a repand leaf* [C18 from L *repandus* bent backwards, from RE- + *pandus* curved] > **reˈpandly** *adv*

reparable (ˈrɛpərəbᵊl, ˈrɛprə-) *adj* able to be repaired, recovered, or remedied [C16 from L *reparābilis*, from *reparāre* to REPAIR[1]] > **ˈreparably** *adv*

reparation (ˌrɛpəˈreɪʃən) *n* **1** the act or process of making amends **2** (*usually pl*) compensation exacted as an indemnity from a defeated nation by the victors **3** the act or process of repairing or state of having been repaired [C14 *reparacioun*, ult. from L *reparāre* to REPAIR[1]] > **reparative** (rɪˈpærətɪv) *or* **reˈparatory** *adj*

repartee (ˌrɛpɑːˈtiː) *n* **1** a sharp, witty, or aphoristic remark made as a reply **2** skill in making sharp witty replies [C17 from F *repartie*, from *repartir* to retort, from RE- + *partir* to go away]

repast (rɪˈpɑːst) *n* a meal or the food provided at a meal: *a light repast* [C14 from OF, from *repaistre* to feed, from LL *repāscere*, from L RE- + *pāscere* to feed, pasture (of animals)]

repatriate *vb* (riːˈpætrɪˌeɪt), **repatriates, repatriating, repatriated** (*tr*) **1** to send back (a refugee, prisoner of war, etc) to the country of his birth or citizenship **2** to send back (a sum of money previously invested abroad) to its country of origin ▷ *n* (riːˈpætrɪɪt) **3** a person who has been repatriated [C17 from LL *repatriāre*, from L RE- + *patria* fatherland] > **reˌpatriˈation** *n*

repay (rɪˈpeɪ) *vb* **repays, repaying, repaid 1** to pay back (money, etc) to (a person); refund or reimburse **2** to make a return for (something): *to repay kindness* > **reˈpayable** *adj* > **reˈpayment** *n*

repeal (rɪˈpiːl) *vb* (*tr*) **1** to annul or rescind officially; revoke: *these laws were repealed* ▷ *n* **2** an instance or the process of repealing; annulment [C14 from OF *repeler*, from RE- + *apeler* to call, APPEAL] > **reˈpealable** *adj* > **reˈpealer** *n*

repeat (rɪˈpiːt) *vb* **1** (when *tr, may take a clause as object*) to do or experience (something) again once or several times, esp to say or write (something) again **2** (*intr*) to occur more than once: *the last figure repeats* **3** (*tr; may take a clause as object*) to reproduce (the words, sounds, etc) uttered by someone else; echo **4** (*tr*) to utter (a poem, etc) from memory; recite **5** (*intr*) (of food) to be tasted again after ingestion as the result of belching **6** (*tr; may take a clause as object*) to tell to another person (the secrets imparted to one by someone else) **7** (*intr*) (of a clock) to strike the hour or quarter-hour just past **8** (*intr*) *US* to vote (illegally) more than once in a single election **9 repeat oneself** to say or do the same thing more than once, esp so as to be tedious ▷ *n* **10a** the act or an instance of repeating **10b** (*as modifier*): *a repeat performance* **11** a word, action, etc, that is repeated **12** an order made out for goods, etc, that duplicates a previous order **13** *radio, television* a broadcast of a programme which has been broadcast before **14** *music* a passage that is an exact restatement of the passage preceding it [C14 from OF *repeter*, from L *repetere*, from RE- + *petere* to seek] > **reˈpeatable** *adj*

USAGE Since *again* is part of the meaning of *repeat*, it is better in writing not to say that something is *repeated again*

repeated (rɪˈpiːtɪd) *adj* done, made, or said again and again; continual > **reˈpeatedly** *adv*

repeater (rɪˈpiːtə) *n* **1** a person or thing that repeats **2** Also called: **repeating firearm** a firearm capable of discharging several shots without reloading **3** a timepiece that strikes the hour or quarter-hour just past, when a spring is pressed **4** a device that amplifies incoming electrical signals and retransmits them

repeating decimal *n* another name for **recurring decimal**

repechage (ˌrɛpɪˈʃɑːʒ) *n* a heat of a competition, esp in rowing or fencing, in which eliminated contestants have another chance to qualify for the next round or the final [C19 from F *repêchage*, lit.: fishing out again, from RE- + *pêcher* to fish + -AGE]

repel (rɪˈpɛl) *vb* **repels, repelling, repelled** (*mainly tr*) **1** to force or drive back (something or somebody) **2** (*also intr*) to produce a feeling of aversion or distaste in (someone or something); be disgusting (to) **3** to be effective in keeping away, controlling, or resisting: *a spray that repels flies* **4** to have no affinity for; fail to mix with or absorb: *water and oil repel each other* **5** to disdain to accept (something); turn away from or spurn: *she repelled his advances* [C15 from L *repellere*, from RE- + *pellere* to push] > **reˈpeller** *n* > **reˈpellingly** *adv*

USAGE See at **repulse**

repellent (rɪˈpɛlənt) *adj* **1** distasteful or repulsive **2** driving or forcing away or back; repelling ▷ *n also* **repellant 3** something, esp a chemical substance, that repels: *insect repellent* **4** a substance with which fabrics are treated to increase their resistance to water > **reˈpellence** *or* **reˈpellency** *n* > **reˈpellently** *adv*

repent[1] (rɪˈpɛnt) *vb* to feel remorse (for); be contrite (about); show penitence (for) [C13 from OF *repentir*, from RE- + *pentir*, from L *paenitēre* to repent] > **reˈpenter** *n*

repent[2] (ˈriːpᵊnt) *adj bot* lying or creeping along the ground: *repent stems* [C17 from L *rēpere* to creep]

repentance (rɪˈpɛntəns) *n* **1** remorse or contrition for one's past actions **2** an act or the process of being repentant; penitence > **reˈpentant** *adj*

repercussion (ˌriːpəˈkʌʃən) *n* **1** (*often pl*) a result or consequence of an action or event: *the repercussions of the war are still felt* **2** a recoil after impact; a rebound **3** a reflection, esp of sound; echo or reverberation [C16 from L *repercussiō*, from *repercutere* to strike back] > **ˌreperˈcussive** *adj*

repertoire (ˈrɛpəˌtwɑː) *n* **1** all the works collectively that a company, actor, etc, is competent to perform **2** the entire stock of things available in a field or of a kind **3 in repertoire** denoting the performance of two or more plays, etc, by the same company in the same venue on different evenings over a period of time: *"Tosca" returns to Leeds next month in repertoire with "Wozzeck"* [C19 from F, from LL *repertōrium* inventory; see REPERTORY]

repertory (ˈrɛpətərɪ, -trɪ) *n, pl* **repertories 1** the entire stock of things available in a field or of a kind; repertoire **2** a place where a stock of things is kept; repository **3** short for **repertory company** [C16 from LL *repertōrium* storehouse, from L *reperīre* to obtain, from RE- + *parere* to bring forth] > **repertorial** (ˌrɛpəˈtɔːrɪəl) *adj*

repertory company *n* a theatrical company that performs plays from a repertoire. US name: **stock company**

repetend (ˈrɛpɪˌtɛnd) *n* **1** *maths* the digit in a recurring decimal that repeats itself **2** anything repeated [C18 from L *repetendum* what is to be repeated, from *repetere* to REPEAT]

répétiteur *French* (repetitœr) *n* a member of an opera company who coaches the singers

repetition (ˌrɛpɪˈtɪʃən) *n* **1** the act or an instance of repeating; reiteration **2** a thing, word, action, etc, that is repeated **3** a replica or copy > **repetitive** (rɪˈpɛtɪtɪv) *adj*

repetitious (ˌrɛpɪˈtɪʃəs) *adj* characterized by unnecessary repetition > **ˌrepeˈtitiously** *adv* > **ˌrepeˈtitiousness** *n*

repetitive strain *or* **stress injury** *n* a condition, characterized by arm or wrist pains, that can affect musicians, computer operators, etc, who habitually perform awkward hand movements. Abbrev: **RSI**

repine (rɪˈpaɪn) *vb* **repines, repining, repined** (*intr*) to be fretful or low-spirited through discontent [C16 from RE- + PINE[2]]

replace (rɪˈpleɪs) *vb* **replaces, replacing, replaced** (*tr*) **1** to take the place of; supersede **2** to substitute a person or thing for (another which has ceased to fulfil its function); put in place of: *to replace an old pair of shoes* **3** to

Rr

restore to its rightful place > **re'placeable** *adj* > **re'placer** *n*
replacement (rɪ'pleɪsmənt) *n* **1** the act or process of replacing **2** a person or thing that replaces another
replay *n* ('riː,pleɪ) **1** Also called: **action replay** a showing again of a sequence of action in slow motion immediately after it happens **2** a second match between a pair or group of contestants ▷ *vb* (riː'pleɪ) **3** to play again (a record, sporting contest, etc)
replenish (rɪ'plɛnɪʃ) *vb* (*tr*) **1** to make full or complete again by supplying what has been used up **2** to put fresh fuel on (a fire) [C14 from OF *replenir*, from RE- + *plenir*, from L *plēnus* full] > **re'plenisher** *n* > **re'plenishment** *n*
replete (rɪ'pliːt) *adj* (*usually postpositive*) **1** (often foll by *with*) copiously supplied (with); abounding (in) **2** having one's appetite completely or excessively satisfied; gorged; satiated [C14 from L *replētus*, from *replēre*, from RE- + *plēre* to fill] > **re'pletely** *adv* > **re'pleteness** *n* > **re'pletion** *n*
replevin (rɪ'plɛvɪn) *law* ▷ *n* **1** the recovery of goods unlawfully taken, made subject to establishing the validity of the recovery in a legal action and returning the goods if the decision is adverse **2** (formerly) a writ of replevin ▷ *vb* **3** another word for **replevy** [C15 from Anglo-F, from OF *replevir* to give security for, from RE- + *plevir* to PLEDGE]
replevy (rɪ'plɛvɪ) *law* ▷ *vb* **replevies, replevying, replevied** (*tr*) **1** to recover possession of (goods) by replevin ▷ *n, pl* **replevies 2** another word for **replevin** [C15 from OF *replevir*; *see* REPLEVIN] > **re'pleviable** *or* **re'plevisable** *adj*
replica ('rɛplɪkə) *n* an exact copy or reproduction, esp on a smaller scale [C19 from It., lit.: a reply, from *replicare*, from L: to bend back, repeat]
replicate *vb* ('rɛplɪ,keɪt), **replicates, replicating, replicated** (*mainly tr*) **1** (*also intr*) to make or be a copy (of); reproduce **2** to fold (something) over on itself; bend back ▷ *adj* ('rɛplɪkɪt) **3** folded back on itself: *a replicate leaf* [C19 from L *replicātus* bent back; see REPLICA] > **,repli'cation** *n* > **'replicative** *adj*
reply (rɪ'plaɪ) *vb* **replies, replying, replied** (*mainly intr*) **1** to make answer (to) in words or writing or by an action; respond **2** (*tr; takes a clause as object*) to say (something) in answer: *he replied that he didn't want to come* **3** *law* to answer a defendant's plea **4** to return (a sound); echo ▷ *n, pl* **replies 5** an answer; response **6** the answer made by a plaintiff or petitioner to a defendant's case [C14 from OF *replier* to fold again, reply, from L *replicāre*, from RE- + *plicāre* to fold] > **re'plier** *n*
repo ('riːpəʊ) *n inf* short for: **1** repurchase agreement **2a** repossession of property **2b** (*as modifier*): *a repo car*
repoint (,riː'pɔɪnt) *vb* (*tr*) to repair the joints of (brickwork, masonry, etc) with mortar or cement
report (rɪ'pɔːt) *n* **1** an account prepared after investigation and published or broadcast **2** a statement made widely known; rumour: *according to report, he is not dead* **3** an account of the deliberations of a committee, body, etc: *a report of parliamentary proceedings* **4** *Brit* a statement on the progress of each schoolchild **5** a written account of a case decided at law **6** comment on a person's character or actions; reputation: *he is of good report here* **7** a sharp loud noise, esp one made by a gun ▷ *vb* (when *tr, may take a clause as object*; when *intr*, often foll by *on*) **8** to give an account (of); describe **9** to give an account of the results of an investigation (into): *to report on housing conditions* **10** (of a committee, legislative body, etc) to make a formal report on (a bill) **11** (*tr*) to complain about (a person), esp to a superior **12** to present (oneself) or be present at an appointed place or for a specific purpose: *report to the manager's office* **13** (*intr*) to say or show that one is (in a certain state): *to report fit* **14** (*intr*; foll by *to*) to be responsible (to) and under the authority (of) **15** (*intr*) to act as a reporter **16** *law* to take down in writing details of (the proceedings of a court of law, etc) as a record or for publication [C14 from OF, from *reporter*, from L *reportāre*, from RE- + *portāre* to carry] > **re'portable** *adj* > **re'portedly** *adv*
reportage (rɪ'pɔːtɪdʒ, ,rɛpɔː'tɑːʒ) *n* **1** the act or process of reporting news or other events of general interest **2** a journalist's style of reporting
reported speech *n* another term for **indirect speech**
reporter (rɪ'pɔːtə) *n* **1** a person who reports, esp one employed to gather news for a newspaper or broadcasting organization **2** a person authorized to report the proceedings of a legislature
report stage *n* the stage preceding the third reading in the passage of a bill through Parliament
repose[1] (rɪ'pəʊz) *n* **1** a state of quiet restfulness; peace or tranquillity **2** dignified calmness of manner; composure ▷ *vb* **reposes, reposing, reposed 3** to lie or lay down at rest **4** (*intr*) to lie when dead, as in the grave **5** (*intr*; foll by *on*, *in*, etc) *formal* to be based (on): *your plan reposes on a fallacy* [C15 from OF *reposer*, from LL *repausāre*, from RE- + *pausāre* to stop] > **re'posal** *n* > **re'poser** *n* > **re'poseful** *adj* > **re'posefully** *adv*
repose[2] (rɪ'pəʊz) *vb* **reposes, reposing, reposed** (*tr*) **1** to put (trust) in a person or thing **2** to place or put (an object) somewhere [C15 from L *repōnere* to store up, from RE- + *pōnere* to put] > **re'posal** *n*
reposition (,riːpə'zɪʃən) *n* **1** the act or process of depositing or storing ▷ *vb* (*tr*) **2** to place in a new position **3** to target (a product or brand) at a new market by changing its image
repository (rɪ'pɒzɪtərɪ, -trɪ) *n, pl* **repositories 1** a place or container in which things can be stored for safety **2** a place where things are kept for exhibition; museum **3** a place of burial; sepulchre **4** a person to whom a secret is entrusted; confidant [C15 from L *repositōrium*, from *repōnere* to place]
repossess (,riːpə'zɛs) *vb* (*tr*) to take back possession of (property), esp for nonpayment of money due under a hire-purchase agreement > **repossession** (,riːpə'zɛʃən) *n* > **,repos'sessor** *n*
repoussé (rə'puːseɪ) *adj* **1** raised in relief, as a design on a thin piece of metal hammered through from the underside ▷ *n* **2** a design or surface made in this way [C19 from F, from *repousser*, from RE- + *pousser* to PUSH]
repp (rɛp) *n* a variant spelling of **rep**[1]
reprehend (,rɛprɪ'hɛnd) *vb* (*tr*) to find fault with; criticize [C14 from L *reprehendere* to hold fast, rebuke, from RE- + *prendere* to grasp] > **,repre'hender** *n* > **,repre'hension** *n*
reprehensible (,rɛprɪ'hɛnsɪbᵊl) *adj* open to criticism or rebuke; blameworthy [C14 from LL *reprehensibilis*, from L *reprehendere*; see REPREHEND] > **,repre,hensi'bility** *n* > **,repre'hensibly** *adv*
represent (,rɛprɪ'zɛnt) *vb* (*tr*) **1** to stand as an equivalent of; correspond to **2** to act as a substitute or proxy (for) **3** to act as or be the authorized delegate or agent for (a person, country, etc): *an MP represents his constituency* **4** to serve or use as a means of expressing: *letters represent the sounds of speech* **5** to exhibit the characteristics of; exemplify; typify: *romanticism in music is represented by Beethoven* **6** to present an image of through the medium of a picture or sculpture; portray **7** to bring clearly before the mind **8** to set forth in words; state or explain **9** to describe as having a specified character or quality: *he represented her as a saint* **10** to act out the part of on stage; portray [C14 from L *repraesentāre* to exhibit, from RE- + *praesentāre* to PRESENT[2]] > **,repre'sentable** *adj* > **,repre,senta'bility** *n*
re-present (,riːprɪ'zɛnt) *vb* (*tr*) to present again > **re-presentation** (,riː,prɛzən'teɪʃən) *n*
representation (,rɛprɪzɛn'teɪʃən) *n* **1** the act or an instance of representing or the state of being represented **2** anything that represents, such as a

verbal or pictorial portrait **3** anything that is represented, such as an image brought clearly to mind **4** the principle by which delegates act for a constituency **5** a body of representatives **6** an instance of acting for another in a particular capacity, such as executor **7** a dramatic production or performance **8** (*often pl*) a statement of facts, true or alleged, esp one set forth by way of remonstrance or expostulation

representational (ˌrɛprɪzɛnˈteɪʃənᵊl) *adj* **1** *art* depicting objects, scenes, etc, directly as seen; naturalistic **2** of or relating to representation

representationalism (ˌrɛprɪzɛnˈteɪʃənəˌlɪzəm) *or* **representationism** *n* **1** *philosophy* the doctrine that in perceptions of objects what is before the mind is not the object but a representation of it ▷ Cf **presentationism** **2** *art* the practice of depicting objects, scenes, etc, directly as seen > ˌ**represenˌtationalˈistic** *adj* > ˌ**represenˈtationist** *n, adj*

representative (ˌrɛprɪˈzɛntətɪv) *n* **1** a person or thing that represents another **2** a person who represents and tries to sell the products or services of a firm **3** a typical example **4** a person representing a constituency in a deliberative, legislative, or executive body, esp (*cap*) a member of the **House of Representatives** (the lower house of Congress) ▷ *adj* **5** serving to represent; symbolic **6a** exemplifying a class or kind; typical **6b** containing or including examples of all the interests, types, etc, in a group **7** acting as deputy or proxy for another **8** representing a constituency or the whole people in the process of government: *a representative council* **9** of or relating to the political representation of the people: *representative government* **10** of or relating to a mental picture or representation > ˌ**repreˈsentatively** *adv* > ˌ**repreˈsentativeness** *n*

repress (rɪˈprɛs) *vb* (*tr*) **1** to keep (feelings, etc) under control; suppress or restrain **2** to put into a state of subjugation: *to repress a people* **3** *psychol* to banish (unpleasant thoughts) from one's conscious mind [C14 from L *reprimere* to press back, from RE- + *premere* to PRESS[1]] > **reˈpressed** *adj* > **reˈpresser** *or* **reˈpressor** *n* > **reˈpressible** *adj* > **reˈpression** *n* > **reˈpressive** *adj*

reprieve (rɪˈpriːv) *vb* **reprieves, reprieving, reprieved** (*tr*) **1** to postpone or remit the punishment of (a person, esp one condemned to death) **2** to give temporary relief to (a person or thing), esp from otherwise irrevocable harm ▷ *n* **3** a postponement or remission of punishment **4** a warrant granting a postponement **5** a temporary relief from pain or harm; respite [C16 from OF *repris* (something) taken back, from *reprendre*, from L *reprehendere*; ?also infl. by obs. E *repreve* to reprove] > **reˈprievable** *adj* > **reˈpriever** *n*

reprimand (ˈrɛprɪˌmɑːnd) *n* **1** a reproof or formal admonition; rebuke ▷ *vb* **2** (*tr*) to admonish or rebuke, esp formally [C17 from F *réprimande*, from L *reprimenda* (things) to be repressed; see REPRESS] > ˌ**repriˈmanding** *adj*

reprint *n* (ˈriːˌprɪnt) **1** a reproduction in print of any matter already published **2** a reissue of a printed work using the same type, plates, etc, as the original ▷ *vb* (riːˈprɪnt) **3** (*tr*) to print again > **reˈprinter** *n*

reprisal (rɪˈpraɪzᵊl) *n* **1** the act or an instance of retaliation in any form **2** (*often pl*) retaliatory action against an enemy in wartime **3** (formerly) the forcible seizure of the property or subjects of one nation by another [C15 from OF *reprisaille*, from OIt., from *riprendere* to recapture, from L *reprehendere*; see REPREHEND]

reprise (rɪˈpriːz) *music* ▷ *n* **1** the repeating of an earlier theme ▷ *vb* **reprises, reprising, reprised** **2** to repeat (an earlier theme) [C14 from OF, from *reprendre* to take back, from L *reprehendere*; see REPREHEND]

repro (ˈriːprəʊ) *n, pl* **repros** **1** short for **reproduction** (sense 2): *repro furniture* **2** short for **reproduction proof**

reproach (rɪˈprəʊtʃ) *vb* (*tr*) **1** to impute blame to (a person) for an action or fault; rebuke ▷ *n* **2** the act of reproaching **3** rebuke or censure; reproof **4** disgrace or shame: *to bring reproach upon one's family* **5** **above** *or* **beyond reproach** perfect; beyond criticism [C15 from OF *reprochier*, from L RE- + *prope* near] > **reˈproachable** *adj* > **reˈproacher** *n* > **reˈproachingly** *adv*

reproachful (rɪˈprəʊtʃfʊl) *adj* full of or expressing reproach > **reˈproachfully** *adv* > **reˈproachfulness** *n*

reprobate (ˈrɛprəʊˌbeɪt) *adj* **1** morally unprincipled; depraved **2** *Christianity* condemned to eternal punishment in hell ▷ *n* **3** an unprincipled, depraved, or damned person **4** a disreputable or roguish person ▷ *vb* **reprobates, reprobating, reprobated** (*tr*) **5** to disapprove of; condemn **6** (of God) to condemn to eternal punishment in hell [C16 from LL *reprobātus* held in disfavour, from L RE- + *probāre* to test, APPROVE] > **reprobacy** (ˈrɛprəbəsɪ) *n* > ˈ**reproˌbater** *n* > ˌ**reproˈbation** *n*

reprocess (riːˈprəʊsɛs) *vb* (*tr*) to treat again (something already made and used) in order to make it reusable in some form > **reˈprocessing** *n, adj*

reproduce (ˌriːprəˈdjuːs) *vb* **reproduces, reproducing, reproduced** (*mainly tr*) **1** to make a copy, representation, or imitation of; duplicate **2** (*also intr*) *biol* to undergo or cause to undergo a process of reproduction **3** to produce again; bring back into existence again; re-create **4** (*intr*) to come out (well, badly, etc) when copied > ˌ**reproˈducer** *n* > ˌ**reproˈducible** *adj* > ˌ**reproˈducibly** *adv* > ˌ**reproˌduciˈbility** *n*

reproduction (ˌriːprəˈdʌkʃən) *n* **1** *biol* any of various processes, either sexual or asexual, by which an animal or plant produces one or more individuals similar to itself **2a** an imitation or facsimile of a work of art **2b** (*as modifier*): *a reproduction portrait* **3** the quality of sound from an audio system **4** the act or process of reproducing

reproduction proof *n printing* a proof of very good quality used for photographic reproduction to make a printing plate

reproductive (ˌriːprəˈdʌktɪv) *adj* of, relating to, characteristic of, or taking part in reproduction > ˌ**reproˈductively** *adv* > ˌ**reproˈductiveness** *n*

reprography (rɪˈprɒgrəfɪ) *n* the art or process of copying, reprinting, or reproducing printed material > **reprographic** (ˌrɛprəˈgræfɪk) *adj* > ˌ**reproˈgraphically** *adv*

reproof (rɪˈpruːf) *n* an act or expression of rebuke or censure. Also: **reproval** (rɪˈpruːvᵊl) [C14 *reproffe*, from OF *reprove*, from LL *reprobāre* to disapprove of; see REPROBATE]

re-proof (riːˈpruːf) *vb* (*tr*) **1** to treat (a coat, jacket, etc) so as to renew its texture, waterproof qualities, etc **2** to provide a new proof of (a book, galley, etc)

reprove (rɪˈpruːv) *vb* **reproves, reproving, reproved** (*tr*) to rebuke or scold [C14 from OF *reprover*, from LL *reprobāre*, from L RE- + *probāre* to examine] > **reˈprovable** *adj* > **reˈprover** *n* > **reˈprovingly** *adv*

reptant (ˈrɛptənt) *adj biol* creeping, crawling, or lying along the ground [C17 from L *reptāre* to creep]

reptile (ˈrɛptaɪl) *n* **1** any of the cold-blooded vertebrates characterized by lungs, an outer covering of horny scales or plates, and young produced in eggs, such as the tortoises, turtles, snakes, lizards, and crocodiles **2** a grovelling insignificant person: *you miserable little reptile!* ▷ *adj* **3** creeping, crawling, or squirming [C14 from LL *reptilis* creeping, from L *rēpere* to crawl] > **reptilian** (rɛpˈtɪlɪən) *n, adj*

Repton (ˈrɛptᵊn) *n* **Humphry** 1752–1818, English landscape gardener

republic (rɪˈpʌblɪk) *n* **1** a form of government in which the people or their elected representatives possess the supreme power **2** a political or national unit possessing such a form of government **3** a constitutional form in which the head of state is an elected or nominated president [C17 from F *république*, from L *rēspublica*, lit.: the

Rr

public thing, from *rēs* thing + *publica* PUBLIC]

republican (rɪˈpʌblɪkən) *adj* **1** of, resembling, or relating to a republic **2** supporting or advocating a republic ▷ *n* **3** a supporter or advocate of a republic

Republican (rɪˈpʌblɪkən) *adj* **1** of, belonging to, or relating to a Republican Party **2** of, belonging to, or relating to the Irish Republican Army ▷ *n* **3** a member or supporter of a Republican Party **4** a member or supporter of the Irish Republican Army

republicanism (rɪˈpʌblɪkəˌnɪzəm) *n* **1** the principles or theory of republican government **2** support for a republic **3** (*often cap*) support for a Republican Party

Republican Party *n* **1** one of the two major political parties in the US: established around 1854 **2** any of a number of political parties in other countries, usually so named to indicate their opposition to monarchy

Republic of Ireland *n* See **Ireland**[1] (sense 2)

repudiate (rɪˈpjuːdɪˌeɪt) *vb* **repudiates, repudiating, repudiated** (*tr*) **1** to reject the authority or validity of; refuse to accept or ratify **2** to refuse to acknowledge or pay (a debt) **3** to cast off or disown (a son, lover, etc) [C16 from L *repudiāre* to put away, from *repudium* separation, divorce, from RE- + *pudēre* to be ashamed] > **reˈpudiable** *adj* > **reˌpudiˈation** *n* > **reˈpudiative** *adj* > **reˈpudiˌator** *n*

repugnant (rɪˈpʌgnənt) *adj* **1** repellent to the senses; causing aversion **2** distasteful; offensive; disgusting **3** contradictory; inconsistent or incompatible [C14 from L *repugnāns* resisting, from *repugnāre*, from RE- + *pugnāre* to fight] > **reˈpugnance** *n* > **reˈpugnantly** *adv*

repulse (rɪˈpʌls) *vb* **repulses, repulsing, repulsed** (*tr*) **1** to drive back or ward off (an attacking force); repel; rebuff **2** to reject with coldness or discourtesy: *she repulsed his advances* ▷ *n* **3** the act or an instance of driving back or warding off; rebuff **4** a cold discourteous rejection or refusal [C16 from L *repellere* to drive back] > **reˈpulser** *n*

USAGE Some people think that the use of *repulse* in sentences such as *he was repulsed by what he saw* is incorrect and that the correct word is *repel*

repulsion (rɪˈpʌlʃən) *n* **1** a feeling of disgust or aversion **2** *physics* a force separating two objects, such as the force between two like electric charges

repulsive (rɪˈpʌlsɪv) *adj* **1** causing or occasioning repugnance; loathsome; disgusting or distasteful **2** tending to repel, esp by coldness and discourtesy **3** *physics* concerned with, producing, or being a repulsion > **reˈpulsively** *adv* > **reˈpulsiveness** *n*

repurchase (riːˈpɜːtʃɪs) *vb* **1** (*tr*) to buy back or buy again (goods, securities, assets, etc) ▷ *n* **2** an act or instance of repurchasing

reputable (ˈrɛpjʊtəbᵊl) *adj* **1** having a good reputation; honoured, trustworthy, or respectable **2** (of words) acceptable as good usage; standard > **ˈreputably** *adv*

reputation (ˌrɛpjʊˈteɪʃən) *n* **1** the estimation in which a person or thing is generally held; opinion **2** a high opinion generally held about a person or thing; esteem **3** notoriety or fame, esp for some specified characteristic [C14 from L *reputātiō*, from *reputāre* to calculate; see REPUTE]

repute (rɪˈpjuːt) *vb* **reputes, reputing, reputed** **1** (*tr*; *usually passive*) to consider (a person or thing) to be as specified: *he is reputed to be rich* ▷ *n* **2** public estimation; reputation: *a writer of little repute* [C15 from OF *reputer*, from L *reputāre*, from RE- + *putāre* to think]

reputed (rɪˈpjuːtɪd) *adj* (*prenominal*) generally reckoned or considered; supposed: *the reputed writer of two epic poems* > **reˈputedly** *adv*

request (rɪˈkwɛst) *vb* (*tr*) **1** to express a desire for, esp politely; ask for or demand: *to request a bottle of wine* ▷ *n* **2** the act or an instance of requesting, esp in the form of a written statement, etc; petition or solicitation **3 by request** in accordance with someone's desire **4 in request** in demand; popular: *he is in request all over the world* **5 on request** on the occasion of a demand or request: *application forms are available on request* [C14 from OF *requeste*, from Vulgar L *requaerere*; see REQUIRE, QUEST] > **reˈquester** *n*

request stop *n* a point on a route at which a bus, etc, will stop only if signalled to do so. US equivalent: **flag stop**

Requiem (ˈrɛkwɪəm) *n* **1** *RC Church* a Mass celebrated for the dead **2** a musical setting of this Mass **3** any piece of music composed or performed as a memorial to a dead person [C14 from L *requiēs* rest, from the introit, *Requiem aeternam dona eis* Rest eternal grant unto them]

requiem shark *n* any of a family of sharks occurring mostly in tropical seas and characterized by a nictitating membrane

requiescat (ˌrɛkwɪˈɛskæt) *n* a prayer for the repose of the souls of the dead [L, from *requiescat in pace* may he rest in peace]

require (rɪˈkwaɪə) *vb* **requires, requiring, required** (*mainly tr*; *may take a clause as object or an infinitive*) **1** to have need of; depend upon; want **2** to impose as a necessity; make necessary: *this work requires precision* **3** (*also intr*) to make formal request (for); insist upon **4** to call upon or oblige (a person) authoritatively; order or command: *to require someone to account for his actions* [C14 from OF *requerre*, via Vulgar L from L *requīrere* to seek to know; also infl. by *quaerere* to seek] > **reˈquirer** *n*

USAGE The use of *require to* as in *I require to see the manager* or *you require to complete a special form* is thought by many people to be incorrect: *I need to see the manager; you are required to complete a special form*

requirement (rɪˈkwaɪəmənt) *n* **1** something demanded or imposed as an obligation **2** a thing desired or needed **3** the act or an instance of requiring

requisite (ˈrɛkwɪzɪt) *adj* **1** absolutely essential; indispensable ▷ *n* **2** something indispensable; necessity [C15 from L *requīsītus* sought after, from *requīrere* to seek for] > **ˈrequisitely** *adv*

requisition (ˌrɛkwɪˈzɪʃən) *n* **1** a request or demand, esp an authoritative or formal one **2** an official form on which such a demand is made **3** the act of taking something over, esp temporarily for military or public use ▷ *vb* (*tr*) **4** to demand and take for use, esp by military or public authority **5** (*may take an infinitive*) to require (someone) formally to do (something): *to requisition a soldier to drive an officer's car* > **ˌrequiˈsitionary** *adj* > **ˌrequiˈsitionist** *n*

requite (rɪˈkwaɪt) *vb* **requites, requiting, requited** (*tr*) to make return to (a person for a kindness or injury); repay with a similar action [C16 RE- + obs. *quite* to discharge, repay; see QUIT] > **reˈquitable** *adj* > **reˈquital** *n* > **reˈquitement** *n* > **reˈquiter** *n*

reredos (ˈrɪədɒs) *n* **1** a screen or wall decoration at the back of an altar **2** another word for **fireback** [C14 from OF *areredos*, from *arere* behind + *dos* back, from L *dorsum*]

rerun *vb* (riːˈrʌn), **reruns, rerunning, reran, rerun** (*tr*) **1** to broadcast or put on (a film, etc) again **2** to run (a race, etc) again ▷ *n* (ˈriːˌrʌn) **3** a film, etc, that is broadcast again; repeat **4** a race that is run again **5** *computing* the repeat of a part of a computer program

res (reɪs) *n, pl* **res** *Latin* a thing, matter, or object

res. *abbrev for:* **1** residence **2** resides **3** resigned **4** resolution

resale price maintenance (ˈriːseɪl) *n* the practice by which a manufacturer establishes a fixed or minimum price for the resale of a brand product by retailers or other distributors. US equivalent: **fair trade** Abbrev: **rpm**

reschedule (riːˈʃɛdjuːl; *also, esp US* -ˈskɛdʒʊəl) *vb* (*tr*) **1** to change the time, date, or schedule of **2** to arrange a revised schedule for repayment of (a debt)

rescind (rɪˈsɪnd) *vb* (*tr*) to annul or repeal [C17 from L *rēscindere* to cut off, from *re-* (intensive) + *scindere* to cut]

> **re'scindable** *adj* > **re'scinder** *n* > **re'scindment** *n*
rescission (rɪ'sɪʒən) *n* **1** the act of rescinding **2** *law* the right to have a contract set aside if it has been entered into mistakenly, as a result of misrepresentation, undue influence, etc
rescript ('riː,skrɪpt) *n* **1** (in ancient Rome) a reply by the emperor to a question on a point of law **2** any official announcement or edict; a decree **3** something rewritten [C16 from L *rēscriptum* reply, from *rēscribere* to write back]
rescue ('rɛskjuː) *vb* **rescues, rescuing, rescued** (*tr*) **1** to bring (someone or something) out of danger, etc; deliver or save **2** to free (a person) from legal custody by force **3** *law* to seize (goods) by force ▷ *n* **4a** the act or an instance of rescuing **4b** (*as modifier*): *a rescue party* **5** the forcible removal of a person from legal custody **6** *law* the forcible seizure of goods or property [C14 *rescowen*, from OF *rescourre*, from RE- + *escourre* to pull away, from L *excutere* to shake off, from *quatere* to shake] > **'rescuer** *n*
research (rɪ'sɜːtʃ) *n* **1** systematic investigation to establish facts or collect information on a subject ▷ *vb* **2** to carry out investigations into (a subject, etc) [C16 from OF *recercher* to seek, search again, from RE- + *cercher* to SEARCH] > **re'searchable** *adj* > **re'searcher** *n*
research and development *n* a commercial company's application of scientific research to develop new products. Abbrev: **R&D**
reseat (riː'siːt) *vb* (*tr*) **1** to show (a person) to a new seat **2** to put a new seat on (a chair, etc) **3** to provide new seats for (a theatre, etc) **4** to re-form the seating of (a valve)
resect (rɪ'sɛkt) *vb* (*tr*) *surgery* to cut out part of (a bone, organ, or other structure or part) [C17 from L *resecāre*, from RE- + *secāre* to cut]
resection (rɪ'sɛkʃən) *n* **1** *surgery* excision of part of a bone, organ, or other part **2** *surveying* a method of fixing the position of a point by making angular observations to three fixed points > **re'sectional** *adj*
resemblance (rɪ'zɛmbləns) *n* **1** the state or quality of resembling; likeness or similarity **2** the degree or extent to which a likeness exists **3** semblance; likeness > **re'semblant** *adj*
resemble (rɪ'zɛmbᵊl) *vb* **resembles, resembling, resembled** (*tr*) to possess some similarity to; be like [C14 from OF *resembler*, from RE- + *sembler* to look like, from L *similis* like] > **re'sembler** *n*
resent (rɪ'zɛnt) *vb* (*tr*) to feel bitter, indignant, or aggrieved at [C17 from F *ressentir*, from RE- + *sentir* to feel, from L *sentīre* to perceive; see SENSE] > **re'sentful** *adj* > **re'sentment** *n*
reserpine ('rɛsəpɪn) *n* an insoluble alkaloid, extracted from the roots of a rauwolfia, used medicinally to lower blood pressure and as a sedative and tranquillizer [C20 from G *Reserpin*, prob. from the NL name of the plant]
reservation (,rɛzə'veɪʃən) *n* **1** the act or an instance of reserving **2** something reserved, esp accommodation or a seat **3** (*often pl*) a stated or unstated qualification of opinion that prevents one's wholehearted acceptance of a proposal, etc **4** an area of land set aside, esp (in the US) for Native American peoples **5** *Brit* the strip of land between the two carriageways of a dual carriageway **6** the act or process of keeping back, esp for oneself; withholding **7** *law* a right or interest retained by the grantor in property dealings
reserve (rɪ'zɜːv) *vb* **reserves, reserving, reserved** (*tr*) **1** to keep back or set aside, esp for future use or contingency; withhold **2** to keep for oneself; retain: *I reserve the right to question these men later* **3** to obtain or secure by advance arrangement: *I have reserved two tickets for tonight's show* **4** to delay delivery of (a judgment) ▷ *n* **5a** something kept back or set aside, esp for future use or contingency **5b** (*as modifier*): *a reserve stock* **6** the state or condition of being reserved: *I have plenty in reserve* **7** a tract of land set aside for a special purpose: *a nature reserve* **8** *Austral & NZ* a public park **9** the usual Canadian name for **reservation** (sense 4) **10** *sport* a substitute **11** (*often pl*) **11a** a part of an army not committed to immediate action in a military engagement **11b** that part of a nation's armed services not in active service **12** coolness or formality of manner; restraint, silence, or reticence **13** (*often pl*) *finance* liquid assets or a portion of capital not invested or a portion of profits not distributed by a bank or business enterprise and held to meet future liabilities or contingencies **14 without reserve** without reservations; fully [C14 from OF *reserver*, from L *reservāre*, from RE- + *servāre* to keep] > **re'servable** *adj* > **re'server** *n*
re-serve (riː'sɜːv) *vb* **re-serves, re-serving, re-served** (*tr*) to serve again
reserve bank *n* one of the twelve banks forming part of the US Federal Reserve System
reserve currency *n* foreign currency that is acceptable as a medium of international payments and is held in reserve by many countries
reserved (rɪ'zɜːvd) *adj* **1** set aside for use by a particular person **2** cool or formal in manner; restrained or reticent **3** destined; fated: *a man reserved for greatness* **4** *Brit* denoting matters that are the responsibility of the national parliament rather than a devolved assembly: *defence is a reserved issue* > **reservedly** (rɪ'zɜːvɪdlɪ) *adv* > **re'servedness** *n*
reserved list *n Brit* a list of retired naval, army, or air-force officers available for recall to active service in an emergency
reserved occupation *n Brit* an occupation from which one will not be called up for military service in time of war
reserve-grade *adj Austral* denoting a sporting team of the second rank in a club
reserve price *n Brit* the minimum price acceptable to the owner of property being auctioned or sold. Also called (esp Scot and US): **upset price**
reserve tranche *n* the quota of 25 per cent to which a member of the IMF has unconditional access. Prior to 1978 it was paid in gold and known as the **gold tranche**
reservist (rɪ'zɜːvɪst) *n* one who serves in the reserve formations of a nation's armed forces
reservoir ('rɛzə,vwɑː) *n* **1** a natural or artificial lake or large tank used for collecting and storing water for community use **2** *biol* a cavity in an organism containing fluid **3** a place where a great stock of anything is accumulated **4** a large supply of something: *a reservoir of talent* [C17 from F *réservoir*, from *réserver* to RESERVE]
reservoir rock *n* porous and permeable rock containing producible oil or gas in its pore spaces
reset[1] *vb* (riː'sɛt), **resets, resetting, reset** (*tr*) **1** to set again (a broken bone, matter in type, a gemstone, etc) **2** to restore (a gauge, etc) to zero ▷ *n* ('riː,sɛt) **3** the act or an instance of setting again **4** a thing that is set again > **re'setter** *n*
reset[2] *Scot* ▷ *vb* (riː'sɛt), **resets, resetting, reset 1** to receive or handle goods knowing they have been stolen ▷ *n* ('riːsɛt) **2** the receiving of stolen goods [C14 from OF *receter*, from L *receptāre*, from *recipere* to receive] > **re'setter** *n*
res gestae ('dʒɛstiː) *pl n* **1** things done or accomplished; achievements **2** *law* incidental facts and circumstances that are admissible in evidence because they explain the matter at issue [L]
Resht (rɛʃt) *n* a variant of **Rasht**
reside (rɪ'zaɪd) *vb* **resides, residing, resided** (*intr*) *formal* **1** to live permanently (in a place); have one's home (in): *he resides in London* **2** (of things, qualities, etc) to be inherently present (in); be vested (in): *political power resides in military strength* [C15 from L *residēre* to sit back, from RE- + *sedēre* to sit] > **re'sider** *n*

Rr

residence (ˈrɛzɪdəns) *n* **1** the place in which one resides; abode or home **2** a large imposing house; mansion **3** the fact of residing in a place or a period of residing **4 in residence 4a** actually resident: *the Queen is in residence* **4b** designating a creative artist resident and active for a set period at a college, gallery, etc: *writer in residence*

residency (ˈrɛzɪdənsɪ) *n, pl* **residencies 1** a variant of **residence 2** a regular series of concerts by a band or singer at one venue **3** *US & Canad* the period, following internship, during which a physician undergoes specialized training **4** (in India, formerly) the official house of the governor general at the court of a native prince

resident (ˈrɛzɪdənt) *n* **1** a person who resides in a place **2** (esp formerly) a representative of the British government in a British protectorate **3** (in India, formerly) a representative of the British governor general at the court of a native prince **4** a bird or animal that does not migrate **5** *Brit & NZ* a junior doctor, esp a house officer, who lives in the hospital in which he or she works **6** *US & Canad* a physician who lives in the hospital while undergoing specialist training after completing his or her internship ▷ *adj* **7** living in a place; residing **8** living or staying at a place in order to discharge a duty, etc **9** (of qualities, etc) existing or inherent (in) **10** (of birds and animals) not in the habit of migrating > ˈ**residentship** *n*

residential (ˌrɛzɪˈdɛnʃəl) *adj* **1** suitable for or allocated for residence: *a residential area* **2** relating to residence > ˌ**resiˈdentially** *adv*

residential school *n* (in Canada) a boarding school maintained by the Canadian government for Native American and Inuit children from sparsely populated settlements

residentiary (ˌrɛzɪˈdɛnʃərɪ) *adj* **1** residing in a place, esp officially **2** obliged to reside in an official residence: *a residentiary benefice* ▷ *n, pl* **residentiaries 3** a member of the clergy obliged to reside in the place of his or her official appointment

residual (rɪˈzɪdjʊəl) *adj* **1** of, relating to, or designating a residue or remainder; remaining; leftover **2** *US* of or relating to the payment of residuals ▷ *n* **3** something left over as a residue; remainder **4** *statistics* **4a** the difference between the mean of a set of observations and one particular observation **4b** the difference between the numerical value of one particular observation and the theoretical result **5** (*often pl*) payment made to an actor, musician, etc, for subsequent use of film in which the person appears > **reˈsidually** *adv*

residual unemployment *n* the unemployment that remains in periods of full employment, as a result of those mentally, physically, or emotionally unfit to work

residuary (rɪˈzɪdjʊərɪ) *adj* **1** of, relating to, or constituting a residue; residual **2** *law* entitled to the residue of an estate after payment of debts and distribution of specific gifts

residue (ˈrɛzɪˌdjuː) *n* **1** matter remaining after something has been removed **2** *law* what is left of an estate after the discharge of debts and distribution of specific gifts [C14 from OF *residu*, from L *residuus* remaining over, from *residēre* to stay behind]

residuum (rɪˈzɪdjʊəm) *n, pl* **residua** (-jʊə) a more formal word for **residue**

resign (rɪˈzaɪn) *vb* **1** (when *intr*, often foll by *from*) to give up tenure of (a job, office, etc) **2** (*tr*) to reconcile (oneself) to; yield: *to resign oneself to death* **3** (*tr*) to give up (a right, claim, etc); relinquish [C14 from OF *resigner*, from L *resignāre* to unseal, destroy, from RE- + *signāre* to seal] > **reˈsigner** *n*

re-sign (riːˈsaɪn) *vb* to sign again

resignation (ˌrɛzɪgˈneɪʃən) *n* **1** the act of resigning **2** a formal document stating one's intention to resign **3** a submissive unresisting attitude; passive acquiescence

resigned (rɪˈzaɪnd) *adj* characteristic of or proceeding from an attitude of resignation; acquiescent or submissive > **resignedly** (rɪˈzaɪnɪdlɪ) *adv* > **reˈsignedness** *n*

resile (rɪˈzaɪl) *vb* **resiles, resiling, resiled** (*intr*) to spring or shrink back; recoil or resume original shape [C16 from OF *resilir*, from L *resilīre* to jump back, from RE- + *salīre* to jump] > **reˈsilement** *n*

resilient (rɪˈzɪlɪənt) *adj* **1** (of an object) capable of regaining its original shape or position after bending, stretching, or other deformation; elastic **2** (of a person) recovering easily and quickly from illness, hardship, etc > **reˈsilience** *or* **reˈsiliency** *n* > **reˈsiliently** *adv*

resin (ˈrɛzɪn) *n* **1** any of a group of solid or semisolid amorphous compounds that are obtained directly from certain plants as exudations **2** any of a large number of synthetic, usually organic, materials that have a polymeric structure, esp such a substance in a raw state before it is moulded or treated with plasticizer, etc ▷ *vb* **3** (*tr*) to treat or coat with resin [C14 from OF *resine*, from L *rēsīna*, from Gk *rhētinē* resin from a pine] > ˈ**resinous** *adj* > ˈ**resinously** *adv* > ˈ**resinousness** *n*

resinate (ˈrɛzɪˌneɪt) *vb* **resinates, resinating, resinated** (*tr*) to impregnate with resin

resipiscence (ˌrɛsɪˈpɪsəns) *n* *literary* acknowledgment that one has been mistaken [C16 from LL *resipiscentia*, from *resipiscere* to recover one's senses, from L *sapere* to know] > ˌ**resiˈpiscent** *adj*

resist (rɪˈzɪst) *vb* **1** to stand firm (against); not yield (to); fight (against) **2** (*tr*) to withstand the deleterious action of; be proof against: *to resist corrosion* **3** (*tr*) to oppose; refuse to accept or comply with: *to resist arrest* **4** (*tr*) to refrain from, esp in spite of temptation (esp in **cannot resist (something)**) ▷ *n* **5** a substance used to protect something, esp a coating that prevents corrosion [C14 from L *resistere*, from RE- + *sistere* to stand firm] > **reˈsister** *n* > **reˈsistible** *adj* > **reˌsistiˈbility** *n* > **reˈsistibly** *adv* > **reˈsistless** *adj*

resistance (rɪˈzɪstəns) *n* **1** the act or an instance of resisting **2** the capacity to withstand something, esp the body's natural capacity to withstand disease **3a** the opposition to a flow of electric current through a circuit component, medium, or substance. It is measured in ohms. Symbol: R **3b** (*as modifier*): *a resistance thermometer* **4** any force that tends to retard or oppose motion: *air resistance; wind resistance* **5 line of least resistance** the easiest, but not necessarily the best or most honourable, course of action **6** See **passive resistance** > **reˈsistant** *adj, n*

Resistance (rɪˈzɪstəns) *n* **the** an illegal organization fighting for national liberty in a country under enemy occupation

resistance thermometer *n* an accurate type of thermometer in which temperature is calculated from the resistance of a coil of wire or of a semiconductor placed at the point at which the temperature is to be measured

Resistencia (*Spanish* rɛsisˈtenθja) *n* a city in NE Argentina, on the Paraná River. Pop: 280 000 (1999 est)

resistivity (ˌriːzɪsˈtɪvɪtɪ) *n* **1** the electrical property of a material that determines the resistance of a piece of given dimensions. It is measured in ohms. Former name: **specific resistance 2** the power or capacity to resist; resistance

resistor (rɪˈzɪstə) *n* an electrical component designed to introduce a known value of resistance into a circuit

resit *vb* (riːˈsɪt), **resits, resitting, resat** (*tr*) **1** to sit (an examination) again ▷ *n* (ˈriːsɪt) **2** an examination which one must sit again

res judicata (ˌdʒuːdɪˈkɑːtə) *or* **res adjudicata** *n* *law* a matter already adjudicated upon that cannot be raised again [L]

Resnais (*French* rɛnɛ) *n* **Alain** (alɛ̃) born 1922, French film director, whose films include *Hiroshima mon amour* (1959), *L'Année dernière à Marienbad* (1961), *La Vie est un roman* (1983), and *On Connaît la Chanson* (1998)

resoluble (rɪ'zɒljʊbᵊl, 'rɛzəl-) *adj* another word for **resolvable**

re-soluble (riː'sɒljʊbᵊl) *adj* capable of being dissolved again > **re-'solubleness** *or* **re-,solu'bility** *n* > **re-'solubly** *adv*

resolute ('rɛzə,luːt) *adj* **1** firm in purpose or belief; steadfast **2** characterized by resolution; determined: *a resolute answer* [C16 from L *resolutus*, from *resolvere* to RESOLVE] > **'reso,lutely** *adv* > **'reso,luteness** *n*

resolution (,rɛzə'luːʃən) *n* **1** the act or an instance of resolving **2** firmness or determination **3** something resolved or determined; decision **4** a formal expression of opinion by a meeting **5** a judicial decision on some matter; verdict; judgment **6** the act of separating something into its constituent parts or elements **7** *med* subsidence of the symptoms of a disease, esp the disappearance of inflammation without pus **8** *music* the process in harmony whereby a dissonant note or chord is followed by a consonant one **9** the ability of a television or film image to reproduce fine detail **10** *physics* another word for **resolving power** > **,reso'lutioner** *or* **,reso'lutionist** *n*

resolvable (rɪ'zɒlvəbᵊl) *or* **resoluble** *adj* able to be resolved or analysed > **re,solva'bility, re,solu'bility** *or* **re'solvableness, re'solubleness** *n*

resolve (rɪ'zɒlv) *vb* **resolves, resolving, resolved** (*mainly tr*) **1** (*takes a clause as object or an infinitive*) to decide or determine firmly **2** to express (an opinion) formally, esp by a vote **3** (*also intr; usually foll by into*) to separate or cause to separate (into) (constituent parts) **4** (*usually reflexive*) to change; alter: *the ghost resolved itself into a tree* **5** to make up the mind of; cause to decide: *the tempest resolved him to stay at home* **6** to find the answer or solution to **7** to explain away or dispel: *to resolve a doubt* **8** to bring to an end; conclude: *to resolve an argument* **9** *med* to cause (an inflammation) to subside, esp without the formation of pus **10** *music* (*also intr*) to follow (a dissonant note or chord) by one producing a consonance **11** *physics* to distinguish between (separate parts) of (an image) as in a microscope, telescope, or other optical instrument ▷ *n* **12** something determined or decided; resolution: *he had made a resolve to work all day* **13** firmness of purpose; determination: *nothing can break his resolve* [C14 from L *resolvere* to unfasten, reveal, from RE- + *solvere* to loosen] > **re'solvable** *adj* > **re,solva'bility** *n* > **re'solver** *n*

resolved (rɪ'zɒlvd) *adj* fixed in purpose or intention; determined > **resolvedly** (rɪ'zɒlvɪdlɪ) *adv* > **re'solvedness** *n*

resolvent (rɪ'zɒlvənt) *adj* **1** serving to dissolve or separate something into its elements; resolving ▷ *n* **2** a drug or agent able to reduce swelling or inflammation

resolving power *n* **1** Also called: **resolution** *physics* the ability of a microscope or telescope to produce separate images of closely placed objects **2** *photog* the ability of an emulsion to show up fine detail in an image

resonance ('rɛzənəns) *n* **1** the condition or quality of being resonant **2** sound produced by a body vibrating in sympathy with a neighbouring source of sound **3** the condition of a body or system when it is subjected to a periodic disturbance of the same frequency as the natural frequency of the body or system **4** amplification of speech sounds by sympathetic vibration in the bone structure of the head and chest, resounding in the cavities of the nose, mouth, and pharynx **5** *electronics* the condition of an electrical circuit when the frequency is such that the capacitive and inductive reactances are equal in magnitude **6** *med* the sound heard when percussing a hollow bodily structure, esp the chest or abdomen **7** *chem* the phenomenon in which the electronic structure of a molecule can be represented by two or more hypothetical structures involving single, double, and triple chemical bonds **8** *physics* the condition of a system in which there is a sharp maximum probability for the absorption of electromagnetic radiation or capture of particles [C16 from L *resonāre* to RESOUND]

resonant ('rɛzənənt) *adj* **1** resounding or re-echoing **2** producing resonance: *resonant walls* **3** full of, or intensified by, resonance: *a resonant voice* > **'resonantly** *adv*

resonate ('rɛzə,neɪt) *vb* **resonates, resonating, resonated** **1** to resound or cause to resound; reverberate **2** *chem, electronics* to exhibit or cause to exhibit resonance **3** (*intr; foll by with*) to be understood or receive a sympathetic response: *themes which will resonate with voters* **4** (*intr; foll by with*) to be filled with: *simple words that seem to resonate with mystery and beauty* [C19 from L *resonāre*] > **,reso'nation** *n*

resonator ('rɛzə,neɪtə) *n* any body or system that displays resonance, esp a tuned electrical circuit or a conducting cavity in which microwaves are generated by a resonant current

resorb (rɪ'sɔːb) *vb* (*tr*) to absorb again [C17 from L *resorbēre*, from RE- + *sorbēre* to suck in] > **re'sorbent** *adj* > **re'sorptive** *adj*

resorcinol (rɪ'zɔːsɪ,nɒl) *n* a colourless crystalline phenol, used in making dyes, drugs, resins, and adhesives. Formula: $C_6H_4(OH)_2$ [C19 NL, from RESIN + *orcinol*, a crystalline solid] > **re'sorcinal** *adj*

resorption (rɪ'sɔːpʃən) *n* **1** the process of resorbing or the state of being resorbed **2** *geol* the partial or complete remelting of a mineral by magma, resulting from changes in temperature, pressure, or magma composition

resort (rɪ'zɔːt) *vb* (*intr*) **1** (usually foll by *to*) to have recourse (to) for help, use, etc: *to resort to violence* **2** to go, esp often or habitually: *to resort to the beach* ▷ *n* **3** a place to which many people go for recreation, etc: *a holiday resort* **4** the use of something as a means, help, or recourse **5** **last resort** the last possible course of action open to one [C14 from OF *resortir*, from RE- + *sortir* to emerge] > **re'sorter** *n*

re-sort (riː'sɔːt) *vb* (*tr*) to sort again

resound (rɪ'zaʊnd) *vb* (*intr*) **1** to ring or echo with sound; reverberate **2** to make a prolonged echoing noise: *the trumpet resounded* **3** (of sounds) to echo or ring **4** to be widely famous: *his fame resounded throughout India* [C14 from OF *resoner*, from L *resonāre* to sound again]

re-sound (riː'saʊnd) *vb* to sound or cause to sound again

resounding (rɪ'zaʊndɪŋ) *adj* **1** clear and emphatic: *a resounding vote of confidence* **2** resonant; reverberating: *a resounding slap* > **re'soundingly** *adv*

resource (rɪ'zɔːs, -'sɔːs) *n* **1** capability, ingenuity, and initiative; quick-wittedness: *a man of resource* **2** (*often pl*) a source of economic wealth, esp of a country or business enterprise **3** a supply or source of aid or support; something resorted to in time of need **4** a means of doing something; expedient [C17 from OF *ressourse* relief, from *resourdre*, from L *resurgere*, from RE- + *surgere* to rise] > **re'sourceless** *adj*

resourceful (rɪ'zɔːsfʊl, -'sɔːs-) *adj* ingenious, capable, and full of initiative > **re'sourcefully** *adv* > **re'sourcefulness** *n*

respect (rɪ'spɛkt) *n* **1** an attitude of deference, admiration, or esteem; regard **2** the state of being honoured or esteemed **3** a detail, point, or characteristic: *they differ in some respects* **4** reference or relation ((esp in **in respect of, with respect to**) **5** polite or kind regard; consideration: *respect for people's feelings* **6** (*often pl*) an expression of esteem or regard (esp in **pay one's respects**) ▷ *vb* (*tr*) **7** to have an attitude of esteem towards: *to respect one's elders* **8** to pay proper attention to;

Rr

not violate: *to respect Swiss neutrality* **9** *arch* to concern or refer to [C14 from L *rēspicere* to look back, pay attention to, from RE- + *specere* to look] > **re'specter** *n*

respectable (rɪ'spɛktəbᵊl) *adj* **1** having or deserving the respect of other people; estimable; worthy **2** having good social standing or reputation **3** having socially or conventionally acceptable morals, etc: *a respectable woman* **4** relatively or fairly good; considerable: *a respectable salary* **5** fit to be seen by other people; presentable > **re,specta'bility** *n* > **re'spectably** *adv*

respectful (rɪ'spɛktfʊl) *adj* full of, showing, or giving respect > **re'spectfully** *adv* > **re'spectfulness** *n*

respecting (rɪ'spɛktɪŋ) *prep* concerning; regarding

respective (rɪ'spɛktɪv) *adj* belonging or relating separately to each of several people or things; several: *we took our respective ways home* > **re'spectiveness** *n*

respectively (rɪ'spɛktɪvlɪ) *adv* (in listing a number of items or attributes that refer to another list) separately in the order given: *he gave Janet and John a cake and a chocolate respectively*

Respighi (*Italian* res'piːgi) *n* **Ottorino** (otto'riːno) 1879–1936, Italian composer, noted esp for his suites *The Fountains of Rome* (1917) and *The Pines of Rome* (1924)

respirable ('rɛspɪrəbᵊl) *adj* **1** able to be breathed **2** suitable or fit for breathing > **,respira'bility** *n*

respiration (,rɛspɪ'reɪʃən) *n* **1** the process in living organisms of taking in oxygen from the surroundings and giving out carbon dioxide **2** the chemical breakdown of complex organic substances that takes place in the cells and tissues of animals and plants, during which energy is released and carbon dioxide produced > **respiratory** ('rɛspɪrətərɪ, -trɪ) *or* **,respi'rational** *adj*

▷ www.osrc.org

respirator ('rɛspɪ,reɪtə) *n* **1** an apparatus for providing long-term artificial respiration **2** a device worn over the mouth and nose to prevent inhalation of noxious fumes or to warm cold air before it is breathed

respiratory failure *n* a condition in which the respiratory system is unable to provide an adequate supply of oxygen or to remove carbon dioxide efficiently

respiratory quotient *n biol* the ratio of the volume of carbon dioxide expired to the volume of oxygen consumed by an organism, tissue, or cell in a given time

respiratory syncytial virus *n* a myxovirus causing infections of the nose and throat, esp in young children. It is thought to be involved in some cot deaths. Abbreviation: **RSV**

respiratory system *n* the specialized organs, collectively, concerned with external respiration: in humans and other mammals it includes the trachea, bronchi, bronchioles, lungs, and diaphragm

respire (rɪ'spaɪə) *vb* **respires, respiring, respired** **1** to inhale and exhale (air); breathe **2** (*intr*) to undergo the process of respiration [C14 from L *rēspīrāre* to exhale, from RE- + *spīrāre* to breathe]

respite ('rɛspɪt, -paɪt) *n* **1** a pause from exertion; interval of rest **2** a temporary delay **3** a temporary stay of execution; reprieve ▷ *vb* **respites, respiting, respited** **4** (*tr*) to grant a respite to; reprieve [C13 from OF *respit*, from L *respectus* a looking back; see RESPECT]

resplendent (rɪ'splɛndənt) *adj* having a brilliant or splendid appearance [C15 from L *rēsplendēre*, from RE- + *splendēre* to shine] > **re'splendence** *or* **re'splendency** *n* > **re'splendently** *adv*

respond (rɪ'spɒnd) *vb* **1** to state or utter (something) in reply **2** (*intr*) to act in reply; react: *to respond by issuing an invitation* **3** (*intr*; foll by *to*) to react favourably: *this patient will respond to treatment* **4** an archaic word for **correspond** ▷ *n* **5** *archit* a pilaster or an engaged column that supports an arch or a lintel **6** *Christianity* a choral anthem chanted in response to a lesson read [C14 from OF *respondre*, from L *rēspondēre* to return like for like, from RE- + *spondēre* to pledge] > **re'spondence** *or* **re'spondency** *n* > **re'sponder** *n*

respondent (rɪ'spɒndənt) *n* **1** *law* a person against whom a petition is brought ▷ *adj* **2** a less common word for **responsive**

response (rɪ'spɒns) *n* **1** the act of responding; reply or reaction **2** *bridge* a bid replying to a partner's bid or double **3** (*usually pl*) *Christianity* a short sentence or phrase recited or sung in reply to the officiant at a church service **4** *electronics* the ratio of the output to the input level of an electrical device **5** a glandular, muscular, or electrical reaction that arises from stimulation of the nervous system [C14 from L *rēsponsum* answer, from *rēspondēre* to RESPOND] > **re'sponseless** *adj*

responser *or* **responsor** (rɪ'spɒnsə) *n* a radio or radar receiver used to receive and display signals from a transponder

responsibility (rɪ,spɒnsɪ'bɪlɪtɪ) *n, pl* **responsibilities** **1** the state or position of being responsible **2** a person or thing for which one is responsible

responsible (rɪ'spɒnsɪbᵊl) *adj* **1** (*postpositive*; usually foll by *for*) having control or authority (over) **2** (*postpositive*; foll by *to*) being accountable for one's actions and decisions (to): *responsible to one's commanding officer* **3** (of a position, duty, etc) involving decision and accountability **4** (often foll by *for*) being the agent or cause (of some action): *responsible for a mistake* **5** able to take rational decisions without supervision; accountable for one's own actions **6** able to meet financial obligations; of sound credit [C16 from L *rēsponsus*, from *rēspondēre* to RESPOND] > **re'sponsibleness** *n* > **re'sponsibly** *adv*

responsive (rɪ'spɒnsɪv) *adj* **1** reacting or replying quickly or favourably, as to a suggestion, initiative, etc **2** (of an organism) reacting to a stimulus > **re'sponsively** *adv* > **re'sponsiveness** *n*

responsory (rɪ'spɒnsərɪ) *n, pl* **responsories** an anthem or chant recited or sung after a lesson in a church service [C15 from LL *rēsponsōrium*, from L *rēspondēre* to answer]

rest[1] (rɛst) *n* **1a** relaxation from exertion or labour **1b** (*as modifier*): *a rest period* **2** repose; sleep **3** any relief or refreshment, as from worry **4** calm; tranquillity **5** death regarded as repose: *eternal rest* **6** cessation from motion **7** **at rest** **7a** not moving **7b** calm **7c** dead **7d** asleep **8** a pause or interval **9** a mark in a musical score indicating a pause of specific duration **10** *prosody* a pause at the end of a line; caesura **11** a shelter or lodging: *a seaman's rest* **12** a thing or place on which to put something for support or to steady it **13** *billiards, snooker* any of various special poles sometimes used as supports for the cue **14** **come to rest** to slow down and stop **15** **lay to rest** to bury (a dead person) **16** **set (someone's mind) at rest** to reassure (someone) or settle (someone's mind) ▷ *vb* **17** to take or give rest, as by sleeping, lying down, etc **18** to place or position (oneself, etc) for rest or relaxation **19** (*tr*) to place or position for support or steadying: *to rest one's elbows on the table* **20** (*intr*) to be at ease; be calm **21** to cease or cause to cease from motion or exertion **22** (*intr*) to remain without further attention or action: *let the matter rest* **23** to direct (one's eyes) or (of one's eyes) to be directed: *her eyes rested on the child* **24** to depend or cause to depend; base; rely: *the whole argument rests on one crucial fact* **25** (*intr*; foll by *with, on, upon*, etc) to be a responsibility (of): *it rests with us to apportion blame* **26** *law* to finish the introduction of evidence in (a case) **27** to put pastry in a cool place to allow the gluten to contract **28** **rest on one's oars** to stop doing anything for a time [OE *ræst, reste*, of Gmc origin] > **'rester** *n*

rest[2] (rɛst) *n* (usually preceded by *the*) **1** something left or remaining; remainder: *the rest of the bacon* **2** the others: *the rest of the world* ▷ *vb* **3** (*copula*) to continue to be (as specified); remain: *rest assured* [C15 from OF *rester* to

remain, from L *rēstāre*, from RE- + *stāre* to stand]
rest area *n Austral & NZ* a motorists' stopping place, usually off a highway, equipped with tables, seats, etc
restaurant ('rɛstəˌrɒŋ, 'rɛstrɒŋ) *n* a commercial establishment where meals are prepared and served to customers [c19 from F, from *restaurer* to RESTORE]
restaurant car *n Brit* a railway coach in which meals are served. Also called: **dining car**
restaurateur (ˌrɛstərə'tɜː) *n* a person who owns or runs a restaurant [c18 via F from LL *restaurātor*, from L *restaurāre* to RESTORE]

USAGE Although the spelling *restauranteur* occurs frequently, it is a misspelling and should be avoided

rest-cure *n* **1** a rest taken as part of a course of medical treatment, so as to relieve stress, anxiety, etc **2** an easy time or assignment: usually used with a negative: *it's no rest-cure, I assure you*
restful ('rɛstfʊl) *adj* **1** giving or conducive to rest **2** being at rest; tranquil; calm > **'restfully** *adv* > **'restfulness** *n*
restharrow ('rɛstˌhærəʊ) *n* any of a genus of Eurasian plants with tough leguminous stems and roots [c16 from *rest*, var. of ARREST (to hinder, stop) + HARROW]
resting ('rɛstɪŋ) *adj* **1** not moving or working; at rest **2** *euphemistic* (of an actor) out of work **3** (esp of plant spores) undergoing a period of dormancy before germination
restitution (ˌrɛstɪ'tjuːʃən) *n* **1** the act of giving back something that has been lost or stolen **2** *law* compensating for loss or injury by reverting as far as possible to the original position **3** the return of an object or system to its original state, esp after elastic deformation [c13 from L *rēstitūtiō*, from *rēstituere* to rebuild, from RE- + *statuere* to set up] > **'restiˌtutive** *or* **ˌresti'tutory** *adj*
restive ('rɛstɪv) *adj* **1** restless, nervous, or uneasy **2** impatient of control or authority [c16 from OF *restif* balky, from *rester* to remain] > **'restively** *adv* > **'restiveness** *n*
restless ('rɛstlɪs) *adj* **1** unable to stay still or quiet **2** ceaselessly active or moving: *the restless wind* **3** worried; anxious; uneasy **4** not restful; without repose: *a restless night* > **'restlessly** *adv* > **'restlessness** *n*
rest mass *n* the mass of an object that is at rest relative to an observer. It is the mass used in Newtonian mechanics
restoration (ˌrɛstə'reɪʃən) *n* **1** the act of restoring to a former or original condition, place, etc **2** the giving back of something lost, stolen, etc **3** something restored, replaced, or reconstructed **4** a model or representation of an extinct animal, etc **5** (*usually cap*) *Brit history* the re-establishment of the monarchy in 1660 or the reign of Charles II (1660–85)
▷ www.bbc.co.uk/history/timelines/britain/stu_charles_ii.shtml
▷ www.britainexpress.com/History/Cromwell_and_Restoration.htm
restorative (rɪ'stɒrətɪv) *adj* **1** tending to revive or renew health, spirits, etc ▷ *n* **2** anything that restores or revives, esp a drug
restorative justice *n* a method of dealing with convicted criminals in which they are urged to accept responsibility for their offences through meeting victims, making amends to victims or the community, etc
restore (rɪ'stɔː) *vb* **restores, restoring, restored** (*tr*) **1** to return (something) to its original or former condition **2** to bring back to health, good spirits, etc **3** to return (something lost, stolen, etc) to its owner **4** to reintroduce or re-enforce: *to restore discipline* **5** to reconstruct (an extinct animal, etc) [c13 from OF, from L *rēstaurāre* to rebuild, from RE- + -*staurāre*, as in *instaurāre* to renew] > **re'storable** *adj* > **re'storer** *n*
restrain (rɪ'streɪn) *vb* (*tr*) **1** to hold (someone) back from some action, esp by force **2** to deprive (someone) of liberty, as by imprisonment **3** to limit or restrict [c14 *restreyne*, from OF *restreindre*, from L *rēstringere*, from RE- + *stringere* to draw, bind] > **re'strainable** *adj* > **restrainedly** (rɪ'streɪnɪdlɪ) *adv* > **re'strainer** *n*
restraining order *n US law* an order issued by a civil court to a potential abuser to keep away from those named in the order
restraint (rɪ'streɪnt) *n* **1** the ability to control or moderate one's impulses, passions, etc **2** the act of restraining or the state of being restrained **3** something that restrains; restriction [c15 from OF *restreinte*, from *restreindre* to RESTRAIN]
restraint of trade *n* action interfering with the freedom to compete in business
restrict (rɪ'strɪkt) *vb* (often foll by *to*) to confine or keep within certain, often specified, limits or selected bounds [c16 from L *rēstrictus* bound up, from *rēstringere*; see RESTRAIN]
restricted (rɪ'strɪktɪd) *adj* **1** limited or confined **2** not accessible to the general public or (esp US) out of bounds to military personnel **3** *Brit* denoting a zone in which a speed limit or waiting restrictions for vehicles apply > **re'strictedly** *adv* > **re'strictedness** *n*
restriction (rɪ'strɪkʃən) *n* **1** something that restricts; a restrictive measure, law, etc **2** the act of restricting or the state of being restricted > **re'strictionist** *n, adj*
restrictive (rɪ'strɪktɪv) *adj* **1** restricting or tending to restrict **2** *grammar* denoting a relative clause or phrase that restricts the number of possible referents of its antecedent. The relative clause in *Americans who live in New York* is restrictive; the relative clause in *Americans, who are generally extrovert*, is nonrestrictive > **re'strictively** *adv* > **re'strictiveness** *n*
restrictive practice *n Brit* **1** a trading agreement against the public interest **2** a practice of a union or other group tending to limit the freedom of other workers or employers
rest room *n* a room in a public building with toilets, washbasins, and, sometimes, couches
restructure (riː'strʌktʃə) *vb* (*tr*) to organize (a system, business, society, etc) in a different way: *radical attempts to restructure the economy* > **re'structuring** *n*
result (rɪ'zʌlt) *n* **1** something that ensues from an action, policy, etc; outcome; consequence **2** a number, quantity, or value obtained by solving a mathematical problem **3** *US* a decision of a legislative body **4** (*often pl*) the final score or outcome of a sporting contest **5** a favourable result, esp a victory or success ▷ *vb* (*intr*) **6** (often foll by *from*) to be the outcome or consequence (of) **7** (foll by *in*) to issue or terminate (in a specified way, etc); end: *to result in tragedy* [c15 from L *resultāre* to rebound, spring from, from RE- + *saltāre* to leap]
resultant (rɪ'zʌltənt) *adj* **1** that results; resulting ▷ *n* **2** *maths, physics* a single vector that is the vector sum of two or more other vectors
resume (rɪ'zjuːm) *vb* **resumes, resuming, resumed** **1** to begin again or go on with (something interrupted) **2** (*tr*) to occupy again, take back, or recover: *to resume one's seat; resume the presidency* **3** *arch* to summarize; make a résumé of [c15 from L *resūmere*, from RE- + *sūmere* to take up] > **re'sumable** *adj* > **re'sumer** *n*
résumé ('rɛzjʊˌmeɪ) *n* **1** a short descriptive summary, as of events, etc **2** *US & Canad* another name for **curriculum vitae** [c19 from F, from *résumer* to RESUME]
resumption (rɪ'zʌmpʃən) *n* the act of resuming or beginning again [c15 via OF from LL *resumptiō*, from L *resūmere* to RESUME] > **re'sumptive** *adj* > **re'sumptively** *adv*
resupinate (rɪ'sjuːpɪnɪt) *adj bot* (of plant parts) reversed or inverted in position, so as to appear to be upside down [c18 from L *resupīnātus* bent back, from *resupīnāre*, from RE- + *supīnāre* to place on the back] > **reˌsupi'nation** *n*

Rr

resurge (rɪ'sɜːdʒ) *vb* **resurges, resurging, resurged** (*intr*) *rare* to rise again as if from the dead [C16 from L *resurgere* to rise again, reappear, from RE- + *surgere* to lift, arise]

resurgent (rɪ'sɜːdʒənt) *adj* rising again, as to new life, vigour, etc: *resurgent nationalism* > **re'surgence** *n*

resurrect (ˌrɛzə'rɛkt) *vb* **1** to rise or raise from the dead; bring or be brought back to life **2** (*tr*) to bring back into use or activity; revive **3** (*tr*) *facetious* (formerly) to exhume and steal (a body) from its grave

resurrection (ˌrɛzə'rɛkʃən) *n* **1** a supposed act or instance of a dead person coming back to life **2** belief in the possibility of this as part of a religious or mystical system **3** the condition of those who have risen from the dead: *we shall all live in the resurrection* **4** (*usually cap*) *Christian theol* the rising again of Christ from the tomb three days after his death **5** (*usually cap*) the rising again from the dead of all men at the Last Judgment **6** the revival of something: *a resurrection of an old story* [C13 via OF from LL *resurrectiō*, from L *resurgere* to rise again] > ˌ**resur'rectional** *or* ˌ**resur'rectionary** *adj*

resurrectionism (ˌrɛzə'rɛkʃəˌnɪzəm) *n* belief that men will rise again from the dead, esp according to Christian doctrine

resurrectionist (ˌrɛzə'rɛkʃənɪst) *n* **1** *facetious* (formerly) a body snatcher **2** a person who believes in the Resurrection

resurrection plant *n* any of several unrelated desert plants that form a tight ball when dry and unfold and bloom when moistened

resuscitate (rɪ'sʌsɪˌteɪt) *vb* **resuscitates, resuscitating, resuscitated** (*tr*) to restore to consciousness; revive [C16 from L *resuscitāre*, from RE- + *suscitāre* to raise, from *sub-* up from below + *citāre* to rouse, from *citus* quick] > **reˌsusci'tation** *n* > **re'suscitative** *adj* > **re'susciˌtator** *n*

ret (rɛt) *vb* **rets, retting, retted** (*tr*) to moisten or soak (flax, hemp, etc) in order to separate the fibres from the woody tissue by beating [C15 of Gmc origin]

retable (rɪ'teɪbᵊl) *n* an ornamental screenlike structure above and behind an altar [C19 from F, from Sp. *retablo*, from L *retrō* behind + *tabula* board]

retail ('riːteɪl) *n* **1** the sale of goods individually or in small quantities to consumers ▷ Cf **wholesale** ▷ *adj* **2** of, relating to, or engaged in such selling: *retail prices* ▷ *adv* **3** in small amounts or at a retail price ▷ *vb* **4** to sell or be sold in small quantities to consumers **5** (rɪ'teɪl) (*tr*) to relate (gossip, scandal, etc) in detail [C14 from OF *retaillier*, from RE- + *taillier* to cut; see TAILOR] > '**retailer** *n*

retail price index *n* a measure of the changes in the average level of retail prices of selected goods, usually on a monthly basis. Abbrev: **RPI**

retail therapy *n jocular* the action of shopping for clothes, etc, esp to cheer oneself up

retain (rɪ'teɪn) *vb* (*tr*) **1** to keep in one's possession **2** to be able to hold or contain: *soil that retains water* **3** (of a person) to be able to remember (information, etc) without difficulty **4** to hold in position **5** to keep for one's future use, as by paying a retainer or nominal charge **6** *law* to engage the services of (a barrister) by payment of a preliminary fee [C14 from OF *retenir*, from L *retinēre* to hold back, from RE- + *tenēre* to hold] > **re'tainable** *adj* > **re'tainment** *n*

retained object *n grammar* a direct or indirect object of a passive verb. The phrase *the drawings* in *she was given the drawings* is a retained object

retainer (rɪ'teɪnə) *n* **1** *history* a supporter or dependant of a person of rank **2** a servant, esp one who has been with a family for a long time **3** a clip, frame, or similar device that prevents a part of a machine, etc, from moving **4** a fee paid in advance to secure first option on the services of a barrister, jockey, etc **5** a reduced rent paid for a flat, etc, to reserve it for future use

retaining wall *n* a wall constructed to hold back earth, loose rock, etc. Also called: **revetment**

retake *vb* (riː'teɪk), **retakes, retaking, retook, retaken** (*tr*) **1** to take back or capture again: *to retake a fortress* **2** *films* to shoot (a scene) again **3** to tape (a recording) again ▷ *n* ('riːˌteɪk) **4** *films* a rephotographed scene **5** a retaped recording > **re'taker** *n*

retaliate (rɪ'tælɪˌeɪt) *vb* **retaliates, retaliating, retaliated** (*intr*) **1** to take retributory action, esp by returning some injury or wrong in kind **2** to cast (accusations) back upon a person [C17 from LL *retāliāre*, from L RE- + *tālis* of such kind] > **reˌtali'ation** *n* > **re'taliative** *or* **re'taliatory** *adj*

retard *vb* (rɪ'tɑːd) **1** (*tr*) to delay or slow down (the progress or speed) of (something) ▷ *n* ('riːtɑːd) **2** *US offensive* a retarded person **3** *US offensive* a foolish person [C15 from OF *retarder*, from L *retardāre*, from RE- + *tardāre* to make slow, from *tardus* sluggish]

retardant (rɪ'tɑːdᵊnt) *n* **1** a substance that reduces the rate of a chemical reaction ▷ *adj* **2** having a slowing effect

retardation (ˌriːtɑː'deɪʃən) *or* **retardment** (rɪ'tɑːdmənt) *n* **1** the act of retarding or the state of being retarded **2** something that retards > **re'tardative** *or* **re'tardatory** *adj*

retarded (rɪ'tɑːdɪd) *adj* underdeveloped, usually mentally and esp having an IQ of 70 to 85

retarder (rɪ'tɑːdə) *n* **1** a person or thing that retards **2** a substance added to slow down the rate of a chemical change, such as one added to cement to delay its setting

retch (rɛtʃ, riːtʃ) *vb* **1** (*intr*) to undergo an involuntary spasm of ineffectual vomiting ▷ *n* **2** an involuntary spasm of ineffectual vomiting [OE *hrǣcan*; rel. to ON *hrǣkja* to spit]

retd *abbrev for*: **1** retired **2** retained **3** returned

rete ('riːtɪ) *n, pl* **retia** ('riːʃɪə, -tɪə) *anat* any network of nerves or blood vessels; plexus [C14 (referring to a metal network used with an astrolabe): from L *rēte* net] > **retial** ('riːʃɪəl) *adj*

retention (rɪ'tɛnʃən) *n* **1** the act of retaining or state of being retained **2** the capacity to hold or retain liquid, etc **3** the capacity to remember **4** *pathol* the abnormal holding within the body of urine, faeces, etc **5** *commerce* a sum of money owed to a contractor but not paid for an agreed period as a safeguard against the appearance of any faults **6** (*pl*) *account* profits earned by a company but not distributed as dividends; retained earnings [C14 from L *retentiō*, from *retinēre* to RETAIN]

retentive (rɪ'tɛntɪv) *adj* having the capacity to retain or remember > **re'tentively** *adv* > **re'tentiveness** *n*

Réti ('reɪtɪ) *n* **Richard** 1889–1929, Hungarian chess player and theorist; influential in enunciating the theories of the hypermodern school

retiarius (ˌriːtɪ'ɛərɪəs, ˌriːʃɪ-) *n, pl* **retiarii** (-'ɛərɪˌaɪ) (in ancient Rome) a gladiator armed with a net and trident [L, from *rēte* net]

reticent ('rɛtɪsənt) *adj* not communicative; not saying all that one knows; taciturn; reserved [C19 from L *reticēre* to keep silent, from RE- + *tacēre* to be silent] > '**reticence** *n* > '**reticently** *adv*

> USAGE This word is quite commonly used nowadays as a synonym of *reluctant* and followed by *to* and a verb. In careful writing it is advisable to avoid this use, since many people would regard it as mistaken

reticle ('rɛtɪkᵊl) *or* (*less commonly*) **reticule** *n* a network of fine lines, wires, etc, placed in the focal plane of an optical instrument [C17 from L *rēticulum* a little net, from *rēte* net]

reticulate *adj* (rɪ'tɪkjʊlɪt) *also* **reticular** **1** in the form of a network or having a network of parts: *a reticulate leaf* ▷ *vb* (rɪ'tɪkjʊˌleɪt), **reticulates, reticulating, reticulated** **2** to form or be formed into a net [C17 from LL *rēticulātus* made like a net] > **re'ticulately** *adv* > **reˌticu'lation** *n*

reticule ('rɛtɪˌkjuːl) *n* **1** (formerly) a woman's small bag or purse, usually with a drawstring and made of net, beading, brocade, etc **2** a less common variant of **reticle** [C18 from F *réticule*, from L *rēticulum* RETICLE]

reticulum (rɪˈtɪkjʊləm) *n, pl* **reticula** (-lə) **1** any fine network, esp one in the body composed of cells, fibres, etc **2** the second compartment of the stomach of ruminants [C17 from L: little net, from *rēte* net]

retiform (ˈriːtɪˌfɔːm, ˈrɛt-) *adj rare* netlike; reticulate [C17 from L *rēte* net + *forma* shape]

retina (ˈrɛtɪnə) *n, pl* **retinas** *or* **retinae** (-ˌniː) the light-sensitive membrane forming the inner lining of the posterior wall of the eyeball [C14 from Med. L, ?from L *rēte* net] > **ˈretinal** *adj*

retinene (ˈrɛtɪˌniːn) *n* a yellow pigment, the aldehyde of vitamin A, that is involved in the formation of rhodopsin [C20 from RETINA + -ENE]

retinitis (ˌrɛtɪˈnaɪtɪs) *n* inflammation of the retina [C20 from NL, from RETINA + -ITIS]

retinoscopy (ˌrɛtɪˈnɒskəpɪ) *n ophthalmol* a procedure for detecting errors of refraction in the eye by means of an instrument (**retinoscope**) that reflects a beam of light from a mirror into the eye > **retinoscopic** (ˌrɛtɪnəˈskɒpɪk) *adj* > **ˌretinoˈscopically** *adv* > **ˌretiˈnoscopist** *n*

retinue (ˈrɛtɪˌnjuː) *n* a body of aides and retainers attending an important person [C14 from OF *retenue*, from *retenir* to RETAIN]

retiral (rɪˈtaɪərᵊl) *n esp Scot* the act of retiring; retirement

retire (rɪˈtaɪə) *vb* **retires, retiring, retired** (*mainly intr*) **1** (*also tr*) to give up or to cause (a person) to give up his or her work, esp on reaching pensionable age **2** to go away, as into seclusion, for recuperation, etc **3** to go to bed **4** to recede or disappear: *the sun retired behind the clouds* **5** to withdraw from a sporting contest, esp because of injury **6** (*also tr*) to pull back (troops, etc) from battle or (of troops, etc) to fall back **7** (*tr*) to remove (money, bonds, shares, etc) from circulation [C16 from F *retirer*, from OF RE- + *tirer* to pull, draw] > **reˈtired** *adj* > **reˈtirer** *n*

retirement (rɪˈtaɪəmənt) *n* **1a** the act of retiring from one's work, office, etc **1b** (*as modifier*): *retirement age* **2** the period of being retired from work: *she had many plans for her retirement* **3** seclusion from the world; privacy **4** the act of going away or retreating

retirement pension *n* a pension given to a person who has retired from regular employment, whether paid by the state, arising from the person's former employment, or the product of investment in a personal or stakeholder pension scheme

retiring (rɪˈtaɪərɪŋ) *adj* shunning contact with others; shy; reserved > **reˈtiringly** *adv*

retool (riːˈtuːl) *vb* **1** to replace, re-equip, or rearrange the tools in (a factory, etc) **2** (*tr*) *chiefly US & Canad* to revise or reorganize

retort[1] (rɪˈtɔːt) *vb* **1** (when *tr, takes a clause as object*) to utter (something) quickly, wittily, or angrily, in response **2** to use (an argument) against its originator ▷ *n* **3** a sharp, angry, or witty reply **4** an argument used against its originator [C16 from L *retorquēre*, from RE- + *torquēre* to twist, wrench] > **reˈtorter** *n*

retort[2] (rɪˈtɔːt) *n* **1** a glass vessel with a long tapering neck that is bent down, used for distillation **2** a vessel used for heating ores in the production of metals or heating coal to produce gas ▷ *vb* **3** (*tr*) to heat in a retort [C17 from F *retorte*, from Med. L *retorta*, from L *retorquēre* to twist back; see RETORT[1]]

retouch (riːˈtʌtʃ) *vb* (*tr*) **1** to restore, correct, or improve (a painting, make-up, etc) with new touches **2** *photog* to alter (a negative or print) by painting over blemishes or adding details ▷ *n* **3** the art or practice of retouching **4** a detail that is the result of retouching **5** a photograph, painting, etc, that has been retouched > **reˈtoucher** *n*

retrace (rɪˈtreɪs) *vb* **retraces, retracing, retraced** (*tr*) **1** to go back over (one's steps, a route, etc) again **2** to go over (a past event) in the mind; recall **3** to go over (a story, account, etc) from the beginning

re-trace (riːˈtreɪs) *vb* **re-traces, re-tracing, re-traced** (*tr*) to trace (a map, etc) again

retract (rɪˈtrækt) *vb* **1** (*tr*) to draw in (a part or appendage): *a snail can retract its horns; to retract the landing gear of an aircraft* **2** to withdraw (a statement, opinion, charge, etc) as invalid or unjustified **3** to go back on (a promise or agreement) [C16 from L *retractāre* to withdraw, from *tractāre*, from *trahere* to drag] > **reˈtractable** *or* **reˈtractible** *adj* > **reˈtraction** *n* > **reˈtractive** *adj*

retractile (rɪˈtræktaɪl) *adj* capable of being drawn in: *the retractile claws of a cat* > **retractility** (ˌriːtrækˈtɪlɪtɪ) *n*

retractor (rɪˈtræktə) *n* **1** *anat* any of various muscles that retract an organ or part **2** *surgery* an instrument for holding back an organ or part **3** a person or thing that retracts

retral (ˈriːtrəl, ˈrɛtrəl) *adj rare* at, near, or towards the back [C19 from L *retrō* backwards] > **ˈretrally** *adv*

retread *vb* (riːˈtrɛd), **retreads, retreading, retreaded** **1** (*tr*) another word for **remould** (sense 2) ▷ *n* (ˈriːˌtrɛd) **2** another word for **remould** (sense 3) **3** *NZ sl* a pensioner who has resumed employment, esp in the same profession as formerly **4** a film, piece of music, etc, that is a superficially altered version of an earlier original

re-tread (riːˈtrɛd) *vb* **re-treads, re-treading, re-trod, re-trodden** *or* **re-trod** (*tr*) to tread (one's steps, etc) again

retreat (rɪˈtriːt) *vb* (*mainly intr*) **1** *mil* to withdraw or retire in the face of or from action with an enemy **2** to retire or withdraw, as to seclusion or shelter **3** (of a person's features) to slope back; recede **4** (*tr*) *chess* to move (a piece) back ▷ *n* **5** the act of retreating or withdrawing **6** *mil* **6a** a withdrawal or retirement in the face of the enemy **6b** a bugle call signifying withdrawal or retirement **7** retirement or seclusion **8** a place to which one may retire for religious contemplation **9** a period of seclusion, esp for religious contemplation **10** an institution for the care and treatment of the mentally ill, infirm, elderly, etc [C14 from OF *retret*, from *retraire* to withdraw, from L *retrahere* to pull back]

Rr

retrench (rɪˈtrɛntʃ) *vb* **1** to reduce (costs); economize **2** (*tr*) to shorten, delete, or abridge [C17 from OF *retrenchier*, from RE- + *trenchier* to cut, from L *truncāre* to lop] > **reˈtrenchment** *n*

retribution (ˌrɛtrɪˈbjuːʃən) *n* **1** the act of punishing or taking vengeance for wrongdoing, sin, or injury **2** punishment or vengeance [C14 via OF from Church L *retribūtiō*, from L *retribuere*, from RE- + *tribuere* to pay] > **retributive** (rɪˈtrɪbjʊtɪv) *adj* > **reˈtributively** *adv*

retrieval (rɪˈtriːvᵊl) *n* **1** the act or process of retrieving **2** the possibility of recovery, restoration, or rectification **3** a computer operation that recalls data from a file

retrieve (rɪˈtriːv) *vb* **retrieves, retrieving, retrieved** (*mainly tr*) **1** to get or fetch back again; recover **2** to bring back to a more satisfactory state; revive **3** to rescue or save **4** to recover or make newly available (stored information) from a computer system **5** (*also intr*) (of dogs) to find and fetch (shot game, etc) **6** *tennis, etc* to return successfully (a shot difficult to reach) **7** to recall; remember ▷ *n* **8** the act of retrieving **9** the chance of being retrieved [C15 from OF *retrover*, from RE- + *trouver* to find, ?from Vulgar L *tropāre* (unattested) to compose] > **reˈtrievable** *adj*

retriever (rɪˈtriːvə) *n* **1** one of a breed of large dogs that can be trained to retrieve game **2** any dog used to retrieve shot game **3** a person or thing that retrieves

retro (ˈrɛtrəʊ) *n, pl* **retros** **1** short for **retrorocket** ▷ *adj* **2** denoting something associated with or revived from the past: *retro fashion*

retro- *prefix* **1** back or backwards: *retroactive* **2** located behind: *retrochoir* [from L *retrō* behind, backwards]

retroact (ˈrɛtrəʊˌækt) *vb* (*intr*) **1** to act in opposition **2** to influence or have reference to past events > ˌ**retro'action** *n*

retroactive (ˌrɛtrəʊ'æktɪv) *adj* **1** applying or referring to the past: *retroactive legislation* **2** effective from a date or for a period in the past > ˌ**retro'actively** *adv* > ˌ**retroac'tivity** *n*

retrocede (ˌrɛtrəʊ'siːd) *vb* **retrocedes, retroceding, retroceded 1** (*tr*) to give back; return **2** (*intr*) to go back; recede > **retrocession** (ˌrɛtrəʊ'sɛʃən) *or* ˌ**retro'cedence** *n* > ˌ**retro'cessive** *or* ˌ**retro'cedent** *adj*

retrochoir ('rɛtrəʊˌkwaɪə) *n* the space in a large church or cathedral behind the high altar

retrofire ('rɛtrəʊˌfaɪə) *n* **1** the act of firing a retrorocket **2** the moment at which it is fired

retrofit ('rɛtrəʊˌfɪt) *vb* **retrofits, retrofitting, retrofitted** (*tr*) to equip (a vehicle, piece of equipment, etc) with new parts, safety devices, etc, after manufacture

retroflex ('rɛtrəʊˌflɛks) *or* **retroflexed** *adj* **1** bent or curved backwards **2** *phonetics* of or involving retroflexion [C18 from L *retrōflexus*, from *retrōflectere*, from RETRO- + *flectere* to bend]

retroflexion *or* **retroflection** (ˌrɛtrəʊ'flɛkʃən) *n* **1** the act or condition of bending or being bent backwards **2** the act of turning the tip of the tongue upwards and backwards in the articulation of a vowel or a consonant

retrograde ('rɛtrəʊˌgreɪd) *adj* **1** moving or bending backwards **2** (esp of order) reverse or inverse **3** tending towards an earlier worse condition; declining or deteriorating **4** *astron* **4a** occurring or orbiting in a direction opposite to that of the earth's motion around the sun ▷ Cf **direct** (sense 18) **4b** occurring or orbiting in a direction around a planet opposite to the planet's rotational direction **4c** appearing to move in a clockwise direction due to the rotational period exceeding the period of revolution around the sun: *Venus has retrograde rotation* ▷ *vb* **retrogrades, retrograding, retrograded** (*intr*) **5** to move in a retrograde direction; retrogress [C14 from L *retrōgradī*, from *gradi* to walk, go] > ˌ**retrogra'dation** *n* > '**retroˌgradely** *adv*

retrogress (ˌrɛtrəʊ'grɛs) *vb* (*intr*) **1** to go back to an earlier, esp worse, condition; degenerate or deteriorate **2** to move backwards; recede [C19 from L *retrōgressus* having moved backwards; see RETROGRADE] > ˌ**retro'gression** *n* > ˌ**retro'gressive** *adj* > ˌ**retro'gressively** *adv*

retrorocket ('rɛtrəʊˌrɒkɪt) *n* a small auxiliary rocket engine on a larger rocket, missile, or spacecraft, that produces thrust in the opposite direction to the direction of flight in order to decelerate. Often shortened to **retro**

retrorse (rɪ'trɔːs) *adj* (esp of plant parts) pointing backwards [C19 from L *retrōrsus*, from *retrōversus* turned back, from RETRO- + *vertere* to turn] > **re'trorsely** *adv*

retrospect ('rɛtrəʊˌspɛkt) *n* the act of surveying things past (often in **in retrospect**) [C17 from L *retrōspicere* to look back, from RETRO- + *specere* to look] > ˌ**retro'spection** *n*

retrospective (ˌrɛtrəʊ'spɛktɪv) *adj* **1** looking or directed backwards, esp in time; characterized by retrospection **2** applying to the past; retroactive ▷ *n* **3** an exhibition of an artist's life's work > ˌ**retro'spectively** *adv*

retroussé (rə'truːseɪ) *adj* (of a nose) turned up [C19 from F *retrousser* to tuck up]

retroversion (ˌrɛtrəʊ'vɜːʃən) *n* **1** the act of turning or condition of being turned backwards **2** the condition of a part or organ, esp the uterus, that is turned backwards > '**retroˌverted** *adj*

Retrovir ('rɛtrəʊˌvɪə) *n trademark* a brand name for **zidovudine**

retrovirus ('rɛtrəʊˌvaɪrəs) *n* any of several viruses that are able to reverse the normal flow of genetic information from DNA to RNA by transcribing RNA into DNA: many retroviruses are known to cause cancer in animals: *a primate retrovirus* > '**retroˌviral** *adj*

retsina (rɛt'siːnə) *n* a Greek wine flavoured with resin [Mod. Gk, from It. *resina* RESIN]

retune (riː'tjuːn) *vb* **retunes, retuning, retuned** (*tr*) **1** to tune (a musical instrument) differently or again **2** to tune (a radio, television, etc) to another frequency

return (rɪ'tɜːn) *vb* **1** (*intr*) to come back to a former place or state **2** (*tr*) to give, take, or carry back; replace or restore **3** (*tr*) to repay or recompense, esp with something of equivalent value: *return the compliment* **4** (*tr*) to earn or yield (profit or interest) as an income from an investment or venture **5** (*intr*) to come back or revert in thought or speech: *I'll return to that later* **6** (*intr*) to recur or reappear: *the symptoms have returned* **7** to answer or reply **8** (*tr*) to vote into office; elect **9** (*tr*) *law* (of a jury) to deliver or render (a verdict) **10** (*tr*) to submit (a report, etc) about (someone or something) to someone in authority **11** (*tr*) *cards* to lead back (the suit led by one's partner) **12** (*tr*) *ball games* to hit, throw, or play (a ball) back **13 return thanks** (of Christians) to say grace before a meal ▷ *n* **14** the act or an instance of coming back **15** something that is given or sent back, esp unsatisfactory merchandise or a theatre ticket for resale **16** the act or an instance of putting, sending, or carrying back; replacement or restoration **17** (*often pl*) the yield or profit from an investment or venture **18** the act or an instance of reciprocation or repayment (esp in **in return for**) **19** a recurrence or reappearance **20** an official report, esp of the financial condition of a company **21a** a form (a **tax return**) on which a statement of one's taxable income is made **21b** the statement itself **22** (*often pl*) a statement of the votes counted at an election **23** an answer or reply **24** *Brit* short for **return ticket 25** *archit* a part of a building that forms an angle with the façade **26** *law* a report by a bailiff or other officer on the outcome of a formal document such as a writ, summons, etc **27** *cards* a lead of a card in the suit that one's partner has previously led **28** *ball games* the act of playing or throwing a ball, etc, back **29 by return (of post)** *Brit* by the next post back to the sender **30 many happy returns (of the day)** a conventional birthday greeting ▷ *adj* **31** of, relating to, or characterized by a return: *a return visit* **32** denoting a second, reciprocal occasion: *a return match* [C14 from OF *retorner*; see RE-, TURN] > **re'turnable** *adj*

return crease *n cricket* one of two lines marked at right angles to each bowling crease, from inside which a bowler must deliver the ball

returned serviceman *n Austral & NZ* a serviceman who has served abroad. Also (Austral and Canad): **returned man**

returner (rɪ'tɜːnə) *n* **1** a person or thing that returns **2** a person who goes back to work after a break, esp a woman who has had children

returning officer *n* (in Britain, Canada, Australia, etc) an official in charge of conducting an election in a constituency, etc

return ticket *n Brit, Austral, & NZ* a ticket entitling a passenger to travel to his or her destination and back

retuse (rɪ'tjuːs) *adj bot* having a rounded apex and a central depression [C18 from L *retundere* to make blunt, from RE- + *tundere* to pound]

Retz (*French* rɛs) *n* **Gilles de** See (Gilles de) **Rais**

Reuben ('ruːbɪn) *n Old Testament* **1** the eldest son of Jacob and Leah: one of the 12 patriarchs of Israel (Genesis 29:30) **2** the Israelite tribe descended from him **3** the territory of this tribe, lying to the northeast of the Dead Sea. Douay spelling: **Ruben**

reunify (riː'juːnɪˌfaɪ) *vb* **reunifies, reunifying, reunified** (*tr*) to bring together again (something, esp a country previously divided) > ˌ**reunifi'cation** *n*

reunion (riː'juːnjən) *n* **1** the act of coming together again **2** the state or condition of having been brought

together again **3** a gathering of relatives, friends, or former associates
Réunion (riːˈjuːnjən; *French* reynjɔ̃) *n* an island in the Indian Ocean, in the Mascarene Islands: an overseas region of France, having been in French possession since 1642. Capital: Saint-Denis. Pop: 733 000 (2001 est). Area: 2510 sq km (970 sq miles)
reunite (ˌriːjuːˈnaɪt) *vb* **reunites, reuniting, reunited** to bring or come together again > ˌ**reuˈnitable** *adj*
Reus (*Spanish* rɛus) *n* a city in NE Spain, northwest of Tarragona: became commercially important after the establishment of an English colony (about 1750). Pop: 86 864 (1991)
Reuter (ˈrɔɪtə) *n* Baron **Paul Julius von** (paul ˈjuːliʊs fɔn) original name *Israel Beer Josaphat*. 1816–99, German telegrapher, who founded a news agency in London (1851)
Reutlingen (*German* ˈrɔytlɪŋən) *n* a city in SW Germany, in Baden-Württemberg: founded in the 11th century; an Imperial free city from 1240 until 1802; textile industry. Pop: 109 882 (1999 est)
rev (rɛv) *inf* ▹ *n* **1** revolution per minute ▹ *vb* **revs, revving, revved 2** (often foll by *up*) to increase the speed of revolution of (an engine)
rev. *abbrev for:* **1** revenue **2** reverse(d) **3** review **4** revise(d) **5** revision **6** revolution **7** revolving
Rev. *abbrev for:* **1** *Bible* Revelation (of Saint John the Divine) **2** Reverend
Reval (ˈreːval) *n* the German name for **Tallinn**
revalue (riːˈvæljuː) *or US* **revaluate** *vb* **revalues, revaluing, revalued** *or US* **revaluates, revaluating, revaluated 1** to adjust the exchange value of (a currency), esp upwards ▹ Cf **devalue 2** (*tr*) to make a fresh valuation of > **reˌvaluˈation** *n*
revamp (riːˈvæmp) *vb* (*tr*) **1** to patch up or renovate; repair or restore ▹ *n* **2** something that has been renovated or revamped **3** the act or process of revamping [C19 from RE- + VAMP²]
revanchism (rɪˈvæntʃɪzəm) *n* **1** a foreign policy aimed at revenge or the regaining of lost territories **2** support for such a policy [C20 from F *revanche* REVENGE] > **reˈvanchist** *n, adj*
rev counter *n Brit* an informal name for **tachometer**
Revd *abbrev for* Reverend
reveal (rɪˈviːl) *vb* (*tr*) **1** (*may take a clause as object or an infinitive*) to disclose (a secret); divulge **2** to expose to view or show (something concealed) **3** (of God) to disclose (divine truths) ▹ *n* **4** *archit* the vertical side of an opening in a wall, esp the side of a window or door between the frame and the front of the wall [C14 from OF *reveler*, from L *revēlāre* to unveil, from RE- + *vēlum* a VEIL] > **reˈvealable** *adj* > **reˈvealer** *n* > **reˈvealment** *n*
revealed religion *n* **1** religion based on the revelation by God to man of ideas that he would not have arrived at by reason alone **2** religion in which the existence of God depends on revelation
revealing (rɪˈviːlɪŋ) *adj* **1** of significance or import: *a very revealing experience* **2** showing more of the body than is usual: *a revealing costume* > **reˈvealingly** *adv*
reveille (rɪˈvælɪ) *n* **1** a signal, given by a bugle, drum, etc, to awaken soldiers or sailors in the morning **2** the hour at which this takes place [C17 from F *réveillez!* awake! from RE- + OF *esveillier* to be wakeful, ult. from L *vigilāre* to keep watch]
revel (ˈrɛvᵊl) *vb* **revels, revelling, revelled** *or US* **revels, reveling, reveled** (*intr*) **1** (foll by *in*) to take pleasure or wallow: *to revel in success* **2** to take part in noisy festivities; make merry ▹ *n* **3** (*often pl*) an occasion of noisy merrymaking [C14 from OF *reveler* to be merry, noisy, from L *rebellāre* to revolt] > ˈ**reveller** *n*
revelation (ˌrɛvəˈleɪʃən) *n* **1** the act or process of disclosing something previously secret or obscure, esp something true **2** a fact disclosed or revealed, esp in a dramatic or surprising way **3** *Christianity* God's disclosure of his own nature and his purpose for mankind [C14 from Church L *revēlātiō*, from L *revēlāre* to REVEAL] > ˌ**reveˈlatory** *or* ˌ**reveˈlational** *adj*
Revelation (ˌrɛvəˈleɪʃən) *n* (*popularly, often pl*) the last book of the New Testament, containing visionary descriptions of heaven, and of the end of the world. Also called: the **Apocalypse**, the **Revelation of Saint John the Divine**
revelationist (ˌrɛvəˈleɪʃənɪst) *n* a person who believes that God has revealed certain truths to man
revelry (ˈrɛvᵊlrɪ) *n, pl* **revelries** noisy or unrestrained merrymaking
revenant (ˈrɛvɪnənt) *n* something, esp a ghost, that returns [C19 from F: ghost, from *revenir*, from L *revenīre*, from RE- + *venīre* to come]
revenge (rɪˈvɛndʒ) *n* **1** the act of retaliating for wrongs or injury received; vengeance **2** something done as a means of vengeance **3** the desire to take vengeance **4** a return match, regarded as a loser's opportunity to even the score ▹ *vb* **revenges, revenging, revenged** (*tr*) **5** to inflict equivalent injury or damage for (injury received) **6** to take vengeance for (oneself or another); avenge [C14 from OF *revenger*, from LL *revindicāre*, from RE- + *vindicāre* to VINDICATE] > **reˈvenger** *n* > **reˈvenging** *adj* > **reˈvengingly** *adv*
revengeful (rɪˈvɛndʒfʊl) *adj* full of or characterized by desire for vengeance; vindictive > **reˈvengefully** *adv* > **reˈvengefulness** *n*
revenue (ˈrɛvɪˌnjuː) *n* **1** the income accruing from taxation to a government **2a** a government department responsible for the collection of government revenue **2b** (*as modifier*): *revenue men* **3** the gross income from a business enterprise, investment, etc **4** a particular item of income **5** a source of income [C16 from OF, from *revenir* to return, from L *revenīre*; see REVENANT]
revenue cutter *n* a small lightly armed boat used to enforce customs regulations and catch smugglers
reverb (ˈriːvɜːb; rɪˈvɜːb) *n* an electronic device that creates artificial acoustics
reverberate (rɪˈvɜːbəˌreɪt) *vb* **reverberates, reverberating, reverberated 1** (*intr*) to resound or re-echo **2** to reflect or be reflected many times **3** (*intr*) to rebound or recoil **4** (*intr*) (of the flame or heat in a reverberatory furnace) to be deflected onto the metal or ore on the hearth **5** (*tr*) to heat, melt, or refine (a metal or ore) in a reverberatory furnace [C16 from L *reverberāre*, from RE- + *verberāre* to beat, from *verber* a lash] > **reˈverberantly** *adv* > **reˌverberˈation** *n* > **reˈverberative** *adj* > **reˈverbeˌrator** *n* > **reˈverberatory** *adj*
reverberation time *n* a measure of the acoustic properties of a room, equal to the time taken for a sound to fall in intensity by 60 decibels. It is usually measured in seconds
reverberatory furnace *n* a metallurgical furnace having a curved roof that deflects heat onto the charge so that the fuel is not in direct contact with the ore
revere (rɪˈvɪə) *vb* **reveres, revering, revered** (*tr*) to be in awe of and respect deeply; venerate [C17 from L *reverērī*, from RE- + *verērī* to fear, be in awe of]
Revere (rɪˈvɪə) *n* **Paul** 1735–1818, American patriot and silversmith, best known for his night ride on April 18, 1775, to warn the Massachusetts colonists of the coming of the British troops
reverence (ˈrɛvərəns) *n* **1** a feeling or attitude of profound respect, usually reserved for the sacred or divine **2** an outward manifestation of this feeling, esp a bow or act of obeisance **3** the state of being revered or commanding profound respect ▹ *vb* **reverences, reverencing, reverenced 4** (*tr*) to revere or venerate
Reverence (ˈrɛvərəns) *n* (preceded by *Your* or *His*) a title sometimes used to address or refer to a Roman Catholic priest

Rr

reverend ('rɛvərənd) *adj* **1** worthy of reverence **2** relating to or designating a clergyman ▷ *n* **3** *inf* a clergyman [C15 from L *reverendus* fit to be revered]

Reverend ('rɛvərənd) *adj* a title of respect for a clergyman. Abbrev: **Rev., Revd**

> USAGE *Reverend* with a surname alone (*Reverend Smith*), as a term of address ("*Yes, Reverend*"), or in the greeting of a letter (*Dear Rev. Mr Smith*) are all generally considered to be wrong usage. Preferred are (*the*) *Reverend John Smith* or *Reverend Mr Smith* and *Dear Mr Smith*

reverent ('rɛvərənt, 'rɛvrənt) *adj* feeling, expressing, or characterized by reverence [C14 from L *reverēns* respectful] > **'reverently** *adv*

reverential (ˌrɛvə'rɛnʃəl) *adj* resulting from or showing reverence > ˌ**rever'entially** *adv*

reverie ('rɛvərɪ) *n* **1** an act or state of absent-minded daydreaming: *to fall into a reverie* **2** a piece of instrumental music suggestive of a daydream **3** *arch* a fanciful or visionary notion; daydream [C14 from OF *resverie* wildness, from *resver* to behave wildly, from ?]

revers (rɪ'vɪə) *n, pl* **revers** (-'vɪəz) (*usually pl*) the turned-back lining of part of a garment, esp of a lapel or cuff [C19 from F, lit.: REVERSE]

reversal (rɪ'vɜːsᵊl) *n* **1** the act or an instance of reversing **2** a change for the worse; reverse **3** the state of being reversed **4** the annulment of a judicial decision, esp by an appeal court

reverse (rɪ'vɜːs) *vb* **reverses, reversing, reversed** (*mainly tr*) **1** to turn or set in an opposite direction, order, or position **2** to change into something different or contrary; alter completely: *reverse one's policy* **3** (*also intr*) to move or cause to move backwards or in an opposite direction: *to reverse a car* **4** to run (machinery, etc) in the opposite direction to normal **5** to turn inside out **6** *law* to revoke or set aside (a judgment, decree, etc); annul **7 reverse the charge(s)** to make a telephone call at the recipient's expense ▷ *n* **8** the opposite or contrary of something **9** the back or rear side of something **10** a change to an opposite position, state, or direction **11** a change for the worse; setback or defeat **12a** the mechanism or gears by which machinery, a vehicle, etc, can be made to reverse its direction **12b** (*as modifier*): *reverse gear* **13** the side of a coin bearing a secondary design **14a** printed matter in which normally black or coloured areas, esp lettering, appear white, and vice versa **14b** (*as modifier*): *reverse plates* **15 in reverse** in an opposite or backward direction **16 the reverse of** emphatically not; not at all: *he was the reverse of polite when I called* ▷ *adj* **17** opposite or contrary in direction, position, order, nature, etc; turned backwards **18** back to front; inverted **19** operating or moving in a manner contrary to that which is usual **20** denoting or relating to a mirror image [C14 from OF, from L *reversus*, from *revertere* to turn back] > **re'versely** *adv* > **re'verser** *n*

reverse-charge *adj* (*prenominal*) (of a telephone call) made at the recipient's expense

reverse osmosis *n* a technique for purifying water, in which pressure is applied to force liquid through a semipermeable membrane in the opposite direction to that in normal osmosis

reverse takeover *n finance* the purchase of a larger company by a smaller company, esp of a public company by a private company

reverse transcriptase (træn'skrɪpteɪz) *n* an enzyme present in retroviruses that copies RNA into DNA, thus reversing the usual flow of genetic information in which DNA is copied into RNA

reverse video *n computing* highlighting by reversing the colours of normal characters and background on a visual display unit

reversible (rɪ'vɜːsɪbᵊl) *adj* **1** capable of being reversed: *a reversible decision* **2** capable of returning to an original condition **3** *chem, physics* capable of assuming or producing either of two possible states and changing from one to the other: *a reversible reaction* **4** (of a fabric or garment) woven, printed, or finished so that either side may be used as the outer side ▷ *n* **5** a reversible garment, esp a coat > **reˌversi'bility** *n* > **re'versibly** *adv*

reversing lights *pl n* lights on the rear of a motor vehicle that go on when the vehicle is being reversed

reversion (rɪ'vɜːʃən) *n* **1** a return to an earlier condition, practice, or belief; act of reverting **2** *biol* the return of individuals, organs, etc, to a more primitive condition or type **3** *property law* **3a** an interest in an estate that reverts to the grantor or his or her heirs at the end of a period, esp at the end of the life of a grantee **3b** an estate so reverting **3c** the right to succeed to such an estate **4** the benefit payable on the death of a life-insurance policyholder > **re'versionary** *or* **re'versional** *adj*

reversionary bonus *n insurance* a bonus added to the sum payable on death or at the maturity of a with-profits assurance policy

revert (rɪ'vɜːt) *vb* (*intr; foll by to*) **1** to go back to a former practice, condition, belief, etc: *he reverted to his old wicked ways* **2** to take up again or come back to a former topic **3** *biol* (of individuals, organs, etc) to return to a more primitive, earlier, or simpler condition or type **4** *property law* (of an estate or interest in land) to return to its former owner or his or her heirs **5 revert to type** to resume characteristics that were thought to have disappeared [C13 from L *revertere*, from RE- + *vertere* to turn] > **re'verter** *n* > **re'vertible** *adj*

> USAGE Since *back* is part of the meaning of *revert*, it is better not to say that someone *reverts back* to a certain type of behaviour

revet (rɪ'vɛt) *vb* **revets, revetting, revetted** to face (a wall or embankment) with stones [C19 from F *revêt*, from OF *revestir* to reclothe; see REVETMENT]

revetment (rɪ'vɛtmənt) *n* **1** a facing of stones, sandbags, etc, to protect a wall, embankment, or earthworks **2** another name for **retaining wall** [C18 from F *revêtement*, lit.: a reclothing, from *revêtir*; ult. from L RE- + *vestīre* to clothe]

review (rɪ'vjuː) *vb* (*mainly tr*) **1** to look at or examine again: *to review a situation* **2** to look back upon (a period of time, sequence of events, etc); remember: *he reviewed his achievements with pride* **3** to inspect, esp formally or officially: *the general reviewed his troops* **4** *law* to re-examine (a decision) judicially **5** to write a critical assessment of (a book, film, play, concert, etc), esp as a profession ▷ *n* **6** Also called: **reviewal** the act or an instance of reviewing **7** a general survey or report: *a review of the political situation* **8** a critical assessment of a book, film, play, concert, etc, esp one printed in a newspaper or periodical **9** a publication containing such articles **10** a second consideration; re-examination **11** a retrospective survey **12** a formal or official inspection **13** a US and Canad word for **revision** (sense 2) **14** *law* judicial re-examination of a case, esp by a superior court **15** a less common spelling of **revue** [C16 from F, from *revoir* to see again, from L RE- + *vidēre* to see] > **re'viewer** *n*

revile (rɪ'vaɪl) *vb* **reviles, reviling, reviled** to use abusive or scornful language against (someone or something) [C14 from OF *reviler*, from RE- + *vil* VILE] > **re'vilement** *n* > **re'viler** *n*

revise (rɪ'vaɪz) *vb* **revises, revising, revised 1** (*tr*) to change or amend: *to revise one's opinion* **2** *Brit* to reread (a subject or notes on it) so as to memorize it, esp for an examination **3** (*tr*) to prepare a new version or edition of (a previously printed work) ▷ *n* **4** the act, process, or result of revising; revision [C16 from L *revīsere*, from RE- + *vīsere* to inspect, from *vidēre* to see] > **re'visal** *n* > **re'viser** *n*

Revised Standard Version *n* a revision by American

scholars of the American Standard Version of the Bible. The New Testament was published in 1946 and the entire Bible in 1953

Revised Version *n* a revision of the Authorized Version of the Bible by two committees of British scholars, the New Testament being published in 1881 and the Old in 1885

revision (rɪˈvɪʒən) *n* **1** the act or process of revising **2** *Brit* the process of rereading a subject or notes on it, esp for an examination **3** a corrected or new version of a book, article, etc > **reˈvisionary** *adj*

revisionism (rɪˈvɪʒəˌnɪzəm) *n* **1** (*sometimes cap*) **1a** a moderate, nonrevolutionary version of Marxism developed in Germany around 1900 **1b** (in Marxist-Leninist ideology) any dangerous departure from the true interpretation of Marx's teachings **2** the advocacy of revision of some political theory, etc > **reˈvisionist** *n, adj*

revisory (rɪˈvaɪzərɪ) *adj* of, relating to, or having the power of revision

revitalize *or* **revitalise** (riːˈvaɪtəˌlaɪz) *vb* **revitalizes, revitalizing, revitalized** *or* **revitalises, revitalising, revitalised** (*tr*) to restore vitality or animation to

revival (rɪˈvaɪvəl) *n* **1** the act or an instance of reviving or the state of being revived **2** an instance of returning to life or consciousness; restoration of vigour or vitality **3** a renewed use, acceptance of, or interest in (past customs, styles, etc): *the Gothic revival* **4** a new production of a play that has not been recently performed **5** a reawakening of faith **6** an evangelistic meeting or meetings intended to effect such a reawakening in those present

revivalism (rɪˈvaɪvəˌlɪzəm) *n* **1** a movement that seeks to reawaken faith **2** the tendency or desire to revive former customs, styles, etc > **reˈvivalist** *n* > **reˌvivalˈistic** *adj*

revive (rɪˈvaɪv) *vb* **revives, reviving, revived** **1** to bring or be brought back to life, consciousness, or strength: *revived by a drop of whisky* **2** to give or assume new vitality; flourish again or cause to flourish again **3** to make or become operative or active again: *the youth movement was revived* **4** to bring or come back to mind **5** (*tr*) *theatre* to mount a new production of (an old play) [C15 from OF *revivre* to live again, from L *revīvere*, from RE- + *vīvere* to live] > **reˈvivable** *adj* > **reˌvivaˈbility** *n* > **reˈviver** *n* > **reˈviving** *adj*

revivify (rɪˈvɪvɪˌfaɪ) *vb* **revivifies, revivifying, revivified** (*tr*) to give new life or spirit to > **reˌvivifiˈcation** *n*

revocable (ˈrɛvəkəbəl) *or* **revokable** (rɪˈvəʊkəbəl) *adj* capable of being revoked > **ˌrevocaˈbility** *or* **reˌvokaˈbility** *n* > **ˈrevocably** *or* **reˈvokably** *adv*

revocation (ˌrɛvəˈkeɪʃən) *n* **1** the act of revoking or state of being revoked **2a** the cancellation or annulment of a legal instrument **2b** the withdrawal of an offer, power of attorney, etc > **revocatory** (ˈrɛvəkətərɪ, -trɪ) *adj*

revoice (riːˈvɔɪs) *vb* **revoices, revoicing, revoiced** (*tr*) **1** to utter again; echo **2** to adjust the design of (an organ pipe or wind instrument) as after disuse or to conform with modern pitch

revoke (rɪˈvəʊk) *vb* **revokes, revoking, revoked** **1** (*tr*) to take back or withdraw; cancel; rescind **2** (*intr*) *cards* to break a rule by failing to follow suit when able to do so ▷ *n* **3** *cards* the act of revoking [C14 from L *revocāre* to call back, withdraw, from RE- + *vocāre* to call] > **reˈvoker** *n*

revolt (rɪˈvəʊlt) *n* **1** a rebellion or uprising against authority **2** **in revolt** in the process or state of rebelling ▷ *vb* **3** (*intr*) to rise up in rebellion against authority **4** (*usually passive*) to feel or cause to feel revulsion, disgust, or abhorrence [C16 from F *révolter*, from OIt. *rivoltare* to overturn, ult. from L *revolvere* to roll back]

revolting (rɪˈvəʊltɪŋ) *adj* **1** causing revulsion; nauseating, disgusting, or repulsive **2** *inf* unpleasant or nasty > **reˈvoltingly** *adv*

revolute (ˈrɛvəˌluːt) *adj* (esp of the margins of a leaf) rolled backwards and downwards [C18 from L *revolūtus* rolled back; see REVOLVE]

revolution (ˌrɛvəˈluːʃən) *n* **1** the overthrow or repudiation of a regime or political system by the governed **2** (in Marxist theory) the inevitable, violent transition from one system of production in a society to the next **3** a far-reaching and drastic change, esp in ideas, methods, etc **4a** movement in or as if in a circle **4b** one complete turn in such a circle: *33 revolutions per minute* **5a** the orbital motion of one body, such as a planet, around another **5b** one complete turn in such motion **6** a cycle of successive events or changes [C14 via OF from LL *revolūtiō*, from L *revolvere* to REVOLVE]

revolutionary (ˌrɛvəˈluːʃənərɪ) *n, pl* **revolutionaries** **1** a person who advocates or engages in revolution ▷ *adj* **2** relating to or characteristic of a revolution **3** advocating or engaged in revolution **4** radically new or different: *a revolutionary method of making plastics*

Revolutionary (ˌrɛvəˈluːʃənərɪ) *adj* **1** *chiefly US* of or relating to the War of American Independence (1775–83) **2** of or relating to any of various other Revolutions, esp the **Russian Revolution** (1917) or the **French Revolution** (1789)

revolutionist (ˌrɛvəˈluːʃənɪst) *n* **1** a less common word for a **revolutionary** ▷ *adj* **2** of or relating to revolution or revolutionaries

revolutionize *or* **revolutionise** (ˌrɛvəˈluːʃəˌnaɪz) *vb* **revolutionizes, revolutionizing, revolutionized** *or* **revolutionises, revolutionising, revolutionised** (*tr*) **1** to bring about a radical change in: *science has revolutionized civilization* **2** to inspire or infect with revolutionary ideas: *they revolutionized the common soldiers* **3** to cause a revolution in (a country, etc) > **ˌrevoˈlutionˌizer** *or* **ˌrevoˈlutionˌiser** *n*

revolve (rɪˈvɒlv) *vb* **revolves, revolving, revolved** **1** to move or cause to move around a centre or axis; rotate **2** (*intr*) to occur periodically or in cycles **3** to consider or be considered **4** (*intr; foll by around or about*) to be centred or focused (upon): *Juliet's thoughts revolved around Romeo* ▷ *n* **5** *theatre* a circular section of a stage that can be rotated by electric power to provide a scene change [C14 from L *revolvere*, from RE- + *volvere* to roll, wind] > **reˈvolvable** *adj*

revolver (rɪˈvɒlvə) *n* a pistol having a revolving multichambered cylinder that allows several shots to be discharged without reloading

revolving (rɪˈvɒlvɪŋ) *adj* **1** moving round a central axis: *revolving door* **2** (of a fund) constantly added to from income from its investments to offset outgoing payments **3** (of a letter of credit, loan, etc) available to be repeatedly drawn on by the beneficiary provided that a specified amount is never exceeded

revue (rɪˈvjuː) *n* a light entertainment consisting of topical sketches, songs, dancing, etc [C20 from F; see REVIEW]

revulsion (rɪˈvʌlʃən) *n* **1** a sudden violent reaction in feeling, esp one of extreme loathing **2** the act or an instance of drawing back or recoiling from something **3** *obsolete* the diversion of disease from one part of the body to another by cupping, counterirritants, etc [C16 from L *revulsiō* a pulling away, from *revellere*, from RE- + *vellere* to pull, tear]

revulsive (rɪˈvʌlsɪv) *adj* **1** of or causing revulsion ▷ *n* **2** *med* a counterirritant > **reˈvulsively** *adv*

reward (rɪˈwɔːd) *n* **1** something given in return for a deed or service rendered **2** a sum of money offered, esp for help in finding a criminal or for the return of lost or stolen property **3** profit or return **4** something received in return for good or evil; deserts ▷ *vb* **5** (*tr*) to give something to (someone), esp in gratitude for (a service rendered); recompense [C14 from OF *rewarder*, from RE- + *warder* to care for, guard, of Gmc origin] > **reˈwardless** *adj*

reward claim *n Austral history* a claim granted to a miner who discovered gold in a new area

rewarding (rɪ'wɔːdɪŋ) *adj* giving personal satisfaction; gratifying

rewa-rewa ('reɪwə'reɪwə) *n* a tall tree of New Zealand, yielding reddish timber [c19 from Maori]

rewind *vb* (riː'waɪnd), **rewinds, rewinding, rewound** **1** (*tr*) to wind back, esp a film or tape onto the original reel ▷ *n* ('riːˌwaɪnd, riː'waɪnd) **2** something rewound **3** the act of rewinding > **re'winder** *n*

rewire (riː'waɪə) *vb* **rewires, rewiring, rewired** (*tr*) to provide (a house, engine, etc) with new wiring > **re'wirable** *adj*

reword (riː'wɜːd) *vb* (*tr*) to alter the wording of; express differently

rework (riː'wɜːk) *vb* (*tr*) **1** to use again in altered form **2** to rewrite or revise **3** to reprocess for use again

rewrite *vb* (riː'raɪt), **rewrites, rewriting, rewrote, rewritten** (*tr*) **1** to write (material) again, esp changing the words or form ▷ *n* ('riːˌraɪt) **2** *computing* to return (data) to a store when it has been erased during reading **3** something rewritten

Rex (rɛks) *n* king: part of the official title of a king, now used chiefly in documents, legal proceedings, on coins, etc ▷ Cf **Regina**[1] [L]

Rexine ('rɛksiːn) *n trademark* a form of artificial leather

Reye's syndrome (raɪz, reɪz) *n* a rare metabolic disease in children that can be fatal, involving damage to the brain, liver, and kidneys [c20 after R.D.K. *Reye* (1912–78), Austral paediatrician]

Reykjavik ('reɪkjəˌviːk) *n* the capital and chief port of Iceland, situated in the southwest: its buildings are heated by natural hot water. Pop: 109 184 (1999 est) ▷ www.rvk.is

Reynard *or* **Renard** ('rɛnəd, 'rɛnɑːd) *n* a name for a fox, used in fables, etc

Reynaud (*French* rɛno) *n* **Paul** (pɔl) 1878–1966, French statesman: premier during the defeat of France by Germany (1940); later imprisoned by the Germans

Reynolds ('rɛnəldz) *n* **1** **Albert** born 1935, Irish politician: leader of the Fianna Fáil party and prime minister of the Republic of Ireland (1994–96) **2** Sir **Joshua** 1723–92, English portrait painter. He was the first president of the Royal Academy (1768): the annual lectures he gave there, published as *Discourses*, are important contributions to art theory and criticism

Reynosa (*Spanish* re'nosa) *n* a city in E Mexico, in Tamaulipas state on the Rio Grande. Pop: 398 000 (2000 est)

RF *abbrev for* radio frequency

RFC *abbrev for:* **1** Royal Flying Corps **2** Rugby Football Club

RFID *abbrev for* radio-frequency identity (*or* identification): a method of security tagging used in shops, etc

RGN (in Britain) *abbrev for* Registered General Nurse

RGS *abbrev for* Royal Geographical Society

rh *or* **RH** *abbrev for* right hand

Rh **1** *the chemical symbol for* rhodium ▷ **2** *abbrev for* rhesus (esp in **Rh factor**)

RHA *abbrev for:* **1** Regional Health Authority **2** Royal Horse Artillery

rhabdomancy ('ræbdəˌmænsɪ) *n* divination for water or mineral ore by means of a rod or wand [c17 via LL from LGk *rhabdomanteia*, from Gk *rhabdos* rod + *manteia* divination] > **'rhabdoˌmantist** *or* **'rhabdoˌmancer** *n*

rhachis ('reɪkɪs) *n, pl* **rhachises** *or* **rhachides** ('rækɪˌdiːz, 'reɪ-) a variant spelling of **rachis**

Rhadamanthus *or* **Rhadamanthys** (ˌrædə'mænθəs) *n Greek myth* one of the judges of the dead in the underworld > **ˌRhada'manthine** *adj*

Rhaetia ('riːʃɪə) *n* an Alpine province of ancient Rome including parts of present-day Tyrol and E Switzerland

Rhaetian Alps *pl n* a section of the central Alps along E Switzerland's borders with Austria and Italy. Highest peak: Piz Bernina, 4049 m (13 284 ft)

rhapsodic (ræp'sɒdɪk) *adj* **1** of or like a rhapsody **2** lyrical or romantic

rhapsodize *or* **rhapsodise** ('ræpsəˌdaɪz) *vb* **rhapsodizes, rhapsodizing, rhapsodized** *or* **rhapsodises, rhapsodising, rhapsodised** **1** to speak or write (something) with extravagant enthusiasm **2** (*intr*) to recite or write rhapsodies > **'rhapsodist** *n*

rhapsody ('ræpsədɪ) *n, pl* **rhapsodies** **1** *music* a composition free in structure and highly emotional in character **2** an expression of ecstatic enthusiasm **3** (in ancient Greece) an epic poem or part of an epic recited by a rhapsodist **4** a literary work composed in an intense or exalted style **5** rapturous delight or ecstasy [c16 via L from Gk *rhapsōidia*, from *rhaptein* to sew together + *ōidē* song]

rhatany ('rætənɪ) *n, pl* **rhatanies** **1** either of two South American leguminous shrubs that have thick fleshy roots **2** the dried roots used as an astringent ▷ Also called: **krameria** [c19 from NL *rhatānia*, ult. from Quechua *ratánya*]

rhea (rɪə) *n* either of two large fast-running flightless birds inhabiting the open plains of S South America. They are similar to but smaller than the ostrich [c19 NL; arbitrarily after RHEA]

Rhea ('rɪə) *n Greek myth* a Titaness, wife of Cronus and mother of several of the gods, including Zeus: a fertility goddess. Roman counterpart: **Ops**

Rhea Silvia *or* **Rea Silvia** ('sɪlvɪə) *n Roman myth* the mother of Romulus and Remus by Mars. See also **Ilia**

rhebuck *or* **rhebok** ('riːbʌk) *n, pl* **rhebucks, rhebuck** *or* **rheboks, rhebok** an antelope of southern Africa, having woolly brownish-grey hair [c18 Afrik., from Du. *reebok* ROEBUCK]

Rhee (riː) *n* **Syngman** ('sɪŋmən) 1875–1965, Korean statesman, leader of the campaign for independence from Japan; first president of South Korea (1948–60). Popular unrest forced his resignation

Rheims (riːmz; *French* rɛ̃s) *n* a variant spelling of **Reims**

Rhein (raɪn) *n* the German name for the **Rhine**

Rheinland ('raɪnlant) *n* the German name for the **Rhineland**

Rheinland-Pfalz ('raɪnlant'pfalts) *n* the German name for **Rhineland-Palatinate**

Rhenish ('rɛnɪʃ, 'riː-) *adj* **1** of or relating to the River Rhine or the lands adjacent to it ▷ *n* **2** another word for **hock**[2]

rhenium ('riːnɪəm) *n* a dense silvery-white metallic element that has a high melting point. Symbol: Re; atomic no.: 75; atomic wt.: 186.2 [c19 NL, from *Rhēnus* the Rhine]

rheo- *combining form* indicating stream, flow, or current: *rheostat* [from Gk *rheos* stream, anything flowing, from *rhein* to flow]

rheology (rɪ'ɒlədʒɪ) *n* the branch of physics concerned with the flow and change of shape of matter, esp the viscosity of liquids > **rheological** (ˌriːə'lɒdʒɪkᵊl) *adj* > **rhe'ologist** *n*

rheostat ('rɪəˌstæt) *n* a variable resistance, usually a coil of wire with a terminal at one end and a sliding contact that moves along the coil to tap off the current > **ˌrheo'static** *adj*

Rhesus ('riːsəs) *n Greek myth* a king of Thrace, who arrived in the tenth year of the Trojan War to aid Troy. Odysseus and Diomedes stole his horses because an oracle had said that if they drank from the River Xanthus, Troy would not fall

rhesus baby ('riːsəs) *n* a baby suffering from haemolytic disease at birth as its red blood cells (which are Rh positive) have been attacked in the womb by antibodies from its Rh negative mother. Technical name: **erythroblastosis fetalis** [c20 see RH FACTOR]

rhesus factor *n* See **Rh factor**

rhesus monkey *n* a macaque monkey of S Asia [c19 NL, arbitrarily from Gk *Rhesos*, mythical Thracian king]

rhetoric (ˈrɛtərɪk) *n* **1** the study of the technique of using language effectively **2** the art of using speech to persuade, influence, or please; oratory **3** excessive ornamentation and contrivance in spoken or written discourse; bombast **4** speech or discourse that pretends to significance but lacks true meaning: *mere rhetoric* [c14 via L from Gk *rhētorikē* (*tekhnē*) (the art of) rhetoric, from *rhētōr* teacher of rhetoric, orator]
▹ http://humanities.byu.edu/rhetoric/silva.htm

rhetorical (rɪˈtɒrɪkᵊl) *adj* **1** concerned with effect or style rather than content or meaning; bombastic **2** of or relating to rhetoric or oratory > **rheˈtorically** *adv*

rhetorical question *n* a question to which no answer is required: used esp for dramatic effect. An example is *Who knows?* (with the implication *Nobody knows*)

rhetorician (ˌrɛtəˈrɪʃən) *n* **1** a teacher of rhetoric **2** a stylish or eloquent writer or speaker **3** a pompous or extravagant speaker

rheum (ruːm) *n* a watery discharge from the eyes or nose [c14 from OF *reume*, ult. from Gk *rheuma* bodily humour, stream, from *rhein* to flow] > **ˈrheumy** *adj*

rheumatic (ruːˈmætɪk) *adj* **1** of, relating to, or afflicted with rheumatism ▹ *n* **2** a person afflicted with rheumatism [c14 ult. from Gk *rheumatikos*, from *rheuma* a flow; see RHEUM] > **rheuˈmatically** *adv*

rheumatic fever *n* a disease characterized by inflammation and pain in the joints

rheumatics (ruːˈmætɪks) *n* (*functioning as sing*) *inf* rheumatism

rheumatism (ˈruːməˌtɪzəm) *n* any painful disorder of joints, muscles, or connective tissue [c17 from L *rheumatismus* catarrh, from Gk *rheumatismos*; see RHEUM]

rheumatoid (ˈruːməˌtɔɪd) *adj* (of symptoms) resembling rheumatism

rheumatoid arthritis *n* a chronic disease characterized by inflammation and swelling of joints (esp in the hands, wrists, knees, and feet), muscle weakness, and fatigue

rheumatology (ˌruːməˈtɒlədʒɪ) *n* the study of rheumatic diseases > **rheumatological** (ˌruːmətəˈlɒdʒɪkᵊl) *adj*

Rh factor *n* an antigen commonly found in human blood: the terms **Rh positive** and **Rh negative** are used to indicate its presence or absence. It may cause a haemolytic reaction, esp during pregnancy or following transfusion of blood that does not contain this antigen. Full name: **rhesus factor** [after the rhesus monkey, in which it was first discovered]

rhinal (ˈraɪnᵊl) *adj* of or relating to the nose

Rhine (raɪn) *n* a river in central and W Europe, rising in SE Switzerland: flows through Lake Constance north through W Germany and west through the Netherlands to the North Sea. Length: about 1320 km (820 miles). Dutch name: **Rijn** French name: **Rhin** (rɛ̃) German name: **Rhein**

Rhineland (ˈraɪnˌlænd, -lənd) *n* the region of Germany surrounding the Rhine. German name: **Rheinland**

Rhineland-Palatinate *n* a state of W Germany: formed in 1946 from the S part of the Prussian Rhine province, the Palatinate, and parts of Rhine-Hesse and Hesse-Nassau; part of West Germany until 1990: agriculture (with extensive vineyards) and tourism are important. Capital: Mainz. Pop: 4 030 800 (2000 est). Area: 19 832 sq km (7657 sq miles). German name: **Rheinland-Pfalz**

rhinestone (ˈraɪnˌstəʊn) *n* an imitation gem made of paste [c19 translation of F *caillou du Rhin*, referring to Strasbourg, where such gems were made]

Rhine wine (raɪn) *n* any wine produced along the Rhine, characteristically a white table wine

rhinitis (raɪˈnaɪtɪs) *n* inflammation of the mucous membrane that lines the nose > **rhinitic** (raɪˈnɪtɪk) *adj*

rhino[1] (ˈraɪnəʊ) *n, pl* **rhinos** *or* **rhino** short for **rhinoceros**

rhino[2] (ˈraɪnəʊ) *n Brit* a slang word for **money** [c17 from ?]

rhino- *or before a vowel* **rhin-** *combining form* the nose: *rhinology* [from Gk *rhis*, *rhin*]

rhinoceros (raɪˈnɒsərəs, -ˈnɒsrəs) *n, pl* **rhinoceroses** *or* **rhinoceros** any of several mammals constituting a family of SE Asia and Africa and having either one horn on the nose, like the **Indian rhinoceros**, or two horns, like the African **white rhinoceros**. They have a very thick skin and a massive body [c13 via L from Gk *rhinokerōs*, from *rhis* nose + *keras* horn] > **rhinocerotic** (ˌraɪnəʊsɪˈrɒtɪk) *adj*

rhinology (raɪˈnɒlədʒɪ) *n* the branch of medical science concerned with the nose > **rhinological** (ˌraɪnᵊˈlɒdʒɪkᵊl) *adj* > **rhiˈnologist** *n*

rhinoplasty (ˈraɪnəʊˌplæstɪ) *n* plastic surgery of the nose > ˌ**rhinoˈplastic** *adj*

rhinoscopy (raɪˈnɒskəpɪ) *n med* examination of the nasal passages, esp with a special instrument called a **rhinoscope** (ˈraɪnəʊˌskəʊp)

rhizo- *or before a vowel* **rhiz-** *combining form* root: *rhizocarpous* [from Gk *rhiza*]

rhizocarpous (ˌraɪzəʊˈkɑːpəs) *adj* **1** (of plants) producing subterranean flowers and fruit **2** (of plants) having perennial roots but stems and leaves that wither

rhizoid (ˈraɪzɔɪd) *n* any of various hairlike structures that function as roots in mosses, ferns, and related plants > **rhiˈzoidal** *adj*

rhizome (ˈraɪzəʊm) *n* a thick horizontal underground stem whose buds develop into new plants. Also called: **rootstock, rootstalk** [c19 from NL *rhizoma*, from Gk, from *rhiza* a root] > **rhizomatous** (raɪˈzɒmətəs, -ˈzəʊ-) *adj*

rhizopod (ˈraɪzəʊˌpɒd) *n* **1** any of various protozoans characterized by naked protoplasmic processes (pseudopodia) ▹ *adj* **2** of, relating to, or belonging to rhizopods

rho (rəʊ) *n, pl* **rhos** the 17th letter in the Greek alphabet (Ρ, ρ)

rhodamine (ˈrəʊdəˌmiːn, -mɪn) *n* any one of a group of synthetic red or pink basic dyestuffs used for wool and silk [c20 from RHODO- + AMINE]

Rhode Island (rəʊd) *n* a state of the northeastern US, bordering on the Atlantic: the smallest state in the US; mainly low-lying and undulating, with an indented coastline in the east and uplands in the northwest. Capital: Providence. Pop: 1 048 319 (2000). Area: 2717 sq km (1049 sq miles). Abbreviations: **R.I.** or (with zip code) **RI**

Rhode Island Red *n* a breed of domestic fowl, originating in America, that has a dark reddish-brown plumage and produces brown eggs

Rhodes[1] (rəʊdz) *n* **1** a Greek island in the SE Aegean Sea, about 16 km (10 miles) off the Turkish coast: the largest of the Dodecanese and the most easterly island in the Aegean. Capital: Rhodes. Pop: 70 000 (latest est). Area: 1400 sq km (540 sq miles) **2** a port on this island, in the NE: founded in 408 BC; of great commercial and political importance in the 3rd century BC; suffered several earthquakes, notably in 225, when the Colossus was destroyed. Pop: 41 000 (latest est) ▹ Ancient Greek name **Rhodos** Modern Greek name: **Ródhos**

Rhodes[2] (rəʊdz) *n* **Cecil John** 1853–1902, British colonial financier and statesman in South Africa. He made a fortune in diamond and gold mining and, as prime minister of the Cape Colony (1890–96), he helped to extend British territory. He established the annual **Rhodes scholarships** to Oxford

Rhodesia (rəʊˈdiːʃə, -zɪə) *n* a former name (1964–79) for **Zimbabwe** > **Rhoˈdesian** *adj, n*

Rhodesia and Nyasaland *n* **Federation of** a federation

Rr

consisting of Northern Rhodesia, Southern Rhodesia, and Nyasaland, which existed from 1953 to 1963

Rhodesian man *n* a type of early man, occurring in Africa in late Pleistocene times and resembling Neanderthal man

Rhodes scholarship (rəʊdz) *n* one of 72 scholarships founded by Cecil Rhodes, awarded annually to Commonwealth and US students to study at Oxford University > **Rhodes scholar** *n*

Rhodian ('rəʊdɪən) *adj* **1** of or relating to the island of Rhodes ▷ *n* **2** a native or inhabitant of Rhodes

rhodium ('rəʊdɪəm) *n* a hard silvery-white element of the platinum metal group. Used as an alloying agent to harden platinum and palladium. Symbol: Rh; atomic no.: 45; atomic wt.: 102.90 [C19 NL, from Gk *rhodon* rose, from the pink colour of its compounds]

rhodo- *or before a vowel* **rhod-** *combining form* rose or rose-coloured: *rhododendron; rhodolite* [from Gk *rhodon* rose]

rhodochrosite (ˌrəʊdəʊ'krəʊsaɪt) *n* a pink, red, grey, or brown mineral that consists of manganese carbonate in hexagonal crystalline form. Formula: $MnCO_3$ [C19 from Gk *rhodokhrōs*, from *rhodon* rose + *khrōs* colour]

rhododendron (ˌrəʊdə'dɛndrən) *n* any of various shrubs native to S Asia but widely cultivated in N temperate regions. They are mostly evergreen and have clusters of showy red, purple, pink, or white flowers [C17 from L: oleander, from Gk, from *rhodon* rose + *dendron* tree]

rhodolite ('rɒdəˌlaɪt) *n* a pale violet or red variety of garnet, used as a gemstone

rhodonite ('rɒdəˌnaɪt) *n* a brownish translucent mineral consisting of manganese silicate in crystalline form with calcium, iron, or magnesium sometimes replacing the manganese. It is used as an ornamental stone, glaze, and pigment [C19 from G *Rhodonit*, from Gk *rhodon* rose + -ITE[1]]

Rhodope Mountains ('rɒdəpɪ, rɒ'dəʊ-) *pl n* a mountain range in SE Europe, in the Balkan Peninsula extending along the border between Bulgaria and Greece. Highest peak: Golyam Perelik (Bulgaria), 2191 m (7188 ft)

rhodopsin (rəʊ'dɒpsɪn) *n* a red pigment in the rods of the retina in vertebrates. Also called: **visual purple.** See also **iodopsin** [C20 from RHODO- + Gk *opsis* sight + -IN]

Rhodos ('rɔðɔs) *n* the Ancient Greek name for **Rhodes**

rhomb (rɒm) *n* another name for **rhombus**

rhombencephalon (ˌrɒmbɛn'sɛfəˌlɒn) *n* the part of the brain that develops from the posterior portion of the embryonic neural tube. Nontechnical name: **hindbrain** [C20 from RHOMBUS + ENCEPHALON]

rhombic aerial *n* a directional travelling-wave aerial, usually horizontal, consisting of two conductors forming a rhombus

rhombohedral (ˌrɒmbəʊ'hiːdrəl) *adj* **1** of or relating to a rhombohedron **2** *crystallog* another term for **trigonal** (sense 2)

rhombohedron (ˌrɒmbəʊ'hiːdrən) *n, pl* **rhombohedrons** *or* **rhombohedra** (-drə) a six-sided prism whose sides are parallelograms [C19 from RHOMBUS + -HEDRON]

rhomboid ('rɒmbɔɪd) *n* **1** a parallelogram having adjacent sides of unequal length ▷ *adj also* **rhom'boidal** **2** having such a shape [C16 from LL, from Gk *rhomboeidēs* shaped like a RHOMBUS]

rhombus ('rɒmbəs) *n, pl* **rhombuses** *or* **rhombi** (-baɪ) an oblique-angled parallelogram having four equal sides. Also called: **rhomb** [C16 from Gk *rhombos* something that spins; rel. to *rhembein* to whirl] > **'rhombic** *adj*

rhonchus ('rɒŋkəs) *n, pl* **rhonchi** (-kaɪ) a rattling or whistling respiratory sound resembling snoring, caused by secretions in the trachea or bronchi [C19 from L, from Gk *rhenkhos* snoring]

Rhondda ('rɒndə) *n* an urban area in S Wales, in Rhondda Cynon Taff county borough on two branches of the **Rhondda Valley**: developed into a major coal-mining centre after 1807 and grew to a population of 167 900 in 1924: the last coal mine closed in 1990. Pop: 59 947 (1991)

Rhondda Cynon Taff ('rɒndə 'kʊnən 'tæf) *n* a county borough in S Wales, created from part of Mid Glamorgan in 1996. Pop: 231 952 (2001). Area: 558 sq km (215 sq miles)

Rhône (rəʊn) *n* **1** a river in W Europe, rising in S Switzerland in the **Rhône glacier** and flowing to Lake Geneva, then into France through gorges between the Alps and Jura and south to its delta on the Gulf of Lions: important esp for hydroelectricity and for wine production along its valley. Length: 812 km (505 miles) **2** a department of E central France, in the Rhône-Alpes region. Capital: Lyons. Pop: 1 578 869 (1999). Area: 3233 sq km (1261 sq miles)

Rhône-Alpes (*French* ronalp) *n* a region of E France: mainly mountainous, rising to the edge of the Massif Central in the west and the French Alps in the east; drained by the Rivers Rhône, Saône, and Isère

RHS *abbrev for:* **1** Royal Historical Society **2** Royal Horticultural Society **3** Royal Humane Society
▷ www.rhs.org.uk

rhubarb ('ruːbɑːb) *n* **1** any of several temperate and subtropical plants, esp **common garden rhubarb,** which has long green and red acid-tasting edible leafstalks, usually eaten sweetened and cooked **2** the leafstalks of this plant **3** a related plant of central Asia, having a bitter-tasting underground stem that can be dried and used as a laxative or astringent **4** *US & Canad sl* a heated discussion or quarrel ▷ *interj, n, vb* **5** the noise made by actors to simulate conversation, esp by repeating the word *rhubarb* [C14 from OF *reubarbe*, from Med. L *reubarbum*, prob. var. of *rha barbarum*, from *rha* rhubarb (from Gk, ?from *Rha*, ancient name of the Volga) + L *barbarus* barbarian]

rhumb (rʌm) *n* short for **rhumb line**

rhumba ('rʌmbə, 'rʊm-) *n, pl* **rhumbas** a variant spelling of **rumba**

rhumb line *n* **1** an imaginary line on the surface of a sphere that intersects all meridians at the same angle **2** the course navigated by a vessel or aircraft that maintains a uniform compass heading [C16 from OSp. *rumbo*, apparently from MDu. *ruum* space, ship's hold, infl. by RHOMBUS]

rhyme *or* (*arch*) **rime** (raɪm) *n* **1** identity of the terminal sounds in lines of verse or in words **2** a word that is identical to another in its terminal sound: *"while" is a rhyme for "mile"* **3** a piece of poetry, esp having corresponding sounds at the ends of the lines **4** **rhyme or reason** sense, logic, or meaning ▷ *vb* **rhymes, rhyming, rhymed** *or* **rimes, riming, rimed** **5** to use (a word) or (of a word) to be used so as to form a rhyme **6** to render (a subject) into rhyme **7** to compose (verse) in a metrical structure ▷ See also **eye rhyme** [C12 from OF *rime*, ult. from OHG *rīm* a number; spelling infl. by RHYTHM]

rhymester, rimester ('raɪmstə), **rhymer,** *or* **rimer** *n* a poet, esp one considered to be mediocre; poetaster or versifier

rhyming slang *n* slang in which a word is replaced by another word or phrase that rhymes with it; e.g. *apples and pears* meaning *stairs*

rhyolite ('raɪəˌlaɪt) *n* a fine-grained igneous rock consisting of quartz, feldspars, and mica or amphibole [C19 *rhyo-* from Gk *rhuax* a stream of lava + -LITE] > **rhyolitic** (ˌraɪə'lɪtɪk) *adj*

Rhys (riːs) *n* **Jean** (**Ella Gwendolen Rees Williams**) ?1890–1979, Welsh novelist and short-story writer, born in Dominica. Her novels include *Voyage in the Dark* (1934), *Good Morning, Midnight* (1939), and *Wide Sargasso Sea* (1966)

rhythm ('rɪðəm) *n* **1a** the arrangement of the durations of and accents on the notes of a melody, usually laid out into regular groups (**bars**) of beats **1b** any specific arrangement of such groupings; time: *quadruple rhythm* **2** (in poetry) **2a** the arrangement of words into a sequence of stressed and unstressed or long and short syllables **2b** any specific such arrangement; metre **3** (in painting, sculpture, etc) a harmonious sequence or pattern of masses alternating with voids, of light alternating with shade, of alternating colours, etc **4** any sequence of regularly recurring functions or events, such as certain physiological functions of the body, as the cardiac rhythm of the heart beat [C16 from L *rhythmus*, from Gk *rhuthmos*; rel. to *rhein* to flow]

rhythm and blues *n (functioning as sing)* any of various kinds of popular music derived from or influenced by the blues. Abbrev: **R&B**
▷ www.rhythm-n-blues.org

rhythmic ('rɪðmɪk) *or* **rhythmical** ('rɪðmɪkᵊl) *adj* of, relating to, or characterized by rhythm, as in movement or sound; metrical, periodic, or regularly recurring > **'rhythmically** *adv* > **rhythmicity** (rɪð'mɪsɪtɪ) *n*

rhythm method *n* a method of contraception by restricting sexual intercourse to those days in a woman's menstrual cycle on which conception is considered least likely to occur

rhythm section *n* those instruments in a band or group (usually piano, double bass, and drums) whose prime function is to supply the rhythm

RI *abbrev for:* **1** Regina et Imperatrix [L: Queen and Empress] **2** Rex et Imperator [L: King and Emperor] **3** Royal Institution **4** religious instruction

ria (rɪə) *n* a long narrow inlet of the seacoast, being a former valley that was submerged by the sea [C19 from Sp., from *rio* river]

Rialto (rɪ'æltəʊ) *n* an island in Venice, Italy, linked with San Marco Island by the **Rialto Bridge** (1590) over the Grand Canal: the business centre of medieval and renaissance Venice

riata *or* **reata** (rɪ'ɑːtə) *n South & West US* a lariat or lasso [C19 from American Sp., from Sp. *reatar* to tie together again, from RE- + *atar* to tie, from L *aptāre* to fit]

rib[1] (rɪb) *n* **1** any of the 24 elastic arches of bone that together form the chest wall in man. All are attached behind to the thoracic part of the spinal column **2** the corresponding bone in other vertebrates **3** a cut of meat including one or more ribs **4** a part or element similar in function or appearance to a rib, esp a structural member or a ridge **5** a structural member in a wing that extends from the leading edge to the trailing edge **6** a projecting moulding or band on the underside of a vault or ceiling **7** one of a series of raised rows in knitted fabric **8** a raised ornamental line on the spine of a book where the stitching runs across it **9** any of the transverse stiffening timbers or joists forming the frame of a ship's hull **10** any of the larger veins of a leaf **11** a vein of ore in rock **12** a projecting ridge of a mountain; spur ▷ *vb* **ribs, ribbing, ribbed** *(tr)* **13** to furnish or support with a rib or ribs **14** to mark with or form into ribs or ridges **15** to knit plain and purl stitches alternately in order to make raised rows in (knitting) [OE *ribb*; rel. to OHG *rippi*, ON *rif* REEF[1]] > **'ribless** *adj*

rib[2] (rɪb) *vb* **ribs, ribbing, ribbed** *(tr) inf* to tease or ridicule [C20 short for *rib-tickle* (vb)]

RIBA *abbrev for* Royal Institute of British Architects

ribald ('rɪbᵊld) *adj* **1** coarse, obscene, or licentious, usually in a humorous or mocking way ▷ *n* **2** a ribald person [C13 from OF *ribauld*, from *riber* to live licentiously, of Gmc origin]

ribaldry ('rɪbᵊldrɪ) *n* ribald language or behaviour

riband *or* **ribband** ('rɪbənd) *n* a ribbon, esp one awarded for some achievement [C14 var. of RIBBON]

Ribbentrop (*German* 'rɪbəntrɔp) *n* **Joachim von** ('joːaxɪm fɔn) 1893–1946, German Nazi politician: foreign minister under Hitler (1938–45). He was hanged after conviction as a war criminal at Nuremberg

ribbing ('rɪbɪŋ) *n* **1** a framework or structure of ribs **2** a pattern of ribs in woven or knitted material **3** *inf* teasing

Ribble ('rɪbᵊl) *n* a river in NW England, flowing south and west through Lancashire to the Irish Sea. Length: 121 km (75 miles)

ribbon ('rɪbᵊn) *n* **1** a narrow strip of fine material, esp silk, used for trimming, tying, etc **2** something resembling a ribbon; a long strip **3** a long thin flexible band of metal used as a graduated measure, spring, etc **4** a long narrow strip of ink-impregnated cloth for making the impression of type characters on paper in a typewriter, etc **5** *(pl)* ragged strips or shreds (esp in **torn to ribbons**) **6** a small strip of coloured cloth signifying membership of an order or award of military decoration, prize, etc **7** a small, usually looped, strip of coloured cloth worn to signify support for a charity or cause: *a red AIDS ribbon* ▷ *vb (tr)* **8** to adorn with a ribbon or ribbons **9** to mark with narrow ribbon-like marks [C14 *ryban*, from OF *riban*, apparently of Gmc origin]

ribbon development *n Brit* the building of houses in a continuous row along a main road

ribbonfish ('rɪbᵊn,fɪʃ) *n, pl* **ribbonfish** *or* **ribbonfishes** any of various soft-finned deep-sea fishes that have an elongated compressed body

ribbonwood ('rɪbᵊn,wʊd) *n* a small evergreen malvaceous tree of New Zealand. Its wood is used in furniture making. Also: **lacebark**

ribcage ('rɪb,keɪdʒ) *n* the bony structure of the ribs and their connective tissue that encloses the lungs, heart, etc

Ribeirão Prêto (*Portuguese* riβi'rɐ̃u 'pretu) *n* a city in SE Brazil, in São Paulo state. Pop: 416 186 (1991)

Ribera (*Spanish* ri'βera) *n* **José de** (xo'se de) also called *Jusepe de Ribera*, Italian nickname *Lo Spagnoletto* (The Little Spaniard). 1591–1652, Spanish artist, living in Italy. His religious pictures often dwell on horrible suffering, presented in realistic detail

Rr

riboflavin *or* **riboflavine** (,raɪbəʊ'fleɪvɪn) *n* a vitamin of the B complex that occurs in green vegetables, milk, fish, egg yolk, liver, and kidney: used as a yellow or orange food colouring (**E 101**). Also called: **vitamin B_2** [C20 from RIBOSE + FLAVIN]

ribonuclease (,raɪbəʊ'njuːklɪ,eɪz) *n* any of a group of enzymes that catalyse the hydrolysis of RNA [C20 from RIBONUCLE(IC ACID) + -ASE]

ribonucleic acid (,raɪbəʊnjuː'kliːɪk, -'kleɪ-) *n* the full name of **RNA** [C20 from RIBO(SE) + NUCLEIC ACID]

ribose ('raɪbəʊz, -bəʊs) *n* a sugar that occurs in RNA and riboflavin [C20 changed from *arabinose*, from (GUM) ARAB(IC) + -IN + -OSE[2]]

ribosomal RNA (,raɪbə'səʊməl) *n* a type of RNA thought to form the component of ribosomes on which the translation of messenger RNA into protein chains is accomplished. Shortened to **rRNA**

ribosome ('raɪbə,səʊm) *n* any of numerous minute particles in the cytoplasm of cells that contain RNA and protein and are the site of protein synthesis [C20 from RIBO(NUCLEIC ACID) + -SOME[3]] > ,**ribo'somal** *adj*

rib-tickler *n* a very amusing joke or story > **'rib-,tickling** *adj*

ribwort ('rɪb,wɜːt) *n* a Eurasian plant that has lancelike ribbed leaves. Also called: **ribgrass** See also **plantain**[1]

Ricardo (rɪ'kɑːdəʊ) *n* **David** 1772–1823, British economist. His main work is *Principles of Political Economy and Taxation* (1817)

Riccio ('rɪtsɪəʊ) *n* a variant of **Rizzio**

rice (raɪs) *n* **1** an erect grass that grows in warm climates on wet ground and has yellow oblong edible grains that become white when polished **2** the grain of this plant ▷ *vb* **rices, ricing, riced 3** *(tr) US & Canad* to sieve (potatoes or other vegetables) to a coarse mashed consistency [C13 *rys*, via F, It., & L from Gk *orūza*, of Oriental origin]

▷ www.riceweb.org
▷ www.virtualcities.com/ons/orec/1orice.htm

Rice (raɪs) *n* **Elmer**, original name *Elmer Reizenstein*. 1892–1967, US dramatist. His plays include *The Adding Machine* (1923) and *Street Scene* (1929), which was made into a musical by Kurt Weill in 1947

rice bowl *n* **1** a small bowl used for eating rice **2** a fertile rice-producing region

rice paper *n* **1** a thin edible paper made from the straw of rice, on which macaroons and similar cakes are baked **2** a thin delicate Chinese paper made from the **rice-paper plant**, the pith of which is pared and flattened into sheets

ricercare (ˌriːtʃəˈkɑːreɪ) *or* **ricercar** (ˈriːtʃəˌkɑː) *n, pl* **ricercari** (-ˈkɑːriː) *or* **ricercars** (in music of the 16th and 17th centuries) **1** an elaborate polyphonic composition making extensive use of contrapuntal imitation and usually very slow in tempo **2** an instructive composition to illustrate instrumental technique; étude [It., lit.: to seek again]

rich (rɪtʃ) *adj* **1a** well supplied with wealth, property, etc; owning much **1b** (*as collective n*; preceded by *the*): *the rich* **2** (when *postpositive*, usually foll by *in*) having an abundance of natural resources, minerals, etc: *a land rich in metals* **3** producing abundantly; fertile: *rich soil* **4** (when *postpositive*, foll by *in* or *with*) well supplied (with desirable qualities); abundant (in): *a country rich with cultural interest* **5** of great worth or quality: *a rich collection of antiques* **6** luxuriant or prolific: *a rich growth of weeds* **7** expensively elegant, elaborate, or fine; costly: *a rich display* **8** (of food) having a large proportion of flavoursome or fatty ingredients **9** having a full-bodied flavour: *a rich ruby port* **10** (of a smell) pungent or fragrant **11** (of colour) intense or vivid; deep: *a rich red* **12** (of sound or a voice) full, mellow, or resonant **13** (of a fuel-air mixture) containing a relatively high proportion of fuel **14** very amusing or ridiculous: *a rich joke* ▷ *n* **15** See **riches** [OE *rīce* (orig. of persons: great, mighty), of Gmc origin, ult. from Celtic]

Rich (rɪtʃ) *n* **1** **Adrienne** born 1929, US poet and feminist writer; her volumes of poetry include *Snapshots of a Daughter-in-Law* (1963) and *Diving Into the Wreck* (1973) **2** **Buddy**, real name *Bernard Rich*. 1917–87, US jazz drummer and band leader

Richard (ˈrɪtʃəd) *n* Sir **Cliff**, real name *Harry Rodger Webb*. born 1940, British pop singer. Film musicals include *The Young Ones* (1961) and *Summer Holiday* (1962)

Richard I (ˈrɪtʃəd) *n* nicknamed *Coeur de Lion* or *the Lion-Heart*. 1157–99, king of England (1189–99); a leader of the third crusade (joining it in 1191). On his way home, he was captured in Austria (1192) and held to ransom. After a brief return to England, where he was crowned again (1194), he spent the rest of his life in France

Richard II *n* 1367–1400, king of England (1377–99), whose reign was troubled by popular discontent and baronial opposition. He was forced to abdicate in favour of Henry Bolingbroke, who became Henry IV

Richard III *n* 1452–85, king of England (1483–85), notorious as the suspected murderer of his two young nephews in the Tower of London. He proved an able administrator until his brief reign was ended by his death at the hands of Henry Tudor (later Henry VII) at the battle of Bosworth Field

Richards (ˈrɪtʃədz) *n* **1** **I(vor) A(rmstrong)** 1893–1979, British literary critic and linguist, who, with C. K. Ogden, wrote *The Meaning of Meaning* (1923) and devised Basic English **2** Sir **Gordon** 1904–86, British jockey **3** Sir **Viv**, full name *Isaac Vivian Alexander Richards*. born 1952, West Indian cricketer; captained the West Indies (1985–91)

Richardson (ˈrɪtʃədsən) *n* **1** **Dorothy M(iller)** 1873–1957, British novelist, a pioneer of stream-of-consciousness writing: author of the novel sequence *Pilgrimage* (14 vols, 1915–67) **2** **Henry Handel** pen name of *Ethel Florence Lindesay Richardson*, 1870–1946, Australian novelist; author of the trilogy *The Fortunes of Richard Mahony* (1917–29) **3** Sir **Owen Willans** 1879–1959, British physicist; a pioneer in the study of atomic physics: Nobel prize for physics 1928 **4** Sir **Ralph** (**David**) 1902–83, British stage and screen actor **5** **Samuel** 1689–1761, British novelist whose psychological insight and use of the epistolary form exerted a great influence on the development of the novel. His chief novels are *Pamela* (1740) and *Clarissa* (1747)

Richelieu (ˈrɪʃəˌljɜː; *French* riʃəljø) *n* **Armand Jean du Plessis** (armɑ̃ ʒɑ̃ dy plɛsi) 1585–1642, French statesman and cardinal, principal minister to Louis XIII and virtual ruler of France (1624–42). He destroyed the power of the Huguenots and strengthened the crown in France and the role of France in Europe

Richelieu River (ˈrɪʃəˌljɜː; *French* riʃəljø) *n* a river in E Canada, in S Quebec, rising in Lake Champlain and flowing north to the St Lawrence River. Length: 338 km (210 miles)

riches (ˈrɪtʃɪz) *pl n* wealth; an abundance of money, valuable possessions, or property

Richler (ˈrɪʃlə) *n* **Mordecai** born 1931, Canadian novelist. His novels include *St Urbain's Horseman* (1971), *Solomon Gursky Was Here* (1990), and *Barney's Version* (1997)

richly (ˈrɪtʃlɪ) *adv* **1** in a rich or elaborate manner: *a richly decorated carving* **2** fully and appropriately: *he was richly rewarded*

Richmond (ˈrɪtʃmənd) *n* **1** a borough of Greater London, on the River Thames: formed in 1965 by the amalgamation of Barnes, Richmond, and Twickenham; site of Hampton Court Palace and the Royal Botanic Gardens at Kew. Pop: 172 327 (2001). Area: 55 sq km (21 sq miles). Official name: **Richmond-upon-Thames** **2** a town in N England, in North Yorkshire: Norman castle. Pop: 7862 (1991) **3** a port in E Virginia, the state capital, at the falls of the James River: developed after the establishment of a trading post (1637); scene of the Virginia Conventions of 1774 and 1775; Confederate capital in the American Civil War. Pop: 197 790 (2000) **4** a county of SW New York City: coextensive with Staten Island borough; consists of Staten Island and several smaller islands

Richter *n* **1** (ˈrɪktə) **Burton** born 1931, US physicist: shared the 1976 Nobel prize for physics with Samuel Tring for discovering the subatomic particle known as the J/psi particle **2** (*German* ˈrɪçtər) **Johann Friedrich** (joˈhan ˈfriːdrɪç), wrote under the name *Jean Paul*. 1763–1825, German romantic novelist. His works include *Hesperus* (1795) and *Titan* (1800–03) **3** (*Russian* ˈrixtɪr) **Sviatoslav** (svɪtaˈslaf) 1915–97, Ukrainian concert pianist

Richter scale (ˈrɪxtə) *n* a scale for expressing the magnitude of an earthquake, ranging from 0 to over 8 [c20 after Charles *Richter* (1900–85), US seismologist]

RICHTER AND MERCALLI SCALES

The Richter Scale is used to measure an earthquake's magnitude and the Mercalli Scale is used to measure its intensity.

MERCALLI	RICHTER	CHARACTERISTICS
1	< 3.5	detected only by seismograph
2	3.5	noticed only by people at rest
3	4.2	similar to vibrations from a large goods vehicle
4	4.5	felt indoors; rocks parked cars

5	4.8	generally felt; awakens sleepers
6	5.4	trees sway; causes some damage
7	6.1	causes general alarm; building walls crack
8	6.5	walls collapse
9	6.9	some houses collapse; cracks appear in ground
10	7.3	buildings destroyed; rails buckle
11	8.1	most buildings destroyed; landslides
12	8.1+	total destruction of area

▷ www.psigate.ac.uk/newsite/earth-gateway.html
▷ www.earthquakes.bgs.ac.uk

Richthofen (*German* 'rɪçtho:fən) *n* Baron **Manfred von** ('manfre:t fɔn), nickname *the Red Baron*. 1892–1918, German aviator; commander during World War I of the 11th Chasing Squadron (**Richthofen's Flying Circus**). He was credited with 80 air victories before he was shot down

rick[1] (rɪk) *n* **1** a large stack of hay, corn, etc, built in a regular-shaped pile, esp with a thatched top ▷ *vb* **2** (*tr*) to stack into ricks [OE *hrēac*]

rick[2] (rɪk) *n* **1** a wrench or sprain, as of the back ▷ *vb* **2** (*tr*) to wrench or sprain (a joint, a limb, the back, etc) [c18 var. of *wrick*]

rickets ('rɪkɪts) *n* (*functioning as sing or pl*) a disease mainly of children, characterized by softening of developing bone, and hence bow legs, caused by a deficiency of vitamin D [c17 from ?]

rickettsia (rɪ'kɛtsɪə) *n, pl* **rickettsiae** (-sɪˌi:) *or* **rickettsias** any of a group of parasitic bacteria, that live in the tissues of ticks, mites, etc, and cause disease when transmitted to humans and other animals [c20 after Howard T. *Ricketts* (1871–1910), US pathologist] > **rick'ettsial** *adj*

rickettsial disease *n* any of several acute infectious diseases, such as typhus, caused by ticks, mites, or body lice infected with rickettsiae

rickety ('rɪkɪtɪ) *adj* **1** (of a structure, piece of furniture, etc) likely to collapse or break **2** feeble **3** resembling or afflicted with rickets [c17 from RICKETS] > **'ricketiness** *n*

rickrack *or* **ricrac** ('rɪkˌræk) *n* a zigzag braid used for trimming [c20 reduplication of RACK[1]]

rickshaw ('rɪkʃɔ:) *or* **ricksha** ('rɪkʃə) *n* **1** Also called: **jinrikisha** a small two-wheeled passenger vehicle drawn by one or two men, used in parts of Asia **2** Also called: **trishaw** a similar vehicle with three wheels, propelled by a man pedalling as on a tricycle [c19 shortened from JINRIKISHA]

ricochet ('rɪkəˌʃeɪ, 'rɪkəˌʃɛt) *vb* **ricochets** (-ˌʃeɪz), **ricocheting** (-ˌʃeɪɪŋ), **ricocheted** (-ˌʃeɪd) *or* **ricochets** (-ˌʃɛts), **ricochetting** (-ˌʃɛtɪŋ), **ricochetted** (-ˌʃɛtɪd) **1** (*intr*) (esp of a bullet) to rebound from a surface, usually with a whining or zipping sound ▷ *n* **2** the motion or sound of a rebounding object, esp a bullet **3** an object that ricochets [c18 from F]

ricotta (rɪ'kɒtə) *n* a soft white unsalted cheese made from sheep's milk [It., from L *recocta* recooked, from *recoquere*, from RE- + *coquere* to COOK]

RICS *abbrev for* Royal Institution of Chartered Surveyors

rictus ('rɪktəs) *n, pl* **rictus** *or* **rictuses** **1** the gape or cleft of an open mouth or beak **2** a fixed or unnatural grin or grimace as in horror or death [c18 from L, from *ringī* to gape] > **'rictal** *adj*

rid (rɪd) *vb* **rids, ridding, rid** *or* **ridded** (*tr*) **1** (foll by *of*) to relieve from something disagreeable or undesirable; make free (of) **2** **get rid of** to relieve or free oneself of (something unpleasant or undesirable) [c13 (meaning: to clear land): from ON *rythja*]

riddance ('rɪdəns) *n* the act of getting rid of something; removal (esp in **good riddance**)

ridden ('rɪdən) *vb* **1** the past participle of **ride** ▷ *adj* **2** (*in combination*) afflicted or dominated by something specified: *disease-ridden*

riddle[1] ('rɪdəl) *n* **1** a question, puzzle, or verse so phrased that ingenuity is required for elucidation of the answer or meaning **2** a person or thing that puzzles, perplexes, or confuses ▷ *vb* **riddles, riddling, riddled** **3** to solve, explain, or interpret (a riddle) **4** (*intr*) to speak in riddles [OE *rǣdelle, rǣdelse*, from *rǣd* counsel] > **'riddler** *n*

riddle[2] ('rɪdəl) *vb* **riddles, riddling, riddled** (*tr*) **1** (usually foll by *with*) to pierce or perforate with numerous holes: *riddled with bullets* **2** to put through a sieve; sift **3** to fill or pervade: *the report was riddled with errors* ▷ *n* **4** a sieve, esp a coarse one used for sand, grain, etc [OE *hriddel* a sieve] > **'riddler** *n*

ride (raɪd) *vb* **rides, riding, rode, ridden** **1** to sit on and control the movements of (a horse or other animal) **2** (*tr*) to sit on and propel (a bicycle or similar vehicle) **3** (*intr; often foll by on or in*) to be carried along or travel on or in a vehicle: *she rides to work on the bus* **4** (*tr*) to travel over or traverse: *they rode the countryside in search of shelter* **5** (*tr*) to take part in by riding: *to ride a race* **6** to travel through or be carried across (sea, sky, etc): *the small boat rode the waves; the moon was riding high* **7** (*tr*) *US & Canad* to cause to be carried: *to ride someone out of town* **8** (*intr*) to be supported as if floating: *the candidate rode to victory on his new policies* **9** (*intr*) (of a vessel) to lie at anchor **10** (*tr*) (of a vessel) to be attached to (an anchor) **11** (*tr*) **11a** *sl* to have sexual intercourse with (someone) **11b** (of a male animal) to copulate with; mount **12** (*tr; usually passive*) to tyrannize over or dominate: *ridden by fear* **13** (*tr*) *inf* to persecute, esp by constant or petty criticism: *don't ride me so hard* **14** (*intr*) *inf* to continue undisturbed: *let it ride* **15** (*tr*) to endure successfully; ride out **16** (*tr*) to yield slightly to (a punch, etc) to lessen its impact **17** (*intr; often foll by on*) (of a bet) to remain placed: *let your winnings ride on the same number* **18** **ride again** *inf* to return to a former activity or scene **19** **ride for a fall** to act in such a way as to invite disaster **20** **riding high** confident, popular, and successful ▷ *n* **21** a journey or outing on horseback or in a vehicle **22** a path specially made for riding on horseback **23** transport in a vehicle; lift: *can you give me a ride to the station?* **24** a device or structure, such as a roller coaster at a fairground, in which people ride for pleasure or entertainment **25** *sl* an act of sexual intercourse **26** *sl* a partner in sexual intercourse **27** **take for a ride** *inf* **27a** to cheat, swindle, or deceive **27b** to take (someone) away in a car and murder him [OE *rīdan*] > **'ridable** *or* **'rideable** *adj*

Rideau Hall ('ri:dəʊ) *n* (in Canada) the official residence of the Governor General, in Ottawa

ride out *vb* (*tr, adv*) to endure successfully; survive (esp in **ride out the storm**)

rider ('raɪdə) *n* **1** a person or thing that rides **2** an additional clause, amendment, or stipulation added to a document, esp (in Britain) a legislative bill at its third reading **3** *Brit* a statement made by a jury in addition to its verdict, such as a recommendation for mercy **4** any of various objects or devices resting on or strengthening something else > **'riderless** *adj*

ride up *vb* (*intr, adv*) to work away from the proper position: *her new skirt rode up*

ridge (rɪdʒ) *n* **1** a long narrow raised land formation with sloping sides **2** any long narrow raised strip or elevation, as on a fabric or in ploughed land **3** *anat* any elongated raised margin or border on a bone, tissue, etc **4a** the top of a roof at the junction of two sloping sides **4b** (*as modifier*): *a ridge tile* **5** *meteorol* an elongated area of high pressure, esp an extension of an anticyclone ▷ Cf **trough** (sense 4) ▷ *vb* **ridges, ridging, ridged** **6** to form into a ridge or ridges [OE *hrycg*] > **'ridgeˌlike** *adj* > **'ridgy** *adj*

ridgepole ('rɪdʒˌpəʊl) *n* **1** a timber along the ridge of a roof, to which the rafters are attached **2** the horizontal pole at the apex of a tent

ridgeway ('rɪdʒ,weɪ) *n Brit* a road or track along a ridge, esp one of great antiquity

ridgy-didge ('rɪdʒɪ,dɪdʒ) *adj Austral inf* genuine; correct: *a full, ridgy-didge Aussie bloke*

ridicule ('rɪdɪ,kjuːl) *n* **1** language or behaviour intended to humiliate or mock ▷ *vb* **ridicules, ridiculing, ridiculed** **2** *(tr)* to make fun of or mock [c17 from F, from L *rīdiculus*, from *rīdēre* to laugh]

ridiculous (rɪ'dɪkjʊləs) *adj* worthy of or exciting ridicule; absurd, preposterous, laughable, or contemptible [c16 from L *rīdiculōsus*, from *rīdēre* to laugh] > **ri'diculousness** *n*

riding[1] ('raɪdɪŋ) *n* **1a** the art or practice of horsemanship **1b** *(as modifier)*: *a riding school* **2** a track for riding

riding[2] ('raɪdɪŋ) *n* **1** *(cap when part of a name)* any of the three former administrative divisions of Yorkshire: **North Riding, East Riding,** and **West Riding** **2** (in Canada) a parliamentary constituency [from OE *thriding*, from ON *thrithjungr* a third]

riding crop *n* a short whip with a handle at one end for opening gates

riding lamp *or* **light** *n* a light on a boat or ship showing that it is at anchor

Ridley ('rɪdlɪ) *n* **Nicholas** ?1500–55, English bishop, who helped to revise the liturgy under Edward VI. He was burnt at the stake for refusing to disavow his Protestant beliefs when Mary I assumed the throne

Riefenstahl (*German* 'riːfənʃtaːl) *n* **Leni** ('leːni) 1902–2003, German photographer and film director, best known for her Nazi propaganda films, such as *Triumph of the Will* (1934)

Riemann (*German* 'riːman) *n* **Georg Friedrich Bernhard** ('geːɔrk 'friːdrɪç 'bɛrnhart) 1826–66, German mathematician whose non-Euclidean geometry was used by Einstein as a basis for his general theory of relativity

riempie ('rɪmpɪ) *n S African* a leather thong or lace used mainly to make chair seats [c19 Afrik., dim. of *riem*, from Du.: RIM]

riesling ('riːzlɪŋ, 'raɪz-) *n* **1** a white wine from the Rhine valley in Germany and from certain districts in other countries **2** the grape used to make this wine [c19 from G, from earlier *Rüssling*, from ?]

rife (raɪf) *adj (postpositive)* **1** of widespread occurrence; current **2** very plentiful; abundant **3** (foll by *with*) abounding (in): *a garden rife with weeds* [OE *rīfe*] > **'rifely** *adv* > **'rifeness** *n*

riff (rɪf) *jazz, rock* ▷ *n* **1** an ostinato played over changing harmonies ▷ *vb* **2** *(intr)* to play riffs [c20 prob. altered from REFRAIN[2]]

riffle ('rɪfᵊl) *vb* **riffles, riffling, riffled** **1** (when *intr*, often foll by *through*) to flick rapidly through (pages of a book, etc) **2** to shuffle (cards) by halving the pack and flicking the corners together **3** to cause or form a ripple on water ▷ *n* **4** *US & Canad* **4a** a rapid in a stream **4b** a rocky shoal causing a rapid **4c** a ripple on water **5** *mining* a contrivance on the bottom of a sluice, containing grooves for trapping particles of gold **6** the act or an instance of riffling [c18 prob. from RUFFLE[1], infl. by RIPPLE[1]]

riffraff ('rɪf,ræf) *n (sometimes functioning as pl)* worthless people, esp collectively; rabble [c15 *rif and raf*, from OF *rif et raf*; rel. to *rifler* to plunder, and *rafle* a sweeping up]

rifle[1] ('raɪfᵊl) *n* **1a** a firearm having a long barrel with a spirally grooved interior, which imparts to the bullet spinning motion and thus greater accuracy over a longer range **1b** *(as modifier)*: *rifle fire* **2** (formerly) a large cannon with a rifled bore **3** one of the grooves in a rifled bore **4** *(pl)* **4a** a unit of soldiers equipped with rifles **4b** *(cap when part of a name)*: *the King's Own Rifles* ▷ *vb* **rifles, rifling, rifled** *(tr)* **5** to make spiral grooves inside the barrel of (a gun) [c18 from OF *rifler* to scratch; rel. to Low G *rifeln* from *riefe* groove, furrow]

rifle[2] ('raɪfᵊl) *vb* **rifles, rifling, rifled** *(tr)* **1** to search (a house, safe, etc) and steal from it; ransack **2** to steal and carry off: *to rifle goods* [c14 from OF *rifler* to plunder, scratch, of Gmc origin] > **'rifler** *n*

riflebird ('raɪfᵊl,bɜːd) *n* any of various Australian birds of paradise whose plumage has a metallic sheen

rifleman ('raɪfᵊlmən) *n, pl* **riflemen** **1** a person skilled in the use of a rifle, esp a soldier **2** a wren of New Zealand

rifle range *n* an area used for target practice with rifles

rifling ('raɪflɪŋ) *n* **1** the cutting of spiral grooves on the inside of a firearm's barrel **2** the series of grooves so cut

rift (rɪft) *n* **1** a gap or space made by cleaving or splitting **2** *geol* a long narrow zone of faulting resulting from tensional stress in the earth's crust **3** a gap between two cloud masses; break or chink **4** a break in friendly relations between people, nations, etc ▷ *vb* **5** to burst or cause to burst open; split [c13 from ON]

rift valley *n* a long narrow valley resulting from the subsidence of land between two faults

rig (rɪg) *vb* **rigs, rigging, rigged** *(tr)* **1** *naut* to equip (a vessel, mast, etc) with (sails, rigging, etc) **2** *naut* to set up or prepare ready for use **3** to put the components of (an aircraft, etc) into their correct positions **4** to manipulate in a fraudulent manner, esp for profit: *to rig prices* ▷ *n* **5** *naut* the distinctive arrangement of the sails, masts, etc, of a vessel **6** the installation used in drilling for and exploiting natural gas and oil deposits: *an oil rig* **7** apparatus or equipment **8** *chiefly US & Canad* an articulated lorry ▷ See also **rig out, rig up** [c15 of Scand. origin; rel. to Norwegian *rigga* to wrap]

Riga ('riːgə) *n* the capital of Latvia, on the **Gulf of Riga** at the mouth of the Western Dvina on the Baltic Sea: a port and major trading centre since Viking times. Pop: 788 283 (2000 est)

▷ www.virtualriga.com/default.asp

rigadoon (,rɪgə'duːn) *n* **1** an old Provençal couple dance, light and graceful, in lively duple time **2** a piece of music composed for or in the rhythm of this dance [c17 from F, allegedly after *Rigaud*, a dancing master at Marseilles]

rigamarole ('rɪgəmə,rəʊl) *n* a variant of **rigmarole**

-rigged *adj (in combination)* (of a sailing vessel) having a rig of a certain kind: *ketch-rigged; schooner-rigged*

rigger ('rɪgə) *n* **1** a workman who rigs vessels, etc **2** *rowing* a bracket on a boat to support a projecting rowlock **3** a person skilled in the use of pulleys, cranes, etc

rigging ('rɪgɪŋ) *n* **1** the shrouds, stays, etc, of a vessel **2** the bracing wires, struts, and lines of a biplane, etc **3** any form of lifting gear

right (raɪt) *adj* **1** in accordance with accepted standards of moral or legal behaviour, justice, etc: *right conduct* **2** correct or true: *the right answer* **3** appropriate, suitable, or proper: *the right man for the job* **4** most favourable or convenient: *the right time to act* **5** in a satisfactory condition: *things are right again now* **6** indicating or designating the correct time: *the clock is right* **7** correct in opinion or judgment **8** sound in mind or body **9** *(usually prenominal)* of, designating, or located near the side of something or someone that faces east when the front is turned towards the north **10** *(usually prenominal)* worn on a right hand, foot, etc **11** *(sometimes cap)* of, designating, belonging to, or relating to the political or intellectual right (see sense 36) **12** *(sometimes cap)* conservative: *the right wing of the party* **13** *geom* **13a** formed by or containing a line or plane perpendicular to another line or plane **13b** having the axis perpendicular to the base: *a right circular cone* **13c** straight: *a right line* **14** relating to or designating the side of cloth worn or facing outwards **15** **in one's right mind** sane **16** **she'll be right** *Austral & NZ inf* that's all right; not to worry **17** **the right side of**

17a in favour with: *you'd better stay on the right side of him* **17b** younger than: *she's still on the right side of fifty* **18 too right** *Austral & NZ inf* an exclamation of agreement ▷ *adv* **19** in accordance with correctness or truth: *to guess right* **20** in the appropriate manner: *do it right next time!* **21** in a straight line: *right to the top* **22** in the direction of the east from the point of view of a person or thing facing north **23** absolutely or completely: *he went right through the floor* **24** all the way: *the bus goes right into town* **25** without delay: *I'll be right over* **26** exactly or precisely: *right here* **27** in a manner consistent with a legal or moral code: *do right by me* **28** in accordance with propriety; fittingly: *it serves you right* **29** to good or favourable advantage: *it all came out right in the end* **30** (esp in religious titles) most or very: *right reverend* **31 right, left, and centre** on all sides ▷ *n* **32** any claim, title, etc, that is morally just or legally granted as allowable or due to a person: *I know my rights* **33** anything that accords with the principles of legal or moral justice **34** the fact or state of being in accordance with reason, truth, or accepted standards (esp in **in the right**) **35** the right side, direction, position, area, or part: *the right of the army* **36** (*often cap* and preceded by *the*) the supporters or advocates of social, political, or economic conservatism or reaction **37** *boxing* **37a** a punch with the right hand **37b** the right hand **38** (*often pl*) *finance* the privilege of a company's shareholders to subscribe for new issues of the company's shares on advantageous terms **39 by right** (*or* **rights**) properly: *by rights you should be in bed* **40 in one's own right** having a claim or title oneself rather than through marriage or other connection **41 to rights** consistent with justice or orderly arrangement: *he put the matter to rights* ▷ *vb* (*mainly tr*) **42** (*also intr*) to restore to or attain a normal, esp an upright, position: *the raft righted in a few seconds* **43** to make (something) accord with truth or facts **44** to restore to an orderly state or condition **45** to compensate for or redress (esp in **right a wrong**) ▷ *interj* **46** an expression of agreement or compliance [OE *riht, reoht*] > **'rightable** *adj* > **'righter** *n* > **'rightness** *n*

right about *n* **1** a turn executed through 180° ▷ *adj, adv* **2** in the opposite direction

right angle *n* **1** the angle between radii of a circle that cut off on the circumference an arc equal in length to one quarter of the circumference; an angle of 90° or $\pi/2$ radians **2 at right angles** perpendicular or perpendicularly > **'right-ˌangled** *adj*

right-angled triangle *n* a triangle one angle of which is a right angle. US and Canad name: **right triangle**

right ascension *n astron* the angular distance measured eastwards along the celestial equator from the vernal equinox to the point at which the celestial equator intersects a great circle passing through the celestial pole and the heavenly object in question

right away *adv* without delay

righteous ('raɪtʃəs) *adj* **1a** characterized by, proceeding from, or in accordance with accepted standards of morality or uprightness: *a righteous man* **1b** (*as collective n*; preceded by *the*): *the righteous* **2** morally justifiable or right: *righteous indignation* [OE *rihtwīs*, from RIGHT + WISE[2]] > **'righteously** *adv* > **'righteousness** *n*

rightful ('raɪtfʊl) *adj* **1** in accordance with what is right **2** (*prenominal*) having a legally or morally just claim: *the rightful owner* **3** (*prenominal*) held by virtue of a legal or just claim: *my rightful property* > **'rightfully** *adv*

right-hand *adj* (*prenominal*) **1** of, located on, or moving towards the right: *a right-hand bend* **2** for use by the right hand **3 right-hand man** one's most valuable assistant

right-handed *adj* **1** using the right hand with greater skill or ease than the left **2** performed with the right hand **3** made for use by the right hand **4** turning from left to right > **ˌright-'handedness** *n*

rightist ('raɪtɪst) *adj* **1** of, tending towards, or relating to the political right or its principles ▷ *n* **2** a person who supports or belongs to the political right > **'rightism** *n*

rightly ('raɪtlɪ) *adv* **1** in accordance with the true facts **2** in accordance with principles of justice or morality **3** with good reason: *he was rightly annoyed with her* **4** properly or suitably **5** (*used with a negative*) *inf* with certainty (usually in **I don't rightly know**)

right-minded *adj* holding opinions or principles that accord with what is right or with the opinions of the speaker

righto *or* **right oh** ('raɪt'əʊ) *sentence substitute Brit inf* an expression of agreement or compliance

right off *adv* immediately; right away

right of way *n, pl* **rights of way** **1** the right of one vehicle or vessel to take precedence over another, as laid down by law or custom **2a** the legal right of someone to pass over another's land, acquired by grant or by long usage **2b** the path used by this right **3** US the strip of land over which a power line, road, etc, extends

right-on *adj inf* modern, trendy, and socially aware or relevant: *right-on green politics*

Right Reverend *adj* (in Britain) a title of respect for an Anglican or Roman Catholic bishop

rights issue *n stock exchange* an issue of new shares offered by a company to its existing shareholders on favourable terms

rightsize ('raɪtˌsaɪz) *vb* to restructure (an organization) to cut costs and improve effectiveness without ruthlessly downsizing

right-thinking ('raɪtˌθɪŋkɪŋ) *adj* possessing reasonable and generally acceptable opinions

rightward ('raɪtwəd) *adj* **1** situated on or directed towards the right ▷ *adv* **2** a variant of **rightwards**

rightwards ('raɪtwədz) *or* **rightward** *adv* towards or on the right

right whale *n* a large whalebone whale which is grey or black, has a large head and no dorsal fin, and is hunted as a source of whalebone and oil. See also **bowhead** [C19 ? because it was *right* for hunting]

right wing *n* **1** (*often cap*) the conservative faction of an assembly, party, etc **2** the part of an army or field of battle on the right from the point of view of one facing the enemy **3a** the right-hand side of the field of play from the point of view of a team facing its opponent's goal **3b** a player positioned in this area in any of various games ▷ *adj* **right-wing** **4** of, belonging to, or relating to the right wing > **'right-'winger** *n*

Rr

Rigi ('riːgɪ) *n* a mountain in the Alps of N central Switzerland, between Lakes Lucerne, Zug, and Lauerz

rigid ('rɪdʒɪd) *adj* **1** physically inflexible or stiff: *a rigid piece of plastic* **2** rigorously strict: *rigid rules* [C16 from L *rigidus*, from *rigēre* to be stiff] > **ri'gidity** *n* > **'rigidly** *adv*

rigidify (rɪ'dʒɪdɪˌfaɪ) *vb* **rigidifies, rigidifying, rigidified** to make or become rigid

rigmarole ('rɪgməˌrəʊl) *or* **rigamarole** *n* **1** any long complicated procedure **2** a set of incoherent or pointless statements [C18 from earlier *ragman roll* a list, prob. a roll used in a medieval game, wherein characters were described in verse, beginning with *Ragemon le bon* Ragman the good]

rigor ('raɪgɔː, 'rɪgə) *n* **1** *med* a sudden feeling of chilliness, often accompanied by shivering: it sometimes precedes a fever **2** ('rɪgə) *pathol* rigidity of a muscle **3** a state of rigidity assumed in reaction to shock [see RIGOUR]

rigor mortis ('rɪgə 'mɔːtɪs) *n pathol* the stiffness of joints and muscular rigidity of a dead body [C19 L, lit.: rigidity of death]

rigorous ('rɪgərəs) *adj* **1** harsh, strict, or severe: *rigorous discipline* **2** severely accurate: *rigorous book-keeping* **3** (esp of weather) extreme or harsh **4** *maths, logic* (of a proof) making the validity of each step explicit > **'rigorously** *adv*

rigour *or US* **rigor** ('rɪgə) *n* **1** harsh but just treatment or action **2** a severe or cruel circumstance: *the rigours of* *famine* **3** strictness, harshness, or severity of character **4** strictness in judgment or conduct [c14 from L *rigor*]

rig out *vb* **1** (*tr, adv; often foll by with*) to equip or fit out (with): *his car is rigged out with gadgets* **2** to dress or be dressed: *rigged out smartly* ▷ *n* **rigout 3** *inf* a person's clothing or costume, esp a bizarre outfit

rig up *vb* (*tr, adv*) to erect or construct, esp as a temporary measure: *cameras were rigged up*

Rig-Veda (rɪg'veɪdə) *n* a compilation of Hindu poems dating from 2000 BC or earlier [c18 from Sansk. *rigveda*, from *ric* song of praise + VEDA]

Rijeka (rɪ'ɛkə; *Serbo-Croat* ri'jɛka) *n* a port in Croatia: an ancient town, changing hands many times before passing to Yugoslavia in 1947 until Croatia became independent in 1991. Pop: 147 709 (2001). Italian name: **Fiume**

Rijksmuseum ('raɪxsmju:ˌzɪəm) *n* a museum in Amsterdam housing the national art collection of the Netherlands

▷ www.rijksmuseum.nl

Rijn (rɛjn) *n* the Dutch name for the **Rhine**

Rijswijk ('raɪsvaɪk; *Dutch* 'rɛjswɛjk) *n* a town in the SW Netherlands, in South Holland province on the SE outskirts of The Hague: scene of the signing (1697) of the **Treaty of Rijswijk** ending the War of the Grand Alliance. Pop: 48 000 (1991). English name: **Ryswick**

rile (raɪl) *vb* **riles, riling, riled** (*tr*) **1** to annoy or anger **2** *US & Canad* to agitate (water, etc) [c19 var. of ROIL]

Riley ('raɪlɪ) *n* **Bridget (Louise)** born 1931, British painter, best known for her black-and-white op art paintings of the 1960s

Rilke ('rɪlkə) *n* **Rainer Maria** ('raɪnər ma'ri:a) 1875–1926, Austro-German poet, born in Prague. Author of intense visionary lyrics, notably in the *Duino Elegies* (1922) and *Sonnets to Orpheus* (1923)

rill (rɪl) *n* **1** a brook or stream **2** a channel or gulley, such as one formed during soil erosion **3** Also: **rille** one of many winding cracks on the moon [c15 from Low G *rille*]

rim (rɪm) *n* **1** the raised edge of an object, esp of something more or less circular such as a cup or crater **2** the peripheral part of a wheel, to which the tyre is attached **3** *basketball* the hoop from which the net is suspended ▷ *vb* **rims, rimming, rimmed** (*tr*) **4** to put a rim on (a pot, cup, wheel, etc) **5** *sl* to lick, kiss, or suck the anus of (one's sexual partner) [OE *rima*]

Rimbaud (*French* rɛ̃bo) *n* **Arthur** (artyr) 1854–91, French poet, whose work, culminating in the prose poetry of *Illuminations* (published 1884), greatly influenced the symbolists. *A Season in Hell* (1873) draws on his tempestuous homosexual affair with Verlaine, after which he abandoned writing (aged about 20) and spent the rest of his life travelling

rime[1] (raɪm) *n* **1** frost formed by the freezing of water droplets in fog onto solid objects ▷ *vb* **rimes, riming, rimed 2** (*tr*) to cover with rime or something resembling rime [OE *hrīm*]

rime[2] (raɪm) *n, vb* **rimes, riming, rimed** an archaic spelling of **rhyme**

rim-fire *adj* **1** (of a cartridge) having the primer in the rim of the base **2** (of a firearm) adapted for such cartridges

Rimini ('rɪmɪnɪ) *n* a port and resort in NE Italy, in Emilia-Romagna on the N Adriatic coast. Pop: 131 062 (2000 est). Ancient name: **Ariminum**

rimose (raɪ'məʊs, -'məʊz) *adj* (esp of plant parts) having the surface marked by a network of cracks [c18 from L *rīmōsus*, from *rīma* a split]

Rimsky-Korsakov ('rɪmskɪ'kɔ:səkɒf; *Russian* 'rimskij'kɔrsəkəf) *n* **Nikolai Andreyevich** (nika'laj an'drjejɪvitʃ) 1844–1908, Russian composer; noted for such works as the orchestral suite *Scheherazade* (1888) and the opera *Le Coq d'or* (first performed in 1910)

rimu ('ri:mu:) *n* a New Zealand tree. Also called: **red pine** [from Maori]

rimy ('raɪmɪ) *adj* **rimier, rimiest** coated with rime

rind (raɪnd) *n* **1** a hard outer layer or skin on bacon, cheese, etc **2** the outer layer of a fruit or of the spore-producing body of certain fungi **3** the outer layer of the bark of a tree [OE *rinde*]

rinderpest ('rɪndəˌpɛst) *n* an acute contagious viral disease of cattle, characterized by severe inflammation of the intestinal tract and diarrhoea [c19 from G *Rinderpest* cattle pest]

ring[1] (rɪŋ) *n* **1** a circular band of a precious metal often set with gems and worn upon the finger as an adornment or as a token of engagement or marriage **2** any object or mark that is circular in shape **3** a circular path or course: *to run around in a ring* **4** a group of people or things standing or arranged so as to form a circle: *a ring of spectators* **5** an enclosed space, usually circular in shape, where circus acts are performed **6** a square raised platform, marked off by ropes, in which contestants box or wrestle **7 the ring** the sport of boxing **8 throw one's hat in the ring** to announce one's intention to be a candidate or contestant **9** a group of people usually operating illegally and covertly: *a drug ring; a paedophile ring* **10** (esp at country fairs) an enclosure where horses, cattle, and other livestock are paraded and auctioned **11** an area reserved for betting at a racecourse **12** a circular strip of bark cut from a tree or branch **13** a single turn in a spiral **14** *geom* the area of space lying between two concentric circles **15** *maths* a set that is subject to two binary operations, addition and multiplication, such that the set is a commutative group under addition and is closed under multiplication, this latter operation being associative **16** *bot* short for **annual ring 17** *chem* a closed loop of atoms in a molecule **18** *astron* any of the thin circular bands of small bodies orbiting a giant planet, esp Saturn **19 run rings round** *inf* to outclass completely ▷ *vb* **rings, ringing, ringed** (*tr*) **20** to surround with, or as if with, or form a ring **21** to mark a bird with a ring or clip for subsequent identification **22** to fit a ring in the nose of (a bull, etc) so that it can be led easily **23** to ringbark [OE *hring*] > **ringed** *adj*

ring[2] (rɪŋ) *vb* **rings, ringing, rang, rung 1** to emit or cause to emit a resonant sound, characteristic of certain metals when struck **2** to cause (a bell, etc) to emit a ringing sound by striking it once or repeatedly or (of a bell) to emit such a sound **3a** (*tr*) to cause (a large bell) to emit a ringing sound by pulling on a rope attached to a wheel on which the bell swings back and forth, being sounded by a clapper inside it **3b** (*intr*) (of a bell) to sound by being swung in this way **4** (*intr*) (of a building, place, etc) to be filled with sound: *the church rang with singing* **5** (*intr; foll by for*) to call by means of a bell, etc: *to ring for the butler* **6** Also: **ring up** *chiefly Brit* to call (a person) by telephone **7** (*tr*) to strike or tap (a coin) in order to assess its genuineness by the sound produced **8** *sl* to change the identity of (a stolen vehicle) by using the licence plate, serial number, etc, of another, usually disused, vehicle **9** (*intr*) (of the ears) to have or give the sensation of humming or ringing **10 ring a bell** to bring something to the mind or memory: *that rings a bell* **11 ring down the curtain 11a** to lower the curtain at the end of a theatrical performance **11b** (foll by *on*) to put an end (to) **12 ring false** to give the impression of being false **13 ring true** to give the impression of being true ▷ *n* **14** the act of or a sound made by ringing **15** a sound produced by or suggestive of a bell **16** any resonant or metallic sound: *the ring of trumpets* **17** *inf, chiefly Brit* a telephone call **18** the complete set of bells in a tower or belfry: *a ring of eight bells* **19** an inherent quality or characteristic: his words had the ring of sincerity ▷ See also **ring in, ring off,** etc [OE *hringan*]

USAGE *Rang* and *sang* are the correct forms of the past tenses of *ring* and *sing*, although *rung* and *sung* are still heard informally and dialectally: *he rung (rang) the bell*

ringbark ('rɪŋˌbɑːk) *vb (tr)* to kill (a tree) by cutting away a strip of bark from around the trunk

ring binder *n* a loose-leaf binder with metal rings that can be opened to insert perforated paper

ringbolt ('rɪŋˌbəʊlt) *n* a bolt with a ring fitted through an eye attached to the bolt head

ringdove ('rɪŋˌdʌv) *n* **1** another name for **wood pigeon** **2** an Old World turtledove, having a black neck band

ringed plover *n* a European shorebird with a greyish-brown back, white underparts, a black throat band, and orange legs

ringer ('rɪŋə) *n* **1** a person or thing that rings a bell, etc **2** Also called: **dead ringer** *sl* a person or thing that is almost identical to another **3** *sl* a stolen vehicle the identity of which has been changed by the use of the licence plate, serial number, etc, of another, usually disused, vehicle **4** *chiefly US* a contestant, esp a horse, entered in a competition under false representations of identity, record, or ability **5** *Austral* a stockman; station hand **6** *Austral* the fastest shearer in a shed **7** *Austral inf* the fastest or best at anything **8** a quoit thrown so as to encircle a peg **9** such a throw

ring-fence *vb* **1** to assign (money, a grant, fund, etc) to one particular purpose, so as to restrict its use: *to ring-fence a financial allowance* **2** to oblige (a person or organization) to use money for a particular purpose: *to ring-fence a local authority* ▷ *n* **ring fence** **3** an agreement, contract, etc, in which the use of money is restricted to a particular purpose

ring finger *n* the third finger, esp of the left hand, on which a wedding ring is worn

ring in *vb (adv)* **1** *(intr) chiefly Brit* to report to someone by telephone **2** *(tr)* to accompany the arrival of with bells (esp in **ring in the new year**) ▷ *n* **ring-in** **3** *Austral & NZ inf* a person or thing that is not normally a member of a particular group; outsider

ringing tone *n Brit* a sequence of pairs of tones heard by the dialler on a telephone when the number dialled is ringing ▷ Cf **engaged tone, dialling tone**

ringleader ('rɪŋˌliːdə) *n* a person who leads others in unlawful or mischievous activity

ringlet ('rɪŋlɪt) *n* **1** a lock of hair hanging down in a spiral curl **2** a butterfly that occurs in S Europe and has dark brown wings marked with small black-and-white eyespots > **'ringleted** *adj*

ring main *n* a domestic electrical supply in which outlet sockets are connected to the mains supply through a continuous closed circuit (**ring circuit**)

ringmaster ('rɪŋˌmɑːstə) *n* the master of ceremonies in a circus

ring-necked *adj* (of animals, esp birds and snakes) having a band of distinctive colour around the neck

ring-necked pheasant *n* a common pheasant originating in Asia. The male has a bright plumage with a band of white around the neck and the female is mottled brown

ring off *vb (intr, adv) chiefly Brit* to terminate a telephone conversation by replacing the receiver; hang up

ring out *vb (adv)* **1** *(tr)* to accompany the departure of with bells (esp in **ring out the old year**) **2** *(intr)* to send forth a loud resounding noise

ring ouzel *n* a European thrush common in rocky areas. The male has a blackish plumage and the female is brown

ring road *n* a main road that bypasses a town or town centre. US names: **belt, beltway**

ringside ('rɪŋˌsaɪd) *n* **1** the row of seats nearest a boxing or wrestling ring **2a** any place affording a close uninterrupted view **2b** *(as modifier)*: *a ringside seat*

ringtail ('rɪŋˌteɪl) *n Austral* any of several tree-living phalangers having curling prehensile tails used to grasp branches while climbing

ring up *vb (adv)* **1** *chiefly Brit* to make a telephone call (to) **2** *(tr)* to record on a cash register **3** **ring up the curtain** **3a** to begin a theatrical performance **3b** (often foll by *on*) to make a start (on)

ringworm ('rɪŋˌwɜːm) *n* any of various fungal infections of the skin or nails, often appearing as itching circular patches. Also called: **tinea**

rink (rɪŋk) *n* **1** an expanse of ice for skating on, esp one that is artificially prepared and under cover **2** an area for roller-skating on **3** a building or enclosure for ice-skating or roller-skating **4** *bowls* a strip of the green on which a game is played **5** *curling* the strip of ice on which the game is played **6** (in bowls and curling) the players on one side in a game [c14 (Scots): from OF *renc* row]

rinkhals ('rɪŋkˌhæls) *or* **ringhals** ('rɪŋgˌhæls) *n, pl* **rinkhals, rinkhalses, ringhals** *or* **ringhalses** a venomous snake of southern Africa, which can spit venom over 2 m (7 ft) [Afrik., lit.: ring neck]

rink rat *n Canad sl* a youth who helps with odd chores around an ice-hockey rink in return for free admission to games, etc

rinse (rɪns) *vb* **rinses, rinsing, rinsed** *(tr)* **1** to remove soap from (clothes, etc) by applying clean water in the final stage in washing **2** to wash lightly, esp without using soap **3** to give a light tint to (hair) ▷ *n* **4** the act or an instance of rinsing **5** *hairdressing* a liquid preparation put on the hair when wet to give a tint to it: *a blue rinse* [c14 from OF *rincer*, from L *recens* fresh] > **'rinser** *n*

Rio Branco (*Portuguese* 'riu 'brəŋku) *n* **1** a city in W Brazil, capital of Acre state. Pop: 226 054 (2000) **2** a river in Brazil, flowing south to the Rio Negro. Length: 644 km (400 miles)

Río Bravo (*Spanish* 'rio 'braβo) *n* the Mexican name for the **Rio Grande**

Rr

Rio de Janeiro ('riːəʊ də dʒə'nɪərəʊ) *or* **Rio** *n* **1** a port in SE Brazil, on Guanabara Bay: the country's chief port and its capital from 1763 to 1960; backed by mountains, notably Sugar Loaf Mountain; founded by the French in 1555 and taken by the Portuguese in 1567. Pop: 5 850 544 (2000), with a conurbation of 9 888 000 (1995 est). Related noun: **Cariocan** **2** a state of E Brazil. Capital: Rio de Janeiro. Pop: 14 367 225 (2000). Area: 42 911 sq km (16 568 sq miles)

Río de la Plata ('riːəʊ də lɑː 'plɑːtə) *n* See **Plata**

Río de Oro (*Spanish* 'rio ðe 'oro) *n* a former region of W Africa: comprised the S part of the Spanish Sahara (now Western Sahara)

Rio Grande *n* **1** ('riːəʊ 'grænd, 'grændɪ) a river in North America, rising in SW Colorado and flowing southeast to the Gulf of Mexico, forming the border between the US and Mexico. Length: about 3030 km (1885 miles). Mexican name: **Río Bravo** **2** (*Portuguese* 'riu 'grəndi) a port in SE Brazil, in SE Rio Grande do Sul state: serves as the port for Pôrto Alegre. Pop: 157 608 (1991)

Rio Grande do Norte (*Portuguese* 'riu 'grəndi du 'nɔrti) *n* a state of NE Brazil, on the Atlantic: much of it is semiarid plateau. Capital: Natal. Pop: 2 770 730 (2000 est). Area: 53 014 sq km (20 469 sq miles)

Rio Grande do Sul (*Portuguese* 'riu 'grəndi du 'sul) *n* a state of S Brazil, on the Atlantic. Capital: Pôrto Alegre. Pop: 10 178 970 (2000). Area: 282 183 sq km (108 951 sq miles)

rioja (rɪ'əʊxə) *n* a red or white wine, with a distinctive vanilla bouquet and flavour, produced around the Ebro river in central N Spain [c20 from *La Rioja*, the area where it is produced]

Río Negro ('riːəʊ 'neɪgrəʊ, 'nɛg-; *Spanish* 'rio 'neɣro) *n* See **Negro**[2]

riot ('raɪət) *n* **1a** a disturbance made by an unruly mob or (in law) three or more persons **1b** (*as modifier*): *a riot shield* **2** unrestrained revelry **3** an occasion of boisterous merriment **4** *sl* a person who occasions boisterous merriment **5** a dazzling display: *a riot of colour* **6** *hunting* the indiscriminate following of any scent by hounds **7** *arch* wanton lasciviousness **8 run riot 8a** to behave without restraint **8b** (of plants) to grow profusely ▷ *vb* **9** (*intr*) to take part in a riot **10** (*intr*) to indulge in unrestrained revelry **11** (*tr; foll by away*) to spend (time or money) in wanton or loose living [C13 from OF *riote* dispute, from *ruihoter* to quarrel, prob. from *ruir* to make a commotion, from L *rugīre* to roar] > **'rioter** *n*

Riot Act *n* **1** *criminal law* (formerly, in England) a statute of 1715 by which persons committing a riot had to disperse within an hour of the reading of the act by a magistrate **2 read the riot act to** to warn or reprimand severely

riotous ('raɪətəs) *adj* **1** proceeding from or of the nature of riots or rioting **2** characterized by wanton revelry: *riotous living* **3** characterized by unrestrained merriment: *riotous laughter* > **'riotously** *adv* > **'riotousness** *n*

riot shield *n* (in Britain) a shield used by police controlling crowds

rip¹ (rɪp) *vb* **rips, ripping, ripped 1** to tear or be torn violently or roughly **2** (*tr; foll by off or out*) to remove hastily or roughly **3** (*intr*) *inf* to move violently or precipitously **4** (*intr; foll by into*) *inf* to pour violent abuse (on) **5** (*tr*) to saw or split (wood) in the direction of the grain **6** (*tr*) *inf computing* to copy (music or software) without permission or making any payment **7 let rip** to act or speak without restraint ▷ *n* **8** a tear or split **9** short for **ripsaw** ▷ See also **rip off** [C15 ?from Flemish *rippen*]

rip² (rɪp) *n* short for **riptide** [C18 ?from RIP¹]

rip³ (rɪp) *n inf, arch* **1** a debauched person **2** an old worn-out horse [C18 ?from *rep*, shortened from REPROBATE]

RIP *abbrev for* requiescat *or* requiescant in pace [L: may he, she, *or* they rest in peace]

riparian (raɪ'pɛərɪən) *adj* **1** of, inhabiting, or situated on the bank of a river **2** denoting or relating to the legal rights of the owner of land on a river bank, such as fishing ▷ *n* **3** *property law* a person who owns land on a river bank [C19 from L, from *rīpa* river bank]

ripcord ('rɪp,kɔːd) *n* **1** a cord that when pulled opens a parachute from its pack **2** a cord on the gas bag of a balloon that when pulled enables gas to escape and the balloon to descend

ripe (raɪp) *adj* **1** (of fruit, grain, etc) mature and ready to be eaten or used **2** mature enough to be eaten or used: *ripe cheese* **3** fully developed in mind or body **4** resembling ripe fruit, esp in redness or fullness: *a ripe complexion* **5** (*postpositive; foll by for*) ready or eager (to undertake or undergo an action) **6** (*postpositive; foll by for*) suitable: *the time is not yet ripe* **7** mature in judgment or knowledge **8** advanced but healthy (esp in **a ripe old age**) **9** *sl* **9a** complete; thorough **9b** excessive; exorbitant **10** *sl* slightly indecent; risqué [OE *rīpe*] > **'ripely** *adv* > **'ripeness** *n*

ripen ('raɪpᵊn) *vb* to make or become ripe

ripieno (,rɪpɪ'eɪnəʊ) *n, pl* **ripieni** (-niː) *or* **ripienos** *music* a supplementary instrument or player [It.]

rip off *vb* (*tr*) **1** to tear roughly (from) **2** (*adv*) *sl* to steal from or cheat (someone) ▷ *n* **rip-off 3** *sl* a grossly overpriced article **4** *sl* the act of stealing or cheating

Ripon ('rɪpᵊn) *n* a city in N England, in North Yorkshire: cathedral (12th–16th centuries). Pop: 13 806 (1991 est)

riposte (rɪ'pɒst, rɪ'pəʊst) *n* **1** a swift sharp reply in speech or action **2** *fencing* a counterattack made immediately after a successful parry ▷ *vb* **ripostes, riposting, riposted 3** (*intr*) to make a riposte [C18 from F, from It., from *rispondere* to reply]

ripper ('rɪpə) *n* **1** a person or thing that rips **2** a murderer who dissects or mutilates the victim's body **3** *inf, chiefly Austral & NZ* a fine or excellent person or thing

ripping ('rɪpɪŋ) *adj arch Brit sl* excellent; splendid > **'rippingly** *adv*

ripple¹ ('rɪpᵊl) *n* **1** a slight wave or undulation on the surface of water **2** a small wave or undulation in fabric, hair, etc **3** a sound reminiscent of water flowing quietly in ripples: *a ripple of laughter* **4** *electronics* an oscillation of small amplitude superimposed on a steady value **5** *US & Canad* another word for **riffle** (sense 4) ▷ *vb* **ripples, rippling, rippled 6** (*intr*) to form ripples or flow with an undulating motion **7** (*tr*) to stir up (water) so as to form ripples **8** (*tr*) to make ripple marks **9** (*intr*) (of sounds) to rise and fall gently [C17 ?from RIP¹] > **'rippler** *n* > **'rippling** *or* **'ripply** *adj*

ripple² ('rɪpᵊl) *n* **1** a special kind of comb designed to separate the seed from the stalks in flax or hemp ▷ *vb* **ripples, rippling, rippled 2** (*tr*) to comb with this tool [C14 of Gmc origin] > **'rippler** *n*

ripple effect *n* the repercussions of an event or situation experienced far beyond its immediate location

ripple mark *n* one of a series of small wavy ridges of sand formed by waves on a beach, by a current in a sandy riverbed, or by wind on land: sometimes found fossilized on bedding planes of sedimentary rock

rip-roaring *adj inf* characterized by excitement, intensity, or boisterous behaviour

ripsaw ('rɪp,sɔː) *n* a handsaw for cutting along the grain of timber

ripsnorter ('rɪp,snɔːtə) *n sl* a person or thing noted for intensity or excellence > **'rip,snorting** *adj*

riptide ('rɪp,taɪd) *n* **1** Also called: **rip** a stretch of turbulent water in the sea, caused by the meeting of currents **2** Also called: **rip current** a strong current, esp one flowing outwards from the shore

RISC *computing abbrev for* reduced instruction set computer

rise (raɪz) *vb* **rises, rising, rose, risen** ('rɪzᵊn) (*mainly intr*) **1** to get up from a lying, sitting, kneeling, or prone position **2** to get out of bed, esp to begin one's day: *he always rises early* **3** to move from a lower to a higher position or place **4** to ascend or appear above the horizon: *the sun is rising* **5** to increase in height or level: *the water rose above the normal level* **6** to attain higher rank, status, or reputation: *he will rise in the world* **7** to be built or erected: *those blocks of flats are rising fast* **8** to appear: *new troubles rose to afflict her* **9** to increase in strength, degree, etc: *the wind is rising* **10** to increase in amount or value: *house prices are always rising* **11** to swell up: *dough rises* **12** to become erect, stiff, or rigid: *the hairs on his neck rose in fear* **13** (of one's stomach or gorge) to manifest nausea **14** to revolt: *the people rose against their oppressors* **15** to slope upwards: *the ground rises beyond the lake* **16** to be resurrected **17** to originate: *that river rises in the mountains* **18** (of a session of a court, legislative assembly, etc) to come to an end **19** *angling* (of fish) to come to the surface of the water **20** (often foll by *to*) *inf* to respond (to teasing, etc) ▷ *n* **21** the act or an instance of rising **22** an increase in height **23** an increase in rank, status, or position **24** an increase in amount, cost, or value **25** an increase in degree or intensity **26** *Brit* an increase in salary or wages. US and Canad word: **raise 27** the vertical height of a step or of a flight of stairs **28** the vertical height of a roof above the walls or columns **29** *angling* the act or instance of fish coming to the surface of the water to take flies, etc **30** the beginning, origin, or source **31** a piece of rising ground; incline **32 get** *or* **take a rise out of** *sl* to provoke an angry or petulant reaction from **33 give rise to** to cause the development of [OE *rīsan*]

riser ('raɪzə) *n* **1** a person who rises, esp from bed: *an early riser* **2** the vertical part of a stair **3** a vertical pipe, esp one within a building

rise to *vb* (*intr, prep*) to respond adequately to (the demands of something, esp a testing challenge)

risibility (ˌrɪzɪˈbɪlɪtɪ) *n, pl* **risibilities** **1** a tendency to laugh **2** hilarity; laughter

risible (ˈrɪzɪbᵊl) *adj* **1** having a tendency to laugh **2** causing laughter; ridiculous [C16 from LL *rīsibilis*, from L *rīdēre* to laugh] > **ˈrisibly** *adv*

rising (ˈraɪzɪŋ) *n* **1** a rebellion; revolt **2** the leaven used to make dough rise in baking ▷ *adj (prenominal)* **3** increasing in rank, status, or reputation: *a rising young politician* **4** growing up to adulthood: *the rising generation* ▷ *adv* **5** *inf* approaching: *he's rising 50*

rising damp *n* capillary movement of moisture from the ground into the walls of buildings, resulting in damage up to a level of 3 feet

rising trot *n* a horse's trot in which the rider rises from the saddle every second beat

risk (rɪsk) *n* **1** the possibility of incurring misfortune or loss **2** *insurance* **2a** chance of a loss or other event on which a claim may be filed **2b** the type of such an event, such as fire or theft **2c** the amount of the claim should such an event occur **2d** a person or thing considered with respect to the characteristics that may cause an insured event to occur **3** **at risk** vulnerable **4** **take** *or* **run a risk** to proceed in an action without regard to the possibility of danger involved ▷ *vb (tr)* **5** to expose to danger or loss **6** to act in spite of the possibility of (injury or loss): *to risk a fall in climbing* [C17 from F, from It., from *rischiare* to be in peril, from Gk *rhiza* cliff (from the hazards of sailing along rocky coasts)]

risk capital *n chiefly Brit* capital invested in an issue of ordinary shares, esp of a speculative enterprise. Also called: **venture capital**

risk factor *n med* a factor, such as a habit or an environmental condition, that predisposes an individual to develop a particular disease

risky (ˈrɪskɪ) *adj* **riskier, riskiest** involving danger > **ˈriskily** *adv* > **ˈriskiness** *n*

risotto (rɪˈzɒtəʊ) *n, pl* **risottos** a dish of rice cooked in stock and served variously with tomatoes, cheese, chicken, etc [C19 from It., from *riso* RICE]

risqué (ˈrɪskeɪ) *adj* bordering on impropriety or indecency: *a risqué joke* [C19 from F *risquer* to hazard, RISK]

rissole (ˈrɪsəʊl) *n* a mixture of minced cooked meat coated in egg and breadcrumbs and fried [C18 from F, prob. ult. from L *russus* red]

risus sardonicus (ˈriːsəs sɑːˈdɒnɪkəs) *n pathol* fixed contraction of the facial muscles resulting in a peculiar distorted grin, caused esp by tetanus. Also called: **trismus cynicus** (ˈtrɪzməs ˈsɪnɪkəs) [C17 NL, lit.: sardonic laugh]

rit. *music abbrev for:* **1** ritardando **2** ritenuto

Ritalin (ˈrɪtəlɪn) *n trademark* a preparation of methylphenidate, a drug related to amphetamine, used to treat attention deficit disorder in children

ritardando (ˌrɪtɑːˈdændəʊ) *adj, adv* another term for **rallentando** Abbrev: **rit** [C19 from It., from *ritardare* to slow down]

rite (raɪt) *n* **1** a formal act prescribed or customary in religious ceremonies: *the rite of baptism* **2** a particular body of such acts, esp of a particular Christian Church: *the Latin rite* **3** a Christian Church: *the Greek rite* [C14 from L *rītus* religious ceremony]

ritenuto (ˌrɪtəˈnuːtəʊ) *adj, adv music* **1** held back momentarily **2** Abbrev: **rit** another term for **rallentando** [C19 from It., from L *retinēre* to hold back]

rite of passage *n* a ceremony performed in some cultures at times when an individual changes his status, as at puberty and marriage

ritornello (ˌrɪtəˈnɛləʊ) *n, pl* **ritornellos** *or* **ritornelli** (-liː) *music* a short piece of instrumental music interpolated in a song [It., lit.: a little return]

ritual (ˈrɪtjʊəl) *n* **1** the prescribed or established form of a religious or other ceremony **2** such prescribed forms in general or collectively **3** stereotyped activity or behaviour **4** any formal act, institution, or procedure that is followed consistently: *the ritual of the law* ▷ *adj* **5** of or characteristic of religious, social, or other rituals [C16 from L *rītuālis*, from *rītus* RITE] > **ˈritually** *adv*

ritualism (ˈrɪtjʊəˌlɪzəm) *n* **1** exaggerated emphasis on the importance of rites and ceremonies **2** the study of rites and ceremonies, esp magical or religious ones > **ˈritualist** *n*

ritualistic (ˌrɪtjʊəˈlɪstɪk) *adj* of, relating to, or suggestive of ritualism > **ˌritualˈistically** *adv*

ritualize *or* **ritualise** (ˈrɪtjʊəˌlaɪz) *vb* **ritualizes, ritualizing, ritualized** *or* **ritualises, ritualising, ritualised** **1** *(intr)* to engage in ritualism or devise rituals **2** *(tr)* to make (something) into a ritual

ritzy (ˈrɪtsɪ) *adj* **ritzier, ritziest** *sl* luxurious or elegant [C20 after the hotels established by César Ritz (1850–1918), Swiss hotelier] > **ˈritzily** *adv* > **ˈritziness** *n*

rival (ˈraɪvᵊl) *n* **1a** a person, organization, team, etc, that competes with another for the same object or in the same field **1b** *(as modifier)*: *rival suitors* **2** a person or thing that is considered the equal of another: *she is without rival in the field of physics* ▷ *vb* **rivals, rivalling, rivalled** *or US* **rivals, rivaling, rivaled** *(tr)* **3** to be the equal or near equal of: *an empire that rivalled Rome* **4** to try to equal or surpass [C16 from L *rīvalis*, lit.: one who shares the same brook, from *rīvus* a brook]

rivalry (ˈraɪvəlrɪ) *n, pl* **rivalries** **1** the act of rivalling **2** the state of being a rival or rivals

rive (raɪv) *vb* **rives, riving, rived; rived** *or* **riven** (ˈrɪvᵊn) *(usually passive)* **1** to split asunder: *a tree riven by lightning* **2** to tear apart: *riven to shreds* [C13 from ON *rīfa*]

river (ˈrɪvə) *n* **1a** a large natural stream of fresh water flowing along a definite course, usually into the sea, being fed by tributary streams **1b** *(as modifier)*: *river traffic* **1c** *(in combination)*: *riverside; riverbed.* Related adjs: **fluvial, potamic** **2** any abundant stream or flow: *a river of blood* [C13 from OF, from L *rīpārius* of a river bank, from *rīpa* bank] > **ˈriverless** *adj*

Rivera (*Spanish* riˈβera) *n* **Diego** (ˈdjeɣo) 1886–1957, Mexican painter, noted for his monumental murals in public buildings, which are influenced by Aztec art and depict revolutionary themes

riverine (ˈrɪvəˌraɪn) *adj* **1** of, like, relating to, or produced by a river **2** located or dwelling near a river; riparian

river red gum *n* a large Australian red gum tree, *Eucalyptus camaldulensis*, growing along river banks

Rivers (ˈrɪvəz) *n* a state of S Nigeria, in the Niger River Delta on the Gulf of Guinea. Capital: Port Harcourt. Pop: 4 103 372 (1995 est). Area: 21 850 sq km (8436 sq miles)

Riverside (ˈrɪvəˌsaɪd) *n* a city in SW California. Pop: 255 166 (2000)

rivet (ˈrɪvɪt) *n* **1** a short metal pin for fastening two or more pieces together, having a head at one end, the other end being hammered flat after being passed through holes in the pieces ▷ *vb* **rivets, riveting, riveted** *(tr)* **2** to join by riveting **3** to hammer in order to form into a head **4** *(often passive)* to cause to be fixed, as in fascinated attention, horror, etc: *to be riveted to the spot* [C14 from OF, from *river* to fasten, from ?] > **ˈriveter** *n* > **ˈriveting** *adj*

riviera (ˌrɪvɪˈɛərə) *n* a coastal region reminiscent of the Riviera

Riviera (ˌrɪvɪˈɛərə) *n* the Mediterranean coastal region between Cannes, France, and La Spezia, Italy: contains some of Europe's most popular resorts [C18 from Italian literally: shore, ultimately from Latin *rīpa* bank, shore]

rivière (ˌrɪvɪˈɛə) *n* a necklace the diamonds or other precious stones of which gradually increase in size up to a large centre stone [C19 from F: brook, RIVER]

rivulet (ˈrɪvjʊlɪt) *n* a small stream [C16 from It. *rivoletto*, from L *rīvulus*, from *rīvus* stream]

Riyadh (rɪˈjɑːd) *n* the joint capital (with Mecca) of Saudi

Arabia, situated in a central oasis: the largest city in the country. Pop: 2 800 000 (1996 est)
▷ www.vvtel.com/vvtravels/saudi_arabia-su/007_guides/02_cities

riyal (rɪ'jɑːl) *n* the standard monetary unit of Qatar, Saudi Arabia, and Yemen [from Ar. *riyāl*, from Sp. *real*]

Rizal[1] (*Spanish* ri'θal) *n* another name for **Pasay**

Rizal[2] (*Spanish* ri'θal) *n* **Jose** (xo'se) 1861–96, Philippine nationalist, executed by the Spanish during the Philippine revolution of 1896

Rizzio ('rɪtsɪəʊ) *or* **Riccio** *n* **David** ?1533–66, Italian musician and courtier who became the secretary and favourite of Mary, Queen of Scots. He was murdered at the instigation of a group of nobles, including Mary's husband, Darnley

RL *abbrev for* Rugby League

rly *abbrev for* railway

rm *abbrev for:* **1** ream **2** room

RM *abbrev for:* **1** Royal Mail **2** Royal Marines **3** (in Canada) Rural Municipality

RMA *abbrev for* Royal Military Academy (Sandhurst)

RME *abbrev for* Religious and Moral Education

rms *abbrev for* root mean square

Rn *the chemical symbol for* radon

RN *abbrev for:* **1** (in Canada) Registered Nurse **2** Royal Navy

RNA *n biochem* ribonucleic acid; any of a group of nucleic acids, present in all living cells, that play an essential role in the synthesis of proteins

RNAS *abbrev for:* **1** Royal Naval Air Service(s) **2** Royal Naval Air Station

RNIB (in Britain) *abbrev for* Royal National Institute for the Blind

RNID (in Britain) *abbrev for* Royal National Institute for Deaf People

RNLI *abbrev for* Royal National Lifeboat Institution

RNZAF *abbrev for* Royal New Zealand Air Force
▷ www.airforce.mil.nz

RNZN *abbrev for* Royal New Zealand Navy
▷ www.navy.mil.nz

roach[1] (rəʊtʃ) *n, pl* **roaches** *or* **roach** a European freshwater food fish having a deep compressed body and reddish ventral and tail fins [C14 from OF *roche*, from ?]

roach[2] (rəʊtʃ) *n* **1** short for **cockroach** **2** *sl* the butt of a cannabis cigarette

roach[3] (rəʊtʃ) *n naut* the curve at the foot of a square sail [C18 from ?]

roach clip *n sl* a small clip resembling tweezers, used to hold the butt of a cannabis cigarette, in order to avoid burning one's fingers

road (rəʊd) *n* **1a** an open way, usually surfaced with tarmac or concrete, providing passage from one place to another **1b** (*as modifier*): *road traffic; a road sign* **1c** (*in combination*): *the roadside* **2a** a street **2b** (*cap when part of a name*): *London Road* **3** *Brit* one of the tracks of a railway **4** a way, path, or course: *the road to fame* **5** (*often pl*) *naut* Also called: **roadstead** a partly sheltered anchorage **6** a drift or tunnel in a mine, esp a level one **7** **hit the road** *sl* to start or resume travelling **8** **one for the road** *inf* a last alcoholic drink before leaving **9** **on the road** **9a** travelling about; on tour **9b** leading a wandering life **10** **take (to) the road** to begin a journey or tour [OE *rād*; rel. to *rīdan* to RIDE] > **'roadless** *adj*

road allowance *n Canad* land reserved by the government to be used for public roads

roadblock ('rəʊd,blɒk) *n* a barrier set up across a road by the police or military, in order to stop a fugitive, inspect traffic, etc

road-fund licence *n Brit* a paper disc showing that the tax in respect of a motor vehicle has been paid [C20 from the former *road fund* for the maintenance of public highways]

road hog *n inf* a selfish or aggressive driver

roadholding ('rəʊd,həʊldɪŋ) *n* the extent to which a motor vehicle is stable and does not skid, esp on sharp bends or wet roads

roadhouse ('rəʊd,haʊs) *n* a pub, restaurant, etc, that is situated at the side of a road

road hump *n* the official name for **sleeping policeman**

roadie ('rəʊdɪ) *n inf* a person who transports and sets up equipment for a band or group [C20 shortened from *road manager*]

road map *n* **1** a map intended for drivers, showing roads, distances, etc in a country or area **2** a plan or guide for future actions

road metal *n* crushed rock, broken stone, etc, used to construct a road

road movie *n* a genre of film in which the chief character takes to the road, esp to escape the law, his own past, etc

road pricing *n* the practice of charging motorists for using certain stretches of road, in order to reduce congestion

road rage *n* aggressive behaviour by a motorist in response to the actions of another road user

roadroller ('rəʊd,rəʊlə) *n* a motor vehicle with heavy rollers for compressing road surfaces during road-making

road show *n* **1** *radio* **1a** a live programme, usually with some audience participation, transmitted from a radio van taking a particular show on the road **1b** the personnel and equipment needed for such a show **2** a group of entertainers on tour **3** any occasion when an organization attracts publicity while touring or visiting: *the royal road show*

roadstead ('rəʊd,stɛd) *n naut* another word for **road** (sense 5)

roadster ('rəʊdstə) *n* **1** an open car, esp one seating only two **2** a kind of bicycle

road tax *n* a tax paid, usually annually, on motor vehicles in use on the roads

road test *n* **1** a test to ensure that a vehicle is roadworthy, esp after repair or servicing, by driving it on roads **2** a test of something in actual use ▷ *vb* **road-test** (*tr*) **3** to test (a vehicle, etc) in this way

road train *n Austral* a truck pulling one or more large trailers, esp on western roads

roadway ('rəʊd,weɪ) *n* **1** the surface of a road **2** the part of a road that is used by vehicles

roadwork ('rəʊd,wɜːk) *n* sports training by running along roads

roadworks ('rəʊd,wɜːks) *pl n* repairs to a road or cable under a road, esp when forming a hazard or obstruction to traffic

roadworthy ('rəʊd,wɜːðɪ) *adj* (of a motor vehicle) mechanically sound; fit for use on the roads > **'road,worthiness** *n*

roam (rəʊm) *vb* **1** to travel or walk about with no fixed purpose or direction ▷ *n* **2** the act of roaming [C13 from ?] > **'roamer** *n*

roan (rəʊn) *adj* **1** (of a horse) having a bay (**red roan**), chestnut (**strawberry roan**), or black (**blue roan**) coat sprinkled with white hairs ▷ *n* **2** a horse having such a coat **3** a soft sheepskin leather used in bookbinding, etc [C16 from OF, from Sp. *roano*, prob. from Gothic *rauths* red]

Roanoke Island ('rəʊə,nəʊk) *n* an island off the coast of North Carolina: site of the first attempted English settlement in America. Length: 19 km (12 miles). Average width: 5 km (3 miles)

roar (rɔː) *vb* (*mainly intr*) **1** (of lions and other animals) to utter characteristic loud growling cries **2** (*also tr*) (of people) to utter (something) with a loud deep cry, as in anger or triumph **3** to laugh in a loud hearty unrestrained manner **4** (of horses) to breathe with laboured rasping sounds **5** (of the wind, waves, etc) to blow or break loudly and violently, as during a storm **6** (of a fire) to burn fiercely with a roaring sound **7** (*tr*) to bring (oneself) into a certain condition by roaring: *to roar oneself hoarse* ▷ *n* **8** a loud deep cry, uttered by a person or crowd, esp in anger or triumph **9** a prolonged loud cry of certain animals, esp lions **10** any similar noise made by a fire, the wind, waves, an engine, etc **11** a loud unrestrained burst of laughter [OE *rārian*] > ˈ**roarer** *n*

roaring (ˈrɔːrɪŋ) *adj* **1** *inf* very brisk and profitable (esp in **a roaring trade**) ▷ *adv* **2** noisily or boisterously (esp in **roaring drunk**) ▷ *n* **3** a loud prolonged cry > ˈ**roaringly** *adv*

roast (rəʊst) *vb* (*mainly tr*) **1** to cook (meat or other food) by dry heat, usually with added fat and esp in an oven **2** to brown or dry (coffee, etc) by exposure to heat **3** *metallurgy* to heat (an ore) in order to produce a concentrate that is easier to smelt **4** to heat (oneself or something) to an extreme degree, as when sunbathing, etc **5** (*intr*) to be excessively and uncomfortably hot **6** (*tr*) *inf* to criticize severely ▷ *n* **7** something that has been roasted, esp meat [c13 from OF *rostir*, of Gmc origin] > ˈ**roaster** *n*

roasting (ˈrəʊstɪŋ) *inf* ▷ *adj* **1** extremely hot ▷ *n* **2** severe criticism

rob (rɒb) *vb* **robs, robbing, robbed 1** to take something from (someone) illegally, as by force **2** (*tr*) to plunder (a house, etc) **3** (*tr*) to deprive unjustly: *to be robbed of an opportunity* [c13 from OF *rober*, of Gmc origin] > ˈ**robber** *n*

Robbe-Grillet (*French* rɔbgrijɛ) *n* **Alain** (alɛ̃) born 1922, French novelist and screenwriter. Author of *The Voyeur* (1955), *Jealousy* (1957), and *Djinn* (1981): he is one of the leading practitioners of the antinovel

Robben Island (ˈrɒbᵊn) *n* a small island in South Africa, 11 km (7 miles) off the Cape Peninsula: formerly used by the South African government to house political prisoners

robbery (ˈrɒbərɪ) *n, pl* **robberies 1** *criminal law* the stealing of property from a person by using or threatening to use force **2** the act or an instance of robbing

Robbia (ˈrəʊbɪə; *Italian* ˈrobbja) *n* **1 Andrea della** (anˈdrɛːa ˈdɛlla) 1435–1525, Florentine sculptor, best known for his polychrome reliefs and his statues of infants in swaddling clothes **2** his uncle, **Luca della** (ˈluːka ˈdɛlla) ?1400–82, Florentine sculptor, who perfected a technique of enamelling terra cotta for reliefs

Robbins (ˈrɒbɪnz) *n* **Jerome** 1918–98, US ballet dancer and choreographer. He choreographed the musicals *The King and I* (1951) and *West Side Story* (1957)

robe (rəʊb) *n* **1** any loose flowing garment, esp the official vestment of a peer, judge, or academic **2** a dressing gown or bathrobe ▷ *vb* **robes, robing, robed 3** to put a robe, etc, on (oneself or someone else) [c13 from OF; of Gmc origin]

Robert I (ˈrɒbət) *n* known as *Robert the Bruce*. 1274–1329, king of Scotland (1306–29): he defeated the English army of Edward II at Bannockburn (1314) and gained recognition of Scotland's independence (1328)

Robert II *n* 1316–90, king of Scotland (1371–90)

Robert III *n* ?1337–1406, king of Scotland (1390–1406), son of Robert II

Roberts (ˈrɒbəts) *n* **1 Frederick Sleigh**, 1st Earl. 1832–1914, British field marshal. He was awarded the Victoria Cross (1858) for his service during the Indian Mutiny and was commander in chief (1899–1900) in the second Boer War **2 Julia** born 1967, US film actress; her films include *Pretty Woman* (1990), *Notting Hill* (1999), *Erin Brockovich* (2000), which earned her an Academy Award, and *Mona Lisa Smile* (2003)

Robertson screw (ˈrɒbətsᵊn) *n trademark* a screw having a square hole in the head into which a screwdriver with a square point (**Robertson screwdriver** (*trademark*)) fits [c20 after its inventor P. L. Robertson (1896–1951), a Canad industrialist]

Robeson (ˈrəʊbsən) *n* **Paul** 1898–1976, US bass singer, actor, and leader in the Black civil rights movement

Robespierre (ˈrəʊbzpjɛə; *French* rɔbzpjɛr) *n* **Maximilien François Marie Isidore de** (maksimiljɛ̃ frɑ̃swa mari izidɔr də) 1758–94, French revolutionary and Jacobin leader: established the Reign of Terror as a member of the Committee of Public Safety (1793–94): executed in the coup d'état of Thermidor (1794)

Robey (ˈrəʊbɪ) *n* Sir **George**, original name *George Edward Wade*, known as *the prime minister of mirth*. 1869–1954, British music-hall comedian, who also appeared in films

robin (ˈrɒbɪn) *n* **1** Also called: **robin redbreast** a small Old World songbird related to the thrushes. The adult has a brown back, orange-red breast and face, and grey underparts **2** a North American thrush similar to but larger than the Old World robin [c16 arbitrary use of name *Robin*]

Robin Goodfellow (ˈrɒbɪn ˈɡʊdˌfɛləʊ) *n* another name for **puck²**

Robin Hood *n* a legendary English outlaw, who lived in Sherwood Forest (in the reign of Richard I) and robbed the rich to give to the poor

robinia (rəˈbɪnɪə) *n* any tree of the leguminous genus *Robinia*, esp the locust tree

Robinson (ˈrɒbɪnsən) *n* **1 Edward G**, real name *Emanuel Goldenberg*. 1893–1973, US film actor, born in Romania, famous esp for gangster roles. His films include *Little Caesar* (1930), *Brother Orchid* (1940), *Double Indemnity* (1944), and *All My Sons* (1948) **2 Edward Arlington** 1869–1935, US poet, author of narrative verse, often based on Arthurian legend. His works include *Collected Poems* (1922), *The Man Who Died Twice* (1924), and *Tristram* (1927) **3 (William) Heath** 1872–1944, British cartoonist and book illustrator, best known for his comic drawings of fantastic machines **4 John (Arthur Thomas)** 1919–83, British bishop and theologian, best known for his controversial *Honest to God* (1963), which popularized radical theological discussion. He was suffragan Bishop of Woolwich (1959–69) **5 Mary** born 1944, Irish barrister and politician: president of Ireland 1990–97; UN high commissioner for human rights (1997–2001) **6 "Sugar" Ray**, real name *Walker Smith*. 1921–89, US boxer, winner of the world middleweight championship on five separate occasions

roborant (ˈrəʊbərənt, ˈrɒb-) *adj* **1** tending to fortify or increase strength ▷ *n* **2** a drug or agent that increases strength [c17 from L *roborāre* to strengthen, from *rōbur* an oak]

robot (ˈrəʊbɒt) *n* **1** any automated machine programmed to perform specific mechanical functions in the manner of a human **2** (*modifier*) automatic: *a robot pilot* **3** a person who works or behaves like a machine **4** *S African* a set of traffic lights [c20 (used in R.U.R., a play by Karel ČAPEK) from Czech *robota* work] > roˈ**botic** *adj* > ˈ**robot-ˌlike** *adj*

robot bomb *n* another name for the **V-1**

robot dancing *or* **robotic dancing** (rəʊˈbɒtɪk) *n* a dance of the 1980s, characterized by jerky, mechanical movements. Also called: **robotics**

robotics (rəʊˈbɒtɪks) *n* (*functioning as sing*) **1** the science or technology of designing, building, and using robots **2** another name for **robot dancing**

Rob Roy (ˈrɒb ˈrɔɪ) *n* real name *Robert Macgregor*. 1671–1734, Scottish outlaw

Robson¹ (ˈrɒbsən) *n* **Mount** a mountain in SW Canada, in E British Columbia: the highest peak in the Canadian Rockies. Height: 3954 m (12 972 ft)

Robson² (ˈrɒbsən) *n* **1 Bobby**, full name *Robert William* born 1933, English footballer and manager of England (1982–90) **2 Bryan** born 1957, English footballer and manager: captain of England (1982–90) **3** Dame **Flora** 1902–84, English stage and film actress

Rr

robust (rəʊ'bʌst, 'rəʊbʌst) *adj* **1** strong in constitution **2** sturdily built: *a robust shelter* **3** requiring or suited to physical strength: *a robust sport* **4** (esp of wines) having a full-bodied flavour **5** rough or boisterous **6** (of thought, intellect, etc) straightforward [c16 from L *rōbustus*, from *rōbur* an oak, strength] > ro'**bustly** *adv*

robusta (rəʊ'bʌstə) *n* **1** a species of coffee tree, *Coffea canephora* **2** coffee or coffee beans obtained from this plant [from L *rōbustus* robust]

robustious (rəʊ'bʌstʃəs) *adj arch* **1** rough; boisterous **2** strong, robust, or stout > ro'**bustiously** *adv* > ro'**bustiousness** *n*

robustness (rəʊ'bʌstnɪs) *n* **1** the quality of being robust **2** *computing* the ability of a computer system to cope with errors during execution

roc (rɒk) *n* (in Arabian legend) a bird of enormous size and power [c16 from Ar., from Persian *rukh*]

ROC *abbrev for* Royal Observer Corps

Roca ('rəʊkə) *n* **Cape** a cape in SW central Portugal, near Lisbon: the westernmost point of continental Europe

rocaille (rɒ'kaɪ) *n* decorative rock or shell work, esp as ornamentation in a rococo fountain, grotto, or interior [from F, from *roc* ROCK[1]]

rocambole ('rɒkəm,bəʊl) *n* a variety of alliaceous plant whose garlic-like bulb is used for seasoning [c17 from F, from G *Rockenbolle*, lit.: distaff bulb (with reference to its shape)]

Rocard (*French* rɔkaːr) *n* **Michel** born 1930, French politician: prime minister of France (1988–91)

Rochdale ('rɒtʃ,deɪl) *n* **1** a town in NW England, in Rochdale unitary authority, Greater Manchester: former centre of the textile industry. Pop: 94 313 (1991) **2** a unitary authority in NW England, in Greater Manchester. Pop: 205 233 (2001). Area: 159 sq km (61 sq miles)

Rochelle salt (rɒ'ʃɛl) *n* a white crystalline double salt used in Seidlitz powder. Formula: $KNaC_4H_4O_6.4H_2O$ [c18 after LA ROCHELLE]

roche moutonnée (rəʊʃ ,muːtə'neɪ) *n, pl* **roches moutonnées** (rəʊʃ ,muːtə'neɪz) a rounded mass of rock smoothed and striated by ice that has flowed over it [c19 F, lit.: fleecy rock, from *mouton* sheep]

Rochester[1] ('rɒtʃɪstə) *n* **1** a city in SE England, in Medway unitary authority, Kent, on the River Medway. Pop: 23 971 (1991) **2** a city in NW New York State, on Lake Ontario. Pop: 219 773 (2000) **3** a city in the US, in Minnesota: site of the Mayo Clinic. Pop: 85 806 (2000)

Rochester[2] ('rɒtʃɪstə) *n* **2nd Earl of**, title of *John Wilmot*. 1647–80, English poet, wit, and libertine. His poems include satires, notably *A Satire against Mankind* (1675), love lyrics, and bawdy verse

rochet ('rɒtʃɪt) *n* a white surplice with tight sleeves, worn by bishops, abbots, and certain other Church dignitaries [c14 from OF, from *roc* coat, of Gmc origin]

rock[1] (rɒk) *n* **1** *geol* any aggregate of minerals that makes up part of the earth's crust. It may be unconsolidated, such as a sand, clay, or mud, or consolidated, such as granite, limestone, or coal **2** any hard mass of consolidated mineral matter, such as a boulder **3** *US, Canad, & Austral* a stone **4** a person or thing suggesting a rock, esp in being dependable, unchanging, or providing firm foundation **5** *Brit* a hard sweet, typically a long brightly coloured peppermint-flavoured stick, sold esp in holiday resorts **6** *sl* a jewel, esp a diamond **7** *sl* another name for **crack** (sense 28) **8 on the rocks 8a** in a state of ruin or destitution **8b** (of drinks, esp whisky) served with ice [c14 from OF *roche*, from ?]

rock[2] (rɒk) *vb* **1** to move or cause to move from side to side or backwards and forwards **2** to reel or sway or cause (someone) to reel or sway, as with a violent shock or emotion **3** (*tr*) to shake or move (something) violently **4** (*intr*) to dance in the rock-and-roll style ▷ *n* **5** a rocking motion **6** short for **rock and roll 7** Also called: **rock music** any of various styles of pop music having a heavy beat, derived from rock and roll. See also **rock up** [OE *roccian*]

Rock (rɒk) *n* **1 the** an informal name for **Gibraltar 2 the** a Canadian informal name for **Newfoundland**

rockabilly ('rɒkə,bɪlɪ) *n* a fast, spare style of White rock music which originated in the mid-1950s in the US South [c20 from ROCK (AND ROLL) + (HILL)BILLY]

Rockall ('rɒkɔːl) *n* an uninhabited British island in the N Atlantic, 354 km (220 miles) W of the Outer Hebrides. Area: 0.07 ha (0.18 acres)

rock and roll *or* **rock'n'roll** *n* **1a** a type of pop music originating in the 1950s as a blend of rhythm and blues and country and western **1b** (*as modifier*): *the rock-and-roll era* **2** dancing performed to such music, with exaggerated body movements stressing the beat ▷ *vb* **3** (*intr*) to perform this dance > **rock and roller** *or* **rock'n'roller** *n*

▷ www.reasontorock.com
▷ www.allmusic.com
▷ www.dotmusic.com

rock bass (bæs) *n* an eastern North American freshwater food fish, related to the sunfish family

rock bottom *n* **a** the lowest possible level **b** (*as modifier*): *rock-bottom prices*

rock-bound *adj* hemmed in or encircled by rocks. Also (poetic): **rock-girt**

rock cake *n* a small cake containing dried fruit and spice, with a rough surface supposed to resemble a rock

rock cod *n Austral* **1** any of various marine fishes found in rocky habitats in Australian waters. NZ **2** another name for **blue cod**

rock crystal *n* a pure transparent colourless quartz, used in electronic and optical equipment

rock dove *or* **pigeon** *n* a common dove from which domestic and feral pigeons are descended

Rockefeller ('rɒkə,fɛlə) *n* **1 John D(avison)** 1839–1937, US industrialist and philanthropist **2** his son, **John D(avison)** 1874–1960, US capitalist and philanthropist **3** his son, **Nelson (Aldrich)** 1908–79, US politician; governor of New York State (1958–74); vice president (1974–76)

rocker ('rɒkə) *n* **1** any of various devices that transmit or operate with a rocking motion. See also **rocker arm 2** another word for **rocking chair 3** either of two curved supports on the legs of a chair on which it may rock **4a** an ice skate with a curved blade **4b** the curve itself **5** a rock-music performer, fan, or song **6** *Brit* an adherent of a youth movement rooted in the 1950s, characterized by motorcycle trappings **7 off one's rocker** *sl* crazy

rocker arm *n* a lever that rocks about a pivot, esp a lever in an internal-combustion engine that transmits the motion of a pushrod or cam to a valve

rockery ('rɒkərɪ) *n, pl* **rockeries** a garden constructed with rocks, esp one where alpine plants are grown

rocket[1] ('rɒkɪt) *n* **1** a self-propelling device, esp a cylinder containing a mixture of solid explosives, used as a firework, distress signal, etc **2a** any vehicle that carries its own fuel and oxidant to burn in a rocket engine, esp one used to carry a spacecraft, etc **2b** (*as modifier*): *rocket launcher* **3** *Brit & NZ inf* a severe reprimand (esp in **get a rocket**) ▷ *vb* **rockets, rocketing, rocketed 4** (*tr*) to propel (a missile, spacecraft, etc) by means of a rocket **5** (*intr*; foll by *off, away*, etc) to move off at high speed **6** (*intr*) to rise rapidly: *he rocketed to the top* [c17 from OF, from It. *rochetto*, dim. of *rocca* distaff, of Gmc origin]

rocket[2] ('rɒkɪt) *n* any of several plants of the mustard family, typically having yellowish flowers, such as **London rocket** and **yellow rocket**. See also **arugula, wall rocket** [c16 from F *roquette*, from It. *rochetta*, from L *ērūca* hairy plant]

rocket engine *n* a reaction engine in which a fuel and

oxidizer are burnt in a combustion chamber, the products of combustion expanding through a nozzle and producing thrust

rocketry ('rɒkɪtrɪ) *n* the science and technology of the design, operation, maintenance, and launching of rockets

rocket scientist *n* a person of considerable intelligence and ability (esp in the phrase **not exactly a rocket scientist**) > '**rocket** '**science** *n*

rockfish ('rɒk,fɪʃ) *n, pl* **rockfish** *or* **rockfishes** **1** any of various fishes that live among rocks, such as the goby, bass, etc **2** *Brit* any of several coarse fishes when used as food, esp the dogfish or wolffish

Rockford ('rɒkfəd) *n* a city in N Illinois, on the Rock River. Pop: 150 115 (2000)

rock garden *n* a garden featuring rocks or rockeries

Rockhampton (rɒk'hæmptən, -'hæmtən) *n* a port in Australia, in E Queensland on the Fitzroy River. Pop: 65 868 (1993)

Rockies ('rɒkɪz) *pl n* another name for the **Rocky Mountains**

rocking chair *n* a chair set on curving supports so that the sitter may rock backwards and forwards

Rockingham ('rɒkɪŋəm) *n* **Marquess of,** title of *Charles Watson-Wentworth.* 1730–82, British statesman and leader of the Whig opposition, whose members were known as the **Rockingham Whigs**; prime minister (1765–66; 1782) He opposed the war with the American colonists

rocking horse *n* a toy horse mounted on a pair of rockers on which a child can rock to and fro in a seesaw movement

rocking stone *n* a boulder so delicately poised that it can be rocked

rockling ('rɒklɪŋ) *n, pl* **rocklings** *or* **rockling** a small gadoid fish which has an elongated body with barbels around the mouth and occurs mainly in the North Atlantic Ocean [C17 from ROCK[1] + -LING[1]]

rock lobster *n* another name for the **spiny lobster**

rock melon *n US, Austral, & NZ* another name for **cantaloupe**

rock pigeon *n* another name for **rock dove**

rock plant *n* any plant that grows on rocks or in rocky ground

rock rabbit *n S African* another name for **dassie.** See **hyrax**

rockrose ('rɒk,rəʊz) *n* any of various shrubs or herbaceous plants cultivated for their yellow-white or reddish roselike flowers

rock salmon *n Brit* a former term for **rockfish** (sense 2)

rock salt *n* another name for **halite**

rock snake *or* **python** *n* any large Australasian python of the genus *Liasis*

rock tripe *n Canad* any of various edible lichens that grow on rocks and are used in the North as a survival food

rock up *vb (intr, adv) S African* to arrive late or unannounced.

Rockwell ('rɒk,wɛl, -wəl) *n* **Norman** 1894–1978, US illustrator, noted esp for magazine covers

rock wool *n* another name for **mineral wool**

rocky[1] ('rɒkɪ) *adj* **rockier, rockiest** **1** consisting of or abounding in rocks: *a rocky shore* **2** unyielding: *rocky determination* **3** hard like rock: *rocky muscles* > '**rockiness** *n*

rocky[2] ('rɒkɪ) *adj* **rockier, rockiest** **1** weak or unstable **2** *inf* (of a person) dizzy; nauseated > '**rockily** *adv* > '**rockiness** *n*

Rocky Mountains *or* **Rockies** *pl n* the chief mountain system of W North America, extending from British Columbia to New Mexico: forms the Continental Divide. Highest peak: Mount Elbert, 4399 m (14 431 ft). Mount McKinley (6194 m (20 320 ft)), in the Alaska Range, is not strictly part of the Rocky Mountains

Rocky Mountain spotted fever *n* an acute rickettsial disease characterized by high fever, chills, pain in muscles and joints, etc. It is caused by the bite of an infected tick

rococo (rə'kəʊkəʊ) *n (often cap)* **1** a style of architecture and decoration that originated in France in the early 18th century, characterized by elaborate but graceful ornamentation **2** an 18th-century style of music characterized by prettiness and extreme use of ornamentation **3** any florid or excessively ornamental style ▷ *adj* **4** denoting, being in, or relating to the rococo **5** florid or excessively elaborate [C19 from F, from ROCAILLE, from *roc* ROCK[1]]

▷ www.artchive.com/ftp_site_reg.htm

▷ www.artlex.com/ArtLex/r/rococo.htmlm

rod (rɒd) *n* **1** a slim cylinder of metal, wood, etc **2** a switch or bundle of switches used to administer corporal punishment **3** any of various staffs of insignia or office **4** power, esp of a tyrannical kind: *a dictator's iron rod* **5** a straight slender shoot or stem of a woody plant **6** See **fishing rod** **7** Also called: **pole, perch** **7a** a unit of length equal to 5½ yards **7b** a unit of square measure equal to 30¼ square yards **8** *surveying* another name (esp US) for **staff[1]** (sense 8) **9** Also called: **retinal rod** any of the elongated cylindrical cells in the retina of the eye, which are sensitive to dim light but not to colour **10** any rod-shaped bacterium **11** *US* a slang name for **pistol** **12** short for **hot rod** [OE *rodd*] > '**rod,like** *adj*

Rodchenko (rɒd'tʃɛŋkəʊ) *n* **Alexander** (**Mikhailovich**) 1891–1956, Soviet painter, sculptor, designer, and photographer, noted for his abstract geometrical style: a member of the constructivist movement

rode (rəʊd) *vb* the past tense of **ride**

rodent ('rəʊdᵊnt) *n* **a** any of the relatively small placental mammals having constantly growing incisor teeth specialized for gnawing. The group includes rats, mice, squirrels, etc **b** *(as modifier)*: *rodent characteristics* [C19 from L *rōdere* to gnaw] > '**rodent-,like** *adj*

rodent ulcer *n* a slow-growing malignant tumour on the face, usually occurring at the edge of the eyelids, lips, or nostrils

Rr

rodeo ('rəʊdɪ,əʊ) *n, pl* **rodeos** *chiefly US & Canad* **1** a display of the skills of cowboys, including bareback riding **2** the rounding up of cattle for branding, etc **3** an enclosure for cattle that have been rounded up [C19 from Sp., from *rodear* to go around, from *rueda* a wheel, from L *rota*]

Roderic ('rɒdərɪk) *n* See **Rory O'Connor**

Rodgers ('rɒdʒəz) *n* **Richard** 1902–79, US composer of musical comedies. He collaborated with the librettist Lorenz Hart on such musicals as *A Connecticut Yankee* (1927), *On Your Toes* (1936), and *Pal Joey* (1940). After Hart's death his librettist was Oscar Hammerstein II. Two of their musicals, *Oklahoma!* (1943) and *South Pacific* (1949), received the Pulitzer Prize

Ródhos ('rɔðɔs) *n* transliteration of the Modern Greek name for **Rhodes**

Rodin (*French* rɔdɛ̃) *n* **Auguste** (ogyst) 1840–1917, French sculptor, noted for his portrayal of the human form. His works include *The Kiss* (1886), *The Burghers of Calais* (1896), and *The Thinker* (1905)

Rodney ('rɒdnɪ) *n* **George Brydges,** 1st Baron Rodney. 1719–92, English admiral: captured Martinique (1762): defeated the Spanish at Cape St Vincent (1780) and the French under Admiral de Grasse off Dominica (1782), restoring British superiority in the Caribbean

rodomontade (,rɒdəmɒn'teɪd, -'tɑːd) *literary* ▷ *n* **1a** boastful words or behaviour **1b** *(as modifier)*: *rodomontade behaviour* ▷ *vb* **rodomontades, rodomontading, rodomontaded** **2** *(intr)* to boast or rant [C17 from F, from It. *rodomonte* a boaster, from *Rodomonte,* the name of a braggart king of Algiers in epic poems]

Rodrigo (rɒ'driːgəʊ) *n* **Joaquín** 1902–99, Spanish composer. His works include *Concierto de Aranjuez* (1940) for guitar and orchestra and *Concierto Pastorale* (1978)

roe[1] (rəʊ) *n* **1** Also called: **hard roe** the ovary of a female fish filled with mature eggs **2** Also called: **soft roe** the testis of a male fish filled with mature sperm [c15 from MDu. *roge*, from OHG *roga*]

roe[2] (rəʊ) *n, pl* **roes** *or* **roe** short for **roe deer** [OE *rā(ha)*]

Roe (rəʊ) *n* **Richard** *law* (formerly) the defendant in a fictitious action, Doe versus Roe, to test a point of law. See also **Doe**

roebuck (ˈrəʊ,bʌk) *n, pl* **roebucks** *or* **roebuck** the male of the roe deer

roe deer *n* a small graceful deer of woodlands of Europe and Asia. The antlers are small and the summer coat is reddish-brown

Roeg (ˈrəʊəg) *n* **Nic(olas)** born 1928, British film director and cinematographer. Films include *Walkabout* (1970), *Don't Look Now* (1972), *Insignificance* (1984), and *The Witches* (1990)

roentgen *or* **röntgen** (ˈrɒntgən, -tjən, ˈrɛnt-) *n* a unit of dose of electromagnetic radiation equal to the dose that will produce in air a charge of 0.258×10^{-3} coulomb on all ions of one sign [c19 after W. K. ROENTGEN]

Roentgen *or* **Röntgen** (ˈrɒntgən, -tjən, ˈrɛnt-; *German* ˈrœntgən) *n* **Wilhelm Konrad** (ˈvɪlhɛlm ˈkɔnraːt) 1845–1923, German physicist, who in 1895 discovered X-rays: Nobel prize for physics 1901

roentgen ray *n* a former name for **X-ray**

Roeselare (ˈruːsəlaːrə) *n* the Flemish name for **Roulers**

Roethke (ˈrɛtkə) *n* **Theodore** 1908–63, US poet, whose books include *Words for the Wind* (1957) and *The Far Field* (1964)

rogation (rəʊˈgeɪʃən) *n* (*usually pl*) *Christianity* a solemn supplication, esp in a form of ceremony prescribed by the Church [c14 from L *rogātiō*, from *rogāre* to ask, make supplication]

Rogation Days *pl n* April 25 (the **Major Rogation**) and the Monday, Tuesday, and Wednesday before Ascension Day, observed by Christians as days of solemn supplication and marked by processions and special prayers

roger (ˈrɒdʒə) *interj* **1** (used in signalling, telecommunications, etc) message received **2** an expression of agreement ▷ *vb* **3** *taboo sl* (of a man) to copulate (with) [c20 from the name *Roger*, representing R for *received*]

Rogers (ˈrɒdʒəz) *n* **1** **Ginger**, real name *Virginia McMath*. 1911–95, US dancer and film actress, who partnered Fred Astaire **2** **Richard**, Baron Rogers of Riverside. born 1933, British architect. His works include the Pompidou Centre in Paris (1971–77; with Renzo Piano), the Lloyd's building in London (1986), and the Millennium Dome in Greenwich, London **3** **William Penn Adair**, known as *Will*. 1879–1935, US actor, newspaper columnist, and humorist in the homespun tradition

Roget (ˈrɒʒeɪ) *n* **Peter Mark** 1779–1869, English physician, who on retirement devised a *Thesaurus of English Words and Phrases* (1852), a classified list of synonyms

rogue (rəʊg) *n* **1** a dishonest or unprincipled person, esp a man **2** *often jocular* a mischievous or wayward person, often a child **3** a crop plant which is inferior, diseased, or of a different, unwanted variety **4a** any inferior or defective specimen **4b** (*as modifier*): *rogue heroin* **5** *arch* a vagrant **6a** an animal of vicious character that leads a solitary life **6b** (*as modifier*): *a rogue elephant* ▷ *vb* **rogues, roguing, rogued** **7** (*tr*) to rid (a field or crop) of plants that are inferior, diseased, etc [c16 from ?]

roguery (ˈrəʊgərɪ) *n, pl* **rogueries** **1** behaviour characteristic of a rogue **2** a roguish or mischievous act

rogues' gallery *n* **1** a collection of photographs of known criminals kept by the police for identification purposes **2** a group of undesirable people

rogue state *n* a state that conducts its policy in a dangerously unpredictable way, disregarding international law or diplomacy

rogue trader *n* a person who makes deals without due regard for normal business practices and controls

roguish (ˈrəʊgɪʃ) *adj* **1** dishonest or unprincipled **2** mischievous > **ˈroguishly** *adv*

roil (rɔɪl) *vb* **1** (*tr*) to make (a liquid) cloudy or turbid by stirring up dregs or sediment **2** (*intr*) (esp of a liquid) to be agitated **3** (*intr*) *dialect* to be noisy **4** (*tr*) *now rare* another word for **rile** (sense 1) [c16 from ?]

roister (ˈrɔɪstə) *vb* (*intr*) **1** to engage in noisy or unrestrained merrymaking **2** to brag, bluster, or swagger [c16 from OF *rustre* lout, from *ruste* uncouth, from L *rusticus* rural] > **ˈroisterer** *n* > **ˈroisterous** *adj* > **ˈroisterously** *adv*

Roland (ˈrəʊlənd) *n* **1** the greatest of the legendary 12 peers or paladins (of whom Oliver was another) in attendance on Charlemagne **2** **a Roland for an Oliver** an effective retort or retaliation

role *or* **rôle** (rəʊl) *n* **1** a part or character in a play, film, etc, to be played by an actor or actress **2** *psychol* the part played by a person in a particular social setting, influenced by his expectation of what is appropriate **3** usual function: *what is his role in the organization?* [c17 from F *rôle* ROLL, an actor's script]

role model *n* a person regarded by others, esp younger people, as a good example to follow

role-playing *n* *psychol* activity in which a person imitates, consciously or unconsciously, a role uncharacteristic of himself. See also **psychodrama**

Rolf (rɒlf) *or* **Rolf the Ganger** *n* other names for **Rollo**

Rolfe (rɒlf) *n* **Frederick William**, also known as *Baron Corvo*. 1860–1913, British novelist. His best-known work is *Hadrian the Seventh* (1904)

roll (rəʊl) *vb* **1** to move or cause to move along by turning over and over **2** to move or cause to move along on wheels or rollers **3** to flow or cause to flow onwards in an undulating movement **4** (*intr*) (of animals, etc) to turn onto the back and kick **5** (*intr*) to extend in undulations: *the hills roll down to the sea* **6** (*intr*; usually foll by *around*) to move or occur in cycles **7** (*intr*) (of a planet, the moon, etc) to revolve in an orbit **8** (*intr*; foll by *on, by,* etc) to pass or elapse: *the years roll by* **9** to rotate or cause to rotate wholly or partially: *to roll one's eyes* **10** to curl, cause to curl, or admit of being curled, so as to form a ball, tube, or cylinder **11** to make or form by shaping into a ball, tube, or cylinder: *to roll a cigarette* **12** (often foll by *out*) to spread or cause to spread out flat or smooth under or as if under a roller: *to roll pastry* **13** to emit or utter with a deep prolonged reverberating sound: *the thunder rolled continuously* **14** to trill or cause to be trilled: *to roll one's r's* **15** (*intr*) (of a vessel, aircraft, rocket, etc) to turn from side to side around the longitudinal axis **16** to cause (an aircraft) to execute a roll or (of an aircraft) to execute a roll (sense 34) **17** (*intr*) to walk with a swaying gait, as when drunk **18** *chiefly US* to throw (dice) **19** (*intr*) to operate or begin to operate: *the presses rolled* **20** (*intr*) *inf* to make progress: *let the good times roll* **21** (*tr*) *inf, chiefly US & NZ* to rob (a helpless person) ▷ *n* **22** the act or an instance of rolling **23** anything rolled up in a cylindrical form: *a roll of newspaper* **24** an official list or register, esp of names: *an electoral roll* **25** a rounded mass: *rolls of flesh* **26** a cylinder used to flatten something; roller **27** a small cake of bread for one person **28** a flat pastry or cake rolled up with a meat (**sausage roll**), jam (**jam roll**), or other filling **29** a swell or undulation on a surface: *the roll of the hills* **30** a swaying, rolling, or unsteady movement or gait **31** a deep prolonged reverberating sound: *the roll of thunder* **32** a trilling sound; trill **33** a very rapid beating of the sticks on a drum **34** a flight manoeuvre in which an aircraft makes one complete rotation about its longitudinal axis without loss of height or change in direction **35** *sl* an act of sexual intercourse or petting (esp in **a roll in the hay**) **36** *US sl* an amount of money, esp a wad of paper money **37 on a roll** *sl* experiencing continued good luck or success **38 strike off the roll(s) 38a** to expel from membership **38b** to debar (a solicitor) from practising, usually because of dishonesty ▷ See also **roll in, roll on,** etc [c14 *rollen*, from OF *roler*, from L *rotulus*, dim. of *rota* a wheel]

Rolland (*French* rɔlɑ̃) *n* **Romain** (rɔmɛ̃) 1866–1944, French novelist, dramatist, and essayist, known for his novels about a musical genius, *Jean-Christophe*, (1904–12): Nobel prize for literature 1915

rollbar (ˈrəʊlˌbɑː) *n* a bar that reinforces the frame of a car used for racing, rallying, etc, to protect the driver if the car should turn over

roll call *n* the reading aloud of an official list of names, those present responding when their names are read out

rolled gold *n* a metal, such as brass, coated with a thin layer of gold. Also (US): **filled gold**

rolled-steel joist *n* a steel beam, esp one with a cross section in the form of a letter H or I. Abbrev: **RSJ**

roller (ˈrəʊlə) *n* **1** a cylinder having an absorbent surface and a handle, used for spreading paint **2** Also called: **garden roller** a heavy cast-iron cylinder on an axle to which a handle is attached; used for flattening lawns **3** a long heavy wave of the sea, advancing towards the shore **4** a hardened cylinder of precision-ground steel that forms one of the rolling components of a roller bearing or of a linked driving chain **5** a cylinder fitted on pivots, used to enable heavy objects to be easily moved **6** *printing* a cylinder, usually of hard rubber, used to ink a plate before impression **7** any of various other cylindrical devices that rotate about a cylinder, used for any of various purposes **8** a small cylinder onto which a woman's hair may be rolled to make it curl **9** *med* a bandage consisting of a long strip of muslin rolled tightly into a cylindrical form before application **10** any of various Old World birds, such as the **European roller**, that have a blue, green, and brown plumage, a slightly hooked bill, and an erratic flight **11** (*often cap*) a variety of tumbler pigeon **12** a person or thing that rolls **13** short for **steamroller**

rollerball (ˈrəʊləˌbɔːl) *n* a pen having a small moving nylon, plastic, or metal ball as a writing point

roller bearing *n* a bearing in which a shaft runs on a number of hardened-steel rollers held within a cage

Rollerblade (ˈrəʊləˌbleɪd) *n trademark* a type of roller skate in which the wheels are set in a single straight line under the boot

roller chain *n engineering* a chain for transmitting power in which each link consists of two free-moving rollers held in position by pins connected to sideplates

roller coaster *n* another term for **big dipper**

roller derby *n* a race on roller skates, esp one involving aggressive tactics

roller skate *n* **1** a device having straps for fastening to a shoe and four small wheels that enable the wearer to glide swiftly over a floor ▷ *vb* **roller-skate, roller-skates, roller-skating, roller-skated 2** (*intr*) to move on roller skates > **roller skater** *n*

roller towel *n* **1** a towel with the two ends sewn together, hung on a roller **2** a towel wound inside a roller enabling a clean section to be pulled out when needed

rollick (ˈrɒlɪk) *vb* **1** (*intr*) to behave in a carefree or boisterous manner ▷ *n* **2** a boisterous or carefree escapade [c19 Scot dialect, prob. from ROMP + FROLIC]

rollicking[1] (ˈrɒlɪkɪŋ) *adj* boisterously carefree [c19 from ROLLICK]

rollicking[2] (ˈrɒlɪkɪŋ) *n Brit inf* a very severe telling-off [c20 from ROLLICK (vb) (in former sense: to be angry, make a fuss); ? infl. by BOLLOCKING]

roll in *vb* (*mainly intr*) **1** (*adv*) to arrive in abundance or in large numbers **2** (*adv*) *inf* to arrive at one's destination **3 be rolling in** (*prep*) *sl* to abound or luxuriate in (wealth, money, etc)

rolling (ˈrəʊlɪŋ) *adj* **1** having gentle rising and falling slopes: *rolling country* **2** progressing by stages or by occurrences in different places in succession: *a rolling strike* **3** subject to regular review and updating: *a rolling plan for overseas development* **4** reverberating: *rolling thunder* **5** *sl* extremely rich **6** that may be turned up or down: *a rolling hat brim* ▷ *adv* **7** *sl* swaying or staggering (in **rolling drunk**)

rolling launch *n marketing* the process of introducing a product onto a market gradually ▷ Cf **roll out** (sense 3)

rolling mill *n* **1** a mill or factory where ingots of heated metal are passed between rollers to produce sheets or bars of a required cross section and form **2** a machine having rollers that may be used for this purpose

rolling pin *n* a cylinder with handles at both ends used for rolling dough, pastry, etc, out flat

rolling stock *n* the wheeled vehicles collectively used on a railway, including the locomotives, coaches, etc

rolling stone *n* a restless or wandering person

Rolling Stones *pl n* **the** British rock group (formed 1962): comprising Mick Jagger, Keith Richards (born 1943; guitar, vocals), Brian Jones (1942–69; guitar), Charlie Watts (born 1941; drums), Bill Wyman (born 1936; bass guitar; now retired), and subsequently Mick Taylor (born 1948; guitar; with the group 1969–74) and Ron Wood (born 1947; guitar; with the group from 1975). See also (Michael Philip) **Jagger**

Rollins (ˈrɒlɪnz) *n* **Sonny,** original name *Theodore Walter Rollins.* born 1930, US jazz tenor saxophonist, noted for his improvisation

rollmop (ˈrəʊlˌmɒp) *n* a herring fillet rolled, usually around onion slices, and pickled in spiced vinegar [c20 from G *Rollmops*, from *rollen* to ROLL + *Mops* pug dog]

rollneck (ˈrəʊlˌnɛk) *adj* **1** (of a garment) having a high neck that may be rolled over ▷ *n* **2** a rollneck sweater or other garment

Rollo (ˈrɒləʊ) *n* ?860–?930 AD, Norse war leader who received from Charles the Simple a fief that formed the basis of the duchy of Normandy. Also called: **Rolf, Rolf the Ganger**

roll of honour *n* a list of those who have died in war for their country

roll on *vb* **1** *Brit* used to express the wish that an eagerly anticipated event or date will come quickly: *roll on Saturday* ▷ *adj* **roll-on 2** (of a deodorant, etc) dispensed by means of a revolving ball fitted into the neck of the container ▷ *n* **roll-on 3** a woman's foundation garment, made of elasticized material and having no fastenings

roll-on/roll-off *adj* denoting a cargo ship or ferry designed so that vehicles can be driven on and off

roll out *vb* (*tr, adv*) **1** to cause (pastry) to become flatter and thinner by pressure with a rolling pin **2** to show (a new type of aircraft) to the public for the first time **3** to launch (a new film, product, etc) in a series of successive waves, as over the whole country ▷ *n* **roll-out 4** a presentation to the public of a new aircraft, product, etc; a launch

roll over *vb* (*adv*) **1** (*intr*) to overturn **2** (*intr*) (of an animal, esp a dog) to lie on its back while kicking its legs in the air **3** (*intr*) to capitulate **4** (*tr*) to allow (a loan, prize, etc) to continue in force for a further period ▷ *n* **rollover 5** an instance of such continuance of a loan, prize, etc

roll-top desk *n* a desk having a slatted wooden panel that can be pulled down over the writing surface when not in use

roll up *vb* (*adv*) **1** to form or cause to form a cylindrical shape **2** (*tr*) to wrap (an object) round on itself or on an axis: *to roll up a map* **3** (*intr*) *inf* to arrive, esp in a vehicle **4** (*intr*) to proceed or develop **5** (*intr*) *Austral* to assemble;

Rr

congregate ▷ *n* **roll-up** **6** *Brit inf* a cigarette made by hand from loose tobacco and cigarette papers **7** *Austral* the number attending a meeting, etc

Rolodex ('rəʊlə,dɛks) *n trademark, chiefly US* a small file for holding names, addresses, and telephone numbers, consisting of cards attached horizontally to a rotatable central cylinder

roly-poly ('rəʊlɪ'pəʊlɪ) *adj* **1** plump, buxom, or rotund ▷ *n, pl* **roly-polies** **2** *Brit* a strip of suet pastry spread with jam, fruit, or a savoury mixture, rolled up, and baked or steamed [C17 apparently by reduplication from *roly*, from ROLL]

ROM (rɒm) *n computing acronym for* read only memory: a storage device that holds data permanently and cannot be altered by the programmer

rom. *printing abbrev for* roman (type)

Rom. *abbrev for:* **1** Roman **2** Romance (languages) **3** Romania(n) **4** *Bible* Romans

Roma[1] ('ro:ma) *n* the Italian name for **Rome**

Romagna (*Italian* ro'maɲɲa) *n* an area of N Italy: part of the Papal States up to 1860

Romaic (rəʊ'meɪɪk) *obs* ▷ *n* **1** the modern Greek vernacular ▷ *adj* **2** of or relating to Greek [C19 from Gk *Rhōmaikos* Roman, with reference to the Eastern Roman Empire]

Romains (*French* rɔmɛ̃) *n* **Jules** (ʒyl) pseudonym of *Louis Farigoule*. 1885–1972, French poet, dramatist, and novelist. His works include the novel *Men of Good Will* (1932–46)

roman ('rəʊmən) *adj* **1** of, relating to, or denoting a vertical style of printing type: the usual form of type for most printed matter ▷ Cf **italic** ▷ *n* **2** roman type [C16 so called because the style of letters is that used in ancient Roman inscriptions]

Roman ('rəʊmən) *adj* **1** of or relating to Rome or its inhabitants in ancient or modern times **2** of or relating to Roman Catholicism or the Roman Catholic Church ▷ *n* **3** a citizen or inhabitant of ancient or modern Rome

roman à clef *French* (rɔmɑ̃ a kle) *n, pl* ***romans à clef*** (rɔmɑ̃ a kle) a novel in which real people are depicted under fictitious names [lit.: novel with a key]

Roman alphabet *n* the alphabet evolved by the ancient Romans for the writing of Latin, derived ultimately from the Phoenicians. The alphabet serves for writing most of the languages of W Europe

Roman blind *n* a window blind consisting of a length of material which, when drawn up, gathers into horizontal folds from the bottom

Roman candle *n* a firework that produces a continuous shower of sparks punctuated by coloured balls of fire [C19 it originated in Italy]

Roman Catholic *adj* **1** of or relating to the Roman Catholic Church ▷ *n* **2** a member of this Church ▷ Often shortened to **Catholic** > **Roman Catholicism** *n*

Roman Catholic Church *n* the Christian Church over which the pope presides, with administrative headquarters in the Vatican. Also called: **Catholic Church, Church of Rome**
▷ http://www.vatican.va/

romance *n* (rə'mæns, 'rəʊmæns) **1** a love affair **2** love, esp romantic love idealized for its purity or beauty **3** a spirit of or inclination for adventure or mystery **4** a mysterious, exciting, sentimental, or nostalgic quality, esp one associated with a place **5** a narrative in verse or prose, written in a vernacular language in the Middle Ages, dealing with adventures of chivalrous heroes **6** any similar narrative work dealing with events and characters remote from ordinary life **7** a story, novel, film, etc, dealing with love, usually in an idealized or sentimental way **8** an extravagant, absurd, or fantastic account **9** a lyrical song or short instrumental composition having a simple melody ▷ *vb* (rə'mæns), **romances, romancing, romanced** **10** (*intr*) to tell, invent, or write extravagant or romantic fictions **11** (*intr*) to tell extravagant or improbable lies **12** (*intr*) to have romantic thoughts **13** (*intr*) (of a couple) to indulge in romantic behaviour **14** (*tr*) to be romantically involved with [C13 *romauns*, from OF *romans*, ult. from L *Rōmānicus* Roman] > **ro'mancer** *n*

Romance (rə'mæns, 'rəʊmæns) *adj* **1** denoting, relating to, or belonging to the languages derived from Latin, including Italian, Spanish, Portuguese, French, and Romanian **2** denoting a word borrowed from a Romance language ▷ *n* **3** this group of languages

Roman Empire *n* **1** the territories ruled by ancient Rome. At its height the Roman Empire included W and S Europe, N Africa, and SW Asia. In 395 AD it was divided into the **Eastern Roman Empire,** whose capital was Byzantium, and the **Western Roman Empire,** whose capital was Rome **2** the government of Rome and its dominions by the emperors from 27 BC **3** the Byzantine Empire **4** the Holy Roman Empire
▷ www.roman-empire.net

Romanesque (,rəʊmə'nɛsk) *adj* **1** denoting or having the style of architecture used in W and S Europe from the 9th to the 12th century, characterized by the rounded arch and massive-masonry wall construction **2** denoting a corresponding style in painting, sculpture, etc [C18 see ROMAN, -ESQUE]
▷ www.britainexpress.com/architecture

Roman holiday *n* entertainment or pleasure that depends on the suffering of others [C19 from Byron's poem *Childe Harold* (IV, 141)]

Romania (rəʊ'meɪnɪə), **Rumania**, *or* **Roumania** *n* a republic in SE Europe, bordering on the Black Sea: united in 1861; became independent in 1878; Communist government set up in 1945; became a socialist republic in 1965; a more democratic regime was installed after a revolution in 1989. It consists chiefly of a great central arc of the Carpathian Mountains and Transylvanian Alps, with the plains of Walachia, Moldavia, and Dobriya on the south and east and the Pannonian Plain in the west. Official language: Romanian. Religion: Romanian Orthodox (Christian) majority. Currency: leu. Capital: Bucharest. Pop: 22 413 000 (2001 est). Area: 237 500 sq km (91 699 sq miles)
▷ www.guv.ro
▷ www.ministerulturismului.ro
▷ www.romaniatourism.com

Romanian (rəʊ'meɪnɪən), **Rumanian,** *or* **Roumanian** *n* **1** the official language of Romania **2** a native, citizen, or inhabitant of Romania ▷ *adj* **3** relating to, denoting, or characteristic of Romania, its people, or their language

Romanic (rəʊ'mænɪk) *adj* another word for **Roman** or **Romance**

Romanism ('rəʊmə,nɪzəm) *n* Roman Catholicism, esp when regarded as excessively or superstitiously ritualistic > **'Romanist** *n*

Romanize *or* **Romanise** ('rəʊmə,naɪz) *vb* **Romanizes, Romanizing, Romanized** *or* **Romanises, Romanising, Romanised** **1** (*tr*) to impart a Roman Catholic character to (a ceremony, etc) **2** (*intr*) to be converted to Roman Catholicism **3** (*tr*) to transcribe (a language) into the Roman alphabet > **,Romani'zation** *or* **,Romani'sation** *n*

Roman law *n* the system of jurisprudence of ancient Rome, codified under Justinian and forming the basis of many modern legal systems

Roman nose *n* a nose having a high prominent bridge

Roman numerals *pl n* the letters used by the Romans for the representation of cardinal numbers, still used occasionally today. The integers are represented by the following letters: I (= 1), V (= 5), X (= 10), L (= 50), C (= 100), D (= 500), and M (= 1000). VI = 6 (V + I) but IV = 4 (V – I)

Roman Numerals

Although in the Western world we use the Arabic numerical system – 0, 1, 2, 3, etc – the Roman system of writing numerals still survives in a number of areas. Roman numerals are used to show the order of monarchs – e.g. King Edward VII – and to distinguish ships that share the same name – e.g. Queen Mary II. They are also to be seen on many watch and clock faces and are sometimes employed in publishing and television to indicate copyright dates.

Unlike the Arabic system, the Roman system does not have a symbol for zero. Also, numeral order within a number sometimes indicates subtraction rather than addition.

The roman system of numbering lives on in the many Latin prefixes used to indicate numerical concepts. Some examples of which are: octogenarian, decade, century, bicep, and quadruped.

I
This symbol is used to indicate 1. **II** = 2 and **III** = 3.

V
This simple system changes when we get to 4 and 5. The Romans used **V** to indicate 5 and **IV** to indicate 4. This illustrates the Roman rule whereby a smaller number placed in front of a larger number indicates subtraction.

X
X represents 10. **IX** means 9 (based on the subtraction rule). **XXIV** = 24 and **XXXVII** = 37, etc

L
L represents 50. The subtraction rule means that **XL** = 40. 60 is represented by **LX**, 70 by **LXX**, and 80 by **LXXX**.

C
C represent 100 and 90 (using the subtraction rule) is **XC**. **CC** = 200. **CCC** = 300.

D
D represents 500 and **CD** stands for 400.

M
M represents 1000. **MM** represents 2000 and so on. The year of publication of this dictionary is **MMIV** (2004).

ª A convention that is now no longer used employed a horizontal line to indicate that the number below should be multiplied by 1000. This system is no longer used as the largest numbers expressed in Roman numerals are usually dates which use the system outlined above.

NOTE

The use of **IV** to mean 4 is not quite universal. It has been a convention, commonly adhered to since timepieces were first built during the early Renaissance, that clock and watch faces using Roman numerals depict the numeral 4 as **IIII**. There are some notable exceptions though. Big Ben and the clock in the South Transept of Norwich Cathedral both use **IV** instead of **IIII**, as does the Cathedral at San Sebastian in Spain.

▷ www.unc.edu/~rowlett/units/roman.html
▷ www.wilkiecollins.demon.co.uk/roman/front.htm
▷ www.novaroma.org/via_romana/numbers.html

Romano (*Italian* roˈmaːno) *n* See **Giulio Romano**

Romanov (ˈrəʊmənɒf; *Russian* raˈmanəf) *n* any of the Russian imperial dynasty that ruled from the crowning (1613) of Mikhail Fyodorovich to the abdication (1917) of Nicholas II during the February Revolution

Romansch *or* **Romansh** (rəʊˈmænʃ) *n* a group of Romance dialects spoken in the Swiss canton of Grisons; an official language of Switzerland since 1938 [c17 from Romansch, lit.: Romance language]

romantic (rəʊˈmæntɪk) *adj* **1** of, relating to, imbued with, or characterized by romance **2** evoking or given to thoughts and feelings of love, esp idealized or sentimental love: *a romantic setting* **3** impractical, visionary, or idealistic: *a romantic scheme* **4** *often euphemistic* imaginary or fictitious: *a romantic account of one's war service* **5** (*often cap*) of or relating to a movement in European art, music, and literature in the late 18th and early 19th centuries, characterized by an emphasis on feeling and content rather than order and form ▷ *n* **6** a person who is romantic, as in being idealistic, amorous, or soulful **7** a person whose tastes in art, literature, etc, lie mainly in romanticism **8** (*often cap*) a poet, composer, etc, of the romantic period or whose main inspiration is romanticism [c17 from F, from obs. *romant* story, romance, from OF *romans* ROMANCE] > **roˈmantically** *adv*
▷ http://classicalmus.hispeed.com/romantic.html

romanticism (rəʊˈmæntɪˌsɪzəm) *n* **1** (*often cap*) the theory, practice, and style of the romantic art, music, and literature of the late 18th and early 19th centuries, usually opposed to classicism **2** romantic attitudes, ideals, or qualities > **roˈmanticist** *n*
▷ www.artchive.com/ftp_site_reg.htm
▷ www.artcyclopedia.com/history/romanticism.html
▷ www.artlex.com/ArtLex/r/romanticism.html

romanticize *or* **romanticise** (rəʊˈmæntɪˌsaɪz) *vb* **romanticizes, romanticizing, romanticized** *or* **romanticises, romanticising, romanticised** **1** (*intr*) to think or act in a romantic way **2** (*tr*) to interpret according to romantic precepts **3** to make or become romantic, as in style > **roˌmanticiˈzation** *or* **roˌmanticiˈsation** *n*

Romany *or* **Romani** (ˈrɒmənɪ, ˈrəʊ-) *n* **1a** (*pl* **Romanies** *or* **Romanis**) another name for a **Gypsy** **1b** (*as modifier*): *Romany customs* **2** the language of the Gypsies, belonging to the Indic branch of the Indo-European family [c19 from Romany *romani* (adj) Gypsy, ult. from Sansk. *domba* man of a low caste of musicians, of Dravidian origin]

romanza (rəʊˈmænzə) *n* a short instrumental piece of songlike character [It.]

romaunt (rəˈmɔːnt) *n arch* a verse romance [c16 from OF; see ROMANTIC]

Romberg (ˈrɒmbɜːg) *n* **Sigmund** 1887–1951, US composer of operettas, born in Hungary. He wrote *The Student Prince* (1924) and *The Desert Song* (1926)

Rome (rəʊm) *n* **1** the capital of Italy, on the River Tiber: includes the independent state of the Vatican City; traditionally founded by Romulus on the Palatine Hill in 753 BC, later spreading to six other hills east of the Tiber; capital of the Roman Empire; a great cultural and artistic centre, esp during the Renaissance. Pop: 2 643 581 (2000 est). Italian name: **Roma** **2** the Roman Empire **3** the Roman Catholic Church or Roman Catholicism
▷ www.comune.roma.it/eng/index.asp

Romeo (ˈrəʊmɪəʊ) *n, pl* **Romeos** an ardent male lover [after the hero of Shakespeare's *Romeo and Juliet* (1594)]

Romish (ˈrəʊmɪʃ) *adj usually derog* of or resembling Roman Catholic beliefs or practices

Rommel (*German* ˈrɔməl) *n* **Erwin** (ˈɛrviːn), nicknamed *the Desert Fox*. 1891–1944, German field marshal, noted for his brilliant generalship in N Africa in World War II. Later a commander in N France, he committed suicide after being implicated in the officers' plot against Hitler

Romney ('rɒmnɪ, 'rʌm-) *n* **George** 1734–1802, English painter, who painted more than 50 portraits of Lady Hamilton in various historical roles

Romney Marsh ('rɒmnɪ, 'rʌm-) *n* **1** a marshy area of SE England, on the Kent coast between New Romney and Rye: includes Dungeness **2** a type of hardy British sheep from this area, with long wool, bred for mutton

romp (rɒmp) *vb (intr)* **1** to play or run about wildly, boisterously, or joyfully **2 romp home** (*or* **in**) to win a race, etc, easily ▷ *n* **3** a noisy or boisterous game or prank **4** an instance of sexual activity between two or more people that is entered into light-heartedly and without emotional commitment: *naked sex romps* **5** *arch* a playful or boisterous child, esp a girl **6** an easy victory [C18 prob. var. of RAMP, from OF *ramper* to crawl, climb]

rompers ('rɒmpəz) *pl n* **1** a one-piece baby garment consisting of trousers and a bib with straps **2** NZ *old-fashioned* a type of costume worn by schoolgirls for games and gymnastics

Romulus ('rɒmjʊləs) *n Roman myth* the founder of Rome, suckled with his twin brother Remus by a she-wolf after they were abandoned in infancy. Their parents were Rhea Silvia and Mars. Romulus later killed Remus in an argument over the new city

Roncesvalles ('rɒnsə,vælz; *Spanish* rɔnθez'βaʎes) *n* a village in N Spain, in the Pyrenees: a nearby pass was the scene of the defeat of Charlemagne and death of Roland in 778. French name: **Roncevaux** (rɔ̃svo)

rondavel (ˌrɒn'dɑːvəl) *n S African* a circular, often thatched, building with a conical roof [from ?]

rondeau ('rɒndəʊ) *n, pl* **rondeaux** (-dəʊ, -dəʊz) a poem consisting of 13 or 10 lines with two rhymes and having the opening words of the first line used as an unrhymed refrain [C16 from OF, from *rondel* a little round, from *rond* ROUND]

rondel ('rɒndᵊl) *n* a rondeau consisting of three stanzas of 13 or 14 lines with a two-line refrain appearing twice or three times [C14 from OF, lit.: a little circle, from *rond* ROUND]

rondo ('rɒndəʊ) *n, pl* **rondos** a piece of music in which a refrain is repeated between episodes: often constitutes the form of the last movement of a sonata or concerto [C18 from It., from F RONDEAU]

Rondônia (*Portuguese* rõ'donja) *n* a state of W Brazil: consists chiefly of tropical rainforest; a centre of the Amazon rubber boom until about 1912. Capital: Pôrto Velho. Pop: 1 377 792 (2000). Area: 243 043 sq km (93 839 sq miles). Former name (until 1956): **Guaporé**

rone (rəʊn) *or* **ronepipe** *n Scot* a drainpipe for carrying rainwater from a roof [C19 from ?]

Ronsard (*French* rɔ̃sar) *n* **Pierre de** (pjɛr də) 1524–85, French poet, foremost of the *Pléiade*

röntgen ('rɒntgən, -tjən, 'rɛnt-) *n* a variant spelling of **roentgen**

Röntgen ('rɒntgən, -tjən, 'rɛnt-; *German* 'rœntgən) *n* a variant spelling of (Wilhelm Konrad) **Roentgen**

roo (ruː) *n Austral inf* a kangaroo

roo bars *pl n Austral* another name for **bull bars**

rood (ruːd) *n* **1a** a crucifix, esp one set on a beam or screen at the entrance to the chancel of a church **1b** (*as modifier*): *rood screen* **2** the Cross on which Christ was crucified **3** a unit of area equal to one quarter of an acre or 0.10117 hectare **4** a unit of area equal to 40 square rods [OE *rōd*]

Roodepoort-Maraisburg ('ruːdə,pʊət mə'reɪsbɜːg) *n* an industrial city in NE South Africa, on the Witwatersrand. Pop: 162 632 (1991)

roof (ruːf) *n, pl* **roofs** (ruːfs, ruːvz) **1a** a structure that covers or forms the top of a building **1b** (*in combination*): *the rooftop* **1c** (*as modifier*): *a roof garden* **2** the top covering of a vehicle, oven, or other structure: *the roof of a car* **3** *anat* any structure that covers an organ or part: *the roof of the mouth* **4** a highest or topmost point or part: *Mount Everest is the roof of the world* **5** a house or other shelter: *a poor man's roof* **6 hit** (*or* **raise** *or* **go through**) **the roof** *inf* to get extremely angry ▷ *vb* **7** (*tr*) to provide or cover with a roof or rooflike part [OE *hrōf*] > '**roofer** *n* > '**roofless** *adj*

roof garden *n* a garden on a flat roof of a building

roofie ('ruːfɪ) *n* a tablet of flunitrazepam used as an illegal drug, often in combination with alcohol or other drugs [C20 from *Rophy*, street name for *Rohypnol*, a tradename for flunitrazepam]

roofing ('ruːfɪŋ) *n* **1** material used to construct a roof **2** the act of constructing a roof

roof rack *n* a rack attached to the roof of a motor vehicle for carrying luggage, skis, etc

rooftree ('ruːf,triː) *n* another name for **ridgepole**

rooibos ('rɔɪ,bɒs, 'rʊɪ,bɒs) *n* any of various South African trees with red leaves [from Afrik. *rooi* red + *bos* bush]

rooibos tea *n S African* a tealike drink made from the leaves of the rooibos

rooikat ('rɔɪ,kæt, 'rʊɪ,kæt) *n* a South African lynx [from Afrik. *rooi* red + *kat* cat]

rooinek ('rɔɪ,nɛk, 'rʊɪ,nɛk) *n S African* a contemptuous name for an **Englishman** [C19 Afrik., lit.: red neck]

rook[1] (rʊk) *n* **1** a large Eurasian passerine bird, with a black plumage and a whitish base to its bill **2** *sl* a swindler or cheat, esp one who cheats at cards ▷ *vb* **3** (*tr*) *sl* to overcharge, swindle, or cheat [OE *hrōc*]

rook[2] (rʊk) *n* a chesspiece that may move any number of unoccupied squares in a straight line, horizontally or vertically. Also called: **castle** [C14 from OF *rok*, ult. from Ar. *rukhkh*]

rookery ('rʊkərɪ) *n, pl* **rookeries** **1** a group of nesting rooks **2** a clump of trees containing rooks' nests **3a** a breeding ground or communal living area of certain other birds or mammals, esp penguins or seals **3b** a colony of any such creatures **4** *arch* an overcrowded slum

rookie ('rʊkɪ) *n inf* a newcomer, esp a raw recruit in the army [C20 changed from RECRUIT]

room (ruːm, rʊm) *n* **1** space or extent, esp unoccupied or unobstructed space for a particular purpose: *is there room to pass?* **2** an area within a building enclosed by a floor, a ceiling, and walls or partitions **3** (*functioning as sing or pl*) the people present in a room: *the whole room was laughing* **4** (foll by *for*) opportunity or scope: *room for manoeuvre* **5** (*pl*) a part of a house, hotel, etc, that is rented out as separate accommodation: *living in dingy rooms in Dalry* ▷ *vb* **6** (*intr*) to occupy or share a room or lodging: *where does he room?* [OE *rūm*] > '**roomer** *n*

roomful ('ruːm,fʊl, 'rʊm-) *n, pl* **roomfuls** a number or quantity sufficient to fill a room: *a roomful of furniture*

rooming house *n US & Canad* a house having self-contained furnished rooms or flats for renting

roommate ('ruːm,meɪt, 'rʊm-) *n* a person with whom one shares a room or lodging

room service *n* service in a hotel providing meals, drinks, etc, in guests' rooms

roomy ('ruːmɪ, 'rʊmɪ) *adj* **roomier, roomiest** spacious > '**roomily** *adv* > '**roominess** *n*

Rooney ('ruːnɪ) *n* **Wayne** born 1985, English footballer; he plays for Everton (from 2002) and England (from 2003)

Roosevelt ('rəʊzə,vɛlt) *n* **1** (**Anna**) **Eleanor** 1884–1962, US writer, diplomat, and advocate of liberal causes: delegate to the United Nations (1945–52) **2** her husband, **Franklin Delano** ('dɛlə,nəʊ), known as FDR. 1882–1945, 32nd president of the US (1933–45); elected four times. He instituted major reforms (the **New Deal**) to counter the economic crisis of the 1930s and was a forceful leader during World War II **3 Theodore** 1858–1919, 26th president of the US (1901–09). A proponent of extending military power, he won for the US the right to build the Panama Canal (1903). He won the Nobel peace prize

(1906), for mediating in the Russo-Japanese war

roost (ru:st) *n* **1** a place, perch, branch, etc, where birds, esp domestic fowl, rest or sleep **2** a temporary place to rest or stay ▷ *vb* **3** (*intr*) to rest or sleep on a roost **4** (*intr*) to settle down or stay **5 come home to roost** to have unfavourable repercussions [OE *hrōst*]

Roost (ru:st) *n* **the** a powerful current caused by conflicting tides around the Shetland and Orkney Islands [C16 from ON *röst*]

rooster (ˈru:stə) *n chiefly US & Canad* the male of the domestic fowl; a cock

root[1] (ru:t) *n* **1a** the organ of a higher plant that anchors the rest of the plant in the ground and absorbs water and mineral salts from the soil **1b** any of the branches of such an organ **2** (loosely) any plant part, such as a tuber, that is similar to a root in function or appearance **3a** the essential part or nature of something: *your analysis strikes at the root of the problem* **3b** (*as modifier*): *the root cause of the problem* **4** *anat* the embedded portion of a tooth, nail, hair, etc **5** origin or derivation **6** (*pl*) a person's sense of belonging in a community, place, etc, esp the one in which he was born or brought up **7** *Bible* a descendant **8** *linguistics* the form of a word that remains after removal of all affixes **9** *maths* a quantity that when multiplied by itself a certain number of times equals a given quantity: *3 is a cube root of 27* **10** Also called: **solution** *maths* a number that when substituted for the variable satisfies a given equation **11** *music* (in harmony) the note forming the foundation of a chord **12** *Austral & NZ sl* sexual intercourse **13 root and branch** (*adv*) entirely; utterly ▷ Related adj: **radical** ▷ *vb* **14** (*intr*) Also: **take root** to establish a root and begin to grow **15** (*intr*) Also: **take root** to become established, embedded, or effective **16** (*tr*) to embed with or as if with a root or roots **17** *Austral & NZ sl* to have sexual intercourse (with) ▷ See also **root out, roots** [OE *rōt*, from ON] > ˈ**rooter** *n* > ˈ**root,like** *adj* > ˈ**rooty** *adj* > ˈ**rootiness** *n*

root[2] (ru:t) *vb* (*intr*) **1** (of a pig) to burrow in or dig up the earth in search of food, using the snout **2** (foll by *about, around, in*, etc) *inf* to search vigorously but unsystematically [C16 changed (through infl. of ROOT[1]) from earlier *wroot*, from OE *wrōtan*; rel. to OE *wrōt* snout] > ˈ**rooter** *n*

root[3] (ru:t) *vb* (*intr*; usually foll by *for*) *inf* to give support to (a contestant, team, etc), as by cheering [C19 ? var. of Scot *rout* to make a loud noise, from ON *rauta* to roar]

root beer *n US & Canad* an effervescent drink made from extracts of various roots and herbs

root canal *n* the passage in the root of a tooth through which its nerves and blood vessels enter the pulp cavity

root-canal therapy *n* another name for **root treatment**

root climber *n* any of various climbing plants, such as the ivy, that adhere to a supporting structure by means of small roots growing from the side of the stem

root crop *n* a crop, as of turnips or beets, cultivated for the food value of its roots

rooted (ˈru:tɪd) *adj* **1** having roots **2** deeply felt: *rooted objections*

root ginger *n* the raw underground stem of the ginger plant used finely chopped or grated, esp in Chinese dishes

root hair *n* any of the hollow hairlike outgrowths of the outer cells of a root, just behind the tip, that absorb water and salts from the soil

rooting compound *n horticulture* a substance, usually a powder, containing auxins in which plant cuttings are dipped in order to promote root growth

rootle (ˈru:tᵊl) *vb* **rootles, rootling, rootled** (*intr*) *Brit* another word for **root**[2]

rootless (ˈru:tlɪs) *adj* having no roots, esp (of a person) having no ties with a particular place

rootlet (ˈru:tlɪt) *n* a small root

root mean square *n* the square root of the average of the squares of a set of numbers or quantities: *the root mean square of* 1, 2, *and* 4 *is* $\sqrt{[(1^2 + 2^2 + 4^2)/3]} = \sqrt{7}$. Abbrev: **rms**

root nodule *n* a swelling on the root of a leguminous plant, such as clover, that contains bacteria capable of nitrogen fixation

root out *vb* (*tr, adv*) to remove or eliminate completely: *we must root out inefficiency*

roots (ru:ts) *adj* (of popular music) going back to the origins of a style, esp in being genuine and unpretentious: *roots rock* > ˈ**rootsy** *adj*

rootserver (ˈru:t,sɜ:və) *n* any of a small number of important large servers on the Internet that match addresses at the top-domain level

roots music *n* **1** another name for **world music** **2** reggae, esp when regarded as authentic and uncommercialized

rootstock (ˈru:t,stɒk) *n* **1** another name for **rhizome** **2** another name for **stock** (sense 7) **3** *biol* a basic structure from which offshoots have developed

root treatment *n dentistry* a procedure, used for treating an abscess at the tip of the root of a tooth, in which the pulp is removed and a filling (**root filling**) inserted in the root canal. Also called: **root-canal therapy**

ropable *or* **ropeable** (ˈrəʊpəbᵊl) *adj* **1** capable of being roped **2** *Austral & NZ inf* **2a** angry **2b** wild or intractable: *a ropable beast*

rope (rəʊp) *n* **1a** a fairly thick cord made of intertwined hemp or other fibres or of wire or other strong material **1b** (*as modifier*): *a rope ladder* **2** a row of objects fastened to form a line: *a rope of pearls* **3** a quantity of material wound in the form of a cord **4** a filament or strand, esp of something viscous or glutinous: *a rope of slime* **5 give (someone) enough** (*or* **plenty of**) **rope to hang himself** (*or* **herself**) to allow (someone) to accomplish his or her own downfall by his or her own foolish acts **6 know the ropes** to have a thorough understanding of a particular sphere of activity **7 on the ropes** **7a** *boxing* driven against the ropes enclosing the ring by an opponent's attack **7b** in a hopeless position **8 the rope** **8a** a rope halter used for hanging **8b** death by hanging ▷ *vb* **ropes, roping, roped** **9** (*tr*) to bind or fasten with or as if with a rope **10** (*tr*; usually foll by *off*) to enclose or divide by means of a rope **11** (when *intr*, foll by *up*) *mountaineering* to tie (climbers) together with a rope [OE *rāp*]

Rr

rope in *vb* (*tr, adv*) **1** *Brit* to persuade to take part in some activity **2** *US & Canad* to trick or entice into some activity

rope's end *n* a short piece of rope, esp as formerly used for flogging sailors

ropewalk (ˈrəʊp,wɔ:k) *n* a long narrow usually covered path or shed where ropes are made

ropey *or* **ropy** (ˈrəʊpɪ) *adj* **ropier, ropiest** **1** *Brit inf* **1a** inferior **1b** slightly unwell **2** (of a viscous or sticky substance) forming strands **3** resembling a rope > ˈ**ropily** *adv* > ˈ**ropiness** *n*

Roquefort (ˈrɒkfɔ:) *n* a blue-veined cheese with a strong flavour, made from ewe's and goat's milk [C19 after *Roquefort*, village in S France]

roquet (ˈrəʊkɪ) *croquet* ▷ *vb* **roquets** (-kɪz), **roqueting** (-kɪɪŋ), **roqueted** (-kɪd) **1** to drive one's ball against (another person's ball) in order to be allowed to croquet ▷ *n* **2** the act of roqueting [C19 var. of CROQUET]

Roraima (*Portuguese* rɔˈraima) *n* a state of N Brazil: chiefly rainforest. Capital: Boa Vista. Pop: 324 152 (2000). Area: 230 104 sq km (89 740 sq miles)

ro-ro (ˈrəʊrəʊ) *adj acronym for* roll-on/roll-off

rorqual (ˈrɔ:kwəl) *n* any of several whalebone whales that have a dorsal fin and a series of grooves along the throat and chest. Also called: **finback** [C19 from F, from Norwegian *rörhval*, from ON *reytharhvalr*, from *reythr* (from *rauthr* red) + *hvalr* whale]

Rorschach test (ˈrɔ:ʃɑ:k) *n psychol* a personality test consisting of a number of unstructured inkblots presented for interpretation [C20 after Hermann

Rorschach (1884–1922), Swiss psychiatrist]

rort (rɔːt) *Austral inf* ▷ *n* **1** a rowdy party or celebration **2** a fraud; deception ▷ *vb (tr)* **3** to take unfair advantage of (something): *our voting system can be rorted* [c20 back formation from E dialect *rorty* (in the sense: good, splendid)] > **'rorty** *adj*

rorter ('rɔːtə) *n Austral inf* a small-scale confidence trickster

Rory O'Connor (ˌrɔːrɪ əʊ'kɒnə) *n* Also called *Roderic.* ?1116–98, king of Connaught and last High King of Ireland

Rosa[1] ('rəʊzə; *Italian* 'rɔːza) *n* **Monte** ('mɒntɪ; *Italian* 'monte) a mountain between Italy and Switzerland: the highest in the Pennine Alps. Height: 4634 m (15 204 ft)

Rosa[2] (*Italian* 'rɔːza) *n* **Salvator** ('salvatɔr) 1615–73, Italian artist, noted esp for his romantic landscapes

rosace ('rəʊzeɪs) *n* **1** another name for **rose window** **2** another name for **rosette** [c19 from F, from L *rosāceus* ROSACEOUS]

rosacea (rəʊ'zeɪʃə) *n* a chronic inflammatory disease causing the skin of the face to become abnormally flushed and sometimes pustular. Also called: **acne rosacea**

rosaceous (rəʊ'zeɪʃəs) *adj* **1** of or belonging to the Rosaceae, a family of plants typically having white, yellow, pink, or red five-petalled flowers. The family includes the rose, strawberry, blackberry, and many fruit trees **2** like a rose, esp, rose-coloured [c18 from L *rosāceus* composed of roses, from *rosa* ROSE[1]]

rosarian (rəʊ'zɛərɪən) *n* a person who cultivates roses, esp professionally

Rosario (rəʊ'sɑːrɪəʊ; *Spanish* rɔ'sarjo) *n* an inland port in E Argentina, on the Paraná River: the second largest city in the country; industrial centre. Pop: 1 000 000 (1999 est)

rosarium (rəʊ'zɛərɪəm) *n, pl* **rosariums** *or* **rosaria** (-'zɛərɪə) a rose garden [c19 NL]

rosary ('rəʊzərɪ) *n, pl* **rosaries** **1** *RC Church* **1a** a series of prayers counted on a string of beads, usually five or 15 decades of Aves, each decade beginning with a Paternoster and ending with a Gloria **1b** a string of 55 or 165 beads used to count these prayers as they are recited **2** (in other religions) a similar string of beads used in praying **3** an archaic word for a **garland** (of flowers, etc) [c14 from L *rosārium* rose garden, from *rosārius* of roses, from *rosa* ROSE[1]]

Roscius ('rɒskɪəs, -sɪəs) *n* **1** full name *Quintus Roscius Gallus.* died 62 BC, Roman actor **2** any actor

Roscommon (rɒs'kɒmən) *n* **1** an inland county of N central Republic of Ireland, in Connacht: economy based on cattle and sheep farming. County town: Roscommon. Pop: 51 975 (1996). Area: 2463 sq km (951 sq miles) **2** a former name for **Galway** (sense 3)

rose[1] (rəʊz) *n* **1a** a shrub or climbing plant having prickly stems, compound leaves, and fragrant flowers **1b** (*in combination*): *rosebush* **2** the flower of any of these plants **3** any of various similar plants, such as the Christmas rose **4a** a purplish-pink colour **4b** (*as adj*): *rose paint* **5** a rose, or a representation of one, as the national emblem of England **6a** a cut for a gemstone, having a hemispherical faceted crown and a flat base **6b** a gem so cut **7** a perforated cap fitted to a watering can or hose, causing the water to issue in a spray **8** a design or decoration shaped like a rose; rosette **9** Also called: **ceiling rose** *electrical engineering* a circular boss attached to a ceiling through which the flexible lead of an electric-light fitting passes **10** *history* See **red rose, white rose** **11** **bed of roses** a situation of comfort or ease **12** **under the rose** in secret; privately; sub rosa ▷ *vb* **roses, rosing, rosed** **13** (*tr*) to make rose-coloured; cause to blush or redden [OE, from L *rosa*, prob. from Gk *rhodon* rose] > **'rose,like** *adj*

rose[2] (rəʊz) *vb* the past tense of **rise**

rosé ('rəʊzeɪ) *n* any pink wine, made either by removing the skins of red grapes after only a little colour has been extracted or by mixing red and white wines [c19 from F, lit.: pink, from L *rosa* ROSE[1]]

roseate ('rəʊzɪˌeɪt) *adj* **1** of the colour rose or pink **2** excessively or idealistically optimistic

rosebay ('rəʊzˌbeɪ) *n* **1** any of several rhododendrons **2** **rosebay willowherb** a perennial plant that has spikes of deep pink flowers and is widespread in N temperate regions **3** another name for **oleander**

Rosebery ('rəʊzbərɪ, -brɪ) *n* **Earl of**, title of *Archibald Philip Primrose.* 1847–1929, British Liberal statesman; prime minister (1894–95)

rosebud ('rəʊzˌbʌd) *n* **1** the bud of a rose **2** *literary* a pretty young woman

rose campion *n* a European plant widely cultivated for its pink flowers. Its stems and leaves are covered with white woolly down. Also called: **dusty miller**

rose chafer *or* **beetle** *n* a British beetle that has a greenish-golden body with a metallic lustre and feeds on plants

rose-coloured *adj* **1** of the colour rose; rosy **2** Also: **rose-tinted** excessively optimistic **3** **see through rose-coloured** *or* **rose-tinted glasses** (*or* **spectacles**) to view in an excessively optimistic light

rose-cut *adj* (of a gemstone) cut with a hemispherical faceted crown and a flat base

rosehip ('rəʊzˌhɪp) *n* the berry-like fruit of a rose plant

rosella (rəʊ'zɛlə) *n* any of various Australian parrots [c19 prob. alteration of *Rose-hiller*, after *Rose Hill*, Parramatta, near Sydney]

rosemary ('rəʊzmərɪ) *n, pl* **rosemaries** an aromatic European shrub widely cultivated for its grey-green evergreen leaves, which are used in cookery and in the manufacture of perfumes. It is the traditional flower of remembrance [c15 earlier *rosmarine*, from L *rōs* dew + *marīnus* marine; modern form infl. by folk etymology, as if ROSE[1] + *Mary*]

Rosenberg ('rəʊzənbɜːg) *n* **1** **Alfred** 1893–1946, German Nazi politician and writer, who devised much of the racial ideology of Nazism: hanged for war crimes **2** **Isaac** 1890–1918, British poet and painter, best known for his poems about life in the trenches during World War I: died in action **3** **Julius** 1918–53, US spy, who, with his wife **Ethel** (1914–53), was executed for passing information about nuclear weapons to the Russians

rose of Sharon ('ʃærən) *n* a creeping shrub native to SE Europe but widely cultivated, having large yellow flowers. Also called: **Aaron's beard**

roseola (rəʊ'ziːələ) *n pathol* **1** a feverish condition of young children (caused by the human herpes virus) that lasts for some five days, during the last two of which the patient has a rose-coloured rash **2** any red skin rash, esp **roseola infantum**, a rash in young children [c19 from NL, dim. of L *roseus* rosy] > **ro'seolar** *adj*

rosery ('rəʊzərɪ) *n, pl* **roseries** a bed or garden of roses

Rosetta (rəʊ'zɛtə) *n* the former name of **Rashid**

Rosetta stone *n* a basalt slab discovered in 1799 at Rosetta, dating to the reign of Ptolemy V (196 BC) and carved with parallel inscriptions in hieroglyphics, Egyptian demotic, and Greek, which provided the key to the decipherment of ancient Egyptian texts

rosette (rəʊ'zɛt) *n* **1** a decoration resembling a rose, esp an arrangement of ribbons in a rose-shaped design worn as a badge or presented as a prize **2** another name for **rose window** **3** *bot* a circular cluster of leaves growing from the base of a stem [c18 from OF: a little ROSE[1]]

rose-water *n* **1** scented water made by the distillation of rose petals or by impregnation with oil of roses **2** (*modifier*) elegant or delicate, esp excessively so

rose window *n* a circular window, esp one that has ornamental tracery radiating from the centre to form a symmetrical roselike pattern. Also called: **wheel window, rosette**

rosewood ('rəʊz,wʊd) *n* the hard dark wood of any of various tropical trees. It has a roselike scent and is used in cabinetwork

Rosh Hashanah *or* **Rosh Hashana** ('rɒʃ hə'ʃɑːnə; *Hebrew* 'rɔʃ haʃa'na) *n* the Jewish New Year festival, celebrated on the first and second of Tishri [from Heb., lit.: beginning of the year, from *rōsh* head + *hash-shānāh* year]

Rosicrucian (,rəʊzɪ'kruːʃən) *n* **1** a member of a society professing esoteric religious doctrines, venerating the rose and Cross as symbols of Christ's Resurrection and Redemption, and claiming various occult powers ▷ *adj* **2** of or designating the Rosicrucians or Rosicrucianism [c17 from L *Rosa Crucis* Rose of the Cross, translation of the G name Christian *Rosenkreuz*, supposed founder of the society]

rosin ('rɒzɪn) *n* **1** Also called: **colophony** a translucent brittle amber substance produced in the distillation of crude turpentine oleoresin and used esp in making varnishes, printing inks, and sealing waxes and for treating the bows of stringed instruments **2** (not in technical usage) another name for **resin** (sense 1) ▷ *vb* **3** (*tr*) to treat or coat with rosin [c14 var. of RESIN] > '**rosiny** *adj*

Roskilde (*Danish* 'rɔskilə) *n* a city in Denmark, on NE Sjælland west of Copenhagen: capital of Denmark from the 10th century to 1443; scene of the signing (1658) of the **Peace of Roskilde** between Denmark and Sweden. Pop: 49 080 (1990)

ROSPA ('rɒspə) *n* (in Britain) *acronym for* Royal Society for the Prevention of Accidents

Ross (rɒs) *n* **1** **Diana** born 1944, US singer: lead vocalist (1961–69) with Motown group the Supremes, whose hits include "Baby Love" (1964). Her subsequent recordings include *Lady Sings the Blues* (film soundtrack, 1972) and *Chain Reaction* (1986) **2** Sir **James Clark** 1800–62, British naval officer; explorer of the Arctic and Antarctic. He located the north magnetic pole (1831) and discovered the Ross Sea during an Antarctic voyage (1839–43) **3** his uncle, Sir **John** 1777–1856, Scottish naval officer and Arctic explorer **4** Sir **Ronald** 1857–1932, English bacteriologist, who discovered the transmission of malaria by mosquitoes: Nobel prize for physiology or medicine 1902

Ross and Cromarty (rɒs ənd 'krɒmətɪ) *n* (until 1975) a county of N Scotland, including the island of Lewis and many islets: now split between the Highland and Western Isles council areas

Ross Dependency *n* a section of Antarctica administered by New Zealand: includes the coastal regions of Victoria Land and King Edward VII Land, the Ross Sea and islands, and the Ross Ice Shelf. Area: about 414 400 sq km (160 000 sq miles)

Rossellini (rɒsə'liːnɪ) *n* **Roberto** 1906–77, Italian film director. His films include *Rome, Open City* (1945), *Paisà* (1946), and *L'Amore* (1948)

Rossetti (rɒ'zɛtɪ) *n* **1** **Christina Georgina** 1830–94, British poet **2** her brother, **Dante Gabriel** 1828–82, British poet and painter: a leader of the Pre-Raphaelites

Rossini (rɒ'siːnɪ) *n* **Gioacchino Antonio** (dʒoak'kiːno an'tɔːnjo) 1792–1868, Italian composer, esp of operas, such as *The Barber of Seville* (1816) and *William Tell* (1829)

Ross Island *n* an island in the W Ross Sea: contains the active volcano Mount Erebus

Rossiya (ra'siːjə) *n* transliteration of the Russian name for **Russia**

Ross Sea *n* a large arm of the S Pacific in Antarctica, incorporating the Ross Ice Shelf and lying between Victoria Land and the Edward VII Peninsula

Rostand (*French* rɔstɑ̃) *n* **Edmond** (ɛdmɔ̃) 1868–1918, French playwright and poet in the romantic tradition; best known for his verse drama *Cyrano de Bergerac* (1897)

roster ('rɒstə) *n* **1** a list or register, esp one showing the order of people enrolled for duty **2** *marketing* the list of advertising agencies regularly used by a particular company ▷ *vb* **2** (*tr*) to place on a roster [c18 from Du. *rooster* grating or list (the lined paper looking like a grid)]

Rostock ('rɒstɒk) *n* a port in NE Germany, in Mecklenburg-West Pomerania on the Warnow estuary 13 km (8 miles) from the Baltic and its outport, Warnemünde: formerly the chief port of East Germany; university (1419). Pop: 205 900 (1999 est)

Rostov *or* **Rostov-on-Don** ('rɒstɒv) *n* a port in S Russia, on the River Don 48 km (30 miles) from the Sea of Azov: industrial centre. Pop: 1 017 300 (1999 est)

Rostropovich (,rɒstrə'pəʊvɪtʃ; *Russian* rəstra'pɔvitʃ) *n* **Mstislav Leopoldovich** ('mɪstɪslɑːv; *Russian* msti'slaf lea'pɔldavitʃ) born 1927, Soviet cellist, composer, and conductor; became a US citizen in 1978 after losing Soviet citizenship (restored in 1990)

rostrum ('rɒstrəm) *n, pl* **rostrums** *or* **rostra** (-trə) **1** any platform on which public speakers stand to address an audience **2** a platform in front of an orchestra on which the conductor stands **3** another word for **ram** (sense 5) **4** the prow of an ancient Roman ship **5** *biol, zool* a beak or beaklike part [c16 from L *rōstrum* beak, ship's prow, from *rōdere* to nibble, gnaw; in pl, *rōstra* orator's platform, because this platform in the Roman forum was adorned with the prows of captured ships] > '**rostral** *adj*

rosy ('rəʊzɪ) *adj* **rosier, rosiest** **1** of the colour rose or pink **2** having a healthy pink complexion: *rosy cheeks* **3** optimistic, esp excessively so: *a rosy view of social improvements* **4** resembling or abounding in roses > '**rosily** *adv* > '**rosiness** *n*

rot (rɒt) *vb* **rots, rotting, rotted** **1** to decay or cause to decay as a result of bacterial or fungal action **2** (*intr;* usually foll by *off* or *away*) to crumble (off) or break (away), as from decay or long use **3** (*intr*) to become weak or depressed through inertia, confinement, etc; languish: *rotting in prison* **4** to become or cause to become morally degenerate ▷ *n* **5** the process of rotting or the state of being rotten **6** something decomposed. Related adj: **putrid** **7** short for **dry rot** **8** *pathol* any putrefactive decomposition of tissues **9** a condition in plants characterized by decay of tissues, caused by bacteria, fungi, etc **10** *vet science* a contagious fungal disease of the feet of sheep **11** (*also interj*) nonsense; rubbish [OE *rotian* (vb); rel. to ON, *rotna;* c13 (n), from ON]

rota ('rəʊtə) *n chiefly Brit* a register of names showing the order in which people take their turn to perform certain duties [c17 from L: a wheel]

Rota ('rəʊtə) *n RC Church* the supreme ecclesiastical tribunal

rotachute ('rəʊtəʃuːt) *n* a device serving the same purpose as a parachute, in which the canopy is replaced by freely revolving rotor blades, used for the delivery of stores or recovery of missiles

rotaplane ('rəʊtə,pleɪn) *n* an aircraft that derives its lift from freely revolving rotor blades

rotary ('rəʊtərɪ) *adj* **1** operating by rotation **2** turning; revolving ▷ *n, pl* **rotaries** **3** a part of a machine that rotates about an axis **4** *US & Canad* another term for **roundabout** (sense 2) [c18 from Med. L *rotārius*, from L *rota* wheel]

Rotary Club *n* any of the local clubs that form **Rotary International,** an international association of professional and businessmen founded in the US in 1905 to promote community service > **Rotarian** (rəʊ'tɛərɪən) *n, adj*

rotary engine *n* **1** an internal-combustion engine having radial cylinders that rotate about a fixed crankshaft **2** an engine, such as a turbine or wankel engine, in which power is transmitted directly to rotating components

Rr

rotary plough *or* **tiller** *n* an implement with a series of blades mounted on a power-driven shaft which rotates so as to break up soil

rotary press *n* a machine for printing from a revolving cylindrical forme, usually onto a continuous strip of paper

rotary table *n* a chain or gear-driven unit, mounted in the derrick floor which rotates the drill pipe and bit

rotate *vb* (rəʊ'teɪt), **rotates, rotating, rotated 1** to turn or cause to turn around an axis; revolve or spin **2** to follow or cause to follow a set sequence **3** (of a position, presidency, etc) to pass in turn from one eligible party to each of the other eligible parties **4** (of staff) to replace or be replaced in turn ▷ *adj* ('rəʊteɪt) **5** *bot* designating a corolla the petals of which radiate like the spokes of a wheel > **ro'tatable** *adj*

rotating (rəʊ'teɪtɪŋ) *adj* **1** revolving around a central axis, line, or point: *the rotating blades of a helicopter* **2** passing in turn to each of two or more eligible parties: *the rotating presidency of the European Union*

rotation (rəʊ'teɪʃən) *n* **1** the act of rotating; rotary motion **2** a regular cycle of events in a set order or sequence **3** a planned sequence of cropping according to which the crops grown in successive seasons on the same land are varied so as to make a balanced demand on its resources of fertility **4** the spinning motion of a body, such as a planet, about an internal axis **5** *maths* **5a** a circular motion of a configuration about a given point, without a change in shape **5b** a transformation in which the coordinate axes are rotated by a fixed angle about the origin > **ro'tational** *adj*

rotator (rəʊ'teɪtə) *n* **1** a person, device, or part that rotates or causes rotation **2** *anat* any of various muscles that revolve a part on its axis

rotatory ('rəʊtətərɪ, -trɪ) *or (less commonly)* **rotative** *adj* of, possessing, or causing rotation > **'rotatorily** *adv*

Rotavator ('rəʊtəˌveɪtə) *n trademark* a mechanical cultivator with rotating blades [C20 from ROTA(RY) + (CULTI)VATOR] > **'Rotaˌvate** *vb (tr)*

rote (rəʊt) *n* **1** a habitual or mechanical routine or procedure **2** **by rote** by repetition; by heart (often in **learn by rote**) [C14 from ?]

rotenone ('rəʊtɪˌnəʊn) *n* a white odourless crystalline substance extracted from the roots of derris: a powerful insecticide [C20 from Japanese *rōten* derris + -ONE]

ROTFL *text messaging abbrev for* rolling on the floor laughing

rotgut ('rɒtˌgʌt) *n facetious sl* alcoholic drink, esp spirits, of inferior quality

Roth (rɒθ) *n* **Philip** born 1933, US novelist. His works include *Goodbye, Columbus* (1959), *Portnoy's Complaint* (1969), *My Life as a Man* (1974), *Sabbath's Theater* (1995), and *The Human Stain* (2000)

Rotherham ('rɒðərəm) *n* **1** an industrial town in N England, in Rotherham unitary authority, South Yorkshire. Pop: 121 380 (1991) **2** a unitary authority in N England, in South Yorkshire. Pop: 248 176 (2001). Area: 283 sq km (109 sq miles)

Rothermere ('rɒðəˌmɪə) *n* **Viscount** title of *Harold Sidney Harmsworth*. 1868–1940, British newspaper magnate

Rothesay ('rɒθsɪ) *n* a town in SW Scotland, in Argyll and Bute, on the E coast of Bute Island. Pop: 5264 (1991)

Rothko ('rɒθkəʊ) *n* **Mark** 1903–70, US abstract expressionist painter, born in Russia

Rothschild ('rɒθtʃaɪld, 'rɒθs-) *n* a powerful family of European Jewish bankers, prominent members of which were **1** **Lionel Nathan**, Baron de Rothschild. 1809–79, British banker and first Jewish member of Parliament **2** his grandfather **Meyer Amschel** ('maɪər 'amʃəl) 1743–1812, German financier and founder of the Rothschild banking firm **3** his son, **Nathan Meyer**, Baron de Rothschild. 1777–1836, British banker, born in Germany

rotifer ('rəʊtɪfə) *n* a minute aquatic multicellular invertebrate having a ciliated wheel-like organ used in feeding and locomotion: common constituents of freshwater plankton. Also called: **wheel animalcule** [C18 from NL *Rotifera*, from L *rota* wheel + *ferre* to bear] > **rotiferal** (rəʊ'tɪfərəl) *or* **ro'tiferous** *adj*

rotisserie (rəʊ'tɪsərɪ) *n* **1** a rotating spit on which meat, poultry, etc, can be cooked **2** a shop or restaurant where meat is roasted to order [C19 from F, from OF *rostir* to ROAST]

rotogravure (ˌrəʊtəʊgrə'vjʊə) *n* **1** a printing process using cylinders with many small holes, from which ink is transferred to a moving web of paper, etc, in a rotary press **2** printed material produced in this way, esp magazines [C20 from L *rota* wheel + GRAVURE]

rotor ('rəʊtə) *n* **1** the rotating member of a machine or device, such as the revolving arm of the distributor of an internal-combustion engine **2** a rotating device having radiating blades projecting from a hub which produces thrust to lift and propel a helicopter [C20 shortened form of ROTATOR]

Rotorua (ˌrəʊtə'ruːə) *n* a city in New Zealand, on N central North Island at the SW end of Lake Rotorua: centre of forestry; noted for volcanic activity. Pop: 54 700 (1994)

rotten ('rɒtᵊn) *adj* **1** decomposing, decaying, or putrid **2** breaking up, esp through age or hard use: *rotten ironwork* **3** morally corrupt **4** disloyal or treacherous **5** *inf* unpleasant: *rotten weather* **6** *inf* unsatisfactory or poor: *rotten workmanship* **7** *inf* miserably unwell **8** *inf* distressed and embarrassed: *I felt rotten breaking the bad news to him* ▷ *adv inf* **9** extremely; very much: *men fancy her rotten* [C13 from ON *rottin*; rel. to OE *rotian* to ROT] > **'rottenly** *adv* > **'rottenness** *n*

rotten borough *n* (before the Reform Act of 1832) any of certain English parliamentary constituencies with few or no electors

rottenstone ('rɒtᵊnˌstəʊn) *n* a much-weathered limestone, rich in silica: used in powdered form for polishing metal

rotter ('rɒtə) *n sl, chiefly Brit* a worthless, unpleasant, or despicable person

Rotterdam ('rɒtəˌdæm) *n* a port in the SW Netherlands, in South Holland province: the second largest city of the Netherlands and one of the world's largest ports; oil refineries, shipbuilding yards, etc Pop: 592 665 (1999 est)

Rottweiler ('rɒtˌwaɪlə, -ˌvaɪlə) *n* **1** a breed of large dog with a smooth black and tan coat, noted for strength and aggression **2** *(often not cap)* **2a** an aggressive and unscrupulous person **2b** *(as modifier)*: *rottweiler politics* [G, from *Rottweil*, town in Swabia where the breed originated]

rotund (rəʊ'tʌnd) *adj* **1** rounded or spherical in shape **2** plump **3** sonorous or grandiloquent [C18 from L *rotundus* round, from *rota* wheel] > **ro'tundity** *n* > **ro'tundly** *adv*

rotunda (rəʊ'tʌndə) *n* a circular building or room, esp one that has a dome [C17 from It. *rotonda*, from L *rotundus* round, from *rota* a wheel]

Rouault (ruː'əʊ; *French* rwo) *n* **Georges** (ʒɔrʒ) 1871–1958, French expressionist artist. His work is deeply religious; it includes much stained glass

Roubaix (*French* rubɛ) *n* a city in N France near the Belgian border: forms, with Tourcoing, a large industrial conurbation. Pop: 97 746 (1990)

Roubiliac *or* **Roubillac** (rubijak) *n* **Louis-François** (lwifrɑ̃swa) ?1695–1762, French sculptor: lived chiefly in England: his sculptures include the statue of Handel in Vauxhall Gardens (1737)

rouble *or* **ruble** ('ruːbᵊl) *n* the standard monetary unit of Belarus, Russia, and Tajikistan [C16 from Russian *rubl* silver bar, from ORussian *rublĭ* bar, block of wood, from *rubiti* to cut up]

roué ('ru:eɪ) *n* a debauched or lecherous man; rake [c19 from F, lit.: one broken on the wheel; with reference to the fate deserved by a debauchee]

Rouen (*French* rwɑ̃) *n* a city in N France, on the River Seine: the chief river port of France; became capital of the duchy of Normandy in 912; scene of the burning of Joan of Arc (1431); university (1964). Pop: 106 035 (1999)

rouge (ru:ʒ) *n* **1** a red powder or cream, used as a cosmetic for adding redness to the cheeks **2** short for **jeweller's rouge** ▷ *vb* **rouges, rouging, rouged 3** (*tr*) to apply rouge to [c18 F: red, from L *rubeus*]

rouge et noir ('ru:ʒ eɪ 'nwɑ:) *n* a card game in which the players put their stakes on any of two red and two black diamond-shaped spots marked on the table [F, lit.: red and black]

Rouget de Lisle (*French* ruʒɛ də lil) *n* **Claude Joseph** (klod ʒozɛf) 1760–1836, French army officer: composer of the *Marseillaise* (1792), the French national anthem

rough (rʌf) *adj* **1** (of a surface) not smooth; uneven or irregular **2** (of ground) covered with scrub, boulders, etc **3** denoting or taking place on uncultivated ground: *rough grazing* **4** shaggy or hairy **5** turbulent: *a rough sea* **6** (of performance or motion) uneven; irregular: *a rough engine* **7** (of behaviour or character) rude, coarse, or violent **8** harsh or sharp: *rough words* **9** *inf* severe or unpleasant: *a rough lesson* **10** (of work, etc) requiring physical rather than mental effort **11** *inf* ill: *he felt rough after an evening of heavy drinking* **12** unfair: *rough luck* **13** harsh or grating to the ear **14** without refinement, luxury, etc **15** not perfected in any detail; rudimentary: *rough workmanship; rough justice* **16** not prepared or dressed: *rough gemstones* **17** (of a guess, etc) approximate **18** having the sound of *h*; aspirated **19 rough on** *inf, chiefly Brit* **19a** severe towards **19b** unfortunate for (a person) **20 the rough side of one's tongue** harsh words; a rebuke ▷ *n* **21** rough ground **22** a sketch or preliminary piece of artwork **23** unfinished or crude state (esp in **in the rough**) **24 the rough** *golf* the part of the course bordering the fairways where the grass is untrimmed **25** *inf* a violent person; thug **26** the unpleasant side of something (esp in **take the rough with the smooth**) ▷ *adv* **27** roughly **28 sleep rough** to spend the night in the open; be without shelter ▷ *vb* (*tr*) **29** to make rough; roughen **30** (foll by *out, in,* etc) to prepare (a sketch, report, etc) in preliminary form **31 rough it** *inf* to live without the usual comforts of life ▷ See also **rough up** [OE *rūh*] > **'roughly** *adv* > **'roughness** *n*

roughage ('rʌfɪdʒ) *n* **1** the coarse indigestible constituents of food, which provide bulk to the diet and promote normal bowel function **2** any rough material

rough-and-ready *adj* **1** crude, unpolished, or hastily prepared, but sufficient for the purpose **2** (of a person) without formality or refinement

rough-and-tumble *n* **1** a fight or scuffle without rules ▷ *adj* **2** characterized by disorderliness and disregard for rules

rough breathing *n* (in Greek) the sign (ʽ) placed over an initial letter, indicating that (in ancient Greek) it was pronounced with an *h*

roughcast ('rʌf,kɑ:st) *n* **1** a mixture of plaster and small stones used to cover the surface of an external wall **2** any rough or preliminary form, model, etc ▷ *adj* **3** covered with roughcast ▷ *vb* **roughcasts, roughcasting, roughcast 4** to apply roughcast to (a wall, etc) **5** to prepare in rough > **'rough,caster** *n*

rough-cut *n* a first basic edited version of a film with the scenes in sequence and the soundtrack synchronized

rough diamond *n* **1** an unpolished diamond **2** an intrinsically trustworthy or good person with uncouth manners or dress

rough-dry *adj* **1** (of clothes or linen) dried ready for pressing ▷ *vb* **rough-dries, rough-drying, rough-dried 2** (*tr*) to dry (clothes, etc) without ironing them

roughen ('rʌfᵊn) *vb* to make or become rough

rough-hew *vb* **rough-hews, rough-hewing, rough-hewed; rough-hewed** *or* **rough-hewn** (*tr*) to cut or shape roughly without finishing the surface

roughhouse ('rʌf,haʊs) *n sl* rough, disorderly, or noisy behaviour

roughish ('rʌfɪʃ) *adj* somewhat rough

roughneck ('rʌf,nɛk) *n sl* **1** a rough or violent person; thug **2** a worker in an oil-drilling operation

rough puff pastry *n* a rich flaky pastry

roughrider ('rʌf,raɪdə) *n* a rider of wild or unbroken horses

roughshod ('rʌf,ʃɒd) *adj* **1** (of a horse) shod with rough-bottomed shoes to prevent sliding ▷ *adv* **2 ride roughshod over** to domineer over or act with complete disregard for

rough stuff *n inf* violence

rough trade *n sl* (in homosexual use) a tough or violent sexual partner, esp one casually picked up

rough up *vb* (*tr, adv*) **1** *inf* to treat violently; beat up **2** to cause (feathers, hair, etc) to stand up by rubbing against the grain

roulade (ru:'lɑ:d) *n* **1** something cooked in the shape of a roll, esp a slice of meat **2** an elaborate run in vocal music [c18 from F, lit.: a rolling, from *rouler* to ROLL]

Roulers (ru:'lɛəz; *French* rulɛrs) *n* a city in NW Belgium, in West Flanders province: electronics. Pop: 53 617 (1995 est). Flemish name: **Roeselare**

roulette (ru:'lɛt) *n* **1** a gambling game in which a ball is dropped onto a spinning horizontal wheel divided into numbered slots, with players betting on the slot into which the ball will fall **2** a toothed wheel for making a line of perforations **3** a curve generated by a point on one curve rolling on another ▷ *vb* **roulettes, rouletting, rouletted** (*tr*) **4** to use a roulette on (something), as in engraving, making stationery, etc [c18 from F, from *rouelle*, dim. of *roue* a wheel, from L *rota*]

Roumania (ru:'meɪnɪə) *n* a variant of **Romania** > **Rou'manian** *adj, n*

round (raʊnd) *adj* **1** having a flat circular shape, as a hoop **2** having the shape of a ball **3** curved; not angular **4** involving or using circular motion **5** (*prenominal*) complete: *a round dozen* **6** *maths* **6a** forming or expressed by a whole number, with no fraction **6b** expressed to the nearest ten, hundred, or thousand: *in round figures* **7** (of a sum of money) considerable **8** fully depicted or developed, as a character in a book **9** full and plump: *round cheeks* **10** (of sound) full and sonorous **11** (of pace) brisk; lively **12** (*prenominal*) (of speech) candid; unmodified: *a round assertion* **13** (of a vowel) pronounced with rounded lips ▷ *n* **14** a round shape or object **15 in the round 15a** in full detail **15b** *theatre* with the audience all round the stage **16** a session, as of a negotiation: *a round of talks* **17** a series: *a giddy round of parties* **18 the daily round** the usual activities of one's day **19** a stage of a competition: *he was eliminated in the first round* **20** (*often pl*) a series of calls: *a milkman's round* **21** a playing of all the holes on a golf course **22** a single turn of play by each player, as in a card game **23** one of a number of periods in a boxing, wrestling, or other match **24** a single discharge by a gun **25** a bullet or other charge of ammunition **26** a number of drinks bought at one time for a group of people **27a** a single slice of bread **27b** a sandwich made from two slices of bread **28** a general outburst of applause, etc **29** movement in a circle **30** *music* a part song in which the voices follow each other at equal intervals at the same pitch **31** a sequence of bells rung in order of treble to tenor **32** a cut of beef from the thigh **33 go** *or* **make the rounds 33a** to go from place to place, as in making social calls **33b** (of information, rumour, etc) to be

Rr

passed around, so as to be generally known ▷ *prep* **34** surrounding, encircling, or enclosing: *a band round her head* **35** on all or most sides of: *to look round one* **36** on or outside the circumference or perimeter of **37** from place to place in: *driving round Ireland* **38** reached by making a partial circuit about: *the shop round the corner* **39** revolving round (a centre or axis): *the earth's motion round its axis* ▷ *adv* **40** on all or most sides **41** on or outside the circumference or perimeter: *the racing track is two miles round* **42** to all members of a group: *pass the food round* **43** in rotation or revolution: *the wheels turn round* **44** by a circuitous route: *the road to the farm goes round by the pond* **45** to a specific place: *she came round to see me* **46** **all year round** throughout the year ▷ *vb* **47** to make or become round **48** (*tr*) to encircle; surround **49** to move or cause to move with turning motion: *to round a bend* **50** (*tr*) **50a** to pronounce (a speech sound) with rounded lips **50b** to purse (the lips) ▷ See also **round down, round off,** etc [c13 from OF *ront*, from L *rotundus* round, from *rota* a wheel] > **'roundish** *adj* > **'roundness** *n*

USAGE See at **around**

roundabout ('raʊndəˌbaʊt) *n* **1** *Brit* a revolving circular platform provided with wooden animals, seats, etc, on which people ride for amusement; merry-go-round **2** a road junction in which traffic streams circulate around a central island. US and Canad name: **traffic circle** ▷ *adj* **3** indirect; devious ▷ *adv, prep* **round about** **4** on all sides: *spectators standing round about* **5** approximately: *at round about 5 o'clock*

round dance *n* **1** a dance in which the dancers form a circle **2** a ballroom dance, such as the waltz, in which couples revolve

round down *vb* (*tr, adv*) to lower (a number) to the nearest whole number or ten, hundred, or thousand below it

rounded ('raʊndɪd) *adj* **1** round or curved **2** mature or complete **3** (of the lips) pursed **4** (of a speech sound) articulated with rounded lips

roundel ('raʊndᵊl) *n* **1** a form of rondeau consisting of three stanzas each of three lines with a refrain after the first and the third **2** a circular identifying mark in national colours on military aircraft **3** a small circular window, medallion, etc **4** a round plate of armour used to protect the armpit **5** another word for **roundelay** [c13 from OF *rondel*; see RONDEL]

roundelay ('raʊndɪˌleɪ) *n* **1** Also called: **roundel** a slow medieval dance performed in a circle **2** a song in which a line or phrase is repeated as a refrain [c16 from OF *rondelet* a little rondel, from *rondel*; also infl. by LAY[4]]

rounders ('raʊndəz) *n* (*functioning as sing*) *Brit* a ball game in which players run between posts after hitting the ball, scoring a **rounder** if they run round all four before the ball is retrieved
▷ www.roundersonline.net

round file *slang* ▷ *n* **1** a wastepaper basket ▷ *vb* **round-file** **2** to throw into a wastepaper basket; discard; reject

Roundhead ('raʊndˌhɛd) *n English history* a supporter of Parliament against Charles I during the Civil War [referring to their short-cut hair]

roundhouse ('raʊndˌhaʊs) *n* **1** *US & Canad* a building in which railway locomotives are serviced, radial tracks being fed by a central turntable **2** *US boxing sl* a swinging punch or style of punching **3** an obsolete word for **jail** **4** *obs* a cabin on the quarterdeck of a sailing ship

rounding ('raʊndɪŋ) *n computing* a process in which a number is approximated as the closest number that can be expressed using the number of bits or digits available

roundly ('raʊndlɪ) *adv* **1** frankly, bluntly, or thoroughly: *to be roundly criticized* **2** in a round manner or so as to be round

round off *vb* (*tr, adv*) **1** (often foll by *with*) to complete, esp agreeably: *we rounded off the evening with a brandy* **2** to make less jagged

round on *vb* (*intr, prep*) to attack or reply to (someone) with sudden irritation or anger

round robin *n* **1** a petition or protest having the signatures in a circle to disguise the order of signing **2** a tournament in which each player plays against every other player

round-shouldered *adj* denoting a faulty posture characterized by drooping shoulders and a slight forward bending of the back

roundsman ('raʊndzmən) *n, pl* **roundsmen** **1** *Brit* a person who makes rounds, as for inspection or to deliver goods **2** *Austral & NZ* a reporter covering a particular district or topic

round table *n* **a** a meeting of parties or people on equal terms for discussion **b** (*as modifier*): *a round-table conference*

Round Table *n* **the** **1** (in Arthurian legend) the circular table of King Arthur, enabling his knights to sit around it without any having precedence **2** Arthur and his knights collectively **3** one of an organization of clubs of young business and professional men who meet in order to further charitable work

round-the-clock *adj* (*or as adv* **round the clock**) throughout the day and night

round tower *n* a freestanding circular stone belfry built in Ireland from the 10th century beside a monastery and used as a place of refuge

round trip *n* a trip to a place and back again, esp returning by a different route

roundtripping ('raʊndˌtrɪpɪŋ) *n finance* a form of trading in which a company borrows a sum of money from one source and takes advantage of a short-term rise in interest rates to make a profit by lending it to another

round up *vb* (*tr, adv*) **1** to gather together: *to round ponies up* **2** to raise (a number) to the nearest whole number or ten, hundred, or thousand above it ▷ *n* **roundup** **3** the act of gathering together livestock, esp cattle, so that they may be branded, counted, or sold **4** any similar act of bringing together: *a roundup of today's news*

roundworm ('raʊndˌwɜːm) *n* a nematode worm that is a common intestinal parasite of man and pigs

roup (raʊp) *Scot & N English dialect* ▷ *vb* (*tr*) **1** to sell by auction ▷ *n* **2** an auction [c16 (orig.: to shout): of Scand. origin]

rouse (raʊz) *vb* **rouses, rousing, roused** **1** to bring (oneself or another person) out of sleep, etc, or (of a person) to come to consciousness in this way **2** (*tr*) to provoke: *to rouse someone's anger* **3** **rouse oneself** to become energetic **4** to start or cause to start from cover: *to rouse game birds* **5** (*intr*; foll by *on*) *Austral* to scold or rebuke [c15 (in sense of hawks ruffling their feathers): from ?] > **'rouser** *n*

rouseabout ('raʊzəˌbaʊt) *n* **1** Also called: **rousie** *Austral & NZ* an unskilled labourer in a shearing shed **2** a variant of **roustabout** (sense 1)

rousing ('raʊzɪŋ) *adj* tending to excite; lively or vigorous: *a rousing chorus* > **'rousingly** *adv*

Rousseau (*French* ruso) *n* **1** **Henri** (ɑ̃ri), known as *le Douanier*. 1844–1910, French painter, who created bold dreamlike pictures, often of exotic landscapes in a naive style. Among his works are *Sleeping Gypsy* (1897) and *Jungle with a Lion* (1904–06). He also worked as a customs official **2** **Jean Jacques** (ʒɑ̃ ʒak) 1712–78, French philosopher and writer, born in Switzerland, who strongly influenced the theories of the French Revolution and the romantics. Many of his ideas spring from his belief in the natural goodness of man, whom he felt was warped by society. His works include *Du contrat social* (1762), *Émile* (1762), and his *Confessions* (1782) **3** **Théodore** (teɔdɔr) 1812–67, French landscape painter: leader of the Barbizon school

Roussillon (*French* rusijɔ̃) *n* a former province of S France: united with Aragon in 1172; passed to the French crown in 1659; now forms part of the region of Languedoc-Roussillon

roust (raʊst) *vb* (*tr*; often foll by *out*) to rout or stir, as out of bed [C17 ?from ROUSE]

roustabout (ˈraʊstəˌbaʊt) *n* **1** an unskilled labourer, esp on an oil rig **2** *Austral & NZ* a variant of **rouseabout** (sense 1)

rout[1] (raʊt) *n* **1** an overwhelming defeat **2** a disorderly retreat **3** a noisy rabble **4** *law* a group of three or more people proceeding to commit an illegal act **5** *arch* a large party or social gathering ▷ *vb* **6** (*tr*) to defeat and cause to flee in confusion [C13 from Anglo-Norman *rute*, from OF: disorderly band, from L *ruptus*, from *rumpere* to burst]

rout[2] (raʊt) *vb* **1** to dig over or turn up (something), esp (of an animal) with the snout; root **2** (*tr*; usually foll by *out* or *up*) to find by searching **3** (*tr*; usually foll by *out*) to drive out: *they routed him out of bed at midnight* **4** (*tr*; often foll by *out*) to hollow or gouge out **5** (*intr*) to search, poke, or rummage [C16 var. of ROOT[2]]

route (ruːt) *n* **1** the choice of roads taken to get to a place **2** a regular journey travelled **3** (*cap*) *US* a main road between cities: *Route 66* ▷ *vb* **routes, routeing, routed** (*tr*) **4** to plan the route of; send by a particular route [C13 from OF *rute*, from Vulgar L *rupta via* (unattested), lit.: a broken (established) way, from L *ruptus*, from *rumpere* to break]

> USAGE When adding *-ing* to the verb, it is preferable to retain the *e* in order to distinguish it from *routing*, deriving from *rout*, 'to defeat' or *rout*, 'to dig, rummage': *...the routeing of buses from the city centre to the suburbs*. The spelling *routing* in this sense is, however, sometimes found, especially in American English

routemarch (ˈruːtˌmɑːtʃ) *n* **1** *mil* a long training march **2** *inf* any long exhausting walk

router (ˈraʊtə) *n* any of various tools or machines for hollowing out, cutting grooves, etc

routine (ruːˈtiːn) *n* **1** a usual or regular method of procedure, esp one that is unvarying **2** *computing* a program or part of a program performing a specific function: *an input routine* **3** a set sequence of dance steps **4** *inf* a hackneyed or insincere speech ▷ *adj* **5** relating to or characteristic of routine [C17 from OF, from *route* a customary way, ROUTE] > **rouˈtinely** *adv*

roux (ruː) *n* a mixture of equal amounts of fat and flour, heated, blended, and used as a basis for sauces [F: brownish, from L *russus* RUSSET]

rove[1] (rəʊv) *vb* **roves, roving, roved 1** to wander about (a place) with no fixed direction; roam **2** (*intr*) (of the eyes) to look around; wander ▷ *n* **3** the act of roving [C15 *roven* (in archery) to shoot at a target chosen at random (C16 to wander, stray), from ON]

rove[2] (rəʊv) *vb* **roves, roving, roved 1** (*tr*) to pull out and twist (fibres of wool, cotton, etc) lightly, as before spinning ▷ *n* **2** wool, cotton, etc, thus prepared [C18 from ?]

rove[3] (rəʊv) *vb* a past tense and past participle of **reeve**[2]

rover[1] (ˈrəʊvə) *n* **1** a person who roves **2** *archery* a mark selected at random for use as a target **3** *Australian rules football* a player without a fixed position who, with the ruckmen, forms the ruck [C15 from ROVE[1]]

rover[2] (ˈrəʊvə) *n* a pirate or pirate ship [C14 prob. from MDu. or MLow G, from *roven* to rob]

Rover *or* **Rover Scout** (ˈrəʊvə) *n Brit* the former name for **Venture Scout**

roving commission *n* authority or power given in a general area, without precisely defined terms of reference

row[1] (rəʊ) *n* **1** an arrangement of persons or things in a line: *a row of chairs* **2** *chiefly Brit* a street, esp a narrow one lined with identical houses **3** a line of seats, as in a cinema, theatre, etc **4** *maths* a horizontal linear arrangement of numbers, quantities, or terms **5** a horizontal rank of squares on a chessboard or draughtboard **6 a hard row to hoe** a difficult task or assignment **7 in a row** in succession; one after the other: *he won two gold medals in a row* [OE *rāw*, *rǣw*]

row[2] (rəʊ) *vb* **1** to propel (a boat) by using oars **2** (*tr*) to carry (people, goods, etc) in a rowing boat **3** to be propelled by means of (oars or oarsmen) **4** (*intr*) to take part in the racing of rowing boats as a sport **5** (*tr*) to race against in a boat propelled by oars: *Oxford row Cambridge every year* ▷ *n* **6** an act, instance, period, or distance of rowing **7** an excursion in a rowing boat [OE *rōwan*] > **ˈrower** *n*

▷ www.worldrowing.com

row[3] (raʊ) *n* **1** a noisy quarrel **2** a noisy disturbance: *we couldn't hear the music for the row next door* **3** a reprimand ▷ *vb* **4** (*intr*; often foll by *with*) to quarrel noisily **5** (*tr*) *arch* to reprimand [C18 from ?]

rowan (ˈrəʊən, ˈraʊ-) *n* another name for the (European) **mountain ash** [C16 of Scand. origin]

rowdy (ˈraʊdɪ) *adj* **rowdier, rowdiest 1** tending to create noisy disturbances; rough, loud, or disorderly: *a rowdy gang of football supporters* ▷ *n, pl* **rowdies 2** a person who behaves in such a fashion [C19 orig. US sl, ? rel. to ROW[3]] > **ˈrowdily** *adv* > **ˈrowdiness** *or* **ˈrowdyism** *n*

Rowe (rəʊ) *n* **Nicholas** 1674–1718, English dramatist, who produced the first critical edition of Shakespeare; poet laureate (1715–18). His plays include *Tamerlane* (1702) and *The Fair Penitent* (1703)

rowel (ˈraʊəl) *n* **1** a small spiked wheel attached to a spur **2** *vet science obsolete* a piece of leather inserted under the skin of a horse to allow drainage ▷ *vb* **rowels, rowelling, rowelled** *or US* **rowels, roweling, roweled** (*tr*) **3** to goad (a horse) using a rowel **4** *vet science* to insert a rowel in (the skin of a horse) to cause a discharge [C14 from OF *roel* a little wheel, from *roe* a wheel, from L *rota*]

rowing boat (ˈrəʊɪŋ) *n chiefly Brit* a small pleasure boat propelled by one or more pairs of oars. Usual US and Canad word: **rowboat**

rowing machine (ˈrəʊɪŋ) *n* a device with oars and a sliding seat, resembling a sculling boat, used to provide exercise

Rowlandson (ˈrəʊləndsən) *n* **Thomas** 1756–1827, English caricaturist, noted for the vigour of his attack on sordid aspects of contemporary society and on statesmen such as Napoleon

Rowley (ˈrəʊlɪ, ˈraʊ-) *n* **Thomas** ?1586–?1642, English dramatist, who collaborated with John Ford and Thomas Dekker on *The Witch of Edmonton* (1621) and with Thomas Middleton on *The Changeling* (1622)

Rowling (ˈrəʊlɪŋ) *n* **J(oanne) K(athleen)** born 1965, British novelist; author of the bestselling series of children's books featuring the boy wizard Harry Potter, which began with *Harry Potter and the Philosopher's Stone* (1995)

rowlock (ˈrɒlək) *n* a swivelling device attached to the gunwale of a boat that holds an oar in place. Usual US and Canad word: **oarlock**

Roxas y Acuña (*Spanish* ˈroxas i aˈkuɲa) *n* **Manuel** (maˈnwel) 1892–1948, Philippine statesman; first president of the Republic of the Philippines (1946–48)

Roxburghshire (ˈrɒksbərəʃɪə, -ʃə) *n* (until 1975) a county of SE Scotland, now part of Scottish Borders council area

royal (ˈrɔɪəl) *adj* **1** of, relating to, or befitting a king, queen, or other monarch; regal **2** (*prenominal; often cap*) established by, chartered by, under the patronage of, or in the service of royalty: *the Royal Society of St George* **3** being a member of a royal family **4** above the usual or normal in standing, size, quality, etc **5** *inf* unusually good or impressive; first-rate **6** *naut* just above the topgallant (in **royal mast**) ▷ *n* **7** (*sometimes cap*) a member of a royal family **8** Also: **royal stag** a stag with antlers having 12 or more branches **9** *naut* a sail set next above the topgallant, on a royal mast **10** a size of printing paper, 20 by 25 inches [C14 from OF *roial*, from L *rēgālis* fit

Rr

for a king, from *rēx* king; cf. REGAL] > '**royally** *adv*

Royal Academy *n* a society founded by George III in 1768 to foster a national school of painting, sculpture, and design in England. Full name: **Royal Academy of Arts**
▷ www.royalacademy.org.uk

Royal Air Force *n* the air force of Great Britain. Abbrev: **RAF**
▷ www.raf.mod.uk

Royal and Ancient Club *n* **the** a golf club, headquarters of the sport's ruling body, based in St Andrews, Scotland. Abbrev: **R&A**

royal assent *n Brit & Canad* the formal signing of an act of Parliament by the sovereign, by which it becomes law

royal blue *n* **a** a deep blue colour **b** (*as adj*): *a royal-blue carpet*

Royal Commission *n* (in Britain and Canada) a body set up by the monarch on the recommendation of the prime minister to gather information about the operation of existing laws or to investigate any social, educational, or other matter

royal fern *n* a fern of damp regions, having large fronds up to 2 metres (7 feet) in height

royal flush *n poker* a hand made up of the five top honours of a suit

royalist ('rɔɪəlɪst) *n* **1** a supporter of a monarch or monarchy, esp during the English Civil War **2** *inf* an extreme reactionary: *an economic royalist* ▷ *adj* **3** of or relating to royalists > '**royalism** *n*

royal jelly *n* a substance secreted by the pharyngeal glands of worker bees and fed to all larvae when very young and to larvae destined to become queens throughout their development

Royal Leamington Spa *n* the official name of **Leamington Spa**

Royal Marines *pl n Brit* a corps of soldiers specially trained in amphibious warfare. Abbrev: **RM**

Royal Mint *n* a British organization having the sole right to manufacture coins since the 16th century. In 1968 it moved from London to Llantrisant in Wales

Royal National Theatre *n* a theatre complex in London, on the S bank of the Thames (opened 1976). The prefix Royal was added in 1988. It houses the Royal National Theatre Company

Royal Navy *n* the navy of Great Britain. Abbrev: **RN**
▷ www.royal-navy.mod.uk

royal palm *n* any of several palm trees of tropical America, having a tall trunk with a tuft of feathery pinnate leaves

royal standard *n* a flag bearing the arms of the British sovereign, flown only when she or he is present

royal tennis *n* another name for **real tennis**

royalty ('rɔɪəltɪ) *n, pl* **royalties 1** the rank, power, or position of a king or queen **2a** royal persons collectively **2b** a person who belongs to a royal family **3** any quality characteristic of a monarch **4** a percentage of the revenue from the sale of a book, performance of a theatrical work, use of a patented invention or of land, etc, paid to the author, inventor, or proprietor

royal warrant *n* an authorization to a tradesman to supply goods to a royal household

Royce (rɔɪs) *n* **Josiah** 1855–1916, US philosopher of monistic idealism. In his ethical studies he emphasized the need for individual loyalty to the world community

rozzer ('rɒzə) *n sl* a policeman [c19 from ?]

RPG *abbrev for* report program generator: a business-oriented computer programming language

RPI (in Britain) *abbrev for* retail price index

rpm *abbrev for:* **1** resale price maintenance **2** revolutions per minute

RPV *abbrev for* remotely piloted vehicle

RR *abbrev for:* **1** Right Reverend **2** *Canad & US* railroad **3** *Canad & US* rural route

-rrhagia *n combining form* (in pathology) an abnormal discharge: *menorrhagia* [from Gk *-rrhagia* a bursting forth, from *rhēgnunai* to burst]

-rrhoea *or esp US* **-rrhea** *n combining form* (in pathology) a flow: *diarrhoea* [from NL, from Gk *-rrhoia*, from *rhein* to flow]

rRNA *abbrev for* ribosomal RNA

RRP *abbrev for* recommended retail price

RRSP (in Canada) *abbrev for* Registered Retirement Plan

Rs *symbol for* rupees

RS (in Britain) *abbrev for* Royal Society
▷ www.royalsoc.ac.uk

RSA *abbrev for:* **1** Republic of South Africa **2** (in New Zealand) Returned Services Association **3** Royal Scottish Academician **4** Royal Scottish Academy **5** Royal Society of Arts
▷ www.rsa.org.uk

RSFSR (formerly) *abbrev for* Russian Soviet Federative Socialist Republic

RSI *abbrev for* repetitive strain injury

RSL (in Australia) *abbrev for* Returned Services League

RSM *abbrev for:* **1** regimental sergeant major **2** Royal School of Music **3** Royal Society of Medicine
▷ www.rsm.ac.uk

RSNZ *abbrev for* Royal Society of New Zealand
▷ www.rsnz.govt.nz

RSPB (in Britain) *abbrev for* Royal Society for the Protection of Birds
▷ www.rspb.org.uk

RSPCA (in England, Wales, and Australia) *abbrev for* Royal Society for the Prevention of Cruelty to Animals
▷ www.rspca.org.uk
▷ www.rspca.org.au

RSV *abbrev for* Revised Standard Version (of the Bible)

RSVP *abbrev for* répondez s'il vous plaît [F: please reply]

rt *abbrev for* right

RTE *abbrev for* Radio Telefis Éireann [Irish Gaelic: Irish Radio and Television]

Rt Hon. *abbrev for* Right Honourable

Ru *the chemical symbol for* ruthenium

RU *abbrev for* Rugby Union

Ruanda-Urundi (rʊ'ændəʊ'rʊndɪ) *n* a former territory of central Africa: part of German East Africa from 1890; a League of Nations mandate under Belgian administration from 1919; a United Nations trusteeship from 1946; divided into the independent states of Rwanda and Burundi in 1962

rub (rʌb) *vb* **rubs, rubbing, rubbed 1** to apply pressure and friction to (something) with a backward and forward motion **2** to move (something) with pressure along, over, or against (a surface) **3** to chafe or fray **4** (*tr*) to bring into a certain condition by rubbing: *rub it clean* **5** (*tr*) to spread with pressure, esp in order to cause to be absorbed: *she rubbed ointment into his back* **6** (*tr*) to mix (fat) into flour with the fingertips, as in making pastry **7** (foll by *off, out, away*, etc) to remove or be removed by rubbing: *the mark would not rub off the chair* **8** (*intr*) *bowls* (of a bowl) to be slowed or deflected by an uneven patch on the green **9** (*tr; often foll by together*) to move against each other with pressure and friction (esp in **rub one's hands,** often a sign of glee, keen anticipation, or satisfaction, and **rub noses,** a greeting among Inuit) **10 rub (up) the wrong way** to arouse anger in; annoy ▷ *n* **11** the act of rubbing **12** (preceded by *the*) an obstacle or difficulty (esp in **there's the rub**) **13** something that hurts the feelings or annoys; cut; rebuke **14** *bowls* an uneven patch in the green ▷ See also **rub along, rub down,** etc [c15 ?from Low G *rubben*, from ?]

Rub' al Khali ('rʊb æl 'kɑːlɪ) *n* a desert in S Arabia, mainly in Saudi Arabia, extending southeast from Nejd to Hadramaut and northeast from Yemen to the United Arab Emirates. Area: about 777 000 sq km (300 000 sq miles). English names: **Great Sandy Desert, Empty Quarter** Also called: **Ar Rimal, Dahna**

rub along *vb (intr, adv) Brit* 1 to continue in spite of difficulties 2 to maintain an amicable relationship; not quarrel

rubato (ruːˈbɑːtəʊ) *music* ▷ *n, pl* **rubatos** 1 flexibility of tempo in performance ▷ *adj, adv* 2 to be played with a flexible tempo [C19 from It. *tempo rubato*, lit.: stolen time, from *rubare* to ROB]

rubber[1] (ˈrʌbə) *n* 1 Also called: **India rubber, gum elastic, caoutchouc** a cream to dark brown elastic material obtained by coagulating and drying the latex from certain plants, esp the rubber tree 2 any of a large variety of elastomers produced from natural rubber or by synthetic means 3 *chiefly Brit* a piece of rubber used for erasing something written; eraser 4 a cloth, pad, etc, used for polishing 5 a person who rubs something in order to smooth, polish, or massage 6 *(often pl) chiefly US & Canad* a rubberized waterproof overshoe 7 *sl* a condom 8 *(modifier)* made of or producing rubber: *a rubber ball; a rubber factory* [C17 from RUB + -ER[1]; the tree was so named because its product was used for rubbing out writing] > ˈ**rubbery** *adj*

rubber[2] (ˈrʌbə) *n* 1 *bridge, whist, etc* 1a a match of three games 1b the deal that wins such a match 2 a series of matches or games in any of various sports [C16 from ?]

rubber band *n* a continuous loop of thin rubber, used to hold papers, etc, together. Also called: **elastic band**

rubber cement *n* any of a number of adhesives made by dissolving rubber in a solvent such as benzene

rubberize *or* **rubberise** (ˈrʌbəˌraɪz) *vb* **rubberizes, rubberizing, rubberized** *or* **rubberises, rubberising, rubberised** *(tr)* to coat or impregnate with rubber

rubberneck (ˈrʌbəˌnɛk) *sl* ▷ *n* 1 a person who stares or gapes inquisitively 2 a sightseer or tourist ▷ *vb* 3 *(intr)* to stare in a naive or foolish manner

rubber plant *n* 1 a plant with glossy leathery leaves that grows as a tall tree in India and Malaya but is cultivated as a house plant in Europe and North America 2 any of several tropical trees, the sap of which yields crude rubber

rubber stamp *n* 1 a device used for imprinting dates, etc, on forms, invoices, etc 2 automatic authorization of a payment, proposal, etc 3 a person who makes such automatic authorizations; a cipher or person of little account ▷ *vb* **rubber-stamp** *(tr)* 4 to imprint (forms, invoices, etc) with a rubber stamp 5 *inf* to approve automatically

rubber tree *n* a tropical American tree cultivated throughout the tropics, esp in Malaya, for the latex of its stem, which is the major source of commercial rubber

rubbing (ˈrʌbɪŋ) *n* an impression taken of an incised or raised surface by laying paper over it and rubbing with wax, graphite, etc

rubbing alcohol *n* denatured alcohol used in massage, as an antiseptic, etc

rubbish (ˈrʌbɪʃ) *n* 1 worthless, useless, or unwanted matter 2 discarded or waste matter; refuse 3 foolish words or speech; nonsense ▷ *vb* 4 *(tr) inf* to criticize; attack verbally [C14 *robys*, from ?] > ˈ**rubbishy** *adj*

rubble (ˈrʌbᵊl) *n* 1 fragments of broken stones, bricks, etc 2 debris from ruined buildings 3 Also called: **rubblework** masonry constructed of broken pieces of rock, stone, etc [C14 *robyl*; ? rel. to RUBBISH, or to ME *rubben* to rub] > ˈ**rubbly** *adj*

Rubbra (ˈrʌbrə) *n* **(Charles) Edmund** 1901–86, English composer of works in a traditional idiom

rubby *or* **rubbie** (ˈrʌbɪ) *n, pl* **rubbies** *Canad sl* 1 rubbing alcohol, esp when mixed with cheap wine for drinking 2 a person who drinks such mixtures, esp a derelict alcoholic

rub down *vb (adv)* 1 to dry or clean (a horse, athlete, oneself, etc) vigorously, esp after exercise 2 to make or become smooth by rubbing 3 *(tr)* to prepare (a surface) for painting by rubbing it with sandpaper ▷ *n* **rubdown** 4 the act of rubbing down

rube (ruːb) *n US sl* an unsophisticated countryman [C20 prob. from the name *Reuben*]

rubella (ruːˈbɛlə) *n* a mild contagious viral disease, somewhat similar to measles, characterized by cough, sore throat, and skin rash. Also called: **German measles** [C19 from NL, from L *rubellus* reddish, from *rubeus* red]

rubellite (ˈruːbɪˌlaɪt, ruːˈbɛl-) *n* a red transparent variety of tourmaline, used as a gemstone [C18 from L *rubellus* reddish]

Rubens (ˈruːbɪnz) *n* Sir **Peter Paul** 1577–1640, Flemish painter, regarded as the greatest exponent of the Baroque: appointed (1609) painter to Archduke Albert of Austria, who gave him many commissions, artistic and diplomatic. He was knighted by Charles I of England in 1629. His prolific output includes the triptych in Antwerp Cathedral, *Descent from the Cross* (1611–14), *The Rape of the Sabines* (1635), and his *Self-Portrait* (?1639)

rubeola (ruːˈbiːələ) *n* the technical name for **measles** [C17 from NL, from L *rubeus* reddish]

Rubicon (ˈruːbɪkən) *n* 1 a stream in N Italy: in ancient times the boundary between Italy and Cisalpine Gaul. By leading his army across it and marching on Rome in 49 BC, Julius Caesar broke the law that a general might not lead an army out of the province to which he was posted and so committed himself to civil war with the senatorial party 2 *(sometimes not capital)* a point of no return 3 a penalty in piquet by which the score of a player who fails to reach 100 points in six hands is added to his opponent's 4 **cross** *(or* **pass***)* the Rubicon. to commit oneself irrevocably to some course of action

rubicund (ˈruːbɪkənd) *adj* of a reddish colour; ruddy; rosy [C16 from L *rubicundus*, from *rubēre* to be ruddy, from *ruber* red] > **rubicundity** (ˌruːbɪˈkʌndɪtɪ) *n*

rubidium (ruːˈbɪdɪəm) *n* a soft highly reactive radioactive element of the alkali metal group. It is used in electronic valves, photocells, and special glass. Symbol: Rb; atomic no.: 37; atomic wt.: 85.47; half-life of ^{87}Rb: 5×10^{11} years [C19 from NL, from L *rubidus* dark red, with reference to the two red lines in its spectrum] > ruˈ**bidic** *adj*

rubidium-strontium dating *n* a technique for determining the age of minerals based on the occurrence in natural rubidium of a fixed amount of the radioisotope ^{87}Rb which decays to the stable strontium isotope ^{87}Sr with a half-life of 5×10^{11} years

rubiginous (ruːˈbɪdʒɪnəs) *adj* rust-coloured [C17 from L *rūbīginōsus*, from *rūbīgō* rust, from *ruber* red]

rub in *vb (tr, adv)* 1 to spread with pressure, esp in order to cause to be absorbed 2 **rub it in** *inf* to harp on something distasteful to a person

Rubinstein (ˈruːbɪnˌstaɪn) *n* 1 **Anton Grigorevich** (anˈtɔn griˈgɔrjɪvitʃ) 1829–94, Russian composer and pianist 2 **Artur** (ˈartur) 1886–1982, US pianist, born in Poland

ruble (ˈruːbᵊl) *n* a variant spelling of **rouble**

rub off *vb* 1 to remove or be removed by rubbing 2 *(intr; often foll by* on *or* onto*)* to have an effect through close association or contact: *her crude manners have rubbed off on you*

rub out *vb (tr, adv)* 1 to remove or be removed with a rubber 2 *US sl* to murder

rubric (ˈruːbrɪk) *n* 1 a title, heading, or initial letter in a book, manuscript, or section of a legal code, esp one printed or painted in red ink or in some similarly distinguishing manner 2 a set of rules of conduct or procedure 3 a set of directions for the conduct of Christian church services, often printed in red in a prayer book or missal [C15 *rubrike* red ochre, red lettering, from L *rubrīca (terra)* red (earth), ruddle, from *ruber* red] > ˈ**rubrical** *adj* > ˈ**rubrically** *adv*

ruby (ˈruːbɪ) *n, pl* **rubies** 1 a deep red transparent precious variety of corundum: used as a gemstone, in lasers, and for bearings and rollers in watchmaking **2a** the deep-red colour of a ruby **2b** (*as adj*): *ruby lips* **3a** something resembling, made of, or containing a ruby **3b** (*as modifier*): *a ruby necklace* **4** (*modifier*) denoting a fortieth anniversary: *our ruby wedding* [C14 from OF *rubi*, from L *rubeus*, from *ruber* red]

RUC *abbrev for* (the former) Royal Ulster Constabulary, now superseded by the Police Service of Northern Ireland

ruche (ru:ʃ) *n* a strip of pleated or frilled lawn, lace, etc, used to decorate blouses, dresses, etc [C19 from F, lit.: beehive, from Med. L *rūsca* bark of a tree, of Celtic origin]

ruching (ˈru:ʃɪŋ) *n* **1** material used for a ruche **2** a ruche or ruches collectively

ruck[1] (rʌk) *n* **1** a large number or quantity; mass, esp of undistinguished people or things **2** (in a race) a group of competitors who are well behind the leaders **3** *rugby* a loose scrum that forms around the ball when it is on the ground **4** *Australian rules football* the three players who do not have fixed positions but follow the ball closely ▷ *vb* **5** (*intr*) *rugby* to try to win the ball by mauling and scrummaging [C13 (meaning "heap of firewood"): ?from ON]

ruck[2] (rʌk) *n* **1** a wrinkle, crease, or fold ▷ *vb* **2** (usually foll by *up*) to become or make wrinkled, creased, or puckered [C18 of Scand. origin; rel. to ON *hrukka*]

ruckman (ˈrʌkmən) *n, pl* **ruckmen** *Australian rules football* either of two players who, with the rover, form the ruck

ruck-rover *n Australian rules football* a player playing a role midway between that of the rover and the ruckmen

rucksack (ˈrʌkˌsæk) *n* a large bag, usually having two straps, carried on the back and often used by climbers, campers, etc. Also called: **backpack** [C19 from G, lit.: back sack]

ruction (ˈrʌkʃən) *n inf* **1** an uproar; noisy or quarrelsome disturbance **2** (*pl*) an unpleasant row; trouble [C19 ? changed from INSURRECTION]

rudaceous (ru:ˈdeɪʃəs) *adj* (of conglomerate, breccia, and similar rocks) composed of coarse-grained material [C20 from L *rudis* coarse, rough + -ACEOUS]

Ruda Śląska (ˈru:də ˈʃlanskə) *n* a town in SW Poland: coalmining. Pop: 159 665 (1999 est)

rudbeckia (rʌdˈbɛkɪə) *n* any of a genus of North American plants of the composite family, cultivated for their showy flowers, which have golden-yellow rays and green or black conical centres. See also **black-eyed Susan** [C18 NL, after Olaus *Rudbeck* (1630–1702), Swedish botanist]

rudd (rʌd) *n* a European freshwater fish, having a compressed dark greenish body and reddish ventral and tail fins [C17 prob. from dialect *rud* red colour, from OE *rudu* redness]

rudder (ˈrʌdə) *n* **1** *naut* a pivoted vertical vane that projects into the water at the stern and can be used to steer a vessel **2** a vertical control surface attached to the rear of the fin used to steer an aircraft **3** anything that guides or directs [OE *rōther*] > ˈ**rudderless** *adj*

rudderpost (ˈrʌdəˌpəʊst) *n naut* **1** a postlike member at the forward edge of a rudder **2** the part of the stern frame of a vessel to which a rudder is fitted

ruddle (ˈrʌdᵊl), **raddle,** *or* **reddle** *n* **1** a red ochre, used esp to mark sheep ▷ *vb* **ruddles, ruddling, ruddled** **2** (*tr*) to mark (sheep) with ruddle [C16 dim. formed from OE *rudu* redness; see RUDD]

ruddy (ˈrʌdɪ) *adj* **ruddier, ruddiest** **1** (of the complexion) having a healthy reddish colour **2** coloured red or pink: *a ruddy sky* ▷ *adv, adj inf, chiefly Brit* **3** (intensifier) bloody; damned: *a ruddy fool* [OE *rudig*, from *rudu* redness] > ˈ**ruddily** *adv* > ˈ**ruddiness** *n*

rude (ru:d) *adj* **1** insulting or uncivil; discourteous; impolite **2** lacking refinement; coarse or uncouth **3** vulgar or obscene: *a rude joke* **4** unexpected and unpleasant: *a rude awakening* **5** roughly or crudely made: *we made a rude shelter on the island* **6** rough or harsh in sound, appearance, or behaviour **7** humble or lowly **8** (*prenominal*) robust or sturdy: *in rude health* **9** (*prenominal*) approximate or imprecise: *a rude estimate* [C14 via OF from L *rudis* coarse, unformed] > ˈ**rudely** *adv* > ˈ**rudeness** *or* (*inf*) ˈ**rudery** *n*

ruderal (ˈru:dərəl) *n* **1** a plant that grows on waste ground ▷ *adj* **2** growing in waste places [C19 from NL *rūderālis*, from L *rūdus* rubble]

rudiment (ˈru:dɪmənt) *n* **1** (*often pl*) the first principles or elementary stages of a subject **2** (*often pl*) a partially developed version of something **3** *biol* an organ or part in an embryonic or vestigial state [C16 from L *rudīmentum* a beginning, from *rudis* unformed]

rudimentary (ˌru:dɪˈmɛntərɪ, -trɪ) *or* **rudimental** *adj* **1** basic; fundamental **2** incompletely developed; vestigial: *rudimentary leaves* > ˌ**rudiˈmentarily** *or* (*less commonly*) ˌ**rudiˈmentally** *adv*

rudish (ˈru:dɪʃ) *adj* somewhat rude

Rudolf (ˈru:dɒlf) *n* **Lake** the former name (until 1979) of (Lake) **Turkana**

Rudolf I *or* **Rudolph I** (ˈru:dɒlf) *n* 1218–91, king of Germany (1273–91): founder of the Hapsburg dynasty based on the duchies of Styria and Austria

rue[1] (ru:) *vb* **rues, ruing, rued** **1** to feel sorrow, remorse, or regret for (one's own wrongdoing, past events, etc) ▷ *n* **2** *arch* sorrow, pity, or regret [OE *hrēowan*] > ˈ**ruer** *n*

rue[2] (ru:) *n* an aromatic Eurasian shrub with small yellow flowers and evergreen leaves which yield an acrid volatile oil, formerly used medicinally as a narcotic and stimulant. Archaic name: **herb of grace** [C14 from OF, from L *rūta*, from Gk *rhutē*]

rueful (ˈru:fʊl) *adj* **1** feeling or expressing sorrow or regret: *a rueful face* **2** inspiring sorrow or pity > ˈ**ruefully** *adv* > ˈ**ruefulness** *n*

ruff[1] (rʌf) *n* **1** a circular pleated or fluted collar of lawn, muslin, etc, worn by both men and women in the 16th and 17th centuries **2** a natural growth of long or coloured hair or feathers around the necks of certain animals or birds **3** an Old World shore bird of the sandpiper family, the male of which has a large erectile ruff of feathers in the breeding season [C16 back formation from RUFFLE[1]] > ˈ**ruffˌlike** *adj*

ruff[2] (rʌf) *cards* ▷ *n, vb* **1** another word for **trump**[1] (senses 1, 4) ▷ *n* **2** an old card game similar to whist [C16 from OF *roffle*; ? changed from It. *trionfa* TRUMP[1]]

ruffe *or* **ruff** (rʌf) *n* a European freshwater teleost fish of the perch family, having a single spiny dorsal fin [C15 ? alteration of ROUGH (referring to its scales)]

ruffian (ˈrʌfɪən) *n* a violent or lawless person; hoodlum [C16 from OF *rufien*, from It. *ruffiano* pander] > ˈ**ruffianism** *n* > ˈ**ruffianly** *adj*

ruffle[1] (ˈrʌfᵊl) *vb* **ruffles, ruffling, ruffled** **1** to make, be, or become irregular or rumpled: *a breeze ruffling the water* **2** to annoy, irritate, or be annoyed or irritated **3** (*tr*) to make into a ruffle; pleat **4** (of a bird) to erect (its feathers) in anger, display, etc **5** (*tr*) to flick (cards, pages, etc) rapidly ▷ *n* **6** an irregular or disturbed surface **7** a strip of pleated material used as a trim **8** *zool* another name for **ruff**[1] (sense 2) **9** annoyance or irritation [C13 of Gmc origin; cf. MLow G *ruffelen* to crumple, ON *hrufla* to scratch]

ruffle[2] (ˈrʌfᵊl) *n* **1** a low continuous drumbeat ▷ *vb* **ruffles, ruffling, ruffled** **2** (*tr*) to beat (a drum) with a low repetitive beat [C18 from earlier *ruff*, imit.]

rufous (ˈru:fəs) *adj* reddish-brown [C18 from L *rūfus*]

rufty-tufty (ˌrʌftɪˈtʌftɪ) *adj sl* rugged in appearance or manner

rug (rʌg) *n* **1** a floor covering, smaller than a carpet and made of thick wool or of other material, such as an animal skin **2** *chiefly Brit* a blanket, esp one used for travellers **3** *sl* a wig **4** **pull the rug out from under** to betray, expose, or leave defenceless [C16 of Scand. origin]

ruga ('ru:gə) *n, pl* **rugae** (-dʒi:) (*usually pl*) *anat* a fold, wrinkle, or crease [c18 L]
rugby *or* **rugby football** ('rʌgbɪ) *n* **1** a form of football played with an oval ball in which the handling and carrying of the ball is permitted. Also called: **rugger.** See also **rugby league, rugby union** **2** *Canad* another name for **Canadian football** [after the public school at *Rugby*, where it was first played]
Rugby ('rʌgbɪ) *n* a town in central England, in E Warwickshire: famous public school, founded in 1567. Pop: 61 106 (1991) > '**Rugbeian** *adj, n*
rugby head *n NZ derogatory sl* a male follower of rugby culture
rugby league *n* a form of rugby football played between teams of 13 players
▷ http://world.rleague.com
rugby union *n* a form of rugby football played between teams of 15 players
▷ www.irfu.com
▷ www.irfb.com
rugged ('rʌgɪd) *adj* **1** having an uneven or jagged surface **2** rocky or steep: *rugged scenery* **3** (of the face) strong-featured or furrowed **4** rough, severe, or stern in character **5** without refinement or culture; rude: *rugged manners* **6** involving hardship; harsh: *he leads a rugged life in the mountains* **7** difficult or hard: *a rugged test* **8** (of equipment, machines, etc) designed to withstand rough treatment or use in rough conditions **9** *chiefly US & Canad* sturdy or strong; robust [c14 from ON] > '**ruggedly** *adv* > '**ruggedness** *n*
rugger ('rʌgə) *n chiefly Brit* an informal name for **rugby**
rugose ('ru:gəʊs, -gəʊz) *adj* wrinkled: *rugose leaves* [c18 from L *rūgōsus*, from *rūga* wrinkle] > '**rugosely** *adv* > **rugosity** (ru:'gɒsɪtɪ) *n*
rug rat *n US & Canad inf* a young child not yet walking
Ruhr (rʊə; *German* ru:r) *n* the chief coalmining and industrial region of Germany: in North Rhine-Westphalia around the valley of the **River Ruhr** (a tributary of the Rhine 235 km (146 miles) long). German name: **Ruhrgebiet** ('ru:rgə,bi:t)
ruin ('ru:ɪn) *n* **1** a destroyed or decayed building or town **2** the state of being destroyed or decayed **3** loss of wealth, position, etc, or something that causes such loss; downfall **4** something that is severely damaged: *his life was a ruin* **5** a person who has suffered a downfall, bankruptcy, etc **6** *arch* loss of her virginity by a woman outside marriage ▷ *vb* **7** (*tr*) to bring to ruin; destroy **8** (*tr*) to injure or spoil: *the town has been ruined with tower blocks* **9** (*intr*) *arch or poetic* to fall into ruins; collapse **10** (*tr*) *arch* to seduce and abandon (a woman) [c14 from OF *ruine*, from L *ruīna* a falling down, from *ruere* to fall violently]
ruination (,ru:ɪ'neɪʃən) *n* **1** the act of ruining or the state of being ruined **2** something that causes ruin
ruinous ('ru:ɪnəs) *adj* causing, tending to cause, or characterized by ruin or destruction > '**ruinously** *adv* > '**ruinousness** *n*
Ruisdael *or* **Ruysdael** ('ri:zda:l, -deɪl, 'raɪz-; *Dutch* 'rœizda:l) *n* **Jacob van** ('ja:kɔp van) ?1628–82, Dutch landscape painter
rule (ru:l) *n* **1** an authoritative regulation or direction concerning method or procedure, as for a court of law, legislative body, game, or other activity: *judges' rules; play according to the rules* **2** the exercise of governmental authority or control: *the rule of Caesar* **3** the period of time in which a monarch or government has power: *his rule lasted 100 days* **4** a customary form or procedure: *he made a morning swim his rule* **5** (usually preceded by *the*) the common order of things: *violence was the rule rather than the exception* **6** a prescribed method or procedure for solving a mathematical problem **7** any of various devices with a straight edge for guiding or measuring; ruler: *a carpenter's rule* **8** *printing* **8a** a printed or drawn character in the form of a long thin line **8b** another name for **dash**[1] (sense 12): *en rule; em rule* **8c** a strip of metal used to print such a line **9** *Christianity* a systematic body of prescriptions followed by members of a religious order **10** *law* an order by a court or judge **11** **as a rule** normally or ordinarily ▷ *vb* **rules, ruling, ruled** **12** to exercise governing or controlling authority over (a people, political unit, individual, etc) **13** (when *tr, often takes a clause as object*) to decide authoritatively; decree: *the chairman ruled against the proposal* **14** (*tr*) to mark with straight parallel lines or one straight line **15** (*tr*) to restrain or control **16** (*intr*) to be customary or prevalent: *chaos rules in this school* **17** (*intr*) to be pre-eminent or superior: *football rules in the field of sport* **18** **rule the roost** (*or* **roast**) to be pre-eminent; be in charge [c13 from OF *riule*, from L *rēgula* a straight edge] > '**rulable** *adj*
rule of three *n* a mathematical rule asserting that the value of one unknown quantity in a proportion is found by multiplying the denominator of each ratio by the numerator of the other
rule of thumb *n* **a** a rough and practical approach, based on experience, rather than theory **b** (*as modifier*): *a rule-of-thumb decision*
rule out *vb* (*tr, adv*) **1** to dismiss from consideration **2** to make impossible; preclude
ruler ('ru:lə) *n* **1** a person who rules or commands **2** Also called: **rule** a strip of wood, metal, or other material, having straight edges, used for measuring and drawing straight lines
Rules (ru:lz) *pl n* **1** short for **Australian Rules** (football) **2** **the Rules** *English history* the neighbourhood around certain prisons in which trusted prisoners were allowed to live under specified restrictions
ruling ('ru:lɪŋ) *n* **1** a decision of someone in authority, such as a judge **2** one or more parallel ruled lines ▷ *adj* **3** controlling or exercising authority **4** predominant
rum[1] (rʌm) *n* spirit made from sugar cane [c17 ? shortened from c16 *rumbullion*, from ?]
rum[2] (rʌm) *adj* **rummer, rummest** *Brit sl* strange; peculiar; odd [c19 ?from Romany *rom* man] > '**rumly** *adv* > '**rumness** *n*
Rumania (ru:'meɪnɪə) *n* a variant of **Romania** > **Ru'manian** *adj, n*
rumba *or* **rhumba** ('rʌmbə, 'rʊm-) *n* **1** a rhythmic and syncopated Cuban dance in duple time **2** a ballroom dance derived from this **3** a piece of music composed for or in the rhythm of this dance [c20 from Sp.: lavish display, from ?]
rumble ('rʌmb[ə]l) *vb* **rumbles, rumbling, rumbled** **1** to make or cause to make a deep resonant sound: *thunder rumbled in the sky* **2** (*intr*) to move with such a sound: *the train rumbled along* **3** (*tr*) to utter with a rumbling sound: *he rumbled an order* **4** (*tr*) *Brit sl* to find out about (someone or something): *the police rumbled their plans* **5** (*intr*) *US sl* to be involved in a gang fight ▷ *n* **6** a deep resonant sound **7** a widespread murmur of discontent **8** *US, Canad, & NZ sl* a gang fight [c14 ?from MDu. *rummelen*] > '**rumbler** *n* > '**rumbling** *adj*
rumble seat *n* a folding outside seat at the rear of some early cars; dicky
rumbustious (rʌm'bʌstʃəs) *adj* boisterous or unruly [c18 prob. var. of ROBUSTIOUS] > **rum'bustiously** *adv* > **rum'bustiousness** *n*
rumen ('ru:mɛn) *n, pl* **rumens** *or* **rumina** (-mɪnə) the first compartment of the stomach of ruminants, in which food is partly digested before being regurgitated as cud [c18 from L: gullet]
Rumford ('rʌmfəd) *n* **Count** See (Benjamin) **Thompson**
ruminant ('ru:mɪnənt) *n* **1** any of a suborder of artiodactyl mammals which chew the cud and have a stomach of four compartments. The suborder includes deer, antelopes, cattle, sheep, and goats **2** any other animal that chews the cud, such as a camel ▷ *adj* **3** of,

Rr

relating to, or belonging to this suborder **4** (of members of this suborder and related animals, such as camels) chewing the cud; ruminating **5** meditating or contemplating in a slow quiet way

ruminate (ˈruːmɪˌneɪt) *vb* **ruminates, ruminating, ruminated 1** (of ruminants) to chew (the cud) **2** (when *intr*, often foll by *upon*, *on*, etc) to meditate or ponder (upon) [C16 from L *rūmināre* to chew the cud, from RUMEN] > ˌ**rumiˈnation** *n* > ˈ**ruminative** *adj* > ˈ**ruminatively** *adv* > ˈ**rumiˌnator** *n*

rummage (ˈrʌmɪdʒ) *vb* **rummages, rummaging, rummaged 1** (when *intr*, often foll by *through*) to search (through) while looking for something, often causing disorder ▷ *n* **2** an act of rummaging **3** a jumble of articles [C14 (in the sense: to pack a cargo): from OF *arrumage*, from *arrumer* to stow in a ship's hold, prob. of Gmc origin] > ˈ**rummager** *n*

rummage sale *n* **1** the US and Canad term for **jumble sale 2** *US* a sale of unclaimed property

rummer (ˈrʌmə) *n* a drinking glass having an ovoid bowl on a short stem [C17 from Du. *roemer* a glass for drinking toasts, from *roemen* to praise]

rummy (ˈrʌmɪ) *or* **rum** *n* a card game based on collecting sets and sequences [C20 ?from RUM[2]]

rumour *or US* **rumor** (ˈruːmə) *n* **1a** information, often a mixture of truth and untruth, passed around verbally **1b** (*in combination*): *a rumourmonger* **2** gossip or hearsay ▷ *vb* **3** (*tr; usually passive*) to pass around or circulate in the form of a rumour: *it is rumoured that the Queen is coming* [C14 via OF from L *rūmor* common talk]

rump (rʌmp) *n* **1** the hindquarters of a mammal, not including the legs **2** the rear part of a bird's back, nearest to the tail **3** a person's buttocks **4** Also called: **rump steak** a cut of beef from behind the loin **5** an inferior remnant [C15 from ON] > ˈ**rumpless** *adj*

Rumpelstiltskin (ˌrʌmpəlˈstɪltskɪn) *n* a dwarf in a German folktale who aids the king's bride on condition that she give him her first child or guess the dwarf's name. She guesses correctly and in his rage he destroys himself

rumple (ˈrʌmpəl) *vb* **rumples, rumpling, rumpled 1** to make or become crumpled or dishevelled ▷ *n* **2** a wrinkle, fold, or crease [C17 from MDu. *rompelen*; rel. to OE *gerumpen* wrinkled] > ˈ**rumply** *adj*

rumpo (rʌmpəʊ) *n sl* sexual intercourse

Rump Parliament *or* **the Rump** *n English history* the remainder of the Long Parliament after Pride's Purge. It sat from 1648–53

rumpus (ˈrʌmpəs) *n, pl* **rumpuses** a noisy, confused, or disruptive commotion [C18 from ?]

rumpus room *n* a room used for noisy activities, such as parties or children's games

rumpy-pumpy (ˈrʌmpɪˈpʌmpɪ) *n inf* sexual intercourse

Rumsfeld (ˈrʌmsˌfɛlt, ˈrʌmz-) *n* **Donald H** born 1932, US Republican politician and businessman: US Secretary of Defense from 2001

run (rʌn) *vb* **runs, running, ran, run 1** (*intr*) **1a** (of a two-legged creature) to move on foot at a rapid pace so that both feet are off the ground for part of each stride **1b** (of a four-legged creature) to move at a rapid gait **2** (*tr*) to pass over (a distance, route, etc) in running: *to run a mile* **3** (*intr*) to run in or finish a race as specified, esp in a particular position: *John is running third* **4** (*tr*) to perform as by running: *to run an errand* **5** (*intr*) to flee; run away **6** (*tr*) to bring into a specified state by running: *to run oneself to a standstill* **7** (*tr*) to track down or hunt (an animal): *to run a fox to earth* **8** (*tr*) to set (animals) loose on (a field or tract of land) so as to graze freely: *he ran stock on that pasture last year* **9** (*intr*; often foll by *over*, *round*, or *up*) to make a short trip or brief visit: *I'll run over this afternoon* **10** (*intr*) to move quickly and easily on wheels by rolling, or in any of certain other ways: *a sledge running over snow* **11** to move or cause to move with a specified result: *to run a ship aground; run into a tree* **12** (often foll by *over*) to move or pass or cause to move or pass quickly: *to run one's eyes over a page* **13** (*tr*; foll by *into*, *out of*, *through*, etc) to force, thrust, or drive: *she ran a needle into her finger* **14** (*tr*) to drive or maintain and operate (a vehicle) **15** (*tr*) to give a lift to (someone) in a vehicle: *he ran her to the station* **16** to ply or cause to ply between places on a route: *the bus runs from Piccadilly to Golders Green* **17** to function or cause to function: *the engine is running smoothly* **18** (*tr*) to manage: *to run a company* **19** to perform or carry out: *to run tests* **20** to extend or continue or cause to extend or continue in a particular direction, for a particular duration or distance, etc: *the road runs north; the play ran for two years* **21** (*intr*) *law* to have legal force or effect: *the house lease runs for two more years* **22** (*tr*) to be subjected to, be affected by, or incur: *to run a risk; run a temperature* **23** (*intr*; often foll by *to*) to be characterized (by); tend or incline: *to run to fat* **24** (*intr*) to recur persistently or be inherent: *red hair runs in my family* **25** to cause or allow (liquids) to flow or (of liquids) to flow: *the well has run dry* **26** (*intr*) to melt and flow: *the wax grew hot and began to run* **27** *metallurgy* **27a** to melt or fuse **27b** (*tr*) to cast (molten metal): *to run lead into ingots* **28** (*intr*) (of waves, tides, rivers, etc) to rise high, surge, or be at a specified height: *a high sea was running that night* **29** (*intr*) to be diffused: *the colours in my dress ran when I washed it* **30** (*intr*) (of stitches) to unravel or come undone or (of a garment) to have stitches unravel or come undone **31** (*intr*) (of growing creepers, etc) to trail, spread, or climb: *ivy running over a cottage wall* **32** (*intr*) to spread or circulate quickly: *a rumour ran through the town* **33** (*intr*) to be stated or reported: *his story runs as follows* **34** to publish or print or be published or printed in a newspaper, magazine, etc: *they ran his story in the next issue* **35** (often foll by *for*) *chiefly US & Canad* to be a candidate or present as a candidate for political or other office: *Jones is running for president* **36** (*tr*) to get past or through: *to run a blockade* **37** (*tr*) to deal in (arms, etc), esp by importing illegally: *he runs guns for the rebels* **38** *naut* to sail (a vessel, esp a sailing vessel) or (of such a vessel) to be sailed with the wind coming from astern **39** (*intr*) (of fish) to migrate upstream from the sea, esp in order to spawn **40** (*tr*) *cricket* to score (a run or number of runs) by hitting the ball and running between the wickets **41** (*tr*) *billiards, etc* to make (a number of successful shots) in sequence **42** (*tr*) *golf* to hit (the ball) so that it rolls along the ground **43** (*tr*) *bridge* to cash (all one's winning cards in a long suit) successively ▷ *n* **44** an act, instance, or period of running **45** a gait, pace, or motion faster than a walk: *she went off at a run* **46** a distance covered by running or a period of running: *a run of ten miles* **47** an instance or period of travelling in a vehicle, esp for pleasure: *to go for a run in the car* **48** free and unrestricted access: *we had the run of the house* **49a** a period of time during which a machine, computer, etc, operates **49b** the amount of work performed in such a period **50** a continuous or sustained period: *a run of good luck* **51** a continuous sequence of performances: *the play had a good run* **52** *cards* a sequence of winning cards in one suit: *a run of spades* **53** tendency or trend: *the run of the market* **54** type, class, or category: *the usual run of graduates* **55** (usually foll by *on*) a continuous and urgent demand: *a run on the dollar* **56** a series of unravelled stitches, esp in tights; ladder **57** the characteristic pattern or direction of something: *the run of the grain on wood* **58a** a period during which water or other liquid flows **58b** the amount of such a flow **59** a pipe, channel, etc, through which water or other liquid flows **60** *US* a small stream **61** a steeply inclined course, esp a snow-covered one used for skiing **62** an enclosure for domestic fowls or other animals: *a chicken run* **63** (esp in Australia and New Zealand) a tract of land for grazing livestock **64** the migration of fish upstream in order to spawn **65** *mil* **65a** a mission in a warplane **65b** Also called: **bombing run** an approach by a bomber to a target

66 the movement of an aircraft along the ground during takeoff or landing **67** *music* a rapid scalelike passage of notes **68** *cricket* a score of one, normally achieved by both batsmen running from one end of the wicket to the other after one of them has hit the ball **69** *baseball* an instance of a batter touching all four bases safely, thereby scoring **70** *golf* the distance that a ball rolls after hitting the ground **71** **a run for (one's) money** *inf* **71a** a close competition **71b** pleasure derived from an activity **72** **in the long run** as the eventual outcome of a series of events, etc **73** **in the short run** as the immediate outcome of a series of events, etc **74** **on the run** **74a** escaping from arrest; fugitive **74b** in rapid flight; retreating: *the enemy is on the run* **74c** hurrying from place to place **75** **the runs** *sl* diarrhoea ▷ See also **runabout, run across,** etc [OE *runnen*, p.p. of *(ge)rinnan*]

runabout (ˈrʌnəˌbaʊt) *n* **1** a small light vehicle or aeroplane ▷ *vb* **run about** **2** *(intr, adv)* to move busily from place to place

run across *vb (intr, prep)* to meet unexpectedly; encounter by chance

run along *vb (intr, adv)* (often said patronizingly) to go away; leave

run around *inf* ▷ *vb (intr, adv)* **1** (often foll by *with*) to associate habitually (with) **2** to behave in a fickle or promiscuous manner ▷ *n* **run-around** **3** deceitful or evasive treatment of a person (esp in **give** *or* **get the run-around**)

run away *vb (intr, adv)* **1** to take flight; escape **2** to go away; depart **3** (of a horse) to gallop away uncontrollably **4** **run away with** **4a** to abscond or elope with: *he ran away with his boss's daughter* **4b** to make off with; steal **4c** to escape from the control of: *his enthusiasm ran away with him* **4d** to win easily or be assured of victory in (a competition): *he ran away with the race* ▷ *n* **runaway** **5a** a person or animal that runs away **5b** *(as modifier)*: *a runaway horse* **6** the act or an instance of running away **7** *(modifier)* rising rapidly, as prices: *runaway inflation* **8** *(modifier)* (of a race, victory, etc) easily won

runcible spoon (ˈrʌnsɪbəl) *n* a forklike utensil with two broad prongs and one sharp curved prong [*runcible* coined by Edward Lear, in a nonsense poem (1871)]

Runcorn (ˈrʌŋˌkɔːn) *n* a town in NW England, in Halton unitary authority, N Cheshire, on the Manchester Ship Canal: port and industrial centre; designated a new town in 1964. Pop: 64 154 (1991)

run down *vb (mainly adv)* **1** to allow (an engine, etc) to lose power gradually and cease to function or (of an engine, etc) to do this **2** to decline or reduce in number or size: *the firm ran down its sales force* **3** *(tr; usually passive)* to tire, sap the strength of, or exhaust: *he was thoroughly run down* **4** *(tr)* to criticize adversely; decry **5** *(tr)* to hit and knock to the ground with a moving vehicle **6** *(tr) naut* to collide with and cause to sink **7** *(tr)* to pursue and find or capture: *to run down a fugitive* **8** *(tr)* to read swiftly or perfunctorily: *he ran down their list of complaints* ▷ *adj* **run-down** **9** tired; exhausted **10** worn-out, shabby, or dilapidated ▷ *n* **rundown** **11** a brief review, résumé, or summary **12** the process of a mechanism coming gradually to a standstill after the power is removed **13** a reduction in number or size

Rundstedt (ˈrʊndstɛt; *German* ˈrʊntʃtɛt) *n* **Karl Rudolf Gerd von** (karl ˈruːdɔlf gɛrt fɔn) 1875–1953, German field marshal; directed the conquest of Poland and France in World War II; commander of the Western Front (1942–44); led the Ardennes counteroffensive (Dec 1944)

rune (ruːn) *n* **1** any of the characters of an ancient Germanic alphabet, in use, esp in Scandinavia, from the 3rd century AD to the end of the Middle Ages **2** any obscure piece of writing using mysterious symbols **3** a kind of Finnish poem or a stanza in such a poem [OE *rūn*, from ON *rūn* secret] > ˈ**runic** *adj*

rung[1] (rʌŋ) *n* **1** one of the bars or rods that form the steps of a ladder **2** a crosspiece between the legs of a chair, etc **3** *naut* a spoke on a ship's wheel or a handle projecting from the periphery [OE *hrung*] > ˈ**rungless** *adj*

rung[2] (rʌŋ) *vb* the past participle of **ring**[2]

USAGE See at **ring**

run in *vb (adv)* **1** to run (an engine) gently, usually when it is new **2** *(tr)* to insert or include **3** *(intr)* (of an aircraft) to approach a point or target **4** *(tr) inf* to take into custody; arrest ▷ *n* **run-in** **5** *inf* an argument or quarrel **6** an approach to the end of an event, etc: *the run-in for the championship* **7** *printing* matter inserted in an existing paragraph

run into *vb (prep, mainly intr)* **1** *(also tr)* to collide with or cause to collide with: *her car ran into a tree* **2** to encounter unexpectedly **3** *(also tr)* to be beset by: *the project ran into financial difficulties* **4** to extend to; be of the order of: *debts running into thousands*

runnel (ˈrʌnəl) *n literary* a small stream [C16 from OE *rynele*; rel. to RUN]

runner (ˈrʌnə) *n* **1** a person who runs, esp an athlete **2** a messenger for a bank, etc **3** a person engaged in the solicitation of business **4** a person on the run; fugitive **5a** a person or vessel engaged in smuggling **5b** *(in combination)*: *a gunrunner* **6** a person who operates, manages, or controls something **7a** either of the strips of metal or wood on which a sledge runs **7b** the blade of an ice skate **8** a roller or guide for a sliding component **9** *bot* **9a** Also called: **stolon** a slender stem, as of the strawberry, that arches down to the ground and propagates by producing roots and shoots at the nodes or tip **9b** a plant that propagates in this way **10** a strip of lace, linen, etc, placed across a table or dressing table for protection and decoration **11** another word for **rocker** (on a rocking chair) **12** **do a runner** *sl* to run away in order to escape trouble or to avoid paying for something

runner bean *n* another name for **scarlet runner**

runner-up *n, pl* **runners-up** a contestant finishing a race or competition in second place

running (ˈrʌnɪŋ) *adj* **1** maintained continuously; incessant: *running commentary* **2** *(postpositive)* without interruption; consecutive: *he lectured for two hours running* **3** denoting or relating to the scheduled operation of a public vehicle: *the running time of a train* **4** accomplished at a run: *a running jump* **5** moving or slipping easily, as a rope or a knot **6** (of a wound, etc) discharging pus **7** prevalent; current: *running prices* **8** repeated or continuous: *a running design* **9** (of plants, plant stems, etc) creeping along the ground **10** flowing: *running water* **11** (of handwriting) having the letters run together ▷ *n* **12** management or organization: *the running of a company* **13** operation or maintenance: *the running of a machine* **14** competition or competitive situation (in **in the running, out of the running**) **15** **make the running** to set the pace in a competition or race

running board *n* a footboard along the side of a vehicle, esp an early motorcar

running head *or* **title** *n printing* a heading printed at the top of every page of a book

running light *n naut* one of several lights displayed by vessels operating at night

running mate *n* **1** *US* a candidate for the subordinate of two linked positions, esp a candidate for the vice-presidency **2** a horse that pairs another in a team

running repairs *pl n* repairs that do not, or do not greatly, interrupt operations

runny (ˈrʌnɪ) *adj* **runnier, runniest** **1** tending to flow; liquid **2** (of the nose) exuding mucus

Runnymede (ˈrʌnɪˌmiːd) *n* a meadow on the S bank of the Thames near Windsor, where King John met his rebellious barons in 1215 and acceded to Magna Carta

run off *vb (adv)* **1** *(intr)* to depart in haste **2** *(tr)* to produce quickly, as copies on a duplicating machine **3** to drain (liquid) or (of liquid) to be drained **4** *(tr)* to decide (a race) by a run-off **5** **run off with** **5a** to steal; purloin **5b** to elope with ▷ *n* **run-off** **6** an extra race, contest, election, etc, to decide the winner after a tie **7** NZ grazing land for store cattle **8** that portion of rainfall that runs into streams as surface water rather than being absorbed into groundwater or evaporating **9** the overflow of a liquid from a container

run-of-the-mill *adj* ordinary, average, or undistinguished in quality, character, or nature

run on *vb (adv)* **1** *(intr)* to continue without interruption **2** to write with linked-up characters **3** *printing* to compose text matter without indentation or paragraphing ▷ *n* **run-on** **4** *printing* **4a** text matter composed without indenting **4b** an additional quantity required in excess of the originally stated amount, whilst the job is being produced **5a** a word added at the end of a dictionary entry whose meaning can be easily inferred from the definition of the headword **5b** *(as modifier): a run-on entry*

run out *vb (adv)* **1** *(intr; often foll by of)* to exhaust (a supply of something) or (of a supply) to become exhausted **2** *(intr)* to become no longer valid; expire: *my passport has run out* **3** **run out on** *inf* to desert or abandon **4** *(tr) cricket* to dismiss (a running batsman) by breaking the wicket with the ball, or with the ball in the hand, while he or she is out of his or her ground ▷ *n* **run-out** **5** *cricket* dismissal of a batsman by running him or her out

run over *vb* **1** *(tr, adv)* to knock down (a person) with a moving vehicle **2** *(intr)* to overflow the capacity of (a container) **3** *(intr, prep)* to examine hastily or make a rapid survey of **4** *(intr, prep)* to exceed (a limit): *we've run over our time*

runt (rʌnt) *n* **1** the smallest and weakest young animal in a litter, esp the smallest piglet in a litter **2** *derog* an undersized or inferior person **3** a large pigeon, originally bred for eating [c16 from ?] > **'runtish** *or* **'runty** *adj* > **'runtiness** *n*

run through *vb* **1** *(tr, adv)* to transfix with a sword or other weapon **2** *(intr, prep)* to exhaust (money) by wasteful spending **3** *(intr, prep)* to practise or rehearse: *let's run through the plan* **4** *(intr, prep)* to examine hastily ▷ *n* **run-through** **5** a practice or rehearsal **6** a brief survey

run time *n computing* the time during which a computer program is executed

run to *vb (intr, prep)* to be sufficient for: *my income doesn't run to luxuries*

run up *vb (tr, adv)* **1** to amass; incur: *to run up debts* **2** to make by sewing together quickly **3** to hoist: *to run up a flag* ▷ *n* **run-up** **4** an approach run by an athlete for the long jump, pole vault, etc **5** a preliminary or preparatory period: *the run-up to the election*

runway ('rʌnˌweɪ) *n* **1** a hard level roadway from which aircraft take off and on which they land **2** *forestry, US & Canad* a chute for sliding logs down **3** *chiefly US* a narrow ramp extending from the stage into the audience in a theatre, etc esp as used by models in a fashion show

Runyon ('rʌnjən) *n* **(Alfred) Damon** 1884–1946, US short-story writer, best known for his humorous tales about racy Broadway characters. His story collections include *Guys and Dolls* (1932), which became the basis of a musical (1950)

RUOK *text messaging abbrev for* are you OK?

rupee (ruːˈpiː) *n* the standard monetary unit of India, Mauritius, Nepal, Pakistan, the Seychelles, and Sri Lanka [c17 from Hindi *rupaīyā*, from Sansk. *rūpya* coined silver, from *rūpa* shape, beauty]

Rupert ('ruːpət) *n* **Prince** 1619–82, German-born nephew of Charles I: Royalist general during the Civil War (until 1646) and commander of the Royalist fleet (1648–50). After the Restoration he was an admiral of the English fleet in wars against the Dutch

Rupert's Land *n* (formerly, in Canada) the territories granted by Charles II to the Hudson's Bay Company in 1670 and ceded to the Canadian Government in 1870, comprising all the land watered by rivers flowing into Hudson Bay

rupiah (ruːˈpiːə) *n, pl* **rupiah** *or* **rupiahs** the standard monetary unit of Indonesia [from Hindi: RUPEE]

rupture ('rʌptʃə) *n* **1** the act of breaking or bursting or the state of being broken or burst **2** a breach of peaceful or friendly relations **3** *pathol* **3a** the breaking or tearing of a bodily structure or part **3b** another word for **hernia** ▷ *vb* **ruptures, rupturing, ruptured** **4** to break or burst **5** to affect or be affected with a rupture or hernia **6** to undergo or cause to undergo a breach in relations or friendship [c15 from L *ruptūra*, from *rumpere* to burst forth] > **'rupturable** *adj*

rural ('rʊərəl) *adj* **1** of, relating to, or characteristic of the country or country life **2** living in the country **3** of, relating to, or associated with farming ▷ Cf **urban** [c15 via OF from L *rūrālis*, from *rūs* the country] > **'ruralism** *n* > **'ruralist** *n* > **ru'rality** *n* > **'rurally** *adv*

rural dean *n chiefly Brit* a clergyman having authority over a group of parishes

rural district *n* (formerly) a rural division of a county

ruralize *or* **ruralise** ('rʊərəˌlaɪz) *vb* **ruralizes, ruralizing, ruralized** *or* **ruralises, ruralising, ruralised** **1** *(tr)* to make rural in character, appearance, etc **2** *(intr)* to go into the country to live > **ˌrurali'zation** *or* **ˌrurali'sation** *n*

rural route *n US & Canad* a mail service or route in a rural area, the mail being delivered by car or van

Rurik *or* **Ryurik** ('rʊərɪk) *n* died 879. Varangian (Scandinavian Viking) leader who founded the Russian monarchy. He gained control over Novgorod (?862) and his dynasty, the **Rurikids**, ruled until 1598

Ruritania (ˌrʊərɪ'teɪnɪə, -njə) *n* **1** an imaginary kingdom of central Europe: setting of several novels by Anthony Hope, esp *The Prisoner of Zenda* (1894) **2** any setting of adventure, romance, and intrigue > **ˌRuri'tanian** *adj, n*

ruse (ruːz) *n* an action intended to mislead, deceive, or trick; stratagem [c15 from OF: trick, esp to evade capture, from *ruser* to retreat, from L *recūsāre* to refuse]

Ruse ('ruːseɪ) *n* a city in NE Bulgaria, on the River Danube: the chief river port and one of the largest industrial centres in Bulgaria. Pop: 166 467 (1999 est)

rush[1] (rʌʃ) *vb* **1** to hurry or cause to hurry; hasten **2** *(tr)* to make a sudden attack upon (a fortress, position, person, etc) **3** (when *intr*, often foll by *at, in,* or *into*) to proceed or approach in a reckless manner **4** **rush one's fences** to proceed with precipitate haste **5** *(intr)* to come, flow, swell, etc, quickly or suddenly: *tears rushed to her eyes* **6** *(tr) sl* to cheat, esp by grossly overcharging **7** *(tr) US & Canad* to make a concerted effort to secure the agreement, participation, etc, of (a person) **8** *(intr) American football* to gain ground by running forwards with the ball ▷ *n* **9** the act or condition of rushing **10** a sudden surge towards someone or something: *a gold rush* **11** a sudden surge of sensation, esp from a drug **12** a sudden demand ▷ *adj (prenominal)* **13** requiring speed or urgency: *a rush job* **14** characterized by much movement, business, etc: *a rush period* [c14 *ruschen*, from OF *ruser* to put to flight, from L *recūsāre* to refuse] > **'rusher** *n*

rush[2] (rʌʃ) *n* **1** an annual or perennial plant growing in wet places and typically having grasslike cylindrical leaves and small green or brown flowers **2** something valueless; a trifle; straw: *not worth a rush* **3** short for **rush light** [OE *risce, rysce*] > **'rushˌlike** *adj* > **'rushy** *adj*

Rush (rʌʃ) *n* **Geoffrey** born 1951, Australian stage and film actor, best known for his starring role in the film *Shine* (1996)

Rushdie ('rʊʃdɪ) *n* **(Ahmed) Salman** (sʌl'mɑːn) born 1947, British writer, born in India, whose novels include

Midnight's Children (1981), which won the Booker prize, *Shame* (1983), and *The Ground Beneath Her Feet* (1998). His novel *The Satanic Verses* (1988) was regarded as blasphemous by many Muslims and he was forced into hiding (1989) when the Ayatollah Khomeini called for his death

rushes ('rʌʃɪz) *pl n* (*sometimes sing*) (in film-making) the initial prints of a scene or scenes before editing, usually prepared daily

rush hour *n* a period at the beginning and end of the working day when large numbers of people are travelling to or from work

rush light *or* **candle** *n* a narrow candle, formerly in use, made of the pith of various types of rush dipped in tallow

Rushmore ('rʌʃmɔː) *n* **Mount** a mountain in W South Dakota, in the Black Hills: a national memorial, with the faces of Washington, Lincoln, Jefferson, and Roosevelt carved into its side by Gutzon Borglum between 1927 and 1941. Height: 1841 m (6040 ft)

rusk (rʌsk) *n* a light bread dough, sweet or plain, baked twice until it is brown, hard, and crisp: often given to babies [c16 from Sp. or Port. *rosca* screw, bread shaped in a twist, from ?]

Rusk (rʌsk) *n* (**David**) **Dean** 1909–94, US statesman: secretary of state (1961–69) He defended US military involvement in Vietnam and opposed recognition of communist China

Ruskin ('rʌskɪn) *n* **John** 1819–1900, English art critic and social reformer. He was a champion of the Gothic Revival and the Pre-Raphaelites and saw a close connection between art and morality. From about 1860 he argued vigorously for social and economic planning. His works include *Modern Painters* (1843–60), *The Stones of Venice* (1851–53), *Unto this Last* (1862), *Time and Tide* (1867), and *Fors Clavigera* (1871–84)

Russ. *abbrev for* Russia(n)

Russell ('rʌsᵊl) *n* **1** **Bertrand** (**Arthur William**), 3rd Earl. 1872–1970, British philosopher and mathematician. His books include *Principles of Mathematics* (1903), *Principia Mathematica* (1910–13) with A. N. Whitehead, *Introduction to Mathematical Philosophy* (1919), *The Problems of Philosophy* (1912), *The Analysis of Mind* (1921), and *An Enquiry into Meaning and Truth* (1940): Nobel prize for literature 1950 **2** **George William**, pen name *A. E.*. 1867–1935, Irish poet and journalist **3** **Henry Norris** 1877–1957, US astronomer and astrophysicist, who originated one form of the Hertzsprung–Russell diagram **4** **John**, 1st Earl. 1792–1878, British statesman; prime minister (1846–52; 1865–66) He led the campaign to carry the 1832 Reform Act **5** **Ken** born 1927, British film director. His films include *Women in Love* (1969), *The Music Lovers* (1970), *The Boy Friend* (1971), *Valentino* (1977), *Gothic* (1986), and *The Rainbow* (1989)

russet ('rʌsɪt) *n* **1** brown with a yellowish or reddish tinge **2** a rough homespun fabric, reddish-brown in colour, formerly in use for clothing **3** any of various apples with rough brownish-red skins ▷ *adj* **4** *arch* simple; homely; rustic: *a russet life* **5** of the colour russet: *russet hair* [c13 from Anglo-Norman, from OF *rosset*, from *rous*, from L *russus*; rel. to L *ruber* red] > '**russety** *adj*

Russia ('rʌʃə) *n* (full name **Russian Federation**) **1** the largest country in the world, covering N Eurasia and bordering on the Pacific and Arctic Oceans and the Baltic, Black, and Caspian Seas: originating from the principality of Muscovy in the 17th century, it expanded to become the Russian Empire; the Tsar was overthrown in 1917 and the Communist Russian Soviet Federative Socialist Republic was created; this merged with neighbouring Soviet Republics in 1922 to form the Soviet Union; on the disintegration of the Soviet Union in 1991 the Russian Federation was established as an independent state. Official language: Russian. Religion: nonreligious and Russian orthodox Christian. Currency: rouble. Capital: Moscow. Pop: 144 417 000 (2001 est). Area: 17 074 984 sq km (6 592 658 sq miles) **2** another name for the **Russian Empire** **3** another name for the former **Soviet Union** **4** another name for the former **Russian Soviet Federative Socialist Republic** ▷ Russian name **Rossiya**
▷ www.russia-travel.com

Russia leather *n* a smooth dyed leather made from calfskin and scented with birch tar oil, originally produced in Russia

Russian ('rʌʃən) *n* **1** the official language of Russia, and of the former Soviet Union: an Indo-European language belonging to the Eastbranch **2** a native or inhabitant of Russia ▷ *adj* **3** of, relating to, or characteristic of Russia, its people, or their language

Russian Alphabet

Letter		Transliteration
А	а	a
Б	б	b
В	в	v
Г	г	g
Д	д	d
Е	е	e. ye
Ж	ж	zh, ž
З	з	z
И	и	5
Й	й	", y, j, i
К	к	k
Л	л	l
М	м	m
Н	н	n
О	о	o
П	п	p
Р	р	r
С	с	s
Т	т	t
У	у	u
Ф	ф	f
Х	х	kh, x
Ц	ц	ta, c
Ч	ч	ch, č
Ш	ш	sh, š
Щ	щ	shch, šč
Ъ	ъ	"
Ы	ы	y, i
Ь	ь	'
Э	э	e, eh
Ю	ю	yu, ju
Я	я	ya, ja

Russian doll *n* a hollow wooden figure, usually representing a Russian peasant woman, that comes apart to reveal a similar smaller figure, which itself contains another, and so on

Russian Empire *n* the tsarist empire in Asia and E Europe, overthrown by the Russian Revolution of 1917
▷ http://all-photo.ru/empire/index.en.html
▷ http://feefhs.org/maps/ruse/mapiruse.html

Russian Federation *n* See **Russia**

Russianize *or* **Russianise** ('rʌʃəˌnaɪz) *vb* **Russianizes, Russianizing, Russianized** *or* **Russianises, Russianising, Russianised** to make or become Russian in style, etc > ˌ**Russiani'zation** *or* ˌ**Russiani'sation** *n*

Russian Orthodox Church *n* the national church of Russia, constituting a branch of the Eastern Church

presided over by the Patriarch of Moscow
▷ www.russian-orthodox-church.org.ru/en.htm

Russian roulette *n* **1** an act of bravado in which each person in turn spins the cylinder of a revolver loaded with only one cartridge and presses the trigger with the barrel against his own head **2** any foolish or potentially suicidal undertaking

Russian salad *n* a salad of cold diced cooked vegetables mixed with mayonnaise and pickles

Russian Soviet Federative Socialist Republic *n* (formerly) the largest administrative division of the Soviet Union. Abbreviation: **RSFSR**

Russian Turkestan *n* See **Turkestan**

Russian Zone *n* another name for the **Soviet Zone**

Russo- (ˈrʌsəʊ) *combining form* Russia or Russian: *Russo-Japanese*

rust (rʌst) *n* **1** a reddish-brown oxide coating formed on iron or steel by the action of oxygen and moisture **2** Also called: **rust fungus** *plant pathol* **2a** any of a group of fungi which are parasitic on cereal plants, conifers, etc **2b** any of various plant diseases characterized by reddish-brown discoloration of the leaves and stem, esp that caused by the rust fungi **3a** a strong brown colour, sometimes with a reddish or yellowish tinge **3b** (*as adj*): *a rust carpet* **4** any corrosive or debilitating influence, esp lack of use ▷ *vb* **5** to become or cause to become coated with a layer of rust **6** to deteriorate or cause to deteriorate through some debilitating influence or lack of use: *he allowed his talent to rust over the years* [OE *rūst*] > ˈ**rustless** *adj*

rust belt *n* an area where heavy industry is in decline, esp in the Midwest of the US

rustic (ˈrʌstɪk) *adj* **1** of, characteristic of, or living in the country; rural **2** having qualities ascribed to country life or people; simple; unsophisticated: *rustic pleasures* **3** crude, awkward, or uncouth **4** made of untrimmed branches: *a rustic seat* **5** (of masonry, etc) having a rusticated finish ▷ *n* **6** a person who comes from or lives in the country **7** an unsophisticated, simple, or clownish person from the country **8** Also called: **rusticwork** brick or stone having a rough finish [C16 from OF *rustique*, from L *rūsticus*, from *rūs* the country] > ˈ**rustically** *adv* > **rusticity** (rʌˈstɪsɪtɪ) *n*

rusticate (ˈrʌstɪˌkeɪt) *vb* **rusticates, rusticating, rusticated 1** to banish or retire to the country **2** to make or become rustic in style, etc **3** (*tr*) *archit* to finish (an exterior wall) with large blocks of masonry separated by deep joints **4** (*tr*) *Brit* to send down from university for a specified time as a punishment [C17 from L *rūsticārī*, from *rūs* the country] > ˌ**rustiˈcation** *n* > ˈ**rustiˌcator** *n*

rusticated (ˈrʌstɪˌkeɪtɪd) *or* **rusticating** (ˈrʌstɪˌkeɪtɪŋ) *n* (in New Zealand) a wide type of weatherboarding used in older houses

rustle¹ (ˈrʌsᵊl) *vb* **rustles, rustling, rustled 1** to make or cause to make a low crisp whispering or rubbing sound, as of dry leaves or paper **2** to move with such a sound ▷ *n* **3** such a sound or sounds [OE *hrūxlian*]

rustle² (ˈrʌsᵊl) *vb* **rustles, rustling, rustled 1** *chiefly US & Canad* to steal (cattle, horses, etc) **2** *inf, US & Canad* to move swiftly and energetically [C19 prob. special use of RUSTLE¹ (in the sense: to move with a quiet sound)] > ˈ**rustler** *n*

rustle up *vb* (*tr, adv*) *Inf* **1** to prepare (a meal, etc) rapidly, esp at short notice **2** to forage for and obtain

rustproof (ˈrʌstˌpruːf) *adj* treated against rusting

rusty (ˈrʌstɪ) *adj* **rustier, rustiest 1** covered with, affected by, or consisting of rust: *a rusty machine* **2** of the colour rust **3** discoloured by age: *a rusty coat* **4** (of the voice) tending to croak **5** old-fashioned in appearance: *a rusty old gentleman* **6** impaired in skill or knowledge by inaction or neglect **7** (of plants) affected by the rust fungus > ˈ**rustily** *adv* > ˈ**rustiness** *n*

rut¹ (rʌt) *n* **1** a groove or furrow in a soft road, caused by wheels **2** a narrow or predictable way of life; dreary or undeviating routine (esp in **in a rut**) ▷ *vb* **ruts, rutting, rutted 3** (*tr*) to make a rut in [C16 prob. from F *route* road]

rut² (rʌt) *n* **1** a recurrent period of sexual excitement and reproductive activity in certain male ruminants ▷ *vb* **ruts, rutting, rutted 2** (*intr*) (of male ruminants) to be in a period of sexual excitement and activity [C15 from OF *rut* noise, roar, from L *rugītus*, from *rugīre* to roar]

rutabaga (ˌruːtəˈbeɪgə) *n* the US and Canad name for **swede** [C18 from Swedish dialect *rotabagge*, lit.: root bag]

rutaceous (ruːˈteɪʃəs) *adj* of, relating to, or belonging to a family of tropical and temperate flowering plants many of which have aromatic leaves. The family includes rue and citrus trees [C19 from NL *Rutaceae*, from L *rūta* RUE²]

ruth (ruːθ) *n arch* **1** pity; compassion **2** repentance; remorse [C12 from *rewen* to RUE¹]

Ruth (ruːθ) *n* **1** *Old Testament* **1a** a Moabite woman, who married a Hebrew and on his death remained with her mother-in-law Naomi, later becoming the wife of Boaz **1b** the book in which these events are recounted **2 George Herman,** nicknamed *Babe*. 1895–1948, US baseball player

Ruthenia (ruːˈθiːnɪə) *n* a region of E Europe on the south side of the Carpathian Mountains: belonged to Hungary from the 14th century, to Czechoslovakia from 1918 to 1939, and was ceded to the former Soviet Union in 1945; in 1991 it became part of the newly independent Ukraine. Also called: **Carpatho-Ukraine**

ruthenium (ruːˈθiːnɪəm) *n* a hard brittle white element of the platinum metal group. It is used to harden platinum and palladium. Symbol: Ru; atomic no.: 44; atomic wt.: 101.07 [C19 from Med. L *Ruthenia* Russia, where it was discovered]

rutherford (ˈrʌðəfəd) *n* a former unit of activity equal to the quantity of a radioactive nuclide required to produce one million disintegrations per second. Abbrev: **rd** [C20 after E RUTHERFORD]

Rutherford (ˈrʌðəfəd) *n* **1 Ernest**, 1st Baron. 1871–1937, British physicist, born in New Zealand, who discovered the atomic nucleus (1909) Nobel prize for chemistry 1908 **2** Dame **Margaret** 1892–1972, British stage and screen actress. Her films include *Passport to Pimlico* (1949), *Murder She Said* (1962), and *The VIPs* (1963) **3 Mark,** original name *William Hale White*. 1831–1913, British novelist and writer, whose work deals with his religious uncertainties: best known for *The Autobiography of Mark Rutherford* (1881) and the novel *The Revolution in Tanner's Lane* (1887)

rutherfordium (ˌrʌðəˈfɔːdɪəm) *n* the US name for the element with the atomic no. 104. Soviet name **kurchatovium** Symbol: Rf [C20 after E. RUTHERFORD]

ruthful (ˈruːθfʊl) *adj arch* full of or causing sorrow or pity > ˈ**ruthfully** *adv* > ˈ**ruthfulness** *n*

ruthless (ˈruːθlɪs) *adj* feeling or showing no mercy; hardhearted > ˈ**ruthlessly** *adv* > ˈ**ruthlessness** *n*

rutile (ˈruːtaɪl) *n* a mineral consisting of titanium(IV) oxide (TiO_2) in tetragonal crystalline form. It is an important source of titanium [C19 via F from G *Rutil*, from L *rutilus* red, glowing]

Rutland (ˈrʌtlənd) *n* an inland county of central England: the smallest of the historical English counties, it became part of Leicestershire in 1974 but was reinstated as an independent unitary authority in 1997: mainly agricultural. Administrative centre: Oakham. Pop: 34 560 (2001). Area: 394 sq km (152 sq miles)

ruttish (ˈrʌtɪʃ) *adj* **1** (of an animal) in a condition of rut **2** lascivious or salacious > ˈ**ruttishly** *adv* > ˈ**ruttishness** *n*

rutty (ˈrʌtɪ) *adj* **ruttier, ruttiest** full of ruts or holes: *a rutty track* > ˈ**ruttily** *adv* > ˈ**ruttiness** *n*

Ruwenzori (ˌruːwɛnˈzɔːrɪ) *n* a mountain range in

central Africa, on the border between Uganda and the Democratic Republic of Congo (formerly Zaïre) between Lakes Edward and Albert: generally thought to be Ptolemy's "Mountains of the Moon". Highest peak: Mount Stanley, 5109 m (16 763 ft)

Ruysdael ('ri:zdɑ:l, -deɪl, 'raɪz-; *Dutch* 'rœizda:l) *n* a variant spelling of **Ruisdael**

Ruyter ('raɪtə; *Dutch* 'rœitər) *n* **Michiel Adriaanszoon de** (mi:'xi:l ˌa:dri'a:nsun də) 1607–76, Dutch admiral, noted for actions in the Anglo-Dutch wars in 1652–53, 1665–67, 1672, and 1673, when he prevented an Anglo-French invasion

RV *abbrev for:* **1** *chiefly US* recreational vehicle **2** Revised Version (of the Bible)

Rwanda[1] (rʊ'ændə) *n* a republic in central Africa: part of German East Africa from 1899 until 1917, when Belgium took over the administration; became a republic in 1961 after the successful Hutu revolt against the Tutsi (1959); fighting between the ethnic groups has broken out repeatedly since independence, culminating in the genocide of Tutsis by Hutus in 1994. Official languages: Rwanda, French, and English. Religion: Roman Catholic, African Protestant, Muslim, and animist. Currency: Rwanda franc. Capital: Kigali. Pop: 7 313 000 (2001 est). Area: 26 338 sq km (10 169 sq miles). Former name (until 1962): **Ruanda** > **R'wandan** *adj, n*

▹ www.rwanda1.com
▹ www.rwanda1.com/government/tourism.htm

-ry *suffix forming nouns* a variant of **-ery**: *dentistry*

Ryazan (*Russian* rɪ'zanj) *n* a city in W central Russia: capital of a medieval principality; oil refineries and engineering industries. Pop: 531 300 (1999 est)

Rybinsk (*Russian* 'ribinsk) *n* a city in W central Russia, on the River Volga: an important river port, terminal of the Mariinsk Waterway (between Saint Petersburg and the Volga) at the SE end of the **Rybinsk Reservoir** (area: 4700 sq km (1800 sq miles)). Pop: 241 800 (1999 est). Former names: **Shcherbakov** (from the Revolution until 1957), **Andropov** (1984–91)

Rydal ('raɪdᵊl) *n* a village in NW England, in Cumbria on **Rydal Water** (a small lake). **Rydal Mount**, home of Wordsworth from 1813 to 1850, is situated here

Ryder ('raɪdə) *n* **Susan**, Baroness Ryder of Warsaw. 1923–2000, British philanthropist; founder of the Sue Ryder Foundation for the Sick and Disabled, which is funded by a chain of charity shops: married to Leonard Cheshire

Ryder Cup *n* **the** the trophy awarded in a professional golfing competition between teams representing Europe and the US [c20 after Samuel *Ryder* (1859–1936), Brit businessman and golf patron]

rye (raɪ) *n* **1** a tall hardy widely cultivated annual grass having bristly flower spikes and light brown grain **2** the grain of this grass, used in making flour and whisky, and as a livestock food **3** Also called: (esp US): **rye whiskey** whisky distilled from rye **4** *US* short for **rye bread** [OE *ryge*]

Rye (raɪ) *n* a resort in SE England, in East Sussex: one of the Cinque Ports. Pop: 3708 (1991)

rye bread *n* any of various breads made entirely or partly from rye flour, often with caraway seeds

rye-grass *n* any of various grasses native to Europe, N Africa, and Asia, and widely cultivated as forage crops. They have flattened flower spikes and hairless leaves

Ryle (raɪl) *n* **1 Gilbert** 1900–76, British philosopher. His works include *The Concept of Mind* (1949) **2** Sir **Martin** 1918–84, British astronomer, noted for his research on radio astronomy: Astronomer Royal 1972–82; shared the Nobel prize for physics in 1974

Ryswick ('rɪzwɪk) *n* the English name for **Rijswijk**

Ryukyu Islands (rɪ'u:kju:) *pl n* a chain of 55 islands in the W Pacific, extending almost 650 km (400 miles) from S Japan to N Taiwan: an ancient kingdom, under Chinese rule from the late 14th century, invaded by Japan in the early 17th century, under full Japanese sovereignty from 1879 to 1945, and US control from 1945 to 1972; now part of Japan again. They are subject to frequent typhoons. Chief town: Naha City (on Okinawa). Pop: 1 318 000 (2000 est). Area: 2196 sq km (849 sq miles)

Ryurik ('rʊərɪk) *n* a variant spelling of **Rurik**

Ss

s *or* **S** (ɛs) *n, pl* **s's, S's,** *or* **Ss 1** the 19th letter of the English alphabet **2** a speech sound represented by this letter, either voiceless, as in *sit*, or voiced, as in *dogs* **3a** something shaped like an S **3b** (*in combination*): *an S-bend in a road*

s *symbol for* second (of time)

S *symbol for:* **1** small **2** Society **3** South **4** *chem* sulphur **5** *physics* **5a** entropy **5b** siemens **5c** strangeness **6** *currency* (the former) schilling

s. *abbrev for:* **1** shilling **2** singular **3** son **4** succeeded

s. *or* **S.** *music abbrev for* soprano

S. *abbrev for:* **1** (*pl* **SS**) Saint **2** school **3** Signor

-s[1] *or* **-es** *suffix* forming the plural of most nouns: *boys; boxes* [from OE *-as*, pl. nominative and accusative ending of some masc nouns]

-s[2] *or* **-es** *suffix* forming the third person singular present indicative tense of verbs: *he runs* [from OE (northern dialect) *-es, -s*, orig. the ending of the second person singular]

-'s *suffix* **1** forming the possessive singular of nouns and some pronouns: *man's; one's* **2** forming the possessive plural of nouns whose plurals do not end in *-s: children's*. (The possessive plural of nouns ending in *s* and of some singular nouns is formed by the addition of an apostrophe after the final *s: girls'; for goodness' sake*.) **3** forming the plural of numbers, letters, or symbols: *20's* **4** *inf* contraction of *is* or *has: it's gone* **5** *inf* contraction of *us* with *let: let's* **6** *inf* contraction of *does* in some questions: *what's he do?* [senses 1, 2: assimilated contraction from ME *-es*, from OE, masc and neuter genitive sing; sense 3, equivalent to -s[1]]

SA *abbrev for:* **1** Salvation Army **2** South Africa **3** South America **4** South Australia **5** *Sturmabteilung:* the Nazi terrorist militia

Saadi (sɑːˈdiː) *n* a variant spelling of **Sadi**

Saar (sɑː; *German* zaːr) *n* **1** a river in W Europe, rising in the Vosges Mountains and flowing north to the Moselle River in Germany. Length: 246 km (153 miles). French name: **Sarre 2 the Saar** another name for **Saarland**

Saarbrücken (*German* zaːrˈbrykən) *n* an industrial city in W Germany, capital of Saarland state, on the Saar River. Pop: 186 402 (1999 est)

Saarinen (ˈsɑːrɪnən) *n* **Eero** (ˈeɪrəʊ) 1910–61, US architect, born in Finland. His works include the US Embassy, London (1960)

Saarland (*German* ˈzaːrlant) *n* a state of W Germany: formed in 1919; under League of Nations administration until 1935; occupied by France (1945–57); part of West Germany (1957–90): contains rich coal deposits and is a major industrial region. Capital: Saarbrücken. Pop: 1 071 500 (2000 est). Area: 2567 sq km (991 sq miles)

Saba (ˈsɑːbə) *n* **1** an island in the NE Caribbean, in the Netherlands Antilles. Pop: 1704 (2000 est). Area: 13 sq km (5 sq miles) **2** another name for **Sheba**[1] (sense 1)

Sabadell (*Spanish* saβaˈðɛl) *n* a town in NE Spain, near Barcelona: textile manufacturing. Pop: 184 859 (1998 est)

sabadilla (ˌsæbəˈdɪlə) *n* **1** a tropical American liliaceous plant **2** the bitter brown seeds of this plant, which contain the alkaloid veratrine used in insecticides [C19 from Sp. *cebadilla*, dim. of *cebada* barley, from L *cibāre* to feed, from *cibus* food]

Sabaean *or* **Sabean** (səˈbiːən) *n* **1** an inhabitant or native of ancient Saba **2** the ancient Semitic language of Saba ▷ *adj* **3** of or relating to ancient Saba, its inhabitants, or their language [C16 from L *Sabaeus*, from Gk *Sabaios* belonging to Saba (Sheba)]

Sabah (ˈsɑːbɑː) *n* a state of Malaysia, occupying N Borneo and offshore islands in the South China and Sulu Seas: became a British protectorate in 1888; gained independence and joined Malaysia in 1963. Capital:

Kota Kinabalu. Pop: 2 449 389 (2000). Area: 76 522 sq km (29 545 sq miles). Former name (until 1963): **North Borneo**

Sabatier (*French* sabatje) *n* **Paul** (pɔl) 1854–1941, French chemist, who discovered a process for the hydrogenation of organic compounds: shared the Nobel prize for chemistry (1912)

sabbat ('sæbæt, -ət) *n* another word for **Sabbath** (sense 4)

Sabbatarian (ˌsæbə'tɛərɪən) *n* **1** a person advocating the strict religious observance of Sunday **2** a person who observes Saturday as the Sabbath ▷ *adj* **3** of the Sabbath or its observance [c17 from LL *sabbatārius* a Sabbath-keeper] > ˌ**Sabba'tarianism** *n*
▷ http://www.sabbatarian.com/

Sabbath ('sæbəθ) *n* **1** the seventh day of the week, Saturday, devoted to worship and rest from work in Judaism and in certain Christian Churches **2** Sunday, observed by Christians as the day of worship and rest **3** (*not cap*) a period of rest **4** Also called: **sabbat, witches' Sabbath** a midnight meeting for practitioners of witchcraft or devil worship [OE *sabbat*, from L, from Gk *sabbaton*, from Heb., from *shābath* to rest]

sabbatical (sə'bætɪkᵊl) *adj* **1** denoting a period of leave granted to university staff, teachers, etc, esp originally every seventh year: *a sabbatical year* ▷ *n* **2** any sabbatical period [c16 from Gk *sabbatikos*; see SABBATH]

Sabbatical (sə'bætɪkᵊl) *adj* of, relating to, or appropriate to the Sabbath as a day of rest and religious observance

SABC *abbrev for* South African Broadcasting Corporation
▷ www.sabc.co.za

saber ('seɪbə) *n, vb* the US spelling of **sabre**

sabin ('sæbɪn, 'seɪ-) *n physics* a unit of acoustic absorption [c20 introduced by Wallace C. *Sabine* (1868–1919), US physicist]

Sabin ('seɪbɪn) *n* **Albert Bruce** 1906–93, US microbiologist, born in Poland. He developed the **Sabin vaccine** (1955), taken orally to immunize against poliomyelitis

Sabine ('sæbaɪn) *n* **1** a member of an ancient people who lived in central Italy ▷ *adj* **2** of or relating to this people or their language

sabkha ('sæbxə, -kə) *n* a flat coastal plain with a salt crust, common in Arabia [c19 from Ar.]

sable ('seɪbᵊl) *n, pl* **sables** *or* **sable 1** a marten of N Asian forests, with dark brown luxuriant fur **2a** the highly valued fur of this animal **2b** (*as modifier*): *a sable coat* **3 American sable** the brown, slightly less valuable fur of the American marten **4** a dark brown to yellowish-brown colour ▷ *adj* **5** of the colour of sable fur **6** black; dark **7** (*usually postpositive*) *heraldry* of the colour black [c15 from OF, from OHG *zobel*, of Slavic origin]

Sable ('seɪbᵊl) *n* **Cape 1** a cape at the S tip of Florida: the southernmost point of continental US **2** the southernmost point of Nova Scotia, Canada

sable antelope *n* a large black E African antelope with long backward-curving horns

Sable Island pony *n* a variety of wild pony found on Sable Island, Nova Scotia.

sabot ('sæbəʊ) *n* **1** a shoe made from a single block of wood **2** a shoe with a wooden sole and a leather or cloth upper **3** *Austral* a small sailing boat with a shortened bow [c17 from F, prob. from OF *savate* an old shoe, also infl. by *bot* BOOT¹]

sabotage ('sæbəˌtɑːʒ) *n* **1** the deliberate destruction, disruption, or damage of equipment, a public service, etc, as by enemy agents, dissatisfied employees, etc **2** any similar action ▷ *vb* **sabotages, sabotaging, sabotaged 3** (*tr*) to destroy or disrupt, esp by secret means [c20 from F, from *saboter* to spoil through clumsiness (lit.: to clatter in sabots)]

saboteur (ˌsæbə'tɜː) *n* a person who commits sabotage [c20 from F]

sabra ('sɑːbrə) *n* a native-born Israeli Jew [from Heb. *Sabēr* prickly pear, common plant in the coastal areas of the country]

sabre *or US* **saber** ('seɪbə) *n* **1** a stout single-edged cavalry sword, having a curved blade **2** a sword used in fencing, having a narrow V-shaped blade ▷ *vb* **sabres, sabring, sabred** *or US* **sabers, sabering, sabered 3** (*tr*) to injure or kill with a sabre [c17 via F from G (dialect) *Sabel*, from MHG *sebel*, ?from Magyar *szablya*]

sabre-rattling *n, inf* an aggressive display of military power

sabre-toothed tiger *or* **cat** *n* any of various extinct felines with long curved upper canine teeth

sac (sæk) *n* a pouch, bag, or pouchlike part in an animal or plant [c18 from F, from L *saccus*; see SACK¹] > **saccate** ('sækɪt, -eɪt) *adj* > '**sac**ˌ**like** *adj*

saccharide ('sækəˌraɪd) *n* any sugar or other carbohydrate, esp a simple sugar

saccharimeter (ˌsækə'rɪmɪtə) *n* any instrument for measuring the strength of sugar solutions > ˌ**saccha'rimetry** *n*

saccharin ('sækərɪn) *n* a very sweet white crystalline slightly soluble powder used as a nonfattening sweetener [c19 from SACCHARO- + -IN]

saccharine ('sækəˌriːn) *adj* **1** excessively sweet; sugary: *a saccharine smile* **2** of the nature of or containing sugar or saccharin

saccharo- *or before a vowel* **sacchar-** *combining form* sugar [via L from Gk *sakkharon*, ult. from Sansk. *śarkarā* sugar]

saccharose ('sækəˌrəʊz, -ˌrəʊs) *n* a technical name for **sugar** (sense 1)

saccule ('sækjuːl) *or* **sacculus** ('sækjʊləs) *n* **1** a small sac **2** the smaller of the two parts of the membranous labyrinth of the internal ear ▷ Cf **utricle** [c19 from L *sacculus* dim. of *saccus* SACK¹]

sacerdotal (ˌsæsə'dəʊtᵊl) *adj* of, relating to, or characteristic of priests [c14 from L *sacerdōtālis*, from *sacerdōs* priest, from *sacer* sacred] > ˌ**sacer'dota**ˌ**lism** *n* > ˌ**sacer'dotally** *adv*

Ss

sachem ('seɪtʃəm) *n* **1** *US* a leader of a political party or organization **2** another name for **sagamore** [c17 from Amerind *s'chim* chief]

sachet ('sæʃeɪ) *n* **1** a small sealed envelope, usually made of plastic, for containing shampoo, etc **2a** a small soft bag containing perfumed powder, placed in drawers to scent clothing **2b** the powder contained in such a bag [c19 from OF: a little bag, from *sac* bag; see SACK¹]

Sachs (*German* zaks) *n* **1 Hans** (hans) 1494–1576, German master shoemaker and Meistersinger, portrayed by Wagner in *Die Meistersinger von Nürnberg* **2 Nelly** (**Leonie**) 1891–1970, German Jewish poet and dramatist, who escaped from Nazi Germany and settled in Sweden. Her works include *Eli: A Mystery Play of the Sufferings of Israel* (1951) and 'O the Chimneys', a poem about the Nazi extermination camps. Nobel prize for literature 1966 jointly with Shmuel Yosef Agnon

Sachsen ('zaksən) *n* the German name for **Saxony**

sack¹ (sæk) *n* **1** a large bag made of coarse cloth, thick paper, etc, used as a container **2** Also called: **sackful** the amount contained in a sack **3a** a woman's loose tube-shaped dress **3b** Also called: **sacque** (sæk) a woman's full loose hip-length jacket **4 the sack** *inf* dismissal from employment **5** a slang word for **bed** **6 hit the sack** *sl* to go to bed ▷ *vb* (*tr*) **7** *inf* to dismiss from employment **8** to put into a sack or sacks [OE *sacc*, from L *saccus* bag, from Gk *sakkos*] > '**sack**ˌ**like** *adj*

sack² (sæk) *n* **1** the plundering of a place by an army or mob **2** *American football* a tackle on a quarterback that brings him or her down before he or she has passed the ball ▷ *vb* (*tr*) **3** to plunder and partially destroy (a place) **4** *American football* to tackle and bring down (a quarterback) before he or she has passed the ball [c16

from F *mettre à sac*, lit.: to put (loot) in a sack, from L *saccus* SACK[1] > **'sacker** *n*
sack[3] (sæk) *n arch except in trademarks* any dry white wine from SW Europe [C16 *wyne seck*, from F *vin sec* dry wine, from L *siccus* dry]
sackbut ('sæk,bʌt) *n* a medieval form of trombone [C16 from F *saqueboute*, from OF *saquer* to pull + *bouter* to push]
sackcloth ('sæk,klɒθ) *n* **1** coarse cloth such as sacking **2** garments made of such cloth, worn formerly to indicate mourning **3** **sackcloth and ashes** a public display of extreme grief
sacking ('sækɪŋ) *n* coarse cloth used for making sacks, woven from flax, hemp, jute, etc
sack race *n* a race in which the competitors' legs and often bodies are enclosed in sacks
Sacks (sæks) *n* **Jonathan** (**Henry**) born 1948, British rabbi; Commonwealth chief rabbi from 1991
Sackville ('sækvɪl) *n* **Thomas,** 1st Earl of Dorset. 1536–1608, English poet, dramatist, and statesman. He collaborated with Thomas Norton on the early blank-verse tragedy *Gorboduc* (1561)
Sackville-West (,sækvɪl 'wɛst) *n* **Victoria** (**Mary**), known as *Vita*. 1892–1962, British writer and gardener, whose works include the novel *The Edwardians* (1930) and the poem *The Land* (1931). She is also noted for the gardens at Sissinghurst Castle, Kent. Married to Harold Nicolson
sacral[1] ('seɪkrəl) *adj* of or associated with sacred rites [C19 from L *sacrum* sacred object]
sacral[2] ('seɪkrəl) *adj* of or relating to the sacrum [C18 from NL *sacrālis* of the SACRUM]
sacrament ('sækrəmənt) *n* **1** an outward sign combined with a prescribed form of words and regarded as conferring grace upon those who receive it. The Protestant sacraments are baptism and the Lord's Supper. In the Roman Catholic and Eastern Churches they are baptism, penance, confirmation, the Eucharist, holy orders, matrimony, and the anointing of the sick (formerly extreme unction) **2** (*often cap*) the Eucharist **3** the consecrated elements of the Eucharist, esp the bread **4** something regarded as possessing a sacred significance **5** a pledge [C12 from Church L *sacrāmentum* vow, from L *sacrāre* to consecrate]
sacramental (,sækrə'mɛntᵊl) *adj* **1** of or having the nature of a sacrament ▷ *n* **2** *RC Church* a sacrament-like ritual action, such as the sign of the cross or the use of holy water > **,sacra'menta,lism** *n* > **sacramentality** (,sækrəmɛn'tælɪtɪ) *n*
Sacramento (,sækrə'mɛntəʊ) *n* **1** an inland port in N central California, capital of the state at the confluence of the American and Sacramento Rivers: became a boom town in the gold rush of the 1850s. Pop: 407 018 (2000) **2** a river in N California, flowing generally south to San Francisco Bay. Length: 615 km (382 miles)
sacrarium (sæ'krɛərɪəm) *n, pl* **sacraria** (-'krɛərɪə) **1** the sanctuary of a church **2** *RC Church* a place near the altar of a church where materials used in the sacred rites are deposited or poured away [C18 from L, from *sacer* sacred]
sacred ('seɪkrɪd) *adj* **1** exclusively devoted to a deity or to some religious ceremony or use **2** worthy of or regarded with reverence and awe **3** connected with or intended for religious use: *sacred music* **4** **sacred to** dedicated to [C14 from L *sacrāre* to set apart as holy, from *sacer* holy] > **'sacredly** *adv* > **'sacredness** *n*
sacred cow *n inf* a person, custom, etc, held to be beyond criticism [alluding to the Hindu belief that cattle are sacred]
sacred mushroom *n* **1** any of various hallucinogenic mushrooms that have been eaten in rituals in various parts of the world **2** a mescal button, used in a similar way
sacred site *n Austral inf* a place of great significance
sacrifice ('sækrɪ,faɪs) *n* **1** a surrender of something of value as a means of gaining something more desirable or of preventing some evil **2** a ritual killing of a person or animal with the intention of propitiating or pleasing a deity **3** a symbolic offering of something to a deity **4** the person, animal, or object killed or offered **5** loss entailed by giving up or selling something at less than its value **6** *chess* the act or an instance of sacrificing a piece ▷ *vb* **sacrifices, sacrificing, sacrificed** **7** to make a sacrifice (of) **8** *chess* to permit or force one's opponent to capture a piece freely, as in playing a gambit: *he sacrificed his queen and checkmated his opponent on the next move* [C13 via OF from L *sacrificium*, from *sacer* holy + *facere* to make] > **'sacri,ficer** *n*
sacrificial (,sækrɪ'fɪʃəl) *adj* used in or connected with a sacrifice > **,sacri'ficially** *adv*
sacrilege ('sækrɪlɪdʒ) *n* **1** the misuse or desecration of anything regarded as sacred or as worthy of extreme respect **2** the act or an instance of taking anything sacred for secular use [C13 from OF, from L, from *sacrilegus* temple-robber, from *sacra* sacred things + *legere* to take] > **sacrilegist** (,sækrɪ'liːdʒɪst) *n*
sacrilegious (,sækrɪ'lɪdʒəs) *adj* **1** of, relating to, or involving sacrilege **2** guilty of sacrilege > **,sacri'legiously** *adv*
sacring bell ('seɪkrɪŋ) *n chiefly RC Church* a small bell rung at the elevation of the Host and chalice during Mass
sacristan ('sækrɪstən) *or* **sacrist** ('sækrɪst, 'seɪ-) *n* **1** a person who has charge of the contents of a church **2** a less common word for **sexton** [C14 from Med. L *sacristānus*, ult. from L *sacer* holy]
sacristy ('sækrɪstɪ) *n, pl* **sacristies** a room attached to a church or chapel where the sacred vessels, vestments, etc, are kept [C17 from Med. L *sacristia*; see SACRISTAN]
sacroiliac (,seɪkrəʊ'ɪlɪ,æk) *anat* ▷ *adj* **1** of or relating to the sacrum and ilium or their articulation ▷ *n* **2** the joint where these bones meet
sacrosanct ('sækrəʊ,sæŋkt) *adj* very sacred or holy [C17 from L *sacrōsanctus* made holy by sacred rite, from *sacer* holy + *sanctus*, from *sancīre* to hallow] > **,sacro'sanctity** *n*
sacrum ('seɪkrəm) *n, pl* **sacra** (-krə) the large wedge-shaped bone, consisting of five fused vertebrae, in the lower part of the back [C18 from L *os sacrum* holy bone, because it was used in sacrifices, from *sacer* holy]
sad (sæd) *adj* **sadder, saddest** **1** feeling sorrow; unhappy **2** causing, suggestive, or expressive of such feelings: *a sad story* **3** unfortunate; shabby: *her clothes were in a sad state* **4** *Brit inf* ludicrously contemptible; pathetic: *a sad, boring little wimp* [OE *sæd* weary] > **'sadly** *adv* > **'sadness** *n*
SAD *abbrev for* **seasonal affective disorder**
Sadat (sə'dæt) *n* (**Mohammed**) **Anwar El** ('ænwɑː ɛl) 1918–81, Egyptian statesman: president of Egypt (1970–81); assassinated; Nobel peace prize jointly with Begin 1978
sadden ('sædᵊn) *vb* to make or become sad
saddle ('sædᵊl) *n* **1** a seat for a rider, usually made of leather, placed on a horse's back and secured with a girth under the belly **2** a similar seat on a bicycle, tractor, etc **3** a back pad forming part of the harness of a packhorse **4** anything that resembles a saddle in shape, position, or function **5** a cut of meat, esp mutton, consisting of both loins **6** the part of a horse or similar animal on which a saddle is placed **7** the part of the back of a domestic chicken that is nearest to the tail **8** another word for **col** (sense 1) **9** **in the saddle** in a position of control ▷ *vb* **saddles, saddling, saddled** **10** (sometimes foll by *up*) to put a saddle on (a horse) **11** (*intr*) to mount into the saddle **12** (*tr*) to burden: *I didn't ask to be saddled with this job* [OE *sadol, sædel*] > **'saddle-,like** *adj*
saddleback ('sædᵊl,bæk) *n* a marking resembling a saddle on the backs of various animals > **'saddle-,backed** *adj*
saddlebag ('sædᵊl,bæg) *n* a pouch or small bag attached to the saddle of a horse, bicycle, etc

saddlebill ('sædᵊl,bɪl) *n* a large black-and-white stork of tropical Africa, having a heavy red bill with a black band around the middle. Also called: **jabiru**
saddlebow ('sædᵊl,bəʊ) *n* the pommel of a saddle
saddlecloth ('sædᵊl,klɒθ) *n* a light cloth put under a horse's saddle, so as to prevent rubbing
saddle horse *n* a lightweight horse kept for riding only
saddler ('sædlə) *n* a person who makes, deals in, or repairs saddles and other leather equipment for horses
saddle roof *n* a roof that has a ridge and two gables
saddlery ('sædlərɪ) *n, pl* **saddleries** 1 saddles, harness, and other leather equipment for horses collectively 2 the business, work, or place of work of a saddler
saddle soap *n* a soft soap containing neat's-foot oil used to preserve and clean leather
saddletree ('sædᵊl,triː) *n* the frame of a saddle
saddo ('sædəʊ) *n, pl* **saddos, saddoes** *Brit sl* a socially inadequate or pathetic person [c20 from SAD (sense 4) + -O]
Sadducee ('sædjʊ,siː) *n Judaism* a member of an ancient Jewish sect that was opposed to the Pharisees, denying the resurrection of the dead and the validity of oral tradition [OE *saddūcēas*, via L & Gk from LHeb. *ṣāddūqi*, prob. from *Ṣadoq* Zadok, high priest and supposed founder of the sect] > ,**Saddu'cean** *adj*
Sade (sɑːd) *n* Comte **Donatien Alphonse François de** (dɔnasjɛ̃ alfɔ̃s frɑ̃swa də), known as the *Marquis de Sade*. 1740–1814, French soldier and writer, whose exposition of sexual perversion gave rise to the term sadism
sadhu *or* **saddhu** ('sɑːduː) *n* a Hindu wandering holy man [Sansk., from *sādhu* good]
Sadi *or* **Saadi** (sɑː'diː) *n* original name *Sheikh Muslih Addin*. ?1184–1292, Persian poet. His best-known works are *Gulistān* (Flower Garden) and *Būstān* (Tree Garden), long moralistic poems in prose and verse
sadiron ('sæd,aɪən) *n* a heavy iron, pointed at both ends for pressing clothes [c19 from SAD (in the obs. sense: heavy) + IRON]
sadism ('seɪdɪzəm) *n* the gaining of pleasure or sexual gratification from the infliction of pain and mental suffering on another person ▷ Cf **masochism** [c19 from F, after the Marquis de SADE] > '**sadist** *n* > **sadistic** (sə'dɪstɪk) *adj* > **sa'distically** *adv*
Sadler's Wells ('sædləz wɛlz) *n* (*functioning as singular*) a theatre in London. It was renovated in 1931 by Lilian Bayliss and became the home of the Sadler's Wells Opera Company and the Sadler's Wells Ballet (now the Royal Ballet) [named after the medicinal *wells* on the site and its owner Thomas *Sadler*, who founded the original theatre on the site]
▷ www.sadlers-wells.com
sadomasochism (,seɪdəʊ'mæsə,kɪzəm) *n* 1 the combination of sadistic and masochistic elements in one person 2 sexual practice in which one partner adopts a sadistic role and the other a masochistic one > ,**sadomaso'chistic** *adj*
Sadowa ('sɑːdəʊvə) *n* a village in the Czech Republic, in NE Bohemia: scene of the decisive battle of the Austro-Prussian war (1866) in which the Austrians were defeated by the Prussians. Czech name: **Sadová** ('sadɔvaː)
SADS (sædz) *n acronym for* sudden adult death syndrome: the sudden death of an apparently healthy adult, for which no cause can be found at postmortem [late c20 by analogy with SIDS (sudden infant death syndrome)]
s.a.e. *abbrev for* stamped addressed envelope
safari (sə'fɑːrɪ) *n, pl* **safaris** 1 an overland journey or hunting expedition, esp in Africa 2 the people, animals, etc, that go on the expedition [c19 from Swahili: journey, from Ar., from *safara* to travel]
safari park *n* an enclosed park in which lions and other wild animals are kept uncaged in the open and can be viewed by the public from cars, etc
safari suit *n* an outfit made of tough cotton, denim, etc, consisting of a bush jacket with matching trousers, shorts, or skirt
safe (seɪf) *adj* 1 affording security or protection from harm: *a safe place* 2 (*postpositive*) free from danger: *you'll be safe here* 3 secure from risk: *a safe investment* 4 worthy of trust: *a safe companion* 5 tending to avoid controversy or risk: *a safe player* 6 not dangerous: *water safe to drink* 7 **on the safe side** as a precaution ▷ *adv* 8 in a safe condition: *the children are safe in bed now* 9 **play safe** to act in a way least likely to cause danger, controversy, or defeat ▷ *n* 10 a strong container, usually of metal and provided with a secure lock, for storing money or valuables 11 a small cupboard-like container for storing food [c13 from OF *salf*, from L *salvus*] > '**safely** *adv* > '**safeness** *n*
safe-breaker *n* a person who breaks open and robs safes. Also called: **safe-cracker**
safe-conduct *n* 1 a document giving official permission to travel through a region, esp in time of war 2 the protection afforded by such a document
safe-deposit *or* **safety-deposit** *n* a a place with facilities for the safe storage of money b (*as modifier*): *a safe-deposit box*
safeguard ('seɪf,gɑːd) *n* 1 a person or thing that ensures protection against danger, injury, etc 2 a safe-conduct ▷ *vb* 3 (*tr*) to protect
safe house *n* a place used secretly by undercover agents, terrorists, etc, as a refuge
safekeeping ('seɪf'kiːpɪŋ) *n* the act of keeping or state of being kept in safety
safe period *n inf* the period during the menstrual cycle when conception is considered least likely to occur
safe seat *n* a Parliamentary seat that at an election is sure to be held by the same party as held it before
safe sex *n* sexual intercourse using physical protection, such as a condom, or nonpenetrative methods to prevent the spread of such diseases as AIDS
safety ('seɪftɪ) *n, pl* **safeties** 1 the quality of being safe 2 freedom from danger or risk of injury 3 a contrivance designed to prevent injury 4 *American football* Also called: **safetyman** either of two players who defend the area furthest back in the field
safety belt *n* 1 another name for **seat belt** (sense 1) 2 a belt or strap worn by a person working at a great height to prevent him from falling
safety curtain *n* a curtain made of fireproof material that can be lowered to separate the auditorium and stage in a theatre to prevent the spread of a fire
safety factor *n* the ratio of the breaking stress of a material to the calculated maximum stress in use. Also called: **factor of safety**
safety glass *n* glass that if broken will not shatter
Safety Islands *pl n* a group of three small French islands in the Atlantic, off the coast of French Guiana. French name: **Îles du Salut**
safety lamp *n* an oil-burning miner's lamp in which the flame is surrounded by a metal gauze to prevent it from igniting combustible gas
safety match *n* a match that will light only when struck against a specially prepared surface
safety net *n* 1 a net used in a circus to catch high-wire and trapeze artistes if they fall 2 any means of protection from hardship or loss
safety pin *n* a spring wire clasp with a covering catch, made so as to shield the point when closed
safety razor *n* a razor with a guard over the blade or blades to prevent deep cuts
safety touch *n Canadian football* a two-point play
safety valve *n* 1 a valve in a pressure vessel that allows fluid to escape at excess pressure 2 a harmless outlet for emotion, etc
saffian ('sæfɪən) *n* leather tanned with sumach and usually dyed a bright colour [c16 via Russian & Turkish

Ss

from Persian *sakhtiyān* goatskin, from *sakht* hard]

safflower (ˈsæflaʊə) *n* **1** a thistle-like Eurasian annual plant having large heads of orange-yellow flowers and yielding a dye and an oil used in paints, medicines, etc **2** a red dye used for cotton and for colouring foods and cosmetics [c16 via Du. *saffloer* or G *safflor* from OF *saffleur*]

saffron (ˈsæfrən) *n* **1** an Old World crocus having purple or white flowers with orange stigmas **2** the dried stigmas of this plant, used to flavour or colour food **3 meadow saffron** another name for **autumn crocus** **4a** an orange to orange-yellow colour **4b** (*as adj*): *a saffron dress* [c13 from OF *safran*, from Med. L *safranum*, from Ar. *za'farān*]

Safi (*French* safi) *n* a port in W Morocco, 170 km (105 miles) northwest of Marrakech, to which it is the nearest port. Pop: 364 648 (1994)

Safid Rud (sæˈfiːd ˈruːd) *n* a river in N Iran, flowing northeast to a delta on the Caspian Sea. Length: about 785 km (490 miles)

S Afr *abbrev for* South Africa(n)

safranine *or* **safranin** (ˈsæfrənɪn) *n* any of a class of azine dyes used for textiles [c19 from F *safran* SAFFRON + -INE[2]]

sag (sæg) *vb* **sags, sagging, sagged** (*mainly intr*) **1** (*also tr*) to sink or cause to sink in parts, as under weight or pressure: *the bed sags in the middle* **2** to fall in value: *prices sagged to a new low* **3** to hang unevenly **4** (of courage, etc) to weaken ▷ *n* **5** the act or an instance of sagging: *a sag in profits* **6** *naut* the extent to which a vessel's keel sags at the centre [c15 from ON] > **ˈsaggy** *adj*

saga (ˈsɑːgə) *n* **1** any of several medieval prose narratives written in Iceland and recounting the exploits of a hero or a family **2** any similar heroic narrative **3** a series of novels about several generations or members of a family **4** *inf* a series of events or a story stretching over a long period [c18 from ON: a narrative]

sagacious (səˈgeɪʃəs) *adj* having or showing sagacity; wise [c17 from L *sagāx*, from *sāgīre* to be astute] > **saˈgaciously** *adv*

sagacity (səˈgæsɪtɪ) *n* foresight, discernment, or keen perception; ability to make good judgments

sagamore (ˈsægəˌmɔː) *n* (among some North American Indians) a chief or eminent man [c17 from Amerind *sāgimau*, lit.: he overcomes]

Sagan (*French* sagɑ̃) *n* **1 Carl** (**Edward**) 1934–96, US astronomer and writer on scientific subjects; presenter of the television series *Cosmos* (1980) **2 Françoise** (frɑ̃swɑːz), original name *Françoise Quoirez*. born 1935, French writer, best-known for the novels *Bonjour Tristesse* (1954) and *Aimez-vous Brahms?* (1959)

sage[1] (seɪdʒ) *n* **1** a man revered for his profound wisdom ▷ *adj* **2** profoundly wise or prudent [c13 from OF, from L *sapere* to be sensible] > **ˈsagely** *adv* > **ˈsageness** *n*

sage[2] (seɪdʒ) *n* **1** a perennial Mediterranean plant having grey-green leaves and purple, blue, or white flowers **2** the leaves of this plant, used in cooking for flavouring **3** short for **sagebrush** [c14 from OF *saulge*, from L *salvia*, from *salvus* in good health (from its curative properties)]

sagebrush (ˈseɪdʒˌbrʌʃ) *n* any of a genus of aromatic plants of W North America, having silver-green leaves and large clusters of small white flowers

saggar *or* **sagger** (ˈsægə) *n* a clay box in which ceramic wares are placed during firing [c17 ? alteration of SAFEGUARD]

Saghalien (səˈgɑːljən) *n* a variant of **Sakhalin**

sagittal suture (ˈsædʒɪtᵊl) *n* a serrated line on the top of the skull that marks the junction of the two parietal bones

Sagittarius (ˌsædʒɪˈtɛərɪəs) *n*, *Latin genitive* **Sagittarii** (ˌsædʒɪˈtɛərɪˌaɪ) **1** *astron* a S constellation **2** Also called: the **Archer** *astrol* the ninth sign of the zodiac. The sun is in this sign between Nov 22 and Dec 21 [c14 from L: an archer, from *sagitta* an arrow] > **Sagittarian** (ˌsædʒɪˈtɛərɪən) *adj*

sagittate (ˈsædʒɪˌteɪt) *adj* (esp of leaves) shaped like the head of an arrow [c18 from NL *sagittātus*, from L *sagitta* arrow]

sago (ˈseɪgəʊ) *n* a starchy cereal obtained from the powdered pith of a palm (**sago palm**), used for puddings and as a thickening agent [c16 from Malay *sāgū*]

saguaro (səˈgwɑːrəʊ) *n*, *pl* **saguaros** a giant cactus of desert regions of Arizona, S California, and Mexico [Mexican Sp., var. of *sahuaro*, an Indian name]

Saguenay (ˌsægəˈneɪ) *n* a river in SE Canada in S Quebec, rising as the Péribonca River on the central plateau and flowing south, then east to the St Lawrence. Length: 764 km (475 miles)

Sagunto (*Spanish* saˈɣunto) *n* an industrial town in E Spain, near Valencia: allied to Rome and made a heroic resistance to the Carthaginian attack led by Hannibal (219–218 BC). Pop: 57 300 (latest est). Ancient name: **Saguntum** (səˈguːntəm)

Sahara (səˈhɑːrə) *n* a desert in N Africa, extending from the Atlantic to the Red Sea and from the Mediterranean to central Mali, Niger, Chad, and the Sudan: the largest desert in the world, occupying over a quarter of Africa; rises to over 3300 m (11 000 ft) in the central mountain system of the Ahaggar and Tibesti massifs; large reserves of iron ore, oil, and natural gas. Area: 9 100 000 sq km (3 500 000 sq miles). Average annual rainfall: less than 254 mm (10 in). Highest recorded temperature: 58°C (136.4°F) > **Saˈharan** *n*, *adj*

sahib (ˈsɑːhɪb) *n* (in India) a form of address placed after a man's name, used as a mark of respect [c17 from Urdu, from Ar. *çāhib*, lit.: friend]

said[1] (sɛd) *adj* **1** (*prenominal*) (in contracts, etc) aforesaid ▷ *vb* **2** the past tense and past participle of **say**

said[2] (ˈsɑːɪd) *n* a variant of **sayyid**

Saida (ˈsɑːɪdə) *n* a port in SW Lebanon, on the Mediterranean: on the site of ancient Sidon; terminal of the Trans-Arabian pipeline from Saudi Arabia. Pop: 100 000 (1991 est)

saiga (ˈsaɪgə) *n* either of two species of antelope of the plains of central Asia, having a slightly elongated nose [c19 from Russian]

Saigon (saɪˈgɒn) *n* the former name (until 1976) of **Ho Chi Minh City**

sail (seɪl) *n* **1** an area of fabric, usually Terylene or nylon (formerly canvas), with fittings for holding it in any suitable position to catch the wind, used for propelling certain kinds of vessels, esp over water **2** a voyage on such a vessel: *a sail down the river* **3** a vessel with sails or such vessels collectively: *to travel by sail* **4** a ship's sails collectively **5** something resembling a sail in shape, position, or function, such as the part of a windmill that is turned by the wind **6 in sail** having the sail set **7 make sail 7a** to run up the sail or to run up more sail **7b** to begin a voyage **8 set sail 8a** to embark on a voyage by ship **8b** to hoist sail **9 under sail 9a** with sail hoisted **9b** under way ▷ *vb* (*mainly intr*) **10** to travel in a boat or ship: *we sailed to Le Havre* **11** to begin a voyage: *we sail at 5 o'clock* **12** (of a vessel) to move over the water **13** (*tr*) to manoeuvre or navigate a vessel: *he sailed the schooner up the channel* **14** (*tr*) to sail over: *she sailed the Atlantic single-handed* **15** (often foll by *over*, *through*, etc) to move fast or effortlessly: *we sailed through customs* **16** to move along smoothly; glide **17** (often foll by *in* or *into*) *inf* **17a** to begin (something) with vigour **17b** to make an attack (on) violently [OE *segl*] > **ˈsailable** *adj* > **ˈsailless** *adj*
▷ www.sailing.org

sailboard (ˈseɪlˌbɔːd) *n* the craft used for windsurfing, consisting of a moulded board to which a mast bearing a single sail is attached

sailboarding (ˈseɪlˌbɔːdɪŋ) *n* another name for **windsurfing**

sailcloth ('seɪl,klɒθ) *n* **1** any of various fabrics from which sails are made **2** a canvas-like cloth used for clothing, etc

sailer ('seɪlə) *n* a vessel, with specified sailing characteristics: *a good sailer*

sailfish ('seɪl,fɪʃ) *n, pl* **sailfish** *or* **sailfishes** **1** any of several large game fishes of warm and tropical seas. They have an elongated upper jaw and a long sail-like dorsal fin **2** another name for **basking shark**

sailing ship *n* a large sailing vessel

sailor ('seɪlə) *n* **1** any member of a ship's crew, esp one below the rank of officer **2** a person who sails, esp with reference to the likelihood of his becoming seasick: *a good sailor*

sailplane ('seɪl,pleɪn) *n* a high-performance glider

sainfoin ('sænfɔɪn) *n* a Eurasian perennial plant, widely grown as a forage crop, having pale pink flowers and curved pods [c17 from F, from Med. L *sānum faenum* wholesome hay, referring to its former use as a medicine]

Sainsbury ('seɪnzbrɪ) *n* **David John,** Baron. born 1940, British businessman and politician, chief executive of the Sainsbury supermarket chain from 1992; science minister from 1998

saint (seɪnt; *unstressed* sənt) *n* **1** a person who after death is formally recognized by a Christian Church as having attained a specially exalted place in heaven and the right to veneration **2** a person of exceptional holiness **3** *(pl) Bible* the collective body of those who are righteous in God's sight ▷ *vb* **4** *(tr)* to recognize formally as a saint [c12 from OF, from L *sanctus* holy, from *sancīre* to hallow] > **'sainthood** *n* > **'saintlike** *adj*

Saint Agnes' Eve *n, usually abbreviated to* **St Agnes' Eve** the night of Jan 20, when according to tradition a woman can discover the identity of her future husband by performing certain rites

Saint Albans ('ɔːlbənz) *n, usually abbreviated to* **St Albans** a city in SE England, in W Hertfordshire: founded in 948 AD around the Benedictine abbey first built in Saxon times on the site of the martyrdom (about 303 AD) of St Alban; present abbey built in 1077; Roman ruins. Pop: 80 376 (1991). Latin name: **Verulamium**

Saint Andrews *n, usually abbreviated to* **St Andrews** a city in E Scotland, in Fife on the North Sea: the oldest university in Scotland (1411); famous golf links. Pop: 11 136 (1991)

Saint Andrew's Cross *n, usually abbreviated to* **St Andrew's Cross** **1** a diagonal cross with equal arms **2** a white diagonal cross on a blue ground

Saint Anthony's fire *n, usually abbreviated to* **St Anthony's fire** *pathol* another name for **ergotism** or **erysipelas**

Saint Augustine ('ɔːgəs,tiːn) *n, usually abbreviated to* **St Augustine** a resort in NE Florida, on the Intracoastal Waterway: the oldest town in North America (1565); the northernmost outpost of the Spanish colonial empire for over 200 years. Pop: 11 692 (1990)

Saint Austell ('ɔːstəl) *n, usually abbreviated to* **St Austell** a town in SW England, in S Cornwall on **St Austell Bay** (an inlet of the English Channel): centre for the now-declining china clay industry; the Eden Project, a rainforest environment in the world's largest greenhouse, is nearby; administratively part of St Austell with Fowey since 1968. Pop (with Fowey): 21 622 (1991)

Saint Bernard *n, usually abbreviated to* **St Bernard** a large breed of dog with a dense red-and-white coat, formerly used as a rescue dog in mountainous areas

Saint Bernard Pass *n, usually abbreviated to* **St Bernard Pass** either of two passes over the Alps: the **Great St Bernard Pass,** 2472 m (8110 ft) high, east of Mont Blanc between Italy and Switzerland, or the **Little St Bernard Pass,** 2157 m (7077 ft) high, south of Mont Blanc between Italy and France

Saint-Brieuc (*French* sɛ̃briø) *n, usually abbreviated to* **St-Brieuc** a market town in NW France, near the N coast of Brittany. Pop: 47 370 (1990)

Saint Catharines *n, usually abbreviated to* **St Catharines** an industrial city in S central Canada, in S Ontario on the Welland Canal. Pop: 130 926 (1996)

Saint Christopher *n, usually abbreviated to* **St Christopher** another name for **Saint Kitts**

Saint Christopher-Nevis *n, usually abbreviated to* **St Christopher-Nevis** the official name of **Saint Kitts-Nevis**

Saint Clair (klɛə) *n, usually abbreviated to* **St Clair Lake** a lake between SE Michigan and Ontario: linked with Lake Huron by the **St Clair River** and with Lake Erie by the Detroit River. Area: 1191 sq km (460 sq miles)

Saint-Cloud (*French* sɛ̃klu) *n, usually abbreviated to* **St-Cloud** a residential suburb of Paris: former royal palace; Sèvres porcelain factory. Pop: 28 670 (1990)

Saint Croix (krɔɪ) *n, usually abbreviated to* **St Croix** an island in the Caribbean, the largest of the Virgin Islands of the US: purchased by the US in 1917. Chief town: Christiansted. Pop: 53 234 (2000). Area: 207 sq km (80 sq miles). Also called: **Santa Cruz** ('sæntə 'kruːz)

Saint Croix River *n, usually abbreviated to* **St Croix River** a river on the border between the northeast US and SE Canada, flowing from the Chiputneticook Lakes to Passamaquoddy Bay, forming the border between Maine, US, and New Brunswick, Canada. Length: 121 km (75 miles)

Saint David's *n, usually abbreviated to* **St David's** a town in SW Wales, in Pembrokeshire: its cathedral was a place of pilgrimage in medieval times. Pop: 1627 (1991)

Saint-Denis (*French* sɛ̃dni) *n, usually abbreviated to* **St-Denis** **1** a town in N France, on the Seine: 12th-century Gothic abbey church, containing the tombs of many French monarchs; an industrial suburb of Paris. Pop: 89 988 (1990) **2** the capital of the French overseas region of Réunion, a port on the N coast. Pop: 131 557 (1999)

Ss

Sainte-Beuve (*French* sɛ̃tbœv) *n* **Charles Augustin** (ʃarl ogystɛ̃) 1804–69, French critic, best known for his collections of essays *Port Royal* (1840–59) and *Les Causeries du Lundi* (1851–62)

sainted ('seɪntɪd) *adj* **1** canonized **2** like a saint in character or nature **3** hallowed or holy

Sainte Foy (seɪnt 'fɔɪ, sənt) *n, usually abbreviated to* **Ste Foy** a SW suburb of Quebec, on the St Lawrence River. Pop: 71 133 (1991)

Saint Elias Mountains *pl n, usually abbreviated to* **St Elias Mountains** a mountain range between SE Alaska and the SW Yukon, Canada. Highest peak: Mount Logan, 6050 m (19 850 ft)

Saint Elmo's fire ('ɛlməʊz) *n, usually abbreviated to* **St Elmo's fire** (not in technical usage) a luminous region that sometimes appears around church spires, the masts of ships, etc

Saint-Étienne (*French* sɛ̃tetjɛn) *n, usually abbreviated to* **St-Étienne** a town in E central France: a major producer of textiles and armaments. Pop: 179 755 (1999)

Saint-Exupéry (*French* sɛ̃tɛgzyperi) *n* **Antoine de** (ɑ̃twan də) 1900–44, French novelist and aviator. His novels of aviation include *Vol de nuit* (1931) and *Terre des hommes* (1939). He also wrote the fairy tale *Le Petit Prince* (1943)

Saint Gall (*French* sɛ̃ gal) *n, usually abbreviated to* **St Gall** **1** a canton of NE Switzerland. Capital: St Gall. Pop: 447 600 (2000 est). Area: 2012 sq km (777 sq miles) **2** a town in NE Switzerland, capital of St Gall canton: an important educational centre in the Middle Ages. Pop: 75 541 (1994). German name: **Sankt Gallen** (zaŋkt 'galən)

Saint George's *n, usually abbreviated to* **St George's** the capital of Grenada, a port in the southwest. Pop: 4621 (1991)

Saint George's Channel *n, usually abbreviated to* **St George's Channel** a strait between Wales and Ireland, linking the Irish Sea with the Atlantic. Length: about

160 km (100 miles). Width: up to 145 km (90 miles)

Saint Gotthard ('gɒtəd) *n, usually abbreviated to* **St Gotthard** **1** a range of the Lepontine Alps in SE central Switzerland **2** a pass over the St Gotthard mountains, in S Switzerland. Height: 2114 m (6935 ft)

Saint Helena (ˌsɛntɪ'li:nə) *n, usually abbreviated to* **St Helena** a volcanic island in the SE Atlantic, forming (with its dependencies Tristan da Cunha and Ascension) a UK Overseas Territory: discovered by the Portuguese in 1502 and annexed by England in 1651; scene of Napoleon's exile and death. Capital: Jamestown. Pop: 5157 (1994 est). Area: 122 sq km (47 sq miles)

Saint Helens *n, usually abbreviated to* **St Helens** **1** a town in NW England, in St Helens unitary authority, Merseyside: glass industry. Pop: 176 845 (2001) **2** a unitary authority in NW England, in Merseyside. Pop: 181 000 (1994 est). Area: 130 sq km (50 sq miles) **3** a volcanic peak in S Washington state; it erupted in 1980 after lying dormant from 1857

Saint Helier ('hɛlɪə) *n, usually abbreviated to* **St Helier** a market town and resort in the Channel Islands, on the S coast of Jersey. Pop: 27 523 (1996)

Saint James's Palace *n, usually abbreviated to* **St James's Palace** a palace in Pall Mall, London: residence of British monarchs from 1697 to 1837

Saint John *n, usually abbreviated to* **St John** **1** a port in E Canada, at the mouth of the St John River: the largest city in New Brunswick. Pop: 90 457 (1991) **2** an island in the Caribbean, in the Virgin Islands of the US Pop: 4197 (2000). Area: 49 sq km (19 sq miles) **3** **Lake** a lake in Canada, in S Quebec: drained by the Saguenay River. Area: 971 sq km (375 sq miles) **4** a river in E North America, rising in Maine, US, and flowing northeast to New Brunswick, Canada, then generally southeast to the Bay of Fundy. Length: 673 km (418 miles)

Saint-John Perse ('sɪndʒən 'pɜ:s) *n* See (Saint-John) **Perse**

Saint John's *n, usually abbreviated to* **St John's** **1** a port in Canada, capital of Newfoundland, on the E coast of the Avalon Peninsula. Pop: 101 936 (1996) **2** the capital of Antigua and Barbuda: a port on the NW coast of the island of Antigua. Pop: 21 514 (1991)
 ▹ www.antigua-barbuda.org/Agjohn01.htm

Saint John's wort *n, usually abbreviated to* **St John's wort** **1** any of various shrubs or perennial herbaceous plants of a genus having yellow flowers **2** a herbal remedy made from a species of this plant, used to treat mild depression ▹ See also **hypericum**

Saint-Just (*French* sɛ̃ʒyst) *n* **Louis Antoine Léon de** (lwi ɑ̃twan leɔ̃ də) 1767–94, French Revolutionary leader and orator. A member of the Committee of Public Safety (1793–94), he was guillotined with Robespierre

Saint Kilda ('kɪldə) *n, usually abbreviated to* **St Kilda** **1** a group of volcanic islands in the Atlantic, in the Outer Hebrides: uninhabited since 1930; bird sanctuary **2** Also called: **Hirta** the main island of this group

Saint Kitts (kɪts) *n, usually abbreviated to* **St Kitts** an island in the E Caribbean, in the Leeward Islands: part of the state of St Kitts-Nevis. Capital: Basseterre. Pop: 35 340 (1995 est). Area: 168 sq km (65 sq miles). Also called: **Saint Christopher**

Saint Kitts-Nevis *n, usually abbreviated to* **St Kitts-Nevis** an independent state in the E Caribbean; comprises the two islands of St Kitts and Nevis: with the island of Anguilla formed a colony (1882–1967) and a British associated state (1967–83); Anguilla formally separated from the group in 1983; gained full independence in 1983 as a member of the Commonwealth. Official language: English. Religion: Protestant majority. Currency: E Caribbean dollar. Capital: Basseterre. Pop: 42 300 (1998 est). Area: 262 sq km (101 sq miles)
 ▹ www.stkittsnevis.net
 ▹ www.stkitts-tourism.com
 ▹ http://web.idirect.com/~stkitts

Saint Laurent (*French* sɛ̃ lɔrɑ̃) *n, usually abbreviated to* **St Laurent** a W suburb of Montreal, Canada. Pop: 72 402 (1991)

Saint-Laurent (*French* sɛ̃lɔrɑ̃) *n* **Yves** (iv), full name *Yves-Mathieu*. born 1936, French couturier: popularized trousers for women for all occasions

Saint Lawrence *n, usually abbreviated to* **St Lawrence** **1** a river in SE Canada, flowing northeast from Lake Ontario, forming part of the border between Canada and the US, to the Gulf of St Lawrence: commercially one of the most important rivers in the world as the easternmost link of the St Lawrence Seaway. Length: 1207 km (750 miles). Width at mouth: 145 km (90 miles) **2** **Gulf of** a deep arm of the Atlantic off the E coast of Canada between Newfoundland and the mainland coasts of Quebec, New Brunswick, and Nova Scotia

Saint Lawrence Seaway *n, usually abbreviated to* **St Lawrence Seaway** an inland waterway of North America, passing through the Great Lakes, the St Lawrence River, and connecting canals and locks: one of the most important waterways in the world. Length: 3993 km (2480 miles)

Saint Leger ('lɛdʒə) *n, usually abbreviated to* **St Leger the** an annual horse race run at Doncaster, England, since 1776

Saint Leonard ('lɛnəd) *n, usually abbreviated to* **St Leonard** a N suburb of Montreal, Canada. Pop: 82 200 (latest est)

Saint-Lô (*French* sɛ̃lo) *n, usually abbreviated to* **St-Lô** a market town in NW France: a Calvinist stronghold in the 16th century. Pop: 22 819 (1990)

Saint Louis ('lʊɪs) *n, usually abbreviated to* **St Louis** a port in E Missouri, on the Mississippi River near its confluence with the Missouri: the largest city in the state; university; major industrial centre. Pop: 348 189 (2000)

Saint-Louis (*French* sɛ̃lwi) *n, usually abbreviated to* **St-Louis** a port in NW Senegal, on an island at the mouth of the Senegal River: the first French settlement in W Africa (1689); capital of Senegal until 1958. Pop: 180 000 (1998 est)

Saint Lucia ('lu:ʃə) *n, usually abbreviated to* **St Lucia** an island state in the Caribbean, in the Windward Islands group of the Lesser Antilles: a volcanic island; gained self-government in 1967 as a British Associated State; attained full independence within the Commonwealth in 1979. Official language: English. Religion: Roman Catholic majority. Currency: E Caribbean dollar. Capital: Castries. Pop: 158 000 (2001 est). Area: 616 sq km (238 sq miles)
 ▹ www.stlucia.gov.lc
 ▹ www.st-lucia.com
 ▹ www.stlucia.org

saintly ('seɪntlɪ) *adj* like, relating to, or suitable for a saint > **'saintlily** *adv* > **'saintliness** *n*

Saint Martin *n, usually abbreviated to* **St Martin** an island in the E Caribbean, in the Leeward Islands: administratively divided since 1648, the north belonging to France (as a dependency of Guadeloupe) and the south belonging to the Netherlands (as part of the Netherlands Antilles); salt industry. Pop: (French) 29 078 (1999); (Dutch) 41 718 (2000 est). Areas: (French) 52 sq km (20 sq miles); (Dutch) 33 sq km (13 sq miles). Dutch name: **Sint Maarten**

Saint-Maur-des-Fossés (*French* sɛ̃mɔrdefose) *n, usually abbreviated to* **St-Maur-des-Fossés** a town in N France, on the River Marne: a residential suburb of SE Paris. Pop: 77 492 (1990)

Saint-Mihiel (*French* sɛ̃mjɛl) *n, usually abbreviated to* **St-Mihiel** a village in NE France, on the River Meuse: site of a battle in World War I, in which the American army launched its first offensive in France

Saint Moritz (mə'rɪts) *n, usually abbreviated to* **St Moritz** a village in E Switzerland, in Graubünden canton in the Upper Engadine, at an altitude of 1856 m (6089 ft):

sports and tourist centre. Pop: 5335 (1990 est)

Saint-Nazaire (*French* sɛ̃nazɛr) *n, usually abbreviated to* **St-Nazaire** a port in NW France, at the mouth of the River Loire: German submarine base in World War II; shipbuilding. Pop: 64 812 (1990)

Saint-Ouen (*French* sɛ̃twɛ̃) *n, usually abbreviated to* **St-Ouen** a town in N France, on the Seine: an industrial suburb of Paris; famous flea market. Pop: 42 611 (1990)

Saint Paul *n, usually abbreviated to* **St Paul** a port in SE Minnesota, capital of the state, at the head of navigation of the Mississippi: now contiguous with Minneapolis (the Twin Cities). Pop: 287 151 (2000)

saintpaulia (sənt'pɔːlɪə) *n* another name for **African violet** [c20 NL, after Baron W. von *Saint Paul*, G soldier (died 1910), who discovered it]

Saint Paul's *n, usually abbreviated to* **St Paul's** a cathedral in central London, built between 1675 and 1710 to replace an earlier cathedral destroyed during the Great Fire (1666): regarded as Wren's masterpiece

Saint Peter's *n, usually abbreviated to* **St Peter's** the basilica of the Vatican City, built between 1506 and 1615 to replace an earlier church: the largest church in the world, 188 m (615 ft) long, and chief pilgrimage centre of Europe; designed by many architects, notably Bramante, Raphael, Sangallo, Michelangelo, and Bernini

Saint Petersburg ('piːtəz,bɜːg) *n, usually abbreviated to* **St Petersburg** **1** a city and port in Russia, on the Gulf of Finland at the mouth of the Neva River: founded by Peter the Great in 1703 and built on low-lying marshes subject to frequent flooding; capital of Russia from 1712 to 1918; a cultural and educational centre, with a university (1819); a major industrial centre, with engineering, shipbuilding, chemical, textile, and printing industries. Pop: 4 169 400 (1999 est). Former names: **Petrograd** (1914–24), **Leningrad** (1924–91) **2** a city and resort in W Florida, on Tampa Bay. Pop: 235 988 (1996 est)

Saint Pierre (*French* sɛ̃ pjɛr) *n, usually abbreviated to* **St Pierre** a former town on the coast of the French island of Martinique, destroyed by the eruption of Mont Pelée in 1902

Saint Pierre and Miquelon (,mɪkə'lɒn; *French* miklɔ̃) *n, usually abbreviated to* **St Pierre and Miquelon** an archipelago in the Atlantic, off the S coast of Newfoundland: an overseas department of France, the only remaining French possession in North America; consists of the islands of St Pierre, with most of the population, and Miquelon, about ten times as large; fishing industries. Capital: St Pierre. Pop: 6392 (1990). Area: 242 sq km (94 sq miles)

Saint Pölten ('pɜːltən) *n* See **Sankt Pölten**

Saint-Quentin (*French* sɛ̃kɑ̃tɛ̃) *n, usually abbreviated to* **St-Quentin** a town in N France, on the River Somme: textile industry. Pop: 62 085 (1990)

Saint-Saëns (*French* sɛ̃sɑ̃s) *n* (**Charles**) **Camille** (kamij) 1835–1921, French composer, pianist, and organist. His works include the symphonic poem *Danse Macabre* (1874), the opera *Samson and Delilah* (1877), the humorous orchestral suite *Carnival of Animals* (1886), five symphonies, and five piano concertos

saint's day *n Christianity* a day in the church calendar commemorating a saint

Saint-Simon (*French* sɛ̃simɔ̃) *n* **1** **Comte de** (kɔ̃t də), title of *Claude Henri de Rouvroy*. 1760–1825, French social philosopher, generally regarded as the founder of French socialism. Among his arguments were that society should be reorganized along industrial lines and that scientists should be the new spiritual leaders. His most important work is *Nouveau Christianisme* (1825) **2** **Duc de** (dyk də), title of *Louis de Rouvroy*. 1675–1755, French soldier, statesman, and writer: his *Mémoires* are an outstanding account of the period 1694–1723, during the reigns of Louis XIV and Louis XV

Saint Thomas *n, usually abbreviated to* **St Thomas** **1** an island in the E Caribbean, in the Virgin Islands of the US Capital: Charlotte Amalie. Pop: 51 181 (2000). Area: 83 sq km (28 sq miles) **2** the former name (1921–37) of **Charlotte Amalie**

Saint Vincent *n, usually abbreviated to* **St Vincent** **1** **Cape** a headland at the SW extremity of Portugal: scene of several important naval battles, notably in 1797, when the British defeated the French and Spanish **2** **Gulf** a shallow inlet of SE South Australia, to the east of the Yorke Peninsula: salt industry

Saint Vincent and the Grenadines *n, usually abbreviated to* **St Vincent and the Grenadines** an island state in the Caribbean, in the Windward Islands of the Lesser Antilles: comprises the island of St Vincent and the Northern Grenadines; formerly a British associated state (1969–79); gained full independence in 1979 as a member of the Commonwealth. Official language: English. Religion: Protestant majority. Currency: Caribbean dollar. Capital: Kingstown. Pop: 113 000 (2001 est). Area: 389 sq km (150 sq miles)
▷ www.svgtourism.com
▷ www.ualberta.ca/~amitchel/stvg.html

Saint Vitus's dance ('vaɪtəsɪz) *n, usually abbreviated to* **St Vitus's dance** *pathol* a nontechnical name for **Sydenham's chorea**

Saipan (saɪ'pæn) *n* an island in the W Pacific, administrative centre of the US associated territory of the Northern Mariana Islands; captured by the Americans and used as an air base until the end of World War II. Pop: 62 392 (2000). Area: 180 sq km (70 sq miles)

Saïs ('seɪɪs) *n* (in ancient Egypt) a city in the W Nile delta; the royal capital of the 24th dynasty (about 730–715 BC) and the 26th dynasty (about 664–525 BC) > **Saite** ('seɪaɪt) *n* > **Saitic** (seɪ'ɪtɪk) *adj*

saith (sɛθ) *vb* (used with *he, she,* or *it*) *arch* a form of the present tense of **say**

saithe (seɪθ) *n Brit* another name for **coalfish** [c19 from ON]

Sakai (sɑː'kaɪ) *n* a port in S Japan, on S Honshu on Osaka Bay: an industrial satellite of Osaka. Pop: 802 965 (1995)

sake[1] (seɪk) *n* **1** benefit or interest (esp in **for** (**someone's** *or* **one's own**) **sake**) **2** the purpose of obtaining or achieving (esp in **for the sake of** (**something**)) **3** used in various exclamations of impatience, urgency, etc: *for heaven's sake* [c13 (in the phrase *for the sake of*, prob. from legal usage): from OE *sacu* lawsuit (hence, a cause)]

sake[2], **saké,** *or* **saki** ('sækɪ) *n* a Japanese alcoholic drink made from fermented rice [c17 from Japanese]

saker ('seɪkə) *n* a large falcon of E Europe and Asia [c14 *sagre*, from OF *sacre*, from Ar. *saqr*]

Sakhalin (*Russian* səxa'lin) *or* **Saghalien** *n* an island in the Sea of Okhotsk, off the SE coast of Russia north of Japan: fishing, forestry, and mineral resources (coal and petroleum). Capital: Yuzhno-Sakhalinsk. Pop: 598 000 (2000 est). Area: 76 000 sq km (29 300 sq miles). Japanese name (1905–24): **Karafuto**

Sakha Republic (*Russian* 'saxa) *n* an administrative division in E Russia, in NE Siberia on the Arctic Ocean: the coldest inhabited region of the world; it has rich mineral resources. Capital: Yakutsk. Pop: 977 000 (2000 est). Area: 3 103 200 sq km (1 197 760 sq miles). Former names: **Yakut Republic, Yakutia**

Sakharov (*Russian* za'xarəf) *n* **Andrei** (an'drjej) 1921–89, Soviet physicist and human-rights campaigner: Nobel peace prize 1975

saki ('sɑːkɪ) *n* **1** any of several small mostly arboreal New World monkeys having a long bushy tail **2** another name for **sake**[2] [sense 1: c20 F, from Tupi *saqi*]

Saki ('sɑːkɪ) *n* pen name of (Hector Hugh) **Munro**

sal (sæl) *n* a pharmacological term for **salt** (sense 3) [L]

Ss

salaam (sə'lɑːm) *n* **1** a Muslim salutation consisting of a deep bow with the right palm on the forehead **2** a salutation signifying peace ▷ *vb* **3** to make a salaam (to) [C17 from Ar. *salām* peace, from *assalām 'alaikum* peace be to you]

salable ('seɪləbᵊl) *adj* the US spelling of **saleable**

salacious (sə'leɪʃəs) *adj* **1** having an excessive interest in sex **2** (of books, etc) erotic, bawdy, or lewd [C17 from L *salax* fond of leaping, from *salīre* to leap] > **sa'laciously** *adv* > **sa'laciousness** *or* **salacity** (sə'læsɪtɪ) *n*

salad ('sæləd) *n* **1** a dish of raw vegetables, such as lettuce, tomatoes, etc, served as a separate course with cold meat, eggs, etc, or as part of a main course **2** any dish of cold vegetables or fruit served with a dressing: *potato salad* **3** any green vegetable or herb used in such a dish [C15 from OF *salade*, from OProvençal *salada*, from *salar* to season with salt, from L *sal* salt]

salad days *pl n* a period of youth and inexperience

salad dressing *n* a sauce for salad, such as oil and vinegar or mayonnaise

salade niçoise (sæ'lɑːd niː'swɑːz) *n* a cold dish consisting of a variety of ingredients, usually including hard-boiled eggs, anchovy fillets, olives, tomatoes, and sometimes tuna fish [C20 from F, lit.: salad of or from NICE]

Saladin ('sælədɪn) *n* Arabic name *Salah-ed-Din Yusuf ibn-Ayyub*. ?1137–93, sultan of Egypt and Syria and opponent of the Crusaders. He defeated the Christians near Tiberias (1187) and captured Acre, Jerusalem, and Ashkelon. He fought against Richard I of England and Philip II of France during the Third Crusade (1189–92)

Salado (*Spanish* sa'laðo) *n* **1** a river in N Argentina, rising in the Andes as the Juramento and flowing southeast to the Paraná River. Length: 2012 km (1250 miles) **2** a river in W Argentina, rising near the Chilean border as the Desaguadero and flowing south to the Colorado River. Length: about 1365 km (850 miles)

Salamanca (*Spanish* sala'maŋka) *n* a city in W Spain: a leading cultural centre of Europe till the end of the 16th century; market town. Pop: 158 457 (1998 est)

salamander ('sælə,mændə) *n* **1** any of various amphibians of central and S Europe. They have an elongated body, and only return to water to breed **2** *chiefly US & Canad* any amphibian with a tail, as the newt **3** a mythical reptilian creature supposed to live in fire **4** an elemental fire-inhabiting being [C14 from OF *salamandre*, from L *salamandra*, from Gk]

Salambria (sə'læmbrɪə, ,sɑːlɑːm'brɪə) *n* a river in N Greece, in Thessaly, rising in the Pindus Mountains and flowing southeast and east to the Gulf of Salonika. Length: about 200 km (125 miles). Ancient name: **Peneus** Modern Greek name: **Piniós**

salami (sə'lɑːmɪ) *n* a highly seasoned type of sausage, usually flavoured with garlic [C19 from It., pl of *salame*, from Vulgar L *salāre* (unattested) to salt, from L *sal* salt]

Salamis ('sæləmɪs) *n* an island in the Saronic Gulf, Greece: scene of the naval battle in 480 BC, in which the Greeks defeated the Persians. Pop: 20 000 (latest est). Area: 95 sq km (37 sq miles)

sal ammoniac *n* another name for **ammonium chloride**

salaried ('sælərɪd) *adj* earning or yielding a salary: *a salaried worker; salaried employment*

salary ('sælərɪ) *n, pl* **salaries** **1** a fixed payment made by an employer, often monthly, for professional or office work ▷ Cf **wage** ▷ *vb* **salaries, salarying, salaried** **2** (*tr*) to pay a salary to [C14 from Anglo-Norman *salarie*, from L *salārium* the sum given to Roman soldiers to buy salt, from *sal* salt]

Salazar (*Portuguese* sələ'zar) *n* **Antonio de Oliveira** (ən'tɔnju 'də: oli'vəirə) 1889–1970, Portuguese statesman; dictator (1932–68)

salchow ('sælkəʊ) *n figure skating* a jump from the inner backward edge of one foot with one, two, or three full turns in the air, returning to the outer backward edge of the opposite foot [C20 after Ulrich *Salchow* (1877–1949), Swedish figure skater, who originated it]

Salduba (sæl'duːbə, 'sældəbə) *n* the pre-Roman name for **Zaragoza**

sale (seɪl) *n* **1** the exchange of goods, property, or services for an agreed sum of money or credit **2** the amount sold **3** the opportunity to sell: *there was no sale for luxuries* **4a** an event at which goods are sold at reduced prices, usually to clear old stocks **4b** (*as modifier*): *sale bargains* **5** an auction [OE *sala*, from ON *sala*]

Sale (seɪl) *n* **1** a town in NW England, in Trafford unitary authority, Greater Manchester: a residential suburb of Manchester. Pop: 57 824 (1991) **2** a city in SE Australia, in SE Victoria: centre of an agricultural region. Pop: 13 858 (1991)

Salé (*French* sale) *n* a port in NW Morocco, on the Atlantic adjoining Rabat. Pop: 504 420 (1994)

saleable *or US* **salable** ('seɪləbᵊl) *adj* fit for selling or capable of being sold > **,salea'bility** *or US* **,sala'bility** *n*

Salem ('seɪləm) *n* **1** a city in S India, in Tamil Nadu: textile industries. Pop: 366 712 (1991) **2** a city in NE Massachusetts, on the Atlantic: scene of the execution of 19 people after the witch hunts of 1692. Pop: 38 091 (1990) **3** a city in the NW USA, the state capital of Oregon: food-processing. Pop: 136 924 (2000) **4** an Old Testament name for **Jerusalem** (Genesis 14:18; Psalms 76:2)

sale of work *n* a sale of articles, often handmade, the proceeds of which benefit a charity or charities

sale or return *n* an arrangement by which a retailer pays only for goods sold, returning those that are unsold

Salerno (*Italian* sa'lɛrno) *n* a port in SW Italy, in Campania on the **Gulf of Salerno**: first medical school of medieval Europe. Pop: 142 055 (2000 est)

saleroom ('seɪl,ruːm, -,rʊm) *n chiefly Brit* a room where objects are displayed for sale, esp by auction

salesclerk ('seɪlz,klɜːk) *n US & Canad* a shop assistant

salesman ('seɪlzmən) *n, pl* **salesmen** **1** Also called: **saleswoman** (*fem*), **salesgirl** (*fem*), *or* **salesperson** a person who sells merchandise or services in a shop **2** short for **travelling salesman**

salesmanship ('seɪlzmənʃɪp) *n* **1** the technique of, skill, or ability in selling **2** the work of a salesman

sales pitch *or* **talk** *n* an argument or other persuasion used in selling

sales resistance *n* opposition of potential customers to selling, esp aggressive selling

sales tax *n* a tax levied on retail sales receipts and added to selling prices by retailers

sales trader *n stock exchange* a person employed by a market maker, or his or her firm, to find clients

Salford ('sɔːlfəd, 'sɒl-) *n* **1** a city in NW England in Salford unitary authority, Greater Manchester, on the Manchester Ship Canal: a major centre of the cotton industry in the 19th century; extensive dock area, now redeveloped, includes the Lowry arts centre; university (1967). Pop: 79 755 (1991) **2** a unitary authority in NW England, in Greater Manchester. Pop: 216 119 (2001). Area: 97 sq km (37 sq miles)

Salian ('seɪlɪən) *adj* **1** denoting or relating to a group of Franks (the **Salii**) who settled in the Netherlands in the 4th century AD ▷ *n* **2** a member of this group

salicin ('sælɪsɪn) *n* a crystalline water-soluble glucoside obtained from the bark of poplar trees and used as a medical analgesic [C19 from F, from L *salix* willow]

Salic law ('sælɪk) *n history* **1** the code of laws of the Salian Franks and other Germanic tribes **2** a law excluding women from succession to the throne in certain countries, such as France

salicylate (sə'lɪsɪ,leɪt) *n* any salt or ester of salicylic acid

salicylic acid (,sælɪ'sɪlɪk) *n* a white crystalline substance with a sweet taste and bitter aftertaste, used in the manufacture of aspirin, and as a fungicide [C19 *salicyl* (from F, from L *salix* a willow + -YL) + -IC]

salient ('seɪlɪənt) *adj* 1 conspicuous or striking: *a salient feature* 2 projecting outwards at an angle of less than 180° 3 (esp of animals) leaping ▷ *n* 4 *mil* a projection of the forward line into enemy-held territory 5 a salient angle [C16 from L *salīre* to leap] > **'salience** *or* **'saliency** *n* > **'saliently** *adv*

salientian (ˌseɪlɪ'ɛnʃɪən) *n* 1 any of an order of vertebrates with no tail and long hind legs adapted for hopping, as the frog or the toad ▷ *adj* 2 of or belonging to this order [C19 from NL *Salientia*, lit.: leapers, from L *salīre* to leap]

Salieri (*Italian* ˌsal'jeri) *n* **Antonio** (an'tonjo) 1750–1825, Italian composer and conductor, who worked in Vienna (from 1766). The suggestion that he poisoned Mozart has no foundation

salina (sə'laɪnə) *n* a salt marsh or lake [C17 from Sp., from Med. L: salt pit, from LL *salīnus* SALINE]

saline ('seɪlaɪn) *adj* 1 of, consisting of, or containing common salt: *a saline taste* 2 *med* of or relating to a saline 3 of, consisting of, or containing any chemical salt, esp sodium chloride ▷ *n* 4 *med* a solution of sodium chloride in water [C15 from LL *salīnus*, from L *sal* salt] > **salinity** (sə'lɪnɪtɪ) *n*

Salinger ('sælɪndʒə) *n* **J(erome) D(avid)** born 1919, US writer, noted particularly for his novel of adolescence *The Catcher in the Rye* (1951) His first novel for 34 years, *Hapworth 16, 1924* was published in 1997

salinometer (ˌsælɪ'nɒmɪtə) *n* a hydrometer for determining the amount of salt in a solution > ˌ**sali'nometry** *n*

Salisbury[1] ('sɔːlzbərɪ, -brɪ) *n* 1 the former name (until 1982) of **Harare** 2 a city in S Australia: an industrial suburb of N Adelaide. Pop: 112 344 (1998 est) 3 a city in S England, in SE Wiltshire: nearby Old Sarum was the site of an Early Iron Age hill fort; its cathedral (1220–58) has the highest spire in England. Pop: 39 268 (1991). Ancient name: **Sarum** Official name: **New Sarum**

Salisbury[2] ('sɔːlzbərɪ, -brɪ) *n* **Robert Gascoyne Cecil** ('gæskɔɪn), 3rd Marquess of Salisbury 1830–1903, British statesman; Conservative prime minister (1885–86; 1886–92; 1895–1902). His greatest interest was in foreign and imperial affairs

Salisbury Plain *n* an open chalk plateau in S England, in Wiltshire: site of Stonehenge; military training area. Average height: 120 m (400 ft)

saliva (sə'laɪvə) *n* the secretion of salivary glands, consisting of a clear usually slightly acid aqueous fluid of variable composition [C17 from L, from ?] > **salivary** (sə'laɪvərɪ) *adj*

salivary gland *n* any of the glands in mammals that secrete saliva

salivate ('sælɪˌveɪt) *vb* **salivates, salivating, salivated** 1 (*intr*) to secrete saliva, esp an excessive amount 2 (*tr*) to cause (an animal, etc) to produce saliva, as by the administration of mercury > ˌ**sali'vation** *n*

Salk (sɔːlk) *n* **Jonas Edward** 1914–95, US virologist: developed an injected vaccine against poliomyelitis (1954)

sallee *or* **sally** ('sælɪ) *n Austral* 1 a SE Australian eucalyptus tree with pale grey bark 2 any of various acacia trees [prob. from Abor.]

sallow[1] ('sæləʊ) *adj* 1 (esp of human skin) of an unhealthy pale or yellowish colour ▷ *vb* 2 (*tr*) to make sallow [OE *salu*] > **'sallowish** *adj* > **'sallowness** *n*

sallow[2] ('sæləʊ) *n* 1 any of several small willow trees, esp the common sallow, which has large catkins that appear before the leaves 2 a twig or the wood of any of these trees [OE *sealh*] > **'sallowy** *adj*

Sallust ('sæləst) *n* full name *Gaius Sallustius Crispus*. 86–?34 BC, Roman historian and statesman, noted for his histories of the Catiline conspiracy and the Roman war against the Numidian king Jugurtha

sally ('sælɪ) *n, pl* **sallies** 1 a sudden sortie, esp by troops 2 a sudden outburst or emergence into action or expression 3 an excursion 4 a jocular retort ▷ *vb* **sallies, sallying, sallied** (*intr*) 5 to make a sudden violent sortie 6 (often foll by *forth*) to go out on an expedition, etc 7 to come or set out in an energetic manner 8 to rush out suddenly [C16 from OF *saillie*, from *saillir* to dash forwards, from L *salīre* to leap]

Sally Lunn (lʌn) *n* a flat round cake made from a sweet yeast dough [C19 said to be after an 18th-century E baker who invented it]

salmagundi (ˌsælmə'gʌndɪ) *n* 1 a mixed salad dish of cooked meats, eggs, beetroot, etc, popular in 18th-century England 2 a miscellany [C17 from F *salmigondis*, ?from It. *salami conditi* pickled salami]

salmon ('sæmən) *n, pl* **salmons** *or* **salmon** 1 a soft-finned fish of the Atlantic and the Pacific, which is an important food fish. Salmon occur in cold and temperate waters and many species migrate to fresh water to spawn 2 *Austral* any of several unrelated fish [C13 from OF *saumon*, from L *salmō*] > **'salmoˌnoid** *adj*

salmonella (ˌsælmə'nɛlə) *n, pl* **salmonellae** (-ˌliː) any of a genus of rod-shaped aerobic bacteria including many species which cause food poisoning [C19 NL, after Daniel E. *Salmon* (1850–1914), US veterinary surgeon]

salmon ladder *n* a series of steps designed to enable salmon to move upstream to their breeding grounds

Salome (sə'ləʊmɪ) *n New Testament* the daughter of Herodias, at whose instigation she beguiled Herod by her seductive dancing into giving her the head of John the Baptist

salon ('sælɒn) *n* 1 a room in a large house in which guests are received 2 an assembly of guests in a fashionable household, esp a gathering of major literary, artistic, and political figures 3 a commercial establishment in which hairdressers, etc, carry on their businesses 4a a hall for exhibiting works of art 4b such an exhibition, esp one showing the work of living artists [C18 from F, from It. *salone*, augmented form of *sala* hall, of Gmc origin]

Salonika *or* **Salonica** (sə'lɒnɪkə) *n* the English name for **Thessaloníki**

saloon (sə'luːn) *n* 1 Also called: **saloon bar** *Brit* another word for **lounge** (sense 5) 2 a large public room on a passenger ship 3 any large public room used for a purpose: *a dancing saloon* 4 *chiefly US & Canad* a place where alcoholic drink is sold and consumed 5 a closed two-door or four-door car with four to six seats. US, Canad, and NZ name: **sedan** [C18 from F SALON]

Salop ('sæləp) *n* a former name (1974–80) of **Shropshire** > **Salopian** (sə'ləʊpjən) *n, adj*

salopettes (ˌsælə'pɛts) *pl n* a garment worn for skiing, consisting of quilted trousers held up by shoulder straps [C20 from F]

salpiglossis (ˌsælpɪ'glɒsɪs) *n* any of a genus of plants, some species of which are cultivated for their bright funnel-shaped flowers [C19 NL, from Gk *salpinx* trumpet + *glōssa* tongue]

salpingitis (ˌsælpɪn'dʒaɪtɪs) *n* inflammation of a Fallopian tube [C19 from SALPINX -ITIS]

salpinx ('sælpɪŋks) *n, pl* **salpinges** (sæl'pɪndʒiːz) *anat* another name for **Fallopian tube** or **Eustachian tube** [C19 from Gk: trumpet] > **salpingectomy** (ˌsælpɪn'dʒɛktəmɪ) *n*

salsa ('sælsə) *n* 1 a type of Latin American big-band dance music 2 a dance performed to this 3 *cookery* a spicy Mexican tomato-based sauce [C20 from Sp.: sauce]

▷ www.salsaweb.com

salsify ('sælsɪfɪ) *n, pl* **salsifies** 1 Also called: **oyster plant, vegetable oyster** a Mediterranean plant having grasslike leaves, purple flower heads, and a long white edible taproot 2 the root of this plant, which tastes of

Ss

oysters and is eaten as a vegetable [C17 from F, from It. *sassefrica*, from LL, from L *saxum* rock + *fricāre* to rub]

sal soda *n* the crystalline decahydrate of sodium carbonate, $Na_2CO_3.10H_2O$

salt (sɔːlt) *n* **1** a white powder or colourless crystalline solid, consisting mainly of sodium chloride and used for seasoning and preserving food **2** (*modifier*) preserved in, flooded with, containing, or growing in salt or salty water: *salt pork* **3** *chem* any of a class of crystalline solid compounds that are formed from, or can be regarded as formed from, an acid and a base **4** liveliness or pungency: *his wit added salt to the discussion* **5** dry or laconic wit **6** an experienced sailor **7** short for **saltcellar** **8** **rub salt into someone's wounds** to make someone's pain, shame, etc, even worse **9** **salt of the earth** a person or group of people regarded as the finest of their kind **10** **with a grain** (*or* **pinch**) **of salt** with reservations **11** **worth one's salt** worthy of one's pay ▷ *vb* (*tr*) **12** to season or preserve with salt **13** to scatter salt over (an iced road, etc) to melt the ice **14** to add zest to **15** (often foll by *down* or *away*) to preserve or cure with salt **16** *chem* to treat with salt **17** to give a false appearance of value to, esp to introduce valuable ore fraudulently into (a mine, sample, etc) ▷ *adj* **18** not sour, sweet, or bitter; salty ▷ See also **salt away, salts** [OE *sealt*] > **'salt,like** *adj* > **'saltness** *n*

SALT (sɔːlt) *n acronym for* Strategic Arms Limitation Talks *or* Treaty

Salta (*Spanish* 'salta) *n* a city in NW Argentina: thermal springs. Pop: 457 223 (1999 est)

saltation (sæl'teɪʃən) *n* **1** *biol* an abrupt variation in the appearance of an organism, species, etc **2** *geol* the leaping movement of sand or soil particles carried in water or by the wind **3** a sudden abrupt movement [C17 from L *saltātiō* a dance, from *saltāre* to leap about] > **saltatorial** (ˌsæltə'tɔːrɪəl) *or* **'saltatory** *adj*

salt away *or* (*less commonly*) **down** *vb* (*tr, adv*) to hoard or save (money, valuables, etc)

saltbush ('sɔːltˌbʊʃ) *n* any of certain shrubs that grow in alkaline desert regions

salt cake *n* an impure form of sodium sulphate used in the manufacture of detergents, glass, and ceramic glazes

saltcellar ('sɔːltˌsɛlə) *n* **1** a small container for salt used at the table **2** *Brit inf* either of the two hollows formed above the collarbones [changed (through infl. of cellar) from C15 *salt saler*; *saler* from OF *saliere* container for salt, from L *salārius* belonging to salt, from *sal* salt]

salt dome *or* **plug** *n* a domelike structure of stratified rocks containing a central core of salt

Salteaux *or* **Saulteaux** ('səutəu) *n* a member of a Native Canadian people of Manitoba [from Ojibwa]

salted ('sɔːltɪd) *adj* seasoned, preserved, or treated with salt

salt flat *n* a flat expanse of salt left by the total evaporation of a body of water

saltie ('sɔːltɪ) *n Austral inf* a saltwater crocodile

saltigrade ('sæltɪˌgreɪd) *adj* (of animals) adapted for moving in a series of jumps [C19 from NL *Saltigradae*, name formerly applied to jumping spiders, from L *saltus* a leap + *gradī* to move]

Saltillo (*Spanish* sal'tiʎo) *n* a city in N Mexico, capital of Coahuila state: resort and commercial centre of a mining region. Pop: 560 000 (2000 est)

saltings ('sɔːltɪŋz) *pl n* meadow land or marsh that is periodically flooded by sea water

saltire *or* **saltier** ('sɔːlˌtaɪə) *n heraldry* an ordinary consisting of a diagonal cross on a shield [C14 *sawturoure*, from OF *sauteour* cross-shaped barricade, from *saulter* to jump, from L *saltāre*]

Salt Lake City *n* a city in N central Utah, near the Great Salt Lake at an altitude of 1330 m (4300 ft): state capital; founded in 1847 by the Mormons as world capital of the Mormon Church; University of Utah (1850). Pop: 181 743 (2000)

salt lick *n* **1** a place where wild animals go to lick salt deposits **2** a block of salt given to domestic animals to lick **3** *Austral & NZ* a soluble cake of minerals used to supplement the diet of farm animals

Salto (*Spanish* 'salto) *n* a port in NW Uruguay, on the Uruguay River: Uruguay's second largest city. Pop: 77 400 (latest est)

saltpan ('sɔːltˌpæn) *n* a shallow basin, usually in a desert region, containing salt, gypsum, etc, that was deposited from an evaporated salt lake

saltpetre *or US* **saltpeter** (ˌsɔːlt'piːtə) *n* **1** another name for **potassium nitrate** **2** short for **Chile saltpetre** [C16 from OF *salpetre*, from L *sal petrae* salt of rock]

salt pork *n* pork, esp taken from the back and belly, that has been cured with salt

salts (sɔːlts) *pl n* **1** *med* any of various mineral salts, such as magnesium sulphate, for use as a cathartic **2** short for **smelling salts** **3** **like a dose of salts** *inf* very quickly

saltus ('sæltəs) *n, pl* **saltuses** a break in the continuity of a sequence [L: a leap]

saltwater ('sɔːltˌwɔːtə) *adj* of or inhabiting salt water, esp the sea: *saltwater fishes*

saltworks ('sɔːltˌwɜːks) *n* (*functioning as sing*) a building or factory where salt is produced

saltwort ('sɔːltˌwɜːt) *n* any of various plants, of beaches and salt marshes, having prickly leaves, striped stems, and small green flowers. Also called: **glasswort, kali**

salty ('sɔːltɪ) *adj* **saltier, saltiest** **1** of, tasting of, or containing salt **2** (esp of humour) sharp **3** relating to life at sea > **'saltiness** *n*

salubrious (sə'luːbrɪəs) *adj* conducive or favourable to health [C16 from L, from *salūs* health] > **sa'lubriously** *adv* > **sa'lubrity** *n*

Saluki (sə'luːkɪ) *n* a tall breed of hound with a smooth coat and long fringes on the ears and tail [C19 from Ar. *salūqīy* of Saluq, an ancient Arabian city]

salutary ('sæljʊtərɪ) *adj* **1** promoting or intended to promote an improvement: *a salutary warning* **2** promoting or intended to promote health [C15 from L *salūtāris* wholesome, from *salūs* safety] > **'salutarily** *adv*

salutation (ˌsæljʊ'teɪʃən) *n* **1** an act, phrase, gesture, etc, that serves as a greeting **2** a form of words used as an opening to a speech or letter, such as *Dear Sir* [C14 from L *salūtātiō*, from *salūtāre* to greet; see SALUTE]

salutatory (sə'luːtətərɪ) *adj* of, relating to, or resembling a salutation > **sa'lutatorily** *adv*

salute (sə'luːt) *vb* **salutes, saluting, saluted** **1** (*tr*) to address or welcome with friendly words or gestures of respect, such as bowing **2** (*tr*) to acknowledge with praise: *we salute your gallantry* **3** *mil* to pay formal respect, as by raising the right arm ▷ *n* **4** the act of saluting **5** a formal military gesture of respect [C14 from L *salūtāre* to greet, from *salūs* wellbeing] > **sa'luter** *n*

salvable ('sælvəbᵊl) *adj* capable of or suitable for being saved or salvaged [C17 from LL *salvāre* to save, from *salvus* safe]

Salvador ('sælvəˌdɔː; *Portuguese* salva'dor) *n* a port in E Brazil, capital of Bahia state: founded in 1549 as capital of the Portuguese colony, which it remained until 1763; a major centre of the African slave trade in colonial times. Pop: 2 439 881 (2000). Former name: **Bahia** Official name: **São Salvador da Bahia de Todos os Santos** (sɐ̃u salva'dor 'də: ba'ia 'də: 'toːduʃ uʃ 'sɐntuʃ) > **ˌSalva'dorian** *n, adj*

salvage ('sælvɪdʒ) *n* **1** the act, process, or business of rescuing vessels or their cargoes from loss at sea **2a** the act of saving any goods or property in danger of damage or destruction **2b** (*as modifier*): *a salvage operation* **3** the goods or property so saved **4** compensation paid for the salvage of a vessel or its cargo **5** the proceeds from the sale of salvaged goods ▷ *vb* **salvages, salvaging,**

salvaged (*tr*) 6 to save or rescue (goods or property) from fire, shipwreck, etc 7 to gain (something beneficial) from a failure [c17 from OF, from Med. L *salvāgium*, from *salvāre* to SAVE[1]] > 'salvageable *adj* > 'salvager *n*

salvation (sæl'veɪʃən) *n* **1** the act of preserving or the state of being preserved from harm **2** a person or thing that is the means of preserving from harm **3** *Christianity* deliverance by redemption from the power of sin [c13 from OF, from LL *salvātiō*, from L *salvātus* saved, from *salvāre* to SAVE[1]]

Salvation Army *n* a Christian body founded in 1865 by William Booth and organized on quasi-military lines for evangelism and social work among the poor ▷ http://www1.salvationarmy.org/

salvationist (sæl'veɪʃənɪst) *n* **1** a member of an evangelical sect emphasizing the doctrine of salvation **2** (*often cap*) a member of the Salvation Army

salve (sælv, sɑːv) *n* **1** an ointment for wounds, etc **2** anything that heals or soothes ▷ *vb* **salves, salving, salved** (*tr*) **3** to apply salve to (a wound, etc) **4** to soothe, comfort, or appease [OE *sealf*]

salver ('sælvə) *n* a tray, esp one of silver, on which food, letters, visiting cards, etc, are presented [c17 from F *salve*, from Sp. *salva* tray from which the king's taster sampled food, from L *salvāre* to SAVE[1]]

salvia ('sælvɪə) *n* any of a genus of herbaceous plants or small shrubs, such as the sage, grown for their medicinal or culinary properties or for ornament [c19 from L: SAGE[2]]

salvo ('sælvəʊ) *n, pl* **salvos** *or* **salvoes** **1** a discharge of fire from weapons in unison, esp on a ceremonial occasion **2** concentrated fire from many weapons, as in a naval battle **3** an outburst, as of applause [c17 from It. *salva*, from OF *salve*, from L *salvē!* greetings!, ult. from *salvus* safe]

Salvo ('sælvəʊ) *n, pl* **Salvos** *Austral sl* a member of the Salvation Army

sal volatile (vɒ'lætɪlɪ) *n* a solution of ammonium carbonate in alcohol and aqueous ammonia, used as smelling salts. Also called: **spirits of ammonia** [c17 from NL: volatile salt]

Salween ('sælwiːn) *n* a river in SW Asia, rising in the Tibetan Plateau and flowing east and south through SW China and Myanmar to the Gulf of Martaban. Length: 2400 km (1500 miles)

Salzburg ('sæltsbɜːg; *German* 'zaltsbʊrk) *n* **1** a city in W Austria, capital of Salzburg province: 7th-century Benedictine abbey; a centre of music since the Middle Ages and birthplace of Mozart; tourist centre. Pop: 144 816 (2001) **2** a state of W Austria. Pop: 518 580 (2001). Area: 7154 sq km (2762 sq miles)

Salzgitter (*German* zalts'gɪtər) *n* an industrial city in central Germany, in SE Lower Saxony. Pop: 113 700 (1999 est)

SAM (sæm) *n acronym for* surface-to-air missile

Sam. *Bible abbrev for* Samuel

S.Am. *abbrev for* South America(n)

Samar ('sɑːmə) *n* an island in the E central Philippines, separated from S Luzon by the San Bernardino Strait: the third largest island in the republic. Capital: Catbalogan. Pop: 1 300 000 (latest est). Area: 13 080 sq km (5050 sq miles)

samara (sə'mɑːrə, 'sæmərə) *n* a dry winged one-seeded fruit: occurs in the ash, maple, etc. Also called: **key fruit** [c16 from NL, from L: seed of an elm]

Samara (*Russian* sa'marə) *n* a port in SW Russia, on the River Volga: centre of an important industrial complex; oil refining. Pop: 1 168 000 (1999 est). Former name (1935–91): **Kuibyshev** *or* **Kuybyshev**

Samaria (sə'mɛərɪə) *n* **1** the region of ancient Palestine that extended from Judaea to Galilee and from the Mediterranean to the River Jordan; the N kingdom of Israel **2** the capital of this kingdom; constructed northwest of Shechem in the 9th century BC

Samaritan (sə'mærɪtᵊn) *n* **1** a native or inhabitant of Samaria **2** short for **Good Samaritan** **3** (in the UK) a member of a voluntary organization (**the Samaritans**) that offers counselling to people in despair, esp by telephone

samarium (sə'mɛərɪəm) *n* a silvery metallic element of the lanthanide series used in carbon-arc lighting, as a doping agent in laser crystals, and as a neutron-absorber. Symbol: Sm; atomic no.: 62; atomic wt.: 150.35 [c19 from NL, from mineral, *samarskite*, after Col. von *Samarski*, 19th-century Russian inspector of mines + -IUM]

Samarkand ('sæmə,kænd; *Russian* səmar'kant) *n* a city in E Uzbekistan: under Tamerlane it became the chief economic and cultural centre of central Asia, on trade routes from China and India (the "silk road"). Pop: 388 000 (1998 est). Ancient name: **Maracanda**

samba ('sæmbə) *n, pl* **sambas** **1** a modern ballroom dance from Brazil in bouncy duple time **2** a piece of music composed for or in the rhythm of this dance ▷ *vb* **sambas, sambaing, sambaed** **3** (*intr*) to perform such a dance [Port., of African origin]

sambar *or* **sambur** ('sæmbə) *n, pl* **sambars, sambar** *or* **samburs, sambur** a S Asian deer with three-tined antlers [c17 from Hindi, from Sansk. *śambarra*, from ?]

Sambre (*French* sɑ̃brə) *n* a river in W Europe, rising in N France and flowing east into Belgium to join the Meuse at Namur. Length: 190 km (118 miles)

Sam Browne belt (,sæm 'braʊn) *n* a military officer's wide belt supported by a strap passing from the left side of the belt over the right shoulder [c20 after Sir *Samuel J. Browne* (1824–1901), British general, who devised it]

same (seɪm) *adj* (usually preceded by *the*) **1** being the very one: *she is wearing the same hat* **2a** being the one previously referred to **2b** (*as n*): *a note received about same* **3a** identical in kind, quantity, etc: *two girls of the same age* **3b** (*as n*): *we'd like the same* **4** unchanged in character or nature: *his attitude is the same as ever* **5** **all the same** **5a** Also: **just the same** nevertheless; yet **5b** immaterial: *it's all the same to me* ▷ *adv* **6** in an identical manner [c12 from ON *samr*] > '**sameness** *n*

> USAGE The use of *same* as in *if you send us your order for the materials, we will deliver same tomorrow* is common in business and official English. In general English, however, this use of the word is best avoided, as it may sound rather stilted: *may I borrow your book? I will return it* (not *same*) *tomorrow*

samfoo ('sæmfuː) *n* a style of dress worn by Chinese women, consisting of a waisted blouse and trousers [from Chinese *sam* dress + *foo* trousers]

Sami ('sɑːmɪ) *n* **1** (*pl* **Sami** *or* **Samis**) a member of the indigenous people of Lapland **2** the language of this people, belonging to the Finno-Ugric family ▷ *adj* **3** of or relating to this people or their language.

> USAGE The indigenous people of Lapland prefer to be called *Sami*, although Lapp is still in widespread use

Samian ('seɪmɪən) *adj* **1** of or relating to Samos, an island in the Aegean, or its inhabitants ▷ *n* **2** a native or inhabitant of Samos

Samian ware *n* a fine earthenware pottery, reddish-brown or black in colour, found in large quantities on Roman sites [c19 after the island of SAMOS, source of a reddish earth similar to that from which the pottery was made]

samisen ('sæmɪ,sɛn) *n* a Japanese plucked stringed instrument with a long neck and a rectangular soundbox [Japanese, from Chinese *san-hsien*, from *san* three + *hsien* string]

samite ('sæmaɪt) *n* a heavy fabric of silk, often woven with gold or silver threads, used in the Middle Ages [c13 from OF *samit*, from Med. L *examitum*, from Gk, from *hexamitos* having six threads]

samizdat (*Russian* səmiz'dat) *n* (formerly, in the Soviet Union) **a** a system of clandestine printing and distribution of banned literature **b** (*as modifier*): *a samizdat publication* [from Russian]

▷ www.nongnu.org/samizdat

Samnium ('sæmnɪəm) *n* an ancient country of central Italy inhabited by Oscan-speaking Samnites: corresponds to the present-day regions of Abruzzi, Molise, and part of Campania

Samoa (sə'məʊə) *n* **1** an independent state occupying four inhabited islands and five uninhabited islands in the S Pacific archipelago of the Samoa Islands: established as a League of Nations mandate under New Zealand administration in 1920 and a UN trusteeship in 1946; gained independence as Western Samoa in 1962 as the first fully independent Polynesian state; officially changed its name to Samoa in 1997; a member of the Commonwealth. Languages: Samoan and English. Religion: Christian. Currency: tala. Capital: Apia. Pop: 179 000 (2001 est). Area 2841 sq km (1097 sq miles) **2** Also called: **Samoa Islands** a group of islands in the S Pacific, northeast of Fiji: an independent kingdom until the mid 19th century, when it was divided administratively into **American Samoa** (in the east) and **German Samoa** (in the west); the latter was mandated to New Zealand in 1919 and gained full independence in 1962 as Western Samoa, now **Samoa** (sense 1) Area: 3038 sq km (1173 sq miles) > **Sa'moan** *adj*, *n*

▷ www.samoa.net.ws/govtsamoapress
▷ www.visitsamoa.ws
▷ www.samoa.co.uk

Samoa Islands *pl n* a group of islands in the S Pacific, northeast of Fiji: an independent kingdom until the mid 19th century, when it was divided administratively into **American Samoa** (in the east) and **German Samoa** (in the west); the latter was mandated to New Zealand in 1919 and gained full independence in 1962 as Western Samoa (now called **Samoa**). Area: 3038 sq km (1173 sq miles)

Samos ('seɪmɒs) *n* a Greek island in the E Aegean Sea, off the SW coast of Turkey: a leading commercial centre of ancient Greece. Pop: 41 965 (1991). Area: 492 sq km (190 sq miles)

samosa (sə'məʊsə) *n, pl* **samosas** *or* **samosa** (in Indian cookery) a small, fried, triangular spiced meat or vegetable pasty [c20 from Hindi]

Samothrace ('sæmə,θreɪs) *n* a Greek island in the NE Aegean Sea: mountainous. Pop: 4000 (latest est)

samovar ('sæmə,vɑː) *n* (esp in Russia) a metal urn for making tea, in which the water is usually heated by an inner container [c19 from Russian, from *samo-* self + *varit'* to boil]

Samoyed (,sæmə'jɛd) *n* **1** (*pl* **Samoyed** *or* **Samoyeds**) a member of a group of peoples who live chiefly in the area of the N Urals: related to the Finns **2** the languages of these peoples **3** (sə'mɔɪɛd) a white or cream breed of dog having a dense coat and a tightly curled tail [c17 from Russian *Samoed*]

samp (sæmp) *n S African* crushed maize used for porridge [from Amerind *nasaump* softened by water]

sampan ('sæmpæn) *n* a small skiff, widely used in the Orient, that is propelled by oars [c17 from Chinese, from *san* three + *pan* board]

samphire ('sæm,faɪə) *n* **1** an umbelliferous plant of Eurasian coasts, having fleshy divided leaves and clusters of small greenish-white flowers **2 golden samphire** a Eurasian coastal plant with fleshy leaves and yellow flower heads **3 marsh samphire** another name for **glasswort** (sense 1) **4** any of several other plants of coastal areas [c16 *sampiere*, from F *herbe de Saint Pierre* Saint Peter's herb]

sample ('sɑːmpᵊl) *n* **1a** a small part of anything, intended as representative of the whole **1b** (*as modifier*): *a sample bottle* **2** Also called: **sampling** *statistics* a set of individuals or items selected from a population and analysed to test hypotheses about or yield estimates of the population ▷ *vb* **samples, sampling, sampled 3** (*tr*) to take a sample or samples of **4** *music* **4a** to take a short extract from (one record) and mix it into a different backing track **4b** to record (a sound) and feed it into a computerized synthesizer so that it can be reproduced at any pitch [c13 from OF *essample*, from L *exemplum* EXAMPLE]

sampler ('sɑːmplə) *n* **1** a person who takes samples **2** a piece of embroidery done to show the embroiderer's skill in using many different stitches **3** *music* a piece of electronic equipment used for sampling **4** a recording comprising a collection of tracks from other albums, to stimulate interest in the featured products

sampling ('sɑːmplɪŋ) *n* **1** the process of selecting a random sample **2** a variant of **sample** (sense 2) **3** *music* the process of taking a short extract from a record and mixing it into a different backing track

sampling distribution *n statistics* the distribution of a random, experimentally obtained sample

Sampras ('sæmp,ræs) *n* **Pete** born 1971, US tennis player: US singles champion (1990, 1993, 1995, 1996); Wimbledon singles champion (1993–95, 1997–99, 2000)

Samson ('sæmsən) *n* **1** a judge of Israel, who performed feats of strength until he was betrayed by his mistress Delilah (Judges 13–16) **2** any man of outstanding physical strength

Samsun (*Turkish* 'sɑmsun) *n* a port in N Turkey, on the Black Sea. Pop: 338 387 (1997). Ancient name: **Amisus** (əmiːsəs)

Samuel ('sæmjʊəl) *n Old Testament* **1** a Hebrew prophet, seer, and judge, who anointed the first two kings of the Israelites (I Samuel 1–3; 8–15) **2** either of the two books named after him, **I** and **II Samuel**

samurai ('sæmʊ,raɪ) *n, pl* **samurai 1** the Japanese warrior caste from the 11th to the 19th centuries **2** a member of this aristocratic caste [c19 from Japanese]

▷ www.samurai-archives.com

samurai bond *n finance* a bond issued in Japan and denominated in yen, available for purchase by nonresidents of Japan ▷ Cf **shogun bond**

San[1] (sɑːn) *n* **1** an aboriginal people of southern Africa **2** a group of the Khoisan languages.

San[2] (sɑːn) *n* a river in E central Europe, rising in the W Ukraine and flowing northwest across SE Poland to the Vistula River. Length: about 450 km (280 miles)

San'a *or* **Sanaa** (sɑː'nɑː) *n* the administrative capital of Yemen, on the central plateau at an altitude of 2350 m (7700 ft): formerly the capital of North Yemen. Pop: 972 000 (1995 est)

▷ http://members.aol.com/yalnet/sanaa.htm

San Antonio (sæn æn'təʊnɪ,əʊ) *n* a city in S Texas: site of the Alamo; the leading town in Texas until about 1930. Pop: 1 144 646 (2000) > **San Antonian** *adj*, *n*

sanative ('sænətɪv) *adj*, *n* a less common word for **curative** [c15 from Med. L *sānātīvus*, from L *sānāre* to heal, from *sānus* healthy]

sanatorium (,sænə'tɔːrɪəm) *or US* **sanitarium** *n, pl* **sanatoriums** *or* **sanatoria** (-rɪə) **1** an institution for the medical care and recuperation of persons who are chronically ill **2** *Brit* a room as in a boarding school where sick pupils may receive treatment [c19 from NL, from L *sānāre* to heal]

San Bernardino (sæn ,bɜːnə'diːnəʊ) *n* a city in SE California: founded in 1851 by Mormons from Salt Lake City. Pop: 185 401 (2000)

San Bernardino Pass *n* a pass over the Lepontine Alps in SE Switzerland. Highest point: 2062 m (6766 ft)

San Blas ('sɑːn 'blɑːs) *n* **1 Isthmus of** the narrowest part

of the Isthmus of Panama. Width: about 50 km (30 miles) **2 Gulf of** an inlet of the Caribbean on the N coast of Panama
San Cristóbal (*Spanish* saŋ kri'stoβal) *n* **1** Also called: **Chatham Island** an island in the Pacific, in the Galápagos Islands. Area: 505 sq km (195 sq miles) **2** a city in SW Venezuela: founded in 1561 by Spanish conquistadores. Pop: 307 184 (2000 est)
sanctified ('sæŋktɪˌfaɪd) *adj* **1** consecrated or made holy **2** sanctimonious
sanctify ('sæŋktɪˌfaɪ) *vb* **sanctifies, sanctifying, sanctified** (*tr*) **1** to make holy **2** to free from sin **3** to sanction (an action or practice) as religiously binding: *to sanctify a marriage* **4** to declare or render (something) productive of or conductive to holiness or grace [C14 from LL *sanctificāre*, from L *sanctus* holy + *facere* to make] > ˌ**sanctifi'cation** *n* > '**sanctiˌfier** *n*
sanctimonious (ˌsæŋktɪ'məʊnɪəs) *adj* affecting piety or making a display of holiness [C17 from L *sanctimonia* sanctity, from *sanctus* holy] > ˌ**sancti'moniously** *adv* > ˌ**sancti'moniousness** *or* '**sanctimony** *n*
sanction ('sæŋkʃən) *n* **1** authorization **2** aid or encouragement **3** something, such as an ethical principle, that imparts binding force to a rule, oath, etc **4** the penalty laid down in a law for contravention of its provisions **5** (*often pl*) a coercive measure, esp one taken by one or more states against another guilty of violating international law ▷ *vb* (*tr*) **6** to give authority to **7** to confirm [C16 from L *sanctiō* the establishment of an inviolable decree, from *sancīre* to decree]
sanctitude ('sæŋktɪˌtjuːd) *n* saintliness; holiness
sanctity ('sæŋktɪtɪ) *n, pl* **sanctities 1** the condition of being sanctified; holiness **2** anything regarded as sanctified or holy **3** the condition of being inviolable: *the sanctity of marriage* [C14 from OF *saincteté*, from L *sanctitās*, from *sanctus* holy]
sanctuary ('sæŋktjʊərɪ) *n, pl* **sanctuaries 1** a holy place **2** a consecrated building or shrine **3** *Old Testament* **3a** the Israelite temple at Jerusalem **3b** the tabernacle in which the Ark was enshrined **4** the chancel, or that part of a sacred building surrounding the main altar **5a** a sacred building where fugitives were formerly entitled to immunity from arrest or execution **5b** the immunity so afforded **6** a place of refuge **7** a place, protected by law, where animals can live and breed without interference [C14 from OF *sainctuarie*, from LL *sanctuārium* repository for holy things, from L *sanctus* holy]
sanctuary lamp *n Christianity* a lamp, usually red, placed in a prominent position in the sanctuary of a church, which, when lit, indicates the presence of the Blessed Sacrament
sanctum ('sæŋktəm) *n, pl* **sanctums** *or* **sancta** (-tə) **1** a sacred or holy place **2** a room or place of total privacy [C16 from L, from *sanctus* holy]
sanctum sanctorum (sæŋk'tɔːrəm) *n* **1** *Bible* another term for the **holy of holies 2** *often facetious* an especially private place [C14 from L, lit.: holy of holies, rendering Heb. *qōdesh haqqodāshīm*]
Sanctus ('sæŋktəs) *n* **1** *liturgy* the hymn that occurs immediately after the preface in the celebration of the Eucharist **2** a musical setting of this [C14 from the hymn, *Sanctus sanctus sanctus* Holy, holy, holy, from L *sancīre* to consecrate]
Sanctus bell *n chiefly RC Church* a bell rung as the opening words of the Sanctus are pronounced
sand (sænd) *n* **1** loose material consisting of rock or mineral grains, esp rounded grains of quartz, between 0.05 and 2 mm in diameter **2** (*often pl*) a sandy area, esp on the seashore or in a desert **3a** a greyish-yellow colour **3b** (*as adj*): *sand upholstery* **4** the grains of sandlike material in an hourglass **5** *US inf* courage **6 the sands are running out** there is not much time left before the end ▷ *vb* **7** (*tr*) to smooth or polish the surface of with sandpaper or sand **8** (*tr*) to sprinkle or cover with or as if with sand **9** to fill or cause to fill with sand: *the channel sanded up* [OE] > '**sandˌlike** *adj*
Sand (*French* sɑ̃d) *n* **George** (ʒɔrʒ), pen name of *Amandine Aurore Lucie Dupin*. 1804–76, French novelist, best known for such pastoral novels as *La Mare au diable* (1846) and *François le Champi* (1847–48) and for her works for women's rights to independence
Sandage ('sændɪdʒ) *n* **Allan Rex** born 1926, US astronomer, who discovered the first quasar (1961)
Sandakan (sɑːn'dɑːkɑːn) *n* a port in Malaysia, on the NE coast of Sabah: capital (until 1947) of North Borneo. Pop: 223 432 (1991)
sandal ('sændᵊl) *n* **1** a light shoe consisting of a sole held on the foot by thongs, straps, etc **2** a strap passing over the instep or around the ankle to keep a low shoe on the foot **3** another name for **sandalwood** [C14 from L *sandalium*, from Gk, from *sandalon* sandal] > '**sandalled** *adj*
sandalwood ('sændᵊlˌwʊd) *or* **sandal** *n* **1** any of a genus of evergreen hemiparasitic trees, esp the **white sandalwood**, of S Asia and Australia, having hard light-coloured heartwood **2** the wood of any of these trees, which is used for carving, is burned as incense, and yields an aromatic oil used in perfumery **3** any of various similar trees or their wood, esp a leguminous tree of SE Asia having dark red wood used as a dye [C14 *sandal*, from Med. L, from LGk *sandanon*, from Sansk. *candana* sandalwood]
Sandalwood Island *n* the former name for **Sumba**
sandarac *or* **sandarach** ('sændəˌræk) *n* **1** either of two coniferous trees of NW Africa, having hard fragrant dark wood **2** a brittle pale yellow transparent resin obtained from the bark of this tree and used in making varnish and incense [C16 *sandaracha*, from L *sandaraca* red pigment, from Gk *sandarakē*]
sandbag ('sændˌbæg) *n* **1** a sack filled with sand used for protection against gunfire, floodwater, etc, or as ballast in a balloon, etc **2** a bag filled with sand and used as a weapon ▷ *vb* **sandbags, sandbagging, sandbagged** (*tr*) **3** to protect or strengthen with sandbags **4** to hit with or as if with a sandbag **5** *finance* to obstruct (an unwelcome takeover bid) by having prolonged talks in the hope that a more acceptable bidder will come forward > '**sandˌbagger** *n*
sandbank ('sændˌbæŋk) *n* a bank of sand in a sea or river, that may be exposed at low tide
sand bar *n* a ridge of sand in a river or sea, built up by the action of tides, currents, etc, and often exposed at low tide
sandblast ('sændˌblɑːst) *n* **1** a jet of sand blown from a nozzle under air or steam pressure ▷ *vb* **2** (*tr*) to clean or decorate (a surface) with a sandblast > '**sandˌblaster** *n*
sand-blind *adj* not completely blind ▷ Cf **stone-blind** [C15 changed (through infl. of SAND) from OE *samblind* (unattested), from *sam-* half, + BLIND] > '**sand-ˌblindness** *n*
sandbox ('sændˌbɒks) *n* **1** a container on a railway locomotive from which sand is released onto the rails to assist the traction **2** a container of sand for small children to play in
sandboy ('sændˌbɔɪ) *n* **happy** (*or* **jolly**) **as a sandboy** very happy; high-spirited
Sandburg ('sændbɜːg, 'sænbɜːg) *n* **Carl** 1878–1967, US writer, noted esp for his poetry, often written in free verse
sand castle *n* a mass of sand moulded into a castle-like shape, esp by a child on the beach
sand eel *or* **lance** *n* a silvery eel-like marine spiny-finned fish found burrowing in sand or shingle. Popular name: **launce**
sander ('sændə) *n* **1** a power-driven tool for smoothing surfaces by rubbing with an abrasive disc **2** a person

Ss

who uses such a sanding device

sanderling ('sændəlɪŋ) *n* a small sandpiper that frequents sandy shores [c17 ?from SAND + OE *erthling, eorthling* inhabitant of earth]

sand flea *n* another name for the **chigoe** or **sand hopper**

sandfly ('sænd,flaɪ) *n, pl* **sandflies** **1** any of various small mothlike dipterous flies: the bloodsucking females transmit diseases including leishmaniasis **2** any of various similar flies

sandgrouse ('sænd,graʊs) *n* a bird of dry regions of the Old World, having very short feet, a short bill, and long pointed wings and tail

sand hopper *n* any of various small hopping crustaceans, common in intertidal regions of seashores. Also called: **beach flea, sand flea**

Sandhurst ('sænd,hɜːst) *n* a village in S England, in Bracknell unitary authority, Berkshire: seat of the Royal Military Academy for the training of officer cadets in the British Army. Pop: 19 153 (1991)

San Diego (,sæn dɪ'eɪgəʊ) *n* a port in S California, on the Pacific: naval base; two universities. Pop: 1 223 400 (2000)

sandman ('sænd,mæn) *n, pl* **sandmen** (in folklore) a magical person supposed to put children to sleep by sprinkling sand in their eyes

sand martin *n* a small brown European songbird with white underparts: it nests in tunnels bored in sand, river banks, etc

sandpaper ('sænd,peɪpə) *n* **1** a strong paper coated with sand or other abrasive material for smoothing and polishing ▷ *vb* **2** (*tr*) to polish or grind (a surface) with or as if with sandpaper

sandpiper ('sænd,paɪpə) *n* **1** any of numerous N hemisphere shore birds having a long slender bill and legs and cryptic plumage **2** any other bird of the family which includes snipes and woodcocks

sandpit ('sænd,pɪt) *n* **1** a shallow pit or container holding sand for children to play in **2** a pit from which sand is extracted

Sandringham ('sændrɪŋəm) *n* a village in E England, in Norfolk near the E shore of the Wash: site of **Sandringham House,** a residence of the royal family

Sandrocottus (,sændrəʊ'kɒtəs) *n* the Greek name of **Chandragupta**

sandshoe ('sænd,ʃuː) *n* a light canvas shoe with a rubber sole

sandstone ('sænd,stəʊn) *n* any of a group of common sedimentary rocks consisting of sand grains consolidated with such materials as quartz, haematite, and clay minerals

sandstorm ('sænd,stɔːm) *n* a strong wind that whips up clouds of sand, esp in a desert

sand trap *n* another name (esp US) for **bunker** (sense 2)

sand viper *n* a S European viper having a yellowish-brown coloration with a zigzag pattern along the back

Sandwell ('sændwɛl) *n* a unitary authority in central England, in West Midlands. Pop: 282 901 (2001). Area: 86 sq km (33 sq miles)

sandwich ('sænwɪdʒ, -wɪtʃ) *n* **1** two or more slices of bread, usually buttered, with a filling of meat, cheese, etc **2** anything that resembles a sandwich in arrangement ▷ *vb* (*tr*) **3** to insert tightly between two other things **4** to put into a sandwich **5** to place between two dissimilar things [c18 after 4th Earl of *Sandwich* (1718–92), who ate sandwiches rather than leave the gambling table for meals]

sandwich board *n* one of two connected boards that are hung over the shoulders in front of and behind a person to display advertisements

sandwich course *n* any of several courses consisting of alternate periods of study and industrial work

Sandwich Islands *pl n* the former name of **Hawaii**

sandwich man *n* a man who carries sandwich boards

sandwort ('sænd,wɜːt) *n* **1** any of various plants which grow in dense tufts on sandy soil and have white or pink solitary flowers **2** any of various related plants

sandy ('sændɪ) *adj* **sandier, sandiest** **1** consisting of, containing, or covered with sand **2** (esp of hair) reddish-yellow **3** resembling sand in texture > **'sandiness** *n*

sand yacht *n* a wheeled boat with sails, built to be propelled over sand by the wind

sandy blight *n Austral inf* any inflammation and irritation of the eye

sane (seɪn) *adj* **1** free from mental disturbance **2** having or showing reason or sound sense [c17 from L *sānus* healthy] > **'sanely** *adv* > **'saneness** *n*

San Fernando (*Spanish* san fɛr'nando) *n* **1** a port in Trinidad and Tobago, on Trinidad on the Gulf of Paria: the second-largest town in the country. Pop: 30 100 (1990) **2** an inland port in W Venezuela, on the Apure River. Pop: 84 180 (latest est). Official name: **San Fernando de Apure** **3** a port in SW Spain, on the Isla de León SE of Cádiz; site of an arsenal (founded 1790) and of the most southerly observatory in Europe. Pop: 85 191 (1991)

Sanforized *or* **Sanforised** ('sænfə,raɪzd) *adj trademark* (of a fabric) preshrunk using a patented process

San Francisco (,sæn fræn'sɪskəʊ) *n* a port in W California, situated around the Golden Gate: developed rapidly during the California gold rush; a major commercial centre and one of the world's finest harbours. Pop: 776 733 (2000) > **San Franciscan** *n, adj*

San Francisco Bay *n* an inlet of the Pacific in W California, linked with the open sea by the Golden Gate strait. Length: about 80 km (50 miles). Greatest width: 19 km (12 miles)

sang (sæŋ) *vb* the past tense of **sing**

USAGE See at **ring**

sanger ('sæŋə) *n Austral sl* a sandwich. Also called: **sango**

Sanger ('sæŋə) *n* **1** **Frederick** born 1918, English biochemist, who determined the molecular structure of insulin: awarded two Nobel prizes for chemistry (1958; 1980) **2** **Margaret** (**Higgins**) 1883–1966, US leader of the birth- control movement

sang-froid (*French* sɑ̃frwa) *n* composure; self-possession [c18 from F, lit.: cold blood]

sangoma (sæŋ'gəʊmə) *n, pl* **sangomas** *S African* a witch doctor [from Bantu]

Sangraal (sæŋ'greɪl), **Sangrail,** *or* **Sangreal** ('sæŋgrɪəl) *n* another name for the **Holy Grail**

Sangre de Cristo Mountains ('sæŋgrɪ də 'krɪstəʊ) *pl n* a mountain range in S Colorado and N New Mexico: part of the Rocky Mountains. Highest peak: Blanca Peak, 4364 m (14 317 ft)

sangria (sæŋ'griːə) *n* a Spanish drink of red wine, sugar, and orange or lemon juice, sometimes laced with brandy [Sp.: a bleeding]

sanguinary ('sæŋgwɪnərɪ) *adj* **1** accompanied by much bloodshed **2** bloodthirsty **3** consisting of or stained with blood [c17 from L *sanguinārius*] > **'sanguinarily** *adv* > **'sanguinariness** *n*

sanguine ('sæŋgwɪn) *adj* **1** cheerful and confident; optimistic **2** (esp of the complexion) ruddy in appearance **3** blood-red ▷ *n* **4** a red pencil containing ferric oxide, used in drawing [c14 from L *sanguineus* bloody, from *sanguis* blood] > **'sanguinely** *adv* > **'sanguineness** *n*

sanguineous (sæŋ'gwɪnɪəs) *adj* **1** of, containing, or associated with blood **2** a less common word for **sanguine** > **san'guineousness** *n*

Sanhedrin ('sænɪdrɪn) *n Judaism* the supreme judicial, ecclesiastical, and administrative council of the Jews in New Testament times [c16 from LHeb., from Gk *sunedrion* council, from *sun-* SYN- + *hedra* seat]

sanies ('seɪnɪ,iːz) *n pathol* a thin greenish foul-smelling discharge from a wound, ulcer, etc, containing pus and blood [c16 from L, from ?]
San Ildefonso (*Spanish* san ilde'fɔnso) *n* a town in central Spain, near Segovia: site of the 18th-century summer palace of the kings of Spain. Also called: **La Granja**
sanitarium (,sænɪ'tɛərɪəm) *n, pl* **sanitariums** *or* **sanitaria** (-rɪə) the US word for **sanatorium** [c19 from L *sānitās* health]
sanitary ('sænɪtərɪ) *adj* **1** of or relating to health and measures for the protection of health **2** free from dirt, germs, etc; hygienic [c19 from F *sanitaire*, from L *sānitās* health] > **sanitarian** (,sænɪ'tɛərɪən) *n* > **'sanitariness** *n*
sanitary engineering *n* the branch of civil engineering associated with the supply of water, disposal of sewage, and other public health services > **sanitary engineer** *n*
sanitary towel *or esp US* **napkin** *n* an absorbent pad worn externally by women during menstruation to absorb the menstrual flow
sanitation (,sænɪ'teɪʃən) *n* the study and use of practical measures for the preservation of public health
sanitize *or* **sanitise** ('sænɪ,taɪz) *vb* **sanitizes, sanitizing, sanitized** *or* **sanitises, sanitising, sanitised** (*tr*) **1** *chiefly US & Canad* to make hygienic, as by sterilizing **2** to omit unpleasant details from (a news report, document, etc) to make it more palatable to the recipients > **,saniti'zation** *or* **,saniti'sation** *n*
sanity ('sænɪtɪ) *n* **1** the state of being sane **2** good sense or soundness of judgment [c15 from L *sānitās* health, from *sānus* healthy]
San Jose (,sæn həʊ'zeɪ) *n* a city in W central California: a leading world centre of the fruit drying and canning industry. Pop: 894 943 (2000)
San José (*Spanish* saŋ xo'se) *n* the capital of Costa Rica, on the central plateau: a major centre of coffee production in the mid-19th century; University of Costa Rica (1843). Pop: 344 349 (2000 est)
▷ www.msj.co.cr
San Juan (*Spanish* saŋ 'xwan) *n* **1** the capital and chief port of Puerto Rico, on the NE coast; University of Puerto Rico; manufacturing centre. Pop: 421 958 (2000) **2** a city in W Argentina: almost completely destroyed by an earthquake in 1944. Pop: 120 000 (1999 est)
San Juan Bautista (*Spanish* saŋ 'xwan bau'tista) *n* the former name of **Villahermosa**
San Juan Islands (sæn 'wɑːn, 'hwɑːn) *pl n* a group of islands between NW Washington, US, and SE Vancouver Island, Canada: administratively part of Washington
San Juan Mountains *pl n* a mountain range in SW Colorado and N New Mexico: part of the Rocky Mountains. Highest peak: Uncompahgre Peak, 4363 m (14 314 ft)
sank (sæŋk) *vb* the past tense of **sink**
Sankey ('sæŋkɪ) *n* **Ira David** 1840–1908, US evangelist and hymnodist, noted for his revivalist campaigns in Britain and the US with D. L. Moody
Sankt Pölten (*German* zaŋkt 'pœltən) *n, usually abbreviated to* **St Pölten** a city in NE Austria, the capital of Lower Austria state. Pop: 50 026 (1991)
San Luis Potosí (*Spanish* san 'lwis poto'si) *n* **1** a state of central Mexico: mainly high plateau; economy based on mining (esp silver) and agriculture. Capital: San Luis Potosí. Pop: 2 296 363 (2000). Area: 62 849 sq km (24 266 sq miles) **2** an industrial city in central Mexico, capital of San Luis Potosí state, at an altitude of 1850 m (6000 ft). Pop: 628 134 (2000 est)
San Marino (,sæn mə'riːnəʊ) *n* a republic in S central Europe in the Apennines, forming an enclave in Italy: the smallest republic in Europe, according to tradition founded by St Marinus in the 4th century. Official language: Italian. Religion: Roman Catholic majority. Currency: euro. Capital: San Marino. Pop: 27 200 (2001 est). Area: 62 sq km (24 sq miles) > **San Marinese** (,sæn ,mærɪ'niːz) *or* **Sammarinese** (sə,mærɪ'niːz) *adj, n*
▷ www.sanmarinosite.com
San Martín (*Spanish* san mar'tin) *n* **José de** (xo'se de) 1778–1850, South American patriot, who played an important part in gaining independence for Argentina, Chile, and Peru. He was protector of Peru (1821–22)
Sanmicheli (*Italian* sanmi'kɛːli) *n* **Michele** (mi'kɛːle) ?1484–1559, Italian mannerist architect
San Pedro Sula (*Spanish* san 'peðro 'sula) *n* a city in NW Honduras: the country's chief industrial centre. Pop: 452 100 (1999 est)
San Remo (*Italian* san 'rɛːmo) *n* a port and resort in NW Italy, in Liguria on the slopes of the Maritime Alps; flower market. Pop: 60 800 (latest est)
sans (sænz) *prep* an archaic word for **without** [c13 from OF *sanz*, from L *sine* without, but prob. also infl. by L *absentiā* in the absence of]
Sans. *or* **Sansk.** *abbrev for* Sanskrit
San Salvador (sæn 'sælvə,dɔː; *Spanish* san salβa'ðɔr) *n* the capital of El Salvador, situated in the SW central part: became capital in 1841; ruined by earthquakes in 1854 and 1873; university (1841). Pop: 422 570 (1992)
San Salvador Island *n* an island in the central Bahamas: the first land in the New World seen by Christopher Columbus (1492). Area: 156 sq km (60 sq miles). Also called: **Watling Island**
sans-culotte (,sænzkjʊ'lɒt) *n* **1** (during the French Revolution) **1a** (originally) a revolutionary of the poorer class **1b** (later) any revolutionary **2** any revolutionary extremist [c18 from F, lit.: without knee breeches, because the revolutionaries wore pantaloons or trousers rather than knee breeches]
San Sebastián (,sæn sə'bæstjən; *Spanish* san seβas'tjan) *n* a port and resort in N Spain on the Bay of Biscay: former summer residence of the Spanish court. Pop: 169 933 (1991)
sansevieria (,sænsɪ'vɪərɪə) *n* any of a genus of herbaceous perennial plants of Old World tropical regions: some are cultivated as house plants for their bayonet-like leaves; others yield a useful fibre [NL, after Raimondo di Sangro (1710–71), It. scholar and prince of *San Severo*]
Sanskrit ('sænskrɪt) *n* an ancient language of India. It is the oldest recorded member of the Indic branch of the Indo-European family of languages. Although it is used only for religious purposes, it is one of the official languages of India [c17 from Sansk. *samskrta* perfected, lit.: put together] > **San'skritic** *adj*
sans serif *or* **sanserif** (sæn'sɛrɪf) *n* a style of printer's typeface in which the characters have no serifs
San Stefano (,sæn stɪ'fɑːnəʊ) *n* a village in NW Turkey, near Istanbul on the Sea of Marmara: scene of the signing (1878) of the treaty ending the Russo-Turkish War. Turkish name: **Yeşilköy**
Santa ('sæntə) *n inf* short for **Santa Claus**
Santa Ana *n* **1** (*Spanish* 'santa 'ana) a city in NW El Salvador: the second largest city in the country; coffee-processing industry. Pop: 202 337 (1992) **2** ('sæntə 'ænə) a city in SW California: commercial and processing centre of a rich agricultural region. Pop: 337 977 (2000)
Santa Catalina ('sæntə ,kætᵊ'liːnə) *n* an island in the Pacific, off the coast of SW California: part of Los Angeles county: resort. Area: 181 sq km (70 sq miles). Also called: **Catalina Island**
Santa Catarina (*Portuguese* 'santə kətə'rinə) *n* a state of S Brazil, on the Atlantic: consists chiefly of the Great Escarpment. Capital: Florianópolis. Pop: 5 333 284 (2000). Area: 95 985 sq km (37 060 sq miles)
Santa Clara (*Spanish* 'santa 'klara) *n* a city in W central Cuba: sugar and tobacco industries. Pop: 205 400 (1994 est)

Santa Claus ('sæntə ˌklɔːz) *n* the legendary patron saint of children, commonly identified with Saint Nicholas. Often shortened to **Santa** Also called: **Father Christmas**

Santa Cruz ('sæntə 'kruːz; *Spanish* 'santa 'kruθ) *n* **1** a province of S Argentina, on the Atlantic: consists of a large part of Patagonia, with the forested foothills of the Andes in the west. Capital: Río Gallegos. Pop: 206 897 (2000 est). Area: 243 940 sq km (94 186 sq miles) **2** a city in E Bolivia: the second largest town in Bolivia. Pop: 1 016 137 (2000 est) **3** another name for **Saint Croix**

Santa Cruz de Tenerife ('sæntə 'kruːz də ˌtɛnə'riːf; *Spanish* 'santa 'kruθ de tene'rife) *n* a port and resort in the W Canary Islands, on NE Tenerife: oil refinery. Pop: 211 930 (1998 est)

Santa Fe *n* **1** ('sæntə 'feɪ) a city in N central New Mexico, capital of the state: one of the oldest European settlements in North America, founded in 1610 as the capital of the Kingdom of New Mexico; developed trade with the US by the Santa Fe Trail in the early 19th century. Pop: 62 514 (1994 est) **2** (*Spanish* 'santa 'fe) an inland port in E Argentina, on the Salado River: University of the Littoral (1920). Pop: 400 000 (1999 est) > **'Santa 'Fean** *adj, n*

Santa Gertrudis ('sæntə gə'truːdɪs) *n* one of a breed of red beef cattle developed in Texas

Santa Isabel (*Spanish* 'santa isa'βɛl) *n* the former name (until 1973) of **Malabo**

Santa Maria *n* **1** (*Portuguese* 'səntə ma'ria) a city in S Brazil, in Rio Grande do Sul state. Pop: 230 464 (2000) **2** (*Spanish* 'santa ma'ria) an active volcano in SW Guatemala. Height: 3768 m (12 362 ft)

Santa Marta (*Spanish* 'santa 'marta) *n* a port in NW Colombia, on the Caribbean: the oldest city in Colombia, founded in 1525; terminus of the Atlantic railway from Bogotá (opened 1961). Pop: 359 147 (1999 est)

Santa Maura ('santa 'maura) *n* the Italian name for **Levkás**

Santander (*Spanish* santan'dɛr) *n* a port and resort in N Spain, on an inlet of the Bay of Biscay: noted for its prehistoric collection from nearby caves; shipyards and an oil refinery. Pop: 184 165 (1998 est)

Santarém (*Portuguese* sənta'rə̃j) *n* a port in N Brazil, in Pará state where the Tapajós River flows into the Amazon. Pop: 186 518 (2000)

Santa Rosa de Copán (*Spanish* 'santa 'rɔsa de ko'pan) *n* a village in W Honduras: noted for the ruined Mayan city of Copán, which lies to the west

Santayana (ˌsæntɪ'ænə) *n* **George** 1863–1952, US philosopher, poet, and critic, born in Spain. His works include *The Life of Reason* (1905–06) and *The Realms of Being* (1927–40)

Santee (sæn'tiː) *n* a river in SE central South Carolina, formed by the union of the Congaree and Wateree Rivers: flows southeast to the Atlantic; part of the **Santee-Wateree-Catawba River System** an inland waterway 866 km (538 miles) long. Length: 230 km (143 miles)

Santiago (ˌsæntɪ'ɑːgəʊ; *Spanish* san'tjaɣo) *n* **1** the capital of Chile, at the foot of the Andes: commercial and industrial centre; two universities. Pop (urban area): 4 640 635 (1999 est). Official name: **Santiago de Chile** (de 'tʃile) **2** a city in the N Dominican Republic. Pop: 365 463 (1993). Official name: **Santiago de los Caballeros** (de los kaβa'ʎeros)

▹ www.ciudad.cl

Santiago de Compostela (*Spanish* de kɔmpɔs'tela) *n* a city in NW Spain: place of pilgrimage since the 9th century and the most visited (after Jerusalem and Rome) in the Middle Ages; cathedral built over the tomb of the apostle St James. Pop: 87 472 (1991). Latin name: **Campus Stellae** ('kæmpəs 'stɛliː)

Santiago de Cuba (*Spanish* de 'kuβa) *n* a port in SE Cuba, on **Santiago Bay** (a large inlet of the Caribbean): capital of Cuba until 1589; university (1947); industrial centre. Pop: 440 084 (1994 est)

Santiago del Estero (*Spanish* del es'tero) *n* a city in N Argentina: the oldest continuous settlement in Argentina, founded in 1553 by Spaniards from Peru. Pop: 202 876 (1999 est)

Santo Domingo ('sæntəʊ də'mɪŋgəʊ; *Spanish* 'santo ðo'miŋgo) *n* **1** the capital and chief port of the Dominican Republic, on the S coast: the oldest continuous European settlement in the Americas, founded in 1496; university (1538). Pop (capital district): 2 138 262 (1993). Former name (1936–61): **Ciudad Trujillo** **2** the former name (until 1844) of the **Dominican Republic** **3** another name (esp in colonial times) for **Hispaniola**

▹ www.sdq.com

santonica (sæn'tɒnɪkə) *n* **1** an oriental wormwood plant **2** the dried flower heads of this plant, formerly used as a vermifuge ▹ Also called: **wormseed** [c17 NL, from LL *herba santonica* herb of the *Santones* (prob. wormwood), from L *Santonī* a people of Aquitania]

santonin ('sæntənɪn) *n* a white crystalline soluble substance extracted from the dried flower heads of santonica and used in medicine as an anthelmintic [c19 from SANTONICA + -IN]

Santos (*Portuguese* 'səntuʃ) *n* a port in S Brazil, in São Paulo state: the world's leading coffee port. Pop: 415 553 (2000)

São Francisco (*Portuguese* sə̃un frə̃'sisku) *n* a river in E Brazil, rising in SW Minas Gerais state and flowing northeast, then southeast to the Atlantic northeast of Aracajú. Length: 3200 km (1990 miles)

São Luís (*Portuguese* sə̃un 'lwis) *or* **São Luíz** ('lwiʃ) *n* a port in NE Brazil, capital of Maranhão state, on the W coast of São Luís Island: founded in 1612 by the French and taken by the Portuguese in 1615. Pop (urban area): 834 968 (2000)

São Miguel (*Portuguese* sə̃un mi'ɣɛl) *n* an island in the E Azores: the largest of the group. Pop: 126 388 (1991 est). Area: 854 sq km (333 sq miles)

Saône (*French* son) *n* a river in E France, rising in Lorraine and flowing generally south to join the Rhône at Lyon, as its chief tributary: canalized for 375 km (233 miles) above Lyon; linked by canals with the Rhine, Marne, Seine, and Loire Rivers. Length: 480 km (298 miles)

Saône-et-Loire (*French* sonelwar) *n* a department of central France, in Burgundy region. Capital: Mâcon. Pop: 554 893 (1999). Area: 8627 sq km (3365 sq miles)

São Paulo (*Portuguese* sə̃un 'paulu) *n* **1** a state of SE Brazil: consists chiefly of tableland draining west into the Paraná River. Capital: São Paulo. Pop: 36 966 527 (2000). Area: 247 239 sq km (95 459 sq miles) **2** a city in S Brazil, capital of São Paulo state: the largest city and industrial centre in Brazil, with one of the busiest airports in the world; three universities; rapidly expanding population. Pop: 25 000 (1874); 2 017 025 (1950); 9 785 640 (2000)

Saorstat Eireann ('sɛəstɑːt 'ɛərən) *n* the Gaelic name for the **Irish Free State**

São Salvador (*Portuguese* sə̃un salva'dor) *n* short for **São Salvador da Bahia de Todos os Santos,** the official name for **Salvador**

São Tomé e Principe (*Portuguese* sə̃un tu'mɛ 'ɛː 'prə̃sipə) *n* a republic in the Gulf of Guinea, off the W coast of Africa, on the Equator: consists of the islands of Principe and São Tomé; colonized by the Portuguese in the late 15th century; became independent in 1975. Official language: Portuguese. Religion: Roman Catholic majority. Currency: dobra. Capital: São Tomé. Pop: 147 000 (2001 est). Area: 1001 sq km (386 sq miles)

▹ www.saotome.st

▹ www.sao-tome.com/english.html

sap[1] (sæp) *n* **1** a solution of mineral salts, sugars, etc, that circulates in a plant **2** any vital body fluid **3** energy; vigour **4** *sl* a gullible person **5** another name for **sapwood** ▷ *vb* **saps, sapping, sapped** (*tr*) **6** to drain of sap [OE *sæp*]

sap[2] (sæp) *n* **1** a deep and narrow trench used to approach or undermine an enemy position ▷ *vb* **saps, sapping, sapped 2** to undermine (a fortification, etc) by digging saps **3** (*tr*) to weaken [C16 *zappe*, from It. *zappa* spade, from ?]

sapele (səˈpiːlɪ) *n* **1** any of various W African trees yielding a hard timber resembling mahogany **2** the timber of such a tree, used to make furniture [C20 West African name]

sapid (ˈsæpɪd) *adj* **1** having a pleasant taste **2** agreeable or engaging [C17 from L *sapidus*, from *sapere* to taste] > **sapidity** (səˈpɪdɪtɪ) *n*

sapient (ˈseɪpɪənt) *adj often used ironically* wise or sagacious [C15 from L *sapere* to taste] > **ˈsapience** *n* > **ˈsapiently** *adv*

sapiential (ˌseɪpɪˈɛnʃəl) *adj* showing, having, or providing wisdom

sapling (ˈsæplɪŋ) *n* **1** a young tree **2** *literary* a youth

sapodilla (ˌsæpəˈdɪlə) *n* **1** a large tropical American evergreen tree, the latex of which yields chicle **2** Also called: **sapodilla plum** the edible brown rough-skinned fruit of this tree [C17 from Sp. *zapotillo*, dim. of *zapote* sapodilla fruit, from Nahuatl *tsapotl*]

saponaceous (ˌsæpəʊˈneɪʃəs) *adj* resembling soap [C18 from NL, from L *sāpō* soap]

saponify (səˈpɒnɪˌfaɪ) *vb* **saponifies, saponifying, saponified** *chem* **1** to undergo or cause to undergo a process in which a fat is converted into a soap by treatment with alkali **2** to undergo or cause to undergo a reaction in which an ester is hydrolysed to an acid and an alcohol as a result of treatment with an alkali [C19 from F *saponifier*, from L *sāpō* soap] > **saponifiable** *adj* > **saˌponifiˈcation** *n*

saponin (ˈsæpənɪn) *n* any of a group of plant glycosides with a steroid structure that foam when shaken and are used in detergents [C19 from F *saponine*, from L *sāpō* soap]

sappanwood *or* **sapanwood** (ˈsæpənˌwʊd) *n* **1** a small tree of S Asia producing wood that yields a red dye **2** the wood of this tree [C16 *sapan*, via Du. from Malay *sapang*]

sapper (ˈsæpə) *n* **1** a soldier who digs trenches, etc **2** (in the British Army) a private of the Royal Engineers

Sapper (ˈsæpə) *n* real name *Herman Cyril McNeile*. 1888–1937, British novelist, author of the popular thriller *Bull-dog Drummond* (1920) and its sequels

Sapphic (ˈsæfɪk) *adj* **1** *prosody* denoting a metre associated with Sappho **2** of or relating to Sappho or her poetry **3** lesbian ▷ *n* **4** *prosody* a verse, line, or stanza written in the Sapphic form of classical lyric poetry

Sapphira (sæˈfaɪrə) *n New Testament* the wife of Ananias, who together with her husband was struck dead for fraudulently concealing their wealth from the Church (Acts 5)

sapphire (ˈsæfaɪə) *n* **1a** any precious corundum gemstone that is not red, esp the highly valued transparent blue variety **1b** (*as modifier*): *a sapphire ring* **2a** the blue colour of sapphire **2b** (*as adj*): *sapphire eyes* **3** (*modifier*) denoting a forty-fifth anniversary: *our sapphire wedding* [C13 *safir*, from OF, from L *sapphīrus*, from Gk *sappheiros*, ?from Sansk. *śanipriya*, lit.: beloved of the planet Saturn]

Sappho (ˈsæfəʊ) *n* 6th century BC, Greek lyric poetess of Lesbos

Sapporo (ˈsɑːpəʊˌrəʊ) *n* a city in N Japan, on W Hokkaido: commercial centre; university (1918). Pop: 1 756 968 (1995)

sappy (ˈsæpɪ) *adj* **sappier, sappiest 1** (of plants) full of sap **2** full of energy or vitality

sapro- *or before a vowel* **sapr-** *combining form* indicating dead or decaying matter: *saprogenic* [from Gk *sapros* rotten]

saprogenic (ˌsæprəʊˈdʒɛnɪk) *or* **saprogenous** (sæˈprɒdʒɪnəs) *adj* **1** producing or resulting from decay **2** growing on decaying matter

saprophyte (ˈsæprəʊˌfaɪt) *n* any plant that lives and feeds on dead organic matter > **saprophytic** (ˌsæprəʊˈfɪtɪk) *adj*

saprotroph (ˈsæprəʊtrəʊf) *n* any organism that lives and feeds on dead organic matter. Also called: **saprobe, saprobiont** > **saprotrophic** (ˌsæprəʊˈtrəʊfɪk) *adj* > **ˌsaproˈtrophically** *adv*

saprozoic (ˌsæprəʊˈzəʊɪk) *adj* (of animals or plants) feeding on dead organic matter

sapsucker (ˈsæpˌsʌkə) *n* either of two North American woodpeckers that have white wing patches and feed on the sap from trees

sapwood (ˈsæpˌwʊd) *n* the soft wood, just beneath the bark in tree trunks, that consists of living tissue

sarabande *or* **saraband** (ˈsærəˌbænd) *n* **1** a decorous 17th-century courtly dance **2** a piece of music composed for or in the rhythm of this dance, in slow triple time [C17 from F *sarabande*, from Sp. *zarabanda*, from ?]

Saracen (ˈsærəsᵊn) *n* **1** *history* a member of one of the nomadic Arabic tribes, esp of the Syrian desert **2a** a Muslim, esp one who opposed the crusades **2b** (in later use) any Arab ▷ *adj* **3** of or relating to Arabs of either of these periods, regions, or types [C13 from OF *Sarrazin*, from LL *Saracēnus*, from LGk *Sarakēnos*, ?from Ar. *sharq* sunrise] > **Saracenic** (ˌsærəˈsɛnɪk) *adj*

Saragossa (ˌsærəˈgɒsə) *n* the English name for **Zaragoza**

Sarah (ˈsɛərə) *n Old Testament* the wife of Abraham and mother of Isaac (Genesis 17:15–22)

Sarajevo (*Serbo-Croat* ˈsarajɛvɔ) *or* **Serajevo** *n* the capital of Bosnia-Herzegovina: developed as a Turkish town in the 15th century; capital of the Turkish and Austro-Hungarian administrations in 1850 and 1878 respectively; scene of the assassination of Archduke Franz Ferdinand in 1914, precipitating World War I; besieged by Bosnian Serbs (1992–95). Pop: 360 000 (1997 est)

Saramago (*Portuguese* ˌsaraˈmɑgo) *n* **José** born 1922, Portuguese novelist and writer; his works include the novel *O ano da morte de Ricardo Reis* (1984): Nobel prize for literature 1998

Saransk (*Russian* saˈransk) *n* a city in W central Russia, capital of the Mordovian Republic: university (1957). Pop: 316 600 (1999 est)

Saratov (*Russian* saˈratəf) *n* an industrial city in W Russia, on the River Volga: university (1919). Pop: 881 000 (1999 est)

Sarawak (səˈrɑːwək) *n* a state of Malaysia, on the NW coast of Borneo on the South China Sea: granted to Sir James Brooke by the Sultan of Brunei in 1841 as a reward for helping quell a revolt; mainly agricultural. Capital: Kuching. Pop: 2 012 616 (2000). Area: about 121 400 sq km (48 250 sq miles)

Sarazen (ˈsærəzən) *n* **Gene,** original name *Eugenio Saraceni*. 1902–99, US golfer; won seven major tournaments between 1922 and 1935

sarcasm (ˈsɑːkæzəm) *n* **1** mocking or ironic language intended to convey scorn or insult **2** the use or tone of such language [C16 from LL *sarcasmus*, from Gk, from *sarkazein* to rend the flesh, from *sarx* flesh]

sarcastic (sɑːˈkæstɪk) *adj* **1** characterized by sarcasm **2** given to the use of sarcasm > **sarˈcastically** *adv*

sarcenet *or* **sarsenet** (ˈsɑːsnɪt) *n* a fine soft silk fabric used for clothing, ribbons, etc [C15 from OF *sarzinet*, from *Sarrazin* SARACEN]

sarco- *or before a vowel* **sarc-** *combining form* indicating flesh: *sarcoma* [from Gk *sark-*, *sarx* flesh]

sarcocarp (ˈsɑːkəʊˌkɑːp) *n bot* the fleshy mesocarp of such fruits as the peach or plum

Ss

sarcoma (sɑːˈkəʊmə) *n, pl* **sarcomata** (-mətə) *or* **sarcomas** *pathol* a usually malignant tumour arising from connective tissue [C17 via NL from Gk *sarkōma* fleshy growth] > **sarˈcomatous** *adj*

sarcomatosis (sɑːˌkəʊməˈtəʊsɪs) *n pathol* a condition characterized by the development of several sarcomas at various bodily sites [C19 see SARCOMA, -OSIS]

sarcophagus (sɑːˈkɒfəgəs) *n, pl* **sarcophagi** (-ˌgaɪ) *or* **sarcophaguses** a stone or marble coffin or tomb, esp one bearing sculpture or inscriptions [C17 via L from Gk *sarkophagos* flesh-devouring; from the type of stone used, which was believed to destroy the flesh of corpses]

sarcoplasm (ˈsɑːkəʊˌplæzəm) *n* the cytoplasm of a muscle fibre > **ˌsarcoˈplasmic** *adj*

sarcous (ˈsɑːkəs) *adj* (of tissue) muscular or fleshy [C19 from Gk *sarx* flesh]

sard (sɑːd) *or* **sardius** (ˈsɑːdɪəs) *n* an orange, red, or brown variety of chalcedony, used as a gemstone. Also called: **sardine** [C14 from L *sarda*, from Gk *sardios* stone from Sardis]

sardar *or* **sirdar** (səˈdɑː) *n* (in India) **1** a title used before the name of Sikh men **2** a leader [Hindi, from Persian]

Sardegna (sarˈdeɲɲa) *n* the Italian name for **Sardinia**

sardine[1] (sɑːˈdiːn) *n, pl* **sardines** *or* **sardine** **1** any of various small food fishes of the herring family, esp a young pilchard **2** **like sardines** very closely crowded together [C15 via OF from L *sardīna*, dim. of *sarda* a fish suitable for pickling]

sardine[2] (ˈsɑːdiːn) *n* another name for **sard** [C14 from LL *sardinus*, from Gk *sardinos lithos* Sardian stone, from *Sardeis* Sardis]

Sardinia (sɑːˈdɪnɪə) *n* the second-largest island in the Mediterranean: forms, with offshore islands, an administrative region of Italy; ceded to Savoy by Austria in 1720 in exchange for Sicily and formed the Kingdom of Sardinia with Piedmont; became part of Italy in 1861. Capital: Cagliari. Pop: 1 651 888 (2000 est). Area: 24 089 sq km (9301 sq miles). Italian name: **Sardegna**

Sardinian (sɑːˈdɪnɪən) *adj* **1** of or relating to Sardinia, its inhabitants, or their language ▷ *n* **2** a native or inhabitant of Sardinia **3** the spoken language of Sardinia, sometimes regarded as a dialect of Italian but containing many loan words from Spanish

Sardis (ˈsɑːdɪs) *or* **Sardes** (ˈsɑːdiːz) *n* an ancient city of W Asia Minor: capital of Lydia

sardonic (sɑːˈdɒnɪk) *adj* characterized by irony, mockery, or derision [C17 from F, from L, from Gk *sardonios* derisive, lit.: of Sardinia, alteration of Homeric *sardanios* scornful (laughter or smile)] > **sarˈdonically** *adv* > **sarˈdonicism** *n*

sardonyx (ˈsɑːdənɪks) *n* a variety of chalcedony with alternating reddish-brown and white parallel bands [C14 via L from Gk *sardonux*, ?from *sardion* SARD + *onux* nail]

Sardou (*French* sardu) *n* **Victorien** (viktɔrjɛ̃) 1831–1908, French dramatist. His plays include *Fédora* (1882) and *La Tosca* (1887), the source of Puccini's opera

SARFU *abbrev for* South African Rugby Football Union

Sargasso Sea *n* a calm area of the N Atlantic, between the Caribbean and the Azores, where there is an abundance of floating seaweed of the genus *Sargassum*

sargassum (sɑːˈgæsəm) *or* **sargasso** (sɑːˈgæsəʊ) *n* a floating brown seaweed having ribbon-like fronds containing air sacs, esp abundant in the Sargasso Sea [C16 from Port. *sargaço* from ?]

sarge (sɑːdʒ) *n inf* sergeant

Sargent (ˈsɑːdʒənt) *n* **1** Sir (**Harold**) **Malcolm** (**Watts**) 1895–1967, English conductor **2** **John Singer** 1856–1925, US painter, esp of society portraits; in London from 1885

Sargeson (ˈsɑːdʒəsᵊn) *n* **Frank** 1903–82, New Zealand short-story writer and novelist. His work includes the short-story collection *That Summer and Other Stories* (1946) and the novel *I Saw in my Dream* (1949)

Sargodha (sɑːˈgəʊdə) *n* a city in NE Pakistan: grain market. Pop (urban area): 455 300 (1998)

Sargon II (ˈsɑːgɒn) *n* died 705 BC, king of Assyria (722–705). He developed a policy of transporting conquered peoples to distant parts of his empire

sari *or* **saree** (ˈsɑːrɪ) *n, pl* **saris** *or* **sarees** the traditional dress of women of India, Pakistan, etc, consisting of a very long piece of cloth swathed around the body [C18 from Hindi *sārī*, from Sansk. *śāṭī*]

Sark (sɑːk) *n* an island in the English Channel in the Channel Islands, consisting of **Great Sark** and **Little Sark**, connected by an isthmus: ruled by a hereditary seigneur or dame. Pop: 550 (1996) Area: 5 sq km (2 sq miles). French name: **Sercq**

Sarka (ˈzɑːkə) *n* a variant spelling of **Zarqa**

sarking (ˈsɑːkɪŋ) *n Scot, northern English, & NZ* flat planking supporting the roof cladding of a building [C15 in England: from Scot *sark* shirt]

sarky (ˈsɑːkɪ) *adj* **sarkier, sarkiest** *Brit inf* sarcastic

Sarmatia (sɑːˈmeɪʃɪə) *n* the ancient name of a region between the Volga and Vistula Rivers now covering parts of Poland, Belarus, and SW Russia > **Sarˈmatian** *n, adj* > **Sarmatic** (sɑːˈmætɪk) *adj*

sarmentose (sɑːˈmɛntəʊs) *or* **sarmentous** (sɑːˈmɛntəs) *adj* (of plants such as the strawberry) having stems in the form of runners [C18 from L *sarmentōsus* full of twigs, from *sarmentum* brushwood, from *sarpere* to prune]

sarmie (ˈsɑːmɪ) *n S African children's sl* a sandwich [C20 from SARNIE]

Sarnen (*German* ˈzarnən) *n* a town in central Switzerland, capital of Obwalden demicanton: resort. Pop: 7200 (latest est)

Sarnia (ˈsɑːnɪə) *n* an inland port in S central Canada, in SW Ontario at the S end of Lake Huron: oil refineries. Pop: 74 376 (1991)

sarnie (ˈsɑːnɪ) *n Brit inf* a sandwich [C20 prob. from N or dialect pronunciation of first syllable of *sandwich*]

sarod (sæˈrəʊd) *n* an Indian stringed musical instrument that may be played with a bow or plucked [C19 from Hindi]

sarong (səˈrɒŋ) *n* **1** a garment worn by men and women in the Malay Archipelago, Sri Lanka, etc, consisting of a long piece of cloth tucked around the waist or under the armpits **2** a western adaptation of this garment, worn by women as beachwear [C19 from Malay, lit.: sheath]

Saronic Gulf (səˈrɒnɪk) *n* an inlet of the Aegean on the SE coast of Greece. Length: about 80 km (50 miles). Width: about 48 km (30 miles). Also called: (Gulf of) **Aegina**

saros (ˈseɪrɒs) *n* a cycle of about 18 years 11 days (6585.32 days) in which eclipses of the sun and moon occur in the same sequence [C19 from Gk, from Babylonian *šāru* 3600 (years); modern use apparently based on mistaken interpretation of *šāru* as a period of 18½ years]

Saros (ˈsɑːrɒs) *n* **Gulf of** an inlet of the Aegean in NW Turkey, north of the Gallipoli Peninsula. Length: 59 km (37 miles). Width: 35 km (22 miles)

Sarpedon (sɑːˈpiːdɒn) *n Greek myth* a son of Zeus and Laodameia, or perhaps Europa, and king of Lycia. He was slain by Patroclus while fighting on behalf of the Trojans

Sarraute (*French* sarot) *n* **Nathalie** (natali) 1900–99, French novelist, noted as an exponent of the antinovel. Her novels include *Portrait of a Man Unknown* (1948), *Martereau* (1953), and *Ici* (1995)

Sarre (sar) *n* the French name for the **Saar**

sarrusophone (səˈruːzəˌfəʊn) *n* a wind instrument resembling the oboe but made of brass [C19 after *Sarrus*, F bandmaster, who invented it (1856)]

SARS (sɑːz) *n acronym for* severe acute respiratory syndrome; a severe viral infection of the lungs characterized by high fever, a dry cough, and breathing difficulties. It is contagious, having an airborne mode of transmission

sarsaparilla (ˌsɑːsəpəˈrɪlə) *n* **1** any of a genus of tropical American prickly climbing plants having large aromatic roots and heart-shaped leaves **2** the dried roots of any of these plants, formerly used as a medicine **3** a nonalcoholic drink prepared from these roots [C16 from Sp. *sarzaparrilla*, from *zarza* a bramble + *-parrilla*, from *parra* a climbing plant]

sarsen (ˈsɑːsᵊn) *n* **1** *geol* a boulder of silicified sandstone, probably of Tertiary age **2** such a stone used in a megalithic monument ▷ Also called: **greywether** [C17 prob. a var. of SARACEN]

sarsenet (ˈsɑːsnɪt) *n* a variant spelling of **sarcenet**

Sarthe (*French* sart) *n* a department of NW France, in Pays de la Loire region. Capital: Le Mans. Pop: 529 851 (1999). Area: 6245 sq km (2436 sq miles)

Sarto (*Italian* ˈsarto) *n* **Andrea del** (anˈdrɛːa del) 1486–1531, Florentine painter. His works include *The Nativity of the Virgin* (1514) in the church of Sant' Annunziata, Florence

sartorial (sɑːˈtɔːrɪəl) *adj* **1** of or relating to a tailor or to tailoring **2** *anat* of the sartorius [C19 from LL *sartōrius* from L *sartor* a patcher, from *sarcīre* to patch] > **sarˈtorially** *adv*

sartorius (sɑːˈtɔːrɪəs) *n, pl* **sartorii** (-ˈtɔːrɪˌaɪ) *anat* a long ribbon-shaped muscle that aids in flexing the knee [C18 NL, from *sartorius musculus*, lit.: tailor's muscle, because it is used when one sits in the cross-legged position in which tailors traditionally sat while sewing]

Sartre (*French* sartrə) *n* **Jean-Paul** (ʒɑ̃pɔl) 1905–80, French philosopher, novelist, and dramatist; chief French exponent of atheistic existentialism. His works include the philosophical essay *Being and Nothingness* (1943), the novels *Nausea* (1938) and *Les Chemins de la liberté* (1945–49), a trilogy, and the plays *Les Mouches* (1943), *Huis clos* (1944), and *Les Mains sales* (1948)

Sarum (ˈsɛərəm) *n* the ancient name of **Salisbury** (sense 3)

Sarum use *n* the distinctive local rite or system of rites used at Salisbury cathedral in late medieval times

SAS *abbrev for* Special Air Service

Sasebo (ˈsɑːsəˌbəʊ) *n* a port in SW Japan, on NW Kyushu on Omura Bay: naval base. Pop: 244 879 (1995)

saser (ˈseɪzə) *n* a device for amplifying ultrasound, working on a similar principle to a laser [C20 *s(ound) a(mplification) by s(timulated) e(mission) of r(adiation)*]

sash¹ (sæʃ) *n* a long piece of ribbon, etc, worn around the waist or over one shoulder, as a symbol of rank [C16 from Ar. *shāsh* muslin]

sash² (sæʃ) *n* **1** a frame that contains the panes of a window or door **2** a complete frame together with panes of glass ▷ *vb* **3** (*tr*) to furnish with a sash, sashes, or sash windows [C17 orig. pl *sashes*, var. of *shashes*, from CHASSIS]

sashay (sæˈʃeɪ) *vb* (*intr*) *inf, chiefly US & Canad* **1** to move, walk, or glide along casually **2** to move or walk in a showy way; parade [C19 from an alteration of *chassé*, a gliding dance step]

sash cord *n* a strong cord connecting a sash weight to a sliding sash

sashimi (ˈsæʃɪmɪ) *n* a Japanese dish of thin fillets of raw fish [C19 from Japanese *sashi* pierce + *mi* flesh]

sash saw *n* a small tenon saw used for cutting sashes

sash weight *n* a weight used to counterbalance the weight of a sliding sash in a sash window and thus hold it in position at any height

sash window *n* a window consisting of two sashes placed one above the other so that they can be slid past each other

Saskatchewan (sæsˈkætʃɪwən) *n* **1** a province of W Canada: consists of Canadian Shield in the north and open prairie in the south; economy based chiefly on agriculture and mineral resources. Capital: Regina. Pop: 1 015 800 (2001 est). Area: 651 900 sq km (251 700 sq miles). Abbreviations: **Sask, SK** **2** a river in W Canada, formed by the confluence of the North and South Saskatchewan Rivers: flows east to Lake Winnipeg. Length: 596 km (370 miles) > **Saskatchewanian** (sæsˌkætʃəˈwɒnɪən) *n, adj*

▷ www.gov.sk.ca

▷ www.sasktourism.com

Saskatoon (ˌsæskəˈtuːn) *n* a city in W Canada, in S Saskatchewan on the South Saskatchewan River: oil refining; university (1907). Pop: 193 647 (1996)

sasquatch (ˈsæsˌkwætʃ) *n* (in Canadian folklore) in British Columbia, a hairy beast or manlike monster said to leave huge footprints [from Amerind]

sass (sæs) *US & Canad inf* ▷ *n* **1** impudent talk or behaviour ▷ *vb* (*intr*) **2** to talk or answer back in such a way [C20 back formation from SASSY]

sassaby (ˈsæsəbɪ) *n, pl* **sassabies** an African antelope of grasslands and semideserts, having angular curved horns [C19 from Bantu *tshêsêbê*]

sassafras (ˈsæsəˌfræs) *n* **1** an aromatic deciduous tree of North America, having three-lobed leaves and dark blue fruits **2** the aromatic dried root bark of this tree, used as a flavouring, and yielding **sassafras oil** **3** *Austral* any of several unrelated trees having a similar fragrant bark [C16 from Sp. *sasafras*, from ?]

Sassari (*Italian* ˈsassari) *n* a city in NW Sardinia, Italy: the second-largest city on the island; university (1565). Pop: 120 803 (2000 est)

Sassenach (ˈsæsəˌnæx) *n Scot & occasionally Irish* an English person or Lowland Scot [C18 from Gaelic *Sassunach*, from LL *saxonēs* Saxons]

Sassoon (sæˈsuːn) *n* **1** **Siegfried** (**Lorraine**) 1886–1967, British poet and novelist, best known for his poems of the horrors of war collected in *Counterattack* (1918) and *Satirical Poems* (1926). He also wrote a semi-fictitious autobiographical trilogy *The Memoirs of George Sherston* (1928–36) **2** **Vidal** born 1928, British hair stylist: founder and chairman of Vidal Sassoon Inc

sassy (ˈsæsɪ) *adj* **sassier, sassiest** *US & Canad inf* insolent; impertinent [C19 var. of SAUCY] > **ˈsassily** *adv* > **ˈsassiness** *n*

sat (sæt) *vb* the past tense and past participle of **sit**

Sat. *abbrev for:* **1** Saturday **2** Saturn

Satan (ˈseɪtᵊn) *n* the devil, adversary of God, and tempter of mankind: sometimes identified with Lucifer (Luke 4:5–8) [OE, from LL, from Gk, from Heb.: plotter, from *sātan* to plot against]

satanic (səˈtænɪk) *adj* **1** of or relating to Satan **2** supremely evil or wicked > **saˈtanically** *adv*

Satanism (ˈseɪtᵊˌnɪzəm) *n* **1** the worship of Satan **2** a form of such worship which includes blasphemous parodies of Christian prayers, etc **3** a satanic disposition > **ˈSatanist** *n, adj*

SATB *abbrev for* soprano, alto, tenor, bass: a combination of voices in choral music

satchel (ˈsætʃəl) *n* a rectangular bag, usually made of leather or cloth and provided with a shoulder strap, used for carrying school books [C14 from OF *sachel*, from LL *saccellus*, from L *saccus* SACK¹] > **ˈsatchelled** *adj*

sate¹ (seɪt) *vb* **sates, sating, sated** (*tr*) **1** to satisfy (a desire or appetite) fully **2** to supply beyond capacity or desire [OE *sadian*]

sate² (sæt, seɪt) *vb arch* a past tense and past participle of **sit**

sateen (sæˈtiːn) *n* a glossy linen or cotton fabric that resembles satin [C19 changed from SATIN, on the model of VELVETEEN]

satellite (ˈsætᵊˌlaɪt) *n* **1** a celestial body orbiting around a planet or star: *the earth is a satellite of the sun* **2** a man-made device orbiting around the earth, moon, or another planet transmitting to earth scientific information or used for communication **3** a country or political unit under the domination of a foreign power **4** a subordinate area that is dependent upon a larger

Ss

adjacent town **5** (*modifier*) subordinate to or dependent upon another: *a satellite nation* **6** (*modifier*) of, used in, or relating to the transmission of television signals from a satellite to the house: *a satellite dish aerial* [C16 from L *satelles* an attendant, prob. of Etruscan origin]

satellite navigation system *n computing* a computer-operated system of navigation that uses signals from orbiting satellites and mapping data to pinpoint the user's position and plot a subsequent course. Often shortened to **satnav**

satiable ('seɪʃɪəbᵊl) *adj* capable of being satiated > ˌ**satia'bility** *n* > '**satiably** *adv*

satiate ('seɪʃɪˌeɪt) *vb* **satiates, satiating, satiated** (*tr*) **1** to fill or supply beyond capacity or desire **2** to supply to capacity [C16 from L *satiāre* to satisfy, from *satis* enough] > ˌ**sati'ation** *n*

Satie (*French* sati) *n* **Erik** (**Alfred Leslie**) (erik) 1866–1925, French composer, noted for his eccentricity, experimentalism, and his direct and economical style. His music, including numerous piano pieces and several ballets, exercised a profound influence upon other composers, such as Debussy and Ravel

satiety (sə'taɪɪtɪ) *n* the state of being satiated [C16 from L *satietās*, from *satis* enough]

satin ('sætɪn) *n* **1** a fabric of silk, rayon, etc, closely woven to show much of the warp, giving a smooth glossy appearance **2** (*modifier*) like satin in texture: *a satin finish* [C14 via OF from Ar. *zaitūnī*, Ar. rendering of Chinese *Tseutung* (now Tsinkiang), port from which the cloth was prob. first exported] > '**satiny** *adj*

satinet *or* **satinette** (ˌsætɪ'nɛt) *n* a thin satin or satin-like fabric [C18 from F: small satin]

satinflower ('sætɪnˌflaʊə) *n* another name for **greater stitchwort** (see **stitchwort**)

satinwood ('sætɪnˌwʊd) *n* **1** a tree that occurs in the East Indies and has hard wood with a satiny texture **2** the wood of this tree, used in veneering, marquetry, etc

satire ('sætaɪə) *n* **1** a novel, play, etc, in which topical issues, folly, or evil are held up to scorn by means of ridicule **2** the genre constituted by such works **3** the use of ridicule, irony, etc, to create such an effect [C16 from L *satira* a mixture, from *satur* sated, from *satis* enough]

satirical (sə'tɪrɪkᵊl) *or* **satiric** *adj* **1** of, relating to, or containing satire **2** given to the use of satire > **sa'tirically** *adv*

satirist ('sætərɪst) *n* **1** a person who writes satire **2** a person given to the use of satire

satirize *or* **satirise** ('sætəˌraɪz) *vb* **satirizes, satirizing, satirized** *or* **satirises, satirising, satirised** to deride (a person or thing) by means of satire > ˌ**satiri'zation** *or* ˌ**satiri'sation** *n*

satisfaction (ˌsætɪs'fækʃən) *n* **1** the act of satisfying or state of being satisfied **2** the fulfilment of a desire **3** the pleasure obtained from such fulfilment **4** a source of fulfilment **5** compensation for a wrong done or received **6** *RC Church, Church of England* the performance of a penance **7** *Christianity* the atonement for sin by the death of Christ

satisfactory (ˌsætɪs'fæktərɪ) *adj* **1** adequate or suitable; acceptable **2** giving satisfaction **3** constituting or involving atonement or expiation for sin > ˌ**satis'factorily** *adv*

satisfice ('sætɪsˌfaɪs) *vb* **satisfices, satisficing, satisficed** **1** (*intr*) to act in such a way as to satisfy the minimum requirements for achieving a particular result **2** (*tr*) *obs* to satisfy [C16 altered from SATISFY] > '**satisˌficer** *n*

satisficing behaviour *n econ* the form of behaviour demonstrated by firms who seek satisfactory profits and satisfactory growth rather than maximum profits

satisfy ('sætɪsˌfaɪ) *vb* **satisfies, satisfying, satisfied** (*mainly tr*) **1** (*also intr*) to fulfil the desires or needs of (a person) **2** to provide amply for (a need or desire) **3** to convince **4** to dispel (a doubt) **5** to make reparation to or for **6** to discharge or pay off (a debt) to (a creditor) **7** to fulfil the requirements of; comply with: *you must satisfy the terms of your lease* **8** *maths, logic* to fulfil the conditions of (a theorem, assumption, etc); to yield a truth by substitution of the given value [C15 from OF *satisfier*, from L *satisfacere*, from *satis* enough + *facere* to make] > '**satisˌfiable** *adj* > '**satisˌfying** *adj* > '**satisˌfyingly** *adv*

Sato Eisaku ('sɑːtəʊ eɪsaku) *n* 1901–75, Japanese statesman: prime minister (1964–72). During his term of office Japan became a major economic power. He shared the Nobel peace prize (1974) for opposing the proliferation of nuclear weapons

satori (sə'tɔːrɪ) *n Zen Buddhism* a state of sudden intuitive enlightenment [from Japanese]

satrap ('sætrəp) *n* **1** (in ancient Persia) a provincial governor **2** a subordinate ruler [C14 from L *satrapa*, from Gk *satrapēs*, from OPersian *khshathrapāvan*, lit.: protector of the land]

satrapy ('sætrəpɪ) *n, pl* **satrapies** the province, office, or period of rule of a satrap

SATs (sæts) *pl n Brit education acronym for* standard assessment tasks: see **assessment tests**

satsuma (sæt'suːmə) *n* **1** a small citrus tree cultivated, esp in Japan, for its edible fruit **2** the fruit of this tree, which has easily separable segments [from SATSUMA]

Satsuma ('sætsʊˌmɑː) *n* a former province of SW Japan, on S Kyushu: famous for its porcelain

saturable ('sætʃərəbᵊl) *adj chem* capable of being saturated > ˌ**satura'bility** *n*

saturate *vb* ('sætʃəˌreɪt), **saturates, saturating, saturated** **1** to fill, soak, or imbue totally **2** to make (a chemical compound, solution, etc) saturated or (of a compound, etc) to become saturated **3** (*tr*) *mil* to bomb or shell heavily ▷ *adj* ('sætʃərɪt, -ˌreɪt) **4** saturated [C16 from L *saturāre*, from *satur* sated, from *satis* enough]

saturated ('sætʃəˌreɪtɪd) *adj* **1** (of a solution or solvent) containing the maximum amount of solute that can normally be dissolved at a given temperature and pressure **2** (of a chemical compound) containing no multiple bonds: *a saturated hydrocarbon* **3** (of a fat) containing a high proportion of fatty acids having single bonds **4** (of a vapour) containing the maximum amount of gaseous material at a given temperature and pressure

saturation (ˌsætʃə'reɪʃən) *n* **1** the act of saturating or the state of being saturated **2** *chem* the state of a chemical compound, solution, or vapour when it is saturated **3** *meteorol* the state of the atmosphere when it can hold no more water vapour at its particular temperature and pressure **4** the attribute of a colour that enables an observer to judge its proportion of pure chromatic colour **5** the level beyond which demand for a product or service is not expected to rise ▷ *modifier* **6** denoting the maximum possible intensity of coverage of an area: *saturation bombing*

saturation point *n* the point at which no more can be absorbed, accommodated, used, etc

Saturday ('sætədɪ) *n* the seventh and last day of the week: the Jewish Sabbath [OE *sæternes dæg*, translation of L *Sāturnī diēs* day of Saturn]

Saturn[1] ('sætɜːn) *n* the Roman god of agriculture and vegetation. Greek counterpart: **Cronus**

Saturn[2] ('sætɜːn) *n* **1** the sixth planet from the sun, around which revolve planar concentric rings (**Saturn's rings**) consisting of small frozen particles **2** the alchemical name for **lead**[2] > **Saturnian** (sæ'tɜːnɪən) *adj*

▷ www.solarviews.com/eng/saturn.htm
▷ http://nssdc.gsfc.nasa.gov/planetary/planets

Saturnalia (ˌsætə'neɪlɪə) *n, pl* **Saturnalia** *or* **Saturnalias** **1** an ancient Roman festival celebrated in December:

renowned for its general merrymaking **2** (*sometimes not cap*) a period or occasion of wild revelry [c16 from L *Sāturnālis* relating to SATURN[1]] > ˌ**Saturˈnalian** *adj*

saturnine (ˈsætəˌnaɪn) *adj* **1** having a gloomy temperament **2** *arch* **2a** of or relating to lead **2b** having lead poisoning [c15 from F *saturnin*, from Med. L *sāturnīnus* (unattested), from L *Sāturnus* Saturn, from the gloomy influence attributed to the planet Saturn] > ˈ**saturˌninely** *adv*

satyagraha (ˈsɔːtjɑːgrɔːhɑː) *n* the policy of nonviolent resistance adopted by Mahatma Gandhi to oppose British rule in India [via Hindi from Sansk., lit.: insistence on truth, from *satya* truth + *agraha* fervour]

satyr (ˈsætə) *n* **1** *Greek myth* one of a class of sylvan deities, represented as goatlike men who drank and danced in the train of Dionysus and chased the nymphs **2** a man who has strong sexual desires **3** any of various butterflies, having dark wings often marked with eyespots [c14 from L *satyrus*, from Gk *saturos*] > **satyric** (səˈtɪrɪk) *adj*

satyriasis (ˌsætɪˈraɪəsɪs) *n* a neurotic compulsion in men to have sexual intercourse with many women without being able to have lasting relationships with them [c17 via NL from Gk *saturiasis*]

sauce (sɔːs) *n* **1** any liquid or semiliquid preparation eaten with food to enhance its flavour **2** anything that adds piquancy **3** *US & Canad* stewed fruit **4** *inf* impudent language or behaviour ▷ *vb* **sauces, saucing, sauced** (*tr*) **5** to prepare (food) with sauce **6** to add zest to **7** *inf* to be saucy to [c14 via OF from L *salsus* salted, from *sal* salt]
▷ www.dressings-sauces.org/recipefile.html
▷ www.recipesource.com/side-dishes/sauces
▷ http://whatscookingamerica.net/History/SauceHistory.htm

saucepan (ˈsɔːspən) *n* a metal or enamel pan with a long handle and often a lid, used for cooking food

saucer (ˈsɔːsə) *n* **1** a small round dish on which a cup is set **2** any similar dish [c14 from OF *saussier* container for SAUCE] > ˈ**saucerful** *n*

saucy (ˈsɔːsɪ) *adj* **saucier, sauciest 1** impertinent **2** pert; jaunty: *a saucy hat* > ˈ**saucily** *adv* > ˈ**sauciness** *n*

Saud (saʊd) *n* full name *Saud ibn Abdul-Aziz*. 1902–69, king of Saudi Arabia (1953–64); son of Ibn Saud. He was deposed by his brother Faisal

Saudi Arabia (ˈsɔːdɪ, ˈsaʊ-) *n* a kingdom in SW Asia, occupying most of the Arabian peninsula between the Persian Gulf and the Red Sea: founded in 1932 by Ibn Saud, who united Hejaz and Nejd; consists mostly of desert plateau; large reserves of petroleum and natural gas. Official language: Arabic. Official religion: (Sunni) Muslim. Currency: riyal. Capital: Riyadh (royal), Jidda (administrative). Pop: 22 757 000 (2001 est). Area: 2 260 353 sq km (872 722 sq miles) > **Saudi** *or* **Saudi Arabian** *adj, n*
▷ www.saudinf.com

sauerkraut (ˈsaʊəˌkraʊt) *n* finely shredded cabbage which has been fermented in brine [G, from *sauer* sour + *Kraut* cabbage]

sauger (ˈsɔːgə) *n* a small North American pikeperch with a spotted dorsal fin: valued as a food and game fish [c19 from ?]

Saul (sɔːl) *n* **1** *Old Testament* the first king of Israel (?1020–1000 BC). He led Israel successfully against the Philistines, but became afflicted with madness and died by his own hand; succeeded by David **2** *New Testament* the name borne by Paul prior to his conversion (Acts 9: 1–30)

sault (suː) *n Canad* a waterfall or rapids [c17 from Canad F, from F *saut* a leap]

Sault Sainte Marie (ˈsuː seɪnt məˈriː) *n, usually abbreviated to* **Sault Ste Marie 1** an inland port in central Canada, in Ontario on the St Mary's River, which links Lake Superior and Lake Huron, opposite Sault Ste Marie, Michigan: canal bypassing the rapids completed in 1895. Pop: 80 054 (1996) **2** an inland port in NE Michigan, opposite Sault Ste Marie, Ontario: canal around the rapids completed in 1855, enlarged and divided in 1896 and 1919 (popularly called **Soo Canals**). Pop: 14 689 (1990)

sauna (ˈsɔːnə) *n* **1** an invigorating bath originating in Finland in which the bather is subjected to hot steam, usually followed by a cold plunge **2** the place in which such a bath is taken [c20 from Finnish]

Saunders (ˈsɔːndəz) *n* Dame **Cicely** born 1918, British philanthropist: founded St Christopher's Hospice in 1967 for the care of the terminally ill, upon which the modern hospice movement is modelled. Her books include *Living with Dying* (1983)

saunter (ˈsɔːntə) *vb* **1** (*intr*) to walk in a casual manner; stroll ▷ *n* **2** a leisurely pace or stroll [c17 (meaning: to wander aimlessly), c15 (to muse): from ?] > ˈ**saunterer** *n*

-saur *or* **-saurus** *n combining form* lizard: *dinosaur* [from NL *saurus*]

saurian (ˈsɔːrɪən) *adj* **1** of or resembling a lizard ▷ *n* **2** a former name for **lizard** [c15 from NL *Sauria*, from Gk *sauros*]

saury (ˈsɔːrɪ) *n, pl* **sauries** a fish of tropical and temperate seas, having an elongated body and long toothed jaws. Also called: **skipper** [c18 ?from LL *saurus*, from ?]

sausage (ˈsɒsɪdʒ) *n* **1** finely minced meat, esp pork or beef, mixed with fat, cereal, and seasonings (**sausage meat**), and packed into a tube-shaped edible casing **2** *Scot* sausage meat **3** an object shaped like a sausage **4 not a sausage** nothing at all [c15 from OF *saussiche*, from LL *salsīcia*, from L *salsus* salted; see SAUCE]
▷ www.sausagefans.com
▷ www.fsis.usda.gov/OA/pubs/sausages.htm

sausage dog *n* an informal name for **dachshund**

sausage roll *n Brit* a roll of sausage meat in pastry

Saussure (*French* sosyr) *n* **Ferdinand de** (fɛrdinɑ̃ də) 1857–1913, Swiss linguist. He pioneered structuralism in linguistics and the separation of scientific language description from historical philological studies

sauté (ˈsəʊteɪ) *vb* **sautés, sautéing** *or* **sautéeing, sautéed 1** to fry (food) quickly in a little fat ▷ *n* **2** a dish of sautéed food, esp meat that is browned and then cooked in a sauce ▷ *adj* **3** sautéed until lightly brown: *sauté potatoes* [c19 from F: tossed, from *sauter* to jump, from L, from *salīre* to spring]

Sauvignon Blanc (ˈsəʊvɪnjɒn blɒŋk) *n* **1** a white grape grown in the Bordeaux and Loire regions of France and in New Zealand and elsewhere **2** any of various white wines made from this grape

Sava (ˈsɑːvə) *or* **Save** (sɑːv) *n* a river in SE Europe, rising in NW Slovenia and flowing east and south to the Danube at Belgrade. Length: 940 km (584 miles)

savage (ˈsævɪdʒ) *adj* **1** wild; untamed: *savage beasts* **2** ferocious in temper: *a savage dog* **3** uncivilized; crude: *savage behaviour* **4** (of peoples) nonliterate or primitive: *a savage tribe* **5** (of terrain) rugged and uncultivated ▷ *n* **6** a member of a nonliterate society, esp one regarded as primitive **7** a fierce or vicious person or animal ▷ *vb* **savages, savaging, savaged** (*tr*) **8** to criticize violently **9** to attack ferociously and wound [c13 from OF *sauvage*, from L *silvāticus* belonging to a wood, from *silva* a wood] > ˈ**savagely** *adv* > ˈ**savageness** *n*

Savage (ˈsævɪdʒ) *n* **Michael Joseph** 1872-1940, New Zealand statesman; prime minister of New Zealand (1935-40)

Savage Island *n* another name for **Niue**

savagery (ˈsævɪdʒrɪ) *n, pl* **savageries 1** an uncivilized condition **2** a savage act or nature **3** savages collectively

Savaii (sɑːˈvaɪiː) *n* the largest island in Samoa: mountainous and volcanic. Pop: 45 050 (1991). Area: 1174 sq km (662 sq miles)

savanna *or* **savannah** (səˈvænə) *n* open grasslands,

Ss

usually with scattered bushes or trees, characteristic of much of tropical Africa [c16 from Sp. *zavana*, from Amerind *zabana*]

Savannah (sə'vænə) *n* **1** a port in the US, in E Georgia, near the mouth of the Savannah River: port of departure of the *Savannah* for Liverpool (1819), the first steamship to cross the Atlantic. Pop: 131 510 (2000) **2** a river in the southeastern US, formed by the confluence of the Tugaloo and Seneca Rivers in NW South Carolina: flows southeast to the Atlantic. Length: 505 km (314 miles)

savant ('sævənt) *n* a man of great learning; sage [c18 from F, from *savoir* to know, from L *sapere* to be wise] > **'savante** *fem n*

savate (sə'væt) *n* a form of boxing in which blows may be delivered with the feet as well as the hands [c19 from F, lit.: old worn-out shoe]

save[1] (seɪv) *vb* **saves, saving, saved 1** (*tr*) to rescue, preserve, or guard (a person or thing) from danger or harm **2** to avoid the spending, waste, or loss of (money, possessions, etc) **3** (*tr*) to deliver from sin; redeem **4** (often foll by *up*) to set aside or reserve (money, goods, etc) for future use **5** (*tr*) to treat with care so as to avoid or lessen wear or degeneration **6** (*tr*) to prevent the necessity for; obviate the trouble of **7** (*tr*) *soccer, hockey, etc* to prevent (a goal) by stopping (a struck ball or puck) ▷ *n* **8** *soccer, hockey, etc* the act of saving a goal **9** *computing* an instruction to write information from the memory onto a tape or disk [c13 from OF *salver*, via LL from L *salvus* safe] > **'savable** *or* **'saveable** *adj* > **'saver** *n*

save[2] (seɪv) *arch* ▷ *prep* **1** (often foll by *for*) Also: **saving** with the exception of ▷ *conj* **2** but [c13 *sauf*, from OF, from L *salvō*, from *salvus* safe]

save as you earn *n* (in Britain) a savings scheme operated by the government, in which monthly contributions earn tax-free interest. Abbrev: **SAYE**

saveloy ('sævɪˌlɔɪ) *n* a smoked sausage made from salted pork, coloured red with saltpetre [c19 prob. via F from It. *cervellato*, from *cervello* brain, from L, from *cerebrum* brain]

Savery ('seɪvərɪ) *n* **Thomas** ?1650–1715, English engineer, who built (1698) the first practical steam engine, used to pump water from mines

savin *or* **savine** ('sævɪn) *n* **1** a small spreading juniper bush of Europe, N Asia, and North America **2** the oil derived from the shoots and leaves of this plant, formerly used in medicine to treat rheumatism, etc [c14 from OF *savine*, from L *herba Sabīna* the Sabine plant]

saving ('seɪvɪŋ) *adj* **1** tending to save or preserve **2** redeeming or compensating (esp in **saving grace**) **3** thrifty or economical **4** *law* denoting or relating to an exception or reservation: *a saving clause in an agreement* ▷ *n* **5** preservation or redemption **6** economy or avoidance of waste **7** reduction in cost or expenditure **8** anything saved **9** (*pl*) money saved for future use ▷ *prep* **10** with the exception of ▷ *conj* **11** except > **'savingly** *adv*

savings bank *n* a bank that accepts the savings of depositors and pays interest on them

savings ratio *n econ* the ratio of personal savings to disposable income, esp using the difference between national figures for disposable income and consumer spending as a measure of savings

saviour *or US* **savior** ('seɪvjə) *n* a person who rescues another person or a thing from danger or harm [c13 *saveour*, from OF, from Church L *Salvātor* the Saviour]

Saviour *or US* **Savior** ('seɪvjə) *n Christianity* Jesus Christ regarded as the saviour of men from sin

Savoie (*French* savwa) *n* **1** a department of E France, in Rhône-Alpes region. Capital: Chambéry. Pop: 373 258 (1999). Area: 6188 sq km (2413 sq miles) **2** the French name for **Savoy**

savoir-faire ('sævwɑː'fɛə) *n* the ability to do the right thing in any situation [F, lit.: a knowing how to do]

Savona (*Italian* sa'voːna) *n* a port in NW Italy, in Liguria on the Mediterranean: an important centre of the Italian iron and steel industry. Pop: 69 806 (1990)

Savonarola (*Italian* savona'rɔːla) *n* **Girolamo** (dʒi'rɔːlamo) 1452–98, Italian religious and political reformer. As a Dominican prior in Florence he preached against contemporary sinfulness and moral corruption. When the Medici were expelled from the city (1494) he instituted a severely puritanical republic but lost the citizens' support after being excommunicated (1497). He was hanged and burned as a heretic

savory ('seɪvərɪ) *n, pl* **savories 1** any of numerous aromatic plants, including the **winter savory** and **summer savory**, of the Mediterranean region, having narrow leaves and white, pink, or purple flowers **2** the leaves of any of these plants, used as a potherb [c14 prob. from OE *sætherie*, from L *saturēia*, from ?]

savour *or US* **savor** ('seɪvə) *n* **1** the quality in a substance that is perceived by the sense of taste or smell **2** a specific taste or smell: *the savour of lime* **3** a slight but distinctive quality or trace **4** the power to excite interest: *the savour of wit has been lost* ▷ *vb* **5** (*intr*; often foll by *of*) to possess the taste or smell (of) **6** (*intr*; often foll by *of*) to have a suggestion (of) **7** (*tr*) to season **8** (*tr*) to taste or smell, esp appreciatively **9** (*tr*) to relish or enjoy [c13 from OF *savour*, from L *sapor* taste, from *sapere* to taste] > **'savourless** *or US* **'savorless** *adj*

savoury *or US* **savory** ('seɪvərɪ) *adj* **1** attractive to the sense of taste or smell **2** salty or spicy: *a savoury dish* **3** pleasant **4** respectable ▷ *n, pl* **savouries** *or US* **savories 5** *chiefly Brit* a savoury dish served as an hors d'oeuvre or dessert [c13 *savure*, from OF, from *savourer* to SAVOUR] > **'savouriness** *or US* **'savoriness** *n*

savoy (sə'vɔɪ) *n* a cultivated variety of cabbage having a compact head and wrinkled leaves [c16 after the SAVOY region]

Savoy[1] (sə'vɔɪ) *n* an area of SE France, bordering on Italy, mainly in the Savoy Alps: a duchy in the late Middle Ages and part of the Kingdom of Sardinia from 1720 to 1860, when it became part of France. French name: **Savoie**

Savoy[2] (sə'vɔɪ) *n* a noble family of Italy that ruled over the duchy of Savoy and became the royal house of Italy (1861–1946): the oldest reigning dynasty in Europe before the dissolution of the Italian monarchy

Savoy Alps *pl n* a range of the Alps in SE France. Highest peak: Mont Blanc, 4807 m (15 772 ft)

Savoyard (sə'vɔɪɑːd; *French* savwajar) *n* **1** a native of Savoy **2** the dialect of French spoken in Savoy ▷ *adj* **3** of or relating to Savoy, its inhabitants, or their dialect

savvy ('sævɪ) *sl* ▷ *vb* **savvies, savvying, savvied 1** to understand or get the sense of (an idea, etc) ▷ *n* **2** comprehension ▷ *adj* **savvier, savviest 3** *chiefly US* shrewd [c18 corruption of Sp. *sabe (usted)* (you) know, from *saber* to know, from L *sapere* to be wise]

saw[1] (sɔː) *n* **1** any of various hand tools for cutting wood, metal, etc, having a blade with teeth along one edge **2** any of various machines or devices for cutting by use of a toothed blade, such as a power-driven toothed band of metal ▷ *vb* **saws, sawing, sawed; sawed** *or* **sawn 3** to cut with a saw **4** to form by sawing **5** to cut as if wielding a saw: *to saw the air* **6** to move (an object) from side to side as if moving a saw [OE *sagu*: rel. to L *secare* to cut] > **'sawer** *n* > **'saw,like** *adj*

saw[2] (sɔː) *vb* the past tense of **see**[1]

saw[3] (sɔː) *n* a wise saying, maxim, or proverb [OE *sagu* a saying]

sawbones ('sɔːˌbəʊnz) *n, pl* **sawbones** *or* **sawboneses** *sl* a surgeon or doctor

sawdust ('sɔːˌdʌst) *n* particles of wood formed by sawing

sawfish ('sɔːˌfɪʃ) *n, pl* **sawfish** *or* **sawfishes** a sharklike ray of subtropical coastal waters, having a serrated bladelike mouth

sawfly ('sɔːˌflaɪ) *n, pl* **sawflies** any of various

hymenopterous insects, the females of which have a sawlike ovipositor

sawhorse ('sɔːˌhɔːs) *n* a stand for timber during sawing

sawmill ('sɔːˌmɪl) *n* an industrial establishment where timber is sawn into planks, etc

sawn (sɔːn) *vb* a past participle of **saw**[1]

sawn-off *or esp US* **sawed-off** *adj (prenominal)* (of a shotgun) having the barrel cut short, mainly to facilitate concealment of the weapon

saw-off *n Canad sl* **1** a compromise **2** a deadlocked situation

saw set *n* a tool used for setting the teeth of a saw, consisting of a clamp used to bend each tooth at a slight angle to the plane of the saw, alternate teeth being bent in the same direction

sawyer ('sɔːjə) *n* a person who saws timber for a living [c14 *sawier*, from SAW[1] + *-ier*, var. of -ER[1]]

sax (sæks) *n inf* short for **saxophone**

Saxe[1] (saks) *n* the French name for **Saxony**

Saxe[2] (*French* saks) *n* **Hermann Maurice** (ɛrman mɔris) comte de Saxe. 1696–1750, French marshal born in Saxony: he distinguished himself in the War of the Austrian Succession (1740–48)

saxe blue (sæks) *n* **a** a light greyish-blue colour **b** (*as adj*): *a saxe-blue dress* [c19 from F *Saxe* Saxony, source of a dye of this colour]

Saxe-Coburg-Gotha (sæks'kəʊbɜːg'gəʊθə) *n* the ruling house of the former German duchy of Saxe-Coburg-Gotha (until 1918) and the name of the British royal family (1901–17) through Prince Albert
▷ www.royal.gov.uk/output/Page128.asp

saxhorn ('sæksˌhɔːn) *n* a valved brass instrument used chiefly in brass and military bands, having a tube of conical bore. It resembles the tuba [c19 after Adolphe *Sax* (see SAXOPHONE), who invented it (1845)]

saxicolous (sæk'sɪkələs) *adj* living on or among rocks: *saxicolous plants*. Also: **saxicole** ('sæksɪˌkəʊl), **saxatile** ('sæksəˌtaɪl) [c19 from NL *saxicolus*, from L *saxum* rock + *colere* to dwell]

saxifrage ('sæksɪˌfreɪdʒ) *n* a plant having small white, yellow, purple, or pink flowers [c15 from LL *saxifraga*, lit.: rock-breaker (probably alluding to its ability to dissolve kidney stones), from L *saxum* rock + *frangere* to break]

Saxo Grammaticus ('sæksəʊ grə'mætɪkəs) *n* ?1150–?1220, Danish chronicler, noted for his *Gesta Danorum*, a history of Denmark down to 1185, written in Latin, which is partly historical and partly mythological, and contains the Hamlet (Amleth) legend

Saxon ('sæksən) *n* **1** a member of a West Germanic people who raided and settled parts of S Britain in the fifth and sixth centuries AD **2** a native or inhabitant of Saxony **3a** the Low German dialect of Saxony **3b** any of the West Germanic dialects spoken by the ancient Saxons ▷ *adj* **4** of or characteristic of the ancient Saxons, the Anglo-Saxons, or their descendants **5** of or characteristic of Saxony, its inhabitants, or their Low German dialect [c13 (replacing OE *Seaxe*): via OF from LL *Saxon-*, *Saxo*, from Gk; of Gmc origin]
▷ www.anglo-saxons.net
▷ www.bbc.co.uk/history/ancient/anglo_saxons/index.shtml

Saxony ('sæksənɪ) *n* **1** a state in E Germany, formerly part of East Germany. Pop: 4 459 700 (2000 est) **2** a former duchy and electorate in SE and central Germany, whose territory changed greatly over the centuries **3** (in the early Middle Ages) any territory inhabited or ruled by Saxons ▷ Compare **Saxony-Anhalt, Lower Saxony** German name: **Sachsen** French name: **Saxe**

Saxony-Anhalt ('sæksənɪ 'ɑːnhɑːlt) *n* a state of E Germany: created in 1947 from the state of Anhalt and those parts of Prussia formerly ruled by the duchy of Saxony: part of East Germany until 1990. Capital: Magdeburg. Pop: 2 648 700 (2000 est)

saxophone ('sæksəˌfəʊn) *n* a keyed single-reed wind instrument of mellow tone colour, used mainly in jazz and dance music. Often shortened to **sax** [c19 after Adolphe *Sax* (1814–94), Belgian musical-instrument maker, who invented it (1846)] > **saxophonic** (ˌsæksə'fɒnɪk) *adj* > **saxophonist** (sæk'sɒfənɪst) *n*

say (seɪ) *vb* **says, saying, said** (*mainly tr*) **1** to speak, pronounce, or utter **2** (*also intr*) to express (an idea, etc) in words; tell **3** (*also intr; may take a clause as object*) to state (an opinion, fact, etc) positively **4** to recite: *to say grace* **5** (*may take a clause as object*) to report or allege: *they say we shall have rain today* **6** (*may take a clause as object*) to suppose: *let us say that he is lying* **7** (*may take a clause as object*) to convey by means of artistic expression **8** to make a case for: *there is much to be said for it* **9 go without saying** to be so obvious as to need no explanation **10 I say!** *inf, chiefly Brit* an exclamation of surprise **11 not to say** even **12 that is to say** in other words **13 to say the least** at the very least ▷ *adv* **14** approximately: *there were, say, 20 people present* **15** for example: *choose a number, say, four* ▷ *n* **16** the right or chance to speak: *let him have his say* **17** authority, esp to influence a decision: *he has a lot of say* **18** a statement of opinion: *you've had your say* ▷ *interj* **19** *US & Canad inf* an exclamation to attract attention or express surprise [OE *secgan*] > **'sayer** *n*

Sayan Mountains (sɑː'jæn) *pl n* a mountain range in S central Russia, in S Siberia. Highest peak: Munku-Sardyk, 3437 m (11 457 ft)

SAYE (in Britain) *abbrev for* save as you earn

Sayers ('seɪəz) *n* **Dorothy L(eigh)** 1893–1957, English detective-story writer

saying ('seɪɪŋ) *n* a maxim, adage, or proverb

say-so *n inf* **1** an arbitrary assertion **2** an authoritative decision **3** the authority to make a final decision

sayyid ('saɪɪd) *or* **said** *n* **1** a Muslim claiming descent from Mohammed's grandson Husain **2** a Muslim honorary title [c17 from Ar.: lord]

Sb *the chemical symbol for* antimony [from NL *stibium*]

SBE *abbrev for* Southern British English

SBU *abbrev for* strategic business unit: a division within an organization responsible for marketing its own range of products

sc *printing abbrev for* small capitals

Sc *the chemical symbol for* scandium

SC *abbrev for:* **1** Signal Corps **2** *Canad* Social Credit

sc. *abbrev for:* **1** scale **2** scene **3** scilicet

scab (skæb) *n* **1** the dried crusty surface of a healing skin wound or sore **2** a contagious disease of sheep, a form of mange, caused by a mite **3** a fungal disease of plants characterized by crusty spots on the fruits, leaves, etc **4** *derog* **4a** Also called: **blackleg** a person who refuses to support a trade union's actions, esp strikes **4b** (*as modifier*): *scab labour* **5** a despicable person ▷ *vb* **scabs, scabbing, scabbed** (*intr*) **6** to become covered with a scab **7** to replace a striking worker [OE *sceabb*]

scabbard ('skæbəd) *n* a holder for a bladed weapon such as a sword or bayonet [c13 *scauberc*, from Norman F *escaubers*, (pl) of Gmc origin]

scabby ('skæbɪ) *adj* **scabbier, scabbiest 1** *pathol* having an area of the skin covered with scabs **2** *pathol obs* having scabies **3** *inf* despicable > **'scabbily** *adv* > **'scabbiness** *n*

scabies ('skeɪbiːz) *n* a contagious skin infection caused by a mite, characterized by intense itching and inflammation [c15 from L: scurf, from *scabere* to scratch]

scabious[1] ('skeɪbɪəs) *adj* **1** having or covered with scabs **2** of, relating to, or resembling scabies [c17 from L *scabiōsus*, from SCABIES]

scabious[2] ('skeɪbɪəs) *n* any of a genus of plants of the Mediterranean region, having blue, red, or whitish dome-shaped flower heads [c14 from Med. L *scabiōsa herba* the scabies plant, referring to its use in treating scabies]

scabrous ('skeɪbrəs) *adj* 1 roughened because of small projections 2 indecent or salacious: *scabrous humour* 3 difficult to deal with [c17 from L *scaber* rough] > '**scabrously** *adv*

scad (skæd) *n, pl* **scad** *or* **scads** any of various marine fishes having a deeply forked tail, such as the large mackerel [c17 from ?]

scads (skædz) *pl n inf* a large amount or number [c19 from ?]

Scafell Pike (skɔː'fɛl) *n* a mountain in NW England, in Cumbria in the Lake District: the highest peak in England. Height: 978 m (3209 ft)

scaffold ('skæfəld) *n* 1 a temporary framework that is used to support workmen and materials during the erection, repair, etc, of a building 2 a raised wooden platform on which plays are performed, tobacco, etc, is dried, or (esp formerly) criminals are executed ▷ *vb* (*tr*) 3 to provide with a scaffold 4 to support by means of a scaffold [c14 from OF *eschaffaut*, from Vulgar L *catafalicum* (unattested)] > '**scaffolder** *n*

scaffolding ('skæfəldɪŋ) *n* 1 a scaffold or system of scaffolds 2 the building materials used to make scaffolds

Scala ('skaːlə) *n* **La** See **La Scala**

scalable ('skeɪləbᵊl) *adj* capable of being climbed > '**scalableness** *n* > '**scalably** *adv*

scalar ('skeɪlə) *n* 1 a quantity, such as time or temperature, that has magnitude but not direction 2 *maths* an element of a field associated with a vector space ▷ *adj* 3 having magnitude but not direction [c17 (meaning: resembling a ladder): from L *scālāris*, from *scāla* ladder]

scalar product *n* the product of two vectors to form a scalar, whose value is the product of the magnitudes of the vectors and the cosine of the angle between them. Also called: **dot product**

scalawag ('skælə,wæg) *n* a variant of **scallywag**

scald¹ (skɔːld) *vb* 1 to burn or be burnt with or as if with hot liquid or steam 2 (*tr*) to subject to the action of boiling water, esp so as to sterilize 3 (*tr*) to heat (a liquid) almost to boiling point 4 to plunge (tomatoes, etc) into boiling water in order to skin them more easily ▷ *n* 5 the act or result of scalding 6 an abnormal condition in plants, caused by exposure to excessive sunlight, gases, etc [c13 via OF from LL *excaldāre* to wash in warm water, from *calida (aqua)* warm (water), from *calēre* to be warm] > '**scalder** *n*

scald² (skɔːld) *n* a variant spelling of **skald**

scaldfish ('skɔːld,fɪʃ, 'skaːld-) *n, pl* **scaldfish** *or* **scaldfishes** a small European flatfish, covered with large fragile scales

scale¹ (skeɪl) *n* 1 any of the numerous plates, made of various substances, covering the bodies of fishes 2a any of the horny or chitinous plates covering a part or the entire body of certain reptiles and mammals 2b any of the numerous minute structures covering the wings of lepidoptera 3 a thin flat piece or flake 4 a thin flake of dead epidermis shed from the skin 5 a specialized leaf or bract, esp the protective covering of a bud or the dry membranous bract of a catkin 6 See **scale insect** 7 any oxide formed on a metal when heated 8 tartar formed on the teeth 9 another name for **limescale** ▷ *vb* **scales, scaling, scaled** 10 (*tr*) to remove the scales or coating from 11 to peel off or cause to peel off in flakes or scales 12 (*intr*) to shed scales 13 to cover or become covered with scales, incrustation, etc [c14 from OF *escale*, of Gmc origin]

scale² (skeɪl) *n* 1 (*often pl*) a machine or device for weighing 2 one of the pans of a balance 3 **tip the scales** 3a to exercise a decisive influence 3b (foll by *at*) to amount in weight (to) ▷ *vb* **scales, scaling, scaled** (*tr*) 4 to weigh with or as if with scales [c13 from ON *skāl* bowl]

scale³ (skeɪl) *n* 1 a sequence of marks either at regular intervals, or representing equal steps, used as a reference in making measurements 2 a measuring instrument having such a scale 3a the ratio between the size of something real and that of a representation of it 3b (*as modifier*): *a scale model* 4 a line, numerical ratio, etc, for showing this ratio 5 a progressive or graduated table of things, wages, etc: *a wage scale for carpenters* 6 an established standard 7 a relative degree or extent: *he entertained on a grand scale* 8 *music* a group of notes taken in ascending or descending order, esp within the compass of one octave 9 *maths* the notation of a given number system: *the decimal scale* ▷ *vb* **scales, scaling, scaled** 10 to climb to the top of (a height) by or as if by a ladder 11 (*tr*) to make or draw (a model, etc) according to a particular ratio of proportionate reduction 12 (*tr*; usually foll by *up* or *down*) to increase or reduce proportionately in size, etc 13 (*intr*) *Austral inf* to ride on public transport without paying a fare [c15 via It. from L *scāla* ladder]

scaleboard ('skeɪl,bɔːd) *n* a very thin piece of board, used for backing a picture, etc

scale insect *n* a small insect which typically lives and feeds on plants and secretes a protective scale around itself. Many species are pests

scalene ('skeɪliːn) *adj* 1 *maths* (of a triangle) having all sides of unequal length 2 *anat* of or relating to any of the scalenus muscles [c17 from LL *scalēnus* with unequal sides, from Gk *skalēnos*]

scalenus (skə'liːnəs) *n, pl* **scaleni** (-naɪ) *anat* any one of the three muscles situated on each side of the neck extending from the cervical vertebrae to the first or second pair of ribs [c18 from NL; see SCALENE]

scaling ladder *n* a ladder used to climb high walls, esp one used formerly to enter a besieged town, fortress, etc

scallion ('skæljən) *n* any of various onions, such as the spring onion, that have a small bulb and long leaves and are eaten in salads [c14 from Anglo-F *scalun*, from L *Ascalōnia (caepa)* Ascalonian (onion), from *Ascalo* Ascalon, a Palestinian port]

scallop ('skɒləp, 'skæl-) *n* 1 any of various marine bivalves having a fluted fan-shaped shell 2 the edible adductor muscle of certain of these molluscs 3 either of the shell valves of any of these molluscs 4 a scallop shell in which fish, esp shellfish, is cooked and served 5 one of a series of curves along an edge 6 the shape of a scallop shell used as the badge of a pilgrim, esp in the Middle Ages 7 *chiefly Austral* a potato cake fried in batter ▷ *vb* 8 (*tr*) to decorate (an edge) with scallops 9 to bake (food) in a scallop shell or similar dish [c14 from OF *escalope* shell, of Gmc origin] > '**scalloper** *n* > '**scalloping** *n*

scally ('skælɪ) *n, pl* **scallies** *Northwest English dialect* a rascal; rogue [c20 from SCALLYWAG]

scallywag ('skælɪ,wæg) *n inf* a scamp; rascal ▷ Also: **scalawag, scallawag** [c19 (orig. undersized animal): from ?]

scalp (skælp) *n* 1 *anat* the skin and subcutaneous tissue covering the top of the head 2 *hist* (among North American Indians) a part of this removed as a trophy from a slain enemy 3 a trophy or token signifying conquest 4 *Scot dialect* a projection of bare rock from vegetation ▷ *vb* (*tr*) 5 to cut the scalp from 6 *inf, chiefly US* to purchase and resell (securities) quickly so as to make several small profits 7 *inf* to buy (tickets) cheaply and resell at an inflated price [c13 prob. from ON] > '**scalper** *n*

scalpel ('skælpᵊl) *n* a surgical knife with a short thin blade [c18 from L *scalpellum*, from *scalper* a knife, from *scalpere* to scrape]

scaly ('skeɪlɪ) *adj* **scalier, scaliest** 1 resembling or covered in scales 2 peeling off in scales > '**scaliness** *n*

scaly anteater *n* another name for **pangolin**

Scamander (skə'mændə) *n* the ancient name for the **Menderes** (sense 2)

scamp¹ (skæmp) *n* 1 an idle mischievous person 2 a

mischievous child [c18 from *scamp* (vb) to be a highway robber, prob. from MDu. *schampen* to decamp, from OF *escamper*, from L *campus* field] > ˈ**scampish** *adj*

scamp² (skæmp) *vb* a less common word for **skimp** > ˈ**scamper** *n*

scamper (ˈskæmpə) *vb* **1** (*intr*) to run about playfully **2** (often foll by *through*) to hurry through (a place, task, etc) ▷ *n* **3** the act of scampering [c17 prob. from *scamp* (vb); see SCAMP¹]

scampi (ˈskæmpɪ) *n* (*usually functioning as sing*) large prawns, usually eaten fried in breadcrumbs [It.: pl of *scampo* shrimp, from ?]

scamto (ˈskæmtəʊ) *n S African* the argot of urban South African Blacks [c20 from ?]

scan (skæn) *vb* **scans, scanning, scanned 1** (*tr*) to scrutinize minutely **2** (*tr*) to glance at quickly **3** (*tr*) *prosody* to read or analyse (verse) according to the rules of metre and versification **4** (*intr*) *prosody* to conform to the rules of metre and versification **5** (*tr*) *electronics* to move a beam of light, electrons, etc, in a predetermined pattern over (a surface or region) to obtain information, esp to reproduce a television image **6** (*tr*) to examine data stored on (magnetic tape, etc), usually in order to retrieve information **7** to examine or search (a prescribed region) by systematically varying the direction of a radar or sonar beam **8** *med* to obtain an image of (a part of the body) by means of a scanner ▷ *n* **9** the act or an instance of scanning **10** *med* **10a** the examination of a part of the body by means of a scanner: *a brain scan; an ultrasound scan* **10b** the image produced by a scanner [c14 from LL *scandere* to scan (verse), from L: to climb] > ˈ**scannable** *adj*

scandal (ˈskændᵊl) *n* **1** a disgraceful action or event: *his negligence was a scandal* **2** censure or outrage arising from an action or event **3** a person whose conduct causes reproach or disgrace **4** malicious talk, esp gossip **5** *law* a libellous action or statement [c16 from LL *scandalum* stumbling block, from Gk *skandalon* a trap] > ˈ**scandalous** *adj* > ˈ**scandalously** *adv*

scandalize *or* **scandalise** (ˈskændəˌlaɪz) *vb* **scandalizes, scandalizing, scandalized** *or* **scandalises, scandalising, scandalised** (*tr*) to shock, as by improper behaviour > ˌ**scandaliˈzation** *or* ˌ**scandaliˈsation** *n*

scandalmonger (ˈskændᵊlˌmʌŋgə) *n* a person who spreads or enjoys scandal, gossip, etc

Scandinavia (ˌskændɪˈneɪvɪə) *n* **1** Also called: **the Scandinavian Peninsula** the peninsula of N Europe occupied by Norway and Sweden **2** the countries of N Europe, esp considered as a cultural unit and including Norway, Sweden, Denmark, and often Finland, Iceland, and the Faeroe Islands > ˌ**Scandiˈnavian** *adj, n*

scandium (ˈskændɪəm) *n* a rare silvery-white metallic element occurring in minute quantities in numerous minerals. Symbol: Sc; atomic no.: 21; atomic wt.: 44.96 [c19 from NL, from L *Scandia* Scandinavia, where discovered]

scanner (ˈskænə) *n* **1** a person or thing that scans **2** a device, usually electronic, used to measure or sample the distribution of some quantity or condition in a particular system, region, or area **3** an aerial or similar device designed to transmit or receive signals, esp radar signals, inside a given solid angle of space **4** any device used in medical diagnosis to obtain an image of an internal organ or part **5** short for **optical scanner**

scanning electron microscope *n* a type of electron microscope that produces a three-dimensional image

scansion (ˈskænʃən) *n* the analysis of the metrical structure of verse [c17 from L: climbing up, from *scandere* to climb]

scant (skænt) *adj* **1** scarcely sufficient: *he paid her scant attention* **2** (*prenominal*) bare: *a scant ten inches* **3** (*postpositive*; foll by *of*) having a short supply (of) ▷ *vb* (*tr*) **4** to limit in size or quantity **5** to provide with a limited supply of **6** to treat in an inadequate manner ▷ *adv* **7** scarcely; barely [c14 from ON *skamt*, from *skammr* short] > ˈ**scantly** *adv*

scantling (ˈskæntlɪŋ) *n* **1** a piece of sawn timber, such as a rafter, that has a small cross section **2** the dimensions of a piece of building material or the structural parts of a ship or aircraft **3** a building stone **4** a small quantity or amount [c16 changed (through infl. of SCANT & -LING¹) from earlier *scantillon* a carpenter's gauge, from OF *escantillon*, ult. from L *scandere* to climb]

scanty (ˈskæntɪ) *adj* **scantier, scantiest 1** limited; barely enough **2** inadequate **3** lacking fullness > ˈ**scantily** *adv* > ˈ**scantiness** *n*

Scapa Flow (ˈskæpə) *n* an extensive landlocked anchorage off the N coast of Scotland, in the Orkney Islands: major British naval base in both World Wars. Length: about 24 km (15 miles). Width: 13 km (8 miles)

scape *or* **'scape** (skeɪp) *vb* **scapes, scaping, scaped,** *n* an archaic word for **escape**

-scape *suffix forming nouns* indicating a scene or view of something: *seascape* [from LANDSCAPE]

scapegoat (ˈskeɪpˌgəʊt) *n* **1** a person made to bear the blame for others **2** *Bible* a goat symbolically laden with the sins of the Israelites and sent into the wilderness ▷ *vb* **3** (*tr*) to make a scapegoat of [c16 from ESCAPE + GOAT, coined by William Tyndale to translate Biblical Heb. *azāzēl* (prob.) goat for Azazel, mistakenly thought to mean "goat that escapes"]

scapegrace (ˈskeɪpˌgreɪs) *n* a mischievous person [c19 from SCAPE + GRACE, alluding to a person who lacks God's grace]

scaphocephalic (ˌskæfɪsɪˈfælɪk) *adj* having a head that is abnormally long and narrow as a result of the two paretal bones on the top of the skull closing prematurely. Compare **dolichocephalic, brachycephalic** > ˈ**scaphoˌcephaly** *or* > ˈ**scaphoˌcephalism** *n*

scaphoid (ˈskæfɔɪd) *adj anat* a boat-shaped bone in the wrist [c18 via NL from Gk *skaphoeidēs*, from *skaphē* boat]

scapula (ˈskæpjʊlə) *n, pl* **scapulae** (-liː) *or* **scapulas** either of two large flat triangular bones, one on each side of the back part of the shoulder in man. Nontechnical name: **shoulder blade** [c16 from LL: shoulder]

scapular (ˈskæpjʊlə) *adj* **1** *anat* of or relating to the scapula ▷ *n* **2** part of the monastic habit worn by members of many Christian religious orders, consisting of a piece of woollen cloth worn over the shoulders, and hanging down to the ankles **3** two small rectangular pieces of cloth joined by tapes passing over the shoulders and worn in token of affiliation to a religious order **4** any of the small feathers of a bird that lie along the shoulder ▷ Also called (for senses 2 and 3): **scapulary**

scar¹ (skɑː) *n* **1** any mark left on the skin or other tissue following the healing of a wound, etc **2** a permanent change in a person's character resulting from emotional distress **3** the mark on a plant indicating the former point of attachment of a part **4** a mark of damage ▷ *vb* **scars, scarring, scarred 5** to mark or become marked with a scar **6** (*intr*) to heal leaving a scar [c14 via LL from Gk *eskhara* scab]

scar² (skɑː) *n* an irregular elongated trenchlike feature on a land surface that often exposes bedrock [c14 from ON *sker* low reef]

scarab (ˈskærəb) *n* **1** any scarabaeid beetle, esp the **sacred scarab**, regarded by the ancient Egyptians as divine **2** the scarab as represented on amulets, etc [c16 from L *scarabaeus*]

scarabaeid (ˌskærəˈbiːɪd) *n* **1** any of a family of beetles including the sacred scarab and other dung beetles, the chafers, and rhinoceros beetles ▷ *adj* **2** of or belonging to this family [c19 from NL]

Scaramouch (ˈskærəˌmuːʃ) *n* a stock character who appears as a boastful coward in commedia dell'arte [c17

Ss

via F from It. *Scaramuccia*, from *scaramuccia* a SKIRMISH]

Scarborough ('skɑːbrə) *n* a fishing port and resort in NE England, in North Yorkshire on the North Sea: developed as a spa after 1660; ruined 12th-century castle. Pop: 38 809 (1991)

scarce (skɛəs) *adj* **1** rarely encountered **2** insufficient to meet the demand **3 make oneself scarce** *inf* to go away ▷ *adv* **4** *arch or literary* scarcely [C13 from OF *scars*, from Vulgar L *excarpsus* (unattested) plucked out, from L *excerpere* to select] > **'scarceness** *n*

scarcely ('skɛəslɪ) *adv* **1** hardly at all; only just **2** *often used ironically* probably or definitely not: *that is scarcely justification for your actions.*

USAGE Since *scarcely*, *hardly*, and *barely* already have negative force, it is unnecessary to use another negative word with them: *he had hardly had* (not *he hadn't hardly had*) *time to think; there was scarcely any* (not *scarcely no*) *bread left*. When *scarcely*, *hardly*, and *barely* are used at the beginning of a sentence, as in *Scarcely had I arrived...*, the following clause should be introduced by *when*: *Scarcely had I arrived when I was asked to chair a meeting*. The word *before* is quite often used instead, and this would generally be considered correct. However, use of the word *than*, though increasingly common, is still thought by many to be incorrect. See also at **sooner**

scarcity ('skɛəsɪtɪ) *n, pl* **scarcities 1** inadequate supply **2** rarity or infrequent occurrence

scare (skɛə) *vb* **scares, scaring, scared 1** to fill or be filled with fear or alarm **2** (*tr; often foll by* *away* or *off*) to drive (away) by frightening **3** (*tr; foll by* *up*) *US & Canad inf* **3a** to produce (a meal) quickly from whatever is available **3b** to manage to find (something) quickly or with difficulty: *brewers need to scare up more sales* ▷ *n* **4** a sudden attack of fear or alarm **5** a period of general fear or alarm ▷ *adj* **6** causing (needless) fear or alarm: *a scare story* [C12 from ON *skirra*] > **'scarer** *n*

scarecrow ('skɛəˌkrəʊ) *n* **1** an object, usually in the shape of a man, made out of sticks and old clothes to scare birds away from crops **2** a person or thing that appears frightening **3** *inf* an untidy-looking person

scaremonger ('skɛəˌmʌŋgə) *n* a person who delights in spreading rumours of disaster > **'scareˌmongering** *n*

scarf[1] (skɑːf) *n, pl* **scarves** *or* **scarfs** a rectangular, triangular, or long narrow piece of cloth worn around the head, neck, or shoulders for warmth or decoration [C16 from ?]

scarf[2] (skɑːf) *n, pl* **scarfs 1** Also called: **scarf joint, scarfed joint** a lapped joint between two pieces of timber made by notching the ends and strapping or gluing the two pieces together **2** the end of a piece of timber shaped to form such a joint **3** *whaling* an incision made along a whale before stripping off the blubber ▷ *vb* (*tr*) **4** to join (two pieces of timber) by means of a scarf **5** to make a scarf on (a piece of timber) **6** to cut a scarf in (a whale) [C14 prob. from ON]

scarfskin ('skɑːfˌskɪn) *n* the outermost layer of the skin; epidermis or cuticle [C17 from SCARF[1] (in the sense: an outer covering)]

scarify ('skɛərɪˌfaɪ, 'skærɪ-) *vb* **scarifies, scarifying, scarified** (*tr*) **1** *surgery* to make tiny punctures or superficial incisions in (the skin or other tissue), as for inoculating **2** *agriculture* to break up and loosen (soil) to a shallow depth **3** to wound with harsh criticism [C15 via OF from L *scarīfāre* to scratch open, from Gk *skariphasthai* to draw, from *skariphos* a pencil] > **ˌscarifiˈcation** *n* > **'scariˌfier** *n*

scarlatina (ˌskɑːləˈtiːnə) *n* the technical name for **scarlet fever** [C19 from NL, from It. *scarlattina*, dim. of *scarlatto* scarlet]

Scarlatti (skɑːˈlætɪ) *n* **1 Alessandro** (alesˈsandro) ?1659–1725, Italian composer; regarded as the founder of modern opera **2** his son, (**Giuseppe**) **Domenico** (doˈmeːniko) 1685–1757, Italian composer and harpsichordist, in Portugal and Spain from 1720. He wrote over 550 single-movement sonatas for harpsichord, many of them exercises in virtuoso technique

scarlet ('skɑːlɪt) *n* **1** a vivid orange-red colour **2** cloth or clothing of this colour ▷ *adj* **3** of the colour scarlet **4** sinful or immoral [C13 from OF *escarlate* fine cloth, from ?]

scarlet fever *n* an acute communicable disease characterized by fever, strawberry-coloured tongue, and a rash starting on the neck and chest and spreading to the abdomen and limbs. Technical name: **scarlatina**

scarlet letter *n* (esp among US Puritans) a scarlet letter *A* formerly worn by a person convicted of adultery

scarlet pimpernel *n* a weedy plant, related to the primrose, having small red, purple, or white star-shaped flowers that close in bad weather. Also called: **shepherd's** (or **poor man's**) **weatherglass**

scarlet runner *n* a climbing perennial bean plant of South America, having scarlet flowers: widely cultivated for its long green edible pods containing edible seeds. Also: **runner bean**

scarlet woman *n* **1** a sinful woman described in the Bible (Rev 17), interpreted as a symbol of pagan Rome or of the Roman Catholic Church **2** any sexually promiscuous woman

scarp (skɑːp) *n* **1** a steep slope, esp one formed by erosion or faulting **2** *fortifications* the side of a ditch cut nearest to a rampart ▷ *vb* **3** (*tr; often passive*) to wear or cut so as to form a steep slope [C16 from It. *scarpa*]

scarper ('skɑːpə) *Brit sl* ▷ *vb* **1** (*intr*) to depart in haste ▷ *n* **2** a hasty departure [from ?]

Scarron (*French* skarɔ̃) *n* **Paul** (pɔl) 1610–60, French comic dramatist and novelist, noted particularly for his picaresque novel *Le Roman comique* (1651–57)

Scart *or* **SCART** (skɑːt) *n* *electronics* **a** a 21-pin plug-and-socket system which carries picture, sound, and other signals, used especially in home entertainment systems **b** (*as modifier*): *a Scart cable* [C20 after Syndicat des Constructeurs des Appareils Radiorécepteurs et Téléviseurs, the company that designed it]

scarves (skɑːvz) *n* a plural of **scarf**[1]

scary ('skɛərɪ) *adj* **scarier, scariest** *inf* **1** causing fear or alarm **2** timid

scat[1] (skæt) *vb* **scats, scatting, scatted** (*intr; usually imperative*) *inf* to go away in haste [C19 ?from a hiss + *cat*, used to frighten away cats]

scat[2] (skæt) *n* **1** a type of jazz singing characterized by improvised vocal sounds instead of words ▷ *vb* **scats, scatting, scatted 2** (*intr*) to sing jazz in this way [C20 ? imit.]

scathe (skeɪð) *vb* **scathes, scathing, scathed** (*tr*) **1** *rare* to attack with severe criticism **2** *arch or dialect* to injure ▷ *n* **3** *arch or dialect* harm [OE *sceatha*]

scathing ('skeɪðɪŋ) *adj* **1** harshly critical; scornful **2** damaging > **'scathingly** *adv*

scatology (skæˈtɒlədʒɪ) *n* **1** the scientific study of excrement, esp in medicine and in palaeontology **2** obscenity or preoccupation with obscenity, esp in the form of references to excrement [C19 from Gk *skat-* excrement + -LOGY] > **scatological** (ˌskætəˈlɒdʒɪkᵊl) *adj*

scatter ('skætə) *vb* **1** (*tr*) to throw about in various directions **2** to separate and move or cause to separate and move in various directions **3** to deviate or cause to deviate in many directions, as in the refraction of light ▷ *n* **4** the act of scattering **5** a substance or a number of objects scattered about [C13 prob. a var. of SHATTER] > **'scatterer** *n*

scatterbrain ('skætəˌbreɪn) *n* a person who is incapable of serious thought or concentration > **'scatterˌbrained** *adj*

scatter diagram *n statistics* a representation by a Cartesian graph of the correlation between two quantities, such as height and weight

scattering ('skætərɪŋ) *n* **1** a small amount **2** *physics* the process in which particles, atoms, etc, are deflected as a result of collision

scattershot ('skætəˌʃɒt) *adj* random; haphazard: *their approach to conservation is scattershot and unscientific*

scatty ('skætɪ) *adj* **scattier, scattiest** *Brit inf* **1** empty-headed or thoughtless **2** distracted (esp in **drive someone scatty**) [c20 from SCATTERBRAINED] > **'scattily** *adv* > **'scattiness** *n*

scaup *or* **scaup duck** (skɔːp) *n* either of two diving ducks, the **greater scaup** or the **lesser scaup**, of Europe and America, having a black-and-white plumage in the male [c16 Scot var. of SCALP]

scavenge ('skævɪndʒ) *vb* **scavenges, scavenging, scavenged 1** to search for (anything usable) among discarded material **2** (*tr*) to purify (a molten metal) by bubbling a suitable gas through it **3** to clean up filth from (streets, etc)

scavenger ('skævɪndʒə) *n* **1** a person who collects things discarded by others **2** any animal that feeds on decaying organic matter **3** a person employed to clean the streets [c16 from Anglo-Norman *scawager*, from OF *escauwage* examination, from *escauwer* to scrutinize, of Gmc origin] > **'scavengery** *n*

ScD *abbrev for* Doctor of Science

SCE (in Scotland) *abbrev for* Scottish Certificate of Education: either of two public examinations in specific subjects taken as school-leaving qualifications or as qualifying examinations for entry into a university, college, etc

scena ('ʃeɪnə) *n, pl* **scene** (-ˌneɪ) a solo vocal piece of dramatic style and large scope, esp in opera [c19 It., from L *scēna* scene]

scenario (sɪ'nɑːrɪˌəʊ) *n, pl* **scenarios 1** a summary of the plot of a play, etc, including information about its characters, scenes, etc **2** a predicted sequence of events [c19 via It. from L *scēnārium*, from *scēna*; see SCENE]

scene (siːn) *n* **1** the place where an action or event, real or imaginary, occurs **2** the setting for the action of a play, novel, etc **3** an incident or situation, real or imaginary, esp as described or represented **4a** a subdivision of an act of a play, in which the setting is fixed **4b** a single event, esp a significant one, in a play **5** *films* a shot or series of shots that constitutes a unit of the action **6** the backcloths, etc, for a play or film set **7** the prospect of a place, landscape, etc **8** a display of emotion **9** *inf* the environment for a specific activity: *the fashion scene* **10** *inf* interest or chosen occupation: *classical music is not my scene* **11** *rare* the stage **12 behind the scenes** out of public view [c16 from L *scēna* theatrical stage, from Gk *skēnē* tent, stage]

scene dock *or* **bay** *n* a place in a theatre where scenery is stored, usually near the stage

scenery ('siːnərɪ) *n, pl* **sceneries 1** the natural features of a landscape **2** *theatre* the painted backcloths, etc, used to represent a location in a theatre or studio [c18 from It. SCENARIO]

scenic ('siːnɪk) *adj* **1** of or relating to natural scenery **2** having beautiful natural scenery: *a scenic drive* **3** of or relating to the stage or stage scenery **4** (in painting, etc) representing a scene > **'scenically** *adv*

scenic railway *n* a miniature railway used for amusement in a park, zoo, etc

scenic reserve *n* NZ an area of natural beauty, set aside for public recreation

scent (sɛnt) *n* **1** a distinctive smell, esp a pleasant one **2** a smell left in passing, by which a person or animal may be traced **3** a trail, clue, or guide **4** an instinctive ability for detecting **5** another word (esp Brit) for **perfume** ▷ *vb* **6** (*tr*) to recognize by or as if by the smell **7** (*tr*) to have a suspicion of: *I scent foul play* **8** (*tr*) to fill with odour or fragrance **9** (*intr*) (of hounds, etc) to hunt by the sense of smell **10** to smell (at): *the dog scented the air* [c14 from OF *sentir* to sense, from L *sentīre* to feel] > **'scented** *adj*

sceptic *or arch & US* **skeptic** ('skɛptɪk) *n* **1** a person who habitually doubts the authenticity of accepted beliefs **2** a person who mistrusts people, ideas, etc, in general **3** a person who doubts the truth of religion [c16 from L *scepticus*, from Gk *skeptikos* one who reflects upon, from *skeptesthai* to consider] > **'sceptical** *or arch & US* **'skeptical** *adj* > **'sceptically** *or arch & US* **'skeptically** *adv* > **'scepticism** *or arch & US* **'skepticism** *n*

Sceptic *or arch & US* **Skeptic** ('skɛptɪk) *n* **1** a member of one of the ancient Greek schools of philosophy, esp that of Pyrrho, who believed that real knowledge of things is impossible ▷ *adj* **2** of or relating to the Sceptics > **'Scepticism** *or arch & US* **'Skepticism** *n*
▷ http://users.ox.ac.uk/~shil0124/serious/scepticism.html

sceptre *or US* **scepter** ('sɛptə) *n* **1** a ceremonial staff held by a monarch as the symbol of authority **2** imperial authority; sovereignty [c13 from OF *sceptre*, from L, from Gk *skeptron* staff] > **'sceptred** *or US* **'sceptered** *adj*

Schaerbeek (*Flemish* 'sxaːrbeːk) *n* a city in central Belgium: an industrial suburb of Brussels. Pop: 105 692 (2000 est)

Schaffhausen (*German* ʃaːf'hauzən) *n* **1** a small canton of N Switzerland. Pop: 73 600 (2000 est). Area: 298 sq km (115 sq miles) **2** a town in N Switzerland, capital of Schaffhausen canton, on the Rhine. Pop: 35 000 (latest est). French name: **Schaffhouse**

Schama ('ʃɑːmə) *n* **Simon** (**Michael**) born 1945, British historian, art critic, and broadcaster, based in the US; his work includes *The Embarrassment of Riches* (1987), *Landscape and Memory* (1995), and the BBC television series *A History of Britain* (2000–02)

Schaumburg-Lippe (*German* 'ʃaumbʊrk'lɪpə) *n* a former state of NW Germany, between Westphalia and Hanover: part of Lower Saxony since 1946

schedule ('ʃɛdjuːl; *also, esp US* 'skɛdʒʊəl) *n* **1** a plan of procedure for a project **2** a list of items: *a schedule of fixed prices* **3** a list of times; timetable **4** a list of tasks to be performed, esp within a set period **5** *law* a list or inventory ▷ *vb* **schedules, scheduling, scheduled** (*tr*) **6** to make a schedule of or place in a schedule **7** to plan to occur at a certain time [c14 earlier *cedule, sedule* via OF from LL *schedula* small piece of paper, from L *scheda* sheet of paper]

scheduled castes *pl n* certain classes in Indian society officially granted special concessions. See **Harijan**

scheduled territories *pl n* **the** another name for **sterling area**

Scheele (*Swedish* 'ʃeːlə) *n* **Karl Wilhelm** (kɑːrl 'vilhɛlm) 1742–86, Swedish chemist. He discovered oxygen, independently of Priestley, and many other substances

scheelite ('ʃiːlaɪt) *n* a white, brownish, or greenish mineral, usually fluorescent, consisting of calcium tungstate with some tungsten often replaced by molybdenum. It is an important source of tungsten [c19 from G *Scheelit*, after K. W. SCHEELE]

Scheldt (ʃɛlt, skɛlt) *n* a river in W Europe, rising in NE France and flowing north and northeast through W Belgium to Antwerp, then northwest to the North Sea in the SW Netherlands. Length: 435 km (270 miles). Flemish and Dutch name: **Schelde** ('sxɛldɛ) French name: **Escaut**

Schelling (*German* 'ʃɛlɪŋ) *n* **Friedrich Wilhelm Joseph von** ('friːdrɪç 'vɪlhɛlm 'joːzɛf fɔn) 1775–1854, German

Ss

philosopher. He expanded Fichte's idea that there is one reality, the infinite and absolute Ego, by regarding nature as an absolute being working towards self-consciousness. His works include *Ideas towards a Philosophy of Nature* (1797) and *System of Transcendental Idealism* (1800)

schema ('ski:mə) *n, pl* **schemata** (-mətə) **1** a plan, diagram, or scheme **2** (in the philosophy of Kant) a rule or principle that enables the understanding to unify experience **3** *logic* **3a** a syllogistic figure **3b** a representation of the form of an inference [c19 from Gk: form]

schematic (skɪ'mætɪk) *adj* **1** of or relating to the nature of a diagram, plan, or schema ▷ *n* **2** a schematic diagram, esp of an electrical circuit, etc > **sche'matically** *adv*

schematize *or* **schematise** ('ski:mə,taɪz) *vb* **schematizes, schematizing, schematized** *or* **schematises, schematising, schematised** (*tr*) to form into or arrange in a scheme > **'schema,tism** *n* > **,schemati'zation** *or* **,schemati'sation** *n*

scheme (ski:m) *n* **1** a systematic plan for a course of action **2** a systematic arrangement of parts **3** a secret plot **4** a chart, diagram, or outline **5** an astrological diagram giving the aspects of celestial bodies **6** *chiefly Brit* a plan formally adopted by a commercial enterprise or governmental body, as for pensions, etc **7** Short for **housing scheme** ▷ *vb* **schemes, scheming, schemed** **8** (*tr*) to devise a system for **9** to form intrigues (for) in an underhand manner [c16 from L *schema*, from Gk *skhēma* form] > **'schemer** *n*

scheming ('ski:mɪŋ) *adj* **1** given to making plots; cunning ▷ *n* **2** intrigues

Schengen Convention *or* **Agreement** ('ʃɛŋən) *n* an agreement, signed in 1985, but not implemented until 1995, to abolish border controls within Europe: thirteen countries had acceded by 1995; the UK is not a signatory

scherzando (skɛə'tsændəʊ) *music* ▷ *adj, adv* **1** to be performed in a light-hearted manner ▷ *n, pl* **scherzandi** (-di:) *or* **scherzandos** **2** a movement, passage, etc, directed to be performed in this way [It., lit.: joking; see SCHERZO]

scherzo ('skɛətsəʊ) *n, pl* **scherzos** *or* **scherzi** (-tsi:) a brisk lively movement, developed from the minuet, with a contrastive middle section (a trio) [It.: joke, of Gmc origin]

Schiaparelli (*Italian* skjapa'rɛlli) *n* **1 Elsa** ('elsa) 1896–1973, Italian couturière, noted esp for the dramatic colours of her designs **2 Giovanni Virginio** (dʒo'vanni vir'dʒi:njo) 1835–1910, Italian astronomer, who discovered the asteroid Hesperia (1861) and the so-called canals of Mars (1877)

Schick test (ʃɪk) *n med* a skin test to determine immunity to diphtheria [c20 after Bela *Schick* (1877–1967), US paediatrician]

Schiedam (*Dutch* sxi:'dɑm) *n* a port in the SW Netherlands, in South Holland province west of Rotterdam: gin distilleries. Pop: 72 515 (1994)

Schiele (*German* 'ʃi:lə) *n* **Egon** ('e:gɔn) 1890–1918, Austrian painter and draughtsman: a leading exponent of Austrian expressionism

Schiff (ʃɪf) *n* **Andras** ('ɑndrəs) born 1953, Hungarian concert pianist

Schiller (*German* 'ʃɪlər) *n* **Johann Christoph Friedrich von** (jo'han 'krɪstɔf 'fri:drɪç fɔn) 1759–1805, German poet, dramatist, historian, and critic. His concern with the ideal freedom of the human spirit to rise above the constraints placed upon it is reflected in his great trilogy *Wallenstein* (1800) and in *Maria Stuart* (1800)

schilling ('ʃɪlɪŋ) *n* the former standard monetary unit of Austria; replaced by the euro in 2002 [c18 from G: SHILLING]

schism ('skɪzəm, 'sɪz-) *n* **1** the division of a group into opposing factions **2** the factions so formed **3** division within or separation from an established Church, not necessarily involving differences in doctrine [c14 from Church L *schisma*, from Gk *skhisma* a cleft, from *skhizein* to split]

schismatic (skɪz'mætɪk, sɪz-) *or* **schismatical** *adj* **1** of or promoting schism ▷ *n* **2** a person who causes schism or belongs to a schismatic faction > **schis'matically** *adv*

schist (ʃɪst) *n* any metamorphic rock that can be split into thin layers [c18 from F *schiste*, from L *lapis schistos* stone that may be split, from Gk *skhizein* to split] > **'schistose** *adj*

schistosome ('ʃɪstə,səʊm) *n* any of a genus of blood flukes which cause disease in man and domestic animals. Also called: **bilharzia** [c19 from NL *Schistosoma*; see SCHIST, -SOME[3]]

schistosomiasis (,ʃɪstəsəʊ'maɪəsɪs) *n* a disease caused by infestation of the body with schistosomes. Also called: **bilharziasis**

schizanthus (skɪz'ænθəs) *n* a flowering annual plant, native to Chile, that has finely divided leaves [c19 NL from Gk *skhizein* to cut + *anthos* flower]

schizo ('skɪtsəʊ) *offens* ▷ *adj* **1** schizophrenic ▷ *n, pl* **schizos** **2** a schizophrenic person

schizo- *or before a vowel* **schiz-** *combining form* indicating a cleavage, split, or division: *schizophrenia* [from Gk *skhizein* to split]

schizocarp ('skɪzə,kɑ:p) *n bot* a dry fruit that splits into two or more one-seeded portions at maturity > **,schizo'carpous** *adj*

schizoid ('skɪtsɔɪd) *adj* **1** *psychol* denoting a personality disorder characterized by extreme shyness and oversensitivity **2** *inf* characterized by conflicting or contradictory ideas, attitudes, etc ▷ *n* **3** a person who has a schizoid personality

schizomycete (,skɪtsəʊmaɪ'si:t) *n* (formerly) any microscopic organism of the now obsolete class *Schizomycetes*, which included the bacteria

schizophrenia (,skɪtsəʊ'fri:nɪə) *n* **1** any of a group of psychotic disorders characterized by progressive deterioration of the personality, withdrawal from reality, hallucinations, emotional instability, etc **2** *inf* behaviour that seems to be motivated by contradictory or conflicting principles [c20 from SCHIZO- + Gk *phrēn* mind] > **,schizo'phrenic** *adj, n*

schizothymia (,skɪtsəʊ'θaɪmɪə) *n psychiatry* the condition of being schizoid or introverted. It encompasses elements of schizophrenia [c20 NL, from SCHIZO- + *-thymia*, from Gk *thumos* spirit] > **,schizo'thymic** *adj*

Schlegel (*German* 'ʃle:gəl) *n* **1 August Wilhelm von** ('aʊgʊst 'vɪlhɛlm fɔn) 1767–1845, German romantic critic and scholar, noted particularly for his translations of Shakespeare **2** his brother, **Friedrich von** ('fri:drɪç fɔn) 1772–1829, German philosopher and critic; a founder of the romantic movement in Germany

Schlesien ('ʃle:zɪən) *n* the German name for **Silesia**

Schlesinger ('ʃlɛzɪŋə) *n* **John (Richard)** 1926–2003, British film and theatre director. Films include *Billy Liar* (1963), *Midnight Cowboy* (1969), *Sunday Bloody Sunday* (1971), and *Eye for an Eye* (1995)

Schleswig (*German* 'ʃle:svɪç) *n* **1** a fishing port in N Germany, in Schleswig-Holstein state: on an inlet of the Baltic. Pop: 26 820 (latest est) **2** a former duchy, in the S Jutland Peninsula: annexed by Prussia in 1864; N part returned to Denmark after a plebiscite in 1920; S part forms part of the German state of Schleswig-Holstein. Danish name: **Slesvig**

Schleswig-Holstein (*German* 'ʃle:svɪç'hɔlʃtain) *n* a state of N Germany, formerly in West Germany: drained chiefly by the River Elbe; mainly agricultural. Capital: Kiel. Pop: 2 777 300 (2000). Area: 15 658 sq km (6045 sq miles)

Schlick (ʃlɪk) *n* **Moritz** 1882–1936, German philosopher, working in Austria, who founded (1924) the Vienna Circle to develop the doctrine of logical positivism. His works include the *General Theory of Knowledge* (1918) and *Problems of Ethics* (1930)

Schlieffen (*German* 'ʃliːfən) *n* **Alfred** ('alfreːt), Count von Schlieffen. 1833–1913, German field marshal, who devised the **Schlieffen Plan** (1905): it was intended to ensure German victory over a Franco-Russian alliance by holding off Russia with minimal strength and swiftly defeating France by a massive flanking movement through the Low Countries. In a modified form, it was unsuccessfully employed in World War I (1914)

Schliemann (*German* 'ʃliːman) *n* **Heinrich** ('hainrɪç) 1822–90, German archaeologist, who discovered nine superimposed city sites of Troy (1871–90). He also excavated the site of Mycenae (1876)

schlieren ('ʃlɪərən) *n* **1** *physics* visible streaks produced in a transparent fluid as a result of variations in the fluid's density **2** streaks or platelike masses of mineral in a rock mass [G, pl of *Schliere* streak]

schmaltz *or* **schmalz** (ʃmælts, ʃmɔːlts) *n* excessive sentimentality [c20 from G (*Schmalz*) & Yiddish: melted fat, from OHG *smalz*] > '**schmaltzy** *or* '**schmalzy** *adj*

schmick (ʃmɪk) *adj Austral inf* excellent, elegant, or stylish [c20 from ?]

Schmidt (ʃmɪt) *n* **Helmut** (**Heinrich Waldemar**) ('hɛlmuːt) born 1918, German Social Democrat statesman; chancellor of West Germany (1974–82)

Schmidt telescope *or* **camera** (ʃmɪt) *n* a catadioptric telescope designed to produce a very sharp image of a large area of sky in one photographic exposure [c20 after B. V. *Schmidt* (1879–1935), Estonian-born G inventor]

Schnabel ('ʃnɑːbᵊl) *n* **Artur** ('artʊr) 1882–1951, US pianist and composer, born in Austria

schnapper ('ʃnæpə) *n* a variant spelling of **snapper** (senses 1, 2)

schnapps *or* **schnaps** (ʃnæps) *n* **1** a Dutch spirit distilled from potatoes **2** (in Germany) any strong spirit [c19 from G *Schnaps*, from *schnappen* to SNAP]

schnauzer ('ʃnaʊtsə) *n* a wire-haired breed of dog of the terrier type, originally from Germany, with a greyish coat [c19 from G *Schnauze* snout]

Schnittke ('ʃnɪtkə) *n* **Alfred** 1934–98, Russian composer: his works include four symphonies, four violin concertos, choral, chamber, and film music

schnitzel ('ʃnɪtsəl) *n* a thin slice of meat, esp veal [G: cutlet, from *schnitzen* to carve, *schnitzeln* to whittle]

schnorkel ('ʃnɔːkᵊl) *n, vb* **schnorkels, schnorkelling, schnorkelled** a less common variant of **snorkel**

schnozzle ('ʃnɒzᵊl) *n chiefly US* a slang word for **nose** [alteration of Yiddish *shnoitsl*, from G *Schnauze* snout]

Schoenberg *or* **Schönberg** ('ʃɜːnbɜːg; *German* 'ʃøːnbɛrk) *n* **Arnold** ('arnɔlt) 1874–1951, Austrian composer and musical theorist, in the US after 1933. The harmonic idiom of such early works as the string sextet *Verklärte Nacht* (1899) gave way to his development of atonality, as in the song cycle *Pierrot Lunaire* (1912), and later of the twelve-tone technique. He wrote many choral, orchestral, and chamber works and the unfinished opera *Moses and Aaron*

scholar ('skɒlə) *n* **1** a learned person, esp in the humanities **2** a person, esp a child, who studies; pupil **3** a student receiving a scholarship **4** *S African* a school pupil [c14 from OF *escoler*, via LL from L *schola* SCHOOL[1]] > '**scholarly** *adj* > '**scholarliness** *n*

scholarship ('skɒləʃɪp) *n* **1** academic achievement; learning **2a** financial aid provided for a scholar because of academic merit **2b** the position of a student who gains this financial aid **2c** (*as modifier*): *a scholarship student* **3** the qualities of a scholar

scholastic (skə'læstɪk) *adj* **1** of or befitting schools, scholars, or education **2** pedantic or precise **3** (*often cap*) characteristic of or relating to the medieval Schoolmen ▷ *n* **4** a student or pupil **5** a person who is given to logical subtleties **6** (*often cap*) a disciple or adherent of scholasticism; Schoolman **7** a Jesuit student who is undergoing a period of probation prior to commencing his theological studies [c16 via L from Gk *skholastikos* devoted to learning, ult. from *skholē* SCHOOL[1]] > **scho'lastically** *adv*

scholasticism (skə'læstɪ,sɪzəm) *n* (*sometimes cap*) the system of philosophy, theology, and teaching that dominated medieval western Europe and was based on the writings of the Church Fathers and Aristotle

scholiast ('skəʊlɪ,æst) *n* a medieval annotator, esp of classical texts [c16 from LGk, ult. from Gk *skholē* school] > ,**scholi'astic** *adj*

Schönberg ('ʃɜːnbɜːg; *German* 'ʃøːnbɛrk) *n* See **Schoenberg**

Schongauer (*German* 'ʃoːngauər) *n* **Martin** ('martiːn) ?1445–91, German painter and engraver

school[1] (skuːl) *n* **1a** an institution or building at which children and young people receive education **1b** (*as modifier*): *school day* **1c** (*in combination*): *schoolwork* **2** any educational institution or building **3** a faculty or department specializing in a particular subject: *a law school* **4** the staff and pupils of a school **5** the period of instruction in a school or one session of this: *he stayed after school to do extra work* **6** a place or sphere of activity that instructs: *the school of hard knocks* **7** a body of people or pupils adhering to a certain set of principles, doctrines, or methods **8** a group of artists, writers, etc, linked by the same style, teachers, or aims **9** a style of life: *a gentleman of the old school* **10** *inf* a group assembled for a common purpose, esp gambling or drinking ▷ *vb* (*tr*) **11** to train or educate in or as in a school **12** to discipline or control [OE *scōl*, from L *schola* school, from Gk *skholē* leisure spent in the pursuit of knowledge]

school[2] (skuːl) *n* **1** a group of fish or other aquatic animals that swim together ▷ *vb* **2** (*intr*) to form such a group [OE *scolu* SHOAL[2]]

Ss

school board *n* **1** *English history* an elected board of ratepayers who provided elementary schools (**board schools**) **2** (in the US and Canada) a local board of education

schoolboy ('skuːl,bɔɪ) *or* (*fem*) **schoolgirl** *n* a child attending school

schoolhouse ('skuːl,haʊs) *n* **1** a building used as a school **2** a house attached to a school

schoolie ('skuːlɪ) *n Austral sl* **1** a schoolteacher **2** a high school student **3** a holiday away from home in which large numbers of school leavers join together

Schoolies Week ('skuːliːz) *n* (in Australia) a week when large numbers of school leavers gather together for a holiday away from home after the end of their final exams

schooling ('skuːlɪŋ) *n* **1** education, esp when received at school **2** the process of teaching or being taught in a school **3** the training of an animal, esp of a horse for dressage

schoolman ('skuːlmən) *n, pl* **schoolmen** (*sometimes cap*) a scholar versed in the learning of the **Schoolmen**, the masters in the universities of the Middle Ages who were versed in scholasticism

schoolmarm ('skuːl,mɑːm) *n inf* **1** a woman schoolteacher **2** any woman considered to be prim or old-fashioned > '**school,marmish** *adj*

schoolmaster ('skuːl,mɑːstə) *or* (*fem*) **schoolmistress** *n* **1** a person who teaches in or runs a school **2** a person or thing that acts as an instructor

schoolmate ('skuːl,meɪt) *or* **schoolfellow** *n* a companion at school; fellow pupil

school of arts *n Austral* a public building in a small town: orig one used for adult education

school prawn *n Austral* an olive-green prawn common to

the E coast of Australia, *Metapenaeus macleayi*

Schools (sku:lz) *pl n* **1** **the Schools** the medieval Schoolmen collectively **2** (at Oxford University) **2a** the University building in which examinations are held **2b** *inf* the Second Public Examination for the degree of Bachelor of Arts

school shark *n Austral* an Australian shark resembling the tope, *Notogaleus australis*

schoolteacher ('sku:l,ti:tʃə) *n* a person who teaches in a school > **'school,teaching** *n*

school year *n* **1** a twelve-month period, usually of three terms, during which pupils remain in the same class **2** the time during this period when the school is open

schooner ('sku:nə) *n* **1** a sailing vessel with at least two masts, with all lower sails rigged fore-and-aft, and with the main mast stepped aft **2** *Brit* a large glass for sherry **3** *US, Canad, Austral, & NZ* a large glass for beer [c18 from ?]

Schopenhauer (*German* 'ʃo:pənhauər) *n* **Arthur** ('artʊr) 1788–1860, German pessimist philosopher. In his chief work, *The World as Will and Idea* (1819), he expounded the view that will is the creative primary factor and idea the secondary receptive factor

schottische (ʃɒ'ti:ʃ) *n* **1** a 19th-century German dance resembling a slow polka **2** a piece of music composed for or in the manner of this dance [c19 from G *der schottische Tanz* the Scottish dance]

Schottky effect ('ʃɒtkɪ) *n physics* a reduction in the energy required to remove an electron from a solid surface in a vacuum when an electric field is applied to the surface [c20 after W. *Schottky* (1886–1976), G physicist]

Schouten Islands ('ʃaʊtᵊn) *pl n* a group of islands in the Pacific, off the N coast of Papua New Guinea. Pop: 25 490 (latest est). Area: 3185 sq km (1230 sq miles)

Schreiner ('ʃraɪnə) *n* **Olive** (**Emilie Albertina**) 1855–1920, South African novelist and feminist writer, whose works include the autobiographical *The Story of an African Farm* (1883) and *Women and Labour* (1911)

Schröder (*German* 'ʃrødɜ:r) *n* **Gerhard** ('gerhɑt) born 1944, German Social Democrat politician; chancellor of Germany from 1998

Schrödinger (*German* 'ʃrø:dɪŋər) *n* **Erwin** ('ɛrvi:n) 1887–1961, Austrian physicist, who discovered the wave equation: shared the Nobel prize for physics 1933

Schubert ('ʃu:bət) *n* **Franz** (**Peter**) (frants) 1797–1828, Austrian composer; the originator and supreme exponent of the modern German lied. His many songs include the cycles *Die Schöne Müllerin* (1823) and *Die Winterreise* (1827). His other works include symphonies and much piano and chamber music including string quartets and the *Trout* piano quintet (1819)

Schumacher (*German* 'ʃu:maxər) *n* **1** **Ernst Friedrich** (ɛrnst 'fri:drɪç) 1911–77, British economist, born in Germany. He is best known for his book *Small is Beautiful* (1973) **2** **Michael** born 1969, German motor racing driver, who has won more Grand Prix races than any other; Formula One world champion (1994, 1995, 2000, 2001, 2002, 2003)

Schuman *n* **1** (*French* ʃuman) **Robert** (rɔbɛr) 1886–1963, French statesman; prime minister (1947–48). He proposed (1950) pooling the coal and steel resources of W Europe **2** ('ʃu:mən) **William** (**Howard**) 1910–91, US composer

Schumann ('ʃu:mən) *n* **1** **Elisabeth** (e'li:zabɛt) 1885–1952, German soprano, noted esp for her interpretations of lieder **2** **Robert Alexander** ('ro:bɛrt alɛ'ksandər) 1810–56, German romantic composer, noted esp for his piano music, such as *Carneval* (1835) and *Kreisleriana* (1838), his songs, and four symphonies

schuss (ʃʊs) *skiing* ▷ *n* **1** a straight high-speed downhill run ▷ *vb* **2** (*intr*) to perform a schuss [G: SHOT[1]]

Schütz (*German* ʃyts) *n* **Heinrich** ('hainrɪç) 1585–1672, German composer, esp of church music and madrigals

schwa *or* **shwa** (ʃwɑ:) *n* **1** a central vowel represented in the International Phonetic Alphabet by (ə). The sound occurs in unstressed syllables in English, as in *around* and *sofa* **2** the symbol (ə) used to represent this sound [c19 via G from Heb. *shewā*, a diacritic indicating lack of a vowel sound]

Schwaben ('ʃva:bən) *n* the German name for **Swabia**

Schwarzkopf (*German* 'ʃvartskɔpf) *n* **Elisabeth** (e'li:zabɛt) born 1915, Austro-British operatic soprano, born in Germany

Schwarzwald ('ʃvartsvalt) *n* the German name for the **Black Forest**

Schweinfurt (*German* 'ʃvainfʊrt) *n* a city in central Germany, in N Bavaria on the River Main. Pop: 54 520 (1991)

Schweitzer ('ʃwaɪtsə, 'ʃvaɪt-) *n* **Albert** 1875–1965, Franco-German medical missionary, philosopher, theologian, and organist, born in Alsace. He took up medicine in 1905 and devoted most of his life after 1913 to a medical mission at Lambaréné, Gabon: Nobel peace prize 1952

Schweiz (ʃvaits) *n* the German name for **Switzerland**

Schwerin (*German* ʃve'ri:n) *n* a city in N Germany, in Mecklenburg-West Pomerania on **Lake Schwerin**. Pop: 104 200 (1999 est)

Schwitters (*German* 'ʃvɪtərs) *n* **Kurt** (kʊrt) 1887–1948, German dadaist painter and poet, noted for his collages composed of discarded materials

Schwyz (*German* ʃvi:ts) *n* **1** a canton of central Switzerland: played an important part in the formation of the Swiss confederation, to which it gave its name. Capital: Schwyz. Pop: 128 200 (2000 est). Area: 908 sq km (351 sq miles) **2** a town in E central Switzerland, capital of Schwyz canton: tourism. Pop: 12 740 (1990)

sci. *abbrev for*: **1** science **2** scientific

sciatic (saɪ'ætɪk) *adj* **1** *anat* of or relating to the hip or the hipbone **2** of or afflicted with sciatica [c16 from F, from LL, from L *ischiadicus* relating to pain in the hip, from Gk, from *iskhia* hip-joint]

sciatica (saɪ'ætɪkə) *n* a form of neuralgia characterized by intense pain along the body's longest nerve (**sciatic nerve**), extending from the back of the thigh down to the calf of the leg [c15 from LL *sciatica*; see SCIATIC]

science ('saɪəns) *n* **1** the systematic study of the nature and behaviour of the material and physical universe, based on observation, experiment, and measurement **2** the knowledge so obtained or the practice of obtaining it **3** any particular branch of this knowledge: *the applied sciences* **4** any body of knowledge organized in a systematic manner **5** skill or technique **6** *arch* knowledge [c14 via OF from L *scientia* knowledge, from *scīre* to know]

- ▷ www.scicentral.com
- ▷ www.100TopScienceSites.com
- ▷ www.sciencedaily.com
- ▷ www.treasure-troves.com
- ▷ www.science.gov
- ▷ www.scitechresources.gov
- ▷ www.howstuffworks.com
- ▷ http://vlib.org/Science.html
- ▷ http://gill.stanford.edu/collect/science
- ▷ www.getscience.co.uk
- ▷ www.eurekalert.org

Finding Science Resources on the Internet

The Internet has a vast amount of information on the sciences available to academics, professional researchers, and laypeople alike. Finding reliable and free data should not be difficult although a few points need to be borne in mind

The material should be up to date.
Small organizations and departments within academic institutions sometimes encounter funding difficulties and are unable to continue with their researches. Make sure to look at the 'Last updated' section of the main website page before using any data. Try clicking on the links to make sure that they have been maintained properly and do not result in error messages.

Ideally information should be obtained from websites run by universities, research institutes, and other reputable organizations.
Websites maintained by individuals may not be up to date and comprehensive. It is also possible that the prejudices of those maintaining the websites will be reflected in the content and list of links.

A number of useful websites for science and technology resources have been listed below. Brief descriptions of the data provided are also given.

▷ www.science.gov
A gateway to information resources at the US government science agencies. There are links to authoritative science websites and databases of technical reports, journal articles, conference proceedings, and other published materials.

▷ www.scitechresources.gov
An online catalogue that provides the scientist, engineer, and technologist with access to key US Government web resources, expertise, services, laboratories, and information centres

▷ www.100TopScienceSites.com
Links to 100 websites plus brief descriptions of the content.

▷ www.sciencedaily.com
News releases submitted by leading universities and other research organizations around the world.

▷ www.eurekalert.org
An online press service run by the American Association for the Advancement of Science and providing science-related news to the news media. There is also a searchable archive.

▷ www.howstuffworks.com
Clear and concise explanations for the layman of processes, systems, machines, and natural phenomena. Voted one of *Time* magazine's 50 best websites in 2002 and 2003.

▷ www.getscience.co.uk
A portal with links to a variety of websites mainly for those for whom science is an interest rather than a profession.

▷ http://vlib.org/Science.html
Maintained by the Virtual Library, the oldest catalogue of the World Wide Web, this portal has hundreds of links to individual websites and gateway directories.

▷ http://gill.stanford.edu/collect/science
A portal maintained by Standford University Libraries and Academic Information Resources. Provides links to thousands of science and technology websites around the world.

science fiction *n* **a** a literary genre that makes imaginative use of scientific knowledge **b** (*as modifier*): *a science-fiction writer*

Science Museum *n* a museum in London, originating from 1852 and given its present name and site in 1899: contains collections relating to the history of science, technology, and industry

science park *n* an area where scientific research and commercial development are carried on in cooperation

scienter (saɪˈɛntə) *adv law* knowingly; wilfully [from L]

sciential (saɪˈɛnʃəl) *adj* **1** of or relating to science **2** skilful or knowledgeable

scientific (ˌsaɪənˈtɪfɪk) *adj* **1** (*prenominal*) of, derived from, or used in science: *scientific equipment* **2** (*prenominal*) occupied in science: *scientific manpower* **3** conforming with the methods used in science > ˌ**scienˈtifically** *adv*

scientism (ˈsaɪənˌtɪzəm) *n* **1** the application of the scientific method **2** the uncritical application of scientific methods to inappropriate fields of study > ˌ**scienˈtistic** *adj*

scientist (ˈsaɪəntɪst) *n* a person who studies or practises any of the sciences or who uses scientific methods

Scientology (ˌsaɪənˈtɒlədʒɪ) *n trademark* the philosophy of the Church of Scientology, a nondenominational movement founded in the US in the 1950s, which emphasizes self-knowledge as a means of realizing full spiritual potential [C20 from L *scient(ia)* SCIENCE + -LOGY] > ˌ**Scienˈtologist** *n*

sci-fi (ˈsaɪˈfaɪ) *n* short for **science fiction**

scilicet (ˈsɪlɪˌsɛt) *adv* namely: used esp in explaining an obscure text or supplying a missing word [L: from *scīre licet* it is permitted to know]

scilla (ˈsɪlə) *n* any of a genus of liliaceous plants having small bell-shaped flowers. See also **squill** (sense 3) [C19 via L from Gk *skilla*]

Scilly Isles, Scilly Islands (ˈsɪlɪ), *or* **Scillies** (ˈsɪlɪz) *pl n* a group of about 140 small islands (only five inhabited) off the extreme SW coast of England: tourist centre. Capital: Hugh Town. Pop: 2153 (2001). Area: 16 sq km (6 sq miles) > **Scillonian** (sɪˈləʊnɪən) *adj, n*

scimitar (ˈsɪmɪtə) *n* an oriental sword with a curved blade broadening towards the point [C16 from OIt., prob. from Persian *shimshīr*, from ?]

scintigraphy (ˌsɪnˈtɪɡrəfɪ) *n med* a diagnostic technique using a radioactive tracer and scintillation counter for producing pictures (**scintigrams**) of internal parts of the body [C20 from SCINTI(LLATION) + -GRAPHY]

scintilla (sɪnˈtɪlə) *n* a minute amount; hint, trace, or particle [C17 from L: a spark]

scintillate (ˈsɪntɪˌleɪt) *vb* **scintillates, scintillating, scintillated** (*mainly intr*) **1** (*also tr*) to give off (sparks); sparkle **2** to be animated or brilliant **3** *physics* to give off flashes of light as a result of the impact of photons [C17 from L *scintillāre*, from *scintilla* a spark] > ˈ**scintillant** *adj*

scintillating (ˈsɪntɪˌleɪtɪŋ) *adj* **1** sparkling; twinkling **2** animated or brilliant

scintillation (ˌsɪntɪˈleɪʃən) *n* **1** the act of scintillating **2** a spark or flash **3** the twinkling of stars **4** *physics* a flash of light produced when a material scintillates

scintillation counter *n* an instrument for detecting and measuring the intensity of high-energy radiation. It consists of a phosphor with which particles collide producing flashes of light that are converted into pulses of electric current that are counted by electronic equipment

sciolism (ˈsaɪəˌlɪzəm) *n rare* the practice of opinionating on subjects of which one has only superficial knowledge [C19 from LL *sciolus* someone with a smattering of knowledge, from L *scīre* to know] > ˈ**sciolist** *n* > ˌ**scioˈlistic** *adj*

scion (ˈsaɪən) *n* **1** a descendant or young member of a family **2** a shoot of a plant used to form a graft [C14 from OF *cion*, of Gmc origin]

Scipio ('skɪpɪˌəʊ, 'sɪpɪˌəʊ) *n* **1** full name *Publius Cornelius Scipio Africanus Major.* 237–183 BC, Roman general. He commanded the Roman invasion of Carthage in the Second Punic War, defeating Hannibal at Zama (202) **2** full name *Publius Cornelius Scipio Aemilianus Africanus Minor.* ?185–129 BC, Roman statesman and general; the grandson by adoption of Scipio Africanus Major. He commanded an army against Carthage in the last Punic War and razed the city to the ground (146). He became the leader (132) of the opposition in Rome to popular reforms

scirrhus ('sɪrəs) *n, pl* **scirrhi** (-raɪ) *or* **scirrhuses** *pathol* a hard cancerous growth composed of fibrous tissues [C17 from NL, from L *scirros*, from Gk, from *skiros* hard] > **scirrhoid** ('sɪrɔɪd) *adj*

scission ('sɪʃən) *n* the act or an instance of cutting, splitting, or dividing [C15 from LL *scissiō*, from *scindere* to split]

scissor ('sɪzə) *vb* to cut (an object) with scissors

scissors ('sɪzəz) *pl n* **1** Also called: **pair of scissors** a cutting instrument used for cloth, hair, etc, having two crossed pivoted blades that cut by a shearing action **2** a wrestling hold in which the legs are wrapped round the opponent's body or head and squeezed **3** any gymnastic feat in which the legs cross and uncross in a scissor-like movement [C14 *sisoures*, from OF *cisoires*, from Vulgar L *cīsōria* (unattested), ult. from L *caedere* to cut]

scissors kick *n* a type of swimming kick in which one leg is moved forward and the other bent back and they are then brought together again in a scissor-like action

sciurine ('saɪjʊrɪn, -ˌraɪn) *adj* of or belonging to a family of rodents inhabiting most parts of the world except Australia and southern South America: includes squirrels, marmots, and chipmunks [C19 from L *sciūrus*, from Gk *skiouros* squirrel, from *skia* a shadow + *oura* a tail]

sclera ('sklɪərə) *n* the firm white fibrous membrane that forms the outer covering of the eyeball. Also called: **sclerotic** [C19 from NL, from Gk *sklēros* hard] > **scle'ritis** *n*

sclerenchyma (sklɪə'rɛŋkɪmə) *n* a supporting tissue in plants consisting of dead cells with very thick lignified walls [C19 from SCLERO- + PARENCHYMA]

sclero- *or before a vowel* **scler-** *combining form* **1** indicating hardness: *sclerosis* **2** of the sclera: *sclerotomy* [from Gk *sklēros* hard]

scleroderma (ˌsklɪərəʊ'dɜːmə) *or* **sclerodermia** (ˌsklɪərəʊ'dɜːmɪə) *n* a chronic disease common among women, characterized by thickening and hardening of the skin

scleroma (sklɪə'rəʊmə) *n, pl* **scleromata** (-mətə) *pathol* any small area of abnormally hard tissue, esp in a mucous membrane [C17 from NL, from Gk, from *sklēroun* to harden, from *sklēros* hard]

scleroprotein (ˌsklɪərəʊ'prəʊtiːn) *n* any of a group of insoluble stable proteins such as keratin that occur in skeletal and connective tissues. Also called: **albuminoid**

sclerosis (sklɪə'rəʊsɪs) *n, pl* **scleroses** (-siːz) **1** *pathol* a hardening or thickening of organs, tissues, or vessels from inflammation, degeneration, or (esp on the inner walls of arteries) deposition of fatty plaques **2** the hardening of a plant cell wall or tissue [C14 via Med. L from Gk *sklērōsis* a hardening]

sclerotic (sklɪə'rɒtɪk) *adj* **1** of or relating to the sclera **2** of, relating to, or having sclerosis [C16 from Med. L *sclērōticus*, from Gk; see SCLEROMA]

sclerous ('sklɪərəs) *adj anat, pathol* hard; bony; indurated [C19 from Gk *sklēros* hard]

SCM (in Britain) *abbrev for:* **1** State Certified Midwife **2** Student Christian Movement

scody ('skəʊdɪ) *adj NZ inf* unkempt; dirty: *they lived in a scody student flat* [C20 from ?]

scoff[1] (skɒf) *vb* **1** (*intr*; often foll by *at*) to speak contemptuously (about); mock **2** (*tr*) *obs* to regard with derision ▷ *n* **3** an expression of derision **4** an object of derision [C14 prob. from ON] > **'scoffer** *n* > **'scoffing** *adj, n*

scoff[2] (skɒf) *inf, chiefly Brit* ▷ *vb* **1** to eat (food) fast and greedily ▷ *n* **2** food or rations [C19 var of *scaff* food]

scold (skəʊld) *vb* **1** to find fault with or reprimand (a person) harshly **2** (*intr*) to use harsh or abusive language ▷ *n* **3** a person, esp a woman, who constantly finds fault [C13 from ON SKALD] > **'scolder** *n* > **'scolding** *n*

scoliosis (ˌskɒlɪ'əʊsɪs) *n pathol* an abnormal lateral curvature of the spine [C18 from NL, from Gk: a curving, from *skolios* bent] > **scoliotic** (ˌskɒlɪ'ɒtɪk) *adj*

scollop ('skɒləp) *n, vb* a variant spelling of **scallop**

scombroid ('skɒmbrɔɪd) *adj* **1** of, relating to, or belonging to the *Scombroidea*, a suborder of marine spiny-finned fishes having a forked powerful tail: includes the mackerels, tunnies, and sailfish ▷ *n* **2** any fish belonging to the suborder *Scombroidea* [C19 from Gk *skombros* a mackerel; see -OID]

sconce[1] (skɒns) *n* **1** a bracket fixed to a wall for holding candles or lights **2** a flat candlestick with a handle [C14 from OF *esconse* hiding place, lantern, or from LL *sconsa*, from *absconsa* dark lantern]

sconce[2] (skɒns) *n* a small protective fortification, such as an earthwork [C16 from Du. *schans*, from MHG *schanze* bundle of brushwood]

scone (skɒn, skəʊn) *n* a light plain doughy cake made from flour with very little fat, cooked in an oven or (esp originally) on a griddle [C16 Scot, ?from MDu. *schoonbrot* fine bread]

Scone (skuːn) *n* a parish in Perth and Kinross, E Scotland, consisting of the two villages of New Scone and Old Scone, formerly the site of the Pictish capital and the stone upon which medieval Scottish kings were crowned. The stone was removed to Westminster Abbey by Edward I in 1296; it was returned to Scotland in 1996 and placed in Edinburgh Castle. Scone Palace was rebuilt in the Neo-Gothic style in the 19th century

scooby doo (ˌskuːbɪ 'duː) *n Brit, rhyming slang* a clue: *I don't have a scooby doo what you're talking about.* Often shortened to: **scooby** [C20 from *Scooby Doo*, a cartoon character on children's television]

scoop (skuːp) *n* **1** a utensil used as a shovel or ladle, esp a small shovel with deep sides and a short handle, used for taking up flour, etc **2** a utensil with a long handle and round bowl used for dispensing liquids, etc **3** anything that resembles a scoop in action, such as the bucket on a dredge **4** a utensil used for serving mashed potatoes, ice cream, etc **5** a spoonlike surgical instrument for extracting foreign matter, etc, from the body **6** the quantity taken up by a scoop **7** the act of scooping, dredging, etc **8** a hollow cavity **9** *sl* a large quick gain, as of money **10** a news story reported in one newspaper before all the others ▷ *vb* (*mainly tr*) **11** (often foll by *up*) to take up and remove (an object or substance) with or as if with a scoop **12** (often foll by *out*) to hollow out with or as if with a scoop **13** to win (a prize, award, or large amount of money) **14** to beat (rival newspapers) in uncovering a news item [C14 via MDu. *schōpe* from Gmc] > **'scooper** *n* > **'scoopˌful** *n*

scoot (skuːt) *vb* **1** to go or cause to go quickly or hastily; dart or cause to dart off or away ▷ *n* **2** the act of scooting [C19 (US): from ?]

scooter ('skuːtə) *n* **1** a child's vehicle consisting of a low footboard on wheels, steered by handlebars **2** See **motor scooter**

Scopas ('skəʊpəs) *n* 4th century BC, Greek sculptor and architect

scope (skəʊp) *n* **1** opportunity for exercising the faculties or abilities: *scope for private enterprise* **2** range of view or grasp **3** the area covered by an activity, topic, etc: *the scope of his thesis was vast* **4** *naut* slack left in an anchor cable **5** *logic* the part of a formula that follows a quantifier or an operator **6** *inf* short for **telescope, microscope, oscilloscope,** etc **7** *arch* purpose [C16 from It.

scopo goal, from L *scopus*, from Gk *skopos* target]

-scope *n combining form* indicating an instrument for observing or detecting: *microscope* [from NL *-scopium*, from Gk *-skopion*, from *skopein* to look at] > **-scopic** *adj combining form*

scopolamine (skəˈpɒləˌmiːn) *n* a colourless viscous liquid alkaloid extracted from certain plants, such as henbane: used in preventing travel sickness and as a sedative and truth serum. Also called: **hyoscine** [c20 *scopol-* from NL *scopolia Japonica* Japanese belladonna (from which the alkaloid is extracted), after G. A. *Scopoli* (1723–88), It. naturalist, + AMINE]

Scopus (ˈskəʊpəs) *n* **Mount** a mountain in central Israel, east of Jerusalem: a N extension of the Mount of Olives; site of the Hebrew University (1925). Height: 834 m (2736 ft)

-scopy *n combining form* indicating a viewing or observation: *microscopy* [from Gk *-skopia*, from *skopein* to look at]

scorbutic (skɔːˈbjuːtɪk) *adj* of or having scurvy [c17 from NL *scorbūticus*, from Med. L *scorbūtus*, prob. of Gmc origin] > **scorˈbutically** *adv*

scorch (skɔːtʃ) *vb* **1** to burn or become burnt, esp so as to affect the colour, taste, etc **2** to wither or parch or cause to wither from exposure to heat **3** *(intr) inf* to be very hot: *it is scorching outside* **4** *(tr) inf* to criticize harshly ▷ *n* **5** a slight burn **6** a mark caused by the application of too great heat **7** *horticulture* a mark on fruit, etc, caused by pests or insecticides [c15 prob. from ON *skorpna* to shrivel up] > **ˈscorching** *adj*

scorched earth policy *n* **1** the policy in warfare of removing or destroying everything that might be useful to an invading enemy **2** *business* a manoeuvre by a company expecting an unwelcome takeover bid in which apparent profitability is greatly reduced by a reversible operation, such as borrowing at an exorbitant interest rate

scorcher (ˈskɔːtʃə) *n* **1** a person or thing that scorches **2** something caustic **3** *inf* a very hot day **4** *Brit inf* something remarkable

score (skɔː) *n* **1** a numerical record of a competitive game or match **2** the total number of points made by a side or individual in a game **3** the act of scoring, esp a point or points **4** **the score** *inf* the actual situation **5** a group or set of twenty: *three score years and ten* **6** *(usually pl; foll by of)* lots: *I have scores of things to do* **7** *music* **7a** the printed form of a composition in which the instrumental or vocal parts appear on separate staves vertically arranged on large pages (**full score**) or in a condensed version, usually for piano (**short score**) or voices and piano (**vocal score**) **7b** the incidental music for a film or play **7c** the songs, music, etc, for a stage or film musical **8** a mark or notch, esp one made in keeping a tally **9** an account of amounts due **10** an amount recorded as due **11** a reason: *the book was rejected on the score of length* **12** a grievance **13a** a line marking a division or boundary **13b** *(as modifier)*: *score line* **14** **over the score** *inf* excessive; unfair **15** **settle** *or* **pay off a score** **15a** to avenge a wrong **15b** to repay a debt ▷ *vb* **scores, scoring, scored** **16** to gain (a point or points) in a game or contest **17** *(tr)* to make a total score of **18** to keep a record of the score (of) **19** *(tr)* to be worth (a certain amount) in a game **20** *(tr)* to record by making notches in **21** to make (cuts, lines, etc) in or on **22** *(intr) sl* to obtain something desired, esp to purchase an illegal drug **23** *(intr) sl* (of men) to be successful in seducing a person **24** *(tr)* **24a** to arrange (a piece of music) for specific instruments or voices **24b** to write the music for (a film, play, etc) **25** to achieve (success or an advantage): *your idea scored with the boss* [OE *scora*] > **ˈscorer** *n*

scoreboard (ˈskɔːˌbɔːd) *n sport, etc* a board for displaying the score of a game or match

scorecard (ˈskɔːˌkɑːd) *n* **1** a card on which scores are recorded, as in golf **2** a card identifying the players in a sports match, esp cricket

score off *vb (intr, prep)* to gain an advantage at someone else's expense

scoria (ˈskɔːrɪə) *n, pl* **scoriae** (-rɪˌiː) **1** a rough cindery crust on top of solidified lava flows containing numerous vesicles **2** refuse obtained from smelted ore [c17 from L: dross, from Gk *skōria*, from *skōr* excrement]

scorify (ˈskɔːrɪˌfaɪ) *vb* **scorifies, scorifying, scorified** to remove (impurities) from metals by forming scoria > **ˌscorifiˈcation** *n* > **ˈscoriˌfier** *n*

scoring (ˈskɔːrɪŋ) *n* another name for **orchestration** (see **orchestrate**)

scorn (skɔːn) *n* **1** open contempt for a person or thing **2** an object of contempt or derision ▷ *vb* **3** to treat with contempt or derision **4** *(tr)* to reject with contempt [c12 *schornen*, from OF *escharnir*, of Gmc origin] > **ˈscorner** *n* > **ˈscornful** *adj* > **ˈscornfully** *adv*

Scorpio (ˈskɔːpɪˌəʊ) *n* **1** Also called: **Scorpius** *astron* a large S constellation **2** Also called: the **Scorpion** *astrol* the eighth sign of the zodiac. The sun is in this sign between about Oct 23 and Nov 21 [L: SCORPION]

scorpion (ˈskɔːpɪən) *n* **1** an arachnid of warm dry regions, having a segmented body with a long tail terminating in a venomous sting **2** **false scorpion** a small nonvenomous arachnid that superficially resembles the scorpion but lacks the long tail **3** *Bible* a barbed scourge (I Kings 12:11) [c13 via OF from L *scorpiō*, from Gk *skorpios*, from ?]

Scorpion (ˈskɔːpɪən) *n* **the** the constellation Scorpio, the eighth sign of the zodiac

scorpion fish *n* any of a genus of fish of temperate and tropical seas, having venomous spines on the dorsal and anal fins

Scorsese (skɔːˈseɪzɪ) *n* **Martin** born 1942, US film director, whose films include *Taxi Driver* (1976), *Raging Bull* (1980), *The Last Temptation of Christ* (1988), *Casino* (1995), and *Gangs of New York* (2002)

Ss

Scot (skɒt) *n* **1** a native or inhabitant of Scotland **2** a member of a tribe of Celtic raiders from the north of Ireland who eventually settled in N Britain during the 5th and 6th centuries

Scot *abbrev for:* **1** Scotch (whisky) **2** Scotland **3** Scottish

scot and lot *n Brit history* a municipal tax paid by burgesses that came to be regarded as a qualification for the borough franchise in parliamentary elections [c13 *scot* tax, from Gmc]

scotch¹ (skɒtʃ) *vb (tr)* **1** to put an end to; crush: *bad weather scotched our plans* **2** *obs* to cut or score ▷ *n* **3** *arch* a gash **4** a line marked down, as for hopscotch [c15 from ?]

scotch² (skɒtʃ) *vb* **1** *(tr)* to block, prop, or prevent from moving with or as if with a wedge ▷ *n* **2** a block or wedge to prevent motion [c17 from ?]

Scotch¹ (skɒtʃ) *adj* **1** another word for **Scottish** ▷ *n* **2** the Scots or their language.

> USAGE In Scotland, *Scotch* is not used outside fixed expressions such as *Scotch whisky*, *Scotch broth*, etc. The use of *Scotch* for *Scots* or *Scottish* is otherwise felt to be incorrect, especially when applied to people

Scotch² (skɒtʃ) *n* whisky distilled from fermented malted barley and made in Scotland. Also called: **Scotch whisky**

Scotch broth *n Brit* a thick soup made from mutton or beef stock, vegetables, and pearl barley

Scotch egg *n Brit* a hard-boiled egg enclosed in a layer of sausage meat, covered in egg and crumbs, and fried

Scotchman (ˈskɒtʃmən) *or (fem)* **Scotchwoman** *n, pl* **Scotchmen** *or* **Scotchwomen** *(regarded as bad usage by the Scots)* another word for **Scotsman** or **Scotswoman**

Scotch mist *n* **1** a heavy wet mist **2** drizzle

Scotch snap *n music* a rhythmic pattern consisting of a short note followed by a long one. Also called: **Scotch catch**

Scotch terrier *n* another name for **Scottish terrier**

scoter ('skəʊtə) *n, pl* **scoters** *or* **scoter** a sea duck of northern regions. The male plumage is black with white patches around the head and eyes [C17 from ?]

scot-free *adv, adj (predicative)* without harm, loss, or penalty [C16 see SCOT AND LOT]

Scotland ('skɒtlənd) *n* a country that is part of the United Kingdom, occupying the north of Great Britain: the English and Scottish thrones were united under one monarch in 1603 and the parliaments in 1707: a separate Scottish parliament was established in 1999. Scotland consists of the Highlands in the north, the central Lowlands, and hilly uplands in the south; has a deeply indented coastline, about 800 offshore islands (mostly in the west), and many lochs. Capital: Edinburgh. Pop: 5 062 011 (2001). Area: 78 768 sq km (30 412 sq miles). Related adjs: **Scots, Caledonian, Scottish**
▷ www.scotland.gov.uk
▷ www.visitscotland.com

Scotland Yard *n* the headquarters of the police force of metropolitan London. Official name: **New Scotland Yard**

scotoma (skɒ'təʊmə) *n, pl* **scotomas** *or* **scotomata** (-mətə) **1** *pathol* a blind spot **2** *psychol* a mental blind spot [C16 via Med. L from Gk *skotōma* giddiness, from *skotoun* to make dark, from *skotos* darkness]

Scots (skɒts) *adj* **1** of or characteristic of Scotland, its people, their English dialects, or their Gaelic language ▷ *n* **2** any of the English dialects spoken or written in Scotland

Scotsman ('skɒtsmən) *or (fem)* **Scotswoman** *n, pl* **Scotsmen** *or* **Scotswomen** a native or inhabitant of Scotland

Scots pine *or* **Scotch pine** *n* **1** a coniferous tree of Europe and W and N Asia, having blue-green needle-like leaves and brown cones with a small prickle on each scale **2** the wood of this tree

Scott (skɒt) *n* **1** Sir **George Gilbert** 1811–78, British architect, prominent in the Gothic revival. He restored many churches and cathedrals and designed the Albert Memorial (1863) and St Pancras Station (1865) **2** his grandson, **Sir Giles Gilbert** 1880–1960, British architect, whose designs include the Anglican cathedral in Liverpool (1904–78) and the new Waterloo Bridge (1939–45) **3** **Paul (Mark)** 1920–78, British novelist, who is best known for the series of novels known as the "Raj Quartet": *The Jewel in the Crown* (1966), *The Day of the Scorpion* (1968), *The Towers of Silence* (1972), and *A Division of the Spoils* (1975). *Staying On* (1977) won the Booker Prize **4** Sir **Peter (Markham)** 1909–89, British naturalist, wildlife artist, and conservationist, noted esp for his paintings of birds. He founded (1946) the Slimbridge refuge for waterfowl in Gloucestershire **5** his father, **Robert Falcon** 1868–1912, British naval officer and explorer of the Antarctic. He commanded two Antarctic expeditions (1901–04; 1910–12) and reached the South Pole on Jan 18, 1912, shortly after Amundsen; he and the rest of his party died on the return journey **6** Sir **Walter** 1771–1832, Scottish romantic novelist and poet. He is remembered chiefly for the "Waverley" historical novels, including *Waverley* (1814), *Rob Roy* (1817), *The Heart of Midlothian* (1818), inspired by Scottish folklore and history, and *Ivanhoe* (1819), *Kenilworth* (1821), *Quentin Durward* (1823), and *Redgauntlet* (1824). His narrative poems include *The Lay of the Last Minstrel* (1805), *Marmion* (1808), and *The Lady of the Lake* (1810)

Scotticism ('skɒtɪˌsɪzəm) *n* a Scottish idiom, word, etc

Scottie *or* **Scotty** ('skɒtɪ) *n, pl* **Scotties** **1** See **Scottish terrier** **2** *inf* a Scotsman

Scottish ('skɒtɪʃ) *adj* of, relating to, or characteristic of Scotland, its people, their Gaelic language, or their English dialects

Scottish Borders *n* a council area in SE Scotland, on the English border: created in 1996, it has the same boundaries as the former Borders Region: it is mainly hilly, with agriculture (esp sheep farming) the chief economic activity. Administrative centre: Newtown St Boswells. Pop: 106 764 (2001). Area: 4734 sq km (1827 sq miles)

Scottish Certificate of Education *n* See **SCE**

Scottish Gaelic *n* the Goidelic language of the Celts of Scotland, used esp in the Highlands and Western Isles

Scottish National Party *n* a political party advocating the independence of Scotland. Abbrev: **SNP**

Scottish terrier *n* a small but sturdy long-haired breed of terrier, usually with a black coat

Scotus ('skəʊtəs) *n* See **Duns Scotus**

scoundrel ('skaʊndrəl) *n* a worthless or villainous person [C16 from ?]

scour[1] ('skaʊə) *vb* **1** to clean or polish (a surface) by washing and rubbing **2** to remove dirt from or have the dirt removed from **3** *(tr)* to clear (a channel) by the force of water **4** *(tr)* to remove by or as if by rubbing **5** *(tr)* to cause (livestock) to purge their bowels ▷ *n* **6** the act of scouring **7** the place scoured, esp by running water **8** something that scours, such as a cleansing agent **9** *(often pl)* prolonged diarrhoea in livestock, esp cattle [C13 via MLow G *schūren*, from OF *escurer*, from LL *excūrāre* to cleanse, from *cūrāre*; see CURE] > **'scourer** *n*

scour[2] ('skaʊə) *vb* **1** to range over (territory), as in making a search **2** to move swiftly or energetically over (territory) [C14 from ON *skūr*]

scourge (skɜːdʒ) *n* **1** a person who harasses or causes destruction **2** a means of inflicting punishment or suffering **3** a whip used for inflicting punishment or torture ▷ *vb* **scourges, scourging, scourged** *(tr)* **4** to whip **5** to punish severely [C13 from Anglo-F, from OF *escorgier* (unattested) to lash, from *es-* EX-[1] + L *corrigia* whip] > **'scourger** *n*

scourings ('skaʊərɪŋz) *pl n* **1** the residue left after cleaning grain **2** residue that remains after scouring

scouse (skaʊs) *n Liverpool dialect* a stew made from left-over meat [C19 shortened from LOBSCOUSE]

Scouse (skaʊs) *Brit inf* ▷ *n* **1** Also: **Scouser** a person who comes from Liverpool **2** the dialect spoken by such a person ▷ *adj* **3** of or from Liverpool [C20 from SCOUSE]

scout[1] (skaʊt) *n* **1** a person, ship, or aircraft sent out to gain information **2** *mil* a person or unit despatched to reconnoitre the position of the enemy, etc **3** the act or an instance of scouting **4** (esp at Oxford University) a college servant **5** *inf* a fellow ▷ *vb* **6** to examine or observe (anything) in order to obtain information **7** *(tr; sometimes foll by out or up)* to seek **8** *(intr; foll by about or around)* to go in search (for) [C14 from OF *ascouter* to listen to, from L *auscultāre* to AUSCULTATE] > **'scouter** *n*

scout[2] (skaʊt) *vb* to reject (a person, etc) with contempt [C17 from ON *skūta* derision]

Scout (skaʊt) *n (sometimes not cap)* a boy or (in some countries) a girl who is a member of a worldwide movement (the **Scout Association**) founded as the Boy Scouts in England in 1908 by Lord Baden-Powell > **'Scouting** *n*

Scouter ('skaʊtə) *n* the leader of a troop of Scouts. Also called (esp formerly): **Scoutmaster**

scow (skaʊ) *n* an unpowered barge used for freight, etc; lighter [C18 via Du. *schouw* from Low G *schalde*]

scowl (skaʊl) *vb* **1** *(intr)* to contract the brows in a threatening or angry manner ▷ *n* **2** a gloomy or threatening expression [C14 prob. from ON] > **'scowler** *n*

scrabble ('skræbᵊl) *vb* **scrabbles, scrabbling, scrabbled** **1** *(intr; often foll by about or at)* to scrape (at) or grope (for), as with hands or claws **2** to struggle (with) **3** *(intr; often foll by for)* to struggle to gain possession **4** to scribble

▷ *n* **5** the act or an instance of scrabbling **6** a scribble **7** a disorderly struggle [C16 from MDu. *shrabbelen*, frequentative of *shrabben* to scrape] > ˈ**scrabbler** *n*

Scrabble (ˈskræbᵊl) *n trademark* a game in which words are formed by placing lettered tiles in a pattern similar to a crossword puzzle
▷ www.scrabble.com

scrag (skræg) *n* **1** a thin or scrawny person or animal **2** the lean end of a neck of veal or mutton **3** *inf* the neck of a human being ▷ *vb* **scrags, scragging, scragged 4** (*tr*) *inf* to wring the neck of [C16 ? var. of CRAG]

scraggly (ˈskræglɪ) *adj* **scragglier, scraggliest** *chiefly US* untidy or irregular

scraggy (ˈskrægɪ) *adj* **scraggier, scraggiest 1** lean or scrawny **2** rough; unkempt > ˈ**scraggily** *adv* > ˈ**scragginess** *n*

scram¹ (skræm) *vb* **scrams, scramming, scrammed** (*intr; often imperative*) *inf* to go away hastily [C20 from SCRAMBLE]

scram² (skræm) *n* **1** an emergency shutdown of a nuclear reactor ▷ *vb* **scrams, scramming, scrammed 2** (of a nuclear reactor) to shut down or be shut down in an emergency [C20 ?from SCRAM¹]

scramble (ˈskræmbᵊl) *vb* **scrambles, scrambling, scrambled 1** (*intr*) to climb or crawl, esp by using the hands to aid movement **2** to proceed hurriedly or in a disorderly fashion **3** (*intr; often foll by for*) to compete with others, esp in a disordered manner **4** (*intr; foll by through*) to deal with hurriedly **5** (*tr*) to throw together in a haphazard manner **6** (*tr*) to collect in a hurried or disorganized manner **7** (*tr*) to cook (eggs that have been whisked up with milk) in a pan containing a little melted butter **8** *mil* to order (a crew or aircraft) to take off immediately or (of a crew or aircraft) to take off immediately **9** (*tr*) to render (speech) unintelligible during transmission by means of an electronic scrambler ▷ *n* **10** the act of scrambling **11** a climb or trek over difficult ground **12** a disorderly struggle, esp to gain possession **13** *mil* an immediate preparation for action, as of crew, aircraft, etc **14** *Brit* a motorcycle rally in which competitors race across rough open ground [C16 blend of SCRABBLE & RAMP]

scrambler (ˈskræmblə) *n* an electronic device that renders speech unintelligible during transmission, by altering frequencies

Scranton (ˈskræntən) *n* an industrial city in NE Pennsylvania: university (1888). Pop: 77 189 (1996 est)

scrap¹ (skræp) *n* **1** a small piece of something larger; fragment **2** an extract from something written **3a** waste material or used articles, esp metal, often collected and reprocessed **3b** (*as modifier*): *scrap iron* **4** (*pl*) pieces of discarded food ▷ *vb* **scraps, scrapping, scrapped** (*tr*) **5** to discard as useless [C14 from ON *skrap*]

scrap² (skræp) *inf* ▷ *n* **1** a fight or argument ▷ *vb* **scraps, scrapping, scrapped 2** (*intr*) to quarrel or fight [C17 ?from SCRAPE]

scrapbook (ˈskræpˌbʊk) *n* a book or album of blank pages in which to mount newspaper cuttings, pictures, etc

scrape (skreɪp) *vb* **scrapes, scraping, scraped 1** to move (a rough or sharp object) across (a surface), esp to smooth or clean **2** (*tr; often foll by away or off*) to remove (a layer) by rubbing **3** to produce a harsh or grating sound by rubbing against (a surface, etc) **4** (*tr*) to injure or damage by rough contact: *to scrape one's knee* **5** (*intr*) to be very economical (esp in **scrimp and scrape**) **6** (*intr*) to draw the foot backwards in making a bow **7 scrape acquaintance with** to contrive an acquaintance with ▷ *n* **8** the act of scraping **9** a scraped place **10** a harsh or grating sound **11** *inf* an awkward or embarrassing predicament **12** *inf* a conflict or struggle [OE *scrapian*] > ˈ**scraper** *n*

scraperboard (ˈskreɪpəˌbɔːd) *n* thin card covered with a layer of china clay and a top layer of Indian ink, which can be scraped away with a special tool to leave a white line

scrape through *vb* (*adv*) **1** (*intr*) to manage or survive with difficulty **2** to succeed in with difficulty or by a narrow margin

scrape together *or* **up** *vb* (*tr, adv*) to collect with difficulty: *to scrape together money for a new car*

scrapheap (ˈskræpˌhiːp) *n* **1** a pile of discarded material **2 on the scrapheap** (of people or things) having outlived their usefulness

scrappy (ˈskræpɪ) *adj* **scrappier, scrappiest** fragmentary; disjointed > ˈ**scrappily** *adv*

scratch (skrætʃ) *vb* **1** to mark or cut (the surface of something) with a rough or sharp instrument **2** (often foll by *at, out, off*, etc) to scrape (the surface of something), as with claws, nails, etc **3** to scrape (the surface of the skin) with the nails, as to relieve itching **4** to chafe or irritate (a surface, esp the skin) **5** to make or cause to make a grating sound **6** (*tr; sometimes foll by out*) to erase by or as if by scraping **7** (*tr*) to write or draw awkwardly **8** (*intr; sometimes foll by along*) to earn a living, manage, etc, with difficulty **9** to withdraw (an entry) from a race, (US) election, etc ▷ *n* **10** the act of scratching **11** a slight injury **12** a mark made by scratching **13** a slight grating sound **14** (in a handicap sport) a competitor or the status of a competitor who has no allowance **15a** the line from which competitors start in a race **15b** (formerly) a line drawn on the floor of a prize ring at which the contestants stood to begin fighting **16** *billiards, etc* a lucky shot **17 from scratch** *inf* from the very beginning **18 up to scratch** (*usually used with a negative*) *inf* up to standard ▷ *adj* **19** *sport* (of a team) assembled hastily **20** (in a handicap sport) with no allowance or penalty **21** *inf* rough or haphazard [C15 via OF *escrater* from Gmc] > ˈ**scratcher** *n* > ˈ**scratchy** *adj*

scratchcard (ˈskrætʒˌkɑːd) *n* a ticket that reveals whether or not the holder is eligible for a prize when the surface is removed by scratching

scratch file *n computing* a temporary store for use during the execution of a program

scratching (ˈskrætʃɪŋ) *n* a percussive effect obtained by rotating a gramophone record manually: a disc-jockey and dub technique

scratch pad *n* **1** *chiefly US & Canad* a notebook, esp one with detachable leaves **2** *computing* a small semiconductor memory for temporary storage

scratch video *n* the recycling of images from films or television to make collages

scrawl (skrɔːl) *vb* **1** to write or draw (words, etc) carelessly or hastily ▷ *n* **2** careless or scribbled writing or drawing [C17 ? a blend of SPRAWL & CRAWL¹] > ˈ**scrawly** *adj*

scrawny (ˈskrɔːnɪ) *adj* **scrawnier, scrawniest 1** very thin and bony **2** meagre or stunted [C19 var. of dialect *scranny*] > ˈ**scrawnily** *adv* > ˈ**scrawniness** *n*

scream (skriːm) *vb* **1** to utter or emit (a sharp piercing cry or similar sound), esp as of fear, pain, etc **2** (*intr*) to laugh wildly **3** (*intr*) to speak, shout, or behave in a wild manner **4** (*tr*) to bring (oneself) into a specified state by screaming: *she screamed herself hoarse* **5** (*intr*) to be extremely conspicuous: *these orange curtains scream; you need something more restful* ▷ *n* **6** a sharp piercing cry or sound, esp one denoting fear or pain **7** *inf* a person or thing that causes great amusement [C13 from Gmc]

screamer (ˈskriːmə) *n* **1** a person or thing that screams **2** a goose-like aquatic bird, such as the **crested screamer** of tropical and subtropical South America **3** *inf* (in printing) an exclamation mark **4** someone or something that raises screams of laughter or astonishment **5** *US & Canad sl* a sensational headline **6** *Austral sl* a person or thing that is excellent of its kind

scree (skriː) *n* an accumulation of rock fragments at the

Ss

foot of a cliff or hillside, often forming a sloping heap [OE *scrīthan* to slip; rel. to ON *skrītha* to slide]

screech[1] (skriːtʃ) *n* **1** a shrill or high-pitched sound or cry ▷ *vb* **2** to utter with or produce a screech [C16 var. of earlier *scritch*, imit.] > **'screecher** *n* > **'screechy** *adj*

screech[2] (skriːtʃ) *n Canad sl* (esp in Newfoundland) a dark rum [?from SCREECH[1]]

screech owl *n* **1** *Brit* another name for **barn owl** **2** a small North American owl having a reddish-brown or grey plumage

screed (skriːd) *n* **1** a long or prolonged speech or piece of writing **2** a strip of wood, plaster, or metal placed on a surface to act as a guide to the thickness of the cement or plaster coat to be applied **3** a mixture of cement, sand, and water applied to a concrete slab, etc, to give a smooth surface finish [C14 prob. var. of OE *scrēade* shred]

screen (skriːn) *n* **1** a light movable frame, panel, or partition serving to shelter, divide, hide, etc **2** anything that serves to shelter, protect, or conceal **3** a frame containing a mesh that is placed over a window to keep out insects **4** a decorated partition, esp in a church around the choir **5** a sieve **6** the wide end of a cathode-ray tube, esp in a television set, on which a visible image is formed **7** a white or silvered surface, placed in front of a projector to receive the enlarged image of a film or of slides **8 the screen** the film industry or films collectively **9** *photog* a plate of ground glass in some types of camera on which the image of a subject is focused **10** men or ships deployed around and ahead of a larger military formation to warn of attack **11** *electronics* See **screen grid** ▷ *vb* (*tr*) **12** (sometimes foll by *off*) to shelter, protect, or conceal **13** to sieve or sort **14** to test or check (an individual or group) so as to determine suitability for a task, etc **15** to examine for the presence of a disease, weapons, etc **16** to provide with a screen or screens **17** to project (a film) onto a screen, esp for public viewing [C15 from OF *escren* (F *écran*)] > **'screenable** *adj* > **'screener** *n* > **'screenful** *n*

screenager ('skriːnˌeɪdʒə) *n inf* a teenager who is dully conversant with and skilled in the use of computers and other electronic devices [C20 from SCREEN + (TEEN) AGER]

screen grid *n electronics* an electrode placed between the control grid and anode of a valve which acts as an electrostatic shield, thus increasing the stability of the device. Sometimes shortened to **screen**

screenings ('skriːnɪŋz) *pl n* refuse separated by sifting

screening test *n* a simple test performed on a large number of people to identify those who have or are likely to develop a specified disease

screenplay ('skriːnˌpleɪ) *n* the script for a film, including instructions for sets and camera work

screen process *n* a method of printing using a fine mesh of silk, nylon, etc, treated with an impermeable coating except in the areas through which ink is subsequently forced onto the paper behind. Also called: **silk-screen printing**

screensaver ('skriːnseɪvə) *n computing* a computer program that reduces screen damage resulting from an unchanging display, when the computer is switched on but not in use, by blanking the screen or generating moving patterns, pictures, etc

screenwriter ('skriːnˌraɪtə) *n* a person who writes screenplays

screw (skruː) *n* **1** a device used for fastening materials together, consisting of a threaded shank that has a slotted head by which it may be rotated so as to cut its own thread **2** Also called: **screw-bolt** a threaded cylindrical rod that engages with a similarly threaded cylindrical hole **3** a thread in a cylindrical hole corresponding with that on the screw with which it is designed to engage **4** anything resembling a screw in shape or spiral form **5** a twisting movement of or resembling that of a screw **6** Also called: **screw-back** *billiards, etc* a stroke in which the cue ball moves backward after striking the object ball **7** another name for **propeller** (sense 1) **8** *sl* a prison guard **9** *Brit sl* salary, wages, or earnings **10** *Brit* a small amount of salt, tobacco, etc, in a twist of paper **11** *sl* a person who is mean with money **12** *sl* an old or worthless horse **13** (*often pl*) *sl* force or compulsion (esp in **put the screws on**) **14** *sl* sexual intercourse **15 have a screw loose** *inf* to be insane ▷ *vb* **16** (*tr*) to rotate (a screw or bolt) so as to drive it into or draw it out of a material **17** (*tr*) to cut a screw thread in (a rod or hole) with a tap or die or on a lathe **18** to turn or cause to turn in the manner of a screw **19** (*tr*) to attach or fasten with a screw or screws **20** (*tr*) *inf* to take advantage of; cheat **21** (*tr; often foll by up*) *inf* to distort or contort: *he screwed his face into a scowl* **22** (*tr; often foll by from or out of*) *inf* to coerce or force out of; extort **23** *sl* to have sexual intercourse (with) **24** (*tr*) *sl* to burgle **25 have one's head screwed on the right way** *inf* to be sensible ▷ See also **screw up** [C15 from F *escroe*, from Med. L *scrōfa* screw, from L: sow, presumably because the thread of the screw is like the spiral of the sow's tail] > **'screwer** *n*

screwball ('skruːˌbɔːl) *sl, chiefly US & Canad* ▷ *n* **1** an odd or eccentric person ▷ *adj* **2** odd; eccentric

screwdriver ('skruːˌdraɪvə) *n* **1** a tool used for turning screws, usually having a steel shank with a flattened square-cut tip that fits into a slot in the head of the screw **2** an alcoholic beverage consisting of orange juice and vodka

screwed (skruːd) *adj* **1** fastened by a screw or screws **2** having spiral grooves like a screw **3** twisted or distorted **4** *Brit sl* drunk

screw eye *n* a wood screw with its shank bent into a ring

screw pine *n* any of various tropical Old World plants having a spiral mass of pineapple-like leaves and conelike fruits

screw propeller *n* an early form of ship's propeller in which an Archimedes' screw is used to produce thrust by accelerating a flow of water

screw top *n* **1** a bottle top that screws onto the bottle, allowing the bottle to be resealed after use **2** a bottle with such a top > **'screw-ˌtop** *adj*

screw up *vb* (*tr, adv*) **1** to twist out of shape or distort **2** to summon up: *to screw up one's courage* **3** (*also intr*) *inf* to mishandle or bungle

screwy ('skruːɪ) *adj* **screwier, screwiest** *inf* odd, crazy, or eccentric

Scriabin *or* **Skryabin** ('skrɪəbɪn; *Russian* 'skrjabin) *n* **Aleksandr Nikolayevich** (alɪk'sandr nika'lajɪvitʃ) 1872–1915, Russian composer, whose works came increasingly to express his theosophic beliefs. He wrote many piano works; his orchestral compositions include *Prometheus* (1911)

scribble ('skrɪbᵊl) *vb* **scribbles, scribbling, scribbled** **1** to write or draw in a hasty or illegible manner **2** to make meaningless or illegible marks (on) **3** *derog or facetious* to write poetry, novels, etc ▷ *n* **4** hasty careless writing or drawing **5** meaningless or illegible marks [C15 from Med. L *scrībillāre* to write hastily, from L *scrībere* to write] > **'scribbler** *n* > **'scribbly** *adj*

scribbly gum *n Austral* a eucalypt with smooth white bark, marked with random patterns made by wood-boring insects

scribe (skraɪb) *n* **1** a person who copies documents, esp a person who made handwritten copies before the invention of printing **2** a clerk or public copyist **3** *Bible* a recognized scholar and teacher of the Jewish Law ▷ *vb* **scribes, scribing, scribed** **4** to score a line on (a surface) with a pointed instrument, as in metalworking [(in the senses: writer, etc) C14 from L *scrība* clerk, from *scrībere* to write; C17 (vb): ?from INSCRIBE] > **'scribal** *adj*

Scribe (*French* skrib) *n* **Augustin Eugène** (ogystɛ̃ øʒɛn) 1791–1861, French author or coauthor of over 350 vaudevilles, comedies, and libretti for light opera

scriber ('skraɪbə) *n* a pointed steel tool used to score materials as a guide to cutting, etc. Also called: **scribe**

scrim (skrɪm) *n* a fine open-weave fabric, used in upholstery, lining, building, and in the theatre to create the illusion of a solid wall [c18 from ?]

scrimmage ('skrɪmɪdʒ) *n* **1** a rough or disorderly struggle **2** *American football* the clash of opposing linemen at every down ▷ *vb* **scrimmages, scrimmaging, scrimmaged 3** (*intr*) to engage in a scrimmage **4** (*tr*) to put (the ball) into a scrimmage [c15 from earlier *scrimish*, var. of SKIRMISH] > '**scrimmager** *n*

scrimp (skrɪmp) *vb* **1** (when *intr*, sometimes foll by *on*) to be very sparing in the use (of) (esp in **scrimp and save**) **2** (*tr*) to treat meanly: *he is scrimping his children* [c18 Scot, from ?] > '**scrimpy** *adj* > '**scrimpiness** *n*

scrimshank ('skrɪm,ʃæŋk) *vb* (*intr*) *Brit mil sl* to shirk work [c19 from ?]

scrimshaw ('skrɪm,ʃɔː) *n* **1** the art of decorating or carving shells, bone, ivory, etc, done by sailors as a leisure activity **2** an article or articles made in this manner [c19 from ?]

scrip[1] (skrɪp) *n* **1** a written certificate, list, etc **2** a small scrap, esp of paper with writing on it **3** *finance* **3a** a certificate representing a claim to part of a share of stock **3b** the shares issued by a company (**scrip** or **bonus issue**) without charge and distributed among existing shareholders [c18 in some senses, prob. from SCRIPT; otherwise, short for *subscription receipt*]

scrip[2] (skrɪp) *or* **script** *n inf* a medical prescription [c20 from PRESCRIPTION]

script (skrɪpt) *n* **1** handwriting as distinguished from print **2** the letters, characters, or figures used in writing by hand **3** any system or style of writing **4** written copy for the use of performers in films and plays **5** *law* an original or principal document **6** an answer paper in an examination **7** *computing* a series of instructions that is executed by a computer program **8** another word for **scrip**[2] ▷ *vb* **9** (*tr*) to write a script for [c14 from L *scriptum* something written, from *scrībere* to write]

script kiddie *n slang* a child or teenager who gains illegal access to computer systems, often by using hacking programs downloaded from the Internet

scriptorium (skrɪp'tɔːrɪəm) *n, pl* **scriptoriums** *or* **scriptoria** (-rɪə) a room, esp in a monastery, set apart for the copying of manuscripts [from Med. L]

scripture ('skrɪptʃə) *n* a sacred, solemn, or authoritative book or piece of writing [c13 from L *scriptūra* written material, from *scrībere* to write] > '**scriptural** *adj*

Scripture ('skrɪptʃə) *n* **1** Also called: **Holy Scripture, Holy Writ, the Scriptures** *Christianity* the Old and New Testaments **2** any book or body of writings, esp when regarded as sacred by a particular religious group

scriptwriter ('skrɪpt,raɪtə) *n* a person who prepares scripts, esp for a film > '**script,writing** *n*

scrivener ('skrɪvnə) *n arch* **1** a person who writes out deeds, etc **2** a notary [c14 from *scrivein* clerk, from OF *escrivain*, ult. from L *scrība* SCRIBE]

scrod (skrɒd) *n US* a young cod or haddock [c19 ? from obs. Du. *schrood*, from MDu. *schrode* SHRED (n); the name perhaps refers to the method of preparing the fish for cooking]

scrofula ('skrɒfjʊlə) *n pathol* (*no longer in technical use*) tuberculosis of the lymphatic glands. Also called (formerly): (the) **king's evil** [c14 from Med. L, from LL *scrōfulae* swollen glands in the neck, lit.: little sows (sows were thought to be particularly prone to the disease), from L *scrōfa* sow] > '**scrofulous** *adj*

scroggin ('skrɒgɪn) *n NZ inf* a home-made high-calorie sweetmeat eaten by people walking in the bush [c20 from ?]

scroll (skrəʊl) *n* **1** a roll of parchment, etc, usually inscribed with writing **2** an ancient book in the form of a roll of parchment, papyrus, etc **3** a decorative carving or moulding resembling a scroll ▷ *vb* **4** (*tr*) to saw into scrolls **5** to roll up like a scroll **6** *computing* to move (text) on a screen in order to view a section that cannot be fitted into a single display [c15 *scrowle*, from *scrowe*, from OF *escroe* scrap of parchment, but also infl. by ROLL]

scroll saw *n* a saw with a narrow blade for cutting intricate ornamental curves in wood

scrollwork ('skrəʊl,wɜːk) *n* ornamental work in scroll-like patterns

Scrooge (skruːdʒ) *n* a mean or miserly person [c19 after a character in Dickens' story *A Christmas Carol* (1843)]

scrophulariaceous (,skrɒfjʊ,lɛərɪ'eɪʃəs) *adj* of or belonging to the *Scrophulariaceae*, a family of plants including figwort, snapdragon, foxglove, and mullein [c19 from NL (*herba*) *scrophularia* scrofula (plant), from the use of such plants in treating scrofula]

scrotum ('skrəʊtəm) *n, pl* **scrota** (-tə) *or* **scrotums** the pouch of skin containing the testes in most mammals [c16 from L] > '**scrotal** *adj*

scrounge (skraʊndʒ) *vb* **scrounges, scrounging, scrounged** *inf* **1** (when *intr*, sometimes foll by *around*) to search in order to acquire (something) without cost **2** to obtain or seek to obtain (something) by begging [c20 var. of dialect *scrunge* to steal, from ?] > '**scrounger** *n*

scrub[1] (skrʌb) *vb* **scrubs, scrubbing, scrubbed 1** to rub (a surface, etc) hard, with or as if with a brush, soap, and water, in order to clean it **2** to remove (dirt) by rubbing, esp with a brush and water **3** (*intr*; foll by *up*) (of a surgeon) to wash the hands and arms thoroughly before operating **4** (*tr*) to purify (a gas) by removing impurities **5** (*tr*) *inf* to delete or cancel ▷ *n* **6** the act of or an instance of scrubbing [c14 from MLow G *schrubben*, or MDu. *schrobben*]

scrub[2] (skrʌb) *n* **1a** vegetation consisting of stunted trees, bushes, and other plants growing in an arid area **1b** (*as modifier*): *scrub vegetation* **2** an area of arid land covered with such vegetation **3a** an animal of inferior breeding or condition **3b** (*as modifier*): *a scrub bull* **4** a small person **5** anything stunted or inferior **6** *sport, US & Canad* a player not in the first team **7 the scrub** *Austral inf* a remote or uncivilized place ▷ *adj* (*prenominal*) **8** small or inferior **9** *sport, US* **9a** (of a player) not in the first team **9b** (of a team) composed of such players [c16 var. of SHRUB[1]]

scrubber ('skrʌbə) *n* **1** a person or thing that scrubs **2** an apparatus for purifying a gas **3** *derog sl* a promiscuous woman

scrubby ('skrʌbɪ) *adj* **scrubbier, scrubbiest 1** covered with or consisting of scrub **2** (of trees, etc) stunted in growth **3** *Brit inf* messy

scrubland ('skrʌb,lænd) *n* an area of scrub vegetation

scrub turkey *n* another term for **megapode**

scrub typhus *n* a disease characterized by severe headache, skin rash, chills, and swelling of the lymph nodes, caused by the bite of mites infected with a microorganism: occurs mainly in Asia and Australia

scruff[1] (skrʌf) *n* the nape of the neck (esp in **by the scruff of the neck**) [c18 var. of *scuft*, ?from ON *skoft* hair]

scruff[2] (skrʌf) *n inf* **1** an untidy scruffy person **2** a disreputable person; ruffian

scruffy ('skrʌfɪ) *adj* **scruffier, scruffiest** unkempt or shabby

scrum (skrʌm) *n* **1** *rugby* the act or method of restarting play when the two opposing packs of forwards group together with heads down and arms interlocked and push to gain ground while the scrum half throws the ball in and the hookers attempt to scoop it out to their own team **2** *inf* a disorderly struggle ▷ *vb* **scrums, scrumming, scrummed 3** (*intr*; usually foll by *down*) *rugby* to form a scrum [c19 from SCRUMMAGE]

scrum half *n rugby* **1** a player who puts in the ball at scrums and tries to get it away to his three-quarter backs **2** this position in a team

scrummage (ˈskrʌmɪdʒ) *n, vb* **scrummages, scrummaging, scrummaged 1** *rugby* another word for **scrum 2** a variant of **scrimmage** [C19 var. of SCRIMMAGE]

scrump (skrʌmp) *vb dialect* to steal (apples) from an orchard or garden [var. of SCRIMP]

scrumptious (ˈskrʌmpʃəs) *adj inf* very pleasing; delicious [C19 prob. changed from SUMPTUOUS] > **ˈscrumptiously** *adv*

scrumpy (ˈskrʌmpɪ) *n* a rough dry cider, brewed esp in the West Country of England [from *scrump*, var. of SCRIMP (in obs. sense: withered), referring to the apples used]

scrunch (skrʌntʃ) *vb* **1** to crumple or crunch or to be crumpled or crunched ▷ *n* **2** the act or sound of scrunching [C19 var. of CRUNCH]

scruncheon *or* **scrunchion** (ˈskrʌntʃən) *n Canad* (in Newfoundland) a small crisp piece of fried pork fat [origin unknown]

scrunchie (ˈskrʌntʃɪ) *n* a loop of elastic covered loosely with fabric, used to hold the hair in a ponytail

scruple (ˈskruːpᵊl) *n* **1** (*often pl*) a doubt or hesitation as to what is morally right in a certain situation **2** *arch* a very small amount **3** a unit of weight equal to 20 grains (1.296 grams) ▷ *vb* **scruples, scrupling, scrupled 4** (*obs when tr*) to have doubts (about), esp from a moral compunction [C16 from L *scrūpulus* a small weight, from *scrūpus* rough stone]

scrupulous (ˈskruːpjʊləs) *adj* **1** characterized by careful observation of what is morally right **2** very careful or precise [C15 from L *scrūpulōsus* punctilious] > **ˈscrupulously** *adv* > **ˈscrupulousness** *n*

scrutineer (ˌskruːtɪˈnɪə) *n* a person who examines, esp one who scrutinizes the conduct of an election poll

scrutinize *or* **scrutinise** (ˈskruːtɪˌnaɪz) *vb* **scrutinizes, scrutinizing, scrutinized** *or* **scrutinises, scrutinising, scrutinised** (*tr*) to examine carefully or in minute detail > **ˈscrutiˌnizer** *or* **ˈscrutiˌniser** *n*

scrutiny (ˈskruːtɪnɪ) *n, pl* **scrutinies 1** close or minute examination **2** a searching look **3** (in the early Christian Church) a formal testing that catechumens had to undergo before being baptized [C15 from LL *scrūtinium* an investigation, from *scrūtārī* to search (orig. referring to rag-and-bone men), from *scrūta* rubbish]

scry (skraɪ) *vb* **scries, scrying, scried** (*intr*) to divine, esp by crystal gazing [C16 from DESCRY]

scuba (ˈskjuːbə) *n* an apparatus used in skin diving, consisting of a cylinder or cylinders containing compressed air attached to a breathing apparatus [C20 from the initials of *self-contained underwater breathing apparatus*]

scud (skʌd) *vb* **scuds, scudding, scudded** (*intr*) **1** (esp of clouds) to move along swiftly and smoothly **2** *naut* to run before a gale ▷ *n* **3** the act of scudding **4a** a formation of low ragged clouds driven by a strong wind beneath rain-bearing clouds **4b** a sudden shower or gust of wind [C16 prob. of Scand. origin]

scuff (skʌf) *vb* **1** to drag (the feet) while walking **2** to scratch (a surface) or (of a surface) to become scratched **3** (*tr*) *US* to poke at (something) with the foot ▷ *n* **4** the act or sound of scuffing **5** a rubbed place caused by scuffing **6** a backless slipper [C19 prob. imit.]

scuffle (ˈskʌfᵊl) *vb* **scuffles, scuffling, scuffled** (*intr*) **1** to fight in a disorderly manner **2** to move by shuffling ▷ *n* **3** a disorderly struggle **4** the sound made by scuffling [C16 of Scand. origin; cf. Swedish *skuff*, *skuffa* to push]

scull (skʌl) *n* **1** a single oar moved from side to side over the stern of a boat to propel it **2** one of a pair of short-handled oars, both of which are pulled by one oarsman **3** a racing shell propelled by an oarsman or oarsmen pulling two oars **4** an act, instance, period, or distance of sculling ▷ *vb* **5** to propel (a boat) with a scull [C14 from ?] > **ˈsculler** *n*

scullery (ˈskʌlərɪ) *n, pl* **sculleries** *chiefly Brit* a small room or part of a kitchen where washing-up, vegetable preparation, etc, is done [C15 from Anglo-Norman *squillerie*, from OF, from *escuele* a bowl, from L *scutella*, from *scutra* a flat tray]

Scullin (ˈskʌlɪn) *n* **James Henry** 1876–1953, Australian statesman; prime minister of Australia (1929–31)

scullion (ˈskʌljən) *n* **1** a mean or despicable person **2** *arch* a servant employed to work in a kitchen [C15 from OF *escouillon* cleaning cloth, from *escouve* a broom, from L *scōpa* a broom, twig]

sculpt (skʌlpt) *vb* **1** a variant of **sculpture 2** (*intr*) to practise sculpture ▷ Also: **sculp** [C19 from F *sculpter*, from L *sculpere* to carve]

sculptor (ˈskʌlptə) *or* (*fem*) **sculptress** *n* a person who practises sculpture

sculpture (ˈskʌlptʃə) *n* **1** the art of making figures or designs in relief or the round by carving wood, moulding plaster, etc, or casting metals, etc **2** works or a work made in this way **3** ridges or indentations as on a shell, formed by natural processes ▷ *vb* **sculptures, sculpturing, sculptured** (*mainly tr*) **4** (*also intr*) to carve, cast, or fashion (stone, bronze, etc) three-dimensionally **5** to portray (a person, etc) by means of sculpture **6** to form in the manner of sculpture **7** to decorate with sculpture [C14 from L *sculptūra* a carving] > **ˈsculptural** *adj*

▷ http://dir.yahoo.com/Arts/Visual_Arts/Sculpture
▷ www.sculptor.org
▷ www.bluffton.edu/~sullivanm/index

sculpturesque (ˌskʌlptʃəˈrɛsk) *adj* resembling sculpture > **ˌsculpturˈesquely** *adv*

scum (skʌm) *n* **1** a layer of impure matter that forms on the surface of a liquid, often as the result of boiling or fermentation **2** the greenish film of algae and similar vegetation surface of a stagnant pond **3** the skin of oxides or impurities on the surface of a molten metal **4** waste matter **5** a worthless person or group of people ▷ *vb* **scums, scumming, scummed 6** (*tr*) to remove scum from **7** (*intr*) *rare* to form a layer of or become covered with scum [C13 of Gmc origin] > **ˈscummy** *adj*

scumbag (ˈskʌmˌbæg) *n sl* an offensive or despicable person [C20 ?from earlier US sense: condom, from US slang *scum* semen + bag]

scumble (ˈskʌmbᵊl) *vb* **scumbles, scumbling, scumbled 1** (in painting and drawing) to soften or blend (an outline or colour) with an upper coat of opaque colour, applied very thinly **2** to produce an effect of broken colour on doors, panelling, etc, by exposing coats of paint below the top coat ▷ *n* **3** the upper layer of colour applied in this way [C18 prob. from SCUM]

scuncheon (ˈskʌntʃən) *n* the inner part of a door jamb or window frame [C15 from OF *escoinson*, from *coin* angle]

scungy (ˈskʌndʒɪ) *adj* **scungier, scungiest** *Austral & NZ sl* miserable; sordid; dirty [C20 from ?]

scunner (ˈskʌnə) *dialect, chiefly Scot* ▷ *vb* **1** (*intr*) to feel aversion **2** (*tr*) to produce a feeling of aversion in ▷ *n* **3** a strong aversion (often in **take a scunner**) **4** an object of dislike; nuisance [C14 from Scot *skunner*, from ?]

Scunthorpe (ˈskʌnˌθɔːp) *n* a town in E England, in North Lincolnshire unitary authority, Lincolnshire: developed rapidly after the discovery of local iron ore in the late 19th century; iron and steel industries have declined. Pop: 75 982 (1991)

scup (skʌp) *n* a common fish of American coastal regions of the Atlantic [C19 from Amerind *mishcup*, from *mishe* big + *kuppe* close together; from the form of the scales]

scupper[1] (ˈskʌpə) *n naut* a drain or spout allowing water on the deck of a vessel to flow overboard [C15 *skopper*, from ?]

scupper[2] (ˈskʌpə) *vb* (*tr*) *Brit sl* **1** to overwhelm, ruin, or disable **2** to sink (one's ship) deliberately [C19 from ?]

scurf (skɜːf) *n* **1** another name for **dandruff 2** flaky or scaly matter adhering to or peeling off a surface [OE *scurf*] > 'scurfy *adj*

scurrilous ('skʌrɪləs) *adj* **1** grossly or obscenely abusive or defamatory **2** characterized by gross or obscene humour [C16 from L *scurrīlis* derisive, from *scurra* buffoon] > **scurrility** (skə'rɪlɪtɪ) *n* > **'scurrilously** *adv*

scurry ('skʌrɪ) *vb* **scurries, scurrying, scurried 1** to move about hurriedly **2** (*intr*) to whirl about ▷ *n, pl* **scurries 3** the act or sound of scurrying **4** a brisk light whirling movement, as of snow [C19 prob. from *hurry-scurry*, from HURRY]

scurvy ('skɜːvɪ) *n* **1** a disease caused by a lack of vitamin C, characterized by anaemia, spongy gums, and bleeding beneath the skin ▷ *adj* **scurvier, scurviest 2** mean or despicable [C16 see SCURF] > **'scurvily** *adv* > **'scurviness** *n*

scurvy grass *n* any of various plants of Europe and North America, formerly used to treat scurvy

scut (skʌt) *n* the short tail of animals such as the deer and rabbit [C15 prob. from ON]

scutage ('skjuːtɪdʒ) *n* (in feudal society) a payment sometimes exacted by a lord from his vassal in lieu of military service [C15 from Med. L *scūtāgium*, lit.: shield dues, from L *scūtum* a shield]

Scutari *n* **1** ('skuːtərɪ, skuː'tɑːrɪ) the former name of **Üsküdar 2** (sku'tari) the Italian name for **Shkodër**

scutate ('skjuːteɪt) *adj* **1** (of animals) covered with large bony or horny plates **2** *bot* shaped like a round shield [C19 from L *scūtātus* armed with a shield, from *scūtum* a shield]

scutcheon ('skʌtʃən) *n* **1** a variant of **escutcheon 2** any rounded or shield-shaped structure

scutch grass (skʌtʃ) *n* another name for **couch grass** [var. of COUCH GRASS]

scute (skjuːt) *n zool* a horny plate that makes up part of the exoskeleton in armadillos, turtles, etc [C14 (the name of a F coin; C19 in zoological sense): from L *scūtum* shield]

scutellum (skjuː'tɛləm) *n, pl* **scutella** (-lə) *biol* **1** the last of three plates into which an insect's thorax is divided **2** one of the scales on the tarsus of a bird's leg **3** an outgrowth from a germinating grass seed that probably represents the cotyledon [C18 from NL: a little shield, from L *scūtum* a shield] > **scutellate** ('skjuːtɪˌleɪt, -lɪt) *adj*

scutter ('skʌtə) *vb, n Brit inf* scurry [C18 prob. from SCUTTLE², with -ER¹ as in SCATTER]

scuttle¹ ('skʌtᵊl) *n* **1** See **coal scuttle 2** *dialect, chiefly Brit* a shallow basket, esp for carrying vegetables **3** the part of a motorcar body lying immediately behind the bonnet [OE *scutel* trencher, from L *scutella* bowl, dim. of *scutra* platter]

scuttle² ('skʌtᵊl) *vb* **scuttles, scuttling, scuttled 1** (*intr*) to run or move about with short hasty steps ▷ *n* **2** a hurried pace or run [C15 ?from SCUD, infl. by SHUTTLE]

scuttle³ ('skʌtᵊl) *vb* **scuttles, scuttling, scuttled** (*tr*) **1** *naut* to cause (a vessel) to sink by opening the seacocks or making holes in the bottom **2** to give up (hopes, plans, etc) ▷ *n* **3** *naut* a small hatch or its cover [C15 (n): via OF from Sp. *escotilla* a small opening, from *escote* opening in a piece of cloth, from *escotar* to cut out]

scuttlebutt ('skʌtᵊlˌbʌt) *n naut* **1** a drinking fountain **2** (formerly) a cask of drinking water aboard a ship **3** *chiefly US sl* gossip

scutum ('skjuːtəm) *n, pl* **scuta** (-tə) **1** the middle of three plates into which an insect's thorax is divided **2** another word for **scute** [L: shield]

scuzzy ('skʌzɪ) *adj* **scuzzier, scuzziest** *sl, chiefly US* unkempt, dirty, or squalid [C20 ?from *disgusting* or ?from blend of *scum & fuzz*]

Scylla ('sɪlə) *n* **1** *Greek myth* a sea nymph transformed into a sea monster believed to drown sailors navigating the Strait of Messina ▷ Cf **Charybdis 2 between Scylla and Charybdis** in a predicament in which avoidance of either of two dangers means exposure to the other

scythe (saɪð) *n* **1** a long-handled implement for cutting grass, etc, having a curved sharpened blade that moves in a plane parallel to the ground ▷ *vb* **scythes, scything, scythed 2** (*tr*) to cut (grass, etc) with a scythe [OE *sigthe*]

Scythia ('sɪðɪə) *n* an ancient region of SE Europe and Asia, north of the Black Sea: now part of the Ukraine > **'Scythian** *adj, n*

SD *abbrev for:* **1** South Dakota **2** Also: **sd** *statistics* standard deviation

S. Dak. *abbrev for* South Dakota

SDI *abbrev for* Strategic Defense Initiative. See **Star Wars**

SDK *computing abbrev for* software development kit

SDLP *abbrev for* Social Democratic and Labour Party

SDP *abbrev for* Social Democratic Party

SDRs *finance abbrev for* special drawing rights

Se *the chemical symbol for* selenium

SE *symbol for* southeast(ern)

sea (siː) *n* **1a** (usually preceded by *the*) the mass of salt water on the earth's surface as differentiated from the land. Related adjs.: **marine, maritime 1b** (*as modifier*): *sea air* **2** (*cap when part of place name*) **2a** one of the smaller areas of ocean: *the Irish Sea* **2b** a large inland area of water: *the Caspian Sea* **3** turbulence or swell: *heavy seas* **4** (*cap when part of a name*) *astron* any of many huge dry plains on the surface of the moon: *Sea of Serenity*. See also **mare² 5** anything resembling the sea in size or apparent limitlessness **6 at sea 6a** on the ocean **6b** in a state of confusion **7 go to sea** to become a sailor **8 put (out) to sea** to embark on a sea voyage [OE *sǣ*]

sea anchor *n naut* any device, such as a bucket, dragged in the water to keep a vessel heading into the wind or reduce drifting

sea anemone *n* any of various coelenterates having a polypoid body with oral rings of tentacles

sea bag *n* a canvas bag used by a seaman for his belongings

sea bass (bæs) *n* any of various American coastal fishes having an elongated body with a long spiny dorsal fin almost divided into two

sea bird *n* a bird such as a gull, that lives on the sea

seaboard ('siːˌbɔːd) *n* land bordering on the sea

Seaborg ('siːbɔːg) *n* **Glenn Theodore** 1912–99, US chemist and nuclear physicist. With E.M. McMillan, he discovered several transuranic elements, including plutonium (1940), curium, and americium (1944), and shared a Nobel prize for chemistry 1951

seaborgium ('siːbɔːgɪəm) *n* a synthetic transuranic element, synthesized and identified in 1974. Symbol: Sg; atomic no.: 106 [C20 after Glenn SEABORG]

seaborne ('siːˌbɔːn) *adj* **1** carried on or by the sea **2** transported by ship

sea bream *n* a fish of European seas, valued as a food fish

sea breeze *n* a wind blowing from the sea to the land, esp during the day when the land surface is warmer

sea change *n* a seemingly magical change [from Ariel's song "Full Fathom Five" in *The Tempest* (1611)]

seacoast ('siːˌkəʊst) *n* land bordering on the sea; a coast

seacock ('siːˌkɒk) *n naut* a valve in the hull of a vessel below the water line for admitting sea water or for pumping out bilge water

sea cow *n* **1** a dugong or manatee **2** an archaic name for the **walrus**

sea cucumber *n* an echinoderm having an elongated body covered with a leathery skin and a cluster of tentacles at the oral end

sea dog *n* an experienced or old sailor

Sea-Doo ('siːˌduː) *n Canad trademark* a small self-propelled watercraft for one person.

sea eagle *n* any of various fish-eating eagles of coastal areas, esp the **European sea eagle,** having a brown plumage and white tail

seafarer (ˈsiːˌfɛərə) *n* **1** a traveller who goes by sea **2** a sailor

seafaring (ˈsiːˌfɛərɪŋ) *adj (prenominal)* **1** travelling by sea **2** working as a sailor ▷ *n* **3** the act of travelling by sea **4** the work of a sailor

seafood (ˈsiːˌfuːd) *n* edible saltwater fish or shellfish
▷ www.seafoodrecipe.com/default.asp
▷ www.seafoodchoices.com
▷ www.aboutseafood.com

seafront (ˈsiːˌfrʌnt) *n* a built-up area facing the sea

sea-girt *adj literary* surrounded by the sea

seagoing (ˈsiːˌɡəʊɪŋ) *adj* intended for or used at sea

sea green *n* **a** a moderate green colour, sometimes with a bluish or yellowish tinge **b** *(as adj): a sea-green carpet*

sea gull *n* **1** a popular name for the **gull** (the bird) **2** *NZ inf* a casual dock worker

seahenge (ˌsiːˈhɜndʒ) *n* an early Bronze Age timber circle discovered in the sands at Holme-next-the-Sea, Norfolk, in 1998; removed for conservation [from SEA + (STONE) HENGE]

sea holly *n* a European plant of sandy shores, having bluish-green stems and blue flowers

sea horse *n* **1** a marine teleost fish of temperate and tropical waters, having a bony-plated body, a prehensile tail, and a horselike head and swimming in an upright position **2** an archaic name for the **walrus** **3** a fabled sea creature with the tail of a fish and the front parts of a horse

sea-island cotton *n* **1** a cotton plant of the Sea Islands, off the Florida coast, widely cultivated for its fine long fibres **2** the fibre of this plant or the material woven from it

Sea Islands *pl n* a chain of islands in the Atlantic off the coasts of South Carolina, Georgia, and Florida

sea kale *n* a European coastal plant with broad fleshy leaves and white flowers: cultivated for its edible asparagus-like shoots ▷ Cf **kale**

seal[1] (siːl) *n* **1** a device impressed on a piece of wax, etc, fixed to a letter, etc, as a mark of authentication **2** a stamp, ring, etc, engraved with a device to form such an impression **3** a substance, esp wax, so placed over an envelope, etc, that it must be broken before the object can be opened or used **4** any substance or device used to close or fasten tightly **5** a small amount of water contained in the trap of a drain to prevent the passage of foul smells **6** anything that gives a pledge or confirmation **7** a token; sign: *seal of death* **8** a decorative stamp sold in aid of charity **9** *RC Church* Also called: **seal of confession** the obligation never to reveal anything said in confession **10** **set one's seal on** (*or* **to**) **10a** to mark with one's sign or seal **10b** to endorse ▷ *vb (tr)* **11** to affix a seal to, as proof of authenticity, etc **12** to stamp with or as if with a seal **13** to approve or authorize **14** (sometimes foll by *up*) to close or secure with or as if with a seal: *to seal one's lips* **15** (foll by *off*) to enclose (a place) with a fence, etc **16** to decide irrevocably **17** to close tightly so as to render airtight or watertight **18** to subject (the outside of meat, etc) to fierce heat so as to retain the juices during cooking **19** to paint (a porous material) with a nonporous coating **20** *Austral* to cover (a road) with bitumen, asphalt, tarmac, etc [C13 *seel*, from OF, from L *sigillum* little figure, from *signum* a sign] > ˈ**sealable** *adj*

seal[2] (siːl) *n* **1** a fish-eating mammal with four flippers which is aquatic but comes on shore to breed **2** sealskin ▷ *vb* **3** *(intr)* to hunt for seals [OE *seolh*] > ˈ**sealer** *n* > ˈ**seal-**ˌ**like** *adj*

sea lane *n* an established route for ships

sealant (ˈsiːlənt) *n* **1** any substance, such as wax, used for sealing documents, bottles, etc **2** any of a number of substances used for stopping leaks, waterproofing wood, etc

sea lavender *n* any of various plants found on temperate salt marshes, having spikes of white, pink, or mauve flowers

sealed-beam *adj* (esp of a car headlight) having a lens and prefocused reflector sealed in the lamp vacuum

sealed road *n Austral & NZ* a road surfaced with bitumen or some other hard material

sea legs *pl n Inf* **1** the ability to maintain one's balance on board ship **2** the ability to resist seasickness

sea level *n* the level of the surface of the sea with respect to the land, taken to be the mean level between high and low tide

sea lily *n* any of various echinoderms in which the body consists of a long stalk bearing a central disc with delicate radiating arms

sealing wax *n* a hard material made of shellac, turpentine, and pigment that softens when heated

sea lion *n* any of various large eared seals, such as the **Californian sea lion**, of the N Pacific, often used as a performing animal

Sea Lord *n* (in Britain) either of the two serving naval officers (**First** and **Second Sea Lords**) who sit on the admiralty board of the Ministry of Defence

seal ring *n* another term for **signet ring**

sealskin (ˈsiːlˌskɪn) *n* **a** the skin or pelt of a fur seal, esp when dressed with the outer hair removed and the underfur dyed dark brown **b** *(as modifier): a sealskin coat*

Sealyham terrier (ˈsiːlɪəm) *n* a short-legged wire-haired breed of terrier with a medium-length white coat [C19 after *Sealyham*, village in S Wales]

seam (siːm) *n* **1** the line along which pieces of fabric, etc, are joined, esp by stitching **2** a ridge or line made by joining two edges **3** a stratum of coal, ore, etc **4** a linear indentation, such as a wrinkle or scar **5** *(modifier) cricket* of or relating to a style of bowling in which the bowler utilizes the stitched seam round the ball in order to make it swing in flight and after touching the ground: *a seam bowler* **6** **bursting at the seams** full to overflowing ▷ *vb* **7** *(tr)* to join or sew together by or as if by a seam **8** to mark or become marked with or as if with a seam or wrinkle [OE]

seaman (ˈsiːmən) *n, pl* **seamen** **1** a naval rating trained in seamanship **2** a man who serves as a sailor **3** a person skilled in seamanship > ˈ**seamanly** *adj, adv* > ˈ**seaman-**ˌ**like** *adj*

seamanship (ˈsiːmənʃɪp) *n* skill in and knowledge of the work of navigating, maintaining, and operating a vessel

Seami (siːˈɑːmɪ) *n* a variant spelling of **Zeami**

sea mile *n* a unit of distance used in navigation, defined as the length of one minute of arc, measured along the meridian, in the latitude of the position. Its actual length varies slightly with latitude, but is about 1853 metres (6080 feet). See also **nautical mile**

seamless (ˈsiːmlɪs) *adj* **1** (of a garment) having no seams **2** continuous or flowing: *seamless output; a seamless performance*

sea mouse *n* any of various large worms having a broad flattened body covered dorsally with a dense mat of iridescent hairlike setae

seamstress (ˈsɛmstrɪs) *or (rarely)* **sempstress** (ˈsɛmpstrɪs) *n* a woman who sews and makes clothes, esp professionally

seamy (ˈsiːmɪ) *adj* **seamier, seamiest** showing the least pleasant aspect; sordid > ˈ**seaminess** *n*

Seanad Éireann (ˈʃænəð ˈeːrən) *n* (in the Republic of Ireland) the upper chamber of parliament [from Irish, lit.: senate of Ireland]

seance *or* **séance** (ˈseɪɑ̃ns) *n* a meeting at which spiritualists attempt to receive messages from the spirits of the dead [C19 from F, lit.: a sitting, from OF *seoir* to sit, from L *sedēre*]

sea otter *n* a large marine otter of N Pacific coasts, formerly hunted for its thick brown fur

sea pink *n* another name for **thrift** (the plant)
seaplane ('siːˌpleɪn) *n* any aircraft that lands on and takes off from water
seaport ('siːˌpɔːt) *n* **1** a port or harbour accessible to seagoing vessels **2** a town or city located at such a place
SEAQ ('siːˌæk) *n acronym for* Stock Exchange Automated Quotations: an electronic system that collects and displays information needed to trade in equities
sear (sɪə) *vb (tr)* **1** to scorch or burn the surface of **2** to brand with a hot iron **3** to cause to wither **4** *rare* to make unfeeling ▷ *adj* **5** *poetic* dried up [OE *sēarian* to become withered, from *sēar* withered]
search (sɜːtʃ) *vb* **1** to look through (a place, etc) thoroughly in order to find someone or something **2** *(tr)* to examine (a person) for concealed objects **3** to look at or examine (something) closely: *to search one's conscience* **4** *(tr; foll by out)* to discover by investigation **5** *surgery* to probe (a wound, etc) **6** *computing* to review (a file) to locate specific information **7** *arch* to penetrate **8** **search me** *inf* I don't know ▷ *n* **9** the act or an instance of searching **10** the examination of a vessel by the right of search **11** **right of search** *international law* the right possessed by the warships of a belligerent state to search merchant vessels to ascertain whether ship or cargo is liable to seizure [C14 from OF *cerchier*, from LL *circāre* to go around, from L *circus* circle] > '**searchable** *adj* > '**searcher** *n*
search engine *n computing* a service provided on the Internet that carries out searches and locates information on the Internet
searching ('sɜːtʃɪŋ) *adj* keenly penetrating: *a searching look* > '**searchingly** *adv*
searchlight ('sɜːtʃˌlaɪt) *n* **1** a device that projects a powerful beam of light in a particular direction **2** the beam of light produced by such a device
search party *n* a group of people taking part in an organized search, as for a lost, missing, or wanted person
search warrant *n* a written order issued by a justice of the peace authorizing a constable to enter and search premises for stolen goods, etc
Searle (sɜːl) *n* **Ronald** (**William Fordham**) born 1920, British cartoonist, best known as the creator of the schoolgirls of St Trinian's
seascape ('siːˌskeɪp) *n* a sketch, etc, of the sea
sea scorpion *n* any of various northern marine fishes having a tapering body and a large head covered with bony plates and spines
Sea Scout *n* a Scout belonging to any of a number of Scout troops whose main activities are canoeing, sailing, etc
sea serpent *n* a huge legendary creature of the sea resembling a snake or dragon
sea shanty *n* another name for **shanty**[2]
seashell ('siːʃɛl) *n* the empty shell of a marine mollusc
seashore ('siːʃɔː) *n* **1** land bordering on the sea **2** *law* the land between the marks of high and low water
seasick ('siːˌsɪk) *adj* suffering from nausea and dizziness caused by the motion of a ship at sea > '**sea,sickness** *n*
seaside ('siːˌsaɪd) *n* **a** any area bordering on the sea, esp one regarded as a resort **b** *(as modifier)*: *a seaside hotel*
sea snail *n* a small spiny-finned fish of cold seas, having a soft scaleless tadpole-shaped body with the pelvic fins fused into a sucker
sea snake *n* a venomous snake of tropical seas that swims by means of a laterally compressed oarlike tail
season ('siːzᵊn) *n* **1** one of the four equal periods into which the year is divided by the equinoxes and solstices. These periods (spring, summer, autumn, and winter) have characteristic weather conditions, and occur at opposite times of the year in the N and S hemispheres **2** a period of the year characterized by particular conditions or activities: *the rainy season* **3** the period during which any particular species of animal, bird, or fish is legally permitted to be caught or killed: *open season on red deer* **4** a period during which a particular entertainment, sport, etc, takes place: *the football season* **5** any definite or indefinite period **6** any of the major periods into which the ecclesiastical calendar is divided, such as Lent or Easter **7** fitting or proper time **8** **in good season** early enough **9** **in season** **9a** (of game) permitted to be killed **9b** (of fresh food) readily available **9c** Also: **in** *or* **on heat** (of some female mammals) sexually receptive **9d** appropriate ▷ *vb* **10** *(tr)* to add herbs, salt, pepper, or spice to (food) **11** *(tr)* to add zest to **12** (in the preparation of timber) to undergo or cause to undergo drying **13** *(tr; usually passive)* to make or become experienced: *seasoned troops* **14** *(tr)* to mitigate or temper [C13 from OF *seson*, from L *satiō* a sowing, from *serere* to sow] > '**seasoned** *adj* > '**seasoner** *n*
seasonable ('siːzənəbᵊl) *adj* **1** suitable for the season: *a seasonable Christmas snow scene* **2** taking place at the appropriate time > '**seasonableness** *n* > '**seasonably** *adv*
seasonal ('siːzənᵊl) *adj* of, relating to, or occurring at a certain season or seasons of the year: *seasonal labour* > '**seasonally** *adv*
seasonal affective disorder *n* a state of depression sometimes experienced by people in winter, thought to be related to lack of sunlight. Abbrev: **SAD**
seasoning ('siːzənɪŋ) *n* **1** something that enhances the flavour of food, such as salt or herbs **2** another term (not now in technical usage) for **drying**
season ticket *n* a ticket for a series of events, number of journeys, etc, within a limited time, usually obtained at a reduced rate
sea squirt *n* a minute primitive marine animal, most of which are sedentary, having a saclike body with openings through which water enters and leaves
sea swallow *n* a popular name for **tern**
seat (siːt) *n* **1** a piece of furniture designed for sitting on, such as a chair or sofa **2** the part of a chair, bench, etc, on which one sits **3** a place to sit, esp one that requires a ticket: *I have two seats for the film tonight* **4** the buttocks **5** the part of a garment covering the buttocks **6** the part or area serving as the base of an object **7** the part or surface on which the base of an object rests **8** the place or centre in which something is located: *a seat of government* **9** a place of abode, esp a country mansion **10** a membership or the right to membership in a legislative or similar body **11** *chiefly Brit* a parliamentary constituency **12** the manner in which a rider sits on a horse ▷ *vb* **13** *(tr)* to bring to or place on a seat **14** *(tr)* to provide with seats **15** *(tr; often passive)* to place or centre: *the ministry is seated in the capital* **16** *(tr)* to set firmly in place **17** *(tr)* to fix or install in a position of power **18** *(intr)* (of garments) to sag in the area covering the buttocks: *your skirt has seated badly* [OE *gesete*]
seat belt *n* **1** Also called: **safety belt** a belt or strap worn in a vehicle to restrain forward motion in the event of a collision **2** a similar belt or strap worn in an aircraft at takeoff and landing
seating ('siːtɪŋ) *n* **1** the act of providing with a seat or seats **2a** the provision of seats, as in a theatre, etc **2b** *(as modifier)*: *seating arrangements* **3** material used for covering seats **4** a surface on which a part, such as a valve, is supported
Seaton Valley ('siːtᵊn) *n* a region in NE England, in SE Northumberland: consists of a group of former coal-mining villages. Pop: 46 140 (latest est)
sea trout *n* a silvery marine variety of the brown trout that migrates to fresh water to spawn
Seattle (sɪ'ætᵊl) *n* a port in W Washington, on the isthmus between Lake Washington and Puget Sound: the largest city in the state and chief commercial centre of the Northwest; two universities. Pop: 563 374 (2000)
sea urchin *n* any echinoderm such as the **edible sea**

Ss

urchin, having a globular body enclosed in a rigid spiny test and occurring in shallow marine waters

sea vegetables *pl n* edible seaweed

sea wall *n* a wall or embankment built to prevent encroachment or erosion by the sea

seaward ('siːwəd) *adv* **1** Also called: **seawards** towards the sea ▷ *adj* **2** directed or moving towards the sea **3** (esp of a wind) coming from the sea

seaway ('siːˌweɪ) *n* **1** a waterway giving access to an inland port **2** a vessel's progress **3** a route across the sea

seaweed ('siːˌwiːd) *n* any of numerous multicellular marine algae that grow on the seashore, in salt marshes, in brackish water, or submerged in the ocean

seaworthy ('siːˌwɜːðɪ) *adj* in a fit condition or ready for a sea voyage > **'seaˌworthiness** *n*

sebaceous (sɪ'beɪʃəs) *adj* **1** of or resembling sebum, fat, or tallow **2** secreting fat [C18 from LL *sēbāceus*, from SEBUM]

sebaceous glands *pl n* the small glands in the skin that secrete sebum into hair follicles and onto most of the body surface except the soles of the feet and the palms of the hands

Sebastian (sɪ'bæstjən) *n* **Saint** died ?288 AD, Christian martyr. According to tradition, he was first shot with arrows and then beaten to death. Feast day: Jan 20

Sebastopol (sɪ'bæstəpəl) *n* the English name for **Sevastopol**

seborrhoea *or esp US* **seborrhea** (ˌsɛbə'rɪə) *n* any disease of the skin characterized by excessive secretion of sebum

sebum ('siːbəm) *n* the oily secretion of the sebaceous glands that acts as a lubricant for the hair and skin and provides some protection against bacteria [C19 from NL, from L: tallow]

sec[1] (sɛk) *adj* **1** (of wines) dry **2** (of champagne) of medium sweetness [C19 from F, from L *siccus*]

sec[2] (sɛk) *n inf* short for **second**[2]: *wait a sec*

sec[3] (sɛk) *abbrev for* secant

SEC *abbrev for* Securities and Exchange Commission

sec. *abbrev for:* **1** second (of time) **2** secondary **3** secretary **4** section **5** sector

secant ('siːkənt) *n* **1** (of an angle) a trigonometric function that in a right-angled triangle is the ratio of the length of the hypotenuse to that of the adjacent side; the reciprocal of cosine. Abbrev: **sec** **2** a line that intersects a curve [C16 from L *secāre* to cut]

secateurs ('sɛkətəz) *pl n chiefly Brit* a small pair of shears for pruning, having a pair of pivoted handles and usually a single cutting blade that closes against a flat surface [C19 pl of F *sécateur*, from L *secāre* to cut]

secede (sɪ'siːd) *vb* **secedes, seceding, seceded** (*intr;* often foll by *from*) (of a person, section, etc) to make a formal withdrawal of membership, as from a political alliance, etc [C18 from L *sēcēdere* to withdraw, from *sē-* apart + *cēdere* to go] > **se'ceder** *n*

secession (sɪ'sɛʃən) *n* **1** the act of seceding **2** (*often cap*) *chiefly US* the withdrawal in 1860–61 of 11 Southern states from the Union to form the Confederacy, precipitating the American Civil War [C17 from L *sēcessiō* a withdrawing, from *sēcēdere* to SECEDE] > **se'cessionˌism** *n* > **se'cessionist** *n, adj*

sech (ʃɛk, sɛtʃ, 'sɛk'eɪtʃ) *n* hyperbolic secant

seclude (sɪ'kluːd) *vb* **secludes, secluding, secluded** (*tr*) **1** to remove from contact with others **2** to shut off or screen from view [C15 from L *sēclūdere* to shut off, from *sē-* + *claudere* to imprison]

secluded (sɪ'kluːdɪd) *adj* **1** kept apart from the company of others: *a secluded life* **2** private > **se'cludedly** *adv* > **se'cludedness** *n*

seclusion (sɪ'kluːʒən) *n* **1** the act of secluding or the state of being secluded **2** a secluded place [C17 from Med. L *sēclūsiō*; see SECLUDE]

second[1] ('sɛkənd) *adj* (*usually prenominal*) **1a** coming directly after the first in numbering or counting order, position, time, etc; being the ordinal number of *two:* often written 2nd **1b** (*as n*): *the second in line* **2** graded or ranked between the first and third levels **3** alternate: *every second Thursday* **4** extra: *a second opportunity* **5** resembling a person or event from an earlier period of history: *a second Wagner* **6** of lower quality; inferior **7** denoting the lowest but one forward ratio of a gearbox in a motor vehicle **8** *music* denoting a musical part, voice, or instrument subordinate to or lower in pitch than another (the first): *the second tenors* **9** **at second hand** by hearsay ▷ *n* **10** *Brit education* an honours degree of the second class, usually further divided into an upper and lower designation. Full term: **second-class honours degree** **11** the lowest but one forward ratio of a gearbox in a motor vehicle **12** (in boxing, duelling, etc) an attendant who looks after a competitor **13** a speech seconding a motion or the person making it **14** *music* the interval between one note and another lying next above or below it in the diatonic scale **15** (*pl*) goods of inferior quality **16** (*pl*) *inf* a second helping of food **17** (*pl*) the second course of a meal ▷ *vb* (*tr*) **18** to give aid or backing to **19** (in boxing, etc) to act as second to (a competitor) **20** to express formal support for (a motion already proposed) ▷ *adv* **21** Also: **secondly** in the second place ▷ *sentence connector* **22** Also: **secondly** as the second point [C13 via OF from L *secundus* coming next in order, from *sequī* to follow] > **'seconder** *n*

second[2] ('sɛkənd) *n* **1a** 1/60 of a minute of time **1b** the basic SI unit of time: the duration of 9 192 631 770 periods of radiation corresponding to the transition between two hyperfine levels of the ground state of caesium-133. Symbol: s **2** 1/60 of a minute of angle. Symbol: ″ **3** a very short period of time [C14 from OF, from Med. L *pars minūta secunda* the second small part (a minute being the first small part of an hour); see SECOND[1]]

second[3] (sɪ'kɒnd) *vb* (*tr*) *Brit* **1** to transfer (an employee) temporarily to another branch, etc **2** *mil* to transfer (an officer) to another post [C19 from F *en second* in second rank (or position)] > **se'condment** *n*

secondary ('sɛkəndərɪ) *adj* **1** one grade or step after the first **2** derived from or depending on what is primary or first: *a secondary source* **3** below the first in rank, importance, etc **4** (*prenominal*) of or relating to the education of young people between the ages of 11 and 18: *secondary education* **5** (of the flight feathers of a bird's wing) growing from the ulna **6a** being the part of an electric circuit, such as a transformer or induction coil, in which a current is induced by a changing current in a neighbouring coil: *a secondary coil* **6b** (of a current) flowing in such a circuit **7** *chem* **7a** (of an amine) containing the group NH **7b** (of a salt) derived from a tribasic acid by replacement of two acidic hydrogen atoms with metal atoms ▷ *n, pl* **secondaries** **8** a person or thing that is secondary **9** a subordinate, deputy, or inferior **10** a secondary coil, winding, inductance, or current in an electric circuit **11** *ornithol* any of the flight feathers that grow from the ulna of a bird's wing **12** *astron* a celestial body that orbits around a specified primary body: *the moon is the secondary of the earth* **13** *American football* **13a** (usually preceded by *the*) cornerbacks and safeties collectively **13b** their area in the field **14** short for **secondary colour** > **'secondarily** *adv* > **'secondariness** *n*

secondary cell *n* an electric cell that can be recharged and can therefore be used to store electrical energy in the form of chemical energy

secondary colour *n* a colour formed by mixing two primary colours

secondary emission *n physics* the emission of electrons (**secondary electrons**) from a solid as a result of bombardment with a beam of electrons, ions, or metastable atoms

secondary picketing *n* the picketing by striking workers of a factory, distribution outlet, etc, that supplies goods to or distributes goods from their employer

secondary sexual characteristic *n* any of various features distinguishing individuals of different sex but not directly concerned in reproduction. Examples are the antlers of a stag and the beard of a man

second ballot *n* an electoral procedure in which, after a first ballot, candidates at the bottom of the poll are eliminated and another ballot is held among the remaining candidates

second-best *adj* **1** next to the best **2 come off second best** *inf* to be worsted by someone ▷ *n* **3 second best** an inferior alternative

second chamber *n* the upper house of a bicameral legislative assembly

second childhood *n* dotage; senility (esp in **in his, her,** etc, **second childhood**)

second class *n* **1** the class or grade next in value, quality, etc, to the first ▷ *adj* (**second-class** *when prenominal*) **2** of the class or grade next to the best in quality, etc **3** shoddy or inferior **4** of or denoting the class of accommodation in a hotel or on a train, etc, lower in quality and price than first class **5** (in Britain) of mail that is processed more slowly than first-class mail **6** *education* See **second**[1] (sense 10) ▷ *adv* **7** by second-class mail, transport, etc

second-class citizen *n* a person whose rights and opportunities are treated as less important than those of other people in the same society

Second Coming *n* the prophesied return of Christ to earth at the Last Judgment

second cousin *n* the child of a first cousin of either of one's parents

second-degree burn *n pathol* a burn in which blisters appear on the skin

seconde (sɪˈkɒnd) *n* the second of eight positions from which a parry or attack can be made in fencing [c18 from F *seconde parade* the second parry]

Second Empire *n* the style of furniture and decoration of the Second Empire in France (1852–70), reviving the Empire style, but with fussier ornamentation
▷ http://ah.bfn.org/a/archsty/sec
▷ www.bc.edu/bc_org/avp/cas/fnart/arch

second fiddle *n inf* **1a** the second violin in a string quartet or an orchestra **1b** the musical part assigned to such an instrument **2** a person who has a secondary status

second floor *n Brit* the storey of a building immediately above the first and two floors up from the ground. US and Canad term: **third floor**

second generation *n* **1** offspring of parents born in a given country **2** (*modifier*) of a refined stage of development in manufacture: *a second-generation robot*

second *or* **secondary growth** *n* natural regrowth of a forest after fire, cutting, etc

second hand *n* a pointer on the face of a timepiece that indicates the seconds

second-hand *adj* **1** previously owned or used **2** not from an original source or experience **3** dealing in or selling goods that are not new: *a second-hand car dealer* ▷ *adv* **4** from a source of previously owned or used goods: *he prefers to buy second-hand* **5** not directly: *he got the news second-hand*

second language *n* **1** a language other than the mother tongue used for business transactions, teaching, debate, etc **2** a language that is officially recognized in a country, other than the main national language

second lieutenant *n* an officer holding the lowest commissioned rank in the armed forces of certain nations

secondly (ˈsɛkəndlɪ) *adv* another word for **second**[1], usually used to precede the second item in a list of topics

second nature *n* a habit, characteristic, etc, long practised or acquired so as to seem innate

second person *n* a grammatical category of pronouns and verbs used when referring to or describing the individual or individuals being addressed

second-rate *adj* **1** not of the highest quality; mediocre **2** second in importance, etc

second reading *n* the second presentation of a bill in a legislative assembly, as to approve its general principles (in Britain), or to discuss a committee's report on it (in the US)

second sight *n* the alleged ability to foresee the future, see actions taking place elsewhere, etc
> ˈ**second-**ˈ**sighted** *adj*

second string *n* **1** *chiefly Brit* an alternative course of action, etc, intended to come into use should the first fail (esp in **a second string to one's bow**) **2** *chiefly US & Canad* a substitute or reserve player or team

second thought *n* (*usually pl*) a revised opinion or idea on a matter already considered

second wind (wɪnd) *n* **1** the return of the ability to breathe at a comfortable rate, esp following a period of exertion **2** renewed ability to continue in an effort

secrecy (ˈsiːkrɪsɪ) *n, pl* **secrecies 1** the state or quality of being secret **2** the state of keeping something secret **3** the ability or tendency to keep things secret

secret (ˈsiːkrɪt) *adj* **1** kept hidden or separate from the knowledge of others. Related adj: **cryptic 2** known only to initiates: *a secret password* **3** hidden from general view or use: *a secret garden* **4** able or tending to keep things private or to oneself **5** operating without the knowledge of outsiders: *a secret society* ▷ *n* **6** something kept or to be kept hidden **7** something unrevealed; a mystery **8** an underlying explanation, reason, etc: *the secret of success* **9** a method, plan, etc, known only to initiates **10** *liturgy* a prayer said by the celebrant of the Mass after the offertory and before the preface [c14 via OF from L *sēcrētus* concealed, from *sēcernere* to sift]
> ˈ**secretly** *adv*

Ss

secret agent *n* a person employed in espionage

secretaire (ˌsɛkrɪˈtɛə) *n* an enclosed writing desk, usually having an upper cabinet section [c19 from F; see SECRETARY]

secretariat (ˌsɛkrɪˈtɛərɪət) *n* **1a** an office responsible for the secretarial, clerical, and administrative affairs of a legislative body or international organization **1b** the staff of such an office **2** a body of secretaries **3** a secretary's place of work; office **4** the position of a secretary [c19 via F from Med. L *sēcrētāriātus*, from *sēcrētārius* SECRETARY]

secretary (ˈsɛkrətrɪ) *n, pl* **secretaries 1** a person who handles correspondence, keeps records, and does general clerical work for an individual, organization, etc **2** the official manager of the day-to-day business of a society or board **3** (in Britain) a senior civil servant who assists a government minister **4** (in the US) the head of a government administrative department **5** (in Britain) See **secretary of state 6** Another name for **secretaire** [c14 from Med. L *sēcrētārius*, from L *sēcrētum* something hidden; see SECRET] > **secretarial** (ˌsɛkrɪˈtɛərɪəl) *adj* > ˈ**secretaryship** *n*

secretary bird *n* a large African long-legged bird of prey having a crest and tail of long feathers and feeding chiefly on snakes

secretary-general *n, pl* **secretaries-general** a chief administrative official, as of the United Nations

secretary of state *n* **1** (in Britain) the head of any of several government departments **2** (in the US) the head of the government department in charge of foreign affairs (**State Department**)

secrete[1] (sɪˈkriːt) *vb* **secretes, secreting, secreted** (of a cell, organ, etc) to synthesize and release (a secretion) [c18 back formation from SECRETION] > **se'cretor** *n* > **se'cretory** *adj*

secrete² (sɪ'kri:t) *vb* **secretes, secreting, secreted** (*tr*) to put in a hiding place [c18 var. of obs. *secret* to hide away]

secretion (sɪ'kri:ʃən) *n* **1** a substance that is released from a cell, esp a glandular cell **2** the process involved in producing and releasing such a substance from the cell [c17 from Med. L *sēcrētiō*, from L: a separation]

secretive ('si:krɪtɪv) *adj* inclined to secrecy > **'secretively** *adv* > **'secretiveness** *n*

secretory (sɪ'kri:tərɪ) *adj* of, relating to, or producing a secretion: *secretory function*

secret police *n* a police force that operates relatively secretly to check subversion or political dissent

secret service *n* a government agency or department that conducts intelligence or counterintelligence operations

sect (sɛkt) *n* **1** a subdivision of a larger religious group (esp the Christian Church as a whole) the members of which have to some extent diverged from the rest by developing deviating beliefs, practices, etc **2** *often disparaging* **2a** a schismatic religious body **2b** a religious group regarded as extreme or heretical **3** a group of people with a common interest, doctrine, etc [c14 from L *secta* faction, from *sequī* to follow]

-sect *vb combining form* to cut or divide, esp into a specified number of parts: *trisect* [from L *sectus* cut, from *secāre* to cut]

sectarian (sɛk'tɛərɪən) *adj* **1** of, relating to, or characteristic of sects or sectaries **2** adhering to a particular sect, faction, or doctrine **3** narrow-minded, esp as a result of adherence to a particular sect ▷ *n* **4** a member of a sect or faction, esp one who is intolerant towards other sects, etc > **sec'tarian,ism** *n*

sectary ('sɛktərɪ) *n, pl* **sectaries** **1** a member of a sect, esp a religous sect **2** a member of a Nonconformist denomination, esp one that is small [c16 from Med. L *sectārius*, from L *secta* SECT]

section ('sɛkʃən) *n* **1** a part cut off or separated from the main body of something **2** a part or subdivision of a piece of writing, book, etc: *the sports section of the newspaper* **3** one of several component parts **4** a distinct part of a country, community, etc **5** *US & Canad* an area one mile square **6** NZ a plot of land for building, esp in a suburban area **7** the section of a railway track that is controlled by a particular signal box **8** the act or process of cutting or separating by cutting **9** a representation of an object cut by an imaginary vertical plane so as to show its construction and interior **10** *geom* a plane surface formed by cutting through a solid **11** a thin slice of biological tissue, etc, prepared for examination by a microscope **12** a segment of an orange or other citrus fruit **13** a small military formation **14** *Austral & NZ* a fare stage on a bus, tram, etc **15** *music* **15a** an extended division of a composition or movement: *the development section* **15b** a division in an orchestra, band, etc, containing instruments belonging to the same class: *the brass section* **16** Also called: **signature, gathering** a folded printing sheet or sheets ready for gathering and binding **17** **on section** NZ (of a trainee teacher) working under supervision in a school ▷ *vb* (*tr*) **18** to cut or divide into sections **19** to cut through so as to reveal a section **20** (in drawing, esp mechanical drawing) to shade so as to indicate sections **21** *Brit* to commit (someone) to a psychiatric hospital under the terms of a certain section of the Mental Health Act [c16 from L *sectiō*, from *secāre* to cut]

sectional ('sɛkʃənᵊl) *adj* **1** composed of several sections **2** of or relating to a section **3** of or concerned with a particular group within a community, esp to the exclusion of others > **'sectiona,lize** *or* **'sectiona,lise** *vb* (*tr*) > **'sectionally** *adv*

sectionalism ('sɛkʃənə,lɪzəm) *n* excessive or narrow-minded concern for local or regional interests > **'sectionalist** *n, adj*

sector ('sɛktə) *n* **1** a part or subdivision, esp of a society or an economy: *the private sector* **2** *geom* either portion of a circle included between two radii and an arc **3** a measuring instrument consisting of two graduated arms hinged at one end **4** a part or subdivision of an area of military operations **5** *computing* the smallest addressable portion of the track on a magnetic tape, disk, or drum store [c16 from LL: sector, from L: a cutter, from *secāre* to cut] > **'sectoral** *adj*

sectorial (sɛk'tɔ:rɪəl) *adj* **1** of or relating to a sector **2** *zool* adapted for cutting: *the sectorial teeth of carnivores*

secular ('sɛkjʊlə) *adj* **1** of or relating to worldly as opposed to sacred things **2** not concerned with or related to religion **3** not within the control of the Church **4** (of an education, etc) having no particular religious affinities **5** (of clerics) not bound by religious vows to a monastic or other order **6** occurring or appearing once in an age or century **7** lasting for a long time **8** *astron* occurring slowly over a long period of time ▷ *n* **9** a member of the secular clergy [c13 from OF *seculer*, from LL *saeculāris* temporal, from L: concerning an age, from *saeculum* an age] > **secularity** (,sɛkjʊ'lærɪtɪ) *n* > **'secularly** *adv*

secularism ('sɛkjʊlə,rɪzəm) *n* **1** *philosophy* a doctrine that rejects religion, esp in ethics **2** the attitude that religion should have no place in civil affairs > **'secularist** *n, adj*

secularize *or* **secularise** ('sɛkjʊlə,raɪz) *vb* **secularizes, secularizing, secularized** *or* **secularises, secularising, secularised** (*tr*) **1** to change from religious or sacred to secular functions, etc **2** to dispense from allegiance to a religious order **3** *law* to transfer (property) from ecclesiastical to civil possession or use > **,seculari'zation** *or* **,seculari'sation** *n*

secund (sɪ'kʌnd) *adj bot* having parts arranged on or turned to one side of the axis [c18 from L *secundus* following, from *sequī* to follow]

Secunderabad (sə'kʌndərə,bæd, -,bɑ:d) *n* a former town in S central India, in N Andra Pradesh: one of the largest British military stations in India: now part of Hyderabad city

secure (sɪ'kjʊə) *adj* **1** free from danger, damage, etc **2** free from fear, care, etc **3** in safe custody **4** not likely to fail, become loose, etc **5** able to be relied on: *a secure investment* **6** *arch* overconfident ▷ *vb* **secures, securing, secured** **7** (*tr*) to obtain: *I will secure some good seats* **8** (when *intr*, often foll by *against*) to make or become free from danger, fear, etc **9** (*tr*) to make fast or firm **10** (when *intr*, often foll by *against*) to make or become certain: *this plan will secure your happiness* **11** (*tr*) to assure (a creditor) of payment, as by giving security **12** (*tr*) to make (a military position) safe from attack **13** *naut* to make (a vessel or its contents) safe or ready by battening down hatches, etc [c16 from L *sēcūrus* free from care] > **se'curable** *adj* > **se'curely** *adv* > **se'curement** *n* > **se'curer** *n*

secure unit *n* an establishment providing secure accommodation, education and training, psychiatric help, etc for offenders and people who are mentally ill

Securities and Investment Board *n* a British regulatory body set up in 1986 to oversee London's financial markets, each of which has its own self-regulatory organization. Abbrev: **SIB**

securitization *or* **securitisation** (sɪ,kjʊərɪtaɪ'zeɪʃən) *n finance* the use of such securities as eurobonds to enable investors to lend directly to borrowers with a minimum of risk but without using banks as intermediaries

security (sɪ'kjʊərɪtɪ) *n, pl* **securities** **1** the state of being secure **2** assured freedom from poverty or want: *he needs the security of a permanent job* **3** a person or thing that secures, guarantees, etc **4** precautions taken to ensure against theft, espionage, etc **5** (*often pl*) **5a** a certificate of creditorship or property carrying the right to receive interest or dividend, such as shares or bonds **5b** the financial asset represented by such a certificate **6** the specific asset that a creditor can claim in the event of default on an obligation **7** something given or pledged to secure the fulfilment of a promise or obligation **8** the protection of data to ensure that only authorised personnel have access to computer files

security blanket *n* **1** a policy of temporary secrecy by police or those in charge of security, in order to protect a person, place, etc, threatened with danger, from further risk **2** a baby's blanket, soft toy, etc, to which a baby or young child becomes very attached, using it as a comforter **3** *inf* anything used or thought of as providing reassurance: *unemployment cover is an added security blanket*

Security Council *n* an organ of the United Nations established to maintain world peace

security guard *n* someone employed to protect buildings, people, etc, and to collect and deliver large sums of money

security risk *n* a person deemed to be a threat to state security in that he or she could be open to pressure, have subversive political beliefs, etc

secy. *or* **sec'y.** *abbrev for* secretary

sedan (sɪ'dæn) *n* **1** *US, Canad, & NZ* a saloon car **2** short for **sedan chair** [C17 from ?]

Sedan (*French* sədɑ̃; *English* sɪ'dæn) *n* a town in NE France, on the River Meuse: passed to France in 1642; a Protestant stronghold (16th–17th centuries); scene of a French defeat (1870) during the Franco-Prussian War and of a battle (1940) in World War II, which began the German invasion of France. Pop: 22 400 (1990)

sedan chair *n* a closed chair for one passenger, carried on poles by two bearers, commonly used in the 17th and 18th centuries

sedate[1] (sɪ'deɪt) *adj* **1** habitually calm and composed in manner **2** sober or decorous [C17 from L *sēdāre* to soothe] > **se'dately** *adv* > **se'dateness** *n*

sedate[2] (sɪ'deɪt) *vb* **sedates, sedating, sedated** (*tr*) to administer a sedative to [C20 back formation from SEDATIVE]

sedation (sɪ'deɪʃən) *n* **1** a state of calm or reduced nervous activity **2** the administration of a sedative

sedative ('sɛdətɪv) *adj* **1** having a soothing or calming effect **2** of or relating to sedation ▷ *n* **3** *med* a sedative drug or agent [C15 from Med. L *sēdātīvus*, from L *sēdātus* assuaged; see SEDATE[1]]

Seddon ('sɛdᵊn) *n* **Richard John,** known as *King Dick*. 1845–1906, New Zealand statesman, born in England; prime minister of New Zealand (1893–1906)

sedentary ('sɛdᵊntərɪ) *adj* **1** characterized by or requiring a sitting position: *sedentary work* **2** tending to sit about without taking much exercise **3** (of animals) moving about very little **4** (of animals) not migratory [C16 from L *sedentārius*, from *sedēre* to sit] > **'sedentarily** *adv* > **'sedentariness** *n*

Seder ('seɪdə) *n Judaism* a ceremonial meal on the first night or first two nights of Passover [from Heb. *sēdher* order]

sedge (sɛdʒ) *n* a grasslike plant growing on wet ground and having rhizomes, triangular stems, and minute flowers in spikelets [OE *secg*] > **'sedgy** *adj*

Sedgemoor ('sɛdʒ,mʊə) *n* a low-lying plain in SW England, in central Somerset: scene of the defeat (1685) of the Duke of Monmouth

sedge warbler *n* a European songbird of reed beds and swampy areas, having a streaked brownish plumage with white eye stripes

Sedgwick ('sɛdʒwɪk) *n* **Adam** 1785–1873, English geologist; played a major role in establishing parts of the geological time scale, esp the Cambrian and Devonian periods

sedilia (sɛ'daɪlɪə) *n* (*functioning as sing*) the group of three seats, each called a **sedile** (sɛ'daɪlɪ) on the south side of a sanctuary where the celebrant and ministers sit during High Mass [C18 from L, from *sedīle* a chair, from *sedēre* to sit]

sediment ('sɛdɪmənt) *n* **1** matter that settles to the bottom of a liquid **2** material that has been deposited from water, ice, or wind [C16 from L *sedimentum* a settling, from *sedēre* to sit] > **,sedimen'tation** *n*

sedimentary (,sɛdɪ'mɛntərɪ) *adj* **1** characteristic of, resembling, or containing sediment **2** (of rocks) formed by the accumulation of mineral and organic fragments that have been deposited by water, ice, or wind > **,sedi'mentarily** *adv*

sedimentation tank *n* a tank into which sewage is passed to allow suspended solid matter to separate out

sedition (sɪ'dɪʃən) *n* **1** speech or behaviour directed against the peace of a state **2** an offence that tends to undermine the authority of a state **3** an incitement to public disorder [C14 from L *sēditiō* discord, from *sēd-* apart + *itiō* a going, from *īre* to go] > **se'ditionary** *n, adj*

seditious (sɪ'dɪʃəs) *adj* **1** of, like, or causing sedition **2** inclined to or taking part in sedition

seduce (sɪ'dju:s) *vb* **seduces, seducing, seduced** (*tr*) **1** to persuade to engage in sexual intercourse **2** to lead astray, as from the right action **3** to win over, attract, or lure [C15 from L *sēdūcere* to lead apart] > **se'ducible** *adj*

seducer (sɪ'dju:sə) *or* (*fem*) **seductress** (sɪ'dʌktrɪs) *n* a person who entices, allures, or seduces, esp one who entices another to engage in sexual intercourse

seduction (sɪ'dʌkʃən) *n* **1** the act of seducing or the state of being seduced **2** a means of seduction

seductive (sɪ'dʌktɪv) *adj* tending to seduce or capable of seducing; enticing; alluring > **se'ductively** *adv* > **se'ductiveness** *n*

sedulous ('sɛdjʊləs) *adj* assiduous; diligent [C16 from L *sēdulus*, from ?] > **sedulity** (sɪ'dju:lɪtɪ) *or* **'sedulousness** *n* > **'sedulously** *adv*

Ss

sedum ('si:dəm) *n* a rock plant having thick fleshy leaves and clusters of white, yellow, or pink flowers [C15 from L: houseleek]

see[1] (si:) *vb* **sees, seeing, saw, seen** **1** to perceive with the eyes **2** (when *tr*, *may take a clause as object*) to understand: *I explained the problem but he could not see it* **3** (*tr*) to perceive with any or all of the senses: *I hate to see you so unhappy* **4** (*tr; may take a clause as object*) to foresee: *I can see what will happen if you don't help* **5** (when *tr*, *may take a clause as object*) to ascertain or find out (a fact): *see who is at the door* **6** (when *tr*, *takes a clause as object;* when *intr*, *foll by* to) to make sure (of something) or take care (of something): *see that he gets to bed early* **7** (when *tr*, *may take a clause as object*) to consider, deliberate, or decide: *see if you can come next week* **8** (*tr*) to have experience of: *he had seen much unhappiness in his life* **9** (*tr*) to allow to be in a specified condition: *I cannot stand by and see a child in pain* **10** (*tr*) to be characterized by: *this period of history has seen much unrest* **11** (*tr*) to meet or pay a visit to: *to see one's solicitor* **12** (*tr*) to receive: *the Prime Minister will see the deputation now* **13** (*tr*) to frequent the company of: *she is seeing a married man* **14** (*tr*) to accompany: *I saw her to the door* **15** (*tr*) to refer to or look up: *for further information see the appendix* **16** (in gambling, esp in poker) to match (another player's bet) or match the bet of (another player) by staking an equal sum **17 as far as I can see** to the best of my judgment **18 see fit** (*takes an infinitive*) to consider proper, etc: *I don't see fit to allow her to come here* **19 see (someone) hanged** *or* **damned first** *inf* to refuse absolutely to do what one has been asked **20 see you, see you later,** *or* **be seeing you** an expression of farewell ▷ See also **see about, see into,** etc [OE *sēon*]

see[2] (si:) *n* the diocese of a bishop, or the place within it where his or her cathedral is situated [c13 from OF *sed*, from L *sēdēs* a seat]

see about *vb (intr, prep)* **1** to take care of: *he couldn't see about the matter because he was ill* **2** to investigate: *to see about a new car*

Seebeck effect ('si:bɛk) *n* the phenomenon in which a current is produced in a circuit containing two or more different metals when the junctions between the metals are maintained at different temperatures. Also called: **thermoelectric effect** [c19 after Thomas *Seebeck* (1770–1831), G physicist]

seed (si:d) *n* **1** *bot* a mature fertilized plant ovule, consisting of an embryo and its food store surrounded by a protective seed coat (testa). Related adj: **seminal** **2** the small hard seedlike fruit of plants such as wheat **3** (loosely) any propagative part of a plant, such as a tuber, spore, or bulb **4** the source, beginning, or germ of anything: *the seeds of revolt* **5** *chiefly Bible* descendants: *the seed of Abraham* **6** an archaic term for **sperm** or **semen** **7** *sport* a seeded player **8** *chem* a small crystal added to a supersaturated solution to induce crystallization **9** **go** *or* **run to seed 9a** (of plants) to produce and shed seeds **9b** to lose vigour, usefulness, etc ▷ *vb* **10** to plant (seeds, grain, etc) in (soil): *we seeded this field with oats* **11** *(intr)* (of plants) to form or shed seeds **12** *(tr)* to remove the seeds from (fruit, etc) **13** *(tr) chem* to add a small crystal to (a supersaturated solution) in order to cause crystallization **14** *(tr)* to scatter certain substances, such as silver iodide, in (clouds) in order to cause rain **15** *(tr)* to arrange (the draw of a tournament) so that outstanding teams or players will not meet in the early rounds [OE *sǣd*] > **'seeder** *n* > **'seedless** *adj*

seedbed ('si:d,bɛd) *n* **1** a plot of land in which seedlings are grown before being transplanted **2** the place where something develops

seedcake ('si:d,keɪk) *n* a sweet cake flavoured with caraway seeds and lemon rind or essence

seed capital *n finance* a small amount of capital required to finance the research necessary to produce a business plan for a new company

seed coral *n* small pieces of coral used in jewellery, etc

seed corn *n* **1** the good quality ears or kernels of corn that are used as seed **2** assets that are expected to provide future benefits

seed leaf *n* the nontechnical name for **cotyledon**

seedling ('si:dlɪŋ) *n* a very young plant produced from a seed

seed money *n* money used for the establishment of an enterprise

seed oyster *n* a young oyster, esp a cultivated oyster, ready for transplantation

seed pearl *n* a tiny pearl weighing less than a quarter of a grain

seed pod *n* a carpel or pistil enclosing the seeds of a plant, esp a flowering plant

seed potato *n* a potato tuber used for planting

seed vessel *n bot* a dry fruit, such as a capsule

seedy ('si:dɪ) *adj* **seedier, seediest** **1** shabby in appearance: *seedy clothes* **2** (of a plant) at the stage of producing seeds **3** *inf* not physically fit > **'seedily** *adv* > **'seediness** *n*

Seeger ('si:gə) *n* **Pete** born 1919. US folk singer and songwriter, noted for his protest songs, which include "We shall Overcome" (1960), "Where have all the Flowers gone?" (1961) and "If I had a Hammer" (1962)

seeing ('si:ɪŋ) *n* **1** the sense or faculty of sight **2** *astron* the condition of the atmosphere with respect to observation of stars, planets, etc ▷ *conj* **3** *(subordinating; often foll by* that*)* in light of the fact (that).

> USAGE The use of *seeing as how* as in *seeing as (how) the bus is always late, I don't need to hurry* is generally thought to be incorrect or nonstandard

seeing-eye dog *n* the US name for **guide dog**

see into *vb (intr, prep)* to discover the true nature of: *I can't see into your thoughts*

seek (si:k) *vb* **seeks, seeking, sought** *(mainly tr)* **1** *(when intr, often foll by* for *or* after*)* to try to find by searching: *to seek a solution* **2** *(also intr)* to try to obtain or acquire: *to seek happiness* **3** to attempt (to do something): *I'm only seeking to help* **4** *(also intr)* to inquire about or request (something) **5** to resort to: *to seek the garden for peace* [OE *sēcan*] > **'seeker** *n*

seek out *vb (tr, adv)* to search hard for and find a specific person or thing: *she sought out her friend from amongst the crowd*

Seeland ('ze:lant) *n* the German name for **Sjælland**

seem (si:m) *vb (may take an infinitive)* **1** *(copula)* to appear to the mind or eye; look: *the car seems to be running well* **2** to appear to be: *there seems no need for all this nonsense* **3** used to diminish the force of a following infinitive to be polite, more noncommittal, etc: *I can't seem to get through to you* [c12 ?from ON *soma* to beseem, from *sœmr* befitting]

> USAGE See at **like**

seeming ('si:mɪŋ) *adj* **1** *(prenominal)* apparent but not actual or genuine ▷ *n* **2** outward or false appearance > **'seemingly** *adv*

seemly ('si:mlɪ) *adj* **seemlier, seemliest** **1** proper or fitting **2** *obs* pleasing in appearance ▷ *adv* **3** *arch* decorously [c13 from ON *sœmiligr*, from *sœmr* befitting]

seen (si:n) *vb* the past participle of **see**[1]

see off *vb (tr, adv)* **1** to be present at the departure of (a person making a journey) **2** *inf* to cause to leave or depart, esp by force

seep (si:p) *vb* **1** *(intr)* to pass gradually or leak as if through small openings ▷ *n* **2** a small spring or place where water, oil, etc, has oozed through the ground [OE *sīpian*] > **'seepage** *n*

seer[1] (sɪə) *n* **1** a person who can supposedly see into the future **2** a person who professes supernatural powers **3** a person who sees

seer[2] (sɪə) *n* a varying unit of weight used in India, usually about two pounds or one kilogram [from Hindi]

seersucker ('sɪə,sʌkə) *n* a light cotton, linen, or other fabric with a crinkled surface and often striped [c18 from Hindi *śīrśakar*, from Persian *shīr o shakkar*, lit.: milk and sugar]

seesaw ('si:,sɔ:) *n* **1** a plank balanced in the middle so that two people seated on the ends can ride up and down by pushing on the ground with their feet **2** the pastime of riding up and down on a seesaw **3** an up-and-down or back-and-forth movement ▷ *vb* **4** *(intr)* to move up and down or back and forth in such a manner [c17 reduplication of SAW[1], alluding to the movement from side to side, as in sawing]

seethe (si:ð) *vb* **seethes, seething, seethed** **1** *(intr)* to boil or to foam as if boiling **2** *(intr)* to be in a state of extreme agitation, esp through anger **3** *(tr)* to soak in liquid **4** *(tr) arch* to cook by boiling [OE *sēothan*]

seething ('si:ðɪŋ) *adj* **1** boiling or foaming as if boiling **2** crowded and full of restless activity **3** in a state of extreme agitation, esp through anger

see through *vb* **1** *(tr)* to help out in time of need or trouble **2** *(tr, adv)* to remain with until the end or completion: *let's see the job through* **3** *(intr, prep)* to perceive the true nature of: *I can see through your evasion* ▷ *adj* **see-through** **4** partly or wholly transparent or translucent, esp (of clothes) in a titillating way

Seferis (sə'fɛərɪs) *n* **George** pen name of *Georgios Seferiades*. 1900–71, Greek poet and diplomat: Nobel prize for literature 1963

Sefton ('sɛftᵊn) *n* a unitary authority in NW England, in Merseyside. Pop: 282 956 (2001). Area: 150 sq km (58 sq miles)

segment *n* ('sɛgmənt) **1** *maths* **1a** a part of a line or curve between two points **1b** a part of a plane or solid figure cut off by an intersecting line, plane, or planes **2** one of several parts or sections into which an object is divided **3** *zool* any of the parts into which the body or appendages of an annelid or arthropod are divided **4** *linguistics* a speech sound considered in isolation ▷ *vb* (sɛg'mɛnt) **5** to cut or divide (a whole object) into segments [C16 from L *segmentum*, from *secāre* to cut] > **seg'mental** *adj* > **'segmentary** *adj*

segmentation (ˌsɛgmɛn'teɪʃən) *n* **1** the act or an instance of dividing into segments **2** *embryol* another name for **cleavage** (sense 4)

Segovia[1] (sɪ'gəʊvɪə; *Spanish* se'ɣoβja) *n* a town in central Spain: site of a Roman aqueduct, still in use, and the fortified palace of the kings of Castile (the Alcázar). Pop: 58 060 (1991)

Segovia[2] (sɪ'gəʊvɪə; *Spanish* se'ɣoβja) *n* **Andrés** (an'dres), Marquis of Salobreña. 1893–1987, Spanish classical guitarist

Segrè (sə'greɪ) *n* **Emilio** (ɛm'iːlɪəʊ) 1905–89, US physicist, born in Italy, who was the first to produce an artificial element. He shared the Nobel prize for physics (1959) with Owen Chamberlain for their discovery (1955) of the antiproton

segregate ('sɛgrɪˌgeɪt) *vb* **segregates, segregating, segregated 1** to set or be set apart from others or from the main group **2** (*tr*) to impose segregation on (a racial or minority group) **3** *genetics* to undergo or cause to undergo segregation [C16 from L *sēgregāre*, from *sē-* apart + *grex* a flock] > **'segreˌgative** *adj* > **'segreˌgator** *n*

segregation (ˌsɛgrɪ'geɪʃən) *n* **1** the act of segregating or state of being segregated **2** *sociol* the practice or policy of creating separate facilities within the same society for the use of a particular group **3** *genetics* the separation at meiosis of the two members of any pair of alleles into separate gametes > **ˌsegre'gational** *adj* > **ˌsegre'gationist** *n*

segue ('seɪgwɪ) *vb* **segues, segueing, segued** (*intr*) **1** (often foll by *into*) to proceed from one piece of music to another without a break ▷ *n* **2** the practice or an instance of segueing [from It: follows, from *seguire* to follow, from L *sequī*]

seguidilla (ˌsɛgɪ'diːljə) *n* **1** a Spanish dance in a fast triple rhythm **2** a piece of music composed for or in the rhythm of this dance [Sp.: a little dance, from *seguida* a dance, from *seguir* to follow, from L *sequī*]

seiche (seɪʃ) *n* a tide-like movement of a body of water caused by barometric pressure, earth tremors, etc [C19 from Swiss F, from ?]

Seidlitz powder *or* **powders** ('sɛdlɪts) *n* a laxative consisting of two powders, tartaric acid and a mixture of sodium bicarbonate and Rochelle salt (sodium potassium tartrate) [C19 after *Seidlitz*, a village in Bohemia with mineral springs having similar laxative effects]

seif dune (seɪf) *n* (in deserts, esp the Sahara) a long ridge of blown sand, often several miles long [*seif*, from Ar.: sword, from the shape of the dune]

seigneur (sɛ'njɜː; *French* sɛɲœr) *n* a feudal lord, esp in France and New France [C16 from OF, from Vulgar L *senior*, from L: an elderly man; see SENIOR] > **sei'gneurial** *adj*

seigneury ('seɪnjərɪ) *n, pl* **seigneuries** the estate of a seigneur

seignior ('seɪnjə) *n* **1** a less common name for a **seigneur** **2** (in England) the lord of a seigniory [C14 from Anglo-F *segnour*] > **seigniorial** (seɪ'njɔːrɪəl) *adj*

seigniory ('seɪnjərɪ) *or* **signory** ('siːnjərɪ) *n, pl* **seigniories** *or* **seignories 1** less common names for a **seigneury** **2** (in England) the fee or manor of a seignior; a feudal domain **3** the authority of a seignior

seine (seɪn) *n* **1** a large fishing net that hangs vertically in the water by means of floats at the top and weights at the bottom ▷ *vb* **seines, seining, seined 2** to catch (fish) using this net [OE *segne*, from L *sagēna*, from Gk *sagēnē*]

Seine (seɪn; *French* sɛn) *n* a river in N France, rising on the Plateau de Langres and flowing northwest through Paris to the English Channel: the second longest river in France, linked by canal with the Rivers Somme, Scheldt, Meuse, Rhine, Saône, and Loire. Length: 776 km (482 miles)

Seine-et-Marne (*French* sɛnemarn) *n* a department of N central France, in Île-de-France region. Capital: Melun. Pop: 1 193 767 (1999). Area: 5931 sq km (2313 sq miles)

Seine-Maritime (*French* sɛnmaritim) *n* a department of N France, in Haute-Normandie region. Capital: Rouen. Pop: 1 239 138 (1999). Area: 6342 sq km (2473 sq miles)

Seine-Saint-Denis (*French* sɛnsɛ̃dni) *n* a department of N central France, in Île-de-France region. Capital: Bobigny. Pop: 1 382 861 (1999). Area: 236 sq km (92 sq miles)

seise *or US* **seize** (siːz) *vb* **seises, seising, seised** *or US* **seizes, seizing, seized** to put into legal possession of (property, etc) > **'seiser** *n*

seisin *or US* **seizin** ('siːzɪn) *n* *property law* feudal possession of an estate in land [C13 from OF *seisine*, from *seisir* to SEIZE]

seismic ('saɪzmɪk) *adj* relating to or caused by earthquakes or artificially produced earth tremors

seismo- *or before a vowel* **seism-** *combining form* earthquake: *seismology* [from Gk *seismos*]

seismograph ('saɪzməˌgrɑːf) *n* an instrument that registers and records earthquakes. A **seismogram** is the record from such an instrument > **seismographic** (ˌsaɪzmə'græfɪk) *adj* > **seismographer** (saɪz'mɒgrəfə) *n* > **seis'mography** *n*

seismology (saɪz'mɒlədʒɪ) *n* the branch of geology concerned with the study of earthquakes and seismic waves > **seismologic** (ˌsaɪzmə'lɒdʒɪk) *or* **ˌseismo'logical** *adj* > **ˌseismo'logically** *adv* > **seis'mologist** *n*

seize[1] (siːz) *vb* **seizes, seizing, seized** (*mainly tr*) **1** (also *intr*, foll by *on*) to take hold of quickly; grab **2** (sometimes foll by *on* or *upon*) to grasp mentally, esp rapidly: *she immediately seized his idea* **3** to take mental possession of: *alarm seized the crowd* **4** to take possession of rapidly and forcibly: *the thief seized the woman's purse* **5** to take legal possession of **6** to take by force or capture: *the army seized the undefended town* **7** to take immediate advantage of: *to seize an opportunity* **8** *naut* to bind (two ropes together) **9** (*intr*; often foll by *up*) (of mechanical parts) to become jammed, esp because of excessive heat [C13 *saisen*, from OF *saisir*, from Med. L *sacīre* to position, of Gmc origin] > **'seizable** *adj*

Ss

seize[2] (siːz) *vb* **seizes, seizing, seized** the US spelling of **seise**

seizure ('siːʒə) *n* **1** the act or an instance of seizing or the state of being seized **2** *pathol* a sudden manifestation or recurrence of a disease, such as an epileptic convulsion

Sekondi (ˌsɛkən'diː) *n* a port in SW Ghana, 8 km (5 miles) northeast of Takoradi: linked administratively with Takoradi in 1946. Pop (with Takoradi): 103 600 (latest est)

selachian (sɪ'leɪkɪən) *adj* of or belonging to a large subclass of cartilaginous fishes including the sharks, rays, dogfish, and skates [C19 from NL *Selachiī*, from Gk *selakhē* a shark]

Selangor (sə'læŋə) *n* a state of Peninsular Malaysia, on the Strait of Malacca: established as a British protectorate in 1874, became a Federated Malay State in 1896 and part of Malaysia in 1946; tin producer. Capital: Shah Alam. Pop: 3 617 527 (2000 est). Area: 8203 sq km (3167 sq miles)

Selby ('sɛlbɪ) *n* an inland port in N England, in North Yorkshire, on the River Ouse: centre for a coalfield since 1983: agricultural products. Pop: 15 292 (1991)

seldom ('sɛldəm) *adv* rarely [OE *seldon*]

select (sɪ'lɛkt) *vb* **1** to choose (someone or something) in preference to another or others ▷ *adj also* **selected** 2 chosen in preference to others 3 of particular quality 4 limited as to membership or entry: *a select gathering* ▷ *n Austral history* 5 a piece of land acquired by a free-selector 6 the process of free-selection [c16 from L *sēligere* to sort, from *sē-* apart + *legere* to choose] > **se'lectness** *n* > **se'lector** *n*

select committee *n* (in Britain) a small committee of members of parliament, set up to investigate and report on a specified matter

selection (sɪ'lɛkʃən) *n* 1 the act or an instance of selecting or the state of being selected 2 a thing or number of things that have been selected 3 a range from which something may be selected: *a good selection of clothes* 4 *biol* the process by which certain organisms or characters are reproduced and perpetuated in the species in preference to others

selective (sɪ'lɛktɪv) *adj* 1 of or characterized by selection 2 tending to choose carefully or characterized by careful choice 3 *electronics* occurring at or operating at a particular frequency or band of frequencies > **se'lectively** *adv*

selectivity (sɪˌlɛk'tɪvɪtɪ) *n* 1 the state or quality of being selective 2 the degree to which a radio receiver, etc, can respond to the frequency of a desired signal

Selene (sɪ'li:nɪ) *n* the Greek goddess of the moon. Roman counterpart: **Luna**

selenite ('sɛlɪˌnaɪt) *n* a colourless glassy variety of gypsum

selenium (sɪ'li:nɪəm) *n* a nonmetallic element that exists in several allotropic forms. The common form is a grey crystalline solid that is photoconductive, photovoltaic, and semiconducting: used in photocells, solar cells, and in xerography. Symbol: Se; atomic no.: 34; atomic wt.: 78.96 [c19 from NL, from Gk *selēnē* moon; by analogy to TELLURIUM (from L *tellus* earth)]

seleno- *or before a vowel* **selen-** *combining form* denoting the moon: *selenography* [from Gk *selēnē* moon]

selenography (ˌsi:lɪ'nɒgrəfɪ) *n* the branch of astronomy concerned with the description and mapping of the surface features of the moon > ˌ**sele'nographer** *n* > **selenographic** (sɪˌli:nəʊ'græfɪk) *adj*

Seles ('sɛlɛʃ, -lɛz) *n* **Monica** born 1973, US tennis player, born in Yugoslavia

Seleucia (sɪ'lu:ʃɪə) *n* 1 an ancient city in Mesopotamia, on the River Tigris: founded by Seleucus Nicator in 312 BC; became the chief city of the Seleucid empire; sacked by the Romans around 162 AD 2 an ancient city in SE Asia Minor, on the River Calycadnus (modern Goksu Nehri): captured by the Turks in the 13th century; site of present-day Silifke (Turkey). Official name: **Seleucia Tracheotis** (ˌtrækɪ'əʊtɪs) *or* **Trachea** (trə'kɪə) 3 an ancient port in Syria, on the River Orontes: the port of Antioch, of military importance during the wars between the Ptolemies and Seleucids; largely destroyed by earthquake in 526; site of present-day Samandağ (Turkey). Official name: **Seleucia Pieria** (paɪ'i:rɪə)

Seleucus I (sɪ'lu:kəs) *n* surname *Nicator*. ?358–280 BC, Macedonian general under Alexander the Great, who founded the Seleucid kingdom

self (sɛlf) *n, pl* **selves** 1 the distinct individuality or identity of a person or thing 2 a person's typical bodily make-up or personal characteristics: *she's looking her old self again* 3 one's own welfare or interests: *he only thinks of self* 4 an individual's consciousness of his or her own identity or being 5 a bird, animal, etc, that is a single colour throughout ▷ *pron* 6 *not standard* myself, yourself, etc: *seats for self and wife* ▷ *adj* 7 of the same colour or material 8 *obs* the same [OE *seolf*]

self- *combining form* 1 of oneself or itself: *self-defence* 2 by, to, in, due to, for, or from the self: *self-employed; self-respect* 3 automatic or automatically: *self-propelled*

self-abnegation *n* the denial of one's own interests in favour of the interests of others

self-absorption *n* 1 preoccupation with oneself to the exclusion of others 2 *physics* the process in which some of the radiation emitted by a material is absorbed by the material itself

self-abuse *n* 1 disparagement or misuse of one's own abilities, etc 2 a censorious term for **masturbation**

self-acting *adj* not requiring an external influence or control to function; automatic

self-addressed *adj* 1 addressed for return to the sender 2 directed to oneself: *a self-addressed remark*

self-aggrandizement *n* the act of increasing one's own power, importance, etc > ˌ**self-ag'granˌdizing** *adj*

self-appointed *adj* having assumed authority without the agreement of others: *a self-appointed critic*

self-assertion *n* the act or an instance of putting forward one's own opinions, etc, esp in an aggressive or conceited manner > ˌ**self-as'serting** *adj* > ˌ**self-as'sertive** *adj*

self-assurance *n* confidence in the validity, value, etc, of one's own ideas, opinions, etc > ˌ**self-as'sured** *adj* > ˌ**self-as'suredly** *adv*

self-centred *adj* totally preoccupied with one's own concerns > ˌ**self-'centredness** *n*

self-certification *n* (in Britain) a formal assertion by a worker to his or her employer that absence from work for up to seven days was due to sickness

self-coloured *adj* 1 having only a single and uniform colour: *a self-coloured dress* 2 (of cloth, etc) having the natural or original colour

self-command *n* another term for **self-control**

self-confessed *adj* according to one's own testimony or admission: *a self-confessed liar*

self-confidence *n* confidence in one's own powers, judgment, etc > ˌ**self-'confident** *adj* > ˌ**self-'confidently** *adv*

self-conscious *adj* 1 unduly aware of oneself as the object of the attention of others 2 conscious of one's existence > ˌ**self-'consciously** *adv* > ˌ**self-'consciousness** *n*

self-contained *adj* 1 containing within itself all parts necessary for completeness 2 (of a flat) having its own kitchen, bathroom, and lavatory not shared by others 3 able or tending to keep one's feelings, thoughts, etc, to oneself > ˌ**self-con'tainedness** *n*

self-contradictory *adj logic* (of a proposition) both asserting and denying a given proposition

self-control *n* the ability to exercise restraint or control over one's feelings, emotions, reactions, etc > ˌ**self-con'trolled** *adj*

self-deception *or* **self-deceit** *n* the act or an instance of deceiving oneself > ˌ**self-de'ceptive** *adj*

self-defence *n* 1 the act of defending oneself, one's actions, ideas, etc 2 boxing as a means of defending the person (esp in **noble art of self-defence**) 3 *law* the right to defend one's person, family, or property against attack or threat of attack > ˌ**self-de'fensive** *adj*

self-denial *n* the denial or sacrifice of one's own desires > ˌ**self-de'nying** *adj*

self-deprecating *or* **self-depreciating** *adj* having a tendency to disparage oneself

self-determination *n* 1 the ability to make a decision for oneself without influence from outside 2 the right of a nation or people to determine its own form of government > ˌ**self-de'termined** *adj* > ˌ**self-de'termining** *adj*

self-discipline *n* the act of disciplining or power to discipline one's own feelings, desires, etc > ˌ**self-'disciplined** *adj*

self-drive *adj* denoting or relating to a hired car that is driven by the hirer

self-educated *adj* 1 educated through one's own efforts without formal instruction 2 educated at one's own expense

self-effacement *n* the act of making oneself, one's actions, etc, inconspicuous, esp because of timidity > ˌ**self-efˈfacing** *adj*
self-employed *adj* earning one's living in one's own business or through freelance work, rather than as the employee of another > ˌ**self-emˈployment** *n*
self-esteem *n* **1** respect for or a favourable opinion of oneself **2** an unduly high opinion of oneself
self-evident *adj* containing its own evidence or proof without need of further demonstration > ˌ**self-ˈevidence** *n* > ˌ**self-ˈevidently** *adv*
self-existent *adj philosophy* existing independently of any other being or cause
self-explanatory *adj* understandable without explanation; self-evident
self-expression *n* the expression of one's own personality, feelings, etc, as in painting or poetry > ˌ**self-exˈpressive** *adj*
self-government *n* **1** the government of a country, nation, etc, by its own people **2** the state of being self-controlled > ˌ**self-ˈgoverned** *adj* > ˌ**self-ˈgoverning** *adj*
self-harm *n* the practice of cutting or otherwise wounding oneself, usually considered as indicating psychological disturbance > ˌ**self-ˈharming** *n*
selfheal (ˈsɛlfˌhiːl) *n* **1** a low-growing European herbaceous plant with tightly clustered violet-blue flowers and reputedly having healing powers **2** any of several other plants thought to have healing powers
self-help *n* **1** the act or state of providing the means to help oneself without relying on the assistance of others **2a** the practice of solving one's problems by joining or forming a group designed to help those suffering from a particular problem **2b** (*as modifier*): *a self-help group*
self-image *n* one's own idea of oneself or sense of one's worth
self-important *adj* having or showing an unduly high opinion of one's own abilities, importance, etc > ˌ**self-imˈportantly** *adv* > ˌ**self-imˈportance** *n*
self-improvement *n* the improvement of one's status, position, education, etc, by one's own efforts
self-induced *adj* **1** induced or brought on by oneself or itself **2** *electronics* produced by self-induction
self-induction *n* the production of an electromotive force in a circuit when the magnetic flux linked with the circuit changes as a result of a change in current in the same circuit
self-indulgent *adj* tending to indulge one's own desires, etc > ˌ**self-inˈdulgence** *n*
self-interest *n* **1** one's personal interest or advantage **2** the act or an instance of pursuing one's own interest > ˌ**self-ˈinterested** *adj*
selfish (ˈsɛlfɪʃ) *adj* **1** chiefly concerned with one's own interest, advantage, etc, esp to the exclusion of the interests of others **2** relating to or characterized by self-interest > ˈ**selfishly** *adv* > ˈ**selfishness** *n*
self-justification *n* the act or an instance of justifying or providing excuses for one's own behaviour, etc
selfless (ˈsɛlflɪs) *adj* having little concern for one's own interests > ˈ**selflessly** *adv* > ˈ**selflessness** *n*
self-loading *adj* (of a firearm) utilizing some of the force of the explosion to eject the empty shell and replace it with a new one > ˌ**self-ˈloader** *n*
self-love *n* the instinct to seek one's own well-being or to further one's own interest
self-made *adj* **1** having achieved wealth, status, etc, by one's own efforts **2** made by oneself
self-opinionated *adj* **1** having an unduly high regard for oneself or one's own opinions **2** clinging stubbornly to one's own opinions
self-pity *n* the act or state of pitying oneself, esp in an exaggerated or self-indulgent manner > ˌ**self-ˈpitying** *adj* > ˌ**self-ˈpityingly** *adv*
self-pollination *n* the transfer of pollen from the anthers to the stigma of the same flower or of another flower on the same plant > ˌ**self-ˈpolliˌnated** *adj*
self-possessed *adj* having control of one's emotions, etc > ˌ**self-posˈsession** *n*
self-preservation *n* the preservation of oneself from danger or injury
self-pronouncing *adj* (in a phonetic transcription) of or denoting a word that, except for marks of stress, keeps the letters of its ordinary orthography to represent its pronunciation
self-propelled *adj* (of a vehicle) provided with its own source of tractive power rather than requiring an external means of propulsion > ˌ**self-proˈpelling** *adj*
self-raising *adj* (of flour) having a raising agent, such as baking powder, already added
self-realization *n* the realization or fulfilment of one's own potential or abilities
self-regard *n* **1** concern for one's own interest **2** proper esteem for oneself
self-regulating organization *n* one of several British organizations set up in 1986 under the auspices of the Securities and Investment Board to regulate the activities of London investment markets. Abbrev: **SRO**
self-reliance *n* reliance on one's own abilities, decisions, etc > ˌ**self-reˈliant** *adj*
self-reproach *n* the act of finding fault with or blaming oneself > ˌ**self-reˈproachful** *adj*
self-respect *n* a proper sense of one's own dignity and integrity > ˌ**self-reˈspecting** *adj*
self-restraint *n* restraint imposed by oneself on one's own feelings, desires, etc
self-righteous *adj* having an exaggerated awareness of one's own virtuousness > ˌ**self-ˈrighteously** *adv* > ˌ**self-ˈrighteousness** *n*
self-rule *n* another term for **self-government** (sense 1)
self-sacrifice *n* the sacrifice of one's own desires, etc, for the sake of duty or for the well-being of others > ˌ**self-ˈsacriˌficing** *adj*
selfsame (ˈsɛlfˌseɪm) *adj* (*prenominal*) the very same
self-satisfied *adj* having or showing a complacent satisfaction with oneself, one's own actions, behaviour, etc > ˌ**self-ˌsatisˈfaction** *n*
self-sealing *adj* (esp of an envelope) designed to become sealed with the application of pressure only
self-seeking *n* **1** the act or an instance of seeking one's own profit or interest ▷ *adj* **2** having or showing an exclusive preoccupation with one's own profit or interest: *a self-seeking attitude* > ˌ**self-ˈseeker** *n*
self-service *adj* **1** of or denoting a shop, restaurant, petrol station, etc, where the customer serves himself ▷ *n* **2** the practice of serving oneself, as in a shop, etc
self-serving *adj* habitually seeking one's own advantage, esp at the expense of others
self-sown *adj* (of plants) growing from seed dispersed by any means other than by the agency of man or animals. Also: **self-seeded**
self-starter *n* **1** an electric motor used to start an internal-combustion engine **2** the switch that operates this motor **3** a person who is strongly motivated and shows initiative, esp at work
self-styled *adj* (*prenominal*) claiming to be of a specified nature, quality, profession, etc: *a self-styled expert*
self-sufficient *or* **self-sufficing** *adj* **1** able to provide for or support oneself without the help of others **2** *rare* having undue confidence in oneself > ˌ**self-sufˈficiency** *n* > ˌ**self-sufˈficiently** *adv*
self-supporting *adj* **1** able to support or maintain oneself without the help of others **2** able to stand up or hold firm without support, props, attachments, etc
self-tender *n* an offer by a company to buy back some or all of its shares from its shareholders, esp as a protection against an unwelcome takeover bid
self-will *n* stubborn adherence to one's own will,

desires, etc, esp at the expense of others > ˌ**self-'willed** *adj*

self-winding *adj* (of a wrist watch) having a mechanism in which a rotating or oscillating weight rewinds the mainspring

Seljuk (sɛl'dʒuːk) *n* **1** a member of any of the pre-Ottoman Turkish dynasties ruling over large parts of Asia in the 11th, 12th, and 13th centuries AD ▹ *adj* **2** of or relating to these dynasties [C19 from Turkish]

Selkirk ('sɛlˌkɜːk) *n* **Alexander** original name *Alexander Selcraig*. 1676–1721, Scottish sailor, who was marooned on one of the islets of Juan Fernández and is regarded as the prototype of Defoe's *Robinson Crusoe*

Selkirk Mountains *pl n* a mountain range in SW Canada, in SE British Columbia. Highest peak: Mount Sir Sandford, 3533 m (11 590 ft)

Selkirkshire ('sɛlkɜːkˌʃɪə, -ʃə) *n* (until 1975) a county of SE Scotland, now part of Scottish Borders

sell (sɛl) *vb* **sells, selling, sold 1** to dispose of or transfer or be disposed of or transferred to a purchaser in exchange for money or other consideration **2** to deal in (objects, property, etc): *he sells used cars* **3** (*tr*) to give up or surrender for a price or reward: *to sell one's honour* **4** to promote or facilitate the sale of (objects, property, etc): *publicity sells many products* **5** to gain acceptance of: *to sell an idea* **6** (*intr*) to be in demand on the market: *these dresses sell well* **7** (*tr*) *inf* to deceive **8 sell down the river** *inf* to betray **9 sell oneself 9a** to convince someone else of one's potential or worth **9b** to give up one's moral standards, etc **10 sell short 10a** *inf* to belittle **10b** *finance* to sell securities or goods without owning them in anticipation of buying them before delivery at a lower price ▹ *n* **11** the act or an instance of selling: *a soft sell* **12** *inf* a hoax or deception ▹ See also **sell off, sell out,** etc [OE *sellan* to lend, deliver] > **'sellable** *adj* > **'seller** *n*

Sella (*French* sela) *n* **Phillipe** (filip) French Rugby Union football player; played 111 internationals (1982–95), making him France's most capped player

Sellafield ('sɛləˌfiːld) *n* the site of an atomic power station and nuclear reprocessing plant in NW England, in W Cumbria. Former name: **Windscale**

sell-by date *n* **1** a date printed on the packaging of perishable goods, indicating the date after which the goods should not be offered for sale **2 past one's sell-by date** *inf* beyond one's prime

Sellers ('sɛləz) *n* **Peter** 1925–80, English radio, stage, and film actor and comedian: noted for his gift of precise vocal mimicry, esp in *The Goon Show* (with Spike Milligan and Harry Secombe; BBC Radio, 1952–60) His films include *I'm All Right, Jack* (1959), *The Millionairess* (1961), *The Pink Panther* (1963), *Dr Strangelove* (1964), and *Being There* (1979)

sell in *vb* (*adverb*) **1** to sell (new products) to a retail outlet to be sold to the public **2** to use the established system to one's advantage, rather than attempting to fight against it

selling race *or* **plate** *n* a horse race in which the winner must be offered for sale at auction

sell off *vb* (*tr, adv*) to sell (remaining or unprofitable items), esp at low prices

Sellotape ('sɛləˌteɪp) *n* **1** *trademark* a type of transparent adhesive tape ▹ *vb* **Sellotapes, Sellotaping, Sellotaped** (*tr*) **2** to seal or stick using adhesive tape

sell out *vb* (*adv*) **1** Also (*chiefly Brit*): **sell up** to dispose of (something) completely by selling **2** (*tr*) *inf* to betray **3** (*intr*) *inf* to abandon one's principles, standards, etc ▹ *n* **sellout 4** *inf* a performance for which all tickets are sold **5** a commercial success **6** *inf* a betrayal

sell-through *adj* **1** (of prerecorded video cassettes) sold without first being available for hire only ▹ *n* **2** the sale of prerecorded video cassettes in this way

sell up *vb* (*adv*) *chiefly Brit* **1** (*tr*) to sell all (the possessions) of (a bankrupt debtor) in order to discharge his debts **2** (*intr*) to sell a business

selsyn ('sɛlsɪn) *n* another name for **synchro** [from SEL(F-) + SYN(CHRONOUS)]

Seltzer ('sɛltsə) *n* **1** a natural effervescent water with a high content of minerals **2** a similar synthetic water, used as a beverage [C18 changed from G *Selterser Wasser* water from (*Nieder*) *Selters*, district where mineral springs are located, near Wiesbaden, Germany]

selva ('sɛlvə) *n* **1** dense equatorial forest, esp in the Amazon basin, characterized by tall broad-leaved evergreen trees **2** a tract of such forest [C19 from Sp. & Port., from L *silva* forest]

selvage *or* **selvedge** ('sɛlvɪdʒ) *n* **1** the finished nonfraying edge of a length of woven fabric **2** a similar strip of material allowed in fabricating a metal or plastic article [C15 from SELF + EDGE] > **'selvaged** *adj*

selves (sɛlvz) *n* **a** the plural of **self b** (*in combination*): *ourselves, yourselves, themselves*

semantic (sɪ'mæntɪk) *adj* **1** of or relating to the meanings of different words or symbols **2** of or relating to semantics [C19 from Gk *sēmantikos* having significance, from *sēmainein* to signify, from *sēma* a sign] > **se'mantically** *adv*

semantics (sɪ'mæntɪks) *n* (*functioning as sing*) **1** the branch of linguistics that deals with the study of meaning **2** the study of the relationships between signs and symbols and what they represent **3** *logic* the principles that determine the truth-values of the formulas in a logical system > **se'manticist** *n*

semaphore ('sɛməˌfɔː) *n* **1** an apparatus for conveying information by means of visual signals, as with flags, etc **2** a system of signalling by holding a flag in each hand and moving the arms to designated positions for each letter of the alphabet ▹ *vb* **semaphores, semaphoring, semaphored 3** to signal (information) by means of semaphore [C19 via F, from Gk *sēma* a signal + -PHORE] > **semaphoric** (ˌsɛmə'fɒrɪk) *adj*

Semarang (sə'mɑːrɑːŋ) *n* a port in S Indonesia, in N Java on the Java Sea. Pop: 1 365 500 (1995 est)

semasiology (sɪˌmeɪsɪ'ɒlədʒɪ) *n* another name for **semantics** [C19 from Gk *sēmasia* meaning, from *sēmainein* to signify + -LOGY]

sematic (sɪ'mætɪk) *adj* (of the conspicuous coloration of certain animals) acting as a warning [C19 from Gk *sēma* a sign]

semblance ('sɛmbləns) *n* **1** outward appearance, esp without any inner substance **2** a resemblance [C13 from OF, from *sembler* to seem, from L *simulāre* to imitate, from *similis* like]

Semele ('sɛmɪlɪ) *n* *Greek myth* mother of Dionysus by Zeus

sememe ('siːmiːm) *n* *linguistics* the meaning of a morpheme [C20 (coined in 1933 by L. Bloomfield, US linguist): from Gk *sēma* a sign + -EME]

semen ('siːmɛn) *n* **1** the thick whitish fluid containing spermatozoa that is ejaculated from the male genital tract **2** another name for **sperm**[1] [C14 from L: seed]

Semeru *or* **Semeroe** (sə'mɛruː) *n* a volcano in Indonesia: the highest peak in Java. Height: 3676 m (12 060 ft)

semester (sɪ'mɛstə) *n* **1** either of two divisions of the academic year **2** (in German universities) a session of six months [C19 via G from L *sēmestris* half-yearly, from *sex* six + *mensis* a month]

semi ('sɛmɪ) *n, pl* **semis** *inf* **1** *Brit* short for **semidetached (house) 2** short for **semifinal**

semi- *prefix* **1** half: *semicircle* **2** partially, partly, or almost: *semiprofessional* **3** occurring twice in a specified period of time: *semiweekly* [from L]

semiannual (ˌsɛmɪ'ænjʊəl) *adj* **1** occurring every half-year **2** lasting for half a year > ˌ**semi'annually** *adv*

semiarid (ˌsɛmɪ'ærɪd) *adj* characterized by scanty rainfall and scrubby vegetation, often occurring in continental interiors

semiautomatic (ˌsɛmɪˌɔːtə'mætɪk) *adj* **1** partly

automatic **2** (of a firearm) self-loading but firing only one shot at each pull of the trigger ▷ *n* **3** a semiautomatic firearm > ˌ**semiˌautoˈmatically** *adv*

semibreve (ˈsɛmɪˌbriːv) *n music* a note, now the longest in common use, having a time value that may be divided by any power of 2 to give all other notes. Usual US and Canad name: **whole note**

semicircle (ˈsɛmɪˌsɜːkᵊl) *n* **1a** one half of a circle **1b** half the circumference of a circle **2** anything having the shape or form of half a circle > **semicircular** (ˌsɛmɪˈsɜːkjʊlə) *adj*

semicircular canal *n anat* any of the three looped fluid-filled membranous tubes, at right angles to one another, that comprise the labyrinth of the ear

semicolon (ˌsɛmɪˈkəʊlən) *n* the punctuation mark **;** used to indicate a pause intermediate in value or length between that of a comma and that of a full stop

semiconductor (ˌsɛmɪkənˈdʌktə) *n* **1** a substance, such as germanium or silicon, that has an electrical conductivity that increases with temperature **2a** a device, such as a transistor or integrated circuit, that depends on the properties of such a substance **2b** (*as modifier*): *a semiconductor diode*

semiconscious (ˌsɛmɪˈkɒnʃəs) *adj* not fully conscious > ˌ**semiˈconsciously** *adv* > ˌ**semiˈconsciousness** *n*

semidetached (ˌsɛmɪdɪˈtætʃt) *adj* **a** (of a building) joined to another building on one side by a common wall **b** (*as n*): *they live in a semidetached*

semifinal (ˌsɛmɪˈfaɪnᵊl) *n* **a** the round before the final in a competition **b** (*as modifier*): *the semifinal draw* > ˌ**semiˈfinalist** *n*

semifluid (ˌsɛmɪˈfluːɪd) *adj* **1** having properties between those of a liquid and those of a solid ▷ *n* **2** a substance that has such properties because of high viscosity: *tar is a semifluid* ▷ Also: **semiliquid**

semiliterate (ˌsɛmɪˈlɪtərɪt) *adj* **1** hardly able to read or write **2** able to read but not to write

semilunar (ˌsɛmɪˈluːnə) *adj* shaped like a crescent or half-moon

semilunar valve *n anat* either of two crescent-shaped valves, one in the aorta and one in the pulmonary artery, that prevent regurgitation of blood into the heart

seminal (ˈsɛmɪnəl) *adj* **1** potentially capable of development **2** highly original and important **3** rudimentary or unformed **4** of or relating to semen: *seminal fluid* **5** *biol* of or relating to seed [c14 from LL *sēminālis* belonging to seed, from L *sēmen* seed] > ˈ**seminally** *adv*

seminar (ˈsɛmɪˌnɑː) *n* **1** a small group of students meeting regularly under the guidance of a tutor, professor, etc **2** one such meeting or the place in which it is held **3** a higher course for postgraduates **4** any group or meeting for holding discussions or exchanging information [c19 via G from L *sēminārium* SEMINARY]

seminary (ˈsɛmɪnərɪ) *n, pl* **seminaries 1** an academy for the training of priests, etc **2** *arch* a private secondary school, esp for girls [c15 from L *sēminārium* a nursery garden, from *sēmen* seed] > ˌ**semiˈnarial** *adj* > **seminarian** (ˌsɛmɪˈnɛərɪən) *n*

seminiferous (ˌsɛmɪˈnɪfərəs) *adj* **1** containing, conveying, or producing semen **2** (of plants) bearing or producing seeds

seminoma (ˌsɛmɪˈnəʊmə) *n, pl* **seminomas** *or* **seminomata** (-mətə) a malignant tumour of the testicle [c20 from F *seminome*, from L *sēmen* seed]

semiotics (ˌsɛmɪˈɒtɪks) *n* (*functioning as sing*) **1** the study of signs and symbols, esp the relations between written or spoken signs and their referents in the physical world or the world of ideas **2** the scientific study of the symptoms of disease ▷ Also called: **semiology** [from Gk *sēmeiōtikos*, from *sēmeion* a sign] > ˌ**semiˈotic** *adj*

Semipalatinsk (*Russian* sɪmipaˈlatinsk) *n* a city in NE Kazakhstan on the Irtysh River; an important communications centre. Pop: 269 600 (1999)

semipermeable (ˌsɛmɪˈpɜːmɪəbᵊl) *adj* (esp of a cell membrane) selectively permeable > ˌ**semiˌpermeaˈbility** *n*

semiprecious (ˌsɛmɪˈprɛʃəs) *adj* (of certain stones) having commercial value, but less than a precious stone

semiprofessional (ˌsɛmɪprəˈfɛʃənᵊl) *adj* **1** (of a person) engaged in an activity or sport part-time but for pay **2** (of an activity or sport) engaged in by semiprofessional people **3** of or relating to a person whose activities are professional in some respects ▷ *n* **4** a semiprofessional person > ˌ**semiproˈfessionally** *adv*

semiquaver (ˈsɛmɪˌkweɪvə) *n music* a note having the time value of one-sixteenth of a semibreve. Usual US and Canad name: **sixteenth note**

Semiramis (sɛˈmɪrəmɪs) *n* the legendary founder of Babylon and wife of Ninus, king of Assyria, which she ruled with great skill after his death

semirigid (ˌsɛmɪˈrɪdʒɪd) *adj* **1** partly but not wholly rigid **2** (of an airship) maintaining shape by means of a main supporting keel and internal gas pressure

semiskilled (ˌsɛmɪˈskɪld) *adj* partly skilled or trained but not sufficiently so to perform specialized work

semisolid (ˌsɛmɪˈsɒlɪd) *adj* having a viscosity and rigidity intermediate between that of a solid and a liquid

semisolus (ˌsɛmɪˈsəʊləs) *n* an advertisement that appears on the same page as another advertisement but not adjacent to it

semisweet (ˈsɛmɪˌswiːt) *adj* (of biscuits, etc) slightly sweetened

Semite (ˈsiːmaɪt) *n* a member of the group of peoples who speak a Semitic language, including the Jews and Arabs as well as the ancient Babylonians, Assyrians, and Phoenicians [c19 from NL *sēmīta* descendant of Shem, via Gk *Sēm*, from Heb. SHEM]

Ss

Semitic (sɪˈmɪtɪk) *n* **1** a branch or subfamily of the Afro-Asiatic family of languages that includes Arabic, Hebrew, Aramaic, and such ancient languages as Phoenician ▷ *adj* **2** denoting or belonging to this group of languages **3** denoting or characteristic of any of the peoples speaking a Semitic language, esp the Jews or the Arabs **4** another word for **Jewish**

semitone (ˈsɛmɪˌtəʊn) *n* an interval denoting the pitch difference between certain adjacent degrees of the diatonic scale (**diatonic semitone**) or between one note and its sharpened or flattened equivalent (**chromatic semitone**); minor second. Also called (US and Canad): **half step** Cf **whole tone** > **semitonic** (ˌsɛmɪˈtɒnɪk) *adj*

semitrailer (ˌsɛmɪˈtreɪlə) *n* a type of trailer or articulated lorry that has wheels only at the rear, the front end being supported by the towing vehicle

semitropical (ˌsɛmɪˈtrɒpɪkᵊl) *adj* partly tropical > ˌ**semiˈtropics** *pl n*

semivowel (ˈsɛmɪˌvaʊəl) *n phonetics* a vowel-like sound that acts like a consonant. In English and many other languages the chief semivowels are (w) in *well* and (j), represented as *y*, in *yell*. Also called: **glide**

semiyearly (ˌsɛmɪˈjɪəlɪ) *adj* another word for **semiannual**

Semmelweis (ˈsɛməlˌvaɪs) *n* **Ignaz Philipp** 1818–65, Hungarian obstetrician, who discovered the cause of puerperal infection and pioneered the use of antiseptics

semolina (ˌsɛməˈliːnə) *n* the large hard grains of wheat left after flour has been bolted, used for puddings, soups, etc [c18 from It. *semolino*, dim. of *semola* bran, from L *simila* very fine wheat flour]

Sempach (*German* ˈzɛmpax) *n* a village in central Switzerland, in Lucerne canton on **Lake Sempach**: scene of the victory (1386) of the Swiss over the Hapsburgs

sempervivum (ˌsɛmpəˈvaɪvəm) *n* any of a genus of hardy perennials including the houseleek [c16 (used of the houseleek, adopted c18 by Linnaeus (1707–78), Swedish botanist, for the genus): L, from *sempervivus* ever-living]

sempiternal (ˌsɛmpɪˈtɜːnᵊl) *adj literary* everlasting; eternal [c15 from OF, from LL *sempiternālis*, from L, from *semper* always + *aeternus* ETERNAL] > ˌ**sempiˈternally** *adv*

semplice (ˈsɛmplɪtʃɪ) *adj, adv music* to be performed in a simple manner [It.: simple, from L *simplex*]

sempre (ˈsɛmprɪ) *adv music* (preceding a tempo or dynamic marking) always; consistently. It is used to indicate that a specified volume, tempo, etc, is to be sustained throughout a piece or passage [It.: always, from L *semper*]

sempstress (ˈsɛmpstrɪs) *n* a rare word for **seamstress**

Semtex (ˈsɛmtɛks) *n* a pliable plastic explosive [orig. a trade name]

Sen. *or* **sen.** *abbrev for:* **1** senator **2** senior

senate (ˈsɛnɪt) *n* **1** any legislative body considered to resemble a Senate **2** the main governing body at some universities [c13 from L *senātus* council of the elders, from *senex* an old man]

Senate (ˈsɛnɪt) *n (sometimes not cap)* **1** the upper chamber of the legislatures of the US, Canada, Australia, and many other countries **2** the legislative council of ancient Rome

senator (ˈsɛnətə) *n* **1** *(often cap)* a member of a Senate or senate **2** any legislator > **senatorial** (ˌsɛnəˈtɔːrɪəl) *adj*

send (sɛnd) *vb* **sends, sending, sent 1** *(tr)* to cause or order (a person or thing) to be taken, directed, or transmitted to another place: *to send a letter* **2** (when *intr*, foll by *for*; when *tr, takes an infinitive*) to dispatch a request or command (for something or to do something): *he sent for a bottle of wine* **3** *(tr)* to direct or cause to go to a place or point: *his blow sent the champion to the floor* **4** *(tr)* to bring to a state or condition: *this noise will send me mad* **5** *(tr; often foll by forth, out, etc)* to cause to issue: *his cooking sent forth a lovely smell* **6** *(tr)* to cause to happen or come: *misery sent by fate* **7** to transmit (a message) by radio **8** *(tr) sl* to move to excitement or rapture: *this music really sends me* ▷ *n* **9** another word for **swash** (sense 4) [OE *sendan*] > ˈ**sendable** *adj* > ˈ**sender** *n*

Sendai (sɛnˈdaɪ) *n* a city in central Japan, on NE Honshu: university (1907). Pop: 971 263 (1995)

send down *vb (tr, adv)* **1** *Brit* to expel from a university **2** *inf* to send to prison

sendoff (ˈsɛndˌɒf) *n inf* **1** a demonstration of good wishes to a person about to set off on a journey, etc ▷ *vb* **send off** *(tr, adv)* **2** to cause to depart **3** *soccer, rugby, etc* (of the referee) to dismiss (a player) from the field of play for some offence **4** *inf* to give a sendoff to

send up *vb (tr, adv)* **1** *sl* to send to prison **2** *Brit inf* to make fun of, esp by doing an imitation or parody of ▷ *n* **send-up 3** *Brit inf* a parody or imitation

Seneca (ˈsɛnɪkə) *n* **1 Lucius Annaeus** (əˈniːəs), called *the Younger*. ?4 BC–65 AD, Roman philosopher, statesman, and dramatist; tutor and adviser to Nero. He was implicated in a plot to murder Nero and committed suicide. His works include Stoical essays on ethical subjects and tragedies that had a considerable influence on Elizabethan drama **2** his father, **Marcus** (ˈmɑːkəs) or **Lucius Annaeus,** called *the Elder* or *the Rhetorician*. ?55 BC–?39 AD, Roman writer on oratory and history

Senegal (ˌsɛnɪˈgɔːl) *n* a republic in West Africa, on the Atlantic: made part of French West Africa in 1895; became fully independent in 1960; mostly low-lying, with semidesert in the north and tropical forest in the southwest. Official language: French. Religion: Muslim majority. Currency: franc. Capital: Dakar. Pop: 10 285 000 (2001 est). Area: 197 160 sq km (76 124 sq miles) > **Senegalese** (ˌsɛnɪgəˈliːz) *adj, n*
▷ www.senegal-tourism.com
▷ www.earth2000.com

Senegambia (ˌsɛnəˈgæmbɪə) *n* a region of W Africa, between the Senegal and Gambia Rivers: now mostly in Senegal

Senegambia Confederation *n* an economic and political union (1982–89) between Senegal and The Gambia

senescent (sɪˈnɛsᵊnt) *adj* **1** growing old **2** characteristic of old age [c17 from L *senēscere* to grow old, from *senex* old] > **seˈnescence** *n*

seneschal (ˈsɛnɪʃəl) *n* **1** a steward of the household of a medieval prince or nobleman **2** *Brit* a cathedral official [c14 from OF, from Med. L *siniscalcus*, of Gmc origin]

senile (ˈsiːnaɪl) *adj* **1** of or characteristic of old age **2** mentally or physically weak or infirm on account of old age [c17 from L *senīlis*, from *senex* an old man] > **senility** (sɪˈnɪlɪtɪ) *n*

senile dementia *n* dementia starting in old age with no precipitating physical cause

senior (ˈsiːnjə) *adj* **1** higher in rank or length of service **2** older in years: *senior citizens* **3** of or relating to maturity or old age: *senior privileges* **4** *education* **4a** of or designating more advanced or older pupils **4b** of or relating to a secondary school **4c** *US* denoting a student in the last year of school or university ▷ *n* **5** a senior person **6** a senior pupil, student, etc [c14 from L: older, from *senex* old]

Senior (ˈsiːnjə) *adj chiefly US* being the older: used to distinguish the father from the son: *Charles Parker, Senior*. Abbrevs: **Sr., Sen**

senior aircraftman *n* a rank in the Royal Air Force comparable to that of a private in the army, though not the lowest rank in the Royal Air Force

senior citizen *n* an old age pensioner

senior common room *n* (in British universities, colleges, etc) a common room for the use of academic staff

seniority (ˌsiːnɪˈɒrɪtɪ) *n, pl* **seniorities 1** the state of being senior **2** precedence in rank, etc, due to senior status

senior moment *n jocular* a lapse of memory common in elderly people

senior service *n Brit* the Royal Navy

Senlac (ˈsɛnlæk) *n* a hill in Sussex: site of the Battle of Hastings in 1066

senna (ˈsɛnə) *n* **1** any of a genus of tropical plants having typically yellow flowers and long pods **2 senna leaf** the dried leaflets of any of these plants, used as a cathartic and laxative **3 senna pods** the dried fruits of any of these plants, used as a cathartic and laxative [c16 via NL from Ar. *sanā*]

Senna (ˈsɛnə) *n* **Ayrton** (ˈɛətən) 1960–94, Brazilian racing driver: world champion (1988, 1990, 1991)

Sennacherib (sɛˈnækərɪb) *n* died 681 BC, king of Assyria (705–681); son of Sargon II. He invaded Judah twice, defeated Babylon, and rebuilt Nineveh

Sennar (ˈsɛnɑː, sɛˈnɑː) *n* **1** a region of the E Sudan, between the White Nile and the Blue Nile: a kingdom from the 16th to 19th centuries **2** a town in this region, on the Blue Nile: the nearby **Sennar Dam** (1925) supplies irrigation water to Gezira. Pop: 8000 (latest est)

sennight *or* **se'nnight** (ˈsɛnaɪt) *n* an archaic word for **week** [OE *seofan nihte*; see SEVEN, NIGHT]

señor (sɛˈnjɔː; *Spanish* seˈɲor) *n, pl* **señors** *or* **señores** (*Spanish* -ˈɲores) a Spaniard: a title of address equivalent to *Mr* when placed before a name or *sir* when used alone [Sp., from L *senior* an older man, SENIOR]

señora (sɛˈnjɔːrə; *Spanish* seˈɲora) *n, pl* **señoras** (-rəz; *Spanish* -ras) a married Spanish woman: a title of address equivalent to *Mrs* when placed before a name or *madam* when used alone

señorita (ˌsɛnjɔːˈriːtə; *Spanish* ˌseɲoˈrita) *n, pl* **señoritas** (-təz; *Spanish* -tas) an unmarried Spanish woman: title of address equivalent to *Miss* when placed before a name or *madam* or *miss* when used alone

sensation (sɛnˈseɪʃən) *n* **1** the power of perceiving through the senses **2** a physical experience resulting from the stimulation of one of the sense organs **3** a general feeling or awareness: *a sensation of fear* **4** a state of widespread public excitement: *his announcement caused a sensation* **5** anything that causes such a state: *your speech was a sensation* [C17 from Med. L, from LL *sensātus* endowed with SENSE]

sensational (sɛnˈseɪʃənᵊl) *adj* **1** causing or intended to cause intense feelings, esp of curiosity, horror, etc: *sensational disclosures in the press* **2** *inf* extremely good: *a sensational skater* **3** of or relating to the faculty of sensation > **senˈsationally** *adv*

sensationalism (sɛnˈseɪʃənᵊˌlɪzəm) *n* **1** the use of sensational language, etc, to arouse an intense emotional response **2** such sensational matter itself **3** *philosophy* the doctrine that knowledge cannot go beyond the analysis of experience > **senˈsationalist** *n* > **senˌsationalˈistic** *adj*

sensationalize *or* **sensationalise** (sɛnˈseɪʃənᵊˌlaɪz) *vb* **sensationalizes, sensationalizing, sensationalized** *or* **sensationalises, sensationalising, sensationalised** (*tr*) to cause (events, esp in newspaper reports) to seem more vivid, shocking, etc, than they really are

sense (sɛns) *n* **1** any of the faculties by which the mind receives information about the external world or the state of the body. The five traditional senses are sight, hearing, touch, taste, and smell **2** the ability to perceive **3** a feeling perceived through one of the senses: *a sense of warmth* **4** a mental perception or awareness: *a sense of happiness* **5** moral discernment: *a sense of right and wrong* **6** (*sometimes pl*) sound practical judgment or intelligence **7** reason or purpose: *what is the sense of going out?* **8** meaning: *what is the sense of this proverb?* **9** specific meaning; definition: *in what sense are you using the word?* **10** an opinion or consensus **11** *maths* one of two opposite directions in which a vector can operate **12 make sense** to be understandable **13 take leave of one's senses** *inf* to go mad ▷ *vb* **senses, sensing, sensed** (*tr*) **14** to perceive through one or more of the senses **15** to apprehend or detect without or in advance of the evidence of the senses **16** to understand **17** *computing* **17a** to test or locate the position of (a part of computer hardware) **17b** to read (data) [C14 from L *sēnsus*, from *sentīre* to feel]

sense datum *n* a unit of sensation, such as a sharp pain, detached both from any information it may convey and from its putative source in the external world

senseless (ˈsɛnslɪs) *adj* **1** foolish: *a senseless plan* **2** lacking in feeling; unconscious **3** lacking in perception > **ˈsenselessly** *adv* > **ˈsenselessness** *n*

sense organ *n* a structure in animals that is specialized for receiving external or internal stimuli and transmitting them in the form of nervous impulses to the brain

sensibility (ˌsɛnsɪˈbɪlɪtɪ) *n, pl* **sensibilities 1** the ability to perceive or feel **2** (*often pl*) the capacity for responding to emotion, etc **3** (*often pl*) the capacity for responding to aesthetic stimuli **4** discernment; awareness **5** (*usually pl*) emotional or moral feelings: *cruelty offends most people's sensibilities*

sensible (ˈsɛnsɪbᵊl) *adj* **1** having or showing good sense or judgment **2** (of clothing) serviceable; practical **3** having the capacity for sensation; sensitive **4** capable of being apprehended by the senses **5** perceptible to the mind **6** (sometimes foll by *of*) having perception; aware: *sensible of your kindness* **7** readily perceived: *a sensible difference* [C14 from OF, from LL *sēnsibilis*, from L *sentīre* to sense] > **ˈsensibleness** *n* > **ˈsensibly** *adv*

sensitive (ˈsɛnsɪtɪv) *adj* **1** having the power of sensation **2** responsive to or aware of feelings, moods, etc **3** easily irritated; delicate **4** affected by external conditions or stimuli **5** easily offended **6** of or relating to the senses or the power of sensation **7** capable of registering small differences or changes in amounts, etc: *a sensitive instrument* **8** *photog* responding readily to light: *a sensitive emulsion* **9** *chiefly US* connected with matters affecting national security **10** (of a stock market or prices) quickly responsive to external influences [C14 from Med. L *sēnsitīvus*, from L *sentīre* to feel] > **ˈsensitively** *adv* > **ˌsensiˈtivity** *n*

sensitive plant *n* a tropical American mimosa plant, the leaflets and stems of which fold if touched

sensitize *or* **sensitise** (ˈsɛnsɪˌtaɪz) *vb* **sensitizes, sensitizing, sensitized** *or* **sensitises, sensitising, sensitised 1** to make or become sensitive **2** (*tr*) to render (an individual) sensitive to a drug, etc **3** (*tr*) *photog* to make (a material) sensitive to light by coating it with a photographic emulsion often containing special chemicals, such as dyes > **ˌsensitiˈzation** *or* **ˌsensitiˈsation** *n* > **ˈsensiˌtizer** *or* **ˈsensiˌtiser** *n*

sensitometer (ˌsɛnsɪˈtɒmɪtə) *n* an instrument for measuring the sensitivity to light of a photographic material over a range of exposures

sensor (ˈsɛnsə) *n* anything, such as a photoelectric cell, that receives a signal or stimulus and responds to it [C19 from L *sēnsus* perceived, from *sentīre* to observe]

sensorimotor (ˌsɛnsərɪˈməʊtə) *or* **sensomotor** (ˌsɛnsəˈməʊtə) *adj* of or relating to both the sensory and motor functions of an organism or to the nerves controlling them

sensorium (sɛnˈsɔːrɪəm) *n, pl* **sensoriums** *or* **sensoria** (-rɪə) **1** the area of the brain considered responsible for receiving and integrating sensations from the outside world **2** *physiol* the entire sensory and intellectual apparatus of the body [C17 from LL, from L *sēnsus* felt, from *sentīre* to perceive]

sensory (ˈsɛnsərɪ) *adj* of or relating to the senses or the power of sensation [C18 from L *sensōrius*, from *sentīre* to feel]

sensual (ˈsɛnsjʊəl) *adj* **1** of or relating to any of the senses or sense organs; bodily **2** strongly or unduly inclined to gratification of the senses **3** tending to arouse the bodily appetites, esp the sexual appetite [C15 from LL *sensuālis*, from L *sēnsus* SENSE] > **ˈsensually** *adv*

Ss

sensualism (ˈsɛnsjʊəˌlɪzəm) *n* **1** the quality or state of being sensual **2** the doctrine that the ability to gratify the senses is the only criterion of goodness

sensuality (ˌsɛnsjʊˈælɪtɪ) *n, pl* **sensualities 1** the quality or state of being sensual **2** excessive indulgence in sensual pleasures > **sensualist** (ˈsɛnsjʊəlɪst) *n*

sensuous (ˈsɛnsjʊəs) *adj* **1** aesthetically pleasing to the senses **2** appreciative of qualities perceived by the senses **3** of or derived from the senses [C17, but not common until C19 apparently coined by Milton to avoid the sexual overtones of SENSUAL] > **ˈsensuously** *adv* > **ˈsensuousness** *n*

sent (sɛnt) *vb* the past tense and past participle of **send**

sentence (ˈsɛntəns) *n* **1** a sequence of words capable of standing alone to make an assertion, ask a question, or give a command, usually consisting of a subject and a predicate **2** the judgment formally pronounced upon a person convicted in criminal proceedings, esp the decision as to what punishment is to be imposed **3** *music* a passage or division of a piece of music, usually consisting of two or more contrasting musical phrases and ending in a cadence **4** *arch* a proverb, maxim, or aphorism ▷ *vb* **sentences, sentencing, sentenced 5** (*tr*) to pronounce sentence on (a convicted person) in a court of law [C13 via OF from L *sententia* a way of thinking, from *sentīre* to feel] > **sentential** (sɛnˈtɛnʃəl) *adj*

sentence connector *n* a word or phrase that introduces a clause or sentence and serves as a transition between it and a previous clause or sentence, as for example *also* in *I'm buying eggs and also I'm looking for a dessert for tonight*

sentence substitute *n* a word or phrase, esp one traditionally classified as an adverb, that is used in place of a finite sentence, such as *yes, no, certainly,* and *never*

sentencing circle *n* a method of dispensing justice amongst native Canadian peoples involving discussion between offenders, victims, and members of the community

sententious (sɛnˈtɛnʃəs) *adj* **1** characterized by or full of aphorisms or axioms **2** constantly using aphorisms, etc **3** tending to indulge in pompous moralizing [C15 from L *sententiōsus* full of meaning, from *sententia*; see SENTENCE] > **senˈtentiously** *adv* > **senˈtentiousness** *n*

sentient (ˈsɛnʃənt, ˈsɛntɪənt) *adj* **1** having the power of sense perception or sensation; conscious ▷ *n* **2** *rare* a sentient person or thing [C17 from L *sentiēns* feeling, from *sentīre* to perceive] > **sentience** (ˈsɛnʃəns) *n*

sentiment (ˈsɛntɪmənt) *n* **1** susceptibility to tender or romantic emotion: *she has too much sentiment to be successful* **2** (*often pl*) a thought, opinion, or attitude **3** exaggerated or mawkish feeling or emotion **4** an expression of response to deep feeling, esp in art **5** a feeling or awareness: *a sentiment of pity* **6** a mental attitude determined by feeling: *there is a strong revolutionary sentiment in his country* **7** a feeling conveyed, or intended to be conveyed, in words [C17 from Med. L *sentīmentum*, from L *sentīre* to feel]

sentimental (ˌsɛntɪˈmɛntᵊl) *adj* **1** tending to indulge the emotions excessively **2** making a direct appeal to the emotions, esp to romantic feelings **3** relating to or characterized by sentiment > **ˌsentiˈmentaˌlism** *n* > **ˌsentiˈmentalist** *n* > **ˌsentiˈmentally** *adv*

sentimentality (ˌsɛntɪmɛnˈtælɪtɪ) *n, pl* **sentimentalities** **1** the state, quality, or an instance of being sentimental **2** an act, statement, etc, that is sentimental

sentimentalize *or* **sentimentalise** (ˌsɛntɪˈmɛntᵊˌlaɪz) *vb* **sentimentalizes, sentimentalizing, sentimentalized** *or* **sentimentalises, sentimentalising, sentimentalised** to make sentimental or behave sentimentally > **ˌsentiˌmentaliˈzation** *or* **ˌsentiˌmentaliˈsation** *n*

sentimental value *n* the value of an article in terms of its sentimental associations for a particular person

sentinel (ˈsɛntɪnᵊl) *n* **1** a person, such as a sentry, assigned to keep guard ▷ *vb* **sentinels, sentinelling, sentinelled** *or US* **sentinels, sentineling, sentineled** (*tr*) **2** to guard as a sentinel **3** to post as a sentinel [C16 from OF *sentinelle*, from OIt., from *sentina* watchfulness, from *sentire* to notice, from L]

sentry (ˈsɛntrɪ) *n, pl* **sentries** a soldier who guards or prevents unauthorized access to a place, etc [C17 ? shortened from obs. *centrinel*, C16 var. of SENTINEL]

sentry box *n* a small shelter with an open front in which a sentry may stand to be sheltered from the weather

senza (ˈsɛntsɑː) *prep music* omitting [It.]

Seoul (səʊl) *n* the capital of South Korea, in the west on the Han River: capital of Korea from 1392 to 1910, then seat of the Japanese administration until 1945; became capital of South Korea in 1948; cultural and educational centre. Pop: 10 229 262 (1995)
▷ http://welcome.seoul.go.kr
▷ http://english.seoul.go.kr

sepal (ˈsɛpᵊl) *n* any of the separate parts of the calyx of a flower [C19 from NL *sepalum*: *sep-* from Gk *skepē* a covering + *-alum*, from NL *petalum* PETAL]

-sepalous *adj combining form* having sepals of a specified type or number: *polysepalous* > **-sepaly** *n combining form*

separable (ˈsɛpərəbᵊl) *adj* able to be separated, divided, or parted > **ˌseparaˈbility** *or* **ˈseparableness** *n* > **ˈseparably** *adv*

separate *vb* (ˈsɛpəˌreɪt), **separates, separating, separated** **1** (*tr*) to act as a barrier between: *a range of mountains separates the two countries* **2** to part or be parted from a mass or group **3** (*tr*) to discriminate between: *to separate the men from the boys* **4** to divide or be divided into component parts **5** to sever or be severed **6** (*intr*) (of a married couple) to cease living together ▷ *adj* (ˈsɛprɪt, ˈsɛpərɪt) **7** existing or considered independently: *a separate problem* **8** disunited or apart **9** set apart from the main body or mass **10** distinct, individual, or particular **11** solitary or withdrawn [C15 from L *sēparāre*, from *sē-* apart + *parāre* to obtain] > **ˈseparately** *adv* > **ˈseparateness** *n* > **ˈseparative** *adj* > **ˈsepaˌrator** *n*

separates (ˈsɛprɪts, ˈsɛpərɪts) *pl n* **1** women's outer garments that only cover part of the body; skirts, blouses, jackets, etc **2** the discrete elements of a hi-fi system sold separately

separate school *n* **1** (in certain Canadian provinces) a school for a large religious minority financed by provincial grants in addition to the education tax **2** a Roman Catholic school

separation (ˌsɛpəˈreɪʃən) *n* **1** the act of separating or state of being separated **2** the place or line where a separation is made **3** a gap that separates **4** *family law* the cessation of cohabitation between a man and wife, either by mutual agreement or under a decree of a court

separation anxiety *n psychoanal* a state of distress felt at the prospect of being separated from a familiar or beloved person

separatist (ˈsɛpərətɪst) *n* **a** a person who advocates secession from an organization, federation, union, etc **b** (*as modifier*): *a separatist movement* > **ˈseparaˌtism** *n*

Sephardi (sɪˈfɑːdiː) *n, pl* **Sephardim** (-dɪm) *Judaism* **1** a Jew of Spanish, Portuguese, or North African descent **2** the pronunciation of Hebrew used by these Jews, and of Modern Hebrew as spoken in Israel ▷ Cf **Ashkenazi** [C19 from LHeb., from Heb. *sepharad* a region mentioned in Obadiah 20, thought to have been Spain] > **Seˈphardic** *adj*

sepia (ˈsiːpɪə) *n* **1** a dark reddish-brown pigment obtained from the inky secretion of the cuttlefish **2** a brownish tone imparted to a photograph, esp an early one **3** a brownish-grey to dark yellowish-brown colour **4** a drawing or photograph in sepia ▷ *adj* **5** of the colour sepia or done in sepia: *a sepia print* [C16 from L: a cuttlefish, from Gk]

sepoy (ˈsiːpɔɪ) *n* (formerly) an Indian soldier in the service of the British [C18 from Port. *sipaio*, from Urdu *sipāhī*, from Persian: horseman, from *sipāh* army]

seppuku (sɛˈpuːkuː) *n* another word for **hara-kiri** [from Japanese, from Chinese *ch'ieh* to cut + *fu* bowels]

sepsis (ˈsɛpsɪs) *n* the presence of pus-forming bacteria in the body [C19 via NL from Gk *sēpsis* a rotting]

sept (sɛpt) *n* **1** *anthropol* a clan that believes itself to be descended from a common ancestor **2** a branch of a tribe, esp in Ireland or Scotland [C16 ? a var. of SECT]

Sept. *abbrev for:* **1** September **2** Septuagint

septa (ˈsɛptə) *n* the plural of **septum**

septal (ˈsɛptəl) *adj* of or relating to a septum

September (sɛpˈtɛmbə) *n* the ninth month of the year, consisting of 30 days [OE, from L: the seventh (month) according to the original calendar of ancient Rome, from *septem* seven]

septenary (ˈsɛptɪnərɪ) *adj* **1** of or relating to the number seven **2** forming a group of seven ▷ *n, pl* **septenaries** **3** the number seven **4** a group of seven things **5** a period of seven years [C16 from L *septēnārius*, from *septēnī* seven each, from *septem* seven]

septennial (sɛpˈtɛnɪəl) *adj* **1** occurring every seven years **2** relating to or lasting seven years [C17 from L, from *septem* seven + *annus* a year]

septet (sɛpˈtɛt) *n* **1** *music* a group of seven singers or instrumentalists or a piece of music composed for such a group **2** a group of seven people or things [C19 from G, from L *septem* seven]

septic (ˈsɛptɪk) *adj* **1** of or caused by sepsis **2** of or caused by putrefaction ▷ *n* **3** *Austral & NZ inf* short for **septic tank** [C17 from L *sēpticus*, from Gk, from *sēptos* decayed, from *sēpein* to make rotten] > **'septically** *adv* > **septicity** (sɛp'tɪsɪtɪ) *n*

septicaemia *or US* **septicemia** (ˌsɛptɪ'si:mɪə) *n* a condition caused by pus-forming microorganisms in the blood. Nontechnical name: **blood poisoning** [c19 from NL, from Gk *sēptik(os)* SEPTIC + -AEMIA] > ˌ**septi'caemic** *or US* ˌ**septi'cemic** *adj*

septic tank *n* a tank, usually below ground, for containing sewage to be decomposed by anaerobic bacteria. Also called (Austral): **septic system**

septillion (sɛp'tɪljən) *n, pl* **septillions** *or* **septillion** **1** (in Britain, France, and Germany) the number represented as one followed by 42 zeros (10^{42}) **2** (in the US and Canada) the number represented as one followed by 24 zeros (10^{24}). Brit word: **quadrillion** [c17 from F, from *sept* seven + *-illion*, on the model of *million*] > **sep'tillionth** *adj, n*

septime ('sɛpti:m) *n* the seventh of eight basic positions from which a parry or attack can be made in fencing [c19 from L *septimus* seventh, from *septem* seven]

septuagenarian (ˌsɛptjʊədʒɪ'nɛərɪən) *n* **1** a person who is from 70 to 79 years old ▷ *adj* **2** being between 70 and 79 years old **3** of or relating to a septuagenarian [c18 from L, from *septuāgintā* seventy]

Septuagesima (ˌsɛptjʊə'dʒɛsɪmə) *n* the third Sunday before Lent [c14 from Church L *septuāgēsima (dīes)* the seventieth (day)]

Septuagint ('sɛptjʊəˌdʒɪnt) *n* the principal Greek version of the Old Testament, including the Apocrypha, believed to have been translated by 70 or 72 scholars [c16 from L *septuāgintā* seventy]

septum ('sɛptəm) *n, pl* **septa** *biol, anat* a dividing partition between two tissues or cavities [c18 from L *saeptum* wall, from *saepīre* to enclose]

septuple ('sɛptjʊpᵊl) *adj* **1** seven times as much or as many **2** consisting of seven parts or members ▷ *vb* **septuples, septupling, septupled** **3** (*tr*) to multiply by seven [c17 from LL *septuplus*, from *septem* seven] > **septuplicate** (sɛp'tju:plɪkɪt) *n, adj*

sepulchral (sɪ'pʌlkrəl) *adj* **1** suggestive of a tomb; gloomy **2** of or relating to a sepulchre > **se'pulchrally** *adv*

sepulchre *or US* **sepulcher** ('sɛpəlkə) *n* **1** a burial vault, tomb, or grave **2** Also called: **Easter sepulchre** an alcove in some churches in which the Eucharistic elements were kept from Good Friday until Easter ▷ *vb* **sepulchres, sepulchring, sepulchred** *or US* **sepulchers, sepulchering, sepulchered** **3** (*tr*) to bury in a sepulchre [c12 from OF *sépulcre*, from L *sepulcrum*, from *sepelīre* to bury]

sepulture ('sɛpəltʃə) *n* the act of placing in a sepulchre [c13 via OF from L *sepultūra*, from *sepultus* buried, from *sepelīre* to bury]

seq. *abbrev for:* **1** sequel **2** sequens [L: the following (one)]

sequel ('si:kwəl) *n* **1** anything that follows from something else **2** a consequence **3** a novel, play, etc, that continues a previously related story [c15 from LL *sequēla*, from L *sequī* to follow]

sequela (sɪ'kwi:lə) *n, pl* **sequelae** (-li:) (*often pl*) *med* **1** any abnormal bodily condition or disease arising from a pre-existing disease **2** any complication of a disease [c18 from L: SEQUEL]

sequence ('si:kwəns) *n* **1** an arrangement of two or more things in a successive order **2** the successive order of two or more things: *chronological sequence* **3** an action or event that follows another or others **4a** *cards* a set of three or more consecutive cards, usually of the same suit **4b** *bridge* a set of two or more consecutive cards **5** *music* an arrangement of notes or chords repeated several times at different pitches **6** *maths* an ordered set of numbers or other mathematical entities in one-to-one correspondence with the integers 1 to *n* **7** a section of a film constituting a single continuous uninterrupted episode **8** *biochem* the unique order of amino acids in a protein or of nucleotides in DNA or RNA ▷ *vb* (*tr*) **9** to arrange in a sequence [c14 from Med. L *sequentia* that which follows, from L *sequī* to follow]

sequence of tenses *n grammar* the sequence according to which the tense of a subordinate verb in a sentence is determined by the tense of the principal verb, as in *I believe he is lying, I believed he was lying*, etc

sequencing ('si:kwənsɪŋ) *n biochem* the procedure of determining the order of amino acids in the polypeptide chain of a protein (**protein sequencing**) or of nucleotides in a DNA section comprising a gene (**gene sequencing**)

sequent ('si:kwənt) *adj* **1** following in order or succession **2** following as a result ▷ *n* **3** something that follows [c16 from L *sequēns*, from *sequī* to follow] > **'sequently** *adv*

sequential (sɪ'kwɛnʃəl) *adj* **1** characterized by or having a regular sequence **2** another word for **sequent** > **sequentiality** (sɪˌkwɛnʃɪ'ælɪtɪ) *n* > **se'quentially** *adv*

sequential access *n* a method of reading data from a computer file by reading through the file from the beginning

sequester (sɪ'kwɛstə) *vb* (*tr*) **1** to remove or separate **2** (*usually passive*) to retire into seclusion **3** *law* to take (property) temporarily out of the possession of its owner, esp until creditors are satisfied or a court order is complied with **4** *international law* to appropriate (enemy property) [c14 from LL *sequestrāre* to surrender for safekeeping, from L *sequester* a trustee]

sequestrate (sɪ'kwɛstreɪt) *vb* **sequestrates, sequestrating, sequestrated** (*tr*) *law* a variant of **sequester** (sense 3) [c16 from LL *sequestrāre* to SEQUESTER] > **sequestrator** ('si:kwɛsˌtreɪtə) *n*

sequestration (ˌsi:kwɛ'streɪʃən) *n* **1** the act of sequestering or state of being sequestered **2** *law* the sequestering of property **3** *chem* the effective removal of ions from a solution by coordination with another type of ion or molecule to form complexes

sequestrum (sɪ'kwɛstrəm) *n, pl* **sequestra** (-trə) *pathol* a detached piece of dead bone that often migrates to a wound, etc [c19 from NL, from L: something deposited] > **se'questral** *adj*

Ss

sequin ('si:kwɪn) *n* **1** a small piece of shiny often coloured metal foil, usually round, used to decorate garments, etc **2** a gold coin formerly minted in Italy [c17 via F from It. *zecchino*, from *zecca* mint, from Ar. *sikkah* die for striking coins] > **'sequined** *adj*

sequoia (sɪ'kwɔɪə) *n* either of two giant Californian coniferous trees, the **redwood,** or the **big tree** or **giant sequoia** [c19 NL, after *Sequoya*, known also as George Guess, (?1770–1843), American Indian scholar and leader]

Sequoia National Park *n* a national park in central California, in the Sierra Nevada Mountains: established in 1890 to protect groves of giant sequoias, some dating back 4000 years. Area: 1556 sq km (601 sq miles)

sérac ('sɛræk) *n* a pinnacle of ice among crevasses on a glacier, usually on a steep slope [c19 from Swiss F: a variety of white cheese (hence the ice that resembles it), from Med. L *serācium*, from L *serum* whey]

seraglio (sɛ'rɑ:lɪˌəʊ) *or* **serail** (sə'raɪ) *n, pl* **seraglios** *or* **serails** **1** the harem of a Muslim house or palace **2** a sultan's palace, esp in the former Turkish empire [c16 from It. *serraglio* animal cage, from Med. L *serrāculum* bolt, from L *sera* a door bar; associated also with Turkish *seray* palace]

Serajevo (*Serbo-Croat* 'sɛrajɛvɔ) *n* a variant of **Sarajevo**

Seram *or* **Ceram** (sɪ'ræm) *n* an island in Indonesia, in the Moluccas, separated from New Guinea by the **Ceram Sea**: mountainous and densely forested. Area: 17 150 sq km (6622 sq miles). Also called: **Serang** (sə'ræŋ)

serape (sə'rɑ:pɪ) *n* **1** a blanket-like shawl, often of brightly coloured wool, worn by men in Latin America **2** a large shawl worn around the shoulders by women as a fashion garment [c19 Mexican Sp.]

seraph ('sɛrəf) *n, pl* **seraphs** *or* **seraphim** (-əfɪm) *theol* a member of the highest order of angels in the celestial hierarchies, often depicted as the winged head of a child [c17 back formation from pl *seraphim*, via LL from Heb.] > **seraphic** (sɪ'ræfɪk) *adj*

Serapis ('sɛrəpɪs) *n* a Graeco-Egyptian god combining attributes of Apis and Osiris

Serb (sɜːb) *n, adj* another word for **Serbian** [c19 from Serbian *Srb*]

Serbia ('sɜːbɪə) *n* a constituent republic of the Union of Serbia and Montenegro: declared a kingdom in 1882; precipitated World War I by the conflict with Austria; became part of the Kingdom of the Serbs, Croats, and Slovenes (later called Yugoslavia) in 1918; with Montenegro formed the Federal Republic of Yugoslavia when the other constituent republics became independent in 1991–92; a new Union of Serbia and Montenegro formed in 2002; the autonomous region of Kosovo has been administered by the UN since the conflict of 1999. Capital: Belgrade. Pop: 5 762 954 (1997 est). Area: 88 361 sq km (34 109 sq miles). Former name: **Servia** Serbian name: **Srbija**

Serbian ('sɜːbɪən) *adj* **1** of, relating to, or characteristic of Serbia, its people, or their dialect of Serbo-Croat ▷ *n* **2** the dialect of Serbo-Croat spoken in Serbia **3** a native or inhabitant of Serbia

Serbo-Croat *or* **Serbo-Croatian** ('sɜːbəʊ-) *n* **1** the language of the Serbs and the Croats. The Serbian dialect is usually written in the Cyrillic alphabet, the Croatian in Roman ▷ *adj* **2** of or relating to this language

Sercq (sɛrk) *n* the French name for **Sark**

sere¹ (sɪə) *adj* **1** *arch* dried up ▷ *vb* **seres, sering, sered,** *n* **2** a rare spelling of **sear** [OE *sēar*]

sere² (sɪə) *n* the series of changes occurring in the ecological succession of a community [c20 from SERIES]

Seremban (sə'rɛmbən) *n* a town in Peninsular Malaysia, capital of Negri Sembilan state. Pop: 182 584 (1991)

serenade (ˌsɛrɪ'neɪd) *n* **1** a piece of music characteristically played outside the house of a woman **2** a piece of music suggestive of this **3** an extended composition in several movements similar to the modern suite ▷ *vb* **serenades, serenading, serenaded** **4** (*tr*) to play a serenade for (someone) **5** (*intr*) to play a serenade [c17 from F *sérénade*, from It. *serenata*, from *sereno* peaceful, from L *serēnus*; also infl. in meaning by It. *sera* evening, from L *sērus* late] > ˌ**sere'nader** *n*

serendipity (ˌsɛrən'dɪpɪtɪ) *n* the faculty of making fortunate discoveries by accident [c18 coined by Horace Walpole, from the Persian fairytale *The Three Princes of Serendip*, in which the heroes possess this gift] > ˌ**seren'dipitous** *adj*

serene (sɪ'riːn) *adj* **1** peaceful or tranquil; calm **2** clear or bright: *a serene sky* **3** (*often cap*) honoured: *His Serene Highness* [c16 from L *serēnus*] > **se'renely** *adv* > **serenity** (sɪ'rɛnɪtɪ) *n*

serf (sɜːf) *n* (esp in medieval Europe) an unfree person, esp one bound to the land [c15 from OF, from L *servus* a slave] > '**serfdom** *or* '**serfhood** *n*

serge (sɜːdʒ) *n* **1** a twill-weave woollen or worsted fabric used for clothing **2** a similar twilled cotton, silk, or rayon fabric [c14 from OF *sarge*, from Vulgar L *sārica* (unattested), from L *sēricum*, from Gk *sērikon* silk, ult. from *sēr* silkworm]

sergeant ('sɑːdʒənt) *n* **1** a noncommissioned officer in certain armies, air forces, and marine corps, usually ranking immediately above a corporal **2a** (in Britain) a police officer ranking between constable and inspector **2b** (in the US) a police officer ranking below a captain **3** a court or municipal officer who has ceremonial duties ▷ Also: **serjeant** [c12 from OF *sergent*, from L *serviēns*, lit.: serving, from *servīre* to SERVE]

sergeant at arms *n* an officer of a legislative or fraternal body responsible for maintaining internal order. Also: **sergeant, serjeant at arms**

Sergeant Baker ('beɪkə) *n* a large brightly coloured Australian sea fish

sergeant major *n* the chief administrative noncommissioned officer of a military headquarters. See also **warrant officer**

Sergipe (*Portuguese* ser'ʒipi) *n* a state of NE Brazil: the smallest Brazilian state; a centre of resistance to Dutch conquest (17th century). Capital: Aracajú. Pop: 1 779 522 (2000). Area: 13 672 sq km (8492 sq miles)

Sergt *abbrev for* Sergeant

serial ('sɪərɪəl) *n* **1** a novel, film, etc, presented in instalments at regular intervals **2** a publication, regularly issued and consecutively numbered ▷ *adj* **3** of or resembling a series **4** published or presented as a serial **5** of or relating to such publication or presentation **6** *computing* of or operating on items of information, etc, in the order in which they occur **7** of or using the techniques of serialism [c19 from NL *seriālis*, from L *seriēs* SERIES] > '**serially** *adv*

serialism ('sɪərɪəˌlɪzəm) *n* (in 20th-century music) the use of a sequence of notes in a definite order as a thematic basis for a composition. See also **twelve-tone**
▷ www.usc.edu/dept/polish_music/578/aug05.html

serialize *or* **serialise** ('sɪərɪəˌlaɪz) *vb* **serializes, serializing, serialized** *or* **serialises, serialising, serialised** (*tr*) to publish or present in the form of a serial > ˌ**seriali'zation** *or* ˌ**seriali'sation** *n*

serial killer *n* a person who carries out a series of murders, selecting victims at random or according to a perverse pattern

serial monogamy *n* the practice of having a number of long-term monogamous romantic or sexual relationships or marriages in succession

serial number *n* any of the consecutive numbers assigned to machines, tools, books, etc

serial port *n computing* (on a computer) a socket that can be used for connecting devices that send data one bit at a time; often used for connecting the mouse or a modem

seriate ('sɪərɪɪt) *adj* forming a series

seriatim (ˌsɪərɪ'ætɪm) *adv* one after another in order [c17 from Med. L, from L *seriēs* SERIES]

sericeous (sɪ'rɪʃəs) *adj bot* **1** covered with a layer of small silky hairs: *a sericeous leaf* **2** silky [c18 from LL *sēriceus* silken, from L *sēricus*; see SERGE]

sericulture ('sɛrɪˌkʌltʃə) *n* the rearing of silkworms for the production of raw silk [c19 via F; *seri-* from L *sēricum* silk, ult. from Gk *sēr* a silkworm] > ˌ**seri'cultural** *adj* > ˌ**seri'culturist** *n*

series ('sɪəriːz) *n, pl* **series** **1** a group or succession of related things, usually arranged in order **2** a set of radio or television programmes having the same characters but different stories **3** a set of books having the same format, related content, etc, published by one firm **4** a set of stamps, coins, etc, issued at a particular time **5** *maths* the sum of a finite or infinite sequence of numbers or quantities **6** *electronics* an arrangement of two or more components connected in a circuit so that the same current flows in turn through each of them (esp in **in series**) ▷ Cf **parallel** (sense 10) **7** *geol* a stratigraphical unit that represents the rocks formed during an epoch [c17 from L: a row, from *serere* to link]

series-wound ('sɪəriːzˌwaʊnd) *adj* (of a motor or generator) having the field and armature circuits connected in series

serif ('sɛrɪf) *n printing* a small line at the extremities of a main stroke in a type character [c19 ?from Du. *schreef* dash, prob. of Gmc origin]

serigraph ('sɛrɪˌgrɑːf) *n* a colour print made by an adaptation of the silk-screen process [c19 from *seri-*, from L *sēricum* silk + -GRAPH] > **serigraphy** (sə'rɪgrəfɪ) *n*

serin ('sɛrɪn) *n* any of various small yellow-and-brown finches of parts of Europe [C16 from F, ?from OProvençal *sirena* a bee-eater, from L *sīrēn*, a kind of bird, from SIREN]

seringa (sə'rɪŋgə) *n* **1** any of a Brazilian genus of trees that yield rubber **2** a deciduous tree of southern Africa with a graceful shape [C18 from Port., var. of SYRINGA]

Seringapatam (sə,rɪŋgəpə'tæm) *n* a small town in S India, in Karnataka on **Seringapatam Island** in the Cauvery River: capital of Mysore from 1610 to 1799, when it was besieged and captured by the British. Pop: 21 902 (1991 est)

seriocomic (,sɪərɪəʊ'kɒmɪk) *adj* mixing serious and comic elements > ,**serio'comically** *adv*

serious ('sɪərɪəs) *adj* **1** grave in nature or disposition: *a serious person* **2** marked by deep feeling; sincere: *is he serious or joking?* **3** concerned with important matters: *a serious conversation* **4** requiring effort or concentration: *a serious book* **5** giving rise to fear or anxiety: *a serious illness* **6** *inf* worthy of regard because of substantial quantity or quality: *serious money; serious wine* **7** *inf* extreme or remarkable: *a serious haircut* [C15 from LL *sēriōsus*, from L *sērius*] > '**seriousness** *n*

seriously ('sɪərɪəslɪ) *adv* **1** in a serious manner or to a serious degree **2** *inf* extremely or remarkably: *seriously tall*

serjeant ('sɑːdʒənt) *n* a variant spelling of **sergeant**

serjeant at law *n* (formerly, in England) a barrister of a special rank. Also: **serjeant, sergeant at law, sergeant**

sermon ('sɜːmən) *n* **1a** an address of religious instruction or exhortation, often based on a passage from the Bible, esp one delivered during a church service **1b** a written version of such an address **2** a serious speech, esp one administering reproof [C12 via OF from L *sermō* discourse, prob. from *serere* to join together]

sermonize *or* **sermonise** ('sɜːmə,naɪz) *vb* **sermonizes, sermonizing, sermonized** *or* **sermonises, sermonising, sermonised** to address (a person or audience) as if delivering a sermon > '**sermon,izer** *or* '**sermon,iser** *n*

Sermon on the Mount *n Bible* a major discourse delivered by Christ, including the Beatitudes and the Lord's Prayer (Matthew 5–7)

sero- *combining form* indicating a serum: *serology*

seroconvert (,sɪərəʊkən'vɜːt) *vb* (*intr*) (of an individual) to produce antibodies specific to, and in response to the presence in the blood of, a particular antigen, such as a virus or vaccine > ,**serocon'version** *n*

serology (sɪ'rɒlədʒɪ) *n* the branch of science concerned with serums > **serologic** (,sɪərə'lɒdʒɪk) *or* ,**sero'logical** *adj*

seropositive (,sɪərəʊ'pɒzɪtɪv) *adj* (of a person whose blood has been tested for a specific disease, such as AIDS) showing a serological reaction indicating the presence of the disease

serotine ('sɛrə,taɪn) *adj* **1** *biol* produced, flowering, or developing late in the season ▷ *n* **2** a reddish-coloured European insectivorous bat [C16 from L *sērōtinus* late, from *sērus* late; applied to the bat because it flies late in the evening]

serotonin (,sɛrə'təʊnɪn) *n* a compound that occurs in the brain, intestines, and blood platelets and induces vasoconstriction

serotype ('sɪərəʊ,taɪp) *n med* a category into which material, usually a bacterium, is placed based on its serological activity, esp in terms of the antigens it contains or the antibodies produced against it

serous ('sɪərəs) *adj* of, producing, or containing serum [C16 from L *serōsus*] > **serosity** (sɪ'rɒsɪtɪ) *n*

serous fluid *n* a thin watery fluid found in many body cavities

serous membrane *n* any of the smooth moist delicate membranes, such as the pleura, that line the closed cavities of the body and secrete a watery exudate

serow ('sɛrəʊ) *n* either of two antelopes of mountainous regions of S and SE Asia, having a dark coat and conical backward-pointing horns [C19 from native name *s'-ro* Tibetan goat]

Seroxat ('sɛ,rɒksæt) *n trademark* a drug that prolongs the action of serotonin in the brain; used to treat depression and social anxiety

serpent ('sɜːpənt) *n* **1** a literary word for **snake** **2** *Bible* a manifestation of Satan as a guileful tempter (Genesis 3:1–5) **3** a sly or unscrupulous person **4** an obsolete wind instrument resembling a snake in shape [C14 via OF from L *serpēns* a creeping thing, from *serpere* to creep]

serpentine[1] ('sɜːpən,taɪn) *adj* **1** of, relating to, or resembling a serpent **2** twisting; winding [C14 from LL *serpentīmus*, from *serpēns* SERPENT]

serpentine[2] ('sɜːpən,taɪn) *n* any of several secondary minerals, consisting of hydrated magnesium silicate, that are green to brown in colour and greasy to the touch [C15 *serpentyn*, from Med. L *serpentīnum* SERPENTINE[1]; referring to the snakelike patterns of these minerals]

serpigo (sɜː'paɪgəʊ) *n pathol* any progressive skin eruption, such as ringworm or herpes [C14 from Med. L, from L *serpere* to creep]

SERPS *or* **Serps** (sɜːps) *n* (in Britain) *acronym for* state earnings-related pension scheme

serrate *adj* ('sɛrɪt, -eɪt) **1** (of leaves) having a margin of forward pointing teeth **2** having a notched or sawlike edge ▷ *vb* (sɛ'reɪt), **serrates, serrating, serrated** **3** (*tr*) to make serrate [C17 from L *serrātus* saw-shaped, from *serra* a saw]

serrated *adj* (sə'reɪtɪd) having a notched or sawlike edge

serration (sɛ'reɪʃən) *n* **1** the state or condition of being serrated **2** a row of toothlike projections on an edge **3** a single notch

serried ('sɛrɪd) *adj* in close or compact formation: *serried ranks of troops* [C17 from OF *serré* close-packed, from *serrer* to shut up]

serriform ('sɛrɪ,fɔːm) *adj biol* resembling a notched or sawlike edge [*serri-*, from L *serra* saw]

serrulate ('sɛrʊ,leɪt, -lɪt) *adj* (esp of leaves) minutely serrate [C18 from NL *serrulātus*, from L *serrula* dim. of *serra* a saw] > ,**serru'lation** *n*

Sertorius (sɜː'tɔːrɪəs) *n* **Quintus** ('kwɪntəs) ?123–72 BC, Roman soldier who fought with Marius in Gaul (102) and led an insurrection in Spain against Sulla until he was assassinated

serum ('sɪərəm) *n, pl* **serums** *or* **sera** (-rə) **1** Also called: **blood serum** blood plasma from which the clotting factors have been removed **2** antitoxin obtained from the blood serum of immunized animals **3** *physiol, zool* clear watery fluid, esp that exuded by serous membranes **4** a less common word for **whey** [C17 from L: whey]

serum albumin *n* a form of albumin that is the most abundant protein constituent of blood plasma

serum hepatitis *n* a former name for **hepatitis B**

serum sickness *n* an allergic reaction, such as vomiting, skin rash, etc, that sometimes follows 2–3 weeks after an injection of a foreign serum

serval ('sɜːvəl) *n, pl* **servals** *or* **serval** a slender feline mammal of the African bush, having an orange-brown coat with black spots [C18 via F from LL *cervālis* staglike, from L *cervus* a stag]

servant ('sɜːvənt) *n* **1** a person employed to work for another, esp one who performs household duties **2** See **public servant** [C13 via OF from *servant* serving, from *servir* to SERVE]

serve (sɜːv) *vb* **serves, serving, served** **1** to be in the service of (a person) **2** to render or be of service to (a person, cause, etc); help **3** to attend to (customers) in a shop, etc **4** (*tr*) to provide (guests, etc) with food, drink, etc: *she served her guests with cocktails* **5** to distribute or provide (food, etc) for guests, etc: *do you serve coffee?* **6** (*tr; sometimes foll by up*) to present (food, etc) in a specified manner: *peaches served with cream* **7** (*tr*) to provide with a

Ss

regular supply of **8** (*tr*) to work actively for: *to serve the government* **9** (*tr*) to pay homage to: *to serve God* **10** to suit: *this will serve my purpose* **11** (*intr; may take an infinitive*) to function: *this wood will serve to build a fire* **12** to go through (a period of service, enlistment, etc) **13** (*intr*) (of weather, conditions, etc) to be suitable **14** (*tr*) Also: **service** (of a male animal) to copulate with (a female animal) **15** *tennis, squash, etc* to put (the ball) into play **16** (*tr*) to deliver (a legal document) to (a person) **17** (*tr*) *naut* to bind (a rope, etc) with fine cord to protect it from chafing, etc **18** **serve (a person) right** *inf* to pay (a person) back, esp for wrongful or foolish treatment or behaviour ▷ *n* **19** *tennis, squash, etc* short for **service** **20** *Austral inf* hostile or critical remarks [C13 from OF *servir*, from L *servīre*, from *servus* a slave] > **'servable** *or* **'serveable** *adj*

server ('sɜːvə) *n* **1** a person who serves **2** *RC Church* a person who assists the priest at Mass **3** something that is used in serving food and drink **4** the player who serves in racket games **5** *computing* a computer or program that supplies data or resources to other machines on a network

Servetus (sɜː'viːtəs) *n* **Michael,** Spanish name *Miguel Serveto*. 1511–53, Spanish theologian and physician. He was burnt at the stake by order of Calvin for denying the doctrine of the Trinity and the divinity of Christ

Servia ('sɜːvɪə) *n* the former name of **Serbia** > **'Servian** *adj, n*

service ('sɜːvɪs) *n* **1** an act of help or assistance **2** an organized system of labour and material aids used to supply the needs of the public: *telephone service* **3** the supply, installation, or maintenance of goods carried out by a dealer **4** the state of availability for use by the public (esp in **into** *or* **out of service**) **5** a periodic overhaul made on a car, etc **6** the act or manner of serving guests, customers, etc, in a shop, hotel, etc **7** a department of public employment and its employees: *civil service* **8** employment in or performance of work for another: *in the service of his firm* **9a** one of the branches of the armed forces **9b** (*as modifier*): *service life* **10** the state or duties of a domestic servant (esp in **in service**) **11** the act or manner of serving food **12** a set of dishes, cups, etc, for use at table **13** public worship carried out according to certain prescribed forms: *divine service* **14** the prescribed form according to which a specific kind of religious ceremony is to be carried out: *the burial service* **15** *tennis, squash, etc* **15a** the act, manner, or right of serving a ball **15b** the game in which a particular player serves: *he has lost his service* **16** the serving of a writ, summons, etc, upon a person **17** (of male animals) the act of mating **18** (*modifier*) of or for the use of servants or employees **19** (*modifier*) serving the public rather than producing goods: *service industry* ▷ *vb* **services, servicing, serviced** (*tr*) **20** to provide service or services to **21** to make fit for use **22** to supply with assistance **23** to overhaul (a car, machine, etc) **24** (of a male animal) to mate with (a female) **25** *Brit* to meet interest on (debt) ▷ See also **services** [C12 *servise*, from OF, from L *servitium* condition of a slave, from *servus* a slave]

serviceable ('sɜːvɪsəbᵊl) *adj* **1** capable of or ready for service **2** capable of giving good service > ˌ**servicea'bility** *n* > **'serviceably** *adv*

service area *n* a place on a motorway providing garage services, restaurants, toilet facilities, etc

service car *n NZ* a bus operating on a long-distance route

service charge *n* a percentage of a bill, as at a hotel, added to the total to pay for service

service contract *n* a contract between an employer and a senior employee, esp a director, executive, etc

service flat *n Brit* a flat in which domestic services are provided by the management. Also called (esp Austral): **serviced flat**

serviceman ('sɜːvɪsmən) *n, pl* **servicemen** **1** a person who serves in the armed services of a country **2** a man employed to service and maintain equipment > **'serviceˌwoman** *fem n*

service road *n Brit* a narrow road running parallel to a main road and providing access to houses, shops, etc, situated along its length

services ('sɜːvɪsɪz) *pl n* **1** work performed for remuneration **2** (usually preceded by *the*) the armed forces **3** (*sometimes sing*) *econ* commodities, such as banking, that are mainly intangible and usually consumed concurrently with their production **4** a system of providing the public with gas, water, etc

service station *n* a place that supplies fuel, oil, etc, for motor vehicles and often carries out repairs, servicing, etc

service tree *n* **1** Also called: **sorb** a Eurasian rosaceous tree, cultivated for its white flowers and brown edible apple-like fruits **2** **wild service tree** a similar and related Eurasian tree [*service* from OE *syrfe*, from Vulgar L *sorbea* (unattested), from L *sorbus* sorb]

serviette (ˌsɜːvɪ'ɛt) *n Brit & Canad* a small square of cloth or paper used while eating to protect the clothes, etc [C15 from OF, from *servir* to SERVE; on the model of OUBLIETTE]

servile ('sɜːvaɪl) *adj* **1** obsequious or fawning in attitude or behaviour **2** of or suitable for a slave **3** existing in or relating to a state of slavery **4** (when *postpositive*, foll by *to*) submitting or obedient [C14 from L *servīlis*, from *servus* slave] > **servility** (sɜː'vɪlɪtɪ) *n*

serving ('sɜːvɪŋ) *n* a portion or helping of food or drink

servitor ('sɜːvɪtə) *n arch* a person who serves another [C14 from OF, from LL, from L *servīre* to SERVE]

servitude ('sɜːvɪˌtjuːd) *n* **1** the state or condition of a slave **2** the state or condition of being subjected to or dominated by a person or thing **3** *law* a burden attaching to an estate for the benefit of an adjoining estate or of some definite person. See also **easement** [C15 via OF from L *servitūdō*, from *servus* a slave]

servlet ('sɜːvlɪt) *n computing* a small program that runs on a web server often accessing databases in response to client input [C20 from SERV(ER) + (APP)LET]

servo ('sɜːvəʊ) *adj* **1** (*prenominal*) of or activated by a servomechanism: *servo brakes* ▷ *n, pl* **servos** **2** *inf* short for **servomechanism** [from *servomotor* from F, from L *servus* slave + F *moteur* motor]

servomechanism ('sɜːvəʊˌmɛkəˌnɪzəm) *n* a mechanical or electromechanical system for control of the position or speed of an output transducer

servomotor ('sɜːvəʊˌməʊtə) *n* any motor that supplies power to a servomechanism

servqual ('sɜːvˌkwɒl) *n marketing* the provision of high-quality products by an organization backed by a high level of service for consumers [C20 from SERV(ICE) + QUAL(ITY)]

sesame ('sɛsəmɪ) *n* **1** a tropical herbaceous plant of the East Indies, cultivated, esp in India, for its small oval seeds **2** the seeds of this plant, used in flavouring bread and yielding an edible oil (**benne oil** or **gingili**) [C15 from L *sēsamum*, from Gk *sēsamon*, *sēsamē*, of Semitic origin]

sesamoid ('sɛsəˌmɔɪd) *adj anat* **1** of or relating to various small bones formed in tendons, such as the patella **2** of or relating to any of various small cartilages, esp those of the nose [C17 from L *sēsamoīdēs* like sesame (seed), from Gk]

sesh (sɛʃ) *n sl* short for **session**

Sesostris I (sɛ'sɒstrɪs) *n* 20th century BC, king of Egypt of the 12th dynasty. He conquered Nubia and brought ancient Egypt to the height of its prosperity. The funerary complex at Lisht was built during his reign

sesqui- *prefix* **1** indicating one and a half: *sesquicentennial* **2** (in a chemical compound) indicating a ratio of two to three [from L, contraction of SEMI- + *as* AS² + *-que* and]

sesquicentennial (ˌsɛskwɪsɛn'tɛnɪəl) *adj* **1** of a period of 150 years ▷ *n* **2** a period of 150 years **3** a 150th anniversary or its celebration > ˌsesquicen'tennially *adv*

sessile ('sɛsaɪl) *adj* **1** (of flowers or leaves) having no stalk **2** (of animals such as the barnacle) permanently attached [C18 from L *sēssilis* concerning sitting, from *sedēre* to sit] > **sessility** (sɛ'sɪlɪtɪ) *n*

sessile oak *n* another name for the **durmast**

session ('sɛʃən) *n* **1** the meeting of a court, legislature, judicial body, etc, for the execution of its function or the transaction of business **2** a single continuous meeting of such a body **3** a series or period of such meetings **4** *education* **4a** the time during which classes are held **4b** a school or university year **5** *Presbyterian Church* the body presiding over a local congregation and consisting of the minister and elders **6** a meeting of a group of musicians to record in a studio **7** any period devoted to an activity [C14 from L *sessiō* a sitting, from *sedēre* to sit] > **'sessional** *adj*

Sessions ('sɛʃənz) *n* **Roger** (**Huntington**) 1896–1985, US composer

sesterce ('sɛstəs) *or* **sestertius** (sɛ'stɜːtɪəs) *n* a silver or, later, bronze coin of ancient Rome worth a quarter of a denarius [C16 from L *sēstertius* a coin worth two and a half asses, from *sēmis* half + *tertius* a third]

sestet (sɛ'stɛt) *n* **1** *prosody* the last six lines of a sonnet **2** another word for **sextet** (sense 1) [C19 from It., from *sesto* sixth, from L, from *sex* six]

sestina (sɛ'stiːnə) *n* an elaborate verse form of Italian origin in which the six final words of the lines in the first stanza are repeated in a different order in each of the remaining five stanzas [C19 from It., from *sesto* sixth, from L *sextus*]

Sestos ('sɛstɒs) *n* a ruined town in NW Turkey, at the narrowest point of the Dardanelles: N terminus of the bridge of boats built by Xerxes in 481 BC for the crossing of his armies of invasion

set[1] (sɛt) *vb* **sets, setting, set** (*mainly tr*) **1** to put or place in position or into a specified state or condition: *to set someone free* **2** (*also intr*; foll by *to* or *on*) to put or be put (to); apply or be applied: *he set fire to the house* **3** to put into order or readiness for use: *to set the table for dinner* **4** (*also intr*) to put, form, or be formed into a jelled, firm, or rigid state: *the jelly set in three hours* **5** (*also intr*) to put or be put into a position that will restore a normal state: *to set a broken bone* **6** to adjust (a clock or other instrument) to a position **7** to establish: *we have set the date for our wedding* **8** to prescribe (an undertaking, course of study, etc): *the examiners have set "Paradise Lost"* **9** to arrange in a particular fashion, esp an attractive one: *she set her hair* **10** Also: **set to music** to provide music for (a poem or other text to be sung) **11** Also: **set up** *printing* to arrange or produce (type, film, etc) from (text or copy) **12** to arrange (a stage, television studio, etc) with scenery and props **13** to describe (a scene or the background to a literary work, etc) in words: *his novel is set in Russia* **14** to present as a model of good or bad behaviour (esp in **set an example**) **15** (foll by *on* or *by*) to value (something) at a specified price or estimation of worth: *he set a high price on his services* **16** (*also intr*) to give or be given a particular direction: *his course was set to the East* **17** (*also intr*) to rig (a sail) or (of a sail) to be rigged so as to catch the wind **18** (*intr*) (of the sun, moon, etc) to disappear beneath the horizon **19** to leave (dough, etc) in one place so that it may prove **20** to sink (the head of a nail) below the surface surrounding it by using a nail set **21** *computing* to give (a binary circuit) the value 1 **22** (of plants) to produce (fruits, seeds, etc) after pollination or (of fruits or seeds) to develop after pollination **23** to plant (seeds, seedlings, etc) **24** to place (a hen) on (eggs) for the purpose of incubation **25** (*intr*) (of a gun dog) to turn in the direction of game **26** *bridge* to defeat (one's opponents) in their attempt to make a contract **27** a dialect word for **sit** ▷ *n* **28** the act of setting or the state of being set **29** a condition of firmness or hardness **30** bearing, carriage, or posture: *the set of a gun dog when pointing* **31** the scenery and other props used in a dramatic production, film, etc **32** Also called: **set width** *printing* **32a** the width of the body of a piece of type **32b** the width of the lines of type in a page or column **33** *psychol* a temporary bias disposing an organism to react to a stimulus in one way rather than in others **34** a seedling, cutting, or similar part that is ready for planting: *onion sets* **35** a variant spelling of **sett** ▷ *adj* **36** fixed or established by authority or agreement: *set hours of work* **37** (*usually postpositive*) rigid or inflexible: *she is set in her ways* **38** unmoving; fixed: *a set expression on his face* **39** conventional, artificial, or stereotyped: *she made her apology in set phrases* **40** (*postpositive*; foll by *on* or *upon*) resolute in intention: *he is set upon marrying* **41** (of a book, etc) prescribed for students' preparation for an examination ▷ See also **set about, set against,** etc [OE *settan*, causative of *sittan* to SIT]

set[2] (sɛt) *n* **1** a number of objects or people grouped or belonging together, often having certain features or characteristics in common: *a set of coins* **2** a group of people who associate together, etc: *he's part of the jet set* **3** *maths* a collection of numbers, objects, etc, that are treated as an entity: {3, the moon} is the set the two members of which are the number 3 and the moon **4** any apparatus that receives or transmits television or radio signals **5** *tennis, squash, etc* one of the units of a match, in tennis, one in which one player or pair of players must win at least six games: *Hingis lost the first set* **6a** the number of couples required for a formation dance **6b** a series of figures that make up a formation dance **7a** a band's or performer's concert repertoire on a given occasion: *the set included no new songs* **7b** a continuous performance: *the Who played two sets* **8 make a dead set at 8a** to attack by arguing or ridiculing **8b** (of a woman) to try to gain the affections of (a man) ▷ *vb* **sets, setting, set 9** (*intr*) (in square and country dancing) to perform a sequence of steps while facing towards another dancer **10** (*usually tr*) to divide into sets: *in this school we set our older pupils for English* [C14 (in the obs. sense: a religious sect): from OF *sette*, from L *secta* SECT; later sense infl. by the verb SET[1]]

seta ('siːtə) *n, pl* **setae** (-tiː) (in invertebrates and plants) any bristle or bristle-like appendage [C18 from L] > **setaceous** (sɪ'teɪʃəs) *adj*

set about *vb* (*intr, prep*) **1** to start or begin **2** to attack physically or verbally

set against *vb* (*tr, prep*) **1** to balance or compare **2** to cause to be unfriendly to

set aside *vb* (*tr, adv*) **1** to reserve for a special purpose **2** to discard or quash ▷ *n* **set-aside 3a** (in the European Union) a scheme in which a proportion of farmland is taken out of production in order to reduce surpluses or maintain or increase prices of a specific crop **3b** (*as modifier*): *set-aside land*

set back *vb* (*tr, adv*) **1** to hinder; impede **2** *inf* to cost (a person) a specified amount ▷ *n* **setback 3** anything that serves to hinder or impede **4** a recession in the upper part of a high building **5** a steplike shelf where a wall is reduced in thickness

set down *vb* (*tr, adv*) **1** to record **2** to judge or regard: *he set him down as an idiot* **3** (foll by *to*) to attribute: *his attitude was set down to his illness* **4** to rebuke **5** to snub **6** *Brit* to allow (passengers) to alight from a bus, etc

set forth *vb* (*adv*) *formal or arch* **1** (*tr*) to state, express, or utter **2** (*intr*) to start out on a journey

Seth (sɛθ) *n Old Testament* Adam's third son, given by God in place of the murdered Abel (Genesis 4:25)

SETI ('sɛtɪ) *n acronym for* Search for Extraterrestrial Intelligence; a scientific programme attempting, by radio transmissions, to make contact with beings from other planets

▷ http://setiathome.ssl.berkeley.edu

Ss

setiferous (sɪ'tɪfərəs) *or* **setigerous** (sɪ'tɪdʒərəs) *adj biol* bearing bristles [C19 see SETA, -FEROUS, -GEROUS]

set in *vb (intr, adv)* **1** to become established: *the winter has set in* **2** (of wind) to blow or (of current) to move towards shore ▷ *adj* **set-in** **3** (of a part) made separately and then added to a larger whole: *a set-in sleeve*

setline ('sɛt,laɪn) *n* any of various types of fishing line that consist of a long suspended line having shorter hooked and baited lines attached

set off *vb (adv)* **1** *(intr)* to embark on a journey **2** *(tr)* to cause (a person) to act or do something, such as laugh **3** *(tr)* to cause to explode **4** *(tr)* to act as a foil or contrast to: *that brooch sets your dress off well* **5** *(tr) accounting* to cancel a credit on (one account) against a debit on another ▷ *n* **setoff** **6** anything that serves as a counterbalance **7** anything that serves to contrast with or enhance something else; foil **8** a cross claim brought by a debtor that partly offsets the creditor's claim

set-off *n printing* a fault in which ink is transferred from a heavily inked or undried printed sheet to the sheet next to it in a pile

set on *vb* **1** *(prep)* Also: **set upon** to attack or cause to attack: *they set the dogs on him* **2** *(tr, adv)* to instigate or incite; urge

Seton ('siːtᵊn) *n* **Ernest Thompson** 1860–1946, US author and illustrator of animal books, born in England

Seto Naikai ('sɛtəʊ 'naɪkaɪ) *n* transliteration of the Japanese name for the **Inland Sea**

setose ('siːtəʊs) *adj biol* covered with setae; bristly [C17 from L *saetōsus*, from *saeta* a bristle]

set out *vb (adv, mainly tr)* **1** to present, arrange, or display **2** to give a full account of: *he set out the matter in full* **3** to plan or lay out (a garden, etc) **4** *(intr)* to begin or embark on an undertaking, esp a journey

set piece *n* **1** a work of literature, music, etc, often having a conventional or prescribed theme, intended to create an impressive effect **2** a display of fireworks **3** *sport* a rehearsed team manoeuvre usually attempted at a restart of play

setscrew ('sɛt,skruː) *n* a screw that fits into the boss or hub of a wheel, coupling, cam, etc, and prevents motion of the part relative to the shaft on which it is mounted

set square *n* a thin flat piece of plastic, metal, etc, in the shape of a right-angled triangle, used in technical drawing

sett *or* **set** (sɛt) *n* **1** a small rectangular paving block made of stone **2** the burrow of a badger **3a** a square in a pattern of tartan **3b** the pattern itself [C19 var. of SET[1] (n)]

settee (sɛ'tiː) *n* a seat, for two or more people, with a back and usually with arms [C18 changed from SETTLE[2]]

setter ('sɛtə) *n* any of various breeds of large long-haired gun dog trained to point out game by standing rigid

set theory *n maths* the branch of mathematics concerned with the properties and interrelationships of sets

setting ('sɛtɪŋ) *n* **1** the surroundings in which something is set **2** the scenery, properties, or background used to create the location for a stage play, film, etc **3** *music* a composition consisting of a certain text and music arranged for it **4** the metal mounting and surround of a gem **5** the tableware, cutlery, etc, for a single place at table **6** any of a set of points on a scale or dial that can be selected to control the speed, temperature, etc, at which a machine operates

settle[1] ('sɛtᵊl) *vb* **settles, settling, settled** **1** *(tr)* to put in order: *he settled his affairs before he died* **2** to arrange or be arranged in a fixed or comfortable position: *he settled himself by the fire* **3** *(intr)* to come to rest or a halt: *a bird settled on the hedge* **4** to take up or cause to take up residence: *the family settled in the country* **5** to establish or become established in a way of life, job, etc **6** *(tr)* to migrate to and form a community; colonize **7** to make or become quiet, calm, or stable **8** to cause (sediment) to sink to the bottom, as in a liquid, or (of sediment) to sink thus **9** to subside or cause to subside: *the dust settled* **10** (sometimes foll by *up*) to pay off or account for (a bill, debt, etc) **11** *(tr)* to decide or dispose of: *to settle an argument* **12** *(intr; often foll by on or upon)* to agree or fix: *to settle upon a plan* **13** *(tr; usually foll by on or upon)* to secure (title, property, etc) to a person: *he settled his property on his wife* **14** to determine (a legal dispute, etc) by agreement of the parties without resort to court action (esp in **settle out of court**) [OE *setlan*] > **'settleable** *adj*

settle[2] ('sɛtᵊl) *n* a seat, for two or more people, usually made of wood with a high back and arms, and sometimes having a storage space in the boxlike seat [OE *setl*]

settle down *vb (adv, mainly intr)* **1** *(also tr)* to make or become quiet and orderly **2** (often foll by *to*) to apply oneself diligently: *please settle down to work* **3** to adopt an orderly and routine way of life, esp after marriage

settle for *vb (intr, prep)* to accept or agree to in spite of dispute or dissatisfaction

settlement ('sɛtᵊlmənt) *n* **1** the act or state of settling or being settled **2** the establishment of a new region; colonization **3** a place newly settled; colony **4** a community formed by members of a group, esp of a religious sect **5** a public building used to provide educational and general welfare facilities for persons living in deprived areas **6** a subsidence of all or part of a structure **7a** the payment of an outstanding account, invoice, charge, etc **7b** *(as modifier)*: *settlement day* **8** an agreement reached in matters of finance, business, etc **9** *law* **9a** a conveyance, usually to trustees, of property to be enjoyed by several persons in succession **9b** the deed conveying such property

settler ('sɛtlə) *n* a person who settles in a new country or a colony

settlings ('sɛtlɪŋz) *pl n* any matter that has settled at the bottom of a liquid

set to *vb (intr, adv)* **1** to begin working **2** to start fighting ▷ *n* **set-to** **3** *inf* a brief disagreement or fight

set-top box *n* a device that converts the signals from a digital television broadcast into a form which can be viewed on a standard analogue television set

Setúbal (*Portuguese* sə'tuβal) *n* a port in SW Portugal, on **Setúbal Bay** south of Lisbon: an earthquake in 1755 destroyed most of the old town. Pop: 83 550 (1991)

set up *vb (adv, mainly tr)* **1** *(also intr)* to put into a position of power, etc **2** *(also intr)* to begin or enable (someone) to begin (a new venture), as by acquiring or providing means, etc **3** to build or construct: *to set up a shed* **4** to raise or produce: *to set up a wail* **5** to advance or propose: *to set up a theory* **6** to restore the health of: *the sea air will set you up again* **7** to establish (a record) **8** *inf* to cause (a person) to be blamed, accused, etc ▷ *n* **setup** **9** *inf* the way in which anything is organized or arranged **10** *sl* an event the result of which is prearranged: *it's a setup* **11** a prepared arrangement of materials, machines, etc, for a job or undertaking ▷ *adj* **set-up** **12** physically well-built

Seurat (*French* sœra) *n* **Georges** (ʒɔrʒ) 1859–91, French neoimpressionist painter. He developed the pointillist technique of painting, characterized by brilliant luminosity, as in *Dimanche à la Grande-Jatte* (1886)

Sevan (sɛ'vɑːn) *n* **Lake** a lake in Armenia at an altitude of 1914 m (6279 ft). Area: 1417 sq km (547 sq miles)

Sevastopol (*Russian* sɪvas'tɔpəlj) *n* a port, resort, and naval base in the S Ukraine, in the Crimea, on the Black Sea: captured and destroyed by British, French, and Turkish forces after a siege of 11 months (1854–55) during the Crimean War; taken by the Germans after a siege of 8 months (1942) during World War II. Pop: 356 000 (1998 est). English name: **Sebastopol**

seven ('sɛvᵊn) *n* **1** the cardinal number that is the sum of six and one and is a prime number **2** a numeral, 7, VII, etc, representing this number **3** the amount or quantity that is one greater than six **4** anything representing, represented by, or consisting of seven units, such as a playing card with seven symbols on it **5** Also called: **seven o'clock** seven hours after noon or midnight ▷ *determiner* **6a** amounting to seven: *seven swans a-swimming* **6b** (*as pron*): *you've eaten seven already* ▷ See also **sevens** [OE *seofon*]

Seven against Thebes *pl n Greek myth* the seven members of an expedition undertaken to regain for Polynices, a son of Oedipus, his share in the throne of Thebes from his usurping brother Eteocles. The seven are usually listed as Polynices, Adrastus, Amphiaraus, Capaneus, Hippomedon, Tydeus, and Parthenopaeus. The campaign failed and the warring brothers killed each other in single combat before the Theban walls. See also **Adrastus**

seven deadly sins *pl n* a fuller name for the **deadly sins**

sevenfold ('sɛv^{ə}n,fəʊld) *adj* **1** equal to or having seven times as many or as much **2** composed of seven parts ▷ *adv* **3** by or up to seven times as many or as much

Seven Hills of Rome *pl n* the hills on which the ancient city of Rome was built: the Palatine, Capitoline, Quirinal, Caelian, Aventine, Esquiline, and Viminal

sevens ('sɛv^{ə}nz) *n* (*functioning as sing*) a rugby union match or competition played with seven players on each side

seven seas *pl n* the oceans of the world considered as the N and S Pacific, the N and S Atlantic, and the Arctic, Antarctic, and Indian Oceans

seven-segment display *n* an arrangement of seven bars forming a square figure of eight, used in electronic displays of alphanumeric characters: any letter or figure can be represented by illuminating selected bars

Seven Sleepers *pl n* seven Christian youths from Ephesus who were walled up in a cave by the Emperor Decius in 250 AD and, according to legend, slept for 187 years

seventeen ('sɛv^{ə}n'tiːn) *n* **1** the cardinal number that is the sum of ten and seven and is a prime number **2** a numeral, 17, XVII, etc, representing this number **3** the amount or quantity that is seven more than ten **4** something represented by, representing, or consisting of 17 units ▷ *determiner* **5a** amounting to seventeen: *seventeen attempts* **5b** (*as pron*): *seventeen were sold* [OE *seofontīene*] > **'seven'teenth** *adj, n*

seventh ('sɛv^{ə}nθ) *adj* **1** (*usually prenominal*) **1a** coming after the sixth and before the eighth in numbering, position, etc; being the ordinal number of *seven*: often written 7th **1b** (*as n*): *she left on the seventh* ▷ *n* **2a** one of seven equal parts of an object, quantity, measurement, etc **2b** (*as modifier*): *a seventh part* **3** the fraction equal to one divided by seven (1/7) **4** *music* **4a** the interval between one note and another seven notes away from it in a diatonic scale **4b** one of two notes constituting such an interval in relation to the other ▷ *adv* **5** Also: **seventhly** after the sixth person, event, etc

Seventh-Day Adventist *n* a member of that branch of the Adventists which constituted itself as a separate body after the expected Second Coming of Christ failed to be realized in 1844. They believe that Christ's coming is imminent and observe Saturday instead of Sunday as their Sabbath

▷ www.adventist.org/

seventh heaven *n* **1** the final state of eternal bliss **2** a state of supreme happiness

seventy ('sɛv^{ə}ntɪ) *n, pl* **seventies** **1** the cardinal number that is the product of ten and seven **2** a numeral, 70, LXX, etc, representing this number **3** (*pl*) the numbers 70–79, esp the 70th to the 79th year of a person's life or of a particular century **4** the amount or quantity that is seven times as big as ten **5** something represented by, representing, or consisting of 70 units ▷ *determiner* **6a** amounting to seventy: *the seventy varieties of fabric* **6b** (*as pron*): *to invite seventy to the wedding* [OE *seofontig*] > **'seventieth** *adj, n*

Seven Wonders of the World *pl n* the seven structures considered by ancient and medieval scholars to be the most wondrous of the ancient world. The list varies, but generally consists of the Pyramids of Egypt, the Hanging Gardens of Babylon, Phidias' statue of Zeus at Olympia, the temple of Artemis at Ephesus, the mausoleum of Halicarnassus, the Colossus of Rhodes, and the Pharos (or lighthouse) of Alexandria

▷ www.unmuseum.org/wonders.htm

Seven Years' War *n* the war (1756–63) of Britain and Prussia, who emerged in the ascendant, against France and Austria, resulting from commercial and colonial rivalry between Britain and France and from the conflict in Germany between Prussia and Austria

▷ www.militaryheritage.com/7yrswar.htm

▷ www.usahistory.com/wars/sevenyrs.htm

sever ('sɛvə) *vb* **1** to put or be put apart **2** to divide or be divided into parts **3** (*tr*) to break off or dissolve (a tie, relationship, etc) [c14 *severen*, from OF, from L *sēparāre* to SEPARATE] > **'severable** *adj*

several ('sɛvrəl) *determiner* **1a** more than a few: *several people objected* **1b** (*as pronoun; functioning as pl*): *several of them know* ▷ *adj* **2** (*prenominal*) various; separate: *the members with their several occupations* **3** (*prenominal*) distinct; different: *three several times* **4** *law* capable of being dealt with separately [c15 via Anglo-F from Med. L *sēparālis*, from L *sēpār*, from *sēparāre* to SEPARATE]

severally ('sɛvrəlɪ) *adv* **1** separately or distinctly **2** each in turn

severalty ('sɛvrəltɪ) *n, pl* **severalties** **1** the state of being several or separate **2** (usually preceded by *in*) *property law* the tenure of property, esp land, in a person's own right

severance ('sɛvərəns) *n* **1** the act of severing or state of being severed **2** a separation **3** *law* the division into separate parts of a joint estate, contract, etc

Ss

severance pay *n* compensation paid by a firm to employees for loss of employment

severe (sɪ'vɪə) *adj* **1** rigorous or harsh in the treatment of others: *a severe parent* **2** serious in appearance or manner **3** critical or dangerous: *a severe illness* **4** causing discomfort by its harshness: *severe weather* **5** strictly restrained in appearance: *a severe way of dressing* **6** hard to perform or accomplish: *a severe test* [c16 from L *sevērus*] > **se'verely** *adv* > **severity** (sɪ'vɛrɪtɪ) *n*

Severn ('sɛv^{ə}n) *n* **1** a river in E Wales and W England, rising in Powys and flowing northeast and east into England, then south to the Bristol Channel. Length: about 290 km (180 miles) **2** a river in SE central Canada, in Ontario, flowing northeast to Hudson Bay. Length: about 676 km (420 miles)

Severnaya Zemlya (*Russian* 'sjevɪrnəjə zɪm'lja) *n* an archipelago in the Arctic Ocean off N central Russia

Severus (sɪ'vɪərəs) *n* **Lucius Septimius** (sɛp'tɪmɪəs) 146–211 AD, Roman soldier and emperor (193–211). He waged war successfully against the Parthians (197–202) and spent his last years in Britain (208–11)

Seveso (sɛ'veɪsəʊ) *n* a town in N Italy, near Milan: evacuated in 1976 after contamination by a poisonous cloud of dioxin gas released from a factory

Sévigné (*French* seviɲe) *n* **Marquise de,** title of *Marie de Rabutin-Chantal*. 1626–96, French letter writer. Her correspondence with her daughter and others provides a vivid account of society during the reign of Louis XIV

Seville (sə'vɪl) *n* a port in SW Spain, on the Guadalquivir River: chief town of S Spain under the Vandals and Visigoths (5th–8th centuries); centre of Spanish colonial trade (16th–17th centuries); tourist centre. Pop: 701 927 (1998 est). Ancient name: **Hispalis** Spanish name: **Sevilla** (se'βiʎa)

Seville orange *n* **1** an orange tree of tropical and semitropical regions: grown for its bitter fruit, which is used to make marmalade **2** the fruit of this tree

Sèvres (*French* sɛvrə) *n* porcelain ware manufactured at Sèvres, near Paris, from 1756, characterized by the use of clear colours and elaborate decorative detail

sew (səʊ) *vb* **sews, sewing, sewed; sewn** *or* **sewed 1** to join or decorate (pieces of fabric, etc) by means of a thread repeatedly passed through with a needle **2** (*tr*; often foll by *on* or *up*) to attach, fasten, or close by sewing **3** (*tr*) to make (a garment, etc) by sewing ▷ See also **sew up** [OE *sēowan*]

sewage ('su:ɪdʒ) *n* waste matter from domestic or industrial establishments that is carried away in sewers or drains [c19 back formation from SEWER[1]]

sewage farm *n* a place where sewage is treated, esp for use as manure

Seward ('sju:əd) *n* **William Henry** 1801–72, US statesman; secretary of state (1861–69) He was a leading opponent of slavery and was responsible for the purchase of Alaska (1867)

Seward Peninsula ('sju:əd) *n* a peninsula of W Alaska, on the Bering Strait. Length: about 290 km (180 miles)

Sewell ('su:əl) *n* **Henry** 1807–79, New Zealand statesman, born in England: first prime minister of New Zealand (1856)

sewer[1] (sʊə) *n* **1** a drain or pipe, esp one that is underground, used to carry away surface water or sewage ▷ *vb* **2** (*tr*) to provide with sewers [c15 from OF, from *essever* to drain, from Vulgar L *exaquāre* (unattested), from L EX-[1] + *aqua* water]

sewer[2] ('səʊə) *n* a person or thing that sews

sewerage ('sʊərɪdʒ) *n* **1** an arrangement of sewers **2** the removal of surface water or sewage by means of sewers **3** another word for **sewage**

sewing ('səʊɪŋ) *n* **a** a piece of cloth, etc, that is sewn or to be sewn **b** (*as modifier*): *sewing basket*

sewing machine *n* any machine designed to sew material. It is now usually driven by electric motor but is sometimes operated by a foot treadle or by hand

sewn (səʊn) *vb* a past participle of **sew**

sew up *vb* (*tr, adv*) **1** to fasten or mend completely by sewing **2** *US* to acquire sole use or control of **3** *inf* to complete or negotiate successfully: *to sew up a deal*

sex (sɛks) *n* **1** the sum of the characteristics that distinguish organisms on the basis of their reproductive function **2** either of the two categories, male or female, into which organisms are placed on this basis **3** short for **sexual intercourse 4** feelings or behaviour resulting from the urge to gratify the sexual instinct **5** sexual matters in general ▷ *modifier* **6** of or concerning sexual matters: *sex education* **7** based on or arising from the difference between the sexes: *sex discrimination* ▷ *vb* **8** (*tr*) to ascertain the sex of [c14 from L *sexus*]

sex- *combining form* six: *sexcentenary* [from L]

sexagenarian (ˌsɛksədʒɪ'nɛərɪən) *n* **1** a person from 60 to 69 years old ▷ *adj* **2** being from 60 to 69 years old **3** of or relating to a sexagenarian [c18 from L, from *sexāgēnī* sixty each, from *sexāgintā* sixty]

Sexagesima (ˌsɛksə'dʒɛsɪmə) *n* the second Sunday before Lent [c16 from L: sixtieth, from *sexāgintā* sixty]

sexagesimal (ˌsɛksə'dʒɛsɪməl) *adj* **1** relating to or based on the number 60: *sexagesimal measurement of angles* ▷ *n* **2** a fraction in which the denominator is some power of 60

sexaholic (ˌsɛksə'hɒlɪk) *n inf* a person who is addicted to sex [c20 from SEX + -HOLIC]

sex-and-shopping *adj* (*prenomial*) (of a novel) belonging to a genre of novel in which the central character, a woman, has a number of sexual encounters, and the author mentions the name of many upmarket products

sex appeal *n* the quality or power of attracting the opposite sex

sexcentenary (ˌsɛksɛn'ti:nərɪ) *adj* **1** of or relating to 600 or a period of 600 years **2** of or celebrating a 600th anniversary ▷ *n, pl* **sexcentenaries 3** a 600th anniversary or its celebration [c18 from L *sexcentēnī* six hundred each]

sex chromosome *n* either of the chromosomes determining the sex of animals

sexed (sɛkst) *adj* **1** (*in combination*) having a specified degree of sexuality: *undersexed* **2** of, relating to, or having sexual differentiation

sex hormone *n* an animal hormone affecting development and growth of reproductive organs and related parts

sexism ('sɛksɪzəm) *n* discrimination on the basis of sex, esp the oppression of women by men > **'sexist** *n, adj*

sexless ('sɛkslɪs) *adj* **1** having or showing no sexual differentiation **2** having no sexual desires **3** sexually unattractive

sex linkage *n genetics* the condition in which a gene is located on a sex chromosome so that the character controlled by the gene is associated with either of the sexes > **'sex-ˌlinked** *adj*

sex object *n* someone, esp a woman, regarded only from the point of view of someone else's sexual desires

sexology (sɛk'sɒlədʒɪ) *n* the study of sexual behaviour in human beings > **sex'ologist** *n* > **sexological** (ˌsɛksə'lɒdʒɪkəl) *adj*

sexpartite (sɛks'pɑ:taɪt) *adj* **1** (esp of vaults, arches, etc) divided into or composed of six parts **2** involving six participants

sex shop *n* a shop selling aids to sexual activity, pornographic material, etc

sext (sɛkst) *n chiefly RC Church* the fourth of the seven canonical hours of the divine office or the prayers prescribed for it [c15 from Church L *sexta hōra* the sixth hour]

sextan ('sɛkstən) *adj* (of a fever) marked by paroxysms that recur after an interval of five days [c17 from Med. L *sextana* (*febris*) (fever) of the sixth (day)]

sextant ('sɛkstənt) *n* **1** an instrument used in navigation and consisting of a telescope through which a sighting of a heavenly body is taken, with protractors for determining its angular distance above the horizon **2** a sixth part of a circle [c17 from L *sextāns* one sixth of a unit]

sextet *or* **sextette** (sɛks'tɛt) *n* **1** *music* a group of six singers or instrumentalists or a piece of music composed for such a group **2** a group of six people or things [c19 var. of SESTET]

sex-text *inf* ▷ *vb* **1** (*tr*) to send a text message of a sexual nature to (someone) ▷ *n* **2** a text message of a sexual nature

sextillion (sɛks'tɪljən) *n, pl* **sextillions** *or* **sextillion 1** (in Britain, France, and Germany) the number represented as one followed by 36 zeros (10^{36}) **2** (in the US and Canada) the number represented as one followed by 21 zeros (10^{21}) [c17 from F, from SEX- + *-illion*, on the model of SEPTILLION]

sexto ('sɛkstəʊ) *n, pl* **sextos** another word for **sixmo**

sexton ('sɛkstən) *n* a person employed to act as caretaker of a church and often also as a bell-ringer, grave-digger, etc [c14 from OF, from Med. L *sacristānus* SACRISTAN]

sextuple ('sɛkstjʊpəl) *n* **1** a quantity or number six times as great as another ▷ *adj* **2** six times as much or as many **3** consisting of six parts or members [c17 L *sextus* sixth + *-uple*, as in QUADRUPLE]

sextuplet ('sɛkstjʊplɪt) *n* **1** one of six offspring at one birth **2** a group of six **3** *music* a group of six notes played in a time value of four

sexual ('sɛksjʊəl) *adj* **1** of or characterized by sex **2** (of reproduction) characterized by the union of male and female gametes ▷ Cf **asexual** (sense 2) [c17 from LL *sexuālis*] > **sexuality** (ˌsɛksjʊˈælɪtɪ) *n* > **ˈsexually** *adv*

sexual harassment *n* the persistent unwelcome directing of sexual remarks and looks, and unnecessary physical contact, at a person, usually a woman, esp in the work place

sexual intercourse *n* the sexual act in which the male's erect penis is inserted into the female's vagina; copulation; coitus

sexually transmitted disease *n* any of various diseases, such as syphilis or gonorrhoea, that are transmitted by sexual intercourse. Also called: **venereal disease**

sexual selection *n* an evolutionary process in animals, in which selection by females of males with certain characters results in the preservation of these characters in the species

sex up *vb* (*tr, adv*) *inf* to make (something) more interesting or exciting: *the BBC decided to sex up the book's title*

sex worker *n* a prostitute

sexy (ˈsɛksɪ) *adj* **sexier, sexiest** *inf* **1** provoking or intended to provoke sexual interest: *a sexy dress* **2** feeling sexual interest; aroused **3** interesting, exciting, or trendy: *a sexy project; a sexy new car* > **ˈsexily** *adv* > **ˈsexiness** *n*

Seychelles (seɪˈʃɛl, -ˈʃɛlz) *pl n* a group of volcanic islands in the W Indian Ocean: taken by the British from the French in 1744: became an independent republic within the Commonwealth in 1976, incorporating the British Indian Ocean Territory islands of Aldabra, Farquhar and Desroches. Languages: Creole, English, and French. Religion: Roman Catholic majority. Currency: rupee. Capital: Victoria. Pop: 80 600 (2001 est). Area: 455 sq km (176 sq miles)
▷ www.seychelles.com
▷ www.sey.net
▷ www.seychelles-online.com.sc

Seyhan (seɪˈhɑːn) *n* another name for **Adana**

Seymour (ˈsiːmɔː) *n* **Jane** ?1509–37, third wife of Henry VIII of England; mother of Edward VI

sf *or* **sfz** *music abbrev for* sforzando

SF *or* **sf** *abbrev for* science fiction

SFA *abbrev for:* **1** Scottish Football Association **2** sweet Fanny Adams. See **fanny adams**

Sfax (sfæks) *n* a port in E Tunisia, on the Gulf of Gabès: the second largest town in Tunisia; commercial centre of a phosphate region. Pop: 230 900 (1994)

SFO *abbrev for* Serious Fraud Office: the department of the British government which investigates cases of serious financial fraud

Sforza (*Italian* ˈsfɔrtsa) *n* **1** Count **Carlo** (ˈkarlo) 1873–1952, Italian statesman; leader of the anti-Fascist opposition **2 Francesco** (franˈtʃesko) 1401–66, duke of Milan (1450–66) **3** his father **Giacomuzzo** (dʒakoˈmuttso) or **Muzio** (ˈmuttsjo), original name *Attendolo*. 1369–1424, Italian condottiere and founder of the dynasty that ruled Milan (1450–1535) **4 Lodovico** (lodoˈviːko), called *the Moor*. 1451–1508, duke of Milan (1494–1500), but effective ruler from 1480; patron of Leonardo da Vinci

sforzando (sfɔːˈtsɑːndəʊ) *or* **sforzato** (sfɔːˈtsɑːtəʊ) *music* ▷ *adj, adv* **1** to be played with strong initial attack. Abbrevs: **sf, sfz** ▷ *n* **2** a symbol, mark, etc, indicating this [C19 from It., from *sforzare* to force, from Vulgar L *fortiāre* (unattested) to FORCE]

SFW (in South Africa) *abbrev for* Skellenbosch Farmers' Winery, South Africa's leading wine producer

SG *abbrev for* solicitor general

sgd *abbrev for* signed

SGML *abbrev for* standard generalized mark-up language: an international standard for defining the structure and formatting of electronic texts

sgraffito (sgræˈfiːtəʊ) *n, pl* **sgraffiti** (-tɪ) **1** a technique in mural or ceramic decoration in which the top layer of glaze, plaster, etc, is incised with a design to reveal parts of the ground **2** such a decoration [C18 from It., from *sgraffire* to scratch]

's Gravenhage (sxraːvənˈhaːxə) *n* the Dutch name for (The) **Hague**

Sgt *abbrev for* Sergeant

sh (*spelling pron* ʃʃʃ) *interj* an exclamation to request silence or quiet

Shaanxi (ˈʃænˈʃiː) *or* **Shensi** *n* a province of NW China: one of the earliest centres of Chinese civilization; largely mountainous. Capital: Xi An. Pop: 32 970 000 (2000 est). Area: 195 800 sq km (75 598 sq miles)

Shaba (ˈʃɑːbə) *n* a region of SE Democratic Republic of Congo (formerly Zaïre): site of a secessionist movement during the 1960s and again declared itself independent in 1993; important for hydroelectric power and rich mineral resources (copper and tin ore). Pop: 4 125 000 (1998 est). Area: 496 964 sq km (191 878 sq miles). Former name (until 1972): **Katanga**

shabby (ˈʃæbɪ) *adj* **shabbier, shabbiest** **1** threadbare or dilapidated in appearance **2** wearing worn and dirty clothes **3** mean or unworthy: *shabby treatment* **4** dirty or squalid [C17 from OE *sceabb* scab] > **ˈshabbily** *adv* > **ˈshabbiness** *n*

Shache (ˈʃæˈtʃeɪ), **Soche**, *or* **So-ch'e** *n* a town in W China, in the W Xinjiang Uygur AR: a centre of the caravan trade between China, India, and Transcaspian areas. Also called: **Yarkand**

shack (ʃæk) *n* **1** a roughly built hut ▷ *vb* **2** See **shack up** [C19 ?from dialect *shackly* ramshackle, from dialect *shack* to shake]

shackle (ˈʃækᵊl) *n* **1** (*often pl*) a metal ring or fastening, usually part of a pair used to secure a person's wrists or ankles **2** (*often pl*) anything that confines or restricts freedom **3** a U-shaped bracket, the open end of which is closed by a bolt (**shackle pin**), used for securing ropes, chains, etc ▷ *vb* **shackles, shackling, shackled** (*tr*) **4** to confine with or as if with shackles **5** to fasten or connect with a shackle [OE *sceacel*] > **ˈshackler** *n*

Shackleton (ˈʃækəltən) *n* Sir **Ernest Henry** 1874–1922, British explorer. He commanded three expeditions to the Antarctic (1907–09; 1914–17; 1921–22), during which the south magnetic pole was located (1909)

shack-shack *n Caribbean* **1** the dried pod of a tree, esp of the flamboyant tree, which rattles in the wind **2** a pair of maracas made from dried coconut shells or gourds containing stones or seeds **3** a child's rattle [from *sheke-sheke*, the Yoruban name for the flamboyant tree]

shack up *vb* (*intr, adv; usually foll by with*) *sl* to live, esp with a lover

shad (ʃæd) *n, pl* **shad** *or* **shads** any of various herring-like food fishes that migrate from the sea to fresh water to spawn [OE *sceadd*]

Shadbolt (ˈʃædˌbəʊlt) *n* **Maurice** born 1932, New Zealand novelist

shaddock (ˈʃædək) *n* another name for **pomelo** (sense 1) [C17 after Captain *Shaddock*, who brought its seed from the East Indies to Jamaica in 1696]

shade (ʃeɪd) *n* **1** relative darkness produced by the blocking out of light **2** a place made relatively darker or cooler than other areas by the blocking of light, esp sunlight **3** a position of relative obscurity **4** something used to provide a shield or protection from a direct source of light, such as a lampshade **5** a darker area indicated in a painting, drawing, etc, by shading **6** a colour that varies slightly from a standard colour: *a darker shade of green* **7** a slight amount: *a shade of difference* **8** *literary* a ghost ▷ *vb* **shades, shading, shaded** (*mainly tr*) **9** to screen or protect from heat, light, view, etc **10** to make darker or dimmer **11** to represent (a darker area) in (a painting, etc), by means of hatching, etc **12** (*also intr*) to change or cause to change slightly **13** to lower (a price) slightly [OE *sceadu*] > **ˈshadeless** *adj*

shades (ʃeɪdz) *pl n* **1** gathering darkness at nightfall **2** *sl*

Ss

sunglasses **3** (*often cap;* preceded by *the*) a literary term for **Hades** **4** (foll by *of*) undertones: *shades of my father!*

shading ('ʃeɪdɪŋ) *n* the graded areas of tone, lines, dots, etc, indicating light and dark in a painting or drawing

shadoof (ʃə'du:f) *n* a mechanism for raising water, consisting of a pivoted pole with a bucket at one end and a counterweight at the other, esp as used in Egypt [c19 from Egyptian Ar.]

shadow ('ʃædəʊ) *n* **1** a dark image or shape cast on a surface by the interception of light rays by an opaque body **2** an area of relative darkness **3** the dark portions of a picture **4** a hint or faint semblance: *beyond a shadow of a doubt* **5** a remnant or vestige: *a shadow of one's past self* **6** a reflection **7** a threatening influence: *a shadow over one's happiness* **8** a spectre **9** an inseparable companion **10** a person who trails another in secret, such as a detective **11** *med* a dark area on an X-ray film representing an opaque structure or part **12** (in Jungian psychology) the archetype that represents man's animal ancestors **13** *arch* shelter **14** (*modifier*) *Brit* designating a member or members of the main opposition party in Parliament who would hold ministerial office if their party were in power: *shadow cabinet* ▷ *vb* (*tr*) **15** to cast a shadow over **16** to make dark or gloomy **17** to shade from light **18** to follow or trail secretly **19** (often foll by *forth*) to represent vaguely [OE *sceadwe,* oblique case of *sceadu* shade] > **'shadower** *n*

shadow-box *vb* (*intr*) *boxing* to practise blows and footwork against an imaginary opponent > **'shadow-,boxing** *n*

shadowgraph ('ʃædəʊ,grɑ:f) *n* **1** a silhouette made by casting a shadow on a lighted surface **2** another name for **radiograph**

shadow play *n* a theatrical entertainment using shadows thrown by puppets or actors onto a lighted screen

shadow price *n econ* the calculated price of a good or service for which no market price exists

shadowy ('ʃædəʊɪ) *adj* **1** dark; shady **2** resembling a shadow in faintness **3** illusory or imaginary **4** mysterious or secretive: *a shadowy underworld figure* > **'shadowiness** *n*

Shadrach ('ʃædræk, 'ʃeɪ-) *n Old Testament* one of Daniel's three companions, who, together with Meshach and Abednego, was miraculously saved from destruction in Nebuchadnezzar's fiery furnace (Daniel 3:12–30)

shady ('ʃeɪdɪ) *adj* **shadier, shadiest** **1** shaded **2** affording or casting a shade **3** quiet or concealed **4** *inf* questionable as to honesty or legality > **'shadily** *adv* > **'shadiness** *n*

SHAEF (ʃeɪf) (in WWII) *n acronym for* Supreme Headquarters Allied Expeditionary Forces

Shaffer ('ʃæfə) *n* Sir **Peter** born 1926, British dramatist. His plays include *The Royal Hunt of the Sun* (1964), *Equus* (1973), *Amadeus* (1979), and *The Gift of the Gorgon* (1992)

shaft (ʃɑ:ft) *n* **1** the long narrow pole that forms the body of a spear, arrow, etc **2** something directed at a person in the manner of a missile **3** a ray or streak, esp of light **4** a rod or pole forming the handle of a hammer, golf club, etc **5** a revolving rod that transmits motion or power **6** one of the two wooden poles by which an animal is harnessed to a vehicle **7** *anat* the middle part of a long bone **8** the middle part of a column or pier, between the base and the capital **9** *archit* a column that supports a vaulting rib, sometimes one of a set **10** a vertical passageway through a building, as for a lift **11** a vertical passageway into a mine **12** *ornithol* the central rib of a feather **13** an archaic or literary word for **arrow** ▷ *vb* **14** *US & Canad sl* to trick or cheat [OE *sceaft*]

Shaftesbury ('ʃɑ:ftsbərɪ, -brɪ) *n* **1** **1st Earl of,** title of *Anthony Ashley Cooper.* 1621–83, English statesman, a major figure in the Whig opposition to Charles II **2** **7th Earl of,** title of *Anthony Ashley Cooper.* 1801–85, English evangelical churchman and social reformer. He promoted measures to improve conditions in mines (1842), factories (1833; 1847; 1850), and schools

shag[1] (ʃæg) *n* **1** a matted tangle, esp of hair, etc **2** a napped fabric, usually a rough wool **3** shredded coarse tobacco [OE *sceacga*]

shag[2] (ʃæg) *n* another name for the **green cormorant** (*Phalacrocorax aristotelis*) [c16 special use of SHAG[1], with reference to its crest]

shag[3] (ʃæg) *Brit sl* ▷ *vb* **shags, shagging, shagged** **1** to have sexual intercourse with (a person) **2** (*tr;* often foll by *out; usually passive*) to exhaust ▷ *n* **3** an act of sexual intercourse [c20 from ?]

shaggable ('ʃægəbᵊl) *adj Brit sl* sexually attractive

shaggy ('ʃægɪ) *adj* **shaggier, shaggiest** **1** having or covered with rough unkempt fur, hair, wool, etc: *a shaggy dog* **2** rough or unkempt > **'shaggily** *adv* > **'shagginess** *n*

shaggy dog story *n inf* a long rambling joke ending in a deliberate anticlimax, such as a pointless punch line

shagreen (ʃæ'gri:n) *n* **1** the rough skin of certain sharks and rays, used as an abrasive **2** a rough grainy leather made from certain animal hides [c17 from F *chagrin,* from Turkish *çagri* rump]

shagtastic (ʃæg'tæstɪk) *adj Brit sl* **1** sexually attractive; sexy **2** excellent; wonderful [c20 from SHAG[3] + (FAN)TASTIC]

shah (ʃɑ:) *n* a ruler of certain Middle Eastern countries, esp (formerly) Iran [c16 from Persian: king] > **'shahdom** *n*

Shah Jahan (dʒə'hɑ:n) *n* 1592–1666, Mogul emperor (1628–58). During his reign the finest monuments of Mogul architecture in India were built, including the Taj Mahal and the Pearl Mosque at Agra

Shahjahanpur (,ʃɑ:dʒə,hɑ:n'pʊə) *n* a city in N India, in central Uttar Pradesh: founded in 1647 in the reign of Shah Jahan. Pop: 237 713 (1991)

Shah of Iran (ʃɑ:) *n* See (Mohammed Reza) **Pahlavi**[1]

shahtoosh (ʃɑ:'tu:ʃ) *n* a soft wool that comes from the protected Tibetan antelope [c19 Persian *šāh* king + Kashmiri *tośá* material]

Shaka *or* **Chaka** ('ʃaka) *n* died 1828, Zulu military leader, who founded the Zulu Empire in southern Africa

shake (ʃeɪk) *vb* **shakes, shaking, shook, shaken** **1** to move or cause to move up and down or back and forth with short quick movements **2** to sway or totter or cause to sway or totter **3** to clasp or grasp (the hand) of (a person) in greeting, agreement, etc: *he shook John's hand* **4** **shake hands** to clasp hands in greeting, agreement, etc **5** **shake on it** *inf* to shake hands in agreement, reconciliation, etc **6** to bring or come to a specified condition by or as if by shaking: *he shook free and ran* **7** (*tr*) to wave or brandish: *he shook his sword* **8** (*tr;* often foll by *up*) to rouse or agitate **9** (*tr*) to shock, disturb, or upset: *he was shaken by the news* **10** (*tr*) to undermine or weaken: *the crisis shook his faith* **11** to mix (dice) by rattling in a cup or the hand before throwing **12** *Austral old-fashioned sl* to steal **13** (*tr*) *US & Canad inf* to get rid of **14** *music* to perform a trill on (a note) **15** **shake in one's shoes** to tremble with fear or apprehension **16** **shake one's head** to indicate disagreement or disapproval by moving the head from side to side ▷ *n* **17** the act or an instance of shaking **18** a tremor or vibration **19** **the shakes** *inf* a state of uncontrollable trembling or a condition that causes it, such as a fever **20** *inf* a very short period of time: *in half a shake* **21** a fissure or crack in timber or rock **22** an instance of shaking dice before casting **23** *music* another word for **trill** (sense 1) **24** an informal name for **earthquake** **25** short for **milk shake** **26** **no great shakes** *inf* of no great merit or value ▷ See also **shake down, shake off, shake up** [OE *sceacan*] > **'shakable** *or* **'shakeable** *adj*

shake down *vb* (*adv*) **1** to fall or settle or cause to fall or settle by shaking **2** (*tr*) *US sl* to extort money from, esp by blackmail **3** (*tr*) *inf, chiefly US* to submit (a vessel, etc) to a shakedown test **4** (*intr*) to go to bed, esp to a makeshift bed ▷ *n* **shakedown 5** *US sl* a swindle or act of extortion **6** a makeshift bed, esp of straw, blankets, etc **7** *inf, chiefly US* **7a** a voyage to test the performance of a ship or aircraft or to familiarize the crew with their duties **7b** (*as modifier*): *a shakedown run*

shake off *vb* (*adv*) **1** to remove or be removed with or as if with a quick movement: *she shook off her depression* **2** (*tr*) to escape from; elude: *they shook off the police*

shaker (ˈʃeɪkə) *n* **1** a person or thing that shakes **2** a container from which a condiment is shaken **3** a container in which the ingredients of alcoholic drinks are shaken together

Shakers (ˈʃeɪkəz) *pl n* **the** an American millenarian sect, founded in 1747 as an offshoot of the Quakers, given to ecstatic shaking and practising common ownership of property

Shakespeare (ˈʃeɪkspɪə) *n* **William** 1564–1616, English dramatist and poet. He was born and died at Stratford-upon-Avon but spent most of his life as an actor and playwright in London. His plays with approximate dates of composition are: *Henry VI, Parts I–III* (1590–92); *Richard III* (1592); *The Comedy of Errors* (1592); *Titus Andronicus* (1593); *The Taming of the Shrew* (1593); *The Two Gentlemen of Verona* (1593); *Love's Labour's Lost* (1594); *Romeo and Juliet* (1595); *Richard II* (1595); *A Midsummer Night's Dream* (1595); *King John* (1596); *The Merchant of Venice* (1596); *Henry IV, Parts I–II* (1597); *Much Ado about Nothing* (1598); *The Merry Wives of Windsor* (1598); *Henry V* (1599); *Julius Caesar* (1599); *As You Like It* (1599); *Twelfth Night* (1599); *Hamlet* (1600); *Troilus and Cressida* (1601); *All's Well that ends Well* (1602); *Measure for Measure* (1604); *Othello* (1604); *King Lear* (1605); *Macbeth* (1605); *Antony and Cleopatra* (1606); *Coriolanus* (1607); *Timon of Athens* (1607); *Pericles* (1608); *Cymbeline* (1609); *The Winter's Tale* (1610); *The Tempest* (1611); and, possibly in collaboration with John Fletcher, *Henry VIII* (1612) and *Two Noble Kinsmen* (1613). His *Sonnets*, variously addressed to a fair young man and a dark lady, were published in 1609

Shakespearean *or* **Shakespearian** (ʃeɪkˈspɪərɪən) *adj* **1** of, relating to, or characteristic of Shakespeare or his works ▷ *n* **2** a student of or specialist in Shakespeare's works

Shakespearean sonnet *n* a sonnet form developed in 16th-century England and employed by Shakespeare, having the rhyme scheme a b a b c d c d e f e f g g

shake up *vb* (*tr, adv*) **1** to shake in order to mix **2** to reorganize drastically **3** to stir **4** to restore the shape of (a pillow, etc) **5** *inf* to shock mentally or physically ▷ *n* **shake-up 6** *inf* a radical reorganization

Shakhty (*Russian* ˈʃaxtɪ) *n* an industrial city in W Russia: the chief town of the E Donets Basin; a major coal-mining centre. Pop: 224 400 (1999 est)

shako (ˈʃækəʊ) *n, pl* **shakos** *or* **shakoes** a tall usually cylindrical military headdress, having a plume and often a peak [c19 via F from Hungarian *csákó*, from MHG *zacke* a sharp point]

shaky (ˈʃeɪkɪ) *adj* **shakier, shakiest 1** tending to shake or tremble **2** liable to prove defective **3** uncertain or questionable: *your arguments are very shaky* > ˈ**shakily** *adv* > ˈ**shakiness** *n*

shale (ʃeɪl) *n* a dark fine-grained sedimentary rock formed by compression of successive layers of clay-rich sediment [OE *scealu* shell] > ˈ**shaly** *adj*

shale oil *n* an oil distilled from shales and used as fuel

shall (ʃæl; *unstressed* ʃəl) *vb past* **should** (takes an infinitive without *to* or an implied infinitive) used as an auxiliary: **1** (esp with I or *we* as subject) to make the future tense: *we shall see you tomorrow* ▷ Cf **will**[1] (sense 1) **2** (with *you, he, she, it, they*, or a noun as subject) **2a** to indicate determination on the part of the speaker, as in issuing a threat: *you shall pay for this!* **2b** to indicate compulsion, now esp in official documents **2c** to indicate certainty or inevitability: *our day shall come* **3** (*with any noun or pronoun as subject, esp in conditional clauses or clauses expressing doubt*) to indicate nonspecific futurity: *I don't think I shall ever see her again* [OE *sceal*]

> **USAGE** The usual rule given for the use of *shall* and *will* is that where the meaning is one of an action in the future, *shall* is used with I and *we* and *will* with all other subjects: *I shall go tomorrow*; *they will be there now*. Where the meaning involves command, obligation, or determination, the reverse is true: *it shall be done*; *I will definitely go*. However, *shall* has largely been ousted in favour of *will*, which has become the commonest form of the future with all subjects

shallop (ˈʃæləp) *n* a light boat used for rowing in shallow water [c16 from F *chaloupe*, from Du. *sloep* sloop]

shallot (ʃəˈlɒt) *n* **1** an alliaceous plant cultivated for its edible bulb **2** the bulb of this plant, which divides into small sections and is used in cooking for flavouring [c17 from OF, from *eschaloigne*, from L *Ascalōnia caepa* Ascalonian onion, from *Ascalon*, a Palestinian town]

shallow (ˈʃæləʊ) *adj* **1** having little depth **2** lacking intellectual or mental depth or subtlety ▷ *n* **3** (*often pl*) a shallow place in a body of water ▷ *vb* **4** to make or become shallow [c15 rel. to OE *sceald* shallow] > ˈ**shallowly** *adv* > ˈ**shallowness** *n*

shalom aleichem *Hebrew* (ʃaˈlɔm aˈlexɛm) *sentence substitute* peace be to you: used by Jews as a greeting or farewell. Often shortened to **shalom**

shalt (ʃælt) *vb arch or dialect* (used with the pronoun *thou*) a singular form of the present tense (indicative mood) of **shall**

shalwar (ˈʃæwɑː) *pl n* loose-fitting trousers tapering to a narrow fit around the ankles, worn in the Indian subcontinent, often with a kameez [from Urdu and Persian *shalwār*]

Ss

sham (ʃæm) *n* **1** anything that is not what it appears to be **2** something false or fictitious that purports to be genuine **3** a person who pretends to be something other than he or she is ▷ *adj* **4** counterfeit or false ▷ *vb* **shams, shamming, shammed 5** to assume the appearance of (something); counterfeit: *to sham illness* [c17 ? a N English dialect var. of SHAME]

shaman (ˈʃæmən) *n* **1** a priest of shamanism **2** a medicine man of a similar religion, esp among certain tribes of North American Indians [c17 from Russian *shaman*, ult. from Sansk. *śrama* religious exercise]

shamanism (ˈʃæməˌnɪzəm) *n* **1** the religion of certain peoples of northern Asia, based on the belief that the world is pervaded by good and evil spirits who can be influenced or controlled only by the shamans **2** any similar religion involving forms of spiritualism > ˈ**shamanist** *n, adj*

▷ www.shamanism.co.uk/
▷ www.faqs.org/faqs/shamanism/overview/

Shamash (ˈʃɑːmæʃ) *n* the sun god of Assyria and Babylonia [from Akkadian: sun]

shamateur (ˈʃæmətə) *n* a sportsperson who is officially an amateur but accepts payment [c20 from SHAM + AMATEUR]

shamble (ˈʃæmb°l) *vb* **shambles, shambling, shambled 1** (*intr*) to walk or move along in an awkward or unsteady way ▷ *n* **2** an awkward or unsteady walk [c17 from *shamble* (adj) ungainly, ?from *shamble legs* legs resembling those of a meat vendor's table; see SHAMBLES] > ˈ**shambling** *adj, n*

shambles (ˈʃæmb°lz) *n* (*functioning as sing or pl*) **1** a place of great disorder: *the room was a shambles after the party* **2** a place where animals are brought to be slaughtered

3 any place of slaughter or carnage [c14 *shamble* table used by meat vendors, from OE *sceamel* stool, from LL *scamellum* a small bench, from L *scamnum* stool]

shambolic (ʃæm'bɒlɪk) *adj inf* completely disorganized; chaotic [c20 from SHAMBLES]

shame (ʃeɪm) *n* **1** a painful emotion resulting from an awareness of having done something dishonourable, unworthy, etc **2** capacity to feel such an emotion **3** ignominy or disgrace **4** a person or thing that causes this **5** an occasion for regret, disappointment, etc: *it's a shame you can't come with us* **6 put to shame 6a** to disgrace **6b** to surpass totally ▷ *vb* **shames, shaming, shamed** (*tr*) **7** to cause to feel shame **8** to bring shame on **9** (often foll by *into*) to compel through a sense of shame **10 name and shame** See **name** (sense 8) ▷ *interj* **11** *S African inf* **11a** an expression of sympathy **11b** an expression of pleasure or endearment [OE *scamu*] > '**shamable** *or* '**shameable** *adj*

shamefaced ('ʃeɪm,feɪst) *adj* **1** bashful or modest **2** showing a sense of shame [c16 alteration of earlier *shamefast*, from OE *sceamfaest*] > **shamefacedly** (ʃeɪm'feɪsɪdlɪ) *adv*

shameful ('ʃeɪmfʊl) *adj* causing or deserving shame > '**shamefully** *adv* > '**shamefulness** *n*

shameless ('ʃeɪmlɪs) *adj* **1** having no sense of shame **2** without decency or modesty > '**shamelessly** *adv* > '**shamelessness** *n*

Shamir (ʃæ'mɪə) *n* **Yitzhak** ('jɪtʒæk) born 1915, Israeli statesman, born in Poland: prime minister (1983–84; 1986–92): foreign minister (1980–83; 1984–86)

shammy ('ʃæmɪ) *n, pl* **shammies** *inf* another word for **chamois** (sense 3) Also called: **shammy leather** [c18 variant of CHAMOIS]

Shamo ('ʃɑː'məʊ) *n* transliteration of the Chinese name for the **Gobi**

shampoo (ʃæm'puː) *n* **1** a preparation of soap or detergent to wash the hair **2** a similar preparation for washing carpets, etc **3** the process of shampooing ▷ *vb* **shampoos, shampooing, shampooed** (*tr*) **4** to wash (the hair, etc) with such a preparation [c18 from Hindi, from *chāmpnā* to knead]

shamrock ('ʃæm,rɒk) *n* a plant having leaves divided into three leaflets: the national emblem of Ireland [c16 from Irish Gaelic *seamrōg*, dim. of *seamar* clover]

shamus ('ʃɑːməs, 'ʃeɪ-) *n, pl* **shamuses** *US sl* a police or private detective [prob. from *shammes* caretaker of a synagogue, infl. by Irish *Séamas* James]

Shandong ('ʃæn'dʌŋ) *or* **Shantung** *n* a province of NE China, on the Yellow Sea and the Gulf of Chihli: part of the earliest organized state of China (1520–1030 BC); consists chiefly of the fertile plain of the lower Yellow River, with mountains over 1500 m (5000 ft) high in the centre. Capital: Jinan. Pop: 90 790 000 (2000 est). Area: 153 300 sq km (59 189 sq miles)

shandy ('ʃændɪ) *n, pl* **shandies** an alcoholic drink made of beer and ginger beer or lemonade [c19 from ?]

Shang (ʃæŋ) *n* **1** the dynasty ruling in China from about the 18th to the 12th centuries BC ▷ *adj* **2** of or relating to the pottery produced during the Shang dynasty
▷ www.chinaknowledge.org/History/Myth/shang.htm

shanghai ('ʃæŋhaɪ, ʃæŋ'haɪ) *sl* ▷ *vb* **shanghais, shanghaiing, shanghaied** (*tr*) **1** to kidnap (a man or seaman) for enforced service at sea **2** to force or trick (someone) into doing something, etc **3** *Austral & NZ* to shoot with a catapult ▷ *n* **4** *Austral & NZ* a catapult [c19 from the city of SHANGHAI; from the forceful methods formerly used to collect crews for voyages to the Orient]

Shanghai ('ʃæŋ'haɪ) *n* a port in E China, in SE Jiangsu near the estuary of the Yangtze: the largest city in China and one of the largest ports in the world; a major cultural and industrial centre, with two universities. Pop: 8 937 175 (1999 est)

Shangri-la (ʃæŋgrɪ'lɑː) *n* a remote or imaginary utopia [c20 from the name of an imaginary valley in the Himalayas, from *Lost Horizon* (1933), a novel by James Hilton]

shank (ʃæŋk) *n* **1** *anat* the shin **2** the corresponding part of the leg in vertebrates other than man **3** a cut of meat from the top part of an animal's shank **4** the main part of a tool, between the working part and the handle **5** the part of a bolt between the thread and the head **6** the ring or stem on the back of some buttons **7** the stem or long narrow part of a key, hook, spoon handle, nail, etc **8** the band of a ring as distinguished from the setting **9** the part of a shoe connecting the wide part of the sole with the heel **10** *printing* the body of a piece of type ▷ *vb* **11** (*intr*) (of fruits, roots, etc) to show disease symptoms, esp discoloration **12** (*tr*) *golf* to mishit (the ball) with the foot of the shaft [OE *scanca*]

Shankar ('ʃæŋkɑː) *n* **Ravi** ('rɑːviː) born 1920, Indian sitarist

Shankaracharya ('ʃʌŋkərɑː'tʃɑːrjə) *or* **Shankara** ('ʃʌŋkərə) *n* 9th century AD, Hindu philosopher and teacher; chief exponent of Vedanta philosophy

Shankly ('ʃæŋklɪ) *n* **Bill** 1913–81, Scottish footballer and manager of Liverpool FC (1959–74)

shanks's pony *or US* **shanks's mare** ('ʃæŋksɪz) *n inf* one's own legs as a means of transportation

Shannon[1] ('ʃænən) *n* a river in the Republic of Ireland, rising in NW Co Cavan and flowing south to the Atlantic by an estuary 113 km (70 miles) long: the longest river in the Republic of Ireland. Length: 260 km (161 miles)

Shannon[2] ('ʃænən) *n* **Claude** (**Elwood**) 1916–2000, US mathematician, who first developed information theory

shanny ('ʃænɪ) *n, pl* **shannies** a European blenny of rocky coastal waters [c19 from ?]

Shansi ('ʃæn'siː) *n* a variant transliteration of the Chinese name for **Shanxi**

Shan State (ʃɑːn, ʃæn) *n* an administrative division of E Myanmar: formed in 1947 from the joining of the Federation of Shan States with the Wa States; consists of the **Shan plateau** crossed by forested mountain ranges reaching over 2100 m (7000 ft). Pop: 4 416 000 (1994 est). Area: 149 743 sq km (57 816 sq miles)

shan't (ʃɑːnt) *contraction of* shall not

Shantou *or* **Shantow** ('ʃæn'taʊ) *n* a port in SE China, in E Guangdong near the mouth of the Han River: became a treaty port in 1869. Pop: 831 949 (1999 est). Also called: **Swatow**

shantung (ʃæn'tʌŋ) *n* **1** a heavy silk fabric with a knobbly surface **2** a cotton or rayon imitation of this [c19 after SHANTUNG]

Shantung ('ʃæn'tʌŋ) *n* a variant transliteration of the Chinese name for **Shandong**

shanty[1] ('ʃæntɪ) *n, pl* **shanties 1** a ramshackle hut; crude dwelling **2** *Austral* a public house, esp an unlicensed one [c19 from Canad F *chantier* cabin built in a lumber camp, from OF *gantier* GANTRY]

shanty[2] ('ʃæntɪ) *or* **chanty** *n, pl* **shanties** *or* **chanties** a song originally sung by sailors, esp a rhythmic one forming an accompaniment to work [c19 from F *chanter* to sing; see CHANT]

shantytown ('ʃæntɪ,taʊn) *n* a town or section of a town or city inhabited by very poor people living in shanties

Shanxi ('ʃæn'ʃiː) *or* **Shansi** *n* a province of N China: China's richest coal reserves and much heavy industry. Capital: Taiyuan. Pop: 32 970 000 (2000 est). Area: 157 099 sq km (60 656 sq miles)

shape (ʃeɪp) *n* **1** the outward form of an object defined by outline **2** the figure or outline of the body of a person **3** a phantom **4** organized or definite form: *my plans are taking shape* **5** the form that anything assumes **6** pattern; mould **7** condition or state of efficiency: *to be in good shape* **8 out of shape 8a** in bad physical condition

8b bent, twisted, or deformed **9 take shape** to assume a definite form ▷ *vb* **shapes, shaping, shaped 10** (when *intr*, often foll by *into* or *up*) to receive or cause to receive shape or form **11** (*tr*) to mould into a particular pattern or form **12** (*tr*) to plan, devise, or prepare: *to shape a plan of action* ▷ See also **shape up** [OE *gesceap*, lit.: that which is created, from *scieppan* to create] > **'shapable** *or* **'shapeable** *adj* > **'shaper** *n*

SHAPE (ʃeɪp) *n acronym for* Supreme Headquarters Allied Powers Europe

-shaped (ʃeɪpt) *adj combining form* having the shape of: *an L-shaped room; a pear-shaped figure*

shapeless ('ʃeɪplɪs) *adj* **1** having no definite shape or form: *a shapeless mass* **2** lacking a symmetrical or aesthetically pleasing shape: *a shapeless figure* > **'shapelessness** *n*

shapely ('ʃeɪplɪ) *adj* **shapelier, shapeliest** (esp of a woman's body or legs) pleasing or attractive in shape > **'shapeliness** *n*

shape up *vb* (*intr, adv*) *Inf* **1** to proceed or develop satisfactorily **2** to develop a definite or proper form

shard (ʃɑːd) *or* **sherd** *n* **1** a broken piece or fragment of a brittle substance, esp of pottery **2** *zool* a tough sheath, scale, or shell, esp the elytra of a beetle [OE *sceard*]

share¹ (ʃɛə) *n* **1** a part or portion of something owned or contributed by a person or group **2** (*often pl*) any of the equal parts, usually of low par value, into which the capital stock of a company is divided **3 go shares** *inf* to share (something) with another or others ▷ *vb* **shares, sharing, shared 4** (*tr*; often foll by *out*) to divide or apportion, esp equally **5** (when *intr*, often foll by *in*) to receive or contribute a portion of: *we can share the cost of the petrol* **6** to join with another or others in the use of (something): *can I share your umbrella?* [OE *scearu*] > **'sharable** *or* **'shareable** *adj* > **'sharer** *n*

share² (ʃɛə) *n* short for **ploughshare** [OE *scear*]

sharecrop ('ʃɛəˌkrɒp) *vb* **sharecrops, sharecropping, sharecropped** *chiefly US* to cultivate (farmland) as a sharecropper

sharecropper ('ʃɛəˌkrɒpə) *n chiefly US* a farmer, esp a tenant farmer, who pays over a proportion of a crop or crops as rent

shared ownership *n* (in Britain) a form of house purchase whereby the purchaser buys a proportion of the dwelling, usually from a local authority or housing association, and rents the rest

share-farmer *n chiefly Austral* a farmer who pays a fee to another in return for use of land to raise crops, etc

shareholder ('ʃɛəˌhəʊldə) *n* the owner of one or more shares in a company

share index *n* an index showing the movement of share prices. See **FT Index**

share market *n* the usual NZ and Austral name for **stock exchange**

share-milker *n* (in New Zealand) a person who lives on a dairy farm and milks the farmer's herd in return for an agreed share of the profits

share option *n* a scheme giving employees an option to buy shares in the company for which they work at a favourable price or discount

share premium *n Brit* the excess of the amount actually subscribed for an issue of corporate capital over its par value

share shop *n* a stockbroker, bank, or other financial intermediary that handles the buying and selling of shares for members of the public, esp during a privatization issue

shareware ('ʃɛəˌwɛə) *n computing* software available to all users without the need for a licence and for which a token fee is requested

sharia *or* **sheria** (ʃə'riːə) *n* the body of doctrines that regulate the lives of those who profess Islam [Ar.]

sharif (ʃæ'riːf) *n* a variant transliteration of **sherif**

shark¹ (ʃɑːk) *n* any of various usually ferocious fishes, with a long body, two dorsal fins, and rows of sharp teeth [c16 from ?] > **'sharkˌlike** *adj*

shark² (ʃɑːk) *n* a person who preys on or victimizes others, esp by swindling or extortion [c18 prob. from G *Schurke* rogue]

shark repellent *pl n* **1** any of various substances used by divers to deter shark attack **2** (*pl*) *finance* another name for **porcupine provisions**

sharkskin ('ʃɑːkˌskɪn) *n* a smooth glossy fabric of acetate rayon, used for sportswear, etc

shark watcher *n inf* a business consultant who assists companies in identifying and preventing unwelcome takeover bids

Sharon¹ ('ʃærən) *n* **Plain of** a plain in W Israel, between the Mediterranean and the hills of Samaria, extending from Haifa to Tel Aviv

Sharon² (ʃæ'rɒn) *n* **Ariel** ('ærɪəl) born 1928, Israeli politician and soldier; Likud prime minister from 2001

sharon fruit ('ʃærən) *n* another name for **persimmon** (sense 2)

sharp (ʃɑːp) *adj* **1** having a keen edge suitable for cutting **2** having an edge or point **3** involving a sudden change, esp in direction: *a sharp bend* **4** moving, acting, or reacting quickly, etc: *sharp reflexes* **5** clearly defined **6** mentally acute; keen-witted; attentive **7** sly or artful: *sharp practice* **8** bitter or harsh: *sharp words* **9** shrill or penetrating: *a sharp cry* **10** having an acrid taste **11** keen; biting: *a sharp wind* **12** *music* **12a** (*immediately postpositive*) denoting a note that has been raised in pitch by one chromatic semitone: *F sharp* **12b** (of an instrument, voice, etc) out of tune by being too high in pitch ▷ Cf **flat¹** (sense 20) **13** *inf* **13a** stylish **13b** too smart **14 at the sharp end** involved in the most competitive or difficult aspect of any activity ▷ *adv* **15** in a sharp manner **16** exactly: *six o'clock sharp* **17** *music* **17a** higher than a standard pitch **17b** out of tune by being too high in pitch: *she sings sharp* ▷ Cf **flat¹** (sense 25) ▷ *n* **18** *music* **18a** an accidental that raises the pitch of a note by one chromatic semitone. Usual symbol: ♯ **18b** a note affected by this accidental ▷ Cf **flat¹** (sense 31) **19** a thin needle with a sharp point **20** *inf* a sharper ▷ *vb* **21** (*tr*) *music* the usual US and Canad word for **sharpen** [OE *scearp*] > **'sharply** *adv* > **'sharpness** *n*

Sharp (ʃɑːp) *n* **Cecil (James)** 1859–1924, British musician, best known for collecting, editing, and publishing English folk songs

sharpbender ('ʃɑːpˌbɛndə) *n inf* an organization that has been underperforming its competitors but suddenly becomes more successful, often as a result of new management or changes in its business strategy [c20 from the sharp upward bend in its sales or profits]

sharpen ('ʃɑːpᵊn) *vb* **1** to make or become sharp or sharper **2** *music* to raise the pitch of (a note), esp by one semitone > **'sharpener** *n*

sharper ('ʃɑːpə) *n* a person who cheats or swindles; fraud

Sharpeville ('ʃɑːpvɪl) *n* a town in E South Africa: scene of riots in 1960, when 69 demonstrators died, 1984, and 1985, when 19 died

sharpish ('ʃɑːpɪʃ) *adj* **1** rather sharp ▷ *adv* **2** *inf* quickly; fairly sharply: *quick sharpish*

sharp-set *adj* **1** set to give an acute cutting angle **2** keenly hungry **3** keen or eager

sharpshooter ('ʃɑːpˌʃuːtə) *n* an expert marksman > **'sharpˌshooting** *n*

sharp-tongued *adj* bitter or critical in speech; sarcastic

sharp-witted *adj* having or showing a keen intelligence; perceptive > **ˌsharp-'wittedly** *adv* > **ˌsharp-'wittedness** *n*

Shasta daisy ('ʃæstə) *n* a plant widely cultivated for its large white daisy-like flowers

shastra ('ʃɑːstrə), **shaster** ('ʃɑːstə), *or* **sastra** ('ʃɑːstrə) *n* any of the sacred writings of Hinduism [c17 from

Ss

Sansk. *śāstra*, from *śās* to teach]

shat (ʃæt) *vb taboo* a past tense and past participle of **shit**

Shatt-al-Arab (ˈʃætælˈærəb) *n* a river in SE Iraq, formed by the confluence of the Tigris and Euphrates Rivers: flows southeast as part of the border between Iraq and Iran to the Persian Gulf. Length: 193 km (120 miles)

shatter (ˈʃætə) *vb* **1** to break or be broken into many small pieces **2** (*tr*) to impair or destroy: *his nerves were shattered by the torture* **3** (*tr*) to dumbfound or thoroughly upset: *she was shattered by the news* **4** (*tr*) *inf* to cause to be tired out or exhausted [c12 ? obscurely rel. to SCATTER] > **ˈshattered** *adj* > **ˈshattering** *adj* > **ˈshatteringly** *adv*

shatterproof (ˈʃætəˌpruːf) *adj* designed to resist shattering

shave (ʃeɪv) *vb* **shaves, shaving, shaved; shaved** *or* **shaven** (*mainly tr*) **1** (*also intr*) to remove (the beard, hair, etc) from (the face, head, or body) by scraping the skin with a razor **2** to cut or trim very closely **3** to reduce to shavings **4** to remove thin slices from (wood, etc) with a sharp cutting tool **5** to touch or graze in passing **6** *inf* to reduce (a price) by a slight amount ▷ *n* **7** the act or an instance of shaving **8** any tool for scraping **9** a thin slice or shaving [OE *sceafan*] > **ˈshavable** *or* **ˈshaveable** *adj*

shaveling (ˈʃeɪvlɪŋ) *n arch* **1** *derog* a priest or clergyman with a shaven head **2** a young fellow; youth

shaven (ˈʃeɪvᵊn) *adj* **a** closely shaved or tonsured **b** (*in combination*): *clean-shaven*

shaver (ˈʃeɪvə) *n* **1** a person or thing that shaves **2** Also called: **electric razor, electric shaver** an electrically powered implement for shaving, having rotating blades behind a fine metal comb **3** *inf* a youngster, esp a young boy

Shavian (ˈʃeɪvɪən) *adj* **1** of or like George Bernard Shaw (1856–1950), Irish dramatist, his works, ideas, etc ▷ *n* **2** an admirer of Shaw or his works

shaving (ˈʃeɪvɪŋ) *n* **1** a thin paring or slice, esp of wood, that has been shaved from something ▷ *modifier* **2** used when shaving the face, etc: *shaving cream*

Shavuot *or* **Shabuoth** (ʃəˈvuːəs, -əʊs; *Hebrew* ʃavuːˈɔt) *n* the Hebrew name for **Pentecost** (sense 2) [from Heb. *shābhūʿōth*, pl of *shābhūaʿ* week]

Shaw (ʃɔː) *n* **1** **Artie,** original name *Arthur Arshawsky*. born 1910, US jazz clarinettist, band leader, and composer **2** **George Bernard,** often known as *GBS*. 1856–1950, Irish dramatist and critic, in England from 1876. He was an active socialist and became a member of the Fabian Society but his major works are effective as satiric attacks rather than political tracts. These include *Arms and the Man* (1894), *Candida* (1894), *Man and Superman* (1903), *Major Barbara* (1905), *Pygmalion* (1913), *Back to Methuselah* (1921), and *St. Joan* (1923): Nobel prize for literature 1925 **3** **Richard Norman** 1831–1912, English architect **4** **Thomas Edward** the name assumed by (T E) **Lawrence** after 1927

shawl (ʃɔːl) *n* a piece of fabric or knitted or crocheted material worn around the shoulders by women or wrapped around a baby [c17 from Persian *shāl*]

shawm (ʃɔːm) *n music* a medieval form of the oboe with a conical bore and flaring bell [c14 *shalmye*, from OF *chalemie*, ult. from L *calamus* a reed, from Gk *kalamos*]

shay (ʃeɪ) *n* a dialect word for **chaise** [c18 back formation from CHAISE, mistaken for pl]

Shcheglovsk (*Russian* ʃtʃɪgˈlɔfsk) *n* the former name (until 1932) of **Kemerovo**

Shcherbakov (*Russian* ʃtʃɪrbaˈkɔf) *n* a former name (from the Revolution until 1957) of **Rybinsk**

she (ʃiː) *pron* (*subjective*) **1** refers to a female person or animal: *she is a doctor* **2** refers to things personified as feminine, such as cars, ships, and nations **3** *Austral & NZ* a pronoun often used instead of *it*, as in **she'll be right** (it will be all right) ▷ *n* **4a** a female person or animal **4b** (*in combination*): *she-cat* [OE *sīe*, accusative of *sēo*, fem. demonstrative pron]

shea (ʃɪə) *n* **1** a tropical African tree with oily seeds **2** **shea butter** the white butter-like fat obtained from the seeds of this plant and used as food, etc [c18 from W African *si*]

sheading (ˈʃiːdɪŋ) *n* any of the six subdivisions of the Isle of Man [var. of *shedding*]

sheaf (ʃiːf) *n, pl* **sheaves** **1** a bundle of reaped but unthreshed corn tied with one or two bonds **2** a bundle of objects tied together **3** the arrows contained in a quiver ▷ *vb* **4** (*tr*) to bind or tie into a sheaf [OE *sceaf*]

shear (ʃɪə) *vb* **shears, shearing, sheared** *or* (*arch, Austral, & NZ*) *sometimes* **shore; sheared** *or* **shorn** **1** (*tr*) to remove (the fleece or hair) of (sheep, etc) by cutting or clipping **2** to cut or cut through (something) with shears or a sharp instrument **3** *engineering* to cause (a part, member, etc) to deform or fracture or (of a part, etc) to deform or fracture as a result of excess torsion **4** (*tr; often foll by of*) to strip or divest: *to shear someone of his power* **5** (when *intr*, foll by *through*) to move through (something) by or as if by cutting ▷ *n* **6** the act, process, or an instance of shearing **7** a shearing of a sheep or flock of sheep: *a sheep of two shears* **8** a form of deformation or fracture in which parallel planes in a body slide over one another **9** *physics* the deformation of a body, part, etc, expressed as the lateral displacement between two points in parallel planes divided by the distance between the planes **10** either one of the blades of a pair of shears, scissors, etc ▷ See also **shears** [OE *sceran*] > **ˈshearer** *n*

shearling (ˈʃɪəlɪŋ) *n* **1** a young sheep after its first shearing **2** the skin of such an animal

shear pin *n* an easily replaceable pin in a machine designed to break and stop the machine if the stress becomes too great

shears (ʃɪəz) *pl n* **1a** large scissors, as for cutting cloth, jointing poultry, etc **1b** a large scissor-like and usually hand-held cutting tool with flat blades, as for cutting hedges **2** any of various analogous cutting implements

shearwater (ˈʃɪəˌwɔːtə) *n* any of several oceanic birds specialized for an aerial or aquatic existence

sheatfish (ˈʃiːtˌfɪʃ) *n, pl* **sheatfish** *or* **sheatfishes** another name for **European catfish** (see **silurid** (sense 1)) [c16 var. of *sheathfish*; ? infl. by G *Schaid* sheatfish]

sheath (ʃiːθ) *n, pl* **sheaths** (ʃiːðz) **1** a case or covering for the blade of a knife, sword, etc **2** any similar close-fitting case **3** *biol* an enclosing or protective structure **4** the protective covering on an electric cable **5** a figure-hugging dress with a narrow tapering skirt **6** another name for **condom** [OE *scēath*]

sheathe (ʃiːð) *vb* **sheathes, sheathing, sheathed** (*tr*) **1** to insert (a knife, sword, etc) into a sheath **2** (esp of cats) to retract (the claws) **3** to surface with or encase in a sheath or sheathing

sheathing (ˈʃiːðɪŋ) *n* **1** any material used as an outer layer, as on a ship's hull **2** boarding, etc, used to cover a timber frame

sheath knife *n* a knife carried in or protected by a sheath

sheave[1] (ʃiːv) *vb* **sheaves, sheaving, sheaved** (*tr*) to gather or bind into sheaves

sheave[2] (ʃiːv) *n* a wheel with a grooved rim, esp one used as a pulley [c14 of Gmc origin]

sheaves (ʃiːvz) *n* the plural of **sheaf**

Sheba[1] (ˈʃiːbə) *n* **1** Also called: **Saba** the ancient kingdom of the Sabeans: a rich trading nation dealing in gold, spices, and precious stones (I Kings 10) **2** the region inhabited by this nation, located in the SW corner of the Arabian peninsula: modern Yemen

Sheba[2] (ˈʃiːbə) *n* **Queen of** *Old Testament* a queen of the Sabeans, who visited Solomon (I Kings 10:1–13)

shebang (ʃɪˈbæŋ) *n sl, chiefly US & Canad* a situation or affair (esp in **the whole shebang**) [c19 from ?]

shebeen *or* **shebean** (ʃəˈbiːn) *n* **1** *Irish, Scot, & S African* a place where alcoholic drink is sold illegally **2** (in Ireland) alcohol, esp home-distilled whiskey, sold without a licence **3** (in South Africa) a place where Black African men engage in social drinking [C18 from Irish Gaelic *síbín* beer of poor quality]

shebeen king *or* (*fem*) **shebeen queen** *n* (in South Africa) the proprietor of a shebeen

Shechem ('ʃɛkəm, -ɛm) *n* the ancient name of **Nablus**

shed¹ (ʃɛd) *n* **1** a small building or lean-to of light construction, used for storage, shelter, etc **2** a large roofed structure, esp one with open sides, used for storage, repairing locomotives, etc **3** *Austral & NZ* the building in which sheep are shorn [OE *sced*; prob. var. of *scead* shelter]

shed² (ʃɛd) *vb* **sheds, shedding, shed** (*mainly tr*) **1** to pour forth or cause to pour forth: *to shed tears* **2 shed light on** *or* **upon** to clarify (a problem, etc) **3** to cast off or lose: *the snake shed its skin* **4** (of a lorry) to drop (its load) on the road by accident **5** to repel: *this coat sheds water* **6** to abolish or get rid of (jobs, workers, etc) **7** to separate or divide a group of sheep: *a good dog can shed his sheep in minutes* **8** *dialect* to make a parting in (the hair) ▷ *n* **9** short for **watershed** **10** the action of separating or dividing a group of sheep: *the old dog was better at the shed than the young one* [OE *sceadan*] > '**shedable** *or* '**sheddable** *adj*

she'd (ʃiːd) *contraction of* she had *or* she would

shedder ('ʃɛdə) *n* **1** a person or thing that sheds **2** an animal, such as a llama, snake, or lobster, that moults

shedful ('ʃɛdfʊl) *n* **1** the quantity or amount contained in a shed **2** *inf* a lot: *a shedful of helpful hints*

shed hand *n chiefly Austral* an unskilled worker in a sheepshearing shed

shedload ('ʃɛd,ləʊd) *n slang* a very large amount or number

shed out *vb* (*tr, adv*) NZ to separate off (sheep that have lambed) and move them to better pasture

sheen (ʃiːn) *n* **1** a gleaming or glistening brightness; lustre **2** *poetic* splendid clothing ▷ *adj* **3** *rare* beautiful [OE *sciene*] > '**sheeny** *adj*

sheep (ʃiːp) *n, pl* **sheep** **1** any of a genus of ruminant mammals having transversely ribbed horns and a narrow face **2 Barbary sheep** another name for **aoudad** **3** a meek or timid person **4 separate the sheep from the goats** to pick out the members of a group who are superior in some respects [OE *sceap*] > '**sheep,like** *adj*

sheepcote ('ʃiːp,kəʊt) *n chiefly Brit* another word for **sheepfold**

sheep-dip *n* **1** any of several liquid disinfectants and insecticides in which sheep are immersed **2** a deep trough containing such a liquid

sheepdog ('ʃiːp,dɒg) *n* **1** a dog used for herding sheep **2** any of various breeds of dog reared originally for herding sheep. See **Old English sheepdog, Shetland sheepdog**

sheepdog trial *n* (*often pl*) a competition in which sheepdogs are tested in their tasks

sheepfold ('ʃiːp,fəʊld) *n* a pen or enclosure for sheep

sheepish ('ʃiːpɪʃ) *adj* **1** abashed or embarrassed, esp through looking foolish **2** resembling a sheep in timidity > '**sheepishly** *adv* > '**sheepishness** *n*

sheepo ('ʃiːpəʊ) *n, pl* **sheepos** NZ a person employed to bring sheep to the catching pen in a shearing shed

sheep's eyes *pl n old-fashioned* amorous or inviting glances

sheepshank ('ʃiːp,ʃæŋk) *n* a knot made in a rope to shorten it temporarily

sheepskin ('ʃiːp,skɪn) *n* **a** the skin of a sheep, esp when used for clothing, etc **b** (*as modifier*): *a sheepskin coat*

sheepwalk ('ʃiːp,wɔːk) *n chiefly Brit* a tract of land for grazing sheep

sheer¹ (ʃɪə) *adj* **1** perpendicular; very steep: *a sheer cliff* **2** (of textiles) so fine as to be transparent **3** (*prenominal*) absolute: *sheer folly* **4** *obs* bright ▷ *adv* **5** steeply **6** completely or absolutely [OE *scīr*] > '**sheerly** *adv* > '**sheerness** *n*

sheer² (ʃɪə) *vb* (foll by *off* or *away* (*from*)) **1** to deviate or cause to deviate from a course **2** (*intr*) to avoid an unpleasant person, thing, topic, etc ▷ *n* **3** *naut* the position of a vessel relative to its mooring [C17 ? var. of SHEAR]

sheerlegs *or* **shearlegs** ('ʃɪə,lɛgz) *n* (*functioning as sing*) a device for lifting weights consisting of two spars lashed together at the upper ends from which a lifting tackle is suspended. Also called: **shears** [C19 var. of *shear legs*]

Sheerness (ʃɪə'nɛs) *n* a port and resort in SE England, in N Kent at the junction of the Medway estuary and the Thames: administratively part of Queenborough in Sheppey since 1968

sheet¹ (ʃiːt) *n* **1** a large rectangular piece of cloth, generally one of a pair used as inner bedclothes **2a** a thin piece of a substance such as paper or glass, usually rectangular in form **2b** (*as modifier*): *sheet iron* **3** a broad continuous surface: *a sheet of water* **4** a newspaper, esp a tabloid **5** a piece of printed paper to be folded into a section for a book ▷ *vb* **6** (*tr*) to provide with, cover, or wrap in a sheet [OE *sciete*]

sheet² (ʃiːt) *n naut* a line or rope for controlling the position of a sail relative to the wind [OE *scēata* corner of a sail]

sheet anchor *n* **1** *naut* a large strong anchor for use in emergency **2** a person or thing to be relied on in an emergency [C17 from earlier *shute anker*, from *shoot* (obs) the sheet of a sail]

sheet bend *n* a knot used esp for joining ropes of different sizes

sheeting ('ʃiːtɪŋ) *n* fabric from which sheets are made

sheet lightning *n* lightning that appears as a broad sheet, caused by the reflection of more distant lightning

sheet metal *n* metal in the form of a sheet, the thickness being intermediate between that of plate and that of foil

sheet music *n* **1** the printed or written copy of a short composition or piece **2** music in its written or printed form

Sheffield ('ʃɛfiːld) *n* **1** a city in N England, in Sheffield unitary authority, South Yorkshire on the River Don: important centre of steel manufacture and of the cutlery industry; Sheffield university (1905) and Sheffield Hallam University (1992). Pop: 431 607 (1991) **2** a unitary authority in N England, in South Yorkshire. Pop: 513 234 (2001). Area: 368 sq km (142 sq miles)

sheikh *or* **sheik** (ʃeɪk) *n* (in Muslim countries) **a** the head of an Arab tribe, village, etc **b** a religious leader [C16 from Ar. *shaykh* old man] > '**sheikhdom** *or* '**sheikdom** *n*

sheila ('ʃiːlə) *n Austral & NZ old-fashioned* an informal word for **girl** or **woman** [C19 from the girl's name *Sheila*]

shekel *or* **shequel** ('ʃɛkᵊl) *n* **1** the standard monetary unit of modern Israel, divided into 100 agorot **2** any of several former coins and units of weight of the Near East **3** (*often pl*) *inf* any coin or money [C16 from Heb. *sheqel*]

Shelburne ('ʃɛlbɜːn) *n* **2nd Earl of,** title of *William Petty Fitzmaurice*, also called (from 1784) *1st Marquess of Lansdowne*. 1737–1805, British statesman; prime minister (1782–83)

shelduck ('ʃɛl,dʌk) *or* (*masc*) **sheldrake** ('ʃɛl,dreɪk) *n, pl* **shelducks, shelduck** *or* **sheldrakes, sheldrake** any of various large usually brightly coloured gooselike ducks of the Old World [C14 *shel*, prob. from dialect *sheld* pied]

shelf (ʃɛlf) *n, pl* **shelves** **1** a thin flat plank of wood, metal, etc, fixed horizontally against a wall, etc, for the purpose of supporting objects **2** something resembling this in shape or function **3** the objects placed on a shelf: *a shelf of books* **4** a projecting layer of ice, rock, etc, on land or in the sea **5** See **off the shelf** **6 on the shelf** put aside or abandoned; used esp of unmarried women

Ss

considered to be past the age of marriage [OE *scylfe* ship's deck] > **'shelf,like** *adj*

shelf life *n* the length of time a packaged food, etc, will last without deteriorating

shell (ʃɛl) *n* **1** the protective outer layer of an egg, esp a bird's egg **2** the hard outer covering of many molluscs **3** any other hard outer layer, such as the exoskeleton of many arthropods **4** the hard outer layer of some fruits, esp of nuts **5** any hard outer case **6** a hollow artillery projectile filled with explosive primed to explode either during flight or on impact **7** a small-arms cartridge **8** a pyrotechnic cartridge designed to explode in the air **9** *rowing* a very light narrow racing boat **10** the external structure of a building, esp one that is unfinished **11** *physics* **11a** a class of electron orbits in an atom in which the electrons have the same principal quantum number and little difference in their energy levels **11b** an analogous energy state of nucleons in certain theories (**shell models**) of the structure of the atomic nucleus **12 come** (*or* **bring**) **out of one's shell** to become (or help to become) less shy and reserved ▷ *vb* **13** to divest or be divested of a shell, husk, etc **14** to separate or be separated from an ear, husk, etc **15** (*tr*) to bombard with artillery shells ▷ See also **shell out** [OE *sciell*] > **'shell-less** *adj* > **'shell-,like** *adj* > **'shelly** *adj*

she'll (ʃiːl; *unstressed* ʃɪl) *contraction of* she will *or* she shall

shellac (ʃə'læk, 'ʃɛlæk) *n* **1** a yellowish resin secreted by the lac insect, esp a commercial preparation of this used in varnishes, polishes, etc **2** Also called: **shellac varnish** a varnish made by dissolving shellac in ethanol or a similar solvent ▷ *vb* **shellacs, shellacking, shellacked** (*tr*) **3** to coat (an article) with a shellac varnish [C18 SHELL + LAC[1], translation of F *laque en écailles*, lit.: lac in scales, that is, in thin plates]

shellback ('ʃɛl,bæk) *n* an experienced or old sailor

shell company *n business* **1** a near-defunct company, esp one with a stock-exchange listing, used as a vehicle for a thriving company **2** a company that has ceased to trade but retains its registration and is sold for a small sum to enable its new owners to avoid the cost and trouble of registering a new company

Shelley ('ʃɛlɪ) *n* **1 Mary** (**Wollstonecraft**) ('wʊlstən,krɑːft) 1797–1851, British writer; author of *Frankenstein* (1818); the daughter of William Godwin and Mary Wollstonecraft, she eloped with Percy Bysshe Shelley **2 Percy Bysshe** (bɪʃ) 1792–1822, British romantic poet. His works include *Queen Mab* (1813), *Prometheus Unbound* (1820), and *The Triumph of Life* (1824). He wrote an elegy on the death of Keats, *Adonais* (1821), and shorter lyrics, including the odes 'To the West Wind' and 'To a Skylark' (both 1820). He was drowned in the Ligurian Sea while sailing from Leghorn to La Spezia

shellfire ('ʃɛl,faɪə) *n* the firing of artillery shells

shellfish ('ʃɛl,fɪʃ) *n, pl* **shellfish** *or* **shellfishes** any aquatic invertebrate having a shell or shell-like carapace, esp such an animal used as human food. Examples are crustaceans such as crabs and lobsters and molluscs such as oysters

shell out *vb* (*adv*) *inf* to pay out or hand over (money)

shell program *n computing* a basic low-cost computer program that provides a framework within which the user can develop the program to suit his personal requirements

shellproof ('ʃɛl,pruːf) *adj* designed, intended, or able to resist shellfire

shell shock *n* loss of sight, etc, resulting from psychological strain during prolonged engagement in warfare > **'shell-,shocked** *adj*

shell suit *n* a lightweight tracksuit consisting of an inner cotton layer covered by a waterproof nylon layer

Shelta ('ʃɛltə) *n* a secret language used by some itinerant travelling people in Ireland and parts of Britain, based on systematically altered Gaelic [C19 from earlier *sheldrū*, ? an arbitrary alteration of OIrish *bēlre* speech]

shelter ('ʃɛltə) *n* **1** something that provides cover or protection, as from weather or danger **2** the protection afforded by such a cover **3** the state of being sheltered ▷ *vb* **4** (*tr*) to provide with or protect by a shelter **5** (*intr*) to take cover, as from rain **6** (*tr*) to act as a shelter for [C16 from ?] > **'shelterer** *n*

sheltered ('ʃɛltəd) *adj* **1** protected from wind or weather **2** protected from outside influences: *a sheltered upbringing* **3** specially designed to provide a safe environment for the elderly, handicapped, or disabled: *sheltered housing*

sheltie *or* **shelty** ('ʃɛltɪ) *n, pl* **shelties** another name for **Shetland pony** or **Shetland sheepdog** [C17 prob. from Orkney dialect *sjalti*, from ON *Hjalti* Shetlander, from *Hjaltland* Shetland]

shelve[1] (ʃɛlv) *vb* **shelves, shelving, shelved** (*tr*) **1** to place on a shelf **2** to provide with shelves **3** to put aside or postpone from consideration **4** to dismiss or cause to retire [C16 from *shelves*, pl of SHELF] > **'shelver** *n*

shelve[2] (ʃɛlv) *vb* **shelves, shelving, shelved** (*intr*) to slope away gradually [C16 from ?]

shelves (ʃɛlvz) *n* the plural of **shelf**

shelving ('ʃɛlvɪŋ) *n* **1** material for making shelves **2** a set of shelves; shelves collectively

Shem (ʃɛm) *n Old Testament* the eldest of Noah's three sons (Genesis 10:21). Douay spelling: **Sem** (sɛm)

shemozzle (ʃɪ'mɒzᵊl) *n inf* a noisy confusion or dispute; uproar [C19 ?from Yiddish *shlimazl* misfortune]

shenanigan (ʃɪ'nænɪgən) *n inf* **1** (*usually pl*) roguishness; mischief **2** an act of treachery; deception [C19 from ?]

Shensi ('ʃɛn'siː) *n* a variant transliteration of the Chinese name for **Shaanxi**

Shenyang ('ʃɛn'jæŋ) *n* a walled city in NE China in S Manchuria, capital of Liaoning province: capital of the Manchu dynasty from 1644–1912; seized by the Japanese in 1931. Pop: 3 876 289 (1999 est). Former name: **Mukden**

she-oak *n* any of various Australian trees of the genus *Casuarina*. See **casuarina** [C18 *she* (in the sense: inferior) + OAK]

Sheol ('ʃiːəʊl, -ɒl) *n Bible* **1** the abode of the dead **2** (*often not cap*) hell [C16 from Heb. *shĕ'ōl*]

Shepard ('ʃɛpəd) *n* **Alan Bartlett, Jr** 1923–98, US naval officer; first US astronaut in space (1961)

shepherd ('ʃɛpəd) *n* **1** a person employed to tend sheep. Fem equivalent: **shepherdess** **2** a person, such as a clergyman, who watches over a group of people ▷ *vb* (*tr*) **3** to guide or watch over in the manner of a shepherd **4** *Australian rules, rugby, etc* to prevent opponents from tackling (a member of one's own team) by blocking their path: illegal in rugby

shepherd dog *n* another term for **sheepdog** (sense 1)

shepherd's pie *n Brit & Canad* a baked dish of minced meat covered with mashed potato

shepherd's-purse *n* a plant having small white flowers and flattened triangular seed pods

shepherd's weatherglass *n Brit* another name for the **scarlet pimpernel**

Sheppey ('ʃɛpɪ) *n* **Isle of** an island in SE England, off the N coast of Kent in the Thames estuary: separated from the mainland by **The Swale**, a narrow channel. Chief towns: Sheerness, Minster. Pop: 31 854 (latest est) Area: 80 sq km (30 sq miles)

sherang (ʃə'ræŋ) *n* **head sherang** *Austral and NZ inf* the boss; person in authority: *who is the head sherang around here?* [C20 from Anglo-Indian *serang* boatswain]

Sheraton[1] ('ʃɛrətən) *n* **Thomas** 1751–1806, English furniture maker, author of the influential *Cabinet-Maker and Upholsterer's Drawing Book* (1791)

Sheraton[2] ('ʃɛrətən) *adj* denoting furniture made by or in the style of Thomas Sheraton, characterized by lightness, elegance, and the extensive use of inlay

sherbet ('ʃɜːbət) *n* **1** a fruit-flavoured slightly effervescent powder, eaten as a sweet or used to make a drink **2** another word (esp US and Canad) for **sorbet** (sense 1) **3** *Austral sl* beer **4** a cooling Oriental drink of sweetened fruit juice [c17 from Turkish, from Persian, from Ar. *sharbah* drink, from *shariba* to drink]

Sherborne ('ʃɛ:bɔ:n) *n* a town in S England in Dorset: noted for its medieval abbey, ruined medieval castle, and Sherborne Castle a mansion built by Sir Walter Raleigh in 1594. Pop: 7606 (1991)

Sherbrooke ('ʃɜ:,brʊk) *n* a city in E Canada, in S Quebec: industrial and commercial centre. Pop: 76 786 (1996)

sherd (ʃɜ:d) *n* a variant of **shard**

Sheridan ('ʃɛrɪdən) *n* **1** **Philip Henry** 1831–88, American Union cavalry commander in the Civil War. He forced Lee's surrender to Grant (1865) **2** **Richard Brinsley** ('brɪnzlɪ) 1751–1816, Irish dramatist, politician, and orator, noted for his comedies of manners *The Rivals* (1775), *School for Scandal* (1777), and *The Critic* (1779)

sherif *or* **shereef** (ʃɛ'ri:f) *or* **sharif** *n Islam* **1** a descendant of Mohammed through his daughter Fatima **2** an honorific title accorded to any Muslim ruler [c16 from Ar. *sharīf* noble]

sheriff ('ʃɛrɪf) *n* **1** (in the US) the chief elected law-enforcement officer in a county **2** (in Canada) a municipal official who enforces court orders, escorts convicted criminals to prison, etc **3** (in England and Wales) the chief executive officer of the Crown in a county, having chiefly ceremonial duties **4** (in Scotland) a judge in any of the sheriff courts **5** (in New Zealand) an officer of the High Court [OE *scīrgerēfa*, from *scīr* SHIRE + *gerēfa* REEVE[1]] > '**sheriffdom** *n*

sheriff court *n* (in Scotland) a court having jurisdiction to try all but the most serious crimes and to deal with most civil actions

Sherman ('ʃɜ:mən) *n* **William Tecumseh** (tɪ'kʌmsə) 1820–91, American Union commander during the Civil War. He led the victorious march through Georgia (1864), becoming commander of the army in 1869

Sherpa ('ʃɜ:pə) *n, pl* **Sherpas** *or* **Sherpa** a member of a people of Mongolian origin living on the southern slopes of the Himalayas in Nepal, noted as mountaineers

Sherrington ('ʃɛrɪŋtən) *n* Sir **Charles Scott** 1857–1952, English physiologist, noted for his work on reflex action, published in *The Integrative Action of the Nervous System* (1906): shared the Nobel prize for physiology or medicine with Adrian (1932)

sherry ('ʃɛrɪ) *n, pl* **sherries** a fortified wine, originally only from the Jerez region of southern Spain [c16 from earlier *sherris* (assumed to be pl), from Sp. *Xeres*, now *Jerez*]

's Hertogenbosch (*Dutch* shɛrto:xən'bɔs) *n* a city in the S Netherlands, capital of North Brabant province: birthplace of Hieronymus Bosch. Pop: 128 009 (1999 est). Also called: **Den Bosch** French name: **Bois-le-Duc**

sherwani (ʃɛə'wɑ:nɪ) *n* a long coat closed up to the neck, worn by men in India [Hindi]

Sherwood ('ʃɜ:,wʊd) *n* **Robert Emmet** 1896–1955, US dramatist. His plays include *The Petrified Forest* (1935), *Idiot's Delight* (1936), and *There shall be no Night* (1940)

Sherwood Forest ('ʃɜ:,wʊd) *n* an ancient forest in central England, in Nottinghamshire: formerly a royal hunting ground and much more extensive; famous as the home of Robin Hood

she's (ʃi:z) *contraction of* she is *or* she has

Shetland ('ʃɛtlənd) *n or* **Shetland Islands** *pl n* a group of about 100 islands (fewer than 20 inhabited), off the N coast of Scotland, which constitute an island authority of Scotland: a Norse dependency from the 8th century until 1472; noted for the breeding of Shetland ponies, knitwear manufacturing, and fishing; oil-related industries. Administrative centre: Lerwick. Pop: 21 988 (2001). Area: 1426 sq km (550 sq miles). Official name (until 1974): **Zetland**

Shetland pony *n* a very small sturdy breed of pony with a long shaggy mane and tail. Also called: **sheltie**

Shetland sheepdog *n* a small dog similar in appearance to a collie. Also called: **sheltie**

Shevardnadze (ʃɛvəd'nɑ:dzə) *n* **Eduard** (**Amvrosiyevich**) born 1928, Georgian statesman; president of Georgia 1995–2003; Soviet minister of foreign affairs (1985–91), who played an important part in arms negotiations with the US; president of the Georgian state council (1992–95)

shew (ʃəʊ) *vb* **shews, shewing, shewed; shewn** *or* **shewed** an archaic spelling of **show**

shewbread *or* **showbread** ('ʃəʊ,brɛd) *n Bible* the loaves of bread placed every Sabbath on the table beside the altar of incense in the tabernacle or temple of ancient Israel

SHF *or* **shf** *radio abbrev for* superhigh frequency

Shiah *or* **Shia** ('ʃi:ə) *n* **1** one of the two main branches of Islam (the other being the Sunni), now mainly in Iran, which regards Mohammed's cousin Ali and his successors as the true imams ▹ *adj* **2** designating or characteristic of this sect or its beliefs and practices [c17 from Ar. *shīʽah* sect, from *shāʽa* to follow]

shiatsu (ʃi:'ætsu:) *n* a type of massage in which pressure is applied to the same points of the body as in acupuncture. Also called: **acupressure** [Japanese from Chinese *chǐ* finger + *yā* pressure]

shibboleth ('ʃɪbə,lɛθ) *n* **1** a slogan or catch phrase, usually considered outworn, characteristic of a particular party or sect **2** a custom, phrase, or use of language that acts as a test of belonging to, or as a stumbling block to joining a particular social class, profession, etc [c14 from Heb., lit.: ear of grain; the word is used in the Old Testament by the Gileadites as a test word for the Ephraimites, who could not pronounce the sound *sh*]

shickered ('ʃɪkəd) *adj Austral & NZ old-fashioned sl* drunk; intoxicated [via Yiddish from Heb.]

shied (ʃaɪd) *vb* the past tense and past participle of **shy**[1] and **shy**[2]

shield (ʃi:ld) *n* **1** any protection used to intercept blows, missiles, etc, such as a tough piece of armour carried on the arm **2** any similar protective device **3** *heraldry* a pointed stylized shield used for displaying armorial bearings **4** anything that resembles a shield in shape, such as a prize in a sports competition **5** *physics* a structure of concrete, lead, etc, placed around a nuclear reactor **6** a broad stable plateau of ancient Precambrian rocks forming the rigid nucleus of a particular continent **7** **the shield** NZ the Ranfurly Shield, a trophy competed for by provincial rugby teams ▹ *vb* **8** (*tr*) to protect, hide, or conceal (something) from danger or harm [OE *sceld*] > '**shield,like** *adj*

Shield (ʃi:ld) *n* **the** *Canad* another term for the **Canadian Shield**

shield match *n* **1** *Austral* a cricket match for the former Sheffield Shield **2** NZ a rugby match for the Ranfurly Shield

Shields (ʃɪ:ldz) *n* **Carol (Ann)** 1935–2003, Canadian novelist and writer. Her fiction includes *Happenstance* (1980), *The Stone Diaries* (1995), and *Unless* (2001)

shield volcano *n* a broad volcano built up from the repeated nonexplosive eruption of basalt to form a low dome or shield, usually having a large caldera at the summit

shieling ('ʃi:lɪŋ) *or* **shiel** (ʃi:l) *n chiefly Scot* **1** a temporary shelter used by people tending cattle on high or remote ground **2** pasture land for the grazing of cattle in summer [c16 from earlier *shiel*, from ME *shale* hut, from ?]

shier ('ʃaɪə) *adj* a comparative of **shy**[1]

shiest ('ʃaɪɪst) *adj* a superlative of **shy**[1]

shift (ʃɪft) *vb* **1** to move or cause to move from one place or position to another **2** (*tr*) to change for another or

Ss

others **3** to change (gear) in a motor vehicle **4** (*intr*) (of a sound or set of sounds) to alter in a systematic way **5** (*intr*) to provide for one's needs (esp in **shift for oneself**) **6** to remove or be removed, esp with difficulty: *no detergent can shift these stains* **7** (*intr*) *sl* to move quickly **8** (*tr*) *computing* to move (bits held in a store location) to the left or right ▷ *n* **9** the act or an instance of shifting **10** a group of workers who work for a specific period **11** the period of time worked by such a group **12** an expedient, contrivance, or artifice **13** an underskirt or dress with little shaping [OE *sciftan*] > **'shifter** *n*

shiftless ('ʃɪftlɪs) *adj* lacking in ambition or initiative > **'shiftlessness** *n*

shifty ('ʃɪftɪ) *adj* **shiftier, shiftiest 1** given to evasions **2** furtive in character or appearance > **'shiftily** *adv* > **'shiftiness** *n*

shigella (ʃɪ'gɛlə) *n* any of a genus of rod-shaped bacteria, some species of which cause dysentery [c20 after K. *Shiga* (1870–1957), Japanese bacteriologist, who discovered them]

shiitake (ʃiɪ'tɑːkeɪ) *or* **shitake** *n, pl* **shiitake** *or* **shitake** a kind of mushroom widely used in Oriental cookery [c20 from Japanese *shii* tree + *take* mushroom]

Shiite ('ʃiːaɪt) *or* **Shiah** *Islam* ▷ *n* **1** an adherent of Shiah ▷ *adj* **2** of or relating to Shiah > **Shiism** ('ʃiːɪzəm) *n* > **Shiitic** (ʃiː'ɪtɪk) *adj*

Shijiazhuang ('ʃiːdʒɑː'dʒwæŋ), **Shihchiachuang**, *or* **Shihkiachwang** (ʃiːtʃjɑː'tʃwæŋ) *n* a city in NE China, capital of Hebei province: textile manufacturing. Pop: 1 338 796 (1999 est)

Shikoku ('ʃiːkəʊˌkuː) *n* the smallest of the four main islands of Japan, separated from Honshu by the Inland Sea: forested and mountainous. Pop: 4 154 000 (2000 est). Area: 17 759 sq km (6857 sq miles)

shillelagh *or* **shillala** (ʃə'leɪlə, -lɪ) *n* (in Ireland) a stout club or cudgel [c18 from Irish Gaelic *sail* cudgel + *éille* leash, thong]

shilling ('ʃɪlɪŋ) *n* **1** a former British or Australian silver or cupronickel coin worth one twentieth of a pound, not minted in Britain since 1970. Abbrevs: **s., sh 2** the standard monetary unit of Kenya, Somalia, Tanzania, and Uganda [OE *scilling*]

Shillong (ʃɪ'lɒŋ) *n* a city in NE India, capital of Meghalaya: situated on the **Shillong Plateau** at an altitude of 1520 m (4987 ft); destroyed by earthquake in 1897 and rebuilt. Pop: 131 719 (1991)

shillyshally ('ʃɪlɪˌʃælɪ) *inf* ▷ *vb* **shillyshallies, shillyshallying, shillyshallied 1** (*intr*) to be indecisive, esp over unimportant matters ▷ *adv* **2** in an indecisive manner ▷ *adj* **3** indecisive or hesitant ▷ *n, pl* **shillyshallies 4** vacillation [c18 from *shill I shall I*, by reduplication of *shall I*] > **'shillyˌshallier** *n*

Shiloh ('ʃaɪləʊ) *n* a town in central ancient Palestine, in Canaan on the E slope of Mount Ephraim: keeping place of the tabernacle and the ark; destroyed by the Philistines

shily ('ʃaɪlɪ) *adv* a less common spelling of **shyly** See **shy**[1]

shim (ʃɪm) *n* **1** a thin washer or strip often used with a number of similar washers or strips to adjust a clearance for gears, etc ▷ *vb* **shims, shimming, shimmed 2** (*tr*) to modify clearance on (a gear, etc) by use of shims [c18 from ?]

shimmer ('ʃɪmə) *vb* **1** (*intr*) to shine with a glistening or tremulous light ▷ *n* **2** a faint, glistening, or tremulous light [OE *scimerian*] > **'shimmering** *or* **'shimmery** *adj*

shimmy ('ʃɪmɪ) *n, pl* **shimmies 1** an American ragtime dance with much shaking of the hips and shoulders **2** abnormal wobbling motion in a motor vehicle, esp in the front wheels or steering ▷ *vb* **shimmies, shimmying, shimmied** (*intr*) **3** to dance the shimmy **4** to vibrate or wobble [c19 changed from CHEMISE, mistaken for pl]

Shimonoseki (ʃɪmənəʊ'sɛkɪ) *n* a port in SW Japan, on SW Honshu: scene of the peace treaty (1895) ending the Sino-Japanese War; a heavy industrial centre. Pop: 259 791 (1995)

shin (ʃɪn) *n* **1** the front part of the lower leg **2** the front edge of the tibia **3** *chiefly Brit* a cut of beef, the lower foreleg ▷ *vb* **shins, shinning, shinned 4** (when *intr*, often foll by *up*) to climb (a pole, tree, etc) by gripping with the hands or arms and the legs and hauling oneself up **5** (*tr*) to kick (a person) in the shins [OE *scinu*]

Shinar ('ʃaɪnə) *n Old Testament* the southern part of the valley of the Tigris and Euphrates, often identified with Sumer; Babylonia

shinbone ('ʃɪnˌbəʊn) *n* the nontechnical name for **tibia** (sense 1)

shindig ('ʃɪnˌdɪg) *or* **shindy** ('ʃɪndɪ) *n, pl* **shindigs** *or* **shindies** *sl* **1** a noisy party, dance, etc **2** a quarrel or commotion [c19 var. of SHINTY]

shine (ʃaɪn) *vb* **shines, shining, shone 1** (*intr*) to emit light **2** (*intr*) to glow or be bright with reflected light **3** (*tr*) to direct the light of (a lamp, etc): *he shone the torch in my eyes* **4** (*tr*; *pt & pp* **shined**) to cause to gleam by polishing: *to shine shoes* **5** (*intr*) to excel: *she shines at tennis* **6** (*intr*) to appear clearly ▷ *n* **7** the state or quality of shining; sheen; lustre **8** *inf* a liking or fancy (esp in **take a shine to**) [OE *scīnan*]

shiner ('ʃaɪnə) *n* **1** something that shines, such as a polishing device **2** any of numerous small North American freshwater cyprinid fishes **3** *inf* a black eye **4** *NZ old-fashioned inf* a tramp

shingle[1] ('ʃɪŋgᵊl) *n* **1** a thin rectangular tile, esp one made of wood, that is laid with others in overlapping rows to cover a roof or a wall **2** a woman's short-cropped hairstyle **3** *US & Canad* a small signboard fixed outside the office of a doctor, lawyer, etc ▷ *vb* **shingles, shingling, shingled** (*tr*) **4** to cover (a roof or a wall) with shingles **5** to cut (the hair) in a short-cropped style [c12 *scingle*, from LL *scindula* a split piece of wood, from L *scindere* to split] > **'shingler** *n*

shingle[2] ('ʃɪŋgᵊl) *n* **1** coarse gravel, esp the pebbles found on beaches **2** a place or area strewn with shingle [c16 of Scand. origin] > **'shingly** *adj*

shingles ('ʃɪŋgᵊlz) *n* (*functioning as sing*) an acute viral disease characterized by inflammation, pain, and skin eruptions along the course of affected nerves. Technical names: **herpes zoster, zoster** [c14 from Med. L *cingulum* girdle, rendering Gk *zōnē* zone]

shinny ('ʃɪnɪ) *n Canad* a kind of hockey either played on ice with skates, or without skates on the street without nets [c20 from SHIN]

Shinto ('ʃɪntəʊ) *n* the indigenous religion of Japan, incorporating the worship of a number of ethnic divinities [c18 from Japanese: the way of the gods, from Chinese *shên* gods + *tao* way] > **'Shintoism** *n* > **'Shintoist** *n, adj*

▷ www.jinja.or.jp/english/

shinty ('ʃɪntɪ) *n* **1** a game resembling hockey played with a ball and sticks curved at the lower end **2** (*pl* **shinties**) the stick used in this game [c17 ? from Scot Gaelic *sinteag* a pace, bound]

▷ http://shinty.com

shiny ('ʃaɪnɪ) *adj* **shinier, shiniest 1** glossy or polished; bright **2** (of clothes or material) worn to a smooth and glossy state, as by continual rubbing > **'shininess** *n*

ship (ʃɪp) *n* **1** a vessel propelled by engines or sails for navigating on the water, esp a large vessel **2** *naut* a large sailing vessel with three or more square-rigged masts **3** the crew of a ship **4** short for **airship** or **spaceship 5 when one's ship comes in** (*or* **home**) when one has become successful ▷ *vb* **ships, shipping, shipped 6** to place, transport, or travel on any conveyance, esp aboard a ship **7** (*tr*) *naut* to take (water) over the side **8** to bring or go aboard a vessel: *to ship oars* **9** (*tr*; often foll by *off*) *inf* to send away: *they shipped the children off to boarding school* **10** (*intr*) to engage to serve aboard a ship: *I shipped* *aboard a Liverpool liner* [OE *scip*] > '**shippable** *adj*

-ship *suffix forming nouns* **1** indicating state or condition: *fellowship* **2** indicating rank, office, or position: *lordship* **3** indicating craft or skill: *scholarship* [OE *-scipe*]
▹ http://routesinternational.com/ships.htm#general
▹ www.imo.org/HOME.html
▹ www.janes.com/transport/digests/ship.shtml

shipboard ('ʃɪpˌbɔːd) *n* (*modifier*) taking place, used, or intended for use aboard a ship: *a shipboard encounter*

shipbuilder ('ʃɪpˌbɪldə) *n* a person or business engaged in building ships > '**shipˌbuilding** *n*

ship chandler *n* a person or business dealing in supplies for ships > **ship chandlery** *n*

Shipka Pass ('ʃɪpkə) *n* a pass over the Balkan Mountains in central Bulgaria: scene of a bloody Turkish defeat in the Russo-Turkish War (1877–78). Height: 1334 m (4376 ft)

shipload ('ʃɪpˌləʊd) *n* the quantity carried by a ship

shipmaster ('ʃɪpˌmɑːstə) *n* the master or captain of a ship

shipmate ('ʃɪpˌmeɪt) *n* a sailor who serves on the same ship as another

shipment ('ʃɪpmənt) *n* **1a** goods shipped together as part of the same lot: *a shipment of grain* **1b** (*as modifier*): *a shipment schedule* **2** the act of shipping cargo

ship money *n English history* a tax levied to finance the fitting out of warships: abolished 1640

ship of the line *n naut* (formerly) a warship large enough to fight in the first line of battle

shipowner ('ʃɪpˌəʊnə) *n* a person who owns or has shares in a ship or ships

shipper ('ʃɪpə) *n* a person or company in the business of shipping freight

shipping ('ʃɪpɪŋ) *n* **1a** the business of transporting freight, esp by ship **1b** (*as modifier*): *a shipping magnate; shipping line* **2** ships collectively: *there is a lot of shipping in the Channel*

ship's biscuit *n* another name for **hardtack**

shipshape ('ʃɪpʃeɪp) *adj* **1** neat; orderly ▹ *adv* **2** in a neat and orderly manner

shipworm ('ʃɪpˌwɜːm) *n* any of a genus of wormlike marine bivalve molluscs that bore into wooden piers, ships, etc, by means of drill-like shell valves

shipwreck ('ʃɪpˌrɛk) *n* **1** the partial or total destruction of a ship at sea **2** a wrecked ship or part of such a ship **3** ruin or destruction: *the shipwreck of all my hopes* ▹ *vb* (*tr*) **4** to wreck or destroy (a ship) **5** to bring to ruin or destruction [OE *scipwræc*, from SHIP + *wræc* something driven by the sea]

shipwright ('ʃɪpˌraɪt) *n* an artisan skilled in one or more of the tasks required to build vessels

shipyard ('ʃɪpˌjɑːd) *n* a place or facility for the building, maintenance, and repair of ships

shiralee (ˌʃɪrə'liː) *n Austral sl* a swagman's bundle [from ?]

Shiraz[1] (ʃɪə'rɑːz) *n* a city in SW Iran, at an altitude of 1585 m (5200 ft): an important Muslim cultural centre in the 14th century; university (1948); noted for fine carpets. Pop: 1 053 025 (1996)

Shiraz[2] (ʃɪə'rɑːz) *n* the Austral name for **Syrah** [from SHIRAZ[1], where the wine supposedly originated]

shire ('ʃaɪə) *n* **1a** one of the British counties **1b** (*in combination*): *Yorkshire* **2** (in Australia) a rural district having its own local council **3** See **shire horse** **4** **the Shires** the Midland counties of England, famous for hunting, etc [OE *scīr* office]

Shiré ('ʃɪəreɪ) *n* a river in E central Africa, flowing from Lake Malawi through Malawi and Mozambique to the Zambezi. Length: 596 km (370 miles)

Shiré Highlands *pl n* an upland area of S Malawi. Average height: 900 m (3000 ft)

shire horse *n* a large heavy breed of carthorse with long hair on the fetlocks

shirk (ʃɜːk) *vb* **1** to avoid discharging (work, a duty, etc); evade ▹ *n also* **shirker** **2** a person who shirks [c17 prob. from G *Schurke* rogue. See SHARK[2]]

shirr (ʃɜː) *vb* **1** to gather (fabric) into two or more parallel rows to decorate a dress, blouse, etc, often using elastic thread **2** (*tr*) to bake (eggs) out of their shells ▹ *n also* **shirring** **3** a series of gathered rows decorating a dress, blouse, etc [c19 from ?]

shirt (ʃɜːt) *n* **1** a garment worn on the upper part of the body, esp by men, usually having a collar and sleeves and buttoning up the front **2** short for **nightshirt** **3** **keep your shirt on** *inf* refrain from losing your temper **4** **put** *or* **lose one's shirt on** *inf* to bet or lose all one has on (a horse, etc) [OE *scyrte*]

shirting ('ʃɜːtɪŋ) *n* fabric used in making men's shirts

shirt-lifter *n derog sl* a male homosexual

shirtsleeve ('ʃɜːtˌsliːv) *n* **1** the sleeve of a shirt **2** **in one's shirtsleeves** not wearing a jacket

shirt-tail *n* the part of a shirt that extends below the waist

shirtwaister ('ʃɜːtˌweɪstə) *or US* **shirtwaist** *n* a woman's dress with a tailored bodice resembling a shirt

shirty ('ʃɜːtɪ) *adj* **shirtier, shirtiest** *sl, chiefly Brit* bad-tempered or annoyed [c19 ? based on such phrases as *to get someone's shirt out* to annoy someone] > '**shirtily** *adv*

shish kebab ('ʃiːʃ kə'bæb) *n* a dish consisting of small pieces of meat and vegetables threaded onto skewers and grilled [from Turkish *şiş kebab*, from *şiş* skewer; see KEBAB]

shit (ʃɪt) *taboo* ▹ *vb* **shits, shitting; shitted, shit,** *or* **shat** **1** to defecate **2** (usually foll by *on*) *sl* to give the worst possible treatment (to) ▹ *n* **3** faeces; excrement **4** an act of defecation **5** *sl* rubbish; nonsense **6** *sl* an obnoxious or worthless person ▹ *interj* **7** *sl* an exclamation expressing anger, disgust, etc [OE *scite* (unattested) dung, *scītan* to defecate, of Gmc origin] > '**shitty** *adj*

shitake (ʃɪ'tɑːkeɪ) *n* a variant of **shiitake**

shitload ('ʃɪtləʊd) *n sl* a lot: *a shitload of money*

shit-stir *vb* (*intr*) *sl* to make trouble > '**shit-ˌstirrer** *n*

Shittim ('ʃɪtɪm) *n Old Testament* the site to the east of the Jordan and northeast of the Dead Sea where the Israelites encamped before crossing the Jordan (Numbers 25:1–9)

Ss

shiv (ʃɪv) *n* a variant of **chiv**

Shiva ('ʃiːvə, 'ʃɪvə) *n* a variant spelling of **Siva**

shivaree (ˌʃɪvə'riː) *n* a variant spelling (esp US and Canad) of **charivari**

shiver[1] ('ʃɪvə) *vb* (*intr*) **1** to shake or tremble, as from cold or fear ▹ *n* **2** the act of shivering; a tremulous motion **3** **the shivers** an attack of shivering, esp through fear or illness [c13 *chiveren*, ? var. of *chevelen* to chatter (used of teeth), from OE *ceafl* jowl] > '**shiverer** *n* > '**shivering** *n, adj* > '**shivery** *adj*

shiver[2] ('ʃɪvə) *vb* **1** to break or cause to break into fragments ▹ *n* **2** a splintered piece [c13 of Gmc origin]

Shizuoka (ˌʃiːzuː'əʊkə) *n* a city in central Japan, on S Honshu: a centre for green tea; university (1949). Pop: 474 089 (1995)

Shkodër (*Albanian* 'ʃkodər) *n* a market town in NW Albania, on **Lake Shkodër**: an Illyrian capital in the first millennium BC. Pop: 83 700 (1991 est). Italian name: **Scutari**

shoal[1] (ʃəʊl) *n* **1** a stretch of shallow water **2** a sandbank or rocky area, esp one that is visible at low water ▹ *vb* **3** to make or become shallow **4** (*intr*) *naut* to sail into shallower water ▹ *adj also* **shoaly** **5** a less common word for **shallow** [OE *sceald* shallow]

shoal[2] (ʃəʊl) *n* **1** a large group of certain aquatic animals, esp fish **2** a large group of people or things ▹ *vb* **3** (*intr*) to collect together in such a group [OE *scolu*]

shock[1] (ʃɒk) *vb* **1** to experience or cause to experience extreme horror, disgust, surprise, etc: *the atrocities shocked us* **2** to cause a state of shock in (a person) **3** to come or cause to come into violent contact ▹ *n* **4** a sudden and violent jarring blow or impact **5** something that causes a sudden and violent disturbance in the emotions **6** *pathol* a state of bodily collapse, as from severe bleeding, burns, fright, etc **7** Also: **electric shock** pain and muscular spasm as the physical reaction to an electric current passing through the body [c16 from OF *choc*, from *choquier* to make violent contact with, of Gmc origin] > **'shockable** *adj* > **,shocka'bility** *n*

shock² (ʃɒk) *n* **1** a number of sheaves set on end in a field to dry **2** a pile or stack of unthreshed corn ▹ *vb* **3** *(tr)* to set up (sheaves) in shocks [c14 prob. of Gmc origin]

shock³ (ʃɒk) *n* a thick bushy mass, esp of hair [c19 ?from SHOCK²]

shock absorber *n* any device designed to absorb mechanical shock, esp one fitted to a motor vehicle to damp the recoil of the road springs

shocker ('ʃɒkə) *n inf* **1** a person or thing that shocks **2** a sensational novel, film, or play

shockheaded ('ʃɒk,hɛdɪd) *adj* having a head of bushy or tousled hair

shock-horror *adj facetious* (esp of newspaper headlines) sensationalistic: *shock-horror stories about the British diet*

shocking ('ʃɒkɪŋ) *adj* **1** causing shock, horror, or disgust **2 shocking pink 2a** of a garish shade of pink **2b** *(as n)*: *dressed in shocking pink* **3** *inf* very bad or terrible: *shocking weather* > **'shockingly** *adv*

Shockley ('ʃɒklɪ) *n* **William Bradfield** 1910–89, US physicist, born in Britain, who shared the Nobel prize for physics (1956) with John Bardeen and Walter Brattain for developing the transistor. He also held controversial views on the connection between race and intelligence

shockproof ('ʃɒk,pru:f) *adj* capable of absorbing shock without damage

shock therapy *or* **treatment** *n* the treatment of certain psychotic conditions by injecting drugs or by passing an electric current through the brain (**electroconvulsive therapy**) to produce convulsions or coma

shock troops *pl n* soldiers specially trained and equipped to carry out an assault

shock wave *n* a region across which there is a rapid pressure, temperature, and density rise caused by a body moving supersonically in a gas or by a detonation. See also **sonic boom**

shod (ʃɒd) *vb* the past participle of **shoe**

shoddy ('ʃɒdɪ) *adj* **shoddier, shoddiest 1** imitating something of better quality **2** of poor quality ▹ *n, pl* **shoddies 3** a yarn or fabric made from wool waste or clippings **4** anything of inferior quality that is designed to simulate superior quality [c19 from ?] > **'shoddily** *adv* > **'shoddiness** *n*

shoe (ʃu:) *n* **1a** one of a matching pair of coverings shaped to fit the foot, esp one ending below the ankle, having an upper of leather, plastic, etc, on a sole and heel of heavier material **1b** *(as modifier)*: *shoe cleaner* **2** anything resembling a shoe in shape, function, position, etc, such as a horseshoe **3** a band of metal or wood on the bottom of the runner of a sledge **4** *engineering* a lining to protect from wear: see **brake shoe 5 be in (a person's) shoes** *inf* to be in (another person's) situation ▹ *vb* **shoes, shoeing, shod** *(tr)* **6** to furnish with shoes **7** to fit (a horse) with horseshoes **8** to furnish with a hard cover, such as a metal plate, for protection against friction or bruising [OE *scōh*]

shoeblack ('ʃu:,blæk) *n* (esp formerly) a person who shines boots and shoes

shoehorn ('ʃu:,hɔ:n) *n* **1** a smooth curved implement of horn, metal, plastic, etc, inserted at the heel of a shoe to ease the foot into it ▹ *vb (tr)* **2** to cram (people or things) into a small space

shoelace ('ʃu:,leɪs) *n* a cord for fastening shoes

shoe leather *n* **1** leather used to make shoes **2 save shoe leather** to avoid wearing out shoes, as by taking a bus rather than walking

shoemaker ('ʃu:,meɪkə) *n* a person who makes or repairs shoes or boots > **'shoe,making** *n*

shoer ('ʃu:ə) *n rare* a person who shoes horses; farrier

shoeshine ('ʃu:ʃaɪn) *n* the act or an instance of polishing a pair of shoes

shoestring ('ʃu:,strɪŋ) *n* **1** another word for **shoelace 2** *inf* a very small or petty amount of money (esp in **on a shoestring**)

shoetree ('ʃu:,tri:) *n* a wooden or metal form inserted into a shoe or boot to stretch it or preserve its shape

shofar *or* **shophar** (*Hebrew* ʃɔ'far) *n, pl* **shofars, shophars** *or* **shofroth, shophroth** (*Hebrew* -'frɔt) *Judaism* a ram's horn sounded on certain religious occasions [from Heb. *shōphār* ram's horn]

shogun ('ʃəʊ,gu:n) *n Japanese history* (from about 1192 to 1867) any of a line of hereditary military dictators who relegated the emperors to a position of purely theoretical supremacy [c17 from Japanese, from Chinese *chiang chün* general, from *chiang* to lead + *chün* army] > **'shogunate** *n*

shogun bond *n* a bond sold on the Japanese market by a foreign institution and denominated in a foreign currency ▹ Cf **samurai bond**

Sholapur ('ʃəʊlə,pʊə) *n* a city in SW India, in S Maharashtra: major textile centre. Pop: 604 215 (1991)

Sholem Aleichem *n* See (Sholem) **Aleichem**

Sholokhov (*Russian* 'ʃɔləxəf) *n* **Mikhail Aleksandrovich** (mixa'il alɪk'sandrəvitʃ) 1905–84, Soviet author, noted particularly for *And Quiet flows the Don* (1934) and *The Don flows Home to the Sea* (1940), describing the effect of the Revolution and civil war on the life of the Cossacks: Nobel prize for literature 1965

shone (ʃɒn; *US* ʃəʊn) *vb* a past tense and past participle of **shine**

shonky ('ʃɒŋkɪ) *adj* **shonkier, shonkiest** *Austral and NZ inf* **1** of dubious integrity or legality **2** unreliable; unsound [c19 perhaps from Yiddish *shonniker* or from SH(ODDY) + (W)ONKY]

shoo (ʃu:) *sentence substitute* **1** go away!: used to drive away unwanted or annoying people, animals, etc ▹ *vb* **shoos, shooing, shooed 2** *(tr)* to drive away by or as if by crying "shoo" **3** *(intr)* to cry "shoo" [c15 imit.]

shoo-in *n* **1** a person or thing that is certain to win or succeed **2** a match or contest that is easy to win

shook¹ (ʃʊk) *n* **1** a set of parts ready for assembly, esp of a barrel **2** a group of sheaves piled together on end; shock [c18 from ?]

shook² (ʃʊk) *vb* the past tense of **shake**

shoon (ʃu:n) *n dialect, chiefly Scot* a plural of **shoe**

shoot (ʃu:t) *vb* **shoots, shooting, shot 1** *(tr)* to hit, wound, damage, or kill with a missile discharged from a weapon **2** to discharge (a missile or missiles) from a weapon **3** to fire (a weapon) or (of a weapon) to be fired **4** to send out or be sent out as if from a weapon: *he shot questions at her* **5** *(intr)* to move very rapidly **6** *(tr)* to slide or push into or out of a fastening: *to shoot a bolt* **7** to emit (a ray of light) or (of a ray of light) to be emitted **8** *(tr)* to go or pass quickly over or through: *to shoot rapids* **9** *(intr)* to hunt game with a gun for sport **10** *(tr)* to pass over (an area) in hunting game **11** *(intr)* (of a plant) to produce (buds, branches, etc) **12** to photograph or record (a sequence, etc) **13** *(tr; usually passive)* to variegate or streak, as with colour **14** *soccer, hockey, etc* to hit or propel (the ball, etc) towards the goal **15** *(tr) sport, chiefly US & Canad* to score (strokes, etc): *he shot 72 on the first round* **16** *(tr)* to measure the altitude of (a celestial body) **17** (often foll by *up*) *sl* to inject (someone, esp oneself) with (a drug, esp heroin) **18 shoot a line** *sl* **18a** to boast **18b** to tell a lie **19 shoot oneself in the foot** *inf* to damage one's own cause inadvertently ▹ *n* **20** the act of shooting **21** the action or motion of something that is shot **22** the first aerial part of a plant to develop from a germinating seed **23** any new growth of a plant, such as a bud, etc

24 *chiefly Brit* a meeting or party organized for hunting game with guns **25** an area where game can be hunted with guns **26** a steep descent in a stream; rapid **27** *inf* a photographic assignment **28 the whole shoot** *sl* everything ▷ *interj* **29** *US & Canad* an exclamation expressing disbelief, scepticism, disappointment, etc ▷ See also **shoot down, shoot through** [OE *scēotan*]
▷ www.issf-shooting.org

shoot down *vb (tr, adv)* **1** to shoot callously **2** to defeat or disprove: *he shot down her argument*

shoot-'em-up *or* **shoot-em-up** *n inf* **1** a type of computer game, the object of which is to shoot as many enemies, targets, etc as possible **2** a fast-moving film involving many gunfights, battles, etc

shooter ('ʃuːtə) *n* **1** a person or thing that shoots **2** *sl* a gun

shooting box *n* a small country house providing accommodation for a shooting party. Also called: **shooting lodge**

shooting brake *n Brit* another name for **estate car**

shooting star *n inf* a meteor

shooting stick *n* a device that resembles a walking stick, having a spike at one end and a folding seat at the other

shoot through *vb (intr, adv) Austral inf* to leave; go away

shop (ʃɒp) *n* **1** a place, esp a small building, for the retail sale of goods and services **2** an act or instance of shopping **3** a place for the performance of a specified type of work; workshop **4 all over the shop** *inf* **4a** in disarray: *his papers were all over the shop* **4b** in every direction: *I've searched for it all over the shop* **5 shut up shop 5a** to close business at the end of the day or permanently **5b** to become defensive or inactive **6 talk shop** *inf* to discuss one's business, profession, etc, esp on a social occasion ▷ *vb* **shops, shopping, shopped 7** *(intr; often foll by for)* to visit a shop or shops in search of (goods) with the intention of buying them **8** *(tr) sl, chiefly Brit* to inform on (someone), esp to the police [OE *sceoppa* stall]

shop around *vb (intr, adv) Inf* **1** to visit a number of shops or stores to compare goods and prices **2** to consider a number of possibilities before making a choice

shop assistant *n* a person who serves in a shop

shop floor *n* **1** the part of a factory housing the machines and men directly involved in production **2** workers, esp factory workers organized in a union

shopkeeper ('ʃɒpˌkiːpə) *n* a person who owns or manages a shop or small store > '**shopˌkeeping** *n*

shoplifter ('ʃɒpˌlɪftə) *n* a customer who steals goods from a shop > '**shopˌlifting** *n*

shopper ('ʃɒpə) *n* **1** a person who buys goods in a shop **2** a bag for shopping

shopping ('ʃɒpɪŋ) *n* **1** a number or collection of articles purchased **2** the act or an instance of making purchases

shopping basket *n* **1** a metal or plastic container with one or two handles, used to carry shopping in a shop **2** the list of items an Internet shopper chooses to buy at one time from a website

shopping cart *n* the usual US and Canad word for **shopping basket**

shopping centre *n* **1** a purpose-built complex of stores, restaurants, etc **2** the area of a town where most of the shops are situated

shopping mall *n* a large enclosed shopping centre

shopping plaza *n chiefly US & Canad* a shopping centre, esp a small group of stores built as a strip

shopsoiled ('ʃɒpˌsɔɪld) *adj* worn, faded, etc, from being displayed in a shop or store

shop steward *n* an elected representative of the union workers in a shop, factory, etc

shoptalk ('ʃɒpˌtɔːk) *n* conversation concerning one's work, esp when carried on outside business hours

shopwalker ('ʃɒpˌwɔːkə) *n Brit* a person employed by a departmental store to supervise sales personnel, assist customers, etc

shoran ('ʃɔːræn) *n* a short-range radar system by which an aircraft, ship, etc, can accurately determine its position [C20 *sho(rt-)ra(nge) n(avigation)*]

shore[1] (ʃɔː) *n* **1** the land along the edge of a sea, lake, or wide river. Related adj: **littoral 2a** land, as opposed to water **2b** *(as modifier)*: *shore duty* **3** *law* the tract of coastland lying between the ordinary marks of high and low water **4** *(often pl)* a country: *his native shores* [C14 prob. from MLow G, MDu. *schōre*]

shore[2] (ʃɔː) *n* **1** a prop or beam used to support a wall, building, etc ▷ *vb* **shores, shoring, shored 2** *(tr; often foll by up)* to make safe with or as if with a shore [C15 from MDu. *schōre*] > '**shoring** *n*

shore[3] (ʃɔː) *vb arch, Austral, & NZ* a past tense of **shear**

shore bird *n* any of various birds that live close to water, esp plovers, sandpipers, etc. Also called (Brit): **wader**

shore leave *n naval* **1** permission to go ashore **2** time spent ashore during leave

shoreless ('ʃɔːlɪs) *adj* **1** without a shore suitable for landing **2** *poetic* boundless; vast

shoreline ('ʃɔːˌlaɪn) *n* the edge of a body of water

shoreward ('ʃɔːwəd) *adj* **1** near or facing the shore ▷ *adv also* **shorewards 2** towards the shore

shorn (ʃɔːn) *vb* a past participle of **shear**

short (ʃɔːt) *adj* **1** of little length; not long **2** of little height; not tall **3** of limited duration **4** deficient: *the number of places laid at the table was short by four* **5** *(postpositive; often foll by of or on)* lacking (in) or needful (of): *I'm always short of money* **6** concise; succinct **7** (of drinks) consisting chiefly of a spirit, such as whisky **8** *cricket* (of a fielding position) near the batsman: *short leg* **9** lacking in the power of retentiveness: *a short memory* **10** abrupt to the point of rudeness: *the salesgirl was very short with him* **11** (of betting odds) almost even **12** *finance* **12a** not possessing the securities or commodities that have been sold under contract and therefore obliged to make a purchase before the delivery date **12b** of or relating to such sales, which depend on falling prices for profit **13** *phonetics* **13a** denoting a vowel of relatively brief temporal duration **13b** (in popular usage) denoting the qualities of the five English vowels represented orthographically in the words *pat, pet, pit, pot, put,* and *putt* **14** *prosody* **14a** denoting a vowel that is phonetically short or a syllable containing such a vowel **14b** (of a vowel or syllable in verse) not carrying emphasis or accent **15** (of pastry) crumbly in texture **16 in short supply** scarce **17 short and sweet** unexpectedly brief **18 short for** an abbreviation for ▷ *adv* **19** abruptly: *to stop short* **20** briefly or concisely **21** rudely or curtly **22** *finance* without possessing the securities or commodities at the time of their contractual sale: *to sell short* **23 caught** *or* **taken short** having a sudden need to urinate or defecate **24 go short** not to have a sufficient amount, etc **25 short of** except: *nothing short of a miracle can save him now* ▷ *n* **26** anything that is short **27** a drink of spirits **28** *phonetics, prosody* a short vowel or syllable **29** *finance* **29a** a short contract or sale **29b** a short seller **30** a short film, usually of a factual nature **31** See **short circuit 32 Scot** *inf* as a shortened form: *he is called JR for short* **33 in short 33a** as a summary **33b** in a few words ▷ *vb* **34** See **short circuit** (sense 2) ▷ See also **shorts** [OE *scort*] > '**shortness** *n*

short-acting *adj* (of a drug) quickly effective, but requiring regularly repeated doses for long-term treatment ▷ Cf **intermediate-acting, long-acting**

shortage ('ʃɔːtɪdʒ) *n* a deficiency or lack in the amount needed, expected, or due; deficit

shortbread ('ʃɔːtˌbrɛd) *n* a rich crumbly biscuit made with a large proportion of butter

shortcake ('ʃɔːtˌkeɪk) *n* **1** shortbread **2** a dessert made of layers of biscuit or cake filled with fruit and cream

short-change *vb* **short-changes, short-changing, short-changed** (*tr*) **1** to give less than correct change to **2** *sl* to treat unfairly or dishonestly, esp by giving less than is expected or deserved

short circuit *n* **1** a faulty or accidental connection between two points of different potential in an electric circuit, establishing a path of low resistance through which an excessive current can flow ▹ *vb* **short-circuit** **2** to develop or cause to develop a short circuit **3** (*tr*) to bypass (a procedure, etc) **4** (*tr*) to hinder or frustrate (plans, etc) ▹ Sometimes (for senses 1, 2) shortened to **short**

shortcoming (ˈʃɔːtˌkʌmɪŋ) *n* a failing, defect, or deficiency

short corner *n* *hockey* another name for **penalty corner**

short covering *n* the purchase of securities or commodities by a short seller to meet delivery requirements

shortcrust pastry (ˈʃɔːtˌkrʌst) *n* a basic type of pastry that has a crisp but crumbly texture. Also: **short pastry**

short cut *n* **1** a route that is shorter than the usual one **2** a means of saving time or effort ▹ *vb* **short-cut, short-cuts, short-cutting, short-cut** **3** (*intr*) to use a short cut

short-dated *adj* (of a gilt-edged security) having less than five years to run before redemption ▹ Cf **medium-dated, long-dated**

short-day *adj* (of plants) able to flower only if exposed to short periods of daylight, each followed by a long dark period ▹ Cf **long-day**

shorten (ˈʃɔːtᵊn) *vb* **1** to make or become short or shorter **2** (*tr*) *naut* to reduce the area of (sail) **3** (*tr*) to make (pastry, etc) short, by adding fat **4** *gambling* to cause (the odds) to lessen or (of odds) to become less

shortening (ˈʃɔːtᵊnɪŋ) *n* butter or other fat, used in a dough, etc, to make the mixture short

Shorter Catechism *n* *chiefly Presbyterian Church* the more widely used of two catechisms of religious instruction drawn up in 1647

shortfall (ˈʃɔːtˌfɔːl) *n* **1** failure to meet a goal or a requirement **2** the amount of such a failure

shorthand (ˈʃɔːtˌhænd) *n* **a** a system of rapid handwriting employing simple strokes and other symbols to represent words or phrases **b** (*as modifier*): *a shorthand typist*
▹ http://pitmanshorthand.homestead.com

short-handed *adj* **1** lacking the usual or necessary number of assistants, workers, etc **2** *sport, US & Canad* with less than the full complement of players

shorthand typist *n* *Brit* a person skilled in the use of shorthand and in typing. US and Canad name: **stenographer**

short head *n* *horse racing* a distance shorter than the length of a horse's head

shorthorn (ˈʃɔːtˌhɔːn) *n* a short-horned breed of cattle with several regional varieties

shortie *or* **shorty** (ˈʃɔːtɪ) *n, pl* **shorties** *inf* **a** a person or thing that is extremely short **b** (*as modifier*): *a shortie nightdress*

short list *chiefly Brit* ▹ *n* **1** Also called (Scot): **short leet** a list of suitable applicants for a job, post, etc, from which the successful candidate will be selected ▹ *vb* **short-list** (*tr*) **2** to put (someone) on a short list

short-lived *adj* living or lasting only for a short time

shortly (ˈʃɔːtlɪ) *adv* **1** in a short time; soon **2** briefly **3** in a curt or rude manner

short-order *adj* *chiefly US* of or connected with food that is easily and quickly prepared

short-range *adj* of small or limited extent in time or distance: *a short-range forecast*

shorts (ʃɔːts) *pl n* **1** trousers reaching the top of the thigh or partway to the knee, worn by both sexes for sport, etc **2** *chiefly US & Canad* men's underpants that usually reach mid-thigh **3** short-dated gilt-edged securities **4** short-term bonds **5** securities or commodities that have been sold short **6** a livestock feed containing a large proportion of bran and wheat germ

short selling *n* *finance* the practice of selling commodities, securities, currencies, etc that one does not have in the expectation that falling prices will enable one to buy them in at a profit before they have to be delivered

short shrift *n* **1** brief and unsympathetic treatment **2** (formerly) a brief period allowed to a condemned prisoner to make confession **3** **make short shrift of** to dispose of quickly

short-sighted *adj* **1** relating to or suffering from myopia **2** lacking foresight: *a short-sighted plan* > ˌ**short-ˈsightedly** *adv* > ˌ**short-ˈsightedness** *n*

short-spoken *adj* tending to be abrupt in speech

short story *n* a prose narrative of shorter length than the novel

short-tempered *adj* easily moved to anger

short-term *adj* **1** of, for, or extending over a limited period **2** *finance* extending over, maturing within, or required within a short period of time, usually twelve months: *short-term credit; short-term capital*

short-termism (-ˈtɜːmɪzəm) *n* the tendency to focus attention on short-term gains, often at the expense of long-term success or stability

short time *n* the state or condition of working less than the normal working week, esp because of a business recession

short ton *n* the full name for **ton**[1] (sense 2)

short-waisted *adj* unusually short from the shoulders to the waist

short wave *n* **a** a radio wave with a wavelength in the range 10–100 metres **b** (*as modifier*): *a short-wave broadcast*

short-winded *adj* **1** tending to run out of breath, esp after exertion **2** (of speech or writing) terse or abrupt

Shostakovich (ˌʃɒstəˈkəʊvɪtʃ; *Russian* ʃəstaˈkɔvitʃ) *n* **Dmitri Dmitriyevich** (ˈdmitrij ˈdmitrijɪvitʃ) 1906–75, Soviet composer, noted esp for his 15 symphonies and his chamber music

shot[1] (ʃɒt) *n* **1** the act or an instance of discharging a projectile **2** (*pl* **shot**) a solid missile, such as an iron ball or a lead pellet, discharged from a firearm **3a** small round pellets of lead collectively, as used in cartridges **3b** metal in the form of coarse powder or small pellets **4** the distance that a discharged projectile travels or is capable of travelling **5** a person who shoots, esp with regard to his or her ability: *he is a good shot* **6** *inf* an attempt **7** *inf* a guess **8** any act of throwing or hitting something, as in certain sports **9** the launching of a rocket, etc, esp to a specified destination: *a moon shot* **10a** a single photograph **10b** a length of film taken by a single camera without breaks **11** *inf* an injection, as of a vaccine or narcotic drug **12** *inf* a glass of alcoholic drink, esp spirits **13** *sport* a heavy metal ball used in the shot put **14** **call the shots** *sl* to have control over an organization, etc **15** **have a shot at** *inf* to attempt **16** **like a shot** very quickly, esp willingly **17** **shot in the arm** *inf* anything that regenerates, increases confidence or efficiency, etc **18** **shot in the dark** a wild guess [OE *scot*]

shot[2] (ʃɒt) *vb* **1** the past tense and past participle of **shoot** ▹ *adj* **2** (of textiles) woven to give a changing colour effect: *shot silk* **3** streaked with colour

shotgun (ˈʃɒtˌgʌn) *n* **1** a shoulder firearm with unrifled bore used mainly for hunting small game **2** *American football* an offensive formation in which the quarterback lines up for a snap unusually far behind the line of scrimmage ▹ *adj* **3** *chiefly US* involving coercion or duress: *a shotgun merger*

shotgun wedding *n* *inf* a wedding into which one or both partners are coerced, usually because the woman is pregnant

shot put *n* an athletic event in which contestants hurl or put a heavy metal ball or shot as far as possible > 'shot-,putter *n*

shotten ('ʃɒtᵊn) *adj* 1 (of fish, esp herring) having recently spawned 2 *arch* worthless [C15 from obs. p.p. of SHOOT]

shot tower *n* a building formerly used in the production of shot, in which molten lead was graded and dropped from a great height into water, thus cooling it and forming the shot

should (ʃʊd) *vb* the past tense of **shall**: used as an auxiliary verb to indicate that an action is considered by the speaker to be obligatory (*you should go*) or to form the subjunctive mood with I or *we* (*I should like to see you; if I should be late*) [OE *sceold*]

USAGE The use of *should of* instead of *should have* in phrases such as *I should of known better* is nonstandard, and should be avoided in writing

shoulder ('ʃəʊldə) *n* 1 the part of the vertebrate body where the arm or a corresponding forelimb joins the trunk 2 the joint at the junction of the forelimb with the pectoral girdle 3 a cut of meat including the upper part of the foreleg 4 *printing* the flat surface of a piece of type from which the face rises 5 the part of a garment that covers the shoulder 6 anything that resembles a shoulder in shape or position 7 the strip of unpaved land that borders a road 8 **a shoulder to cry on** a person one turns to for sympathy with one's troubles 9 **give (someone) the cold shoulder** *inf* 9a to treat in a cold manner; snub 9b to ignore or shun 10 **put one's shoulder to the wheel** *inf* to work very hard 11 **rub shoulders with** *inf* to mix with socially or associate with 12 **shoulder to shoulder** 12a side by side 12b in a corporate effort ▷ *vb* 13 (*tr*) to bear or carry (a burden, etc) as if on one's shoulders 14 to push (something) with or as if with the shoulder 15 (*tr*) to lift or carry on the shoulders 16 **shoulder arms** *mil* to bring the rifle vertically close to the right side with the muzzle uppermost [OE *sculdor*]

shoulder blade *n* the nontechnical name for **scapula**

shoulder strap *n* a strap over the shoulders, as to hold up a garment or to support a bag, etc

shouldn't ('ʃʊdᵊnt) *contraction of* should not

shouldst (ʃʊdst) *or* **shouldest** ('ʃʊdɪst) *vb arch or dialect* (used with the pronoun *thou*) a form of the past tense of **shall**

shout (ʃaʊt) *n* 1 a loud cry, esp to convey emotion or a command 2 *inf* 2a a round, esp of drinks 2b one's turn to buy a round of drinks 3 *inf* a greeting (to family, friends, etc) sent to a radio station for broadcasting ▷ *vb* 4 to utter (something) in a loud cry 5 (*intr*) to make a loud noise 6 (*tr*) *Austral & NZ inf* to treat (someone or a group of people) to (something, esp a drink) [C14 prob. from ON *skūta* taunt] > '**shouter** *n*

shout down *vb* (*tr, adv*) to drown, overwhelm, or silence by talking loudly

shove (ʃʌv) *vb* **shoves, shoving, shoved** 1 to give a thrust or push to (a person or thing) 2 (*tr*) to give a violent push to 3 (*intr*) to push one's way roughly 4 (*tr*) *inf* to put (something) somewhere: *shove it in the bin* ▷ *n* 5 the act or an instance of shoving ▷ See also **shove off** [OE *scūfan*] > '**shover** *n*

shove-halfpenny *n Brit* a game in which players try to propel coins, originally old halfpennies, with the hand into lined sections of a wooden board

shovel ('ʃʌvᵊl) *n* 1 an instrument for lifting or scooping loose material, such as earth, coal, etc, consisting of a curved blade or a scoop attached to a handle 2 any machine or part resembling a shovel in action 3 Also called: **shovelful** the amount that can be contained in a shovel ▷ *vb* **shovels, shovelling, shovelled** *or US* **shovels, shoveling, shoveled** 4 to lift (earth, etc) with a shovel 5 (*tr*) to clear or dig (a path) with or as if with a shovel 6 (*tr*) to gather, load, or unload in a hurried or careless way [OE *scofl*] > '**shoveller** *or US* '**shoveler** *n*

shoveler ('ʃʌvələ) *n* a duck of ponds and marshes, having a spoon-shaped bill, a blue patch on each wing, and in the male a green head, white breast, and reddish-brown body

shovelhead ('ʃʌvᵊl,hɛd) *n* a common shark of the Atlantic and Pacific Oceans, having a shovel-shaped head

shove off *vb* (*intr, adv; often imperative*) 1 to move from the shore in a boat 2 *inf* to go away; depart

show (ʃəʊ) *vb* **shows, showing, showed; shown** *or* **showed** 1 to make, be, or become visible or noticeable: *to show one's dislike* 2 (*tr*) to exhibit: *he showed me a picture* 3 (*tr*) to indicate or explain; prove: *to show that the earth moves round the sun* 4 (*tr*) to present (oneself or itself) in a specific character: *to show oneself to be trustworthy* 5 (*tr*; foll by *how* and an infinitive) to instruct by demonstration: *show me how to swim* 6 (*tr*) to indicate: *a barometer shows changes in the weather* 7 (*tr*) to grant or bestow: *to show favour to someone* 8 (*intr*) to appear: *to show to advantage* 9 to exhibit, display, or offer (goods, etc) for sale: *three artists were showing at the gallery* 10 (*tr*) to allege, as in a legal document: *to show cause* 11 to present (a film, etc) or (of a play, etc) to be presented, as at a theatre or cinema 12 (*tr*) to guide or escort: *please show me to my room* 13 **show in** *or* **out** to conduct a person into or out of a room or building by opening the door for him or her 14 (*intr*) *inf* to arrive ▷ *n* 15 a display or exhibition 16 a public spectacle 17 an ostentatious display 18 a theatrical or other entertainment 19 a trace or indication 20 *obstetrics* a discharge of blood at the onset of labour 21 *US, Austral, & NZ inf* a chance (esp in **give someone a show**) 22 *sl, chiefly Brit* a thing or affair (esp in **good show, bad show**, etc) 23 **for show** in order to attract attention 24 **run the show** *inf* to take charge of or manage an affair, business, etc 25 **steal the show** *inf* to be looked upon as the most interesting, popular, etc, esp unexpectedly ▷ See also **show off, show up** [OE *scēawian*]

Ss

showboat ('ʃəʊ,bəʊt) *n* 1 a paddle-wheel river steamer with a theatre and a repertory company ▷ *vb* 2 (*intr*) to perform or behave in a showy flamboyant way

showbread ('ʃəʊ,brɛd) *n* a variant spelling of **shewbread**

show business *n* the entertainment industry, including theatre, films, television, and radio. Informal term: **show biz**

show card *n commerce* a card containing a tradesman's advertisement; poster

showcase ('ʃəʊ,keɪs) *n* 1 a glass case used to display objects in a museum or shop 2 a setting in which anything may be displayed to best advantage ▷ *vb* **showcases, showcasing, showcased** 3 (*tr*) to display or exhibit

show day *n* (in Australia) a public holiday in a state on the date of its annual agricultural and industrial show

showdown ('ʃəʊ,daʊn) *n* 1 *inf* an action that brings matters to a head or acts as a conclusion 2 *poker* the exposing of the cards in the players' hands at the end of the game

shower[1] ('ʃaʊə) *n* 1 a brief period of rain, hail, sleet, or snow 2 a sudden abundant fall or downpour, as of tears, sparks, or light 3 a rush: *a shower of praise* 4a a kind of bath in which a person stands upright and is sprayed with water from a nozzle 4b the room, booth, etc, containing such a bath. Full name: **shower bath** 5 *Brit sl* a derogatory term applied to a person or group 6 *US, Canad, Austral, & NZ* a party held to honour and present gifts to a person, as to a prospective bride 7 a large number of particles formed by the collision of a cosmic-ray particle with a particle in the atmosphere 8 *NZ* a light fabric put over a tea table to protect the food from flies, etc ▷ *vb* **9** (*tr*) to sprinkle or spray with or as if with a shower **10** (often with *it* as subject) to fall or cause to fall in the form of a shower **11** (*tr*) to give (gifts, etc) in abundance or present (a person) with (gifts, etc): *they showered gifts on him* **12** (*intr*) to take a shower [OE *scūr*] > **'showery** *adj*

shower² ('ʃəʊə) *n* a person or thing that shows

showgirl ('ʃəʊˌgɜːl) *n* a girl who appears in variety shows, nightclub acts, etc

show house *n* a house on a newly built estate that is decorated and furnished for prospective buyers to view

showing ('ʃəʊɪŋ) *n* **1** a presentation, exhibition, or display **2** manner of presentation

showjumping ('ʃəʊˌdʒʌmpɪŋ) *n* the riding of horses in competitions to demonstrate skill in jumping over or between various obstacles > **'show-jumper** *n*
▷ www.horsesport.org
▷ www.bsja.co.uk

showman ('ʃəʊmən) *n, pl* **showmen 1** a person who presents or produces a theatrical show, etc **2** a person skilled at presenting anything in an effective manner > **'showmanship** *n*

shown (ʃəʊn) *vb* a past participle of **show**

show off *vb* (*adv*) **1** (*tr*) to exhibit or display so as to invite admiration **2** (*intr*) *inf* to behave in such a manner as to make an impression ▷ *n* **show-off 3** *inf* a person who makes a vain display of himself or herself

showpiece ('ʃəʊˌpiːs) *n* **1** anything displayed or exhibited **2** anything prized as a very fine example of its type

showplace ('ʃəʊˌpleɪs) *n* a place exhibited or visited for its beauty, historic interest, etc

showroom ('ʃəʊˌruːm, -ˌrʊm) *n* a room in which goods for sale, such as cars, are on display

show up *vb* (*adv*) **1** to reveal or be revealed clearly **2** (*tr*) to expose or reveal the faults or defects of by comparison **3** (*tr*) *inf* to put to shame; embarrass **4** (*intr*) *inf* to appear or arrive

showy ('ʃəʊɪ) *adj* **showier, showiest 1** gaudy or ostentatious **2** making an imposing display > **'showily** *adv* > **'showiness** *n*

shrank (ʃræŋk) *vb* a past tense of **shrink**

shrapnel ('ʃræpnᵊl) *n* **1** a projectile containing a number of small pellets or bullets exploded before impact **2** fragments from this type of shell [c19 after H. *Shrapnel* (1761–1842), E army officer, who invented it]

shred (ʃrɛd) *n* **1** a long narrow strip or fragment torn or cut off **2** a very small piece or amount ▷ *vb* **shreds, shredding, shredded** *or* **shred 3** (*tr*) to tear or cut into shreds [OE *scread*] > **'shredder** *n*

Shreveport ('ʃriːvˌpɔːt) *n* a city in NW Louisiana, on the Red River: centre of an oil and natural-gas region. Pop: 200 145 (2000)

shrew (ʃruː) *n* **1** Also called: **shrewmouse** a small mouselike long-snouted insectivorous mammal **2** a bad-tempered or mean-spirited woman [OE *scrēawa*]

shrewd (ʃruːd) *adj* **1** astute and penetrating, often with regard to business **2** artful: *a shrewd politician* **3** *obs* piercing: *a shrewd wind* [c14 from *shrew* (obs. vb) to curse, from SHREW] > **'shrewdly** *adv* > **'shrewdness** *n*

shrewish ('ʃruːɪʃ) *adj* (esp of a woman) bad-tempered and nagging

Shrewsbury ('ʃrəʊzbərɪ, -brɪ, 'ʃruːz-) *n* a town in W central England, administrative centre of Shropshire, on the River Severn: strategically situated near the Welsh border; market town. Pop: 90 900 (1991)

shriek (ʃriːk) *n* **1** a shrill and piercing cry ▷ *vb* **2** to produce or utter (words, sounds, etc) in a shrill piercing tone [c16 prob. from ON *skrækja* to screech] > **'shrieker** *n*

shrieval ('ʃriːvᵊl) *adj* of or relating to a sheriff

shrievalty ('ʃriːvəltɪ) *n, pl* **shrievalties 1** the office or term of office of a sheriff **2** the jurisdiction of a sheriff [c16 from arch. *shrieve* sheriff, on the model of *mayoralty*]

shrift (ʃrɪft) *n arch* the act or an instance of shriving or being shriven. See also **short shrift** [OE *scrift*, from L *scriptum* SCRIPT]

shrike (ʃraɪk) *n* an Old World songbird having a heavy hooked bill and feeding on smaller animals which it sometimes impales on thorns, etc. Also called: **butcherbird** [OE *scrīc* thrush]

shrill (ʃrɪl) *adj* **1** sharp and high-pitched in quality **2** emitting a sharp high-pitched sound ▷ *vb* **3** to utter (words, sounds, etc) in a shrill tone [c14 prob. from OE *scralletan*] > **'shrillness** *n* > **'shrilly** *adv*

shrimp (ʃrɪmp) *n* **1** any of a genus of chiefly marine decapod crustaceans having a slender flattened body with a long tail and a single pair of pincers **2** *inf* a diminutive person, esp a child ▷ *vb* **3** (*intr*) to fish for shrimps [c14 prob. of Gmc origin] > **'shrimper** *n*

shrine (ʃraɪn) *n* **1** a place of worship hallowed by association with a sacred person or object **2** a container for sacred relics **3** the tomb of a saint or other holy person **4** a place or site venerated for its association with a famous person or event **5** *RC Church* a building, alcove, or shelf arranged as a setting for a statue, picture, etc, of Christ, the Virgin Mary, or a saint ▷ *vb* **shrines, shrining, shrined 6** short for **enshrine** [OE *scrīn*, from L *scrīnium* bookcase] > **'shrineˌlike** *adj*

shrink (ʃrɪŋk) *vb* **shrinks, shrinking; shrank** *or* **shrunk; shrunk** *or* **shrunken 1** to contract or cause to contract as from wetness, heat, cold, etc **2** to become or cause to become smaller in size **3** (*intr; often foll by from*) **3a** to recoil or withdraw: *to shrink from the sight of blood* **3b** to feel great reluctance (at) ▷ *n* **4** the act or an instance of shrinking **5** a slang word for **psychiatrist** [OE *scrincan*] > **'shrinkable** *adj* > **'shrinker** *n* > **'shrinking** *adj*

shrinkage ('ʃrɪŋkɪdʒ) *n* **1** the act or fact of shrinking **2** the amount by which anything decreases in size, value, weight, etc **3** *commerce* the loss of merchandise through shoplifting or damage

shrinking violet *n inf* a shy person

shrink-wrap *vb* **shrink-wraps, shrink-wrapping, shrink-wrapped** (*tr*) to package a product in a flexible plastic wrapping designed to shrink about its contours to protect and seal it

shrive (ʃraɪv) *vb* **shrives, shriving; shrove** *or* **shrived; shriven** ('ʃrɪvᵊn) *or* **shrived** *chiefly RC Church* **1** to hear the confession of (a penitent) **2** (*tr*) to impose a penance upon (a penitent) and grant him or her absolution **3** (*intr*) to confess one's sins to a priest in order to obtain forgiveness [OE *scrīfan*, from L *scrībere* to write] > **'shriver** *n*

shrivel ('ʃrɪvᵊl) *vb* **shrivels, shrivelling, shrivelled** *or US* **shrivels, shriveling, shriveled 1** to make or become shrunken and withered **2** to lose or cause to lose vitality [c16 prob. of Scand. origin]

Shropshire ('ʃrɒpʃɪə, -ʃə) *n* **1** a county of W central England: Telford and Wrekin became an independent unitary authority in 1998; mainly agricultural. Administrative centre: Shrewsbury. Pop (excluding Telford and Wrekin): 283 240 (2001). Area (excluding Telford and Wrekin): 3201 sq km (1236 sq miles) **2** a breed of medium-sized sheep having a dense fleece, originating from Shropshire and Staffordshire, England

shroud (ʃraʊd) *n* **1** a garment or piece of cloth used to wrap a dead body **2** anything that envelops like a garment: *a shroud of mist* **3** a protective covering for a piece of equipment **4** *astronautics* a streamlined protective covering used to protect the payload during a rocket-powered launch **5** *naut* one of a pattern of ropes or cables used to stay a mast ▷ *vb* (*tr*) **6** to wrap in a shroud **7** to cover, envelop, or hide [OE *scrūd* garment] > **'shroudless** *adj*

shrove (ʃrəʊv) *vb* a past tense of **shrive**

Shrovetide ('ʃrəʊvˌtaɪd) *n* the Sunday, Monday, and Tuesday before Ash Wednesday, formerly a time when confessions were made for Lent

shrub[1] (ʃrʌb) *n* a woody perennial plant, smaller than a tree, with several major branches arising from near the base of the main stem [OE *scrybb*] > '**shrub,like** *adj*

shrub[2] (ʃrʌb) *n* a mixed drink of rum, fruit juice, sugar, and spice [c18 from Ar. *sharāb*, var. of *shurb* drink; see SHERBET]

▷ www.ngpc.state.ne.us/wildlife/shrubs.html
▷ http://forums2.gardenweb.com/forums/shrubs
▷ http://doityourself.com/shrubs

shrubbery ('ʃrʌbərɪ) *n, pl* **shrubberies** **1** a place where a number of shrubs are planted **2** shrubs collectively

shrubby ('ʃrʌbɪ) *adj* **shrubbier, shrubbiest** **1** consisting of, planted with, or abounding in shrubs **2** resembling a shrub > '**shrubbiness** *n*

shrug (ʃrʌg) *vb* **shrugs, shrugging, shrugged** **1** to draw up and drop (the shoulders) abruptly in a gesture expressing indifference, ignorance, etc ▷ *n* **2** the gesture so made [c14 from ?]

shrug off *vb (tr, adv)* **1** to minimize the importance of; dismiss **2** to get rid of

shrunk (ʃrʌŋk) *vb* a past participle and past tense of **shrink**

shrunken ('ʃrʌŋk^{ə}n) *vb* **1** a past participle of **shrink** ▷ *adj* **2** (*usually prenominal*) reduced in size

shtoom (ʃtʊm) *adj sl* silent, dumb (esp in **keep shtoom**) [from Yiddish, from G *stumm* silent]

shuck (ʃʌk) *n* **1** the outer covering of something, such as the husk of a grain of maize, a pea pod, or an oyster shell ▷ *vb (tr)* **2** to remove the shucks from [c17 US dialect, from ?] > '**shucker** *n*

shucks (ʃʌks) *interj US & Canad inf* an exclamation of disappointment, annoyance, etc

shudder ('ʃʌdə) *vb* **1** (*intr*) to shake or tremble suddenly and violently, as from horror, fear, aversion, etc ▷ *n* **2** a convulsive shiver [c18 from MLow G *schōderen*] > '**shuddering** *adj* > '**shudderingly** *adv* > '**shuddery** *adj*

shuffle ('ʃʌf^{ə}l) *vb* **shuffles, shuffling, shuffled** **1** to walk or move (the feet) with a slow dragging motion **2** to change the position of (something), esp in order to deceive others **3** (*tr*) to mix together in a careless manner: *he shuffled the papers nervously* **4** to mix up (cards in a pack) to change their order **5** (*intr*) to behave in an evasive or underhand manner **6** (when *intr*, often foll by *into* or *out of*) to move or cause to move clumsily: *he shuffled out of the door* ▷ *n* **7** the act or an instance of shuffling **8** a rearrangement: *a Cabinet shuffle* **9** a dance or dance step with short dragging movements of the feet [c16 prob. from Low G *schüffeln*] > '**shuffler** *n*

shuffleboard ('ʃʌf^{ə}l,bɔːd) *n* a game in which players push wooden or plastic discs with a long cue towards numbered scoring sections marked on a floor, esp a ship's deck

shuffle off *vb (tr, adv)* to thrust off or put aside: *shuffle off responsibility*

shuffle play *n* a facility on a compact disc player that selects tracks at random from one or more compact discs

shufty *or* **shufti** ('ʃʊftɪ, 'ʃʌftɪ) *n, pl* **shufties** *Brit sl* a look; peep [c20 from Ar.]

heraldry ('ʃuː'fuː) *n* transliteration of the Chinese name for **Kashi**

shun (ʃʌn) *vb* **shuns, shunning, shunned** (*tr*) to avoid deliberately [OE *scunian*, from ?]

shunt (ʃʌnt) *vb* **1** to turn or cause to turn to one side **2** *railways* to transfer (rolling stock) from track to track **3** *electronics* to divert or be diverted through a shunt **4** (*tr*) to evade by putting off onto someone else ▷ *n* **5** the act or an instance of shunting **6** a railway point **7** *electronics* a low-resistance conductor connected in parallel across a part of a circuit to provide an alternative path for a known fraction of the current **8** *med* a channel that bypasses the normal circulation of the blood **9** *Brit inf* a collision that occurs when a vehicle runs into the back of the vehicle in front [c13 ?from *shunen* to SHUN]

shunt-wound ('ʃʌnt,waʊnd) *adj electrical engineering* (of a motor or generator) having the field and armature circuits connected in parallel

shush (ʃʊʃ) *interj* **1** be quiet! hush! ▷ *vb* **2** to silence or calm (someone) by or as if by saying "shush" [c20 reduplication of SH, infl. by HUSH]

Shushan ('ʃuːʃæn) *n* the Biblical name for **Susa**

shut (ʃʌt) *vb* **shuts, shutting, shut** **1** to move (something) so as to cover an aperture: *to shut a door* **2** to close (something) by bringing together the parts: *to shut a book* **3** (*tr*; often foll by *up*) to close or lock the doors of: *to shut up a house* **4** (*tr*; foll by *in, out*, etc) to confine, enclose, or exclude **5** (*tr*) to prevent (a business, etc) from operating **6** **shut the door on** **6a** to refuse to think about **6b** to render impossible ▷ *adj* **7** closed or fastened ▷ *n* **8** the act or time of shutting ▷ See also **shutdown, shut-off**, etc [OE *scyttan*]

shutdown ('ʃʌt,daʊn) *n* **1a** the closing of a factory, shop, etc **1b** (*as modifier*): *shutdown costs* ▷ *vb* **shut down** (*adv*) **2** to cease or cause to cease operation **3** (*tr*) to close by lowering

Shute (ʃuːt) *n* **Nevil**, real name *Nevil Shute Norway*. 1899–1960, English novelist, in Australia after World War II: noted for his novels set in Australia, esp *A Town like Alice* (1950) and *On the Beach* (1957)

shuteye ('ʃʌt,aɪ) *n* a slang term for **sleep**

shut-in *n chiefly US* **a** a person confined indoors by illness **b** (*as modifier*): *a shut-in patient*

shut-off *n* **1** a device that shuts something off, esp a machine control **2** a stoppage or cessation ▷ *vb* **shut off** (*tr, adv*) **3** to stem the flow of **4** to block off the passage through **5** to isolate or separate

shutout ('ʃʌt,aʊt) *n* **1** a less common word for a **lockout** **2** *sport* a match in which the opposition does not score ▷ *vb* **shut out** (*tr, adv*) **3** to keep out or exclude **4** to conceal from sight: *we planted trees to shut out the view of the road*

Ss

shutter ('ʃʌtə) *n* **1** a hinged doorlike cover, often louvred and usually one of a pair, for closing off a window **2** **put up the shutters** to close business at the end of the day or permanently **3** *photog* an opaque shield in a camera that, when tripped, admits light to expose the film or plate for a predetermined period, usually a fraction of a second **4** *music* one of the louvred covers over the mouths of organ pipes, operated by the swell pedal **5** a person or thing that shuts ▷ *vb (tr)* **6** to close with a shutter or shutters **7** to equip with a shutter or shutters

shuttering ('ʃʌtərɪŋ) *n* another word (esp Brit) for **formwork**

shuttle ('ʃʌt^{ə}l) *n* **1** a bobbin-like device used in weaving for passing the weft thread between the warp threads **2** a small bobbin-like device used to hold the thread in a sewing machine, etc **3a** a bus, train, aircraft, etc, that plies between two points **3b** short for **space shuttle** **4a** the movement between various countries of a diplomat in order to negotiate with rulers who refuse to meet each other **4b** (*as modifier*): *shuttle diplomacy* **5** *badminton, etc* short for **shuttlecock** ▷ *vb* **shuttles, shuttling, shuttled** **6** to move or cause to move by or as if by a shuttle [OE *scytel* bolt]

shuttlecock ('ʃʌt^{ə}l,kɒk) *n* **1** a light cone consisting of a cork stub with feathered flights, struck to and fro in badminton and battledore **2** anything moved to and fro, as in an argument

shut up *vb (adv)* **1** (*tr*) to prevent all access to **2** (*tr*) to confine or imprison **3** *inf* to cease to talk or make a noise or cause to cease to talk or make a noise: often used in commands

shwa (ʃwɑː) *n* a variant spelling of **schwa**

shy[1] (ʃaɪ) *adj* **shyer, shyest** *or* **shier, shiest** **1** not at ease in the company of others **2** easily frightened; timid **3** (*often foll by of*) watchful or wary **4** (*foll by of*) *inf, chiefly US & Canad* short (of) **5** (*in combination*) showing reluctance or disinclination: *workshy* ▷ *vb* **shies, shying, shied** (*intr*) **6** to move suddenly, as from fear: *the horse shied at the snake in the road* **7** (*usually foll by off or away*) to draw back ▷ *n, pl* **shies 8** a sudden movement, as from fear [OE *sceoh*] > **'shyer** *n* > **'shyly** *adv* > **'shyness** *n*

shy² (ʃaɪ) *vb* **shies, shying, shied 1** to throw (something) with a sideways motion ▷ *n, pl* **shies 2** a quick throw **3** *inf* a gibe **4** *inf* an attempt [C18 of Gmc origin] > **'shyer** *n*

Shylock ('ʃaɪˌlɒk) *n* a heartless or demanding creditor [C19 after *Shylock*, the heartless usurer in Shakespeare's *The Merchant of Venice* (1596)]

shyster ('ʃaɪstə) *n sl, chiefly US* a person, esp a lawyer or politician, who uses discreditable methods [C19 prob. based on *Scheuster*, a disreputable 19th-cent. New York lawyer]

si (siː) *n music* the syllable used in the fixed system of solmization for the note B [C14 see GAMUT]

Si¹ (ʃiː) *or* **Si Kiang** *n* a variant transliteration of the Chinese name for the **Xi**

Si² *the chemical symbol for* silicon

SI 1 *symbol for* Système International (d'Unités). See **SI unit 2** *NZ abbrev for* South Island
▷ www.bipm.fr/en/si

sial ('saɪəl) *n* the silicon-rich and aluminium-rich rocks of the earth's continental upper crust [C20 *si(licon)* + *al(uminium)*] > **sialic** (saɪ'ælɪk) *adj*

Sialkot (sɪ'ælkɒt) *n* a city in NE Pakistan: shrine of Guru Nanak. Pop (urban area): 417 597 (1988)

Siam (saɪ'æm, 'saɪæm) *n* **1** the former name (until 1939 and 1945–49) of **Thailand 2 Gulf of** an arm of the South China Sea between the Malay Peninsula and Indochina

siamang ('saɪəˌmæŋ) *n* a large black gibbon of Sumatra and the Malay Peninsula, having the second and third toes united [C19 from Malay]

Siamese (ˌsaɪə'miːz) *n, pl* **Siamese 1** See **Siamese cat** ▷ *adj* **2** characteristic of, relating to, or being a Siamese twin ▷ *adj, n, pl* **Siamese 3** another word for **Thai**

Siamese cat *n* a short-haired breed of cat with a tapering tail, blue eyes, and dark ears, mask, tail, and paws

Siamese fighting fish *n* a brightly coloured labyrinth fish of Thailand and Malaysia: the males are very pugnacious

Siamese twins *pl n* (*not in technical usage*) another name for **conjoined twins**

Sian (ʃɑːn) *n* a variant transliteration of the Chinese name for **Xi An**

Siang (ʃɑːŋ) *n* a variant transliteration of the Chinese name for the **Xiang**

Siangtan ('ʃɑːŋ'tɑːn) *n* a variant transliteration of the Chinese name for **Xiangtan**

sib (sɪb) *n* **1** a blood relative **2** a brother or sister; sibling **3** kinsmen collectively; kindred [OE *sibb*]

SIB (in Britain) *abbrev for* (the former) Securities and Investments Board

Sibelius (sɪ'beɪlɪəs) *n* **Jean** (ʒɑn) 1865–1957, Finnish composer, noted for his seven symphonies, his symphonic poems, such as *Finlandia* (1900) and *Tapiola* (1925), and his violin concerto (1905)

Siberia (saɪ'bɪərɪə) *n* a vast region of Russia and N Kazakhstan: extends from the Ural Mountains to the Pacific and from the Arctic Ocean to the borders with China and Mongolia; colonized after the building of the Trans-Siberian Railway. Area: 13 807 037 sq km (5 330 896 sq miles) > **Si'berian** *n, adj*

sibilant ('sɪbɪlənt) *adj* **1** *phonetics* relating to or denoting the consonants (s, z, ʃ, ʒ), all pronounced with a characteristic hissing sound **2** having a hissing sound ▷ *n* **3** a sibilant consonant [C17 from L *sībilāre* to hiss, imit.] > **'sibilance** *or* **'sibilancy** *n* > **'sibilantly** *adv*

sibilate ('sɪbɪˌleɪt) *vb* **sibilates, sibilating, sibilated** to pronounce or utter (words or speech) with a hissing sound > **ˌsibi'lation** *n*

Sibiu (*Romanian* si'biu) *n* an industrial town in W central Romania: originally a Roman city, refounded by German colonists in the 12th century. Pop: 168 949 (1997 est). German name: **Hermannstadt** Hungarian name: **Nagyszeben**

sibling ('sɪblɪŋ) *n* **a** a person's brother or sister **b** (*as modifier*): *sibling rivalry* [C19 specialized modern use of OE *sibling* relative, from SIB]

sibyl ('sɪbɪl) *n* **1** (in ancient Greece and Rome) any of a number of women believed to be oracles or prophetesses **2** a witch, fortune-teller, or sorceress [C13 ult. from Gk *Sibulla*, from ?] > **sibylline** ('sɪbɪˌlaɪn) *adj*

sic¹ (sɪk) *adv* so or thus: inserted in brackets in a text to indicate that an odd or questionable reading is what was actually written or printed [L]

sic² (sɪk) *vb* **sics, sicking, sicked** (*tr*) **1** to attack: used only in commands, as to a dog **2** to urge (a dog) to attack [C19 dialect var. of SEEK]

Sica (*Italian* 'siːka) **Vittorio de** See (Vittorio) **de Sica**

siccative ('sɪkətɪv) *n* a substance added to a liquid to promote drying: used in paints and some medicines [C16 from LL *siccātīvus*, from L *siccāre* to dry up, from *siccus* dry]

Sichuan ('sɪ'tʃwɑːn) *or* **Szechwan** *n* a province of SW China: the most populous administrative division in the country, esp in the central Red Basin, where it is crossed by three main tributaries of the Yangtze. Capital: Chengdu. Pop: 83 290 000 (2000 est). Area: about 569 800 sq km (220 000 sq miles)

Sicilia (si'tʃiːlja) *n* the Latin and Italian name for **Sicily**

siciliano (ˌsiːtʃiː'ljɑːnəʊ) *n, pl* **sicilianos 1** an old dance in six-beat or twelve-beat time **2** a piece of music composed for or in the rhythm of this dance [It.]

Sicily ('sɪsɪlɪ) *n* the largest island in the Mediterranean, separated from the tip of SW Italy by the Strait of Messina: administratively an autonomous region of Italy; settled by Phoenicians, Greeks, and Carthaginians before the Roman conquest of 241 BC; under Normans (12th–13th centuries); formed the **Kingdom of the Two Sicilies** with Naples in 1815; mountainous and volcanic. Capital: Palermo. Pop: 5 087 794 (2000 est). Area: 25 460 sq km (9830 sq miles). Latin names: **Sicilia, Trinacria** Italian name: **Sicilia** > **Sicilian** (sɪ'sɪlɪən) *adj, n*

sick¹ (sɪk) *adj* **1** inclined or likely to vomit **2a** suffering from ill health **2b** (*as collective n; preceded by the*): *the sick* **3a** of or used by people who are unwell: *sick benefits* **3b** (*in combination*): *a sickroom* **4** deeply affected with a mental or spiritual feeling akin to physical sickness: *sick at heart* **5** mentally or spiritually disturbed **6** *inf* delighting in or catering for the macabre: *sick humour* **7** Also: **sick and tired** (*often foll by of*) *inf* disgusted or weary: *I am sick of his everlasting laughter* **8** (*often foll by for*) weary with longing: *I am sick for my own country* **9** pallid or sickly **10** not in working order ▷ *n, vb* **11** an informal word for **vomit** [OE *sēoc*] > **'sickish** *adj*

sick² (sɪk) *vb* a variant spelling of **sic²**

sickbay ('sɪkˌbeɪ) *n* a room for the treatment of the sick or injured, as on board a ship or at a boarding school

sick building syndrome *n* a group of symptoms, such as headaches, eye irritation, and lethargy, that may be experienced by workers in offices with limited ventilation

sicken ('sɪkən) *vb* **1** to make or become nauseated or disgusted **2** (*intr; often foll by for*) to show symptoms (of an illness) > **'sickener** *n*

sickening ('sɪkənɪŋ) *adj* **1** causing sickness or revulsion **2** *inf* extremely annoying > **'sickeningly** *adv*

Sickert ('sɪkət) *n* **Walter Richard** 1860–1942, British impressionist painter, esp of scenes of London music halls

sick headache *n* **1** a headache accompanied by nausea

2 a nontechnical name for **migraine**

sickie ('sɪkɪ) *n inf* a day of sick leave from work [C20 from SICK[1] + -IE]

sickle ('sɪkᵊl) *n* an implement for cutting grass, corn, etc, having a curved blade and a short handle [OE *sicol*, from L *sēcula*]

sick leave *n* leave of absence from work through illness

sicklebill ('sɪkᵊl,bɪl) *n* any of various birds having a markedly curved bill, such as certain hummingbirds and birds of paradise

sickle-cell anaemia *n* a hereditary form of anaemia occurring mainly in Black populations, in which a large number of red blood cells become sickle-shaped

sick list *n* **1** a list of the sick, esp in the army or navy **2 on the sick list** ill

sickly ('sɪklɪ) *adj* **sicklier, sickliest 1** disposed to frequent ailments; not healthy; weak **2** of or caused by sickness **3** (of a smell, taste, etc) causing revulsion or nausea **4** (of light or colour) faint or feeble **5** mawkish; insipid ▷ *adv* **6** in a sick or sickly manner > '**sickliness** *n*

sick-making *adj inf* galling; sickening

sickness ('sɪknɪs) *n* **1** an illness or disease **2** nausea or queasiness **3** the state or an instance of being sick

sick pay *n* wages paid to an employee while he or she is on sick leave

sic transit gloria mundi *Latin* ('sɪk 'trænsɪt 'glɔːrɪ,ɑː 'mʊndiː) thus passes the glory of the world

Sicyon ('sɪsɪ,ɒn, 'sɪsɪən) *n* an ancient city in S Greece, in the NE Peloponnese near Corinth: declined after 146 BC

sidalcea (sɪ'dælsɪə) *n* any of a genus of hardy perennial plants with pink flowers. Also called **Greek mallow** [from NL]

Siddhartha (sɪ'dɑːtə) *n* the personal name of the **Buddha**

Siddons ('sɪdᵊnz) *n* **Sarah** 1755–1831, English tragedienne

side (saɪd) *n* **1** a line or surface that borders anything **2** *geom* **2a** any line segment forming part of the perimeter of a plane geometric figure **2b** another name for **face** (sense 13) **3** either of two parts into which an object, surface, area, etc, can be divided: *the right side and the left side* **4** either of the two surfaces of a flat object: *the right and wrong side of the cloth* **5** a surface or part of an object that extends vertically: *the side of a cliff* **6** either half of a human or animal body, esp the area around the waist: *I have a pain in my side* **7** the area immediately next to a person or thing: *he stood at her side* **8** a district, point, or direction within an area identified by reference to a central point: *the south side of the city* **9** the area at the edge of a room, road, etc **10** aspect or part: *look on the bright side* **11** one of two or more contesting factions, teams, etc **12** a page in an essay, etc **13** a position, opinion, etc, held in opposition to another in a dispute **14** line of descent: *he gets his brains from his mother's side* **15** *inf* a television channel **16** *billiards, etc* spin imparted to a ball by striking it off-centre with the cue **17** *Brit sl* insolence or pretentiousness: *to put on side* **18 on one side** set apart from the rest, as provision for emergencies, etc **19 on the side 19a** apart from or in addition to the main object **19b** as a sideline **19c** *US* as a side dish **20 take sides** to support one group, opinion, etc, as against another ▷ *adj* **21** being on one side; lateral **22** from or viewed as if from one side **23** directed towards one side **24** subordinate or incidental: *side road* ▷ *vb* **sides, siding, sided 25** (*intr*; usually foll by *with*) to support or associate oneself (with a faction, interest, etc) [OE *sīde*]

side arms *pl n* weapons carried on the person, by belt or holster, such as a sword, pistol, etc

sideband ('saɪd,bænd) *n* the frequency band either above (**upper sideband**) or below (**lower sideband**) the carrier frequency, within which fall the components produced by modulation of a carrier wave

sideboard ('saɪd,bɔːd) *n* a piece of furniture intended to stand at the side of a dining room, with drawers, cupboards, and shelves to hold silver, china, linen, etc

sideboards ('saɪd,bɔːdz) *pl n* another term for **sideburns**

sideburns ('saɪd,bɜːnz) *pl n* a man's whiskers grown down either side of the face in front of the ears. Also called: **sideboards, side whiskers,** (*Austral*) **sidelevers**

sidecar ('saɪd,kɑː) *n* a small car attached on one side to a motorcycle, the other side being supported by a single wheel

side chain *n chem* a group of atoms bound to an atom, usually a carbon atom, that forms part of a larger chain or ring in a molecule

-sided *adj* (*in combination*) having a side or sides as specified: *three-sided; many-sided*

side deal *n* a transaction between two people for their private benefit, which is subsidiary to a contract negotiated by them on behalf of the organizations they represent

side dish *n* a portion of food served in addition to the main dish

side drum *n* a small double-headed drum carried at the side with snares that produce a rattling effect

side effect *n* **1** any unwanted nontherapeutic effect caused by a drug **2** any secondary effect, esp an undesirable one

side-foot *soccer* ▷ *n* **1** a shot or pass played with the side of the foot ▷ *vb* **2** (*tr*) to strike (a ball) with the side of the foot

sidekick ('saɪd,kɪk) *n inf* a close friend or follower who accompanies another on adventures, etc

sidelight ('saɪd,laɪt) *n* **1** light coming from the side **2** a side window **3** either of the two navigational running lights used by vessels at night, a red light on the port and a green on the starboard **4** *Brit* either of two small lights on the front of a motor vehicle **5** additional or incidental information

sideline ('saɪd,laɪn) *n* **1** *sport* a line that marks the side boundary of a playing area **2** a subsidiary interest or source of income **3** an auxiliary business activity or line of merchandise ▷ *vb* **sidelines, sidelining, sidelined 4** (*tr*) *chiefly US & Canad* to prevent (a player) from taking part in a game

Ss

sidelines ('saɪd,laɪnz) *pl n* **1** *sport* the area immediately outside the playing area, where substitute players sit **2** the peripheral areas of any region, organization, etc

sidelong ('saɪd,lɒŋ) *adj* (*prenominal*) **1** directed or inclining to one side **2** indirect or oblique ▷ *adv* **3** from the side; obliquely

sidereal (saɪ'dɪərɪəl) *adj* **1** of or involving the stars **2** determined with reference to one or more stars: *the sidereal day* [C17 from L *sīdereus*, from *sīdus* a star] > **si'dereally** *adv*

sidereal day *n* See **day** (sense 5)

sidereal period *n astron* the period of revolution of a body about another with respect to one or more stars

sidereal time *n* time based upon the rotation of the earth with respect to a particular star, the **sidereal day** being the unit of measurement

sidereal year *n* See **year** (sense 5)

siderite ('saɪdə,raɪt) *n* **1** a pale yellow to brownish-black mineral consisting chiefly of iron(II) carbonate. It occurs mainly in ore veins and sedimentary rocks and is an important source of iron. Formula: $FeCO_3$ **2** a meteorite consisting principally of metallic iron

sidero- *or before a vowel* **sider-** *combining form* indicating iron: *siderolite* [from Gk *sidēros*]

siderolite ('saɪdərə,laɪt) *n* a meteorite consisting of a mixture of iron, nickel, and such ferromagnesian minerals as olivine

siderosis (,saɪdə'rəʊsɪs) *n* a lung disease caused by breathing in fine particles of iron or other metallic dust

siderostat ('saɪdərəʊ,stæt) *n* an astronomical instrument consisting of a plane mirror rotated by a clock mechanism about two axes so that light from a celestial body, esp the sun, is reflected along a constant direction for a long period of time [c19 from *sidero-*, from L *sidus* a star + -STAT]

side-saddle *n* **1** a riding saddle originally designed for women riders in skirts who sit with both legs on the near side of the horse ▷ *adv* **2** on or as if on a side-saddle

sideshow ('saɪd,ʃəʊ) *n* **1** a small show or entertainment offered in conjunction with a larger attraction, as at a circus or fair **2** a subordinate event or incident

sideslip ('saɪd,slɪp) *n* **1** a sideways skid, as of a motor vehicle ▷ *vb* **sideslips, sideslipping, sideslipped** **2** another name for **slip**[1] (sense 11)

sidesman ('saɪdzmən) *n, pl* **sidesmen** *Church of England* a man elected to help the parish church-warden

side-splitting *adj* **1** producing great mirth **2** (of laughter) uproarious or very hearty

sidestep ('saɪd,stɛp) *vb* **sidesteps, sidestepping, sidestepped** **1** to step aside from or out of the way of (something) **2** (*tr*) to dodge or circumvent ▷ *n* **side step** **3** a movement to one side, as in dancing, boxing, etc > **'side,stepper** *n*

sidestroke ('saɪd,strəʊk) *n* a type of swimming stroke in which the swimmer lies sideways in the water making a scissors kick with his or her legs

sideswipe ('saɪd,swaɪp) *n* **1** a glancing blow or hit along or from the side **2** an unexpected criticism of someone or something while discussing another subject ▷ *vb* **sideswipes, sideswiping, sideswiped** **3** to strike (someone) with a glancing blow from the side > **'side,swiper** *n*

sidetrack ('saɪd,træk) *vb* **1** to distract or be distracted from a main subject or topic ▷ *n* **2** *US & Canad* a railway siding **3** a digression

side-valve engine *n* a type of internal-combustion engine in which the inlet and exhaust valves are in the cylinder block at the side of the pistons

sidewalk ('saɪd,wɔːk) *n* the US and Canad word for **pavement**

sidewall ('saɪd,wɔːl) *n* either of the sides of a pneumatic tyre between the tread and the rim

sideward ('saɪdwəd) *adj* **1** directed or moving towards one side ▷ *adv also* **sidewards** **2** towards one side

sideways ('saɪd,weɪz) *adv* **1** moving, facing, or inclining towards one side **2** from one side; obliquely **3** with one side forward ▷ *adj* (*prenominal*) **4** moving or directed to or from one side **5** towards or from one side

side whiskers *pl n* another name for **sideburns**

sidewinder ('saɪd,waɪndə) *n* **1** a North American rattlesnake that moves forwards by a sideways looping motion **2** *boxing, US* a heavy swinging blow from the side

Sidi-bel-Abbès (*French* sidibɛlabɛs) *n* a city in NW Algeria: headquarters of the Foreign Legion until Algerian independence (1962). Pop: 180 260 (1998)

siding ('saɪdɪŋ) *n* **1** a short stretch of railway track connected to a main line, used for storing rolling stock **2** a short railway line giving access to the main line for freight from a factory, etc **3** *US & Canad* material attached to the outside of a building to make it weatherproof

sidle ('saɪdᵊl) *vb* **sidles, sidling, sidled** (*intr*) **1** to move in a furtive or stealthy manner **2** to move along sideways [c17 back formation from obs. *sideling* sideways]

Sidmouth ('sɪdmʊθ) *n* **1st Viscount** See (Henry) **Addington**

Sidney *or* **Sydney** ('sɪdnɪ) *n* **1** **Algernon** 1622–83, English Whig politician, beheaded for his supposed part in the Rye House Plot to assassinate Charles II and the future James II: author of *Discourses Concerning Government* (1689) **2** Sir **Philip** 1554–86, English poet, courtier, and soldier. His works include the pastoral romance *Arcadia* (1590), the sonnet sequence *Astrophel and Stella* (1591), and *The Defence of Poesie* (1595), one of the earliest works of literary criticism in English

Sidon ('saɪdᵊn) *n* the chief city of ancient Phoenicia: founded in the third millennium BC; wealthy through trade and the making of glass and purple dyes; now the Lebanese city of Saïda > **Sidonian** (saɪ'dəʊnɪən) *adj, n*

Sidra ('sɪdrə) *n* **Gulf of** a wide inlet of the Mediterranean on the N coast of Libya

SIDS *abbrev for* sudden infant death syndrome. See **cot death**

Siegbahn ('siːgbɑːn) *n* **1** **Kai** ('kaɪ) born 1918, Swedish physicist who worked on electron spectroscopy: Nobel prize for physics 1981 **2** his father, **Karl Manne Georg** (kɑːrl 'manə 'jeːɔrj) 1886–1978, Swedish physicist, who discovered the M series in X-ray spectroscopy: Nobel prize for physics 1924

siege (siːdʒ) *n* **1a** the offensive operations carried out to capture a fortified place by surrounding it and deploying weapons against it **1b** (*as modifier*): *siege warfare* **2** a persistent attempt to gain something **3** *obs* a seat or throne **4** **lay siege to** **4a** to besiege **4b** to importune [c13 from OF *sege* a seat, from Vulgar L *sēdicāre* (unattested) to sit down, from L *sedēre*]

siege mentality *n* a state of mind in which a person believes that he or she is being constantly oppressed or attacked

Siegen ('siːgən) *n* a city in NW Germany, in North Rhine-Westphalia: manufacturing centre: birthplace of Rubens. Pop: 110 847 (1999 est)

Siegfried ('siːgfriːd; *German* 'ziːkfriːt) *n* *German myth* a German prince, the son of Sigmund and husband of Kriemhild, who, in the *Nibelungenlied*, assumes possession of the treasure of the Nibelungs by slaying the dragon that guards it, wins Brunhild for King Gunther, and is eventually killed by Hagen. Norse equivalent: **Sigurd**

siemens ('siːmənz) *n, pl* **siemens** the derived SI unit of electrical conductance equal to 1 reciprocal ohm. Symbol: S. Formerly called: **mho**

Siemens ('siːmənz) *n* **1** **Ernst Werner von** (ɛrnst 'vɛrnər fɔn) 1816–92, German engineer, inventor, and pioneer in telegraphy. Among his inventions are the self-excited dynamo and an electrolytic refining process **2** his brother, Sir **William**, original name *Karl Wilhelm Siemens*. 1823–83, British engineer, born in Germany, who invented the open-hearth process for making steel

Siena (sɪ'ɛnə; *Italian* 'sjɛːna) *n* a walled city in central Italy, in Tuscany: founded by the Etruscans; important artistic centre (13th–14th centuries); university (13th century). Pop: 58 278 (1990)

Sienkiewicz (*Polish* ʃɛŋ'kjɛvitʃ) *n* **Henryk** ('xɛnrik) 1846–1916, Polish novelist. His best-known works are *Quo Vadis?* (1896), set in Nero's Rome, and the war trilogy *With Fire and Sword* (1884), *The Deluge* (1886), and *Pan Michael* (1888), set in 17th-century Poland: Nobel prize for literature 1905

sienna (sɪ'ɛnə) *n* **1** a natural earth containing ferric oxide used as a yellowish-brown pigment when untreated (**raw sienna**) or a reddish-brown pigment when roasted (**burnt sienna**) **2** the colour of this pigment [c18 from It. *terra di Siena* earth of SIENA]

sierra (sɪ'ɛərə) *n* a range of mountains with jagged peaks, esp in Spain or America [c17 from Sp., lit.: saw, from L *serra*] > **si'erran** *adj*

Sierra Leone (sɪ'ɛərə lɪ'əʊnɪ, lɪ'əʊn) *n* a republic in W Africa, on the Atlantic: became a British colony in 1808 and gained independence (within the Commonwealth) in 1961; declared a republic in 1971; became a one-party state in 1978; military coups in 1991 and 1997; multiparty democracy restored in 1998 but civil war continued until 2002; consists of coastal swamps rising to a plateau in the east. Official language: English. Religion: Muslim majority and animist. Currency: leone. Capital: Freetown. Pop: 5 427 000 (2001 est). Area: 71 740 sq km (27 699 sq miles) > **Sierra Leonean** *adj, n*
▷ www.sierraleone.gov.sl

Sierra Madre (*Spanish* ˈsjɛrra ˈmaðre) *n* (*functioning as singular*) the main mountain system of Mexico, extending for 2500 km (1500 miles) southeast from the N border: consists of the **Sierra Madre Oriental** in the east, the **Sierra Madre Occidental** in the west, and the **Sierra Madre del Sur** in the south. Highest peak: Citlaltépetl, 5699 m (18 698 ft)

Sierra Morena (*Spanish* ˈsjɛrra moˈrena) *n* (*functioning as singular*) a mountain range in SW Spain, between the Guadiana and Guadalquivir Rivers. Highest peak: Estrella, 1299 m (4262 ft)

Sierra Nevada *n* (*functioning as singular*) **1** (sɪˈɛərə nɪˈvɑːdə) a mountain range in E California, parallel to the Coast Ranges. Highest peak: Mount Whitney, 4418 m (14 495 ft) **2** (*Spanish* ˈsjɛrra neˈβaða) a mountain range in SE Spain, mostly in Granada and Almería provinces. Highest peak: Cerro de Mulhacén, 3478 m (11 411 ft)

siesta (sɪˈɛstə) *n* a rest or nap, usually taken in the early afternoon, as in hot countries [c17 from Sp., from L *sexta hōra* the sixth hour, i.e. noon]

sieve (sɪv) *n* **1** a device for separating lumps from powdered material, straining liquids, etc, consisting of a container with a mesh or perforated bottom through which the material is shaken or poured ▷ *vb* **sieves, sieving, sieved 2** to pass or cause to pass through a sieve **3** (*tr; often foll by out*) to separate or remove (lumps, materials, etc) by use of a sieve [OE *sife*] > ˈ**sieve**ˌ**like** *adj*

Sieyès (*French* sjejɛs) *n* **Emmanuel Joseph** (ɛmanɥɛl ʒozɛf), called *Abbé Sieyès*. 1748–1836, French statesman, political theorist, and churchman, who became prominent during the Revolution following the publication of his pamphlet *Qu'est-ce que le tiers état?* (1789). He was instrumental in bringing Napoleon I to power (1799)

sift (sɪft) *vb* **1** (*tr*) to sieve (sand, flour, etc) in order to remove the coarser particles **2** to scatter (something) over a surface through a sieve **3** (*tr*) to separate with or as if with a sieve **4** (*tr*) to examine minutely: *to sift evidence* **5** (*intr*) to move as if through a sieve [OE *siftan*] > ˈ**sifter** *n*

siftings (ˈsɪftɪŋz) *pl n* material or particles separated out by or as if by a sieve

sigh (saɪ) *vb* **1** (*intr*) to draw in and exhale audibly a deep breath as an expression of weariness, relief, etc **2** (*intr*) to make a sound resembling this **3** (*intr; often foll by for*) to yearn, long, or pine **4** (*tr*) to utter or express with sighing ▷ *n* **5** the act or sound of sighing [OE *sīcan*, from ?] > ˈ**sigher** *n*

sight (saɪt) *n* **1** the power or faculty of seeing; vision. Related adj: **visual 2** the act or an instance of seeing **3** the range of vision: *within sight of land* **4** point of view; judgment: *in his sight she could do no wrong* **5** a glimpse or view (esp in **catch** *or* **lose sight of**) **6** anything that is seen **7** (*often pl*) anything worth seeing: *the sights of London* **8** *inf* anything unpleasant or undesirable to see: *his room was a sight!* **9** any of various devices or instruments used to assist the eye in making alignments or directional observations, esp such a device used in aiming a gun **10** an observation or alignment made with such a device **11 a sight** *inf* a great deal: *she's a sight too good for him* **12 a sight for sore eyes** a person or thing that one is pleased or relieved to see **13 at** *or* **on sight 13a** as soon as seen **13b** on presentation: *a bill payable at sight* **14 know by sight** to be familiar with the appearance of without having personal acquaintance **15 not by a long sight** *inf* on no account **16 set one's sights on** to have (a specified goal) in mind **17 sight unseen** without having seen the object at issue: *to buy a car sight unseen* ▷ *vb* **18** (*tr*) to see, view, or glimpse **19** (*tr*) **19a** to furnish with a sight or sights **19b** to adjust the sight of **20** to aim (a firearm) using the sight [OE *sihth*] > ˈ**sightable** *adj*

sighted (ˈsaɪtɪd) *adj* **1** not blind **2** (*in combination*) having sight of a specified kind: *short-sighted*

sighting (ˈsaɪtɪŋ) *n* **1** an occasion on which something is seen, esp something rare or unusual **2** another name for **sight** (sense 10)

sighting shot *n* an experimental shot made to assist gunmen in setting their sights

sightless (ˈsaɪtlɪs) *adj* **1** blind **2** invisible > ˈ**sightlessly** *adv* > ˈ**sightlessness** *n*

sightly (ˈsaɪtlɪ) *adj* **sightlier, sightliest** pleasing or attractive to see > ˈ**sightliness** *n*

sight-read (ˈsaɪtˌriːd) *vb* **sight-reads, sight-reading, sight-read** (-ˌrɛd) to sing or play (music in a printed or written form) without previous preparation > ˈ**sight-**ˌ**reader** *n* > ˈ**sight-**ˌ**reading** *n*

sightscreen (ˈsaɪtˌskriːn) *n cricket* a large screen placed near the boundary behind the bowler to help the batsman see the ball

sightsee (ˈsaɪtˌsiː) *vb* **sightsees, sightseeing, sightsaw, sightseen** to visit the famous or interesting sights of (a place) > ˈ**sight**ˌ**seer** *n*

sightseeing (ˈsaɪtˌsiːɪŋ) *n inf* **a** the activity of visiting the famous or interesting sights of a place **b** (*as modifier*): *sightseeing trip*

Sigismund (ˈsɪgɪsmənd) *n* 1368–1437, king of Hungary (1387–1437) and of Bohemia (1419–37); Holy Roman Emperor (1411–37). He helped to end the Great Schism in the Church; implicated in the death of Huss

sigla (ˈsɪglə) *n* the list of symbols used in a book, usually collected together as part of the preliminaries [L: pl of *siglum*, dim. of *signum* sign]

sigma (ˈsɪgmə) *n* **1** the 18th letter in the Greek alphabet (Σ, σ, or, when final, ς), a consonant, transliterated as *S* **2** *maths* the symbol Σ, indicating summation of the numbers of quantities indicated [c17 from Gk]

sigma notation *n* an algebraic notation in which a capital Greek sigma (Σ) is used to indicate that all values of the expression following the sigma are to be added together (usually for values of a variable between specified limits)

sigmoid (ˈsɪgmɔɪd) *or* **sigmoidal** *adj* **1** shaped like the letter S **2** of or relating to the sigmoid colon of the large intestine [c17 from Gk *sigmoeidēs* sigma-shaped]

sigmoid flexure *n* the S-shaped bend in the final portion of the large intestine

Sigmund (ˈsɪgmənd, ˈsiːgmʊnd; *German* ˈziːkmʊnt) *n* **1** *Norse myth* the father of the hero Sigurd **2** Also called: **Siegmund** (*German* ˈziːkmʊnt) *German myth* king of the Netherlands, father of Siegfried

sign (saɪn) *n* **1** something that indicates a fact, condition, etc, that is not immediately or outwardly observable **2** an action or gesture intended to convey information, a command, etc **3a** a board, placard, etc, displayed in public and intended to inform, warn, etc **3b** (*as modifier*): *a sign painter* **4** an arbitrary mark or device that stands for a word, phrase, etc **5** *maths, logic* **5a** any symbol used to indicate an operation: *a plus sign* **5b** the positivity or negativity of a number, expression, etc **6** an indication or vestige: *the house showed no signs of being occupied* **7** a portentous or significant event **8** the scent or spoor of an animal **9** *med* any objective evidence of the presence of a disease or disorder **10** *astrol* See **sign of the zodiac** ▷ *vb* **11** to write (one's name) as a signature to (a document, etc) in attestation, confirmation, etc **12** (*intr; often foll by to*) to make a sign **13** to engage or be engaged by written agreement, as a player for a team, etc **14** (*tr*) to outline in gestures a sign over, esp the sign of the cross **15** (*tr*) to indicate by or as if by a sign; betoken ▷ See also **sign away, sign in,** etc [c13 from OF, from L *signum* a sign] > ˈ**signable** *adj* > ˈ**signer** *n*

Signac (*French* siɲak) *n* **Paul** (pɔl) 1863–1935, French neoimpressionist painter, influenced by Seurat

signal (ˈsɪgnᵊl) *n* **1** any sign, gesture, etc, that serves to communicate information **2** anything that acts as an incitement to action: *the rise in prices was a signal for rebellion*

Ss

3a a variable parameter, such as a current or electromagnetic wave, by which information is conveyed through an electronic circuit, etc **3b** the information so conveyed **3c** *(as modifier)*: *a signal generator* ▷ *adj* **4** distinguished or conspicuous **5** used to give or act as a signal ▷ *vb* **signals, signalling, signalled** *or US* **signals, signaling, signaled 6** to communicate (a message, etc) to (a person) [c16 from OF *seignal*, from Med. L *signāle*, from L *signum* sign] > **'signaller** *or US* **'signaler** *n*

signal box *n* **1** a building containing signal levers for all the railway lines in its section **2** a control point for a large area of a railway system

signalize *or* **signalise** ('sɪgnə,laɪz) *vb* **signalizes, signalizing, signalized** *or* **signalises, signalising, signalised** *(tr)* **1** to make noteworthy **2** to point out carefully

signally ('sɪgnəlɪ) *adv* conspicuously or especially

signalman ('sɪgnᵊlmən) *n, pl* **signalmen** a railway employee in charge of the signals and points within a section

signal-to-noise ratio *n* the ratio of one parameter, such as power of a wanted signal, to the same parameter of the noise at a specified point in an electronic circuit, etc

signatory ('sɪgnətərɪ, -trɪ) *n, pl* **signatories 1** a person who has signed a document such as a treaty or an organization, state, etc, on whose behalf such a document has been signed ▷ *adj* **2** having signed a document, treaty, etc [c17 from L *signātōrius* concerning sealing, from *signāre* to seal, from *signum* a mark]

signature ('sɪgnɪtʃə) *n* **1** the name of a person or a mark or sign representing his or her name **2** the act of signing one's name **3a** a distinctive mark, characteristic, etc, that identifies a person or thing **3b** *(as modifier)*: *a signature fragrance* **4** *music* See **key signature, time signature 5** *printing* **5a** a sheet of paper printed with several pages that upon folding will become a section or sections of a book **5b** such a sheet so folded **5c** a mark, esp a letter, printed on the first page of a signature [c16 from OF, from Med. L *signātura*, from L *signāre* to sign]

signature tune *n Brit* a melody used to introduce or identify a television or radio programme, a performer, etc

sign away *vb (tr, adv)* to dispose of by or as if by signing a document

signboard ('saɪn,bɔːd) *n* a board carrying a sign or notice, esp one used to advertise a product, event, etc

signet ('sɪgnɪt) *n* **1** a small seal, esp one as part of a finger ring **2** a seal used to stamp or authenticate documents **3** the impression made by such a seal [c14 from Med. L *signētum* a little seal, from L *signum* a sign]

signet ring *n* a finger ring bearing a signet

significance (sɪg'nɪfɪkəns) *n* **1** consequence or importance **2** something expressed or intended **3** the state or quality of being significant **4** *statistics* a measure of the confidence that can be placed in a result as not being merely a matter of chance

significant (sɪg'nɪfɪkənt) *adj* **1** having or expressing a meaning **2** having a covert or implied meaning **3** important or momentous **4** *statistics* of or relating to a difference between a result derived from a hypothesis and its observed value that is too large to be attributed to chance [c16 from L *significāre* to SIGNIFY] > **sig'nificantly** *adv*

significant figures *pl n* **1** the figures of a number that express a magnitude to a specified degree of accuracy: *3.14159 to four significant figures is 3.142* **2** the number of such figures: *3.142 has four significant figures*

significant other *n US inf* a spouse or lover

signification (,sɪgnɪfɪ'keɪʃən) *n* **1** meaning or sense **2** the act of signifying

signify ('sɪgnɪ,faɪ) *vb* **signifies, signifying, signified** (when *tr, may take a clause as object*) **1** *(tr)* to indicate or suggest **2** *(tr)* to imply or portend: *the clouds signified the coming storm* **3** *(tr)* to stand as a symbol, sign, etc (for) **4** *(intr)* to be important [c13 from OF, from L *significāre*, from *signum* a mark + *facere* to make] > **sig'nificative** *adj* > **'signi,fier** *n*

sign in *vb (adv)* **1** to sign or cause to sign a register, as at a hotel, club, etc **2** to make or become a member, as of a club

signing ('saɪnɪŋ) *n* a specific set of manual signs used to communicate with deaf people

sign language *n* any system of communication by manual signs or gestures, such as one used by deaf people

sign off *vb (adv)* **1** *(intr)* to announce the end of a radio or television programme, esp at the end of a day **2** *(tr)* (of a doctor) to declare (someone) unfit for work, because of illness **3** *(intr) Brit* to terminate one's claim to social security benefits

sign of the zodiac *n* any of the 12 equal areas into which the zodiac can be divided, named after the 12 zodiacal constellations. In astrology, it is thought that a person's attitudes to life can be correlated with the sign in which the sun lay at the moment of their birth. Also called: **sign, star sign, sun sign**

sign on *vb (adv)* **1** *(tr)* to hire or employ **2** *(intr)* to commit oneself to a job, activity, etc **3** *(intr) Brit* to claim social security benefits

signor *or* **signior** ('siːnjɔː; *Italian* siɲ'ɲor) *n, pl* **signors** *or* **signori** (*Italian* -'ɲori) an Italian man: usually used before a name as a title equivalent to *Mr*

signora (siːn'jɔːrə; *Italian* siɲ'ɲora) *n, pl* **signoras** *or* **signore** (*Italian* -re) a married Italian woman: a title of address equivalent to *Mrs* when placed before a name or *madam* when used alone [It., fem of SIGNORE]

signore (siːn'jɔːreɪ; *Italian* siɲ'ɲore) *n, pl* **signori** (-rɪ; *Italian* -ri) an Italian man: a title of respect equivalent to *sir* when used alone [It., ult. from L *senior* an elder, from *senex* an old man]

Signorelli (*Italian* siɲɲo'rɛlli) *n* **Luca** ('luːka) ?1441–1523, Italian painter, noted for his frescoes

Signoret (*French* siɲɔrɛ) *n* **Simone** (simɔ̃), original name *Simone Kaminker*. 1921–85, French stage and film actress, whose films include *La Ronde* (1950), *Casque d'Or* (1952), *Room at the Top* (1958), and *Ship of Fools* (1965): married the actor and singer Yves Montand (1921–91)

signorina (,siːnjɔː'riːnə; *Italian* siɲɲo'rina) *n, pl* **signorinas** *or* **signorine** (*Italian* -ne) an unmarried Italian woman: a title of address equivalent to *Miss* when placed before a name or *madam* or *miss* when used alone [It., dim. of SIGNORA]

signory ('siːnjərɪ) *n, pl* **signories** a variant spelling of **seigniory**

sign out *vb (adv)* to sign (one's name) to indicate that one is leaving a place: *he signed out for the evening*

signpost ('saɪn,pəʊst) *n* **1** a post bearing a sign that shows the way, as at a roadside **2** something that serves as a clue or indication ▷ *vb (tr; usually passive)* **3** to mark with signposts **4** to indicate direction towards

sign up *vb (adv)* to enlist or cause to enlist, as for military service

Sigurd ('sɪgʊəd; *German* 'ziːgʊrt) *n Norse myth* a hero who killed the dragon Fafnir to gain the treasure of Andvari, won Brynhild for Gunnar by deception, and then was killed by her when she discovered the fraud. His wife was Gudrun. German counterpart: **Siegfried**

Sihanouk ('sɪənʊk) *n* King **Norodom** (,nɒrə'dɒm) born 1922, Cambodian statesman; king of Cambodia (1941–55 and from 1993); prime minister (1955–60), after which he became head of state. He was deposed in 1970 but reinstated (1975–76) following the victory of the Khmer Rouge in the civil war. He was head of state in exile from 1982; returned in 1991 and became monarch once again in 1993 under a new constitution

sika ('si:kə) *n* a Japanese forest-dwelling deer, now introduced into Britain, having a brown coat and a large white patch on the rump [from Japanese *shika*]

Sikang ('ʃi:'kæŋ) *n* a former province of W China: established in 1928 from part of W Sichuan and E Tibet; dissolved in 1955

Sikh (si:k) *n* **1** a member of an Indian religion that separated from Hinduism and was founded in the 16th century, that teaches monotheism and rejects the authority of the Vedas ▹ *adj* **2** of or relating to the Sikhs or their religious beliefs [c18 from Hindi, lit.: disciple, from Sansk. *śiksati* he studies] > **'Sikh,ism** *n*

▹ www.sikhnet.com/
▹ www.sikhs.org/
▹ www.sikhseek.com/

Si Kiang ('ʃi: 'kjæŋ, kaɪ'æŋ) *n* See **Xi**

Siking ('si:'kɪŋ) *n* a former name for **Xi An**

Sikkim ('sɪkɪm) *n* a state of NE India: under British control (1861–1947); became an Indian protectorate in 1950 and an Indian state in 1975; lies in the Himalayas, rising to 8600 m (28 216 ft) at Kanchenjunga in the north. Capital: Gangtok. Pop: 540 493 (2001). Area: 7096 sq km (2740 sq miles) > **,Sikki'mese** *adj, n*

Sikorski (sɪ'kɔ:ski:) *n* **Władysław** ('vlædɪslæf) 1881–1943, Polish general and statesman: prime minister (1922–23) and prime minister of the Polish government in exile during World War II: died in an air crash

Sikorsky (sɪ'kɔ:skɪ) *n* **Igor** 1889–1972, US aeronautical engineer, born in Russia. He designed and flew the first four-engined aircraft (1913) and designed the first successful helicopter (1939)

silage ('saɪlɪdʒ) *n* any crop harvested while green for fodder and kept succulent by partial fermentation in a silo. Also called: **ensilage** [c19 alteration (infl. by SILO) of ENSILAGE]

sild (sɪld) *n* any of various small young herrings, esp when prepared and canned in Norway [Norwegian]

silence ('saɪləns) *n* **1** the state or quality of being silent **2** the absence of sound or noise **3** refusal or failure to speak, etc, when expected: *his silence on their promotion was alarming* **4** a period of time without noise **5** oblivion or obscurity ▹ *vb* **silences, silencing, silenced** (*tr*) **6** to bring to silence **7** to put a stop to: *to silence all complaint*

silencer ('saɪlənsə) *n* **1** any device designed to reduce noise, esp the device in the exhaust system of a motor vehicle. US and Canad name: **muffler 2** a device fitted to the muzzle of a firearm to deaden the report **3** a person or thing that silences

silene (saɪ'li:nɪ) *n* any of a genus of plants with pink or white flowers and slender leaves [c18 NL, from L]

silent ('saɪlənt) *adj* **1** characterized by an absence or near absence of noise or sound: *a silent house* **2** tending to speak very little or not at all **3** unable to speak **4** failing to speak, communicate, etc, when expected: *the witness chose to remain silent* **5** not spoken or expressed **6** (of a letter) used in the orthography of a word but no longer pronounced in that word: *the "k" in "know" is silent* **7** denoting a film that has no accompanying soundtrack [c16 from L *silēns*, from *silēre* to be quiet] > **'silently** *adv* > **'silentness** *n*

silent cop *n Austral sl* a small raised hemispherical marker in the middle of a crossroads

silent majority *n* a presumed moderate majority of the citizens who are too passive to make their views known

Silenus (saɪ'li:nəs; 'sileɪnəs) *n Greek myth* **1** chief of the satyrs and foster father to Dionysus **2** *pl* **Sileni** (saɪ'li:naɪ; 'sileɪni:) (*often not cap*) one of a class of woodland deities, closely similar to the satyrs

Silesia (saɪ'li:ʃɪə) *n* a region of central Europe around the upper and middle Oder valley: mostly annexed by Prussia in 1742 but became almost wholly Polish in 1945; rich coal and iron-ore deposits. Polish name: **Śląsk** Czech name: **Slezsko** German name: **Schlesien** > **Si'lesian** *adj, n*

silex ('saɪlɛks) *n* a type of heat-resistant glass made from fused quartz [c16 from L: hard stone]

silhouette (,sɪlu:'ɛt) *n* **1** the outline of a solid figure as cast by its shadow **2** an outline drawing filled in with black, often a profile portrait cut out of black paper and mounted on a light ground ▹ *vb* **silhouettes, silhouetting, silhouetted 3** (*tr*) to cause to appear in silhouette [c18 after Étienne de *Silhouette* (1709–67), F politician]

silica ('sɪlɪkə) *n* the dioxide of silicon (SiO_2), occurring naturally as quartz. It is a refractory insoluble material used in the manufacture of glass, ceramics, and abrasives [c19 NL, from L *silex* hard stone]

silica gel *n* an amorphous form of silica capable of absorbing large quantities of water: used esp in drying gases and oils

silicate ('sɪlɪkɪt, -,keɪt) *n* a salt or ester that can be regarded as derived from silicic acid. Silicates constitute a large proportion of the earth's minerals and are present in cement and glass

siliceous *or* **silicious** (sɪ'lɪʃəs) *adj* **1** of, relating to, or containing abundant silica: *a siliceous clay* **2** (of plants) growing in soil rich in silica

silicic (sɪ'lɪsɪk) *adj* of or containing silicon or an acid obtained from silicon

silicic acid *n* a white gelatinous substance obtained by adding an acid to a solution of sodium silicate. It is best regarded as hydrated silica

silicify (sɪ'lɪsɪ,faɪ) *vb* **silicifies, silicifying, silicified** to convert or be converted into silica: *silicified wood* > **si,licifi'cation** *n*

silicon ('sɪlɪkən) *n* **a** a brittle metalloid element that exists in two allotropic forms; occurs principally in sand, quartz, granite, feldspar, and clay. It is usually a grey crystalline solid but is also found as a brown amorphous powder. It is used in transistors, solar cells, and alloys. Its compounds are widely used in glass manufacture and the building industry. Symbol: Si; atomic no.: 14; atomic wt.: 28.09 **b** (*modifier; sometimes cap*) denoting an area of a country that contains much high-technology industry [c19 from SILICA, on the model of *boron, carbon*]

Ss

Silicon Alley *n* an area of New York City in which industries associated with information technology are concentrated

silicon carbide *n* an extremely hard bluish-black insoluble crystalline substance produced by heating carbon with sand at a high temperature and used as an abrasive and refractory material. Very pure crystals are used as semiconductors. Formula: SiC

silicon chip *n* another term for **chip** (sense 7)

silicon-controlled rectifier *n* a semiconductor rectifier whose forward current between two electrodes, the anode and cathode, is initiated by means of a signal applied to a third electrode, the gate. The current subsequently becomes independent of the signal. Also called: **thyristor**

silicone ('sɪlɪ,kəʊn) *n chem* **a** any of a large class of polymeric synthetic materials that usually have resistance to temperature, water, and chemicals, and good insulating and lubricating properties, making them suitable for wide use as oils, water repellents, resins, etc **b** (*as modifier*): *silicone rubber*

Silicon Fen *n* an area of Cambridgeshire, esp around the city of Cambridge, in which industries associated with information technology are concentrated

Silicon Glen *n* a collective term for the industries in Scotland associated with information technology, esp those concentrated in the central conurbation between Glasgow and Edinburgh

Silicon Valley *n* **1** an industrial strip in W California, extending S of San Francisco, in which the US information technology industry is concentrated **2** any area in which industries associated with information technology are concentrated

silicosis (ˌsɪlɪˈkəʊsɪs) *n pathol* a form of pneumoconiosis caused by breathing in tiny particles of silica, quartz, or slate, and characterized by shortness of breath

siliqua (sɪˈliːkwə, ˈsɪlɪkwə) *or* **silique** (sɪˈliːk, ˈsɪlɪk) *n, pl* **siliquae** (-ˈliːkwiː), **siliquas,** *or* **siliques** the long dry dehiscent fruit of cruciferous plants, such as the wallflower [C18 via F from L *siliqua* a pod] > **siliquose** (ˈsɪlɪˌkwəʊs) *or* **siliquous** (ˈsɪlɪkwəs) *adj*

silk (sɪlk) *n* **1** the very fine soft lustrous fibre produced by a silkworm to make its cocoon **2a** thread or fabric made from this fibre **2b** (*as modifier*): *a silk dress* **3** a garment made of this **4** a very fine fibre produced by a spider to build its web, nest, or cocoon **5** the tuft of long fine styles on an ear of maize **6** *Brit* **6a** the gown worn by a Queen's (or King's) Counsel **6b** *inf* a Queen's (or King's) Counsel **6c** **take silk** to become a Queen's (or King's) Counsel [OE *sioluc;* ult. from Chinese *ssŭ* silk] > **ˈsilkˌlike** *adj*

▹ www.silkroadproject.org/silkroad

silk cotton *n* another name for **kapok**

silk-cotton tree *n* any of a genus of tropical trees having seeds covered with silky hairs from which kapok is obtained. Also called: **kapok tree**

silken (ˈsɪlkən) *adj* **1** made of silk **2** resembling silk in smoothness or gloss **3** dressed in silk **4** soft and delicate

silk hat *n* a man's top hat covered with silk

silkworm (ˈsɪlkˌwɜːm) *n* **1** the larva of the Chinese moth that feeds on the leaves of the mulberry tree: widely cultivated as a source of silk **2** any of various similar or related larvae

silky (ˈsɪlkɪ) *adj* **silkier, silkiest 1** resembling silk in texture; glossy **2** made of silk **3** (of a voice, manner, etc) suave; smooth **4** *bot* covered with long fine soft hairs: *silky leaves* > **ˈsilkily** *adv* > **ˈsilkiness** *n*

silky oak *n* any of an Australian genus of trees having divided leaves and showy clusters of orange, red, or white flowers: cultivated in the tropics as shade trees

sill (sɪl) *n* **1** a shelf at the bottom of a window inside a room **2** a horizontal piece along the outside lower member of a window, that throws water clear of the wall below **3** the lower horizontal member of a window or door frame **4** a horizontal member placed on top of a foundation wall in order to carry a timber framework **5** a mass of igneous rock, situated between two layers of older sedimentary rock [OE *syll*]

sillabub (ˈsɪləˌbʌb) *n* a variant spelling of **syllabub**

Sillanpää (*Finnish* ˈsillampæː) *n* **Frans Eemil** (frans ˈeːmil) 1888–1964, Finnish writer, noted for his novels *Meek Heritage* (1919) and *The Maid Silja* (1931): Nobel prize for literature 1939

Sillitoe (ˈsɪlɪtəʊ) *n* **Alan** born 1928, British novelist. His best-known works include *Saturday Night and Sunday Morning* (1958) and *The Loneliness of the Long Distance Runner* (1959)

silly (ˈsɪlɪ) *adj* **sillier, silliest 1** lacking in good sense; absurd **2** frivolous, trivial, or superficial **3** feeble-minded **4** dazed, as from a blow ▹ *n* **5** (*modifier*) *cricket* (of a fielding position) near the batsman's wicket: *silly mid-on* **6** (*pl* **sillies**) Also called: **silly-billy** *inf* a foolish person [C15 (in the sense: pitiable, hence the later senses: foolish): from OE *sǣlig* (unattested) happy, from *sǣl* happiness] > **ˈsilliness** *n*

silly season *n Brit* a period, usually during the summer months, when journalists fill space reporting on frivolous events and activities

silo (ˈsaɪləʊ) *n, pl* **silos 1** a pit, trench, or tower, often cylindrical in shape, in which silage is made and stored **2** an underground position in which missile systems are sited for protection [C19 from Sp., ? of Celtic origin]

Siloam (saɪˈləʊəm, sɪ-) *n Bible* a pool in Jerusalem where Jesus cured a man of his blindness (John 9)

Silone (*Italian* siˈloːne) *n* **Ignazio** (iɲˈɲattsjo) 1900–78, Italian writer, noted for his humanitarian socialistic novels, *Fontamara* (1933) and *Bread and Wine* (1937)

silt (sɪlt) *n* **1** a fine deposit of mud, clay, etc, esp one in a river or lake ▹ *vb* **2** (usually foll by *up*) to fill or become filled with silt; choke [C15 from ON] > **silˈtation** *n* > **ˈsilty** *adj*

Silurian (saɪˈlʊərɪən) *adj* **1** of or formed in the third period of the Palaeozoic era, which lasted for 25 million years, during which fishes first appeared ▹ *n* **2** **the** the Silurian period or rock system [C19 from *Silures,* a Welsh tribe who opposed the Romans]

silurid (saɪˈlʊərɪd) *n* **1** any freshwater teleost fish of the family Siluridae, such as the **European catfish**, which has an elongated body, naked skin, and a long anal fin ▹ *adj* **2** of, relating to, or belonging to the family Siluridae [C19 from L *silūrus,* from Gk *silouros* a river fish]

silva (ˈsɪlvə) *n* a variant spelling of **sylva**

silvan (ˈsɪlvən) *adj, n* a variant spelling of **sylvan**

Silvanus *or* **Sylvanus** (sɪlˈveɪnəs) *n Roman myth* the Roman god of woodlands, fields, and flocks. Greek counterpart: **Pan** [L: from *silva* woodland]

silver (ˈsɪlvə) *n* **1a** a ductile malleable brilliant greyish-white element having the highest electrical and thermal conductivity of any metal. It occurs free and in argentite and other ores: used in jewellery, tableware, coinage, electrical contacts, and electroplating. Symbol: Ag; atomic no.: 47; atomic wt.: 107.870 **1b** (*as modifier*): *a silver coin.* Related adj: **argent** **2** coin made of, or having the appearance of, this metal **3** cutlery, whether made of silver or not **4** any household articles made of silver **5** short for **silver medal** **6a** a brilliant or light greyish-white colour **6b** (*as adj*): *silver hair* ▹ *adj* **7** well-articulated: *silver speech* **8** (*prenominal*) denoting the 25th in a series: *a silver wedding anniversary* ▹ *vb* **9** (*tr*) to coat with silver or a silvery substance: *to silver a spoon* **10** to become or cause to become silvery in colour [OE *siolfor*] > **ˈsilvering** *n*

silver age *n* **1** (in Greek and Roman mythology) the second of the world's major epochs, inferior to the preceding golden age **2** the postclassical period of Latin literature, occupying the early part of the Roman imperial era

silver beet *n* an Australian and New Zealand variety of beet, cultivated for its edible leaves with white stems

silver bell *n* any of various deciduous trees of North America and China, having white bell-shaped flowers. Also called: **snowdrop tree**

silver birch *n* a tree of N temperate regions of the Old World, having silvery-white peeling bark

silver bromide *n* a yellowish powder that darkens when exposed to light: used in making photographic emulsions. Formula: AgBr

silver chloride *n* a white powder that darkens on exposure to light: used in making photographic emulsions and papers. Formula: AgCl

silver disc *n* (in Britain) an album certified to have sold 60 000 copies or a single certified to have sold 200 000 copies

silver-eye *n Austral & NZ* another name for **waxeye** or **white-eye**

silver fern *n NZ* **1** another name for **ponga** **2** a formalized spray of fern leaf, silver on a black background: the symbol of New Zealand sporting teams

Silver Ferns *pl n* **the** the women's international netball team of New Zealand

silver fir *n* any of various fir trees the leaves of which have a silvery undersurface

silverfish (ˈsɪlvəˌfɪʃ) *n, pl* **silverfish** *or* **silverfishes 1** a silver variety of the goldfish **2** any of various other silvery fishes, such as the moonfish **3** any of various small primitive wingless insects that have long antennae and tail appendages and occur in buildings, feeding on food scraps, book-bindings, etc

silver fox *n* **1** an American red fox in a colour phase in which the fur is black with long silver-tipped hairs **2** the valuable fur or pelt of this animal

silver-gilt *n* silver covered with a thin film of gold

silver goal *n soccer* (in certain competitions) a goal scored in a full half of extra time that is played if a match is drawn. This goal counts as the winner if it is the only goal scored in the full half or full period of extra time

silver iodide *n* a yellow powder that darkens on exposure to light: used in photography and artificial rainmaking. Formula: AgI

silver lining *n* a hopeful aspect of an otherwise desperate or unhappy situation (esp in the phrase **every cloud has a silver lining**)

silver medal *n* a medal of silver awarded to a competitor who comes second in a contest or race

silver nitrate *n* a white crystalline soluble poisonous substance used in making photographic emulsions and as a medical antiseptic and astringent. Formula: $AgNO_3$

silver plate *n* **1** a thin layer of silver deposited on a base metal **2** articles, esp tableware, made of silver plate ▷ *vb* **silver-plate, silver-plates, silver-plating, silver-plated 3** (*tr*) to coat (a metal, object, etc) with silver, as by electroplating

silver screen *n* **the** *inf* **1** films collectively or the film industry **2** the screen onto which films are projected

silver service *n* (in restaurants) a style of serving food using a spoon and fork in one hand like a pair of tongs

silverside (ˈsɪlvəˌsaɪd) *n* **1** *Brit & NZ* a cut of beef below the aitchbone and above the leg **2** a small marine or freshwater teleost fish related to the grey mullets

silversmith (ˈsɪlvəˌsmɪθ) *n* a craftsman who makes or repairs articles of silver > ˈ**silverˌsmithing** *n*

silver surfer *n inf* an older, esp retired, person who uses the Internet

silver thaw *n Canad* **1** a freezing rainstorm **2** another name for **glitter** (sense 7)

silverware (ˈsɪlvəˌwɛə) *n* articles, esp tableware, made of or plated with silver

silverweed (ˈsɪlvəˌwiːd) *n* **1** a rosaceous perennial creeping plant with silvery pinnate leaves and yellow flowers **2** any of various twining shrubs of SE Asia and Australia, having silvery leaves and showy purple flowers

silvery (ˈsɪlvərɪ) *adj* **1** of or having the appearance of silver: *the silvery moon* **2** containing or covered with silver **3** having a clear ringing sound > ˈ**silveriness** *n*

silviculture (ˈsɪlvɪˌkʌltʃə) *n* the branch of forestry that is concerned with the cultivation of trees [C20 *silvi-*, from L *silva* woodland + CULTURE] > ˌ**silviˈcultural** *adj* > ˌ**silviˈculturist** *n*

sim (sɪm) *n* a computer game that simulates an activity, such as playing a sport or flying an aircraft

sima (ˈsaɪmə) *n* **1** the silicon-rich and magnesium-rich rocks of the earth's oceanic crust **2** the earth's continental lower crust [C20 from SI(LICA) + MA(GNESIA)]

Simbirsk (*Russian* simˈbirsk) *n* a city in W central Russia on the River Volga: birthplace of Lenin (V I Ulyanov). Pop: 671 700 (1999 est). Former name (1924–91): **Ulyanovsk**

Simenon (ˈsɪmənɒn; *French* simnɔ̃) *n* **Georges** (ʒɔrʒ) 1903–89, Belgian novelist. He wrote over two hundred novels, including the detective series featuring Maigret

Simeon (ˈsɪmɪən) *n* **1a** *Old Testament* the second son of Jacob and Leah, one of the Hebrew patriarchs **1b** the tribe descended from him **1c** the territory once occupied by this tribe in the extreme south of the land of Canaan **2** *New Testament* a devout Jew, who recognized the infant Jesus as the Messiah and uttered the canticle *Nunc Dimittis* over him in the Temple (Luke 2:25–35)

Simeon Stylites (staɪˈlaɪtiːz) *n* **Saint** ?390–459 AD, Syrian monk, first of the ascetics who lived on pillars. Feast day: Jan 5 or Sept 1

Simferopol (*Russian* simfɪˈrɔpəlj) *n* a city in the S Ukraine on the S Crimean Peninsula: a Scythian town in the 1st century BC; seized by the Russians in 1736. Pop: 341 000 (1998 est)

simian (ˈsɪmɪən) *adj* **1** of or resembling a monkey or ape ▷ *n* **2** a monkey or ape [C17 from L *sīmia* an ape, prob. from Gk *sīmos* flat-nosed]

similar (ˈsɪmɪlə) *adj* **1** showing resemblance in qualities, characteristics, or appearance; alike but not identical **2** *geom* (of two or more figures) having corresponding angles equal and all corresponding sides in the same ratio [C17 from OF, from L *similis*] > **similarity** (ˌsɪmɪˈlærɪtɪ) *n* > ˈ**similarly** *adv*

> USAGE *As* should not be used after *similar*: *Wilson held a similar position to Jones* (not *a similar position as Jones*); *the system is similar to the one in France* (not *similar as in France*)

simile (ˈsɪmɪlɪ) *n* a figure of speech that expresses the resemblance of one thing to another of a different category, usually introduced by *as* or *like* ▷ Cf **metaphor** [C14 from L *simile* something similar, from *similis* like]

similitude (sɪˈmɪlɪˌtjuːd) *n* **1** likeness **2** a thing or sometimes a person that is like or the counterpart of another **3** *arch* a simile or parable [C14 from L *similitūdō*, from *similis* like]

Simla (ˈsɪmlə) *n* a city in N India, capital of Himachal Pradesh state: summer capital of India (1865–1939); hill resort and health centre. Pop: 109 860 (1991)

simmer (ˈsɪmə) *vb* **1** to cook (food) gently at or just below the boiling point **2** (*intr*) to be about to break out in rage or excitement ▷ *n* **3** the act, sound, or state of simmering [C17 ? imit.]

simmer down *vb* (*adv*) **1** (*intr*) *inf* to grow calmer, as after intense rage **2** (*tr*) to reduce the volume of (a liquid) by boiling slowly

Ss

simnel cake (ˈsɪmnᵊl) *n Brit* a fruit cake with a layer of marzipan, traditionally eaten at Lent or Easter [C13 *simenel*, from OF, from L *simila* fine flour, prob. of Semitic origin]

Simon (ˈsaɪmən) *n* **1** the original name of (Saint) **Peter** **2** *New Testament* **2a** See **Simon Zelotes** **2b** a relative of Jesus, who may have been identical with Simon Zelotes (Matthew 13:55) **2c** Also called: **Simon the Tanner** a Christian of Joppa with whom Peter stayed (Acts of the Apostles 9:43) **3 John** (**Allsebrook**), 1st Viscount Simon. 1873–1954, British statesman and lawyer. He was Liberal home secretary (1915–16) and, as a leader of the National Liberals, foreign secretary (1931–35), home secretary (1935–37), Chancellor of the Exchequer (1937–40), Lord Chancellor (1940–45) **4** (**Marvin**) **Neil** born 1927, US dramatist and librettist: his plays include *Barefoot in the Park* (1963) and *London Suite* (1995) **5 Paul** born 1942, US pop singer and songwriter. His albums include: with Art Garfunkel (born 1941), *Bridge over Troubled Water* (1970); and, solo, *Graceland* (1986), *The Rhythm of the Saints* (1990), and *You're the One* (2000)

Simonides (saɪˈmɒnɪˌdiːz) *n* ?556–?468 BC, Greek lyric poet and epigrammatist, noted for his odes to victory

Simon Magus *n New Testament* a Samaritan sorcerer, probably from Gitta, of the 1st century AD. After being converted to Christianity, he tried to buy miraculous powers from the apostles (Acts of the Apostles 8:9–24). He is also identified as the founder of a Gnostic sect

Simon Peter *n New Testament* the full name of the apostle Peter, a combination of his original name and the name given him by Christ (Matthew 16:17–18)

simon-pure (ˈsaɪmən-) *adj rare* real; authentic [C19 from *the real Simon Pure*, a character in the play *A Bold Stroke for a*

Wife (1717) by Susannah Centlivre (1669–1723), who is impersonated by another character in some scenes]

simony (ˈsaɪmənɪ) *n Christianity* the practice, now usually regarded as a sin, of buying or selling spiritual or Church benefits such as pardons, relics, etc [c13 from OF *simonie*, from LL *sīmōnia*, from SIMON MAGUS]

Simon Zelotes (zɪˈləʊtiːz) *n* **Saint** one of the 12 apostles, who had probably belonged to the Zealot party before becoming a Christian (Luke 6:15). Owing to a misinterpretation of two similar Aramaic words he is also, but mistakenly, called *the Canaanite* (Matthew 10:4). Feast day: Oct 28 or May 10

simoom (sɪˈmuːm) *or* **simoon** (sɪˈmuːn) *n* a strong suffocating sand-laden wind of the deserts of Arabia and North Africa [from Ar. *samūm* poisonous, from Aramaic *sammā* poison]

simpatico (sɪmˈpɑːtɪˌkəʊ) *adj inf* **1** pleasant or congenial **2** of similar mind or temperament [It.: from *simpatia* SYMPATHY]

simper (ˈsɪmpə) *vb* **1** (*intr*) to smile coyly, affectedly, or in a silly self-conscious way **2** (*tr*) to utter (something) in such a manner ▷ *n* **3** a simpering smile; smirk [c16 prob. from Du. *simper* affected] > **ˈsimpering** *adj* > **ˈsimperingly** *adv*

simple (ˈsɪmpᵊl) *adj* **1** easy to understand or do: *a simple problem* **2** plain; unadorned: *a simple dress* **3** not combined or complex: *a simple mechanism* **4** unaffected or unpretentious: *despite his fame, he remained a simple man* **5** sincere; frank: *her simple explanation was readily accepted* **6** of humble condition or rank: *the peasant was of simple birth* **7** feeble-minded **8** (*prenominal*) without additions or modifications: *the witness told the simple truth* **9** (*prenominal*) straightforward: *a simple case of mumps* **10** *chem* (of a substance) consisting of only one chemical compound **11** *maths* (of an equation) containing variables to the first power only **12** *biol* **12a** not divided into parts: *a simple leaf* **12b** formed from only one ovary: *simple fruit* **13** *music* relating to or denoting a time where the number of beats per bar may be two, three, or four ▷ *n arch* **14** a simpleton **15** a plant having medicinal properties [c13 via OF from L *simplex* plain] > **simplicity** (sɪmˈplɪsɪtɪ) *n*

simple fraction *n* a fraction in which the numerator and denominator are both integers. Also called: **common fraction, vulgar fraction**

simple fracture *n* a fracture in which the broken bone does not pierce the skin

simple harmonic motion *n* a form of periodic motion of a particle, etc, in which the acceleration is always directed towards some equilibrium point and is proportional to the displacement from this point. Abbrev: **SHM**

simple-hearted *adj* free from deceit; frank

simple interest *n* interest paid on the principal alone ▷ Cf **compound interest**

simple machine *n* a simple device for altering the magnitude or direction of a force. The six basic types are the lever, wheel and axle, pulley, screw, wedge, and inclined plane

simple-minded *adj* **1** stupid; foolish; feeble-minded **2** unsophisticated; artless > **ˌsimple-ˈmindedly** *adv* > **ˌsimple-ˈmindedness** *n*

simple sentence *n* a sentence consisting of a single main clause

simpleton (ˈsɪmpᵊltən) *n* a foolish or ignorant person

simplify (ˈsɪmplɪˌfaɪ) *vb* **simplifies, simplifying, simplified** (*tr*) **1** to make less complicated or easier **2** *maths* to reduce (an equation, fraction, etc) to its simplest form [c17 via F from Med. L *simplificāre*, from L *simplus* simple + *facere* to make] > **ˌsimplifiˈcation** *n*

simplistic (sɪmˈplɪstɪk) *adj* **1** characterized by extreme simplicity **2** making unrealistically simple judgments or analyses > **ˈsimplism** *n* > **simˈplistically** *adv*

> USAGE Since *simplistic* already has 'too' as part of its meaning, some people object to something being referred to as *too simplistic* or *oversimplistic*, and it is best to avoid such uses in serious writing

Simplon Pass (ˈsɪmplɒn) *n* a pass over the Lepontine Alps in S Switzerland, between Brig (Switzerland) and Iselle (Italy). Height: 2009 m (6590 ft)

simply (ˈsɪmplɪ) *adv* **1** in a simple manner **2** merely **3** absolutely; altogether: *a simply wonderful holiday* **4** (*sentence modifier*) frankly

Simpson (ˈsɪmpsᵊn, ˈsɪmsᵊn) *n* **1** Sir **James Young** 1811–70, Scottish obstetrician, who pioneered the use of chloroform as an anaesthetic **2** **Wallis** (**Warfield**) (ˈwɒlɪs) See **Edward VIII**

Simpson Desert (ˈsɪmpsən) *n* an uninhabited arid region in central Australia, mainly in the Northern Territory. Area: about 145 000 sq km (56 000 sq miles)

simulacrum (ˌsɪmjʊˈleɪkrəm) *n, pl* **simulacra** (-krə) *arch* **1** any image or representation of something **2** a superficial likeness [c16 from L: likeness, from *simulāre* to imitate, from *similis* like]

simulate *vb* (ˈsɪmjʊˌleɪt), **simulates, simulating, simulated** (*tr*) **1** to make a pretence of: *to simulate anxiety* **2** to reproduce the conditions of (a situation, etc), as in carrying out an experiment: *to simulate weightlessness* **3** to have the appearance of ▷ *adj* (ˈsɪmjʊlɪt, -ˌleɪt) **4** *arch* assumed [c17 from L *simulāre* to copy, from *similis* like] > **ˌsimuˈlation** *n* > **ˈsimulative** *adj*

simulated (ˈsɪmjʊˌleɪtɪd) *adj* **1** (of fur, leather, pearls, etc) being an imitation of the genuine article, usually made from cheaper material **2** (of actions, emotions, etc) imitated; feigned

simulator (ˈsɪmjʊˌleɪtə) *n* **1** any device that simulates specific conditions for the purposes of research or operator training: *space simulator* **2** a person who simulates

simulcast (ˈsɪməlˌkɑːst) *vb* **1** (*tr*) to broadcast (a programme, etc) simultaneously on radio and television ▷ *n* **2** a programme, etc, so broadcast [c20 from SIMUL(TANEOUS) + (BROAD)CAST]

simultaneous (ˌsɪməlˈteɪnɪəs) *adj* occurring, existing, or operating at the same time [c17 on the model of INSTANTANEOUS from L *simul* at the same time] > **ˌsimulˈtaneously** *adv* > **ˌsimulˈtaneousness** *or* **simultaneity** (ˌsɪməltəˈniːɪtɪ) *n*

simultaneous equations *pl n* a set of equations that are all satisfied by the same values of the variables, the number of variables being equal to the number of equations

sin¹ (sɪn) *n* **1a** transgression of God's known will or any principle or law regarded as embodying this **1b** the condition of estrangement from God arising from such transgression **2** any serious offence, as against a religious or moral principle **3** any offence against a principle or standard **4** **live in sin** *inf* (of an unmarried couple) to live together ▷ *vb* **sins, sinning, sinned** (*intr*) **5** to commit a sin **6** (usually foll by *against*) to commit an offence (against a person, etc) [OE *synn*] > **ˈsinner** *n*

sin² (saɪn) *maths abbrev for* sine

SIN *or* **S.I.N.** (in Canada) *abbrev for* Social Insurance Number

Sinai (ˈsaɪnaɪ) *n* **1** a mountainous peninsula of NE Egypt at the N end of the Red Sea, between the Gulf of Suez and the Gulf of Aqaba: occupied by Israel in 1967; fully restored by 1982 **2** **Mount** the mountain where Moses received the Law from God (Exodus 19–20): often identified as Jebel Musa, sometimes as Jebel Serbal, both on the S Sinai Peninsula > **Sinaitic** (ˌsaɪnɪˈɪtɪk) *or* **Sinaic** (sɪˈneɪɪk)

Sinaloa (ˌsiːnəˈləʊə, ˌsɪn-; *Spanish* sinaˈloa) *n* a state of W Mexico. Capital: Culiacán. Pop: 2 534 835 (2000). Area: 58 092 sq km (22 425 sq miles)

sinanthropus (sɪnˈænθrəpəs) *n* a primitive apelike man of the genus *Sinanthropus*, now considered a subspecies of *Homo erectus* [c20 from NL, from LL *Sīnae* the Chinese + *-anthropus*, from Gk *anthrōpos* man]

Sinatra (sɪˈnɑːtrə) *n* **Francis Albert**, known as *Frank*. 1915–98, US popular singer and film actor. His recordings include "One for My Baby (and One More for the Road)" (1955) and "My Way" (1969)

sin bin *n* **1** (in certain sports) an area off the field of play where a player who has committed a foul can be sent to sit for a specified period **2** *inf* a separate unit for disruptive schoolchildren

since (sɪns) *prep* **1** during or throughout the period of time after: *since May it has only rained once* ▷ *conj (subordinating)* **2** (sometimes preceded by *ever*) continuously from or starting from the time when **3** seeing that; because ▷ *adv* **4** since that time: *I haven't seen him since* [OE *sīththan*, lit.: after that]

USAGE See at **ago**

sincere (sɪnˈsɪə) *adj* **1** not hypocritical or deceitful; genuine: *sincere regret* **2** *arch* pure; unmixed [c16 from L *sincērus*] > **sinˈcerely** *adv* > **sincerity** (sɪnˈsɛrɪtɪ) *or* **sinˈcereness** *n*

sinciput (ˈsɪnsɪˌpʌt) *n, pl* **sinciputs** *or* **sincipita** (sɪnˈsɪpɪtə) *anat* the forward upper part of the skull [c16 from L: half a head, from SEMI- + *caput* head] > **sinˈcipital** *adj*

Sinclair (sɪŋˈklɛə, ˈsɪŋklɛə) *n* **1** Sir **Clive** (**Marles**) born 1940, British electronics engineer, inventor, and entrepreneur, who produced such electronic goods as pocket calculators and some of the first home computers; however, the Sinclair C5, a small light electric vehicle for one person, proved a commercial failure **2** **Upton** (**Beall**) 1878–1968, US novelist, whose *The Jungle* (1906) exposed the working and sanitary conditions of the Chicago meat-packing industry and prompted the passage of food inspection laws

Sind (sɪnd) *n* a province of SE Pakistan, mainly in the lower Indus valley: formerly a province of British India; became a province of Pakistan in 1947; divided in 1955 between Hyderabad and Khairpur; reunited as a province in 1970. Capital: Karachi. Pop: 29 991 000 (1998 est). Area: 140 914 sq km (54 407 sq miles)

sine[1] (saɪn) *n* (of an angle) a trigonometric function that in a right-angled triangle is the ratio of the length of the opposite side to that of the hypotenuse [c16 from L *sinus* a bend; in NL, *sinus* was mistaken as a translation of Ar. *jiba* sine (from Sansk. *jīva*, lit.: bowstring) because of confusion with Ar. *jaib* curve]

sine[2] (ˈsaɪnɪ) *prep* (esp in Latin phrases or legal terms) lacking; without

sinecure (ˈsaɪnɪˌkjʊə) *n* **1** a paid office or post involving minimal duties **2** a Church benefice to which no spiritual charge is attached [c17 from Med. L (*beneficium*) *sine cūrā* (benefice) without cure (of souls), from L *sine* without + *cūra* cure] > **ˈsineˌcurism** *n* > **ˈsineˌcurist** *n*

sine curve (saɪn) *n* a curve of the equation $y = \sin x$. Also called: **sinusoid**

sine die *Latin* (ˈsaɪnɪ ˈdaɪɪ) *adv, adj* without a day fixed [lit.: without a day]

sine qua non *Latin* (ˈsaɪnɪ kweɪ ˈnɒn) *n* an essential requirement [lit.: without which not]

sinew (ˈsɪnjuː) *n* **1** *anat* another name for **tendon** **2** (*often pl*) **2a** a source of strength or power **2b** a literary word for **muscle** [OE *sionu*] > **ˈsinewless** *adj*

sine wave (saɪn) *n* any oscillation, such as an alternating current, whose waveform is that of a sine curve

sinewy (ˈsɪnjʊɪ) *adj* **1** consisting of or resembling a tendon or tendons **2** muscular **3** (esp of language, style, etc) forceful **4** (of meat, etc) tough > **ˈsinewiness** *n*

sinfonia (ˌsɪnfəˈnɪə) *n, pl* **sinfonie** (-ˈniːeɪ) *or* **sinfonias** **1** another word for **symphony** (senses 2, 3) **2** (*cap when part of a name*) a symphony orchestra [It.]

sinfonietta (ˌsɪnfənˈjɛtə) *n* **1** a short or light symphony **2** (*cap. when part of a name*) a small symphony orchestra [It.: a little symphony]

sinful (ˈsɪnfʊl) *adj* **1** having committed or tending to commit sin: *a sinful person* **2** characterized by or being a sin: *a sinful act* > **ˈsinfully** *adv* > **ˈsinfulness** *n*

sing (sɪŋ) *vb* **sings, singing, sang, sung** **1** to produce or articulate (sounds, words, a song, etc) with musical intonation **2** (when *intr*, often foll by *to*) to perform (a song) to the accompaniment (of): *to sing to a guitar* **3** (*intr;* foll by *of*) to tell a story in song (about): *I sing of a maiden* **4** (*intr*) to perform songs for a living **5** (*intr*) (esp of certain birds and insects) to utter calls or sounds reminiscent of music **6** (when *intr*, usually foll by *of*) to tell (something), esp in verse: *the poet who sings of the war* **7** (*intr*) to make a whining, ringing, or whistling sound: *the arrow sang past his ear* **8** (*intr*) (of the ears) to experience a continuous ringing **9** (*tr*) to bring to a given state by singing: *to sing a child to sleep* **10** (*intr*) *sl, chiefly US* to confess or act as an informer ▷ *n* **11** *inf* an act or performance of singing ▷ See also **sing out** [OE *singan*] > **ˈsingable** *adj* > **ˈsinging** *adj, n*

USAGE See at **ring**

sing. *abbrev for* singular

Singapore (ˌsɪŋəˈpɔː, ˌsɪŋgə-) *n* **1** a republic in SE Asia, occupying one main island and about 58 small islands at the S end of the Malay Peninsula: established as a British trading post in 1819 and became part of the Straits Settlements in 1826; occupied by the Japanese (1942–45); a British colony from 1946, becoming self-governing in 1959; part of the Federation of Malaysia from 1963 to 1965, when it became an independent republic (within the Commonwealth). Official languages: Chinese, Malay, English, and Tamil. Religion: Buddhist, Taoist, traditional beliefs, and Muslim. Currency: Singapore dollar. Capital: Singapore. Pop: 3 322 000 (2001 est). Area: 646 sq km (250 sq miles) **2** the capital of the republic of Singapore: a major international port; administratively not treated as a city > **ˌSingaˈporean** *adj, n*

▷ www.gov.sg
▷ www.visitsingapore.com

singe (sɪndʒ) *vb* **singes, singeing, singed** **1** to burn or be burnt superficially; scorch: *to singe one's clothes* **2** (*tr*) to burn the ends of (hair, etc) **3** (*tr*) to expose (a carcass) to flame to remove bristles or hair ▷ *n* **4** a superficial burn [OE *sengan*]

singer (ˈsɪŋə) *n* **1** a person who sings, esp one who earns a living by singing **2** a singing bird

Singer (ˈsɪŋə) *n* **1** **Isaac Bashevis** 1904–91, US writer of Yiddish novels and short stories; born in Poland. His works include *Satan in Goray* (1935), *The Family Moscat* (1950), the autobiographical *In my Father's Court* (1966), and *The King of the Fields* (1989): Nobel prize for literature 1978 **2** **Isaac Merrit** 1811–75, US inventor, who originated and developed an improved chain-stitch sewing machine (1852)

Singh (sɪŋ) *n* a title assumed by a Sikh when he becomes a full member of the community [from Hindi, from Sansk. *sinhá* a lion]

Singhalese (ˌsɪŋəˈliːz) *n, pl* **Singhaleses** *or* **Singhalese**, *adj* a variant spelling of **Sinhalese**

singing telegram *n* **a** a service by which a person is employed to present greetings or congratulations by singing **b** the greetings or congratulations presented thus

single (ˈsɪŋgᵊl) *adj* (*usually prenominal*) **1** existing alone; solitary: *upon the hill stood a single tower* **2** distinct from other things **3** composed of one part **4** designed or sufficient for one user: *a single bed* **5** (*also postpositive*) unmarried **6** connected with the condition of being unmarried: *he led a single life* **7** (esp of combat) involving

Ss

two individuals **8** even one: *there wasn't a single person on the beach* **9** (of a flower) having only one set or whorl of petals **10** single-minded: *a single devotion to duty* **11** *rare* honest or sincere ▷ *n* **12** something forming one individual unit **13** (*often pl*) **13a** an unmarried person **13b** (*as modifier*): *singles bar* **14** a gramophone record, CD, or cassette with a short recording, usually of pop music, on it **15** *cricket* a hit from which one run is scored **16a** *Brit* a pound note **16b** *US & Canad* a dollar note **17** See **single ticket** ▷ *vb* **singles, singling, singled 18** (*tr*; usually foll by *out*) to select from a group of people or things: *he singled him out for special mention* ▷ See also **singles** [c14 from OF *sengle*, from L *singulus* individual] > **'singleness** *n*

single-acting *adj* (of a reciprocating engine or pump) having a piston or pistons pressurized on one side only

single-breasted *adj* (of a garment) having the fronts overlapping only slightly and with one row of fastenings

single cream *n* cream having a low fat content that does not thicken with beating

single-decker *n Brit inf* a bus with only one passenger deck

single-end *n Scot* a dwelling consisting of a single room

single entry *n* **a** a book-keeping system in which transactions are entered in one account only **b** (*as modifier*): *a single-entry account*

single file *n* a line of persons, animals, or things ranged one behind the other

single-foot *n* **1** a rapid showy gait of a horse in which each foot strikes the ground separately ▷ *vb* **2** to move or cause to move at this gait

single-handed *adj, adv* **1** unaided or working alone: *a single-handed crossing of the Atlantic* **2** having or operated by one hand or one person only > **ˌsingle-'handedly** *adv* > **ˌsingle-'handedness** *n*

single-lens reflex *n* See **reflex camera**

single-minded *adj* having but one aim or purpose; dedicated > **ˌsingle-'mindedly** *adv* > **ˌsingle-'mindedness** *n*

single parent *n* **a** a person who has a dependent child or dependent children and who is widowed, divorced, or unmarried **b** (*as modifier*): *a single-parent family*. Also called (NZ): **solo parent**

single-parent family *n* a household consisting of at least one dependent child and the mother or father, the other parent being dead or permanently absent. Also called: **one-parent family**

singles ('sɪŋgᵊlz) *pl n tennis, etc* a match played with one person on each side

singles bar *n* a bar or club that is a social meeting place for single people

single-sex *adj* (of schools, etc) admitting members of one sex only

single sideband transmission *n* a method of transmitting radio waves in which either the upper or the lower sideband is transmitted, the carrier being either wholly or partially suppressed

singlestick ('sɪŋgᵊlˌstɪk) *n* **1** a wooden stick used instead of a sword for fencing **2** fencing with such a stick **3** any short heavy stick

singlet ('sɪŋglɪt) *n* **1** a sleeveless undergarment covering the body from the shoulders to the hips **2** a garment worn with shorts by athletes, boxers, etc [c18 from SINGLE, on the model of *doublet*]

single ticket *n Brit* a ticket entitling a passenger to travel only to his or her destination, without returning

singleton ('sɪŋgᵊltən) *n* **1** *bridge, etc* an original holding of one card only in a suit **2** a single object, etc, distinguished from a pair or group **3** *maths* a set containing only one member **4** a person who is neither married nor in a relationship [c19 from SINGLE, on the model of SIMPLETON]

single-track *adj* **1** (of a railway) having only a single pair of lines, so that trains can travel in only one direction at a time **2** (of a road) only wide enough for one vehicle

Single Transferable Vote *n* (*modifier*) of or relating to a system of voting in which voters list the candidates in order of preference. Abbrev: **STV** See **proportional representation**

singletree ('sɪŋgᵊlˌtriː) *n US & Austral* another word for **swingletree**

singly ('sɪŋglɪ) *adv* **1** one at a time; one by one **2** apart from others; separately; alone

sing out *vb* (*tr, adv*) to call out in a loud voice; shout

singsong ('sɪŋˌsɒŋ) *n* **1** an accent or intonation that is characterized by an alternately rising and falling rhythm, such as in a person's voice **2** *Brit* an informal session of singing, esp of popular songs ▷ *adj* **3** having a monotonous rhythm: *a singsong accent*

singular ('sɪŋgjʊlə) *adj* **1** remarkable; extraordinary: *a singular feat* **2** unusual; odd: *a singular character* **3** unique **4** denoting a word or an inflected form of a word indicating that one referent is being referred to or described **5** *logic* (of a proposition) referring to a specific thing or person ▷ *n* **6** *grammar* **6a** the singular number **6b** a singular form of a word [c14 from L *singulāris* single] > **'singularly** *adv*

singularity (ˌsɪŋgjʊ'lærɪtɪ) *n, pl* **singularities 1** the state or quality of being singular **2** something distinguishing a person or thing from others **3** something unusual **4** *maths* a point at which a function is not differentiable although it is differentiable in a neighbourhood of that point **5** *astron* a hypothetical point in space-time at which matter is infinitely compressed to infinitesimal volume

singularize *or* **singularise** ('sɪŋgjʊləˌraɪz) *vb* **singularizes, singularizing, singularized** *or* **singularises, singularising, singularised** (*tr*) **1** to make (a word, etc) singular **2** to make conspicuous > **ˌsingulari'zation** *or* **ˌsingulari'sation** *n*

singultus (sɪŋ'gʌltəs) *n, pl* **singultuses** a technical name for **hiccup** [c18 from L, lit.: a sob]

sinh (ʃaɪn, sɪnʃ) *n* hyperbolic sine [c20 from SIN(E)[1] + H(YPERBOLIC)]

Sinhailien ('ʃɪn'haɪ'ljɛn) *n* a variant transliteration of the Chinese name for **Lianyungang**

Sinhalese (ˌsɪnhə'liːz) *or* **Singhalese** *n* **1** (*pl* **Sinhaleses** *or* **Sinhalese**) a member of a people living chiefly in Sri Lanka, where they constitute the majority of the population **2** the language of this people: the official language of Sri Lanka ▷ *adj* **3** of or relating to this people or their language

Sining ('ʃiː'nɪŋ) *n* variant transliteration of the Chinese name for **Xining**

sinister ('sɪnɪstə) *adj* **1** threatening or suggesting evil or harm: *a sinister glance* **2** evil or treacherous **3** (*usually postpositive*) *heraldry* of, on, or starting from the left side from the bearer's point of view **4** *arch* located on the left side [c15 from L *sinister* on the left-hand side, considered by Roman augurs to be the unlucky one] > **'sinisterly** *adv* > **'sinisterness** *n*

sinistral ('sɪnɪstrəl) *adj* **1** of or located on the left side, esp the left side of the body **2** a technical term for **left-handed 3** (of the shells of certain molluscs) coiling in a clockwise direction from the apex > **'sinistrally** *adv*

sinistrorse ('sɪnɪˌstrɔːs, ˌsɪnɪ'strɔːs) *adj* (of some climbing plants) growing upwards in a spiral from right to left [c19 from L *sinistrōrsus* turned towards the left, from *sinister* on the left + *vertere* to turn] > **ˌsinis'trorsal** *adj*

Sinitic (sɪ'nɪtɪk) *n* **1** a branch of the Sino-Tibetan family of languages, consisting of the various dialects of Chinese ▷ *adj* **2** belonging to this group of languages

sink (sɪŋk) *vb* **sinks, sinking, sank; sunk** *or* **sunken 1** to descend or cause to descend, esp beneath the surface of a liquid **2** (*intr*) to appear to move down towards or descend below the horizon **3** (*intr*) to slope downwards

4 (*intr; often foll by in or into*) to pass into a specified lower state or condition: *to sink into apathy* 5 to make or become lower in volume, pitch, etc 6 to make or become lower in value, price, etc 7 (*intr*) to become weaker in health, strength, etc 8 (*intr*) to seep or penetrate 9 (*tr*) to dig, cut, drill, bore, or excavate (a hole, shaft, etc) 10 (*tr*) to drive into the ground: *to sink a stake* 11 (*tr; usually foll by in or into*) 11a to invest (money) 11b to lose (money) in an unwise investment 12 (*tr*) to pay (a debt) 13 (*intr*) to become hollow: *his cheeks had sunk during his illness* 14 (*tr*) to hit or propel (a ball) into a hole, pocket, etc: *he sank a 15-foot putt* 15 (*tr*) *Brit inf* to drink, esp quickly: *he sank three pints in half an hour* 16 **sink or swim** to take risks where the alternatives are loss or success ▷ *n* 17 a fixed basin, esp in a kitchen, made of stone, metal, etc, used for washing 18 a place of vice or corruption 19 an area of ground below that of the surrounding land, where water collects 20 *physics* a device by which energy is removed from a system: *a heat sink* ▷ *adj* 21 *inf* (of a housing estate or school) deprived or having low standards of achievement [OE *sincan*] > **'sinkable** *adj*

sinker ('sɪŋkə) *n* 1 a weight attached to a fishing line, net, etc, to cause it to sink in water 2 a person who sinks shafts, etc

sinkhole ('sɪŋkˌhəʊl) *n* 1 Also called (esp in Britain): **swallow hole** a depression in the ground surface, esp in limestone, where a surface stream disappears underground 2 a place into which foul matter runs

Sinkiang-Uighur Autonomous Region ('sɪn'kjæŋ 'wiːgʊə) *n* a variant transliteration of the Chinese name for the **Xinjiang Uygur Autonomous Region**

sink in *vb* (*intr, adv*) to enter or penetrate the mind: *eventually the news sank in*

sinking ('sɪŋkɪŋ) *n* **a** a feeling in the stomach caused by hunger or uneasiness **b** (*as modifier*): *a sinking feeling*

sinking fund *n* a fund accumulated out of a business enterprise's earnings or a government's revenue and invested to repay a long-term debt

sinless ('sɪnlɪs) *adj* free from sin or guilt; pure > **'sinlessly** *adv* > **'sinlessness** *n*

Sinn Féin ('ʃɪn 'feːn) *n* an Irish republican political movement founded about 1905 and linked to the revolutionary Irish Republican Army [c20 from Irish Gaelic: we ourselves] > **'Sinn 'Féiner** *n* > **'Sinn 'Féinism** *n*

Sino- *combining form* Chinese: *Sino-Tibetan; Sinology* [from F, from LL *Sīnae* the Chinese, from LGk, from Ar. *Sīn* China, prob. from Chinese *Ch'in*]

Sinology (saɪ'nɒlədʒɪ) *n* the study of Chinese history, language, culture, etc > **Sinological** (ˌsaɪnə'lɒdʒɪkᵊl) *adj* > **Si'nologist** *n* > **Sinologue** ('saɪnəˌlɒg) *n*

Sino-Tibetan ('saɪnəʊ-) *n* 1 a family of languages that includes most of the languages of China, as well as Tibetan, Burmese, and possibly Thai ▷ *adj* 2 belonging or relating to this family of languages

sinsemilla (ˌsɪnsə'miːljə) *n* 1 a type of marijuana with a very high narcotic content 2 the plant from which it is obtained, a strain of *Cannabis sativa* [c20 from American Sp., lit.: without seed]

sinter ('sɪntə) *n* 1 a whitish porous incrustation, usually consisting of silica, that is deposited from hot springs 2 the product of a sintering process ▷ *vb* 3 (*tr*) to form large particles, lumps, or masses from (metal powders) by heating or pressure or both [c18 from G *Sinter* CINDER]

Sint Maarten (sɪnt 'maːrtə) *n* the Dutch name for **Saint Martin**

Sintra ('sɪntrə) *n* a town in central Portugal, near Lisbon, in the Sintra mountains: noted for its castles and palaces and the beauty of its setting: tourism. Former name: **Cintra**

sinuate ('sɪnjʊɪt, -ˌeɪt) *adj* 1 Also: **sinuous** (of leaves) having a strongly waved margin 2 another word for **sinuous** [c17 from L *sinuātus* curved] > **'sinuately** *adv*

Sinŭiju (sɪˌnuːɪ'dʒuː) *n* a port in North Korea, on the Yalu River opposite Andong, China: developed by the Japanese during their occupation (1910–45); industrial centre. Pop: 289 000 (latest est)

sinuous ('sɪnjʊəs) *adj* 1 full of turns or curves 2 devious; not straightforward 3 supple [c16 from L *sinuōsus* winding, from *sinus* a curve] > **'sinuously** *adv* > **sinuosity** (ˌsɪnjʊ'ɒsɪtɪ) *n*

sinus ('saɪnəs) *n, pl* **sinuses** 1 *anat* 1a any bodily cavity or hollow space 1b a large channel for venous blood, esp between the brain and the skull 1c any of the air cavities in the cranial bones 2 *pathol* a passage leading to a cavity containing pus [c16 from L: a curve]

sinusitis (ˌsaɪnə'saɪtɪs) *n* inflammation of the membrane lining a sinus, esp a nasal sinus

sinusoid ('saɪnəˌsɔɪd) *n* 1 any of the irregular terminal blood vessels that replace capillaries in certain organs, such as the liver, heart, spleen, and pancreas 2 another name for **sine curve** ▷ *adj* 3 resembling a sinus [c19 from F *sinusoïde*. See SINUS, -OID]

sinusoidal projection *n* an equal-area map projection on which all parallels are straight lines and all except the prime meridian are sine curves, often used to show tropical latitudes

Sion *n* 1 (*French* sjɔ̃) a town in SW Switzerland, capital of Valais canton, on the River Rhône. Pop: 24 538 (1990). Latin name: **Sedunum** 2 ('saɪən) a variant of **Zion**

Siouan ('suːən) *n* a family of North American Indian languages, including Sioux

Sioux (suː) *n* 1 (*pl* **Sioux** (suː, suːz)). a member of a group of North American Indian peoples 2 any of the languages of the Sioux [from F, shortened from *Nadowessioux*]

sip (sɪp) *vb* **sips, sipping, sipped** 1 to drink (a liquid) by taking small mouthfuls ▷ *n* 2 a small quantity of a liquid taken into the mouth and swallowed 3 an act of sipping [c14 prob. from Low G *sippen*] > **'sipper** *n*

siphon *or* **syphon** ('saɪfᵊn) *n* 1 a tube placed with one end at a certain level in a vessel of liquid and the other end outside the vessel below this level, so that atmospheric pressure forces the liquid through the tube and out of the vessel 2 See **soda siphon** 3 *zool* any of various tubular organs in different aquatic animals, such as molluscs, through which water passes ▷ *vb* 4 (*often foll by off*) to draw off through or as if through a siphon [c17 from L *sīphō*, from Gk *siphōn*] > **'siphonal** *or* **siphonic** (saɪ'fɒnɪk) *adj*

Ss

siphon bottle *n* another name (esp US) for **soda siphon**

siphonophore ('saɪfənəˌfɔː) *n* any of an order of marine colonial hydrozoans, including the Portuguese man-of-war [c19 from NL, from Gk *siphōnophoros* tube-bearing]

Siple ('saɪpᵊl) *n* **Mount** a mountain in Antarctica, on the coast of Byrd Land. Height: 3100 m (10 171 ft)

sippet ('sɪpɪt) *n* a small piece of something, esp a piece of toast or fried bread eaten with soup or gravy [c16 used as dim. of SOP]

sir (sɜː) *n* 1 a formal or polite term of address for a man 2 *arch* a gentleman of high social status [c13 var. of SIRE]

Sir (sɜː) *n* 1 a title of honour placed before the name of a knight or baronet: *Sir Walter Raleigh* 2 *arch* a title placed before the name of a figure from ancient history

Siracusa (sira'kuːza) *n* the Italian name for **Syracuse**

Siraj-ud-daula (sɪ'rɑːdʒʊd'daʊlə) *n* ?1728–57, Indian leader who became the Great Mogul's deputy in Bengal (1756); opponent of English colonization. He captured Calcutta (1756) from the English and many of his prisoners suffocated in a crowded room that became known as the Black Hole of Calcutta. He was defeated (1757) by a group of Indian nobles in alliance with Robert Clive

sirdar ('sɜːdɑː) *n* 1 a general or military leader in Pakistan and India 2 (formerly) the title of the British commander in chief of the Egyptian Army 3 a variant of

sardar [from Hindi *sardār*, from Persian, from *sar* head + *dār* possession]

sire ('saɪə) *n* **1** a male parent, esp of a horse or other domestic animal **2** a respectful term of address, now used only in addressing a male monarch ▷ *vb* **sires, siring, sired 3** (*tr*) (esp of a domestic animal) to father [C13 from OF, from L *senior* an elder, from *senex* an old man]

siren ('saɪərən) *n* **1** a device for emitting a loud wailing sound, esp as a warning or signal, consisting of a rotating perforated metal drum through which air or steam is passed under pressure **2** (*sometimes cap*) *Greek myth* one of several sea nymphs whose singing was believed to lure sailors to destruction on the rocks the nymphs inhabited **3** a woman considered to be dangerously alluring or seductive **4** an aquatic eel-like salamander of North America, having external gills, no hind limbs, and reduced forelimbs [C14 from OF *sereine*, from L *sīrēn*, from Gk *seirēn*]

sirenian (saɪ'ri:nɪən) *adj* **1** of or belonging to the *Sirenia*, an order of aquatic herbivorous placental mammals having forelimbs modified as paddles and a horizontally flattened tail: contains only the dugong and manatees ▷ *n* **2** an animal belonging to this order; sea cow

Siret (sɪ'rɛt) *n* a river in SE Europe, rising in the Ukraine and flowing southeast through E Romania to the Danube. Length: about 450 km (280 miles)

Sirius ('sɪrɪəs) *n* the brightest star in the sky, lying in the constellation Canis Major. Also called: the **Dog Star** [C14 via L from Gk *Seirios*, from ?]

sirloin ('sɜ:ˌlɔɪn) *n* a prime cut of beef from the loin, esp the upper part [C16 *surloyn*, from OF *surlonge*, from *sur* above + *longe*, from *loigne* LOIN]

sirocco (sɪ'rɒkəʊ) *n, pl* **siroccos** a hot oppressive and often dusty wind usually occurring in spring, beginning in N Africa and reaching S Europe [C17 from It., from Ar. *sharq* east wind]

sironize *or* **sironise** ('saɪrəˌnaɪz) *vb* **sironizes, sironizing, sironized** *or* **sironises, sironising, sironised** (*tr*) *Austral* to treat (a woollen fabric) chemically to prevent it wrinkling after being washed [C20 from (C)SIRO + -*n*- + -IZE]

siroset ('saɪrəʊˌsɛt) *adj Austral* of or relating to the chemical treatment of woollen fabrics to give a permanent-press effect, or a garment so treated

sirrah ('sɪrə) *n arch* a contemptuous term used in addressing a man or boy [C16 prob. var. of SIRE]

sirree (sə'ri:) *interj* (*sometimes cap*) *US inf* an exclamation used with *yes* or *no*

sirup ('sɪrəp) *n US* a less common spelling of **syrup**

sis[1] (sɪs) *n inf* short for **sister**

sis[2] (sɪs) *interj S African inf* an exclamation of disgust [Afrik.]

SIS (in Britain) *abbrev for* Secret Intelligence Service. Also called: **MI6**

sisal ('saɪsᵊl) *n* **1** a Mexican agave plant cultivated for its large fleshy leaves, which yield a stiff fibre used for making rope **2** the fibre of this plant ▷ Also called: **sisal hemp** [C19 from Mexican Sp., after *Sisal*, a port in Yucatán, Mexico]

Sisera ('sɪsərə) *n* a defeated leader of the Canaanites, who was assassinated by Jael (Judges 4:17–21)

siskin ('sɪskɪn) *n* **1** a yellow-and-black Eurasian finch **2 pine siskin** a North American finch, having a streaked yellowish-brown plumage [C16 from MDu. *sīseken*, from MLow G *sīsek*]

Sisley ('sɪslɪ; *French* sislɛ) *n* **Alfred** (alfrɛd) 1839–99, French painter, esp of landscapes; one of the originators of impressionism

sissy *or* **cissy** ('sɪsɪ) *n, pl* **sissies 1** an effeminate, weak, or cowardly boy or man ▷ *adj* **2** effeminate, weak, or cowardly

sister ('sɪstə) *n* **1** a female person having the same parents as another person **2** a female person who belongs to the same group, trade union, etc, as another or others **3** a senior nurse **4** *chiefly RC Church* a nun or a title given to a nun **5** a woman fellow member of a religious body **6** (*modifier*) belonging to the same class, fleet, etc, as another or others: *a sister ship* **7** (*modifier*) *biol* denoting any of the cells or cell components formed by division of a parent cell or cell component: *sister nuclei* [OE *sweostor*]

sisterhood ('sɪstəˌhʊd) *n* **1** the state of being related as a sister or sisters **2** a religious body or society of sisters

sister-in-law *n, pl* **sisters-in-law 1** the sister of one's husband or wife **2** the wife of one's brother

sisterly ('sɪstəlɪ) *adj* of or suitable to a sister, esp in showing kindness > **'sisterliness** *n*

Sistine Chapel ('sɪstaɪn, -ti:n) *n* the chapel of the pope in the Vatican at Rome, built for Sixtus IV and decorated with frescoes by Michelangelo and others [Sistine, from Italian *Sistino* relating to *Sisto* Sixtus (Pope Sixtus IV)]

sistrum ('sɪstrəm) *n, pl* **sistra** (-trə) a musical instrument of ancient Egypt consisting of a metal rattle [C14 via L from Gk *seistron*, from *seiein* to shake]

Sisyphean (ˌsɪsɪ'fi:ən) *adj* **1** relating to Sisyphus **2** actually or seemingly endless and futile

Sisyphus ('sɪsɪfəs) *n Greek myth* a king of Corinth, punished in Hades for his misdeeds by eternally having to roll a heavy stone up a hill: every time he approached the top, the stone escaped his grasp and rolled to the bottom

sit (sɪt) *vb* **sits, sitting, sat** (*mainly intr*) **1** (*also tr;* when *intr*, often foll by *down, in,* or *on*) to adopt a posture in which the body is supported on the buttocks and the torso is more or less upright: *to sit on a chair* **2** (*tr*) to cause to adopt such a posture **3** (of an animal) to adopt or rest in a posture with the hindquarters lowered to the ground **4** (of a bird) to perch or roost **5** (of a hen or other bird) to cover eggs to hatch them **6** to be situated or located **7** (of the wind) to blow from the direction specified **8** to adopt and maintain a posture for one's portrait to be painted, etc **9** to occupy or be entitled to a seat in some official capacity, as a judge, etc **10** (of a deliberative body) to be in session **11** to remain inactive or unused: *his car sat in the garage* **12** (of a garment) to fit or hang as specified: *that dress sits well on you* **13** to weigh, rest, or lie as specified: *greatness sits easily on him* **14** (*tr*) *chiefly Brit* to take (an examination): *he's sitting his bar finals* **15** (usually foll by *for*) *chiefly Brit* to be a candidate (for a qualification): *he's sitting for a BA* **16** (*intr; in combination*) to look after a specified person or thing for someone else: *granny-sit* **17** (*tr*) to have seating capacity for **18 sit tight** *inf* **18a** to wait patiently **18b** to maintain one's stand, opinion, etc, firmly ▷ See also **sit back, sit down,** etc [OE *sittan*]

SIT *text messaging abbrev for* stay in touch

sitar (sɪ'tɑ:) *n* a stringed musical instrument, esp of India, having a long neck, a rounded body, and movable frets [from Hindi *sitār*, lit.: three-stringed] > **si'tarist** *n*

sit back *vb* (*intr, adv*) to relax, as when action should be taken: *many people just sit back and ignore the problems of today*

sitcom ('sɪtˌkɒm) *n* an informal term for **situation comedy**

sit down *vb* (*adv*) **1** to adopt or cause (oneself or another) to adopt a sitting posture **2** (*intr;* foll by *under*) to suffer (insults, etc) without protests or resistance ▷ *n* **sit-down 3** a form of civil disobedience in which demonstrators sit down in a public place **4** See **sit-down strike** ▷ *adj* **sit-down 5** (of a meal, etc) eaten while sitting down at a table

sit-down strike *n* a strike in which workers refuse to leave their place of employment until a settlement is reached

site (saɪt) *n* **1a** the piece of land where something was, is, or is intended to be located: *a building site* **1b** (*as modifier*): *site office* **2** *computing* an Internet location where information relating to a specific subject or group of subjects can be accessed ▷ *vb* **sites, siting, sited 3** (*tr*) to locate or install (something) in a specific place [C14 from L *situs* situation, from *sinere* to be placed]

site map *n computing* a plan of a website showing its contents and where it can be viewed

sith (sɪθ) *adv, conj, prep* an archaic word for **since** [OE *siththa*]

sit-in *n* **1** a form of civil disobedience in which demonstrators occupy seats in a public place and refuse to move **2** another term for **sit-down strike** ▷ *vb* **sit in** (*intr, adv*) **3** (often foll by *for*) to deputize (for) **4** (foll by *on*) to take part (in) as a visitor or guest **5** to organize or take part in a sit-in

Sitka (ˈsɪtkə) *n* a town in SE Alaska, in the Alexander Archipelago on W Baranof Island: capital of Russian America (1804–67) and of Alaska (1867–1906). Pop: 8588 (1990)

sitkamer (ˈsɪtˌkɑːmə) *n S African* a sitting room [from Afrik.]

sitka spruce (ˈsɪtkə) *n* a tall North American spruce tree having yellowish-green needle-like leaves [from SITKA]

sit on *vb* (*intr, prep*) **1** to be a member of (a committee, etc) **2** *inf* to suppress **3** *inf* to check or rebuke

sit out *vb* (*tr, adv*) **1** to endure to the end: *I sat out the play although it was terrible* **2** to remain seated throughout (a dance, etc)

Sitsang (ˈsiːˈtsæŋ) *n* a Chinese name for **Tibet**

sitter (ˈsɪtə) *n* **1** a person or animal that sits **2** a person who is posing for his or her portrait to be painted, etc **3** a broody hen that is sitting on its eggs to hatch them **4** (*in combination*) a person who looks after a specified person or thing for someone else: *flat-sitter* **5** *US* short for **baby-sitter 6** anyone, other than the medium, taking part in a seance **7** anything that is extremely easy, such as an easy catch in cricket

Sitter (ˈsɪtə) *n* **Willem de** (ˈwɪləm də) 1872–1934, Dutch astronomer, who calculated the size of the universe and conceived of it as expanding

sitting (ˈsɪtɪŋ) *n* **1** a continuous period of being seated: *I read his novel at one sitting* **2** such a period in a restaurant, canteen, etc: *dinner will be served in two sittings* **3** the act or period of posing for one's portrait to be painted, etc **4** a meeting, esp of an official body, to conduct business **5** the incubation period of a bird's eggs during which the mother sits on them ▷ *adj* **6** in office: *a sitting councillor* **7** seated: *in a sitting position*

Sitting Bull *n* Indian name *Tatanka Yotanka*. ?1831–90, American Indian chief of the Teton Dakota Sioux. Resisting White encroachment on his people's hunting grounds, he led the Sioux tribes against the US Army in the Sioux War (1876–77) in which Custer was killed. The hunger of the Sioux, whose food came from the diminishing buffalo, forced his surrender (1881). He was killed during renewed strife

sitting duck *n inf* a person or thing in a defenceless or vulnerable position. Also called: **sitting target**

sitting room *n* a room in a private house or flat used for relaxation and entertainment of guests

sitting tenant *n* a tenant occupying a house, flat, etc

situate (ˈsɪtjʊˌeɪt) *vb* **situates, situating, situated 1** (*tr; often passive*) to place ▷ *adj* **2** (now used esp in legal contexts) situated [C16 from LL *situāre* to position, from L *situs* a SITE]

situation (ˌsɪtjʊˈeɪʃən) *n* **1** physical placement, esp with regard to the surroundings **2a** state of affairs **2b** a complex or critical state of affairs in a novel, play, etc **3** social or financial status, position, or circumstances **4** a position of employment > ˌ**situˈational** *adj*

> USAGE *Situation* is often used in contexts in which it is redundant or imprecise. Typical examples are: *the company is in a crisis situation* or *people in a job situation*. In neither example does *situation* add to the meaning and should be left out

situation comedy *n* (on television or radio) a comedy series involving the same characters in various day-to-day situations which are developed as separate stories for each episode. Also called: **sitcom**

▷ www.eigo-i.com/tv/sitcom

sit up *vb* (*adv*) **1** to raise (oneself or another) from a recumbent to an upright posture **2** (*intr*) to remain out of bed and awake, esp until a late hour **3** (*intr*) *inf* to become suddenly interested: *devaluation of the dollar made the money market sit up* ▷ *n* **sit-up 4** a physical exercise in which the body is brought into a sitting position from one of lying on the back. Also called: **trunk curl**

Sitwell (ˈsɪtwəl) *n* **1** Dame **Edith** 1887–1964, English poet and critic, noted esp for her collection *Façade* (1922) **2** her brother, Sir **Osbert** 1892–1969, English writer, best known for his five autobiographical books (1944–50) **3** his brother, Sir **Sacheverell** (səˈʃɛvərəl) 1897–1988, English poet and writer of books on art, architecture, music, and travel

sitz bath (sɪts, zɪts) *n* a bath in which the buttocks and hips are immersed in hot water [half translation of G *Sitzbad*, from *Sitz* seat + *Bad* bath]

SI unit *n* any of the units adopted for international use under the Système International d'Unités, now employed for all scientific and most technical purposes. There are seven fundamental units: the metre, kilogram, second, ampere, kelvin, candela, and mole; and two supplementary units: the radian and the steradian. All other units are derived by multiplication or division of these units

SI Units

Base and Supplementary SI Units

Physical quantity	*Name of SI unit*	*Symbol for SI unit*
length	meter	m
mass	kilogram	kg
time	second	s
electric current	ampere	A
thermodynamic temperature	kelvin	K
luminous intensity	candela	cd
amount of substance	mole	mol
*plane angle	radian	rad
*solid angle	steradian	sr

*supplementary units

Derived SI Units with Special Names

Physical quantity	*Name of SI unit*	*Symbol for SI unit*
frequency	hertz	Hz
energy	joule	J
force	newton	N
power	watt	W
pressure	pascal	Pa
electric charge	coulomb	C
electric potential difference	volt	V

electric resistance	ohm	W
electric conductance	siemens	S
electric capacitance	farad	F
magnetic flux	weber	Wb
inductance	henry	H
magnetic flux density	tesla	T
luminous flux	lumen	lm
illuminance (illumination)	lux	lx
absorbed dose	gray	Gy
activity	becquerel	Bq
dose equivalent	sievert	Sv

DECIMAL MULTIPLES AND SUBMULTIPLES USED WITH SI UNITS

Submultiple	*Prefix*	*Symbol*	*Multiple*	*Prefix*	*Symbol*
10^{-1}	deci-	d	101	deca-	da
10^{-2}	centi-	c	102	hecto-	h
10^{-3}	milli-	m	103	kilo-	k
10^{-6}	micro-	m	106	mega-	M
10^{-9}	nano-	n	109	giga-	G
10^{-12}	pico-	p	1012	tera-	T
10^{-15}	femto-	f	1015	peta-	P
10^{-18}	atto-	a	1018	exa-	E
10^{-21}	zepto-	z	1021	zetta-	Z
10^{-24}	yocto-	y	1024	yotta-	Y

Siva ('siːvə) *n Hinduism* the destroyer, one of the three chief divinities of the later Hindu pantheon [from Sansk. *Śiva*, lit.: the auspicious (one)] > **'Siva,ism** *n*

Sivas (*Turkish* 'sivɑs) *n* a city in central Turkey, at an altitude of 1347 m (4420 ft): one of the chief cities in Asia Minor in ancient times; scene of the national congress (1919) leading to the revolution that established modern Turkey. Pop: 232 352 (1997)

six (sɪks) *n* **1** the cardinal number that is the sum of five and one **2** a numeral, 6, VI, etc, representing this number **3** something representing, represented by, or consisting of six units, such as a playing card with six symbols on it **4** Also: **six o'clock** six hours after noon or midnight **5** *cricket* **5a** a stroke from which the ball crosses the boundary without bouncing **5b** the six runs scored for such a stroke **6** a division of a Brownie Guide or Cub Scout pack **7** **at sixes and sevens** **7a** in disagreement **7b** in a state of confusion **8** **knock (someone) for six** *inf* to upset or overwhelm (someone) completely **9** **six of one and half a dozen of the other** a situation in which the alternatives are considered equivalent ▷ *determiner* **10a** amounting to six: *six nations* **10b** (*as pron*): *set the table for six* [OE *siex*]

Six (*French* sis) *n* **Les** (le) a group of six young composers in France, who from about 1916 formed a temporary association. Its members were Darius Milhaud, Arthur Honegger, Francis Poulenc, Georges Auric, Louis Durey, and Germaine Tailleferre

Six Counties *pl n* the historic counties of Northern Ireland, which no longer have a local government function

sixer ('sɪksə) *n* the leader of a group of six Cub Scouts or Brownie Guides

sixfold ('sɪks,fəʊld) *adj* **1** equal to or having six times as many or as much **2** composed of six parts ▷ *adv* **3** by or up to six times as many or as much

sixmo ('sɪksməʊ) *n, pl* **sixmos** **1** a book size resulting from folding a sheet of paper into six leaves or twelve pages, each one sixth the size of the sheet. Often written: **6mo, 6°**. Also called: **sexto** **2** a book this size

Six Nations *pl n* (in North America) the Indian confederacy of the Cayugas, Mohawks, Oneidas, Onondagas, Senecas, and Tuscaroras. Also called: **Iroquois** See also **Five Nations**

six-pack *n inf* **1** a package containing six units, esp six cans of beer **2** a highly developed set of abdominal muscles in a man

sixpence ('sɪkspəns) *n* (formerly) a small British cupronickel coin with a face value of six old pennies, worth 2½ pence

six-shooter *n US inf* a revolver with six chambers. Also called: **six-gun**

sixte (sɪkst) *n* the sixth of eight basic positions from which a parry or attack can be made in fencing [from F: (the) sixth (parrying position), from L *sextus* sixth]

sixteen ('sɪks'tiːn) *n* **1** the cardinal number that is the sum of ten and six **2** a numeral, 16, XVI, etc, representing this number **3** something represented by, representing, or consisting of 16 units ▷ *determiner* **4a** amounting to sixteen: *sixteen tons* **4b** (*as pron*): *sixteen are known to the police* [OE *sextyne*] > **'six'teenth** *adj, n*

sixteenmo ('sɪks'tiːnməʊ) *n, pl* **sixteenmos** a book size resulting from folding a sheet of paper into 16 leaves or 32 pages. Often written: **16mo, 16°** Also called: **sextodecimo**

sixteenth note *n* the usual US and Canad name for **semiquaver**

sixth (sɪksθ) *adj* **1** (*usually prenominal*) **1a** coming after the fifth and before the seventh in numbering, position, time, etc; being the ordinal number of *six*: often written 6th **1b** (*as n*): *the sixth to go* ▷ *n* **2a** one of six parts of an object, quantity, measurement, etc **2b** (*as modifier*): *a sixth part* **3** the fraction equal to one divided by six (1/6) **4** *music* **4a** the interval between one note and another six notes away from it in the diatonic scale **4b** one of two notes constituting such an interval in relation to the other ▷ *adv* **5** Also: **sixthly** after the fifth person, position, etc ▷ *sentence connector* **6** Also: **sixthly** as the sixth point

sixth form *n* (in England and Wales) **a** the most senior level in a secondary school to which pupils, usually above the legal leaving age, may proceed to take A levels, retake GCSEs, etc **b** (*as modifier*): *a sixth-form college* > **'sixth-,former** *n*

sixth sense *n* any supposed means of perception, such as intuition, other than the five senses of sight, hearing, touch, taste, and smell

Sixtus V *n* original name *Felice Peretti*. 1520–90, Italian ecclesiastic; pope (1585–90). He is noted for vigorous administrative reforms that contributed to the Counter-Reformation

sixty ('sɪkstɪ) *n, pl* **sixties** **1** the cardinal number that is the product of ten and six **2** a numeral, 60, LX, etc, representing sixty **3** something represented by, representing, or consisting of 60 units ▷ *determiner* **4a** amounting to sixty: *sixty soldiers* **4b** (*as pron*): *sixty are dead* [OE *sixtig*] > **'sixtieth** *adj, n*

sixty-fourmo (,sɪkstɪ'fɔːməʊ) *n, pl* **sixty-fourmos** a book size resulting from folding a sheet of paper into 64 leaves or 128 pages, each one sixty-fourth the size of the sheet. Often written **64mo, 64°**

sixty-fourth note *n* the usual US and Canad name for **hemidemisemiquaver**

sixty-nine *n* another term for **soixante-neuf**

sizable *or* **sizeable** ('saɪzəbᵊl) *adj* quite large > **'sizably** *or* **'sizeably** *adv*

size[1] (saɪz) *n* **1** the dimensions, amount, or extent of something **2** large dimensions, etc **3** one of a series of graduated measurements, as of clothing: *she takes size 4 shoes* **4** *inf* state of affairs as summarized: *he's bankrupt, that's the size of it* ▷ *vb* **sizes, sizing, sized** **5** to sort according to size **6** (*tr*) to cut to a particular size or sizes

[c13 from OF *sise*, shortened from *assise* ASSIZE] > 'sizer *n*
size² (saɪz) *n* **1** Also called: **sizing** a thin gelatinous mixture, made from glue, clay, or wax, that is used as a sealer on paper or plaster surfaces ▷ *vb* **sizes, sizing, sized** **2** (*tr*) to treat or coat (a surface) with size [c15 ?from OF *sise*; see SIZE¹]
sized (saɪzd) *adj* of a specified size: *medium-sized*
sizeism ('saɪzɪzəm) *n* discrimination on the basis of a person's size, esp against people considered to be overweight [c20 from SIZE¹ + -ISM, on the model of RACISM]
size up *vb* (*adv*) **1** (*tr*) *inf* to make an assessment of (a person, problem, etc) **2** to conform to or make so as to conform to certain specifications of dimension
sizzle ('sɪzəl) *vb* **sizzles, sizzling, sizzled** (*intr*) **1** to make the hissing sound characteristic of frying fat **2** *inf* to be very hot **3** *inf* to be very angry ▷ *n* **4** a hissing sound [c17 imit.] > '**sizzler** *n* > '**sizzling** *adj*
SJ *abbrev for* Society of Jesus
SJA *abbrev for* Saint John's Ambulance (Brigade *or* Association)
Sjælland (*Danish* 'sjɛlan) *n* the Danish name for **Zealand**
sjambok ('ʃæmbʌk) *n* (in South Africa) a heavy whip of rhinoceros or hippopotamus hide [c19 from Afrik., ult. from Urdu *chābuk* horsewhip]
SK *abbrev for* Saskatchewan
ska (skɑː) *n* a type of West Indian pop music: a precursor of reggae [c20 from ?]
skaapsteker ('skɑːpˌstɪəkə) *n* any of several back-fanged venomous South African snakes [from Afrik. *skaap* sheep + *steek* to pierce]
Skagen ('skɑːgən) *n* **Cape** another name for the **Skaw**
Skagerrak ('skægəˌræk) *n* an arm of the North Sea between Denmark and Norway, merging with the Kattegat in the southeast
skald *or* **scald** (skɔːld) *n* (in ancient Scandinavia) a bard or minstrel [from ON, from ?] > '**skaldic** *or* '**scaldic** *adj*
skanky ('skæŋkɪ) *adj* **skankier, skankiest** *sl* **1** dirty, foul-smelling, or unattractive **2** promiscuous > '**skankiness** *n*
Skara Brae ('skærə) *n* a neolithic village in NE Scotland, in the Orkney Islands: one of Europe's most perfectly preserved Stone Age villages, buried by a sand dune until uncovered by a storm in 1850
Skase ('skeɪs) ▷ *n* **do a Skase** *Austral inf* to skip the country while owing a large amount of money [c20 after the Austral businessman Christopher *Skase* (1948–2001), who fled Australia after the collapse of his business empire, owing millions of dollars]
skat (skæt) *n* a three-handed card game using 32 cards, popular in German-speaking communities [c19 from G, from It. *scarto* played cards, from *scartare* to discard, from L *charta* CARD¹]
skate¹ (skeɪt) *n* **1** See **roller skate, ice skate** **2** the steel blade or runner of an ice skate **3** such a blade fitted with straps for fastening to a shoe **4** **get one's skates on** to hurry ▷ *vb* **skates, skating, skated** (*intr*) **5** to glide swiftly on skates **6** to slide smoothly over a surface **7** **skate on thin ice** to place oneself in a dangerous situation [c17 via Du. from OF *éschasse* stilt, prob. of Gmc origin] > '**skater** *n*
skate² (skeɪt) *n, pl* **skate** *or* **skates** any of a family of large rays of temperate and tropical seas, having two dorsal fins, a short spineless tail, and a long snout [c14 from ON *skata*]
skateboard ('skeɪtˌbɔːd) *n* **1** a board mounted on roller-skate wheels, usually ridden while standing up ▷ *vb* **2** (*intr*) to ride on a skateboard > '**skateˌboarder** *n* > '**skateˌboarding** *n*
▷ http://skateboard.about.com
skate over *vb* (*intr, prep*) **1** to cross on or as if on skates **2** to avoid dealing with (a matter) fully
Skaw (skɔː) *n* **the** a cape at the extreme N tip of Denmark. Also called: (Cape) **Skagen**
skean-dhu (ˌskiːən'duː) *n* a dirk worn in the stocking as part of Highland dress [c19 from Gaelic *sgian dubh* black knife]
skedaddle (skɪ'dædəl) *inf* ▷ *vb* **skedaddles, skedaddling, skedaddled** **1** (*intr*) to run off hastily ▷ *n* **2** a hasty retreat [c19 from ?]
skeet (skiːt) *n* a form of clay-pigeon shooting in which targets are hurled from two traps at varying speeds and angles [c20 changed from ON *skeyti* a thrown object, from *skjōta* to shoot]
skein (skeɪn) *n* **1** a length of yarn, etc, wound in a long coil **2** something resembling this, such as a lock of hair **3** a flock of geese flying [c15 from OF *escaigne*, from ?]
skeletal muscle *n* another name for **striped muscle**
skeleton ('skɛlɪtən) *n* **1** a hard framework consisting of inorganic material that supports and protects the soft parts of an animal's body: may be internal, as in vertebrates, or external, as in arthropods **2** *inf* a very thin emaciated person or animal **3** the essential framework of any structure, such as a building or leaf **4** an outline consisting of bare essentials: *the skeleton of a novel* **5** (*modifier*) reduced to a minimum: *a skeleton staff* **6** **skeleton in the cupboard** *or US & Canad* **closet** a scandalous fact or event in the past that is kept secret [c16 via NL from Gk: something desiccated, from *skellein* to dry up] > '**skeletal** *or* '**skeleton-ˌlike** *adj*
skeletonize *or* **skeletonise** ('skɛlɪtəˌnaɪz) *vb* **skeletonizes, skeletonizing, skeletonized** *or* **skeletonises, skeletonising, skeletonised** (*tr*) **1** to reduce to a minimum framework or outline **2** to create the essential framework of
skeleton key *n* a key with the serrated edge filed down so that it can open numerous locks. Also called: **passkey**
skelm ('skɛləm) *n S African inf* a villain or crook [Afrik]
Skelmersdale ('skɛlməzˌdeɪl) *n* a town in NW England, in Lancashire: designated a new town in 1962. Pop: 42 104 (1991)
Skelton ('skɛltən) *n* **John** ?1460–1529, English poet celebrated for his short rhyming lines using the rhythms of colloquial speech
skep (skɛp) *n* **1** a beehive, esp one constructed of straw **2** *now chiefly dialect* a large basket of wickerwork or straw [OE *sceppe*]
skeptic ('skɛptɪk) *n, adj* an archaic and the usual US spelling of **sceptic**
skerrick ('skɛrɪk) *n US, Austral, & NZ* a small fragment or amount (esp in **not a skerrick**) [c20 N English dialect, prob. of Scand. origin]
skerry ('skɛrɪ) *n, pl* **skerries** *chiefly Scot* **1** a small rocky island **2** a reef [c17 Orkney dialect, from ON *sker* scar (rock formation)]
sketch (skɛtʃ) *n* **1** a rapid drawing or painting **2** a brief usually descriptive essay or other literary composition **3** a short play, often comic, forming part of a revue **4** a short evocative piece of instrumental music **5** any brief outline ▷ *vb* **6** to make a rough drawing (of) **7** (*tr; often foll by out*) to make a brief description of [c17 from Du. *schets*, via It. from L *schedius* hastily made, from Gk *skhedios* unprepared] > '**sketcher** *n*
sketchbook ('skɛtʃˌbʊk) *n* **1** a book of plain paper containing sketches or for making sketches in **2** a book of literary sketches
sketchy ('skɛtʃɪ) *adj* **sketchier, sketchiest** **1** existing only in outline **2** superficial or slight > '**sketchily** *adv* > '**sketchiness** *n*
skew (skjuː) *adj* **1** placed in or turning into an oblique position or course **2** *machinery* having a component that is at an angle to the main axis of an assembly: *a skew bevel gear* **3** *maths* composed of or being elements that are neither parallel nor intersecting **4** (of a statistical distribution) not having equal probabilities above and below the mean **5** distorted or biased ▷ *n* **6** an oblique,

slanting, or indirect course or position ▷ *vb* **7** to take or cause to take an oblique course or direction **8** (*intr*) to look sideways **9** (*tr*) to distort [c14 from OF *escuer* to shun, of Gmc origin] > **'skewness** *n*

skewback ('skjuː,bæk) *n archit* the sloping surface on both sides of a segmental arch that takes the thrust

skewbald ('skjuː,bɔːld) *adj* **1** marked or spotted in white and any colour except black ▷ *n* **2** a horse with this marking [c17 see SKEW, PIEBALD]

skewer (skjʊə) *n* **1** a long pin for holding meat in position while being cooked, etc **2** a similar pin having some other function ▷ *vb* **3** (*tr*) to drive a skewer through or fasten with a skewer [c17 prob. from dialect *skiver*]

skewwhiff ('skjuː'wɪf) *adj* (*postpositive*) *Brit inf* not straight [c18 prob. infl. by ASKEW]

ski (skiː) *n, pl* **skis** *or* **ski** **1a** one of a pair of wood, metal, or plastic runners that are used for gliding over snow **1b** (*as modifier*): *a ski boot* **2** a water-ski ▷ *vb* **skis, skiing; skied** *or* **ski'd** **3** (*intr*) to travel on skis [c19 from Norwegian, from ON *skíth* snowshoes] > **'skier** *n* > **'skiing** *n*

▷ www.fis-ski.com

skibob ('skiːbɒb) *n* a vehicle made of two short skis, the forward one having a steering handle and the rear one supporting a low seat, for gliding down snow slopes > **'skibobber** *n*

skid (skɪd) *vb* **skids, skidding, skidded** **1** to cause (a vehicle) to slide sideways or (of a vehicle) to slide sideways while in motion, esp out of control **2** (*intr*) to slide without revolving, as the wheel of a moving vehicle after sudden braking ▷ *n* **3** an instance of sliding, esp sideways **4** a support on which heavy objects may be stored and moved short distances by sliding **5** a shoe or drag used to apply pressure to the metal rim of a wheel to act as a brake [c17 ? of Scand. origin]

Skidoo ('skɪduː) *n Canad, trademark* another name for **snowmobile**

skid row (rəʊ) *or* **skid road** *n sl, chiefly US & Canad* a dilapidated section of a city inhabited by vagrants, etc

skied[1] (skaɪd) *vb* the past tense and past participle of **sky**

skied[2] (skiːd) *vb* a past tense and past participle of **ski**

Skien (*Norwegian* 'ʃeːən) *n* a port in S Norway, on the **Skien River**: one of the oldest towns in Norway; timber industry. Pop: 47 870 (1990)

skiff (skɪf) *n* a small narrow boat [c18 from F *esquif*, from OIt. *schifo* a boat, of Gmc origin]

skiffle ('skɪfᵊl) *n* a style of popular music of the 1950s, played chiefly on guitars and improvised percussion instruments [c20 from ?]

skijoring (skiː'dʒɔːrɪŋ, -'jɔːrɪŋ) *n* a sport in which a skier is pulled over snow or ice, usually by a horse [Norwegian *skikjöring*, lit.: ski-driving] > **ski'jorer** *n*

ski jump *n* **1** a high ramp overhanging a slope from which skiers compete to make the longest jump ▷ *vb* **ski-jump** **2** (*intr*) to perform a ski jump > **ski jumper** *n*

Skikda ('skɪkdɑː) *n* a port in NE Algeria, on an inlet of the Mediterranean: founded by the French in 1838 on the site of a Roman city. Pop: 152 335 (1998). Former name: **Philippeville**

skilful *or US* **skillful** ('skɪlfʊl) *adj* **1** possessing or displaying accomplishment or skill **2** involving or requiring accomplishment or skill > **'skilfully** *or US* **'skillfully** *adv*

ski lift *n* any device for carrying skiers up a slope, such as a chairlift

skill (skɪl) *n* **1** special ability in a sport, etc, esp ability acquired by training **2** something, esp a trade or technique, requiring special training or manual proficiency [c12 from ON *skil* distinction] > **'skill-less** *or* **'skilless** *adj*

skilled (skɪld) *adj* **1** demonstrating accomplishment or special training **2** (*prenominal*) involving skill or special training: *a skilled job*

skillet ('skɪlɪt) *n* **1** a small frying pan **2** *chiefly Brit* a >n [c15 prob. from *skele* bucket, from ON]

skilly ('skɪlɪ) *n chiefly Brit* a thin soup or gruel [c19 from *skilligallee*, from ?]

skim (skɪm) *vb* **skims, skimming, skimmed** **1** (*tr*) to remove floating material from the surface of (a liquid), as with a spoon: *to skim milk* **2** to glide smoothly or lightly over (a surface) **3** (*tr*) to throw (something) in a path over a surface, so as to bounce or ricochet: *to skim stones over water* **4** (when *intr*, usually foll by *through*) to read (a book) in a superficial manner ▷ *n* **5** the act or process of skimming **6** material skimmed off a liquid, esp off milk **7** any thin layer covering a surface [c15 *skimmen*, prob. from *scumen* to skim]

skimmed milk *n* milk from which the cream has been removed. Also called: **skim milk**

skimmer ('skɪmə) *n* **1** a person or thing that skims **2** any of several mainly tropical coastal aquatic birds having a bill with an elongated lower mandible for skimming food from the surface of the water **3** a flat perforated spoon used for skimming fat from liquids

skimmia ('skɪmɪə) *n* any of a genus of rutaceous shrubs grown for their ornamental red berries and evergreen foliage [c18 NL from Japanese (*mijama-*) *shikimi*, a native name of the plant]

skimp (skɪmp) *vb* **1** to be extremely sparing or supply (someone) sparingly **2** to perform (work, etc) carelessly or with inadequate materials [c17 ? a combination of SCANT & SCRIMP]

skimpy ('skɪmpɪ) *adj* **skimpier, skimpiest** **1** made of too little material **2** excessively thrifty; mean > **'skimpily** *adv* > **'skimpiness** *n*

skin (skɪn) *n* **1** the tissue forming the outer covering of the vertebrate body: it consists of two layers, the outermost of which may be covered with hair, scales, feathers, etc **2** a person's complexion: *a fair skin* **3** any similar covering in a plant or lower animal **4** any coating or film, such as one that forms on the surface of a liquid **5** the outer covering of a fur-bearing animal, dressed and finished with the hair on **6** a container made from animal skin **7** the outer covering surface of a vessel, rocket, etc **8** a person's skin regarded as his or her life: *to save one's skin* **9** (*often pl*) *inf* (in jazz or pop use) a drum **10** *inf* short for **skinhead** **11** **by the skin of one's teeth** only just **12** **get under one's skin** *inf* to irritate **13** **no skin off one's nose** *inf* not a matter that affects one adversely **14** **skin and bone** extremely thin **15** **thick** (*or* **thin**) **skin** an insensitive (*or* sensitive) nature ▷ *vb* **skins, skinning, skinned** **16** (*tr*) to remove the outer covering from (fruit, etc) **17** (*tr*) to scrape a small piece of skin from (a part of oneself) in falling, etc: *he skinned his knee* **18** (often foll by *over*) to cover (something) with skin or a skinlike substance or (of something) to become covered in this way **19** (*tr*) *sl* to swindle ▷ *adj* **20** of or for the skin: *skin cream* [OE *scinn*] > **'skinless** *adj* > **'skin,like** *adj*

skin-deep *adj* **1** superficial; shallow ▷ *adv* **2** superficially

skin diving *n* the sport or activity of diving and underwater swimming without wearing a diver's costume > **'skin-,diver** *n*

skin flick *n sl* a film containing much nudity and explicit sex for sensational purposes

skinflint ('skɪn,flɪnt) *n* an ungenerous or niggardly person [c18 referring to a person so avaricious that he would skin (swindle) a flint]

skinful ('skɪn,fʊl) *n, pl* **skinfuls** *sl* sufficient alcoholic drink to make one drunk

skin graft *n* a piece of skin removed from one part of the body and surgically grafted at the site of a severe burn or similar injury

skinhead ('skɪn,hɛd) *n* **1** a member of a group of White youths, noted for their closely cropped hair, aggressive behaviour, and overt racism **2** a closely cropped hairstyle

skink (skɪŋk) *n* any of a family of lizards commonest in tropical Africa and Asia, having an elongated body covered with smooth scales [C16 from L *scincus* a lizard, from Gk *skinkos*]

skinned (skɪnd) *adj* **1** stripped of the skin **2a** having a skin as specified **2b** *(in combination): thick-skinned*

Skinner ('skɪnə) *n* **B**(urrhus) **F**(rederic) 1904–90, US behavioural psychologist. His "laws of learning", derived from experiments with animals, have been widely applied to education and behaviour therapy

skinny ('skɪnɪ) *adj* **skinnier, skinniest 1** lacking in flesh; thin **2** consisting of or resembling skin

skint (skɪnt) *adj (usually postpositive) Brit sl* without money [var. of *skinned*, p.p. of SKIN]

skin test *n med* any test to determine immunity to a disease or hypersensitivity by introducing a small amount of the test substance beneath the skin

skintight ('skɪn'taɪt) *adj* (of garments) fitting tightly over the body; clinging

skip[1] (skɪp) *vb* **skips, skipping, skipped 1** (when *intr*, often foll by *over, into*, etc) to spring or move lightly, esp to move by hopping from one foot to the other **2** *(intr)* to jump over a skipping-rope **3** to cause (a stone, etc) to skim over a surface or (of a stone) to move in this way **4** to omit (intervening matter): *he skipped a chapter of the book* **5** *(intr; foll by through) inf* to read or deal with quickly or superficially **6 skip it!** *inf* it doesn't matter! **7** *(tr) inf* to miss deliberately: *to skip school* **8** *(tr) inf, chiefly US & Canad* to leave (a place) in haste: *to skip town* ▷ *n* **9** a skipping movement or gait **10** the act of passing over or omitting [C13 prob. from ON]

skip[2] (skɪp) *n, vb* **skips, skipping, skipped** *inf* short for **skipper**[1]

skip[3] (skɪp) *n* **1** a large open container for transporting building materials, etc **2** a cage used as a lift in mines, etc [C19 var. of SKEP]

ski pants *pl n* stretch trousers, worn for skiing or as a fashion garment, kept taut by a strap under the foot

skip distance *n* the shortest distance between a transmitter and a receiver that will permit reception of radio waves of a specified frequency by one reflection from the ionosphere

skipjack ('skɪp,dʒæk) *n, pl* **skipjack** *or* **skipjacks 1** Also called: **skipjack tuna** an important food fish that has a striped abdomen and occurs in all tropical seas **2 black skipjack** a small spotted tuna of Indo-Pacific seas

skiplane ('skiː,pleɪn) *n* an aircraft fitted with skis to enable it to land on and take off from snow

skipper[1] ('skɪpə) *n* **1** the captain of any vessel **2** the captain of an aircraft **3** a leader, as of a sporting team ▷ *vb* **4** to act as skipper (of) [C14 from MLow G, MDu. *schipper* shipper]

skipper[2] ('skɪpə) *n* **1** a person or thing that skips **2** a small butterfly having a hairy mothlike body and erratic darting flight

skipping ('skɪpɪŋ) *n* the act of jumping over a rope that is held either by the person jumping or by two other people, as a game or for exercise

skipping-rope *n Brit* a cord, usually having handles at each end, that is held in the hands and swung round and down so that the holder or others can jump over it

Skipton ('skɪptən) *n* a market town in N England, in North Yorkshire: 11th-century castle. Pop: 13 583 (1991)

skip-tooth saw *n* a saw with alternate teeth absent

skip zone *n* a region surrounding a broadcasting station that cannot receive transmissions either directly or by reflection off the ionosphere

skirl (skɜːl) *Scot & N English dialect* ▷ *vb* **1** *(intr)* (esp of bagpipes) to emit a shrill sound ▷ *n* **2** the sound of bagpipes [C14 prob. from ON]

skirmish ('skɜːmɪʃ) *n* **1** a minor short-lived military engagement **2** any brisk clash or encounter ▷ *vb* **3** *(intr; often foll by with)* to engage in a skirmish [C14 from OF *eskirmir*, of Gmc origin] > '**skirmisher** *n*

Skíros ('skirɔs) *n* transliteration of the Modern Greek name for **Skyros**

skirt (skɜːt) *n* **1** a garment hanging from the waist, worn chiefly by women and girls **2** the part of a dress below the waist **3** Also called: **apron** a circular flap, as round the base of a hovercraft **4** the flaps on a saddle **5** *Brit* a cut of beef from the flank **6** *(often pl)* an outlying area **7 bit of skirt** *sl* a girl or woman ▷ *vb* **8** *(tr)* to form the edge of **9** *(tr)* to provide with a border **10** (when *intr*, foll by *around, along*, etc) to pass (by) or be situated (near) the outer edge of (an area, etc) **11** *(tr)* to avoid (a difficulty, etc): *he skirted the issue* **12** *chiefly Austral & NZ* to trim the ragged edges from (a fleece) [C13 from ON *skyrta* shirt] > '**skirted** *adj*

skirting ('skɜːtɪŋ) *n* **1** a border, esp of wood or tiles, fixed round the base of an interior wall to protect it **2** material used for skirts

skirting board *n* a skirting made of wood

skirtings ('skɜːtɪŋz) *pl n* ragged edges trimmed from the fleece of a sheep

ski stick *or* **pole** *n* a stick, usually with a metal point, used by skiers to gain momentum and maintain balance

skit (skɪt) *n* **1** a brief satirical theatrical sketch **2** a short satirical piece of writing [C18 rel. to earlier verb *skit* to move rapidly, hence to score a satirical hit, prob. of Scand. origin]

skite[1] (skaɪt) *Scot dialect* ▷ *vb* **skites, skiting, skited 1** *(intr)* to slide or slip, as on ice **2** *(tr)* to strike with a sharp blow ▷ *n* **3** an instance of slipping or sliding **4** a sharp blow [C18 from ?]

skite[2] (skaɪt) *Austral & NZ inf* ▷ *vb* **skites, skiting, skited** *(intr)* **1** to boast ▷ *n* **2** boastful talk **3** a person who boasts [C19 from Scot & N English dialect]

ski tow *n* a device for pulling skiers uphill, usually a motor-driven rope grasped by the skier while riding on his skis

skitter ('skɪtə) *vb* **1** *(intr; often foll by off)* to move or run rapidly or lightly **2** to skim or cause to skim lightly and rapidly **3** *(intr) angling* to draw a bait lightly over the surface of water [C19 prob. from dialect *skite* to dash about]

skittish ('skɪtɪʃ) *adj* **1** playful, lively, or frivolous **2** difficult to handle or predict [C15 prob. from ON] > '**skittishly** *adv* > '**skittishness** *n*

skittle ('skɪtᵊl) *n* **1** a wooden or plastic pin, typically widest just above the base **2** *(pl; functioning as sing)* Also called (esp US): **ninepins** a bowling game in which players knock over as many skittles as possible by rolling a wooden ball at them [C17 from ?]

skive[1] (skaɪv) *vb* **skives, skiving, skived** *(tr)* to shave or remove the surface of (leather) [C19 of Scand. origin, from *skifa*] > '**skiver** *n*

skive[2] (skaɪv) *vb* **skives, skiving, skived** (when *intr*, often foll by *off*) *Brit inf* to evade (work or responsibility) [C20 from ?] > '**skiver** *n*

skivvy[1] ('skɪvɪ) *n, pl* **skivvies 1** *chiefly Brit, often contemptuous* a servant, esp a female; drudge ▷ *vb* **skivvies, skivvying, skivvied 2** *(intr) Brit* to work as a skivvy [C20 from ?]

skivvy[2] ('skɪvɪ) *n, pl* **skivvies** *Austral & NZ* a lightweight sweater-like garment with long sleeves and a polo neck [from ?]

skol (skɒl) *or* **skoal** (skəʊl) *sentence substitute* good health! (a drinking toast) [C16 from Danish *skaal* bowl, of Scand. origin, from *skal*]

skookum ('skuːkəm) *adj W Canad* large or big [from Chinook Jargon]

Skopje ('skɔːpjɛ) *n* the capital of (the Former Yugoslav

Ss

Republic of) Macedonia, on the Vardar River: became capital of Serbia in 1346 and of Macedonia in 1945; suffered a severe earthquake in 1963; university (1949). Pop: 541 280 (1994). Serbo-Croat name: **Skoplje** ('skɔpljɛ) Turkish name (1392–1913): **Üsküb**
▷ www.skopjeonline.com.mk
▷ www.b-info.com/places/Macedonia

Skryabin *n* a variant spelling of **Scriabin**

Skt., Skt., Skr., *or* **Skr.** *abbrev for* Sanskrit

skua ('skjuːə) *n* any of various predatory aquatic gull-like birds having a dark plumage and long tail [C17 from NL, from Faeroese *skūgvur*, of Scand. origin, from *skūfr*]

skulduggery *or US* **skullduggery** (skʌl'dʌgərɪ) *n inf* underhand dealing; trickery [C18 from earlier Scot *skulduddery*, from ?]

skulk (skʌlk) *vb (intr)* **1** to move stealthily so as to avoid notice **2** to lie in hiding; lurk **3** to shirk duty or evade responsibilities ▷ *n* **4** a person who skulks **5** *obs* a pack of foxes [C13 from ON] > **'skulker** *n*

skull (skʌl) *n* **1** the bony skeleton of the head of vertebrates **2** *often derog* the head regarded as the mind or intelligence: *to have a dense skull* **3** a picture of a skull used to represent death or danger [C13 from ON]

skull and crossbones *n* a picture of the human skull above two crossed thighbones, formerly on the pirate flag, now used as a warning of danger or death

skullcap ('skʌl,kæp) *n* **1** a rounded brimless hat fitting the crown of the head **2** the top part of the skull **3** any of a genus of perennial plants, that have helmet-shaped flowers

skunk (skʌŋk) *n, pl* **skunks** *or* **skunk** **1** any of various American mammals having a black-and-white coat and bushy tail: they eject an unpleasant-smelling fluid from the anal gland when attacked **2** *inf* a despicable person [C17 of Amerind origin]

skunk cabbage *n* a low-growing fetid aroid swamp plant of E North America, having broad leaves and minute flowers enclosed in a greenish spathe

sky (skaɪ) *n, pl* **skies** **1** *(sometimes pl)* the apparently dome-shaped expanse extending upwards from the horizon that is blue or grey during the day and black at night **2** outer space, as seen from the earth **3** *(often pl)* weather, as described by the appearance of the upper air: *sunny skies* **4** heaven **5** *inf* the highest level of attainment: *the sky's the limit* **6** **to the skies** extravagantly ▷ *vb* **skies, skying, skied** **7** *rowing* to lift (the blade of an oar) too high before a stroke **8** *(tr) sport inf* to hit (a ball) high in the air [C13 from ON *sky̆*]

sky blue *n, adj* (of) a light or pale blue colour

skydiving ('skaɪ,daɪvɪŋ) *n* the sport of parachute jumping, in which participants perform manoeuvres before opening the parachute > **'sky,dive** *vb* **'sky,dives, 'sky,diving, 'sky,dived** *or US* **'sky,dove; 'sky,dived** > **'sky,diver** *n*
▷ www.fai.org/parachuting

Skye (skaɪ) *n* a mountainous island off the NW coast of Scotland, the largest island of the Inner Hebrides: tourist centre. Chief town: Portree. Pop: 7500 (latest est). Area: 1735 sq km (670 sq miles)

Skye terrier *n* a short-legged long-bodied breed of terrier with long wiry hair and erect ears

sky-high *adj, adv* **1** at or to an unprecedented level: *prices rocketed sky-high* ▷ *adv* **2** high into the air **3** **blow sky-high** to destroy

skyjack ('skaɪ,dʒæk) *vb (tr)* to hijack (an aircraft) [C20 from SKY + (HI)JACK]

skylark ('skaɪ,lɑːk) *n* **1** an Old World lark, noted for singing while hovering at a great height ▷ *vb* **2** *(intr) inf* to romp or play jokes

skylight ('skaɪ,laɪt) *n* a window placed in a roof or ceiling to admit daylight. Also called: **fanlight**

skyline ('skaɪ,laɪn) *n* **1** the line at which the earth and sky appear to meet **2** the outline of buildings, trees, etc, seen against the sky

sky marshal *n* an armed security guard on a commercial aircraft

sky pilot *n sl* a clergyman, esp a chaplain

skyrocket ('skaɪ,rɒkɪt) *n* **1** another word for **rocket**[1] (sense 1) ▷ *vb* **2** *(intr) inf* to rise rapidly, as in price

Skyros ('skiːrɒs) *n* a Greek island in the Aegean, the largest island in the N Sporades. Pop: 3000 (latest est). Area: 199 sq km (77 sq miles). Modern Greek name: **Skíros**

skysail ('skaɪ,seɪl) *n naut* a square sail set above the royal on a square-rigger

skyscraper ('skaɪ,skreɪpə) *n* a tall multistorey building

sky show *n Austral* a fireworks display

skyward ('skaɪwəd) *adj* **1** directed or moving towards the sky ▷ *adv* **2** Also: **skywards** towards the sky

skywriting ('skaɪ,raɪtɪŋ) *n* **1** the forming of words in the sky by the release of smoke or vapour from an aircraft **2** the words so formed > **'sky,writer** *n*

slab (slæb) *n* **1** a broad flat thick piece of wood, stone, or other material **2** a thick slice of cake, etc **3** any of the outside parts of a log that are sawn off while the log is being made into planks **4** *Austral & NZ* **4a** a rough-hewn wooden plank **4b** *(as modifier)*: *a slab hut* **5** *inf, chiefly Brit* an operating or mortuary table **6** *Austral inf* a pack of 24 cans, esp of beer ▷ *vb* **slabs, slabbing, slabbed** *(tr)* **7** to cut or make into a slab or slabs **8** to saw slabs from (a log) [C13 from ?]

slack[1] (slæk) *adj* **1** not tight, tense, or taut **2** negligent or careless **3** (esp of water, etc) moving slowly **4** (of trade, etc) not busy **5** *phonetics* another term for **lax** (sense 4) ▷ *adv* **6** in a slack manner ▷ *n* **7** a part of a rope, etc, that is slack: *take in the slack* **8** a period of decreased activity ▷ *vb* **9** to neglect (one's duty, etc) **10** (often foll by *off*) to loosen ▷ See also **slacks** [OE *slæc, sleac*] > **'slackly** *adv* > **'slackness** *n*

slack[2] (slæk) *n* small pieces of coal with a high ash content [C15 prob. from MLow G *slecke*]

slacken ('slækən) *vb* (often foll by *off*) **1** to make or become looser **2** to make or become slower, less intense, etc

slacker ('slækə) *n* a person who evades work or duty; shirker

slacks (slæks) *pl n* informal trousers worn by both sexes

slack water *n* the period of still water around the turn of the tide, esp at low tide

slag (slæg) *n* **1** Also called: **cinder** the fused material formed during the smelting or refining of metals. It usually consists of a mixture of silicates with calcium, phosphorus, sulphur, etc **2** a mass of rough fragments of rock derived from a volcanic eruption **3** a mixture of shale, clay, coal dust, etc, produced during coal mining **4** *Brit sl* a coarse or dissipated woman or girl ▷ *vb* **slags, slagging, slagged** **5** *(tr; sometimes foll by off) sl* to make disparaging comments about; slander [C16 from MLow G *slagge*, ?from *slagen* to slay] > **'slagging** *n* > **'slaggy** *adj*

slag heap *n* a hillock of waste matter from coal mining, etc

slain (sleɪn) *vb* the past participle of **slay**

slake (sleɪk) *vb* **slakes, slaking, slaked** **1** *(tr) literary* to satisfy (thirst, desire, etc) **2** *(tr) poetic* to cool or refresh **3** to undergo or cause to undergo the process in which lime reacts with water to produce calcium hydroxide [OE *slacian*, from *slæc* SLACK[1]] > **'slakable** *or* **'slakeable** *adj*

slaked lime *n* another name for **calcium hydroxide**

slalom ('slɑːləm) *n skiing, canoeing, etc* a race over a winding course marked by artificial obstacles [Norwegian, from *slad* sloping + *lom* path]

slam[1] (slæm) *vb* **slams, slamming, slammed** **1** to cause (a door or window) to close noisily or (of a door, etc) to close in this way **2** *(tr)* to throw (something) down violently **3** *(tr) sl* to criticize harshly **4** *(intr; usually foll* by *into* or *out of*) *inf* to go (into or out of a room, etc) in violent haste or anger **5** (*tr*) to strike with violent force **6** (*tr*) *inf* to defeat easily ▷ *n* **7** the act or noise of slamming [C17 of Scand. origin]

slam² (slæm) *n* **a** the winning of all (**grand slam**) or all but one (**little** *or* **small slam**) of the 13 tricks at bridge or whist **b** the bid to do so in bridge [C17 from ?]

slam³ (slæm) *n* a poetry contest in which entrants compete with each other by reciting their work and are awarded points by the audience [C20 from ?]

slam-dance *vb* **slam-dances, slam-dancing, slam-danced** (*intr*) to hurl oneself repeatedly into or through a crowd at a rock-music concert

slammer (ˈslæmə) *n* **the** *sl* prison

slander (ˈslɑːndə) *n* **1** *law* **1a** defamation in some transient form, as by spoken words, gestures, etc **1b** a slanderous statement, etc **2** any defamatory words spoken about a person ▷ *vb* **3** to utter or circulate slander (about) [C13 via Anglo-F from OF *escandle*, from LL *scandalum* a cause of offence; see SCANDAL] > ˈ**slanderer** *n* > ˈ**slanderous** *adj*

slang (slæŋ) *n* **1a** vocabulary, idiom, etc, that is not appropriate to the standard form of a language or to formal contexts and may be restricted as to social status or distribution **1b** (*as modifier*): *a slang word* ▷ *vb* **2** to abuse (someone) with vituperative language [C18 from ?] > ˈ**slangy** *adj* > ˈ**slangily** *adv* > ˈ**slanginess** *n*

slant (slɑːnt) *vb* **1** to incline or be inclined at an oblique or sloping angle **2** (*tr*) to write or present (news, etc) with a bias **3** (*intr; foll by towards*) (of a person's opinions) to be biased ▷ *n* **4** an inclined or oblique line or direction **5** a way of looking at something **6** a bias or opinion, as in an article **7** **on a** (*or* **the**) **slant** sloping ▷ *adj* **8** oblique; sloping [C17 short for ASLANT, prob. of Scand. origin] > ˈ**slanting** *adj*

slantwise (ˈslɑːntˌwaɪz) *or* **slantways** *adv, adj* (*prenominal*) in a slanting or oblique direction

slap (slæp) *n* **1** a sharp blow or smack, as with the open hand, something flat, etc **2** the sound made by or as if by such a blow **3** (**a bit of**) **slap and tickle** *Brit inf* sexual play **4** **a slap in the face** an insult or rebuff **5** **a slap on the back** congratulation ▷ *vb* **slaps, slapping, slapped** **6** (*tr*) to strike (a person or thing) sharply, as with the open hand or something flat **7** (*tr*) to bring down (the hand, etc) sharply **8** (when *intr*, usually foll by *against*) to strike (something) with or as if with a slap **9** (*tr*) *inf, chiefly Brit* to apply in large quantities, haphazardly, etc: *she slapped butter on the bread* **10** **slap on the back** to congratulate ▷ *adv inf* **11** exactly: *slap on time* **12** forcibly or abruptly: *to fall slap on the floor* [C17 from Low G *slapp*, G *Schlappe*, imit.]

slap bass *n* a rock or jazz style of playing the electric or double bass in which the strings are plucked and released so as to vibrate sharply against the fretboard or fingerboard

slapdash (ˈslæpˌdæʃ) *adv* **1** in a careless, hasty, or haphazard manner ▷ *adj* **2** careless, hasty, or haphazard ▷ *n* **3** slapdash activity or work

slap-happy *adj* **slap-happier, slap-happiest** *inf* **1** cheerfully irresponsible or careless **2** dazed or giddy from or as if from repeated blows

slaphead (ˈslæpˌhɛd) *n derog sl* a bald person [C20 from ?]

slapstick (ˈslæpˌstɪk) *n* **1a** comedy characterized by horseplay and physical action **1b** (*as modifier*): *slapstick humour* **2** a pair of paddles formerly used in pantomime to strike a blow with a loud sound but without injury

slap-up *adj* (*prenominal*) *Brit inf* (esp of meals) lavish; excellent; first-class

slash (slæʃ) *vb* (*tr*) **1** to cut or lay about (a person or thing) with sharp sweeping strokes, as with a sword, etc **2** to lash with a whip **3** to make large gashes in: *to slash tyres* **4** to reduce (prices, etc) drastically **5** to criticize harshly **6** to slit (the outer fabric of a garment) so that the lining material is revealed **7** to clear (scrub or undergrowth) by cutting ▷ *n* **8** a sharp sweeping stroke, as with a sword or whip **9** a cut or rent made by such a stroke **10** a decorative slit in a garment revealing the lining material **11** *US & Canad* littered wood chips that remain after trees have been cut down **12** another name for **solidus** **13** *Brit sl* the act of urinating [C14 *slaschen*, ?from OF *esclachier* to break]

slashdot effect (ˈslæʃˌdɒt) *n computing* a temporary surge in the numbers visiting a website and consequent service slowdown or even server crash that sometimes arises as a result of a new link being set up from a more popular website [C21 from the conventions of website addresses, featuring slashes and dots]

slasher (ˈslæʃə) *n* **1** a person or thing that slashes **2** *Austral & NZ* a tool or machine used for cutting scrub or undergrowth in the bush

slasher movie *n sl* a film in which victims, usually women, are slashed with knives, razors, etc. Also called: **stalk-and-slash movie**

slashing (ˈslæʃɪŋ) *adj* aggressively or harshly critical (esp in **slashing attack**)

Śląsk (ʃlɔ̃sk) *n* the Polish name for **Silesia**

slat (slæt) *n* **1** a narrow thin strip of wood or metal, as used in a Venetian blind, etc **2** a movable or fixed aerofoil attached to the leading edge of an aircraft wing to increase lift [C14 from OF *esclat* splinter, from *esclater* to shatter]

slate¹ (sleɪt) *n* **1a** a compact fine-grained metamorphic rock that can be split into thin layers and is used as a roofing and paving material **1b** (*as modifier*): *a slate tile* **2** a roofing tile of slate **3** (formerly) a writing tablet of slate **4** a dark grey colour **5** *chiefly US & Canad* a list of candidates in an election **6** **clean slate** a record without dishonour **7** **have a slate loose** *Brit & Irish inf* to be eccentric or crazy **8** **on the slate** *Brit inf* on credit ▷ *vb* **slates, slating, slated** (*tr*) **9** to cover (a roof) with slates **10** *chiefly US* to enter (a person's name) on a list, esp on a political slate ▷ *adj* **11** of the colour slate [C14 from OF *esclate*, from *esclat* a fragment] > ˈ**slaty** *adj*

slate² (sleɪt) *vb* **slates, slating, slated** (*tr*) *inf, chiefly Brit* to criticize harshly [C19 prob. from SLATE¹] > ˈ**slating** *n*

slater (ˈsleɪtə) *n* **1** a person trained in laying roof slates **2** another name for **woodlouse**

slather (ˈslɑːðə) *n* **1** (*usually pl*) *inf, chiefly US & Canad* a large quantity **2** **open slather** *Austral & NZ sl* a free-for-all [C19 from ?]

slattern (ˈslætən) *n* a slovenly woman or girl [C17 prob. from *slattering*, from dialect *slatter* to slop] > ˈ**slatternly** *adj* > ˈ**slatternliness** *n*

slaughter (ˈslɔːtə) *n* **1** the killing of animals, esp for food **2** the savage killing of a person **3** the indiscriminate or brutal killing of large numbers of people, as in war ▷ *vb* (*tr*) **4** to kill (animals), esp for food **5** to kill in a brutal manner **6** to kill indiscriminately or in large numbers **7** to defeat resoundingly [OE *sleaht*] > ˈ**slaughterer** *n* > ˈ**slaughterous** *adj*

slaughterhouse (ˈslɔːtəˌhaʊs) *n* a place where animals are butchered for food; abattoir

Slav (slɑːv) *n* a member of any of the peoples of E Europe or NW Asia who speak a Slavonic language [C14 from Med. L *Sclāvus* a captive Slav; see SLAVE]

slave (sleɪv) *n* **1** a person legally owned by another and having no freedom of action or right to property **2** a person who is forced to work for another against his or her will **3** a person under the domination of another person or some habit or influence **4** a drudge **5** a device that is controlled by or that duplicates the action of another similar device ▷ *vb* **slaves, slaving, slaved** **6** (*intr*; often foll by *away*) to work like a slave [C13 via OF from Med. L *Sclāvus* a Slav, one held in bondage (the Slavonic races were frequently conquered in the Middle Ages), from LGk *Sklabos* a Slav]

Ss

Slave Coast *n* the coast of W Africa between the Volta River and Mount Cameroon, chiefly along the Bight of Benin: the main source of African slaves (16th–19th centuries)

slave cylinder *n* a small cylinder containing a piston that operates the brake shoes or pads in hydraulic brakes or the working part in any other hydraulically operated system

slave-driver *n* **1** (esp formerly) a person forcing slaves to work **2** an employer who demands excessively hard work from his or her employees

slaveholder ('sleɪvˌhəʊldə) *n* a person who owns slaves > **'slaveˌholding** *n*

slaver[1] ('sleɪvə) *n* **1** an owner of or dealer in slaves **2** another name for **slave ship**

slaver[2] ('slævə) *vb (intr)* **1** to dribble saliva **2** (often foll by *over*) **2a** to fawn or drool (over someone) **2b** to show great desire (for) ▷ *n* **3** saliva dribbling from the mouth **4** *inf* drivel [C14 prob. from Low Du.] > **'slaverer** *n*

Slave River *n* a river in W Canada, in the Northwest Territories and NE Alberta, flowing from Lake Athabaska northwest to Great Slave Lake. Length: about 420 km (260 miles). Also called: **Great Slave River**

slavery ('sleɪvərɪ) *n* **1** the state or condition of being a slave **2** the subjection of a person to another person, esp in being forced into work **3** the condition of being subject to some influence or habit **4** work done in harsh conditions for low pay

slave ship *n* a ship used to transport slaves, esp formerly from Africa to the New World

Slave State *n US history* any of the 15 Southern states in which slavery was legal until the Civil War

slave trade *n* the business of trading in slaves, esp the transportation of Black Africans to America from the 16th to 19th centuries > **'slave-ˌtrader** *n* > **'slave-ˌtrading** *n*

▷ www.spartacus.schoolnet.co.uk/slavery.htm

▷ http://webworld.unesco.org/slave_quest/en

slavey ('sleɪvɪ) *n Brit inf* a female general servant

Slavey ('sleɪvɪ) *n* a member of a Dene Native Canadian people of northern Canada [from Athapascan]

Slavic ('slɑːvɪk) *n, adj* another word (esp US) for **Slavonic**

slavish ('sleɪvɪʃ) *adj* **1** of or befitting a slave **2** being or resembling a slave **3** unoriginal; imitative > **'slavishly** *adv*

Slavkov ('slafkɔf) *n* the Czech name for **Austerlitz**

Slavonia (slə'vəʊnɪə) *n* a region in Croatia, mainly between the Drava and Sava Rivers > **Sla'vonian** *adj, n*

Slavonic (slə'vɒnɪk) *or esp US* **Slavic** *n* **1** a branch of the Indo-European family of languages, usually divided into three subbranches: **South Slavonic** (including Bulgarian), **East Slavonic** (including Russian), and **West Slavonic** (including Polish and Czech) ▷ *adj* **2** of or relating to this group of languages **3** of or relating to the people who speak these languages

slaw (slɔː) *n chiefly US & Canad* short for **coleslaw** [C19 from Danish *sla*, short for *salade* SALAD]

slay (sleɪ) *vb* **slays, slaying, slew, slain** *(tr)* **1** *arch or literary* to kill, esp violently **2** *sl* to impress (someone of the opposite sex) [OE *slēan*] > **'slayer** *n*

SLCM *abbrev for* sea-launched cruise missile: a type of cruise missile that can be launched from either a submarine or a surface ship

sleaze (sliːz) *n inf* **1** sleaziness **2** dishonest, disreputable, or immoral behaviour, esp of public officials or employees: *political sleaze*

sleazy ('sliːzɪ) *adj* **sleazier, sleaziest 1** disreputable: *a sleazy nightclub* **2** flimsy, as cloth [C17 from ?] > **'sleazily** *adv* > **'sleaziness** *n*

sledge[1] (slɛdʒ) *or esp US & Canad* **sled** (slɛd) *n* **1** Also called: **sleigh** a vehicle mounted on runners, drawn by horses or dogs, for transporting people or goods, esp over snow **2** a light wooden frame used, esp by children, for sliding over snow ▷ *vb* **sledges, sledging, sledged 3** to convey, travel, or go by sledge [C17 from MDu. *sleedse*; C14 *sled*, from MLow G, from ON *slethi*] > **'sledger** *n*

sledge[2] (slɛdʒ) *n* short for **sledgehammer**

sledge[3] (slɛdʒ) *vb* **sledges, sledging, sledged** *(tr) inf* to bait (an opponent, esp a batsman in cricket) in order to upset his or her concentration [from ?]

sledgehammer ('slɛdʒˌhæmə) *n* **1** a large heavy hammer with a long handle used with both hands for heavy work such as breaking rocks, etc **2** *(modifier)* resembling the action of a sledgehammer in power, etc: *a sledgehammer blow* [C15 *sledge*, from OE *slecg* a large hammer]

sleek (sliːk) *adj* **1** smooth and shiny **2** polished in speech or behaviour **3** (of an animal or bird) having a shiny healthy coat or feathers **4** (of a person) having a prosperous appearance ▷ *vb (tr)* **5** to make smooth and glossy, as by grooming, etc **6** (usually foll by *over*) to gloss (over) [C16 var. of SLICK] > **'sleekly** *adv* > **'sleekness** *n* > **'sleeky** *adj*

sleep (sliːp) *n* **1** a periodic state of physiological rest during which consciousness is suspended **2** *bot* the nontechnical name for **nyctitropism 3** a period spent sleeping **4** a state of quiescence or dormancy **5** a poetic word for **death** ▷ *vb* **sleeps, sleeping, slept 6** *(intr)* to be in or as in the state of sleep **7** *(intr)* (of plants) to show nyctitropism **8** *(intr)* to be inactive or quiescent **9** *(tr)* to have sleeping accommodation for (a certain number): *the boat could sleep six* **10** *(tr; foll by away)* to pass (time) sleeping **11** *(intr) poetic* to be dead **12 sleep on it** to give (something) extended consideration, esp overnight ▷ See also **sleep around, sleep in,** etc [OE *slǣpan*]

▷ www.sleepfoundation.org

▷ www.stanford.edu/~dement

sleep around *vb (intr, adv) inf* to be sexually promiscuous

sleeper ('sliːpə) *n* **1** a person, animal, or thing that sleeps **2** a railway sleeping car or compartment **3** *Brit* one of the blocks supporting the rails on a railway track **4** a heavy timber beam, esp one that is laid horizontally on the ground **5** *chiefly Brit* a small plain gold circle worn in a pierced ear lobe to prevent the hole from closing up **6** *inf* a person or thing that achieves unexpected success after an initial period of obscurity **7** a spy planted in advance for future use

sleep in *vb (intr, adv)* **1** *Brit* to sleep longer than usual **2** to sleep at the place of one's employment

sleeping bag *n* a large well-padded bag designed for sleeping in, esp outdoors

sleeping car *n* a railway carriage fitted with compartments containing bunks for people to sleep in

sleeping partner *n* a partner in a business who does not play an active role. Also called: **silent partner**

sleeping pill *n* a pill or tablet containing a sedative drug, such as a barbiturate, used to induce sleep

sleeping policeman *n* a bump built across a road to deter motorists from speeding. Official name: **road hump**

sleeping sickness *n* **1** Also called: **African sleeping sickness** an African disease transmitted by the bite of the tsetse fly, characterized by fever and sluggishness **2** Also called: **sleepy sickness** an epidemic viral form of encephalitis characterized by extreme drowsiness. Technical name: **encephalitis lethargica**

sleepless ('sliːplɪs) *adj* **1** without sleep or rest: *a sleepless journey* **2** unable to sleep **3** always alert **4** *chiefly poetic* always active or moving > **'sleeplessly** *adv* > **'sleeplessness** *n*

sleep off *vb (tr, adv) inf* to lose by sleeping: *to sleep off a hangover*

sleep out *vb (intr, adv)* **1** (esp of a tramp) to sleep in the open air **2** to sleep away from the place of one's employment ▷ *n* **sleep-out 3** *Austral* an area of a veranda partitioned off so that it may be used as a bedroom **4** NZ a small building for sleeping that is separate from the rest of a house

sleepover ('sli:pˌəʊvə) *n inf* an instance of spending the night at someone else's home

sleepwalk ('sli:pˌwɔ:k) *vb (intr)* to walk while asleep > **'sleepˌwalker** *n* > **'sleepˌwalking** *n, adj*

sleep with *vb (intr, prep)* to have sexual intercourse and (usually) spend the night with. Also: **sleep together**

sleepy ('sli:pɪ) *adj* **sleepier, sleepiest 1** inclined to or needing sleep **2** characterized by or exhibiting drowsiness, etc **3** conducive to sleep **4** without activity or bustle: *a sleepy town* > **'sleepily** *adv* > **'sleepiness** *n*

sleet (sli:t) *n* **1** partly melted falling snow or hail or (esp US) partly frozen rain **2** *chiefly US* the thin coat of ice that forms when sleet or rain freezes on cold surfaces ▷ *vb* **3** *(intr)* to fall as sleet [C13 of Gmc origin] > **'sleety** *adj*

sleeve (sli:v) *n* **1** the part of a garment covering the arm **2** a tubular piece that is shrunk into a cylindrical bore to reduce its bore or to line it with a different material **3** a tube fitted externally over two cylindrical parts in order to join them **4** a flat cardboard container to protect a gramophone record. US name: **jacket 5** (**have a few tricks**) **up one's sleeve** (to have options, etc) secretly ready **6 roll up one's sleeves** to prepare oneself for work, a fight, etc ▷ *vb* **sleeves, sleeving, sleeved 7** *(tr)* to provide with a sleeve or sleeves [OE *slīf, slēf*] > **'sleeveless** *adj* > **'sleeveˌlike** *adj*

sleeve board *n* a small ironing board for pressing sleeves, fitted onto an ironing board or table

sleeving ('sli:vɪŋ) *n electronics, chiefly Brit* tubular flexible insulation into which bare wire can be inserted

sleigh (sleɪ) *n* **1** another name for **sledge**[1] (sense 1) ▷ *vb* **2** *(intr)* to travel by sleigh [C18 from Du. *slee*, var. of *slede* SLEDGE[1]]

sleight (slaɪt) *n arch* **1** skill; dexterity **2** a trick or stratagem **3** cunning [C14 from ON *slægth*, from *slǣgr* SLY]

sleight of hand *n* **1** manual dexterity used in performing conjuring tricks **2** the performance of such tricks

slender ('slɛndə) *adj* **1** of small width relative to length or height **2** (esp of a person's figure) slim and well-formed **3** small or inadequate in amount, size, etc: *slender resources* **4** (of hopes, etc) feeble **5** very small: *a slender margin* [C14 *slendre*, from ?] > **'slenderly** *adv* > **'slenderness** *n*

slenderize or **slenderise** ('slɛndəˌraɪz) *vb* **slenderizes, slenderizing, slenderized** or **slenderises, slenderising, slenderised** *chiefly US & Canad* to make or become slender

slept (slɛpt) *vb* the past tense and past participle of **sleep**

Slesvig ('sle:svi) *n* the Danish name for **Schleswig**

sleuth (slu:θ) *n* **1** an informal word for **detective 2** short for **sleuthhound** (sense 1) ▷ *vb* **3** *(tr)* to track or follow [C19 short for *sleuthhound*, from C12 *sleuth* trail, from ON *sloth*]

sleuthhound ('slu:θˌhaʊnd) *n* **1** a dog trained to track people, esp a bloodhound **2** an informal word for **detective**

S level *n Brit* a public examination in a subject taken for the General Certificate of Education: usually taken at the same time as A2 levels as an additional qualification

slew[1] (slu:) *vb* the past tense of **slay**

slew[2] *or esp US* **slue** (slu:) *vb* **1** to twist or be twisted sideways, esp awkwardly **2** *naut* to cause (a mast) to rotate in its step or (of a mast) to rotate in its step ▷ *n* **3** the act of slewing [C18 from ?]

slew[3] (slu:) *n* a variant spelling (esp US) of **slough**[1] (sense 2)

slew[4] or **slue** (slu:) *n inf, chiefly US & Canad* a great number [C20 from Irish Gaelic *sluagh*]

Slezsko ('slɛskɔ) *n* the Czech name for **Silesia**

slice (slaɪs) *n* **1** a thin flat piece cut from something having bulk: *a slice of pork* **2** a share or portion: *a slice of the company's revenue* **3** any of various utensils having a broad flat blade and resembling a spatula **4** (in golf, tennis, etc) **4a** the flight of a ball that travels obliquely **4b** the action of hitting such a shot **4c** the shot so hit ▷ *vb* **slices, slicing, sliced 5** to divide or cut (something) into parts or slices **6** (when *intr*, usually foll by *through*) to cut in a clean and effortless manner **7** (when *intr*, foll by *into* or *through*) to move or go (through something) like a knife **8** (usually foll by *off, from, away*, etc) to cut or be cut (from) a larger piece **9** *(tr)* to remove by use of a slicing implement **10** to hit (a ball) with a slice [C14 from OF *esclice* a piece split off, from *esclicier* to splinter] > **'sliceable** *adj* > **'slicer** *n*

slick (slɪk) *adj* **1** flattering and glib: *a slick salesman* **2** adroitly devised or executed: *a slick show* **3** *inf, chiefly US & Canad* shrewd; sly **4** *inf* superficially attractive: *a slick publication* **5** *chiefly US & Canad* slippery ▷ *n* **6** a slippery area, esp a patch of oil floating on water ▷ *vb (tr)* **7** *chiefly US & Canad* to make smooth or sleek [C14 prob. from ON] > **'slickly** *adv* > **'slickness** *n*

slicker ('slɪkə) *n* **1** *inf* a sly or untrustworthy person (esp in **city slicker**) **2** *US & Canad* a shiny raincoat, esp an oilskin

slide (slaɪd) *vb* **slides, sliding, slid** (slɪd); **slid** or **slidden** ('slɪdᵊn) **1** to move or cause to move smoothly along a surface in continual contact with it: *doors that slide open* **2** *(intr)* to lose grip or balance: *he slid on his back* **3** *(intr; usually foll by into, out of, away from*, etc) to pass or move unobtrusively: *she slid into the room* **4** *(intr;* usually foll by *into)* to go (into a specified condition) by degrees, etc: *he slid into loose living* **5** (foll by *in, into*, etc) to move (an object) unobtrusively or (of an object) to move in this way: *he slid the gun into his pocket* **6 let slide** to allow to deteriorate: *to let things slide* ▷ *n* **7** the act or an instance of sliding **8** a smooth surface, as of ice or mud, for sliding on **9** a construction incorporating an inclined smooth slope for sliding down in playgrounds, etc **10** a thin glass plate on which specimens are mounted for microscopical study **11** Also called: **diapositive, transparency** a positive photograph on a transparent base, mounted in a frame, that can be viewed by means of a slide projector **12** Also called: **hair slide** *chiefly Brit* an ornamental clip to hold hair in place **13** *machinery* a sliding part or member **14** *music* a portamento **15** *music* the sliding curved tube of a trombone that is moved in or out **16** *music* **16a** a tube placed over a finger held against the frets of a guitar to produce a portamento **16b** the style of guitar playing using a slide **17** *geol* **17a** the rapid downward movement of a large mass of earth, rocks, etc **17b** the mass of material involved in this descent. See also **landslide** [OE *slīdan*] > **'slidable** *adj* > **'slider** *n*

slide over *vb (intr, prep)* **1** to cross as if by sliding **2** to avoid dealing with (a matter) fully

slide rule *n* a mechanical calculating device consisting of two strips, one sliding along a central groove in the other, each strip graduated in two or more logarithmic scales of numbers, trigonometric functions, etc

sliding scale *n* a variable scale according to which specified wages, prices, etc, fluctuate in response to changes in some other factor

slier ('slaɪə) *adj* a comparative of **sly**

sliest ('slaɪɪst) *adj* a superlative of **sly**

slight (slaɪt) *adj* **1** small in quantity or extent **2** of small importance **3** slim and delicate **4** lacking in strength or substance ▷ *vb (tr)* **5** to show disregard for (someone); snub **6** to treat as unimportant or trifling **7** *US* to devote inadequate attention to (work, duties, etc) ▷ *n* **8** an act or omission indicating supercilious neglect [C13 from ON *slēttr* smooth] > **'slightingly** *adv* > **'slightness** *n*

slightly ('slaɪtlɪ) *adv* in small measure or degree

Sligo ('slaɪgəʊ) *n* **1** a county of NW Republic of Ireland, on the Atlantic: has a deeply indented low-lying coast; livestock and dairy farming. County town: Sligo. Pop:

Ss

55 821 (1996). Area: 1795 sq km (693 sq miles) **2** a port in NW Republic of Ireland, county town of Co Sligo on **Sligo Bay**. Pop: 17 300 (1991)

slily ('slaılı) *adv* a variant spelling of **slyly**

slim (slım) *adj* **slimmer, slimmest 1** small in width relative to height or length **2** poor; meagre: *slim chances of success* ▷ *vb* **3** to make or become slim, esp by diets and exercise **4** (*tr*) to reduce in size: *the workforce was slimmed* [c17 from Du.: crafty, from MDu. *slimp* slanting] > **'slimmer** *n* > **'slimming** *n* > **'slimness** *n*

Slim[1] (slım) *n* the E African name for **AIDS** [from its wasting effects]

Slim[2] (slım) *n* **William Joseph**, 1st Viscount. 1891–1970, British field marshal, who commanded (1943–45) the 14th Army in the reconquest of Burma (now called Myanmar) from the Japanese; governor general of Australia (1953–60)

slim down *vb* (*adv*) **1** to make or become slim, esp intentionally **2** to make (an organization) more efficient or (of an organization) to become more efficient, esp by cutting staff ▷ *n* **slimdown 3** an instance of an organization slimming down

slime (slaım) *n* **1** soft thin runny mud or filth **2** any moist viscous fluid, esp when noxious or unpleasant **3** a mucous substance produced by various organisms, such as fish, slugs, and fungi ▷ *vb* **slimes, sliming, slimed** (*tr*) **4** to cover with slime [OE *slīm*]

slimline ('slım,laın) *adj* slim or conducive to slimness

slimy ('slaımı) *adj* **slimier, slimiest 1** characterized by, covered with, secreting, or resembling slime **2** offensive or repulsive **3** *chiefly Brit* characterized by servility

sling[1] (slıŋ) *n* **1** a simple weapon consisting of a loop of leather, etc, in which a stone is whirled and then let fly **2** a rope or strap by which something may be secured or lifted **3** *med* a wide piece of cloth suspended from the neck for supporting an injured hand or arm **4** a loop or band attached to an object for carrying **5** the act of slinging ▷ *vb* **slings, slinging, slung 6** (*tr*) to hurl with or as if with a sling **7** to attach a sling or slings to (a load, etc) **8** (*tr*) to carry or hang loosely from or as if from a sling: *to sling washing from the line* **9** (*tr*) *inf* to throw [c13 ?from ON] > **'slinger** *n*

sling[2] (slıŋ) *n* a mixed drink with a spirit base, usually sweetened [c19 from ?]

slingback ('slıŋ,bæk) *n* a shoe with a strap instead of a full covering for the heel

sling off *vb* (*intr, adv; often foll by at*) *Austral & NZ inf* to mock; deride; jeer (at)

slingshot ('slıŋ,ʃɒt) *n* **1** the US and Canad name for **catapult** (sense 1) **2** another name for **sling**[1] (sense 1)

slink (slıŋk) *vb* **slinks, slinking, slunk 1** (*intr*) to move or act in a furtive manner from or as if from fear, guilt, etc **2** (*intr*) to move in a sinuous alluring manner **3** (*tr*) (of animals, esp cows) to give birth to prematurely ▷ *n* **4** an animal, esp a calf, born prematurely [OE *slincan*]

slinky ('slıŋkı) *adj* **slinkier, slinkiest** *inf* **1** moving in a sinuously graceful or provocative way **2** (of clothes) figure-hugging > **'slinkily** *adv* > **'slinkiness** *n*

slip[1] (slıp) *vb* **slips, slipping, slipped 1** to move or cause to move smoothly and easily **2** (*tr*) to place, insert, or convey quickly or stealthily **3** (*tr*) to put on or take off easily or quickly: *to slip on a sweater* **4** (*intr*) to lose balance and slide unexpectedly: *he slipped on the ice* **5** to let loose or be let loose **6** to be released from (something) **7** (*tr*) to let go (mooring or anchor lines) over the side **8** (when *intr*, often foll by *from* or *out of*) to pass out of (the mind or memory) **9** (*intr*) to move or pass swiftly or unperceived: *to slip quietly out of the room* **10** (*intr*; sometimes foll by *up*) to make a mistake **11** Also: **sideslip** to cause (an aircraft) to slide sideways or (of an aircraft) to slide sideways **12** (*intr*) to decline in health, mental ability, etc **13** (*intr*) (of an intervertebral disc) to become displaced from the normal position **14** (*tr*) to dislocate (a bone) **15** (of animals) to give birth to (offspring) prematurely **16** (*tr*) to pass (a stitch) from one needle to another without knitting it **17a** (*tr*) to operate (the clutch of a motor vehicle) so that it partially disengages **17b** (*intr*) (of the clutch of a motor vehicle) to fail to engage, esp as a result of wear **18 let slip 18a** to allow to escape **18b** to say unintentionally ▷ *n* **19** the act or an instance of slipping **20** a mistake or oversight: *a slip of the pen* **21** a moral lapse or failing **22** a woman's sleeveless undergarment, worn as a lining for a dress **23** a pillowcase **24** See **slipway 25** *cricket* **25a** the position of the fielder who stands a little way behind and to the offside of the wicketkeeper **25b** the fielder himself or herself **26** the relative movement of rocks along a fault plane **27** *metallurgy, crystallog* the deformation of a metallic crystal caused when one part glides over another part along a plane **28** a landslide **29** the deviation of a propeller from its helical path through a fluid **30** another name for **sideslip** (sense 1) **31 give someone the slip** to elude or escape from someone ▷ See also **slip up** [c13 from MLow G or Du. *slippen*] > **'slipless** *adj*

slip[2] (slıp) *n* **1** a narrow piece; strip **2** a small piece of paper: *a receipt slip* **3** a part of a plant that, when detached from the parent, will grow into a new plant; cutting **4** a young slender person: *a slip of a child* **5** *printing* **5a** a long galley **5b** a galley proof ▷ *vb* **slips, slipping, slipped 6** (*tr*) to detach (portions of stem, etc) from (a plant) for propagation [c15 prob. from MLow G, MDu. *slippe* to cut, strip]

slip[3] (slıp) *n* clay mixed with water to a creamy consistency, used for decorating or patching a ceramic piece [OE *slyppe* slime]

slipcase ('slıp,keıs) *n* a protective case for a book or set of books that is open at one end so that only the spines of the books are visible

slipcover ('slıp,kʌvə) *n* *US & Canad* **1** a loose cover **2** a book jacket; dust cover

slipe (slaıp) *n* *NZ* **a** wool removed from the pelt of a slaughtered sheep by immersion in a chemical bath **b** (*as modifier*): *slipe wool* [c14 in England: from *slype* to strip, skin]

slipknot ('slıp,nɒt) *n* **1** Also called: **running knot** a nooselike knot tied so that it will slip along the rope round which it is made **2** a knot that can be easily untied by pulling one free end

slip-on *adj* **1** (of a garment or shoe) made so as to be easily and quickly put on or taken off ▷ *n* **2** a slip-on garment or shoe

slipover ('slıp,əʊvə) *adj* **1** of or denoting a garment that can be put on easily over the head ▷ *n* **2** such a garment, esp a sleeveless pullover

slippage ('slıpıdʒ) *n* **1** the act or an instance of slipping **2** the amount of slipping or the extent to which slipping occurs **3a** an instance of not reaching a target, etc **3b** the extent of this

slipped disc *n* *pathol* a herniated intervertebral disc, often resulting in pain because of pressure on the spinal nerves

slipper ('slıpə) *n* **1** a light shoe of some soft material, for wearing around the house **2** a woman's evening shoe ▷ *vb* **3** (*tr*) *inf* to hit or beat with a slipper > **'slippered** *adj*

slipper bath *n* a bath in the shape of a slipper, with a covered end

slipperwort ('slıpə,wɜːt) *n* another name for **calceolaria**

slippery ('slıpərı, -prı) *adj* **1** causing or tending to cause objects to slip: *a slippery road* **2** liable to slip from the grasp, etc **3** not to be relied upon: *a slippery character* **4** (esp of a situation) unstable [c16 prob. coined by Coverdale to translate G *schlipfferig* in Luther's Bible (Psalm 35:6)] > **'slipperiness** *n*

slippery elm *n* **1** a North American tree, having notched winged fruits and a mucilaginous inner bark **2** the bark of this tree, used medicinally as a demulcent ▷ Also called: **red elm**

slippy ('slɪpɪ) *adj* **slippier, slippiest** 1 *inf or dialect* another word for **slippery** (senses 1, 2) 2 *Brit inf* alert; quick > '**slippiness** *n*

slip rail *n Austral & NZ* a rail in a fence that can be slipped out of place to make an opening

slip road *n Brit* a short road connecting a motorway to another road

slipshod ('slɪp,ʃɒd) *adj* 1 (of an action) negligent; careless 2 (of a person's appearance) slovenly; down-at-heel [C16 from SLIP[1] + SHOD]

slipstream ('slɪp,striːm) *n* Also called: **airstream a** the stream of air forced backwards by an aircraft propeller **b** a stream of air behind any moving object

slip up *inf* ▷ *vb (intr, adv)* 1 to make a blunder or mistake ▷ *n* **slip-up** 2 a mistake or mishap

slipware ('slɪp,wɛə) *n* pottery that has been decorated with slip and glazed

slipway ('slɪp,weɪ) *n* 1 the sloping area in a shipyard, containing the ways 2 the ways on which a vessel is launched

slit (slɪt) *vb* **slits, slitting, slit** *(tr)* 1 to make a straight long incision in 2 to cut into strips lengthwise ▷ *n* 3 a long narrow cut 4 a long narrow opening [OE *slītan* to slice] > '**slitter** *n*

slither ('slɪðə) *vb* 1 to move or slide or cause to move or slide unsteadily, as on a slippery surface 2 *(intr)* to travel with a sliding motion ▷ *n* 3 a slithering motion [OE *slidrian*, from *slīdan* to slide] > '**slithery** *adj*

slit trench *n mil* a narrow trench dug for the protection of a small number of people

sliver ('slɪvə) *n* 1 a thin piece that is cut or broken off lengthwise 2 a loose fibre obtained by carding ▷ *vb* 3 to divide or be divided into splinters 4 *(tr)* to form (wool, etc) into slivers [C14 from *sliven* to split]

Sloan (sləʊn) *n* **John** 1871–1951, US painter and etcher, a leading member of the group of realistic painters known as the Ash Can School. His pictures of city scenes include *McSorley's Bar* (1912) and *Backyards, Greenwich Village* (1914)

Sloane Ranger (sləʊn) *n* (in Britain) *inf* a young upper-class person having a home in London and in the country, characterized as wearing expensive informal clothes. Also called: **Sloane** [C20 pun on *Sloane* Square, London, and *Lone Ranger*, television cowboy character]

slob (slɒb) *n* 1 *inf* a slovenly, unattractive, and lazy person 2 *Irish* mire [C19 from Irish Gaelic *slab* mud] > '**slobbish** *adj*

slobber ('slɒbə) *or* **slabber** *vb* 1 to dribble (saliva, food, etc) from the mouth 2 *(intr)* to speak or write mawkishly 3 *(tr)* to smear with matter dribbling from the mouth ▷ *n* 4 liquid or saliva spilt from the mouth 5 maudlin language or behaviour [C15 from MLow G, MDu. *slubberen*] > '**slobberer** *or* '**slabberer** *n* > '**slobbery** *or* '**slabbery** *adj*

sloe (sləʊ) *n* 1 the small sour blue-black fruit of the blackthorn 2 another name for **blackthorn** [OE *slāh*]

sloe-eyed *adj* having dark slanted or almond-shaped eyes

sloe gin *n* gin flavoured with sloe juice

slog (slɒg) *vb* **slogs, slogging, slogged** 1 to hit with heavy blows, as in boxing 2 *(intr)* to work hard; toil 3 *(intr; foll by down, up, along, etc)* to move with difficulty 4 *cricket* to take large swipes at the ball ▷ *n* 5 a tiring walk 6 long exhausting work 7 a heavy blow or swipe [C19 from ?] > '**slogger** *n*

slogan ('sləʊgən) *n* 1 a distinctive or topical phrase used in politics, advertising, etc 2 *Scot history* a Highland battle cry [C16 from Gaelic *sluagh-ghairm* war cry]

slommock ('slɒmək) *vb (intr) Midland English dialect* to walk assertively with a hip-rolling gait

sloop (sluːp) *n* a single-masted sailing vessel, rigged fore-and-aft [C17 from Du. *sloep*]

sloot (sluːt) *n S African* a ditch for irrigation or drainage [from Afrik., from Du. *sluit, sluis* SLUICE]

slop[1] (slɒp) *vb* **slops, slopping, slopped** 1 (when *intr*, often foll by *about*) to cause (liquid) to splash or spill or (of liquid) to splash or spill 2 *(intr; foll by along, through*, etc) to tramp (through) mud or slush 3 *(tr)* to feed slop or swill to: *to slop the pigs* 4 *(tr)* to ladle or serve, esp clumsily 5 *(intr; foll by over) inf, chiefly US & Canad* to be unpleasantly effusive ▷ *n* 6 a puddle of spilt liquid 7 *(pl)* wet feed, esp for pigs, made from kitchen waste, etc 8 *(pl)* waste food or liquid refuse 9 *(often pl) inf* liquid or semiliquid food of low quality 10 soft mud, snow, etc [C14 prob. from OE *-sloppe* in *cūsloppe* COWSLIP]

slop[2] (slɒp) *n* 1 *(pl)* sailors' clothing and bedding issued from a ship's stores 2 any loose article of clothing, esp a smock 3 *(pl)* shoddy manufactured clothing [OE *oferslop* surplice]

slop basin *n* a bowl or basin into which the dregs from teacups are emptied at the table

slope (sləʊp) *vb* **slopes, sloping, sloped** 1 to lie or cause to lie at a slanting or oblique angle 2 *(intr)* (esp of natural features) to follow an inclined course: *many paths sloped down the hillside* 3 *(intr; foll by off, away*, etc) to go furtively 4 *(tr) mil* (formerly) to hold (a rifle) in the slope position ▷ *n* 5 an inclined portion of ground 6 *(pl)* hills or foothills 7 any inclined surface or line 8 the degree or amount of such inclination 9 *maths* (of a line) the tangent of the angle between the line and another line parallel to the *x*-axis 10 (formerly) the position adopted for military drill when the rifle is rested on the shoulder [C15 short for *aslope*, ?from the p.p. of OE *āslūpan* to slip away] > '**sloper** *n* > '**sloping** *adj*

slop out *vb (intr, adv)* (of prisoners) to empty chamber pots and collect water for washing

sloppy ('slɒpɪ) *adj* **sloppier, sloppiest** 1 (esp of the ground, etc) wet; slushy 2 *inf* careless; untidy 3 *inf* mawkishly sentimental 4 (of food or drink) watery and unappetizing 5 splashed with slops 6 (of clothes) loose; baggy > '**sloppily** *adv* > '**sloppiness** *n*

Ss

slosh (slɒʃ) *n* 1 watery mud, snow, etc 2 *Brit sl* a heavy blow 3 the sound of splashing liquid ▷ *vb* 4 *(tr; foll by around, on, in*, etc) *inf* to throw or pour (liquid) 5 (when *intr*, often foll by *about* or *around*) *Inf* **5a** to shake or stir (something) in a liquid **5b** (of a person) to splash (around) in water, etc 6 *(tr) Brit sl* to deal a heavy blow to 7 (usually foll by *about* or *around*) *inf* to shake (a container of liquid) or (of liquid within a container) to be shaken [C19 var. of SLUSH, infl. by SLOP[1]] > '**sloshy** *adj*

sloshed (slɒʃt) *adj chiefly Brit sl* drunk

slot[1] (slɒt) *n* 1 an elongated aperture or groove, such as one in a vending machine for inserting a coin 2 *inf* a place in a series or scheme ▷ *vb* **slots, slotting, slotted** 3 *(tr)* to furnish with a slot or slots 4 (usually foll by *in* or *into*) to fit or adjust in a slot 5 *inf* to situate or be situated in a series [C13 from OF *esclot* the depression of the breastbone, from ?] > '**slotter** *n*

slot[2] (slɒt) *n* the trail of an animal, esp a deer [C16 from OF *esclot* horse's hoofprint, prob. of Scand. origin]

sloth (sləʊθ) *n* 1 any of a family of shaggy-coated arboreal edentate mammals, such as the three-toed sloth or ai or the two-toed sloth or unau, of Central and South America. They are slow-moving, hanging upside down by their long arms and feeding on vegetation 2 reluctance to exert oneself [OE *slǣwth*, from *slǣw*, var. of *slāw* slow]

sloth bear *n* a bear of forests of S India and Sri Lanka, having an elongated snout specialized for feeding on termites

slothful ('sləʊθfʊl) *adj* lazy; indolent > '**slothfully** *adv* > '**slothfulness** *n*

slot machine *n* a machine, esp one for gambling, activated by placing a coin in a slot

slouch (slaʊtʃ) *vb* **1** (*intr*) to sit or stand with a drooping bearing **2** (*intr*) to walk or move with an awkward slovenly gait **3** (*tr*) to cause (the shoulders) to droop ▷ *n* **4** a drooping carriage **5** (*usually used in negative constructions*) *inf* an incompetent or slovenly person: *he's no slouch at football* [C16 from ?] > **'slouching** *adj*

slouch hat *n* any soft hat with a brim that can be pulled down over the ears, esp an Australian army hat with the left side of the brim turned up

slough[1] (slaʊ) *n* **1** a hollow filled with mud; bog **2** (slu:) Also: **slew** (esp US), **slue** *North American* a large hole where water collects or a marshy inlet **3** despair or degradation [OE *slōh*] > **'sloughy** *adj*

slough[2] (slʌf) *n* **1** any outer covering that is shed, such as the dead outer layer of the skin of a snake, the cellular debris in a wound, etc ▷ *vb* **2** (often foll by *off*) to shed (a skin, etc) or (of a skin, etc) to be shed [C13 of Gmc origin] > **'sloughy** *adj*

Slough (slaʊ) *n* **1** an industrial town in SE central England, in Slough unitary authority, Berkshire; food products, high-tech industries. Pop: 118 008 (1998 est) **2** a unitary authority in SE central England, in Berkshire. Pop: 119 070 (2001). Area: 28 sq km (11 sq miles)

slough off (slʌf) *vb* (*tr, adv*) to cast off (cares, etc)

Slovak ('sləʊvæk) *adj* **1** of or characteristic of Slovakia, its people, or their language ▷ *n* **2** the official language of Slovakia. Slovak is closely related to Czech; they are mutually intelligible **3** a native or inhabitant of Slovakia

Slovakia (sləʊ'vækɪə) *n* a country in central Europe: part of Hungary from the 11th century until 1918, when it united with Bohemia and Moravia to form Czechoslovakia; it became independent in 1993 and joined the EU in 2004. Official language: Slovak. Religion: Roman Catholic majority. Currency: koruna. Capital: Bratislava. Pop: 5 410 000 (2001 est). Area: 49 036 sq km (18 940 sq miles) > **Slo'vakian** *adj, n*
▷ www.sacr.sk
▷ www.slovakia.org
▷ slovakia.eunet.sk

sloven ('slʌvᵊn) *n* a person who is habitually negligent in appearance, hygiene, or work [C15 prob. rel. to Flemish *sloef* dirty, Du. *slof* negligent]

Slovene (sləʊ'vi:n) *adj* **1** Also **Slovenian** of or characteristic of Slovenia, its people, or their language ▷ *n* **2** Also **Slovenian** the official language of Slovenia **3** a native or inhabitant of Slovenia

Slovenia (sləʊ'vi:nɪə) *n* a republic in S central Europe: settled by the Slovenes in the 6th century; joined Yugoslavia in 1918 and became an autonomous republic in 1946; became fully independent in 1992 and joined the EU in 2004; rises over 2800 m (9000 ft) in the Julian Alps. Official language: Slovene. Religion: Roman Catholic majority. Currency: tolar. Capital: Ljubljana. Pop: 1 991 000 (2001 est). Area: 20 251 sq km (7819 sq miles)
▷ www.sigov.si
▷ www.slovenia-tourism.si
▷ www.tourist-board.si
▷ www.matkurja.com/eng/country-info

slovenly ('slʌvənlɪ) *adj* **1** frequently or habitually unclean or untidy **2** negligent and careless: *slovenly manners* ▷ *adv* **3** in a negligent or slovenly manner > **'slovenliness** *n*

slow (sləʊ) *adj* **1** performed or occurring during a comparatively long interval of time **2** lasting a comparatively long time: *a slow journey* **3** characterized by lack of speed: *a slow walker* **4** (*prenominal*) adapted to or productive of slow movement: *the slow lane of a motorway* **5** (of a clock, etc) indicating a time earlier than the correct time **6** not readily responsive to stimulation: *a slow mind* **7** dull or uninteresting: *the play was very slow* **8** not easily aroused: *a slow temperament* **9** lacking promptness or immediacy: *a slow answer* **10** unwilling to perform an action or enter into a state: *slow to anger* **11** behind the times **12** (of trade, etc) unproductive; slack **13** (of a fire) burning weakly **14** (of an oven) cool **15** *photog* requiring a relatively long time of exposure to produce a given density: *a slow lens* **16** *sport* (of a court, track, etc) tending to reduce the speed of the ball or the competitors **17** *cricket* (of a bowler, etc) delivering the ball slowly, usually with spin ▷ *adv* **18** in a manner characterized by lack of speed; slowly ▷ *vb* **19** (often foll by *up, down*, etc) to decrease or cause to decrease in speed, efficiency, etc [OE *slāw* sluggish] > **'slowly** *adv* > **'slowness** *n*

slowcoach ('sləʊ,kəʊtʃ) *n Brit inf* a person who moves or works slowly. US and Canad equivalent: **slowpoke**

slow handclap *n Brit* slow rhythmic clapping, esp used by an audience to indicate dissatisfaction or impatience

slow march *n mil* a march in **slow time**, usually 65 or 75 paces to the minute

slow match *or* **fuse** *n* a match or fuse that burns slowly without flame

slow-mo *or* **slo-mo** ('sləʊ,məʊ) *n, adj inf* short for **slow motion** *or* **slow-motion**

slow motion *n* **1** *films, television, etc* action that is made to appear slower than normal by passing the film through the camera at a faster rate or by replaying a video recording more slowly ▷ *adj* **slow-motion** **2** of or relating to such action **3** moving or functioning at considerably less than usual speed

slow virus *n* a type of virus-like disease-causing agents known as prions that are present in the body for a long time before they become active or infectious

slowworm ('sləʊ,wɜ:m) *n* a Eurasian legless lizard with a brownish-grey snakelike body. Also called: **blindworm**

SLR *abbrev for* single-lens reflex: see **reflex camera**

SLSC *Austral abbrev for* Surf Life Saving Club

slub (slʌb) *n* **1** a lump in yarn or fabric, often made intentionally to give a knobbly effect **2** a loosely twisted roll of fibre prepared for spinning ▷ *vb* **slubs, slubbing, slubbed** **3** (*tr*) to draw out and twist (a sliver of fibre) ▷ *adj* **4** (of material) having an irregular appearance [C18 from ?]

sludge (slʌdʒ) *n* **1** soft mud, snow, etc **2** any deposit or sediment **3** a surface layer of ice that is not frozen solid but has a slushy appearance **4** (in sewage disposal) the solid constituents of sewage that are removed for purification [C17 prob. rel. to SLUSH] > **'sludgy** *adj*

slue[1] (slu:) *n, vb* **slues, sluing, slued** a variant spelling (esp US) of **slew**[2]

slue[2] (slu:) *n* a variant spelling of **slough**[1] (sense 2)

slug[1] (slʌg) *n* **1** any of various terrestrial gastropod molluscs in which the body is elongated and the shell is absent or very much reduced **2** any of various other invertebrates having a soft slimy body, esp the larvae of certain sawflies [C15 (in the sense: a slow person or animal): prob. from ON]

slug[2] (slʌg) *n* **1** an fps unit of mass; the mass that will acquire an acceleration of 1 foot per second per second when acted upon by a force of 1 pound **2** *metallurgy* a metal blank from which small forgings are worked **3** a bullet **4** *chiefly US & Canad* a metal token for use in slot machines, etc **5** *printing* **5a** a thick strip of type metal that is used for spacing **5b** a metal strip containing a line of characters as produced by a Linotype machine **6** a draught of a drink, esp an alcoholic one [C17 (bullet), C19 (printing): ?from SLUG[1], with allusion to the shape of the animal]

slug[3] (slʌg) *vb* **slugs, slugging, slugged** **1** *chiefly US & Canad* to hit very hard and solidly **2** (*tr*) *Austral & NZ inf* to charge (someone) an exorbitant price ▷ *n* **3** *US & Canad* a heavy blow **4** *Austral & NZ inf* an exorbitant price [C19 ?from SLUG[2] (bullet)]

sluggard ('slʌgəd) *n* **1** a person who is habitually indolent ▷ *adj* **2** lazy [c14 *slogarde*] > '**sluggardly** *adj*
sluggish ('slʌgɪʃ) *adj* **1** lacking energy; inactive **2** functioning at below normal rate or level **3** exhibiting poor response to stimulation > '**sluggishly** *adv* > '**sluggishness** *n*
sluice (slu:s) *n* **1** Also called: **sluiceway** a channel that carries a rapid current of water, esp one that has a sluicegate to control the flow **2** the body of water controlled by a sluicegate **3** See **sluicegate** **4** *mining* an inclined trough for washing ore **5** an artificial channel through which logs can be floated ▷ *vb* **sluices, sluicing, sluiced** **6** (*tr*) to draw out or drain (water, etc) from (a pond, etc) by means of a sluice **7** (*tr*) to wash or irrigate with a stream of water **8** (*tr*) *mining* to wash in a sluice **9** (*tr*) to send (logs, etc) down a sluice **10** (*intr*; often foll by *away* or *out*) (of water, etc) to run or flow from or as if from a sluice **11** (*tr*) to provide with a sluice [c14 from OF *escluse*, from LL *exclūsa aqua* water shut out, from L *exclūdere* to shut out] > '**sluice,like** *adj*
sluicegate ('slu:s,geɪt) *n* a valve or gate fitted to a sluice to control the rate of flow of water. See also **floodgate** (sense 1)
slum (slʌm) *n* **1** a squalid overcrowded house, etc **2** (*often pl*) a squalid section of a city, characterized by inferior living conditions **3** (*modifier*) of or characteristic of slums: *slum conditions* ▷ *vb* **slums, slumming, slummed** (*intr*) **4** to visit slums, esp for curiosity **5** Also: **slum it** to suffer conditions below those to which one is accustomed [c19 orig. sl, from ?] > '**slummy** *adj*
slumber ('slʌmbə) *vb* **1** (*intr*) to sleep, esp peacefully **2** (*intr*) to be quiescent or dormant **3** (*tr*; foll by *away*) to spend (time) sleeping ▷ *n* **4** (*sometimes pl*) sleep **5** a dormant or quiescent state [OE *slūma* sleep (n)] > '**slumberer** *n* > '**slumbering** *adj*
slumberous ('slʌmbərəs) *or* **slumbrous** *adj chiefly poetic* **1** sleepy; drowsy **2** inducing sleep > '**slumberously** *adv* > '**slumberousness** *n*
slump (slʌmp) *vb* (*intr*) **1** to sink or fall heavily and suddenly **2** to relax ungracefully **3** (of business activity, etc) to decline suddenly **4** (of health, interest, etc) to deteriorate or decline suddenly ▷ *n* **5** a sudden or marked decline or failure, as in progress or achievement **6** a decline in commercial activity, prices, etc; depression **7** the act of slumping [c17 prob. of Scand. origin]
slung (slʌŋ) *vb* the past tense and past participle of **sling**[1]
slunk (slʌŋk) *vb* the past tense and past participle of **slink**
slur (slɜ:) *vb* **slurs, slurring, slurred** (*mainly tr*) **1** (often foll by *over*) to treat superficially, hastily, or without due deliberation **2** (*also intr*) to pronounce or utter (words, etc) indistinctly **3** to speak disparagingly of **4** *music* to execute (a melodic interval of two or more notes) smoothly, as in legato performance ▷ *n* **5** an indistinct sound or utterance **6** a slighting remark **7** a stain or disgrace, as upon one's reputation **8** *music* **8a** a performance or execution of a melodic interval of two or more notes in a part **8b** the curved line (⁀ or ‿) indicating this [c15 prob. from MLow G]
slurp (slɜ:p) *inf* ▷ *vb* **1** to eat or drink (something) noisily ▷ *n* **2** a sound produced in this way [c17 from MDu. *slorpen* to sip]
slurry ('slʌrɪ) *n, pl* **slurries** a suspension of solid particles in a liquid, as in a mixture of cement, coal dust, manure, meat, etc with water [c15 *slory*]
slush (slʌʃ) *n* **1** any watery muddy substance, esp melting snow **2** *inf* sloppily sentimental language ▷ *vb* **3** (*intr*; often foll by *along*) to make one's way through or as if through slush [c17 rel. to Danish *slus* sleet, Norwegian *slusk* slops] > '**slushy** *adj* > '**slushiness** *n*
slush fund *n* a fund for financing political or commercial corruption
slushy ('slʌʃɪ) *adj* **slushier, slushiest** of, resembling, or consisting of slush > '**slushiness** *n*
slut (slʌt) *n* **1** a dirty slatternly woman **2** an immoral woman [c14 from ?] > '**sluttish** *adj* > '**sluttishness** *n*
Sluter (*Dutch* 'sly:tər) *n* **Claus** (klaʊs) ?1345–1406, Dutch sculptor, working in Burgundy, whose realism influenced many sculptors and painters in 15th-century Europe. He is best known for the portal sculptures and the *Well of Moses* in the Carthusian monastery at Champnol
sly (slaɪ) *adj* **slyer, slyest** *or* **slier, sliest** **1** crafty; artful: *a sly dodge* **2** insidious; furtive: *a sly manner* **3** roguish: *sly humour* ▷ *n* **4** **on the sly** in a secretive manner [c12 from ON *slǣgr* clever, lit.: able to strike, from *slā* to slay] > '**slyly** *or* '**slily** *adv* > '**slyness** *n*
slype (slaɪp) *n* a covered passage in a church that connects the transept to the chapterhouse [c19 prob. from MFlemish *slijpen* to slip]
Sm *the chemical symbol for* samarium
SM *abbrev for* **1** sergeant major **2** sadomasochism
smack[1] (smæk) *n* **1** a smell or flavour that is distinctive though faint **2** a distinctive trace: *the smack of corruption* **3** a small quantity, esp a taste **4** a slang word for **heroin** ▷ *vb* (*intr*; foll by *of*) **5** to have the characteristic smell or flavour (of something): *to smack of the sea* **6** to have an element suggestive (of something): *his speeches smacked of bigotry* [OE *smæc*]
smack[2] (smæk) *vb* **1** (*tr*) to strike or slap smartly, with or as if with the open hand **2** to strike or send forcibly or loudly or to be struck or sent forcibly or loudly **3** to open and close (the lips) loudly, esp to show pleasure ▷ *n* **4** a sharp resounding slap or blow with something flat, or the sound of such a blow **5** a loud kiss **6** a sharp sound made by the lips, as in enjoyment **7** **have a smack at** *inf, chiefly Brit* to attempt **8** **smack in the eye** *inf, chiefly Brit* a snub or setback ▷ *adv inf* **9** directly; squarely **10** sharply and unexpectedly [c16 from MLow G or MDu. *smacken*, prob. imit.]
smack[3] (smæk) *n* a sailing vessel, usually sloop-rigged, used in coasting and fishing along the British coast [c17 from Low G *smack* or Du. *smak*, from ?]
smacker ('smækə) *n sl* **1** a loud kiss; smack **2** a pound note or dollar bill
smackhead ('smæk,hɛd) *n Brit sl* a person who is addicted to heroin
small (smɔ:l) *adj* **1** limited in size, number, importance, etc **2** of little importance or on a minor scale: *a small business* **3** lacking in moral or mental breadth or depth: *a small mind* **4** modest or humble: *small beginnings* **5** of low or inferior status, esp socially **6** **feel small** to be humiliated **7** (of a child or animal) young; not mature **8** unimportant; trivial: *a small matter* **9** of or designating the ordinary modern minuscule letter used in printing and cursive writing **10** lacking great strength or force: *a small effort* **11** in fine particles: *small gravel* ▷ *adv* **12** into small pieces: *cut it small* **13** in a small or soft manner ▷ *n* **14** (often preceded by *the*) an object, person, or group considered to be small: *the small or the large?* **15** a small slender part, esp of the back **16** (*pl*) *inf, chiefly Brit* items of personal laundry, such as underwear [OE *smæl*] > '**smallish** *adj* > '**smallness** *n*
small arms *pl n* portable firearms of relatively small calibre
small beer *n inf, chiefly Brit* people or things of no importance
small change *n* **1** coins, esp those of low value **2** a person or thing that is not outstanding or important
small circle *n* a circular section of a sphere that does not contain the centre of the sphere
small claims court *n Brit & Canad* a local court with jurisdiction to try civil actions involving small claims
small fry *pl n* **1** people or things regarded as unimportant **2** young children **3** young or small fishes

Ss

small goods *pl n Austral & NZ* meats bought from a delicatessen, such as sausages
smallholding ('smɔːlˌhəʊldɪŋ) *n* a holding of agricultural land smaller than a small farm > **'smallˌholder** *n*
small hours *pl n* **the** the early hours of the morning, after midnight and before dawn
small intestine *n* the longest part of the alimentary canal, in which digestion is completed ▷ Cf **large intestine**
small-minded *adj* narrow-minded; intolerant > **ˌsmall-'mindedly** *adv* > **ˌsmall-'mindedness** *n*
smallpox ('smɔːlˌpɒks) *n* a highly contagious viral disease characterized by high fever and a rash changing to pustules, which dry up and form scabs that are cast off, leaving pitted depressions. Technical name: **variola**
small print *n* matter in a contract, etc, printed in small type, esp when considered to be a trap for the unwary
small-scale *adj* **1** of limited size or scope **2** (of a map, model, etc) giving a relatively small representation of something
small screen *n* an informal name for **television**
small slam *n bridge* another name for **little slam**
small talk *n* light conversation for social occasions
small-time *adj inf* insignificant; minor: *a small-time criminal* > **'small-'timer** *n*
smalt (smɔːlt) *n* **1** a type of silica glass coloured deep blue with cobalt oxide **2** a pigment made by crushing this glass, used in colouring enamels [C16 via F from It. *smalto* coloured glass, of Gmc origin]
smarm (smɑːm) *vb Brit inf* **1** (*tr; often foll by down*) to flatten (the hair, etc) with grease **2** (*when intr, foll by up to*) to ingratiate oneself (with) [C19 from ?]
smarmy ('smɑːmɪ) *adj* **smarmier, smarmiest** *Brit inf* obsequiously flattering or unpleasantly suave > **'smarmily** *adv* > **'smarminess** *n*
smart (smɑːt) *adj* **1** astute, as in business **2** quick, witty, and often impertinent in speech: *a smart talker* **3** fashionable; chic: *a smart hotel* **4** well-kept; neat **5** causing a sharp stinging pain **6** vigorous or brisk **7** (of systems) operating as if by human intelligence by using automatic computer control **8** (of a weapon, etc) containing a device which enables it to be guided to its target: *smart bombs* ▷ *vb* (*mainly intr*) **9** to feel, cause, or be the source of a sharp stinging physical pain or keen mental distress: *he smarted under their abuse* **10** (often foll by *for*) to suffer a harsh penalty ▷ *n* **11** a stinging pain or feeling ▷ *adv* **12** in a smart manner ▷ See also **smarts** [OE *smeortan*] > **'smartly** *adv* > **'smartness** *n*
Smart (smɑːt) *n* **Christopher** 1722–71, British poet, author of *A Song to David* (1763) and *Jubilate Agno* (written 1758–63, published 1939). He was confined (1756–63) for religious mania and died in a debtors' prison
smart aleck ('ælɪk) *n inf* **a** an irritatingly oversmart person **b** (*as modifier*): *a smart-aleck remark* [C19 from *Aleck, Alec*, short for *Alexander*] > **'smart-ˌalecky** *adj*
smart card *n* a plastic card with integrated circuits used for storing and processing computer data. Also called: **laser card, intelligent card**
smart drug *n* any of various drugs that are claimed to improve the intelligence or memory of the person taking them
smarten ('smɑːtᵊn) *vb* (usually foll by *up*) **1** (*intr*) to make oneself neater **2** (*tr*) to make quicker or livelier
smart money *n* **1** money bet or invested by experienced gamblers or investors **2** money paid in order to extricate oneself from an unpleasant situation or agreement, esp from military service **3** *law* damages awarded to a plaintiff where the wrong was aggravated by fraud, malice, etc
smartphone ('smɑːtˌfəʊn) *n computing* a wireless telephone with added computer features that may enable it to interact with computerized systems, send and receive e-mails, and access the web
smarts (smɑːts) *pl n sl, chiefly US* know-how, intelligence, or wits: *street smarts*
smart set *n* (*functioning as sing or pl*) fashionable people considered as a group
smash (smæʃ) *vb* **1** to break into pieces violently and usually noisily **2** (*when intr*, foll by *against, through, into*, etc) to throw or crash (against) vigorously, causing shattering: *he smashed the equipment* **3** (*tr*) to hit forcefully and suddenly **4** (*tr*) *tennis, etc* to hit (the ball) fast and powerfully, esp with an overhead stroke **5** (*tr*) to defeat (persons, theories, etc) **6** to make or become bankrupt **7** (*intr*) to collide violently; crash ▷ *n* **8** an act, instance, or sound of smashing or the state of being smashed **9** a violent collision, esp of vehicles **10** a total failure or collapse, as of a business **11** *tennis, etc* a fast and powerful overhead stroke **12** *inf* **12a** something having popular success **12b** (*in combination*): *smash-hit* ▷ *adv* **13** with a smash ▷ See also **smash-up** [C18 prob. from SM(ACK[2] + M)ASH] > **'smashable** *adj*
smash-and-grab *adj inf* of or relating to a robbery in which a shop window is broken and the contents removed
smashed (smæʃt) *adj sl* drunk or under the influence of a drug
smasher ('smæʃə) *n inf, chiefly Brit* a person or thing that is very attractive or outstanding
smashing ('smæʃɪŋ) *adj inf, chiefly Brit* excellent or first-rate: *we had a smashing time*
smash-up *inf* ▷ *n* **1** a bad collision, esp of cars ▷ *vb* **smash up 2** (*tr, adv*) to damage to the point of complete destruction: *they smashed the place up*
smatter ('smætə) *n* **1** a smattering ▷ *vb* **2** (*tr*) *arch* to dabble in [C14 (in the sense: to prattle): from ?] > **'smatterer** *n*
smattering ('smætərɪŋ) *n* **1** a slight or superficial knowledge **2** a small amount
smear (smɪə) *vb* (*mainly tr*) **1** to bedaub or cover with oil, grease, etc **2** to rub over or apply thickly **3** to rub so as to produce a smudge **4** to slander **5** (*intr*) to be or become smeared or dirtied ▷ *n* **6** a dirty mark or smudge **7a** a slanderous attack **7b** (*as modifier*): *smear tactics* **8** a preparation of blood, secretions, etc, smeared onto a glass slide for examination under a microscope [OE *smeoru* (n)] > **'smeary** *adj* > **'smearily** *adv* > **'smeariness** *n*
smear test *n med* another name for **Pap test**
smectic ('smɛktɪk) *adj chem* (of a substance) existing in or having a mesomorphic state in which the molecules are oriented in layers [C17 via L from Gk *smēktikos*, from *smēkhein* to wash; from the soaplike consistency of a smectic substance]
smegma ('smɛgmə) *n physiol* a whitish sebaceous secretion that accumulates beneath the prepuce [C19 via L from Gk *smēgma* detergent, from *smekhein* to wash]
smell (smɛl) *vb* **smells, smelling, smelt** *or* **smelled 1** (*tr*) to perceive the scent of (a substance) by means of the olfactory nerves **2** (*copula*) to have a specified smell: *the curry smells very spicy* **3** (*intr; often foll by of*) to emit an odour (of): *the park smells of flowers* **4** (*intr*) to emit an unpleasant odour **5** (*tr; often foll by out*) to detect through shrewdness or instinct **6** (*intr*) to have or use the sense of smell; sniff **7** (*intr; foll by of*) to give indications (of): *he smells of money* **8** (*intr; foll by around, about*, etc) to search, investigate, or pry **9** (*copula*) to be or seem to be untrustworthy ▷ *n* **10** that sense (olfaction) by which scents or odours are perceived. Related adj: **olfactory 11** anything detected by the sense of smell **12** a trace or indication **13** the act or an instance of smelling [C12 from ?] > **'smeller** *n*
smelling salts *pl n* a pungent preparation containing crystals of ammonium carbonate that has a stimulant action when sniffed in cases of faintness, headache, etc
smelly ('smɛlɪ) *adj* **smellier, smelliest** having a strong or

unpleasant smell > 'smelliness *n*

smelt¹ (smɛlt) *vb* (*tr*) to extract (a metal) from (an ore) by heating [c15 from MLow G, MDu. *smelten*]

smelt² (smɛlt) *n, pl* **smelt** *or* **smelts** a marine or freshwater salmonoid food fish having a long silvery body and occurring in temperate and cold northern waters [OE *smylt*]

smelt³ (smɛlt) *vb* a past tense and past participle of **smell**

smelter ('smɛltə) *n* **1** a person engaged in smelting **2** Also called: **smeltery** an industrial plant in which smelting is carried out

Smetana (*Czech* 'smɛtana) *n* **Bedřich** ('bɛdrʒix) 1824–84, Czech composer, founder of his country's national school of music. His works include *My Fatherland* (1874–79), a cycle of six symphonic poems, and the opera *The Bartered Bride* (1866)

smew (smjuː) *n* a merganser of N Europe and Asia, having a male plumage of white with black markings [c17 from ?]

smidgen *or* **smidgin** ('smɪdʒən) *n inf, chiefly US* a very small amount [c20 from ?]

smilax ('smaɪlæks) *n* **1** any of a genus of climbing shrubs having slightly lobed leaves, small greenish or yellow flowers, and berry-like fruits: includes the sarsaparilla plant and greenbrier **2** a fragile, much branched vine of southern Africa: cultivated for its glossy green foliage [c17 via L from Gk: bindweed]

smile (smaɪl) *n* **1** a facial expression characterized by an upturning of the corners of the mouth, usually showing amusement, friendliness, etc **2** favour or blessing: *the smile of fortune* ▷ *vb* **smiles, smiling, smiled 3** (*intr*) to wear or assume a smile **4** (*intr; foll by at*) **4a** to look (at) with a kindly expression **4b** to look derisively (at) **4c** to bear (troubles, etc) patiently **5** (*intr; foll by on or upon*) to show approval **6** (*tr*) to express by means of a smile: *she smiled a welcome* **7** (*tr; often foll by away*) to drive away or change by smiling **8 come up smiling** to recover cheerfully from misfortune [c13 prob. from ON] > '**smiler** *n* > '**smiling** *adj* > '**smilingly** *adv*

Smiles (smaɪlz) *n* **Samuel** 1812–1904, British writer: author of the didactic work *Self-Help* (1859)

smiley ('smaɪlɪ) *adj* **1** given to smiling; cheerful **2** depicting a smile: *a smiley badge* ▷ *n* **3** any of a group of symbols depicting a smile, or other facial expression, used in electronic mail

smirch (smɜːtʃ) *vb* (*tr*) **1** to dirty; soil ▷ *n* **2** the act of smirching or state of being smirched **3** a smear or stain [c15 *smorchen*, from ?]

smirk (smɜːk) *n* **1** a smile expressing scorn, smugness, etc, rather than pleasure ▷ *vb* **2** (*intr*) to give such a smile **3** (*tr*) to express with such a smile [OE *smearcian*] > '**smirker** *n* > '**smirking** *adj* > '**smirkingly** *adv*

smite (smaɪt) *vb* **smites, smiting, smote; smitten** *or* **smit** (smɪt) (*mainly tr*) *now arch in most senses* **1** to strike with a heavy blow **2** to damage with or as if with blows **3** to affect severely: *smitten with flu* **4** to afflict in order to punish **5** (*intr; foll by on*) to strike forcibly or abruptly: *the sun smote down on him* [OE *smītan*] > '**smiter** *n*

smith (smɪθ) *n* **1a** a person who works in metal **1b** (*in combination*): *a silversmith* **2** See **blacksmith** [OE]

Smith (smɪθ) *n* **1 Adam** 1723–90, Scottish economist and philosopher, whose influential book *The Wealth of Nations* (1776) advocated free trade and private enterprise and opposed state interference **2 Bessie**, known as *Empress of the Blues*. 1894–1937, US blues singer and songwriter **3 Delia** born 1941, British cookery writer and broadcaster: her publications include *The Complete Cookery Course* (1982) and *Delia's How to Cook* (1998–99) **4 F.E.** See (1st Earl of) **Birkenhead 5 Harvey** born 1938, British showjumper **6 Ian (Douglas)** born 1919, Zimbabwean statesman; prime minister of Rhodesia (1964–79). He declared independence from Britain unilaterally (1965) **7 John** ?1580–1631, English explorer and writer, who helped found the North American colony of Jamestown, Virginia. He was reputedly saved by the Indian chief's daughter Pocahontas from execution by her tribe. Among his works is a *Description of New England* (1616) **8 Joseph** 1805–44, US religious leader; founder of the Mormon Church **9 Stevie**, real name *Florence Margaret Smith*. 1902–71, British poet. Her works include *Novel on Yellow Paper* (1936), and the poems 'A Good Time was had by All' (1937) and 'Not Waving but Drowning' (1957) **10 Sydney** 1771–1845, British clergyman and writer, noted for *The Letters of Peter Plymley* (1807–08), in which he advocated Catholic emancipation **11 Will(ard) Christopher** born 1968, US film actor and rap singer; star of the television series *The Fresh Prince of Bel Air* (1990–96) and the films *Men In Black* (1997), *Wild Wild West* (1999), and *Ali* (2001) **12 William** 1769–1839, English geologist, who founded the science of stratigraphy by proving that rock strata could be dated by the fossils they contained

smithereens (ˌsmɪðə'riːnz) *pl n* little shattered pieces or fragments [c19 from Irish Gaelic *smidirīn*, from *smiodar*]

smithery ('smɪθərɪ) *n, pl* **smitheries 1** the trade or craft of a blacksmith **2** a rare word for **smithy**

Smithson ('smɪθsən) *n* **James** original name *James Lewes Macie*. 1765–1829, English chemist and mineralogist, who left a bequest to found the Smithsonian Institution

smithy ('smɪðɪ) *n, pl* **smithies** a place in which metal, usually iron or steel, is worked by heating and hammering; forge [OE *smiththe*]

smitten ('smɪtᵊn) *vb* **1** a past participle of **smite** ▷ *adj* **2** (*postpositive*) affected by love (for)

smock (smɒk) *n* **1** any loose protective garment, worn by artists, laboratory technicians, etc **2** a woman's loose blouselike garment, reaching to below the waist, worn over slacks, etc **3** Also called: **smock frock** a loose protective overgarment decorated with smocking, worn formerly esp by farm workers **4** *arch* a woman's loose undergarment ▷ *vb* **5** to ornament (a garment) with smocking [OE *smocc*] > '**smock,like** *adj*

smocking ('smɒkɪŋ) *n* ornamental needlework used to gather and stitch material in a honeycomb pattern so that the part below the gathers hangs in even folds

smog (smɒg) *n* a mixture of smoke, fog, and chemical fumes [c20 from SM(OKE + F)OG¹] > '**smoggy** *adj*

smoke (sməʊk) *n* **1** the product of combustion, consisting of fine particles of carbon carried by hot gases and air **2** any cloud of fine particles suspended in a gas **3a** the act of smoking tobacco, esp as a cigarette **3b** the duration of smoking such substances **4** *inf* a cigarette or cigar **5** something with no concrete or lasting substance: *everything turned to smoke* **6** a thing or condition that obscures **7 go** *or* **end up in smoke 7a** to come to nothing **7b** to burn up vigorously **7c** to flare up in anger ▷ *vb* **smokes, smoking, smoked 8** (*intr*) to emit smoke or the like, sometimes excessively or in the wrong place **9** to draw in on (a burning cigarette, etc) and exhale the smoke **10** (*tr*) to bring (oneself) into a specified state by smoking **11** (*tr*) to subject or expose to smoke **12** (*tr*) to cure (meat, fish, etc) by treating with smoke **13** (*tr*) to fumigate or purify the air of (rooms, etc) **14** (*tr*) to darken (glass, etc) by exposure to smoke ▷ See also **smoke out** [OE *smoca* (n)] > '**smokable** *or* '**smokeable** *adj*

Smoke (sməʊk) *n* **the** short for the **Big Smoke**

smoke and mirrors *n* irrelevant or misleading information serving to obscure the truth of a situation [c20 reference to the use of smoke and mirrors in conjuring illusions]

smoke-dried *adj* (of fish, etc) cured in smoke

smoked rubber *n* a type of crude natural rubber in the form of brown sheets obtained by coagulating latex with an acid, rolling it into sheets, and drying over open

Ss

wood fires. It is the main raw material for natural rubber products

smokeho ('sməʊkəʊ) *n* a variant spelling of **smoko**

smokehouse ('sməʊk,haʊs) *n* a building or special construction for curing meat, fish, etc, by smoking

smokeless ('sməʊklɪs) *adj* having or producing little or no smoke: *smokeless fuel*

smokeless zone *n* an area where only smokeless fuels are permitted to be used

smoke out *vb (tr, adv)* **1** to subject to smoke in order to drive out of hiding **2** to bring into the open: *they smoked out the plot*

smoker ('sməʊkə) *n* **1** a person who habitually smokes tobacco **2** Also called: **smoking compartment** a compartment of a train where smoking is permitted **3** an informal social gathering, as at a club

smoke screen *n* **1** *mil* a cloud of smoke produced to obscure movements **2** something said or done in order to hide the truth

smokestack ('sməʊk,stæk) *n* a tall chimney that conveys smoke into the air

smokestack industry *n inf* any of the traditional British industries, esp heavy engineering or manufacturing, as opposed to such modern industries as electronics

smoking jacket *n* (formerly) a man's comfortable jacket of velvet, etc, closed by a tie belt or fastenings, worn at home

smoko *or* **smokeho** ('sməʊkəʊ) *n, pl* **smokos** *or* **smokehos** *Austral & NZ inf* **1** a short break from work for tea, a cigarette, etc **2** refreshment taken during this break

smoky ('sməʊkɪ) *adj* **smokier, smokiest 1** emitting or resembling smoke **2** emitting smoke excessively or in the wrong place: *a smoky fireplace* **3** having the flavour of having been cured by smoking **4** made dirty or hazy by smoke: *a smoky atmosphere* > **'smokily** *adv* > **'smokiness** *n*

Smoky Mountains *pl n* See **Great Smoky Mountains**

smolder ('sməʊldə) *vb, n* the US spelling of **smoulder**

Smolensk (*Russian* sma'ljɛnsk; *English* 'smɒlɛnsk) *n* a city in W Russia, on the Dnieper River: a major commercial centre in medieval times; scene of severe fighting (1941 and 1943) in World War II. Pop: 355 700 (1999 est)

Smollett ('smɒlɪt) *n* **Tobias George** 1721–71, Scottish novelist, whose picaresque satires include *Roderick Random* (1748), *Peregrine Pickle* (1751), and *Humphry Clinker* (1771)

smolt (sməʊlt) *n* a young salmon at the stage when it migrates from fresh water to the sea [c14 Scot, from ?]

smooch (smu:tʃ) *sl* ▷ *vb (intr)* **1** Also (Austral and NZ): **smoodge, smooge** (of two people) to kiss and cuddle **2** *Brit* to dance very slowly and amorously with one's arms around another person or (of two people) to dance together in such a way ▷ *n* **3** the act of smooching [c20 var. of dialect *smouch*, imit.]

smoodge *or* **smooge** (smu:dʒ) *vb* **smoodges, smoodging, smoodged** *or* **smooges, smooging, smooged** *(intr) Austral & NZ* **1** another word for **smooch** (sense 1) **2** to seek to ingratiate oneself

smooth (smu:ð) *adj* **1** without bends or irregularities **2** silky to the touch: *smooth velvet* **3** lacking roughness of surface; flat **4** tranquil or unruffled: *smooth temper* **5** lacking obstructions or difficulties **6a** suave or persuasive, esp as suggestive of insincerity **6b** (*in combination*): *smooth-tongued* **7** (of the skin) free from hair **8** of uniform consistency: *smooth batter* **9** free from jolts: *smooth driving* **10** not harsh or astringent: *a smooth wine* **11** having all projections worn away: *smooth tyres* **12** *phonetics* without preliminary aspiration **13** *physics* (of a plane, etc) regarded as being frictionless ▷ *adv* **14** in a calm or even manner ▷ *vb (mainly tr)* **15** (*also intr; often foll by down*) to make or become flattened or without roughness **16** (often foll by *out* or *away*) to take or rub (away) in order to make smooth: *she smoothed out the creases in her dress* **17** to make calm; soothe **18** to make easier: *smooth his path* ▷ *n* **19** the smooth part of something **20** the act of smoothing **21** *tennis, etc* the side of a racket on which the binding strings form a continuous line ▷ See also **smooth over** [OE *smōth*] > **'smoother** *n* > **'smoothly** *adv* > **'smoothness** *n*

smoothbore ('smu:ð,bɔ:) *n (modifier)* (of a firearm) having an unrifled bore: *a smoothbore shotgun* > **'smooth,bored** *adj*

smooth breathing *n* (in Greek) the sign (') placed over an initial vowel, indicating that (in ancient Greek) it was not pronounced with an *h*

smoothen ('smu:ðən) *vb* to make or become smooth

smooth hound *n* any of several small sharks of North Atlantic coastal regions

smoothie *or* **smoothy** ('smu:ðɪ) *n, pl* **smoothies 1** *sl, usually derog* a person, esp a man, who is suave or slick, esp in speech, dress, or manner **2** a smooth thick drink made from puréed fresh fruit and yoghurt, ice cream, or milk

smoothing iron *n* a former name for **iron** (sense 3)

smooth muscle *n* muscle that is capable of slow rhythmic involuntary contractions: occurs in the walls of the blood vessels, etc

smooth over *vb (tr)* to ease or gloss over: *to smooth over a difficulty*

smooth snake *n* any of several slender nonvenomous European snakes having very smooth scales and a reddish-brown coloration

smooth-spoken *adj* speaking or spoken in a gently persuasive or competent manner

smooth-tongued *adj* suave or persuasive in speech

smorgasbord ('smɔ:gəs,bɔ:d) *n* a variety of cold or hot savoury dishes served in Scandinavia as hors d'oeuvres or as a buffet meal [Swedish, from *smörgås* sandwich + *bord* table]

smote (sməʊt) *vb* the past tense of **smite**

smother ('smʌðə) *vb* **1** to suffocate or stifle by cutting off or being cut off from the air **2** (*tr*) to surround (with) or envelop (in): *he smothered her with love* **3** (*tr*) to extinguish (a fire) by covering so as to cut it off from the air **4** to be or cause to be suppressed or stifled: *smother a giggle* **5** (*tr*) to cook or serve (food) thickly covered with sauce, etc ▷ *n* **6** anything, such as a cloud of smoke, that stifles **7** a profusion or turmoil [OE *smorian* to suffocate] > **'smothery** *adj*

smothered mate *n chess* checkmate given by a knight when the king is prevented from moving by surrounding men

smoulder *or US* **smolder** ('sməʊldə) *vb (intr)* **1** to burn slowly without flame, usually emitting smoke **2** (esp of anger, etc) to exist in a suppressed state **3** to have strong repressed feelings, esp anger ▷ *n* **4** a smouldering fire [c14 from *smolder* (n), from ?]

SMP (in Britain) *abbrev for* statutory maternity pay

smudge (smʌdʒ) *vb* **smudges, smudging, smudged 1** to smear or soil or cause to do so **2** (*tr*) *chiefly US & Canad* to fill (an area) with smoke in order to drive insects away ▷ *n* **3** a smear or dirty mark **4** a blurred form or area: *that smudge in the distance is a quarry* **5** *chiefly US & Canad* a smoky fire for driving insects away or protecting plants from frost [c15 from ?] > **'smudgy** *adj* > **'smudgily** *adv* > **'smudginess** *n*

smug (smʌg) *adj* **smugger, smuggest** excessively self-satisfied or complacent [c16 of Gmc origin] > **'smugly** *adv* > **'smugness** *n*

smuggle ('smʌgᵊl) *vb* **smuggles, smuggling, smuggled 1** to import or export (prohibited or dutiable goods) secretly **2** (*tr; often foll by* into *or* out of) to bring or take secretly, as against the law or rules [c17 from Low G *smukkelen* & Du. *smokkelen*, ?from OE *smūgen* to creep] > **'smuggler** *n* > **'smuggling** *n*

smut (smʌt) *n* **1** a small dark smudge or stain, esp one caused by soot **2** a speck of soot or dirt **3** something obscene or indecent **4a** any of various fungal diseases of flowering plants, esp cereals, in which black sooty masses of spores cover the affected parts **4b** any parasitic fungus that causes such a disease ▷ *vb* **smuts, smutting, smutted 5** to mark or become marked or smudged, as with soot **6** to affect (grain, etc) or (of grain) to be affected with smut [OE *smitte;* associated with SMUDGE, SMUTCH] > **'smutty** *adj* > **'smuttily** *adv* > **'smuttiness** *n*

smutch (smʌtʃ) *vb* **1** (*tr*) to smudge; mark ▷ *n* **2** a mark; smudge **3** soot; dirt [c16 prob. from MHG *smutzen* to soil] > **'smutchy** *adj*

Smuts (smʌts) *n* **Jan Christiaan** (jan 'kristi,an) 1870–1950, South African statesman; prime minister (1919–24; 1939–48). He fought for the Boers during the Boer War, then worked for Anglo-Boer reconciliation and served the Allies during World Wars I and II

Smyrna ('smɜːnə) *n* an ancient city on the W coast of Asia Minor: a major trading centre in the ancient world; a centre of early Christianity. Modern name: **Izmir**

Sn *the chemical symbol for* tin [from NL *stannum*]

snack (snæk) *n* **1** a light quick meal eaten between or in place of main meals **2** a sip or bite ▷ *vb* **3** (*intr*) to eat a snack [c15 prob. from MDu. *snacken*, var. of *snappen* to snap]

snack bar *n* a place where light meals or snacks can be obtained, often with a self-service system

snaffle ('snæfᵊl) *n* **1** Also called: **snaffle bit** a simple jointed bit for a horse ▷ *vb* **snaffles, snaffling, snaffled** (*tr*) **2** *Brit inf* to steal or take for oneself **3** to equip or control with a snaffle [c16 from ?]

snafu (snæ'fuː) *sl, chiefly mil* ▷ *n* **1** confusion or chaos regarded as the normal state ▷ *adj* **2** (*postpositive*) confused or muddled up, as usual ▷ *vb* **snafus, snafuing, snafued 3** (*tr*) *US & Canad* to throw into chaos [c20 from *s(ituation) n(ormal): a(ll) f(ucked) u(p)*]

snag[1] (snæg) *n* **1** a difficulty or disadvantage: *the snag is that I have nothing suitable to wear* **2** a sharp protuberance, such as a tree stump **3** a small loop or hole in a fabric caused by a sharp object **4** *chiefly US & Canad* a tree stump in a riverbed that is dangerous to navigation **5** *US & Canad* a standing dead tree, esp one used as a perch by an eagle ▷ *vb* **snags, snagging, snagged 6** (*tr*) to hinder or impede **7** (*tr*) to tear or catch (fabric) **8** (*intr*) to develop a snag **9** (*intr*) *chiefly US & Canad* (of a boat) to strike a snag **10** (*tr*) *chiefly US & Canad* to clear (a stretch of water) of snags **11** (*tr*) *US* to seize (an opportunity, etc) [c16 of Scand. origin] > **'snaggy** *adj*

snag[2] (snæg) *n* (*usually pl*) *Austral sl* a sausage [from ?]

snaggletooth ('snægᵊl,tuːθ) *n, pl* **snaggleteeth** a tooth that is broken or projecting

snail (sneɪl) *n* **1** any of numerous terrestrial or freshwater gastropod molluscs with a spirally coiled shell, esp the **garden snail 2** any other gastropod with a spirally coiled shell, such as a whelk **3** a slow-moving person or animal [OE *snægl*] > **'snail-,like** *adj*

snail mail *n inf* **1** the conventional postal system, as opposed to electronic mail ▷ *vb* **snail-mail 2** (*tr*) to send by the conventional postal system, rather than by electronic mail [c20 so named because of the relative slowness of the conventional postal system]

snail's pace *n* a very slow speed or rate

snake (sneɪk) *n* **1** a reptile having a scaly cylindrical limbless body, fused eyelids, and a jaw modified for swallowing large prey: includes venomous forms such as cobras and rattlesnakes, large nonvenomous constrictors (boas and pythons), and small harmless types such as the grass snake **2** Also: **snake in the grass** a deceitful or treacherous person **3** anything resembling a snake in appearance or action **4** (in the European Union) a group of currencies, any one of which can only fluctuate within narrow limits, but each can fluctuate more against other currencies **5** a tool in the form of a long flexible wire for unblocking drains ▷ *vb* **snakes, snaking, snaked 6** (*intr*) to glide or move like a snake **7** (*tr*) to move in or follow (a sinuous course) [OE *snaca*] > **'snake,like** *adj*

snakebird ('sneɪk,bɜːd) *n* another name for **darter** (the bird)

snakebite ('sneɪk,baɪt) *n* **1** a bite inflicted by a snake, esp a venomous one **2** a drink of cider and lager

snake charmer *n* an entertainer, esp in Asia, who charms or appears to charm snakes by playing music

Snake River *n* a river in the northwestern US, rising in NW Wyoming and flowing west through Idaho, turning north as part of the border between Idaho and Oregon, and flowing west to the Columbia River near Pasco, Washington. Length: 1670 km (1038 miles)

snakeroot ('sneɪk,ruːt) *n* **1** any of various North American plants the roots or rhizomes of which have been used as a remedy for snakebite **2** the rhizome or root of any such plant

snakes and ladders *n* (*functioning as sing*) a board game in which players move counters along a series of squares according to throws of a dice. A ladder provides a short cut to a square nearer the finish and a snake obliges a player to return to a square nearer the start

snake's head *n* a European fritillary plant of damp meadows, having purple-and-white flowers

snakeskin ('sneɪk,skɪn) *n* the skin of a snake, esp when made into a leather valued for handbags, shoes, etc

snaky ('sneɪkɪ) *adj* **snakier, snakiest 1** of or like a snake **2** treacherous or insidious **3** infested with snakes **4** *Austral & NZ sl* angry or bad-tempered > **'snakily** *adv* > **'snakiness** *n*

snap (snæp) *vb* **snaps, snapping, snapped 1** to break or cause to break suddenly, esp with a sharp sound **2** to make or cause to make a sudden sharp cracking sound **3** (*intr*) to give way or collapse suddenly, esp from strain **4** to move, close, etc, or cause to move, close, etc, with a sudden sharp sound **5** to move or cause to move in a sudden or abrupt way **6** (*intr; often foll by* *at* or *up*) to seize something suddenly or quickly **7** (when *intr*, often foll by *at*) to bite at (something) bringing the jaws rapidly together **8** to speak (words) sharply or abruptly **9** to take a snapshot of (something) **10** (*tr*) *American football* to put (the ball) into play by sending it back from the line of scrimmage **11 snap one's fingers at** *inf* **11a** to dismiss with contempt **11b** to defy **12 snap out of it** *inf* to recover quickly, esp from depression or anger ▷ *n* **13** the act of breaking suddenly or the sound produced by a sudden breakage **14** a sudden sharp sound, esp of bursting, popping, or cracking **15** a catch, clasp, or fastener that operates with a snapping sound **16** a sudden grab or bite **17** a thin crisp biscuit: *ginger snaps* **18** *inf* See **snapshot 19** *inf* vigour, liveliness, or energy **20** *inf* a task or job that is easy or profitable to do **21** a short spell or period, esp of cold weather **22** *Brit* a card game in which the word *snap* is called when two cards of equal value are turned up on the separate piles dealt by each player **23** *American football* the start of each play when the centre passes the ball back from the line of scrimmage to a teammate **24** (*modifier*) done on the spur of the moment: *a snap decision* **25** (*modifier*) closed or fastened with a snap ▷ *adv* **26** with a snap ▷ *interj* **27a** *cards* the word called while playing snap **27b** an exclamation used to draw attention to the similarity of two things ▷ See also **snap up** [c15 from MLow G or MDu. *snappen* to seize] > **'snapless** *adj* > **'snappingly** *adv*

snapdragon ('snæp,drægən) *n* any of several plants of the genus *Antirrhinum* having spikes of showy white, yellow, pink, red, or purplish flowers. Also called: **antirrhinum**

snap fastener *n* another name for **press stud**

snapper ('snæpə) *n, pl* **snapper** *or* **snappers 1** any large

Ss

sharp-toothed percoid food fish of warm and tropical coastal regions. See also **red snapper** 2 a food fish of Australia and New Zealand that has a pinkish body covered with blue spots 3 another name for the **snapping turtle** 4 a person or thing that snaps ▷ Also (for sense 1, 2): **schnapper**

snapping turtle *n* any large aggressive North American river turtle having powerful hooked jaws and a rough shell. Also called: **snapper**

snappy ('snæpɪ) *adj* **snappier, snappiest** 1 Also: **snappish** apt to speak sharply or irritably 2 Also: **snappish** apt to snap or bite 3 crackling in sound: *a snappy fire* 4 brisk, sharp, or chilly: *a snappy pace* 5 smart and fashionable: *a snappy dresser* 6 **make it snappy** *sl* hurry up! > '**snappily** *adv* > '**snappiness** *n*

snap ring *n mountaineering* another name for **karabiner**

snapshot ('snæpˌʃɒt) *n* an informal photograph taken with a simple camera. Often shortened to **snap**

snap shot *n sport* a sudden, fast shot at goal

snap up *vb (tr, adv)* 1 to avail oneself of eagerly and quickly: *she snapped up the bargains* 2 to interrupt abruptly

snare[1] (snɛə) *n* 1 a device for trapping birds or small animals, esp a flexible loop that is drawn tight around the prey 2 a surgical instrument for removing certain tumours, consisting of a wire loop that may be drawn tight around their base to sever them 3 anything that traps or entangles someone or something unawares ▷ *vb* **snares, snaring, snared** *(tr)* 4 to catch (birds or small animals) with a snare 5 to catch or trap in or as if in a snare [OE *sneare*] > '**snarer** *n*

snare[2] (snɛə) *n music* a set of gut strings wound with wire fitted against the lower drumhead of a snare drum. They produce a rattling sound when the drum is beaten [C17 from MDu. *snaer* or MLow G *snare* string]

snare drum *n music* a cylindrical drum with two drumheads, the upper of which is struck and the lower fitted with a snare. See **snare**[2]

snarky ('snɒːkɪ) *adj* **snarkier, snarkiest** *inf* unpleasant and scornful [C20 from SARCASTIC + NASTY]

snarl[1] (snɑːl) *vb* 1 *(intr)* (of an animal) to growl viciously, baring the teeth 2 to speak or express (something) viciously ▷ *n* 3 a vicious growl or facial expression 4 the act of snarling [C16 of Gmc origin] > '**snarler** *n* > '**snarling** *adj* > '**snarly** *adj*

snarl[2] (snɑːl) *n* 1 a tangled mass of thread, hair, etc 2 a complicated or confused state or situation 3 a knot in wood ▷ *vb* 4 (often foll by *up*) to be, become, or make tangled or complicated 5 *(tr; often foll by up)* to confuse mentally 6 *(tr)* to emboss (metal) by hammering on a tool held against the under surface [C14 from ON] > '**snarler** *n* > '**snarly** *adj*

snarl-up *n inf, chiefly Brit* a confusion, obstruction, or tangle, esp a traffic jam

snatch (snætʃ) *vb* 1 *(tr)* to seize or grasp (something) suddenly or peremptorily: *he snatched the chocolate* 2 *(intr; usually foll by at)* to seize or attempt to seize suddenly 3 *(tr)* to take hurriedly: *to snatch some sleep* 4 *(tr)* to remove suddenly: *she snatched her hand away* 5 *(tr)* to gain, win, or rescue, esp narrowly: *they snatched victory in the closing seconds* ▷ *n* 6 an act of snatching 7 a fragment or incomplete part: *snatches of conversation* 8 a brief spell: *snatches of time off* 9 *weightlifting* a lift in which the weight is raised in one quick motion from the floor to an overhead position 10 *sl, chiefly US* an act of kidnapping 11 *Brit sl* a robbery: *a diamond snatch* [C13 *snacchen*] > '**snatcher** *n*

snatchy ('snætʃɪ) *adj* **snatchier, snatchiest** disconnected or spasmodic > '**snatchily** *adv*

snazzy ('snæzɪ) *adj* **snazzier, snazziest** *inf* (esp of clothes) stylishly and often flashily attractive [C20 ?from SN(APPY + J)AZZY] > '**snazzily** *adv* > '**snazziness** *n*

Snead (sniːd) *n* **Sam(uel Jackson)** born 1912, U.S. golfer; winner of seven major tournaments between 1938 and 1951 including three Masters titles (1949, 1952, 1954)

sneak (sniːk) *vb* 1 *(intr; often foll by along, off, in, etc)* to move furtively 2 *(intr)* to behave in a cowardly or underhand manner 3 *(tr)* to bring, take, or put stealthily 4 *(intr) inf, chiefly Brit* to tell tales (esp in schools) 5 *(tr) inf* to steal 6 *(intr; foll by off, out, away, etc) inf* to leave unobtrusively ▷ *n* 7 a person who acts in an underhand or cowardly manner, esp as an informer 8a a stealthy act 8b *(as modifier): a sneak attack* [OE *snīcan* to creep] > '**sneaky** *adj* > '**sneakily** *adv* > '**sneakiness** *n*

sneakers ('sniːkəz) *pl n chiefly US & Canad* canvas shoes with rubber soles worn informally

sneaking ('sniːkɪŋ) *adj* 1 acting in a furtive or cowardly way 2 secret: *a sneaking desire to marry a millionaire* 3 slight but nagging (esp in **a sneaking suspicion**) > '**sneakingly** *adv*

sneak thief *n* a person who steals paltry articles from premises, which he or she enters through open doors, windows, etc

sneer (snɪə) *n* 1 a facial expression of scorn or contempt, typically with the upper lip curled 2 a scornful or contemptuous remark or utterance ▷ *vb* 3 *(intr)* to assume a facial expression of scorn or contempt 4 to say or utter (something) in a scornful manner [C16 ?from Low Du.] > '**sneerer** *n* > '**sneering** *adj, n*

sneeze (sniːz) *vb* **sneezes, sneezing, sneezed** 1 *(intr)* to expel air and nasal secretions from the nose involuntarily, esp as the result of irritation of the nasal mucous membrane ▷ *n* 2 the act or sound of sneezing [OE *fnēosan* (unattested)] > '**sneezer** *n* > '**sneezy** *adj*

sneeze at *vb (intr, prep; usually with a negative) inf* to dismiss lightly: *his offer is not to be sneezed at*

sneezewood ('sniːzˌwʊd) *n* 1 a South African tree 2 its exceptionally hard wood, used for furniture, gateposts and railway sleepers

sneezewort ('sniːzˌwɜːt) *n* a Eurasian plant having daisy-like flowers and long grey-green leaves, which cause sneezing when powdered

snick (snɪk) *n* 1 a small cut; notch 2 *cricket* 2a a glancing blow off the edge of the bat 2b the ball so hit ▷ *vb (tr)* 3 to cut a small corner or notch in (material, etc) 4 *cricket* to hit (the ball) with a snick [C18 prob. of Scand. origin]

snicker ('snɪkə) *n, vb* 1 another word (esp US and Canad) for **snigger** ▷ *vb* 2 *(intr)* (of a horse) to whinny [C17 prob. imit.]

Snicket ('snɪkət) *n* **Lemony** ('lɛmənɪ) See (Daniel) **Handler**

Snickometer (snɪ'kɒmɪtə) *n trademark, cricket* a device, which uses sound waves recorded by the stump microphone, employed by TV commentators to determine whether or not a batsman has made contact with the ball [C20 from SNICK (sense 2) + -METER]

snide (snaɪd) *adj* 1 Also: **snidey** ('snaɪdɪ) (of a remark, etc) maliciously derogatory 2 counterfeit ▷ *n* 3 *sl* sham jewellery [C19 from ?] > '**snidely** *adv* > '**snideness** *n*

sniff (snɪf) *vb* 1 to inhale through the nose, usually in short rapid audible inspirations, as for clearing a congested nasal passage or for taking a drug 2 (when *intr*, often foll by *at*) to perceive or attempt to perceive (a smell) by inhaling through the nose ▷ *n* 3 the act or sound of sniffing 4 a smell perceived by sniffing, esp a faint scent ▷ See also **sniff at, sniff out** [C14 prob. rel. to *snivelen* to snivel] > '**sniffer** *n* > '**sniffing** *n, adj*

sniff at *vb (intr, prep)* to express contempt or dislike for

sniffer dog *n* a police dog trained to detect drugs or explosives by smell

sniffle ('snɪfᵊl) *vb* **sniffles, sniffling, sniffled** 1 *(intr)* to breathe audibly through the nose, as when the nasal passages are congested ▷ *n* 2 the act, sound, or an instance of sniffling > '**sniffler** *n* > '**sniffly** *adj*

sniffles ('snɪfᵊlz) *or* **snuffles** *pl n inf* **the** a cold in the head

sniff out *vb (tr, adv)* to detect through shrewdness or instinct

sniffy ('snɪfɪ) *adj* **sniffier, sniffiest** *inf* contemptuous or disdainful > '**sniffily** *adv* > '**sniffiness** *n*

snifter ('snɪftə) *n* **1** a pear-shaped glass with a bowl that narrows towards the top so that the aroma of brandy or a liqueur is retained **2** *inf* a small quantity of alcoholic drink [C19 ?from dialect *snifter* to sniff, ? of Scand. origin]

snig (snɪg) *vb* **snigs, snigging, snigged** (*tr*) *NZ* to drag (a felled log) by a chain or cable [from E dialect]

snigger ('snɪgə) *n* **1** a sly or disrespectful laugh, esp one partly stifled ▷ *vb* (*intr*) **2** to utter such a laugh [C18 var. of SNICKER] > '**sniggering** *n, adj*

snigging chain *n Austral & NZ* a chain attached to a log when being hauled out of the bush

snip (snɪp) *vb* **snips, snipping, snipped 1** to cut or clip with a small quick stroke or a succession of small quick strokes, esp with scissors or shears ▷ *n* **2** the act of snipping **3** the sound of scissors or shears closing **4** Also called: **snipping** a small piece of anything **5** a small cut made by snipping **6** *chiefly Brit* an informal word for **bargain 7** *inf* something easily done; cinch ▷ See also **snips¹** [C16 from Low G, Du. *snippen*]

snipe (snaɪp) *n, pl* **snipe** *or* **snipes 1** any of a genus of birds, such as the common snipe, of marshes and river banks, having a long straight bill **2** a shot, esp a gunshot, fired from a place of concealment ▷ *vb* **snipes, sniping, sniped 3** (when *intr*, often foll by *at*) to attack (a person or persons) with a rifle from a place of concealment **4** (*intr*; often foll by *at*) to criticize a person or persons from a position of security **5** (*intr*) to hunt or shoot snipe [C14 from ON *snīpa*] > '**sniper** *n*

snipefish ('snaɪp,fɪʃ) *n, pl* **snipefish** *or* **snipefishes** a teleost fish of tropical and temperate seas, having a deep body, long snout, and a single long dorsal fin. Also called: **bellows fish**

snippet ('snɪpɪt) *n* a small scrap or fragment of fabric, news, etc > '**snippetiness** *n* > '**snippety** *adj*

snips¹ (snɪps) *pl n* a small pair of shears used for cutting sheet metal

snips² (snɪps) *pl n biochemistry inf* differences in single pairs of purine and purimidine bases in the nucleotides of DNA that occur between individuals and comprise the most common type of variation in the human genome. Analysis of snips is important in the identification of genes responsible for disease [C20 from *s(ingle) n(uclot)i(de) p(olymorphism)s*]

snitch (snɪtʃ) *sl* ▷ *vb* **1** (*tr*) to steal; take, esp in an underhand way **2** (*intr*) to act as an informer ▷ *n* **3** an informer **4** the nose [C17 from ?]

snitchy ('snɪtʃɪ) *adj* **snitchier, snitchiest** *NZ inf* bad-tempered or irritable

snivel ('snɪvᵊl) *vb* **snivels, snivelling, snivelled** *or US* **snivels, sniveling, sniveled 1** (*intr*) to sniffle as a sign of distress **2** to utter (something) tearfully; whine **3** (*intr*) to have a runny nose ▷ *n* **4** an instance of snivelling [C14 *snivelen*] > '**sniveller** *n* > '**snivelling** *adj, n*

snob (snɒb) *n* **1a** a person who strives to associate with those of higher social status and who behaves condescendingly to others **1b** (*as modifier*): *snob appeal* **2** a person having similar pretensions with regard to his or her tastes, etc: *an intellectual snob* [C18 (in the sense: shoemaker; hence, C19 a person who flatters those of higher station, etc): from ?] > '**snobbery** *n* > '**snobbish** *adj* > '**snobbishly** *adv*

SNOBOL ('snəʊbɒl) *n* String Oriented Symbolic Language: a computer-programming language for handling strings of symbols

Sno-Cat ('snəʊ,kæt) *n trademark* a type of snowmobile

snoek (snʊk) *n* a South African edible marine fish [Afrik., from Du. *snoek* pike]

snoep (snʊp) *adj S African inf* mean or tight-fisted [Afrik., lit.: greedy]

snog (snɒg) *Brit sl* ▷ *vb* **snogs, snogging, snogged 1** to kiss and cuddle (someone) ▷ *n* **2** the act of kissing and cuddling: *a quick snog* [from ?]

snood (snuːd) *n* **1** a pouchlike hat, often of net, loosely holding a woman's hair at the back **2** a headband, esp one formerly worn by young unmarried women in Scotland [OE *snōd*; from ?]

snook¹ (snuːk) *n, pl* **snook** *or* **snooks 1** any of a genus of large game fishes of tropical American marine and fresh waters **2** *Austral* the sea pike [C17 from Du. *snoek* pike]

snook² (snuːk) *n Brit* a rude gesture, made by putting one thumb to the nose with the fingers of the hand outstretched (esp in **cock a snook**) [C19 from ?]

snooker ('snuːkə) *n* **1** a game played on a billiard table with 15 red balls, six balls of other colours, and a white cue ball. The object is to pot the balls in a certain order **2** a shot in which the cue ball is left in a position such that another ball blocks the target ball ▷ *vb* (*tr*) **3** to leave (an opponent) in an unfavourable position by playing a snooker **4** to place (someone) in a difficult situation **5** (*often passive*) to thwart; defeat [C19 from ?]
▷ www.worldsnooker.com

snoop (snuːp) *inf* ▷ *vb* **1** (*intr*; often foll by *about* or *around*) to pry into the private business of others ▷ *n* **2** a person who pries into the business of others **3** an act or instance of snooping [C19 from Du. *snoepen* to eat furtively] > '**snooper** *n* > '**snoopy** *adj*

snooperscope ('snuːpə,skəʊp) *n mil, US* an instrument that enables the user to see objects in the dark by illuminating the object with infrared radiation

snoot (snuːt) *n sl* the nose [C20 var. of SNOUT]

snooty ('snuːtɪ) *adj* **snootier, snootiest** *inf* **1** aloof or supercilious **2** snobbish: *a snooty restaurant* > '**snootily** *adv* > '**snootiness** *n*

snooze (snuːz) *inf* ▷ *vb* **snoozes, snoozing, snoozed 1** (*intr*) to take a brief light sleep ▷ *n* **2** a nap [C18 from ?] > '**snoozer** *n* > '**snoozy** *adj*

snore (snɔː) *vb* **snores, snoring, snored 1** (*intr*) to breathe through the mouth and nose while asleep with snorting sounds caused by vibration of the soft palate ▷ *n* **2** the act or sound of snoring [C14 imit.] > '**snorer** *n*

Ss

snorkel ('snɔːkᵊl) *n* **1** a device allowing a swimmer to breathe while face down on the surface of the water, consisting of a bent tube fitting into the mouth and projecting above the surface **2** (on a submarine) a retractable vertical device containing air-intake and exhaust pipes for the engines and general ventilation ▷ *vb* **snorkels, snorkelling, snorkelled** *or US* **snorkels, snorkeling, snorkeled 3** (*intr*) to swim with a snorkel [C20 from G *Schnorchel*]

Snorri Sturluson ('snɔːrɪ 'stɜːləsᵊn) *n* 1179–1241, Icelandic historian and poet; author of *Younger* or *Prose Edda* (?1222), containing a collection of Norse myths and a treatise on poetry, and the *Heimskringla* sagas of the Norwegian kings from their mythological origins to the 12th century

snort (snɔːt) *vb* **1** (*intr*) to exhale forcibly through the nostrils, making a characteristic noise **2** (*intr*) (of a person) to express contempt or annoyance by such an exhalation **3** (*tr*) to utter in a contemptuous or annoyed manner **4** *sl* to inhale (a powdered drug) through the nostrils ▷ *n* **5** a forcible exhalation of air through the nostrils, esp (of persons) as a noise of contempt **6** *sl* an instance of snorting a drug [C14 *snorten*] > '**snorting** *n, adj* > '**snortingly** *adv*

snorter ('snɔːtə) *n* **1** a person or animal that snorts **2** *Brit sl* something outstandingly impressive or difficult

snot (snɒt) *n* (*usually considered vulgar*) **1** nasal mucus or discharge **2** *sl* a contemptible person [OE *gesnot*]

snotty ('snɒtɪ) *adj* **snottier, snottiest** (*considered vulgar*) **1** dirty with nasal discharge **2** *sl* contemptible; nasty **3** snobbish; conceited > '**snottily** *adv* > '**snottiness** *n*

snout (snaʊt) *n* **1** the part of the head of a vertebrate, esp a mammal, consisting of the nose, jaws, and surrounding region **2** the corresponding part of the head of such insects as weevils **3** anything projecting like a snout, such as a nozzle **4** *sl* a person's nose **5** *Brit sl* a cigarette or tobacco **6** *sl* an informer [C13 of Gmc origin] > **'snouted** *adj* > **'snoutless** *adj* > **'snout,like** *adj*

snout beetle *n* another name for **weevil**

snow (snəʊ) *n* **1** precipitation from clouds in the form of flakes of ice crystals formed in the upper atmosphere **2** a layer of snowflakes on the ground **3** a fall of such precipitation **4** anything resembling snow in whiteness, softness, etc **5** the random pattern of white spots on a television or radar screen, occurring when the signal is weak **6** *sl* cocaine ▷ *vb* **7** (*intr*, with *it* as subject) to be the case that snow is falling **8** (*tr*; usually passive, foll by *over*, *under*, *in*, or *up*) to cover or confine with a heavy fall of snow **9** (often with *it* as subject) to fall or cause to fall as or like snow **10** (*tr*) *US & Canad sl* to overwhelm with elaborate often insincere talk **11 be snowed under** to be overwhelmed, esp with paperwork [OE *snāw*] > **'snowless** *adj* > **'snow,like** *adj*

Snow (snəʊ) *n* **C(harles) P(ercy)**, Baron. 1905–80, British novelist and physicist. His novels include the series *Strangers and Brothers* (1949–70)

snow apple *n* a Canadian variety of eating apple

snowball ('snəʊ,bɔːl) *n* **1** snow pressed into a ball for throwing, as in play **2** a drink made of advocaat and lemonade ▷ *vb* **3** (*intr*) to increase rapidly in size, importance, etc **4** (*tr*) to throw snowballs at

snowball tree *n* any of several shrubs of the genus *Viburnum*, with spherical clusters of white or pinkish flowers

snowberry ('snəʊbərɪ) *n, pl* **snowberries 1** a shrub cultivated for its small pink flowers and white berries **2** Also called: **waxberry** any of the berries of such a plant

snow-blind *adj* having temporarily impaired vision because of the intense reflection of sunlight from snow > **snow blindness** *n*

snowblower ('snəʊ,bləʊə) *n* a snow-clearing machine that draws the snow in and blows it away

snowboard ('snəʊ,bɔːd) *n* a shaped board, resembling a skateboard without wheels, on which a person can stand to slide across snow [C20 on the model of SURFBOARD] > **'snow,boarding** *n*

snowbound ('snəʊ,baʊnd) *adj* confined to one place by heavy falls or drifts of snow; snowed in

snow bunting *n* a bunting of northern and arctic regions, having a white plumage with dark markings on the wings, back, and tail

snowcap ('snəʊ,kæp) *n* a cap of snow, as on top of a mountain

snowcapped ('snəʊ,kæpt) *adj* (of a mountain, hill, etc) having a cap of snow on the top

Snowdon ('snəʊdən) *n* a mountain in NW Wales, in Gwynedd: the highest peak in Wales. Height: 1085 m (3560 ft)

Snowdonia (snəʊ'dəʊnɪə) *n* **1** a massif in NW Wales, in Gwynedd, the highest peak being Snowdon **2** a national park in NW Wales, in Gwynedd and Conwy: includes the Snowdonia massif in the north. Area: 2189 sq km (845 sq miles)

snowdrift ('snəʊ,drɪft) *n* a bank of deep snow driven together by the wind

snowdrop ('snəʊ,drɒp) *n* a Eurasian plant having drooping white bell-shaped flowers that bloom in early spring

snowfall ('snəʊ,fɔːl) *n* **1** a fall of snow **2** *meteorol* the amount of snow received in a specified place and time

snow fence *n* a lath-and-wire fence put up in winter beside windy roads to prevent snowdrifts

snowfield ('snəʊ,fiːld) *n* a large area of permanent snow

snowflake ('snəʊ,fleɪk) *n* **1** one of the mass of small thin delicate arrangements of ice crystals that fall as snow **2** any of various European plants that have white nodding bell-shaped flowers

snow goose *n* a North American goose having a white plumage with black wing tips

snow gum *n* any of several eucalypts of mountainous regions of SE Australia

snow-in-summer *n* a plant of SE Europe and Asia having white flowers and downy stems and leaves: cultivated as a rock plant

snow leopard *n* a large feline mammal of mountainous regions of central Asia, closely related to the leopard but having a long pale brown coat marked with black rosettes

snow lily *n Canad* another name for **dogtooth violet**

snow line *n* the altitudinal or latitudinal limit of permanent snow

snowman ('snəʊ,mæn) *n, pl* **snowmen** a figure resembling a man, made of packed snow

snowmobile ('snəʊmə,biːl) *n* a motor vehicle for travelling on snow, esp one with caterpillar tracks and front skis

snowplough *or esp US* **snowplow** ('snəʊ,plaʊ) *n* an implement or vehicle for clearing away snow

snowshoe ('snəʊ,ʃuː) *n* **1** a device to facilitate walking on snow, esp a racket-shaped frame with a network of thongs stretched across it ▷ *vb* **snowshoes, snowshoeing, snowshoed 2** (*intr*) to walk or go using snowshoes > **'snow,shoer** *n*

snowstorm ('snəʊ,stɔːm) *n* a storm with heavy snow

snow tyre *n* a motor-vehicle tyre with deep treads to give improved grip on snow and ice

snow-white *adj* **1** white as snow **2** pure as white snow

snowy ('snəʊɪ) *adj* **snowier, snowiest 1** covered with or abounding in snow: *snowy hills* **2** characterized by snow: *snowy weather* **3** resembling snow in whiteness, purity, etc > **'snowily** *adv* > **'snowiness** *n*

Snowy Mountains *pl n* a mountain range in SE Australia, part of the Australian Alps: famous hydroelectric scheme. Also called (Austral informal): **the Snowy, the Snowies** > **Snowy Mountain** *adj*

snowy owl *n* a large owl of tundra regions, having a white plumage flecked with brown

Snowy River *n* a river in SE Australia, rising in SE New South Wales: waters diverted through a system of dams and tunnels across the watershed into the Murray and Murrumbidgee Rivers for hydroelectric power and to provide water for irrigation. Length: 426 km (265 miles)

SNP *abbrev for* Scottish National Party

Snr *or* **snr** *abbrev for* senior

snub (snʌb) *vb* **snubs, snubbing, snubbed** (*tr*) **1** to insult (someone) deliberately **2** to stop or check the motion of (a boat, horse, etc) by taking turns of a rope around a post ▷ *n* **3** a deliberately insulting act or remark **4** *naut* an elastic shock absorber attached to a mooring line ▷ *adj* **5** short and blunt. See also **snub-nosed** [C14 from ON *snubba* to scold] > **'snubber** *n* > **'snubby** *adj*

snub-nosed *adj* **1** having a short turned-up nose **2** (of a pistol) having an extremely short barrel

snuff[1] (snʌf) *vb* **1** (*tr*) to inhale through the nose **2** (when *intr*, often foll by *at*) (esp of an animal) to examine by sniffing ▷ *n* **3** an act or the sound of snuffing [C16 prob. from MDu. *snuffen* to snuffle, ult. imit.] > **'snuffer** *n*

snuff[2] (snʌf) *n* **1** finely powdered tobacco, esp for sniffing up the nostrils **2** a small amount of this **3 up to snuff** *inf* **3a** in good health or in good condition **3b** *chiefly Brit* not easily deceived ▷ *vb* **4** (*intr*) to use or inhale snuff [C17 from Du. *snuf*, shortened from *snuftabale*, lit.: tobacco for snuffing]

snuff[3] (snʌf) *vb* (*tr*) **1** (often foll by *out*) to extinguish (a light from a candle) **2** to cut off the charred part of (the wick of a candle, etc) **3** (usually foll by *out*) *inf* to put an end to **4 snuff it** *Brit inf* to die ▷ *n* **5** the burned portion of the wick of a candle [C14 *snoffe*, from ?]

snuffbox ('snʌf,bɒks) *n* a container, often of elaborate ornamental design, for holding small quantities of snuff

snuff-dipping *n* the practice of absorbing nicotine by holding in one's mouth, between the cheek and the gum, a small amount of tobacco

snuffer ('snʌfə) *n* **1** a cone-shaped implement for extinguishing candles **2** (*pl*) an instrument resembling a pair of scissors for trimming the wick or extinguishing the flame of a candle

snuffle ('snʌfᵊl) *vb* **snuffles, snuffling, snuffled 1** (*intr*) to breathe noisily or with difficulty **2** to say or speak in a nasal tone **3** (*intr*) to snivel ▷ *n* **4** an act or the sound of snuffling **5** a nasal voice **6 the snuffles** a condition characterized by snuffling [C16 from Low G or Du. *snuffelen*] > **'snuffly** *adj*

snuff movie *or* **film** *n sl* a pornographic film in which an unsuspecting actress or actor is murdered as the climax of the film

snuffy ('snʌfɪ) *adj* **snuffier, snuffiest 1** of or resembling snuff **2** covered with or smelling of snuff **3** disagreeable > **'snuffiness** *n*

snug (snʌg) *adj* **snugger, snuggest 1** comfortably warm and well protected; cosy: *the children were snug in bed* **2** small but comfortable: *a snug cottage* **3** well ordered; compact: *a snug boat* **4** sheltered and secure: *a snug anchorage* **5** fitting closely and comfortably **6** offering safe concealment ▷ *n* **7** (in Britain and Ireland) one of the bars in certain pubs, offering intimate seating for only a few persons ▷ *vb* **snugs, snugging, snugged 8** to make or become comfortable and warm [C16 (in the sense: prepared for storms (used of a ship)) from O Icelandic *snöggr* short-haired, from Swedish *snygg* tidy] > **'snugly** *adv* > **'snugness** *n*

snuggery ('snʌgərɪ) *n, pl* **snuggeries 1** a cosy and comfortable place or room **2** another name for **snug** (sense 7)

snuggle ('snʌgᵊl) *vb* **snuggles, snuggling, snuggled 1** (usually *intr*; usually foll by *down*, *up*, or *together*) to nestle into or draw close to (somebody or something) for warmth or from affection ▷ *n* **2** the act of snuggling [C17 frequentative of SNUG (vb)]

so¹ (səʊ) *adv* **1** (foll by an adjective or adverb and a correlative clause often introduced by *that*) to such an extent: *the river is so dirty that it smells* **2** (*used with a negative*; it replaces the first *as* in an equative comparison) to the same extent as: *she is not so old as you* **3** (intensifier): *it's so lovely* **4** in the state or manner expressed or implied: *they're happy and will remain so* **5** (*not used with a negative*; foll by an auxiliary verb or *do*, *have*, or *be* used as main verbs) also: *I can speak Spanish and so can you* **6** *dialect* indeed: used to contradict a negative statement: *"you didn't phone her." "I did so!"* **7** *arch* provided that **8 and so on** *or* **forth** and continuing similarly **9 or so** approximately: *fifty or so people came to see me* **10 so be it** used to express agreement or resignation **11 so much 11a** a certain degree or amount (of) **11b** a lot (of): *it's just so much nonsense* **12 so much for 12a** no more can or need be said about **12b** used to express contempt for something that has failed ▷ *conj* (*subordinating*; often foll by *that*) **13** in order (that): *to die so that you might live* **14** with the consequence (that): *he was late home, so that there was trouble* **15 so as** (*takes an infinitive*) in order (to): *to diet so as to lose weight* ▷ *sentence connector* **16** in consequence: *she wasn't needed, so she left* **17** thereupon: *and so we ended up in France* **18 so what!** *inf* what importance does that have? ▷ *pron* **19** used to substitute for a clause or sentence, which may be understood: *you'll stop because I said so* ▷ *adj* **20** (used with *is*, *was*, etc) factual: *it can't be so* ▷ *interj* **21** an exclamation of surprise, etc [OE *swā*]

so² (səʊ) *n music* a variant spelling of **soh**

soak (səʊk) *vb* **1** to make, become, or be thoroughly wet or saturated, esp by immersion in a liquid **2** (when *intr*, usually foll by *in* or *into*) (of a liquid) to penetrate or permeate **3** (*tr*; usually foll by *in* or *up*) (of a permeable solid) to take in (a liquid) by absorption: *the earth soaks up rainwater* **4** (*tr*; foll by *out* or *out of*) to remove by immersion in a liquid: *she soaked the stains out of the dress* **5** *inf* to drink excessively or make or become drunk **6** (*tr*) *sl* to overcharge ▷ *n* **7** the act of immersing in a liquid or the period of immersion **8** the liquid in which something may be soaked **9** *Austral* a natural depression holding rainwater, esp just beneath the surface of the ground **10** *sl* a person who drinks to excess [OE *sōcian* to cook] > **'soaker** *n* > **'soaking** *n, adj* > **'soakingly** *adv*

soakaway ('səʊkə,weɪ) *n* a pit filled with rubble, etc, into which waste water drains

so-and-so *n, pl* **so-and-sos** *inf* **1** a person whose name is forgotten or ignored **2** *euphemistic* a person or thing regarded as unpleasant: *which so-and-so broke my razor?*

Soane (səʊn) *n* Sir **John** 1753–1837, British architect. His work includes Dulwich College Art Gallery (1811–14) and his own house in Lincoln's Inn Fields, London (1812–13), which is now the Sir John Soane's Museum

soap (səʊp) *n* **1** a cleaning agent made by reacting animal or vegetable fats or oils with potassium or sodium hydroxide. Soaps act by emulsifying grease and lowering the surface tension of water, so that it more readily penetrates open materials such as textiles **2** any metallic salt of a fatty acid, such as palmitic or stearic acid **3** *sl* flattery or persuasive talk (esp in **soft soap**) **4** *inf* short for **soap opera 5 no soap** *sl* not possible ▷ *vb* (*tr*) **6** to apply soap to **7** (often foll by *up*) *sl* to flatter [OE *sāpe*] > **'soapless** *adj* > **'soap,like** *adj*

soapberry ('səʊp,bɛrɪ) *n, pl* **soapberries 1** any of various chiefly tropical American trees having pulpy fruit containing saponin **2** the fruit of any of these trees

soapbox ('səʊp,bɒks) *n* **1** a box or crate for packing soap **2** a crate used as a platform for speech-making **3** a child's home-made racing cart

soapie *or* **soapy** ('səʊpɪ) *n Austral* an informal word for **soap opera**

soap opera *n* a serialized drama, usually dealing with domestic themes, broadcast on radio or television. Often shortened to **soap** [C20 so called because manufacturers of soap were typical sponsors]

▷ www.soapcity.com

▷ www.bbc.co.uk/puresoap

soapstone ('səʊp,stəʊn) *n* a massive compact soft variety of talc, used for making table tops, hearths, ornaments, etc. Also called: **steatite**

soapsuds ('səʊp,sʌdz) *pl n* foam or lather made from soap > **'soap,sudsy** *adj*

soapwort ('səʊp,wɜːt) *n* a Eurasian plant having rounded clusters of fragrant pink or white flowers and leaves that were formerly used as a soap substitute. Also called: **bouncing Bet**

soapy ('səʊpɪ) *adj* **soapier, soapiest 1** containing or covered with soap: *soapy water* **2** resembling or characteristic of soap **3** *sl* flattering > **'soapily** *adv* > **'soapiness** *n*

soar (sɔː) *vb* (*intr*) **1** to rise or fly upwards into the air **2** (of a bird, aircraft, etc) to glide while maintaining altitude by the use of ascending air currents **3** to rise or increase in volume, size, etc: *soaring prices* [C14 from OF *essorer*, from Vulgar L *exaurāre* (unattested) to expose to the breezes, from L EX-¹ + *aura* breeze] > **'soarer** *n* > **'soaring** *n, adj* > **'soaringly** *adv*

Soares (*Portuguese* 'swarɪʃ) *n* **Mário** ('mərju) born 1924, Portuguese statesman; prime minister of Portugal (1976–77; 1978–80; 1983–86); president of Portugal (1986–96)

sob (sɒb) *vb* **sobs, sobbing, sobbed 1** (*intr*) to weep with convulsive gasps **2** (*tr*) to utter with sobs **3** to cause (oneself) to be in a specified state by sobbing: *to sob oneself* *to sleep* ▷ *n* **4** a convulsive gasp made in weeping [C12 prob. from Low G] > **'sobbing** *n, adj*

soba ('səʊbə) *pl n* (in Japanese cookery) noodles made from buckwheat flour [Japanese]

sober ('səʊbə) *adj* **1** not drunk **2** not given to excessive indulgence in drink or any other activity **3** sedate and rational: *a sober attitude to a problem* **4** (of colours) plain and dull or subdued **5** free from exaggeration or speculation: *he told us the sober truth* ▷ *vb* **6** (usually foll by *up*) to make or become less intoxicated [C14 *sobre*, from OF, from L *sōbrius*] > **'sobering** *n, adj* > **'soberly** *adv*

Sobers ('səʊbəz) *n* Sir **Garfield St Auburn,** known as *Garry*. born 1936, West Indian (Barbadian) cricketer; one of the finest all-rounders of all time

sobriety (səʊ'braɪətɪ) *n* **1** the state or quality of being sober **2** the quality of refraining from excess **3** the quality of being serious or sedate

sobriety coach *n* a person who helps someone who has been dependent on alcohol or drugs to maintain an abstinent lifestyle

sobriquet *or* **soubriquet** ('səʊbrɪˌkeɪ) *n* a humorous epithet, assumed name, or nickname [C17 from F *soubriquet*, from ?]

sob story *n* a tale of personal distress intended to arouse sympathy

Soc. *or* **soc.** *abbrev for:* **1** socialist **2** society

soca ('səʊkə) *n* a mixture of soul and calypso music typical of the E Caribbean [C20 a blend of *soul* + *calypso*]

socage ('sɒkɪdʒ) *n English legal history* the tenure of land by certain services, esp of an agricultural nature [C14 from Anglo-F, from *soc* SOKE]

so-called *adj* **a** (*prenominal*) designated or styled by the name or word mentioned, esp (in the speaker's opinion) incorrectly: *a so-called genius* **b** (also used parenthetically after a noun): *these experts, so-called, are no help*

soccer ('sɒkə) *n* **a** a game in which two teams of eleven players try to kick or head a ball into their opponents' goal, only the goalkeeper on either side being allowed to touch the ball with his or her hands and arms, except in the case of throw-ins **b** (*as modifier*): *a soccer player* ▷ Also called: **Association Football** [C19 from *Assoc(iation Football)* + -ER[1]]

socceroo (ˌsɒkə'ruː) *n, pl* **socceroos** *Austral sl* a member of the Australian men's national soccer team [C20 from SOCCER + (KANGAR)OO]

Soche *or* **So-ch'e** ('səʊ'tʃɛ) *n* a variant transliteration of the Chinese name for **Shache**

Sochi (*Russian* 'sɔtʃi) *n* a city and resort in SW Russia, in the Krasnodar Territory on the Black Sea: hot mineral springs. Pop: 359 300 (1995 est)

sociable ('səʊʃəbᵊl) *adj* **1** friendly or companionable **2** (of an occasion) providing the opportunity for friendliness and conviviality ▷ *n* **3** *chiefly US* a social **4** a type of open carriage with two seats facing each other [C16 via F from L, from *sociāre* to unite, from *socius* an associate] > ˌ**socia'bility** *n* > **'sociably** *adv*

social ('səʊʃəl) *adj* **1** living or preferring to live in a community rather than alone **2** denoting or relating to human society or any of its subdivisions **3** of or characteristic of the behaviour and interaction of persons forming groups **4** relating to or having the purpose of promoting companionship, communal activities, etc: *a social club* **5** relating to or engaged in social services: *a social worker* **6** relating to or considered appropriate to a certain class of society **7** (esp of certain species of insects) living together in organized colonies: *social bees* **8** (of plant species) growing in clumps ▷ *n* **9** an informal gathering, esp of an organized group [C16 from L *sociālis* companionable, from *socius* a comrade] > **'socially** *adv*

Social and Liberal Democrats *pl n* (in Britain) a political party formed in 1988 by the merging of the Liberal Party and part of the Social Democratic Party; in 1989 it changed its name to the Liberal Democrats

social anthropology *n* the branch of anthropology that deals with cultural and social phenomena such as kinship systems or beliefs

social capital *n* the network of social connections that exist between people, and their shared values and norms of behaviour, which enable and encourage mutually advantageous social cooperation

Social Chapter *n* the section of the **Maastricht Treaty** concerning working conditions, consultation of workers, employment rights, and social security

Social Charter *n* a declaration of the rights, minimum wages, maximum hours, etc, of workers in the European Union, codified in the Maastricht Treaty (1992)

social climber *n* a person who seeks advancement to a higher social class, esp by obsequious behaviour > **social climbing** *n*

social contract *or* **compact** *n* (in the theories of Locke, Hobbes, Rousseau, and others) an agreement, entered into by individuals, that results in the formation of the state, the prime motive being the desire for protection, which entails the surrender of some personal liberties

Social Credit *n* **1** (esp in Canada) a right-wing Populist political party, movement, or doctrine **2** **Social Credit League** (in New Zealand) a middle-of-the-road political party, in favour of free enterprise **3** **Social Credit Rally** (in Canada) a political party formed in 1963 from a splinter group of the Social Credit Party

social democrat *n* **1** any socialist who believes in the gradual transformation of capitalism into democratic socialism **2** (*usually cap*) a member of a Social Democratic Party > **social democracy** *n*

Social Democratic and Labour Party *n* a Northern Irish political party, which advocates peaceful union with the Republic of Ireland. Abbrev: **SDLP**

Social Democratic Party *n* **1** (in Britain, 1981–90) a political party founded by ex-members of the Labour Party. It formed an alliance with the Liberal Party and continued in a reduced form after many members left to join the Social and Liberal Democrats in 1988 **2** one of the two major political parties in Germany, favouring gradual reform **3** any of the parties in many other countries similar to that of Germany

social dumping *n* the practice of allowing employers to lower wages and reduce employees' benefits in order to attract and retain employment and investment

social engineering *n* the manipulation of the social position and function of individuals in order to manage change in a society

social exclusion *n sociol* the failure of society to provide certain individuals and groups with those rights and benefits normally available to its members, such as employment, adequate housing, health care, education and training, etc

social fund *n* (in Britain) a social security fund from which loans or payments may be made to people in cases of extreme need

social inclusion *n sociol* the provision of certain rights to all individuals and groups in society, such as employment, adequate housing, health care, education and training, etc

social insurance *n* government insurance providing coverage for the unemployed, the injured, the old, etc: usually financed by contributions from employers and employees

Social Insurance Number *n Canad* an identification number issued to individuals by the government in connection with income tax and social insurance

socialism ('səʊʃəˌlɪzəm) *n* **1** an economic theory or system in which the means of production, distribution, and exchange are owned by the community collectively, usually through the state ▷ Cf **capitalism** **2** any of various social or political theories or movements in which the common welfare is to be achieved through the establishment of a socialist economic system **3** (in Leninist theory) a transitional stage in the development of a society from capitalism to communism: characterized by the distribution of income according to work rather than need

socialist ('səʊʃəlɪst) *n* **1** a supporter or advocate of socialism or any party promoting socialism (**socialist party**) ▷ *adj* **2** of, implementing, or relating to socialism **3** (*sometimes cap*) of or relating to socialists or a socialist party > ˌ**socia'listic** *adj*

Socialist International *n* an international association of largely anti-Communist Social Democratic Parties founded in Frankfurt in 1951

socialist realism *n* (in Communist countries, esp formerly) the doctrine that art, literature, etc, should present an idealized portrayal of reality, which glorifies the achievements of the Communist Party

socialite ('səʊʃəˌlaɪt) *n* a person who is or seeks to be prominent in fashionable society

sociality (ˌsəʊʃɪ'ælɪtɪ) *n, pl* **socialities 1** the tendency of groups and persons to develop social links and live in communities **2** the quality or state of being social

socialize *or* **socialise** ('səʊʃəˌlaɪz) *vb* **socializes, socializing, socialized** *or* **socialises, socialising, socialised 1** (*intr*) to behave in a friendly or sociable manner **2** (*tr*) to prepare for life in society **3** (*tr*) *chiefly US* to alter or create so as to be in accordance with socialist principles

social market *n* **a** an economic system in which industry and commerce are run by private enterprise within limits set by the government to ensure equality of opportunity and social and environmental responsibility **b** (*as modifier*): *a social-market economy*

social realism *n* **1** the use of realist art, literature, etc, as a medium for social or political comment **2** another name for **socialist realism**

social science *n* **1** the study of society and of the relationship of individual members within society, including economics, history, political science, psychology, anthropology, and sociology **2** any of these subjects studied individually > **social scientist** *n*

▷ www.sosig.ac.uk/social_science_general/

▷ http://bitbucket.icaap.org/

social secretary *n* **1** a member of an organization who arranges its social events **2** a personal secretary who deals with private correspondence, etc

social security *n* **1** public provision for the economic welfare of the aged, unemployed, etc, esp through pensions and other monetary assistance **2** (*often cap*) a government programme designed to provide such assistance

social services *pl n* welfare activities organized by the state or a local authority and carried out by trained personnel

social studies *n* (*functioning as sing*) the study of how people live and organize themselves in society, embracing geography, history, economics, and other subjects

social welfare *n* **1** social services provided by a state for the benefit of its citizens **2** (*caps*) (in New Zealand) a government department concerned with pensions and benefits for the elderly, the sick, etc

▷ www.sosig.ac.uk/social_welfare/

▷ www.eswin.net

▷ www.unfpa.org

social work *n* any of various social services designed to alleviate the conditions of the poor and aged and to increase the welfare of children > **social worker** *n*

societal (sə'saɪətᵊl) *adj* of or relating to society, esp human society > **so'cietally** *adv*

societal marketing *n* **1** marketing that takes into account society's long-term welfare **2** the marketing of a social or charitable cause, such as an anti-apartheid campaign

society (sə'saɪətɪ) *n, pl* **societies 1** the totality of social relationships among organized groups of human beings or animals **2** a system of human organizations generating distinctive cultural patterns and institutions **3** such a system with reference to its mode of social and economic organization or its dominant class: *middle-class society* **4** those with whom one has companionship **5** an organized group of people associated for some specific purpose or on account of some common interest: *a learned society* **6a** the privileged class of people in a community, esp as considered superior or fashionable **6b** (*as modifier*): *a society woman* **7** the social life and intercourse of such people: *to enter society* **8** companionship: *I enjoy her society* **9** *ecology* a small community of plants within a larger association [C16 via OF *societé* from L *societās*, from *socius* a comrade]

Society Islands *pl n* a group of islands in the S Pacific: administratively part of French Polynesia; consists of the Windward Islands and the Leeward Islands; became a French protectorate in 1843 and a colony in 1880. Pop: 189 524 (1996). Area: 1595 sq km (616 sq miles)

Society of Jesus *n* the religious order of the Jesuits, founded by Ignatius Loyola

socio- *combining form* denoting social or society: *socioeconomic; sociopolitical; sociology*

sociobiology (ˌsəʊsɪəʊbaɪ'ɒlədʒɪ) *n* the study of social behaviour in animals and humans > ˌ**sociobi'ologist** *n*

socioeconomic (ˌsəʊsɪəʊˌiːkə'nɒmɪk, -ˌɛkə-) *adj* of, relating to, or involving both economic and social factors > ˌ**socioˌeco'nomically** *adv*

sociolinguistics (ˌsəʊsɪəʊlɪŋ'gwɪstɪks) *n* (*functioning as sing*) the study of language in relation to its social context > ˌ**socio'linguist** *n*

sociology (ˌsəʊsɪ'ɒlədʒɪ) *n* the study of the development, organization, functioning, and classification of human societies > **sociological** (ˌsəʊsɪə'lɒdʒɪkᵊl) *adj* > ˌ**soci'ologist** *n*

▷ www.sosig.ac.uk/sociology

▷ www2.fmg.uva.nl/sociosite/topics/sociologists.html

sociometry (ˌsəʊsɪ'ɒmɪtrɪ) *n* the study of sociological relationships within groups > **sociometric** (ˌsəʊsɪə'mɛtrɪk) *adj* > ˌ**soci'ometrist** *n*

sociopath ('səʊsɪəˌpæθ) *n psychiatry* another term for **psychopath** > ˌ**socio'pathic** *adj* > **sociopathy** (ˌsəʊsɪ'ɒpəθɪ) *n*

sociopolitical (ˌsəʊsɪəʊpə'lɪtɪkᵊl) *adj* of or involving both political and social factors

sock[1] (sɒk) *n* **1** a cloth covering for the foot, reaching to between the ankle and knee and worn inside a shoe **2** an insole put in a shoe, as to make it fit better **3** a light shoe worn by actors in ancient Greek and Roman comedy **4 pull one's socks up** *Brit inf* to make a determined effort, esp to improve one's behaviour or performance **5 put a sock in it** *Brit sl* be quiet! [OE *socc* a light shoe, from L *soccus*, from Gk *sukkhos*]

sock[2] (sɒk) *sl* ▷ *vb* **1** (*usually tr*) to hit with force **2 sock it to** *sl* to make a forceful impression on ▷ *n* **3** a forceful blow [C17 from ?]

socket ('sɒkɪt) *n* **1** a device into which an electric plug can be inserted in order to make a connection in a circuit **2** *chiefly Brit* such a device mounted on a wall and connected to the electricity supply; power point **3** a part with an opening or hollow into which some other part can be fitted **4** *anat* **4a** a bony hollow into which a part or structure fits: *an eye socket* **4b** the receptacle of a ball-and-socket joint ▷ *vb* **5** (*tr*) to furnish with or place into a socket [C13 from Anglo-Norman *soket* a little ploughshare, from *soc*, of Celtic origin]

socket set *n* a set of tools consisting of a handle into which various interchangeable heads can be fitted

sockeye ('sɒkˌaɪ) *n* a Pacific salmon having red flesh and valued as a food fish. Also called: **red salmon** [by folk etymology from *sukkegh*, of Amerind origin]

socle ('səʊkᵊl) *n* another name for **plinth** (sense 1) [C18 via F from It. *zoccolo*, from L *socculus* a little shoe, from *soccus* a SOCK[1]]

Socotra (sə'kəʊtrə) *n* an island in the Indian Ocean, about 240 km (150 miles) off Cape Guardafui, Somalia: administratively part of Yemen. Capital: Tamrida. Area: 3100 sq km (1200 sq miles)

Socrates ('sɒkrəˌtiːz) *n* ?470–399 BC, Athenian philosopher, whose beliefs are known only through the writings of his pupils Plato and Xenophon. He taught that virtue was based on knowledge, which was attained by a dialectical process that took into account many aspects of a stated hypothesis. He was indicted for impiety and corruption of youth (399) and was condemned to death. He refused to flee and died by drinking hemlock

Socratic (sɒ'krætɪk) *adj* **1** of or relating to Socrates, his methods, etc ▷ *n* **2** a person who follows the teachings of Socrates > **So'cratically** *adv* > **So'cratiˌcism** *n* > **Socratist** ('sɒkrətɪst) *n*

Socratic irony *n philosophy* a means by which the feigned ignorance of a questioner leads the person answering to expose his own ignorance

Socratic method *n philosophy* the method of instruction by question and answer used by Socrates in order to elicit from his pupils truths he considered to be implicitly known by all rational beings

sod[1] (sɒd) *n* **1** a piece of grass-covered surface soil held together by the roots of the grass; turf **2** *poetic* the ground ▷ *vb* **sods, sodding, sodded 3** *(tr)* to cover with sods [C15 from Low G]

sod[2] (sɒd) *sl, chiefly Brit* ▷ *n* **1** a person considered to be obnoxious **2** a jocular word for a **person 3 sod all** *sl* nothing ▷ *interj* **4 sod it** a strong exclamation of annoyance. See also **sod off** [C19 shortened from SODOMITE] > **'sodding** *adj*

soda ('səʊdə) *n* **1** any of a number of simple inorganic compounds of sodium, such as sodium carbonate (**washing soda**), sodium bicarbonate (**baking soda**), and sodium hydroxide (**caustic soda**) **2** See **soda water 3** *US & Canad* a fizzy drink [C16 from Med. L, from *sodanum* barilla, a plant that was burned to obtain a type of sodium carbonate, ?from Ar.]

soda ash *n* the anhydrous commercial form of sodium carbonate

soda bread *n* a type of bread leavened with sodium bicarbonate combined with milk and cream of tartar

soda fountain *n US & Canad* **1** a counter that serves drinks, snacks, etc **2** an apparatus dispensing soda water

sodality (səʊ'dælɪtɪ) *n, pl* **sodalities 1** *RC Church* a religious society **2** fellowship [C16 from L *sodālitās* fellowship, from *sodālis* a comrade]

sodamide ('səʊdəˌmaɪd) *n* a white crystalline compound used as a dehydrating agent and in making sodium cyanide. Formula: $NaNH_2$

soda siphon *n* a sealed bottle containing and dispensing soda water. The water is forced up a tube reaching to the bottom of the bottle by the pressure of gas above the water

soda water *n* an effervescent beverage made by charging water with carbon dioxide under pressure. Sometimes shortened to **soda**

sodden ('sɒdᵊn) *adj* **1** completely saturated **2a** dulled, esp by excessive drinking **2b** *(in combination): a drink-sodden mind* **3** doughy, as bread is when improperly cooked ▷ *vb* **4** to make or become sodden [C13 *soden*, p.p. of SEETHE] > **'soddenness** *n*

Soddy ('sɒdɪ) *n* **Frederick** 1877–1956, English chemist, whose work on radioactive disintegration led to the discovery of isotopes: Nobel prize for chemistry 1921

sodium ('səʊdɪəm) *n* **a** a very reactive soft silvery-white element of the alkali metal group occurring principally in common salt, Chile saltpetre, and cryolite. It is used in the production of chemicals, in metallurgy, and, alloyed with potassium, as a cooling medium in nuclear reactors. Symbol: Na; atomic no.: 11; atomic wt.: 22.99 **b** *(as modifier): sodium light* [C19 NL, from SODA + -IUM]

sodium amytal *n* another name for **Amytal**

sodium benzoate *n* a white crystalline soluble compound used in preserving food (**E 211**), as an antiseptic, and in making dyes

sodium bicarbonate *n* a white crystalline soluble compound used in effervescent drinks, baking powders, fire-extinguishers, and in medicine as an antacid; sodium hydrogen carbonate. Formula: $NaHCO_3$. Systematic name: **sodium hydrogencarbonate.** Also called: **bicarbonate of soda, baking soda**

sodium carbonate *n* a colourless or white odourless soluble crystalline compound used in the manufacture of glass, ceramics, soap, and paper, and as a cleansing agent. Formula: Na_2CO_3

sodium chlorate *n* a colourless crystalline soluble compound used as a bleaching agent, antiseptic, and weedkiller. Formula: $NaClO_3$

sodium chloride *n* common table salt; a soluble colourless crystalline compound widely used as a seasoning and preservative for food and in the manufacture of chemicals, glass, and soap. Formula: NaCl. Also called: **salt**

sodium cyanide *n* a white odourless crystalline soluble poisonous compound used for extracting gold and silver from their ores and for case-hardening steel. Formula: NaCN

sodium glutamate ('gluːtəˌmeɪt) *n* another name for **monosodium glutamate**

sodium hydrogencarbonate *n* the systematic name for **sodium bicarbonate**

sodium hydroxide *n* a white strongly alkaline solid used in the manufacture of rayon, paper, aluminium, soap, and sodium compounds. Formula: NaOH. Also called: **caustic soda**

sodium hyposulphite *n* another name (not in technical usage) for **sodium thiosulphate**

sodium lamp *n* another name for **sodium-vapour lamp**

sodium nitrate *n* a white crystalline soluble solid compound used in matches, explosives, and rocket propellants, as a fertilizer, and as a curing salt for preserving food (**E 251**). Formula: $NaNO_3$

Sodium Pentothal *n trademark* another name for **thiopental sodium**

sodium silicate *n* **1** Also called: **soluble glass** See **water glass 2** any sodium salt of a silicic acid

sodium sulphate *n* a solid white substance used in making glass, detergents, and pulp. Formula: Na_2SO_4. See **salt cake** and **Glauber's salt**

sodium thiosulphate *n* a white soluble substance used in photography as a fixer to dissolve unchanged silver halides and also to remove excess chlorine from chlorinated water. Formula: $Na_2S_2O_3$. Also called (not in technical usage): **sodium hyposulphite, hypo**

sodium-vapour lamp *n* a type of electric lamp consisting of a glass tube containing neon and sodium vapour at low pressure through which an electric current is passed to give an orange light: used in street lighting

sod off *sl, chiefly Brit* ▷ *interj* **1** a forceful expression of dismissal ▷ *vb* **sods, sodding, sodded 2** *(intr, adv)* to go away

Sodom ('sɒdəm) *n* **1** *Old Testament* a city destroyed by God for its wickedness that, with Gomorrah, traditionally typifies depravity (Genesis 19:24) **2** this city as representing homosexuality **3** any place notorious for depravity: *Vienna was a Sodom of licentiousness*

sodomite ('sɒdəˌmaɪt) *n* a person who practises sodomy

sodomize *or* **sodomise** ('sɒdəˌmaɪz) *vb* **sodomizes, sodomizing, sodomized** *or* **sodomises, sodomising, sodomised** (*tr*) to be the active partner in anal intercourse with (a person)

sodomy ('sɒdəmɪ) *n* anal intercourse committed by a man with another man or a woman [c13 via OF *sodomie* from L (Vulgate) *Sodoma* Sodom]

Sod's law (sɒdz) *n inf* a facetious precept stating that if something can go wrong or turn out inconveniently it will

Soekarno (suː'kɑːnəʊ) *n* a variant spelling of (Achmed) **Sukarno**

Soembawa (suːm'bɑːwə) *n* a variant spelling of **Sumbawa**

soever (səʊ'ɛvə) *adv* in any way at all: used to emphasize or make less precise a word or phrase, usually in combination with *what, where, when, how*, etc, or else separated by intervening words ▷ Cf **whatsoever**

sofa ('səʊfə) *n* an upholstered seat with back and arms for two or more people [c17 (in the sense: dais upholstered as a seat): from Ar. *suffah*]

soffit ('sɒfɪt) *n* the underside of a part of a building or a structural component, such as an arch, beam, stair, etc [c17 via F from It. *soffitto*, from L *suffixus* something fixed underneath, from *suffigere*, from *sub-* under + *figere* to fasten]

Sofia ('səʊfɪə) *n* the capital of Bulgaria, in the west: colonized by the Romans in 29 AD; became capital of Bulgaria in 1879; university (1880). Pop: 1 122 302 (1999 est). Ancient name: **Serdica** Bulgarian name: **Sofiya** ('sɔfiˌja)
▷ www.sofia.bg

S. of Sol. *Bible abbrev for* Song of Solomon

soft (sɒft) *adj* **1** easy to dent, work, or cut without shattering; malleable **2** not hard; giving little or no resistance to pressure or weight **3** fine, light, smooth, or fluffy to the touch **4** gentle; tranquil **5** (of music, sounds, etc) low and pleasing **6** (of light, colour, etc) not excessively bright or harsh **7** (of a breeze, climate, etc) temperate, mild, or pleasant **8** slightly blurred; not sharply outlined: *soft focus* **9** (of a diet) consisting of easily digestible foods **10** kind or lenient, often excessively so **11** easy to influence or impose upon **12** prepared to compromise; not doctrinaire: *the soft left* **13** *inf* feeble or silly; simple (often in **soft in the head**) **14** unable to endure hardship, esp through pampering **15** physically out of condition; flabby: *soft muscles* **16** loving; tender: *soft words* **17** *inf* requiring little exertion; easy: *a soft job* **18** *chem* (of water) relatively free of mineral salts and therefore easily able to make soap lather **19** (of a drug such as cannabis) nonaddictive **20** *phonetics* (not in technical usage) denoting the consonants *c* and *g* in English when they are pronounced as palatal or alveolar fricatives or affricates (s, dʒ, ʃ, ð, tʃ) before *e* and *i*, rather than as velar stops (k, g) **21** *finance, chiefly US* (of prices, a market, etc) unstable and tending to decline **22** (of currency) in relatively little demand, esp because of a weak balance of payments situation **23** (of radiation, such as X-rays and ultraviolet radiation) having low energy and not capable of deep penetration of materials **24** related to the performance of nonspecific generalized tasks: *soft skills such as customer services and office support* **25** **soft on** *or* **about 25a** gentle, sympathetic, or lenient towards **25b** feeling affection or infatuation for ▷ *adv* **26** in a soft manner: *to speak soft* ▷ *n* **27** a soft object, part, or piece **28** *inf* See **softie** ▷ *sentence substitute arch* **29** quiet! **30** wait! [OE *sōfte*] > **'softly** *adv* > **'softness** *n*

softa ('sɒftə) *n* a Muslim student of divinity and jurisprudence, esp in Turkey [c17 from Turkish, from Persian *sōkhtah* aflame (with love of learning)]

softball ('sɒftˌbɔːl) *n* a variation of baseball using a larger softer ball, pitched underhand
▷ www.internationalsoftball.com

soft ball *n cookery* a term used for sugar syrup boiled to a consistency at which it may be rubbed into balls after dipping in cold water

soft-boiled *adj* (of an egg) boiled for a short time so that the yolk is still soft

soft coal *n* another name for **bituminous coal**

soft commodities *pl n* nonmetal commodities, such as cocoa, sugar, and grains, bought and sold on a futures market. Also called: **softs**

soft-core *adj* (of pornography) suggestive and titillating through not being totally explicit

soft-cover *adj* a less common word for **paperback**

soft drink *n* a nonalcoholic drink

soften ('sɒfᵊn) *vb* **1** to make or become soft or softer **2** to make or become more gentle > **'softener** *n*

softening of the brain *n* an abnormal softening of the tissues of the cerebrum characterized by mental impairment

soft-focus lens *n photog* a lens designed to produce an image that is slightly out of focus: typically used for portrait work

soft furnishings *pl n Brit* curtains, hangings, rugs, etc

soft goods *pl n* textile fabrics and related merchandise. Also called (US and Canad): **dry goods**

soft-headed *adj* **1** *inf* feeble-minded; stupid; simple **2** (of a stick or hammer for playing a percussion instrument) having a soft head > **ˌsoft-'headedness** *n*

softhearted (ˌsɒft'hɑːtɪd) *adj* easily moved to pity > **ˌsoft'heartedly** *adv* > **ˌsoft'heartedness** *n*

softie *or* **softy** ('sɒftɪ) *n, pl* **softies** *inf* a person who is sentimental, weakly foolish, or lacking in physical endurance

soft landing *n* **1** a landing by a spacecraft on a celestial body at a sufficiently low velocity for the equipment or occupants to remain unharmed **2** a painless resolution of a problem **3** a gentle economic slowdown in which a recession is avoided ▷ Cf **hard landing**

soft option *n* in a number of choices, the one involving the least difficulty or exertion

soft palate *n* the posterior fleshy portion of the roof of the mouth

soft paste *n* **a** artificial porcelain made from clay, bone ash, etc **b** (*as modifier*): *softpaste porcelain*

soft-pedal *vb* **soft-pedals, soft-pedalling, soft-pedalled** *or US* **soft-pedals, soft-pedaling, soft-pedaled** (*tr*) **1** to mute the tone of (a piano) by depressing the soft pedal **2** *inf* to make (something, esp something unpleasant) less obvious by deliberately failing to emphasize or allude to it ▷ *n* **soft pedal 3** a foot-operated lever on a piano, the left one of two, that either moves the whole action closer to the strings so that the hammers strike with less force or causes fewer of the strings to sound

soft porn *n inf* soft-core pornography

softs (sɒfts) *pl n* another name for **soft commodities**

soft science *n* a science, such as sociology or anthropology, that deals with humans as its principle subject matter, and is therefore not generally considered to be based on rigorous experimentation

soft sell *n* a method of selling based on indirect suggestion or inducement

soft shoulder *or* **verge** *n* a soft edge along the side of a road that is unsuitable for vehicles to drive on

soft skills *pl n* desirable qualities for certain forms of employment that do not depend on acquired knowledge: they include common sense, the ability to deal with people, and a positive flexible attitude

soft soap *n* **1** *med* Also called: **green soap** a soft or liquid alkaline soap used in treating certain skin disorders **2** *inf* flattering, persuasive, or cajoling talk ▷ *vb* **soft-soap 3** *inf* to use such talk on (a person)

soft-spoken *adj* **1** speaking or said with a soft gentle voice **2** able to persuade or impress by glibness of tongue
soft spot *n* a sentimental fondness (esp in **have a soft spot for**)
soft touch *n inf* a person easily persuaded or imposed on, esp to lend money
software ('sɒftˌwɛə) *n computing* the programs that can be used with a particular computer system ▷ Cf **hardware** (sense 2)
softwood ('sɒftˌwʊd) *n* **1** the open-grained wood of any of numerous coniferous trees, such as pine and cedar **2** any tree yielding this wood
Sogdiana (ˌsɒgdɪ'ɑːnə) *n* a region of ancient central Asia. Its chief city was Samarkand > '**Sogdian** *adj, n*
soggy ('sɒgɪ) *adj* **soggier, soggiest 1** soaked with liquid **2** (of bread, pastry, etc) moist and heavy **3** *inf* lacking in spirit or positiveness [c18 prob. from dialect *sog* marsh, from ?] > '**soggily** *adv* > '**sogginess** *n*
soh *or* **so** (səʊ) *n music* (in tonic sol-fa) the name used for the fifth note or dominant of any scale [c14 later variant of *sol*; see GAMUT]
Soho ('səʊhəʊ) *n* a district of central London, in the City of Westminster: a foreign quarter since the late 17th century, now chiefly known for restaurants, nightclubs, striptease clubs, etc
soi-disant *French* (swadizɑ̃) *adj* so-called; self-styled [lit.: calling oneself]
soigné *or* (*fem*) **soignée** ('swɑːnjeɪ) *adj* well-groomed; elegant [F, from *soigner* to take good care of, of Gmc origin]
soil[1] (sɔɪl) *n* **1** the top layer of the land surface of the earth that is composed of disintegrated rock particles, humus, water, and air **2** a type of this material having specific characteristics: *loamy soil* **3** land, country, or region: *one's native soil* **4 the soil** life and work on a farm; land: *he belonged to the soil* **5** any place or thing encouraging growth or development [c14 from Anglo-Norman, from L *solium* a seat, but confused with L *solum* the ground]
soil[2] (sɔɪl) *vb* **1** to make or become dirty or stained **2** (*tr*) to pollute with sin or disgrace; sully; defile ▷ *n* **3** the state or result of soiling **4** refuse, manure, or excrement [c13 from OF *soillier* to defile, from *soil* pigsty, prob. from L *sūs* a swine]
soil[3] (sɔɪl) *vb* (*tr*) to feed (livestock) green fodder to fatten or purge them [c17 ?from obs. vb (c16) *soil* to manure, from SOIL[2] (n)]
soil pipe *n* a pipe that conveys sewage or waste water from a toilet, etc, to a soil drain or sewer
soiree ('swɑːreɪ) *n* an evening party or gathering, usually at a private house, esp where guests listen to, play, or dance to music [c19 from F, from OF *soir* evening, from L *sērum* a late time, from *sērus* late]
Soissons (*French* swasɔ̃) *n* a city in N France, on the Aisne River: has Roman remains and an 11th-century abbey. Pop: 32 144 (1990)
soixante-neuf *French* (swasɑ̃tnœf) *n* a sexual activity in which two people simultaneously stimulate each other's genitalia with their mouths. Also called: **sixty-nine** [lit.: sixty-nine, from the position adopted by the participants]
sojourn ('sɒdʒɜːn, 'sʌdʒ-) *n* **1** a temporary stay ▷ *vb* **2** (*intr*) to stay or reside temporarily [c13 from OF *sojorner*, from Vulgar L *subdiurnāre* (unattested) to spend a day, from L *sub-* during + LL *diurnum* day] > '**sojourner** *n*
soke (səʊk) *n English legal history* **1** the right to hold a local court **2** the territory under the jurisdiction of a particular court [c14 from Med. L *sōca*, from OE *sōcn* a seeking]
Sokoto ('səʊkəˌtəʊ) *n* **1** a state of NW Nigeria. Capital: Sokoto. Pop: 4 524 162 (1992 est). Area: 65 735 sq km (25 380 sq miles) **2** a town in NW Nigeria, capital of Sokoto state: capital of the Fulah Empire in the 19th century; Muslim place of pilgrimage. Pop: 204 900 (1997 est)
sol[1] (sɒl) *n music* the syllable used in the fixed system of solmization for the note G [c14 see GAMUT]
sol[2] (sɒl) *n* a colloid that has a continuous liquid phase, esp one in which a solid is suspended in a liquid [c20 shortened from SOLUTION]
Sol (sɒl) *n* **1** the Roman god personifying the sun **2** a poetic word for the **sun**
Sol. *abbrev for:* **1** Also: **Solr** solicitor **2** *Bible* Solomon
sola *Latin* ('səʊlə) *adj* the feminine form of ***solus***
solace ('sɒlɪs) *n* **1** comfort in misery, disappointment, etc **2** something that gives comfort or consolation ▷ *vb* **solaces, solacing, solaced** (*tr*) **3** to give comfort or cheer to (a person) in time of sorrow, distress, etc **4** to alleviate (sorrow, misery, etc) [c13 from OF *solas*, from L *sōlātium* comfort, from *sōlārī* to console] > '**solacer** *n*
solan *or* **solan goose** ('səʊlən) *n* an archaic name for the **gannet** [c15 *soland*, from ON]
solanaceous (ˌsɒlə'neɪʃəs) *adj* of or relating to the Solanaceae, a family of plants having typically tubular flowers, protruding anthers, and often poisonous or narcotic properties: includes the potato, tobacco, and several nightshades [c19 from NL *Sōlānāceae*, from L *sōlānum* nightshade]
Solana (**Madariaga**) (səʊ'lɑːnə) *n* **Javier** ('hævɪeɪ) born 1942, Spanish socialist politician; minister for foreign affairs (1992–95), secretary-general of NATO (1995–99), and EU high representative for foreign policy from 1999
solanum (səʊ'leɪnəm) *n* any tree, shrub, or herbaceous plant of the mainly tropical solanaceous genus *Solanum:* includes the potato and certain nightshades [c16 from L: nightshade]
solar ('səʊlə) *adj* **1** of or relating to the sun **2** operating by or utilizing the energy of the sun: *solar cell* **3** *astron* determined from the motion of the earth relative to the sun: *solar year* **4** *astrol* subject to the influence of the sun [c15 from L *sōlāris*, from *sōl* the sun]
solar cell *n* a cell that produces electricity from the sun's rays, used esp in spacecraft
solar constant *n* the rate at which the sun's energy is received per unit area at the top of the earth's atmosphere when the sun is at its mean distance from the earth and atmospheric absorption has been corrected for
solar day *n* See under **day** (sense 6)
solar energy *n* energy obtained from solar power
solar flare *n* a brief powerful eruption of intense high-energy radiation from the sun's surface, associated with sunspots and causing radio and magnetic disturbances on earth
solarium (səʊ'lɛərɪəm) *n, pl* **solariums** *or* **solaria** (-'lɛərɪə) **1** a room built largely of glass to afford exposure to the sun **2** a bed equipped with ultraviolet lights used for acquiring an artificial suntan **3** an establishment offering such facilities [c19 from L: a terrace, from *sōl* sun]
solar month *n* See under **month** (sense 4)
solar plexus *n* **1** *anat* the network of nerves situated behind the stomach that supply the abdominal organs. Also called: **coeliac plexus 2** (not in technical usage) the part of the stomach beneath the diaphragm; pit of the stomach [c18 referring to resemblance between the radial network of nerves & ganglia & the rays of the sun]
solar power *n* radiation from the sun used to heat a fluid or to generate electricity using solar cells
solar system *n* the system containing the sun and the bodies held in its gravitational field, including the planets (Mercury, Venus, earth, Mars, Jupiter, Saturn, Uranus, Neptune, Pluto), the asteroids, and comets
▷ www.solarviews.com
▷ www.the-solar-system.net
▷ http://ssd.jpl.nasa.gov

Solar System

Mercury
DISTANCE FROM THE SUN = 57,909,175 km
VOLUME (Earth = 1) = 0.054
SIDEREAL ROTATION PERIOD = 58.646225 earth days
SIDEREAL ORBIT PERIOD = 0.2408467 sidereal years
MASS = 0.3302 X 10 g
INCLINATION OF EQUATOR TO ORBIT = 0.0 degrees
NUMBER OF MOONS = 0

Venus
DISTANCE FROM THE SUN = 108,208,930 km
VOLUME (Earth = 1) = 0.88
SIDEREAL ROTATION PERIOD = 243.0187 earth days (retrograde)
SIDEREAL ORBIT PERIOD = 0.61519726 sidereal years
MASS = 4.8690 X 10 g
INCLINATION OF EQUATOR TO ORBIT = 177.3 degrees
NUMBER OF MOONS = 0

Earth
DISTANCE FROM THE SUN = 149,597,890 km
SIDEREAL ROTATION PERIOD = 0.99726968 earth day
SIDEREAL ORBIT PERIOD = 1.0000174 sidereal years
MASS = 5.9742 X 10 g
INCLINATION OF EQUATOR TO ORBIT = 23.45 degrees
NUMBER OF MOONS = 1
NAME OF MOON:
The Moon

Mars
DISTANCE FROM THE SUN = 227,936,640 km
VOLUME (Earth = 1) = 0.149
SIDEREAL ROTATION PERIOD = 1.02595675earth days
SIDEREAL ORBIT PERIOD = 1.8808476 sidereal years
MASS = 0.64191 X 10 g
INCLINATION OF EQUATOR TO ORBIT =25.19 degrees
NUMBER OF MOONS = 2
NAMES OF MOONS:
Phobos
Deimos

Jupiter
DISTANCE FROM THE SUN = 778,412,010 km
VOLUME (Earth = 1) = 1316
SIDEREAL ROTATION PERIOD = 0.41354 earth day
SIDEREAL ORBIT PERIOD = 11.862615 sidereal years
MASS = 1,898.7 X 10 g
INCLINATION OF EQUATOR TO ORBIT = 3.12 degrees
NUMBER OF MOONS = 61
NAMES OF MOONS:
Metis
Adrastea
Amalthea
Thebe
Io
Europa
Ganymede
Callisto
Themisto
Leda
Himalia
Lysithea
Elara
S/2000 J11
Iocaste
Praxidike
Harpalyke
Ananke
Isonoe
Erinome
Taygete
Chaldene
Carme
Pasiphae
S/2002 J1
Kalkyke
Megaclite
Sinope
Callirhoe
Euporie
Kale
Orthosie
Thyone
Euanthe
Hermippe
Pasithee
Eurydome
Aitne
Sponde
Autonoe
S/2003 J1
S/2003 J2
S/2003 J3
S/2003 J4
S/2003 J5
S/2003 J6
S/2003 J7
S/2003 J8
S/2003 J9
S/2003 J10
S/2003 J11
S/2003 J12
S/2003 J13
S/2003 J14
S/2003 J15
S/2003 J16
S/2003 J17
S/2003 J18
S/2003 J19
S/2003 J20
S/2003 J21

Saturn
DISTANCE FROM THE SUN = 1,426,725,400 km
VOLUME (Earth = 1) = 755
SIDEREAL ROTATION PERIOD = 0.44401 earth day
SIDEREAL ORBIT PERIOD = 29.447498 sidereal years
MASS = 568.51 X 10 g
INCLINATION OF EQUATOR TO ORBIT = 26.73 degrees
NUMBER OF MOONS = 30
NAMES OF MOONS:
Pan
Atlas
Prometheus
Pandora
Epimetheus
Janus
Mimas
Enceladus
Tethys
Telesto
Calypso
Dione
Helene
Rhea
Titan
Hyperion
Iapetus

Phoebe
Ymir
Paaliaq
Siarnaq
Tarvos
Kiviuq
Ijiraq
Thrym
Skadi
Mundilfari
Erriapo
Albiorix
Suttung
S/2003 S1

Uranus
DISTANCE FROM THE SUN = 2,870,972,200 km
VOLUME (Earth = 1) = 52
SIDEREAL ROTATION PERIOD = 0.71833 earth day
SIDEREAL ORBIT PERIOD = 84.016846 sidereal years
MASS = 86.849 x 10 g
INCLINATION OF EQUATOR TO ORBIT = 97.86 degrees
NUMBER OF MOONS = 21
NAMES OF MOONS:
Cordelia
Ophelia
Bianca
Cressida
Desdemona
Juliet
Portia
Rosalind
Belinda
Puck
Miranda
Ariel
Umbriel
Titania
Oberon
Caliban
Stephano
Trinculo
Sycorax
Prospero
Setebos

Neptune
DISTANCE FROM THE SUN = 4,498,252,900 km
VOLUME (Earth = 1) = 44
SIDEREAL ROTATION PERIOD = 0.67125 earth day
SIDEREAL ORBIT PERIOD = 164.79132 sidereal years
MASS = 102.44 x 10 g
INCLINATION OF EQUATOR TO ORBIT = 29.58 degrees
NUMBER OF MOONS = 11
NAMES OF MOONS:
Naiad
Thalassa
Despina
Galatea
Larissa
Proteus
Triton
Nereid
S/2002 N1
S/2002 N2
S/2002 N3

Pluto
DISTANCE FROM THE SUN = 5,906,376,200 km
VOLUME (Earth = 1) = 0.005
SIDEREAL ROTATION PERIOD = 6.38718 earth days (retrograde)
SIDEREAL ORBIT PERIOD = 247.92065 sidereal years
MASS = 0.013 x 10 g
EQUATORIAL INCLINATION = 119.61 degrees
NUMBER OF MOONS = 1
NAME OF MOON:
Charon

▷ http://solarsystem.nasa.gov/features/planets

solar wind (wɪnd) *n* the stream of charged particles, such as protons, emitted by the sun at high velocities, its intensity increasing during periods of solar activity

solar year *n* See under **year** (sense 4)

solatium (səʊˈleɪʃɪəm) *n, pl* **solatia** (-ʃɪə) *law, chiefly US & Scot* compensation awarded for injury to the feelings as distinct from physical suffering and pecuniary loss [C19 from L: see SOLACE]

sold (səʊld) *vb* **1** the past tense and past participle of **sell** ▷ *adj* **2** **sold on** *sl* uncritically attached to or enthusiastic about

solder (ˈsɒldə; *US* ˈsɒdər) *n* **1** an alloy used for joining two metal surfaces by melting the alloy so that it forms a thin layer between the surfaces **2** something that joins things together firmly; a bond ▷ *vb* **3** to join or mend or be joined or mended with or as if with solder [C14 via OF from L *solidāre* to strengthen, from *solidus* solid] > ˈ**solderable** *adj* > ˈ**solderer** *n*

soldering iron *n* a hand tool consisting of a handle fixed to a copper tip that is heated and used to melt and apply solder

soldier (ˈsəʊldʒə) *n* **1a** a person who serves or has served in an army **1b** Also called: **common soldier** a noncommissioned member of an army as opposed to a commissioned officer **2** a person who works diligently for a cause **3** *zool* an individual in a colony of social insects, esp ants, that has powerful jaws adapted for defending the colony, crushing food, etc ▷ *vb* **4** (*intr*) to serve as a soldier [C13 from OF *soudier*, from *soude* (army) pay, from LL *solidus* a gold coin, from L: firm] > ˈ**soldierly** *adj*

soldier of fortune *n* a man who seeks money or adventure as a soldier; mercenary

soldier on *vb* (*intr, adv*) to persist in one's efforts in spite of difficulties, pressure, etc

soldiery (ˈsəʊldʒərɪ) *n, pl* **soldieries** **1** soldiers collectively **2** a group of soldiers **3** the profession of being a soldier

sole[1] (səʊl) *adj* **1** (*prenominal*) being the only one; only **2** (*prenominal*) of or relating to one individual or group and no other: *sole rights* **3** *law* having no wife or husband **4** an archaic word for **solitary** [C14 from OF *soule*, from L *sōlus* alone] > ˈ**soleness** *n*

sole[2] (səʊl) *n* **1** the underside of the foot **2** the underside of a shoe **3a** the bottom of a furrow **3b** the bottom of a plough **4** the underside of a golf-club head ▷ *vb* **soles, soling, soled** (*tr*) **5** to provide (a shoe) with a sole [C14 via OF from L *solea* sandal]

sole[3] (səʊl) *n, pl* **sole** *or* **soles** any of various tongue-shaped flatfishes, esp the **European sole**: most common in warm seas and highly valued as food fishes [C14 via OF from Vulgar L *sola* (unattested), from L *solea* a sandal (from the fish's shape)]

sole-charge school *n* *NZ* a rural school with only one teacher

solecism (ˈsɒlɪˌsɪzəm) *n* **1a** the nonstandard use of a grammatical construction **1b** any mistake, incongruity, or absurdity **2** a violation of good manners [C16 from L *soloecismus*, from Gk, from *soloikos* speaking incorrectly, from *Soloi* an Athenian colony of Cilicia where the inhabitants spoke a corrupt form of Greek] > ˈ**solecist** *n* > ˌ**sole**ˈ**cistic** *adj* > ˌ**sole**ˈ**cistically** *adv*

solely ('səʊllɪ) *adv* **1** only; completely **2** without others; singly **3** for one thing only

solemn ('sɒləm) *adj* **1** characterized or marked by seriousness or sincerity: *a solemn vow* **2** characterized by pomp, ceremony, or formality **3** serious, glum, or pompous **4** inspiring awe: *a solemn occasion* **5** performed with religious ceremony **6** gloomy or sombre: *solemn colours* [c14 from OF *solempne*, from L *sōllemnis* appointed, ?from *sollus* whole] > **'solemnly** *adv* > **'solemnness** *or* **'solemness** *n*

solemnify (sə'lɛmnɪ,faɪ) *vb* **solemnifies, solemnifying, solemnified** (*tr*) to make serious or grave > **so,lemnifi'cation** *n*

solemnity (sə'lɛmnɪtɪ) *n, pl* **solemnities 1** the state or quality of being solemn **2** (*often pl*) solemn ceremony, observance, etc **3** *law* a formality necessary to validate a deed, contract, etc

solemnize *or* **solemnise** ('sɒləm,naɪz) *vb* **solemnizes, solemnizing, solemnized** *or* **solemnises, solemnising, solemnised** (*tr*) **1** to celebrate or observe with rites or formal ceremonies, as a religious occasion **2** to celebrate or perform the ceremony of (marriage) **3** to make solemn or serious **4** to perform or hold (ceremonies, etc) in due manner > **,solemni'zation** *or* **,solemni'sation** *n* > **'solem,nizer** *or* **'solem,niser** *n*

solenodon (sə'lɛnədən) *n* either of two rare shrewlike nocturnal mammals of the Caribbean having a long hairless tail and an elongated snout [c19 from NL, from L *sōlēn* sea mussel (from Gk: pipe) + Gk *odōn* tooth]

solenoid ('səʊlɪ,nɔɪd) *n* **1** a coil of wire, usually cylindrical, in which a magnetic field is set up by passing a current through it **2** a coil of wire, partially surrounding an iron core, that is made to move inside the coil by the magnetic field set up by a current: used to convert electrical to mechanical energy, as in the operation of a switch [c19 from F *solénoïde*, from Gk *sōlēn* a tube] > **,sole'noidal** *adj*

Solent ('səʊlənt) *n* **the** a strait of the English Channel between the coast of Hampshire, on the English mainland, and the Isle of Wight. Width: up to 6 km (4 miles)

Soleure (sɔlœr) *n* the French name for **Solothurn**

sol-fa ('sɒl'fɑː) *n* **1** short for **tonic sol-fa** ▷ *vb* **sol-fas, sol-faing, sol-faed 2** *US* to use tonic sol-fa syllables in singing (a tune) [c16 see GAMUT]

solfatara (,sɒlfə'tɑːrə) *n* a volcanic vent emitting only sulphurous gases and water vapour or sometimes hot mud [c18 from It.: a sulphurous volcano near Naples, from *solfo* sulphur]

solfeggio (sɒl'fɛdʒɪəʊ) *or* **solfège** (sɒl'fɛʒ) *n, pl* **solfeggi** (-'fɛdʒiː), **solfeggios,** *or* **solfèges** *music* **1** a voice exercise in which runs, scales, etc, are sung to the same syllable or syllables **2** solmization, esp the French or Italian system, in which the names correspond to the notes of the scale of C major [c18 from It. *solfeggiare* to use the syllables sol-fa; see GAMUT]

soli ('səʊlɪ) *adj, adv music* (of a piece or passage) (to be performed) by or with soloists

solicit (sə'lɪsɪt) *vb* **solicits, soliciting, solicited 1** (when *intr*, foll by *for*) to make a request, application, etc, to (a person for business, support, etc) **2** to accost (a person) with an offer of sexual relations in return for money **3** to provoke or incite (a person) to do something wrong or illegal [c15 from OF *solliciter* to disturb, from L *sollicitāre* to harass, from *sollus* whole + *ciēre* to excite] > **so,lici'tation** *n*

solicitor (sə'lɪsɪtə) *n* **1** (in Britain) a lawyer who advises clients on matters of law, draws up legal documents, prepares cases for barristers, etc **2** (in the US) an officer responsible for the legal affairs of a town, city, etc **3** a person who solicits > **so'licitor,ship** *n*

Solicitor General *n, pl* **Solicitors General 1** (in Britain) the law officer of the Crown ranking next to the Attorney General (in Scotland to the Lord Advocate) and acting as his assistant **2** (in New Zealand) the government's chief lawyer

solicitous (sə'lɪsɪtəs) *adj* **1** showing consideration, concern, attention, etc **2** keenly anxious or willing; eager [c16 from L *sollicitus* anxious; see SOLICIT] > **so'licitousness** *n*

solicitude (sə'lɪsɪ,tjuːd) *n* **1** the state or quality of being solicitous **2** (*often pl*) something that causes anxiety or concern **3** anxiety or concern

solid ('sɒlɪd) *adj* **1** of, concerned with, or being a substance in a physical state in which it resists changes in size and shape ▷ Cf **gas** (sense 1), **liquid** (sense 1) **2** consisting of matter all through **3** of the same substance all through: *solid rock* **4** sound; proved or provable: *solid facts* **5** reliable or sensible; upstanding: *a solid citizen* **6** firm, strong, compact, or substantial: *a solid table; solid ground* **7** (of a meal or food) substantial **8** (*often postpositive*) without interruption or respite: *solid bombardment* **9** financially sound or solvent: *a solid institution* **10** strongly linked or consolidated: *a solid relationship* **11 solid for** unanimously in favour of **12** *geom* having or relating to three dimensions **13** (of a word composed of two or more elements) written or printed as a single word without a hyphen **14** *printing* with no space or leads between lines of type **15** (of a writer, work, etc) adequate; sensible **16** of or having a single uniform colour or tone **17** *Austral* excessively severe or unreasonable ▷ *n* **18** *geom* **18a** a closed surface in three-dimensional space **18b** such a surface together with the volume enclosed by it **19** a solid substance, such as wood, iron, or diamond **20** (*pl*) solid food, as opposed to liquid: *babies are messy eaters when they start on solids* [c14 from OF *solide*, from L *solidus* firm] > **solidity** (sə'lɪdɪtɪ) *n* > **'solidly** *adv* > **'solidness** *n*

solidago (,sɒlɪ'deɪgəʊ) *n, pl* **solidagos** any plant of a chiefly American genus, which includes the goldenrods [c18 via NL from Med. L *soldago* a plant reputed to have healing properties, from *soldāre* to strengthen, from L *solidāre*, from *solidus* solid]

solid angle *n* an area subtended in three dimensions by lines intersecting at a point on a sphere whose radius is the distance to the point. See also **steradian**

solidarity (,sɒlɪ'dærɪtɪ) *n, pl* **solidarities** unity of interests, sympathies, etc, as among members of the same class

solid fuel *n* **1** a fuel, such as coal or coke, that is a solid rather than an oil or gas **2** Also called: **solid propellant** a rocket fuel that is a solid rather than a liquid or a gas

solid geometry *n* the branch of geometry concerned with three-dimensional geometric figures

solidify (sə'lɪdɪ,faɪ) *vb* **solidifies, solidifying, solidified 1** to make or become solid or hard **2** to make or become strong, united, determined, etc > **so,lidifi'cation** *n* > **so'lidi,fier** *n*

solid-state *n* (*modifier*) **1** (of an electronic device) activated by a semiconductor component in which current flow is through solid material rather than in a vacuum **2** of, concerned with, characteristic of, or consisting of solid matter

solid-state physics *n* (*functioning as sing*) the branch of physics concerned with the properties of solids, such as superconductivity, photoconductivity, and ferromagnetism

solidus ('sɒlɪdəs) *n, pl* **solidi** (-,daɪ) **1** Also called: **diagonal, oblique, separatrix, shilling mark, slash, stroke, virgule** a short oblique stroke used in text to separate items of information, such as days, months, and years in dates (*18/7/80*), alternative words (*and/or*), numerator from denominator in fractions (*55/103*), etc **2** a gold coin of the Byzantine empire [c14 from LL *solidus* (*nummus*) a gold coin (from *solidus* solid); in Med. L, *solidus* referred to a shilling and was indicated by a long *s*, which ult. became the virgule]

solifluction *or* **solifluxion** (ˈsɒlɪˌflʌkʃən, ˈsəʊlɪ-) *n* slow downhill movement of soil, saturated with meltwater, over a permanently frozen subsoil in tundra regions [c20 from L *solum* soil + *fluctio* act of flowing]

Solihull (ˌsəʊlɪˈhʌl) *n* **1** a town in central England, in Solihull unitary authority in the S West Midlands near Birmingham: mainly residential. Pop: 94 531 (1991) **2** a unitary authority in central England, in the West Midlands. Pop: 199 521 (2001). Area: 180 sq km (70 sq miles)

soliloquize *or* **soliloquise** (səˈlɪləˌkwaɪz) *vb* **soliloquizes, soliloquizing, soliloquized** *or* **soliloquises, soliloquising, soliloquised** (*intr*) to utter a soliloquy > **soˈliloquist** *n* > **soˈliloˌquizer** *or* **soˈliloˌquiser** *n*

soliloquy (səˈlɪləkwɪ) *n, pl* **soliloquies** **1** the act of speaking alone or to oneself, esp as a theatrical device **2** a speech in a play that is spoken in soliloquy [c17 via LL *sōliloquium*, from L *sōlus* sole + *loquī* to speak]

> **USAGE** *Soliloquy* is sometimes wrongly used where *monologue* is meant. Both words refer to a long speech by one person, but a *monologue* can be addressed to other people, whereas in a *soliloquy* the speaker is always talking to himself or herself

Soliman (ˈsɒlɪmən) *n* a variant spelling of **Suleiman I**

Solimões (suliˈmõəʃ) *n* **the** the Brazilian name for the Amazon from the Peruvian border to the Rio Negro

Solingen (*German* ˈzoːlɪŋən) *n* a city in W Germany, in North Rhine-Westphalia: a major European centre of the cutlery industry. Pop: 165 400 (1999 est)

solipsism (ˈsɒlɪpˌsɪzəm) *n philosophy* the extreme form of scepticism which denies the possibility of any knowledge other than of one's own existence [c19 from L *sōlus* alone + *ipse* self] > **ˈsolipsist** *n, adj* > **ˌsolipˈsistic** *adj*

solitaire (ˈsɒlɪˌtɛə, ˌsɒlɪˈtɛə) *n* **1** Also called: **pegboard** a game played by one person, esp one involving moving and taking pegs in a pegboard with the object of being left with only one **2** the US name for **patience** (the card game) **3** a gem, esp a diamond, set alone in a ring **4** any of several extinct birds related to the dodo **5** any of several dull grey North American songbirds [c18 from OF: SOLITARY]

solitary (ˈsɒlɪtərɪ, -trɪ) *adj* **1** following or enjoying a life of solitude: *a solitary disposition* **2** experienced or performed alone: *a solitary walk* **3** (of a place) unfrequented **4** (*prenominal*) single; sole: *a solitary cloud* **5** having few companions; lonely **6** (of animals) not living in organized colonies or large groups: *solitary bees* **7** (of flowers) growing singly ▷ *n, pl* **solitaries** **8** a person who lives in seclusion; hermit **9** *inf* short for **solitary confinement** [c14 from L *sōlitārius*, from *sōlus* SOLE[1]] > **ˈsolitarily** *adv* > **ˈsolitariness** *n*

solitary confinement *n* isolation imposed on a prisoner, as by confinement in a special cell

solitude (ˈsɒlɪˌtjuːd) *n* **1** the state of being solitary or secluded **2** *poetic* a solitary place [c14 from L *sōlitūdō*, from *sōlus* alone, SOLE[1]] > **ˌsoliˈtudinous** *adj*

solmization *or* **solmisation** (ˌsɒlmɪˈzeɪʃən) *n music* a system of naming the notes of a scale by syllables instead of letters, which assigns the names *ut* (or *do*), *re*, *mi*, *fa*, *sol*, *la*, *si* (or *ti*) to the degrees of the major scale of C (**fixed system**) or (excluding the syllables *ut* and *si*) to the major scale in any key (**movable system**) See also **tonic sol-fa** [c18 from F *solmisation*, from *solmiser* to use the sol-fa syllables, from SOL[1] + MI]

solo (ˈsəʊləʊ) *n, pl* **solos** **1** (*pl* **solos** *or* **soli** (-liː)) a musical composition for one performer with or without accompaniment **2** any of various card games in which each person plays on his or her own, such as solo whist **3** a flight in which an aircraft pilot is unaccompanied **4a** any performance carried out by an individual without assistance **4b** (*as modifier*): *a solo attempt* ▷ *adj* **5** *music* unaccompanied: *a sonata for cello solo* ▷ *adv* **6** by oneself; alone: *to fly solo* ▷ *vb* **7** (*intr*) to operate an aircraft alone [c17 via It. from L *sōlus* alone] > **soloist** (ˈsəʊləʊɪst) *n*

Solomon (ˈsɒləmən) *n* 10th century BC, king of Israel, son of David and Bathsheba, credited with great wisdom > **Solomonic** (ˌsɒləˈmɒnɪk) *or* **Solomonian** (ˌsɒləˈməʊnɪən) *adj*

Solomon Gundy (ˈsɒləmən ˈɡʌndɪ) *n Canad* a dish of salted marinated herring in vinegar and spices [from SALMAGUNDI]

Solomon Islands *pl n* an independent state in the SW Pacific comprising an archipelago extending for almost 1450 km (900 miles) in a northwest–southeast direction: the northernmost islands of the archipelago (Buka and Bougainville) form part of Papua New Guinea; the main islands are Guadalcanal, Malaita, San Cristobal, New Georgia, Santa Isabel, and Choiseul: a member of the Commonwealth. Official language: English. Religion: Christian majority. Currency: Solomon Islands dollar. Capital: Honiara. Pop: 480 000 (2001 est). Area: 29 785 sq km (11 500 sq miles)
▷ www.solomons.com
▷ www.commerce.gov.sb/Tourism

Solomon's seal *n* **1** another name for **Star of David** **2** any of several plants of N temperate regions, having greenish or yellow paired flowers, long narrow waxy leaves, and prominent leaf scars [c16 translation of Med. L *sigillum Solomonis*, ?from resemblance of the leaf scars to seals]

Solon (ˈsəʊlən) *n* ?638–?559 BC, Athenian statesman, who introduced economic, political, and legal reforms. *adj*

so long *sentence substitute* **1** *inf* farewell; goodbye ▷ *adv* **2** *S African sl* for the time being; meanwhile

solo parent *n* NZ the usual name for **single parent**

Solothurn (*German* ˈzoːlotʊrn) *n* **1** a canton of NW Switzerland. Capital: Solothurn. Pop: 243 900 (2000 est). Area: 793 sq km (306 sq miles) **2** a town in NW Switzerland, capital of Solothurn canton, on the Aare River. Pop: 15 480 (1990 est) ▷ French name **Soleure**

solo whist *n* a version of whist for four players acting independently, each of whom may bid to win or lose a fixed number of tricks

solstice (ˈsɒlstɪs) *n* **1** either the shortest day of the year (**winter solstice**) or the longest day of the year (**summer solstice**) **2** either of the two points on the ecliptic at which the sun is overhead at the tropic of Cancer or Capricorn at the summer and winter solstices [c13 via OF from L *sōlstitium*, lit.: the (apparent) standing still of the sun, from *sōl* sun + *sistere* to stand still] > **solstitial** (sɒlˈstɪʃəl) *adj*

Solti (ˈʃɒltɪ) *n* Sir **Georg** (ˈɡeːɔrk) 1912–97, British conductor, born in Hungary

soluble (ˈsɒljʊbəl) *adj* **1** (of a substance) capable of being dissolved, esp easily dissolved **2** capable of being solved or answered [c14 from LL *solūbilis*, from L *solvere* to dissolve] > **ˌsoluˈbility** *n* > **ˈsolubly** *adv*

solus (ˈsəʊləs) *adj* **1** alone; separate **2** of or denoting the position of an advertising poster or press advertisement that is separated from competing advertisements: *a solus position* **3** of or denoting a retail outlet, such as a petrol station, that sells the products of one company exclusively: *a solus site* **4** (*fem* **sola**) alone; by oneself (formerly used in stage directions) [c17 from L *sōlus* alone]

solute (ˈsɒljuːt) *n* **1** the substance in a solution that is dissolved ▷ *adj* **2** *bot, now rare* loose or unattached; free [c16 from L *solūtus* free, from *solvere* to release]

solution (səˈluːʃən) *n* **1** a homogeneous mixture of two or more substances in which the molecules or atoms of the substances are completely dispersed **2** the act or process of forming a solution **3** the state of being dissolved (esp in **in solution**) **4** a mixture of substances in which one or more components are present as small particles with colloidal dimension: *a colloidal solution* **5** a specific answer to or way of answering a problem **6** the act or process of solving a problem **7** *maths* **7a** the unique set of values that yield a true statement when substituted for the variables in an equation **7b** a member of a set of assignments of values to variables under which a given statement is satisfied; a member of a solution set [C14 from L *solūtiō* an unloosing, from *solūtus*; see SOLUTE]

solution set *n* another name for **truth set**

Solutrean (sə'lu:trɪən) *adj* of or relating to an Upper Palaeolithic culture of Europe [C19 after *Solutré*, village in central France where traces of this culture were orig. found]

solvation (sɒl'veɪʃən) *n* the process in which there is some chemical association between the molecules of a solute and those of the solvent

Solvay process ('sɒlveɪ) *n* an industrial process for manufacturing sodium carbonate. Carbon dioxide is passed into a solution of sodium chloride saturated with ammonia. Sodium bicarbonate is precipitated and heated to form the carbonate [C19 after Ernest *Solvay* (1838–1922), Belgian chemist who invented it]

solve (sɒlv) *vb* **solves, solving, solved** (*tr*) **1** to find the explanation for or solution to (a mystery, problem, etc) **2** *maths* **2a** to work out the answer to (a problem) **2b** to obtain the roots of (an equation) [C15 from L *solvere* to loosen] > **'solvable** *adj*

solvent ('sɒlvənt) *adj* **1** capable of meeting financial obligations **2** (of a substance, esp a liquid) capable of dissolving another substance ▷ *n* **3** a liquid capable of dissolving another substance **4** something that solves [C17 from L *solvēns* releasing, from *solvere* to free] > **'solvency** *n*

solvent abuse *n* the deliberate inhaling of intoxicating fumes given off by certain solvents

Solway Firth ('sɒlweɪ) *n* an inlet of the Irish Sea between SW Scotland and NW England. Length: about 56 km (35 miles)

Solyman ('sɒlɪmən) *n* a variant spelling of **Suleiman I**

Solzhenitsyn (ˌsɒlʒə'nɪtsɪn; *Russian* səlʒə'nitsin) *n* **Alexander Isayevich** (alɪk'sandr i'sajɪvitʃ) born 1918, Russian novelist. His books include *One Day in the Life of Ivan Denisovich* (1962), *The First Circle* (1968), *Cancer Ward* (1968), *August 1914* (1971), *The Gulag Archipelago* (1974), and *October 1916* (1985). His works criticize the Soviet regime and he was imprisoned (1945–53) and exiled to Siberia (1953–56). He was deported to the West from the Soviet Union in 1974; all charges against him were dropped in 1991 and he returned to Russia in 1994. Nobel prize for literature 1970

Som. *abbrev for* Somerset

soma¹ ('səʊmə) *n, pl* **somata** (-mətə) *or* **somas** the body of an organism, as distinct from the germ cells [C19 via NL from Gk *sōma* the body]

soma² ('səʊmə) *n* an intoxicating plant juice drink used in Vedic rituals [from Sansk.]

Somali (səʊ'mɑ:lɪ) *n* **1** (*pl* **Somalis** *or* **Somali**) a member of a tall dark-skinned people inhabiting Somalia **2** the Cushitic language of this people ▷ *adj* **3** of, relating to, or characteristic of Somalia, the Somalis, or their language

Somalia (səʊ'mɑ:lɪə) *n* a republic in NE Africa, on the Indian Ocean and the Gulf of Aden: the north became a British protectorate in 1884; the east and south were established as an Italian protectorate in 1889; gained independence and united as the Somali Republic in 1960. In 1991 the former British Somaliland region in the north unilaterally declared itself independent as the Republic of Somaliland but this has not been recognized officially. Official languages: Arabic and Somali. Official religion: (Sunni) Muslim. Currency: Somali shilling. Capital: Mogadishu. Pop: 7 489 000 (2001 est). Area: 637 541 sq km (246 154 sq miles) > **So'malian** *adj, n*
▷ http://goafrica.about.com/cs/countriesaz/index_3.htm

Somaliland (səʊ'mɑ:lɪˌlænd) *n* a former region of E Africa, between the equator and the Gulf of Aden: includes Somalia, Djibouti, and SE Ethiopia

somatic (səʊ'mætɪk) *adj* **1** of or relating to the soma: *somatic cells* **2** of or relating to an animal body or body wall as distinct from the viscera, limbs, and head **3** of or relating to the human body as distinct from the mind: *a somatic disease* [C18 from Gk *sōmatikos* concerning the body, from *sōma* the body] > **so'matically** *adv*

somato- *or before a vowel* **somat-** *combining form* body: *somatotype* [from Gk *sōma*, *sōmat-* body]

somatogenic (səˌmætəʊ'dʒɛnɪk) *adj* *med* originating in the cells of the body: of organic, rather than mental, origin: *a somatogenic disorder*

somatotype ('səʊmətəˌtaɪp) *n* a type or classification of physique or body build. See **endomorph, mesomorph, ectomorph**

sombre *or US* **somber** ('sɒmbə) *adj* **1** dismal; melancholy: *a sombre mood* **2** dim, gloomy, or shadowy **3** (of colour, clothes, etc) sober, dull, or dark [C18 from F, from Vulgar L *subumbrāre* (unattested) to shade, from L *sub* beneath + *umbra* shade] > **'sombrely** *or US* **'somberly** *adv* > **'sombreness** *or US* **'somberness** *n* > **sombrous** ('sɒmbrəs) *adj*

sombrero (sɒm'brɛərəʊ) *n, pl* **sombreros** a hat with a wide brim, as worn in Mexico [C16 from Sp., from *sombrero de sol* shade from the sun]

some (sʌm; *unstressed* səm) *determiner* **1a** (a) certain unknown or unspecified: *some people never learn* **1b** (*as pron; functioning as sing or pl*): *some can teach and others can't* **2a** an unknown or unspecified quantity or amount of: *there's some rice on the table; he owns some horses* **2b** (*as pron; functioning as sing or pl*): *we'll buy some* **3a** a considerable number or amount of: *he lived some years afterwards* **3b** a little: *show him some respect* **4** (*usually stressed*) *inf* an impressive or remarkable: *that was some game!* ▷ *adv* **5** about; approximately: *some thirty pounds* **6** a certain amount (more) (in **some more** and (*inf*) **and then some**) **7** *US, not standard* to a certain degree or extent: *I like him some* [OE *sum*]

-some¹ *suffix forming adjectives* characterized by; tending to: *awesome; tiresome* [OE *-sum*]

-some² *suffix forming nouns* indicating a group of a specified number of members: *threesome* [OE *sum*, special use of SOME (determiner)]

-some³ (-səʊm) *n combining form* a body: *chromosome* [from Gk *sōma* body]

somebody ('sʌmbədɪ) *pron* **1** some person; someone ▷ *n, pl* **somebodies** **2** a person of great importance: *he is somebody in this town.*

USAGE See at **everyone**

someday ('sʌmˌdeɪ) *adv* at some unspecified time in the (distant) future

somehow ('sʌmˌhaʊ) *adv* **1** in some unspecified way **2** Also: **somehow or other** by any means that are necessary

someone ('sʌmˌwʌn, -wən) *pron* some person; somebody.

USAGE See at **everyone**

someplace ('sʌmˌpleɪs) *adv US & Canad inf* in, at, or to some unspecified place or region

somersault *or* **summersault** ('sʌməˌsɔ:lt) *n* **1a** a forward roll in which the head is placed on the ground and the trunk and legs are turned over it **1b** a similar roll in a backward direction **2** an acrobatic feat in which either of these rolls is performed in midair, as in diving or gymnastics **3** a complete reversal of opinion, policy, etc ▷ *vb* **4** (*intr*) to perform a somersault [C16 from OF *soubresault*, prob. from OProvençal *sobresaut*, from *sobre* over (from L *super*) + *saut* a jump, leap (from L *saltus*)]

Somerset[1] (ˈsʌməsɪt, -ˌsɛt) *n* a county of SW England, on the Bristol Channel: the Mendip Hills lie in the north and Exmoor in the west: the geographical and ceremonial county includes the unitary authorities of North Somerset and Bath and North East Somerset (both part of Avon county from 1975 until 1996): mainly agricultural (esp dairying and fruit). Administrative centre: Taunton. Pop (excluding unitary authorities): 498 093 (2001). Area (excluding unitary authorities): 3452 sq km (1332 sq miles)

Somerset[2] (ˈsʌməsɛt) *n* **1st Duke of,** title of *Edward Seymour*. ?1500–52, English statesman, protector of England (1547–49) during Edward VI's minority. He defeated the Scots (1547) and furthered the Protestant Reformation: executed

something (ˈsʌmθɪŋ) *pron* **1** an unspecified or unknown thing; some thing: *take something warm with you* **2** **something or other** one unspecified thing or an alternative thing **3** an unspecified or unknown amount: *something less than a hundred* **4** an impressive or important person, thing, or event: *isn't that something?* ▷ *adv* **5** to some degree; a little; somewhat: *to look something like me* **6** (foll by an *adj*) *inf* (intensifier): *it hurts something awful* **7** **something else** *sl, chiefly US* a remarkable person or thing

-something *n combining form* **a** a person whose age can be approximately expressed by a specified decade **b** (*as modifier*): *the thirtysomething market* [c20 from the US television series *thirtysomething*]

sometime (ˈsʌmˌtaɪm) *adv* **1** at some unspecified point of time ▷ *adj* **2** (*prenominal*) having been at one time; former: *the sometime President*.

> **USAGE** *Sometime* as a single word should only be used to refer to an unspecified point in time. When referring to a considerable length of time, you should use *some time*. Compare: *it was some time after, that the rose garden was planted*, ie after a considerable period of time, with *it was sometime after, that the rose garden was planted*, ie at some unspecified point after the move, but not necessarily a long time after

sometimes (ˈsʌmˌtaɪmz) *adv* **1** now and then; from time to time **2** *obs* formerly; sometime

someway (ˈsʌmˌweɪ) *adv* in some unspecified manner

somewhat (ˈsʌmˌwɒt) *adv* (*not used with a negative*) rather; a bit: *she found it somewhat odd*

somewhere (ˈsʌmˌwɛə) *adv* **1** in, to, or at some unknown or unspecified place or point: *somewhere in England; somewhere between 3 and 4 o'clock* **2** **get somewhere** *inf* to make progress

Somme (*French* sɔm) *n* **1** a department of N France, in Picardy region. Capital: Amiens. Pop: 555 551 (1999). Area: 6277 sq km (2448 sq miles) **2** a river in N France, rising in Aisne department and flowing west to Amiens, then northwest to the English Channel: scene of heavy fighting in World War I. Length: 245 km (152 miles)

sommelier (ˈsʌməlˌjeɪ) *n* a wine waiter [F: butler, via OF from OProvençal *saumalier* pack-animal driver, from LL *sagma* a packsaddle, from Gk]

somnambulate (sɒmˈnæmbjʊˌleɪt) *vb* **somnambulates, somnambulating, somnambulated** (*intr*) to walk while asleep [c19 from L *somnus* sleep + *ambulāre* to walk] > **somˈnambulance** *n* > **somˈnambulant** *adj, n* > **somˌnambuˈlation** *n* > **somˈnambuˌlator** *n*

somnambulism (sɒmˈnæmbjʊˌlɪzəm) *n* a condition characterized by walking while asleep or in a hypnotic trance. Also called: **noctambulism** > **somˈnambulist** *n*

somniferous (sɒmˈnɪfərəs) *or* **somnific** *adj rare* tending to induce sleep

somnolent (ˈsɒmnələnt) *adj* **1** drowsy; sleepy **2** causing drowsiness [c15 from L *somnus* sleep] > **ˈsomnolence** *or* **ˈsomnolency** *n* > **ˈsomnolently** *adv*

Somnus (ˈsɒmnəs) *n* the Roman god of sleep. Greek counterpart: **Hypnos**

son (sʌn) *n* **1** a male offspring; a boy or man in relation to his parents **2** a male descendant **3** (*often cap*) a familiar term of address for a boy or man **4** a male from a certain country, environment, etc: *a son of the circus* ▷ Related adj: **filial** [OE *sunu*] > **ˈsonless** *adj*

Son (sʌn) *n Christianity* the second person of the Trinity, Jesus Christ

sonant (ˈsəʊnənt) *adj* **1** *phonetics* denoting a voiced sound capable of forming a syllable or syllable nucleus **2** inherently possessing, exhibiting, or producing a sound **3** *rare* resonant; sounding ▷ *n* **4** *phonetics* a voiced sound belonging to the class of frictionless continuants or nasals (l, r, m, n, ŋ) considered from the point of view of being a vowel and, in this capacity, able to form a syllable or syllable nucleus [c19 from L *sonāns* sounding, from *sonāre* to make a noise, resound] > **ˈsonance** *n*

sonar (ˈsəʊnɑː) *n* a communication and position-finding device used in underwater navigation and target detection using echolocation [c20 from *so(und) na(vigation and) r(anging)*]

sonata (səˈnɑːtə) *n* **1** an instrumental composition, usually in three or more movements, for piano alone (**piano sonata**) or for any other instrument with or without piano accompaniment (**violin sonata, cello sonata,** etc) See also **sonata form** **2** a one-movement keyboard composition of the baroque period [c17 from It., from *sonare* to sound, from L]

sonata form *n* a musical structure consisting of an expanded ternary form whose three sections (exposition, development, and recapitulation), followed by a coda, are characteristic of the first movement in a sonata, symphony, string quartet, concerto, etc

sondage (sɒnˈdɑːʒ) *n, pl* **sondages** (-ˈdɑːʒɪz, -ˈdɑːʒ) *archaeol* a deep trial trench for inspecting stratigraphy [c20 from F: a sounding, from *sonder* to sound]

sonde (sɒnd) *n* a rocket, balloon, or probe used for observing in the upper atmosphere [c20 from F: plummet, plumb line; see SOUND[3]]

Sondheim (ˈsɒndhaɪm) *n* **Stephen (Joshua)** born 1930, US songwriter. He wrote the lyrics for *West Side Story* (1957), the score for *Company* (1971), and both for *A Little Night Music* (1973), *Into the Woods* (1987), and *Passion* (1994)

sone (səʊn) *n* a unit of loudness equal to 40 phons [c20 from L *sonus* a sound]

son et lumière (ˈsɒn eɪ ˈluːmɪˌɛə) *n* an entertainment staged at night at a famous building, historical site, etc, whereby the history of the location is presented by means of lighting effects, sound effects, and narration [F, lit.: sound and light]

song (sɒŋ) *n* **1a** a piece of music, usually employing a verbal text, composed for the voice, esp one intended for performance by a soloist **1b** the whole repertory of such pieces **1c** (*as modifier*): *a song book* **2** poetical composition; poetry **3** the characteristic tuneful call or sound made by certain birds or insects and also whales and bats **4** the act or process of singing: *they raised their voices in song* **5** **for a song** at a bargain price **6** **on song** *Brit inf* performing at peak efficiency or ability [OE *sang*]

Song (sʊŋ) *n* the Pinyin transliteration of the Chinese name for **Sung**

song and dance *n inf* **1** *Brit* a fuss, esp one that is unnecessary **2** *US & Canad* a long or elaborate story or explanation

songbird (ˈsɒŋˌbɜːd) *n* **1** any of a suborder of passerine birds having highly developed vocal organs and, in most, a musical call **2** any bird having a musical call

song cycle *n* any of several groups of songs written during and after the Romantic period, each series relating a story or grouped around a central motif

Songhua (ˈsʌŋˈwɑː) *n* a river in NE China, rising in SE

Jilin province and flowing north and northeast to the Amur River near Tongjiang: the chief river of Manchuria and largest tributary of the Amur; frozen from November to April. Length: over 1300 km (800 miles). Also called: **Sungari**

Song Koi *or* **Song Coi** ('sɒŋ 'kɔɪ) *n* transliteration of the Vietnamese name for the **Red River** (sense 3)

songololo (ˌsɒŋgɒ'lɒlɒ) *n, pl* **songololos** *S African* a millipede [from Nguni, from *ukusonga* to roll up]

songster ('sɒŋstə) *n* **1** a singer or poet **2** a singing bird; songbird > '**songstress** *fem n*

song thrush *n* a common Old World thrush with a spotted breast, noted for its song

songwriter ('sɒŋˌraɪtə) *n* a person who composes songs in a popular idiom

sonic ('sɒnɪk) *adj* **1** of, involving, or producing sound **2** having a speed about equal to that of sound in air [c20 from L *sonus* sound]

sonic barrier *n* another name for **sound barrier**

sonic boom *n* a loud explosive sound caused by the shock wave of an aircraft, etc, travelling at supersonic speed

sonic depth finder *n* an instrument for detecting the depth of water or of a submerged object by means of sound waves; Fathometer

sonics ('sɒnɪks) *n (functioning as sing) physics* the study of mechanical vibrations in matter

son-in-law *n, pl* **sons-in-law** the husband of one's daughter

sonnet ('sɒnɪt) *prosody* ▷ *n* **1** a verse form consisting of 14 lines in iambic pentameter with a fixed rhyme scheme, usually divided into octave and sestet or, in the English form, into three quatrains and a couplet ▷ *vb* **2** *(intr)* to compose sonnets **3** *(tr)* to celebrate in a sonnet [c16 via It. from OProvençal *sonet* a little poem, from *son* song, from L *sonus* a sound]

sonneteer (ˌsɒnɪ'tɪə) *n* a writer of sonnets

sonny ('sʌnɪ) *n, pl* **sonnies** *often patronizing* a familiar term of address to a boy or man

sonobuoy ('səʊnəˌbɔɪ) *n* a buoy equipped to detect underwater noises and transmit them by radio [SONIC + BUOY]

Son of Man *n Bible* a title of Jesus Christ

sonoluminescence (ˌsəʊnəʊˌlu:mɪ'nɛsəns) *n* luminescence produced by ultrasound

Sonora (*Spanish* so'nora) *n* a state of NW Mexico, on the Gulf of California: consists of a narrow coastal plain rising inland to the Sierra Madre Occidental; an important mining area in colonial times. Capital: Hermosillo. Pop: 2 213 370 (2000). Area: 184 934 sq km (71 403 sq miles)

sonorant ('sɒnərənt) *n phonetics* **1** one of the frictionless continuants or nasals (l, r, m, n, ŋ) having consonantal or vocalic functions depending on its situation within the syllable **2** either of the two consonants represented in English orthography by *w* or *y* and regarded as either consonantal or vocalic articulations of the vowels (i:) and (u:)

sonorous (sə'nɔ:rəs, 'sɒnərəs) *adj* **1** producing or capable of producing sound **2** (of language, sound, etc) deep or resonant **3** (esp of speech) high-flown; grandiloquent [c17 from L *sonōrus* loud, from *sonor* a noise] > **sonority** (sə'nɒrɪtɪ) *n* > **so'norously** *adv* > **so'norousness** *n*

sonsy *or* **sonsie** ('sɒnsɪ) *adj* **sonsier, sonsiest** *Scot, Irish, & English dialect* **1** plump; buxom **2** cheerful; good-natured **3** lucky [c16 from Gaelic *sonas* good fortune]

Sontag ('sɒntæg) *n* **Susan** born 1933, US intellectual and essayist, noted esp for her writings on modern culture. Her works include 'Notes on Camp' (1964), 'Against Interpretation' (1968), *On Photography* (1977), *Illness as Metaphor* (1978), and the novel *The Volcano Lover* (1992)

Soo Canals (su:) *pl n* **the** the two ship canals linking Lakes Superior and Huron. There is a canal on the Canadian and on the US side of the rapids of the St Mary's River. See also **Sault Sainte Marie**

Soochow ('su:'tʃaʊ) *n* a variant transliteration of the Chinese name for **Suzhou**

sook (sʊk) *n* **1** *SW English dialect* a baby **2** *derog* a coward [?from OE *sūcan* to suck, infl. by Welsh *swci swead* tame]

sool (su:l) *vb (tr) Austral & NZ sl* **1** to incite (esp a dog) to attack **2** to attack > '**sooler** *n*

soon (su:n) *adv* **1** in or after a short time; in a little while; before long **2** **as soon as** at the very moment that: *as soon as she saw him* **3** **as soon ... as** used to indicate that the second alternative is not preferable to the first: *I'd just as soon go by train as drive* [OE *sōna*]

sooner ('su:nə) *adv* **1** the comparative of **soon**: *he came sooner than I thought* **2** rather; in preference: *I'd sooner die than give up* **3** **no sooner ... than** immediately after or when: *no sooner had he got home than the rain stopped* **4** **sooner or later** eventually; inevitably.

> USAGE *When* is sometimes used instead of *than* after *no sooner*, but this use is generally regarded as incorrect: *no sooner had he arrived than* (not *when*) *the telephone rang*

Soong *or* **Song** (sʊŋ) *n* an influential Chinese family, notably **Soong Ch'ing-ling** (1890–1981), who married **Sun Yat-sen** and became a vice-chairman of the People's Republic of China (1959); and **Soong Mei-ling** (1898–2003), who married **Chiang Kai-shek**

soot (sʊt) *n* **1** finely divided carbon deposited from flames during the incomplete combustion of organic substances such as coal ▷ *vb* **2** *(tr)* to cover with soot [OE *sōt*]

sooth (su:θ) *arch or poetic* ▷ *n* **1** truth or reality (esp in **in sooth**) ▷ *adj* **2** true or real [OE *sōth*]

soothe (su:ð) *vb* **soothes, soothing, soothed** **1** *(tr)* to make calm or tranquil **2** *(tr)* to relieve or assuage (pain, longing, etc) **3** *(intr)* to bring tranquillity or relief [c16 (in the sense: to mollify): from OE *sōthian* to prove] > '**soother** *n* > '**soothing** *adj* > '**soothingly** *adv* > '**soothingness** *n*

Ss

soothsayer ('su:θˌseɪə) *n* a seer or prophet

sooty ('sʊtɪ) *adj* **sootier, sootiest** **1** covered with soot **2** resembling or consisting of soot > '**sootily** *adv* > '**sootiness** *n*

sop (sɒp) *n* **1** *(often pl)* food soaked in a liquid before being eaten **2** a concession, bribe, etc, given to placate or mollify: *a sop to one's feelings* **3** *inf* a stupid or weak person ▷ *vb* **sops, sopping, sopped** **4** *(tr)* to dip or soak (food) in liquid **5** (when *intr*, often foll by *in*) to soak or be soaked **6** *(tr; often foll by up)* to mop or absorb (liquid) as with a sponge [OE *sopp*]

SOP *abbrev for* standard operating procedure

sop. *abbrev for* soprano

Sophia (səʊ'faɪə) *n* 1630–1714, electress of Hanover (1658–1714), in whom the Act of Settlement (1701) vested the English Crown. She was a granddaughter of James I of England and her son became George I of Great Britain and Ireland

sophism ('sɒfɪzəm) *n* an instance of sophistry ▷ Cf **paralogism** [c14 from L *sophisma*, from Gk: ingenious trick, from *sophizesthai* to use clever deceit, from *sophos* wise]

sophist ('sɒfɪst) *n* **1** a person who uses clever or quibbling but unsound arguments **2** one of the pre-Socratic philosophers who were prepared to enter into debate on any subject however specious [c16 from L *sophista*, from Gk *sophistēs* a wise man, from *sophizesthai* to act craftily]

sophistic (sə'fɪstɪk) *or* **sophistical** *adj* **1** of or relating to sophists or sophistry **2** consisting of sophisms or sophistry; specious > **so'phistically** *adv*

sophisticate *vb* (sə'fɪstɪˌkeɪt), **sophisticates, sophisticating, sophisticated** **1** *(tr)* to make (someone) less natural or innocent, as by education **2** to pervert or corrupt (an argument, etc) by sophistry 3 (*tr*) to make more complex or refined 4 *rare* to falsify (a text, etc) by alterations ▷ *n* (səˈfɪstɪˌkeɪt, -kɪt) 5 a sophisticated person [c14 from Med. L *sophisticāre*, from L *sophisticus* sophistic] > **soˌphistiˈcation** *n* > **soˈphistiˌcator** *n*

sophisticated (səˈfɪstɪˌkeɪtɪd) *adj* 1 having refined or cultured tastes and habits 2 appealing to sophisticates: *a sophisticated restaurant* 3 unduly refined or cultured 4 pretentiously or superficially wise 5 (of machines, methods, etc) complex and refined

sophistry (ˈsɒfɪstrɪ) *n, pl* **sophistries** 1a a method of argument that is seemingly plausible though actually invalid and misleading 1b the art of using such arguments 2 subtle but unsound or fallacious reasoning 3 an instance of this

Sophocles (ˈsɒfəˌkliːz) *n* ?496–406 BC, Greek dramatist; author of seven extant tragedies: *Ajax, Antigone, Oedipus Rex, Trachiniae, Electra, Philoctetes*, and *Oedipus at Colonus*

sophomore (ˈsɒfəˌmɔː) *n chiefly US & Canad* a second-year student at a secondary (high) school or college [c17 ?from earlier *sophumer*, from *sophum*, var. of SOPHISM, + -ER[1]]

Sophy *or* **Sophi** (ˈsəʊfɪ) *n, pl* **Sophies** (formerly) a title of the Persian monarchs [c16 from L *sophī* wise men, from Gk *sophos* wise]

-sophy *n combining form* indicating knowledge or an intellectual system: *philosophy* [from Gk, from *sophia* wisdom, from *sophos* wise] > **-sophic** *or* **-sophical** *adj combining form*

soporific (ˌsɒpəˈrɪfɪk) *adj also (arch)* **ˌsoporˈiferous** 1 inducing sleep 2 drowsy; sleepy ▷ *n* 3 a drug or other agent that induces sleep [c17 from F, from L *sopor* sleep + -FIC]

sopping (ˈsɒpɪŋ) *adj* completely soaked; wet through. Also: **sopping wet**

soppy (ˈsɒpɪ) *adj* **soppier, soppiest** 1 wet or soggy 2 *Brit inf* silly or sentimental 3 **soppy on** *Brit inf* foolishly charmed or affected by > **ˈsoppily** *adv* > **ˈsoppiness** *n*

sopranino (ˌsɒprəˈniːnəʊ) *n, pl* **sopraninos** a the instrument with the highest possible pitch in a family of instruments b (*as modifier*): *a sopranino recorder* [It., dim. of SOPRANO]

soprano (səˈprɑːnəʊ) *n, pl* **sopranos** *or* **soprani** (-ˈprɑːniː) 1 the highest adult female voice 2 the voice of a young boy before puberty 3 a singer with such a voice 4 the highest part of a piece of harmony 5a the highest or second highest instrument in a family of instruments 5b (*as modifier*): *a soprano saxophone* ▷ See also **treble** [c18 from It., from *sopra* above, from L *suprā*]

soprano clef *n* the clef that establishes middle C as being on the bottom line of the staff

Sopwith (ˈsɒpwɪθ) *n* Sir **Thomas Octave Murdoch** 1888–1989, British aircraft designer, who built the Sopwith Camel biplane used during World War I. He was chairman (1935–63) of the Hawker Siddeley Group, which developed the Hurricane fighter

Sorata (*Spanish* soˈrata) *n* **Mount** a mountain in W Bolivia, in the Andes: the highest mountain in the Cordillera Real, with two peaks, Ancohuma, 6550 m (21 490 ft), and Illampu, 6485 m (21 276 ft)

sorb (sɔːb) *n* 1 another name for **service tree** 2 any of various related trees, esp the mountain ash 3 Also called: **sorb apple** the fruit of any of these trees [c16 from L *sorbus*]

sorbefacient (ˌsɔːbɪˈfeɪʃənt) *adj* 1 inducing absorption ▷ *n* 2 a sorbefacient drug [c19 from L *sorbē(re)* to absorb + -FACIENT]

sorbet (ˈsɔːbeɪ, -bɪt) *n* 1 a water ice made from fruit juice, egg whites, etc 2 a US word for **sherbet** (sense 1) [c16 from F, from OIt. *sorbetto*, from Turkish *şerbet*, from Ar. *sharbah* a drink]

sorbic acid (ˈsɔːbɪk) *n* a white crystalline carboxylic acid found in berries of the mountain ash and used to inhibit the growth of moulds and as an additive (**E 200**) for certain synthetic coatings [c19 from SORB (the tree), from its discovery in berries of the mountain ash]

sorbitol (ˈsɔːbɪˌtɒl) *n* a white crystalline alcohol, found in certain fruits and berries and manufactured by the catalytic hydrogenation of sucrose: used as a sweetener (**E 420**) and in the manufacture of ascorbic acid and synthetic resins [c19 from SORB + -ITOL]

Sorbonne (*French* sɔrbɔn) *n* **the** a part of the University of Paris containing the faculties of science and literature: founded in 1253 by Robert de Sorbon as a theological college; given to the university in 1808

sorbo rubber (ˈsɔːbəʊ) *n Brit* a spongy form of rubber [c20 from ABSORB]

sorcerer (ˈsɔːsərə) *or (fem)* **sorceress** (ˈsɔːsərɪs) *n* a person who seeks to control and use magic powers; a wizard or magician [c16 from OF *sorcier*, from Vulgar L *sortiārius* (unattested) caster of lots, from L *sors* lot]

sorcery (ˈsɔːsərɪ) *n, pl* **sorceries** the art, practices, or spells of magic, esp black magic [c13 from OF *sorcerie*, from *sorcier* SORCERER]

sordid (ˈsɔːdɪd) *adj* 1 dirty, foul, or squalid 2 degraded; vile; base 3 selfish and grasping: *sordid avarice* [c16 from L *sordidus*, from *sordēre* to be dirty] > **ˈsordidly** *adv* > **ˈsordidness** *n*

sordino (sɔːˈdiːnəʊ) *n, pl* **sordini** (-niː) 1 a mute for a stringed or brass musical instrument 2 any of the dampers in a piano 3 **con sordino** *or* **sordini** a musical direction to play with a mute 4 **senza sordino** *or* **sordini** a musical direction to remove or play without the mute or (on the piano) with the sustaining pedal pressed down [It.: from *sordo* deaf, from L *surdus*]

sore (sɔː) *adj* 1 (esp of a wound, injury, etc) painfully sensitive; tender 2 causing annoyance: *a sore point* 3 resentful; irked 4 urgent; pressing: *in sore need* 5 (*postpositive*) grieved; distressed 6 causing grief or sorrow ▷ *n* 7 a painful or sensitive wound, injury, etc 8 any cause of distress or vexation ▷ *adv* 9 *arch* direly; sorely (now only in such phrases as **sore afraid**) [OE *sār*] > **ˈsoreness** *n*

sorehead (ˈsɔːˌhɛd) *n inf, chiefly US & Canad* a peevish or disgruntled person

sorely (ˈsɔːlɪ) *adv* 1 painfully or grievously: *sorely wounded* 2 pressingly or greatly: *to be sorely taxed*

Sorenstam (ˈsɔːrənstəm) *n* **Annika** (ˈænɪka) born 1970, Swedish golfer; winner of the US Women's Open (1995, 1996), the LPGA Championship (2003), and the British Women's Open (2003)

sorghum (ˈsɔːgəm) *n* any grass of the Old World genus *Sorghum*, having glossy seeds: cultivated for grain, hay, and as a source of syrup [c16 from NL, from It. *sorgo*, prob. from Vulgar L *Syricum grānum* (unattested) Syrian grain]

Sorocaba (*Portuguese* soroˈkaba) *n* a city in S Brazil, in São Paulo state: industrial centre. Pop: 487 907 (2000)

soroptimist (səˈrɒptɪmɪst) *n* a member of Soroptimist International, an organization of clubs for professional and executive businesswomen

sororal (səˈrɔːrəl) *adj* of or relating to a sister or sisters [c17 from L *soror* sister]

sorority (səˈrɒrɪtɪ) *n, pl* **sororities** *chiefly US* a social club or society for university women [c16 from Med. L *sorōritās*, from L *soror* sister]

sorption (ˈsɔːpʃən) *n* the process in which one substance takes up or holds another; adsorption or absorption [c20 back formation from ABSORPTION, ADSORPTION]

sorrel[1] (ˈsɒrəl) *n* 1a a light brown to brownish-orange colour 1b (*as adj*): *a sorrel carpet* 2 a horse of this colour [c15 from OF *sorel*, from *sor* a reddish brown, of Gmc origin]

sorrel[2] (ˈsɒrəl) *n* 1 any of several plants of Eurasia and North America, having acid-tasting leaves used in salads and sauces 2 short for **wood sorrel** [c14 from OF *surele*, from *sur* sour, of Gmc origin]

Sorrento (sə'rɛntəʊ; *Italian* sor'rɛnto) *n* a port in SW Italy, in Campania on a mountainous peninsula between the Bay of Naples and the Gulf of Salerno: a resort since Roman times. Pop: 17 500 (1990)

sorrow ('sɒrəʊ) *n* **1** the feeling of sadness, grief, or regret associated with loss, bereavement, sympathy for another's suffering, etc **2** a particular cause or source of this **3** Also called: **sorrowing** the outward expression of grief or sadness ▷ *vb* **4** (*intr*) to mourn or grieve [OE *sorg*] > '**sorrowful** *adj* > '**sorrowfully** *adv* > '**sorrowfulness** *n*

sorry ('sɒrɪ) *adj* **sorrier, sorriest 1** (*usually postpositive; often foll by* for) feeling or expressing pity, sympathy, grief, or regret: *I feel sorry for him* **2** pitiful, wretched, or deplorable: *a sorry sight* **3** poor; paltry: *a sorry excuse* **4** affected by sorrow; sad **5** causing sorrow or sadness ▷ *interj* **6** an exclamation expressing apology [OE *sārig*] > '**sorrily** *adv* > '**sorriness** *n*

sort (sɔːt) *n* **1** a class, group, kind, etc, as distinguished by some common quality or characteristic **2** *inf* a type of character, nature, etc: *he's a good sort* **3** *Austral sl* a person, esp a girl **4** a more or less definable or adequate example: *it's a sort of review* **5** (*often pl*) *printing* any of the individual characters making up a fount of type **6** *arch* manner; way: *in this sort we struggled home* **7 after a sort** to some extent **8 of sorts** *or* **of a sort 8a** of an inferior kind **8b** of an indefinite kind **9 out of sorts** not in normal good health, temper, etc **10 sort of** in some way or other; as it were; rather ▷ *vb* **11** (*tr*) to arrange according to class, type, etc **12** (*tr*) to put (something) into working order **13** to arrange (computer information) by machine in an order convenient to the user **14** (*intr*) *arch* to agree; accord [c14 from OF, from Med. L *sors* kind, from L: fate] > '**sortable** *adj* > '**sorter** *n*

USAGE See at **kind**

sort code *n* a sequence of numbers printed on a cheque or embossed on a bank or building-society card that identifies the branch holding the account

sortie ('sɔːtɪ) *n* **1a** (of troops, etc) the act of attacking from a contained or besieged position **1b** the troops doing this **2** an operational flight made by one aircraft **3** a short or relatively short return trip ▷ *vb* **sorties, sortieing, sortied 4** (*intr*) to make a sortie [c17 from F: a going out, from *sortir* to go out]

sortilege ('sɔːtɪlɪdʒ) *n* the act or practice of divination by drawing lots [c14 via OF from Med. L *sortilegium*, from L *sortilegus* a soothsayer, from *sors* fate + *legere* to select]

sort out *vb* (*tr, adv*) **1** to find a solution to (a problem, etc), esp to make clear or tidy: *to sort out the mess* **2** to take or separate, as from a larger group: *to sort out the likely ones* **3** to organize into an orderly and disciplined group **4** *inf* to beat or punish

SOS *n* **1** an internationally recognized distress signal in which the letters SOS are repeatedly spelt out, as by radiotelegraphy: used esp by ships and aircraft **2** a message broadcast in an emergency for people otherwise unobtainable **3** *inf* a call for help

sosatie (sə'sɑːtɪ) *n S African* curried meat on skewers [from Afrik., from Du.]

Sosnowiec (*Polish* sɔs'nɔvjɛts) *n* an industrial town in S Poland. Pop: 244 102 (1999 est)

so-so *inf* ▷ *adj* **1** (*postpositive*) neither good nor bad ▷ *adv* **2** in an average or indifferent manner

sostenuto (ˌsɒstə'nuːtəʊ) *adj, adv music* to be performed in a smooth sustained manner [c18 from It., from *sostenere* to sustain, from L *sustinēre*]

sot (sɒt) *n* **1** a habitual or chronic drunkard **2** a person stupefied by or as if by drink [OE, from Med. L *sottus*] > '**sottish** *adj*

soteriology (sɒˌtɪərɪ'ɒlədʒɪ) *n Christian theol* the doctrine of salvation [c19 from Gk *sōtēria* deliverance (from *sōtēr* a saviour) + -LOGY]

Soto *n* See (Hernando) **De Soto**

sotto voce ('sɒtəʊ 'vəʊtʃɪ) *adv* (of speaking or singing) in an undertone [c18 from It.: under (one's) voice]

sou (suː) *n* **1** a former French coin of low denomination **2** a very small amount of money: *I haven't a sou* [c19 from F, from OF *sol*, from L: SOLIDUS]

soubrette (suː'brɛt) *n* **1** a minor female role in comedy, often that of a pert lady's maid **2** any pert or flirtatious girl [c18 from F: maidservant, from Provençal, from *soubret* conceited, from *soubra* to exceed, from L *superāre* to surmount]

soubriquet ('səʊbrɪˌkeɪ) *n* a variant spelling of **sobriquet**

Soudan (sudɑ̃) *n* the French name for the **Sudan**

soufflé ('suːfleɪ) *n* **1** a light fluffy dish made with beaten egg whites combined with cheese, fish, etc **2** a similar sweet or savoury cold dish, set with gelatine ▷ *adj also* **souffléed 3** made light and puffy, as by beating and cooking [c19 from F, from *souffler* to blow, from L *sufflāre*]

Soufrière (*French* sufrjɛr) *n* **1** a volcano in the Caribbean, on N St Vincent: erupted in 1902, killing about 2000 people. Height: 1234 m (4048 ft) **2** a volcano in the Caribbean, on S Montserrat: the highest point on the island. Height: 915 m (3002 ft) **3** a volcano in the Caribbean, on Guadeloupe. Height: 1484 m (4869 ft)

sough (saʊ) *vb* **1** (*intr*) (esp of the wind) to make a sighing sound ▷ *n* **2** a soft continuous murmuring sound [OE *swōgan* to resound]

sought (sɔːt) *vb* the past tense and past participle of **seek**

souk (suːk) *n* an open-air marketplace in Muslim countries, esp North Africa and the Middle East [from Ar.]

soukous ('suːkʊs) *n* a style of African popular music that originated in the Democratic Republic of Congo, characterized by syncopated rhythms and intricate contrasting guitar melodies [c20 ? from F *secouer* to shake]

soul (səʊl) *n* **1** the spirit or immaterial part of man, the seat of human personality, intellect, will, and emotions: regarded as an entity that survives the body after death **2** *Christianity* the spiritual part of a person, capable of redemption from sin through divine grace **3** the essential part or fundamental nature of anything **4** a person's feelings or moral nature **5a** Also called: **soul music** a type of Black music resulting from the addition of jazz, gospel, and pop elements to the urban blues style **5b** (*as modifier*): *a soul singer* **6** (*modifier*) of or relating to Black Americans and their culture: *soul food* **7** nobility of spirit or temperament: *a man of great soul* **8** an inspiring or leading figure, as of a movement **9** a person regarded as typifying some characteristic or quality: *the soul of discretion* **10** a person; individual: *an honest soul* **11 upon my soul!** an exclamation of surprise [OE *sāwol*]

▷ www.jazzinamerica.org

▷ www.bluesandsoul.co.uk

soul-destroying *adj* (of an occupation, situation, etc) unremittingly monotonous

soul food *n inf* food, such as chitterlings, yams, etc, traditionally eaten by African-Americans

soulful ('səʊlfʊl) *adj* expressing profound thoughts or feelings > '**soulfully** *adv* > '**soulfulness** *n*

soulless ('səʊllɪs) *adj* **1** lacking humanizing qualities or influences; mechanical: *soulless work* **2** (of a person) lacking in sensitivity or nobility > '**soullessness** *n*

soul mate *n* a person for whom one has a deep affinity, esp a lover, wife, husband, etc

soul-searching *n* **1** deep or critical examination of one's motives, actions, beliefs, etc ▷ *adj* **2** displaying the characteristics of this

sound[1] (saʊnd) *n* **1a** a periodic disturbance in the pressure or density of a fluid or in the elastic strain of a solid, produced by a vibrating object. It travels as longitudinal waves **1b** (*as modifier*): *a sound wave* **2** the sensation produced by such a periodic disturbance in the organs of hearing **3** anything that can be heard

4 (*modifier*) of or relating to radio as distinguished from television: *sound broadcasting* 5 a particular instance or type of sound: *the sound of running water* 6 volume or quality of sound: *a radio with poor sound* 7 the area or distance over which something can be heard: *within the sound of Big Ben* 8 impression or implication: *I don't like the sound of that* 9 (*often pl*) *sl* music, esp rock, jazz, or pop ▷ *vb* 10 to cause (an instrument, etc) to make a sound or (of an instrument, etc) to emit a sound 11 to announce or be announced by a sound: *to sound the alarm* 12 (*intr*) (of a sound) to be heard 13 (*intr*) to resonate with a certain quality or intensity: *to sound loud* 14 (*copula*) to give the impression of being as specified: *to sound reasonable* 15 (*tr*) to pronounce distinctly or audibly: *to sound one's consonants* [C13 from OF *soner* to make a sound, from L *sonāre*, from *sonus* a sound] > **'soundable** *adj*

sound[2] (saʊnd) *adj* 1 free from damage, injury, decay, etc 2 firm; substantial: *a sound basis* 3 financially safe or stable: *a sound investment* 4 showing good judgment or reasoning; wise: *sound advice* 5 valid, logical, or justifiable: *a sound argument* 6 holding approved beliefs; ethically correct; honest 7 (of sleep) deep; peaceful; unbroken 8 thorough: *a sound examination* ▷ *adv* 9 soundly; deeply: now archaic except when applied to sleep [OE *sund*] > **'soundly** *adv* > **'soundness** *n*

sound[3] (saʊnd) *vb* 1 to measure the depth of (a well, the sea, etc) by plumb line, sonar, etc 2 to seek to discover (someone's views, etc), as by questioning 3 (*intr*) (of a whale, etc) to dive downwards swiftly and deeply 4 *med* 4a to probe or explore (a bodily cavity or passage) by means of a sound 4b to examine (a patient) by means of percussion and auscultation ▷ *n* 5 *med* an instrument for insertion into a bodily cavity or passage to dilate strictures, dislodge foreign material, etc ▷ See also **sound out** [C14 from OF *sonder*, from *sonde* sounding line, prob. of Gmc origin] > **'sounder** *n*

sound[4] (saʊnd) *n* 1 a relatively narrow channel between two larger areas of sea or between an island and the mainland 2 an inlet or deep bay of the sea 3 the air bladder of a fish [OE *sund* swimming, narrow sea]

Sound (saʊnd) *n* **the** a strait between SW Sweden and Sjælland (Denmark), linking the Kattegat with the Baltic: busy shipping lane; spanned by a bridge in 2000. Length: 113 km (70 miles). Narrowest point: 5 km (3 miles). Danish name: **Øresund** Swedish name: **Öresund**

soundalike ('saʊndəˌlaɪk) *n* **a** a person or thing that sounds like another, often well-known, person or thing **b** (*as modifier*): *a soundalike band*

sound barrier *n* (not in technical usage) a hypothetical barrier to flight at or above the speed of sound, when a sudden large increase in drag occurs. Also called: **sonic barrier**

sound bite *n* a short pithy sentence or phrase extracted from a longer speech for use on radio or television

soundbox ('saʊndˌbɒks) *n* the resonating chamber of the hollow body of a violin, guitar, etc

sound effect *n* any sound artificially produced, reproduced from a recording, etc, to create a theatrical effect, as in plays, films, etc

sounding[1] ('saʊndɪŋ) *adj* 1 resounding; resonant 2 having an imposing sound and little content; pompous: *sounding phrases*

sounding[2] ('saʊndɪŋ) *n* 1 (*sometimes pl*) the act or process of measuring depth of water or examining the bottom of a river, lake, etc, as with a sounding line 2 an observation or measurement of atmospheric conditions, as made using a sonde 3 (*often pl*) measurements taken by sounding 4 (*pl*) a place where a sounding line will reach the bottom, esp less than 100 fathoms in depth

sounding board *n* 1 Also called: **soundboard** a thin wooden board in a violin, piano, etc, serving to amplify the vibrations produced by the strings passing across it 2 Also called: **soundboard** a thin screen suspended over a pulpit, stage, etc, to reflect sound towards an audience 3 a person, group, experiment, etc, used to test a new idea, policy, etc

sounding line *n* a line marked off to indicate its length and having a **sounding lead** at one end. It is dropped over the side of a vessel to determine the depth of the water

soundless ('saʊndlɪs) *adj* extremely still or silent > **'soundlessness** *n*

sound out *vb* (*tr, adv*) to question (someone) in order to discover (opinions, facts, etc)

soundpost ('saʊndˌpəʊst) *n music* a small wooden post in guitars, violins, etc, that joins the front to the back and helps support the bridge

soundproof ('saʊndˌpruːf) *adj* 1 not penetrable by sound ▷ *vb* 2 (*tr*) to render soundproof

sound spectrograph *n* an electronic instrument that produces a record (**sound spectrogram**) of the frequencies and intensities of the components of a sound

sound system *n* 1 any system of sounds, as in the speech of a language 2 integrated equipment for producing amplified sound, as in a hi-fi or mobile disco, or as a public-address system on stage

soundtrack ('saʊndˌtræk) *n* 1 the recorded sound accompaniment to a film 2 a narrow strip along the side of a spool of film, which carries the sound accompaniment

sound wave *n* a wave that propagates sound

soup (suːp) *n* 1 a liquid food made by boiling or simmering meat, fish, vegetables, etc 2 *inf* a photographic developer 3 *inf* anything resembling soup, esp thick fog 4 a slang name for **nitroglycerine** 5 **in the soup** *sl* in trouble or difficulties [C17 from OF *soupe*, from LL *suppa*, of Gmc origin] > **'soupy** *adj*
▷ www.souprecipe.com/default.asp
▷ www.greatrecipesonline.com/dir/Soup

soupçon *French* (supsɔ̃) *n* a slight amount; dash [C18 from F, ult. from L *suspicio* SUSPICION]

soup kitchen *n* 1 a place or mobile stall where food and drink, esp soup, is served to destitute people 2 *mil* a mobile kitchen

soup plate *n* a deep plate with a wide rim, used esp for drinking soup

soup up *vb* (*tr, adv*) *sl* to modify the engine of (a car or motorcycle) in order to increase its power. Also: **hot up**, (esp US and Canad) **hop up**

sour ('saʊə) *adj* 1 having or denoting a sharp biting taste like that of lemon juice or vinegar 2 made acid or bad, as in the case of milk, by the action of microorganisms 3 having a rancid or unwholesome smell 4 (of a person's temperament) sullen, morose, or disagreeable 5 (esp of the weather) harsh and unpleasant 6 disagreeable; distasteful: *a sour experience* 7 (of land, etc) lacking in fertility, esp due to excessive acidity 8 (of petrol, gas, etc) containing a relatively large amount of sulphur compounds 9 **go** *or* **turn sour** to become unfavourable or inharmonious: *his marriage went sour* ▷ *n* 10 something sour 11 *chiefly US* an iced drink usually made with spirits, lemon juice, and ice: *a whiskey sour* 12 an acid used in bleaching clothes or in curing skins ▷ *vb* 13 to make or become sour [OE *sūr*] > **'sourish** *adj* > **'sourly** *adv* > **'sourness** *n*

source (sɔːs) *n* 1 the point or place from which something originates 2a a spring that forms the starting point of a stream 2b the area where the headwaters of a river rise 3 a person, group, etc, that creates, issues, or originates something: *the source of a complaint* 4a any person, book, organization, etc, from which information, evidence, etc, is obtained 4b (*as modifier*): *source material* 5 anything, such as a story or work of art, that provides a model or inspiration for a later work **6** **at source** at the point of origin ▷ *vb* **sources, sourcing, sourced** (*tr*) **7** to establish an originator or source of (a product, etc) **8** to determine the source of a news report or story **9** (foll by *from*) to originate from [c14 from OF *sors*, from *sourdre* to spring forth, from L *surgere* to rise]

source code *n computing* the original form of a computer program before it is converted into a machine-readable code

source program *n computing* an original computer program written by a programmer that is converted into the equivalent object program, written in machine language

sour cherry *n* **1** a Eurasian tree with white flowers: cultivated for its tart red fruits **2** the fruit

sour cream *n* cream soured by lactic acid bacteria, used in making salads, dips, etc

sourdough ('saʊə,dəʊ) ▷ *adj* **1** (of bread) made with fermented dough used as leaven ▷ *n* **2** (in the Western US, Canada, and Alaska) an old-time prospector or pioneer

sour gourd *n* **1** a large tree of N Australia, having gourdlike fruit **2** the acid-tasting fruit **3** the fruit of the baobab tree

sour grapes *n* (*functioning as sing*) the attitude of affecting to despise something because one cannot have it oneself

sourpuss ('saʊə,pʊs) *n inf* a person who is habitually gloomy or sullen

sourveld ('saʊə,fɛlt) *n* (in South Africa) a type of grazing characterized by long coarse grass [from Afrik. *suur* sour + *veld* grassland]

Sousa ('suːzə) *n* **John Philip** 1854–1932, US bandmaster and composer of military marches, such as *The Stars and Stripes Forever* (1897) and *The Liberty Bell* (1893)

sousaphone ('suːzə,fəʊn) *n* a large tuba that encircles the player's body and has a bell facing forwards [c20 after J. P. Sousa] > '**sousa,phonist** *n*

souse (saʊs) *vb* **souses, sousing, soused** **1** to plunge (something) into water or other liquid **2** to drench or be drenched **3** (*tr*) to pour or dash (liquid) over (a person or thing) **4** to steep or cook (food) in a marinade **5** (*tr*) *sl* to make drunk ▷ *n* **6** the liquid used in pickling **7** the act or process of sousing **8** *sl* a drunkard [c14 from OF *sous*, of Gmc origin]

Sousse (suːs), **Susa**, *or* **Susah** *n* a port in E Tunisia, on the Mediterranean: founded by the Phoenicians in the 9th century BC. Pop: 125 000 (1994). Ancient name: **Hadrumetum** (,hædrə'miːtəm)

soutane (suː'tæn) *n RC Church* a priest's cassock [c19 from F, from OIt. *sottana*, from Med. L *subtanus* (adj) (worn) beneath, from L *subtus* below]

souterrain ('suːtə,reɪn) *n archaeol* an underground chamber or passage [c18 from F]

south (saʊθ) *n* **1** one of the four cardinal points of the compass, at 180° from north and 90° clockwise from east and anticlockwise from west **2** the direction along a meridian towards the South Pole **3** **the south** (*often cap*) any area lying in or towards the south **4** (*usually cap*) *cards* the player or position corresponding to south on the compass ▷ *adj* **5** in, towards, or facing the south **6** (esp of the wind) from the south ▷ *adv* **7** in, to, or towards the south [OE *sūth*]

South (saʊθ) *n* **the 1** the southern part of England, generally regarded as lying to the south of an imaginary line between the Wash and the Severn **2** (in the US) **2a** the states south of the Mason-Dixon Line that formed the Confederacy during the Civil War **2b** the Confederacy itself **3** the countries of the world that are not economically and technically advanced ▷ *adj* **4** of or denoting the southern part of a specified country, area, etc

South Africa *n* **Republic of** a republic occupying the southernmost part of the African continent: the Dutch Cape Colony (1652) was acquired by Britain in 1806 and British victory in the Boer War resulted in the formation of the Union of South Africa in 1910, which became a republic in 1961; implementation of the apartheid system began in 1948 and was abolished, following an intense civil rights campaign, in 1993 with multiracial elections held in 1994; a member of the Commonwealth, it withdrew in 1961 but was re-admitted in 1994. Mainly plateau with mountains in the south and east. Mineral production includes gold, diamonds, coal, and copper. Official languages: Afrikaans; English; Ndebele; Pedi; South Sotho; Swazi; Tsonga; Tswana; Venda; Xhosa; Zulu. Religion: Christian majority. Currency: rand. Capitals: Cape Town (legislative), Pretoria (administrative), Bloemfontein (judicial). Pop: 43 586 000 (2001 est). Area: 1 221 044 sq km (471 445 sq miles). Former name (1910–61): **Union of South Africa** > **South African** *adj, n*
▷ www.gov.za
▷ www.southafrica.net
▷ www.satour.org

South America *n* the fourth largest of the continents, bordering on the Caribbean in the north, the Pacific in the west, and the Atlantic in the east and joined to Central America by the Isthmus of Panama. It is dominated by the Andes Mountains, which extend over 7250 km (4500 miles) and include many volcanoes; ranges from dense tropical jungle, desert, and temperate plains to the cold wet windswept region of Tierra del Fuego. It comprises chiefly developing countries undergoing great changes. Pop: 317 846 000 (1996). Area: 17 816 600 sq km (6 879 000 sq miles) > **South American** *adj, n*

Southampton (saʊθ'æmptən, -'hæmp-) *n* **1** a port in S England, in Southampton unitary authority, Hampshire on **Southampton Water** (an inlet of the English Channel): chief English passenger port; university (1952); shipyards and oil refinery. Pop: 210 138 (1991) **2** a unitary authority in S England, in Hampshire. Pop: 217 478 (2001). Area: 49 sq km (19 sq miles)

Southampton Island *n* an island in N Canada, in Nunavut at the entrance to Hudson Bay: inhabited chiefly by Inuit. Area: 49 470 sq km (19 100 sq miles)

South Arabia *n* **Federation of** the former name (1963–67) of **South Yemen** (excluding Aden) > **South Arabian** *adj, n*

South Australia *n* a state of S central Australia, on the Great Australian Bight: generally arid, with the Great Victoria Desert in the west central part, the Lake Eyre basin in the northeast, and the Flinders Ranges, Murray River basin, and salt lakes in the southeast. Capital: Adelaide. Pop: 1 493 070 (1999 est). Area: 984 395 sq km (380 070 sq miles) > **South Australian** *adj, n*
▷ www.sa.gov.au
▷ www.tourism.sa.gov.au

South Ayrshire ('ɛəʃɪə, -ʃə) *n* a council area of SW Scotland, on the Firth of Clyde: comprises the S part of the historical county of Ayrshire; formerly part of Strathclyde Region (1975–96): chiefly agricultural, with fishing and tourism. Administrative centre: Ayr. Pop: 112 097 (2001). Area: 1202 sq km (464 sq miles)

South Bend *n* a city in the US, in N Indiana: university (1842). Pop: 107 789 (2000)

southbound ('saʊθ,baʊnd) *adj* going or leading towards the south

south by east *n* **1** one point on the compass east of south ▷ *adj, adv* **2** in, from, or towards this direction

south by west *n* **1** one point on the compass west of south ▷ *adj, adv* **2** in, from, or towards this direction

South Carolina *n* a state of the southeastern US, on the Atlantic: the first state to secede from the Union in 1860; consists largely of low-lying coastal plains, rising

Ss

in the northwest to the Blue Ridge Mountains; the largest US textile producer. Capital: Columbia. Pop: 4 012 012 (2000). Area: 78 282 sq km (30 225 sq miles). Abbreviation and zip code: **SC** > **South Carolinian** *adj, n*

South China Sea *n* part of the Pacific surrounded by SE China, Vietnam, the Malay Peninsula, Borneo, and the Philippines

Southcott ('saʊθkɒt) *n* **Joanna** 1750–1814, British religious fanatic, who claimed that she would give birth to the second Messiah

South Dakota *n* a state of the western US: lies mostly in the Great Plains; the chief US producer of gold and beryl. Capital: Pierre. Pop: 754 844 (2000). Area: 196 723 sq km (75 955 sq miles). Abbreviations: **S Dak.** or (with zip code) **SD** > **South Dakotan** *adj, n*

Southdown ('saʊθˌdaʊn) *n* an English breed of sheep with short wool and a greyish-brown face and legs [C18 so called because it was originally bred on the SOUTH DOWNS]

South Downs *pl n* a range of low hills in S England, extending from E Hampshire to East Sussex

southeast (ˌsaʊθ'iːst; *naut* ˌsaʊ'iːst) *n* **1** the point of the compass or the direction midway between south and east **2** (*often cap*; *usually preceded by* the) any area lying in or towards this direction ▷ *adj also* **southeastern** **3** (*sometimes cap*) of or denoting the southeastern part of a specified country, area, etc **4** in, towards, or facing the southeast **5** (esp of the wind) from the southeast ▷ *adv* **6** in, to, or towards the southeast > ˌ**south'easternmost** *adj*

Southeast (ˌsaʊθ'iːst) *n* (usually preceded by *the*) the southeastern part of Britain, esp the London area

Southeast Asia *n* a region including Brunei, Cambodia, Indonesia, Laos, Malaysia, Myanmar, the Philippines, Thailand, and Vietnam > **Southeast Asian** *adj, n*

southeast by east *n* **1** one point on the compass north of southeast ▷ *adj, adv* **2** in, from, or towards this direction

southeast by south *n* **1** one point on the compass south of southeast ▷ *adj, adv* **2** in, from, or towards this direction

southeaster (ˌsaʊθ'iːstə; *naut* ˌsaʊ'iːstə) *n* a strong wind or storm from the southeast

southeasterly (ˌsaʊθ'iːstəlɪ; *naut* ˌsaʊ'iːstəlɪ) *adj, adv* **1** in, towards, or (esp of the wind) from the southeast ▷ *n, pl* **southeasterlies** **2** a strong wind or storm from the southeast

southeastward (ˌsaʊθ'iːstwəd; *naut* ˌsaʊ'iːstwəd) *adj* **1** towards or (esp of a wind) from the southeast ▷ *n* **2** a direction towards or area in the southeast ▷ *adv* **3** Also: **southeastwards** towards the southeast

Southend-on-Sea (ˌsaʊθ'ɛnd-) *n* **1** a town in SE England, in SE Essex on the Thames estuary: one of England's largest resorts, extending for about 11 km (7 miles) along the coast. Pop: 158 517 (1991) **2** a unitary authority in SE England, in Essex. Pop: 160 256 (2001). Area: 42 sq km (16 sq miles)

souther ('saʊðə) *n* a strong wind or storm from the south

southerly ('sʌðəlɪ) *adj* **1** of or situated in the south ▷ *adv, adj* **2** towards the south **3** from the south ▷ *n, pl* **southerlies** **4** a wind from the south > '**southerliness** *n*

southern ('sʌðən) *adj* **1** in or towards the south **2** (of a wind, etc) coming from the south **3** native to or inhabiting the south > '**southern,most** *adj*

Southern ('sʌðən) *adj* of, relating to, or characteristic of the south of a particular region or country

Southern Alps *pl n* a mountain range in New Zealand, on South Island: the highest range in Australasia. Highest peak: Mount Cook, 3764 m (12 349 ft)

Southern Cross *n* a small constellation in the S hemisphere (lying in the Milky Way near Centaurus) whose four brightest stars form a cross. It is represented on the national flags of Australia and New Zealand

Southerner ('sʌðənə) *n* (*sometimes not cap*) a native or inhabitant of the south of any specified region, esp the South of England or the Southern states of the US

southern hemisphere *n* (*often caps*) that half of the earth lying south of the equator

Southern Ireland *n* See **Ireland**[1] (sense 2)

southern lights *pl n* another name for **aurora australis**

Southern Ocean *n* another name for the **Antarctic Ocean**

Southern Rhodesia *n* the former name (until 1964) of **Zimbabwe** > **Southern Rhodesian** *adj, n*

Southern Uplands *pl n* a hilly region extending across S Scotland: includes the Lowther, Moorfoot, and Lammermuir hills

Southey ('saʊðɪ, 'sʌðɪ) *n* **Robert** 1774–1843, English poet, a friend of Wordsworth and Coleridge, attacked by Byron; poet laureate (1813–43)

South Georgia *n* an island in the S Atlantic, about 1300 km (800 miles) southeast of the Falkland Islands, part of the UK Overseas Territory of **South Georgia and the South Sandwich Islands.** Area: 3755 sq km (1450 sq miles) > **South Georgian** *adj*

South Glamorgan *n* a former county of S Wales, formed in 1974 from parts of Glamorgan and Monmouthshire plus the county borough of Cardiff: replaced in 1996 by the county boroughs of Cardiff and Vale of Glamorgan

South Gloucestershire *n* a unitary authority of SW England, in Gloucestershire: formerly (1975–96) part of the county of Avon. Pop: 245 644 (2001). Area: 510 sq km (197 sq miles)

South Holland *n* a province of the SW Netherlands, on the North Sea: lying mostly below sea level, it has a coastal strip of dunes and is drained chiefly by distributaries of the Rhine, with large areas of reclaimed land; the most densely populated province in the country, intensively cultivated and industrialized. Capital: The Hague. Pop: 3 397 700 (2000 est). Area: 3196 sq km (1234 sq miles). Dutch name: **Zuidholland**

southing ('saʊðɪŋ) *n* **1** *navigation* movement, deviation, or distance covered in a southerly direction **2** *astron* a south or negative declination

South Island *n* **the** the largest island of New Zealand, separated from the North Island by Cook Strait. Pop: 942 213 (2001). Area: 153 947 sq km (59 439 sq miles)

South Korea *n* a republic in NE Asia: established as a republic in 1948; invaded by North Korea and Chinese Communists in 1950 but division remained unchanged at the end of the war (1953); includes over 3000 islands; rapid industrialization. Language: Korean. Religions: Buddhist, Confucianist, Shamanist, and Chondokyo. Currency: won. Capital: Seoul. Pop: 47 676 000 (2001 est). Area: 98 477 sq km (38 022 sq miles). Korean name: **Hanguk** > **South Korean** *adj, n*
▷ www.cwd.go.kr/warp/app/home/en_home
▷ http://english.tour2korea.com

South Lanarkshire ('lænəkʃɪə, -ʃə) *n* a council area of S Scotland, comprising the S part of the historical county of Lanarkshire: included within Strathclyde Region from 1975 to 1996: has uplands in the S and part of the Glasgow conurbation in the N: mainly agricultural. Administrative centre: Hamilton. Pop: 302 216 (2001). Area: 1771 sq km (684 sq miles)
▷ www.southlanddc.govt.nz
▷ www.southland.org.nz

South Orkney Islands *pl n* a group of islands in the S Atlantic, southeast of Cape Horn: formerly a dependency of the Falkland Islands; part of British Antarctic Territory since 1962. Area: 621 sq km (240 sq miles)

South Ossetia (ə'siːʃə) *n* a region in Georgia on the S slopes of the Caucasus Mountains; in 1990 it voted to join Russia, leading to armed conflict with Georgian forces; it became an autonomous region in 1997. Capital: Tskhinvali. Pop: 99 800 (1990). Area: 3900 sq km (1500 sq miles). Georgian name: **Tskhinvali** Also called: **South Ossetian Autonomous Region**

southpaw (ˈsaʊθˌpɔː) *inf* ▷ *n* **1** a left-handed boxer **2** any left-handed person ▷ *adj* **3** of or relating to a southpaw

South Pole *n* **1** the southernmost point on the earth's axis, at the latitude of 90°S **2** *astron* the point of intersection, in the constellation Octans, of the earth's extended axis and the southern half of the celestial sphere **3** (*usually not capitals*) the south-seeking pole of a freely suspended magnet

Southport (ˈsaʊθˌpɔːt) *n* a town and resort in NW England, in Sefton unitary authority, Merseyside on the Irish Sea. Pop: 90 959 (1991)

South Saskatchewan *n* a river in S central Canada, rising in S Alberta and flowing east and northeast to join the North Saskatchewan River, forming the Saskatchewan River. Length: 1392 km (865 miles)

South Sea Bubble *n Brit history* the financial crash that occurred in 1720 after the **South Sea Company** had taken over the national debt in return for a monopoly of trade with the South Seas, causing feverish speculation in their stocks
▷ www.dal.ca/~dmcneil/sketch.html
▷ www.historyhouse.com/in_history/south_sea

South Sea Islands *pl n* the islands in the S Pacific that constitute Oceania

South Seas *pl n* the seas south of the equator

South Shetland Islands *pl n* a group of islands in the S Atlantic, north of the Antarctic Peninsula: formerly a dependency of the Falkland Islands; part of British Antarctic Territory since 1962. Area: 4662 sq km (1800 sq miles)

South Shields *n* a port in NE England, in South Tyneside unitary authority, Tyne and Wear on the Tyne estuary opposite North Shields. Pop: 83 704 (1991)

south-southeast *n* **1** the point on the compass or the direction midway between southeast and south ▷ *adj, adv* **2** in, from, or towards this direction

south-southwest *n* **1** the point on the compass or the direction midway between south and southwest ▷ *adj, adv* **2** in, from, or towards this direction

South Tyneside (ˈtaɪnˌsaɪd) *n* a unitary authority of NE England, in Tyne and Wear. Pop: 152 785 (2001). Area: 64 sq km (25 sq miles)

South Tyrol *or* **Tirol** *n* a former part of the Austrian state of Tyrol: ceded to Italy in 1919, becoming the Bolzano and Trento provinces of the Trentino-Alto Adige Autonomous Region. Area: 14 037 sq km (5420 sq miles)

South Vietnam *n* a former republic (1955–76) occupying the S of present-day Vietnam on the South China Sea and the Gulf of Siam > **South Vietnamese** *adj, n*

southward (ˈsaʊθwəd; *naut* ˈsʌðəd) *adj* **1** situated, directed, or moving towards the south ▷ *n* **2** the southward part, direction, etc ▷ *adv* **3** Also: **southwards** towards the south

Southwark (ˈsʌðək) *n* a borough of S central Greater London, on the River Thames: site of the Globe Theatre, now reconstructed; the former docks and warehouses have been redeveloped. Pop: 244 867 (2001). Area: 29 sq km (11 sq miles)

Southwell (ˈsaʊθwɛl) *n* **Saint Robert** ?1561–95, English poet and Roman Catholic martyr, who was imprisoned, tortured, and executed for his Jesuit activities. His best known poem is 'The Burning Babe'

southwest (ˌsaʊθˈwɛst; *naut* ˌsaʊˈwɛst) *n* **1** the point of the compass or the direction midway between west and south **2** (*often cap*; usually preceded by *the*) any area lying in or towards this direction ▷ *adj also* **southwestern** **3** (*sometimes cap*) of or denoting the southwestern part of a specified country, area, etc: *southwest Italy* **4** in or towards the southwest **5** (esp of the wind) from the southwest ▷ *adv* **6** in, to, or towards the southwest > ˌ**south'westernmost** *adj*

Southwest (ˌsaʊθˈwɛst) *n* (usually preceded by *the*) the southwestern part of Britain, esp Cornwall, Devon, and Somerset

South West Africa *n* another name for **Namibia**

southwest by south *n* **1** one point on the compass south of southwest ▷ *adj, adv* **2** in, from, or towards this direction

southwest by west *n* **1** one point on the compass north of southwest ▷ *adj, adv* **2** in, from, or towards this direction

southwester (ˌsaʊθˈwɛstə; *naut* ˌsaʊˈwɛstə) *n* a strong wind or storm from the southwest

southwesterly (ˌsaʊθˈwɛstəlɪ; *naut* ˌsaʊˈwɛstəlɪ) *adj, adv* **1** in, towards, or (esp of a wind) from the southwest ▷ *n, pl* **southwesterlies** **2** a wind or storm from the southwest

southwestward (ˌsaʊθˈwɛstwəd; *naut* ˌsaʊˈwɛstwəd) *adj* **1** from or towards the southwest ▷ *adv* **2** Also: **southwestwards** towards the southwest ▷ *n* **3** a direction towards or area in the southwest

South Yemen *n* a former republic in SW Arabia, on the Gulf of Aden; now a part of Yemen: became a republic in 1967; merged with North Yemen in 1990. Official name (1967–90): **People's Democratic Republic of Yemen** Name from 1963 to 1967 (excluding Aden): (Federation of) South Arabia. See also **Yemen, North Yemen**

South Yorkshire *n* a metropolitan county of N England, administered since 1986 by the unitary authorities of Barnsley, Doncaster, Sheffield, and Rotherham. Area: 1560 sq km (602 sq miles)

Soutine (*French* sutin) *n* **Chaim** (ˈxaɪɪm) 1893–1943, French expressionist painter, born in Russia; noted for his portraits and still lifes, esp of animal carcasses

souvenir (ˌsuːvəˈnɪə, ˈsuːvəˌnɪə) *n* **1** an object that recalls a certain place, occasion, or person; memento **2** *rare* a thing recalled ▷ *vb* **3** (*tr*) *Austral & NZ sl* to steal or keep for one's own use; purloin [C18 from F, from (*se*) *souvenir* to remember, from L *subvenīre* to come to mind]

Ss

sou'wester (saʊˈwɛstə) *n* a waterproof hat having a very broad rim behind, worn esp by seamen [C19 a contraction of SOUTHWESTER]

sovereign (ˈsɒvrɪn) *n* **1** a person exercising supreme authority, esp a monarch **2** a former British gold coin worth one pound sterling ▷ *adj* **3** supreme in rank or authority: *a sovereign lord* **4** excellent or outstanding: *a sovereign remedy* **5** of or relating to a sovereign **6** independent of outside authority: *a sovereign state* [C13 from OF *soverain*, from Vulgar L *superānus* (unattested), from L *super* above; also infl. by REIGN] > ˈ**sovereignly** *adv*

sovereigntist (ˈsɒvrəntɪst) (in Canada) ▷ *n* **1** a supporter of sovereignty association ▷ *adj* **2** supporting sovereignty association

sovereignty (ˈsɒvrəntɪ) *n, pl* **sovereignties** **1** supreme and unrestricted power, as of a state **2** the position, dominion, or authority of a sovereign **3** an independent state

sovereignty association *n* (in Canada) a proposed arrangement by which Quebec would become independent but would maintain a formal association with Canada

Sovetsk (*Russian* saˈvjɛtsk) *n* a town in W Russia, in the Kaliningrad Region on the Neman River: scene of the signing of the treaty (1807) between Napoleon I and Tsar Alexander I; passed from East Prussia to the Soviet Union in 1945. Former name (until 1945): **Tilsit**

soviet (ˈsəʊvɪət, ˈsɒv-) *n* **1** (in the former Soviet Union) an elected government council at the local, regional, and national levels, culminating in the Supreme Soviet ▷ *adj* **2** of or relating to a soviet [C20 from Russian *sovyet* council, from ORussian sŭvětŭ] > ˈ**sovieˌtism** *n*

Soviet ('səʊvɪət, 'sɒv-) *adj* of or relating to the former Soviet Union, its people, or its government

Soviet Central Asia *n* the region of the former Soviet Union now occupied by Kazakhstan, Kyrgyzstan, Tajikistan, Turkmenistan, and Uzbekistan. Also called: **Russian Turkestan, West Turkestan**

sovietize *or* **sovietise** ('səʊvɪɪˌtaɪz, 'sɒv-) *vb* **sovietizes, sovietizing, sovietized** *or* **sovietises, sovietising, sovietised** (*tr*) (*often cap*) **1** to bring (a country, person, etc) under Soviet control or influence **2** to cause (a country) to conform to the Soviet model in its social, political, and economic structure > ˌ**sovietiˈzation** *or* ˌ**sovietiˈsation** *n*

Soviet Russia *n* (formerly) another name for the **Russian Soviet Federative Socialist Republic** or the **Soviet Union**

Soviets ('səʊvɪəts, 'sɒv-) *pl n* the people or government of the former Soviet Union

Soviet Union *n* a former federal republic in E Europe and central and N Asia: the revolution of 1917 achieved the overthrow of the Russian monarchy and the USSR was established in 1922 as a Communist state. It was the largest country in the world, occupying a seventh of the total land surface. The collapse of Communist rule in 1991 was followed by declarations of independence by many of the constituent republics and the break-up of the Soviet Union. Official name: **Union of Soviet Socialist Republics** Also called: **Russia, Soviet Russia** Abbreviation: **USSR**

Soviet Zone *n* that part of Germany occupied by Soviet forces in 1945–49: transformed into the German Democratic Republic in 1949–50. Also called: **Russian Zone**

sow[1] (səʊ) *vb* **sows, sowing, sowed; sown** *or* **sowed 1** to scatter or place (seed, a crop, etc) in or on (a piece of ground, field, etc) so that it may grow: *to sow wheat; to sow a strip of land* **2** (*tr*) to implant or introduce: *to sow a doubt in someone's mind* [OE *sāwan*] > '**sower** *n*

sow[2] (saʊ) *n* **1** a female adult pig **2** the female of certain other animals, such as the mink **3** *metallurgy* **3a** the channels for leading molten metal to the moulds in casting pig iron **3b** iron that has solidified in these channels [OE *sugu*]

Soweto (sə'wɛtəʊ, -'weɪtəʊ) *n* a contiguous group of Black African townships southwest of Johannesburg, South Africa: the largest purely Black African urban settlement in southern Africa: scene of riots (1976) following protests against the use of Afrikaans in schools for Black African children. Area: 62 sq km (24 sq miles). Pop: 1 098 094 (1996) [c20 from *so(uth) we(st) to(wnship)*]

sown (səʊn) *vb* a past participle of **sow**[1]

sow thistle (saʊ) *n* any of various plants of an Old World genus, having milky juice, prickly leaves, and heads of yellow flowers

soya bean ('sɔɪə) *or US & Canad* **soybean** ('sɔɪˌbiːn) *n* **1** an Asian bean plant cultivated for its nutritious seeds, for forage, and to improve the soil **2** the seed, used as food, forage, and as the source of an oil [c17 *soya*, via Du. from Japanese *shōyu*, from Chinese *chiang yu*, from *chiang* paste + *yu* sauce]

Soyinka (sɔ'jɪŋkə) *n* **Wole** ('wɔːle) born 1934, Nigerian dramatist, novelist, poet, and literary critic. His works include the plays *The Strong Breed* (1963), *The Road* (1965), and *Kongi's Harvest* (1966), the novel *The Interpreters* (1965), and the political essays *The Burden of Memory, the Muse of Forgiveness* (1999); forced into exile by the military regime (1993–98). Nobel prize for literature 1986

soy sauce (sɔɪ) *n* a salty dark brown sauce made from fermented soya beans, used esp in Chinese cookery. Also called: **soya sauce**

sozzled ('sɒzəld) *adj* an informal word for **drunk** [c19 ?from obs. *sozzle* stupor]

SP *abbrev for* starting price

sp. *abbrev for:* **1** special **2** (*pl* **spp.**) species **3** specific

Sp. *abbrev for:* **1** Spain **2** Spaniard **3** Spanish

spa (spɑː) *n* a mineral spring or a place or resort where such a spring is found [c17 after Spa]

Spa (spɑː) *n* a town in E Belgium, in Liège province: a resort with medicinal mineral springs (discovered in the 14th century). Pop: 10 140 (1991)

Spaak (spɑːk) *n* **Paul Henri** (pɔl ɑ̃ri) 1899–1972, Belgian statesman, first socialist premier of Belgium (1937–38); a leading advocate of European unity, he was president of the consultative assembly of the Council of Europe (1949–51) and secretary-general of NATO (1957–61)

space (speɪs) *n* **1** the unlimited three-dimensional expanse in which all material objects are located. Related adj: **spatial 2** an interval of distance or time between two points, objects, or events **3** a blank portion or area **4a** unoccupied area or room: *there is no space for a table* **4b** (*in combination*): *space-saving*. Related adj: **spacious 5a** the region beyond the earth's atmosphere containing other planets, stars, galaxies, etc; universe **5b** (*as modifier*): *a space probe* **6** a seat or place, as on a train, aircraft, etc **7** *printing* a piece of metal, less than type-high, used to separate letters or words **8** *music* any of the gaps between the lines that make up the staff **9** Also called: **spacing** *Telegraphy*. the period of time that separates characters in Morse code ▷ *vb* **spaces, spacing, spaced** (*tr*) **10** to place or arrange at intervals or with spaces between **11** to divide into or by spaces: *to space one's time evenly* **12** *printing* to separate (letters, words, or lines) by the insertion of spaces [c13 from OF *espace*, from L *spatium*] > '**spacer** *n*

space age *n* **1** the period in which the exploration of space has become possible ▷ *adj* **space-age 2** (*usually prenominal*) futuristic or ultramodern

space-bar *n* a horizontal bar on a typewriter that is depressed in order to leave a space between words, letters, etc

space capsule *n* a vehicle, sometimes carrying people or animals, designed to obtain scientific information from space, planets, etc, and be recovered on returning to earth

spacecraft ('speɪsˌkrɑːft) *n* a manned or unmanned vehicle designed to orbit the earth or travel to celestial objects

spaced out *adj sl* intoxicated through or as if through taking a drug. Often shortened to **spaced**

space heater *n* a heater used to warm the air in an enclosed area, such as a room

Space Invaders *n trademark* a video or computer game, the object of which is to destroy attacking alien spacecraft

spaceman ('speɪsˌmæn) *or* (*fem*) **spacewoman** *n, pl* **spacemen** *or* (*fem*) **spacewomen** a person who travels in outer space

space platform *n* another name for **space station**

spaceport ('speɪsˌpɔːt) *n* a base equipped to launch, maintain, and test spacecraft

space probe *n* a vehicle, such as a satellite, equipped to obtain scientific information, normally transmitted back to earth by radio, about a planet, conditions in space, etc

spaceship ('speɪsˌʃɪp) *n* a manned spacecraft

space shuttle *n* any of a series of reusable US space vehicles (*Columbia* (exploded 2003), *Challenger* (exploded 1986), *Discovery*, *Atlantis*, *Endeavor*) that can be launched into earth orbit transporting astronauts and equipment for a period of observation, research, etc, before re-entry and an unpowered landing on a runway; the first operational flight was in 1982

space station *n* any large manned artificial satellite designed to orbit the earth during a long period of time thus providing a base for scientific research in space and a construction site, launch pad, and docking arrangements for spacecraft

spacesuit ('speɪsˌsuːt, -ˌsjuːt) *n* a sealed and pressurized suit worn by astronauts providing an artificial atmosphere, acceptable temperature, radiocommunication link, and protection from radiation

space-time *or* **space-time continuum** *n physics* the four-dimensional continuum having three spatial coordinates and one time coordinate that together completely specify the location of a particle or an event

spacewalk ('speɪsˌwɔːk) *n* **1** the act or an instance of floating and manoeuvring in space, outside but attached by a lifeline to a spacecraft. Technical name: **extravehicular activity** ▷ *vb* **2** (*intr*) to engage in this activity

spacey ('speɪsɪ) *adj* **spacier, spaciest** *sl* vague and dreamy, as if under the influence of drugs [C20 SPACE + -EY]

Spacey ('speɪsɪ) *n* **Kevin,** original name *Kevin Spacey Fowler*. born 1959, US actor; films include *Glengarry Glen Ross* (1992), *The Usual suspects* (1995), *American Beauty* (1999), which earned him an Academy Award, and *The Shipping News* (2001)

spacial ('speɪʃəl) *adj* a variant spelling of **spatial**

spacing ('speɪsɪŋ) *n* **1** the arrangement of letters, words, spaces, etc, on a page **2** the arrangement of objects in a space

spacious ('speɪʃəs) *adj* having a large capacity or area > '**spaciously** *adv* > '**spaciousness** *n*

SPAD (spæd) *n acronym for* signal passed at danger: an incident in which a train goes through a red light

spade[1] (speɪd) *n* **1** a tool for digging, typically consisting of a flat rectangular steel blade attached to a long wooden handle **2** something resembling a spade **3** a cutting tool for stripping the blubber from a whale or skin from a carcass **4** **call a spade a spade** to speak plainly and frankly ▷ *vb* **spades, spading, spaded** **5** (*tr*) to use a spade on [OE *spadu*] > '**spader** *n*

spade[2] (speɪd) *n* **1a** the black symbol on a playing card resembling a heart-shaped leaf with a stem **1b** a card with one or more of these symbols or (*when pl*) the suit of cards so marked, usually the highest ranking of the four **2** a derogatory word for a **Black**[1] **3** **in spades** *inf* in an extreme or emphatic way [C16 from It. *spada* sword, used as an emblem on playing cards, from L *spatha*, from Gk *spathē* blade]

spadework ('speɪdˌwɜːk) *n* dull or routine preparatory work

spadix ('speɪdɪks) *n, pl* **spadices** (speɪ'daɪsiːz) a spike of small flowers on a fleshy stem, the whole usually being surrounded by a spathe [C18 from L: pulled-off branch of a palm, with its fruit, from Gk: torn-off frond]

spaghetti (spə'gɛtɪ) *n* pasta in the form of long strings [C19 from It.: little cords, from *spago* a cord]

spaghetti junction *n* a junction, usually between motorways, in which there are a large number of intersecting roads used by a large volume of high-speed traffic [C20 from the nickname given to the Gravelly Hill Interchange, Birmingham, where the M6, A38M, A38, and A5127 intersect]

spaghetti western *n* a cowboy film made in Europe, esp by an Italian director

▷ www.everything2.com/index.pl?node=Spaghetti%20western
▷ www.plume-noire.com/movies/cult/spaghettiwesterns.html

spahi *or* **spahee** ('spɑːhiː, 'spɑːiː) *n, pl* **spahis** *or* **spahees** **1** (formerly) an irregular cavalryman in the Turkish army **2** (formerly) a member of a body of native Algerian cavalry in the French army [C16 from OF, from Turkish *sipahi*, from Persian *sipāhī* soldier]

Spain (speɪn) *n* a kingdom of SW Europe, occupying the Iberian peninsula between the Mediterranean and the Atlantic: a leading European power in the 16th century, with many overseas possessions, esp in the New World; became a republic in 1931; under the fascist dictatorship of Franco following the Civil War (1936–39) until his death in 1975; a member of the European Union. It consists chiefly of a central plateau (the Meseta), with the Pyrenees and the Cantabrian Mountains in the north and the Sierra Nevada in the south. Official language: Castilian Spanish, with Catalan, Galician, and Basque official regional languages. Religion: Roman Catholic majority. Currency: euro. Capital: Madrid. Pop: 40 144 000 (2001). Area: 504 748 sq km (194 883 sq miles). Spanish name: **España**

▷ www.tourspain.es
▷ www.tizz.com/spain
▷ www.spaintour.com

spake (speɪk) *vb arch* a past tense of **speak**

Spalato ('spaːlato) *n* the Italian name for **Split**

Spalding ('spɔːldɪŋ) *n* a town in E England, in S Lincolnshire: noted for its bulbfields. Pop: 18 731 (1991)

spam (spæm) *computing sl* ▷ *vb* **spams, spamming, spammed** **1** to send unsolicited electronic mail simultaneously to a number of newsgroups on the Internet ▷ *n* **2** unsolicited electronic mail sent in this way [C20 from the repeated use of the word *Spam* in a popular sketch from the Brit television show *Monty Python's Flying Circus*, first broadcast in 1969] > '**spammer** *n* > '**spamming** *n*

Spam (spæm) *n trademark* a kind of tinned luncheon meat, made largely from pork

spammie ('spæmɪ) *n Northern English dialect* a love bite

span[1] (spæn) *n* **1** the interval, space, or distance between two points, such as the ends of a bridge or arch **2** the complete duration or extent: *the span of his life* **3** *psychol* the amount of material that can be processed in a single mental act: *span of attention* **4** short for **wingspan** **5** a unit of length based on the width of an expanded hand, usually taken as nine inches ▷ *vb* **spans, spanning, spanned** (*tr*) **6** to stretch or extend across, over, or around **7** to provide with something that spans: *to span a river with a bridge* **8** to measure or cover, esp with the extended hand [OE *spann*]

span[2] (spæn) *n* a team of horses or oxen, esp two matched animals [C16 (in the sense: yoke): from MDu.: something stretched, from *spannen* to stretch]

span[3] (spæn) *vb arch or dialect* a past tense of **spin**

Span. *abbrev for* Spanish

spandrel *or* **spandril** ('spændrəl) *n archit* **1** an approximately triangular surface bounded by the outer curve of an arch and the adjacent wall **2** the surface area between two adjacent arches and the horizontal cornice above them [C15 *spaundrell*, from Anglo-F *spaundre*, from OF *spandre* to spread]

spangle ('spæŋgᵊl) *n* **1** a small thin piece of metal or other shiny material used as a decoration, esp on clothes; sequin **2** any glittering or shiny spot or object ▷ *vb* **spangles, spangling, spangled** **3** (*intr*) to glitter or shine with or like spangles **4** (*tr*) to cover with spangles [C15 dim. of *spange*, ?from MDu.: clasp] > '**spangly** *adj*

Spaniard ('spænjəd) *n* a native or inhabitant of Spain

spaniel ('spænjəl) *n* **1** any of several breeds of gundog with long drooping ears and a silky coat **2** an obsequiously devoted person [C14 from OF *espaigneul* Spanish (dog), from OProvençal *espanhol*, ult. from L *Hispāniolus* Spanish]

Spanish ('spænɪʃ) *n* **1** the official language of Spain, Mexico, and most countries of South and Central America (except Brazil), as well as several other countries. Spanish is an Indo-European language belonging to the Romance group **2** **the Spanish** (*functioning as pl*) the natives, citizens, or inhabitants of Spain ▷ *adj* **3** of or relating to the Spanish language or

Ss

its speakers 4 of or relating to Spain or Spaniards

Spanish America *n* the parts of America colonized by Spaniards from the 16th century onwards and now chiefly Spanish-speaking: includes all of South America (except Brazil, Guyana, French Guiana, and Surinam), Central America (except Belize), Mexico, Cuba, Puerto Rico, the Dominican Republic, and a number of small Caribbean islands

Spanish-American *adj* 1 of or relating to any of the Spanish-speaking countries or peoples of the Americas ▷ *n* 2 a native or inhabitant of Spanish America 3 a Spanish-speaking person in the US

Spanish customs *or* **practices** *pl n inf* irregular practices among a group of workers to gain increased financial allowances, reduced working hours, etc

Spanish fly *n* 1 a European blister beetle, the dried body of which yields cantharides 2 another name for **cantharides**

Spanish Guinea *n* the former name (until 1964) of **Equatorial Guinea**

Spanish guitar *n* the classic form of the guitar; a six-stringed instrument with a waisted body and a central sound hole

Spanish Main *n* 1 the mainland of Spanish America, esp the N coast of South America 2 the Caribbean Sea, the S part of which in colonial times was the haunt of pirates

Spanish Morocco *n* a former Spanish colony on the N coast of Morocco: part of the kingdom of Morocco since 1956 > **Spanish Moroccan** *adj, n*

Spanish moss *n* 1 an epiphytic plant growing in tropical and subtropical regions as long bluish-grey strands suspended from the branches of trees 2 a tropical lichen growing as long trailing green threads from the branches of trees

Spanish omelette *n* an omelette containing green peppers, onions, tomato, etc

Spanish rice *n* rice cooked with tomatoes, onions, green peppers, etc

Spanish Sahara *n* the former name (until 1975) of **Western Sahara**

Spanish West Africa *n* a former overseas territory of Spain in NW Africa: divided in 1958 into the overseas provinces of Ifni and Spanish Sahara > **Spanish West African** *adj, n*

spank[1] (spæŋk) *vb* 1 (*tr*) to slap with the open hand, esp on the buttocks ▷ *n* 2 one or a series of these slaps [C18 prob. imit.]

spank[2] (spæŋk) *vb* (*intr*) to go at a quick and lively pace [C19 back formation from SPANKING[2]]

spanker ('spæŋkə) *n* 1 a person or thing that spanks 2 *naut* a fore-and-aft sail or a mast that is aftermost in a sailing vessel 3 *inf* something outstandingly fine or large

spanking[1] ('spæŋkɪŋ) *n* a series of spanks, usually as a punishment for children

spanking[2] ('spæŋkɪŋ) *adj* (*prenominal*) 1 *inf* outstandingly fine, smart, large, etc 2 quick and energetic 3 (esp of a breeze) fresh and brisk

spanner ('spænə) *n* 1 a steel hand tool with jaws or a hole, designed to grip a nut or bolt head 2 **spanner in the works** *Brit inf* an impediment or annoyance [C17 from G, from *spannen* to stretch]

span roof *n* a roof consisting of two equal sloping sides

spanspek (ˌspæn'spɛk) *n S African* the sweet melon [C19 possibly from Afrik.: literally, Spanish bacon]

spar[1] (spɑː) *n* 1 any piece of nautical gear resembling a pole and used as a mast, boom, gaff, etc 2 a principal supporting structural member of an aerofoil that runs from tip to tip or root to tip [C13 from ON *sperra* beam]

spar[2] (spɑː) *vb* **spars, sparring, sparred** (*intr*) 1 *boxing & martial arts* to box using light blows, as in training 2 to dispute or argue 3 (of gamecocks, etc) to fight with the feet or spurs ▷ *n* 4 an unaggressive fight 5 an argument or wrangle [OE, ? from SPUR]

spar[3] (spɑː) *n* any of various minerals, such as feldspar, that are light-coloured, crystalline, and easily cleavable [C16 from MLow G *spar*]

sparaxis (spər'æksɪs) *n* a South African plant of the iris family, having lacerated spathes and showy flowers [C19 NL, from Gk, from *sparassō* to tear]

spare (spɛə) *vb* **spares, sparing, spared** 1 (*tr*) to refrain from killing, punishing, or injuring 2 (*tr*) to release or relieve, as from pain, suffering, etc 3 (*tr*) to refrain from using: *spare the rod, spoil the child* 4 (*tr*) to be able to afford or give: *I can't spare the time* 5 (*usually passive*) (esp of Providence) to allow to survive: *I'll see you next year if we are spared* 6 (*intr*) *now rare* to act or live frugally 7 **not spare oneself** to exert oneself to the full 8 **to spare** more than is required: *two minutes to spare* ▷ *adj* 9 (*often immediately postpositive*) in excess of what is needed; additional 10 able to be used when needed: *a spare part* 11 (of a person) thin and lean 12 scanty or meagre 13 (*postpositive*) *Brit sl* upset, angry, or distracted (esp in **go spare**) ▷ *n* 14 a duplicate kept as a replacement in case of damage or loss 15 a spare tyre 16 *tenpin bowling* 16a the act of knocking down all the pins with the two bowls of a single frame 16b the score thus made [OE *sparian* to refrain from injuring] > '**sparely** *adv* > '**spareness** *n* > '**sparer** *n*

spare-part surgery *n* surgical replacement of defective or damaged organs by transplant or insertion of artficial devices

sparerib (ˌspɛə'rɪb) *n* a cut of pork ribs with most of the meat trimmed off

spare tyre *n* 1 an additional tyre carried by a motor vehicle in case of puncture 2 *Brit sl* a deposit of fat just above the waist

sparing ('spɛərɪŋ) *adj* 1 (sometimes foll by *of*) economical or frugal (with) 2 scanty; meagre 3 merciful or lenient > '**sparingly** *adv* > '**sparingness** *n*

spark[1] (spɑːk) *n* 1 a fiery particle thrown out or left by burning material or caused by the friction of two hard surfaces 2a a momentary flash of light accompanied by a sharp crackling noise, produced by a sudden electrical discharge through the air or some other insulating medium between two points 2b the electrical discharge itself 2c (*as modifier*): *a spark gap* 3 anything that serves to animate or kindle 4 a trace or hint: *a spark of interest* 5 vivacity, enthusiasm, or humour 6 a small piece of diamond, as used in cutting glass ▷ *vb* 7 (*intr*) to give off sparks 8 (*intr*) (of the sparking plug or ignition system of an internal-combustion engine) to produce a spark 9 (*tr; often foll by off*) to kindle or animate ▷ See also **sparks** [OE *spearca*]

spark[2] (spɑːk) *n* 1 *rare* a fashionable or gallant young man 2 **bright spark** *Brit, usually ironic* a person who appears clever or witty [C16 (in the sense: beautiful or witty woman): ? of Scand. origin] > '**sparkish** *adj*

Spark (spɑːk) *n* Dame **Muriel** (**Sarah**) born 1918, British novelist and writer; her novels include *Memento Mori* (1959), *The Prime of Miss Jean Brodie* (1961), *A Far Cry from Kensington* (1988), *Symposium* (1990), and *The Finishing School* (2004)

spark gap *n* the space between two electrodes across which a spark can jump

sparkie ('spɑːkɪ) *n* an informal name for an electrician

sparking plug *n* a device screwed into the cylinder head of an internal-combustion engine to ignite the explosive mixture by means of an electric spark. Also called: **spark plug**

sparkle ('spɑːkᵊl) *vb* **sparkles, sparkling, sparkled** 1 to issue or reflect or cause to issue or reflect bright points of light 2 (*intr*) (of wine, mineral water, etc) to effervesce 3 (*intr*) to be vivacious or witty ▷ *n* 4 a point of light, spark, or gleam 5 vivacity or wit [C12 *sparklen*, frequentative of *sparken* to SPARK[1]]

sparkler ('spɑːklə) *n* **1** a type of firework that throws out sparks **2** *inf* a sparkling gem

sparkling wine *n* a wine made effervescent by carbon dioxide gas added artificially or produced naturally by secondary fermentation

spark plug *n* another name for **sparking plug**

sparks (spɑːks) *n (functioning as sing) Inf* **1** an electrician **2** a radio officer, esp on a ship

sparky ('spɑːkɪ) *adj* **sparkier, sparkiest** lively, vivacious, spirited

sparring partner ('spɑːrɪŋ) *n* **1** a person who practises with a boxer during training **2** a person with whom one has friendly arguments

sparrow ('spærəʊ) *n* **1** any of various weaverbirds, esp the house sparrow, having a brown or grey plumage and feeding on seeds or insects **2** *US & Canad* any of various North American finches, such as the chipping sparrow, that have a dullish streaked plumage ▷ See also **hedge sparrow, tree sparrow** [OE *spearwa*]

sparrowgrass ('spærəʊˌgrɑːs) *n* a dialect or popular name for **asparagus**

sparrowhawk ('spærəʊˌhɔːk) *n* any of several small hawks of Eurasia and N Africa that prey on smaller birds

sparrow hawk *n* a very small North American falcon, closely related to the kestrels

sparse (spɑːs) *adj* scattered or scanty; not dense [C18 from L *sparsus*, from *spargere* to scatter] > **'sparsely** *adv* > **'sparseness** *or* **'sparsity** *n*

Sparta ('spɑːtə) *n* an ancient Greek city in the S Peloponnese, famous for the discipline and military prowess of its citizens and for their austere way of life ▷ www.sikyon.com/Sparta/history_eg.html

Spartacus ('spɑːtəkəs) *n* died 71 BC, Thracian slave, who led an ultimately unsuccessful revolt of gladiators against Rome (73–71 BC)

Spartan ('spɑːtᵊn) *adj* **1** of or relating to Sparta or its citizens **2** *(sometimes not cap)* very strict or austere: *a Spartan upbringing* **3** *(sometimes not cap)* possessing courage and resolve ▷ *n* **4** a citizen of Sparta **5** *(sometimes not cap)* a disciplined or brave person

spasm ('spæzəm) *n* **1** an involuntary muscular contraction, esp one resulting in cramp or convulsion **2** a sudden burst of activity, emotion, etc [C14 from L *spasmus*, from Gk *spasmos* a cramp, from *span* to tear]

spasmodic (spæz'mɒdɪk) *or (rarely)* **spasmodical** *adj* **1** taking place in sudden brief spells **2** of or characterized by spasms [C17 NL, from Gk *spasmos* SPASM] > **spas'modically** *adv*

Spassky ('spæskɪ; *Russian* 'spaskij) *n* **Boris** (ba'ris) born 1937, Russian chess player; world champion (1969–72)

spastic ('spæstɪk) *n* **1** a person who is affected by spasms or convulsions, esp one who has cerebral palsy **2** *offens sl* a clumsy, incapable, or incompetent person ▷ *adj* **3** affected by or resembling spasms **4** *offens sl* clumsy, incapable, or incompetent [C18 from L *spasticus*, from Gk, from *spasmos* SPASM] > **'spastically** *adv* > **spas'ticity** (spæs'tɪsɪtɪ) *n*

spat[1] (spæt) *n* **1** *now rare* a slap or smack **2** a slight quarrel ▷ *vb* **spats, spatting, spatted** **3** *rare* to slap (someone) **4** *(intr) US, Canad, & NZ* to have a slight quarrel [C19 prob. imit.]

spat[2] (spæt) *vb* a past tense and past participle of **spit**[1]

spat[3] (spæt) *n* another name for **gaiter** (sense 2) [C19 short for SPATTERDASH]

spat[4] (spæt) *n* **1** a larval oyster or similar bivalve mollusc **2** such oysters or other molluscs collectively [C17 from Anglo-Norman *spat*]

spatchcock ('spætʃˌkɒk) *n* **1** a chicken or game bird split down the back and grilled ▷ *vb (tr)* **2** to interpolate (words, a story, etc) into a sentence, narrative, etc, esp inappropriately [C18 ? var. of *spitchcock* eel when prepared & cooked]

spate (speɪt) *n* **1** a fast flow, rush, or outpouring: *a spate of words* **2** *chiefly Brit* a sudden flood: *the rivers were in spate* **3** *chiefly Brit* a sudden heavy downpour [C15 (Scot & N English): from ?]

spathe (speɪð) *n* a large bract that encloses the inflorescence of aroid plants and palms [C18 from L *spatha*, from Gk *spathē* a blade] > **spathaceous** (spə'θeɪʃəs) *adj*

spathic ('spæθɪk) *or* **spathose** ('spæθəʊs) *adj* (of minerals) resembling spar, esp in having good cleavage [C18 from G *Spat* SPAR[3]]

spatial *or* **spacial** ('speɪʃəl) *adj* **1** of or relating to space **2** existing or happening in space > **spatiality** (ˌspeɪʃɪ'ælɪtɪ) *n* > **'spatially** *adv*

spatiotemporal (ˌspeɪʃɪəʊ'tɛmpərəl) *adj* **1** of or existing in both space and time **2** of or concerned with space-time > ˌ**spatio'temporally** *adv*

spatter ('spætə) *vb* **1** to scatter or splash (a substance, esp a liquid) or (of a substance) to splash (something) in scattered drops: *to spatter mud on the car; mud spattered in her face* **2** *(tr)* to sprinkle, cover, or spot (with a liquid) **3** *(tr)* to slander or defame **4** *(intr)* to shower or rain down: *bullets spattered around them* ▷ *n* **5** the sound of spattering **6** something spattered, such as a spot or splash **7** the act or an instance of spattering [C16 imit.]

spatterdash ('spætəˌdæʃ) *n* **1** *US* another name for **roughcast** **2** *(pl)* long leather leggings worn in the 18th century, as to protect from mud when riding [C17 see SPATTER, DASH[1]]

spatula ('spætjʊlə) *n* a utensil with a broad flat blade, used for lifting, spreading, or stirring foods, etc [C16 from L: a broad piece, from *spatha* a flat wooden implement; see SPATHE] > **'spatular** *adj*

spatulate ('spætjʊlɪt) *adj* **1** shaped like a spatula; having thickened rounded ends: *spatulate fingers* **2** Also: **spathulate** *bot* having a narrow base and a broad rounded apex

spavin ('spævɪn) *n* enlargement of the hock of a horse by a bony growth (**bony spavin**) or fluid accumulation in the joint (**bog spavin**), often resulting in lameness [C15 from OF *espavin*, from ?] > **'spavined** *adj*

Ss

spawn (spɔːn) *n* **1** the mass of eggs deposited by fish, amphibians, or molluscs **2** *often derog* offspring, product, or yield **3** *bot* the nontechnical name for **mycelium** ▷ *vb* **4** (of fish, amphibians, etc) to produce or deposit (eggs) **5** *often derog* (of people) to produce (offspring) **6** *(tr)* to produce or engender [C14 from Anglo-Norman *espaundre*, from OF *spandre* to spread out] > **'spawner** *n*

spay (speɪ) *vb (tr)* to remove the ovaries, and usually the uterus, from (a female animal) [C15 from OF *espeer* to cut with the sword, from *espee* sword, from L *spatha*]

spaza shop ('spɑːzə) *n S African sl* a small informal shop in a township, often run from a private house [from slang, dummy, camouflaged]

SPCK (in Britain) *abbrev for* Society for Promoting Christian Knowledge

speak (spiːk) *vb* **speaks, speaking, spoke, spoken** **1** to make (verbal utterances); utter (words) **2** to communicate or express (something) in or as if in words **3** *(intr)* to deliver a speech, discourse, etc **4** *(tr)* to know how to talk in (a language or dialect): *he does not speak German* **5** *(intr)* to make a characteristic sound: *the clock spoke* **6** *(intr)* (of hounds used in hunting) to give tongue; bark **7** *(tr) naut* to hail and communicate with (another vessel) at sea **8** *(intr)* (of a musical instrument) to produce a sound **9** **on speaking terms** on good terms; friendly **10** **so to speak** in a manner of speaking; as it were **11** **speak one's mind** to express one's opinions frankly and plainly **12** **to speak of** of a significant or worthwhile nature: *no support to speak of* ▷ See also **speak for, speak out, speak to** [OE *specan*] > **'speakable** *adj*

speakeasy ('spiːkˌiːzɪ) *n, pl* **speakeasies** *US* a place where alcoholic drink was sold illicitly during Prohibition

speaker ('spi:kə) *n* **1** a person who speaks, esp at a formal occasion **2** See **loudspeaker** > **'speakership** *n*

Speaker ('spi:kə) *n* the presiding officer in any of numerous legislative bodies

speak for *vb (intr, prep)* **1** to speak as a representative of (other people) **2** **speak for itself** to be so evident that no further comment is necessary **3** **speak for yourself** *inf* (used as an imperative) do not presume that other people agree with you

speaking ('spi:kɪŋ) *adj* **1** *(prenominal)* eloquent, impressive, or striking **2a** able to speak **2b** *(in combination)* able to speak a particular language: *French-speaking*

speaking clock *n Brit* a telephone service that gives a verbal statement of the time

speaking in tongues *n* another term for **gift of tongues**

speaking tube *n* a tube for conveying a person's voice from one room or building to another

speak out *or* **up** *vb (intr, adv)* **1** to state one's beliefs, objections, etc, bravely and firmly **2** to speak more loudly and clearly

speak to *vb (intr, prep)* **1** to address (a person) **2** to reprimand **3** *formal* to give evidence of or comments on (a subject)

spear[1] (spɪə) *n* **1** a weapon consisting of a long shaft with a sharp pointed end of metal, stone, or wood that may be thrown or thrust **2** a similar implement used to catch fish **3** another name for **spearman** ▷ *vb* **4** to pierce (something) with or as if with a spear [OE *spere*]

spear[2] (spɪə) *n* a shoot, stalk, or blade, as of grass [C16 prob. var. of SPIRE[1], infl. by SPEAR[1]]

spear grass *n* **1** Also called: **wild Spaniard** a New Zealand grass with sharp leaves that grows on mountains **2** any of various other grasses with sharp stiff blades or seeds

spear gun *n* a device for shooting spears underwater

spearhead ('spɪəˌhɛd) *n* **1** the pointed head of a spear **2** the leading force in a military attack **3** any person or thing that leads or initiates an attack, campaign, etc ▷ *vb* **4** *(tr)* to lead or initiate (an attack, campaign, etc)

spearman ('spɪəmən) *n, pl* **spearmen** a soldier armed with a spear

spearmint ('spɪəmɪnt) *n* a purple-flowered mint plant of Europe, having leaves that yield an oil used for flavouring

Spears (spɪəz) *n* **Britney** ('brɪtnɪ) born 1981, US pop singer; records include the single "Baby One More Time" (1998) and the album *Britney* (2001)

spec (spɛk) *n* **1** **on spec** *inf* as a speculation or gamble: *all the tickets were sold so I went to the theatre on spec* ▷ *adj* **2** *(prenominal) Austral & NZ inf* speculative: *a spec developer*

spec. *abbrev for:* **1** specification **2** speculation

speccy ('spɛkɪ) *adj* **speccier, specciest** *sl* wearing spectacles

special ('spɛʃəl) *adj* **1** distinguished from, set apart from, or excelling others of its kind **2** *(prenominal)* designed or reserved for a particular purpose **3** not usual or commonplace **4** *(prenominal)* particular or primary: *his special interest was music* ▷ *n* **5** a special person or thing, such as an extra edition of a newspaper or a train reserved for a particular purpose **6** a dish or meal given prominence, esp at a low price, in a café, etc **7** short for **special constable** **8** *US, Canad, Austral, & NZ inf* an item in a store advertised at a reduced price ▷ *vb* **specials, specialling, specialled** *(tr)* **9** (of a nurse) to give (a gravely ill patient) constant individual care **10** *NZ inf* to advertise and sell (an item) at a reduced price [C13 from OF *especial*, from L *speciālis* individual, special, from *speciēs* appearance] > **'specially** *adv* > **'specialness** *n*

Special Branch *n* (in Britain) the department of the police force that is concerned with political security

special clearing *n banking* (in Britain) the clearing of a cheque through a bank in less than the usual three days, for an additional charge

special constable *n* a person recruited for temporary or occasional police duties, esp in time of emergency

special delivery *n* the delivery of a piece of mail outside the time of a scheduled delivery

special drawing rights *pl n (sometimes caps)* the reserve assets of the International Monetary Fund on which member nations may draw

special effects *pl n Films.* techniques used in the production of scenes that cannot be achieved by normal techniques

▷ www.howstuffworks.com/blue-screen.htm

▷ www.cinefex.com

special forces *pl n* elite, highly trained military forces, specially selected to work on difficult missions

specialist ('spɛʃəlɪst) *n* a person who specializes in a particular activity, field of research, etc > **'specialˌism** *n* > **ˌspecial'istic** *adj*

specialist registrar *n* a hospital doctor senior to a house officer but junior to a consultant, specializing in medicine (**medical specialist registrar**), surgery (**surgical specialist registrar**), or some subspeciality of either

speciality (ˌspɛʃɪ'ælɪtɪ) *or esp US & Canad* **specialty** *n, pl* **specialities** *or esp US & Canad* **specialties** **1** a special interest or skill **2a** a service or product specialized in, as at a restaurant **2b** *(as modifier): a speciality dish* **3** a special feature or characteristic

specialize *or* **specialise** ('spɛʃəˌlaɪz) *vb* **specializes, specializing, specialized** *or* **specialises, specialising, specialised** **1** *(intr)* to train in or devote oneself to a particular area of study, occupation, or activity **2** *(usually passive)* to cause (organisms or parts) to develop in a way most suited to a particular environment or way of life or (of organisms, etc) to develop in this way **3** *(tr)* to modify for a special use or purpose > **ˌspeciali'zation** *or* **ˌspeciali'sation** *n*

special licence *n Brit* a licence permitting a marriage to take place by dispensing with the usual legal conditions

special needs *or* **special educational needs** *pl n* **a** the educational requirements of pupils or students suffering from any of a wide range of physical disabilities, medical conditions, intellectual difficulties, or emotional problems, including deafness, blindness, dyslexia, learning difficulties, and behavioural problems **b** *(as modifier): special-needs teachers*

special pleading *n law* **1** a pleading that alleges new facts that offset those put forward by the other side rather than directly admitting or denying those facts **2** a pleading that emphasizes the favourable aspects of a case while omitting the unfavourable

special school *n Brit* a school for children who are unable to benefit from ordinary schooling because they have learning difficulties, physical or mental handicaps, etc

special team *n American football* any of several predetermined permutations of the players within a team that play in situations, such as kickoffs and attempts at field goals, where the standard offensive and defensive formations are not appropriate

specialty ('spɛʃəltɪ) *n, pl* **specialties** **1** *law* a formal contract or obligation expressed in a deed **2** a variant (esp US and Canad) of **speciality**

speciation (ˌspi:ʃɪ'eɪʃən) *n* the evolutionary development of a biological species

specie ('spi:ʃi:) *n* **1** coin money, as distinguished from bullion or paper money **2** **in specie** **2a** (of money) in coin **2b** in kind [C16 from L *in speciē* in kind]

species ('spi:ʃi:z; *Latin* 'spi:ʃɪˌi:z) *n, pl* **species** **1** *biol* **1a** any of the taxonomic groups into which a genus is divided, the members of which are capable of interbreeding. Abbrev: **sp** **1b** the animals of such a group **1c** any group of related animals or plants not necessarily of this taxonomic rank **2** *(modifier)* denoting a plant that is a natural member of a species rather than a hybrid or cultivar: *a species clematis* **3** *logic* a group of objects or individuals, all sharing common attributes, that forms a subdivision of a genus **4** a kind, sort, or variety: *a species of treachery* **5** *chiefly RC Church* the outward form of the bread and wine in the Eucharist **6** *obs* an outward appearance or form [C16 from L: appearance, from *specere* to look]

specific (spɪˈsɪfɪk) *adj* **1** explicit, particular, or definite **2** relating to a specified or particular thing: *a specific treatment for arthritis* **3** of or relating to a biological species **4** (of a disease) caused by a particular pathogenic agent **5** *physics* **5a** characteristic of a property of a substance, esp in relation to the same property of a standard reference substance: *specific gravity* **5b** characteristic of a property of a substance per unit mass, length, area, etc: *specific heat* **5c** (of an extensive physical quantity) divided by mass: *specific volume* **6** denoting a tariff levied at a fixed sum per unit of weight, quantity, volume, etc, irrespective of value ▷ *n* **7** (*sometimes pl*) a designated quality, thing, etc **8** *med* any drug used to treat a particular disease [C17 from Med. L *specificus*, from L SPECIES] > **speˈcifically** *adv* > **specificity** (ˌspɛsɪˈfɪsɪtɪ) *n*

specification (ˌspɛsɪfɪˈkeɪʃən) *n* **1** the act or an instance of specifying **2** (in patent law) a written statement accompanying an application for a patent that describes the nature of an invention **3** a detailed description of the criteria for the constituents, construction, appearance, performance, etc, of a material, apparatus, etc, or of the standard of workmanship required in its manufacture **4** an item, detail, etc, specified

specific charge *n physics* the charge-to-mass ratio of an elementary particle

specific gravity *n* the ratio of the density of a substance to that of water

specific heat capacity *n* the heat required to raise unit mass of a substance by unit temperature interval under specified conditions, such as constant pressure. Also called: **specific heat**

specific humidity *n* the mass of water vapour in a sample of moist air divided by the mass of the sample

specific volume *n physics* the volume of matter per unit mass

specify (ˈspɛsɪˌfaɪ) *vb* **specifies, specifying, specified** (*tr; may take a clause as object*) **1** to refer to or state specifically **2** to state as a condition **3** to state or include in the specification of [C13 from Med. L *specificāre* to describe] > ˈ**speciˌfiable** *adj* > **specificative** (ˈspɛsɪfɪˌkeɪtɪv) *adj*

specimen (ˈspɛsɪmɪn) *n* **1a** an individual, object, or part regarded as typical of its group or class **1b** (*as modifier*): *a specimen page* **2** *med* a sample of tissue, blood, urine, etc, taken for diagnostic examination or evaluation **3** the whole or a part of an organism, plant, rock, etc, collected and preserved as an example of its class, species, etc **4** *inf, often derog* a person [C17 from L: mark, proof, from *specere* to look at]

specious (ˈspiːʃəs) *adj* **1** apparently correct or true, but actually wrong or false **2** deceptively attractive in appearance [C14 (orig.: fair): from L *speciōsus* plausible, from *speciēs* outward appearance, from *specere* to look at] > ˈ**speciously** *adv* > **speciosity** (ˌspiːʃɪˈɒsɪtɪ) *or* ˈ**speciousness** *n*

speck (spɛk) *n* **1** a very small mark or spot **2** a small or tiny piece of something ▷ *vb* **3** (*tr*) to mark with specks or spots [OE *specca*]

speckle (ˈspɛkᵊl) *n* **1** a small mark usually of a contrasting colour, as on the skin, eggs, etc ▷ *vb* **speckles, speckling, speckled** **2** (*tr*) to mark with or as if with speckles [C15 from MDu. *spekkel*] > ˈ**speckled** *adj*

specs (spɛks) *pl n inf* short for **spectacles**

spectacle (ˈspɛktəkᵊl) *n* **1** a public display or performance, esp a showy or ceremonial one **2** a thing or person seen, esp an unusual or ridiculous one: *he makes a spectacle of himself* **3** a strange or interesting object or phenomenon [C14 via OF from L *spectaculum* a show, from *spectāre* to watch, from *specere* to look at]

spectacles (ˈspɛktəkᵊlz) *pl n* a pair of glasses for correcting defective vision. Often (informal) shortened to **specs** > ˈ**spectacled** *adj*

spectacular (spɛkˈtækjʊlə) *adj* **1** of or resembling a spectacle; impressive, grand, or dramatic **2** unusually marked or great: *a spectacular increase* ▷ *n* **3** a lavishly produced performance > **specˈtacularly** *adv*

spectate (spɛkˈteɪt) *vb* **spectates, spectating, spectated** (*intr*) to be a spectator; watch [C20 back formation from SPECTATOR]

spectator (spɛkˈteɪtə) *n* a person viewing anything; onlooker; observer [C16 from L, from *spectāre* to watch; see SPECTACLE]

spectator sport *n* a sport that attracts more people as spectators than as participants

Spector (ˈspɛktə) *n* **Phil** born 1940, US record producer and songwriter, noted for the densely orchestrated "Wall of Sound" in his work with groups such as the Ronettes and the Crystals: arrested on a murder charge 2003

spectra (ˈspɛktrə) *n* the plural of **spectrum**

spectral (ˈspɛktrəl) *adj* **1** of or like a spectre **2** of or relating to a spectrum > **spectrality** (spɛkˈtrælɪtɪ) *n* > ˈ**spectrally** *adv*

spectral type *or* **class** *n* any of various groups into which stars are classified according to characteristic spectral lines and bands

spectre *or US* **specter** (ˈspɛktə) *n* **1** a ghost; phantom; apparition **2** an unpleasant or menacing mental image: *the spectre of redundancy* [C17 from L *spectrum*, from *specere* to look at]

spectro- *combining form* indicating a spectrum: *spectrogram*

spectrograph (ˈspɛktrəʊˌgrɑːf) *n* a spectroscope or spectrometer that produces a photographic record (**spectrogram**) of a spectrum. See also **sound spectrograph** > ˌ**spectroˈgraphic** *adj* > ˌ**spectroˈgraphically** *adv* > **spectrography** (spɛkˈtrɒgrəfɪ) *n*

spectroheliograph (ˌspɛktrəʊˈhiːlɪəˌgrɑːf) *n* an instrument used to take a photograph (**spectroheliogram**) of the sun in light of a particular wavelength, usually that of calcium or hydrogen, to show the distribution of the element over the surface and in the atmosphere > ˌ**spectroˌhelioˈgraphic** *adj*

spectrometer (spɛkˈtrɒmɪtə) *n* any instrument for producing a spectrum, esp one in which wavelength, energy, intensity, etc, can be measured. See also **mass spectrometer** > **spectrometric** (ˌspɛktrəʊˈmɛtrɪk) *adj* > **specˈtrometry** *n*

spectrophotometer (ˌspɛktrəʊfəʊˈtɒmɪtə) *n* an instrument for producing or recording a spectrum and measuring the photometric intensity of each wavelength present > **spectrophotometric** (ˌspɛktrəʊˌfəʊtəˈmɛtrɪk) *adj* > ˌ**spectrophoˈtometry** *n*

spectroscope (ˈspɛktrəˌskəʊp) *n* any of a number of instruments for dispersing electromagnetic radiation and thus forming or recording a spectrum > **spectroscopic** (ˌspɛktrəˈskɒpɪk) *or* ˌ**spectroˈscopical** *adj*

spectroscopy (spɛkˈtrɒskəpɪ) *n* the science and practice of using spectrometers and spectroscopes and of analysing spectra > **specˈtroscopist** *n*

spectrum (ˈspɛktrəm) *n, pl* **spectra** **1** the distribution of colours produced when white light is dispersed by a prism or diffraction grating. There is a continuous change in wavelength from red, the longest wavelength, to violet, the shortest. Seven colours are usually distinguished: violet, indigo, blue, green, yellow, orange, and red **2** the whole range of

Ss

electromagnetic radiation with respect to its wavelength or frequency **3** any particular distribution of electromagnetic radiation often showing lines or bands characteristic of the substance emitting the radiation or absorbing it **4** any similar distribution or record of the energies, velocities, masses, etc, of atoms, ions, electrons, etc: *a mass spectrum* **5** any range or scale, as of capabilities, emotions, or moods **6** another name for an **afterimage** [C17 from L: image, from *spectāre* to observe, from *specere* to look at]

spectrum analysis *n* the analysis of a spectrum to determine the properties of its source

specular (ˈspɛkjʊlə) *adj* **1** of, relating to, or having the properties of a mirror **2** of or relating to a speculum [C16 from L *speculāris*, from *speculum* a mirror, from *specere* to look at]

speculate (ˈspɛkjʊˌleɪt) *vb* **speculates, speculating, speculated 1** (when *tr, takes a clause as object*) to conjecture without knowing the complete facts **2** (*intr*) to buy or sell securities, property, etc, in the hope of deriving capital gains **3** (*intr*) to risk loss for the possibility of considerable gain **4** (*intr*) NZ in rugby football, to make an emergency undirected forward kick at the ball [C16 from L *speculārī* to spy out, from *specula* a watchtower, from *specere* to look at]

speculation (ˌspɛkjʊˈleɪʃən) *n* **1** the act or an instance of speculating **2** a supposition, theory, or opinion arrived at through speculating **3** investment involving high risk but also possible high profits > ˈ**speculative** *adj*

speculator (ˈspɛkjʊˌleɪtə) *n* **1** a person who speculates **2** NZ *rugby* an undirected kick of the ball

speculum (ˈspɛkjʊləm) *n, pl* **specula** (-lə) *or* **speculums 1** a mirror, esp one made of polished metal for use in a telescope, etc **2** *med* an instrument for dilating a bodily cavity or passage to permit examination of its interior **3** a patch of distinctive colour on the wing of a bird [C16 from L: mirror, from *specere* to look at]

sped (spɛd) *vb* a past tense and past participle of **speed**

speech (spiːtʃ) *n* **1a** the act or faculty of speaking **1b** (*as modifier*): *speech therapy* **2** that which is spoken; utterance **3** a talk or address delivered to an audience **4** a person's characteristic manner of speaking **5** a national or regional language or dialect **6** *linguistics* another word for **parole** [OE *spēc*]

speech day *n Brit* (in schools) an annual day on which prizes are presented, speeches are made by guest speakers, etc

speechify (ˈspiːtʃɪˌfaɪ) *vb* **speechifies, speechifying, speechified** (*intr*) **1** to make a speech or speeches **2** to talk pompously and boringly > ˈ**speechiˌfier** *n*

speechless (ˈspiːtʃlɪs) *adj* **1** not able to speak **2** temporarily deprived of speech **3** not expressed or able to be expressed in words: *speechless fear* > ˈ**speechlessly** *adv* > ˈ**speechlessness** *n*

speed (spiːd) *n* **1** the act or quality of acting or moving fast; rapidity **2** the rate at which something moves, is done, or acts **3** *physics* **3a** a scalar measure of the rate of movement of a body expressed either as the distance travelled divided by the time taken (**average speed**) or the rate of change of position with respect to time at a particular point (**instantaneous speed**) **3b** another word for **velocity** (sense 2) **4** a rate of rotation, usually expressed in revolutions per unit time **5a** a gear ratio in a motor vehicle, bicycle, etc **5b** (*in combination*): *a three-speed gear* **6** *photog* a numerical expression of the sensitivity to light of a particular type of film, paper, or plate. See also **ISO rating 7** *photog* a measure of the ability of a lens to pass light from an object to the image position **8** a slang word for **amphetamine 9** *arch* prosperity or success **10 at speed** quickly **11 up to speed 11a** operating at an acceptable or competitive level **11b** in possession of all the relevant or necessary information ▹ *vb* **speeds, speeding; sped** *or* **speeded 12** to move or go or cause to move or go quickly **13** (*intr*) to drive (a motor vehicle) at a high speed, esp above legal limits **14** (*tr*) to help further the success or completion of **15** (*intr*) *sl* to take or be under the influence of amphetamines **16** (*intr*) to operate or run at a high speed **17** *arch* **17a** (*intr*) to prosper or succeed **17b** (*tr*) to wish success to ▹ See also **speed up** [OE *spēd* (orig. in the sense: success)] > ˈ**speeder** *n*

speedball (ˈspiːdˌbɔːl) *n sl* a mixture of heroin with amphetamine or cocaine

speedboat (ˈspiːdˌbəʊt) *n* a high-speed motorboat

speed camera *n* a fixed camera that photographs vehicles breaking the speed limit on a certain stretch of road

speed chess *n* a form of chess in which each player's game is limited to a total stipulated time, usually half an hour; the first player to exceed the time limit loses

speed dating *n* a method of meeting potential partners in which each participant has only a few minutes to talk to each of his or her dates before being moved on to the next one. At the end of the event, participants decide which dates they would like to see again

speed limit *n* the maximum permitted speed at which a vehicle may travel on certain roads

speedo (ˈspiːdəʊ) *n, pl* **speedos** an informal name for **speedometer**

speed of light *n* the speed at which electromagnetic radiation travels in a vacuum; $2.997\,924\,58 \times 10^8$ metres per second exactly. Symbol: *c* Also called (not in technical usage): **velocity of light**

speedometer (spɪˈdɒmɪtə) *n* a device fitted to a vehicle to measure and display the speed of travel. See also **mileometer**

speed ramp *n Brit* a raised band across a road, designed to make motorists reduce their speed, esp in built-up areas

speed up *vb* (*adv*) **1** to increase or cause to increase in speed or rate; accelerate ▹ *n* **speed-up 2** an instance of this; acceleration.

USAGE The past tense and past participle of *speed up* is *speeded up* not *sped up*

speedway (ˈspiːdˌweɪ) *n* **1** the sport of racing on light powerful motorcycles round cinder tracks **2** the track or stadium where such races are held **3** *US & Canad* **3a** a racetrack for cars **3b** a road on which fast driving is allowed

▹ www.speedwaygp.com
▹ www.british-speedway.co.uk

speedwell (ˈspiːdˌwɛl) *n* any of various temperate plants, such as the **heath speedwell** and the **germander speedwell**, having small blue or pinkish-white flowers

speedy (ˈspiːdɪ) *adj* **speedier, speediest 1** characterized by speed **2** done or decided without delay > ˈ**speedily** *adv* > ˈ**speediness** *n*

spek (spɛk) *n S African* bacon [from Afrik., from Du.]

speleology *or* **spelaeology** (ˌspiːlɪˈɒlədʒɪ) *n* **1** the scientific study of caves **2** the sport or pastime of exploring caves [C19 from L *spēlaeum* cave] > **speleological** *or* **spelaeological** (ˌspiːlɪəˈlɒdʒɪkᵊl) *adj* > ˌ**speleˈologist** *or* ˌ**spelaeˈologist** *n*

spell[1] (spɛl) *vb* **spells, spelling; spelt** *or* **spelled 1** to write or name in correct order the letters that comprise the conventionally accepted form of (a word) **2** (*tr*) (of letters) to go to make up the conventionally established form of (a word) when arranged correctly: *d-o-g spells dog* **3** (*tr*) to indicate or signify: *such actions spell disaster* ▹ See also **spell out** [C13 from OF *espeller*, of Gmc origin] > ˈ**spellable** *adj*

spell[2] (spɛl) *n* **1** a verbal formula considered as having magical force **2** any influence that can control the mind or character; fascination **3** a state induced as by the pronouncing of a spell; trance: *to break the spell* **4 under a spell** held in or as if in a spell [OE *spell* speech]

spell[3] (spɛl) *n* **1** an indeterminate, usually short, period of time: *a spell of cold weather* **2** a period or tour of duty after which one person or group relieves another **3** *Scot, Austral, & NZ* a period or interval of rest ▷ *vb* **4** *(tr)* to take over from (a person) for an interval of time; relieve temporarily [OE *spelian* to take the place of, from ?]

spellbind ('spɛl,baɪnd) *vb* **spellbinds, spellbinding, spellbound** *(tr)* to cause to be spellbound; entrance or enthral > **'spell,binder** *n*

spellbound ('spɛl,baʊnd) *adj* having one's attention held as though one is bound by a spell

spellchecker ('spɛl,tʃɛkə) *n computing* a program that highlights any word in a word-processed document that is not recognized as being correctly spelt

speller ('spɛlə) *n* **1** a person who spells words in the manner specified: *a bad speller* **2** a book designed to teach or improve spelling

spelling ('spɛlɪŋ) *n* **1** the act or process of writing words by using the letters conventionally accepted for their formation; orthography **2** the art or study of orthography **3** the way in which a word is spelt **4** the ability of a person to spell

spelling bee *n* a contest in which players are required to spell words

spell out *vb (tr, adv)* **1** to make clear, distinct, or explicit; clarify in detail: *let me spell out the implications* **2** to read laboriously or with difficulty, working out each word letter by letter **3** to discern by study; puzzle out

spelt[1] (spɛlt) *vb* a past tense and past participle of **spell**[1]

spelt[2] (spɛlt) *n* a species of wheat that was formerly much cultivated and was used to develop present-day cultivated wheats [OE]

spelter ('spɛltə) *n* impure zinc [C17 prob. from MDu. *speauter*, from ?]

spelunker (spɪ'lʌŋkə) *n* a person whose hobby is the exploration of caves [C20 from L *spēlunca*, from Gk *spēlunx* a cave] > **spe'lunking** *n*

Spence (spɛns) *n* Sir **Basil** (**Unwin**) 1907–76, Scottish architect, born in India; designed Coventry Cathedral (1951)

spencer[1] ('spɛnsə) *n* **1** a short fitted coat or jacket **2** a woman's knitted vest [C18 after Earl *Spencer* (1758–1834)]

spencer[2] ('spɛnsə) *n naut* a large loose-footed gaffsail on a square-rigger or barque [C19 ?from a proper name]

Spencer ('spɛnsə) *n* **1 Herbert** 1820–1903, English philosopher, who applied evolutionary theory to the study of society, favouring laissez-faire doctrines **2** Sir **Stanley** 1891–1959, English painter, noted esp for his paintings of Christ in a contemporary English setting

Spencer Gulf *n* an inlet of the Indian Ocean in S Australia, between the Eyre and Yorke Peninsulas. Length: about 320 km (200 miles). Greatest width: about 145 km (90 miles)

spend (spɛnd) *vb* **spends, spending, spent 1** to pay out (money, wealth, etc) **2** *(tr)* to concentrate (time, effort, etc) upon an object, activity, etc **3** *(tr)* to pass (time) in a specific way, place, etc **4** *(tr)* to use up completely: *the hurricane spent its force* **5** *(tr)* to give up (one's blood, life, etc) in a cause [OE *spendan*, from L *expendere*; infl. also by OF *despendre* to spend; see EXPEND, DISPENSE] > **'spendable** *adj* > **'spender** *n*

Spender ('spɛndə) *n* Sir **Stephen** 1909–95, English poet and critic, who played an important part in the left-wing literary movement of the 1930s. His works include *Journals 1939–83* (1985) and *Collected Poems* (1985)

spendthrift ('spɛnd,θrɪft) *n* **1** a person who spends money in an extravagant manner ▷ *adj* **2** *(usually prenominal)* of or like a spendthrift

Spengler ('spɛŋlə; *German* 'ʃpɛŋlər) *n* **Oswald** ('ɔsvalt) 1880–1936, German philosopher of history, noted for *The Decline of the West* (1918–22), which argues that civilizations go through natural cycles of growth and decay

Spenser ('spɛnsə) *n* **Edmund** ?1552–99, English poet celebrated for *The Faerie Queene* (1590; 1596), an allegorical romance. His other verse includes the collection of eclogues *The Shepheardes Calendar* (1579) and the marriage poem *Epithalamion* (1594)

Spenserian (spɛn'sɪərɪən) *adj* **1** relating to or characteristic of Edmund Spenser or his poetry ▷ *n* **2** a student or imitator of Edmund Spenser

Spenserian stanza *n prosody* the stanza form used by the poet Spenser in his poem *The Faerie Queene*, consisting of eight lines in iambic pentameter and a concluding Alexandrine, rhyming a b a b b c b c **c**

spent (spɛnt) *vb* **1** the past tense and past participle of **spend** ▷ *adj* **2** used up or exhausted; consumed **3** (of a fish) exhausted by spawning

sperm[1] (spɜːm) *n, pl* **sperms** *or* **sperm 1** another name for **semen 2** a male reproductive cell; male gamete [C14 from LL *sperma*, from Gk]

sperm[2] (spɜːm) *n* short for **sperm whale, spermaceti,** or **sperm oil**

-sperm *n combining form* (in botany) a seed: *gymnosperm* > **-spermous** *or* **-spermal** *adj combining form*

spermaceti (,spɜːmə'sɛtɪ, -'siːtɪ) *n* a white waxy substance obtained from oil from the head of the sperm whale [C15 from Med. L *sperma cētī* whale's sperm, from *sperma* SPERM[1] + L *cētus* whale, from Gk *kētos*]

spermatic (spɜː'mætɪk), **spermic** ('spɜːmɪk), *or* **spermous** ('spɜːməs) *adj* **1** of or relating to spermatozoa: *spermatic fluid* **2** of or relating to the testis: *the spermatic artery* [C16 from LL *spermaticus*, from Gk *spermatikos* concerning seed, from *sperma* seed] > **sper'matically** *adv*

spermatid ('spɜːmətɪd) *n zool* any of four immature male gametes that are formed from a spermatocyte, each of which develops into a spermatozoon

spermato-, spermo- *or before a vowel* **spermat-, sperm-** *combining form* **1** indicating sperm: *spermatozoon* **2** indicating seed: *spermatophyte* [from Gk *sperma, spermat-* seed]

spermatocyte ('spɜːmətəʊ,saɪt) *n* an immature male germ cell

spermatogenesis (,spɜːmətəʊ'dʒɛnɪsɪs) *n* the formation and maturation of spermatozoa in the testis > **spermatogenetic** (,spɜːmətəʊdʒɪ'nɛtɪk) *adj*

spermatogonium (,spɜːmətə'gəʊnɪəm) *n, pl* **spermatogonia** (-nɪə) *zool* an immature male germ cell that divides to form many spermatocytes

spermatophyte ('spɜːmətəʊ,faɪt) *or* **spermophyte** *n* (in traditional classifications) any seed-bearing plant. Former name: **phanerogam** > **spermatophytic** (,spɜːmətəʊ'fɪtɪk) *adj*

spermatozoon (,spɜːmətəʊ'zəʊɒn) *n, pl* **spermatozoa** (-zəʊə) any of the male reproductive cells released in the semen during ejaculation. Also called: **sperm, zoosperm** > **,spermato'zoal, ,spermato'zoan,** *or* **,spermato'zoic** *adj*

spermicide ('spɜːmɪ,saɪd) *n* any agent that kills spermatozoa > **,spermi'cidal** *adj*

sperm oil *n* an oil obtained from the head of the sperm whale, used as a lubricant

spermous ('spɜːməs) *adj* **1** of or relating to the sperm whale or its products **2** another word for **spermatic**

sperm whale *n* a large toothed whale, having a square-shaped head and hunted for sperm oil, spermaceti, and ambergris. Also called: **cachalot** [C19 short for SPERMACETI *whale*]

spew (spjuː) *vb* **1** to eject (the contents of the stomach) involuntarily through the mouth; vomit **2** to spit (spittle, phlegm, etc) out of the mouth **3** (usually foll by *out*) to send or be sent out in a stream: *flames spewed out* ▷ *n* **4** something ejected from the mouth ▷ Also (archaic): **spue** [OE *spīwan*] > **'spewer** *n*

Spey (speɪ) *n* a river in E Scotland, flowing generally northeast through the Grampian Mountains to the

Ss

Moray Firth: salmon fishing. Length: 172 km (107 miles)

Speyer (*German* 'ʃpaiər) *n* a port in SW Germany, in Rhineland-Palatinate on the Rhine: the scene of 50 imperial diets. Pop: 47 450 (1991). English name: **Spires**

SPF *abbrev for* sun protection factor: an indicator of how effectively a lotion, cosmetic, etc, protects the skin from the harmful rays of the sun

sp. gr. *abbrev for* specific gravity

sphagnum ('sfægnəm) *n* any moss of the genus *Sphagnum*, of temperate bogs: layers of these mosses decay to form peat. Also called: **peat moss, bog moss** [C18 from NL, from Gk *sphagnos* a variety of moss] > '**sphagnous** *adj*

sphairee (sfaɪriː) *n Austral* a game resembling tennis played with wooden bats and a perforated plastic ball [from Gk *sphaira* a ball]

sphalerite ('sfæləˌraɪt, 'sfeɪlə-) *n* a yellow to brownish-black mineral consisting mainly of zinc sulphide in cubic crystalline form: the chief source of zinc. Formula: ZnS. Also called: **zinc blende** [C19 from Gk *sphaleros* deceitful, from *sphallein* to cause to stumble]

sphene (sfiːn) *n* a brown, yellow, green, or grey lustrous mineral consisting of calcium titanium silicate in monoclinic crystalline form. Also called: **titanite** [C19 from F *sphène*, from Gk *sphēn* a wedge, alluding to its crystals]

sphenoid ('sfiːnɔɪd) *adj also* **sphenoidal** 1 wedge-shaped 2 of or relating to the sphenoid bone ▷ *n* 3 See **sphenoid bone**

sphenoid bone *n* the large butterfly-shaped compound bone at the base of the skull

sphere (sfɪə) *n* 1 *maths* 1a a three-dimensional closed surface such that every point on the surface is equidistant from a given point, the centre 1b the solid figure bounded by this surface or the space enclosed by it 2 any object having approximately this shape; a globe 3 the night sky considered as a vaulted roof; firmament 4 any heavenly object such as a planet, natural satellite, or star 5 (in the Ptolemaic or Copernican systems of astronomy) one of a series of revolving hollow globes, arranged concentrically, on whose transparent surfaces the sun, the moon, the planets, and fixed stars were thought to be set 6 a particular field of activity; environment 7 a social class or stratum of society ▷ *vb* **spheres, sphering, sphered** (*tr*) *chiefly poetic* 8 to surround or encircle 9 to place aloft or in the heavens [C14 from LL *sphēra*, from L *sphaera* globe, from Gk *sphaira*] > '**spheral** *adj*

-sphere *n combining form* 1 having the shape or form of a sphere: *bathysphere* 2 indicating a spherelike enveloping mass: *atmosphere* > **-spheric** *adj combining form*

spherical ('sfɛrɪkᵊl) *or* **spheric** *adj* 1 shaped like a sphere 2 of or relating to a sphere: *spherical geometry* 3 *geom* formed on the surface of or inside a sphere: *a spherical triangle* 4a of or relating to heavenly bodies 4b of or relating to the spheres of the Ptolemaic or the Copernican system > '**spherically** *adv* > '**sphericalness** *n*

spherical aberration *n physics* a defect of optical systems that arises when light striking a mirror or lens near its edge is focused at different points on the axis to the light striking near the centre. The effect occurs when the mirror or lens has spherical surfaces

spherical angle *n* an angle formed at the intersection of two great circles of a sphere

spherical coordinates *pl n* three coordinates that define the location of a point in space in terms of its radius vector, *r*, the angle, θ, which this vector makes with one axis, and the angle, ϕ, which the plane of this vector makes with a mutually perpendicular axis

spherical trigonometry *n* the branch of trigonometry concerned with the measurement of the angles and sides of spherical triangles

spheroid ('sfɪərɔɪd) *n* 1 another name for **ellipsoid of revolution** ▷ *adj* 2 shaped like but not exactly a sphere > **spher'oidal** *adj* > ˌ**spheroid'icity** *n*

spherometer (sfɪə'rɒmɪtə) *n* an instrument for measuring the curvature of a surface

spherule ('sfɛruːl) *n* a very small sphere [C17 from LL *sphaerula*] > '**spherular** *adj*

spherulite ('sfɛrʊˌlaɪt) *n* any of several spherical masses of radiating needle-like crystals of one or more minerals occurring in rocks such as obsidian > **spherulitic** (ˌsfɛrʊ'lɪtɪk) *adj*

sphincter ('sfɪŋktə) *n anat* a ring of muscle surrounding the opening of a hollow organ or body and contracting to close it [C16 from LL, from Gk *sphinkter*, from *sphingein* to grip tightly] > '**sphincteral** *adj*

sphinx (sfɪŋks) *n, pl* **sphinxes** *or* **sphinges** ('sfɪndʒiːz) 1 any of a number of huge stone statues built by the ancient Egyptians, having the body of a lion and the head of a man 2 an inscrutable person

Sphinx (sfɪŋks) *n* **the** 1 *Greek myth* a monster with a woman's head and a lion's body. She lay outside Thebes, asking travellers a riddle and killing them when they failed to answer it. Oedipus answered the riddle and the Sphinx then killed herself 2 the huge statue of a sphinx near the pyramids at El Gîza in Egypt [C16 via L from Gk, apparently from *sphingein* to hold fast]

sphragistics (sfrə'dʒɪstɪks) *n* (*functioning as sing*) the study of seals and signet rings [C19 from Gk *sphragistikos*, from *sphragizein* to seal, from *sphragis* a seal] > **sphra'gistic** *adj*

sphygmo- *or before a vowel* **sphygm-** *combining form* indicating the pulse: *sphygmograph* [from Gk *sphugmos* pulsation, from *sphuzein* to throb]

sphygmograph ('sfɪgməʊˌgrɑːf) *n med* an instrument for making a recording (**sphygmogram**) of variations in blood pressure and pulse > **sphygmographic** (ˌsfɪgməʊ'græfɪk) *adj* > **sphygmography** (sfɪg'mɒgrəfɪ) *n*

sphygmomanometer (ˌsfɪgməʊmə'nɒmɪtə) *n med* an instrument for measuring arterial blood pressure

spicate ('spaɪkeɪt) *adj bot* having, arranged in, or relating to spikes: *a spicate inflorescence* [C17 from L *spīcātus* having spikes, from *spīca* a point]

spiccato (spɪ'kɑːtəʊ) *music* ▷ *n* 1 a style of playing a bowed stringed instrument in which the bow bounces lightly off the strings ▷ *adj, adv* 2 (to be played) in this manner [It.: detached]

spice (spaɪs) *n* 1a any of a variety of aromatic vegetable substances, such as ginger, cinnamon, or nutmeg, used as flavourings 1b these substances collectively 2 something that represents or introduces zest, charm, or gusto 3 *rare* a small amount ▷ *vb* **spices, spicing, spiced** (*tr*) 4 to prepare or flavour (food) with spices 5 to introduce charm or zest into [C13 from OF *espice*, from LL *speciēs* (pl) spices, from L *speciēs* (sing) kind; also associated with LL *spīcea* (unattested) fragrant herb, from L *spīceus* having spikes of foliage]
▷ www.culinarycafe.com/Spices_Herbs

spicebush ('spaɪsˌbʊʃ) *n* a North American shrub having aromatic leaves and bark

Spice Islands *pl n* the former name of the **Moluccas**

spick-and-span *or* **spic-and-span** ('spɪkən'spæn) *adj* 1 extremely neat and clean 2 new and fresh [C17 shortened from *spick-and-span-new*, from obs. *spick* spike + *span-new*, from ON *spānnȳr* absolutely new]

spicule ('spɪkjuːl) *n* 1 Also called: **spiculum** a small slender pointed structure or crystal, esp any of the calcareous or siliceous elements of the skeleton of sponges, corals, etc 2 *astron* a spiked ejection of hot gas above the sun's surface [C18 from L *spiculum* small, sharp point] > **spiculate** ('spɪkjʊˌleɪt, -lɪt) *adj*

spicy ('spaɪsɪ) *adj* **spicier, spiciest** 1 seasoned with or containing spice 2 highly flavoured; pungent 3 *inf* suggestive of scandal or sensation > '**spicily** *adv* > '**spiciness** *n*

spider ('spaɪdə) *n* 1 any of various predatory

silk-producing arachnids, having four pairs of legs and a rounded unsegmented body **2** any of various similar or related arachnids **3** any implement or tool having the shape of a spider **4** any part of a machine having a number of radiating spokes, tines, or arms **5** Also called: **octopus** *Brit* a cluster of elastic straps fastened at a central point and used to hold a load on a car rack, motorcycle, etc **6** *snooker, etc* a rest having long legs, used to raise the cue above the level of the height of the ball **7** *computing* a program that is capable of performing sophisticated recursive searches on the Internet [OE *spīthra*] > '**spidery** *adj*

spider crab *n* any of various crabs having a small triangular body and very long legs

spiderman ('spaɪdəˌmæn) *n, pl* **spidermen** *inf, chiefly Brit* a person who erects the steel structure of a building

spider mite *n* any of various plant-feeding mites, esp the **red spider mite,** which is a serious orchard pest

spider monkey *n* **1** any of several arboreal New World monkeys of Central and South America, having very long legs, a long prehensile tail, and a small head **2** **woolly spider monkey** a rare related monkey of SE Brazil

spider plant *n* any of various house plants having long narrow leaves with a light central stripe

spiderwort ('spaɪdəˌwɜːt) *n* **1** any of various American plants having blue, purplish, or pink flowers and widely grown as house plants. See also **tradescantia** **2** any of various similar or related plants

spiel (ʃpiːl) *n* **1** glib plausible talk, associated esp with salesmen ▹ *vb* **2** (*intr*) to deliver a prepared spiel **3** (*tr; usually foll by off*) to recite (a prepared oration) [c19 from G *Spiel* play] > '**spieler** *n*

Spielberg ('spiːlbɜːg) *n* **Steven** born 1947, US film director, noted esp for the commercial success of such films as *Jaws* (1975), *Close Encounters of the Third Kind* (1977), *Raiders of the Lost Ark* (1981) and its sequels, E.T. (1982), and *Jurassic Park* (1993). Other films include *The Color Purple* (1986), *Schindler's List* (1993), *Saving Private Ryan* (1998), and *Catch Me If You Can* (2003)

spier ('spaɪə) *n arch* a person who spies or scouts

spiffing ('spɪfɪŋ) *adj Brit sl, old-fashioned* excellent; splendid [c19 prob. from dialect *spiff* spruce, smart]

spiffy ('spɪfɪ) *adj* **spiffier, spiffiest** *US & Canad sl* smart; stylish [c19 from dialect *spiff* smartly dressed] > '**spiffily** *adv*

spigot ('spɪgət) *n* **1** a stopper for the vent hole of a cask **2** a tap, usually of wood, fitted to a cask **3** a US name for **tap**[2] (sense 1) **4** a short projection on one component designed to fit into a hole on another, esp the male part of a joint between two pipes [c14 prob. from OProvençal *espiga* a head of grain, from L *spīca* a point]

spike[1] (spaɪk) *n* **1** a sharp point **2** any sharp-pointed object, esp one made of metal **3** a long metal nail **4** (*pl*) shoes with metal projections on the sole and heel for greater traction, as used by athletes **5** *Brit sl* another word for **dosshouse** ▹ *vb* **spikes, spiking, spiked** (*tr*) **6** to secure or supply with or as with spikes **7** to render ineffective or block the intentions of; thwart **8** to impale on a spike **9** to add alcohol to (a drink) **10** *volleyball* to hit (a ball) sharply downwards with an overarm motion from the front of one's own court into the opposing court **11** (formerly) to render (a cannon) ineffective by blocking its vent with a spike **12** **spike (someone's) guns** to thwart (someone's) purpose [c13 *spyk*] > '**spiky** *adj*

spike[2] (spaɪk) *n bot* **1** an inflorescence consisting of a raceme of sessile flowers as in the gladiolus and sedge **2** an ear of wheat, etc [c14 from L *spīca* ear of corn]

spikelet ('spaɪklɪt) *n bot* a small spike, esp the inflorescence of most grasses and sedges

spikenard ('spaɪknɑːd, 'spaɪkəˌnɑːd) *n* **1** an aromatic Indian plant, having rose-purple flowers **2** an aromatic ointment obtained from this plant **3** any of various similar or related plants **4** a North American plant having small green flowers and an aromatic root ▹ Also called (for senses 1, 2): **nard** [c14 from Med. L *spīca nardī*; see SPIKE[2], NARD]

spile (spaɪl) *n* **1** a heavy timber stake or pile **2** *US* a spout for tapping sap from the sugar maple tree **3** a plug or spigot ▹ *vb* **spiles, spiling, spiled** (*tr*) **4** to provide or support with a spile **5** *US* to tap (a tree) with a spile [c16 prob. from MDu. *spile* peg]

spill[1] (spɪl) *vb* **spills, spilling; spilt** *or* **spilled** (*mainly tr*) **1** (when *intr*, usually foll by *from, out of*, etc) to fall or cause to fall from or as from a container, esp unintentionally **2** to disgorge (contents, occupants, etc) or (of contents, occupants, etc) to be disgorged **3** to shed (blood) **4** Also: **spill the beans** *inf* to divulge something confidential **5** *naut* to let (wind) escape from a sail or (of the wind) to escape from a sail ▹ *n* **6** *inf* a fall or tumble **7** short for **spillway** **8** a spilling of liquid, etc, or the amount spilt **9** *Austral* the declaring of several political jobs vacant when one higher up becomes so [OE *spillan* to destroy] > '**spillage** *n* > '**spiller** *n*

spill[2] (spɪl) *n* a splinter of wood or strip of twisted paper with which pipes, fires, etc, are lit [c13 of Gmc origin]

Spillane (spɪ'leɪn) *n* **Mickey,** original name *Frank Morrison Spillane*. born 1918, US detective-story writer, best known for his books featuring the detective Mike Hammer, for example *I, the Jury* (1947) and *The Twisted Thing* (1966)

spillikin, spilikin ('spɪlɪkɪn), *or* **spellican** ('spɛlɪkən) *n* a thin strip of wood, cardboard, or plastic, esp one used in spillikins

spillikins ('spɪlɪkɪnz) *n* (*functioning as sing*) *Brit* a game in which players try to pick each spillikin from a heap without moving any of the others. Also called: **jackstraws**

spill over *vb* **1** (*intr, adv*) to overflow or be forced out of an area, container, etc ▹ *n* **spillover** *chiefly US & Canad* **2** the act of spilling over **3** the excess part of something

spillway ('spɪlˌweɪ) *n* a channel that carries away surplus water, as from a dam

spilt (spɪlt) *vb* a past tense and past participle of **spill**[1]

spin (spɪn) *vb* **spins, spinning, spun** **1** to rotate or cause to rotate rapidly, as on an axis **2a** to draw out and twist (natural fibres, as of silk or cotton) into a long continuous thread **2b** to make such a thread or filament from (synthetic resins, etc), usually by forcing through a nozzle **3** (of spiders, silkworms, etc) to form (webs, cocoons, etc) from a silky fibre exuded from the body **4** (*tr*) to shape (metal) into a rounded form on a lathe **5** (*tr*) *inf* to tell (a tale, story, etc) by drawing it out at great length (esp in **spin a yarn**) **6** to bowl, pitch, hit, or kick (a ball) so that it rotates in the air and changes direction or speed on bouncing, or (of a ball) to be projected in this way **7** (*intr*) (of wheels) to revolve rapidly without causing propulsion **8** to cause (an aircraft) to dive in a spiral descent or (of an aircraft) to dive in a spiral descent **9** (*intr; foll by along*) to drive or travel swiftly **10** (*tr*) Also: **spin-dry** to rotate (clothes) in a washing machine in order to extract surplus water **11** (*intr*) to reel or grow dizzy, as from turning around: *my head is spinning* **12** (*intr*) to fish by drawing a revolving lure through the water **13** (*intr*) *inf* to present news or information in a way that creates a favourable impression ▹ *n* **14** a swift rotating motion; instance of spinning **15** *physics* **15a** the intrinsic angular momentum of an elementary particle or atomic nucleus **15b** a quantum number determining values of this angular momentum **16** a condition of loss of control of an aircraft or an intentional flight manoeuvre in which the aircraft performs a continuous spiral descent **17** a spinning motion imparted to a ball, etc **18** *inf* a short or fast drive, ride, etc, esp in a car, for pleasure **19** *inf* the practice of presenting news or information in a way that creates a favourable impression **20** *Austral & NZ inf* a period of a specified kind of fortune: *a bad spin* **21** **flat spin** *inf, chiefly Brit* a state of agitation or confusion **22** **on the spin** *inf* one after another: *they have lost two finals on the spin* ▷ See also **spin out** [OE *spinnan*]

spina bifida ('spaɪnə 'bɪfɪdə) *n* a congenital condition in which the meninges of the spinal cord protrude through a gap in the backbone, sometimes causing enlargement of the skull and paralysis [NL; see SPINE, BIFID]

spinach ('spɪnɪdʒ, -ɪtʃ) *n* **1** an annual plant cultivated for its dark green edible leaves **2** the leaves, eaten as a vegetable [C16 from OF *espinache*, from OSp., from Ar. *isfānākh*, from Persian]

spinal ('spaɪn°l) *adj* **1** of or relating to the spine or the spinal cord ▷ *n* **2** short for **spinal anaesthesia** > **'spinally** *adv*

spinal anaesthesia *n* **1** anaesthesia of the lower half of the body produced by injecting an anaesthetic beneath the arachnoid membrane ▷ Cf **epidural** (sense 2) **2** loss of sensation in part of the body as the result of injury of the spinal cord

spinal canal *n* the passage through the spinal column that contains the spinal cord

spinal column *n* a series of contiguous or interconnecting bony or cartilaginous segments that surround and protect the spinal cord. Also called: **spine, vertebral column** Nontechnical name: **backbone**

spinal cord *n* the thick cord of nerve tissue within the spinal canal, which together with the brain forms the central nervous system

▷ www.spinalcord.uab.edu

▷ www.spinalcord.org

spin bowler *n* another name for **spinner** (sense 2b)

spindle ('spɪnd°l) *n* **1** a rod or stick that has a notch in the top, used to draw out natural fibres for spinning into thread, and a long narrow body around which the thread is wound when spun **2** one of the thin rods or pins bearing bobbins upon which spun thread is wound in a spinning machine **3** any of various parts in the form of a rod, esp a rotating rod that acts as an axle, etc **4** a piece of wood that has been turned, such as a table leg **5** a small square metal shaft that passes through the lock of a door and to which the door knobs or handles are fixed **6** *biol* a spindle-shaped structure formed in a cell during mitosis or meiosis which draws the duplicated chromosomes apart during cell division **7** a device consisting of a sharp upright spike on a pedestal on which bills, order forms, etc, are impaled ▷ *vb* **spindles, spindling, spindled** **8** (*tr*) to form into a spindle or equip with spindles **9** (*intr*) *rare* (of a plant, stem, shoot, etc) to grow rapidly and become elongated and thin [OE *spinel*]

spindlelegs ('spɪnd°l,lɛgz) *or* **spindleshanks** *n* **1** (*functioning as pl*) long thin legs **2** (*functioning as sing*) a person who has such legs

spindle tree *n* any of various shrubs or trees of Europe and W Asia, typically having red fruits and yielding a hard wood formerly used in making spindles

spindly ('spɪndlɪ) *adj* **spindlier, spindliest** tall, slender, and frail; attenuated

spin doctor *n inf* a person who provides a favourable slant to an item of news, potentially unpopular policy, etc, esp on behalf of a political personality or party [C20 from the spin given to a ball in various sports to make it go in the desired direction]

spindrift ('spɪn,drɪft) *n* spray blown up from the sea. Also: **spoondrift** [C16 Scot var. of *spoondrift*, from *spoon* to scud + DRIFT]

spin-dry *vb* **spin-dries, spin-drying, spin-dried** (*tr*) to extract water from (wet washing) by spinning in a washing machine or spin-dryer

spin-dryer *n* a device that extracts water from clothes, etc, by spinning them in a perforated drum

spine (spaɪn) *n* **1** the spinal column **2** the sharply pointed tip or outgrowth of a leaf, stem, etc **3** *zool* a hard pointed process or structure, such as the quill of a porcupine **4** the back of a book, record sleeve, etc **5** a ridge, esp of a hill **6** strength of endurance, will, etc **7** anything resembling the spinal column in function or importance; main support or feature [C14 from OF *espine* spine, from L *spīna* thorn, backbone] > **spined** *adj*

spine-chiller *n* a book, film, etc, that arouses terror > **'spine-,chilling** *adj*

spinel (spɪ'nɛl) *n* any of a group of hard glassy minerals of variable colour consisting of oxides of aluminium, magnesium, iron, zinc, or manganese: used as gemstones [C16 from F *spinelle*, from It. *spinella*, dim. of *spina* a thorn, from L; so called from the shape of the crystals]

spineless ('spaɪnlɪs) *adj* **1** lacking a backbone **2** having no spiny processes: *spineless stems* **3** lacking character, resolution, or courage > **'spinelessly** *adv* > **'spinelessness** *n*

spinet (spɪ'nɛt, 'spɪnɪt) *n* a small type of harpsichord having one manual [C17 from It. *spinetta*, ? from Giovanni *Spinetti*, 16th-cent. It. maker of musical instruments & its supposed inventor]

spinifex ('spɪnɪ,fɛks) *n* **1** Also called: **porcupine grass** *Austral* any of various coarse spiny-leaved inland grasses **2** any of various SE Asian grasses having pointed leaves and spiny seed heads [C19 from NL, from L *spīna* a thorn + *-fex* maker, from *facere* to make]

spinnaker ('spɪnəkə; *naut* 'spæŋkə) *n* a large light triangular racing sail set from the foremast of a yacht [C19 prob. from SPIN + (MO)NIKER, but traditionally from *Sphinx*, the yacht that first adopted this type of sail]

spinner ('spɪnə) *n* **1** a person or thing that spins **2** *cricket* **2a** a ball that is bowled with a spinning motion **2b** a bowler who specializes in bowling such balls **3** a streamlined fairing that fits over the hub of an aircraft propeller **4** a fishing lure with a fin or wing that revolves

spinneret ('spɪnə,rɛt) *n* **1** any of several organs in spiders and certain insects through which silk threads are exuded **2** a finely perforated dispenser through which a liquid is extruded in the production of synthetic fibres

spinney ('spɪnɪ) *n chiefly Brit* a small wood or copse [C16 from OF *espinei*, from *espine* thorn, from L *spīna*]

spinning ('spɪnɪŋ) *n* **1** the act or process of spinning **2** the act or technique of casting and drawing a revolving lure through the water so as to imitate a live fish, etc

spinning jenny *n* an early type of spinning frame with several spindles, invented in 1764

spinning wheel *n* a wheel-like machine for spinning at home, having one hand- or foot-operated spindle

spin-off *n* **1** any product or development derived incidentally from the application of existing knowledge or enterprise **2** a book, film, or television series derived from a similar successful book, film, or television series

spinose ('spaɪnəʊs, spaɪ'nəʊs) *adj* (esp of plants) bearing many spines [C17 from L *spīnōsus* prickly, from *spīna* a thorn]

spin out *vb* (*tr, adv*) **1** to extend or protract (a story, etc) by including superfluous detail **2** to spend or pass (time) **3** to contrive to cause (money, etc) to last as long as possible

Spinoza (spɪ'nəʊzə) *n* **Baruch** (bə'ruːk) 1632–77, Dutch philosopher who constructed a holistic metaphysical system derived from a series of hypotheses that he judged self-evident. His chief work is *Ethics* (1677)

spinster ('spɪnstə) *n* **1** an unmarried woman **2** a woman regarded as being beyond the age of marriage

3 (formerly) a woman who spins thread for her living [C14 (in the sense: a person, esp a woman, whose occupation is spinning; C17 a woman still unmarried): from SPIN + -STER] > '**spinster,hood** *n* > '**spinsterish** *adj*

spiny ('spaɪnɪ) *adj* **spinier, spiniest 1** (of animals) having or covered with quills or spines **2** (of plants) covered with spines; thorny **3** troublesome; puzzling > '**spininess** *n*

spiny anteater *n* another name for **echidna**

spiny-finned *adj* (of certain fishes) having fins that are supported by stiff bony spines

spiny lobster *n* any of various large edible marine decapod crustaceans having a very tough spiny carapace. Also called: **rock lobster, crawfish, langouste**

spiracle ('spaɪərəkᵊl, 'spaɪrə-) *n* **1** any of several paired apertures in the cuticle of an insect, by which air enters and leaves the trachea **2** a small paired rudimentary gill slit in skates, rays, and related fishes **3** any similar respiratory aperture, such as the blowhole in whales [C14 (orig.: breath): from L *spīrāculum* vent, from *spīrāre* to breathe] > **spiracular** (spɪ'rækjʊlə) *adj* > **spi'raculate** *adj*

spiraea *or esp US* **spirea** (spaɪ'rɪə) *n* any of various rosaceous plants having sprays of small white or pink flowers. See also **meadowsweet** (sense 2) [C17 via L from Gk *speiraia*, from *speira* SPIRE²]

spiral ('spaɪərəl) *n* **1** *geom* one of several plane curves formed by a point winding about a fixed point at an ever-increasing distance from it **2** a curve that lies on a cylinder or cone, at a constant angle to the line segments making up the surface; helix **3** something that pursues a winding, usually upward, course or that displays a twisting form or shape **4** a flight manoeuvre in which an aircraft descends describing a helix of comparatively large radius with the angle of attack within the normal flight range **5** *econ* a continuous upward or downward movement in economic activity or prices, caused by interaction between prices, wages, demand, and production ▷ *adj* **6** having the shape of a spiral ▷ *vb* **spirals, spiralling, spiralled** *or US* **spirals, spiraling, spiraled 7** to assume or cause to assume a spiral course or shape **8** (*intr*) to increase or decrease with steady acceleration: *prices continue to spiral* [C16 via F from Med. L *spīrālis*, from L *spīra* a coil; see SPIRE²] > '**spirally** *adv*

spiral galaxy *n* a galaxy consisting of an ellipsoidal nucleus of old stars from opposite sides of which arms, containing younger stars, spiral outwards around the nucleus

spirant ('spaɪrənt) *adj* **1** *phonetics* another word for **fricative** ▷ *n* **2** a fricative consonant [C19 from L *spīrāns* breathing, from *spīrāre* to breathe]

spire¹ ('spaɪə) *n* **1** Also called: **steeple** a tall structure that tapers upwards to a point, esp one on a tower or roof or one that forms the upper part of a steeple **2** a slender tapering shoot or stem **3** the apical part of any tapering formation; summit ▷ *vb* **spires, spiring, spired 4** (*intr*) to assume the shape of a spire; point up **5** (*tr*) to furnish with a spire or spires [OE *spīr* blade] > '**spiry** *adj*

spire² ('spaɪə) *n* **1** any of the coils or turns in a spiral structure **2** the apical part of a spiral shell [C16 from L *spīra* a coil, from Gk *speira*]

Spires (spaɪəz) *n* the English name for **Speyer**

spirillum (spaɪ'rɪləm) *n, pl* **spirilla** (-lə) **1** any bacterium having a curved or spirally twisted rodlike body **2** any bacterium of the genus *Spirillum*, such as *S. minus*, which causes ratbite fever [C19 from NL, lit.: a little coil, from *spīra* a coil]

spirit¹ ('spɪrɪt) *n* **1** the force or principle of life that animates the body of living things **2** temperament or disposition: *truculent in spirit* **3** liveliness; mettle: *they set to it with spirit* **4** the fundamental, emotional, and activating principle of a person; will: *the experience broke his spirit* **5** a sense of loyalty or dedication: *team spirit* **6** the prevailing element; feeling: *a spirit of joy pervaded the atmosphere* **7** state of mind or mood; attitude: *he did it in the wrong spirit* **8** (*pl*) an emotional state, esp with regard to exaltation or dejection: *in high spirits* **9** a person characterized by some activity, quality, or disposition: *a leading spirit of the movement* **10** the deeper more significant meaning as opposed to a pedantic interpretation: *the spirit of the law* **11** a person's intangible being as contrasted with his physical presence: *I shall be with you in spirit* **12a** an incorporeal being, esp the soul of a dead person **12b** (*as modifier*): *spirit world* ▷ *vb* (*tr*) **13** (usually foll by *away* or *off*) to carry off mysteriously or secretly **14** (often foll by *up*) to impart animation or determination to [C13 from OF *esperit*, from L *spīritus* breath, spirit] > '**spiritless** *adj*

spirit² ('spɪrɪt) *n* **1** (*often pl*) any distilled alcoholic liquor, such as whisky or gin **2** *chem* **2a** an aqueous solution of ethanol, esp one obtained by distillation **2b** the active principle or essence of a substance, extracted as a liquid, esp by distillation **3** *pharmacol* a solution of a volatile substance, esp a volatile oil, in alcohol **4** *alchemy* any of the four substances sulphur, mercury, sal ammoniac, or arsenic [C14 special use of SPIRIT¹, name applied to alchemical substances (as in sense 4), hence extended to distilled liquids]

▷ http://thatsthespirit.com

▷ www.webtender.com

Spirit ('spɪrɪt) *n* **the a** another name for the **Holy Spirit b** God, esp when regarded as transcending material limitations

spirited ('spɪrɪtɪd) *adj* **1** displaying animation, vigour, or liveliness **2** (*in combination*) characterized by mood, temper, or disposition as specified: *high-spirited; public-spirited* > '**spiritedly** *adv* > '**spiritedness** *n*

spirit gum *n* a glue made from gum dissolved in ether used to affix a false beard, etc

spiritism ('spɪrɪ,tɪzəm) *n* a less common word for **spiritualism** > '**spiritist** *n* > ,**spirit'istic** *adj*

spirit lamp *n* a lamp that burns methylated or other spirits instead of oil

spirit level *n* a device for setting horizontal surfaces, consisting of a block of material in which a sealed tube partially filled with liquid is set so that the air bubble rests between two marks on the tube when the block is horizontal

spiritous ('spɪrɪtəs) *adj* a variant of **spirituous**

spirits of ammonia *n* (*functioning as sing or pl*) another name for **sal volatile**

spirits of hartshorn *n* (*functioning as sing or pl*) a solution of ammonia gas in water. See **ammonium hydroxide** Also called: **aqueous ammonia**

spirits of salt *n* (*functioning as sing or pl*) a solution of hydrochloric acid in water

spiritual ('spɪrɪtjʊəl) *adj* **1** relating to the spirit or soul and not to physical nature or matter; intangible **2** of or relating to sacred things, the Church, religion, etc **3** standing in a relationship based on communication between souls or minds: *a spiritual father* **4** having a mind or emotions of a high and delicately refined quality ▷ *n* **5** Also called: **Negro spiritual** a type of religious song originating among Black slaves in the American South **6** (*often pl*) the sphere of religious, spiritual, or ecclesiastical matters, or such matters in themselves > ,**spiritu'ality** *n* > '**spiritually** *adv*

spiritualism ('spɪrɪtjʊə,lɪzəm) *n* **1** the belief that the disembodied spirits of the dead, surviving in another world, can communicate with the living in this world, esp through mediums **2** the doctrines and practices associated with this belief **3** *philosophy* the belief that because reality is to some extent immaterial it is therefore spiritual **4** any doctrine that prefers the spiritual to the material > '**spiritualist** *n*

spiritualize *or* **spiritualise** ('spɪrɪtjʊə,laɪz)

Ss

vb **spiritualizes, spiritualizing, spiritualized** *or* **spiritualises, spiritualising, spiritualised** (*tr*) to make spiritual or infuse with spiritual content > **ˌspirituaIiˈzation** *or* **ˌspiritualiˈsation** *n* > **ˈspiritualˌizer** *or* **ˈspiritualˌiser** *n*

spirituel (ˌspɪrɪtjʊˈɛl) *adj* having a refined and lively mind or wit. Also (fem): **spirituelle** [c17 from F]

spirituous (ˈspɪrɪtjʊəs) *adj* **1** characterized by or containing alcohol **2** (of a drink) being a spirit > **spirituosity** (ˌspɪrɪtjʊˈɒsɪtɪ) *or* **ˈspirituousness** *n*

spirochaete *or US* **spirochete** (ˈspaɪrəʊˌkiːt) *n* any of a group of spirally coiled rodlike bacteria that includes the causative agent of syphilis [c19 from NL, from *spiro-*, from L *spira*, from Gk *speira* a coil + *chaeta*, from Gk *khaitē* long hair]

spirograph (ˈspaɪrəˌgrɑːf) *n med* an instrument for recording the movements of breathing [c20 NL, from *spiro-*, from L *spīrāre* to breathe + -GRAPH] > **ˌspiroˈgraphic** *adj*

spirogyra (ˌspaɪrəˈdʒaɪrə) *n* any of various green freshwater multicellular algae containing spirally coiled chloroplasts [c20 from NL, from *spiro-*, from L *spīra*, from Gk *speira* a coil + Gk *guros* a circle]

spirt (spɜːt) *n* a variant spelling of **spurt**

spiry (ˈspaɪərɪ) *adj poetic* of spiral form; helical

spit[1] (spɪt) *vb* **spits, spitting, spat** *or* **spit** **1** (*intr*) to expel saliva from the mouth; expectorate **2** (*intr*) *inf* to show disdain or hatred by spitting **3** (of a fire, hot fat, etc) to eject (sparks, etc) violently and with an explosive sound **4** (*intr*) to rain very lightly **5** (*tr*; often foll by *out*) to eject or discharge (something) from the mouth: *he spat the food out* **6** (*tr*; often foll by *out*) to utter (short sharp words or syllables), esp in a violent manner **7** **spit it out!** *Brit inf* a command given to someone to speak forthwith ▷ *n* **8** another name for **spittle** **9** a light or brief fall of rain, snow, etc **10** the act or an instance of spitting **11** *inf, chiefly Brit* another word for **spitting image** [OE *spittan*] > **ˈspitter** *n*

spit[2] (spɪt) *n* **1** a pointed rod on which meat is skewered and roasted before or over an open fire **2** Also called: **rotisserie, rotating spit** a similar device fitted onto a cooker **3** an elongated often hooked strip of sand or shingle projecting from a shore ▷ *vb* **spits, spitting, spitted** **4** (*tr*) to impale on or transfix with or as if with a spit [OE *spitu*]

spit and polish *n inf* punctilious attention to neatness, discipline, etc, esp in the armed forces

spite (spaɪt) *n* **1** maliciousness; venomous ill will **2** an instance of such malice; grudge **3** **in spite of** (*prep*) in defiance of; regardless of; notwithstanding ▷ *vb* **spites, spiting, spited** (*tr*) **4** to annoy in order to vent spite [c13 var. of DESPITE] > **ˈspiteful** *adj*

spitfire (ˈspɪtˌfaɪə) *n* a person given to outbursts of spiteful temper, esp a woman or girl

Spithead (ˌspɪtˈhɛd) *n* an extensive anchorage between the mainland of England and the Isle of Wight, off Portsmouth

Spitsbergen (ˈspɪtsˌbɜːgən) *n* another name for **Svalbard**

spitting image *n inf* a person who bears a strong physical resemblance to another. Also called: **spit, spit and image** [c19 modification of *spit and image*, from SPIT[1] (as in *the very spit of* the exact likeness of)]

spitting snake *n* another name for the **rinkhals**

spittle (ˈspɪtᵊl) *n* **1** the fluid secreted in the mouth; saliva **2** Also called: **cuckoo spit, frog spit** the frothy substance secreted on plants by the larvae of certain froghoppers [OE *spǣtl* saliva]

spittoon (spɪˈtuːn) *n* a receptacle for spittle, usually in a public place

spitz (spɪts) *n* any of various breeds of dog characterized by a stocky build, a pointed muzzle, erect ears, and a tightly-curled tail [c19 from G *Spitz*, from *spitz* pointed]

Spitz (spɪts) *n* **Mark** born 1950, US swimmer, who won seven gold medals at the 1972 Olympic Games

spiv (spɪv) *n Brit sl* a person who makes a living by underhand dealings or swindling; black marketeer [c20 back formation from dialect *spiving* smart] > **ˈspivvy** *adj*

splake (spleɪk) *n* a type of hybrid trout bred by Canadian zoologists [from *sp(eckled)* + *lake (trout)*]

splanchnic (ˈsplæŋknɪk) *adj* of or relating to the viscera: *a splanchnic nerve* [c17 from NL *splanchnicus*, from Gk, from *splankhna* the entrails]

splash (splæʃ) *vb* **1** to scatter (liquid) about in blobs; spatter **2** to descend or cause to descend upon in scattered blobs: *he splashed his jacket; rain splashed against the window* **3** to make (one's way) by or as if by splashing: *he splashed through the puddle* **4** (*tr*) to print (a story or photograph) prominently in a newspaper ▷ *n* **5** an instance or sound of splashing **6** an amount splashed **7** a mark or patch created by or as if by splashing **8** *inf* an extravagant display, usually for effect (esp in **make a splash**) **9** a small amount of soda water, etc, added to an alcoholic drink **10** **splash out** spend extravagantly [c18 alteration of PLASH] > **ˈsplashy** *adj*

splashdown (ˈsplæʃˌdaʊn) *n* **1** the controlled landing of a spacecraft on water at the end of a space flight **2** the time scheduled for this event ▷ *vb* **splash down** **3** (*intr, adv*) (of a spacecraft) to make a splashdown

splat[1] (splæt) *n* a wet slapping sound [c19 imit.]

splat[2] (splæt) *n* a wide flat piece of wood, esp one that is the upright central part of a chair back [c19 ? rel. to OE *splātan* to split]

splatter (ˈsplætə) *vb* **1** to splash with small blobs ▷ *n* **2** a splash of liquid, mud, etc

splatter movie *n sl* a film in which the main feature is the graphic and gory murder of numerous victims

splay (spleɪ) *adj* **1** spread out; broad and flat **2** turned outwards in an awkward manner ▷ *vb* **3** to spread out; turn out or expand ▷ *n* **4** a surface of a wall that forms an oblique angle to the main flat surfaces, esp at a doorway or window opening [c14 short for DISPLAY]

splayfoot (ˈspleɪˌfʊt) *n, pl* **splayfeet** *pathol* another word for **flatfoot** > **ˈsplayˌfooted** *adj*

spleen (spliːn) *n* **1** a spongy highly vascular organ situated near the stomach in man. It forms lymphocytes, produces antibodies, and filters bacteria and foreign particles from the blood **2** the corresponding organ in other animals **3** spitefulness or ill humour: *to vent one's spleen* **4** *arch* the organ in the human body considered to be the seat of the emotions **5** *arch* another word for **melancholy** [c13 from OF *esplen*, from L *splēn*, from Gk] > **ˈspleenish** *or* **ˈspleeny** *adj*

spleenwort (ˈspliːnˌwɜːt) *n* any of various ferns that often grow on walls

splendent (ˈsplɛndənt) *adj arch* **1** shining brightly; lustrous: *a splendent sun* **2** famous; illustrious [c15 from L *splendēns* brilliant, from *splendēre* to shine]

splendid (ˈsplɛndɪd) *adj* **1** brilliant or fine, esp in appearance **2** characterized by magnificence **3** glorious or illustrious: *a splendid reputation* **4** brightly gleaming; radiant: *splendid colours* **5** very good or satisfactory: *a splendid time* [c17 from L *splendidus*, from *splendēre* to shine] > **ˈsplendidly** *adv* > **ˈsplendidness** *n*

splendiferous (splɛnˈdɪfərəs) *adj facetious* grand; splendid: *a really splendiferous meal* [c15 from Med. L *splendiferus*, from L *splendor* radiance + *ferre* to bring]

splendour *or US* **splendor** (ˈsplɛndə) *n* **1** the state or quality of being splendid **2** **sun in splendour** *heraldry* a representation of the sun with rays and a human face

splenetic (splɪˈnɛtɪk) *adj* **1** of or relating to the spleen **2** spiteful or irritable; peevish ▷ *n* **3** a spiteful or irritable person > **spleˈnetically** *adv*

splenic (ˈsplɛnɪk, ˈspliː-) *adj* **1** of, relating to, or in the spleen **2** having a disease or disorder of the spleen

splenius (ˈspliːnɪəs) *n, pl* **splenii** (-nɪˌaɪ) either of two muscles at the back of the neck that rotate, flex, and extend the head and neck [C18 via NL from Gk *splēnion* a plaster] > '**splenial** *adj*

splenomegaly (ˌspliːnəʊˈmɛɡəlɪ) *n* abnormal enlargement of the spleen [C20 NL, from Gk *splēn* spleen + *megal-*, stem of *megas* big]

splice (splaɪs) *vb* **splices, splicing, spliced** (*tr*) **1** to join (two ropes) by intertwining the strands **2** to join up the trimmed ends of (two pieces of wire, film, etc) with solder or an adhesive material **3** to join (timbers) by overlapping and binding or bolting the ends together **4** (*passive*) *inf* to enter into marriage: *the couple got spliced* **5 splice the mainbrace** *naut hist* to issue and partake of an extra allocation of alcoholic spirits ▷ *n* **6** a join made by splicing **7** the place where such a join occurs **8** the wedge-shaped end of a cricket-bat handle that fits into the blade [C16 prob. from MDu. *splissen*] > '**splicer** *n*

spline (splaɪn) *n* **1** any one of a series of narrow keys formed longitudinally around a shaft that fit into corresponding grooves in a mating part: used to prevent movement between two parts, esp in transmitting torque **2** a long narrow strip of wood, metal, etc; slat **3** a thin narrow strip made of wood, metal, or plastic fitted into a groove in the edge of a board, tile, etc, to connect it to another ▷ *vb* **splines, splining, splined 4** (*tr*) to provide (a shaft, part, etc) with splines [C18 East Anglian dialect; ? rel. to OE *splin* spindle]

splint (splɪnt) *n* **1** a rigid support for restricting movement of an injured part, esp a broken bone **2** a thin sliver of wood, esp one used to light cigars, a fire, etc **3** a thin strip of wood woven with others to form a chair seat, basket, etc **4** *vet science* inflammation of the small bones alongside the cannon bone of a horse ▷ *vb* **5** to apply a splint to (a broken arm, etc) [C13 from MLow G *splinte*]

splinter ('splɪntə) *n* **1** a small thin sharp piece of wood, glass, etc, broken off from a whole **2** a metal fragment from a shell, bomb, etc, thrown out during an explosion ▷ *vb* **3** to reduce or be reduced to sharp fragments **4** to break or be broken off in small sharp fragments [C14 from MDu. *splinter*; see SPLINT] > '**splintery** *adj*

splinter group *n* a number of members of an organization, political party, etc, who split from the main body and form an independent association of their own

split (splɪt) *vb* **splits, splitting, split 1** to break or cause to break, esp forcibly, by cleaving into separate pieces, often into two roughly equal pieces **2** to separate or be separated from a whole: *he split a piece of wood from the block* **3** to separate or be separated into factions, usually through discord **4** (often foll by *up*) to separate or cause to separate through a disagreement **5** (when *tr*, often foll by *up*) to divide or be divided among two or more persons: *split up the pie among us* **6** *sl* to depart; leave: *let's split* **7** (*tr*) to separate (something) into its components by interposing something else: *to split a word with hyphens* **8** (*intr*; usually foll by *on*) *sl* to betray; inform: *he split on me to the cops* **9** (*tr*) *US politics* to mark (a ballot, etc) so as to vote for the candidates of more than one party: *he split the ticket* **10 split one's sides** to laugh very heartily ▷ *n* **11** the act or process of splitting **12** a gap or rift caused or a piece removed by the process of splitting **13** a breach or schism in a group or the faction resulting from such a breach **14** a dessert of sliced fruit and ice cream, covered with whipped cream, nuts, etc: *banana split* **15** See **Devonshire split 16** *tenpin bowling* a formation of the pins after the first bowl in which there is a large gap between two pins or groups of pins **17** *inf* an arrangement or process of dividing up loot or money ▷ *adj* **18** having been split; divided: *split logs* **19** having a split or splits: *hair with split ends* ▷ See also **splits, split up** [C16 from MDu. *splitten* to cleave] > '**splitter** *n*

Split (*Serbo-Croat* split) *n* a port and resort in W Croatia on the Adriatic: remains of the palace of Diocletian (295–305). Pop: 173 692 (2001). Italian name: **Spalato**

split infinitive *n* (in English grammar) an infinitive used with another word between *to* and the verb itself, as in *to really finish it*.

> USAGE The often quoted 'rule' against placing an adverb between *to* and its verb seems to be honoured more in the breach than the observance. Although it is true that a split infinitive may result in a clumsy sentence (*he decided to firmly and definitively deal with the problem*), this is not enough to justify the absolute condemnation that this practice has attracted in some circles. Indeed, very often the most natural position for the adverb is between *to* and the verb (*he decided to really try next time*) and to change it would result in an artificial and awkward construction (*he decided really to try next time*). And one of the most well known catchphrases of the time enshrines the split infinitive: 'to boldly go where no man has gone before'. Many people therefore maintain that the split infinitive is not in itself a grammatical error, but a matter of style. Nevertheless, many writers prefer to avoid it in formal written English, since readers with a more traditional point of view are likely to view this type of construction as incorrect

split-level *adj* (of a house, room, etc) having the floor level of one part about half a storey above the floor level of an adjoining part

split pea *n* a pea dried and split and used in soups, pease pudding, or as a vegetable

split personality *n* **1** the tendency to change rapidly in mood or temperament **2** a nontechnical term for **multiple personality**

split pin *n* a metal pin made by bending double a wire, often of hemispherical section, so that it can be passed through a hole in a nut, shaft, etc, to secure another part by bending back the ends of the wire

split ring *n* a steel ring having two helical turns, often used as a key ring

split run *n Canad* a divided print run of a periodical in which a number of copies contain advertisements not included in the rest, esp a Canadian edition of a US magazine which contains Canadian advertisements but no Canadian editorial content.

splits (splɪts) *n* (*functioning as sing*) (in gymnastics, etc) the act of sinking to the floor to achieve a sitting position in which both legs are straight, pointing in opposite directions, and at right angles to the body

split-screen technique *n* a cinematic device by which two or more complete images are projected simultaneously onto separate parts of the screen. Also called: **split screen**

split second *n* **1** an extremely small period of time; instant ▷ *adj* **split-second** (*prenominal*) **2** made or arrived at in an extremely short time: *a split-second decision* **3** depending upon minute precision: *split-second timing*

split shift *n* a work period divided into two parts that are separated by an interval longer than a normal rest period

splitting ('splɪtɪŋ) *adj* **1** (of a headache) intolerably painful; acute **2** (of the head) assailed by an overpowering unbearable pain

split up *vb* (*adv*) **1** (*tr*) to separate out into parts; divide **2** (*intr*) to become parted through disagreement: *they split up after years of marriage* **3** to break down or be capable of being broken down into constituent parts ▷ *n* **split-up 4** the act or an instance of separating

splodge (splɒdʒ) *n* **1** a large irregular spot or blot ▷ *vb* **splodges, splodging, splodged 2** (*tr*) to mark (something) with such a blot or blots [C19 alteration of earlier SPLOTCH] > **'splodgy** *adj*

splotch (splɒtʃ) *n, vb* the usual US word for **splodge** [C17 ? a blend of SPOT + BLOTCH] > **'splotchy** *adj*

splurge (splɜːdʒ) *n* **1** an ostentatious display, esp of wealth **2** a bout of unrestrained extravagance ▷ *vb* **splurges, splurging, splurged 3** (often foll by *out*) to spend (money) extravagantly [C19 from ?]

splutter ('splʌtə) *vb* **1** to spit out (saliva, food particles, etc) from the mouth in an explosive manner, as through choking or laughing **2** to utter (words) with spitting sounds, as through rage or choking **3** to eject or be ejected in an explosive manner: *sparks spluttered from the fire* **4** (*tr*) to bespatter (a person) with tiny particles explosively ejected ▷ *n* **5** the process or noise of spluttering **6** spluttering incoherent speech **7** anything ejected through spluttering [C17 var. of SPUTTER, infl. by SPLASH] > **'splutterer** *n*

Spock (spɒk) *n* **Benjamin,** known as *Dr Spock*. 1903–98, US paediatrician, whose *The Common Sense Book of Baby and Child Care* (1946) has influenced the upbringing of children throughout the world

spode (spəʊd) *n* (*sometimes cap*) china or porcelain manufactured by Josiah Spode (1754–1827), English potter, or his company
▷ www.someonespecial.com/cgi-bin/someone/spode.html

spoil (spɔɪl) *vb* **spoils, spoiling, spoilt** *or* **spoiled 1** (*tr*) to cause damage to (something), in regard to its value, beauty, usefulness, etc **2** (*tr*) to weaken the character of (a child) by complying unrestrainedly with its desires **3** (*intr*) (of perishable substances) to become unfit for consumption or use **4** (*intr*) *sport* to disrupt the play or style of an opponent, as to prevent him from settling into a rhythm **5** *arch* to strip (a person or place) of (property) by force **6 be spoiling for** to have an aggressive desire for (a fight, etc) ▷ *n* **7** waste material thrown up by an excavation **8** any treasure accumulated by a person **9** *obs* the act of plundering ▷ See also **spoils** [C13 from OF *espoillier*, from L *spoliāre* to strip, from *spolium* booty]

spoilage ('spɔɪlɪdʒ) *n* **1** the act or an instance of spoiling or the state or condition of being spoilt **2** an amount of material that has been wasted by being spoilt: *considerable spoilage*

spoiler ('spɔɪlə) *n* **1** a plunderer or robber **2** a person or thing that causes spoilage or corruption **3** a device fitted to an aircraft wing to increase drag and reduce lift **4** a similar device fitted to a car **5** *sport* a competitor who adopts spoiling tactics **6** a magazine, newspaper, etc, produced specifically to coincide with the production of a rival magazine, newspaper, etc, in order to divert public interest and reduce its sales

spoils (spɔɪlz) *pl n* **1** (*sometimes sing*) valuables seized by violence, esp in war **2** *chiefly US* the rewards and benefits of public office regarded as plunder for the winning party or candidate. See also **spoils system**

spoilsport ('spɔɪl,spɔːt) *n inf* a person who spoils the pleasure of other people

spoils system *n chiefly US* the practice of filling appointive public offices with friends and supporters of the ruling political party

spoilt (spɔɪlt) *vb* a past tense and past participle of **spoil**

Spokane (spəʊ'kæn) *n* a city in E Washington: commercial centre of an agricultural region. Pop: 195 629 (2000)

spoke[1] (spəʊk) *vb* **1** the past tense of **speak 2** *arch or dialect* a past participle of **speak**

spoke[2] (spəʊk) *n* **1** a radial member of a wheel, joining the hub to the rim **2** a radial projection from the rim of a wheel, as in a ship's wheel **3** a rung of a ladder **4 put a spoke in someone's wheel** *Brit* to thwart someone's plans ▷ *vb* **spokes, spoking, spoked 5** (*tr*) to equip with or as if with spokes [OE *spaca*]

spoken ('spəʊkən) *vb* **1** the past participle of **speak** ▷ *adj* **2** uttered in speech **3** (*in combination*) having speech as specified: *soft-spoken* **4 spoken for** engaged or reserved

spokeshave ('spəʊk,ʃeɪv) *n* a small plane with two handles, one on each side of its blade, used for shaping cylindrical wooden surfaces, such as spokes

spokesman ('spəʊksmən), **spokesperson** ('spəʊks,pɜːsᵊn), *or* **spokeswoman** ('spəʊks,wʊmən) *n, pl* **spokesmen, spokespersons** *or* **spokespeople,** *or* **spokeswomen** a person authorized to speak on behalf of another person or group

spoliation (,spəʊlɪ'eɪʃən) *n* **1** the act or an instance of despoiling or plundering **2** the authorized plundering of neutral vessels on the seas by a belligerent state in time of war **3** *law* the material alteration of a document so as to render it invalid **4** *English ecclesiastical law* the taking of the fruits of a benefice by a person not entitled to them [C14 from L *spoliātiō*, from *spoliāre* to SPOIL] > **spoliatory** ('spəʊlɪətərɪ, -trɪ) *adj*

spondee ('spɒndiː) *n prosody* a metrical foot consisting of two long syllables (– –) [C14 from OF *spondée*, from L *spondēus*, from Gk, from *spondē* ritual libation; from use of spondee in the music for such ceremonies] > **spondaic** (spɒn'deɪɪk) *adj*

spondylitis (,spɒndɪ'laɪtɪs) *n* inflammation of the vertebrae [C19 from NL, from Gk *spondulos* vertebra; see -ITIS]

sponge (spʌndʒ) *n* **1** any of various multicellular typically marine animals, usually occurring in complex sessile colonies, in which the porous body is supported by a fibrous, calcareous, or siliceous skeletal framework **2** a piece of the light porous highly absorbent elastic skeleton of certain sponges, used in bathing, cleaning, etc **3** any of a number of light porous elastic materials resembling a sponge **4** another word for **sponger** (sense 1) **5** *inf* a person who indulges in heavy drinking **6** leavened dough, esp before kneading **7** See **sponge cake 8** Also called: **sponge pudding** *Brit* a light steamed or baked spongy pudding **9** porous metal capable of absorbing large quantities of gas: *platinum sponge* **10** a rub with a sponge **11 throw in the sponge** (*or* **towel**) See **throw in** (sense 3) ▷ *vb* **sponges, sponging, sponged 12** (*tr; often foll by off or down*) to clean (something) by wiping or rubbing with a damp or wet sponge **13** (*tr; usually foll by off, away, out*, etc) to remove (marks, etc) by rubbing with a damp or wet sponge or cloth **14** (when *tr*, often foll by *up*) to absorb (liquids, esp when spilt) in the manner of a sponge **15** (*intr*) to go collecting sponges **16** (foll by *off*) to get (something) from someone by presuming on his or her generosity: *to sponge a meal off someone* **17** (foll by *off* or *on*) to obtain one's subsistence, etc, unjustifiably (from): *he sponges off his friends* [OE, from L *spongia*, from Gk] > **'spongy** *adj*

sponge bag *n* a small waterproof bag made of plastic, etc, that holds toilet articles, used esp when travelling

sponge bath *n* a washing of the body with a wet sponge or cloth, without immersion in water

sponge cake *n* a light porous cake, made of eggs, sugar, flour, and flavourings, without any fat

sponger ('spʌndʒə) *n* **1** *inf* a person who lives off other people by continually taking advantage of their generosity; parasite or scrounger **2** a person or ship employed in collecting sponges

spongiform ('spʌndʒɪ,fɔːm) *adj* **1** resembling a sponge in appearance, esp in having many holes **2** denoting diseases characterized by this appearance of affected tissues

sponsion ('spɒnʃən) *n* **1** the act or process of becoming surety; sponsorship **2** (*often pl*) *international law* an unauthorized agreement made by a public officer, requiring ratification by his or her government **3** any act or promise, esp one made on behalf of someone else

[c17 from L *sponsiō*, from *spondēre* to pledge]

sponson ('spɒnsən) *n* **1** *naval* an outboard support for a gun, etc **2** a structural projection from the side of a paddle steamer for supporting a paddle wheel **3** a float or flotation chamber along the gunwale of a boat or ship **4** a structural unit attached to a helicopter fuselage by struts, housing the landing gear and flotation bags [c19 ?from EXPANSION]

sponsor ('spɒnsə) *n* **1** a person or group that promotes either another person or group in an activity or the activity itself, either for profit or for charity **2** *chiefly US & Canad* a person or business firm that pays the costs of a radio or television programme in return for advertising time **3** a legislator who presents and supports a bill, motion, etc **4** Also called: **godparent** **4a** an authorized witness who makes the required promises on behalf of a person to be baptized and thereafter assumes responsibility for his Christian upbringing **4b** a person who presents a candidate for confirmation ▷ *vb* **5** (*tr*) to act as a sponsor for [c17 from L, from *spondēre* to promise solemnly] > **sponsorial** (spɒn'sɔːrɪəl) *adj* > **'sponsor,ship** *n*

sponsored ('spɒnsəd) *adj* denoting an activity organized to raise money for a charity in which sponsors agree to donate money on completion of the activity by participants

spontaneity (,spɒntə'niːɪtɪ, -'neɪ-) *n, pl* **spontaneities** **1** the state or quality of being spontaneous **2** (*often pl*) the exhibiting of spontaneous actions, impulses, or behaviour

spontaneous (spɒn'teɪnɪəs) *adj* **1** occurring, produced, or performed through natural processes without external influence **2** arising from an unforced personal impulse; voluntary; unpremeditated **3** (of plants) growing naturally; indigenous [c17 from LL *spontāneus*, from L *sponte* voluntarily] > **spon'taneously** *adv* > **spon'taneousness** *n*

spontaneous combustion *n* the ignition of a substance or body as a result of internal oxidation processes, without the application of an external source of heat

spontaneous generation *n* a theory, now discredited, stating that living organisms could arise directly and rapidly from nonliving material. Also called: **abiogenesis**

spoof (spuːf) *inf* ▷ *n* **1** a mildly satirical mockery or parody; lampoon **2** a good-humoured deception or trick ▷ *vb* **3** to indulge in a spoof of (a person or thing) [c19 coined by A. Roberts (1852–1933), E comedian] > **'spoofer** *n*

spook (spuːk) *inf* ▷ *n* **1** a ghost **2** *US & Canad* a spy **3** a strange or frightening person ▷ *vb* (*tr*) *US & Canad* **4** to frighten: *to spook horses; to spook a person* **5** (of a ghost) to haunt [c19 Du. *spook*, from MLow G *spōk* ghost] > **'spooky** *adj*

spool (spuːl) *n* **1** a device around which magnetic tape, film, cotton, etc, can be wound, with plates at top and bottom to prevent it from slipping off **2** anything round which other materials, esp thread, are wound ▷ *vb* **3** (sometimes foll by *up*) to wind or be wound onto a spool [c14 of Gmc origin]

spoon (spuːn) *n* **1** a utensil having a shallow concave part, usually elliptical in shape, attached to a handle, used in eating or serving food, stirring, etc **2** Also called: **spoonbait** an angling lure consisting of a bright piece of metal which swivels on a trace to which are attached a hook or hooks **3** *golf* a former name for a No 3 wood **4** **be born with a silver spoon in one's mouth** to inherit wealth or social standing **5** *rowing* a type of oar blade that is curved at the edges and tip ▷ *vb* **6** (*tr*) to scoop up or transfer (food, liquid, etc) from one container to another with or as if with a spoon **7** (*intr*) *old-fashioned sl* to kiss and cuddle **8** *sport* to hit (a ball) with a weak lifting motion, as in golf, cricket, etc [OE *spōn* splinter]

spoonbill ('spuːn,bɪl) *n* any of several wading birds of warm regions, having a long horizontally flattened bill

spoondrift ('spuːn,drɪft) *n* a less common spelling of **spindrift**

spoonerism ('spuːnə,rɪzəm) *n* the transposition of the initial consonants or consonant clusters of a pair of words, often resulting in an amusing ambiguity, such as *hush my brat* for *brush my hat* [c20 after W. A. *Spooner* (1844–1930), E clergyman renowned for this]

spoon-feed *vb* **spoon-feeds, spoon-feeding, spoon-fed** (*tr*) **1** to feed with a spoon **2** to overindulge or spoil **3** to provide (a person) with ready-made opinions, judgments, etc

spoonful ('spuːn,fʊl) *n, pl* **spoonfuls** **1** the amount that a spoon is able to hold **2** a small quantity

spoony *or* **spooney** ('spuːnɪ) *inf, old-fashioned* ▷ *adj* **spoonier, spooniest** **1** foolishly or stupidly amorous ▷ *n, pl* **spoonies** **2** a fool or silly person, esp one in love

spoor (spʊə, spɔː) *n* **1** the trail of an animal or person, esp as discernible to the eye ▷ *vb* **2** to track (an animal) by following its trail [c19 from Afrik., from MDu. *spor*; rel. to OE *spor* track]

Sporades ('spɒrə,diːz) *pl n* two groups of Greek islands in the Aegean: the **Northern Sporades**, lying northeast of Euboea, and the **Southern Sporades**, which include the Dodecanese and lie off the SW coast of Turkey

sporadic (spə'rædɪk) *adj* **1** occurring at irregular points in time; intermittent: *sporadic firing* **2** scattered; isolated: *a sporadic disease* [c17 from Med. L *sporadicus*, from Gk, from *sporas* scattered] > **spo'radically** *adv*

sporangium (spə'rændʒɪəm) *n, pl* **sporangia** (-dʒɪə) any organ, esp in fungi, in which asexual spores are produced [c19 from NL, from SPORO- + Gk *angeion* receptacle] > **spo'rangial** *adj*

Ss

spore (spɔː) *n* **1** a reproductive body, produced by bacteria, fungi, some protozoans and many plants, that develops into a new individual. A **sexual spore** is formed after the fusion of gametes and an **asexual spore** is the result of asexual reproduction **2** a germ cell, seed, dormant bacterium, or similar body ▷ *vb* **spores, sporing, spored** **3** (*intr*) to produce, carry, or release spores [c19 from NL *spora*, from Gk: a sowing; rel. to Gk *speirein* to sow]

spore case *n* the nontechnical name for **sporangium**

sporo- *or before a vowel* **spor-** *combining form* spore: *sporophyte* [from NL *spora*]

sporogenesis (,spɔːrəʊ'dʒɛnɪsɪs, ,spɒ-) *n* the process of spore formation in plants and animals > **sporogenous** (spɔː'rɒdʒɪnəs, spɒ-) *adj*

sporogonium (,spɔːrəʊ'gəʊnɪəm, ,spɒ-) *n, pl* **sporogonia** (-nɪə) the sporophyte of mosses and liverworts, consisting of a spore-bearing capsule on a short stalk that arises from the parent plant

sporophyll *or* **sporophyl** ('spɔːrəʊfɪl, 'spɒ-) *n* a leaf in ferns and other spore-bearing plants that bears the sporangia

sporophyte ('spɔːrəʊ,faɪt, 'spɒ-) *n* the diploid form of plants that have alternation of generations. It produces asexual spores > **sporophytic** (,spɔːrə'fɪtɪk, ,spɒ-) *adj*

-sporous *adj combining form* (in botany) having a specified type or number of spores

sporozoan (,spɔːrə'zəʊən, ,spɒ-) *n* **1** any parasitic protozoan of a phylum that includes the malaria parasite ▷ *adj* **2** of or relating to the sporozoans

sporran ('spɒrən) *n* a large pouch, usually of fur, worn hanging from a belt in front of the kilt in Scottish Highland dress [c19 from Scot Gaelic *sporan* purse]

sport (spɔːt) *n* **1** an individual or group activity pursued for exercise or pleasure, often taking a competitive form **2** such activities considered collectively **3** any pastime indulged in for pleasure **4** the pleasure derived from a pastime, esp hunting, shooting, or fishing **5** playful or good-humoured joking: *to say a thing in sport* **6** derisive mockery or the object of such mockery: *to make sport of someone* **7** someone or something that is controlled by external influences: *the sport of fate* **8** *inf* (sometimes qualified by *good, bad*, etc) a person who reacts cheerfully in the face of adversity, esp a good loser **9** *inf* a person noted for being scrupulously fair and abiding by the rules of a game **10** *inf* a person who leads a merry existence, esp a gambler: *he's a bit of a sport* **11** *Austral & NZ inf* a form of address used esp between males **12** *biol* **12a** an animal or plant that differs conspicuously from other organisms of the same species, usually because of a mutation **12b** an anomalous characteristic of such an organism ▷ *vb* **13** (*tr*) *inf* to wear or display in an ostentatious or proud manner: *she was sporting a new hat* **14** (*intr*) to skip about or frolic happily **15** to amuse (oneself), esp in outdoor physical recreation **16** (*intr*; often foll by *with*) *arch* to make fun (of) **17** (*intr*) *biol* to produce or undergo a mutation ▷ See also **sports** [c15 *sporten*, var. of *disporten* to DISPORT] > **'sporter** *n* > **'sportful** *adj* > **'sportfully** *adv* > **'sportfulness** *n*

sporting ('spɔːtɪŋ) *adj* **1** (*prenominal*) of, relating to, or used or engaged in a sport or sports **2** relating or conforming to sportsmanship; fair **3** of or relating to gambling **4** willing to take a risk > **'sportingly** *adv*

sportive ('spɔːtɪv) *adj* **1** playful or joyous **2** done in jest rather than seriously > **'sportively** *adv* > **'sportiveness** *n*

sports (spɔːts) *n* **1** (*modifier*) relating to, concerned with, or used in sports: *sports equipment* **2** Also called: **sports day** *Brit* a meeting held at a school or college for competitions in various athletic events

sports cap *n* **1** a hat designed for sports or to look sporty **2** a special top for a bottle, designed to aid drinking without spilling

sports car *n* a production car designed for speed and manoeuvrability, having a low body and usually seating only two persons

sportscast ('spɔːtsˌkɑːst) *n US* a broadcast consisting of sports news > **'sportsˌcaster** *n*

sports jacket *n* a man's informal jacket, made esp of tweed. Also called (US, Austral, and NZ): **sports coat**

sportsman ('spɔːtsmən) *n, pl* **sportsmen** **1** a man who takes part in sports, esp of the outdoor type **2** a person who exhibits fairness, generosity, observance of the rules, and good humour when losing > **'sportsman-ˌlike** *or* **'sportsmanly** *adj* > **'sportsmanˌship** *n*

sports medicine *n* the branch of medicine concerned with injuries sustained through sport

sportswear ('spɔːtsˌwɛə) *n* clothes worn for sport or outdoor leisure wear

sportswoman ('spɔːtsˌwʊmən) *n, pl* **sportswomen** a woman who takes part in sports, esp of the outdoor type

sport utility vehicle *or* **sports utility vehicle** *n chiefly US* a powerful four-wheel drive vehicle suitable for rough terrain. Sometimes shortened to **sport utility** *or* **sports utility** Abbrev: **SUV**

sporty ('spɔːtɪ) *adj* **sportier, sportiest** **1** (of a person) fond of sport or outdoor activities **2** (of clothes) having the appearance of sportswear **3** (of a car) having the performance or appearance of a sports car > **'sportily** *adv* > **'sportiness** *n*

sporule ('spɒruːl) *n* a very small spore [c19 from NL *sporula*]

spot (spɒt) *n* **1** a small mark on a surface, such as a circular patch or stain, differing in colour or texture from its surroundings **2** a location: *this is the exact spot* **3** a blemish of the skin, esp a pimple or one occurring through some disease **4** a blemish on the character of a person; moral flaw **5** *inf* a place of entertainment: *a night spot* **6** *inf, chiefly Brit* a small quantity or amount: *a spot of lunch* **7** *inf* an awkward situation: *that puts me in a spot* **8** a short period between regular television or radio programmes that is used for advertising **9** a position or length of time in a show assigned to a specific performer **10** short for **spotlight** **11** (in billiards) **11a** Also called: **spot ball** the white ball that is distinguished from the plain by a mark or spot **11b** the player using this ball **12** *billiards, snooker, etc* one of the marked places where the ball is placed **13** (*modifier*) **13a** denoting or relating to goods, currencies, or securities available for immediate delivery and payment: *spot goods*. See also **spot price** **13b** involving immediate cash payment: *spot sales* **14** **change one's spots** (*used mainly in negative constructions*) to reform one's character **15** **high spot** an outstanding event: *the high spot of the holiday* **16** **knock spots off** to outstrip or outdo with ease **17** **on the spot** **17a** immediately **17b** at the place in question **17c** in the best position to deal with a situation **17d** in an awkward predicament **17e** (*as modifier*): *our on-the-spot reporter* **18** **tight spot** a serious, difficult, or dangerous situation **19** **weak spot** **19a** some aspect of a character or situation that is susceptible to criticism **19b** a flaw in a person's knowledge ▷ *vb* **spots, spotting, spotted** **20** (*tr*) to observe or perceive suddenly; discern **21** to put stains or spots upon (something) **22** (*intr*) (of some fabrics) to be susceptible to spotting by or as if by water: *silk spots easily* **23** *billiards* to place (a ball) on one of the spots **24** to look out for and note (trains, talent, etc) **25** (*intr*) to rain slightly; spit [c12 (in the sense: moral blemish): from G] > **'spotless** *adj* > **'spotlessly** *adv* > **'spotlessness** *n*

spot check *n* **1** a quick random examination **2** a check made without prior warning ▷ *vb* **spot-check** **3** (*tr*) to perform a spot check on

spot height *n* a mark on a map indicating the height of a hill, mountain, etc

spotlight ('spɒtˌlaɪt) *n* **1** a powerful light focused so as to illuminate a small area **2** **the** the focus of attention ▷ *vb* **spotlights, spotlighting, spotlit** *or* **spotlighted** (*tr*) **3** to direct a spotlight on **4** to focus attention on

spot-on *adj Brit inf* absolutely correct; very accurate

spot price *n* the price of goods, currencies, or securities that are offered for immediate delivery and payment

spotted ('spɒtɪd) *adj* **1** characterized by spots or marks, esp in having a pattern of spots **2** stained or blemished; soiled or bespattered

spotted dick *or* **dog** *n Brit* a steamed or boiled suet pudding containing dried fruit and shaped into a roll

spotted fever *n* any of various severe febrile diseases characterized by small irregular spots on the skin

spotted gum *n* **1** an Australian eucalyptus tree **2** the wood of this tree, used for shipbuilding, sleepers, etc

spotted mackerel *n* a small mackerel, *Scomberomorus queenslandicus*, of northern Australian waters

spotter ('spɒtə) *n* **1a** a person or thing that watches or observes **1b** (*as modifier*): *a spotter plane* **2** a person who makes a hobby of watching for and noting numbers or types of trains, buses, etc: *a train spotter* **3** *mil* a person who advises adjustment of fire on a target by observations **4** a person, esp one engaged in civil defence, who watches for enemy aircraft

spottie ('spɒtɪ) *n NZ* a young deer of up to three months of age

spotty ('spɒtɪ) *adj* **spottier, spottiest** **1** abounding in or characterized by spots or marks, esp on the skin **2** not consistent or uniform; irregular or uneven > **'spottily** *adv* > **'spottiness** *n*

spot-weld *vb* **1** (*tr*) to join (two pieces of metal) by small circular welds by means of heat, usually electrically generated, and pressure ▷ *n* **2** a weld so formed > **'spot-ˌwelder** *n*

spousal ('spaʊzᵊl) *n* **1** (*often pl*) **1a** the marriage ceremony **1b** a wedding ▷ *adj* **2** of or relating to marriage > **'spousally** *adv*

spouse *n* (spaʊs, spaʊz) **1** a person's partner in marriage. Related adj: **spousal** ▷ *vb* (spaʊz, spaʊs), **spouses, spousing, spoused 2** *(tr) obs* to marry [c12 from OF *spus* (masc), *spuse* (fem), from L *sponsus, sponsa* betrothed man or woman, from *spondēre* to promise solemnly]

spout (spaʊt) *vb* **1** to discharge (a liquid) in a continuous jet or in spurts, esp through a narrow gap or under pressure, or (of a liquid) to gush thus **2** (of a whale, etc) to discharge air through the blowhole in a spray at the surface of the water **3** *inf* to utter (a stream of words) on a subject ▷ *n* **4** a tube, pipe, chute, etc, allowing the passage or pouring of liquids, grain, etc **5** a continuous stream or jet of liquid **6** short for **waterspout 7 up the spout** *sl* **7a** ruined or lost: *any hope of rescue is right up the spout* **7b** pregnant [c14 ?from MDu. *spouten*, from ON *spyta* to spit] > **'spouter** *n*

spouting ('spaʊtɪŋ) *n* NZ **a** a rainwater downpipe on the exterior of a building **b** such pipes collectively

SPQR *abbrev for* Senatus Populusque Romanus [L: the Senate and People of Rome]

sprag (spræg) *n* **1** a chock or steel bar used to prevent a vehicle from running backwards on an incline **2** a support or post used in mining [c19 from ?]

sprain (spreɪn) *vb* **1** *(tr)* to injure (a joint) by a sudden twisting or wrenching of its ligaments ▷ *n* **2** the injury, characterized by swelling and temporary disability [c17 from ?]

sprang (spræŋ) *vb* a past tense of **spring**

sprat (spræt) *n* **1** Also called: **brisling** a small marine food fish of the herring family **2** any of various small or young herrings [c16 var. of OE *sprott*]

sprawl (sprɔːl) *vb* **1** *(intr)* to sit or lie in an ungainly manner with one's limbs spread out **2** to fall down or knock down with the limbs spread out in an ungainly way **3** to spread out or cause to spread out in a straggling fashion: *his handwriting sprawled all over the paper* ▷ *n* **4** the act or an instance of sprawling **5** a sprawling posture or arrangement of items **6a** the urban area formed by the expansion of a town or city into surrounding countryside: *the urban sprawl* **6b** the process by which this has happened [OE *spreawlian*] > **'sprawling** *or* **'sprawly** *adj*

spray[1] (spreɪ) *n* **1** fine particles of a liquid **2a** a liquid, such as perfume, paint, etc, designed to be discharged from an aerosol or atomizer: *hair spray* **2b** the aerosol or atomizer itself **3** a quantity of small objects flying through the air: *a spray of bullets* ▷ *vb* **4** to scatter (liquid) in the form of fine particles **5** to discharge (a liquid) from an aerosol or atomizer **6** *(tr)* to treat or bombard with a spray: *to spray the lawn* [c17 from MDu. *sprāien*] > **'sprayer** *n*

spray[2] (spreɪ) *n* **1** a single slender shoot, twig, or branch that bears buds, leaves, flowers, or berries **2** an ornament or floral design like this [c13 of Gmc origin]

spray gun *n* a device that sprays a fluid in a finely divided form by atomizing it in an air jet

spread (sprɛd) *vb* **spreads, spreading, spread 1** to extend or unfold or be extended or unfolded to the fullest width: *she spread the map* **2** to extend or cause to extend over a larger expanse: *the milk spread all over the floor; the political unrest spread over several years* **3** to apply or be applied in a coating: *butter does not spread very well when cold* **4** to distribute or be distributed over an area or region **5** to display or be displayed in its fullest extent: *the landscape spread before us* **6** *(tr)* to prepare (a table) for a meal **7** *(tr)* to lay out (a meal) on a table **8** to send or be sent out in all directions; disseminate or be disseminated: *someone was spreading rumours; the disease spread quickly* **9** (of rails, wires, etc) to force or be forced apart **10** to increase the breadth of (a part), esp to flatten the head of a rivet by pressing, hammering, or forging **11** *(tr) agriculture* **11a** to lay out (hay) in a relatively thin layer to dry **11b** to scatter (seed, manure, etc) over an area **12** *(tr; often foll by around) inf* to make (oneself) agreeable to a large number of people ▷ *n* **13** the act or process of spreading; diffusion, dispersion, expansion, etc **14** *inf* the wingspan of an aircraft **15** an extent of space or time; stretch: *a spread of 50 years* **16** *inf, chiefly US & Canad* a ranch or large tract of land **17** the limit of something fully extended: *the spread of a bird's wings* **18** a covering for a table or bed **19** *inf* a large meal or feast, esp when it is laid out on a table **20** a food which can be spread on bread, etc: *salmon spread* **21** two facing pages in a book or other publication **22** a widening of the hips and waist: *middle-age spread* ▷ *adj* **23** extended or stretched out, esp to the fullest extent [OE *sprǣdan*] > **'spreadable** *adj* > **'spreader** *n*

spread betting *n* a form of gambling in which stakes are placed not on the results of contests but on the number of points scored, etc. Winnings and losses are calculated according to the accuracy or inaccuracy of the prediction

spread eagle *n* **1** the representation of an eagle with outstretched wings, used as an emblem of the US **2** an acrobatic skating figure

spread-eagle *adj also* **spread-eagled 1** lying or standing with arms and legs outstretched ▷ *vb* **spread-eagles, spread-eagling, spread-eagled 2** to assume or cause to assume the shape of a spread eagle **3** *(intr) skating* to execute a spread eagle

spreadsheet ('sprɛdʃiːt) *n* a computer program that allows easy entry and manipulation of figures, equations, and text: used esp for financial planning

sprechgesang (*German* 'ʃprɛçgəzaŋ) *n music* a type of vocalization between singing and recitation [c20 from G *Sprechgesang*, lit.: speaking-song]

spree (spriː) *n* **1** a session of considerable overindulgence, esp in drinking, squandering money, etc **2** a romp [c19 ? changed from Scot *spreath* plundered cattle, ult. from L *praeda* booty]

sprig (sprɪg) *n* **1** a shoot, twig, or sprout of a tree, shrub, etc; spray **2** an ornamental device resembling a spray of leaves or flowers **3** Also called: **dowel pin** a small wire nail without a head **4** *inf, rare* a youth **5** *inf, rare* a person considered as the descendant of an established family, social class, etc **6** NZ another word for **stud**[1] (sense 5) ▷ *vb* **sprigs, sprigging, sprigged** *(tr)* **7** to fasten or secure with sprigs **8** to ornament (fabric, etc) with a design of sprigs [c15 prob. of Gmc origin] > **'sprigger** *n* > **'spriggy** *adj*

sprightly ('spraɪtlɪ) *adj* **sprightlier, sprightliest 1** full of vitality; lively and active ▷ *adv* **2** *obs* in an active or lively manner [c16 from *spright*, var. of SPRITE + -LY[1]] > **'sprightliness** *n*

spring (sprɪŋ) *vb* **springs, springing, sprang** *or* **sprung; sprung 1** to move or cause to move suddenly upwards or forwards in a single motion **2** to release or be released from a forced position by elastic force: *the bolt sprang back* **3** *(tr)* to leap or jump over **4** *(intr)* to come or arise suddenly **5** *(intr)* (of a part of a mechanism, etc) to jump out of place **6** to make (wood, etc) warped or split or (of wood, etc) to become warped or split **7** to happen or cause to happen unexpectedly: *to spring a surprise* **8** *(intr; usually foll by from)* to originate; be descended: *the idea sprang from a chance meeting; he sprang from peasant stock* **9** *(intr; often foll by up)* to come into being or appear suddenly: *factories springing up* **10** *(tr)* (of a gundog) to rouse (game) from cover **11** *(intr)* (of game or quarry) to start or rise suddenly from cover **12** to explode (a mine) or (of a mine) to explode **13** *(tr)* to provide with a spring or springs **14** *(tr) inf* to arrange the escape of (someone) from prison **15** *(intr) arch or poetic* (of daylight or dawn) to begin to appear ▷ *n* **16** the act or an instance of springing **17** a leap, jump, or bound **18a** the quality of resilience; elasticity **18b** *(as modifier)*: *spring steel* **19** the act or an instance of moving rapidly back from a position of tension **20a** a natural outflow of ground water, as forming the source of a stream **20b** (*as modifier*): *spring water* **21a** a device, such as a coil or strip of steel, that stores potential energy when it is compressed, stretched, or bent and releases it when the restraining force is removed **21b** (*as modifier*): *a spring mattress* **22** a structural defect such as a warp or bend **23a** (*sometimes cap*) the season of the year between winter and summer, astronomically from the March equinox to the June solstice in the N hemisphere and from the September equinox to the December solstice in the S hemisphere **23b** (*as modifier*): *spring showers*. Related adj: **vernal** **24** the earliest or freshest time of something **25** a source or origin **26** Also called: **spring line** *naut* a mooring line, usually one of a pair that cross amidships [OE *springan*] > **'springless** *adj* > **'spring,like** *adj*

spring balance *or esp US* **spring scale** *n* a device in which an object to be weighed is attached to the end of a helical spring, the extension of which indicates the weight of the object on a calibrated scale

springboard ('sprɪŋ,bɔːd) *n* **1** a flexible board, usually projecting low over the water, used for diving **2** a similar board used for gaining height or momentum in gymnastics **3** *Austral & NZ* a board inserted into the trunk of a tree at some height above the ground on which a lumberjack stands to chop down the tree **4** anything that serves as a point of departure or initiation

springbok ('sprɪŋ,bʌk) *n, pl* **springbok** *or* **springboks** an antelope of semidesert regions of southern Africa, which moves in leaps [C18 from Afrik., from Du. *springen* to spring + *bok* goat]

Springbok ('sprɪŋ,bʌk, -,bɒk) *n* a person who has represented South Africa at rugby union

spring chicken *n* **1** *chiefly US* a young chicken, tender for cooking, esp one from two to ten months old **2** **he** *or* **she is no spring chicken** *inf* he or she is no longer young

spring-clean *vb* **1** to clean (a house) thoroughly: traditionally at the end of winter ▷ *n* **2** an instance of this > **,spring-'cleaning** *n*

springe (sprɪndʒ) *n* **1** a snare set to catch small wild animals or birds and consisting of a loop attached to a bent twig or branch under tension ▷ *vb* **springes, springeing, springed** **2** (*tr*) to catch (animals or birds) with this [C13 rel. to OE *springan* to spring]

springer ('sprɪŋə) *n* **1** a person or thing that springs **2** short for **springer spaniel** **3** *archit* **3a** the first and lowest stone of an arch **3b** the impost of an arch

springer spaniel *n* either of two breeds of spaniel with a slightly domed head and ears of medium length

Springfield ('sprɪŋ,fiːld) *n* **1** a city in S Massachusetts, on the Connecticut River: the site of the US arsenal and armoury (1794–1968), which developed the Springfield and Garand rifles. Pop: 152 082 (2000) **2** a city in SW Missouri. Pop: 151 580 (2000) **3** a city in central Illinois, capital of the state: the home and burial place of Abraham Lincoln. Pop: 111 454 (2000)

springhaas ('sprɪŋ,hɑːs) *n, pl* **springhaas** *or* **springhase** (-,hɑːzə) a small S and E African nocturnal kangaroo-like rodent [from Afrik.: spring hare]

springing ('sprɪŋɪŋ) *n* *archit* the level where an arch or vault rises from a support

spring lock *n* a type of lock having a spring-loaded bolt, a key being required only to unlock it

spring onion *n* an immature form of the onion, widely cultivated for its tiny bulb and long green leaves which are eaten in salads, etc. Also called: **scallion**

spring roll *n* a Chinese dish consisting of a savoury mixture rolled up in a thin pancake and fried

Springs (sprɪŋz) *n* a city in E South Africa: developed around a coal mine established in 1885 and later became a major world gold-mining centre, now with uranium extraction. Pop (urban area): 160 795 (1996)

Springsteen ('sprɪŋ,stiːn) *n* **Bruce** born 1949, US rock singer, songwriter, and guitarist. His albums include *Born to Run* (1975), *Darkness on the Edge of Town* (1978), and *Born in the USA* (1984), *The Ghost of Tom Joad* (1995), and *The Rising* (2002)

springtail ('sprɪŋ,teɪl) *n* any of various primitive wingless insects having a forked springing organ

spring tide *n* **1** either of the two tides that occur at or just after new moon and full moon: the greatest rise and fall in tidal level ▷ Cf **neap tide** **2** any great rush or flood

springtime ('sprɪŋ,taɪm) *n* **1** Also called: **springtide** the season of spring **2** the earliest, usually the most attractive, period of the existence of something

springy ('sprɪŋɪ) *adj* **springier, springiest** **1** possessing or characterized by resilience or bounce **2** (of a place) having many springs of water > **'springily** *adv* > **'springiness** *n*

sprinkle ('sprɪŋkᵊl) *vb* **sprinkles, sprinkling, sprinkled** **1** to scatter (liquid, powder, etc) in tiny particles or droplets over (something) **2** (*tr*) to distribute over (something): *the field was sprinkled with flowers* **3** (*intr*) to drizzle slightly ▷ *n* **4** the act or an instance of sprinkling or a quantity that is sprinkled **5** a slight drizzle [C14 prob. from MDu. *sprenkelen*] > **'sprinkler** *n*

sprinkler system *n* a fire-extinguishing system that releases water from overhead nozzles opened automatically by a temperature rise

sprinkling ('sprɪŋklɪŋ) *n* a small quantity or amount: *a sprinkling of common sense*

sprint (sprɪnt) *n* **1** *athletics* a short race run at top speed **2** a fast finishing speed at the end of a longer race, as in running or cycling, etc **3** any quick run ▷ *vb* **4** (*intr*) to go at top speed, as in running, cycling, etc [C16 of Scand. origin] > **'sprinter** *n*

sprit (sprɪt) *n* *naut* a light spar pivoted at the mast and crossing a fore-and-aft quadrilateral sail diagonally to the peak [OE *spreot*]

sprite (spraɪt) *n* **1** (in folklore) a nimble elflike creature, esp one associated with water **2** a small dainty person [C13 from OF *esprit*, from L *spīritus* SPIRIT[1]]

spritsail ('sprɪt,seɪl; *naut* 'sprɪtsəl) *n* *naut* a sail mounted on a sprit or bowsprit

spritzer ('sprɪtsə) *n* a drink, usually white wine, with soda water added [from G *spritzen* to splash]

sprocket ('sprɒkɪt) *n* **1** Also called: **sprocket wheel** a relatively thin wheel having teeth projecting radially from the rim, esp one that drives or is driven by a chain **2** an individual tooth on such a wheel **3** a cylindrical wheel with teeth on one or both rims for pulling film through a camera or projector [C16 from ?]

sprog (sprɒg) *n* *sl* **1** a child; baby **2** (esp in RAF) a new recruit

sprout (spraʊt) *vb* **1** (of a plant, seed, etc) to produce (new leaves, shoots, etc) **2** (*intr*; often foll by *up*) to begin to grow or develop ▷ *n* **3** a new shoot or bud **4** something that grows like a sprout **5** See **Brussels sprout** [OE *sprūtan*]

spruce[1] (spruːs) *n* **1** any coniferous tree of a N temperate genus, cultivated for timber and for ornament. They grow in a pyramidal shape and have needle-like leaves and light-coloured wood. See also **Norway spruce** **2** the wood of any of these trees [C17 short for *Spruce fir*, from C14 *Spruce* Prussia, changed from *Pruce*, via OF from L *Prussia*]

spruce[2] (spruːs) *adj* neat, smart, and trim [C16 ?from *Spruce leather*, a fashionable leather imported from Prussia; see SPRUCE[1]] > **'sprucely** *adv* > **'spruceness** *n*

spruce beer *n* an alcoholic drink made of fermented molasses flavoured with spruce twigs and cones

spruce grouse *n* a game bird, *Dendragapus canadensis*, occurring in Canadian coniferous forests.

spruce up *vb* **spruces, sprucing, spruced** (*adv*) to make (oneself, a person, or thing) smart and neat

sprue[1] (spruː) *n* **1** a vertical channel in a mould through which plastic or molten metal is introduced or out of which it flows when the mould is filled **2** plastic or metal that solidifies in a sprue [c19 from ?]

sprue[2] (spruː) *n* a chronic disease, esp of tropical climates, characterized by diarrhoea and emaciation [c19 from Du. *spruw*]

spruik (ˈspruːɪk) *vb (intr) Austral sl* to describe or hold forth like a salesman; spiel or advertise loudly [c20 from ?] > **ˈspruiker** *n*

spruit (spreɪt) *n S African* a small tributary stream or watercourse [Afrik. *sprint* offshoot, tributary]

sprung (sprʌŋ) *vb* a past tense and past participle of **spring**

sprung rhythm *n prosody* a type of poetic rhythm characterized by metrical feet of irregular composition, each having one strongly stressed syllable, often the first, and an indefinite number of unstressed syllables

spry (spraɪ) *adj* **spryer, spryest** *or* **sprier, spriest** active and brisk; nimble [c18 ? of Scand. origin] > **ˈspryly** *adv* > **ˈspryness** *n*

spud (spʌd) *n* **1** an informal word for **potato** **2** a narrow-bladed spade for cutting roots, digging up weeds, etc ▷ *vb* **spuds, spudding, spudded** **3** *(tr)* to eradicate (weeds) with a spud **4** *(intr)* to drill the first foot of an oil well [c15 *spudde* short knife, from ?; applied later to a digging tool, & hence to a potato]

spuddle (ˈspʌdᵊl) *n Southwest English dialect* a feeble movement

Spud Island *n* a slang name for **Prince Edward Island**

spue (spjuː) *vb* **spues, spuing, spued** an archaic spelling of **spew** > **ˈspuer** *n*

spume (spjuːm) *n* **1** foam or surf, esp on the sea; froth ▷ *vb* **spumes, spuming, spumed** **2** *(intr)* to foam [c14 from OF *espume*, from L *spūma*] > **ˈspumous** *or* **ˈspumy** *adj*

spun (spʌn) *vb* **1** the past tense and past participle of **spin** ▷ *adj* **2** formed or manufactured by spinning: *spun gold; spun glass*

spunk (spʌŋk) *n* **1** *inf* courage or spirit **2** *Brit* a slang word for **semen** **3** touchwood or tinder [c16 (in the sense: a spark): from Scot Gaelic *spong* tinder, sponge, from L *spongia* sponge] > **ˈspunky** *adj* > **ˈspunkily** *adv*

spun silk *n* shiny yarn or fabric made from silk waste

spur (spɜː) *n* **1** a pointed device or sharp spiked wheel fixed to the heel of a rider's boot to enable him to urge his horse on **2** anything serving to urge or encourage **3** a sharp horny projection from the leg in male birds, such as the domestic cock **4** a pointed process in any of various animals **5** a tubular extension at the base of the corolla in flowers such as larkspur **6** a short or stunted branch of a tree **7** a ridge projecting laterally from a mountain or mountain range **8** another name for **groyne** **9** Also called: **spur track** a railway branch line or siding **10** a short side road leading off a main road **11** a sharp cutting instrument attached to the leg of a gamecock **12 on the spur of the moment** on impulse **13 win one's spurs** **13a** to prove one's ability; gain distinction **13b** *history* to earn a knighthood ▷ *vb* **spurs, spurring, spurred** **14** *(tr)* to goad or urge with or as if with spurs **15** *(intr)* to go or ride quickly; press on **16** *(tr)* to provide with a spur or spurs [OE *spura*]

spurge (spɜːdʒ) *n* any of various plants that have milky sap and small flowers typically surrounded by conspicuous bracts [c14 from OF *espurge*, from *espurgier* to purge, from L *expurgāre* to cleanse]

spur gear *or* **wheel** *n* a gear having involuted teeth either straight or helically cut on a cylindrical surface

spurious (ˈspjʊərɪəs) *adj* **1** not genuine or real **2** (of a plant part or organ) resembling another part in appearance only; false: *a spurious fruit* **3** *rare* illegitimate [c17 from L *spurius* of illegitimate birth] > **ˈspuriously** *adv* > **ˈspuriousness** *n*

spurn (spɜːn) *vb* **1** to reject (a person or thing) with contempt **2** (when *intr*, often foll by *against*) *arch* to kick (at) ▷ *n* **3** an instance of spurning **4** *arch* a kick or thrust [OE *spurnan*] > **ˈspurner** *n*

spurt *or* **spirt** (spɜːt) *vb* **1** to gush or cause to gush forth in a sudden stream or jet **2** *(intr)* to make a sudden effort ▷ *n* **3** a sudden stream or jet **4** a short burst of activity, speed, or energy [c16 ? rel. to MHG *sprützen* to squirt]

Sputnik (ˈspʊtnɪk, ˈspʌt-) *n* any of a series of Soviet artificial satellites, **Sputnik 1** (launched in 1957) being the first man-made satellite to orbit the earth [c20 from Russian, lit.: fellow traveller, from *s-* with + *put* path + *-nik*, suffix indicating agent]

sputter (ˈspʌtə) *vb* **1** another word for **splutter** (senses 1–3) **2** *physics* **2a** to undergo or cause to undergo a process in which atoms of a solid are removed from its surface by the impact of high-energy ions **2b** to coat (a metal) onto (a solid surface) by this process ▷ *n* **3** the process or noise of sputtering **4** incoherent stammering speech **5** something ejected while sputtering [c16 from Du. *sputteren*, imit.] > **ˈsputterer** *n*

sputum (ˈspjuːtəm) *n, pl* **sputa** (-tə) saliva ejected from the mouth, esp mixed with mucus [c17 from L: spittle, from *spuere* to spit out]

spy (spaɪ) *n, pl* **spies** **1** a person employed by a state or institution to obtain secret information from rival countries, organizations, companies, etc **2** a person who keeps secret watch on others **3** *obs* a close view ▷ *vb* **spies, spying, spied** **4** *(intr;* usually foll by *on)* to keep a secret or furtive watch (on) **5** *(intr)* to engage in espionage **6** *(tr)* to catch sight of; descry [c13 *spien*, from OF *espier*, of Gmc origin]

spyglass (ˈspaɪˌglɑːs) *n* a small telescope

spy out *vb (tr, adv)* **1** to discover by careful observation **2** to make a close scrutiny of

sq *or* **sq.** *abbrev for:* **1** sequence **2** square **3** *(pl* **sqq***)* the following one [from L *sequens*]

Sq. *abbrev for:* **1** Squadron **2** Square

SQL *abbrev for* structured query language: a computer programming language used for database management

squab (skwɒb) *n, pl* **squabs** *or* **squab** **1** a young unfledged bird, esp a pigeon **2** a short fat person **3a** a well-stuffed bolster or cushion **3b** a sofa ▷ *adj* **4** (of birds) unfledged **5** short and fat [c17 prob. of Gmc origin] > **ˈsquabby** *adj*

squabble (ˈskwɒbᵊl) *vb* **squabbles, squabbling, squabbled** **1** *(intr)* to quarrel over a small matter ▷ *n* **2** a petty quarrel [c17 prob. of Scand. origin] > **ˈsquabbler** *n*

squad (skwɒd) *n* **1** the smallest military formation, typically a dozen soldiers, esp a drill formation **2** any small group of people engaged in a common pursuit **3** *sport* a number of players from which a team is to be selected [c17 from OF *esquade*, from OSp. *escuadra*, from *escuadrar* to SQUARE, from the square formations used]

squaddie *or* **squaddy** (ˈskwɒdɪ) *n, pl* **squaddies** *Brit sl* a private soldier [c20 from SQUAD]

squadron (ˈskwɒdrən) *n* **1** a subdivision of a naval fleet detached for a particular task **2** a cavalry unit comprising two or more troops **3** the basic tactical and administrative air force unit comprising two or more flights [c16 from It. *squadrone* soldiers drawn up in square formation, from *squadro* square]

squadron leader *n* an officer holding commissioned rank, between flight lieutenant and wing commander in the air forces of Britain and certain other countries

squalamine (ˈskweɪləˌmiːn) *n* a steroid derivative found in sharks; it has antibiotic properties and inhibits cell division and may be useful in cancer and AIDS treatments [c20 from NL *squalus*, genus name of the shark]

squalene (ˈskweɪˌliːn) *n biochemistry* a terpene first found in the liver of sharks but also present in the livers of most higher animals [c20 from NL *squalus*, genus name of the shark]

squalid ('skwɒlɪd) *adj* **1** dirty and repulsive, esp as a result of neglect or poverty **2** sordid [c16 from L *squālidus*, from *squālēre* to be stiff with dirt] > **squa'lidity** *or* **'squalidness** *n* > **'squalidly** *adv*

squall[1] (skwɔːl) *n* **1** a sudden strong wind or brief turbulent storm **2** any sudden commotion ▷ *vb* **3** (*intr*) to blow in a squall [c18 ? a special use of SQUALL[2]] > **'squally** *adj*

squall[2] (skwɔːl) *vb* **1** (*intr*) to cry noisily; yell ▷ *n* **2** a shrill or noisy yell or howl [c17 prob. of Scand. origin] > **'squaller** *n*

squalor ('skwɒlə) *n* the condition or quality of being squalid; disgusting filth [c17 from L]

squama ('skweɪmə) *n, pl* **squamae** (-miː) *biol* a scale or scalelike structure [c18 from L] > **squamate** ('skweɪmeɪt) *adj* > **squa'mation** *n* > **'squamose** *or* **'squamous** *adj*

squander ('skwɒndə) *vb* (*tr*) **1** to spend wastefully or extravagantly; dissipate ▷ *n* **2** an obsolete word for **scatter** [c16 from ?] > **'squanderer** *n*

square (skwɛə) *n* **1** a plane geometric figure having four equal sides and four right angles **2** any object, part, or arrangement having this or a similar shape **3** an open area in a town, sometimes including the surrounding buildings, which may form a square **4** *maths* the product of two equal factors; the second power: *9 is the square of 3, written* 3^2 **5** an instrument having two strips of wood, metal, etc, set in the shape of a T or L, used for constructing or testing right angles **6** *cricket* the closely-cut area in the middle of a ground on which wickets are prepared **7** *inf* a person who is old-fashioned in views, customs, appearance, etc **8** *obs* a standard, pattern, or rule **9** **back to square one** indicating a return to the starting point because of failure, lack of progress, etc **10** **on the square 10a** at right angles **10b** *inf* honestly and openly **11** **out of square 11a** not at right angles or not having a right angle **11b** not in order or agreement ▷ *adj* **12** being a square in shape or section **13** having or forming one or more right angles or being at right angles to something **14a** (*prenominal*) denoting a measure of area of any shape: *a circle of four square feet* **14b** (*immediately postpositive*) denoting a square having a specified length on each side: *a board four feet square* **15** fair and honest (esp in **a square deal**) **16** straight, even, or level: *a square surface* **17** *cricket* at right angles to the wicket: *square leg* **18** *soccer, hockey, etc* in a straight line across the pitch: *a square pass* **19** *naut* (of the sails of a square-rigged ship) set at right angles to the keel **20** *inf* old-fashioned **21** stocky or sturdy: *square shoulders* **22** (*postpositive*) having no remaining debts or accounts to be settled **23** (*prenominal*) unequivocal or straightforward: *a square contradiction* **24** (*postpositive*) neat and tidy **25** *maths* (of a matrix) having the same number of rows and columns **26** **all square** on equal terms; even in score **27** **square peg (in a round hole)** *inf* a person or thing that is a misfit ▷ *vb* **squares, squaring, squared** (*mainly tr*) **28** to make into a square or similar shape **29** *maths* to raise (a number or quantity) to the second power **30** to test or adjust for deviation with respect to a right angle, plane surface, etc **31** (sometimes foll by *off*) to divide into squares **32** to position so as to be rectangular, straight, or level: *to square the shoulders* **33** (sometimes foll by *up*) to settle (debts, accounts, etc) **34** to level (the score) in a game, etc **35** (*also intr; often* foll by *with*) to agree or cause to agree: *your ideas don't square with mine* **36** to arrange (something) or come to an arrangement with (someone) as by bribery **37** **square the circle** to attempt the impossible (in reference to the insoluble problem of constructing a square having exactly the same area as a given circle) ▷ *adv* **38** in order to be square **39** at right angles **40** *soccer, hockey, etc* in a straight line across the pitch: *to pass the ball square* **41** *inf* squarely ▷ See also **square away, square off, square up** [c13 from OF *esquare*, from Vulgar L *exquadra* (unattested), from L *quadrāre* to make square] > **'squareness** *n* > **'squarer** *n*

square away *vb* (*adv*) **1** to set the sails of (a square-rigged ship) at right angles to the keel **2** (*tr*) *US & Canad* to make neat and tidy

square-bashing *n Brit mil sl* drill on a barracks square

square bracket *n* **1** either of a pair of characters [ ], used to enclose a section of writing or printing to separate it from the main text **2** Also called: **bracket** either of these characters used as a sign of aggregation in mathematical or logical expressions

square dance *n* **1** any of various formation dances in which the couples form squares ▷ *vb* **square-dance, square-dances, square-dancing, square-danced 2** (*intr*) to perform such a dance > **'square-ˌdancer** *n*

▷ www.squaredanceworld.com

▷ www.dosado.com

square knot *n* another name for **reef knot**

square leg *n cricket* **1** a fielding position on the on side approximately at right angles to the batsman **2** a person who fields in this position

squarely ('skwɛəlɪ) *adv* **1** in a direct way; straight: *he hit me squarely on the nose* **2** in an honest, frank, and just manner **3** at right angles

square meal *n* a substantial meal consisting of enough to satisfy

square measure *n* a unit or system of units for measuring areas

square number *n* an integer, such as 1, 4, 9, or 16, that is the square of an integer

square off *vb* (*intr, adv*) to assume a posture of offence or defence, as in boxing

square of opposition *n logic* the diagrammatic representation of the relationships between the four types of proposition found in the syllogism

square-rigged *adj naut* rigged with square sails. See **square sail**

square root *n* a number or quantity that when multiplied by itself gives a given number or quantity: *the square roots of 4 are 2 and −2*

square sail *n naut* a rectangular or square sail set on a horizontal yard rigged more or less at right angles to the keel

square shooter *n inf, chiefly US* an honest or frank person > **square shooting** *adj*

square up *vb* (*adv*) **1** to pay or settle (bills, debts, etc) **2** *inf* to arrange or be arranged satisfactorily **3** (*intr; foll by to*) to prepare to be confronted (with), esp courageously **4** (*tr; foll by to*) to adopt a position of readiness to fight (an opponent) **5** *Scot* to tidy up

squarrose ('skwærəʊz, 'skwɒ-) *adj* **1** *biol* having a rough surface, caused by projecting hairs, scales, etc **2** *bot* having or relating to parts that are recurved [c18 from L *squarrōsus* scabby]

squash[1] (skwɒʃ) *vb* **1** to press or squeeze or be pressed or squeezed in or down so as to crush, distort, or pulp **2** (*tr*) to suppress or overcome **3** (*tr*) to humiliate or crush (a person), esp with a disconcerting retort **4** (*intr*) to make a sucking, splashing, or squelching sound **5** (often foll by *in* or *into*) to enter or insert in a confined space ▷ *n* **6** *Brit* a still drink made from fruit juice or fruit syrup diluted with water **7** a crush, esp of people in a confined space **8** something squashed **9** the act or sound of squashing or the state of being squashed **10** Also called: **squash rackets** a game for two or four players played in an enclosed court with a small rubber ball and light long-handled rackets **11** Also called: **squash tennis** a similar game played with larger rackets and a larger pneumatic ball [c16 from OF *esquasser*, from Vulgar L *exquassāre* (unattested), from L EX-[1] + *quassāre* to shatter] > **'squasher** *n*

▷ www.worldsquash.org

squash[2] (skwɒʃ) *n, pl* **squashes** *or* **squash** *US & Canad* **1** any of various marrow-like plants, the fruits of which have a hard rind surrounding edible flesh **2** the fruit, eaten as a vegetable [C17 of Amerind origin, from *askutasquash*, lit.: green vegetable eaten green]

squashy ('skwɒʃɪ) *adj* **squashier, squashiest 1** easily squashed; pulpy: *a squashy peach* **2** soft and wet; marshy: *squashy ground* > '**squashily** *adv* > '**squashiness** *n*

squat (skwɒt) *vb* **squats, squatting, squatted** (*intr*) **1** to rest in a crouching position with the knees bent and the weight on the feet **2** to crouch down, esp in order to hide **3** *law* to occupy land or property to which the occupant has no legal title ▷ *adj* **4** Also: **squatty** short and broad ▷ *n* **5** a squatting position **6** a house occupied by squatters [C13 from OF *esquater*, from *es-* EX-[1] + *catir* to press together, from Vulgar L *coactīre* (unattested), from L *cōgere* to compress] > '**squatly** *adv* > '**squatness** *n*

squatter ('skwɒtə) *n* **1** a person who occupies property or land to which he or she has no legal title **2** (in Australia) **2a** a grazier with extensive holdings **2b** *history* a person occupying land as tenant of the Crown **3** (in New Zealand) a 19th-century settler who took up large acreage on a crown lease

squat thrust *n* an exercise in which the hands are kept on the floor with the arms held straight while the legs are straightened out behind and quickly drawn in towards the body again

squattocracy (skwɒ'tɒkrəsɪ) *n Austral* squatters collectively, regarded as rich and influential. See **squatter** (sense 2a) [C19 from SQUATTER + -CRACY]

squaw (skwɔː) *n* **1** *offens* a North American Indian woman **2** *sl, usually facetious* a woman or wife [C17 of Amerind origin]

squawk (skwɔːk) *n* **1** a loud raucous cry; screech **2** *inf* a loud complaint ▷ *vb* **3** to utter (with) a squawk **4** (*intr*) *inf* to complain loudly [C19 imit.] > '**squawker** *n*

squaw man *n derog* a White man married to a North American Indian woman

squeak (skwiːk) *n* **1** a short shrill cry or high-pitched sound **2** *inf* an escape (esp in **narrow squeak, near squeak**) **3** *inf* (*usually used with a negative*) a word; a slight sound ▷ *vb* **4** to make or cause to make a squeak **5** (*intr; usually foll by through* or *by*) to pass with only a narrow margin: *to squeak through an examination* **6** (*intr*) *inf* to confess information about oneself or another **7** (*tr*) to utter with a squeak [C17 prob. of Scand. origin] > '**squeaky** *adj* > '**squeakily** *adv* > '**squeakiness** *n*

squeaky-clean *adj* **1** (of hair) washed so clean that wet strands squeak when rubbed **2** completely clean **3** *inf, derog* (of a person) cultivating a virtuous and wholesome image

squeal (skwiːl) *n* **1** a high shrill yelp, as of pain **2** a screaming sound ▷ *vb* **3** to utter (with) a squeal **4** (*intr*) *sl* to confess information about another **5** (*intr*) *inf, chiefly Brit* to complain loudly [C13 *squelen*, imit.] > '**squealer** *n*

squeamish ('skwiːmɪʃ) *adj* **1** easily sickened or nauseated **2** easily shocked; prudish **3** easily frightened: *squeamish about spiders* [C15 from Anglo-F *escoymous*, from ?] > '**squeamishly** *adv* > '**squeamishness** *n*

squeegee ('skwiːdʒiː) *n* **1** an implement with a rubber blade used for wiping away surplus water from a surface, such as a windowpane **2** any of various similar devices used in photography for pressing water out of wet prints or negatives or for squeezing prints onto a glazing surface ▷ *vb* **squeegees, squeegeeing, squeegeed 3** to remove (liquid) from (something) by use of a squeegee [C19 prob. imit., infl. by SQUEEZE]

squeeze (skwiːz) *vb* **squeezes, squeezing, squeezed** (*mainly tr*) **1** to grip or press firmly, esp so as to crush or distort **2** to crush or press (something) so as to extract (a liquid): *to squeeze juice from an orange; to squeeze an orange* **3** to apply gentle pressure to, as in affection or reassurance: *he squeezed her hand* **4** to push or force in a confined space: *to squeeze six lettuces into one box; to squeeze through a crowd* **5** to hug closely **6** to oppress with exacting demands, such as excessive taxes **7** to exert pressure on (someone) in order to extort (something): *to squeeze money out of a victim by blackmail* **8** *bridge, whist* to lead a card that forces (opponents) to discard potentially winning cards ▷ *n* **9** the act or an instance of squeezing or of being squeezed **10** a hug or handclasp **11** a crush of people in a confined space **12** *chiefly Brit* a condition of restricted credit imposed by a government to counteract price inflation **13** an amount extracted by squeezing: *a squeeze of lemon juice* **14** *inf* pressure brought to bear in order to extort something (esp in **put the squeeze on**) **15** *commerce* any action taken by a trader or traders on a market that forces buyers to make purchases and prices to rise **16** Also called: **squeeze play** *bridge, whist* a manoeuvre that forces opponents to discard potentially winning cards [C16 from ME *queysen* to press, from OE *cwȳsan*] > '**squeezable** *adj* > '**squeezer** *n*

squeezy ('skwiːzɪ) *adj* **squeezier, squeeziest** (of bottles, tubes, mops, etc) designed to be squeezed, especially in order to extract something

squelch (skwɛltʃ) *vb* **1** (*intr*) to walk laboriously through soft wet material or with wet shoes, making a sucking noise **2** (*intr*) to make such a noise **3** (*tr*) to crush completely; squash **4** (*tr*) *inf* to silence, as by a crushing retort ▷ *n* **5** a squelching sound **6** something that has been squelched **7** *inf* a crushing remark [C17 imit.] > '**squelcher** *n* > '**squelchy** *adj*

squib (skwɪb) *n* **1** a firework that burns with a hissing noise and culminates in a small explosion **2** a short witty attack; lampoon **3** **damp squib** something intended but failing to impress ▷ *vb* **squibs, squibbing, squibbed 4** (*intr*) to sound, move, or explode like a squib **5** (*intr*) to let off or shoot a squib **6** to write a squib against (someone) [C16 prob. imit. of a light explosion]

squid (skwɪd) *n, pl* **squid** *or* **squids** any of various ten-limbed pelagic cephalopod molluscs of most seas, having a torpedo-shaped body ranging from about 10 centimetres to 16.5 metres long. See also **cuttlefish** [C17 from ?]

squiffy ('skwɪfɪ) *adj* **squiffier, squiffiest** *Brit inf* slightly drunk [C19 from ?]

squiggle ('skwɪgᵊl) *n* **1** a mark or movement in the form of a wavy line; curlicue **2** an illegible scrawl ▷ *vb* **squiggles, squiggling, squiggled 3** (*intr*) to wriggle **4** (*intr*) to form or draw squiggles **5** (*tr*) to make into squiggles [C19 ? a blend of SQUIRM + WIGGLE] > '**squiggler** *n* > '**squiggly** *adj*

squilgee ('skwɪldʒiː) *n* a variant spelling of **squeegee** [C19 ?from SQUEEGEE, infl. by SQUELCH]

squill (skwɪl) *n* **1** Also called: **sea squill** a Mediterranean plant of the lily family **2** any of various related Old World plants **3** Also called: **scilla** the bulb of the sea squill, which is sliced and dried; formerly used medicinally, as an expectorant [C14 from L *squilla* sea onion, from Gk *skilla*, from ?]

squinch (skwɪntʃ) *n* a small arch, corbelling, etc, across an internal corner of a tower, used to support a spire, etc. Also called: **squinch arch** [C15 from obs. *scunch*, from ME *sconcheon*, from OF *escoinson*, from *es-* EX-[1] + *coin* corner]

squint (skwɪnt) *vb* **1** (*usually intr*) to cross or partly close (the eyes) **2** (*intr*) to have a squint **3** (*intr*) to look or glance sideways or askance ▷ *n* **4** the nontechnical name for **strabismus 5** the act or an instance of squinting; glimpse **6** a narrow oblique opening in a wall or pillar of a church to permit a view of the main altar from a side aisle or transept **7** *inf* a quick look; glance ▷ *adj* **8** having a squint **9** *inf* askew; crooked [C14 short for ASQUINT] > '**squinter** *n* > '**squinty** *adj*

squire ('skwaɪə) *n* **1** a country gentleman in England, esp the main landowner in a rural community **2** *feudal history* a young man of noble birth, who attended upon a

Ss

knight **3** *rare* a man who courts or escorts a woman **4** *inf, chiefly Brit* a term of address used by one man to another ▷ *vb* **squires, squiring, squired 5** (*tr*) (of a man) to escort (a woman) [C13 from OF *esquier*; see ESQUIRE]

squirearchy *or* **squirarchy** ('skwaɪəˌrɑːkɪ) *n, pl* **squirearchies** *or* **squirarchies 1** government by squires **2** squires collectively, esp as a political or social force > **squire'archal, squir'archal** *or* **squire'archical, squir'archical** *adj*

squireen (skwaɪ'riːn) *or* **squireling** ('skwaɪəlɪŋ) *n rare* a petty squire [C19 from SQUIRE + *-een*, Anglo-Irish dim. suffix]

squirm (skwɜːm) *vb* (*intr*) **1** to move with a wriggling motion; writhe **2** to feel deep mental discomfort, guilt, embarrassment, etc ▷ *n* **3** a squirming movement [C17 imit. (? infl. by WORM)] > **'squirmer** *n* > **'squirmy** *adj*

squirrel ('skwɪrəl) *n, pl* **squirrels** *or* **squirrel 1** any of various arboreal rodents having a bushy tail and feeding on nuts, seeds, etc **2** any of various related rodents, such as a ground squirrel or a marmot **3** the fur of such an animal **4** *inf* a person who hoards things ▷ *vb* **squirrels, squirrelling, squirrelled** *or US* **squirrels, squirreling, squirreled 5** (*tr*; usually foll by *away*) *inf* to store for future use; hoard [C14 from OF *esquireul*, from LL *sciūrus*, from Gk *skiouros*, from *skia* shadow + *oura* tail]

squirrel cage *n* **1** a cage consisting of a cylindrical framework that is made to rotate by a small animal running inside the framework **2** a repetitive purposeless task, way of life, etc **3** Also called: **squirrel-cage motor** *electrical engineering* the rotor of an induction motor with a cylindrical winding having copper bars around the periphery parallel to the axis

squirt (skwɜːt) *vb* **1** to force (a liquid) or (of a liquid) to be forced out of a narrow opening **2** (*tr*) to cover or spatter with liquid so ejected ▷ *n* **3** a jet or amount of liquid so ejected **4** the act or an instance of squirting **5** an instrument used for squirting **6** *inf* **6a** a person regarded as insignificant or contemptible **6b** a short person [C15 imit.] > **'squirter** *n*

squirting cucumber *n* a hairy plant of the Mediterranean region, having a fruit that discharges seeds explosively when ripe

squish (skwɪʃ) *vb* **1** (*tr*) to crush, esp so as to make a soft splashing noise **2** (*intr*) (of mud, etc) to make a splashing noise ▷ *n* **3** a soft squashing sound [C17 imit.] > **'squishy** *adj*

squit (skwɪt) *n Brit sl* **1** an insignificant person **2** nonsense [C19 var. of SQUIRT]

squiz (skwɪz) *n, pl* **squizzes** *Austral & NZ sl* a look or glance, esp an inquisitive one [C20 ? blend of SQUINT + QUIZ]

sr *maths abbrev for* steradian

Sr *abbrev for:* **1** (after a name) senior **2** Señor **3** Sir **4** Sister (religious) **5** *the chemical symbol for* strontium

Sra *abbrev for* Señora

SRA (in Britain) *abbrev for* Strategic Rail Authority

Srbija ('sᵊrbija) *n* the Serbian name for **Serbia**

Sri Lanka (ˌsriː 'læŋkə) *n* a republic in S Asia, occupying the island of Ceylon: settled by the Sinhalese from S India in about 550 BC; became a British colony 1802; gained independence in 1948, becoming a republic within the Commonwealth in 1972. Exports include tea, cocoa, cinnamon, and copra. Official languages: Sinhalese and Tamil; English is also widely spoken. Religion: Hinayana Buddhist majority. Currency: Sri Lanka rupee. Capital: Colombo (administrative), Sri Jayewardenepura Kotte (legislative). Pop: 19 399 000 (2001 est). Area: 65 610 sq km (25 332 sq miles). Official name (since 1978): **Democratic Socialist Republic of Sri Lanka** Former name (until 1972): **Ceylon** > **Sri Lankan** *adj, n*
▷ www.priu.gov.lk
▷ www.lanka.net/ctb

Srinagar (sriː'nʌgə) *n* a city in N India, the summer capital of the state of Jammu and Kashmir, at an altitude of 1600 m (5250 ft) on the Jhelum River: seat of the University of Jammu and Kashmir (1948). Pop: 586 038 (1991)

SRN (formerly, in Britain) *abbrev for* State Registered Nurse

SRO *abbrev for:* **1** standing room only **2** (in Britain) Statutory Rules and Orders **3** self-regulatory organization

Srta *abbrev for* Señorita

SS *abbrev for:* **1** Saints **2** a paramilitary organization within the Nazi party that provided Hitler's bodyguard, security forces, concentration-camp guards, etc [G *Schutzstaffel* protection squad] **3** steamship

SSE *symbol for* south-southeast

ssp. (*pl* **sspp.**) *biol abbrev for* subspecies

SSR (formerly) *abbrev for* Soviet Socialist Republic

SST *abbrev for* supersonic transport

SSW *symbol for* south-southwest

St *abbrev for:* **1** Saint (all entries that are usually preceded by *St* are in this dictionary listed alphabetically under **Saint**) **2** statute **3** Strait **4** Street

st. *abbrev for:* **1** stanza **2** statute **3** stone **4** *cricket* stumped by

s.t. *abbrev for* short ton

-st *suffix* a variant of **-est²**

Sta (in the names of places or churches) *abbrev for* Saint (female) [It. *Santa*]

stab (stæb) *vb* **stabs, stabbing, stabbed 1** (*tr*) to pierce or injure with a sharp pointed instrument **2** (*tr*) (of a sharp pointed instrument) to pierce or wound **3** (when *intr*, often foll by *at*) to make a thrust (at); jab **4** (*tr*) to inflict with a sharp pain **5 stab in the back 5a** (*vb*) to damage the reputation of (a person, esp a friend) in a surreptitious way **5b** (*n*) a treacherous action or remark that causes the downfall of or injury to a person ▷ *n* **6** the act or an instance of stabbing **7** an injury or rift made by stabbing **8** a sudden sensation, esp an unpleasant one: *a stab of pity* **9** *inf* an attempt (esp in **make a stab at**) [C14 from *stabbe* stab wound] > **'stabber** *n*

Stabat Mater ('stɑːbæt 'mɑːtə) *n* **1** *RC Church* a Latin hymn commemorating the sorrows of the Virgin Mary at the crucifixion **2** a musical setting of this hymn [from opening words, lit.: the mother was standing]

stabile ('steɪbaɪl) *n* **1** *arts* a stationary abstract construction, usually of wire, metal, wood, etc ▷ *adj* **2** fixed; stable **3** resistant to chemical change [C18 from L *stabilis*]

stability (stə'bɪlɪtɪ) *n, pl* **stabilities 1** the quality of being stable **2** the ability of an aircraft to resume its original flight path after inadvertent displacement

stabilize *or* **stabilise** ('steɪbɪˌlaɪz) *vb* **stabilizes, stabilizing, stabilized** *or* **stabilises, stabilising, stabilised 1** to make or become stable or more stable **2** to keep or be kept stable **3** (*tr*) to put or keep (an aircraft, vessel, etc) in equilibrium by one or more special devices or (of an aircraft, etc) to become stable > **ˌstabili'zation** *or* **ˌstabili'sation** *n*

stabilizer *or* **stabiliser** ('steɪbɪˌlaɪzə) *n* **1** any device for stabilizing an aircraft **2** a substance added to something to maintain it in a stable or unchanging state, such as an additive that preserves the texture of food **3** *naut* **3a** a system of pairs of fins projecting from the hull of a ship and controllable to counteract roll **3b** See **gyrostabilizer 4** either of a pair of small wheels fitted to the back wheel of a bicycle to help a beginner to maintain balance **5** *econ* a measure, such as progressive taxation, interest-rate control, or unemployment benefit, used to restrict swings in prices, employment, production, etc, in a free economy **6** a person or thing that stabilizes

stable¹ ('steɪbᵊl) *n* **1** a building, usually consisting of stalls, for the lodging of horses or other livestock **2** the animals lodged in such a building, collectively **3a** the racehorses belonging to a particular establishment or owner **3b** the establishment itself **3c** (*as modifier*): *stable companion* **4** *inf* a source of training, such as a school, theatre, etc: *the two athletes were out of the same stable* **5** a number of people considered as a source of a particular talent: *a stable of writers* **6** (*modifier*) of, relating to, or suitable for a stable: *stable door* ▷ *vb* **stables, stabling, stabled 7** to put, keep, or be kept in a stable [c13 from OF *estable* cowshed, from L *stabulum* shed, from *stāre* to stand]

stable² (ˈsteɪbᵊl) *adj* **1** steady in position or balance; firm **2** lasting: *a stable relationship* **3** steadfast or firm of purpose **4** (of an elementary particle, etc) not undergoing decay; not radioactive **5** (of a chemical compound) not readily partaking in a chemical change [c13 from OF *estable*, from L *stabilis* steady, from *stāre* to stand] > ˈ**stableness** *n* > ˈ**stably** *adv*

stableboy (ˈsteɪbᵊlˌbɔɪ), **stablegirl** (ˈsteɪbᵊlˌgɜl), *or* **stableman** (ˈsteɪbᵊlˌmæn, -mən) *n, pl* **stableboys, stablegirls,** *or* **stablemen** a boy, girl, or man who works in a stable

stable door *n* a door with an upper and lower leaf that may be opened separately. US and Canad equivalent: **Dutch door**

Stableford (ˈsteɪbᵊlfəd) *n golf* **a** a scoring system in which points are awarded according to the number of strokes taken at each hole, whereby a hole completed in one stroke over par counts as one point, a hole completed in level par counts as two points, etc **b** (*as modifier*): *a Stableford competition* ▷ Cf **match play, stroke play** [c20 after its inventor Dr Frank *Stableford* (1870–1959), E amateur golfer]

stable lad or **stable lass** *n* a person who looks after the horses in a racing stable

stabling (ˈsteɪblɪŋ) *n* stable buildings or accommodation

stablish (ˈstæblɪʃ) *vb* an archaic variant of **establish**

Stabroek (*Dutch* ˈsta:bru:k) *n* the former name (until 1812) of **Georgetown** (sense 1)

staccato (stəˈkɑ:təʊ) *adj* **1** *music* (of notes) short, clipped, and separate **2** characterized by short abrupt sounds, as in speech: *a staccato command* ▷ *adv* **3** (esp used as a musical direction) in a staccato manner [c18 from It., from *staccare* to detach, shortened from *distaccare*]

stachys (ˈstækɪs) *n* any plant of the herbaceous genus *Stachys*. See also **woundwort** [c16 from L, from Gk: ear of corn]

stack (stæk) *n* **1** an ordered pile or heap **2** a large orderly pile of hay, straw, etc, for storage in the open air **3** (*often pl*) compactly spaced bookshelves, used to house collections of books in an area usually prohibited to library users **4** a number of aircraft circling an airport at different altitudes, awaiting their signal to land **5** a large amount **6** *mil* a pile of rifles or muskets in the shape of a cone **7** *Brit* a measure of coal or wood equal to 108 cubic feet **8** See **chimney stack, smokestack 9** a vertical pipe, such as the funnel of a ship or the soil pipe attached to the side of a building **10** a high column of rock, esp one isolated from the mainland by the erosive action of the sea **11** an area in a computer memory for temporary storage ▷ *vb* (*tr*) **12** to place in a stack; pile **13** to load or fill up with piles of something: *to stack a lorry with bricks* **14** to control a number of aircraft waiting to land at an airport so that each flies at a different altitude **15 stack the cards** to prearrange the order of a pack of cards secretly so as to cheat [c13 from ON *stakkr* haystack, of Gmc origin] > ˈ**stackable** *adj* > ˈ**stacker** *n*

stacked (stækt) *adj sl* a variant of **well-stacked**

stadholder *or* **stadtholder** (ˈstædˌhəʊldə) *n* **1** the chief magistrate of the former Dutch republic or any of its provinces (from about 1580 to 1802) **2** a viceroy or governor of a province [c16 from Du. *stad houder*, from *stad* city + *houder* holder]

stadia¹ (ˈsteɪdɪə) *n* **1** measurement of distance using a telescopic surveying instrument and a graduated staff calibrated to correspond with the distance from the observer **2** the two parallel cross hairs or **stadia hairs** in the eyepiece of the instrument used **3** the staff used [c19 prob. from STADIA²]

stadia² (ˈsteɪdɪə) *n* a plural of **stadium**

stadium (ˈsteɪdɪəm) *n, pl* **stadiums** *or* **stadia 1** a sports arena with tiered seats for spectators **2** (in ancient Greece) a course for races, usually located between two hills providing slopes for tiers of seats **3** an ancient Greek measure of length equivalent to about 607 feet or 184 metres [c16 via L from Gk *stadion*, changed from *spadion* racecourse, from *spān* to pull; infl. by Gk *stadios* steady]

Staël (*French* stal) *n* **Madame de** full name *Baronne Anne Louise Germaine* (née *Necker*) *de Staël-Holstein*. 1766–1817, French writer, whose works, esp *De l'Allemagne* (1810), anticipated French romanticism

staff¹ (stɑ:f) *n, pl* **staffs** *for senses 1–4;* **staffs** *or* **staves** *for senses 5–9* **1** a group of people employed by a company, individual, etc, for executive, clerical, sales work, etc **2** (*modifier*) attached to or provided for the staff of an establishment: *a staff doctor* **3** the body of teachers or lecturers of an educational institution **4** *mil* the officers appointed to assist a commander, service, or central headquarters organization **5** a stick with some special use, such as a walking stick or an emblem of authority **6** something that sustains or supports: *bread is the staff of life* **7** a pole on which a flag is hung **8** *chiefly Brit* a graduated rod used in surveying, esp for sighting to with a levelling instrument **9** Also called: **stave** *music* **9a** the system of horizontal lines grouped into sets of five (four in plainsong) upon which music is written. The spaces between them are employed in conjunction with a clef in order to give a graphic indication of pitch **9b** any set of five lines in this system together with its clef: *the treble staff* ▷ *vb* **10** (*tr*) to provide with a staff [OE *stæf*]

staff² (stɑ:f) *n US* a mixture of plaster and hair used to cover the external surface of temporary structures and for decoration [c19 from ?]

Staffa (ˈstæfə) *n* an island in W Scotland, in the Inner Hebrides west of Mull: site of Fingal's Cave

staff corporal *n* a noncommissioned rank in the British Army above that of staff sergeant and below that of warrant officer

staff nurse *n* (formerly in Britain) a qualified nurse ranking immediately below a sister

staff officer *n* a commissioned officer serving on the staff of a commander, service, or central headquarters

Stafford¹ (ˈstæfəd) *n* a market town in central England, administrative centre of Staffordshire. Pop: 61 885 (1991)

Stafford² (ˈstæfəd) *n* Sir **Edward William** 1819–1901, New Zealand statesman, born in Scotland: prime minister of New Zealand (1856–61; 1865–69; 1872)

Staffordshire (ˈstæfədˌʃɪə, -ʃə) *n* a county of central England: lowlands in the east and south rise to the Pennine uplands in the north; important in the history of industry, coal and iron having been worked at least as early as the 13th century. In 1974 the industrial area in the S passed to the new county of West Midlands; Stoke-on-Trent became an independent unitary authority in 1997. Administrative centre: Stafford. Pop (excluding Stoke-on-Trent): 806 737 (2001). Area (excluding Stoke-on-Trent): 2624 sq km (1013 sq miles)

Staffordshire bull terrier *n* a breed of smooth-coated terrier with a stocky frame and generally a pied or brindled coat

Staffs. (stæfs) *abbrev for* Staffordshire

staff sergeant *n mil* **1** *Brit* a noncommissioned officer holding a rank between sergeant and warrant officer and employed on administrative duties **2** *US* a noncommissioned officer who ranks: **2a** (in the Army) above sergeant and below sergeant first class **2b** (in the Air Force) above airman first class and below technical sergeant **2c** (in the Marine Corps) above sergeant and below gunnery sergeant

stag (stæg) *n* **1** the adult male of a deer **2** a man unaccompanied by a woman at a social gathering **3** *stock exchange, Brit* a speculator who applies for shares in a new issue in anticipation of a rise in its price and thus a quick profit on resale **4** (*modifier*) (of a social gathering) attended by men only ▷ *adv* **5** without a female escort ▷ *vb* **stags, stagging, stagged** (*tr*) **6** *stock exchange* to apply for (shares in a new issue) with the intention of selling them for a quick profit when trading commences [OE *stagga* (unattested); rel. to ON *steggr* male bird]

stag beetle *n* any of various beetles, the males of which have large branched mandibles

stage (steɪdʒ) *n* **1** a distinct step or period of development, growth, or progress **2** a raised area or platform **3** the platform in a theatre where actors perform **4 the** the theatre as a profession **5** any scene regarded as a setting for an event or action **6** a portion of a journey or a stopping place after such a portion **7** short for **stagecoach** **8** *Brit* a division of a bus route for which there is a fixed fare **9** one of the separate propulsion units of a rocket that can be jettisoned when it has burnt out **10** a small stratigraphical unit; a subdivision of a rock series or system **11** the platform on a microscope on which the specimen is mounted for examination **12** *electronics* a part of a complex circuit, esp a transistor with the associated elements required to amplify a signal in an amplifier **13 by** *or* **in easy stages** not hurriedly: *he learned French by easy stages* ▷ *vb* **stages, staging, staged** (*tr*) **14** to perform (a play), esp on a stage: *to stage "Hamlet"* **15** to set the action of (a play) in a particular time or place **16** to plan, organize, and carry out (an event) [c13 from OF *estage* position, from Vulgar L *staticum* (unattested), from L *stāre* to stand]

stagecoach (ˈsteɪdʒˌkəʊtʃ) *n* a large four-wheeled horse-drawn vehicle formerly used to carry passengers, mail, etc, on a regular route

stagecraft (ˈsteɪdʒˌkrɑːft) *n* skill in or the art of writing or staging plays

stage direction *n* an instruction to an actor or director, written into the script of a play

stage door *n* a door at a theatre leading backstage

stage fright *n* nervousness or panic that may beset a person about to appear in front of an audience

stagehand (ˈsteɪdʒˌhænd) *n* a person who sets the stage, moves props, etc, in a theatrical production

stage left *n* the part of the stage to the left of a performer facing the audience

stage-manage *vb* **stage-manages, stage-managing, stage-managed** **1** to work as stage manager (for a play, etc) **2** (*tr*) to arrange, present, or supervise from behind the scenes

stage manager *n* a person who supervises the stage arrangements of a theatrical production

stager (ˈsteɪdʒə) *n* **1** a person of experience; veteran (esp in **old stager**) **2** an archaic word for **actor**

stage right *n* the part of the stage to the right of a performer facing the audience

stage-struck *adj* infatuated with the glamour of theatrical life, esp with the desire to act

stage whisper *n* **1** a loud whisper from one actor to another onstage intended to be heard by the audience **2** any loud whisper that is intended to be overheard

stagflation (stægˈfleɪʃən) *n* a situation in which inflation is combined with stagnant or falling output and employment [c20 blend of *stagnation* + *inflation*]

stagger (ˈstægə) *vb* **1** (*usually intr*) to walk or cause to walk unsteadily as if about to fall **2** (*tr*) to astound or overwhelm, as with shock: *I am staggered by his ruthlessness* **3** (*tr*) to place or arrange in alternating or overlapping positions or time periods to prevent confusion or congestion: *a staggered junction; to stagger holidays* **4** (*intr*) to falter or hesitate: *his courage staggered in the face of the battle* ▷ *n* **5** the act or an instance of staggering [c13 from dialect *stacker*, from ON *staka* to push] > **ˈstaggerer** *n* > **ˈstaggering** *adj* > **ˈstaggeringly** *adv*

staggered directorships *pl n business* a defence against unwelcome takeover bids in which a company resolves that its directors should serve staggered terms of office and that no director can be removed from office without just cause, thus preventing a bidder from controlling the board for some years

staggers (ˈstægəz) *n* (*functioning as sing or pl*) **1** a form of vertigo associated with decompression sickness **2** Also called: **blind staggers** a disease of horses and some other domestic animals characterized by a swaying unsteady gait, caused by infection or lesions of the central nervous system

staghorn fern (ˈstægˌhɔːn) *n* any of various tropical and subtropical ferns of the genus *Platycerium* with fronds resembling antlers

staging (ˈsteɪdʒɪŋ) *n* any temporary structure used in the process of building, esp the horizontal platforms supported by scaffolding

staging area *n* a checkpoint or regrouping area for military formations in transit

staging post *n* a place where a journey is usually broken, esp a stopover on a flight

Stagira (stəˈdʒaɪrə) *n* an ancient city on the coast of Chalcidice in Macedonia: the birthplace of Aristotle

stagnant (ˈstægnənt) *adj* **1** (of water, etc) standing still; without flow or current **2** brackish and foul from standing still **3** stale, sluggish, or dull from inaction **4** not growing or developing; static [c17 from L *stagnāns*, from *stagnāre* to be stagnant, from *stagnum* a pool] > **ˈstagnancy** *n*

stagnate (stægˈneɪt) *vb* **stagnates, stagnating, stagnated** (*intr*) to be or become stagnant > **stagˈnation** *n*

stag night *or* **party** *n* a party for men only, esp one held for a man just before he is married

stagy *or US* **stagey** (ˈsteɪdʒɪ) *adj* **stagier, stagiest** excessively theatrical or dramatic > **ˈstagily** *adv* > **ˈstaginess** *n*

staid (steɪd) *adj* of a settled, sedate, and steady character [c16 obs. p.p. of STAY[1]] > **ˈstaidly** *adv* > **ˈstaidness** *n*

stain (steɪn) *vb* (*mainly tr*) **1** to mark or discolour with patches of something that dirties **2** to dye with a penetrating dyestuff or pigment **3** to bring disgrace or shame on: *to stain one's honour* **4** to colour (specimens) for microscopic study by treatment with a dye or similar reagent **5** (*intr*) to produce indelible marks or discoloration: *does ink stain?* ▷ *n* **6** a spot, mark, or discoloration **7** a moral taint; blemish or slur **8** a dye or similar reagent, used to colour specimens for microscopic study **9** a solution or liquid used to penetrate the surface of a material, esp wood, and impart a rich colour without covering up the surface or grain **10** any dye used to colour textiles and hides [c14 *steynen* (vb), shortened from *disteynen* to remove colour from, from OF *desteindre* to discolour, ult. from L *tingere* to tinge] > **ˈstainable** *adj* > **ˌstainaˈbility** *n* > **ˈstainer** *n*

stained glass *n* **a** glass that has been coloured, as by fusing with a film of metallic oxide or burning pigment into the surface **b** (*as modifier*): *a stained-glass window*

stained glass ceiling *n* a situation in a church organization in which promotion for a female member of the clergy appears to be possible, but discrimination prevents it

Stainer (ˈsteɪnə) *n* Sir **John** 1840–1901, British composer and organist, noted for his sacred music, esp the oratorio *The Crucifixion* (1887)

Staines (steɪnz) *n* a town in SE England, in N Surrey on the River Thames. Pop: 51 167 (1991)

stainless ('steɪnlɪs) *adj* **1** resistant to discoloration, esp that resulting from corrosion; rust-resistant: *stainless steel* **2** having no blemish: *stainless reputation* > **'stainlessly** *adv*

stainless steel *n* **a** a type of steel resistant to corrosion as a result of the presence of large amounts of chromium **b** (*as modifier*): *stainless-steel cutlery*

stair (stɛə) *n* **1** one of a flight of stairs **2** a series of steps: *a narrow stair* ▷ See also **stairs** [OE *stæger*]

staircase ('stɛə,keɪs) *n* a flight of stairs, its supporting framework, and, usually, a handrail or banisters

stairs (stɛəz) *pl n* **1** a flight of steps leading from one storey or level to another, esp indoors **2 below stairs** *Brit* in the servants' quarters

stairway ('stɛə,weɪ) *n* a means of access consisting of stairs; staircase or flight of steps

stairwell ('stɛə,wɛl) *n* a vertical shaft or opening that contains a staircase

stake[1] (steɪk) *n* **1** a stick or metal bar driven into the ground as a marker, part of a fence, support for a plant, etc **2** one of a number of vertical posts that fit into sockets around a flat truck or railway wagon to hold the load in place **3** a method or the practice of executing a person by binding him or her to a stake in the centre of a pile of wood that is then set on fire **4 pull up stakes** to leave one's home or resting place and move on ▷ *vb* **stakes, staking, staked** (*tr*) **5** to tie, fasten, or tether with or to a stake **6** (often foll by *out* or *off*) to fence or surround with stakes **7** (often foll by *out*) to lay (a claim) to land, rights, etc **8** to support with a stake [OE *staca* pin]

stake[2] (steɪk) *n* **1** the money or valuables that a player must hazard in order to buy into a gambling game or make a bet **2** an interest, often financial, held in something: *a stake in the company's future* **3** (*often pl*) the money that a player has available for gambling **4** (*often pl*) a prize in a race, etc, esp one made up of contributions from contestants or owners **5** (*pl*) a horse race in which all owners of competing horses contribute to the prize **6** *US & Canad inf* short for **grubstake 7 at stake** at risk: *lives are at stake* **8 raise the stakes 8a** to increase the amount of money or valuables hazarded in a gambling game **8b** to increase the costs, risks, or considerations involved in taking an action or reaching a conclusion ▷ *vb* **stakes, staking, staked** (*tr*) **9** to hazard (money, etc) on a result **10** to invest in or support with money, etc: *to stake a business* [c16 from ?]

Staked Plain *n* another name for the **Llano Estacado**

stakeholder ('steɪk,haʊldə) *n* **1** a person or group owning a significant percentage of a company's shares **2** a person or group not owning shares in an enterprise but affected by or having an interest in its operations, such as the employees, customers, local community, etc ▷ *adj* **3** of or relating to policies intended to allow people to participate in and benefit from decisions made by enterprises in which they have a stake: *a stakeholder economy* > **'stake,holding** *n, adj*

stakeholder pension *n* (in Britain) a flexible pension scheme with low charges, in which contributors can stop and restart payments and switch funds to another scheme without paying a penalty

stakeout ('steɪkaʊt) *chiefly US & Canad sl* ▷ *n* **1** a police surveillance **2** an area or house kept under such surveillance ▷ *vb* **stake out 3** (*tr, adv*) to keep under surveillance

Stakhanovism (stæ'kænə,vɪzəm) *n* (in the former Soviet Union) a system designed to raise production by offering incentives to efficient workers [c20 after A. G. *Stakhanov* (1906–77), Soviet miner, the worker first awarded benefits under the system in 1935] > **Sta'khanov,ite** *n, adj*

stalactite ('stæləkˌtaɪt) *n* a cylindrical mass of calcium carbonate hanging from the roof of a limestone cave: formed by precipitation from continually dripping water ▷ Cf **stalagmite** [c17 from NL *stalactites*, from Gk *stalaktos* dripping, from *stalassein* to drip] > **stalactiform** (stə'læktɪ,fɔːm) *adj* > **stalactitic** (ˌstælək'tɪtɪk) *or* **ˌstalac'titical** *adj*

stalag ('stælæg) *n* a German prisoner-of-war camp in World War II, esp for men from the ranks [short for *Stammlager* base camp]

stalagmite ('stæləg,maɪt) *n* a cylindrical mass of calcium carbonate projecting upwards from the floor of a limestone cave: formed by precipitation from continually dripping water ▷ Cf **stalactite** [c17 from NL *stalagmites*, from Gk *stalagmos* dripping; rel. to Gk *stalassein* to drip] > **stalagmitic** (ˌstæləg'mɪtɪk) *or* **ˌstalag'mitical** *adj*

stale[1] (steɪl) *adj* **1** (esp of food) hard, musty, or dry from being kept too long **2** (of beer, etc) flat and tasteless from being kept open too long **3** (of air) stagnant; foul **4** uninteresting from overuse: *stale clichés* **5** no longer new: *stale news* **6** lacking in energy or ideas through overwork or lack of variety **7** *banking* (of a cheque) not negotiable by a bank as a result of not having been presented within six months of being written **8** *law* (of a claim, etc) having lost its effectiveness or force, as by failure to act or by the lapse of time ▷ *vb* **stales, staling, staled 9** to make or become stale [c13 (orig. applied to liquor in the sense: well matured): prob. from OF *estale* (unattested) motionless, of Frankish origin] > **'staleness** *n*

stale[2] (steɪl) *vb* **stales, staling, staled 1** (*intr*) (of livestock) to urinate ▷ *n* **2** the urine of horses or cattle [c15 ?from OF *estaler* to stand in one position]

stale bull *n business* a dealer or speculator who holds unsold commodities after a rise in market prices but who cannot trade because there are no buyers at the new levels and because his financial commitments prevent him from making further purchases

stalemate ('steɪl,meɪt) *n* **1** a chess position in which any of a player's possible moves would place his king in check: in this position the game ends in a draw **2** a situation in which two opposing forces find that further action is impossible or futile; deadlock ▷ *vb* **stalemates, stalemating, stalemated 3** (*tr*) to subject to a stalemate [c18 from obs. *stale*, from OF *estal* STALL[1] + (CHECK)MATE]

Stalin[1] ('stɑːlɪn) *n* **1** Also called: **Stalino** a former name (from after the Revolution until 1961) of **Donetsk 2** the former name (1950–61) of **Braşov 3** the former name (1949–56) of **Varna**

Stalin[2] ('stɑːlɪn) *n* **Joseph** original name *Iosif Vissarionovich Dzhugashvili*. 1879–1953, Soviet leader; general secretary of the Communist Party of the Soviet Union (1922–53) He succeeded Lenin as head of the party and created a totalitarian state, crushing all opposition, esp in the great purges of 1934–37. He instigated rapid industrialization and the collectivization of agriculture and established the Soviet Union as a world power

Stalinabad (*Russian* stəlina'bat) *n* the former name (1929–61) of **Dushanbe**

Stalingrad ('stɑːlɪn,græd; *Russian* stəlin'grat) *n* the former name (1925–61) of **Volgograd**

Stalinism ('stɑːlɪ,nɪzəm) *n* the theory and form of government associated with Joseph Stalin: a variant of Marxism-Leninism characterized by totalitarianism, rigid bureaucracy, and loyalty to the state > **'Stalinist** *n, adj*

Stalinogrod (*Polish* stali'nɔgrɔt) *n* the former name (1953–56) for **Katowice**

Stalin Peak *n* a former name for **Kommunizma Peak**

Stalinsk (*Russian* 'stalinsk) *n* the former name (1932–61) of **Novokuznetsk**

stalk[1] (stɔːk) *n* **1** the main stem of a herbaceous plant

Ss

2 any of various subsidiary plant stems, such as a leafstalk or flower stalk 3 a slender supporting structure in animals such as crinoids and barnacles 4 any long slender supporting shaft or column [c14 prob. dim. from OE *stalu* upright piece of wood] > **stalked** *adj* > **'stalk,like** *adj*

stalk² (stɔːk) *vb* 1 to follow or approach (game, prey, etc) stealthily and quietly 2 to pursue persistently and, sometimes, attack (a person with whom one is obsessed, often a celebrity) 3 to spread over (a place) in a menacing or grim manner: *fever stalked the camp* 4 (*intr*) to walk in a haughty, stiff, or threatening way 5 to search (a piece of land) for prey ▷ *n* 6 the act of stalking 7 a stiff or threatening stride [OE *bestealcian* to walk stealthily] > **'stalker** *n*

stalk-and-slash movie *n* another name for **slasher movie**

stalking-horse *n* 1 a horse or an imitation one used by a hunter to hide behind while stalking 2 something serving as a means of concealing plans; pretext 3 a candidate put forward to divide the opposition or mask the candidacy of another person for whom the stalking-horse would then withdraw

stalky ('stɔːkɪ) *adj* **stalkier, stalkiest** 1 like a stalk; slender and tall 2 having or abounding in stalks > **'stalkily** *adv* > **'stalkiness** *n*

stall¹ (stɔːl) *n* 1a a compartment in a stable or shed for a single animal 1b another name for **stable¹** (sense 1) 2 a small often temporary stand or booth for the sale of goods 3 (in a church) 3a one of a row of seats usually divided by armrests or a small screen, for the choir or clergy 3b a pen 4 an instance of an engine stalling 5 a condition of an aircraft in flight in which a reduction in speed or an increase in the aircraft's angle of attack causes a sudden loss of lift resulting in a downward plunge 6 any small room or compartment 7 *Brit* 7a a seat in a theatre or cinema, usually fixed to the floor 7b (*pl*) the area of seats on the ground floor of a theatre or cinema nearest to the stage or screen 8 a tubelike covering for a finger 9 (*pl*) short for **starting stalls** ▷ *vb* 10 to cause (a motor vehicle or its engine) to stop, usually by incorrect use of the clutch or incorrect adjustment of the fuel mixture, or (of an engine or motor vehicle) to stop, usually for these reasons 11 to cause (an aircraft) to go into a stall or (of an aircraft) to go into a stall 12 to stick or cause to stick fast, as in mud or snow 13 (*tr*) to confine (an animal) in a stall [OE *steall* a place for standing]

stall² (stɔːl) *vb* 1 to employ delaying tactics towards (someone); be evasive ▷ *n* 2 an evasive move; pretext [c16 from Anglo-F *estale* bird used as a decoy, infl. by STALL¹]

stall-feed *vb* **stall-feeds, stall-feeding, stall-fed** (*tr*) to keep and feed (an animal) in a stall, esp as an intensive method of fattening it for slaughter

stallholder ('stɔːl,həʊldə) *n* a person who sells goods at a market stall

stallion ('stæljən) *n* an uncastrated male horse, esp one used for breeding [c14 *staloun*, from OF *estalon*, of Gmc origin]

stalwart ('stɔːlwət) *adj* 1 strong and sturdy; robust 2 solid, dependable, and courageous 3 resolute and firm ▷ *n* 4 a stalwart person, esp a supporter [OE *stǣlwirthe* serviceable, from *stǣl*, from *stathol* support + *wierthe* WORTH] > **'stalwartly** *adv* > **'stalwartness** *n*

Stambul *or* **Stamboul** (stæm'buːl) *n* the old part of Istanbul, Turkey, south of the Golden Horn: the site of ancient Byzantium; sometimes used as a name for the whole city

stamen ('steɪmɛn) *n, pl* **stamens** *or* **stamina** the male reproductive organ of a flower, consisting of a stalk (filament) bearing an anther in which pollen is produced [c17 from L: the warp in an upright loom, from *stāre* to stand] > **staminiferous** (,stæmɪ'nɪfərəs) *adj*

Stamford ('stæmfəd) *n* a city in SW Connecticut, on Long Island Sound: major chemical research laboratories. Pop: 117 083 (2000)

Stamford Bridge *n* a village in N England, east of York: site of a battle (1066) in which King Harold of England defeated his brother Tostig and King Harald Hardrada of Norway, three weeks before the Battle of Hastings

stamina¹ ('stæmɪnə) *n* enduring energy, strength, and resilience [c19 identical with STAMINA², from L *stāmen* thread, hence the threads of life spun out by the Fates, hence energy, etc]

stamina² ('stæmɪnə) *n* a plural of **stamen**

staminate ('stæmɪnɪt, -,neɪt) *adj* (of plants) having stamens, esp having stamens but no carpels; male

stammer ('stæmə) *vb* 1 to speak or say (something) in a hesitant way, esp as a result of a speech disorder or through fear, stress, etc ▷ *n* 2 a speech disorder characterized by involuntary repetitions and hesitations [OE *stamerian*] > **'stammerer** *n* > **'stammering** *n, adj*

stamp (stæmp) *vb* 1 (when *intr*, often foll by *on*) to bring (the foot) down heavily (on the ground, etc) 2 (*intr*) to walk with heavy or noisy footsteps 3 (*intr*; foll by *on*) to repress or extinguish: *he stamped on criticism* 4 (*tr*) to impress or mark (a device or sign) on (something) 5 to mark (something) with an official seal or device: *to stamp a passport* 6 (*tr*) to fix or impress permanently: *the date was stamped on her memory* 7 (*tr*) to affix a postage stamp to 8 (*tr*) to distinguish or reveal: *that behaviour stamps him as a cheat* 9 to pound or crush (ores, etc) ▷ *n* 10 the act or an instance of stamping 11a See **postage stamp** 11b a mark applied to postage stamps for cancellation 12 a similar piece of gummed paper used for commercial or trading purposes 13 a block, die, etc, used for imprinting a design or device 14 a design, device, or mark that has been stamped 15 a characteristic feature or trait; hallmark: *the stamp of authenticity* 16 a piece of gummed paper or other mark applied to official documents to indicate payment, validity, ownership, etc 17 *Brit inf* a national insurance contribution, formerly recorded by means of a stamp on an official card 18 type or class: *men of his stamp* 19 an instrument or machine for crushing or pounding ores, etc, or the pestle in such a device ▷ See also **stamp out** [OE *stampe*] > **'stamper** *n*

stamp duty *or* **tax** *n* a tax on legal documents, publications, etc, the payment of which is certified by the attaching or impressing of official stamps

stampede (stæm'piːd) *n* 1 an impulsive headlong rush of startled cattle or horses 2 headlong rush of a crowd 3 any sudden large-scale action, such as a rush of people to support a candidate 4 *W US & Canad* a rodeo event featuring fairground and social elements ▷ *vb* **stampedes, stampeding, stampeded** 5 to run away or cause to run away in a stampede [c19 from American Sp. *estampida*, from Sp.: a din, from *estampar* to stamp, of Gmc origin] > **stam'peder** *n*

stamping ground *n* a habitual or favourite meeting or gathering place

stamp mill *n* a machine for crushing ore

stamp out *vb* (*tr, adv*) 1 to put out or extinguish by stamping: *to stamp out a fire* 2 to suppress by force: *to stamp out a rebellion*

stance (stæns, stɑːns) *n* 1 the manner and position in which a person or animal stands 2 *sport* the posture assumed when about to play the ball, as in golf, cricket, etc 3 emotional or intellectual attitude: *a leftist stance* 4 *chiefly Scot* a place where a vehicle waits: *taxi stance* [c16 via F from It. *stanza* place for standing, from L *stāns*, from *stāre* to stand]

stanch (stɑːntʃ) *vb* a variant of **staunch²**

stanchion ('stɑːnʃən) *n* 1 any vertical pole, beam, rod, etc, used as a support ▷ *vb* **2** (*tr*) to provide or support with a stanchion or stanchions [C15 from OF *estanchon*, from *estance*, from Vulgar L *stantia* (unattested) a standing, from L *stāre* to stand]

stand (stænd) *vb* **stands, standing, stood** (*mainly intr*) **1** (*also tr*) to be or cause to be in an erect or upright position **2** to rise to, assume, or maintain an upright position **3** (*copula*) to have a specified height when standing: *to stand six feet tall* **4** to be situated or located: *the house stands in the square* **5** to be in a specified state or condition: *to stand in awe of someone* **6** to adopt or remain in a resolute position or attitude **7** (*may take an infinitive*) to be in a specified position: *I stand to lose money in this venture* **8** to remain in force or continue in effect: *my orders stand* **9** to come to a stop or halt, esp temporarily **10** (of water, etc) to collect and remain without flowing **11** (often foll by *at*) (of a score, account, etc) to indicate the specified position: *the score stands at 20 to 1* **12** (*also tr*; when *intr*, foll by *for*) to tolerate or bear: *I won't stand for your nonsense; I can't stand spiders* **13** (*tr*) to resist; survive: *to stand the test of time* **14** (*tr*) to submit to: *to stand trial* **15** (often foll by *for*) *chiefly Brit* to be or become a candidate: *stand for Parliament* **16** to navigate in a specified direction: *we were standing for Madeira* **17** (of a gun dog) to point at game **18** to halt, esp to give action, repel attack, or disrupt an enemy advance when retreating **19** (*tr*) *inf* to bear the cost of; pay for: *to stand someone a drink* **20 stand a chance** to have a hope or likelihood of winning, succeeding, etc **21 stand fast** to maintain one's position firmly **22 stand one's ground** to maintain a stance or position in the face of opposition **23 stand still 23a** to remain motionless **23b** (foll by *for*) *US* to tolerate: *I won't stand still for your threats* **24 stand to (someone)** *Irish inf* to be useful to (someone): *your knowledge of English will stand to you* ▷ *n* **25** the act or an instance of standing **26** an opinion, esp a resolutely held one: *he took a stand on capital punishment* **27** a halt or standstill **28** a place where a person or thing stands **29** *Austral & NZ* **29a** a position on the floor of a shearing shed allocated to one shearer **29b** the shearer's equipment **30** a structure on which people can sit or stand **31** a frame or rack on which such articles as coats and hats may be hung **32** a small table or piece of furniture where articles may be placed or stored: *a music stand* **33** a supporting framework, esp for a tool or instrument **34** a stall, booth, or counter from which goods may be sold **35** a halt to give action, etc, esp during a retreat and having some duration or success **36** *cricket* an extended period at the wicket by two batsmen **37** a growth of plants in a particular area, esp trees in a forest or a crop in a field **38** a stop made by a touring theatrical company, pop group, etc, to give a performance (esp in **one-night stand**) **39** (of a gun dog) the act of pointing at game ▷ See also **stand by, stand down,** etc [OE *standan*] > **'stander** *n*

standard ('stændəd) *n* **1** an accepted or approved example of something against which others are judged or measured **2** (*often pl*) a principle of propriety, honesty, and integrity **3** a level of excellence or quality **4** any distinctive flag or device, etc, as of a nation, sovereign, or special cause, etc, or the colours of a cavalry regiment **5** a flag or emblem formerly used to show the central or rallying point of an army in battle **6** the commodity or commodities in which is stated the value of a basic monetary unit: *the gold standard; the silver standard* **7** an authorized model of a unit of measure or weight **8** a unit of board measure equal to 1980 board feet **9** (in coinage) the prescribed proportion by weight of precious metal and base metal that each coin must contain **10** an upright pole or beam, esp one used as a support **11a** a piece of furniture consisting of an upright pole or beam on a base or support **11b** (*as modifier*): *a standard lamp* **12a** a plant, esp a fruit tree, that is trained so that it has an upright stem free of branches **12b** (*as modifier*): *a standard cherry* **13** a song or piece of music that has remained popular for many years **14** a form or grade in an elementary school ▷ *adj* **15** of the usual, regularized, medium, or accepted kind: *a standard size* **16** of recognized authority, competence, or excellence: *the standard work on Greece* **17** denoting or characterized by idiom, vocabulary, etc, that is regarded as correct and acceptable by educated native speakers **18** *Brit* (formerly) (of eggs) of a size that is smaller than *large* and larger than *medium* [C12 from OF *estandart* gathering place, flag to mark such a place, prob. of Gmc origin]

standard assessment tasks *pl n Brit education* the formal name for assessment tests. Acronym: **SATs**

standard-bearer *n* **1** a man who carries a standard **2** a leader of a cause or party

standard cell *n* a voltaic cell producing a constant and accurately known electromotive force that can be used to calibrate voltage-measuring instruments

standard cost *n* the predetermined budgeted cost of a manufacturing process against which actual costs are compared

standard deviation *n statistics* a measure of dispersion obtained by extracting the square root of the mean of the squared deviations of the observed values from their mean in a frequency distribution

standard error of the mean *n statistics* the standard deviation of the distribution of means of samples chosen from a larger population; equal to the standard deviation of the whole population divided by the square root of the sample size

standard function *n computing* a subprogram provided by a translator that carries out a task, for example the computation of a mathematical function, such as sine, square root, etc

standard gauge *n* **1** a railway track with a distance of 4 ft 8½ in (1.435 m) between the lines; used on most railways ▷ *adj* **standard-gauge** *or* **standard-gauged 2** of, relating to, or denoting a railway with a standard gauge

standard generalized mark-up language *n* See **SGML**

Standard Grade *n* (in Scotland) an examination designed to test skills and the application of knowledge, which replaced O grade

standardize *or* **standardise** ('stændə,daɪz) *vb* **standardizes, standardizing, standardized** *or* **standardises, standardising, standardised 1** to make or become standard **2** (*tr*) to test by or compare with a standard > **,standardi'zation** *or* **,standardi'sation** *n* > **'standard,izer** *or* **'standard,iser** *n*

standard model *n physics* a theory of fundamental interactions in which the electromagnetic, weak, and strong interactions are described in terms of the exchange of virtual particles

standard of living *n* a level of subsistence or material welfare of a community, class, or person

standard time *n* the official local time of a region or country determined by the distance from Greenwich of a line of longitude passing through the area

stand by *vb* (*intr*) **1** (*adv*) to be available and ready to act if needed **2** (*adv*) to be present as an onlooker or without taking any action: *he stood by at the accident* **3** (*prep*) to be faithful to: *to stand by one's principles* ▷ *n* **stand-by 4a** a person or thing that is ready for use or can be relied on in an emergency **4b** (*as modifier*): *stand-by provisions* **5 on stand-by** in a state of readiness for action or use ▷ *adj* **stand-by 6** not booked in advance but awaiting or subject to availability: *a stand-by ticket*

stand down *vb* (*adv*) **1** (*intr*) to resign or withdraw, esp in favour of another **2** (*intr*) to leave the witness box in a court of law after giving evidence **3** *chiefly Brit* to go or be taken off duty

Ss

stand for *vb* (*intr, prep*) **1** to represent or mean **2** *chiefly Brit* to be or become a candidate for **3** to support or recommend **4** *inf* to tolerate or bear: *he won't stand for it*

stand in *vb* **1** (*intr, adv; usually foll by for*) to act as a substitute **2** **stand (someone) in good stead** to be of benefit or advantage to (someone) ▷ *n* **stand-in 3a** a person or thing that serves as a substitute **3b** (*as modifier*): *a stand-in teacher* **4** a person who substitutes for an actor during intervals of waiting or in dangerous stunts

standing ('stændɪŋ) *n* **1** social or financial position, status, or reputation: *a man of some standing* **2** length of existence, experience, etc **3** (*modifier*) used to stand in or on: *standing room* ▷ *adj* **4** *athletics* **4a** (of the start of a race) begun from a standing position **4b** (of a jump, leap, etc) performed from a stationary position without a run-up **5** (*prenominal*) permanent, fixed, or lasting **6** (*prenominal*) still or stagnant: *a standing pond* **7** *printing* (of type) set and stored for future use

standing army *n* a permanent army of paid soldiers maintained by a nation

standing order *n* **1** Also called: **banker's order** an instruction to a bank by a depositor to pay a stated sum at regular intervals ▷ Cf **direct debit 2** a rule or order governing the procedure, conduct, etc, of an organization **3** *mil* one of a number of orders which have long-term validity

standing rigging *n* the stays, shrouds, and other more or less fixed, though adjustable, ropes that support the masts of a sailing vessel

standing wave *n* *physics* a wave that has unchanging amplitude at each point along its axis. Also called: **stationary wave**

Standish ('stændɪʃ) *n* **Myles (or Miles) ?1584–1656, English military leader of the Pilgrim Fathers at Plymouth, New England**

standoff ('stænd,ɒf) *n* **1** *US & Canad* the act or an instance of standing off or apart **2** a deadlock or stalemate **3** *rugby* short for **stand-off half** ▷ *vb* **stand off** (*adv*) **4** (*intr*) to navigate a vessel so as to avoid the shore, an obstruction, etc **5** (*tr*) to keep or cause to keep at a distance **6** (*intr*) to reach a deadlock or stalemate **7** (*tr*) to dismiss (workers), esp temporarily

stand-off half *n* *rugby* **1** a player who acts as a link between his or her scrum half and three-quarter backs **2** this position ▷ Also called: **fly half**

standoffish (,stænd'ɒfɪʃ) *adj* reserved, haughty, or aloof > **,stand'offishness** *n*

stand on *vb* (*intr*) **1** (*adv*) to continue to navigate a vessel on the same heading **2** (*prep*) to insist on: *to stand on ceremony*

stand out *vb* (*intr, adv*) **1** to be distinctive or conspicuous **2** to refuse to agree or comply: *they stood out for a better price* **3** to protrude or project **4** to navigate a vessel away from a port, harbour, etc ▷ *n* **standout 5** *inf* **5a** a person or thing that is distinctive or outstanding **5b** (*as modifier*): *the standout track from the album*

stand over *vb* (*tr, prep*) **1** to supervise closely **2** *Austral & NZ inf* to threaten or intimidate

standover man ('stænd,əʊvə) *n* *Austral* a person who extorts money by intimidation

standpipe ('stænd,paɪp) *n* **1** a vertical pipe, open at the upper end, attached to a pipeline or tank serving to limit the pressure head to that of the height of the pipe **2** a temporary freshwater outlet installed in a street when household water supplies are cut off

standpoint ('stænd,pɔɪnt) *n* a physical or mental position from which things are viewed

standstill ('stænd,stɪl) *n* a complete cessation of movement; halt: *come to a standstill*

stand to *vb* **1** (*adv*) *mil* to assume positions or cause to assume positions to resist a possible attack **2** **stand to reason** to conform with the dictates of reason: *it stands to reason that which is not good is evil!*

stand up *vb* (*adv*) **1** (*intr*) to rise to the feet **2** (*intr*) to resist or withstand wear, criticism, etc **3** (*tr*) *inf* to fail to keep an appointment with, esp intentionally **4** **stand up for** to support, side with, or defend **5** **stand up to 5a** to confront or resist courageously **5b** to withstand or endure (wear, criticism, etc) ▷ *adj* **stand-up** (*prenominal*) **6** having or being in an erect position: *a stand-up collar* **7** done, taken, etc, while standing: *a stand-up meal* **8** (of comedy or a comedian) performed or performing solo ▷ *n* **stand-up 9** a stand-up comedian **10** stand-up comedy

Stanford ('stænfəd) *n* Sir **Charles (Villiers)** 1852–1924, Anglo-Irish composer and conductor, who as a teacher at the Royal College of Music had much influence on the succeeding generation of composers: noted esp for his church music, oratorios, and cantatas

Stanford-Binet test (-bɪ'neɪ) *n* *psychol* a revision, esp for US use, of the Binet-Simon scale designed to measure mental ability by comparing the performance of an individual with the average performance for his age group. See also **Binet-Simon scale, intelligence test** [c20 after *Stanford University*, California, & Alfred *Binet* (1857–1911), F psychologist]

stanhope ('stænəp) *n* a light one-seater carriage with two or four wheels [c18 after Fitzroy *Stanhope* (1787–1864), E clergyman for whom it was first built]

Stanislavsky *or* **Stanislavski** (,stænɪ'slævskɪ; *Russian* stəni'slafskij) *n* **Konstantin** (kənstan'tin) 1863–1938, Russian actor and director, cofounder of the Moscow Art Theatre (1897). He is famous for his theory of acting, known as the Method, which directs the actor to find the truth within himself about the role he is playing

Stanisław (*Polish* 'staniswaf) *or* **Stanislaus** ('stænɪslaʊs) *n* **Saint** 1030–79, the patron saint of Poland. As Bishop of Cracow (1072–79) he excommunicated King Bolesław II, who arranged his murder. Feast day: May 11

stank (stæŋk) *vb* a past tense of **stink**

Stanley[1] ('stænlɪ) *n* **1** the capital of the Falkland Islands, in NE East Falkland Island: scene of fighting in the Falklands War of 1982. Pop: 1557 (1991) **2** a town in NE England, in N Durham. Pop: 18 905 (1991) **3** **Mount** a mountain in central Africa, between Uganda and the Democratic Republic of Congo (formerly Zaïre): the highest peak of the Ruwenzori range. Height: 5109 m (16 763 ft). Congolese name: **Ngaliema Mountain**

Stanley[2] ('stænlɪ) *n* Sir **Henry Morton** 1841–1904, British explorer and journalist, who led an expedition to Africa in search of Livingstone, whom he found on Nov 10, 1871. He led three further expeditions in Africa (1874–77; 1879–84; 1887–89) and was instrumental in securing Belgian sovereignty over the Congo Free State

Stanley Falls *pl n* the former name of **Boyoma Falls**

Stanley knife *n* *trademark* a type of knife used for carpet fitting, etc, consisting of a thick hollow metal handle with a short, very sharp, replaceable blade inserted in one end [c19 after F. T. *Stanley*, US businessman and founder of the Stanley Rule and Level Company]

Stanley Pool *n* a lake between the Democratic Republic of Congo (formerly Zaïre) and Congo-Brazzaville, formed by a widening of the River Congo. Area: 829 sq km (320 sq miles). Congolese name: **Pool Malebo**

Stanleyville ('stænlɪ,vɪl) *n* the former name (until 1966) of **Kisangani**

stann- *combining form* denoting tin: *stannite* [from LL *stannum* tin]

Stannaries ('stænərɪz) *n* **the** a tin-mining district of Devon and Cornwall, formerly under the jurisdiction of special courts

stannary ('stænərɪ) *n, pl* **stannaries** a place or region where tin is mined or worked [c15 from Med. L *stannāria*, from LL *stannum* tin]

stannic ('stænɪk) *adj* of or containing tin, esp in the tetravalent state; designating a tin(IV) compound [c18 from LL *stannum* tin]

stannite ('stænaɪt) *n* a grey metallic mineral that consists of a sulphide of tin, copper, and iron and is a source of tin. Formula: Cu_2FeSnS_4 [c19 from LL *stannum* tin + -ITE[1]]

stannous ('stænəs) *adj* of or containing tin, esp in the divalent state; designating a tin(II) compound

Stanovoi Range *or* **Stanovoy Range** (*Russian* stəna'vɔj) *n* a mountain range in SE Russia; forms part of the watershed between rivers flowing to the Arctic and the Pacific. Highest peak: Mount Skalisty, 2482 m (8143 ft)

Stans (*German* ʃtans) *n* a town in central Switzerland, capital of Nidwalden demicanton, 11 km (7 miles) southeast of Lucerne: tourist centre. Pop: 5700 (latest est)

stanza ('stænzə) *n* **1** *prosody* a fixed number of verse lines arranged in a definite metrical pattern, forming a unit of a poem **2** *US & Austral* a half or a quarter in a football match [c16 from It.: halting place, from Vulgar L *stantia* (unattested) station, from L *stāre* to stand] > '**stanzaed** *adj* > **stanzaic** (stæn'zeɪɪk) *adj*

stapelia (stə'piːlɪə) *n* any of various fleshy cactus-like leafless African plants having large fetid flowers [c18 from NL, after J. B. van *Stapel* (died 1636), Du. botanist]

stapes ('steɪpiːz) *n, pl* **stapes** *or* **stapedes** (stæ'piːdiːz) the stirrup-shaped bone that is the innermost of three small bones in the middle ear of mammals. Nontechnical name: **stirrup bone** Cf **incus, malleus** [c17 via NL from Med. L, ? var. of *stapeda* stirrup, infl. by L *stāre* to stand + *pēs* a foot]

staphylo- *combining form* **1** uvula: *staphyloplasty* **2** resembling a bunch of grapes: *staphylococcus* [from Gk *staphulē* bunch of grapes, uvula]

staphylococcus (ˌstæfɪləʊ'kɒkəs) *n, pl* **staphylococci** (-'kɒkaɪ, -'kɒkiː) any spherical Gram-positive bacterium of the genus *Staphylococcus*, typically occurring in clusters and causing boils, infection in wounds, and septicaemia. Often shortened to **staph** > ˌ**staphylo'coccal** *adj*

staphyloplasty ('stæfɪləʊˌplæstɪ) *n* plastic surgery or surgical repair involving the soft palate or the uvula > ˌ**staphylo'plastic** *adj*

staple[1] ('steɪpᵊl) *n* **1** a short length of thin wire bent into a square U-shape, used to fasten papers, cloth, etc **2** a short length of stiff wire formed into a U-shape with pointed ends, used for holding a hasp to a post, securing electric cables, etc ▷ *vb* **staples, stapling, stapled 3** (*tr*) to secure (papers, wire, etc) with staples [OE *stapol* prop, of Gmc origin] > '**stapler** *n*

staple[2] ('steɪpᵊl) *adj* **1** of prime importance; principal: *staple foods* **2** (of a commodity) forming a predominant element in the product, consumption, or trade of a nation, region, etc ▷ *n* **3** a staple commodity **4** a main constituent; integral part **5** *chiefly US & Canad* a principal raw material produced or grown in a region **6** the fibre of wool, cotton, etc, graded as to length and degree of fineness ▷ *vb* **staples, stapling, stapled 7** (*tr*) to arrange or sort (wool, cotton, etc) according to length and fineness [c15 from MDu. *stapel* warehouse]

staple gun *n* a mechanism that fixes staples to a surface

star (stɑː) *n* **1** any of a vast number of celestial objects visible in the clear night sky as points of light **2a** a hot gaseous mass, such as the sun, that radiates energy, esp as light and infrared radiation, and in some cases as ultraviolet, radio waves, and X-rays **2b** (*as modifier*): *a star catalogue*. Related adjs: **astral, sidereal, stellar 3** *astrol* **3a** a celestial body, esp a planet, supposed to influence events, personalities, etc **3b** (*pl*) another name for **horoscope** (sense 1) **4** an emblem shaped like a conventionalized star, often used as a symbol of rank, an award, etc **5** a small white blaze on the forehead of an animal, esp a horse **6a** a distinguished or glamorous celebrity, often from the entertainment world **6b** (*as modifier*): *star quality* **7** another word for **asterisk 8 see stars** to see or seem to see bright moving pinpoints of light, as from a blow on the head, increased blood pressure, etc ▷ *vb* **stars, starring, starred 9** (*tr*) to mark or decorate with a star or stars **10** to feature or be featured as a star: *"Greed" starred Erich von Stroheim; Olivier starred in "Hamlet"* [OE *steorra*] > '**starless** *adj* > '**star**ˌ**like** *adj*

Stara Zagora (*Bulgarian* 'stara za'gɔra) *n* a city in central Bulgaria: ceded to Bulgaria by Turkey in 1877. Pop: 147 939 (1999 est)

starboard ('stɑːbəd, -ˌbɔːd) *n* **1** the right side of an aeroplane or vessel when facing the nose or bow ▷ Cf **port**[2] (sense 1) ▷ *adj* **2** relating to or on the starboard ▷ *vb* **3** to turn or be turned towards the starboard [OE *stēorbord*, lit.: steering side, from *stēor* steering paddle + *bord* side; from the fact that boats were formerly steered by a paddle held over the right-hand side]

starburst ('stɑːˌbɜːst) *n* **1** a pattern of rays or lines radiating from a light source **2** *photog* a lens attachment which produces a starburst effect

starch (stɑːtʃ) *n* **1** a polysaccharide composed of glucose units that occurs widely in plant tissues in the form of storage granules **2** a starch obtained from potatoes and some grain: it is fine white powder that, in solution with water, is used to stiffen fabric **3** any food containing a large amount of starch, such as rice and potatoes **4** stiff or pompous formality ▷ *vb* **5** (*tr*) to stiffen with or soak in starch [OE *stercan* (unattested except by the p.p. *sterced*) to stiffen] > '**starcher** *n*

Star Chamber *n* **1** *English history* the Privy Council sitting as a court of equity; abolished 1641 **2** (*sometimes not caps*) any arbitrary tribunal dispensing summary justice **3** (*sometimes not caps*) (in Britain, in a Conservative government) a group of senior ministers who make the final decision on the public spending of each government department

starch-reduced *adj* (of food, esp bread) having the starch content reduced, as in proprietary slimming products

starchy ('stɑːtʃɪ) *adj* **starchier, starchiest 1** of or containing starch **2** extremely formal, stiff, or conventional: *a starchy manner* **3** stiffened with starch > '**starchily** *adv* > '**starchiness** *n*

star connection *n* a connection used in a polyphase electrical device or system of devices in which the windings each have one end connected to a common junction, the **star point**, and the other end to a separate terminal

star-crossed *adj* dogged by ill luck; destined to misfortune

stardom ('stɑːdəm) *n* **1** the fame and prestige of being a star in films, sport, etc **2** the world of celebrities

stardust ('stɑːˌdʌst) *n* **1** a large number of distant stars appearing to the observer as a cloud of dust **2** a dreamy romantic or sentimental quality or feeling

stare (stɛə) *vb* **stares, staring, stared 1** (*intr*) (often foll by *at*) to look or gaze fixedly, often with hostility or rudeness **2** (*intr*) to stand out as obvious; glare **3 stare one in the face** to be glaringly obvious or imminent ▷ *n* **4** the act or an instance of staring [OE *starian*] > '**starer** *n*

starfish ('stɑːˌfɪʃ) *n, pl* **starfish** *or* **starfishes** any of various echinoderms, typically having a flattened body covered with a flexible test and five arms radiating from a central disc

star fruit *n* another name for **carambola**

starfucker ('stɑːˌfʌkə) *offensive taboo slang* ▷ *n* **1** a person who seeks to have sexual relations with celebrities; groupie **2** a person who seeks to associate with famous or powerful people > '**star**ˌ**fucking** *n*

stargaze ('stɑːˌgeɪz) *vb* **stargazes, stargazing, stargazed** (*intr*) **1** to observe the stars **2** to daydream > '**star**ˌ**gazer** *n* > '**star**ˌ**gazing** *n, adj*

Ss

stark (stɑːk) *adj* **1** (*usually prenominal*) devoid of any elaboration; blunt: *the stark facts* **2** grim; desolate: *a stark landscape* **3** (*usually prenominal*) utter; absolute: *stark folly* **4** *arch* severe; violent **5** *arch or poetic* rigid, as in death (esp in **stiff and stark, stark dead**) **6** short for **stark-naked** ▷ *adv* **7** completely: *stark mad* **8** *rare* starkly [OE *stearc* stiff] > **'starkly** *adv* > **'starkness** *n*

Stark *n* **1** (stɑːk) Dame **Freya** (**Madeline**) ('freɪə) 1893–1993, British traveller and writer, whose many books include *The Southern Gates of Arabia* (1936), *Beyond Euphrates* (1951), and *The Journey's Echo* (1963) **2** (*German* ʃtark) **Johannes** (jo'hanəs) 1874–1957, German physicist, who discovered the splitting of the lines of a spectrum when the source of light is subjected to a strong electrostatic field (**Stark effect**, 1913): Nobel prize for physics 1919

Starkey ('stɑːkɪ) *n* **David** born 1945, British historian and broadcaster, noted for his books and television series on the Tudor period

stark-naked *adj* completely naked. Informal word (*postpositive*): **starkers** [C13 *stert naket*, lit.: tail naked; *stert*, from OE *steort* tail]

starlet ('stɑːlɪt) *n* **1** a young actress who is projected as a potential star **2** a small star

starlight ('stɑːˌlaɪt) *n* **1** the light emanating from the stars ▷ *adj also* **starlighted** **2** of or like starlight **3** Also: **starlit** ('stɑːˌlɪt) illuminated by starlight

starling ('stɑːlɪŋ) *n* any gregarious passerine songbird of an Old World family, esp the **common starling**, which has a blackish iridescent plumage and a short tail [OE *stærlinc*, from *stær* starling + *-line* -LING[1]]

star-of-Bethlehem *n* **1** Also: **starflower** a Eurasian liliaceous plant having narrow leaves and starlike white flowers **2** any of several similar and related plants

Star of David *n* an emblem symbolizing Judaism and consisting of a six-pointed star formed by superimposing one inverted equilateral triangle upon another of equal size

Starr (stɑː) *n* **1** (**Myra**) **Belle** 1848–89, US outlaw, a famous rustler of horses and cattle **2** **Ringo**, original name *Richard Starkey*. born 1940, British rock musician; drummer (1962–70) with the Beatles

starry ('stɑːrɪ) *adj* **starrier, starriest** **1** filled, covered with, or illuminated by stars **2** of, like, or relating to a star or stars > **'starriness** *n*

starry-eyed *adj* given to naive wishes, judgments, etc; full of unsophisticated optimism

Stars and Stripes *n* (*functioning as sing*) **the** the national flag of the United States of America, consisting of 50 white stars representing the present states on a blue field and seven red and six white horizontal stripes representing the original states. Also called: the **Star-Spangled Banner**

star sapphire *n* a sapphire showing a starlike figure in reflected light because of its crystalline structure

star sign *n* another name for **sign of the zodiac**

Star-Spangled Banner *n* **the** **1** the national anthem of the United States of America **2** another term for the **Stars and Stripes**

star stream *n* one of two main streams of stars that, because of the rotation of the Milky Way, appear to move in opposite directions

star-studded *adj* featuring a large proportion of well-known performers: *a star-studded cast*

start (stɑːt) *vb* **1** to begin or cause to begin (something or to do something); come or cause to come into being, operation, etc: *he started a quarrel; they started to work* **2** (when *intr*, sometimes foll by *on*) to make or cause to make a beginning of (a process, series of actions, etc): *they started on the project* **3** (sometimes foll by *up*) to set or be set in motion: *he started up the machine* **4** (*intr*) to make a sudden involuntary movement, as from fright; jump **5** (*intr*; sometimes foll by *up, away*, etc) to spring or jump suddenly from a position or place **6** to establish or be established; set up: *to start a business* **7** (*tr*) to support (someone) in the first part of a venture, career, etc **8** to work or cause to work loose **9** to enter or be entered in a race **10** (*intr*) to flow violently from a source: *wine started from a hole in the cask* **11** (*tr*) to rouse (game) from a hiding place, lair, etc **12** (*intr*) (esp of eyes) to bulge; pop **13** (*intr*) *Brit inf* to commence quarrelling or causing a disturbance **14** **to start with** in the first place ▷ *n* **15** the beginning or first part of a journey, series of actions or operations, etc **16** the place or time of starting, as of a race or performance **17** a signal to proceed, as in a race **18** a lead or advantage, either in time or distance, in a competitive activity: *he had an hour's start on me* **19** a slight involuntary movement, as through fright, surprise, etc: *she gave a start as I entered* **20** an opportunity to enter a career, undertake a project, etc **21** *inf* a surprising incident **22** **for a start** in the first place ▷ See also **start in, start off**, etc [OE *styrtan*]

starter ('stɑːtə) *n* **1** Also called: **self-starter** a device for starting an internal-combustion engine, usually consisting of a powerful electric motor that engages with the flywheel **2** a person who supervises and signals the start of a race **3** a competitor who starts in a race or contest **4** *inf, chiefly Austral* an acceptable or practicable proposition, plan, idea, etc **5** *chiefly Brit* the first course of a meal **6** (*modifier*) designed to be used by a novice: *a starter kit* **7** **for starters** *sl* in the first place **8** **under starter's orders** **8a** (of horses in a race) awaiting the start signal **8b** (of a person) eager or ready to begin

starter home *n* a compact flat or house marketed by price and size specifications to suit the requirements of first-time home buyers

start in *vb* (*adv*) to undertake (something or doing something); commence or begin

starting block *n* one of a pair of adjustable devices with pads or blocks against which a sprinter braces his feet in crouch starts

starting gate *n* **1** a movable barrier so placed on the starting line of a racecourse that the raising of it releases all the contestants simultaneously **2** the US name for **starting stalls**

starting grid *n* *motor racing* a marked section of the track at the start where the cars line up according to their times in practice, the fastest occupying the front position

starting price *n* (esp in horse racing) the latest odds offered by bookmakers at the start of a race

starting rate *n* (in Britain) a rate of income tax below the basic rate

starting stalls *pl n Brit* a line of stalls in which horses are enclosed at the start of a race and from which they are released by the simultaneous springing open of retaining barriers at the front of each stall

startle ('stɑːtᵊl) *vb* **startles, startling, startled** to be or cause to be surprised or frightened, esp so as to start involuntarily [OE *steartlian* to stumble]

startling ('stɑːtlɪŋ) *adj* causing surprise or fear; striking; astonishing > **'startlingly** *adv*

start off *vb* (*adv*) **1** (*intr*) to set out on a journey **2** to be or make the first step in (an activity); initiate: *he started the show off with a lively song* **3** (*tr*) to cause (a person) to act or do something, such as to laugh, to tell stories, etc

start on *vb* (*intr, prep*) *Brit inf* to pick a quarrel with; upbraid

start out *vb* (*intr, adv*) **1** to set out on a journey **2** to take the first steps, as in life, one's career, etc: *he started out as a salesman* **3** to take the first actions in an activity in a particular way or with a specified aim: *they started out wanting a house, but eventually bought a flat*

start up *vb* (*adv*) **1** to come or cause to come into being for the first time; originate **2** (*intr*) to spring or jump suddenly **3** to set in or go into motion, activity, etc: *he started up the engine* ▷ *n* **start-up** **4a** a recently launched project or business enterprise **4b** (*as modifier*): *start-up grants; an Internet start-up company*

starve (stɑːv) *vb* **starves, starving, starved** **1** to die or cause to die from lack of food **2** to deprive (a person or animal) or (of a person, etc) to be deprived of food **3** (*intr*) *inf* to be very hungry **4** (foll by *of* or *for*) to deprive or be deprived (of something), esp so as to cause suffering or malfunctioning: *the engine was starved of fuel* **5** (*tr*; foll by *into*) to bring (to) a specified condition by starving: *to starve someone into submission* **6** *arch or dialect* to be or cause to be extremely cold [OE *steorfan* to die] > **star'vation** *n*

starveling ('stɑːvlɪŋ) *arch* ▷ *n* **1a** a starving or poorly fed person, animal, etc **1b** (*as modifier*): *a starveling child* ▷ *adj* **2** insufficient; meagre; scant

Star Wars *n* (*functioning as sing*) (in the US) a proposed system of artificial satellites armed with lasers to destroy enemy missiles in space. Official name: **Strategic Defense Initiative** [c20 popularly named after the science-fiction film *Star Wars* (1977)]

starwort ('stɑːˌwɜːt) *n* **1** any of several plants with star-shaped flowers, esp the stitchwort **2** any of several aquatic plants having a star-shaped rosette of floating leaves

stash (stæʃ) *vb* **1** (*tr*; often foll by *away*) *inf* to put or store (money, valuables, etc) in a secret place, as for safekeeping ▷ *n* **2** *inf, chiefly US & Canad* a secret store or the place where this is hidden **3** *sl* drugs kept for personal consumption [c20 from ?]

stasis ('steɪsɪs) *n* **1** *pathol* a stagnation in the normal flow of bodily fluids, such as the blood or urine **2** a state or condition in which there is no action or progress [c18 via NL from Gk: a standing, from *histanai* to cause to stand]

-stat *n combining form* indicating a device that causes something to remain stationary or constant: *thermostat* [from Gk *-statēs*, from *histanai* to cause to stand]

state (steɪt) *n* **1** the condition of a person, thing, etc, with regard to main attributes **2** the structure or form of something: *a solid state* **3** any mode of existence **4** position in life or society; estate **5** ceremonious style, as befitting wealth or dignity: *to live in state* **6** a sovereign political power or community **7** the territory occupied by such a community **8** the sphere of power in such a community: *affairs of state* **9** (*often cap*) one of a number of areas or communities having their own governments and forming a federation under a sovereign government, as in the US **10** (*often cap*) the body politic of a particular sovereign power, esp as contrasted with a rival authority such as the Church **11** *obs* a class or order; estate **12** *inf* a nervous, upset, or excited condition (esp in **in a state**) **13** **lie in state** (of a body) to be placed on public view before burial **14** **state of affairs** a situation; circumstances or condition ▷ *modifier* **15** controlled or financed by a state: *state university* **16** of, relating to, or concerning the State: *State trial* **17** involving ceremony or concerned with a ceremonious occasion: *state visit* ▷ *vb* **states, stating, stated** (*tr; may take a clause as object*) **18** to articulate in words; utter **19** to declare formally or publicly [c13 from OF *estat*, from L *status* a standing, from *stāre* to stand] > **'statable** *or* **'stateable** *adj* > **'statehood** *n*
▷ www.sosig.ac.uk/roads/subject-listing/World-cat/state.html

state bank *n* (in the US) a commercial bank incorporated under a State charter and not required to be a member of the Federal Reserve System

statecraft ('steɪtˌkrɑːft) *n* the art of conducting public affairs; statesmanship

state duma *n* another name for **duma** (sense 3)

state house *n NZ* a house built by the government and rented to a **state tenant.** Brit equivalent: **council house**

Statehouse ('steɪtˌhaʊs) *n* (in the US) the building which houses a state legislature

stateless ('steɪtlɪs) *adj* **1** without nationality: *stateless persons* **2** without a state or states > **'statelessness** *n*

stately ('steɪtlɪ) *adj* **statelier, stateliest** **1** characterized by a graceful, dignified, and imposing appearance or manner ▷ *adv* **2** in a stately manner > **'stateliness** *n*

stately home *n Brit* a large mansion, esp one open to the public

statement ('steɪtmənt) *n* **1** the act of stating **2** something that is stated, esp a formal prepared announcement or reply **3** *law* a declaration of matters of fact **4** an account containing a summary of bills or invoices and displaying the total amount due **5** an account prepared by a bank for a client, usually at regular intervals, to show all credits and debits and the balance at the end of the period **6** a computer instruction written in a source language, such as FORTRAN, which is converted into one or more machine-code instructions by a compiler **7** *logic* the content of a sentence that affirms or denies something and may be true or false **8** *Brit education* a legally binding account of the provisions that will be made to meet the needs of a pupil with special educational needs ▷ *vb* (*tr; usually passive*) **9** to supply a legally binding account of the provisions that will be made to meet the needs of (a pupil with special educational needs)

statement of attainment *n Brit education* a programme of specific objectives that pupils should achieve within their own levels of attainment in a particular subject

statement of claim *n law* (in England) the first pleading made by the plaintiff in a High Court action

Staten Island ('stæt^ən) *n* an island in SE New York State, in New York Harbor: a borough of New York city; heavy industry. Pop: 378 977 (1990). Area: 155 sq km (60 sq miles)

state of the art *n* **1** the level of knowledge and development achieved in a technique, science, etc, esp at present ▷ *adj* **state-of-the-art** (*prenominal*) **2** the most recent and therefore considered the best; up-to-the-minute: *a state-of-the-art amplifier*

State Registered Nurse *n* (formerly, in Britain) a nurse who had extensive training and was qualified to perform all nursing services. See **Registered General Nurse**

stateroom ('steɪtˌruːm, -ˌrʊm) *n* **1** a private cabin or room on a ship, train, etc **2** *chiefly Brit* a large room in a palace or other building for use on state occasions

States (steɪts) *n* (*functioning as sing or pl*) **the** an informal name for the **United States of America**

state school *n* any school maintained by the state, in which education is free

stateside ('steɪtˌsaɪd) *adj, adv* (*sometimes cap*) *US* of, in, to, or towards the US

statesman ('steɪtsmən) *n, pl* **statesmen** **1** a political leader whose wisdom, integrity, etc, win great respect **2** a person active and influential in the formulation of high government policy > **'statesman-ˌlike** *or* **'statesmanly** *adj* > **'statesmanship** *n* > **'statesˌwoman** *fem n*

state socialism *n* a variant of socialism in which the power of the state is employed for the purpose of creating an egalitarian society by means of public control of major industries, banks, etc > **state socialist** *n*

state trooper *n US* a state policeman

static ('stætɪk) *adj also* **statical** **1** not active or moving; stationary **2** (of a weight, force, or pressure) acting but causing no movement **3** of or concerned with forces that do not produce movement **4** relating to or causing stationary electric charges; electrostatic **5** of or relating to interference in the reception of radio or television transmissions **6** of or concerned with statics **7** *computing* (of a memory) not needing its contents refreshed periodically ▷ *n* **8** random hissing or crackling or a speckled picture caused by interference in the reception of radio or television transmissions **9** electric sparks or crackling produced by friction [C16 from NL *staticus*, from Gk *statikos* causing to stand, from *histanai* to stand] > **'statically** *adv*

statice ('stætɪsɪ) *n* another name for **sea lavender**

static electricity *n* electricity that is not dynamic or flowing as a current

statics ('stætɪks) *n* (*functioning as sing*) the branch of mechanics concerned with the forces that produce a state of equilibrium in a system

station ('steɪʃən) *n* **1** the place or position at which a thing or person stands **2a** a place along a route or line at which a bus, train, etc, stops for fuel or to pick up or let off passengers or goods, esp one with ancillary buildings and services **2b** (*as modifier*): *a station buffet* **3a** the headquarters or local offices of an organization such as the police or fire services **3b** (*as modifier*): *a station sergeant*. See **police station, fire station** **4** a building, depot, etc, with special equipment for some particular purpose: *power station; petrol station* **5** *mil* a place of duty: *an action station* **6** *navy* **6a** a location to which a ship or fleet is assigned for duty **6b** an assigned location for a member of a ship's crew **7** a television or radio channel **8** a position or standing, as in a particular society or organization **9** the type of one's occupation; calling **10** (in British India) a place where the British district officials or garrison officers resided **11** *biol* the habitat occupied by a particular animal or plant **12** *Austral & NZ* a large sheep or cattle farm **13** (*sometimes cap*) *RC Church* **13a** one of the stations of the Cross **13b** any of the churches (**station churches**) in Rome used as points of assembly for religious processions and ceremonies on particular days (**station days**) ▷ *vb* **14** (*tr*) to place in or assign to a station [C14 via OF from L *statiō* a standing still, from *stāre* to stand]

stationary ('steɪʃənərɪ) *adj* **1** not moving; standing still **2** not able to be moved **3** showing no change: *the doctors said his condition was stationary* **4** tending to remain in one place [C15 from L *statiōnārius*, from *statiō* STATION]

> USAGE This word, which is always an adjective, is occasionally wrongly used where 'paper products' are meant: *in the stationery* (not *stationary*) *cupboard*

stationary orbit *n astronautics* a synchronous orbit lying in or approximately in the plane of the equator

stationary wave *n* another name for **standing wave**

stationer ('steɪʃənə) *n* a person who sells stationery or a shop where stationery is sold [C14 from Med. L *stationarius* a person having a regular station, hence a shopkeeper (esp a bookseller) as distinguished from an itinerant tradesman; see STATION]

stationery ('steɪʃənərɪ) *n* any writing materials, such as paper, envelopes, pens, ink, rulers, etc

> USAGE See at **stationary**

station house *n chiefly US* a house that is situated by or serves as a station, esp as a police or fire station

stationmaster ('steɪʃən,mɑːstə) *n* the senior official in charge of a railway station

Stations of the Cross *pl n RC Church* **1** a series of 14 crosses, often accompanied by 14 pictures or carvings, arranged around the walls of a church, to commemorate 14 stages in Christ's journey to Calvary **2** a devotion of 14 prayers relating to each of these stages

station wagon *n* another name (less common in Britain) for **estate car**

statism ('steɪtɪzəm) *n* the theory or practice of concentrating economic and political power in the state > **'statist** *n*

statistic (stə'tɪstɪk) *n* a datum capable of exact numerical representation, such as the correlation coefficient of two series or the standard deviation of a sample. See also **parameter**[2] > **sta'tistical** *adj* > **sta'tistically** *adv* > **statistician** (,stætɪ'stɪʃən) *n*

statistical mechanics *n* (*functioning as sing*) the study of the properties of physical systems as predicted by the statistical behaviour of their constituent particles

statistics (stə'tɪstɪks) *n* **1** (*functioning as sing*) a science concerned with the collection, classification, and interpretation of quantitative data and with the application of probability theory to the analysis and estimation of population parameters **2** the quantitative data themselves [C18 (orig. "science dealing with facts of a state"): via G *Statistik*, from NL *statisticus* concerning state affairs, from L *status* STATE]
▷ www.stat.ufl.edu/vlib/statistics.html
▷ www.statsoftinc.com/textbook/stathome.html
▷ www.sosig.ac.uk/statistics

Statius ('steɪʃɪəs) *n* **Publius Papinius** ('pʌblɪəs pə'pɪnɪəs) ?45–96 AD, Roman poet; author of the collection *Silvae* and of two epics, *Thebais* and the unfinished *Achilleis*

stator ('steɪtə) *n* the stationary part of a rotary machine or device, esp of a motor or generator [C20 from L: one who stands (by), from *stāre* to stand]

statoscope ('stætə,skəʊp) *n* a very sensitive form of aneroid barometer used to detect and measure small variations in atmospheric pressure, such as one used in an aircraft to indicate small changes in altitude

statuary ('stætjʊərɪ) *n* **1** statues collectively **2** the art of making statues ▷ *adj* **3** of or for statues [C16 from L *statuārius*]

statue ('stætjuː) *n* a wooden, stone, metal, plaster, or other sculpture of a human or animal figure, usually life-size or larger [C14 via OF from L *statua*, from *statuere* to set up; see STATUTE]

statuesque (,stætjʊ'ɛsk) *adj* like a statue, esp in possessing great formal beauty or dignity > **,statu'esquely** *adv* > **,statu'esqueness** *n*

statuette (,stætjʊ'ɛt) *n* a small statue

stature ('stætʃə) *n* **1** height, esp of a person or animal when standing **2** the degree of development of a person: *the stature of a champion* **3** intellectual or moral greatness: *a man of stature* [C13 via OF from L *statūra*, from *stāre* to stand]

status ('steɪtəs) *n*, *pl* **statuses** **1** a social or professional position, condition, or standing **2** the relative position or standing of a person or thing **3** a high position or standing: *he has acquired a new status in that job* **4** the legal standing or condition of a person **5** a state of affairs [C17 from L: posture, from *stāre* to stand]

status asthmaticus (æs'mætɪkəs) *n* a severe attack of asthma in which the patient may die from respiratory failure if not treated with inhaled oxygen or other appropriate measures

status epilepticus (,ɛpɪ'lɛptɪkəs) *n* a condition in which repeated epileptic seizures occur without the patient gaining consciousness between them. If untreated for a prolonged period it can lead to long-term disability or death

status Indian *n* (in Canada) a registered member of an Indian band who is recognized by the federal government as having specific rights and privileges

status quo (kwəʊ) *n* (usually preceded by *the*) the existing state of affairs [Latin lit.: the state in which]

status symbol *n* a possession which is regarded as proof of the owner's social position, wealth, prestige, etc

status zero *n* the condition of young people who are out of school but not in further education or training, permanently or regularly out of work, and dropping out of the mainstream of society

statute ('stætjuːt) *n* **1a** an enactment of a legislative body expressed in a formal document **1b** this document **2** a permanent rule made by a body or institution [C13 from OF *estatut*, from LL *statūtum*, from L *statuere* to set up, decree, ult. from *stāre* to stand]

statute book *n chiefly Brit* a register of enactments

passed by the legislative body of a state: *not on the statute book*

statute law *n* **1** a law enacted by a legislative body **2** a particular example of this ▷ Cf **common law, equity**

statute mile *n* a legal or formal name for **mile** (sense 1)

statute of limitations *n* a legislative enactment prescribing the period of time within which proceedings must be instituted to enforce a right or bring an action at law

statutory ('stætjʊtərɪ, -trɪ) *adj* **1** of, relating to, or having the nature of a statute **2** prescribed or authorized by statute **3** (of an offence) **3a** recognized by statute **3b** subject to a punishment or penalty prescribed by statute > '**statutorily** *adv*

statutory order *n* a statute that applies further legislation to an existing act

Stauffenberg ('ʃtaʊfən,bɜːg) *n* **Claus** (klaʊs), Graf von. 1907–44, German army officer, who tried to assassinate Hitler (1944). He and his fellow conspirators were executed

staunch[1] (stɔːntʃ) *adj* **1** loyal, firm, and dependable: *a staunch supporter* **2** solid or substantial in construction **3** *rare* (of a ship, etc) watertight; seaworthy [c15 (orig.: watertight): from OF *estanche*, from *estanchier* to STANCH] > '**staunchly** *adv* > '**staunchness** *n*

staunch[2] (stɔːntʃ) *or* **stanch** (stɑːntʃ) *vb* **1** to stem the flow of (a liquid, esp blood) or (of a liquid) to stop flowing **2** to prevent the flow of a liquid, esp blood, from (a hole, wound, etc) [c14 from OF *estanchier*, from Vulgar L *stanticāre* (unattested) to cause to stand, from L *stāre* to halt] > '**staunchable** *or* '**stanchable** *adj* > '**stauncher** *or* '**stancher** *n*

Stavanger (*Norwegian* sta'vaŋər) *n* a port in SW Norway: canning and shipbuilding industries. Pop: 108 818 (2000 est)

stave (steɪv) *n* **1** any one of a number of long strips of wood joined together to form a barrel, bucket, boat hull, etc **2** any of various bars, slats, or rods, usually of wood, such as a rung of a ladder **3** any stick, staff, etc **4** a stanza or verse of a poem **5** *music* **5a** *Brit* an individual group of five lines and four spaces used in staff notation **5b** another word for **staff**[1] (sense 9) ▷ *vb* **staves, staving, staved** *or* **stove 6** (often foll by *in*) to break or crush (the staves of a boat, barrel, etc) or (of the staves of a boat) to be broken or crushed **7** (*tr*; usually foll by *in*) to burst or force (a hole in something) **8** (*tr*) to provide (a ladder, chair, etc) with staves [c14 back formation from *staves*, pl. of STAFF[1]]

stave off *vb* (*tr, adv*) to avert or hold off, esp temporarily: *to stave off hunger*

staves (steɪvz) *n* a plural of **staff**[1] or **stave**

stavesacre ('steɪvz,eɪkə) *n* **1** a Eurasian ranunculaceous plant having poisonous seeds **2** the seeds, which have strong emetic and cathartic properties [c14 *staphisagre*, from L *staphis agria*, from Gk, from *staphis* raisin + *agria* wild]

Stavropol (*Russian* 'stavrəpəlj) *n* **1** a city in SW Russia: founded as a fortress in 1777. Pop: 345 100 (1999 est). Former name (1940–44): **Voroshilovsk 2** the former name (until 1964) of **Togliatti**

stay[1] (steɪ) *vb* **1** (*intr*) to continue or remain in a certain place, position, etc: *to stay outside* **2** (*copula*) to continue to be; remain: *to stay awake* **3** (*intr*; often foll by *at*) to reside temporarily: *to stay at a hotel* **4** (*tr*) to remain for a specified period: *to stay the weekend* **5** (*intr*) *Scot & S African* to reside permanently or habitually; live **6** *arch* to stop or cause to stop **7** (*intr*) to wait, pause, or tarry **8** (*tr*) to delay or hinder **9** (*tr*) **9a** to discontinue or suspend (a judicial proceeding) **9b** to hold in abeyance or restrain from enforcing (an order, decree, etc) **10** to endure (something testing or difficult, such as a race): *stay the course* **11** (*tr*) to hold back or restrain: *to stay one's anger* **12** (*tr*) to satisfy or appease (an appetite, etc) temporarily ▷ *n* **13** the act of staying or sojourning in a place or the period during which one stays **14** the act of stopping or restraining or state of being stopped, etc **15** the suspension of a judicial proceeding, etc: *stay of execution* [c15 *staien*, from Anglo-F *estaier* to stay, from OF *ester* to stay, from L *stāre* to stand] > '**stayer** *n*

stay[2] (steɪ) *n* **1** anything that supports or steadies, such as a prop or buttress **2** a thin strip of metal, plastic, bone, etc, used to stiffen corsets, etc. See also **stays** (sense 1) ▷ *vb* (*tr*) *arch* **3** (often foll by *up*) to prop or hold **4** (often foll by *up*) to comfort or sustain **5** (foll by *on* or *upon*) to cause to rely or depend [c16 from OF *estaye*, of Gmc origin]

stay[3] (steɪ) *n* a rope, cable, or chain, usually one of a set, used for bracing uprights, such as masts, funnels, flagpoles, chimneys, etc; guy ▷ See also **stays** (senses 2, 3) [OE *stæg*]

stay-at-home *adj* **1** (of a person) enjoying a quiet, settled, and unadventurous use of leisure ▷ *n* **2** a stay-at-home person

staying power *n* endurance; stamina

stays (steɪz) *pl n* **1** old-fashioned corsets with bones in them **2** a position of a sailing vessel relative to the wind so that the sails are luffing or aback **3 miss** *or* **refuse stays** (of a sailing vessel) to fail to come about

staysail ('steɪ,seɪl; *naut* 'steɪsᵊl) *n* an auxiliary sail, often triangular, set on a stay

STD *abbrev for:* **1** Doctor of Sacred Theology **2** sexually transmitted disease **3** subscriber trunk dialling

STD code *n Brit* a code of four or more digits, other than those comprising a subscriber's local telephone number, that determines the routing of a call [c20 *s(ubscriber) t(runk) d(ialling)*]

Ste *abbrev for* Saint (female) [F *Sainte*]

stead (stɛd) *n* **1** (preceded by *in*) *rare* the place, function, or position that should be taken by another: *to come in someone's stead* **2 stand** (**someone**) **in good stead** to be useful or of good service to (someone) ▷ *vb* **3** (*tr*) *arch* to help or benefit [OE *stede*]

Stead (stɛd) *n* **Christina** (**Ellen**) 1902–83, Australian novelist. Her works include *Seven Poor Men of Sydney* (1934), *The Man who Loved Children* (1940), and *Cotters' England* (1966)

steadfast *or* **stedfast** ('stɛdfəst, -,fɑːst) *adj* **1** (esp of a person's gaze) fixed in intensity or direction; steady **2** unwavering or determined in purpose, loyalty, etc: *steadfast resolve* > '**steadfastly** *or* '**stedfastly** *adv* > '**steadfastness** *or* '**stedfastness** *n*

steading ('stɛdɪŋ) *n* another name for **farmstead**

steady ('stɛdɪ) *adj* **steadier, steadiest 1** not able to be moved or disturbed easily; stable **2** free from fluctuation **3** not easily excited; imperturbable **4** staid; sober **5** regular; habitual: *a steady drinker* **6** continuous: *a steady flow* **7** *naut* (of a vessel) keeping upright, as in heavy seas ▷ *vb* **steadies, steadying, steadied 8** to make or become steady ▷ *adv* **9** in a steady manner **10 go steady** *inf* to date one person regularly ▷ *n, pl* **steadies 11** *inf* one's regular boyfriend or girlfriend ▷ *interj* **12** *naut* an order to the helmsman to stay on a steady course **13** a warning to keep calm, be careful, etc **14** *Brit* a command to get set to start, as in a race: *ready, steady, go!* [c16 from STEAD + -Y[1]] > '**steadily** *adv* > '**steadiness** *n* > '**steadying** *adj*

steady state *n physics* the condition of a system when some or all of the quantities describing it are independent of time but not necessarily in thermodynamic or chemical equilibrium

steady-state theory *n* a theory postulating that the universe exists throughout time in a steady state such that the average density of matter does not vary with distance or time. Matter is continuously created in the space left by the receding stars and galaxies of the expanding universe ▷ Cf **big-bang theory**

steak (steɪk) *n* **1** See **beefsteak** **2** any of various cuts of beef, for braising, stewing, etc **3** a thick slice of pork, veal, cod, salmon, etc **4** minced meat prepared in the same way as steak: *hamburger steak* [C15 from ON *steik* roast]

steakhouse (ˈsteɪkˌhaʊs) *n* a restaurant that has steaks as its speciality

steak tartare (tɑːˈtɑː) *or* **tartar** *n* raw minced steak, mixed with onion, seasonings, and raw egg. Also called: **tartare steak, tartar steak**

steal (stiːl) *vb* **steals, stealing, stole, stolen** **1** to take (something) from someone, etc, without permission or unlawfully, esp in a secret manner **2** (*tr*) to obtain surreptitiously **3** (*tr*) to appropriate (ideas, etc) without acknowledgment, as in plagiarism **4** to move or convey stealthily: *they stole along the corridor* **5** (*intr*) to pass unnoticed: *the hours stole by* **6** (*tr*) to win or gain by strategy or luck, as in various sports: *to steal a few yards* ▷ *n inf* **7** the act of stealing **8** something stolen or acquired easily or at little cost [OE *stelan*] > **ˈstealer** *n*

stealth (stɛlθ) *n* **1** the act or characteristic of moving with extreme care and quietness, esp so as to avoid detection **2** cunning or underhand procedure or dealing [C13 *stelthe*; see STEAL, -TH[1]] > **ˈstealthy** *adj*

Stealth (stɛlθ) *n* (*modifier*) *inf* denoting or referring to technology that aims to reduce the radar, thermal, and acoustic recognizability of aircraft and missiles

Stealth bomber *or* **plane** *n* a type of US military aircraft using advanced technology to render it virtually undetectable to sight, radar, or infrared sensors

stealth tax *n Brit inf* an indirect tax, such as that on fuel or pension funds, esp one of which people are unaware or that is felt to be unfair

steam (stiːm) *n* **1** the gas or vapour into which water is changed when boiled **2** the mist formed when such gas or vapour condenses in the atmosphere **3** any vaporous exhalation **4** *inf* power, energy, or speed **5 get up steam** **5a** (of a ship, etc) to work up a sufficient head of steam in a boiler to drive an engine **5b** *inf* to go quickly **6 let off steam** *inf* to release pent-up energy, feelings, etc **7 under one's own steam** without the assistance of others **8** (*modifier*) driven, operated, heated, powered, etc, by steam: *a steam radiator* **9** (*modifier*) treated by steam: *steam-ironed* **10** (*modifier*) *Humorous.* old-fashioned; outmoded: *steam radio* ▷ *vb* **11** to emit or be emitted as steam **12** (*intr*) to generate steam, as a boiler, etc **13** (*intr*) to move or travel by steam power, as a ship, etc **14** (*intr*) *inf* to proceed quickly and sometimes forcefully **15** to cook or be cooked in steam **16** (*tr*) to treat with steam or apply steam to, as in cleaning, pressing clothes, etc ▷ See also **steam up** [OE]

steam bath *n* **1** a room or enclosure that can be filled with steam in which people bathe to induce sweating and refresh or cleanse themselves **2** an act of taking such a bath

steamboat (ˈstiːmˌbəʊt) *n* a boat powered by a steam engine

steam boiler *n* a vessel in which water is boiled to generate steam

steam engine *n* an engine that uses steam to produce mechanical work, esp one in which steam from a boiler is expanded in a cylinder to drive a reciprocating piston

steamer (ˈstiːmə) *n* **1** a boat or ship driven by steam engines **2** a vessel used to cook food by steam **3** *Austral sl* a rough clash between sports teams

steaming (ˈstiːmɪŋ) *adj* **1** very hot **2** *inf* angry **3** *sl* drunk ▷ *n* **4** *inf* robbery, esp of passengers in a railway carriage or bus, by a large gang of armed youths

steam iron *n* an electric iron that emits steam from channels in the iron face to facilitate pressing and ironing, the steam being produced from water contained within the iron

steam jacket *n engineering* a jacket containing steam that surrounds and heats a cylinder

steam organ *n* a type of organ powered by steam, once common at fairgrounds, played either by a keyboard or by a moving punched card. US name: **calliope**

steam point *n* the temperature at which the maximum vapour pressure of water is equal to one atmosphere (1.01325×10^5 N/m^2). It has the value of 100° on the Celsius scale

steam reforming *n chem* a process in which methane from natural gas is heated, with steam, usually with a catalyst, to produce a mixture of carbon monoxide and hydrogen used in organic synthesis and as a fuel

steamroller (ˈstiːmˌrəʊlə) *n* **1a** a steam-powered vehicle with heavy rollers used for compressing road surfaces during road-making **1b** another word for **roadroller** **2a** an overpowering force or person that overcomes all opposition **2b** (*as modifier*): *steamroller tactics* ▷ *vb* **3** (*tr*) to crush (opposition, etc) by overpowering force

steamship (ˈstiːmˌʃɪp) *n* a ship powered by one or more steam engines

steam shovel *n* a steam-driven mechanical excavator

steam turbine *n* a turbine driven by steam

steam up *vb* (*adv*) **1** to cover (windows, etc) or (of windows, etc) to become covered with a film of condensed steam **2** (*tr*; *usually passive*) *sl* to excite or make angry: *he's all steamed up about the delay*

steamy (ˈstiːmɪ) *adj* **steamier, steamiest** **1** of, resembling, full of, or covered with steam **2** *inf* lustful or erotic: *steamy nightlife* > **ˈsteaminess** *n*

steapsin (stɪˈæpsɪn) *n biochem* a pancreatic lipase [C19 from Gk *stear* fat + PEPSIN]

stearic (stɪˈærɪk) *adj* **1** of or relating to suet or fat **2** of, consisting of, containing, or derived from stearic acid

stearic acid *n* a colourless odourless insoluble waxy carboxylic acid used for making candles and suppositories. Formula: $CH_3(CH_2)_{16}COOH$. Systematic name: **octadecanoic acid**

stearin *or* **stearine** (ˈstɪərɪn) *n* **1** Also called: **tristearin** a colourless crystalline ester of glycerol and stearic acid, present in fats and used in soap and candles **2** another name for **stearic acid** **3** fat in its solid form [C19 from F *stéarine*, from Gk *stear* fat + -IN]

steatite (ˈstɪəˌtaɪt) *n* another name for **soapstone** [C18 from L *steatītēs*, from Gk *stear* fat + -ITE[1]] > **steatitic** (ˌstɪəˈtɪtɪk) *adj*

steato- *combining form* denoting fat [from Gk *stear, steat-* fat, tallow]

steatolysis (ˌstɪəˈtɒlɪsɪs) *n physiol* **1** the digestive process whereby fats are emulsified and then hydrolysed to fatty acids and glycerine **2** the breaking down of fat

steatopygia (ˌstɪətəʊˈpɪdʒɪə, -ˈpaɪ-) *or* **steatopyga** (ˌstɪətəʊˈpaɪgə) *n* excessive fatness of the buttocks [C19 from NL, from STEATO- + Gk *pugē* the buttocks] > **ˌsteatoˈpygic** *or* **steatopygous** (ˌstɪəˈtɒpɪgəs) *adj*

Stębark (ˈstɛmbark) *n* the Polish name for **Tannenberg**

stedfast (ˈstɛdfəst, -ˌfɑːst) *adj* a less common spelling of **steadfast**

steed (stiːd) *n arch or literary* a horse, esp one that is spirited or swift [OE *stēda* stallion]

steel (stiːl) *n* **1a** any of various alloys based on iron containing carbon and often small quantities of other elements such as sulphur, manganese, chromium, and nickel. Steels exhibit a variety of properties, such as strength, malleability, etc, depending on their composition and the way they have been treated **1b** (*as modifier*): *steel girders*. See also **stainless steel** **2** something that is made of steel **3** a steel stiffener in a corset, etc **4** a ridged steel rod used for sharpening knives **5** the quality of hardness, esp with regard to a person's character or attitudes **6** *Canad* a railway track or line **7 cold steel** bladed weapons ▷ *vb* (*tr*) **8** to fit, plate, edge, or point with steel **9** to make hard and unfeeling: *he steeled his heart against her sorrow; he steeled himself for the blow*

[OE *stēli*] > **'steely** *adj* > **'steeliness** *n*
Steel (sti:l) *n* **Danielle,** full name *Danielle Fernande Schüelein-Steel.* born 1950, US writer of romantic fiction
steel band *n music* a type of band, popular in the Caribbean Islands, consisting mainly of percussion instruments made from oil drums, hammered or embossed to obtain different notes
steel blue *n* **a** a dark bluish-grey colour **b** (*as adj*): *steel-blue eyes*
Steele (sti:l) *n* Sir **Richard** 1672–1729, British essayist and dramatist, born in Ireland; with Joseph Addison he was the chief contributor to the periodicals *The Tatler* (1709–11) and *The Spectator* (1711–12)
steel engraving *n* **a** a method or art of engraving (letters, etc) on a steel plate **b** a print made from such a plate
steel grey *n* **a** a dark grey colour, usually slightly purple **b** (*as adj*): *a steel-grey suit*
steelhead ('sti:l,hɛd) *n, pl* **steelheads** *or* **steelhead** a silvery North Pacific variety of the rainbow trout
steelpan ('sti:l,pæn) *n* a metal percussion instrument made from the bottom of an oil drum, hammered or embossed to obtain different notes
steel wool *n* a tangled or woven mass of fine steel fibres, used for cleaning or polishing
steelworks ('sti:l,wɜ:ks) *n* (*functioning as sing or pl*) a plant in which steel is made from iron ore and rolled or forged into bars, sheets, etc > **'steel,worker** *n*
steelyard ('sti:l,jɑ:d) *n* a portable balance consisting of a pivoted bar with two unequal arms. The load is suspended from the shorter one and the bar is returned to the horizontal by sliding a weight along the longer, graduated arm
Steen (steɪn) *n* **Jan** (jɑn) 1626–79, Dutch genre painter
steenbok ('sti:n,bɒk) *n, pl* **steenboks** *or* **steenbok** a small antelope of central and southern Africa, having a reddish-brown coat and straight horns [c18 from Afrik., from Du. *steen* stone + *bok* BUCK[1]]
steenbras ('sti:n,brɑ:s) *n S African* a variety of edible marine fish [Afrik., from Du. *steen* stone + *brasen* bream]
steep[1] (sti:p) *adj* **1a** having or being a slope or gradient approaching the perpendicular **1b** (*as n*): *the steep* **2** *inf* (of a fee, price, demand, etc) unduly high; unreasonable (esp in **that's a bit steep**) **3** *inf* excessively demanding or ambitious: *a steep task* **4** *Brit inf* (of a statement) extreme or far-fetched [OE *steap*] > **'steeply** *adv* > **'steepness** *n*
steep[2] (sti:p) *vb* **1** to soak or be soaked in a liquid in order to soften, cleanse, extract an element, etc **2** (*tr; usually passive*) to saturate; imbue: *steeped in ideology* ▷ *n* **3** an instance or the process of steeping or the condition of being steeped **4** a liquid or solution used for the purpose of steeping something [OE *stēpan*] > **'steeper** *n*
steepen ('sti:pᵊn) *vb* to become or cause to become steep or steeper
steeple ('sti:pᵊl) *n* **1** a tall ornamental tower that forms the superstructure of a church, temple, etc **2** such a tower with the spire above it **3** any spire or pointed structure [OE *stēpel*] > **'steepled** *adj*
steeplechase ('sti:pᵊl,tʃeɪs) *n* **1** a horse race over a course equipped with obstacles to be jumped **2** a track race in which the runners have to leap hurdles, a water jump, etc **3** *arch* **3a** a horse race across a stretch of open countryside including obstacles to be jumped **3b** a rare word for **point-to-point** ▷ *vb* **steeplechases, steeplechasing, steeplechased 4** (*intr*) to take part in a steeplechase > **'steeple,chaser** *n* > **'steeple,chasing** *n*
steeplejack ('sti:pᵊl,dʒæk) *n* a person trained and skilled in the construction and repair of steeples, chimneys, etc
steer[1] (stɪə) *vb* **1** to direct the course of (a vehicle or vessel) with a steering wheel, rudder, etc **2** (*tr*) to guide with tuition: *his teachers steered him through his exams* **3** (*tr*) to direct the movements or course of (a person, conversation, etc) **4** to pursue (a specified course) **5** (*intr*) (of a vessel, vehicle, etc) to admit of being guided in a specified fashion: *this boat does not steer properly* **6** **steer clear of** to keep away from; shun ▷ *n* **7** *chiefly US* guidance; information (esp in **a bum steer**) [OE *stieran*] > **'steerable** *adj* > **'steerer** *n*
steer[2] (stɪə) *n* a castrated male ox or bull; bullock [OE *stēor*]
steerage ('stɪərɪdʒ) *n* **1** the cheapest accommodation on a passenger ship, originally the compartments containing steering apparatus **2** an instance or the practice of steering and its effect on a vessel or vehicle
steerageway ('stɪərɪdʒ,weɪ) *n naut* enough forward movement to allow a vessel to be steered
steering committee *n* a committee set up to prepare and arrange topics to be discussed, the order of business, etc, for a legislative assembly or other body
steering wheel *n* a wheel turned by the driver of a motor vehicle, ship, etc, when he wishes to change direction
steersman ('stɪəzmən) *n, pl* **steersmen** the helmsman of a vessel
Stefansson ('stɛfənsən) *n* **Vilhjalmur** ('vɪl,hjaʊmɛr) 1879–1962, Canadian explorer, noted for his books on the Inuit
Steffens ('stɛfənz) *n* (**Joseph**) **Lincoln** 1866–1936, US political analyst, known for his exposure of political corruption
stegosaur ('stɛgə,sɔ:) *or* **stegosaurus** (,stɛgə'sɔ:rəs) *n* any of various quadrupedal herbivorous dinosaurs of Jurassic and early Cretaceous times, having an armour of bony plates [c19 from Gk *stegos* roof + -SAUR]
Steiermark ('ʃtaiər,mark) *n* the German name for **Styria**
stein (staɪn) *n* an earthenware beer mug, esp of a German design [from G *Stein*, lit.: stone]
Stein *n* **1** (staɪn) **Gertrude** 1874–1946, US writer, resident in Paris (1903–1946) Her works include *Three Lives* (1908) and *The Autobiography of Alice B. Toklas* (1933) **2** (*German* ʃtain) **Heinrich Friedrich Carl** ('hainrɪç 'fri:drɪç karl), Baron Stein. 1757–1831, Prussian statesman, who contributed greatly to the modernization of Prussia and played a major role in the European coalition against Napoleon (1813–15) **3** (sti:n) **Jock,** real name *John.* 1922–85, Scottish footballer and manager: managed Celtic (1965–78) and Scotland (1978–85)
Steinbeck ('staɪnbɛk) *n* **John** (**Ernst**) 1902–68, US writer, noted for his novels about agricultural workers, esp *The Grapes of Wrath* (1939): Nobel prize for literature 1962
steinbok ('staɪn,bɒk) *n, pl* **steinboks** *or* **steinbok** a variant of **steenbok**
Steiner ('staɪnə; *German* 'ʃtainər) *n* **Rudolf** ('ru:dɔlf) 1861–1925, Austrian philosopher, founder of anthroposophy. He was particularly influential in education. See also **anthroposophy**
Steinitz ('staɪnɪts; *German* 'ʃtainɪts) *n* **Wilhelm** ('vɪlhɛlm) 1836–1900, US chess player, born in Prague; world champion (1866–94)
Steinway ('staɪnweɪ) *n* **Henry** (**Engelhard**), original name *Heinrich Engelhardt Steinweg.* 1797–1871, US piano maker, born in Germany
stele ('sti:lɪ, sti:l) *n, pl* **stelae** ('sti:li:) *or* **steles** **1** an upright stone slab or column decorated with figures or inscriptions, common in prehistoric times **2** a prepared vertical surface that has a commemorative inscription or design, esp one on the face of a building **3** the conducting tissue of the stems and roots of plants, which is in the form of a cylinder ▷ Also called (for senses 1, 2): **stela** [c19 from Gk *stēlē*] > **'stelar** *adj*
stellar ('stɛlə) *adj* **1** of, relating to, or resembling a star or stars **2** of or relating to star entertainers **3** *inf* outstanding or immense: *companies are registering stellar profits* [c17 from LL *stellāris*, from L *stella* star]
stellar evolution *n astron* the sequence of changes that occurs in a star as it ages

Ss

stellate ('stɛlɪt, -eɪt) *or* **stellated** *adj* resembling a star in shape; radiating from the centre: *a stellate arrangement of petals* [C16 from L *stellātus* starry, from *stellāre* to stud with stars, from *stella* a star] > '**stellately** *adv*

stellular ('stɛljʊlə) *adj* **1** displaying or abounding in small stars: *a stellular pattern* **2** resembling a little star or little stars [C18 from LL *stellula*, dim. of L *stella* star] > '**stellularly** *adv*

stem[1] (stɛm) *n* **1** the main axis of a plant, which bears the leaves, axillary buds, and flowers and contains a hollow cylinder of vascular tissue **2** any similar subsidiary structure in such plants that bears a flower, fruit, or leaf **3** a corresponding structure in algae and fungi **4** any long slender part, such as the hollow part of a tobacco pipe between the bit and the bowl **5** the main line of descent or branch of a family **6** any shank or cylindrical pin or rod, such as the pin that carries the winding knob on a watch **7** *linguistics* the form of a word that remains after removal of all inflectional affixes **8** the main, usually vertical, stroke of a letter or of a musical note such as a minim **9a** the main upright timber or structure at the bow of a vessel **9b** the very forward end of a vessel (esp in **from stem to stern**) ▷ *vb* **stems, stemming, stemmed 10** (*intr;* usually foll by *from*) to be derived; originate **11** (*tr*) to make headway against (a tide, wind, etc) **12** (*tr*) to remove or disengage the stem or stems from [OE *stemn*] > '**stem,like** *adj*

stem[2] (stɛm) *vb* **stems, stemming, stemmed 1** (*tr*) to restrain or stop (the flow of something) by or as if by damming up **2** (*tr*) to pack tightly or stop up **3** *skiing* to manoeuvre (a ski or skis), as in performing a stem ▷ *n* **4** *skiing* a technique in which the heel of one ski or both skis is forced outwards from the direction of movement in order to slow down or turn [C15 *stemmen*, from ON *stemma*]

Stem (stɛm) *n* **die** the South African national anthem until 1991, when it was joined by 'Nkosi Sikele' iAfrica' [C19 from Afrik., the call]

stem cell *n histology* an undifferentiated cell that gives rise to specialized cells, such as blood cells. A focus for much recent cloning research

stem ginger *n* choice pieces of the underground stem of the ginger plant which are crystallized or preserved in syrup and eaten as a sweetmeat

stemma ('stɛmə) *n* a family tree; pedigree [C19 via L from Gk *stema* garland, wreath, from *stephein* to crown, wreathe]

stemmed (stɛmd) *adj* **1a** having a stem **1b** (*in combination*): *a long-stemmed glass* **2** having had the stem or stems removed

stem turn *n skiing* a turn in which the heel of one ski is stemmed and the other ski is brought parallel. Also called: **stem**

stench (stɛntʃ) *n* a strong and extremely offensive odour; stink [OE *stenc*]

stencil ('stɛnsᵊl) *n* **1** a device for applying a design, characters, etc, to a surface, consisting of a thin sheet of plastic, metal, etc, in which the design or characters have been cut so that ink or paint can be applied through the incisions onto the surface **2** a design or characters produced in this way ▷ *vb* **stencils, stencilling, stencilled** *or US* **stencils, stenciling, stenciled** (*tr*) **3** to mark (a surface) with a stencil **4** to produce (characters or a design) with a stencil [C14 *stanselen* to decorate with bright colours, from OF *estenceler*, from *estencele* a spark, from L *scintilla*]

Stendhal (*French* stɛ̃dal) *n* original name *Marie Henri Beyle*. 1783–1842, French writer, who anticipated later novelists in his psychological analysis of character. His two chief novels are *Le Rouge et le noir* (1830) and *La Chartreuse de Parme* (1839)

Sten gun (stɛn) *n* a light 9mm sub-machine-gun formerly used in the British Army [C20 from S & T (initials of Shepherd & Turpin, the inventors) + *-en*, as in BREN GUN]

steno- *or before a vowel* **sten-** *combining form* indicating narrowness or contraction: *stenography; stenosis* [from Gk *stenos* narrow]

stenograph ('stɛnə,grɑːf) *n* **1** any of various keyboard machines for writing in shorthand **2** any character used in shorthand ▷ *vb* **3** (*tr*) to record (minutes, letters, etc) in shorthand

stenographer (stə'nɒgrəfə) *n* the US & Canad name for **shorthand typist**

stenography (stə'nɒgrəfɪ) *n* **1** the act or process of writing in shorthand by hand or machine **2** matter written in shorthand > **stenographic** (,stɛnə'græfɪk) *adj*

stenosis (stɪ'nəʊsɪs) *n, pl* **stenoses** (-siːz) *pathol* an abnormal narrowing of a bodily canal or passage [C19 via NL from Gk *stenōsis*, ult. from *stenos* narrow] > **stenotic** (stɪ'nɒtɪk) *adj*

Stenotype ('stɛnə,taɪp) *n* **1** *trademark* a machine with a keyboard for recording speeches, etc, in a phonetic shorthand **2** any machine resembling this **3** the phonetic symbol typed in one stroke of such a machine

stenotypy ('stɛnə,taɪpɪ) *n* a form of shorthand in which alphabetic combinations are used to represent groups of sounds or short common words > '**steno,typist** *n*

stent (stɛnt) *n med* a tube of plastic or sprung metal mesh placed inside a hollow tube to reopen it or keep it open; uses in surgery include preventing a blood vessel from closing, esp after angioplasty, and assisting healing after an anastomosis [C19 after Charles *Stent* (1807–85), English dentist]

Stentor ('stɛntɔː) *n* **1** *Greek myth* a Greek herald with a powerful voice who died after he lost a shouting contest with Hermes, herald of the gods **2** (*not cap*) any person with an unusually loud voice

stentorian (stɛn'tɔːrɪən) *adj* (of the voice, etc) uncommonly loud: *stentorian tones* [C17 after STENTOR]

step (stɛp) *n* **1** the act of raising the foot and setting it down again in coordination with the transference of the weight of the body **2** the distance or space covered by such a motion **3** the sound made by such a movement **4** the impression made by such movement of the foot; footprint **5** the manner of walking or moving the feet; gait: *a proud step* **6** a sequence of foot movements that make up a particular dance or part of a dance: *the steps of the waltz* **7** any of several paces or rhythmic movements in marching, dancing, etc: *the goose step* **8** (*pl*) a course followed by a person in walking or as walking: *they followed in their leader's steps* **9** one of a sequence of separate consecutive stages in the progression towards some goal **10** a rank or grade in a series or scale **11** an object or device that offers support for the foot when ascending or descending **12** (*pl*) a flight of stairs, esp out of doors **13** (*pl*) another name for **stepladder 14** a very short easily walked distance: *it is only a step* **15** *music* a melodic interval of a second **16** an offset or change in the level of a surface similar to the step of a stair **17** a strong block or frame bolted onto the keel of a vessel and fitted to receive the base of a mast **18** a ledge cut in mining or quarrying excavations **19 break step** to cease to march in step **20 in step 20a** marching, dancing, etc, in conformity with a specified pace or moving in unison with others **20b** *inf* in agreement or harmony **21 keep step** to remain walking, marching, dancing, etc, in unison or in a specified rhythm **22 out of step 22a** not moving in conformity with a specified pace or in accordance with others **22b** *inf* not in agreement; out of harmony **23 step by step** with care and deliberation; gradually **24 take steps** to undertake measures (to do something) **25 watch one's step 25a** *inf* to conduct oneself with caution and good behaviour **25b** to walk or move carefully ▷ *vb* **steps, stepping, stepped 26** (*intr*) to move by raising the foot and then setting it down in a different position, transferring the weight of the body to this foot and repeating the process with the other foot **27** (*intr; often foll by in, out, etc*) to move or go on foot, esp for a short distance: *step this way* **28** (*intr*) *inf, chiefly US* to move, often in an attractive graceful manner, as in dancing: *he can really step around* **29** (*intr; usually foll by on or upon*) to place or press the foot; tread: *to step on the accelerator* **30** (*intr; usually foll by into*) to enter (into a situation) apparently with ease: *she stepped into a life of luxury* **31** (*tr*) to walk or take (a number of paces, etc): *to step ten paces* **32** (*tr*) to perform the steps of: *they step the tango well* **33** (*tr*) to set or place (the foot) **34** (*tr; usually foll by off or out*) to measure (some distance of ground) by stepping **35** (*tr*) to arrange in or supply with a series of steps so as to avoid coincidence or symmetry **36** (*tr*) to raise (a mast) and fit it into its step ▷ See also **step down, step in,** etc [OE *stepe, stæpe*] > '**step,like** *adj*

Step (stɛp) *n trademark* **a** a set of aerobic exercises designed to improve the cardiovascular system, which consists of stepping on and off a special box of adjustable height **b** (*as modifer*): *Step aerobics*

step- *combining form* indicating relationship through the previous marriage of a spouse or parent: *stepson; stepfather* [OE *stēop-*]

stepbrother ('stɛp,brʌðə) *n* a son of one's stepmother or stepfather by a union with someone other than one's father or mother

stepchild ('stɛp,tʃaɪld) *n, pl* **stepchildren** a stepson or stepdaughter

stepdaughter ('stɛp,dɔːtə) *n* a daughter of one's husband or wife by a former union

step down *vb* (*adv*) **1** (*tr*) to reduce gradually **2** (*intr*) *inf* to resign or abdicate (from a position) **3** (*intr*) *inf* to assume an inferior or less senior position ▷ *adj* **step-down** (*prenominal*) **4** (of a transformer) reducing a high voltage to a lower voltage ▷ Cf **step-up** (sense 3) ▷ *n* **step-down** **5** *inf* a decrease in quantity or size

stepfather ('stɛp,fɑːðə) *n* a man who has married one's mother after the death or divorce of one's father

stephanotis (,stɛfə'nəʊtɪs) *n* any of various climbing shrubs of Madagascar and Malaya, cultivated for their fragrant white waxy flowers [C19 via NL from Gk: fit for a crown, from *stephanos* a crown]

Stephen ('stiːvᵊn) *n* **1** ?1097–1154, king of England (1135–54); grandson of William the Conqueror. He seized the throne on the death of Henry I, causing civil war with Henry's daughter Matilda. He eventually recognized her son (later Henry II) as his successor **2 Saint** died ?35 AD, the first Christian martyr. Feast day: Dec 26 or 27 **3 Saint,** Hungarian name *István*. ?975–1038 AD, first king of Hungary as Stephen I (997–1038). Feast day: Aug 16 or 20 **4** Sir **Leslie** 1832–1904, English biographer, critic, and first editor of the *Dictionary of National Biography*; father of the novelist Virginia Woolf

Stephenson ('stiːvənsən) *n* **1 George** 1781–1848, British inventor of the first successful steam locomotive (1814); constructed the first railway line to carry passengers, the Stockton and Darlington Railway (opened 1825) **2** his son, **Robert** 1803–59, British engineer, noted for his construction of railway bridges and viaducts, esp the tubular bridge over the Menai Strait

step in *vb* **1** (*intr, adv*) *inf* to intervene or involve oneself ▷ *adj* **step-in** **2** (*prenominal*) (of garments, etc) put on by being stepped into; without fastenings **3** (of a ski binding) engaging automatically when the boot is positioned on the ski ▷ *n* **step-in** **4** (*often pl*) a step-in garment, esp underwear

stepladder ('stɛp,lædə) *n* a folding portable ladder that is made of broad flat steps fixed to a supporting frame hinged at the top to another supporting frame

stepmother ('stɛp,mʌðə) *n* a woman who has married one's father after the death or divorce of one's mother

step on *vb* (*intr, prep*) **1** to place or press the foot on **2** *inf* to behave harshly or contemptuously towards **3 step on it** *inf* to go more quickly; hurry up

step out *vb* (*intr, adv*) **1** to go outside or leave a room, etc, esp briefly **2** to begin to walk more quickly and take longer strides **3** *US & Canad inf* to withdraw from involvement

step-parent ('stɛp,pɛərənt) *n* a stepfather or stepmother > '**step-,parenting** *n*

steppe (stɛp) *n* (*often pl*) an extensive grassy plain usually without trees [C17 from ORussian *step* lowland]

stepper ('stɛpə) *n* a person who or animal that steps, esp a horse or a dancer

Steppes (stɛps) *pl n* **the 1** the huge grasslands of Eurasia, chiefly in Ukraine and Russia **2** another name for **Kyrgyz Steppe**

stepping stone *n* **1** one of a series of stones acting as footrests for crossing streams, marshes, etc **2** a circumstance that assists progress towards some goal

stepsister ('stɛp,sɪstə) *n* a daughter of one's stepmother or stepfather by a union with someone other than one's father or mother

stepson ('stɛp,sʌn) *n* a son of one's husband or wife by a former union

step up *vb* (*adv*) *Inf* **1** (*tr*) to increase or raise by stages; accelerate **2** (*intr*) to make progress or effect an advancement; be promoted ▷ *adj* **step-up** (*prenominal*) **3** (of a transformer) increasing a low voltage to a higher voltage ▷ Cf **step-down** (sense 4) ▷ *n* **step-up** **4** *inf* an increment in quantity, size, etc

-ster *suffix forming nouns* **1** indicating a person who is engaged in a certain activity: *prankster; songster* **2** indicating a person associated with or being something specified: *mobster; youngster* [OE *-estre*]

steradian (stə'reɪdɪən) *n* an SI unit of solid angle; the angle that, having its vertex in the centre of a sphere, cuts off an area of the surface of the sphere equal to the square of the length of the radius. Symbol: sr [C19 from STEREO- + RADIAN]

Ss

stercoraceous (,stɜːkə'reɪʃəs) *adj* of, relating to, or consisting of dung or excrement [C18 from L *stercus* dung + -ACEOUS]

stere (stɪə) *n* a unit used to measure volumes of stacked timber equal to one cubic metre (35.315 cubic feet) [C18 from F *stère*, from Gk *stereos* solid]

stereo ('stɛrɪəʊ, 'stɪər-) *adj* **1** short for **stereophonic** or **stereoscopic** ▷ *n, pl* **stereos** **2** stereophonic sound: *to broadcast in stereo* **3** a stereophonic record player, tape recorder, etc **4** *photog* **4a** stereoscopic photography **4b** a stereoscopic photograph **5** *printing* short for **stereotype** [C20 shortened form]

stereo- *or sometimes before a vowel* **stere-** *combining form* indicating three-dimensional quality or solidity: *stereoscope* [from Gk *stereos* solid]

stereochemistry (,stɛrɪəʊ'kɛmɪstrɪ, ,stɪər-) *n* the study of the spatial arrangement of atoms in molecules and its effect on chemical properties

stereograph ('stɛrɪə,grɑːf, 'stɪər-) *n* two almost identical pictures, or one special picture, that when viewed through special glasses or a stereoscope form a single three-dimensional image. Also called: **stereogram**

stereoisomer (,stɛrɪəʊ'aɪsəmə, ,stɪər-) *n chem* an isomer that exhibits stereoisomerism

stereoisomerism (,stɛrɪəʊaɪ'sɒmə,rɪzəm, ,stɪər-) *n chem* isomerism caused by differences in the spatial arrangement of atoms in molecules

stereophonic (,stɛrɪə'fɒnɪk, ,stɪər-) *adj* (of a system for recording, reproducing, or broadcasting sound) using two or more separate microphones to feed two or more loudspeakers through separate channels in order to give a spatial effect to the sound. Often shortened to **stereo** > **,stereo'phonically** *adv* > **stereophony** (,stɛrɪ'ɒfənɪ, ,stɪər-) *n*

stereoscope (ˈstɛrɪəˌskəʊp, ˈstɪər-) *n* an optical instrument for viewing two-dimensional pictures, giving an illusion of depth and relief. It has a binocular eyepiece through which two slightly different pictures of an object are viewed, one with each eye > **stereoscopic** (ˌstɛrɪəˈskɒpɪk, ˌstɪər-) *adj*

stereoscopy (ˌstɛrɪˈɒskəpɪ, ˌstɪər-) *n* **1** the viewing or appearance of objects in or as if in three dimensions **2** the study and use of the stereoscope > ˌ**stereˈoscopist** *n*

stereospecific (ˌstɛrɪəʊspɪˈsɪfɪk, ˌstɪər-) *adj chem* relating to or having fixed position in space, as in the spatial arrangements of atoms in certain polymers

stereotype (ˈstɛrɪəˌtaɪp, ˈstɪər-) *n* **1a** a method of producing cast-metal printing plates from a mould made from a forme of type **1b** the plate so made **2** another word for **stereotypy** **3** an idea, convention, etc, that has grown stale through fixed usage **4** a standardized image or conception of a type of person, etc ▷ *vb* **stereotypes, stereotyping, stereotyped** (*tr*) **5a** to make a stereotype of **5b** to print from a stereotype **6** to impart a fixed usage or convention to > ˈ**stereoˌtyper** *or* ˈ**stereoˌtypist** *n*

stereotyped (ˈstɛrɪəˌtaɪpt, ˈstɪər-) *adj* **1** lacking originality or individuality; conventional; trite **2** reproduced from or on a stereotype printing plate

stereotypy (ˈstɛrɪəˌtaɪpɪ, ˈstɪər-) *n* **1** the act or process of making stereotype printing plates **2** a tendency to think or act in rigid, repetitive, and often meaningless patterns

stereovision (ˈstɛrɪəʊˌvɪʒən, ˈstɪər-) *n* the perception or exhibition of three-dimensional objects in three dimensions

steric (ˈstɛrɪk, ˈstɪər-) *or* **sterical** *adj chem* of or caused by the spatial arrangement of atoms in a molecule [C19 from STEREO- + -IC]

sterile (ˈstɛraɪl) *adj* **1** unable to produce offspring; permanently infertile **2** free from living, esp pathogenic, microorganisms **3** (of plants or their parts) not producing or bearing seeds, fruit, spores, stamens, or pistils **4** lacking inspiration or vitality; fruitless [C16 from L *sterilis*] > ˈ**sterilely** *adv* > **sterility** (stɛˈrɪlɪtɪ) *n*

sterilize *or* **sterilise** (ˈstɛrɪˌlaɪz) *vb* **sterilizes, sterilizing, sterilized** *or* **sterilises, sterilising, sterilised** (*tr*) to render sterile; make infertile or barren > ˌ**steriliˈzation** *or* ˌ**steriliˈsation** *n* > ˈ**steriˌlizer** *or* ˈ**steriˌliser** *n*

sterling (ˈstɜːlɪŋ) *n* **1a** British money: *pound sterling* **1b** (*as modifier*): *sterling reserves* **2** the official standard of purity of British coins **3a** short for **sterling silver** **3b** (*as modifier*): *a sterling bracelet* **4** an article or articles manufactured from sterling silver ▷ *adj* **5** (*prenominal*) genuine and reliable: first-class: *sterling quality* [C13 prob. from OE *steorra* star + -LING[1]; referring to a small star on early Norman pennies]

sterling area *n* a group of countries that use sterling as a medium of international payments. Also called: **scheduled territories**

sterling silver *n* **1** an alloy containing not less than 92.5 per cent of silver **2** sterling-silver articles collectively

Sterlitamak (*Russian* stjerlitəˈmak) *n* an industrial city in W Russia, in the Bashkir Republic. Pop: 263 600 (1999 est)

stern[1] (stɜːn) *adj* **1** showing uncompromising or inflexible resolve; firm or authoritarian **2** lacking leniency or clemency **3** relentless; unyielding: *the stern demands of parenthood* **4** having an austere or forbidding appearance or nature [OE *styrne*] > ˈ**sternly** *adv* > ˈ**sternness** *n*

stern[2] (stɜːn) *n* **1** the rear or after part of a vessel, opposite the bow or stem **2** the rear part of any object ▷ *adj* **3** relating to or located at the stern [C13 from ON *stjórn* steering]

Stern (stɜːn) *n* **Isaac** 1920–2001, US concert violinist, born in Russia

Sternberg (ˈstɜːnˌbɜːg, ˈʃtɜːn-) *n* See (Joseph) **von Sternberg**

Sterne (stɜːn) *n* **Laurence** 1713–68, English novelist, born in Ireland, author of *The Life and Opinions of Tristram Shandy, Gentleman* (1759–67) and *A Sentimental Journey through France and Italy* (1768)

sternforemost (ˈstɜːnˈfɔːməʊst) *adv naut* backwards

sternmost (ˈstɜːnˌməʊst) *adj naut* **1** farthest to the stern; aftmost **2** nearest the stern

sternpost (ˈstɜːnˌpəʊst) *n naut* the main upright timber or structure at the stern of a vessel

stern sheets *pl n naut* the part of an open boat near the stern

sternum (ˈstɜːnəm) *n, pl* **sterna** (-nə) *or* **sternums** **1** (in man) a long flat vertical bone in front of the thorax, to which are attached the collarbone and the first seven pairs of ribs. Nontechnical name: **breastbone** **2** the corresponding part in many other vertebrates [C17 via NL from Gk *sternon* breastbone] > ˈ**sternal** *adj*

sternutation (ˌstɜːnjʊˈteɪʃən) *n* a sneeze or the act of sneezing [C16 from LL *sternūtāre* to sneeze, from *sternuere* to sputter (of a light)]

sternutator (ˈstɜːnjʊˌteɪtə) *n* a substance that causes sneezing, coughing, and tears; used in chemical warfare > **sternutatory** (stɜːˈnjuːtətərɪ, -trɪ) *adj, n*

sternwards (ˈstɜːnwədz) *or* **sternward** *adv naut* towards the stern; astern

sternway (ˈstɜːnˌweɪ) *n naut* movement of a vessel sternforemost

stern-wheeler *n* a vessel, esp a river boat, propelled by a large paddle wheel at the stern

steroid (ˈstɪərɔɪd, ˈstɛr-) *n biochem* any of a large group of organic compounds containing a characteristic chemical ring system, including sterols, bile acids, many hormones, and the D vitamins [C20 from STEROL + -OID] > **steˈroidal** *adj*

sterol (ˈstɛrɒl) *n biochem* any of a group of natural steroid alcohols, such as cholesterol and ergosterol, that are waxy insoluble substances [C20 shortened from CHOLESTEROL, ERGOSTEROL, etc]

stertorous (ˈstɜːtərəs) *adj* **1** marked by heavy snoring **2** breathing in this way [C19 from L *stertere* to snore] > ˈ**stertorously** *adv* > ˈ**stertorousness** *n*

stet (stɛt) *n* **1** a word or mark indicating that certain deleted typeset or written matter is to be retained ▷ *vb* **stets, stetting, stetted** **2** (*tr*) to mark (matter) thus [L, lit.: let it stand]

stethoscope (ˈstɛθəˌskəʊp) *n med* an instrument for listening to the sounds made within the body, typically consisting of a hollow disc that transmits the sound through hollow tubes to earpieces [C19 from F, from Gk *stēthos* breast + -SCOPE] > **stethoscopic** (ˌstɛθəˈskɒpɪk) *adj* > **stethoscopy** (stɛˈθɒskəpɪ) *n*

Stetson (ˈstɛtsᵊn) *n trademark* a type of felt hat with a broad brim and high crown, worn mainly by cowboys [C20 after John *Stetson* (1830–1906), US hat-maker]

Stettin (ʃtɛˈtiːn) *n* the German name for **Szczecin**

stevedore (ˈstiːvɪˌdɔː) *n* **1** a person employed to load or unload ships ▷ *vb* **stevedores, stevedoring, stevedored** **2** to load or unload (a ship, ship's cargo, etc) [C18 from Sp. *estibador* a packer, from *estibar* to load (a ship), from L *stīpāre* to pack full]

Stevenage (ˈstiːvənɪdʒ) *n* a town in SE England, in N Hertfordshire on the Great North Road: developed as the first of the new towns (1946). Pop: 76 064 (1991)

Stevenson (ˈstiːvənsən) *n* **1** **Adlai Ewing** (ˈædleɪ ˈjuːɪŋ) 1900–68, US statesman: twice defeated as Democratic presidential candidate (1952; 1956); US delegate at the United Nations (1961–65) **2** **Robert Louis** (**Balfour**) 1850–94, Scottish writer: his novels include *Treasure Island* (1883), *Kidnapped* (1886), and *The Master of Ballantrae* (1889)

stew[1] (stjuː) *n* **1a** a dish of meat, fish, or other food, cooked by stewing **1b** (*as modifier*): *stew pot* **2** *inf* a difficult or worrying situation or a troubled state (esp in **in a stew**) **3** a heterogeneous mixture: *a stew of people of every race* **4** (*usually pl*) *arch* a brothel ▷ *vb* **5** to cook or cause to cook by long slow simmering **6** (*intr*) *inf* to be troubled or agitated **7** (*intr*) *inf* to be oppressed with heat or crowding **8** to cause (tea) to become bitter or (of tea) to become bitter through infusing for too long **9** **stew in one's own juice** to suffer unaided the consequences of one's actions [C14 *stuen* to take a very hot bath, from OF *estuver*, from Vulgar L *extūfāre* (unattested), from EX-[1] + (unattested) *tūfus* vapour, from Gk *tuphos*]

stew² (stju:) *n Brit* **1** a fishpond or fishtank **2** an artificial oyster bed [C14 from OF *estui*, from *estoier* to confine, ult. from L *studium* STUDY]

steward (stjʊəd) *n* **1** a person who administers the property, house, finances, etc, of another **2** a person who manages the eating arrangements, staff, or service at a club, hotel, etc **3** a waiter on a ship or aircraft **4** a mess attendant in a naval mess **5** a person who helps to supervise some event or proceedings in an official capacity **6** short for **shop steward** ▷ *vb* **7** to act or serve as a steward (of something) [OE *stigweard*, from *stig* hall + *weard* WARD] > **'stewardship** *n*

stewardess ('stjʊədɪs, ˌstjʊə'dɛs) *n* a woman steward on an aircraft or ship

Stewart ('stjʊət) *n* **1** the usual spelling for the royal house of **Stuart** before the reign of Mary Queen of Scots (Mary Stuart) **2** Sir **Jackie,** full name *John Young Stewart* born 1939, Scottish motor-racing driver: world champion 1969, 1971, and 1973 **3** **James** (**Maitland**) 1908–97, US film actor, known for his distinctive drawl; appeared in many films including *Destry Rides Again* (1939), *It's a Wonderful Life* (1946), *The Glenn Miller Story* (1953), and *Vertigo* (1958)

Stewart Island *n* the third largest island of New Zealand, in the SW Pacific off the S tip of South Island. Pop: 450 (latest est). Area: 1735 sq km (670 sq miles)

stewed (stju:d) *adj* **1** (of meat, fish, etc) cooked by stewing **2** *Brit* (of tea) bitter through having been left to infuse for too long **3** a slang word for **drunk** (sense 1)

Steyr (*German* 'ʃtaiər) *n* an industrial city in N central Austria, in Upper Austria. Pop: 39 542 (1991)

stg *abbrev for* sterling

sthenic ('sθɛnɪk) *adj* abounding in energy or bodily strength; active or strong [C18 from NL *sthenicus*, from Gk *sthenos* force, on the model of *asthenic*]

Stheno ('sθi:nəʊ, 'sθɛnəʊ) *n Greek myth* one of the three Gorgons

stibine ('stɪbaɪn) *n* **1** a colourless poisonous gas with an offensive odour: made by the action of hydrochloric acid on an alloy of antimony and zinc **2** any one of a class of stibine derivatives in which one or more hydrogen atoms have been replaced by organic groups [C19 from L *stibium* antimony + -INE[2]]

stibnite ('stɪbnaɪt) *n* a soft greyish mineral consisting of antimony sulphide in crystalline form: the chief ore of antimony [C19 from obs. *stibine* stibnite + -ITE[1]]

-stichous *adj combining form* having a certain number of rows [from LL *-stichus*, from Gk *-stikhos*, from *stikhos* row]

stick¹ (stɪk) *n* **1** a small thin branch of a tree **2a** any long thin piece of wood **2b** such a piece of wood having a characteristic shape for a special purpose: *a walking stick; a hockey stick* **2c** a baton, wand, staff, or rod **3** an object or piece shaped like a stick: *a stick of celery* **4** In full: **control stick** the lever by which a pilot controls the movements of an aircraft **5** *inf* the lever used to change gear in a motor vehicle **6** *naut* a mast or yard **7a** a group of bombs arranged to fall at intervals across a target **7b** a number of paratroops jumping in sequence **8** *sl* **8a** verbal abuse, criticism: *I got some stick for that blunder* **8b** physical power, force (esp in **give it some stick**) **9** (*usually pl*) a piece of furniture: *these few sticks are all I have* **10** (*pl*) *inf* a rural area considered remote or backward (esp in **in the sticks**) **11** (*pl*) *hockey* a declaration made by the umpire if a player's stick is above the shoulders **12** (*pl*) goalposts **13** *inf* a dull boring person **14** (usually preceded by *old*) *inf* a familiar name for a person: *not a bad old stick* **15** punishment; beating **16** **in a cleft stick** in a difficult position **17** **wrong end of the stick** a complete misunderstanding of a situation, explanation, etc ▷ *vb* **sticks, sticking, sticked** **18** to support (a plant) with sticks; stake [OE *sticca*]

stick² (stɪk) *vb* **sticks, sticking, stuck** **1** (*tr*) to pierce or stab with or as if with something pointed **2** to thrust or push (a sharp or pointed object) or (of a sharp or pointed object) to be pushed into or through another object **3** (*tr*) to fasten in position by pushing or forcing a point into something: *to stick a peg in a hole* **4** (*tr*) to fasten in position by or as if by pins, nails, etc: *to stick a picture on the wall* **5** (*tr*) to transfix or impale on a pointed object **6** (*tr*) to cover with objects piercing or set in the surface **7** (when *intr*, foll by *out, up, through*, etc) to put forward or be put forward; protrude or cause to protrude: *to stick one's head out* **8** (*tr*) *inf* to place or put in a specified position: *stick your coat on this chair* **9** to fasten or be fastened by or as if by an adhesive substance: *stick the pages together; they won't stick* **10** (*tr*) *inf* to cause to become sticky **11** (when *tr*, *usually passive*) to come or cause to come to a standstill: *stuck in a traffic jam; the wheels stuck* **12** (*intr*) to remain for a long time: *the memory sticks in my mind* **13** (*tr*) *sl, chiefly Brit* to tolerate; abide: *I can't stick that man* **14** (*intr*) to be reluctant **15** (*tr; usually passive*) *inf* to cause to be at a loss; baffle or puzzle: *I was totally stuck for an answer* **16** (*tr*) *sl* to force or impose something unpleasant on: *they stuck me with the bill* **17** (*tr*) to kill by piercing or stabbing **18** **stick to the ribs** *inf* (of food) to be hearty and satisfying ▷ *n* **19** the state or condition of adhering **20** *inf* a substance causing adhesion **21** *obs* something that causes delay or stoppage ▷ See also **stick around, stick by,** etc [OE *stician*]

Ss

stick around *or* **about** *vb* (*intr, adv*) *inf* to remain in a place, esp awaiting something

stick by *vb* (*intr, prep*) to remain faithful to; adhere to

sticker ('stɪkə) *n* **1** an adhesive label, poster, or paper **2** a person or thing that sticks **3** a persevering or industrious person **4** something prickly, such as a thorn, that clings to one's clothing, etc **5** *inf* something that perplexes **6** *inf* a knife used for stabbing or piercing

stick fighting *n Caribbean* a form of combat between two trained fighters, each of whom uses a stick with both hands at the midpoint, to hit the opponent's head and body

stickhandle ('stɪkˌhændəl) *vb* **stickhandles, stickhandling, stickhandled** *ice hockey* to manoeuvre (the puck) deftly

sticking plaster *n* a thin cloth with an adhesive substance on one side, used for covering slight or superficial wounds

stick insect *n* any of various mostly tropical insects that have an elongated cylindrical body and long legs and resemble twigs

stick-in-the-mud *n inf* a conservative person who lacks initiative or imagination

stickle ('stɪkəl) *vb* **stickles, stickling, stickled** (*intr*) **1** to dispute stubbornly, esp about minor points **2** to refuse to agree or concur, esp by making petty stipulations [C16 *stightle* (in the sense: to arbitrate): frequentative of OE *stihtan* to arrange]

stickleback ('stɪkəlˌbæk) *n* any of various small fishes that have a series of spines along the back and occur in cold and temperate northern regions [C15 from OE *stickel* prick, sting + BACK]

stickler ('stɪklə) *n* **1** (usually foll by *for*) a person who makes insistent demands: *a stickler for accuracy* **2** a problem or puzzle

stick out *vb (adv)* **1** to project or cause to project **2** *(tr) inf* to endure (something disagreeable) (esp in **stick it out**) **3 stick out a mile** *or* **like a sore thumb** *inf* to be extremely obvious **4 stick out for** to insist on (a demand), refusing to yield until it is met

stick shift *n US & Canad* **1a** a manually operated transmission system in a motor vehicle **1b** a motor vehicle having manual transmission **2** a gear lever

stick to *vb (prep, mainly intr)* **1** *(also tr)* to adhere or cause to adhere to **2** to continue constantly at **3** to remain faithful to **4** not to move or digress from: *the speaker stuck closely to his subject* **5 stick to someone's fingers** *inf* to be stolen by someone

stick-up *n* **1** *sl, chiefly US* a robbery at gunpoint; hold-up ▷ *vb* **stick up** *(adv)* **2** *(tr) sl, chiefly US* to rob, esp at gunpoint **3** *(intr; foll by for) inf* to support or defend: *stick up for oneself*

sticky ('stɪkɪ) *adj* **stickier, stickiest 1** covered or daubed with an adhesive or viscous substance: *sticky fingers* **2** having the property of sticking to a surface **3** (of weather or atmosphere) warm and humid; muggy **4** *inf* difficult, awkward, or painful: *a sticky business* **5** (of a website) encouraging users to stay on the website or to visit it repeatedly ▷ *vb* **stickies, stickying, stickied 6** *(tr) inf* to make sticky > **'stickily** *adv* > **'stickiness** *n*

stickybeak ('stɪkɪˌbiːk) *Austral & NZ inf* ▷ *n* **1** an inquisitive person ▷ *vb* **2** *(intr)* to pry

sticky end *n inf* an unpleasant finish or death (esp in **come to** *or* **meet a sticky end**)

sticky wicket *n* **1** a cricket pitch that is rapidly being dried by the sun after rain and is particularly conducive to spin **2** *inf* a difficult or awkward situation

Stieglitz ('stiːglɪts) *n* **Alfred** 1864–1946, US photographer, whose work helped to develop photography as an art: among his best photographs are those of his wife Georgia O'Keeffe. He was also well known as a promoter of modern art

stiff (stɪf) *adj* **1** not easily bent; rigid; inflexible **2** not working or moving easily or smoothly: *a stiff handle* **3** difficult to accept in its severity or harshness: *a stiff punishment* **4** moving with pain or difficulty; not supple: *a stiff neck* **5** difficult; arduous: *a stiff climb* **6** unrelaxed or awkward; formal **7** firmer than liquid in consistency; thick or viscous **8** powerful; strong: *a stiff breeze; a stiff drink* **9** excessively high: *a stiff price* **10** lacking grace or attractiveness **11** stubborn or stubbornly maintained: *a stiff fight* **12** *obs* tightly stretched; taut **13** *sl* intoxicated **14 stiff with** *inf* amply provided with ▷ *n* **15** *sl* a corpse **16** *sl* anything thought to be a loser or a failure; flop ▷ *adv* **17** completely or utterly: *bored stiff; frozen stiff* ▷ *vb* **18** *(intr) sl* to fail: *the film stiffed* **19** *(tr) sl, chiefly US* to cheat or swindle [OE *stīf*] > **'stiffish** *adj* > **'stiffly** *adv* > **'stiffness** *n*

stiffen ('stɪfᵊn) *vb* **1** to make or become stiff or stiffer **2** *(intr)* to become suddenly tense or unyielding > **'stiffener** *n*

stiff-necked *adj* haughtily stubborn or obstinate

stifle ('staɪfᵊl) *vb* **stifles, stifling, stifled 1** *(tr)* to smother or suppress: *stifle a cough* **2** to feel or cause to feel discomfort and difficulty in breathing **3** to prevent or be prevented from breathing so as to cause death **4** *(tr)* to crush or stamp out [c14 var. of *stuflen*, prob. from OF *estouffer* to smother]

stigma ('stɪgmə) *n, pl* **stigmas** *or* **stigmata** ('stɪgmətə, stɪg'mɑːtə) **1** a distinguishing mark of social disgrace: *the stigma of having been in prison* **2** a small scar or mark such as a birthmark **3** *pathol* any mark on the skin, such as one characteristic of a specific disease **4** *bot* the receptive surface of a carpel where deposited pollen germinates **5** *zool* **5a** a pigmented eyespot in some invertebrates **5b** the spiracle of an insect **6** *arch* a mark branded on the skin **7** *(pl) Christianity* marks resembling the wounds of the crucified Christ, believed to appear on the bodies of certain individuals [c16 via L from Gk: brand, from *stizein* to tattoo]

stigmatic (stɪg'mætɪk) *adj* **1** relating to or having a stigma or stigmata **2** another word for **anastigmatic** ▷ *n also* **stigmatist** ('stɪgmətɪst) **3** *chiefly RC Church* a person marked with the stigmata

stigmatism ('stɪgməˌtɪzəm) *n* **1** *physics* the state or condition of being anastigmatic **2** *pathol* the condition resulting from or characterized by stigmata

stigmatize *or* **stigmatise** ('stɪgməˌtaɪz) *vb* **stigmatizes, stigmatizing, stigmatized** *or* **stigmatises, stigmatising, stigmatised** *(tr)* **1** to mark out or describe (as something bad) **2** to mark with a stigma or stigmata > **ˌstigmati'zation** *or* **ˌstigmati'sation** *n* > **'stigmaˌtizer** *or* **'stigmaˌtiser** *n*

stilbene ('stɪlbiːn) *n* a colourless or slightly yellow crystalline unsaturated hydrocarbon used in the manufacture of dyes [c19 from Gk *stilbos* glittering + -ENE]

stilboestrol *or US* **stilbestrol** (stɪl'biːstrəl) *n* a synthetic hormone having derivatives with oestrogenic properties. Also called: **diethylstilboestrol** [c20 from STILBENE + OESTRUS + -OL[1]]

stile[1] (staɪl) *n* **1** a set of steps or rungs in a wall or fence to allow people, but not animals, to pass over **2** short for **turnstile** [OE *stigel*]

stile[2] (staɪl) *n* a vertical framing member in a door, window frame, etc [c17 prob. from Du. *stijl* pillar, ult. from L *stilus* writing instrument]

stiletto (stɪ'lɛtəʊ) *n, pl* **stilettos 1** a small dagger with a slender tapered blade **2** a sharply pointed tool used to make holes in leather, cloth, etc **3** Also called: **spike heel, stiletto heel** a very high heel on a woman's shoe, tapering to a very narrow tip ▷ *vb* **stilettoes, stilettoeing, stilettoed 4** *(tr)* to stab with a stiletto [c17 from It., from *stilo* a dagger, from L *stilus* a stake, pen]

Stilicho ('stɪlɪkəʊ) *n* **Flavius** ('fleɪvɪəs) ?365–408 AD, Roman general and statesman, born a Vandal. As the guardian of Emperor Theodosius' son Honorius, he was effective ruler of the Western Roman Empire (395–408), which he defended against the Visigoths

still[1] (stɪl) *adj* **1** *(usually predicative)* motionless; stationary **2** undisturbed or tranquil; silent and calm **3** not sparkling or effervescent **4** gentle or quiet; subdued **5** *obs* (of a child) dead at birth ▷ *adv* **6** continuing now or in the future as in the past: *do you still love me?* **7** up to this or that time; yet: *I still don't know your name* **8** (often used with a comparative) even or yet: *still more insults* **9** quietly or without movement: *sit still* **10** *poetic & dialect* always ▷ *n* **11** *poetic* silence or tranquillity: *the still of the night* **12a** a still photograph, esp of a scene from a film **12b** *(as modifier): a still camera* ▷ *vb* **13** to make or become still, quiet, or calm **14** *(tr)* to allay or relieve: *her fears were stilled* ▷ *sentence connector* **15** even then; nevertheless: *he is rich but he is still not happy* [OE *stille*] > **'stillness** *n*

still[2] (stɪl) *n* an apparatus for carrying out distillation, used esp in the manufacture of spirits [c16 from OF *stiller* to drip, from L *stillāre*, from *stilla* a drip]

stillage ('stɪlɪdʒ) *n* **1** a frame or stand for keeping things off the ground, such as casks in a brewery **2** a container in which goods, machinery, etc, are transported [c16 prob. from Du. *stillagie* frame, scaffold, from *stellen* to stand; see -AGE]

stillborn ('stɪlˌbɔːn) *adj* **1** (of a fetus) dead at birth **2** (of an idea, plan, etc) fruitless; abortive; unsuccessful > **'stillˌbirth** *n*

still life *n, pl* **still lifes 1a** a painting or drawing of inanimate objects, such as fruit, flowers, etc **1b** *(as modifier): a still-life painting* **2** the genre of such paintings

still room *n Brit* **1** a room in which distilling is carried out **2** a pantry or storeroom, as in a large house

Stillson wrench ('stɪlsᵊn) *n trademark* a large wrench having adjustable jaws that are tightened by increasing the pressure on the handle

stilly *adv* ('stɪllɪ) **1** *arch or literary* quietly or calmly ▷ *adj* ('stɪlɪ) **2** *poetic* still, quiet, or calm

stilt (stɪlt) *n* **1** either of a pair of two long poles with footrests on which a person stands and walks, as used by circus clowns **2** a long post or column that is used with others to support a building above ground level **3** any of several shore birds similar to the avocets but having a straight bill ▷ *vb* **4** (*tr*) to raise or place on or as if on stilts [C14 (in the sense: crutch, handle of a plough): rel. to Low G *stilte* pole]

stilted ('stɪltɪd) *adj* **1** (of speech, writing, etc) formal, pompous, or bombastic **2** not flowing continuously or naturally: *stilted conversation* **3** *archit* (of an arch) having vertical piers between the impost and the springing > **'stiltedly** *adv* > **'stiltedness** *n*

Stilton ('stɪltən) *n trademark* either of two rich cheeses, blue-veined (**blue Stilton**) or white (**white Stilton**), both very strong in flavour [C18 named after *Stilton*, Cambridgeshire, where it was orig. sold]

Stilwell ('stɪlwɛl) *n* **Joseph W(arren)**, known as *Vinegar Joe*. 1883–1946, US general, who was (1941–44) Chiang Kai-shek's chief of staff and commander of all US forces in China, Burma (Myanmar), and India

stimulant ('stɪmjʊlənt) *n* **1** a drug or similar substance that increases physiological activity, esp of a particular organ **2** any stimulating agent or thing ▷ *adj* **3** stimulating [C18 from L *stimulāns* goading, from *stimulāre* to urge on]

stimulate ('stɪmjʊˌleɪt) *vb* **stimulates, stimulating, stimulated** **1** (*tr*) to arouse or quicken the activity or senses of **2** (*tr*) *physiol* to excite (a nerve, organ, etc) with a stimulus **3** (*intr*) to act as a stimulant or stimulus [C16 from L *stimulāre*] > **'stimuˌlating** *adj* > **ˌstimu'lation** *n* > **'stimulative** *adj, n* > **'stimuˌlator** *n*

stimulus ('stɪmjʊləs) *n, pl* **stimuli** (-ˌlaɪ, -ˌliː) **1** something that stimulates or acts as an incentive **2** any drug, agent, electrical impulse, or other factor able to cause a response in an organism [C17 from L: a cattle goad]

Stine (staɪn) *n* **R(obert) L(awrence)** born 1943, U.S. writer, noted for his numerous bestselling horror novels for older children, esp those in the *Goosebumps* and *Fear Street* series

sting (stɪŋ) *vb* **stings, stinging, stung** **1** (of certain animals and plants) to inflict a wound on (an organism) by the injection of poison **2** to feel or cause to feel a sharp mental or physical pain **3** (*tr*) to goad or incite (esp in **sting into action**) **4** (*tr*) *inf* to cheat, esp by overcharging ▷ *n* **5** a skin wound caused by the poison injected by certain insects or plants **6** pain caused by or as if by the sting of a plant or animal **7** a mental pain or pang: *a sting of conscience* **8** a sharp pointed organ, such as the ovipositor of a wasp, by which poison can be injected **9** the ability to sting: *a sharp sting in his criticism* **10** something as painful or swift of action as a sting: *the sting of death* **11** a sharp stimulus or incitement **12** *sl* a swindle or fraud **13** *sl* a police trap, esp one whereby a person is enticed into committing a crime for which he is then arrested [OE *stingan*] > **'stinger** *n* > **'stinging** *adj*

stinging nettle *n* See **nettle** (sense 1)

stingray ('stɪŋˌreɪ) *n* any of various rays having a whiplike tail bearing a serrated venomous spine capable of inflicting painful weals

stingy[1] ('stɪndʒɪ) *adj* **stingier, stingiest** **1** unwilling to spend or give **2** insufficient or scanty [C17 (? in the sense: ill-tempered): ?from *stinge*, dialect var. of STING] > **'stingily** *adv* > **'stinginess** *n*

stingy[2] ('stɪŋɪ) *adj* **stingier, stingiest** *inf* stinging or capable of stinging

stink (stɪŋk) *n* **1** a strong foul smell; stench **2** *sl* a great deal of trouble (esp in **make** *or* **raise a stink**) **3** **like stink** intensely; furiously ▷ *vb* **stinks, stinking, stank** *or* **stunk; stunk** (*mainly intr*) **4** to emit a foul smell **5** *sl* to be thoroughly bad or abhorrent: *this town stinks* **6** *inf* to have a very bad reputation: *his name stinks* **7** to be of poor quality **8** (foll by *of* or *with*) *sl* to have or appear to have an excessive amount (of money) **9** (*tr*; usually foll by *up*) *inf* to cause to stink ▷ See also **stink out** [OE *stincan*] > **'stinky** *adj*

stink bomb *n* a small glass globe which releases a liquid with an offensive smell when broken

stinker ('stɪŋkə) *n* **1** a person or thing that stinks **2** *sl* a difficult or very unpleasant person or thing **3** *sl* something of very poor quality **4** *inf* any of several fulmars or related birds that feed on carrion

stinkhorn ('stɪŋkˌhɔːn) *n* any of various fungi having an unpleasant odour

stinking ('stɪŋkɪŋ) *adj* **1** having a foul smell **2** *inf* unpleasant or disgusting **3** (*postpositive*) *sl* very drunk **4** **cry stinking fish** to decry something, esp one's own products ▷ *adv* **5** *inf* (intensifier, expressing contempt): *stinking rich* > **'stinkingly** *adv* > **'stinkingness** *n*

stinko ('stɪŋkəʊ) *adj* (*postpositive*) *sl* drunk

stink out *vb* (*tr, adv*) **1** to drive out or away by a foul smell **2** *Brit* to cause to stink: *the smell of orange peel stinks out the room*

stinkweed ('stɪŋkˌwiːd) *n* **1** Also called: **wall mustard** a plant, naturalized in Britain and S and central Europe, having pale yellow flowers and a disagreeable smell when bruised **2** any of various other ill-smelling plants

stinkwood ('stɪŋkˌwʊd) *n* **1** any of various trees having offensive-smelling wood, esp a southern African lauraceous tree yielding a hard wood used for furniture **2** the heavy durable wood of any of these trees

stint[1] (stɪnt) *vb* **1** to be frugal or miserly towards (someone) with (something) **2** *arch* to stop or check (something) ▷ *n* **3** an allotted or fixed amount of work **4** a limitation or check [OE *styntan* to blunt] > **'stinter** *n*

stint[2] (stɪnt) *n* any of various small sandpipers of a chiefly northern genus [OE]

Ss

stipe (staɪp) *n* **1** a stalk in plants that bears reproductive structures, esp the stalk bearing the cap of a mushroom **2** the stalk that bears the leaflets of a fern or the thallus of a seaweed **3** *zool* any stalklike part; stipes [C18 via F from L *stīpes* tree trunk]

stipel ('staɪp[ə]l) *n* a small paired leaflike structure at the base of certain leaflets; secondary stipule [C19 via NL from L *stipula*, dim. of *stīpes* a log] > **stipellate** (staɪ'pɛlɪt, -eɪt) *adj*

stipend ('staɪpɛnd) *n* a fixed or regular amount of money paid as a salary or allowance, as to a clergyman [C15 from OF *stipende*, from L *stīpendium* tax, from *stips* a contribution + *pendere* to pay out]

stipendiary (staɪ'pɛndɪərɪ) *adj* **1** receiving or working for regular pay: *a stipendiary magistrate* **2** paid for by a stipend ▷ *n, pl* **stipendiaries** **3** a person who receives regular payment [C16 from L *stīpendiārius* concerning tribute, from *stīpendium* STIPEND]

stipes ('staɪpiːz) *n, pl* **stipites** ('stɪpɪˌtiːz) *zool* **1** the second maxillary segment in insects and crustaceans **2** the eyestalk of a crab or similar crustacean **3** any similar stemlike structure [C18 from L; see STIPE] > **stipiform** ('staɪpɪˌfɔːm) *or* **stipitiform** ('stɪpɪtɪˌfɔːm) *adj*

stipple ('stɪp[ə]l) *vb* **stipples, stippling, stippled** (*tr*) **1** to draw, engrave, or paint using dots or flecks **2** to apply paint, powder, etc, to (something) with many light dabs ▷ *n also* **stippling** **3** the technique of stippling or a picture produced by or using stippling [C18 from Du. *stippelen*, from *stippen* to prick, from *stip* point] > **'stippler** *n*

stipulate ('stɪpjʊˌleɪt) *vb* **stipulates, stipulating, stipulated** **1** (*tr; may take a clause as object*) to specify, often as a condition of an agreement **2** (*intr*; foll by *for*) to insist (on) as a term of an agreement **3** (*tr; may take a clause as object*) to guarantee or promise [C17 from L *stipulārī*, prob. from OL *stipulus* firm] > **ˌstipu'lation** *n* > **'stipuˌlator** *n*

stipule ('stɪpju:l) *n* a small paired usually leaflike outgrowth occurring at the base of a leaf or its stalk [C18 from L; see STIPE] > **stipular** ('stɪpjʊlə) *adj*

stir[1] (stɜ:) *vb* **stirs, stirring, stirred** **1** to move an implement such as a spoon around in (a liquid) so as to mix up the constituents **2** to change or cause to change position; disturb or be disturbed **3** (*intr; often foll by from*) to venture or depart (from one's usual or preferred place) **4** (*intr*) to be active after a rest; be up and about **5** (*tr*) to excite or stimulate, esp emotionally **6** to move (oneself) briskly or vigorously; exert (oneself) **7** (*tr*) to rouse or awaken: *to stir someone from sleep; to stir memories* **8** (when *tr*, foll by *up*) to cause or incite others to cause (trouble, arguments, etc) **9** **stir one's stumps** to move or become active ▷ *n* **10** the act or an instance of stirring or the state of being stirred **11** a strong reaction, esp of excitement: *his publication caused a stir* **12** a slight movement ▷ See also **stir up** [OE *styrian*]

stir[2] (stɜ:) *n* **1** a slang word for **prison**: *in stir* **2** **stir-crazy** *sl, chiefly US & Canad* mentally disturbed as a result of being in prison [C19 from ?]

Stir. *abbrev for* Stirlingshire

stir-fry *vb* **stir-fries, stir-frying, stir-fried** **1** to cook (chopped meat, vegetables, etc) rapidly by stirring them in a wok or frying pan over a high heat ▷ *n, pl* **stir-fries** **2** a dish cooked in this way

stirk (stɜ:k) *n* **1** a heifer of 6 to 12 months old **2** a yearling heifer or bullock [OE *stierc*]

Stirling[1] ('stɜ:lɪŋ) *n* **1** a city in central Scotland, in Stirling council area on the River Forth: its castle was a regular residence of many Scottish monarchs between the 12th century and 1603. Pop: 30 515 (1991) **2** a council area of central Scotland, created from part of Central Region in 1996; includes most of the historical county of Stirlingshire: the Forth valley rises to the Grampian Mountains in the N. Administrative centre: Stirling. Pop: 86 212 (2001). Area: 2173 sq km (839 sq miles)

Stirling[2] ('stɜ:rlɪŋ) *n* Sir **James** 1926–92, British architect; buildings include the Neue Staatsgalerie in Stuttgart (1977–84)

Stirlingshire ('stɜ:lɪŋʃɪə, -ʃə) *n* a former county of central Scotland: mostly became part of Central Region in 1975: now covered by the council areas of Stirling, Falkirk, and East Dunbartonshire

stirps (stɜ:ps) *n, pl* **stirpes** ('stɜ:pi:z) **1** *genealogy* a line of descendants from an ancestor **2** *bot* a race or variety [C17 from L: root, family origin]

stirrer ('stɜ:rə) *n* **1** a person or thing that stirs **2** *inf* a person who deliberately causes trouble **3** *Austral & NZ inf* a political activist or agitator

stirring ('stɜ:rɪŋ) *adj* **1** exciting the emotions; stimulating **2** active, lively, or busy > **'stirringly** *adv*

stirrup ('stɪrəp) *n* **1** Also called: **stirrup iron** either of two metal loops on a riding saddle, with a flat footpiece through which a rider puts his foot for support. They are attached to the saddle by **stirrup leathers** **2** a U-shaped support or clamp **3** *naut* one of a set of ropes fastened to a yard at one end and having a thimble at the other through which a footrope is reeved for support [OE *stigrāp*, from *stīg* step + *rāp* rope]

stirrup cup *n* a cup containing an alcoholic drink offered to a horseman ready to ride away

stirrup pump *n* a hand-operated pump, the base of the cylinder of which is placed in a bucket of water: used in fighting fires

stir up *vb* (*tr, adv*) to set in motion; instigate: *he stirred up trouble*

stitch (stɪtʃ) *n* **1** a link made by drawing a thread through material by means of a needle **2** a loop of yarn formed around an implement used in knitting, crocheting, etc **3** a particular method of stitching or shape of stitch **4** a sharp spasmodic pain in the side resulting from running or exercising **5** (*usually used with a negative*) *inf* the least fragment of clothing: *he wasn't wearing a stitch* **6** *agriculture* the ridge between two furrows **7** **drop a stitch** to allow a loop of wool to fall off a knitting needle accidentally while knitting **8** **in stitches** *inf* laughing uncontrollably ▷ *vb* **9** (*tr*) to sew, fasten, etc, with stitches **10** (*intr*) to be engaged in sewing **11** (*tr*) to bind together (the leaves of a book, pamphlet, etc) with wire staples or thread ▷ *n, vb* **12** an informal word for **suture** (senses 1b, 5) [OE *stice* sting] > **'stitcher** *n*

▷ www.petitpoint.com/References/stitchTypes.htm

stitch up *vb* (*tr, adv*) **1** to join or mend by means of stitches or sutures **2** *sl* **2a** to incriminate (someone) on a false charge by manufacturing evidence **2b** to betray, cheat, or defraud **3** *sl* to prearrange (something) in a clandestine manner ▷ *n* **stitch-up** **4** *sl* a matter that has been prearranged clandestinely

stitchwort ('stɪtʃ,wɜ:t) *n* any of several low-growing N temperate herbaceous plants having small white star-shaped flowers

stiver ('staɪvə) *n* **1** a former Dutch coin worth one twentieth of a guilder **2** a small amount, esp of money [C16 from Du. *stuiver*]

stoa ('stəʊə) *n, pl* **stoae** ('stəʊi:) *or* **stoas** a covered walk that has a colonnade on one or both sides, esp as in ancient Greece [C17 from Gk]

stoat (stəʊt) *n* a small Eurasian mammal, closely related to the weasels, having a brown coat and a black-tipped tail: in the northern parts of its range it has a white winter coat and is then known as an ermine [C15 from ?]

stochastic (stɒ'kæstɪk) *adj* **1** *statistics* **1a** (of a random variable) having a probability distribution, usually with finite variance **1b** (of a process) involving a random variable the successive values of which are not independent **1c** (of a matrix) square with non-negative elements that add to unity in each row **2** *rare* involving conjecture [C17 from Gk *stokhastikos* capable of guessing, from *stokhazesthai* to aim at, conjecture, from *stokhos* a target]

stock (stɒk) *n* **1a** (*sometimes pl*) the total goods or raw material kept on the premises of a shop or business **1b** (*as modifier*): *a stock book* **2** a supply of something stored for future use **3** *finance* **3a** the capital raised by a company through the issue and subscription of shares entitling their holders to dividends, partial ownership, and usually voting rights **3b** the proportion of such capital held by an individual shareholder **3c** the shares of a specified company or industry **4** standing or status **5a** farm animals, such as cattle and sheep, bred and kept for their meat, skins, etc **5b** (*as modifier*): *stock farming* **6** the trunk or main stem of a tree or other plant **7** *horticulture* **7a** a rooted plant into which a scion is inserted during grafting **7b** a plant or stem from which cuttings are taken **8** the original type from which a particular race, family, group, etc, is derived **9** a race, breed, or variety of animals or plants **10** (*often pl*) a small pen in which a single animal can be confined **11** a line of descent **12** any of the major subdivisions of the human species; race or ethnic group **13** the part of a rifle, etc, into which the barrel is set: held by the firer against the shoulder **14** the handle of something, such as a whip or fishing rod **15** the main body of a tool, such as the block of a plane **16** short for **diestock, gunstock,** or **rolling stock** **17** (formerly) the part of a plough to which the irons and handles were attached **18** the main upright part of a supporting structure **19** a liquid or broth in which meat, fish, bones, or vegetables have been simmered for a long time **20** film material before exposure and processing **21** Also called: **gillyflower** any of several plants such as **evening** or **night-scented stock**, of the Mediterranean region: cultivated for their brightly coloured flowers **22** **Virginian stock** a similar and related North American plant **23** a long usually white neckcloth wrapped around the neck, worn in the 18th century and as part of modern riding dress **24a** the repertoire of plays available to a repertory company **24b** (*as modifier*): *a stock play* **25** a log or block of wood **26** See **laughing stock** **27** **in stock** **27a** stored on the premises or available for sale or use **27b** supplied with goods of a specified kind **28** **out of stock** **28a** not immediately available for sale or use **28b** not having goods of a specified kind immediately available **29** **take stock** **29a** to make an inventory **29b** to make a general appraisal, esp of prospects, resources, etc **30** **take stock in** to attach importance to ▷ *adj* **31** staple; standard: *stock sizes in clothes* **32** (*prenominal*) being a cliché; hackneyed: *a stock phrase* ▷ *vb* **33** (*tr*) to keep (goods) for sale **34** (*intr; usually foll by up or up on*) to obtain a store of (something) for future use or sale: *to stock up on beer* **35** (*tr*) to supply with live animals, fish, etc: *to stock a farm* **36** (*intr*) (of a plant) to put forth new shoots **37** (*tr*) *obs* to punish by putting in the stocks ▷ See also **stocks** [OE *stocc* trunk (of a tree), stem, stick (the various senses developed from these meanings, as trunk of a tree, hence line of descent; structures made of timber; a store of timber or other goods for future use, hence an aggregate of goods, animals, etc)] > **'stocker** *n*

stockade (stɒ'keɪd) *n* **1** an enclosure or barrier of stakes and timbers ▷ *vb* **stockades, stockading, stockaded** **2** (*tr*) to surround with a stockade [C17 from Sp. *estacada*, from *estaca* a stake, of Gmc origin]

stockbreeder ('stɒk,bri:də) *n* a person who breeds or rears livestock as an occupation > **'stock,breeding** *n*

stockbroker ('stɒk,brəʊkə) *n* a person who buys and sells securities on a commission basis for customers > **'stock,brokerage** *or* **'stock,broking** *n*

stockbroker belt *n Brit inf* the area outside a city, esp London, in which rich commuters live

stock car *n* **1** a car, usually a production saloon, strengthened and modified for a form of racing in which the cars often collide **2** *US & Canad* a railway wagon for carrying livestock

stock dove *n* a European dove, smaller than the wood pigeon and having a grey plumage

stock exchange *n* **1a** a highly organized market facilitating the purchase and sale of securities and operated by professional stockbrokers and market makers according to fixed rules **1b** a place where securities are regularly traded **1c** (*as modifier*): *a stock-exchange operator; stock-exchange prices* **2** the prices or trading activity of a stock exchange: *the stock exchange fell heavily today* ▷ Also called: **stock market**

▷ www.londonstockexchange.com
▷ www.tse.or.jp/english/index.shtml
▷ www.euronext.com
▷ www.nyse.com
▷ www.asx.com.au
▷ www.hsi.com
▷ www.nzx.com
▷ www.tse.com
▷ www.jse.co.za

stockfish ('stɒk,fɪʃ) *n, pl* **stockfish** *or* **stockfishes** fish cured by splitting and drying in the air

Stockhausen (*German* 'ʃtɔkhauzən) *n* **Karlheinz** (karl'haints) born 1928, German composer, whose avant-garde music exploits advanced serialization, electronic sounds, group improvization, and vocal and instrumental timbres and techniques. Works include *Gruppen* (1959) for three orchestras, *Stimmung* (1968) for six vocalists, and the operas *Donnerstag* (1980) and *Freitag* (1996)

stockholder ('stɒk,həʊldə) *n* **1** an owner of corporate capital stock **2** *Austral* a person who keeps livestock > **'stock,holding** *n*

Stockholm ('stɒkhəʊm; *Swedish* 'stɔkhɔlm) *n* the capital of Sweden, a port in the E central part at the outflow of Lake Mälar into the Baltic: situated partly on the mainland and partly on islands; traditionally founded about 1250; university (1877). Pop: 743 703 (2000 est)

▷ www.sverigeturism.se/smorgasbord/index.html

stockhorse ('stɒk,hɔ:s) *n Austral* a stockman's horse

stockinet (,stɒkɪ'nɛt) *n* a machine-knitted elastic fabric used, esp formerly, for stockings, underwear, etc [C19 ?from earlier *stocking-net*]

stocking ('stɒkɪŋ) *n* **1** one of a pair of close-fitting garments made of knitted yarn to cover the foot and part or all of the leg **2** something resembling this in position, function, etc **3** **in (one's) stocking** *or* **stockinged feet** wearing stockings or socks but no shoes [C16 from dialect *stock* stocking + -ING[1]] > **'stockinged** *adj*

stocking cap *n* a conical knitted cap, often with a tassel

stocking filler *n Brit* a present of a size suitable for inclusion in a Christmas stocking

stock in trade *n* **1** goods in stock necessary for carrying on a business **2** anything constantly used by someone as a part of his or her profession, occupation, or trade: *friendliness is the salesman's stock in trade*

stockist ('stɒkɪst) *n commerce, Brit* a dealer who undertakes to maintain stocks of a specified product at or above a certain minimum in return for favourable buying terms granted by the manufacturer of the product

stockjobber ('stɒk,dʒɒbə) *n* **1** *Brit* (formerly) a wholesale dealer on a stock exchange who sold securities to brokers without transacting directly with the public. See **market maker** **2** *US, disparaging* a stockbroker, esp one dealing in worthless securities > **'stock,jobbery** *or* **'stock,jobbing** *n*

stockman ('stɒkmən, -,mæn) *n, pl* **stockmen** **1a** a man engaged in the rearing or care of farm livestock, esp cattle **1b** an owner of cattle or other livestock **2** *US & Canad* a man employed in a warehouse or stockroom

stock market *n* another name for **stock exchange**

stockpile ('stɒk,paɪl) *vb* **stockpiles, stockpiling, stockpiled** **1** to acquire and store a large quantity of (something) ▷ *n* **2** a large store or supply accumulated for future use > **'stock,piler** *n*

Stockport ('stɒk,pɔ:t) *n* **1** a town in NW England, in Stockport unitary authority, Greater Manchester: an early textile centre and scene of several labour disturbances in the early 19th century; engineering, electronics. Pop: 132 813 (1991) **2** a unitary authority in NW England, in Greater Manchester. Pop: 84 544 (2001). Area: 126 sq km (49 sq miles)

stockpot ('stɒk,pɒt) *n chiefly Brit* a pot in which stock for soup, etc, is made or kept

stockroom ('stɒk,ru:m, -,rʊm) *n* a room in which a stock of goods is kept, as in a shop or factory

stock route *n Austral & NZ* a route designated for droving sheep or cattle

stocks (stɒks) *pl n* **1** *history* an instrument of punishment consisting of a heavy wooden frame with holes in which the feet, hands, or head of an offender were locked **2** a frame used to support a boat while under construction **3** *naut* a vertical post or shaft at the forward edge of a rudder, extended upwards for attachment to the steering controls **4** **on the stocks** in preparation or under construction

stock-still *adv* absolutely still; motionless

stocktaking ('stɒk,teɪkɪŋ) *n* **1** the examination, counting, and valuing of goods on hand in a shop or business **2** a reassessment of one's current situation, progress, prospects, etc

Stockton[1] ('stɒktən) *n* an inland port in central California, on the San Joaquin River: seat of the University of the Pacific (1851). Pop: 243 771 (2000)

Stockton[2] ('stɒktən) *n* **1st Earl of** title of (Maurice Harold) **Macmillan**

Ss

Stockton-on-Tees *n* 1 a former port and industrial centre in NE England, in Stockton-on-Tees unitary authority, Co Durham, on the River Tees: famous for the **Stockton-Darlington Railway** (1825), the first passenger-carrying railway in the world; now mainly residential. Pop: 83 576 (1991) 2 a unitary authority in NE England, in Co Durham and North Yorkshire: created in 1996 from part of Cleveland county. Pop: 178 405 (2001). Area: 195 sq km (75 sq miles)

stock watering *n business* the creation of more new shares in a company than is justified by its assets

stock whip *n* a whip with a long lash and a short handle, used to herd cattle, etc

stocky ('stɒkɪ) *adj* **stockier, stockiest** (usually of a person) thickset; sturdy > '**stockily** *adv* > '**stockiness** *n*

stockyard ('stɒk,jɑːd) *n* a large yard with pens or covered buildings where farm animals are assembled, sold, etc

stodge (stɒdʒ) *inf* ▷ *n* 1 heavy filling starchy food 2 a dull person or subject ▷ *vb* **stodges, stodging, stodged** 3 to stuff (oneself or another) with food [c17 ? blend of STUFF + *podge*, from *podgy* fat]

stodgy ('stɒdʒɪ) *adj* **stodgier, stodgiest** 1 (of food) heavy or uninteresting 2 excessively formal and conventional [c19 from STODGE] > '**stodgily** *adv* > '**stodginess** *n*

stoep (stuːp) *n S African* a veranda [from Afrik., from Du.]

stoic ('stəʊɪk) *n* 1 a person who maintains stoical qualities ▷ *adj* 2 a variant of **stoical**

Stoic ('stəʊɪk) *n* 1 a member of the ancient Greek school of philosophy founded by Zeno, holding that virtue and happiness can be attained only by submission to destiny and the natural law, and that pleasure and pain should be treated with indifference ▷ *adj* 2 of or relating to the doctrines of the Stoics [c16 via L from Gk *stōikos*, from *stoa*, the porch in Athens where Zeno taught]

stoical ('stəʊɪkᵊl) *adj* characterized by impassivity or resignation > '**stoically** *adv*

stoichiometry *or* **stoicheiometry** (,stɔɪkɪ'ɒmɪtrɪ) *n* the branch of chemistry concerned with the proportions in which elements are combined in compounds and the quantitative relationships between reactants and products in chemical reactions [c19 from Gk *stoikheion* element + -METRY] > ,**stoichio'metric** *or* ,**stoicheio'metric** *adj*

stoicism ('stəʊɪ,sɪzəm) *n* 1 indifference to pleasure and pain 2 (*cap.*) the philosophy of the Stoics

stoke (stəʊk) *vb* **stokes, stoking, stoked** 1 to feed, stir, and tend (a fire, furnace, etc) 2 (*tr*) to tend the furnace of; act as a stoker for [c17 back formation from STOKER]

stoked (stəʊkt) *adj NZ inf* very pleased; elated: *really stoked to have got the job*

stokehold ('stəʊk,həʊld) *n naut* 1 a coal bunker for a ship's furnace 2 the hold for a ship's boilers; fire room

stokehole ('stəʊk,həʊl) *n* 1 another word for **stokehold** 2 a hole in a furnace through which it is stoked

Stoke-on-Trent *n* 1 a city in central England, in Stoke-on-Trent unitary authority, Staffordshire on the River Trent: a centre of the pottery industry; university (1992). Pop: 266 543 (1991) 2 a unitary authority in central England, in N Staffordshire. Pop: 240 643 (2001). Area: 93 sq km (36 sq miles)

stoker ('stəʊkə) *n* a person employed to tend a furnace, as on a steamship [c17 from Du., from *stoken* to stoke]

Stoker ('stəʊkə) *n* **Bram,** original name *Abraham Stoker*. 1847–1912, Irish novelist, author of *Dracula* (1897)

stoke up *vb* (*adv*) 1 to feed and tend (a fire, etc) with fuel 2 (*intr*) to fill oneself with food

Stokowski (stə'kɒfskɪ) *n* **Leopold** 1887–1977, US conductor, born in Britain. He did much to popularize classical music with orchestral transcriptions and film appearances, esp in *Fantasia* (1940)

stokvel ('stɒk,fɛl) *n S African* a savings pool or syndicate, usually among Black people, in which funds are combined for mutual support or entertainment [c20 from ?]

STOL (stɒl) *n* 1 a system in which an aircraft can take off and land in a short distance 2 an aircraft using this system ▷ Cf **VTOL** [c20 *s(hort) t(ake)o(ff and) l(anding)*]

stole¹ (stəʊl) *vb* the past tense of **steal**

stole² (stəʊl) *n* 1 a long scarf or shawl, worn by women 2 a long narrow scarf worn by various officiating clergymen [OE *stole*, from L *stola*, from Gk *stolē* clothing]

stolen ('stəʊlən) *vb* the past participle of **steal**

stolen generation *n Austral* Aboriginal children removed from their families and placed in institutions or fostered by White families

stolid ('stɒlɪd) *adj* showing little or no emotion or interest [c17 from L *stolidus* dull] > **stolidity** (stɒ'lɪdɪtɪ) *or* '**stolidness** *n* > '**stolidly** *adv*

stolon ('stəʊlən) *n* 1 a long horizontal stem as of the currents, that grows along the surface of the soil and propagates by producing roots and shoots at the nodes or tip 2 a branching structure in lower animals, esp the anchoring rootlike part of colonial organisms [c17 from L *stolō* shoot] > **stoloniferous** (,stəʊlə'nɪfərəs) *adj*

Stolypin (,stʌlɪ'pjɪn) *n* **Petr Arkadievich** 1863–1911, Russian conservative statesman: prime minister (1906–11) He instituted agrarian reforms but was ruthless in suppressing rebellion: assassinated

stoma ('stəʊmə) *n, pl* **stomata** 1 *bot* an epidermal pore in plant leaves, that controls the passage of gases into and out of a plant 2 *zool, anat* a mouth or mouthlike part 3 *surgery* an artificial opening made in a tubular organ, esp the colon or ileum. See **colostomy, ileostomy** [c17 via NL from Gk: mouth]

stomach ('stʌmək) *n* 1 (in vertebrates) the enlarged muscular saclike part of the alimentary canal in which food is stored until it has been partially digested. Related adj: **gastric** 2 the corresponding organ in invertebrates 3 the abdominal region 4 desire, appetite, or inclination: *I have no stomach for arguments* ▷ *vb* (*tr; used mainly in negative constructions*) 5 to tolerate; bear: *I can't stomach his bragging* 6 to eat or digest: *he cannot stomach oysters* [c14 from OF *stomaque*, from L *stomachus*, from Gk *stomakhos*, from *stoma* mouth]

stomachache ('stʌmək,eɪk) *n* pain in the stomach, as from acute indigestion. Also called: **stomach upset, upset stomach**

stomacher ('stʌməkə) *n* a decorative V-shaped panel of stiff material worn over the chest and stomach by men and women in the 16th century, later only by women

stomachic (stə'mækɪk) *adj also* **stomachical** 1 stimulating gastric activity 2 of or relating to the stomach ▷ *n* 3 a stomachic medicine

stomach pump *n med* a suction device or siphon for removing stomach contents by a tube inserted through the mouth

stomata ('stəʊmətə, 'stɒm-, stəʊ'mɑːtə) *n* the plural of **stoma**

stomatitis (,stəʊmə'taɪtɪs, ,stɒm-) *n* inflammation of the mouth > **stomatitic** (,stəʊmə'tɪtɪk, ,stɒm-) *adj*

stomato- *or before a vowel* **stomat-** *combining form* indicating the mouth or a mouthlike part: *stomatology* [from Gk *stoma, stomat-*]

stomatology (,stəʊmə'tɒlədʒɪ) *n* the branch of medicine concerned with the mouth > **stomatological** (,stəʊmətə'lɒdʒɪkᵊl) *adj*

-stome *n combining form* indicating a mouth or opening resembling a mouth: *peristome* [from Gk *stoma* mouth, & *stomion* little mouth]

-stomous *adj combining form* having a specified type of mouth

stomp (stɒmp) *vb* 1 (*intr*) to tread or stamp heavily ▷ *n* 2 a rhythmic stamping jazz dance [var. of STAMP] > '**stomper** *n*

stompie ('stɒmpɪ) *n S African sl* 1 a cigarette butt 2 a

short man [Afrik. *stomp* stamp]
-stomy *n combining form* indicating a surgical operation performed to make an artificial opening into or for a specified part: *cytostomy* [from Gk *-stomia*, from *stoma* mouth]
stone (stəʊn) *n* **1** the hard compact nonmetallic material of which rocks are made **2** a small lump of rock; pebble **3** short for **gemstone** **4a** a piece of rock designed or shaped for some particular purpose **4b** (*in combination*): *gravestone; millstone* **5a** something that resembles a stone **5b** (*in combination*): *hailstone* **6** the woody central part of such fruits as the peach and plum, that contains the seed; endocarp **7** any similar hard part of a fruit, such as the stony seed of a date **8** (*pl* **stone**) *Brit* a unit of weight, used esp to express human body weight, equal to 14 pounds or 6.350 kilograms **9** Also called: **granite** the rounded heavy mass of granite or iron used in the game of curling **10** *pathol* a nontechnical name for **calculus** **11** *printing* a table with a very flat iron or stone surface upon which pages are composed **12** (*modifier*) relating to or made of stone: *a stone house* **13** (*modifier*) made of stoneware: *a stone jar* **14** **cast a stone (at)** cast aspersions (upon) **15** **heart of stone** an obdurate or unemotional nature **16** **leave no stone unturned** to do everything possible to achieve an end ▷ *vb* **stones, stoning, stoned** (*tr*) **17** to throw stones at, esp to kill **18** to remove the stones from **19** to furnish or provide with stones [OE *stān*] > **'stoner** *n*
stone- *prefix* very, completely: *stone-blind, stone-cold* [from STONE in sense of "like a stone"]
Stone (stəʊn) *n* **Oliver** born 1946, US film director and screenwriter: his films include *Platoon* (1986), *Born on the Fourth of July* (1989), *JFK* (1991), *Nixon* (1995), and *Any Given Sunday* (1999)
Stone Age *n* **1** a period in human culture identified by the use of stone implements ▷ *modifier* **Stone-Age** **2** (*sometimes not caps*) of or relating to this period
stone-blind *adj* completely blind ▷ Cf **sand-blind**
stonechat ('stəʊn,tʃæt) *n* an Old World songbird having a black plumage with a reddish-brown breast [c18 from its cry, which sounds like clattering pebbles]
stone-cold *adj* **1** completely cold **2** **stone-cold sober** completely sober
stonecrop ('stəʊn,krɒp) *n* any of various N temperate plants having fleshy leaves and typically red, yellow, or white flowers
stone curlew *n* any of several brownish shore birds having a large head and eyes. Also called: **thick-knee**
stonecutter ('stəʊn,kʌtə) *n* **1** a person who is skilled in cutting and carving stone **2** a machine used to dress stone > **'stone,cutting** *n*
stoned (stəʊnd) *adj sl* under the influence of drugs or alcohol
stone-deaf *adj* completely deaf
stonefish ('stəʊn,fɪʃ) *n, pl* **stonefish** *or* **stonefishes** a venomous tropical marine fish that resembles a piece of rock on the seabed
stonefly ('stəʊn,flaɪ) *n, pl* **stoneflies** any of various insects, in which the larvae are aquatic, living beneath stones
stone fruit *n* the nontechnical name for **drupe**
Stonehenge (,stəʊn'hɛndʒ) *n* a prehistoric ruin in S England, in Wiltshire on Salisbury Plain: constructed over the period of roughly 3000–1600 BC; one of the most important megalithic monuments in Europe; believed to have had religious and astronomical purposes
stonemason ('stəʊn,meɪsᵊn) *n* a person who is skilled in preparing stone for building > **'stone,masonry** *n*
stone pine *n* a pine tree with a short bole and radiating branches forming an umbrella shape
Stones (stəʊnz) *pl n* **the** See **Rolling Stones**
Stone sheep *or* **Stone's sheep** *n* a wild sheep found in the Yukon and the northern Rocky Mountains [c19 after the US naturalist Andrew Jackson Stone, who first discovered the breed in 1896]
stone's throw *n* a short distance
stonewall (,stəʊn'wɔːl) *vb* **1** (*intr*) *cricket* (of a batsman) to play defensively **2** to obstruct (an investigation, etc), esp by giving uncommunicative answers to questioning **3** to obstruct or hinder (parliamentary business) > **,stone'waller** *n*
stoneware ('stəʊn,wɛə) *n* **1** a hard opaque pottery, fired at a very high temperature ▷ *adj* **2** made of stoneware
stonewashed ('stəʊn,wɒʃt) *adj* (of clothes or fabric) given a worn faded look by being subjected to the abrasive action of many small pieces of pumice
stonework ('stəʊn,wɜːk) *n* **1** any structure or part of a building made of stone **2** the process of dressing or setting stones > **'stone,worker** *n*
Stoney ('stəʊnɪ) *n* a member of a Native Canadian people of Alberta [from Siouan]
stonkered ('stɒŋkəd) *adj sl* completely exhausted or beaten [c20 from *stonker* to beat, from ?]
stony *or* **stoney** ('stəʊnɪ) *adj* **stonier, stoniest** **1** of or resembling stone **2** abounding in stone or stones **3** unfeeling or obdurate **4** short for **stony-broke** > **'stonily** *adv* > **'stoniness** *n*
stony-broke *adj Brit sl* completely without money; penniless
stony-hearted *adj* unfeeling; hardhearted > **,stony-'heartedness** *n*
stood (stʊd) *vb* the past tense and past participle of **stand**
stooge (stuːdʒ) *n* **1** an actor who feeds lines to a comedian or acts as his or her butt **2** *sl* someone who is taken advantage of by another ▷ *vb* **stooges, stooging, stooged** **3** (*intr*) *sl* to act as a stooge [c20 from ?]
stook (stuːk) *n* **1** a number of sheaves set upright in a field to dry with their heads together ▷ *vb* **2** (*tr*) to set up (sheaves) in stooks [c15 var. of *stouk*, of Gmc origin] > **'stooker** *n*
stool (stuːl) *n* **1** a backless seat or footrest consisting of a small flat piece of wood, etc, resting on three or four legs, a pedestal, etc **2** a rootstock or base of a plant from which shoots, etc, are produced **3** a cluster of shoots growing from such a base **4** *chiefly US* a decoy used in hunting **5** waste matter evacuated from the bowels **6** a lavatory seat **7** (in W Africa, esp Ghana) a chief's throne **8** **fall between two stools** **8a** to fail through vacillation between two alternatives **8b** to be in an unsatisfactory situation through not belonging to either of two categories or groups ▷ *vb* (*intr*) **9** (of a plant) to send up shoots from the base of the stem, rootstock, etc **10** to lure wildfowl with a decoy [OE *stōl*]
stool ball *n* a game resembling cricket, still played by girls and women in Sussex, England
stool pigeon *n* **1** an informer for the police **2** *sl* a person acting as a decoy [c19 from use of pigeon fixed to a stool as a decoy]
stoop[1] (stuːp) *vb* (*mainly intr*) **1** (*also tr*) to bend (the body) forward and downward **2** to carry oneself with head and shoulders habitually bent forward **3** (often foll by *to*) to abase or degrade oneself **4** (often foll by *to*) to condescend; deign **5** (of a bird of prey) to swoop down ▷ *n* **6** the act, position, or characteristic of stooping **7** a lowering from a position of dignity or superiority **8** a downward swoop, esp of a bird of prey [OE *stūpan*] > **'stooping** *adj*
stoop[2] (stuːp) *n US* an open porch or small platform with steps leading up to it at the entrance to a building [c18 from Du. *stoep*, of Gmc origin]
stop (stɒp) *vb* **stops, stopping, stopped** **1** to cease from doing or being (something); discontinue **2** to cause (something moving) to halt or (of something moving) to come to a halt **3** (*tr*) to prevent the continuance or completion of **4** (*tr; often foll by from*) to prevent or

restrain: *to stop George from fighting* **5** (*tr*) to keep back: *to stop supplies* **6** (*tr*) to intercept or hinder in transit: *to stop a letter* **7** (*tr*; often foll by *up*) to block or plug, esp so as to close: *to stop up a pipe* **8** (*tr*; often foll by *up*) to fill a hole or opening in: *to stop up a wall* **9** (*tr*) to staunch or stem: *to stop a wound* **10** (*tr*) to instruct a bank not to honour (a cheque) **11** (*tr*) to deduct (money) from pay **12** (*tr*) *Brit* to provide with punctuation **13** (*tr*) *boxing* to beat (an opponent) by a knockout **14** (*tr*) *inf* to receive (a blow, hit, etc) **15** (*intr*) to stay or rest: *we stopped at the Robinsons'* **16** (*tr*) *rare* to defeat, beat, or kill **17** (*tr*) *music* **17a** to alter the vibrating length of (a string on a violin, guitar, etc) by pressing down on it at some point with the finger **17b** to alter the vibrating length of an air column in a wind instrument by closing (a finger hole, etc) **17c** to produce (a note) in this manner **18** *bridge* to have a protecting card or winner in (a suit in which one's opponents are strong) **19 stop at nothing** to be prepared to do anything; be unscrupulous or ruthless ▷ *n* **20** an arrest of movement or progress **21** the act of stopping or the state of being stopped **22** a place where something halts or pauses: *a bus stop* **23** a stay in or as if in the course of a journey **24** the act or an instance of blocking or obstructing **25** a plug or stopper **26** a block, screw, etc, that prevents, limits, or terminates the motion of a mechanism or moving part **27** *Brit* a punctuation mark, esp a full stop **28** *music* **28a** the act of stopping the string, finger hole, etc, of an instrument **28b** a set of organ pipes or harpsichord strings that may be allowed to sound as a group by muffling or silencing all other such sets **28c** a knob, lever, or handle on an organ, etc, that is operated to allow sets of pipes to sound **28d** an analogous device on a harpsichord or other instrument with variable registers, such as an electronic instrument **29 pull out all the stops 29a** to play at full volume **29b** to spare no effort **30** Also called: **stop consonant** *phonetics* any of a class of consonants articulated by first making a complete closure at some point of the vocal tract and then releasing it abruptly with audible plosion **31** Also called: **f-stop** *photog* **31a** a setting of the aperture of a camera lens, calibrated to the corresponding f-number **31b** another name for **diaphragm** (sense 4) **32** Also called: **stopper** *bridge* a protecting card or winner in a suit in which one's opponents are strong ▷ See also **stop off, stop out, stopover** [C14 from OE *stoppian* (unattested), as in *forstoppian* to plug the ear, ult. from LL *stuppāre* to stop with tow, from L *stuppa* tow, from Gk *stuppē*] > **'stoppable** *adj*

stopbank ('stɒpbæŋk) *n* NZ an embankment to prevent flooding

stop bath *n* a weakly acidic solution used to stop the action of a developer on a film, plate, or paper before the material is immersed in fixer

stopcock ('stɒpˌkɒk) *n* a valve used to control or stop the flow of a fluid in a pipe

stope (stəʊp) *n* **1** a steplike excavation made in a mine to extract ore ▷ *vb* **stopes, stoping, stoped 2** to mine (ore, etc) in stopes [C18 prob. from Low G *stope*]

Stopes (stəʊps) *n* **Marie Carmichael** 1880–1958, English pioneer of birth control, who established the first birth-control clinic in Britain (1921)

stopgap ('stɒpˌgæp) *n* **a** a temporary substitute **b** (*as modifier*): *a stopgap programme*

stop-go *adj Brit* (of economic policy) characterized by deliberate alternate expansion and contraction of aggregate demand in an effort to curb inflation and eliminate balance-of-payments deficits, and yet maintain full employment

stoplight ('stɒpˌlaɪt) *n* **1** a red light on a traffic signal indicating that vehicles or pedestrians coming towards it should stop **2** another word for **brake light**

stop-loss *adj business* of or relating to an order to a broker in a commodity or security market to close an open position at a specified price in order to limit any loss

stop-motion *n* **a** a technique used in animation and photography in which a subject is filmed then adjusted a frame at a time **b** (*as modifier*): *stop-motion animation*

stop off *vb* also **stop in,** (esp US) **stop by 1** (*intr, adv*; often foll by *at*) to halt and call somewhere, as on a visit or errand, esp en route to another place ▷ *n* **stopoff 2a** a break in a journey **2b** (*as modifier*): *stopoff point*

stop out *vb* (*adv*) **1** (*tr*) to cover (part of the area) of a piece of cloth, printing plate, etc, to prevent it from being dyed, etched, etc **2** (*intr*) to remain out of a house, esp overnight

stopover ('stɒpˌəʊvə) *n* **1** a stopping place on a journey ▷ *vb* **stop over 2** (*intr, adv*) to make a stopover

stoppage ('stɒpɪdʒ) *n* **1** the act of stopping or the state of being stopped **2** something that stops or blocks **3** a deduction of money, as from pay **4** an organized cessation of work, as during a strike

stoppage time *n soccer, rugby, etc* another name for **injury time**

Stoppard ('stɒpɑːd) *n* Sir **Tom,** original name *Thomas Strausser.* born 1937, British playwright, born in Czechoslovakia: his works include *Rosencrantz and Guildenstern are Dead* (1967), *Travesties* (1974), *Hapgood* (1988), *The Invention of Love* (1997), and the trilogy *The Coast of Utopia* (2002)

stopped (stɒpt) *adj* (of a pipe, esp an organ pipe) closed at one end and thus sounding an octave lower than an open pipe of the same length

stopper ('stɒpə) *n* **1** Also called: **stopple** a plug or bung for closing a bottle, pipe, duct, etc **2** a person or thing that stops or puts an end to something **3** *bridge* another name for **stop** (sense 32) ▷ *vb* **4** (*tr*) Also: **stopple** to close or fit with a stopper

stopping ('stɒpɪŋ) *n* **1** *Brit inf* a dental filling ▷ *adj* **2** *chiefly Brit* making many stops in a journey: *a stopping train*

stop press *n Brit* **1** news items inserted into a newspaper after the printing has been started **2** the space regularly left blank for this

stopwatch ('stɒpˌwɒtʃ) *n* a type of watch used for timing sporting events, etc, accurately, having a device for stopping the hands instantly

storage ('stɔːrɪdʒ) *n* **1** the act of storing or the state of being stored **2** space or an area reserved for storing **3** a charge made for storing **4** *computing* **4a** the act or process of storing information in a computer memory or on a disk, etc **4b** (*as modifier*): *storage capacity*

storage battery *n* another name (esp US) for **accumulator** (sense 1)

storage capacity *n* the maximum number of bits, bytes, words, etc, that can be held in a memory system such as that of a computer or of the brain

storage device *n* a piece of computer equipment, such as a magnetic tape, disk, drum, etc, in or on which information can be stored

storage heater *n* an electric device capable of accumulating and radiating heat generated by off-peak electricity

storax ('stɔːræks) *n* **1** any of numerous trees or shrubs of tropical and subtropical regions, having drooping showy white flowers **2** a vanilla-scented solid resin obtained from one of these trees, formerly used as incense and in perfumery and medicine **3** a liquid aromatic balsam obtained from liquidambar trees and used in perfumery and medicine [C14 via LL from Gk *sturax*]

store (stɔː) *vb* **stores, storing, stored 1** (*tr*) to keep, set aside, or accumulate for future use **2** (*tr*) to place in a warehouse, depository, etc, for safekeeping **3** (*tr*) to supply, provide, or stock **4** (*intr*) to be put into storage **5** *computing* to enter or retain (information) in a storage device ▷ *n* **6a** an establishment for the retail sale of goods and services **6b** (*in combination*): *storefront* **7** a large supply or stock kept for future use **8** short for **department store** **9a** a storage place such as a warehouse or depository **9b** (*in combination*): *storeman* **10** the state of being stored (esp in **in store**) **11** a large amount or quantity **12** *computers, chiefly Brit* another name for **memory** (sense 7) **13** **in store** forthcoming or imminent **14** **lay, put,** *or* **set store by** to value or reckon as important ▷ *adj* **15** (of cattle, sheep, etc) bought lean to be fattened up for market ▷ See also **stores** [C13 from OF *estor*, from *estorer* to restore, from L *instaurāre* to refresh] > '**storable** *adj*

Store Bælt ('sdo:rə 'bɛld) *n* the Danish name for the **Great Belt**

store card *n* another name for **charge card**

storehouse ('stɔ:ˌhaʊs) *n* a place where things are stored

storekeeper ('stɔ:ˌki:pə) *n* a manager, owner, or keeper of a store > '**storeˌkeeping** *n*

store of value *n econ* the function of money that enables goods and services to be paid for a considerable time after they have been acquired

storeroom ('stɔ:ˌru:m, -ˌrʊm) *n* **1** a room in which things are stored **2** room for storing

stores (stɔ:z) *pl n* supply or stock of something, esp essentials, for a specific purpose

storey *or esp US* **story** ('stɔ:rɪ) *n, pl* **storeys** *or* **stories** **1** a floor or level of a building **2** a set of rooms on one level [C14 from Anglo-L *historia*, picture, from L: narrative, prob. from the pictures on medieval windows]

Storey ('stɔ:rɪ) *n* **David** (**Malcolm**) born 1933, British novelist and dramatist. His best-known works include the novels *This Sporting Life* (1960) and *A Serious Man* (1998) and the plays *In Celebration* (1969), *Home* (1970), and *Stages* (1992)

storeyed *or US* **storied** ('stɔ:rɪd) *adj* **a** having a storey or storeys **b** (*in combination*): *a two-storeyed house*

storied ('stɔ:rɪd) *adj* **1** recorded in history or in a story **2** decorated with narrative scenes

stork (stɔ:k) *n* any of a family of large wading birds, chiefly of warm regions of the Old World, having very long legs and a long stout pointed bill, and typically having a white-and-black plumage [OE *storc*]

storksbill ('stɔ:ksˌbɪl) *n* a plant related to the geranium, having pink or reddish-purple flowers and fruits with a beaklike process

storm (stɔ:m) *n* **1a** a violent weather condition of strong winds, rain, hail, thunder, lightning, blowing sand, snow, etc **1b** (*as modifier*): *storm cloud* **1c** (*in combination*): *stormproof* **2** *meteorol* a wind of force 10 on the Beaufort scale, reaching speeds of 55 to 63 mph **3** a strong or violent reaction: *a storm of protest* **4** a direct assault on a stronghold **5** a heavy discharge or rain, as of bullets or missiles **6** short for **storm window** **7** **storm in a teacup** *Brit* a violent fuss or disturbance over a trivial matter **8** **take by storm** **8a** to capture or overrun by a violent assault **8b** to overwhelm and enthral ▷ *vb* **9** to attack or capture (something) suddenly and violently **10** (*intr*) to be vociferously angry **11** (*intr*) to move or rush violently or angrily **12** (*intr; with it as subject*) to rain, hail, or snow hard and be very windy, often with thunder and lightning [OE]

stormbound ('stɔ:mˌbaʊnd) *adj* detained or harassed by storms

storm centre *n* **1** the centre of a cyclonic storm, etc, where pressure is lowest **2** the centre of any disturbance or trouble

storm cloud *n* **1** a heavy dark cloud presaging rain or a storm **2** a herald of disturbance, anger, etc: *the storm clouds of war*

storm-cock *n* another name for **mistle thrush**

storm cone *n Brit* a canvas cone hoisted as a warning of (and indication of the nature of) high winds

storm door *n* an additional door outside an ordinary door, providing extra insulation against wind, cold, rain, etc

storming ('stɔ:mɪŋ) *adj inf* characterized by or displaying dynamism, speed, and energy: *a storming performance*

storm lantern *n* another name for **hurricane lamp**

Stormont ('stɔ:mənt) *n* a suburb of Belfast: site of Parliament House (1928–30), formerly the seat of the parliament of Northern Ireland (1922–72) and since 1998 of the Northern Ireland assembly, and Stormont Castle, formerly the residence of the prime minister of Northern Ireland and since 1998 the office of the province's first minister

storm trooper *n* **1** a member of the Nazi SA **2** a member of a force of shock troops

storm window *n* **1** an additional window fitted outside an ordinary window to provide insulation against wind, cold, rain, etc **2** a type of dormer window

stormy ('stɔ:mɪ) *adj* **stormier, stormiest** **1** characterized by storms **2** involving or characterized by violent disturbance or emotional outburst > '**stormily** *adv* > '**storminess** *n*

stormy petrel *n* **1** Also called: **storm petrel** any of various small petrels typically having dark plumage and paler underparts **2** a person who brings or portends trouble

Stornoway ('stɔ:nəˌweɪ) *n* a port in NW Scotland, on the E coast of Lewis in the Outer Hebrides, administrative centre of the Western Isles. Pop: 5975 (1991)

Storting *or* **Storthing** ('stɔ:tɪŋ) *n* the parliament of Norway [C19 Norwegian, from *stor* great + *thing* assembly]

story[1] ('stɔ:rɪ) *n, pl* **stories** **1** a narration of a chain of events told or written in prose or verse **2** Also called: **short story** a piece of fiction, briefer and usually less detailed than a novel **3** Also called: **story line** the plot of a book, film, etc **4** an event that could be the subject of a narrative **5** a report or statement on a matter or event **6** the event or material for such a report **7** *inf* a lie, fib, or untruth **8** **cut** (*or* **make**) **a long story short** to leave out details in a narration **9** **the same old story** *inf* the familiar or regular course of events **10** **the story goes** it is commonly said or believed ▷ *vb* **stories, storying, storied** (*tr*) **11** to decorate (a pot, wall, etc) with scenes from history or legends [C13 from Anglo-F *estorie*, from L *historia*; see HISTORY]

Ss

story[2] ('stɔ:rɪ) *n, pl* **stories** another spelling (esp US) of **storey**

storyboard ('stɔ:rɪˌbɔ:d) *n* (in films, television, etc) a series of sketches or photographs showing the sequence of shots or images planned for a film

storybook ('stɔ:rɪˌbʊk) *n* **1** a book containing stories, esp for children ▷ *adj* **2** unreal or fantastic: *a storybook world*

storyteller ('stɔ:rɪˌtɛlə) *n* **1** a person who tells stories **2** *inf* a liar > '**storyˌtelling** *n*

Stoss (*German* ʃto:s) *n* **Viet** (faɪət) ?1445–1533, German Gothic sculptor and woodcarver. His masterpiece is the high altar in the Church of St Mary, Cracow (1477–89)

stoup *or* **stoop** (stu:p) *n* **1** a small basin for holy water **2** *dialect* a bucket or cup [C14 (in the sense: bucket): from ON]

Stour (staʊə) *n* **1** Also called: **Great Stour** a river in S England, in Kent, rising in the Weald and flowing N to the North Sea: separates the Isle of Thanet from the mainland **2** any of several smaller rivers in England

Stourbridge ('staʊəˌbrɪdʒ) *n* an industrial town in W central England, in Dudley unitary authority, West Midlands. Pop: 55 624 (1991)

stoush (staʊʃ) *Austral & NZ sl* ▷ *vb* **1** (*tr*) to hit or punch ▷ *n* **2** fighting, violence, or a fight [C19 from ?]

stout (staʊt) *adj* **1** solidly built or corpulent **2** (*prenominal*) resolute or valiant: *stout fellow* **3** strong, substantial, and robust **4** **a stout heart** courage; resolution ▷ *n* **5** strong porter highly flavoured with malt [c14 from OF *estout* bold, of Gmc origin] > **'stoutly** *adv* > **'stoutness** *n*

Stout (staʊt) *n* Sir **Robert** 1844–1930, New Zealand statesman, born in Scotland: prime minister of New Zealand (1884–87)

stouthearted (ˌstaʊt'hɑːtɪd) *adj* valiant; brave > **ˌstout'heartedly** *adv* > **ˌstout'heartedness** *n*

stove[1] (stəʊv) *n* **1** another word for **cooker** (sense 1) **2** any heating apparatus, such as a kiln [OE *stofa* bathroom]

stove[2] (stəʊv) *vb* a past tense and past participle of **stave**

stove enamel *n* a type of enamel made heatproof by treatment in a stove

stovepipe ('stəʊvˌpaɪp) *n* **1** a pipe that serves as a flue to a stove **2** Also called: **stovepipe hat** a man's tall silk hat

stow (stəʊ) *vb* (*tr*) **1** (often foll by *away*) to pack or store **2** to fill by packing **3** *naut* to pack or put away (cargo, sails, etc) **4** to have enough room for **5** (*usually imperative*) *Brit sl* to cease from: *stow your noise!* [OE *stōwian* to keep, from *stōw* a place]

Stow (stəʊ) *n* **John** 1525–1605, English antiquary, noted for his *Survey of London and Westminster* (1598; 1603)

stowage ('stəʊɪdʒ) *n* **1** space, room, or a charge for stowing goods **2** the act or an instance of stowing or the state of being stowed **3** something that is stowed

stowaway ('stəʊəˌweɪ) *n* **1** a person who hides aboard a vehicle, ship, or aircraft in order to gain free passage ▷ *vb* **stow away 2** (*intr, adv*) to travel in such a way

Stowe (stəʊ) *n* **Harriet Elizabeth Beecher** 1811–96, US writer, whose bestselling novel *Uncle Tom's Cabin* (1852) contributed to the antislavery cause

STP *abbrev for:* **1** Professor of Sacred Theology [from L: *Sanctae Theologiae Professor*] **2** *trademark* scientifically treated petroleum: an oil substitute promising renewed power for an internal-combustion engine **3** standard temperature and pressure ▷ *n* **4** a synthetic hallucinogenic drug related to mescaline [sense 4 from humorous reference to the extra power resulting from scientifically treated petroleum]

Strabane (strə'bæn) *n* a district of W Northern Ireland, in Co Tyrone. Pop: 38 248 (2001). Area: 862 sq km (333 sq miles)

strabismus (strə'bɪzməs) *n* abnormal alignment of one or both eyes, characterized by a turning inwards or outwards from the nose: caused by paralysis of an eye muscle, etc. Also called: **squint** [c17 via NL from Gk *strabismos*, from *strabizein* to squint, from *strabos* cross-eyed] > **stra'bismal, stra'bismic,** *or* **stra'bismical** *adj*

Strabo ('streɪbəʊ) *n* ?63 BC–?23 AD, Greek geographer and historian, noted for his *Geographica*

Strachey ('streɪtʃɪ) *n* (**Giles**) **Lytton** 1880–1932, English biographer and critic, best known for *Eminent Victorians* (1918) and *Queen Victoria* (1921)

straddle ('strædᵊl) *vb* **straddles, straddling, straddled** **1** (*tr*) to have one leg, part, or support on each side of **2** (*tr*) *US & Canad inf* to be in favour of both sides of (something) **3** (*intr*) to stand, walk, or sit with the legs apart **4** (*tr*) to spread (the legs) apart **5** *gunnery* to fire a number of shots slightly beyond and slightly short of (a target) to determine the correct range **6** (*intr*) (in poker, of the second player after the dealer) to double the ante before looking at one's cards ▷ *n* **7** the act or position of straddling **8** a noncommittal attitude or stand **9** *business* a contract or option permitting its purchaser either to sell or buy securities or commodities within a specified period of time at specified prices **10** *athletics* a high-jumping technique in which the body is parallel with the bar and the legs straddle it at the highest point of the jump **11** (in poker) the stake put up after the ante in poker by the second player after the dealer [c16 from obs. *strad-* (OE *strode*), past stem of STRIDE] > **'straddler** *n*

Stradivari (ˌstrædɪ'vɑːrɪ) *n* **Antonio** (an'tɔːnjo) ?1644–1737, Italian violin, viola, and cello maker

Stradivarius (ˌstrædɪ'vɛərɪəs) *n* any of a number of violins manufactured by Antonio Stradivari or his family. Often shortened to (informal) **Strad**

strafe (streɪf, strɑːf) *vb* **strafes, strafing, strafed** (*tr*) **1** to machine-gun (troops, etc) from the air **2** *sl* to punish harshly ▷ *n* **3** an act or instance of strafing [c20 from G *strafen* to punish] > **'strafer** *n*

Strafford ('stræfəd) *n* **Thomas Wentworth,** Earl of. 1593–1641, English statesman. As lord deputy of Ireland (1632–39) and a chief adviser to Charles I, he was a leading proponent of the king's absolutist rule. He was impeached by Parliament and executed

straggle ('strægᵊl) *vb* **straggles, straggling, straggled** (*intr*) **1** to go, come, or spread in a rambling or irregular way **2** to linger behind or wander from a main line or part [c14 from ?] > **'straggler** *n* > **'straggly** *adj*

straight (streɪt) *adj* **1** not curved or crooked; continuing in the same direction without deviating **2** straightforward, outright, or candid: *a straight rejection* **3** even, level, or upright **4** in keeping with the facts; accurate **5** honest, respectable, or reliable **6** accurate or logical: *straight reasoning* **7** continuous; uninterrupted **8** (esp of an alcoholic drink) undiluted; neat **9** not crisp, kinked, or curly: *straight hair* **10** correctly arranged; orderly **11** (of a play, acting style, etc) straightforward or serious **12** *boxing* (of a blow) delivered with an unbent arm: *a straight left* **13** (of the cylinders of an internal-combustion engine) in line, rather than in a V-formation or in some other arrangement: *a straight eight* **14** a slang word for **heterosexual** **15** *inf* no longer owing or being owed something: *if you buy the next round we'll be straight* **16** *sl* conventional in views, customs, appearance, etc **17** *sl* not using narcotics ▷ *adv* **18** in a straight line or direct course **19** immediately; at once: *he came straight back* **20** in an even, level, or upright position **21** without cheating, lying, or unreliability: *tell it to me straight* **22** continuously; uninterruptedly **23** (often foll by *out*) frankly; candidly: *he told me straight out* **24** **go straight** *inf* to reform after having been dishonest or a criminal ▷ *n* **25** the state of being straight **26** a straight line, form, part, or position **27** *Brit* a straight part of a racetrack **28** *poker* **28a** five cards that are in sequence irrespective of suit **28b** a hand containing such a sequence **28c** (*as modifier*): *a straight flush* **29** *sl* a conventional person **30** *sl* a heterosexual person **31** *sl* a cigarette containing only tobacco, without marijuana, etc [c14 from p.p. of OE *streccan* to stretch] > **'straightly** *adv* > **'straightness** *n*

straight and narrow *n inf* the proper, honest, and moral path of behaviour

straight angle *n* an angle of 180°

straightaway *adv* (ˌstreɪtə'weɪ). *also* **straight away** **1** at once ▷ *n* ('streɪtəˌweɪ) **2** the US word for **straight** (sense 27)

straight chair *n* a straight-backed side chair

straightedge ('streɪtˌɛdʒ) *n* a stiff strip of wood or metal with one edge straight, used for ruling and testing straight lines

straighten ('streɪtᵊn) *vb* (sometimes foll by *up* or *out*) **1** to make or become straight **2** (*tr*) to make neat or tidy > **'straightener** *n*

straighten out *vb* (*adv*) **1** to make or become less complicated or confused **2** *US & Canad* to reform or become reformed

straight face *n* a serious facial expression, esp one that conceals the impulse to laugh > **'straight-'faced** *adj*

straight fight *n* a contest between two candidates only

straight flush *n* (in poker) five consecutive cards of the same suit

straightforward (ˌstreɪt'fɔːwəd) *adj* **1** (of a person) honest, frank, or simple **2** *chiefly Brit* (of a task, etc) simple; easy ▷ *adv, adj* **3** in a straight course > **ˌstraight'forwardly** *adv* > **ˌstraight'forwardness** *n*

straightjacket ('streɪtˌdʒækɪt) *n* a less common spelling of **straitjacket**

straight-laced *adj* a variant spelling of **strait-laced**

straight man *n* a subsidiary actor who acts as stooge to a comedian

straight-out *adj US inf* **1** complete; thoroughgoing **2** frank or honest

straight razor *n* another name for **cut-throat** (sense 2)

straightway ('streɪtˌweɪ) *adv arch* at once

strain[1] (streɪn) *vb* **1** to draw or be drawn taut; stretch tight **2** to exert, tax, or use (resources) to the utmost extent **3** to injure or damage or be injured or damaged by overexertion: *he strained himself* **4** to deform or be deformed as a result of a stress **5** (*intr*) to make intense or violent efforts; strive **6** to subject or be subjected to mental tension or stress **7** to pour or pass (a substance) or (of a substance) to be poured or passed through a sieve, filter, or strainer **8** (*tr*) to draw off or remove (one part of a substance or mixture from another) by or as if by filtering **9** (*tr*) to clasp tightly; hug **10** (*intr; foll by at*) to push, pull, or work with violent exertion (upon) ▷ *n* **11** the act or an instance of straining **12** the damage resulting from excessive exertion **13** an intense physical or mental effort **14** (*often pl*) *music* a theme, melody, or tune **15** a great demand on the emotions, resources, etc **16** a way of speaking; tone of voice: *don't go on in that strain* **17** tension or tiredness resulting from overwork, worry, etc; stress **18** *physics* the change in dimension of a body under load expressed as the ratio of the total deflection or change in dimension to the original unloaded dimension [C13 from OF *estreindre* to press together, from L *stringere* to bind tightly]

strain[2] (streɪn) *n* **1** the main body of descendants from one ancestor **2** a group of organisms within a species or variety, distinguished by one or more minor characteristics **3** a variety of bacterium or fungus, esp one used for a culture **4** a streak; trace **5** *arch* a kind, type, or sort [OE *strēon*]

strained (streɪnd) *adj* **1** (of an action, expression, etc) not natural or spontaneous **2** (of an atmosphere, relationship, etc) not relaxed; tense

strainer ('streɪnə) *n* **1** a sieve used for straining sauces, vegetables, tea, etc **2** a gauze or simple filter used to strain liquids

strait (streɪt) *n* **1** (*often pl*) a narrow channel of the sea linking two larger areas of sea **2** (*often pl*) a position of acute difficulty (often in **in dire** *or* **desperate straits**) **3** *arch* a narrow place or passage ▷ *adj* **4** *arch* (of spaces, etc) affording little room [C13 from OF *estreit* narrow, from L *strictus* constricted, from *stringere* to bind tightly] > '**straitly** *adv* > '**straitness** *n*

straiten ('streɪtᵊn) *vb* **1** (*tr; usually passive*) to embarrass or distress, esp financially **2** (*tr*) to limit, confine, or restrict **3** *arch* to make or become narrow

straitjacket ('streɪtˌdʒækɪt) *n* **1** Also: **straightjacket** a jacket made of strong canvas material with long sleeves for binding the arms of violent prisoners or mental patients **2** a restriction or limitation ▷ *vb* **3** (*tr*) to confine in or as if in a straitjacket

strait-laced *or* **straight-laced** *adj* prudish or puritanical

Straits Settlements (streɪts) *n* (formerly) a British crown colony of SE Asia that included Singapore, Penang, Malacca, Labuan, and some smaller islands

strake (streɪk) *n* **1a** a curved metal plate forming part of the metal rim on a wooden wheel **1b** any metal plate let into a rubber tyre **2** Also called: **streak** *naut* one of a continuous range of planks or plates forming the side of a vessel [C14 rel. to OE *streccan* to stretch]

Stralsund (*German* 'ʃtraːlzʊnt) *n* a port in NE Germany, in Mecklenburg-West Pomerania on a strait of the Baltic: one of the leading towns of the Hanseatic League. Pop: 71 620 (1991)

stramonium (strəˈməʊnɪəm) *n* **1** a preparation of the dried leaves and flowers of the thorn apple, containing hyoscyamine and formerly used as a drug to treat asthma **2** another name for **thorn apple** (sense 1) [C17 from NL, from ?]

strand[1] (strænd) *vb* **1** to leave or drive (ships, fish, etc) aground or ashore or (of ships, etc) to be left or driven ashore **2** (*tr; usually passive*) to leave helpless, as without transport, money, etc ▷ *n* **3** *chiefly poetic* a shore or beach [OE]

strand[2] (strænd) *n* **1** a set of or one of the individual fibres or threads of string, wire, etc, that form a rope, cable, etc **2** a single length of string, hair, wool, wire, etc **3** a string of pearls or beads **4** a constituent element of something ▷ *vb* **5** (*tr*) to form (a rope, cable, etc) by winding strands together [C15 from ?]

Strand (strænd) *n* **the** a street in W central London, parallel to the Thames: famous for its hotels and theatres

strange (streɪndʒ) *adj* **1** odd, unusual, or extraordinary; peculiar **2** not known, seen, or experienced before; unfamiliar **3** not easily explained **4** (usually foll by *to*) inexperienced (in) or unaccustomed (to): *strange to a task* **5** not of one's own kind, locality, etc; alien; foreign **6** shy; distant; reserved **7** **strange to say** it is unusual or surprising (that) **8** *physics* **8a** denoting a particular flavour of quark **8b** denoting or relating to a hypothetical form of matter composed of such quarks: *strange matter; a strange star* ▷ *adv* **9** *not standard* in a strange manner [C13 from OF *estrange*, from L *extrāneus* foreign; see EXTRANEOUS] > '**strangely** *adv*

strangeness ('streɪndʒnɪs) *n* **1** the state or quality of being strange **2** *physics* a property of certain elementary particles characterized by a quantum number (**strangeness number**) conserved in strong but not in weak interactions

stranger ('streɪndʒə) *n* **1** any person whom one does not know **2** a person who is new to a particular locality, from another region, town, etc **3** a guest or visitor **4** (foll by *to*) a person who is unfamiliar (with) or new (to) something: *he is no stranger to computing*

Ss

strangle ('stræŋgᵊl) *vb* **strangles, strangling, strangled** (*tr*) **1** to kill by compressing the windpipe; throttle **2** to prevent or inhibit the growth or development of: *to strangle originality* **3** to suppress (an utterance) by or as if by swallowing suddenly: *to strangle a cry* ▷ See also **strangles** [C13 via OF, ult. from Gk *strangalē* a halter] > '**strangler** *n*

stranglehold ('stræŋgᵊlˌhəʊld) *n* **1** a wrestling hold in which a wrestler's arms are pressed against his opponent's windpipe **2** complete power or control over a person or situation

strangles ('stræŋgᵊlz) *n* (*functioning as sing*) an acute infectious bacterial disease of horses, characterized by inflammation of the respiratory tract. Also called: **equine distemper**

strangulate ('stræŋgjʊˌleɪt) *vb* **strangulates, strangulating, strangulated** (*tr*) **1** to constrict (a hollow organ, vessel, etc) so as to stop the flow of air, blood, etc, through it **2** another word for **strangle** > ˌ**stranguˈlation** *n*

strangury ('stræŋgjʊrɪ) *n* *pathol* painful excretion of urine, drop by drop [C14 from L *strangūria*, from Gk, from *stranx* a drop squeezed out + *ouron* urine]

Stranraer (strænˈrɑː) *n* a market town in SW Scotland, in W Dumfries and Galloway: fishing port with a ferry service to Northern Ireland. Pop: 11 348 (1991)

strap (stræp) *n* **1** a long strip of leather or similar material, for binding trunks, baggage, etc **2** a strip of leather or similar material used for carrying, lifting, or holding **3** a loop of leather, rubber, etc, suspended from the roof in a bus or train for standing passengers to hold on to **4** a razor strop **5** short for **shoulder strap** **6** *business* a triple option on a security or commodity consisting of one put option and two call options at the same price and for the same period ▷ Cf **strip²** (sense 4) **7** *Irish, derog sl* a shameless or promiscuous woman **8 the strap** a beating with a strap as a punishment ▷ *vb* **straps, strapping, strapped** (*tr*) **9** to tie or bind with a strap **10** to beat with a strap **11** to sharpen with a strap or strop [C16 var. of STROP]

straphanger (ˈstræpˌhæŋə) *n inf* a passenger in a bus, train, etc, who has to travel standing, esp holding on to a strap > **ˈstrapˌhanging** *n*

strapping (ˈstræpɪŋ) *adj* (*prenominal*) tall and sturdy [C17 from STRAP (in the arch. sense: to work vigorously)]

strapwork (ˈstræpˌwɜːk) *n archit* decorative work resembling interlacing straps

Strasbourg (*French* strasbur; *English* ˈstræzbɜːg) *n* a city in NE France, on the Rhine: the chief French inland port; under German rule (1870–1918); university (1567); seat of the Council of Europe and of the European Parliament. Pop: 263 940 (1999). German name: **Strassburg** (ˈʃtraːsbʊrk)

strata (ˈstrɑːtə) *n* a plural of **stratum**

> USAGE *Strata* is sometimes wrongly used as a singular noun: *this stratum* (not *strata*) *of society is often disregarded*

stratagem (ˈstrætɪdʒəm) *n* a plan or trick, esp to deceive an enemy [C15 ult. from Gk *stratēgos* a general, from *stratos* an army + *agein* to lead]

strategic (strəˈtiːdʒɪk) *or* **strategical** *adj* **1** of or characteristic of strategy **2** important to strategy **3** (of weapons, esp missiles) directed against an enemy's homeland rather than used on a battlefield ▷ Cf **tactical** > **straˈtegically** *adv*

strategics (strəˈtiːdʒɪks) *n* (*functioning as sing*) strategy, esp in a military sense

strategist (ˈstrætɪdʒɪst) *n* a specialist or expert in strategy

strategy (ˈstrætɪdʒɪ) *n, pl* **strategies 1** the art or science of the planning and conduct of a war **2** a particular long-term plan for success, esp in politics, business, etc **3** a plan or stratagem [C17 from F *stratégie*, from Gk *stratēgia* function of a general; see STRATAGEM]

Stratford-on-Avon *or* **Stratford-upon-Avon** (ˈstrætfəd) *n* a market town in central England, in SW Warwickshire on the River Avon: the birthplace and burial place of William Shakespeare and home of the Royal Shakespeare Company; tourist centre. Pop: 22 231 (1991)

strath (stræθ) *n Scot* a flat river valley [C16 from Scot & Irish Gaelic *srath*]

Strathclyde Region (ˌstræθˈklaɪd) *n* a former local government region in W Scotland: formed in 1975 from Glasgow, Renfrewshire, Lanarkshire, Buteshire, Dunbartonshire, and parts of Argyllshire, Ayrshire, and Stirlingshire; replaced in 1996 by the council areas of Glasgow, Renfrewshire, East Renfrewshire, Inverclyde, North Lanarkshire, South Lanarkshire, Argyll and Bute, East Dunbartonshire, West Dunbartonshire, North Ayrshire, South Ayrshire, and East Ayrshire

strathspey (stræθˈspeɪ) *n* **1** a Scottish dance with gliding steps, slower than a reel **2** a piece of music composed for or in the rhythm of this dance [after *Strathspey*, valley of the river Spey]

strati- *combining form* indicating stratum or strata: *stratigraphy*

straticulate (strəˈtɪkjʊlɪt, -ˌleɪt) *adj* (of a rock formation) composed of very thin even strata [C19 from NL *strāticulum* (unattested), dim. of L *strātum* something strewn; see STRATUS] > **straˌticuˈlation** *n*

stratification (ˌstrætɪfɪˈkeɪʃən) *n* **1** the arrangement of sedimentary rocks in distinct layers (strata), each layer representing the sediment deposited over a specific period **2** the act of stratifying or state of being stratified

stratify (ˈstrætɪˌfaɪ) *vb* **stratifies, stratifying, stratified 1** to form or be formed in layers or strata **2** *sociol* to divide (a society) into status groups or (of a society) to develop such groups [C17 from F *stratifier*, from NL *stratificāre*, from L STRATUM] > **ˈstratiˌfied** *adj*

stratigraphy (strəˈtɪgrəfɪ) *n* **1** the study of the composition, relative positions, etc, of rock strata in order to determine their geological history **2** *archaeol* a vertical section through the earth showing the relative positions of the human artefacts and therefore the chronology of successive levels of occupation > **stratigraphic** (ˌstrætɪˈgræfɪk) *or* **ˌstratiˈgraphical** *adj*

stratocumulus (ˌstrætəʊˈkjuːmjʊləs) *n, pl* **stratocumuli** (-ˌlaɪ) *meteorol* a uniform stretch of cloud containing dark grey globular masses

stratopause (ˈstrætəˌpɔːz) *n meteorol* the transitional zone of maximum temperature between the stratosphere and the mesosphere

stratosphere (ˈstrætəˌsfɪə) *n* the atmospheric layer lying between the troposphere and the mesosphere, in which temperature generally increases with height > **stratospheric** (ˌstrætəˈsfɛrɪk) *or* **ˌstratoˈspherical** *adj*

stratum (ˈstrɑːtəm) *n, pl* **strata** *or* **stratums 1** (*usually pl*) any of the distinct layers into which sedimentary rocks are divided **2** *biol* a single layer of tissue or cells **3** a layer of any material, esp one of several parallel layers **4** a layer of ocean or atmosphere either naturally or arbitrarily demarcated **5** a level of a social hierarchy [C16 via NL from L: something strewn, from *sternere* to scatter] > **ˈstratal** *adj*

> USAGE See at **strata**

stratus (ˈstreɪtəs) *n, pl* **strati** (-taɪ) a grey layer cloud [C19 via NL from L: strewn, from *sternere* to extend]

Straus (straʊs) *n* **Oscar** (ɔskar) 1870–1954, French composer, born in Austria, noted for such operettas as *Waltz Dream* (1907) and *The Chocolate Soldier* (1908)

Strauss (straʊs; *German* ʃtraʊs) *n* **1 David Friedrich** (ˈdaːfɪt ˈfriːdrɪç) 1808–74, German Protestant theologian: in his *Life of Jesus* (1835–36) he treated the supernatural elements of the story as myth **2 Johann** (joˈhan) 1804–49, Austrian composer, noted for his waltzes **3** his son, **Johann,** called the *Waltz King*. 1825–99, Austrian composer, whose works include *The Blue Danube Waltz* (1867) and the operetta *Die Fledermaus* (1874) **4 Richard** (ˈrɪçart) 1864–1949, German composer, noted esp for his symphonic poems, including *Don Juan* (1889) and *Till Eulenspiegel* (1895), his operas, such as *Elektra* (1909) and *Der Rosenkavalier* (1911), and his *Four Last Songs* (1948)

Stravinsky (*Russian* straˈvinskij) *n* **Igor Fyodorovich** (ˈigərj ˈfjɔdərəvitʃ) 1882–1971, US composer, born in Russia. He created ballet scores, such as *The Firebird* (1910), *Petrushka* (1911), and *The Rite of Spring* (1913), for Diaghilev. These were followed by neoclassical works, including *Oedipus Rex* (1927) and the *Symphony of Psalms* (1930). The 1950s saw him reconciled to serial techniques, which he employed in such works as the *Canticum Sacrum* (1955), the ballet *Agon* (1957), and *Requiem Canticles* (1966)

straw (strɔː) *n* **1a** stalks of threshed grain, esp of wheat, rye, oats, or barley, used in plaiting hats, baskets, etc, or as fodder **1b** (*as modifier*): *a straw hat* **2** a single dry or ripened stalk, esp of a grass **3** a long thin hollow paper or plastic tube, used for sucking up liquids into the mouth **4** (*usually used with a negative*) anything of little value or importance: *I wouldn't give a straw for our chances* **5** a measure or remedy that one turns to in desperation (esp in **clutch** *or* **grasp at a straw** *or* **straws**) **6a** a pale yellow colour **6b** (*as adj*): *straw hair* **7 draw the short straw** to be the person to whom an unpleasant task falls **8 straw in the wind** a hint or indication **9 the last straw** a small incident, setback, etc, that coming after others proves insufferable [OE *streaw*] > **ˈstrawy** *adj*

Straw (strɔː) *n* **Jack,** full name *John Whitaker Straw* born

1946, British Labour politician; Home Secretary (1997–2001); foreign secretary from 2001

strawberry ('strɔːbərɪ, -brɪ) *n, pl* **strawberries** 1 any of various low-growing rosaceous plants which have red edible fruits and spread by runners 2a the fruit of any of these plants, consisting of a sweet fleshy receptacle bearing small seedlike parts (the true fruits) 2b (*as modifier*): *strawberry ice cream* 3a a purplish-red colour 3b (*as adj*): *strawberry shoes* [OE *streawberige*; ?from the strawlike appearance of the runners]

strawberry blonde *adj* 1 (of hair) reddish blonde ▷ *n* 2 a woman with such hair

strawberry mark *n* a soft vascular red birthmark. Also called: **strawberry**

strawberry tomato *n* 1 a tropical annual plant having bell-shaped whitish-yellow flowers and small edible round yellow berries 2 the fruit of this plant, eaten fresh or made into preserves or pickles ▷ Also called: **Cape gooseberry**

strawberry tree *n* a S European evergreen tree having white or pink flowers and red strawberry-like berries. See also **arbutus**

strawboard ('strɔːˌbɔːd) *n* a board made of compressed straw and adhesive

strawflower ('strɔːˌflaʊə) *n* an Australian plant in which the coloured bracts retain their colour when the plant is dried. See also **immortelle**

straw man *n chiefly US* 1 a figure of a man made from straw 2 a person of little substance 3 a person used as a cover for some dubious plan or enterprise

straw poll *or esp US, Canad, & NZ* **vote** *n* an unofficial poll or vote taken to determine the opinion of a group or the public on some issue

Strawson ('strɔːsən) *n* Sir **Peter** (**Frederick**) born 1919, British philosopher. His early work deals with the relationship between language and logic, his later work with metaphysics. His books include *The Bounds of Sense* (1966), *Freedom and Resentment* (1974), and *Entity and Identity* (1997)

strawweight ('strɔːˌweɪt) *n* **a** a professional boxer weighing not more than 47.6 kg (105 pounds) **b** (*as modifier*): *the strawweight title* ▷ Also called: **mini-flyweight**

stray (streɪ) *vb* (*intr*) 1 to wander away, as from the correct path or from a given area 2 to wander haphazardly 3 to digress from the point, lose concentration, etc 4 to deviate from certain moral standards ▷ *n* 5a a domestic animal, fowl, etc, that has wandered away from its place of keeping and is lost 5b (*as modifier*): *stray dogs* 6 a lost or homeless person, esp a child: *waifs and strays* 7 an occurrence, specimen, etc, that is out of place or outside the usual pattern ▷ *adj* 8 scattered, random, or haphazard [C14 from OF *estraier*, from Vulgar L *estragāre* (unattested), from L *extrā-* outside + *vagāri* to roam] > **'strayer** *n*

Strayhorn ('streɪˌhɔːn) *n* **Billy**, full name *William Strayhorn*. 1915–67, US jazz composer and pianist, noted esp for his association (1939–67) with Duke Ellington

strays (streɪz) *pl n* 1 Also called: **stray capacitance** *electronics* undesired capacitance in equipment 2 another word for **static** (sense 8)

streak (striːk) *n* 1 a long thin mark, stripe, or trace of some contrasting colour 2 (of lightning) a sudden flash 3 an element or trace, as of some quality or characteristic 4 a strip, vein, or layer 5 a short stretch or run, esp of good or bad luck 6 *inf* an act or the practice of running naked through a public place ▷ *vb* 7 (*tr*) to mark or daub with a streak or streaks 8 (*intr*) to form streaks or become streaked 9 (*intr*) to move rapidly in a straight line 10 (*intr*) *inf* to run naked through a public place in order to shock or amuse [OE *strica*] > **streaked** *adj* > **'streaker** *n* > **'streakˌlike** *adj*

streaky ('striːkɪ) *adj* **streakier, streakiest** 1 marked with streaks 2 occurring in streaks 3 (of bacon) having alternate layers of meat and fat 4 of varying or uneven quality > **'streakiness** *n*

stream (striːm) *n* 1 a small river; brook 2 any steady flow of water or other fluid 3 something that resembles a stream in moving continuously in a line or particular direction 4 a rapid or unbroken flow of speech, etc: *a stream of abuse* 5 *Brit, Austral, & NZ* any of several parallel classes of schoolchildren, or divisions of children within a class, grouped together because of similar ability 6 **go** (*or* **drift**) **with the stream** to conform to the accepted standards 7 **on** (*or* **off**) **stream** 7a (of an industrial plant, manufacturing process, etc) in (*or* not in) operation or production 7b available (*or* not available) or in existence (*or* not in existence) ▷ *vb* 8 to emit or be emitted in a continuous flow: *his nose streamed blood* 9 (*intr*) to move in unbroken succession, as a crowd of people, vehicles, etc 10 (*intr*) to float freely or with a waving motion: *bunting streamed in the wind* 11 (*tr*) to unfurl (a flag, etc) 12 *Brit education* to group or divide (children) in streams [OE] > **'streamlet** *n*

streamer ('striːmə) *n* 1 a long narrow flag or part of a flag 2 a long narrow coiled ribbon of coloured paper that becomes unrolled when tossed 3 a stream of light, esp one appearing in some forms of the aurora 4 *journalism* a large heavy headline printed across the width of a page 5 *computing* another word for **tape streamer**

streamline ('striːmˌlaɪn) *n* 1 a contour on a body that offers the minimum resistance to a gas or liquid flowing around it ▷ *vb* **streamlines, streamlining, streamlined** 2 (*tr*) to make streamlined

streamlined ('striːmˌlaɪnd) *adj* 1 offering or designed to offer the minimum resistance to the flow of a gas or liquid 2 made more efficient, esp by simplifying

stream of consciousness *n* 1 *psychol* the continuous flow of ideas, thoughts, and feelings forming the content of an individual's consciousness 2 a literary technique that reveals the flow of thoughts and feelings of characters through long passages of soliloquy

streamy ('striːmɪ) *adj* **streamier, streamiest** *chiefly poetic* 1 (of an area, land, etc) having many streams 2 flowing or streaming

Streep (striːp) *n* **Meryl**, original name *Mary Louise Streep*. born 1949, US actress. Her films include *The Deerhunter* (1978), *Kramer vs Kramer* (1979), *The French Lieutenant's Woman* (1981), *Sophie's Choice* (1982), *Out of Africa* (1986), *Dancing at Lughnasa* (1999), and *The Hours* (2002)

street (striːt) *n* 1a a public road that is usually lined with buildings, esp in a town: *Oxford Street* 1b (*as modifier*): *a street directory* 2 the buildings lining a street 3 the part of the road between the pavements, used by vehicles 4 the people living, working, etc, in a particular street 5 (*modifier*) of or relating to the urban counterculture 6 **on the streets** 6a earning a living as a prostitute 6b homeless 7 (**right**) **up one's street** *inf* (just) what one knows or likes best 8 **streets ahead of** *inf* superior to, more advanced than, etc 9 **streets apart** *inf* markedly different [OE *strǣt*, from L *via strāta* paved way (*strāta*, from *strātus*, p.p. of *sternere* to stretch out)]

street Arab *n literary & old-fashioned* a homeless child, esp one who survives by begging and stealing; urchin

streetcar ('striːtˌkɑː) *n* the usual US and Canad name for **tram** (sense 1)

street credibility *n* a command of the style, knowledge, etc, associated with urban counter-culture. Often shortened to **street cred** > **ˌstreet-'credible** *adj*

street cry *n* (*often pl*) the cry of a street hawker

street furniture *n* pieces of equipment, such as street lights and pillar boxes, placed in the street for the benefit of the public

street value *n* the monetary worth of a commodity, usually an illicit one, considered as the price it would

Ss

fetch when sold to the ultimate user

streetwalker ('stri:t,wɔ:kə) *n* a prostitute who solicits on the streets > '**street,walking** *n, adj*

streetwear ('stri:t,wɛə) *n* fashionable casual clothes

streetwise ('stri:t,waɪz) *adj* adept at surviving in an urban, poor, and often criminal environment

Streicher ('ʃtraɪkə) *n* **Julius** 1885–1946, German Nazi journalist and politician, who spread anti-Semitic propaganda as editor of *Der Stürmer* (1923–45) He was hanged as a war criminal

Streisand ('straɪsænd) *n* **Barbra** born 1942, US singer, actress, and film director: the films she has acted in include *Funny Girl* (1968) and *A Star is Born* (1976); her films as actress and director include *Yentl* (1983), *Prince of Tides* (1990), and *The Mirror has Two Faces* (1996)

strelitzia (strɛ'lɪtsɪə) *n* any of various southern African perennial herbaceous plants, cultivated for their showy flowers: includes the bird-of-paradise flower [c18 after Charlotte of Mecklenburg-*Strelitz* (1744–1818), queen of George III of Great Britain & Ireland]

strength (strɛŋθ) *n* **1** the state or quality of being physically or mentally strong **2** the ability to withstand or exert great force, stress, or pressure **3** something regarded as beneficial or a source of power: *their chief strength is technology* **4** potency, as of a drink, drug, etc **5** power to convince; cogency: *the strength of an argument* **6** degree of intensity or concentration of colour, light, sound, flavour, etc **7** the full or part of the full complement as specified: *at full strength; below strength* **8 from strength to strength** with ever-increasing success **9 in strength** in large numbers **10 on the strength of** on the basis of or relying upon **11 the strength of** *Austral & NZ inf* the essential facts about [OE *strengthu*]

strengthen ('strɛŋθən) *vb* to make or become stronger > '**strengthener** *n*

strenuous ('strɛnjʊəs) *adj* **1** requiring or involving the use of great energy or effort **2** characterized by great activity, effort, or endeavour [c16 from L *strēnuus* brisk] > '**strenuously** *adv* > '**strenuousness** *n*

strep (strɛp) *n inf* short for **streptococcus**

strepitoso (,strɛpɪ'təʊsəʊ) *adv music* boisterously [It.]

strepto- *combining form* **1** indicating a shape resembling a twisted chain: *streptococcus* **2** indicating streptococcus [from Gk *streptos* twisted, from *strephein* to twist]

streptocarpus (,strɛptəʊ'kɑ:pəs) *n* any of various mostly African plants having spirally-twisted capsules [c19 from NL, from Gk *streptos* twisted + *karpos* fruit]

streptococcus (,strɛptəʊ'kɒkəs) *n, pl* **streptococci** (-'kɒkaɪ, -'kɒki:, -'kɒksi:) any spherical bacterium of the genus *Streptococcus*, typically occurring in chains and including many pathogenic species. Often shortened to **strep** > **streptococcal** (,strɛptəʊ'kɒkᵊl) *or* **streptococcic** (,strɛptəʊ'kɒksɪk) *adj*

streptomycin (,strɛptəʊ'maɪsɪn) *n* an antibiotic obtained from the bacterium *Streptomyces griseus*: used in the treatment of tuberculosis and other bacterial infections

streptothricin (,strɛptəʊ'θraɪsɪn) *n* an antibiotic produced by the bacterium *Streptomyces lavendulae*

Stresemann (*German* 'ʃtresəman) *n* **Gustav** 1878–1929, German statesman; chancellor (1923) and foreign minister (1923–29) of the Weimar Republic. He gained (1926) Germany's admission to the League of Nations and shared the Nobel peace prize (1926) with Aristide Briand

stress (strɛs) *n* **1** special emphasis or significance **2** mental, emotional, or physical strain or tension **3** emphasis placed upon a syllable by pronouncing it more loudly than those that surround it **4** such emphasis as part of a rhythm in music or poetry **5** a syllable so emphasized **6** *physics* **6a** force or a system of forces producing deformation or strain **6b** the force acting per unit area ▷ *vb* (*tr*) **7** to give emphasis or prominence to **8** to pronounce (a word or syllable) more loudly than those that surround it **9** to subject to stress [c14 *stresse*, shortened from DISTRESS] > '**stressful** *adj*

-stress *suffix forming nouns* indicating a woman who performs or is engaged in a certain activity: *songstress; seamstress* [from -ST(E)R + -ESS]

stressor ('strɛsə) *n* an event, experience, etc, that causes stress

stretch (strɛtʃ) *vb* **1** to draw out or extend or be drawn out or extended in length, area, etc **2** to extend or be extended to an undue degree, esp so as to distort or lengthen permanently **3** to extend (the limbs, body, etc) **4** (*tr*) to reach or suspend (a rope, etc) from one place to another **5** (*tr*) to draw tight; tighten **6** (often foll by *out, forward*, etc) to reach or hold (out); extend **7** (*intr;* usually foll by *over*) to extend in time: *the course stretched over three months* **8** (*intr;* foll by *for, over*, etc) (of a region, etc) to extend in length or area **9** (*intr*) (esp of a garment) to be capable of expanding, as to a larger size: *socks that will stretch* **10** (*tr*) to put a great strain upon or extend to the limit **11** to injure (a muscle, tendon, etc) by means of a strain or sprain **12** (*tr;* often foll by *out*) to make do with (limited resources): *to stretch one's budget* **13** (*tr*) *inf* to expand or elaborate (a story, etc) beyond what is credible or acceptable **14** (*tr; often passive*) to extend, as to the limit of one's abilities or talents **15** *arch or sl* to hang or be hanged by the neck **16 stretch a point 16a** to make a concession or exception not usually made **16b** to exaggerate ▷ *n* **17** the act of stretching or state of being stretched **18** a large or continuous expanse or distance: *a stretch of water* **19** extent in time, length, area, etc **20a** capacity for being stretched, as in some garments **20b** (*as modifier*): *stretch pants* **21** the section or sections of a racecourse that are straight, esp the final section leading to the finishing line **22** *sl* a term of imprisonment **23 at a stretch** *chiefly Brit* **23a** with some difficulty; by making a special effort **23b** if really necessary or in extreme circumstances **23c** at one time: *he sometimes read for hours at a stretch* [OE *streccan*] > '**stretchable** *adj* > ,**stretcha'bility** *n*

stretcher ('strɛtʃə) *n* **1** a device for transporting the ill, wounded, or dead, consisting of a frame covered by canvas or other material **2** a strengthening often decorative member joining the legs of a chair, table, etc **3** the wooden frame on which canvas is stretched and fixed for oil painting **4** a tie beam or brace used in a structural framework **5** a brick or stone laid horizontally with its length parallel to the length of a wall **6** *rowing* a fixed board across a boat on which a rower braces his or her feet **7** *Austral & NZ* a camp bed ▷ *vb* (*tr*) **8** to transport (a sick or injured person) on a stretcher

stretcher-bearer *n* a person who helps to carry a stretcher, esp in wartime

stretch limo *n inf* a limousine that has been lengthened to provide extra seating accommodation and more legroom. In full: **stretch limousine**

stretchmarks ('strɛtʃ,mɑ:ks) *pl n* marks that remain visible on the abdomen after its distension, esp in pregnancy

stretchy ('strɛtʃɪ) *adj* **stretchier, stretchiest** characterized by elasticity > '**stretchiness** *n*

Stretford ('strɛtfəd) *n* an industrial town in NW England, in Trafford unitary authority, Greater Manchester. Pop: 43 953 (1991)

stretto ('strɛtəʊ) *n, pl* **strettos** *or* **stretti** (-ti:) **1** (in a fugue) the close overlapping of two parts or voices, the second one entering before the first has completed its statement **2** Also called: **stretta** a concluding passage, played at a faster speed than earlier material [c17 from It., from L *strictus* tightly bound; see STRICT]

strew (stru:) *vb* **strews, strewing, strewed; strewn** *or*

strewed to spread or scatter or be spread or scattered, as over a surface or area [OE *streowian*] > '**strewer** *n*

strewth (struːθ) *interj* an expression of surprise or dismay [c19 alteration of *God's truth*]

stria ('straɪə) *n, pl* **striae** ('straɪiː) (*often pl*) **1** Also called: **striation** *geol* any of the parallel scratches or grooves on the surface of a rock caused by abrasion resulting from the passage of a glacier or fine ridges and grooves caused by irregular growth **2** *biol, anat* a narrow band of colour or a ridge, groove, or similar linear mark **3** *archit* a narrow channel, such as a flute on the shaft of a column [c16 from L: a groove]

striate *adj* ('straɪɪt), *also* **striated 1** marked with striae; striped ▷ *vb* ('straɪeɪt), **striates, striating, striated 2** (*tr*) to mark with striae [c17 from L *striāre* to make grooves]

striation (straɪ'eɪʃən) *n* **1** an arrangement or pattern of striae **2** the condition of being striate **3** another word for **stria** (sense 1)

stricken ('strɪkən) *adj* **1** laid low, as by disease or sickness **2** deeply affected, as by grief, love, etc **3** *arch* wounded or injured **4 stricken in years** made feeble by age [c14 p.p. of STRIKE] > '**strickenly** *adv*

strict (strɪkt) *adj* **1** adhering closely to specified rules, ordinances, etc **2** complied with or enforced stringently; rigorous: *a strict code of conduct* **3** severely correct in attention to conduct or morality: *a strict teacher* **4** (of a punishment, etc) harsh; severe **5** (*prenominal*) complete; absolute: *strict secrecy* [c16 from L *strictus*, from *stringere* to draw tight] > '**strictly** *adv* > '**strictness** *n*

strict implication *n logic* a form of implication in which the proposition "if A then B" is true only when B is deducible from A

stricture ('strɪktʃə) *n* **1** a severe criticism; censure **2** *pathol* an abnormal constriction of a tubular organ or part [c14 from L *strictūra* contraction; see STRICT] > '**strictured** *adj*

stride (straɪd) *n* **1** a long step or pace **2** the space measured by such a step **3** a striding gait **4** an act of forward movement by an animal **5** progress or development (esp in **make rapid strides**) **6** a regular pace or rate of progress: *to get into one's stride*; *to be put off one's stride* **7** Also: **stride piano** *jazz* a piano style characterized by single bass notes on the first and third beats and chords on the second and fourth **8** (*pl*) *inf, chiefly Austral inf* men's trousers **9 take (something) in one's stride** to do (something) without difficulty or effort ▷ *vb* **strides, striding, strode, stridden** ('strɪdᵊn) **10** (*intr*) to walk with long regular or measured paces, as in haste, etc **11** (*tr*) to cover or traverse by striding: *he strode thirty miles* **12** (often foll by *over, across*, etc) to cross (over a space, obstacle, etc) with a stride **13** *arch or poetic* to straddle or bestride [OE *strīdan*] > '**strider** *n*

strident ('straɪdᵊnt) *adj* **1** (of a shout, voice, etc) loud or harsh **2** urgent, clamorous, or vociferous: *strident demands* [c17 from L *strīdēns*, from *strīdēre* to make a grating sound] > '**stridence** *or* '**stridency** *n* > '**stridently** *adv*

stridor ('straɪdɔː) *n* **1** *pathol* a high-pitched whistling sound made during respiration, caused by obstruction of the air passages **2** *chiefly literary* a harsh or shrill sound [c17 from L; see STRIDENT]

stridulate ('strɪdjʊˌleɪt) *vb* **stridulates, stridulating, stridulated** (*intr*) (of insects such as the cricket) to produce sounds by rubbing one part of the body against another [c19 back formation from *stridulation*, from L *strīdulus* creaking, from *strīdēre* to make a harsh noise] > ˌ**stridu'lation** *n* > '**striduˌlator** *n*

stridulous ('strɪdjʊləs) *or* **stridulant** *adj* **1** making a harsh, shrill, or grating noise **2** *pathol* of, relating to, or characterized by stridor > '**stridulousness** *or* '**stridulance** *n*

strife (straɪf) *n* **1** angry or violent struggle; conflict **2** rivalry or contention, esp of a bitter kind **3** *Austral & NZ inf* trouble or discord of any kind **4** *arch* striving [c13 from OF *estrif*, prob. from *estriver* to STRIVE]

strigil ('strɪdʒɪl) *n* a curved blade used by the ancient Romans and Greeks to scrape the body after bathing [c16 from L *strigilis*, from *stringere* to graze]

strigose ('straɪgəʊs) *adj* **1** *bot* bearing stiff hairs or bristles **2** *zool* marked with fine closely set grooves or ridges [c18 via NL *strigōsus*, from *striga* a bristle, from L: grain cut down]

strike (straɪk) *vb* **strikes, striking, struck 1** to deliver (a blow or stroke) to (a person) **2** to come or cause to come into sudden or violent contact (with) **3** (*tr*) to make an attack on **4** to produce (fire, sparks, etc) or (of fire, sparks, etc) to be produced by ignition **5** to cause (a match) to light by friction or (of a match) to be lighted **6** to press (the key of a piano, organ, etc) or to sound (a specific note) in this or a similar way **7** to indicate (a specific time) by the sound of a hammer striking a bell or by any other percussive sound **8** (of a venomous snake) to cause injury by biting **9** (*tr*) to affect or cause to affect deeply, suddenly, or radically: *her appearance struck him as strange* **10** (*past participle* **struck** *or* **stricken**) (*tr; passive*; usually foll by *with*) to render incapable or nearly so: *stricken with grief* **11** (*tr*) to enter the mind of: *it struck me that he had become very quiet* **12** (*past participle* **struck** *or* **stricken**) to render: *struck dumb* **13** (*tr*) to be perceived by; catch: *the glint of metal struck his eye* **14** to arrive at or come upon (something), esp suddenly or unexpectedly: *to strike the path for home; to strike upon a solution* **15** (*intr*; sometimes foll by *out*) to set (out) or proceed, esp upon a new course: *to strike out for the coast* **16** (*tr; usually passive*) to afflict with a disease, esp unexpectedly: *he was struck with polio* **17** (*tr*) to discover or come upon a source of (ore, petroleum, etc) **18** (*tr*) (of a plant) to produce or send down (a root or roots) **19** (*tr*) to take apart or pack up; break (esp in **strike camp**) **20** (*tr*) to take down or dismantle (a stage set, etc) **21** (*tr*) *naut* **21a** to lower or remove (a specified piece of gear) **21b** to haul down or dip (a flag, sail, etc) in salute or in surrender **22** to attack (an objective) **23** to impale the hook in the mouth of (a fish) by suddenly tightening or jerking the line after the bait has been taken **24** (*tr*) to form or impress (a coin, metal, etc) by or as if by stamping **25** to level (a surface) by use of a flat board **26** (*tr*) to assume or take up (an attitude, posture, etc) **27** (*intr*) (of workers in a factory, etc) to cease work collectively as a protest against working conditions, low pay, etc **28** (*tr*) to reach by agreement: *to strike a bargain* **29** (*tr*) to form (a jury, esp a special jury) by cancelling certain names among those nominated for jury service until only the requisite number remains **30 strike home 30a** to deliver an effective blow **30b** to achieve the intended effect **31 strike it rich** *inf* **31a** to discover an extensive deposit of a mineral, petroleum, etc **31b** to have an unexpected financial success ▷ *n* **32** an act or instance of striking **33** a cessation of work, as a protest against working conditions or low pay: *on strike* **34** a military attack, esp an air attack on a surface target: *air strike* **35** *baseball* a pitched ball judged good but missed or not swung at, three of which cause a batter to be out **36** Also called: **ten-strike** *tenpin bowling* **36a** the act or an instance of knocking down all the pins with the first bowl of a single frame **36b** the score thus made **37** a sound made by striking **38** the mechanism that makes a clock strike **39** the discovery of a source of ore, petroleum, etc **40** the horizontal direction of a fault, rock stratum, etc **41** *angling* the act or an instance of striking **42** *inf* an unexpected or complete success, esp one that brings financial gain **43 take strike** *cricket* (of a batsman) to prepare to play a ball delivered by the bowler ▷ See also **strike down, strike off,** etc [OE *strīcan*]

strikebound ('straɪkˌbaʊnd) *adj* (of a factory, etc) closed or made inoperative by a strike

strikebreaker ('straɪkˌbreɪkə) *n* a person who tries to

Ss

make a strike ineffectual by working or by taking the place of those on strike > ˈ**strike,breaking** *n, adj*
strike down *vb (tr, adv)* to cause to die, esp suddenly: *he was struck down in his prime*
strike off *vb (tr)* **1** to remove or erase from (a list, record, etc) by or as if by a stroke of the pen **2** *(adv)* to cut off or separate by or as if by a blow: *she was struck off from the inheritance*
strike out *vb (adv)* **1** *(tr)* to remove or erase **2** *(intr)* to start out or begin: *to strike out on one's own* **3** *baseball* to put out or be put out on strikes **4** *(intr) US inf* to fail utterly
strike pay *n* money paid to strikers from the funds of a trade union
striker (ˈstraɪkə) *n* **1** a person who is on strike **2** the hammer in a timepiece that rings a bell or alarm **3** any part in a mechanical device that strikes something, such as the firing pin of a gun **4** *soccer, inf* an attacking player, esp one who generally positions himself or herself near the opponent's goal in the hope of scoring **5** *cricket* the batsman who is about to play a ball
strike up *vb (adv)* **1** (of a band, orchestra, etc) to begin to play or sing **2** *(tr)* to bring about; cause to begin: *to strike up a friendship*
striking (ˈstraɪkɪŋ) *adj* **1** attracting attention; fine; impressive: *a striking beauty* **2** conspicuous; noticeable: *a striking difference* > ˈ**strikingly** *adv* > ˈ**strikingness** *n*
striking circle *n hockey* the semicircular area in front of each goal, which an attacking player must have entered before scoring a goal
Strimmer (ˈstrɪmə) *n trademark* an electrical tool for trimming the edges of lawns
Strimon (ˈstrimɔn) *n* a transliteration of the Greek name for the **Struma**
Strindberg (ˈstrɪndbɜːg; *Swedish* ˈstrɪndbærj) *n* **August** (ˈaugʊst) 1849–1912, Swedish dramatist and novelist, whose plays include *The Father* (1887), *Miss Julie* (1888), and *The Ghost Sonata* (1907)
Strine (straɪn) *n* a humorous transliteration of Australian pronunciation, as in *Gloria Soame* for *glorious home* [c20 a jocular rendering of the Australian pronunciation of *Australian*]
string (strɪŋ) *n* **1** a thin length of cord, twine, fibre, or similar material used for tying, hanging, binding, etc **2** a group of objects threaded on a single strand: *a string of beads* **3** a series or succession of things, events, etc: *a string of oaths* **4** a number, chain, or group of similar things, animals, etc, owned by or associated with one person or body: *a string of girlfriends* **5** a tough fibre or cord in a plant **6** *music* a tightly stretched wire, cord, etc, found on stringed instruments, such as the violin, guitar, and piano **7** short for **bowstring** **8** *archit* short for **string course** or **stringer** (sense 1) **9** *(pl; usually preceded by the)* **9a** violins, violas, cellos, and double basses collectively **9b** the section of a symphony orchestra constituted by such instruments **10** a group of characters that can be treated as a unit by a computer program **11** *physics* a one-dimensional entity postulated to be a fundamental component of matter in some theories of particle physics. See also **cosmic string** **12** *(pl)* complications or conditions (esp in **no strings attached**) **13** *(modifier)* composed of stringlike strands woven in a large mesh: *a string bag; a string vest* **14** **first** (**second**, etc) **string** a person or thing regarded as a primary (secondary, etc) source of strength **15** **keep on a string** to have control or a hold over (a person), esp emotionally **16** **pull strings** *inf* to exert power or influence, esp secretly or unofficially **17** **pull the strings** to have real or ultimate control of something ▷ *vb* **strings, stringing, strung** **18** *(tr)* to provide with a string or strings **19** *(tr)* to suspend or stretch from one point to another **20** *(tr)* to thread on a string **21** *(tr)* to form or extend in a line or series **22** (foll by *out*) to space or spread out at intervals **23** *(tr; usually foll by up) inf* to kill (a person) by hanging **24** *(tr)* to remove the stringy parts from (vegetables, esp beans) **25** *(intr)* (esp of viscous liquids) to become stringy or ropey **26** *(tr; often foll by up)* to cause to be tense or nervous [OE *streng*] > ˈ**string,like** *adj*
string along *vb (adv) Inf* **1** *(intr; often foll by with)* to agree or appear to be in agreement (with) **2** *(intr; often foll by with)* to accompany **3** to deceive or hoax, esp in order to gain time
stringboard (ˈstrɪŋ,bɔːd) *n* a skirting that covers the ends of the steps in a staircase. Also called: **stringer**
string course *n archit* an ornamental projecting band or continuous moulding along a wall. Also called: **cordon**
stringed (strɪŋd) *adj* (of musical instruments) having or provided with strings
stringendo (strɪnˈdʒɛndəʊ) *adj, adv music* to be performed with increasing speed [It., from *stringere* to compress, from L: to draw tight]
stringent (ˈstrɪndʒənt) *adj* **1** requiring strict attention to rules, procedure, detail, etc **2** *finance* characterized by or causing a shortage of credit, loan capital, etc [c17 from L *stringere* to bind] > ˈ**stringency** *n* > ˈ**stringently** *adv*
stringer (ˈstrɪŋə) *n* **1** *archit* **1a** a long horizontal beam that is used for structural purposes **1b** another name for **stringboard** **2** *naut* a longitudinal structural brace for strengthening the hull of a vessel **3** a journalist retained by a newspaper or news service on a part-time basis to cover a particular town or area
stringhalt (ˈstrɪŋ,hɔːlt) *n vet science* a sudden spasmodic lifting of the hind leg of a horse. Also called: **springhalt** [c16 prob. STRING + HALT[2]]
stringpiece (ˈstrɪŋ,piːs) *n* a long horizontal timber beam used to strengthen or support a framework
string quartet *n music* **1** an instrumental ensemble consisting of two violins, one viola, and one cello **2** a piece of music for such a group
string tie *n* a very narrow tie
stringy (ˈstrɪŋɪ) *adj* **stringier, stringiest** **1** made of strings or resembling strings **2** (of meat, etc) fibrous **3** (of a person's build) wiry; sinewy **4** (of liquids) forming in strings > ˈ**stringily** *adv* > ˈ**stringiness** *n*
stringy-bark *n Austral* any of several eucalyptus trees having fibrous bark
strip[1] (strɪp) *vb* **strips, stripping, stripped** **1** to take or pull (the covering, clothes, etc) off (oneself, another person, or thing) **2** *(intr)* **2a** to remove all one's clothes **2b** to perform a striptease **3** *(tr)* to denude or empty completely **4** *(tr)* to deprive: *he was stripped of his pride* **5** *(tr)* to rob or plunder **6** *(tr)* to remove (paint, etc) from (a surface, furniture, etc): *stripped pine* **7** *(tr)* to pull out the old coat of hair from (dogs of certain long- and wire-haired breeds) **8a** to remove the leaves from the stalks of (tobacco, etc) **8b** to separate the leaves from the stems of (tobacco, etc) **9** *(tr) agriculture* to draw the last milk from (a cow) **10** to dismantle (an engine, mechanism, etc) **11** to tear off or break (the thread) from (a screw, bolt, etc) or (the teeth) from (a gear) **12** (often foll by *down*) to remove the accessories from (a motor vehicle): *his car was stripped down* ▷ *n* **13** the act or an instance of undressing or of performing a striptease [OE *bestriepan* to plunder]
strip[2] (strɪp) *n* **1** a relatively long, flat, narrow piece of something **2** short for **airstrip** **3** the clothes worn by the members of a team, esp a football team **4** *business* a triple option on a security or commodity consisting of one call option and two put options at the same price and for the same period ▷ Cf **strap** (sense 6) **5** **tear (someone) off a strip** *inf* to rebuke (someone) angrily ▷ *vb* **strips, stripping, stripped** **6** to cut or divide into strips [c15 from MDu. *strīpe* STRIPE[1]]
strip cartoon *n* a sequence of drawings in a newspaper, magazine, etc, relating a humorous story or an adventure. Also called: **comic strip**
strip club *n* a small club in which striptease

performances regularly take place

stripe[1] (straɪp) *n* **1** a relatively long band of colour or texture that differs from the surrounding material or background **2** a fabric having such bands **3** a strip, band, or chevron worn on a uniform, etc, esp to indicate rank **4** *chiefly US & Canad* kind; type: *a man of a certain stripe* ▷ *vb* **stripes, striping, striped 5** (*tr*) to mark with stripes [c17 prob. from MDu. *strīpe*] > **striped** *adj*

stripe[2] (straɪp) *n* a stroke from a whip, rod, cane, etc [c15 ?from MLow G *strippe*]

striped muscle *n* a type of contractile tissue that is marked by transverse striations. Also called: **skeletal muscle, striated muscle**

strip lighting *n* electric lighting by means of long glass tubes that are fluorescent lamps or that contain long filaments

stripling (ˈstrɪplɪŋ) *n* a lad [c13 from STRIP[2] + -LING[1]]

strip mining *n* another term (esp US) for **opencast mining**

stripper (ˈstrɪpə) *n* **1** a striptease artiste **2** a person or thing that strips **3** a device or substance for removing paint, varnish, etc

strip-search *vb* **1** (*tr*) (of police, customs officials, etc) to strip (a prisoner or suspect) naked to search him or her for contraband, narcotics, etc ▷ *n* **2** a search that involves stripping a person naked > **ˈstrip-ˌsearching** *n*

striptease (ˈstrɪpˌtiːz) *n* **a** a form of erotic entertainment in which a person gradually undresses to music **b** (*as modifier*): *a striptease club* > **ˈstripˌteaser** *n*

stripy *or* **stripey** (ˈstraɪpɪ) *adj* **stripier, stripiest** marked by or with stripes; striped

strive (straɪv) *vb* **strives, striving, strove, striven** (ˈstrɪvᵊn) **1** (*may take a clause as object or an infinitive*) to make a great and tenacious effort **2** (*intr*) to fight; contend [c13 from OF *estriver*, of Gmc origin] > **ˈstriver** *n*

strobe (strəʊb) *n* short for **strobe lighting** or **stroboscope**

strobe lighting *n* **1** a high-intensity flashing beam of light produced by rapid electrical discharges in a tube or by a perforated disc rotating in front of an intense light source **2** the use of or the apparatus for producing such light. Sometimes shortened to **strobe**

strobilus (ˈstrəʊbɪləs) *or* **strobile** (ˈstrəʊbaɪl) *n, pl* **strobiluses, strobili** (-bɪlaɪ), *or* **strobiles** *bot* the technical name for **cone** (sense 3) [c18 via LL from Gk *strobilos* a fir cone]

stroboscope (ˈstrəʊbəˌskəʊp) *n* **1** an instrument producing an intense flashing light, the frequency of which can be synchronized with some multiple of the frequency of rotation, vibration, or operation of an object, etc, making it appear stationary. Sometimes shortened to **strobe 2** a similar device synchronized with the shutter of a camera so that a series of still photographs can be taken of a moving object [c19 from *strobo-*, from Gk *strobos* a whirling + -SCOPE] > **stroboscopic** (ˌstrəʊbəˈskɒpɪk) *or* **ˌstroboˈscopical** *adj* > **ˌstroboˈscopically** *adv*

strode (strəʊd) *vb* the past tense of **stride**

Stroessner (ˈstrəʊsnə) *n* **Alfredo** born 1912, Paraguayan soldier and politician; president (1954–89): deposed in a military coup

stroganoff (ˈstrɒgəˌnɒf) *n* a dish of sliced beef cooked with onions and mushrooms, served in a sour-cream sauce. Also called: **beef stroganoff** [c19 after Count *Stroganoff*, 19th-century Russian diplomat]

Stroheim (ˈstrəʊˌhaɪm, ˈʃtrəʊ-) *n* See (Erich) **von Stroheim**

stroke (strəʊk) *n* **1** the act or an instance of striking; a blow, knock, or hit **2** a sudden action, movement, or occurrence: *a stroke of luck* **3** a brilliant or inspired act or feat: *a stroke of genius* **4** *pathol* apoplexy; rupture of a blood vessel in the brain resulting in loss of consciousness, often followed by paralysis, or embolism or thrombosis affecting a cerebral vessel **5a** the striking of a clock **5b** the hour registered by this: *on the stroke of three* **6** a mark made by a writing implement **7** another name for **solidus** (sense 1), used esp when dictating or reading aloud **8** a light touch or caress, as with the fingers **9** a pulsation, esp of the heart **10** a single complete movement or one of a series of complete movements **11** *sport* the act or manner of striking the ball with a club, bat, etc **12** any one of the repeated movements used by a swimmer **13** a manner of swimming, esp one of several named styles such as the crawl **14a** any one of a series of linear movements of a reciprocating part, such as a piston **14b** the distance travelled by such a part from one end of its movement to the other **15** a single pull on an oar or oars in rowing **16** manner or style of rowing **17** the oarsman who sits nearest the stern of a shell, facing the cox, and sets the rate of rowing **18 a stroke (of work)** (*usually used with a negative*) a small amount of work **19 at a stroke** with one action **20 off one's stroke** performing or working less well than usual **21 on the stroke** punctually ▷ *vb* **strokes, stroking, stroked 22** (*tr*) to touch, brush, etc lightly or gently **23** (*tr*) to mark a line or a stroke on or through **24** to act as the stroke of (a racing shell) **25** (*tr*) *sport* to strike (a ball) with a smooth swinging blow [OE *strācian*]
▷ www.neuro.wustl.edu/stroke
▷ http://209.107.44.93/NationalStroke/default.htm

stroke play *n golf* **a** scoring by counting the strokes taken **b** (*as modifier*): *a strokeplay tournament* ▷ Also called: **medal play** Cf **match play, Stableford**

stroll (strəʊl) *vb* **1** to walk about in a leisurely manner **2** (*intr*) to wander about ▷ *n* **3** a leisurely walk [c17 prob. from dialect G *strollen*, from ?]

stroller (ˈstrəʊlə) *n* the usual US, Canad, and Austral word for **pushchair**

stroma (ˈstrəʊmə) *n, pl* **stromata** (-mətə) *biol* **1** the gel-like matrix of chloroplasts and certain cells **2** the fibrous connective tissue forming the matrix of the mammalian ovary and testis **3** a dense mass of hyphae that is produced by certain fungi and gives rise to spore-producing bodies [c19 via NL from LL: a mattress, from Gk] > **stromatic** (strəʊˈmætɪk) *or* **ˈstromatous** *adj*

Stromboli (ˈstrɒmbəlɪ) *n* an island in the Tyrrhenian Sea, in the Lipari Islands off the N coast of Sicily: famous for its active volcano, 927 m (3040 ft) high

Strombolian (strɒmˈbəʊlɪən) *adj* relating to or denoting a type of volcanic eruption characterized by repeated fountains or jetting of fluid lava into the air

strong (strɒŋ) *adj* **1** involving or possessing strength **2** solid or robust; not easily broken or injured **3** resolute or morally firm **4** intense in quality; not faint or feeble: *a strong voice; a strong smell* **5** easily defensible; incontestable or formidable **6** concentrated; not weak or diluted **7a** (*postpositive*) containing or having a specified number: *a navy 40 000 strong* **7b** (*in combination*): *a 40 000-strong navy* **8** having an unpleasantly powerful taste or smell **9** having an extreme or drastic effect: *strong discipline* **10** emphatic or immoderate: *strong language* **11** convincing, effective, or cogent **12** (of a colour) having a high degree of saturation or purity; produced by a concentrated quantity of colouring agent **13** *grammar* **13a** of or denoting a class of verbs, in certain languages including the Germanic languages, whose conjugation shows vowel gradation, as *sing, sang, sung* **13b** belonging to any part-of-speech class, in various languages, whose inflections follow the less regular of two possible patterns ▷ Cf **weak** (sense 10) **14** (of a wind, current, etc) moving fast **15** (of a syllable) accented or stressed **16** (of an industry, etc) firm in price or characterized by firm or increasing prices **17** (of certain acids and bases) producing high concentrations of hydrogen or hydroxide ions in aqueous solution **18 have a strong stomach** not to be prone to nausea

Ss

▷ *adv* **19** *inf* in a strong way; effectively: *going strong* **20 come on strong** to make a forceful or exaggerated impression [OE *strang*] > **'strongly** *adv* > **'strongness** *n*
strong-arm *inf* ▷ *n* **1** (*modifier*) of or involving physical force or violence: *strong-arm tactics* ▷ *vb* **2** (*tr*) to show violence towards
strongbox ('strɒŋ,bɒks) *n* a box or safe in which valuables are locked for safety
strong breeze *n meteorol* a wind of force 6 on the Beaufort scale, reaching speeds of 25 to 31 mph
strong drink *n* alcoholic drink
strong-eye dog *n NZ* See **eye dog**
strong gale *n meteorol* a wind of force 9 on the Beaufort scale, reaching speeds of 47 to 54 mph
stronghold ('strɒŋ,həʊld) *n* **1** a defensible place; fortress **2** a major centre or area of predominance
strong interaction *or* **force** *n physics* an interaction between elementary particles responsible for the forces between nucleons in the nucleus. Also called: **strong nuclear interaction** *or* **force** See **interaction** (sense 2) ▷ Cf **weak interaction**
strong-minded *adj* having strength of mind; firm, resolute, and determined > **,strong-'mindedly** *adv* > **,strong-'mindedness** *n*
strong point *n* something at which one excels; forte
strongroom ('strɒŋ,ru:m, -,rʊm) *n* a specially designed room in which valuables are locked for safety
strong-willed *adj* having strength of will
strontium ('strɒntɪəm) *n* a soft silvery-white element of the alkaline earth group of metals. The radioisotope **strontium-90**, with a half-life of 28.1 years, is used in nuclear power sources and is a hazardous nuclear fallout product. Symbol: Sr; atomic no.: 38; atomic wt.: 87.62 [C19 from NL, after *Strontian*, in the Highlands of Scotland, where discovered]
strontium unit *n* a unit expressing the concentration of strontium-90 in an organic medium, such as soil, bone, etc, relative to the concentration of calcium in the medium
strop (strɒp) *n* **1** a leather strap or an abrasive strip for sharpening razors **2** a rope or metal band around a block or deadeye for support **3** *inf* a temper tantrum: *he threw a strop and stormed off* ▷ *vb* **strops, stropping, stropped 4** (*tr*) to sharpen (a razor, etc) on a strop [C14 (in nautical use: a strip of rope): via MLow G or MDu. *strop*, ult. from L *stroppus*, from Gk *strophos* cord]
strophanthin (strəʊ'fænθɪn) *n* a toxic glycoside or mixture of glycosides obtained from the ripe seeds of certain species of strophanthus [C19 NL, from STROPHANTH(US) + -IN]
strophanthus (strəʊ'fænθəs) *n* **1** any of various small trees or shrubs of tropical Africa and Asia, having strap-shaped twisted petals **2** the seeds of any of these plants [C19 NL, from Gk *strophos* twisted cord + *anthos* flower]
strophe ('strəʊfɪ) *n prosody* (in ancient Greek drama) **a** the first of two movements made by a chorus during the performance of a choral ode **b** the first part of a choral ode sung during this movement ▷ See **antistrophe, epode** [C17 from Gk: a verse, lit.: a turning, from *strephein* to twist] > **strophic** ('strɒfɪk, 'strəʊ-) *adj*
stroppy ('strɒpɪ) *adj* **stroppier, stroppiest** *Brit inf* angry or awkward [C20 changed & shortened from OBSTREPEROUS] > **'stroppily** *adv* > **'stroppiness** *n*
strove (strəʊv) *vb* the past tense of **strive**
strow (strəʊ) *vb* **strows, strowing, strowed; strown** *or* **strowed** an archaic variant of **strew**
struck (strʌk) *vb* **1** the past tense and past participle of **strike** ▷ *adj* **2** *chiefly US & Canad* (of an industry, factory, etc) shut down or otherwise affected by a labour strike
structural ('strʌktʃərəl) *adj* **1** of, relating to, or having structure or a structure **2** of, relating to, or forming part of the structure of a building **3** of or relating to the structure and deformation of the earth's crust **4** of or relating to the structure of organisms **5** *chem* of or involving the arrangement of atoms in molecules > **'structurally** *adv*
structural formula *n* a chemical formula showing the composition and structure of a molecule
structuralism ('strʌktʃərə,lɪzəm) *n* **1** an approach to social sciences and to literature in terms of oppositions, contrasts, and hierarchical structures, esp as they might reflect universal mental characteristics or organizing principles **2** an approach to linguistics that analyses and describes the structure of language, as distinguished from its comparative and historical aspects > **'structuralist** *n, adj*
structural linguistics *n* (*functioning as sing*) a descriptive approach to an analysis of language on the basis of its structure as reflected by irreducible units of phonological, morphological, and semantic features
structural unemployment *n econ* unemployment resulting from changes in the structure of an industry as a result of changes in either technology or taste
structure ('strʌktʃə) *n* **1** a complex construction or entity **2** the arrangement and interrelationship of parts in a construction **3** the manner of construction or organization **4** *chem* the arrangement of atoms in a molecule of a chemical compound **5** *geol* the way in which a mineral, rock, etc, is made up of its component parts ▷ *vb* **structures, structuring, structured** (*tr*) **6** to impart a structure to [C15 from L *structūra*, from *struere* to build]
structured interview *n marketing* an interview in which the respondent answers only "yes", "no", or "don't know"
strudel ('stru:dəl) *n* a thin sheet of filled dough rolled up and baked: *apple strudel* [G, from MHG *strodel* whirlpool, from the way the pastry is rolled]
struggle ('strʌgᵊl) *vb* **struggles, struggling, struggled** (*intr*) **1** (*usually foll by for or against; may take an infinitive*) to exert strength, energy, and force; work or strive **2** to move about strenuously so as to escape from something confining **3** to contend, battle, or fight **4** to go or progress with difficulty ▷ *n* **5** a laboured or strenuous exertion or effort **6** a fight or battle **7** the act of struggling **8 the struggle** *S African* the concerted opposition to apartheid [C14 from ?] > **'struggling** *adj*
strum (strʌm) *vb* **strums, strumming, strummed 1** to sound (the strings of a guitar, etc) with a downward or upward sweep of the thumb or of a plectrum **2** to play (chords, a tune, etc) in this way [C18 prob. imit.] > **'strummer** *n*
struma ('stru:mə) *n, pl* **strumae** (-mi:) **1** an abnormal enlargement of the thyroid gland; goitre **2** *bot* a swelling, esp at the base of a moss capsule **3** another word for **scrofula** [C16 from L: scrofulous tumour, from *struere* to heap up] > **strumous** ('stru:məs) *or* **strumose** ('stru:məʊs) *adj*
Struma ('stru:mə) *n* a river in S Europe, rising in SW Bulgaria near Sofia and flowing generally southeast through Greece to the Aegean. Length: 362 km (225 miles). Greek names: **Strimon, Strymon**
strumpet ('strʌmpɪt) *n arch* a prostitute or promiscuous woman [C14 from ?]
strung (strʌŋ) *vb* **1** a past tense and past participle of **string** ▷ *adj* **2a** (of a piano, etc) provided with strings **2b** (*in combination*): *gut-strung* **3 highly strung** very nervous or volatile in character
strung up *adj* (*postpositive*) *inf* tense or nervous
strut (strʌt) *vb* **struts, strutting, strutted 1** (*intr*) to walk in a pompous or arrogant manner; swagger **2** (*tr*) to support or provide with struts ▷ *n* **3** a structural member, esp as part of a framework **4** an affected, proud, or stiff walk [C14 *strouten* (in the sense: swell, stand out; C16 to walk stiffly), from OE *strūtian* to stand

stiffly] > **'strutter** *n* > **'strutting** *adj* > **'struttingly** *adv*

struthious ('struːθɪəs) *adj* **1** (of birds) related to or resembling the ostrich **2** of, relating to, or designating all flightless birds [c18 from LL *strūthiō*, from Gk *strouthiōn*, from *strouthos* ostrich]

Struve ('struːvə) *n* **Otto** 1897–1963, US astronomer, born in Russia, noted for his work in stellar spectroscopy and his discovery (1937) of interstellar hydrogen

strychnine ('strɪkniːn) *n* a white crystalline very poisonous alkaloid, obtained from the plant nux vomica: formerly used in small quantities as a stimulant [c19 via F from NL *Strychnos*, from Gk *strukhnos* nightshade]

Strymon ('straɪmən) *n* transliteration of the Greek name for the **Struma**

Stuart ('stjʊət) *n* **1** the royal house that ruled in Scotland from 1371 to 1714 and in England from 1603 to 1714. See also **Stewart** (sense 1) **2 Charles Edward,** called *the Young Pretender* or *Bonnie Prince Charlie*. 1720–88, pretender to the British throne. He led the Jacobite Rebellion (1745–46) in an attempt to re-establish the Stuart succession **3** his father, **James Francis Edward,** called *the Old Pretender*. 1688–1766, pretender to the British throne; son of James II (James VII of Scotland) and his second wife, Mary of Modena. He made two unsuccessful attempts to realize his claim to the throne (1708; 1715) **4 Mary** See **Mary, Queen of Scots**
▹ www.royal.gov.uk/output/Page74.asp
▹ www.wsu.edu:8080/~dee/ENLIGHT/ENGLAND.HTM

stub (stʌb) *n* **1** a short piece remaining after something has been cut, removed, etc: *a cigar stub* **2** the residual piece or section of a receipt, ticket, cheque, etc **3** the usual US and Canad word for **counterfoil** **4** any short projection or blunted end **5** the stump of a tree or plant ▹ *vb* **stubs, stubbing, stubbed** (*tr*) **6** to strike (one's toe, foot, etc) painfully against a hard surface **7** (usually foll by *out*) to put (out a cigarette or cigar) by pressing the end against a surface **8** to clear (land) of stubs **9** to dig up (the roots) of (a tree or bush) [OE *stubb*]

stub axle *n* a short axle that carries one of the front steered wheels of a motor vehicle

stubble ('stʌbᵊl) *n* **1a** the stubs of stalks left in a field where a crop has been harvested **1b** (*as modifier*): *a stubble field* **2** any bristly growth [c13 from OF *estuble*, from L *stupula*, var. of *stipula* stalk] > **'stubbled** *or* **'stubbly** *adj*

stubble-jumper *n* *Canad sl* a prairie grain farmer

stubborn ('stʌbᵊn) *adj* **1** refusing to comply, agree, or give in **2** difficult to handle, treat, or overcome **3** persistent and dogged [c14 *stoborne*, from ?] > **'stubbornly** *adv* > **'stubbornness** *n*

Stubbs (stʌbz) *n* **George** 1724–1806, English painter, noted esp for his pictures of horses

stubby ('stʌbɪ) *adj* **stubbier, stubbiest** **1** short and broad; stumpy or thickset **2** bristling and stiff ▹ *n* **3** *Austral sl* Also: **stubbie** a small bottle of beer > **'stubbily** *adv* > **'stubbiness** *n*

stucco ('stʌkəʊ) *n, pl* **stuccoes** *or* **stuccos** **1** a weather-resistant mixture of dehydrated lime, powdered marble, and glue, used in decorative mouldings on buildings **2** any of various types of cement or plaster used for coating outside walls **3** Also called: **stuccowork** decorative work moulded in stucco ▹ *vb* **stuccoes** *or* **stuccos, stuccoing, stuccoed** **4** (*tr*) to apply stucco to [c16 from It., of Gmc origin]

stuck (stʌk) *vb* **1** the past tense and past participle of **stick²** ▹ *adj* **2** *inf* baffled or nonplussed **3** (foll by *on*) *sl* keen (on) or infatuated (with) **4 get stuck in** *or* **into** *inf* **4a** to perform (a task) with determination **4b** to attack (a person)

stuck-up *adj inf* conceited, arrogant, or snobbish > **'stuck-'upness** *n*

stud¹ (stʌd) *n* **1** a large-headed nail or other projection protruding from a surface, usually as decoration **2** a type of fastener consisting of two discs at either end of a short shank, used to fasten shirtfronts, collars, etc **3** a vertical member used with others to construct the framework of a wall **4** the crossbar in the centre of a link of a heavy chain **5** one of a number of rounded projections on the sole of a boot or shoe to give better grip, as on a football boot ▹ *vb* **studs, studding, studded** (*tr*) **6** to provide, ornament, or make with studs **7** to dot or cover (with): *the park was studded with daisies* **8** to provide or support (a wall, partition, etc) with studs [OE *studu*]

stud² (stʌd) *n* **1** a group of pedigree animals, esp horses, kept for breeding purposes **2** any male animal kept principally for breeding purposes, esp a stallion **3** a farm or stable where a stud is kept **4** the state or condition of being kept for breeding purposes: *at stud; put to stud* **5** (*modifier*) of or relating to such animals or the place where they are kept: *a stud farm; a stud horse* **6** *sl* a virile or sexually active man **7** short for **stud poker** [OE *stōd*]

studbook ('stʌdˌbʊk) *n* a written record of the pedigree of a purebred stock, esp of racehorses

studding ('stʌdɪŋ) *n* **1** studs collectively, esp as used to form a wall or partition **2** material used to form or serve as studs

studdingsail ('stʌdɪŋˌseɪl; *naut* 'stʌnsᵊl) *n naut* a light auxiliary sail set outboard on spars on either side of a square sail. Also called: **stunsail, stuns'l** [c16 *studding*, ?from MLow G, MDu. *stōtinge*, from *stōten* to thrust]

student ('stjuːdᵊnt) *n* **1a** a person following a course of study, as in a school, college, university, etc **1b** (*as modifier*): *student teacher* **2** a person who makes a thorough study of a subject [c15 from L *studēns* diligent, from *studēre* to be zealous]

Student's t *n* a statistic often used to test the hypothesis that a random sample of normally distributed observations has a given mean [after *Student*, pen name of W. S. Gosset (1876–1937), Brit mathematician]

studenty ('stjuːdᵊntɪ) *adj inf, sometimes derog* denoting or exhibiting the characteristics believed typical of an undergraduate student

studhorse ('stʌdˌhɔːs) *n* another word for **stallion**

studied ('stʌdɪd) *adj* carefully practised, designed, or premeditated: *a studied reply* > **'studiedly** *adv* > **'studiedness** *n*

studio ('stjuːdɪəʊ) *n, pl* **studios** **1** a room in which an artist, photographer, or musician works **2** a room used to record television or radio programmes, make films, etc **3** (*pl*) the premises of a radio, television, or film company [c19 from It., lit.: study, from L *studium* diligence]

studio couch *n* an upholstered couch, usually backless, convertible into a double bed

studio flat *n* a flat with one main room

studious ('stjuːdɪəs) *adj* **1** given to study **2** of a serious, thoughtful, and hard-working character **3** showing deliberation, care, or precision [c14 from L *studiōsus* devoted to, from *studium* assiduity] > **'studiously** *adv* > **'studiousness** *n*

stud poker *n* a variety of poker in which the first card is dealt face down before each player and the next four are dealt face up (**five-card stud**) or in which the first two cards and the last card are dealt face down and the intervening four cards are dealt face up (**seven-card stud**)

study ('stʌdɪ) *vb* **studies, studying, studied** **1** to apply the mind to the learning or understanding of (a subject), esp by reading **2** (*tr*) to investigate or examine, as by observation, research, etc **3** (*tr*) to look at minutely; scrutinize **4** (*tr*) to give much careful or critical thought to **5** to take a course in (a subject), as at a college **6** (*tr*) to try to memorize: *to study a part for a play* **7** (*intr*) to meditate or contemplate; reflect ▹ *n, pl* **studies** **8a** the act or process of studying **8b** (*as modifier*): *study*

Ss

group **9** a room used for studying, reading, writing, etc **10** (*often pl*) work relating to a particular discipline: *environmental studies* **11** an investigation and analysis of a subject, institution etc **12** a product of studying, such as a written paper or book **13** a drawing, sculpture, etc, executed for practice or in preparation for another work **14** a musical composition intended to develop one aspect of performing technique **15** *inf* **in a brown study** in a reverie or daydream [c13 from OF *estudie*, from L *studium* zeal, from *studēre* to be diligent]

stuff (stʌf) *vb* (*mainly tr*) **1** to pack or fill completely; cram **2** (*intr*) to eat large quantities **3** to force, shove, or squeeze: *to stuff money into a pocket* **4** to fill (food such as poultry or tomatoes) with a stuffing **5** to fill (an animal's skin) with material so as to restore the shape of the live animal **6** *sl* to have sexual intercourse with (a woman) **7** *US & Canad* to fill (a ballot box) with fraudulent votes **8** *sl* to ruin, frustrate, or defeat ▷ *n* **9** the raw material or fabric of something **10** woollen cloth or fabric **11** any general or unspecified substance or accumulation of objects **12** stupid or worthless actions, speech, etc **13** subject matter, skill, etc: *he knows his stuff* **14** a slang word for **money** **15** *sl* a drug, esp cannabis **16** *inf* **do one's stuff** to do what is expected of one **17** **that's the stuff** that is what is needed **18** *Brit sl* a girl or woman considered sexually (esp in **bit of stuff**) [c14 from OF *estoffe*, from *estoffer* to furnish, of Gmc origin] > **'stuffer** *n*

stuffed (stʌft) *adj* **1** filled with something, esp (of poultry and other food) filled with stuffing **2** (foll by *up*) having the nasal passages blocked with mucus **3** **get stuffed!** *Brit sl* an exclamation of contemptuous anger or annoyance against another person

stuffed shirt *n inf* a pompous person

stuff gown *n Brit* a woollen gown worn by a barrister who has not taken silk

stuffing ('stʌfɪŋ) *n* **1** the material with which something is stuffed **2** a mixture of ingredients with which poultry, meat, etc, is stuffed before cooking **3** **knock the stuffing out of** (**someone**) to cause (someone) to lose his or her enthusiasm or confidence

stuffing box *n* a small chamber in which packing is compressed around a reciprocating or rotating rod or shaft to form a seal

stuffy ('stʌfɪ) *adj* **stuffier, stuffiest** **1** lacking fresh air **2** excessively dull, staid, or conventional **3** (of the nasal passages) blocked with mucus > **'stuffily** *adv* > **'stuffiness** *n*

stultify ('stʌltɪˌfaɪ) *vb* **stultifies, stultifying, stultified** (*tr*) **1** to make useless, futile, or ineffectual, esp by routine **2** to cause to appear absurd or inconsistent [c18 from L *stultus* stupid + *facere* to make] > **ˌstultifi'cation** *n* > **'stultiˌfier** *n*

stum (stʌm) (in wine-making) ▷ *n* **1** a less common word for **must²** **2** partly fermented wine added to fermented wine as a preservative ▷ *vb* **stums, stumming, stummed** **3** to preserve (wine) by adding stum [c17 from Du. *stom* dumb]

stumble ('stʌmbᵊl) *vb* **stumbles, stumbling, stumbled** (*intr*) **1** to trip or fall while walking or running **2** to walk in an awkward, unsteady, or unsure way **3** to make mistakes or hesitate in speech or actions **4** (foll by *across* or *upon*) to come (across) by accident ▷ *n* **5** a false step, trip, or blunder **6** the act of stumbling [c14 rel. to Norwegian *stumla*, Danish dialect *stumle*] > **'stumbler** *n* > **'stumbling** *adj* > **'stumblingly** *adv*

stumbling block *n* any impediment or obstacle

stumer ('stjuːmə) *n* **1** *sl* a forgery or cheat **2** *Irish dialect* a poor bargain **3** *Scot* a stupid person **4** **come a stumer** *Austral sl* to crash financially [from ?]

stump (stʌmp) *n* **1** the base of a tree trunk left standing after the tree has been felled or has fallen **2** the part of something, such as a tooth, limb, or blade, that remains after a larger part has been removed **3** (*often pl*) *inf, facetious* a leg (esp in **stir one's stumps**) **4** *cricket* any of three upright wooden sticks that, with two bails laid across them, form a wicket (the **stumps**) **5** Also called: **tortillon** a short sharply-pointed stick of cork or rolled paper or leather, used in drawing and shading **6** a heavy tread or the sound of heavy footsteps **7** a platform used by an orator when addressing a meeting ▷ *vb* **8** (*tr*) to stop, confuse, or puzzle **9** (*intr*) to plod or trudge heavily **10** (*tr*) *cricket* to dismiss (a batsman) by breaking his wicket with the ball or with the ball in the hand while he is out of his crease **11** *chiefly US & Canad* to campaign or canvass (an area), esp by political speech-making [c14 from MLow G *stump*] > **'stumper** *n*

stump up *vb* (*adv*) *Brit inf* to give (the money required)

stumpy ('stʌmpɪ) *adj* **stumpier, stumpiest** **1** short and thickset like a stump; stubby **2** full of stumps > **'stumpiness** *n*

stun (stʌn) *vb* **stuns, stunning, stunned** (*tr*) **1** to render unconscious, as by a heavy blow or fall **2** to shock or overwhelm **3** to surprise or astound ▷ *n* **4** the state or effect of being stunned [c13 *stunen*, from OF *estoner* to daze, ult. from L EX-¹ + *tonāre* to thunder]

stung (stʌŋ) *vb* the past tense and past participle of **sting**

stunk (stʌŋk) *vb* a past tense and past participle of **stink**

stunner ('stʌnə) *n inf* a person or thing of great beauty, quality, size, etc

stunning ('stʌnɪŋ) *adj inf* very attractive, impressive, astonishing, etc > **'stunningly** *adv*

stunsail *or* **stuns'l** ('stʌnsᵊl) *n* another word for **studdingsail**

stunt¹ (stʌnt) *vb* **1** (*tr*) to prevent or impede (the growth or development) of (a plant, animal, etc) ▷ *n* **2** the act or an instance of stunting **3** a person, animal, or plant that has been stunted [c17 (as vb: to check the growth of): ?from c15 *stont* of short duration, from OE *stunt* foolish; sense prob. infl. by ON *stuttr* dwarfed] > **'stunted** *adj* > **'stuntedness** *n*

stunt² (stʌnt) *n* **1** a feat of daring or skill **2a** an acrobatic or dangerous piece of action in a film, etc **2b** (*as modifier*): *a stunt man* **3** anything spectacular or unusual done for attention ▷ *vb* **4** (*intr*) to perform a stunt or stunts [c19 US student slang, from ?]

stupa ('stuːpə) *n* a domed edifice housing Buddhist or Jain relics [c19 from Sansk.: dome]

stupe (stjuːp) *n med* a hot damp cloth, usually sprinkled with an irritant, applied to the body to relieve pain by counterirritation [c14 from L *stuppa* flax, from Gk *stuppē*]

stupefacient (ˌstjuːpɪ'feɪʃɪənt) *n* **1** a drug that causes stupor ▷ *adj* **2** of, relating to, or designating this type of drug [c17 from L *stupefaciēns*, from *stupēre* to be stunned + *facere* to make]

stupefaction (ˌstjuːpɪ'fækʃən) *n* **1** astonishment **2** the act of stupefying or the state of being stupefied

stupefy ('stjuːpɪˌfaɪ) *vb* **stupefies, stupefying, stupefied** (*tr*) **1** to render insensitive or lethargic **2** to confuse or astound [c16 from OF *stupefier*, from L *stupefacere*; see STUPEFACIENT] > **'stupeˌfying** *adj*

stupendous (stjuː'pɛndəs) *adj* astounding, wonderful, huge, etc [c17 from L *stupēre* to be amazed] > **stu'pendously** *adv* > **stu'pendousness** *n*

stupid ('stjuːpɪd) *adj* **1** lacking in common sense, perception, or intelligence **2** (*usually postpositive*) dazed or stupefied: *stupid from lack of sleep* **3** slow-witted **4** trivial, silly, or frivolous ▷ *n* **5** *inf* a stupid person [c16 from F *stupide*, from L *stupidus* silly, from *stupēre* to be amazed] > **stu'pidity** *or* **'stupidness** *n*

stupor ('stjuːpə) *n* **1** a state of unconsciousness **2** mental dullness; torpor [c17 from L, from *stupēre* to be aghast] > **'stuporous** *adj*

sturdy ('stɜːdɪ) *adj* **sturdier, sturdiest** **1** healthy, strong, and vigorous: *the league newcomers mounted a sturdy challenge* **2** strongly built; stalwart [c13 (in the sense: rash, harsh): from OF *estordi* dazed, from *estordir* to stun] > **'sturdily** *adv* > **'sturdiness** *n*

sturgeon ('stɜːdʒən) *n* any of various primitive bony fishes of temperate waters of the N hemisphere, having an elongated snout and rows of spines along the body [C13 from OF *estourgeon*, of Gmc origin]

Sturt (stɜːt) *n* **Charles** 1795–1869, English explorer, who led three expeditions (1828–29; 1829; 1844–45) into the Australian interior, discovering the Darling River (1828)

Sturt's desert pea *n Austral* the desert pea [named after Charles STURT

stutter ('stʌtə) *vb* **1** to speak (a word, phrase, etc) with recurring repetition of consonants, esp initial ones **2** to make (an abrupt sound) repeatedly: *the gun stuttered* ▷ *n* **3** the act or habit of stuttering **4** a stuttering sound [C16] > **'stutterer** *n* > **'stuttering** *n, adj* > **'stutteringly** *adv*

Stuttgart (*German* 'ʃtʊtgart) *n* an industrial city in W Germany, capital of Baden-Württemberg state, on the River Neckar: developed around a stud farm (*Stuotgarten*) of the Counts of Württemberg. Pop: 581 200 (2000)

Stuyvesant ('staɪvɪsᵊnt) *n* **Peter** ?1610–72, Dutch colonial administrator of New Netherland (later New York) (1646–64)

sty (staɪ) *n, pl* **sties 1** a pen in which pigs are housed **2** any filthy or corrupt place ▷ *vb* **sties, stying, stied 3** to enclose or be enclosed in a sty [OE *stig*]

stye *or* **sty** (staɪ) *n, pl* **styes** *or* **sties** inflammation of a sebaceous gland of the eyelid [C15 *styanye* (mistaken as *sty on eye*), from OE *stīgend* rising, hence swelling, + *ye* eye]

Stygian ('stɪdʒɪən) *adj* **1** of or relating to the Styx **2** *chiefly literary* dark, gloomy, or hellish [C16 from L *Stygius*, from Gk *Stugios*, from *Stux* STYX]

style (staɪl) *n* **1** a form of appearance, design, or production; type or make **2** the way in which something is done: *good style* **3** the manner in which something is expressed or performed, considered as separate from its intrinsic content, meaning, etc **4** a distinctive, formal, or characteristic manner of expression in words, music, painting, etc **5** elegance or refinement of manners, dress, etc **6** prevailing fashion in dress, looks, etc **7** a fashionable or ostentatious mode of existence: *to live in style* **8** the particular mode of orthography, punctuation, design, etc, followed in a book, journal, etc, or in a printing or publishing house **9** *chiefly Brit* the distinguishing title or form of address of a person or firm **10** *bot* the stalk of a carpel bearing the stigma **11** a method of expressing or calculating dates. See **Old Style, New Style 12** another word for **stylus** (sense 1) **13** the arm of a sundial ▷ *vb* **styles, styling, styled** (*mainly tr*) **14** to design, shape, or tailor: *to style hair* **15** to adapt or make suitable for **16** to make consistent or correct according to a printing or publishing style **17** to name or call; designate: *to style a man a fool* [C13 from L *stylus*, *stilus* writing implement, hence characteristics of the writing, style] > **'stylar** *adj* > **'styler** *n*

stylebook ('staɪl,bʊk) *n* a book containing rules and examples of punctuation, typography, etc, for the use of writers, editors, and printers

stylet ('staɪlɪt) *n surgery* **1** a wire for insertion into a catheter, etc, to maintain its rigidity during passage **2** a slender probe [C17 from F *stilet*, from OIt. STILETTO; infl. by L *stylus* style]

styling mousse *n* a light foamy substance applied to the hair before styling in order to retain the style

stylish ('staɪlɪʃ) *adj* having style; smart; fashionable > **'stylishly** *adv* > **'stylishness** *n*

stylist ('staɪlɪst) *n* **1** a person who performs, writes, or acts with attention to style **2** a designer of clothes, décor, etc **3** a hairdresser who styles hair

stylistic (staɪ'lɪstɪk) *adj* of or relating to style, esp artistic or literary style > **sty'listically** *adv*

stylite ('staɪlaɪt) *n Christianity* one of a class of recluses who in ancient times lived on the top of high pillars [C17 from LGk *stulitēs*, from Gk *stulos* a pillar] > **stylitic** (staɪ'lɪtɪk) *adj*

stylize *or* **stylise** ('staɪlaɪz) *vb* **stylizes, stylizing, stylized** *or* **stylises, stylising, stylised** (*tr*) to give an established stylistic form to > **,styli'zation** *or* **,styli'sation** *n*

stylo- *or before a vowel* **styl-** *combining form* **1** (in biology) a style **2** indicating a column or point: *stylobate; stylograph* [from Gk *stulos* column]

stylobate ('staɪlə,beɪt) *n* a continuous horizontal course of masonry that supports a colonnade [C17 from L *stylobatēs*, from Gk *stulos* pillar + *-batēs*, from *bainein* to walk]

stylograph ('staɪlə,grɑːf) *n* a fountain pen having a fine hollow tube as the writing point instead of a nib [C19 from STYL(US) + -GRAPH]

styloid ('staɪlɔɪd) *adj* **1** resembling a stylus **2** *anat* of or relating to a projecting process of the temporal bone [C18 from NL *styloides*, from Gk *stuloeidēs* like a stylus; infl. by Gk *stulos* pillar]

stylops ('staɪlɒps) *n, pl* **stylopes** (-lə,piːz) any of various insects living as a parasite in other insects, esp bees and wasps [C19 NL, from Gk, from *stulos* a pillar + *ōps* an eye, from the fact that the male has stalked eyes]

stylus ('staɪləs) *n, pl* **styli** (-laɪ) *or* **styluses 1** Also called: **style** a pointed instrument for engraving, drawing, or writing **2** a tool used in ancient times for writing on wax tablets, which was pointed at one end and blunt at the other for erasing **3** Also called: **needle** a device attached to the cartridge in the pick-up arm of a record player that rests in the groove in the record, transmitting the vibrations to the sensing device in the cartridge [C18 from L, var. of *stilus* writing implement]

stymie *or* **stymy** ('staɪmɪ) *vb* **stymies, stymieing** *or* **stymying, stymied** (*tr; often passive*) **1** to hinder or thwart **2** *golf* (formerly) to impede with a stymie ▷ *n, pl* **stymies 3** *golf* (formerly) a situation in which an opponent's ball is blocking the line between the hole and the ball about to be played **4** a situation of obstruction [C19 from ?]

styptic ('stɪptɪk) *adj* **1** contracting the blood vessels or tissues ▷ *n* **2** a styptic drug [C14 via LL, from Gk *stuptikos* capable of contracting, from *stuphein* to contract]

styrene ('staɪriːn) *n* a colourless oily volatile flammable liquid made from ethylene and benzene. It readily polymerizes and is used in making synthetic plastics and rubbers. Formula: $C_6H_5CH{:}CH_2$. Systematic name: **phenylethene** [C20 from Gk *sturax* tree of the genus *Styrax* + -ENE]

Styria ('stɪərɪə) *n* a mountainous state of SE Austria: rich mineral resources. Capital: Graz. Pop: 1 185 911 (2000). Area: 16 384 sq km (6326 sq miles). German name: **Steiermark**

Styrofoam ('staɪrə,fəʊm) *n trademark* (*sometimes not cap*) a light form of expanded polystyrene [C20 from POLYSTYRENE + FOAM]

Styx (stɪks) *n Greek myth* a river in Hades across which Charon ferried the souls of the dead [from Gk *Stux*; related to *stugein* to hate]

suable ('sjuːəbᵊl) *adj* liable to be sued in a court > **,sua'bility** *n*

Suakin ('suːɑːkɪn) *n* a port in the NE Sudan, on the Red Sea: formerly the chief port of the African Red Sea; now obstructed by a coral reef. Pop: 5511 (latest est)

suasion ('sweɪʒən) *n* a rare word for **persuasion** [C14 from L *suāsiō*, from *suādēre* to PERSUADE] > **'suasive** *adj*

suave (swɑːv) *adj* (esp of a man) displaying smoothness and sophistication in manner; urbane [C16 from L *suāvis* sweet] > **'suavely** *adv* > **suavity** ('swɑːvɪtɪ) *or* **'suaveness** *n*

sub (sʌb) *n* **1** short for several words beginning with *sub-*, such as **subeditor, submarine, subordinate, subscription,** and **substitute 2** *Brit inf* an advance payment of wages or salary. Formal term: **subsistence allowance** ▷ *vb* **subs, subbing, subbed 3** (*intr*) to serve or

Ss

act as a substitute **4** *Brit inf* to grant or receive (an advance payment of wages or salary) **5** *(tr) inf* short for **subedit**

sub. *abbrev for:* **1** subeditor **2** *music* subito **3** subscription **4** substitute

sub- *prefix* **1** situated under or beneath: *subterranean* **2** secondary in rank; subordinate: *subeditor* **3** falling short of; less than or imperfectly: *subarctic; subhuman* **4** forming a subdivision or subordinate part: *subcommittee* **5** (in chemistry) **5a** indicating that a compound contains a relatively small proportion of a specified element: *suboxide* **5b** indicating that a salt is basic salt: *subacetate* [from L *sub*]

subacid (sʌbˈæsɪd) *adj* (esp of some fruits) moderately acid or sour > **subacidity** (ˌsʌbəˈsɪdɪtɪ) *or* **subˈacidness** *n*

subadar *or* **subahdar** (ˈsuːbəˌdɑː) *n* (formerly) the chief native officer of a company of Indian soldiers in the British service [c17 via Urdu from Persian, from *sūba* province + *-dār* holding]

subalpine (sʌbˈælpaɪn) *adj* **1** situated in or relating to the regions at the foot of mountains **2** (of plants) growing below the tree line in mountainous regions

subaltern (ˈsʌbᵊltən) *n* **1** a commissioned officer below the rank of captain in certain armies, esp the British ▷ *adj* **2** of inferior position or rank **3** *logic* (of a proposition) particular, esp in relation to a universal of the same quality [c16 from LL *subalternus*, from L SUB- + *alternus* alternate, from *alter* the other]

subalternation (ˌsʌbɔːltəˈneɪʃən) *n logic* the relation between a universal and a particular proposition of the same quality where the universal proposition implies the particular proposition

subantarctic (ˌsʌbæntˈɑːktɪk) *adj* of or relating to latitudes immediately north of the Antarctic Circle

subaqua (ˌsʌbˈækwə) *adj* of or relating to underwater sport: *subaqua swimming*

subaqueous (sʌbˈeɪkwɪəs, -ˈækwɪ-) *adj* occurring, formed, or used under water

subarctic (sʌbˈɑːktɪk) *adj* of or relating to latitudes immediately south of the Arctic Circle

subatomic (ˌsʌbəˈtɒmɪk) *adj* **1** of, relating to, or being a particle making up an atom or a process occurring within atoms **2** having dimensions smaller than atomic dimensions

Subatomic Particles

PARTICLE	SYMBOL	CHARGE	MASS	SPIN
Gauge Bosons				
photon	v	0	0	1
gluon	g	0	0	1
W boson	W^-	–1	80 400	1
Z boson	Z^0	0	91 200	1
Quarks				
up	u	+2/3	5.1	½
down	d	–1/3	10.2	½
charm	c	+2/3	1500	½
strange	s	–1/3	200	½
top	t	+2/3	179870	½
bottom	b	–1/3	8690	½
Leptons				
electron	e^-	–1	0.511	½
neutrino (electron)	ν_e	0	0	½
muon	μ^-	–1	105.66	½
neutrino (muon)	ν_μ	0	0	½
tau	τ^-	-1	1 784 000	½
neutrino (tau)	ν_τ	0	0	½
Baryons				
proton	p	+1	938.26	½
neutron	n	0	939.55	½
xi particle	Ξ^0	0	1314.9	½
	Ξ^-	–1	1321.3	½
sigma particle	Σ^+	+1	1189.5	½
	Σ^0	0	1192.5	½
	Σ^-	–1	1197.4	½
lambda particle	Λ	0	1115.5	½
omega particle	Ω^-	–1	1672.5	¾
Mesons				
kaon	κ^-	–1	493.8	0
	κ^+	+1	493.8	0
pion	π^+	+1	139.6	0
	π^0	0	135	0
	π^-	–1	139.6	0
phi particle	Φ	0	1020	1
psi particle	Ψ	0	3095	1
eta particle	η^0	0	548.8	0

NOTE: masses are given in MeV/c^2 (1 Mev/c^2 = 1.78 × 10–30 kg)

subbasement (ˈsʌbˌbeɪsmənt) *n* a storey of a building beneath the main basement

subclass (ˈsʌbˌklɑːs) *n* **1** a principal subdivision of a class **2** *biol* a taxonomic group that is a subdivision of a class **3** *maths* another name for **subset**

subclavian (sʌbˈkleɪvɪən) *adj anat* (of an artery, vein, etc) below the clavicle [c17 from NL *subclāvius*, from L SUB- + *clavis* key]

subclinical (sʌbˈklɪnɪkᵊl) *adj med* of or relating to the stage in the course of a disease before the symptoms are first noted > **subˈclinically** *adv*

subconscious (sʌbˈkɒnʃəs) *adj* **1** acting or existing without one's awareness ▷ *n* **2** *psychol* that part of the mind on the fringe of consciousness which contains material it is possible to become aware of by redirecting attention > **subˈconsciously** *adv* > **subˈconsciousness** *n*

subcontinent (sʌbˈkɒntɪnənt) *n* a large land mass that is a distinct part of a continent, such as India is of Asia > **subcontinental** (ˌsʌbkɒntɪˈnɛntᵊl) *adj*

subcontract *n* (sʌbˈkɒntrækt) **1** a subordinate contract under which the supply of materials, labour, etc, is let out to someone other than a party to the main contract ▷ *vb* (ˌsʌbkənˈtrækt) **2** *(intr; often foll by for)* to enter into or make a subcontract **3** *(tr)* to let out (work) on a subcontract > ˌ**subconˈtractor** *n*

subcontrary (sʌbˈkɒntrərɪ) *logic* ▷ *adj* **1** (of a pair of propositions) related such that they cannot both be false at once, although they may be true together ▷ *n, pl* **subcontraries** **2** a statement which cannot be false when a given statement is false

subcritical (sʌbˈkrɪtɪkᵊl) *adj physics* (of a nuclear reaction, power station, etc) having or involving a chain reaction that is not self-sustaining; not yet critical

subculture (ˈsʌbˌkʌltʃə) *n* a subdivision of a national culture or an enclave within it with a distinct integrated network of behaviour, beliefs, and attitudes > **subˈcultural** *adj*

subcutaneous (ˌsʌbkjuːˈteɪnɪəs) *adj med* situated, used, or introduced beneath the skin > ˌ**subcuˈtaneously** *adv*

subdeacon (ˌsʌbˈdiːkən) *n chiefly RC Church* **1** a cleric who assists at High Mass **2** (formerly) a person ordained to the lowest of the major orders

subdivide (ˌsʌbdɪˈvaɪd, ˈsʌbdɪˌvaɪd) *vb* **subdivides, subdividing, subdivided** to divide (something) resulting from an earlier division > **ˈsubdiˌvision** *n*

subdominant (sʌbˈdɒmɪnənt) *music* ▷ *n* **1** the fourth degree of a major or minor scale **2** a key or chord based on this ▷ *adj* **3** of or relating to the subdominant

subdue (səb'dju:) *vb* **subdues, subduing, subdued** (*tr*) **1** to establish ascendancy over by force **2** to overcome and bring under control, as by intimidation or persuasion **3** to hold in check or repress (feelings, etc) **4** to render less intense or less conspicuous [C14 *sobdue*, from OF *soduire* to mislead, from L *subdūcere* to remove; infl. by L *subdere* to subject] > **sub'duable** *adj* > **sub'dual** *n*
subdued (səb'dju:d) *adj* **1** cowed, passive, or shy **2** gentle or quiet: *a subdued whisper* **3** (of colours, lighting, etc) not harsh or bright
subdural (sʌb'djʊərəl) *adj anat* between the dura mater and the arachnoid: *subdural haematoma*
subedit (sʌb'ɛdɪt) *vb* **subedits, subediting, subedited** to edit and correct (written or printed material)
subeditor (sʌb'ɛdɪtə) *n* a person who checks and edits copy, esp on a newspaper
subequatorial (sʌbˌɛkwə'tɔ:rɪəl) *adj* in or characteristic of regions immediately north or south of equatorial regions
suberose ('sju:bəˌrəʊs), **subereous** (sju:'bɛrɪəs), *or* **suberic** (sju:'bɛrɪk) *adj bot* relating to, resembling, or consisting of cork; corky [C19 from L *sūber* cork + -OSE[1]]
subfamily ('sʌbˌfæmɪlɪ) *n, pl* **subfamilies** **1** *biol* a taxonomic group that is a subdivision of a family **2** a subdivision of a family of languages
subfusc ('sʌbfʌsk) *adj* **1** devoid of brightness or appeal; drab, dull, or dark ▷ *n* **2** (at Oxford University) formal academic dress [C18 from L *subfuscus* dusky, from *fuscus* dark]
subgenus ('sʌbˌdʒi:nəs, -ˌdʒɛn-) *n, pl* **subgenera** (-'dʒɛnərə) *or* **subgenuses** *biol* a subdivision of a genus that is of higher rank than a species > **subgeneric** (ˌsʌbdʒə'nɛrɪk) *adj*
subheading ('sʌbˌhɛdɪŋ) *or* **subhead** *n* **1** the heading or title of a subdivision or subsection of a printed work **2** a division subordinate to a main heading or title
subhuman (sʌb'hju:mən) *adj* **1** of or designating animals below man (*Homo sapiens*) in evolutionary development **2** less than human
subindex (sʌb'ɪndɛks) *n, pl* **subindices** (-dɪˌsi:z) *or* **subindexes** another word for **subscript** (sense 2)
subitize *or* **subitise** ('sʌbɪˌtaɪz) *vb* **subitizes, subitizing, subitized** *or* **subitises, subitising, subitised** *psychol* to perceive the number of (a group of items) at a glance and without counting: *the maximum number of items that can be subitized is about five* [C20 from L *subitus* sudden + -IZE]
subito ('su:bɪˌtəʊ) *adv music* suddenly; immediately [C18 via It. from L: suddenly, from *subitus* sudden, from *subīre* to approach]
subj. *abbrev for:* **1** subject **2** subjective(ly) **3** subjunctive
subjacent (sʌb'dʒeɪsᵊnt) *adj* **1** forming a foundation; underlying **2** lower than [C16 from L *subjacēre* to lie close, be under] > **sub'jacency** *n* > **sub'jacently** *adv*
subject *n* ('sʌbdʒɪkt) **1** the predominant theme or topic, as of a book, discussion, etc **2** any branch of learning considered as a course of study **3** *grammar, logic* a word, phrase, etc, about which something is predicated or stated in a sentence; for example, *the cat* in the sentence *The cat catches mice* **4** a person or thing that undergoes experiment, treatment, etc **5** a person under the rule of a monarch, government, etc **6** an object, figure, scene, etc, as portrayed by an artist or photographer **7** *philosophy* **7a** that which thinks or feels as opposed to the object of thinking and feeling; the self or the mind **7b** a substance as opposed to its attributes **8** Also called: **theme** *music* the principal motif of a fugue, the basis from which the musical material is derived in a sonata-form movement, or the recurrent figure in a rondo **9** *logic* the term of a proposition about which something is asserted **10** an originating motive **11** **change the subject** to select a new topic of conversation ▷ *adj* ('sʌbdʒɪkt) (*usually postpositive;* foll by *to*) **12** being under the power or sovereignty of a ruler, government, etc: *subject peoples* **13** showing a tendency (towards): *a child subject to indiscipline* **14** exposed or vulnerable: *subject to ribaldry* **15** conditional upon: *the results are subject to correction* ▷ *adv* ('sʌbdʒɪkt) **16** **subject to** (*prep*) under the condition that: *we accept, subject to her agreement* ▷ *vb* (səb'dʒɛkt) (*tr*) **17** (foll by *to*) to cause to undergo: *they subjected him to torture* **18** (*often passive;* foll by *to*) to expose or render vulnerable or liable (to some experience): *he was subjected to great danger* **19** (foll by *to*) to bring under the control or authority (of): *to subject a soldier to discipline* **20** *rare* to present for consideration; submit [C14 from L *subjectus* brought under, from *subicere* to place under, from SUB- + *jacere* to throw] > **sub'jectable** *adj* > **sub'jection** *n*
subjective (səb'dʒɛktɪv) *adj* **1** of, proceeding from, or relating to the mind of the thinking subject and not the nature of the object being considered **2** of, relating to, or emanating from a person's emotions, prejudices, etc **3** relating to the inherent nature of a person or thing; essential **4** existing only as perceived and not as a thing in itself **5** *med* (of a symptom, condition, etc) experienced only by the patient and incapable of being recognized or studied by anyone else **6** *grammar* denoting a case of nouns and pronouns, esp in languages having only two cases, that identifies the subject of a finite verb and (in formal use in English) is selected for predicate complements, as in *It is I* ▷ *n* **7** *grammar* **7a** the subjective case **7b** a subjective word or speech element ▷ Cf **objective** > **sub'jectively** *adv* > ˌ**subjec'tivity** *or* **sub'jectiveness** *n*
subjectivism (səb'dʒɛktɪˌvɪzəm) *n philosophy* the doctrine that there are no absolute moral values but that these are variable in the same way that taste is > **sub'jectivist** *n*
subjoin (sʌb'dʒɔɪn) *vb* (*tr*) to add or attach at the end of something spoken, written, etc [C16 from F *subjoindre*, from L *subjungere* to add to, from *sub-* in addition + *jungere* to join] > **sub'joinder** *n*
sub judice ('dʒu:dɪsɪ) *adj* (*usually postpositive*) before a court of law or a judge; under judicial consideration [L]
subjugate ('sʌbdʒʊˌgeɪt) *vb* **subjugates, subjugating, subjugated** (*tr*) **1** to bring into subjection **2** to make subservient or submissive [C15 from LL *subjugāre* to subdue, from L SUB- + *jugum* yoke] > **'subjugable** *adj* > ˌ**subju'gation** *n* > **'subjuˌgator** *n*
subjunctive (səb'dʒʌŋktɪv) *grammar* ▷ *adj* **1** denoting a mood of verbs used when the content of the clause is being doubted, supposed, feared true, etc, rather than being asserted. In the following sentence, *were* is in the subjunctive: *I'd think seriously about it if I were you* ▷ Cf **indicative** ▷ *n* **2a** the subjunctive mood **2b** a verb in this mood [C16 via LL *subjunctīvus*, from L *subjungere* to SUBJOIN] > **sub'junctively** *adv*
sublease *n* ('sʌbˌli:s) **1** a lease of property made by a lessee or tenant of that property ▷ *vb* (sʌb'li:s), **subleases, subleasing, subleased** **2** to grant a sublease of (property); sublet **3** (*tr*) to obtain or hold by sublease > **sublessee** (ˌsʌblɛ'si:) *n* > **sublessor** (ˌsʌblɛ'sɔ:) *n*
sublet (sʌb'lɛt) *vb* **sublets, subletting, sublet** **1** to grant a sublease of (property) **2** to let out (work, etc) under a subcontract
sublieutenant (ˌsʌblə'tɛnənt) *n* the most junior commissioned officer in the Royal Navy and certain other navies > ˌ**sublieu'tenancy** *n*
sublimate ('sʌblɪˌmeɪt) *vb* **sublimates, sublimating, sublimated** **1** *psychol* to direct the energy of (a primitive impulse) into activities that are socially more acceptable **2** (*tr*) to make purer; refine ▷ *n* **3** *chem* the material obtained when a substance is sublimed [C16 from L *sublīmāre* to elevate, from *sublīmis* lofty; see SUBLIME] > ˌ**subli'mation** *n*
sublime (sə'blaɪm) *adj* **1** of high moral, intellectual, or spiritual value; noble; exalted **2** inspiring deep

veneration or awe **3** unparalleled; supreme **4** *poetic* of proud bearing or aspect **5** *arch* raised up ▷ *n* **the sublime** **6** something that is sublime **7** the ultimate degree or perfect example: *the sublime of folly* ▷ *vb* **sublimes, subliming, sublimed** **8** (*tr*) to make higher or purer **9** to change or cause to change directly from a solid to a vapour or gas without first melting **10** to undergo or cause to undergo this process followed by a reverse change directly from a vapour to a solid: *to sublime iodine onto glass* [C14 from L *sublīmis* lofty, ?from *sub-* up to + *līmen* lintel] > **sub'limely** *adv* > **sublimity** (sə'blɪmɪtɪ) *n*

subliminal (sʌb'lɪmɪnᵊl) *adj* **1** resulting from processes of which the individual is not aware **2** (of stimuli) less than the minimum intensity or duration required to elicit a response [C19 from L *sub-* below + *līmen* threshold] > **sub'liminally** *adv*

subliminal advertising *n* advertising on film or television that employs subliminal images to influence the viewer unconsciously

sublingual (sʌb'lɪŋgwəl) *adj anat* situated beneath the tongue

sublunary (sʌb'lu:nərɪ) *adj* **1** between the moon and the earth **2** of or relating to the earth [C16 via LL, from L SUB- + *lūna* moon]

sub-machine-gun *n* a portable automatic or semiautomatic light gun with a short barrel, designed to be fired from the hip or shoulder

submarginal (sʌb'mɑ:dʒɪnᵊl) *adj* **1** below the minimum requirements **2** (of land) infertile and unprofitable > **sub'marginally** *adv*

submarine ('sʌbmə,ri:n, ,sʌbmə'ri:n) *n* **1** a vessel, esp a warship, capable of operating below the surface of the sea **2** (*modifier*) **2a** of or relating to a submarine: *a submarine captain* **2b** below the surface of the sea: *a submarine cable* > **submariner** (sʌb'mærɪnə) *n*
▷ www.howstuffworks.com/submarine.htm

submaxillary gland (,sʌbmæk'sɪlərɪ) *n* (in mammals) either of a pair of salivary glands situated on each side behind the lower jaw

submediant (sʌb'mi:dɪənt) *music* ▷ *n* **1** the sixth degree of a major or minor scale **2** a key or chord based on this ▷ *adj* **3** of or relating to the submediant

submerge (səb'mɜ:dʒ) *or* **submerse** (səb'mɜ:s) *vb* **submerges, submerging, submerged** *or* **submerses, submersing, submersed** **1** to plunge, sink, or dive or cause to plunge, sink, or dive below the surface of water, etc **2** (*tr*) to cover with water or other liquid **3** (*tr*) to hide; suppress **4** (*tr*) to overwhelm, as with work, etc [C17 from L *submergere*] > **sub'mergence** *or* **sub'mersion** *n*

submersible (səb'mɜ:sɪbᵊl) *or* **submergible** (səb'mɜ:dʒɪbᵊl) *adj* **1** able to be submerged **2** capable of operating under water, etc ▷ *n* **3** a vessel designed to operate under water for short periods **4** a submarine designed and equipped to carry out work below the level that divers can work > **sub,mersi'bility** *or* **sub,mergi'bility** *n*

subminiature (sʌb'mɪnɪətʃə) *adj* smaller than miniature

subminiature camera *n* a pocket-sized camera, usually using 16 millimetre film

submission (səb'mɪʃən) *n* **1** an act or instance of submitting **2** something submitted; a proposal, etc **3** the quality or condition of being submissive **4** the act of referring a document, etc, for the consideration of someone else

submissive (səb'mɪsɪv) *adj* of, tending towards, or indicating submission, humility, or servility > **sub'missively** *adv* > **sub'missiveness** *n*

submit (səb'mɪt) *vb* **submits, submitting, submitted** **1** (often foll by *to*) to yield (oneself), as to the will of another person, a superior force, etc **2** (foll by *to*) to subject or be voluntarily subjected (to analysis, treatment, etc) **3** (*tr*; often foll by *to*) to refer (something to someone) for judgment or consideration **4** (*tr*; *may take a clause as object*) to state, contend, or propose deferentially **5** (*intr*; often foll by *to*) to defer or accede (to the decision, etc, of another) [C14 from L *submittere* to place under] > **sub'mittable** *or* **sub'missible** *adj* > **sub'mittal** *n* > **sub'mitter** *n*

submultiple (sʌb'mʌltɪpᵊl) *n* **1** a number that can be divided into another number an integral number of times without a remainder: *three is a submultiple of nine* ▷ *adj* **2** being a submultiple of a quantity or number

subnormal (sʌb'nɔ:məl) *adj* **1** less than the normal **2** having a low intelligence ▷ *n* **3** a subnormal person > **subnormality** (,sʌbnɔ:'mælɪtɪ) *n*

subnuclear (sʌb'nju:klɪə) *adj* in or smaller than the nucleus of an atom

suborbital (sʌb'ɔ:bɪtᵊl) *adj* **1** (of a rocket, missile, etc) having a flight path that is less than an orbit of the earth or other celestial body **2** *anat* situated beneath the orbit of the eye

suborder ('sʌb,ɔ:də) *n biol* a subdivision of an order > **sub'ordinal** *adj*

subordinate *adj* (sə'bɔ:dɪnɪt) **1** of lesser order or importance **2** under the authority or control of another: *a subordinate functionary* ▷ *n* (sə'bɔ:dɪnɪt) **3** a person or thing that is subordinate ▷ *vb* (sə'bɔ:dɪ,neɪt), **subordinates, subordinating, subordinated** (*tr*; usually foll by *to*) **4** to put in a lower rank or position (than) **5** to make subservient: *to subordinate mind to heart* [C15 from Med. L *subordināre*, from L SUB- + *ordō* rank] > **sub'ordinately** *adv* > **sub,ordi'nation** *n* > **sub'ordinative** *adj*

subordinate clause *n grammar* a clause with an adjectival, adverbial, or nominal function, rather than one that functions as a separate sentence in its own right

subordinating conjunction *n* a conjunction that introduces subordinate clauses, such as *if*, *because*, *although*, and *until*

suborn (sə'bɔ:n) *vb* (*tr*) **1** to bribe, incite, or instigate (a person) to commit a wrongful act **2** *law* to induce (a witness) to commit perjury [C16 from L *subornāre*, from *sub-* secretly + *ornāre* to furnish] > **subornation** (,sʌbɔ:'neɪʃən) *n* > **subornative** (sʌ'bɔ:nətɪv) *adj* > **sub'orner** *n*

Subotica (*Serbo-Croat* 'subɔtitsa) *n* a town in NE Serbia and Montenegro, in Serbia near the border with Hungary: agricultural and industrial centre. Pop: 100 386 (1991). Hungarian name: **Szabadka**

suboxide (sʌb'ɒksaɪd) *n* an oxide of an element containing less oxygen than the common oxide formed by the element: *carbon suboxide*, C_2O_3

subplot ('sʌb,plɒt) *n* a subordinate or auxiliary plot in a novel, play, film, etc

subpoena (səb'pi:nə) *n* **1** a writ issued by a court of justice requiring a person to appear before the court at a specified time ▷ *vb* **subpoenas, subpoenaing, subpoenaed** **2** (*tr*) to serve with a subpoena [C15 from L: under penalty]

subrogate ('sʌbrə,geɪt) *vb* **subrogates, subrogating, subrogated** (*tr*) *law* to put (one person or thing) in the place of another in respect of a right or claim [C16 from L *subrogāre*, from *sub-* in place of + *rogāre* to ask]

subrogation (,sʌbrə'geɪʃən) *n law* the substitution of one person or thing for another, esp the placing of a surety who has paid the debt in the place of the creditor, entitling him to payment from the original debtor

sub rosa ('rəʊzə) *adv* in secret [L, lit.: under the rose; from use of the rose in ancient times as a token of secrecy]

subroutine ('sʌbru:,ti:n) *n* a section of a computer program that is stored only once but can be used at several different points in the program. Also called: **procedure**

sub-Saharan *adj* in, of, or relating to Africa south of the Sahara desert

subscribe (səbˈskraɪb) *vb* **subscribes, subscribing, subscribed** 1 (usually foll by *to*) to pay or promise to pay (money) as a contribution (to a fund, for a magazine, etc), esp at regular intervals 2 to sign (one's name, etc) at the end of a document 3 (*intr; foll by to*) to give support or approval: *to subscribe to the theory of reincarnation* [c15 from L *subscrībere* to write underneath] > **subˈscriber** *n*

subscriber trunk dialling *n Brit* a service by which telephone subscribers can obtain trunk calls by dialling direct without the aid of an operator. Abbrev: **STD**

subscript (ˈsʌbskrɪpt) *printing* ▷ *adj* 1 (of a character) written or printed below the base line ▷ Cf **superscript** ▷ *n* 2 Also called: **subindex** a subscript character

subscription (səbˈskrɪpʃən) *n* 1 a payment or promise of payment for consecutive issues of a magazine, newspaper, book, etc, over a specified period of time 2a the advance purchase of tickets for a series of concerts, etc 2b (*as modifier*): *a subscription concert* 3 money paid or promised, as to a charity, or the fund raised in this way 4 an offer to buy shares or bonds issued by a company 5 the act of signing one's name to a document, etc 6 a signature or other appendage attached to the bottom of a document, etc 7 agreement or acceptance expressed by or as if by signing one's name 8 a signed document, statement, etc 9 *chiefly Brit* the membership dues or fees paid to a society or club 10 an advance order for a new product 11a the sale of books, etc, prior to publishing 11b (*as modifier*): *a subscription edition* > **subˈscriptive** *adj* > **subˈscriptively** *adv*

subsequence (ˈsʌbsɪkwəns) *n* 1 the fact or state of being subsequent 2 a subsequent incident or occurrence

subsequent (ˈsʌbsɪkwənt) *adj* occurring after; succeeding [c15 from L *subsequēns* following on, from *subsequī*, from *sub-* near + *sequī* to follow] > **ˈsubsequently** *adv* > **ˈsubsequentness** *n*

subserve (səbˈsɜːv) *vb* **subserves, subserving, subserved** (*tr*) to be helpful or useful to [c17 from L *subservīre* to be subject to, from SUB- + *servīre* to serve]

subservient (səbˈsɜːvɪənt) *adj* 1 obsequious 2 serving as a means to an end 3 a less common word for **subordinate** (sense 2) [c17 from L *subserviēns* complying with, from *subservīre* to SUBSERVE] > **subˈserviently** *adv* > **subˈservience** *or* **subˈserviency** *n*

subset (ˈsʌbˌsɛt) *n* a mathematical set contained within a larger set

subshrub (ˈsʌbˌʃrʌb) *n* a small bushy plant that is woody except for the tips of the branches

subside (səbˈsaɪd) *vb* **subsides, subsiding, subsided** (*intr*) 1 to become less loud, excited, violent, etc; abate 2 to sink or fall to a lower level 3 (of the surface of the earth, etc) to cave in; collapse 4 (of sediment, etc) to sink or descend to the bottom; settle [c17 from L *subsīdere* to settle down] > **subˈsider** *n*

subsidence (səbˈsaɪdᵊns, ˈsʌbsɪdᵊns) *n* 1 the act or process of subsiding or the condition of having subsided 2 *geol* the gradual sinking of landforms to a lower level.

subsidiarity (səbˌsɪdɪˈærɪtɪ) *n* the principle of devolving political decisions to the lowest practical level

subsidiary (səbˈsɪdɪərɪ) *adj* 1 serving to aid or supplement; auxiliary 2 of lesser importance; subordinate ▷ *n, pl* **subsidiaries** 3 a subsidiary person or thing 4 Also called: **subsidiary company** a company with at least half of its capital stock owned by another company [c16 from L *subsidiārius* supporting, from *subsidium* SUBSIDY] > **subˈsidiarily** *adv* > **subˈsidiariness** *n*

subsidize *or* **subsidise** (ˈsʌbsɪˌdaɪz) *vb* **subsidizes, subsidizing, subsidized** *or* **subsidises, subsidising, subsidised** (*tr*) 1 to aid or support with a subsidy 2 to obtain the aid of by means of a subsidy > **ˌsubsidiˈzation** *or* **ˌsubsidiˈsation** *n* > **ˈsubsiˌdizer** *or* **ˈsubsiˌdiser** *n*

subsidy (ˈsʌbsɪdɪ) *n, pl* **subsidies** 1 a financial aid supplied by a government, as to industry, for public welfare, the balance of payments, etc 2 *English history* a financial grant made originally for special purposes by Parliament to the Crown 3 any monetary aid, grant, or contribution [c14 from Anglo-Norman *subsidie*, from L *subsidium* assistance, from *subsidēre* to remain, from *sub-* down + *sedēre* to sit]

subsist (səbˈsɪst) *vb* (*mainly intr*) 1 (often foll by *on*) to be sustained; manage to live: *to subsist on milk* 2 to continue in existence 3 (foll by *in*) to lie or reside by virtue (of); consist 4 (*tr*) *obs* to provide with support [c16 from L *subsistere* to stand firm] > **subˈsistent** *adj*

subsistence (səbˈsɪstəns) *n* 1 the means by which one maintains life 2 the act or condition of subsisting

subsistence farming *n* a type of farming in which most of the produce (**subsistence crop**) is consumed by the farmer and his family

subsistence level *n* a standard of living barely adequate to support life

subsistence wage *n* the lowest wage upon which a worker and his or her family can survive

subsoil (ˈsʌbˌsɔɪl) *n* 1 Also called: **undersoil** the layer of soil beneath the surface soil and overlying the bedrock ▷ *vb* 2 (*tr*) to plough (land) to a depth so as to break up the subsoil

subsonic (sʌbˈsɒnɪk) *adj* being, having, or travelling at a velocity below that of sound

subspecies (ˈsʌbˌspiːʃiːz) *n, pl* **subspecies** *biol* a subdivision of a species: usually occurs because of isolation within a species

subst. *abbrev for*: 1 substantive 2 substitute

substance (ˈsʌbstəns) *n* 1 the tangible basic matter of which a thing consists 2 a specific type of matter, esp a homogeneous material with definite or fairly definite chemical composition 3 the essence, meaning, etc, of a discourse, thought, or written article 4 solid or meaningful quality: *an education of substance* 5 material density or body: *free space has no substance* 6 material possessions or wealth: *a man of substance* 7 *philosophy* the supposed immaterial substratum of anything that can receive modifications and in which attributes and accidents inhere 8 **in substance** with regard to the salient points [c13 via OF from L *substantia*, from *substāre*, from SUB- + *stāre* to stand]

substandard (sʌbˈstændəd) *adj* 1 below an established or required standard 2 another word for **nonstandard**

substantial (səbˈstænʃəl) *adj* 1 of a considerable size or value: *substantial funds* 2 worthwhile; important; telling: *a substantial reform* 3 having wealth or importance: *a substantial member of the community* 4 (of food or a meal) sufficient and nourishing 5 solid or strong: *a substantial door* 6 real; actual; true: *substantial evidence* 7 of or relating to the basic or fundamental substance or aspects of a thing ▷ *n* 8 (*often pl*) *rare* an essential or important element > **substantiality** (səbˌstænʃɪˈælɪtɪ) *or* **subˈstantialness** *n* > **subˈstantially** *adv*

substantialism (səbˈstænʃəˌlɪzəm) *n philosophy* the doctrine that a substantial reality underlies phenomena > **subˈstantialist** *n*

substantiate (səbˈstænʃɪˌeɪt) *vb* **substantiates, substantiating, substantiated** (*tr*) 1 to establish as valid or genuine 2 to give form or real existence to [c17 from NL *substantiāre*, from L *substantia* SUBSTANCE] > **subˌstantiˈation** *n*

substantive (ˈsʌbstəntɪv) *n* 1 *grammar* a noun or pronoun used in place of a noun ▷ *adj* 2 of, relating to, containing, or being the essential element of a thing 3 having independent function, resources, or existence 4 of substantial quantity 5 solid in foundation or basis 6 *grammar* denoting, relating to, or standing in place of a noun 7 (səbˈstæntɪv) (of a dye or colour) staining the material directly without use of a mordant [c15 from LL

Ss

substantīvus, from L *substāre* to stand beneath] > **substantival** (ˌsʌbstənˈtaɪvᵊl) *adj* > ˌ**substanˈtivally** *adv* > ˈ**substantively** *adv*

substantive rank *n* a permanent rank in the armed services

substation (ˈsʌbˌsteɪʃən) *n* **1** a subsidiary station **2** an installation at which electrical energy is received from one or more power stations for conversion from alternating to direct current, stepping down the voltage, or switching before distribution by a low-tension network

substituent (sʌbˈstɪtjʊənt) *n* **1** *chem* an atom or group that replaces another atom or group in a molecule or can be regarded as replacing an atom in a parent compound ▷ *adj* **2** substituted or substitutable [C19 from L *substituere* to SUBSTITUTE]

substitute (ˈsʌbstɪˌtjuːt) *vb* **substitutes, substituting, substituted 1** (often foll by *for*) to serve or cause to serve in place of another person or thing **2** *chem* to replace (an atom or group in a molecule) with (another atom or group) ▷ *n* **3a** a person or thing that serves in place of another, such as a player in a game who takes the place of an injured colleague **3b** (*as modifier*): *a substitute goalkeeper* [C16 from L *substituere*, from *sub-* in place of + *statuere* to set up] > ˌ**substiˈtutable** *adj* > ˈ**substiˌtutive** *adj*

USAGE Although *substitute* and *replace* have the same meaning, the structures they are used in are different. You replace A *with* B, while you substitute B *for* A. Accordingly, *he replaced the worn tyre with a new one*, and *he substituted a new tyre for the worn one* are both correct ways of saying the same thing

substitution (ˌsʌbstɪˈtjuːʃən) *n* **1** the act of substituting or state of being substituted **2** something or someone substituted

substrate (ˈsʌbstreɪt) *n* **1** *biochem* the substance upon which an enzyme acts **2** another word for **substratum**

substratum (sʌbˈstrɑːtəm, -ˈstreɪ-) *n, pl* **substrata** (-ˈstrɑːtə, -ˈstreɪtə) **1** any layer or stratum lying underneath another **2** a basis or foundation; groundwork [C17 from NL, from L *substrātus* strewn beneath, from *substernere* to spread under] > **subˈstrative** *or* **subˈstratal** *adj*

substructure (ˈsʌbˌstrʌktʃə) *n* **1** a structure, pattern, etc, that forms the basis of anything **2** a structure forming a foundation or framework for a building or other construction > **subˈstructural** *adj*

subsume (səbˈsjuːm) *vb* **subsumes, subsuming, subsumed** (*tr*) **1** to incorporate (an idea, case, etc) under a comprehensive or inclusive classification **2** to consider (an instance of something) as part of a general rule [C16 from NL *subsumere*, from L SUB- + *sumere* to take] > **subˈsumable** *adj* > **subsumption** (səbˈsʌmpʃən) *n*

subtemperate (sʌbˈtɛmpərɪt) *adj* of or relating to the colder temperate regions

subtenant (sʌbˈtɛnənt) *n* a person who rents or leases property from a tenant > **subˈtenancy** *n*

subtend (səbˈtɛnd) *vb* (*tr*) **1** *geom* to be opposite to and delimit (an angle or side) **2** (of a bract, stem, etc) to have (a bud or similar part) growing in its axil [C16 from L *subtendere* to extend beneath]

subterfuge (ˈsʌbtəˌfjuːdʒ) *n* a stratagem employed to conceal something, evade an argument, etc [C16 from LL *subterfugium*, from L *subterfugere* to escape by stealth, from *subter* secretly + *fugere* to flee]

subterminal (sʌbˈtɜːmɪnᵊl) *adj* almost at an end

subterranean (ˌsʌbtəˈreɪnɪən) *adj* **1** Also: **subterraneous, subterrestrial** situated, living, or operating below the surface of the earth **2** existing or operating in concealment [C17 from L *subterrāneus*, from SUB- + *terra* earth] > ˌ**subterˈraneanly** *or* ˌ**subterˈraneously** *adv*

subtext (ˈsʌbˌtɛkst) *n* **1** an underlying theme in a piece of writing **2** a message which is not stated directly but can be inferred

subtile (ˈsʌtᵊl) *adj* a rare spelling of **subtle** > ˈ**subtilely** *adv* > **subtility** (sʌbˈtɪlɪtɪ) *or* ˈ**subtileness** *n* > ˈ**subtilty** *n*

subtilize *or* **subtilise** (ˈsʌtɪˌlaɪz) *vb* **subtilizes, subtilizing, subtilized** *or* **subtilises, subtilising, subtilised 1** (*tr*) to bring to a purer state; refine **2** to debate subtly **3** (*tr*) to make (the mind, etc) keener > ˌ**subtiliˈzation** *or* ˌ**subtiliˈsation** *n*

subtitle (ˈsʌbˌtaɪtᵊl) *n* **1** an additional subordinate title given to a literary or other work **2** (*often pl*) **2a** text superimposed on a film or television broadcast, either a translation of foreign dialogue or as an aid for the hard of hearing **2b** Also called: **caption** explanatory text on a silent film ▷ *vb* **subtitles, subtitling, subtitled 3** (*tr; usually passive*) to provide a subtitle for

subtle (ˈsʌtᵊl) *adj* **1** not immediately obvious or comprehensible **2** difficult to detect or analyse, often through being delicate or highly refined: *a subtle scent* **3** showing or making or capable of showing or making fine distinctions of meaning **4** marked by or requiring mental acuteness or ingenuity; discriminating **5** delicate or faint: *a subtle shade* **6** cunning or wily: *a subtle rogue* **7** operating or executed in secret: *a subtle intrigue* [C14 from OF *soutil*, from L *subtīlis* finely woven] > ˈ**subtleness** *n* > ˈ**subtly** *adv*

subtlety (ˈsʌtᵊltɪ) *n, pl* **subtleties 1** the state or quality of being subtle; delicacy **2** a fine distinction **3** something subtle

subtonic (sʌbˈtɒnɪk) *n* *music* the seventh degree of a major or minor scale

subtotal (sʌbˈtəʊtᵊl, ˈsʌbˌtəʊtᵊl) *n* **1** the total made up by a column of figures, etc, forming part of the total made up by a larger column ▷ *vb* **subtotals, subtotalling, subtotalled** *or US* **subtotals, subtotaling, subtotaled 2** to work out a subtotal for (a column, etc)

subtract (səbˈtrækt) *vb* **1** to calculate the difference between (two numbers or quantities) by subtraction **2** to remove (a part of a thing, quantity, etc) from the whole [C16 from L *subtractus* withdrawn, from *subtrahere* to draw away from beneath] > **subˈtracter** *n* > **subˈtractive** *adj*

subtraction (səbˈtrækʃən) *n* **1** the act or process of subtracting **2** a mathematical operation in which the difference between two numbers or quantities is calculated

subtrahend (ˈsʌbtrəˌhɛnd) *n* the number to be subtracted from another number (the **minuend**) [C17 from L *subtrahendus*, from *subtrahere* to SUBTRACT]

subtropics (sʌbˈtrɒpɪks) *pl n* the region lying between the tropics and temperate lands > **subˈtropical** *adj*

subulate (ˈsuːbjʊlɪt, -ˌleɪt) *adj* (esp of plant parts) tapering to a point; awl-shaped [C18 from NL *subulatus* like an awl, from L *sūbula* awl]

suburb (ˈsʌbɜːb) *n* a residential district situated on the outskirts of a city or town [C14 from L *suburbium*, from *sub-* close to + *urbs* a city]

suburban (səˈbɜːbᵊn) *adj* **1** of, in, or inhabiting a suburb or the suburbs **2** characteristic of a suburb or the suburbs **3** *mildly derog* narrow or unadventurous in outlook > **suˈburbanˌite** *n* > **suˈburbanˌize** *or* **suˈburbanˌise** *vb* (*tr*)

suburbia (səˈbɜːbɪə) *n* **1** suburbs or the people living in them considered as an identifiable community or class in society **2** the life, customs, etc, of suburbanites

subvention (səbˈvɛnʃən) *n* **1** a grant, aid, or subsidy, as from a government **2** *sport* a fee paid indirectly to a supposedly amateur athlete for appearing at a meeting [C15 from LL *subventiō* assistance, from L *subvenīre*, from *sub-* under + *venīre* to come]

subversion (səbˈvɜːʃən) *n* **1** the act or an instance of subverting a legally constituted government, institution, etc **2** the state of being subverted;

destruction or ruin [C14 from LL *subversiō* destruction, from L *subvertere* to overturn]

subversive (səb'vɜːsɪv) *adj* **1** liable to subvert or overthrow a government, legally constituted institution, etc ▷ *n* **2** a person engaged in subversive activities, etc > **sub'versively** *adv* > **sub'versiveness** *n*

subvert (səb'vɜːt) *vb* (*tr*) **1** to bring about the complete downfall or ruin of (something existing by a system of law, etc) **2** to undermine the moral principles of (a person, etc) [C14 from L *subvertere* to overturn] > **sub'verter** *n*

subway ('sʌbˌweɪ) *n* **1** *Brit* an underground tunnel enabling pedestrians to cross a road, railway, etc **2** an underground tunnel for traffic, power supplies, etc **3** an underground railway

succedaneum (ˌsʌksɪ'deɪnɪəm) *n, pl* **succedanea** (-nɪə) *obs* something that is used as a substitute, esp any medical drug or agent that may be taken or prescribed in place of another [C17 from L *succēdāneus* following after; see SUCCEED] > ˌ**succe'daneous** *adj*

succeed (sək'siːd) *vb* **1** (*intr*) to accomplish an aim, esp in the manner desired **2** (*intr*) to happen in the manner desired: *the plan succeeded* **3** (*intr*) to acquit oneself satisfactorily or do well, as in a specified field **4** (when *intr*, often foll by *to*) to come next in order (after someone or something) **5** (when *intr*, often foll by *to*) to take over an office, post, etc (from a person) **6** (*intr*; usually foll by *to*) to come into possession (of property, etc); inherit **7** (*intr*) to have a result according to a specified manner: *the plan succeeded badly* [C15 from L *succēdere* to follow after] > **suc'ceeder** *n* > **suc'ceedingly** *adv*

success (sək'sɛs) *n* **1** the favourable outcome of something attempted **2** the attainment of wealth, fame, etc **3** an action, performance, etc, that is characterized by success **4** a person or thing that is successful [C16 from L *successus* an outcome; see SUCCEED]

successful (sək'sɛsfʊl) *adj* **1** having succeeded in one's endeavours **2** marked by a favourable outcome **3** having obtained fame, wealth, etc > **suc'cessfully** *adv* > **suc'cessfulness** *n*

succession (sək'sɛʃən) *n* **1** the act or an instance of one person or thing following another **2** a number of people or things following one another in order **3** the act, process, or right by which one person succeeds to the office, etc, of another **4** the order that determines how one person or thing follows another **5** a line of descent to a title, etc **6** **in succession** in a manner such that one thing is followed uninterruptedly by another [C14 from L *successio*; see SUCCEED] > **suc'cessional** *adj*

successive (sək'sɛsɪv) *adj* **1** following another without interruption **2** of or involving succession: *a successive process* > **suc'cessively** *adv* > **suc'cessiveness** *n*

successor (sək'sɛsə) *n* a person or thing that follows, esp a person who succeeds another

succinct (sək'sɪŋkt) *adj* marked by brevity and clarity; concise [C15 from L *succinctus* girt about, from *succingere* to gird from below] > **suc'cinctly** *adv* > **suc'cinctness** *n*

succinic acid (sʌk'sɪnɪk) *n* a colourless odourless water-soluble acid found in plant and animal tissues, deriving from amber. Formula: $HOOC(CH_2)_2COOH$. Systematic name: **butanedioic acid** [C19 from L *succinum* amber]

succotash ('sʌkəˌtæʃ) *n* *US & Canad* a mixture of cooked sweet corn kernels and lima beans, served as a vegetable [C18 of Amerind origin, from *msiquatash*, lit.: broken pieces]

succour *or US* **succor** ('sʌkə) *n* **1** help or assistance, esp in time of difficulty **2** a person or thing that provides help ▷ *vb* **3** (*tr*) to give aid to [C13 from OF *sucurir*, from L *succurrere* to hurry to help]

succubus ('sʌkjʊbəs) *n, pl* **succubi** (-ˌbaɪ) **1** Also called: **succuba** a female demon fabled to have sexual intercourse with sleeping men ▷ Cf **incubus** **2** any evil demon [C16 from Med. L, from LL *succuba* harlot, from L *succubāre* to lie beneath]

succulent ('sʌkjʊlənt) *adj* **1** juicy **2** (of plants) having thick fleshy leaves or stems ▷ *n* **3** a plant that can exist in arid or salty conditions by using water stored in its fleshy tissues [C17 from L *succulentus*, from *sūcus* juice] > '**succulence** *or* '**succulency** *n* > '**succulently** *adv*

succumb (sə'kʌm) *vb* (*intr*; often foll by *to*) **1** to give way to the force (of) or desire (for) **2** to be fatally overwhelmed (by disease, etc); die (of) [C15 from L *succumbere* to be overcome, from SUB- + *-cumbere*, from *cubāre* to lie down]

succursal (sʌ'kɜːsᵊl) *adj* **1** (esp of a religious establishment) subsidiary ▷ *n* **2** a subsidiary establishment [C19 from F, from Med. L *succursus*, from L *succurrere* to SUCCOUR]

such (sʌtʃ) (often foll by a corresponding subordinate clause introduced by *that* or *as*) ▷ *determiner* **1a** of the sort specified or understood: *such books* **1b** (*as pronoun*): *such is life; robbers, rapists, and such* **2** so great; so much: *such a help* **3** **as such** **3a** in the capacity previously specified or understood: *a judge as such hasn't so much power* **3b** in itself or themselves: *intelligence as such can't guarantee success* **4** **such and such** specific, but not known or named: *at such and such a time* **5** **such as** **5a** for example: *animals, such as tigers* **5b** of a similar kind as; like: *people such as your friend* **5c** of the (usually small) amount, etc: *the food, such as there was, was excellent* **6** **such that** so that: used to express purpose or result: *power such that it was effortless* ▷ *adv* **7** (intensifier): *such a nice person* [OE *swilc*]

suchlike ('sʌtʃˌlaɪk) *adj* **1** (*prenominal*) of such a kind; similar: *John, Ken, and other suchlike idiots* ▷ *n* **2** such or similar persons or things: *hyenas, jackals, and suchlike*

Su-chou ('suː'tʃaʊ) *n* a variant transliteration of the Chinese name for **Suzhou**

Süchow ('ʃuː'tʃaʊ) *n* a variant transliteration of the Chinese name for **Xuzhou**

suck (sʌk) *vb* **1** to draw (a liquid or other substance) into the mouth by creating a partial vacuum in the mouth **2** to draw in (fluid, etc) by or as if by a similar action: *plants suck moisture from the soil* **3** to drink milk from (a mother's breast); suckle **4** (*tr*) to extract fluid content from (a solid food): *to suck a lemon* **5** (*tr*) to take into the mouth and moisten, dissolve, or roll around with the tongue: *to suck one's thumb* **6** (*tr*; often foll by *down, in*, etc) to draw by using irresistible force **7** (*intr*) (of a pump) to draw in air because of a low supply level or leaking valves, etc **8** (*tr*) to assimilate or acquire (knowledge, comfort, etc) **9** (*intr*) *sl* to be contemptible or disgusting ▷ *n* **10** the act or an instance of sucking **11** something that is sucked, esp milk from the mother's breast **12** **give suck to** to give (a baby or young animal) milk from the breast or udder **13** an attracting or sucking force **14** a sound caused by sucking ▷ See also **suck in, sucks, suck up to** [OE *sūcan*]

sucker ('sʌkə) *n* **1** a person or thing that sucks **2** *sl* a person who is easily deceived or swindled **3** *sl* a person who cannot resist the attractions of a particular type of person or thing: *he's a sucker for blondes* **4** a young animal that is not yet weaned **5** *zool* an organ specialized for sucking or adhering **6** a cup-shaped device, generally made of rubber, that may be attached to articles allowing them to adhere to a surface by suction **7** *bot* **7a** a strong shoot that arises in a mature plant from a root, rhizome, or the base of the main stem **7b** a short branch of a parasitic plant that absorbs nutrients from the host **8** a pipe or tube through which a fluid is drawn by suction **9** any of various small mainly North American cyprinoid fishes having a large sucking mouth **10** any of certain fishes that have sucking discs, esp the sea snail **11** a piston in a suction pump or the valve in such a piston ▷ *vb* **12** (*tr*) to strip the suckers from (a plant) **13** (*intr*) (of a plant) to produce suckers

suck in *vb (adv)* **1** *(tr)* to attract by using an inexorable force, inducement, etc **2** to draw in (one's breath) sharply

suckle ('sʌkᵊl) *vb* **suckles, suckling, suckled 1** to give (a baby or young animal) milk from the breast or (of a baby, etc) to suck milk from the breast **2** *(tr)* to bring up; nurture [C15 prob. back formation from SUCKLING] > '**suckler** *n*

suckling ('sʌklɪŋ) *n* **1** an infant or young animal that is still taking milk from the mother **2** a very young child [C15 see SUCK, -LING[1]]

Suckling ('sʌklɪŋ) *n* Sir **John** 1609–42, English Cavalier poet and dramatist

sucks (sʌks) *interj Sl* **1** an expression of disappointment **2** an exclamation of defiance or derision (esp in **yah boo sucks to you**)

suck up to *vb (intr, adv + prep) inf* to flatter for one's own profit; toady

sucrase ('sjuːkreɪz) *n* another name for **invertase** [C19 from F *sucre* sugar + -ASE]

sucre (*Spanish* 'sukre) *n* the former (until 2000) standard monetary unit of Ecuador; replaced by the US dollar [C19 after Antonio José de SUCRE]

Sucre[1] (*Spanish* 'sukre) *n* the legal capital of Bolivia, in the south central part of the country in the E Andes: university (1624). Pop: 192 238 (2000 est). Former name (until 1839): **Chuquisaca**

Sucre[2] (*Spanish* 'sukre) *n* **Antonio José de** (an'tonjo xo'se de) 1795–1830, South American liberator, born in Venezuela, who assisted Bolivar in the colonial revolt against Spain; first president of Bolivia (1826–28)

sucrose ('sjuːkrəʊz, -krəʊs) *n* the technical name for **sugar** (sense 1) [C19 F *sucre* sugar + -OSE[2]]

suction ('sʌkʃən) *n* **1** the act or process of sucking **2** the force produced by a pressure difference, as the force holding a sucker onto a surface **3** the act or process of producing such a force [C17 from LL *suctiō* a sucking, from L *sūgere* to suck] > '**suctional** *adj*

suction pump *n* a pump for raising water or a similar fluid by suction. It usually consists of a cylinder containing a piston fitted with a flap valve

suctorial (sʌk'tɔːrɪəl) *adj* **1** specialized for sucking or adhering **2** relating to or possessing suckers or suction [C19 from NL *suctōrius*, from L *sūgere* to suck]

Sudan (suː'dɑːn, -'dæn) *n* **1** a republic in NE Africa, on the Red Sea: the largest country in Africa; conquered by Mehemet Ali of Egypt (1820–22) and made an Anglo-Egyptian condominium in 1899 after joint forces defeated the Mahdist revolt; became a republic in 1956; civil war has been waged between separatists, in the mainly Christian south, and the government since independence, apart from a period of peace (1972–83). It consists mainly of a plateau, with the Nubian Desert in the north. Official language: Arabic. Official religion: Muslim; there are large Christian and animist minorities. Currency: Sudanese dinar. Capital: Khartoum. Pop: 36 080 000 (2001 est). Area: 2 505 805 sq km (967 491 sq miles). Former name (1899–1956): **Anglo-Egyptian Sudan** French name: **Soudan 2 the** a region stretching across Africa south of the Sahara and north of the tropical zone: inhabited chiefly by Negroid tribes rather than Arabs > **Sudanese** (ˌsuːdᵊ'niːz) *adj, n*
▷ www.sudan.net
▷ http://sudanhome.com

sudarium (sjʊ'dɛərɪəm) *n, pl* **sudaria** (-'dɛərɪə) another word for **sudatorium** [C17 from L, from *sūdāre* to sweat]

sudatorium (ˌsjuːdə'tɔːrɪəm) *or* **sudatory** *n, pl* **sudatoria** (-'tɔːrɪə) *or* **sudatories** a room, esp in a Roman bathhouse, where sweating is induced by heat [C18 from L, from *sūdāre* to sweat]

sudatory ('sjuːdətərɪ, -trɪ) *adj* **1** relating to or producing sweating ▷ *n, pl* **sudatories 2** a sudatory agent **3** another word for **sudatorium**

Sudbury ('sʌdbərɪ, -brɪ) *n* a city in central Canada, in Ontario: a major nickel-mining centre. Pop: 92 059 (1996)

sudd (sʌd) *n* floating masses of reeds and weeds that occur on the White Nile and obstruct navigation [C19 from Ar., lit.: obstruction]

sudden ('sʌdᵊn) *adj* **1** occurring or performed quickly and without warning **2** marked by haste; abrupt **3** *rare* rash; precipitate ▷ *n* **4** *arch* an abrupt occurrence (in **on a sudden**) **5 all of a sudden** without warning; unexpectedly [C13 via F from LL *subitāneus*, from L *subitus* unexpected, from *subīre* to happen unexpectedly, from *sub-* secretly + *īre* to go] > '**suddenness** *n*

sudden adult death syndrome *n* the unexpected death of a young adult, usually due to undetected inherited heart disease. Also called: **sudden death syndrome, sudden cardiac death** Abbrevs: **SADS, SDS, SCD**

sudden death *n* **1** (in sports, etc) an extra game or contest to decide the winner of a tied competition **2** an unexpected or quick death

sudden infant death syndrome *n* a technical name for **cot death** Abbrev: **SIDS**

suddenly ('sʌdᵊnlɪ) *adv* quickly and without warning

Sudetenland (suː'deɪtᵊnˌlænd) *n* a mountainous region of the N Czech Republic: part of Czechoslovakia (1919–38; 1945–93); occupied by Germany (1938–45). Also called: **the Sudeten**

Sudetes (suː'diːtiːz) *or* **Sudeten Mountains** *pl n* a mountain range in E central Europe, along the N border of the Czech Republic, extending into Germany and Poland: rich in minerals, esp coal. Highest peak: Schneekoppe, 1603 m (5259 ft)

sudor ('sjuːdɔː) *n* a technical name for **sweat** [L] > **sudoral** ('sjuːdərəl) *adj*

sudoriferous (ˌsjuːdə'rɪfərəs) *adj* producing or conveying sweat. Also: ˌ**sudo'riparous** [C16 via NL from SUDOR + L *ferre* to bear] > ˌ**sudor'iferousness** *n*

sudorific (ˌsjuːdə'rɪfɪk) *adj* **1** producing or causing sweating ▷ *n* **2** a sudorific agent [C17 from NL *sūdōrificus*, from SUDOR + L *facere* to make]

suds (sʌdz) *pl n* **1** the bubbles on the surface of water in which soap, detergents, etc, have been dissolved; lather **2** soapy water [C16 prob. from MDu. *sudse* marsh] > '**sudsy** *adj*

sue (sjuː, suː) *vb* **sues, suing, sued 1** to institute legal proceedings (against) **2** to make suppliant requests of (someone for something) [C13 from OF *sivre*, from L *sequī* to follow] > '**suer** *n*

Sue (*French* sy) *n* **Eugène** (øʒɛn) original name *Marie-Joseph Sue*. 1804–57, French novelist, whose works, notably *Les mystères de Paris* (1842–43) and *Le juif errant* (1844–45), were among the first to reflect the impact of the industrial revolution on France

suede (sweɪd) *n* **a** a leather with a fine velvet-like nap on the flesh side, produced by abrasive action **b** *(as modifier): a suede coat* [C19 from F *gants de Suède*, lit.: gloves from Sweden]

suet ('suːɪt, 'sjuːɪt) *n* a hard waxy fat around the kidneys and loins in sheep, cattle, etc, used in cooking and making tallow [C14 from OF *seu*, from L *sēbum*] > '**suety** *adj*

Suetonius (swiː'təʊnɪəs) *n* full name *Gaius Suetonius Tranquillus*. 75–150 AD, Roman biographer and historian, whose chief works were *Concerning Illustrious Men* and *The Lives of the Caesars* (from Julius Caesar to Domitian)

suet pudding *n Brit* any of a variety of puddings made with suet and steamed or boiled

Suez ('suːɪz) *n* **1** a port in NE Egypt, at the head of the Gulf of Suez at the S end of the Suez Canal: an ancient trading site and a major naval station under the Ottoman Empire; port of departure for pilgrims to Mecca; oil-refining centre. It suffered severely in the Arab-Israeli conflicts of 1967 and 1973. Pop: 417 610 (1996) **2 Isthmus of** a strip of land in NE Egypt, between the

Mediterranean and the Red Sea: links Africa and Asia and is crossed by the Suez Canal **3 Gulf of** the NW arm of the Red Sea: linked with the Mediterranean by the Suez Canal

▷ www.bbc.co.uk/history/timelines/britain/post_suez.shtml

▷ www.fas.org/man/dod-101/ops/suez.htm

Suez Canal *n* a sea-level canal in NE Egypt, crossing the Isthmus of Suez and linking the Mediterranean with the Red Sea: built (1854–69) by de Lesseps with French and Egyptian capital; nationalized in 1956 by the Egyptians. Length: 163 km (101 miles)

Suff. *abbrev for* **1** Suffolk **2** Suffragan

suffer ('sʌfə) *vb* **1** to undergo or be subjected to (pain, punishment, etc) **2** (*tr*) to undergo or experience (anything): *to suffer a change of management* **3** (*intr*) to be set at a disadvantage: *this author suffers in translation* **4** (*tr*) *arch* to tolerate; permit (someone to do something): *suffer the little children to come unto me* **5 suffer from 5a** to be ill with, esp recurrently **5b** to be given to: *he suffers from a tendency to exaggerate* [C13 from OF *soffrir*, from L *sufferre*, from SUB- + *ferre* to bear] > **'sufferer** *n*

sufferable ('sʌfərəbᵊl, 'sʌfrə-) *adj* able to be tolerated or suffered; endurable

sufferance ('sʌfərəns, 'sʌfrəns) *n* **1** tolerance arising from failure to prohibit; tacit permission **2** capacity to endure pain, injury, etc **3** the state or condition of suffering **4 on sufferance** tolerated with reluctance [C13 via OF from LL *sufferentia* endurance, from L *sufferre* to SUFFER]

suffering ('sʌfərɪŋ, 'sʌfrɪŋ) *n* **1** the pain, misery, or loss experienced by a person who suffers **2** the state or an instance of enduring pain, etc

suffice (sə'faɪs) *vb* **suffices, sufficing, sufficed 1** to be adequate or satisfactory for (something) **2 suffice it to say that** (*takes a clause as object*) let us say no more than that; I shall just say that [C14 from OF *suffire*, from L *sufficere* from *sub-* below + *facere* to make]

sufficiency (sə'fɪʃənsɪ) *n, pl* **sufficiencies 1** the quality or condition of being sufficient **2** an adequate amount **3** *arch* efficiency

sufficient (sə'fɪʃənt) *adj* **1** enough to meet a need or purpose; adequate **2** *logic* (of a condition) assuring the truth of a statement; requiring but not necessarily caused by some other state of affairs ▷ Cf **necessary** (sense 3b) **3** *arch* competent; capable ▷ *n* **4** a sufficient quantity [C14 from L *sufficiens* supplying the needs of, from *sufficere* to SUFFICE] > **suf'ficiently** *adv*

suffix *n* ('sʌfɪks) **1** *grammar* an affix that follows the stem to which it is attached, as for example *-s* and *-ness* in *dogs* and *softness* ▷ Cf **prefix** (sense 1) **2** anything added at the end of something else ▷ *vb* ('sʌfɪks, sə'fɪks) **3** (*tr*) *grammar* to add (a morpheme) as a suffix to a word [C18 from NL *suffixum*, from L *suffixus* fastened below, from *suffigere* to fasten below]

suffocate ('sʌfə,keɪt) *vb* **suffocates, suffocating, suffocated 1** to kill or be killed by the deprivation of oxygen, as by obstruction of the air passage **2** to block the air passages or have the air passages blocked **3** to feel or cause to feel discomfort from heat and lack of air [C16 from L *suffōcāre*, from SUB- + *faucēs* throat] > **'suffo,cating** *adj* > **,suffo'cation** *n*

Suffolk ('sʌfək) *n* a county of SE England, on the North Sea: its coast is flat and marshy, indented by broad tidal estuaries. Administrative centre: Ipswich. Pop: 668 548 (2001). Area: 3800 sq km (1467 sq miles)

Suffolk punch *n* a breed of draught horse with a chestnut coat and short legs

suffragan ('sʌfrəgən) *adj* **1a** (of any bishop of a diocese) subordinate to and assisting his superior archbishop or metropolitan **1b** (of any assistant bishop) assisting the bishop of his diocese but having no ordinary jurisdiction in that diocese ▷ *n* **2** a suffragan bishop [C14 from Med. L *suffragāneus*, from *suffrāgium* assistance, from L: suffrage] > **'suffraganship** *n*

suffrage ('sʌfrɪdʒ) *n* **1** the right to vote, esp in public elections; franchise **2** the exercise of such a right; casting a vote **3** a short intercessory prayer [C14 from L *suffrāgium*]

suffragette (,sʌfrə'dʒɛt) *n* a female advocate of the extension of the franchise to women, esp a militant one, as in Britain at the beginning of the 20th century [C20 from SUFFRAG(E) + -ETTE]

▷ www.cjbooks.demon.co.uk/suffrage.htm

▷ www.san.beck.org/GPJ19-Suffragettes.html

suffragist ('sʌfrədʒɪst) *n* an advocate of the extension of the franchise, esp to women > **'suffragism** *n*

suffruticose (sə'fru:tɪ,kəʊz) *adj* (of a plant) having a permanent woody base and herbaceous branches [C18 from NL *suffruticōsus*, from L SUB- + *frutex* shrub]

suffuse (sə'fju:z) *vb* **suffuses, suffusing, suffused** (*tr; usually passive*) to spread or flood through or over (something) [C16 from L *suffūsus* overspread with, from *suffundere*, from SUB- + *fundere* to pour] > **suffusion** (sə'fju:ʒən) *n* > **suf'fusive** *adj*

Sufi ('su:fɪ) *n, pl* **Sufis** an adherent of any of various Muslim mystical orders or teachings, which emphasize the direct personal experience of God [C17 from Ar. *ṣūfīy*, lit.: (man) of wool; prob. from the ascetic's woollen garments] > **'Sufic** *adj* > **'Sufism** *n*

sugar ('ʃʊgə) *n* **1** Also called: **sucrose, saccharose** a white crystalline sweet carbohydrate, a disaccharide, found in many plants: used esp as a sweetening agent in food and drinks. Related adj: **saccharine 2** any of a class of simple water-soluble carbohydrates, such as sucrose, lactose, and fructose **3** *inf, chiefly US & Canad* a term of affection, esp for one's sweetheart ▷ *vb* **4** (*tr*) to add sugar to; make sweet **5** (*tr*) to cover or sprinkle with sugar **6** (*intr*) to produce sugar **7 sugar the pill** *or* **medicine** to make something unpleasant more agreeable by adding something pleasant [C13 *suker*, from OF *çucre*, from Med. L *zuccārum*, ult. from Sansk. *śarkarā*] > **'sugared** *adj*

▷ www.britishsugar.co.uk

▷ www.sugar.org

Sugar ('ʃʊgə) *n* Sir **Alan** (**Michael**) born 1947, British electronics entrepreneur; chairman of Amstrad from 1968

sugar beet *n* a variety of beet cultivated for its white roots from which sugar is obtained

sugar candy *n* **1** Also called: **rock candy** large crystals of sugar formed by suspending strings in a strong sugar solution that hardens on the strings, used chiefly for sweetening coffee **2** *chiefly US* confectionery; sweets

sugar cane *n* a coarse perennial grass of Old World tropical regions, having tall stout canes that yield sugar: widely cultivated in tropical regions

sugar-coat *vb* (*tr*) **1** to coat or cover with sugar **2** to cause to appear more attractive

sugar diabetes *n* an informal name for **diabetes mellitus**

sugar glider *n* a common Australian phalanger that glides from tree to tree feeding on insects and nectar

sugaring off *n Canad* the boiling down of maple sap to produce sugar, traditionally a social event in early spring

sugar loaf *n* **1** a large conical mass of hard refined sugar **2** something resembling this

Sugar Loaf Mountain *n* a mountain in SE Brazil, in Rio de Janeiro on Guanabara Bay. Height: 390 m (1280 ft). Portuguese name: **Pão de Açúcar**

sugar maple *n* a North American maple tree, grown as a source of sugar, which is extracted from the sap, and for its hard wood

sugar of lead (lɛd) *n* another name for **lead acetate**

sugar pie *n Canad* an open pie with a brown sugar filling

Ss

sugarplum ('ʃʊgəˌplʌm) *n* a crystallized plum

sugary ('ʃʊgərɪ) *adj* **1** of, like, or containing sugar **2** excessively sweet **3** deceptively pleasant; insincere > '**sugariness** *n*

Suger (suː'ʒɛə) *n* 1081–1151, French ecclesiastic and statesman, who acted as adviser to Louis VI and regent (1147–49) to Louis VII. As abbot of Saint-Denis (1122–51) he influenced the development of Gothic architecture

suggest (sə'dʒɛst) *vb (tr; may take a clause as object)* **1** to put forward (a plan, idea, etc) for consideration: *I suggest Smith for the post; a plan suggested itself* **2** to evoke (a person, thing, etc) in the mind by the association of ideas: *that painting suggests home to me* **3** to give an indirect or vague hint of: *his face always suggests his peace of mind* [c16 from L *suggerere* to bring up] > **sug'gester** *n*

suggestible (sə'dʒɛstɪbᵊl) *adj* **1** easily influenced by ideas provided by other persons **2** characteristic of something that can be suggested > **sugˌgesti'bility** *n*

suggestion (sə'dʒɛstʃən) *n* **1** something that is suggested **2** a hint or indication: *a suggestion of the odour of violets* **3** *psychol* the process whereby the mere presentation of an idea to a receptive individual leads to the acceptance of that idea. See also **autosuggestion**

suggestive (sə'dʒɛstɪv) *adj* **1** *(postpositive; foll by of)* conveying a hint (of something) **2** tending to suggest something improper or indecent > **sug'gestively** *adv* > **sug'gestiveness** *n*

Suharto (sʊ'hɑːtəʊ) *n* **T N J** born 1921, Indonesian general and statesman; president (1968–98)

suicidal (ˌsuːɪ'saɪdᵊl, ˌsjuː-) *adj* **1** involving, indicating, or tending towards suicide **2** liable to result in suicide: *a suicidal attempt* **3** liable to destroy one's own interests or prospects; dangerously rash > ˌ**sui'cidally** *adv*

suicide ('suːɪˌsaɪd, 'sjuː-) *n* **1** the act or an instance of killing oneself intentionally **2** the self-inflicted ruin of one's own prospects or interests: *a merger would be financial suicide* **3** a person who kills himself or herself intentionally **4** *(modifier)* reckless; extremely dangerous: *a suicide mission* **5** *(modifier)* (of an action) undertaken or (of a person) undertaking an action in the knowledge that it will result in the death of the person performing it in order that maximum damage may be inflicted: *suicide bomber* [c17 from NL *suīcīdium*, from L *suī* of oneself + *-cīdium*, from *caedere* to kill]

sui generis (ˌsuːaɪ 'dʒɛnərɪs) *adj* unique [L, lit.: of its own kind]

suint ('suːɪnt, swɪnt) *n* a water-soluble substance found in the fleece of sheep, formed from dried perspiration [c18 from F *suer* to sweat, from L *sūdāre*]

Suisse (sɥis) *n* the French name for **Switzerland**

suit (suːt, sjuːt) *n* **1** any set of clothes of the same or similar material designed to be worn together, now usually (for men) a jacket with matching trousers or (for women) a jacket with matching or contrasting skirt or trousers **2** *(in combination)* any outfit worn for a specific purpose: *a spacesuit* **3** any set of items, such as parts of personal armour **4** any of the four sets of 13 cards in a pack of playing cards, being spades, hearts, diamonds, and clubs **5** a civil proceeding; lawsuit **6** the act or process of suing in a court of law **7** a petition or appeal made to a person of superior rank or status or the act of making such a petition **8** a man's courting of a woman **9** *sl* an executive, manager, or bureaucrat, esp one considered faceless or dull **10 follow suit 10a** to play a card of the same suit as the card played immediately before it **10b** to act in the same way as someone else **11 strong** *or* **strongest suit** something that one excels in ▷ *vb* **12** to make or be fit or appropriate for: *that dress suits your figure* **13** to meet the requirements or standards (of) **14** to be agreeable or acceptable to (someone) **15 suit oneself** to pursue one's own intentions without reference to others [c13 from OF *sieute* set of things, from *sivre* to follow]

suitable ('suːtəbᵊl, 'sjuːt-) *adj* appropriate; proper; fit > ˌ**suita'bility** *or* '**suitableness** *n* > '**suitably** *adv*

suitcase ('suːtˌkeɪs, 'sjuːt-) *n* a portable rectangular travelling case for clothing, etc

suite (swiːt) *n* **1** a series of items intended to be used together; set **2** a set of connected rooms in a hotel **3** a matching set of furniture, esp of two armchairs and a settee **4** a number of attendants or followers **5** *music* **5a** an instrumental composition consisting of several movements in the same key based on or derived from dance rhythms, esp in the baroque period **5b** an instrumental composition in several movements less closely connected than a sonata [c17 from F, from OF *sieute*; see SUIT]

suiting ('suːtɪŋ, 'sjuːt-) *n* a fabric used for suits

suitor ('suːtə, 'sjuːt-) *n* **1** a man who courts a woman; wooer **2** *law* a person who brings a suit in a court of law; plaintiff [c13 from Anglo-Norman *suter*, from L *secūtor* follower, from *sequī* to follow]

Suiyüan ('swiː'yɑːn) *n* a former province in N China: now part of the Inner Mongolian Autonomous Region

Sukarnapura (sʊˌkɑːnə'pʊərə) *n* a former name of **Jayapura**

Sukarno *or* **Soekarno** (suː'kɑːnəʊ) *n* **Achmed** ('ɑːkmɛd) 1901–70, Indonesian statesman; first president of the Republic of Indonesia (1945–67)

Sukarno Peak *n* a former name of (Mount) **Jaya**

Sukarnoputri (suːˌkɑːnəʊ'puːtrɪ) *n* **Megawati** ('mɛgəˌwɒtɪ) born 1949, Indonesian politician; president of Indonesia from 2001: daughter of Achmed Sukarno

Sukhumi *(Russian* su'xumi) *n* a port and resort in W Georgia, on the Black Sea: site of an ancient Greek colony. Pop: 112 000 (1993)

sukiyaki (ˌsuːkɪ'jɑːkɪ) *n* a Japanese dish consisting of very thinly sliced beef or other meat, vegetables, and seasonings cooked together quickly, usually at the table [from Japanese]

Sukkoth *or* **Succoth** ('sʊkəʊt, -kəʊθ; *Hebrew* suː'kɔt) *n* an eight-day Jewish harvest festival beginning on Tishri 15, which commemorates the period when the Israelites lived in the wilderness. Also called: **Feast of Tabernacles** [from Heb., lit.: tabernacles]

Sulawesi (ˌsuːlə'weɪsɪ) *n* an island in E Indonesia: mountainous and forested, with volcanoes and hot springs. Pop: 14 768 400 (1999 est). Area (including adjacent islands): 229 108 sq km (88 440 sq miles). Also called: **Celebes**

sulcate ('sʌlkeɪt) *adj biol* marked with longitudinal parallel grooves [c18 via L *sulcātus* from *sulcāre* to plough, from *sulcus* a furrow]

sulcus ('sʌlkəs) *n, pl* **sulci** (-saɪ) **1** a linear groove, furrow, or slight depression **2** any of the narrow grooves on the surface of the brain that mark the cerebral convolutions [c17 from L]

Suleiman I (ˌsuːlɪ'mɑːn, -leɪ-), **Soliman**, *or* **Solyman** *n* called *the Magnificent* ?1495–1566, sultan of the Ottoman Empire (1520–66), whose reign was noted for its military power and cultural achievements

sulf- *combining form* a US variant of **sulph-**

sulfur ('sʌlfə) *n* the US spelling of **sulphur**

sulk (sʌlk) *vb* **1** *(intr)* to be silent and resentful because of a wrong done to one; brood sullenly: *the child sulked after being slapped* ▷ *n* **2** *(often pl)* a state or mood of feeling resentful or sullen: *he's in a sulk; he's got the sulks* **3** Also: **sulker** a person who sulks [c18 ? back formation from SULKY[1]]

sulky[1] ('sʌlkɪ) *adj* **sulkier, sulkiest 1** sullen, withdrawn, or moody, through or as if through resentment **2** dull or dismal: *sulky weather* [c18 ?from obs. *sulke* sluggish] > '**sulkily** *adv* > '**sulkiness** *n*

sulky[2] ('sʌlkɪ) *n, pl* **sulkies** a light two-wheeled vehicle for one person, usually drawn by one horse [c18 from SULKY[1]]

Sulla ('sʌlə) *n* full name *Lucius Cornelius Sulla Felix*. 138–78 BC, Roman general and dictator (82–79). He introduced reforms to strengthen the power of the Senate

sullage ('sʌlɪdʒ) *n* **1** filth or waste, esp sewage **2** sediment deposited by running water [C16 ?from F *souiller* to sully]

sullen ('sʌlən) *adj* **1** unwilling to talk or be sociable; sulky; morose **2** sombre; gloomy: *a sullen day* ▷ *n* **3** (*pl*) *arch* a sullen mood [C16 ?from Anglo-F *solain* (unattested), ult. rel. to L *sōlus* alone] > **'sullenly** *adv* > **'sullenness** *n*

Sullivan ('sʌlɪvᵊn) *n* **1** Sir **Arthur** (**Seymour**) 1842–1900, English composer who wrote operettas, such as *HMS Pinafore* (1878) and *The Mikado* (1885), with W. S. Gilbert as librettist **2 Louis** (**Henri**) 1856–1924, US pioneer of modern architecture: he coined the slogan "form follows function"

Sullom Voe ('sʌləm vəʊ) *n* a deep coastal inlet in the Shetland Islands, on the N coast of Mainland. It is used for the storage and transshipment of oil

sully ('sʌlɪ) *vb* **sullies, sullying, sullied** (*tr*) to stain or tarnish (a reputation, etc) or (of a reputation) to become stained or tarnished [C16 prob. from F *souiller* to soil]

Sully ('sʌlɪ; *French* sylli) *n* **Maximilien de Béthune** (maksimiljɛ̃ də betyn), Duc de Sully. 1559–1641, French statesman; minister of Henry IV. He helped restore the finances of France after the Wars of Religion

Sully-Prudhomme (*French* sylli prydɔm) *n* **René François Armand** (rəne frɑ̃swa armɑ̃) 1839–1907, French poet: Nobel prize for literature 1901

sulph- *or US* **sulf-** *combining form* containing sulphur: *sulphate*

sulpha *or US* **sulfa drug** ('sʌlfə) *n* any of a group of sulphonamides that inhibit the activity of bacteria and are used to treat bacterial infections

sulphadiazine *or US* **sulfadiazine** (ˌsʌlfə'daɪəˌziːn) *n* an important sulpha drug used chiefly in combination with an antibiotic [from SULPH- + DIAZ(O) + -INE[2]]

sulphanilamide *or US* **sulfanilamide** (ˌsʌlfə'nɪləˌmaɪd) *n* a white crystalline compound formerly used in the treatment of bacterial infections [from SULPH- + ANIL(INE) + AMIDE]

sulphate *or US* **sulfate** ('sʌlfeɪt) *n* **1** any salt or ester of sulphuric acid ▷ *vb* **sulphates, sulphating, sulphated** *or US* **sulfates, sulfating, sulfated** **2** (*tr*) to treat with a sulphate or convert into a sulphate **3** to undergo or cause to undergo the formation of a layer of lead sulphate on the plates of an accumulator [C18 from NL *sulfātum*] > **sul'phation** *or US* **sul'fation** *n*

sulphide *or US* **sulfide** ('sʌlfaɪd) *n* a compound of sulphur with a more electropositive element

sulphite *or US* **sulfite** ('sʌlfaɪt) *n* any salt or ester of sulphurous acid > **sulphitic** *or US* **sulfitic** (sʌl'fɪtɪk) *adj*

sulphonamide *or US* **sulfonamide** (sʌl'fɒnəˌmaɪd) *n* any of a class of organic compounds that are amides of sulphonic acids containing the group $-SO_2NH_2$ or a group derived from this. An important class of sulphonamides are the sulpha drugs

sulphone *or US* **sulfone** ('sʌlfəʊn) *n* any of a class of organic compounds containing the divalent group SO_2 linked to two other organic groups

sulphonic *or US* **sulfonic acid** (sʌl'fɒnɪk) *n* any of a large group of strong organic acids that contain the group $-SO_2OH$ and are used in the manufacture of dyes and drugs

sulphonmethane *or US* **sulfonmethane** (ˌsʌlfɒn'miːθeɪn) *n* a colourless crystalline compound used medicinally as a hypnotic. Formula: $C_7H_{16}O_4S_2$

sulphur *or US* **sulfur** ('sʌlfə) *n* **a** an allotropic nonmetallic element, occurring free in volcanic regions and in combined state in gypsum, pyrite, and galena. It is used in the production of sulphuric acid, in the vulcanization of rubber, and in fungicides. Symbol: S; atomic no.: 16; atomic wt.: 32.066 **b** (*as modifier*): *sulphur springs* [C14 *soufre*, from OF, from L *sulfur*] > **sulphuric** *or US* **sulfuric** (sʌl'fjʊərɪk) *adj*

sulphurate *or US* **sulfurate** ('sʌlfjʊˌreɪt) *vb* **sulphurates, sulphurating, sulphurated** (*tr*) to combine or treat with sulphur or a sulphur compound > ˌ**sulphu'ration** *or US* ˌ**sulfu'ration** *n*

sulphur-bottom *n* another name for **blue whale**

sulphur-crested cockatoo *n* a large Australian white parrot, *Kakatoe galerita*, with a yellow erectile crest. Also called: **white cockatoo**

sulphur dioxide *n* a colourless soluble pungent gas. It is both an oxidizing and a reducing agent and is used in the manufacture of sulphuric acid, the preservation of foodstuffs (**E 220**), bleaching, and disinfecting. Formula: SO_2. Systematic name: **sulphur(IV) oxide**

sulphureous *or US* **sulfureous** (sʌl'fjʊərɪəs) *adj* **1** another word for **sulphurous** (sense 1) **2** of the yellow colour of sulphur

sulphuretted *or US* **sulfureted hydrogen** ('sʌlfjʊˌrɛtɪd) *n* another name for **hydrogen sulphide**

sulphuric acid *n* a colourless dense oily corrosive liquid used in accumulators and in the manufacture of fertilizers, dyes, and explosives. Formula: H_2SO_4. Systematic name: **tetraoxosulphuric(VI) acid**

sulphurize, sulphurise, *or US* **sulfurize** ('sʌlfjʊˌraɪz) *vb* **sulphurizes, sulphurizing, sulphurized, sulphurises, sulphurising, sulphurised** *or US* **sulfurizes, sulfurizing, sulfurized** (*tr*) to combine or treat with sulphur or a sulphur compound > ˌ**sulphuri'zation,** ˌ**sulphuri'sation,** *or US* ˌ**sulfuri'zation** *n*

sulphurous *or US* **sulfurous** ('sʌlfərəs) *adj* **1** Also: **sulphureous** of, relating to, or resembling sulphur: *a sulphurous colour* **2** (sʌl'fjʊərəs) of or containing sulphur with an oxidation state of 4: *sulphurous acid* **3** of or relating to hellfire **4** hot-tempered > **'sulphurously** *or US* **'sulfurously** *adv* > **'sulphurousness** *or US* **'sulfurousness** *n*

sulphurous acid *n* an unstable acid produced when sulphur dioxide dissolves in water: used as a preservative for food and a bleaching agent. Formula: H_2SO_3. Systematic name: **sulphuric(IV) acid**

sulphur trioxide *n* a colourless reactive fuming solid that forms sulphuric acid with water. Formula: SO_3. Systematic name: **sulphur(VI) oxide**

sultan ('sʌltən) *n* **1** the sovereign of a Muslim country, esp of the former Ottoman Empire **2** a small domestic fowl with a white crest and heavily feathered legs and feet: originated in Turkey [C16 from Med. L *sultānus*, from Ar. *sultān* rule, from Aramaic *salita* to rule]

sultana (sʌl'tɑːnə) *n* **1a** the dried fruit of a small white seedless grape, originally produced in SW Asia; seedless raisin **1b** the grape itself **2** Also called: **sultaness** a wife, concubine, or female relative of a sultan **3** a mistress; concubine [C16 from It., fem of *sultano* SULTAN]

sultanate ('sʌltəˌneɪt) *n* **1** the territory or a country ruled by a sultan **2** the office, rank, or jurisdiction of a sultan

sultry ('sʌltrɪ) *adj* **sultrier, sultriest** **1** (of weather or climate) oppressively hot and humid **2** characterized by or emitting oppressive heat **3** displaying or suggesting passion; sensual: *sultry eyes* [C16 from obs. *sulter* to swelter + -Y[1]] > **'sultrily** *adv* > **'sultriness** *n*

Sulu Archipelago ('suːluː) *n* a chain of over 500 islands in the SW Philippines, separating the Sulu Sea from the Celebes Sea: formerly a sultanate, ceded to the Philippines in 1940. Capital: Jolo. Pop: 555 240 (latest est). Area: 2686 sq km (1037 sq miles)

Sulu Sea *n* part of the W Pacific between Borneo and the central Philippines

sum (sʌm) *n* **1** the result of the addition of numbers, quantities, objects, etc **2** one or more columns or rows of numbers to be added, subtracted, multiplied, or divided **3** *maths* the limit of the first *n* terms of a

Ss

converging infinite series as *n* tends to infinity **4** a quantity, esp of money: *he borrows enormous sums* **5** the essence or gist of a matter (esp in **in sum, in sum and substance**) **6** a less common word for **summary** **7** (*modifier*) complete or final (esp in **sum total**) ▷ *vb* **sums, summing, summed 8** (often foll by *up*) to add or form a total of (something) **9** (*tr*) to calculate the sum of (the terms in a sequence) ▷ See also **sum up** [C13 *summe*, from OF, from L *summa* the top, sum, from *summus* highest, from *super* above]

sumach *or US* **sumac** (ˈsuːmæk, ˈʃuː-) *n* **1** any of various temperate or subtropical shrubs or small trees, having compound leaves and red hairy fruits. See also **poison sumach 2** a preparation of powdered leaves of certain species of sumach, used in dyeing and tanning **3** the wood of any of these plants [C14 via OF from Ar. *summāq*]

Sumatra (sʊˈmɑːtrə) *n* a mountainous island in W Indonesia, in the Greater Sunda Islands, separated from the Malay Peninsula by the Strait of Malacca: Dutch control began in the 16th century; joined Indonesia in 1945. Pop: 24 284 400 (1999 est). Area: 473 606 sq km (182 821 sq miles) > **Suˈmatran** *adj, n*

Sumba (ˈsuːmbə) *n* an island in Indonesia, in the Lesser Sunda Islands, separated from Flores by the **Sumba Strait**: formerly important for sandalwood exports. Pop: 355 073 (1990). Area: 11 153 sq km (4306 sq miles). Former name: **Sandalwood Island**

Sumbawa *or* **Soembawa** (suːmˈbɑːwə) *n* a mountainous island in Indonesia, in the Lesser Sunda Islands, between Lombok and Flores Islands. Pop: 373 000 (1990 est). Area: 14 750 sq km (5695 sq miles)

Sumer (ˈsuːmə) *n* the S region of Babylonia; seat of a civilization of city-states that reached its height in the 3rd millennium BC

Sumerian (suːˈmɪərɪən, -ˈmɛər-) *n* **1** a member of a people who established a civilization in Sumer during the 4th millennium BC **2** the extinct language of this people ▷ *adj* **3** of or relating to ancient Sumer, its inhabitants, or their language or civilization
▷ www.crystalinks.com/sumerlanguage.html
▷ www.islandnet.com/~edonon/Sumer.htm

summa cum laude (ˈsʊmɑː kʊm ˈlaʊdeɪ) *adv, adj chiefly US* with the utmost praise: the highest designation for achievement in examinations. In Britain it is sometimes used to designate a first-class honours degree [from L]

summarize *or* **summarise** (ˈsʌməˌraɪz) *vb* **summarizes, summarizing, summarized** *or* **summarises, summarising, summarised** (*tr*) to make or be a summary of; express concisely > **ˌsummariˈzation** *or* **ˌsummariˈsation** *n* > **ˈsummaˌrizer, ˈsummaˌriser,** *or* **ˈsummarist** *n*

summary (ˈsʌmərɪ) *n, pl* **summaries 1** a brief account giving the main points of something ▷ *adj* (*usually prenominal*) **2** performed arbitrarily and quickly, without formality: *a summary execution* **3** (of legal proceedings) short and free from the complexities and delays of a full trial **4 summary jurisdiction** the right a court has to adjudicate immediately upon some matter **5** giving the gist or essence [C15 from L *summārium*, from *summa* SUM] > **ˈsummarily** *adv* > **ˈsummariness** *n*

summary offence *n* an offence that is triable in a magistrates' court

summation (sʌˈmeɪʃən) *n* **1** the act or process of determining a sum; addition **2** the result of such an act or process **3** a summary **4** *US law* the concluding statements made by opposing counsel in a case before a court [C18 from Med. L *summātiō*, from *summāre* to total, from L *summa* SUM] > **sumˈmational** *adj* > **ˈsummative** *adj*

summative assessment *n Brit education* general assessment of a pupil's achievements over a range of subjects by means of a combined appraisal of formative assessments

summer (ˈsʌmə) *n* **1** (*sometimes cap*) **1a** the warmest season of the year, between spring and autumn, astronomically from the June solstice to the September equinox in the N hemisphere and at the opposite time of year in the S hemisphere **1b** (*as modifier*): *summer flowers*. Related adj: **aestival 2** the period of hot weather associated with the summer **3** a time of blossoming, greatest happiness, etc **4** *chiefly poetic* a year represented by this season: *a child of nine summers* ▷ *vb* **5** (*intr*) to spend the summer (at a place) **6** (*tr*) to keep or feed (farm animals) during the summer: *they summered their cattle on the mountain slopes* [OE *sumor*] > **ˈsummerly** *adj* > **ˈsummery** *adj*

summerhouse (ˈsʌməˌhaʊs) *n* a small building in a garden or park, used for shade or recreation in the summer

summer pudding *n Brit* a pudding made by filling a bread-lined basin with a purée of fruit

summersault (ˈsʌməˌsɔːlt) *n, vb* a variant spelling of **somersault**

summer school *n* a school, academic course, etc, held during the summer

summer solstice *n* **1** the time at which the sun is at its northernmost point in the sky (southernmost point in the S hemisphere). It occurs about June 21 (December 22 in the S hemisphere) **2** *astron* the point on the celestial sphere, opposite the **winter solstice,** at which the ecliptic is furthest north from the celestial equator

summertime (ˈsʌməˌtaɪm) *n* the period or season of summer

summer time *n Brit* any daylight-saving time, esp British Summer Time

summerweight (ˈsʌməˌweɪt) *adj* (of clothes) suitable in weight for wear in the summer

summing-up *n* **1** a review or summary of the main points of an argument, speech, etc **2** concluding statements made by a judge to the jury before they retire to consider their verdict

summit (ˈsʌmɪt) *n* **1** the highest point or part, esp of a mountain; top **2** the highest possible degree or state; peak or climax: *the summit of ambition* **3** the highest level, importance, or rank: *a meeting at the summit* **4a** a meeting of chiefs of governments or other high officials **4b** (*as modifier*): *a summit conference* [C15 from OF *somet*, dim. of *som*, from L *summum*; see SUM]

summon (ˈsʌmən) *vb* (*tr*) **1** to order to come; send for, esp to attend court, by issuing a summons **2** to order or instruct (to do something) or call (to something): *the bell summoned them to their work* **3** to call upon to meet or convene **4** (often foll by *up*) to muster or gather (one's strength, courage, etc) **5** *arch* to call upon to surrender [C13 from L *summonēre* to give a discreet reminder, from *monēre* to advise]

summons (ˈsʌmənz) *n, pl* **summonses 1** a call, signal, or order to do something, esp to attend at a specified place or time **2a** an official order requiring a person to attend court, either to answer a charge or to give evidence **2b** the writ making such an order **3** a call or command given to the members of an assembly to convene a meeting ▷ *vb* **4** to take out a summons against (a person) [C13 from OF *somonse*, from *somondre* to SUMMON]

summum bonum *Latin* (ˈsʊmʊm ˈbɒnʊm) *n* the principle of goodness in which all moral values are included or from which they are derived; highest or supreme good

sumo (ˈsuːməʊ) *n* the national style of wrestling of Japan, in which two contestants of great height and weight attempt to force each other to touch the ground with any part of the body except the soles of the feet or to step out of the ring [from Japanese *sumō*]

sump (sʌmp) *n* **1** a receptacle, as in the crankcase of an internal-combustion engine, into which liquids, esp lubricants, can drain to form a reservoir **2** another name for **cesspool** (sense 1) **3** *mining* a depression at the bottom of a shaft where water collects [c17 from MDu. *somp* marsh]

sumpter ('sʌmptə) *n arch* a packhorse, mule, or other beast of burden [c14 from OF *sometier* driver of a baggage horse, from Vulgar L *sagmatārius* (unattested), from LL *sagma* packsaddle]

sumptuary ('sʌmptjʊərɪ) *adj* relating to or controlling expenditure or extravagance [c17 from L *sumptuārius* concerning expense, from *sumptus* expense, from *sūmere* to spend]

sumptuous ('sʌmptjʊəs) *adj* **1** expensive or extravagant: *sumptuous costumes* **2** magnificent; splendid: *a sumptuous scene* [c16 from OF *somptueux*, from L *sumptuōsus* costly, from *sumptus*; see SUMPTUARY] > '**sumptuously** *adv* > '**sumptuousness** *n*

Sumter ('sʌmtə) *n* See **Fort Sumter**

sum up *vb* (*adv*) **1** to summarize (the main points of an argument, etc) **2** (*tr*) to form a quick opinion of: *I summed him up in five minutes*

Sumy (*Russian* 'sumi) *n* a city in the Ukraine, on the River Pysol: site of early Slav settlements. Pop: 299 800 (1998 est)

sun (sʌn) *n* **1** the star that is the source of heat and light for the planets in the solar system. Related adj: **solar** **2** any star around which a planetary system revolves **3** the sun as it appears at a particular time or place: *the winter sun* **4** the radiant energy, esp heat and light, received from the sun; sunshine **5** a person or thing considered as a source of radiant warmth, glory, etc **6** a pictorial representation of the sun, often depicted with a human face **7** *poetic* a year or a day **8** *poetic* a climate **9** *arch* sunrise or sunset (esp in **from sun to sun**) **10** **catch the sun** to become slightly sunburnt **11** **place in the sun** a prominent or favourable position **12** **take** *or* **shoot the sun** *naut* to measure the altitude of the sun in order to determine latitude **13** **touch of the sun** slight sunstroke **14** **under** *or* **beneath the sun** on earth; at all: *nobody under the sun eats more than you* ▹ *vb* **suns, sunning, sunned** **15** to expose (oneself) to the sunshine **16** (*tr*) to expose to the sunshine in order to warm, etc [OE *sunne*]

▹ www.solarviews.com/eng/sun.htm

▹ www.michielb.nl/sun/kaft.htm

▹ www.hao.ucar.edu/public/education/education.html

Sun. *abbrev for* Sunday

sunbaked ('sʌn,beɪkt) *adj* **1** (esp of roads, etc) dried or cracked by the sun's heat **2** baked hard by the heat of the sun: *sunbaked bricks*

sun bath *n* the exposure of the body to the rays of the sun or a sun lamp, esp in order to get a suntan

sunbathe ('sʌn,beɪð) *vb* **sunbathes, sunbathing, sunbathed** (*intr*) to bask in the sunshine, esp in order to get a suntan > '**sun,bather** *n*

sunbeam ('sʌn,biːm) *n* a beam, ray, or stream of sunlight > '**sun,beamed** *or* '**sun,beamy** *adj*

Sunbelt ('sʌn,bɛlt) *n* the southern states of the USA

sunbird ('sʌn,bɜːd) *n* any of various small songbirds of tropical regions of the Old World, esp Africa, having a long slender curved bill and a bright plumage in the males

sunblock ('sʌn,blɒk) *n* another name for **sunscreen**

sunbonnet ('sʌn,bɒnɪt) *n* a hat that shades the face and neck from the sun, esp one of cotton with a projecting brim, now worn esp by babies

sunburn ('sʌn,bɜːn) *n* **1** inflammation of the skin caused by overexposure to the sun **2** another word for **suntan** > '**sun,burnt** *or* '**sun,burned** *adj*

sunburst ('sʌn,bɜːst) *n* **1** a burst of sunshine, as through a break in the clouds **2** a pattern or design resembling that of the sun **3** a jewelled brooch with this pattern

Sunbury-on-Thames ('sʌnbərɪ, -brɪ) *n* a town in SE England, in N Surrey. Pop: 27 392 (1991)

sun-cured *adj* cured or preserved by exposure to the sun

sundae ('sʌndɪ, -deɪ) *n* ice cream topped with a sweet sauce, nuts, whipped cream, etc [c20 from ?]

Sunda Islands ('sʌndə) *pl n* a chain of islands in the Malay Archipelago, consisting of the **Greater Sunda Islands** (chiefly Sumatra, Java, Borneo, and Sulawesi) and **Nusa Tenggara** (formerly the Lesser Sunda Islands)

Sunda Strait *n* a strait between Sumatra and Java, linking the Java Sea with the Indian Ocean. Narrowest point: about 26 km (16 miles)

Sunday ('sʌndɪ) *n* the first day of the week and the Christian day of worship [OE *sunnandæg*, translation of L *diēs sōlis* day of the sun, translation of Gk *hēmera hēliou*]

Sunday best *n* one's best clothes, esp regarded as those most suitable for churchgoing

Sunday school *n* **1a** a school for the religious instruction of children on Sundays, usually held in a church hall **1b** (*as modifier*): *a Sunday-school outing* **2** the members of such a school

sunder ('sʌndə) *arch or literary* ▹ *vb* **1** to break or cause to break apart or in pieces ▹ *n* **2** **in sunder** into pieces; apart [OE *sundrian*]

Sunderland ('sʌndələnd) *n* **1** a city and port in NE England, in Sunderland unitary authority, Tyne and Wear at the mouth of the River Wear: formerly known for shipbuilding now has car manufacturing, chemicals; university (1992). Pop: 183 310 (1991) **2** a unitary authority in NE England, in Tyne and Wear. Pop: 280 807 (2001). Area: 138 sq km (53 sq miles)

sundew ('sʌn,djuː) *n* any of several bog plants having leaves covered with sticky hairs that trap and digest insects [c16 translation of L *ros solis*]

sundial ('sʌn,daɪəl) *n* a device indicating the time during the hours of sunlight by means of a stationary arm (the **gnomon**) that casts a shadow onto a plate or surface marked in hours

sun disc *n* a disc symbolizing the sun, esp one flanked by two serpents and the extended wings of a vulture: a religious figure in ancient Egypt

sundog ('sʌn,dɒg) *n* another word for **parhelion**

sundown ('sʌn,daʊn) *n* another name for **sunset**

sundowner ('sʌn,daʊnə) *n* **1** *Austral sl* a tramp, esp one who seeks food and lodging at sundown when it is too late to work **2** *inf, chiefly Brit* an alcoholic drink taken at sunset

sundress ('sʌn,drɛs) *n* a dress for hot weather that exposes the shoulders, arms, and back

sun-dried *adj* dried or preserved by exposure to the sun

sundry ('sʌndrɪ) *determiner* **1** several or various; miscellaneous ▹ *pron* **2** **all and sundry** everybody, individually and collectively ▹ *n, pl* **sundries** **3** (*pl*) miscellaneous unspecified items **4** another word for **extra** (sense 6) [OE *syndrig* separate]

Sundsvall (*Swedish* 'sʊndsval) *n* a port in E Sweden, on the Gulf of Bothnia: icebound in winter; cellulose industries. Pop: 94 815 (1994)

sunfast ('sʌn,fɑːst) *adj chiefly US & Canad* not fading in sunlight

sunfish ('sʌn,fɪʃ) *n, pl* **sunfish** *or* **sunfishes** **1** any of various large fishes of temperate and tropical seas, esp one which has a large rounded compressed body, long pointed dorsal and anal fins, and a fringelike tail fin **2** any of various small predatory North American freshwater percoid fishes, typically having a compressed brightly coloured body

sunflower ('sʌn,flaʊə) *n* **1** any of several American plants having very tall thick stems, large flower heads with yellow rays, and seeds used as food, esp for poultry. See also **Jerusalem artichoke** **2** **sunflower seed oil** the oil extracted from sunflower seeds, used as a salad oil, in margarine, etc

sung (sʌŋ) *vb* **1** the past participle of **sing** ▹ *adj* **2** produced by singing: *a sung syllable.*

USAGE See at **ring**

Sung *or* **Song** (sʊŋ) *n* an imperial dynasty of China

Ss

(960–1279 AD), notable for its art, literature, and philosophy
Sungari ('sʊŋgərɪ) *n* another name for the **Songhua**
Sungkiang ('sʊŋ'kjæŋ, -kaɪ'æŋ) *n* a former province of NE China: now part of the Inner Mongolian AR
sunglass ('sʌn,glɑːs) *n* another name for **burning glass**
sunglasses ('sʌn,glɑːsɪz) *pl n* glasses with darkened or polarizing lenses that protect the eyes from the sun's glare
sun-god *n* **1** the sun considered as a personal deity **2** a deity associated with the sun or controlling its movements
sunk (sʌŋk) *vb* **1** a past participle of **sink** ▷ *adj* **2** *inf* with all hopes dashed; ruined
sunken ('sʌŋkən) *vb* **1** a past participle of **sink** ▷ *adj* **2** unhealthily hollow: *sunken cheeks* **3** situated at a lower level than the surrounding or usual one: *a sunken bath* **4** situated under water; submerged **5** depressed; low: *sunken spirits*
sunk fence *n* another name for **ha-ha²**
Sun King *n* **the** an epithet of **Louis XIV**
sun lamp *n* **1** a lamp that generates ultraviolet rays, used for obtaining an artificial suntan, for muscular therapy, etc **2** a lamp used in film studios, etc, to give an intense beam of light by means of parabolic mirrors
sunless ('sʌnlɪs) *adj* **1** without sun or sunshine **2** gloomy; depressing > **'sunlessly** *adv*
sunlight ('sʌnlaɪt) *n* **1** the light emanating from the sun **2** an area or the time characterized by sunshine > **'sunlit** *adj*
sun lounge *or US* **sun parlor** *n* a room with large windows positioned to receive as much sunlight as possible
Sunna ('sʌnə) *n* the body of traditional Islamic law accepted by most orthodox Muslims as based on the words and acts of Mohammed [C18 from Ar. *sunnah* rule]
Sunni ('sʌnɪ) *n* **1** one of the two main branches of orthodox Islam (the other being the Shiah), consisting of those who acknowledge the authority of the Sunna **2** (*pl* **Sunnis** *or* **Sunni**) an adherent to this branch of Islam
sunnies ('sʌnɪz) *pl n* an informal name for **sunglasses**
Sunnite ('sʌnaɪt) *n* a less common word for Sunni (sense 2)
sunny ('sʌnɪ) *adj* **sunnier, sunniest 1** full of or exposed to sunlight **2** radiating good humour **3** of or resembling the sun > **'sunnily** *adv* > **'sunniness** *n*
sunrise ('sʌn,raɪz) *n* **1** the daily appearance of the sun above the horizon **2** the atmospheric phenomena accompanying this appearance **3** Also called (esp US): **sunup** the time at which the sun rises at a particular locality
sunrise industry *n* any of the high-technology industries, such as electronics, that hold promise of future development
sunroof ('sʌn,ruːf) *or* **sunshine roof** *n* a panel, often translucent, that may be opened in the roof of a car
sunscreen ('sʌn,skriːn) *n* a cream or lotion applied to exposed skin to protect it from harmful ultraviolet radiation from the sun. Also called: **sunblock**
sunset ('sʌn,sɛt) *n* **1** the daily disappearance of the sun below the horizon **2** the atmospheric phenomena accompanying this disappearance **3** Also called: **sundown** the time at which the sun sets at a particular locality **4** the final stage or closing period, as of a person's life
sunshade ('sʌn,ʃeɪd) *n* a device, esp a parasol or awning, serving to shade from the sun
sunshine ('sʌn,ʃaɪn) *n* **1** the light received directly from the sun **2** the warmth from the sun **3** a sunny area **4** a light-hearted or ironic term of address > **'sun,shiny** *adj*
sun sign *n* another name for **sign of the zodiac**
sunspot ('sʌn,spɒt) *n* **1** any of the dark cool patches that appear on the surface of the sun and last about a week **2** *inf* a sunny holiday resort **3** *Austral* a small cancerous spot produced by overexposure to the sun
sunstroke ('sʌn,strəʊk) *n* heatstroke caused by prolonged exposure to intensely hot sunlight
sunsuit ('sʌn,suːt, -,sjuːt) *n* a child's outfit consisting of a brief top and shorts or skirt
suntan ('sʌn,tæn) *n* **a** a brownish colouring of the skin caused by the formation of the pigment melanin within the skin on exposure to the ultraviolet rays of the sun or a sun lamp. Often shortened to **tan b** (*as modifier*): *suntan oil* > **'sun,tanned** *adj*
suntrap ('sʌn,træp) *n* a very sunny sheltered place
sunward ('sʌnwəd) *adj* **1** directed or moving towards the sun ▷ *adv* **2** Also: **sunwards** towards the sun
Sun Yat-sen ('sʊn 'jɑːt'sɛn) *n* 1866–1925, Chinese statesman, who was instrumental in the overthrow of the Manchu dynasty and was the first president of the Republic of China (1911). He reorganized the Kuomintang
Suomi ('suɔmi) *n* the Finnish name for **Finland**
sup¹ (sʌp) *vb* **sups, supping, supped** (*intr*) *arch* to have supper [C13 from OF *soper*]
sup² (sʌp) *vb* **sups, supping, supped 1** to partake of (liquid) by swallowing a little at a time **2** *Scot & N English dialect* to drink ▷ *n* **3** a sip [OE *sūpan*]
sup. *abbrev for:* **1** above [from L *supra*] **2** superior **3** *grammar* superlative
super (suːpə) *adj* **1** *inf* outstanding; exceptional ▷ *n* **2** petrol with a high octane rating **3** *inf* a supervisor **4** *Austral & NZ inf* superannuation benefits **5** *Austral & NZ inf* superphosphate ▷ *interj* **6** *Brit inf* an enthusiastic expression of approval [from L: above]
super- *prefix* **1** placed above or over: *superscript* **2** surpassing others; outstanding: *superstar* **3** of greater size, extent, quality, etc: *supermarket* **4** beyond a standard or norm: *supersonic* **5** indicating that a chemical compound contains a specified element in a higher proportion than usual: *superphosphate* [from L *super* above]
superable ('suːpərəbᵊl) *adj* able to be surmounted or overcome [C17 from L *superābilis*, from *superāre* to overcome] > **,supera'bility** *or* **'superableness** *n* > **'superably** *adv*
superannuate (,suːpər'ænjʊ,eɪt) *vb* **superannuates, superannuating, superannuated** (*tr*) **1** to pension off **2** to discard as obsolete or old-fashioned
superannuated (,suːpər'ænjʊ,eɪtɪd) *adj* **1** discharged, esp with a pension, owing to age or illness **2** too old to serve usefully **3** obsolete [C17 from Med. L *superannātus* aged more than one year, from L SUPER- + *annus* a year]
superannuation (,suːpər,ænjʊ'eɪʃən) *n* **1a** the amount deducted regularly from employees' incomes in a contributory pension scheme **1b** the pension finally paid **2** the act or process of superannuating or the condition of being superannuated
superb (sʊ'pɜːb, sjʊ-) *adj* **1** surpassingly good; excellent **2** majestic or imposing **3** magnificently rich; luxurious [C16 from OF *superbe*, from L *superbus* distinguished, from *super* above] > **su'perbly** *adv* > **su'perbness** *n*
superbike ('suːpə,baɪk) *n* a high-performance motorcycle
Super Bowl *n American football* the championship game held annually between the best team of the American Football Conference and that of the National Football Conference
superbug ('suːpə,bʌg) *n inf* an infective microorganism that has become resistant to antibiotics
supercalender (,suːpə'kæləndə) *n* **1** a calender that gives a high gloss to paper ▷ *vb* **2** (*tr*) to finish (paper) in this way > **,super'calendered** *adj*
supercargo (,suːpə'kɑːgəʊ) *n, pl* **supercargoes** an officer on a merchant ship who supervises commercial matters and is in charge of the cargo [C17 changed from Sp.

sobrecargo, from *sobre* over + *cargo* CARGO]

supercharge ('su:pə,tʃɑ:dʒ) *vb* **supercharges, supercharging, supercharged** (*tr*) **1** to increase the intake pressure of (an internal-combustion engine) with a supercharger; boost **2** to charge (the atmosphere, a remark, etc) with an excess amount of (tension, emotion, etc) **3** to apply pressure to (a fluid); pressurize

supercharger ('su:pə,tʃɑ:dʒə) *n* a device that increases the mass of air drawn into an internal-combustion engine by raising the intake pressure. Also called: **blower, booster**

superciliary (,su:pə'sɪlɪərɪ) *adj* over the eyebrow or a corresponding region in lower animals [c18 from NL *superciliaris*, from L, from SUPER- + *cilium* eyelid]

supercilious (,su:pə'sɪlɪəs) *adj* displaying arrogant pride, scorn, or indifference [c16 from L, from *supercilium* eyebrow] > ,**super'ciliously** *adv* > ,**super'ciliousness** *n*

superclass ('su:pə,klɑ:s) *n* a taxonomic group that is a subdivision of a subphylum

supercolumnar (,su:pəkə'lʌmnə) *adj archit* **1** having one colonnade above another **2** placed above a colonnade or a column > ,**supercol,umni'ation** *n*

superconductivity (,su:pə,kɒndʌk'tɪvɪtɪ) *n physics* the property of certain substances that have no electrical resistance. In metals it occurs at very low temperatures; higher-temperature superconductivity occurs in some ceramic materials > **superconduction** (,su:pəkən'dʌkʃən) *n* > ,**supercon'ductive** *or* ,**supercon'ducting** *adj* > ,**supercon'ductor** *n*

supercontinent ('su:pə,kɒntɪnənt) *n* a great landmass thought to have existed in the geological past and to have split into smaller landmasses, which drifted and formed the present continents

supercool (,su:pə'ku:l) *vb chem* to cool or be cooled without freezing or crystallization to a temperature below that at which freezing or crystallization should occur

supercritical (,su:pə'krɪtɪkəl) *adj* **1** *physics* (of a fluid) brought to a temperature and pressure higher than its critical temperature and pressure, so that its physical and chemical properties change **2** *nuclear physics* of or containing more than the critical mass

superdense theory (,su:pə'dɛns) *n astron* another name for the **big-bang theory**

super-duper ('su:pə'du:pə) *adj inf* extremely pleasing, impressive, etc: often used as an exclamation

superego (,su:pər'i:gəʊ, -'ɛgəʊ) *n, pl* **superegos** *psychoanal* that part of the unconscious mind that acts as a conscience for the ego

superelevation (,su:pər,ɛlɪ'veɪʃən) *n* **1** another name for **bank**[2] (sense 8) **2** the difference between the heights of the sides of a road or railway track on a bend

supereminent (,su:pər'ɛmɪnənt) *adj* of distinction, dignity, or rank superior to that of others; pre-eminent > ,**super'eminence** *n* > ,**super'eminently** *adv*

supererogation (,su:pər,ɛrə'geɪʃən) *n* **1** the performance of work in excess of that required or expected **2** *RC Church* supererogatory prayers, devotions, etc

supererogatory (,su:pərɛ'rɒgətərɪ, -trɪ) *adj* **1** performed to an extent exceeding that required or expected **2** exceeding what is needed; superfluous **3** *RC Church* of or relating to prayers, good works, etc, performed over and above those prescribed as obligatory [c16 from Med. L *superērogātōrius*, from L *supererogāre* to spend over and above]

superfamily ('su:pə,fæmɪlɪ) *n, pl* **superfamilies** **1** *biol* a subdivision of a suborder **2** any analogous group, such as a group of related languages

superfecundation (,su:pə,fi:kən'deɪʃən) *n physiol* the fertilization of two or more ova, produced during the same menstrual cycle, by sperm ejaculated during two or more acts of sexual intercourse

superfetation (,su:pəfi:'teɪʃən) *n physiol* the presence in the uterus of two fetuses developing from ova fertilized at different times [c17 *superfetate*, from L *superfētāre* to fertilize when already pregnant, from *fētus* offspring]

superficial (,su:pə'fɪʃəl) *adj* **1** of, near, or forming the surface: *superficial bruising* **2** displaying a lack of thoroughness or care: *a superficial inspection* **3** only outwardly apparent rather than genuine or actual: *the similarity was merely superficial* **4** of little substance or significance: *superficial differences* **5** lacking profundity: *the film's plot was quite superficial* **6** (of measurements) involving only the surface area [c14 from LL *superficiālis* of the surface, from L SUPERFICIES] > **superficiality** (,su:pə,fɪʃɪ'ælɪtɪ) *n* > ,**super'ficially** *adv*

superficies (,su:pə'fɪʃi:z) *n, pl* **superficies** **1** a surface or outer face **2** the outward form of a thing [c16 from L: upper side]

superfine (,su:pə'faɪn) *adj* **1** of exceptional fineness or quality **2** excessively refined > ,**super'fineness** *n*

superfix ('su:pə,fɪks) *n linguistics* a type of feature distinguishing the meaning or grammatical function of one word or phrase from that of another, as stress does for example between the noun *conduct* and the verb *conduct*

superfluid (,su:pə'flu:ɪd) *n* **1** *physics* a fluid in a state characterized by a very low viscosity, high thermal conductivity, high capillarity, etc. The only known example is that of liquid helium at temperatures close to absolute zero ▷ *adj* **2** being or relating to a superfluid > ,**superflu'idity** *n*

superfluity (,su:pə'flu:ɪtɪ) *n* **1** the condition of being superfluous **2** a quantity or thing that is in excess of what is needed **3** a thing that is not needed [c14 from OF *superfluité*, via LL from L *superfluus* SUPERFLUOUS]

superfluous (su:'pɜ:fluəs) *adj* **1** exceeding what is sufficient or required **2** not necessary or relevant; uncalled for [c15 from L *superfluus* overflowing, from *fluere* to flow] > **su'perfluously** *adv* > **su'perfluousness** *n* Ss

Super-G *n skiing* a type of slalom in which the course is shorter than in a standard slalom and the obstacles are farther apart than in a giant slalom [c20 from SUPER- + G(IANT)]

supergiant ('su:pə,dʒaɪənt) *n* any of a class of extremely bright stars which have expanded to a large diameter and are eventually likely to explode as supernovas

superglue ('su:pə,glu:) *n* any of various adhesives that quickly make an exceptionally strong bond

supergrass ('su:pə,grɑ:s) *n* an informer whose information implicates a large number of people

supergravity (,su:pə'grævɪtɪ) *n physics* any of various theories in which supersymmetry is applied to the theory of gravitation

superheat (,su:pə'hi:t) *vb* (*tr*) **1** to heat (a vapour, esp steam) to a temperature above its saturation point for a given pressure **2** to heat (a liquid) to a temperature above its boiling point without boiling occurring **3** to heat excessively; overheat > ,**super'heater** *n*

superheavy (,su:pə'hɛvɪ) *adj physics* denoting or relating to elements of high atomic number (above 109) postulated to exist with special stability as a consequence of the shell model of the nucleus

superheavyweight (,su:pə'hɛvɪ,weɪt) *n* an amateur boxer weighing more than 91 kg

superheterodyne receiver (,su:pə'hɛtərə,daɪn) *n* a radio receiver that combines two radio-frequency signals by heterodyne action, to produce a signal above the audible frequency limit. Sometimes shortened to **superhet** [c20 from SUPER(SONIC) + HETERODYNE]

superhigh frequency ('su:pə,haɪ) *n* a radio-frequency band or radio frequency lying between 30 000 and 3000 megahertz

superhuman (,su:pə'hju:mən) *adj* **1** having powers above and beyond those of mankind **2** exceeding normal human ability or experience > ˌ**superˈhumanly** *adv*

superimpose (ˌsu:pərɪmˈpəʊz) *vb* **superimposes, superimposing, superimposed** (*tr*) **1** to set or place on or over something else **2** (usually foll by *on* or *upon*) to add (to) > ˌ**superˌimpoˈsition** *n*

superinduce (ˌsu:pərɪnˈdju:s) *vb* **superinduces, superinducing, superinduced** (*tr*) to introduce as an additional feature, factor, etc > **superinduction** (ˌsu:pərɪnˈdʌkʃən) *n*

superintend (ˌsu:pərɪnˈtɛnd) *vb* to undertake the direction or supervision (of); manage [c17 from Church L *superintendere*, from L SUPER- + *intendere* to give attention to] > ˌ**superinˈtendence** *n*

superintendent (ˌsu:pərɪnˈtɛndənt) *n* **1** a person who directs and manages an organization, office, etc **2** (in Britain) a senior police officer higher in rank than an inspector but lower than a chief superintendent **3** (in the US) the head of a police department **4** *chiefly US & Canad* a caretaker, esp of a block of apartments ▷ *adj* **5** of or relating to supervision; superintending [c16 from Church L *superintendens* overseeing] > ˌ**superinˈtendency** *n*

superior (su:ˈpɪərɪə) *adj* **1** greater in quality, quantity, etc **2** of high or extraordinary worth, merit, etc **3** higher in rank or status **4** displaying a conscious sense of being above or better than others; supercilious **5** (*often postpositive*; foll by *to*) not susceptible (to) or influenced (by) **6** placed higher up; further from the base **7** *astron* (of a planet) having an orbit further from the sun than the orbit of the earth **8** (of a plant ovary) situated above the calyx and other floral parts **9** *printing* (of a character) written or printed above the line; superscript ▷ *n* **10** a person or thing of greater rank or quality **11** *printing* a character set in a superior position **12** (*often cap*) the head of a community in a religious order [c14 from L, from *superus* placed above, from *super* above] > **suˈperioress** *fem n* > **superiority** (su:ˌpɪərɪˈɒrɪtɪ) *n*

USAGE *Superior* should not be used with *than*: *he is a better* (not *a superior*) *poet than his brother*; *his poetry is superior to* (not *than*) *his brother's*

Superior (su:ˈpɪərɪə, sju:-) *n* **Lake** a lake in the N central US and S Canada: one of the largest freshwater lakes in the world and westernmost of the Great Lakes. Area: 82 362 sq km (31 800 sq miles)

superior court *n* **1** (in England) a higher court not subject to control by any other court except by way of appeal. See also **Supreme Court of Judicature** **2** (in several states of the US) a court of general jurisdiction ranking above the inferior courts and below courts of last resort

superiority complex *n inf* an inflated estimate of one's own merit, usually manifested in arrogance

superior planet *n* any of the six planets (Mars, Jupiter, Saturn, Uranus, Neptune, and Pluto) whose orbit lies outside that of the earth

superlative (su:ˈpɜ:lətɪv) *adj* **1** of outstanding quality, degree, etc; supreme **2** *grammar* denoting the form of an adjective or adverb that expresses the highest or a very high degree of quality. In English this is usually marked by the suffix *-est* or the word *most*, as in *loudest* or *most loudly* **3** (of language or style) excessive; exaggerated ▷ *n* **4** a thing that excels all others or is of the highest quality **5** *grammar* the superlative form of an adjective or adverb **6** the highest degree; peak [c14 from OF *superlatif*, via LL from L *superlātus* extravagant, from *superferre* to carry beyond] > **suˈperlatively** *adv* > **suˈperlativeness** *n*

superlunar (ˌsu:pəˈlu:nə) *adj* beyond the moon; celestial > ˌ**superˈlunary** *adj*

superman (ˈsu:pəˌmæn) *n, pl* **supermen** **1** (in the philosophy of Nietzsche) an ideal man who would rise above good and evil and who represents the goal of human evolution **2** any man of apparently superhuman powers

supermarket (ˈsu:pəˌmɑ:kɪt) *n* a large self-service store selling food and household supplies

supermembrane (ˌsu:pəˈmɛmbreɪn) *n physics* a type of membrane postulated in certain theories of elementary particles that involve supersymmetry

supermini (ˈsu:pəˌmɪnɪ) *n* a small car, usually a hatchback, that is economical to run but has a high level of performance

supermodel (ˈsu:pəˌmɒdᵊl) *n* a very successful and well-known photographic or catwalk model
▷ www.supermodelguide.com
▷ www.supermodels.it

supermundane (ˌsu:pəˈmʌndeɪn) *adj* elevated above earthly things

supernal (su:ˈpɜ:nᵊl, sju:-) *adj literary* **1** divine; celestial **2** of, from above, or from the sky [c15 from Med. L *supernālis*, from L *supernus* that is on high, from *super* above] > **suˈpernally** *adv*

supernatant (ˌsu:pəˈneɪtᵊnt) *adj* **1** floating on the surface or over something **2** *chem* (of a liquid) lying above a sediment or precipitate [c17 from L *supernatāre* to float, from SUPER- + *natāre* to swim] > ˌ**supernaˈtation** *n*

supernatural (ˌsu:pəˈnætʃərəl) *adj* **1** of or relating to things that cannot be explained according to natural laws **2** of or caused as if by a god; miraculous **3** of or involving occult beings **4** exceeding the ordinary; abnormal ▷ *n* **5** **the supernatural** supernatural forces, occurrences, and beings collectively > ˌ**superˈnaturally** *adv* > ˌ**superˈnaturalness** *n*

supernaturalism (ˌsu:pəˈnætʃərəlɪzəm) *n* **1** the quality or condition of being supernatural **2** belief in supernatural forces or agencies as producing effects in this world > ˌ**superˈnaturalist** *n, adj* > ˌ**superˌnaturalˈistic** *adj*

supernormal (ˌsu:pəˈnɔ:məl) *adj* greatly exceeding the normal > **supernormality** (ˌsu:pənɔ:ˈmælɪtɪ) *n* > ˌ**superˈnormally** *adv*

supernova (ˌsu:pəˈnəʊvə) *n, pl* **supernovae** (-vi:) *or* **supernovas** a star that explodes owing to instabilities following the exhaustion of its nuclear fuel, becoming for a few days up to one hundred million times brighter than the sun ▷ Cf **nova**

supernumerary (ˌsu:pəˈnju:mərərɪ) *adj* **1** exceeding a regular or proper number; extra **2** functioning as a substitute or assistant with regard to a regular body or staff ▷ *n, pl* **supernumeraries** **3** a person or thing that exceeds the required or regular number **4** a substitute or assistant **5** an actor who has no lines, esp a nonprofessional one [c17 from LL *supernumerārius*, from L SUPER- + *numerus* number]

supernurse (ˈsu:pəˌnɜ:s) *n* (in Britain) an informal name for **consultant nurse**

superorder (ˈsu:pərˌɔ:də) *n biol* a subdivision of a subclass

superordinate (ˌsu:pərˈɔ:dɪnɪt) *adj* **1** of higher status or condition ▷ *n* **2** a person or thing that is superordinate **3** a word the meaning of which includes the meaning of another word or words: *"red" is the superordinate of "scarlet" and "crimson"*

superphosphate (ˌsu:pəˈfɒsfeɪt) *n* **1** a mixture of the diacid calcium salt of orthophosphoric acid with calcium sulphate and small quantities of other phosphates: used as a fertilizer **2** a salt of phosphoric acid formed by incompletely replacing its acidic hydrogen atoms

superpose (ˌsu:pəˈpəʊz) *vb* **superposes, superposing, superposed** (*tr*) *geom* to transpose (the coordinates of one geometric figure) to coincide with those of another [c19 from F *superposer*, from L *superpōnere*, from *pōnere* to place]

superposition (ˌsu:pəpəˈzɪʃən) *n* **1** the act of superposing or state of being superposed **2** *geol* the principle that in any sequence of sedimentary rocks that has not been disturbed the lowest strata are the oldest

superpower ('su:pə,paʊə) *n* **1** an extremely powerful state, such as the US **2** extremely high power, esp electrical or mechanical > **'super,powered** *adj*

supersaturated (,su:pə'sætʃə,reɪtɪd) *adj* **1** (of a solution) containing more solute than a saturated solution **2** (of a vapour) containing more material than a saturated vapour > **,super,satu'ration** *n*

superscribe (,su:pə'skraɪb) *vb* **superscribes, superscribing, superscribed** (*tr*) to write (an inscription, name, etc) above, on top of, or outside [C16 from L *superscrībere*, from *scrībere* to write] > **superscription** (,su:pə'skrɪpʃən) *n*

superscript ('su:pə,skrɪpt) *printing* ▷ *adj* **1** (of a character) written or printed above the line; superior ▷ Cf **subscript** ▷ *n* **2** a superscript or superior character [C16 from L *superscriptus*]

supersede (,su:pə'si:d) *vb* **supersedes, superseding, superseded** (*tr*) **1** to take the place of (something old-fashioned or less appropriate); supplant **2** to replace in function, office, etc; succeed **3** to discard or set aside or cause to be set aside as obsolete or inferior [C15 via OF from L *supersedēre* to sit above] > **,super'sedence** *n* > **supersedure** (,su:pə'si:dʒə) *n* > **supersession** (,su:pə'sɛʃən) *n*

supersex ('su:pə,sɛks) *n genetics* a sterile organism in which the ratio between the sex chromosomes is disturbed

supersonic (,su:pə'sɒnɪk) *adj* being, having, or capable of a velocity in excess of the velocity of sound > **,super'sonically** *adv*

supersonics (,su:pə'sɒnɪks) *n (functioning as sing)* **1** the study of supersonic motion **2** a less common name for **ultrasonics**

superstar ('su:pə,stɑ:) *n* an extremely popular film star, pop star, etc > **'super,stardom** *n*

superstition (,su:pə'stɪʃən) *n* **1** irrational belief usually founded on ignorance or fear and characterized by obsessive reverence for omens, charms, etc **2** a notion, act, or ritual that derives from such belief **3** any irrational belief, esp with regard to the unknown [C15 from L *superstitiō*, from *superstāre* to stand still by something (as in amazement)]

superstitious (,su:pə'stɪʃəs) *adj* **1** disposed to believe in superstition **2** of or relating to superstition > **,super'stitiously** *adv* > **,super'stitiousness** *n*

superstore ('su:pə,stɔ:) *n* a large supermarket

superstratum (,su:pə'strɑ:təm, -'streɪ-) *n, pl* **superstrata** (-tə) *or* **superstratums** *geol* a layer or stratum overlying another layer or similar structure

superstring ('su:pə,strɪŋ) *n physics* a type of string postulated in certain theories of elementary particles that involve supersymmetry

superstructure ('su:pə,strʌktʃə) *n* **1** the part of a building above its foundation **2** any structure or concept erected on something else **3** *naut* any structure above the main deck of a ship with sides flush with the sides of the hull **4** the part of a bridge supported by the piers and abutments > **'super,structural** *adj*

supersymmetry (,su:pə'sɪmɪtrɪ) *n physics* a symmetry of elementary particles having a higher order than that in the standard model, postulated to encompass the behaviour of both bosons and fermions

supertanker ('su:pə,tæŋkə) *n* a large fast tanker of more than 275 000 tons capacity

supertax ('su:pə,tæks) *n* a tax levied in addition to the basic tax, esp on incomes above a certain level

superteacher ('su:pə,ti:tʃə) *n Brit education* an informal name for an **advanced skills teacher**

supertonic (,su:pə'tɒnɪk) *n music* **1** the second degree of a major or minor scale **2** a key or chord based on this

Super Twelve *n* an annual international southern hemisphere Rugby Union tournament between club teams from South Africa, Australia, and New Zealand

supervene (,su:pə'vi:n) *vb* **supervenes, supervening, supervened** (*intr*) **1** to follow closely; ensue **2** to occur as an unexpected or extraneous development [C17 from L *supervenīre* to come upon] > **,super'venience** *or* **supervention** (,su:pə'vɛnʃən) *n* > **,super'venient** *adj*

supervise ('su:pə,vaɪz) *vb* **supervises, supervising, supervised** (*tr*) **1** to direct or oversee the performance or operation of **2** to watch over so as to maintain order, etc [C16 from Med. L *supervidēre*, from L SUPER- + *vidēre* to see] > **supervision** (,su:pə'vɪʒən) *n*

supervisor ('su:pə,vaɪzə) *n* **1** a person who manages or supervises **2** a foreman or forewoman **3** (in some British universities) a tutor supervising the work, esp research work, of a student **4** (in some US schools) an administrator running a department of teachers > **'super,visorship** *n* > **'super,visory** *adj*

supinate ('su:pɪ,neɪt, 'sju:-) *vb* **supinates, supinating, supinated** to turn (the hand and forearm) so that the palm faces up or forwards [C19 from L *supīnāre* to lay on the back, from *supīnus* supine] > **,supi'nation** *n*

supine *adj* (su:'paɪn, sju:-; 'su:paɪn, 'sju:-) **1** lying or resting on the back with the face, palm, etc, upwards **2** displaying no interest or animation; lethargic ▷ *n* ('su:paɪn, 'sju:-) **3** *grammar* a noun form derived from a verb in Latin, often used to express purpose with verbs of motion [C15 from L *supīnus* rel. to *sub* under, up; (in grammatical sense) from L *verbum supīnum* supine word (from ?)] > **su'pinely** *adv* > **su'pineness** *n*

supper ('sʌpə) *n* **1** an evening meal, esp a light one **2** an evening social event featuring a supper **3 sing for one's supper** to obtain something by performing a service [C13 from OF *soper*] > **'supperless** *adj*

Suppiluliumas I (,sʌpɪlʌlɪ'u:məs) *n* king of the Hittites (?1375–?1335 BC); founder of the Hittite empire

supplant (sə'plɑ:nt) *vb* (*tr*) to take the place of, often by trickery or force [C13 via OF from L *supplantāre* to trip up, from *sub-* from below + *planta* sole of the foot] > **sup'planter** *n*

Ss

supple ('sʌpᵊl) *adj* **1** bending easily without damage **2** capable of or showing easy or graceful movement; lithe **3** mentally flexible; responding readily **4** disposed to agree, sometimes to the point of servility ▷ *vb* **supples, suppling, suppled 5** *rare* to make or become supple [C13 from OF *souple*, from L *supplex* bowed] > **'suppleness** *n*

supplejack ('sʌpᵊl,dʒæk) *n* **1** a North American twining woody vine that has greenish-white flowers and purple fruits **2** a liliaceous plant of New Zealand having tough climbing vines **3** a tropical American woody vine having strong supple wood **4** any of various other vines with strong supple stems **5** *US* a walking stick made from the wood of the tropical supplejack

supplement *n* ('sʌplɪmənt) **1** an addition designed to complete, make up for a deficiency, etc **2** a section appended to a publication to supply further information, correct errors, etc **3** a magazine or section inserted into a newspaper or periodical, such as one issued every week **4** *geom* **4a** either of a pair of angles whose sum is 180° **4b** an arc of a circle that when added to another arc forms a semicircle ▷ *vb* ('sʌplɪ,mɛnt) **5** (*tr*) to provide a supplement to, esp in order to remedy a deficiency [C14 from L *supplēmentum*, from *supplēre* to SUPPLY] > **,supplemen'tation** *n*

supplementary (,sʌplɪ'mɛntərɪ) *adj* **1** Also (*less commonly*): **supplemental** (,sʌplə'mɛntᵊl) forming or acting as a supplement ▷ *n, pl* **supplementaries 2** a person or thing that is a supplement > **,supple'mentarily** *or* (*less commonly*) **,supple'mentally** *adv*

supplementary angle *n* either of two angles whose sum is 180° ▷ Cf **complementary angle**

suppliant ('sʌplɪənt) *adj* **1** expressing entreaty or supplication ▷ *n, adj* **2** another word for **supplicant** [C15 from F *supplier* to beseech, from L *supplicāre* to kneel in entreaty or supplication] > **'suppliantly** *adv*

supplicant ('sʌplɪkənt) *or* **suppliant** *n* **1** a person who supplicates ▷ *adj* **2** entreating humbly; supplicating [c16 from L *supplicāns* beseeching]

supplicate ('sʌplɪˌkeɪt) *vb* **supplicates, supplicating, supplicated 1** to make a humble request to (someone); plead **2** (*tr*) to ask for or seek humbly [c15 from L *supplicāre* to beg on one's knees] > **'suppliˌcatory** *adj*

supplication (ˌsʌplɪ'keɪʃən) *n* **1** the act of supplicating **2** a humble entreaty or petition; prayer

supply[1] (sə'plaɪ) *vb* **supplies, supplying, supplied 1** (*tr*; often foll by *with*) to furnish with something required **2** (*tr*; often foll by *to* or *for*) to make available or provide (something desired or lacking): *to supply books to the library* **3** (*tr*) to provide for adequately; satisfy: *who will supply their needs?* **4** to serve as a substitute, usually temporary, in (another's position, etc): *there are no clergymen to supply the pulpit* **5** (*tr*) *Brit* to fill (a vacancy, position, etc) ▷ *n, pl* **supplies 6a** the act of providing or something provided **6b** (*as modifier*): *a supply dump* **7** (*often pl*) an amount available for use; stock **8** (*pl*) food, equipment, etc, needed for a campaign or trip **9** *econ* **9a** willingness and ability to offer goods and services for sale **9b** the amount of a commodity that producers are willing and able to offer for sale at a specified price ▷ Cf **demand** (sense 9) **10** *mil* **10a** the management and disposal of food and equipment **10b** (*as modifier*): *supply routes* **11** (*often pl*) a grant of money voted by a legislature for government expenses **12** (in Parliament and similar legislatures) the money voted annually for the expenses of the civil service and armed forces **13a** a person who acts as a temporary substitute **13b** (*as modifier*): *a supply vicar* **14** a source of electricity, gas, etc [c14 from OF *souppleier*, from L *supplēre* to complete, from *sub-* up + *plēre* to fill] > **sup'pliable** *adj* > **sup'plier** *n*

supply[2] ('sʌplɪ) *or* **supplely** ('sʌpᵊlɪ) *adv* in a supple manner

supply-side economics (sə'plaɪ-) *n* (*functioning as sing*) a school of economic thought that emphasizes the importance to a strong economy of policies that remove impediments to supply

▷ www.econlib.org/library/Enc/SupplySideEconomics.html

▷ www.auburn.edu/~johnspm/gloss/supply_side.html

support (sə'pɔːt) *vb* (*tr*) **1** to carry the weight of **2** to bear (pressure, weight, etc) **3** to provide the necessities of life for (a family, person, etc) **4** to tend to establish (a theory, statement, etc) by providing new facts **5** to speak in favour of (a motion) **6** to give aid or courage to **7** to give approval to (a cause, principle, etc); subscribe to **8** to endure with forbearance: *I will no longer support bad behaviour* **9** to give strength to; maintain: *to support a business* **10** (in a concert) to perform earlier than (the main attraction) **11** *films, theatre* **11a** to play a subordinate role to **11b** to accompany (the feature) in a film programme **12** to act or perform (a role or character) ▷ *n* **13** the act of supporting or the condition of being supported **14** a thing that bears the weight or part of the weight of a construction **15** a person who or thing that furnishes aid **16** the means of maintenance of a family, person, etc **17** a band or entertainer not topping the bill **18** (often preceded by *the*) an actor or group of actors playing subordinate roles **19** *med* an appliance worn to ease the strain on an injured bodily structure or part **20** Also: **athletic support** a more formal term for **jockstrap** [c14 from OF *supporter*, from L *supportāre* to bring, from *sub-* up + *portāre* to carry] > **sup'portable** *adj* > **sup'portive** *adj*

supporter (sə'pɔːtə) *n* **1** a person who or thing that acts as a support **2** a person who backs a sports team, politician, etc **3** a garment or device worn to ease the strain on or restrict the movement of a bodily structure or part **4** *heraldry* a figure or beast in a coat of arms depicted as holding up the shield

supporting (sə'pɔːtɪŋ) *adj* **1** (of a role) being a fairly important but not leading part **2** (of an actor or actress) playing a supporting role

suppose (sə'pəʊz) *vb* **supposes, supposing, supposed** (*tr; may take a clause as object*) **1** to presume (something) to be true without certain knowledge: *I suppose he meant to kill her* **2** to consider as a possible suggestion for the sake of discussion, etc: *suppose that he wins* **3** (of theories, etc) to imply the inference or assumption (of): *your policy supposes full employment* [c14 from OF *supposer*, from Med. L *suppōnere*, from L: to substitute, from SUB- + *pōnere* to put] > **sup'posable** *adj* > **sup'poser** *n*

supposed (sə'pəʊzd, -'pəʊzɪd) *adj* **1** (*prenominal*) presumed to be true without certain knowledge **2** (*prenominal*) believed to be true on slight grounds; highly doubtful **3** (sə'pəʊzd) (*postpositive; foll by to*) expected or obliged (to): *I'm supposed to be there* **4** (sə'pəʊzd) (*postpositive; used in negative; foll by to*) expected or obliged not (to): *you're not supposed to walk on the grass* > **supposedly** (sə'pəʊzɪdlɪ) *adv*

supposition (ˌsʌpə'zɪʃən) *n* **1** the act of supposing **2** a fact, theory, etc, that is supposed > ˌ**suppo'sitional** *adj* > ˌ**suppo'sitionally** *adv*

suppositious (ˌsʌpə'zɪʃəs) *adj* deduced from supposition; hypothetical > ˌ**suppo'sitiously** *adv* > ˌ**suppo'sitiousness** *n*

supposititious (səˌpɒzɪ'tɪʃəs) *adj* substituted with intent to mislead or deceive > **supˌposi'titiously** *adv* > **supˌposi'titiousness** *n*

suppositive (sə'pɒzɪtɪv) *adj* **1** of, involving, or arising out of supposition **2** *grammar* denoting a conjunction introducing a clause expressing a supposition, as for example *if, supposing,* or *provided that* ▷ *n* **3** *grammar* a suppositive conjunction > **sup'positively** *adv*

suppository (sə'pɒzɪtərɪ, -trɪ) *n, pl* **suppositories** *med* a solid medication for insertion into the vagina, rectum, or urethra, where it melts and releases the active substance [c14 from Med. L *suppositōrium*, from L *suppositus* placed beneath]

suppress (sə'prɛs) *vb* (*tr*) **1** to put an end to; prohibit **2** to hold in check; restrain: *I was obliged to suppress a smile* **3** to withhold from circulation or publication: *to suppress seditious pamphlets* **4** to stop the activities of; crush: *to suppress a rebellion* **5** *electronics* **5a** to reduce or eliminate (unwanted oscillations) in a circuit **5b** to eliminate (a particular frequency or frequencies) in a signal **6** *psychiatry* to resist consciously (an idea or a desire entering one's mind) [c14 from L *suppressus* held down, from *supprimere* to restrain, from *sub-* down + *premere* to press] > **sup'pressible** *adj* > **sup'pressive** *adj* > **sup'presser** *n*

suppressant (sə'prɛsənt) *adj* **1** tending to suppress or restrain an action or condition ▷ *n* **2** a suppressant drug or agent: *a cough suppressant*

suppression (sə'prɛʃən) *n* **1** the act or process of suppressing or the condition of being suppressed **2** *psychiatry* the conscious avoidance of unpleasant thoughts

suppressor (sə'prɛsə) *n* **1** a person or thing that suppresses **2** a device fitted to an electrical appliance to suppress unwanted electrical interference to audiovisual signals

suppurate ('sʌpjʊˌreɪt) *vb* **suppurates, suppurating, suppurated** (*intr*) *pathol* (of a wound, sore, etc) to discharge pus; fester [c16 from L *suppūrāre*, from SUB- + *pūs* pus] > ˌ**suppu'ration** *n* > **'suppurative** *adj*

supra- *prefix* over, above, beyond, or greater than: *supranational* [from L *suprā* above]

supraliminal (ˌsuːprə'lɪmɪnᵊl, ˌsjuː-) *adj* of or relating to any stimulus that is above the threshold of sensory awareness > ˌ**supra'liminally** *adv*

supramolecular (ˌsuːprəmə'lɛkjʊlə, ˌsjuː-) *adj* **1** more complex than a molecule **2** consisting of more than one molecule

supranational (ˌsuːprəˈnæʃnᵊl, ˌsjuː-) *adj* beyond the authority or jurisdiction of one national government: *the supranational institutions of the EU* > ˌ**supraˈnationalism** *n*

supraorbital (ˌsuːprəˈɔːbɪtᵊl, ˌsjuː-) *adj anat* situated above the orbit

suprarenal (ˌsuːprəˈriːnᵊl, ˌsjuː-) *adj anat* situated above a kidney

suprarenal gland *n* another name for **adrenal gland**

supremacist (sʊˈprɛməsɪst, sjʊ-) *n* **1** a person who promotes or advocates the supremacy of any particular group ▷ *adj* **2** characterized by belief in the supremacy of any particular group > **suˈpremacism** *or* **suˈprematism** *n*

supremacy (sʊˈprɛməsɪ, sjʊ-) *n* **1** supreme power; authority **2** the quality or condition of being supreme

supreme (sʊˈpriːm, sjʊ-) *adj* **1** of highest status or power **2** (*usually prenominal*) of highest quality, importance, etc **3** greatest in degree; extreme: *supreme folly* **4** (*prenominal*) final or last, ultimate: *the supreme judgment* [C16 from L *suprēmus* highest, from *superus* that is above, from *super* above] > **suˈpremely** *adv*

Supreme Being *n* God

Supreme Court *n* (in the US) **1** the highest Federal court **2** (in many states) the highest state court

Supreme Court of Judicature *n* (in England) a court formed in 1873 by the amalgamation of several superior courts into two divisions, the High Court of Justice and the Court of Appeal

supreme sacrifice *n* **the** the sacrifice of one's life

Supreme Soviet *n* (in the former Soviet Union) **1** the bicameral legislature, comprising the **Soviet of the Union** and the **Soviet of the Nationalities** **2** a similar legislature in each former Soviet republic

supremo (sʊˈpriːməʊ, sjʊ-) *n, pl* **supremos** *Brit inf* a person in overall authority [C20 from SUPREME]

Supt *or* **supt** *abbrev for* superintendent

sur-[1] *prefix* over; above; beyond: *surcharge; surrealism* ▷ Cf **super-** [from OF, from L SUPER-]

sur-[2] *prefix* a variant of **sub-** before *r*: *surrogate*

Sur (sʊə) *n* transliteration of the Arabic name for **Tyre**

sura (ˈsʊərə) *n* any of the 114 chapters of the Koran [C17 from Ar. *sūrah* section]

Surabaya *or* **Surabaja** (ˌsʊərəˈbaɪə) *n* a port in Indonesia, on E Java on the **Surabaya Strait**: the country's second port and chief naval base; university (1954); fishing and ship-building industries; oil refinery. Pop: 2 701 300 (1995 est)

surah (ˈsʊərə) *n* a twill-weave fabric of silk or rayon [C19 from F pronunciation of *Surat*, a port in W India where orig. made]

Surakarta (ˌsʊərəˈkɑːtə) *n* a town in Indonesia, on central Java: textile manufacturing. Pop: 516 500 (1995 est)

sural (ˈsjʊərəl) *adj anat* of or relating to the calf of the leg [C17 via NL from L *sūra* calf]

Surat (sʊˈræt, ˈsʊərət) *n* a port in W India, in W Gujarat: a major port in the 17th century; textile manufacturing. Pop: 1 498 817 (1991)

surbase (ˈsɜːˌbeɪs) *n* the uppermost part, such as a moulding, of a pedestal, base, or skirting

surcease (sɜːˈsiːs) *arch* ▷ *n* **1** cessation or intermission ▷ *vb* **surceases, surceasing, surceased** **2** to desist from (some action) **3** to cease or cause to cease [C16 from earlier *sursesen*, from OF *surseoir*, from L *supersedēre* to sit above]

surcharge *n* (ˈsɜːˌtʃɑːdʒ) **1** a charge in addition to the usual payment, tax, etc **2** an excessive sum charged, esp when unlawful **3** an extra and usually excessive burden or supply **4** an overprint that alters the face value of a postage stamp ▷ *vb* (sɜːˈtʃɑːdʒ, ˈsɜːˌtʃɑːdʒ), **surcharges, surcharging, surcharged** (*tr*) **5** to charge an additional sum, tax, etc **6** to overcharge (a person) for something **7** to put an extra physical burden upon; overload **8** to fill to excess; overwhelm **9** *law* to insert credits that have been omitted in (an account) **10** to overprint a surcharge on (a stamp)

surcingle (ˈsɜːˌsɪŋgᵊl) *n* a girth for a horse which goes around the body, used esp with a racing saddle [C14 from OF *surcengle*, from *sur-* over + *cengle* a belt, from L *cingulum*]

surcoat (ˈsɜːˌkəʊt) *n* **1** a tunic, often embroidered with heraldic arms, worn by a knight over his armour during the Middle Ages **2** (formerly) an outer coat or other garment

surculose (ˈsɜːkjʊˌləʊs) *adj* (of a plant) bearing suckers [C19 from L *surculōsus* woody, from *surculus* twig, from *sūrus* a branch]

surd (sɜːd) *n* **1** *maths* a number containing an irrational root, such as 2√3; irrational number **2** *phonetics* a voiceless consonant, such as (t) ▷ *adj* **3** of or relating to a surd [C16 from L *surdus* muffled]

sure (ʃʊə, ʃɔː) *adj* **1** (sometimes foll by *of*) free from hesitancy or uncertainty (with regard to a belief, conviction, etc): *we are sure of the accuracy of the data; I am sure that he is lying* **2** (foll by *of*) having no doubt, as of the occurrence of a future state or event: *sure of success* **3** always effective; unfailing: *a sure remedy* **4** reliable in indication or accuracy: *a sure criterion* **5** (of persons) worthy of trust or confidence: *a sure friend* **6** not open to doubt: *sure proof* **7** admitting of no vacillation or doubt: *he is sure in his beliefs* **8** bound to be or occur; inevitable: *victory is sure* **9** (*postpositive*) bound inevitably (to be or do something); certain: *she is sure to be there* **10** physically secure or dependable: *a sure footing* **11** **be sure** (*usually imperative or dependent imperative; takes a clause as object or an infinitive*, sometimes with *to* replaced by *and*) to be careful or certain: *be sure and shut the door; be sure to shut the door* **12** **for sure** without a doubt; surely **13** **make sure** **13a** (*takes a clause as object*) to make certain; ensure **13b** (foll by *of*) to establish or confirm power or possession (over) **14** **sure enough** *inf* as might have been confidently expected; definitely: often used as a sentence substitute **15** **to be sure** **15a** without doubt; certainly **15b** it has to be acknowledged; admittedly ▷ *adv* **16** (*sentence modifier*) *US & Canad inf* without question; certainly ▷ *sentence substitute* **17** *US & Canad inf* willingly; yes [C14 from OF *seur*, from L *sēcūrus* SECURE] > ˈ**sureness** *n*

sure-fire *adj* (*usually prenominal*) *inf* certain to succeed or meet expectations; assured

sure-footed *adj* **1** unlikely to fall, slip, or stumble **2** not likely to err or fall > ˌ**sure-ˈfootedly** *adv* > ˌ**sure-ˈfootedness** *n*

surely (ˈʃʊəlɪ, ˈʃɔː-) *adv* **1** without doubt; assuredly **2** without fail; inexorably (esp in **slowly but surely**) **3** (*sentence modifier*) am I not right in thinking that?; I am sure that: *surely you don't mean it?* **4** *rare* in a sure manner **5** *arch* safely; securely ▷ *sentence substitute* **6** *chiefly US & Canad* willingly; yes

sure thing *inf* ▷ *sentence substitute* **1** *chiefly US* used to express enthusiastic assent ▷ *n* **2** something guaranteed to be successful

surety (ˈʃʊətɪ, ˈʃʊərɪtɪ) *n, pl* **sureties** **1** a person who assumes legal responsibility for another's debt or obligation and himself becomes liable if the other defaults **2** security given against loss or damage or as a guarantee that an obligation will be met **3** *obs* the quality or condition of being sure **4** **stand surety** to act as a surety [C14 from OF *seurte*, from L *sēcūritās* security] > ˈ**suretyship** *n*

surf (sɜːf) *n* **1** waves breaking on the shore or on a reef **2** foam caused by the breaking of waves ▷ *vb* (*intr*) **3** to take part in surfing **4a** *computing* (on the Internet) to move freely from website to website (esp in the phrase

Ss

surf the Net) **4b** to move freely between TV channels or radio stations **5** *inf* to be carried on top of something: *that guy's surfing the audience* [C17 prob. var. of SOUGH]

surface ('sɜːfɪs) *n* **1a** the exterior face of an object or one such face **1b** (*as modifier*): *surface gloss* **2** the area or size of such a face **3** material resembling such a face, with length and width but without depth **4a** the superficial appearance as opposed to the real nature **4b** (*as modifier*): *a surface resemblance* **5** *geom* **5a** the complete boundary of a solid figure **5b** a continuous two-dimensional configuration **6a** the uppermost level of the land or sea **6b** (*as modifier*): *surface transportation* **7** **come to the surface** to emerge; become apparent **8** **on the surface** to all appearances ▷ *vb* **surfaces, surfacing, surfaced** **9** to rise or cause to rise to or as if to the surface (of water, etc) **10** (*tr*) to treat the surface of, as by polishing, smoothing, etc **11** (*tr*) to furnish with a surface **12** (*intr*) to become apparent; emerge **13** (*intr*) *inf* **13a** to wake up **13b** to get up [C17 from F, from *sur* on + *face* FACE] > '**surfacer** *n*

surface-active *adj* (of a substance, esp a detergent) capable of lowering the surface tension of a liquid. See also **surfactant**

surface mail *n* mail transported by land or sea ▷ Cf **airmail**

surface structure *n generative grammar* a representation of a string of words or morphemes as they occur in a sentence, together with labels and brackets that represent syntactic structure ▷ Cf **deep structure**

surface tension *n* **1** a property of liquids caused by intermolecular forces near the surface leading to the apparent presence of a surface film and to capillarity, etc **2** a measure of this

surface-to-air *adj* of or relating to a missile launched from the surface of the earth against airborne targets

surfactant (sɜː'fæktənt) *n* **1** Also called: **surface-active agent** a substance, such as a detergent, that can reduce the surface tension of a liquid and thus allow it to foam or penetrate solids; a wetting agent ▷ *adj* **2** having the properties of a surfactant [C20 *surf(ace)-act(ive) a(ge)nt*]

surfboard ('sɜːfˌbɔːd) *n* a long narrow board used in surfing

surfboat ('sɜːfˌbəʊt) *n* a boat with a high bow and stern and flotation chambers, equipped for use in rough surf

surfcasting ('sɜːfˌkɑːstɪŋ) *n* fishing from the shore by casting into the surf > '**surfˌcaster** *n*

surfeit ('sɜːfɪt) *n* **1** (usually foll by *of*) an excessive amount **2** overindulgence, esp in eating or drinking **3** disgust, nausea, etc, caused by such overindulgence ▷ *vb* **4** (*tr*) to supply or feed excessively; satiate **5** (*intr*) *arch* to eat, drink, or be supplied to excess [C13 from F *sourfait*, from *sourfaire* to overdo, from SUR-[1] + *faire*, from L *facere* to do]

surfie ('sɜːfɪ) *n Austral & NZ sl* a young person whose main interest in life is surfing

surfing ('sɜːfɪŋ) *n* the sport of riding towards shore on the crest of a wave by standing or lying on a surfboard > '**surfer** *or* '**surfˌrider** *n*

▷ www.aspeurope.com

surf mat *n Austral inf* a small inflatable rubber mattress used to ride on waves

surg. *abbrev for:* **1** surgeon **2** surgery **3** surgical

surge (sɜːdʒ) *n* **1** a strong rush or sweep; sudden increase: *a surge of anger* **2** the rolling swell of the sea **3** a heavy rolling motion or sound: *the surge of the trumpets* **4** an undulating rolling surface, as of hills **5** a billowing cloud or volume **6** *naut* a temporary release or slackening of a rope or cable **7** a large momentary increase in the voltage or current in an electric circuit **8** an instability or unevenness in the power output of an engine ▷ *vb* **surges, surging, surged** **9** (*intr*) (of waves, the sea, etc) to rise or roll with a heavy swelling motion **10** (*intr*) to move like a heavy sea **11** *naut* to slacken or temporarily release (a rope or cable) from a capstan or (of a rope, etc) to be slackened or released and slip back **12** (*intr*) (of an electric current or voltage) to undergo a large momentary increase **13** (*tr*) *rare* to cause to move in or as if in a wave or waves [C15 from L *surgere* to rise, from *sub-* up + *regere* to lead] > '**surger** *n*

surgeon ('sɜːdʒən) *n* **1** a medical practitioner who specializes in surgery **2** a medical officer in the Royal Navy [C14 from Anglo-Norman *surgien*, from OF *cirurgien*; see SURGERY]

surgeonfish ('sɜːdʒənˌfɪʃ) *n, pl* **surgeonfish** *or* **surgeonfishes** any of various tropical marine spiny-finned fishes, having a compressed brightly coloured body with knifelike spines at the base of the tail

surgeon general *n, pl* **surgeons general** **1** (esp in the British and US armies and navies) the senior officer of the medical service **2** the head of the US public health service

surgery ('sɜːdʒərɪ) *n, pl* **surgeries** **1** the branch of medicine concerned with manual or operative procedures, esp incision into the body **2** the performance of such procedures by a surgeon **3** *Brit* a place where, or time when, a doctor, dentist, etc, can be consulted **4** *Brit* an occasion when an MP, lawyer, etc, is available for consultation **5** *US & Canad* an operating theatre [C14 via OF from L *chirurgia*, from Gk *kheirurgia*, from *kheir* hand + *ergon* work]

▷ www.nlm.nih.gov/medlineplus/surgery.html
▷ www.contemporarysurgery.com/links.html

surgical ('sɜːdʒɪkᵊl) *adj* of, relating to, involving, or used in surgery > '**surgically** *adv*

surgical boot *n* a specially designed boot or shoe that compensates for deformities of the foot or leg

surgical spirit *n* methylated spirit used medically for sterilizing

Suribachi (ˌsʊərɪ'bɑːtʃɪ) *n* **Mount** a volcanic hill in the Volcano Islands, on Iwo Jima: site of a US victory (1945) over the Japanese in World War II

suricate ('sjʊərɪˌkeɪt) *n* another name for **slender-tailed meerkat** (see **meerkat**) [C18 from F *surikate*, prob. from a native South African word]

surimi (ˌsuː'riːmɪ) *n* a blended seafood product made from precooked fish, restructured into stick shapes

Surinam (ˌsʊərɪ'næm) *n* a republic in NE South America, on the Atlantic: became a self-governing part of the Netherlands in 1954 and fully independent in 1975. Official languages: Dutch; English is also widely spoken. Religion: Hindu, Christian, and Muslim. Currency: guilder. Capital: Paramaribo. Pop: 434 000 (2001 est). Area: 163 820 sq km (63 251 sq miles). Former names: **Dutch Guiana, Netherlands Guiana**

▷ www.parbo.com
▷ www.escapeartist.com/suriname/suriname.htm

surly ('sɜːlɪ) *adj* **surlier, surliest** **1** sullenly ill-tempered or rude **2** (of an animal) ill-tempered or refractory [C16 from obs. *sirly* haughty] > '**surlily** *adv* > '**surliness** *n*

surmise *vb* (sɜː'maɪz), **surmises, surmising, surmised** **1** (when *tr, may take a clause as object*) to infer (something) from incomplete or uncertain evidence ▷ *n* (sɜː'maɪz, 'sɜːmaɪz) **2** an idea inferred from inconclusive evidence [C15 from OF, from *surmettre* to accuse, from L *supermittere* to throw over] > **surmisedly** (sɜː'maɪzɪdlɪ) *adv*

surmount (sɜː'maʊnt) *vb* (*tr*) **1** to prevail over; overcome **2** to ascend and cross to the opposite side of **3** to lie on top of or rise above **4** to put something on top of or above [C14 from OF *surmonter*, from SUR-[1] + *monter* to mount] > **sur'mountable** *adj*

surname ('sɜːˌneɪm) *n* **1** Also called: **last name, second name** a family name as opposed to a first or Christian name **2** (formerly) a descriptive epithet attached to a person's name to denote a personal characteristic, profession, etc; nickname ▷ *vb* **surnames, surnaming,**

surnamed 3 (*tr*) to furnish with or call by a surname > **'sur,namer** *n*

surpass (sɜː'pɑːs) *vb* (*tr*) 1 to be greater than in degree, extent, etc 2 to be superior to in achievement or excellence 3 to overstep the limit or range of: *the theory surpasses my comprehension* [C16 from F *surpasser*, from SUR-[1] + *passer* to PASS] > **sur'passable** *adj*

surpassing (sɜː'pɑːsɪŋ) *adj* 1 exceptional; extraordinary ▷ *adv* 2 *obs or poetic* (intensifier): *surpassing fair* > **sur'passingly** *adv*

surplice ('sɜːplɪs) *n* a loose wide-sleeved liturgical vestment of linen, reaching to the knees, worn over the cassock by clergymen, choristers, and acolytes [C13 from OF *sourpelis*, from Med. L *superpellīcium*, from SUPER- + *pellīcium* coat made of skins, from L *pellis* a skin]

surplus ('sɜːpləs) *n*, *pl* **surpluses** 1 a quantity or amount in excess of what is required 2 *accounting* 2a an excess of total assets over total liabilities 2b an excess of actual net assets over the nominal value of capital stock 2c an excess of revenues over expenditures 3 *econ* 3a an excess of government revenues over expenditures 3b an excess of receipts over payments on the balance of payments ▷ *adj* 4 being in excess; extra [C14 from OF, from Med. L *superplūs*, from L SUPER- + *plūs* more]

surprise (sə'praɪz) *vb* **surprises, surprising, surprised** (*tr*) 1 to cause to feel amazement or wonder 2 to encounter or discover unexpectedly or suddenly 3 to capture or assault suddenly and without warning 4 to present with something unexpected, such as a gift 5 (foll by *into*) to provoke (someone) to unintended action by a trick, etc 6 (often foll by *from*) to elicit by unexpected behaviour or by a trick: *to surprise information from a prisoner* ▷ *n* 7 the act or an instance of surprising; the act of taking unawares 8 a sudden or unexpected event, gift, etc 9 the feeling or condition of being surprised; astonishment 10 (*modifier*) causing, characterized by, or relying upon surprise: *a surprise move* 11 **take by surprise** 11a to come upon suddenly and without warning 11b to capture unexpectedly or catch unprepared 11c to astonish; amaze [C15 from OF, from *surprendre* to overtake, from SUR-[1] + L *prehendere* to grasp] > **sur'prisal** *n* > **sur'prised** *adj* > **surprisedly** (sə'praɪzɪdlɪ) *adv*

surprising (sə'praɪzɪŋ) *adj* causing surprise; unexpected or amazing > **sur'prisingly** *adv*

surra ('sʊərə) *n* a tropical febrile disease of cattle, horses, camels, and dogs [from Marathi, a language of India]

surrealism (sə'rɪə,lɪzəm) *n* (*sometimes cap*) a movement in art and literature in the 1920s, which developed esp from Dada, characterized by the evocative juxtaposition of incongruous images in order to include unconscious and dream elements [C20 from F *surréalisme*, from SUR-[1] + *réalisme* realism] > **sur'real** *adj* > **sur'realist** *n*, *adj* > **sur,real'istic** *adj*
▷ www.artchive.com/ftp_site_reg.htm

surrebutter (,sɜːrɪ'bʌtə) *n* *law* (in pleading) the plaintiff's reply to the defendant's rebutter > **,surre'buttal** *n*

surrejoinder (,sɜːrɪ'dʒɔɪndə) *n* *law* (in pleading) the plaintiff's reply to the defendant's rejoinder

surrender (sə'rɛndə) *vb* 1 (*tr*) to relinquish to another under duress or on demand: *to surrender a city* 2 (*tr*) to relinquish or forego (an office, position, etc), esp as a voluntary concession to another: *he surrendered his place to a lady* 3 to give (oneself) up physically, as to an enemy 4 to allow (oneself) to yield, as to a temptation, influence, etc 5 (*tr*) to give up (hope, etc) 6 (*tr*) *law* to give up or restore (an estate), esp to give up a lease before expiration of the term 7 **surrender to bail** to present oneself at court at the appointed time after having been on bail ▷ *n* 8 the act or instance of surrendering 9 *insurance* the voluntary discontinuation of a life policy by its holder in return for a consideration (the **surrender value**) 10 *law* 10a the yielding up or restoring of an estate, esp the giving up of a lease before its term has expired 10b the giving up to the appropriate authority of a fugitive from justice 10c the act of surrendering or being surrendered to bail 10d the deed by which a legal surrender is effected [C15 from OF *surrendre* to yield]

surreptitious (,sʌrəp'tɪʃəs) *adj* 1 done, acquired, etc, in secret or by improper means 2 operating by stealth [C15 from L *surreptīcius* furtive, from *surripere* to steal, from *sub-* secretly + *rapere* to snatch] > **,surrep'titiously** *adv* > **,surrep'titiousness** *n*

surrey ('sʌrɪ) *n* a light four-wheeled horse-drawn carriage having two or four seats [C19 from *Surrey cart*, after SURREY[1] where orig. made]

Surrey[1] ('sʌrɪ) *n* a county of SE England, on the River Thames: urban in the northeast; crossed from east to west by the North Downs and drained by tributaries of the Thames. Administrative centre: Kingston upon Thames. Pop: 1 059 015 (2001). Area: 1679 sq km (648 sq miles)

Surrey[2] ('sʌrɪ) *n* **Earl of**, title of *Henry Howard*. ?1517–47, English courtier and poet; one of the first in England to write sonnets. He was beheaded for high treason

surrogate *n* ('sʌrəgɪt) 1 a person or thing acting as a substitute 2 *chiefly Brit* a deputy, such as a clergyman appointed to deputize for a bishop in granting marriage licences 3 (in some US states) a judge with jurisdiction over the probate of wills, etc 4 (*modifier*) of, relating to, or acting as a surrogate: *a surrogate pleasure* ▷ *vb* ('sʌrə,geɪt), **surrogates, surrogating, surrogated** (*tr*) 5 to put in another's position as a deputy, substitute, etc [C17 from L *surrogāre* to substitute] > **'surrogateship** *n* > **,surro'gation** *n*

surrogate motherhood *or* **surrogacy** ('sʌrəgəsɪ) *n* the role of a woman who bears a child on behalf of a childless couple, either by artificial insemination or implantation of an embryo > **surrogate mother** *n*

surround (sə'raʊnd) *vb* (*tr*) 1 to encircle or enclose or cause to be encircled or enclosed 2 to deploy forces on all sides of (a place or military formation), so preventing access or retreat 3 to exist around: *the people who surround her* ▷ *n* 4 *chiefly Brit* a border, esp the area of uncovered floor between the walls of a room and the carpet or around an opening or panel 5 *chiefly US* 5a a method of capturing wild beasts by encircling the area in which they are believed to be 5b the area so encircled [C15 *surrounden* to overflow, from OF *suronder*, from LL, from L SUPER- + *undāre* to abound, from *unda* a wave] > **sur'rounding** *adj*

Ss

surroundings (sə'raʊndɪŋz) *pl n* the conditions, scenery, etc, around a person, place, or thing; environment

sursum corda ('sɜːsəm 'kɔːdə) *n* 1 *RC Church* a Latin versicle meaning *Lift up your hearts*, said by the priest at Mass 2 a cry of exhortation, hope, etc

surtax ('sɜː,tæks) *n* 1 a tax, usually highly progressive, levied on the amount by which a person's income exceeds a specific level 2 an additional tax on something that has already been taxed ▷ *vb* 3 (*tr*) to assess for liability to surtax; charge with an extra tax

Surtees ('sɜːtiːz) *n* 1 **John** born 1934, British racing motorcyclist and motor-racing driver. He was motorcycling world champion (1956, 1958–60) and world champion motor-racing driver (1964), the only man to have been world champion in both sports 2 **Robert Smith** 1803–64, British journalist and novelist, who satirized the sporting life of the English gentry in such works as *Jorrocks's Jaunts and Jollities* (1838)

surtitles ('sɜː,taɪtᵊlz) *pl n* brief translations of the text of an opera or play that is being sung or spoken in a foreign language, projected above the stage

surtout ('sɜːtuː) *n* a man's overcoat resembling a frock coat, popular in the late 19th century [C17 from F, from *sur* over + *tout* all]

surveillance (sɜːˈveɪləns) *n* close observation or supervision over a person, group, etc, esp one in custody or under suspicion [C19 from F, from *surveiller* to watch over, from SUR-[1] + *veiller* to keep watch (from L *vigilāre*; see VIGIL)] > **surˈveillant** *adj, n*

survey *vb* (sɜːˈveɪ, ˈsɜːveɪ) **1** (*tr*) to view or consider in a comprehensive or general way **2** (*tr*) to examine carefully, in order to or as if to appraise condition and value **3** to plot a detailed map of (an area of land) by measuring or calculating distances and height **4** *Brit* to inspect a building to determine its condition and value **5** to examine a vessel thoroughly in order to determine its seaworthiness **6** (*tr*) to run a statistical survey on (incomes, opinions, etc) ▷ *n* (ˈsɜːveɪ) **7** a comprehensive or general view **8** a critical, detailed, and formal inspection **9** *Brit* an inspection of a building to determine its condition and value **10** a report incorporating the results of such an inspection **11a** a body of surveyors **11b** an area surveyed [C15 from F *surveoir*, from SUR-[1] + *veoir* to see, from L *vidēre*]

surveying (sɜːˈveɪɪŋ) *n* **1** the study or practice of making surveys of land **2** the setting out on the ground of the positions of proposed construction or engineering works

▷ www.fig.net/figtree/links/siteindex.htm

surveyor (sɜːˈveɪə) *n* **1** a person whose occupation is to survey land or buildings. See also **quantity surveyor** **2** *chiefly Brit* a person concerned with the official inspection of something for purposes of measurement and valuation **3** a person who carries out surveys, esp of ships (**marine surveyor**) to determine seaworthiness, etc **4** a customs official **5** *arch* a supervisor > **surˈveyorship** *n*

surveyor's measure *n* the system of measurement based on the **surveyor's chain** (66 feet) as a unit

survival (səˈvaɪvᵊl) *n* **1** a person or thing that survives, such as a custom **2a** the act or fact of surviving or condition of having survived **2b** (*as modifier*): *survival kit*

survival bag *n* a large plastic bag carried by climbers for use in an emergency as protection against exposure

survivalist (səˈvaɪvəlɪst) *n chiefly US* **a** a person who believes in ensuring his or her personal survival of a catastrophic event by arming himself or herself and often by living in the wild **b** (*as modifier*): *survivalist weapons* > **surˈvivalˌism** *n*

survival of the fittest *n* a popular term for **natural selection**

survive (səˈvaɪv) *vb* **survives, surviving, survived** **1** (*tr*) to live after the death of (another) **2** to continue in existence or use after (a passage of time, adversity, etc) **3** *inf* to endure (something): *I don't know how I survive such an awful job* [C15 from OF *sourvivre*, from L *supervīvere*, from SUPER- + *vīvere* to live] > **surˈvivor** *n*

sus (sʌs) *Brit sl* ▷ *n* **1** short for **suspicion**, with reference to former police powers (**sus laws**) of detaining for questioning, searching, etc, any person suspected of criminal intent: *he was picked up on sus* ▷ *vb* **susses, sussing, sussed** **2** a variant spelling of **suss** (sense 2)

Susa (ˈsuːsə) *n* an ancient city north of the Persian Gulf: capital of Elam and of the Persian Empire; flourished as a Greek polis under the Seleucids and Parthians. Biblical name: **Shushan**

Susah *or* **Susa** (ˈsuːzə) *n* other names for **Sousse**

Susanna (suːˈzænə) *n Apocrypha* **1** the wife of Joachim, who was condemned to death for adultery because of a false accusation, but saved by Daniel's sagacity **2** the book of the Apocrypha containing this story

susceptance (səˈsɛptəns) *n physics* the imaginary component of the admittance [C19 from *suscept(ibility)* + -ANCE]

susceptibility (səˌsɛptəˈbɪlɪtɪ) *n, pl* **susceptibilities** **1** the quality or condition of being susceptible **2** the ability or tendency to be impressed by emotional feelings **3** (*pl*) emotional sensibilities; feelings **4** *physics* **4a** Also called: **electric susceptibility** (of a dielectric) the amount by which the relative permittivity differs from unity **4b** Also called: **magnetic susceptibility** (of a magnetic medium) the amount by which the relative permeability differs from unity

susceptible (səˈsɛptəbᵊl) *adj* **1** (*postpositive; foll by* of *or* to) yielding readily (to); capable (of): *hypotheses susceptible of refutation; susceptible to control* **2** (*postpositive; foll by* to) liable to be afflicted (by): *susceptible to colds* **3** easily impressed emotionally [C17 from LL *susceptibilis*, from L *suscipere* to take up] > **susˈceptibly** *adv*

sushi (ˈsuːʃɪ) *n* a Japanese dish consisting of small cakes of cold rice with a topping, esp of raw fish [Japanese]

suslik (ˈsʌslɪk) *or* **souslik** *n* a central Eurasian ground squirrel having large eyes and small ears [from Russian]

suspect *vb* (səˈspɛkt) **1** (*tr*) to believe guilty of a specified offence without proof **2** (*tr*) to think false, questionable, etc: *she suspected his sincerity* **3** (*tr; may take a clause as object*) to surmise to be the case; think probable: *to suspect fraud* **4** (*intr*) to have suspicion ▷ *n* (ˈsʌspɛkt) **5** a person under suspicion ▷ *adj* (ˈsʌspɛkt) **6** causing or open to suspicion [C14 from L *suspicere* to mistrust, from SUB- + *specere* to look]

suspend (səˈspɛnd) *vb* **1** (*tr*) to hang from above **2** (*tr; passive*) to cause to remain floating or hanging: *a cloud of smoke was suspended over the town* **3** (*tr*) to render inoperative or cause to cease, esp temporarily **4** (*tr*) to hold in abeyance; postpone action on **5** (*tr*) to debar temporarily from privilege, office, etc, as a punishment **6** (*tr*) *chem* to cause (particles) to be held in suspension in a fluid **7** (*tr*) *music* to continue (a note) until the next chord is sounded, with which it usually forms a dissonance. See **suspension** (sense 11) **8** (*intr*) to cease payment, as from incapacity to meet financial obligations [C13 from L *suspendere* from SUB- + *pendere* to hang] > **susˈpendible** *or* **susˈpensible** *adj* > **susˌpendiˈbility** *n*

suspended animation *n* a temporary cessation of the vital functions, as by freezing an organism

suspended sentence *n* a sentence of imprisonment that is not served by an offender unless he commits a further offence during its currency

suspender (səˈspɛndə) *n* **1** (*often pl*) *Brit* **1a** an elastic strap attached to a belt or corset having a fastener at the end, for holding up women's stockings **1b** a similar fastener attached to a garter worn by men in order to support socks **2** (*pl*) the US and Canad name for **braces** **3** a person or thing that suspends, such as one of the vertical cables in a suspension bridge

suspender belt *n* a belt with suspenders hanging from it to hold up women's stockings

suspense (səˈspɛns) *n* **1** the condition of being insecure or uncertain **2** mental uncertainty; anxiety: *their father's illness kept them in a state of suspense* **3** excitement felt at the approach of the climax: *a play of terrifying suspense* **4** the condition of being suspended [C15 from Med. L *suspensum* delay, from L *suspendere* to hang up] > **susˈpenseful** *adj*

suspense account *n book-keeping* an account in which entries are made until determination of their proper disposition

suspension (səˈspɛnʃən) *n* **1** an interruption or temporary revocation: *the suspension of a law* **2** a temporary debarment, as from position, privilege, etc **3** a deferment, esp of a decision, judgment, etc **4** *law* a postponement of execution of a sentence or the deferring of a judgment, etc **5** cessation of payment of business debts, esp as a result of insolvency **6** the act of suspending or the state of being suspended **7** a system of springs, shock absorbers, etc, that supports the body of a wheeled or tracked vehicle and insulates it from shocks transmitted by the wheels **8** a device or structure, usually a wire or spring, that serves to suspend or support something, such as the pendulum of a clock **9** *chem* a dispersion of fine solid or liquid particles in a fluid, the particles being supported by buoyancy. See also **colloid** **10** the process by which eroded particles of rock are transported in a river **11** *music* one or more notes of a chord that are prolonged until a subsequent chord is sounded, usually to form a dissonance

suspension bridge *n* a bridge suspended from cables or chains that hang between two towers and are anchored at both ends

suspensive (sə'spɛnsɪv) *adj* **1** having the power of deferment; effecting suspension **2** causing, characterized by, or relating to suspense > **sus'pensively** *adv* > **sus'pensiveness** *n*

suspensory (sə'spɛnsərɪ) *n, pl* **suspensories** **1** Also called: **suspensor** *anat* a ligament or muscle that holds a structure or part in position **2** *med* a bandage, sling, etc, for supporting a dependent part ▷ *adj* **3** suspending or supporting **4** *anat* (of a ligament or muscle) supporting or holding a structure or part in position

suspicion (sə'spɪʃən) *n* **1** the act or an instance of suspecting; belief without sure proof, esp that something is wrong **2** the feeling of mistrust of a person who suspects **3** the state of being suspected: *to be shielded from suspicion* **4** a slight trace **5** **above suspicion** in such a position that no guilt may be thought or implied, esp through having an unblemished reputation **6** **on suspicion** as a suspect **7** **under suspicion** regarded with distrust [C14 from OF *sospeçon*, from L *suspīciō* distrust, from *suspicere*; see SUSPECT] > **sus'picional** *adj*

suspicious (sə'spɪʃəs) *adj* **1** exciting or liable to excite suspicion; questionable **2** disposed to suspect something wrong **3** indicative or expressive of suspicion > **sus'piciously** *adv* > **sus'piciousness** *n*

Susquehanna (ˌsʌskwɪ'hænə) *n* a river in the eastern US, rising in Otsego Lake and flowing generally south to Chesapeake Bay at Havre de Grace: the longest river in the eastern US Length: 714 km (444 miles)

suss (sʌs) *inf* ▷ *vb (tr)* **1** (often foll by *out*) to attempt to work out (a situation, person's character, etc), esp using one's intuition **2** Also: **sus** to become aware of; suspect (esp in **suss it**) ▷ *n* **3** sharpness of mind; social astuteness [C20 shortened from SUSPECT]

sussed (sʌst) *adj Brit inf* well-informed; aware

Sussex ('sʌsɪks) *n* **1** (until 1974) a county of SE England, now divided into the separate counties of East Sussex and West Sussex **2** (in Anglo-Saxon England) the kingdom of the South Saxons, which became a shire of the kingdom of Wessex in the early 9th century AD **3** a breed of red beef cattle originally from Sussex **4** a heavy and long-established breed of domestic fowl used principally as a table bird

sustain (sə'steɪn) *vb (tr)* **1** to hold up under; withstand: *to sustain great provocation* **2** to undergo (an injury, loss, etc); suffer: *to sustain a broken arm* **3** to maintain or prolong: *to sustain a discussion* **4** to support physically from below **5** to provide for or give support to, esp by supplying necessities: *to sustain one's family* **6** to keep up the vitality or courage of **7** to uphold or affirm the justice or validity of: *to sustain a decision* **8** to establish the truth of; confirm ▷ *n* **9** *music* the prolongation of a note, by playing technique or electronics [C13 via OF from L *sustinēre* to hold up] > **sus'tained** *adj* > **sustainedly** (sə'steɪnɪdlɪ) *adv* > **sus'tainer** *n* > **sus'taining** *adj* > **sus'tainment** *n*

sustainable (sə'steɪnəbᵊl) *adj* **1** capable of being sustained **2** (of economic development, energy sources, etc) capable of being maintained at a steady level without exhausting natural resources or causing severe ecological damage: *sustainable development*

sustaining pedal *n music* a foot-operated lever on a piano that keeps the dampers raised from the strings when keys are released, allowing them to continue to vibrate

sustenance ('sʌstənəns) *n* **1** means of sustaining health or life; nourishment **2** means of maintenance; livelihood **3** Also: **sustention** (sə'stɛnʃən) the act or process of sustaining or the quality of being sustained [C13 from OF *sostenance*, from *sustenir* to SUSTAIN]

sustentation (ˌsʌstɛn'teɪʃən) *n* a less common word for **sustenance** [C14 from L *sustentātio*, from *sustentāre*, frequentative of *sustinēre* to SUSTAIN]

susurrate ('sjuːsəˌreɪt) *vb* **susurrates, susurrating, susurrated** *(intr) literary* to make a soft rustling sound; whisper; murmur [C17 from L *susurrāre* to whisper] > ˌ**susur'ration** *or* **susurrus** (sjuː'sʌrəs) *n*

Sutcliffe ('sʌtˌklɪf) *n* **Herbert** 1894–1978, English cricketer, who played for Yorkshire; scorer of 149 centuries and 1000 runs in a season 24 times

Suth. *abbrev for* Sutherland

Sutherland[1] ('sʌðələnd) *n* (until 1975) a county of N Scotland, now part of Highland

Sutherland[2] ('sʌðələnd) *n* **1** **Graham** 1903–80, English artist, noted for his work as an official war artist (1941–44), for his tapestry *Christ in Majesty* (1962) in Coventry Cathedral, and for his portraits **2** Dame **Joan**, known as *La Stupenda*. born 1926, Australian operatic soprano

Sutherland Falls *n* a waterfall in New Zealand, on SW South Island. Height: 580 m (1904 ft)

Sutlej ('sʌtlɪdʒ) *n* a river in S Asia, rising in SW Tibet and flowing west through the Himalayas: crosses Himachal Pradesh and the Punjab (India), enters Pakistan, and joins the Chenab west of Bahawalpur: the longest of the five rivers of the Punjab. Length: 1368 km (850 miles)

sutler ('sʌtlə) *n* (formerly) a merchant who accompanied an army in order to sell provisions to the soldiers [C16 from obs. Du. *soeteler*, ult. from MHG *sudelen* to do dirty work]

sutra ('suːtrə) *n* **1** *Hinduism* Sanskrit sayings or collections of sayings on Vedic doctrine dating from about 200 AD onwards **2** *(modifier) Hinduism* **2a** of or relating to the last of the Vedic literary periods, from about 500 to 100 BC: *the sutra period* **2b** of or relating to the sutras or compilations of sutras of about 200 AD onwards **3** *Buddhism* collections of dialogues and discourses of classic Mahayana Buddhism dating from the 2nd to the 6th century AD [C19 from Sansk.: list of rules]

Ss

suttee (sʌ'tiː, 'sʌtiː) *n* **1** the former Hindu custom whereby a widow burnt herself to death on her husband's funeral pyre **2** a widow performing this [C18 from Sansk. *satī* virtuous woman, from *sat* good] > **sut'teeism** *n*

Sutton ('sʌtᵊn) *n* a borough of S Greater London. Pop: 179 667 (2001). Area: 43 sq km (17 sq miles)

Sutton Coldfield (-'kəʊldˌfiːld) *n* a town in central England, in Birmingham unitary authority, West Midlands; a residential suburb of Birmingham. Pop: 106 001 (1991)

Sutton-in-Ashfield (-'æʃˌfiːld) *n* a market town in N central England, in W Nottinghamshire. Pop: 37 890 (1991)

suture ('suːtʃə) *n* **1** *surgery* **1a** catgut, silk thread, or wire used to stitch together two bodily surfaces **1b** the surgical seam formed after stitching **2** *anat* a type of immovable joint, esp between the bones of the skull (**cranial suture**) **3** a seam or joining, as in sewing **4** *zool* a line of junction in a mollusc shell ▷ *vb* **sutures, suturing, sutured** **5** *(tr) surgery* to join (the edges of a wound, etc) by means of sutures [C16 from L *sūtūra*, from *suere* to sew] > **'sutural** *adj*

Suu Kyi *n* See **Aung San Suu Kyi**

SUV *abbrev for* sport (*or* sports) utility vehicle

Suva ('suːvə) *n* the capital and chief port of Fiji, on the SE coast of Viti Levu; popular tourist resort; University of

the South Pacific (1968). Pop: 167 421 (1996)
Suvorov (*Russian* su'vɔrəf) *n* **Aleksandr Vasilyevich** (alɪk'sandr va'siljɪvitʃ) 1729–1800, Russian field marshal, who fought successfully against the Turks (1787–91), the Poles (1794), and the French in Italy (1798–99)
Suwannee (sʊ'wɒnɪ) *or* **Swanee** *n* a river in the southeastern US, rising in SE Georgia and flowing across Florida to the Gulf of Mexico at **Suwannee Sound** Length: about 400 km (250 miles)
suzerain ('su:zə,reɪn) *n* **1a** a state or sovereign exercising some degree of dominion over a dependent state, usually controlling its foreign affairs **1b** (*as modifier*): *a suzerain power* **2a** a feudal overlord **2b** (*as modifier*): *suzerain lord* [c19 from F, from *sus* above (from L *sursum* turned upwards) + *-erain*, as in *souverain* sovereign]
suzerainty ('su:zərəntɪ) *n, pl* **suzerainties** **1** the position, power, or dignity of a suzerain **2** the relationship between suzerain and subject
Suzhou ('su:'dʒəʊ), **Su-chou**, *or* **Soochow** *n* a city in E China, in S Jiangsu on the Grand Canal: noted for its gardens; produces chiefly silk. Pop: 845 687 (1999 est). Also called: **Wuhsien**
sv *abbrev for:* **1** sailing vessel **2** side valve **3** sub verbo *or* voce [L: under the word *or* voice]
Svalbard (*Norwegian* 'sva:lbar) *n* a Norwegian archipelago in the Arctic Ocean, about 650 km (400 miles) north of Norway: consists of the main group (Spitsbergen, North East Land, Edge Island, Barents Island, and Prince Charles Foreland) and a number of outlying islands; sovereignty long disputed but granted to Norway in 1920; coal mining. Administrative centre: Longyearbyen. Area: 62 050 sq km (23 958 sq miles). Also called: **Spitsbergen**
svelte (svɛlt, sfɛlt) *adj* attractively or gracefully slim; slender [c19 from F, from It. *svelto*, from *svellere* to pull out, from L *ēvellere*]
Svengali (svɛn'gɑ:lɪ) *n* a person who controls another's mind, usually with sinister intentions [after a character in George Du Maurier's novel *Trilby* (1894)]
Sverdlovsk (*Russian* svɪr'dlɔfsk) *n* the former name (1924–91) of **Yekaterinburg**
Sverige ('sværjə) *n* the Swedish name for **Sweden**
Svevo (*Italian* 'svevo) *n* **Italo** (ɪ'talo), original name *Ettore Schnitz*. 1861–1928, Italian novelist and short-story writer, best known for the novel *Confessions of Zeno* (1923)
SVGA *computing abbrev for* Super Video Graphics Array. See also **VGA**
Svizzera ('zvittsera) *n* the Italian name for **Switzerland**
Svizzra ('zvitsra) *n* the Romansch name for **Switzerland**
SVQ *abbrev for* Scottish Vocational Qualification
SW **1** *symbol for* southwest(ern) **2** *abbrev for* short wave
Sw. *abbrev for* **1** Sweden **2** Swedish
swab (swɒb) *n* **1** *med* **1a** a small piece of cotton, gauze, etc, for use in applying medication, cleansing a wound, or obtaining a specimen of a secretion, etc **1b** the specimen so obtained **2** a mop for cleaning floors, decks, etc **3** a brush used to clean a firearm's bore **4** *sl* an uncouth or worthless fellow ▹ *vb* **swabs, swabbing, swabbed** **5** (*tr*) to clean or medicate with or as if with a swab **6** (*tr; foll by up*) to take up with a swab [c16 prob. from MDu. *swabbe* mop] > **'swabber** *n*
Swabia ('sweɪbɪə) *n* a region and former duchy (from the 10th century to 1313) of S Germany, now part of Baden-Württemberg and Bavaria: part of West Germany until 1990. German name: **Schwaben** ('ʃva:bᵊn) > **'Swabian** *adj, n*
swaddle ('swɒdᵊl) *vb* **swaddles, swaddling, swaddled** (*tr*) **1** to wind a bandage round **2** to wrap (a baby) in swaddling clothes **3** to restrain as if by wrapping with bandages; smother ▹ *n* **4** *chiefly US* swaddling clothes [c15 from OE *swæthel* swaddling clothes]
swaddling clothes *pl n* **1** long strips of linen or other cloth formerly wrapped round a newly born baby **2** restrictions or supervision imposed on the immature
swaddy *or* **swaddie** ('swɒdɪ) *n Brit sl, old-fashioned* a soldier [c19 from E dialect *swad* country bumpkin, soldier]
swag (swæg) *n* **1** *sl* property obtained by theft or other illicit means **2** *sl* goods; valuables **3** an ornamental festoon of fruit, flowers, or drapery or a representation of this **4** a swaying movement; lurch **5** *Austral & NZ inf* a swagman's pack containing personal belongings, etc **6** **swags of** *Austral & NZ inf* lots of ▹ *vb* **swags, swagging, swagged** **7** *chiefly Brit* to lurch or sag or cause to lurch or sag **8** (*tr*) to adorn or arrange with swags [c17 ? of Scand. origin]
swage (sweɪdʒ) *n* **1** a shaped tool or die used in forming cold metal by hammering, pressing, etc ▹ *vb* **swages, swaging, swaged** **2** (*tr*) to form (metal) with a swage [c19 from F *souage*, from ?] > **'swager** *n*
swage block *n* an iron block with holes, grooves, etc, to assist in the cold-working of metal
swagger ('swægə) *vb* **1** (*intr*) to walk or behave in an arrogant manner **2** (*intr; often foll by about*) to brag loudly ▹ *n* **3** an arrogant gait or manner ▹ *adj* **4** *Brit inf, rare* elegantly fashionable [c16 prob. from SWAG] > **'swaggerer** *n* > **'swaggering** *adj* > **'swaggeringly** *adv*
swagger stick *or esp Brit* **swagger cane** *n* a short cane or stick carried on occasion mainly by army officers
swaggie ('swægɪ) *n Austral sl* short for **swagman**
swagman ('swæg,mæn, -mən) *n, pl* **swagmen** *Austral & NZ inf* a tramp or vagrant worker who carries his possessions on his back. Also called: **swaggie**
Swahili (swɑ:'hi:lɪ) *n* **1** a language of E Africa that is an official language of Kenya and Tanzania and is widely used as a lingua franca throughout E and central Africa. Also called: **Kiswahili** **2** (*pl* **Swahilis** *or* **Swahili**) a member of a people speaking this language, living chiefly in Zanzibar. Also called: **Mswahili** (*pl* **Waswahili**) ▹ *adj* **3** of or relating to the Swahilis or their language [c19 from Ar. *sawāhil* coasts] > **Swa'hilian** *adj*
swain (sweɪn) *n arch or poetic* **1** a male lover or admirer **2** a country youth [OE *swān* swineherd]
swallow¹ ('swɒləʊ) *vb* (*mainly tr*) **1** to pass (food, drink, etc) through the mouth to the stomach by means of the muscular action of the oesophagus **2** (*often foll by up*) to engulf or destroy as if by ingestion **3** *inf* to believe gullibly: *he will never swallow such an excuse* **4** to refrain from uttering or manifesting: *to swallow one's disappointment* **5** to endure without retaliation **6** to enunciate (words, etc) indistinctly; mutter **7** (*often foll by down*) to eat or drink reluctantly **8** (*intr*) to perform or simulate the act of swallowing, as in gulping ▹ *n* **9** the act of swallowing **10** the amount swallowed at any single time; mouthful **11** *rare* another word for **throat** or **gullet** [OE *swelgan*] > **'swallowable** *adj* > **'swallower** *n*
swallow² ('swɒləʊ) *n* any of various passerine songbirds having long pointed wings, a forked tail, short legs, and a rapid flight [OE *swealwe*]
swallow dive *n* a type of dive in which the diver arches back while in the air, keeping his legs straight and together and his arms outstretched, finally entering the water headfirst. US and Canad equivalent: **swan dive**
swallow hole *n chiefly Brit* another word for **sinkhole** (sense 1)
swallowtail ('swɒləʊ,teɪl) *n* **1** any of various butterflies of Europe, having a tail-like extension of each hind wing **2** the forked tail of a swallow or similar bird **3** short for **swallow-tailed coat** > **'swallow-,tailed** *adj*
swallow-tailed coat *n* another name for **tail coat**
swam (swæm) *vb* the past tense of **swim**
swami ('swɑ:mɪ) *n, pl* **swamies** *or* **swamis** (in India) a title of respect for a Hindu saint or religious teacher [c18 from Hindi *svāmī*, from Sansk. *svāmin* master, from *sva* one's own]

swamp (swɒmp) *n* **1** permanently waterlogged ground that is usually overgrown and sometimes partly forested ▷ Cf **marsh** ▷ *vb* **2** to drench or submerge or be drenched or submerged **3** *naut* to cause (a boat) to sink or fill with water or (of a boat) to sink or fill with water **4** to overburden or overwhelm or be overburdened or overwhelmed, as by excess work or great numbers **5** (*tr*) to render helpless [C17 prob. from MDu. *somp*] > **'swampy** *adj*

swamp boat *n* a shallow-draught boat powered by an aeroplane engine mounted on a raised structure for use in swamps. Also called: **airboat**

swamp cypress *n* a North American deciduous coniferous tree that grows in swamps. Also called: **bald cypress**

swamp fever *n* **1** Also called: **equine infectious anaemia** a viral disease of horses **2** *US* another name for **malaria**

swampland ('swɒmp,lænd) *n* a permanently waterlogged area; marshland

swan (swɒn) *n* **1** any of various large aquatic birds having a long neck and usually a white plumage **2** *rare, literary* **2a** a poet **2b** (*cap when part of a title or epithet*): *the Swan of Avon* (Shakespeare) ▷ *vb* **swans, swanning, swanned 3** (*intr; usually foll by around or about*) *inf* to wander idly [OE] > **'swan,like** *adj*

Swan[1] (swɒn) *n* a river in SW Western Australia, rising as the Avon northeast of Narrogin and flowing northwest and west to the Indian Ocean below Perth. Length: about 240 km (150 miles)

Swan[2] (swɒn) *n* Sir **Joseph Wilson** 1828–1914, English physicist and chemist, who developed the incandescent electric light (1880) independently of Edison

swan dive *n* the US and Canad name for **swallow dive**

Swanee ('swɒnɪ) *n* a variant spelling of **Suwannee**

swank (swæŋk) *inf* ▷ *vb* **1** (*intr*) to show off or swagger ▷ *n* **2** Also called: **swankpot** *Brit* a swaggering or conceited person **3** *chiefly US* showy elegance or style **4** swagger; ostentation ▷ *adj* **5** another word (esp US) for **swanky** [C19 ?from MHG *swanken* to sway]

swanky ('swæŋkɪ) *adj* **swankier, swankiest** *inf* **1** expensive and showy; stylish: *a swanky hotel* **2** boastful or conceited > **'swankily** *adv* > **'swankiness** *n*

Swanndri *or* **Swandri** ('swɒn,draɪ) *n pl* **-dris** *trademark NZ* an all-weather heavy woollen shirt. Also called: **swannie** ('swɒnɪ)

swan neck *n* a tube, rail, etc, curved like a swan's neck

swannery ('swɒnərɪ) *n, pl* **swanneries** a place where swans are kept and bred

swan's-down *n* **1** the fine soft down feathers of a swan, used to trim powder puffs, clothes, etc **2** a thick soft fabric of wool with silk, cotton, or rayon, used for infants' clothing, etc **3** a cotton fabric with a heavy nap

Swansea ('swɒnzɪ) *n* **1** a port in S Wales, in Swansea county on an inlet of the Bristol Channel (**Swansea Bay**); a metallurgical and oil-refining centre; university (1920) Pop: 171 038 (1991) **2** a county of S Wales on the Bristol Channel, created in 1996 from part of West Glamorgan: includes the Swansea conurbation and the Gower peninsula. Administrative centre: Swansea. Pop: 223 293 (2001). Area: 378 sq km (146 sq miles)

swan song *n* **1** the last act, publication, etc, of a person before retirement or death **2** the song that a dying swan is said to sing

swan-upping *n Brit* **1** the practice or action of marking nicks in swans' beaks as a sign of ownership **2** the annual swan-upping of royal cygnets on the River Thames

swap *or* **swop** (swɒp) *vb* **swaps, swapping, swapped** *or* **swops, swopping, swopped 1** to trade or exchange (something or someone) for another ▷ *n* **2** an exchange **3** something that is exchanged **4** *finance* Also called: **swap option, swaption** a contract in which the parties to it exchange liabilities on outstanding debts, often exchanging fixed-interest-rate for floating-rate debts (**debt swap**), either as a means of debt management or in trading (**swap trading**) [C14 (in the sense: to shake hands on a bargain, strike): prob. imit.] > **'swapper** *or* **'swopper** *n*

SWAPO *or* **Swapo** ('swɑːpəʊ) *n acronym for* South-West Africa People's Organization

swaption ('swɒpʃən) *n* another name for **swap** (sense 4)

swaraj (swə'rɑːdʒ) *n* (in British India) self-government; independence [C20 from Sansk. *svarāj*, from *sva* self + *rājya* rule] > **swa'rajism** *n* > **swa'rajist** *n, adj*

sward (swɔːd) *n* **1** turf or grass or a stretch of turf or grass ▷ *vb* **2** to cover or become covered with grass [OE *sweard* skin]

swarf (swɔːf, swɑːf) *n* **1** material removed by cutting or grinding tools in the machining of metals, stone, etc **2** radioactive metal waste from a nuclear power station **3** small fragments of disintegrating spacecraft orbiting the earth [C16 of Scand. origin]

swarm[1] (swɔːm) *n* **1** a group of bees, led by a queen, that has left the parent hive to start a new colony **2** a large mass of small animals, esp insects **3** a throng or mass, esp when moving or in turmoil ▷ *vb* **4** (*intr*) (of small animals, esp bees) to move in or form a swarm **5** (*intr*) to congregate, move about or proceed in large numbers **6** (when *intr*, often foll by *with*) to overrun or be overrun (with): *swarming with rats* **7** (*tr*) to cause to swarm [OE *swearm*]

swarm[2] (swɔːm) *vb* (when *intr*, usually foll by *up*) to climb (a ladder, etc) by gripping with the hands and feet: *the boys swarmed up the rigging* [C16 from ?]

swart (swɔːt) *or* **swarth** (swɔːθ) *adj arch or dialect* swarthy [OE *sweart*]

swarthy ('swɔːðɪ) *adj* **swarthier, swarthiest** dark-hued or dark-complexioned [C16 from obs. *swarty*] > **'swarthily** *adv* > **'swarthiness** *n*

swash (swɒʃ) *vb* **1** (*intr*) (esp of water or things in water) to wash or move with noisy splashing **2** (*tr*) to dash (a liquid, esp water) against or upon **3** (*intr*) *arch* to swagger ▷ *n* **4** Also called: **send** the dashing movement or sound of water, as of waves on a beach **5** Also called: **swash channel** a channel of moving water cutting through or running behind a sandbank **6** *arch* swagger or bluster [C16 prob. imit.]

Ss

swashbuckler ('swɒʃ,bʌklə) *n* **1** a swaggering or flamboyant adventurer **2** a film, book, play, etc, depicting excitement and adventure, esp in a historical setting [C16 from SWASH (in archaic sense: to make the noise of a sword striking a shield) + BUCKLER] > **'swash,buckling** *adj*

swash letter *n printing* a decorative letter, esp an ornamental italic capital [C17 from *aswash* aslant]

swastika ('swɒstɪkə) *n* **1** a primitive religious symbol or ornament in the shape of a Greek cross, usually having the ends of the arms bent at right angles **2** this symbol with clockwise arms, the emblem of Nazi Germany [C19 from Sansk. *svastika*, from *svasti* prosperity; from belief that it brings good luck]

swat (swɒt) *vb* **swats, swatting, swatted** (*tr*) **1** to strike or hit sharply: *to swat a fly* ▷ *n* **2** a sharp or violent blow ▷ Also: **swot** [C17 N English dialect & US var. of SQUAT] > **'swatter** *n*

Swat (swɒt) *n* **1** a former princely state of NW India: passed to Pakistan in 1947 **2** a river in Pakistan, rising in the north and flowing south to the Kabul River north of Peshawar. Length: about 640 km (400 miles)

swatch (swɒtʃ) *n* **1** a sample of cloth or other material **2** a number of such samples, usually fastened together in book form [C16 Scot & N English, from ?]

swath (swɔːθ) *or* **swathe** (sweɪð) *n, pl* **swaths** (swɔːðz) *or* **swathes 1** the width of one sweep of a scythe or of the blade of a mowing machine **2** the strip cut by these in one course **3** the quantity of cut grass, hay, etc, left in one such course **4** a long narrow strip or belt [OE *swæth*]

swathe (sweɪð) *vb* **swathes, swathing, swathed** (*tr*) **1** to bandage (a wound, limb, etc), esp completely **2** to wrap a band, garment, etc, around, esp so as to cover completely; swaddle **3** to envelop ▷ *n* **4** a bandage or wrapping **5** a variant spelling of **swath** [OE *swathian*]

Swatow (ˈswɒˈtaʊ) *n* a variant transliteration of the Chinese name for **Shantou**

sway (sweɪ) *vb* **1** (*usually intr*) to swing or cause to swing to and fro: *the door swayed in the wind* **2** (*usually intr*) to lean or incline or cause to lean or incline to one side or in different directions in turn **3** (*usually intr*) to vacillate or cause to vacillate between two or more opinions **4** to be influenced or swerve or influence or cause to swerve to or from a purpose or opinion **5** *arch or poetic* to rule or wield power (over) ▷ *n* **6** control; power **7** a swinging or leaning movement **8** *arch* dominion; governing authority **9** **hold sway** to be master; reign [c16 prob. from ON *sveigja* to bend]

sway-back *n* an abnormal sagging or concavity of the spine in older horses and a neurological disease of young lambs > **ˈsway-ˌbacked** *adj*

Swaziland (ˈswɑːzɪˌlænd) *n* a kingdom in southern Africa: made a protectorate of the Transvaal by Britain in 1894; gained independence in 1968; a member of the Commonwealth. Official languages: Swazi and English. Religion: Christian majority, traditional beliefs. Currency: lilangeni (plural emalangeni). Capital: Mbabane (administrative), Lobamba (legislative). Pop: 1 104 000 (2001 est). Area: 17 363 sq km (6704 sq miles)

▷ www.gov.sz

▷ www.mintour.gov.sz

Swazi Territory *n* the former name of **KaNgwane**

swear (swɛə) *vb* **swears, swearing, swore, sworn** **1** to declare or affirm (a statement) as true, esp by invoking a deity, etc, as witness **2** (foll by *by*) **2a** to invoke (a deity, etc) by name as a witness or guarantee to an oath **2b** to trust implicitly; have complete confidence (in) **3** (*intr; often foll by at*) to curse, blaspheme, or use swearwords **4** (when *tr, may take a clause as object or an infinitive*) to promise solemnly on oath; vow **5** (*tr*) to assert or affirm with great emphasis or earnestness **6** (*intr*) to give evidence or make any statement or solemn declaration on oath **7** to take an oath in order to add force or solemnity to (a statement or declaration) ▷ *n* **8** a period of swearing [OE *swerian*] > **ˈswearer** *n*

swear in *vb* (*tr, adv*) to administer an oath to (a person) on his or her assuming office, entering the witness box to give evidence, etc

swear off *vb* (*intr, prep*) to promise to abstain from something: *to swear off drink*

swearword (ˈswɛəˌwɜːd) *n* a socially taboo word of a profane, obscene, or insulting character

sweat (swɛt) *n* **1** the secretion from the sweat glands, esp when profuse and visible, as during strenuous activity, from excessive heat, etc; commonly called perspiration **2** the act or process of secreting this fluid **3** the act of inducing the exudation of moisture **4** drops of moisture given forth or gathered on the surface of something **5** *inf* a state or condition of worry or eagerness (esp in **in a sweat**) **6** *sl* drudgery or hard labour: *mowing lawns is a real sweat!* **7** *sl, chiefly Brit* a soldier, esp one who is old and experienced **8** **no sweat!** *sl* an expression conveying consent or assurance ▷ *vb* **sweats, sweating, sweat** *or* **sweated** **9** to secrete (sweat) through the pores of the skin, esp profusely **10** (*tr*) to make wet or stain with sweat **11** to give forth or cause to give forth (moisture) in droplets: *the maple sweats sap* **12** (*intr*) to collect and condense moisture on an outer surface: *a glass of beer sweating* **13** (*intr*) (of a liquid) to pass through a porous surface in droplets **14** (of tobacco leaves, hay, etc) to exude moisture and, sometimes, begin to ferment or to cause (tobacco leaves, etc) to exude moisture **15** (*tr*) to heat (food, esp vegetables) slowly in butter in a tightly closed >n **16** (*tr*) to join (pieces of metal) by pressing together and heating **17** (*tr*) to heat (solder) until it melts **18** (*tr*) to heat (partially fused metal) to extract an easily fusible constituent **19** *inf* to suffer anxiety, impatience, or distress **20** *inf* to overwork or be overworked **21** (*tr*) *inf* to employ at very low wages and under bad conditions **22** (*tr*) *inf* to extort, esp by torture: *to sweat information out of a captive* **23** (*intr*) *inf* to suffer punishment: *you'll sweat for this!* **24** **sweat blood** *inf* **24a** to work very hard **24b** to be filled with anxiety or impatience ▷ See also **sweat off, sweat out, sweats** [OE *swætan* to sweat, from *swāt* sweat]

sweatband (ˈswɛtˌbænd) *n* **1** a band of material set in a hat or cap to protect it from sweat **2** a piece of cloth tied around the forehead to keep sweat out of the eyes or around the wrist to keep the hands dry, as in sports

sweated (ˈswɛtɪd) *adj* **1** made by exploited labour: *sweated goods* **2** (of workers, etc) forced to work in poor conditions for low pay

sweater (ˈswɛtə) *n* **1** a garment made of knitted or crocheted material covering the upper part of the body, esp a heavy one worn for warmth **2** a person or thing that sweats **3** an employer who overworks and underpays his or her employees

sweat gland *n* any of the coiled tubular subcutaneous glands that secrete sweat

sweating sickness *n* an acute infectious febrile disease that was widespread in Europe during the late 15th century, characterized by profuse sweating

sweat lodge *n* (among native North American peoples) a structure in which water is poured onto hot stones to make the occupants sweat for religious or medicinal purposes

sweat off *or* **away** *vb* (*tr, adv*) *inf* to get rid of (weight) by strenuous exercise or sweating

sweat out *vb* (*tr, adv*) **1** to cure or lessen the effects of (a cold, respiratory infection, etc) by sweating **2** *inf* to endure (hardships) for a time (often in **sweat it out**) **3** **sweat one's guts out** *inf* to work extremely hard

sweat pants *pl n* loose thick cotton trousers with elasticated ankles and an elasticated or drawstring waist, worn esp by athletes warming up or training

sweats (swɛts) *pl n* sweatshirts and sweat-suit trousers: *jeans and sweats*

sweatshirt (ˈswɛtˌʃɜːt) *n* a long-sleeved knitted cotton sweater worn by athletes, etc

sweatshop (ˈswɛtˌʃɒp) *n* a workshop where employees work long hours under bad conditions for low wages

sweat suit *n* a suit worn by athletes for training comprising knitted cotton trousers and a light cotton sweater

sweaty (ˈswɛtɪ) *adj* **sweatier, sweatiest** **1** covered with sweat; sweating **2** smelling of or like sweat **3** causing sweat > **ˈsweatily** *adv* > **ˈsweatiness** *n*

swede (swiːd) *n* **1** a Eurasian plant cultivated for its bulbous edible root, which is used as a vegetable and as cattle fodder **2** the root of this plant ▷ Also called: **Swedish turnip** [c19 so called after being introduced into Scotland from Sweden in the 18th century]

Swede (swiːd) *n* a native, citizen, or inhabitant of Sweden

Sweden (ˈswiːdᵊn) *n* a kingdom in NW Europe, occupying the E part of the Scandinavian Peninsula, on the Gulf of Bothnia and the Baltic: first united during the Viking period (8th–11th centuries); neutral in both world wars; a member of the European Union. About 50 per cent of the total area is forest and 9 per cent lakes. Exports include timber, pulp, paper, iron ore, and steel. Official language: Swedish. Official religion: Church of Sweden (Lutheran). Currency: krona. Capital: Stockholm. Pop: 8 888 000 (2001 est). Area: 449 793 sq km

(173 665 sq miles). Swedish name: **Sverige**
▷ www.sweden.gov.se
▷ www.visit-sweden.com

Swedenborg ('swi:dᵊn,bɔ:g; *Swedish* 'sve:dənbɔrj) *n* **Emanuel** (e'manuel) original surname *Svedberg*. 1688–1772, Swedish scientist and theologian, whose mystical ideas became the basis of a religious movement

Swedish ('swi:dɪʃ) *adj* **1** of, relating to, or characteristic of Sweden, its people, or their language ▷ *n* **2** the official language of Sweden

Sweelinck (*Dutch* 'swe:lɪŋk) *n* **Jan Pieterszoon** (jɑn 'pi:tər,zo:n) 1562–1621, Dutch composer and organist, whose organ works are important for being the first to incorporate independent parts for the pedals

sweep (swi:p) *vb* **sweeps, sweeping, swept 1** to clean or clear (a space, chimney, etc) with a brush, broom, etc **2** (often foll by *up*) to remove or collect (dirt, rubbish, etc) with a brush, broom, etc **3** to move in a smooth or continuous manner, esp quickly or forcibly: *cars swept along the road* **4** to move in a proud or dignified fashion: *she swept past* **5** to spread or pass rapidly across, through, or along (a region, area, etc): *the news swept through the town* **6** (*tr*) to direct (the gaze, line of fire, etc) over; survey **7** (*tr; foll by away or off*) to overwhelm emotionally: *she was swept away by his charm* **8** to brush or lightly touch (a surface, etc): *the dress swept along the ground* **9** (*tr;* often foll by *away*) to convey, clear, or abolish, esp with strong or continuous movements: *the sea swept the sandcastle away; secondary modern schools were swept away* **10** (*intr*) to extend gracefully or majestically, esp in a wide circle: *the plains sweep down to the sea* **11** to search (a body of water) for mines, etc, by dragging **12** (*tr*) to win overwhelmingly, esp in an election: *Labour swept the country* **13** (*tr*) to propel (a boat) with sweeps **14 sweep the board 14a** (in gambling) to win all the cards or money **14b** to win every event or prize in a contest **15 sweep** (**something**) **under the carpet** to conceal (something, esp a problem) in the hope that it will be overlooked by others ▷ *n* **16** the act or an instance of sweeping; removal by or as if by a brush or broom **17** a swift or steady movement, esp in an arc **18** the distance, arc, etc, through which something, such as a pendulum, moves **19** a wide expanse or scope: *the sweep of the plains* **20** any curving line or contour **21** short for **sweepstake 22a** a long oar used on an open boat **22b** *Austral* a person steering a surf boat with such an oar at the stern **23** any of the sails of a windmill **24** *electronics* a steady horizontal or circular movement of an electron beam across or around the fluorescent screen of a cathode-ray tube **25** a curving driveway **26** *chiefly Brit* See **chimney sweep 27** another name for **swipe** (sense 6) **28 clean sweep 28a** an overwhelming victory or success **28b** a complete change; purge: *to make a clean sweep* [C13 *swepen*] > '**sweepy** *adj*

sweeper ('swi:pə) *n* **1** a person employed to sweep, such as a roadsweeper **2** any device for sweeping: *a carpet sweeper* **3** *soccer* a player who supports the main defenders, as by intercepting loose balls, etc

sweep hand *n horology* a long hand that registers seconds or fractions of seconds on the perimeter of the dial

sweeping ('swi:pɪŋ) *adj* **1** comprehensive and wide-ranging: *sweeping reforms* **2** indiscriminate or without reservations: *sweeping statements* **3** decisive or overwhelming: *a sweeping victory* **4** taking in a wide area: *a sweeping glance* **5** driving steadily onwards, esp over a large area: *a sweeping attack* > '**sweepingly** *adv* > '**sweepingness** *n*

sweep-saw *n* a saw with a thin blade that can be used for cutting curved shapes

sweepstake ('swi:p,steɪk) *or esp US* **sweepstakes** *n* **1a** a lottery in which the stakes of the participants constitute the prize **1b** the prize itself **2** any event involving such a lottery, esp a horse race ▷ Often shortened to **sweep** [C15 orig. referring to someone who *sweeps* or takes all the stakes in a game]

sweet (swi:t) *adj* **1** having or denoting a pleasant taste like that of sugar **2** agreeable to the senses or the mind: *sweet music* **3** having pleasant manners; gentle: *a sweet child* **4** (of wine, etc) having a relatively high sugar content; not dry **5** (of foods) not decaying or rancid: *sweet milk* **6** not salty: *sweet water* **7** free from unpleasant odours: *sweet air* **8** containing no corrosive substances: *sweet soil* **9** (of petrol) containing no sulphur compounds **10** sentimental or unrealistic **11** *jazz* performed with a regular beat, with the emphasis on clearly outlined melody and little improvisation **12** *arch* respected; dear (used in polite forms of address): *sweet sir* **13** smooth and precise; perfectly executed: *a sweet shot* **14 at one's own sweet will** as it suits oneself alone **15 keep** (**someone**) **sweet** to ingratiate oneself in order to ensure cooperation **16 sweet on** fond of or infatuated with ▷ *adv* **17** *inf* in a sweet manner ▷ *n* **18** a sweet taste or smell; sweetness in general **19** (*often pl*) *Brit* any of numerous kinds of confectionery consisting wholly or partly of sugar, esp of sugar boiled and crystallized (**boiled sweets**) **20** *Brit* any sweet dish served as a dessert **21** dear; sweetheart (used as a form of address) **22** anything that is sweet **23** (*often pl*) a pleasurable experience, state, etc: *the sweets of success* [OE *swēte*] > '**sweetish** *adj* > '**sweetly** *adv* > '**sweetness** *n*
▷ www.completechocolate.com

Sweet *n* **Henry** 1845–1912, English philologist; a pioneer of modern phonetics. His books include *A History of English Sounds* (1874)

sweet alyssum *n* a Mediterranean plant having clusters of small fragrant white or violet flowers. See also **alyssum**

sweet-and-sour *adj* (of food) cooked in a sauce made from sugar and vinegar and other ingredients

sweet bay *n* a small tree of SE North America, belonging to the magnolia family and having large fragrant white flowers. Sometimes shortened to **bay**

sweetbread ('swi:t,brɛd) *n* the pancreas or the thymus gland of an animal, used for food [C16 SWEET + BREAD, ? from OE *brǣd* meat]

sweetbrier ('swi:t,braɪə) *n* a Eurasian rose having a tall bristly stem, fragrant leaves, and single pink flowers. Also called: **eglantine**

sweet cherry *n* either of two types of cherry tree that are cultivated for their edible sweet fruit

sweet chestnut *n* See **chestnut** (sense 1)

sweet cicely ('sɪsəlɪ) *n* **1** Also called: **myrrh** an aromatic European plant, having compound leaves and clusters of small white flowers **2** the leaves, formerly used in cookery for their flavour of aniseed **3** any of various related plants of Asia and America, having aromatic roots

sweet corn *n* **1** a variety of maize whose kernels are rich in sugar and eaten as a vegetable when young **2** the unripe ears of maize, esp the sweet kernels removed from the cob, cooked as a vegetable

sweeten ('swi:tᵊn) *vb* (*mainly tr*) **1** (*also intr*) to make or become sweet or sweeter **2** to mollify or soften (a person) **3** to make more agreeable **4** (*also intr*) *chem* to free or be freed from unpleasant odours, acidic or corrosive substances, or the like

sweetener ('swi:tᵊnə) *n* **1** a sweetening agent, esp one that does not contain sugar **2** *inf* a bribe **3** *inf* a financial inducement

sweetening ('swi:tᵊnɪŋ) *n* something that sweetens

sweet flag *n* an aroid marsh plant, having swordlike leaves, small greenish flowers, and aromatic roots. Also called: **calamus**

sweet gale *n* a shrub of northern swamp regions, having yellow catkin-like flowers and aromatic leaves.

Also called: **bog myrtle** Often shortened to **gale**

sweet gum *n* **1** a North American liquidambar tree, having prickly spherical fruit clusters and fragrant sap: the wood (called **satin walnut**) is used to make furniture **2** the sap of this tree ▷ Also called: **red gum**

sweetheart ('swiːtˌhɑːt) *n* **1** a person loved by another **2** *inf* a lovable, generous, or obliging person **3** a term of endearment

sweetheart agreement *n Austral inf* an industrial agreement on pay and conditions concluded without resort to arbitration

sweetie ('swiːtɪ) *n inf* **1** sweetheart; darling: used as a term of endearment **2** *Brit* another word for **sweet** (sense 19) **3** *chiefly Brit* an endearing person **4** a large seedless variety of grapefruit that has a green-to-yellow rind and juicy sweet pulp

sweeting ('swiːtɪŋ) *n* **1** a variety of sweet apple **2** an archaic word for **sweetheart**

sweet marjoram *n* another name for **marjoram** (sense 1)

sweetmeat ('swiːtˌmiːt) *n* a sweetened delicacy, such as a preserve, sweet, or, formerly, a cake or pastry

sweet pea *n* a climbing plant of S Europe, widely cultivated for its butterfly-shaped fragrant flowers of delicate pastel colours

sweet pepper *n* **1** a pepper plant with large bell-shaped fruits that are eaten unripe (**green pepper**) or ripe (**red pepper**) **2** the fruit of this plant

sweet potato *n* **1** a twining plant of tropical America, cultivated in the tropics for its edible fleshy yellow root **2** the root of this plant

sweet shop *n chiefly Brit* a shop solely or largely selling sweets, esp boiled sweets

sweetsop ('swiːtˌsɒp) *n* **1** a small West Indian tree, having yellowish-green fruit **2** the fruit, which has a sweet edible pulp ▷ Also called: **custard apple**

sweet spot *n sport* the centre area of a racket, golf club, etc, from which the cleanest shots are made

sweet-talk *inf* ▷ *vb* **1** to coax, flatter, or cajole (someone) ▷ *n* **sweet talk 2** cajolery; coaxing

sweet tooth *n* a strong liking for sweet foods

sweetveld ('swiːtˌfɛlt) *n* (in South Africa) a type of grazing characterized by high-quality grass [pron. from Afrik. *soetveld*]

sweet william ('wɪljəm) *n* a widely cultivated Eurasian plant with flat clusters of white, pink, red, or purple flowers

swell (swɛl) *vb* **swells, swelling, swelled; swollen** *or* **swelled 1** to grow or cause to grow in size, esp as a result of internal pressure **2** to expand or cause to expand at a particular point or above the surrounding level; protrude **3** to grow or cause to grow in size, amount, intensity, or degree: *the party is swelling with new recruits* **4** to puff or be puffed up with pride or another emotion **5** (*intr*) (of seas or lakes) to rise in waves **6** (*intr*) to well up or overflow **7** (*tr*) to make (a musical phrase) increase gradually in volume and then diminish ▷ *n* **8a** the undulating movement of the surface of the open sea **8b** a succession of waves or a single large wave **9** a swelling or being swollen; expansion **10** an increase in quantity or degree; inflation **11** a bulge; protuberance **12** a gentle hill **13** *inf* a person very fashionably dressed **14** *inf* a man of high social or political standing **15** *music* a crescendo followed by an immediate diminuendo **16** Also called: **swell organ** *music* **16a** a set of pipes on an organ housed in a box (**swell box**) fitted with a shutter operated by a pedal, which can be opened or closed to control the volume **16b** the manual on an organ controlling this ▷ *adj* **17** *inf* stylish or grand **18** *sl* excellent; first-class [OE *swellan*]

swelled head *or* **swollen head** *n inf* an inflated view of one's own worth, often caused by sudden success > **swelled-headed, swell-headed,** *or* **swollen-headed** *adj*

swelling ('swɛlɪŋ) *n* **1** the act of expansion or inflation **2** the state of being or becoming swollen **3** a swollen or inflated part or area **4** an abnormal enlargement of a bodily structure or part, esp as the result of injury ▷ Related adj: **tumescent**

swelter ('swɛltə) *vb* **1** (*intr*) to suffer under oppressive heat, esp to sweat and feel faint **2** (*tr*) *rare* to cause to suffer under oppressive heat ▷ *n* **3** a sweltering condition (esp in **in a swelter**) **4** oppressive humid heat [c15 *swelten*, from OE *sweltan* to die]

sweltering ('swɛltərɪŋ) *adj* oppressively hot and humid: *a sweltering day* > **'swelteringly** *adv*

swept (swɛpt) *vb* the past tense and past participle of **sweep**

sweptback ('swɛptˌbæk) *adj* (of an aircraft wing) inclined backwards towards the rear of the fuselage

sweptwing ('swɛptˌwɪŋ) *adj* (of an aircraft, etc) having wings swept (usually) backwards

swerve (swɜːv) *vb* **swerves, swerving, swerved 1** to turn or cause to turn aside, usually sharply or suddenly, from a course ▷ *n* **2** the act, instance, or degree of swerving [OE *sweorfan* to scour] > **'swervable** *adj* > **'swerver** *n* > **'swerving** *adj*

Sweyn (sweɪn) *n* known as *Sweyn Forkbeard*. died 1014, king of Denmark (?986–1014). He conquered England, forcing Ethelred II to flee (1013); father of Canute

SWG *abbrev for* Standard Wire Gauge; a notation for the diameters of metal rods or thickness of metal sheet ranging from 16 mm to 0.02 mm or from 0.5 inch to 0.001 inch

swift (swɪft) *adj* **1** moving or able to move quickly; fast **2** occurring or performed quickly or suddenly; instant **3** (*postpositive; foll by to*) prompt to act or respond: *swift to take revenge* ▷ *adv* **4a** swiftly or quickly **4b** (*in combination*): *swift-moving* ▷ *n* **5** any of various insectivorous birds of the Old World. They have long narrow wings and spend most of the time on the wing **6** any of certain North American lizards of the iguana family that can run very rapidly **7** the main cylinder in a carding machine **8** an expanding circular frame used to hold skeins of silk, wool, etc [OE, from *swīfan* to turn] > **'swiftly** *adv* > **'swiftness** *n*

Swift (swɪft) *n* **1 Graham Colin** born 1949, British writer: his novels include *Waterland* (1983), *Last Orders* (1996), which won the Booker prize, and *The Light of Day* (2002) **2 Jonathan** 1667–1745, Anglo-Irish satirist and churchman, who became dean of St. Patrick's, Dublin, in 1713. His works include *A Tale of a Tub* (1704) and *Gulliver's Travels* (1726)

swiftlet ('swɪftlɪt) *n* any of various small swifts of an Asian genus that often live in caves and use echolocation

swig (swɪg) *inf* ▷ *n* **1** a large swallow or deep drink, esp from a bottle ▷ *vb* **swigs, swigging, swigged 2** to drink (some liquid) deeply, esp from a bottle [c16 from ?] > **'swigger** *n*

swiler ('swaɪlə) *n Canad* (in Newfoundland) a seal hunter [variant of SEALER[2]]

swill (swɪl) *vb* **1** to drink large quantities of (liquid, esp alcoholic drink); guzzle **2** (*tr; often foll by out*) *chiefly Brit* to drench or rinse in large amounts of water **3** (*tr*) to feed swill to (pigs, etc) ▷ *n* **4** wet feed, esp for pigs, consisting of kitchen waste, skimmed milk, etc **5** refuse, esp from a kitchen **6** a deep drink, esp beer **7** any liquid mess **8** the act of swilling [OE *swilian* to wash out] > **'swiller** *n*

swim (swɪm) *vb* **swims, swimming, swam, swum 1** (*intr*) to move along in water by means of movements of the body, esp the arms and legs, or (in the case of fish) tail and fins **2** (*tr*) to cover (a distance or stretch of water) in this way **3** (*tr*) to compete in (a race) in this way **4** (*intr*) to be supported by and on a liquid; float **5** (*tr*) to use (a particular stroke) in swimming **6** (*intr*) to move

smoothly, usually through air or over a surface **7** (*intr*) to reel or seem to reel: *my head swam; the room swam around me* **8** (*intr; often foll by in or with*) to be covered or flooded with water or other liquid **9** (*intr; often foll by in*) to be liberally supplied (with): *he's swimming in money* **10** (*tr*) to cause to float or swim **11 swim with** (*or* **against**) **the stream** *or* **tide** to conform to (or resist) prevailing opinion ▷ *n* **12** the act, an instance, or period of swimming **13** any graceful gliding motion **14** a condition of dizziness; swoon **15** a pool in a river good for fishing **16 in the swim** *inf* fashionable or active in social or political activities [OE *swimman*] > **'swimmable** *adj* > **'swimmer** *n* > **'swimming** *n, adj*
▷ www.fina.org

swim bladder *n ichthyol* another name for **air bladder** (sense 1)

swimmeret ('swɪməˌrɛt) *n* any of the small paired appendages on the abdomen of crustaceans, used chiefly in locomotion

swimming bath *n* (*often pl*) an indoor swimming pool

swimming costume *or* **bathing costume** *n chiefly Brit* any garment worn for swimming or sunbathing, such as a woman's one-piece garment covering most of the torso but not the limbs

swimmingly ('swɪmɪŋlɪ) *adv* successfully, effortlessly, or well (esp in **go swimmingly**)

swimming pool *n* an artificial pool for swimming

swimsuit ('swɪmˌsuːt, -ˌsjuːt) *n* a woman's one-piece swimming garment that leaves the arms and legs bare

Swinburne ('swɪnˌbɜːn) *n* **Algernon Charles** 1837–1909, English lyric poet and critic

swindle ('swɪndᵊl) *vb* **swindles, swindling, swindled 1** to cheat (someone) of money, etc; defraud **2** (*tr*) to obtain (money, etc) by fraud ▷ *n* **3** a fraudulent scheme or transaction [C18 back formation from G *Schwindler*, from *schwindeln*, from OHG *swintilōn*, from *swintan* to disappear] > **'swindler** *n*

swindle sheet *n* a slang term for **expense account**

Swindon ('swɪndən) *n* **1** a town in S England, in NE Wiltshire: railway workshops, high technology. Pop: 145 236 (1991) **2** a unitary authority in S England, in Wiltshire. Pop: 80 061 (2001). Area: 230 sq km (89 sq miles)

swine (swaɪn) *n* **1** (*pl* **swine** *or* **swines**) a coarse or contemptible person **2** (*pl* **swine**) another name for a **pig** [OE *swīn*] > **'swinish** *adj* > **'swinishly** *adv* > **'swinishness** *n*

swine fever *n* an infectious viral disease of pigs, characterized by fever and diarrhoea

swineherd ('swaɪnˌhɜːd) *n arch* a person who looks after pigs

swing (swɪŋ) *vb* **swings, swinging, swung 1** to move or cause to move rhythmically to and fro, as a free-hanging object; sway **2** (*intr*) to move, walk, etc, with a relaxed and swaying motion **3** to pivot or cause to pivot, as on a hinge **4** to move or cause to move in a curve: *the car swung around the bend* **5** to move or cause to move by suspending or being suspended **6** to hang or be hung so as to be able to turn freely **7** (*intr*) *sl* to be hanged: *he'll swing for it* **8** to alter or cause to alter habits, a course, etc **9** (*tr*) *inf* to influence or manipulate successfully: *I hope he can swing the deal* **10** (*tr; foll by up*) to raise or hoist, esp in a sweeping motion **11** (*intr; often foll by at*) to hit out or strike (at), esp with a sweeping motion **12** (*tr*) to wave (a weapon, etc) in a sweeping motion; flourish **13** to arrange or play (music) with the rhythmically flexible and compulsive quality associated with jazz **14** (*intr*) (of popular music, esp jazz, or of the musicians who play it) to have this quality **15** *sl* to be lively and modern **16** (*intr*) *cricket* to bowl (a ball) with swing or (of a ball) to move with a swing **17 swing the lead** *inf* to malinger or make up excuses ▷ *n* **18** the act or manner of swinging or the distance covered while swinging: *a wide swing* **19** a sweeping stroke or blow **20** *boxing* a wide punch from the side similar to but longer than a hook **21** *cricket* the lateral movement of a bowled ball through the air **22** any free-swaying motion **23** any curving movement; sweep **24** something that swings or is swung, esp a suspended seat on which a person may swing back and forth **25** a kind of popular dance music influenced by jazz, usually played by big bands and originating in the 1930s **26** *prosody* a steady distinct rhythm or cadence in prose or verse **27** *inf* the normal round or pace: *the swing of things* **28a** a fluctuation, as in some business activity, voting pattern, etc **28b** (*modifier*) able to bring about a swing in a voting pattern **29** *Canad* (in the North) a train of freight sleighs or canoes **30** *chiefly US* a circular tour **31 go with a swing** to go well; be successful **32 in full swing** at the height of activity **33 swings and roundabouts** equal advantages and disadvantages [OE *swingan*]
▷ www.jazzinamerica.org

swingboat ('swɪŋˌbəʊt) *n* a piece of fairground equipment consisting of a boat-shaped carriage for swinging in

swing bridge *n* a low bridge that can be rotated about a vertical axis to permit the passage of ships, etc

swinge (swɪndʒ) *vb* **swinges, swingeing** *or* **swinging, swinged** (*tr*) *arch* to beat, flog, or punish [OE *swengan*]

swingeing ('swɪndʒɪŋ) *adj chiefly Brit* punishing; severe

swinger ('swɪŋə) *n sl* **1** a person regarded as being modern and lively **2** a person who swaps sexual partners in a group, esp habitually

swinging ('swɪŋɪŋ) *adj* **1** moving rhythmically to and fro **2** *slang* modern and lively > **'swingingly** *adv*

swingle ('swɪŋgᵊl) *n* **1** a flat-bladed wooden instrument used for beating and scraping flax or hemp to remove coarse matter from it ▷ *vb* **swingles, swingling, swingled 2** (*tr*) to use a swingle on [OE *swingel* stroke]

swingletree ('swɪŋgᵊlˌtriː) *n* a crossbar in a horse's harness to which the ends of the traces are attached. Also called: **whippletree**

Ss

swing shift *n US & Canad inf* the usual US and Canad term for **back shift**

swing-wing *adj* **1** of or relating to a variable-geometry aircraft ▷ *n* **2a** such an aircraft **2b** either of the two wings of such an aircraft

Swinney ('swɪnɪ) *n* **John** (**Ramsay**) born 1964, Scottish politician; leader of the Scottish National Party from 2000–2004

swipe (swaɪp) *vb* **swipes, swiping, swiped 1** (when *intr*, usually foll by *at*) *inf* to hit hard with a sweeping blow **2** (*tr*) *sl* to steal **3** (*tr*) to pass a machine-readable card, such as a credit card, debit card, etc, through a machine that electronically interprets the information encoded on it, usu in a magnetic strip ▷ *n* **4** *inf* a hard blow **5** an unexpected criticism of someone or something while discussing another subject **6** Also called: **sweep** a type of lever for raising and lowering a weight, such as a bucket in a well [C19 ? rel. to SWEEP]

swipe card *n* a credit card, identity card, etc, with a magnetic strip that holds encoded information that can be electronically interpreted as it is passed through the slot of a machine designed to read it

swirl (swɜːl) *vb* **1** to turn or cause to turn in a twisting spinning fashion **2** (*intr*) to be dizzy; swim: *my head was swirling* ▷ *n* **3** a whirling or spinning motion, esp in water **4** a whorl; curl **5** the act of swirling or stirring **6** dizzy confusion or disorder [C15 prob. from Du. *zwirrelen*] > **'swirling** *adj* > **'swirly** *adj*

swish (swɪʃ) *vb* **1** to move with or make or cause to move with or make a whistling or hissing sound **2** (*intr*) (esp of fabrics) to rustle **3** (*tr*) *sl, now rare* to whip; flog **4** (*tr; foll by off*) to cut with a swishing blow ▷ *n* **5** a hissing or rustling sound or movement **6** a rod for flogging or a blow from this ▷ *adj* **7** *inf, chiefly Brit* fashionable; smart:

a swish gentlemen's club [c18 imit.] > **'swishy** *adj*

Swiss (swɪs) *adj* **1** of, relating to, or characteristic of Switzerland, its inhabitants, or their dialects of German, French, and Italian ▷ *n, pl* **Swiss 2** a native, inhabitant, or citizen of Switzerland

Swiss chard *n* another name for **chard**

Swiss cheese plant *n* See **monstera**

swiss roll *n* a sponge cake spread with jam, cream, or some other filling, and rolled up

switch (swɪtʃ) *n* **1** a mechanical, electrical, or electronic device for opening or closing a circuit or for diverting a current from one part of a circuit to another **2** a swift and usually sudden shift or change **3** an exchange or swap **4** a flexible rod or twig, used esp for punishment **5** the sharp movement or blow of such an instrument **6** a tress of false hair used to give added length or bulk to a woman's own hair-style **7** the tassel-like tip of the tail of cattle and certain other animals **8** any of various card games in which the suit is changed during play **9** *US & Canad* a railway siding **10** *US & Canad* a railway point **11** *Austral inf* short for **switchboard** (sense 1) ▷ *vb* **12** to shift, change, turn aside, or change the direction of (something) **13** to exchange (places); replace (something by something else) **14** *chiefly US & Canad* to transfer (rolling stock) from one railway track to another **15** (*tr*) to cause (an electric current) to start or stop flowing or to change its path by operating a switch **16** (*tr*) to lash or whip with or as if with a switch ▷ See also **switch off, switch on** [c16 ?from MDu. *swijch* twig] > **'switcher** *n*

switchback ('swɪtʃˌbæk) *n* **1** a mountain road, railway, or track which rises and falls sharply many times or a sharp rise and fall on such a road, railway, or track **2** another word (esp Brit) for **big dipper**

switchblade *or* **switchblade knife** ('swɪtʃˌbleɪd) *n* another name (esp US and Canad) for **flick knife**

switchboard ('swɪtʃˌbɔːd) *n* **1** an installation in a telephone exchange, office, etc, at which the interconnection of telephone lines is manually controlled **2** an assembly of switchgear for the control of power supplies in an installation or building

switched-on *adj inf* well-informed or aware of what is up to date

switchgear ('swɪtʃˌɡɪə) *n electrical engineering* any of several devices used for opening and closing electric circuits, esp those that pass high currents

switchman ('swɪtʃmən) *n, pl* **switchmen** the US and Canad name for **pointsman**

switch off *vb* (*adv*) **1** to cause (a device) to stop operating as by moving a switch, knob, etc **2** *inf* to cease to interest or be interested; make or become bored, alienated, etc

switch on *vb* (*adv*) **1** to cause (a device) to operate as by moving a switch, knob, or lever **2** (*tr*) *inf* to produce (charm, tears, etc) suddenly or automatically **3** (*tr*) *inf* (now dated) to make up-to-date, esp in outlook, dress, etc

swither ('swɪðə) *Scot* ▷ *vb* (*intr*) **1** to hesitate; vacillate; be perplexed ▷ *n* **2** hesitation; perplexity; agitation [c16 from ?]

Swithin *or* **Swithun** ('swɪðɪn, 'swɪθ-) *n* **Saint** died 862 AD, English ecclesiastic: bishop of Winchester (?852–862). Feast day: July 15

Switz. *or* **Swit.** *abbrev for* Switzerland

Switzer ('swɪtsə) *n* a less common word for **Swiss** [c16 from MHG, from *Swīz* Switzerland]

Switzerland ('swɪtsələnd) *n* a federal republic in W central Europe: the cantons of Schwyz, Uri, and Unterwalden formed a defensive league against the Hapsburgs in 1291, later joined by other cantons; gained independence in 1499; adopted a policy of permanent neutrality from 1516; a leading centre of the Reformation in the 16th century. It lies in the Jura Mountains and the Alps, with a plateau between the two ranges. Official languages: German, French, and Italian; Romansch minority. Religion: mostly Protestant and Roman Catholic. Currency: Swiss franc. Capital: Bern. Pop: 7 222 000 (2001 est). Area: 41 288 sq km (15 941 sq miles). German name: **Schweiz** French name: **Suisse** Italian name: **Svizzera** Latin name: **Helvetia** (hɛl'viːʃə)

▷ www.admin.ch

▷ www.switzerlandtourism.ch

▷ www.eda.admin.ch/london_emb/e/home.html

swivel ('swɪvᵊl) *n* **1** a coupling device which allows an attached object to turn freely **2** such a device made of two parts which turn independently, such as a compound link of a chain **3a** a pivot on which is mounted a gun that may be swung horizontally from side to side **3b** Also called: **swivel gun** the gun itself ▷ *vb* **swivels, swivelling, swivelled** *or US* **swivels, swiveling, swiveled 4** to turn or swing on or as if on a pivot **5** (*tr*) to provide with, secure by, or support with a swivel [c14 from OE *swīfan* to turn]

swivel chair *n* a chair, the seat of which is joined to the legs by a swivel and which thus may be spun round

swivel pin *n* another name for **kingpin** (sense 2)

swiz *or* **swizz** (swɪz) *n Brit inf* a swindle or disappointment; swizzle

swizzle ('swɪzᵊl) *n* **1** an alcoholic drink containing gin or rum **2** *Brit inf* a swiz ▷ *vb* **swizzles, swizzling, swizzled 3** (*tr*) to stir a swizzle stick in (a drink) **4** *Brit inf* to swindle; cheat [c19 from ?]

swizzle stick *n* a small rod used to agitate an effervescent drink to facilitate the escape of carbon dioxide

swob (swɒb) *n, vb* **swobs, swobbing, swobbed** a less common word for **swab**

swollen ('swəʊlən) *vb* **1** a past participle of **swell** ▷ *adj* **2** tumid or enlarged as by swelling **3** turgid or bombastic > **'swollenness** *n*

swoon (swuːn) *vb* (*intr*) **1** a literary word for **faint 2** to become ecstatic ▷ *n* **3** an instance of fainting ▷ Also (archaic or dialect): **swound** (swaʊnd) [OE *geswōgen* insensible, p.p. of *swōgan* (unattested except in compounds) suffocate] > **'swooning** *adj*

swoop (swuːp) *vb* **1** (*intr; usually foll by down, on, or upon*) to sweep or pounce suddenly **2** (*tr; often foll by up, away, or off*) to seize or scoop suddenly ▷ *n* **3** the act of swooping **4** a swift descent [OE *swāpan* to sweep]

swoosh (swʊʃ) *vb* **1** to make or cause to make a rustling or swirling sound, esp when moving or pouring out ▷ *n* **2** a swirling or rustling sound or movement [c20 imit.]

swop (swɒp) *vb* **swops, swopping, swopped,** *n* a variant spelling of **swap**

sword (sɔːd) *n* **1** a thrusting, striking, or cutting weapon with a long blade having one or two cutting edges, a hilt, and usually a crosspiece or guard **2** such a weapon worn on ceremonial occasions as a symbol of authority **3** something resembling a sword, such as the snout of a swordfish **4 the sword 4a** violence or power, esp military power **4b** death; destruction: *to put to the sword* [OE *sweord*]

swordbearer ('sɔːdˌbɛərə) *n* an official who carries a ceremonial sword

sword dance *n* a dance in which the performers dance nimbly over swords on the ground or brandish them in the air > **sword dancer** *n* > **sword dancing** *n*

swordfish ('sɔːdˌfɪʃ) *n, pl* **swordfish** *or* **swordfishes** a large fish with a very long upper jaw: valued as a food and game fish

sword grass *n* any of various grasses and other plants having sword-shaped sharp leaves

sword knot *n* a loop on the hilt of a sword by which it was attached to the wrist, now purely decorative

sword lily *n* another name for **gladiolus**

Sword of Damocles *n* a situation in which disaster

might strike at any moment [see DAMOCLES]
swordplay ('sɔːdˌpleɪ) *n* **1** the action or art of fighting with a sword **2** verbal sparring
swordsman ('sɔːdzmən) *n, pl* **swordsmen** one who uses or is skilled in the use of a sword > **'swordsmanship** *n*
swordstick ('sɔːdˌstɪk) *n* a hollow walking stick containing a short sword or dagger
swordtail ('sɔːdˌteɪl) *n* any of several small freshwater fishes of Central America having a long swordlike tail
swore (swɔː) *vb* the past tense of **swear**
sworn (swɔːn) *vb* **1** the past participle of **swear** ▷ *adj* **2** bound, pledged, or made inveterate, by or as if by an oath: *a sworn statement; he was sworn to God*
swot[1] (swɒt) *Brit inf* ▷ *vb* **swots, swotting, swotted** **1** (often foll by *up*) to study (a subject) intensively, as for an examination; cram ▷ *n* **2** Also called: **swotter** a person who works or studies hard **3** hard work or grind ▷ Also: **swat** [c19 var. of SWEAT (n)]
swot[2] (swɒt) *vb* **swots, swotting, swotted,** *n* a variant of **swat**
SWOT (swɒt) *n acronym for* strengths, weaknesses, opportunities, and threats: an analysis of a product made before it is marketed
swotty ('swɒtɪ) *adj* **swottier, swottiest** *Brit inf* given to studying hard, esp to the exclusion of other activities
swounds *or* **'swounds** (zwaʊndz, zaʊndz) *interj arch* less common spellings of **zounds**
swum (swʌm) *vb* the past participle of **swim**
swung (swʌŋ) *vb* the past tense and past participle of **swing**
swy (swaɪ) *n Austral* another name for **two-up** [c20 from G *zwei* two]
Syal (saɪˌæl) *n* **Meera** ('mɪərə) born 1964, British actress and writer of Punjabi origin, who appeared in the TV comedy series *Goodness Gracious Me* (1998) and *The Kumars at No. 42* (2001–02); her screenplays include *Bhaji on the Beach* (1993)
Sybaris ('sɪbərɪs) *n* a Greek colony in S Italy, on the Gulf of Taranto: notorious for its luxurious living, founded about 720 BC and sacked in 510 > **'Sybarite** *n* > **Sybaritic** (ˌsɪbə'rɪtɪk) *adj*
sybarite ('sɪbəˌraɪt) *n* **1** (*sometimes cap*) a devotee of luxury and the sensual vices ▷ *adj* **2** luxurious; sensuous [c16 from L *Sybarīta*, from Gk *Subaritēs* inhabitant of SYBARIS] > **sybaritic** (ˌsɪbə'rɪtɪk) *adj* > **ˌsyba'ritically** *adv* > **'sybaritism** *n*
sycamore ('sɪkəˌmɔː) *n* **1** a Eurasian maple tree, naturalized in Britain and North America, having five-lobed leaves and two-winged fruits **2** *US & Canad* an American plane tree. See **plane tree** **3** Also sycomore, a tree of N Africa and W Asia, having an edible figlike fruit [c14 from OF *sicamor*, from L *sȳcomorus*, from Gk, from *sukon* fig + *moron* mulberry]
syconium (saɪ'kəʊnɪəm) *n, pl* **syconia** (-nɪə) *bot* the fleshy fruit of the fig, consisting of an enlarged receptacle [c19 from NL, from Gk *sukon* fig]
sycophant ('sɪkəfənt) *n* a person who uses flattery to win favour from individuals wielding influence; toady [c16 from L *sȳcophanta*, from Gk *sukophantēs*, lit.: person showing a fig, apparently referring to the fig sign used in accusation, from *sukon* fig + *phainein* to show; sense prob. developed from "accuser" to "informer, flatterer"] > **'sycophancy** *n* > **sycophantic** (ˌsɪkə'fæntɪk) *adj* > **ˌsyco'phantically** *adv*
sycosis (saɪ'kəʊsɪs) *n* chronic inflammation of the hair follicles, esp those of the beard [c16 via NL from Gk *sukōsis*, from *sukon* fig]
Sydenham's chorea ('sɪdᵊnəmz) *n* a form of chorea affecting children, often associated with rheumatic fever. Nontechnical name: **Saint Vitus's dance** [after T. *Sydenham* (1624–89), E physician]
Sydney[1] ('sɪdnɪ) *n* **1** a port in SE Australia, capital of New South Wales, on an inlet of the S Pacific: the largest city in Australia and the first British settlement, established as a penal colony in 1788; developed rapidly after 1820 with the discovery of gold in its hinterland; large wool market; three universities. Pop (urban area): 3 276 207 (1998 est) **2** a port in SE Canada, in Nova Scotia on NE Cape Breton Island: capital of Cape Breton Island until 1820, when the island united administratively with Nova Scotia. Pop: 26 063 (1991)
Sydney[2] ('sɪdnɪ) *n* a variant spelling of (Sir Philip) **Sidney**
Syene (saɪ'iːnɪ) *n* transliteration of the Ancient Greek name for **Aswan**
syenite ('saɪəˌnaɪt) *n* a light-coloured coarse-grained igneous rock consisting of feldspars with hornblende [c18 from F, from L *syēnītēs lapis* stone from *Syene* (Aswan), where orig. quarried] > **syenitic** (ˌsaɪə'nɪtɪk) *adj*
Syktyvkar (*Russian* siktif'kar) *n* a city in NW Russia, capital of the Komi Republic: timber industry. Pop: 230 900 (1999 est)
syllabary ('sɪləbərɪ) *n, pl* **syllabaries** **1** a table or list of syllables **2** a set of symbols used in certain writing systems, such as one used for Japanese, in which each symbol represents a spoken syllable [c16 from NL *syllabārium*, from L *syllaba* SYLLABLE]
syllabi ('sɪləˌbaɪ) *n* a plural of **syllabus**
syllabic (sɪ'læbɪk) *adj* **1** of or relating to syllables or the division of a word into syllables **2** denoting a kind of verse line based on a specific number of syllables rather than being regulated by stresses or quantities **3** (of a consonant) constituting a syllable ▷ *n* **4** a syllabic consonant > **syl'labically** *adv*
syllabify (sɪ'læbɪˌfaɪ) *or* **syllabicate** *vb* **syllabifies, syllabifying, syllabified** *or* **syllabicates, syllabicating, syllabicated** (*tr*) to divide (a word) into its constituent syllables > **sylˌlabifi'cation** *or* **sylˌlabi'cation** *n*
syllable ('sɪləbᵊl) *n* **1** a combination or set of one or more units of sound in a language that must consist of a sonorous element (a sonant or vowel) and may or may not contain less sonorous elements (consonants or semivowels) flanking it: for example "paper" has two syllables **2** (in the writing systems of certain languages, esp ancient ones) a symbol or set of symbols standing for a syllable **3** the least mention: *don't breathe a syllable of it* **4** **in words of one syllable** simply; bluntly ▷ *vb* **syllables, syllabling, syllabled** **5** to pronounce syllables of (a text); articulate **6** (*tr*) to write down in syllables [c14 via OF from L *syllaba*, from Gk *sullabē*, from *sullambanein* to collect together]
syllabub *or* **sillabub** ('sɪləˌbʌb) *n* **1** a spiced drink made of milk with rum, port, brandy, or wine, often hot **2** *Brit* a cold dessert made from milk or cream beaten with sugar, wine, and lemon juice [c16 from ?]
syllabus ('sɪləbəs) *n, pl* **syllabuses** *or* **syllabi** (-ˌbaɪ) **1** an outline of a course of studies, text, etc **2** *Brit, Austral, & NZ* **2a** the subjects studied for a particular course **2b** a list of these subjects [c17 from LL, erroneously from L *sittybus* parchment strip giving title and author, from Gk *sittuba*]
syllepsis (sɪ'lɛpsɪs) *n, pl* **syllepses** (-siːz) **1** (in grammar or rhetoric) the use of a single sentence construction in which a verb, adjective, etc, is made to cover two syntactical functions, as *have* in *she and they have promised to come* **2** another word for **zeugma** [c16 from LL, from Gk *sullēpsis*, from *sul-* SYN- + *lēpsis*, from *lambanein* to take] > **syl'leptic** *adj* > **syl'leptically** *adv*
syllogism ('sɪləˌdʒɪzəm) *n* **1** a deductive inference consisting of two premises and a conclusion, all of which are categorical propositions. The subject of the conclusion is the **minor term** and its predicate the **major term;** the **middle term** occurs in both premises but not the conclusion. There are 256 such arguments but only 24 are valid. *Some men are mortal; some men are angelic; so some mortals are angelic* is invalid, while *some temples are in ruins; all ruins are fascinating; so some temples are fascinating* is valid.

Ss

Here *fascinating*, *in ruins*, and *temples* are respectively major, middle, and minor terms **2** a piece of deductive reasoning from the general to the particular [C14 via L from Gk *sullogismos*, from *sullogizesthai* to reckon together, from *logos* a discourse] > ˌ**syllo'gistic** *adj* > '**sylloˌgize** *or* '**sylloˌgise** *vb*

sylph (sɪlf) *n* **1** a slender graceful girl or young woman **2** any of a class of imaginary beings assumed to inhabit the air [C17 from NL *sylphus*, prob. coined from L *silva* wood + Gk *numphē* nymph] > '**sylphˌlike** *adj*

sylva *or* **silva** ('sɪlvə) *n, pl* **sylvas** *or* **sylvae** (-viː) the trees growing in a particular region [C17 from L *silva* a wood]

sylvan *or* **silvan** ('sɪlvən) *chiefly poetic* ▷ *adj* **1** of or consisting of woods or forests **2** in woods or forests **3** idyllically rural or rustic ▷ *n* **4** an inhabitant of the woods, esp a spirit [C16 from L *silvānus*, from *silva* forest]

sylvanite ('sɪlvəˌnaɪt) *n* a silver-white mineral consisting of a compound of tellurium with gold and silver in the form of elongated crystals [C18 from (TRAN)SYLVAN(IA) + -ITE[1], with reference to the region where first found]

Sylvanus (sɪl'veɪnəs) *n* a variant spelling of **Silvanus**

Sylvester II (sɪl'vɛstə) *n* original name *Gerbert of Aurillac*. *c* 940–1003 AD, French ecclesiastic and scholar; pope (999–1003): noted for his achievements in mathematics and astronomy

sylviculture ('sɪlvɪˌkʌltʃə) *n* a variant spelling of **silviculture**

sym- *prefix* a variant of **syn-** before *b*, *p*, and *m*

symbiont ('sɪmbɪˌɒnt) *n* an organism living in a state of symbiosis [C19 from Gk *sumbioun* to live together, from *bioun* to live] > ˌ**symbi'ontic** *adj* > ˌ**symbi'ontically** *adv*

symbiosis (ˌsɪmbɪ'əʊsɪs) *n* **1** a close and usually obligatory association of two organisms of different species that live together, often to their mutual benefit **2** a similar relationship between persons or groups [C19 via NL from Gk: a living together] > ˌ**symbi'otic** *adj*

symbol ('sɪmbᵊl) *n* **1** something that represents or stands for something else, usually by convention or association, esp a material object used to represent something abstract **2** an object, person, etc, used in a literary work, film, etc, to stand for or suggest something else with which it is associated **3** a letter, figure, or sign used in mathematics, music, etc, to represent a quantity, phenomenon, operation, function, etc ▷ *vb* **symbols, symbolling, symbolled** *or US* **symbols, symboling, symboled** **4** (*tr*) another word for **symbolize** [C15 from Church L *symbolum*, from Gk *sumbolon* sign, from *sumballein* to throw together, from SYN- + *ballein* to throw]

symbolic (sɪm'bɒlɪk) *or* **symbolical** *adj* **1** of or relating to a symbol or symbols **2** serving as a symbol **3** characterized by the use of symbols or symbolism > **sym'bolically** *adv*

symbolic logic *n* another name for **formal logic**

symbolism ('sɪmbəˌlɪzəm) *n* **1** the representation of something in symbolic form or the attribution of symbolic character to something **2** a system of symbols or symbolic representation **3** a symbolic significance or quality **4** (*often cap*) a late 19th-century movement in art that sought to express mystical or abstract ideas through the symbolic use of images

symbolist ('sɪmbəlɪst) *n* **1** a person who uses or can interpret symbols, esp as a means to revealing aspects of truth and reality **2** an artist or writer who practises symbolism in his or her work **3** (*usually cap*) a writer associated with the symbolist movement **4** (*often cap*) an artist associated with the symbolist movement ▷ *adj* **5** of, relating to, or characterizing symbolism or symbolists > ˌ**symbol'istic** *adj* > ˌ**symbol'istically** *adv*

symbolist movement *n* (*usually cap*) a movement beginning in French and Belgian poetry towards the end of the 19th century with Mallarmé, Valéry, Verlaine, Rimbaud, and others, and seeking to express states of mind rather than objective reality by the power of words and images to suggest as well as denote

symbolize *or* **symbolise** ('sɪmbəˌlaɪz) *vb* **symbolizes, symbolizing, symbolized** *or* **symbolises, symbolising, symbolised** **1** (*tr*) to serve as or be a symbol of **2** (*tr; usually foll by by*) to represent by a symbol or symbols **3** (*intr*) to use symbols **4** (*tr*) to treat or regard as symbolic > ˌ**symboli'zation** *or* ˌ**symboli'sation** *n*

symbol retailer *n* any member of a voluntary group of independent retailers, often using a common name or symbol, formed to obtain better prices from wholesalers or manufacturers in competition with supermarket chains. Also called: **voluntary retailer**

symmetrical (sɪ'mɛtrɪkᵊl) *adj* possessing or displaying symmetry

symmetry ('sɪmɪtrɪ) *n, pl* **symmetries** **1** similarity, correspondence, or balance among systems or parts of a system **2** *maths* an exact correspondence in position or form about a given point, line, or plane **3** beauty or harmony of form based on a proportionate arrangement of parts [C16 from L *symmetria*, from Gk *summetria* proportion, from SYN- + *metron* measure]

Symonds ('sɪməndz) *n* **John Addington** ('ædɪŋtən) 1840–93, English writer, noted for his *Renaissance in Italy* (1875–86) and for studies of homosexuality

Symons ('saɪmənz) *n* **Arthur** 1865–1945, English poet and critic, who helped to introduce the French symbolists to England

sympathectomy (ˌsɪmpə'θɛktəmɪ) *n, pl* **sympathectomies** the surgical excision or chemical destruction (**chemical sympathectomy**) of one or more parts of the sympathetic nervous system [C20 from SYMPATHETIC + -ECTOMY]

sympathetic (ˌsɪmpə'θɛtɪk) *adj* **1** characterized by, feeling, or showing sympathy; understanding **2** in accord with the subject's personality or mood; congenial: *a sympathetic atmosphere* **3** (when *postpositive, often foll by to or towards*) showing agreement (with) or favour (towards) **4** *anat, physiol* of or relating to the division of the autonomic nervous system that acts in opposition to the parasympathetic system accelerating the heartbeat, dilating the bronchi, inhibiting the smooth muscles of the digestive tract, etc ▷ Cf **parasympathetic** **5** relating to vibrations occurring as a result of similar vibrations in a neighbouring body: *sympathetic strings on a sitar* > ˌ**sympa'thetically** *adv*

sympathetic magic *n* a type of magic in which it is sought to produce a large-scale effect, often at a distance, by performing some small-scale ceremony resembling it, such as the pouring of water on an altar to induce rainfall

sympathize *or* **sympathise** ('sɪmpəˌθaɪz) *vb* **sympathizes, sympathizing, sympathized** *or* **sympathises, sympathising, sympathised** (*intr; often foll by with*) **1** to feel or express compassion or sympathy (for); commiserate: *he sympathized with my troubles* **2** to share or understand the sentiments or ideas (of); be in sympathy (with) > '**sympaˌthizer** *or* '**sympaˌthiser** *n*

sympatholytic (ˌsɪmpəθəʊ'lɪtɪk) *med* ▷ *adj* **1a** inhibiting or antagonistic to nerve impulses of the sympathetic nervous system **1b** of or relating to such inhibition ▷ *n* **2** a sympatholytic drug ▷ Cf **sympathomimetic** [C20 from SYMPATH(ETIC) + -LYTIC]

sympathomimetic (ˌsɪmpəθəʊmɪ'mɛtɪk) *med* ▷ *adj* **1** causing a physiological effect similar to that produced by stimulation of the sympathetic nervous system ▷ *n* **2** a sympathomimetic drug ▷ Cf **sympatholytic** [C20 from SYMPATH(ETIC) + MIMETIC]

sympathy ('sɪmpəθɪ) *n, pl* **sympathies** **1** the sharing of another's emotions, esp of sorrow or anguish; compassion **2** affinity or harmony, usually of feelings or interests, between persons or things: *to be in sympathy* *with someone* **3** mutual affection or understanding arising from such a relationship **4** the condition of a physical system or body when its behaviour is similar or corresponds to that of a different system that influences it, such as the vibration of sympathetic strings **5** (*sometimes pl*) a feeling of loyalty, support, or accord, as for an idea, cause, etc **6** *physiol* the relationship between two organs or parts whereby a change in one affects the other [c16 from L *sympathīa*, from Gk, from *sumpathēs*, from SYN- + *pathos* suffering]

sympathy strike *n* a strike organized in support of another strike or cause. Also called: **sympathetic strike**

symphonic poem *n music* an extended orchestral composition, originated by Liszt, based on nonmusical material, such as a work of literature or folk tale. Also called: **tone poem**

symphony ('sɪmfənɪ) *n, pl* **symphonies** **1** an extended large-scale orchestral composition, usually with several movements, at least one of which is in sonata form **2** a piece of instrumental music in up to three very short movements, used as an overture to or interlude in a baroque opera **3** any purely orchestral movement in a vocal work, such as a cantata or oratorio **4** short for **symphony orchestra** **5** anything distinguished by a harmonious composition: *the picture was a symphony of green* **6** *arch* harmony in general; concord [c13 from OF *symphonie*, from L *symphōnia* concord, from Gk, from SYN- + *phōnē* sound] > **symphonic** (sɪm'fɒnɪk) *adj* > **sym'phonically** *adv*

symphony orchestra *n music* an orchestra capable of performing symphonies, esp a large orchestra comprising strings, brass, woodwind, harp and percussion

symphysis ('sɪmfɪsɪs) *n, pl* **symphyses** (-ˌsi:z) **1** *anat, bot* a growing together of parts or structures, such as two bony surfaces joined by an intermediate layer of fibrous cartilage **2** a line marking this growing together **3** *pathol* an abnormal adhesion of two or more parts or structures [c16 via NL from Gk *sumphusis*, from *sumphuein*, from SYN- + *phuein* to grow] > **symphysial** *or* **symphyseal** (sɪm'fɪzɪəl) *adj*

sympodium (sɪm'pəʊdɪəm) *n, pl* **sympodia** (-dɪə) the main axis of growth in the grapevine and similar plants: a lateral branch that arises from just behind the apex of the main stem, which ceases to grow and continues growing in the same direction as the main stem [c19 from NL, from SYN- + Gk *podion* a little foot] > **sym'podial** *adj* > **sym'podially** *adv*

symposium (sɪm'pəʊzɪəm) *n, pl* **symposiums** *or* **symposia** (-zɪə) **1** a conference or meeting for the discussion of some subject, esp an academic topic or social problem **2** a collection of scholarly contributions on a given subject **3** (in classical Greece) a drinking party with intellectual conversation, music, etc [c16 via L from Gk *sumposion*, from *sumpinein* to drink together]

symptom ('sɪmptəm) *n* **1** *med* any sensation or change in bodily function experienced by a patient that is associated with a particular disease **2** any phenomenon or circumstance accompanying something and regarded as evidence of its existence; indication [c16 from LL *symptōma*, from Gk *sumptōma* chance, from *sumpiptein* to occur, from SYN- + *piptein* to fall]

symptomatic (ˌsɪmptə'mætɪk) *adj* **1** (often foll by *of*) being a symptom; indicative: *symptomatic of insanity* **2** of, relating to, or according to symptoms: *a symptomatic analysis* > **ˌsympto'matically** *adv*

symptomatology *or* **symptomology** (ˌsɪmptəmə'tɒlədʒɪ) *n* the branch of medicine concerned with the study and classification of the symptoms of disease

syn. *abbrev for* synonym(ous)

syn- *prefix* **1** with or together: *synecology* **2** fusion: *syngamy* [from Gk *sun* together]

synaeresis (sɪ'nɪərɪsɪs) *n* a variant spelling of **syneresis**

synaesthesia *or US* **synesthesia** (ˌsɪni:s'θi:zɪə) *n* **1** *physiol* a sensation experienced in a part of the body other than the part stimulated **2** *psychol* the subjective sensation of a sense other than the one being stimulated [c19 from NL, from SYN- + *-esthesia*, from Gk *aisthēsis* sensation] > **synaesthetic** *or US* **synesthetic** (ˌsɪni:s'θɛtɪk) *adj*

synagogue ('sɪnəˌgɒg) *n* **1a** a building for Jewish religious services and religious instruction **1b** (*as modifier*): *synagogue services* **2** a congregation of Jews who assemble for worship or religious study **3** the religion of Judaism as organized in such congregations [c12 from OF, from LL *synagōga*, from Gk *sunagōgē* a gathering, from *sunagein* to bring together] > **synagogical** (ˌsɪnə'gɒdʒɪkᵊl) *or* **synagogal** ('sɪnəˌgɒgᵊl) *adj*

synapse ('saɪnæps) *n* the point at which a nerve impulse is relayed from the terminal portion of an axon to the dendrites of an adjacent neuron

synapsis (sɪ'næpsɪs) *n, pl* **synapses** (-si:z) **1** *cytology* the association in pairs of homologous chromosomes at the start of meiosis **2** another word for **synapse** [c19 from NL, from Gk *sunapsis* junction, from *sunaptein* to join together]

synaptic (sɪ'næptɪk) *or* **synaptical** *adj* of or relating to a synapse > **syn'aptically** *adv*

synarthrosis (ˌsɪnɑ:'θrəʊsɪs) *n, pl* **synarthroses** (-si:z) *anat* any of various joints which lack a synovial cavity and are virtually immovable; a fixed joint [c16 via NL from Gk *sunarthrōsis*, from *sunarthrousthai* to be connected by joints, from *sun-* SYN- + *arthron* a joint] > **ˌsynar'throdial** *adj*

sync *or* **synch** (sɪŋk) *films, television, computing* ▷ *vb* **1** an informal word for **synchronize** ▷ *n* **2** an informal word for **synchronization** (esp in **in** *or* **out of sync**)

syncarp ('sɪnkɑ:p) *n bot* a fleshy multiple fruit, formed from two or more carpels of one flower or the aggregated fruits of several flowers [c19 from NL *syncarpium*, from SYN- + Gk *karpos* fruit] **Ss**

syncarpous (sɪn'kɑ:pəs) *adj* **1** (of the ovaries of certain flowering plants) consisting of united carpels **2** of or relating to a syncarp

synchro ('sɪŋkrəʊ) *n, pl* **synchros** **1** Also called: **selsyn** any of a number of electrical devices in which the angular position of a rotating part is transformed into a voltage, or vice versa **2** short for **synchronized swimming**

synchro- *combining form* indicating synchronization: *synchromesh*

synchrocyclotron (ˌsɪŋkrəʊ'saɪkləˌtrɒn) *n* a cyclotron in which the frequency of the electric field is modulated to allow for relativistic effects at high velocities and thus produce higher energies

synchromesh ('sɪŋkrəʊˌmɛʃ) *adj* **1** (of a gearbox, etc) having a system of clutches that synchronizes the speeds of the driving and driven members before engagement to avoid shock in gear changing and to reduce noise and wear ▷ *n* **2** a gear system having these features [c20 shortened from *synchronized mesh*]

synchronic (sɪn'krɒnɪk) *adj* **1** concerned with the events or phenomena at a particular period without considering historical antecedents: *synchronic linguistics* ▷ Cf **diachronic** **2** synchronous > **syn'chronically** *adv*

synchronicity (ˌsɪnkrə'nɪsɪtɪ) *n* an apparently meaningful coincidence in time of two or more similar or identical events that are causally unrelated [c20 coined by Carl Jung from SYNCHRONIC -ITY]

synchronism ('sɪŋkrəˌnɪzəm) *n* **1** the quality or condition of being synchronous **2** a chronological list of historical persons and events, arranged to show parallel or synchronous occurrence **3** the representation in a work of art of one or more incidents that occurred at separate times [c16 from Gk *sunkhronismos*]

synchronistic (ˌsɪŋkrəˈnɪstɪk) *adj* of, relating to, or exhibiting synchronism > ˌ**synchroˈnistically** *adv*

synchronize *or* **synchronise** (ˈsɪŋkrəˌnaɪz) *vb* **synchronizes, synchronizing, synchronized** *or* **synchronises, synchronising, synchronised** **1** (when *intr*, usually foll by *with*) to occur or recur or cause to occur or recur at the same time or in unison **2** to indicate or cause to indicate the same time: *synchronize your watches* **3** (*tr*) *films* to establish (the picture and soundtrack records) in their correct relative position **4** (*tr*) to designate (events) as simultaneous > ˌ**synchroniˈzation** *or* ˌ**synchroniˈsation** *n* > ˈ**synchroˌnizer** *or* ˈ**synchroˌniser** *n*

synchronized swimming *n* a sport in which swimmers move in patterns in time to music. Sometimes shortened to **synchro** *or* **synchro swimming**
▷ www.fina.org

synchronous (ˈsɪŋkrənəs) *adj* **1** occurring at the same time **2** *physics* (of periodic phenomena, such as voltages) having the same frequency and phase **3** occurring or recurring exactly together and at the same rate [C17 from LL *synchronus*, from Gk *sunkhronos*, from SYN- + *khronos* time] > ˈ**synchronously** *adv* > ˈ**synchronousness** *n*

synchronous machine *n* an electrical machine whose rotating speed is proportional to the frequency of the alternating-current supply and independent of the load

synchronous motor *n* an alternating-current motor that runs at a speed that is equal to or is a multiple of the frequency of the supply

synchrony (ˈsɪŋkrənɪ) *n* the state of being synchronous; simultaneity

synchrotron (ˈsɪŋkrəˌtrɒn) *n* a particle accelerator having an electric field of fixed frequency and a changing magnetic field [C20 from SYNCHRO- + (ELEC)TRON]

syncline (ˈsɪŋklaɪn) *n* a downward fold of stratified rock in which the strata slope towards a vertical axis [C19 from SYN- + Gk *klīnein* to lean] > **synˈclinal** *adj*

Syncom (ˈsɪnˌkɒm) *n* a communications satellite in stationary orbit [C20 from *syn(chronous) com(munication)*]

syncopate (ˈsɪŋkəˌpeɪt) *vb* **syncopates, syncopating, syncopated** (*tr*) **1** *music* to modify or treat (a beat, rhythm, note, etc) by syncopation **2** to shorten (a word) by omitting sounds or letters from the middle [C17 from Med. L *syncopāre* to omit a letter or syllable, from LL *syncopa* SYNCOPE] > ˈ**syncoˌpator** *n*

syncopation (ˌsɪŋkəˈpeɪʃən) *n* **1** *music* **1a** the displacement of the usual rhythmic accent away from a strong beat onto a weak beat **1b** a note, beat, rhythm, etc, produced by syncopation **2** another word for **syncope** (sense 2)

syncope (ˈsɪŋkəpɪ) *n* **1** a technical word for a **faint** **2** the omission of sounds or letters from the middle of a word [C16 from LL *syncopa*, from Gk *sunkopē* a cutting off, from SYN- + *koptein* to cut] > **syncopic** (sɪŋˈkɒpɪk) *or* ˈ**syncopal** *adj*

syncretism (ˈsɪŋkrɪˌtɪzəm) *n* **1** the tendency to syncretize **2** the historical tendency of languages to reduce their use of inflection, as in the development of Old English into Modern English [C17 from NL *syncrētismus*, from Gk *sunkrētismos* alliance of Cretans, from *sunkrētizein* to join forces (in the manner of the Cretan towns), from SYN- + *Krēs* a Cretan] > **syncretic** (sɪŋˈkrɛtɪk) *or* ˌ**syncreˈtistic** *adj* > ˈ**syncretist** *n*

syncretize *or* **syncretise** (ˈsɪŋkrɪˌtaɪz) *vb* **syncretizes, syncretizing, syncretized** *or* **syncretises, syncretising, syncretised** to attempt to combine the characteristic teachings, beliefs, or practices of (differing systems of religion or philosophy) > ˌ**syncretiˈzation** *or* ˌ**syncretiˈsation** *n*

syndactyl (sɪnˈdæktɪl) *adj* **1** (of certain animals) having two or more digits fused together ▷ *n* **2** an animal with this arrangement of digits > **synˈdactylism** *n*

syndesmosis (ˌsɪndɛsˈməʊsɪs) *n, pl* **syndesmoses** (-siːz) *anat* a type of joint in which the articulating bones are held together by a ligament of connective tissue [C18 NL, from Gk *sundein* to bind together] > **syndesmotic** (ˌsɪndɛsˈmɒtɪk) *adj*

syndetic (sɪnˈdɛtɪk) *adj* denoting a grammatical construction in which two clauses are connected by a conjunction [C17 from Gk *sundetikos*, from *sundetos* bound together] > **syndesis** (sɪnˈdiːsɪs) *n* > **synˈdetically** *adv*

syndic (ˈsɪndɪk) *n* **1** *Brit* a business agent of some universities or other bodies **2** (in several countries) a government administrator or magistrate with varying powers [C17 via OF from LL *syndicus*, from Gk *sundikos* defendant's advocate, from SYN- + *dikē* justice] > ˈ**syndical** *adj*

syndicalism (ˈsɪndɪkəˌlɪzəm) *n* **1** a revolutionary movement and theory advocating seizure of the means of production and distribution by syndicates of workers, esp by a general strike **2** an economic system resulting from such action > ˈ**syndical** *adj* > ˈ**syndicalist** *adj, n* > ˌ**syndicalˈistic** *adj*

syndicate *n* (ˈsɪndɪkɪt) **1** an association of business enterprises or individuals organized to undertake a joint project **2** a news agency that sells articles, photographs, etc, to a number of newspapers for simultaneous publication **3** any association formed to carry out an enterprise of common interest to its members **4** a board of syndics or the office of syndic ▷ *vb* (ˈsɪndɪˌkeɪt) **syndicates, syndicating, syndicated** **5** (*tr*) to sell (articles, photographs, etc) to several newspapers for simultaneous publication **6** (*tr*) *US* to sell (a programme or programmes) to several local commercial stations **7** to form a syndicate of (people) [C17 from OF *syndicat* office of a SYNDIC] > ˌ**syndiˈcation** *n*

syndicated research *n marketing* a large-scale marketing research project undertaken without being commissioned and subsequently offered to interested parties

syndrome (ˈsɪndrəʊm) *n* **1** *med* any combination of signs and symptoms that are indicative of a particular disease or disorder **2** a symptom, characteristic, or set of symptoms or characteristics indicating the existence of a condition, problem, etc [C16 via NL from Gk *sundromē*, lit.: a running together, from SYN- + *dramein* to run] > **syndromic** (sɪnˈdrɒmɪk) *adj*

syne *or* **syn** (saɪn) *adv, prep, conj* a Scottish word for **since** [C14 prob. rel. to OE *sīth* since]

synecdoche (sɪnˈɛkdəkɪ) *n* a figure of speech in which a part is substituted for a whole or a whole for a part, as in *50 head of cattle* for *50 cows*, or *the army* for *a soldier* [C14 via L from Gk *sunekdokhē*, from SYN- + *ekdokhē* interpretation, from *dekhesthai* to accept] > **synecdochic** (ˌsɪnɛkˈdɒkɪk) *or* ˌ**synecˈdochical** *adj*

synecious (sɪˈniːʃəs) *adj* a variant spelling of **synoecious**

synecology (ˌsɪnɪˈkɒlədʒɪ) *n* the ecological study of communities of plants and animals > **synecologic** (sɪnˌɛkəˈlɒdʒɪk) *or* **synˌecoˈlogical** *adj* > **synˌecoˈlogically** *adv*

syneresis *or* **synaeresis** (sɪˈnɪərɪsɪs) *n* **1** *chem* the process in which a gel contracts on standing and exudes liquid, as in the separation of whey in cheese-making **2** the contraction of two vowels into a diphthong [C16 via LL from Gk *sunairesis* a shortening, from *sunairein* to draw together, from SYN- + *hairein* to take]

synergism (ˈsɪnəˌdʒɪzəm, sɪˈnɜː-) *n* **1** Also called: **synergy** the working together of two or more drugs, muscles, etc, to produce an effect greater than the sum of their individual effects **2** another name for **synergy** (sense 1) [C18 from NL *synergismus*, from Gk *sunergos*, from SYN- + *ergon* work] > ˌ**synerˈgetic** *adj* > ˈ**synergist** *n, adj*

synergy (ˈsɪnədʒɪ) *n, pl* **synergies** **1** Also called: **synergism** the potential ability of individual organizations or groups to be more successful or productive as a result of a merger **2** another name for **synergism** (sense 1) [c19 from NL *synergia*, from Gk *sunergos*; see SYNERGISM] > **sy'nergic** *adj*

synesis ('sɪnɪsɪs) *n* a grammatical construction in which the inflection or form of a word is conditioned by the meaning rather than the syntax, as for example the plural form *have* with the singular noun *group* in the sentence *the group have already assembled* [via NL from Gk *sunesis* union, from *sunienai* to bring together, from SYN- + *hienai* to send]

synesthesia (ˌsɪni:s'θi:zɪə) *n* the usual US spelling of **synaesthesia**

syngamy ('sɪŋgəmɪ) *or* **syngenesis** (sɪn'dʒɛnɪsɪs) *n* reproduction involving the fusion of a male and female haploid gamete. Also called: **sexual reproduction** > **syngamic** (sɪŋ'gæmɪk) *or* **syngamous** ('sɪŋgəməs) *adj*

Synge (sɪŋ) *n* **John Millington** 1871–1909, Irish playwright. His plays, marked by vivid colloquial Irish speech, include *Riders to the Sea* (1904) and *The Playboy of the Western World*, produced amidst uproar at the Abbey Theatre, Dublin, in 1907

synod ('sɪnəd, 'sɪnɒd) *n* **1** a special ecclesiastical council, esp of a diocese, formally convened to discuss ecclesiastical affairs **2** *rare* any council, esp for discussion [c14 from LL *synodus*, from Gk SYN- + *hodos* a way] > **'synodal** *adj*

synodic (sɪ'nɒdɪk) *adj* relating to or involving a conjunction or two successive conjunctions of the same star, planet, or satellite

synodic month *n* See **month** (sense 6)

synoecious *or* **synecious** (sɪ'ni:ʃəs) *adj* (of plants) having male and female organs mixed together on a branch, usually at the tip [c19 SYN- + *-oecious*, from Gk *oikion* dim. of *oikos* house]

synonym ('sɪnənɪm) *n* **1** a word that means the same or nearly the same as another word, such as *bucket* and *pail* **2** a word or phrase used as another name for something, such as *Hellene* for a *Greek* > ˌ**syno'nymic** *or* ˌ**syno'nymical** *adj* > ˌ**syno'nymity** *n*

synonymous (sɪ'nɒnɪməs) *adj* **1** (often foll by *with*) being a synonym (of) **2** (*postpositive; foll by with*) closely associated (with) or suggestive (of): *his name was synonymous with greed* > **syn'onymously** *adv* > **syn'onymousness** *n*

synonymy (sɪ'nɒnɪmɪ) *n, pl* **synonymies 1** the study of synonyms **2** the character of being synonymous; equivalence **3** a list or collection of synonyms, esp one in which their meanings are discriminated **4** *biol* a collection of the synonyms of a species or group

synopsis (sɪ'nɒpsɪs) *n, pl* **synopses** (-si:z) a brief review of a subject; summary [c17 via LL from Gk *sunopsis*, from SYN- + *opsis* view]

synopsize *or* **synopsise** (sɪ'nɒpsaɪz) *vb* **synopsizes, synopsizing, synopsized** *or* **synopsises, synopsising, synopsised** (*tr*) **1** *US* variants of **epitomize 2** *US & Canad* to make a synopsis of

synoptic (sɪ'nɒptɪk) *adj* **1** of or relating to a synopsis **2** (*often cap*) *Bible* **2a** (of the Gospels of Matthew, Mark, and Luke) presenting the narrative of Christ's life, ministry, etc, from a point of view held in common by all three, and with close similarities in content, order, etc **2b** of or relating to these three Gospels **3** *meteorol* concerned with the distribution of meteorological conditions over a wide area at a given time: *a synoptic chart* ▷ *n* **4** (*often cap*) *Bible* **4a** any of the three synoptic Gospels **4b** any of the authors of these [c18 from Gk *sunoptikos*] > **syn'optically** *adv* > **syn'optist** *n*

synovia (saɪ'nəʊvɪə, sɪ-) *n* a transparent viscid lubricating fluid, secreted by the membrane lining joints, tendon sheaths, etc. Also called: **synovial fluid** [c17 from NL, prob. from SYN- + L *ōvum* egg]

synovial (saɪ'nəʊvɪəl, sɪ-) *adj* of or relating to the synovia; (of a joint) surrounded by a synovia-secreting membrane

synovitis (ˌsaɪnəʊ'vaɪtɪs, ˌsɪn-) *n* inflammation of the membrane surrounding a joint > **synovitic** (ˌsaɪnəʊ'vɪtɪk, ˌsɪn-) *adj*

synovium (saɪ'nəʊvɪəm) *n* a membrane that encloses a freely moving joint and secretes the synovia. Also called: **synovial membrane**

synroc ('sɪnˌrɒk) *n* a titanium-ceramic substance that can incorporate nuclear waste in its crystals [from *syn(thetic)* + *roc(k)*]

syntactics (sɪn'tæktɪks) *n* (*functioning as sing*) the branch of semiotics that deals with the formal properties of symbol systems; proof theory

syntagma (sɪn'tægmə) *or* **syntagm** ('sɪnˌtæm) *n, pl* **syntagmata** (-'tægmətə) *or* **syntagms 1** a word or phrase forming a syntactic unit **2** a systematic collection of statements or propositions [c17 from LL, from Gk, from *suntassein* to put in order; see SYNTAX] > ˌ**syntag'matic** *adj*

syntax ('sɪntæks) *n* **1** the branch of linguistics that deals with the grammatical arrangement of words and morphemes in sentences **2** the totality of facts about the grammatical arrangement of words in a language **3** a systematic statement of the rules governing the grammatical arrangement of words and morphemes in a language **4** a systematic statement of the rules governing the properly formed formulas of a logical system [c17 from LL *syntaxis*, from Gk *suntaxis*, from *suntassein* to put in order, from SYN- + *tassein* to arrange] > **syn'tactic** *or* **syn'tactical** *adj* > **syn'tactically** *adv*

synteny (sɪn'tɛnɪ) *n* the presence of two or more genes on the same chromosome [c20 SYN- + Gk *tainia* ribbon] > **syn'tenic** *adj*

synth (sɪnθ) *n* short for **synthesizer**

synthesis ('sɪnθɪsɪs) *n, pl* **syntheses** (-ˌsi:z) **1** the process of combining objects or ideas into a complex whole **2** the combination or whole produced by such a process **3** the process of producing a compound by a chemical reaction or series of reactions, usually from simpler starting materials **4** *linguistics* the use of inflections rather than word order and function words to express the syntactic relations in a language [c17 via L from Gk *sunthesis*, from *suntithenai* to put together, from SYN- + *tithenai* to place] > **'synthesist** *n*

synthesis gas *n chem* **1** a mixture of carbon dioxide, carbon monoxide, and hydrogen formerly made by reacting water gas with steam to enrich the proportion of hydrogen in the synthesis of ammonia **2** a similar mixture of gases made by steam reforming natural gas, used for synthesizing organic chemicals and as a fuel

synthesize ('sɪnθɪˌsaɪz), **synthetize,** *or* **synthesise, synthetise** *vb* **synthesizes, synthesizing, synthesized; synthetizes, synthetizing, synthetized** *or* **synthesises, synthesising, synthesised; synthetises, synthetising, synthetised 1** to combine or cause to combine into a whole **2** (*tr*) to produce by synthesis > ˌ**synthesi'zation,** ˌ**syntheti'zation** *or* ˌ**synthesi'sation,** ˌ**syntheti'sation** *n*

synthesizer ('sɪnθɪˌsaɪzə) *n* **1** an electronic musical instrument, usually operated by means of a keyboard, in which sounds are produced by oscillators, filters, and amplifiers **2** a person or thing that synthesizes

synthespian (ˌsɪn'θɛspɪən) *n* a computer-generated image of a film actor, esp used in place of the real actor when shooting special effects or stunts [c20 from SYN(THETIC) + THESPIAN]

synthetic (sɪn'θɛtɪk) *adj also* **synthetical 1** (of a substance or material) made artificially by chemical reaction **2** not genuine; insincere: *synthetic compassion* **3** denoting languages, such as Latin, whose morphology is characterized by synthesis **4** *philosophy* **4a** (of a proposition) having a truth-value that is not determined solely by virtue of the meanings of the words, as in *all men are arrogant* **4b** contingent ▷ *n* **5** a

Ss

synthetic substance or material [c17 from NL *syntheticus*, from Gk *sunthetikos* expert in putting together, from *suntithenai* to put together; see SYNTHESIS] > **syn'thetically** *adv*

syphilis ('sɪfɪlɪs) *n* a sexually transmitted disease caused by infection with the microorganism *Treponema pallidum*: characterized by an ulcerating chancre, usually on the genitals and progressing through the lymphatic system to nearly all tissues of the body, producing serious clinical manifestations [c18 from NL *Syphilis (sive Morbus Gallicus)* "Syphilis (or the French disease)", title of a poem (1530) by G. Fracastoro, It. physician and poet, in which a shepherd *Syphilus* is portrayed as the first victim of the disease] > **syphilitic** (ˌsɪfɪ'lɪtɪk) *adj* > **'syphiˌloid** *adj*

syphon ('saɪfᵊn) *n, vb* a variant spelling of **siphon**

Syr. *abbrev for* **1** Syria **2** Syriac **3** Syrian

Syracuse *n* **1** ('saɪrəˌkjuːz) a port in SW Italy, in SE Sicily on the Ionian Sea: founded in 734 BC by Greeks from Corinth and taken by the Romans in 212 BC, after a siege of three years. Pop: 126 282 (2000 est). Italian name: **Siracusa** **2** ('sɪrəˌkjuːs) a city in central New York State, on Lake Onondaga: site of the capital of the Iroquois Indian federation. Pop: 147 306 (2000)

Syrah ('saɪrə) **1** a red grape grown in France and Australia, used, often in a blend, for making wine **2** any of various wines made from this grape ▷ Australian name: **Shiraz** [from SHIRAZ[1], the city in Iran where the wine supposedly originated]

Syr Darya (*Russian* sir darj'ja) *n* a river in central Asia, formed from two headstreams rising in the Tian Shan: flows generally west to the Aral Sea: the longest river in central Asia. Length: (from the source of the Naryn) 2900 km (1800 miles). Ancient name: **Jaxartes**

Syria ('sɪrɪə) *n* **1** a republic in W Asia, on the Mediterranean: ruled by the Ottoman Turks (1516–1918); made a French mandate in 1920; became independent in 1944; joined Egypt in the United Arab Republic (1958–61). Official language: Arabic. Religion: Muslim majority. Currency: Syrian pound. Capital: Damascus. Pop: 16 729 000 (2001 est). Area: 185 180 sq km (71 498 sq miles) **2** (formerly) the region between the Mediterranean, the Euphrates, the Taurus, and the Arabian Desert

▷ www.moi-syria.com

▷ www.syriatourism.org

Syriac ('sɪrɪˌæk) *n* a dialect of Aramaic spoken in Syria until about the 13th century AD

Syrian ('sɪrɪən) *adj* **1** of or relating to Syria, its people, or their dialect of Arabic ▷ *n* **2** a native or inhabitant of Syria

syringa (sɪ'rɪŋgə) *n* another name for **mock orange** (sense 1) or **lilac** (sense 1) [c17 from NL, from Gk *surinx* tube, from use of its hollow stems for pipes]

syringe ('sɪrɪndʒ, sɪ'rɪndʒ) *n* **1** *med* a hypodermic syringe or a rubber ball with a slender nozzle, for use in withdrawing or injecting fluids, cleaning wounds, etc **2** any similar device for injecting, spraying, or extracting liquids by means of pressure or suction ▷ *vb* **syringes, syringing, syringed** **3** (*tr*) to cleanse, inject, or spray with a syringe [c15 from LL, from L: SYRINX]

syringomyelia (səˌrɪŋgəʊmaɪ'iːlɪə) *n* a chronic progressive disease of the spinal cord in which cavities form in the grey matter: characterized by loss of the sense of pain and temperature [c19 *syringo-*, from Gk: SYRINX + *-myelia* from Gk *muelos* marrow] > **syringomyelic** (səˌrɪŋgəʊmaɪ'ɛlɪk) *adj*

syrinx ('sɪrɪŋks) *n, pl* **syringes** (sɪ'rɪndʒiːz) *or* **syrinxes** **1** the vocal organ of a bird, situated in the lower part of the trachea **2** (in classical Greek music) a panpipe or set of panpipes [c17 via L from Gk *surinx* pipe] > **syringeal** (sɪ'rɪndʒɪəl) *adj*

Syrinx ('sɪrɪŋks) *n* *Greek myth* a nymph who was changed into a reed to save her from the amorous pursuit of Pan. From this reed Pan then fashioned his musical pipes

syrup ('sɪrəp) *n* **1** a solution of sugar dissolved in water and often flavoured with fruit juice: used for sweetening fruit, etc **2** any of various thick sweet liquids prepared for cooking or table use from molasses, sugars, etc **3** *inf* cloying sentimentality **4** a liquid medicine containing a sugar solution for flavouring or preservation ▷ Also: **sirup** [c15 from Med. L *syrupus*, from Ar. *sharāb* a drink, from *shariba* to drink] > **'syrupy** *adj*

sysop *or* **SYSOP** ('sɪsˌɒp) *n* *computing* a person who runs a system or network [c20 SYS(TEM) + OP(ERATOR)]

syssarcosis (ˌsɪsɑː'kəʊsɪs) *n, pl* **syssarcoses** (-siːz) *anat* the union or articulation of bones by muscle [c17 from NL, from Gk *sussarkōsis*, from *sus-* SYN- + *sarkoun* to become fleshy, from *sarx* flesh] > **syssarcotic** (ˌsɪsɑː'kɒtɪk) *adj*

systaltic (sɪ'stæltɪk) *adj* (esp of the action of the heart) of, relating to, or characterized by alternate contractions and dilations; pulsating [c17 from LL *systalticus*, from Gk, from *sustellein* to contract, from SYN- + *stellein* to place]

system ('sɪstəm) *n* **1** a group or combination of interrelated, interdependent, or interacting elements forming a collective entity; a methodical or coordinated assemblage of parts, facts, etc **2** any scheme of classification or arrangement **3** a network of communications, transportation, or distribution **4** a method or complex of methods: *he has a perfect system at roulette* **5** orderliness; an ordered manner **6** **the system** (*often cap*) society seen as an environment exploiting, restricting, and repressing individuals **7** an organism considered as a functioning entity **8** any of various bodily parts or structures that are anatomically or physiologically related: *the digestive system* **9** one's physiological or psychological constitution: *get it out of your system* **10** any assembly of electronic, mechanical, etc, components with interdependent functions, usually forming a self-contained unit: *a brake system* **11** a group of celestial bodies that are associated as a result of natural laws, esp gravitational attraction: *the solar system* **12** a point of view or doctrine used to interpret a branch of knowledge **13** *mineralogy* one of a group of divisions into which crystals may be placed on the basis of the lengths and inclinations of their axes. Also called: **crystal system** **14** *geol* a stratigraphical unit for the rock strata formed during a period of geological time [c17 from F, from LL *systēma*, from Gk *sustēma*, from SYN- + *histanai* to cause to stand]

systematic (ˌsɪstɪ'mætɪk) *adj* **1** characterized by the use of order and planning; methodical: *a systematic administrator* **2** comprising or resembling a system: *systematic theology* **3** Also: **systematical** *biol* of or relating to taxonomic classification > ˌ**system'atically** *adv* > **'systemaˌtism** *n* > **'systematist** *n*

systematics (ˌsɪstɪ'mætɪks) *n* (*functioning as sing*) the study of systems and the principles of classification and nomenclature

systematize ('sɪstɪməˌtaɪz), **systemize** *or* **systematise, systemise** *vb* **systematizes, systematizing, systematized; systemizes, systemizing, systemized** *or* **systematises, systematising, systematised; systemises, systemising, systemised** (*tr*) to arrange in a system > ˌ**systemati'zation,** ˌ**systemati'sation** *or* ˌ**systemi'zation,** ˌ**systemi'sation** *n* > **'systemaˌtizer, 'systemaˌtiser** *or* **'systeˌmizer, 'systeˌmiser** *n*

system building *n* a method of building in which prefabricated components are used to speed the construction of buildings > ˌ**system 'built** *adj*

Système International d'Unités (*French* sistɛm ɛ̃tɛrnasjɔnal dynite) *n* the International System of units. See **SI unit**

systemic (sɪ'stɛmɪk, -'stiː-) *adj* **1** another word for

systematic (senses 1, 2) **2** *physiol* (of a poison, disease, etc) affecting the entire body **3** (of an insecticide, fungicide, etc) designed to be absorbed by a plant into its tissues ▷ *n* **4** a systemic insecticide, fungicide, etc > **sys'temically** *adv*

systems analysis *n* the analysis of the requirements of a task and the expression of these in a form that permits the assembly of computer hardware and software to perform the task > **systems analyst** *n*

systems engineering *n* the branch of engineering, based on systems analysis and information theory, concerned with the design of integrated systems

systole ('sɪstəlɪ) *n* contraction of the heart, during which blood is pumped into the aorta and the arteries ▷ Cf **diastole** [C16 via LL from Gk *sustolē*, from *sustellein* to contract; see SYSTALTIC] > **systolic** (sɪ'stɒlɪk) *adj*

Syzran (*Russian* 'sizrənj) *n* a port in W central Russia, on the Volga River: oil refining. Pop: 188 100 (1999 est)

syzygy ('sɪzɪdʒɪ) *n, pl* **syzygies** **1** either of the two positions (conjunction or opposition) of a celestial body when sun, earth, and the body lie in a straight line: *the moon is at syzygy when full* **2** *rare* any pair, usually of opposites [C17 from LL, from Gk *suzugia*, from *suzugos* yoked together, from SYN- + *zugon* a yoke] > **syzygial** (sɪ'zɪdʒɪəl), **syzygetic** (ˌsɪzɪ'dʒɛtɪk), *or* **syzygal** ('sɪzɪgəl) *adj* > **ˌsyzy'getically** *adv*

Szabadka ('sɔbɔtkɔ) *n* the Hungarian name for **Subotica**

Szczecin (*Polish* 'ʃtʃɛtʃin) *n* a port in NW Poland, on the River Oder: the busiest Polish port and leading coal exporter; shipbuilding. Pop: 416 988 (1999 est). German name: **Stettin**

Szechwan ('seɪ'tʃwɑ:n) *n* a variant transliteration of the Chinese name for **Sichuan**

Szeged (*Hungarian* 'sɛgɛd) *n* an industrial city in S Hungary, on the Tisza River. Pop: 158 158 (2000 est)

Szell (sɛl) *n* **George** 1897–1970, US conductor, born in Hungary

Szent-Györgyi (sɛnt'dʒɜ:dʒɪ) *n* **Albert** (**von Nagyrapolt**) 1893–1986, US biochemist, born in Hungary, who isolated ascorbic acid and identified it as vitamin C. Nobel prize for physiology or medicine 1937

Szilard ('sɪlɑ:d) *n* **Leo** 1898–1964, US physicist, born in Hungary, who originated the idea of a self-sustaining nuclear chain reaction (1934) He worked on the atomic bomb during World War II but later pressed for the international control of nuclear weapons

Szombathely (*Hungarian* 'sombɔthɛj) *n* a city in W Hungary: site of the Roman capital of Pannonia. Pop: 84 000 (1995 est)

Szymanowski (*Polish* ʃima'nɔfski) *n* **Karol** ('karɔl) 1882–1937, Polish composer, whose works include the opera *King Roger* (1926), two violin concertos, symphonies, piano music, and songs

Szymborska (*Polish* ʃɪm'bɔrskə) *n* **Wisława** (vɪ'swavə) born 1923, Polish poet and writer: Nobel prize for literature 1996.

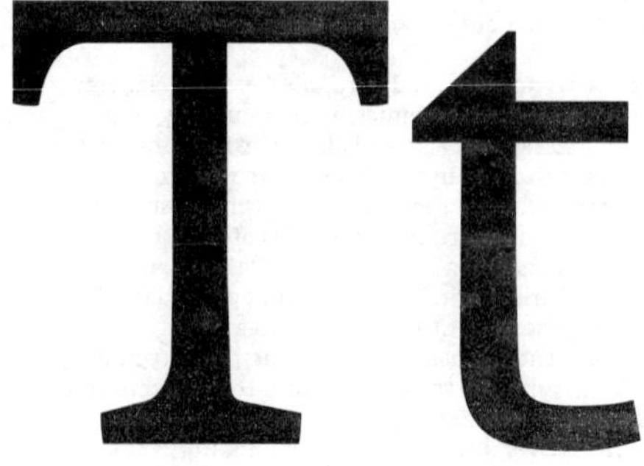

t *or* **T** (tiː) *n, pl* **t's, T's,** *or* **Ts 1** the 20th letter of the English alphabet **2** a speech sound represented by this letter **3** something shaped like a T **4 to a T** in every detail; perfectly

t *symbol for:* **1** *statistics* distribution **2** tonne(s) **3** troy (weight)

T *symbol for:* **1** absolute temperature **2** surface tension **3** tera- **4** tesla **5** *chem* tritium **6** *biochem* thymine

t. *abbrev for:* **1** *commerce* tare **2** teaspoon(ful) **3** temperature **4** *music* tempo **5** *music* Also: **T** tenor **6** *grammar* tense **7** ton(s) **8** transitive

't *contraction of* it

ta (tɑː) *interj Brit inf* thank you [C18 imit. of baby talk]

Ta *the chemical symbol for* tantalum

TA (in Britain) *abbrev for* Territorial Army (now superseded by **TAVR**)

taal (tɑːl) *n S African* language: usually, by implication, Afrikaans [Afrik. from Du.]

Taal (tɑːˈɑːl) *n* an active volcano in the Philippines, on S Luzon on an island in the centre of **Lake Taal.** Height: 300 m (984 ft). Area of lake: 243 sq km (94 sq miles)

tab[1] (tæb) *n* **1** a small flap of material, esp one on a garment for decoration or for fastening to a button **2** any similar flap, such as a piece of paper attached to a file for identification **3** *Brit mil* the insignia on the collar of a staff officer **4** *chiefly US & Canad* a bill, esp for a meal or drinks **5 keep tabs on** *inf* to keep a watchful eye on ▷ *vb* **tabs, tabbing, tabbed 6** (*tr*) to supply with a tab or tabs [C17 from ?]

tab[2] (tæb) *n* short for **tabulator** or **tablet**

TAB *abbrev for:* **1** *Austral & NZ* Totalizator Agency Board **2** typhoid-paratyphoid A and B (vaccine)

tabard (ˈtæbəd) *n* a sleeveless or short-sleeved jacket, esp one worn by a herald, bearing a coat of arms, or by a knight over his armour [C13 from OF *tabart*, from ?]

tabaret (ˈtæbərɪt) *n* a hard-wearing fabric of silk or similar cloth with stripes of satin or moire, used esp for upholstery [C19 ? from TABBY[1]]

Tabasco[1] (təˈbæskəʊ) *n trademark* a very hot red sauce made from matured capsicums

Tabasco[2] (*Spanish* taˈβasko) *n* a state in SE Mexico, on the Gulf of Campeche: mostly flat and marshy with extensive jungles; hot and humid climate. Capital: Villahermosa. Pop: 1 889 367 (2000). Area: 24 661 sq km (9520 sq miles)

tabby[1] (ˈtæbɪ) *n* a fabric with a watered pattern, esp silk or taffeta [C17 from OF *tabis* silk cloth, from Ar. *al-'attabiya*, lit.: the quarter of (Prince) 'Attab, the part of Baghdad where the fabric was first made]

tabby[2] (ˈtæbɪ) *adj* **1** (esp of cats) brindled with dark stripes or wavy markings on a lighter background **2** having a wavy or striped pattern, particularly in colours of grey and brown ▷ *n, pl* **tabbies 3** a tabby cat **4** any female domestic cat [C17 from *Tabby*, pet form of the girl's name *Tabitha*, prob. infl. by TABBY[1]]

tabernacle (ˈtæbəˌnækᵊl) *n* **1** (*often cap*) *Old Testament* **1a** the portable sanctuary in which the ancient Israelites carried the Ark of the Covenant **1b** the Jewish Temple **2** any place of worship that is not called a church **3** *RC Church* a receptacle in which the Blessed Sacrament is kept **4** *chiefly RC Church* a canopied niche **5** *naut* a strong framework for holding the foot of a mast, allowing it to be swung down to pass under low bridges, etc [C13 from L *tabernāculum* a tent, from *taberna* a hut] > ˌ**taberˈnacular** *adj*

tabes (ˈteɪbiːz) *n, pl* **tabes 1** a wasting of a bodily organ or part **2** short for **tabes dorsalis** [C17 from L: a wasting away] > **tabetic** (təˈbɛtɪk) *adj*

tabescent (təˈbɛsᵊnt) *adj* **1** progressively emaciating; wasting away **2** of, relating to, or having tabes [C19 from L *tābēscere*, from TABES] > **ta'bescence** *n*

tabes dorsalis (dɔː'sɑːlɪs) *n* a form of late syphilis that attacks the spinal cord causing degeneration of the nerve fibres, paralysis of the leg muscles, acute abdominal pain, etc [NL, lit.: tabes of the back]

tabla ('tʌblə, 'tɑːblɑː) *n* a musical instrument of India consisting of a pair of drums whose pitches can be varied [Hindu, from Ar. *tabla* drum]

tablature ('tæblətʃə) *n music* any of a number of forms of musical notation, esp for playing the lute, consisting of letters and signs indicating rhythm and fingering [c16 from F, ult. from L *tabulātum* wooden floor, from *tabula* a plank]

table ('teɪbᵊl) *n* **1** a flat horizontal slab or board, usually supported by one or more legs **2a** such a slab or board on which food is served **2b** (*as modifier*): *table linen* **3** food as served in a particular household, etc: *a good table* **4** such a piece of furniture specially designed for any of various purposes: *a bird table* **5a** a company of persons assembled for a meal, game, etc **5b** (*as modifier*): *table talk* **6** any flat or level area, such as a plateau **7** a rectangular panel set below or above the face of a wall **8** *archit* another name for **string course** **9** any of various flat surfaces, as an upper horizontal facet of a cut gem **10** *music* the sounding board of a violin, guitar, etc **11a** an arrangement of words, numbers, or signs, usually in parallel columns **11b** See **multiplication table** **12** a tablet on which laws were inscribed by the ancient Romans, the Hebrews, etc **13** **turn the tables** to cause a complete reversal of circumstances **14** **under the table** **14a** (**under-the-table** *when prenominal*) done illicitly and secretly **14b** *sl* drunk ▷ *vb* **tables, tabling, tabled** (*tr*) **15** to place on a table **16** *Brit* to submit (a bill, etc) for consideration by a legislative body **17** *US* to suspend discussion of (a bill, etc) indefinitely **18** to enter in or form into a list [c12 via OF from L *tabula* a writing tablet]

tableau ('tæbləʊ) *n, pl* **tableaux** (-ləʊ, -ləʊz) *or* **tableaus** **1** See ***tableau vivant*** **2** a pause on stage when all the performers briefly freeze in position **3** any dramatic group or scene [c17 from F, from OF *tablel* a picture, dim. of TABLE]

tableau vivant *French* (tablo vivɑ̃) *n, pl* ***tableaux vivants*** (tablo vivɑ̃) a representation of a scene by a person or group posed silent and motionless [c19, lit.: living picture]

Table Bay *n* the large bay on which Cape Town is situated, on the SW coast of South Africa

tablecloth ('teɪbᵊl,klɒθ) *n* a cloth for covering the top of a table, esp during meals

table d'hôte ('tɑːbᵊl 'dəʊt) *adj* **1** (of a meal) consisting of a set number of courses with limited choice of dishes offered at a fixed price. ▷ Cf **à la carte** ▷ *n, pl* **tables d'hôte** ('tɑːbᵊlz 'dəʊt) **2** a table d'hôte meal or menu [c17 from F, lit.: the host's table]

tableland ('teɪbᵊl,lænd) *n* flat elevated land

table licence *n* a licence authorizing the sale of alcoholic drinks with meals only

Table Mountain *n* a mountain in SW South Africa, overlooking Cape Town and Table Bay: flat-topped and steep-sided. Height: 1087 m (3567 ft)

tablespoon ('teɪbᵊl,spuːn) *n* **1** a spoon, larger than a dessertspoon, used for serving food, etc **2** Also called: **tablespoonful** the amount contained in such a spoon **3** a unit of capacity used in cooking, etc, equal to half a fluid ounce

tablet ('tæblɪt) *n* **1** a medicinal formulation made of a compressed substance **2** a flattish cake of some substance, such as soap **3** a slab of stone, wood, etc, esp one used for inscriptions **4a** a rigid sheet, as of bark, etc, used for similar purposes **4b** (*often pl*) a set of these fastened together **5** a pad of writing paper **6** *Scot* a sweet made from butter, sugar, and condensed milk, usually shaped into flat oblong cakes [c14 from OF *tablete* a little table, from L *tabula* a board]

table tennis *n* a miniature form of tennis played on a table with bats and a hollow ball

▷ www.ittf.com

▷ www.ettu.org

▷ www.usatt.org

table-turning *n* the movement of a table attributed by spiritualists to the power of spirits

tableware ('teɪbᵊl,wɛə) *n* articles such as dishes, plates, knives, forks, etc, used at meals

tabloid ('tæblɔɪd) *n* **1** a newspaper with pages about 30 cm (12 inches) by 40 cm (16 inches), usually with many photographs and a concise and often sensational style **2** (*modifier*) designed to appeal to a mass audience or readership; sensationalist: *the tabloid press; tabloid television* [c20 from earlier *Tabloid*, a trademark for a medicine in tablet form]

taboo *or* **tabu** (tə'buː) *adj* **1** forbidden or disapproved of: *taboo words* **2** (in Polynesia) marked off as sacred and forbidden ▷ *n, pl* **taboos** *or* **tabus** **3** any prohibition resulting from social or other conventions **4** ritual restriction or prohibition, esp of something that is considered holy or unclean ▷ *vb* **5** (*tr*) to place under a taboo [c18 from Tongan *tapu*]

tabor *or* **tabour** ('teɪbə) *n* a small drum used esp in the Middle Ages, struck with one hand while the other held a pipe [c13 from OF *tabour*, ?from Persian *tabīr*]

Tabor ('teɪbə) *n* **Mount** a mountain in N Israel, near Nazareth: traditionally regarded as the mountain where the Transfiguration took place. Height: 588 m (1929 ft)

taboret *or* **tabouret** ('tæbərɪt) *n* **1** a low stool **2** a frame for stretching out cloth while it is being embroidered **3** a small tabor [c17 from F *tabouret*, dim. of TABOR]

Tabriz (tæ'briːz) *n* a city in NW Iran: an ancient city, situated in a volcanic region of hot springs; university (1947); carpet manufacturing. Pop: 1 191 043 (1996). Ancient name: **Tauris** ('tɔːrɪs)

Tt

tabular ('tæbjʊlə) *adj* **1** arranged in systematic or table form **2** calculated from or by means of a table **3** like a table in form; flat [c17 from L *tabulāris* concerning boards, from *tabula* a board] > **'tabularly** *adv*

tabula rasa ('tæbjʊlə 'rɑːsə) *n, pl* **tabulae rasae** ('tæbjʊliː 'rɑːsiː) **1** the mind in its uninformed original state **2** an opportunity for a fresh start; clean slate [L: a scraped tablet]

tabulate *vb* ('tæbjʊ,leɪt), **tabulates, tabulating, tabulated** (*tr*) **1** to set out, arrange, or write in tabular form **2** to form or cut with a flat surface ▷ *adj* ('tæbjʊlɪt, -,leɪt) **3** having a flat surface [c18 from L *tabula* a board] > **'tabulable** *adj* > **,tabu'lation** *n*

tabulator ('tæbjʊ,leɪtə) *n* **1** a device for setting the stops that locate the column margins on a typewriter **2** *computing* a machine that reads data from one medium, such as punched cards, producing lists, tabulations, or totals

tacamahac ('tækəmə,hæk) *or* **tacmahack** *n* **1** any of several strong-smelling resinous gums used in ointments, incense, etc **2** any tree yielding this resin [c16 from Sp. *tacamahaca*, from Nahuatl *tecomahca* aromatic resin]

tacet ('teɪsɛt, 'tæs-) *vb* (*intr*) (on a musical score) a direction indicating that a particular instrument or singer does not take part [c18 from L: it is silent, from *tacēre* to be quiet]

tacheometer (,tækɪ'ɒmɪtə) *or* **tachymeter** *n surveying* a type of theodolite designed for the rapid measurement of distances, elevations, and directions > **,tache'ometry** *n*

tachisme ('tɑːʃɪzəm) *n* a type of action painting in which haphazard dabs and blots of colour are treated as a means of unconscious expression [c20 F, from *tache* stain]

tachistoscope (tæ'kɪstə,skəʊp) *n* an instrument for displaying visual images for very brief intervals, usually a fraction of a second [c20 from Gk *takhistos* swiftest + -SCOPE] > **tachistoscopic** (tæ,kɪstə'skɒpɪk) *adj*
tacho- *combining form* speed: *tachograph; tachometer* [from Gk *takhos*]
tachograph ('tækə,grɑːf) *n* a tachometer that produces a record (**tachogram**) of its readings, esp a device for recording the speed of and distance covered by a vehicle. Often shortened to **tacho**
tachometer (tæ'kɒmɪtə) *n* any device for measuring speed, esp the rate of revolution of a shaft. Tachometers are often fitted to cars to indicate the number of revolutions per minute of the engine > **ta'chometry** *n*
tachy- *or* **tacheo-** *combining form* swift or accelerated: *tachyon* [from Gk *takhus* swift]
tachycardia (,tækɪ'kɑːdɪə) *n* abnormally rapid beating of the heart
tachygraphy (tæ'kɪgrəfɪ) *n* shorthand, esp as used in ancient Rome or Greece
tachymeter (tæ'kɪmɪtə) *n* another name for **tacheometer**
tachyon ('tækɪ,ɒn) *n physics* a hypothetical elementary particle capable of travelling faster than the velocity of light [c20 from TACHY- + -ON]
tachyphylaxis (,tækɪfɪ'læksɪs) *n* very rapid development of tolerance or immunity to the effects of a drug [NL, from TACHY- + *phylaxis* on the model of *prophylaxis;* see PROPHYLACTIC]
tacit ('tæsɪt) *adj* implied or inferred without direct expression; understood: *a tacit agreement* [c17 from L *tacitus*, p.p. of *tacēre* to be silent] > **'tacitly** *adv*
taciturn ('tæsɪ,tɜːn) *adj* habitually silent, reserved, or uncommunicative [c18 from L *taciturnus*, from *tacēre* to be silent] > **,taci'turnity** *n* > **'taci,turnly** *adv*
Tacitus ('tæsɪtəs) *n* **Publius Cornelius** ('pʌblɪəs kɔː'niːljəs) ?55–?120 AD, Roman historian and orator, famous as a prose stylist. His works include the *Histories*, dealing with the period 68–96, and the *Annals*, dealing with the period 14–68
tack¹ (tæk) *n* **1** a short sharp-pointed nail, with a large flat head **2** *Brit* a long loose temporary stitch used in dressmaking, etc **3** See **tailor's-tack** **4** a temporary fastening **5** stickiness **6** *naut* the heading of a vessel sailing to windward, stated in terms of the side of the sail against which the wind is pressing **7** *naut* **7a** a course sailed with the wind blowing from forward of the beam **7b** one such course or a zigzag pattern of such courses **8** *naut* **8a** a sheet for controlling the weather clew of a course **8b** the weather clew itself **9** *naut* the forward lower clew of a fore-and-aft sail **10** a course of action or policy **11** **on the wrong tack** under a false impression ▷ *vb* **12** (*tr*) to secure by a tack or tacks **13** *Brit* to sew (something) with long loose temporary stitches **14** (*tr*) to attach or append **15** *naut* to change the heading of (a sailing vessel) to the opposite tack **16** *naut* to steer (a sailing vessel) on alternate tacks **17** (*intr*) *naut* (of a sailing vessel) to proceed on a different tack or to alternate tacks **18** (*intr*) to follow a zigzag route; keep changing one's course of action [c14 *tak* fastening, nail]
tack² (tæk) *n* riding harness for horses, such as saddles, bridles, etc [c20 shortened from TACKLE]
tacker ('tækə) *n* **1** a person or thing that tacks **2** *Austral sl* a young person; child
tack hammer *n* a light hammer for driving tacks
tackies *or* **takkies** ('tækɪz) *pl n, sing* **tacky** *S African inf* tennis shoes or plimsolls [c20 prob. from TACKY¹, from their nonslip rubber soles]
tackle ('tækᵊl) *n* **1** an arrangement of ropes and pulleys designed to lift heavy weights **2** the equipment required for a particular occupation, etc **3** *naut* the halyards and other running rigging aboard a vessel **4** *sport* a physical challenge to an opponent, as to prevent his or her progress **5** *American football* a defensive lineman ▷ *vb* **tackles, tackling, tackled** **6** (*tr*) to undertake (a task, etc) **7** (*tr*) to confront (esp an opponent) with a difficult proposition **8** *sport* to challenge (an opponent) with a tackle [c13 rel. to MLow G *takel* ship's rigging] > **'tackler** *n*
tack rag *n building trades* a cotton cloth impregnated with an oil, used to remove dust from a surface prior to painting
tacky¹ ('tækɪ) *adj* **tackier, tackiest** slightly sticky or adhesive [c18 from TACK¹ (in the sense: stickiness)] > **'tackily** *adv* > **'tackiness** *n*
tacky² ('tækɪ) *adj* **tackier, tackiest** *inf* **1** shabby or shoddy **2** ostentatious and vulgar **3** *US* (of a person) dowdy; seedy [c19 from dialect *tacky* an inferior horse, from ?] > **'tackiness** *n*
Tacna-Arica (*Spanish* 'taknaa'rika) *n* a coastal desert region of W South America, long disputed by Chile and Peru: divided in 1929 into the Peruvian department of Tacna and the Chilean department of Arica
tacnode ('tæk,nəʊd) *n* another name for **osculation** (sense 1) [c19 from L *tactus* touch (from *tangere* to touch) + NODE]
taco ('tɑːkəʊ) *n pl* **-cos** *Mexican cookery* a tortilla folded into a roll with a filling and usually fried [from Mexican Sp., from Sp.: lit., a snack, a bite to eat]
Tacoma (tə'kəʊmə) *n* a port in W Washington, on Puget Sound: industrial centre. Pop: 193 556 (2000)
tact (tækt) *n* **1** a sense of what is fitting and considerate in dealing with others, so as to avoid giving offence **2** skill in handling difficult situations; diplomacy [c17 from L *tactus* a touching, from *tangere* to touch] > **'tactful** *adj* > **'tactfulness** *n* > **'tactless** *adj* > **'tactlessness** *n*
tactic ('tæktɪk) *n* a piece of tactics; tactical move. See also **tactics**
-tactic *adj combining form* having a specified kind of pattern or arrangement or having an orientation determined by a specified force: *syndiotactic; phototactic* [from Gk *taktikos* relating to order; see TACTICS]
tactical ('tæktɪkᵊl) *adj* **1** of, relating to, or employing tactics: *a tactical error* **2** (of missiles, bombing, etc) for use in or supporting limited military operations; short-range **3** skilful, adroit, or diplomatic > **'tactically** *adv*
tactical voting *n* (in an election) the practice of casting one's vote not for the party of one's choice but for the second strongest contender in a constituency in order to defeat the likeliest winner
tactics ('tæktɪks) *pl n* **1** (*functioning as sing*) *mil* the art and science of the detailed direction and control of movement of forces in battle to achieve an aim or task **2** the manoeuvres used to achieve an aim or task **3** plans followed to achieve a particular short-term aim [c17 from NL *tactica*, from Gk, from *taktikos* concerning arrangement, from *taktos* arranged (for battle), from *tassein* to arrange] > **tac'tician** *n*
tactile ('tæktaɪl) *adj* **1** of, relating to, affecting, or having a sense of touch **2** *now rare* tangible [c17 from L *tactilis*, from *tangere* to touch] > **tactility** (tæk'tɪlɪtɪ) *n*
Tadmor ('tædmɔː) *n* the biblical name for **Palmyra**
tadpole ('tæd,pəʊl) *n* the aquatic larva of frogs, toads, etc, which develops from a limbless tailed form with external gills into a form with internal gills, limbs, and a reduced tail [c15 *taddepol*, from *tadde* toad + *pol* head]
Tadzhik *n* a variant spelling of **Tajik**
Tadzhikistan *or* **Tadjikistan** (tɑː,dʒɪkɪ'stɑːn, -stæn) *n* variant spellings of **Tajikistan**
taedium vitae ('tiːdɪəm 'viːtaɪ, 'vaɪtiː) *n* the feeling that life is boring and dull [L, lit.: weariness of life]
Taegu (tɛ'guː) *n* a city in SE South Korea: textile and agricultural trading centre. Pop: 2 449 139 (1995)
Taejon (tɛ'dʒɒn) *n* a city in W South Korea: market centre of an agricultural region. Pop: 1 272 143 (1995)

tae kwon do ('taɪ 'kwɒn 'dəʊ, 'teɪ) *n* a Korean martial art that resembles karate [c20 Korean *tae* kick + *kwon* fist + *do* way, method]

tael (teɪl) *n* **1** a unit of weight, used in the Far East **2** (formerly) a Chinese monetary unit [c16 from Port., from Malay *tahil* weight, ?from Sansk.]

ta'en (teɪn) *vb* a Scot or poetic contraction of **taken**

taenia *or US* **tenia** ('ti:nɪə) *n, pl* **taeniae** *or US* **teniae** (-nɪ,i:) **1** (in ancient Greece) a headband **2** *archit* the fillet between the architrave and frieze of a Doric entablature **3** *anat* any bandlike structure or part **4** any of a genus of tapeworms [c16 via L from Gk *tainia* narrow strip]

taeniasis *or US* **teniasis** (ti:'naɪəsɪs) *n pathol* infestation with tapeworms of the genus *Taenia*

taffeta ('tæfɪtə) *n* a thin crisp lustrous plain-weave fabric of silk, etc, used esp for women's clothes [c14 from Med. L *taffata*, from Persian *tāftah* spun, from *tāftan* to spin]

taffrail ('tæf,reɪl) *n naut* a rail at the stern of a vessel [c19 changed from earlier *tafferel*, from Du. *taffereel* panel (hence applied to the part of a vessel decorated with carved panels), from *tafel* table]

Taffy ('tæfɪ) *n, pl* **Taffies** a slang word or nickname for a **Welshman** [c17 from the supposed Welsh pronunciation of *Davy* (from *David*, Welsh *Dafydd*), a common Welsh Christian name]

tafia *or* **taffia** ('tæfɪə) *n* a type of rum, esp from Guyana or the Caribbean [c18 from F, from West Indian Creole, prob. from RATAFIA]

Tafilelt (tæ'fi:lɛlt) *or* **Tafilalet** (,tæfɪ'lɑ:lɛt) *n* an oasis in SE Morocco, the largest in the Sahara. Area: about 1300 sq km (500 sq miles)

Taft (tæft) *n* **William Howard** 1857–1930, US statesman; 27th president of the US (1909–13)

tag[1] (tæg) *n* **1** a piece of paper, leather, etc, for attaching to something as a mark or label: *a price tag* **2** Also called: **electronic tag** an electronic device worn by an offender serving a noncustodial sentence, which monitors the offender's whereabouts by means of a link to a central computer through the telephone system **3** a small piece of material hanging from a part or piece **4** a point of metal, etc, at the end of a cord or lace **5** an epithet or verbal appendage, the refrain of a song, the moral of a fable, etc **6** a brief quotation **7** an ornamental flourish **8** the tip of an animal's tail **9** a matted lock of wool or hair **10** *sl* a graffito consisting of a nickname or personal symbol ▷ *vb* **tags, tagging, tagged** (*mainly tr*) **11** to mark with a tag **12** to monitor the whereabouts of (an offender) by means of an electronic tag **13** to add or append as a tag **14** to supply (prose or blank verse) with rhymes **15** (*intr; usually foll by on or along*) to trail (behind) **16** to name or call (someone something) **17** to cut the tags of wool or hair from (an animal) [c15 from ?]

tag[2] (tæg) *n* **1** Also called: **tig** a children's game in which one player chases the others in an attempt to catch one of them who will then become the chaser **2** the act of tagging one's partner in tag wrestling **3** (*modifier*) denoting a wrestling contest between two teams of two wrestlers, in which only one from each team may be in the ring at one time. The contestant outside the ring may change places with his team-mate inside the ring after touching his hand ▷ *vb* **tags, tagging, tagged** (*tr*) **4** to catch (another child) in the game of tag **5** (in tag wrestling) to touch the hand of (one's partner) [c18 ?from TAG[1]]

Tagalog (tə'gɑ:lɒg) *n* **1** (*pl* **Tagalogs** *or* **Tagalog**) a member of a people of the Philippines **2** the language of this people ▷ *adj* **3** of or relating to this people or their language

Taganrog (*Russian* təgan'rɔk) *n* a port in SW Russia, on the **Gulf of Taganrog** (an inlet of the Sea of Azov): founded in 1698 as a naval base and fortress by Peter the Great: industrial centre. Pop: 287 600 (1999 est)

tag end *n* **1** the last part of something **2** a loose end of cloth, thread, etc

tagetes (tæ'dʒi:ti:z) *n, pl* **tagetes** any of a genus of plants with yellow or orange flowers, including the French and African marigolds [from NL, from *Tages*, an Etruscan god]

tagliatelle (,tæljə'tɛlɪ) *n* a form of pasta made in narrow strips [It., from *tagliare* to cut]

tag line *n* **1** an amusing or memorable phrase designed to catch attention in an advert **2** another name for **punch line**

Tagore (tə'gɔ:) *n* **Rabindranath** (rə'bi:ndrə,nɑ:t) 1861–1941, Indian poet and philosopher. His verse collections, written in Bengali and English, include *Gitanjali* (1910; 1912): Nobel prize for literature 1913

Tagus ('teɪgəs) *n* a river in SW Europe, rising in E central Spain and flowing west to the border with Portugal, then southwest to the Atlantic at Lisbon: the longest river of the Iberian Peninsula. Length: 1007 km (626 miles). Portuguese name: **Tejo**. Spanish name: **Tajo**

taha Maori ('tɑ :hə) *n NZ* a Maori perspective or dimension of a subject [Maori]

Tahiti (tə'hi:tɪ) *n* an island in the S Pacific, in the Windward group of the Society Islands: the largest and most important island in French Polynesia; became a French protectorate in 1842 and a colony in 1880. Capital: Papeete. Pop: 115 820 (latest est). Area: 1005 sq km (388 sq miles) > **Tahitian** (tə'hi:tɪən, tə'hi:ʃɪən) *adj, n*

Tahoe ('tɑ:həʊ, 'teɪ-) *n* **Lake** a lake between E California and W Nevada, in the Sierra Nevada Mountains at an altitude of 1899 m (6229 ft). Area: about 520 sq km (200 sq miles)

tahr (tɑ:) *n* any of several goatlike mammals of S and SW Asia, having a shaggy coat and curved horns [from Nepali *thār*]

tahsil (tə'si:l) *n* an administrative division in certain states in India [Urdu, from Ar.: collection]

Tai (taɪ) *adj, n* a variant spelling of **Thai**

TAI *abbrev for* International Atomic Time (*Temps Atomique International*)

taiaha ('taɪə,hɑ:) *n NZ* a carved weapon in the form of a staff, now used in Maori ceremonial oratory [from Maori]

t'ai chi ch'uan ('taɪ dʒi: 'tʃwɑ:n) *n* a Chinese system of callisthenics characterized by coordinated and rhythmic movements. Often shortened to **t'ai chi** ('taɪ 'dʒi:) [Chinese, lit.: great art of boxing]

▷ www.taichichuan.co.uk

Taichung *or* **T'ai-chung** ('taɪ'tʃʊŋ) *n* a city in W Taiwan (Republic of China): commercial centre of an agricultural region. Pop: 940 589 (2000 est)

taiga ('taɪgɑ:) *n* the coniferous forests extending across much of subarctic North America and Eurasia [from Russian, of Turkic origin]

taihoa ('taɪhəʊə) *sentence substitute NZ* hold on! no hurry! [Maori]

taikonaut ('taɪkəʊ,nɔ:t) *n* an astronaut from the People's Republic of China [c20 from Cantonese *taikon(g)* cosmos + -NAUT]

tail[1] (teɪl) *n* **1** the rear part of the vertebrate body that contains an elongation of the vertebral column, esp forming a flexible appendage **2** anything resembling such an appendage; the bottom, lowest, or rear part **3** the last part or parts: *the tail of the storm* **4** the rear part of an aircraft including the fin, tailplane, and control surfaces **5** *astron* the luminous stream of gas and dust particles driven from the head of a comet when close to the sun **6** the rear portion of a bomb, rocket, missile, etc, usually fitted with guiding or stabilizing vanes **7** a line of people or things **8** a long braid or tress of hair: *a pigtail* **9** a final short line in a stanza **10** *inf* a person employed to follow and spy upon another **11** an informal word for **buttocks** **12** *taboo sl* **12a** the female

Tt

genitals **12b** a woman considered sexually (esp in **piece of tail, bit of tail**) **13** the foot of a page **14** the lower end of a pool or part of a stream **15** *inf* the course or track of a fleeing person or animal **16** (*modifier*) coming from or situated in the rear: *a tail wind* **17** **turn tail** to run away; escape **18** **with one's tail between one's legs** in a state of utter defeat or confusion ▷ *vb* **19** to form or cause to form the tail **20** to remove the tail of (an animal) **21** (*tr*) to remove the stalk of **22** (*tr*) to connect (objects, ideas, etc) together by or as if by the tail **23** (*tr*) *inf* to follow stealthily **24** (*intr*) (of a vessel) to assume a specified position, as when at a mooring **25** to build the end of (a brick, joist, etc) into a wall or (of a brick, etc) to have one end built into a wall ▷ See also **tail off, tail out, tails** [OE *tægel*] > **'tailless** *adj*

tail² (teɪl) *law* ▷ *n* **1** the limitation of an estate or interest to a person and the heirs of his body ▷ *adj* **2** (*immediately postpositive*) limited in this way [C15 from OF *taille* a division; see TAILOR] > **'tailless** *adj*

tailback ('teɪl,bæk) *n* a queue of traffic stretching back from an obstruction

tailboard ('teɪl,bɔːd) *n* a board at the rear of a lorry, etc, that can be removed or let down

tail coat *n* **1** a man's black coat having a horizontal cut over the hips and a tapering tail with a vertical slit up to the waist **2** a cutaway frock coat, part of morning dress

tail covert *n* any of the covert feathers of a bird covering the bases of the tail feathers

tail end *n* the last, endmost, or final part

tailgate ('teɪl,geɪt) *n* **1** another name for **tailboard** **2** a door at the rear of a hatchback vehicle ▷ *vb* **tailgates, tailgating, tailgated** **3** to drive very close behind (a vehicle) > **'tail,gater** *n*

tail gate *n* a gate that is used to control the flow of water at the lower end of a lock

tailing ('teɪlɪŋ) *n* the part of a beam, rafter, projecting brick, etc, embedded in a wall

tailings ('teɪlɪŋz) *pl n* waste left over after certain processes, such as from an ore-crushing plant or in milling grain

tail-light ('teɪl,laɪt) *or* **tail lamp** *n* other names for **rear light**

tail off *or* **away** *vb* (*adv; usually intr*) to decrease or cause to decrease in quantity, degree, etc, esp gradually

tailor ('teɪlə) *n* **1** a person who makes, repairs, or alters outer garments, esp menswear. Related adj: **sartorial** **2** a voracious and active marine food fish of Australia ▷ *vb* **3** to cut or style (material, etc) to satisfy certain requirements **4** (*tr*) to adapt so as to make suitable **5** (*intr*) to work as a tailor [C13 from Anglo-Norman *taillour*, from OF *taillier* to cut, from L *tālea* a cutting] > **'tailored** *adj*

tailorbird ('teɪlə,bɜːd) *n* any of several tropical Asian warblers that build nests by sewing together large leaves using plant fibres

tailor-made *adj* **1** made by a tailor to fit exactly **2** perfectly meeting a particular purpose ▷ *n* **3** a tailor-made garment **4** *inf* a factory-made cigarette

tailor's chalk *n* pipeclay used by tailors and dressmakers to mark seams, darts, etc, on material

tailor's-tack *n* one of a series of loose looped stitches used to transfer markings for seams, darts, etc, from a paper pattern to material

tail out *vb* (*tr, adv*) NZ to guide (timber) as it emerges from a circular saw

tailpiece ('teɪl,piːs) *n* **1** an extension or appendage that lengthens or completes something **2** a decorative design at the foot of a page or end of a chapter **3** *music* a piece of wood to which the strings of a violin, etc, are attached at their lower end **4** a short beam or rafter that has one end embedded in a wall

tailpipe ('teɪl,paɪp) *n* a pipe from which exhaust gases are discharged from an engine, esp the terminal pipe of the exhaust system of a motor vehicle

tailplane ('teɪl,pleɪn) *n* a small horizontal wing at the tail of an aircraft to provide longitudinal stability. Also called (esp US): **horizontal stabilizer**

tailrace ('teɪl,reɪs) *n* a channel that carries water away from a water wheel, turbine, etc

tail rotor *n* a small propeller fitted to the rear of a helicopter to counteract the torque reaction of the main rotor and thus prevent the body of the helicopter from rotating in an opposite direction

tails (teɪlz) *pl n* **1** an informal name for **tail coat** ▷ *interj, adv* **2** with the reverse side of a coin uppermost

tailskid ('teɪl,skɪd) *n* **1** a runner under the tail of an aircraft **2** a rear-wheel skid of a motor vehicle

tailspin ('teɪl,spɪn) *n* **1** *aeronautics* another name for **spin** (sense 16) **2** *inf* a state of confusion or panic

tailstock ('teɪl,stɒk) *n* a casting that slides on the bed of a lathe and is locked in position to support the free end of a workpiece

tailwind ('teɪl,wɪnd) *n* a wind blowing in the same direction as the course of an aircraft or ship

Taimyr Peninsula (*Russian* taj'mir) *n* a large peninsula of N central Russia, between the Kara Sea and the Laptev Sea. Also called: **Taymyr Peninsula**

Tainan *or* **T'ai-nan** ('taɪ'næn) *n* a city in the SW Republic of China (Taiwan): an early centre of Chinese emigration from the mainland; largest city and capital of the island (1638–1885); Chengkung University. Pop: 728 060 (2000 est)

Taínaron ('tɛnarɔn) *n* transliteration of the Modern Greek name for (Cape) **Matapan**

Taino ('taɪnəʊ) *n* **1** (*pl* **Tainos** *or* **Taino**) a member of an American Indian people of the West Indies **2** the language of this people

taint (teɪnt) *vb* **1** to affect or be affected by pollution or contamination **2** to tarnish (someone's reputation, etc) ▷ *n* **3** a defect or flaw **4** a trace of contamination or infection [C14 (infl. by *attaint* infected, from ATTAIN) from OF *teindre* to dye, from L *tingere*] > **'taintless** *adj*

taipan ('taɪ,pæn) *n* a large highly venomous Australian snake [C20 from Abor.]

Taipei *or* **T'ai-pei** ('taɪ'peɪ) *n* the capital of the Republic of China (Taiwan), at the N tip of the island: became capital in 1885; industrial centre; two universities. Pop: 2 641 312 (2000 est)
▷ www.taipei.gov.tw/English

Taisho (taɪ'ʃəʊ) *n* **1** the period of Japanese history and artistic style associated with the reign of Emperor Yoshihito (1912–26) **2** the throne name of Yoshihito (1879–1926), emperor of Japan (1912–26)

Taiwan ('taɪ'wɑːn) *n* an island in SE Asia between the East China Sea and the South China Sea, off the SE coast of the People's Republic of China: the principal territory of the Republic of China. Pop: 22 340 000 (2001 est). Former name: **Formosa** > **,Taiwan'ese** *adj, n*
▷ http://gio.gov.tw
▷ www.tbroc.gov.tw

Taiwan Strait *n* another name for **Formosa Strait**

Taiyuan *or* **T'ai-yüan** ('taɪjuː'ɑːn) *n* a city in N China, capital of Shanxi: founded before 450 AD; an industrial centre, surrounded by China's largest reserves of high-grade bituminous coal. Pop: 1 500 000 (1991 est)

Ta'izz (tæ'ɪz, teɪ'iːz) *n* a town in SW Yemen, formerly in North Yemen: agricultural trading centre. Pop: 178 043 (1995 est)

taj (tɑːdʒ) *n* a tall conical cap worn as a mark of distinction by Muslims [via Ar. from Persian: crown]

Tajik *or* **Tadzhik** ('tɑːdʒɪk, tɑː'dʒiːk) *n* **1** a member of a Muslim people of Tajikistan **2** the language of this people

Tajikistan, Tadzhikistan, *or* **Tadjikistan** (tɑː,dʒɪkɪ'stɑːn, -stæn) *n* a republic in central Asia: under Uzbek rule from the 15th century until taken over

by Russia in the 1860s, it became an autonomous Soviet republic in 1929 and gained full independence from the Soviet Union in 1991; it is mainly mountainous. Official language: Tajiki. Religion: believers are mainly Muslim. Currency: somoni. Capital: Dushanbe. Pop: 6 252 000 (2001 est). Area: 143 100 sq km (55 240 sq miles)
▷ http://tajikistan.tajnet.com/english/aboutland.htm
▷ www.tajiktour.tajnet.com

Taj Mahal ('tɑːdʒ mə'hɑːl) *n* a white marble mausoleum in central India, in Agra on the Jumna River: built (1632–43) by the emperor Shah Jahan in memory of his beloved wife, Mumtaz Mahal; regarded as the finest example of Mogul architecture [Urdu, literally: crown of buildings]

Tajo ('taxo) *n* the Spanish name for the **Tagus**

takahe ('tɑːkə,hiː) *n* a rare flightless New Zealand rail. Also called: **notornis** [from Maori]

Takamatsu (,tækə'mætsuː) *n* a port in SW Japan, on NE Shikoku on the Inland Sea. Pop: 330 997 (1995)

Takao (tæ'kaʊ) *n* the Japanese name for **Kaohsiung**

take[1] (teɪk) *vb* **takes, taking, took, taken** (*mainly tr*) **1** (*also intr*) to gain possession of (something) by force or effort **2** to appropriate or steal **3** to receive or accept into a relationship with oneself: *to take a wife* **4** to pay for or buy **5** to rent or lease **6** to obtain by regular payment **7** to win **8** to obtain or derive from a source **9** to assume the obligations of: *to take office* **10** to endure, esp with fortitude: *to take punishment* **11** to adopt as a symbol of duty, etc: *to take the veil* **12** to receive in a specified way: *she took the news very well* **13** to adopt as one's own: *to take someone's part in a quarrel* **14** to receive and make use of: *to take advice* **15** to receive into the body, as by eating, inhaling, etc **16** to eat, drink, etc, esp habitually **17** to have or be engaged in for one's benefit or use: *to take a rest* **18** to work at or study: *to take economics at college* **19** to make, do, or perform (an action) **20** to make use of: *to take an opportunity* **21** to put into effect: *to take measures* **22** (*also intr*) to make a photograph of or admit of being photographed **23** to act or perform **24** to write down or copy: *to take notes* **25** to experience or feel: *to take offence* **26** to consider or regard: *I take him to be honest* **27** to accept as valid: *I take your point* **28** to hold or maintain in the mind: *his father took a dim view of his career* **29** to deal or contend with **30** to use as a particular case: *take hotels for example* **31** (*intr;* often foll by *from*) to diminish or detract: *the actor's bad performance took from the effect of the play* **32** to confront successfully: *the horse took the jump at the third attempt* **33** (*intr*) to have or produce the intended effect: *her vaccination took* **34** (*intr*) (of plants, etc) to start growing successfully **35** to aim or direct: *he took a swipe at his opponent* **36** to deal a blow to in a specified place **37** *arch* to have sexual intercourse with (a woman) **38** to remove from a place **39** to carry along or have in one's possession **40** to convey or transport **41** to use as a means of transport: *I shall take the bus* **42** to conduct or lead **43** to escort or accompany **44** to bring or deliver to a state, position, etc: *his ability took him to the forefront* **45** to seek: *to take cover* **46** to ascertain by measuring, etc: *to take a pulse* **47** (*intr*) (of a mechanism) to catch or engage (a part) **48** to put an end to: *she took her own life* **49** to come upon unexpectedly **50** to contract: *he took a chill* **51** to affect or attack: *the fever took him one night* **52** (*copula*) to become suddenly or be rendered (ill): *he was taken sick* **53** (*also intr*) to absorb or become absorbed by something: *to take a polish* **54** (*usually passive*) to charm: *she was very taken with the puppy* **55** (*intr*) to be or become popular; win favour **56** to require: *that task will take all your time* **57** to subtract or deduct **58** to hold: *the suitcase won't take all your clothes* **59** to quote or copy **60** to proceed to occupy: *to take a seat* **61** (often foll by *to*) to use or employ: *to take steps to ascertain the answer* **62** to win or capture (a trick, piece, etc) **63** *sl* to cheat, deceive, or victimize **64** **take five** (*or* **ten**) *inf, chiefly US & Canad* to take a break of five (or ten) minutes **65** **take it** **65a** to assume; believe **65b** *inf* to stand up to or endure criticism, harsh treatment, etc **66** **take one's time** to use as much time as is needed **67** **take (someone's) name in vain** **67a** to use a name, esp of God, disrespectfully or irreverently **67b** *jocular* to say (someone's) name **68** **take upon oneself** to assume the right to do or responsibility for something ▷ *n* **69** the act of taking **70** the number of quarry killed or captured **71** *inf, chiefly US* the amount of anything taken, esp money **72** *films, music* **72a** one of a series of recordings from which the best will be selected **72b** the process of taking one such recording **72c** a scene photographed without interruption **73** *inf, chiefly US* a version or interpretation: *Cronenberg's harsh take on the sci-fi story* ▷ See also **take after, take against,** etc [OE *tacan*] > '**takable** *or* '**takeable** *adj* > '**taker** *n*

take[2] ('tɑːkɪ) *n* NZ a topic or cause [Maori]

take after *vb* (*intr, prep*) to resemble in appearance, character, behaviour, etc

take against *vb* (*intr, prep*) to start to dislike, esp without good reason

take apart *vb* (*tr, adv*) **1** to separate (something) into component parts **2** to criticize severely

take away *vb* (*tr, adv*) **1** to subtract: *take away four from nine to leave five* ▷ *prep* **2** minus: *nine take away four is five* ▷ *adj* **takeaway** *Brit, Austral, & NZ* **3** sold for consumption away from the premises: *a takeaway meal* **4** selling food for consumption away from the premises: *a takeaway Indian restaurant* ▷ *n* **takeaway** *Brit, Austral, & NZ* **5** a shop or restaurant that sells such food **6** a meal bought at such a shop or restaurant: *we'll have a Chinese takeaway tonight.* Scot word (for senses 3–6): **carry out.** US and Canad word (for senses 3–6): **takeout**

take back *vb* (*adv, mainly tr*) **1** to retract or withdraw (something said, promised, etc) **2** to regain possession of **3** to return for exchange **4** to accept (someone) back (into one's home, affections, etc) **5** to remind one of the past: *that tune really takes me back* **6** (*also intr*) *printing* to move (copy) to the previous line

Tt

take down *vb* (*tr, adv*) **1** to record in writing **2** to dismantle or tear down **3** to lower or reduce in power, arrogance, etc (esp in **take down a peg**) ▷ *adj* **take-down** **4** made or intended to be disassembled

take for *vb* (*tr, prep*) *inf* to consider or suppose to be, esp mistakenly: *the fake coins were taken for genuine; who do you take me for?*

take-home pay *n* the remainder of one's pay after all income tax and other compulsory deductions have been made

take in *vb* (*tr, adv*) **1** to understand **2** to include **3** to receive into one's house in exchange for payment: *to take in lodgers* **4** to make (clothing, etc) smaller by altering seams **5** *inf* to cheat or deceive **6** US to go to: *let's take in a movie tonight*

taken ('teɪkən) *vb* **1** the past participle of **take** ▷ *adj* **2** (*postpositive;* foll by *with*) enthusiastically impressed (by); infatuated (with)

take off *vb* (*adv*) **1** (*tr*) to remove (a garment) **2** (*intr*) (of an aircraft) to become airborne **3** *inf* to set out or cause to set out on a journey: *they took off for Spain* **4** (*tr*) (of a disease) to kill **5** (*tr*) *inf* to mimic **6** (*intr*) *inf* to become successful or popular ▷ *n* **takeoff** **7** the act or process of making an aircraft airborne **8** the stage of a country's economic development when rapid and sustained economic growth is first achieved **9** *inf* an act of mimicry

take on *vb* (*adv, mainly tr*) **1** to employ or hire **2** to assume or acquire: *his voice took on a plaintive note* **3** to agree to do; undertake **4** to compete against; fight **5** (*intr*) *inf* to exhibit great emotion, esp grief

take out *vb* (*tr, adv*) **1** to extract or remove **2** to obtain or secure (a licence, patent, etc) **3** to go out with; escort **4** *bridge* to bid a different suit from (one's partner) in order to rescue him or her from a difficult contract **5** *sl* to kill or destroy **6** *Austral inf* to win, esp in sport **7** **take it** *or* **a lot out of** *inf* to sap the energy or vitality of **8** **take out on** *inf* to vent (anger, etc) on **9** **take someone out of himself** (*or* **herself**) *inf* to make someone forget his or her anxieties, problems, etc ▷ *adj* **takeout** **10** *bridge* of or designating a conventional informatory bid, asking one's partner to bid another suit ▷ *adj, n* **takeout** **11** the US and Canad word for **takeaway** (senses 3–6)

take over *vb* (*adv*) **1** to assume the control or management of **2** *printing* to move (copy) to the next line ▷ *n* **takeover** **3** the act of seizing or assuming power, control, etc

take to *vb* (*intr, prep*) **1** to make for; flee to: *to take to the hills* **2** to form a liking for **3** to have recourse to: *to take to the bottle*

take up *vb* (*adv, mainly tr*) **1** to adopt the study, practice, or activity of: *to take up gardening* **2** to shorten (a garment) **3** to pay off (a note, mortgage, etc) **4** to agree to or accept (an invitation, etc) **5** to pursue further or resume (something): *he took up French where he left off* **6** to absorb (a liquid) **7** to act as a patron to **8** to occupy or fill (space or time) **9** to interrupt, esp in order to contradict or criticize **10** *Austral & NZ* to occupy and break in (uncultivated land): *he took up some hundreds of acres in the back country* **11** **take up on** **11a** to argue with (someone): *can I take you up on two points in your talk?* **11b** to accept what is offered by (someone): *let me take you up on your invitation* **12** **take up with** **12a** to discuss with (someone); refer to **12b** (*intr*) to begin to keep company or associate with ▷ *n* **take-up** **13a** the claiming of something, esp a state benefit **13b** (*as modifier*): *take-up rate*

takin ('tɑːkiːn) *n* a massive bovid mammal of S Asia, having a shaggy coat, short legs, and horns [C19 from Tibetan native name]

taking ('teɪkɪŋ) *adj* **1** charming, fascinating, or intriguing **2** *inf* infectious; catching ▷ *n* **3** something taken **4** (*pl*) receipts; earnings > '**takingly** *adv* > '**takingness** *n*

Takoradi (ˌtɑːkəˈrɑːdɪ) *n* the chief port of Ghana, in the southwest on the Gulf of Guinea: modern harbour opened in 1928. Pop (with Sekondi): 103 600 (1988 est)

talapoin ('tæləˌpɔɪn) *n* **1** a small W African monkey **2** (in Myanmar and Thailand) a Buddhist monk [C16 from F, lit.: Buddhist monk, from Port. *talapão*; orig. jocular, from the appearance of the monkey]

talaria (təˈlɛərɪə) *pl n Greek myth* winged sandals [C16 from L, from *tālāris* belonging to the ankle, from *tālus* ankle]

Talavera de la Reina (*Spanish* talaˈβera ðe la ˈrɛina) *n* a walled town in central Spain, on the Tagus River: scene of the defeat of the French by British and Spanish forces (1809) during the Peninsular War; agricultural processing centre. Pop: 68 640 (1991)

Talbot ('tɒlbət) *n* (**William Henry**) **Fox** 1800–77, British scientist, a pioneer of photography, who developed the calotype process

talc (tælk) *n also* **talcum** **1** See **talcum powder** **2** a soft mineral, consisting of magnesium silicate, used in the manufacture of ceramics and paints and as a filler in talcum powder, etc ▷ *vb* **talcs, talcking, talcked** *or* **talcs, talcing, talced** **3** (*tr*) to apply talc to [C16 from Med. L *talcum*, from Ar. *talq* mica, from Persian *talk*] > '**talcose** *or* '**talcous** *adj*

Talca (*Spanish* 'talka) *n* a city in central Chile: scene of the declaration of Chilean independence (1818). Pop: 174 858 (1999 est)

Talcahuano (*Spanish* talkaˈwano) *n* a port in S central Chile, near Concepción on an inlet of the Pacific: oil refinery. Pop: 269 265 (1999 est)

talcum powder ('tælkəm) *n* a powder made of purified talc, usually scented, used for perfuming the body and for absorbing excess moisture. Often shortened to **talcum** or **talc**

tale (teɪl) *n* **1** a report, narrative, or story **2** one of a group of short stories **3a** a malicious or meddlesome rumour or piece of gossip **3b** (*in combination*): *talebearer; taleteller* **4** a fictitious or false statement **5** **tell tales** **5a** to tell fanciful lies **5b** to report malicious stories, trivial complaints, etc, esp to someone in authority **6** **tell a tale** to reveal something important **7** **tell its own tale** to be self-evident **8** *arch* a number; amount [OE *talu* list]

talent ('tælənt) *n* **1** innate ability, aptitude, or faculty; above average ability: *a talent for cooking; a child with talent* **2** a person or persons possessing such ability **3** any of various ancient units of weight and money **4** *inf* members of the opposite sex collectively: *the local talent* [OE *talente*, from L *talenta*, pl. of *talentum* sum of money, from Gk *talanton* unit of money; in Med. L the sense was extended to ability through the infl. of the parable of the talents (Matthew 25:14–30)] > '**talented** *adj*

talent scout *n* a person whose occupation is the search for talented sportsmen, performers, etc, for engagements as professionals

tales ('teɪliːz) *n law* **1** (*functioning as pl*) a group of persons summoned to fill vacancies on a jury panel **2** (*functioning as sing*) the writ summoning such jurors [C15 from Med. L *tālēs dē circumstantibus* such men from among the bystanders, from L *tālis* such] > '**talesman** *n*

Taliban *or* **Taleban** ('tælɪˌbæn) *n* a militant fundamentalist Islamic organization in Afghanistan [C20 from Ar. *tāliban* seekers]

Taliesin (ˌtælɪˈɛsɪn) *n* 6th century AD, Welsh bard; supposed author of 12 heroic poems in the *Book of Taliesin*

taligrade ('tælɪˌgreɪd) *adj* (of mammals) walking on the outer side of the foot [C20 from NL, from L *tālus* ankle, heel + -GRADE]

talion ('tælɪən) *n* the system or legal principle of making the punishment correspond to the crime; retaliation [C15 via OF from L *tāliō*, from *tālis* such]

talipes ('tælɪˌpiːz) *n* **1** a congenital deformity of the foot by which it is twisted in any of various positions **2** a technical name for **club foot** [C19 NL, from L *tālus* ankle + *pēs* foot]

talipot *or* **talipot palm** ('tælɪˌpɒt) *n* a palm tree of the East Indies, having large leaves that are used for fans, thatching houses, etc [C17 from Bengali: palm leaf, from Sansk. *tālī* fan palm + *pattra* leaf]

talisman ('tælɪzmən) *n, pl* **talismans** **1** a stone or other small object, usually inscribed or carved, believed to protect the wearer from evil influences **2** anything thought to have magical or protective powers [C17 via F or Sp. from Ar. *tilsam*, from Med. Gk *telesma* ritual, from Gk: consecration, from *telein* to perform a rite, complete] > **talismanic** (ˌtælɪzˈmænɪk) *adj*

talk (tɔːk) *vb* **1** (*intr*; often foll by *to* or *with*) to express one's thoughts, feelings, or desires by means of words (to) **2** (*intr*) to communicate by other means: *lovers talk with their eyes* **3** (*intr*; usually foll by *about*) to exchange ideas or opinions (about) **4** (*intr*) to articulate words **5** (*tr*) to give voice to; utter: *to talk rubbish* **6** (*tr*) to discuss: *to talk business* **7** (*intr*) to reveal information **8** (*tr*) to know how to communicate in (a language or idiom): *he talks English* **9** (*intr*) to spread rumours or gossip **10** (*intr*) to make sounds suggestive of talking **11** (*intr*) to be effective or persuasive: *money talks* **12** **now you're talking** *inf* at last you're saying something agreeable **13** **talk big** to boast **14** **talk the talk** to speak convincingly on a particular subject, showing apparent mastery of its jargon and themes; often used in conjunction with the expression *walk the walk*. See also **walk** (sense 13) **15** **you can talk** *inf* **15a** you don't have to worry about doing a particular thing yourself **15b** Also: **you can't talk** you yourself are guilty of offending in the very matter you are upholding or decrying ▷ *n* **16** a speech or lecture **17** an exchange of ideas or thoughts **18** idle chatter, gossip, or rumour **19** a subject of conversation; theme **20** (*often pl*) a conference, discussion, or negotiation **21** a specific manner of speaking: *children's talk* ▷ See also **talk about, talk back,** etc [C13 *talkien*] > '**talker** *n*

talk about *vb* (*intr, prep*) **1** to discuss **2** used informally and often ironically to add emphasis to a statement: *all his plays have such ridiculous plots – talk about good drama!*

talkative ('tɔːkətɪv) *adj* given to talking a great deal > '**talkatively** *adv* > '**talkativeness** *n*

talk back *vb* (*intr, adv*) **1** to answer boldly or impudently **2** NZ to conduct a telephone dialogue for immediate transmission over the air ▷ *n* **talkback 3** *television, radio* a system of telephone links enabling spoken directions to be given during the production of a programme **4** NZ a broadcast telephone dialogue

talk down *vb* (*adv*) **1** (*intr; often foll by* to) to behave (towards) in a superior manner **2** (*tr*) to override (a person) by continuous or loud talking **3** (*tr*) to give instructions to (an aircraft) by radio to enable it to land

talkie ('tɔːkɪ) *n inf* an early film with a soundtrack. Full name: **talking picture**

Talking Book *n trademark* a recording of a book, designed to be used by blind people

talking head *n* (on television) a person, shown only from the shoulders up, who speaks without illustrative material

talking-to *n inf* a session of criticism, as of a subordinate by a person in authority

talk into *vb* (*tr, prep*) to persuade to by talking: *I talked him into buying the house*

talk out *vb* (*tr, adv*) **1** to resolve or eliminate by talking **2** *Brit* to block (a bill, etc) in a legislative body by lengthy discussion **3 talk out of** to dissuade from by talking

talk round *vb* **1** (*tr, adv*) Also: **talk over** to persuade to one's opinion **2** (*intr, prep*) to discuss (a subject), esp without coming to a conclusion

talk shop *vb* to talk about one's profession, esp at a social occasion

tall (tɔːl) *adj* **1** of more than average height **2** (*postpositive*) having a specified height: *five feet tall* [C14 (in the sense: big, comely, valiant)] > '**tallness** *n*

tallage ('tælɪdʒ) *n English history* **a** a tax levied by kings on Crown lands and royal towns **b** a toll levied by a lord upon his tenants or by a feudal lord upon his vassals [C13 from OF *taillage*, from *taillier* to cut; see TAILOR]

Tallahassee (ˌtælə'hæsɪ) *n* a city in N Florida, capital of the state: two universities. Pop: 150 624 (2000)

Tall Blacks *pl n* **the** the international basketball team of New Zealand

tallboy ('tɔːlˌbɔɪ) *n* **1** a high chest of drawers made in two sections placed one on top of the other **2** a fitting on the top of a chimney to prevent downdraughts

Talleyrand-Périgord ('tælɪˌrænd'pɛrɪɡɔː; *French* talɛrɑ̃periɡɔr) *n* **Charles Maurice** (ʃarl mɔris) 1754–1838, French statesman; foreign minister (1797–1807; 1814–15). He secretly negotiated with the Allies against Napoleon I from 1808 and was France's representative at the Congress of Vienna (1815)

Tallinn *or* **Tallin** ('tælɪn) *n* the capital of Estonia, on the Gulf of Finland: founded by the Danes in 1219; a port and naval base. Pop: 404 000 (2000 est). German name: **Reval**

▷ http://tallinn.ee

Tallis ('tælɪs) *n* **Thomas** ?1505–85, English composer and organist; noted for his music for the Anglican liturgy

tallith ('tælɪθ) *n* a shawl with fringed corners worn by Jewish males, esp during religious services [C17 from Heb. *tallīt*]

tall order *n inf* a difficult or unreasonable request

tallow ('tæləʊ) *n* **1** a fatty substance extracted chiefly from the suet of sheep and cattle: used for making soap, candles, food, etc ▷ *vb* **2** (*tr*) to cover or smear with tallow [OE *tælg*, a dye] > '**tallowy** *adj*

tallowwood ('tæləʊˌwʊd) *n Austral* a tall eucalyptus tree having soft fibrous bark and a greasy timber

tall poppy *n Austral inf* a prominent or highly paid person

tall poppy syndrome *n Austral inf* a tendency to disparage any person who has achieved great prominence or wealth

tall ship *n* any square-rigged sailing ship

tall story *n inf* an exaggerated or incredible account of something

tally ('tælɪ) *vb* **tallies, tallying, tallied 1** (*intr*) to correspond one with the other: *the two stories don't tally* **2** (*tr*) to supply with an identifying tag **3** (*intr*) to keep score **4** (*tr*) *obs* to record or mark ▷ *n, pl* **tallies 5** any record of debit, credit, the score in a game, etc **6** *Austral & NZ* the number of sheep shorn in a specified period **7** an identifying label or mark **8** a counterpart or duplicate of something **9** a stick used (esp formerly) as a record of the amount of a debt according to the notches cut in it **10** a notch or mark made on such a stick **11** a mark used to represent a certain number in counting [C15 from Med. L *tālea*, from L: cutting]

tally clerk *n Austral & NZ* a person, esp on a wharf or in an airport, who checks the count of goods being loaded or unloaded

tally-ho (ˌtælɪ'həʊ) *interj* **1** the cry of a participant at a hunt when the quarry is sighted ▷ *n, pl* **tally-hos 2** an instance of crying tally-ho **3** another name for a **four-in-hand** (sense 1) ▷ *vb* **tally-hos, tally-hoing, tally-hoed** *or* **tally-ho'd 4** (*intr*) to make the cry of tally-ho [C18 ?from F *taïaut* cry used in hunting]

tallyman ('tælɪmən) *n, pl* **tallymen 1** a scorekeeper or recorder **2** *dialect* a travelling salesman for a firm specializing in hire-purchase > '**tallyˌwoman** *fem n*

Talmud ('tælmʊd) *n Judaism* the primary source of Jewish religious law, consisting of the Mishnah and the Gemara [C16 from Heb. *talmūdh*, lit.: instruction, from *lāmadh* to learn] > **Tal'mudic** *or* **Tal'mudical** *adj* > '**Talmudism** *n* > '**Talmudist** *n*

▷ http://oru.edu/university/library/guides/talmud.html

▷ http://aishdas.org/webshas/

talon ('tælən) *n* **1** a sharply hooked claw, esp of a bird of prey **2** anything resembling this **3** the part of a lock that the key presses on when it is turned **4** *piquet, etc* the pile of cards left after the deal **5** *archit* another name for **ogee 6** *stock exchange* a printed slip attached to some bearer bonds to enable the holder to apply for a new sheet of coupons [C14 from OF: heel, from L *tālus*] > '**taloned** *adj*

Talos ('teɪlɒs) *n Greek myth* the nephew and apprentice of Daedalus, who surpassed his uncle as an inventor and was killed by him out of jealousy

talus[1] ('teɪləs) *n, pl* **tali** (-laɪ) the bone of the ankle that articulates with the leg bones to form the ankle joint; anklebone [C18 from L: ankle]

talus[2] ('teɪləs) *n, pl* **taluses 1** *geol* another name for **scree 2** *fortifications* the sloping side of a wall [C17 from F, from L *talūtium* slope, ? of Iberian origin]

tam (tæm) *n* short for **tam-o'-shanter**

tamale (tə'mɑːlɪ) *n* a Mexican dish made of minced meat mixed with crushed maize and seasonings, wrapped in maize husks and steamed [C19 erroneously for *tamal*, from Mexican Sp., from Nahuatl *tamalli*]

tamandua (ˌtæmən'dʊə) *n* a small arboreal mammal of Central and South America, having a tubular mouth specialized for feeding on termites. Also called: **lesser anteater** [C17 via Port. from Tupi: ant trapper, from *taixi* ant + *mondê* to catch]

tamarack ('tæməˌræk) *n* **1** any of several North American larches **2** the wood of any of these trees [C19 of Amerind origin]

tamari (tə'mɑːrɪ) *n* a Japanese variety of soy sauce [Japanese]

tamarillo (ˌtæməˈrɪləʊ) *n, pl* **tamarillos** another name for **tree tomato**

tamarin (ˈtæmərɪn) *n* any of numerous small monkeys of South and Central American forests; similar to the marmosets [c18 via F, of Amerind origin]

tamarind (ˈtæmərɪnd) *n* **1** a tropical evergreen tree having yellow flowers and brown pods **2** the fruit of this tree, used as a food and to make beverages and medicines **3** the wood of this tree [c16 from Med. L *tamarindus*, ult. from Ar. *tamr hindī* Indian date]

tamarisk (ˈtæmərɪsk) *n* any of a genus of trees and shrubs of the Mediterranean region and S and SE Asia, having scalelike leaves, slender branches, and feathery flower clusters [c15 from LL *tamariscus*, from L *tamarix*]

Tamatave (*French* tamatav) *n* the former name (until 1979) of **Toamasina**

Tamaulipas (*Spanish* tamauˈlipas) *n* a state of NE Mexico, on the Gulf of Mexico. Capital: Ciudad Victoria. Pop: 2 747 114 (2000). Area: 79 829 sq km (30 822 sq miles)

Tambo (ˈtæmbəʊ) *n* **Oliver** 1917–93, South African politician; president (1977–91) of the African National Congress. He was arrested (1956) with Nelson Mandela but released (1957)

Tambora (ˈtæmbəˌrɑː) *n* a volcano in Indonesia, on N Sumbawa: violent eruption of 1815 reduced its height from about 4000 m (13 000 ft) to 2850 m (9400 ft)

tambour (ˈtæmbʊə) *n* **1** *real tennis* the sloping buttress on one side of the receiver's end of the court **2** a small embroidery frame, consisting of two hoops over which the fabric is stretched while being worked **3** embroidered work done on such a frame **4** a sliding door on desks, cabinets, etc, made of thin strips of wood glued onto a canvas backing **5** *archit* a wall that is circular in plan, esp one that supports a dome or one that is surrounded by a colonnade **6** a drum ▷ *vb* **7** to embroider on a tambour [c15 from F, from *tabour* TABOR]

tamboura (tæmˈbʊərə) *n* a stringed instrument with a long neck used in Indian music to provide a drone [from Persian *tanbūr*, from Ar. *tunbūr*]

tambourin (ˈtæmbʊrɪn) *n* **1** an 18th-century Provençal folk dance **2** a piece of music composed for or in the rhythm of this dance **3** a small drum [c18 from F: a little drum]

tambourine (ˌtæmbəˈriːn) *n* *music* a percussion instrument consisting of a single drumhead of skin stretched over a circular wooden frame hung with pairs of metal discs that jingle when it is struck or shaken [c16 from MFlemish *tamborijn* a little drum, from OF: TAMBOURIN] > ˌ**tambouˈrinist** *n*

Tambov (*Russian* tamˈbɔf) *n* an industrial city in W Russia: founded in 1636 as a Muscovite fort; a major engineering centre. Pop: 315 100 (1999 est)

Tamburlaine (ˈtæmbəˌleɪn) *n* a variant of **Tamerlane**

tame (teɪm) *adj* **1** changed by man from a wild state into a domesticated or cultivated condition **2** (of animals) not fearful of human contact **3** meek or submissive **4** flat, insipid, or uninspiring ▷ *vb* **tames, taming, tamed** (*tr*) **5** to make tame; domesticate **6** to break the spirit of, subdue, or curb **7** to tone down, soften, or mitigate [OE *tam*] > ˈ**tamable** *or* ˈ**tameable** *adj* > ˈ**tamely** *adv* > ˈ**tameness** *n* > ˈ**tamer** *n*

Tamerlane (ˈtæməˌleɪn) *or* **Tamburlaine** *n* Turkic name *Timur* (tiːˈmʊə) ?1336–1405, Mongol conqueror of the area from Mongolia to the Mediterranean; ruler of Samarkand (1369–1405). He defeated the Turks at Angora (1402) and died while invading China

Tameside (ˈteɪmˌsaɪd) *n* a unitary authority of NW England, in Greater Manchester. Pop: 213 045 (2001). Area: 103 sq km (40 sq miles)

Tamil (ˈtæmɪl) *n* **1** (*pl* **Tamils** *or* **Tamil**) a member of a mixed Dravidian and Caucasoid people of S India and Sri Lanka **2** the language of this people ▷ *adj* **3** of or relating to this people or their language

Tamil Nadu (ˈtæmɪl nɑːˈduː) *n* a state of SE India, on the Coromandel Coast: reorganized in 1956 and 1960 and made smaller; consists of a coastal plain backed by hills, including the Nilgiri Hills in the west. Capital: Madras. Pop: 62 110 839 (2001). Area: 130 058 sq km (50 216 sq miles). Former name (until 1968): **Madras**

Tammerfors (tamərˈfɔrs) *n* the Swedish name for **Tampere**

tammy (ˈtæmɪ) *n, pl* **tammies** another word for **tam-o'-shanter**

tam-o'-shanter (ˌtæməˈʃæntə) *n* a Scottish brimless wool or cloth cap with a bobble in the centre [c19 after the hero of Burns's poem *Tam o' Shanter* (1790)]

tamoxifen (təˈmɒksɪˌfɛn) *n* a drug that antagonizes the action of oestrogen and is used to treat breast cancer and some types of infertility in women [c20 from T(RANS-) + AM(INE) + OXY-² + PHEN(OL)]

tamp (tæmp) *vb* (*tr*) **1** to force or pack down firmly by repeated blows **2** to pack sand, earth, etc, into (a drill hole) over an explosive [c17 prob. back formation from *tampin* (obs. var. of TAMPION), taken as a present participle *tamping*]

Tampa (ˈtæmpə) *n* a port and resort in W Florida, on **Tampa Bay** (an arm of the Gulf of Mexico): two universities. Pop: 303 447 (2000)

tamper¹ (ˈtæmpə) *vb* (*intr*) **1** (usually foll by *with*) to interfere or meddle **2** to use bribery or blackmail **3** (usually foll by *with*) to attempt to influence, esp by bribery [c16 alteration of TEMPER (vb)] > ˈ**tamperer** *n*

tamper² (ˈtæmpə) *n* **1** a person or thing that tamps, esp an instrument for packing down tobacco in a pipe **2** a casing around the core of a nuclear weapon to increase its efficiency by reflecting neutrons and delaying the expansion

Tampere (*Finnish* ˈtampɛrɛ) *n* a city in SW Finland: the second largest town in Finland; textile manufacturing. Pop: 193 174 (2000 est). Swedish name: **Tammerfors**

Tampico (*Spanish* tamˈpiko) *n* a port and resort in E Mexico, in Tamaulipas on the Pánuco River: oil refining. Pop: 294 789 (2000 est)

tampion (ˈtæmpɪən) *or* **tompion** *n* a plug placed in a gun's muzzle when the gun is not in use [c15 from F: TAMPON]

tampon (ˈtæmpɒn) *n* **1** a plug of lint, cotton wool, etc, inserted into a wound or body cavity to stop the flow of blood, absorb secretions, etc ▷ *vb* **2** (*tr*) to plug (a wound, etc) with a tampon [c19 via F from OF *tapon* a little plug, of Gmc origin] > **tamponage** (ˈtæmpənɪdʒ) *n*

tam-tam *n* another name for **gong** (sense 1) [from Hindi; see TOM-TOM]

Tamworth (ˈtæmwəθ) *n* **1** a market town in W central England, in SE Staffordshire. Pop: 68 440 (1991) **2** a city in SE Australia, in E central New South Wales: industrial centre of an agricultural region. Pop: 33 900 (latest est)

tan¹ (tæn) *n* **1** the brown colour produced by the skin after exposure to ultraviolet rays, esp those of the sun **2** a yellowish-brown colour **3** short for **tanbark** ▷ *vb* **tans, tanning, tanned 4** to go brown or cause to go brown after exposure to ultraviolet rays **5** to convert (a skin or hide) into leather by treating it with a tanning agent **6** (*tr*) *sl* to beat or flog ▷ *adj* **tanner, tannest 7** of the colour tan [OE *tannian* (unattested as infinitive, attested as *getanned*, p.p.), from Med. L *tannāre*, from *tannum* tanbark, ? of Celtic origin] > ˈ**tannable** *adj* > ˈ**tannish** *adj*

tan² (tæn) *abbrev for* tangent (sense 2)

Tana (ˈtɑːnə) *n* **1 Lake** Also called: (Lake) **Tsana** a lake in NW Ethiopia, on a plateau 1800 m (6000 ft) high: the largest lake of Ethiopia; source of the Blue Nile. Area: 3673 sq km (1418 sq miles) **2** a river in E Kenya, rising in the Aberdare Range and flowing in a wide curve east to the Indian Ocean: the longest river in Kenya. Length:

708 km (440 miles) **3** a river in NE Norway, flowing generally northeast as part of the border between Norway and Finland to the Arctic Ocean by Tana Fjord. Length: about 320 km (200 miles). Finnish name: **Teno**

tanager ('tænədʒə) *n* any of a family of American songbirds having a short thick bill and, in the male, a brilliantly coloured plumage [C19 from NL *tanagra*, based on Amerind *tangara*]

Tanagra ('tænəgrə) *n* a town in ancient Boeotia, famous for terracotta figurines of the same name, first discovered in its necropolis

Tanana ('tænənɑː) *n* a river in central Alaska, rising in the Wrangell Mountains and flowing northwest to the Yukon River. Length: about 765 km (475 miles)

Tananarive (*French* tananariv) *n* the former name of **Antananarivo**

tanbark ('tæn,bɑːk) *n* the bark of certain trees, esp the oak, used as a source of tannin

Tancred ('tæŋkrɪd) *n* died 1112, Norman hero of the First Crusade, who played a prominent part in the capture of Jerusalem (1099)

tandem ('tændəm) *n* **1** a bicycle with two sets of pedals and two saddles, arranged one behind the other for two riders **2** a two-wheeled carriage drawn by two horses harnessed one behind the other **3** a team of two horses so harnessed **4** any arrangement of two things in which one is placed behind the other **5 in tandem** together or in conjunction ▷ *adj* **6** *Brit* used as, used in, or routed through an intermediate automatic telephone exchange ▷ *adv* **7** one behind the other [C18 whimsical use of L *tandem* at length, to indicate a long vehicle]

Tandjungpriok *or* **Tanjungpriok** (,tændʒʊŋ'priːɒk) *n* a port in Indonesia, on the NW coast of Java adjoining the capital, Jakarta: a major shipping and distributing centre for the whole archipelago

tandoori (tæn'dʊərɪ) *n* an Indian method of cooking meat or vegetables on a spit in a clay oven [from Urdu, from *tandoor* an oven]

tang (tæŋ) *n* **1** a strong taste or flavour **2** a pungent or characteristic smell **3** a trace, touch, or hint of something **4** the pointed end of a tool, such as a chisel, file, knife, etc, which is fitted into a handle, shaft, or stock [C14 from ON *tangi* point]

Tang (tæŋ) *n* the imperial dynasty of China from 618–907 AD

tanga ('tæŋgə) *n* **1** a triangular loincloth worn by indigenous peoples in tropical America **2** a type of very brief bikini [from Port., ult. of Bantu origin]

Tanga ('tæŋgə) *n* a port in N Tanzania, on the Indian Ocean: Tanzania's second port. Pop: 187 155 (latest est)

Tanganyika (,tæŋgə'njiːkə) *n* **1** a former state in E Africa: became part of German East Africa in 1884; ceded to Britain as a League of Nations mandate in 1919 and as a UN trust territory in 1946; gained independence in 1961 and united with Zanzibar in 1964 as the United Republic of Tanzania **2 Lake** a lake in central Africa between Tanzania and the Democratic Republic of Congo (formerly Zaïre), bordering also on Burundi and Zambia, in the Great Rift Valley: the longest freshwater lake in the world. Area: 32 893 sq km (12 700 sq miles). Length: 676 km (420 miles) > ,**Tangan'yikan** *adj, n*

tangata tiriti (,tʌŋgɑːtə tɪ'riːtɪ) *n* NZ a Maori term for non-Maori people [Maori, lit.: people of the Treaty (of Waitangi)]

tangata whenua (,tʌŋgɑːtə fə'nuːə) *n* NZ the indigenous Maori people of a particular area of New Zealand or of the country as a whole [Maori, lit.: people of the land]

Tange ('tæŋgə) *n* **Kenzo** born 1913, Japanese architect and town planner. His buildings include the Kurashiki city hall (1960), St Mary's Cathedral in Tokyo (1962–64), and the New Tokyo City Hall (1986). He also produced town plans for Skopje, Macedonia (1965), and Abuja, Nigeria (1979)

tangent ('tændʒənt) *n* **1** a geometric line, curve, plane, or curved surface that touches another curve or surface at one point but does not intersect it **2** (of an angle) a trigonometric function that in a right-angled triangle is the ratio of the length of the opposite side to that of the adjacent side; the ratio of sine to cosine. Abbrev: **tan** **3** *music* a small piece of metal that strikes the string of a clavichord **4 on** *or* **at a tangent** on a completely different or divergent course, esp of thought ▷ *adj* **5a** of or involving a tangent **5b** touching at a single point **6** touching [C16 from L *līnea tangēns* the touching line, from *tangere* to touch] > '**tangency** *n*

tangent galvanometer *n* a galvanometer having a vertical coil of wire with a horizontal magnetic needle at its centre. The current to be measured is passed through the coil and produces a proportional magnetic field which deflects the needle

tangential (tæn'dʒɛnʃəl) *adj* **1** of, being, or in the direction of a tangent **2** *astron* (of velocity) in a direction perpendicular to the line of sight of a celestial object **3** of superficial relevance only; digressive > **tan,genti'ality** *n* > **tan'gentially** *adv*

tangerine (,tændʒə'riːn) *n* **1** an Asian citrus tree cultivated for its small orange-like fruits **2** the fruit of this tree, having sweet spicy flesh **3a** a reddish-orange colour **3b** (*as adj*): *a tangerine door* [C19 from TANGIER]

tangi ('tæŋiː) *n* NZ **1** a Maori funeral ceremony **2** *inf* a lamentation

tangible ('tændʒɪbᵊl) *adj* **1** capable of being touched or felt **2** capable of being clearly grasped by the mind **3** having a physical existence [C16 from LL *tangibilis*, from L *tangere* to touch] > ,**tangi'bility** *n* > '**tangibly** *adv*

Tangier (tæn'dʒɪə) *n* a port in N Morocco, on the Strait of Gibraltar: a Phoenician trading post in the 15th century BC; a neutral international zone (1923–56); made the summer capital of Morocco and a free port in 1962; commercial and financial centre. Pop: 521 735 (1994) > ,**Tange'rine** *n, adj*

Tt

tangle ('tæŋgᵊl) *n* **1** a confused or complicated mass of hairs, lines, fibres, etc, knotted or coiled together **2** a complicated problem, condition, or situation ▷ *vb* **tangles, tangling, tangled** **3** to become or cause to become twisted together in a confused mass **4** (*intr*; often foll by *with*) to come into conflict; contend **5** (*tr*) to involve in matters which hinder or confuse **6** (*tr*) to ensnare or trap, as in a net [C14 *tangilen*, var. of *tagilen*, prob. from ON] > '**tangled** *or* '**tangly** *adj*

tango ('tæŋgəʊ) *n, pl* **tangos** **1** a Latin-American dance characterized by long gliding steps and sudden pauses **2** a piece of music composed for or in the rhythm of this dance ▷ *vb* **tangoes, tangoing, tangoed** **3** (*intr*) to perform this dance [C20 from American Sp., prob. of Niger-Congo origin]

tangram ('tæŋgræm) *n* a Chinese puzzle in which a square, cut into a parallelogram, a square, and five triangles, is formed into figures [C19 ?from Chinese *t'ang* Chinese + -GRAM]

Tangshan ('tæŋ'ʃæn) *n* an industrial city in NE China, in Hebei province. Pop: 1 210 842 (1999 est)

Tanguy (*French* tãgi) *n* **Yves** (iv) 1900–55, US surrealist painter, born in France

tangy ('tæŋɪ) *adj* **tangier, tangiest** having a pungent, fresh, or briny flavour or aroma

tanh (θæn, tænʃ) *n* hyperbolic tangent; a hyperbolic function that is the ratio of sinh to cosh [C20 from TAN(GENT) + H(YPERBOLIC)]

Tanis ('teɪnɪs) *n* an ancient city located in the E part of the Nile delta: abandoned after the 6th century BC; at one time the capital of Egypt. Biblical name: **Zoan**

taniwha ('tʌniːfɑː, 'tænəwɑː) *n* NZ a legendary Maori monster that lives in rivers and lakes [Maori]

Tanjore (tæn'dʒɔː) *n* the former name of **Thanjavur**

Tanjungpriok (ˌtændʒʊŋ'priːɒk) *n* a variant spelling of **Tandjungpriok**

tank (tæŋk) *n* **1** a large container or reservoir for liquids or gases **2** an armoured combat vehicle moving on tracks and armed with guns, etc **3** *Brit or US dialect* a reservoir, lake, or pond **4** *sl, chiefly US* a jail **5** Also called: **tankful** the quantity contained in a tank **6** *Austral* a reservoir formed by excavation and damming ▷ *vb* **7** (*tr*) to put or keep in a tank **8** *sl* to defeat heavily ▷ See also **tank up** [C17 from Gujarati (a language of W India) *tānkh* artificial lake, but infl. also by Port. *tanque*, from *estanque* pond, ult. from Vulgar L *stanticāre* (unattested) to block]

tanka ('tɑːŋkə) *n, pl* **tankas** *or* **tanka** a Japanese verse form consisting of five lines, the first and third having five syllables, the others seven [C19 from Japanese, from *tan* short + *ka* verse]

tankage ('tæŋkɪdʒ) *n* **1** the capacity or contents of a tank or tanks **2** the act of storing in a tank or tanks, or a fee charged for this **3** *agriculture* **3a** fertilizer consisting of the dried and ground residues of animal carcasses **3b** a protein supplement feed for livestock

tankard ('tæŋkəd) *n* a large one-handled drinking vessel sometimes fitted with a hinged lid [C14]

tank engine *or* **locomotive** *n* a steam locomotive that carries its water supply in tanks mounted around its boiler

tanker ('tæŋkə) *n* a ship, lorry, or aeroplane designed to carry liquid in bulk, such as oil

tank farming *n* another name for **hydroponics** > **tank farmer** *n*

tank top *n* a sleeveless upper garment with wide shoulder straps and a low neck [C20 after *tank suits*, one-piece bathing costumes of the 1920s worn in tanks or swimming pools]

tank up *vb* (*adv*) *chiefly Brit* **1** to fill the tank of (a vehicle) with petrol **2** *sl* to imbibe or cause to imbibe a large quantity of alcoholic drink

tank wagon *or esp US & Canad* **tank car** *n* a form of railway wagon carrying a tank for the transport of liquids

Tannenberg (*German* 'tanənbɛrk) *n* a village in N Poland, formerly in East Prussia: site of a decisive defeat of the Teutonic Knights by the Poles in 1410 and of a decisive German victory over the Russians in 1914. Polish name: **Stębark**

tanner[1] ('tænə) *n* a person who tans skins and hides

tanner[2] ('tænə) *n* *Brit* an informal word for **sixpence** [C19 from ?]

tannery ('tænərɪ) *n, pl* **tanneries** a place or building where skins and hides are tanned

▷ www.cudahytanning.com/process.htm

Tannhäuser ('tænˌhɔɪzə) *n* 13th-century German minnesinger, identified with a legendary knight. The legend forms the basis of an opera by Wagner

tannic ('tænɪk) *adj* of, relating to, containing, or produced from tan, tannin, or tannic acid

tannie ('tʌnɪ) *n* *S African* a title of respect used to refer to an elderly woman [Afrik., lit.: aunt]

tannin ('tænɪn) *n* any of a class of yellowish compounds found in many plants and used as tanning agents, mordants, medical astringents, etc. Also called: **tannic acid** [C19 from F *tanin*, from TAN[1]]

Tannoy ('tænɔɪ) *n* *trademark* a type of public-address system

Tans (tænz) *pl n* **the** *Irish inf* short for the **Black and Tans**

tansy ('tænzɪ) *n, pl* **tansies** any of numerous plants having yellow flowers in flat-topped clusters and formerly used in medicine and for seasoning [C15 from OF *tanesie*, from Med. L *athanasia* (from its alleged power to prolong life) from Gk: immortality]

Tanta ('tæntə) *n* a city in N Egypt, on the Nile delta: noted for its Muslim festivals. Pop: 371 010 (1996)

tantalite ('tæntəˌlaɪt) *n* a heavy brownish mineral: it occurs in coarse granite and is an ore of tantalum [C19 from TANTALUM + -ITE[1]]

tantalize *or* **tantalise** ('tæntəˌlaɪz) *vb* **tantalizes, tantalizing, tantalized** *or* **tantalises, tantalising, tantalised** (*tr*) to tease or make frustrated, as by tormenting with the sight of something desired but inaccessible [C16 from TANTALUS] > ˌ**tantaliˈzation** *or* ˌ**tantaliˈsation** *n* > ˈ**tantaˌlizing** *or* ˈ**tantaˌlising** *adj* > ˈ**tantaˌlizingly** *or* ˈ**tantaˌlisingly** *adv*

tantalum ('tæntələm) *n* a hard greyish-white metallic element: used in electrolytic rectifiers and in alloys to increase hardness and chemical resistance, esp in surgical instruments. Symbol: Ta; atomic no.: 73; atomic wt.: 180.95 [C19 after TANTALUS, from the metal's incapacity to absorb acids]

tantalus ('tæntələs) *n* *Brit* a case in which bottles may be locked with their contents tantalizingly visible

Tantalus ('tæntələs) *n* *Greek myth* a king, the father of Pelops, punished in Hades for his misdeeds by having to stand in water that recedes when he tries to drink it and under fruit that moves away as he reaches for it

tantamount ('tæntəˌmaʊnt) *adj* (*postpositive; foll by* to) as good (as); equivalent in effect (to) [C17 from Anglo-F *tant amunter* to amount to as much]

tantara ('tæntərə, tæn'tɑːrə) *n* a fanfare or blast, as on a trumpet or horn [C16 from L *taratantara*, imit. of the sound of the tuba]

tantivy (tæn'tɪvɪ) *adv* **1** at full speed; rapidly ▷ *n, pl* **tantivies** *sentence substitute* **2** a hunting cry, esp at full gallop [C17 ? imit. of galloping hooves]

tant mieux *French* (tɑ̃ mjø) so much the better

tanto ('tæntəʊ) *adv* *music* too much; excessively [It.]

tant pis *French* (tɑ̃ pi) so much the worse

Tantrism ('tæntrɪzəm) *n* **1** a movement within Hinduism combining magical and mystical elements and with sacred writings of its own (**the Tantra**) **2** a similar movement within Buddhism [C18 from Sansk. *tantra*, lit.: warp, hence doctrine] > ˈ**Tantric** *adj* > ˈ**Tantrist** *n*

tantrum ('tæntrəm) *n* (*often pl*) a childish fit of rage; outburst of bad temper [C18 from ?]

Tan-tung ('tæn'tʊŋ) *n* a variant transliteration of the Chinese name for **Andong**

Tanzania (ˌtænzə'nɪə) *n* a republic in E Africa, on the Indian Ocean: formed by the union of the independent states of Tanganyika and Zanzibar in 1964; a member of the Commonwealth. Exports include coffee, tea, sisal, and cotton. Official languages: Swahili and English. Religions: Christian, Muslim, and animist. Currency: Tanzanian shilling. Capital: Dodoma. Pop: 36 232 000 (2001 est). Area: 945 203 sq km (364 943 sq miles) > ˌ**Tanzaˈnian** *adj, n*

▷ www.tanzania.go.tz

▷ www.tanzania-web.com

Tao (taʊ) *n* (in the philosophy of Taoism) **1** that in virtue of which all things happen or exist **2** the rational basis of human conduct **3** the course of life and its relation to eternal truth [Chinese, lit.: path, way]

Taoiseach ('tiːʃæx) *n* the prime mininster of the Irish Republic [from Irish, lit.: leader]

Taoism ('taʊɪzəm) *n* a system of religion and philosophy based on the teachings of Lao Zi and advocating a simple honest life and noninterference with the course of natural events > ˈ**Taoist** *n, adj* > ˌ**Taoˈistic** *adj*

▷ http://taopage.org/

▷ http://crystalinks.com/taoism.html

taonga (ta'ɔŋgə) *n* *NZ* anything highly prized [Maori]

tap[1] (tæp) *vb* **taps, tapping, tapped** **1** to strike (something) lightly and usually repeatedly **2** (*tr*) to produce by striking in this way: *to tap a rhythm* **3** (*tr*) to strike lightly with (something): *to tap one's finger on the desk* **4** (*intr*) to walk with a tapping sound **5** (*tr*) to attach reinforcing pieces to (the toe or heel of a shoe) ▷ *n* **6** a light blow or knock, or the sound made by it **7** the metal piece attached to the toe or heel of a shoe used for tap-dancing **8** short for **tap-dancing** ▷ See also **taps** [C13 *tappen*, prob. from OF *taper*, of Gmc origin]

tap² (tæp) *n* **1** a valve by which a fluid flow from a pipe can be controlled. US names: **faucet, spigot** **2** a stopper to plug a cask or barrel **3** a particular quality of alcoholic drink, esp when contained in casks: *an excellent tap* **4** *Brit* short for **taproom** **5** the withdrawal of fluid from a bodily cavity **6** a tool for cutting female screw threads **7** *electronics, chiefly US & Canad* a connection made at some point between the end terminals of an inductor, resistor, etc. Usual Brit name: **tapping** **8** *stock exchange* **8a** an issue of a government security released slowly onto the market when its market price reaches a predetermined level **8b** (*as modifier*): *tap stock; tap issue* **9** a concealed listening or recording device connected to a telephone or telegraph wire **10** **on tap** **10a** *inf* ready for use **10b** (of drinks) on draught ▷ *vb* **taps, tapping, tapped** (*tr*) **11** to furnish with a tap **12** to draw off with or as if with a tap **13** to cut into (a tree) and draw off sap from it **14** *Brit inf* **14a** to ask (someone) for money: *he tapped me for a fiver* **14b** to obtain (money) from someone **15** to connect a tap to (a telephone or telegraph wire) **16** to make a connection to (a pipe, drain, etc) **17** to cut a female screw thread in (an object or material) by use of a tap **18** *inf* (of a sports team or an employer) to make an illicit attempt to recruit (a player or employee bound by an existing contract) [OE *tæppa*] > **'tapper** *n*

tapa ('tɑːpə) *n* **1** the inner bark of the paper mulberry **2** a cloth made from this in the Pacific islands [C19 from native Polynesian name]

Tapajós (*Portuguese* tapa'ʒɔs) *n* a river in N Brazil, rising in N central Mato Grosso and flowing northeast to the Amazon. Length: about 800 km (500 miles)

tapas ('tæpəs) *pl n* **a** light snacks or appetizers, usually eaten with drinks **b** (*as modifier*): *a tapas bar* [from Sp. *tapa* cover, lid]

tap dance *n* **1** a step dance in which the performer wears shoes equipped with taps that make a rhythmic sound on the stage as he dances ▷ *vb* **tap-dance, tap-dances, tap-dancing, tap-danced** (*intr*) **2** to perform a tap dance > **'tap-ˌdancer** *n* > **'tap-ˌdancing** *n*
▷ www.tapdance.org

tape (teɪp) *n* **1** a long thin strip of cotton, linen, etc, used for binding, fastening, etc **2** a long narrow strip of paper, metal, etc **3** a string stretched across the track at the end of a race course **4** See **magnetic tape, ticker tape, paper tape, tape recording** ▷ *vb* **tapes, taping, taped** (*mainly tr*) **5** (*also intr*) Also: **tape record** to record (speech, music, etc) **6** to furnish with tapes **7** to bind, measure, secure, or wrap with tape **8** (*usually passive*) *Brit inf* to take stock of (a person or situation) [OE *tæppe*] > **'tapeˌlike** *adj* > **'taper** *n*

tape deck *n* **1** a tape recording unit in a hi-fi system **2** the platform supporting the spools, cassettes, or cartridges of a tape recorder, incorporating the motor and the playback, recording, and erasing heads

tape drive *n computing* a device that handles reading from or writing to magnetic tape

tape machine *n* **1** another word for **tape recorder** **2** a telegraphic device that records current stock quotations electronically or on ticker tape. US equivalent: **ticker**

tape measure *n* a tape or length of metal marked off in inches, centimetres, etc, used for measuring. Also called (esp US): **tapeline**

tapenade ('tæpənɑːd) *n* a savoury paste made from capers, olives, and anchovies, with olive oil and lemon juice [C20 F, from Provençal *tapéo* capers]

taper ('teɪpə) *vb* **1** to become or cause to become narrower towards one end **2** (often foll by *off*) to become or cause to become smaller or less significant ▷ *n* **3** a thin candle **4** a thin wooden or waxed strip for transferring a flame; spill **5** a narrowing **6** any feeble light [OE *tapor*, prob. from L *papȳrus* papyrus (from its use as a wick)] > **'taperer** *n* > **'tapering** *adj*

tape recorder *n* an electrical device used for recording sounds on magnetic tape and usually also for reproducing them

tape recording *n* **1** the act of recording on magnetic tape **2** the speech, music, etc, so recorded

taper relief *n* (in Britain) a system of relief from capital gains tax under which the percentage of a chargeable gain considered taxable is reduced for each whole year (from April 1998) that the asset was held by the vendor

tape streamer *n computing* an electromechanical device that enables data to be copied byte by byte from a hard disk onto magnetic tape for security or storage

tapestry ('tæpɪstrɪ) *n, pl* **tapestries** **1** a heavy woven fabric, often in the form of a picture, used for wall hangings, furnishings, etc **2** another word for **needlepoint** (sense 1) **3** a colourful and complicated situation: *the rich tapestry of life* [C15 from OF *tapisserie* carpeting, from OF *tapiz*; see TAPIS] > **'tapestried** *adj*
▷ www.adorabella.com.au/HistoryTapestry.htm
▷ www.bayeuxtapestry.org.uk
▷ www.metmuseum.org/explore/Unicorn/unicorn_inside.htm

tapeworm ('teɪpˌwɜːm) *n* any of a class of parasitic ribbon-like flatworms. The adults inhabit the intestines of vertebrates

taphole ('tæpˌhəʊl) *n* a hole in a furnace for running off molten metal or slag

taphouse ('tæpˌhaʊs) *n now rare* an inn

tapioca (ˌtæpɪ'əʊkə) *n* a beadlike starch obtained from cassava root, used in cooking as a thickening agent, esp in puddings [C18 via Port. from Tupi *tipioca* pressed-out juice, from *tipi* residue + *ok* to squeeze out]

tapir ('teɪpə) *n, pl* **tapirs** *or* **tapir** any of various mammals of South and Central America and SE Asia, having an elongated snout, three-toed hind legs, and four-toed forelegs [C18 from Tupi *tapiira*]

Tt

tapis ('tæpiː) *n, pl* **tapis** **1** tapestry or carpeting, esp as formerly used to cover a table **2** **on the tapis** currently under consideration [C17 from F, from OF *tapiz*, from Gk *tapētion* rug, from *tapēs* carpet]

tappet ('tæpɪt) *n* a mechanical part that reciprocates to receive or transmit intermittent motion [C18 from TAP¹ + -ET]

taproom ('tæpˌruːm, -ˌrʊm) *n* a bar, as in a hotel or pub

taproot ('tæpˌruːt) *n* the main root of plants such as the dandelion, which grows vertically downwards and bears smaller lateral roots

taps (tæps) *n* (*functioning as sing*) **1** *chiefly US* **1a** (in army camps, etc) a signal given on a bugle, drum, etc, indicating that lights are to be put out **1b** any similar signal, as at a military funeral **2** (in the Guide movement) a closing song sung at an evening camp fire or at the end of a meeting

tapster ('tæpstə) *n* **1** *rare* a barman **2** (in W Africa) a man who taps palm trees [OE *tæppestre*, fem. of *tæppere*, from *tappian* to TAP²]

tap water *n* water drawn off through taps from pipes in a house, as distinguished from distilled water, mineral water, etc

tar¹ (tɑː) *n* **1** any of various dark viscid substances obtained by the destructive distillation of organic matter such as coal, wood, or peat **2** another name for **coal tar** ▷ *vb* **tars, tarring, tarred** (*tr*) **3** to coat with tar **4** **tar and feather** to punish by smearing tar and feathers over (someone) **5** **tarred with the same brush** regarded as having the same faults [OE *teoru*] > **'tarry** *adj* > **'tarriness** *n*

tar² (tɑː) *n* an informal word for **seaman** [C17 short for TARPAULIN]

Tara ('tærə, 'tɑːrə) *n* a village in Co Meath near Dublin, by the **Hill of Tara**, the historic seat of the ancient Irish kings

Tarabulus el Gharb (tə'rɑːbələs ɛl 'gɑːb) *n* transliteration of the Arabic name for **Tripoli** (Libya)

Tarabulus esh Sham (tə'rɑːbələs ɛʃ 'ʃæm) *n* transliteration of the Arabic name for **Tripoli** (Lebanon)

taradiddle ('tærəˌdɪdᵊl) *n* a variant spelling of **tarradiddle**

tarakihi *or* **terakihi** ('tærəˌkiːhiː) *n, pl* **tarakihis** a common edible sea fish of New Zealand waters [from Maori]

taramasalata (ˌtærəməsə'lɑːtə) *n* a creamy pale pink paté, made from the roe of grey mullet or smoked cod and served as an hors d'oeuvre [c20 from Mod. Gk, from *tarama* cod's roe]

tarantass (ˌtɑːrən'tæs) *n* a four-wheeled Russian carriage without springs [c19 from Russian *tarantas*]

tarantella (ˌtærən'tɛlə) *n* **1** a peasant dance from S Italy **2** a piece of music composed for or in the rhythm of this dance [c18 from It., from TARANTO]

Tarantino (ˌtærən'tiːnəʊ) *n* **Quentin** born 1963, US film director and screenwriter, noted for violent quirky crime dramas including *Reservoir Dogs* (1993), *Pulp Fiction* (1994), *Jackie Brown* (1998), and *Kill Bill* (2003)

tarantism ('tærənˌtɪzəm) *n* a nervous disorder marked by uncontrollable bodily movement, widespread in S Italy during the 15th to 17th centuries: popularly thought to be caused by the bite of a tarantula [c17 from NL *tarantismus*, from TARANTO]

Taranto (tə'ræntəʊ; *Italian* 'taːranto) *n* a port in SE Italy, in Apulia on the **Gulf of Taranto** (an inlet of the Ionian Sea): the chief city of Magna Graecia; taken by the Romans in 272 BC. Pop: 208 214 (2000 est). Latin name: **Tarentum**

tarantula (tə'ræntjʊlə) *n, pl* **tarantulas** *or* **tarantulae** (-ˌliː) **1** any of various large hairy spiders of tropical America **2** a large hairy spider of S Europe [c16 from Med. L, from OIt. *tarantola*, from TARANTO]

Tarawa (tə'rɑːwə) *n* an atoll in Kiribati, occupying a chain of islets surrounding a lagoon in the W central Pacific: the capital of Kiribati, Bairiki, is on this atoll. Pop: 32 354 (1995)

taraxacum (tə'ræksəkəm) *n* **1** any of a genus of perennial plants of the composite family, such as the dandelion **2** the dried root of the dandelion, used as a laxative, diuretic, and tonic [c18 from Med. L, from Ar. *tarakhshaqūn* wild chicory, ? of Persian origin]

Tarbes (*French* tarb) *n* a town in SW France: noted for the breeding of Anglo-Arab horses. Pop: 50 228 (1990)

tarboosh (tɑː'buːʃ) *n* a felt or cloth brimless cap, usually red and often with a silk tassel, worn by Muslim men [c18 from Ar. *tarbūsh*]

tarboy ('tɑːˌbɔɪ) *n Austral inf* a boy who applies tar to the skin of sheep cut during shearing

Tardenoisian (ˌtɑːdə'nɔɪzɪən) *adj* of or referring to a Mesolithic culture characterized by small flint instruments [c20 after *Tardenois*, France, where implements were found]

tardigrade ('tɑːdɪˌgreɪd) *n* any of various minute aquatic segmented eight-legged invertebrates occurring in soil, ditches, etc. Popular name: **water bear** [c17 via L *tardigradus*, from *tardus* sluggish + *gradī* to walk]

tardy ('tɑːdɪ) *adj* **tardier, tardiest** **1** occurring later than expected **2** slow in progress, growth, etc [c15 from OF *tardif*, from L *tardus* slow] > **'tardily** *adv* > **'tardiness** *n*

tare¹ (tɛə) *n* **1** any of various vetch plants of Eurasia and N Africa **2** the seed of any of these plants **3** *Bible* a weed, thought to be the darnel [c14 from ?]

tare² (tɛə) *n* **1** the weight of the wrapping or container in which goods are packed **2** a deduction from gross weight to compensate for this **3** the weight of an unladen vehicle ▷ *vb* **tares, taring, tared** **4** (*tr*) to weigh (a package, etc) in order to calculate the amount of tare [c15 from OF: waste, from Med. L *tara*, from Ar. *tarhah* something discarded, from *taraha* to reject]

Tarentum (tə'rɛntəm) *n* the Latin name of **Taranto**

targe (tɑːdʒ) *n* an archaic word for **shield** [c13 from OF, of Gmc origin]

target ('tɑːgɪt) *n* **1a** an object or area at which an archer or marksman aims, usually a round flat surface marked with concentric rings **1b** (*as modifier*): *target practice* **2a** any point or area aimed at **2b** (*as modifier*): *target area; target company* **3** a fixed goal or objective **4** a person or thing at which an action or remark is directed or the object of a person's feelings **5** a joint of lamb consisting of the breast and neck **6** (formerly) a small round shield **7** *physics, electronics* **7a** a substance subjected to bombardment by electrons or other particles, or to irradiation **7b** an electrode in a television camera tube whose surface is scanned by the electron beam **8** *electronics* an object detected by the reflection of a radar or sonar signal, etc ▷ *vb* **targets, targeting, targeted** (*tr*) **9** to make a target of **10** to direct or aim: *to target benefits at those most in need* [c14 from OF *targette* a little shield, from OF TARGE]

targetitis (ˌtɑːgɪt'aɪtɪs) *n jocular* the setting of more targets than is strictly necessary for the effective functioning of an organization, esp when it leads to an increase in bureaucracy [c20 TARGET + -ITIS (sense 2)]

tariff ('tærɪf) *n* **1a** a tax levied by a government on imports or occasionally exports **1b** a system or list of such taxes **2** any schedule of prices, fees, fares, etc **3** *chiefly Brit* **3a** a method of charging for the supply of services such as gas and electricity **3b** a schedule of such charges **4** *chiefly Brit* a bill of fare with prices listed; menu ▷ *vb* (*tr*) **5** to set a tariff on **6** to price according to a schedule of tariffs [c16 from It. *tariffa*, from Ar. *ta'rīfa* to inform]

tariff office *n insurance* a company whose premiums are based on a tariff agreed with other insurance companies

Tarim ('tɑː'riːm) *n* a river in NW China, in Xinjiang Uygur AR: flows east along the N edge of the Taklimakan Shama desert, dividing repeatedly and forming lakes among the dunes, finally disappearing in the Lop Nor depression; the chief river of Xinjiang Uygur AR; drains the great **Tarim Basin** between the Tian Shan and Kunlun mountain systems of central Asia, an area of about 906 500 sq km (350 000 sq miles). Length: 2190 km (1360 miles)

Tarkington ('tɑːkɪŋtən) *n* (**Newton**) **Booth** 1869–1946, US novelist. His works include the historical romance *Monsieur Beaucaire* (1900), tales of the Middle West, such as *The Magnificent Ambersons* (1918) and *Alice Adams* (1921), and the series featuring the character Penrod

Tarkovsky (*Russian* 'tɑkɔfskij) *n* **Andrei** ('ɑndrej) 1932–86, Soviet film director, whose films include *Andrei Rublev* (1966), *Solaris* (1971), *Nostalgia* (1983), and *The Sacrifice* (1986)

tarlatan ('tɑːlətən) *n* an open-weave cotton fabric, used for stiffening garments [c18 from F *tarlatane*, var. of *tarnatane* type of muslin, ? of Indian origin]

Tarmac ('tɑːmæk) *n* **1** *trademark* (*often not cap*) a paving material that consists of crushed stone rolled and bound with a mixture of tar and bitumen, esp as used for a road, airport runway, etc. Full name: **Tarmacadam** (ˌtɑːmə'kædəm). See also **macadam** ▷ *vb* **Tarmacs, Tarmacking, Tarmacked** (*tr*) **2** (*usually not cap*) to apply Tarmac to

tarn (tɑːn) *n* a small mountain lake or pool [c14 from ON]

Tarn (*French* tarn) *n* **1** a department of S France, in Midi-Pyrénées region. Capital: Albi. Pop: 343 402 (1999). Area: 5780 sq km (2254 sq miles) **2** a river in SW France, rising in the Massif Central and flowing generally west to the Garonne River. Length: 375 km (233 miles)

tarnation (tɑːˈneɪʃən) *n* a euphemism for **damnation**

Tarn-et-Garonne (*French* tarnegarɔn) *n* a department of SW France, in Midi-Pyrénées region. Capital: Montauban. Pop: 206 034 (1999). Area: 3731 sq km (1455 sq miles)

tarnish (ˈtɑːnɪʃ) *vb* **1** to lose or cause to lose the shine, esp by exposure to air or moisture resulting in surface oxidation; discolour **2** to stain or become stained; taint ▷ *n* **3** a tarnished condition, surface, or film [C16 from OF *ternir* to make dull, from *terne* lustreless of Gmc origin] > ˈ**tarnishable** *adj*

Tarnopol (tarˈnɔpɔl) *n* the Polish name for **Ternopol**

Tarnów (*Polish* ˈtarnuf) *n* an industrial city in SE Poland. Pop: 121 494 (1999 est)

taro (ˈtɑːrəʊ) *n, pl* **taros 1** a plant cultivated in the tropics for its large edible rootstock **2** the rootstock of this plant ▷ Also called: **eddo** [C18 from Tahitian & Maori]

tarot (ˈtærəʊ) *n* **1** one of a special pack of cards, now used mainly for fortune-telling **2** a card in a tarot pack with distinctive symbolic design ▷ *adj* **3** relating to tarot cards [C16 from F, from OIt. *tarocco*, from ?]

tarpan (ˈtɑːpæn) *n* a European wild horse, now extinct [from Tatar]

tarpaulin (tɑːˈpɔːlɪn) *n* **1** a heavy waterproof fabric made of canvas or similar material coated with tar, wax, or paint **2** a sheet of this fabric **3** a hat made of or covered with this fabric, esp a sailor's hat **4** a rare word for **seaman** [C17 prob. from TAR[1] + PALL[1] + -ING[1]]

Tarpeia (tɑːˈpiːə) *n* (in Roman legend) a vestal virgin, who betrayed Rome to the Sabines and was killed by them when she requested a reward

Tarpeian Rock (tɑːˈpiːən) *n* (in ancient Rome) a cliff on the Capitoline hill from which traitors were hurled

tarpon (ˈtɑːpən) *n, pl* **tarpons** *or* **tarpon** a large silvery game fish of warm oceans [C17 ?from Du. *tarpoen*, from ?]

Tarquin (ˈtɑːkwɪn) *n* **1** Latin name *Lucius Tarquinius Priscus* fifth legendary king of Rome (616–578 BC) **2** Latin name *Lucius Tarquinius Superbus* seventh and last legendary king of Rome (534–510 BC)

tarradiddle (ˈtærəˌdɪdᵊl) *n* **1** a trifling lie **2** nonsense; twaddle [C18 from ?]

tarragon (ˈtærəgən) *n* **1** an aromatic plant of the Old World, having leaves which are used as seasoning **2** the leaves of this plant [C16 from OF *targon*, from Med. L *tarcon*, ? ult. from Gk *drakontion* adderwort]

Tarragona (*Spanish* tarraˈɣona) *n* a port in NE Spain, on the Mediterranean: one of the richest seaports of the Roman Empire; destroyed by the Moors (714). Pop: 112 795 (1998 est). Latin name: **Tarraco** (təˈrɑːkəʊ)

Tarrasa (*Spanish* taˈrrasa) *n* a city in NE Spain: textile centre. Pop: 165 654 (1998 est)

tarry (ˈtærɪ) *vb* **tarries, tarrying, tarried 1** (*intr*) to delay; linger **2** (*intr*) to remain temporarily or briefly **3** (*intr*) to wait or stay **4** (*tr*) *arch or poetic* to await [C14 *tarien*, from ?] > ˈ**tarrier** *n*

tarsal (ˈtɑːsᵊl) *adj* **1** of the tarsus or tarsi ▷ *n* **2** a tarsal bone

tarseal (ˈtɑːˌsiːl) *n NZ* **1** the bitumen surface of a road **2 the tarseal** the main highway

Tarshish (ˈtɑːʃɪʃ) *n Old Testament* an ancient port, mentioned in I Kings 10:22, situated in Spain or in one of the Phoenician colonies in Sardinia

tarsia (ˈtɑːsɪə) *n* another term for **intarsia** [C17 from It., from Ar. *tarsi'*]

tarsier (ˈtɑːsɪə) *n* any of several nocturnal arboreal primates of Indonesia and the Philippines, having huge eyes, long hind legs, and digits ending in pads to facilitate climbing [C18 from F, from *tarse* the flat of the foot; see TARSUS]

tarsus (ˈtɑːsəs) *n, pl* **tarsi** (-saɪ) **1** the bones of the ankle and heel, collectively **2** the corresponding part in other mammals and in amphibians and reptiles **3** the connective tissue supporting the free edge of each eyelid **4** the part of an insect's leg that lies distal to the tibia [C17 from NL, from Gk *tarsos* flat surface, instep]

Tarsus (ˈtɑːsəs) *n* **1** a city in SE Turkey, on the Tarsus River: site of ruins of ancient Tarsus, capital of Cilicia, and birthplace of St. Paul. Pop: 190 184 (1997) **2** a river in SE Turkey, in Cilicia, rising in the Taurus Mountains and flowing south past Tarsus to the Mediterranean. Length: 153 km (95 miles). Ancient name: **Cydnus**

tart[1] (tɑːt) *n* a pastry case often having no top crust, with a filling of fruit, custard, etc [C14 from OF *tarte*, from ?]

tart[2] (tɑːt) *adj* **1** (of a flavour, etc) sour; acid **2** cutting; sharp: *a tart remark* [OE *teart* rough] > ˈ**tartly** *adv* > ˈ**tartness** *n*

tart[3] (tɑːt) *n inf* a promiscuous woman, esp a prostitute. See also **tart up** [C19 shortened from SWEETHEART] > ˈ**tarty** *adj*

tartan (ˈtɑːtᵊn) *n* **1a** a design of straight lines, crossing at right angles to give a chequered appearance, esp the distinctive design or designs associated with each Scottish clan **1b** (*as modifier*): *a tartan kilt* **2** a fabric or garment with this design [C16 ?from OF *tertaine* linsey-woolsey, from OSp. *tiritaña* a fine silk fabric, from *tiritar* to rustle] > ˈ**tartaned** *adj*

tartar[1] (ˈtɑːtə) *n* **1** a hard deposit on the teeth, consisting of food, cellular debris, and mineral salts **2** a brownish-red substance consisting mainly of potassium hydrogen tartrate, deposited during the fermentation of wine [C14 from Med. L *tartarum*, from Med. Gk *tartaron*]

tartar[2] (ˈtɑːtə) *n* (*sometimes cap*) a fearsome or formidable person [C16 special use of TARTAR]

Tartar (ˈtɑːtə) *n, adj* a variant spelling of **Tatar**

Tartarean (tɑːˈtɛərɪən) *adj literary* of or relating to Tartarus; infernal

tartar emetic *n* antimony potassium tartrate, a poisonous, crystalline salt used as a mordant and in medicine

Tt

tartaric (tɑːˈtærɪk) *adj* of, containing, or derived from tartar or tartaric acid

tartaric acid *n* a colourless crystalline acid which is found in many fruits: used as a food additive (**E334**) in soft drinks, confectionery, and baking powders, and in tanning and photography. Formula: $(CHOH)_2(COOH)_2$. Systematic name: **2,3-dihydroxybutanedioic acid**

tartar sauce *n* a mayonnaise sauce mixed with hard-boiled egg yolks, chopped herbs, capers, etc [from F *sauce tartare*, from TARTAR]

Tartarus (ˈtɑːtərəs) *n Greek myth* **1** an abyss under Hades where the Titans were imprisoned **2** a part of Hades reserved for evildoers **3** the underworld; Hades **4** a primordial god who became the father of the monster Typhon [C16 from L, from Gk *Tartaros*, of obscure origin]

Tartary (ˈtɑːtərɪ) *n* a variant spelling of **Tatary**

tartlet (ˈtɑːtlɪt) *n Brit* an individual pastry case with a sweet or savoury filling

tartrate (ˈtɑːtreɪt) *n* any salt or ester of tartaric acid

tartrated (ˈtɑːtreɪtɪd) *adj* being in the form of a tartrate

tartrazine (ˈtɑːtrəˌziːn, -zɪn) *n* an azo dye that produces a yellow colour: used as a food additive (**E102**), in drugs, and to dye textiles

Tartu (*Russian* ˈtartu) *n* a city in SE Estonia: became Russian in 1704 after successive Russian, Polish, and Swedish rule; became part of independent Estonia in 1991; university (1632). Pop: 101 000 (2000 est). Former name (11th century until 1918): **Yurev**. German name: **Dorpat**

tart up *vb* (*tr; adv*) *Brit inf* **1** to dress and make (oneself) up in a provocative way **2** to decorate or improve the appearance of: *to tart up a bar*

tarwhine (ˈtɑːˌwaɪn) *n* any of various Australian marine food fishes, esp the sea bream [?from Abor.]

Tarzan (ˈtɑːzən) *n* (*sometimes not cap*) *inf, often ironical* a man with great physical strength, agility, and virility [c20 after the hero of a series of stories by E. R. BURROUGHS]

Tashkent (*Russian* taʃ'kjɛnt) *n* the capital of Uzbekistan: one of the oldest and largest cities in central Asia; cotton textile manufacturing. Pop: 2 124 000 (1998 est)
▷ www.tashkent.org
▷ www.advantour.com/uzbekistan/tashkent.htm
▷ www.uzbekistanembassy.uk.net/main/uzbekistan

tasimeter (tə'sɪmɪtə) *n* a device for measuring small temperature changes. It depends on the changes of pressure resulting from expanding or contracting solids [c19 *tasi-*, from Gk *tasis* tension + -METER] > **tasimetric** (ˌtæsɪ'mɛtrɪk) *adj* > **ta'simetry** *n*

task (tɑːsk) *n* **1** a specific piece of work required to be done **2** an unpleasant or difficult job or duty **3** any piece of work **4 take to task** to criticize or reprove ▷ *vb* (*tr*) **5** to assign a task to **6** to subject to severe strain; tax [c13 from OF *tasche*, from Med. L *tasca*, from *taxa* tax, from L *taxāre* to TAX]

task force *n* **1** a temporary grouping of military units formed to undertake a specific mission **2** any organization set up to carry out a continuing task

taskmaster ('tɑːskˌmɑːstə) *n* a person, discipline, etc, that enforces work, esp hard or continuous work > **'taskˌmistress** *fem n*

taskwork ('tɑːskˌwɜːk) *n* **1** hard or unpleasant work **2** a rare word for **piecework**

Tasman ('tæzmən) *n* **Abel Janszoon** ('abəl 'jansuːn) 1603–59, Dutch navigator, who discovered Tasmania, New Zealand, and the Tonga and Fiji Islands (1642–43)

Tasmania (tæz'meɪnɪə) *n* an island in the S Pacific, south of mainland Australia: forms, with offshore islands, the smallest state of Australia; discovered by the Dutch explorer Tasman in 1642; used as a penal colony by the British (1803–53); mostly forested and mountainous. Capital: Hobart. Pop: 470 260 (1999 est). Area: 68 332 sq km (26 383 sq miles). Former name (1642–1855): **Van Diemen's Land** > **Tas'manian** *adj, n*
▷ www.parliament.tas.gov.au
▷ www.discovertasmania.com.au

Tasmanian devil *n* a small ferocious carnivorous marsupial of Tasmania

Tasmanian tiger *or* **wolf** *n* other names for **thylacine**

Tasman Sea *n* the part of the Pacific between SE Australia and NW New Zealand

tass (tæs) *or* **tassie** ('tæsɪ) *n Scot & N English dialect* **1** a cup or glass **2** its contents [c15 from OF *tasse* cup, from Ar. *tassah* basin, from Persian *tast*]

Tass (tæs) *n* (formerly) the principal news agency of the Soviet Union: replaced in 1992 by Itar Tass [*T(elegrafnoye) a(gentstvo) S(ovetskogo) S(oyuza)* Telegraphic Agency of the Soviet Union]

tassel ('tæsᵊl) *n* **1** a tuft of loose threads secured by a knot or knob, used to decorate soft furnishings, clothes, etc **2** anything resembling this, esp the tuft of stamens at the tip of a maize inflorescence ▷ *vb* **tassels, tasselling, tasselled** *or US* **tassels, tasseling, tasseled** **3** (*tr*) to adorn with tassels **4** (*intr*) (of maize) to produce stamens in a tuft [c13 from OF, from Vulgar L *tassellus* (unattested), changed from L *taxillus* a small die]

Tassie *or* **Tassy** ('tæzɪ) *n pl* **-sies** *Austral inf* **1** Tasmania **2** a native or inhabitant of Tasmania

Tasso (*Italian* 'tasso) *n* **Torquato** (tor'kwaːto) 1544–95, Italian poet, noted for his pastoral idyll *Aminta* (1573) and for *Jerusalem Delivered* (1581), dealing with the First Crusade

taste (teɪst) *n* **1** the sense by which the qualities and flavour of a substance are distinguished by the taste buds **2** the sensation experienced by means of the taste buds **3** the act of tasting **4** a small amount eaten, drunk, or tried on the tongue **5** a brief experience of something: *a taste of the whip* **6** a preference or liking for something **7** the ability to make discerning judgments about aesthetic, artistic, and intellectual matters **8** judgment of aesthetic or social matters according to a generally accepted standard: *bad taste* **9** discretion; delicacy: *that remark lacks taste* ▷ *vb* **tastes, tasting, tasted** **10** to distinguish the taste of (a substance) by means of the taste buds **11** (*usually tr*) to take a small amount of (a food, liquid, etc) into the mouth, esp in order to test the quality **12** (often foll by *of*) to have a specific flavour or taste **13** (when *intr*, usually foll by *of*) to have an experience of (something): *to taste success* **14** (*tr*) an archaic word for **enjoy** [c13 from OF *taster*, ult. from L *taxāre* to appraise] > **'tastable** *adj*

taste bud *n* any of the elevated sensory organs on the surface of the tongue, by means of which the sensation of taste is experienced

tasteful ('teɪstfʊl) *adj* indicating good taste: *a tasteful design* > **'tastefully** *adv* > **'tastefulness** *n*

tasteless ('teɪstlɪs) *adj* **1** lacking in flavour; insipid **2** lacking social or aesthetic taste > **'tastelessly** *adv* > **'tastelessness** *n*

taster ('teɪstə) *n* **1** a person who samples food or drink for quality **2** any device used in tasting or sampling **3** a person employed, esp formerly, to taste food and drink prepared for a king, etc, to test for poison **4** a sample or preview of a product, experience, etc, intended to stimulate interest in the product, experience, etc, itself: *the single serves as a taster for the band's new album*

-tastic *adj combining form jocular* denoting excellence in a specified area: *the funtastic theme park; their poptastic new single* [c20 from (FAN)TASTIC]

tasty ('teɪstɪ) *adj* **tastier, tastiest** **1** having a pleasant flavour **2** *Brit inf* skilful or impressive: *she was a bit tasty with a cutlass* **3** *NZ* (of cheddar cheese) having a strong flavour > **'tastily** *adv* > **'tastiness** *n*

tat¹ (tæt) *vb* **tats, tatting, tatted** to make (something) by tatting [c19 from ?]

tat² (tæt) *n* **1** tatty articles or a tatty condition **2** tasteless articles **3** a tangled mass [c20 back formation from TATTY]

tat³ (tæt) *n* See **tit for tat**

ta-ta (tæ'tɑː) *sentence substitute Brit inf* goodbye; farewell [c19 from ?]

Tatar *or* **Tartar** ('tɑːtə) *n* **1a** a member of a Mongoloid people who established a powerful state in central Asia in the 13th century **1b** a descendant of this people, now scattered throughout Russia and N central Asia **2** any of the Turkic languages spoken by the present-day Tatars ▷ *adj* **3** of or relating to the Tatars [c14 from OF *Tartare*, from Med. L *Tartarus* (associated with L *Tartarus* the underworld), from Persian *Tātār*] > **Tatarian** (tɑː'tɛərɪən), **Tar'tarian** *or* **Tataric** (tɑː'tærɪk), **Tar'taric** *adj*

Tatar Republic *n* a constituent republic of W Russia, around the confluence of the Volga and Kama Rivers. Capital: Kazan. Pop: 3 779 000 (2000 est) Area: 68 000 sq km (26 250 sq miles)

Tatar Strait *n* an arm of the Pacific between the mainland of SE Russia and Sakhalin Island, linking the Sea of Japan with the Sea of Okhotsk. Length: about 560 km (350 miles). Also called: **Gulf of Tatary**

Tatary *or* **Tartary** ('tɑːtərɪ) *n* **1** a historical region (with indefinite boundaries) in E Europe and Asia, inhabited by Bulgars until overrun by the Tatars in the mid-13th century: extended as far east as the Pacific under Genghis Khan **2 Gulf of** another name for the **Tatar Strait**

Tate (teɪt) *n* **1** (**John Orley**) **Allen** 1899–1979, US poet and critic **2** Sir **Henry** 1819–99, British sugar refiner and philanthropist; founder of the Tate Gallery **3 Nahum** ('neɪʊm) 1652–1715, British poet, dramatist, and hymn-writer, born in Ireland: poet laureate (1692–1715). He is best known for writing a version of *King Lear* with a happy ending

Tate Gallery *n* either of two art galleries in London, **Tate**

Britain, built in 1897, and **Tate Modern**, built 1999–2000 ▷ www.tate.org.uk
tater ('teɪtə) *n* a dialect word for **potato**
Tati (*French* tati) *n* **Jacques** (ʒak), real name *Jacques Tatischeff* 1908–82, French film director, pantomimist, and comic actor, creator of the character Monsieur Hulot
tatouay ('tætʊ,eɪ) *n* a large armadillo of South America [c16 from Sp. *tatuay*, from Guarani, from *tatu* armadillo + *ai* worthless (because inedible)]
Tatra Mountains ('tɑːtrə, 'tæt-) *pl n* a mountain range along the border between Slovakia and Poland, extending for about 64 km (40 miles): the highest range of the central Carpathians. Highest peak: Gerlachovka, 2663 m (8737 ft). Also called: **High Tatra**
TATT *abbrev for* tired all the time: used to describe a set of symptoms often reported to doctors by patients
tatter ('tætə) *vb* **1** to make or become ragged or worn to shreds ▷ *n* **2** a torn or ragged piece, esp of material [c14 from ON]
tatterdemalion (,tætədɪ'meɪljən) *n rare* a person dressed in ragged clothes [c17 from TATTER + *-demalion*, from ?]
tattersall ('tætə,sɔːl) *n* a fabric having stripes or bars in a checked or squared pattern [c19 after *Tattersall's*, a horse market in London founded by Richard *Tattersall* (died 1795), Brit horseman; the horse blankets at the market orig. had this pattern]
Tattersall's ('tætə,sɔːlz) *n Austral* **1** Also called (inf): **Tatt's** a lottery now based in Melbourne **2** a name used for sportsmen's clubs [after *Tattersall's* horse market; see TATTERSALL]
tatting ('tætɪŋ) *n* **1** an intricate type of lace made by looping a thread of cotton or linen by means of a hand shuttle **2** the act or work of producing this [c19 from ?]
tattle ('tætᵊl) *vb* **tattles, tattling, tattled 1** (*intr*) to gossip about another's personal matters **2** (*tr*) to reveal by gossiping **3** (*intr*) to talk idly; chat ▷ *n* **4** the act or an instance of tattling **5** a scandalmonger; gossip [c15 (in the sense: to stammer, hesitate): from MDu. *tatelen* to prate, imit.] > **'tattler** *n*
tattletale ('tætᵊl,teɪl) *chiefly US & Canad n* **1** a scandalmonger or gossip **2** another word for **telltale** (sense 1)
tattoo¹ (tæ'tuː) *n, pl* **tattoos 1** (formerly) a signal by drum or bugle ordering the military to return to their quarters **2** a military display or pageant **3** any similar beating on a drum, etc [c17 from Du. *taptoe*, from *tap toe!* turn off the taps! from *tap* tap of a barrel + *toe* to shut]
tattoo² (tæ'tuː) *vb* **tattoos, tattooing, tattooed 1** to make (pictures or designs) on (the skin) by pricking and staining with indelible colours ▷ *n, pl* **tattoos 2** a design made by this process **3** the practice of tattooing [c18 from Tahitian *tatau*] > **tat'tooer** *or* **tat'tooist** *n*
tatty ('tætɪ) *adj* **tattier, tattiest** *chiefly Brit* worn out, shabby, or unkempt [c16 of Scot origin] > **'tattily** *adv* > **'tattiness** *n*
Tatum ('teɪtəm) *n* **1 Art,** full name *Arthur Tatum* 1910–56, US jazz pianist **2 Edward Lawrie** 1909–75, US biochemist, who showed how genes regulate biochemical processes in an organism and demonstrated that bacteria reproduce sexually; Nobel prize for physiology or medicine (1958) with Beadle and Lederberg
tau (tɔː, taʊ) *n* the 19th letter in the Greek alphabet (Τ or τ) [c13 from Gk]
tau cross *n* a cross shaped like the Greek letter tau. Also called: **Saint Anthony's cross**
taught (tɔːt) *vb* the past tense and past participle of **teach**
tauiwi (təʊ'iːwɪ) *n NZ* a Maori term for the non-Maori people of New Zealand [Maori lit.: foreign race]
taunt (tɔːnt) *vb* (*tr*) **1** to provoke or deride with mockery, contempt, or criticism **2** to tease; tantalize ▷ *n* **3** a jeering remark [c16 from F *tant pour tant* like for like] > **'taunting** *adj*
Taunton ('tɔːntən) *n* a market town in SW England, administrative centre of Somerset: scene of Judge Jeffreys' "Bloody Assize" (1685) after the Battle of Sedgemoor. Pop: 55 855 (1991)
tau particle *n physics* a type of elementary particle classified as a lepton
taupe (təʊp) *n* **a** a brownish-grey colour **b** (*as adj*): *a taupe coat* [c20 from F, lit.: mole, from L *talpa*]
Taupo ('taʊpəʊ) *n* **Lake** a lake in New Zealand, on central North Island: the largest lake of New Zealand. Area: 616 sq km (238 sq miles)
Tauranga (taʊ'ræŋə) *n* a port in New Zealand, on NE North Island on the Bay of Plenty: exports dairy produce, meat, and timber. Pop: 76 100 (1994)
taurine ('tɔːraɪn) *adj* of or resembling a bull [c17 from L *taurīnus*, from *taurus* a bull]
tauromachy (tɔː'rɒməkɪ) *n* the art or act of bullfighting [c19 Gk *tauromakhia*, from *tauros* bull + *makhē* fight]
Taurus ('tɔːrəs) *n* **1** *astron* a constellation in the N hemisphere **2** *astrol* Also called: the **Bull** the second sign of the zodiac. The sun is in this sign between about April 20 and May 20 [c14 from L: bull]
Taurus Mountains *pl n* a mountain range in S Turkey, parallel to the Mediterranean coast: crossed by the Cilician Gates; continued in the northeast by the Anti-Taurus range. Highest peak: Kaldi Dağ, 3734 m (12 251 ft)
taut (tɔːt) *adj* **1** tightly stretched; tense **2** showing nervous strain; stressed **3** *chiefly naut* in good order; neat [c14 *tought*] > **'tautly** *adv* > **'tautness** *n*
tauten ('tɔːtᵊn) *vb* to make or become taut
tauto- *or before a vowel* **taut-** *combining form* identical or same: *tautology* [from Gk *tauto*, from *to auto*]
tautog (tɔː'tɒg) *n* a large dark-coloured food fish of the North American coast of the Atlantic Ocean [c17 from Narraganset *tautauog*, pl. of *tautau* sheepshead]
tautology (tɔː'tɒlədʒɪ) *n, pl* **tautologies 1** the use of words that merely repeat elements of the meaning already conveyed, as in *Will these supplies be adequate enough?* in place of *Will these supplies be adequate?* **2** *logic* a statement that is always true, as in *either the sun is out or the sun is not out* [c16 from LL *tautologia*, from Gk, from *tautologos*] > **tautological** (,tɔːtᵊ'lɒdʒɪkᵊl) *or* **tau'tologous** *adj*
tautomerism (tɔː'tɒmə,rɪzəm) *n* the ability of certain chemical compounds to exist as a mixture of two interconvertible isomers in equilibrium [c19 from TAUTO- + ISOMERISM] > **tautomer** ('tɔːtəmə) *n* > **tautomeric** (,tɔːtə'mɛrɪk) *adj*
tautonym ('tɔːtənɪm) *n biol* a taxonomic name in which the generic and specific components are the same, as in *Rattus rattus* (black rat) > **,tauto'nymic** *or* **tautonymous** (tɔː'tɒnəməs) *adj* > **tau'tonymy** *n*
Tavener ('tævənə) *n* Sir **John** (**Kenneth**) born 1944, British composer, whose works include the cantata *The Whale* (1966), the opera *Thérèse* (1979), and the choral work *The Last Discourse* (1998); many of his later works are inspired by the liturgy of the Russian Orthodox Church
tavern ('tævən) *n* **1** a less common word for **pub 2** *US, E Canad, & NZ* a place licensed for the sale and consumption of alcoholic drink [c13 from OF *taverne*, from L *taberna* hut]
taverna (tə'vɜːnə) *n* **1** (in Greece) a guesthouse that has its own bar **2** a Greek restaurant [c20 Mod. Gk, from L *taberna*]
Taverner ('tævənə) *n* **John** ?1495–1545, English composer, esp of church music; best known for the mass *Western Wynde*, based on a secular song
TAVR *abbrev for* Territorial and Army Volunteer Reserve
taw¹ (tɔː) *n* **1** a large marble used for shooting **2** a game

Tt

of marbles **3** the line from which the players shoot in marbles **4** **back to taws** *Austral inf* back to the beginning [c18 from ?]

taw² (tɔː) *vb (tr)* to convert (skins) into leather by treatment with alum and salt rather than by normal tanning processes [OE *tawian*] > **'tawer** *n*

tawa ('tɑːwə) *n* a New Zealand timber tree with edible berries [from Maori]

tawdry ('tɔːdrɪ) *adj* **tawdrier, tawdriest** cheap, showy, and of poor quality: *tawdry jewellery* [c16 *tawdry lace,* shortened & altered from *Seynt Audries lace,* finery sold at the fair of St *Audrey* (Etheldrida), 7th-century queen of Northumbria] > **'tawdrily** *adv* > **'tawdriness** *n*

tawny ('tɔːnɪ) *n* **a** a light brown to brownish-orange colour **b** *(as adj): tawny port* [c14 from OF *tané,* from *taner* to tan] > **'tawniness** *n*

tawny owl *n* a European owl having a reddish-brown plumage and a round head

tawse *or* **taws** (tɔːz) *n chiefly Scot* a leather strap having one end cut into thongs, formerly used as an instrument of punishment by a schoolteacher [c16 prob. pl of obs. *taw* strip of leather; see TAW²]

tax (tæks) *n* **1** a compulsory financial contribution imposed by a government to raise revenue, levied on income or property, on the prices of goods and services, etc **2** a heavy demand on something; strain ▷ *vb (tr)* **3** to levy a tax on (persons, companies, etc) **4** to make heavy demands on; strain **5** to accuse or blame **6** *law* to determine (the amount legally chargeable or allowable to a party to a legal action): *to tax costs* **7** *sl* to demand money or goods from (someone) with menaces [c13 from OF *taxer,* from L *taxāre* to appraise, from *tangere* to touch] > **'taxable** *adj* > **'taxer** *n*

taxation (tæk'seɪʃən) *n* **1** the act or principle of levying taxes or the condition of being taxed **2a** an amount assessed as tax **2b** a tax rate **3** revenue from taxes > **tax'ational** *adj*

tax avoidance *n* reduction or minimization of tax liability by lawful methods

tax credit *n* (in Britain) a social security benefit paid in the form of an additional income tax allowance

tax-deductible *adj* legally deductible from income or wealth before tax assessment

tax disc *n* a paper disc displayed on the windscreen of a motor vehicle showing that the tax due on it has been paid

taxeme ('tæksiːm) *n linguistics* any element of speech that may differentiate one utterance from another with a different meaning, such as the occurrence of a particular phoneme, the presence of a certain intonation, or a distinctive word order [c20 from Gk *taxis* order, arrangement + -EME] > **tax'emic** *adj*

tax evasion *n* reduction or minimization of tax liability by illegal methods

tax exile *n* a person having a high income who chooses to live abroad so as to avoid paying high taxes

tax haven *n* a country or state having a lower rate of taxation than elsewhere

tax holiday *n* a period during which tax concessions are made for some reason; examples include an export incentive or an incentive to start a new business given by some governments, in which a company is excused all or part of its tax liability

taxi ('tæksɪ) *n, pl* **taxis** *or* **taxies** **1** Also called: **cab, taxicab** a car, usually fitted with a taximeter, that may be hired, along with its driver, to carry passengers to any specified destination ▷ *vb* **taxis** *or* **taxies, taxiing** *or* **taxying, taxied** **2** to cause (an aircraft) to move along the ground, esp before takeoff and after landing, or (of an aircraft) to move along the ground in this way **3** *(intr)* to travel in a taxi [c20 shortened from *taximeter cab*]

taxidermy ('tæksɪˌdɜːmɪ) *n* the art or process of preparing, stuffing, and mounting animal skins so that they have a lifelike appearance [c19 from Gk *taxis* arrangement + *-dermy,* from Gk *derma* skin] > ˌ**taxi'dermal** *or* ˌ**taxi'dermic** *adj* > **'taxiˌdermist** *n*

taximeter ('tæksɪˌmiːtə) *n* a meter fitted to a taxi to register the fare, based on the length of the journey [c19 from F *taximètre;* see TAX, -METER]

taxing ('tæksɪŋ) *adj* demanding, onerous, and wearing

taxi rank *n* a place where taxis wait to be hired

taxis ('tæksɪs) *n* **1** the movement of an organism in response to an external stimulus **2** *surgery* the repositioning of a displaced part by manual manipulation only [c18 via NL from Gk: arrangement, from *tassein* to place in order]

-taxis *or* **-taxy** *n combining form* **1** indicating movement towards or away from a specified stimulus: *thermotaxis* **2** order or arrangement: *phyllotaxis* [from NL, from Gk *taxis* order] > **-tactic** *or* **-taxic** *adj combining form*

taxiway ('tæksɪˌweɪ) *n* a marked path along which aircraft taxi to or from a runway, parking area, etc

tax loss *n* a loss sustained by a company that can be set against future profits for tax purposes

taxman ('tæksˌmæn) *n, pl* **-men** **1** a collector of taxes **2** *inf* a tax-collecting body personified

taxon ('tæksɒn) *n, pl* **taxa** ('tæksə) *biol* any taxonomic group or rank [c20 back formation from TAXONOMY]

taxonomy (tæk'sɒnəmɪ) *n* **1** the branch of biology concerned with the classification of organisms into groups based on similarities of structure, origin, etc **2** the science or practice of classification [c19 from F *taxonomie,* from Gk *taxis* order + -NOMY] > **taxonomic** (ˌtæksə'nɒmɪk) *or* ˌ**taxo'nomical** *adj* > ˌ**taxo'nomically** *adv* > **tax'onomist** *n*

taxpayer ('tæksˌpeɪə) *n* a person or organization that pays taxes

tax relief *n* remission of income tax due on a proportion of income earned

tax return *n* a declaration of personal income used as a basis for assessing an individual's liability for taxation

tax shelter *n* a form into which business activities may be organized to minimize taxation

-taxy *n combining form* a variant of **-taxis**

Tay (teɪ) *n* **1** **Firth of** the estuary of the River Tay on the North Sea coast of Scotland. Length: 40 km (25 miles) **2** a river in central Scotland, flowing northeast through Loch Tay, then southeast to the Firth of Tay: the longest river in Scotland; noted for salmon fishing. Length: 193 km (120 miles) **3** **Loch** a lake in central Scotland, in Stirling council area. Length: 23 km (14 miles)

Taylor ('teɪlə) *n* **1** **A(lan) J(ohn) P(ercivale)** 1906–90, British historian whose many works include *The Origins of the Second World War* (1961) **2** **Brook** 1685–1731, English mathematician, who laid the foundations of differential calculus **3** Dame **Elizabeth** born 1932, US film actress, born in England: films include *National Velvet* (1944), *Cat on a Hot Tin Roof* (1958), *Suddenly Last Summer* (1959), *Butterfield 8* (1960), and *Who's Afraid of Virginia Woolf?* (1966), for the last two of which she won Oscars **4** **Frederick Winslow** 1856–1915, US engineer, who pioneered the use of time and motion studies to increase efficiency in industry **5** **Jeremy** 1613–67, English cleric, best known for his devotional manuals *Holy Living* (1650) and *Holy Dying* (1651) **6** **Zachary** 1784–1850, 12th president of the US (1849–50); hero of the Mexican War

Taylor's Gold *n* a variety of pear from New Zealand

Taymyr Peninsula (taɪ'mɪə) *n* a variant spelling of **Taimyr Peninsula**

Tay-Sachs disease (ˌteɪ'sæks) *n* an inherited disorder, caused by a faulty recessive gene, in which lipids accumulate in the brain, leading to mental retardation and blindness [c20 after W. *Tay* (1843–1927), Brit physician, and B. *Sachs* (1858–1944), US neurologist]

Tayside Region ('teɪˌsaɪd) *n* a former local government region in E Scotland: formed in 1975 from Angus, Kinross-shire, and most of Perthshire; replaced in 1996 by the council areas of Angus, City of Dundee, and Perth and Kinross

tazza ('tætsə) *n* a wine cup with a shallow bowl and a circular foot [C19 from It., prob. from Ar. *tassah* bowl]

Tb *the chemical symbol for* terbium

TB *abbrev for:* **1** torpedo boat **2** Also: **tb** tuberculosis

T-bar *n* **1** a T-shaped wrench for use with a socket **2** a T-shaped bar on a ski tow which skiers hold on to while being pulled up slopes

tbc *or* **TBC** *abbrev for* to be confirmed

Tbilisi (dbɪ'li:sɪ) *n* the capital of Georgia, on the Kura River: founded in 458; taken by the Russians in 1801; university (1918); a major industrial centre. Pop: 1 398 968 (1997 est). Russian name: **Tiflis**
▷ www.parliament.ge/~nino/tbilisi.html

T-bone steak *n* a large choice steak cut from the sirloin of beef, containing a T-shaped bone

tbs. *or* **tbsp.** *abbrev for* tablespoon(ful)

TBT *abbrev for* tri-*n*-butyl tin: a biocide used in marine paints to prevent fouling

Tc *the chemical symbol for* technetium

T-cell *n* a type of lymphocyte that matures in the thymus gland and is responsible for killing cells infected by a virus. Also called: **T-lymphocyte**

Tchad (tʃad) *n* the French name for **Chad**

Tchaikovsky (tʃaɪ'kɒfskɪ; *Russian* tʃɪj'kɔfskij) *n* **Pyotr Ilyich** (pjɔtr ilj'jitʃ) 1840–93, Russian composer. His works, which are noted for their expressive melodies, include the *Sixth Symphony* (the *Pathétique;* 1893), ballets, esp *Swan Lake* (1876) and *The Sleeping Beauty* (1889), and operas, including *Eugene Onegin* (1879) and *The Queen of Spades* (1890), both based on works by Pushkin

t distribution *n* See **Student's t**

te *or* **ti** (ti:) *n music* (in tonic sol-fa) the syllable used for the seventh note or subtonic of any scale [later variant of *si;* see GAMUT]

Te *the chemical symbol for* tellurium

tea (ti:) *n* **1** an evergreen shrub of tropical and subtropical Asia, having white fragrant flowers: family *Theaceae* **2a** the dried leaves of this shrub, used to make a beverage by infusion in boiling water **2b** such a beverage, served hot or iced **3a** any of various similar plants or any plants that are used to make a tealike beverage **3b** any such beverage **4** *chiefly Brit* **4a** Also called: **afternoon tea** a light meal eaten in mid-afternoon, usually consisting of tea and cakes, etc **4b** Also called: **high tea** afternoon tea that also includes a light cooked dish **5** *Brit, Austral, & NZ* the main evening meal **6** *US & Canad dated sl* marijuana **7** **tea and sympathy** *inf* a caring attitude, esp to someone in trouble [C17 from Chinese (Amoy) *t'e*, from Ancient Chinese *d'a*]
▷ www.teacouncil.co.uk
▷ www.tea.co.uk
▷ http://coffeetea.about.com
▷ www.nicecupofteaandasitdown.com

tea bag *n* a small bag containing tea leaves, infused in boiling water to make tea

tea ball *n chiefly US* a perforated metal ball filled with tea leaves and used to make tea

tea break *n* a short rest period during working hours during which tea, coffee, etc, is drunk

teacake ('ti:ˌkeɪk) *n Brit* a flat bun, usually eaten toasted and buttered

teach (ti:tʃ) *vb* **teaches, teaching, taught** **1** (*tr; may take a clause as object or an infinitive;* often foll by *how*) to help to learn; tell or show (how) **2** to give instruction or lessons in (a subject) to (a person or animal) **3** (*tr; may take a clause as object or an infinitive*) to cause to learn or understand: *experience taught him that he could not be a journalist* [OE *tǣcan*]
> '**teachable** *adj*

teacher ('ti:tʃə) *n* a person whose occupation is teaching others, esp children

teach-in *n* an informal conference, esp on a topical subject, usually held at a university or college and involving a panel of visiting speakers, lecturers, students, etc

teaching ('ti:tʃɪŋ) *n* **1** the art or profession of a teacher **2** (*sometimes pl*) something taught; precept **3** (*modifier*) denoting a person or institution that teaches: *a teaching hospital* **4** (*modifier*) used in teaching: *teaching aids*
▷ www.sosig.ac.uk/education/teaching_methods

teaching machine *n* a machine that presents information and questions to the user, registers the answers, and indicates whether these are correct or acceptable

tea cloth *n* another name for **tea towel**

tea cosy *n* a covering for a teapot to keep the contents hot

teacup ('ti:ˌkʌp) *n* **1** a cup out of which tea may be drunk **2** Also called: **teacupful** the amount a teacup will hold, about four fluid ounces

tea dance *n* a dance held in the afternoon at which tea is served

teahouse ('ti:ˌhaʊs) *n* a restaurant, esp in Japan or China, where tea and light refreshments are served

teak (ti:k) *n* **1** a large tree of the East Indies **2** the hard resinous yellowish-brown wood of this tree, used for furniture making, etc [C17 from Port. *teca*, from Malayalam *tēkka*]

teakettle ('ti:ˌkɛtᵊl) *n* a kettle for boiling water to make tea

teal (ti:l) *n, pl* **teals** *or* **teal** **1** any of various small freshwater ducks that are related to the mallard **2** a greenish-blue colour [C14]

tea lady *n* a woman employed in a factory, office, etc, to make tea during a tea break

tea leaf *n* **1** the dried leaf of the tea shrub, used to make tea **2** (*usually pl*) shredded parts of these leaves, esp after infusion

tea light *n* a small round candle in a disposable metal container

team (ti:m) *n* (*sometimes functioning as pl*) **1** a group of people organized to work together **2** a group of players forming one of the sides in a sporting contest **3** two or more animals working together, as to pull a vehicle **4** such animals and the vehicle ▷ *vb* **5** (when *intr*, often foll by *up*) to make or cause to make a team **6** (*tr*) *US & Canad* to drag or transport in or by a team **7** (*intr*) *US & Canad* to drive a team [OE *team* offspring]

tea-maker *n* a spoon with a perforated cover used to infuse tea in a cup of boiling water

team-mate *n* a fellow member of a team

team spirit *n* willingness to cooperate as part of a team

teamster ('ti:mstə) *n* **1** a driver of a team of horses **2** *US & Canad* the driver of a lorry

team teaching *n* a system whereby two or more teachers pool their skills, knowledge, etc, to teach combined classes

teamwork ('ti:mˌwɜ:k) *n* **1** the cooperative work done by a team **2** the ability to work efficiently as a team

teapot ('ti:ˌpɒt) *n* a container with a lid, spout, and handle, in which tea is made and from which it is served

teapoy ('ti:pɔɪ) *n* a small table with a tripod base [C19 from Hindi *tipāī*, from Sansk. *tri* three + *pāda* foot]

tear¹ (tɪə) *n* **1** a drop of the secretion of the lacrimal glands. See **tears** **2** something shaped like a hanging drop: *a tear of amber.* Also called: **teardrop** [OE *tēar*]
> '**tearless** *adj*

tear² (tɛə) *vb* **tears, tearing, tore, torn** **1** to cause to come apart or to come apart; rip **2** (*tr*) to make (a hole or split) in (something) **3** (*intr;* often foll by *along*) to hurry or rush **4** (*tr;* usually foll by *away* or *from*) to remove or

Tt

take by force **5** (when *intr*, often foll by *at*) to cause pain, distress, or anguish (to) **6** **tear one's hair** *inf* to be angry, frustrated, very worried, etc ▷ *n* **7** a hole, cut, or split **8** the act of tearing ▷ See also **tear away, tear down,** etc [OE *teran*] > '**tearable** *adj* > '**tearer** *n*

tear away (tɛə) *vb* **1** (*tr, adv*) to persuade (oneself or someone else) to leave ▷ *n* **tearaway 2** *Brit* a reckless impetuous unruly person

tear down (tɛə) *vb* (*tr, adv*) to destroy or demolish

tear duct (tɪə) *n* a short tube in the inner corner of the eyelid through which tears drain into the nose. Technical name: **lacrimal duct**

tearful ('tɪəfʊl) *adj* **1** crying or about to cry **2** tending to produce tears; sad > '**tearfully** *adv* > '**tearfulness** *n*

tear gas (tɪə) *n* a gas that makes the eyes smart and water, causing temporary blindness; used in warfare and to control riots

tearing ('tɛərɪŋ) *adj* violent or furious (esp in **tearing hurry** *or* **rush**)

tear into (tɛə) *vb* (*intr, prep*) *inf* to attack vigorously and damagingly

tear-jerker ('tɪəˌdʒɜːkə) *n inf* an excessively sentimental film, play, book, etc

tearoom ('tiːˌruːm, -ˌrʊm) *n Brit* a restaurant where tea and light refreshments are served. Also called: **teashop**

tea rose *n* any of several varieties of hybrid rose that have pink or yellow flowers with a scent resembling that of tea

tears (tɪəz) *pl n* **1** the clear salty solution secreted by the lacrimal glands that lubricates and cleanses the surface of the eyeball **2** a state of intense frustration (esp in **bored to tears**) **3** **in tears** weeping

tear sheet (tɛə) *n* a page in a newspaper or periodical that is cut or perforated so that it can be easily torn out

teary ('tɪərɪ) *adj* **tearier, teariest 1** characterized by, covered with, or secreting tears **2** given to weeping; tearful > '**tearily** *adv* > '**teariness** *n*

tease (tiːz) *vb* **teases, teasing, teased 1** to annoy (someone) by deliberately offering something with the intention of delaying or withdrawing the offer **2** to vex (someone) maliciously or playfully **3** (*tr*) to separate the fibres of; comb; card **4** (*tr*) to raise the nap of (a fabric) with a teasel **5** another word (esp US and Canad) for **backcomb 6** (*tr*) to loosen or pull apart (biological tissues, etc) ▷ *n* **7** a person or thing that teases **8** the act of teasing ▷ See also **tease out** [OE *tǣsan*] > '**teasing** *adj* > '**teasingly** *adv*

teasel, teazel, *or* **teazle** ('tiːzᵊl) *n* **1** any of various plants (esp the **fuller's teasel**) of Eurasia and N Africa, having prickly leaves and prickly heads of yellow or purple flowers **2a** the dried flower head of the fuller's teasel, used for teasing **2b** any implement used for the same purpose ▷ *vb* **teasels, teaselling, teaselled** *or US* **teasels, teaseling, teaseled 3** (*tr*) to tease (a fabric) [OE *tǣsel*] > '**teaseller** *n*

tease out *vb* (*tr, adv*) to extract (information) with difficulty

teaser ('tiːzə) *n* **1** a person who teases **2** a difficult question **3** a preliminary advertisement in a campaign that attracts attention by making people curious to know what product is being advertised

tea service *or* **set** *n* the china or pottery articles used in serving tea, including a teapot, cups, saucers, etc

teashop ('tiːˌʃɒp) *n Brit* another name for **tearoom**

teaspoon ('tiːˌspuːn) *n* **1** a small spoon used for stirring tea, etc **2** Also called: **teaspoonful** the amount contained in such a spoon **3** a unit of capacity used in cooking, medicine, etc, equal to about 5 ml

teat (tiːt) *n* **1a** the nipple of a mammary gland **1b** (in cows, etc) any of the projections from the udder **2** something resembling a teat such as the rubber mouthpiece of a feeding bottle [C13 from OF *tete*, of Gmc origin]

tea towel *or* **cloth** *n* a towel for drying dishes, etc. US name: **dishtowel**

tea tree *n* any of various trees of Australia and New Zealand that yield an oil used as an antiseptic

tea trolley *n Brit* a trolley from which tea is served

tebi- ('tɛbɪ) *combining form computing* denoting 2^{40}: *tebibyte*. Symbol: Ti [C20 from TE(RA-) + BI(NARY)]

TEC (tɛk) (in Britain) *n acronym for* Training and Enterprise Council. See **Training Agency**

tech (tɛk) *n inf* a technical college

tech. *abbrev for:* **1** technical **2** technology

techie *or* **techy** ('tɛkɪ) *inf* ▷ *n, pl* **techies 1** a person who is skilled in the use of technological devices, such as computing ▷ *adj* **2** of, relating to, or skilled in the use of such devices

technetium (tɛk'niːʃɪəm) *n* a silvery-grey metallic element, artificially produced by bombardment of molybdenum by deuterons. The radioisotope **technetium-99m** is used in radiotherapy. Symbol: Tc; atomic no.: 43; half-life of most stable isotope, ^{97}Tc: 2.6×10^6 years [C20 NL, from Gk *tekhnētos* manmade, from *tekhnasthai* to devise artificially, from *tekhnē* skill]

technic *n* **1** (tɛk'niːk) another word for **technique** **2** ('tɛknɪk) another word for **technics** [C17 from L *technicus*, from Gk *tekhnikos*, from *tekhnē* skill]

technical ('tɛknɪkᵊl) *adj* **1** of or specializing in industrial, practical, or mechanical arts and applied sciences **2** skilled in practical arts rather than abstract thinking **3** relating to a particular field of activity: *the technical jargon of linguistics* **4** existing by virtue of a strict application of the rules or a strict interpretation of the wording: *a technical loophole in the law* **5** of or showing technique: *technical brilliance* > '**technically** *adv* > '**technicalness** *n*

technical college *n Brit* an institution for further education that provides courses in technology, art, secretarial skills, agriculture, etc

technical drawing *n* the study and practice of the basic techniques of draughtsmanship, as employed in mechanical drawing, architecture, etc

technicality (ˌtɛknɪ'kælɪtɪ) *n, pl* **technicalities 1** a petty formal point arising from a strict interpretation of rules, etc **2** the state or quality of being technical **3** technical methods and vocabulary

technical knockout *n boxing* a judgment of a knockout given when a boxer is in the referee's opinion too badly beaten to continue without risk of serious injury

technician (tɛk'nɪʃən) *n* **1** a person skilled in mechanical or industrial techniques or in a particular technical field **2** a person employed in a laboratory, etc, to do mechanical and practical work **3** a person having specific artistic or mechanical skill, esp if lacking flair

Technicolor ('tɛknɪˌkʌlə) *n trademark* the process of producing colour film by means of superimposing synchronized films of the same scene, each of which has a different colour filter

technics ('tɛknɪks) *n* (*functioning as sing*) the study or theory of industry and industrial arts; technology

technikon ('tɛknɪˌkɒn) *n S African* a technical college

technique (tɛk'niːk) *n* **1** a practical method, skill, or art applied to a particular task **2** proficiency in a practical or mechanical skill **3** special facility; knack [C19 from F, from *technique* (adj): see TECHNIC]

techno ('tɛknəʊ) *n* a type of fast disco music, using electronic sounds and having a strong technological influence

▷ www.technopunkmusic.com

techno- *combining form* **1** craft or art: *technology; technography* **2** technological or technical: *technocracy* [from Gk *tekhnē* skill]

technocracy (tɛk'nɒkrəsɪ) *n, pl* **technocracies** government by scientists, engineers, and other such experts > **technocrat** ('tɛknəˌkræt) *n* > ˌ**techno'cratic** *adj*

technology (tɛk'nɒlədʒɪ) *n, pl* **technologies** **1** the application of practical or mechanical sciences to industry or commerce **2** the methods, theory, and practices governing such application **3** the total knowledge and skills available to any human society [C17 from Gk *tekhnologia* systematic treatment, from *tekhnē* skill] > **technological** (ˌtɛknə'lɒdʒɪkᵊl) *adj* > **tech'nologist** *n*

technophile ('tɛknəʊˌfaɪl) *n* **1** a person who is enthusiastic about technology ▷ *adj* **2** enthusiastic about technology

technophobe ('tɛknəʊˌfəʊb) *n* **1** someone who fears the effects of technological development on society or the environment **2** someone who is afraid of using technological devices, such as computers > ˌ**techno'phobic** *adj*

techy¹ ('tɛkɪ) *n, pl* **techies,** *adj* a variant spelling of **techie**

techy² ('tɛtʃɪ) *adj* **techier, techiest** a variant spelling of **tetchy** > **'techily** *adv* > **'techiness** *n*

tectonic (tɛk'tɒnɪk) *adj* **1** denoting or relating to building **2** *geol* **2a** (of landforms, etc) resulting from distortion of the earth's crust due to forces within it **2b** (of processes, movements, etc) occurring within the earth's crust and causing structural deformation [C17 from LL *tectonicus*, from Gk *tektonikos* belonging to carpentry, from *tektōn* a builder]

tectonics (tɛk'tɒnɪks) *n (functioning as sing)* **1** the art and science of construction or building **2** the study of the processes by which the earth's crust has attained its present structure

tectrix ('tɛktrɪks) *n, pl* **tectrices** ('tɛktrɪˌsiːz) *(usually pl) ornithol* another name for **covert** (sense 5) [C19 NL, from L *tector* plasterer, from *tegere* to cover] > **tectricial** (tɛk'trɪʃəl) *adj*

Tecumseh (tɪ'kʌmsə) *n* ?1768–1813, American Indian chief of the Shawnee tribe. He attempted to unite western Indian tribes against the Whites, but was defeated at Tippecanoe (1811). He was killed while fighting for the British in the War of 1812

ted¹ (tɛd) *vb* **teds, tedding, tedded** to shake out (hay), so as to dry it [C15 from ON *tethja*]

ted² (tɛd) *n inf* short for **teddy boy**

tedder ('tɛdə) *n* **1** a machine equipped with a series of small rotating forks for tedding hay **2** a person who teds

Tedder ('tɛdə) *n* **Arthur William,** 1st Baron Tedder of Glenguin. 1890–1967, British marshal of the Royal Air Force; deputy commander under Eisenhower of the Allied Expeditionary Force (1944–45)

teddy ('tɛdɪ) *n, pl* **teddies** a woman's one-piece undergarment, incorporating a chemise top and panties

teddy bear *n* a stuffed toy bear. Often shortened to **teddy** [C20 from *Teddy*, from *Theodore*, after Theodore ROOSEVELT, well known as a hunter of bears]

teddy boy *n* **1** (in Britain, esp in the mid-1950s) one of a cult of youths who wore mock Edwardian fashions **2** any tough or delinquent youth [C20 from *Teddy*, from *Edward*, referring to the Edwardian dress]
▷ www.rockabilly.nl/general/teddyboys.htm

Te Deum (ˌtiː 'diːəm) *n* **1** an ancient Latin hymn in rhythmic prose **2** a musical setting of this hymn **3** a service of thanksgiving in which the recital of this hymn forms a central part [from the L canticle beginning *Tē Deum laudāmus*, lit.: Thee, God, we praise]

tedious ('tiːdɪəs) *adj* causing fatigue or tedium; monotonous > **'tediousness** *n*

tedium ('tiːdɪəm) *n* the state of being bored or the quality of being boring; monotony [C17 from L *taedium*, from *taedēre* to weary]

tee¹ (tiː) *n* **1** a pipe fitting in the form of a letter T, used to join three pipes **2** a metal section with a cross section in the form of a letter T

tee² (tiː) *golf* ▷ *n* **1** an area, often slightly elevated, from which the first stroke of a hole is made **2** a support for a golf ball, usually a small wooden or plastic peg, used when teeing off or in long grass, etc ▷ *vb* **tees, teeing, teed** **3** (when *intr*, often foll by *up*) to position (the ball) ready for striking, on or as if on a tee ▷ See also **tee off** [C17 *teaz*, from ?]

tee³ (tiː) *n* a mark used as a target in certain games such as curling and quoits [C18 ?from T-shaped marks, which may have orig. been used in curling]

tee-hee *or* **te-hee** ('tiː'hiː) *interj* **1** an exclamation of laughter, esp when mocking ▷ *n* **2** a chuckle ▷ *vb* **tee-hees, tee-heeing, tee-heed** *or* **te-hees, te-heeing, te-heed** **3** *(intr)* to snigger or laugh, esp derisively [C14 imit.]

teem¹ (tiːm) *vb (intr; usually foll by with)* to be prolific or abundant (in) [OE *tēman* to produce offspring; rel. to West Saxon *tīeman*; see TEAM]

teem² (tiːm) *vb* **1** *(intr; often foll by down or with rain)* to pour in torrents **2** *(tr)* to pour or empty out [C15 *temen* to empty, from ON *tœma*]

teen (tiːn) *adj inf* another word for **teenage**

teenage ('tiːnˌeɪdʒ) *adj (prenominal)* of or relating to the time in a person's life between the ages of 13 and 19. Also: **teenaged**

teenager ('tiːnˌeɪdʒə) *n* a person between the ages of 13 and 19 inclusive

teens (tiːnz) *pl n* **1** the years of a person's life between the ages of 13 and 19 inclusive **2** all the numbers that end in *-teen*

teeny ('tiːnɪ) *adj* **teenier, teeniest** *inf* extremely small; tiny. Also: **teeny-weeny** ('tiːnɪ'wiːnɪ) *or* **teensy-weensy** ('tiːnzɪ'wiːnzɪ) [C19 var. of TINY]

teenybopper ('tiːnɪˌbɒpə) *n sl* a young teenager, usually a girl, who avidly follows fashions in clothes and pop music [C20 *teeny*, from teenage + *-bopper*; see BOP]

tee off *vb (adv)* **1** *golf* to strike (the ball) from a tee **2** *inf* to begin; start

teepee ('tiːpiː) *n* a variant spelling of **tepee**

Tees (tiːz) *n* a river in N England, rising in the N Pennines and flowing southeast and east to the North Sea at Middlesbrough. Length: 113 km (70 miles)

tee shirt *n* a variant of **T-shirt**

Teesside ('tiːzˌsaɪd) *n* the industrial region around the lower Tees valley and estuary: a county borough, containing Middlesbrough, from 1968 to 1974

teeter ('tiːtə) *vb* **1** to move or cause to move unsteadily; wobble ▷ *n, vb* **2** another word for **seesaw** [C19 from ME *titeren*]

teeth (tiːθ) *n* **1** the plural of **tooth** **2** the most violent part: *the teeth of the gale* **3** the power to produce a desired effect: *that law has no teeth* **4** **get one's teeth into** to become engrossed in **5** **in the teeth of** in direct opposition to; against **6** **to the teeth** to the greatest possible degree: *armed to the teeth* **7** **show one's teeth** to threaten

teethe (tiːð) *vb* **teethes, teething, teethed** *(intr)* to cut one's baby (deciduous) teeth

teething ring *n* a hard ring on which babies may bite while teething

teething troubles *pl n* the problems that arise during the initial stages of a project, etc

teetotal (tiː'təʊtᵊl) *adj* **1** of or practising abstinence from alcoholic drink **2** *dialect* complete [C19 allegedly coined in 1833 by Richard Turner, E advocate of total abstinence from alcohol; prob. from TOTAL, with emphatic reduplication] > **tee'totaller** *n* > **tee'totalism** *n*

teetotum (tiː'təʊtəm) *n arch* a spinning top bearing letters of the alphabet on its four sides [C18 from T *totum*, from T initial on one of the faces + *totum* the name of the toy, from L *tōtum* the whole]

teff (tɛf) *n* an annual grass of NE Africa, grown for its grain [C18 from Amharic *tēf*]

Tt

TEFL ('tɛfᵊl) *n acronym for* Teaching (of) English as a Foreign Language

Teflon ('tɛflɒn) *n* a trademark for **polytetrafluoroethylene**

teg (tɛg) *n* **1** a two-year-old sheep **2** the fleece of a two-year-old sheep [c16 from ?]

tegmen ('tɛgmən) *n, pl* **tegmina** (-mənə) **1** either of the leathery forewings of the cockroach and related insects **2** the delicate inner covering of a seed **3** any similar covering or layer [c19 from L: a cover, from *tegere* to cover] > **'tegminal** *adj*

Tegucigalpa (*Spanish* teɣuθi'ɣalpa) *n* the capital of Honduras, in the south on the Choluteca River: founded about 1579; university (1847). Pop: 988 400 (1999 est)

tegument ('tɛgjʊmənt) *n* a less common word for **integument** [c15 from L *tegumentum* a covering, from *tegere* to cover]

te-hee (tiː'hiː) *interj, n, vb* a variant of **tee-hee**

Tehran *or* **Teheran** (tɛə'rɑːn, -'ræn) *n* the capital of Iran, at the foot of the Elburz Mountains: built on the site of the ancient capital Ray, destroyed by Mongols in 1220; became capital in the 1790s; three universities. Pop: 16 758 845 (1996)
▷ www.farsinet.com/tehran

Tehuantepec (tə'wɑːntəˌpɛk) *n* **Isthmus of** the narrowest part of S Mexico, with the Bay of Campeche on the north coast and the **Gulf of Tehuantepec** (an inlet of the Pacific) on the south coast

Teide (*Spanish* 'tɛiðe) *n* **Pico de** ('piko de) a volcanic mountain in the Canary Islands, on Tenerife. Height: 3718 m (12 198 ft)

te igitur *Latin* (teɪ 'ɪgɪˌtʊə; *English* teɪ 'ɪdʒɪtʊə) *n RC Church* the first prayer of the canon of the Mass, which begins *Te igitur clementissime Pater* (Thee, therefore, most merciful Father)

Teilhard de Chardin (*French* tɛjar də ʃardɛ̃) *n* **Pierre** (pjɛr) 1881–1955, French Jesuit priest, palaeontologist, and philosopher. *The Phenomenon of Man* (1938–40), uses scientific evolution to prove the existence of God

Tejo ('təʒu) *n* the Portuguese name for the **Tagus**

Te Kanawa (teɪ 'kɑːnəwə) *n* Dame **Kiri** ('kɪrɪ) born 1944, New Zealand operatic soprano

tektite ('tɛktaɪt) *n* a small dark glassy object found in several areas around the world, thought to be a product of meteorite impact [c20 from Gk *tēktos* molten]

tel- *combining form* a variant of **tele-** and **telo-** before a vowel

telaesthesia *or US* **telesthesia** (ˌtɛlɪs'θiːzɪə) *n* the alleged perception of events that are beyond the normal range of perceptual processes > **telaesthetic** *or US* **telesthetic** (ˌtɛlɪs'θɛtɪk) *adj*

telamon ('tɛləmən) *n, pl* **telamones** (ˌtɛlə'məʊniːz) *or* **telamons** a column in the form of a male figure, used to support an entablature [c18 via L from Gk, from *tlēnai* to bear]

Telamon ('tɛləmən, -ˌmɒn) *n Greek myth* a king of Salamis; brother of Peleus and father of Teucer and Ajax

Telanaipura (ˌtɛlənaɪ'pʊərə) *n* another name for **Jambi**

telangiectasis (tɪˌlændʒɪ'ɛktəsɪs) *or* **telangiectasia** (tɪˌlændʒɪɛk'teɪzɪə) *n, pl* **telangiectases** (-ˌsiːz) *pathol* an abnormal dilation of the capillaries or terminal arteries producing blotched red spots, esp on the face or thighs [c19 NL, from Gk *telos* end + *angeion* vessel + *ektasis* dilation] > **telangiectatic** (tɪˌlændʒɪɛk'tætɪk) *adj*

Tel Aviv ('tɛl ə'viːv) *n* a city in W Israel, on the Mediterranean: the largest city and chief financial centre in Israel; incorporated the city of Jaffa in 1950; university (1953): the capital of Israel according to the UN and international law. Pop: 348 100 (1999 est). Official name: **Tel Aviv-Jaffa** ('tɛl ə'viːv'dʒæfə)
▷ www.tel-aviv.gov.il

Telcom ('tɛlˌkɒm) *n* the official telephone service in South Africa

tele- *combining form* **1** at or over a distance; distant: *telescope; telekinesis* **2** television: *telecast* **3** by means of or via telephone or television: *telesales* [from Gk *tele* far]

telecast ('tɛləˌkɑːst) *vb* **telecasts, telecasting, telecast** *or* **telecasted 1** to broadcast by television ▷ *n* **2** a television broadcast > **'teleˌcaster** *n*

telecom ('tɛlɪˌkɒm) *or* **telecoms** ('tɛlɪˌkɒmz) *n* (*functioning as sing*) short for **telecommunications**

telecommunications (ˌtɛlɪkəˌmjuːnɪ'keɪʃənz) *n* (*functioning as sing*) the science and technology of communications by telephony, radio, television, etc
▷ www.analysys.com
▷ www.itu.int/home

telecommuting (ˌtɛlɪkə'mjuːtɪŋ) *n* another name for **teleworking** > **ˌtelecom'muter** *n*

teledu ('tɛlɪˌduː) *n* a badger of SE Asia and Indonesia, having dark brown hair with a white stripe along the back and producing a fetid secretion when attacked [c19 from Malay]

telegenic (ˌtɛlɪ'dʒɛnɪk) *adj* having or showing a pleasant television image [c20 from TELE(VISION) + (PHOTO)GENIC] > **ˌtele'genically** *adv*

telegnosis (ˌtɛlə'nəʊsɪs, ˌtɛləg-) *n* knowledge about distant events alleged to have been obtained without the use of any normal sensory mechanism [c20 from TELE- + *-gnosis*, from Gk *gnōsis* knowledge]

Telegonus (tɪ'lɛgənəs) *n Greek myth* a son of Odysseus and Circe, who sought his father and mistakenly killed him, later marrying Odysseus' widow Penelope

telegony (tɪ'lɛgənɪ) *n genetics* the supposed influence of a previous sire on offspring borne by a female to other sires > **telegonic** (ˌtɛlɪ'gɒnɪk) *or* **te'legonous** *adj*

telegram ('tɛlɪˌgræm) *n* a communication transmitted by telegraph

telegraph ('tɛlɪˌgrɑːf) *n* **1a** a device, system, or process by which information can be transmitted over a distance, esp using radio signals or coded electrical signals sent along a transmission line **1b** (*as modifier*): *telegraph pole* ▷ *vb* **2** to send a telegram to (a person or place); wire **3** (*tr*) to transmit or send by telegraph **4** (*tr*) to give advance notice of (anything), esp unintentionally **5** (*tr*) *Canad inf* to cast (votes) illegally by impersonating registered voters > **telegraphist** (tɪ'lɛgrəˌfɪst) *or* **telegrapher** (tɪ'lɛgrəfə) *n* > **ˌtele'graphic** *adj*

telegraph plant *n* a small tropical Asian shrub having small leaflets that turn in various directions during the day and droop at night

telegraphy (tɪ'lɛgrəfɪ) *n* **1** a system of telecommunications involving any process providing reproduction at a distance of written, printed, or pictorial matter **2** the skill or process of operating a telegraph

Telegu ('tɛləˌguː) *n, adj* a variant spelling of **Telugu**

telekinesis (ˌtɛlɪkaɪ'niːsɪs) *n* **1** the movement of a body caused by thought or willpower without the application of a physical force **2** the ability to cause such movement > **telekinetic** (ˌtɛlɪkɪ'nɛtɪk) *adj*

Telemachus (tɪ'lɛməkəs) *n Greek myth* the son of Odysseus and Penelope, who helped his father slay his mother's suitors

Telemann (*German* 'teːləman) *n* **Georg Philipp** ('geːɔrk 'fiːlɪp) 1681–1767, German composer, noted for his prolific output

telemark ('tɛlɪˌmɑːk) *n skiing* a turn in which one ski is placed far forward of the other and turned gradually inwards [c20 after *Telemark*, county in Norway]

telemarketing ('tɛlɪˌmɑːkɪtɪŋ) *n* another name for **telesales** > **'teleˌmarketer** *n*

telematics (ˌtɛlɪ'mætɪks) *n* the branch of science concerned with the use of technological devices to transmit information over long distances [c20 from TELE- + (INFOR)MATICS] > **ˌtele'matic** *adj*

telemedicine ('tɛlɪˌmɛdɪsɪn, -ˌmedsɪn) *n* the treatment of disease or injury by consultation with a specialist in a distant place, esp by means of a computer or satellite link

Telemessage (ˈtɛlɪˌmɛsɪdʒ) *n trademark* a message sent by telephone or telex and delivered in printed form

telemeter (tɪˈlɛmɪtə) *n* **1** any device for recording or measuring a distant event and transmitting the data to a receiver **2** any device used to measure a distance without directly comparing it with a measuring rod, etc ▷ *vb* **3** (*tr*) to obtain and transmit (data) from a distant source > **telemetric** (ˌtɛlɪˈmɛtrɪk) *adj*

telemetry (tɪˈlɛmɪtrɪ) *n* **1** the use of radio waves, telephone lines, etc, to transmit the readings of measuring instruments to a device on which the readings can be indicated or recorded **2** the measurement of linear distance using a tellurometer

telencephalon (ˌtɛlɛnˈsɛfəˌlɒn) *n* the cerebrum together with related parts of the hypothalamus and the third ventricle > **telencephalic** (ˈtɛlɛnsɪˈfælɪk) *adj*

teleology (ˌtɛlɪˈɒlədʒɪ, ˌtiːlɪ-) *n* **1** *philosophy* **1a** the doctrine that there is evidence of purpose or design in the universe, and esp that this provides proof of the existence of a Designer **1b** the belief that certain phenomena are best explained in terms of purpose rather than cause **2** *biol* the belief that natural phenomena have a predetermined purpose and are not determined by mechanical laws [c18 from NL *teleologia*, from Gk *telos* end + -LOGY] > **teleological** (ˌtɛlɪəˈlɒdʒɪkᵊl, ˌtiːlɪ-) *adj* > ˌ**teleˈologist** *n*

teleost (ˈtɛlɪˌɒst, ˈtiːlɪ-) *n* any of a subclass of bony fishes having rayed fins and a swim bladder, as herrings, carps, eels, cod, perches, etc [c19 from NL *teleosteī* (pl) creatures having complete skeletons, from Gk *teleos* complete + *osteon* bone]

telepathy (tɪˈlɛpəθɪ) *n* the communication between people of thoughts, feelings, etc, involving mechanisms that cannot be understood in terms of known scientific laws > **telepathic** (ˌtɛlɪˈpæθɪk) *adj* > **teˈlepathist** *n* > **teˈlepaˌthize** *or* > **teˈlepaˌthise** *vb* (*intr*)

telephone (ˈtɛlɪˌfəʊn) *n* **1** an electrical device for transmitting speech, consisting of a microphone and receiver mounted on a handset **2a** a worldwide system of communications using telephones. The microphone in one telephone converts sound waves into electrical signals that are transmitted along a telephone wire or by radio to one or more distant sets **2b** (*as modifier*): *a telephone exchange* ▷ *vb* **3** to call or talk to (a person) by telephone **4** to transmit (a message, etc) by telephone > **ˈteleˌphoner** *n* > **telephonic** (ˌtɛlɪˈfɒnɪk) *adj*

telephone banking *n* a facility enabling customers to make use of banking services, such as oral payment instructions, account movements, raising loans, etc, over the telephone rather than by personal visit

telephone box *n* an enclosure from which a paid telephone call can be made. Also called: **telephone kiosk, telephone booth**

telephone directory *n* a book listing the names, addresses, and telephone numbers of subscribers in a particular area

telephone number *n* **1** a set of figures identifying the telephone of a particular subscriber, and used in making connections to that telephone **2** (*pl*) extremely large numbers, esp in reference to salaries or prices

telephone selling *n* another name for **telesales**

telephonist (tɪˈlɛfənɪst) *n Brit* a person who operates a telephone switchboard. Also called (esp US): **telephone operator**

telephony (tɪˈlɛfənɪ) *n* a system of telecommunications for the transmission of speech or other sounds

telephotography (ˌtɛlɪfəˈtɒgrəfɪ) *n* the process or technique of photographing distant objects using a telephoto lens

telephoto lens (ˈtɛlɪˌfəʊtəʊ) *n* a compound camera lens in which the focal length is greater than that of a simple lens and thus produces a magnified image of a distant object

telepoint (ˈtɛlɪˌpɔɪnt) *n* **a** a system providing a place where a cordless telephone can be connected to a telephone network **b** a place where a cordless telephone can be connected to a telephone network

teleprinter (ˈtɛlɪˌprɪntə) *n* **1** a telegraph apparatus consisting of a keyboard transmitter, which converts a typed message into coded pulses for transmission along a wire or cable, and a printing receiver, which converts incoming signals and prints out the message. US name: **teletypewriter** **2** a network of such devices: no longer widely used **3** a similar device used for direct input/output of data into a computer at a distant location

Teleprompter (ˈtɛlɪˌprɒmptə) *n trademark* a device for displaying a television script so that the speaker can read it while appearing to look at the camera

Teleran (ˈtɛləˌræn) *n trademark* an electronic navigational aid in which the image of a ground-based radar system is televised to aircraft [c20 from *Tele(vision) R(adar) A(ir) N(avigation)*]

telesales (ˈtɛlɪˌseɪlz) *n* (*functioning as sing*) the selling or attempted selling of a particular commodity or service by a salesperson who makes his or her initial approach by telephone. Also called: **telemarketing, telephone selling**

telescope (ˈtɛlɪˌskəʊp) *n* **1** an optical instrument for making distant objects appear closer by use of a combination of lenses (**refracting telescope**) or lenses and curved mirrors (**reflecting telescope**) **2** any instrument, such as a radio telescope, for collecting, focusing, and detecting electromagnetic radiation from space ▷ *vb* **telescopes, telescoping, telescoped** **3** to crush together or be crushed together, as in a collision **4** to fit together like a set of cylinders that slide into one another, thus allowing extension and shortening **5** to make or become smaller or shorter [c17 from It. *telescopio* or NL *telescopium*, lit.: far-seeing instrument]

telescopic (ˌtɛlɪˈskɒpɪk) *adj* **1** of or relating to a telescope **2** seen through or obtained by means of a telescope **3** visible only with a telescope **4** able to see far **5** having parts that telescope > ˌ**teleˈscopically** *adv*

telescopic sight *n* a telescope mounted on a rifle, etc, used for sighting

telescopy (tɪˈlɛskəpɪ) *n* the branch of astronomy concerned with the use and design of telescopes

teleshopping (ˈtɛlɪˌʃɒpɪŋ) *n* the purchase of goods by telephone or via the Internet

telespectroscope (ˌtɛlɪˈspɛktrəˌskəʊp) *n* a combination of a telescope and a spectroscope, used for spectroscopic analysis of radiation from stars and other celestial bodies

telestereoscope (ˌtɛlɪˈstɪərɪəˌskəʊp, -ˈstɛrɪə-) *n* an optical instrument for obtaining stereoscopic images of distant objects

telestich (tɪˈlɛstɪk, ˈtɛlɪˌstɪk) *n* a short poem in which the last letters of each successive line form a word [c17 from Gk *telos* end + *stikhos* row]

Teletext (ˈtɛlɪˌtɛkst) *n trademark* a form of Videotex in which information is broadcast by a television station and received on an adapted television set. **Ceefax** is provided by the BBC and **Oracle** by ITV

▷ www.teletext.com

telethon (ˈtɛlɪˌθɒn) *n* a lengthy television programme to raise charity funds, etc [c20 from TELE- + MARATHON]

Teletype (ˈtɛlɪˌtaɪp) *n* **1** *trademark* a type of teleprinter **2** (*sometimes not cap*) a network of such devices ▷ *vb* **Teletypes, Teletyping, Teletyped** **3** (*sometimes not cap*) to transmit (a message) by Teletype

teletypewriter (ˌtɛlɪˈtaɪpˌraɪtə, ˈtɛlɪˌtaɪp-) *n* a US name for **teleprinter**

Tt

televangelist (ˌtɛlɪˈvændʒəlɪst) *n US* an evangelical preacher who appears regularly on television, preaching the gospel and appealing for donations from viewers [C20 from TELE(VISION + E)VANGELIST]

televise (ˈtɛlɪˌvaɪz) *vb* **televises, televising, televised 1** to put on television **2** (*tr*) to transmit by television

television (ˈtɛlɪˌvɪʒən) *n* **1** the system or process of producing on a distant screen a series of transient visible images, usually with an accompanying sound signal. Electrical signals, converted from optical images by a camera tube, are transmitted by radio waves or by cable and reconverted into optical images by means of a television tube inside a television set **2** Also called: **television set** a device designed to receive and convert incoming electrical signals into a series of visible images on a screen together with accompanying sound **3** the content, etc, of television programmes **4** the occupation or profession concerned with any aspect of the broadcasting of television programmes **5** (*modifier*) of, relating to, or used in the transmission or reception of video and audio UHF or VHF radio signals: *a television transmitter*. Abbrev: **TV**
▷ www.emmys.com

television tube *n* a cathode-ray tube designed for the reproduction of television pictures. Sometimes shortened to **tube**

televisual (ˌtɛlɪˈvɪʒʊəl, -zjʊ-) *adj* relating to or suitable for production on television > ˌ**teleˈvisually** *adv*

teleworking (ˈtɛlɪˌwɜːkɪŋ) *n* the use of home computers, telephones, etc, to enable a person to work from home while maintaining contact with colleagues, customers, or a central office. Also called: **telecommuting** > ˈ**teleˌworker** *n*

telex (ˈtɛlɛks) *n* **1** an international telegraph service in which teleprinters are rented out to subscribers **2** a teleprinter used in such a service **3** a message transmitted or received by telex ▷ *vb* **4** to transmit (a message) to (a person, etc) by telex [C20 from *tel(eprinter) ex(change)*]

Telford[1] (ˈtɛlfəd) *n* a town in W central England, in Telford and Wrekin unitary authority, Shropshire: designated a new town in 1963. Pop: 119 340 (1991)

Telford[2] (ˈtɛlfəd) *n* **Thomas** 1757–1834, Scottish civil engineer, known esp for his roads and such bridges as the Menai suspension bridge (1825)

Telford and Wrekin *n* a unitary authority in W Central England, in Shropshire. Pop: 158 285 (2001). Area: 289 sq km (112 sq miles)

Telidon (ˈtɛlɪˌdɒn) *n trademark* a Canadian interactive viewdata service

tell[1] (tɛl) *vb* **tells, telling, told 1** (when *tr, may take a clause as object*) to let know or notify **2** (*tr*) to order or instruct **3** (when *intr*, usually foll by *of*) to give an account or narration (of) **4** (*tr*) to communicate by words: *tell lies* **5** (*tr*) to make known: *to tell fortunes* **6** (*intr;* often foll by *of*) to serve as an indication: *her blush told of her embarrassment* **7** (*tr;* used with *can*, etc; *may take a clause as object*) to discover or discern: *I can tell what is wrong* **8** (*tr;* used with *can*, etc) to distinguish or discriminate: *he couldn't tell chalk from cheese* **9** (*intr*) to have or produce an impact, effect, or strain: *every step told on his bruised feet* **10** (*intr;* sometimes foll by *on*) *inf* to reveal secrets or gossip (about) **11** (*tr*) to assure: *I tell you, I've had enough!* **12** (*tr*) to count (votes) **13 tell the time** to read the time from a clock **14 you're telling me** *sl* I know that very well ▷ See also **tell apart, tell off** [OE *tellan*] > ˈ**tellable** *adj*

tell[2] (tɛl) *n* a large mound resulting from the accumulation of rubbish on a long-settled site, esp in the Middle East [C19 from Ar. *tall*]

Tell (tɛl) *n* **William,** German name *Wilhelm Tell* a legendary Swiss patriot, who, traditionally, lived in the early 14th century and was compelled by an Austrian governor to shoot an apple from his son's head with one shot of his crossbow. He did so without mishap

tell apart *vb* (*tr, adv*) to distinguish between

Tell el Amarna (ˈtɛl ɛl əˈmɑːnə) *n* a group of ruins and rock tombs in Upper Egypt, on the Nile below Asyut: site of the capital of Amenhotep IV, built about 1375 BC; excavated from 1891 onwards

teller (ˈtɛlə) *n* **1** a bank cashier **2** a person appointed to count votes **3** a person who tells; narrator

Teller (ˈtɛlə) *n* **Edward** 1908–2003, US nuclear physicist, born in Hungary: a major contributor to the development of the hydrogen bomb (1952)

telling (ˈtɛlɪŋ) *adj* **1** having a marked effect or impact **2** revealing > ˈ**tellingly** *adv*

tell off *vb* (*tr, adv*) **1** *inf* to reprimand; scold **2** to count and select for duty

telltale (ˈtɛlˌteɪl) *n* **1** a person who tells tales about others **2a** an outward indication of something concealed **2b** (*as modifier*): *a telltale paw mark* **3** a device used to monitor a process, machine, etc

tellurian (tɛˈlʊərɪən) *adj* **1** of the earth ▷ *n* **2** (esp in science fiction) an inhabitant of the earth [C19 from L *tellūs* the earth]

telluric[1] (tɛˈlʊərɪk) *adj* of or originating on or in the earth or soil; terrestrial [C19 from L *tellūs* the earth]

telluric[2] (tɛˈlʊərɪk) *adj* of or containing tellurium, esp in a high valence state [C20 from TELLUR(IUM) + -IC]

tellurion *or* **tellurian** (tɛˈlʊərɪən) *n* an instrument that shows how day and night, etc, result from the earth's rotation on its axis, etc [C19 from L *tellūs* the earth]

tellurium (tɛˈlʊərɪəm) *n* a brittle silvery-white nonmetallic element. Symbol: Te; atomic no.: 52; atomic wt.: 127.60 [C19 NL, from L *tellūs* the earth, by analogy with URANIUM]

tellurometer (ˌtɛljʊˈrɒmɪtə) *n surveying* an electronic instrument for measuring distances by the transmission of radio waves [C20 from L *tellūs* the earth + -METER]

Tellus (ˈtɛləs) *n* the Roman goddess of the earth; protectress of marriage, fertility, and the dead

telly (ˈtɛlɪ) *n, pl* **tellies** *inf, chiefly Brit* short for **television**

telo- *or before a vowel* **tel-** *combining form* **1** complete; final; perfect **2** end; at the end [from Gk *telos* end]

telpherage (ˈtɛlfərɪdʒ) *n* an overhead transport system in which an electrically driven truck runs along a rail or cable, the load being suspended in a car beneath. Also called: **telpher** [C19 changed from *telephore*, from TELE- + -PHORE + -AGE]

telson (ˈtɛlsən) *n* the last segment or an appendage on the last segment of the body of crustaceans and arachnids [C19 from Gk: a boundary]

Telugu *or* **Telegu** (ˈtɛləˌguː) *n* **1** a language of SE India, belonging to the Dravidian family of languages **2** (*pl* **Telugus** *or* **Telugu**) a member of the people who speak this language ▷ *adj* **3** of or relating to this people or their language

Telukbetung *or* **Teloekbetoeng** (təˌlʊkbəˈtʊŋ) *n* a port in Indonesia, in S Sumatra on the Sunda Strait. Pop: 284 275 (latest est)

Tema (ˈtiːmə) *n* a port in SE Ghana on the Atlantic: new harbour opened in 1962; oil-refining. Pop (urban area): 300 000 (1998 est)

temazepam (təˈmæzəˌpæm) *n* a benzodiazepine sedative; the gel-like capsule formulation is properly taken orally but has also been melted and injected by drug users

Témbi (ˈtɛmbiː) *n* transliteration of the Modern Greek name for **Tempe**

temblor (ˈtɛmblə, -blɔː) *n, pl* **temblors** *or* **temblores** (tɛmˈblɔːreɪz) *chiefly US* an earthquake or earth tremor [C19 American Sp., from Sp. *temblar* to shake, tremble]

temerity (tɪˈmɛrɪtɪ) *n* rashness or boldness [C15 from L *temeritās* accident, from *temere* at random] > **temerarious** (ˌtɛməˈrɛərɪəs) *adj*

Temesvár ('tɛmɛʃvaːr) *n* the Hungarian name for **Timişoara**
temp (tɛmp) *inf* ▷ *n* **1** a person, esp a typist or other office worker, employed on a temporary basis ▷ *vb (intr)* **2** to work as a temp
temp. *abbrev for:* **1** temperature **2** temporary **3** tempore [L: in the time of]
Tempe ('tɛmpɪ) *n* **Vale of** a wooded valley in E Greece, in Thessaly between the mountains Olympus and Ossa. Modern Greek name: **Témbi**
temper ('tɛmpə) *n* **1** a frame of mind; mood or humour **2** a sudden outburst of anger **3** a tendency to exhibit anger; irritability **4** a mental condition of moderation and calm (esp in **keep one's temper** *or* **lose one's temper**) **5** the degree of hardness, elasticity, etc, of a metal ▷ *vb (tr)* **6** to make more acceptable or suitable by adding something else; moderate: *he tempered his criticism with sympathy* **7** to reduce the brittleness of (a hardened metal) by reheating it and allowing it to cool **8** *music* **8a** to adjust the frequency differences between the notes of a scale on (a keyboard instrument) **8b** to make such an adjustment to the pitches of notes in (a scale) [OE *temprian* to mingle, from L *temperāre* to mix, prob. from *tempus* time] > **'temperable** *adj* > **'temperer** *n*
tempera ('tɛmpərə) *n* **1** a painting medium for powdered pigments, consisting usually of egg yolk and water **2a** any emulsion used as a painting medium, with casein, glue, wax, etc, as a base **2b** the paint made from this **3** the technique of painting with tempera [c19 from It. *pingere a tempera* painting in tempera, from *temperare* to mingle; see TEMPER]
temperament ('tɛmpərəmənt) *n* **1** a person's character, disposition, and tendencies **2** excitability, moodiness, or anger **3** the characteristic way an individual behaves, esp towards other people **4a** an adjustment made to the frequency differences between notes on a keyboard instrument to allow modulation to other keys **4b** any of several systems of such adjustment, esp **equal temperament,** a system giving a scale based on an octave divided into twelve exactly equal semitones **5** *obs* the characteristic way an individual behaves, viewed as the result of the influence of the four humours [c15 from L *temperāmentum* a mixing in proportion, from *temperāre* to TEMPER]
temperamental (ˌtɛmpərə'mɛntᵊl) *adj* **1** easily upset or irritated; excitable **2** of or caused by temperament **3** *inf* working erratically and inconsistently; unreliable > **ˌtempera'mentally** *adv*
temperance ('tɛmpərəns) *n* **1** restraint or moderation, esp in yielding to one's appetites or desires **2** abstinence from alcoholic drink [c14 from L *temperantia*, from *temperāre* to regulate]
temperate ('tɛmpərɪt) *adj* **1** having a climate intermediate between tropical and polar; moderate or mild in temperature **2** mild in quality or character; exhibiting temperance [c14 from L *temperātus*] > **'temperately** *adv* > **'temperateness** *n*
Temperate Zone *n* those parts of the earth's surface lying between the Arctic Circle and the tropic of Cancer and between the Antarctic Circle and the tropic of Capricorn
temperature ('tɛmprɪtʃə) *n* **1** the degree of hotness of a body, substance, or medium, esp as measured on a scale that has one or more fixed reference points **2** *inf* a body temperature in excess of the normal [c16 (orig.: a mingling): from L *temperātūra* proportion, from *temperāre* to TEMPER]
temperature gradient *n* the rate of change in temperature in a given direction
temperature-humidity index *n* an index of the effect on human comfort of temperature and humidity levels, 65 being the highest comfortable level
tempered ('tɛmpəd) *adj* **1** *music* adjusted in accordance with a system of temperament **2** *(in combination)* having a temper or temperament as specified: *ill-tempered*
tempest ('tɛmpɪst) *n* **1** *chiefly literary* a violent wind or storm **2** a violent commotion, uproar, or disturbance [c13 from OF *tempeste*, from L *tempestās* storm, from *tempus* time]
tempestuous (tɛm'pɛstjʊəs) *adj* **1** of or relating to a tempest **2** violent or stormy > **tem'pestuously** *adv* > **tem'pestuousness** *n*
tempi ('tɛmpiː) *n* (in musical senses) the plural of **tempo**
Templar ('tɛmplə) *n* **1** a member of a military order (**Knights of the Temple of Solomon**) founded by Crusaders in Jerusalem around 1118; suppressed in 1312 **2** *(sometimes not cap) Brit* a lawyer who has chambers in the Temple in London [c13 from Med. L *templārius* of the TEMPLE; applied to the order because their house adjoined the site of the Temple of Solomon]
template *or* **templet** ('tɛmplɪt) *n* **1** a gauge or pattern, cut out in wood or metal, used in woodwork, etc, to help shape something accurately **2** a pattern cut out in card or plastic, used to reproduce shapes **3** a short beam that is used to spread a load, as over a doorway **4** *biochem* the molecular structure of a compound that serves as a pattern for the production of another compound [c17 *templet* (later spelling infl. by PLATE), prob. from F, dim. of TEMPLE[3]]
temple[1] ('tɛmpᵊl) *n* **1** a building or place dedicated to the worship of a deity or deities **2** a Mormon church **3** *US* another name for a **synagogue** **4** a Christian church **5** any place or object regarded as a shrine where God makes himself present **6** a building regarded as the focus of an activity, interest, or practice: *a temple of the arts* [OE *tempel*, from L *templum*]
temple[2] ('tɛmpᵊl) *n* the region on each side of the head in front of the ear and above the cheekbone [c14 from OF *temple*, from L *tempora* the temples, from *tempus* temple of the head]
temple[3] ('tɛmpᵊl) *n* the part of a loom that keeps the cloth being woven stretched to the correct width [c15 from F, from L *templum* a small timber] ('tɛmpəl) *n* **1** a building in London that belonged to the Templars: it now houses two law societies **2** any of three buildings erected by the Jews in ancient Jerusalem for the worship of Jehovah
Temple[1] ('tɛmpəl) *n* **1** a building in London that belonged to the Templars: it now houses two law societies **2** any of three buildings erected by the Jews in ancient Jerusalem for the worship of Jehovah
Temple[2] ('tɛmpᵊl) *n* **1** **Shirley,** married name *Shirley Temple Black* born 1928, US film actress and politician. Her films as a child star include *Little Miss Marker* (1934), *Wee Willie Winkie* (1937), and *Heidi* (1937). She was US ambassador to Ghana (1974–76) and to Czechoslovakia (1989–92) **2** Sir **William** 1628–99, English diplomat and essayist. He negotiated the Triple Alliance (1668) and the marriage of William of Orange to Mary II **3** **William** 1881–1944, English prelate and advocate of social reform; archbishop of Canterbury (1942–44)
Temple of Artemis *n* the large temple at Ephesus, on the W coast of Asia Minor: one of the Seven Wonders of the World
tempo ('tɛmpəʊ) *n, pl* **tempos** *or* **tempi** (-piː) **1** the speed at which a piece of music is meant to be played **2** rate or pace [c18 from It., from L *tempus* time]
temporal[1] ('tɛmpərəl) *adj* **1** of or relating to time **2** of secular as opposed to spiritual or religious affairs **3** lasting for a relatively short time **4** *grammar* of or relating to tense or the linguistic expression of time [c14 from L *temporālis*, from *tempus* time] > **'temporally** *adv*
temporal[2] ('tɛmpərəl) *adj anat* of or near the temple or temples [c16 from LL *temporālis* belonging to the temples; see TEMPLE[2]]
temporal bone *n* either of two compound bones

Tt

forming the sides of the skull

temporality (ˌtɛmpəˈrælɪtɪ) *n, pl* **temporalities** 1 the state or quality of being temporal 2 something temporal 3 (*often pl*) a secular possession or revenue belonging to a Church

temporal lobe *n* the laterally protruding portion of each cerebral hemisphere, situated below the parietal lobe and associated with sound perception and interpretation

temporary (ˈtɛmpərərɪ) *adj* 1 not permanent; provisional 2 lasting only a short time ▹ *n, pl* **temporaries** 3 a person employed on a temporary basis [c16 from L *temporārius*, from *tempus* time] > ˈ**temporarily** *adv* > ˈ**temporariness** *n*

temporize *or* **temporise** (ˈtɛmpəˌraɪz) *vb* **temporizes, temporizing, temporized** *or* **temporises, temporising, temporised** (*intr*) 1 to delay, act evasively, or protract a negotiation, etc, esp in order to gain time or effect a compromise 2 to adapt oneself to the circumstances, as by temporary or apparent agreement [c16 from F *temporiser*, from Med. L *temporizāre*, from L *tempus* time] > ˌ**temporiˈzation** *or* ˌ**temporiˈsation** *n* > ˈ**tempoˌrizer** *or* ˈ**tempoˌriser** *n*

tempt (tɛmpt) *vb* (*tr*) 1 to entice to do something, esp something morally wrong or unwise 2 to allure or attract 3 to give rise to a desire in (someone) to do something; dispose 4 to risk provoking (esp in **tempt fate**) [c13 from OF *tempter*, from L *temptāre* to test] > ˈ**temptable** *adj* > ˈ**tempter** *n* > ˈ**temptress** *fem n*

temptation (tɛmpˈteɪʃən) *n* 1 the act of tempting or the state of being tempted 2 a person or thing that tempts

tempting (ˈtɛmptɪŋ) *adj* attractive or inviting: *a tempting meal* > ˈ**temptingly** *adv*

tempus fugit *Latin* (ˈtɛmpəs ˈfjuːdʒɪt) time flies

Temuco (*Spanish* teˈmuko) *n* a city in S Chile: agricultural trading centre. Pop: 253 451 (1999 est)

ten (tɛn) *n* 1 the cardinal number that is the sum of nine and one. It is the base of the decimal number system and the base of the common logarithm 2 a numeral, 10, X, etc, representing this number 3 something representing or consisting of ten units 4 Also called: **ten o'clock** ten hours after noon or midnight ▹ *determiner* 5 amounting to ten. Related adj: **decimal** [OE *tēn*]

tenable (ˈtɛnəbᵊl) *adj* able to be upheld, believed, maintained, or defended [c16 from OF, from *tenir* to hold, from L *tenēre*] > ˌ**tenaˈbility** *or* ˈ**tenableness** *n* > ˈ**tenably** *adv*

tenace (ˈtɛneɪs) *n bridge, whist* a holding of two nonconsecutive high cards of a suit, such as the ace and queen [c17 from F, from Sp. *tenaza* forceps, ult. from L *tenāx* holding fast, from *tenēre* to hold]

tenacious (tɪˈneɪʃəs) *adj* 1 holding firmly: *a tenacious grip* 2 retentive: *a tenacious memory* 3 stubborn or persistent 4 holding together firmly; cohesive 5 tending to stick or adhere [c16 from L *tenāx*, from *tenēre* to hold] > **teˈnaciously** *adv* > **teˈnaciousness** *or* **tenacity** (tɪˈnæsɪtɪ) *n*

tenaculum (tɪˈnækjʊləm) *n, pl* **tenacula** (-lə) a hooked surgical instrument for grasping and holding parts [c17 from LL, from L *tenēre* to hold]

tenancy (ˈtɛnənsɪ) *n, pl* **tenancies** 1 the temporary possession or holding by a tenant of lands or property owned by another 2 the period of holding or occupying such property 3 the period of holding office, a position, etc

tenant (ˈtɛnənt) *n* 1 a person who holds, occupies, or possesses land or property, esp from a landlord 2 a person who has the use of a house, etc, subject to the payment of rent 3 any holder or occupant ▹ *vb* 4 (*tr*) to hold as a tenant [c14 from OF, lit.: (one who is) holding, from *tenir* to hold, from L *tenēre*] > ˈ**tenantable** *adj* > ˈ**tenantless** *adj*

tenant farmer *n* a person who farms land rented from another, the rent usually taking the form of crops or livestock

tenantry (ˈtɛnəntrɪ) *n* 1 tenants collectively 2 the status or condition of being a tenant

tench (tɛntʃ) *n* a European freshwater game fish of the carp family [c14 from OF *tenche*, from LL *tinca*]

Ten Commandments *pl n* **the** *Old Testament* the commandments summarizing the basic obligations of man towards God and his fellow men, delivered to Moses on Mount Sinai engraved on two tables of stone (Exodus 20:1–17)

tend[1] (tɛnd) *vb* (when *intr*, usually foll by *to* or *towards*) 1 (when *tr*, *takes an infinitive*) to have a general disposition (to do something); be inclined: *children tend to prefer sweets to meat* 2 (*intr*) to have or be an influence (towards a specific result) 3 (*intr*) to go or move (in a particular direction): *to tend to the south* [c14 from OF *tendre*, from L *tendere* to stretch]

tend[2] (tɛnd) *vb* 1 (*tr*) to care for 2 (when *intr*, often foll by *on* or *to*) to attend (to) 3 (*tr*) to handle or control 4 (*intr*; often foll by *to*) *inf, chiefly US & Canad* to pay attention [c14 var. of ATTEND]

tendency (ˈtɛndənsɪ) *n, pl* **tendencies** 1 (often foll by *to*) an inclination, predisposition, propensity, or leaning 2 the general course, purport, or drift of something, esp a written work [c17 from Med. L *tendentia*, from L *tendere* to TEND[1]]

tendentious *or* **tendencious** (tɛnˈdɛnʃəs) *adj* having or showing an intentional tendency or bias, esp a controversial one [c20 from TENDENCY] > **tenˈdentiously** *or* **tenˈdenciously** *adv* > **tenˈdentiousness** *or* **tenˈdenciousness** *n*

tender[1] (ˈtɛndə) *adj* 1 easily broken, cut, or crushed; soft 2 easily damaged; vulnerable or sensitive: *at a tender age* 3 having or expressing warm feelings 4 kind or sympathetic: *a tender heart* 5 arousing warm feelings; touching 6 gentle and delicate: *a tender breeze* 7 requiring care in handling: *a tender question* 8 painful or sore 9 sensitive to moral or spiritual feelings 10 (*postpositive; foll by of*) protective: *tender of one's emotions* [c13 from OF *tendre*, from L *tener* delicate] > ˈ**tenderly** *adv* > ˈ**tenderness** *n*

tender[2] (ˈtɛndə) *vb* 1 (*tr*) to give, present, or offer: *to tender a bid* 2 (*intr*; foll by *for*) to make a formal offer or estimate (for a job or contract) 3 (*tr*) *law* to offer (money or goods) in settlement of a debt or claim ▹ *n* 4 the act or an instance of tendering; offer 5 a formal offer to supply specified goods or services at a stated cost or rate 6 something, esp money, used as an official medium of payment: *legal tender* [c16 from Anglo-F *tendre*, from L *tendere* to extend] > ˈ**tenderer** *n*

tender[3] (ˈtɛndə) *n* 1 a small boat towed or carried by a ship 2 a vehicle drawn behind a steam locomotive to carry the fuel and water 3 a person who tends [c15 var. of *attender*]

tenderfoot (ˈtɛndəˌfʊt) *n, pl* **tenderfoots** *or* **tenderfeet** 1 a newcomer, esp to the mines or ranches of the southwestern US 2 (formerly) a beginner in the Scouts or Guides

tenderhearted (ˌtɛndəˈhɑːtɪd) *adj* having a compassionate, kindly, or sensitive disposition

tenderize *or* **tenderise** (ˈtɛndəˌraɪz) *vb* **tenderizes, tenderizing, tenderized** *or* **tenderises, tenderising, tenderised** (*tr*) to make (meat) tender, as by pounding it or adding a substance to break down the fibres > ˌ**tenderiˈzation** *or* ˌ**tenderiˈsation** *n* > ˈ**tenderˌizer** *or* ˈ**tenderˌiser** *n*

tenderloin (ˈtɛndəˌlɔɪn) *n* a tender cut of pork or other meat from between the sirloin and ribs

tendon (ˈtɛndən) *n* a cord or band of tough tissue that attaches a muscle to a bone or some other part; sinew [c16 from Med. L *tendō*, from L *tendere* to stretch]

tendril ('tɛndrɪl) *n* a threadlike part of a leaf or stem that attaches climbing plants to a support by twining or adhering [C16 ?from OF *tendron* tendril (confused with OF *tendron* bud), from Med. L *tendō* TENDON]

Tendulkar (tɛn'dʊlkə) *n* **Sachin** ('sæʃɪn) (**Ramesh**) born 1973, Indian cricketer; captain of India from 1996

tenebrism ('tɛnə,brɪzəm) *n* (*sometimes cap*) a school, style, or method of painting, adopted chiefly by 17th-century Spanish and Neapolitan painters, characterized by large areas of dark colours, usually relieved with a shaft of light > '**tenebrist** *n, adj*

tenebrous ('tɛnəbrəs) *or* **tenebrious** (tə'nɛbrɪəs) *adj* gloomy, shadowy, or dark [C15 from L *tenebrōsus* from *tenebrae* darkness]

Tenedos ('tɛnɪ,dɒs) *n* an island in the NE Aegean, near the entrance to the Dardanelles: in Greek legend the base of the Greek fleet during the siege of Troy. Modern Turkish name: **Bozcaada**

tenement ('tɛnəmənt) *n* **1** Also called: **tenement building** a large building divided into rooms or flats **2** a dwelling place or residence **3** *chiefly Brit* a room or flat for rent **4** *property law* any form of permanent property, such as land, dwellings, offices, etc [C14 from Med. L *tenementum*, from L *tenēre* to hold] > **tenemental** (,tɛnə'mɛntᵊl) *adj*

Tenerife (,tɛnə'ri:f; *Spanish* tene'rife) *n* a Spanish island in the Atlantic, off the NW coast of Africa: the largest of the Canary Islands; volcanic and mountainous; tourism and agriculture. Capital: Santa Cruz. Pop: 560 000 (latest est). Area: 2058 sq km (795 sq miles)

tenesmus (tɪ'nɛzməs) *n* an ineffective painful straining to empty the bowels [C16 from Med. L, from L *tēnesmos*, from Gk, from *teinein* to strain] > **te'nesmic** *adj*

tenet ('tɛnɪt, 'ti:nɪt) *n* a belief, opinion, or dogma [C17 from L, lit.: he (it) holds, from *tenēre* to hold]

tenfold ('tɛn,fəʊld) *adj* **1** equal to or having 10 times as many or as much **2** composed of 10 parts ▷ *adv* **3** by or up to 10 times as many or as much

ten-gallon hat *n* (in the US) a cowboy's broad-brimmed felt hat with a very high crown

Teng Hsiao-ping ('tɛŋ sjaʊ 'pɪŋ) *n* a variant transliteration of the Chinese name for **Deng Xiaoping**

Tengri Khan ('tɛŋgrɪ 'kɑ:n) *n* a mountain in central Asia, on the border between Kyrgyzstan and the Xinjiang Uygur Autonomous Region of W China. Height: 6995 m (22 951 ft)

Tengri Nor ('tɛŋgrɪ 'nɔ:) *n* another name for **Nam Co**

Ten Gurus *pl n* the ten leaders of the Sikh religion, from its founder Guru Nanak (1469–1539) to Guru Govind Singh (1666–1708)

Teniers ('tɛnɪəz) *n* **David** ('dɑ:vɪt), called *the Elder*, 1582–1649, and his son **David,** called *the Younger*, 1610–90, Flemish painters

tenner ('tɛnə) *n inf* **1** *Brit* **1a** a ten-pound note **1b** the sum of ten pounds **2** *US* a ten-dollar bill

Tennessee (,tɛnɪ'si:) *n* **1** a state of the E central US: consists of a plain in the west, rising to the Appalachians and the Cumberland Plateau in the east. Capital: Nashville. Pop: 5 689 283 (2000). Area: 109 412 sq km (42 244 sq miles). Abbreviations: **Tenn.** or (with zip code) **TN** **2** a river in the E central US, flowing southwest from E Tennessee into N Alabama, then west and north to the Ohio River at Paducah: the longest tributary of the Ohio; includes a series of dams and reservoirs under the Tennessee Valley Authority. Length: 1049 km (652 miles) > ,**Tennes'sean** *adj, n*

Tenniel ('tɛnjəl) *n* Sir **John** 1820–1914, English caricaturist, noted for his illustrations to Lewis Carroll's *Alice* books and for his political cartoons in *Punch* (1851–1901)

tennis ('tɛnɪs) *n* **a** a racket game played between two players or pairs of players who hit a ball to and fro over a net on a rectangular court of grass, asphalt, clay, etc. See also **lawn tennis, real tennis, table tennis** **b** (*as modifier*): *tennis court; tennis racket* [C14 prob. from Anglo-F *tenetz* hold (imperative), from OF *tenir* to hold, from L *tenēre*]
▷ www.lta.org.uk
▷ www.atptennis.com

tennis elbow *n* inflammation of the elbow caused by exertion in playing tennis, etc

tennis shoe *n* a rubber-soled canvas shoe tied with laces

Tennyson ('tɛnɪsᵊn) *n* **Alfred,** Lord Tennyson 1809–92, English poet; poet laureate (1850–92). His poems include *The Lady of Shalott* (1832) and *Maud* (1855), and the sequences *In Memoriam* (1850) and *Idylls of the King* (1859–85)

teno- *or before a vowel* **ten-** *combining form* tendon: *tenosynovitis* [from Gk *tenōn*]

Teno ('tɛnɔ) *n* the Finnish name for **Tana** (sense 3)

Tenochtitlán (tɛ,nɔ:tʃti:'tlɑ:n) *n* an ancient city and capital of the Aztec empire on the present site of Mexico City; razed by Cortés in 1521

tenon ('tɛnən) *n* **1** the projecting end of a piece of wood formed to fit into a corresponding mortise in another piece ▷ *vb (tr)* **2** to form a tenon on (a piece of wood) **3** to join with a tenon and mortise [C15 from OF, from *tenir* to hold, from L *tenēre*] > '**tenoner** *n*

tenon saw *n* a small fine-toothed saw with a strong back, used esp for cutting tenons

tenor ('tɛnə) *n* **1** *music* **1a** the male voice intermediate between alto and baritone **1b** a singer with such a voice **1c** a saxophone, horn, etc, intermediate between the alto and baritone or bass **2** general drift of thought; purpose **3** a settled course of progress **4** *arch* general tendency **5** *finance* the time required for a bill of exchange or promissory note to become due for payment **6** *law* **6a** the exact words of a deed, etc **6b** an exact copy [C13 (orig.: general sense): from OF *tenour*, from L *tenor* a holding to a course, from *tenēre* to hold; musical sense via It. *tenore*, referring to the voice part that was continuous, that is, to which the melody was assigned]

Tt

tenor clef *n* the clef that establishes middle C as being on the fourth line of the staff

tenorrhaphy (tɪ'nɒrəfɪ) *n, pl* **tenorrhaphies** *surgery* the union of torn or divided tendons by means of sutures [C19 from TENO- + Gk *raphē* a sewing]

tenosynovitis ('tɛnəʊ,saɪnəʊ'vaɪtɪs) *n* painful swelling and inflammation of tendons, usually of the wrist, often the result of repetitive movements such as typing

tenotomy (tə'nɒtəmɪ) *n, pl* **tenotomies** surgical division of a tendon > **te'notomist** *n*

tenpin bowling ('tɛn,pɪn) *n* a bowling game in which bowls are rolled down a lane to knock over the ten target pins. Also called (esp US and Canad): **tenpins**
▷ www.bowwwling.com
▷ www.btba.org.uk

tenrec ('tɛnrɛk) *n* any of a family of small mammals of Madagascar resembling hedgehogs or shrews [C18 via F from Malagasy *tràndraka*]

TENS (tɛnz) *n acronym for* transcutaneous electrical nerve stimulation: the application of low-voltage electric impulses to the skin to relieve rheumatic pain and provide some pain relief in labour. The pulses are said to stimulate the release of pain-killing endorphins

tense[1] (tɛns) *adj* **1** stretched or stressed tightly; taut or rigid **2** under mental or emotional strain **3** producing mental or emotional strain: *a tense day* **4** *phonetics* Also: **narrow** pronounced with considerable muscular effort, as the vowel (i:) in "beam" ▷ *vb* **tenses, tensing, tensed** (*often foll by up*) **5** to make or become tense [C17 from L *tensus* taut, from *tendere* to stretch] > '**tensely** *adv* > '**tenseness** *n*

tense[2] (tɛns) *n grammar* a category of the verb or verbal inflections, such as present, past, and future, that expresses the temporal relations between what is reported in a sentence and the time of its utterance [C14 from OF *tens* time, from L *tempus*] > ˈ**tenseless** *adj*

tense logic *n logic* the study of temporal relations between propositions, usually pursued by considering the logical properties of symbols representing the tenses of natural languages

tensile (ˈtɛnsaɪl) *adj* **1** of or relating to tension **2** sufficiently ductile to be stretched or drawn out [C17 from NL *tensilis*, from L *tendere* to stretch] > **tensility** (tɛnˈsɪlɪtɪ) *or* ˈ**tensileness** *n*

tensile strength *n* a measure of the ability of a material to withstand a longitudinal stress, expressed as the greatest stress that the material can stand without breaking

tensimeter (tɛnˈsɪmɪtə) *n* a device that measures differences in vapour pressures [C20 from TENSI(ON) + -METER]

tensiometer (ˌtɛnsɪˈɒmɪtə) *n* **1** an instrument for measuring the tensile strength of a wire, beam, etc **2** an instrument used to compare the vapour pressures of two liquids **3** an instrument for measuring the surface tension of a liquid **4** an instrument for measuring the moisture content of soil

tension (ˈtɛnʃən) *n* **1** the act of stretching or the state or degree of being stretched **2** mental or emotional strain; stress **3** a situation or condition of hostility, suspense, or uneasiness **4** *physics* a force that tends to produce an elongation of a body or structure **5** *physics* voltage, electromotive force, or potential difference **6** a device for regulating the tension in a part, string, thread, etc, as in a sewing machine **7** the degree of tightness or looseness with which a person knits [C16 from L *tensiō*, from *tendere* to strain] > ˈ**tensional** *adj* > ˈ**tensionless** *adj*

tensor (ˈtɛnsə, -sɔː) *n* **1** *anat* any muscle that can cause a part to become firm or tense **2** *maths* a set of components, functions of the coordinates of any point in space, that transform linearly between coordinate systems [C18 from NL, lit.: a stretcher] > **tensorial** (tɛnˈsɔːrɪəl) *adj*

tent (tɛnt) *n* **1** a portable shelter of canvas, plastic, etc, supported on poles and fastened to the ground by pegs and ropes **2** something resembling this in function or shape ▷ *vb* **3** (*intr*) to camp in a tent **4** (*tr*) to cover with or as if with a tent or tents **5** (*tr*) to provide with a tent as shelter [C13 from OF *tente*, from L *tentōrium* something stretched out, from *tendere* to stretch] > ˈ**tentage** *n* > ˈ**tented** *adj*

tentacle (ˈtɛntəkᵊl) *n* **1** any of various elongated flexible organs that occur near the mouth in many invertebrates and are used for feeding, grasping, etc **2** any of the hairs on the leaf of an insectivorous plant that are used to capture prey **3** something resembling a tentacle, esp in its ability to reach out or grasp [C18 from NL *tentāculum*, from L *tentāre*, var. of *temptāre* to feel] > ˈ**tentacled** *adj* > **tentacular** (tɛnˈtækjʊlə) *adj*

tentation (tɛnˈteɪʃən) *n* a method of achieving the correct adjustment of a mechanical device by a series of trials [C14 from L *tentātiō*, variant of *temptātiō* TEMPTATION]

tentative (ˈtɛntətɪv) *adj* **1** provisional or experimental **2** hesitant, uncertain, or cautious [C16 from Med. L *tentātīvus*, from L *tentāre* to test] > ˈ**tentatively** *adv* > ˈ**tentativeness** *n*

tenter (ˈtɛntə) *n* **1** a frame on which cloth is stretched in order that it may retain its shape while drying **2** a person who stretches cloth on a tenter ▷ *vb* **3** (*tr*) to stretch (cloth) on a tenter [C14 from Med. L *tentōrium*, from L *tentus* stretched, from *tendere* to stretch]

tenterhook (ˈtɛntəˌhʊk) *n* **1** one of a series of hooks used to hold cloth on a tenter **2 on tenterhooks** in a state of tension or suspense

tenth (tɛnθ) *adj* **1** (*usually prenominal*) **1a** coming after the ninth in numbering, position, etc; being the ordinal number of *ten*: often written 10th **1b** (*as n*): *see you on the tenth* ▷ *n* **2a** one of 10 equal parts of something **2b** (*as modifier*): *a tenth part* **3** the fraction equal to one divided by ten (1/10) ▷ *adv* **4** Also: **tenthly** after the ninth person, position, event, etc [C12 *tenthe*, from OE *tēotha*]

tent stitch *n* another term for **petit point** [C17 from ?]

tenuis (ˈtɛnjʊɪs) *n, pl* **tenues** (ˈtɛnjʊˌiːz) (in classical Greek) a voiceless stop (k, p, t) [C17 from L: thin]

tenuous (ˈtɛnjʊəs) *adj* **1** insignificant or flimsy: *a tenuous argument* **2** slim, fine, or delicate: *a tenuous thread* **3** diluted or rarefied in consistency or density: *a tenuous fluid* [C16 from L *tenuis*] > **tenuity** (tɛˈnjʊɪtɪ) *or* ˈ**tenuousness** *n* > ˈ**tenuously** *adv*

tenure (ˈtɛnjʊə, ˈtɛnjə) *n* **1** the possession or holding of an office or position **2** the length of time an office, position, etc, lasts **3** *chiefly US & Canad* the improved security status of a person after having been in the employ of the same company or institution for a specified period **4** the right to permanent employment until retirement, esp for teachers, etc **5a** the holding of property, esp realty, in return for services rendered, etc **5b** the duration of such holding [C15 from OF, from Med. L *tenitūra*, ult. from L *tenēre* to hold] > **tenˈurial** *adj*

tenuto (tɪˈnjuːtəʊ) *adj, adv music* (of a note) to be held for or beyond its full time value [from It., lit.: held, from *tenere* to hold, from L *tenēre*]

Tenzing Norgay (ˈtɛnsɪŋ ˈnɔːgeɪ) *n* 1914–86, Nepalese mountaineer. With Sir Edmund Hillary, he was the first to reach the summit of Mount Everest (1953)

teocalli (ˌtiːəʊˈkælɪ) *n, pl* **teocallis** any of various truncated pyramids built by the Aztecs as bases for their temples [C17 from Nahuatl, from *teotl* god + *calli* house]

tepee *or* **teepee** (ˈtiːpiː) *n* a cone-shaped tent of animal skins used by American Indians [C19 from Siouan *tīpī*, from *ti* to dwell + *pi* used for]

tephra (ˈtɛfrə) *n chiefly US* solid matter ejected during a volcanic eruption [C20 Gk, lit.: ashes]

Tepic (*Spanish* teˈpik) *n* a city in W central Mexico, capital of Nayarit state: agricultural, trading and processing centre. Pop: 265 681 (2000 est)

tepid (ˈtɛpɪd) *adj* **1** slightly warm; lukewarm **2** relatively unenthusiastic or apathetic [C14 from L *tepidus*, from *tepēre* to be lukewarm] > **tepidity** (tɛˈpɪdɪtɪ) *or* ˈ**tepidness** *n* > ˈ**tepidly** *adv*

tequila (tɪˈkiːlə) *n* **1** a spirit that is distilled in Mexico from an agave plant and forms the basis of many mixed drinks **2** the plant from which this drink is made [C19 from Mexican Sp., from *Tequila*, region of Mexico]

ter- *combining form* three, third, or three times [from L *ter* thrice]

tera- *prefix* **1** denoting 10^{12}: *terameter* **2** Also: **tebi-** denoting 2^{40}: *terabyte* ▷ Symbol: T [from Gk *teras* monster]

USAGE See at **kilo-**

Terai (təˈraɪ) *n* **1** (in India) a belt of marshy land at the foot of mountains, esp at the foot of the Himalayas in N India **2** a felt hat with a wide brim worn in subtropical regions

terat- *or* **terato-** *combining form* indicating a monster or something abnormal: *teratism* [from Gk *terat-*, *teras* monster, prodigy]

teratism (ˈtɛrəˌtɪzəm) *n* a malformed animal or human, esp in the fetal stage; monster

teratogen (ˈtɛrətədʒən, tɪˈrætə-) *n* any substance, organism, or process that causes malformations in a fetus. Teratogens include certain drugs (such as thalidomide), infections (such as German measles), and ionizing radiation > ˌ**teratoˈgenic** *adj*

teratoid (ˈtɛrəˌtɔɪd) *adj biol* resembling a monster

teratology (ˌtɛrəˈtɒlədʒɪ) *n* **1** the branch of medical science concerned with the development of physical abnormalities during the fetal or early embryonic stage **2** the branch of biology concerned with the structure, development, etc, of monsters **3** a collection of tales about mythical or fantastic creatures, monsters, etc > ˌ**teraˈtologist** *n*

teratoma (ˌtɛrəˈtəʊmə) *n, pl* **teratomata** (-mətə) *or* **teratomas** a tumour composed of tissue foreign to the site of growth

terbium (ˈtɜːbɪəm) *n* a soft malleable silvery-grey element of the lanthanide series of metals. Symbol: Tb; atomic no.: 65; atomic wt.: 158.925 [C19 from NL, after *Ytterby*, Sweden, village where discovered] > ˈ**terbic** *adj*

terbium metal *n chem* any of a group of related lanthanides, including terbium, europium, and gadolinium

Ter Borch *or* **Terborch** (*Dutch* tɛr ˈbɔrx) *n* **Gerard** (ˈxeːrɑrt) 1617–81, Dutch genre and portrait painter

terce (tɜːs) *or* **tierce** *n chiefly RC Church* the third of the seven canonical hours, originally fixed at the third hour of the day, about 9 am [C14 var. of TIERCE]

Terceira (*Portuguese* tərˈsirə) *n* an island in the N Atlantic, in the Azores: NATO military air base. Pop: 60 000 (latest est). Area: 397 sq km (153 sq miles)

tercel (ˈtɜːsᵊl) *or* **tiercel** *n* a male falcon or hawk, esp as used in falconry [C14 from OF, from Vulgar L *tertiolus* (unattested), from L *tertius* third, from the tradition that only one egg in three hatched a male chick]

tercentenary (ˌtɜːsɛnˈtiːnərɪ) *or* **tercentennial** *adj* **1** of a period of 300 years **2** of a 300th anniversary ▷ *n, pl* **tercentenaries** *or* **tercentennials** **3** an anniversary of 300 years

tercet (ˈtɜːsɪt, tɜːˈsɛt) *n* a group of three lines of verse that rhyme together or are connected by rhyme with adjacent groups of three lines [C16 from F, from It. *terzetto*, dim. of *terzo* third, from L *tertius*]

terebene (ˈtɛrəˌbiːn) *n* a mixture of hydrocarbons prepared from oil of turpentine and sulphuric acid, used to make paints and varnishes and medicinally as an expectorant and antiseptic [C19 from TEREB(INTH) + -ENE]

terebinth (ˈtɛrɪbɪnθ) *n* a small Mediterranean tree that yields a turpentine [C14 from L *terebinthus*, from Gk *terebinthos* turpentine tree]

terebinthine (ˌtɛrɪˈbɪnθaɪn) *adj* **1** of or relating to terebinth or related plants **2** of, consisting of, or resembling turpentine

teredo (təˈriːdəʊ) *n, pl* **teredos** *or* **teredines** (-dɪˌniːz) any of a genus of marine bivalve molluscs. See **shipworm** [C17 via L from Gk *terēdōn* wood-boring worm; rel. to Gk *tetrainein* to pierce]

Terence (ˈtɛrəns) *n* Latin name *Publius Terentius Afer*. ?190–159 BC, Roman comic dramatist. His six comedies, *Andria*, *Hecyra*, *Heauton Timoroumenos*, *Eunuchus*, *Phormio*, and *Adelphoe*, are based on Greek originals by Menander

Terengganu (tɛrɛŋˈgɑːnuː) *n* a variant spelling of **Trengganu**

Teresa *or* **Theresa** (təˈriːzə; *Spanish* teˈresa) *n* **1 Saint**, known as *Teresa of Avila*. 1515–82, Spanish nun and mystic. She reformed the Carmelite order and founded 17 convents. Her writings include a spiritual autobiography and *The Way to Perfection*. Feast day: Oct 15 **2 Mother**, original name *Agnes Gonxha Bojaxhiu*. 1910–97, Indian Roman Catholic missionary, born in Skopje, now in the Former Yugoslav Republic of Macedonia, of Albanian parents: noted for her work among the starving in Calcutta; Nobel peace prize 1979 ▷ See also **Thérèse de Lisieux**

Tereshkova (*Russian* tɪrɪʃˈkɔvə) *n* **Valentina Vladimirovna** (vəlɪnˈtinə vlaˈdimirəvnə) born 1937, Soviet cosmonaut; first woman in space (1963)

Teresina (*Portuguese* tereˈzina) *n* an inland port in NE Brazil, capital of Piauí state, on the Parnaíba River: chief commercial centre of the Parnaíba valley. Pop: 676 596 (2000). Former name: **Therezina**

terete (ˈtɛriːt) *adj* (esp of plant parts) smooth and usually cylindrical and tapering [C17 from L *teres* smooth, from *terere* to rub]

Terfel (ˈtɜːfəl) *n* **Bryn**, real name *Bryn Terfel Jones*. born 1965, Welsh bass baritone

tergiversate (ˈtɜːdʒɪvəˌseɪt) *vb* **tergiversates, tergiversating, tergiversated** (*intr*) **1** to change sides or loyalties **2** to be evasive or ambiguous [C17 from L *tergiversārī* to turn one's back, from *tergum* back + *vertere* to turn] > ˌ**tergiverˈsation** *n* > ˈ**tergiverˌsator** *n*

tergum (ˈtɜːgəm) *n, pl* **terga** (-gə) a cuticular plate covering the dorsal surface of a body segment of an arthropod [C19 from L: the back] > ˈ**tergal** *adj*

term (tɜːm) *n* **1** a name, expression, or word used for some particular thing, esp in a specialized field of knowledge: *a medical term* **2** any word or expression **3** a limited period of time: *a prison term* **4** any of the divisions of the academic year during which a school, college, etc, is in session **5** a point in time determined for an event or for the end of a period **6** the period at which childbirth is imminent **7** *law* **7a** an estate or interest in land limited to run for a specified period **7b** the duration of an estate, etc **7c** (formerly) a period of time during which sessions of courts of law are held **7d** time allowed to a debtor to settle **8** *maths* any distinct quantity making up a fraction or proportion, or contained in a polynominal, sequence, series, etc **9** *logic* **9a** the word or phrase that forms either the subject or predicate of a proposition **9b** a name or variable, as opposed to a predicate **9c** any of the three subjects or predicates occurring in a syllogism **10** *archit* a sculptured post, esp one in the form of an armless bust or an animal on the top of a square pillar ▷ *vb* **11** (*tr*) to designate; call: *he was termed a thief* ▷ See also **terms** [C13 from OF *terme*, from L *terminus* end] > ˈ**termly** *adj, adv*

> USAGE Many people object to the use of *in terms of* as an all-purpose preposition replacing phrases such as 'as regards', 'about', and so forth in a context such as the following: *in terms of trends in smoking habits, there is good news*. They would maintain that in strict usage it should be used to specify a relationship, as in: *obesity is defined in terms of body mass index, which involves a bit of cumbersome maths*. Nevertheless, despite objections, it is very commonly used as a link phrase, particularly in speech

termagant (ˈtɜːməgənt) *n* a shrewish woman; scold [C13 from earlier *Tervagaunt*, from OF *Tervagan*, from It. *Trivigante*; after an arrogant character in medieval mystery plays who was supposed to be a Muslim deity]

-termer *n* (*in combination*) a person serving a specified length of time in prison: *a short-termer*

terminable (ˈtɜːmɪnəbᵊl) *adj* **1** able to be terminated **2** terminating after a specific period or event > ˌ**terminaˈbility** *or* ˈ**terminableness** *n* > ˈ**terminably** *adv*

terminal (ˈtɜːmɪnᵊl) *adj* **1** of, being, or situated at an end, terminus, or boundary **2** of or occurring after or in a term: *terminal examinations* **3** (of a disease) terminating in death **4** *inf* extreme: *terminal boredom* **5** of or relating to the storage or delivery of freight at a warehouse ▷ *n* **6** a terminating point, part, or place **7a** a point at which current enters or leaves an electrical device, such as a battery or a circuit **7b** a conductor by which current enters or leaves at such a point **8** *computing* a device having input/output links with a computer **9** *archit* **9a** an ornamental carving at the end of a structure **9b** another name for **term** (sense 10) **10a** a point or station at the end of the line of a railway or at an airport, serving as an important access point for passengers or freight **10b** a less common name for **terminus** (sense 2) **11** a reception and departure building at the terminus of a bus, sea, or air transport route **12** a site where raw material is unloaded and

Tt

processed, esp an onshore installation designed to receive offshore oil or gas [C15 from L *terminālis*, from *terminus* end] > '**terminally** *adv*

terminal market *n* a commodity market in a trading centre rather than at a producing centre

terminal velocity *n* **1** the constant maximum velocity reached by a body falling under gravity through a fluid, esp the atmosphere **2** the velocity of a missile or projectile when it reaches its target **3** the maximum velocity attained by a rocket, missile, or shell flying in a parabolic flight path **4** the maximum velocity that an aircraft can attain

terminate ('tɜːmɪˌneɪt) *vb* **terminates, terminating, terminated** (when *intr*, often foll by *in* or *with*) to form, be, or put an end (to); conclude [C16 from L *terminātus* limited, from *termināre* to set boundaries, from *terminus* end] > '**terminative** *adj* > '**termiˌnator** *n*

termination (ˌtɜːmɪ'neɪʃən) *n* **1** the act of terminating or the state of being terminated **2** something that terminates **3** a final result

terminator seed *n* a seed that produces sterile plants, used in some genetically modified crops so that a new supply of seeds has to be bought every year

terminology (ˌtɜːmɪ'nɒlədʒɪ) *n, pl* **terminologies 1** the body of specialized words relating to a particular subject **2** the study of terms [C19 from Med. L *terminus* term from L: end] > **terminological** (ˌtɜːmɪnə'lɒdʒɪkᵊl) *adj*

term insurance *n* life assurance, usually low in cost and offering no cash value, that provides for the payment of a specified sum of money only if the insured dies within a stipulated time

terminus ('tɜːmɪnəs) *n, pl* **termini** (-naɪ) *or* **terminuses 1** the last or final part or point **2** either end of a railway, bus route, etc, or a station or town at such a point **3** a goal aimed for **4** a boundary or boundary marker **5** *archit* another name for **term** (sense 10) [C16 from L: end]

Terminus ('tɜːmɪnəs) *n* the Roman god of boundaries

terminus ad quem *Latin* ('tɜːmɪˌnʊs æd 'kwɛm) *n* the aim or terminal point [lit.: the end to which]

terminus a quo *Latin* ('tɜːmɪˌnʊs ɑː 'kwəʊ) *n* the starting point; beginning [lit.: the end from which]

termitarium (ˌtɜːmɪ'tɛərɪəm) *n, pl* **termitaria** (-ɪə) the nest of a termite colony [C20 from TERMITE + -ARIUM]

termite ('tɜːmaɪt) *n* any of an order of whitish antlike social insects of warm and tropical regions. Some species feed on wood, causing damage to buildings, trees, etc [C18 from NL *termitēs* white ants, pl of *termes*, from L: a woodworm] > **termitic** (tɜː'mɪtɪk) *adj*

termless ('tɜːmlɪs) *adj* **1** without limit or boundary **2** unconditional **3** an archaic word for **indescribable**

termor *or* **termer** ('tɜːmə) *n property law* a person who holds an estate for a term of years or until he or she dies

terms (tɜːmz) *pl n* **1** (usually specified prenominally) the actual language or mode of presentation used: *he described the project in loose terms* **2** conditions of an agreement **3** a sum of money paid for a service **4** (usually preceded by *on*) mutual relationship or standing: *they are on affectionate terms* **5 bring to terms** to cause to agree or submit **6 come to terms** to reach acceptance or agreement **7 in terms of** as expressed by; regarding: *in terms of money he was no better off*

terms of trade *pl n economics, Brit* the ratio of export prices to import prices

tern (tɜːn) *n* any of several aquatic birds related to the gulls, having a forked tail, long narrow wings, and a typically black-and-white plumage [C18 from ON *therna*]

ternary ('tɜːnərɪ) *adj* **1** consisting of three or groups of three **2** *maths* (of a number system) to the base three [C14 from L *ternārius*, from *ternī* three each]

ternary form *n* a musical structure consisting of two contrasting sections followed by a repetition of the first; the form *aba*

ternate ('tɜːnɪt, -neɪt) *adj* **1** (esp of a leaf) consisting of three leaflets or other parts **2** (esp of plants) having groups of three members [C18 from NL *ternātus*, from Med. L *ternāre* to increase threefold] > '**ternately** *adv*

terne (tɜːn) *n* **1** an alloy of lead containing tin and antimony **2** Also called: **terne plate** steel plate coated with this alloy [C16 ?from F *terne* dull, from OF *ternir* to TARNISH]

Terni (*Italian* 'tɛrni) *n* an industrial city in central Italy, in Umbria: site of waterfalls created in Roman times. Pop: 107 770 (2000 est)

Ternopol (*Russian* tɪr'nɔpəlj) *n* a town in the W Ukraine, on the River Seret: formerly under Polish rule. Pop: 235 100 (1998 est). Polish name: **Tarnopol**

terotechnology (ˌtɪərəʊtɛk'nɒlədʒɪ, tɛr-) *n* a branch of technology that utilizes management, financial, and engineering expertise in the installation, efficient operation, and maintenance of equipment and machinery [C20 from Gk *tērein* to care for + TECHNOLOGY]

terpene ('tɜːpiːn) *n* any one of a class of unsaturated hydrocarbons, such as pinene and the carotenes, that are found in the essential oils of many plants, esp conifers [C19 *terp-* from obs. *terpentine* turpentine + -ENE]

terpineol (tɜː'pɪnɪˌɒl) *n* a terpene alcohol with an odour of lilac, existing in three isomeric forms that occur in several essential oils [C20 from TERPENE + -INE[2] + -OL[1]]

Terpsichore (tɜːp'sɪkərɪ) *n* the Muse of the dance and of choral song [C18 via L from Gk, from *terpsikhoros* delighting in the dance, from *terpein* to delight + *khoros* dance]

Terpsichorean (ˌtɜːpsɪkə'rɪən, -'kɔːrɪən) *often used facetiously* ▷ *adj also* **Terpsichoreal 1** of or relating to dancing ▷ *n* **2** a dancer

terra ('tɛrə) *n* (in legal contexts) earth or land [from L]

terra alba ('ælbə) *n* **1** a white finely powdered form of gypsum, used to make paints, paper, etc **2** any of various other white earthy substances, such as kaolin, pipeclay, and magnesia [from L, lit.: white earth]

terrace ('tɛrəs) *n* **1** a horizontal flat area of ground, often one of a series in a slope **2a** a row of houses, usually identical and having common dividing walls, or the street onto which they face **2b** (*cap when part of a street name*): *Grosvenor Terrace* **3** a paved area alongside a building, serving partly as a garden **4** a balcony or patio **5** the flat roof of a house built in a Spanish or Oriental style **6** a flat area bounded by a short steep slope formed by the down-cutting of a river or by erosion **7** (*usually pl*) unroofed tiers around a football pitch on which the spectators stand ▷ *vb* **terraces, terracing, terraced 8** (*tr*) to make into or provide with a terrace or terraces [C16 from OF *terrasse*, from OProvençal *terrassa* pile of earth, from *terra* earth, from L]

terraced house *n Brit* a house that is part of a terrace. US and Canad name: **row house**

terracing ('tɛrəsɪŋ) *n* **1** a series of terraces, esp one dividing a slope into a steplike system of flat narrow fields **2** the act of making a terrace or terraces **3** another name for **terrace** (sense 7)

terra cotta ('kɒtə) *n* **1** a hard unglazed brownish-red earthenware, or the clay from which it is made **2** something made of terra cotta, such as a sculpture **3** a strong reddish-brown to brownish-orange colour [C18 from It., lit.: baked earth] > '**terra-'cotta** *adj*

terra firma ('fɜːmə) *n* the solid earth; firm ground [C17 from L]

terrain (tə'reɪn) *n* a piece of ground, esp with reference to its physical character or military potential: *a rocky terrain* [C18 from F, ult. from L *terrēnum* ground, from *terra* earth]

terra incognita *Latin* ('tɛrə ɪn'kɒgnɪtə) *n* an unexplored or unknown land, region, or area

Terramycin (ˌtɛrə'maɪsɪn) *n trademark* a broad-spectrum antibiotic used in treating various infections

terrapin ('tɛrəpɪn) *n* any of various web-footed reptiles that live on land and in fresh water and feed on small aquatic animals. Also called: **water tortoise** [C17 of Amerind origin]

terrarium (tɛ'rɛərɪəm) *n, pl* **terrariums** *or* **terraria** (-'rɛərɪə) **1** an enclosure for small land animals **2** a glass container, often a globe, in which plants are grown [C19 NL, from L *terra* earth]

terra sigillata (ˌsɪdʒɪ'lɑːtə) *n* **1** a reddish-brown clayey earth found on the Aegean island of Lemnos: formerly used as an astringent and in the making of earthenware pottery **2** any similar earth resembling this **3** earthenware pottery made from this or a similar earth, esp Samian ware [from L: sealed earth]

terrazzo (tɛ'rætsəʊ) *n, pl* **terrazzos** a floor made by setting marble chips into a layer of mortar and polishing the surface [C20 from It.: TERRACE]

terrene (tɛ'riːn) *adj* **1** of the earth; worldly; mundane **2** *rare* of earth; earthy ▷ *n* **3** a land **4** a rare word for **earth** [C14 from Anglo-Norman, from L *terrēnus*, from *terra* earth]

terreplein ('tɛəˌpleɪn) *n* the top of a rampart where guns are placed behind the parapet [C16 from F, from Med. L *terrā plēnus* filled with earth]

terrestrial (tə'rɛstrɪəl) *adj* **1** of the earth **2** of the land as opposed to the sea or air **3** (of animals and plants) living or growing on the land **4** earthly, worldly, or mundane **5** *television* denoting or using signals sent over the earth's surface from a transmitter on land, rather than by satellite ▷ *n* **6** an inhabitant of the earth [C15 from L *terrestris*, from *terra* earth] > **ter'restrially** *adv* > **ter'restrialness** *n*

terrestrial telescope *n* a telescope for use on earth rather than for making astronomical observations. Such telescopes contain an additional lens or prism system to produce an erect image

terret ('tɛrɪt) *n* **1** either of the two rings on a harness through which the reins are passed **2** the ring on a dog's collar for attaching the lead [C15 var. of *toret*, from OF, dim. of *tor* loop]

terre-verte ('tɛəˌvɜːt) *n* **1** a greyish-green pigment used in paints. It is made from a mineral found in greensand and similar rocks ▷ *adj* **2** of a greyish-green colour [C17 from F, lit.: green earth]

terrible ('tɛrəbᵊl) *adj* **1** very serious or extreme **2** *inf* of poor quality; unpleasant or bad **3** causing terror **4** causing awe [C15 from L *terribilis*, from *terrēre* to terrify] > **'terribleness** *n* > **'terribly** *adv*

terricolous (tɛ'rɪkələs) *adj* living on or in the soil [C19 from L *terricola*, from *terra* earth + *colere* to inhabit]

terrier[1] ('tɛrɪə) *n* any of several usually small, active, and short-bodied breeds of dog, originally trained to hunt animals living underground [C15 from OF *chien terrier* earth dog, from Med. L *terrārius* belonging to the earth, from L *terra* earth]

terrier[2] ('tɛrɪə) *n English legal history* a register or survey of land [C15 from OF, from Med. L *terrārius* of the land, from L *terra* land]

terrific (tə'rɪfɪk) *adj* **1** very great or intense **2** *inf* very good; excellent **3** very frightening [C17 from L *terrificus*, from *terrēre* to frighten] > **ter'rifically** *adv*

terrify ('tɛrɪˌfaɪ) *vb* **terrifies, terrifying, terrified** (*tr*) to inspire fear or dread in; frighten greatly [C16 from L *terrificāre*, from *terrēre* to alarm + *facere* to cause]

terrifying ('tɛrɪˌfaɪɪŋ) *adj* causing great fear or dread; extremely frightening > **'terriˌfyingly** *adv*

terrigenous (tɛ'rɪdʒɪnəs) *adj* **1** of or produced by the earth **2** (of geological deposits) formed in the sea from material derived from the land by erosion [C17 from L *terrigenus*, from *terra* earth + *gignere* to beget]

terrine (tɛ'riːn) *n* **1** an oval earthenware cooking dish with a tightly fitting lid used for pâtés, etc **2** the food cooked or served in such a dish, esp pâté **3** another word for **tureen** [C18 earlier form of TUREEN]

territorial (ˌtɛrɪ'tɔːrɪəl) *adj* **1** of or relating to a territory or territories **2** restricted to or owned by a particular territory **3** local or regional **4** *zool* establishing and defending a territory **5** pertaining to a territorial army, providing a reserve of trained men for use in emergency > **ˌterriˌtori'ality** *n* > **ˌterri'torially** *adv*

Territorial (ˌtɛrɪ'tɔːrɪəl) *n* a member of a Territorial Army

Territorial Army *n* (in Britain) a standing reserve army originally organized between 1907 and 1908. Full name: **Territorial and Volunteer Reserve**

territorial waters *pl n* the waters over which a nation exercises jurisdiction and control

territory ('tɛrɪtərɪ) *n, pl* **territories** **1** any tract of land; district **2** the geographical domain under the jurisdiction of a political unit, esp of a sovereign state **3** the district for which an agent, etc, is responsible **4** an area inhabited and defended by an animal or a breeding group of animals **5** an area of knowledge **6** (in football, hockey, etc) the area defended by a team **7** (*often cap*) a region of a country, esp of a federal state, that enjoys less autonomy and a lower status than most constituent parts of the state **8** (*often cap*) a protectorate or other dependency of a country [C15 from L *territōrium* land surrounding a town, from *terra* land]

terror ('tɛrə) *n* **1** great fear, panic, or dread **2** a person or thing that inspires great dread **3** *inf* a troublesome person or thing, esp a child **4** terrorism [C14 from OF *terreur*, from L *terror*, from *terrēre* to frighten] > **'terrorful** *adj* > **'terrorless** *adj*

terrorism ('tɛrəˌrɪzəm) *n* **1** the systematic use of violence and intimidation to achieve some goal **2** the act of terrorizing **3** the state of being terrorized

▷ www.ict.org.il/default.htm

▷ www.un.org/terrorism

terrorist ('tɛrərɪst) *n* **a** a person who employs terror or terrorism, esp as a political weapon **b** (*as modifier*): *terrorist tactics*

terrorize *or* **terrorise** ('tɛrəˌraɪz) *vb* **terrorizes, terrorizing, terrorized** *or* **terrorises, terrorising, terrorised** (*tr*) **1** to coerce or control by violence, fear, threats, etc **2** to inspire with dread; terrify > **ˌterrori'zation** *or* **ˌterrori'sation** *n* > **'terrorˌizer** *or* **'terrorˌiser** *n*

terror-stricken *or* **terror-struck** *adj* in a state of terror

terry ('tɛrɪ) *n, pl* **terries** **1** an uncut loop in the pile of towelling or a similar fabric **2** a fabric with such a pile [C18 ? var. of TERRET]

Terry ('tɛrɪ) *n* **1** Dame **Ellen** 1847–1928, British actress, noted for her Shakespearean roles opposite Sir Henry Irving and for her correspondence with George Bernard Shaw **2** **(John) Quinlan** ('kwɪnlən) born 1937, British architect, noted for his works in neoclassical style, such as the Richmond riverside project (1984)

terse (tɜːs) *adj* **1** neatly brief and concise **2** curt; abrupt [C17 from L *tersus* precise, from *tergēre* to polish] > **'tersely** *adv* > **'terseness** *n*

tertial ('tɜːʃəl) *adj, n* another word for **tertiary** (senses 5, 6) [C19 from L *tertius* third, from *ter* thrice, from *trēs* three]

tertian ('tɜːʃən) *adj* **1** (of a fever) occurring every other day ▷ *n* **2** a tertian fever [C14 from L *febris tertiāna* fever occurring every third day, from *tertius* third]

tertiary ('tɜːʃərɪ) *adj* **1** third in degree, order, etc **2** (of an industry) involving services as opposed to extraction or manufacture, such as transport, finance, etc **3** *RC Church* of or relating to a Third Order **4** *chem* **4a** (of an organic compound) having a functional group attached to a carbon atom that is attached to three other groups **4b** (of an amine) having three organic groups attached to a nitrogen atom **4c** (of a salt) derived from a tribasic acid by replacement of all its acidic hydrogen atoms with metal atoms or electropositive groups **5** *ornithol*,

Tt

rare of or designating any of the small flight feathers attached to the part of the humerus nearest to the body ▷ *n, pl* **tertiaries 6** *ornithol, rare* any of the tertiary feathers **7** *RC Church* a member of a Third Order [C16 from L *tertiārius* containing one third, from *tertius* third]

Tertiary ('tɜːʃərɪ) *adj* **1** of, denoting, or formed in the first period of the Cenozoic era, which lasted for 63 million years ▷ *n* **2 the** the Tertiary period or rock system

tertiary college *n Brit* a college system incorporating the secondary school sixth form and vocational courses

tertiary colour *n* a colour formed by mixing two secondary colours

tertium quid ('tɜːtɪəm) *n* an unknown or indefinite thing related in some way to two known or definite things, but distinct from both [C18 from LL, rendering Gk *triton ti* some third thing]

Tertullian (tɜː'tʌlɪən) *n* Latin name *Quintus Septimius Florens Tertullianus*. ?160–?220 AD, Carthaginian Christian theologian, who wrote in Latin rather than Greek and originated much of Christian terminology

Teruel (*Spanish* te'rwɛl) *n* a city in E central Spain: 15th-century cathedral; scene of fierce fighting during the Spanish Civil War. Pop: 31 000 (1991)

tervalent (tɜː'veɪlənt) *adj chem* another word for **trivalent** > **ter'valency** *n*

Terylene ('tɛrɪˌliːn) *n trademark* a synthetic polyester fibre or fabric. US name (trademark): **Dacron**

terza rima ('tɛətsə 'riːmə) *n, pl* **terze rime** ('tɛətseɪ 'riːmeɪ) a verse form consisting of a series of tercets in which the middle line of one tercet rhymes with the first and third lines of the next [C19 from It., lit.: third rhyme]

TE score (in Australia) *abbrev for* Tertiary Entrance score: a score based on a pupil's performance in secondary school that determines his or her prospects of gaining entrance to tertiary educational institutions

TESL ('tɛsᵊl) *n acronym for* Teaching (of) English as a Second Language

tesla ('tɛslə) *n* the derived SI unit of magnetic flux density equal to a flux of 1 weber in an area of 1 square metre. Symbol: T [C20 after Nikola TESLA]

Tesla ('tɛslə) *n* **Nikola** ('nɪkələ) 1857–1943, US electrical engineer and inventor, born in Smiljan, now in Croatia. His inventions include a transformer, generators, and dynamos

tesla coil *n* a step-up transformer with an air core, used for producing high voltages at high frequencies

TESSA *or* **Tessa** ('tɛsə) (in Britain) *n acronym for* Tax Exempt Special Savings Account; a former (available 1991–99) tax-free savings scheme

tessellate ('tɛsɪˌleɪt) *vb* **tessellates, tessellating, tessellated 1** (*tr*) to construct, pave, or inlay with a mosaic of small tiles **2** (*intr*) (of identical shapes) to fit together exactly [C18 from L *tessellātus* checked, from *tessella* small stone cube, from TESSERA]

tessera ('tɛsərə) *n, pl* **tesserae** (-səˌriː) **1** a small square tile of stone, glass, etc, used in mosaics **2** a die, tally, etc, used in classical times, made of bone or wood [C17 from L, from Ionic Gk *tesseres* four] > **'tesseral** *adj*

Tessin (tɛ'siːn) *n* the German name for **Ticino**

tessitura (ˌtɛsɪ'tʊərə) *n music* the general pitch level of a piece of vocal music [It.: texture, from L *textura*; see TEXTURE]

test¹ (tɛst) *vb* **1** to ascertain (the worth, capability, or endurance) of (a person or thing) by subjection to certain examinations, etc; try **2** (often foll by *for*) to carry out an examination on (a substance, material, or system) to indicate the presence of a substance or the possession of a property: *to test food for arsenic* **3** (*tr*) to put under severe strain: *the long delay tested my patience* **4** (*intr*) to achieve a specified result in a test: *he tested positive for the AIDS virus* ▷ *n* **5** a method, practice, or examination designed to test a person or thing **6** a series of questions or problems designed to test a specific skill or knowledge **7** a standard of judgment; criterion **8a** a chemical reaction or physical procedure for testing a substance, material, etc **8b** a chemical reagent used in such a procedure **8c** the result of the procedure or the evidence gained from it **9** *sport* See **test match 10** *arch* a declaration of truth, loyalty, etc **11** (*modifier*) performed as a test: *test drive* [C14 (in the sense: vessel used in treating metals): from L *testum* earthen vessel] > **'testable** *adj* > **'testing** *adj*

test² (tɛst) *n* the hard outer covering of certain invertebrates and tunicates [C19 from L *testa* shell]

testa ('tɛstə) *n, pl* **testae** (-tiː) the hard outer layer of a seed [C18 from L: shell]

testaceous (tɛ'steɪʃəs) *adj biol* **1** of or possessing a test or testa **2** of the reddish-brown colour of terra cotta [C17 from L *testācens*, from TESTA]

testament ('tɛstəmənt) *n* **1** *law* a will (esp in **last will and testament**) **2** a proof, attestation, or tribute **3a** a covenant instituted between God and man **3b** a copy of either the Old or the New Testament, or of the complete Bible [C14 from L *testamentum* a will, from *testārī* to bear witness, from *testis* a witness] > **ˌtesta'mental** *adj* > **ˌtesta'mentary** *adj*

Testament ('tɛstəmənt) *n* **1** either of the two main parts of the Bible; the Old Testament or the New Testament **2** the New Testament as distinct from the Old

testate ('tɛsteɪt, 'tɛstɪt) *adj* **1** having left a legally valid will at death ▷ *n* **2** a person who dies testate [C15 from L *testārī* to make a will; see TESTAMENT] > **testacy** ('tɛstəsɪ) *n*

testator (tɛ'steɪtə) *or* (*fem*) **testatrix** (tɛ'steɪtrɪks) *n* a person who makes a will, esp one who dies testate [C15 from Anglo-F *testatour*, from LL *testātor*, from L *testārī* to make a will]

test ban *n* an agreement among nations to forgo tests of nuclear weapons

test-bed *n engineering* an area used for testing machinery, etc, under working conditions

test card *or* **pattern** *n* a complex pattern used to test the characteristics of a television transmission system

test case *n* a legal action that serves as a precedent in deciding similar succeeding cases

test-drive *vb* **test-drives, test-driving, test-drove, test-driven** (*tr*) to drive (a car or other motor vehicle) for a limited period in order to assess it

tester¹ ('tɛstə) *n* a person or thing that tests

tester² ('tɛstə) *n* a canopy over a bed [C14 from Med. L *testerium*, from LL *testa* a skull, from L: shell]

testes ('tɛstiːz) *n* the plural of **testis**

testicle ('tɛstɪkᵊl) *n* either of the two male reproductive glands, in most mammals enclosed within the scrotum, that produce spermatozoa [C15 from L *testiculus*, dim. of *testis*] > **testicular** (tɛ'stɪkjʊlə) *adj*

testiculate (tɛ'stɪkjʊlɪt) *adj bot* shaped like testicles: *the testiculate tubers of certain orchids* [C18 from LL *testiculātus*; see TESTICLE]

testify ('tɛstɪˌfaɪ) *vb* **testifies, testifying, testified 1** (when *tr, may take a clause as object*) to state (something) formally as a declaration of fact **2** *law* to declare or give (evidence) under oath, esp in court **3** (when *intr*, often foll by *to*) to be evidence (of); serve as witness (to) **4** (*tr*) to declare or acknowledge openly [C14 from L *testificārī*, from *testis* witness] > **ˌtestifi'cation** *n* > **'testiˌfier** *n*

testimonial (ˌtɛstɪ'məʊnɪəl) *n* **1a** a recommendation of the character, ability, etc, of a person or of the quality of a product or service **1b** (*as modifier*): *testimonial advertising* **2** a formal statement of truth or fact **3** a tribute given for services or achievements **4** a sports match to raise money for a particular player ▷ *adj* **5** of or relating to a testimony or testimonial.

USAGE *Testimonial* is sometimes wrongly used where *testimony* is meant: *his re-election is a testimony* (not *a testimonial*) *to his popularity with his constituents*

testimony (ˈtɛstɪmənɪ) *n, pl* **testimonies** **1** a declaration of truth or fact **2** *law* evidence given by a witness, esp in court under oath **3** evidence testifying to something: *her success was a testimony to her good luck* **4** *Old Testament* the Ten Commandments [C15 from L *testimōnium*, from *testis* witness]

testis (ˈtɛstɪs) *n, pl* **testes** another word for **testicle** [C17 from L, lit.: witness (to masculinity)]

test match *n* (in various sports, esp cricket) an international match, esp one of a series

testosterone (tɛˈstɒstəˌrəʊn) *n* a potent steroid hormone secreted mainly by the testes [C20 from TESTIS + STEROL + -ONE]

test paper *n* **1** *chem* paper impregnated with an indicator for use in chemical tests **2a** the question sheet of a test **2b** the paper completed by a test candidate

test pilot *n* a pilot who flies aircraft of new design to test their performance in the air

test tube *n* **1** a cylindrical round-bottomed glass tube open at one end: used in scientific experiments **2** (*modifier*) made synthetically in, or as if in, a test tube: *a test-tube product*

test-tube baby *n* **1** a fetus that has developed from an ovum fertilized in an artificial womb **2** a baby conceived by artificial insemination

testudinal (tɛˈstjuːdɪnᵊl) *adj* of or resembling a tortoise [C19 from L TESTUDO]

testudo (tɛˈstjuːdəʊ) *n, pl* **testudines** (-dɪˌniːz) a form of shelter used by the ancient Roman army as protection against attack from above, consisting of a mobile arched structure or of overlapping shields held by the soldiers over their heads [C17 from L: a tortoise, from *testa* a shell]

testy (ˈtɛstɪ) *adj* **testier, testiest** irritable or touchy [C14 from Anglo-Norman *testif* headstrong, from OF *teste* head, from LL *testa* skull, from L: shell] > **ˈtestily** *adv* > **ˈtestiness** *n*

tetanus (ˈtɛtənəs) *n* **1** Also called: **lockjaw** an acute infectious disease in which sustained muscular spasm, contraction, and convulsion are caused by the release of toxins from a bacterium **2** *physiol* any tense contraction of a muscle [C16 via L from Gk *tetanos*, ult. from *teinein* to stretch] > **ˈtetanal** *adj* > **ˈtetaˌnoid** *adj*

tetany (ˈtɛtənɪ) *n* an abnormal increase in the excitability of nerves and muscles caused by a deficiency of parathyroid secretion [C19 from F; see TETANUS]

tetchy (ˈtɛtʃɪ) *adj* **tetchier, tetchiest** being or inclined to be cross, irritable, or touchy [C16 prob. from obs. *tetch* defect, from OF *tache* spot, of Gmc origin] > **ˈtetchily** *adv* > **ˈtetchiness** *n*

tête-à-tête (ˌteɪtəˈteɪt) *n, pl* **tête-à-têtes** *or* **tête-à-tête** **1a** a private conversation between two people **1b** (*as modifier*): *a tête-à-tête conversation* **2** a small sofa for two people, esp one that is S-shaped in plan so that the sitters are almost face to face ▷ *adv* **3** intimately; in private [C17 from F, lit.: head to head]

tête-bêche (tɛtˈbɛʃ) *adj philately* (of an unseparated pair of stamps) printed so that one is inverted in relation to the other [C19 from F, from *tête* head + *bêche*, from obs. *béchevet* double-headed (orig. of a bed)]

tether (ˈtɛðə) *n* **1** a rope, chain, etc, by which an animal is tied to a particular spot **2** the range of one's endurance, etc **3** **at the end of one's tether** distressed or exasperated to the limit of one's endurance ▷ *vb* **4** (*tr*) to tie with or as if with a tether [C14 from ON *tjothr*]

Tethys¹ (ˈtiːθɪs, ˈtɛθ-) *n Greek myth* a Titaness and sea goddess, wife of Oceanus

Tethys² (ˈtiːθɪs, ˈtɛθ-) *n* the sea that lay between Laurasia and Gondwanaland, the two supercontinents formed by the first split of the larger supercontinent Pangaea. The Tethys Sea can be regarded as the predecessor of today's smaller Mediterranean. See also **Pangaea**

Teton Range (ˈtiːtᵊn) *n* a mountain range in the N central US, mainly in NW Wyoming. Highest peak: Grand Teton, 4196 m (13 766 ft)

tetra- *or before a vowel* **tetr-** *combining form* four: *tetrameter* [from Gk]

tetrabasic (ˌtɛtrəˈbeɪsɪk) *adj* (of an acid) containing four replaceable hydrogen atoms > **tetrabasicity** (ˌtɛtrəbeɪˈsɪsɪtɪ) *n*

tetrachloromethane (ˈtɛtrəklɔːrəʊˌmiːθeɪn) *n* the systematic name for **carbon tetrachloride**

tetrachord (ˈtɛtrəˌkɔːd) *n music* any of several groups of four notes in descending order, in which the first and last notes form a perfect fourth [C17 from Gk *tetrakhordos* four-stringed] > ˌ**tetraˈchordal** *adj*

tetracyclic (ˌtɛtrəˈsaɪklɪk) *adj chem* containing four rings in its molecular structure

tetracycline (ˌtɛtrəˈsaɪklaɪn, -klɪn) *n* an antibiotic synthesized from chlortetracycline or derived from a bacterium [C20 from TETRA- + CYCL(IC) + -INE²]

tetrad (ˈtɛtræd) *n* a group or series of four [C17 from Gk *tetras*, from *tettares* four]

tetraethyl lead (ˌtɛtrəˈiːθaɪl lɛd) *n* a colourless oily insoluble liquid used in petrol to prevent knocking. Systematic name: **lead tetraethyl**

tetrafluoroethene (ˈtɛtrəˌflʊərəʊˈɛθiːn) *n chem* a dense colourless gas that is polymerized to make polytetrafluorethene (PTFE). Formula: $F_2C{:}CF_2$. Also called: **tetrafluoroethylene** [C20 from TETRA- + FLUORO- + ETHENE]

tetragon (ˈtɛtrəˌgɒn) *n* a less common name for **quadrilateral** (sense 2) [C17 from Gk *tetragōnon*]

tetragonal (tɛˈtrægənᵊl) *adj* **1** *crystallog* relating or belonging to the crystal system characterized by three mutually perpendicular axes of which only two are equal **2** of or shaped like a quadrilateral > **teˈtragonally** *adv*

Tetragrammaton (ˌtɛtrəˈgræmətᵊn) *n Bible* the Hebrew name for God consisting of the four consonants Y H V H (or Y H W H). It is usually transliterated as *Jehovah* or *Yahweh*. Sometimes shortened to **Tetragram** [C14 from Gk, from *tetragrammatos* having four letters]

tetrahedron (ˌtɛtrəˈhiːdrən) *n, pl* **tetrahedrons** *or* **tetrahedra** (-drə) a solid figure having four triangular plane faces. A **regular tetrahedron** has faces that are equilateral triangles [C16 from NL, from LGk *tetraedron*] > ˌ**tetraˈhedral** *adj*

tetralogy (tɛˈtrælədʒɪ) *n, pl* **tetralogies** a series of four related works, as in drama or opera [C17 from Gk *tetralogia*]

tetramerous (tɛˈtræmərəs) *adj biol* having or consisting of four parts [C19 from NL *tetramerus*, from Gk *tetramerēs*]

tetrameter (tɛˈtræmɪtə) *n prosody* **1** a line of verse consisting of four metrical feet **2** a verse composed of such lines

tetraplegia (ˌtɛtrəˈpliːdʒɪə) *n* another name for **quadriplegia** > ˌ**tetraˈplegic** *adj*

tetraploid (ˈtɛtrəˌplɔɪd) *genetics* ▷ *adj* **1** having four times the haploid number of chromosomes in the nucleus ▷ *n* **2** a tetraploid organism, nucleus, or cell

tetrapod (ˈtɛtrəˌpɒd) *n* **1** any vertebrate that has four limbs **2** a device consisting of four arms radiating from a central point: three arms form a supporting tripod and the fourth is vertical

tetrapterous (tɛˈtræptərəs) *adj* having four wings [C19 from NL *tetrapterus*, from Gk *tetrapteros*, from TETRA- + *pteron* wing]

tetrarch (ˈtɛtrɑːk) *n* **1** the ruler of one fourth of a country

Tt

2 a subordinate ruler 3 any of four joint rulers [c14 from Gk *tetrarkhēs*; see TETRA-, -ARCH] > **tetrarchate** (tɛˈtrɑːˌkeɪt, -kɪt) *n* > **teˈtrarchic** *adj* > **ˈtetrarchy** *n*

tetrastich (ˈtɛtrəˌstɪk) *n* a poem, stanza, or strophe that consists of four lines [c16 via L from Gk *tetrastikhon*, from TETRA- + *stikhos* row] > **tetrastichic** (ˌtɛtrəˈstɪkɪk) *or* **tetrastichal** (tɛˈtræstɪkᵊl) *adj*

tetravalent (ˌtɛtrəˈveɪlənt) *adj chem* 1 having a valency of four 2 Also: **quadrivalent** having four valencies > **ˌtetraˈvalency** *n*

Tetrazzini (*Italian* tetratˈtsiːni) *n* **Luisa** (luˈiːza) 1871–1940, Italian coloratura soprano

tetrode (ˈtɛtrəʊd) *n* an electronic valve having four electrodes

tetroxide (tɛˈtrɒksaɪd) *n* any oxide that contains four oxygen atoms per molecule

tetryl (ˈtɛtrɪl) *n* a yellow crystalline explosive solid, trinitrophenylmethylnitramine, used in detonators

Tetuán (tɛˈtwɑːn) *n* a city in N Morocco: capital of Spanish Morocco (1912–56). Pop: 277 516 (1994 est)

Tetzel *or* **Tezel** (ˈtɛtsᵊl) *n* **Johann** (joˈhan) ?1465–1519, German Dominican monk. His preaching on papal indulgences provoked Luther's 95 theses at Wittenberg (1517)

Teucer (ˈtjuːsə) *n Greek myth* 1 a Cretan leader, who founded Troy 2 a son of Telamon and Hesione, who distinguished himself by his archery on the side of the Greeks in the Trojan War

Teucrian (ˈtjuːkrɪən) *n, adj* another word for **Trojan**

Teutoburger Wald (*German* ˈtɔytobʊrgər valt) *n* a low wooded mountain range in N Germany: possible site of the annihilation of three Roman legions by Germans under Arminius in 9 AD

Teuton (ˈtjuːtən) *n* 1 a member of an ancient Germanic people from Jutland who migrated to S Gaul in the 2nd century BC 2 a member of any people speaking a Germanic language, esp a German ▷ *adj* 3 Teutonic [c18 from L *Teutonī* the Teutons, of Gmc origin]

Teutonic (tjuːˈtɒnɪk) *adj* 1 characteristic of or relating to the German people 2 of the ancient Teutons 3 (not used in linguistics) of or relating to the Germanic languages

Tevere (ˈteːvere) *n* the Italian name for the **Tiber**

Tewkesbury (ˈtjuːksbərɪ, -brɪ) *n* a town in W England, in N Gloucestershire at the confluence of the Rivers Severn and Avon: scene of a decisive battle (1471) of the Wars of the Roses in which the Yorkists defeated the Lancastrians; 12th-century abbey. Pop: 9488 (1991)

Tex. *abbrev for* 1 Texan 2 Texas

Texas (ˈtɛksəs) *n* a state of the southwestern US, on the Gulf of Mexico: the second largest state; part of Mexico from 1821 to 1836, when it was declared an independent republic; joined the US in 1845; consists chiefly of a plain, with a wide flat coastal belt rising up to the semiarid Sacramento and Davis Mountains of the southwest; a major producer of cotton, rice, and livestock; the chief US producer of oil and gas; a leading world supplier of sulphur. Capital: Austin. Pop: 20 851 820 (2000). Area: 678 927 sq km (262 134 sq miles). Abbreviations: **Tex.** or (with zip code) **TX** > **ˈTexan** *n, adj*

Tex-Mex (ˈtɛksˌmɛks) *adj* of, relating to, or denoting the Texan version of something Mexican, such as music, food, or language

text (tɛkst) *n* 1 the main body of a printed or written work as distinct from commentary, notes, illustrations, etc 2 the words of something printed, written, or displayed on a visual display unit 3 the original exact wording of a work as distinct from a revision or translation 4 a short passage of the Bible used as a starting point for a sermon 5 the topic or subject of a discussion or work 6 short for **textbook** 7 any novel, play, etc, prescribed as part of a course of study 8 a text message: *send me a text* ▷ *vb* 9 to send (someone) a text message: *text your answer to the following number* [c14 from Med. L *textus* version, from L *textus* texture, from *texere* to compose]

textbook (ˈtɛkstˌbʊk) *n* a book used as a standard source of information on a particular subject or field > **ˈtextˌbookish** *adj*

textile (ˈtɛkstaɪl) *n* 1 any fabric or cloth, esp woven 2 raw material suitable to be made into cloth ▷ *adj* 3 of or relating to fabrics [c17 from L *textilis* woven, from *texere* to weave]

▷ www.textilemuseum.org

text message *n* 1 a message sent in text form, esp by means of a mobile phone 2 a message appearing on a computer screen > **text messaging** *n*

Text Messaging

1	one
2	to, too, *or* two
2DAY	today
2MORO	tomorrow
2NT	tonight
2NITE	tonight
2U	to you
4	for *or* four
4EVA	for ever
8	ate
24/7	twenty-four hours a day, seven days a week
A3	anytime, anywhere, anyplace
AAM	as a matter of fact
AFAIK	as far as I know
AFK	away from keyboard
al2gethr	altogether
aLrIt	all right
aQr8	accurate
ATB	all the best
ATK	at the keyboard
ATM	at the moment
ATTN	attention
B	be
B4	before
B4N	bye for now
BAK	back at keyboard
BBL	be back later
BBS	be back soon
BCNU	be seeing you
BFN	bye for now
BK *or* COZ	because
B4N	bye for now
BRB	be right back
BRT	be right there
BTW	by the way
BWD	backward
BY	busy
C	see
cngrtultns	congratulations
CMIIW	correct me if I'm wrong
CU	see you
CUL8R	see you later
CYA	see ya
DRIB	don't read if busy
dubl	double
duz	does
DWB	don't write back
enuf	enough
EZ	easy
FC	fingers crossed
F2F	face-to-face
FONE	phone
F2T	free to talk

FWD forward
FWIW for what it's worth
FYI for your information
G2G got to go
GMTA great minds think alike
GR8 great
H& hand
H8 hate
HAND have a nice day
IC I see
ICU I see you
IDD indeed
ILU I love you
IMHO in my humble *or* honest opinion
IMO in my opinion
IMNSHO in my not so humble opinion
IOW in other words
IRL in real life
IRW in the real world
IYKWIMAITYD if you know what I mean and I think you do
K okay
KIT keep in touch
L8 late
L8R later
LO hello
LOL laughing out loud
LTNS long time no see
LUV love
M8 mate
MergNC emergency
MLO mellow
MLOD melody
MOB mobile
mRvLS marvellous
MSG message
MT empty
MTNG meeting
NE any
NE1 anyone
NEhng anything
NEwer anywhere
Njoy enjoy
NO1 no-one
NRN no reply necessary
NtRtain entertain
OB obligatory
ofN often
OIC oh I see
oper8n operation
opN open
opRtunET opportunity
PCM please call me
PLS please
PLU people like us
PPL people
PRT party
Q queue
QL cool
QT quiet
R are
reCv receive
RGDS regards
RU are you?
RUOK are you OK?
RUF2T? are you free to talk?
SA essay
SIT stay in touch
SK8 skate
SOM1 someone
S/TH something
THNQ, TY, *or* **T/Y** thank you
THX *or* **TNZ** thanks
Ti2GO time to go
TTYL talk to you later
TX thanks
TXT text
U you
U2 you too
U4E yours for ever
UR your
USU usually
v very
w/ *or* **WIV** with
W8 wait
WADYA what do you
WAN2 want to
WAN2TLK want to talk?
WB welcome back
WK week
WKND weekend
w/o without
WOT what
WTG way to go!
x extra *or* kiss
xample example
XLNT excellent
XOXO hugs and kisses

▷ www.sharpened.net/glossary/acronyms.php

textual ('tɛkstjʊəl) *adj* **1** of or relating to a text or texts **2** based on a text > '**textually** *adv*

textual criticism *n* **1** the scholarly study of manuscripts, esp of the Bible, in an effort to establish the original text **2** literary criticism emphasizing a close analysis of the text

textualism ('tɛkstjʊəˌlɪzəm) *n* **1** doctrinaire adherence to a text, esp of the Bible **2** textual criticism, esp of the Bible > '**textualist** *n, adj*

texture ('tɛkstʃə) *n* **1** the surface of a material, esp as perceived by the sense of touch **2** the structure, appearance, and feel of a woven fabric **3** the general structure and disposition of the constituent parts of something: *the texture of a cake* **4** the distinctive character or quality of something: *the texture of life in America* ▷ *vb* **textures, texturing, textured 5** (*tr*) to give a distinctive texture to [c15 from L *textūra* web, from *texere* to weave] > '**textural** *adj* > '**texturally** *adv*

Tezel ('tɛtsᵊl) *n* a variant spelling of (Johann) **Tetzel**

TGV (ˌtiːdʒiːˈviː, *French* teʒeve) (in France) *abbrev for* train à grande vitesse: a high-speed passenger train

TGWU (in Britain) *abbrev for* Transport and General Workers' Union

Th *the chemical symbol for* thorium

-th[1] *suffix forming nouns* **1** (*from verbs*) indicating an action or its consequence: *growth* **2** (*from adjectives*) indicating a quality: *width* [from OE *-thu, -tho*]

-th[2] *or* **-eth** *suffix* forming ordinal numbers: *fourth; thousandth* [from OE *-(o)tha, -(o)the*]

Thabana-Ntlenyana (tɑːˈbɑːnəᵊnˈtleɪnjənə) *n* a mountain in Lesotho: the highest peak of the Drakensberg Mountains. Height: 3482 m (11 425 ft). Also called: **Thadentsonyane, Thabantshonyana**

Thackeray ('θækərɪ) *n* **William Makepeace** 1811–63, English novelist, born in India. His novels, originally serialized, include *Vanity Fair* (1848), *Pendennis* (1850), *Henry Esmond* (1852), and *The Newcomes* (1855)

Thaddeus *or* **Thadeus** ('θædɪəs) *n New Testament* one of the 12 apostles (Matthew 10:3; Mark 3:18), traditionally identified with Jude

Thadentsonyane (ˌtɑːdənˈtsɒnjənə) *n* another name for **Thabana-Ntlenyana**

Thai (taɪ) *adj* **1** of Thailand, its people, or their language

▷ *n* **2** (*pl* **Thais** *or* **Thai**) a native or inhabitant of Thailand **3** the language of Thailand, sometimes classified as belonging to the Sino-Tibetan family

Thailand ('taɪˌlænd) *n* a kingdom in SE Asia, on the Andaman Sea and the Gulf of Siam: united as a kingdom in 1350 and became a major SE Asian power; consists chiefly of a central plain around the Chao Phraya river system, mountains rising over 2400 m (8000 ft) in the northwest, and rainforest the length of the S peninsula. Official language: Thai. Official religion: (Hinayana) Buddhist. Currency: baht. Capital: Bangkok. Pop: 61 251 000 (2001 est). Area: 513 998 sq km (198 455 sq miles). Former name (until 1939 and 1945–49): **Siam**
▷ www.thaigov.go.th
▷ www.tourismthailand.org
▷ www.tatnews.org/photo_gallery

Thaïs ('θeɪɪs) *n* 4th-century BC Athenian courtesan; mistress of Alexander the Great

thalamus ('θæləməs) *n, pl* **thalami** (-ˌmaɪ) **1** either of the two contiguous egg-shaped masses of grey matter at the base of the brain **2** both of these masses considered as a functional unit **3** the receptacle or torus of a flower [C18 from L, from Gk *thalamos* inner room] > **thalamic** (θə'læmɪk) *adj*

thalassaemia *or US* **thalassemia** (ˌθælə'siːmɪə) *n* a hereditary disease resulting from defects in the synthesis of the red blood pigment haemoglobin [NL, from Gk *thalassa* sea + -AEMIA, it being esp prevalent round the eastern Mediterranean]

thalassic (θə'læsɪk) *adj* of or relating to the sea, esp to small or inland seas [C19 from F *thalassique*, from Gk *thalassa* sea]

thaler ('tɑːlə) *n, pl* **thaler** *or* **thalers** a former German, Austrian, or Swiss silver coin [from G; see DOLLAR]

Thales ('θeɪliːz) *n* ?624–?546 BC, Greek philosopher, mathematician, and astronomer, born in Miletus. He held that water was the origin of all things and he predicted the solar eclipse of May 28, 585 BC

Thalia (θə'laɪə) *n Greek myth* **1** the Muse of comedy and pastoral poetry **2** one of the three Graces, the others are Aglaia and Euphrosyne [C17 via L from Gk, from *thaleia* blooming]

thalidomide (θə'lɪdəˌmaɪd) *n* **a** a drug formerly used as a sedative and hypnotic but withdrawn from use when found to cause abnormalities in developing fetuses **b** (*as modifier*): *a thalidomide baby* [C20 from *thali(mi)do(glutari)mide*]

thallium ('θælɪəm) *n* a soft malleable highly toxic white metallic element. Symbol: Tl; atomic no.: 81; atomic wt.: 204.37 [C19 from NL, from Gk *thallos* a green shoot; from the green line in its spectrum]

thallus ('θæləs) *n, pl* **thalli** ('θælaɪ) *or* **thalluses** the undifferentiated vegetative body of algae, fungi, and lichens [C19 from L, from Gk *thallos* green shoot, from *thallein* to bloom] > '**thalloid** *adj*

thalweg *or* **talweg** ('tɑːlvɛg) *n geog, rare* **1** the longitudinal outline of a riverbed from source to mouth **2** the line of steepest descent from any point on the land surface [C19 from G *Thal* or *Tal* valley + *Weg* way]

Thames *n* **1** (tɛmz) a river in S England, rising in the Cotswolds in several headstreams and flowing generally east through London to the North Sea by a large estuary. Length: 346 km (215 miles). Ancient name: **Tamesis** ('tæməsɪs) **2** (teɪmz, θeɪmz) a river in SE Canada, in Ontario, flowing south to London, then southwest to Lake St Clair. Length: 217 km (135 miles)

than (ðæn; *unstressed* ðən) *conj (coordinating), prep* **1** used to introduce the second element of a comparison, the first element of which expresses difference: *shorter than you* **2** used after adverbs such as *rather* or *sooner* to introduce a rejected alternative in an expression of preference: *rather than be imprisoned, I shall die* [OE *thanne*]

> USAGE In formal English, *than* is usually regarded as a conjunction governing an unexpressed verb: *he does it far better than I (do)*. Which pronoun to use therefore depends on whether it is the subject or object of the unexpressed verb: *she likes him more than I (like him)*; *she likes him more than (she likes) me*. However, in ordinary speech and writing *than* is usually treated as a preposition and is followed by the object form of a pronoun: *my brother is younger than me*

thanatology (ˌθænə'tɒlədʒɪ) *n* the scientific study of death and its related phenomena [C19 from Gk *thanatos* death + -LOGY]

thanatopsis (ˌθænə'tɒpsɪs) *n* a meditation on death, as in a poem [C19 from Gk *thanatos* death + *opsis* a view]

Thanatos ('θænəˌtɒs) *n* the Greek personification of death: son of Nyx, goddess of night. Roman counterpart: **Mors.** ▷ Cf **Eros** > **Thanatotic** (ˌθænə'tɒtɪk) *adj*

thane *or (less commonly)* **thegn** (θeɪn) *n* **1** (in Anglo-Saxon England) a member of an aristocratic class who held land from the king or from another nobleman in return for certain services **2** (in medieval Scotland) a person of rank holding land from the king [OE *thegn*] > **thanage** ('θeɪnɪdʒ) *n*

Thanet ('θænɪt) *n* **Isle of** an island in SE England, in NE Kent, separated from the mainland by two branches of the River Stour: scene of many Norse invasions. Area: 109 sq km (42 sq miles)

thangka ('θæŋkə) *n* (in Tibetan Buddhism) a religious painting on a scroll [from Tibetan]

Thanjavur (ˌtʌndʒə'vʊə) *n* a city in SE India, in E Tamil Nadu: headquarters of the earliest Protestant missions in India. Pop: 202 013 (1991). Former name: **Tanjore**

thank (θæŋk) *vb (tr)* **1** to convey feelings of gratitude to **2** to hold responsible: *he has his creditors to thank for his bankruptcy* [OE *thancian*]

thankful ('θæŋkfʊl) *adj* grateful and appreciative > '**thankfully** *adv* > '**thankfulness** *n*

> USAGE Some people object to the use of *thankfully* to qualify a complete statement, as in *that conflict is, thankfully, over*. However, this use is now very well established, and far more common than e.g. *she drew some smoke in thankfully and settled herself more comfortably on her chair*

thankless ('θæŋklɪs) *adj* **1** receiving no thanks or appreciation **2** ungrateful > '**thanklessly** *adv* > '**thanklessness** *n*

thanks (θæŋks) *pl n* **1** an expression of appreciation or gratitude **2** **thanks to** because of: *thanks to him we lost the match* ▷ *interj* **3** *inf* an exclamation expressing gratitude

thanksgiving ('θæŋksˌgɪvɪŋ; US θæŋks'gɪv-) *n* **1** the act of giving thanks **2** a formal public expression of thanks to God

Thanksgiving Day *n* an annual day of holiday celebrated in thanksgiving to God on the fourth Thursday of November in the United States, and on the second Monday of October in Canada. Often shortened to **Thanksgiving**

Thapsus ('θæpsəs) *n* an ancient town near Carthage in North Africa: site of Caesar's victory over Pompey in 46 BC

thar (tɑː) *n* a native name in Nepal for a species of goatlike mammal

Thar Desert (tɑː) *n* a desert in NW India, mainly in NW Rajasthan state and extending into Pakistan. Area: over 260 000 sq km (100 000 sq miles). Also called: **Indian Desert, Great Indian Desert**

Tharp (θɑːp) *n* **Twyla** ('twaɪlə) born 1941, US choreographer, whose work fuses classical ballet with modern dance

Thásos ('θæsɒs) *n* a Greek island in the N Aegean: colonized by Greeks from Paros in the 7th century BC as a gold-mining centre; under Turkish rule (1455–1912). Pop: 13 110 (latest est). Area: 379 sq km (146 sq miles)

that (ðæt; *unstressed* ðət) *determiner* (*used before a sing n*) **1a** used preceding a noun that has been mentioned or is understood: *that idea of yours* **1b** (*as pronoun*): *don't eat that* **2a** used preceding a noun that denotes something more remote or removed: *that building over there is for sale* **2b** (*as pronoun*): *that is John and this is his wife* **3** used to refer to something that is familiar: *that old chap from across the street* **4** **and** (**all**) **that** *inf* everything connected with the subject mentioned: *he knows a lot about building and that* **5** **at that** (*completive-intensive*) additionally, all things considered, or nevertheless: *I might decide to go at that* **6** **like that** **6a** effortlessly: *he gave me the answer just like that* **6b** of such a nature, character, etc: *he paid for all our tickets — he's like that* **7** **that is** **7a** to be precise **7b** in other words **7c** for example **8** **that's that** there is no more to be done, discussed, etc ▷ *conj* (*subordinating*) **9** used to introduce a noun clause: *I believe that you'll come* **10** used to introduce: **10a** a clause of purpose: *they fought that others might have peace* **10b** a clause of result: *he laughed so hard that he cried* **10c** a clause after an understood sentence expressing desire, indignation, or amazement: *oh, that I had never lived!* ▷ *adv* **11** used to reinforce the specification of a precise degree already mentioned: *go just that fast and you should be safe* **12** Also: **all that** (*usually used with a negative*) *inf* (intensifier): *he wasn't that upset at the news* **13** *dialect* (intensifier): *the cat was that weak after the fight* ▷ *pron* **14** used to introduce a restrictive relative clause: *the book that we want* **15** used to introduce a clause with the verb *to be* to emphasize the extent to which the preceding noun is applicable: *genius that she is, she outwitted the computer* [OE *thæt*]

> USAGE Precise writers maintain a distinction between *that* and *which*. In *the book that is on the table is mine*, the clause *that is on the table* is used to distinguish one particular book (the one on the table) from another or others (which may be anywhere, but not on the table). In *the book, which is on the table, is mine*, the *which* clause is merely descriptive or incidental. The more formal the level of language, the more important it is to preserve the distinction between the two relative pronouns; but in informal or colloquial language they are often used interchangeably

thatch (θætʃ) *n* **1a** Also called: **thatching** a roofing material that consists of straw, reed, etc **1b** a roof made of such a material **2** anything resembling this, such as the hair of the head **3** Also called: **thatch palm** any of various palms with leaves suitable for thatching ▷ *vb* **4** to cover with thatch [OE *theccan* to cover] > '**thatcher** *n*

Thatcher ('θætʃə) *n* **Margaret** (**Hilda**), Baroness (née *Roberts*) born 1925, British stateswoman; leader of the Conservative Party (1975–90); prime minister (1979–90)

Thatcherism ('θætʃəˌrɪzəm) *n* the policies of monetarism, privatization, and self-help promoted by Margaret Thatcher > '**Thatcherˌite** *n, adj*

thaumatology (ˌθɔːmə'tɒlədʒɪ) *n* the study of or a treatise on miracles [C19 from Gk *thaumato-* combining form of *thauma* a wonder, marvel + -LOGY]

thaumatrope ('θɔːməˌtrəʊp) *n* a toy in which partial pictures on the two sides of a card appear to merge when the card is twirled rapidly [C19 from Gk *thaumato-* (see THAUMATOLOGY) + -TROPE] > **thaumatropical** (ˌθɔːmə'trɒpɪkᵊl) *adj*

thaumaturge ('θɔːməˌtɜːdʒ) *n rare* a performer of miracles; magician [C18 from Med. L *thaumaturgus*, from Gk *thaumatourgos* miracle-working] > ˌ**thauma'turgic** *adj* > '**thaumaˌturgy** *n*

thaw (θɔː) *vb* **1** to melt or cause to melt: *the snow thawed* **2** to become or cause to become unfrozen; defrost **3** (*intr*) to be the case that the ice or snow is melting: *it's thawing fast* **4** (*intr*) to become more relaxed or friendly ▷ *n* **5** the act or process of thawing **6** a spell of relatively warm weather, causing snow or ice to melt **7** an increase in relaxation or friendliness [OE *thawian*]

ThD *abbrev for* Doctor of Theology

the[1] (*stressed or emphatic* ðiː; *unstressed before a consonant* ðə; *unstressed before a vowel* ðɪ) *determiner* (*article*) **1** used preceding a noun that has been previously specified: *the pain should disappear soon.* ▷ Cf **a**[1] **2** used to indicate a particular person, object, etc: *ask the man standing outside.* ▷ Cf **a**[1] **3** used preceding certain nouns associated with one's culture, society, or community: *to go to the doctor; to listen to the news* **4** used preceding present participles and adjectives when they function as nouns: *the singing is awful* **5** used preceding titles and certain uniquely specific or proper nouns: *the United States; the Chairman* **6** used preceding a qualifying adjective or noun in certain names or titles: *Edward the First* **7** used preceding a noun to make it refer to its class generically: *the white seal is hunted for its fur* **8** used instead of *my, your, her*, etc, with parts of the body: *take me by the hand* **9** (usually stressed) the best, only, or most remarkable: *Harry's is the club in this town* **10** used with proper nouns when qualified: *written by the young Hardy* **11** another word for **per**: *fifty pence the pound* **12** *often facetious or derog* my; our: *the wife goes out on Thursdays* **13** used preceding a unit of time in phrases or titles indicating an outstanding person, event, etc: *housewife of the year* [ME, from OE *thē*, a demonstrative adjective that later superseded *sē* (masculine singular) and *sēo, sio* (feminine singular)]

the[2] (ðə, ðɪ) *adv* **1** (often foll by *for*) used before comparative adjectives or adverbs for emphasis: *she looks the happier for her trip* **2** used correlatively before each of two comparative adjectives or adverbs to indicate equality: *the sooner you come, the better; the more I see you, the more I love you* [OE *thī, thȳ*]

theanthropism (θiː'ænθrəˌpɪzəm) *n* **1** the ascription of human traits or characteristics to a god or gods **2** *Christian theol* the doctrine of the union of the divine and human natures in the single person of Christ [C19 from Ecclesiastical Gk *theanthrōpos* (from *theos* god + *anthrōpos* man) + -ISM] > **theanthropic** (ˌθiːæn'θrɒpɪk) *adj*

thearchy ('θiːɑːkɪ) *n, pl* **thearchies** rule or government by God or gods; theocracy [C17 from Church Gk *thearkhia*; see THEO-, -ARCHY]

theatre *or US* **theater** ('θɪətə) *n* **1** a building designed for the performance of plays, operas, etc **2** a large room or hall, usually with a raised platform and tiered seats for an audience **3** a room in a hospital equipped for surgical operations **4** plays regarded collectively as a form of art **5** **the theatre** the world of actors, theatrical companies, etc **6** a setting for dramatic or important events **7** writing that is suitable for dramatic presentation: *a good piece of theatre* **8** *US & Austral* the usual word for **cinema** (sense 1) **9** a major area of military activity **10** a circular or semicircular open-air building with tiers of seats [C14 from L *theātrum*, from Gk *theatron* place for viewing, from *theasthai* to look at]

▷ http://vl-theatre.com
▷ www.theatrelinks.com
▷ www.uktw.co.uk
▷ www.artslynx.org/theatre

theatre-in-the-round *n, pl* **theatres-in-the-round** a theatre with seats arranged around a central acting area

theatre of cruelty *n* a type of theatre that seeks to communicate a sense of pain, suffering, and evil, using gesture, movement, sound, and symbolism rather than language

▷ www.theatrelinks.com

theatre of the absurd *n* drama in which normal conventions and dramatic structure are modified in order to present life as irrational
▷ www2.arts.gla.ac.uk/Slavonic/Absurd.htm
▷ www.theatrelinks.com

theatrical (θɪˈætrɪkᵊl) *adj* **1** of or relating to the theatre or dramatic performances **2** exaggerated and affected in manner or behaviour; histrionic > **theˌatriˈcality** *or* **theˈatricalness** *n* > **theˈatrically** *adv*

theatricals (θɪˈætrɪkᵊlz) *pl n* dramatic performances, esp as given by amateurs

theatrics (θɪˈætrɪks) *n* (*functioning as sing*) **1** the art of staging plays **2** exaggerated mannerisms or displays of emotions

Thebaid (ˈθiːbeɪɪd, -bɪ-) *n* the territory around ancient Thebes in Egypt, or sometimes around Thebes in Greece

thebaine (ˈθiːbəˌiːn) *n* a poisonous white crystalline alkaloid, found in opium [C19 from NL *thebaia* opium of Thebes (with reference to Egypt as a chief source of opium) + -INE²]

Thebes (θiːbz) *n* **1** (in ancient Greece) the chief city of Boeotia, destroyed by Alexander the Great (336 BC) **2** (in ancient Egypt) a city on the Nile: at various times capital of Upper Egypt or of the entire country > **Thebaic** (θɪˈbeɪɪk) *adj* > **ˈTheban** *adj, n*

theca (ˈθiːkə) *n, pl* **thecae** (-siː) **1** *bot* an enclosing organ, cell, or spore case **2** *zool* a hard outer covering, such as the container of a coral polyp [C17 from L *thēca*, from Gk *thēkē* case] > **ˈthecate** *adj*

thecodont (ˈθiːkəˌdɒnt) *adj* **1** (of mammals and certain reptiles) having teeth that grow in sockets **2** of or relating to teeth of this type ▷ *n* **3** any of various extinct reptiles of Triassic times, having teeth set in sockets: they gave rise to the dinosaurs, crocodiles, pterodactyls, and birds [C20 NL *Thecodontia*, from Gk *thēkē* case + -ODONT]

thé dansant *French* (te dɑ̃sɑ̃) *n, pl* ***thés dansant*** (te dɑ̃sɑ̃) a dance held while afternoon tea is served, popular in the 1920s and 1930s [lit.: dancing tea]

thee (ðiː) *pron* **1** the objective form of **thou¹** **2** (*subjective*) *rare* refers to the person addressed: used mainly by members of the Society of Friends [OE *thē*]

theft (θɛft) *n* **1** the dishonest taking of property belonging to another person with the intention of depriving the owner permanently of its possession **2** *rare* something stolen [OE *thēofth*]

thegn (θeɪn) *n* a less common variant of **thane**

Theiler (ˈtaɪlə) *n* **Max** 1899–1972, US virologist, born in South Africa, who developed a vaccine against yellow fever. Nobel prize for physiology or medicine 1951

theine (ˈθiːiːn, -ɪn) *n* caffeine, esp when present in tea [C19 from NL *thea* tea + -INE²]

their (ðɛə) *determiner* **1** of or associated in some way with them: *their own clothes; she tried to combat their mocking her* **2** belonging to or associated with people in general: *in many countries they wash their clothes in the river* **3** belonging to or associated with an indefinite antecedent such as *one, whoever,* or *anybody: everyone should bring their own lunch* [C12 from ON *theira*]

USAGE See at **they**

theirs (ðɛəz) *pron* **1** something or someone belonging to or associated with them: *theirs is difficult* **2** something or someone belonging to or associated with an indefinite antecedent such as *one, whoever,* or *anybody: everyone thinks theirs is best* **3** **of theirs** belonging to or associated with them

theism (ˈθiːɪzəm) *n* **1** the belief in one God as the creator and ruler of the universe **2** the belief in the existence of a God or gods [C17 from Gk *theos* god + -ISM] > **ˈtheist** *n, adj* > **theˈistic** *or* **theˈistical** *adj*

them (ðɛm; *unstressed* ðəm) *pron* **1** (*objective*) refers to things or people other than the speaker or people addressed: *I'll kill them; what happened to them?* ▷ *determiner* **2** a nonstandard word for **those:** *three of them oranges* [OE *thǣm*, infl. by ON *theim*]

USAGE See at **me, they**

thematic apperception test *n psychol* a projective test in which drawings of interacting people are shown and the person being tested is asked to make up a story about them

theme (θiːm) *n* **1** an idea or topic expanded in a discourse, discussion, etc **2** (in literature, music, art, etc) a unifying idea, image, or motif, repeated or developed throughout a work **3** *music* a group of notes forming a recognizable melodic unit, often used as the basis of the musical material in a composition **4** a short essay, esp one set as an exercise for a student **5** *grammar* another word for **root¹** (sense 8) or **stem¹** (sense 7) **6** (*modifier*) planned or designed round one unifying subject, image, etc: *a theme holiday* ▷ *vb* **themes, theming, themed** (*tr*) **7** to design, decorate, etc, in accordance with a theme [C13 from L *thema*, from Gk: deposit, from *tithenai* to lay down] > **thematic** (θɪˈmætɪk) *adj*

theme park *n* an area planned as a leisure attraction, in which all the displays, buildings, activities, etc, are based on one subject

theme song *n* **1** a melody used, esp in a film score, to set a mood, introduce a character, etc **2** another term for **signature tune**

Themis (ˈθiːmɪs) *n Greek myth* a goddess of order and justice

Themistocles (θəˈmɪstəˌkliːz) *n* ?527–?460 BC, Athenian statesman, who was responsible for the Athenian victory against the Persians at Salamis (480). He was ostracized in 470

themselves (ðəmˈsɛlvz) *pron* **1a** the reflexive form of *they* or *them* **1b** (intensifier): *the team themselves voted on it* **2** (*preceded by a copula*) their normal or usual selves: *they don't seem themselves any more* **3** Also: **themself** *not standard* a reflexive form of an indefinite antecedent such as *one, whoever,* or *anybody: everyone has to look after themselves*

then (ðɛn) *adv* **1** at that time; over that period of time **2** (*sentence modifier*) in that case; that being so: *then why don't you ask her? go on then, take it* ▷ *sentence connector* **3** after that; with that: *then John left the room* ▷ *n* **4** that time: *from then on* ▷ *adj* **5** (*prenominal*) existing, functioning, etc, at that time: *the then prime minister* [OE *thenne*]

thenar (ˈθiːnɑː) *n* **1** the palm of the hand **2** the fleshy area of the palm at the base of the thumb [C17 via NL from Gk]

thence (ðɛns) *adv* **1** from that place **2** Also: **thenceforth** (ˈðɛnsˈfɔːθ) from that time or event; thereafter **3** therefore [C13 *thannes*, from *thanne*, from OE *thanon*]

thenceforward (ˈðɛnsˈfɔːwəd) *or* **thenceforwards** *adv* from that time or place on

theo- *or before a vowel* **the-** *combining form* indicating God or gods: *theology* [from Gk *theos* god]

theobromine (ˌθiːəʊˈbrəʊmiːn, -mɪn) *n* a white crystalline alkaloid that occurs in tea and cacao: formerly used to treat asthma [C18 from NL *theobroma* genus of trees, lit.: food of the gods]

theocentric (ˌθɪəˈsɛntrɪk) *adj theol* having God as the focal point of attention

theocracy (θɪˈɒkrəsɪ) *n, pl* **theocracies** **1** government by a deity or by a priesthood **2** a community under such government > **ˈtheoˌcrat** *n* > **ˌtheoˈcratic** *adj*

theocrasy (θɪˈɒkrəsɪ) *n* **1** a mingling into one of deities or divine attributes previously regarded as distinct **2** the union of the soul with God in mysticism [C19 from Gk *theokrasia*, from THEO- + *-krasia* from *krasis* a blending]

Theocritus (θɪˈɒkrɪtəs) *n* ?310–?250 BC, Greek poet, born in Syracuse. He wrote the first pastoral poems in Greek literature and was closely imitated by Virgil > **Theˈocritan** or > **Theocritean** (θɪˌɒkrɪˈtiːən) *adj, n*

theodicy (θɪˈɒdɪsɪ) *n, pl* **theodicies** the branch of theology concerned with defending the attributes of God against objections resulting from the existence of physical and moral evil [c18 coined by Leibnitz in F as *théodicée*, from THEO- + Gk *dikē* justice] > **the,odi'cean** *adj*

theodolite (θɪ'ɒdə,laɪt) *n* a surveying instrument for measuring horizontal and vertical angles, consisting of a small tripod-mounted telescope. Also called (in the US and Canada): **transit** [c16 from NL *theodolitus*, from ?] > **theodolitic** (θɪ,ɒdə'lɪtɪk) *adj*

Theodora (,θɪə'dɔːrə) *n* ?500–548 AD, Byzantine empress; wife and counsellor of Justinian I

Theodoric *or* **Theoderic** (θɪ'ɒdərɪk) *n* called *the Great* ?454–526 AD, king of the Ostrogoths and founder of the Ostrogothic kingdom in Italy after his murder of Odoacer (493)

Theodosius I (,θɪə'dəʊsɪəs) *n* called *the Great*. ?346–395 AD, Roman emperor of the Eastern Roman Empire (379–95) and of the Western Roman Empire (392–95)

theogony (θɪ'ɒgənɪ) *n, pl* **theogonies 1** the origin and descent of the gods **2** an account of this [c17 from Gk *theogonia*] > **theogonic** (,θɪə'gɒnɪk) *adj* > **the'ogonist** *n*

theol. *abbrev for:* **1** theologian **2** theological **3** theology

theologian (,θɪə'ləʊdʒɪən) *n* a person versed in or engaged in the study of theology

theological (,θɪə'lɒdʒɪkᵊl) *adj* of, relating to, or based on theology > **,theo'logically** *adv*

theological virtues *pl n* those virtues that are infused into man by a special grace of God, specifically faith, hope, and charity

theologize *or* **theologise** (θɪ'ɒlə,dʒaɪz) *vb* **theologizes, theologizing, theologized** *or* **theologises, theologising, theologised 1** (*intr*) to speculate upon theological subjects or engage in theological study or discussion **2** (*tr*) to render theological or treat from a theological point of view > **the,ologi'zation** *or* **the,ologi'sation** *n* > **the'olo,gizer** *or* **the'olo,giser** *n*

theology (θɪ'ɒlədʒɪ) *n, pl* **theologies 1** the systematic study of the existence and nature of the divine and its relationship to other beings **2** the systematic study of Christian revelation concerning God's nature and purpose **3** a specific system, form, or branch of this study [c14 from LL *theologia*, from L] > **the'ologist** *n*

theomachy (θɪ'ɒməkɪ) *n, pl* **theomachies** a battle among the gods or against them [c16 from Gk *theomakhia*, from THEO- + *makhē* battle]

theomancy ('θiːəʊ,mænsɪ) *n* divination or prophecy by an oracle or by people directly inspired by a god

theomania (,θɪə'meɪnɪə) *n* religious madness, esp when it takes the form of believing oneself to be a god > **,theo'mani,ac** *n*

theophany (θɪ'ɒfənɪ) *n, pl* **theophanies** a visible manifestation of a deity to man [c17 from LL *theophania*, from LGk, from THEO- + *phainein* to show] > **theophanic** (,θɪə'fænɪk) *adj*

Theophrastus (,θɪə'fræstəs) *n* ?372–?287 BC, Greek Peripatetic philosopher, noted esp for his *Characters*, a collection of sketches of moral types

theophylline (,θɪə'fɪliːn, -ɪn) *n* a white crystalline alkaloid that is an isomer of theobromine: it occurs in plants such as tea and is used to treat asthma [c19 from THEO(BROMINE) + PHYLLO- + -INE²]

theorem ('θɪərəm) *n* a statement or formula that can be deduced from the axioms of a formal system by means of its rules of inference [c16 from LL *theōrēma*, from Gk: something to be viewed, from *theōrein* to view] > **theorematic** (,θɪərə'mætɪk) *or* **theoremic** (,θɪə'rɛmɪk) *adj*

theoretical (,θɪə'rɛtɪkᵊl) *or* **theoretic** *adj* **1** of or based on theory **2** lacking practical application or actual existence; hypothetical **3** using or dealing in theory; impractical > **,theo'retically** *adv*

theoretician (,θɪərɪ'tɪʃən) *n* a student or user of the theory rather than the practical aspects of a subject

theoretics (,θɪə'rɛtɪks) *n* (*functioning as sing or pl*) the theory of a particular subject or discipline

theorize *or* **theorise** ('θɪə,raɪz) *vb* **theorizes, theorizing, theorized** *or* **theorises, theorising, theorised** (*intr*) to produce or use theories; speculate > **'theorist** *n* > **,theori'zation** *or* **,theori'sation** *n* > **'theo,rizer** *or* **'theo,riser** *n*

theory ('θɪərɪ) *n, pl* **theories 1** a system of rules, procedures, and assumptions used to produce a result **2** abstract knowledge or reasoning **3** a conjectural view or idea: *I have a theory about that* **4** an ideal or hypothetical situation (esp in **in theory**) **5** a set of hypotheses related by logical or mathematical arguments to explain a wide variety of connected phenomena in general terms: *the theory of relativity* **6** a nontechnical name for **hypothesis** [c16 from LL *theōria*, from Gk: a sight, from *theōrein* to gaze upon]

theory of games *n* a mathematical theory concerned with the optimum choice of strategy in situations involving a conflict of interest. Also called: **game theory**

theosophy (θɪ'ɒsəfɪ) *n* **1** any of various religious or philosophical systems claiming to be based on or to express an intuitive insight into the divine nature **2** the system of beliefs of the Theosophical Society founded in 1875, claiming to be derived from the sacred writings of Brahmanism and Buddhism [c17 from Med. L *theosophia*, from LGk; see THEO-, -SOPHY] > **theosophical** (,θɪə'sɒfɪkᵊl) *or* **,theo'sophic** *adj* > **the'osophist** *n*

Thera ('θɪərə) *n* a Greek island in the Aegean Sea, in the Cyclades: site of a Minoan settlement and of the volcano that ended Minoan civilization on Crete. Pop: 7000 (latest est). Also called: **Santoríni**. Modern Greek name: **Thíra**

therapeutic (,θɛrə'pjuːtɪk) *adj* **1** of or relating to the treatment of disease; curative **2** serving or performed to maintain health: *therapeutic abortion* [c17 from NL *therapeuticus*, from Gk, from *therapeuein* to minister to, from *therapṣ* an attendant] > **,thera'peutically** *adv*

therapeutics (,θɛrə'pjuːtɪks) *n* (*functioning as sing*) the branch of medicine concerned with the treatment of disease

therapy ('θɛrəpɪ) *n, pl* **therapies a** the treatment of physical, mental, or social disorders or disease **b** (*in combination*): *physiotherapy* [c19 from NL *therapia*, from Gk *therapeia* attendance; see THERAPEUTIC] > **'therapist** *n*

Theravada (,θɛrə'vɑːdə) *n* the southern school of Buddhism, the name preferred by Hinayana Buddhists [from Pali: doctrine of the elders]

there (ðɛə) *adv* **1** in, at, or to that place, point, case, or respect: *we never go there; I agree with you there* ▷ *pron* **2** used as a grammatical subject with some verbs, esp *be*, when the true subject follows the verb: *there is a girl in that office* ▷ *adj* **3** (*postpositive*) who or which is in that place or position: *that boy there did it* **4 all there** (*predicative*) of normal intelligence **5 so there** an exclamation that usually follows a declaration of refusal or defiance **6 there you are 6a** an expression used when handing a person something requested or desired **6b** an exclamation of triumph ▷ *n* **7** that place: *near there* ▷ *interj* **8** an expression of sympathy, as in consoling a child: *there, there, dear* [OE *thǣr*]

> USAGE In correct usage, the verb should agree with the subject in such constructions as *there is a man waiting* and *there are several people waiting*. However, where the subject is compound, it is common in speech to use a singular verb, as in *there's a police car and an ambulance outside*

thereabouts ('ðɛərə,baʊts) *or US* **thereabout** *adv* near that place, time, amount, etc

thereafter (,ðɛər'ɑːftə) *adv* from that time on or after that time

thereat (,ðɛər'æt) *adv rare* **1** at that point or time **2** for that reason

Tt

thereby (ˌðɛəˈbaɪ, ˈðɛəˌbaɪ) *adv* **1** by that means; because of that **2** *arch* thereabouts
therefor (ˌðɛəˈfɔː) *adv arch* for this, that, or it
therefore (ˈðɛəˌfɔː) *sentence connector* **1** thus; hence: *those people have their umbrellas up; therefore, it must be raining* **2** consequently; as a result
therefrom (ˌðɛəˈfrɒm) *adv arch* from that or there: *the roads that lead therefrom*
therein (ˌðɛərˈɪn) *adv formal or law* in or into that place, thing, etc
thereinto (ˌðɛərˈɪntuː) *adv formal or law* into that place, circumstance, etc
thereof (ˌðɛərˈɒv) *adv formal or law* **1** of or concerning that or it **2** from or because of that
thereon (ˌðɛərˈɒn) *adv arch* thereupon
Theresa (təˈriːzə; *Spanish* teˈresa) *n* See (Saint) **Teresa**
Thérèse de Lisieux (*French* terɛz də lizjø) *n* **Saint,** known as *the Little Flower of Jesus.* 1873–97, French Carmelite nun, noted for her autobiography, *The Story of a Soul* (1897). Feast day: Oct 3
thereto (ˌðɛəˈtuː) *adv* **1** *formal or law* to that or it **2** *obs* in addition to that
theretofore (ˌðɛətʊˈfɔː) *adv formal or law* before that time; previous to that
thereunder (ˌðɛərˈʌndə) *adv formal or law* **1** (in documents, etc) below that or it; subsequently in that; thereafter **2** under the terms or authority of that
thereupon (ˌðɛərəˈpɒn) *adv* **1** immediately after that; at that point **2** *formal or law* upon that thing, point, subject, etc
therewith (ˌðɛəˈwɪθ, -ˈwɪð) *or* **therewithal** *adv* **1** *formal or law* with or in addition to that **2** a less common word for **thereupon** (sense 1) **3** *arch* by means of or on account of that
Therezina (*Portuguese* tereˈzina) *n* the former name of **Teresina**
therianthropic (ˌθɪərɪənˈθrɒpɪk) *adj* **1** (of certain mythical creatures or deities) having a partly animal, partly human form **2** of or relating to such creatures or deities [c19 from Gk *thērion* wild animal + *anthrōpos* man] > **therianthropism** (ˌθɪərɪˈænθrəˌpɪzəm) *n*
theriomorphic (ˌθɪərɪəʊˈmɔːfɪk) *adj* (esp of a deity) possessing or depicted in the form of a beast [c19 from Gk *thēriomorphos*, from *thērion* wild animal + *morphē* shape]
therm (θɜːm) *n Brit* a unit of heat equal to 100 000 British thermal units. One therm is equal to $1.055\ 056 \times 10^8$ joules [c19 from Gk *thermē* heat]
thermae (ˈθɜːmiː) *pl n* public baths or hot springs, esp in ancient Greece or Rome [c17 from L, from Gk *thermai*, pl. of *thermē* heat]
thermal (ˈθɜːməl) *adj* **1** Also: **thermic** of, caused by, or generating heat **2** hot or warm: *thermal baths* **3** (of garments) specially made so as to have exceptional heat-retaining qualities: *thermal underwear* ▷ *n* **4** a column of rising air caused by local unequal heating of the land surface, and used by gliders and birds to gain height **5** (*pl*) thermal garments, esp underclothes > ˈ**thermally** *adv*
thermal barrier *n* an obstacle to flight at very high speeds as a result of the heating effect of air friction. Also called: **heat barrier**
thermal conductivity *n* a measure of the ability of a substance to conduct heat
thermal efficiency *n* the ratio of the work done by a heat engine to the energy supplied to it
thermal equator *n* an imaginary line round the earth running through the point on each meridian with the highest average temperature
thermal imaging *n* the technique of producing images of people or objects by using the infrared radiation that they emit or reflect > **thermal image** *n*
thermalize *or* **thermalise** (ˈθɜːməˌlaɪz) *vb* **thermalizes, thermalizing, thermalized** *or* **thermalises, thermalising, thermalised** *physics* to undergo or cause to undergo a process in which neutrons lose energy in a moderator and become thermal neutrons > ˌ**thermaliˈzation** *or* ˌ**thermaliˈsation** *n*
thermal neutrons *pl n* slow neutrons that are approximately in thermal equilibrium with a moderator
thermal reactor *n* a nuclear reactor in which most of the fission is caused by thermal neutrons
thermal shock *n* a fluctuation in temperature causing stress in a material. It often results in fracture, esp in brittle materials such as ceramics
thermion (ˈθɜːmɪən) *n physics* an electron or ion emitted by a body at high temperature
thermionic (ˌθɜːmɪˈɒnɪk) *adj* of, relating to, or operated by electrons emitted from materials at high temperatures: *a thermionic valve*
thermionic current *n* an electric current produced between two electrodes as a result of electrons emitted by thermionic emission
thermionic emission *n* the emission of electrons from very hot solids or liquids
thermionics (ˌθɜːmɪˈɒnɪks) *n* (*functioning as sing*) the branch of electronics concerned with the emission of electrons by hot bodies and with devices based on this effect
thermionic valve *or esp US & Canad* **tube** *n* an electronic valve in which electrons are emitted from a heated rather than a cold cathode
thermistor (θɜːˈmɪstə) *n* a semiconductor device having a resistance that decreases rapidly with an increase in temperature. It is used for temperature measurement and control [c20 from THERMO- + (RES)ISTOR]
Thermit (ˈθɜːmɪt) *or* **Thermite** (ˈθɜːmaɪt) *n trademark* a mixture of aluminium powder and a metal oxide, which when ignited produces great heat: used for welding and in incendiary bombs
thermo- *or before a vowel* **therm-** *combining form* related to, caused by, or measuring heat: *thermodynamics; thermophile* [from Gk *thermos* hot, *thermē* heat]
thermobarograph (ˌθɜːməʊˈbærəˌgrɑːf) *n* a device that simultaneously records the temperature and pressure of the atmosphere
thermobarometer (ˌθɜːməʊbəˈrɒmɪtə) *n* an apparatus that provides an accurate measurement of pressure by observation of the change in the boiling point of a fluid
thermochemistry (ˌθɜːməʊˈkɛmɪstrɪ) *n* the branch of chemistry concerned with the study and measurement of the heat evolved or absorbed during chemical reactions > ˌ**thermoˈchemical** *adj* > ˌ**thermoˈchemist** *n*
thermochromism (ˌθɜːməʊˈkrəʊmɪzəm) *n* a phenomenon in which certain dyes made from liquid crystals change colour reversibly when their temperature is changed > ˈ**thermoˌchromy** *n* > ˌ**thermoˈchromic** *adj*
thermocline (ˈθɜːməʊˌklaɪn) *n* a temperature gradient in a thermally stratified body of water, such as a lake
thermocouple (ˈθɜːməʊˌkʌpᵊl) *n* **1** a device for measuring temperature consisting of a pair of wires of different metals or semiconductors joined at both ends. One junction is at the temperature to be measured, the second at a fixed temperature. The electromotive force generated depends upon the temperature difference **2** a similar device with only one junction between two dissimilar metals or semiconductors
thermodynamic (ˌθɜːməʊdaɪˈnæmɪk) *or* **thermodynamical** *adj* **1** of or concerned with thermodynamics **2** determined by or obeying the laws of thermodynamics
thermodynamic equilibrium *n* the condition of a system in which the quantities that specify its properties, such as pressure, temperature, etc, all remain unchanged

thermodynamics (ˌθɜːməʊdaɪˈnæmɪks) *n* (*functioning as sing*) the branch of physical science concerned with the interrelationship and interconversion of different forms of energy

thermodynamic temperature *n* temperature defined in terms of the laws of thermodynamics rather than of the properties of a real material: expressed in kelvins

thermoelectric (ˌθɜːməʊɪˈlɛktrɪk) *or* **thermoelectrical** *adj* **1** of, relating to, used in, or operated by the conversion of heat energy to electrical energy **2** of, relating to, used in, or operated by the conversion of electrical energy

thermoelectric effect *n* another name for the **Seebeck effect**

thermoelectricity (ˌθɜːməʊɪlɛkˈtrɪsɪtɪ) *n* **1** electricity generated by a thermocouple **2** the study of the relationship between heat and electrical energy

thermoelectron (ˌθɜːməʊɪˈlɛktrɒn) *n* an electron emitted at high temperature, as in a thermionic valve

thermogenesis (ˌθɜːməʊˈdʒɛnɪsɪs) *n* the production of heat by metabolic processes > ˌ**thermoˈgenic** *adj*

thermogram (ˈθɜːməʊˌɡræm) *n* **1** *med* a picture produced by thermography, using film sensitive to infrared radiation **2** the record produced by a thermograph

thermograph (ˈθɜːməʊˌɡrɑːf, -ˌɡræf) *n* a type of thermometer that produces a continuous record of a fluctuating temperature

thermography (θɜːˈmɒɡrəfɪ) *n* **1** any writing, printing, or recording process involving the use of heat **2** *med* the measurement and recording of heat produced by a part of the body: used in the diagnosis of tumours, esp of the breast (**mammothermography**), which have increased blood supply and therefore generate more heat than normal tissue ▷ See also **thermogram** > **therˈmographer** *n* > **thermographic** (ˌθɜːməʊˈɡræfɪk) *adj*

thermojunction (ˌθɜːməʊˈdʒʌŋkʃən) *n* a point of electrical contact between two dissimilar metals across which a voltage appears, the magnitude of which depends on the temperature of the contact and the nature of the metals

thermolabile (ˌθɜːməʊˈleɪbɪl) *adj* easily decomposed or subject to a loss of characteristic properties by the action of heat

thermoluminescence (ˌθɜːməʊˌluːmɪˈnɛsəns) *n* phosphorescence of certain materials or objects as a result of heating

thermolysis (θɜːˈmɒlɪsɪs) *n* **1** *physiol* loss of heat from the body **2** the dissociation of a substance as a result of heating > **thermolytic** (ˌθɜːməʊˈlɪtɪk) *adj*

thermomagnetic (ˌθɜːməʊmæɡˈnɛtɪk) *adj* of or concerned with the relationship between heat and magnetism, esp the change in temperature of a body when it is magnetized or demagnetized

thermometer (θəˈmɒmɪtə) *n* an instrument used to measure temperature, esp one in which a thin column of liquid, such as mercury, expands and contracts within a graduated sealed tube > **therˈmometry** *n*

thermonuclear (ˌθɜːməʊˈnjuːklɪə) *adj* **1** involving nuclear fusion **2** involving thermonuclear weapons

thermonuclear reaction *n* a nuclear fusion reaction occurring at a very high temperature: responsible for the energy produced in the sun, nuclear weapons, and fusion reactors

thermophile (ˈθɜːməʊˌfaɪl) *or* **thermophil** (ˈθɜːməʊˌfɪl) *n* **1** an organism, esp a bacterium or plant, that thrives under warm conditions ▷ *adj* **2** thriving under warm conditions > ˌ**thermoˈphilic** *adj*

thermopile (ˈθɜːməʊˌpaɪl) *n* an instrument for detecting and measuring heat radiation or for generating a thermoelectric current. It consists of a number of thermocouple junctions

thermoplastic (ˌθɜːməʊˈplæstɪk) *adj* **1** (of a material, esp a synthetic plastic) becoming soft when heated and rehardening on cooling without appreciable change of properties ▷ *n* **2** a synthetic plastic or resin, such as polystyrene, with these properties

Thermopylae (θəˈmɒpəˌliː) *n* (in ancient Greece) a narrow pass between the mountains and the sea linking Locris and Thessaly: a defensible position on a traditional invasion route from N Greece; scene of a famous battle (480 BC) in which a greatly outnumbered Greek army under Leonidas fought to the death to delay the advance of the Persians during their attempted conquest of Greece

Thermos *or* **Thermos flask** (ˈθɜːməs) *n* *trademark* a type of stoppered vacuum flask used to preserve the temperature of its contents

thermosetting (ˌθɜːməʊˈsɛtɪŋ) *adj* (of a material, esp a synthetic plastic) hardening permanently after one application of heat and pressure

thermosiphon (ˌθɜːməʊˈsaɪfən) *n* a system in which a coolant is circulated by convection caused by a difference in density between the hot and cold portions of the liquid

thermosphere (ˈθɜːməˌsfɪə) *n* an atmospheric layer lying between the mesosphere and the exosphere

thermostable (ˌθɜːməʊˈsteɪbᵊl) *adj* capable of withstanding moderate heat without loss of characteristic properties

thermostat (ˈθɜːməˌstæt) *n* **1** a device that maintains a system at a constant temperature **2** a device that sets off a sprinkler, etc, at a certain temperature > ˌ**thermoˈstatic** *adj* > ˌ**thermoˈstatically** *adv*

thermostatics (ˌθɜːməˈstætɪks) *n* (*functioning as sing*) the branch of science concerned with thermal equilibrium

thermotaxis (ˌθɜːməʊˈtæksɪs) *n* the directional movement of an organism in response to the stimulus of heat > ˌ**thermoˈtaxic** *adj*

thermotropism (ˌθɜːməʊˈtrəʊpɪzəm) *n* the directional growth of a plant in response to the stimulus of heat > ˌ**thermoˈtropic** *adj*

Tt

-thermy *n combining form* indicating heat: *diathermy* [from NL *-thermia*, from Gk *thermē*] > **-thermic** *or* **-thermal** *adj combining form*

theroid (ˈθɪərɔɪd) *adj* of, relating to, or resembling a beast [C19 from Gk *thēroeidēs*, from *thēr* wild animal; see -OID]

Theron (ˈθərɒn) *n* **Charlize** (ˈʃɑːliːz) born 1975, South African film actress; her films include *The Cider House Rules* (1999) and *Monster* (2003), which earned her an Oscar

Theroux (θəˈruː) *n* **Paul** (**Edward**) born 1941, US novelist and travel writer. His novels include *Picture Palace* (1978), *The Mosquito Coast* (1981), and *My Other Life* (1996); travel writings include *The Great Railway Bazaar* (1975)

Thersites (θəˈsaɪtiːz) *n* the ugliest and most evil-tongued fighter on the Greek side in the Trojan War, killed by Achilles

thesaurus (θɪˈsɔːrəs) *n, pl* **thesauruses** *or* **thesauri** (-raɪ) **1** a book containing systematized lists of synonyms and related words **2** a dictionary of selected words or topics **3** *rare* a treasury [C18 from L, Gk: TREASURE]

these (ðiːz) *determiner* **a** the form of **this** used before a plural noun: *these men* **b** (*as pronoun*): *I don't much care for these*

Theseus (ˈθiːsɪəs) *n* *Greek myth* a hero of Attica, noted for slaying the Minotaur and conquering the Amazons > **Thesean** (θɪˈsiːən) *adj*

Thesiger (ˈθɛsɪdʒə) *n* **Wilfred** (**Patrick**) 1910–2003, British writer, who explored the Empty Quarter of Arabia (1945–50) and lived with the Iraqi marsh Arabs (1950–58). His books include *Arabian Sands* (1958), *The Marsh Arabs* (1964), and *My Kenya Days* (1994)

thesis (ˈθiːsɪs) *n, pl* **theses** (-siːz) **1** a dissertation resulting from original research, esp when submitted for a degree or diploma **2** a doctrine maintained in argument **3** a subject for a discussion or essay **4** an unproved statement put forward as a premise in an argument [c16 via LL from Gk: a placing, from *tithenai* to place]

Thespian (ˈθɛspɪən) *adj* **1** of or relating to Thespis **2** (*usually not cap*) of or relating to drama and the theatre; dramatic ▷ *n* (*usually not cap*) **3** *often facetious* an actor or actress

Thespis (ˈθɛspɪs) *n* 6th century BC, Greek poet, regarded as the founder of tragic drama

Thess. *Bible abbrev for* Thessalonians

Thessalonian (ˌθɛsəˈləʊnɪən) *adj* **1** of or relating to ancient Thessalonica (modern Salonika) ▷ *n* **2** an inhabitant of ancient Thessalonica

Thessaloníki (*Greek* θɛsalɔˈniki) *n* a port in NE Greece, in central Macedonia at the head of the **Gulf of Salonika** (an inlet of the Aegean): capital of the Roman province of Macedonia; university (1926). Pop: 377 951 (1991). Latin name: **Thessalonica** (ˌθɛsəˈlɒnɪkə). English name: **Salonika** *or* **Salonica**

Thessaly (ˈθɛsəlɪ) *n* a region of E Central Greece, on the Aegean: an extensive fertile plain, edged with mountains. Pop: 754 893 (2001). Area: 14 037 sq km (5418 sq miles). Modern Greek name: **Thessalía** (ˌθɛsaˈljia) > **Thessalian** (θɛˈseɪlɪən) *adj, n*

theta (ˈθiːtə) *n* the eighth letter of the Greek alphabet (Θ, θ) [c17 from Gk]

Thetford Mines (ˈθɛtfəd) *n* a city in SE Canada, in S Quebec: asbestos industry. Pop: 17 273 (1991)

Thetis (ˈθiːtɪs) *n* one of the Nereids and mother of Achilles by Peleus

theurgy (ˈθiːˌɜːdʒɪ) *n, pl* **theurgies** **1** the intervention of a divine or supernatural agency in the affairs of man **2** beneficent magic as taught by Egyptian Neoplatonists [c16 from LL *theūrgia*, from LGk *theourgia* the practice of magic, from *theo-* THEO- + *-urgia*, from *ergon* work] > **theˈurgic** *or* **theˈurgical** *adj* > **ˈtheurgist** *n*

thew (θjuː) *n* **1** muscle, esp if strong or well-developed **2** (*pl*) muscular strength [OE *thēaw*] > **ˈthewless** *adj* > **ˈthewy** *adj*

they (ðeɪ) *pron* (*subjective*) **1** refers to people or things other than the speaker or people addressed: *they fight among themselves* **2** refers to people in general: *in Australia they have Christmas in the summer* **3** refers to an indefinite antecedent such as *one, whoever*, or *anybody*: *if anyone objects, they can go* [c12 *thei* from ON *their*, masc. nominative pl, equivalent to OE *thā*]

> **USAGE** It was formerly considered correct to use *he, him*, or *his* after pronouns such as *everyone, no-one, anyone*, or *someone* as in *everyone did his best*. Nowadays it is probably more common to use *they, them*, or *their*, in order to avoid referring specifically to one gender, and this use has become acceptable in all but the most formal contexts: *everyone did their best*

they'd (ðeɪd) *contraction of* they would *or* they had

they'll (ðeɪl) *contraction of* they will *or* they shall

they're (ðɛə, ˈðeɪə) *contraction of* they are

they've (ðeɪv) *contraction of* they have

THG *abbrev for* tetrahydrogestrinone: a steroid performance-enhancing drug originally designed to evade drug tests taken by athletes

thi- *combining form* a variant of **thio-**

thiamine (ˈθaɪəˌmiːn, -mɪn) *or* **thiamin** (ˈθaɪəmɪn) *n* a white crystalline vitamin that occurs in the outer coat of rice and other grains. It forms part of the vitamin B complex: deficiency leads to nervous disorders and to the disease beriberi. Also called: **vitamin B_1, aneurin** [c20 THIO- + (VIT)AMIN]

thiazine (ˈθaɪəˌziːn, -ˌzaɪn) *n* any of a group of organic compounds containing a ring system composed of four carbon atoms, a sulphur atom, and a nitrogen atom

thiazole (ˈθaɪəˌzəʊl) *n* **1** a colourless liquid that contains a ring system composed of three carbon atoms, a sulphur atom, and a nitrogen atom **2** any of a group of compounds derived from this substance that are used in dyes

thick (θɪk) *adj* **1** of relatively great extent from one surface to the other: *a thick slice of bread* **2a** (*postpositive*) of specific fatness: *ten centimetres thick* **2b** (*in combination*): *a six-inch-thick wall* **3** having a dense consistency: *thick soup* **4** abundantly covered or filled: *a piano thick with dust* **5** impenetrable; dense: *a thick fog* **6** stupid, slow, or insensitive **7** throaty or badly articulated: *a voice thick with emotion* **8** (of accents, etc) pronounced **9** *inf* very friendly (esp in **thick as thieves**) **10** **a bit thick** *Brit* unfair or excessive ▷ *adv* **11** in order to produce something thick: *to slice bread thick* **12** profusely; in quick succession (esp in **thick and fast**) **13** **lay it on thick** *inf* **13a** to exaggerate a story, etc **13b** to flatter excessively ▷ *n* **14** a thick piece or part **15** **the thick** the busiest or most intense part **16** **through thick and thin** in good times and bad [OE *thicce*] > **ˈthickish** *adj* > **ˈthickly** *adv*

thick client *n computing* a computer having its own hard drive, as opposed to one on a network where most functions are carried out on a central server. See **thin client**

thicken (ˈθɪkən) *vb* **1** to make or become thick or thicker **2** (*intr*) to become more involved: *the plot thickened* > **ˈthickener** *n*

thickening (ˈθɪkənɪŋ) *n* **1** something added to a liquid to thicken it **2** a thickened part or piece

thicket (ˈθɪkɪt) *n* a dense growth of small trees, shrubs, and similar plants [OE *thiccet*]

thickhead (ˈθɪkˌhɛd) *n* **1** a stupid or ignorant person; fool **2** any of a family of Australian and SE Asian songbirds > **ˌthickˈheaded** *adj*

thickie *or* **thicky** (ˈθɪkɪ) *n, pl* **thickies** *Brit sl* a variant of **thicko**

thick-knee *n* another name for **stone curlew**

thickness (ˈθɪknɪs) *n* **1** the state or quality of being thick **2** the dimension through an object, as opposed to length or width **3** a layer

thicko (ˈθɪkəʊ) *n, pl* **thickos** *or* **thickoes** *Brit sl* a slow-witted unintelligent person. Also: **thickie, thicky**

thickset (ˌθɪkˈsɛt) *adj* **1** stocky in build; sturdy **2** densely planted or placed ▷ *n* **3** a rare word for **thicket**

thick-skinned *adj* insensitive to criticism or hints; not easily upset or affected

thick-witted *or* **thick-skulled** *adj* stupid, dull, or slow to learn > **ˌthick-ˈwittedly** *adv* > **ˌthick-ˈwittedness** *n*

thief (θiːf) *n, pl* **thieves** (θiːvz) a person who steals something from another [OE *thēof*] > **ˈthievish** *adj*

Thiers (*French* tjɛr) *n* **Louis Adolphe** (lwi adɔlf) 1797–1877, French statesman and historian. After the Franco-Prussian war, he suppressed the Paris Commune and became first president of the Third Republic (1871–73). His policies made possible the paying off of the war indemnity exacted by Germany

thieve (θiːv) *vb* **thieves, thieving, thieved** to steal (someone's possessions) [OE *thēofian*, from *thēof* thief] > **ˈthievery** *n* > **ˈthieving** *adj*

thigh (θaɪ) *n* **1** the part of the leg between the hip and the knee in man **2** the corresponding part in other vertebrates and insects. Related adj: **femoral** [OE *thēh*]

thighbone (ˈθaɪˌbəʊn) *n* a nontechnical name for the **femur**

thimble (ˈθɪmbᵊl) *n* **1** a cap of metal, plastic, etc, used to protect the end of the finger when sewing **2** any small metal cap resembling this **3** *naut* a loop of metal having a groove at its outer edge for a rope or cable [OE *thȳmel* thumbstall, from *thūma* thumb]

thimbleful (ˈθɪmbᵊlˌfʊl) *n* a very small amount, esp of a liquid

thimblerig (ˈθɪmbᵊlˌrɪg) *n* a game in which the operator rapidly moves about three inverted thimbles, often with sleight of hand, one of which conceals a token, the other player betting on which thimble the token is under [C19 from THIMBLE + RIG (in obs. sense meaning a trick, scheme)] > 'thimble,rigger *n*

Thimbu ('θɪmbu:) *or* **Thimphu** ('θɪmfu:) *n* the capital of Bhutan, in the west in the foothills of the E Himalayas: became the official capital in 1962. Pop: 30 340 (1993 est)

thin (θɪn) *adj* **thinner, thinnest 1** of relatively small extent from one side or surface to the other **2** slim or lean **3** sparsely placed; meagre: *thin hair* **4** of low density: *a thin liquid* **5** weak; poor: *a thin disguise* **6 thin on the ground** few in number; scarce ▷ *adv* **7** in order to produce something thin: *to cut bread thin* ▷ *vb* **thins, thinning, thinned 8** to make or become thin or sparse [OE *thynne*] > '**thinly** *adv* > '**thinness** *n*

thin client *n computing* a computer on a network where most functions are carried out on a central server. See **thick client**

thine (ðaɪn) *determiner arch* **a** (*preceding a vowel*) of or associated with you (thou): *thine eyes* **b** (*as pronoun*): *thine is the greatest burden* [OE *thīn*]

thin-film *adj* (of an electronic component, etc) composed of one or more extremely thin layers of metal, semiconductor, etc

thing (θɪŋ) *n* **1** an object, fact, affair, circumstance, or concept considered as being a separate entity **2** any inanimate object **3** an object or entity that cannot or need not be precisely named **4** *inf* a person or animal: *you poor thing* **5** an event or act **6** a thought or statement **7** *law* property **8** a device, means, or instrument **9** (*often pl*) a possession, article of clothing, etc **10** *inf* a preoccupation or obsession (esp in **have a thing about**) **11** an activity or mode of behaviour satisfying to one's personality (esp in **do one's** (**own**) **thing**) **12 make a thing of** exaggerate the importance of **13 the thing** the latest fashion [OE *thing* assembly]

thing-in-itself *n* (in the philosophy of Immanuel Kant) reality regarded apart from human knowledge and perception

thingumabob *or* **thingamabob** ('θɪŋəmə,bɒb) *n inf* a person or thing the name of which is unknown, temporarily forgotten, or deliberately overlooked. Also: **thingumajig, thingamajig,** *or* **thingummy** [C18 from THING, with humorous suffix]

think (θɪŋk) *vb* **thinks, thinking, thought 1** (*tr; may take a clause as object*) to consider, judge, or believe: *he thinks my ideas impractical* **2** (*intr;* often foll by *about*) to exercise the mind as in order to make a decision; ponder **3** (*intr*) to be capable of conscious thought: *man is the only animal that thinks* **4** to remember; recollect **5** (*intr;* foll by *of*) to make the mental choice (of): *think of a number* **6** (*may take a clause as object or an infinitive*) **6a** to expect; suppose **6b** to be considerate enough (to do something): *he did not think to thank them* **7** (*intr*) to focus the attention on being: *think big* **8 think twice** to consider carefully before deciding ▷ *n* **9** *inf* a careful, open-minded assessment **10** (*modifier*) *inf* characterized by or involving thinkers, thinking, or thought ▷ See also **think over, think up** [OE *thencan*] > '**thinkable** *adj* > '**thinker** *n*

thinking ('θɪŋkɪŋ) *n* **1** opinion or judgment **2** the process of thought ▷ *adj* **3** (*prenominal*) using or capable of using intelligent thought: *thinking people* **4 put on one's thinking cap** to ponder a matter or problem

think over *vb* (*tr, adv*) to ponder or consider

think-tank *n inf* a group of specialists commissioned to undertake intensive study and research into specified problems

think up *vb* (*tr, adv*) to invent or devise

thinner ('θɪnə) *n* (*often pl, functioning as sing*) a solvent, such as turpentine, added to paint or varnish to dilute it, reduce its opacity or viscosity, or increase its penetration

thin-skinned *adj* sensitive to criticism or hints; easily upset or affected: *too thin-skinned for politics*

thio- *or before a vowel* **thi-** *combining form* sulphur, esp denoting the replacement of an oxygen atom with a sulphur atom: *thiol; thiosulphate* [from Gk *theion* sulphur]

thiol ('θaɪɒl) *n* any of a class of sulphur-containing organic compounds with the formula RSH, where R is an organic group

thionine ('θaɪəʊ,ni:n, -,naɪn) *or* **thionin** ('θaɪənɪn) *n* **1** a crystalline derivative of thiazine used as a violet dye to stain microscope specimens **2** any of a class of related dyes [C19 by shortening, from *ergothioneine*]

thiopental sodium (,θaɪəʊ'pɛntæl) *n* a barbiturate drug used as an intravenous general anaesthetic. Also called: **Sodium Pentothal**

thiophen ('θaɪəʊ,fɛn) *or* **thiophene** ('θaɪəʊ,fi:n) *n* a colourless liquid heterocyclic compound found in the benzene fraction of coal tar and manufactured from butane and sulphur

thiosulphate (,θaɪəʊ'sʌlfeɪt) *n* any salt of thiosulphuric acid

thiosulphuric acid (,θaɪəʊsʌl'fjʊərɪk) *n* an unstable acid known only in solutions and in the form of its salts. Formula: $H_2S_2O_3$

thiouracil (,θaɪəʊ'jʊərəsɪl) *n* a white crystalline water-insoluble substance with an intensely bitter taste, used in medicine to treat hyperthyroidism [from THIO- + *uracil* (URO- + AC(ETIC) + -IL(E))]

thiourea (,θaɪəʊ'jʊərɪə) *n* a white crystalline substance used in photographic fixing, rubber vulcanization, and the manufacture of synthetic resins

third (θɜ:d) *adj* (*usually prenominal*) **1a** coming after the second in numbering, position, etc; being the ordinal number of *three:* often written 3rd **1b** (*as n*): *the third got a prize* **2** rated, graded, or ranked below the second level **3** denoting the third from lowest forward ratio of a gearbox in a motor vehicle ▷ *n* **4a** one of three equal parts of an object, quantity, etc **4b** (*as modifier*): *a third part* **5** the fraction equal to one divided by three (1/3) **6** the forward ratio above second of a gearbox in a motor vehicle **7a** the interval between one note and another three notes away from it counting inclusively along the diatonic scale **7b** one of two notes constituting such an interval in relation to the other **8** *Brit* an honours degree of the third and usually the lowest class. Full term: **third class honours degree** ▷ *adv* **9** Also: **thirdly** in the third place [OE *thirda,* var. of *thridda;* rel. to OFrisian *thredda,* OSaxon *thriddio*] > '**thirdly** *adv*

Third Age *n* **the** old age, esp when viewed as a period of opportunity for learning something new or for other new developments: *University of the Third Age*

third class *n* **1** the class or grade next in value, quality, etc, to the second ▷ *adj* (**third-class** *when prenominal*) **2** of the class or grade next in value, quality, etc, to the second ▷ *adv* **3** by third-class transport, etc

third degree *n inf* torture or bullying, esp used to extort confessions or information

third-degree burn *n pathol* the most severe type of burn, involving the destruction of both epidermis and dermis

third dimension *n* the dimension of depth by which a solid object may be distinguished from a two-dimensional drawing or picture of it

third eye *n* the pineal gland, believed by some people to be the source of spiritual insight

third eyelid *n* another name for **nictitating membrane**

Third International *n* another name for **Comintern**

third-line forcing *n* the deprecated practice of forcing a buyer to purchase a supply of a product that he does not want as a condition of supplying him with the product he does want

third man *n cricket* **a** a fielding position on the off side near the boundary behind the batsman's wicket **b** a fielder in this position

Third Market *n stock exchange* a new small market

Tt

designed to meet the needs of young growing British companies for raising capital

Third Order *n RC Church* a religious society of laymen affiliated to one of the religious orders and following a mitigated form of religious rule

third party *n* **1** a person who is involved by chance or only incidentally in a legal proceeding, agreement, or other transaction ▷ *adj* **2** *insurance* providing protection against liability caused by accidental injury or death of other persons

third person *n* a grammatical category of pronouns and verbs used when referring to objects or individuals other than the speaker or his addressee or addressees

third-rate *adj* mediocre or inferior

third reading *n* (in a legislative assembly) **1** *Brit* the process of discussing the committee's report on a bill **2** *US* the final consideration of a bill

Third Way *n* **a** a political ideology that seeks to combine egalitarian and individualist policies, and elements of socialism and capitalism **b** (*as modifier*): *Third-Way government*

Third World *n* the less economically and industrially advanced countries of Africa, Asia, and Latin America collectively. Also called: **developing world**

Thirlmere (ˈθɜːlmɪə) *n* a lake in NW England, in Cumbria in the Lake District: provides part of Manchester's water supply. Length: 6 km (4 miles)

thirst (θɜːst) *n* **1** a craving to drink, accompanied by a feeling of dryness in the mouth and throat **2** an eager longing, craving, or yearning ▷ *vb* (*intr*) **3** to feel a thirst [OE *thyrstan*, from *thurst*]

thirsty (ˈθɜːstɪ) *adj* **thirstier, thirstiest 1** feeling a desire to drink **2** dry; arid **3** (foll by *for*) feeling an eager desire **4** causing thirst > ˈ**thirstily** *adv* > ˈ**thirstiness** *n*

thirteen (ˈθɜːˈtiːn) *n* **1** the cardinal number that is the sum of ten and three and is a prime number **2** a numeral, 13, XIII, etc, representing this number **3** something representing or consisting of 13 units ▷ *determiner* **4a** amounting to thirteen **4b** (*as pronoun*): *thirteen of them fell* [OE *threotēne*] > ˈ**thirˈteenth** *adj, n*

thirteenth chord *n* a chord much used in jazz and pop, consisting of a major or minor triad upon which are superimposed the seventh, ninth, eleventh, and thirteenth above the root. Often shortened to **thirteenth**

thirty (ˈθɜːtɪ) *n, pl* **thirties 1** the cardinal number that is the product of ten and three **2** a numeral, 30, XXX, etc, representing this number **3** (*pl*) the numbers 30-39, esp the 30th to the 39th year of a person's life or of a century **4** the amount or quantity that is three times as big as ten **5** something representing or consisting of 30 units ▷ *determiner* **6a** amounting to thirty **6b** (*as pronoun*): *thirty are broken* [OE *thrītig*] > ˈ**thirtieth** *adj, n*

Thirty-nine Articles *pl n* a set of formulas defining the doctrinal position of the Church of England, drawn up in the 16th century

thirty-second note *n* the usual US and Canad name for **demisemiquaver**

thirty-twomo (ˌθɜːtɪˈtuːməʊ) *n, pl* **thirty-twomos** a book size resulting from folding a sheet of paper into 32 leaves or 64 pages

this (ðɪs) *determiner* (*used before a sing n*) **1a** used preceding a noun referring to something or someone that is closer: *look at this picture* **1b** (*as pronoun*): *take this* **2a** used preceding a noun that has just been mentioned or is understood: *this plan of yours won't work* **2b** (*as pronoun*): *I first saw this on Sunday* **3a** used to refer to something about to be said, read, etc: *consider this argument* **3b** (*as pronoun*): *listen to this* **4a** the present or immediate: *this time you'll know better* **4b** (*as pronoun*): *before this, I was mistaken* **5** *inf* an emphatic form of **a** or **the**[1]: *I saw this big brown bear* **6 this and that** various unspecified and trivial actions, matters, objects, etc **7 with** (*or* **at**) **this** after this ▷ *adv* **8** used with adjectives and adverbs to specify a precise degree that is about to be mentioned: *go just this fast and you'll be safe* [OE *thēs, thēos, this* (masc, fem, neuter sing)]

Thisbe (ˈθɪzbɪ) *n* See **Pyramus and Thisbe**

thistle (ˈθɪsᵊl) *n* any of numerous plants of the composite family, having prickly-edged leaves, dense flower heads, and feathery hairs on the seeds: the national emblem of Scotland [OE *thīstel*] > ˈ**thistly** *adj*

thistledown (ˈθɪsᵊlˌdaʊn) *n* the mass of feathery plumed seeds produced by a thistle

thither (ˈðɪðə) *or* **thitherward** *adv obs or formal* to or towards that place; in that direction [OE *thider*, var. of *thæder*, infl. by *hider* hither]

thitherto (ˌðɪðəˈtuː, ˈðɪðəˌtuː) *adv obs or formal* until that time

thixotropic (ˌθɪksəˈtrɒpɪk) *adj* (of fluids and gels) having a reduced viscosity when stress is applied, as when stirred: *thixotropic paints* [c20 from Gk *thixis* the act of touching + -TROPIC] > **thixotropy** (θɪkˈsɒtrəpɪ) *n* > **thixotrope** (ˈθɪksəˌtrəʊp) *n*

tho' *or* **tho** (ðəʊ) *conj, adv US or poetic* a variant spelling of **though**

thole[1] (θəʊl) *or* **tholepin** (ˈθəʊlˌpɪn) *n* a wooden pin or one of a pair, set upright in the gunwales of a rowing boat to serve as a fulcrum in rowing [OE *tholl*]

thole[2] (θəʊl) *vb* **tholes, tholing, tholed 1** (*tr*) *Scot & N English dialect* to put up with; bear **2** an archaic word for **suffer** [OE *tholian*]

tholos (ˈθəʊlɒs) *n, pl* **tholoi** (-lɔɪ) a dry-stone beehive-shaped tomb associated with the Mycenaean culture of Greece from the 16th to the 12th centuries BC [c17 from Gk]

Thomas (ˈtɒməs) *n* **1 Saint** Also called: **doubting Thomas** one of the twelve apostles, who refused to believe in Christ's resurrection until he had seen his wounds (John 20:24–29). Feast day: July 3 or Dec 21 or Oct 6 **2** (*French* tɔmɑ) **Ambroise** (ɑ̃brwaz) 1811–96, French composer of light operas, including *Mignon* (1866) **3 Dylan** (**Marlais**) (ˈdɪlən) 1914–53, Welsh poet and essayist. His works include the prose *Portrait of the Artist as a Young Dog* (1940), the verse collection *Deaths and Entrances* (1946), and his play for voices *Under Milk Wood* (1954) **4** (**Philip**) **Edward,** pen name *Edward Eastaway*. 1878–1917, British poet and critic: killed in World War I **5 R**(**onald**) **S**(**tuart**) 1913–2000, Welsh poet and clergyman. His collections include *Song at the Year's Turning* (1955), *Not that He Brought Flowers* (1968), and *Laboratories of the Spirit* (1975)

Thomas à Kempis *n* See (Thomas à) **Kempis**

Thomas Becket *n* **Saint** See (Saint Thomas) **Becket**

Thomas of Woodstock *n* 1355–97, youngest son of Edward III, who led opposition to his nephew Richard II (1386–89); arrested in 1397, he died in prison

Thomism (ˈtəʊmɪzəm) *n* the system of philosophy and theology developed by Saint Thomas Aquinas in the 13th century

Thompson (ˈtɒmpsən, ˈtɒmsən) *n* **1 Benjamin,** Count Rumford. 1753–1814, Anglo-American physicist, noted for his work on the nature of heat **2 Daley** born 1958, British athlete: Olympic decathlon champion (1980, 1984) **3 Flora** (**Jane**) 1876–1947, British writer, author of the autobiographical *Lark Rise to Candleford* (1945) **4 Francis** 1859–1907, British poet, best known for the mystical poem *The Hound of Heaven* (1893)

Thompson sub-machine-gun *n trademark* a .45 calibre sub-machine-gun [c20 after John T. *Thompson* (1860–1940), US Army officer, its co-inventor]

Thomson (ˈtɒmsən) *n* **1** Sir **George Paget,** son of Joseph John Thomson. 1892–1975, British physicist, who discovered (1927) the diffraction of electrons by crystals: shared the Nobel prize for physics 1937 **2 James** 1700–48, Scottish poet. He anticipated the romantics' feeling for nature in *The Seasons* (1726–30) **3 James,** pen name *B.V.* 1834–82, British poet, born in Scotland, noted esp for *The*

City of Dreadful Night (1874), reflecting man's isolation and despair **4** Sir **Joseph John** 1856–1940, British physicist. He discovered the electron (1897) and his work on the nature of positive rays led to the discovery of isotopes: Nobel prize for physics 1906 **5 Roy,** 1st Baron Thomson of Fleet. 1894–1976, British newspaper proprietor, born in Canada **6 Virgil** 1896–1989, US composer, music critic, and conductor, whose works include two operas, *Four Saints in Three Acts* (1928) and *The Mother of Us All* (1947), piano sonatas, a cello concerto, songs, and film music **7** Sir **William** See (1st Baron) **Kelvin**

-thon *suffix forming nouns* indicating a large-scale event or operation of a specified kind: *telethon* [C20 on the pattern of MARATHON]

Thonburi (ˌtɒnbʊˈriː) *n* a city in central Thailand, part of Bankok Metropolis on the Chao Phraya River; the national capital (1767–82)

thong (θɒŋ) *n* **1** a thin strip of leather or other material **2** a whip or whiplash, esp one made of leather **3** *US, Canad, & Austral* the usual name for **flip-flop** (sense 5) **4a** a skimpy article of beachwear, worn by men or women, consisting of thin strips of leather or cloth attached to a piece of material that covers the genitals while leaving the buttocks bare **4b** a similar item of underwear [OE *thwang*]

Thor (θɔː) *n Norse myth* the god of thunder, depicted as wielding a hammer, emblematic of the thunderbolt [OE *Thōr*, from ON *thōrr* THUNDER]

thoracic (θɔːˈræsɪk) *adj* of, near, or relating to the thorax

thoracic duct *n* the major duct of the lymphatic system, beginning below the diaphragm and ascending in front of the spinal column to the base of the neck

thoraco- *or before a vowel* **thorac-** *combining form* thorax: *thoracotomy*

thoracoplasty (ˈθɔːrəkəʊˌplæstɪ) *n, pl* **thoracoplasties** **1** plastic surgery of the thorax **2** surgical removal of several ribs or a part of them to permit the collapse of a diseased lung

thorax (ˈθɔːræks) *n, pl* **thoraxes** *or* **thoraces** (ˈθɔːrəˌsiːz, θɔːˈreɪsiːz) **1** the part of the human body enclosed by the ribs **2** the corresponding part in other vertebrates **3** the part of an insect's body between the head and abdomen [C16 via L from Gk *thōrax* breastplate, chest]

Thoreau (ˈθɔːrəʊ, θɔːˈrəʊ) *n* **Henry David** 1817–62, US writer, noted esp for *Walden, or Life in the Woods* (1854), an account of his experiment in living in solitude. A powerful social critic, his essay *Civil Disobedience* (1849) influenced such dissenters as Gandhi

thorium (ˈθɔːrɪəm) *n* a silvery-white radioactive metallic element. It is used in electronic equipment and as a nuclear power source. Symbol: Th; atomic no.: 90; atomic wt.: 232.04 [C19 NL, THOR + -IUM] > ˈ**thoric** *adj*

thorium dioxide *n* a white powder used in incandescent mantles. Also called: **thoria**

thorium series *n* a radioactive series that starts with thorium-232 and ends with lead-208

thorn (θɔːn) *n* **1** a sharp pointed woody extension of a stem or leaf. ▷ Cf **prickle** (sense 1) **2** any of various trees or shrubs having thorns, esp the hawthorn **3** a Germanic character of runic origin (Þ) used in Icelandic to represent the sound of *th*, as in *thin, bath* **4** this same character as used in Old and Middle English to represent this sound **5** a source of irritation (esp in **a thorn in one's side** *or* **flesh**) [OE] > ˈ**thornless** *adj*

Thorn (tɔrn) *n* the German name for **Toruń**

thorn apple *n* **1** a poisonous plant of the N hemisphere, having white funnel-shaped flowers and spiny fruits. US name: **jimson weed** **2** the fruit of certain types of hawthorn

thornbill (ˈθɔːnˌbɪl) *n* **1** any of various South American hummingbirds having a thornlike bill **2** Also called: **thornbill warbler** any of various Australasian wrens **3** any of various other birds with thornlike bills

Thorndike (ˈθɔːnˌdaɪk) *n* **1 Edward Lee** 1874–1949, US psychologist, who worked on animals and proposed that all learnt behaviour is regulated by rewards and punishments (**Thorndike's law** *or* **law of effect**) **2** Dame (**Agnes**) **Sybil** 1882–1976, British actress

thorny (ˈθɔːnɪ) *adj* **thornier, thorniest** **1** bearing or covered with thorns **2** difficult or unpleasant **3** sharp > ˈ**thornily** *adv* > ˈ**thorniness** *n*

thoron (ˈθɔːrɒn) *n* a radioisotope of radon that is a decay product of thorium. Symbol: Tn or ^{220}Rn; atomic no.: 86; half-life: 54.5s [C20 from THORIUM + -ON]

thorough (ˈθʌrə) *adj* **1** carried out completely and carefully **2** (*prenominal*) utter: *a thorough bore* **3** painstakingly careful [OE *thurh*] > ˈ**thoroughly** *adv* > ˈ**thoroughness** *n*

thorough bass (beɪs) *n* a bass part underlying a piece of concerted music. Also called: **basso continuo, continuo** See also **figured bass**

thoroughbred (ˈθʌrəˌbrɛd) *adj* **1** purebred ▷ *n* **2** a pedigree animal; purebred **3** a person regarded as being of good breeding

Thoroughbred (ˈθʌrəˌbrɛd) *n* a British breed of horse the ancestry of which can be traced to English mares and Arab sires

thoroughfare (ˈθʌrəˌfɛə) *n* **1** a road from one place to another, esp a main road **2** way through, access, or passage: *no thoroughfare*

thoroughgoing (ˈθʌrəˌgəʊɪŋ) *adj* **1** extremely thorough **2** (*usually prenominal*) absolute; complete: *thoroughgoing incompetence*

thoroughpaced (ˈθʌrəˌpeɪst) *adj* **1** (of a horse) showing performing ability in all paces **2** thoroughgoing

thorp *or* **thorpe** (θɔːp) *n obs except in place names* a small village [OE]

Thorpe (θɔːp) *n* **1 Ian** born 1982, Australian swimmer; won three gold medals at the 2000 Olympic Games and six gold medals at the 2002 Commonwealth Games **2 James Francis** 1888–1953, American football player and athlete: Olympic pentathlon and decathlon champion (1912)

Thorshavn (*Danish* ˈtɔːrshaun) *n* the capital of the Faeroe Islands, a port on the northernmost island. Pop: 16 474 (2000 est)

Thorvaldsen (*Danish* ˈtɔrvalsən) *n* **Bertel** (ˈbertəl) 1770–1884, Danish neoclassical sculptor

those (ðəʊz) *determiner* the form of **that** used before a plural noun [OE *thās*, pl. of THIS]

Thoth (θəʊθ, təʊt) *n* (in Egyptian mythology) a moon deity, scribe of the gods and protector of learning and the arts

thou[1] (ðaʊ) *pron* (*subjective*) **1** *arch or dialect* refers to the person addressed: used mainly in familiar address **2** (*usually cap*) refers to God when addressed in prayer, etc [OE *thū*]

thou[2] (θaʊ) *n, pl* **thous** *or* **thou** **1** one thousandth of an inch **2** *inf* short for **thousand**

though (ðəʊ) *conj* (*subordinating*) **1** (sometimes preceded by *even*) despite the fact that: *though he tries hard, he always fails* ▷ *adv* **2** nevertheless; however: *he can't dance; he sings well, though* [OE *theah*]

thought (θɔːt) *vb* **1** the past tense and past participle of **think** ▷ *n* **2** the act or process of thinking **3** a concept, opinion, or idea **4** ideas typical of a particular time or place: *German thought in the 19th century* **5** application of mental attention; consideration **6** purpose or intention: *I have no thought of giving up* **7** expectation: *no thought of reward* **8** a small amount; trifle: *you could be a thought more enthusiastic* **9** kindness or regard [OE *thōht*]

thoughtful (ˈθɔːtfʊl) *adj* **1** considerate in the treatment of other people **2** showing careful thought **3** pensive; reflective > ˈ**thoughtfully** *adv* > ˈ**thoughtfulness** *n*

thoughtless (ˈθɔːtlɪs) *adj* **1** inconsiderate **2** having or showing lack of thought: *a thoughtless remark*

Tt

> 'thoughtlessly *adv* > 'thoughtlessness *n*

thought-out *adj* conceived and developed by careful thought: *a well thought-out scheme*

thought transference *n psychol* another name for **telepathy**

thousand ('θaʊzənd) *n* **1** the cardinal number that is the product of 10 and 100 **2** a numeral, 1000, 10^3, M, etc, representing this number **3** (*often pl*) a very large but unspecified number, amount, or quantity **4** something representing or consisting of 1000 units ▷ *determiner* **5a** amounting to a thousand **5b** (*as pronoun*): *a thousand is hardly enough.* Related adj: **millenary** [OE *thūsend*] > 'thousandth *adj, n*

Thousand Guineas *n* (*functioning as sing*), usually written **1,000 Guineas** an annual horse race, restricted to fillies, run at Newmarket in England since 1814

Thousand Island dressing *n* a salad dressing made from mayonnaise with ketchup, chopped gherkins, etc

Thousand Islands *pl n* a group of about 1500 islands between the US and Canada, in the upper St Lawrence River: administratively divided between the US and Canada > **Thousand Island** *adj*

Thrace (θreɪs) *n* **1** an ancient country in the E Balkan Peninsula: successively under the Persians, Macedonians, and Romans **2** a region of SE Europe, corresponding to the S part of the ancient country: divided by the Maritsa River into **Western Thrace** (Greece) and **Eastern Thrace** (Turkey)

Thracian ('θreɪʃɪən) *n* **1** a member of an ancient Indo-European people who lived in Thrace **2** the ancient language spoken by this people ▷ *adj* **3** of or relating to Thrace, its inhabitants, or the extinct Thracian language

thrall (θrɔːl) *n* **1** Also: **thraldom** *or US* **thralldom** ('θrɔːldəm) the state or condition of being in the power of another person **2** a person who is in such a state **3** a person totally subject to some need, desire, appetite, etc ▷ *vb* **4** (*tr*) to enslave or dominate [OE *thrǣl* slave]

thrash (θræʃ) *vb* **1** (*tr*) to beat soundly, as with a whip or stick **2** (*tr*) to defeat totally; overwhelm **3** (*intr*) to beat or plunge about in a wild manner **4** to sail (a boat) against the wind or tide or (of a boat) to sail in this way **5** another word for **thresh** ▷ *n* **6** the act of thrashing; beating **7** *inf* a party ▷ See also **thrash out** [OE *threscan*]

thrasher[1] ('θræʃə) *n* another name for **thresher** (the shark)

thrasher[2] ('θræʃə) *n* any of various brown thrushlike American songbirds

thrashing ('θræʃɪŋ) *n* **1** a physical assault; flogging **2** a convincing defeat

thrash metal *n* a type of very fast very loud rock music that combines elements of heavy metal and punk rock. Often shortened to **thrash**

thrash out *vb* (*tr, adv*) to discuss fully or vehemently, esp in order to come to an agreement

thrasonical (θrə'sɒnɪkᵊl) *adj rare* bragging; boastful [c16 from L *Thrasō* name of boastful soldier in *Eunuchus*, a play by Terence, from Gk *Thrasōn*, from *thrasus* forceful] > thra'sonically *adv*

thrawn (θrɔːn) *adj Scot & N English dialect* **1** crooked or twisted **2** stubborn; perverse [N English dialect, var. of *thrown*, from OE *thrāwan* to twist about, throw]

thread (θrɛd) *n* **1** a fine strand, filament, or fibre of some material **2** a fine cord of twisted filaments, esp of cotton, used in sewing, etc **3** any of the filaments of which a spider's web is made **4** any fine line, stream, mark, or piece **5** the helical ridge on a screw, bolt, nut, etc **6** a very thin seam of coal or vein of ore **7** something acting as the continuous link or theme of a whole: *the thread of the story* **8** the course of an individual's life believed in Greek mythology to be spun, measured, and cut by the Fates ▷ *vb* **9** (*tr*) to pass (thread, film, tape, etc) through (something) **10** (*tr*) to string on a thread: *she threaded the beads* **11** to make (one's way) through or over (something) **12** (*tr*) to produce a screw thread **13** (*tr*) to pervade: *hysteria threaded his account* **14** (*intr*) (of boiling syrup) to form a fine thread when poured from a spoon ▷ See also **threads** [OE *thrǣd*] > 'threader *n* > 'thread,like *adj*

threadbare ('θrɛd,bɛə) *adj* **1** (of cloth, clothing, etc) having the nap worn off so that the threads are exposed; worn out **2** meagre or poor **3** hackneyed: *a threadbare argument* **4** wearing threadbare clothes; shabby

thread mark *n* a mark put into paper money to prevent counterfeiting, consisting of a pattern of silk fibres

Threadneedle Street (,θrɛd'niːdᵊl, 'θrɛd,niːdᵊl) *n* a street in the City of London famous for its banks, including the Bank of England, known as **The Old Lady of Threadneedle Street**

threads (θrɛdz) *pl n sl* clothes

threadworm ('θrɛd,wɜːm) *n* any of various nematodes, esp the pinworm

thready ('θrɛdɪ) *adj* **threadier, threadiest** **1** of or resembling a thread **2** (of the pulse) barely perceptible; weak **3** sounding thin, weak, or reedy > 'threadiness *n*

threat (θrɛt) *n* **1** a declaration of the intention to inflict harm, pain, or misery **2** an indication of imminent harm, danger, or pain **3** a person or thing that is regarded as dangerous or likely to inflict pain or misery [OE]

threaten ('θrɛtᵊn) *vb* **1** (*tr*) to be a threat to **2** to be a menacing indication of (something); portend **3** (when *tr, may take a clause as object*) to express a threat to (a person or people) > 'threatening *adj* > 'threateningly *adv*

three (θriː) *n* **1** the cardinal number that is the sum of two and one and is a prime number **2** a numeral, 3, III, (iii), representing this number **3** something representing or consisting of three units **4** Also called: **three o'clock** three hours after noon or midnight ▷ *determiner* **5a** amounting to three **5b** (*as pronoun*): *three were killed.* Related adjs: **ternary, tertiary, treble, triple** [OE *thrēo*]

three-card trick *n* a game in which players bet on which of three playing cards is the queen

three-colour *adj* of or comprising a colour print or a photomechanical process in which a picture is reproduced by superimposing three prints from half-tone plates in inks corresponding to the three primary colours

three-D *or* **3-D** *n* a three-dimensional effect

three-decker *n* **1a** anything having three levels or layers **1b** (*as modifier*): *a three-decker sandwich* **2** a warship with guns on three decks

three-dimensional *adj* **1** of, having, or relating to three dimensions **2** simulating the effect of depth **3** having volume **4** lifelike

threefold ('θriː,fəʊld) *adj* **1** equal to or having three times as many or as much; triple **2** composed of three parts ▷ *adv* **3** by or up to three times as many or as much

three-legged race *n* a race in which pairs of competitors run with their adjacent legs tied together

threepenny bit *or* **thrupenny bit** ('θrʌpnɪ, -ənɪ, 'θrɛp-) *n* a twelve-sided British coin valued at three old pence, obsolete since 1971

three-phase *adj* (of an electrical circuit, etc) having or using three alternating voltages of the same frequency, displaced in phase by 120°

three-ply *adj* **1** having three layers or thicknesses **2** (of wool, etc) three-stranded

three-point landing *n* an aircraft landing in which the main wheels and the nose or tail wheel touch the ground simultaneously

three-point turn *n* a complete turn of a motor vehicle using forward and reverse gears alternately, and completed after only three movements

three-quarter *adj* **1** being three quarters of something

2 being of three quarters the normal length ▷ *n* 3 *rugby* any of the four players between the fullback and the halfbacks

three-ring circus *n US* 1 a circus with three rings for simultaneous performances 2 a situation of confusion, characterized by a bewildering variety of events or activities

Three Rivers *n* the English name for **Trois Rivières**

three Rs *pl n* **the** the three skills regarded as the fundamentals of education; reading, writing, and arithmetic [from the humorous spelling *reading, 'riting,* and *'rithmetic*]

threescore ('θriːˈskɔː) *determiner* an archaic word for **sixty**

threesome ('θriːsəm) *n* 1 a group of three 2 *golf* a match in which a single player playing his or her own ball competes against two others playing on the same ball 3 any game, etc, for three people 4 (*modifier*) performed by three

thremmatology (ˌθrɛməˈtɒlədʒɪ) *n* the science of breeding domesticated animals and plants [c19 from Gk *thremma* nursling + -LOGY]

threnody ('θrɛnədɪ, 'θriː-) *or* **threnode** ('θriːnəʊd, 'θrɛn-) *n, pl* **threnodies** *or* **threnodes** an ode, song, or speech of lamentation, esp for the dead [c17 from Gk *thrēnōidia,* from *thrēnos* dirge + *ōidē* song] > **threnodic** (θrɪˈnɒdɪk) *adj* > **threnodist** ('θrɛnədɪst, 'θriː-) *n*

thresh (θrɛʃ) *vb* 1 to beat stalks of ripe corn, etc, either with a hand implement or a machine to separate the grain from the husks and straw 2 (*tr*) to beat or strike 3 (*intr;* often foll by *about*) to toss and turn; thrash [OE *threscan*]

thresher ('θrɛʃə) *n* 1 a person who threshes 2 short for **threshing machine** 3 any of a genus of large sharks occurring in tropical and temperate seas. They have a very long whiplike tail

threshing machine *n* a machine for threshing crops

threshold ('θrɛʃəʊld, 'θrɛʃˌhəʊld) *n* 1 a sill, esp one made of stone or hardwood, placed at a doorway 2 any doorway or entrance 3 the starting point of an experience, event, or venture 4 *psychol* the strength at which a stimulus is just perceived: *the threshold of consciousness* 5a a point at which something would stop, take effect, etc 5b (*as modifier*): *threshold price; threshold effect* 6 the minimum intensity or value of a signal, etc, that will produce a response or specified effect 7 (*modifier*) of a pay agreement, clause, etc, that raises wages to compensate for increases in the cost of living. Related adj: **liminal** [OE *therscold*]

threshold agreement *n* an agreement between an employer and employees or their union to increase wages by a specified sum if inflation exceeds a specified level in a specified time

threw (θruː) *vb* the past tense of **throw**

thrice (θraɪs) *adv* 1 three times 2 threefold 3 *arch* greatly [OE *thrīwa, thrīga*]

thrift (θrɪft) *n* 1 wisdom and caution in the management of money 2 Also called: **sea pink** any of a genus of perennial low-growing plants of Europe, W Asia, and North America, having narrow leaves and round heads of pink or white flowers [c13 from ON: success; see THRIVE] > '**thriftless** *adj* > '**thriftlessly** *adv*

thrifty ('θrɪftɪ) *adj* **thriftier, thriftiest** 1 showing thrift; economical or frugal 2 *rare* thriving or prospering > '**thriftily** *adv* > '**thriftiness** *n*

thrill (θrɪl) *n* 1 a sudden sensation of excitement and pleasure 2 a situation producing such a sensation 3 a trembling sensation caused by fear or emotional shock 4 *pathol* an abnormal slight tremor ▷ *vb* 5 to feel or cause to feel a thrill 6 to tremble or cause to tremble; vibrate or quiver [OE *thȳrlian* to pierce, from *thyrel* hole] > '**thrilling** *adj*

thriller ('θrɪlə) *n* 1 a book, film, play, etc, depicting crime, mystery, or espionage in an atmosphere of excitement and suspense 2 a person or thing that thrills

thrips (θrɪps) *n, pl* **thrips** any of various small slender-bodied insects typically having piercing mouthparts [c18 via NL from Gk: woodworm]

thrive (θraɪv) *vb* **thrives, thriving, thrived** *or* **throve, thrived** *or* **thriven** ('θrɪvᵊn) (*intr*) 1 to grow strongly and vigorously 2 to do well; prosper [c13 from ON *thrīfask* to grasp for oneself, from ?]

thro' *or* **thro** (θruː) *prep, adv inf or poetic* variant spellings of **through**

throat (θrəʊt) *n* 1a that part of the alimentary and respiratory tracts extending from the back of the mouth to just below the larynx 1b the front part of the neck 2 something resembling a throat, esp in shape or function: *the throat of a chimney* 3 **cut one's** (**own**) **throat** to bring about one's own ruin 4 **ram** *or* **force** (**something**) **down someone's throat** to insist that someone listen to or accept (something). Related adjs: **guttural, laryngeal** [OE *throtu*]

throaty ('θrəʊtɪ) *adj* **throatier, throatiest** 1 indicating a sore throat; hoarse: *a throaty cough* 2 of or produced in the throat 3 deep, husky, or guttural > '**throatily** *adv*

throb (θrɒb) *vb* **throbs, throbbing, throbbed** (*intr*) 1 to pulsate or beat repeatedly, esp with increased force 2 (of engines, drums, etc) to have a strong rhythmic vibration or beat ▷ *n* 3 a throbbing, esp a rapid pulsation as of the heart: *a throb of pleasure* [c14 ? imit.]

throes (θrəʊz) *pl n* 1 a condition of violent pangs, pain, or convulsions: *death throes* 2 **in the throes of** struggling with great effort with [OE *thrāwu* threat]

thrombin ('θrɒmbɪn) *n biochem* an enzyme that acts on fibrinogen in blood causing it to clot [c19 from THROMB(US) + -IN]

thrombocyte ('θrɒmbəˌsaɪt) *n* another name for a **platelet** > **thrombocytic** (ˌθrɒmbəˈsɪtɪk) *adj*

thromboembolism (ˌθrɒmbəʊˈɛmbəˌlɪzəm) *n* the obstruction of a blood vessel by a thrombus that has become detached from its original site

thrombose ('θrɒmbəʊz) *vb* **thromboses, thrombosing, thrombosed** to become or affect with a thrombus [c19 back formation from THROMBOSIS]

thrombosis (θrɒmˈbəʊsɪs) *n, pl* **thromboses** (-siːz) 1 the formation or presence of a thrombus 2 *inf* short for **coronary thrombosis** [c18 from NL, from Gk: curdling, from *thrombousthai* to clot, from *thrombos* THROMBUS] > **thrombotic** (θrɒmˈbɒtɪk) *adj*

thrombus ('θrɒmbəs) *n, pl* **thrombi** (-baɪ) a clot of coagulated blood that forms within a blood vessel or inside the heart, often impeding the flow of blood [c17 from NL, from Gk *thrombos* lump, from ?]

throne (θrəʊn) *n* 1 the ceremonial seat occupied by a monarch, bishop, etc, on occasions of state 2 the power or rank ascribed to a royal person 3 a person holding royal rank 4 (*pl; often cap*) the third of the nine orders into which the angels are divided in medieval angelology ▷ *vb* **thrones, throning, throned** 5 to place or be placed on a throne [c13 from OF *trone,* from L *thronus,* from Gk *thronos*]

throng (θrɒŋ) *n* 1 a great number of people or things crowded together ▷ *vb* 2 to gather in or fill (a place) in large numbers; crowd 3 (*tr*) to hem in (a person); jostle [OE *gethrang*]

thronner ('θrɒnə) *n N English dialect* a person who is good at doing odd jobs

throstle ('θrɒsᵊl) *n* 1 a poetic name for the **song thrush** 2 a spinning machine for wool or cotton in which the fibres are twisted and wound continuously [OE]

throttle ('θrɒtᵊl) *n* 1 Also called: **throttle valve** any device that controls the quantity of fuel or fuel and air mixture entering an engine 2 an informal or dialect word for **throat** ▷ *vb* **throttles, throttling, throttled** (*tr*) 3 to kill or injure by squeezing the throat 4 to suppress

Tt

5 to control or restrict (a flow of fluid) by means of a throttle valve [C14 *throtelen*, from *throte* THROAT]
> '**throttler** *n*

through (θruː) *prep* 1 going in at one side and coming out at the other side of: *a path through the wood* 2 occupying or visiting several points scattered around in (an area) 3 as a result of; by means of 4 *chiefly US* up to and including: *Monday through Friday* 5 during: *through the night* 6 at the end of; having completed 7 **through with** having finished with (esp when dissatisfied with) ▷ *adj* 8 (*postpositive*) having successfully completed some specified activity 9 (on a telephone line) connected 10 (*postpositive*) no longer able to function successfully in some specified capacity: *as a journalist, you're through* 11 (*prenominal*) (of a route, journey, etc) continuous or unbroken: *a through train* ▷ *adv* 12 through some specified thing, place, or period of time 13 **through and through** thoroughly; completely [OE *thurh*]

through bridge *n civil engineering* a bridge in which the track is carried by the lower horizontal members

throughout (θruːˈaʊt) *prep* 1 right through; through the whole of (a place or a period of time): *throughout the day* ▷ *adv* 2 through the whole of some specified period or area

throughput (ˈθruːˌpʊt) *n* the quantity of raw material or information processed or communicated in a given period, esp by a computer

throughway (ˈθruːˌweɪ) *n US* a thoroughfare, esp a motorway

throve (θrəʊv) *vb* a past tense of **thrive**

throw (θrəʊ) *vb* **throws, throwing, threw, thrown** (*mainly tr*) 1 (*also intr*) to project (something) through the air, esp with a rapid motion of the arm 2 (foll by *in, on, onto*, etc) to put or move suddenly, carelessly, or violently 3 to bring to or cause to be in a specified state or condition, esp suddenly: *the news threw them into a panic* 4 to direct or cast (a shadow, light, etc) 5 to project (the voice) so as to make it appear to come from other than its source 6 to give or hold (a party) 7 to cause to fall or be upset: *the horse threw his rider* 8a to tip (dice) out onto a flat surface 8b to obtain (a specified number) in this way 9 to shape (clay) on a potter's wheel 10 to move (a switch or lever) to engage or disengage a mechanism 11 to be subjected to (a fit) 12 to turn (wood, etc) on a lathe 13 *inf* to baffle or astonish; confuse: *the question threw me* 14 *boxing* to deliver (a punch) 15 *wrestling* to hurl (an opponent) to the ground 16 *inf* to lose (a contest, etc) deliberately 17a to play (a card) 17b to discard (a card) 18 (of an animal) to give birth to (young) 19 to twist or spin (filaments) into thread 20 *Austral inf* (often foll by *at*) to mock or poke fun 21 **throw oneself at** to strive actively to attract the attention or affection of 22 **throw oneself into** to involve oneself enthusiastically in 23 **throw oneself on** to rely entirely upon ▷ *n* 24 the act or an instance of throwing 25 the distance over which anything may be thrown: *a stone's throw* 26 *inf* a chance or try 27 an act or result of throwing dice 28a the eccentricity of a cam 28b the radial distance between the central axis of a crankshaft and the axis of a crankpin forming part of the shaft 29 a decorative blanket or cover 30 *geol* the vertical displacement of rock strata at a fault 31 *physics* the deflection of a measuring instrument as a result of a fluctuation ▷ See also **throwaway, throwback, throw in,** etc [OE *thrāwan* to turn, torment] > '**thrower** *n*

throwaway (ˈθrəʊəˌweɪ) *adj* (*prenominal*) 1 said or done incidentally, esp for rhetorical effect; casual: *a throwaway remark* 2 designed to be discarded after use rather than reused, refilled, etc: *a throwaway carton* ▷ *n* 3 *chiefly US & Canad* a handbill ▷ *vb* **throw away** (*tr, adv*) 4 to get rid of; discard 5 to fail to make good use of; waste

throwback (ˈθrəʊˌbæk) *n* 1a a person, animal, or plant that has the characteristics of an earlier or more primitive type 1b a reversion to such an organism ▷ *vb* **throw back** (*adv*) 2 (*intr*) to revert to an earlier or more primitive type 3 (*tr*; foll by *on*) to force to depend (on): *the crisis threw her back on her faith in God*

throw in *vb* (*tr, adv*) 1 to add at no additional cost 2 to contribute or interpose (a remark, argument, etc) 3 **throw in the sponge** (*or* **towel**) to give in; accept defeat ▷ *n* **throw-in** 4 *soccer, etc* the method of putting the ball into play after it has gone into touch by throwing it to a team-mate

thrown (θrəʊn) *vb* the past participle of **throw**

throw off *vb* (*mainly tr, adv*) 1 to free oneself of; discard 2 to produce or utter in a casual manner 3 to escape from or elude 4 to confuse or disconcert 5 (*intr*; often foll by **at**) *Austral & NZ inf* to deride or ridicule

throw out *vb* (*tr, adv*) 1 to discard or reject 2 to expel or dismiss, esp forcibly 3 to construct (something projecting or prominent) 4 to put forward or offer 5 to utter in a casual or indirect manner 6 to confuse or disconcert 7 to give off or emit 8 *cricket* (of a fielder) to put (the batsman) out by throwing the ball to hit the wicket 9 *baseball* to make a throw to a team-mate who in turn puts out (a base runner)

throw over *vb* (*tr, adv*) to forsake or abandon; jilt

throw together *vb* (*tr, adv*) 1 to assemble hurriedly 2 to cause to become casually acquainted

throw up *vb* (*adv, mainly tr*) 1 to give up; abandon 2 to construct hastily 3 to reveal; produce 4 (*also intr*) *inf* to vomit

thru (θruː) *prep, adv, adj chiefly US* a variant spelling of **through**

thrum[1] (θrʌm) *vb* **thrums, thrumming, thrummed** 1 to strum rhythmically but without expression on (a musical instrument) 2 (*intr*) to drum incessantly: *rain thrummed on the roof* ▷ *n* 3 a repetitive strumming [C16 imit.]

thrum[2] (θrʌm) *n* 1a any of the unwoven ends of warp thread remaining on the loom when the web has been removed 1b such ends of thread collectively 2 a fringe or tassel of short unwoven threads ▷ *vb* **thrums, thrumming, thrummed** 3 (*tr*) to trim with thrums [C14 from OE]

thrush[1] (θrʌʃ) *n* any of a subfamily of songbirds, esp those having a brown plumage with a spotted breast, such as the mistle thrush and song thrush [OE *thrȳsce*]

thrush[2] (θrʌʃ) *n* 1 a fungal disease, esp of infants, characterized by the formation of whitish spots 2 a genital infection caused by the same fungus 3 a softening of the frog of a horse's hoof characterized by degeneration and a thick foul discharge [C17 from ?]

thrust (θrʌst) *vb* **thrusts, thrusting, thrust** 1 (*tr*) to push (someone or something) with force 2 (*tr*) to force upon (someone) or into (some condition or situation): *they thrust responsibilities upon her* 3 (*tr*; foll by *through*) to pierce; stab 4 (*intr*; usually foll by *through* or *into*) to force a passage 5 to make a stab or lunge at ▷ *n* 6 a forceful drive, push, stab, or lunge 7 a force, esp one that produces motion 8a a propulsive force produced by the fluid pressure or the change of momentum of the fluid in a jet engine, rocket engine, etc 8b a similar force produced by a propeller 9 a continuous pressure exerted by one part of an object, structure, etc, against another 10 force, impetus, or drive 11 the essential or most forceful part: *the thrust of the argument* [C12 from ON *thrysta*]

thruster (ˈθrʌstə) *n* 1 a person or thing that thrusts 2 a small rocket engine, esp one used to correct the altitude or course of a spacecraft

thrust fault *n* a fault in which the rocks on the upper side of an inclined fault plane have been displaced upwards; a reverse fault

thrutch (θrʌtʃ) *n N English dialect* a narrow, fast-moving stream

Thucydides (θuːˈsɪdɪˌdiːz) *n* ?460–?395 BC, Greek historian and politician, distinguished for his *History of the Peloponnesian War*

thud (θʌd) *n* **1** a dull heavy sound **2** a blow or fall that causes such a sound ▷ *vb* **thuds, thudding, thudded 3** to make or cause to make such a sound [OE *thyddan* to strike]

thug (θʌg) *n* **1** a tough and violent man, esp a criminal **2** (*sometimes cap*) (formerly) a member of an organization of robbers and assassins in India [c19 from Hindi *thag* thief, from Sansk. *sthaga* scoundrel, from *sthagati* to conceal] > ˈ**thuggery** *n* > ˈ**thuggish** *adj*

thuja *or* **thuya** (ˈθuːjə) *n* any of a genus of coniferous trees of North America and East Asia, having scalelike leaves, small cones, and an aromatic wood [c18 from NL, from Med. L *thuia*, ult. from Gk *thua* an African tree]

Thule (ˈθjuːlɪ) *n* **1** Also called: **ultima Thule** a region believed by ancient geographers to be the northernmost land in the inhabited world: sometimes thought to have been Iceland, Norway, or one of the Shetland Islands **2** an Inuit settlement in NW Greenland: a Danish trading post, founded in 1910, and US air force base

thulium (ˈθjuːlɪəm) *n* a malleable ductile silvery-grey element. The radioisotope **thulium-170** is used as an electron source in portable X-ray units. Symbol: Tm; atomic no.: 69; atomic wt.: 168.93 [c19 NL, from THULE + -IUM]

thumb (θʌm) *n* **1** the first and usually shortest and thickest of the digits of the hand **2** the corresponding digit in other vertebrates **3** the part of a glove shaped to fit the thumb **4 all thumbs** clumsy **5 thumbs down** an indication of refusal or disapproval **6 thumbs up** an indication of encouragement or approval **7 under someone's thumb** at someone's mercy or command ▷ *vb* **8** (*tr*) to touch, mark, or move with the thumb **9** to attempt to obtain (a lift or ride) by signalling with the thumb **10** (when *intr*, often foll by *through*) to flip the pages of (a book, etc) in order to glance at the contents **11 thumb one's nose at** to deride or mock, esp by placing the thumb on the nose with fingers extended [OE *thūma*]

thumb index *n* **1** a series of indentations cut into the fore-edge of a book to facilitate quick reference ▷ *vb* **thumb-index 2** (*tr*) to furnish with a thumb index

thumbnail (ˈθʌmˌneɪl) *n* **1** the nail of the thumb **2** (*modifier*) concise and brief: *a thumbnail sketch* **3** *computing* a small image that can be expanded

thumbnut (ˈθʌmˌnʌt) *n* a wing nut

thumb piano *n* another name for **mbira**

thumbscrew (ˈθʌmˌskruː) *n* **1** an instrument of torture that pinches or crushes the thumbs **2** a screw with projections on its head enabling it to be turned by the thumb and forefinger

thumbstall (ˈθʌmˌstɔːl) *n* a protective sheathlike cover for the thumb

thumbtack (ˈθʌmˌtæk) *n* the US and Canad name for **drawing pin**

thump (θʌmp) *n* **1** the sound of a heavy solid body hitting a comparatively soft surface **2** a heavy blow with the hand ▷ *vb* **3** (*tr*) to strike or beat heavily; pound **4** (*intr*) to throb, beat, or pound violently [c16] > ˈ**thumper** *n*

thumping (ˈθʌmpɪŋ) *adj* (*prenominal*) *sl* huge or excessive: *a thumping loss*

Thun (*German* tuːn) *n* **1** a town in central Switzerland, in Bern canton on Lake Thun. Pop: 36 700 (1990 est) **2** a lake in central Switzerland, formed by a widening of the Aar River. Length: about 17 km (11 miles). Width: 3 km (2 miles). German name: **Thuner See**

thunbergia (θʌnˈbɜːdʒɪə) *n* any of various climbing or dwarf plants of tropical and subtropical Africa and Asia [c19 after K. P. *Thunberg* (1743-1822), Swedish botanist]

thunder (ˈθʌndə) *n* **1** a loud cracking or deep rumbling noise caused by the rapid expansion of atmospheric gases which are suddenly heated by lightning **2** any loud booming sound **3** *rare* a violent threat or denunciation **4 steal someone's thunder** to lessen the effect of someone's idea or action by anticipating it ▷ *vb* **5** to make (a loud sound) or utter (words) in a manner suggesting thunder **6** (*intr*; with *it* as subject) to be the case that thunder is being heard **7** (*intr*) to move fast and heavily: *the bus thundered downhill* **8** (*intr*) to utter vehement threats or denunciation; rail [OE *thunor*] > ˈ**thundery** *adj* > ˈ**thunderer** *n*

Thunder Bay *n* a port in central Canada, in Ontario on Lake Superior: formed in 1970 by the amalgamation of Fort William and Port Arthur; the head of the St Lawrence Seaway for Canada. Pop: 113 662 (1996)

thunderbolt (ˈθʌndəˌbəʊlt) *n* **1** a flash of lightning accompanying thunder **2** the imagined agency of destruction produced by a flash of lightning **3** (in mythology) the destructive weapon wielded by several gods, esp the Greek god Zeus **4** something very startling

thunderclap (ˈθʌndəˌklæp) *n* **1** a loud outburst of thunder **2** something as violent or unexpected as a clap of thunder

thundercloud (ˈθʌndəˌklaʊd) *n* a towering electrically charged cumulonimbus cloud associated with thunderstorms

thunderhead (ˈθʌndəˌhɛd) *n chiefly US* the anvil-shaped top of a cumulonimbus cloud

thundering (ˈθʌndərɪŋ) *adj* (*prenominal*) *sl* very great or excessive: *a thundering idiot*

thunderous (ˈθʌndərəs) *adj* **1** threatening; angry: *a thunderous face* **2** resembling thunder, esp in loudness: *thunderous applause*

thunderstorm (ˈθʌndəˌstɔːm) *n* a storm with thunder and lightning and usually heavy rain or hail

thunderstruck (ˈθʌndəˌstrʌk) *or* **thunderstricken** (ˈθʌndəˌstrɪkən) *adj* **1** completely taken aback; amazed or shocked **2** *rare* struck by lightning

Tt

Thurber (ˈθɜːbə) *n* **James** (**Grover**) 1894–1961, US humorist and illustrator. He contributed drawings and stories to the *New Yorker* and his books include *Is Sex Necessary?* (1929), written with E. B. White

Thurgau (*German* ˈtuːrgau) *n* a canton of NE Switzerland, on Lake Constance: annexed by the confederated Swiss states in 1460. Capital: Frauenfeld. Pop: 227 300 (2000 est). Area: 1007 sq km (389 sq miles). French name: **Thurgovie** (tyrgɔvi)

thurible (ˈθjʊərɪbᵊl) *n* another word for **censer** [c15 from L *tūribulum* censer, from *tūs* incense]

Thuringia (θjʊˈrɪndʒɪə) *n* a state of central Germany, formerly in East Germany. Pop: 2 449 100 (2001 est). German name: **Thüringen** (ˈtyːrɪŋən) > **Thuˈringian** *adj, n*

Thuringian Forest *n* a forested mountainous region in E central Germany, rising over 900 m (3000 ft). German name: **Thüringer Wald** (ˈtyːrɪŋər ˈvalt)

Thurrock (ˈθʌrək) *n* a unitary authority in SE England, in Essex. Pop: 143 042 (2001). Area: 163 sq km (63 sq miles)

Thurs. *abbrev for* Thursday

Thursday (ˈθɜːzdɪ) *n* the fifth day of the week; fourth day of the working week [OE *Thursdæg*, lit.: Thor's day]

Thursday Island *n* an island in Torres Strait, between NE Australia and New Guinea: administratively part of Queensland, Australia. Area: 4 sq km (1.5 sq miles)

thus (ðʌs) *adv* **1** in this manner: *do it thus* **2** to such a degree: *thus far and no further* ▷ *sentence connector* **3** therefore: *We have failed. Thus we have to take the consequences* [OE]

Thutmose I (θʊtˈməʊsə, -məʊs) *n* died *c* 1500 BC, king of Egypt of the 18th dynasty, who extended his territory in Nubia and Syria and enlarged the Temple of Ammon at Karnak

Thutmose III *n* died *c* 1450 BC, king of Egypt of the 18th dynasty, who completed the conquest of Syria and dominated the Middle East. He was also a patron of the arts and a famous athlete

thuya (ˈθuːjə) *n* a variant spelling of **thuja**

thwack (θwæk) *vb* **1** to beat, esp with something flat ▹ *n* **2a** a blow with something flat **2b** the sound made by it [C16 imit.]

thwart (θwɔːt) *vb* **1** to oppose successfully or prevent; frustrate **2** *obs* to be or move across ▹ *n* **3** an oarsman's seat lying across a boat ▹ *adj* **4** passing or being situated across ▹ *prep, adv* **5** *obs* across [C13 from ON *thvert*, from *thverr* transverse]

thy (ðaɪ) *determiner* (*usually preceding a consonant*) *arch or Brit dialect* belonging to or associated in some way with you (thou): *thy goodness* [C12 var. of THINE]

Thyestes (θaɪˈɛstiːz) *n Greek myth* son of Pelops and brother of Atreus, with whose wife he committed adultery. In revenge, Atreus killed Thyestes' sons and served them to their father at a banquet > **Thyestean** *or* **Thyestian** (θaɪˈɛstɪən, ˌθaɪɛˈstiːən) *adj*

thylacine (ˈθaɪləˌsaɪn) *n* an extinct or rare doglike carnivorous marsupial of Tasmania. Also called: **Tasmanian tiger, Tasmanian wolf** [C19 from NL *thȳlacīnus*, from Gk *thulakos* pouch]

thyme (taɪm) *n* any of various small shrubs having a strong odour, small leaves, and white, pink, or red flowers [C14 from OF *thym*, from L *thymum*, from Gk, from *thuein* to make a burnt offering] > **ˈthymy** *adj*

-thymia *n combining form* indicating a certain emotional condition, mood, or state of mind: *cyclothymia* [NL, from Gk *thumos* temper]

thymine (ˈθaɪmiːn) *n* a white crystalline base found in DNA [C19 from THYMIC (see THYMUS) + -INE[2]]

thymol (ˈθaɪmɒl) *n* a white crystalline substance obtained from thyme and used as a fungicide, antiseptic, etc [C19 from THYME + -OL[2]]

thymus (ˈθaɪməs) *n, pl* **thymuses** *or* **thymi** (-maɪ) a glandular organ of vertebrates, consisting in man of two lobes situated below the thyroid. It atrophies with age and is almost nonexistent in the adult [C17 from NL, from Gk *thumos* sweetbread] > **ˈthymic** *adj*

thyratron (ˈθaɪrəˌtrɒn) *n electronics* a gas-filled tube that has three electrodes and can be switched between an 'off' state and an 'on' state. It has been superseded by the thyristor [C20 orig. a trademark, from Gk *thura* door, valve + -TRON]

thyristor (θaɪˈrɪstə) *n* any of a group of semiconductor devices, such as the silicon-controlled rectifier, that can be switched between two states [C20 from THYR(ATRON) + (TRANS)ISTOR]

thyroid (ˈθaɪrɔɪd) *adj* **1** of or relating to the thyroid gland **2** of or relating to the largest cartilage of the larynx ▹ *n* **3** See **thyroid gland 4** Also: **thyroid extract** a preparation of the thyroid gland of certain animals, used to treat hypothyroidism [C18 from NL *thyroidēs*, from Gk *thureoeidēs*, from *thureos* oblong (lit.: door-shaped), from *thura* door]
▹ www.thyroidfoundation.org

thyroid gland *n* an endocrine gland of vertebrates, consisting in man of two lobes near the base of the neck. It secretes hormones that control metabolism and growth

thyrotropin (ˌθaɪrəʊˈtrəʊpɪn) *or* **thyrotrophin** *n* a hormone secreted by the pituitary gland: it stimulates the activity of the thyroid gland [C20 from *thyro-* thyroid + -TROPE + -IN]

thyroxine (θaɪˈrɒksiːn, -sɪn) *or* **thyroxin** (θaɪˈrɒksɪn) *n* the principal hormone produced by the thyroid gland [C19 from *thyro-* thyroid + OXY-[2] + -INE[2]]

thyrse (θɜːs) *or* **thyrsus** (ˈθɜːsəs) *n, pl* **thyrses** *or* **thyrsi** (ˈθɜːsaɪ) *bot* a type of inflorescence, occurring in the lilac and grape, in which the main branch is racemose and the lateral branches cymose [C17 from F: THYRSUS]

thyrsus (ˈθɜːsəs) *n, pl* **thyrsi** (-saɪ) **1** *Greek myth* a staff, usually one tipped with a pine cone, borne by Dionysus (Bacchus) and his followers **2** a variant spelling of **thyrse** [C18 from L, from Gk *thursos* stalk]

thyself (ðaɪˈsɛlf) *pron arch* **a** the reflexive form of *thou* or *thee* **b** (intensifier): *thou, thyself, wouldst know*

ti (tiː) *n music* a variant spelling of **te**

Ti *the chemical symbol for* titanium

Tianjin (ˈtjɛnˈdʒɪn), **Tientsin**, *or* **T'ien-ching** *n* an industrial city in NE China, in Hebei province, on the Grand Canal, 51 km (32 miles) from the Yellow Sea: the third largest city in China; seat of Nankai University (1919). Pop: 4 835 327 (1999 est)

Tian Shan *or* **Tien Shan** (ˈtjɛnˈʃɑːn) *n* a great mountain system of central Asia, in Kyrgyzstan and the Xinjiang Uygur Autonomous Region of W China, extending for about 2500 km (1500 miles). Highest peak: Pobeda Peak, 7439 m (24 406 ft). Russian name: **Tyan-Shan**

tiara (tɪˈɑːrə) *n* **1** a woman's semicircular jewelled headdress for formal occasions **2** a high headdress worn by Persian kings in ancient times **3** a headdress worn by the pope, consisting of a beehive-shaped diadem surrounded by three coronets [C16 via L from Gk, of Oriental origin] > **tiˈaraed** *adj*
▹ www.vam.ac.uk/vastatic/microsites/tiaras/exhibition.html

Tiber (ˈtaɪbə) *n* a river in central Italy, rising in the Tuscan Apennines and flowing south through Rome to the Tyrrhenian Sea. Length: 405 km (252 miles). Ancient name: **Tiberis** (ˈtiːbərɪs). Italian name: **Tevere**

Tiberias (taɪˈbɪərɪˌæs) *n* **1** a resort in N Israel, on the Sea of Galilee: an important Jewish centre after the destruction of Jerusalem by the Romans. Pop: 35 400 (latest est) **2 Lake** another name for the (Sea of) **Galilee**

Tiberius (taɪˈbɪərɪəs) *n* full name *Tiberius Claudius Nero Caesar Augustus*. 42 BC–37 AD, Roman emperor (14–37 AD). He succeeded his father-in-law Augustus after a brilliant military career. He became increasingly tyrannical

Tibesti *or* **Tibesti Massif** (tɪˈbɛstɪ) *n* a mountain range of volcanic origin in NW Chad, in the central Sahara extending for about 480 km (300 miles). Highest peak: Emi Koussi, 3415 m (11 204 ft)

Tibet (tɪˈbɛt) *n* an autonomous region of SW China: Europeans strictly excluded in the 19th century; invaded by China in 1950; rebellion (1959) against Chinese rule suppressed and the Dalai Lama fled to India; military rule imposed (1989–90) after continued demands for independence; consists largely of a vast high plateau between the Himalayas and Kunlun Mountains; formerly a theocracy and the centre of Lamaism. Capital: Lhasa. Pop: 2 620 000 (2000 est). Area: 1 221 601 sq km (471 660 sq miles). Chinese names: **Xizang Autonomous Region, Sitsang**

Tibetan (tɪˈbɛtᵊn) *adj* **1** of or characteristic of Tibet, its people, or their language ▹ *n* **2** a native or inhabitant of Tibet **3** the language of Tibet

tibia (ˈtɪbɪə) *n, pl* **tibiae** (ˈtɪbɪˌiː) *or* **tibias 1** the inner and thicker of the two bones of the human leg below the knee; shinbone **2** the corresponding bone in other vertebrates **3** the fourth segment of an insect's leg [C16 from L: leg, pipe] > **ˈtibial** *adj*

Tibullus (tɪˈbʌləs) *n* **Albius** (ˈælbɪəs) ?54–?19 BC, Roman elegiac poet

Tibur (ˈtaɪbə) *n* the ancient name for **Tivoli**

tic (tɪk) *n* spasmodic twitching of a particular group of muscles [C19 from F, from ?]

tic douloureux (ˈtɪk ˌduːləˈruː) *n* a condition of momentary stabbing pain along the trigeminal nerve [C19 from F, lit.: painful tic]

Ticino (*Italian* tiˈtʃiːno) *n* **1** a canton in S Switzerland: predominantly Italian-speaking and Roman Catholic; mountainous. Capital: Bellinzona. Pop: 308 500 (2000 est). Area: 2810 sq km (1085 sq miles). German name:

Tessin 2 a river in S central Europe, rising in S central Switzerland and flowing southeast and west to Lake Maggiore, then southeast to the River Po. Length: 248 km (154 miles)

tick¹ (tɪk) *n* **1** a recurrent metallic tapping or clicking sound, such as that made by a clock **2** *Brit inf* a moment or instant **3** a mark (✓) used to check off or indicate the correctness of something **4** *commerce* the smallest increment by which a price can fluctuate in a commodity or financial futures market ▷ *vb* **5** to produce a recurrent tapping sound or indicate by such a sound: *the clock ticked the minutes away* **6** (when *tr*, often foll by *off*) to mark or check with a tick **7 what makes someone tick** *inf* the basic drive or motivation of a person ▷ See also **tick off, tick over** [c13 from Low G *tikk* touch]

tick² (tɪk) *n* any of a large group of small parasitic arachnids typically living on the skin of warm-blooded animals and feeding on the blood, etc, of their hosts [OE *ticca*]

tick³ (tɪk) *n* **1** the strong covering of a pillow, mattress, etc **2** *inf* short for **ticking** [c15 prob. from MDu. *tīke*]

tick⁴ (tɪk) *n Brit inf* account or credit (esp in **on tick**) [c17 shortened from TICKET]

tick bird *n* another name for **oxpecker**

tick box *n* (on a form, questionnaire, or test) a square in which one places a tick to show agreement with the accompanying statement

ticker ('tɪkə) *n* **1** *sl* **1a** the heart **1b** a watch **2** a person or thing that ticks **3** the US word for **tape machine**

ticker tape *n* a continuous paper ribbon on which a tape machine prints current stock quotations

ticket ('tɪkɪt) *n* **1a** a piece of paper, cardboard, etc, showing that the holder is entitled to certain rights, such as travel on a train or bus, entry to a place of public entertainment, etc **1b** (*modifier*) concerned with the issue, sale, or checking of tickets: *a ticket collector* **2** a piece of card, cloth, etc, attached to an article showing information such as its price, size, etc **3** a summons served for a parking or traffic offence **4** *inf* the certificate of competence issued to a ship's captain or an aircraft pilot **5** *chiefly US & NZ* the group of candidates nominated by one party in an election; slate **6** *chiefly US* the declared policy of a political party at an election **7** *Brit inf* a certificate of discharge from the armed forces **8** *inf* the right or appropriate thing: *that's the ticket* **9 have (got) tickets on oneself** *Austral inf* to be conceited ▷ *vb* **tickets, ticketing, ticketed** (*tr*) **10** to issue or attach a ticket or tickets to [c17 from OF *etiquet*, from *estiquier* to stick on, from MDu. *steken* to stick]

ticket day *n stock exchange* the day before settling day, when the stockbrokers are given the names of the purchasers

tickets ('tɪkɪts) *pl n S African inf* the end: *it's tickets for him*

tick fever *n* any acute infectious febrile disease caused by the bite of an infected tick

ticking ('tɪkɪŋ) *n* a strong cotton fabric, often striped, used esp for mattress and pillow covers [c17 from TICK³]

ticklace ('tɪkə,læs) *n Canad* (in Newfoundland) a kittiwake [imit. of the bird's cry]

tickle ('tɪkᵊl) *vb* **tickles, tickling, tickled 1** to touch or stroke, so as to produce pleasure, laughter, or a twitching sensation **2** (*tr*) to excite pleasurably; gratify **3** (*tr*) to delight or entertain (often in **tickle one's fancy**) **4** (*intr*) to itch or tingle **5** (*tr*) to catch (a fish, esp a trout) with the hands **6 tickle pink** *or* **to death** *inf* to please greatly ▷ *n* **7** a sensation of light stroking or itching **8** the act of tickling **9** *Canad* (in the Atlantic Provinces) a narrow strait [c14]

tickler ('tɪklə) *n* **1** *inf, chiefly Brit* a difficult problem **2** Also called: **tickler file** *US* a memorandum book **3** a person or thing that tickles

ticklish ('tɪklɪʃ) *adj* **1** sensitive to being tickled **2** delicate or difficult **3** easily upset or offended > '**ticklishly** *adv* > '**ticklishness** *n*

tick off *vb* (*tr, adv*) **1** to mark with a tick **2** *inf, chiefly Brit* to scold; reprimand

tick over *vb* (*intr, adv*) **1** Also: **idle** *Brit* (of an engine) to run at low speed with the throttle control closed and the transmission disengaged **2** to run smoothly without any major changes

ticktack ('tɪk,tæk) *n* **1** *Brit* a system of sign language, mainly using the hands, by which bookmakers transmit their odds to each other at race courses **2** *US* a ticking sound [from TICK¹]

ticktock ('tɪk,tɒk) *n* **1** a ticking sound as made by a clock ▷ *vb* **2** (*intr*) to make a ticking sound

Ticonderoga (,taɪkɒndə'rəʊgə) *n* a village in NE New York State, on Lake George: site of Fort Ticonderoga, scene of battles between the British and French (1758–59) and a strategic point in the War of American Independence

tidal ('taɪdᵊl) *adj* **1** relating to, characterized by, or affected by tides **2** dependent on the tide: *a tidal ferry* > '**tidally** *adv*

tidal energy *n* energy obtained by harnessing tidal power

tidal volume *n* **1** the volume of water associated with a rising tide **2** *physiol* the amount of air passing into and out of the lungs during normal breathing

tidal wave *n* **1** a name (not in technical usage) for **tsunami 2** an unusually large incoming wave, often caused by high winds and spring tides **3** a forceful and widespread movement in public opinion, action, etc

tidbit ('tɪd,bɪt) *n* the usual US spelling of **titbit**

tiddler ('tɪdlə) *n Brit inf* **1** a very small fish, esp a stickleback **2** a small child [c19 from *tittlebat*, childish var. of STICKLEBACK, infl. by TIDDLY¹]

tiddly¹ ('tɪdlɪ) *adj* **tiddlier, tiddliest** *Brit* small; tiny [c19 childish var. of LITTLE]

tiddly² ('tɪdlɪ) *adj sl, chiefly Brit* slightly drunk [c19 (meaning: a drink): from ?]

tiddlywinks ('tɪdlɪ,wɪŋks) *n* (*functioning as sing*) a game in which players try to flick discs of plastic into a cup by pressing them with other larger discs [c19 prob. from TIDDLY¹ + dialect *wink*, var. of WINCH¹]

tide (taɪd) *n* **1** the cyclic rise and fall of sea level caused by the gravitational pull of the sun and moon. There are usually two high tides and two low tides in each lunar day **2** the current, ebb, or flow of water at a specified place resulting from these changes in level **3** See **ebb** (sense 3) and **flood** (sense 3) **4** a widespread tendency or movement **5** a critical point in time; turning point **6** *arch except in combination* a season or time: *Christmastide* **7** *arch* a favourable opportunity **8 the tide is in** (*or* **out**) the sea has reached its highest (*or* lowest) level ▷ *vb* **tides, tiding, tided 9** to carry or be carried with or as if with the tide **10** (*intr*) to ebb and flow like the tide [OE *tīd* time] > '**tideless** *adj*

tideland ('taɪd,lænd) *n US* land between high-water and low-water marks

tideline ('taɪd,laɪn) *n* the mark or line left by the tide when it retreats from its highest point

tidemark ('taɪd,mɑːk) *n* **1** a mark left by the highest or lowest point of a tide **2** *chiefly Brit* a mark showing a level reached by a liquid: *a tidemark on the bath* **3** *inf, chiefly Brit* a dirty mark on the skin, indicating the extent to which someone has washed

tide over *vb* (*tr, adv*) to help to get through (a period of difficulty, distress, etc)

tide-rip *n* another word for **riptide** (sense 1)

tidewaiter ('taɪd,weɪtə) *n* (formerly) a customs officer who boarded and inspected incoming ships

tidewater ('taɪd,wɔːtə) *n* **1** water that advances and recedes with the tide **2** *US* coastal land drained by tidal streams

Tt

tideway ('taɪd,weɪ) *n* a strong tidal current or its channel, esp the tidal part of a river

tidings ('taɪdɪŋz) *pl n* information or news [OE *tīdung*]

tidy ('taɪdɪ) *adj* **tidier, tidiest 1** characterized by or indicating neatness and order **2** *inf* considerable: *a tidy sum of money* ▷ *vb* **tidies, tidying, tidied 3** (when *intr*, usually foll by *up*) to put (things) in order; neaten ▷ *n, pl* **tidies 4a** a small container for odds and ends **4b sink tidy** a container to retain rubbish that might clog the plughole **5** *chiefly US & Canad* an ornamental protective covering for the back or arms of a chair [c13 (in the sense: timely, excellent): from TIDE + -Y[1]] > **'tidily** *adv* > **'tidiness** *n*

tie (taɪ) *vb* **ties, tying, tied 1** (when *tr*, often foll by *up*) to fasten or be fastened with string, thread, etc **2** to make (a knot or bow) in (something) **3** (*tr*) to restrict or secure **4** to equal (the score) of a competitor, etc **5** (*tr*) *inf* to unite in marriage **6** *music* **6a** to execute (two successive notes) as though they formed one note **6b** to connect (two printed notes) with a tie ▷ *n* **7** a bond, link, or fastening **8** a restriction or restraint **9** a string, wire, etc, with which something is tied **10** a long narrow piece of material worn, esp by men, under the collar of a shirt, tied in a knot close to the throat with the ends hanging down the front. US name: **necktie 11a** an equality in score, attainment, etc, in a contest **11b** the match or competition in which such a result is attained **12** a structural member such as a tie beam or tie rod **13** *sport, Brit* a match or game in an eliminating competition: *a cup tie* **14** (*usually pl*) a shoe fastened by means of laces **15** the US and Canad name for **sleeper** (on a railway track) **16** *music* a slur connecting two notes of the same pitch indicating that the sound is to be prolonged for their joint time value ▷ See also **tie in, tie up** [OE *tīgan* to tie]

tie beam *n* a horizontal beam that serves to prevent two other structural members from separating, esp one that connects two corresponding rafters in a roof or roof truss

tie-break *or* **tie-breaker** *n* **1** *tennis* an extra game played to decide the result of a set when the score is 6–6 **2** any method of deciding quickly the result of a drawn contest, esp an extra game, question, etc

tie clasp *n* a clip which holds a tie in place against a shirt. Also called: **tie clip**

tied (taɪd) *adj Brit* **1** (of a public house, retail shop, etc) obliged to sell only the beer, products, etc of a particular producer: *a tied house; tied outlet* **2** (of a house) rented out to the tenant for as long as he or she is employed by the owner **3** (of a loan) made by one nation to another on condition that the money is spent on goods or services provided by the lending nation

tie-dyeing, tie-dye *or* **tie and dye** *n* a method of dyeing textiles to produce patterns by tying sections of the cloth together so that they will not absorb the dye > **'tie-,dyed** *adj*

▷ www.ritdye.com/artoftiedye.asp
▷ www.mendels.com/tiedye.html

tie in *vb* (*adv*) **1** to come or bring into a certain relationship; coordinate ▷ *n* **tie-in 2** a link, relationship, or coordination **3** publicity material, a book, etc, linked to a film, etc **4** *US* **4a** a sale or advertisement offering products of which a purchaser must buy one or more in addition to his purchase **4b** an item sold or advertised in this way **4c** (*as modifier*): *a tie-in sale*

tie line *n* a telephone line between two private branch exchanges or private exchanges that may or may not pass through a main exchange

Tien Shan ('tjɛn'ʃɑːn) *n* a variant transliteration of the Chinese name for the **Tian Shan**

Tientsin ('tjɛn'tsɪn) *n* a variant transliteration of the Chinese name for **Tianjin**

tiepin ('taɪ,pɪn) *n* an ornamental pin of various shapes used to pin the two ends of a tie to a shirt

Tiepolo (*Italian* 'tjɛːpolo; *English* tiː'ɛpə,ləʊ) *n* **Giovanni Battista** (dʒo'vanni bat'tista) 1696–1770, Italian rococo painter, esp of frescoes as in the Residenz at Würzburg

tier[1] (tɪə) *n* **1** one of a set of rows placed one above and behind the other, such as theatre seats **2a** a layer or level **2b** (*in combination*): *a three-tier cake* ▷ *vb* **3** to be or arrange in tiers [c16 from OF *tire* rank, of Gmc origin]

tier[2] ('taɪə) *n* a person or thing that ties

tierce (tɪəs) *n* **1** a variant of **terce 2** the third of eight positions from which a parry or attack can be made in fencing **3** (tɜːs) a sequence of three cards **4** an obsolete measure of capacity equal to 42 wine gallons [c15 from OF, fem of *tiers* third, from L *tertius*]

tiercel ('tɪəsᵊl) *n* a variant of **tercel**

Tierra del Fuego (*Spanish* 'tjɛrra ðɛl 'fweɣo) *n* an archipelago at the S extremity of South America, separated from the mainland by the Strait of Magellan: the west and south belong to Chile, the east to Argentina, and several islands are disputed. Area: 73 643 sq km (28 434 sq miles)

tie up *vb* (*adv*) **1** (*tr*) to bind securely with or as if with string, rope, etc **2** to moor (a vessel) **3** (*tr; often passive*) to engage the attentions of **4** (*tr; often passive*) to conclude (the organization of something) **5** to come or bring to a complete standstill **6** (*tr*) to commit (funds, etc) and so make unavailable for other uses **7** (*tr*) to subject (property) to conditions that prevent sale, alienation, etc ▷ *n* **tie-up 8** a link or connection **9** *chiefly US & Canad* a standstill **10** *chiefly US & Canad* an informal term for **traffic jam**

tiff (tɪf) *n* **1** a petty quarrel **2** a fit of ill humour ▷ *vb* **3** (*intr*) to have or be in a tiff [c18 from ?]

tiffany ('tɪfənɪ) *n, pl* **tiffanies** a sheer fine gauzy fabric [c17 (in the sense: a fine dress worn on Twelfth Night): from OF *tifanie*, from ecclesiastical L *theophania* Epiphany]

Tiffany ('tifənɪ) *n* **Louis Comfort** 1848–1933, US glass-maker and Art-Nouveau craftsman, best known for creating the Favrile style of stained glass

tiffin ('tɪfɪn) *n* (in India) a light meal, esp at midday [c18 prob. from obs. *tiffing*, from *tiff* to sip]

Tiflis (tɪf'liːs) *n* transliteration of the Russian name for **Tbilisi**

tig (tɪg) *n, vb* **tigs, tigging, tigged** another word for **tag[2]** (senses 1, 4)

tiger ('taɪgə) *n* **1** a large feline mammal of forests in most of Asia, having a tawny yellow coat with black stripes **2** a dynamic, forceful, or cruel person **3a** a country, esp in E Asia, that is achieving rapid economic growth **3b** (*as modifier*): *a tiger economy* [c13 from OF *tigre*, from L *tigris*, from Gk, of Iranian origin] > **'tigerish** *adj*

Tiger ('taɪgə) *n* a variant of **TIGR**

tiger beetle *n* any of a family of active predatory beetles, chiefly of warm dry regions, having powerful mandibles and long legs

tiger cat *n* a medium-sized feline mammal of Central and South America, having a dark-striped coat

tiger lily *n* a lily plant of China and Japan cultivated for its flowers, which have black-spotted orange petals

tiger moth *n* any of various moths having wings that are conspicuously marked with stripes and spots

tiger's-eye *or* **tigereye** ('taɪgər,aɪ) *n* a semiprecious golden-brown stone

tiger shark *n* a voracious omnivorous requiem shark of tropical waters, having a striped or spotted body

tiger snake *n* a highly venomous and aggressive Australian snake, usually with dark bands on the back

tight (taɪt) *adj* **1** stretched or drawn so as not to be loose; taut **2** fitting in a close manner **3** held, made, fixed, or closed firmly and securely: *a tight knot* **4a** of close and compact construction or organization, esp so as to be impervious to water, air, etc **4b** *(in combination)*: *airtight* **5** unyielding or stringent **6** cramped or constricted: *a tight fit* **7** mean or miserly **8** difficult and problematic: *a tight situation* **9** hardly profitable: *a tight bargain* **10** *econ* **10a** (of a commodity) difficult to obtain **10b** (of funds, money, etc) difficult and expensive to borrow **10c** (of markets) characterized by excess demand or scarcity **11** (of a match or game) very close or even **12** (of a team or group, esp of a pop group) playing well together, in a disciplined coordinated way **13** *inf* drunk **14** *inf* (of a person) showing tension ▷ *adv* **15** in a close, firm, or secure way [C14 prob. var. of *thight*, from ON *thēttr* close] > **'tightly** *adv* > **'tightness** *n*

tightass ('taɪtˌs) *n sl, chiefly US* an inhibited or excessively self-controlled person > **'tightˌassed** *adj*

tighten ('taɪtᵊn) *vb* to make or become tight or tighter

tightfisted (ˌtaɪt'fɪstɪd) *adj* mean; miserly

tight head *n rugby* the prop on the hooker's right in the front row of a scrum. ▷ Cf **loose head**

tightknit (ˌtaɪt'nɪt) *adj* **1** closely integrated: *a tightknit community* **2** organized carefully

tight-lipped *adj* **1** secretive or taciturn **2** with the lips pressed tightly together, as through anger

tightrope ('taɪtˌrəʊp) *n* a rope stretched taut on which acrobats walk or perform balancing feats > **tightrope walker** *n*

tights (taɪts) *pl n* **1a** Also called: (US) **panty hose,** (Canad and NZ) **pantyhose,** (Austral and NZ) **pantihose** a one-piece clinging garment covering the body from the waist to the feet, worn by women and also by acrobats, dancers, etc **1b** *US & Canad* Also called: **leotards** a similar, tight-fitting garment worn instead of trousers by either sex **2** a similar garment formerly worn by men, as in the 16th century with a doublet

Tiglath-pileser I ('tɪglæθpɪ'li:zə, -paɪ-) *n* king of Assyria (?1116–?1093 BC), who extended his kingdom to the upper Euphrates and defeated the king of Babylonia

Tiglath-pileser III *n* known as *Pulu.* died ?727 BC, king of Assyria (745–727), who greatly extended his empire, subjugating Syria and Palestine

tiglic acid ('tɪglɪk) *n* a syrupy liquid or crystalline unsaturated carboxylic acid, found in croton oil and used in perfumery [C19 *tiglic*, from NL *Croton tiglium* (the croton plant), from ?]

tigon ('taɪgən) *or* **tiglon** ('tɪglɒn) *n* the hybrid offspring of a male tiger and a female lion

TIGR *abbrev for* Treasury Investment Growth Receipts: a bond denominated in dollars and linked to US treasury bonds, the yield on which is taxed in the UK as income when it is cashed or redeemed. Also called: **Tiger**

Tigré *or* **Tigray** ('ti:greɪ) *n* **1** an autonomous region of N Ethiopia, bordering on Eritrea: formerly a separate kingdom. Capital: Mekele. Pop: 3 136 267 (1994). Area: 53 498 sq km (20 656 sq miles) **2** a language of NE Ethiopia, belonging to the SE Semitic subfamily of the Afro-Asiatic family

tigress ('taɪgrɪs) *n* **1** a female tiger **2** a fierce, cruel, or wildly passionate woman

tigridia (taɪ'grɪdɪə) *n* any of various bulbous plants of Mexico, Central America, and tropical S America [C19 from Mod. L, from Gk *tigris* tiger (alluding to the spotted flowers of these plants)]

Tigris ('taɪgrɪs) *n* a river in SW Asia, rising in E Turkey and flowing southeast through Baghdad to the Euphrates in SE Iraq, forming the delta of the Shatt-al-Arab, which flows into the Persian Gulf: part of a canal and irrigation system as early as 2400 BC, with many ancient cities (including Nineveh) on its banks. Length: 1900 km (1180 miles)

Tihwa *or* **Tihua** ('ti:'hwɑ:) *n* a former name for **Urumchi**

Tijuana (ti:'wɑ:nə; *Spanish* ti'xwana) *n* a city in NW Mexico, in Baja California. Pop (urban area): 1 150 000 (2000 est)

tikanga ('tə'kæŋə) *pl n* NZ Maori ways or customs [Maori]

tike (taɪk) *n* a variant spelling of **tyke**

tiki ('ti:ki:) *n* a Maori greenstone neck ornament in the form of a fetus. Also called: **heitiki** [from Maori *heitiki* figure worn round neck]

tiki tour *n* NZ a scenic tour of an area

tikka ('ti:kə) *adj (immediately postpositive) Indian cookery* (of meat, esp chicken or lamb) marinated in spices and then dry-roasted, usually in a clay oven

Tikrit (tɪ'kri:t) *n* a town in N central Iraq on the River Tigris; birthplace of Saladin and Saddam Hussein. Pop: 28 900 (2002 est)

tilak ('tɪlək) *n, pl* **tilak** *or* **tilaks** a coloured spot or mark worn by Hindus, esp on the forehead, often indicating membership of a religious sect, caste, etc, or (in the case of a woman) marital status [from Sansk. *tilaka*]

Tilburg ('tɪlbɜ:g; *Dutch* 'tɪlbyrx) *n* a city in the S Netherlands, in North Brabant: textile industries. Pop: 190 559 (1999 est)

tilbury ('tɪlbərɪ, -brɪ) *n, pl* **tilburies** a light two-wheeled horse-drawn open carriage, seating two people [C19 prob. after the inventor]

Tilbury ('tɪlbərɪ, -brɪ) *n* an area in Essex, on the River Thames: extensive docks; principal container port of the Port of London

tilde ('tɪldə) *n* the diacritical mark (~) placed over a letter to indicate a particular sound, as in Spanish *señor* [C19 from Sp., from L *titulus* title]

Tilden ('tɪldᵊn) *n* **Bill,** full name *William Tatem Tilden,* known as *Big Bill.* 1893–1953, US tennis player: won the US singles championship (1920–25, 1929) and the British singles championship (1920–21, 1930)

tile (taɪl) *n* **1** a thin slab of fired clay, rubber, linoleum, etc, used with others to cover a roof, floor, wall, etc **2** a short pipe made of earthenware, plastic, etc, used with others to form a drain **3** tiles collectively **4** a rectangular block used as a playing piece in mah jong and other games **5 on the tiles** *inf* on a spree, esp of drinking or debauchery ▷ *vb* **tiles, tiling, tiled 6** *(tr)* to cover with tiles [OE *tīgele*, from L *tēgula*] > **'tiler** *n*
▷ www.tiles.org

Tt

tiling ('taɪlɪŋ) *n* **1** tiles collectively **2** something made of or surfaced with tiles

till[1] (tɪl) *conj, prep* short for **until**. Also (not standard): **'til** [OE *til*]

> **USAGE** *Till* is a variant of *until* that is acceptable in all styles of language. *Until* is, however, often preferred at the beginning of a sentence in formal writing: *until his behaviour improves, he cannot become a member*

till[2] (tɪl) *vb (tr)* **1** to cultivate and work (land) for the raising of crops **2** to plough [OE *tilian* to try, obtain] > **'tillable** *adj* > **'tiller** *n*

till[3] (tɪl) *n* a box, case, or drawer into which money taken from customers is put, now usually part of a cash register [C15 *tylle*, from ?]

till[4] (tɪl) *n* a glacial deposit consisting of rock fragments of various sizes. The most common is boulder clay [C17 from ?]

tillage ('tɪlɪdʒ) *n* **1** the act or art of tilling **2** tilled land

tiller[1] ('tɪlə) *n naut* a handle fixed to the top of a rudder to serve as a lever in steering it [C14 from Anglo-F *teiler* beam of a loom, from Med. L *tēlārium*, from L *tēla* web]

tiller[2] ('tɪlə) *n* **1** a shoot that arises from the base of the stem in grasses **2** a less common name for **sapling** ▷ *vb* **3** *(intr)* (of a plant) to produce tillers [OE *telgor* twig]

Till Eulenspiegel ('tɪl 'ɔɪlənʃpi:gᵊl) *n* ?14th century, legendary German peasant, whose pranks became the subject of many tales

Tilley ('tɪlɪ) *n* **Vesta** ('vɛstə), original name *Matilda Alice Powles.* 1864–1952, British music-hall entertainer, best known as a male impersonator

Tillich ('tɪlɪk) *n* **Paul Johannes** 1886–1965, US Protestant theologian and philosopher, born in Germany. His works include *The Courage to Be* (1952) and *Systematic Theology* (1951–63)

Tilsit ('tɪlzɪt) *n* the former name (until 1945) of **Sovetsk**

tilt (tɪlt) *vb* **1** to incline or cause to incline at an angle **2** (*usually intr*) to attack or overthrow (a person) in a tilt or joust **3** (when *intr*, often foll by *at*) to aim or thrust: *to tilt a lance* **4** (*tr*) to forge with a tilt hammer ▷ *n* **5** a slope or angle: *at a tilt* **6** the act of tilting **7** (esp in medieval Europe) **7a** a jousting contest **7b** a thrust with a lance or pole delivered during a tournament **8** an attempt to win a contest **9** See **tilt hammer** **10** **(at) full tilt** at full speed or force [OE *tealtian*] > '**tilter** *n*

tilth (tɪlθ) *n* **1** the act or process of tilling land **2** the condition of soil or land that has been tilled [OE *tilthe*]

tilt hammer *n* a drop hammer with a heavy head; used in forging

tiltyard ('tɪlt,jɑːd) *n* (formerly) an enclosed area for tilting

Tim. *Bible abbrev for* Timothy

Timaru ('tɪmə,ruː) *n* a port and resort in S New Zealand, on E South Island. Pop: 15 350 (1995 est)

timbal *or* **tymbal** ('tɪmbᵊl) *n music* a type of kettledrum [C17 from F *timbale*, from OF *tamballe*, (associated also with *cymbale* cymbal), from OSp. *atabal*, from Ar. *at-tabl* the drum]

timbale (tæm'bɑːl) *n* **1** a mixture of meat, fish, etc, cooked in a mould lined with potato or pastry **2** a straight-sided mould in which such a dish is prepared [C19 from F: kettledrum]

timber ('tɪmbə) *n* **1a** wood, esp when regarded as a construction material. Usual US and Canad word: **lumber** **1b** (*as modifier*): *a timber cottage* **2a** trees collectively **2b** *chiefly US* woodland **3** a piece of wood used in a structure **4** *naut* a frame in a wooden vessel ▷ *vb* **5** (*tr*) to provide with timbers ▷ *sentence substitute* **6** a lumberjack's shouted warning when a tree is about to fall [OE] > '**timbered** *adj* > '**timbering** *n*

timber hitch *n* a knot used for tying a rope round a spar, log, etc, for haulage

Timberlake ('tɪmbə,leɪk) *n* **Justin** born 1981, US pop singer; a member of the boy band NSYNC, he later found success with the bestselling solo album *Justified* (2002)

timber limit *n Canad* **1** the area to which rights of cutting timber, granted by a government licence, are limited **2** another term for **timber line**

timberline ('tɪmbə,laɪn) *n* the altitudinal or latitudinal limit of normal tree growth. See also **tree line**

timber wolf *n* a wolf with a grey brindled coat found in forested northern regions, esp of North America

timberyard ('tɪmbə,jɑːd) *n Brit, Austral, & NZ* an establishment where timber, etc, is stored or sold. US and Canad word: **lumberyard**

timbre ('tɪmbə, 'tæmbə) *n* **1** *phonetics* the distinctive tone quality differentiating one vowel or sonant from another **2** *music* tone colour or quality of sound [C19 from F: note of a bell, from OF: drum, from Med. Gk *timbanon*, from Gk *tumpanon*]

timbrel ('tɪmbrəl) *n chiefly biblical* a tambourine [C16 from OF; see TIMBRE]

Timbuktu (,tɪmbʌk'tuː) *n* **1** a town in central Mali, on the River Niger: terminus of a trans-Saharan caravan route; a great Muslim centre (14th–16th centuries). Pop: 31 925 (latest est). French name: **Tombouctou** **2** any distant or outlandish place: *from here to Timbuktu*

time (taɪm) *n* **1** the continuous passage of existence in which events pass from a state of potentiality in the future, through the present, to a state of finality in the past. Related adj: **temporal** **2** *physics* a quantity measuring duration, usually with reference to a periodic process such as the rotation of the earth or the vibration of electromagnetic radiation emitted from certain atoms. Time is considered as a fourth coordinate required to specify an event. See **space-time continuum** **3** a specific point on this continuum expressed in hours and minutes: *the time is four o'clock* **4** a system of reckoning for expressing time: *Greenwich Mean Time* **5a** a definite and measurable portion of this continuum **5b** (*as modifier*): *time limit* **6a** an accepted period such as a day, season, etc **6b** (*in combination*): *springtime* **7** an unspecified interval; a while **8** (*often pl*) a period or point marked by specific attributes or events: *the Victorian times* **9** a sufficient interval or period: *have you got time to help me?* **10** an instance or occasion: *I called you three times* **11** an occasion or period of specified quality: *have a good time* **12** the duration of human existence **13** the heyday of human life: *in her time she was a great star* **14** a suitable moment: *it's time I told you* **15** the expected interval in which something is done **16** a particularly important moment, esp childbirth or death: *her time had come* **17** (*pl*) indicating a degree or amount calculated by multiplication with the number specified: *ten times three is thirty* **18** (*often pl*) the fashions, thought, etc, of the present age (esp in **ahead of one's time, behind the times**) **19** *Brit* Also: **closing time** the time at which bars, pubs, etc, are legally obliged to stop selling alcoholic drinks **20** *inf* a term in jail (esp in **do time**) **21a** a customary or full period of work **21b** the rate of pay for this period **22** Also (esp US): **metre** **22a** the system of combining beats or pulses in music into successive groupings by which the rhythm of the music is established **22b** a specific system having a specific number of beats in each grouping or bar: *duple time* **23** *music* short for **time value** **24** **against time** in an effort to complete something in a limited period **25** **ahead of time** before the deadline **26** **at one time** **26a** once; formerly **26b** simultaneously **27** **at the same time** **27a** simultaneously **27b** nevertheless; however **28** **at times** sometimes **29** **beat time** to indicate the tempo of a piece of music by waving a baton, hand, etc **30** **for the time being** for the moment; temporarily **31** **from time to time** at intervals; occasionally **32** **have no time for** to have no patience with; not tolerate **33** **in good time** **33a** early **33b** quickly **34** **in no time** very quickly **35** **in one's own time** **35a** outside paid working hours **35b** at one's own rate **36** **in time** **36a** early or at the appointed time **36b** eventually **36c** *music* at a correct metrical or rhythmic pulse **37** **keep time** to observe correctly the accent or rhythmic pulse of a piece of music in relation to tempo **38** **make time** **38a** to find an opportunity **38b** (often foll by *with*) *US inf* to succeed in seducing **39** **on time** **39a** at the expected or scheduled time **39b** *US* payable in instalments **40** **pass the time of day** to exchange casual greetings (with an acquaintance) **41** **time and again** frequently **42** **time off** a period when one is absent from work for a holiday, through sickness, etc **43** **time of one's life** a memorably enjoyable time **44** **time out of mind** from time immemorial **45** (*modifier*) operating automatically at or for a set time: *time lock; time switch* ▷ *vb* **times, timing, timed** (*tr*) **46** to ascertain the duration or speed of **47** to set a time for **48** to adjust to keep accurate time **49** to pick a suitable time for **50** *sport* to control the execution or speed of (an action) ▷ *sentence substitute* **51** the word called out by a publican signalling that it is closing time [OE *tīma*]

time and a half *n* the rate of pay equalling one and a half times the normal rate, often offered for overtime work

time and motion study *n* the analysis of industrial or work procedures to determine the most efficient methods of operation. Also: **time and motion, time study, motion study**

time bomb *n* a bomb containing a timing mechanism that determines the time at which it will detonate

time capsule *n* a container holding articles, documents, etc, representative of the current age, buried for discovery in the future

time charter *n* the hire of a ship or aircraft for a specified period. ▷ Cf **voyage charter**

time clock *n* a clock which records, by punching or stamping **timecards** inserted into it, the time of arrival or departure of people, such as employees in a factory

time-consuming *adj* taking up or involving a great deal of time

time exposure *n* **1** an exposure of a photographic film for a relatively long period, usually a few seconds **2** a photograph produced by such an exposure

time frame *n* the period of time within which certain events are scheduled to occur

time-honoured *adj* having been observed for a long time and sanctioned by custom

time immemorial *n* the distant past beyond memory or record

timekeeper (ˈtaɪmˌkiːpə) *n* **1** a person or thing that keeps or records time **2** an employee who maintains a record of the hours worked by the other employees **3** an employee whose record of punctuality is of a specified nature: *a bad timekeeper* > **ˈtimeˌkeeping** *n*

time-lag *n* an interval between two connected events

time-lapse photography *n* the technique of recording a very slow process on film by exposing single frames at regular intervals. The film is then projected at normal speed

timeless (ˈtaɪmlɪs) *adj* **1** unaffected or unchanged by time; ageless **2** eternal > **ˈtimelessly** *adv* > **ˈtimelessness** *n*

timeline (ˈtaɪmˌlaɪn) *n* **1** a graphic representation showing the passage of time as a line **2** a specified period of time during which something is scheduled to happen

timely (ˈtaɪmlɪ) *adj* **timelier, timeliest,** *adv* at the right or an opportune or appropriate time

time machine *n* (in science fiction) a machine in which people or objects can be transported into the past or the future

time-out *n chiefly US & Canad* **1** *sport* an interruption in play during which players rest, discuss tactics, etc **2** a period of rest; break **3** *computing* a condition that occurs when the amount of time a computer has been instructed to wait for another device to perform a task has expired, usually indicated by an error message ▷ *vb* **time out 4** (of a computer) to stop operating because of a time-out

timepiece (ˈtaɪmˌpiːs) *n* any of various devices, such as a clock, watch, or chronometer, which measure and indicate time

timer (ˈtaɪmə) *n* **1** a device for measuring, recording, or indicating time **2** a switch or regulator that causes a mechanism to operate at a specific time **3** a person or thing that times

time-saving *adj* shortening the length of time required for an operation, activity, etc > **time-saver** *n*

timescale (ˈtaɪmˌskeɪl) *n* the span of time within which certain events occur or are scheduled in relation to any broader period of time

time-sensitive *adj* **1** physically changing as time passes **2** only relevant or applicable for a short period of time

time-served *adj* (of a craftsman or tradesman) having completed an apprenticeship; fully trained and competent

timeserver (ˈtaɪmˌsɜːvə) *n* a person who compromises and changes his or her opinions, way of life, etc, to suit the current fashions

time sharing *n* **1** a system of part ownership of a property for use as a holiday home whereby each participant owns the property for a particular period every year **2** a system by which users at different terminals of a computer can, because of its high speed, apparently communicate with it at the same time

time signal *n* an announcement of the correct time, esp on radio or television

time signature *n music* a sign usually consisting of two figures, one above the other, the upper figure representing the number of beats per bar and the lower one the time value of each beat: it is placed after the key signature

Times Square *n* a square formed by the intersection of Broadway and Seventh Avenue in New York City, extending from 42nd to 45th Street

timetable (ˈtaɪmˌteɪbᵊl) *n* **1** a list or table of events arranged according to the time when they take place; schedule ▷ *vb* **timetables, timetabling, timetabled** (*tr*) **2** to include in or arrange according to a timetable

time value *n music* the duration of a note relative to other notes in a composition and considered in relation to the basic tempo

time warp *n* an imagined distortion of the progress of time so that, for instance, events from the past may appear to be happening in the present

timeworn (ˈtaɪmˌwɔːn) *adj* **1** showing the adverse effects of overlong use or of old age **2** hackneyed; trite

time zone *n* a region throughout which the same standard time is used. There are 24 time zones in the world, demarcated approximately by meridians at 15° intervals, an hour apart

timid (ˈtɪmɪd) *adj* **1** easily frightened or upset, esp by human contact; shy **2** indicating shyness or fear [C16 from L *timidus*, from *timēre* to fear] > **tiˈmidity** *or* **ˈtimidness** *n* > **ˈtimidly** *adv*

timing (ˈtaɪmɪŋ) *n* the regulation of actions or remarks in relation to others to produce the best effect, as in music, the theatre, etc

Timişoara (*Romanian* timiˈʃwara) *n* a city in W Romania: formerly under Turkish and then Hapsburg rule, being allotted to Romania in 1920; scene of violence during the revolution of 1989. Pop: 334 098 (1997 est). Hungarian name: **Temesvár**

timocracy (taɪˈmɒkrəsɪ) *n, pl* **timocracies 1** a political system in which possession of property is a requirement for participation in government **2** a political system in which love of honour is deemed the guiding principle of government [C16 from OF *tymocracie*, ult. from Gk *timokratia*, from *timē* worth, honour, + -CRACY]

Timor (ˈtiːmɔː, ˈtaɪ-) *n* an island in the Malay Archipelago, the largest and easternmost of the Lesser Sunda Islands: the west was a Dutch possession until 1949, when it became part of Indonesia: the east was held by Portugal until 1975, when it declared independence but was immediately invaded by Indonesia; East Timor finally became an independent state in 2002. Area: 30 775 sq km (11 883 sq miles) > **ˌTimoˈrese** *adj, n*

timorous (ˈtɪmərəs) *adj* **1** fearful or timid **2** indicating fear or timidity [C15 from OF *temoros*, from Med. L, from L *timor* fear, from *timēre* to be afraid] > **ˈtimorously** *adv* > **ˈtimorousness** *n*

Timor Sea *n* an arm of the Indian Ocean between Australia and Timor. Width: about 480 km (300 miles)

Timoshenko (ˌtɪməˈʃɛŋkəʊ; *Russian* timaˈʃɛnkə) *n* **Semyon Konstantinovich** (sɪˈmjɔn kənstanˈtinəvitʃ) 1895–1970, Soviet general in World War II

Timothy (ˈtɪməθɪ) *n New Testament* **1 Saint** a disciple of Paul, who became leader of the Christian community at Ephesus. Feast day: Jan 26 or 22 **2** either of the two books addressed to him (in full **The First and Second Epistles of Paul the Apostle to Timothy**)

timothy grass *or* **timothy** *n* a perennial grass of temperate regions having erect stiff stems: grown for hay and pasture [C18 apparently after a *Timothy Hanson*, who brought it to colonial Carolina]

timpani *or* **tympani** (ˈtɪmpənɪ) *pl n* (*sometimes functioning*

Tt

as sing) a set of kettledrums [from It., pl of *timpano* kettledrum, from L: TYMPANUM] > **'timpanist** *or* **'tympanist** *n*

Timur *or* **Timour** (tiː'mʊə) *n* See **Tamerlane**

tin (tɪn) *n* **1** a malleable silvery-white metallic element. It is used extensively in alloys, esp bronze and pewter, and as a noncorroding coating for steel. Symbol: Sn; atomic no.: 50; atomic wt.: 118.69. Related adjs: **stannic, stannous** **2** Also called (esp US and Canad): **can** an airtight sealed container of thin sheet metal coated with tin, used for preserving and storing food or drink **3** any container made of metallic tin **4** Also called: **tinful** the contents of a tin **5** *Brit, Austral, & NZ* galvanized iron: *a tin roof* **6** any metal regarded as cheap or flimsy **7** *Brit* a loaf of bread with a rectangular shape **8** *NZ* a receptacle for home-baked biscuits, etc (esp in **fill her tins** to bake a supply of biscuits, etc) **9 it does exactly what it says on the tin** it lives up to expectations ▷ *vb* **tins, tinning, tinned** (*tr*) **10** to put (food, etc) into a tin or tins; preserve in a tin **11** to plate or coat with tin **12** to prepare (a metal) for soldering or brazing by applying a thin layer of solder to the surface [OE]

tinamou ('tɪnəˌmuː) *n* any of various birds of Central and South America, having small wings and a heavy body [C18 via F from Carib *tinamu*]

Tinbergen ('tɪnˌbɜːgən) *n* **1 Jan** (jæn) 1903–94, Dutch economist, noted for his work on econometrics. He shared (1969) the first Nobel prize for economics with Ragnar Frisch **2** his brother, **Nikolaas** ('nɪkələs) 1907–88, British zoologist, born in the Netherlands; studied animal behaviour, esp instincts, and was one of the founders of ethology; Nobel prize for physiology or medicine 1973

tin can *n* a metal food container, esp when empty

tinctorial (tɪŋk'tɔːrɪəl) *adj* of or relating to colouring, staining, or dyeing [C17 from L *tinctōrius*, from *tingere* to tinge]

tincture ('tɪŋktʃə) *n* **1** a medicinal extract in a solution of alcohol **2** a tint, colour, or tinge **3** a slight flavour, aroma, or trace **4** a colour or metal used on heraldic arms **5** *obs* a dye ▷ *vb* **tinctures, tincturing, tinctured** **6** (*tr*) to give a tint or colour to [C14 from L *tinctūra* a dyeing, from *tingere* to dye]

Tindal *or* **Tindale** ('tɪndᵊl) *n* variant spellings of (William) **Tyndale**

tinder ('tɪndə) *n* **1** dry wood or other easily combustible material used for lighting a fire **2** anything inflammatory or dangerous [OE *tynder*] > **'tindery** *adj*

tinderbox ('tɪndəˌbɒks) *n* **1** a box used formerly for holding tinder, esp one fitted with a flint and steel **2** a person or thing that is particularly touchy or explosive

tine (taɪn) *n* **1** a slender prong, esp of a fork **2** any of the sharp terminal branches of a deer's antler [OE *tind*] > **tined** *adj*

tinea ('tɪnɪə) *n* any fungal skin disease, esp ringworm [C17 from L: worm] > **'tineal** *adj*

tinfoil ('tɪnˌfɔɪl) *n* **1** thin foil made of tin or an alloy of tin and lead **2** thin foil made of aluminium; used for wrapping foodstuffs

ting (tɪŋ) *n* **1** a high metallic sound such as that made by a small bell ▷ *vb* **2** to make or cause to make such a sound [C15 imit.]

Ting (tɪŋ) *n* **Samuel Chao Chung** born 1936, US physicist, who discovered the J/psi particle independently of Burton Richter, with whom he shared (1976) the Nobel prize for physics

ting-a-ling ('tɪŋə'lɪŋ) *n* the sound of a small bell

tinge (tɪndʒ) *n* **1** a slight tint or colouring **2** any slight addition ▷ *vb* **tinges, tingeing** *or* **tinging, tinged** (*tr*) **3** to colour or tint faintly **4** to impart a slight trace to: *her thoughts were tinged with nostalgia* [C15 from L *tingere* to colour]

tingle ('tɪŋgᵊl) *vb* **tingles, tingling, tingled** **1** (*usually intr*) to feel or cause to feel a prickling, itching, or stinging sensation of the flesh, as from a cold plunge ▷ *n* **2** a sensation of tingling [C14 ? a var. of TINKLE] > **'tingler** *n* > **'tingling** *adj* > **'tingly** *adj*

tin god *n* **1** a self-important person **2** a person erroneously regarded as holy or venerable

tin hat *n inf* a steel helmet worn by military personnel

tinker ('tɪŋkə) *n* **1** (esp formerly) a travelling mender of pots and pans **2** a clumsy worker **3** the act of tinkering **4** *Scot & Irish derog* a Gypsy ▷ *vb* **5** (*intr;* foll by *with*) to play, fiddle, or meddle (with machinery, etc), esp while undertaking repairs **6** to mend (pots and pans) as a tinker [C13 *tinkere*, ?from *tink* tinkle, imit.]

tinker's damn *or* **cuss** *n sl* the slightest heed (esp in **not give a tinker's damn** *or* **cuss**)

tinkle ('tɪŋkᵊl) *vb* **tinkles, tinkling, tinkled** **1** to ring with a high tinny sound like a small bell **2** (*tr*) to announce or summon by such a ringing **3** (*intr*) *Brit inf* to urinate ▷ *n* **4** a high clear ringing sound **5** the act of tinkling **6** *Brit inf* a telephone call [C14 imit.] > **'tinkly** *adj*

tin lizzie ('lɪzɪ) *n inf* an old or decrepit car

tinned (tɪnd) *adj* **1** plated, coated, or treated with tin **2** *chiefly Brit* preserved or stored in airtight tins **3** coated with a layer of solder

tinnitus (tɪ'naɪtəs) *n pathol* a ringing, hissing, or booming sensation in one or both ears, caused by infection of the ear, a side effect of certain drugs, etc [C19 from L, from *tinnīre* to ring]

tinny ('tɪnɪ) *adj* **tinnier, tinniest** **1** of or resembling tin **2** cheap or shoddy **3** (of a sound) high, thin, and metallic **4** (of food or drink) flavoured with metal, as from a container **5** *Austral & NZ sl* lucky ▷ *n, pl* **tinnies** **6** *Austral sl* a can of beer > **'tinnily** *adv* > **'tinniness** *n*

tin-opener *n* a small tool for opening tins

Tin Pan Alley *n* **1** originally, a district in New York concerned with the production of popular music **2** the commercial side of show business and pop music

tin plate *n* **1** thin steel sheet coated with a layer of tin that protects the steel from corrosion ▷ *vb* **tin-plate, tin-plates, tin-plating, tin-plated** **2** (*tr*) to coat with a layer of tin

tinpot ('tɪnˌpɒt) *adj* (*prenominal*) *Brit inf* **1** inferior, cheap, or worthless **2** petty; unimportant

tinsel ('tɪnsəl) *n* **1** a decoration consisting of a piece of string with thin strips of metal foil attached along its length **2** a yarn or fabric interwoven with strands of glittering thread **3** anything cheap, showy, and gaudy ▷ *vb* **tinsels, tinselling, tinselled** *or US* **tinsels, tinseling, tinseled** (*tr*) **4** to decorate with or as if with tinsel: *snow tinsels the trees* **5** to give a gaudy appearance to ▷ *adj* **6** made of or decorated with tinsel **7** showily but cheaply attractive; gaudy [C16 from OF *estincele* a spark, from L *scintilla*] > **'tinselly** *adj*

Tinseltown ('tɪnsəlˌtaʊn) *n* an informal name for **Hollywood** [C20 from the insubstantial glitter of the film world]

tinsmith ('tɪnˌsmɪθ) *n* a person who works with tin or tin plate

tin soldier *n* a miniature toy soldier, usually made of lead

tinstone ('tɪnˌstəʊn) *n* another name for **cassiterite**

tint (tɪnt) *n* **1** a shade of a colour, esp a pale one **2** a colour that is softened by the addition of white **3** a tinge **4** a dye for the hair **5** a trace or hint **6** *engraving* uniform shading, produced esp by hatching ▷ *vb* **7** (*tr*) to colour or tinge **8** (*intr*) to acquire a tint [C18 from earlier *tinct*, from L *tingere* to colour] > **'tinter** *n*

Tintagel Head (tɪn'tædʒəl) *n* a promontory in SW England, on the W coast of Cornwall: ruins of **Tintagel Castle**, legendary birthplace of King Arthur

tintinnabulation (ˌtɪntɪˌnæbjʊ'leɪʃən) *n* the act or an instance of the ringing or pealing of bells [from L, from *tintinnāre* to tinkle, from *tinnīre* to ring]

Tintoretto (ˌtɪntəˈrɛtəʊ; *Italian* tintoˈretto) *n* **Il** (il) original name *Jacopo Robusti*. 1518–94, Italian painter of the Venetian school. His works include *Susanna bathing* (?1550) and the fresco cycle in the Scuola di San Rocco, Venice (from 1564)

tinware (ˈtɪnˌwɛə) *n* objects made of tin plate

tin whistle *n* another name for **penny whistle**

tinworks (ˈtɪnˌwɜːks) *n* (*functioning as sing or pl*) a place where tin is mined, smelted, or rolled

tiny (ˈtaɪnɪ) *adj* **tinier, tiniest** very small [c16 *tine*, from ?] > ˈ**tinily** *adv* > ˈ**tininess** *n*

-tion *suffix forming nouns* indicating state, condition, action, process, or result: *election; prohibition* [from OF, from L *-tiō, -tiōn-*]

tip[1] (tɪp) *n* **1** a narrow or pointed end of something **2** the top or summit **3** a small piece forming an end: *a metal tip on a cane* ▷ *vb* **tips, tipping, tipped** (*tr*) **4** to adorn or mark the tip of **5** to cause to form a tip [c15 from ON *typpa*] > ˈ**tipless** *adj*

tip[2] (tɪp) *vb* **tips, tipping, tipped 1** to tilt or cause to tilt **2** (usually foll by *over* or *up*) to tilt or cause to tilt, so as to overturn or fall **3** *Brit* to dump (rubbish, etc) **4 tip one's hat** to raise one's hat in salutation ▷ *n* **5** a tipping or being tipped **6** *Brit* a dump for refuse, etc [c14 from ?] > ˈ**tipper** *n*

tip[3] (tɪp) *n* **1** a payment given for services in excess of the standard charge; gratuity **2** a helpful hint or warning **3** a piece of inside information, esp in betting or investing ▷ *vb* **tips, tipping, tipped 4** to give a tip to [c18 ?from TIP[4]] > ˈ**tipper** *n*

tip[4] (tɪp) *vb* **tips, tipping, tipped** (*tr*) **1** to hit or strike lightly ▷ *n* **2** a light blow [c13 ?from Low G *tippen*]

tip-off *n* **1** a warning or hint, esp given confidentially and based on inside information **2** *basketball* the act or an instance of putting the ball in play by the referee throwing it high between two opposing players ▷ *vb* **tip off 3** (*tr, adv*) to give a hint or warning to

Tipperary (ˌtɪpəˈrɛərɪ) *n* a county of S Republic of Ireland, in Munster province; divided into the North Riding and South Riding: mountainous. County town: Clonmel. Pop: 133 535 (1996). Area: 4255 sq km (1643 sq miles)

tipper truck *or* **lorry** *n* a truck or lorry the rear platform of which can be raised at the front end to enable the load to be discharged

tippet (ˈtɪpɪt) *n* **1** a woman's fur cape for the shoulders **2** the long stole of Anglican clergy worn during a service **3** a long streamer-like part to a sleeve, hood, etc, esp in the 16th century [c14 ?from TIP[1]]

Tippett (ˈtɪpɪt) *n* Sir **Michael** 1905–98, English composer, whose works include the oratorio *A Child of Our Time* (1941) and the operas *The Midsummer Marriage* (1952), *King Priam* (1961), *The Knot Garden* (1970), *The Ice Break* (1976), and *New Year* (1989)

tipping point *n* the moment, event, or stage that marks a decisive change in something or someone

tipple (ˈtɪpᵊl) *vb* **tipples, tippling, tippled 1** to make a habit of taking (alcoholic drink), esp in small quantities ▷ *n* **2** alcoholic drink [c15 back formation from obs. *tippler* tapster, from ?] > ˈ**tippler** *n*

tipstaff (ˈtɪpˌstɑːf) *n* **1** a court official **2** a metal-tipped staff formerly used as a symbol of office [c16 *tipped staff*]

tipster (ˈtɪpstə) *n* a person who sells tips on horse racing, the stock market, etc

tipsy (ˈtɪpsɪ) *adj* **tipsier, tipsiest 1** slightly drunk **2** slightly tilted or tipped; askew [c16 from TIP[2]] > ˈ**tipsily** *adv* > ˈ**tipsiness** *n*

tipsy cake *n Brit* a kind of trifle made from a sponge cake soaked with wine or sherry and decorated with almonds and crystallized fruit

tiptoe (ˈtɪpˌtəʊ) *vb* **tiptoes, tiptoeing, tiptoed** (*intr*) **1** to walk with the heels off the ground **2** to walk silently or stealthily ▷ *n* **3 on tiptoe 3a** on the tips of the toes or on the ball of the foot and the toes **3b** eagerly anticipating something **3c** stealthily or silently ▷ *adv* **4** on tiptoe ▷ *adj* **5** walking or standing on tiptoe

tiptop (ˌtɪpˈtɒp) *adj, adv* **1** at the highest point of health, excellence, etc **2** at the topmost point ▷ *n* **3** the best in quality **4** the topmost point

tipuna *or* **tupuna** (təˈpuːnə) *n* NZ an ancestor [Maori]

tip-up *adj* (*prenominal*) able to be turned upwards around a hinge or pivot: *a tip-up seat*

TIR *abbrev for* Transports Internationaux Routiers [F: International Road Transport]

tirade (taɪˈreɪd) *n* a long angry speech or denunciation [c19 from F, lit.: a pulling, from It. *tirata*, from *tirare* to pull, from ?]

Tiran (tɪˈrɑːn) *n* **Strait of** a strait between the Gulf of Aqaba and the Red Sea. Length: 16 km (10 miles). Width: 8 km (5 miles)

Tirana (tɪˈrɑːnə) *or* **Tiranë** (*Albanian* tiˈranə) *n* the capital of Albania, in the central part 32 km (20 miles) from the Adriatic: founded in the early 17th century by Turks; became capital in 1920; the country's largest city and industrial centre. Pop: 279 000 (1999 est) ▷ www.tirana-online

tire[1] (ˈtaɪə) *vb* **tires, tiring, tired 1** (*tr*) to reduce the energy of, esp by exertion; weary **2** (*tr; often passive*) to reduce the tolerance of; bore or irritate: *I'm tired of the children's chatter* **3** (*intr*) to become wearied or bored; flag [OE *tēorian*, from ?] > ˈ**tiring** *adj*

tire[2] (ˈtaɪə) *n, vb* the US spelling of **tyre**

tired (ˈtaɪəd) *adj* **1** weary; fatigued **2** no longer fresh; hackneyed **3 tired and emotional** *euphemistic* drunk > ˈ**tiredness** *n*

Tiree (taɪˈriː) *n* an island off the W coast of Scotland, in the Inner Hebrides. Pop: 1054 (latest est). Area: 78 sq km (30 sq miles)

tireless (ˈtaɪəlɪs) *adj* unable to be tired > ˈ**tirelessly** *adv* > ˈ**tirelessness** *n*

Tiresias (taɪˈriːsɪˌæs) *n Greek myth* a blind soothsayer of Thebes, who revealed to Oedipus that the latter had murdered his father and married his mother

tiresome (ˈtaɪəsəm) *adj* boring and irritating > ˈ**tiresomely** *adv* > ˈ**tiresomeness** *n*

tirewoman (ˈtaɪəˌwʊmən) *n, pl* **tirewomen** an obsolete term for a lady's maid [c17 from *tire* (obs.) to ATTIRE]

Tîrgu Mureş (*Romanian* ˈtirgu ˈmureʃ) *n* a city in central Romania: manufacturing and cultural centre. Pop: 165 534 (1997 est)

Tirich Mir (ˈtɪərɪtʃ ˈmɪə) *n* a mountain in N Pakistan: highest peak of the Hindu Kush. Height: 7690 m (25 230 ft)

tiring room (ˈtaɪərɪŋ) *n arch* a dressing room

tiro (ˈtaɪrəʊ) *n, pl* **tiros** a variant spelling of **tyro**

Tirol (tɪˈrəʊl, ˈtɪrəʊl; *German* tiˈroːl) *n* a variant spelling of **Tyrol** > **Tirolese** (ˌtɪrəˈliːz) *or* ˌ**Tiroˈlean** *adj, n*

Tirpitz (*German* ˈtɪrpɪts) *n* **Alfred von** (ˈalfreːt fɔn) 1849–1930, German admiral: as secretary of state for the Imperial Navy (1897–1916), he created the modern German navy, which challenged British supremacy at sea

Tiruchirapalli (ˌtɪrətʃɪrəˈpʌlɪ, tɪˌruːtʃɪˈrɑːpəlɪ) *or* **Trichinopoly** *n* an industrial city in S India, in central Tamil Nadu on the Cauvery River: dominated by a rock fortress 83 m (273 ft) high. Pop: 387 223 (1991)

Tirunelveli (ˌtɪrʊˈnɛlvɛlɪ) *n* a city in S India, in Tamil Nadu: site of St Francis Xavier's first preaching in India; textile manufacturing. Pop: 135 825 (1991)

'tis (tɪz) *poetic or dialect contraction of* it is

Tisa (ˈtisa) *n* the Slavonic and Romanian name for the **Tisza**

tisane (tɪˈzæn) *n* an infusion of leaves or flowers [c19 from F, from L *ptisana* barley water]

Tishri *Hebrew* (tɪʃˈriː) *n* (in the Jewish calendar) the seventh month of the year according to biblical

Tt

reckoning and the first month of the civil year, falling in September and October [c19 from Heb.]

Tisiphone (tɪˈsɪfənɪ) *n Greek myth* one of the three Furies; the others are Alecto and Megaera

Tissot (ˈtɪsəʊ) *n* **James Joseph Jacques** 1836–1902, French painter and etcher, best known for scenes of fashionable Victorian life painted in England

tissue (ˈtɪsjuː, ˈtɪʃuː) *n* **1** a part of an organism consisting of a large number of cells having a similar structure and function: *nerve tissue* **2** a thin piece of soft absorbent paper used as a disposable handkerchief, towel, etc **3** See **tissue paper** **4** an interwoven series: *a tissue of lies* **5** a woven cloth, esp of a light gauzy nature ▷ *vb* **tissues, tissuing, tissued** (*tr*) **6** to decorate or clothe with tissue or tissue paper [c14 from OF *tissu* woven cloth, from *tistre* to weave, from L *texere*]

tissue culture *n* **1** the growth of small pieces of animal or plant tissue in a sterile controlled medium **2** the tissue produced

tissue paper *n* very thin soft delicate paper used to wrap breakable goods, as decoration, etc

Tisza (*Hungarian* ˈtisɔ) *n* a river in S central Europe, rising in the W Ukraine and flowing west, forming part of the border between the Ukraine and Romania, then southwest across Hungary into Serbia to join the Danube north of Belgrade. Slavonic and Romanian name: **Tisa**

tit[1] (tɪt) *n* any of numerous small active Old World songbirds, esp the bluetit, great tit, etc. They have a short bill and feed on insects and seeds [c16 ? imit., applied to small animate or inanimate objects]

tit[2] (tɪt) *n* **1** *sl* a female breast **2** a teat or nipple **3** *derog* a young woman **4** *sl* a despicable or unpleasant person [OE *titt*]

Tit. *Bible abbrev for* Titus

titan (ˈtaɪtᵊn) *n* a person of great strength or size [after TITAN]

Titan (ˈtaɪtᵊn) *or (fem)* **Titaness** *n Greek myth* **1** any of a family of primordial gods, the sons and daughters of Uranus (sky) and Gaea (earth) **2** any of the offspring of the children of Uranus and Gaea > **Titanesque** (ˌtaɪtəˈnɛsk) *adj*

Titania (tɪˈtɑːnɪə) *n* **1** (in medieval folklore) the queen of the fairies and wife of Oberon **2** (in classical antiquity) a poetic epithet used of Circe, Diana, Latona, or Pyrrha

titanic (taɪˈtænɪk) *adj* possessing or requiring colossal strength: *a titanic battle*

titanium (taɪˈteɪnɪəm) *n* a strong malleable white metallic element, which is very corrosion-resistant. It is used in the manufacture of strong lightweight alloys, esp aircraft parts. Symbol: Ti; atomic no.: 22; atomic wt.: 47.88 [c18 NL; see TITAN, -IUM]

titanium dioxide *n* a white powder used chiefly as a pigment. Formula: TiO_2. Also called: **titanium oxide, titanic oxide, titania**

titbit (ˈtɪtˌbɪt) *or esp US* **tidbit** *n* **1** a tasty small piece of food; dainty **2** a pleasing scrap of anything, such as scandal [c17 ?from dialect *tid* tender, from ?]

titchy *or* **tichy** (ˈtɪtʃɪ) *adj* **titchier, titchiest** *or* **tichier, tichiest** *Brit sl* very small; tiny [c20 from *tich* or *titch* a small person, from *Little Tich*, stage name of Harry Relph (1867–1928), E actor noted for his small stature]

titfer (ˈtɪtfə) *n Brit sl* a hat [from rhyming slang *tit for tat*]

tit for tat *n* an equivalent given in return or retaliation; blow for blow [c16 from earlier *tip for tap*]

tithe (taɪð) *n* **1** (*often pl*) a tenth part of produce, income, or profits, contributed for the support of the church or clergy **2** any levy, esp of one tenth **3** a tenth or a very small part of anything ▷ *vb* **tithes, tithing, tithed** **4** (*tr*) **4a** to exact or demand a tithe from **4b** to levy a tithe upon **5** (*intr*) to pay a tithe or tithes [OE *teogoth*] > ˈ**tithable** *adj*

tithe barn *n* a large barn where, formerly, the agricultural tithe of a parish was stored

Tithonus (tɪˈθəʊnəs) *n Greek myth* the son of Laomedon of Troy who was loved by the goddess Eos. She asked that he be made immortal but forgot to ask that he be made eternally young. When he aged she turned him into a grasshopper

titi (ˈtiːtiː) *n, pl* **titis** any of a genus of small New World monkeys of South America, having beautifully coloured fur and a long nonprehensile tail [via Sp. from Aymara, lit.: little cat]

Titian (ˈtɪʃən) *n* original name *Tiziano Vecellio*. ?1490–1576, Italian painter of the Venetian school, noted for his religious and mythological works, such as *Bacchus and Ariadne* (1523), and his portraits

Titian red *n* a reddish-yellow colour, as in the hair colour in many of the works of Titian

Titicaca (*Spanish* titiˈkaka) *n* **Lake** a lake between S Peru and W Bolivia, in the Andes: the highest large lake in the world; drained by the Desaguadero River flowing into Lake Poopó. Area: 8135 sq km (3141 sq miles). Altitude: 3809 m (12 497 ft). Depth: 370 m (1214 ft)

titillate (ˈtɪtɪˌleɪt) *vb* **titillates, titillating, titillated** (*tr*) **1** to arouse or excite pleasurably **2** to cause a tickling or tingling sensation in, esp by touching [c17 from L *tītillāre*] > ˈ**titilˌlating** *adj* > ˌ**titilˈlation** *n*

titivate *or* **tittivate** (ˈtɪtɪˌveɪt) *vb* **titivates, titivating, titivated** *or* **tittivates, tittivating, tittivated** to smarten up; spruce up [c19 earlier *tidivate*, ? based on TIDY & CULTIVATE] > ˌ**titiˈvation** *or* ˌ**tittiˈvation** *n*

titlark (ˈtɪtˌlɑːk) *n* another name for **pipit**, esp the meadow pipit [c17 from TIT[1] + LARK[1]]

title (ˈtaɪtᵊl) *n* **1** the distinctive name of a work of art, musical or literary composition, etc **2** a descriptive name or heading of a section of a book, speech, etc **3** See **title page** **4** a name or epithet signifying rank, office, or function **5** a formal designation, such as *Mr* **6** an appellation designating nobility **7** *films* **7a** short for **subtitle** **7b** written material giving credits in a film or television programme **8** *sport* a championship **9** *law* **9a** the legal right to possession of property, esp real property **9b** the basis of such right **9c** the documentary evidence of such right: *title deeds* **10a** any customary or established right **10b** a claim based on such a right **11** a definite spiritual charge or office in the church as a prerequisite for ordination **12** *RC Church* a titular church ▷ *vb* **titles, titling, titled** **13** (*tr*) to give a title to [c13 from OF, from L *titulus*]

title deed *n* a document evidencing a person's legal right or title to property, esp real property

titleholder (ˈtaɪtᵊlˌhəʊldə) *n* a person who holds a title, esp a sporting championship

title page *n* the page in a book that gives the title, author, publisher, etc

title role *n* the role of the character after whom a play, etc, is named

titmouse (ˈtɪtˌmaʊs) *n, pl* **titmice** another name for **tit**[1] [c14 *titemous*, from *tite* (see TIT[1]) + MOUSE]

Tito (ˈtiːtəʊ) *n* **Marshal** original name *Josip Broz*. 1892–1980, Yugoslav statesman, who led the communist guerrilla resistance to German occupation during World War II; prime minister of Yugoslavia (1945–53) and president (1953–80)

Titograd (*Serbo-Croat* ˈtitɔgraːd) *n* the former name (1946–92) of **Podgorica**

titrate (ˈtaɪtreɪt) *vb* **titrates, titrating, titrated** (*tr*) to measure the volume or the concentration of (a solution) by titration [c19 from F *titrer*; see TITRE] > **tiˈtratable** *adj*

titration (taɪˈtreɪʃən) *n* an operation in which a measured amount of one solution is added to a known quantity of another solution until the reaction between the two is complete. If the concentration of one solution is known, that of the other can be calculated

titre *or US* **titer** (ˈtaɪtə) *n* the concentration of a solution as determined by titration [c19 from F *titre* proportion of gold or silver in an alloy, from OF *title* TITLE]

titter ('tɪtə) *vb (intr)* **1** to snigger, esp derisively or in a suppressed way ▷ *n* **2** a suppressed laugh, chuckle, or snigger [c17 imit.] > '**titterer** *n* > '**tittering** *adj*

tittle ('tɪtᵊl) *n* **1** a small mark in printing or writing, esp a diacritic **2** a jot; particle [c14 from Med. L *titulus* label, from L: title]

tittle-tattle *n* **1** idle chat or gossip ▷ *vb* **tittle-tattles, tittle-tattling, tittle-tattled 2** *(intr)* to chatter or gossip > '**tittle-,tattler** *n*

tittup ('tɪtəp) *vb* **tittups, tittupping, tittupped** *or US* **tittups, tittuping, tittuped 1** *(intr)* to prance or frolic ▷ *n* **2** a caper [c18 (in the sense: a horse's gallop): prob. imit.]

titubation (ˌtɪtjʊ'beɪʃən) *n pathol* a disordered gait characterized by stumbling or staggering, often caused by a lesion of the cerebellum [c17 from L *titubātiō*, from *titubāre* to reel]

titular ('tɪtjʊlə) *adj* **1** of, relating to, or of the nature of a title **2** in name only **3** bearing a title **4** *RC Church* designating any of certain churches in Rome to whom cardinals or bishops are attached as their nominal incumbents ▷ *n* **5** the bearer of a title **6** the bearer of a nominal office [c18 from F *titulaire*, from L *titulus* title]

Titus ('taɪtəs) *n* **1** *New Testament* **1a Saint** a Greek disciple and helper of Saint Paul. Feast day: Jan 26 or Aug 25 **1b** the book written to him (in full **The Epistle of Paul the Apostle to Titus**) **2** full name *Titus Flavius Sabinus Vespasianus*. ?40–81 AD, Roman emperor (78–81 AD)

Ti2GO *text messaging abbrev for* time to go

Tiu ('tiːuː) *n* (in Anglo-Saxon mythology) the god of war and the sky. Norse counterpart: **Tyr**

Tivoli ('tɪvəlɪ; *Italian* 'tiːvoli) *n* a town in central Italy, east of Rome: a summer resort in Roman times; contains the Renaissance Villa d'Este and the remains of Hadrian's Villa. Pop: 55 030 (1990). Ancient name: **Tibur**

tizzy ('tɪzɪ) *n, pl* **tizzies** *inf* a state of confusion or excitement. Also called: **tizz, tiz-woz** [c19 from ?]

Tjirebon ('tʃɪərəˌbɒn) *n* a port in S central Indonesia, on N Java on the Java Sea: scene of the signing of the **Tjirebon Agreement** of Indonesian independence (1946) by the Netherlands. Pop: 245 307 (1990)

T-junction *n* a road junction in which one road joins another at right angles but does not cross it

TKO *boxing abbrev for* technical knockout

Tl *the chemical symbol for* thallium

Tlaxcala (*Spanish* tlas'kala) *n* **1** a state of S central Mexico: the smallest Mexican state; formerly an Indian principality, the chief Indian ally of Cortés in the conquest of Mexico. Capital: Tlaxcala. Pop: 961 912 (2000 est). Area: 3914 sq km (1511 sq miles) **2** a city in E central Mexico, on the central plateau, capital of Tlaxcala state: the church of San Francisco (founded 1521 by Cortés) is the oldest in the Americas. Pop: 25 000 (1990 est). Official name: **Tlaxcala de Xicohténcatl**

Tlemcen (*French* tlɛmsɛn) *n* a city in NW Algeria: capital of an Arab kingdom from the 12th to the late 14th century. Pop: 155 162 (1998)

Tm *the chemical symbol for* thulium

TM *abbrev for* transcendental meditation

tmesis (tə'miːsɪs) *n* interpolation of a word or words between the parts of a compound word, as in *every-blooming-where* [c16 via L from Gk, lit.: a cutting, from *temnein* to cut]

TN *abbrev for* Tennessee

TNT *n* 2,4,6-trinitrotoluene; a yellow solid: used chiefly as a high explosive

T-number *or* **T number** *n photog* a function of the f-number of a lens that takes into account the light transmitted by the lens [from *T(otal Light Transmission) Number*]

to (tuː; *unstressed* tʊ, tə) *prep* **1** used to indicate the destination of the subject or object of an action: *he climbed to the top* **2** used to mark the indirect object of a verb: *telling stories to children* **3** used to mark the infinitive of a verb: *he wanted to go* **4** as far as; until: *working from Monday to Friday* **5** used to indicate equality: *16 ounces to the pound* **6** against; upon; onto: *put your ear to the wall* **7** before the hour of: *five minutes to four* **8** accompanied by: *dancing to loud music* **9** as compared with, as against: *the score was eight to three* **10** used to indicate a resulting condition: *they starved to death* ▷ *adv* **11** towards a fixed position, esp (of a door) closed [OE *tō*]

toad (təʊd) *n* **1** any of a group of amphibians similar to frogs but more terrestrial, having a drier warty skin **2** a loathsome person [OE *tādige*, from ?] > '**toadish** *adj*

toadfish ('təʊdˌfɪʃ) *n, pl* **toadfish** *or* **toadfishes** any of various spiny-finned marine fishes of tropical and temperate seas

toadflax ('təʊdˌflæks) *n* a perennial plant having narrow leaves and spurred two-lipped yellow-orange flowers. Also called: **butter-and-eggs**

toad-in-the-hole *n Brit & Austral* a dish made of sausages baked in a batter

toadstone ('təʊdˌstəʊn) *n rare* an intrusive volcanic rock occurring in limestone [c18 ?from a supposed resemblance to a toad's spotted skin]

toadstool ('təʊdˌstuːl) *n (not in technical use)* any basidiomycetous fungus with a capped spore-producing body that is not edible. ▷ Cf **mushroom**

toady ('təʊdɪ) *n, pl* **toadies 1** Also: **toadeater** a person who flatters and ingratiates himself or herself in a servile way; sycophant ▷ *vb* **toadies, toadying, toadied 2** to fawn on and flatter (someone) [c19 shortened from *toadeater*, orig. a quack's assistant who pretended to eat toads, hence a flatterer] > '**toadyish** *adj* > '**toadyism** *n*

Toamasina (*Portuguese* tə̃uma'sinə) *n* a port in E Madagascar, on the Indian Ocean: the country's chief commercial centre. Pop: 127 441 (1993). Former name (until 1979): **Tamatave**

Tt

to and fro *adv*, **to-and-fro** *adj* **1** back and forth **2** here and there > '**toing and** '**froing** *n*

toast¹ (təʊst) *n* **1a** sliced bread browned by exposure to heat **1b** *(as modifier): a toast rack* **2 be toast** *inf* to face certain destruction or defeat ▷ *vb* **3** *(tr)* to brown under a grill or over a fire: *to toast cheese* **4** to warm or be warmed: *to toast one's hands by the fire* [c14 from OF *toster*, from L *tōstus* parched, from *torrēre* to dry with heat]

toast² (təʊst) *n* **1** a tribute or proposal of health, success, etc, given to a person or thing and marked by people raising glasses and drinking together **2** a person or thing honoured by such a tribute or proposal **3** (esp formerly) an attractive woman to whom such tributes are frequently made ▷ *vb* **4** to propose or drink a toast to (a person or thing) **5** *(intr)* to add vocal effects to a prerecorded track: a disc-jockey technique [c17 (in the sense: a lady to whom the company is asked to drink): from TOAST¹, from the idea that the name of the lady would flavour the drink like a piece of spiced toast] > '**toaster** *n*

toaster ('təʊstə) *n* a device, esp an electrical device, for toasting bread

toastmaster ('təʊstˌmɑːstə) *n* a person who introduces speakers, proposes toasts, etc, at public dinners > '**toast,mistress** *fem n*

toasty *or* **toastie** ('təʊstɪ) *n, pl* **toasties** a toasted sandwich ▷ *adj* **toastier, toastiest** tasting or smelling like toast

Tob. *abbrev for* Tobit

tobacco (tə'bækəʊ) *n, pl* **tobaccos** *or* **tobaccoes 1** any of a genus of plants having mildly narcotic properties, one species of which is cultivated as the chief source of commercial tobacco **2** the leaves of certain of these plants dried and prepared for snuff, chewing, or smoking [c16 from Sp. *tabaco*, ?from Taino: leaves rolled for smoking, assumed by the Spaniards to be the name of the plant] > **to'baccoless** *adj*

tobacco mosaic virus *n* the virus that causes mosaic disease in tobacco and related plants: its discovery provided the first evidence of the existence of viruses. Abbrev: **TMV**

tobacconist (tə'bækənɪst) *n chiefly Brit* a person or shop that sells tobacco, cigarettes, pipes, etc

Tobago (tə'beɪgəʊ) *n* an island in the SE Caribbean, northeast of Trinidad: ceded to Britain in 1814; joined with Trinidad in 1888 as a British colony; part of the independent republic of Trinidad and Tobago. Pop: 46 400 (1990) > **Tobagonian** (ˌtəʊbə'gəʊnɪən) *adj, n*

-to-be *adj (in combination)* about to be; future: *a mother-to-be; the bride-to-be*

Tobey ('təʊbɪ) *n* **Mark** 1890–1976, US painter. Influenced by Chinese calligraphy, he devised a style of improvisatory abstract painting called "white writing"

Tobit ('təʊbɪt) *n Old Testament* **1** a pious Jew who was released from blindness through the help of the archangel Raphael **2** a book of the Apocrypha relating this story

toboggan (tə'bɒgən) *n* **1** a light wooden frame on runners used for sliding over snow and ice **2** a long narrow sledge made of a thin board curved upwards at the front ▷ *vb* **toboggans, tobogganing, tobogganed** *(intr)* **3** to ride on a toboggan [C19 from Canad F, of Amerind origin] > **to'bogganer** *or* **to'bogganist** *n* ▷ www.bobsleigh.com

Tobol (*Russian* ta'bɔl) *n* a river in central Asia, rising in N Kazakhstan and flowing northeast into Russia to join the Irtysh River. Length: about 1300 km (800 miles)

Tobolsk (*Russian* ta'bɔljsk) *n* a town in central Russia, at the confluence of the Irtysh and Tobol Rivers: the chief centre for the early Russian colonization of Siberia. Pop: 100 000 (1989 est)

Tobruk (tə'brʊk, təʊ-) *n* a small port in NE Libya, in E Cyrenaica on the Mediterranean coast road: scene of severe fighting in World War II: taken from the Italians by the British in January 1941, from the British by the Germans in June 1942, and finally taken by the British in November 1942

toby ('təʊbɪ) *n, pl* **tobies** *NZ* a water stopcock at the boundary of a street and house section

toby jug *n* a beer mug or jug in the form of a stout seated man wearing a three-cornered hat and smoking a pipe. Also called: **toby** [C19 from the familiar form of the name *Tobias*]

TOC *or* **toc** (tɒk) (in Britain) *n acronym for* train operating company

Tocantins (*Portuguese* tokã'tĩs) *n* **1** a state of N Brazil, created from the northern part of Goiás state in 1988. Capital: Palmas. Pop: 1 155 251 (2000). Area: 278 421 sq km (107 499 sq miles) **2** a river in E Brazil, rising in S central Goiás state and flowing generally north to the Pará River. Length: about 2700 km (1700 miles)

toccata (tə'kɑːtə) *n* a rapid keyboard composition for organ, harpsichord, etc, usually in a rhythmically free style [C18 from It., lit.: touched, from *toccare* to play (an instrument)]

Toc H ('tɒk 'eɪtʃ) *n* a society formed after World War I to encourage Christian comradeship [C20 from the obs. telegraphic code for T.H., initials of *Talbot House*, Poperinge, Belgium, the original headquarters of the society]

Tocharian *or* **Tokharian** (tɒ'kɑːrɪən) *n* **1** a member of an Asian people who lived in the Tarim Basin until around 800 AD **2** the language of this people, known from records in a N Indian script of the 7th and 8th centuries AD [C20 ult. from Gk *Tokharoi*, from ?]

tocopherol (tɒ'kɒfəˌrɒl) *n* any of a group of fat-soluble alcohols that occur in wheat-germ oil, lettuce, egg yolk, etc. Also called: **vitamin E** [C20 from *toco-*, from Gk *tokos* offspring + *-pher-*, from *pherein* to bear + -OL[1]]

Tocqueville ('təʊkvɪl, 'tɒk-; *French* tɔkvil) *n* **Alexis Charles Henri Maurice Clérel de** (alɛksi ʃarl ɑ̃ri mɔris klerɛl də) 1805–59, French politician and political writer. His chief works are *De la Démocratie en Amérique* (1835–40) and *L'Ancien régime et la révolution* (1856)

tocsin ('tɒksɪn) *n* **1** an alarm or warning signal, esp one sounded on a bell **2** an alarm bell [C16 from F, from OF *toquassen*, from OProvençal, from *tocar* to touch + *senh* bell, from L *signum*]

tod (tɒd) *n* **on one's tod** *Brit sl* on one's own [C19 rhyming sl *Tod Sloan/alone*, after *Tod* Sloan, a jockey]

today (tə'deɪ) *n* **1** this day, as distinct from yesterday or tomorrow **2** the present age ▷ *adv* **3** during or on this day **4** nowadays [OE *tō dæge*, lit.: on this day]

Todd (tɒd) *n* Baron **Alexander Robertus** 1907–97, Scottish chemist, noted for his research into the structure of nucleic acids: Nobel prize for chemistry 1957

toddle ('tɒdᵊl) *vb* **toddles, toddling, toddled** *(intr)* **1** to walk with short unsteady steps, as a child **2** (foll by *off*) *jocular* to depart **3** (foll by *round, over*, etc) *jocular* to stroll ▷ *n* **4** the act or an instance of toddling [C16 (Scot & N English): from ?]

toddler ('tɒdlə) *n* a young child, usually between the ages of one and two and a half

toddy ('tɒdɪ) *n, pl* **toddies** **1** a drink made from spirits, esp whisky, hot water, sugar, and usually lemon juice **2** the sap of various palm trees used as a beverage [C17 from Hindi *tārī* juice of the palmyra palm, from *tār* palmyra palm, from Sansk. *tāra*]

to-do (tə'duː) *n, pl* **to-dos** a commotion, fuss, or quarrel

toe (təʊ) *n* **1** any one of the digits of the foot **2** the corresponding part in other vertebrates **3** the part of a shoe, etc, covering the toes **4** anything resembling a toe in shape or position **5** **on one's toes** alert **6** **tread on someone's toes** to offend a person, esp by trespassing on his or her field of responsibility ▷ *vb* **toes, toeing, toed** **7** *(tr)* to touch, kick, or mark with the toe **8** *(tr)* to drive (a nail, etc) obliquely **9** *(intr)* to walk with the toes pointing in a specified direction: *to toe inwards* **10** **toe the line** *or* **mark** to conform to expected attitudes, standards, etc [OE *tā*]

toe and heel *n* a technique used by racing drivers on sharp bends, in which the brake and accelerator are operated simultaneously by the toe and heel of the right foot

toecap ('təʊˌkæp) *n* a reinforced covering for the toe of a boot or shoe

toed (təʊd) *adj* **1** having a part resembling a toe **2** fixed by nails driven in at the foot **3** *(in combination)* having a toe or toes as specified: *five-toed; thick-toed*

toehold ('təʊˌhəʊld) *n* **1** a small foothold to facilitate climbing **2** any means of gaining access, support, etc **3** a wrestling hold in which the opponent's toe is held and his or her leg twisted

toe-in *n* a slight forward convergence given to the wheels of motor vehicles to improve steering

toenail ('təʊˌneɪl) *n* **1** a thin horny translucent plate covering part of the surface of the end joint of each toe **2** *carpentry* a nail driven obliquely ▷ *vb* **3** *(tr) carpentry* to join (beams) by driving nails obliquely

toerag ('təʊˌræg) *n Brit sl* a contemptible or despicable person [C20 orig., a beggar, tramp: from the rags wrapped round their feet]

toe-to-toe *inf adv* **1** in one-to-one combat or in direct competition: *there aren't many fighters willing to go toe-to-toe with him* ▷ *adj* **2** (of battles, confrontations, or contests) involving two people or groups fighting with or competing against each other: *a toe-to-toe battle* ▷ *n* **3** a fight, confrontation, or contest between two people or groups

toey ('təʊɪ) *adj Austral sl* nervous and restless; anxious

toff (tɒf) *n Brit sl* a well-dressed or upper-class person, esp a man [C19 ? var. of TUFT, nickname for a titled student at Oxford University, wearing a cap with a gold tassel]

toffee *or* **toffy** ('tɒfɪ) *n, pl* **toffees** *or* **toffies** 1 a sweet made from sugar or treacle boiled with butter, nuts, etc 2 **for toffee** (preceded by *can't*) *inf* to be incompetent at: *he can't sing for toffee* [c19 var. of earlier *taffy*]

toffee-apple *n* an apple fixed on a stick and coated with a thin layer of toffee

toffee-nosed *adj sl, chiefly Brit* pretentious or supercilious; used esp of snobbish people

toft (tɒft) *n Brit history* 1 a homestead 2 a homestead and its arable land [OE]

tofu ('təʊ,fuː) *n* unfermented soya-bean curd, a food with a soft cheeselike consistency [from Japanese]

tog[1] (tɒg) *inf* ▷ *vb* **togs, togging, togged** 1 (often foll by *up* or *out*) to dress oneself, esp in smart clothes ▷ *n* 2 See **togs** [c18 ?from obs. cant *togemans* coat, from L *toga* TOGA + *-mans*, from ?]

tog[2] (tɒg) *n* **a** a unit of thermal resistance used to measure the power of insulation of a fabric, garment, quilt, etc **b** (*as modifier*): *tog-rating* [c20 arbitrary coinage from TOG[1] (n)]

toga ('təʊgə) *n* 1 a garment worn by citizens of ancient Rome, consisting of a piece of cloth draped around the body 2 a robe of office [c16 from L] > **togaed** ('təʊgəd) *adj*

together (tə'gɛðə) *adv* 1 with cooperation and interchange between constituent elements, members, etc: *we worked together* 2 in or into contact with each other: *to stick papers together* 3 in or into one place; with each other: *the people are gathered together* 4 at the same time 5 considered collectively: *all our wages put together couldn't buy that car* 6 continuously: *working for eight hours together* 7 closely or compactly united or held: *water will hold the dough together* 8 mutually or reciprocally: *to multiply seven and eight together* 9 *inf* organized: *to get things together* ▷ *adj* 10 *sl* self-possessed, competent, and well-organized 11 **together with** (*prep*) in addition to [OE *tōgædre*]

USAGE See at **plus**

togetherness (tə'gɛðənɪs) *n* a feeling of closeness or affection from being united with other people

toggery ('tɒgərɪ) *n inf* clothes; togs

toggle ('tɒgᵊl) *n* 1 a peg or rod at the end of a rope, chain, or cable, for fastening by insertion through an eye in another rope, chain, etc 2 a bar-shaped button inserted through a loop for fastening 3 a toggle joint or a device having such a joint ▷ *vb* **toggles, toggling, toggled** 4 (*tr*) to supply or fasten with a toggle [c18 from ?]

toggle joint *n* a device consisting of two arms pivoted at a common joint and at their outer ends and used to apply pressure by straightening the angle between the two arms

toggle switch *n* 1 an electric switch having a projecting lever that is manipulated in a particular way to open or close a circuit 2 a computer device used to turn a feature on or off

Togliatti (,tɒlɪ'ætɪ) *n* a city in W central Russia, on the Volga River: automobile industry: renamed in honour of Palmiro Togliatti, an Italian communist. Pop: 720 300 (1999 est). Former name (until 1964): **Stavropol** Russian name: **Tolyatti**

Togo[1] ('təʊgəʊ) *n* a republic in West Africa, on the Gulf of Guinea: became French Togoland (a League of Nations mandate) after the division of German Togoland in 1922; independent since 1960. Official language: French. Religion: animist majority. Currency: franc. Capital: Lomé. Pop: 5 153 000 (2001 est). Area: 56 700 sq km (20 900 sq miles) > **Togolese** (,təʊgə'liːz) *adj, n*

▷ www.republicoftogo.com

▷ www.afrika.com/togo

Togo[2] ('təʊgəʊ) *n* Marquis **Heihachiro** (,heɪhɑː'tʃiːrəʊ) 1847–1934, Japanese admiral, who commanded the Japanese fleet in the war with Russia (1904–05)

Togoland ('təʊgəʊ,lænd) *n* a former German protectorate in West Africa on the Gulf of Guinea: divided in 1922 into the League of Nations mandates of British Togoland (west) and French Togoland (east); the former joined Ghana in 1957; the latter became independent as Togo in 1960 > '**Togo,lander** *n*

togs (tɒgz) *pl n Inf* 1 clothes 2 *Austral, NZ, & Irish* a swimming costume [from TOG[1]]

toheroa (,təʊə'rəʊə) *n* a large edible bivalve mollusc of New Zealand with a distinctive flavour [from Maori]

tohunga ('tɒhʊŋə) *n* NZ a Maori priest, the repository of traditional lore

toil[1] (tɔɪl) *n* 1 hard or exhausting work ▷ *vb* (*intr*) 2 to labour 3 to progress with slow painful movements [c13 from Anglo-F *toiler* to struggle, from OF *toeillier* to confuse, from L *tudiculāre* to stir, ult. from *tundere* to beat] > '**toiler** *n*

toil[2] (tɔɪl) *n* 1 (*often pl*) a net or snare 2 *arch* a trap for wild beasts [c16 from OF *toile*, from L *tēla* loom]

toile (twɑːl) *n* 1 a transparent linen or cotton fabric 2 a garment of exclusive design made up in cheap cloth so that alterations can be made [c19 from F, from L *tēla* a loom]

toilet ('tɔɪlɪt) *n* 1 another word for **lavatory** 2 *old-fashioned* the act of dressing and preparing oneself 3 *old-fashioned* a dressing table 4 *rare* costume 5 the cleansing of a wound, etc, after an operation or childbirth [c16 from F *toilette* dress, from TOILE]

toilet paper *or* **tissue** *n* thin absorbent paper, often wound in a roll round a cardboard cylinder (**toilet roll**), used for cleaning oneself after defecation or urination

toiletry ('tɔɪlɪtrɪ) *n, pl* **toiletries** an object or cosmetic used in making up, dressing, etc

toilet set *n* a matching set consisting of a hairbrush, comb, mirror, and clothes brush

toilette (twɑː'lɛt) *n* another word for **toilet** (sense 2) [c16 from F; see TOILET]

toilet water *n* a form of liquid perfume lighter than cologne

toilsome ('tɔɪlsəm) *or* **toilful** *adj* laborious > '**toilsomely** *adv* > '**toilsomeness** *n*

toitoi ('tɔɪtɔɪ) *n* a tall New Zealand grass with feathery seed-heads [from Maori]

Tojo ('təʊdʒəʊ) *n* **Hideki** ('hiːdɛ,kiː) 1885–1948, Japanese soldier and statesman; minister of war (1940–41) and premier (1941–44); hanged as a war criminal

tokamak ('təʊkə,mæk) *n physics* a toroidal reactor used in thermonuclear experiments, in which strong axial magnetic fields keep the plasma from contacting the external walls [c20 from Russian acronym, from *to(roidál'naya) kám(era s) ak(siál'nym magnitnym pólem)*, toroidal chamber with magnetic field]

Tokay (təʊ'keɪ) *n* 1 a sweet wine made near Tokaj, Hungary 2 a variety of grape used to make this 3 a similar wine made elsewhere

Tokelau Islands ('təʊkə,laʊ) *pl n* an island group in the South Pacific composed of three atolls, Nukunono, Atafu, and Fakaofo, which in 1948 was included within the territorial boundaries of New Zealand. Pop: 1577 (1991). Area: about 11 sq km (4 sq miles)

token ('təʊkən) *n* 1 an indication, warning, or sign of something 2 a symbol or visible representation of something 3 something that indicates authority, proof, etc 4 a metal or plastic disc, such as a substitute for currency for use in slot machines 5 a memento 6 a gift voucher that can be used as payment for goods of a specified value 7 (*modifier*) as a matter of form only; nominal: *a token increase in salary* ▷ *vb* 8 (*tr*) to act or serve as a warning or symbol of; betoken [OE *tācen*]

tokenism ('təʊkə,nɪzəm) *n* the practice of making only a token effort or doing no more than the minimum, esp in order to comply with a law > '**toke,nist** *adj*

token money *n* coins having greater face value than the value of their metal content

token strike *n* a brief strike intended to convey strength of feeling on a disputed issue

token vote *n* a Parliamentary vote of money in which the amount quoted is not binding

tokoloshe (ˌtɒkɒˈlɒʃ, -ˈlɒʃɪ) *n* (in Bantu folklore) a malevolent mythical manlike animal. Also called: **tikoloshe** [from Xhosa *uthikoloshe*]

toktokkie (ˈtɒkˌtɒkɪ) *n* a large S African beetle [from Afrik., from Du. *tokken* to tap]

Tokugawa Iyeyasu (ˌtəʊkuːˈgɑːwə ˌiːjeɪˈjɑːsuː) *n* See (Tokugawa) **Iyeyasu**

Tokyo (ˈtəʊkjəʊ, -kɪˌəʊ) *n* the capital of Japan, a port on SE Honshu on **Tokyo Bay** (an inlet of the Pacific): part of the largest conurbation in the world (the Tokyo-Yukohama metropolitan area) of over 25 million people; major industrial centre and the chief cultural centre of Japan. Pop: 7 966 195 (1995)
▹ www.chijihonbu.metro.tokyo.jp/english/index.htm

tolbooth (ˈtəʊlˌbuːθ, -ˌbuːð, ˈtɒl-) *n* **1** *chiefly Scot* a town hall **2** a variant spelling of **tollbooth**

tolbutamide (tɒlˈbjuːtəˌmaɪd) *n* a synthetic crystalline compound used in the treatment of diabetes to lower blood glucose concentrations [c20 from TOL(UENE) + BUT(YRIC ACID) + AMIDE]

told (təʊld) *vb* **1** the past tense and past participle of **tell**[1] ▹ *adj* **2** See **all told**

tole (təʊl) *n* enamelled or lacquered metal ware, popular in the 18th century [from F *tôle* sheet metal, from F (dialect): table, from L *tabula* table]

Toledo *n* **1** (tɒˈleɪdəʊ; *Spanish* toˈleðo) a city in central Spain, on the River Tagus: capital of Visigothic Spain, and of Castile from 1087 to 1560; famous for steel and swords since the first century. Pop: 63 560 (1991). Ancient name: **Toletum** (təˈliːtəm) **2** (təˈliːdəʊ) an inland port in NW Ohio, on Lake Erie: one of the largest coal-shipping ports in the world; transportation and industrial centre; university (1872). Pop: 313 619 (2000) **3** a fine-tapered sword or sword blade

tolerable (ˈtɒlərəbᵊl) *adj* **1** able to be tolerated; endurable **2** permissible **3** *inf* fairly good > ˌ**toleraˈbility** *n* > ˈ**tolerably** *adv*

tolerance (ˈtɒlərəns) *n* **1** the state or quality of being tolerant **2** capacity to endure something, esp pain or hardship **3** the permitted variation in some characteristic of an object or workpiece **4** the capacity to endure the effects of a poison or other substance, esp after it has been taken over a prolonged period

tolerance zone *n* a designated area where prostitutes can work without being arrested

tolerant (ˈtɒlərənt) *adj* **1** able to tolerate the beliefs, actions, etc, of others **2** permissive **3** able to withstand extremes **4** exhibiting tolerance to a drug > ˈ**tolerantly** *adv*

tolerate (ˈtɒləˌreɪt) *vb* **tolerates, tolerating, tolerated** (*tr*) **1** to treat with indulgence or forbearance **2** to permit **3** to be able to bear; put up with **4** to have tolerance for (a drug, etc) [c16 from L *tolerāre* to sustain]

toleration (ˌtɒləˈreɪʃən) *n* **1** the act or practice of tolerating **2** freedom to hold religious opinions that differ from the established religion of a country > ˌ**tolerˈationist** *n*

Tolima (*Spanish* toˈlima) *n* a volcano in W Colombia, in the Andes. Height: 5215 m (17 110 ft)

Tolkien (ˈtɒlkiːn) *n* **J**(ohn) **R**(onald) **R**(euel) 1892–1973, British philologist and writer, born in South Africa. He is best known for *The Hobbit* (1937), the trilogy *The Lord of the Rings* (1954–55), and the posthumously published *The Silmarillion* (1977)

toll[1] (təʊl) *vb* **1** to ring slowly and recurrently **2** (*tr*) to summon or announce by tolling **3** *US & Canad* to decoy (game, esp ducks) ▹ *n* **4** the act or sound of tolling [c15 ? rel. to OE *-tyllan*, as in *fortyllan* to attract]

toll[2] (təʊl, tɒl) *n* **1a** an amount of money levied, esp for the use of certain roads, bridges, etc **1b** (*as modifier*): *toll road; toll bridge* **2** loss or damage incurred through a disaster, etc: *the war took its toll of the inhabitants* **3** (formerly) the right to levy a toll [OE *toln*]

tollbooth *or* **tolbooth** (ˈtəʊlˌbuːθ, -ˌbuːð, ˈtɒl-) *n* a booth or kiosk at which a toll is collected

tollgate (ˈtəʊlˌgeɪt, ˈtɒl-) *n* a gate across a toll road or bridge at which travellers must pay

tollhouse (ˈtəʊlˌhaʊs, ˈtɒl-) *n* a small house at a tollgate occupied by a toll collector

tollie (ˈtɒlɪ) *n, pl* **tollies** *S African* a castrated calf [c19 from Xhosa *ithole* calf on which the horns have begun to appear]

Tolstoy (ˈtɒlstɔɪ; *Russian* talˈstɔj) *n* Leo, Russian name *Count Lev Nikolayevich Tolstoy*. 1828–1910, Russian novelist, short-story writer, and philosopher; author of the two monumental novels *War and Peace* (1865–69) and *Anna Karenina* (1875–77). Following a spiritual crisis in 1879, he adopted a form of Christianity based on a doctrine of nonresistance to evil

Toltec (ˈtɒltɛk) *n, pl* **Toltecs** *or* **Toltec** **1** a member of a Central American Indian people who dominated the valley of Mexico until they were overrun by the Aztecs ▹ *adj also* **Toltecan** **2** of or relating to this people
▹ www.mnsu.edu/emuseum/prehistory/latinamerica/meso/cultures/toltec.html
▹ http://members.aol.com/xiuhcoatl/toltec.htm

tolu (tɒˈluː) *n* an aromatic balsam obtained from a South American tree [c17 after *Santiago de Tolu*, Colombia, from which it was exported]

Toluca (*Spanish* toˈluka) *n* **1** a city in S central Mexico, capital of Mexico state, at an altitude of 2640 m (8660 ft). Pop: 435 000 (2000 est). Official name: **Toluca de Lerdo** (deˈlɛrðo) **2** **Nevado de** (neˈβaðo de) a volcano in central Mexico, in Mexico state near Toluca: crater partly filled by a lake. Height: 4577 m (15 017 ft)

toluene (ˈtɒljʊˌiːn) *n* a colourless volatile flammable liquid obtained from petroleum and coal tar and used as a solvent and in the manufacture of many organic chemicals [c19 from TOLU + -ENE, since it was previously obtained from tolu]

toluic acid (tɒˈljuːɪk) *n* a white crystalline derivative of toluene used in synthetic resins and as an insect repellent [c19 from TOLU(ENE) + -IC]

toluidine (tɒˈljuːɪˌdiːn) *n* an amine derived from toluene, used in making dyes [c19 from TOLU(ENE) + -IDE + -INE[2]]

tom (tɒm) *n* **a** the male of various animals, esp the cat **b** (*as modifier*): *a tom turkey* **c** (*in combination*): *a tomcat* [c16 special use of the short form of *Thomas*, applied to any male, often implying a common or ordinary type of person, etc]

tomahawk (ˈtɒməˌhɔːk) *n* a fighting axe with a stone or iron head, used by the North American Indians [c17 from Algonquian *tamahaac*]

tomato (təˈmɑːtəʊ) *n, pl* **tomatoes** **1** a South American plant widely cultivated for its red fleshy many-seeded fruits **2** the fruit of this plant, eaten in salads, as a vegetable, etc [c17 *tomate*, from Sp., from Nahuatl *tomatl*]

tomb (tuːm) *n* **1** a place, esp a vault beneath the ground, for the burial of a corpse **2** a monument to the dead **3** **the tomb** a poetic term for death [c13 from OF *tombe*, from LL *tumba* burial mound, from Gk *tumbos*]

tombac (ˈtɒmbæk) *n* any of various alloys containing copper and zinc: used for making cheap jewellery, etc [c17 from F, from Du. *tombak*, from Malay *tambâga* copper, apparently from Sansk. *tāmraka*, from *tāmra* dark coppery red]

Tombaugh (ˈtɒmbəʊ) *n* **Clyde William** 1906–97, US astronomer, who discovered (1930) the planet Pluto

tombola (tɒmˈbəʊlə) *n* *Brit* a type of lottery, esp at a fête, in which tickets are drawn from a revolving drum [c19 from It., from *tombolare* to somersault]

Tombouctou (tɔ̃buktu) *n* the French name for **Timbuktu**

tomboy ('tɒm,bɔɪ) *n* a girl who acts or dresses in a boyish way, liking rough outdoor activities > **'tom,boyish** *adj* > **'tom,boyishly** *adv*

tombstone ('tu:m,stəʊn) *n* another word for **gravestone**

Tom Collins *n* a long drink consisting of gin, lime or lemon juice, sugar, and soda water

Tom, Dick, and (or) Harry *n* an ordinary, undistinguished, or common person (esp in **every Tom, Dick, and Harry; any Tom, Dick, or Harry**)

tome (təʊm) *n* **1** a large weighty book **2** one of the several volumes of a work [c16 from F, from L *tomus* section of larger work, from Gk *tomos* a slice, from *temnein* to cut]

-tome *n combining form* indicating an instrument for cutting: *osteotome* [from Gk *tomē* a cutting, *tomos* a slice, from *temnein* to cut]

tomentum (tə'mɛntəm) *n, pl* **tomenta** (-tə) **1** a covering of downy hairs on leaves and other plant parts **2** a network of minute blood vessels occurring in the human brain [c17 NL, from L: stuffing for cushions] > **to'mentose** *adj*

tomfool (,tɒm'fu:l) *n* **a** a fool **b** (*as modifier*): *tomfool ideas* > **,tom'foolishness** *n*

tomfoolery (,tɒm'fu:lərɪ) *n, pl* **tomfooleries 1** foolish behaviour **2** utter nonsense; rubbish

tommy ('tɒmɪ) *n, pl* **tommies** (*often cap*) *Brit inf* a private in the British Army [c19 orig. *Thomas Atkins*, name representing typical private in specimen forms]

Tommy gun *n* an informal name for **Thompson sub-machine-gun**

tommyrot ('tɒmɪ,rɒt) *n* utter nonsense

tomography (tə'mɒgrəfɪ) *n* a technique used to obtain an X-ray photograph of a plane section of the human body or some other object [c20 from Gk *tomē* a cutting + -GRAPHY]

tomorrow (tə'mɒrəʊ) *n* **1** the day after today **2** the future ▷ *adv* **3** on the day after today **4** at some time in the future [OE *tō morgenne*, from *to* on + *morgenne*, dative of *morgen* morning]

Tomsk (*Russian* tɔmsk) *n* a city in central Russia: formerly an important gold-mining town and administrative centre for a large area of Siberia; university (1888); engineering industries. Pop: 481 400 (1999 est)

Tom Thumb *n* **1 General,** stage name of *Charles Stratton*. 1838–83, US midget, exhibited in P. T. Barnum's circus **2** a dwarf; midget [after *Tom Thumb*, the tiny hero of several English folk tales]

tomtit ('tɒm,tɪt) *n Brit* any of various tits, esp the bluetit

tom-tom *n* a drum usually beaten with the hands as a signalling instrument [c17 from Hindi *tamtam*, imit.]

-tomy *n combining form* indicating a surgical cutting of a specified part or tissue: *lobotomy* [from Gk *-tomia*]

ton[1] (tʌn) *n* **1** Also called: **long ton** *Brit* a unit of weight equal to 2240 pounds or 1016.046 909 kilograms **2** Also called: **short ton, net ton** *US & Canad* a unit of weight equal to 2000 pounds or 907.184 kilograms **3** See **metric ton, tonne** a unit of weight equal to 1000 kilograms **4** Also called: **freight ton, measurement ton** a unit of volume or weight used for charging or measuring freight in shipping. It is usually equal to 40 cubic feet, 1 cubic metre, or 1000 kilograms **5** Also called: **displacement ton** a unit used for measuring the displacement of a ship, equal to 35 cubic feet of sea water or 2240 pounds **6** Also called: **register ton** a unit of internal capacity of ships equal to 100 cubic feet ▷ *adv* **7 tons** (intensifier): *the new flat is tons better than the old one* [c14 var. of TUN]

ton[2] (tʌn) *n sl, chiefly Brit* a score or achievement of a hundred, esp a hundred miles per hour, as in a car or on a motorcycle [c20 special use of TON[1] applied to quantities of one hundred]

tonal ('təʊnᵊl) *adj* **1** of or relating to tone **2** of or utilizing the diatonic system; having an established key **3** (of an answer in a fugue) not having the same melodic intervals as the subject, so as to remain in the original key > **'tonally** *adv*

tonality (təʊ'nælɪtɪ) *n, pl* **tonalities 1** *music* **1a** the presence of a musical key in a composition **1b** the system of major and minor keys prevalent in Western music **2** the overall scheme of colours and tones in a painting

Tonbridge ('tʌn,brɪdʒ) *n* a market town in SE England, in SW Kent on the River Medway. Pop: 34 260 (1991)

tondo ('tɒndəʊ) *n, pl* **tondi** (-di:) a circular easel painting or relief carving [c19 from It.: a circle, shortened from *rotondo* round]

tone (təʊn) *n* **1** sound with reference to quality, pitch, or volume **2** short for **tone colour 3** *US & Canad* another word for **note** (sense 10) **4** an interval of a major second; whole tone **5** Also called: **Gregorian tone** any of several plainsong melodies or other chants used in the singing of psalms **6** *linguistics* any of the pitch levels or pitch contours at which a syllable may be pronounced, such as high tone, falling tone, etc **7** the quality or character of a sound: *a nervous tone of voice* **8** general aspect, quality, or style **9** high quality or style: *to lower the tone of a place* **10** the quality of a given colour, as modified by mixture with white or black; shade; tint **11** *physiol* **11a** the normal tension of a muscle at rest **11b** the natural firmness of the tissues and normal functioning of bodily organs in health **12** the overall effect of the colour values and gradations of light and dark in a picture **13** *photog* a colour of a particular area on a negative or positive that can be distinguished from surrounding areas ▷ *vb* **tones, toning, toned 14** (*intr*; often foll by *with*) to be of a matching or similar tone (to) **15** (*tr*) to give a tone to or correct the tone of **16** (*tr*) *photog* to soften or change the colour of the tones of (a photographic image) ▷ See also **tone down, tone up** [c14 from L *tonus*, from Gk *tonos* tension, tone, from *teinein* to stretch] > **'toneless** *adj* > **'tonelessly** *adv*

Tt

tone arm *n* another name for **pick-up**

tone colour *n* the quality of a musical sound that is conditioned or distinguished by the upper partials or overtones present in it

tone-deaf *adj* unable to distinguish subtle differences in musical pitch > **tone deafness** *n*

tone down *vb* (*adv*) to moderate or become moderated in tone: *to tone down an argument*

tone language *n* a language, such as Chinese, in which differences in tone may make differences in meaning

toneme ('təʊni:m) *n linguistics* a phoneme that is distinguished from another phoneme only by its tone [c20] > **to'nemic** *adj*

tone poem *n* another term for **symphonic poem**

toner ('təʊnə) *n* **1** a person or thing that tones **2** a cosmetic preparation that is applied to produce a desired effect, such as to reduce the oiliness of the skin **3** *photog* a chemical solution that softens or alters the tones of a photographic image **4** a powdered chemical used in photocopying machines, which adheres to electrostatically charged areas of a plate or roller and is then transferred onto the paper to form the copy

tone row *or* **series** *n music* a group of notes having a characteristic pattern that forms the basis of the musical material in a serial composition, esp one consisting of the twelve notes of the chromatic scale

tone up *vb* (*adv*) to make or become more vigorous, healthy, etc

tong (tɒŋ) *n* (formerly) a secret society of Chinese Americans [c20 from Chinese (Cantonese) *t'ong* meeting place]

tonga ('tɒŋgə) *n* a light two-wheeled vehicle used in

rural areas of India [c19 from Hindi *tāngā*]

Tonga ('tɒŋə, 'tɒŋgə) *n* a kingdom occupying an archipelago of more than 150 volcanic and coral islands in the SW Pacific, east of Fiji: inhabited by Polynesians; became a British protectorate in 1900 and gained independence in 1970; a member of the Commonwealth. Official languages: Tongan and English. Religion: Christian majority. Currency: pa'anga. Capital: Nuku'alofa. Pop: 101 000 (2001 est). Area: 750 sq km (290 sq miles). Also called: **Friendly Islands** > '**Tongan** *adj, n*

▹ www.pmo.gov.to
▹ www.vacations.tvb.gov.to
▹ www.tonga-island.com

Tongchak (ˌtɒŋ'tʃæk) *n* the former name for **Chondokyo**

tongs (tɒŋz) *pl n* a tool for grasping or lifting, consisting of a hinged, sprung, or pivoted pair of arms or levers, joined at one end. Also called: **pair of tongs** [pl. of OE *tange*]

tongue (tʌŋ) *n* **1** a movable mass of muscular tissue attached to the floor of the mouth in most vertebrates. It is used in tasting, eating, and (in man) speaking. Related adj: **lingual 2** an analogous organ in invertebrates **3** the tongue of certain animals used as food **4** a language, dialect, or idiom: *the English tongue* **5** the ability to speak: *to lose one's tongue* **6** a manner of speaking: *a glib tongue* **7** utterance or voice (esp in **give tongue**) **8** anything which resembles a tongue in shape or function **9** a promontory or spit of land **10** a flap of leather on a shoe **11** *music* the reed of an oboe or similar instrument **12** the clapper of a bell **13** the harnessing pole of a horse-drawn vehicle **14** a projection on a machine part that serves as a guide for assembly, etc **15** a projecting strip along an edge of a board that is made to fit a groove in another board **16 hold one's tongue** to keep quiet **17 on the tip of one's tongue** about to come to mind **18 with (one's) tongue in (one's) cheek** Also: **tongue in cheek** with insincere or ironical intent ▹ *vb* **tongues, tonguing, tongued 19** to articulate (notes on a wind instrument) by tonguing **20** (*tr*) to lick, feel, or touch with the tongue **21** (*tr*) to provide (a board) with a tongue **22** (*intr*) (of a piece of land) to project into a body of water [OE *tunge*] > '**tongueless** *adj* > '**tongue,like** *adj*

tongue-and-groove joint *n* a joint made between two boards by means of a tongue along the edge of one board that fits into a groove along the edge of the other board

tongued (tʌŋd) *adj* **1** having a tongue or tongues **2** (*in combination*) having a manner of speech as specified: *sharp-tongued*

tongue-lash *vb* (*tr*) to reprimand severely; scold > '**tongue-ˌlashing** *n, adj*

tongue-tie *n* a congenital condition in which the tongue has restricted mobility as the result of an abnormally short fraenum

tongue-tied *adj* **1** speechless, esp with embarrassment or shyness **2** having a condition of tongue-tie

tongue twister *n* a sentence or phrase that is difficult to articulate clearly and quickly, such as *Peter Piper picked a peck of pickled pepper*

tonguing ('tʌŋɪŋ) *n* a technique of playing (any nonlegato passage) on a wind instrument by obstructing and uncovering the air passage through the lips with the tongue

tonic ('tɒnɪk) *n* **1** a medicinal preparation intended to improve the functioning of the body or increase the feeling of wellbeing **2** anything that enlivens or strengthens **3** Also called: **tonic water** a mineral water, usually carbonated and containing quinine and often mixed with gin or other alcoholic drinks **4** *music* **4a** the first degree of a major or minor scale and the tonal centre of a piece composed in a particular key **4b** a key or chord based on this ▹ *adj* **5** serving to enliven and invigorate: *a tonic wine* **6** of or relating to a tone or tones **7** *music* of the first degree of a major or minor scale **8** of or denoting the general effect of colour and light and shade in a picture **9** *physiol* of or affecting normal muscular or bodily tone: *a tonic spasm* [c17 from NL *tonicus*, from Gk *tonikos* concerning tone, from *tonos* TONE] > '**tonically** *adv*

tonic accent *n* **1** emphasis imparted to a note by virtue of its having a higher pitch **2** (in some languages) an accent in which emphatic syllables are pronounced on a higher musical pitch

tonicity (təʊ'nɪsɪtɪ) *n* **1** the condition or quality of being tonic **2** another name for **tonus**

tonic sol-fa *n* a method of teaching music, by which syllables are used as names for the notes of the major scale in any key

tonight (tə'naɪt) *n* **1** the night or evening of this present day ▹ *adv* **2** in or during the night or evening of this day **3** *obs* last night [OE *tōniht*]

toning table *n* an exercise table, parts of which move mechanically for a set time in order to exercise specific parts of the body of the person lying on it

tonka bean ('tɒŋkə) *n* **1** a tall tree of tropical America **2** the seeds of this tree, used in the manufacture of perfumes, snuff, etc [c18 prob. from Tupi *tonka*]

Tonkin ('tɒn'kɪn) *or* **Tongking** ('tɒŋ'kɪŋ) *n* **1** a former state of N French Indochina (1883–1946), on the Gulf of Tonkin: forms the largest part of N Vietnam **2 Gulf of** an arm of the South China Sea, bordered by N Vietnam, the Leizhou Peninsula of SW China, and Hainan Island. Length: about 500 km (300 miles)

Tonle Sap ('tɒnlɪ 'sæp) *n* a lake in W central Cambodia, linked with the Mekong River by the **Tonle Sap River** Area: (dry season) about 2600 sq km (1000 sq miles); (rainy season) about 10 000 sq km (3860 sq miles)

tonnage *or* **tunnage** ('tʌnɪdʒ) *n* **1** the capacity of a merchant ship expressed in tons **2** the weight of the cargo of a merchant ship **3** the total amount of shipping of a port or nation **4** a duty on ships based either on their capacity or their register tonnage [c15 from OF, from *tonne* barrel]

tonne (tʌn) *n* a unit of mass equal to 1000 kg or 2204.6 pounds. Also called (not in technical use): **metric ton** [from F]

tonneau ('tɒnəʊ) *n, pl* **tonneaus** *or* **tonneaux** (-nəʊ, -nəʊz) **1** a detachable cover to protect empty passenger seats in an open vehicle **2** *rare* the part of an open car in which the rear passengers sit [c20 from F: special type of vehicle body, from OF *tonnel* cask, from *tonne* tun]

tonometer (təʊ'nɒmɪtə) *n* **1** an instrument for measuring the pitch of a sound, esp one consisting of a set of tuning forks **2** any of various types of instrument for measuring pressure or tension, such as the blood pressure, vapour pressure, etc [c18 from Gk *tonos* TONE + -METER] > **tonometric** (ˌtɒnə'mɛtrɪk, ˌtəʊ-) *adj*

tonsil ('tɒnsəl) *n* either of two small masses of lymphatic tissue situated one on each side of the back of the mouth [c17 from L *tōnsillae* (pl) tonsils, from ?] > '**tonsillar** *adj*

tonsillectomy (ˌtɒnsɪ'lɛktəmɪ) *n, pl* **tonsillectomies** surgical removal of the tonsils

tonsillitis (ˌtɒnsɪ'laɪtɪs) *n* inflammation of the tonsils > **tonsillitic** (ˌtɒnsɪ'lɪtɪk) *adj*

tonsorial (tɒn'sɔːrɪəl) *adj often facetious* of barbering or hairdressing [c19 from L *tōnsōrius* concerning shaving, from *tondēre* to shave]

tonsure ('tɒnʃə) *n* **1** (in certain religions and monastic orders) **1a** the shaving of the head or the crown of the head only **1b** the part of the head left bare by shaving ▹ *vb* **tonsures, tonsuring, tonsured 2** (*tr*) to shave the head of [c14 from L *tōnsūra* a clipping, from *tondēre* to shave] > '**tonsured** *adj*

tontine ('tɒntiːn, tɒn'tiːn) *n* an annuity scheme by

which several subscribers accumulate and invest a common fund out of which they receive an annuity that increases as subscribers die until the last survivor takes the whole [C18 from F, after Lorenzo *Tonti*, Neapolitan banker who devised the scheme]

ton-up *Brit inf* ▷ *adj (prenominal)* **1** (esp of a motorcycle) capable of speeds of a hundred miles per hour or more **2** liking to travel at such speeds: *a ton-up boy* ▷ *n* **3** a person who habitually rides at such speeds

tonus ('təʊnəs) *n* the normal tension of a muscle at rest; tone [C19 from L, from Gk *tonos* TONE]

too (tuː) *adv* **1** as well; in addition; also: *can I come too?* **2** in or to an excessive degree: *I have too many things to do* **3** extremely: *you're too kind* **4** *US & Canad inf* indeed: used to reinforce a command: *you will too do it!* [OE tō]

USAGE See at **very**

took (tʊk) *vb* the past tense of **take**

tool (tuːl) *n* **1a** an implement, such as a hammer, saw, or spade, that is used by hand **1b** a power-driven instrument; machine tool **1c** *(in combination)*: *a toolkit* **2** the cutting part of such an instrument **3** any of the instruments used by a bookbinder to impress a design on a book cover **4** anything used as a means of achieving an end **5** a person used to perform dishonourable or unpleasant tasks for another **6** a necessary medium for or adjunct to one's profession: *numbers are the tools of the mathematician's trade* ▷ *vb* **7** to work, cut, or form (something) with a tool **8** *(tr)* to decorate (a book cover) with a bookbinder's tool **9** *(tr; often foll by up)* to furnish with tools [OE tōl] > **'tooler** *n*

tooling ('tuːlɪŋ) *n* **1** any decorative work done with a tool, esp a design stamped onto a book cover, etc **2** the selection, provision, and setting up of tools for a machining operation

toolkit ('tuːl,kɪt) *n* **1** a set of tools designed to be used together or for a particular purpose **2** software designed to perform a specific function, esp to solve a problem: *your on-line printer toolkit*

tool-maker *n* a person who specializes in the production or reconditioning of precision tools, cutters, etc > **'tool-,making** *n*

tool pusher *n* a foreman who supervises drilling operations on an oil rig

toolroom ('tuːlruːm, -rʊm) *n* a room, such as in a machine shop, where tools are made, stored, etc

toonie *or* **twonie** ('tuːnɪ) *n Canad inf* a Canadian two-dollar coin

tooshie ('tʊʃɪ) *adj Austral sl* angry; upset [from TUSH buttocks, by analogy with ARSEY]

toot (tuːt) *vb* **1** to give or cause to give (a short blast, hoot, or whistle) ▷ *n* **2** the sound made by or as if by a horn, whistle, etc **3** *sl* any drug for snorting, esp cocaine **4** *US & Canad sl* a drinking spree **5** *Austral sl* a lavatory [C16 from MLow G *tuten*, imit.] > **'tooter** *n*

tooth (tuːθ) *n, pl* **teeth** (tiːθ) **1** any of various bonelike structures set in the jaws of most vertebrates and used for biting, tearing, or chewing. Related adj: **dental** **2** any of various similar structures in invertebrates **3** anything resembling a tooth in shape, prominence, or function: *the tooth of a comb* **4** any of the indentations on the margin of a leaf, petal, etc **5** any of the projections on a gear, sprocket, rack, etc **6** taste or appetite (esp in **sweet tooth**) **7** **long in the tooth** old or ageing **8** **tooth and nail** with ferocity and force ▷ *vb* (tuːð, tuːθ) **9** *(tr)* to provide with a tooth or teeth **10** *(intr)* (of two gearwheels) to engage [OE tōth] > **'toothless** *adj* > **'tooth,like** *adj*

toothache ('tuːθ,eɪk) *n* a pain in or about a tooth. Technical name: **odontalgia**

toothbrush ('tuːθ,brʌʃ) *n* a small brush, usually with a long handle, for cleaning the teeth

toothed (tuːθt) *adj* **a** having a tooth or teeth **b** *(in combination)*: *sabre-toothed; six-toothed*

toothed whale *n* any of a suborder of whales having simple teeth and feeding on fish, smaller mammals, etc: includes dolphins and porpoises

toothpaste ('tuːθ,peɪst) *n* a paste used for cleaning the teeth, applied with a toothbrush

toothpick ('tuːθ,pɪk) *n* a small sharp sliver of wood, plastic, etc, used for extracting pieces of food from between the teeth

tooth powder *n* a powder used for cleaning the teeth, applied with a toothbrush

tooth shell *n* another name for the **tusk shell**

toothsome ('tuːθsəm) *adj* of delicious or appetizing appearance, flavour, or smell

toothwort ('tuːθ,wɜːt) *n* **1** a parasitic European plant having no green parts, scaly stems, pinkish flowers, and a rhizome covered with toothlike scales **2** any of a genus of North American or Eurasian plants having rhizomes covered with toothlike projections

toothy ('tuːθɪ) *adj* **toothier, toothiest** having or showing numerous, large, or projecting teeth: *a toothy grin* > **'toothily** *adv* > **'toothiness** *n*

tootle ('tuːtᵊl) *vb* **tootles, tootling, tootled** **1** to toot or hoot softly or repeatedly ▷ *n* **2** a soft hoot or series of hoots [C19 from TOOT] > **'tootler** *n*

Toowoomba (tə'wʊmbə) *n* a city in E Australia, in SE Queensland: agricultural and industrial centre. Pop: 86 968 (1998 est)

top[1] (tɒp) *n* **1** the highest or uppermost part of anything: *the top of a hill* **2** the most important or successful position: *the top of the class* **3** the part of a plant that is above ground: *carrot tops* **4** a thing that forms or covers the uppermost part of anything, esp a lid or cap **5** the highest degree or point: *at the top of his career* **6** the most important person **7** the best part of anything **8** the loudest or highest pitch (esp in **top of one's voice**) **9** another name for **top gear** (sense 1) **10** *cards* the highest card of a suit in a player's hand **11** *sport* **11a** a stroke that hits the ball above its centre **11b** short for **topspin** **12** a platform around the head of a lower mast of a sailing vessel **13** a garment, esp for a woman, that extends from the shoulders to the waist or hips **14** **off the top of one's head** with no previous preparation; extempore **15** **on top of** **15a** in addition to **15b** *inf* in complete control of (a difficult situation, etc) **16** **over the top** **16a** over the parapet or leading edge of a trench **16b** over the limit; lacking restraint or a sense of proportion **17** **the top of the morning** a morning greeting regarded as characteristic of Irishmen ▷ *adj* **18** of, relating to, serving as, or situated on the top ▷ *vb* **tops, topping, topped** *(mainly tr)* **19** to form a top on (something): *to top a cake with cream* **20** to remove the top of or from **21** to reach or pass the top of **22** to be at the top of: *he tops the team* **23** to exceed or surpass **24** *sl* to kill, esp by hanging **25** *(also intr) Sport* **25a** to hit (a ball) above the centre **25b** to make (a stroke) by hitting the ball in this way **26** **top and tail** **26a** to trim off the ends of (fruit or vegetables) before cooking them **26b** to wash a baby's face and bottom without immersion in a bath ▷ See also **top off, top out, tops, top up** [OE *topp*]

top[2] (tɒp) *n* **1** a toy that is spun on its pointed base **2** **sleep like a top** to sleep very soundly [OE, from ?]

topaz ('təʊpæz) *n* **1** a hard glassy mineral consisting of a silicate of aluminium and fluorine in crystalline form. It is yellow, pink, or colourless, and is a valuable gemstone **2** **oriental topaz** a yellowish-brown variety of sapphire **3** **false topaz** another name for **citrine** **4a** a yellowish-brown colour, as in some varieties of topaz **4b** *(as adj)*: *topaz eyes* **5** either of two South American hummingbirds [C13 from OF *topaze*, from L *topazus*, from Gk *topazos*]

top boot *n* a high boot, often with a decorative or contrasting upper section

top brass *n (functioning as pl) inf* the most important or

Tt

high-ranking officials or leaders
topcoat ('tɒp,kəʊt) *n* an outdoor coat worn over a suit, etc
top dog *n inf* the leader or chief of a group
top dollar *n inf* the highest level of payment
top drawer *n* people of the highest standing, esp socially (esp in **out of the top drawer**)
top dressing *n* a surface application of some material, such as fertilizer > **'top-,dress** *vb (tr)*
tope[1] (təʊp) *vb* **topes, toping, toped** to consume (alcoholic drink) as a regular habit, usually in large quantities [C17 from F *toper* to keep an agreement, from Sp. *topar* to take a bet; prob. because a wager was generally followed by a drink] > **'toper** *n*
tope[2] (təʊp) *n* a small grey shark of European coastal waters [C17 from ?]
topee *or* **topi** ('təʊpiː, -pɪ) *n, pl* **topees** *or* **topis** another name for **pith helmet** [C19 from Hindi *topī* hat]
Topeka (tə'piːkə) *n* a city in E central Kansas, capital of the state, on the Kansas River: university (1865). Pop: 122 377 (2000)
Top End *n* **the** *Austral* the northern part of the Northern Territory
top-end *adj* of or relating to the best or most expensive products of their kind: *a range of top-end vehicles*
top-flight *adj* of superior or excellent quality
topgallant (,tɒp'gælənt; *naut* tə'gælənt) *n* **1** a mast on a square-rigger above a topmast or an extension of a topmast **2** a sail set on a yard of a topgallant mast **3** *(modifier)* of or relating to a topgallant
top gear *n* **1** Also called: **top** the highest forward ratio of a gearbox in a motor vehicle **2** the highest speed, greatest energy, etc
top hat *n* a man's hat with a tall cylindrical crown and narrow brim, often made of silk, now worn for some formal occasions
top-hat scheme *n inf* a pension scheme for the senior executives of an organization
top-heavy *adj* **1** unstable through being overloaded at the top **2** *finance* characterized by too much debt capital in relation to revenue or profit; overcapitalized
Tophet *or* **Topheth** ('təʊfɛt) *n Old Testament* a place in the valley immediately to the southwest of Jerusalem; the Shrine of Moloch, where human sacrifices were offered [from Heb. *Tōpheth*]
tophus ('təʊfəs) *n, pl* **tophi** (-faɪ) a deposit of sodium urate in the ear or surrounding a joint: a diagnostic of gout [C16 from L, var. of *tōfus* TUFA, TUFF]
topi[1] ('təʊpiː, -pɪ) *n, pl* **topis** another name for **pith helmet** [C19 from Hindi: hat]
topi[2] ('təʊpɪ) *n, pl* **topi** *or* **topis** a glossy brown African antelope [C19 from Swahili]
topiary ('təʊpɪərɪ) *adj* **1** of, relating to, or characterized by the trimming or training of trees or bushes into artificial decorative shapes ▷ *n, pl* **topiaries 2a** topiary work **2b** a topiary garden **3** the art of topiary [C16 from F *topiaire*, from L *topia* decorative garden work, from Gk *topion* little place, from *topos* place] > **'topiarist** *n*
▷ www.topiaryart.com
topic ('tɒpɪk) *n* **1** a subject or theme of a speech, book, etc **2** a subject of conversation [C16 from L *topica* translating Gk *ta topika*, lit.: matters relating to commonplaces, title of a treatise by Aristotle, from *topoi*, pl. of *topos* place]
topical ('tɒpɪkᵊl) *adj* **1** of, relating to, or constituting current affairs **2** relating to a particular place; local **3** of or relating to a topic or topics **4** (of a drug, ointment, etc) for application to the body surface; local > **topicality** (,tɒpɪ'kælɪtɪ) *n* > **'topically** *adv*
topknot ('tɒp,nɒt) *n* **1** a crest, tuft, chignon, etc, on top of the head **2** any of several European flatfishes
topless ('tɒplɪs) *adj* **1** having no top **2a** denoting a costume which has no covering for the breasts **2b** wearing such a costume
top-level *n (modifier)* of, involving, or by those on the highest level of influence or authority: *top-level talks*
toplofty ('tɒp,lɒftɪ) *adj inf* haughty or pretentious > **'top,loftiness** *n*
topmast ('tɒp,mɑːst; *naut* 'tɒpməst) *n* the mast next above a lower mast on a sailing vessel
topmost ('tɒp,məʊst) *adj* at or nearest the top
top-notch ('tɒp'nɒtʃ) *adj inf* excellent; superb > **'top-'notcher** *n*
topo- *or before a vowel* **top-** *combining form* indicating place or region: *topography* [from Gk *topos* a place]
top off *vb (tr, adv)* to finish or complete, esp with some decisive action
topography (tə'pɒgrəfɪ) *n, pl* **topographies 1** the study or detailed description of the surface features of a region **2** the detailed mapping of the configuration of a region **3** the land forms or surface configuration of a region **4** the surveying of a region's surface features **5** the study or description of the configuration of any object > **to'pographer** *n* > **topographic** (,tɒpə'græfɪk) *or* **,topo'graphical** *adj*
topological group *n maths* a group, such as the set of all real numbers, that constitutes a topological space and in which multiplication and inversion are continuous
topological space *n maths* a set *S* with an associated family of subsets τ that is closed under set union and finite intersection
topology (tə'pɒlədʒɪ) *n* **1** the branch of mathematics concerned with generalization of the concepts of continuity, limit, etc **2** a branch of geometry describing the properties of a figure that are unaffected by continuous distortion **3** *maths* a family of subsets of a given set *S*, such that *S* is a topological space **4** the study of the topography of a given place **5** the anatomy of any specific bodily area, structure, or part > **topologic** (,tɒpə'lɒdʒɪk) *or* **,topo'logical** *adj* > **,topo'logically** *adv* > **to'pologist** *n*
Topolski (to'pɒlskɪ) *n* **'Feliks** ('fiːlɪks) 1907–89, British painter, born in Poland; best known for his sketches and murals, esp for *Memoir of the Century* (1975–89) painted on viaduct arches on London's South Bank
top out *vb (adv)* to place the highest part of a building in position
topper ('tɒpə) *n* **1** an informal name for **top hat 2** a person or thing that tops or excels
topping ('tɒpɪŋ) *n* **1** something that tops something else, esp a sauce or garnish for food ▷ *adj* **2** high or superior in rank, degree, etc **3** *Brit sl* excellent; splendid
topple ('tɒpᵊl) *vb* **topples, toppling, toppled 1** to tip over or cause to tip over, esp from a height **2** *(intr)* to lean precariously or totter **3** *(tr)* to overthrow; oust [C16 frequentative of TOP[1] (vb)]
tops (tɒps) *sl* ▷ *n* **1 the tops** a person or thing of top quality ▷ *adj* **2** *(postpositive)* excellent
topsail ('tɒp,seɪl; *naut* 'tɒpsəl) *n* a square sail carried on a yard set on a topmast
top-secret *adj* classified as needing the highest level of secrecy and security
topside ('tɒp,saɪd) *n* **1** the uppermost side of anything **2** *Brit & NZ* a lean cut of beef from the thigh containing no bone **3** *(often pl)* **3a** the part of a ship's sides above the water line **3b** the parts of a ship above decks
top slicing *n* the act or process of using a specific part of a sum of money for a special purpose, such as assessing a taxable gain
topsoil ('tɒp,sɔɪl) *n* the surface layer of soil
topspin ('tɒp,spɪn) *n tennis, etc* a spin imparted to make a ball bounce or travel exceptionally far, high, or quickly
topsy-turvy ('tɒpsɪ'tɜːvɪ) *adj* **1** upside down **2** in a state of confusion ▷ *adv* **3** in a topsy-turvy manner ▷ *n* **4** a topsy-turvy state [C16 prob. from *tops*, pl. of TOP[1] + obs. *tervy* to turn upside down]
top up *vb (tr, adv) Brit* **1** to raise the level of (a liquid,

powder, etc) in (a container), usually bringing it to the brim of the container **2a** to increase the benefits from (an insurance scheme), esp to increase a pension when a salary rise enables higher premiums to be paid **2b** to add money to (a loan, bank account, etc) in order to keep it at a constant or acceptable level ▷ *n* **top-up 3a** an amount added to something in order to raise it to or maintain it at a desired level **3b** (*as modifier*): *a top-up loan; a top-up policy*

top whack *n inf* the maximum price: *paying top whack for your child's education*

toque (təʊk) *n* **1** a woman's small round brimless hat **2** a chef's tall white hat **3** *Canad* a variant spelling of **tuque** (sense 2) **4** a small plumed hat popular in the 16th century [c16 from F, from OSp. *toca* headdress, prob. from Basque *tauka* hat]

tor (tɔː) *n* a high hill, esp a bare rocky one [OE *torr*]

Torah (ˈtəʊrə) *n* **1a** the Pentateuch **1b** the scroll on which this is written **2** the whole body of traditional Jewish teaching, including the Oral Law [c16 from Heb.: precept, from *yārāh* to instruct]
▷ http://jewfaq.org/torah.htm

Torbay (ˌtɔːˈbeɪ) *n* **1** a unitary authority in SW England, in Devon, consisting of Torquay and two neighbouring coastal resorts. Pop: 129 702 (2001). Area: 63 sq km (24 sq miles) **2** Also: **Tor Bay** an inlet of the English Channel on the coast of SW England, near Torquay

torc (tɔːk) *n* a variant of **torque** (sense 1)

torch (tɔːtʃ) *n* **1** a small portable electric lamp powered by batteries. US and Canad word: **flashlight 2** a wooden or tow shaft dipped in wax or tallow and set alight **3** anything regarded as a source of enlightenment, guidance, etc **4** any apparatus with a hot flame for welding, brazing, etc **5 carry a torch for** to be in love with, esp unrequitedly ▷ *vb* **6** (*tr*) to set fire to, esp deliberately as an act of arson [c13 from OF *torche* handful of twisted straw, from Vulgar L *torca* (unattested), from L *torquēre* to twist]

torchbearer (ˈtɔːtʃˌbɛərə) *n* **1** a person or thing that carries a torch **2** a person who leads or inspires

torchère (tɔːˈʃɛə) *n* a tall stand for holding a candelabrum [c20 from F, from *torche* TORCH]

torchier *or* **torchiere** (ˈtɔːtʃɪə) *n* a standing lamp with a bowl for casting light upwards [c20 from TORCHÈRE]

torch song *n* a sentimental song, usually sung by a woman [c20 from *to carry a torch for (someone)*] > **torch singer** *n*

tore (tɔː) *vb* the past tense of **tear²**

toreador (ˈtɒrɪəˌdɔː) *n* a bullfighter [c17 from Sp., from *torear* to take part in bullfighting, from *toro* a bull, from L *taurus*]

torero (tɒˈrɛərəʊ) *n, pl* **toreros** a bullfighter, esp one who fights on foot [c18 from Sp., from LL *taurārius*, from L *taurus* a bull]

Torfaen (ˈtɔːˌvæn) *n* a county borough of SE Wales, created in 1996 from part of Gwent. Administrative centre: Pontypool. Pop: 90 967 (2001). Area: 290 sq km (112 sq miles)

toric lens (ˈtɒrɪk) *n* a lens used to correct astigmatism, having one of its surfaces shaped like part of a torus so that its focal lengths are different in different meridians

torii (ˈtɔːrɪˌiː) *n, pl* **torii** a gateway at the entrance to a Shinto temple [c19 from Japanese, lit.: a perch for birds]

Torino (toˈriːno) *n* the Italian name for **Turin**

torment *vb* (tɔːˈmɛnt) (*tr*) **1** to afflict with great pain, suffering, or anguish; torture **2** to tease or pester in an annoying way ▷ *n* (ˈtɔːmɛnt) **3** physical or mental pain **4** a source of pain, worry, annoyance, etc [c13 from OF, from L *tormentum*, from *torquēre*] > **torˈmented** *adj* > **torˈmenting** *adj, n* > **torˈmentor** *n*

tormentil (ˈtɔːməntɪl) *n* a perennial plant of Europe and W Asia, having yellow flowers, and an astringent root used in medicine, tanning, and dyeing [c15 from OF *tormentille*, from Med. L *tormentilla*, from L *tormentum* agony; from its use in relieving pain]

torn (tɔːn) *vb* **1** the past participle of **tear² 2 that's torn it** *Brit sl* an unexpected event or circumstance has upset one's plans ▷ *adj* **3** split or cut **4** divided or undecided, as in preference: *torn between staying and leaving*

tornado (tɔːˈneɪdəʊ) *n, pl* **tornadoes** *or* **tornados 1** a violent storm with winds whirling around a small area of extremely low pressure, usually characterized by a dark funnel-shaped cloud causing damage along its path **2** a small but violent squall or whirlwind **3** any violently active or destructive person or thing [c16 prob. alteration of Sp. *tronada* thunderstorm (from *tronar* to thunder, from L *tonāre*) through infl. of *tornar* to turn, from L *tornāre* to turn in a lathe] > **tornadic** (tɔːˈnædɪk) *adj*

toroid (ˈtɔːrɔɪd) *n* **1** *geom* a surface generated by rotating a closed plane curve about a coplanar line that does not intersect the curve **2** the solid enclosed by such a surface. See also **torus** > **toˈroidal** *adj*

Toronto (təˈrɒntəʊ) *n* a city in S central Canada, capital of Ontario, on Lake Ontario: the major industrial centre of Canada; two universities. Pop: 653 734 (1996), with a metropolitan area of 4 338 400 (1995) > **ˌToronˈtonian** *adj, n*

torpedo (tɔːˈpiːdəʊ) *n, pl* **torpedoes 1** a cylindrical self-propelled weapon carrying explosives that is launched from aircraft, ships, or submarines and follows an underwater path to hit its target **2** *obs* a submarine mine **3** *US & Canad* a firework with a percussion cap **4** an electric ray ▷ *vb* **torpedoes, torpedoing, torpedoed** (*tr*) **5** to attack or hit (a ship, etc) with one or a number of torpedoes **6** to destroy or wreck: *to torpedo the administration's plan* [c16 from L: crampfish (whose electric discharges can cause numbness), from *torpēre* to be inactive] > **torˈpedo-ˌlike** *adj*

torpedo boat *n* (formerly) a small high-speed warship designed to carry out torpedo attacks

torpedo tube *n* the tube from which a torpedo is discharged from submarines or ships

torpid (ˈtɔːpɪd) *adj* **1** apathetic; sluggish **2** (of a hibernating animal) dormant **3** unable to move or feel [c17 from L *torpidus*, from *torpēre* to be numb] > **torˈpidity** *n* > **ˈtorpidly** *adv*

torpor (ˈtɔːpə) *n* a state of torpidity [c17 from L: inactivity, from *torpēre* to be motionless]

Torquay (ˌtɔːˈkiː) *n* a town and resort in SW England, in Torbay unitary authority, S Devon. Pop: 61 300 (2000 est)

torque (tɔːk) *n* **1** a necklace or armband made of twisted metal **2** any force that causes rotation [c19 from L *torquēs* necklace & *torquēre* to twist]

torque converter *n* a device for the transmission of power in which an engine-driven impeller transmits its momentum to a fluid held in a sealed container, which in turn drives a rotor. Also called: **hydraulic coupling**

Torquemada (*Spanish* torkeˈmaða) *n* **Tomás de** (toˈmas de) 1420–98, Spanish Dominican monk. As first Inquisitor-General of Spain (1483–98), he was responsible for the burning of some 2000 heretics

torques (ˈtɔːkwiːz) *n* a distinctive band of hair, feathers, skin, or colour around the neck of an animal; a collar [c17 from L: necklace, from *torquēre* to twist] > **torquate** (ˈtɔːkwɪt, -kweɪt) *adj*

torque wrench *n* a type of wrench with a gauge attached to indicate the torque applied

torr (tɔː) *n, pl* **torr** a unit of pressure equal to one millimetre of mercury (133.322 newtons per square metre) [c20 after E. TORRICELLI]

Torrance (ˈtɒrəns) *n* a city in SW California, southwest of Los Angeles: developed rapidly with the discovery of oil. Pop: 137 946 (2000)

Torre del Greco (*Italian* ˈtorre del ˈgrɛːko) *n* a city in SW

Tt

Italy, in Campania near Vesuvius on the Bay of Naples: damaged several times by eruptions. Pop: 100 688 (1992)

torrefy ('tɒrɪˌfaɪ) *vb* **torrefies, torrefying, torrefied** (*tr*) to dry (drugs, ores, etc) by heat [C17 from F *torréfier*, from L *torrefacere*, from *torrēre* to parch + *facere* to make] > **torrefaction** (ˌtɒrɪ'fækʃən) *n*

Torrens ('tɒrənz) *n* **Lake** a shallow salt lake in E central South Australia, about 8 m (25 ft) below sea level. Area: 5776 sq km (2230 sq miles)

Torrens title *n Austral* legal title to land based on record of registration rather than on title deeds [from Sir Robert Richard *Torrens* (1814–84), who introduced the system as premier of South Australia in 1857]

torrent ('tɒrənt) *n* **1** a fast or violent stream, esp of water **2** an overwhelming flow of thoughts, words, sound, etc [C17 from F, from L *torrēns* (n), from *torrēns* (adj) burning, from *torrēre* to burn] > **torrential** (tɒ'rɛnʃəl) *adj*

Torreón (*Spanish* tɔrre'ɔn) *n* an industrial city in N Mexico, in Coahuila state. Pop: 505 000 (2000 est)

Torres Strait ('tɔːrɪz, 'tɒr-) *n* a strait between NE Australia and S New Guinea, linking the Arafura Sea with the Coral Sea. Width: about 145 km (90 miles)

Torricelli (ˌtɒrɪ'tʃɛlɪ) *n* **Evangelista** (evandʒe'lista) 1608–47, Italian physicist and mathematician, who discovered the principle of the barometer

Torricellian tube (ˌtɒrɪ'sɛlɪən) *n* a vertical glass tube partly evacuated and partly filled with mercury, used to measure atmospheric pressure [C17 after E. TORRICELLI]

torrid ('tɒrɪd) *adj* **1** so hot and dry as to parch or scorch **2** arid or parched **3** highly charged emotionally: *a torrid love scene* [C16 from L *torridus*, from *torrēre* to scorch] > **tor'ridity** *or* **'torridness** *n* > **'torridly** *adv*

Torrid Zone *n rare* that part of the earth's surface lying between the tropics of Cancer and Capricorn

torsion ('tɔːʃən) *n* **1a** the twisting of a part by application of equal and opposite torques at either end **1b** the condition of twist and shear stress produced by a torque on a part or component **2** a twisting or being twisted [C15 from OF, from Medical L *torsiō* griping pains, from L *torquēre* to twist, torture] > **'torsional** *adj* > **'torsionally** *adv*

torsion balance *n* an instrument used to measure small forces, esp electric or magnetic forces, by the torsion they produce in a thin wire

torsion bar *n* a metal bar acting as a torsional spring

torsk (tɔːsk) *n, pl* **torsks** *or* **torsk** a food fish of northern coastal waters. Usual US name: **cusk** [C17 of Scand. origin]

torso ('tɔːsəʊ) *n, pl* **torsos** *or* **torsi** (-sɪ) **1** the trunk of the human body **2** a statue of a nude human trunk, esp without the head or limbs [C18 from It.: stalk, stump, from L: THYRSUS]

tort (tɔːt) *n law* a civil wrong or injury arising out of an act or failure to act, independently of any contract, for which an action for damages may be brought [C14 from OF, from Med. L *tortum*, lit.: something twisted, from L *torquēre* to twist]

torte (tɔːt) *n* a rich cake usually decorated or filled with cream, fruit, etc [C16 ult. ?from LL *tōrta* a round loaf, from ?]

Tortelier (*French* tɔrtəlje) *n* **Paul** (pɔl) 1914–90, French cellist and composer

torticollis (ˌtɔːtɪ'kɒlɪs) *n pathol* an abnormal position of the head, usually with the neck bent to one side [C19 NL, from L *tortus* twisted (from *torquēre* to twist) + *collum* neck]

tortilla (tɔː'tiːə) *n Mexican cookery* a kind of thin pancake made from corn meal [C17 from Sp.: a little cake, from *torta* a round cake, from LL]

tortoise ('tɔːtəs) *n* **1** any of a family of herbivorous reptiles having a heavy dome-shaped shell and clawed limbs **2** a slow-moving person **3** another word for **testudo** [C15 prob. from OF *tortue* (infl. by L *tortus* twisted), from Med. L *tortūca*, from LL *tartarūcha* coming from Tartarus (in the underworld), from Gk *tartaroukhos*; from belief that the tortoise originated in the underworld]

tortoiseshell ('tɔːtəsˌʃɛl) *n* **1** the horny yellow-and-brown mottled shell of the hawksbill turtle: used for making ornaments, jewellery, etc **2** a similar synthetic substance **3** a breed of domestic cat having black, cream, and brownish markings **4** any of several butterflies having orange-brown wings with black markings **5a** a yellowish-brown mottled colour **5b** (*as adj*): *a tortoiseshell décor* **6** (*modifier*) made of tortoiseshell

Tortola (tɔː'təʊlə) *n* an island in the NE Caribbean, in the Leeward Islands group: chief island of the British Virgin Islands. Pop: 13 568 (1991). Area: 62 sq km (24 sq miles)

tortricid ('tɔːtrɪsɪd) *n* any of a family of moths, the larvae of which live in leaves, which they roll or tie together [C19 from NL *Tortrīcidae*, from *tortrix*, fem. of *tortor*, lit.: twister, from the leaf-rolling of the larvae, from *torquēre* to twist]

Tortuga (tɔː'tuːgə) *n* an island in the Caribbean, off the NW coast of Haiti: haunt of pirates in the 17th century. Area: 180 sq km (70 sq miles). French name: **La Tortue** (la tɔrty)

tortuous ('tɔːtjʊəs) *adj* **1** twisted or winding **2** devious or cunning **3** intricate > **tortuosity** (ˌtɔːtjʊ'ɒsɪtɪ) *n* > **'tortuously** *adv* > **'tortuousness** *n*

USAGE See at **torture**

torture ('tɔːtʃə) *vb* **tortures, torturing, tortured** (*tr*) **1** to cause extreme physical pain to, esp to extract information, etc: *to torture prisoners* **2** to give mental anguish to **3** to twist into a grotesque form ▷ *n* **4** physical or mental anguish **5** the practice of torturing a person **6** a cause of mental agony [C16 from LL *tortūra* a twisting, from *torquēre* to twist] > **'torturer** *n* > **'torturous** *adj* > **'torturously** *adv*

USAGE The adjective *torturous* is sometimes confused with *tortuous*. A *torturous* experience is one that involves pain, suffering, or discomfort, while a *tortuous* road is one that winds or twists

Toruń (*Polish* 'tɔrunj) *n* an industrial city in N Poland, on the River Vistula: developed around a castle that was founded by the Teutonic Knights in 1230; under Prussian rule (1793–1919). Pop: 206 158 (1999 est). German name: **Thorn**

torus ('tɔːrəs) *n, pl* **tori** (-raɪ) **1** a large convex moulding semicircular in cross section, esp one used on the base of a column **2** *geom* a ring-shaped surface generated by rotating a circle about a coplanar line that does not intersect the circle **3** *bot* another name for **receptacle** (sense 2) [C16 from L: a swelling, from ?] > **toric** ('tɒrɪk) *adj*

Tory ('tɔːrɪ) *n, pl* **Tories** **1** a member or supporter of the Conservative Party in Great Britain or Canada **2** a member of the English political party that opposed the exclusion of James, Duke of York from the royal succession (1679–80). Tory remained the label for conservative interests until they gave birth to the Conservative Party in the 1830s **3** an American supporter of the British cause in the War of American Independence; loyalist. ▷ Cf **Whig** **4** (*sometimes not cap*) an ultraconservative or reactionary ▷ *adj* **5** of, characteristic of, or relating to Tories **6** (*sometimes not cap*) ultraconservative or reactionary [C17 from Irish *tōraidhe* outlaw, from MIrish *tōir* pursuit] > **'Toryish** *adj* > **'Toryism** *n*

tosa ('təʊsə) *n* a large dog, usually red in colour, that is a cross between a mastiff and a Great Dane: originally developed for dog-fighting; it is not recognized as a breed by kennel clubs outside Japan [C20 from the name of a province of Japan]

Toscana (tos'kaːna) *n* the Italian name for **Tuscany**

Toscanini (ˌtɒskəˈniːnɪ) *n* **Arturo** (arˈtuːro) 1867–1957, Italian conductor; musical director of La Scala, Milan, and of the NBC symphony orchestra (1937–57) in New York

tosh (tɒʃ) *n sl, chiefly Brit* nonsense; rubbish [c19 from ?]

toss (tɒs) *vb* **1** (*tr*) to throw lightly, esp with the palm of the hand upwards **2** to fling or be flung about, esp in an agitated or violent way: *a ship tosses in a storm* **3** to discuss or put forward for discussion in an informal way **4** (*tr*) (of a horse, etc) to throw (its rider) **5** (*tr*) (of an animal) to butt with the head or the horns and throw into the air **6** (*tr*) to shake or disturb **7** to toss up a coin with (someone) in order to decide something **8** (*intr*) to move away angrily or impatiently ▷ *n* **9** an abrupt movement **10** a rolling or pitching motion **11** the act or an instance of tossing **12** the act of tossing up a coin. See **toss up** **13** a fall from a horse [c16 of Scand. origin]

tosser (ˈtɒsə) *n Brit sl* a stupid or despicable person [c20 probably from TOSS OFF (to masturbate)]

toss off *vb* (*adv*) **1** (*tr*) to perform, write, etc, quickly and easily **2** (*tr*) to drink at one draught **3** (*intr*) *Brit sl* to masturbate

toss up *vb* (*adv*) **1** to spin (a coin) in the air in order to decide between alternatives by guessing which side will fall uppermost ▷ *n* **toss-up** **2** an instance of tossing up a coin **3** *inf* an even chance or risk

tot[1] (tɒt) *n* **1** a young child; toddler **2** *chiefly Brit* a small amount of anything **3** a small measure of spirits [c18 ? short for *totterer*; see TOTTER]

tot[2] (tɒt) *vb* **tots, totting, totted** (usually foll by *up*) *chiefly Brit* to total; add [c17 shortened from TOTAL or from L *totum* all]

total (ˈtəʊtᵊl) *n* **1** the whole, esp regarded as the complete sum of a number of parts ▷ *adj* **2** complete; absolute **3** (*prenominal*) being or related to a total ▷ *vb* **totals, totalling, totalled** *or US* **totals, totaling, totaled** **4** (when *intr*, sometimes foll by *to*) to amount: *to total six pounds* **5** (*tr*) to add up **6** (*tr*) *sl* to wreck or destroy [c14 from OF, from Med. L *tōtālis*, from L *tōtus* all] > ˈ**totally** *adv*

total football *n* an attacking style of play, popularized by the Dutch national team of the 1970s, in which there are no fixed positions and every outfield player can join in the attack

total internal reflection *n physics* the complete reflection of a light ray at the boundary of two media, when the ray is in the medium with greater refractive index

totalitarian (təʊˌtælɪˈtɛərɪən) *adj* **1** of, denoting, relating to, or characteristic of a dictatorial one-party state that regulates every realm of life ▷ *n* **2** a person who advocates or practises totalitarian policies > **toˌtaliˈtarianism** *n*

totality (təʊˈtælɪtɪ) *n, pl* **totalities** **1** the whole amount **2** the state of being total

totalizator (ˈtəʊtᵊlaɪˌzeɪtə), **totalizer** *or* **totalisator, totaliser** *n* **1** a system of betting on horse races in which the aggregate stake, less tax, etc, is paid out to winners in proportion to their stake **2** the machine that records bets in this system and works out odds, pays out winnings, etc ▷ US and Canad term: **pari-mutuel**

total quality management *n* an approach to the management of an organization that integrates the needs of customers with a deep understanding of the technical details, costs, and human-resource relationships of the organization. Abbrev: **TQM**

totaquine (ˈtəʊtəˌkwiːn, -kwɪn) *n* a mixture of quinine and other alkaloids derived from cinchona bark, used as a substitute for quinine in treating malaria [c20 from NL *tōtaquīna*, from TOTA(L) + Sp. *quina* cinchona bark; see QUININE]

totara (ˈtəʊtərə) *n* a tall coniferous forest tree of New Zealand with durable wood

tote[1] (təʊt) *inf* ▷ *vb* **totes, toting, toted** **1** (*tr*) to carry, convey, or drag ▷ *n* **2** the act of or an instance of toting **3** something toted [c17 from ?] > ˈ**toter** *n*

tote[2] (təʊt) *n* (usually preceded by *the*) *inf* short for **totalizator**

tote bag *n* a large handbag or shopping bag

totem (ˈtəʊtəm) *n* **1** (in some societies, esp among North American Indians) an object, animal, plant, etc, symbolizing a clan, family, etc, often having ritual associations **2** a representation of such an object [c18 from Ojibwa *nintōtēm* mark of my family] > **totemic** (təʊˈtɛmɪk) *adj* > ˈ**totemˌism** *n*

totem pole *n* a pole carved or painted with totemic figures set up by certain North American Indians as a tribal symbol, etc

tother *or* **t'other** (ˈtʌðə) *adj, n arch or dialect* the other [c13 *the tother*, by mistaken division from *thet other* (*thet*, from OE *thæt*, neuter of THE[1])]

totipalmate (ˌtəʊtɪˈpælmɪt, -ˌmeɪt) *adj* (of certain birds) having all four toes webbed [c19 from L *tōtus* entire + *palmate*, from *palmātus* shaped like a hand, from *palma* PALM[1]]

totter (ˈtɒtə) *vb* (*intr*) **1** to move in an unsteady manner **2** to sway or shake as if about to fall **3** to be failing, unstable, or precarious ▷ *n* **4** the act or an instance of tottering [c12 ?from OE *tealtrian* to waver, & MDu. *touteren* to stagger] > ˈ**totterer** *n* > ˈ**tottery** *adj*

totting (ˈtɒtɪŋ) *n Brit* the practice of searching through rubbish for usable or saleable items [c19 from ?]

toucan (ˈtuːkən) *n* any of a family of tropical American fruit-eating birds having a large brightly coloured bill and a bright plumage [c16 from F, from Port. *tucano*, from Tupi *tucana*, prob. imit. of its cry]

touch (tʌtʃ) *n* **1** the sense by which the texture and other qualities of objects can be experienced when they come in contact with a part of the body surface, esp the tips of the fingers. Related adj: **tactile** **2** the quality of an object as perceived by this sense; feel; feeling **3** the act or an instance of something coming into contact with the body **4** a gentle push, tap, or caress **5** a small amount; hint: *a touch of sarcasm* **6** a noticeable effect; influence: *the house needed a woman's touch* **7** any slight stroke or mark **8** characteristic manner or style **9** a detail of some work: *she added a few finishing touches to the book* **10** a slight attack, as of a disease **11** a specific ability or facility **12** the state of being aware of a situation or in contact with someone **13** the state of being in physical contact **14** a trial or test (esp in **put to the touch**) **15** *rugby, soccer, etc* the area outside the touchlines, beyond which the ball is out of play (esp in **in touch**) **16** a scoring hit in fencing **17** an estimate of the amount of gold in an alloy as obtained by use of a touchstone **18** the technique of fingering a keyboard instrument **19** the quality of the action of a keyboard instrument with regard to the ease with which the keys may be depressed **20** *sl* **20a** the act of asking for money, often by devious means **20b** the money received **20c** a person asked for money in this way ▷ *vb* **21** (*tr*) to cause or permit a part of the body to come into contact with **22** (*tr*) to tap, feel, or strike **23** to come or cause to come into contact with **24** (*intr*) to be in contact **25** (*tr; usually used with a negative*) to take hold of (a person or thing), esp in violence **26** to be adjacent to (each other) **27** (*tr*) to move or disturb by handling **28** (*tr*) to have an effect on **29** (*tr*) to produce an emotional response in **30** (*tr*) to affect; concern **31** (*tr; usually used with a negative*) to partake of, eat, or drink **32** (*tr; usually used with a negative*) to handle or deal with: *I wouldn't touch that business* **33** (when *intr*, often foll by *on*) to allude (to) briefly or in passing **34** (*tr*) to tinge or tint slightly: *brown hair touched with gold* **35** (*tr*) to spoil slightly: *blackfly touched the flowers* **36** (*tr*) to mark, as with a brush or pen **37** (*tr*) to compare to in quality or attainment **38** (*tr*) to reach or attain: *he touched the high* *point in his career* **39** *(intr)* to dock or stop briefly: *the ship touches at Tenerife* **40** *(tr) sl* to ask for a loan or gift of money from ▷ See also **touchdown, touch off, touch up** [C13 from OF *tochier*, from Vulgar L *toccāre* (unattested) to strike, prob. imit. of a tapping sound] > **'touchable** *adj* > **'toucher** *n*

touch and go *adj* (**touch-and-go** *when prenominal*) risky or critical

touchdown ('tʌtʃ,daʊn) *n* **1** the moment at which a landing aircraft or spacecraft comes into contact with the landing surface **2** *rugby* the act of placing or touching the ball on the ground behind the goal line, as in scoring a try **3** *American football* a scoring play worth six points, achieved by being in possession of the ball in the opposing team's end zone. Abbrev: **TD** ▷ *vb* **touch down** *(intr, adv)* **4** (of an aircraft, etc) to land **5** *rugby* to place the ball behind the goal line, as when scoring a try

touché (tu:'ʃeɪ) *interj* **1** an acknowledgment of a scoring hit in fencing **2** an acknowledgment of the striking home of a remark, witty reply, etc [from F, lit.: touched]

touched (tʌtʃt) *adj (postpositive)* **1** moved to sympathy or emotion **2** showing slight insanity

touchhole ('tʌtʃ,həʊl) *n* a hole in the breech of early cannon and firearms through which the charge was ignited

touching ('tʌtʃɪŋ) *adj* **1** evoking or eliciting tender feelings ▷ *prep* **2** on the subject of; relating to > **'touchingly** *adv*

touch judge *n* one of the two linesmen in rugby

touchline ('tʌtʃ,laɪn) *n* either of the lines marking the side of the playing area in certain games, such as rugby

touchmark ('tʌtʃ,mɑ:k) *n* a maker's mark stamped on pewter objects

touch-me-not *n* an impatiens with yellow spurred flowers and seed pods that burst open at a touch when ripe. Also called: **noli-me-tangere**

touch off *vb (tr, adv)* **1** to cause to explode, as by touching with a match **2** to cause (a disturbance, violence, etc) to begin

touchpaper ('tʌtʃ,peɪpə) *n* paper soaked in saltpetre for lighting fireworks or firing gunpowder

touch rugby *n* a non-contact version of rugby for seven players in a team, in which the player who is touched must pass the ball

touch screen *n* **a** a visual display unit screen that allows the user to give commands by touching certain areas of the screen with a finger rather than using a keyboard or mouse **b** *(as modifier)*: *a touch-screen computer; a touch-screen game*

touchstone ('tʌtʃ,stəʊn) *n* **1** a criterion or standard **2** a hard dark stone that is used to test gold and silver from the streak they produce on it

touch-tone *adj* of or relating to a telephone dialling system in which each dialling button pressed generates a different pitch, which is transmitted to the exchange

touch-type *vb* **touch-types, touch-typing, touch-typed** *(intr)* to type without looking at the keyboard > **'touch-,typist** *n*

touch up *vb (tr, adv)* **1** to put extra or finishing touches to **2** to enhance, renovate, or falsify by putting extra touches to **3** *Brit sl* to touch or caress (someone)

touchwood ('tʌtʃ,wʊd) *n* something, esp dry wood or fungus material, used as tinder [C16 TOUCH (in the sense: to kindle) + WOOD]

touchy ('tʌtʃɪ) *adj* **touchier, touchiest** **1** easily upset or irritated **2** extremely risky **3** easily ignited > **'touchily** *adv* > **'touchiness** *n*

touchy-feely ('tʌtʃɪ,fi:lɪ) *adj inf, sometimes derog* sensitive and caring

tough (tʌf) *adj* **1** strong or resilient; durable **2** not tender **3** hardy and fit **4** rough or pugnacious **5** resolute or intractable **6** difficult or troublesome to do or deal with: *a tough problem* **7** *inf* unfortunate or unlucky: *it's tough on him* ▷ *n* **8** a rough, vicious, or pugnacious person ▷ *adv* **9** *inf* violently, aggressively, or intractably: *to treat someone tough* ▷ *vb (tr)* **10** *sl* to stand firm, hold out against (a difficulty or difficult situation) (esp in **tough it out**) [OE *tōh*] > **'toughly** *adv* > **'toughness** *n*

toughen ('tʌfən) *vb* to make or become tough or tougher > **'toughener** *n*

tough love *n* the practice of taking a stern attitude towards a relative or friend suffering from an addiction, etc, to help the addict overcome the problem

tough-minded *adj* practical, unsentimental, or intractable > **,tough-'mindedness** *n*

Toul (tu:l) *n* a town in NE France: a leading episcopal see in the Middle Ages. Pop: 17 406 (1982)

Toulon (*French* tulɔ̃) *n* a fortified port and naval base in SE France, on the Mediterranean: naval arsenal developed by Henry IV and Richelieu, later fortified by Vauban. Pop: 159 389 (1999)

Toulouse (tu:'lu:z) *n* a city in S France, on the Garonne River: scene of severe religious strife in the early 13th and mid-16th centuries; university (1229). Pop: 390 413 (1999). Ancient name: **Tolosa** (tə'ləʊsə)

Toulouse-Lautrec (*French* tuluzlotrɛk) *n* **Henri** (**Marie Raymond**) **de** (ɑ̃ri də) 1864–1901, French painter and lithographer, noted for his paintings and posters of the life of Montmartre, Paris

toupee ('tu:peɪ) *n* a hairpiece worn by men to cover a bald place [C18 apparently from F *toupet* forelock, from OF *toup* top, of Gmc origin]

tour (tʊə) *n* **1** an extended journey visiting places of interest along the route **2** *mil* a period of service, esp in one place **3** a short trip, as for inspection **4** a trip made by a theatre company, orchestra, etc, to perform in several places **5** an overseas trip made by a cricket or rugby team, etc, to play in several places ▷ *vb* **6** to make a tour of (a place) **7** *(tr)* to perform (a show) or promote (a product) in several different places [C14 from OF: a turn, from L *tornus* a lathe, from Gk *tornos*]

touraco *or* **turaco** ('tʊərə,kəʊ) *n, pl* **touracos** *or* **turacos** any of a family of brightly coloured crested African birds [C18 of West African origin]

Touraine (*French* turɛn) *n* a former province of NW central France: at its height in the 16th century as an area of royal residences, esp along the Loire. Chief town: Tours

Tourane (tu:'rɑ:n) *n* the former name of **Da Nang**

Tourcoing (*French* turkwɛ̃) *n* a town in NE France: textile manufacturing. Pop: 93 765 (1990)

tour de force *French* (tur də fɔrs) *n, pl* ***tours de force*** (tur) a masterly or brilliant stroke, creation, effect, or accomplishment [lit.: feat of skill or strength]

Touré ('tʊəreɪ) *n* (**Ahmed**) **Sékou** ('seɪku:) 1922–84, president of the Republic of Guinea (1958–84)

tourer ('tʊərə) *n* a large open car with a folding top, usually seating a driver and four passengers. Also called (esp US): **touring car**

tourism ('tʊərɪzəm) *n* tourist travel, esp when regarded as an industry

tourist ('tʊərɪst) *n* **1a** a person who travels for pleasure, usually sightseeing and staying in hotels **1b** *(as modifier)*: *tourist attractions* **2** a person on an excursion or sightseeing tour **3** a member of a touring team **4** Also called: **tourist class** the lowest class of accommodation on a passenger ship or aircraft ▷ *adj* **5** of or relating to tourist accommodation > **tour'istic** *adj*

touristy ('tʊərɪstɪ) *adj inf, often derog* abounding in or designed for tourists

tourmaline ('tʊəmə,li:n) *n* any of a group of hard glassy minerals of variable colour consisting of a complex silicate of boron and aluminium in crystalline form: used in jewellery and optical and electrical equipment [C18 from G *Turmalin*, from Sinhalese *toramalli* carnelian]

Tournai (*French* turnɛ) *n* a city in W Belgium, in Hainaut province on the River Scheldt: under several different European rulers until 1814. Pop: 68 086 (1995 est). Flemish name: **Doornik**

tournament ('tʊənəmənt) *n* **1** a sporting competition in which contestants play a series of games to determine an overall winner **2** a meeting for athletic or other sporting contestants: *an archery tournament* **3** *medieval history* a martial sport or contest in which mounted combatants fought for a prize [C13 from OF *torneiement*, from *torneier* to fight on horseback, lit.: to turn, from the constant wheeling round of the combatants; see TOURNEY]

tournedos ('tʊənəˌdəʊ) *n, pl* **tournedos** (-ˌdəʊz) a thick round steak of beef [from F, from *tourner* to TURN + *dos* back]

Tourneur ('tɜːnə) *n* **Cyril** ?1575–1626, English dramatist; author of *The Atheist's Tragedy* (1611) and, reputedly, of *The Revenger's Tragedy* (1607)

tourney ('tʊənɪ, 'tɔː-) *medieval history* ▷ *n* **1** a knightly tournament ▷ *vb* **2** (*intr*) to engage in a tourney [C13 from OF *torneier*, from Vulgar L *tornidiāre* (unattested) to turn constantly, from L *tornāre* to TURN (in a lathe); see TOURNAMENT]

tourniquet ('tʊənɪˌkeɪ) *n med* any device for constricting an artery of the arm or leg to control bleeding [C17 from F: device that operates by turning, from *tourner* to TURN]

tour operator *n* a person or company that specializes in providing package holidays

Tours (*French* tur) *n* a town in W central France, on the River Loire: nearby is the scene of the defeat of the Arabs in 732, which ended the advance of Islam in W Europe. Pop: 132 820 (1999)

tourtière (ˌtuːrtɪ'ɛə; *French* turtjɛr) *n Canad* a type of meat pie [from French]

tousle ('taʊzᵊl) *vb* **tousles, tousling, tousled** (*tr*) **1** to tangle, ruffle, or disarrange **2** to treat roughly ▷ *n* **3** a disorderly, tangled, or rumpled state **4** a dishevelled or disordered mass, esp of hair [C15 from Low G *tūsen* to shake]

Toussaint L'Ouverture (*French* tusɛ̃ luvɛrtyr) *n* **Pierre Dominique** (pjɛr dɔminik) ?1743–1803, Haitian revolutionary leader. He was made governor of the island by the French Revolutionary government (1794) and expelled the Spanish and British but when Napoleon I proclaimed the re-establishment of slavery he was arrested. He died in prison in France

tout (taʊt) *vb* **1** to solicit (business, customers, etc) or hawk (merchandise), esp in a brazen way **2** (*intr*) **2a** to spy on racehorses being trained in order to obtain information for betting purposes **2b** to sell such information or to take bets, esp in public places ▷ *n* **3** a person who touts **4** Also: **ticket tout** a person who sells tickets for a heavily booked event at inflated prices [C14 (in the sense: to peer, look out): rel. to OE *tȳtan* to peep out] > **'touter** *n*

tout à fait *French* (tut a fɛ) *adv* completely

tout de suite *French* (tud sɥit) *adv* at once

tout le monde *French* (tu lə mɔ̃d) *n* all the world; everyone

tovarisch, tovarich, *or* **tovarish** (tə'vɑːrɪʃ) *n* comrade: a term of address [from Russian]

tow¹ (təʊ) *vb* **1** (*tr*) to pull or drag (a vehicle, boat, etc), esp by means of a rope or cable ▷ *n* **2** the act or an instance of towing **3** the state of being towed (esp in **in tow, on tow**) **4** something towed **5** something used for towing **6** **in tow** in one's charge or under one's influence **7** short for **ski tow** [OE *togian*] > **'towable** *adj* > **'towage** *n*

tow² (təʊ) *n* the coarse and broken fibres of hemp, flax, jute, etc, prepared for spinning [OE *tōw*] > **'towy** *adj*

toward *adj* ('təʊəd) **1** *now rare* in progress; afoot **2** *obs* about to happen; imminent **3** *obs* promising or favourable ▷ *prep* (tə'wɔːd, tɔːd) **4** a variant of **towards** [OE *tōweard*]

towards (tə'wɔːdz, tɔːdz) *prep* **1** in the direction or vicinity of: *towards London* **2** with regard to: *her feelings towards me* **3** as a contribution or help to: *money towards a new car* **4** just before: *towards noon* ▷ Also: **toward**

towbar ('təʊˌbɑː) *n* a rigid metal bar or frame used for towing vehicles

towboat ('təʊˌbəʊt) *n* another word for **tug** (sense 4)

tow-coloured *adj* pale yellow; flaxen

towel ('taʊəl) *n* **1** a piece of absorbent cloth or paper used for drying things **2** **throw in the towel.** See **throw in** (sense 3) ▷ *vb* **towels, towelling, towelled** *or US* **towels, toweling, toweled** **3** (*tr*) to dry or wipe with a towel **4** (*tr*; often foll by *up*) *Austral sl* to assault or beat (a person) [C13 from OF *toaille*, of Gmc origin]

towelling ('taʊəlɪŋ) *n* an absorbent fabric used for making towels, bathrobes, etc

tower ('taʊə) *n* **1** a tall, usually square or circular structure, sometimes part of a larger building and usually built for a specific purpose **2** a place of defence or retreat **3** **tower of strength** a person who gives support, comfort, etc ▷ *vb* **4** (*intr*) to be or rise like a tower; loom [C12 from OF *tur*, from L *turris*, from Gk]

Tower Hamlets *n* a borough of E Greater London, on the River Thames: contains the main part of the East End. Pop: 196 121 (2001). Area: 20 sq km (8 sq miles)

towering ('taʊərɪŋ) *adj* **1** very tall; lofty **2** outstanding, as in importance or stature **3** (*prenominal*) very intense: *a towering rage*

Tower of London *n* a fortress in the City of London, on the River Thames: begun 1078; later extended and used as a palace, the main state prison, and now as a museum containing the crown jewels

towhead ('təʊˌhɛd) *n* **1** a person with blond or yellowish hair **2** a head of such hair [from TOW² (flax)] > ˌ**tow'headed** *adj*

towhee ('taʊˌhiː, 'təʊ-) *n* any of various North American brownish-coloured sparrows [C18 imit.]

towie ('taʊɪ) *n Austral inf* a truck used for towing

towline ('təʊˌlaɪn) *n* another name for **towrope**

town (taʊn) *n* **1** a densely populated urban area, typically smaller than a city and larger than a village **2** a city, borough, or other urban area **3** (in the US) a territorial unit of local government that is smaller than a county; township **4** the nearest town or commercial district **5** London or the chief city of an area **6** the inhabitants of a town **7** **go to town** **7a** to make a supreme or unrestricted effort **7b** *Austral & NZ inf* to lose one's temper **8** **on the town** seeking out entertainments and amusements [OE *tūn* village] > **'townish** *adj*

town clerk *n* **1** (in Britain until 1974) the secretary and chief administrative officer of a town or city **2** (in the US) the official who keeps the records of a town

town crier *n* (formerly) a person employed to make public announcements in the streets

Townes (taʊnz) *n* **Charles Hard** born 1915, US physicist, noted for his research in quantum electronics leading to the invention of the maser and the laser; shared the Nobel prize for physics in 1964

town gas *n* coal gas manufactured for domestic and industrial use

town hall *n* the chief building in which municipal business is transacted, often with a hall for public meetings

town house *n* **1** a terraced house in an urban area, esp a fashionable one **2** a person's town residence as distinct from his or her country residence

townie ('taʊnɪ) *or* **townee** (taʊ'niː) *n inf, often disparaging* a permanent resident in a town, esp as distinct from country dwellers or students

townland ('taʊnlænd) *n Irish* a division of land of various sizes

town planning *n* the comprehensive planning of the

physical and social development of a town. US term: **city planning**

townscape ('taʊnskeɪp) *n* **1** a view of an urban scene **2** an extensive area of urban development

Townshend ('taʊnzɛnd) *n* **1 Charles,** 2nd Viscount. 1674–1738, English politician and agriculturist **2 Pete** born 1945, British rock guitarist, singer, and songwriter: member of the Who (1964–83) and composer of much of their material

township ('taʊnʃɪp) *n* **1** a small town **2** (in the Scottish Highlands) a small crofting community **3** (in the US and Canada) a territorial area, esp a subdivision of a county: often organized as a unit of local government **4** (in Canada) a land-survey area, usually 36 square miles (93 square kilometres) **5** (formerly, in South Africa) a planned urban settlement of Black Africans or Coloured people **6** *English history* **6a** any of the local districts of a large parish **6b** the parish itself

townsman ('taʊnzmən) *n, pl* **townsmen 1** an inhabitant of a town **2** a person from the same town as oneself > **'towns,woman** *fem n*

townspeople ('taʊnz,piːpᵊl) *or* **townsfolk** ('taʊnz,fəʊk) *pl n* the inhabitants of a town; citizens

Townsville ('taʊnzvɪl) *n* a port in E Australia, in NE Queensland on the Coral Sea: centre of a vast agricultural and mining hinterland. Pop: 87 235 (1998 est)

towpath ('təʊ,pɑːθ) *n* a path beside a canal or river, used by people or animals towing boats. Also called: **towing path**

towrope ('təʊ,rəʊp) *n* a rope or cable used for towing a vehicle or vessel. Also called: **towline**

tox-, toxic- *or before a consonant* **toxo-, toxico-** *combining form* indicating poison: *toxaemia* [from L *toxicum*]

toxaemia *or US* **toxemia** (tɒk'siːmɪə) *n* **1** a condition characterized by the presence of bacterial toxins in the blood **2** the condition in pregnancy of pre-eclampsia or eclampsia > **tox'aemic** *or US* **tox'emic** *adj*

toxic ('tɒksɪk) *adj* **1** of or caused by a toxin or poison **2** harmful or deadly [C17 from Medical L *toxicus*, from L *toxicum* poison, from Gk *toxikon* (*pharmakon*) (poison) used on arrows, from *toxon* arrow] > **'toxically** *adv* > **toxicity** (tɒk'sɪsɪtɪ) *n*

toxicant ('tɒksɪkənt) *n* **1** a toxic substance; poison ▷ *adj* **2** poisonous; toxic [C19 from Med. L *toxicāre* to poison]

toxic effect *n* an adverse effect of a drug produced by an exaggeration of the effect that produces the therapeutic response

toxicology (,tɒksɪ'kɒlədʒɪ) *n* the branch of science concerned with poisons, their effects, antidotes, etc > **toxicological** (,tɒksɪkə'lɒdʒɪkᵊl) *or* **,toxico'logic** *adj* > **,toxi'cologist** *n*

toxic shock syndrome *n* a potentially fatal condition in women, characterized by fever, stomachache, a painful rash, and a drop in blood pressure, that is caused by staphylococcal blood poisoning, commonly from a retained tampon

toxin ('tɒksɪn) *n* **1** any of various poisonous substances produced by microorganisms that stimulate the production of neutralizing substances (antitoxins) in the body **2** any other poisonous substance of plant or animal origin

toxin-antitoxin *n* a mixture of a toxin and antitoxin. The diphtheria toxin-antitoxin was formerly used for immunization

toxocariasis (,tɒksəkə'raɪəsɪs) *n* the infection of humans with the larvae of a genus of roundworms, *Toxocara*, of dogs and cats

toxoid ('tɒksɔɪd) *n* a toxin that has been treated to reduce its toxicity and is used in immunization to stimulate production of antitoxins

toxophilite (tɒk'sɒfɪ,laɪt) *formal* ▷ *n* **1** an archer ▷ *adj* **2** of archery [C18 from *Toxophilus*, the title of a book (1545) by Ascham, designed to mean: a lover of the bow, from Gk *toxon* bow + *philos* loving] > **tox'ophily** *n*

toxoplasmosis (,tɒksəʊplæz'məʊsɪs) *n* a protozoal disease characterized by jaundice and convulsions > **,toxo'plasmic** *adj*

toy (tɔɪ) *n* **1** an object designed to be played with **2a** something that is a nonfunctioning replica of something else, esp a miniature one **2b** (*as modifier*): *a toy guitar* **3** any small thing of little value; trifle **4a** something small or miniature, esp a miniature variety of a breed of dog **4b** (*as modifier*): *a toy poodle* ▷ *vb* **5** (*intr; usually foll by with*) to play, fiddle, or flirt [C16 (in the sense: amorous dalliance): from ?]

Toyama ('təʊjɑː,mɑː) *n* a city in central Japan, on W Honshu on **Toyama Bay** (an inlet of the Sea of Japan): chemical and textile centre. Pop: 325 303 (1995)

toy boy *n* the much younger male lover of an older woman

Toynbee ('tɔɪnbɪ) *n* **1 Arnold** 1852–83, British economist and social reformer, after whom **Toynbee Hall,** a residential settlement in East London, is named **2** his nephew, **Arnold Joseph** 1889–1975, British historian. In his chief work, *A Study of History* (1934–61), he attempted to analyse the principles determining the rise and fall of civilizations

toy-toy *or* **toyi-toyi** ('tɔɪ'tɔɪ) *S African* ▷ *n* **1** a dance expressing defiance and protest ▷ *vb (intr)* **2** to dance in this way [from ?]

TPI *abbrev for* tax and price index: a measure of the increase in taxable income needed to compensate for an increase in retail prices

TPWS *abbrev for* train-protection warning system: a rail safety system that warns the driver if the train passes a stop signal

TQM *abbrev for* total quality management

tr *abbrev for:* **1** transitive **2** treasurer

tr. *abbrev for:* **1** translated **2** *music* trill

trabeated ('treɪbɪ,eɪtɪd) *or* **trabeate** ('treɪbɪɪt, -,eɪt) *adj archit* constructed with horizontal beams as opposed to arches [C19 back formation from *trabeation*, from L *trabs* a beam]

trabecula (trə'bɛkjʊlə) *n, pl* **trabeculae** (-,liː) *anat, bot* any of various rod-shaped structures that divide organs into separate chambers [C19 via NL from L: a little beam, from *trabs* a beam] > **tra'becular** *or* **tra'beculate** *adj*

Trabzon ('trɑːbzɔːn) *or* **Trebizond** *n* a port in NE Turkey, on the Black Sea: founded as a Greek colony in the 8th century BC at the terminus of an important trade route from central Europe to Asia. Pop: 182 552 (1997)

trace[1] (treɪs) *n* **1** a mark or other sign that something has been in a place **2** a scarcely detectable amount or characteristic **3** a footprint or other indication of the passage of an animal or person **4** any line drawn by a recording instrument or a record consisting of a number of such lines **5** something drawn, such as a tracing **6** *chiefly US* a beaten track or path ▷ *vb* **traces, tracing, traced 7** (*tr*) to follow, discover, or ascertain the course or development of (something) **8** (*tr*) to track down and find, as by following a trail **9** to copy (a design, map, etc) by drawing over the lines visible through a superimposed sheet of transparent paper **10** (*tr; often foll by out*) **10a** to draw or delineate a plan or diagram of **10b** to outline or sketch (an idea, etc) **11** (*tr*) to decorate with tracery **12** (usually foll by *back*) to follow or be followed to source; date back: *his ancestors trace back to the 16th century* [C13 from F *tracier*, from Vulgar L *tractiāre* (unattested) to drag, from L *tractus*, from *trahere*] > **'traceable** *adj* > **,tracea'bility** *or* **'traceableness** *n* > **'traceably** *adv*

trace[2] (treɪs) *n* **1** either of the two side straps that connect a horse's harness to the swingletree **2** *angling* a length of nylon or, formerly, gut attaching a hook or fly to a line **3 kick over the traces** to escape or defy control

[C14 *trais*, from OF *trait*, ult. from L *trahere* to drag]

trace element *n* any of various chemical elements, such as iron, manganese, zinc, copper, and iodine, that occur in very small amounts in organisms and are essential for many physiological and biochemical processes

trace fossil *n* the fossilized remains of a track, trail, footprint, burrow, etc, of an organism

tracer (ˈtreɪsə) *n* **1** a person or thing that traces **2** a projectile that can be observed when in flight by the burning of chemical substances in its base **3** *med* any radioactive isotope introduced into the body to study metabolic processes, etc, by following its progress with a gamma counter or other detector **4** an investigation to trace missing cargo, mail, etc

tracer bullet *n* a round of small arms ammunition containing a tracer

tracery (ˈtreɪsərɪ) *n, pl* **traceries 1** a pattern of interlacing ribs, esp as used in the upper part of a Gothic window, etc **2** any fine pattern resembling this > ˈ**traceried** *adj*

trachea (trəˈkiːə) *n, pl* **tracheae** (-ˈkiːiː) **1** *anat, zool* the tube that conveys inhaled air from the larynx to the bronchi **2** any of the tubes in insects and related animals that convey air from the spiracles to the tissues [C16 from Med. L, from Gk *trakheia*, shortened from (*artēria*) *trakheia* rough (artery), from *trakhus* rough] > **traˈcheal** *or* **traˈcheate** *adj*

tracheitis (ˌtreɪkɪˈaɪtɪs) *n* inflammation of the trachea

tracheo- *or before a vowel* **trache-** *combining form* denoting the trachea

tracheotomy (ˌtrækɪˈɒtəmɪ) *n, pl* **tracheotomies** surgical incision into the trachea, as performed when the air passage has been blocked

trachoma (trəˈkəʊmə) *n* a chronic contagious disease of the eye caused by a species of chlamydia: a severe form of conjunctivitis that can result in scarring and blindness [C17 from NL, from Gk *trakhōma* roughness, from *trakhus* rough] > **trachomatous** (trəˈkɒmətəs) *adj*

trachyte (ˈtreɪkaɪt, ˈtræ-) *n* a light-coloured fine-grained volcanic rock [C19 from F, from Gk *trakhutēs*, from *trakhus* rough]

tracing (ˈtreɪsɪŋ) *n* **1** a copy made by tracing **2** the act of making a trace **3** a record made by an instrument

track (træk) *n* **1** the mark or trail left by something that has passed by **2** any road or path, esp a rough one **3** a rail or pair of parallel rails on which a vehicle, such as a locomotive, runs **4** a course of action, thought, etc: *don't start on that track again!* **5** a line of motion or travel, such as flight **6** an endless band on the wheels of a tank, tractor, etc, to enable it to move across rough ground **7a** a course for running or racing **7b** (*as modifier*): *track events* **8** *US & Canad* **8a** sports performed on a track **8b** track and field events as a whole **9** a path on a magnetic recording medium, esp magnetic tape, on which music or speech is recorded **10** any of a number of separate sections in the recording on a record, CD, or cassette **11** the distance between the points of contact with the ground of a pair of wheels, as of a motor vehicle **12 keep** (*or* **lose**) **track of** to follow (or fail to follow) the passage, course, or progress of **13 off the track** away from what is correct or true **14 on the track of** on the scent or trail of; pursuing ▷ *vb* **15** to follow the trail of (a person, animal, etc) **16** to follow the flight path of (a satellite, etc) by picking up signals transmitted or reflected by it **17** *US railways* **17a** to provide with a track **17b** to run on a track of (a certain width) **18** (of a camera or camera-operator) to follow (a moving object) while operating **19** to follow a track through (a place): *to track the jungles* **20** (*intr*) (of the pick-up, stylus, etc, of a record player) to follow the groove of a record ▷ See also **tracks** [C15 from OF *trac*, prob. of Gmc origin] > ˈ**tracker** *n*

track down *vb* (*tr, adv*) to find by tracking or pursuing

tracker dog *n* a dog specially trained to search for missing people

track event *n* a competition in athletics, such as relay running or sprinting, that takes place on a running track

tracking (ˈtrækɪŋ) *n* **1** the act or process of following something or someone **2** *electrical engineering* a leakage of electric current between two insulated points caused by dirt, carbon particles, moisture, etc **3** the way wheels on a vehicle are aligned **4** a function of a video cassette recorder, which adjusts the alignment of the heads in order to achieve the best possible audio and video reproduction from each recording

tracking shot *n* a camera shot in which the cameraman follows a specific person or event in the action

tracking station *n* a station that can use a radio or radar beam to follow the path of an object in space or in the atmosphere

tracklaying (ˈtrækˌleɪɪŋ) *adj also* **tracked** (of a vehicle) having an endless jointed metal band around the wheels

track record *n inf* the past record of the accomplishments and failures of a person, business, etc

track rod *n* the rod connecting the two front wheels of a motor vehicle

tracks (træks) *pl n* **1** (*sometimes sing*) marks, such as footprints, etc, left by someone or something that has passed **2 in one's tracks** on the very spot where one is standing **3 make tracks** to leave or depart **4 make tracks for** to go or head towards

track shoe *n* either of a pair of light running shoes fitted with steel spikes for better grip

tracksuit (ˈtrækˌsuːt) *n* a warm suit worn by athletes, etc, esp during training

tract[1] (trækt) *n* **1** an extended area, as of land **2** *anat* a system of organs, glands, etc, that has a particular function: *the digestive tract* **3** *arch* an extended period of time [C15 from L *tractus* a stretching out, from *trahere* to drag]

tract[2] (trækt) *n* a treatise or pamphlet, esp a religious or moralistic one [C15 from L *tractātus* TRACTATE]

tractable (ˈtræktəbᵊl) *adj* **1** easily controlled or persuaded **2** readily worked; malleable [C16 from L *tractābilis*, from *tractāre* to manage, from *trahere* to draw] > ˌ**tractaˈbility** *or* ˈ**tractableness** *n* > ˈ**tractably** *adv*

Tractarianism (trækˈtɛərɪəˌnɪzəm) *n* another name for the **Oxford Movement** [after the series of tracts, *Tracts for the Times*, published between 1833 and 1841, in which the principles of the movement were presented] > **Tracˈtarian** *n, adj*

tractate (ˈtrækteɪt) *n* a treatise [C15 from L *tractātus*, from *tractāre* to handle; see TRACTABLE]

traction (ˈtrækʃən) *n* **1** the act of drawing or pulling, esp by motive power **2** the state of being drawn or pulled **3** *med* the application of a steady pull on a limb, etc, using a system of weights and pulleys or splints **4** adhesive friction, as between a wheel of a motor vehicle and the road [C17 from Med. L *tractiō*, from L *tractus* dragged, from *trahere* to drag] > ˈ**tractional** *adj* > **tractive** (ˈtræktɪv) *adj*

traction engine *n* a steam-powered locomotive used, esp formerly, for drawing heavy loads along roads or over rough ground

traction load *n geol* the solid material that is carried along the bed of a river

tractor (ˈtræktə) *n* **1** a motor vehicle with large rear wheels or endless belt treads, used to pull heavy loads, esp farm machinery **2** a short vehicle with a driver's cab, used to pull a trailer, as in an articulated lorry [C18 from LL: one who pulls, from *trahere* to drag]

Tracy (ˈtreɪsɪ) *n* **Spencer** 1900–67, US film actor. His films include *The Power and the Glory* (1933), *Captains Courageous* (1937) and *Boys' Town* (1938), for the last two of which he

Tt

won Oscars, *Adam's Rib* (1949), and *Bad Day at Black Rock* (1955)

trad (træd) *n* **1** *chiefly Brit* traditional jazz ▷ *adj* **2** short for **traditional**

trade (treɪd) *n* **1** the act or an instance of buying and selling goods and services **2** a personal occupation, esp a craft requiring skill **3** the people and practices of an industry, craft, or business **4** exchange of one thing for something else **5** the regular clientele of a firm or industry **6** amount of custom or commercial dealings; business **7** a specified market or business: *the tailoring trade* **8** an occupation in commerce, as opposed to a profession ▷ *vb* **trades, trading, traded 9** (*tr*) to buy and sell (merchandise) **10** to exchange (one thing) for another **11** (*intr*) to engage in trade **12** (*intr*) to deal or do business (with) ▷ See also **trade-in, trade on** [C14 (in the sense: track, hence, a regular business)] > **'tradable** *or* **'tradeable** *adj*

trade agreement *n* a commercial treaty between two or more nations

trade association *n* an association of organizations in the same trade formed to further their collective interests, esp in negotiating with governments, trade unions, etc

trade cycle *n* the recurrent fluctuation between boom and depression in the economic activity of a capitalist country

trade discount *n* a sum or percentage deducted from the list price of a commodity allowed to a retailer or by one enterprise to another in the same trade

traded option *n stock exchange* an option that can itself be bought and sold on a stock exchange. ▷ Cf **traditional option**

trade down *vb* (*intr, adv*) to sell a large or relatively expensive house, car, etc, and replace it with a smaller or less expensive one

trade gap *n* the amount by which the value of a country's visible imports exceeds that of visible exports; an unfavourable balance of trade

trade-in *n* **1a** a used article given in part payment for the purchase of a new article **1b** a transaction involving such part payment **1c** the valuation put on the article traded in ▷ *vb* **trade in 2** (*tr, adv*) to give (a used article) as part payment for a new article

trademark ('treɪdˌmɑːk) *n* **1a** the name or other symbol used by a manufacturer or dealer to distinguish his products from those of competitors **1b Registered Trademark** one that is officially registered and legally protected **2** any distinctive sign or mark of the presence of a person or animal ▷ *vb* (*tr*) **3** to label with a trademark **4** to register as a trademark

trade name *n* **1** the name used by a trade to refer to a commodity, service, etc **2** the name under which a commercial enterprise operates in business

trade-off *n* an exchange, esp as a compromise

trade on *vb* (*intr, prep*) to exploit or take advantage of: *he traded on her endless patience*

trade plate *n* a numberplate attached temporarily to a vehicle by a dealer, etc, before the vehicle has been registered

trader ('treɪdə) *n* **1** a person who engages in trade **2** a vessel regularly employed in trade **3** *stock exchange, US* a member who operates mainly on his or her own account

trade reference *n* a reference in which one trader gives his or her opinion as to the credit worthiness of another trader in the same trade, esp to a supplier

tradescantia (ˌtrædɛsˈkænʃɪə) *n* any of a genus of plants widely cultivated for their striped variegated leaves [C18 NL, after John *Tradescant* (1608–62), E botanist]

Trades Council *n* (in Britain) an association of the different trade unions in one town or area

trade secret *n* a secret formula, technique, process, etc, known and used to advantage by only one manufacturer

tradesman ('treɪdzmən) *n, pl* **tradesmen 1** a man engaged in trade, esp a retail dealer **2** a skilled worker > **'tradesˌwoman** *fem n*

tradespeople ('treɪdzˌpiːpᵊl) *or* **tradesfolk** ('treɪdzˌfəʊk) *pl n chiefly Brit* people engaged in trade, esp shopkeepers

Trades Union Congress *n* the major association of British trade unions, which includes all the larger unions. Abbrev: **TUC**

trade union *or* **trades union** *n* an association of employees formed to improve their incomes and working conditions by collective bargaining > **trade unionism** *or* **trades unionism** *n* > **trade unionist** *or* **trades unionist** *n*

▷ www.tuc.org.uk
▷ www.actu.asn.au
▷ www.union.org.nz
▷ www.clc-ctc.ca
▷ www.cosatu.org.za

trade up *vb* (*intr, adv*) to sell a small or relatively inexpensive house, car, etc, and replace it with a larger or more expensive one

trade-weighted *adj* (of exchange rates) weighted according to the value of trade between the various countries involved

trade wind (wɪnd) *n* a wind blowing obliquely towards the equator either from the northeast in the N hemisphere or the southeast in the S hemisphere, between latitudes 30° N and S [C17 from *to blow trade* to blow steadily in one direction, from *trade* in the obs. sense: a track]

trading estate *n chiefly Brit* a large area in which a number of commercial or industrial firms are situated. Also called: **industrial estate**

trading post *n* a general store in an unsettled or thinly populated region

tradition (trəˈdɪʃən) *n* **1** the handing down from generation to generation of customs, beliefs, etc **2** the body of customs, thought, etc, belonging to a particular country, people, family, or institution over a long period **3** a specific custom or practice of long standing **4** *Christianity* a doctrine regarded as having been established by Christ or the apostles though not contained in Scripture **5** (*often cap*) *Judaism* a body of laws regarded as having been handed down from Moses orally **6** the beliefs and customs of Islam supplementing the Koran **7** *law, chiefly Roman & Scots* the act of formally transferring ownership of movable property [C14 from L *trāditiō* a handing down, surrender, from *trādere* to give up, transmit, from TRANS- + *dāre* to give] > **tra'ditionless** *adj*

traditional (trəˈdɪʃənᵊl) *adj* **1** of, relating to, or being a tradition **2** of the style of jazz originating in New Orleans, characterized by collective improvisation by a front line of trumpet, trombone, and clarinet > **tra'ditionally** *adv*

traditionalism (trəˈdɪʃənᵊˌlɪzəm) *n* **1** the doctrine that all knowledge originates in divine revelation and is perpetuated by tradition **2** adherence to tradition, esp in religion > **tra'ditionalist** *n, adj* > **traˌditional'istic** *adj*

traditional logic *n* the logic of the late Middle Ages, derived from Aristotelian logic, and concerned esp with the study of the syllogism

traditional option *n stock exchange* an option that once purchased cannot be resold. ▷ Cf **traded option**

traditional weapon *n S African* a weapon having ceremonial tribal significance, such as an assegai or knobkerrie

traduce (trəˈdjuːs) *vb* **traduces, traducing, traduced** (*tr*) to speak badly or maliciously of [C16 from L *trādūcere* to lead over, disgrace] > **tra'ducement** *n* > **tra'ducer** *n*

Trafalgar (trəˈfælgə; *Spanish* trafalˈɣar) *n* **Cape** a cape on

the SW coast of Spain, south of Cádiz: scene of the decisive naval battle (1805) in which the French and Spanish fleets were defeated by the British under Nelson, who was mortally wounded
▷ www.nelsonsnavy.co.uk/battle-of-trafalgar.html
▷ www.napoleonguide.com/battle_trafalgar.htm

traffic (ˈtræfɪk) *n* **1a** the vehicles coming and going in a street, town, etc **1b** (*as modifier*): *traffic lights* **2** the movement of vehicles, people, etc, in a particular place or for a particular purpose: *sea traffic* **3** (usually foll by *with*) dealings or business **4** trade, esp of an illicit kind: *drug traffic* **5** the aggregate volume of messages transmitted through a communications system in a given period **6** *chiefly US* the number of customers patronizing a commercial establishment in a given time period ▷ *vb* **traffics, trafficking, trafficked** (*intr*) **7** (often foll by *in*) to carry on trade or business, esp of an illicit kind **8** (usually foll by *with*) to have dealings [C16 from OF *trafique*, from OIt. *traffico*, from *trafficare* to engage in trade] > ˈ**trafficker** *n*

trafficator (ˈtræfɪˌkeɪtə) *n* (formerly) an illuminated arm on a motor vehicle raised to indicate a left or right turn

traffic calming *n* the use of a series of devices, such as bends and humps in the road, to slow down traffic, esp in residential areas

traffic island *n* a raised area in the middle of a road designed as a guide for traffic flow and to provide a stopping place for pedestrians crossing

traffic jam *n* a number of vehicles so obstructed that they can scarcely move

traffic light *or* **signal** *n* one of a set of coloured lights at crossroads or junctions, to control the flow of traffic

traffic pattern *n* a pattern of permitted lanes in the air around an airport to which an aircraft is restricted

traffic warden *n Brit* a person who is appointed to supervise road traffic and report traffic offences

Trafford (ˈtræfəd) *n* a unitary authority in NW England, in Greater Manchester. Pop: 210 135 (2001). Area: 106 sq km (41 sq miles)

tragacanth (ˈtrægəˌkænθ) *n* **1** any of various spiny plants that yield a substance that is made into a gum **2** the gum obtained from these plants, used in the manufacture of pills and lozenges and in calico printing [C16 from F *tragacante*, from L *tragacantha* goat's thorn, from Gk, from *tragos* goat + *akantha* thorn]

tragedian (trəˈdʒiːdɪən) *or* (*fem*) **tragedienne** (trəˌdʒiːdɪˈɛn) *n* **1** an actor who specializes in tragic roles **2** a writer of tragedy

tragedy (ˈtrædʒɪdɪ) *n, pl* **tragedies 1** a play in which the protagonist falls to disaster through the combination of a personal failing and circumstances with which he cannot deal **2** any dramatic or literary composition dealing with serious or sombre themes and ending with disaster **3** the branch of drama dealing with such themes **4** the unfortunate aspect of something **5** a shocking or sad event; disaster [C14 from OF *tragédie*, from L *tragoedia*, from Gk, from *tragos* goat + *ōidē* song; ?from the goat-satyrs of Peloponnesian plays]

tragic (ˈtrædʒɪk) *or* (*less commonly*) **tragical** *adj* **1** of, relating to, or characteristic of tragedy **2** mournful or pitiable > ˈ**tragically** *adv*

tragic flaw *n* the failing of character in a tragic hero

tragic irony *n* the use of dramatic irony in a tragedy so that the audience is aware that a character's words or actions will bring about a tragic or fatal result, while the character himself is not

tragicomedy (ˌtrædʒɪˈkɒmɪdɪ) *n, pl* **tragicomedies 1** a drama in which aspects of both tragedy and comedy are found **2** an event or incident having both comic and tragic aspects [C16 from F, ult. from LL *tragicōmoedia*] > ˌ**tragiˈcomic** *or* ˌ**tragiˈcomical** *adj*

tragopan (ˈtrægəˌpæn) *n* any of a genus of pheasants of S and SE Asia, having brightly coloured fleshy processes on the head [C19 via L from Gk, from *tragos* goat + PAN]

tragus (ˈtreɪgəs) *n, pl* **tragi** (-dʒaɪ) the fleshy projection that partially covers the entrance to the external ear [C17 from LL, from Gk *tragos* hairy projection of the ear, lit.: goat]

Traherne (trəˈhɜːn) *n* **Thomas** 1637–74, English mystical prose writer and poet. His prose works include *Centuries of Meditations*, which was discovered in manuscript in 1896 and published in 1908

trail (treɪl) *vb* **1** to drag, stream, or permit to drag or stream along a surface, esp the ground **2** to make (a track) through (a place) **3** to follow or hunt (an animal or person) by following marks or tracks **4** (when *intr*, often foll by *behind*) to lag or linger behind (a person or thing) **5** (*intr*) (esp of plants) to extend or droop over or along a surface **6** (*intr*) to be falling behind in a race: *the favourite is trailing at the last fence* **7** (*tr*) to tow (a caravan, etc) behind a motor vehicle **8** (*tr*) to carry (a rifle) at the full length of the right arm in a horizontal position, with the muzzle to the fore **9** (*intr*) to move wearily or slowly **10** (*tr*) (on television or radio) to advertise (a future programme) with short extracts ▷ *n* **11** a print, mark, or scent made by a person, animal, or object **12** the act or an instance of trailing **13** a path, track, or road, esp one roughly blazed **14** something that trails behind or trails in loops or strands **15** the part of a towed gun carriage and limber that connects the two when in movement and rests on the ground as a partial support when unlimbered [C14 from OF *trailler* to tow, from Vulgar L *tragulāre* (unattested), from L *trāgula* dragnet, from *trahere* to drag]

trail away *or* **off** *vb* (*intr, adv*) to make or become fainter, quieter, or weaker

trailblazer (ˈtreɪlˌbleɪzə) *n* **1** a leader or pioneer in a particular field **2** a person who blazes a trail > ˈ**trailˌblazing** *adj, n*

trailer (ˈtreɪlə) *n* **1** a road vehicle, usually two-wheeled, towed by a motor vehicle: used for transporting boats, etc **2** the rear section of an articulated lorry **3** a series of short extracts from a film, used to advertise it in a cinema or on television **4** a person or thing that trails **5** the US and Canad name for **caravan** (sense 1)

trailer park *n US* a mobile-home site

trailer trash *n derog* **a** poor people living in trailer parks in the US **b** (*as modifier*): *trailer-trash culture*

trailing edge *n* the rear edge of a propeller blade or aerofoil. ▷ Cf **leading edge**

train (treɪn) *vb* **1** (*tr*) to guide or teach (to do something), as by subjecting to various exercises or experiences **2** (*tr*) to control or guide towards a specific goal: *to train a plant up a wall* **3** (*intr*) to do exercises and prepare for a specific purpose **4** (*tr*) to improve or curb by subjecting to discipline: *to train the mind* **5** (*tr*) to focus or bring to bear (on something): *to train a telescope on the moon* ▷ *n* **6** a line of coaches or wagons coupled together and drawn by a railway locomotive **7** a sequence or series: *a train of disasters* **8** a procession of people, vehicles, etc, travelling together, such as one carrying equipment in support of a military operation **9** a series of interacting parts through which motion is transmitted: *a train of gears* **10** a fuse or line of gunpowder to an explosive charge, etc **11** something drawn along, such as the long back section of a dress that trails along the floor **12** a retinue or suite [C14 from OF *trahiner*, from Vulgar L *tragīnāre* (unattested) to draw] > ˈ**trainable** *adj*

trainband (ˈtreɪnˌbænd) *n* a company of English militia from the 16th to the 18th century [C17 altered from *trained band*]

trainbearer (ˈtreɪnˌbɛərə) *n* an attendant who holds up the train of a dignitary's robe or bride's gown

trainee (treɪˈniː) *n* **a** a person undergoing training **b** (*as modifier*): *a trainee journalist*

Tt

trainer ('treɪnə) *n* **1** a person who trains athletes **2** a piece of equipment employed in training, such as a simulated aircraft cockpit **3** a person who schools racehorses **4** (*pl*) another name for **training shoes**

training ('treɪnɪŋ) *n* **1a** the process of bringing a person, etc, to an agreed standard of proficiency, etc, by practice and instruction **1b** (*as modifier*): *training college* **2 in training 2a** undergoing physical training **2b** physically fit **3 out of training** physically unfit

Training Agency *n* (in Britain) an organization established in 1989 to replace the **Training Commission**; it provides training and retraining for adult workers and operates the Youth Training Scheme, in England and Wales working through the local **Training and Enterprise Councils** (TECs) and in Scotland through the **Local Enterprise Companies** (LECs) set up in 1990

training shoes *pl n* **1** running shoes for sports training, esp in contrast to studded or spiked shoes worn for the sport itself **2** shoes in the style of those used for sports training. Also called: **trainers**

train oil *n* whale oil obtained from blubber [c16 from earlier *train* or *trane*, from MLow G *trān*, or MDu. *traen* tear, drop]

train smash *n S African inf* a disaster or serious setback (esp in the phrase **it's not a train smash**)

train spotter *n* **1** a person who collects the numbers of railway locomotives **2** *inf* a person who is obsessed with trivial details, esp of a subject generally considered uninteresting

▷ www.wikipedia.org/wiki/Train_spotting

traipse *or* **trapes** (treɪps) *Inf* ▷ *vb* **traipses, traipsing, traipsed** *or* **trapeses, trapesing, trapesed 1** (*intr*) to walk heavily or tiredly ▷ *n* **2** a long or tiring walk; trudge [c16 from ?]

trait (treɪt, treɪ) *n* **1** a characteristic feature or quality distinguishing a particular person or thing **2** *rare* a touch or stroke [c16 from F, from OF: a pulling, from L *tractus*, from *trahere* to drag]

traitor ('treɪtə) *n* a person who is guilty of treason or treachery, in betraying friends, country, a cause, etc [c13 from OF *traitour*, from L *trāditor*, from *trādere* to hand over] > '**traitorous** *adj* > '**traitress** *fem n*

Trajan ('treɪdʒən) *n* Latin name *Marcus Ulpius Traianus*. ?53–117 AD, Roman emperor (98–117). He extended the empire to the east and built many roads, bridges, canals, and towns

trajectory (trə'dʒɛktərɪ) *n, pl* **trajectories 1** the path described by an object moving in air or space, esp the curved path of a projectile **2** *geom* a curve that cuts a family of curves or surfaces at a constant angle [c17 from L *trājectus* cast over, from *trāicere* to throw across]

Tralee (trə'li:) *n* a market town in SW Republic of Ireland, county town of Kerry, near **Tralee Bay** (an inlet of the Atlantic) Pop: 17 200 (1991)

tram (træm) *n* **1** Also called: **tramcar** an electrically driven public transport vehicle that runs on rails let into the surface of the road. US and Canad names: **streetcar, trolley car 2** a small vehicle on rails for carrying loads in a mine; tub [c16 (in the sense: shaft of a cart): prob. from Low G *traam* beam] > '**tramless** *adj*

▷ http://routesinternational.com/buslines.htm

tramline ('træm,laɪn) *n* **1** (*often pl*) Also called: **tramway** the tracks on which a tram runs **2** the route taken by a tram **3** (*often pl*) the outer markings along the sides of a tennis or badminton court

trammel ('træməl) *n* **1** (*often pl*) a hindrance to free action or movement **2** Also called: **trammel net** a fishing net in three sections, the two outer nets having a large mesh and the middle one a fine mesh **3** *rare* a fowling net **4** *US* a shackle for a horse **5** a device for drawing ellipses consisting of a flat sheet having a cruciform slot in which run two pegs attached to a beam **6** (*sometimes pl*) a beam compass **7** a device set in a fireplace to support cooking pots ▷ *vb* **trammels, trammelling, trammelled** *or US* **trammels, trammeling, trammeled** (*tr*) **8** to hinder or restrain **9** to catch or ensnare [c14 from OF *tramail* three-mesh net, from LL *trēmaculum*, from L *trēs* three + *macula* mesh in a net]

tramontane (trə'mɒnteɪn) *adj* **1** being or coming from the far side of the mountains, esp from the other side of the Alps as seen from Italy ▷ *n* **2** an inhabitant of a tramontane country **3** Also called: **tramontana** a cold dry wind blowing south or southwest from the mountains in Italy and the W Mediterranean [c16 from It. *tramontano*, from L *trānsmontānus*, from TRANS- + *montānus*, from *mōns* mountain]

tramp (træmp) *vb* **1** (*intr*) to walk long and far; hike **2** to walk heavily or firmly across or through (a place) **3** (*intr*) to wander about as a vagabond or tramp **4** (*tr*) to traverse on foot, esp laboriously or wearily **5** (*intr*) to tread or trample ▷ *n* **6** a person who travels about on foot, living by begging or doing casual work **7** a long hard walk; hike **8** a heavy or rhythmic tread **9** the sound of heavy treading **10** a merchant ship that does not run on a regular schedule but carries cargo wherever the shippers desire **11** *sl, chiefly US & Canad* a prostitute or promiscuous girl or woman [c14 prob. from MLow G *trampen*] > '**trampish** *adj*

tramper ('træmpə) *n* NZ a person who tramps, or walks long distances, in the bush

tramping ('træmpɪŋ) *n* NZ **1** the leisure activity of walking in the bush **2** (*as modifier*): *tramping boots*

trample ('træmp^ə^l) *vb* **tramples, trampling, trampled** (when *intr*, usually foll by *on, upon*, or *over*) **1** to stamp or walk roughly (on) **2** to encroach (upon) so as to violate or hurt ▷ *n* **3** the action or sound of trampling [c14 frequentative of TRAMP] > '**trampler** *n*

trampoline ('træmpəlɪn, -,li:n) *n* **1** a tough canvas sheet suspended by springs or cords from a frame, used by acrobats, gymnasts, etc ▷ *vb* **trampolines, trampolining, trampolined 2** (*intr*) to exercise on a trampoline [c18 via Sp. from It. *trampolino*, from *trampoli* stilts, of Gmc origin] > '**trampoliner** *or* '**trampolinist** *n*

trance (trɑ:ns) *n* **1** a hypnotic state resembling sleep **2** any mental state in which a person is unaware of the environment, characterized by loss of voluntary movement, rigidity, and lack of sensitivity to external stimuli **3** a dazed or stunned state **4** a state of ecstasy or mystic absorption so intense as to cause a temporary loss of consciousness at the earthly level **5** *spiritualism* a state in which a medium can supposedly be controlled by an intelligence from without as a means of communication with the dead ▷ *vb* **trances, trancing, tranced 6** (*tr*) to put into or as into a trance [c14 from OF *transe*, from *transir* to faint, from L *trānsīre* to go over] > '**trance,like** *adj*

tranche (trɑ:nʃ) *n* an instalment or portion, esp of a loan or share issue [F, lit.: slice]

trannie *or* **tranny** ('trænɪ) *n, pl* **trannies** *inf, chiefly Brit* a transistor radio

tranquil ('træŋkwɪl) *adj* calm, peaceful, or quiet [c17 from L *tranquillus*] > '**tranquilly** *adv*

tranquillity *or US (sometimes)* **tranquility** (træŋ'kwɪlɪtɪ) *n* a state of calm or quietude

tranquillize, tranquillise, *or US* **tranquilize** ('træŋkwɪ,laɪz) *vb* **tranquillizes, tranquillizing; tranquillized, tranquillises, tranquillising, tranquillised,** *or US* **tranquilizes, tranquilizing, tranquilized** to make or become calm or calmer > ,**tranquilli'zation, ,tranquilli'sation,** *or US* **,tranquili'zation** *n*

tranquillizer, tranquilliser *or US* **tranquilizer** ('træŋkwɪ,laɪzə) *n* **1** a drug that calms a person **2** anything that tranquillizes

tranquillo (,træŋ'kwi:ləʊ) *adj music* calm; tranquil [It.]

trans. *abbrev for:* **1** transaction **2** transferred **3** transitive **4** translated **5** translator

trans- *prefix* **1** across, beyond, crossing, on the other side: *transatlantic* **2** changing thoroughly: *transliterate* **3** transcending: *transubstantiation* **4** transversely: *transect* **5** (*often in italics*) indicating that a chemical compound has a molecular structure in which two identical groups or atoms are on opposite sides of a double bond: *trans*-butadiene [from L *trāns* across, through, beyond]

transact (træn'zækt) *vb* to do, conduct, or negotiate (business, a deal, etc) [c16 from L *trānsactus*, from *trānsigere*, lit.: to drive through] > **trans'actor** *n*

transactinide (træns'æktɪˌnaɪd) *n* any artificially produced element with an atomic number greater than 103 [c20]

transaction (træn'zækʃən) *n* **1** something that is transacted, esp a business deal **2** a transacting or being transacted **3** (*pl*) the records of the proceedings of a society, etc > **trans'actional** *adj*

transalpine (trænz'ælpaɪn) *adj* (*prenominal*) **1** situated in or relating to places beyond the Alps, esp from Italy **2** passing over the Alps

Transalpine Gaul *n* (in the ancient world) that part of Gaul northwest of the Alps

transaminase (trænz'æmɪˌneɪz, -ˌneɪs) *n* *biochem* an enzyme that catalyses the transfer of an amino group from one molecule, esp an amino acid, to another, esp a keto acid, in the process of **transamination**

transatlantic (ˌtrænzət'læntɪk) *adj* **1** on or from the other side of the Atlantic **2** crossing the Atlantic

Transcaucasia (ˌtrænskɔː'keɪzjə) *n* a region in central Asia, south of the Caucasus Mountains between the Black and Caspian Seas in Georgia, Armenia, and Azerbaijan: a constituent republic of the Soviet Union from 1918 until 1936 > ˌ**Transcau'casian** *adj, n*

transceiver (træn'siːvə) *n* a device which transmits and receives radio or electronic signals [c20 from TRANS(MITTER) + (RE)CEIVER]

transcend (træn'sɛnd) *vb* **1** to go above or beyond (a limit, expectation, etc), as in degree or excellence **2** (*tr*) to be superior to [c14 from L *trānscendere* to climb over]

transcendent (træn'sɛndənt) *adj* **1** exceeding or surpassing in degree or excellence **2** (in the philosophy of Kant) beyond or before experience **3** *theol* (of God) having existence outside the created world **4** free from the limitations inherent in matter ▷ *n* **5** *philosophy* a transcendent thing > **tran'scendence** *or* **tran'scendency** *n* > **tran'scendently** *adv*

transcendental (ˌtrænsɛn'dɛntᵊl) *adj* **1** transcendent, superior, or surpassing **2** (in the philosophy of Kant) **2a** (of a judgment or logical deduction) being both synthetic and a priori **2b** of or relating to knowledge of the presuppositions of thought **3** *philosophy* beyond our experience of phenomena, although not beyond potential knowledge **4** *theol* supernatural or mystical **5** *maths* **5a** (of a number or quantity) not being a root of any polynomial with rational coefficients **5b** (of a function) not capable of expression in terms of a finite number of arithmetical operations > ˌ**transcen'dentally** *adv*

transcendentalism (ˌtrænsɛn'dɛntəˌlɪzəm) *n* **1a** any system of philosophy, esp that of Kant, holding that the key to knowledge of the nature of reality lies in the critical examination of the processes of reason on which depends the nature of experience **1b** any system of philosophy, esp that of Emerson, that emphasizes intuition as a means to knowledge or the importance of the search for the divine **2** vague philosophical speculation **3** the state of being transcendental **4** something, such as thought or language, that is transcendental > ˌ**transcen'dentalist** *n, adj*

Transcendental Meditation *n* *trademark in the US* a technique, based on Hindu traditions, for relaxing and refreshing the mind and body through the silent repetition of a mantra
▷ http://tm.org/
▷ http://transcendental-meditation.org.uk/
▷ http://suggestibility.org/

transcontinental (ˌtrænzkɒntɪ'nɛntᵊl) *adj* **1** crossing a continent **2** on or from the far side of a continent > ˌ**transconti'nentally** *adv*

transcribe (træn'skraɪb) *vb* **transcribes, transcribing, transcribed** (*tr*) **1** to write, type, or print out fully from speech, notes, etc **2** to transliterate or translate **3** to make an electrical recording of (a programme or speech) for a later broadcast **4** *music* to rewrite (a piece of music) for an instrument or medium other than that originally intended; arrange **5** *computing* **5a** to transfer (information) from one storage device to another **5b** to transfer (information) from a computer to an external storage device [c16 from L *trānscrībere*] > **tran'scribable** *adj* > **tran'scriber** *n*

transcript ('trænskrɪpt) *n* **1** a written, typed, or printed copy or manuscript made by transcribing **2** *chiefly US & Canad* an official record of a student's school progress **3** any reproduction or copy [c13 from L *trānscriptum*, from *trānscrībere* to transcribe]

transcriptase (træn'skrɪpteɪz) *n* See **reverse transcriptase**

transcription (træn'skrɪpʃən) *n* **1** the act or an instance of transcribing or the state of being transcribed **2** something transcribed **3** a representation in writing of the actual pronunciation of a speech sound, word, etc, using phonetic symbols > **tran'scriptional** *or* **tran'scriptive** *adj*

transducer (trænz'djuːsə) *n* any device, such as a microphone or electric motor, that converts one form of energy into another [c20 from L *trānsducere* to lead across]

transect *vb* (træn'sɛkt) (*tr*) **1** to cut or divide crossways ▷ *n* ('trænsɛkt) **2** a sample strip of land used to monitor plant distribution, animal populations, or some other feature, within a given area [c17 from L TRANS- + *secāre* to cut] > **tran'section** *n*

Tt

transept ('trænsɛpt) *n* either of the two wings of a cruciform church at right angles to the nave [c16 from Anglo-L *trānseptum*, from L TRANS- + *saeptum* enclosure] > **tran'septal** *adj*

trans-fatty acid *or* **transfat** *n* a polyunsaturated fatty acid that has been converted from the cis-form by hydrogenation: used in the manufacture of margarine

transfer *vb* (træns'fɜː), **transfers, transferring, transferred** **1** to change or go or cause to change or go from one thing, person, or point to another **2** to change (buses, trains, etc) **3** *law* to make over (property, etc) to another; convey **4** to displace (a drawing, design, etc) from one surface to another **5** (of a football player) to change clubs or (of a club, manager, etc) to sell or release (a player) to another club **6** to leave one school, college, etc, and enrol at another **7** to change (the meaning of a word, etc), esp by metaphorical extension ▷ *n* ('trænsfɜː) **8** the act, process, or system of transferring, or the state of being transferred **9** a person or thing that transfers or is transferred **10** a design or drawing that is transferred from one surface to another **11** *law* the passing of title to property or other right from one person to another; conveyance **12** any document or form effecting or regulating a transfer **13** *chiefly US & Canad* a ticket that allows a passenger to change routes [c14 from L *trānsferre*, from TRANS- + *ferre* to carry] > **trans'ferable** *or* **trans'ferrable** *adj* > **transference** ('trænsfərəns) *n*

transferable vote *n* a vote that is transferred to a second candidate indicated by the voter if the first is eliminated from the ballot

transferee (ˌtrænsfə'riː) *n* **1** *property law* a person to whom property is transferred **2** a person who is transferred

transfer fee *n* a sum of money paid by one football club to another for a transferred player

transferrin (træns'fɜːrɪn) *n biochem* any of a group of blood proteins that transport iron [c20 from TRANS- + FERRO- + -IN]

transfer RNA *n biochem* any of several soluble forms of RNA of low molecular weight, each of which transports a specific amino acid to a ribosome during protein synthesis

transfer station *n NZ* a municipal depot where rubbish is sorted for recycling or relocation to a landfill site

transfiguration (ˌtrænsfɪgjʊ'reɪʃən) *n* a transfiguring or being transfigured

Transfiguration (ˌtrænsfɪgjʊ'reɪʃən) *n* **1** *New Testament* the change in the appearance of Christ that took place before three disciples (Matthew 17:1–9) **2** the Church festival held in commemoration of this on Aug 6

transfigure (træns'fɪgə) *vb* **transfigures, transfiguring, transfigured** (*usually tr*) **1** to change or cause to change in appearance **2** to become or cause to become more exalted [c13 from L *trānsfigūrāre*, from TRANS- + *figūra* appearance] > **trans'figurement** *n*

transfinite number (træns'faɪnaɪt) *n* a cardinal or ordinal number used in the comparison of infinite sets for which several types of infinity can be classified

transfix (træns'fɪks) *vb* **transfixes, transfixing, transfixed** *or* **transfixt** (*tr*) **1** to render motionless, esp with horror or shock **2** to impale or fix with a sharp weapon or other device [c16 from L *trānsfīgere* to pierce through] > **transfixion** (træns'fɪkʃən) *n*

transform *vb* (træns'fɔːm) **1** to alter or be altered in form, function, etc **2** (*tr*) to convert (one form of energy) to another form **3** (*tr*) *maths* to change the form of (an equation, etc) by a mathematical transformation **4** (*tr*) to change (an alternating current or voltage) using a transformer ▷ *n* ('træns,fɔːm) **5** *maths* the result of a mathematical transformation [c14 from L *trānsformāre*] > **trans'formable** *adj* > **trans'formative** *adj*

transformation (ˌtrænsfə'meɪʃən) *n* **1** a change or alteration, esp a radical one **2** a transforming or being transformed **3** *maths* **3a** a change in position or direction of the reference axes in a coordinate system without an alteration in their relative angle **3b** an equivalent change in an expression or equation resulting from the substitution of one set of variables by another **4** *physics* a change in an atomic nucleus to a different nuclide as the result of the emission of either an alpha-particle or a beta-particle **5** *linguistics* another word for **transformational rule** **6** an apparently miraculous change in the appearance of a stage set > ˌ**transfor'mational** *adj*

transformational grammar *n* a grammatical description of a language making essential use of transformational rules

transformational rule *n generative grammar* a rule that converts one phrase marker into another. Taken together, these rules convert the deep structures of sentences into their surface structures

transformer (træns'fɔːmə) *n* **1** a device that transfers an alternating current from one circuit to one or more other circuits, usually with a change of voltage **2** a person or thing that transforms

transfuse (træns'fjuːz) *vb* **transfuses, transfusing, transfused** (*tr*) **1** to permeate or infuse **2a** to inject (blood, etc) into a blood vessel **2b** to give a transfusion to (a patient) [c15 from L *trānsfundere* to pour out] > **trans'fuser** *n* > **trans'fusible** *or* **trans'fusable** *adj* > **trans'fusive** *adj*

transfusion (træns'fjuːʒən) *n* **1** a transfusing **2** the injection of blood, blood plasma, etc, into the blood vessels of a patient

transgender (trænz'dʒɛndə) *adj* attempting or appearing to be a member of the opposite sex

transgenic (trænz'dʒɛnɪk) *adj* (of an animal or plant) containing genetic material artificially transferred from another species

transgress (trænz'grɛs) *vb* **1** to break (a law, etc) **2** to go beyond or overstep (a limit) [c16 from L *trānsgredī*, from TRANS- + *gradī* to step] > **trans'gressor** *n*

transgression (trænz'grɛʃən) *n* **1** a breach of a law, etc; sin or crime **2** a transgressing

transgressive (ˌtrænz'grɛsɪv) *adj* going beyond accepted boundaries of taste, convention, or the law: *transgressive art; transgressive pursuits*

tranship (træn'ʃɪp) *vb* **tranships, transhipping, transhipped** a variant spelling of **transship**

transhumance (træns'hjuːməns) *n* the seasonal migration of livestock to suitable grazing grounds [c20 from F, from *transhumer* to change one's pastures, from Sp. *trashumar*, from L TRANS- + *humus* ground] > **trans'humant** *adj*

transient ('trænzɪənt) *adj* **1** for a short time only; temporary or transitory ▷ *n* **2** a transient person or thing [c17 from L *trānsiēns* going over, from *trānsīre* to pass over] > **'transiently** *adv* > **'transience** *or* **'transiency** *n*

transistor (træn'zɪstə) *n* **1** a semiconductor device, having three or more terminals attached to electrode regions, in which current flowing between two electrodes is controlled by a voltage or current applied to one or more specified electrodes. The device has replaced the valve in most circuits since it is much smaller and works at a much lower voltage **2** *inf* a transistor radio [c20 orig. a trademark, from TRANSFER + RESISTOR, from the transfer of electric signals across a resistor]

transistorize *or* **transistorise** (træn'zɪstəˌraɪz) *vb* **transistorizes, transistorizing, transistorized** *or* **transistorises, transistorising, transistorised** **1** to convert to the use or manufacture of transistors and other solid-state components **2** (*tr*) to equip with transistors and other solid-state components

transit ('trænsɪt, 'trænz-) *n* **1a** the passage or conveyance of goods or people **1b** (*as modifier*): *a transit visa* **2** a change or transition **3** a route **4** *astron* **4a** the passage of a celestial body or satellite across the face of a larger body as seen from the earth **4b** the apparent passage of a celestial body across the meridian **5** **in transit** while being conveyed; during passage ▷ *vb* **6** to make a transit through or over (something) [c15 from L *trānsitus* a going over, from *trānsīre* to pass over]

transit camp *n* a camp in which refugees, soldiers, etc, live temporarily

transit instrument *n* an astronomical instrument used to time the transit of a star, etc, across the meridian

transition (træn'zɪʃən) *n* **1** change or passage from one state or stage to another **2** the period of time during which something changes **3** *music* **3a** a movement from one key to another; modulation **3b** a linking passage between two divisions in a composition; bridge **4** a style of architecture in the late 11th and early 12th centuries, characterized by late Romanesque forms combined with early Gothic details **5** *physics* a change in the configuration of an atomic nucleus, involving either a change in energy level or a transformation to another element or isotope **6** a sentence, passage, etc, that links sections of a written work [c16 from L *transitio*; see TRANSIENT] > **tran'sitional** *adj* > **tran'sitionally** *adv*

transition element *or* **metal** *n chem* any element belonging to one of three series of elements with atomic numbers between 21 and 30, 39 and 48, and 57 and 80. They have an incomplete penultimate electron shell and tend to form complexes

transition temperature *n* the temperature at which a sudden change of physical properties occurs

transitive ('trænsɪtɪv) *adj* **1** *grammar* **1a** denoting an occurrence of a verb when it requires a direct object or denoting a verb that customarily requires a direct object: *"to find" is a transitive verb* **1b** (*as n*): *these verbs are transitives* **2** *logic, maths* having the property that if one object bears a relationship to a second object that also bears the same relationship to a third object, then the first object bears this relationship to the third object: *if x = y and y = z then x = z* ▷ Cf **intransitive** [C16 from LL *trānsitīvus*, from L *trānsitus* a going over; see TRANSIENT] > **'transitively** *adv* > **,transi'tivity** *or* **'transitiveness** *n*

transitory ('trænsɪtərɪ, -trɪ) *adj* of short duration; transient or ephemeral [C14 from Church L *trānsitōrius* passing, from L *trānsitus* a crossing over] > **'transitoriness** *n*

transit theodolite *n* a theodolite the telescope of which can be rotated completely about its horizontal axis

Trans-Jordan *n* the former name (1922–49) of **Jordan** > **,Trans-Jor'danian** *adj, n*

Transkei (træn'skaɪ) *n* a former Bantu homeland in South Africa: the largest of South Africa's Bantu homelands and the first Bantu self-governing territory (1963); declared an independent state in 1976 but this status was not recognized outside South Africa; abolished in 1993 when South African citizenship was restored to its inhabitants. Capital: Umtata > **Trans'keian** *adj, n*

translate (træns'leɪt, trænz-) *vb* **translates, translating, translated 1** to express or be capable of being expressed in another language **2** (*intr*) to act as translator **3** (*tr*) to express or explain in simple or less technical language **4** (*tr*) to interpret or infer the significance of (gestures, symbols, etc) **5** (*tr*) to transform or convert: *to translate hope into reality* **6** to transfer from one place or position to another **7** (*tr*) *theol* to transfer (a person) from one place or plane of existence to another, as from earth to heaven **8** (*tr*) *maths, physics* to move (a figure or body) laterally, without rotation, dilation, or angular displacement [C13 from L *trānslātus* carried over, from *trānsferre* to TRANSFER] > **trans'latable** *adj* > **trans'lator** *n*

translation (træns'leɪʃən, trænz-) *n* **1** something that is or has been translated **2** a translating or being translated **3** *maths* a transformation in which the origin of a coordinate system is moved to another position so that each axis retains the same direction > **trans'lational** *adj*

TRANSLATING ONLINE SOURCES

Although English is the world's lingua franca and much of the Internet's content is in English, there are many foreign-language websites that might be of interest to English speakers. Foreign news sources, for example, can offer a different perspective on events from their counterparts in the English-speaking world.

Not everyone has sufficient knowledge of foreign languages to make the most of such websites but the Internet does offer help in translating texts from foreign languages into English and vice versa.

Two search engines, **Google** and **Alta Vista**, provide easy-to-use software that can translate both keyed-in texts and the content of web pages. Google offers translations to and from the following languages: German, Spanish, Portuguese, Italian, and French. AltaVista also covers these languages as well as Korean, Russian, Chinese, and Japanese.

The services provided by Google and AltaVista are free and the translations are quick. However, it must be borne in mind that automatic translations can never approach the effectiveness of a skilled linguist who understands the structure and subtleties of a language. The meaning of words depends on the context in which they are used but 'understanding' context is not something that translation software can do just yet.

The two search engines mentioned can be found at:

▷ www.google.com/language_tools?hl=en
▷ http://babelfish.altavista.com

transliterate (trænz'lɪtə,reɪt) *vb* **transliterates, transliterating, transliterated** (*tr*) to transcribe (a word, etc) into corresponding letters of another alphabet [C19 TRANS- + -*literate*, from L *līttera* letter] > **,transliter'ation** *n* > **trans'liter,ator** *n*

translocation (,trænzləʊ'keɪʃən) *n* **1** *genetics* the transfer of one part of a chromosome to another part of the same or a different chromosome **2** *bot* the transport of minerals, sugars, etc, in solution within a plant **3** a movement from one position or place to another

translucent (trænz'luːsᵊnt) *adj* allowing light to pass through partially or diffusely; semitransparent [C16 from L *trānslūcēre* to shine through] > **trans'lucence** *or* **trans'lucency** *n* > **trans'lucently** *adv*

translunar (trænz'luːnə) *or* **translunary** (trænz'luːnərɪ) *adj* **1** lying beyond the moon **2** unworldly or ethereal

transmigrate (,trænzmaɪ'greɪt) *vb* **transmigrates, transmigrating, transmigrated** (*intr*) **1** to move from one place, state, or stage to another **2** (of souls) to pass from one body into another at death > **,transmi'gration** *n* > **trans'migratory** *adj*

transmission (trænz'mɪʃən) *n* **1** the act or process of transmitting **2** something that is transmitted **3** the extent to which a body or medium transmits light, sound, etc **4** the transference of motive force or power **5** a system of shafts, gears, etc, that transmits power, esp the arrangement of such parts that transmits the power of the engine to the driving wheels of a motor vehicle **6** the act or process of sending a message, picture, or other information by means of radio waves, electrical signals, light signals, etc **7** a radio or television broadcast [C17 from L *trānsmissiō* a sending across] > **trans'missible** *adj* > **trans'missive** *adj*

transmission density *n physics* a measure of the extent to which a substance transmits light or other electromagnetic radiation

transmission line *n* a coaxial cable, waveguide, etc, that transfers electrical signals from one location to another

transmissivity (,trænzmɪ'sɪvɪtɪ) *n physics* a measure of the ability of a material to transmit radiation

transmit (trænz'mɪt) *vb* **transmits, transmitting, transmitted 1** (*tr*) to pass or cause to go from one place or person to another; transfer **2** (*tr*) to pass on or impart (a disease, etc) **3** (*tr*) to hand down to posterity **4** (*tr; usually passive*) to pass (an inheritable characteristic) from parent to offspring **5** to allow the passage of (particles, energy, etc): *radio waves are transmitted through the atmosphere* **6a** to send out (signals) by means of radio waves or along a transmission line **6b** to broadcast (a radio or television programme) **7** (*tr*) to transfer (a force, motion, etc) from one part of a mechanical system to another [C14 from L *trānsmittere* to send across] > **trans'mittable** *adj* > **trans'mittal** *n*

transmittance (trænz'mɪtᵊns) *n* **1** the act of transmitting **2** Also called: **transmission factor** *physics* a measure of the ability of anything to transmit radiation, equal to the ratio of the transmitted flux to the incident flux

transmitter (trænz'mɪtə) *n* **1** a person or thing that transmits **2** the equipment used for generating and amplifying a radio-frequency carrier, modulating the carrier with information, and feeding it to an aerial for transmission **3** the microphone in a telephone that converts sound waves into audio-frequency electrical signals **4** a device that converts mechanical movements into coded electrical signals transmitted along a telegraph circuit **5** short for **neurotransmitter**

transmogrify (trænz'mɒgrɪ,faɪ) *vb* **transmogrifies, transmogrifying, transmogrified** *(tr) jocular* to change or transform into a different shape, esp a grotesque or bizarre one [C17 from ?] > **trans,mogrifi'cation** *n*

transmontane (,trænzmɒn'teɪn) *adj, n* another word for **tramontane**

transmutation (,trænzmjuː'teɪʃən) *n* **1** the act or an instance of transmuting **2** the change of one chemical element into another by a nuclear reaction **3** the attempted conversion, by alchemists, of base metals into gold or silver > **,transmu'tational** *or* **trans'mutative** *adj*

transmute (trænz'mjuːt) *vb* **transmutes, transmuting, transmuted** *(tr)* **1** to change the form, character, or substance of **2** to alter (an element, metal, etc) by alchemy [C15 via OF from L *trānsmūtāre* to shift, from TRANS- + *mūtāre* to change] > **trans,muta'bility** *n* > **trans'mutable** *adj*

transnational (trænz'næʃənəl) *adj* extending beyond the boundaries, etc, of a single nation

Transnet ('trænz,nɛt) *n S African* the official rail and transport service in South Africa

transoceanic (trænz,əʊʃɪ'ænɪk) *adj* **1** on or from the other side of an ocean **2** crossing an ocean

transom ('trænsəm) *n* **1** a horizontal member across a window **2** a horizontal member that separates a door from a window over it **3** the usual US name for **fanlight** **4** *naut* **4a** a surface forming the stern of a vessel **4b** any of several transverse beams used for strengthening the stern of a vessel [C14 earlier *traversayn*, from OF *traversin*, from TRAVERSE] > **'transomed** *adj*

transonic (træn'sɒnɪk) *adj* of or relating to conditions when travelling at or near the speed of sound

transparency (træns'pærənsɪ) *n, pl* **transparencies** **1** Also called: **transparence** the state of being transparent **2** Also called: **slide** a positive photograph on a transparent base, usually mounted in a frame or between glass plates. It can be viewed by means of a slide projector

transparent (træns'pærənt) *adj* **1** permitting the uninterrupted passage of light; clear **2** easy to see through, understand, or recognize; obvious **3** permitting the free passage of electromagnetic radiation **4** candid, open, or frank [C15 from Med. L *trānspārēre* to show through, from L TRANS- + *pārēre* to appear] > **trans'parently** *adv* > **trans'parentness** *n*

transpire (træn'spaɪə) *vb* **transpires, transpiring, transpired** **1** *(intr)* to come to light; be known **2** *(intr) inf* to happen or occur **3** *physiol* to give off or exhale (water or vapour) through the skin, a mucous membrane, etc **4** (of plants) to lose (water), esp through the stomata of the leaves [C16 from Med. L *trānspīrāre*, from L TRANS- + *spīrāre* to breathe] > **transpiration** (,trænspə'reɪʃən) *n* > **tran'spiratory** *adj*

> USAGE It is sometimes maintained that *transpire* should not be used to mean 'happen' or 'occur', as in *the event transpired late in the evening*, and that the word is properly used to mean 'become known', as in *it transpired later that the thief had been caught*. The word is, however, widely used in the first sense, especially in spoken English

transplant *vb* (træns'plɑːnt) **1** *(tr)* to remove or transfer (esp a plant) from one place to another **2** *(intr)* to be capable of being transplanted **3** *surgery* to transfer (an organ or tissue) from one part of the body or from one person to another ▷ *n* ('træns,plɑːnt) **4** *surgery* **4a** the procedure involved in such a transfer **4b** the organ or tissue transplanted > **trans'plantable** *adj* > **,transplan'tation** *n*

transponder (træn'spɒndə) *n* **1** a type of radio or radar transmitter-receiver that transmits signals automatically when it receives predetermined signals **2** the receiver and transmitter in a communications satellite, relaying signals back to earth [C20 from TRANSMITTER + RESPONDER]

transport *vb* (træns'pɔːt) *(tr)* **1** to carry or cause to go from one place to another, esp over some distance **2** to deport or exile to a penal colony **3** *(usually passive)* to have a strong emotional effect on ▷ *n* ('træns,pɔːt) **4a** the business or system of transporting goods or people **4b** *(as modifier): a modernized transport system* **5** *Brit* freight vehicles generally **6a** a vehicle used to transport goods or people, esp troops **6b** *(as modifier): a transport plane* **7** a transporting or being transported **8** ecstasy, rapture, or any powerful emotion **9** a convict sentenced to be transported [C14 from L *trānsportāre*, from TRANS- + *portāre* to carry] > **trans'portable** *adj* > **trans'porter** *n*

▷ http://europa.eu.int/comm/transport/index_en.html
▷ http://faculty.washington.edu/~jbs/itrans/
▷ http://routesinternational.com/
▷ www.trafficlinq.com/advancedtransportation.htm

transportation (,trænspɔː'teɪʃən) *n* **1** a means or system of transporting **2** the act of transporting or the state of being transported **3** (esp formerly) deportation to a penal colony

transport café ('træns,pɔːt) *n Brit* an inexpensive eating place on a main route, used mainly by long-distance lorry drivers

transpose (træns'pəʊz) *vb* **transposes, transposing, transposed** **1** *(tr)* to alter the positions of; interchange, as words in a sentence **2** *music* to play (notes, music, etc) in a different key from that originally intended **3** *(tr) maths* to move (a term) from one side of an equation to the other with a corresponding reversal in sign [C14 from OF *transposer*, from L *trānspōnere* to remove] > **trans'posable** *adj* > **trans'posal** *n* > **trans'poser** *n* > **transposition** (,trænspə'zɪʃən) *n*

transposing instrument *n* a musical instrument, esp a horn or clarinet, pitched in a key other than C major, but whose music is written down as if its basic scale were C major

transposon (træns'pəʊzɒn) *n genetics* a genetic element that can move from one site in a chromosome to another site in the same or a different chromosome and thus alter the genetic constitution of the organism [C20 TRANSPOS(E) + -ON]

transputer (trænz'pjuːtə) *n computing* a type of fast powerful microchip that is the equivalent of a 32-bit microprocessor with its own RAM facility [C20 from TRANS(ISTOR) + (COM)PUTER]

transsexual *or* **transexual** (trænz'sɛksjʊəl) *n* **1** a person who completely identifies with the opposite sex **2** a person who has undergone medical procedures to alter sexual characteristics to those of the opposite sex

transship (træns'ʃɪp) *or* **tranship** *vb* **transships, transshipping, transshipped** *or* **tranships, transhipping, transhipped** to transfer or be transferred from one vessel or vehicle to another > **trans'shipment** *or* **tran'shipment** *n*

transubstantiation (,trænsəb,stænʃɪ'eɪʃən) *n* **1** (esp in Roman Catholic theology) **1a** the doctrine that the whole substance of the bread and wine changes into the substance of the body and blood of Christ when consecrated in the Eucharist **1b** the mystical process by which this is believed to take place during consecration. ▷ Cf **consubstantiation** **2** a substantial change; transmutation > **,transub,stanti'ationalist** *n*

transude (træn'sjuːd) *vb* **transudes, transuding,**

transuded (of a fluid) to ooze or pass through interstices, pores, or small holes [C17 from NL *trānsūdāre*, from L TRANS- + *sūdāre* to sweat] > **transudation** (ˌtrænsjʊˈdeɪʃən) *n*

transuranic (ˌtrænzjʊˈrænɪk), **transuranian** (ˌtrænzjʊˈreɪnɪən), *or* **transuranium** *adj* **1** (of an element) having an atomic number greater than that of uranium **2** of or having the behaviour of transuranic elements [C20 from TRANS- + *uranic*, from URANIUM]

Transvaal (ˈtrænzvɑːl) *n* former province of NE South Africa: colonized by the Boers after the Great Trek (1836); became a British colony in 1902; joined South Africa in 1910; replaced by new administrative regions in 1994. Capital: Pretoria > **ˈTransˌvaaler** *n* > **Transˈvaalian** *adj*

transversal (trænzˈvɜːsəl) *n* **1** *geom* a line intersecting two or more other lines ▷ *adj* **2** a less common word for **transverse** > **transˈversally** *adv*

transverse (trænzˈvɜːs) *adj* **1** crossing from side to side; athwart; crossways ▷ *n* **2** a transverse piece or object [C16 from L *trānsversus*, from *trānsvertere* to turn across] > **transˈversely** *adv*

transverse colon *n anat* the part of the large intestine passing transversely in front of the liver and stomach

transverse wave *n* a wave, such as an electromagnetic wave, that is propagated in a direction perpendicular to the displacement of the transmitting field or medium

transvestite (trænzˈvɛstaɪt) *n* a person who seeks sexual pleasure from wearing clothes of the opposite sex [C19 from G *Transvestit*, from TRANS- + L *vestītus* clothed, from *vestīre* to clothe] > **transˈvestism** *or* **transˈvestitism** *n*

Transylvania (ˌtrænsɪlˈveɪnɪə) *n* a region of central and NW Romania: belonged to Hungary from the 11th century until 1918; restored to Romania in 1947

Transylvanian Alps (ˌtrænsɪlˈveɪnɪən) *pl n* a mountain range in S Romania; a SW extension of the Carpathian Mountains. Highest peak: Mount Negoiu, 2548 m (8360 ft)

trap[1] (træp) *n* **1** a mechanical device or enclosed place or pit in which something, esp an animal, is caught or penned **2** any device or plan for tricking a person or thing into being caught unawares **3** anything resembling a trap or prison **4** a fitting for a pipe in the form of a U-shaped or S-shaped bend that contains standing water to prevent the passage of gases **5** any similar device **6** a device that hurls clay pigeons into the air to be fired at by trapshooters **7** *greyhound racing* any one of a line of boxlike stalls in which greyhounds are enclosed before the start of a race **8** See **trap door** **9** a light two-wheeled carriage **10** a slang word for **mouth** **11** *golf* an obstacle or hazard, esp a bunker **12** (*pl*) *jazz sl* percussion instruments **13** (*usually pl*) *Austral sl* a policeman ▷ *vb* **traps, trapping, trapped** **14** to catch, take, or pen in or as if in a trap **15** (*tr*) to ensnare by trickery; trick **16** (*tr*) to provide (a pipe) with a trap **17** to set traps in (a place), esp for animals [OE *træppe*] > **ˈtrapˌlike** *adj*

trap[2] (træp) *vb* **traps, trapping, trapped** (*tr*; often foll by *out*) to dress or adorn ▷ See also **traps** [C11 prob. from OF *drap* cloth]

trap[3] (træp) *or* **traprock** (ˈtræpˌrɒk) *n* **1** any fine-grained often columnar dark igneous rock, esp basalt **2** any rock in which oil or gas has accumulated [C18 from Swedish *trappa* stair (from its steplike formation)]

Trapani (*Italian* ˈtraːpani) *n* a port in S Italy, in NW Sicily: Carthaginian naval base, ceded to the Romans after the First Punic War. Pop: 72 840 (1990)

trap door *n* a door or flap flush with and covering an opening, esp in a ceiling

trap-door spider *n* any of various spiders that construct a silk-lined hole in the ground closed by a hinged door of earth and silk

trapes (treɪps) *vb, n* a less common spelling of **traipse**

trapeze (trəˈpiːz) *n* a free-swinging bar attached to two ropes, used by circus acrobats, etc [C19 from F *trapèze*, from NL; see TRAPEZIUM]

trapezium (trəˈpiːzɪəm) *n, pl* **trapeziums** *or* **trapezia** (-zɪə) **1** *chiefly Brit* a quadrilateral having two parallel sides of unequal length. Usual US and Canad name: **trapezoid** **2** *chiefly US & Canad* a quadrilateral having neither pair of sides parallel [C16 via LL from Gk *trapezion*, from *trapeza* table] > **traˈpezial** *adj*

trapezius (trəˈpiːzɪəs) *n, pl* **trapeziuses** either of two flat triangular muscles that rotate the shoulder blades [C18 from NL *trapezius* (*musculus*) trapezium-shaped (muscle)]

trapezoid (ˈtræpɪˌzɔɪd) *n* **1** a quadrilateral having neither pair of sides parallel **2** the usual US and Canad name for **trapezium** [C18 from NL *trapezoidēs*, from LGk *trapezoeidēs* trapezium-shaped, from *trapeza* table]

trapper (ˈtræpə) *n* a person who traps animals, esp for their furs or skins

trappings (ˈtræpɪŋz) *pl n* **1** the accessories and adornments that symbolize a condition, office, etc: *the trappings of success* **2** ceremonial harness for a horse or other animal [C16 from TRAP[2]]

Trappist (ˈtræpɪst) *n* **a** a member of a branch of the Cistercian order of Christian monks, which originated at La Trappe in France in 1664. They are noted for their rule of silence **b** (*as modifier*): *a Trappist monk*

traps (træps) *pl n* belongings; luggage [C19 prob. shortened from TRAPPINGS]

trapshooting (ˈtræpˌʃuːtɪŋ) *n* the sport of shooting at clay pigeons thrown up by a trap > **ˈtrapˌshooter** *n*

trash (træʃ) *n* **1** foolish ideas or talk; nonsense **2** *chiefly US & Canad* useless or unwanted matter or objects; rubbish **3** a literary or artistic production of poor quality **4** *chiefly US & Canad* a poor or worthless person or a group of such people **5** bits that are broken or lopped off, esp the trimmings from trees or plants **6** the dry remains of sugar cane after the juice has been extracted ▷ *vb* **7** to remove the outer leaves and branches from (growing plants, esp sugar cane) **8** *sl* to attack or destroy (someone or something) wilfully or maliciously [C16 from ?]

trashy (ˈtræʃɪ) *adj* **trashier, trashiest** cheap, worthless, or badly made > **ˈtrashily** *adv* > **ˈtrashiness** *n*

Trasimene (ˈtræzɪˌmiːn) *n* **Lake** a lake in central Italy, in Umbria: the largest lake in central Italy; scene of Hannibal's victory over the Romans in 217 BC. Area: 128 sq km (49 sq miles). Italian name: **Trasimeno.** Also called: (Lake) Perugia

trass (træs) *n* a volcanic rock used to make a hydraulic cement [C18 from Du. *tras*, *tarasse*, from It. *terrazza* worthless earth; see TERRACE]

trattoria (ˌtrætəˈrɪə) *n* an Italian restaurant [C19 from It., from *trattore* innkeeper, from F *traiteur*, from OF *tretier* to TREAT]

trauma (ˈtrɔːmə) *n, pl* **traumata** (-mətə) *or* **traumas** **1** *psychol* a powerful shock that may have long-lasting effects **2** *pathol* any bodily injury or wound [C18 from Gk: a wound] > **traumatic** (trɔːˈmætɪk) *adj* > **trauˈmatically** *adv*

traumatize *or* **traumatise** (ˈtrɔːməˌtaɪz) *vb* **traumatizes, traumatizing, traumatized** *or* **traumatises, traumatising, traumatised** **1** (*tr*) to wound or injure (the body) **2** to subject or be subjected to mental trauma > **ˌtraumatiˈzation** *or* **ˌtraumatiˈsation** *n*

travail (ˈtræveɪl) *literary* ▷ *n* **1** painful or excessive labour or exertion **2** the pangs of childbirth; labour ▷ *vb* **3** (*intr*) to suffer or labour painfully, esp in childbirth [C13 from OF *travaillier*, from Vulgar L *tripaliāre* (unattested) to torture, from LL *trepālium* instrument of torture, from L *tripālis* having three stakes]

Travancore (ˌtrævənˈkɔː) *n* a former princely state of S India which joined with Cochin in 1949 to form

Travancore-Cochin: part of Kerala state since 1956
travel ('trævᵊl) *vb* **travels, travelling, travelled** *or US* **travels, traveling, traveled** (*mainly intr*) **1** to go, move, or journey from one place to another **2** (*tr*) to go, move, or journey through or across (an area, region, etc) **3** to go, move, or cover a distance **4** to go from place to place as a salesman **5** (esp of perishable goods) to withstand a journey **6** (of light, sound, etc) to be transmitted or move **7** to progress or advance **8** *basketball* to take an excessive number of steps while holding the ball **9** (of part of a mechanism) to move in a fixed path **10** *inf* to move rapidly ▷ *n* **11a** the act of travelling **11b** (*as modifier*): *a travel brochure*. Related adj: **itinerant** **12** (*usually pl*) a tour or journey **13** the distance moved by a mechanical part, such as the stroke of a piston **14** movement or passage [C14 *travaillen* to make a journey, from OF *travaillier* to TRAVAIL]
travel agency *or* **bureau** *n* an agency that arranges and negotiates flights, holidays, etc, for travellers > **travel agent** *n*
travelled *or US* **traveled** ('trᵊvəld) *adj* having experienced or undergone much travelling
traveller ('trævələ, 'trævlə) *n* **1** a person who travels, esp habitually **2** See **travelling salesman** **3** a part of a mechanism that moves in a fixed course **4** *Austral* a swagman
traveller's cheque *n* a cheque sold by a bank, etc, to the bearer, who signs it on purchase and can cash it abroad by signing it again
traveller's joy *n* a ranunculaceous Old World climbing plant having white flowers and heads of feathery plumed fruits; wild clematis
travelling people *or* **folk** *pl n* (*sometimes caps*) *Brit* Gypsies or other itinerant people: a term used esp by such people of themselves
travelling salesman *n* a salesman who travels within an assigned territory in order to sell merchandise or to solicit orders for the commercial enterprise he represents by direct personal contact with customers
travelling wave *n* **a** a wave carrying energy away from its source **b** (*as modifier*): *a travelling-wave aerial*
travelogue *or US* (*sometimes*) **travelog** ('trævᵊlɒg) *n* a film, lecture, or brochure on travels and travelling
Traven ('trɑːvən) *n* **B(en)**, original name *Albert Otto Max Feige*. ?1882–1969, US novelist, born in Germany and living in Mexico from 1920, who kept his identity secret. His novels, originally written in German, include *The Treasure of the Sierra Madre* (1934)
Travers ('trævɜːz) *n* **Ben(jamin)** 1886–1980, British dramatist, best known for such farces as *Rookery Nook* (1926), *Thark* (1927), and *Plunder* (1928)
traverse ('trævɜːs, trə'vɜːs) *vb* **traverses, traversing, traversed** **1** to pass or go over or back and forth over (something); cross **2** (*tr*) to go against; oppose **3** to move sideways or crosswise **4** (*tr*) to extend or reach across **5** to turn (an artillery gun) laterally or (of an artillery gun) to turn laterally **6** (*tr*) to examine carefully **7** (*tr*) *law* to deny (an allegation) **8** *mountaineering* to move across (a face) horizontally ▷ *n* **9** something being or lying across, such as a transom **10** a gallery or loft inside a building that crosses it **11** an obstruction **12** a protective bank or other barrier across a trench or rampart **13** a railing, screen, or curtain **14** the act or an instance of traversing or crossing **15** *mountaineering* the act or an instance of moving horizontally across a face **16** a path or road across **17** *naut* the zigzag course of a vessel tacking frequently **18** *law* the formal denial of a fact alleged in the opposite party's pleading **19** *surveying* a survey consisting of a series of straight lines, the length of each and the angle between them being measured ▷ *adj* **20** being or lying across; transverse [C14 from OF *traverser*, from LL *trānsversāre*, from L *trānsversus* TRANSVERSE] > **tra'versal** *n* > **'traverser** *n*
travertine ('trævətɪn) *n* a porous rock consisting of calcium carbonate, used for building [C18 from It. *travertino* (infl. by *tra*- TRANS-), from L *lapis Tīburtīnus* Tiburtine stone, from *Tībur*s the district around Tibur (now Tivoli)]
travesty ('trævɪstɪ) *n, pl* **travesties** **1** a farcical or grotesque imitation; mockery ▷ *vb* **travesties, travestying, travestied** (*tr*) **2** to make or be a travesty of [C17 from F *travesti* disguised, from *travestir* to disguise, from It. *travestire*, from *tra*- TRANS- + *vestire* to clothe]
travois (trə'vɔɪ) *n, pl* **travois** (-'vɔɪz) **1** *history* a sled formerly used by the Plains Indians of North America, consisting of two poles joined by a frame and pulled by an animal **2** *Canad* a similar sled used for dragging logs [from Canad F, from F *travail* beam, from L *trabs*]
trawl (trɔːl) *n* **1** Also called: **trawl net** a large net, usually in the shape of a sock or bag, drawn at deep levels behind special boats (trawlers) **2** Also called: **trawl line** a long line to which numerous shorter hooked lines are attached, suspended between buoys **3** the act of trawling ▷ *vb* **4** to catch (fish) with a trawl net or trawl line **5** (*intr; foll by for*) to seek or gather (information, etc) from a wide variety of sources [C17 from MDu. *traghelen* to drag, from L *trāgula* dragnet; see TRAIL]
trawler ('trɔːlə) *n* **1** a vessel used for trawling **2** a person who trawls
tray (treɪ) *n* **1** a thin flat board or plate of metal, plastic, etc, usually with a raised edge, on which things can be carried **2** a shallow receptacle for papers, etc, sometimes forming a drawer in a cabinet or box [OE *trieg*]
TRC *abbrev for* (in South Africa) Truth and Reconciliation Commission: a body established in 1996 to investigate political crimes committed under the apartheid system
treacherous ('trɛtʃərəs) *adj* **1** betraying or likely to betray faith or confidence **2** unstable, unreliable, or dangerous > **'treacherously** *adv* > **'treacherousness** *n*
treachery ('trɛtʃərɪ) *n, pl* **treacheries** **1** the act or an instance of wilful betrayal **2** the disposition to betray [C13 from OF *trecherie*, from *trechier* to cheat]
treacle ('triːkᵊl) *n* **1** Also called: **black treacle**, (US and Canad) **molasses** *Brit* a dark viscous syrup obtained during the refining of sugar **2** *Brit* another name for **golden syrup** **3** anything sweet and cloying [C14 from OF *triacle*, from L *thēriaca* antidote to poison] > **'treacly** *adj*
tread (trɛd) *vb* **treads, treading, trod; trodden** *or* **trod** **1** to walk or trample in, on, over, or across (something) **2** (when *intr*, foll by *on*) to crush or squash by or as if by treading **3** (*intr; sometimes foll by on*) to subdue or repress **4** (*tr*) to do by walking or dancing: *to tread a measure* **5** (*tr*) (of a male bird) to copulate with (a female bird) **6** **tread lightly** to proceed with delicacy or tact **7** **tread water** to stay afloat in an upright position by moving the legs in a walking motion ▷ *n* **8** a manner or style of walking, dancing, etc: *a light tread* **9** the act of treading **10** the top surface of a step in a staircase **11** the outer part of a tyre or wheel that makes contact with the road, esp the grooved surface of a pneumatic tyre **12** the part of a rail that wheels touch **13** the part of a shoe that is generally in contact with the ground [OE *tredan*] > **'treader** *n*
treadle ('trɛdᵊl) *n* **1** a lever operated by the foot to drive a machine ▷ *vb* **treadles, treadling, treadled** **2** to work (a machine) with a treadle [OE *tredel*, from *trǣde* something firm, from *tredan* to tread]
treadmill ('trɛd,mɪl) *n* **1** Also called: **treadwheel** (formerly) an apparatus turned by the weight of men or animals climbing steps on the periphery of a cylinder or wheel **2** a dreary round or routine **3** an exercise machine that consists of a continuous moving belt on which to walk or jog
treas. *abbrev for*: **1** treasurer **2** treasury
treason ('triːzᵊn) *n* **1** betrayal of one's sovereign or

country, esp by attempting to overthrow the government **2** any treachery or betrayal [C13 from OF *traïson*, from L *trāditiō* a handing over; see TRADITION] > **'treasonable** *or* **'treasonous** *adj* > **'treasonably** *adv*

treasure ('trɛʒə) *n* **1** wealth and riches, usually hoarded, esp in the form of money, precious metals, or gems **2** a thing or person that is highly prized or valued ▷ *vb* **treasures, treasuring, treasured** (*tr*) **3** to prize highly as valuable, rare, or costly **4** to store up and save; hoard [C12 from OF *tresor*, from L *thēsaurus* anything hoarded, from Gk *thēsauros*]

treasure hunt *n* a game in which players act upon successive clues to find a hidden prize

treasurer ('trɛʒərə) *n* a person appointed to look after the funds of a society, company, city, or other governing body > **'treasurership** *n*

Treasurer ('trɛʒərə) *n* (in Australia) the minister of finance

treasure-trove *n* **1** *Brit law* valuable articles, such as coins, etc, found hidden and of unknown ownership **2** any valuable discovery [C16 from Anglo-F *tresor trové* treasure found, from OF *tresor* TREASURE + *trover* to find]

treasury ('trɛʒərɪ) *n, pl* **treasuries** **1** a storage place for treasure **2** the revenues or funds of a government, private organization, or individual **3** a place where funds are kept and disbursed **4** a person or thing regarded as a valuable source of information **5** a collection of highly valued poems, etc; anthology **6** Also: **treasure house** a source of valuable items: *a treasury of information* [C13 from OF *tresorie*, from *tresor* TREASURE]

Treasury ('trɛʒərɪ) *n* (in various countries) the government department in charge of finance

Treasury Bench *n* (in Britain) the front bench to the right of the Speaker in the House of Commons, traditionally reserved for members of the Government

treasury note *n* a note issued by a government treasury and generally receivable as legal tender for any debt

treat (tri:t) *n* **1** a celebration, entertainment, gift, or feast given for or to someone and paid for by another **2** any delightful surprise or specially pleasant occasion **3** the act of treating ▷ *vb* **4** (*tr*) to deal with or regard in a certain manner: *she treats school as a joke* **5** (*tr*) to apply treatment to **6** (*tr*) to subject to a process or to the application of a substance **7** (often foll by *to*) to provide (someone) (with) as a treat **8** (*intr*; usually foll by *of*) to deal (with), as in writing or speaking **9** (*intr*) to discuss settlement; negotiate [C13 from OF *tretier*, from L *tractāre* to manage, from *trahere* to drag] > **'treatable** *adj* > **'treater** *n*

treatise ('tri:tɪz) *n* a formal work on a subject, esp one that deals systematically with its principles and conclusions [C14 from Anglo-F *tretiz*, from OF *tretier* to TREAT]

treatment ('tri:tmənt) *n* **1** the application of medicines, surgery, etc, to a patient **2** the manner of handling a person or thing, as in a literary or artistic work **3** the act, practice, or manner of treating **4** **the treatment** *sl* the usual manner of dealing with a particular type of person (esp in **give someone the (full) treatment**)

treaty ('tri:tɪ) *n, pl* **treaties** **1a** a formal agreement between two or more states, such as an alliance or trade arrangement **1b** the document in which such a contract is written **2** any pact or agreement **3** an agreement between two parties concerning the purchase of property at a price privately agreed between them [C14 from OF *traité*, from Med. L *tractātus*, from L: discussion, from *tractāre* to manage; see TREAT]
▷ http://fletcher.tufts.edu/multilaterals.html

treaty port *n* *history* (in China, Japan, and Korea) a city, esp a port, in which foreigners, esp Westerners, were allowed by treaty to conduct trade

Trebizond ('trɛbɪˌzɒnd) *n* a variant of **Trabzon**

treble ('trɛbᵊl) *adj* **1** threefold; triple **2** of or denoting a soprano voice or part or a high-pitched instrument ▷ *n* **3** treble the amount, size, etc **4** a soprano voice or part or a high-pitched instrument **5** the highest register of a musical instrument **6** the high-frequency response of an audio amplifier, esp in a record player or tape recorder **7a** the narrow inner ring on a dartboard **7b** a hit on this ring ▷ *vb* **trebles, trebling, trebled** **8** to make or become three times as much [C14 from OF, from L *triplus* threefold] > **'trebly** *adv, adj*

treble chance *n* a method of betting in football pools in which the chances of winning are related to the number of draws and the number of home and away wins forecast by the competitor

treble clef *n* *music* the clef that establishes G a fifth above middle C as being on the second line of the staff. Symbol: 𝄞

trebuchet ('trɛbjʊˌʃɛt) *or* **trebucket** ('tri:ˌbʌkɪt) *n* a large medieval siege engine consisting of a sling on a pivoted wooden arm set in motion by the fall of a weight [C13 from OF, from *trebuchier* to stumble, from *tre-* TRANS- + *-buchier*, from *buc* trunk of the body, of Gmc origin]

trecento (treɪ'tʃɛntəʊ) *n* the 14th century, esp with reference to Italian art and literature [C19 shortened from It. *mille trecento* one thousand three hundred] > **tre'centist** *n*

tree (tri:) *n* **1** any large woody perennial plant with a distinct trunk giving rise to branches. Related adj: **arboreal** **2** any plant that resembles this **3** a wooden post, bar, etc **4** See **family tree, shoetree, saddletree** **5** *chem* a treelike crystal growth **6** a branching diagrammatic representation of something **7** **at the top of the tree** in the highest position of a profession, etc **8** **up a tree** *US & Canad inf* in a difficult situation; trapped or stumped ▷ *vb* **trees, treeing, treed** (*tr*) **9** to drive or force up a tree **10** to stretch on a shoetree [OE *treo*] > **'treeless** *adj* > **'treelessness** *n* > **'treeˌlike** *adj*
▷ www.british-trees.com
▷ www.wildlifesafari.info
▷ http://homepages.ihug.co.nz/~crysalis
▷ www.ecoworld.org/trees/ecoworld_trees_home.cfm
▷ www.globalforestscience.org

Tree (tri:) *n* Sir **Herbert Beerbohm** 1853–1917, English actor and theatre manager; half-brother of Sir Max Beerbohm. He was noted for his lavish productions of Shakespeare

tree creeper *n* any of a family of small songbirds of the N hemisphere, having a slender downward-curving bill. They creep up trees to feed on insects

tree diagram *n* a diagram in which relationships are represented by lines and nodes having other lines branching off from them

tree fern *n* any of numerous large tropical ferns having a trunklike stem

tree frog *n* any of various arboreal frogs of SE Asia, Australia, and America

treehopper ('tri:ˌhɒpə) *n* any of a family of insects which live among trees and have a large hoodlike thoracic process curving backwards over the body

tree-hugger *n* *inf, derog* an environmental campaigner [C20 from the tactic of embracing trees to prevent their being felled]

tree kangaroo *n* any of several arboreal kangaroos of New Guinea and N Australia, having hind legs and forelegs of a similar length

tree line *n* the zone, at high altitudes or high latitudes, beyond which no trees grow. Trees growing between the timberline and the tree line are typically stunted

treen ('tri:ən) *adj* **1** made of wood; wooden ▷ *n* **2** dishes and other utensils made of wood [OE *trēowen*, from *trēow* tree] > **'treenˌware** *n*

treenail *or* **trenail** ('tri:neɪl, 'trɛnᵊl) *n* a dowel used for pinning planks or timbers together

Tt

tree of heaven *n* another name for **ailanthus**
tree shrew *n* any of a family of small arboreal mammals of SE Asia having large eyes and resembling squirrels
tree sparrow *n* **1** a small European weaverbird similar to the house sparrow but having a brown head **2** a small North American finch
tree surgery *n* the treatment of damaged trees by filling cavities, applying braces, etc > **tree surgeon** *n*
tree toad *n* a less common name for **tree frog**
tree tomato *n* **1** an arborescent shrub of South America bearing red egg-shaped edible fruit **2** the fruit of this plant. Also called: **tamarillo**
tref (treɪf) *adj Judaism* ritually unfit to be eaten [Yiddish, from Heb. *terēphāh*, lit.: torn (i.e., animal meat torn by beasts), from *tāraf* to tear]
trefoil (ˈtrɛfɔɪl) *n* **1** any of a genus of leguminous plants having leaves divided into three leaflets **2** any of various related plants having similar leaves **3** a leaf having three leaflets **4** *archit* an ornament in the form of three arcs arranged in a circle [c14 from Anglo-F *trifoil*, from L *trifolium* three-leaved herb] > ˈ**trefoiled** *adj*
trek (trɛk) *n* **1** a long and often difficult journey **2** *S African* a journey or stage of a journey, esp a migration by ox wagon ▷ *vb* **treks, trekking, trekked** **3** *(intr)* to make a trek [c19 from Afrik., from MDu. *trekken* to travel]
trellis (ˈtrɛlɪs) *n* **1** a structure of latticework, esp one used to support climbing plants ▷ *vb (tr)* **2** to interweave (strips of wood, etc) to make a trellis **3** to provide or support with a trellis [c14 from OF *treliz* fabric of open texture, from LL *trilīcius* woven with three threads, from L TRI- + *līcium* thread] > ˈ**trellis**ˌ**work** *n*
trematode (ˈtrɛməˌtəʊd, ˈtriː-) *n* any of a class of parasitic flatworms, which includes the flukes [c19 from NL *Trematoda*, from Gk *trēmatōdēs* full of holes, from *trēma* hole]
tremble (ˈtrɛmbᵊl) *vb* **trembles, trembling, trembled** *(intr)* **1** to vibrate with short slight movements; quiver **2** to shake involuntarily, as with cold or fear; shiver **3** to experience fear or anxiety ▷ *n* **4** the act or an instance of trembling [c14 from OF *trembler*, from Med. L *tremulāre*, from L *tremulus* quivering, from *tremere* to quake] > ˈ**trembling** *adj* > ˈ**trembly** *adj*
trembler (ˈtrɛmblə) *n* a device that vibrates to make or break an electrical circuit
trembles (ˈtrɛmbᵊlz) *n (functioning as sing)* a disease of cattle and sheep characterized by trembling
trembling poplar *n* another name for **aspen**
tremendous (trɪˈmɛndəs) *adj* **1** vast; huge **2** *inf* very exciting or unusual **3** *inf* (intensifier): *a tremendous help* **4** *arch* terrible or dreadful [c17 from L *tremendus* terrible, lit.: that is to be trembled at, from *tremere* to quake] > **tre**ˈ**mendously** *adv* > **tre**ˈ**mendousness** *n*
tremolo (ˈtrɛməˌləʊ) *n, pl* **tremolos** *music* **1** (in playing the violin, cello, etc) the rapid reiteration of a note or notes to produce a trembling effect **2** (in singing) a fluctuation in pitch **3** a device, as on an organ, that produces a tremolo effect [c19 from It.: quavering, from Med. L *tremulāre* to TREMBLE]
tremor (ˈtrɛmə) *n* **1** an involuntary shudder or vibration **2** any trembling movement **3** a vibrating or trembling effect, as of sound or light **4** a minor earthquake ▷ *vb* **5** *(intr)* to tremble [c14 from L: a shaking, from *tremere* to tremble] > ˈ**tremorous** *adj*
tremulous (ˈtrɛmjʊləs) *adj* **1** vibrating slightly; quavering; trembling **2** showing or characterized by fear, anxiety, excitement, etc [c17 from L *tremulus*, from *tremere* to shake] > ˈ**tremulously** *adv* > ˈ**tremulousness** *n*
trenail (ˈtriːneɪl, ˈtrɛnᵊl) *n* a variant spelling of **treenail**
trench (trɛntʃ) *n* **1** a deep ditch **2** a ditch dug as a fortification, having a parapet of earth ▷ *vb* **3** to make a trench in (a place) **4** *(tr)* to fortify with a trench **5** to slash or be slashed **6** *(intr; foll by on or upon)* to encroach or verge [c14 from OF *trenche* something cut, from *trenchier* to cut, from L *truncāre* to cut off]
trenchant (ˈtrɛntʃənt) *adj* **1** keen or incisive: *trenchant criticism* **2** vigorous and effective: *a trenchant foreign policy* **3** distinctly defined **4** *arch or poetic* sharp [c14 from OF *trenchant* cutting, from *trenchier* to cut; see TRENCH] > ˈ**trenchancy** *n* > ˈ**trenchantly** *adv*
Trenchard (ˈtrɛntʃɑːd) *n* **Hugh Montague,** 1st Viscount. 1873–1956, British air marshal, who as chief of air staff (1918, 1919–27) and marshal of the RAF (1927–29) established the RAF as a fully independent service. As commissioner of the Metropolitan Police (1931–35) he founded the police college at Hendon
trench coat *n* a belted waterproof coat resembling a military officer's coat
trencher (ˈtrɛntʃə) *n* **1** (esp formerly) a wooden board on which food was served or cut **2** Also called: **trencher cap** a mortarboard [c14 *trenchour* knife, plate for carving on, from OF *trencheoir*, from *trenchier* to cut; see TRENCH]
trencherman (ˈtrɛntʃəmən) *n, pl* **trenchermen** a person who enjoys food; hearty eater
trench fever *n* an acute infectious disease characterized by fever and muscular aches and pains and transmitted by lice
trench foot *n* a form of frostbite affecting persons standing for long periods in cold water
trench mortar *or* **gun** *n* a portable mortar used in trench warfare to shoot projectiles at a high trajectory over a short range
trench warfare *n* a type of warfare in which opposing armies face each other in entrenched positions
trend (trɛnd) *n* **1** general tendency or direction **2** fashion; mode ▷ *vb* **3** *(intr)* to take a certain trend [OE *trendan* to turn]
trendsetter (ˈtrɛndˌsɛtə) *n* a person or thing that creates, or may create, a new fashion > ˈ**trend**ˌ**setting** *adj*
trendy (ˈtrɛndɪ) *Brit inf* ▷ *adj* **trendier, trendiest** **1** consciously fashionable ▷ *n, pl* **trendies** **2** a trendy person > ˈ**trendily** *adv* > ˈ**trendiness** *n*
Trengganu *or* **Terengganu** (trɛŋˈɡɑːnuː, tɛrɛŋ-) *n* a state of E Peninsular Malaysia, on the South China Sea: under Thai suzerainty until becoming a British protectorate in 1909; joined the Federation of Malaya in 1948; an isolated forested region; mainly agricultural. Capital: Kuala Trengganu. Pop: 879 691 (2000). Area: 13 020 sq km (5027 sq miles)
Trent (trɛnt) *n* **1** a river in central England, rising in Staffordshire and flowing generally northeast into the Humber: the chief river of the Midlands. Length: 270 km (170 miles) **2** Also: **Trient** the German name for **Trento**
trente et quarante (*French* trɑ̃t e karɑ̃t) *n cards* another name for **rouge et noir** [c17 F, lit.: thirty and forty; from the rule that forty is the maximum number that may be dealt and the winning colour is the one closest to thirty-one]
Trentino-Alto Adige (trɛnˈtiːnəʊˈɑːltəʊ, ˈɑːdɪˌdʒeɪ) *n* a region of N Italy: consists of the part of the Tyrol south of the Brenner Pass, ceded by Austria after World War I. Pop: 936 256 (2000 est). Area: 13 613 sq km (5256 sq miles). Former name (until 1947): **Venezia Tridentina**
Trento (*Italian* ˈtrɛnto) *n* a city in N Italy, in Trentino-Alto Adige region on the Adige River: Roman military base; seat of the Council of Trent. Pop: 104 906 (2000 est). Latin name: **Tridentum.** German name: **Trent**
Trenton (ˈtrɛntən) *n* a city in W New Jersey, capital of the state, on the Delaware River: settled by English Quakers in 1679; scene of the defeat of the British by Washington (1776) during the War of American Independence. Pop: 85 403 (2000)
trepan (trɪˈpæn) *n* **1** *surgery* an instrument resembling a carpenter's brace and bit formerly used to remove circular sections of bone from the skull **2** a tool for

cutting out circular blanks or for making grooves around a fixed centre ▷ *vb* **trepans, trepanning, trepanned** (*tr*) **3** to cut (a hole or groove) with a trepan **4** *surgery* another word for **trephine** [C14 from Med. L *trepanum* rotary saw, from Gk *trupanon* auger, from *trupan* to bore, from *trupa* a hole] > **trepanation** (ˌtrɛpəˈneɪʃən) *n*

trepang (trɪˈpæŋ) *n* any of various large sea cucumbers of tropical Oriental seas, the body walls of which are used as food by the Japanese and Chinese [C18 from Malay *tĕripang*]

trephine (trɪˈfiːn) *n* **1** a surgical sawlike instrument for removing circular sections of bone esp from the skull ▷ *vb* **trephines, trephining, trephined 2** (*tr*) to remove a circular section of bone from (esp the skull) [C17 from F *tréphine*, from obs. E *trefine* TREPAN, allegedly from L *trēs fīnēs*, lit.: three ends] > **trephination** (ˌtrɛfɪˈneɪʃən) *n*

trepidation (ˌtrɛpɪˈdeɪʃən) *n* **1** a state of fear or anxiety **2** a condition of quaking or palpitation, esp one caused by anxiety [C17 from L *trepidātiō*, from *trepidāre* to be in a state of alarm]

trespass (ˈtrɛspəs) *vb* (*intr*) **1** (often foll by *on* or *upon*) to go or intrude (on the property, privacy, or preserves of another) with no right or permission **2** *law* to commit trespass **3** *arch* (often foll by *against*) to sin or transgress ▷ *n* **4** *law* **4a** any unlawful act committed with force, which causes injury to another person, his property or his rights **4b** a wrongful entry upon another's land **5** an intrusion on another's privacy or preserves **6** a sin or offence [C13 from OF *trespas* a passage, from *trespasser* to pass through, ult. from L *passus* a PACE[1]] > **ˈtrespasser** *n*

tress (trɛs) *n* **1** (*often pl*) a lock of hair, esp a long lock of woman's hair **2** a plait or braid of hair ▷ *vb* (*tr*) **3** to arrange in tresses [C13 from OF *trece*, from ?] > **ˈtressy** *adj*

trestle (ˈtrɛsᵊl) *n* **1** a framework in the form of a horizontal member supported at each end by a pair of splayed legs, used to carry scaffold boards, a table top, etc **2a** a framework of timber, metal, or reinforced concrete that is used to support a bridge or ropeway **2b** a bridge constructed of such frameworks [C14 from OF *trestel*, ult. from L *trānstrum* transom]

trestlework (ˈtrɛsᵊlˌwɜːk) *n* an arrangement of trestles, esp one that supports a bridge

trevally (trɪˈvælɪ) *n, pl* **trevallies** *Austral & NZ* any of various food and game fishes of the genus *Caranx* [C19 prob. alteration of *cavally*, from *cavalla* species of tropical fish, from Sp. *caballa* horse]

Trevelyan (trɪˈvɛljən, -ˈvɪl-) *n* **1 George Macaulay** 1876–1962, British historian, noted for his *English Social History* (1944) **2** his father, Sir **George Otto** 1838–1928, British historian and biographer. His works include a biography of his uncle Lord Macaulay (1876)

Trèves (trɛv) *n* the French name for **Trier**

Trevino (trəˈviːnəʊ) *n* **Lee** born 1939, US professional golfer: winner of the US Open Championship (1968; 1971) and the British Open Championship (1971; 1972)

Treviso (*Italian* treˈviːzo) *n* a city in N Italy, in Veneto region: agricultural market centre. Pop: 84 066 (1990)

Trevithick (trəˈvɪθɪk) *n* **Richard** 1771–1833, British engineer, who built the first steam-driven passenger carriage (1801) and the first locomotive to run on smooth wheels on smooth rails (1804)

trews (truːz) *pl n chiefly Brit* close-fitting trousers of tartan cloth [C16 from Scot Gaelic *triubhas*, from OF *trebus*]

trey (treɪ) *n* any card or dice throw with three spots [C14 from OF *treis* three, from L *trēs*]

tri- *prefix* **1** three or thrice: *triaxial; trigon; trisect* **2** occurring every three: *trimonthly* [from L *trēs*, Gk *treis*]

triable (ˈtraɪəbᵊl) *adj* **1** subject to trial in a court of law **2** *rare* able to be tested

triacid (traɪˈæsɪd) *adj* capable of reacting with three molecules of a monobasic acid

triad (ˈtraɪæd) *n* **1** a group of three; trio **2** *chem* an atom, element, group, or ion that has a valency of three **3** *music* a three-note chord consisting of a note and the third and fifth above it **4** an aphoristic literary form used in medieval Welsh and Irish literature [C16 from LL *trias*, from Gk] > **triˈadic** *adj* > **ˈtriadism** *n*

Triad (ˈtraɪæd) *n* any of several Chinese secret societies, esp one involved in criminal activities, such as drug trafficking

triage (ˈtraɪɪdʒ) *n* **1** the action of sorting casualties, patients, etc according to priority **2** the allocating of limited resources on a basis of expediency rather than moral principles [C18 from F; see TRY, -AGE]

trial (ˈtraɪəl, traɪl) *n* **1a** the act or an instance of trying or proving; test or experiment **1b** (*as modifier*): *a trial run* **2** *law* **2a** the judicial examination and determination of the issues in a civil or criminal cause by a competent tribunal **2b** the determination of an accused person's guilt or innocence after hearing evidence and the judicial examination of the issues involved **2c** (*as modifier*): *trial proceedings* **3** an effort or attempt to do something **4** trouble or grief **5** an annoying or frustrating person or thing **6** (*often pl*) a competition for individuals: *sheepdog trials* **7** a motorcycling competition in which the skills of the riders are tested over rough ground **8 on trial 8a** undergoing trial, esp before a court of law **8b** being tested, as before a commitment to purchase ▷ *vb* **trials, trialling, trialled 9** to test or make experimental use of (something): *the idea has been trialled in several schools* [C16 from Anglo-F, from *trier* to TRY] > **ˈtrialling** *n*

trial and error *n* a method of discovery, solving problems, etc, based on practical experiment and experience rather than on theory: *he learned to cook by trial and error*

trial balance *n book-keeping* a statement of all the debit and credit balances in the ledger of a double-entry system, drawn up to test their equality

triallist *or* **trialist** (ˈtraɪəlɪst, ˈtraɪlɪst) *n* **1** a person who takes part in a competition, esp a motorcycle trial **2** *sport* a person who takes part in a preliminary match or heat held to determine selection for an event, a team, etc

Tt

triangle (ˈtraɪˌæŋgᵊl) *n* **1** *geom* a three-sided polygon that can be classified by angle, as in an acute triangle, or by side, as in an equilateral triangle **2** any object shaped like a triangle **3** any situation involving three parties or points of view **4** *music* a percussion instrument consisting of a sonorous metal bar bent into a triangular shape, beaten with a metal stick **5** a group of three [C14 from L *triangulum* (n), from *triangulus* (adj), from TRI- + *angulus* corner] > **triangular** (traɪˈæŋgjʊlə) *adj*

triangle of forces *n physics* a triangle whose sides represent the magnitudes and directions of three forces in equilibrium

triangulate *vb* (traɪˈæŋgjʊˌleɪt), **triangulates, triangulating, triangulated** (*tr*) **1a** to survey by the method of triangulation **1b** to calculate trigonometrically **2** to divide into triangles **3** to make triangular ▷ *adj* (traɪˈæŋgjʊlɪt, -ˌleɪt) **4** marked with or composed of triangles > **triˈangulately** *adv*

triangulation (traɪˌæŋgjʊˈleɪʃən) *n* a method of surveying in which an area is divided into triangles, one side (the base line) and all angles of which are measured and the lengths of the other lines calculated trigonometrically

triangulation station *n* a point on a hilltop, etc, used for triangulation by a surveyor

Triassic (traɪˈæsɪk) *adj* **1** of or formed in the first period of the Mesozoic era, that lasted for 42 million years ▷ *n* **2 the** Also called: **Trias** the Triassic period or rock system [C19 from L *trias* triad, from the three subdivisions]

triathlon (traɪˈæθlɒn) *n* an athletic contest in which each athlete competes in three different events, swimming, cycling, and running [C20 from TRI- + Gk *athlon* contest] > ˌ**triˈathlete** *n*

triatomic (ˌtraɪəˈtɒmɪk) *adj chem* having three atoms in the molecule

tribade (ˈtrɪbɑːd) *n* a lesbian who practises tribadism [C17 from L *tribas*, from Gk *tribein* to rub]

tribadism (ˈtrɪbədɪzəm) *n* a lesbian practice in which one partner lies on top of the other and simulates the male role in heterosexual intercourse

tribalism (ˈtraɪbəˌlɪzəm) *n* **1** the state of existing as a tribe **2** the customs and beliefs of a tribal society **3** loyalty to a tribe > ˈ**tribalist** *n, adj* > ˌ**tribalˈistic** *adj*

tribasic (traɪˈbeɪsɪk) *adj* **1** (of an acid) containing three replaceable hydrogen atoms in the molecule **2** (of a molecule) containing three monovalent basic atoms or groups

tribe (traɪb) *n* **1** a social division of a people, esp of a preliterate people, defined in terms of common descent, territory, culture, etc **2** an ethnic or ancestral division of ancient cultures, esp: **2a** one of the political divisions of the Roman people **2b** any of the 12 divisions of ancient Israel, each of which was believed to be descended from one of the 12 patriarchs **3** *inf* **3a** a large number of persons, animals, etc **3b** a specific class or group of persons **3c** a family, esp a large one **4** *biol* a taxonomic group that is a subdivision of a subfamily [C13 from L *tribus*] > ˈ**tribal** *adj*

tribesman (ˈtraɪbzmən) *n, pl* **tribesmen** a member of a tribe

tribo- *combining form* indicating friction: *triboelectricity* [from Gk *tribein* to rub]

triboelectricity (ˌtraɪbəʊɪlɛkˈtrɪsɪtɪ, -ˌiːlɛk-) *n* electricity generated by friction

tribology (traɪˈbɒlədʒɪ) *n* the study of friction, lubrication, and wear between moving surfaces

triboluminescence (ˌtraɪbəʊˌluːmɪˈnɛsəns) *n* luminescence produced by friction, such as the emission of light when certain crystals are crushed > ˌ**triboˌlumiˈnescent** *adj*

tribrach (ˈtraɪbræk, ˈtrɪb-) *n* a metrical foot of three short syllables [C16 from L *tribrachys*, from Gk, from TRI- + *brakhus* short]

tribromoethanol (traɪˌbrəʊməʊˈɛθəˌnɒl) *n* a soluble white crystalline compound with a slight aromatic odour, used as a general anaesthetic

tribulation (ˌtrɪbjʊˈleɪʃən) *n* **1** a cause of distress **2** a state of suffering or distress [C13 from OF, from Church L *trībulātiō*, from L *trībulāre* to afflict, from *trībulum* a threshing board, from *terere* to rub]

tribunal (traɪˈbjuːnᵊl, trɪ-) *n* **1** a court of justice **2** (in Britain) a special court, convened by the government to inquire into a specific matter **3** a raised platform containing the seat of a judge [C16 from L *tribūnus* TRIBUNE[1]]

tribune[1] (ˈtrɪbjuːn) *n* **1** (in ancient Rome) **1a** an officer elected by the plebs to protect their interests **1b** a senior military officer **2** a person who upholds public rights [C14 from L *tribunus*, prob. from *tribus* tribe] > **tribunate** (ˈtrɪbjʊnɪt) *or* ˈ**tribuneship** *n*

tribune[2] (ˈtrɪbjuːn) *n* **1a** the apse of a Christian basilica that contains the bishop's throne **1b** the throne itself **2** a gallery or raised area in a church **3** *rare* a raised platform; dais [C17 via F from It. *tribuna*, from Med. L *tribūna*, var. of L *tribūnal* TRIBUNAL]

tributary (ˈtrɪbjʊtərɪ) *n, pl* **tributaries 1** a stream, river, or glacier that feeds another larger one **2** a person, nation, or people that pays tribute ▷ *adj* **3** (of a stream, etc) feeding a larger stream **4** given or owed as a tribute **5** paying tribute > ˈ**tributarily** *adv*

tribute (ˈtrɪbjuːt) *n* **1** a gift or statement made in acknowledgment, gratitude, or admiration **2** a payment by one ruler or state to another, usually as an acknowledgment of submission **3** the obligation to pay tribute [C14 from L *tribūtum*, from *tribuere* to grant (orig.: to distribute among the tribes), from *tribus* tribe]

tribute band *n* a group that plays the songs of a band they admire, often dressing in the style of the original band members

trice (traɪs) *n* a moment; instant (esp in **in a trice**) [C15 (in *at* or *in a trice*, in the sense: at one tug): apparent substantive use of *trice* to haul up, from MDu. *trīse* pulley]

tricentenary (ˌtraɪsɛnˈtiːnərɪ) *or* **tricentennial** (ˌtraɪsɛnˈtɛnɪəl) *adj* **1** of a period of 300 years **2** of a 300th anniversary ▷ *n, pl* **tricentenaries** *or* **tricentennials 3** an anniversary of 300 years

triceps (ˈtraɪsɛps) *n, pl* **tricepses** (-sɛpsɪz) *or* **triceps** any muscle having three heads, esp the one that extends the forearm [C16 from L, from TRI- + *caput* head]

trichiasis (trɪˈkaɪəsɪs) *n pathol* an abnormal position of the eyelashes that causes irritation when they rub against the eyeball [C17 via LL from Gk *trikhiasis*, from *thrix* a hair]

trichina (trɪˈkaɪnə) *n, pl* **trichinae** (-niː) a parasitic nematode worm occurring in the intestines of pigs, rats, and man and producing larvae that form cysts in skeletal muscle [C19 from NL, from Gk *trikhinos* relating to hair, from *thrix* a hair] > **trichinous** (ˈtrɪkɪnəs) *adj*

Trichinopoly (ˌtrɪkɪˈnɒpəlɪ) *n* another name for **Tiruchirapalli**

trichinosis (ˌtrɪkɪˈnəʊsɪs) *n* a disease characterized by nausea, fever, diarrhoea, and swelling of the muscles, caused by ingestion of pork infected with trichina larvae [C19 from NL TRICHINA]

trichloride (traɪˈklɔːraɪd) *n* any compound that contains three chlorine atoms per molecule

tricho- *or before a vowel* **trich-** *combining form* indicating hair or a part resembling hair: *trichocyst* [from Gk *thrix* (genitive *trikhos*) hair]

trichology (trɪˈkɒlədʒɪ) *n* the branch of medicine concerned with the hair and its diseases > **triˈchologist** *n*

trichomoniasis (ˌtrɪkəʊməˈnaɪəsɪs) *n* inflammation of the vagina caused by infection with parasitic protozoa [C19 NL]

trichopteran (traɪˈkɒptərən) *n* **1** any insect of the order *Trichoptera*, which comprises the caddis flies ▷ *adj* **2** Also: **trichopterous** (trɪˈkɒptərəs) of or belonging to the order *Trichoptera* [C19 from NL *Trichoptera*, lit.: having hairy wings, from Gk *thrix* a hair + *pteron* wing]

trichosis (trɪˈkəʊsɪs) *n* any abnormal condition or disease of the hair [C19 via NL from Gk *trikhōsis* growth of hair]

trichotomy (traɪˈkɒtəmɪ) *n, pl* **trichotomies 1** division into three categories **2** *theol* the division of man into body, spirit, and soul [C17 prob. from NL *trichotomia*, from Gk *trikhotomein* to divide into three] > **trichotomic** (ˌtrɪkəˈtɒmɪk) *or* **triˈchotomous** *adj*

trichroism (ˈtraɪkrəʊˌɪzəm) *n* a property of biaxial crystals as a result of which they show a difference in colour when viewed along three different axes [C19 from Gk *trikhroos* three-coloured, from TRI- + *khrōma* colour]

trichromatic (ˌtraɪkrəʊˈmætɪk) *or* **trichromic** (traɪˈkrəʊmɪk) *adj* **1** involving the combination of three primary colours **2** of or having normal colour vision **3** having or involving three colours > **triˈchromaˌtism** *n*

trick (trɪk) *n* **1** a deceitful or cunning action or plan **2a** a mischievous, malicious, or humorous action or plan; joke **2b** (*as modifier*): *a trick spider* **3** an illusory or magical feat **4** a simple feat learned by an animal or person **5** an adroit or ingenious device; knack: *a trick of the trade* **6** a habit or mannerism **7** a turn of duty **8** *cards* a batch of cards containing one from each player, usually played in turn and won by the player or side that plays the card with the highest value **9 can't take a trick** *Austral sl* to be consistently unsuccessful or unlucky **10 do the trick** *inf* to produce the desired result **11 how's tricks?** *sl* how are you? **12 turn a trick** *sl* (of a prostitute) to gain a customer

▷ *vb* **13** (*tr*) to defraud, deceive, or cheat (someone) ▷ See also **trick out** [C15 from OF *trique*, from *trikier* to deceive, ult. from L *trīcārī* to play tricks]

trick cyclist *n* **1** a cyclist who performs tricks, such as in a circus **2** a slang term for **psychiatrist**

trickery (ˈtrɪkərɪ) *n, pl* **trickeries** the practice or an instance of using tricks

trickle (ˈtrɪkᵊl) *vb* **trickles, trickling, trickled 1** to run or cause to run in thin or slow streams **2** (*intr*) to move gradually: *the crowd trickled away* ▷ *n* **3** a thin, irregular, or slow flow of something **4** the act of trickling [C14 ? imit.] > ˈ**trickling** *adj*

trickle charger *n* a small mains-operated battery charger, esp one used by car owners

trickle-down *adj* of or concerning the theory that granting concessions such as tax cuts to the rich will benefit all levels of society by stimulating the economy

trick or treat *sentence substitute chiefly US & Canad* a customary cry used by children at Halloween when they call at houses in disguise, indicating that they want a present of sweets, apples, or money and, if refused, will play a trick on the householder

trick out *or* **up** *vb* (*tr, adv*) to dress up; deck out: *tricked out in frilly dresses*

trickster (ˈtrɪkstə) *n* a person who deceives or plays tricks

tricksy (ˈtrɪksɪ) *adj* **tricksier, tricksiest 1** playing tricks habitually; mischievous **2** crafty or difficult to deal with > ˈ**tricksiness** *n*

tricky (ˈtrɪkɪ) *adj* **trickier, trickiest 1** involving snags or difficulties **2** needing careful handling **3** sly; wily: *a tricky dealer* > ˈ**trickily** *adv* > ˈ**trickiness** *n*

triclinic (traɪˈklɪnɪk) *adj* of the crystal system characterized by three unequal axes, no pair of which are perpendicular

triclinium (traɪˈklɪnɪəm) *n, pl* **triclinia** (-ɪə) (in ancient Rome) **1** an arrangement of three couches around a table for reclining upon while dining **2** a dining room [C17 from L, from Gk *triklinion*, from TRI- + *klinē* a couch]

tricolour *or US* **tricolor** (ˈtrɪkələ, ˈtraɪˌkʌlə) *adj also* **tricoloured** *or US* **tricolored** (ˈtraɪˌkʌləd) **1** having or involving three colours ▷ *n* **2** (*often cap*) the French flag, having three stripes in blue, white, and red **3** any flag, badge, etc, with three colours

tricorn (ˈtraɪˌkɔːn) *n also* **tricorne 1** a cocked hat with the brim turned up on three sides ▷ *adj also* **tricornered 2** having three horns or corners [C18 from L *tricornis*, from TRI- + *cornu* horn]

tricot (ˈtrɪkəʊ, ˈtriː-) *n* **1** a thin rayon or nylon fabric knitted or resembling knitting, used for dresses, etc **2** a type of ribbed dress fabric [C19 from F, from *tricoter* to knit, from ?]

tricuspid (traɪˈkʌspɪd) *anat* ▷ *adj also* **tricuspidal 1** having three points, cusps, or segments: *a tricuspid tooth; a tricuspid valve* ▷ *n* **2** a tooth having three cusps

tricycle (ˈtraɪsɪkᵊl) *n* a three-wheeled cycle, esp one driven by pedals > ˈ**tricyclist** *n*

trident (ˈtraɪdᵊnt) *n* a three-pronged spear [C16 from L *tridēns* three-pronged, from TRI- + *dēns* tooth]

Trident (ˈtraɪdᵊnt) *n* a type of US submarine-launched ballistic missile with independently targetable warheads

tridentate (traɪˈdɛnteɪt) *or* **tridental** *adj* having three prongs, teeth, or points

Tridentine (traɪˈdɛntaɪn) *adj* **1a** *history* of the Council of Trent in the 16th century **1b** in accord with Tridentine doctrine: *Tridentine mass* ▷ *n* **2** an orthodox Roman Catholic [C16 from Med. L *Tridentīnus*, from *Tridentum* TRENT]

Tridentum (traɪˈdɛntəm) *n* the Latin name for **Trento**

tried (traɪd) *vb* the past tense and past participle of **try**

triella (traɪˈɛlə) *n* a cumulative bet on horses in three specified races

triennial (traɪˈɛnɪəl) *adj* **1** relating to, lasting for, or occurring every three years ▷ *n* **2** a third anniversary **3** a triennial period, thing, or occurrence [C17 from L TRIENNIUM] > **triˈennially** *adv*

triennium (traɪˈɛnɪəm) *n, pl* **trienniums** *or* **triennia** (-nɪə) a period or cycle of three years [C19 from L, from TRI- + *annus* a year]

Trient (triˈɛnt) *n* the German name for **Trento.** Also: **Trent**

trier (ˈtraɪə) *n* a person or thing that tries

Trier (*German* triːr) *n* a city in W Germany, in the Rhineland-Palatinate on the Moselle River: one of the oldest towns of central Europe, ancient capital of a Celto-Germanic tribe (the **Treveri**); an early centre of Christianity, ruled by powerful archbishops until the 18th century; wine trade; important Roman remains. Pop: 98 750 (1991). Latin name: **Augusta Treverorum** (aʊˈguːstə ˌtrɛvəˈrəʊrəm). French name: **Trèves**

Trieste (triːˈɛst; *Italian* triˈɛste) *n* **1** a port in NE Italy, capital of Friuli-Venezia Giulia region, on the **Gulf of Trieste** at the head of the Adriatic Sea: under Austrian rule (1382–1918); capital of the Free Territory of Trieste (1947–54); important transit port for central Europe. Pop: 216 459 (2000 est). Slovene and Serbo-Croat name: **Trst 2 Free Territory of** a former territory on the N Adriatic: established by the UN in 1947; most of the N part passed to Italy and the remainder to Yugoslavia in 1954

trifacial (traɪˈfeɪʃəl) *adj* another word for **trigeminal**

trifecta (traɪˈfɛktə) *n* a form of betting in which punters select first-, second-, and third-place winners in the correct order

trifid (ˈtraɪfɪd) *adj* divided or split into three parts or lobes [C18 from L *trifidus*, from TRI- + *findere* to split]

trifle (ˈtraɪfᵊl) *n* **1** a thing of little or no value or significance **2** a small amount; bit: *a trifle more enthusiasm* **3** *Brit* a cold dessert made with sponge cake spread with jam or fruit, soaked in sherry, covered with custard and cream ▷ *vb* **trifles, trifling, trifled 4** (*intr; usually foll by with*) to deal (with) as if worthless; dally: *to trifle with a person's affections* **5** to waste (time) frivolously [C13 from OF *trufle* mockery, from *trufler* to cheat] > ˈ**trifler** *n*

trifling (ˈtraɪflɪŋ) *adj* **1** insignificant or petty **2** frivolous or idle > ˈ**triflingly** *adv*

trifocal *adj* (traɪˈfəʊkᵊl) **1** having three focuses **2** having three focal lengths ▷ *n* (traɪˈfəʊkᵊl, ˈtraɪˌfəʊkᵊl) **3** (*pl*) glasses that have trifocal lenses

triforium (traɪˈfɔːrɪəm) *n, pl* **triforia** (-rɪə) an arcade above the arches of the nave, choir, or transept of a church [C18 from Anglo-L, apparently from L TRI- + *foris* a doorway; from the fact that each bay had three openings]

trifurcate (ˈtraɪfɜːkɪt, -ˌkeɪt) *or* **trifurcated** *adj* having three branches or forks [C19 from L *trifurcus*, from TRI- + *furca* a fork]

trig (trɪg) *arch or dialect* ▷ *adj* **1** neat or spruce ▷ *vb* **trigs, trigging, trigged 2** to make or become trim or spruce [C12 (orig.: trusty): from ON] > ˈ**trigly** *adv* > ˈ**trigness** *n*

trig. *abbrev for:* **1** trigonometrical **2** trigonometry

trigeminal (traɪˈdʒɛmɪnᵊl) *adj anat* of or relating to the trigeminal nerve [C19 from L *trigeminus* triplet, from TRI- + *geminus* twin]

trigeminal nerve *n* either one of the fifth pair of cranial nerves, which supply the muscles of the mandible and maxilla. Their ophthalmic branches supply the area around the orbit of the eye, the nasal cavity, and the forehead

trigeminal neuralgia *n pathol* another name for **tic douloureux**

trigger (ˈtrɪgə) *n* **1** a small lever that activates the firing mechanism of a firearm **2** a device that releases a spring-loaded mechanism **3** any event that sets a course of action in motion ▷ *vb* (*tr*) **4** (*usually foll by off*) to give rise (to); set off **5** to fire or set in motion by or as

Tt

by pulling a trigger [c17 *tricker*, from Du. *trekker*, from *trekken* to pull]

triggerfish ('trɪgə,fɪʃ) *n, pl* **triggerfish** *or* **triggerfishes** any of a family of fishes of tropical and temperate seas. They have erectile spines in the first dorsal fin

trigger-happy *adj inf* **1** tending to resort to the use of firearms or violence irresponsibly **2** tending to act rashly

triglyceride (traɪ'glɪsə,raɪd) *n* any ester of glycerol and one or more carboxylic acids, in which each glycerol molecule has combined with three carboxylic acid molecules

triglyph ('traɪ,glɪf) *n archit* a stone block in a Doric frieze, having three vertical channels [c16 via L from Gk *trigluphos*, from TRI- + *gluphē* carving]

trigonal ('trɪgənᵊl) *adj* **1** triangular **2** of the crystal system characterized by three equal axes that are equally inclined and not perpendicular to each other [c16 via L from Gk *trigōnon* triangle]

trigonometric function *n* any of a group of functions of an angle expressed as a ratio of two of the sides of a right-angled triangle containing the angle. The group includes sine, cosine, tangent, etc

trigonometry (,trɪgə'nɒmɪtrɪ) *n* the branch of mathematics concerned with the properties of trigonometric functions and their application to the determination of the angles and sides of triangles: used in surveying, navigation, etc [c17 from NL *trigōnometria*, from Gk *trigōnon* triangle] > **trigonometric** (,trɪgənə'mɛtrɪk) *or* ,**trigono'metrical** *adj*

trig point *n* an informal name for **triangulation station** [from *trigonometric*]

trigraph ('traɪ,grɑːf) *n* a combination of three letters used to represent a single speech sound or phoneme, such as *eau* in French *beau*

trihedral (traɪ'hiːdrəl) *adj* **1** having three plane faces ▷ *n* **2** a figure formed by the intersection of three lines in different planes

trihedron (traɪ'hiːdrən) *n, pl* **trihedrons** *or* **trihedra** (-drə) a figure determined by the intersection of three planes

trike (traɪk) *n* short for **tricycle**

trilateral (traɪ'lætərəl) *adj* having three sides

trilby ('trɪlbɪ) *n, pl* **trilbies** a man's soft felt hat with an indented crown [c19 after *Trilby*, the heroine of a dramatized novel (1893) of that title by George Du Maurier]

trilingual (traɪ'lɪŋgwəl) *adj* **1** able to speak three languages fluently **2** expressed or written in three languages > **tri'lingualism** *n*

trilithon (traɪ'lɪθɒn) *or* **trilith** ('traɪlɪθ) *n* a structure consisting of two upright stones with a third placed across the top, as at Stonehenge [c18 from Gk] > **trilithic** (traɪ'lɪθɪk) *adj*

trill (trɪl) *n* **1** *music* a rapid alternation between a principal note and the note above it **2** a shrill warbling sound, esp as made by some birds **3** the articulation of an (r) sound produced by the rapid vibration of the tongue or the uvula ▷ *vb* **4** to sound, sing, or play (a trill or with a trill) **5** (*tr*) to pronounce (an (r) sound) by the production of a trill [c17 from It. *trillo*, from *trillare*, apparently from MDu. *trillen* to vibrate]

trillion ('trɪljən) *n* **1** the number represented as one followed by twelve zeros (10^{12}); a million million **2** (formerly, in Britain) the number represented as one followed by eighteen zeros (10^{18}); a million million million ▷ *determiner* **3** (preceded by *a* or a numeral) amounting to a trillion [c17 from F, on the model of *million*] > **'trillionth** *n, adj*

trillium ('trɪljəm) *n* any of a genus of herbaceous plants of Asia and North America, having a whorl of three leaves at the top of the stem with a single white, pink, or purple three-petalled flower [c18 from NL, modification by Linnaeus of Swedish *trilling* triplet]

trilobate (traɪ'ləʊbeɪt, 'traɪlə,beɪt) *adj* (esp of a leaf) consisting of or having three lobes or parts

trilobite ('traɪlə,baɪt) *n* any of various extinct marine arthropods abundant in Palaeozoic times, having a segmented exoskeleton divided into three parts [c19 from NL *Trilobītēs*, from Gk *trilobos* having three lobes] > **trilobitic** (,traɪlə'bɪtɪk) *adj*

trilogy ('trɪlədʒɪ) *n, pl* **trilogies** **1** a series of three related works, esp in literature, etc **2** (in ancient Greece) a series of three tragedies performed together [c19 from Gk *trilogia*]

trim (trɪm) *adj* **trimmer, trimmest** **1** neat and spruce in appearance **2** slim; slender **3** in good condition ▷ *vb* **trims, trimming, trimmed** (*mainly tr*) **4** to put in good order, esp by cutting or pruning **5** to shape and finish (timber) **6** to adorn or decorate **7** (sometimes foll by *off* or *away*) to cut so as to remove: *to trim off a branch* **8** to cut down to the desired size or shape **9** *naut* **9a** (*also intr*) to adjust the balance of (a vessel) or (of a vessel) to maintain an even balance, by distribution of ballast, cargo, etc **9b** (*also intr*) to adjust (a vessel's sails) to take advantage of the wind **10** to balance (an aircraft) before flight by adjusting the position of the load or in flight by the use of trim tabs, fuel transfer, etc **11** (*also intr*) to modify (one's opinions, etc) for expediency **12** *inf* to thrash or beat **13** *inf* to rebuke ▷ *n* **14** a decoration or adornment **15** the upholstery and decorative facings of a car's interior **16** proper order or fitness; good shape **17** a haircut that neatens but does not alter the existing hairstyle **18** *naut* **18a** the general set and appearance of a vessel **18b** the difference between the draught of a vessel at the bow and at the stern **18c** the fitness of a vessel **18d** the position of a vessel's sails relative to the wind **19** dress or equipment **20** *US* window-dressing **21** the attitude of an aircraft in flight when the pilot allows the main control surfaces to take up their own positions **22** material that is trimmed off **23** decorative mouldings, such as architraves, picture rails, etc [OE *trymman* to strengthen] > **'trimly** *adv* > **'trimness** *n*

Trim (trɪm) *n* the county town of Meath, Republic of Ireland; 12th-century castle, medieval cathedral; textiles and machinery. Pop: 18 120 (1991)

trimaran ('traɪmə,ræn) *n* a vessel, usually of shallow draught, with two hulls flanking the main hull [c20 from TRI- + (CATA)MARAN]

Trimble ('trɪmbᵊl) *n* (**William**) **David** born 1944, Northern Irish politician; leader of the Ulster Unionist party from 1995, First Minister of Northern Ireland from 1998; Nobel peace prize jointly with John Hume in 1998

trimer ('traɪmə) *n* a polymer or a molecule of a polymer consisting of three identical monomers

trimerous ('trɪmərəs) *adj* **1** having parts in groups of three **2** having three parts

trimester (traɪ'mɛstə) *n* **1** a period of three months **2** (in some US and Canad universities or schools) any of the three academic sessions [c19 from F *trimestre*, from L *trimēstris* of three months] > **tri'mestral** *or* **tri'mestrial** *adj*

trimeter ('trɪmɪtə) *prosody* ▷ *n* **1** a verse line consisting of three metrical feet ▷ *adj* **2** designating such a line

trimethadione (,traɪmɛθə'daɪəʊn) *n* a crystalline compound with a camphor-like odour, used in the treatment of epilepsy

trimetric projection (traɪ'mɛtrɪk) *n* a geometric projection, used in mechanical drawing, in which the three axes are at arbitrary angles, often using different linear scales

trimmer ('trɪmə) *n* **1** a beam attached to truncated joists in order to leave an opening for a staircase, chimney, etc **2** a machine for trimming timber **3** a variable capacitor of small capacitance used for making fine adjustments, etc **4** a person who alters his or her opinions on the grounds of expediency **5** a person who fits out motor vehicles

trimming ('trɪmɪŋ) *n* **1** an extra piece used to decorate or complete **2** (*pl*) usual or traditional accompaniments: *roast turkey with all the trimmings* **3** (*pl*) parts that are cut off

trimolecular (ˌtraɪmə'lɛkjʊlə) *adj chem* of, formed from, or involving three molecules

trimonthly (traɪ'mʌnθlɪ) *adj, adv* every three months

trimorphism (traɪ'mɔːfɪzəm) *n* **1** *biol* the property exhibited by certain species of having or occurring in three different forms **2** the property of certain minerals of existing in three crystalline forms

Trinacria (trɪ'neɪkrɪə, traɪ-) *n* the Latin name for **Sicily** > **Tri'nacrian** *adj*

trinary ('traɪnərɪ) *adj* **1** made up of three parts; ternary **2** going in threes [C15 from LL *trīnārius* of three sorts, from L *trīnī* three each, from *trēs* three]

Trincomalee (ˌtrɪŋkəʊmə'liː) *n* a port in NE Sri Lanka, on the **Bay of Trincomalee** (an inlet of the Bay of Bengal); British naval base until 1957. Pop: 51 000 (latest est)

trine (traɪn) *n* **1** *astrol* an aspect of 120° between two planets **2** anything comprising three parts ▷ *adj* **3** of or relating to a trine **4** threefold; triple [C14 from OF *trin*, from L *trīnus* triple, from *trēs* three] > '**trinal** *adj*

Trinidad ('trɪnɪˌdæd) *n* an island in the West Indies, off the NE coast of Venezuela: colonized by the Spanish in the 17th century and ceded to Britain in 1802; joined with Tobago in 1888 as a British colony; now part of the independent republic of Trinidad and Tobago. Pop: 1 184 106 (1990) > ˌ**Trini'dadian** *adj, n*

Trinidad and Tobago *n* an independent republic in the Caribbean, occupying the two southernmost islands of the Lesser Antilles: became a British colony in 1888 and gained independence in 1962; became a republic in 1976; a member of the Commonwealth. Official language: English. Religion: Christian majority, with a large Hindu minority. Currency: Trinidad and Tobago dollar. Capital: Port of Spain. Pop: 1 298 000 (2001 est). Area: 5128 sq km (1980 sq miles)
▷ www.gov.tt
▷ www.visittnt.com
▷ www.discover-tt.com

Trinitarian (ˌtrɪnɪ'tɛərɪən) *n* **1** a person who believes in the doctrine of the Trinity ▷ *adj* **2** of or relating to the doctrine of the Trinity or those who uphold it > ˌ**Trini'tarianˌism** *n*

trinitroglycerine (traɪˌnaɪtrəʊ'glɪsərɪn) *n* the full name for **nitroglycerine**

trinitrotoluene (traɪˌnaɪtrəʊ'tɒljʊˌiːn) *or* **trinitrotoluol** (traɪˌnaɪtrəʊ'tɒljʊˌɒl) *n* the full name for **TNT**

trinity ('trɪnɪtɪ) *n, pl* **trinities** **1** a group of three **2** the state of being threefold [C13 from OF *trinite*, from LL *trīnitās*, from L *trīnus* triple]

Trinity ('trɪnɪtɪ) *n Christian theol* the union of three persons, the Father, Son, and Holy Spirit, in one Godhead

Trinity Brethren *pl n* the members of Trinity House

Trinity House *n* an association that provides lighthouses, buoys, etc, around the British coast

Trinity Sunday *n* the Sunday after Whit Sunday

Trinity term *n* the summer term at the Inns of Court and certain universities

trinket ('trɪŋkɪt) *n* **1** a small or worthless ornament or piece of jewellery **2** a trivial object; trifle [C16 ? from earlier *trenket* little knife, via OF, from L *truncāre* to lop]

trinomial (traɪ'nəʊmɪəl) *adj* **1** consisting of three terms ▷ *n* **2** *maths* a polynomial consisting of three terms, such as $ax^2 + bx + c$ **3** *biol* the three-part name of an organism that incorporates its genus, species, and subspecies [C18 TRI- + *-nomial* on the model of *binomial*]

trio ('triːəʊ) *n, pl* **trios** **1** a group of three people or things **2** *music* **2a** a group of three singers or instrumentalists or a piece of music composed for such a group **2b** a subordinate section in a scherzo, minuet, etc [C18 from It., ult. from L *trēs* three] ▷ Cf **duo**

triode ('traɪəʊd) *n* **1** an electronic valve having three electrodes, a cathode, an anode, and a grid **2** any electronic device having three electrodes [C20 TRI- + ELECTRODE]

trioecious *or* **triecious** (traɪ'iːʃəs) *adj* (of a plant species) having male, female, and hermaphrodite flowers in three different plants [C18 from NL *trioecia*, from Gk TRI- + *oikos* house]

triolein (traɪ'əʊlɪɪn) *n* a naturally occurring glyceride of oleic acid, found in fats and oils

triolet ('triːəʊˌlɛt) *n* a verse form of eight lines, having the first line repeated as the fourth and seventh and the second line as the eighth, rhyming a b a a a b a b [C17 from F: a little TRIO]

trioxide (traɪ'ɒksaɪd) *n* any oxide that contains three oxygen atoms per molecule

trip (trɪp) *n* **1** an outward and return journey, often for a specific purpose **2** any journey **3** a false step; stumble **4** any slip or blunder **5** a light step or tread **6** a manoeuvre or device to cause someone to trip **7** Also called: **tripper** any catch on a mechanism that acts as a switch **8** *inf* a hallucinogenic drug experience **9** *inf* any stimulating, profound, etc, experience ▷ *vb* **trips, tripping, tripped** **10** (often foll by *up*, or when *intr*, by *on* or *over*) to stumble or cause to stumble **11** to make or cause to make a mistake **12** (*tr*; often foll by *up*) to trap or catch in a mistake **13** (*intr*) to go on a short journey **14** (*intr*) to move or tread lightly **15** (*intr*) *inf* to experience the effects of a hallucinogenic drug **16** (*tr*) to activate a mechanical trip [C14 from OF *triper* to tread, of Gmc origin]

tripartite (traɪ'pɑːtaɪt) *adj* **1** divided into or composed of three parts **2** involving three participants **3** (esp of leaves) consisting of three parts formed by divisions extending almost to the base > **tri'partitely** *adv*

tripe (traɪp) *n* **1** the stomach lining of an ox, cow, etc, prepared for cooking **2** *inf* something silly; rubbish [C13 from OF, from ?]

triphammer ('trɪpˌhæmə) *n* a power hammer that is raised or tilted by a cam and allowed to fall under gravity

triphibious (traɪ'fɪbɪəs) *adj* (esp of military operations) occurring on land, at sea, and in the air [C20 from TRI- + (AM)PHIBIOUS]

triphthong ('trɪfθɒŋ, 'trɪp-) *n* **1** a composite vowel sound during the articulation of which the vocal organs move from one position through a second, ending in a third, as in *fire* **2** a trigraph representing such a composite vowel sound [C16 via NL from Med. Gk *triphthongos*, from TRI- + *phthongos* sound] > **triph'thongal** *adj*

tripinnate (traɪ'pɪnɪt, -eɪt) *adj* (of a bipinnate leaf) having pinnate pinnules

triplane ('traɪˌpleɪn) *n* an aeroplane having three wings arranged one above the other

triple ('trɪpᵊl) *adj* **1** consisting of three parts; threefold **2** (of musical time or rhythm) having three beats in each bar **3** three times as great or as much ▷ *n* **4** a threefold amount **5** a group of three ▷ *vb* **triples, tripling, tripled** **6** to increase threefold; treble [C16 from L *triplus*] > '**triply** *adv*

triple A *n mil* anti-aircraft artillery [referring to the abbrev AAA]

triple crown *n* (*often caps*) *rugby union* a victory by England, Ireland, Scotland, or Wales in all three games against the others in the annual Six Nations Championship

triple jump *n* an athletic event in which the competitor has to perform successively a hop, a step, and a jump in continuous movement

triple point *n chem* the temperature and pressure at which the three phases of a substance are in equilibrium

triplet ('trɪplɪt) *n* **1** a group or set of three similar things

Tt

2 one of three offspring born at one birth **3** *music* a group of three notes played in a time value of two, four, etc **4** *chem* a state of a molecule or free radical in which there are two unpaired electrons [C17 from TRIPLE, on the model of *doublet*]

Triplex ('trɪplɛks) *n Brit trademark* a laminated safety glass, as used in car windows

triplicate *adj* ('trɪplɪkɪt) **1** triple ▷ *vb* ('trɪplɪˌkeɪt), **triplicates, triplicating, triplicated 2** to multiply or be multiplied by three ▷ *n* ('trɪplɪkɪt) **3a** a group of three things **3b** one of such a group **4 in triplicate** written out three times [C15 from L *triplicāre* to triple] > ˌ**tripli'cation** *n*

triploid ('trɪplɔɪd) *adj* **1** having or relating to three times the haploid number of chromosomes: *a triploid organism* ▷ *n* **2** a triploid organism [C19 from Gk *tripl(oos)* triple + (HAPL)OID]

tripod ('traɪpɒd) *n* **1** a three-legged stand to which a camera, etc, can be attached to hold it steady **2** a stand or table having three legs > **tripodal** ('trɪpədᵊl) *adj*

tripoli ('trɪpəlɪ) *n* a lightweight porous siliceous rock used in a powdered form as a polish [C17 after TRIPOLI, in Libya or in Lebanon]

Tripoli ('trɪpəlɪ) *n* **1** the capital and chief port of Libya, in the northwest on the Mediterranean: founded by Phoenicians in about the 7th century BC; the only city that has survived of the three (Oea, Leptis Magna, and Sabratha) that formed the African Tripolis ("three cities"); fishing and manufacturing centre. Pop (urban area): 1 140 000 (1995 est). Ancient name: **Oea** ('iːə) Arabic name: **Tarabulus el Gharb 2** a port in N Lebanon, on the Mediterranean: the second largest town in Lebanon; taken by the Crusaders in 1109 after a siege of five years; oil-refining and manufacturing centre. Pop: 160 000 (1998 est). Ancient name: **Tripolis** Arabic name: **Tarabulus esh Sham**
▷ www.libyaonline.com/libya/cities/tripoli.php

Tripolitania (ˌtrɪpəlɪ'teɪnɪə) *n* the NW part of Libya: established as a Phoenician colony in the 7th century BC; taken by the Turks in 1551 and became one of the Barbary states; under Italian rule from 1912 until World War II > ˌ**Tripoli'tanian** *adj, n*

tripos ('traɪpɒs) *n Brit* the final honours degree examinations at Cambridge University [C16 from L *tripūs*, infl. by Gk noun ending *-os*]

tripper ('trɪpə) *n* **1** *chiefly Brit* a tourist **2** another word for **trip** (sense 7) **3** any device that causes a trip to operate

trippy ('trɪpɪ) *adj* **trippier, trippiest** *inf* suggestive of or resembling the effect produced by a hallucinogenic drug

triptane ('trɪpteɪn) *n* a liquid hydrocarbon used in aviation fuel [C20 shortened & altered from *trimethylbutane*]

Triptolemus (trɪp'tɒlɪməs) *n Greek myth* a favourite of Demeter, sent by her to teach men agriculture

triptych ('trɪptɪk) *n* **1** a set of three pictures or panels, usually hinged so that the two wing panels fold over the larger central one: often used as an altarpiece **2** a set of three hinged writing tablets [C18 from Gk *triptukhos*, from TRI- + *ptux* plate]

triptyque (trɪp'tiːk) *n* a customs permit for the temporary importation of a motor vehicle [C20 from F: TRIPTYCH (from its three sections)]

Tripura ('trɪpʊrə) *n* a state of NE India: formerly a princely state, ruled by the Maharajahs for over 1300 years; became a union territory in 1956 and a state in 1972; extensive jungles. Capital: Agartala. Pop: 3 191 168 (2001). Area: 10 486 sq km (4051 sq miles)

tripwire ('trɪpˌwaɪə) *n* a wire that activates a trap, mine, etc, when tripped over

trireme ('traɪriːm) *n* an ancient Greek galley with three banks of oars on each side [C17 from L *trirēmis*, from TRI- + *rēmus* oar]

trisect (traɪ'sɛkt) *vb (tr)* to divide into three parts, esp three equal parts [C17 TRI- + *-sect* from L *secāre* to cut] > **trisection** (traɪ'sɛkʃən) *n*

trishaw ('traɪˌʃɔː) *n* another name for **rickshaw** (sense 2) [C20 from TRI- + RICKSHAW]

triskelion (trɪ'skɛlɪˌɒn) *n, pl* **triskelia** (trɪ'skɛlɪə) a symbol consisting of three bent limbs or lines radiating from a centre [C19 from Gk *triskelēs* three-legged]

Trismegistus (ˌtrɪsmɪ'dʒɪstəs) *n* See **Hermes Trismegistus**

trismus ('trɪzməs) *n pathol* the state of being unable to open the mouth because of sustained contractions of the jaw muscles, caused by tetanus. Nontechnical name: **lockjaw** [C17 from NL, from Gk *trismos* a grinding]

Tristan ('trɪstən) *or* **Tristram** ('trɪstrəm) *n* (in medieval romance) the nephew of King Mark of Cornwall who fell in love with his uncle's bride, Iseult, after they mistakenly drank a love potion

Tristan da Cunha ('trɪstən də 'kuːnjə) *n* a group of four small volcanic islands in the S Atlantic, about halfway between South Africa and South America: comprises the main island of Tristan and the uninhabited islands of Gough, Inaccessible, and Nightingale; discovered in 1506 by the Portuguese admiral Tristão da Cunha; annexed to Britain in 1816; whole population of Tristan evacuated for two years after the volcanic eruption of 1961. Pop: 288 (1994 est). Area: about 100 sq km (40 sq miles)

triste (triːst) *adj* an archaic word for **sad** [from F]

trisyllable (traɪ'sɪləbᵊl) *n* a word of three syllables > **trisyllabic** (ˌtraɪsɪ'læbɪk) *adj*

trite (traɪt) *adj* hackneyed; dull: *a trite comment* [C16 from L *trītus* worn down, from *terere* to rub] > '**tritely** *adv* > '**triteness** *n*

tritheism ('traɪθɪˌɪzəm) *n theol* belief in three gods, esp in the Trinity as consisting of three distinct gods > '**tritheist** *n, adj*

triticum ('trɪtɪkəm) *n* any of a genus of cereal grasses which includes the wheats [C19 L, lit.: wheat, prob. from *tritum*, supine of *terere* to grind]

tritium ('trɪtɪəm) *n* a radioactive isotope of hydrogen. Symbol: T or ^{3}H; half-life: 12.5 years [C20 NL, from Gk *tritos* third]

triton[1] ('traɪtᵊn) *n* any of various chiefly tropical marine gastropod molluscs having large spiral shells [C16 via L from Gk *tritōn*]

triton[2] ('traɪtɒn) *n physics* a nucleus of an atom of tritium, containing two neutrons and one proton [C20 from TRIT(IUM) + -ON]

Triton ('traɪtᵊn) *n Greek myth* a sea god depicted as having the upper parts of a man with a fish's tail

tritone ('traɪˌtəʊn) *n* a musical interval consisting of three whole tones

triturate ('trɪtjʊˌreɪt) *vb* **triturates, triturating, triturated 1** *(tr)* to grind or rub into a fine powder or pulp ▷ *n* **2** the powder or pulp resulting from this [C17 from LL *trītūrāre* to thresh, from L *trītūra* a threshing, from *terere* to grind] > ˌ**tritu'ration** *n*

triumph ('traɪəmf) *n* **1** the feeling of exultation and happiness derived from a victory or major achievement **2** the act or condition of being victorious; victory **3** (in ancient Rome) a procession held in honour of a victorious general ▷ *vb (intr)* **4** (often foll by *over*) to win a victory or control: *to triumph over one's weaknesses* **5** to rejoice over a victory **6** to celebrate a Roman triumph [C14 from OF *triumphe*, from L *triumphus*, from OL *triumpus*] > **triumphal** (traɪ'ʌmfəl) *adj*

triumphant (traɪ'ʌmfənt) *adj* **1** experiencing or displaying triumph **2** exultant through triumph > **tri'umphantly** *adv*

triumvir (traɪ'ʌmvə) *n, pl* **triumvirs** *or* **triumviri** (-vɪˌriː) (esp in ancient Rome) a member of a triumvirate [C16 from L: one of three administrators, from *trium virōrum* of three men, from *trēs* three + *vir* man] > **tri'umviral** *adj*

triumvirate (traɪˈʌmvɪrɪt) *n* **1** (in ancient Rome) a board of three officials jointly responsible for some task **2** joint rule by three men **3** any group of three men associated in some way **4** the office of a triumvir

triune (ˈtraɪjuːn) *adj* constituting three in one, esp the three persons in one God of the Trinity [C17 TRI- + *-une*, from L *ūnus* one] > **triˈunity** *n*

trivalent (traɪˈveɪlənt, ˈtrɪvələnt) *adj chem* **1** having a valency of three **2** having three valencies. Also: **tervalent** > **triˈvalency** *n*

Trivandrum (trɪˈvændrəm) *n* a city in S India, capital of Kerala, on the Malabar Coast: made capital of the kingdom of Travancore in 1745; University of Kerala (1937). Pop: 524 006 (1991). Official name: **Thiruvananthapuram**

trivet (ˈtrɪvɪt) *n* **1** a stand, usually three-legged and metal, on which cooking vessels are placed over a fire **2** a short metal stand on which hot dishes are placed on a table **3 as right as a trivet** in perfect health [OE *trefet* (infl. by OE *thrifēte* having three feet), from L *tripēs* having three feet]

trivia (ˈtrɪvɪə) *n* (*functioning as sing or pl*) petty details or considerations; trifles; trivialities [from NL, pl of L *trivium* junction of three roads]

trivial (ˈtrɪvɪəl) *adj* **1** of little importance; petty or frivolous: *trivial complaints* **2** ordinary or commonplace; trite: *trivial conversation* **3** *biol, chem* denoting the common name of an organism or substance **4** *biol* denoting the specific name of an organism in binomial nomenclature [C15 from L *triviālis* belonging to the public streets, common, from *trivium* junction of three roads] > **ˈtrivially** *adv* > **ˈtrivialness** *n*

triviality (ˌtrɪvɪˈælɪtɪ) *n, pl* **trivialities** **1** the state or quality of being trivial **2** something, such as a remark, that is trivial

trivialize *or* **trivialise** (ˈtrɪvɪəˌlaɪz) *vb* **trivializes, trivializing, trivialized** *or* **trivialises, trivialising, trivialised** (*tr*) to cause to seem trivial or more trivial; minimize > **ˌtrivialiˈzation** *or* **ˌtrivialiˈsation** *n*

trivium (ˈtrɪvɪəm) *n, pl* **trivia** (-ɪə) (in medieval learning) the arts of grammar, rhetoric, and logic. ▷ Cf **quadrivium** [C19 from Med. L, from L: crossroads]

-trix *suffix forming nouns* indicating a feminine agent, corresponding to nouns ending in *-tor*: *executrix* [from L]

t-RNA *abbrev for* transfer RNA

Troas (ˈtrəʊæs) *n* the region of NW Asia Minor surrounding the ancient city of Troy. Also called: **the Troad** (ˈtrəʊæd)

Trobriand Islands (ˈtrəʊbrɪˌænd) *pl n* a group of coral islands in the Solomon Sea, north of the E part of New Guinea: part of Papua New Guinea. Area: about 440 sq km (170 sq miles) > **Trobriand Islander** *n*

trocar (ˈtrəʊkɑː) *n* a surgical instrument for removing fluid from bodily cavities [C18 from F *trocart*, lit.: with three sides, from *trois* three + *carre* side]

trochal (ˈtrəʊkᵊl) *adj zool* shaped like a wheel [C19 from Gk *trokhos* wheel]

trochanter (trəʊˈkæntə) *n* **1** any of several processes on the upper part of the vertebrate femur, to which muscles are attached **2** the third segment of an insect's leg [C17 via F from Gk *trokhantēr*, from *trekhein* to run]

troche (trəʊʃ) *n med* another name for **lozenge** (sense 1) [C16 from F *trochisque*, from LL *trochiscus*, from Gk *trokhiskos* little wheel, from *trokhos* wheel]

trochee (ˈtrəʊkiː) *n* a metrical foot of two syllables, the first long and the second short [C16 via L from Gk *trokhaios pous*, lit.: a running foot, from *trekhein* to run] > **trochaic** (trəʊˈkeɪɪk) *adj*

trochlea (ˈtrɒklɪə) *n, pl* **trochleae** (-lɪˌiː) any bony or cartilaginous part with a grooved surface over which a bone, etc, may slide or articulate [C17 from L, from Gk *trokhileia* a sheaf of pulleys]

trochlear nerve (ˈtrɒklɪə) *n* either one of the fourth pair of cranial nerves, which supply the superior oblique muscle of the eye

trochoid (ˈtrəʊkɔɪd) *n* **1** the curve described by a fixed point on the radius of a circle as the circle rolls along a straight line ▷ *adj also* **trochoidal** **2** rotating about a central axis **3** *anat* (of a structure or part) resembling or functioning as a pivot or pulley [C18 from Gk *trokhoeidēs* circular, from *trokhos* wheel]

trod (trɒd) *vb* the past tense and a past participle of **tread**

trodden (ˈtrɒdᵊn) *vb* a past participle of **tread**

trode (trəʊd) *vb arch* a past tense of **tread**

troglodyte (ˈtrɒgləˌdaɪt) *n* **1** a cave dweller, esp of prehistoric times **2** *inf* a person who lives alone and appears eccentric [C16 via L from Gk *trōglodutēs* one who enters caves, from *trōglē* hole + *duein* to enter] > **troglodytic** (ˌtrɒgləˈdɪtɪk) *adj*

trogon (ˈtrəʊgɒn) *n* any of an order of birds of tropical regions of America, Africa, and Asia, having a brilliant plumage and long tail. See also **quetzal** (sense 1) [C18 from NL, from Gk *trōgōn*, from *trōgein* to gnaw]

troika (ˈtrɔɪkə) *n* **1** a Russian vehicle drawn by three horses abreast **2** three horses harnessed abreast **3** a triumvirate [C19 from Russian, from *troe* three]

Troilus (ˈtrɔɪləs, ˈtrəʊɪləs) *n Greek myth* the youngest son of King Priam and Queen Hecuba, slain at Troy. In medieval romance he is portrayed as the lover of Cressida

Trois Rivières (*French* trwɑ rivjɛr) *n* a port in central Canada, in Quebec on the St Lawrence River: one of the world's largest centres of newsprint production. Pop: 49 426 (1991), with a metropolitan area of 136 300 (1991). English name: **Three Rivers**

Trojan (ˈtrəʊdʒən) *n* **1** a native or inhabitant of ancient Troy **2** a person who is hard-working and determined ▷ *adj* **3** of or relating to ancient Troy or its inhabitants

Trojan Horse *n* **1** *Greek myth* the huge wooden hollow figure of a horse left outside Troy by the Greeks and dragged inside by the Trojans. The men concealed inside it opened the city to the final Greek assault **2** a trap intended to undermine an enemy **3** *computing* a bug inserted into a program or system designed to be activated after a certain time or a certain number of operations

troll[1] (trəʊl) *vb* **1** *angling* **1a** to draw (a baited line, etc) through the water **1b** to fish (a stretch of water) by trolling **1c** to fish (for) by trolling **2** to roll or cause to roll **3** *arch* to sing (a refrain, chorus, etc) in a loud hearty voice **4** (*intr*) *Brit inf* to walk or stroll ▷ *n* **5** a trolling **6** *angling* a bait or lure used in trolling [C14 from OF *troller* to run about] > **ˈtroller** *n*

troll[2] (trəʊl) *n* (in Scandinavian folklore) one of a class of supernatural creatures that dwell in caves or mountains and are depicted either as dwarfs or as giants [C19 from ON: demon]

trolley (ˈtrɒlɪ) *n* **1** a small table on casters used for conveying food, etc **2** *chiefly Brit* a wheeled cart or stand used for moving heavy items, such as shopping in a supermarket or luggage at a railway station **3** *Brit* (in a hospital) a bed mounted on casters and used for moving patients who are unconscious, etc **4** *Brit* See **trolleybus** **5** *US & Canad* See **trolley car** **6** a device that collects the current from an overhead wire, third rail, etc, to drive the motor of an electric vehicle **7** a pulley or truck that travels along an overhead wire in order to support a suspended load **8** *chiefly Brit* a low truck running on rails, used in factories, mines, etc **9** a truck, cage, or basket suspended from an overhead track or cable for carrying loads in a mine, etc [C19 prob. from TROLL[1]]

trolleybus (ˈtrɒlɪˌbʌs) *n* an electrically driven public-transport vehicle that does not run on rails but takes its power from two overhead wires

trolley car *n* a US and Canad name for **tram** (sense 1)

trollius ('trəʊlɪəs) *n* another name for **globeflower** [from G *Trollblume* globeflower]

trollop ('trɒləp) *n* **1** a promiscuous woman, esp a prostitute **2** an untidy woman; slattern [c17 ?from G dialect *Trolle* prostitute] > '**trollopy** *adj*

Trollope ('trɒləp) *n* **1 Anthony** 1815–82, English novelist. His most successful novels, such as *The Warden* (1855), *Barchester Towers* (1857), and *Dr Thorne* (1858), are those in the Barsetshire series of studies of English provincial life. The Palliser series of political novels includes *Phineas Redux* (1874) and *The Prime Minister* (1876) **2 Joanna** born 1943, British novelist: her works include *The Choir* (1988), *A Village Affair* (1989), *The Rector's Wife* (1991), *The Best of Friends* (1995), and *The Girl From the South* (2002)

trombone (trɒm'bəʊn) *n* a brass instrument, a low-pitched counterpart of the trumpet, consisting of a tube the effective length of which is varied by means of a U-shaped slide [c18 from It., from *tromba* a trumpet, from OHG *trumba*] > **trom'bonist** *n*

trommel ('trɒməl) *n* a revolving cylindrical sieve used to screen crushed ore [c19 from G: a drum]

trompe (trɒmp) *n* an apparatus for supplying the blast of air in a forge, consisting of a thin column down which water falls, drawing in air through side openings [c19 from F, lit.: trumpet]

trompe l'oeil (*French* trɔ̃p lœj) *n, pl* **trompe l'oeils** (trɔ̃p lœj) **1** a painting, etc, giving a convincing illusion of reality **2** an effect of this kind [from F, lit.: deception of the eye]

Tromsø ('trɒmsəʊ; *Norwegian* 'trumsø) *n* a port in N Norway, on a small island between Kvaløy and the mainland: fishing and sealing centre. Pop: 51 218 (1990)

-tron *suffix forming nouns* **1** indicating a vacuum tube **2** indicating an instrument for accelerating atomic particles [from Gk, suffix indicating instrument]

tronc (trɒŋk) *n* a pool into which waiters, etc, pay their tips for later distribution to staff by a **tronc master**, according to agreed percentages [c20 from F: collecting box]

Trondheim ('trɒnd,haɪm; *Norwegian* 'trɔnhɛim) *n* a port in central Norway, on **Trondheim Fjord** (an inlet of the Norwegian Sea): national capital until 1380; seat of the Technical University of Norway. Pop: 148 859 (2000 est). Former name (until the 16th century and from 1930 to 1931): **Nidaros**

tronk (trɒŋk) *n S African inf* a prison [Afrik.]

troop (tru:p) *n* **1** a large group or assembly **2** a subdivision of a cavalry squadron or artillery battery of about platoon size **3** (*pl*) armed forces; soldiers **4** a large group of Scouts comprising several patrols ▹ *vb* **5** (*intr*) to gather, move, or march in or as if in a crowd **6** (*tr*) *mil, chiefly Brit* to parade (the colour or flag) ceremonially [c16 from F *troupe*, from *troupeau* flock, of Gmc origin]

trooper ('tru:pə) *n* **1** a soldier in a cavalry regiment **2** *US & Austral* a mounted policeman **3** *US* a state policeman **4** a cavalry horse **5** *inf, chiefly Brit* a troopship

troopship ('tru:p,ʃɪp) *n* a ship used to transport military personnel

tropaeolum (trəʊ'pi:ələm) *n, pl* **tropaeolums** *or* **tropaeola** (-lə) any of a genus of garden plants, esp the nasturtium [c18 from NL, from L *tropaeum* TROPHY; from the shield-shaped leaves and helmet-shaped flowers]

trope (trəʊp) *n* a word or expression used in a figurative sense [c16 from L *tropus* figurative use of a word, from Gk *tropos* style, turn]

-trope *n combining form* indicating a turning towards, development in the direction of, or affinity to: *heliotrope* [from Gk *tropos* a turn]

trophic ('trɒfɪk) *adj* of nutrition [c19 from Gk *trophikos*, from *trophē* food, from *trephein* to feed]

tropho- *or before a vowel* **troph-** *combining form* indicating nourishment or nutrition: *trophozoite* [from Gk *trophē* food, from *trephein* to feed]

trophoblast ('trɒfə,blæst) *n* the outer layers of cells of the embryo of mammals that absorbs nourishment from the uterine fluids

trophozoite (,trɒfə'zəʊaɪt) *n* the form of a sporozoan protozoan, esp of certain parasites, in the feeding stage

trophy ('trəʊfɪ) *n, pl* **trophies 1** an object such as a silver cup that is symbolic of victory in a contest, esp a sporting contest; prize **2** a memento of success, esp one taken in war or hunting **3** (in ancient Greece and Rome) a memorial to a victory, usually consisting of captured arms raised on the battlefield or in a public place **4** an ornamental carving that represents a group of weapons, etc [c16 from F *trophée*, from L *tropaeum*, from Gk *tropaion*, from *tropē* a turning, defeat of the enemy]

-trophy *n combining form* indicating a certain type of nourishment or growth: *dystrophy* [from Gk *-trophia*, from *trophē* nourishment] > **-trophic** *adj combining form*

tropic ('trɒpɪk) *n* **1** (*sometimes cap*) either of the parallel lines of latitude at about 23½°N (**tropic of Cancer**) and 23½°S (**tropic of Capricorn**) of the equator **2 the tropics** (*often cap*) that part of the earth's surface between the tropics of Cancer and Capricorn **3** *astron* either of the two parallel circles on the celestial sphere having the same latitudes and names as the lines on the earth ▹ *adj* **4** tropical [c14 from LL *tropicus* belonging to a turn, from Gk *tropikos*, from *tropos* a turn; from the belief that the sun turned back at the solstices]

-tropic *adj combining form* turning or developing in response to a certain stimulus: *heliotropic* [from Gk *tropos* a turn]

tropical ('trɒpɪkᵊl) *adj* **1** situated in, used in, characteristic of, or relating to the tropics **2** (of weather) very hot, esp when humid **3** of a trope > ,**tropi'cality** *n* > '**tropically** *adv*

tropical depression *n Caribbean* an area of heavy rains and winds, the first stage in the development of a possible hurricane

Tropical Storms

Cyclones, hurricanes, and typhoons rotate in an anticlockwise direction in the northern hemisphere, and clockwise in the southern hemisphere. The centre of a hurricane or typhoon is called the eye, and it is produced by a strong downdraught of air.

TYPE OF STORM	AREAS AFFECTED	TIME OF YEAR
Hurricane	USA, Caribbean	July to Oct
Typhoon	China, Japan	July to Oct
Cyclone	Indian subcontinent	April to June, Sept to Dec
Tropical cyclone	Philippines, etc	Dec to Mar
Willy-willy	Australia	Dec to Mar

▹ www.spc.ncep.noaa.gov/faq/tornado
▹ www.aoml.noaa.gov/hrd/tcfaq/tcfaqHED.html

tropicbird ('trɒpɪk,bɜ:d) *n* any of various tropical aquatic birds having long tail feathers and a white plumage with black markings

tropism ('trəʊpɪzəm) *n* the response of an organism, esp a plant, to an external stimulus by growth in a direction determined by the stimulus [from Gk *tropos* a turn] > ,**tropis'matic** *adj*

-tropism *or* **-tropy** *n combining form* indicating a tendency to turn or develop in response to a stimulus: *phototropism* [from Gk *tropos* a turn]

tropo- *combining form* indicating change or a turning: *tropophyte* [from Gk *tropos* a turn]

tropopause ('trɒpəˌpɔːz) *n meteorol* the plane of discontinuity between the troposphere and the stratosphere, characterized by a sharp change in the lapse rate

troposphere ('trɒpəˌsfɪə) *n* the lowest atmospheric layer, about 18 kilometres (11 miles) thick at the equator to about 6 km (4 miles) at the Poles, in which air temperature decreases normally with height at about 6.5°C per km > **tropospheric** (ˌtrɒpə'sfɛrɪk) *adj*

-tropous *adj combining form* indicating a turning away: *anatropous* [from Gk *-tropos* concerning a turn]

troppo[1] ('trɒpəʊ) *adv music* too much; excessively. See **non troppo** [It.]

troppo[2] ('trɒpəʊ) *adj Austral sl* mentally affected by a tropical climate

Trossachs ('trɒsəks) *n (functioning as plural or singular)* **the** **1** a narrow wooded valley in central Scotland, between Loch Achray and Loch Katrine: made famous by Sir Walter Scott's descriptions **2** (popularly) the area extending northwards from Loch Ard and Aberfoyle to Lochs Katrine, Achray, and Venachar

trot (trɒt) *vb* **trots, trotting, trotted 1** to move or cause to move at a trot ▷ *n* **2** a gait of a horse in which diagonally opposite legs come down together **3** a steady brisk pace **4** (in harness racing) a race for horses that have been trained to trot fast **5** *chiefly Brit* a small child **6** *US sl* a student's crib **7 on the trot** *inf* **7a** one after the other: *to read two books on the trot* **7b** busy, esp on one's feet **8 the trots** *inf* **8a** diarrhoea **8b** NZ trotting races ▷ See also **trot out** [C13 from OF *trot*, from *troter* to trot, of Gmc origin]

Trot (trɒt) *n inf* a follower of Trotsky; Trotskyist

troth (trəʊθ) *n arch* **1** a pledge of fidelity, esp a betrothal **2** truth (esp in **in troth**) **3** loyalty; fidelity [OE *trēowth*]

trotline ('trɒtˌlaɪn) *n angling* a long line suspended across a stream, river, etc, to which shorter hooked and baited lines are attached

trot out *vb (tr, adv) inf* to bring forward, as for approbation or admiration, esp repeatedly

Trotsky *or* **Trotski** ('trɒtskɪ) *n* **Leon**, original name *Lev Davidovich Bronstein*. 1879–1940, Russian revolutionary and Communist theorist. He was a leader of the November Revolution (1917) and, as commissar of foreign affairs and war (1917–24), largely created the Red Army. He was ousted by Stalin after Lenin's death and deported from Russia (1929); assassinated by a Stalinist agent

Trotskyism ('trɒtskɪˌɪzəm) *n* Trotsky's theory of communism, in which he called for immediate worldwide revolution by the proletariat > '**Trotskyist** *or* '**Trotskyˌite** *n, adj*

trotter ('trɒtə) *n* **1** a horse that is specially trained to trot fast **2** *(usually pl)* the foot of certain animals, esp of pigs

troubadour ('truːbəˌdʊə) *n* any of a class of lyric poets who flourished principally in Provence and N Italy from the 11th to the 13th century, writing chiefly on courtly love [C18 from F, from OProvençal *trobador*, from *trobar* to write verses, ? ult. from L *tropus* TROPE]

trouble ('trʌbᵊl) *n* **1** a state of mental distress or anxiety **2** a state of disorder or unrest: *industrial trouble* **3** a condition of disease, pain, or malfunctioning: *liver trouble* **4** a cause of distress, disturbance, or pain **5** effort or exertion taken to do something **6** liability to suffer punishment or misfortune (esp in **be in trouble**): *he's in trouble with the police* **7** a personal weakness or cause of annoyance: *his trouble is he's too soft* **8** political unrest **9** the condition of an unmarried girl who becomes pregnant (esp in **in trouble**) ▷ *vb* **troubles, troubling, troubled 10** *(tr)* to cause trouble to **11** *(intr; usually with a negative and foll by about)* to put oneself to inconvenience; be concerned: *don't trouble about me* **12** *(intr; usually with a negative)* to take pains; exert oneself **13** *(tr)* to cause inconvenience or discomfort to **14** *(tr; usually passive)* to agitate or make rough: *the seas were troubled* **15** *(tr) Caribbean* to interfere with [C13 from OF *troubler*, from Vulgar L *turbulāre* (unattested), from LL *turbidāre*, ult. from *turba* commotion] > '**troubler** *n*

troublemaker ('trʌbᵊlˌmeɪkə) *n* a person who makes trouble, esp between people > '**troubleˌmaking** *adj, n*

troubleshooter ('trʌbᵊlˌʃuːtə) *n* a person who locates the cause of trouble and removes or treats it > '**troubleˌshooting** *n, adj*

troublesome ('trʌbᵊlsəm) *adj* **1** causing trouble **2** characterized by violence; turbulent > '**troublesomeness** *n*

troublous ('trʌbləs) *adj arch or literary* unsettled; agitated > '**troublously** *adv*

trough (trɒf) *n* **1** a narrow open container, esp one in which food or water for animals is put **2** a narrow channel, gutter, or gulley **3** a narrow depression, as between two waves **4** *meteorol* an elongated area of low pressure **5** a single or temporary low point; depression **6** *physics* the portion of a wave in which the amplitude lies below its average value **7** *econ* the lowest point of the trade cycle [OE *trōh*]

trounce (traʊns) *vb* **trounces, trouncing, trounced** *(tr)* to beat or defeat utterly; thrash [C16 from ?]

troupe (truːp) *n* **1** a company of actors or other performers, esp one that travels ▷ *vb* **troupes, trouping, trouped 2** *(intr)* (esp of actors) to move or travel in a group [C19 from F; see TROOP]

trouper ('truːpə) *n* **1** a member of a troupe **2** a dependable worker or associate

trouser ('traʊzə) *n (modifier)* **1** of or relating to trousers: *trouser buttons* ▷ *vb* **2** *(tr) sl* to take (something, esp money), often surreptitiously or unlawfully

trousers ('traʊzəz) *pl n* a garment shaped to cover the body from the waist to the ankles or knees with separate tube-shaped sections for each leg [C17 from earlier *trouse*, var. of TREWS, infl. by DRAWERS]

trousseau ('truːsəʊ) *n, pl* **trousseaux** *or* **trousseaus** (-səʊz) the clothes, linen, etc, collected by a bride for her marriage [C19 from OF, lit.: a little bundle; see TRUSS]

trout (traʊt) *n, pl* **trout** *or* **trouts** any of various game fishes, mostly of fresh water in northern regions. They are related to the salmon but are smaller and spotted [OE *trūht*, from LL *tructa*, from Gk *troktēs* sharp-toothed fish]

trouvère (truː'vɛə) *n* any of a group of poets of N France during the 12th and 13th centuries who composed chiefly narrative works [C19 from F, from OF *troveor*, from *trover* to compose]

trove (trəʊv) *n* See **treasure-trove**

trow (trəʊ) *vb arch* to think, believe, or trust [OE *treow*]

Trowbridge ('trəʊˌbrɪdʒ) *n* a market town in SW England, administrative centre of Wiltshire: woollen manufacturing. Pop: 29 334 (1991)

trowel ('traʊəl) *n* **1** any of various small hand tools having a flat metal blade attached to a handle, used for scooping or spreading plaster or similar materials **2** a similar tool with a curved blade used by gardeners for lifting plants, etc ▷ *vb* **trowels, trowelling, trowelled** *or US* **trowels, troweling, troweled 3** *(tr)* to use a trowel on [C14 from OF *truele*, from L *trulla* a scoop, from *trua* a stirring spoon]

Troy (trɔɪ) *n* any of nine ancient cities in NW Asia Minor, each of which was built on the ruins of its predecessor. The seventh was the site of the Trojan War (mid-13th century BC). Greek name: **Ilion**. Latin name: **Ilium** Related adj: **Trojan**

Troyes (*French* trwa) *n* an industrial city in NE France: became prosperous through its great fairs in the early Middle Ages. Pop: 59 271 (1990)

troy weight *or* **troy** (trɔɪ) *n* a system of weights used for precious metals and gemstones, based on the grain. 24 grains = 1 pennyweight; 20 pennyweights = 1 (troy) ounce; 12 ounces = 1 (troy) pound [C14 after TROYES, where first used]

trs *printing abbrev for* transpose

Trst (trst) *n* the Slovene and Serbo-Croat name for **Trieste**

truant ('tru:ənt) *n* **1** a person who is absent without leave, esp from school ▷ *adj* **2** being or relating to a truant ▷ *vb* **3** *(intr)* to play truant [C13 from OF: vagabond, prob. of Celtic origin] > '**truancy** *n*

truce (tru:s) *n* **1** an agreement to stop fighting, esp temporarily **2** temporary cessation of something unpleasant [C13 from pl of OE *treow* trow]

Trucial States ('tru:ʃəl) *pl n* a former name (until 1971) of the **United Arab Emirates.** Also called: **Trucial Sheikdoms, Trucial Oman, Trucial Coast**

truck[1] (trʌk) *n* **1** *Brit* a vehicle for carrying freight on a railway; wagon **2** another name (esp US, Canad, Austral, and NZ) for **lorry 3** Also called: **truckload** the amount carried by a truck **4** a frame carrying two or more pairs of wheels attached under an end of a railway coach, etc **5** *naut* a disc-shaped block fixed to the head of a mast having holes for receiving halyards **6** any wheeled vehicle used to move goods ▷ *vb* **7** to convey (goods) in a truck **8** *(intr) chiefly US & Canad* to drive a truck [C17 ? shortened from *truckle* a small wheel]

truck[2] (trʌk) *n* **1** commercial goods **2** dealings (esp in **have no truck with**) **3** commercial exchange **4** *arch* payment of wages in kind **5** miscellaneous articles **6** *inf* rubbish **7** *US & Canad* vegetables grown for market ▷ *vb* **8** *arch* to exchange (goods); barter **9** *(intr)* to traffic or negotiate [C13 from OF *troquer* (unattested) to barter, equivalent to Med. L *trocare*, from ?]

trucker ('trʌkə) *n chiefly US & Canad* **1** a lorry driver **2** a person who arranges for the transport of goods by lorry

truck farm *n US & Canad* a market garden > **truck farmer** *n* > **truck farming** *n*

truckie ('trʌkɪ) *n Austral & NZ inf* a truck driver

trucking ('trʌkɪŋ) *n chiefly US & Canad* the transportation of goods by lorry

truckle ('trʌkᵊl) *vb* **truckles, truckling, truckled** *(intr; usually foll by* to*)* to yield weakly; give in [C17 from obs. *truckle* to sleep in a truckle bed] > '**truckler** *n*

truckle bed *n* a low bed on wheels, stored under a larger bed [C17 from *truckle* small wheel, ult. from L *trochlea* sheaf of a pulley]

truck system *n* a system during the early years of the Industrial Revolution of forcing workers to accept payment of wages in kind

truculent ('trʌkjʊlənt) *adj* **1** defiantly aggressive, sullen, or obstreperous **2** *arch* savage, fierce, or harsh [C16 from L *truculentus*, from *trux* fierce] > '**truculence** *or* '**truculency** *n* > '**truculently** *adv*

Trudeau (tru:'dəʊ) *n* **Pierre Elliott** 1919–2000, Canadian statesman; Liberal prime minister (1968–79; 1980–84)

trudge (trʌdʒ) *vb* **trudges, trudging, trudged 1** *(intr)* to walk or plod heavily or wearily **2** *(tr)* to pass through or over by trudging ▷ *n* **3** a long tiring walk [C16 from ?] > '**trudger** *n*

trudgen ('trʌdʒən) *n* a type of swimming stroke that uses overarm action, as in the crawl, and a scissors kick [C19 after John *Trudgen*, E swimmer, who introduced it]

true (tru:) *adj* **truer, truest 1** not false, fictional, or illusory; factual; conforming with reality **2** *(prenominal)* real; not synthetic **3** faithful and loyal **4** conforming to a required standard, law, or pattern: *a true aim* **5** exactly in tune **6** (of a compass bearing) according to the earth's geographical rather than magnetic poles: *true north* **7** *biol* conforming to the typical structure of a designated type **8** *physics* not apparent or relative ▷ *n* **9** correct alignment (esp in **in true, out of true**) ▷ *adv* **10** truthfully; rightly **11** precisely or unswervingly ▷ *vb* **trues, truing, trued 12** *(tr)* to adjust so as to make true [OE *triewe*] > '**trueness** *n*

true bill *n* (formerly in Britain; now US) the endorsement made on a bill of indictment by a grand jury certifying it to be supported by sufficient evidence to warrant a trial

true-blue *adj* **1** unwaveringly or staunchly loyal ▷ *n* **true blue 2** *chiefly Brit* a staunch royalist or Conservative

true-life *adj* directly comparable to reality: *a true-life story*

truelove ('tru:ˌlʌv) *n* **1** someone truly loved; sweetheart **2** another name for **herb Paris**

truelove knot *or* **true-lovers' knot** *n* a complicated bowknot that is hard to untie, symbolizing ties of love

Trueman ('tru:mən) *n* **Freddy,** full name *Frederick Sewards Trueman.* born 1931, English cricketer, a fast bowler for Yorkshire and England

true north *n* the direction from any point along a meridian towards the North Pole. Also called: **geographic north.** ▷ Cf **magnetic north**

true rib *n* any of the upper seven pairs of ribs in man

true time *n* the time shown by a sundial

Truffaut (*French* tryfo) *n* **François** (frɑ̃swa) 1932–84, French film director of the New Wave. His films include *Les Quatre cents coups* (1959), *Jules et Jim* (1961), *Baisers volés* (1968), and *Le Dernier Métro* (1980)

truffle ('trʌfᵊl) *n* **1** any of various edible subterranean European fungi. They have a tuberous appearance and are regarded as a delicacy **2** Also called: **rum truffle** *chiefly Brit* a sweet resembling this fungus in shape, flavoured with chocolate or rum [C16 from F *truffe*, from OProvençal *trufa*, ult. from L *tūber*]

trug (trʌg) *n* a long shallow basket for carrying flowers, fruit, etc [C16 ? var. of TROUGH]

trugo ('tru:gəʊ) *n Austral* a game similar to croquet, originally improvised in Victoria from the rubber discs used as buffers on railway carriages [from *true go*, when the wheel is hit between the goalposts]

truism ('tru:ɪzəm) *n* an obvious truth; platitude > **tru'istic** *adj*

Trujillo (*Spanish* tru'xijo) *n* a city in NW Peru: founded 1535; university (1824); centre of a district producing rice and sugar cane. Pop: 603 657 (1998 est)

Truk Islands (trʌk) *pl n* a group of islands in the W Pacific, in the E Caroline Islands: administratively part of the US Trust Territory of the Pacific Islands from 1947; became self-governing in 1979 as part of the Federated States of Micronesia; consists of 11 chief islands; a major Japanese naval base during World War II. Pop: 52 870 (1994). Area: 130 sq km (50 sq miles)

trull (trʌl) *n arch* a prostitute; harlot [C16 from G *Trulle*]

truly ('tru:lɪ) *adv* **1** in a true, just, or faithful manner **2** (intensifier): *a truly great man* **3** indeed; really

Truman ('tru:mən) *n* **Harry S** 1884–1972, US Democratic statesman; 33rd president of the US (1945–53) He approved the dropping of the two atomic bombs on Japan (1945), advocated the postwar loan to Britain, and involved the US in the Korean War

trumeau (trʊ'məʊ) *n, pl* **trumeaux** (-məʊz) *archit* a section of a wall or pillar between two openings [from F]

trump[1] (trʌmp) *n* **1** Also called: **trump card 1a** any card from the suit chosen as trumps **1b** this suit itself; trumps **2** a decisive or advantageous move, resource, action, etc **3** *inf* a fine or reliable person ▷ *vb* **4** to play a trump card on (a suit, or a particular card of a suit, that is not trumps) **5** *(tr)* to outdo or surpass ▷ See also **trumps, trump up** [C16 var. of TRIUMPH]

trump[2] (trʌmp) *n arch or literary* **1** a trumpet or the sound produced by one **2 the last trump** the final trumpet call on the Day of Judgment [C13 from OF *trompe*, from OHG *trumpa* trumpet]

trumpery ('trʌmpərɪ) *n, pl* **trumperies 1** foolish talk or actions **2** a useless or worthless article; trinket ▷ *adj* **3** useless or worthless [C15 from OF *tromperie* deceit, from *tromper* to cheat]

trumpet ('trʌmpɪt) *n* **1** a valved brass instrument of brilliant tone consisting of a narrow tube ending in a flared bell **2** any similar instrument, esp a straight instrument used for fanfares, signals, etc **3** a loud sound such as that of a trumpet, esp when made by an animal **4** an eight-foot reed stop on an organ **5** something resembling a trumpet in shape **6** short for **ear trumpet 7 blow one's own trumpet** to boast about one's own skills or good qualities ▷ *vb* **trumpets, trumpeting, trumpeted 8** to proclaim or sound loudly [C13 from OF *trompette* a little TRUMP²]

trumpeter ('trʌmpɪtə) *n* **1** a person who plays the trumpet, esp one whose duty it is to play fanfares, signals, etc **2** any of three birds of South America, having a rounded body, long legs, and a glossy blackish plumage **3** (*sometimes cap*) a breed of domestic fancy pigeon with a long ruff **4** a large silvery-grey Australian marine food and game fish that grunts when taken from the water

trumpeter swan *n* a large swan of W North America, having a white plumage and black bill

trumps (trʌmps) *pl n* **1** (*sometimes sing*) *cards* any one of the four suits that outranks all the other suits for the duration of a deal or game **2 turn up trumps** (of a person) to bring about a happy or successful conclusion, esp unexpectedly

trump up *vb* (*tr, adv*) to invent (a charge, accusation, etc) so as to deceive

truncate *vb* (trʌŋ'keɪt, 'trʌŋkeɪt), **truncates, truncating, truncated 1** (*tr*) to shorten by cutting ▷ *adj* ('trʌŋkeɪt) **2** cut short; truncated **3** *biol* having a blunt end [C15 from L *truncāre* to lop] > **trun'cation** *n*

truncated (trʌŋ'keɪtɪd) *adj* **1** (of a cone, prism, etc) having an apex or end removed by a plane intersection **2** shortened by or as if by cutting off; truncate

truncheon ('trʌntʃən) *n* **1** *chiefly Brit* a club or cudgel formerly carried by a policeman **2** a baton of office [C16 from OF *tronchon* stump, from L *truncus* trunk; see TRUNCATE]

trundle ('trʌndᵊl) *vb* **trundles, trundling, trundled 1** to move heavily on or as if on wheels: *the bus trundled by* ▷ *n* **2** a trundling **3** a small wheel or roller [OE *tryndel*]

trundle bed *n* a less common word for **truckle bed**

trundler ('trʌndlə) *n* NZ **1** a trolley for shopping or one for golf clubs **2** a child's pushchair

trunk (trʌŋk) *n* **1** the main stem of a tree **2** a large strong case or box used to contain clothes, etc, when travelling and for storage **3** the body excluding the head, neck, and limbs; torso **4** the elongated nasal part of an elephant **5** the US and Canad name for **boot**¹ (sense 2) **6** the main stem of a nerve, blood vessel, etc **7** *naut* a watertight boxlike cover within a vessel, such as one used to enclose a centreboard **8** an enclosed duct or passageway for ventilation, etc **9** (*modifier*) of a main road, railway, etc, in a network: *a trunk line* ▷ See also **trunks** [C15 from OF *tronc*, from L *truncus*, from *truncus* (adj) lopped]

trunk call *n chiefly Brit* a long-distance telephone call

trunk curl *n* another name for **sit-up**

trunkfish ('trʌŋk,fɪʃ) *n, pl* **trunkfish** *or* **trunkfishes** any of a family of fishes having the body encased in bony plates

trunk hose *n* a man's puffed-out breeches reaching to the thighs and worn with tights in the 16th century

trunking ('trʌŋkɪŋ) *n* **1** *telecomm* the cables that take a common route through a telephone exchange building **2** plastic housing used to conceal wires, etc; casing **3** the delivery of goods over long distances, esp by road vehicles to local distribution centres

trunk line *n* **1** a direct link between two telephone exchanges or switchboards that are a considerable distance apart **2** the main route or routes on a railway

trunk road *n Brit* a main road, esp one that is suitable for heavy vehicles

trunks (trʌŋks) *pl n* **1** a man's garment worn for swimming, extending from the waist to the thigh **2** shorts worn for some sports **3** *chiefly Brit* men's underpants with legs that reach midthigh

trunnion ('trʌnjən) *n* one of a pair of coaxial projections attached to opposite sides of a container, cannon, etc, to provide a support about which it can turn [C17 from OF *trognon* trunk]

Truro ('trʊərəʊ) *n* a market town in SW England, administrative centre of Cornwall. Pop: 18 966 (1991)

truss (trʌs) *vb* (*tr*) **1** (sometimes foll by *up*) to tie, bind, or bundle **2** to bind the wings and legs of (a fowl) before cooking **3** to support or stiffen (a roof, bridge, etc) with structural members **4** *med* to supply or support with a truss ▷ *n* **5** a structural framework of wood or metal used to support a roof, bridge, etc **6** *med* a device for holding a hernia in place, typically consisting of a pad held in position by a belt **7** a cluster of flowers or fruit growing at the end of a single stalk **8** *naut* a metal fitting fixed to a yard at its centre for holding it to a mast **9** another name for **corbel 10** a bundle or pack **11** *chiefly Brit* a bundle of hay or straw, esp one having a fixed weight of 36, 56, or 60 pounds [C13 from OF *trousse*, from *trousser*, apparently from Vulgar L *torciāre* (unattested), from *torca* (unattested) a bundle]

trust (trʌst) *n* **1** reliance on and confidence in the truth, worth, reliability, etc, of a person or thing; faith. Related adj: **fiducial 2** a group of commercial enterprises combined to control the market for any commodity **3** the obligation of someone in a responsible position **4** custody, charge, or care **5** a person or thing in which confidence or faith is placed **6** commercial credit **7a** an arrangement whereby a person to whom the legal title to property is conveyed (the trustee) holds such property for the benefit of those entitled to the beneficial interest **7b** property that is the subject of such an arrangement. Related adj: **fiduciary 8** (in the British National Health Service) a self-governing hospital, group of hospitals, or other body providing health-care services, which operates as an independent commercial unit within the NHS **9** (*modifier*) of or relating to a trust or trusts ▷ *vb* **10** (*tr; may take a clause as object*) to expect, hope, or suppose **11** (when *tr, may take an infinitive;* when *intr*, often foll by *in* or *to*) to place confidence in (someone to do something); rely (upon) **12** (*tr*) to consign for care **13** (*tr*) to allow (someone to do something) with confidence in his or her good sense or honesty **14** (*tr*) to extend business credit to [C13 from ON *traust*] > '**trustable** *adj* > '**truster** *n*

trust account *n* **1** Also called: **trustee account** a savings account deposited in the name of a trustee who controls it during his lifetime, after which the balance is payable to a prenominated beneficiary **2** property under the control of a trustee or trustees

trustafarian (,trʌstə'fɛərɪən) *n* (*sometimes cap*) *Brit inf* a young person from a wealthy background whose trust fund enables him or her to eschew conventional attitudes to work, dress, drug taking, etc [C20 from TRUST (FUND) + (RAST)AFARIAN]

trustee (trʌ'stiː) *n* **1** a person to whom the legal title to property is entrusted **2** a member of a board that manages the affairs of an institution or organization

trustee in bankruptcy *n* a person entrusted with the administration of a bankrupt's affairs and with realizing his assets for the benefit of the creditors

trustee investment *n stock exchange* an investment in which trustees are authorized to invest money belonging to a trust fund

trusteeship (trʌ'stiːʃɪp) *n* **1** the office or function of a trustee **2a** the administration or government of a territory by a foreign country under the supervision of the **Trusteeship Council** of the United Nations **2b** (*often cap*) any such dependent territory; trust territory

Tt

trustful ('trʌstfʊl) *or* **trusting** *adj* characterized by a tendency or readiness to trust others > '**trustfully** *or* '**trustingly** *adv*
trust fund *n* money, securities, etc, held in trust
trust territory *n (sometimes cap)* another name for a **trusteeship** (sense 2b)
trustworthy ('trʌst,wɜːðɪ) *adj* worthy of being trusted; honest, reliable, or dependable > '**trust,worthily** *adv* > '**trust,worthiness** *n*
trusty ('trʌstɪ) *adj* **trustier, trustiest** 1 faithful or reliable ▷ *n, pl* **trusties** 2 a trustworthy convict given special privileges > '**trustily** *adv* > '**trustiness** *n*
truth (truːθ) *n* 1 the quality of being true, genuine, actual, or factual 2 something that is true as opposed to false 3 a proven or verified fact, principle, etc: *the truths of astronomy* 4 *(usually pl)* a system of concepts purporting to represent some aspect of the world: *the truths of religion* 5 fidelity to a standard or law 6 faithful reproduction or portrayal 7 honesty 8 accuracy, as in the setting of a mechanical instrument 9 loyalty ▷ Related adjs: **veritable, veracious** [OE *triewth*] > '**truthless** *adj*
truth drug *or* **serum** *n inf* any of various drugs supposed to have the property of making people tell the truth, as by relaxing them
truthful ('truːθfʊl) *adj* 1 telling the truth; honest 2 realistic: *a truthful portrayal of the king* > '**truthfully** *adv* > '**truthfulness** *n*
truth-function *n logic* a function that determines the truth-value of a complex sentence solely in terms of the truth-values of the component sentences without reference to their meaning
truth set *n logic, maths* the set of values that satisfy an open sentence, equation, inequality, etc, having no unique solution. Also called: **solution set**
truth table *n* 1 a table, used in logic, indicating the truth-value of a compound statement for every truth-value of its component propositions 2 a similar table, used in transistor technology, to indicate the value of the output signal of a logic circuit for every value of input signal
truth-value *n logic* either of the values, true or false, that may be taken by a statement
try (traɪ) *vb* **tries, trying, tried** 1 (when *tr, may take an infinitive,* sometimes with *to* replaced by *and*) to make an effort or attempt 2 *(tr; often foll by out)* to sample, test, or give experimental use to (something) 3 *(tr)* to put strain or stress on: *he tries my patience* 4 *(tr; often passive)* to give pain, affliction, or vexation to 5a to examine and determine the issues involved in (a cause) in a court of law 5b to hear evidence in order to determine the guilt or innocence of (an accused) 6 *(tr)* to melt (fat, lard, etc) in order to separate out impurities ▷ *n, pl* **tries** 7 an experiment or trial 8 an attempt or effort 9 *rugby* the act of an attacking player touching the ball down behind the opposing team's goal line 10 *American football* an attempt made after a touchdown to score an extra point, as by kicking a goal ▷ See also **try on, try out** [C13 from OF *trier* to sort, from ?]
USAGE See at **and**
trying ('traɪɪŋ) *adj* upsetting, difficult, or annoying > '**tryingly** *adv*
trying plane *n* a plane with a long body for planing the edges of long boards. Also called: **try plane**
try line *n* the line behind which the ball must be placed to score a try in a rugby match
try on *vb (tr, adv)* 1 to put on (a garment) to find out whether it fits, etc 2 **try it on** *inf* to attempt to deceive or fool someone ▷ *n* **try-on** 3 *Brit inf* something done to test out a person's tolerance, etc
try out *vb (adv)* 1 *(tr)* to test or put to experimental use 2 (when *intr*, usually foll by *for*) *US & Canad* (of an athlete, actor, etc) to undergo a test or to submit (an athlete, actor, etc) to a test in order to determine suitability for a place in a team, an acting role, etc ▷ *n* **tryout** 3 *chiefly US & Canad* a trial or test, as of an athlete or actor
trypanosome ('trɪpənə,səʊm) *n* any parasitic flagellate protozoan that lives in the blood of vertebrates and causes sleeping sickness and certain other diseases [C19 from NL *Trypanosoma*, from Gk *trupanon* borer + *sōma* body]
trypanosomiasis (,trɪpənəsə'maɪəsɪs) *n* any infection of an animal or human with a trypanosome
trypsin ('trɪpsɪn) *n* a digestive enzyme in the pancreatic juice: it catalyses the hydrolysis of proteins to peptides [C19 *tryp-*, from Gk *tripsis* a rubbing, from *tribein* to rub + -IN; from the fact that it was orig. produced by rubbing the pancreas with glycerine] > **tryptic** ('trɪptɪk) *adj*
tryptophan ('trɪptə,fæn) *n* an essential amino acid; a component of proteins necessary for growth [C20 from *trypt(ic)*, from TRYPSIN + *-o-* + *-phan*, var. of -PHANE]
trysail ('traɪ,seɪl; *naut* 'traɪsᵊl) *n* a small fore-and-aft sail set on a sailing vessel in foul weather to help keep her head to the wind
try square *n* a device for testing or laying out right angles, usually consisting of a metal blade fixed at right angles to a wooden handle
tryst (trɪst, traɪst) *n arch or literary* 1 an appointment to meet, esp secretly 2 the place of such a meeting or the meeting itself [C14 from OF *triste* lookout post, apparently from ON]
Tsana ('tsɑːnə) *n* **Lake** another name for (Lake) **Tana**
tsar *or* **czar** (zɑː) *n* 1 (until 1917) the emperor of Russia 2 a tyrant; autocrat 3 *inf* a public official charged with responsibility for dealing with a certain problem or issue: *the drugs tsar* [C17 from Russian *tsar*, via Gothic *kaisar* from L: CAESAR] > '**tsardom** *or* '**czardom** *n*
tsarevitch *or* **czarevitch** ('zɑːrəvɪtʃ) *n* a son of a Russian tsar, esp the eldest son [from Russian *tsarevich*, from TSAR + *-evich*, masc. patronymic suffix]
tsarevna *or* **czarevna** (zɑː'rɛvnə) *n* 1 a daughter of a Russian tsar 2 the wife of a Russian tsarevitch [from Russian, from TSAR + *-evna*, fem. patronymic suffix]
tsarina, czarina (zɑː'riːnə) *or* **tsaritsa, czaritza** (zɑː'rɪtsə) *n* the wife of a Russian tsar; Russian empress [from It., Sp. *czarina*, from G *Czarin*]
tsarism *or* **czarism** ('zɑːrɪzəm) *n* a system of government by a tsar > '**tsarist** *or* '**czarist** *n, adj*
Tsaritsyn (*Russian* tsa'ritsin) *n* a former name (until 1925) of **Volgograd**
TSE (in Canada) *abbrev for* Toronto Stock Exchange
Tselinograd (*Russian* tsəlɪna'grat) *n* a former name (1961–94) for **Akmola**
tsetse fly *or* **tzetze fly** ('tsɛtsɪ) *n* any of various bloodsucking African dipterous flies which transmit various diseases, esp sleeping sickness [C19 via Afrik. from Tswana]
T-shirt *or* **tee-shirt** *n* a lightweight simple garment for the upper body, usually short-sleeved [from T-shape formed when laid out flat]
Tshombe ('tʃɒmbɪ) *n* **Moise** (məʊ'iːz) 1919–69, Congolese statesman. He led the secession of Katanga (1960) from the newly independent Congo; forced into exile (1963) but returned (1964–65) as premier of the Congo; died in exile
Tsimshian ('tʃɪmʃɪən) *n* 1 a member of a Native Canadian people of northern British Columbia 2 the Penutian language of this people [C19 from Tsimshian, inside the Skeena River]
Tsinan ('tsiː'næn) *n* a variant transliteration of the Chinese name for **Jinan**
Tsinghai ('tsɪŋ'haɪ) *n* 1 a variant transliteration of the Chinese name for **Qinghai** 2 a variant transliteration of the Chinese name for **Koko Nor**
Tsingtao ('tsɪŋ'taʊ) *n* a variant transliteration of the Chinese name for **Qingdao**
Tsingyuan ('tsɪŋ'jwɑːn) *or* **Ch'ing-yüan** *n* the former name of **Baoding**

Tsitsihar ('tsɪtsɪ,hɑː) *n* a variant transliteration of the Chinese name for **Qiqihar**

TSO *abbrev for* The Stationery Office, formerly His (or Her) Majesty's Stationery Office

tsotsi ('tsɒtsɪ) *n, pl* **tsotsis** *S African inf* a Black street thug or gang member; wide boy [c20 ?from Nguni *tsotsa* to dress flashily]

tsp. *abbrev for* teaspoon

T-square *n* a T-shaped ruler used for drawing horizontal lines and to support set squares when drawing vertical and inclined lines

T-stop *n* a setting of the lens aperture on a camera calibrated photometrically and assigned a T-number

Tsugaru Strait ('tsugɑ,ru) *n* a channel between N Honshu and S Hokkaido islands, Japan. Width: about 30 km (20 miles)

tsunami (tsʊ'nɑːmɪ) *n, pl* **tsunamis** *or* **tsunami** a large, often destructive sea wave produced by a submarine earthquake, subsidence, or volcanic eruption. Sometimes called a tidal wave [from Japanese, from *tsu* port + *nami* wave]

Tsushima ('tsuːʃiː,mɑː) *n* a group of five rocky islands between Japan and South Korea, in the Korea Strait: administratively part of Japan; scene of a naval defeat for the Russians (1905) during the Russo-Japanese war. Pop: 50 810 (latest est). Area: 698 sq km (269 sq miles)

tsutsugamushi disease (,tsʊtsʊgə'mʊʃɪ) *n* one of the five major groups of acute infectious rickettsial diseases affecting man, common in Asia. It is transmitted by the bite of mites [from Japanese, from *tsutsuga* disease + *mushi* insect]

Tsvangirai (tsvæn'gɪərɪ) *n* **Morgan** born 1952, Zimbabwean trade unionist and politician; leader of the Movement for Democratic Change, the main opposition party to President Mugabe's Zanu-PF since 1999

Tswana ('tswɑːnə) *n* **1** (*pl* **Tswana** *or* **Tswanas**) a member of a mixed Negroid and Bushman people of southern Africa, living chiefly in Botswana **2** the language of this people

TT *abbrev for:* **1** teetotal **2** teetotaller **3** telegraphic transfer: a method of sending money abroad by cabled transfer between banks **4** Tourist Trophy (annual motorcycle races held in the Isle of Man) **5** tuberculin-tested

TTA (in Britain) *abbrev for* Teacher Training Agency

TTL *abbrev for:* **1** transistor transistor logic: a method of constructing electronic logic circuits **2** through-the-lens: denoting a system of light metering in cameras

TTS *computing abbrev for* text-to-speech: a technology that allows written text to be output as speech

TU *abbrev for* trade union

Tuamotu Archipelago (,tuːə'məʊtuː) *n* a group of about 80 coral islands in the S Pacific, in French Polynesia. Pop: 15 370 (1996). Area: 860 sq km (332 sq miles). Also called: **Low Archipelago, Paumotu Archipelago**

tuatara (,tuːə'tɑːrə) *n* a lizard-like reptile occurring on certain islands near New Zealand [c19 from Maori, from *tua* back + *tara* spine]

tub (tʌb) *n* **1** a low wide open container, typically round: used in a variety of domestic and industrial situations **2** a small plastic or cardboard container of similar shape for ice cream, margarine, etc **3** another word (esp US) for **bath** (sense 1) **4** Also called: **tubful** the amount a tub will hold **5** a clumsy slow boat or ship **6a** a small vehicle on rails for carrying loads in a mine **6b** a container for lifting coal or ore up a mine shaft ▷ *vb* **tubs, tubbing, tubbed 7** *Brit inf* to wash (oneself) in a tub **8** (*tr*) to keep or put in a tub [c14 from MDu. *tubbe*] > **'tubbable** *adj* > **'tubber** *n*

tuba ('tjuːbə) *n, pl* **tubas** *or* **tubae** (-biː) **1** a valved brass instrument of bass pitch, in which the bell points upwards and the mouthpiece projects at right angles **2** a powerful reed stop on an organ [L]

tubal ('tjuːbᵊl) *adj* **1** of or relating to a tube **2** of, relating to, or developing in a Fallopian tube

Tubal-cain ('tjuːbᵊl,keɪn) *n Old Testament* a son of Lamech, said in Genesis 4:22 to be the first craftsman in metals

tubby ('tʌbɪ) *adj* **tubbier, tubbiest 1** plump **2** shaped like a tub > **'tubbiness** *n*

tube (tjuːb) *n* **1** a long hollow cylindrical object, used for the passage of fluids or as a container **2** a collapsible cylindrical container of soft metal or plastic closed with a cap, used to hold viscous liquids or pastes **3** *anat* **3a** short for **Eustachian tube** or **Fallopian tube 3b** any hollow cylindrical structure **4** (*sometimes cap*) *Brit* **4a the tube** an underground railway system, esp that in London. US and Canad equivalent: **subway 4b** the tunnels through which the railway runs **5** *electronics* **5a** another name for **valve** (sense 3) **5b** See **electron tube, cathode-ray tube, television tube 6** *sl, chiefly US* a television set **7** *Austral sl* a bottle or can of beer **8** *surfing* the cylindrical passage formed when a wave breaks and the crest tips forward ▷ *vb* **tubes, tubing, tubed** (*tr*) **9** to supply with a tube **10** to convey in a tube **11** to shape like a tube [c17 from L *tubus*] > **'tubeless** *adj*

tube foot *n* any of numerous tubular outgrowths of most echinoderms that are used for locomotion, to aid ingestion of food, etc

tubeless tyre *n* a pneumatic tyre in which the outer casing makes an airtight seal with the rim of the wheel so that an inner tube is unnecessary

tuber ('tjuːbə) *n* **1** a fleshy underground stem or root **2** *anat* a raised area; swelling [c17 from L *tūber* hump]

tubercle ('tjuːbəkᵊl) *n* **1** any small rounded nodule or elevation, esp on the skin, on a bone, or on a plant **2** any small rounded pathological lesion, esp one characteristic of tuberculosis [c16 from L *tūberculum* a little swelling]

Tt

tubercle bacillus *n* a rodlike bacterium that causes tuberculosis

tubercular (tjʊ'bɜːkjʊlə) *adj also* **tuberculous 1** of or symptomatic of tuberculosis **2** of or relating to a tubercle **3** characterized by the presence of tubercles ▷ *n* **4** a person with tuberculosis

tuberculate (tjʊ'bɜːkjʊlɪt) *adj* covered with tubercles > **tu,bercu'lation** *n*

tuberculin (tjʊ'bɜːkjʊlɪn) *n* a sterile liquid prepared from cultures of attenuated tubercle bacillus and used in the diagnosis of tuberculosis

tuberculin-tested *adj* (of milk) produced by cows that have been certified as free of tuberculosis

tuberculosis (tjʊ,bɜːkjʊ'ləʊsɪs) *n* a communicable disease caused by infection with the tubercle bacillus, most frequently affecting the lungs [c19 from NL]

tuberose ('tjuːbə,rəʊz) *n* a perennial Mexican agave plant having a tuberous root and fragrant white flowers [c17 from L *tūberōsus* full of lumps; from its root]

tuberous ('tjuːbərəs) *or* **tuberose** ('tjuːbə,rəʊs) *adj* **1** (of plants) forming, bearing, or resembling a tuber or tubers **2** *anat* of or having warty protuberances or tubers [c17 from L *tūberōsus* full of knobs]

tube worm *n* any of various worms that construct and live in a tube of sand, lime, etc

tubifex ('tjuːbɪ,fɛks) *n, pl* **tubifex** *or* **tubifexes** any of a genus of small reddish freshwater worms [c19 from NL, from L *tubus* tube + *facere* to make]

tubing ('tjuːbɪŋ) *n* **1** tubes collectively **2** a length of tube **3** a system of tubes **4** fabric in the form of a tube

Tübingen ('tjuːbɪŋgən) *n* a town in SW Germany, in Baden-Württemberg: university (1477). Pop: 76 040 (latest est)

Tubman ('tʌbmən) *n* **William Vacanarat Shadrach** (və'kænə,ræt 'ʃædræk) 1895–1971, Liberian statesman;

president of Liberia (1944–71)

tub-thumper *n* a noisy, violent, or ranting public speaker > **'tub-,thumping** *adj, n*

Tubuai Islands (,tu:bu:'aɪ) *pl n* a chain of small islands extending about 1400 km (850 miles) in the S Pacific, in French Polynesia; discovered by Captain Cook in 1777; annexed by France in 1880. Pop: 6510 (latest est). Area: 173 sq km (67 sq miles). Also called: **Austral Islands**

tubular ('tju:bjʊlə) *adj* **1** Also: **tubiform** ('tju:bɪ,fɔ:m) having the form of a tube or tubes **2** of or relating to a tube or tubing

tubular bells *pl n* a set of long tubes of brass tuned for use in an orchestra and struck with a mallet to simulate the sound of bells

tubule ('tju:bju:l) *n* any small tubular structure, esp in an animal body [C17 from L *tubulus* a little TUBE]

TUC (in Britain) *abbrev for* Trades Union Congress

tuck (tʌk) *vb* **1** (*tr*) to push or fold into a small confined space or concealed place or between two surfaces **2** (*tr*) to thrust the loose ends or sides of (something) into a confining space, so as to make neat and secure **3** to make a tuck or tucks in (a garment) **4** (*usually tr*) to draw together, contract, or pucker ▷ *n* **5** a tucked object or part **6** a pleat or fold in a part of a garment, usually stitched down **7** the part of a vessel where the planks meet at the sternpost **8** *Brit inf* **8a** food, esp cakes and sweets **8b** (*as modifier*): *a tuck box* **9** a position of the body, as in certain dives, in which the legs are bent with the knees drawn up against the chest and tightly clasped ▷ See also **tuck away, tuck in** [C14 from OE *tūcian* to torment]

tuck away *vb (tr, adv) inf* **1** to eat (a large amount of food) **2** to store, esp in a place difficult to find

tucker[1] ('tʌkə) *n* **1** a person or thing that tucks **2** a detachable yoke of lace, linen, etc, often white, worn over the breast, as of a low-cut dress **3** *Austral inf old-fashioned* an informal word for **food**

tucker[2] ('tʌkə) *vb (tr; often passive;* usually foll by *out) inf, chiefly US & Canad* to weary or tire

tucker-bag *or* **tuckerbox** ('tʌkə,bɒks) *n Austral old-fashioned sl* a bag or box in which food is carried or stored

tucket ('tʌkɪt) *n arch* a flourish on a trumpet [C16 from OF *toquer* to sound (on a drum)]

tuck in *vb (adv)* **1** (*tr*) Also: **tuck into** to put to bed and make snug **2** (*tr*) to thrust the loose ends or sides of (something) into a confining space: *tuck the blankets in* **3** (*intr*) Also: **tuck into** *inf* to eat, esp heartily ▷ *n* **tuck-in** **4** *Brit inf* a meal, esp a large one

tuck shop *n chiefly Brit* a shop, esp one near a school, where cakes and sweets are sold

Tucson ('tu:sɒn) *n* a city in SE Arizona, at an altitude of 700m (2400 ft): resort and seat of the University of Arizona (1891). Pop: 486 699 (2000)

Tucumán (*Spanish* tuku'man) *n* a city in NW Argentina: scene of the declaration (1816) of Argentinian independence from Spain; university (1914). Pop: 519 252 (1999 est)

-tude *suffix forming nouns* indicating state or condition: *plenitude* [from L *-tūdō*]

Tudor ('tju:də) *n* **1** an English royal house (1485–1603), consisting of Henry VII, Henry VIII, Edward VI, Mary I, and Elizabeth I, descended from a Welsh squire, **Owen Tudor** (died 1461) ▷ *adj* **2** denoting a style of architecture of this period, characterized by half-timbered houses

▷ www.artchive.com/ftp_site_reg.htm
▷ www.britainexpress.com/architecture/tudor.htm
▷ www.bbc.co.uk/history/timelines/wales/tudor.shtml
▷ www.2hwy.com/eg/d/dynt.htm

Tues. *abbrev for* Tuesday

Tuesday ('tju:zdɪ) *n* the third day of the week; second day of the working week [OE *tīwesdæg*]

TUF (in New Zealand) *abbrev for* Trade Union Federation

tufa ('tju:fə) *n* a porous rock formed of calcium carbonate deposited from springs [C18 from It. *tufo*, from LL *tōfus*] > **tufaceous** (tju:'feɪʃəs) *adj*

tuff (tʌf) *n* a hard volcanic rock consisting of consolidated fragments of lava [C16 from OF *tuf*, from It. *tufo*; see TUFA] > **tuffaceous** (tʌ'feɪʃəs) *adj*

tuffet ('tʌfɪt) *n* a small mound or low seat [C16 alteration of TUFT]

tuft (tʌft) *n* **1** a bunch of feathers, grass, hair, etc, held together at the base **2** a cluster of threads drawn tightly through upholstery, a quilt, etc, to secure the padding **3** a small clump of trees or bushes **4** (formerly) a gold tassel on the cap worn by titled undergraduates at English universities ▷ *vb* **5** (*tr*) to provide or decorate with a tuft or tufts **6** to form or be formed into tufts **7** to secure with tufts [C14 ?from OF *tufe*, of Gmc origin] > **'tufted** *adj* > **'tufty** *adj*

tufted duck *n* a European lake-dwelling duck, the male of which has a black plumage with white underparts and a long black drooping crest

tug (tʌg) *vb* **tugs, tugging, tugged** **1** (when *intr*, sometimes foll by *at*) to pull or drag with sharp or powerful movements **2** (*tr*) to tow (a vessel) by means of a tug ▷ *n* **3** a strong pull or jerk **4** Also called: **tugboat** a boat with a powerful engine, used for towing barges, ships, etc **5** a hard struggle or fight [C13 rel. to OE *tēon* to TOW[1]] > **'tugger** *n*

Tugela (tu:'geɪlə) *n* a river in E South Africa, rising in the Drakensberg where it forms the **Tugela Falls**, 856 m (2810 ft) high, before flowing east to the Indian Ocean: scene of battles during the Zulu War (1879) and the Boer War (1899–1902). Length: about 500 km (312 miles)

tug-of-love *n* a conflict over custody of a child between divorced parents or between natural parents and foster or adoptive parents

tug-of-war *n* **1** a contest in which two people or teams pull opposite ends of a rope in an attempt to drag the opposition over a central line **2** any hard struggle between two factions

tui ('tu:i:) *n, pl* **tuis** a New Zealand songbird with white feathers at the throat. Also called: **parson bird** [from Maori]

tuition (tju:'ɪʃən) *n* **1** instruction, esp that received individually or in a small group **2** the payment for instruction, esp in colleges or universities [C15 from OF *tuicion*, from L *tuitiō* a guarding, from *tuērī* to watch over] > **tu'itional** *adj*

Tula (*Russian* 'tulə) *n* an industrial city in W central Russia. Pop: 513 100 (1999 est)

tularaemia *or US* **tularemia** (,tu:lə'ri:mɪə) *n* an infectious disease of rodents, transmitted to man by infected ticks or flies or by handling contaminated flesh [C19/20: from NL, from *Tulare*, county in California where first observed] > **,tula'raemic** *or US* **,tula'remic** *adj*

tulip ('tju:lɪp) *n* **1** any of various spring-blooming bulb plants having long broad pointed leaves and single showy bell-shaped flowers **2** the flower or bulb [C17 from NL *tulipa*, from Turkish *tülbend* turban, which the opened bloom was thought to resemble]

tulip tree *n* **1** Also called: **tulip poplar** a North American tree having tulip-shaped greenish-yellow flowers and long conelike fruits **2** a similar and related Chinese tree **3** any of various other trees with tulip-shaped flowers, such as the magnolia

tulipwood ('tju:lɪp,wʊd) *n* **1** the light soft wood of the tulip tree, used in making furniture and veneer **2** any of several woods having streaks of colour

Tull (tʌl) *n* **Jethro** ('dʒɛθrəʊ) 1674–1741, English agriculturalist, who invented the seed drill

Tullamore (tʌlə'mɔ:) *n* the county town of Offaly, Republic of Ireland; food processing and brewing. Pop: 8485 (latest est)

tulle (tju:l) *n* a fine net fabric of silk, rayon, etc [C19 from

F, from *Tulle*, city in S central France, where first manufactured]

tullibee ('tʌlıbi:) *n* a cisco of the Great Lakes of Canada [c19 from French *toulibi*, from Ojibwa]

Tully ('tʌlı) *n* the former English name for (Marcus Tullius) **Cicero**

Tulsa ('tʌlsə) *n* a city in NE Oklahoma, on the Arkansas River: a major oil centre; two universities. Pop: 393 049 (2000)

tumble ('tʌmbᵊl) *vb* **tumbles, tumbling, tumbled** **1** to fall or cause to fall, esp awkwardly, precipitately, or violently **2** (*intr*; usually foll by *about*) to roll or twist, esp in playing **3** (*intr*) to perform leaps, somersaults, etc **4** to move in a heedless or hasty way **5** (*tr*) to polish (gemstones) in a tumbler **6** (*tr*) to disturb, rumple, or toss around ▷ *n* **7** a tumbling **8** a fall or toss **9** a decrease in value, number, etc: *stock markets have taken a tumble* **10** an acrobatic feat, esp a somersault **11** a state of confusion **12** a confused heap or pile ▷ See also **tumble to** [OE *tumbian*]

tumbledown ('tʌmbᵊl,daʊn) *adj* falling to pieces; dilapidated; crumbling

tumble dryer *or* **tumble drier** *n* a machine that dries wet laundry by rotating it in warmed air inside a metal drum. Also called: **tumbler dryer, tumbler**

tumbler ('tʌmblə) *n* **1a** a flat-bottomed drinking glass with no handle or stem **1b** Also called: **tumblerful** its contents **2** a person who performs somersaults and other acrobatic feats **3** another name for **tumble dryer** **4** a box or drum rotated so that the contents (usually gemstones) become smooth and polished **5** the part of a lock that retains or releases the bolt and is moved by the action of a key **6** a lever in a gunlock that receives the action of the mainspring when the trigger is pressed and thus forces the hammer forwards **7** a part that moves a gear in a train of gears into and out of engagement

tumbler switch *n* a small electrical switch incorporating a spring, widely used in lighting

tumble to *vb* (*intr, prep*) *inf* to understand; become aware of: *she tumbled to his plan quickly*

tumbleweed ('tʌmbᵊl,wi:d) *n* any of various densely branched American and Australian plants that break off near the ground on withering and are rolled about by the wind

tumbrel *or* **tumbril** ('tʌmbrəl) *n* **1** a farm cart, esp one that tilts backwards to deposit its load. A cart of this type was used to take condemned prisoners to the guillotine during the French Revolution **2** (formerly) a covered cart used to carry ammunition, tools, etc [c14 *tumberell* ducking stool, from Med. L *tumbrellum*, from OF *tumberel* dump cart, ult. of Gmc origin]

tumefacient (,tju:mı'feıʃıənt) *adj* producing or capable of producing swelling: *a tumefacient drug* [c16 from L *tumefacere* to cause to swell]

tumefy ('tju:mı,faı) *vb* **tumefies, tumefying, tumefied** to make or become tumid; swell or puff up [c16 from F *tuméfier*, from L *tumefacere*] > ,**tume'faction** *n*

tumescent (tju:'mɛsənt) *adj* swollen or becoming swollen [c19 from L *tumescere* to begin to swell, from *tumēre*] > **tu'mescence** *n*

tumid ('tju:mıd) *adj* **1** enlarged or swollen **2** bulging **3** pompous or fulsome in style [c16 from L *tumidus*, from *tumēre* to swell] > **tu'midity** *or* **'tumidness** *n* > **'tumidly** *adv*

tummy ('tʌmı) *n, pl* **tummies** an informal or childish word for **stomach**. Also called: **tum**

tummy tuck *n inf* the surgical removal of abdominal fat and skin for cosmetic purposes

tumour *or US* **tumor** ('tju:mə) *n pathol* **a** any abnormal swelling **b** a mass of tissue formed by a new growth of cells [c16 from L, from *tumēre* to swell] > **'tumorous** *adj*

tumult ('tju:mʌlt) *n* **1** a loud confused noise, as of a crowd; commotion **2** violent agitation or disturbance **3** great emotional agitation [c15 from L *tumultus*, from *tumēre* to swell up]

tumultuous (tju:'mʌltjʊəs) *adj* **1** uproarious, riotous, or turbulent **2** greatly agitated, confused, or disturbed **3** making a loud or unruly disturbance > **tu'multuously** *adv* > **tu'multuousness** *n*

tumulus ('tju:mjʊləs) *n, pl* **tumuli** (-li:) *archaeol* (*no longer in technical usage*) another word for **barrow²** [c17 from L: a hillock, from *tumēre* to swell up]

tun (tʌn) *n* **1** a large beer cask **2** a measure of capacity, usually equal to 252 wine gallons ▷ *vb* **tuns, tunning, tunned** **3** (*tr*) to put into or keep in tuns [OE *tunne*]

tuna¹ ('tju:nə) *n, pl* **tuna** *or* **tunas** **1** Also called: **tunny** any of a genus of large marine spiny-finned fishes, chiefly of warm waters **2** any of various similar and related fishes [c20 from American Sp., from Sp. *atún*, from Ar. *tūn*, from L *thunnus* tunny, from Gk]

tuna² ('tju:nə) *n* any of various tropical American prickly pear cacti [c16 via Sp. from Taino]

tunable *or* **tuneable** ('tju:nəbᵊl) *adj* able to be tuned

Tunbridge Wells ('tʌn,brıdʒ) *n* a town and resort in SE England, in SW Kent: chalybeate spring discovered in 1606; an important social centre in the 17th and 18th centuries. Pop: 60 272 (1991). Official name: **Royal Tunbridge Wells**

tundra ('tʌndrə) *n* a vast treeless zone lying between the ice cap and the timberline of North America and Eurasia and having a permanently frozen subsoil [c19 from Russian, from Lapp *tundar* hill]

tune (tju:n) *n* **1** a melody, esp one for which harmony is not essential **2** the condition of producing accurately pitched notes, intervals, etc (esp in **in tune, out of tune**) **3** accurate correspondence of pitch and intonation between instruments (esp in **in tune, out of tune**) **4** the correct adjustment of a radio, television, etc, with respect to the required frequency **5** a frame of mind; mood **6** **call the tune** to be in control of the proceedings **7** **change one's tune** to alter one's attitude or tone of speech **8** **to the tune of** *inf* to the amount or extent of ▷ *vb* **tunes, tuning, tuned** **9** to adjust (a musical instrument) to a certain pitch **10** to adjust (a note, etc) so as to bring it into harmony or concord **11** (*tr*) to adapt or adjust (oneself); attune **12** (*tr*; often foll by *up*) to make fine adjustments to (an engine, machine, etc) to obtain optimum performance **13** *electronics* to adjust (one or more circuits) for resonance at a desired frequency ▷ See also **tune in, tune up** [c14 var. of TONE] > **'tuner** *n*

tuneful ('tju:nfʊl) *adj* **1** having a pleasant tune; melodious **2** producing a melody or music > **'tunefully** *adv* > **'tunefulness** *n*

tune in *vb* (*adv*; often foll by *to*) **1** to adjust (a radio or television) to receive (a station or programme) **2** *sl* to make or become more aware, knowledgeable, etc (about)

tuneless ('tju:nlıs) *adj* having no melody or tune > **'tunelessly** *adv* > **'tunelessness** *n*

tune up *vb* (*adv*) **1** to adjust (a musical instrument) to a particular pitch **2** to tune (instruments) to a common pitch **3** (*tr*) to adjust (an engine) in (a car, etc) to improve performance ▷ *n* **tune-up** **4** adjustments made to an engine to improve its performance

tung oil (tʌŋ) *n* a fast-drying oil obtained from the seeds of an Asian tree, used in paints, varnishes, etc [partial translation of Chinese *yu t'ung* tung tree oil, from *yu* oil + *t'ung* tung tree]

tungsten ('tʌŋstən) *n* a hard malleable ductile greyish-white element. It is used in lamp filaments, electrical contact points, X-ray targets, and, alloyed with steel, in high-speed cutting tools. Symbol: W; atomic no.: 74; atomic wt.: 183.85. Also called: **wolfram** [c18 from Swedish *tung* heavy + *sten* stone]

tungsten lamp *n* a lamp in which light is produced by a

Tt

tungsten filament heated to incandescence by an electric current. Sometimes small amounts of a halogen, such as iodine, are added to improve the intensity (**tungsten-halogen lamp**)

tungsten steel *n* any of various hard steels containing tungsten and traces of carbon

Tungting *or* **Tung-t'ing** (ˌtʊŋ'tɪŋ) *n* a variant transliteration of the Chinese name for the **Dongting**

Tungusic (tʊŋ'gʊsɪk) *n* a branch or subfamily of the Altaic family of languages, some of which are spoken in NE Asia

Tunguska (*Russian* tun'guskə) *n* any of three rivers in Russia, in central Siberia, all tributaries of the Yenisei: the **Lower** (Nizhnyaya) **Tunguska** 2690 km (1670 miles) long; the **Stony** (Podkamennaya) **Tunguska** 1550 km (960 miles) long; the **Upper** (Verkhnyaya) **Tunguska** which is the lower course of the Angara

tunic ('tjuːnɪk) *n* **1** any of various hip-length or knee-length garments, such as the loose sleeveless garb worn in ancient Greece or Rome, the jacket of some soldiers, or a woman's hip-length garment, worn with a skirt or trousers **2** a covering, lining, or enveloping membrane of an organ or part **3** Also called: **tunicle** a short vestment worn by a bishop or subdeacon [OE *tunice* (unattested except in the accusative case), from L *tunica*]

tunicate ('tjuːnɪkɪt, -ˌkeɪt) *n* **1** any of various minute primitive marine animals having a saclike unsegmented body enclosed in a cellulose-like outer covering ▷ *adj also* **tunicated 2** (esp of a bulb) having concentric layers of tissue [c18 from L *tunicātus* clad in a TUNIC]

tuning ('tjuːnɪŋ) *n music* **1** a set of pitches to which the open strings of a guitar, violin, etc, are tuned **2** the accurate pitching of notes and intervals by a choir, orchestra, etc; intonation

tuning fork *n* a two-pronged metal fork that when struck produces a pure note of constant specified pitch. It is used to tune musical instruments and in acoustics

Tunis ('tjuːnɪs) *n* the capital and chief port of Tunisia, in the northeast on the **Gulf of Tunis** (an inlet of the Mediterranean): dates from Carthaginian times, the ruins of ancient Carthage lying to the northeast; university (1960). Pop: 674 100 (1994)
▷ www.tourismtunisia.com/togo/tunis/tunis.html

Tunisia (tjuː'nɪzɪə, -'nɪsɪə) *n* a republic in N Africa, on the Mediterranean: settled by the Phoenicians in the 12th century BC; made a French protectorate in 1881 and gained independence in 1955. It consists chiefly of the Sahara in the south, a central plateau, and the Atlas Mountains in the north. Exports include textiles, petroleum, and phosphates. Official language: Arabic; French is also widely spoken. Official religion: Muslim. Currency: dinar. Capital: Tunis. Pop: 9 828 000 (1998 est). Area: 164 150 sq km (63 380 sq miles) > **Tu'nisian** *adj, n*
▷ www.tunisiaonline.com
▷ www.tourismtunisia.com

tunnage ('tʌnɪdʒ) *n* a variant spelling of **tonnage**

tunnel ('tʌnᵊl) *n* **1** an underground passageway, esp one for trains or cars **2** any passage or channel through or under something ▷ *vb* **tunnels, tunnelling, tunnelled** *or US* **tunnels, tunneling, tunneled 3** (*tr*) to make or force (a way) through or under (something) **4** (*intr*; foll by *through*, *under*, etc) to make or force a way (through or under something) [c15 from OF *tonel* cask, from *tonne* tun, from Med. L *tonna* barrel, of Celtic origin] > '**tunneller** *or US* '**tunneler** *n*

tunnel diode *n* an extremely stable semiconductor diode, having a very narrow highly doped p-n junction, in which electrons travel across the junction by means of the tunnel effect. Also called: **Esaki diode**

tunnel effect *n physics* the phenomenon in which an object, usually an elementary particle, tunnels through a potential barrier even though it does not have sufficient energy to surmount it

tunnel vision *n* **1** a condition in which peripheral vision is greatly restricted **2** narrowness of viewpoint resulting from concentration on a single idea, opinion, etc

tunny ('tʌnɪ) *n, pl* **tunnies** *or* **tunny** another name for **tuna¹** [c16 from OF *thon*, from OProvençal *ton*, from L *thunnus*, from Gk]

tup (tʌp) *n* **1** *chiefly Brit* a male sheep; ram **2** the head of a pile-driver or steam hammer ▷ *vb* **tups, tupping, tupped 3** (*tr*) (of a ram) to mate with (a ewe) [c14 from ?]

tupelo ('tjuːpɪˌləʊ) *n, pl* **tupelos 1** any of several gum trees of the southern US **2** the light strong wood of any of these trees [c18 from Creek *ito opilwa*, from *ito* tree + *opilwa* swamp]

Tupi (tuː'piː) *n* **1** (*pl* **Tupis** *or* **Tupi**) a member of a South American Indian people of Brazil and Paraguay **2** their language > **Tu'pian** *adj*

tupik ('tuːpək) *n Canad* a tent of seal or caribou skin used for shelter by the Inuit in summer [from Inuktitut]

tuple ('tjʊpᵊl, 'tʌpᵊl) *n computing* a row of values in a relational database

Tupolev (*Russian* tu'pəljif) *n* **Andrei Nikolaievich** (un'drjeɪ njɪkə'lɑjɪvjɪtʃ) 1888–1972, Soviet aircraft designer, who designed the first supersonic passenger aircraft, the TU-144 (tested 1969). He also designed supersonic bombers and the TU-104, one of the first passenger jet aircraft (1955)

tuppence ('tʌpəns) *n Brit* a variant spelling of **twopence** > '**tuppenny** *adj*

Tupperware ('tʌpəweə) *n trademark* a range of plastic containers used for storing food [c20 *Tupper*, US manufacturing company + WARE¹]

tupuna (tə 'puːnə) *n* a variant spelling of **tipuna**

Tupungato (*Spanish* tupuŋ'gato) *n* a mountain on the border between Argentina and Chile, in the Andes. Height: 6550 m (21 484 ft)

tuque (tuːk) *n Canad* **1** a knitted cap with a long tapering end **2** Also called: **toque** a close-fitting knitted hat often with a tassel or pompom [c19 from Canad F, from F: TOQUE]

turaco ('tʊərəˌkəʊ) *n, pl* **turacos** a variant spelling of **touraco**

turangawaewae (təˌrʌŋgə'weɪweɪ) *n NZ* the area that is a person's home [Maori, lit.: standing on one's feet]

Turanian (tjʊ'reɪnɪən) *n, adj* another name for **Ural-Altaic**

turban ('tɜːbᵊn) *n* **1** a man's headdress, worn esp by Muslims, Hindus, and Sikhs, made by swathing a length of linen, silk, etc, around the head or around a caplike base **2** a woman's brimless hat resembling this **3** any headdress resembling this [c16 from Turkish *tülbend*, from Persian *dulband*] > '**turbaned** *adj*

turbary ('tɜːbərɪ) *n, pl* **turbaries 1** land where peat or turf is cut **2** the legal right to cut peat for fuel on a common [c14 from OF *turbarie*, from Med. L *turbāria*, from *turba* peat]

turbellarian (ˌtɜːbɪ'lɛərɪən) *n* **1** any of a class of flatworms having a ciliated epidermis and a simple life cycle ▷ *adj* **2** of or belonging to this class of flatworms [c19 from NL *Turbellāria*, from L *turbellae* (pl) bustle, from *turba* brawl, referring to the swirling motion created in the water]

turbid ('tɜːbɪd) *adj* **1** muddy or opaque, as a liquid clouded with a suspension of particles **2** dense, thick, or cloudy: *turbid fog* **3** in turmoil or confusion [c17 from L *turbidus*, from *turbāre* to agitate, from *turba* crowd] > **tur'bidity** *or* '**turbidness** *n* > '**turbidly** *adv*

turbinate ('tɜːbɪnɪt, -ˌneɪt) *or* **turbinal** ('tɜːbɪnᵊl) *adj also* **turbinated 1** *anat* of any of the scroll-shaped bones on the walls of the nasal passages **2** shaped like a spiral or scroll **3** shaped like an inverted cone ▷ *n* **4** a turbinate bone **5** a turbinate shell [c17 from L *turbō* spinning top] > ˌ**turbi'nation** *n*

turbine ('tɜːbɪn, -baɪn) *n* any of various types of machine in which the kinetic energy of a moving fluid, as water, steam, air, etc, is converted into mechanical energy by causing a bladed rotor to rotate [c19 from F, from L *turbō* whirlwind, from *turbāre* to throw into confusion]

turbine blade *n* any of a number of bladelike vanes assembled around the periphery of a turbine rotor to guide the steam or gas flow

turbit ('tɜːbɪt) *n* a crested breed of domestic pigeon [c17 from L *turbō* spinning top, from the bird's shape]

turbo- *combining form* of, relating to, or driven by a turbine: *turbofan*

turbocharger ('tɜːbəʊˌtʃɑːdʒə) *n* a centrifugal compressor which boosts the intake pressure of an internal-combustion engine, driven by an exhaust-gas turbine fitted to the engine's exhaust manifold

turbofan (ˌtɜːbəʊ'fæn) *n* **1** a type of bypass engine in which a large fan driven by a turbine forces air rearwards around the exhaust gases in order to increase the propulsive thrust **2** an aircraft driven by turbofans **3** the fan in such an engine

turbogenerator (ˌtɜːbəʊ'dʒɛnəˌreɪtə) *n* an electrical generator driven by a steam turbine

turbojet (ˌtɜːbəʊ'dʒɛt) *n* **1** a turbojet engine **2** an aircraft powered by turbojet engines

turbojet engine *n* a gas turbine in which the exhaust gases provide the propulsive thrust to drive an aircraft

turboprop (ˌtɜːbəʊ'prɒp) *n* **1** an aircraft propulsion unit where a propeller is driven by a gas turbine **2** an aircraft powered by turboprops

turbosupercharger (ˌtɜːbəʊ'suːpəˌtʃɑːdʒə) *n obs* a supercharging device for an internal-combustion engine, consisting of a turbine driven by the exhaust gases

turbot ('tɜːbət) *n, pl* **turbot** *or* **turbots** **1** a European flatfish having a speckled scaleless body covered with tubercles. It is highly valued as a food fish **2** any of various similar or related fishes [c13 from OF *tourbot*, from Med. L *turbō*, from L: spinning top, from a fancied similarity in shape]

turbulence ('tɜːbjʊləns) *n* **1** a state or condition of confusion, movement, or agitation **2** *meteorol* local instability in the atmosphere, oceans, or rivers **3** turbulent flow in a liquid or gas

turbulent ('tɜːbjʊlənt) *adj* **1** being in a state of turbulence **2** wild or insubordinate; unruly [c16 from L *turbulentus*, from *turba* confusion] > **'turbulently** *adv*

turd (tɜːd) *n sl* **1** a piece of excrement **2** a contemptible person or thing [OE *tord*]

tureen (tə'riːn) *n* a large deep usually rounded dish with a cover, used for serving soups, stews, etc [c18 from F *terrine* earthenware vessel, from *terrin* made of earthenware, from Vulgar L *terrīnus* (unattested), from L *terra* earth]

turf (tɜːf) *n, pl* **turfs** *or* **turves** **1** the surface layer of fields and pastures, consisting of earth containing a dense growth of grasses with their roots; sod **2** a piece cut from this layer **3** **the turf** **3a** a track where horse races are run **3b** horse racing as a sport or industry **4** an area of knowledge or influence: *he's on home turf when it comes to music* **5** another word for **peat** ▷ *vb* **6** (*tr*) to cover with pieces of turf ▷ See also **turf out** [OE]

turf accountant *n Brit* a formal name for a **bookmaker**

turfman ('tɜːfmən) *n, pl* **turfmen** *chiefly US* a person devoted to horse racing

turf out *vb* (*tr, adv*) *Brit inf* to throw out or dismiss; eject

turf war *n inf* **1** a dispute between criminals or gangs over the right to operate within a particular area **2** any dispute in which parties contest influence or rights

Turgenev (*Russian* tur'gjenɪf) *n* **Ivan Sergeyevich** (i'van sɪr'gjejɪvitʃ) 1818–83, Russian novelist and dramatist. In *A Sportsman's Sketches* (1852) he pleaded for the abolition of serfdom. His novels, such as *Rudin* (1856) and *Fathers and Sons* (1862), are noted for their portrayal of country life and of the Russian intelligentsia. His plays include *A Month in the Country* (1850)

turgescent (tɜː'dʒɛsᵊnt) *adj* becoming or being swollen; inflated; tumid > **tur'gescence** *n*

turgid ('tɜːdʒɪd) *adj* **1** swollen and distended **2** (of language) pompous; bombastic [c17 from L *turgidus*, from *turgēre* to swell] > **tur'gidity** *or* **'turgidness** *n* > **'turgidly** *adv*

turgor ('tɜːgə) *n* the normal rigid state of a cell, caused by pressure of the cell contents against the cell wall [c19 from LL: a swelling, from L *turgēre* to swell]

Turin (tjʊə'rɪn) *n* a city in NW Italy, capital of Piedmont region, on the River Po: became capital of the Kingdom of Sardinia in 1720; first capital (1861–65) of united Italy; university (1405); a major industrial centre, producing most of Italy's cars. Pop: 903 703 (2000 est). Italian name: **Torino**

Turing ('tjʊərɪŋ) *n* **Alan Mathison** 1912–54, English mathematician, who was responsible for formal description of abstract automata, and speculation on computer imitation of humans: a leader of the Allied codebreakers at Bletchley Park during World War II

Turing machine *n* a hypothetical universal computing machine able to modify its original instructions by reading, erasing, or writing a new symbol on a moving tape that acts as its program [c20 after A. M. TURING]

turion ('tʊərɪən) *n* a scaly shoot produced by many aquatic plants: it detaches from the parent plant and remains dormant until the following spring [c17 from F *turion*, from L *turio* shoot]

Turishcheva (*Russian* tu'riʃtʃəvə) *n* **Ludmilla** (lʊd'mɪlə) born 1952, Soviet gymnast: world champion 1970, 1972 (at the Olympic Games), and 1974

Turk (tɜːk) *n* **1** a native, inhabitant, or citizen of Turkey **2** a native speaker of any Turkic language **3** *obs derog* a brutal or domineering person. See also **Young Turk**

Turk. *abbrev for* **1** Turkey **2** Turkish

Turkana (tɜː'kɑːnə) *n* **Lake** a long narrow lake in E Africa, in the Great Rift Valley. Area: 7104 sq km (2743 sq miles) Former name: (Lake) Rudolf

Turkestan *or* **Turkistan** (ˌtɜːkɪ'stɑːn) *n* an extensive region of central Asia between Siberia in the north and Tibet, India, Afghanistan, and Iran in the south: formerly divided into **West** (**Russian**) **Turkestan** (also called Soviet Central Asia), comprising present-day Turkmenistan, Uzbekistan, Tajikistan, and Kyrgyzstan and the S part of Kazakhstan, and **East** (**Chinese**) **Turkestan** consisting of the Xinjiang Uygur Autonomous Region > ˌ**Turke'stani** *adj, n*

turkey ('tɜːkɪ) *n, pl* **turkeys** *or* **turkey** **1** a large bird of North America, having a bare wattled head and neck and a brownish plumage. The male has a fan-shaped tail. A domesticated variety is bred for its flesh **2** *inf* something, esp a film or theatrical production, that fails **3** See **cold turkey** **4** **talk turkey** *sl, chiefly US & Canad* to discuss frankly and practically [c16 shortened from *Turkey cock* (*hen*), used at first to designate the African guinea fowl (apparently because the bird was brought through Turkish territory), later applied by mistake to the American bird]

Turkey ('tɜːkɪ) *n* a republic in W Asia and SE Europe, between the Black Sea, the Mediterranean, and the Aegean: one of the oldest inhabited regions of the world; the centre of the Ottoman Empire; became a republic in 1923. The major Asian part, consisting mainly of an arid plateau, is separated from European Turkey by the Bosporus, Sea of Marmara, and Dardanelles. Official language: Turkish; Kurdish and Arabic minority languages. Religion: Muslim majority. Currency: lira. Capital: Ankara. Pop: 66 229 000 (2001 est). Area: 780 576 sq km (301 380 sq miles)

▷ www.turkey.org

▷ www.turizm.gov.tr

Tt

turkey buzzard *or* **vulture** *n* a New World vulture having a naked red head
turkey cock *n* **1** a male turkey **2** an arrogant person
turkey nest *n Austral* a small earth dam adjacent to, and higher than, a larger earth dam, to feed water by gravity to a cattle trough, etc
Turkey red *n* **1a** a moderate or bright red colour **1b** (*as adj*): *a Turkey-red fabric* **2** a cotton fabric of a bright red colour
Turki ('tɜːkɪ) *adj* **1** of or relating to the Turkic languages **2** of or relating to speakers of these languages ▷ *n* **3** these languages collectively
Turkic ('tɜːkɪk) *n* a branch of the Altaic family of languages, including Turkish, Tatar, etc, members of which are found from Turkey to NE China, esp in Soviet central Asia
Turkish ('tɜːkɪʃ) *adj* **1** of Turkey, its people, or their language ▷ *n* **2** the official language of Turkey, belonging to the Turkic branch of the Altaic family >'**Turkishness** *n*
Turkish bath *n* **1** a type of bath in which the bather sweats freely in hot dry air, is then washed, often massaged, and has a cold plunge or shower **2** (*sometimes pl*) an establishment where such a bath is obtainable
Turkish coffee *n* very strong black coffee
Turkish delight *n* a jelly-like sweet flavoured with flower essences, usually cut into cubes and covered in icing sugar
Turkish towel *n* a rough loose-piled towel
Turkmenistan (ˌtɜːkmɛnɪ'stɑːn) *n* a republic in central Asia; the area has been occupied by a succession of empires; a Turkmen state was established in the 15th century but suffered almost continual civil strife and was gradually conquered by Russia; in 1918 it became a Soviet republic and gained independence from the Soviet Union in 1991: deserts including the **Kara Kum** cover most of the region; agricultural communities are concentrated around oases; there are rich mineral deposits. Official language: Turkmen. Religion: believers are mainly Muslim. Currency: manat. Capital: Ashkhabad. Pop: 5 462 000 (2001 est). Area: 488 100 sq km (186 400 sq miles)
▷ www.turkmenistanembassy.org
Turks and Caicos Islands *pl n* a UK Overseas Territory in the Caribbean, southeast of the Bahamas: consists of the eight **Turks Islands**, separated by the Turks Island Passage from the Caicos group, which has six main islands. Capital: Grand Turk. Pop: 23 000 (1999 est) Area: 430 sq km (166 sq miles)
Turk's-cap lily *n* any of several cultivated lilies that have brightly coloured flowers with reflexed petals
Turk's-head *n* an ornamental turban-like knot
Turku (*Finnish* 'turku) *n* a city and port in SW Finland, on the Gulf of Bothnia: capital of Finland until 1812. Pop: 166 929 (1997 est). Swedish name: **Åbo**
turmeric ('tɜːmərɪk) *n* **1** a tropical Asian plant, *Curcuma longa*, having yellow flowers and an aromatic underground stem **2** the powdered stem of this plant, used as a condiment and as a yellow dye [C16 from OF *terre merite*, from Med. L *terra merita*, lit.: meritorious earth, name applied for obscure reasons to curcuma]
turmeric paper *n chem* paper impregnated with turmeric used as a test for alkalis and for boric acid
turmoil ('tɜːmɔɪl) *n* violent or confused movement; agitation; tumult [C16 ?from TURN + MOIL]
turn (tɜːn) *vb* **1** to move around an axis: *to turn a knob* **2** (sometimes foll by *round*) to change or cause to change positions by moving through an arc of a circle: *he turned the chair to face the light* **3** to change or cause to change in course, direction, etc **4** to go or pass to the other side of (a corner, etc) **5** to assume or cause to assume a rounded, curved, or folded form: *the road turns here* **6** to reverse or cause to reverse position **7** (*tr*) to perform or do by a rotating movement: *to turn a somersault* **8** (*tr*) to shape or cut a thread in (a workpiece) by rotating it on a lathe against a cutting tool **9** (when *intr*, foll by *into* or *to*) to change or convert or be changed or converted **10** (foll by *into*) to change or cause to change in nature, character, etc: *the frog turned into a prince* **11** (*copula*) to change so as to become: *he turned nasty* **12** to cause (foliage, etc) to change colour or (of foliage, etc) to change colour **13** to cause (milk, etc) to become rancid or sour or (of milk, etc) to become rancid or sour **14** to change or cause to change in subject, trend, etc: *the conversation turned to fishing* **15** to direct or apply or be directed or applied: *he turned his attention to the problem* **16** (*intr*; usually foll by *to*) to appeal or apply (to) for help, advice, etc **17** to reach, pass, or progress beyond in age, time, etc: *she has just turned twenty* **18** (*tr*) to cause or allow to go: *to turn an animal loose* **19** to affect or be affected with nausea **20** to affect or be affected with giddiness: *my head is turning* **21** (*tr*) to affect the mental or emotional stability of (esp in **turn (someone's) head**) **22** (*tr*) to release from a container **23** (*tr*) to render into another language **24** (usually foll by *against* or *from*) to transfer or reverse (one's loyalties, affections, etc) **25** (*tr*) to cause (an enemy agent) to become a double agent working for one's own side **26** (*tr*) to bring (soil) from lower layers to the surface **27** to blunt (an edge) or (of an edge) to become blunted **28** (*tr*) to give a graceful form to: *to turn a compliment* **29** (*tr*) to reverse (a cuff, collar, etc) **30** (*intr*) *US* to be merchandised as specified: *shirts are turning well this week* **31** *cricket* to spin (the ball) or (of the ball) to spin **32** **turn a trick** *sl* (of a prostitute) to gain a customer **33** **turn one's hand to** to undertake (something practical) ▷ *n* **34** a turning or being turned **35** a movement of complete or partial rotation **36** a change of direction or position **37** direction or drift: *his thoughts took a new turn* **38** a deviation from a course or tendency **39** the place, point, or time at which a deviation or change occurs **40** another word for **turning** (sense 1) **41** the right or opportunity to do something in an agreed order or succession: *now it's George's turn* **42** a change in nature, condition, etc: *his illness took a turn for the worse* **43** a period of action, work, etc **44** a short walk, ride, or excursion **45** natural inclination: *a speculative turn of mind* **46** distinctive form or style: *a neat turn of phrase* **47** requirement, need, or advantage: *to serve someone's turn* **48** a deed that helps or hinders someone **49** a twist, bend, or distortion in shape **50** *music* a melodic ornament that makes a turn around a note, beginning with the note above, in a variety of sequences **51** a short theatrical act **52** *stock exchange, Brit* the difference between a market maker's bid and offer prices, representing the market maker's profit **53** *inf* a shock or surprise **54** **by turns** one after another; alternately **55** **turn and turn about** one after another; alternately **56** **to a turn** to the proper amount; perfectly ▷ See also **turn down, turn in,** etc [OE *tyrnian*, from OF *torner*, from L *tornāre* to turn in a lathe, from *tornus* lathe, from Gk *tornos* dividers] > '**turner** *n*
turnabout ('tɜːnəˌbaʊt) *n* **1** the act of turning so as to face a different direction **2** a change or reversal of opinion, attitude, etc
turnaround ('tɜːnəˌraʊnd) *n* **1a** the act or process in which a ship, aircraft, etc, unloads at the end of a trip and reloads for the next trip **1b** the time taken for this **2** the total time taken by a vehicle in a round trip **3** a complete reversal of a situation
turnbuckle ('tɜːnˌbʌkᵊl) *n* an open mechanical sleeve usually having a swivel at one end and a thread at the other to enable a threaded wire or rope to be tightened
turncoat ('tɜːnˌkəʊt) *n* a person who deserts one cause or party for the opposite faction
turncock ('tɜːnˌkɒk) *n* (formerly) an official employed to turn on the water for the mains supply

turn down *vb (tr, adv)* **1** to reduce (the volume or brightness) of (something) **2** to reject or refuse **3** to fold down (a collar, sheets, etc) ▷ *adj* **turndown 4** *(prenominal)* designed to be folded down

Turner ('tɜːnə) *n* **1 J(oseph) M(allord) W(illiam)** 1775–1851, British landscape painter; a master of water colours. He sought to convey atmosphere by means of an innovative use of colour and gradations of light **2 Nat** 1800–31, US rebel slave, who led (1831) Turner's Insurrection, the only major slave revolt in US history: executed **3 Robert Edward III,** known as *Ted.* born 1938, US broadcasting executive and yachtsman; chairman of Turner Broadcasting (1970–96), founder of Cable News Network (1980), and vice-chairman of Time Warner from 1996 **4 Tina,** real name *Annie Mae Bullock* born 1940 US rock singer who performed (1958–75) with her then husband Ike Turner (born 1931) and later as a solo act. Her recordings include "River Deep, Mountain High" (1966) and "Simply the Best" (1991)

turn in *vb (adv) inf* **1** *(intr)* to go to bed for the night **2** *(tr)* to hand in; deliver **3** *(tr)* to give up or conclude (something) **4** *(tr)* to record (a score, etc) **5 turn in on oneself** to become preoccupied with one's own problems

turning ('tɜːnɪŋ) *n* **1** a road, river, or path that turns off the main way **2** the point where such a way turns off **3** a bend in a straight course **4** an object made on a lathe **5** the process or skill of turning objects on a lathe **6** *(pl)* the waste produced in turning on a lathe

turning circle *n* the smallest circle in which a vehicle can turn

turning point *n* **1** a moment when the course of events is changed **2** a point at which there is a change in direction or motion

turnip ('tɜːnɪp) *n* **1** a widely cultivated plant of the cabbage family with a large yellow or white edible root **2** the root of this plant, which is eaten as a vegetable [C16 from earlier *turnepe,* ?from TURN (indicating its rounded shape) + *nepe,* from L *nāpus* turnip]

turnkey ('tɜːnˌkiː) *n* **1** *arch* a keeper of the keys, esp in a prison; warder or jailer ▷ *adj* **2** denoting a project, as in civil engineering, in which a single contractor has responsibility for the complete job from the start to the time of installation or occupancy

turn off *vb* **1** *(intr)* to leave (a road, etc) **2** *(intr)* (of a road, etc) to deviate from (another road, etc) **3** *(tr, adv)* to cause (something) to cease operating by turning a knob, pushing a button, etc **4** *(tr) inf* to cause (a person, etc) to feel dislike or distaste for (something): *this music turns me off* **5** *(tr, adv) Brit inf* to dismiss from employment ▷ *n* **turn-off 6** a road or other way branching off from the main thoroughfare **7** *inf* a person or thing that elicits dislike or distaste

turn on *vb* **1** *(tr, adv)* to cause (something) to operate by turning a knob, etc **2** *(intr, prep)* to depend or hinge on: *the success of the party turns on you* **3** *(prep)* to become hostile or to retaliate: *the dog turned on the children* **4** *(tr, adv) inf* to produce (charm, tears, etc) suddenly or automatically **5** *(tr, adv) sl* to arouse emotionally or sexually **6** *(intr, adv) sl* to take or become intoxicated by drugs **7** *(tr, adv) sl* to introduce (someone) to drugs ▷ *n* **turn-on 8** *sl* a person or thing that causes emotional or sexual arousal

turn out *vb (adv)* **1** *(tr)* to cause (something, esp a light) to cease operating by or as if by turning a knob, etc **2** *(tr)* to produce by an effort or process **3** *(tr)* to dismiss, discharge, or expel **4** *(tr)* to empty the contents of, esp in order to clean, tidy, or rearrange **5** *(copula)* to prove to be as specified **6** to end up; result: *it all turned out well* **7** *(tr)* to fit as with clothes: *that woman turns her children out well* **8** *(intr)* to assemble or gather **9** (of a soldier) to parade or to call (a soldier) to parade **10** *(intr) inf* to get out of bed **11** *(intr; foll by for) inf* to make an appearance, esp in a sporting competition: *he was asked to turn out for Liverpool* ▷ *n* **turnout 12** the body of people appearing together at a gathering **13** the quantity or amount produced **14** an array of clothing or equipment

turn over *vb (adv)* **1** to change or cause to change position, esp so as to reverse top and bottom **2** to start (an engine), esp with a starting handle, or (of an engine) to start or function correctly **3** to shift or cause to shift position, as by rolling from side to side **4** *(tr)* to deliver; transfer **5** *(tr)* to consider carefully **6** *(tr)* **6a** to sell and replenish (stock in trade) **6b** to transact business and so generate gross revenue of (a specified sum) **7** *(tr)* to invest and recover (capital) **8** *(tr) sl* to rob ▷ *n* **turnover 9a** the amount of business transacted during a specified period **9b** *(as modifier)*: *a turnover tax* **10** the rate at which stock in trade is sold and replenished **11** a change or reversal of position **12** a small pastry case filled with fruit, jam, etc **13a** the number of workers employed by a firm in a given period to replace those who have left **13b** the ratio between this number and the average number of employees during the same period **14** *banking* the amount of capital funds loaned on call during a specified period ▷ *adj* **turnover 15** *(prenominal)* designed to be turned over

turnpike ('tɜːnˌpaɪk) *n* **1** *history* **1a** a barrier set across a road to prevent passage until a toll had been paid **1b** a road on which a turnpike was operated **2** an obsolete word for **turnstile 3** *US* a motorway for use of which a toll is charged [C15 from TURN + PIKE[2]]

turnround ('tɜːnˌraʊnd) *n* another word for **turnaround**

turnspit ('tɜːnˌspɪt) *n* **1** (formerly) a servant or small dog whose job was to turn a spit **2** a spit that can be so turned

turnstile ('tɜːnˌstaɪl) *n* a mechanical barrier with arms that are turned to admit one person at a time

turnstone ('tɜːnˌstəʊn) *n* a shore bird, related to the plovers and sandpipers, that lifts up stones in search of food

turntable ('tɜːnˌteɪbᵊl) *n* **1** the circular platform that rotates a gramophone record while it is being played **2** a circular platform used for turning locomotives and cars **3** the revolvable platform on a microscope on which specimens are examined

turntable ladder *n Brit* a power-operated extending ladder mounted on a fire engine. US and Canad name: **aerial ladder**

turn to *vb (intr, adv)* to set about a task

turn up *vb (adv)* **1** *(intr)* to arrive or appear **2** to find or be found, esp by accident **3** *(tr)* to increase the flow, volume, etc, of ▷ *n* **turn-up 4** *(often pl) Brit* the turned-up fold at the bottom of some trouser legs. US, Canad and Austral name: **cuff 5** *inf* an unexpected or chance occurrence

turpentine ('tɜːpᵊnˌtaɪn) *n* **1** Also called: **gum turpentine** any of various oleoresins obtained from various coniferous trees and used as the main source of commercial turpentine **2** a sticky oleoresin that exudes from the terebinth tree **3** Also called: **oil of turpentine, spirits of turpentine** a colourless volatile oil distilled from turpentine oleoresin. It is used as a solvent for paints and in medicine **4** Also called: **turpentine substitute, white spirit** *(not in technical usage)* any one of a number of thinners for paints and varnishes, consisting of fractions of petroleum. Related adj: **terebinthine** ▷ *vb* **turpentines, turpentining, turpentined** *(tr)* **5** to treat or saturate with turpentine [C14 *terebentyne,* from Med. L, from L *terebinthīna* turpentine, from *terebinthus* the turpentine tree]

turpentine tree *n* **1** a tropical African tree yielding a hard dark wood and a useful resin **2** either of two Australian evergreen trees that yield resin

turpeth ('tɜːpɪθ) *n* **1** an East Indian plant having roots with purgative properties **2** the root of this plant or the

Tt

drug obtained from it [c14 from Med. L *turbithum*, ult. from Ar. *turbid*]

Turpin ('tɜːpɪn) *n* **Dick** 1706–39, English highwayman

turpitude ('tɜːpɪˌtjuːd) *n* base character or action; depravity [c15 from L *turpitūdō* ugliness, from *turpis* base]

turps (tɜːps) *n* (*functioning as sing*) *Brit* short for **turpentine** (sense 3)

turquoise ('tɜːkwɔɪz, -kwɑːz) *n* **1** a greenish-blue fine-grained mineral consisting of hydrated copper aluminium phosphate. It is used as a gemstone **2a** the colour of turquoise **2b** (*as adj*): *a turquoise dress* [c14 from OF *turqueise* Turkish (stone)]

turret ('tʌrɪt) *n* **1** a small tower that projects from the wall of a building, esp a castle **2a** a self-contained structure, capable of rotation, in which weapons are mounted, esp in tanks and warships **2b** a similar structure on an aircraft **3** (on a machine tool) a turret-like steel structure with tools projecting radially that can be indexed round to bring each tool to bear on the work [c14 from OF *torete*, from *tor* tower, from L *turris*] > '**turreted** *adj*

turret lathe *n* another name for **capstan lathe**

turtle[1] ('tɜːtᵊl) *n* **1** any of various aquatic reptiles, esp those having a flattened shell enclosing the body and flipper-like limbs adapted for swimming **2 turn turtle** to capsize [c17 from F *tortue* TORTOISE (infl. by TURTLE[2])]

turtle[2] ('tɜːtᵊl) *n* an archaic name for **turtledove** [OE *turtla*, from L *turtur*, imit.]

turtleback ('tɜːtᵊlˌbæk) *n* an arched projection over the upper deck of a ship for protection in heavy seas

turtledove ('tɜːtᵊlˌdʌv) *n* **1** any of several Old World doves having a brown plumage with speckled wings and a long dark tail **2** a gentle or loving person [see TURTLE[2]]

turtleneck ('tɜːtᵊlˌnɛk) *n* a round high close-fitting neck on a sweater or the sweater itself

turves (tɜːvz) *n* a plural of **turf**

Tuscan ('tʌskən) *adj* **1** of or relating to Tuscany, its inhabitants, or their dialect of Italian **2** of or denoting one of the five classical orders of architecture: characterized by a column with an unfluted shaft and a capital and base with mouldings but no decoration ▷ *n* **3** a native or inhabitant of Tuscany **4** any of the dialects of Italian spoken in Tuscany

▷ http://ah.bfn.org/a/DCTNRY/t/tuscan.html

Tuscany ('tʌskənɪ) *n* a region of central Italy, on the Ligurian and Tyrrhenian Seas: corresponds roughly to ancient Etruria; a region of numerous small states in medieval times; united in the 15th and 16th centuries under Florence; united with the rest of Italy in 1861. Capital: Florence. Pop: 3 536 392 (2000 est). Area: 22 990 sq km (8876 sq miles). Italian name: **Toscana**

tusche (tʊʃ) *n* a substance used in lithography for drawing the design and as a resist in silk-screen printing and lithography [from G, from *tuschen* to touch up with colour, from F *toucher* to touch]

Tusculum ('tʌskjʊləm) *n* an ancient city in Latium near Rome

tush (tʌʃ) *interj arch* an exclamation of disapproval or contempt [c15 imit.]

tusk (tʌsk) *n* **1** a pointed elongated usually paired tooth in the elephant, walrus, and certain other mammals **2** a tusklike tooth or part **3** a sharp pointed projection ▷ *vb* **4** to stab, tear, or gore with the tusks [OE *tūsc*] > **tusked** *adj*

tusker ('tʌskə) *n* any animal with long tusks

tusk shell *n* any of various burrowing seashore molluscs that have a long narrow tubular shell open at both ends

Tussaud (*French* tyso) *n* **Marie** (mari) 1760–1850, Swiss modeller in wax, who founded a permanent exhibition in London of historical and contemporary figures

tussis ('tʌsɪs) *n* the technical name for a **cough**. See **pertussis** [L: cough] > '**tussive** *adj*

tussle ('tʌsᵊl) *vb* **tussles, tussling, tussled** **1** (*intr*) to fight or wrestle in a vigorous way ▷ *n* **2** a vigorous fight; scuffle; struggle [c15]

tussock ('tʌsək) *n* **1** a dense tuft of vegetation, esp of grass **2** *Austral & NZ* **2a** short for **tussock grass** **2b** the country where tussock grass grows [c16 from ?] > '**tussocky** *adj*

tussock grass *n* any of several pasture grasses

tussore (tʊ'sɔː, 'tʌsə), **tusser** ('tʌsə), *or* (*chiefly US*) **tussah** ('tʌsə) *n* **1** Also called: **wild silk** a coarse silk obtained from an oriental silkworm **2** the silkworm producing this [c17 from Hindi *tasar* shuttle, from Sansk. *tasara* a wild silkworm]

tut (tʌt) *interj, n, vb* **tuts, tutting, tutted** short for **tut-tut**

Tutankhamen (ˌtuːtən'kɑːmɛn, -mən) *or* **Tutankhamun** (ˌtuːtənkɑː'muːn) *n* king (1361–1352 BC) of the 18th dynasty of Egypt. His tomb near Luxor, discovered in 1922, contained many material objects

tutelage ('tjuːtɪlɪdʒ) *n* **1** the act or office of a guardian or tutor **2** instruction or guidance, esp by a tutor **3** the condition of being under the supervision of a guardian or tutor [c17 from L *tūtēla* a caring for, from *tuērī* to watch over]

tutelary ('tjuːtɪlərɪ) *or* **tutelar** ('tjuːtɪlə) *adj* **1** invested with the role of guardian or protector **2** of or relating to a guardian ▷ *n, pl* **tutelaries** *or* **tutelars** **3** a tutelary person, deity, etc

tutor ('tjuːtə) *n* **1** a teacher, usually instructing individual pupils **2** (at universities, colleges, etc) a member of staff responsible for the teaching and supervision of a certain number of students ▷ *vb* **3** to act as a tutor to (someone) **4** (*tr*) to act as guardian to [c14 from L: a watcher, from *tuērī* to watch over] > '**tutorage** *or* '**tutorship** *n*

tutorial (tjuː'tɔːrɪəl) *n* **1** a period of intensive tuition given by a tutor to an individual student or to a small group of students ▷ *adj* **2** of or relating to a tutor

tutsan ('tʌtsən) *n* a woodland shrub of Europe and W Asia, having yellow flowers and reddish-purple fruits [c15 from OF *toute-saine* (unattested), lit.: all healthy]

tutti ('tʊtɪ) *adj, adv music* to be performed by the whole orchestra, choir, etc [c18 from It., pl of *tutto* all, from L *tōtus*]

tutti-frutti ('tuːtɪ'fruːtɪ) *n* **1** (*pl* **tutti-fruttis**) an ice cream or a confection containing small pieces of candied or fresh fruits **2** a preserve of chopped mixed fruits **3** a flavour like that of many fruits combined [from It., lit.: all the fruits]

tut-tut ('tʌt'tʌt) *interj* **1** an exclamation of mild reprimand, disapproval, or surprise ▷ *vb* **tut-tuts, tut-tutting, tut-tutted** **2** (*intr*) to express disapproval by the exclamation of "tut-tut" ▷ *n* **3** the act of tut-tutting

tutty ('tʌtɪ) *n* impure zinc oxide used as a polishing powder [c14 from OF *tutie*, from Ar. *tūtiyā*, prob. from Persian, from Sansk. *tuttha*]

tutu ('tuːtuː) *n* a very short skirt worn by ballerinas, made of projecting layers of stiffened material [from F, changed from the nursery word *cucu* backside, from L *cūlus* the buttocks]

Tutu ('tuːtuː) *n* **Desmond** born 1931, South African clergyman, noted for his opposition to apartheid: Anglican Bishop of Johannesburg (1984–86) and Archbishop of Cape Town (1986–96); chairman of South Africa's Truth and Reconciliation Commission (1995–99). Nobel peace prize 1984

Tutuila (ˌtuːtuː'iːlə) *n* the largest island of American Samoa, in the SW Pacific. Chief town and port: Pago Pago. Pop: 54 108 (2000). Area: 135 sq km (52 sq miles)

Tutuola ('tuːtuːˌəʊlə) *n* **Amos** 1920–97, Nigerian writer: his books include *The Palm-Wine Drinkard* (1952) and *Pauper, Brawler and Slanderer* (1987)

Tuvalu (ˌtuːvə'luː) *n* a country in the SW Pacific, comprising a group of nine coral islands: established as

a British protectorate in 1892. From 1915 until 1975 the islands formed part of the British colony of the Gilbert and Ellice Islands; achieved full independence in 1978; a special member of the Commonwealth (not represented at meetings of Commonwealth heads of state). Languages: English and Tuvaluan. Religion: Christian majority. Currency: Australian dollar; Tuvalu dollars are also used. Capital: Funafuti. Pop: 11 000 (2001 est). Area: 26 sq km (10 sq miles). Former names: **Lagoon Islands, Ellice Islands** > ˌ**Tuva'luan** *adj, n*
▷ www.pacific-travel-guides.com/tuvalu/index.html
▷ www.southpacific.org/text/tuvalu.html

Tuva Republic ('tu:və) *n* a constituent republic of S Russia: mountainous. Capital: Kizyl. Pop: 311 000 (2000 est). Area: 170 500 sq km (65 800 sq miles). Also called: **Tuvinian Autonomous Republic**

tu-whit tu-whoo (tə'wɪt tə'wu:) *interj* an imitation of the sound made by an owl

tuxedo (tʌk'si:dəʊ) *n, pl* **tuxedos** the usual US and Canad name for **dinner jacket** [C19 after a country club in *Tuxedo Park*, New York]

Tuxtla Gutiérrez (*Spanish* 'tustla gu'tjɛrrɛθ) *n* a city in SE Mexico, capital of Chiapas state: agricultural centre. Pop: 425 000 (2000 est)

tuyère ('twi:ɛə, 'twaɪə) *or* **twyer** ('twaɪə) *n* a water-cooled nozzle through which air is blown into a cupola, blast furnace, or forge [C18 from F, from *tuyau* pipe, from OF *tuel*, prob. of Gmc origin]

TV *abbrev for* television

TVEI (in Britain) *abbrev for* technical and vocational educational initiative: a national educational scheme in which pupils gain practical experience in technology and industry often through work placement

Tver (*Russian* tvjerj) *n* a city in central Russia, at the confluence of the Volga and Tversta Rivers: chief port of the upper Volga, linked by canal with Moscow. Pop: 457 100 (1999 est). Former name (1932–91): **Kalinin**

TVM *abbrev for* television movie: a film made specifically for television and not intended for release in cinemas

TVNZ *abbrev for* Television New Zealand

TVP *abbrev for* textured vegetable protein: protein from soya beans or other vegetables spun into fibres and flavoured: used esp as a substitute for meat

TVR *abbrev for* television rating: a measurement of the popularity of a TV programme based on a survey

TVRO *abbrev for* television receive only: an antenna and associated apparatus for reception from a broadcasting satellite

twaddle ('twɒdᵊl) *n* **1** silly, trivial, or pretentious talk or writing ▷ *vb* **twaddles, twaddling, twaddled 2** (*intr*) to talk or write in a silly or pretentious way [C16 *twattle*, var. of *twittle* or *tittle*] > '**twaddler** *n*

twain (tweɪn) *determiner, n* an archaic word for **two** [OE *twēgen*]

Twain (tweɪn) *n* **1 Mark**, pen name of *Samuel Langhorne Clemens*. 1835–1910, US novelist and humorist, famous for his classics *The Adventures of Tom Sawyer* (1876) and *The Adventures of Huckleberry Finn* (1885) **2 Shania** (ʃə'naɪə), real name *Eilleen Regina Edwards*. born 1965, Canadian country-rock singer; her bestselling recordings include *The Woman In Me* (1995) *Come On Over* (1997), and *UP!* (2002)

twang (twæŋ) *n* **1** a sharp ringing sound produced by or as if by the plucking of a taut string **2** the act of plucking a string to produce such a sound **3** a strongly nasal quality in a person's speech ▷ *vb* **4** to make or cause to make a twang **5** to strum (music, a tune, etc) **6** to speak with a nasal voice **7** (*intr*) to be released or move with a twang: *the arrow twanged away* [C16 imit.] > '**twangy** *adj*

'twas (twɒz; *unstressed* twəz) *poetic or dialect contraction of* it was

twat (twæt, twɒt) *n taboo sl* **1** the female genitals **2** a foolish person [from ?]

twayblade ('tweɪˌbleɪd) *n* **1** any of various orchids having a basal pair of unstalked leaves arranged opposite each other **2** any of various other orchids with paired basal leaves [C16 translation of Med. L *bifolium* having two leaves, from obs. *tway* two + BLADE]

tweak (twi:k) *vb* (*tr*) **1** to twist or pinch with a sharp or sudden movement **2** *inf* to make a minor alteration ▷ *n* **3** a tweaking **4** *inf* a minor alteration [OE *twiccian*]

twee (twi:) *adj Brit inf* excessively sentimental, sweet, or pretty [C19 from *tweet*, mincing or affected pronunciation of *sweet*] > '**tweely** *adv*

tweed (twi:d) *n* **1** a thick woollen cloth produced originally in Scotland **2** (*pl*) clothes made of this **3** (*pl*) *Austral inf* trousers [C19 prob. from *tweel*, Scot var. of TWILL, infl. by TWEED]
▷ www.harristweed.org/fabric_hist.htm
▷ www.irishcultureandcustoms.com/AEmblem/Tweed.html

Tweed (twi:d) *n* a river in SE Scotland and NE England, flowing east and forming part of the border between Scotland and England, then crossing into England to enter the North Sea at Berwick. Length: 156 km (97 miles)

Tweeddale ('twi:dˌdeɪl) *n* another name for **Peeblesshire**

Tweedledum and Tweedledee (ˌtwi:dᵊl'dʌm; ˌtwi:dᵊl'di:) *n* any two persons or things that differ only slightly from each other; two of a kind [C19 from the proverbial names of HANDEL and the rival musician Buononcini. The names were popularized by Lewis Carroll's use of them in *Through the Looking Glass* (1872)]

Tweedsmuir ('twi:dzmjʊə) *n* **Baron** title of (John) **Buchan**

tweedy ('twi:dɪ) *adj* **tweedier, tweediest 1** of, made of, or resembling tweed **2** showing a fondness for a hearty outdoor life, usually associated with wearers of tweeds

'tween (twi:n) *poetic or dialect contraction of* between

'tween deck *or* **decks** *n naut* a space between two continuous decks of a vessel

tweet (twi:t) *interj* **1** an imitation of the thin chirping sound made by small birds ▷ *vb* **2** (*intr*) to make this sound [C19 imit.]

tweeter ('twi:tə) *n* a loudspeaker used in high-fidelity systems for the reproduction of high audio frequencies. It is usually employed in conjunction with a woofer [C20 from TWEET]

tweezers ('twi:zəz) *pl n* a small pincer-like instrument for handling small objects, plucking out hairs, etc. Also called: **pair of tweezers, tweezer** (esp US) [C17 pl of *tweezer* (on the model of *scissors*, etc), from *tweeze* case of instruments, from F *étuis*, from OF *estuier* to preserve, ult. from L *studēre* to care about]

Twelfth Day *n* Jan 6, the twelfth day after Christmas and the feast of the Epiphany

twelfth man *n* a reserve player in a cricket team

Twelfth Night *n* **a** the evening of Jan 5, the eve of Twelfth Day **b** the evening of Twelfth Day itself

twelve (twɛlv) *n* **1** the cardinal number that is the sum of ten and two **2** a numeral, 12, XII, etc, representing this number **3** something representing or consisting of 12 units **4** Also called: **twelve o'clock** noon or midnight ▷ *determiner* **5a** amounting to twelve **5b** (*as pronoun*): *twelve have arrived.* Related adj: **duodecimal** [OE *twelf*] > **twelfth** *adj, n*

twelve-inch *n* a gramophone record 12 inches in diameter and played at 45 revolutions per minute, usually containing an extended remix of a single

twelvemo ('twɛlvməʊ) *n, pl* **twelvemos** *bookbinding* another word for **duodecimo**

twelvemonth ('twɛlvˌmʌnθ) *n chiefly Brit* an archaic or dialect word for a **year**

twelve-tone *adj* of or denoting the type of serial music

Tt

which uses as musical material a tone row formed by the 12 semitones of the chromatic scale. See **serialism**

twenty ('twɛntɪ) *n, pl* **twenties** **1** the cardinal number that is the product of ten and two **2** a numeral, 20, XX, etc, representing this number **3** something representing or consisting of 20 units ▷ *determiner* **4a** amounting to twenty: *twenty questions* **4b** *(as pronoun): to order twenty* > '**twentieth** *adj, n* [OE *twēntig*]

twenty-four-seven *adv, often written* **24/7** *inf* twenty-four hours a day, seven days a week; constantly; all the time: *consultants would no longer be available 24/7*

twenty-six counties *pl n* the counties of the Republic of Ireland

twenty-sixer *n Canad inf* a liquor bottle of around 26 ounces (0.750 litre) capacity

twenty-twenty *adj med* (of vision) being of normal acuity: usually written 20/20

'twere (twɜː; *unstressed* twə) *poetic or dialect contraction of* it were

twerp *or* **twirp** (twɜːp) *n inf* a silly, weak-minded, or contemptible person [C20 from ?]

twibill *or* **twibil** ('twaɪˌbɪl) *n* **1** a mattock with a blade shaped like an adze at one end and like an axe at the other **2** *arch* a double-bladed battle-axe [OE, from *twi-* double + *bill* sword]

twice (twaɪs) *adv* **1** two times; on two occasions or in two cases **2** double in degree or quantity: *twice as long* [OE *twiwa*]

Twickenham ('twɪkənəm) *n* a former town in SE England, on the River Thames: part of the Greater London borough of Richmond-upon-Thames since 1965; contains the English Rugby Football Union ground

twiddle ('twɪdᵊl) *vb* **twiddles, twiddling, twiddled** **1** (when *intr*, often foll by *with*) to twirl or fiddle (with), often in an idle way **2** **twiddle one's thumbs** to do nothing; be unoccupied **3** *(intr)* to turn, twirl, or rotate **4** *(intr) rare* to be occupied with trifles ▷ *n* **5** an act or instance of twiddling [C16 prob. a blend of TWIRL + FIDDLE] > '**twiddler** *n*

twig[1] (twɪg) *n* **1** any small branch or shoot of a tree **2** something resembling this, esp a minute branch of a blood vessel [OE *twigge*] > '**twiggy** *adj*

twig[2] (twɪg) *vb* **twigs, twigging, twigged** *Brit inf* **1** to understand (something) **2** to find out or suddenly comprehend (something): *he hasn't twigged yet* [C18 ?from Scot Gaelic *tuig* I understand]

twilight ('twaɪˌlaɪt) *n* **1** the soft diffused light occurring when the sun is just below the horizon, esp following sunset **2** the period in which this light occurs **3** any faint light **4** a period in which strength, importance, etc, are waning **5** *(modifier)* **5a** of or relating to the period towards the end of the day: *the twilight shift* **5b** of or relating to the final phase of a particular era: *the twilight days of the Bush presidency* **5c** denoting irregularity and obscurity: *a twilight existence* [C15 lit.: half light (between day and night), from OE *twi-* half + LIGHT[1]] > **twilit** ('twaɪˌlɪt) *adj*

Twilight of the Gods *n* another term for **Götterdämmerung**

twilight sleep *n med* a state of partial anaesthesia in which the patient retains a slight degree of consciousness

twilight zone *n* **1** any indefinite or transitional condition or area **2** an inner-city area where houses have become dilapidated

twill (twɪl) *adj* **1** (in textiles) of a weave in which the yarns are worked to produce an effect of parallel diagonal lines or ribs ▷ *n* **2** any fabric so woven ▷ *vb* **3** *(tr)* to weave in this fashion [OE *twilic* having a double thread]

'twill (twɪl) *poetic or dialect contraction of* it will

twin (twɪn) *n* **1a** either of two persons or animals conceived at the same time **1b** *(as modifier): a twin brother.* See also **identical** (sense 3), **fraternal** (sense 3) **2a** either of two persons or things that are identical or very similar **2b** *(as modifier): twin carburettors* **3** Also called: **macle** a crystal consisting of two parts each of which has a definite orientation to the other ▷ *vb* **twins, twinning, twinned** **4** to pair or be paired together; couple **5** *(intr)* to bear twins **6** *(intr)* (of a crystal) to form into a twin **7a** *(tr)* to create a reciprocal relation between (two towns in different countries); pair (a town) with another in a different country **7b** *(intr)* (of a town) to be paired in a town in a different country [OE *twinn*] > '**twinning** *n*

twin bed *n* one of a pair of matching single beds

twine (twaɪn) *n* **1** string made by twisting together fibres of hemp, cotton, etc **2** a twining **3** something produced or characterized by twining **4** a twist, coil, or convolution **5** a knot or tangle ▷ *vb* **twines, twining, twined** **6** *(tr)* to twist together; interweave **7** *(tr)* to form by or as if by twining **8** (when *intr*, often foll by *around*) to wind or cause to wind, esp in spirals [OE *twīn*] > '**twiner** *n*

twin-engined *adj* (of an aeroplane) having two engines

twinge (twɪndʒ) *n* **1** a sudden brief darting or stabbing pain **2** a sharp emotional pang ▷ *vb* **twinges, twinging, twinged** **3** to have or cause to have a twinge [OE *twengan* to pinch]

twinkle ('twɪŋkᵊl) *vb* **twinkles, twinkling, twinkled** *(mainly intr)* **1** to emit or reflect light in a flickering manner; shine brightly and intermittently; sparkle **2** (of the eyes) to sparkle, esp with amusement or delight **3** *rare* to move about quickly ▷ *n* **4** a flickering brightness; sparkle **5** an instant [OE *twinclian*] > '**twinkler** *n* > '**twinkly** *adj*

twinkling ('twɪŋklɪŋ) *or* **twink** (twɪŋk) *n* a very short time; instant; moment. Also called: **twinkling of an eye**

Twins (twɪnz) *pl n* **the** the constellation Gemini, the third sign of the zodiac

twin-screw *adj* (of a vessel) having two propellers

twinset ('twɪnˌsɛt) *n Brit* a matching jumper and cardigan

twin town *n* a town that has civic associations, such as reciprocal visits and cultural exchanges, with a foreign town

twin-tub *n* a type of washing machine that has two revolving drums, one for washing and the other for spin-drying

twirl (twɜːl) *vb* **1** to move around rapidly and repeatedly in a circle **2** *(tr)* to twist, wind, or twiddle, often idly: *she twirled her hair around her finger* **3** *(intr; often foll by around or about)* to turn suddenly to face another way ▷ *n* **4** a rotating or being rotated; whirl or twist **5** something wound around or twirled; coil **6** a written flourish [C16 ? a blend of TWIST + WHIRL] > '**twirler** *n*

twirp (twɜːp) *n* a variant spelling of **twerp**

twist (twɪst) *vb* **1** to cause (one end or part) to turn or (of one end or part) to turn in the opposite direction from another; coil or spin **2** to distort or be distorted **3** to wind or twine **4** to force or be forced out of the natural form or position **5** to change for the worse in character, meaning, etc; pervert: *she twisted the statement* **6** to revolve; rotate **7** *(tr)* to wrench with a turning action **8** *(intr)* to follow a winding course **9** *(intr)* to squirm, as with pain **10** *(intr)* to dance the twist **11** *(tr) Brit inf* to cheat; swindle **12** **twist someone's arm** to persuade or coerce someone ▷ *n* **13** a twisting **14** something formed by or as if by twisting **15** a decisive change of direction, aim, meaning, or character **16** (in a novel, play, etc) an unexpected event, revelation, etc **17** a bend: *a twist in the road* **18** a distortion of the original shape or form **19** a jerky pull, wrench, or turn **20** a strange personal characteristic, esp a bad one **21** a confused tangle made by twisting **22** a twisted thread used in sewing where extra strength is needed **23** **the twist** a dance popular in the 1960s, in which dancers vigorously twist the hips

24 a loaf or roll made of pieces of twisted dough **25** a thin sliver of peel from a lemon, lime, etc, twisted and added to a drink **26a** a cigar made by twisting three cigars around one another **26b** chewing tobacco made in the form of a roll by twisting the leaves together **27** *physics* torsional deformation or shear stress or strain **28** *sport, chiefly US & Canad* spin given to a ball in various games **29 round the twist** *Brit sl* mad; eccentric [OE] > **'twisty** *adj*

twist drill *n* a drill bit having two helical grooves running from the point along the shank to clear swarf and cuttings

twister ('twɪstə) *n* **1** *Brit* a swindling or dishonest person **2** a person or thing that twists **3** *US & Canad* an informal name for **tornado** **4** a ball moving with a twisting motion

twist grip *n* a handlebar control in the form of a ratchet-controlled rotating grip

twit[1] (twɪt) *vb* **twits, twitting, twitted** **1** (*tr*) to tease, taunt, or reproach, often in jest ▷ *n* **2** *US & Canad inf* a nervous or excitable state **3** *rare* a reproach; taunt [OE *ætwītan*, from *æt* against + *wītan* to accuse]

twit[2] (twɪt) *n inf, chiefly Brit* a foolish or stupid person; idiot [C19 from TWIT[1] (orig. in the sense: a person given to twitting)]

twitch (twɪtʃ) *vb* **1** to move in a jerky spasmodic way **2** (*tr*) to pull (something) with a quick jerky movement **3** (*intr*) to hurt with a sharp spasmodic pain ▷ *n* **4** a sharp jerking movement **5** a mental or physical twinge **6** a sudden muscular spasm, esp one caused by a nervous condition **7** a loop of cord used to control a horse by drawing it tight about its upper lip [OE *twiccian* to pluck]

twitcher ('twɪtʃə) *n* **1** a person or thing that twitches **2** *inf* a bird-watcher who tries to spot as many rare varieties as possible

twitch grass *n* another name for **couch grass** Sometimes shortened to **twitch** [C16 var. of QUITCH GRASS]

twite (twaɪt) *n* a N European finch with a brown streaked plumage [C16 imit. of its cry]

twitter ('twɪtə) *vb* **1** (*intr*) (esp of a bird) to utter a succession of chirping sounds **2** (*intr*) to talk or move rapidly and tremulously **3** (*intr*) to giggle **4** (*tr*) to utter in a chirping way ▷ *n* **5** a twittering sound **6** the act of twittering **7** a state of nervous excitement (esp in **in a twitter**) [C14 imit.] > **'twitterer** *n* > **'twittery** *adj*

'twixt *or* **twixt** (twɪkst) *poetic or dialect contraction of* betwixt

two (tuː) *n* **1** the cardinal number that is the sum of one and one **2** a numeral, 2, II, (ii), etc, representing this number **3** something representing or consisting of two units **4** Also called: **two o'clock** two hours after noon or midnight **5 in two** in or into two parts **6 put two and two together** to make an inference from available evidence, esp an obvious inference **7 that makes two of us** the same applies to me ▷ *determiner* **8a** amounting to two: *two nails* **8b** (*as pronoun*): *he bought two*. Related adjs: **binary, double, dual** [OE *twā* (fem)]

two-by-four *n* **1** a length of untrimmed timber with a cross section that measures 2 inches by 4 inches **2** a trimmed timber joist with a cross section that measures 1½ inches by 3½ inches

twoccing *or* **twocking** ('twɒkɪŋ) *n Brit sl* the act of breaking into a motor vehicle and driving it away [C20 from *T(aking) W(ithout) O(wner's) C(onsent)*, the legal offence with which car thieves may be charged] > **'twoccer** *or* **'twocker** *n*

two-dimensional *adj* **1** of or having two dimensions **2** having an area but not enclosing any volume **3** lacking in depth

two-edged *adj* **1** having two cutting edges **2** (esp of a remark) having two interpretations, such as *she looks nice when she smiles*

two-faced *adj* deceitful; hypocritical

twofold ('tuːˌfəʊld) *adj* **1** equal to twice as many or twice as much **2** composed of two parts ▷ *adv* **3** doubly

two-four *n Canad inf* a box containing 24 bottles of beer

two-handed *adj* **1** requiring the use of both hands **2** ambidextrous **3** requiring the participation or cooperation of two people

twonie ('tuːnɪ) *n* a variant spelling of **toonie**

two-pack *adj* (of a paint, filler, etc) supplied as two separate components, for example a base and a catalyst, that are mixed together immediately before use

twopence *or* **tuppence** ('tʌpəns) *n Brit* **1** the sum of two pennies **2** (*used with a negative*) something of little value (in **not care** *or* **give twopence**) **3** a former British silver coin

twopenny *or* **tuppenny** ('tʌpənɪ) *adj chiefly Brit* **1** Also: **twopenny-halfpenny** cheap or tawdry **2** (intensifier): *a twopenny damn* **3** worth two pence

two-phase *adj* (of an electrical circuit, device, etc) generating or using two alternating voltages of the same frequency, displaced in phase by 90°

two-piece *adj* **1** consisting of two separate parts, usually matching, as of a garment ▷ *n* **2** such an outfit

two-ply *adj* **1** made of two thicknesses, layers, or strands ▷ *n, pl* **two-plies** **2** a two-ply wood, knitting yarn, etc

Two Sicilies *pl n* **the** a former kingdom of S Italy, consisting of the kingdoms of Sicily and Naples (1061–1860)

two-sided *adj* **1** having two sides or aspects **2** controversial; debatable

twosome ('tuːsəm) *n* **1** two together, esp two people **2** a match between two people

two-step *n* **1** an old-time dance in duple time **2** a piece of music composed for or in the rhythm of this dance

two-stroke *adj* of an internal-combustion engine whose piston makes two strokes for every explosion. US and Canad word: **two-cycle**

Two Thousand Guineas *n* (*functioning as sing*), *usually written* **2000 Guineas the** an annual horse race run at Newmarket since 1809

two-time *vb* **two-times, two-timing, two-timed** *inf* to deceive (someone, esp a lover) by carrying on a relationship with another > ˌ**two-'timer** *n*

two-tone *adj* **1** of two colours or two shades of the same colour **2** (esp of sirens, car horns, etc) producing or consisting of two notes

'twould (twʊd) *poetic or dialect contraction of* it would

two-up *n chiefly Austral* a illegal gambling game in which two coins are tossed or spun

two-way *adj* **1** moving, permitting movement, or operating in either of two opposite directions **2** involving two participants **3** involving reciprocal obligation or mutual action **4** (of a radio, telephone, etc) allowing communications in two directions using both transmitting and receiving equipment

two-way mirror *n* a half-silvered sheet of glass that functions as a mirror when viewed from one side but is translucent from the other

two-way street *n* an arrangement or a situation involving reciprocal obligation or mutual action

TX *abbrev for:* **1** Texas **2** *text messaging* thanks

TXT *text messaging abbrev for* text

-ty[1] *suffix of numerals* denoting a multiple of ten: *sixty; seventy* [from OE *-tig*]

-ty[2] *suffix forming nouns* indicating state, condition, or quality: *cruelty* [from OF *-te*, *-tet*, from L *-tās*, *-tāt-*]

Tyan-Shan ('tjan'ʃan) *n* transliteration of the Russian name for the **Tian Shan**

Tyburn ('taɪbɜːn) *n* (formerly) a place of execution in London, on the **River Tyburn** (a tributary of the Thames, now entirely below ground)

Tyche ('taɪkɪ) *n Greek myth* the goddess of fortune. Roman counterpart: **Fortuna**

Tt

tychism (ˈtaɪkɪzəm) *n philosophy* the theory that chance is an objective reality at work in the universe [from Gk *tukhē* chance]

tycoon (taɪˈkuːn) *n* **1** a businessman of great wealth and power **2** an archaic name for a **shogun** [c19 from Japanese *taikun*, from Chinese *ta* great + *chün* ruler]

tyke *or* **tike** (taɪk) *n* **1** a dog, esp a mongrel **2** *inf* a small or cheeky child **3** *Brit dialect* a rough ill-mannered person **4** *Brit sl often offens* a person from Yorkshire **5** *Austral sl, offens* a Roman Catholic [c14 from ON *tīk* bitch]

Tyler (ˈtaɪlə) *n* **1** **John** 1790–1862, US statesman; tenth president of the US (1841–45) **2** **Wat** (wɒt) died 1381, English leader of the Peasants' Revolt (1381)

tylopod (ˈtaɪləʊˌpɒd) *n* a mammal having padded, rather than hoofed, digits, such as camels and llamas [c19 from NL, from Gk *tulos* knob or *tulē* cushion + -POD]

Tylor (ˈtaɪlə) *n* Sir **Edward Burnett** 1832–1917, British anthropologist; first professor of anthropology at Oxford (1896). His *Primitive Culture* (1871) became a standard work

tympan (ˈtɪmpən) *n* **1** a membrane stretched over a frame or cylinder **2** *printing* packing interposed between the platen and the paper to be printed in order to provide an even impression **3** *archit* another name for **tympanum** [OE *timpana*, from L; see TYMPANUM]

tympani (ˈtɪmpənɪ) *pl n* a variant spelling of **timpani**

tympanic bone (tɪmˈpænɪk) *n* the part of the temporal bone that surrounds the auditory canal

tympanic membrane *n* the thin membrane separating the external ear from the middle ear. It transmits vibrations, produced by sound waves, to the cochlea. Nontechnical name: **eardrum**

tympanites (ˌtɪmpəˈnaɪtiːz) *n* distension of the abdomen caused by an accumulation of gas in the intestinal or peritoneal cavity. Also called: **meteorism, tympany** [c14 from LL, from Gk *tumpanitēs* concerning a drum, from *tumpanon* drum] > **tympanitic** (ˌtɪmpəˈnɪtɪk) *adj*

tympanitis (ˌtɪmpəˈnaɪtɪs) *n* inflammation of the eardrum

tympanum (ˈtɪmpənəm) *n, pl* **tympanums** *or* **tympana** (-nə) **1a** the cavity of the middle ear **1b** another name for **tympanic membrane** **2** any diaphragm resembling that in the middle ear in function **3** *archit* **3a** the recessed space bounded by the cornices of a pediment, esp one that is triangular in shape **3b** the recessed space bounded by an arch and the lintel of a doorway or window below it **4** *music* a tympan or drum **5** a scoop wheel for raising water [c17 from L, from Gk *tumpanon* drum] > **tympanic** (tɪmˈpænɪk) *adj*

Tyndale, Tindal, *or* **Tindale** (ˈtɪndᵊl) *n* **William** ?1492–1536, English Protestant and humanist, who translated the New Testament (1525), the Pentateuch (1530), and the Book of Jonah (1531) into English. He was burnt at the stake as a heretic

Tyndall (ˈtɪndᵊl) *n* **John** 1820–93, Irish physicist, noted for his work on the radiation of heat by gases, the transmission of sound through the atmosphere, and the scattering of light

Tyndall effect *n* the phenomenon in which light is scattered by particles of matter in its path [c19 after John TYNDALL]

Tyndareus (tɪnˈdærɪəs) *n Greek myth* a Spartan king; the husband of Leda

Tyne (taɪn) *n* a river in N England, flowing east to the North Sea. Length: 48 km (30 miles)

Tyne and Wear *n* a metropolitan county of NE England, administered since 1986 by the unitary authorities of Newcastle upon Tyne, North Tyneside, Gateshead, South Tyneside, and Sunderland. Area: 540 sq km (208 sq miles)

Tynemouth (ˈtaɪnˌmaʊθ) *n* a port in NE England, in North Tyneside unitary authority, Tyne and Wear, at the mouth of the River Tyne: includes the port and industrial centre of North Shields; fishing, ship-repairing, and marine engineering. Pop: 20 716 (1991)

Tyneside (ˈtaɪnˌsaɪd) *n* the conurbation on the banks of the Tyne from Newcastle to the coast. Related word: **Geordie**

Tynwald (ˈtɪnwəld, ˈtaɪn-) *n* **the** the Parliament of the Isle of Man [c15 from ON *thingvollr*, from *thing* assembly + *vollr* field]

typ., typo., *or* **typog.** *abbrev for:* **1** typographer **2** typographic(al) **3** typography

typal (ˈtaɪpᵊl) *adj* a rare word for **typical**

type (taɪp) *n* **1** a kind, class, or category, the constituents of which share similar characteristics **2** a subdivision of a particular class; sort: *what type of shampoo do you use?* **3** the general form, plan, or design distinguishing a particular group **4** *inf* a person who typifies a particular quality: *he's the administrative type* **5** *inf* a person, esp of a specified kind: *he's a strange type* **6a** a small block of metal or more rarely wood bearing a letter or character in relief for use in printing **6b** such pieces collectively **7** characters printed from type; print **8** *biol* **8a** the taxonomic group the characteristics of which are used for defining the next highest group **8b** (*as modifier*): *a type genus* **9** See **type specimen** **10** the characteristic device on a coin **11** *chiefly Christian theol* a figure, episode, or symbolic factor resembling some future reality in such a way as to foreshadow or prefigure it ▷ *vb* **types, typing, typed** **12** to write (copy) on a typewriter **13** (*tr*) to be a symbol of; typify **14** (*tr*) to decide the type of **15** (*tr*) *med* to determine the blood group of (a blood sample) **16** (*tr*) *chiefly Christian theol* to foreshadow or serve as a symbol of (some future reality) [c15 from L *typus* figure, from Gk *tupos* image, from *tuptein* to strike]

-type *n combining form* **1** type or form: *archetype* **2** printing type or photographic process: *collotype* [from L *-typus*, from Gk *-typos*, from *tupos* TYPE]

typecast (ˈtaɪpˌkɑːst) *vb* **typecasts, typecasting, typecast** (*tr*) to cast (an actor or actress) in the same kind of role continually, esp because of his or her physical appearance or previous success in such roles: *typecast as a villain*

typeface (ˈtaɪpˌfeɪs) *n* another name for **face** (sense 14)

type founder *n* a person who casts metallic printer's type > **type foundry** *n*

type metal *n printing* an alloy of tin, lead, and antimony, from which type is cast

typescript (ˈtaɪpˌskrɪpt) *n* **1** a typed copy of a document, etc **2** any typewritten material

typeset (ˈtaɪpˌsɛt) *vb* **typesets, typesetting, typeset** (*tr*) *printing* to set (textual matter) in type
▷ www.historybuff.com/library/reftype.html

typesetter (ˈtaɪpˌsɛtə) *n* **1** a person who sets type; compositor **2** a typesetting machine

type specimen *n biol* the original specimen from which a description of a new species is made

typewrite (ˈtaɪpˌraɪt) *vb* **typewrites, typewriting, typewrote, typewritten** to write by means of a typewriter; type

typewriter (ˈtaɪpˌraɪtə) *n* a keyboard machine for writing mechanically in characters resembling print

typewriting (ˈtaɪpˌraɪtɪŋ) *n* **1** the act or skill of using a typewriter **2** copy produced by a typewriter; typescript

typhlitis (tɪfˈlaɪtɪs) *n* inflammation of the caecum [c19 from NL, from Gk *tuphlon* the caecum, from *tuphlos* blind] > **typhlitic** (tɪfˈlɪtɪk) *adj*

Typhoeus (taɪˈfiːəs) *n Greek myth* the son of Gaea and Tartarus who had a hundred dragon heads, which spurted fire, and a bellowing many-tongued voice. He created the whirlwinds and fought with Zeus before the god hurled him beneath Mount Etna > **Tyˈphoean** *adj*

typhoid (ˈtaɪfɔɪd) *pathol* ▷ *adj also* **typhoidal** **1** resembling typhus ▷ *n* **2** short for **typhoid fever** [C19 from TYPHUS + -OID]

typhoid fever *n* an acute infectious disease characterized by high fever, spots, abdominal pain, etc. It is caused by a bacillus ingested with food or water

Typhon ('taɪfɒn) *n Greek myth* a monster and one of the whirlwinds: later confused with his father Typhoeus

typhoon (taɪ'fuːn) *n* a violent tropical storm or cyclone, esp in the China Seas and W Pacific [C16 from Chinese *tai fung* great wind; infl. by Gk *tuphōn* whirlwind] > **typhonic** (taɪ'fɒnɪk) *adj*

typhus ('taɪfəs) *n* any one of a group of acute infectious rickettsial diseases characterized by high fever, skin rash, and severe headache. Also called: **typhus fever** [C18 from NL *tȳphus*, from Gk *tuphos* fever] > **'typhous** *adj*

typical ('tɪpɪkᵊl) *adj* **1** being or serving as a representative example of a particular type; characteristic **2** considered to be an example of some undesirable trait: *that is typical of you!* **3** of or relating to a representative specimen or type **4** conforming to a type **5** *biol* having most of the characteristics of a particular taxonomic group [C17 from Med. L *typicālis*, from LL *typicus* figurative, from Gk *tupikos*, from *tupos* TYPE] > **'typically** *adv* > **'typicalness** *or* **,typi'cality** *n*

typify ('tɪpɪ,faɪ) *vb* **typifies, typifying, typified** (*tr*) **1** to be typical of; characterize **2** to symbolize or represent completely, by or as if by a type [C17 from L *typus* TYPE] > **,typifi'cation** *n*

typist ('taɪpɪst) *n* a person who types, esp for a living

typo ('taɪpəʊ) *n, pl* **typos** *inf* a typographical error. Also called (Brit): **literal**

typographer (taɪ'pɒgrəfə) *n* **1** a person skilled in typography **2** a compositor

typography (taɪ'pɒgrəfɪ) *n* **1** the art, craft, or process of composing type and printing from it **2** the planning, selection, and setting of type for a printed work > **typographical** (,taɪpə'græfɪkᵊl) *or* **,typo'graphic** *adj* > **,typo'graphically** *adv*

typology (taɪ'pɒlədʒɪ) *n* **1** the study of types in archaeology, biology, etc **2** *Christian theol* the doctrine that symbols for events, figures, etc, in the New Testament can be found in the Old Testament > **typological** (,taɪpə'lɒdʒɪkᵊl) *adj* > **ty'pologist** *n*

Tyr *or* **Tyrr** (tjʊə, tɪə) *n Norse myth* the god of war, son of Odin. Anglo-Saxon counterpart: **Tiu**

tyrannical (tɪ'rænɪkᵊl) *or* **tyrannic** *adj* characteristic of or relating to a tyrant or to tyranny; oppressive > **ty'rannically** *adv*

tyrannicide (tɪ'rænɪ,saɪd) *n* **1** the killing of a tyrant **2** a person who kills a tyrant

tyrannize *or* **tyrannise** ('tɪrə,naɪz) *vb* **tyrannizes, tyrannizing, tyrannized** or **tyrannises, tyrannising, tyrannised** (when *intr*, often foll by *over*) to rule or exercise power (over) in a cruel or oppressive manner > **'tyran,nizer** *or* **'tyran,niser** *n*

tyrannosaurus (tɪ,rænə'sɔːrəs) *or* **tyrannosaur** (tɪ'rænə,sɔː) *n* any of various large carnivorous two-footed dinosaurs common in North America in Upper Jurassic and Cretaceous times [C19 from NL, from Gk *turannos* tyrant + -SAUR]

tyranny ('tɪrənɪ) *n, pl* **tyrannies 1a** government by a tyrant; despotism **1b** oppressive and unjust government by more than one person **2** arbitrary, unreasonable, or despotic behaviour or use of authority **3** a tyrannical act [C14 from OF *tyrannie*, from Med. L *tyrannia*, from L *tyrannus* TYRANT] > **'tyrannous** *adj*

tyrant ('taɪrənt) *n* **1** a person who governs oppressively, unjustly, and arbitrarily; despot **2** any person who exercises authority in a tyrannical manner [C13 from OF *tyrant*, from L *tyrannus*, from Gk *turannos*]

tyre *or US* **tire** ('taɪə) *n* **1** a rubber ring placed over the rim of a wheel of a road vehicle to provide traction and reduce road shocks, esp a hollow inflated ring (**pneumatic tyre**) consisting of a reinforced outer casing enclosing an inner tube **2** a metal band or hoop attached to the rim of a wooden cartwheel [C18 var. of C15 *tire*, prob. from archaic var. of ATTIRE]

Tyre *or* **Tyr** ('taɪə) *n* a port in S Lebanon, on the Mediterranean: founded about the 15th century BC; for centuries a major Phoenician seaport, famous for silks and its Tyrian-purple dye; now a small market town. Pop: 70 000 (1991 est). Arabic name: **Sur** > **Tyrian** ('tɪrɪən) *adj, n*

Tyrian purple *n* **1** a deep purple dye obtained from certain molluscs and highly prized in antiquity **2a** a vivid purplish-red colour **2b** (*as adj*): *a Tyrian-purple robe*

tyro *or* **tiro** ('taɪrəʊ) *n, pl* **tyros** *or* **tiros** a novice or beginner [C17 from L *tīrō* recruit]

Tyrol *or* **Tirol** (tɪ'rəʊl, 'tɪrəʊl; *German* ti'roːl) *n* a mountainous state of W Austria: passed to the Hapsburgs in 1363; S part transferred to Italy in 1919. Capital: Innsbruck. Pop: 675 063 (2001). Area: 12 648 sq km (4883 sq miles) > **Tyrolese** (,tɪrə'liːz) *or* **,Tyro'lean** *adj, n*

Tyrone (tɪ'rəʊn) *n* a historical county of W Northern Ireland, occupying almost a quarter of the total area of Northern Ireland; in 1973 its administrative functions were devolved to several district councils

tyrosinase (,taɪrəʊsɪ'neɪz) *n* an enzyme that is a catalyst in the conversion of tyrosine to the pigment melanin

tyrosine ('taɪrə,siːn, -sɪn, 'tɪrə-) *n* an amino acid that is a precursor of the hormones adrenaline and thyroxine and of the pigment melanin [C19 from Gk *turos* cheese + -INE[2]]

tyrothricin (,taɪrəʊ'θraɪsɪn) *n* an antibiotic, obtained from a soil bacterium: applied locally for the treatment of ulcers and abscesses [C20 from NL *Tyrothrix* (genus name), from Gk *turos* cheese + *thrix* hair]

Tyrr (tjʊə, tɪə) *n* a variant spelling of **Tyr**

Tyrrhenian Sea (tɪ'riːnɪən) *n* an arm of the Mediterranean between Italy and the islands of Corsica, Sardinia, and Sicily

Tyumen (*Russian* tju'mjenj) *n* a port in S central Russia, on the Tura River: one of the oldest Russian towns in Siberia; industrial centre with nearby oil and natural gas reserves. Pop: 503 800 (1999 est)

tzar (zɑː) *n* a less common spelling of **tsar**

Tzara ('zɑːrə) *n* **Tristan**, original name *Samuel Rosenstock*. 1896–1963, French poet and essayist, born in Romania, best known as the founder of Dada: author of *The Approximate Man* (1931)

tzatziki (tsæt'sɪkɪ) *n* a Greek dip made from yogurt, chopped cucumber, and mint [C20 from Mod. Gk]

Tzekung ('tsɛ'kʊŋ) *or* **Tzu-kung** ('tsuː'kʊŋ) *n* a variant transliteration of the Chinese name for **Zigong**

tzetze fly ('tsɛtsɪ) *n* a variant spelling of **tsetse fly**

Tzigane (tsɪ'gɑːn, sɪ-) *n* **a** a Gypsy, esp a Hungarian one **b** (*as modifier*): *Tzigane music* [C19 via F from Hungarian *czigány* Gypsy, from ?]

T-zone *n* the T-shaped area of a person's face that includes the forehead, nose, and chin

Tzu-po ('tsuː'pəʊ) *or* **Tzepo** ('tsɛ'pəʊ) *n* a variant transliteration of the Chinese name for **Zibo**

Uu

u *or* **U** (juː) *n, pl* **u's, U's,** *or* **Us 1** the 21st letter and fifth vowel of the English alphabet **2** any of several speech sounds represented by this letter, as in *mute, cut,* or *minus* **3a** something shaped like a U **3b** (*in combination*): *a U-bolt*

U *symbol for*: **1** united **2** unionist **3** university **4** (in Britain) **4a** universal (used to describe a category of film certified as suitable for viewing by anyone) **4b** (*as modifier*): *a U certificate film* **5** *chem* uranium **6** *biochem* uracil ▷ *adj* **7** *Brit inf* (esp of language habits) characteristic of or appropriate to the upper class

U. *abbrev for*: **1** *maths* union **2** unit **3** united **4** university **5** upper

U2 *text messaging abbrev for* you too

UA (in Britain) *abbrev for* unitary authority

UAE *abbrev for* United Arab Emirates

UAM *abbrev for* underwater-to-air missile

UAR *abbrev for* United Arab Republic

UB40 *n* (in Britain) **1** a registration card issued by the Department of Employment to a person registering as unemployed **2** *inf* a person registered as unemployed

Ubangi (juːˈbæŋɡɪ) *n* a river in central Africa, flowing west and south, forming the border between the Democratic Republic of Congo (formerly Zaïre) and the Central African Republic and Congo-Brazzaville, into the River Congo. Length (with the Uele): 2250 km (1400 miles). French name: **Oubangui**

Ubangi-Shari *n* a former name (until 1958) of the **Central African Republic**

U-bend *n* a U-shaped bend in a pipe that traps water in the lower part of the U and prevents the escape of noxious fumes; trap

uber- *or* **über-** (ˈuːbə) *combining form* indicating the highest, greatest, or most extreme example of something: *America's ubernerd, Bill Gates*; *the uber-hip young Bohemians* [c20 from G *über* over, above]

uberrima fides (jʊˈbɛrɪmə ˈfaɪdiːz) *n* another name for **utmost good faith** [L: utmost good faith]

ubiety (juːˈbaɪɪtɪ) *n* the condition of being in a particular place [c17 from L *ubī* where + *-ety*, on the model of *society*]

ubiquitarian (juːˌbɪkwɪˈtɛərɪən) *n* **1** a member of the Lutheran church who holds that Christ is no more present in the elements of the Eucharist than elsewhere, as he is present in all places at all times ▷ *adj* **2** denoting or holding this belief [c17 from L *ubīque* everywhere] > **uˌbiquiˈtarianˌism** *n*

ubiquitous (juːˈbɪkwɪtəs) *adj* having or seeming to have the ability to be everywhere at once [c14 from L *ubīque* everywhere, from *ubī* where] > **uˈbiquitously** *adv* > **uˈbiquity** *n*

U-boat *n* a German submarine, esp in World Wars I and II [from G *U-Boot*, short for *Unterseeboot*, lit.: undersea boat]

UBR *abbrev for* uniform business rate

ubuntu (ʊˈbʊntʊ) *n S African* humanity or fellow feeling; kindness [Nguni]

u.c. *printing abbrev for*: upper case

UCAS (ˈjuːkæs) *n* (in Britain) *acronym for* Universities and Colleges Admission Service
▷ www.ucas.co.uk

UCATT *n* (ˈʌkat) (in Britain) *acronym for* Union of Construction, Allied Trades and Technicians

Ucayali (*Spanish* ukaˈjali) *n* a river in E Peru, flowing north into the Marañón above Iquitos. Length: 1600 km (1000 miles)

Uccello (*Italian* utˈtʃɛllo) *n* **Paolo** (ˈpaːolo) 1397–1475, Florentine painter noted esp for three paintings of *The Battle of San Romano, 1432* (1456–60)

UDA *abbrev for* Ulster Defence Association

Udaipur (uːˈdaɪpʊə, ˈuːdaɪˌpʊə) *n* **1** Also called: **Mewar** a former state of NW India: became part of Rajasthan in

1947 **2** a city in NW India, in S Rajasthan. Pop: 308 571 (1991)

udal ('juːdᵊl) *n law* a form of freehold possession of land existing in northern Europe before the introduction of the feudal system and still used in Orkney and Shetland [c16 Orkney & Shetland dialect, from ON *othal*]

udder ('ʌdə) *n* the large baglike mammary gland of cows, sheep, etc, having two or more teats [OE *ūder*]

UDI *abbrev for* Unilateral Declaration of Independence

Udine (*Italian* 'uːdine) *n* a city in NE Italy, in Friuli-Venezia Giulia region: partially damaged in an earthquake in 1976. Pop: 98 872 (1990)

UDM (in Britain) *abbrev for* Union of Democratic Mineworkers

Udmurt Republic ('ʊdmʊət) *n* a constituent republic of W central Russia, in the basin of the middle Kama. Capital: Izhevsk. Pop: 1 639 000 (1999 est). Area: 42 100 sq km (16 250 sq miles)

udometer (juː'dɒmɪtə) *n* an archaic term for **rain gauge** [c19 from F, from L *ūdus* damp]

udon ('uːdɒn) *n* (in Japanese cookery) large noodles made of wheat flour [Japanese]

UDR *abbrev for* Ulster Defence Regiment

U4E *text messaging abbrev for* yours for ever

UEFA (juː'eɪfə,'juːfə) *n acronym for* Union of European Football Associations

▹ www.uefa.com

Uele ('weɪlə) *n* a river in central Africa, rising near the border between the Democratic Republic of Congo (formerly Zaïre) and Uganda and flowing west to join the Bomu River and form the Ubangi River. Length: about 1100 km (700 miles)

uey ('juːɪ) *n, pl* **ueys** *Austral sl* a U-turn

Ufa (*Russian* u'fa) *n* a city in W central Russia, capital of the Bashkir Republic: university (1957). Pop: 1 088 900 (1999 est)

Uffizi (juː'fɪtsɪ) *n* an art gallery in Florence; built by Giorgio Vasari in the 16th century and opened as a museum in 1765: contains chiefly Italian Renaissance paintings

▹ www.televisual.it/uffizi/indice.html

▹ www.arca.net/uffizi/index1.htm

UFO (*sometimes* 'juːfəʊ) *abbrev for* unidentified flying object

ufology (ˌjuː'fɒlədʒɪ) *n* the study of UFOs > **u'fologist** *n*

Uganda (juː'gændə) *n* a republic in E Africa: British protectorate established in 1894–96; gained independence in 1962 and became a republic in 1963; a member of the Commonwealth. It consists mostly of a savanna plateau with part of Lake Victoria in the southeast and mountains in the southwest, reaching 5109 m (16 763 ft) in the Ruwenzori Range. Official language: English; Swahili, Luganda, and Luo are also widely spoken. Religion: Christian majority. Currency: Ugandan shilling. Capital: Kampala. Pop: 23 986 000 (2001 est). Area: 235 886 sq km (91 076 sq miles) > **U'gandan** *adj, n*

▹ www.government.go.ug

▹ www.visituganda.com

Ugaritic (ˌuːgə'rɪtɪk) *n* **1** an extinct Semitic language of N Syria ▹ *adj* **2** of or relating to this language [c19 after *Ugarit* (modern name: Ras Shamra), an ancient Syrian city-state]

UGC (in Britain) *abbrev for* University Grants Committee

ugh (ʊx, ʊh, ʌx) *interj* an exclamation of disgust, annoyance, or dislike

UGLI ('ʌglɪ) *n, pl* **UGLIS** *or* **UGLIES** *trademark* a large juicy yellow-skinned citrus fruit of the Caribbean: a cross between a tangerine, grapefruit, and orange. Also called: **UGLI fruit** [c20 prob. an alteration of UGLY, from its wrinkled skin]

uglify ('ʌglɪˌfaɪ) *vb* **uglifies, uglifying, uglified** to make or become ugly or more ugly > ˌ**uglifi'cation** *n*

ugly ('ʌglɪ) *adj* **uglier, ugliest 1** of unpleasant or unsightly appearance **2** repulsive or displeasing: *war is ugly* **3** ominous or menacing: *an ugly situation* **4** bad-tempered or sullen: *an ugly mood* [c13 from ON *uggligr* dreadful, from *ugga* fear] > **'uglily** *adv* > **'ugliness** *n*

ugly duckling *n* a person or thing, initially ugly or unpromising, that changes into something beautiful or admirable [from *The Ugly Duckling* by Hans Christian Andersen]

Ugrian ('uːgrɪən, 'juː-) *adj* **1** of or relating to a subdivision of the Turanian people, who include the Samoyeds and Magyars ▹ *n* **2** a member of this group **3** another word for **Ugric** [c19 from ORussian *Ugre* Hungarians]

Ugric ('uːgrɪk, 'juː-) *n* **1** one of the two branches of the Finno-Ugric family of languages, including Hungarian and some languages of NW Siberia ▹ *adj* **2** of or relating to this group of languages or their speakers

UHF *radio abbrev for:* ultrahigh frequency

uh-huh ('ʌhʌ) *sentence substitute inf* a less emphatic variant of **yes**

uhlan ('uːlɑːn) *n history* a member of a body of lancers first employed in the Polish army and later in W European armies [c18 via G from Polish *ułan*, from Turkish *ōlan* young man]

Uhland (*German* 'uːlant) *n* **Johann Ludwig** (jo'han 'luːtvɪç) 1787–1862, German romantic poet, esp of lyrics and ballads

UHT *abbrev for* ultra-heat-treated (milk or cream)

uhuru (uː'huːruː) *n* (esp in E Africa) **1** national independence **2** freedom [c20 from Swahili]

Uigur *or* **Uighur** ('wiːgʊə) *n* **1** (*pl* **Uigur, Uigurs** *or* **Uighur, Uighurs**) a member of a Mongoloid people of NW China and adjacent parts of central Asia **2** the language of this people, belonging to the Turkic branch of the Altaic family > **Ui'gurian, Ui'ghurian** *or* **Ui'guric, Ui'ghuric** *adj*

uillean pipes ('uːlɪən) *pl n* bagpipes developed in Ireland and operated by squeezing bellows under the arm. Also called: **Irish pipes, union pipes** [c19 Irish *píob uilleann*, from *píob* pipe + *uilleann* genitive sing of *uille* elbow]

Uinta Mountains (jʊ'ɪntə) *pl n* a mountain range in NE Utah: part of the Rocky Mountains. Highest peak: Kings Peak, 4123 m (13 528 ft)

uitlander ('eɪtˌlandə, -ˌlæn-) *n* (*sometimes cap*) *S African* a foreigner [c19 Afrik.: outlander]

Ujiji (uː'dʒiːdʒɪ) *n* a town in W Tanzania, on Lake Tanganyika: a former slave and ivory centre; the place where Stanley found Livingstone in 1871. It merged with the neighbouring town of Kigoma to form Kigoma-Ujiji in the 1960s

Ujjain (uː'dʒeɪn) *n* a city in W central India, in Madhya Pradesh: one of the seven sacred cities of the Hindus; a major agricultural trade centre. Pop: 362 266 (1991)

Ujung Pandang ('uːdʒʊŋ pæn'dæŋ) *n* a port in central Indonesia, on SW Sulawesi: an important native port before Portuguese (16th century) and Dutch (17th century) control; capital of Dutch East Indonesia (1946–49); a major Indonesian distribution and transshipment port. Pop: 1 091 800 (1995 est). Also called: **Makasar, Makassar, Macassar**

UK *abbrev for* United Kingdom

ukase (juː'keɪz) *n* **1** (in imperial Russia) an edict of the tsar **2** a rare word for **edict** [c18 from Russian *ukaz*, from *ukazat* to command]

UKCC *abbrev for* United Kingdom Central Council for Nursing, Midwifery, and Health Visiting

Ukr. *abbrev for* Ukraine

Ukraine (juː'kreɪn) *n* **the** a republic in SE Europe, on the Black Sea and the Sea of Azov: ruled by the Khazars (7th–9th centuries), by Ruik princes with the Mongol conquest in the 13th century, then by Lithuania, by Poland, and by Russia; one of the four original republics that formed the Soviet Union in 1922; unilaterally declared independence in 1990, which was recognized

Uu

in 1991: consists chiefly of lowlands; economy based on rich agriculture and mineral resources and on the major heavy industries of the Donets Basin. Official language: Ukrainian. Religion: believers are mainly Christian. Currency: hryvna. Capital: Kiev. Pop: 48 767 000 (2001 est). Area: 603 700 sq km (231 990 sq miles)

▷ www.kmu.gov.ua/control/en
▷ www.brama.com/ukraine
▷ www.new.tour.com.ua
▷ www.uazone.net/Ukraine.html

Ukrainian (juːˈkreɪnɪən) *adj* **1** of or relating to Ukraine, its people, or their language ▷ *n* **2** the official language of Ukraine: an East Slavonic language closely related to Russian **3** a native or inhabitant of Ukraine

ukulele *or* **ukelele** (ˌjuːkəˈleɪlɪ) *n* a small four-stringed guitar, esp of Hawaii [c19 from Hawaiian, lit.: jumping flea]

Ulan Bator (ʊˈlɑːn ˈbɑːtɔː) *n* the capital of Mongolia, in the N central part: developed in the mid-17th century around the Da Khure monastery, residence until 1924 of successive "living Buddhas" (third in rank of Buddhist-Lamaist leaders), and main junction of caravan routes across Mongolia; university (1942); industrial and commercial centre. Pop: 691 000 (2000 est). Former name (until 1924): **Urga** Chinese name: **Kulun**

▷ www.niislel.com
▷ http://ulaanbaatar.net

Ulanova (ʊˈlɑːnəvə) *n* **Galina** (**Sergeyevna**) (gəˈliːnə) 1910–98, Russian ballet dancer, who performed with the Leningrad Kirov ballet (1928–44) and the Moscow Bolshoi Ballet (1944–62)

Ulan-Ude (ʊˈlɑːnʊˈdɛ) *n* an industrial city in SE Russia, capital of the Buryat Republic: an important rail junction. Pop: 371 400 (1999 est). Former name (until 1934): **Verkhne-Udinsk**

Ulbricht (*German* ˈʊlbrɪçt) *n* **Walter** (ˈvaltər) 1893-1973, East German statesman; largely responsible for the establishment and development of East German communism

ulcer (ˈʌlsə) *n* **1** a disintegration of the surface of the skin or a mucous membrane resulting in an open sore that heals very slowly **2** a source or element of corruption or evil [c14 from L *ulcus*]

ulcerate (ˈʌlsəˌreɪt) *vb* **ulcerates, ulcerating, ulcerated** to make or become ulcerous > ˌ**ulceˈration** *n* > ˈ**ulcerative** *adj*

ulcerous (ˈʌlsərəs) *adj* **1** relating to or characterized by ulcers **2** being or having a corrupting influence > ˈ**ulcerously** *adv*

-ule *suffix forming nouns* indicating smallness: *globule* [from L *-ulus*, dim. suffix]

Uleåborg (ˈuːlioˌbɔrjə) *n* the Swedish name for **Oulu**

ulema (ˈuːlɪmə) *n* **1** a body of Muslim scholars or religious leaders **2** a member of this body [c17 from Ar. *'ulamā* scholars, from *'alama* to know]

-ulent *suffix forming adjectives* abundant or full of: *fraudulent* [from L *-ulentus*]

ullage (ˈʌlɪdʒ) *n* **1** the volume by which a liquid container falls short of being full **2a** the quantity of liquid lost from a container due to leakage or evaporation **2b** (in customs terminology) the amount of liquid remaining in a container after such loss [c15 from OF *ouillage* filling of a cask, from *ouil* eye, from L *oculus* eye]

Ullswater (ˈʌlzˌwɔːtə) *n* a lake in NW England, in Cumbria in the Lake District. Length: 12 km (7.5 miles)

Ulm (*German* ʊlm) *n* an industrial city in S Germany, in Baden-Württemberg on the Danube: a free imperial city (1155–1802). Pop: 116 000 (1999 est)

ulna (ˈʌlnə) *n, pl* **ulnae** (-niː) *or* **ulnas** **1** the inner and longer of the two bones of the human forearm **2** the corresponding bone in other vertebrates [c16 from L: elbow] > ˈ**ulnar** *adj*

ulnar nerve *n* a nerve situated along the inner side of the arm and passing close to the surface of the skin near the elbow

ulotrichous (juːˈlɒtrɪkəs) *adj* having woolly or curly hair [c19 from NL *Ulotrichī* (classification applied to humans having this type of hair), from Gk *oulothrix*, from *oulos* curly + *thrix* hair]

ulster (ˈʌlstə) *n* a man's heavy double-breasted overcoat with a belt or half-belt [c19 from ULSTER]

Ulster (ˈʌlstə) *n* **1** a province and former kingdom of N Ireland: passed to the English Crown in 1461; confiscated land given to English and Scottish Protestant settlers in the 17th century, giving rise to serious long-term conflict; partitioned in 1921, six counties forming Northern Ireland and three counties joining the Republic of Ireland. Pop (three Ulster counties of the Republic of Ireland): 234 251 (1996); (six Ulster counties of Northern Ireland): 1 691 800 (1999 est). Area (Republic of Ireland): 8013 sq km (3094 sq miles); (Northern Ireland): 14 121 sq km (5452 sq miles) **2** an informal name for **Northern Ireland**

Ulster Defence Association *n* (in Northern Ireland) a Loyalist paramilitary organization. Abbrev: **UDA**

Ulster Democratic Unionist Party *n* a Northern Irish political party advocating the maintenance of the Union with Great Britain

Ulsterman (ˈʌlstəmən) *n, pl* **Ulstermen** a native or inhabitant of Ulster > ˈ**Ulsterˌwoman** *fem n*

Ulster Unionist Council *n* a Northern Irish political party supporting the Union with Great Britain

ult. *abbrev for:* **1** ultimate(ly) **2** ultimo

ulterior (ʌlˈtɪərɪə) *adj* **1** lying beneath or beyond what is revealed or supposed: *ulterior motives* **2** succeeding, subsequent, or later **3** lying beyond a certain line or point [c17 from L: further, from *ulter* beyond] > **ulˈteriorly** *adv*

ultima (ˈʌltɪmə) *n* the final syllable of a word [from L: the last]

ultimate (ˈʌltɪmɪt) *adj* **1** conclusive in a series or process; final: *an ultimate question* **2** the highest or most significant: *the ultimate goal* **3** elemental, fundamental, or essential **4** most extreme: *the ultimate abuse of human rights* **5** final or total: *the ultimate cost* ▷ *n* **6** the most significant, highest, or greatest thing [c17 from LL *ultimāre* to come to an end, from L *ultimus* last, from *ulter* distant]

ultimately (ˈʌltɪmɪtlɪ) *adv* in the end; at last; finally

ultima Thule (ˈθjuːlɪ) *n* **1** a region believed by ancient geographers to be the northernmost land **2** any distant or unknown region **3** a remote goal or aim [L: the most distant Thule]

ultimatum (ˌʌltɪˈmeɪtəm) *n, pl* **ultimatums** *or* **ultimata** (-tə) **1** a final communication by a party setting forth conditions on which it insists, as during negotiations on some topic **2** any final or peremptory demand or proposal [c18 from NL, neuter of *ultimatus* ULTIMATE]

ultimo (ˈʌltɪˌməʊ) *adv now rare except when abbreviated in formal correspondence* in or during the previous month: *a letter of the 7th ultimo*. Abbrev: **ult** [c16 from L *ultimō* on the last]

ultimogeniture (ˌʌltɪməʊˈdʒɛnɪtʃə) *n law* a principle of inheritance whereby the youngest son succeeds to the estate of his ancestor [c19 *ultimo-* from L *ultimus* last + LL *genitūra* a birth]

ultra (ˈʌltrə) *adj* **1** extreme or immoderate, esp in beliefs or opinions ▷ *n* **2** an extremist [c19 from L: beyond, from *ulter* distant]

ultra- *prefix* **1** beyond or surpassing a specified extent, range, or limit: *ultramicroscopic* **2** extreme or extremely: *ultramodern* [from L *ultrā* beyond]

ultracentrifuge (ˌʌltrəˈsɛntrɪˌfjuːdʒ) *n chem* a

high-speed centrifuge used to separate colloidal solutions

ultraconservative (ˌʌltrəkənˈsɜːvətɪv) *adj* **1** highly reactionary ▷ *n* **2** a reactionary person

ultra-distance *n* (*modifier*) *athletics* covering a distance in excess of 30 miles, often as part of a longer race or competition: *an ultra-distance runner*

ultrafiche (ˈʌltrəˌfiːʃ) *n* a sheet of film, usually the size of a filing card, that is similar to a microfiche but has a much larger number of microcopies [C20 from ULTRA- + F *fiche* small card]

ultrahigh frequency (ˈʌltrəˌhaɪ) *n* a radio-frequency band or radio frequency lying between 3000 and 300 megahertz. Abbrev: **UHF**

ultraism (ˈʌltrəˌɪzəm) *n* extreme philosophy, belief, or action > ˈ**ultraist** *n, adj*

ultramarine (ˌʌltrəməˈriːn) *n* **1** a blue pigment obtained by powdering natural lapis lazuli or made synthetically: used in paints, printing ink, plastics, etc **2** a vivid blue colour ▷ *adj* **3** of the colour ultramarine **4** from across the seas [C17 from Med. L *ultramarinus*, from *ultrā* beyond + *mare* sea; so called because the lapis lazuli from which the pigment was made was imported from Asia]

ultramicroscope (ˌʌltrəˈmaɪkrəˌskəʊp) *n* a microscope used for studying colloids, in which the sample is illuminated from the side and colloidal particles are seen as bright points on a dark background

ultramicroscopic (ˌʌltrəˌmaɪkrəˈskɒpɪk) *adj* **1** too small to be seen with an optical microscope **2** of or relating to an ultramicroscope

ultramodern (ˌʌltrəˈmɒdən) *adj* extremely modern > ˌ**ultraˈmodernism** *n* > ˌ**ultraˈmodernist** *n* > ˌ**ultraˌmodernˈistic** *adj*

ultramontane (ˌʌltrəmɒnˈteɪn) *adj* **1** on the other side of the mountains, esp the Alps, from the speaker or writer **2** of or relating to a movement in the Roman Catholic Church which favours the centralized authority and influence of the pope as opposed to local independence ▷ *n* **3** a person from beyond the mountains, esp the Alps **4** a member of the ultramontane party of the Roman Catholic Church

ultramundane (ˌʌltrəˈmʌndeɪn) *adj* extending beyond the world, this life, or the universe

ultranationalism (ˌʌltrəˈnæʃnəˌlɪzəm) *n* extreme devotion to one's own nation > ˌ**ultraˈnational** *adj* > ˌ**ultraˈnationalist** *adj, n*

ultrashort (ˌʌltrəˈʃɔːt) *adj* (of a radio wave) having a wavelength shorter than 10 metres

ultrasonic (ˌʌltrəˈsɒnɪk) *adj* of, concerned with, or producing waves with the same nature as sound waves but frequencies above audio frequencies > ˌ**ultraˈsonically** *adv*

ultrasonics (ˌʌltrəˈsɒnɪks) *n* (*functioning as sing*) the branch of physics concerned with ultrasonic waves. Also called: **supersonics**

ultrasound (ˈʌltrəˌsaʊnd) *n* ultrasonic waves at frequencies above the audible range (above about 20 kHz), used in cleaning metallic parts, echo sounding, medical diagnosis and therapy, etc

ultrasound scanner *n* a device used to examine an internal bodily structure by the use of ultrasonic waves, esp for the diagnosis of abnormality in a fetus

ultrastructure (ˈʌltrəˌstrʌktʃə) *n* the minute structure of a tissue or cell, as revealed by microscopy

ultraviolet (ˌʌltrəˈvaɪəlɪt) *n* **1** the part of the electromagnetic spectrum with wavelengths shorter than light but longer than X-rays; in the range 0.4×10^{-6} and 1×10^{-8} metres ▷ *adj* **2** of, relating to, or consisting of radiation lying in the ultraviolet: *ultraviolet radiation; ultraviolet spectroscopy*. Abbrev: **UV**

ultraviolet astronomy *n* the study of radiation from celestial sources in the wavelength range 91.2 to 320 nanometres

ultra vires (ˈvaɪriːz) *adv, adj* (*predicative*) *law* beyond the legal power of a person, corporation, agent, etc [L, lit.: beyond strength]

ultravirus (ˌʌltrəˈvaɪrəs) *n* a virus small enough to pass through the finest filter

ululate (ˈjuːljʊˌleɪt) *vb* **ululates, ululating, ululated** (*intr*) to howl or wail, as with grief [C17 from L *ululāre* to howl, from *ulula* screech owl] > ˈ**ululant** *adj* > ˌ**uluˈlation** *n*

Uluru (ˌuːləˈruː) *n* the world's largest monolith, in the Northern Territory of Australia: sacred to local Aboriginal people. Height: 330m (1100 ft). Base circumference: 9 km (5.6 miles). Former name: **Ayers Rock**

Ulyanovsk (*Russian* uljˈjanəfsk) *n* the former name (1924–91) of **Simbirsk**

Ulysses (ˈjuːlɪˌsiːz, juːˈlɪsiːz) *n* the Latin name of **Odysseus**

Umar (ˈuːmɑː) *n* a variant transliteration of the Arabic name for **Omar**

Umayyad (uːˈmaɪjæd) *n* a variant spelling of **Omayyad**

umbel (ˈʌmbəl) *n* an inflorescence, characteristic of umbelliferous plants, in which the flowers arise from the same point in the main stem and have stalks of the same length, to give a cluster with the youngest flowers at the centre [C16 from L *umbella* a sunshade, from *umbra* shade] > **umbellate** (ˈʌmbɪlɪt, -ˌleɪt) *or* **umbellar** (ʌmˈbɛlə) *adj* > **umbellule** (ʌmˈbɛljuːl) *n*

umbelliferous (ˌʌmbɪˈlɪfərəs) *adj* of or belonging to a family of herbaceous plants and shrubs, typically having hollow stems, divided or compound leaves, and flowers in umbels: includes fennel, parsley, carrot, and parsnip [C17 from NL, from L *umbella* sunshade + *ferre* to bear] > **umˈbellifer** *n*

umber (ˈʌmbə) *n* **1** any of various natural brown earths containing ferric oxide together with lime and oxides of aluminium, manganese, and silicon **2** any of the dark brown to greenish-brown colours produced by this pigment **3** *obs* shade ▷ *adj* **4** of, relating to, or stained with umber [C16 from F (*terre d'*)*ombre* or It. (*terra di*) *ombra* shadow (earth), from L *umbra* shade]

Umberto I (*Italian* umˈbɛrto) *n* 1844–1900, king of Italy (1878–1900); son of Victor Emmanuel II: assassinated at Monza

umbilical (ʌmˈbɪlɪkəl, ˌʌmbɪˈlaɪkəl) *adj* **1** of, relating to, or resembling the umbilicus or the umbilical cord **2** in the region of the umbilicus: *an umbilical hernia*

umbilical cord *n* **1** the long flexible tubelike structure connecting a fetus with the placenta **2** any flexible cord, tube, or cable, as between an astronaut walking in space and his spacecraft

umbilicate (ʌmˈbɪlɪkɪt, -ˌkeɪt) *adj* **1** having an umbilicus **2** having a central depression: *an umbilicate leaf* **3** shaped like a navel, as some bacterial colonies > **umˌbiliˈcation** *n*

umbilicus (ʌmˈbɪlɪkəs, ˌʌmbɪˈlaɪkəs) *n, pl* **umbilici** (-ˈbɪlɪˌsaɪ, -bɪˈlaɪsaɪ) **1** *biol* a hollow or navel-like structure, such as the cavity at the base of a gastropod shell **2** *anat* a technical name for the **navel** [C18 from L: navel, centre]

umble pie (ˈʌmbəl) *n* See **humble pie** (sense 1)

umbles (ˈʌmbəlz) *pl n* See **numbles**

umbo (ˈʌmbəʊ) *n, pl* **umbones** (ʌmˈbəʊniːz) *or* **umbos** **1** *bot, anat* a small hump, prominence, or convex area, as in certain mushrooms, bivalve molluscs, and the outer surface of the eardrum **2** a large projecting central boss on a shield, esp on a Saxon shield [C18 from L: projecting piece] > **umbonate** (ˈʌmbənɪt, -ˌneɪt), **umbonal** (ˈʌmbənəl), *or* **umbonic** (ʌmˈbɒnɪk) *adj*

umbra (ˈʌmbrə) *n, pl* **umbrae** (-briː) *or* **umbras** **1** a region of complete shadow resulting from the obstruction of light by an opaque object, esp the shadow cast by the moon onto the earth during a solar eclipse **2** the darker inner region of a sunspot [C16 from L: shade] > ˈ**umbral** *adj*

Uu

umbrage ('ʌmbrɪdʒ) *n* **1** displeasure or resentment; offence (in **give** *or* **take umbrage**) **2** the foliage of trees, considered as providing shade **3** *rare* shadow or shade [c15 from OF, from L *umbrāticus* relating to shade, from *umbra* shade]

umbrageous (ʌm'breɪdʒəs) *adj* **1** shady or shading **2** *rare* easily offended

umbrella (ʌm'brɛlə) *n* **1** a portable device used for protection against rain, snow, etc, and consisting of a light canopy supported on a collapsible metal frame mounted on a central rod **2** the flattened cone-shaped body of a jellyfish **3** a protective shield or screen, esp of aircraft or gunfire **4** anything that has the effect of a protective screen, general cover, or organizing agency [c17 from It. *ombrella*, dim. of *ombra* shade; see UMBRA] > **um'brella-,like** *adj*

umbrella pine *n* another name for **stone pine**

umbrella stand *n* an upright rack or stand for umbrellas

umbrella tree *n* **1** a North American magnolia having long leaves clustered into an umbrella formation at the ends of the branches and having unpleasant-smelling white flowers **2** Also called: **umbrella bush** any of various trees or shrubs having umbrella-shaped leaves or growing in an umbrella-like cluster

Umbria ('ʌmbrɪə; *Italian* 'umbrja) *n* a mountainous region of central Italy, in the valley of the Tiber. Pop: 835 488 (2001 est). Area: 8456 sq km (3265 sq miles)

Umbrian ('ʌmbrɪən) *adj* **1** of or relating to Umbria, its inhabitants, or the ancient language once spoken there **2** of or relating to a Renaissance school of painting that included Raphael ▷ *n* **3** a native or inhabitant of Umbria **4** an extinct language of ancient S Italy

umfazi (ˌʊm'fɑːʒɪ) *n S African* a Black married woman [from Bantu]

umiak *or* **oomiak** ('uːmɪˌæk) *n* a large open boat made of stretched skins, used by the Inuit [c18 from Inuktitut: boat for the use of women]

UML *computing trademark abbrev for:* unified modeling language: a standardized language for describing and visualizing the different parts of software systems; used for designing software

umlaut ('ʊmlaʊt) *n* **1** the mark (¨) placed over a vowel in some languages, such as German, indicating modification in the quality of the vowel **2** (esp in Germanic languages) the change of a vowel within a word brought about by the assimilating influence of a vowel or semivowel in a preceding or following syllable [c19 G, from *um* around (in the sense of changing places) + *Laut* sound]

umlungu (ˌʊm'lʊŋgʊ) *n S African* a White man: used esp as a term of address [from Bantu]

umpie *or* **umpy** ('ʌmpɪ) *n pl* **umpies** *Austral* an informal word for **umpire**

umpire ('ʌmpaɪə) *n* **1** an official who rules on the playing of a game, as in cricket **2** a person who rules on or judges disputes between contesting parties ▷ *vb* **umpires, umpiring, umpired** **3** to act as umpire in (a game, dispute, or controversy) [c15 by mistaken division from *a noumpere*, from OF *nomper* not one of a pair, from *nom-*, *non-* not + *per* equal]

umpteen (ˌʌmp'tiːn) *determiner inf* **a** very many: *umpteen things to do* **b** (*as pronoun*): *umpteen of them came* [c20 from *umpty* a great deal (?from *-enty* as in *twenty*) + *-teen* ten] > **ˌump'teenth** *n, adj*

Umtali (ʊm'tɑːlɪ) *n* the former name (until 1982) of **Mutare**

Umtata (ʌm'tɑːtə) *n* a city in South Africa, in Eastern Cape province; the capital of the former Transkei Bantu homeland. Pop: 80 000 (latest est)

UN *abbrev for* United Nations

un-[1] *prefix* (*freely used with adjectives, participles, and their derivative adverbs and nouns: less frequently used with certain other nouns*) not; contrary to; opposite of: *uncertain; untidiness; unhealthy; unbelief; untruth* [from OE *on-*, *un-*]

un-[2] *prefix forming verbs* **1** denoting reversal of an action or state: *uncover; untangle* **2** denoting removal from, release, or deprivation: *unharness; unthrone* **3** (intensifier): *unloose* [from OE *un-*, *on-*]

'un *or* **un** (ən) *pron* a spelling of **one** intended to reflect a dialectal or informal pronunciation: *that's a big 'un*

unable (ʌn'eɪbᵊl) *adj* (*postpositive; foll by to*) lacking the necessary power, ability, or authority (to do something); not able

unaccented (ˌʌnæk'sɛntɪd) *adj* not stressed or emphasized in pronunciation

unaccountable (ˌʌnə'kaʊntəbᵊl) *adj* **1** allowing of no explanation; inexplicable **2** extraordinary: *an unaccountable fear of heights* **3** not accountable or answerable to > **ˌunacˌcounta'bility** *n* > **ˌunac'countably** *adv*

unaccustomed (ˌʌnə'kʌstəmd) *adj* **1** (foll by *to*) not used (to): *unaccustomed to pain* **2** not familiar > **ˌunac'customedness** *n*

una corda ('uːnə 'kɔːdə) *adj, adv music* (of the piano) to be played with the soft pedal depressed [It., lit.: one string; the pedal moves the mechanism so that only one string of the three tuned to each note is struck by the hammer]

unadopted (ˌʌnə'dɒptɪd) *adj* **1** (of a child) not adopted **2** *Brit* (of a road, etc) not maintained by a local authority

unadvised (ˌʌnəd'vaɪzd) *adj* **1** rash or unwise **2** not having received advice > **unadvisedly** (ˌʌnəd'vaɪzɪdlɪ) *adv* > **ˌunad'visedness** *n*

unaffected[1] (ˌʌnə'fɛktɪd) *adj* unpretentious, natural, or sincere > **ˌunaf'fectedly** *adv* > **ˌunaf'fectedness** *n*

unaffected[2] (ˌʌnə'fɛktɪd) *adj* not affected

Unalaska Island (ˌuːnə'læskə) *n* a large volcanic island in SW Alaska, in the Aleutian Islands. Length: 120 km (75 miles). Greatest width: about 40 km (25 miles)

unalienable (ʌn'eɪljənəbᵊl) *adj law* a variant of **inalienable**

un-American *adj* **1** not in accordance with the aims, ideals, customs, etc, of the US **2** against the interests of the US > **ˌun-A'mericanism** *n*

Unamuno (*Spanish* una'muno) *n* **Miguel de** (mi'ɣel de) 1864–1936, Spanish philosopher and writer

unanimous (juː'nænɪməs) *adj* **1** in complete agreement **2** characterized by complete agreement: *a unanimous decision* [c17 from L, from *ūnus* one + *animus* mind] > **u'nanimously** *adv* > **unanimity** (ˌjuːnə'nɪmɪtɪ) *n*

unapproachable (ˌʌnə'prəʊtʃəbᵊl) *adj* **1** discouraging intimacy, friendliness, etc; aloof **2** inaccessible **3** not to be rivalled > **ˌunap'proachableness** *n* > **ˌunap'proachably** *adv*

unappropriated (ˌʌnə'prəʊprɪˌeɪtɪd) *adj* **1** not set aside for specific use **2** *accounting* designating that portion of the profits of a business enterprise that is retained in the business and not withdrawn by the proprietor **3** (of property) not having been taken into any person's possession or control

unapt (ʌn'æpt) *adj* **1** (*usually postpositive; often foll by for*) not suitable or qualified; unfitted **2** mentally slow **3** (*postpositive; may take an infinitive*) not disposed or likely (to) > **un'aptly** *adv* > **un'aptness** *n*

unarm (ʌn'ɑːm) *vb* a less common word for **disarm**

unarmed (ʌn'ɑːmd) *adj* **1** without weapons **2** (of animals and plants) having no claws, prickles, spines, thorns, or similar structures

unassailable (ˌʌnə'seɪləbᵊl) *adj* **1** not able to be attacked **2** undeniable or irrefutable > **ˌunas'sailableness** *n* > **ˌunas'sailably** *adv*

unassuming (ˌʌnə'sjuːmɪŋ) *adj* modest or unpretentious > **ˌunas'sumingly** *adv* > **ˌunas'sumingness** *n*

unattached (ˌʌnə'tætʃt) *adj* **1** not connected with any specific thing, body, group, etc **2** not engaged or

married **3** (of property) not seized or held as security
unavailing (ˌʌnəˈveɪlɪŋ) *adj* useless or futile > **ˌunaˈvailingly** *adv*
unavoidable (ˌʌnəˈvɔɪdəbᵊl) *adj* **1** unable to be avoided **2** *law* not capable of being declared null and void > **ˌunaˌvoidaˈbility** or **ˌunaˈvoidableness** *n* > **ˌunaˈvoidably** *adv*
unaware (ˌʌnəˈwɛə) *adj* **1** (*postpositive*) not aware or conscious (of): *unaware of the danger he ran across the road* ▷ *adv* **2** a variant of **unawares** > **ˌunaˈwareness** *n*
unawares (ˌʌnəˈwɛəz) *adv* **1** without prior warning or plan: *she caught him unawares* **2** without knowing: *he lost it unawares*
unbacked (ʌnˈbækt) *adj* **1** (of a book, chair, etc) not having a back **2** bereft of support, esp on a financial basis **3** not supported by bets
unbalance (ʌnˈbæləns) *vb* **unbalances, unbalancing, unbalanced** (*tr*) **1** to upset the equilibrium or balance of **2** to disturb the mental stability of (a person or his or her mind) ▷ *n* **3** imbalance or instability
unbalanced (ʌnˈbælənst) *adj* **1** lacking balance **2** irrational or unsound; erratic **3** mentally disordered or deranged **4** biased; one-sided: *unbalanced reporting* **5** (in double-entry book-keeping) not having total debit balances equal to total credit balances
unbar (ʌnˈbɑː) *vb* **unbars, unbarring, unbarred** (*tr*) **1** to take away a bar or bars from **2** to unfasten bars, locks, etc, from (a door); open
unbearable (ʌnˈbɛərəbᵊl) *adj* not able to be borne or endured > **unˈbearably** *adv*
unbeatable (ʌnˈbiːtəbᵊl) *adj* unable to be defeated or outclassed; surpassingly excellent
unbeaten (ʌnˈbiːtᵊn) *adj* **1** having suffered no defeat **2** not worn down; untrodden **3** not mixed or stirred by beating: *unbeaten eggs*
unbecoming (ˌʌnbɪˈkʌmɪŋ) *adj* **1** unsuitable or inappropriate, esp through being unattractive: *an unbecoming hat* **2** (when *postpositive*, usually foll by *of* or an object) not proper or seemly (for): *manners unbecoming a lady* > **ˌunbeˈcomingly** *adv* > **ˌunbeˈcomingness** *n*
unbeknown (ˌʌnbɪˈnəʊn) *adv* (*sentence modifier; foll by to*) without the knowledge (of a person): *unbeknown to him she had left the country*. Also (esp Brit): **unbeknownst** [C17 from arch *beknown* known]
unbelief (ˌʌnbɪˈliːf) *n* disbelief or rejection of belief
unbelievable (ˌʌnbɪˈliːvəbᵊl) *adj* unable to be believed; incredible > **ˌunbeˌlievaˈbility** *n* > **ˌunbeˈlievably** *adv*
unbeliever (ˌʌnbɪˈliːvə) *n* a person who does not believe, esp in religious matters
unbelieving (ˌʌnbɪˈliːvɪŋ) *adj* **1** not believing; sceptical **2** proceeding from or characterized by scepticism > **ˌunbeˈlievingly** *adv*
unbend (ʌnˈbɛnd) *vb* **unbends, unbending, unbent** **1** to release or be released from the restraints of formality and ceremony **2** *inf* to relax (the mind) or (of the mind) to become relaxed **3** to straighten out from an originally bent shape **4** (*tr*) *naut* **4a** to remove (a sail) from a stay, mast, etc **4b** to untie (a rope, etc) or cast (a cable) loose
unbending (ʌnˈbɛndɪŋ) *adj* **1** rigid or inflexible **2** characterized by sternness or severity: *an unbending rule* > **unˈbendingly** *adv* > **unˈbendingness** *n*
unbent (ʌnˈbɛnt) *vb* **1** the past tense and past participle of **unbend** ▷ *adj* **2** not bent or bowed **3** not compelled to give way by force
unbidden (ʌnˈbɪdᵊn) *adj* **1** not ordered or commanded; voluntary or spontaneous **2** not invited or asked
unbind (ʌnˈbaɪnd) *vb* **unbinds, unbinding, unbound** (*tr*) **1** to set free from restraining bonds or chains **2** to unfasten or make loose (a bond, etc)
unblessed (ʌnˈblɛst) *adj* **1** deprived of blessing **2** cursed or evil **3** unhappy or wretched > **unblessedness** (ʌnˈblɛsɪdnɪs) *n*
unblushing (ʌnˈblʌʃɪŋ) *adj* immodest or shameless > **unˈblushingly** *adv*
unbolt (ʌnˈbəʊlt) *vb* (*tr*) **1** to unfasten a bolt of (a door) **2** to undo (the nut) on a bolt
unbolted (ʌnˈbəʊltɪd) *adj* (of grain, meal, or flour) not sifted
unborn (ʌnˈbɔːn) *adj* **1** not yet born or brought to birth **2** still to come in the future: *the unborn world*
unbosom (ʌnˈbʊzəm) *vb* (*tr*) to relieve (oneself) of (secrets, etc) by telling someone [C16 from UN-[2] + BOSOM (in the sense: seat of the emotions)]
unbounded (ʌnˈbaʊndɪd) *adj* having no boundaries or limits > **unˈboundedly** *adv* > **unˈboundedness** *n*
unbowed (ʌnˈbaʊd) *adj* **1** not bowed or bent **2** free or unconquered
unbridled (ʌnˈbraɪdᵊld) *adj* **1** with all restraints removed **2** (of a horse) wearing no bridle > **unˈbridledly** *adv* > **unˈbridledness** *n*
unbroken (ʌnˈbrəʊkən) *adj* **1** complete or whole **2** continuous or incessant **3** undaunted in spirit **4** (of animals, esp horses) not tamed; wild **5** not disturbed or upset: *the unbroken quiet of the afternoon* **6** (of a record, esp at sport) not improved upon > **unˈbrokenly** *adv* > **unˈbrokenness** *n*
unbundling (ʌnˈbʌndlɪŋ) *n commerce* the takeover of a large conglomerate with a view to retaining the core business and selling off some of the subsidiaries to help finance the takeover
unburden (ʌnˈbɜːdᵊn) *vb* (*tr*) **1** to remove a load or burden from **2** to relieve or make free (one's mind, oneself, etc) of a worry, trouble, etc, by revelation or confession
unbutton (ʌnˈbʌtᵊn) *vb* to undo by unfastening (the buttons) of (a garment)
unbuttoned (ʌnˈbʌtᵊnd) *adj* **1** with buttons not fastened **2** *inf* uninhibited; unrestrained: *hours of unbuttoned self-revelation*
uncalled-for (ˌʌnˈkɔːldfɔː) *adj* unnecessary or unwarranted
uncanny (ʌnˈkænɪ) *adj* **1** characterized by apparently supernatural wonder, horror, etc **2** beyond what is normal: *uncanny accuracy* > **unˈcannily** *adv* > **unˈcanniness** *n*
uncap (ʌnˈkæp) *vb* **uncaps, uncapping, uncapped** **1** (*tr*) to remove a cap or top from (a container): *to uncap a bottle* **2** to remove a cap from (the head)
uncared-for (ˌʌnˈkɛədfɔː) *adj* not cared for; neglected
unceremonious (ˌʌnsɛrɪˈməʊnɪəs) *adj* without ceremony; informal, abrupt, rude, or undignified > **ˌuncereˈmoniously** *adv* > **ˌuncereˈmoniousness** *n*
uncertain (ʌnˈsɜːtᵊn) *adj* **1** not able to be accurately known or predicted: *the issue is uncertain* **2** (when *postpositive*, often foll by *of*) not sure or confident (about): *he was uncertain of the date* **3** not precisely determined or decided: *uncertain plans* **4** not to be depended upon: *an uncertain vote* **5** liable to variation; changeable: *the weather is uncertain* **6 in no uncertain terms** **6a** unambiguously **6b** forcefully > **unˈcertainly** *adv*
uncertainty (ʌnˈsɜːtᵊntɪ) *n, pl* **uncertainties** **1** Also: **uncertainness** the state or condition of being uncertain **2** an uncertain matter, contingency, etc
uncertainty principle *n* **the** the principle that energy and time or position and momentum, cannot both be accurately measured simultaneously. Also called: **Heisenberg uncertainty principle, indeterminacy principle**
uncharted (ʌnˈtʃɑːtɪd) *adj* (of a physical or nonphysical region or area) not yet mapped, surveyed, or investigated: *uncharted waters; the uncharted depths of the mind*
unchartered (ʌnˈtʃɑːtəd) *adj* **1** not authorized by charter; unregulated **2** unauthorized, lawless, or irregular

Uu

USAGE *Unchartered* is sometimes mistakenly used where *uncharted* is meant: *We did not want to pioneer in completely uncharted* (not *unchartered*) *territory*

unchristian (ʌnˈkrɪstʃən) *adj* **1** not in accordance with the principles or ethics of Christianity **2** non-Christian or pagan > **unˈchristianly** *adv*

unchurch (ʌnˈtʃɜːtʃ) *vb* (*tr*) **1** to excommunicate **2** to remove church status from (a building)

uncial (ˈʌnsɪəl) *adj* **1** of, relating to, or written in majuscule letters, as used in Greek and Latin manuscripts of the third to ninth centuries, that resemble modern capitals, but are characterized by much greater curvature ▷ *n* **2** an uncial letter or manuscript [C17 from LL *unciāles litterae* letters an inch long, from L *unciālis*, from *uncia* one twelfth, inch] > **ˈuncially** *adv*

uncinate (ˈʌnsɪnɪt, -ˌneɪt) *adj biol* shaped like a hook: *the uncinate process of the ribs of certain vertebrates* [C18 from L *uncīnātus*, from *uncīnus* a hook, from *uncus*]

uncircumcised (ʌnˈsɜːkəmˌsaɪzd) *adj* **1** not circumcised **2** not Jewish; gentile **3** spiritually unpurified > **ˌuncircumˈcision** *n*

uncivil (ʌnˈsɪvəl) *adj* **1** lacking civility or good manners **2** an obsolete word for **uncivilized** > **uncivility** (ˌʌnsɪˈvɪlɪtɪ) *n* > **unˈcivilly** *adv*

uncivilized *or* **uncivilised** (ʌnˈsɪvɪˌlaɪzd) *adj* **1** (of a tribe or people) not yet civilized, esp not having developed a written language **2** lacking culture or sophistication > **unˈcivilˌizedness** *or* **unˈcivilˌisedness** *n*

unclad (ʌnˈklæd) *adj* having no clothes on; naked

unclasp (ʌnˈklɑːsp) *vb* **1** (*tr*) to unfasten the clasp of (something) **2** to release one's grip (upon an object)

uncle (ˈʌŋkəl) *n* **1** a brother of one's father or mother **2** the husband of one's aunt **3** a term of address sometimes used by children for a male friend of their parents **4** *sl* a pawnbroker ▷ Related adj: **avuncular** [C13 from OF *oncle*, from L *avunculus*]

unclean (ʌnˈkliːn) *adj* lacking moral, spiritual, or physical cleanliness > **unˈcleanness** *n*

uncleanly[1] (ʌnˈkliːnlɪ) *adv* in an unclean manner

uncleanly[2] (ʌnˈklɛnlɪ) *adj* characterized by an absence of cleanliness > **unˈcleanliness** *n*

Uncle Sam (sæm) *n* a personification of the government of the United States [C19 apparently a humorous interpretation of the letters stamped on army supply boxes during the War of 1812: *US*]

Uncle Tom (tɒm) *n inf, derog* a Black person whose behaviour towards White people is regarded as servile [C20 after the main character of H. B. Stowe's novel *Uncle Tom's Cabin* (1852)] > **ˈUncle ˈTomˌism** *n*

unclose (ʌnˈkləʊz) *vb* **uncloses, unclosing, unclosed** **1** to open or cause to open **2** to come or bring to light

unclothe (ʌnˈkləʊð) *vb* **unclothes, unclothing, unclothed** *or* **unclad** (*tr*) **1** to take off garments from; strip **2** to uncover or lay bare

unco (ˈʌŋkəʊ) *Scot* ▷ *adj* **uncoer, uncoest** **1** unfamiliar, strange, or odd **2** remarkable or striking ▷ *adv* **3** very; extremely **4 the unco guid** narrow-minded, excessively religious, or self-righteous people ▷ *n pl* **uncos** *or* **uncoes** **5** a novel or remarkable person or thing **6** *obsolete* a stranger **7** (*plural*) news [C15 variant of UNCOUTH]

uncoil (ʌnˈkɔɪl) *vb* to unwind or become unwound; untwist

uncomfortable (ʌnˈkʌmftəbəl) *adj* **1** not comfortable **2** feeling or causing discomfort or unease; disquieting > **unˈcomfortableness** *n* > **unˈcomfortably** *adv*

uncommitted (ˌʌnkəˈmɪtɪd) *adj* not bound or pledged to a specific opinion, course of action, or cause

uncommon (ʌnˈkɒmən) *adj* **1** outside or beyond normal experience, etc **2** in excess of what is normal: *an uncommon liking for honey* ▷ *adv* **3** an archaic word for **uncommonly** (sense 2) > **unˈcommonness** *n*

uncommonly (ʌnˈkɒmənlɪ) *adv* **1** in an uncommon or unusual manner or degree; rarely **2** (intensifier): *you're uncommonly friendly*

uncommunicative (ˌʌnkəˈmjuːnɪkətɪv) *adj* disinclined to talk or give information or opinions > **ˌuncomˈmunicatively** *adv* > **ˌuncomˈmunicativeness** *n*

uncompromising (ʌnˈkɒmprəˌmaɪzɪŋ) *adj* not prepared to give ground or to compromise > **unˈcomproˌmisingly** *adv*

unconcern (ˌʌnkənˈsɜːn) *n* apathy or indifference

unconcerned (ˌʌnkənˈsɜːnd) *adj* **1** lacking in concern or involvement **2** untroubled > **unconcernedly** (ˌʌnkənˈsɜːnɪdlɪ) *adv*

unconditional (ˌʌnkənˈdɪʃənəl) *adj* without conditions or limitations; total: *unconditional surrender* > **ˌunconˈditionally** *adv*

unconditioned (ˌʌnkənˈdɪʃənd) *adj* **1** *psychol* characterizing an innate reflex and the stimulus and response that form parts of it **2** *metaphysics* unrestricted by conditions; absolute **3** without limitations > **ˌunconˈditionedness** *n*

unconformable (ˌʌnkənˈfɔːməbəl) *adj* **1** not conformable or conforming **2** (of rock strata) consisting of a series of younger strata that do not succeed the underlying older rocks in age > **ˌunconˌformaˈbility** *or* **ˌunconˈformableness** *n* > **ˌunconˈformably** *adv* > **ˌunconˈformity** *n*

unconscionable (ʌnˈkɒnʃənəbəl) *adj* **1** unscrupulous or unprincipled: *an unconscionable liar* **2** immoderate or excessive: *unconscionable demands* > **unˈconscionably** *adv*

unconscious (ʌnˈkɒnʃəs) *adj* **1** lacking normal sensory awareness of the environment; insensible **2** not aware of one's actions, behaviour, etc: *unconscious of his bad manners* **3** characterized by lack of awareness or intention: *an unconscious blunder* **4** coming from or produced by the unconscious: *unconscious resentment* ▷ *n* **5** *psychoanal* the part of the mind containing instincts, impulses, images, and ideas that are not available for direct examination > **unˈconsciously** *adv*

unconstitutional (ˌʌnkɒnstɪˈtjuːʃənəl) *adj* at variance with or not permitted by a constitution > **ˌunconstiˌtutionˈality** *n*

unconventional (ˌʌnkənˈvɛnʃənəl) *adj* not conforming to accepted rules or standards > **ˌunconˌventionˈality** *n* > **ˌunconˈventionally** *adv*

uncool (ʌnˈkuːl) *adj sl* **1** unsophisticated; unfashionable **2** excitable; tense; not cool

uncork (ʌnˈkɔːk) *vb* (*tr*) **1** to draw the cork from (a bottle, etc) **2** to release or unleash (emotions, etc)

uncountable (ʌnˈkaʊntəbəl) *adj* **1** too many to be counted; innumerable **2** *linguistics* denoting a noun that does not refer to an isolable object. See **mass noun**

uncounted (ʌnˈkaʊntɪd) *adj* **1** unable to be counted; innumerable **2** not counted

uncouple (ʌnˈkʌpəl) *vb* **uncouples, uncoupling, uncoupled** **1** to disconnect or unfasten or become disconnected or unfastened **2** (*tr*) to set loose; release

uncouth (ʌnˈkuːθ) *adj* lacking in good manners, refinement, or grace [OE *uncūth*, from UN-[1] + *cūth* familiar] > **unˈcouthly** *adv* > **unˈcouthness** *n*

uncover (ʌnˈkʌvə) *vb* **1** (*tr*) to remove the cover, cap, top, etc, from **2** (*tr*) to reveal or disclose: *to uncover a plot* **3** to take off (one's head covering), esp as a mark of respect

uncovered (ʌnˈkʌvəd) *adj* **1** not covered; revealed or bare **2** not protected by insurance, security, etc **3** with hat off, as a mark of respect

UNCTAD *abbrev for* United Nations Conference on Trade and Development

▷ www.unctad.org

unction (ˈʌŋkʃən) *n* **1** *chiefly RC & Eastern Churches* the act of anointing with oil in sacramental ceremonies, in the conferring of holy orders **2** excessive suavity or affected charm **3** an ointment or unguent **4** anything soothing [c14 from L *unctiō* an anointing, from *ungere* to anoint] > **'unctionless** *adj*

unctuous ('ʌŋktjʊəs) *adj* **1** slippery or greasy **2** affecting an oily charm [c14 from Med. L *unctuōsus*, from L *unctum* ointment, from *ungere* to anoint] > **unctuosity** (ˌʌŋktjʊ'ɒsɪtɪ) *or* **'unctuousness** *n* > **'unctuously** *adv*

uncut (ʌn'kʌt) *adj* **1** (of a book) not having the edges of its pages trimmed or slit **2** (of a gemstone) not cut and faceted **3** not abridged

undamped (ʌn'dæmpt) *adj* **1** (of an oscillating system) having unrestricted motion; not damped **2** not repressed, discouraged, or subdued

undaunted (ʌn'dɔːntɪd) *adj* not put off, discouraged, or beaten > **un'dauntedly** *adv* > **un'dauntedness** *n*

undecagon (ʌn'dɛkəˌɡɒn) *n* a polygon having eleven sides [c18 from L *undecim* eleven + -GON]

undeceive (ˌʌndɪ'siːv) *vb* **undeceives, undeceiving, undeceived** (*tr*) to reveal the truth to (someone previously misled or deceived) > **ˌunde'ceivable** *adj* > **ˌunde'ceiver** *n*

undecidability (ˌʌndɪˌsaɪdə'bɪlɪtɪ) *n, pl* **undecidabilities** *maths, logic* the condition of not being open to formal proof or disproof by logical deduction from the axioms of a system

undecided (ˌʌndɪ'saɪdɪd) *adj* **1** not having made up one's mind **2** (of an issue, problem, etc) not agreed or decided upon > **ˌunde'cidedly** *adv* > **ˌunde'cidedness** *n*

undeniable (ˌʌndɪ'naɪəbᵊl) *adj* **1** unquestionably or obviously true **2** of unquestionable excellence: *a man of undeniable character* **3** unable to be resisted or denied > **ˌunde'niableness** *n* > **ˌunde'niably** *adv*

under ('ʌndə) *prep* **1** directly below; on, to, or beneath the underside or base of: *under one's feet* **2** less than: *under forty years* **3** lower in rank than: *under a corporal* **4** subject to the supervision, jurisdiction, control, or influence of **5** subject to (conditions); in (certain circumstances) **6** within a classification of: *a book under theology* **7** known by: *under an assumed name* **8** planted with: *a field under corn* **9** powered by: *under sail* **10** *astrol* during the period that the sun is in (a sign of the zodiac): *born under Aries* ▷ *adv* **11** below; to a position underneath something [OE]

under- *prefix* **1** below or beneath: *underarm; underground* **2** of lesser importance or lower rank: *undersecretary* **3** insufficient or insufficiently: *underemployed* **4** indicating secrecy or deception: *underhand*

underachieve (ˌʌndərə'tʃiːv) *vb* **underachieves, underachieving, underachieved** (*intr*) to fail to achieve a performance appropriate to one's age or talents > **ˌundera'chievement** *n* > **ˌundera'chiever** *n*

underact (ˌʌndər'ækt) *vb* *theatre* to play (a role) without adequate emphasis

underage (ˌʌndər'eɪdʒ) *adj* below the required or standard age, esp below the legal age for voting or drinking

underarm ('ʌndərˌɑːm) *adj* **1** (of a measurement) extending along the arm from wrist to armpit **2** *cricket, tennis, etc* denoting a style of throwing, bowling, or serving in which the hand is swung below shoulder level **3** below the arm ▷ *adv* **4** in an underarm style

underbelly ('ʌndəˌbɛlɪ) *n, pl* **underbellies** **1** the part of an animal's belly nearest to the ground **2** a vulnerable or unprotected part, aspect, or region

underbid (ˌʌndə'bɪd) *vb* **underbids, underbidding, underbid** **1** (*tr*) to submit a bid lower than that of (others) **2** (*tr*) to submit an excessively low bid for **3** *bridge* to bid (one's hand) at a lower level than the strength of the hand warrants: *he underbid his hand*

underbidder ('ʌndəˌbɪdə) *n* **1** the person who makes the highest bid below the top bidder, esp in an auction **2** a person who underbids

underbody ('ʌndəˌbɒdɪ) *n, pl* **underbodies** the underpart of a body, as of an animal or motor vehicle

underbred (ˌʌndə'brɛd) *adj* of impure stock; not thoroughbred > **ˌunder'breeding** *n*

underbuy (ˌʌndə'baɪ) *vb* **underbuys, underbuying, underbought** **1** to buy (stock in trade) in amounts lower than required **2** (*tr*) to buy at a price below that paid by (others) **3** (*tr*) to pay a price less than the true value for

undercapitalize *or* **undercapitalise** (ˌʌndə'kæpɪtəˌlaɪz) *vb* **undercapitalizes, undercapitalizing, undercapitalized** *or* **undercapitalises, undercapitalising, undercapitalised** to provide or issue capital for (a commercial enterprise) in an amount insufficient for efficient operation

undercarriage ('ʌndəˌkærɪdʒ) *n* **1** Also called: **landing gear** the assembly of wheels, shock absorbers, struts, etc, that supports an aircraft on the ground and enables it to take off and land **2** the framework that supports the body of a vehicle, carriage, etc

undercharge (ˌʌndə'tʃɑːdʒ) *vb* **undercharges, undercharging, undercharged** **1** to charge too little for something **2** (*tr*) to load (a gun, cannon, etc) with an inadequate charge

underclass ('ʌndəˌklɑːs) *n* a class beneath the usual social scale consisting of the most disadvantaged people, such as the long-term unemployed

underclothes ('ʌndəˌkləʊðz) *pl n* a variant of **underwear** Also called: **underclothing**

undercoat ('ʌndəˌkəʊt) *n* **1** a coat of paint or other substance applied before the top coat **2** a coat worn under an overcoat **3** *zool* another name for **underfur** ▷ *vb* **4** (*tr*) to apply an undercoat to (a surface)

undercover (ˌʌndə'kʌvə) *adj* done or acting in secret: *undercover operations*

undercroft ('ʌndəˌkrɒft) *n* an underground chamber, such as a church crypt, often with a vaulted ceiling [c14 from *croft* a vault, cavern, ult. from L *crypta* CRYPT]

undercurrent ('ʌndəˌkʌrənt) *n* **1** a current that is not apparent at the surface or lies beneath another current **2** an opinion, emotion, etc, lying beneath apparent feeling or meaning ▷ Also called: **underflow**

undercut *vb* (ˌʌndə'kʌt), **undercuts, undercutting, undercut** **1** to charge less than (a competitor) in order to obtain trade **2** to cut away the under part of (something) **3** *golf, tennis, etc* to hit (a ball) in such a way as to impart backspin ▷ *n* ('ʌndəˌkʌt) **4** the act of cutting underneath **5** a part that is cut away underneath **6** a tenderloin of beef **7** *forestry, chiefly US & Canad* a notch cut in a tree trunk, to ensure a clean break in felling **8** *tennis, golf, etc* a stroke that imparts backspin to the ball

underdaks ('ʌndəˌdæks) *pl n Austral* an informal word for **underpants**

underdevelop (ˌʌndədɪ'vɛləp) *vb* (*tr*) *photog* to process (a film, plate, or paper) in developer for less than the required time, or at too low a temperature, or in an exhausted solution

underdeveloped (ˌʌndədɪ'vɛləpt) *adj* **1** immature or undersized **2** relating to societies in which both the surplus capital and the social organization necessary to advance are lacking **3** *photog* (of a film, etc) processed in developer for less than the required time

underdog ('ʌndəˌdɒɡ) *n* **1** the competitor in a fight or contest who is expected not to win **2** a person in adversity or a position of inferiority

underdone (ˌʌndə'dʌn) *adj* insufficiently or lightly cooked

underdressed (ˌʌndə'drɛst) *adj* wearing clothes that are not elaborate or formal enough for a particular occasion

underemployed (ˌʌndərɪm'plɔɪd) *adj* not fully or adequately employed

underestimate *vb* (ˌʌndər'ɛstɪˌmeɪt), **underestimates, underestimating, underestimated** (*tr*) **1** to make too low an estimate of: *he underestimated the cost* **2** to think insufficiently highly of: *to underestimate a person; underestimate her at your peril* ▷ *n* (ˌʌndər'ɛstɪmɪt) **3** too low

Uu

an estimate > ˌ**underˌestiˈmation** *n*

> **USAGE** *Underestimate* is sometimes wrongly used where *overestimate* is meant: *the importance of his work cannot be overestimated* (not *cannot be underestimated*)

underexpose (ˌʌndərɪkˈspəʊz) *vb* **underexposes, underexposing, underexposed** (*tr*) **1** *photog* to expose (a film, plate, or paper) for too short a period or with insufficient light so as not to produce the required effect **2** (*often passive*) to fail to subject to appropriate or expected publicity > ˌ**underexˈposure** *n*

underfeed (ˌʌndəˈfiːd) *vb* **underfeeds, underfeeding, underfed** (*tr*) **1** to give too little food to **2** to supply (a furnace, engine, etc) with fuel from beneath

underfelt (ˈʌndəˌfɛlt) *n* thick felt laid between floorboards and carpet to increase insulation

underfloor (ˈʌndəˌflɔː) *adj* situated beneath the floor: *underfloor heating*

underfoot (ˌʌndəˈfʊt) *adv* **1** underneath the feet; on the ground **2** in a position of subjugation **3** in the way

underfur (ˈʌndəˌfɜː) *n* the layer of dense soft fur occurring beneath the outer coarser fur in certain mammals, such as the otter and seal. Also called: **undercoat**

undergarment (ˈʌndəˌgɑːmənt) *n* any garment worn under the visible outer clothes, usually next to the skin

undergird (ˌʌndəˈgɜːd) *vb* **undergirds, undergirding, undergirded** *or* **undergirt** (*tr*) to strengthen or reinforce by passing a rope, cable, or chain around the underside of (an object, load, etc) [C16 from UNDER- + GIRD[1]]

underglaze (ˈʌndəˌgleɪz) *adj* **1** *ceramics* applied to pottery or porcelain before the application of glaze ▷ *n* **2** a pigment, etc, applied in this way

undergo (ˌʌndəˈgəʊ) *vb* **undergoes, undergoing, underwent, undergone** (*tr*) to experience, endure, or sustain: *to undergo a change of feelings* [OE] > ˈ**underˌgoer** *n*

undergraduate (ˌʌndəˈgrædjʊɪt) *n* a person studying in a university for a first degree. Sometimes shortened to **undergrad**

underground *adj* (ˈʌndəˌgraʊnd), *adv* (ˌʌndəˈgraʊnd) **1** occurring, situated, used, or going below ground level: *an underground explosion* **2** secret; hidden: *underground activities* ▷ *n* (ˈʌndəˌgraʊnd) **3** a space or region below ground level **4a** a movement dedicated to overthrowing a government or occupation forces, as in the European countries occupied by the German army in World War II **4b** (*as modifier*): *an underground group* **5** (often preceded by *the*) an electric passenger railway operated in underground tunnels. US and Canad equivalent: **subway** **6** (usually preceded by *the*) **6a** any avant-garde, experimental, or subversive movement in popular art, films, music, etc **6b** (*as modifier*): *the underground press*
▷ www.reed.edu/~reyn/transport.html
▷ www.metropla.net/index2.htm

underground railroad *n* (*often cap*) (in the pre-Civil War US) the system established by abolitionists to aid escaping slaves

undergrowth (ˈʌndəˌgrəʊθ) *n* small trees, bushes, ferns, etc, growing beneath taller trees in a wood or forest

underhand (ˈʌndəˌhænd) *adj also* **underhanded** **1** clandestine, deceptive, or secretive **2** *sport* another word for **underarm** ▷ *adv* **3** in an underhand manner or style

underhanded (ˌʌndəˈhændɪd) *adj* another word for **underhand** or **short-handed**

underhung (ˌʌndəˈhʌŋ) *adj* **1** (of the lower jaw) projecting beyond the upper jaw; undershot **2** (of a sliding door, etc) supported at its lower edge by a track or rail

underlay *vb* (ˌʌndəˈleɪ), **underlays, underlaying, underlaid** (*tr*) **1** to place (something) under or beneath **2** to support by something laid beneath **3** to achieve the correct printing pressure all over (a forme block) or to bring (a block) up to type height by adding material, such as paper, beneath it ▷ *n* (ˈʌndəˌleɪ) **4** a lining, support, etc, laid underneath something else **5** *printing* material, such as paper, used to underlay a forme or block **6** felt, rubber, etc, laid beneath a carpet to increase insulation and resilience

underlie (ˌʌndəˈlaɪ) *vb* **underlies, underlying, underlay, underlain** (*tr*) **1** to lie or be placed under or beneath **2** to be the foundation, cause, or basis of: *careful planning underlies all our decisions* **3** to be the root or stem from which (a word) is derived: *"happy" underlies "happiest"* > ˈ**underˌlier** *n*

underline (ˌʌndəˈlaɪn) *vb* **underlines, underlining, underlined** (*tr*) **1** to put a line under **2** to state forcibly; emphasize

underlinen (ˈʌndəˌlɪnən) *n* underclothes, esp when made of linen

underling (ˈʌndəlɪŋ) *n* a subordinate or lackey

underlying (ˌʌndəˈlaɪɪŋ) *adj* **1** concealed but detectable: *underlying guilt* **2** fundamental; basic **3** lying under **4** *finance* (of a claim, liability, etc) taking precedence; prior

undermentioned (ˈʌndəˌmɛnʃənd) *adj* mentioned below or subsequently

undermine (ˌʌndəˈmaɪn) *vb* **undermines, undermining, undermined** (*tr*) **1** (of the sea, wind, etc) to wear away the bottom or base of (land, cliffs, etc) **2** to weaken gradually or insidiously: *insults undermined her confidence* **3** to tunnel or dig beneath > ˌ**underˈminer** *n*

undermost (ˈʌndəˌməʊst) *adj* **1** being the furthest under; lowest ▷ *adv* **2** in the lowest place

underneath (ˌʌndəˈniːθ) *prep, adv* **1** under; beneath ▷ *adj* **2** lower ▷ *n* **3** a lower part, surface, etc [OE *underneothan*, from UNDER + *neothan* below]

undernourish (ˌʌndəˈnʌrɪʃ) *vb* (*tr*) to deprive of or fail to provide with nutrients essential for health and growth > ˌ**underˈnourishment** *n*

underpants (ˈʌndəˌpænts) *pl n* a man's undergarment covering the body from the waist or hips to the thighs or ankles. Often shortened to **pants**

underpass (ˈʌndəˌpɑːs) *n* **1** a section of a road that passes under another road, railway line, etc **2** another word for **subway** (sense 1)

underpay (ˌʌndəˈpeɪ) *vb* **underpays, underpaying, underpaid** to pay (someone) insufficiently > ˌ**underˈpayment** *n*

underpin (ˌʌndəˈpɪn) *vb* **underpins, underpinning, underpinned** (*tr*) **1** to support from beneath, esp by a prop, while avoiding damaging or weakening the superstructure: *to underpin a wall* **2** to give corroboration, strength, or support to

underpinning (ˈʌndəˌpɪnɪŋ) *n* a structure of masonry, concrete, etc, placed beneath a wall to provide support

underplay (ˌʌndəˈpleɪ) *vb* **1** to play (a role) with restraint or subtlety **2** to achieve (an effect) by deliberate lack of emphasis **3** (*intr*) *cards* to lead or follow suit with a lower card when holding a higher one

underprivileged (ˌʌndəˈprɪvɪlɪdʒd) *adj* lacking the rights and advantages of other members of society; deprived

underproduction (ˌʌndəprəˈdʌkʃən) *n* *commerce* production below full capacity or below demand

underproof (ˌʌndəˈpruːf) *adj* (of a spirit) containing less than 57.1 per cent alcohol by volume

underquote (ˌʌndəˈkwəʊt) *vb* **underquotes, underquoting, underquoted** **1** to offer for sale (securities, goods, or services) at a price lower than the market price **2** (*tr*) to quote a price lower than that quoted by (another)

underrate (ˌʌndəˈreɪt) *vb* **underrates, underrating, underrated** (*tr*) to underestimate

underscore (ˌʌndəˈskɔː) *vb* **underscores, underscoring, underscored** (*tr*) **1** to draw or score a line or mark under

2 to stress or reinforce: *to underscore a point*

undersea ('ʌndəˌsiː) *adj, adv also* **underseas** (ˌʌndə'siːz) below the surface of the sea

underseal ('ʌndəˌsiːl) *Brit* ▷ *n* **1** a coating of a tar, etc, applied to the underside of a motor vehicle to retard corrosion ▷ *vb* **2** (*tr*) to apply a coating of underseal to (a vehicle)

undersecretary (ˌʌndə'sɛkrətrɪ) *n, pl* **undersecretaries** **1** (in Britain) **1a** any of various senior civil servants in certain government departments **1b** short for **undersecretary of state**: any of various high officials subordinate only to the minister in charge of a department **2** (in the US) a high government official subordinate only to the secretary in charge of a department

undersell (ˌʌndə'sɛl) *vb* **undersells, underselling, undersold** **1** to sell for less than the usual price **2** (*tr*) to sell at a price lower than that of (another seller) **3** (*tr*) to advertise (merchandise) with moderation or restraint > ˌ**under'seller** *n*

undersexed (ˌʌndə'sɛkst) *adj* having weaker sex urges or responses than is considered normal

undershirt ('ʌndəʃɜːt) *n* the US and Canad name for **vest** (sense 1)

undershoot (ˌʌndə'ʃuːt) *vb* **undershoots, undershooting, undershot** **1** (of a pilot) to cause (an aircraft) to land short of (a runway) or (of an aircraft) to land in this way **2** to shoot a projectile so that it falls short of (a target)

undershorts ('ʌndəʃɔːts) *pl n* another word for **shorts** (sense 2)

undershot ('ʌndəʃɒt) *adj* **1** (of the lower jaw) projecting beyond the upper jaw; underhung **2** (of a water wheel) driven by a flow of water that passes under the wheel rather than over it

underside ('ʌndəˌsaɪd) *n* the bottom or lower surface

undersigned ('ʌndəˌsaɪnd) *n* **1** **the** the person or persons who have signed at the foot of a document, statement, etc ▷ *adj* **2** having signed one's name at the foot of a document, statement, etc

undersized (ˌʌndə'saɪzd) *adj* of less than usual size

underskirt ('ʌndəˌskɜːt) *n* any skirtlike garment worn under a skirt or dress; petticoat

underslung (ˌʌndə'slʌŋ) *adj* suspended below a supporting member, esp (of a motor vehicle chassis) suspended below the axles

understand (ˌʌndə'stænd) *vb* **understands, understanding, understood** **1** (*may take a clause as object*) to know and comprehend the nature or meaning of: *I understand you* **2** (*may take a clause as object*) to realize or grasp (something): *he understands your position* **3** (*tr; may take a clause as object*) to assume, infer, or believe: *I understand you are thinking of marrying* **4** (*tr*) to know how to translate or read: *can you understand Spanish?* **5** (*tr; may take a clause as object; often passive*) to accept as a condition or proviso: *it is understood that children must be kept quiet* **6** (*tr*) to be sympathetic to or compatible with: *we understand each other* [OE *understandan*] > ˌ**under'standable** *adj* > ˌ**under'standably** *adv*

understanding (ˌʌndə'stændɪŋ) *n* **1** the ability to learn, judge, make decisions, etc **2** personal opinion or interpretation of a subject: *my understanding of your predicament* **3** a mutual agreement or compact, esp an informal or private one **4** *chiefly Brit* an unofficial engagement to be married **5** **on the understanding that** providing ▷ *adj* **6** sympathetic, tolerant, or wise towards people **7** possessing judgment and intelligence > ˌ**under'standingly** *adv*

understate (ˌʌndə'steɪt) *vb* **understates, understating, understated** **1** to state (something) in restrained terms, often to obtain an ironic effect **2** to state that (something, such as a number) is less than it is > ˌ**under'statement** *n*

understeer (ˌʌndə'stɪə) *vb* (*intr*) (of a vehicle) to turn less sharply, for a particular movement of the steering wheel, than anticipated

understood (ˌʌndə'stʊd) *vb* **1** the past tense and past participle of **understand** ▷ *adj* **2** implied or inferred **3** taken for granted

understudy ('ʌndəˌstʌdɪ) *vb* **understudies, understudying, understudied** **1** (*tr*) to study (a role or part) so as to be able to replace the usual actor or actress if necessary **2** to act as understudy to (an actor or actress) ▷ *n, pl* **understudies** **3** an actor or actress who studies a part so as to be able to replace the usual actor or actress if necessary **4** anyone who is trained to take the place of another in case of need

undertake (ˌʌndə'teɪk) *vb* **undertakes, undertaking, undertook, undertaken** (*tr*) **1** to contract to or commit oneself to (something) or (to do something): *to undertake a job* **2** to attempt to; agree to start **3** to take (someone) in charge **4** to promise

undertaker ('ʌndəˌteɪkə) *n* a person whose profession is the preparation of the dead for burial or cremation and the management of funerals; funeral director

undertaking ('ʌndəˌteɪkɪŋ) *n* **1** a task, venture, or enterprise **2** an agreement to do something **3** the business of an undertaker

underthings ('ʌndəˌθɪŋz) *pl n* girls' or women's underwear

underthrust ('ʌndəˌθrʌst) *n geol* a reverse fault in which the rocks on the lower surface of a fault plane have moved under the relatively static rocks on the upper surface

undertone ('ʌndəˌtəʊn) *n* **1** a quiet or hushed tone of voice **2** an underlying suggestion in words or actions: *his offer has undertones of dishonesty*

undertow ('ʌndəˌtəʊ) *n* **1** the seaward undercurrent following the breaking of a wave on the beach **2** any strong undercurrent flowing in a different direction from the surface current

undertrick ('ʌndəˌtrɪk) *n bridge* a trick by which a declarer falls short of making his or her contract

undervalue (ˌʌndə'væljuː) *vb* **undervalues, undervaluing, undervalued** (*tr*) to value at too low a level or price > ˌ**underˌvalu'ation** *n* > ˌ**under'valuer** *n*

undervest ('ʌndəˌvɛst) *n Brit* another name for **vest** (sense 1)

underwater ('ʌndə'wɔːtə) *adj* **1** being, occurring, or going under the surface of the water, esp the sea: *underwater exploration* **2** *naut* below the water line of a vessel ▷ *adv* **3** beneath the surface of the water

under way *adj* (*postpositive*) **1** in progress; in operation: *the show was under way* **2** *naut* in motion

underwear ('ʌndəˌwɛə) *n* clothing worn under the outer garments, usually next to the skin

underweight (ˌʌndə'weɪt) *adj* **1** weighing less than is average, expected, or healthy **2** *finance* **2a** having a lower proportion of one's investments in a particular sector of the market than the size of that sector relative to the total market would suggest **2b** (of a fund, etc) disproportionately invested in this way: *pension funds have become underweight of equities*

underwent (ˌʌndə'wɛnt) *vb* the past tense of **undergo**

underwhelm (ˌʌndə'wɛlm) *vb* (*tr*) to make no positive impact on; disappoint [c20 orig. a humorous coinage based on *overwhelm*]

underwhelming (ˌʌndə'wɛlmɪŋ) *adj* failing to make a positive impact or impression; disappointing

underwing ('ʌndəˌwɪŋ) *n* **1** the hind wing of an insect **2** See **red underwing, yellow underwing**

underwood ('ʌndəˌwʊd) *n* a less common word for **undergrowth**

Underwood ('ʌndəˌwʊd) *n* **Rory** born 1963, British Rugby Union football player; played for England (1984–99), becoming Britain's most capped player

Uu

underworld ('ʌndəˌwɜːld) *n* **1a** criminals and their associates **1b** (*as modifier*): *underworld connections* **2** *Greek & Roman myth* the regions below the earth's surface regarded as the abode of the dead

underwrite ('ʌndəˌraɪt, ˌʌndə'raɪt) *vb* **underwrites, underwriting, underwrote, underwritten** (*tr*) **1** *finance* to undertake to purchase at an agreed price any unsold portion of (a public issue of shares, etc) **2** to accept financial responsibility for (a commercial project or enterprise) **3** *insurance* **3a** to sign and issue (an insurance policy) thus accepting liability **3b** to insure (a property or risk) **3c** to accept liability up to (a specified amount) in an insurance policy **4** to write (words, a signature, etc) beneath (other written matter) **5** to support

underwriter ('ʌndəˌraɪtə) *n* **1** a person or enterprise that underwrites public issues of shares, bonds, etc **2a** a person or enterprise that underwrites insurance policies **2b** an employee or agent of an insurance company who determines the premiums payable

undesirable (ˌʌndɪ'zaɪərəbᵊl) *adj* **1** not desirable or pleasant; objectionable ▷ *n* **2** a person or thing considered undesirable > ˌ**undeˌsira'bility** *or* ˌ**unde'sirableness** *n* > ˌ**unde'sirably** *adv*

undetermined (ˌʌndɪ'tɜːmɪnd) *adj* **1** not yet resolved; undecided **2** not known or discovered

undies ('ʌndɪz) *pl n inf* women's underwear

undine ('ʌndiːn) *n* any of various female water spirits [c17 from NL *undina*, from L *unda* a wave]

undisputed world champion *n boxing* a boxer who holds the World Boxing Association and the World Boxing Council world championship titles simultaneously

undistributed (ˌʌndɪ'strɪbjʊtɪd) *adj* **1** *logic* (of a term) referring only to some members of the class designated by the term, as *doctors* in *some doctors are overworked* **2** *business* (of a profit) not paid in dividends to the shareholders of a company but retained to help finance its trading

undo (ʌn'duː) *vb* **undoes, undoing, undid, undone** (*mainly tr*) **1** (*also intr*) to untie, unwrap, or open or become untied, unwrapped, etc **2** to reverse the effects of **3** to cause the downfall of

undoing (ʌn'duːɪŋ) *n* **1** ruin; downfall **2** the cause of downfall: *drink was his undoing*

undone[1] (ʌn'dʌn) *adj* not done or completed; unfinished

undone[2] (ʌn'dʌn) *adj* **1** ruined; destroyed **2** unfastened; untied

undoubted (ʌn'daʊtɪd) *adj* beyond doubt; certain or indisputable > **un'doubtedly** *adv*

undreamed (ʌn'driːmd) *or* **undreamt** (ʌn'drɛmt) *adj* (*often foll by of*) not thought of, conceived, or imagined

undress (ʌn'drɛs) *vb* **1** to take off clothes from (oneself or another) **2** (*tr*) to strip of ornamentation **3** (*tr*) to remove the dressing from (a wound) ▷ *n* **4** partial or complete nakedness **5** informal or normal working clothes or uniform

undressed (ʌn'drɛst) *adj* **1** partially or completely naked **2** (of an animal hide) not fully processed **3** (of food, esp salad) not prepared with sauce or dressing

Undset (*Norwegian* 'unsɛt) *n* **Sigrid** ('sigri) 1882–1949, Norwegian novelist, best known for her trilogy *Kristin Lavransdatter* (1920–22): Nobel prize for literature 1928

undue (ʌn'djuː) *adj* **1** excessive or unwarranted **2** unjust, improper, or illegal **3** (of a debt, bond, etc) not yet payable

undulant ('ʌndjʊlənt) *adj rare* resembling waves; undulating > '**undulance** *n*

undulant fever *n* another name for **brucellosis** [c19 so called because the fever symptoms are intermittent]

undulate *vb* ('ʌndjʊˌleɪt), **undulates, undulating, undulated** **1** to move or cause to move in waves or as if in waves **2** to have or provide with a wavy form or appearance ▷ *adj* ('ʌndjʊlɪt, -ˌleɪt) **3** having a wavy or rippled appearance, margin, or form: *an undulate leaf* [c17 from L from *unda* a wave] > '**unduˌlator** *n* > '**undulatory** *adj*

undulation (ˌʌndjʊ'leɪʃən) *n* **1** the act or an instance of undulating **2** any wave or wavelike form, line, etc

unduly (ʌn'djuːlɪ) *adv* excessively

undying (ʌn'daɪɪŋ) *adj* unending; eternal > **un'dyingly** *adv*

unearned (ʌn'ɜːnd) *adj* **1** not deserved **2** not yet earned

unearned income *n* income from property, investment, etc, comprising rent, interest, and dividends

unearth (ʌn'ɜːθ) *vb* (*tr*) **1** to dig up out of the earth **2** to reveal or discover, esp by exhaustive searching

unearthly (ʌn'ɜːθlɪ) *adj* **1** ghostly; eerie: *unearthly screams* **2** heavenly; sublime: *unearthly music* **3** ridiculous or unreasonable (esp in **unearthly hour**) > **un'earthliness** *n*

uneasy (ʌn'iːzɪ) *adj* **1** (of a person) anxious; apprehensive **2** (of a condition) precarious: *an uneasy truce* **3** (of a thought, etc) disquieting > **un'ease** *n* > **un'easily** *adv* > **un'easiness** *n*

uneatable (ʌn'iːtəbᵊl) *adj* (of food) not fit or suitable for eating, esp because it is rotten or unattractive

uneconomic (ˌʌniːkə'nɒmɪk, ˌʌnɛkə-) *adj* not economic; not profitable

uneconomical (ˌʌniːkə'nɒmɪkᵊl, -ɛkə-) *adj* not economical; wasteful

unemployable (ˌʌnɪm'plɔɪəbᵊl) *adj* unable or unfit to keep a job > ˌ**unemˌploya'bility** *n*

unemployed (ˌʌnɪm'plɔɪd) *adj* **1a** without remunerative employment; out of work **1b** (*as collective n*; preceded by *the*): *the unemployed* **2** not being used; idle

unemployment (ˌʌnɪm'plɔɪmənt) *n* **1** the condition of being unemployed **2** the number of unemployed workers, often as a percentage of the total labour force

unemployment benefit *n* (in Britain, formerly) a regular payment to a person who is out of work: replaced by jobseeker's allowance in 1996. Informal term: **dole**

unequal (ʌn'iːkwəl) *adj* **1** not equal in quantity, size, rank, value, etc **2** (foll by *to*) inadequate; insufficient **3** not evenly balanced **4** (of character, quality, etc) irregular; inconsistent **5** (of a contest, etc) having competitors of different ability

unequalled *or US* **unequaled** (ʌn'iːkwəld) *adj* not equalled; unrivalled; supreme

unequivocal (ˌʌnɪ'kwɪvəkᵊl) *adj* not ambiguous; plain > ˌ**une'quivocally** *adv* > ˌ**une'quivocalness** *n*

unerring (ʌn'ɜːrɪŋ) *adj* **1** not missing the mark or target **2** consistently accurate; certain > **un'erringly** *adv* > **un'erringness** *n*

UNESCO (juː'nɛskəʊ) *n acronym for* United Nations Educational, Scientific, and Cultural Organization ▷ www.unesco.org

uneven (ʌn'iːvən) *adj* **1** (of a surface, etc) not level or flat **2** spasmodic or variable **3** not parallel, straight, or horizontal **4** not fairly matched: *an uneven race* **5** *arch* not equal > **un'evenly** *adv* > **un'evenness** *n*

uneventful (ˌʌnɪ'vɛntfʊl) *adj* ordinary, routine, or quiet > ˌ**une'ventfully** *adv* > ˌ**une'ventfulness** *n*

unexampled (ˌʌnɪg'zɑːmpᵊld) *adj* without precedent or parallel

unexceptionable (ˌʌnɪk'sɛpʃənəbᵊl) *adj* beyond criticism or objection > ˌ**unex'ceptionably** *adv*

unexceptional (ˌʌnɪk'sɛpʃənᵊl) *adj* **1** usual, ordinary, or normal **2** subject to or allowing no exceptions > ˌ**unex'ceptionally** *adv*

unexcited (ˌʌnɪk'saɪtɪd) *adj* **1** not aroused to pleasure, interest, agitation, etc **2** (of an atom, molecule, etc) remaining in its ground state

unexpected (ˌʌnɪk'spɛktɪd) *adj* surprising or unforeseen > ˌ**unex'pectedly** *adv* > ˌ**unex'pectedness** *n*

unfailing (ʌnˈfeɪlɪŋ) *adj* **1** not failing; unflagging **2** continuous **3** sure; certain > **unˈfailingly** *adv* > **unˈfailingness** *n*

unfair (ʌnˈfɛə) *adj* **1** characterized by inequality or injustice **2** dishonest or unethical > **unˈfairly** *adv* > **unˈfairness** *n*

unfaithful (ʌnˈfeɪθfʊl) *adj* **1** not true to a promise, vow, etc **2** not true to a wife, husband, lover, etc, esp in having sexual intercourse with someone else **3** inaccurate; untrustworthy: *unfaithful copy* **4** *obs* not having religious faith > **unˈfaithfully** *adv* > **unˈfaithfulness** *n*

unfamiliar (ˌʌnfəˈmɪljə) *adj* **1** not known or experienced; strange **2** (*postpositive; foll by with*) not familiar > **unfamiliarity** (ˌʌnfəˌmɪlɪˈærɪtɪ) *n* > **unˌfaˈmiliarly** *adv*

unfasten (ʌnˈfɑːsᵊn) *vb* to undo, untie, or open or become undone, untied, or opened

unfathered (ʌnˈfɑːðəd) *adj* **1** having no known father **2** of unknown or uncertain origin

unfathomable (ʌnˈfæðəməbᵊl) *adj* **1** incapable of being fathomed; immeasurable **2** incomprehensible > **unˈfathomableness** *n* > **unˈfathomably** *adv*

unfavourable *or US* **unfavorable** (ʌnˈfeɪvərəbᵊl) *adj* not favourable; adverse or inauspicious > **unˈfavourably** *or US* **unˈfavorably** *adv*

unfazed (ʌnˈfeɪzd) *adj inf* not disconcerted; unperturbed

Unfederated Malay States (ʌnˈfɛdəˌreɪtɪd) *pl n* a former group of native states in the Malay Peninsula that became British protectorates between 1885 and 1909. All except Brunei joined the Malayan Union (later Federation of Malaya) in 1946. Brunei joined the Federation of Malaysia in 1963

unfeeling (ʌnˈfiːlɪŋ) *adj* **1** without sympathy; callous **2** without physical feeling or sensation > **unˈfeelingly** *adv* > **unˈfeelingness** *n*

unfinished (ʌnˈfɪnɪʃt) *adj* **1** incomplete or imperfect **2** (of paint, polish, varnish, etc) without an applied finish; rough **3** (of fabric) unbleached or not processed

unfit (ʌnˈfɪt) *adj* **1** (*postpositive; often foll by for*) unqualified, incapable, or incompetent: *unfit for military service* **2** (*postpositive; often foll by for*) unsuitable or inappropriate: *the ground was unfit for football* **3** in poor physical condition ▷ *vb* **unfits, unfitting, unfitted 4** (*tr*) *rare* to render unfit > **unˈfitly** *adv* > **unˈfitness** *n*

unfix (ʌnˈfɪks) *vb* (*tr*) **1** to unfasten, detach, or loosen **2** to unsettle or disturb

unflappable (ʌnˈflæpəbᵊl) *adj inf* hard to upset; calm; composed > **unˌflappaˈbility** *n* > **unˈflappably** *adv*

unfledged (ʌnˈflɛdʒd) *adj* **1** (of a young bird) not having developed adult feathers **2** immature and undeveloped: *an unfledged lawyer taking his first case*

unflinching (ʌnˈflɪntʃɪŋ) *adj* not shrinking from danger, difficulty, etc > **unˈflinchingly** *adv*

unfold (ʌnˈfəʊld) *vb* **1** to open or spread out or be opened or spread out from a folded state **2** to reveal or be revealed: *the truth unfolds* **3** to develop or expand or be developed or expanded > **unˈfolder** *n*

unfortunate (ʌnˈfɔːtʃənɪt) *adj* **1** causing or attended by misfortune **2** unlucky or unhappy: *an unfortunate character* **3** regrettable or unsuitable: *an unfortunate speech* ▷ *n* **4** an unlucky person

unfortunately (ʌnˈfɔːtʃənɪtlɪ) *adv* (*sentence modifier*) it is regrettable that; unluckily

unfounded (ʌnˈfaʊndɪd) *adj* **1** (of ideas, allegations, etc) baseless; groundless **2** not yet founded or established > **unˈfoundedly** *adv* > **unˈfoundedness** *n*

unfranked income (ʌnˈfræŋkt) *n* any income from an investment that does not qualify as franked investment income

unfreeze (ʌnˈfriːz) *vb* **unfreezes, unfreezing, unfroze, unfrozen 1** to thaw or cause to thaw **2** (*tr*) to relax governmental restrictions on (wages, prices, credit, etc) or on the manufacture or sale of (goods, etc)

unfriended (ʌnˈfrɛndɪd) *adj now rare* without a friend or friends; friendless: *unfriended and alone*

unfriendly (ʌnˈfrɛndlɪ) *adj* **unfriendlier, unfriendliest 1** not friendly; hostile **2** unfavourable or disagreeable ▷ *adv* **3** *rare* in an unfriendly manner > **unˈfriendliness** *n*

unfrock (ʌnˈfrɒk) *vb* (*tr*) to deprive (a person in holy orders) of ecclesiastical status

unfunded debt (ʌnˈfʌndɪd) *n* a short-term floating debt not represented by bonds

unfurl (ʌnˈfɜːl) *vb* to unroll, unfold, or spread out or be unrolled, unfolded, or spread out from a furled state

ungainly (ʌnˈgeɪnlɪ) *adj* **ungainlier, ungainliest 1** lacking grace when moving **2** difficult to move or use; unwieldy [C17 from UN-[1] + obs. or dialect *gainly* graceful] > **unˈgainliness** *n*

Ungaretti (*Italian* uŋgaˈretti) *n* **Giuseppe** (dʒuˈzɛppe) 1888–1970, Italian poet, best known for his collection of war poems *Allegria di naufragi* (1919)

Ungava (ʊŋˈgeɪvə, -ˈgɑː-) *n* a sparsely inhabited region of NE Canada, in N Quebec east of Hudson Bay: part of the Labrador peninsula: rich mineral resources. Area: 911 110 sq km (351 780 sq miles)

ungodly (ʌnˈgɒdlɪ) *adj* **ungodlier, ungodliest 1a** wicked, sinful **1b** (*as collective n; preceded by the*): *the ungodly* **2** *inf* unseemly; outrageous (esp in **an ungodly hour**) > **unˈgodliness** *n*

ungovernable (ʌnˈgʌvənəbᵊl) *adj* not able to be disciplined, restrained, etc: *an ungovernable temper* > **unˈgovernableness** *n* > **unˈgovernably** *adv*

ungual (ˈʌŋgwəl) *adj* **1** of, relating to, or affecting the fingernails or toenails **2** of or relating to an unguis [C19 from L *unguis* nail]

unguarded (ʌnˈgɑːdɪd) *adj* **1** unprotected; vulnerable **2** open; frank **3** incautious > **unˈguardedly** *adv* > **unˈguardedness** *n*

unguent (ˈʌŋgwənt) *n* a less common name for an **ointment** [C15 from L, from *unguere* to anoint]

unguiculate (ʌŋˈgwɪkjʊlɪt, -ˌleɪt) *adj* **1** (of mammals) having claws or nails **2** (of petals) having a clawlike base ▷ *n* **3** an unguiculate mammal [C19 from NL *unguiculātus*, from L *unguiculus*, dim. of *unguis* nail]

unguis (ˈʌŋgwɪs) *n, pl* **ungues** (-gwiːz) **1** a nail, claw, or hoof, or the part of the digit giving rise to it **2** the clawlike base of a petal [C18 from L]

ungulate (ˈʌŋgjʊlɪt, -ˌleɪt) *n* any of a large group of mammals all of which have hooves: divided into odd-toed ungulates (see **perissodactyl**) and even-toed ungulates (see **artiodactyl**) [C19 from LL *ungulātus* having hooves, from *ungula* hoof]

unhallowed (ʌnˈhæləʊd) *adj* **1** not consecrated or holy: *unhallowed ground* **2** sinful

unhand (ʌnˈhænd) *vb* (*tr*) *arch or literary* to release from the grasp

unhappy (ʌnˈhæpɪ) *adj* **unhappier, unhappiest 1** not joyful; sad or depressed **2** unfortunate or wretched: *an unhappy fellow* **3** tactless or inappropriate: *an unhappy remark* > **unˈhappily** *adv* > **unˈhappiness** *n*

UNHCR *abbrev for* United Nations High Commissioner for Refugees

unhealthy (ʌnˈhɛlθɪ) *adj* **unhealthier, unhealthiest 1** characterized by ill health; sick **2** characteristic of, conducive to, or resulting from ill health: *an unhealthy complexion* **3** morbid or unwholesome **4** *inf* dangerous; risky > **unˈhealthily** *adv* > **unˈhealthiness** *n*

unheard (ʌnˈhɜːd) *adj* **1** not heard; not perceived by the ear **2** not listened to: *his warning went unheard* **3** *arch* unheard-of

unheard-of *adj* **1** previously unknown: *an unheard-of actress* **2** without precedent: *an unheard-of treatment* **3** highly offensive: *unheard-of behaviour*

unhinge (ʌnˈhɪndʒ) *vb* **unhinges, unhinging, unhinged** (*tr*) **1** to remove (a door, etc) from its hinges **2** to derange or unbalance (a person, his or her mind, etc) **3** to

Uu

disrupt or unsettle (a process or state of affairs)
unhip (ʌnˈhɪp) *adj sl* not at all fashionable or up to date: *my terminally unhip parents*
unholy (ʌnˈhəʊlɪ) *adj* **unholier, unholiest 1** not holy or sacred **2** immoral or depraved **3** *inf* outrageous or unnatural: *an unholy alliance* > **unˈholiness** *n*
unhook (ʌnˈhʊk) *vb* **1** (*tr*) to remove (something) from a hook **2** (*tr*) to unfasten the hook of (a dress, etc) **3** (*intr*) to become unfastened or be capable of unfastening: *the dress wouldn't unhook*
unhorse (ʌnˈhɔːs) *vb* **unhorses, unhorsing, unhorsed** (*tr*) **1** (*usually passive*) to knock or throw from a horse **2** to overthrow or dislodge, as from a powerful position
unhouseled (ʌnˈhaʊzəld) *adj arch* not having received the Eucharist [C16 from *un-* + obs. *housel* to administer the sacrament, from OE *hūsl* (n), *hūslian* (vb), from ?]
uni (ˈjuːnɪ) *n inf* short for **university**
uni- *combining form* consisting of, relating to, or having only one: *unilateral* [from L *ūnus* one]
Uniat (ˈjuːnɪˌæt) *or* **Uniate** (ˈjuːnɪɪt, -ˌeɪt) *adj* **1** designating any of the Eastern Churches that retain their own liturgy but submit to papal authority ▷ *n* **2** a member of one of these Churches [C19 from Russian *uniyat*, from Polish *unia* union, from LL *ūniō*; see UNION] > **ˈUniˌatism** *n*
uniaxial (ˌjuːnɪˈæksɪəl) *adj* **1** (esp of plants) having an unbranched main axis **2** (of a crystal) having only one direction along which double refraction of light does not occur
unicameral (ˌjuːnɪˈkæmərəl) *adj* of or characterized by a single legislative chamber > **ˌuniˈcameralism** *n* > **ˌuniˈcameralist** *n* > **ˌuniˈcamerally** *adv*
UNICEF (ˈjuːnɪˌsɛf) *n acronym for* United Nations Children's Fund (formerly, United Nations International Children's Emergency Fund)
▷ www.unicef.org
unicellular (ˌjuːnɪˈsɛljʊlə) *adj* (of organisms, such as protozoans and certain algae) consisting of a single cell > **ˌuniˌcelluˈlarity** *n*
Unicode (ˈjuːnɪˌkəʊd) *n computing* a standard character-coding format able to represent characters in a wide range of languages
unicorn (ˈjuːnɪˌkɔːn) *n* **1** an imaginary creature usually depicted as a white horse with one long spiralled horn growing from its forehead **2** *Old Testament* a two-horned animal: mistranslation in the Authorized Version of the original Hebrew [C13 from OF, from L *ūnicornis* one-horned, from *ūnus* one + *cornu* a horn]
unicycle (ˈjuːnɪˌsaɪkᵊl) *n* a one-wheeled vehicle driven by pedals, esp one used in a circus, etc. Also called: **monocycle** [from UNI- + CYCLE, on the model of TRICYCLE] > **ˈuniˌcyclist** *n*
unidirectional (ˌjuːnɪdɪˈrɛkʃənᵊl) *adj* having, moving in, or operating in only one direction
UNIDO (juːˈniːdəʊ) *n acronym for* United Nations Industrial Development Organization
▷ www.unido.org
Unification Church *n* a religious sect founded in 1954 by Sun Myung Moon (born 1920), S Korean industrialist and religious leader
unified field theory *n* any theory capable of describing in one set of equations the properties of gravitational fields, electromagnetic fields, and strong and weak nuclear interactions. No satisfactory theory has yet been found. See also **grand unified theory**
Unified Modeling Language *n trademark* See **UML**
uniform (ˈjuːnɪˌfɔːm) *n* **1** a prescribed identifying set of clothes for the members of an organization, such as soldiers or schoolchildren **2** a single set of such clothes **3** a characteristic feature of some class or group ▷ *adj* **4** unchanging in form, quality, etc: *a uniform surface* **5** alike or like: *a line of uniform toys* ▷ *vb* (*tr*) **6** to fit out (a body of soldiers, etc) with uniforms **7** to make uniform [C16 from L *ūniformis*, from *ūnus* one + *forma* shape] > **ˈuniˌformly** *adv* > **ˈuniˌformness** *n*
▷ www.messdress-britishmilitaria.com
▷ www.uniformology.com
Uniform Business Rate *n* a local tax in the UK paid by businesses, based on a local valuation of their premises and a rate fixed by central government that applies throughout the country. Abbrev: **UBR**
uniformitarianism (ˌjuːnɪˌfɔːmɪˈtɛərɪəˌnɪzəm) *n* the concept that the earth's surface was shaped in the past by gradual processes, such as erosion, and by small sudden changes, such as earthquakes, rather than by sudden divine acts, such as Noah's flood > **ˌuniˌformiˈtarian** *n, adj*
uniformity (ˌjuːnɪˈfɔːmɪtɪ) *n, pl* **uniformities 1** a state or condition in which everything is regular, homogeneous, or unvarying **2** lack of diversity or variation
unify (ˈjuːnɪˌfaɪ) *vb* **unifies, unifying, unified** to make or become one; unite [C16 from Med. L *ūnificāre*, from L *ūnus* one + *facere* to make] > **ˈuniˌfiable** *adj* > **ˌunifiˈcation** *n* > **ˈuniˌfier** *n*
unilateral (ˌjuːnɪˈlætərəl) *adj* **1** of, having, affecting, or occurring on only one side **2** involving or performed by only one party of several: *unilateral disarmament* **3** *law* (of contracts, obligations, etc) made by, affecting, or binding one party only **4** *bot* having or designating parts situated or turned to one side of an axis > **ˌuniˈlateralism** *n* > **ˌuniˈlaterally** *adv*
Unilateral Declaration of Independence *n* a declaration of independence made by a dependent state without the assent of the protecting state. Abbrev: **UDI**
Unimak Island (ˈjuːnɪˌmæk) *n* an island in SW Alaska, in the Aleutian Islands. Length: 113 km (70 miles)
unimpeachable (ˌʌnɪmˈpiːtʃəbᵊl) *adj* unquestionable as to honesty, truth, etc > **ˌunimˈpeachably** *adv*
unimproved (ˌʌnɪmˈpruːvd) *adj* **1** not improved or made better **2** (of land) not cleared, drained, cultivated, etc **3** neglected; unused: *unimproved resources*
unincorporated business (ˌʌnɪnˈkɔːpəreɪtɪd) *n* a privately owned business, often owned by one person who has unlimited liability as the business is not legally registered as a company
uninstall (ˌʌnɪnˈstɔːl) *vb* (*tr*) *computing* to remove (a program)
uninterested (ʌnˈɪntrɪstɪd) *adj* indifferent > **unˈinterestedly** *adv* > **unˈinterestedness** *n*
USAGE See at **disinterested**
union (ˈjuːnjən) *n* **1** the condition of being united, the act of uniting, or a conjunction formed by such an act **2** an association, alliance, or confederation of individuals or groups for a common purpose, esp political **3** agreement or harmony **4** short for **trade union 5** the act or state of marriage or sexual intercourse **6** a device on a flag representing union, such as another flag depicted in the top left corner **7** a device for coupling pipes **8** (*often cap*) **8a** an association of students at a university or college formed to look after the students' interests **8b** the building or buildings housing the facilities of such an organization **9** *maths* a set containing all members of two given sets. Symbol: $\cup$ **10** (in 19th-century England) a number of parishes united for the administration of poor relief **11** *textiles* a piece of cloth or fabric consisting of two different kinds of yarn **12** (*modifier*) of or related to a union, esp a trade union [C15 from Church L *ūniō* oneness, from L *ūnus* one]
Union (ˈjuːnjən) *n* **the 1** *Brit* **1a** the union of England and Wales from 1543 **1b** the union of the English and Scottish crowns (1603–1707) **1c** the union of England and Scotland from 1707 **1d** the political union of Great Britain and Ireland (1801–1920) **1e** the union of Great Britain and Northern Ireland from 1921 **2** *US* **2a** the United States of America **2b** the northern states of the

US during the Civil War **2c** (*as modifier*): *Union supporters*
union catalogue *n* a catalogue listing every publication held at cooperating libraries
Union flag *n* the national flag of the United Kingdom, being a composite design composed of Saint George's Cross (England), Saint Andrew's Cross (Scotland), and Saint Patrick's Cross (Ireland). Often called: **Union Jack**
unionism ('ju:njə,nɪzəm) *n* **1** the principles of trade unions **2** adherence to the principles of trade unions **3** the principle or theory of any union > '**unionist** *n, adj*
Unionist ('ju:njənɪst) *n* **1** (*sometimes not cap*) **1a** (before 1920) a supporter of the Union of all Ireland and Great Britain **1b** (since 1920) a supporter of Union between Britain and Northern Ireland **2** a supporter of the US federal Union, esp during the Civil War ▷ *adj* **3** of, resembling, or relating to Unionists > '**Union,ism** *n*
Unionist Party *n* (formerly, in Northern Ireland) the major Protestant political party, closely identified with the Union with Britain. See also **Ulster Democratic Unionist Party, Ulster Unionist Council**
unionize *or* **unionise** ('ju:njə,naɪz) *vb* **unionizes, unionizing, unionized** *or* **unionises, unionising, unionised** **1** to organize (workers) into a trade union **2** to join or cause to join a trade union **3** (*tr*) to subject to the rules or codes of a trade union > ,**unioni'zation** *or* ,**unioni'sation** *n*
Union Jack *n* a common name for **Union flag**
Union of South Africa *n* the former name (1910–61) of the (Republic of) **South Africa**
Union of Soviet Socialist Republics *n* the official name of the former **Soviet Union**
union pipes *pl n* another name for **uillean pipes**
unipolar (,ju:nɪ'pəʊlə) *adj* **1** of, concerned with, or having a single magnetic or electric pole **2** (of a nerve cell) having a single process **3** (of a transistor) utilizing charge carriers of one polarity only, as in a field-effect transistor > **unipolarity** (,ju:nɪpəʊ'lærɪtɪ) *n*
unique (ju:'ni:k) *adj* **1** being the only one of a particular type **2** without equal or like **3** *inf* very remarkable **4** *maths* **4a** leading to only one result: *the sum of two integers is unique* **4b** having precisely one value: *the unique positive square root of 4 is 2* [C17 via F from L *ūnicus* unparalleled, from *ūnus* one] > **u'niquely** *adv* > **u'niqueness** *n*

> USAGE *Unique* with the meaning 'being the only one' or 'having no equal' describes an absolute state: *a case unique in British law*. In this use it cannot therefore be qualified; something is either *unique* or *not unique*. However, *unique* is also very commonly used in the sense of 'remarkable' or 'exceptional', particularly in the language of advertising, and in this meaning it can be used with words such as *rather*, *quite*, etc. Since many people object to this use, it is best avoided in formal and serious writing

unisex ('ju:nɪ,sɛks) *adj* of or relating to clothing, a hairstyle, hairdressers, etc, that can be worn or used by either sex [C20 from UNI- + SEX]
unisexual (,ju:nɪ'sɛksjʊəl) *adj* **1** of one sex only **2** (of some organisms) having either male or female reproductive organs but not both > ,**uni,sexu'ality** *n* > ,**uni'sexually** *adv*
unison ('ju:nɪsᵊn) *n* **1** *music* **1a** the interval between two sounds of identical pitch **1b** (*modifier*) played or sung at the same pitch: *unison singing* **2** complete agreement (esp in **in unison**) [C16 from LL *ūnisonus*, from UNI- + *sonus* sound] > **u'nisonous, u'nisonal,** *or* **u'nisonant** *adj*
UNISON ('ju:nɪsᵊn) *n* (in Britain) a trade union representing local government, health-care, and other workers: formed in 1993 by the amalgamation of COHSE, NALGO, and NUPE
unit ('ju:nɪt) *n* **1** a single undivided entity or whole **2** any group or individual, esp when regarded as a basic element of a larger whole **3** a mechanical part or assembly of parts that performs a subsidiary function: *a filter unit* **4** a complete system or establishment that performs a specific function: *a production unit* **5** a subdivision of a larger military formation **6** a standard amount of a physical quantity, such as length, mass, etc, multiples of which are used to express magnitudes of that physical quantity: *the second is a unit of time* **7** the amount of a drug, vaccine, etc, needed to produce a particular effect **8** a standard measure used in calculating alcohol intake and its effect **9** the digit or position immediately to the left of the decimal point **10** (*modifier*) having or relating to a value of one: *a unit vector* **11** NZ a self-propelled railcar **12** *Austral & NZ* short for **home unit** [C16 back formation from UNITY, ? on the model of *digit*]

▷ www.psigate.ac.uk/newsite/reference/units.html
▷ www.ex.ac.uk/cimt/dictunit/dictunit.htm
▷ www.unc.edu/~rowlett/units/index.html

unitarian (,ju:nɪ'tɛərɪən) *n* **1** a supporter of unity or centralization in politics ▷ *adj* **2** of or relating to unity or centralization
Unitarian (,ju:nɪ'tɛərɪən) *n* **1** a person who believes that God is one being and rejects the doctrine of the Trinity **2** a member of the Church (**Unitarian Church**) that embodies this system of belief ▷ *adj* **3** of or relating to Unitarians or Unitarianism > ,**Uni'taria,nism** *n*

▷ http://uusc.org/
▷ http://unitarian.org.uk/
▷ http://cuc.ca/
▷ http://anzua.org/
▷ http://unitarian.co.za/

unitary ('ju:nɪtərɪ, -trɪ) *adj* **1** of a unit or units **2** based on or characterized by unity **3** individual; whole
unitary authority *n* (in Britain) a district administered by a single tier of local government
unit character *n genetics* a character inherited as a single unit and dependent on a single gene
unit cost *n* the actual cost of producing one article
unite[1] (ju:'naɪt) *vb* **unites, uniting, united** **1** to make or become an integrated whole or a unity **2** to join, unify or be unified in purpose, action, beliefs, etc **3** to enter or cause to enter into an association or alliance **4** to adhere or cause to adhere; fuse **5** (*tr*) to possess (qualities) in combination or at the same time: *he united charm with severity* [C15 from LL *ūnīre*, from *ūnus* one]
unite[2] ('ju:naɪt, ju:'naɪt) *n* an English gold coin of the Stuart period, originally worth 20 shillings [C17 from obs. *unite* joined, from the union of England & Scotland (1603)]
united (ju:'naɪtɪd) *adj* **1** produced by two or more persons or things in combination or from their union or amalgamation: *a united effort* **2** in agreement **3** in association or alliance > **u'nitedly** *adv* > **u'nitedness** *n*
United Arab Emirates *pl n* a group of seven emirates in SW Asia, on the Persian Gulf: consists of Abu Dhabi, Dubai, Sharjah, Ajman, Umm al Qaiwain, Ras el Khaimah, and Fujairah; a former British protectorate; became fully independent in 1971; consists mostly of flat desert, with mountains in the east; rich petroleum resources. Official language: Arabic. Official religion: Muslim. Currency: dirham. Capital: Abu Dhabi. Pop: 3 108 000 (2001 est). Area: 83 600 sq km (32 300 sq miles). Former name (until 1971): **Trucial States** Abbreviation: **UAE**

▷ www.uaeinteract.com
▷ www.uae.org.ae/tourist/index.htm
▷ www.dubaitourism.co.ae

United Arab Republic *n* the official name (1958–71) of **Egypt**
United Arab States *pl n* a federation (1958–61) between the United Arab Republic and Yemen

Uu

United Church of Canada *n* the largest Protestant denomination in Canada, formed in the 1920s by incorporating some Presbyterians and most Methodists.

United Empire Loyalist *n Canad history* an American colonist who settled in Canada during or after the War of American Independence because of loyalty to the British Crown

United Kingdom *n* a kingdom of NW Europe, consisting chiefly of the island of Great Britain together with Northern Ireland: became the world's leading colonial power in the 18th century: the first country to undergo the Industrial Revolution. It became the **United Kingdom of Great Britain and Northern Ireland** in 1921, after the rest of Ireland became autonomous as the Irish Free State. Primarily it is a trading nation, the chief exports being manufactured goods; joined the Common Market (now the European Union) in January 1973. Official language: English; Gaelic, Welsh, and other minority languages. Religion: Christian majority. Currency: pound sterling. Capital: London. Pop: 58 789 194 (2001). Area: 244 110 sq km (94 251 sq miles). Abbreviation: **UK.** See also **Great Britain**
▹ www.ukonline.gov.uk
▹ www.visitbritain.com

United Kingdom overseas territory *n* any of the territories that are governed by the UK but lie outside the British Isles; many were formerly British **crown colonies**: includes Bermuda, Falkland Islands, Gibraltar, and Montserrat

United Nations *n (functioning as sing or pl)* an international organization of independent states, with its headquarters in New York City, that was formed in 1945 to promote peace and international cooperation and security. Abbrev: **UN**
▹ www.unsystem.org

United Provinces *pl n* **1** a Dutch republic (1581–1795) formed by the union of the seven northern provinces of the Netherlands, which were in revolt against their suzerain, Philip II of Spain **2** short for **United Provinces of Agra and Oudh**: the former name of **Uttar Pradesh**

United States of America *n (functioning as singular or plural)* a federal republic mainly in North America consisting of 50 states and the District of Columbia: colonized principally by the English and French in the 17th century, the native Indians being gradually defeated and displaced; 13 colonies under British rule made the Declaration of Independence in 1776 and became the United States after the War of American Independence. The northern states defeated the South in the Civil War (1861–65). It is the world's most productive industrial nation and also exports agricultural products. It participated reluctantly in World Wars I and II but since the establishment of the United Nations in 1945 has played a major role in international affairs. It consists generally of the Rocky Mountains in the west, the Great Plains in the centre, the Appalachians in the east, deserts in the southwest, and coastal lowlands and swamps in the southeast. Language: predominantly English; Spanish is also widely spoken. Religion: Christian majority. Currency: dollar. Capital: Washington, D.C. Pop: 286 067 000 (2001 est). Area: 9 518 323 sq km (3 675 031 sq miles). Often shortened to: **United States** Abbreviations: **US, USA**
▹ www.whitehouse.gov/government
▹ www.usinfo.state.gov/usa/infousa/travel
▹ www.usatourism.com

unitive (ˈjuːnɪtɪv) *adj* **1** tending to unite or capable of uniting **2** characterized by unity

unitize *or* **unitise** (ˈjuːnɪˌtaɪz) *vb* **unitizes, unitizing, unitized** *or* **unitises, unitising, unitised** *(tr) finance* to convert (an investment trust) into a unit trust
> **ˌunitiˈzation** *or* **ˌunitiˈsation** *n*

unit-linked policy *n* a life-assurance policy the benefits of which are directly in proportion to the number of units purchased on the policyholder's behalf

unit of account *n* **1** *econ* the function of money that enables the user to keep accounts, value transactions, etc **2** a monetary denomination used for accounting purposes, etc, but not necessarily corresponding to any real currency: *the euro is the unit of account of the European Monetary Fund* **3** the unit of currency of a country

unit price *n* a price for foodstuffs, etc, stated or shown as the cost per unit, as per pound, per kilogram, per dozen, etc

unit pricing *n* a system of pricing foodstuffs, etc, in which the cost of a single unit is shown to enable shoppers to see the advantage of buying multipacks

unit trust *n Brit* an investment trust that issues units for public sale, the holders of which are creditors and not shareholders with their interests represented by a trust company independent of the issuing agency. US and Canad equivalent: **mutual fund**

unity (ˈjuːnɪtɪ) *n, pl* **unities 1** the state or quality of being one; oneness **2** the act, state, or quality of forming a whole from separate parts **3** something whole or complete that is composed of separate parts **4** mutual agreement; harmony or concord: *the participants were no longer in unity* **5** uniformity or constancy: *unity of purpose* **6** *maths* **6a** the number or numeral one **6b** a quantity assuming the value of one: *the area of the triangle was regarded as unity* **6c** the element of a set producing no change in a number following multiplication **7** any one of the three principles of dramatic structure by which the action of a play should be limited to a single plot (unity of action), a single location (unity of place), and a single day (unity of time) [C13 from OF *unité*, from L *ūnitās*, from *ūnus* one]

Univ. *abbrev for* University

univalent (ˌjuːnɪˈveɪlənt, juːˈnɪvələnt) *adj* **1** (of a chromosome during meiosis) not paired with its homologue **2** *chem* another word for **monovalent**
> **ˌuniˈvalency** *n*

univalve (ˈjuːnɪˌvælv) *zool* ▹ *adj* **1** relating to or possessing a mollusc shell that consists of a single piece (valve) ▹ *n* **2** a gastropod mollusc

universal (ˌjuːnɪˈvɜːsᵊl) *adj* **1** of or typical of the whole of mankind or of nature **2** common to or proceeding from all in a particular group **3** applicable to or affecting many individuals, conditions, or cases **4** existing or prevailing everywhere **5** applicable or occurring throughout or relating to the universe: *a universal constant* **6** (esp of a language) capable of being used and understood by all **7** embracing or versed in many fields of knowledge, activity, interest, etc **8** *machinery* designed or adapted for a range of sizes, fittings, or uses **9** *logic* (of a statement or proposition) affirming or denying something about every member of a class, as in *all men are wicked* ▹ Cf **particular** (sense 6) **10** *arch* entire; whole ▹ *n* **11** *philosophy* a general term or concept or the type such a term signifies **12** *logic* a universal proposition, statement, or formula **13** a characteristic common to every member of a particular culture or to every human being

> **USAGE** The use of *more universal* as in *his writings have long been admired by fellow scientists, but his latest book should have more universal appeal* is acceptable in modern English usage

universal class *or* **set** *n* (in Boolean algebra) the class containing all points and including all other classes

universal gas constant *n* another name for **gas constant**

universalism (ˌjuːnɪˈvɜːsəˌlɪzəm) *n* **1** a universal feature or characteristic **2** another word for **universality**

Universalism (ˌjuːnɪˈvɜːsəˌlɪzəm) *n* a system of religious beliefs maintaining that all men are predestined for salvation > ˌUniˈversalist *n, adj*

universality (ˌjuːnɪvɜːˈsælɪtɪ) *n* the state or quality of being universal

universalize *or* **universalise** (ˌjuːnɪˈvɜːsəˌlaɪz) *vb* **universalizes, universalizing, universalized** *or* **universalises, universalising, universalised** (*tr*) to make universal > **ˌuniˌversaliˈzation** *or* **ˌuniˌversaliˈsation** *n*

universal joint *or* **coupling** *n* a form of coupling between two rotating shafts allowing freedom of movement in all directions

universally (ˌjuːnɪˈvɜːsəlɪ) *adv* everywhere or in every case: *this principle applies universally*

universal motor *n* an electric motor capable of working on either direct current or single-phase alternating current at approximately the same speed and output

universal time *n* **1** (from 1928) name adopted internationally for Greenwich Mean Time (measured from Greenwich midnight), now split into several slightly different scales, one of which (UT1) is used by astronomers. Abbrev: **UT** **2** Also called: **universal coordinated time** an internationally agreed system for civil timekeeping introduced in 1960 and redefined in 1972 as an atomic timescale. Available from broadcast signals, it has a second equal to the International Atomic Time (TAI) second, the difference between UTC and TAI being an integral number of seconds with leap seconds inserted when necessary to keep it within 0.9 seconds of UT1. Abbrev: **UTC**

universe (ˈjuːnɪˌvɜːs) *n* **1** *astron* the aggregate of all existing matter, energy, and space **2** human beings collectively **3** a province or sphere of thought or activity [C16 from F, from L *ūniversum* the whole world, from *ūniversus* all together, from UNI- + *vertere* to turn]

universe of discourse *n* *logic* the complete range of objects, relations, ideas, etc, that are expressed or implied in a discussion

university (ˌjuːnɪˈvɜːsɪtɪ) *n, pl* **universities** **1** an institution of higher education having authority to award bachelors' and higher degrees, usually having research facilities **2** the buildings, members, staff, or campus of a university [C14 from OF, from Med. L *universitās* group of scholars, from LL: guild, body of men, from L: whole]

▷ www.braintrack.com
▷ www.unesco.org/iau

UNIX (ˈjuːnɪks) *n* *trademark* a multi-user operating system found on many types of computer

unjust (ʌnˈdʒʌst) *adj* not in accordance with accepted standards of fairness or justice; unfair > **unˈjustly** *adv* > **unˈjustness** *n*

unkempt (ʌnˈkɛmpt) *adj* **1** (of the hair) uncombed; dishevelled **2** ungroomed; slovenly: *unkempt appearance* [OE *uncembed*; from UN-[1] + *cembed*, p.p. of *cemban* to comb] > **unˈkemptly** *adv* > **unˈkemptness** *n*

unkind (ʌnˈkaɪnd) *adj* lacking kindness; unsympathetic or cruel > **unˈkindly** *adv* > **unˈkindness** *n*

unknowing (ʌnˈnəʊɪŋ) *adj* **1** not knowing; ignorant **2** (*postpositive*; often foll by *of*) unaware (of) > **unˈknowingly** *adv*

unknown (ʌnˈnəʊn) *adj* **1** not known, understood, or recognized **2** not established, identified, or discovered: *an unknown island* **3** not famous: *some unknown artist* ▷ *n* **4** an unknown person, quantity, or thing **5** *maths* a variable the value of which is to be discovered by solving an equation; a variable in a conditional equation > **unˈknownness** *n*

Unknown Soldier *or* **Warrior** *n* (in various countries) an unidentified soldier who has died in battle and for whom a tomb is established as a memorial to the other unidentified dead of the nation's armed forces

unlace (ʌnˈleɪs) *vb* **unlaces, unlacing, unlaced** (*tr*) **1** to loosen or undo the lacing of (shoes, etc) **2** to unfasten or remove garments, etc, of (oneself or another) by or as if by undoing lacing

unlawful assembly (ʌnˈlɔːfʊl) *n* *law* a meeting of three or more people with the intent of carrying out any unlawful purpose

unlay (ʌnˈleɪ) *vb* **unlays, unlaying, unlaid** (*tr*) to untwist (a rope or cable) to separate its strands

unleaded (ʌnˈlɛdɪd) *adj* **1** (of petrol) containing a reduced amount of tetraethyl lead, in order to reduce environmental pollution ▷ *n* **2** petrol containing a reduced amount of tetraethyl lead

unlearn (ʌnˈlɜːn) *vb* **unlearns, unlearning, unlearnt** *or* **unlearned** (-ˈlɜːnd) to try to forget (something learnt) or to discard (accumulated knowledge)

unlearned (ʌnˈlɜːnɪd) *adj* ignorant or untaught > **unˈlearnedly** *adv*

unlearnt (ʌnˈlɜːnt) *or* **unlearned** (ʌnˈlɜːnd) *adj* **1** denoting knowledge or skills innately present and therefore not learnt **2** not learnt or taken notice of: *unlearnt lessons*

unleash (ʌnˈliːʃ) *vb* (*tr*) **1** to release from or as if from a leash **2** to free from restraint

unleavened (ʌnˈlɛvənd) *adj* (of bread, etc) made from a dough containing no yeast or leavening

unless (ʌnˈlɛs) *conj* (*subordinating*) except under the circumstances that; except on the condition that: *they'll sell it unless he hears otherwise* [C14 *onlesse*, from *on* ON + *lesse* LESS]

unlettered (ʌnˈlɛtəd) *adj* uneducated; illiterate

unlike (ʌnˈlaɪk) *adj* **1** not alike; dissimilar or unequal; different ▷ *prep* **2** not like; not typical of: *unlike his father he lacks intelligence* > **unˈlikeness** *n*

unlikely (ʌnˈlaɪklɪ) *adj* not likely; improbable > **unˈlikeliness** *or* **unˈlikeliˌhood** *n*

unlimber (ʌnˈlɪmbə) *vb* **1** (*tr*) to disengage (a gun) from its limber **2** to prepare (something) for use

unlimited (ʌnˈlɪmɪtɪd) *adj* **1** without limits or bounds: *unlimited knowledge* **2** not restricted, limited, or qualified: *unlimited power* > **unˈlimitedly** *adv* > **unˈlimitedness** *n*

unlisted (ʌnˈlɪstɪd) *adj* **1** not entered on a list **2** the US and Canad word for **ex-directory**

Unlisted Securities Market *n* a market on the London Stock Exchange for trading in shares of smaller companies, who do not wish to comply with the requirements for a full listing. Abbrev: **USM**

unload (ʌnˈləʊd) *vb* **1** to remove a load or cargo from (a ship, lorry, etc) **2** to discharge (cargo, freight, etc) **3** (*tr*) to relieve of a burden or troubles **4** (*tr*) to give vent to (anxiety, troubles, etc) **5** (*tr*) to get rid of or dispose of (esp surplus goods) **6** (*tr*) to remove the charge of ammunition from (a firearm) > **unˈloader** *n*

unlock (ʌnˈlɒk) *vb* **1** (*tr*) to unfasten (a lock, door, etc) **2** (*tr*) to release or let loose **3** (*tr*) to provide the key to: *unlock a puzzle* **4** (*intr*) to become unlocked > **unˈlockable** *adj*

unlooked-for (ˌʌnˈlʊktfɔː) *adj* unexpected; unforeseen

unloose (ʌnˈluːs) *or* **unloosen** *vb* **unlooses, unloosing, unloosed** *or* **unloosens, unloosening, unloosened** (*tr*) **1** to set free; release **2** to loosen or relax (a hold, grip, etc) **3** to unfasten or untie

unlovely (ʌnˈlʌvlɪ) *adj* unpleasant in appearance or character > **unˈloveliness** *n*

unlucky (ʌnˈlʌkɪ) *adj* **1** characterized by misfortune or failure: *an unlucky chance* **2** ill-omened; inauspicious: *an unlucky date* **3** regrettable; disappointing > **unˈluckily** *adv* > **unˈluckiness** *n*

unmake (ʌnˈmeɪk) *vb* **unmakes, unmaking, unmade** (*tr*) **1** to undo or destroy **2** to depose from office or authority **3** to alter the nature of

unman (ʌnˈmæn) *vb* **unmans, unmanning, unmanned** (*tr*) **1** to cause to lose courage or nerve **2** to make effeminate **3** to remove the men from

Uu

unmanly (ʌnˈmænlɪ) *adj* **1** not masculine or virile **2** ignoble, cowardly, or dishonourable ▷ *adv* **3** *arch* in an unmanly manner > **unˈmanliness** *n*
unmanned (ʌnˈmænd) *adj* **1** lacking personnel or crew: *an unmanned ship* **2** (of aircraft, spacecraft, etc) operated by automatic or remote control **3** uninhabited
unmannered (ʌnˈmænəd) *adj* **1** without good manners; rude **2** without mannerisms
unmannerly (ʌnˈmænəlɪ) *adj* **1** lacking manners; discourteous ▷ *adv* **2** *arch* rudely; discourteously > **unˈmannerliness** *n*
unmask (ʌnˈmɑːsk) *vb* **1** to remove (the mask or disguise) from (someone or oneself) **2** to appear or cause to appear in true character > **unˈmasker** *n*
unmeaning (ʌnˈmiːnɪŋ) *adj* **1** having no meaning **2** showing no intelligence; vacant: *an unmeaning face* > **unˈmeaningly** *adv* > **unˈmeaningness** *n*
unmeet (ʌnˈmiːt) *adj literary or arch* unsuitable > **unˈmeetly** *adv* > **unˈmeetness** *n*
unmentionable (ʌnˈmɛnʃənəbᵊl) *adj* **a** unsuitable or forbidden as a topic of conversation **b** (*as n*): *the unmentionable* > **unˈmentionableness** *n* > **unˈmentionably** *adv*
unmentionables (ʌnˈmɛnʃənəbᵊlz) *pl n chiefly humorous* underwear
unmerciful (ʌnˈmɜːsɪfʊl) *adj* **1** showing no mercy; relentless **2** extreme or excessive > **unˈmercifully** *adv* > **unˈmercifulness** *n*
unmindful (ʌnˈmaɪndfʊl) *adj* (*usually postpositive* and foll by *of*) careless or forgetful > **unˈmindfully** *adv* > **unˈmindfulness** *n*
unmissable (ʌnˈmɪsəbᵊl) *adj* (of a film, television programme, etc) so good that it should not be missed
unmistakable *or* **unmistakeable** (ˌʌnmɪsˈteɪkəbᵊl) *adj* not mistakable; clear or unambiguous > **ˌunmisˈtakably** *or* **ˌunmisˈtakeably** *adv*
unmitigated (ʌnˈmɪtɪˌgeɪtɪd) *adj* **1** not diminished in intensity, severity, etc **2** (*prenominal*) (intensifier): *an unmitigated disaster* > **unˈmitiˌgatedly** *adv*
unmoral (ʌnˈmɒrəl) *adj* outside morality; amoral > **unmorality** (ˌʌnməˈrælɪtɪ) *n* > **unˈmorally** *adv*
unmurmuring (ʌnˈmɜːmərɪŋ) *adj* not complaining
unmuzzle (ʌnˈmʌzᵊl) *vb* **unmuzzles, unmuzzling, unmuzzled** (*tr*) **1** to take the muzzle off (a dog, etc) **2** to free from control or censorship
unnatural (ʌnˈnætʃərəl) *adj* **1** contrary to nature; abnormal **2** not in accordance with accepted standards of behaviour or right and wrong: *unnatural love* **3** uncanny; supernatural: *unnatural phenomena* **4** affected or forced: *an unnatural manner* **5** inhuman or monstrous: *an unnatural crime* > **unˈnaturally** *adv* > **unˈnaturalness** *n*
unnecessary (ʌnˈnɛsɪsərɪ) *adj* not necessary > **unˈnecessarily** *adv* > **unˈnecessariness** *n*
unnerve (ʌnˈnɜːv) *vb* **unnerves, unnerving, unnerved** (*tr*) to cause to lose courage, strength, confidence, self-control, etc
unnumbered (ʌnˈnʌmbəd) *adj* **1** countless; innumerable **2** not counted or assigned a number
UNO *abbrev for* United Nations Organization
unoccupied (ʌnˈɒkjʊˌpaɪd) *adj* **1** (of a building) without occupants **2** unemployed or idle **3** (of an area or country) not overrun by foreign troops
unofficial (ˌʌnəˈfɪʃəl) *adj* **1** not official or formal: *an unofficial engagement* **2** not confirmed officially: *an unofficial report* **3** (of a strike) not approved by the strikers' trade union > **ˌunofˈficially** *adv*
unorganized *or* **unorganised** (ʌnˈɔːgəˌnaɪzd) *adj* **1** not arranged into an organized system, structure, or unity **2** (of workers) not unionized **3** nonliving; inorganic
unowned (ʌnˈəʊnd) *adj* **1** unacknowledged **2** without an owner
unpack (ʌnˈpæk) *vb* **1** to remove the packed contents of (a case, trunk, etc) **2** (*tr*) to take (something) out of a packed container **3** (*tr*) to unload: *to unpack a mule* > **unˈpacker** *n*
unpaged (ʌnˈpeɪdʒd) *adj* (of a book) having no page numbers
unparalleled (ʌnˈpærəˌlɛld) *adj* unmatched; unequalled
unparliamentary (ˌʌnpɑːləˈmɛntərɪ) *adj* not consistent with parliamentary procedure or practice > **ˌunparliaˈmentarily** *adv* > **ˌunparliaˈmentariness** *n*
unpeg (ʌnˈpɛg) *vb* **unpegs, unpegging, unpegged** (*tr*) **1** to remove the peg from, esp to unfasten **2** to allow (prices, etc) to rise and fall freely
unpeople (ʌnˈpiːpᵊl) *vb* **unpeoples, unpeopling, unpeopled** (*tr*) to empty of people
unperson (ˈʌnpɜːsᵊn) *n* a person whose existence is officially denied or ignored
unpick (ʌnˈpɪk) *vb* (*tr*) **1** to undo (the stitches) of (a piece of sewing) **2** to unravel or undo (a garment, etc)
unpin (ʌnˈpɪn) *vb* **unpins, unpinning, unpinned** (*tr*) **1** to remove a pin or pins from **2** to unfasten in this way
unpleasant (ʌnˈplɛzᵊnt) *adj* not pleasant or agreeable > **unˈpleasantly** *adv* > **unˈpleasantness** *n*
unplugged (ʌnˈplʌgd) *adj* (of a performer or performance of popular music) using acoustic rather than electric instruments: *Eric Clapton unplugged; an unplugged version of the song*
unplumbed (ʌnˈplʌmd) *adj* **1** unfathomed; unsounded **2** not understood in depth **3** (of a building) having no plumbing
unpolled (ʌnˈpəʊld) *adj* **1** not included in an opinion poll **2** not having voted **3** *arch* unshorn
unpopular (ʌnˈpɒpjʊlə) *adj* not popular with an individual or group of people > **unpopularity** (ˌʌnpɒpjʊˈlærɪtɪ) *n* > **unˈpopularly** *adv*
unpractical (ʌnˈpræktɪkᵊl) *adj* another word for **impractical** > **ˌunpractiˈcality** *n* > **unˈpractically** *adv*
unpractised *or US* **unpracticed** (ʌnˈpræktɪst) *adj* **1** without skill, training, or experience **2** not used or done often or repeatedly **3** not yet tested
unprecedented (ʌnˈprɛsɪˌdɛntɪd) *adj* having no precedent; unparalleled > **unˈpreceˌdentedly** *adv*
unprejudiced (ʌnˈprɛdʒʊdɪst) *adj* not prejudiced or biased; impartial > **unˈprejudicedly** *adv*
unprincipled (ʌnˈprɪnsɪpᵊld) *adj* lacking moral principles; unscrupulous > **unˈprincipledness** *n*
unprintable (ʌnˈprɪntəbᵊl) *adj* unsuitable for printing for reasons of obscenity, libel, etc > **unˈprintableness** *n* > **unˈprintably** *adv*
unprofessional (ˌʌnprəˈfɛʃənᵊl) *adj* **1** contrary to the accepted code of conduct of a profession **2** amateur **3** not belonging to or having the required qualifications for a profession > **ˌunproˈfessionally** *adv*
unprotected sex *n* an act of sexual intercourse or sodomy performed without the use of a condom thus involving the risk of sexually transmitted diseases
unputdownable (ˌʌnpʊtˈdaʊnəbᵊl) *adj* (esp of a novel) so gripping as to be read at one sitting
unqualified (ʌnˈkwɒlɪˌfaɪd) *adj* **1** lacking the necessary qualifications **2** not restricted or modified: *an unqualified criticism* **3** (*usually prenominal*) (intensifier): *an unqualified success* > **unˈqualiˌfiable** *adj*
unquestionable (ʌnˈkwɛstʃənəbᵊl) *adj* **1** indubitable or indisputable **2** not admitting of exception: *an unquestionable ruling* > **unˌquestionaˈbility** *n* > **unˈquestionably** *adv*
unquestioned (ʌnˈkwɛstʃənd) *adj* **1** accepted without question **2** not admitting of doubt or question: *unquestioned power* **3** not questioned or interrogated
unquiet (ʌnˈkwaɪət) *chiefly literary* ▷ *adj* **1** characterized by disorder or tumult: *unquiet times* **2** anxious; uneasy ▷ *n* **3** a state of unrest > **unˈquietly** *adv* > **unˈquietness** *n*
unquote (ʌnˈkwəʊt) *interj* **1** an expression used parenthetically to indicate that the preceding quotation is finished ▷ *vb* **unquotes, unquoting,**

unquoted **2** to close (a quotation), esp in printing
unravel (ʌn'ræv^ə^l) *vb* **unravels, unravelling, unravelled** *or US* **unravels, unraveling, unraveled** **1** (*tr*) to reduce (something knitted or woven) to separate strands **2** (*tr*) to explain or solve: *the mystery was unravelled* **3** (*intr*) to become unravelled
unreactive (ˌʌnrɪ'æktɪv) *adj* (of a substance) not readily partaking in chemical reactions
unread (ʌn'rɛd) *adj* **1** (of a book, etc) not yet read **2** (of a person) having read little
unreadable (ʌn'riːdəb^ə^l) *adj* **1** illegible; undecipherable **2** difficult or tedious to read > **unˌreada'bility** *or* **un'readableness** *n*
unready (ʌn'rɛdɪ) *adj* **1** not ready or prepared **2** slow or hesitant to see or act > **un'readily** *adv* > **un'readiness** *n*
unreal (ʌn'rɪəl) *adj* **1** imaginary or fanciful or seemingly so: *an unreal situation* **2** having no actual existence or substance **3** insincere or artificial > **unreality** (ˌʌnrɪ'ælɪtɪ) *n* > **un'really** *adv*
unreason (ʌn'riːz^ə^n) *n* **1** irrationality or madness **2** something that lacks or is contrary to reason **3** lack of order; chaos
unreasonable (ʌn'riːznəb^ə^l) *adj* **1** immoderate: *unreasonable demands* **2** refusing to listen to reason **3** lacking judgment > **un'reasonableness** *n* > **un'reasonably** *adv*
unreasoning (ʌn'riːzənɪŋ) *adj* not controlled by reason; irrational > **un'reasoningly** *adv*
unregenerate (ˌʌnrɪ'dʒɛnərɪt) *adj also* **unregenerated** **1** unrepentant; unreformed **2** obstinately adhering to one's own views ▷ *n* **3** an unregenerate person > **ˌunre'generacy** *n* > **ˌunre'generately** *adv*
unrelenting (ˌʌnrɪ'lɛntɪŋ) *adj* **1** refusing to relent or take pity **2** not diminishing in determination, speed, effort, force, etc > **ˌunre'lentingly** *adv* > **ˌunre'lentingness** *n*
unreligious (ˌʌnrɪ'lɪdʒəs) *adj* **1** another word for **irreligious** **2** secular > **ˌunre'ligiously** *adv*
unremitting (ˌʌnrɪ'mɪtɪŋ) *adj* never slackening or stopping; unceasing; constant > **ˌunre'mittingly** *adv* > **ˌunre'mittingness** *n*
unreserved (ˌʌnrɪ'zɜːvd) *adj* **1** without reserve; having an open manner **2** without reservation **3** not booked or bookable > **unreservedly** (ˌʌnrɪ'zɜːvɪdlɪ) *adv* > **ˌunre'servedness** *n*
unrest (ʌn'rɛst) *n* **1** a troubled or rebellious state of discontent **2** an uneasy or troubled state
unriddle (ʌn'rɪd^ə^l) *vb* **unriddles, unriddling, unriddled** (*tr*) to solve or puzzle out [C16 from UN-[2] + RIDDLE[1]] > **un'riddler** *n*
unrig (ʌn'rɪg) *vb* **unrigs, unrigging, unrigged** **1** (*tr*) to strip (a vessel) of standing and running rigging **2** *arch or dialect* to undress (someone or oneself)
unrighteous (ʌn'raɪtʃəs) *adj* **1a** sinful; wicked **1b** (*as collective n; preceded by* the): *the unrighteous* **2** not fair or right; unjust > **un'righteously** *adv* > **un'righteousness** *n*
unrip (ʌn'rɪp) *vb* **unrips, unripping, unripped** (*tr*) **1** to rip open **2** *obs* to reveal; disclose
unripe (ʌn'raɪp) *or* **unripened** *adj* **1** not fully matured **2** not fully prepared or developed; not ready > **un'ripeness** *n*
unrivalled *or US* **unrivaled** (ʌn'raɪv^ə^ld) *adj* having no equal; matchless
unroll (ʌn'rəʊl) *vb* **1** to open out or unwind (something rolled, folded, or coiled) or (of something rolled, etc) to become opened out or unwound **2** to make or become visible or apparent, esp gradually; unfold
unruffled (ʌn'rʌf^ə^ld) *adj* **1** unmoved; calm **2** still: *the unruffled seas* > **un'ruffledness** *n*
unruly (ʌn'ruːlɪ) *adj* **unrulier, unruliest** disposed to disobedience or indiscipline > **un'ruliness** *n*
UNRWA ('ʌnrə) *n acronym for* United Nations Relief and Works Agency
▷ www.un.org.unrwa
unsaddle (ʌn'sæd^ə^l) *vb* **unsaddles, unsaddling, unsaddled** **1** to remove the saddle from (a horse, mule, etc) **2** (*tr*) to unhorse
unsaddling enclosure *n* the area at a racecourse where horses are unsaddled after a race and often where awards are given to owners, trainers, and jockeys
unsafe (ʌn'seɪf) *adj* **1** not safe; perilous **2** (of a criminal conviction) based on inadequate or false evidence > **un'safely** *adv*
unsaid (ʌn'sɛd) *adj* not said or expressed; unspoken
unsaturated (ʌn'sætʃəˌreɪtɪd) *adj* **1** not saturated **2** (of a chemical compound, esp an organic compound) containing one or more double or triple bonds and thus capable of undergoing addition reactions **3** (of a fat, esp a vegetable fat) containing a high proportion of fatty acids having double bonds > **ˌunsatu'ration** *n*
unsavoury *or US* **unsavory** (ʌn'seɪvərɪ) *adj* **1** objectionable or distasteful: *an unsavoury character* **2** disagreeable in odour or taste > **un'savourily** *or US* **un'savorily** *adv* > **un'savouriness** *or US* **un'savoriness** *n*
unsay (ʌn'seɪ) *vb* **unsays, unsaying, unsaid** (*tr*) to retract or withdraw (something said or written)
unscathed (ʌn'skeɪðd) *adj* not harmed or injured
unscramble (ʌn'skræmb^ə^l) *vb* **unscrambles, unscrambling, unscrambled** (*tr*) **1** to resolve from confusion or disorderliness **2** to restore (a scrambled message) to an intelligible form > **un'scrambler** *n*
unscrew (ʌn'skruː) *vb* **1** (*tr*) to remove a screw from (an object) **2** (*tr*) to loosen (a screw, lid, etc) by rotating, usually in an anticlockwise direction **3** (*intr*) (esp of an engaged threaded part) to become loosened or separated
unscripted (ʌn'skrɪptɪd) *adj* (of a speech, play, etc) not using or based on a script
unscrupulous (ʌn'skruːpjʊləs) *adj* without scruples; unprincipled > **un'scrupulously** *adv* > **un'scrupulousness** *n*
unseal (ʌn'siːl) *vb* (*tr*) **1** to remove or break the seal of **2** to free (something concealed or closed as if sealed): *to unseal one's lips*

unsealed (ʌn'siːld) *adj Austral & NZ* (of a road) surfaced with road metal not bound by bitumen or other sealant
unseam (ʌn'siːm) *vb* (*tr*) to open or undo the seam of
unseasonable (ʌn'siːzənəb^ə^l) *adj* **1** (esp of the weather) inappropriate for the season **2** untimely; inopportune > **un'seasonableness** *n* > **un'seasonably** *adv*
unseat (ʌn'siːt) *vb* (*tr*) **1** to throw or displace from a seat, saddle, etc **2** to depose from office or position
unseeded (ʌn'siːdɪd) *adj* (of players in various sports) not assigned to a preferential position in the preliminary rounds of a tournament
unseemly (ʌn'siːmlɪ) *adj* **1** not in good style or taste **2** *obs* unattractive ▷ *adv* **3** *rare* in an unseemly manner > **un'seemliness** *n*
unseen (ʌn'siːn) *adj* **1** not observed or perceived; invisible **2** (of passages of writing) not previously seen or prepared ▷ *n* **3** *chiefly Brit* a passage, not previously seen, that is presented to students for translation
unselfish (ʌn'sɛlfɪʃ) *adj* not selfish; generous > **un'selfishly** *adv* > **un'selfishness** *n*
unsettle (ʌn'sɛt^ə^l) *vb* **unsettles, unsettling, unsettled** **1** (*usually tr*) to change or become changed from a fixed or settled condition **2** (*tr*) to confuse or agitate (emotions, the mind, etc) > **un'settlement** *n*
unsettled (ʌn'sɛt^ə^ld) *adj* **1** lacking order or stability: *an unsettled era* **2** unpredictable: *an unsettled climate* **3** constantly changing or moving from place to place: *an unsettled life* **4** (of controversy, etc) not brought to an agreed conclusion **5** (of debts, law cases, etc) not disposed of > **un'settledness** *n*
unsex (ʌn'sɛks) *vb* (*tr*) *chiefly literary* to deprive (a person) of the attributes of his or her sex, esp to make a woman more callous

unshapen (ʌnˈʃeɪpᵊn) *adj* **1** having no definite shape; shapeless **2** deformed; misshapen

unsheathe (ʌnˈʃiːð) *vb* **unsheathes, unsheathing, unsheathed** (*tr*) to draw or pull out (something, esp a weapon) from a sheath

unship (ʌnˈʃɪp) *vb* **unships, unshipping, unshipped 1** to be or cause to be unloaded, discharged, or disembarked from a ship **2** (*tr*) *naut* to remove from a regular place: *to unship oars*

unsighted (ʌnˈsaɪtɪd) *adj* **1** not sighted **2** not having a clear view **3** (of a gun) not equipped with a sight > **unˈsightedly** *adv*

unsightly (ʌnˈsaɪtlɪ) *adj* unpleasant or unattractive to look at; ugly > **unˈsightliness** *n*

unskilful *or US* **unskillful** (ʌnˈskɪlfʊl) *adj* lacking dexterity or proficiency > **unˈskilfully** *or US* **unˈskillfully** *adv* > **unˈskilfulness** *or US* **unˈskillfulness** *n*

unskilled (ʌnˈskɪld) *adj* **1** not having or requiring any special skill or training: *an unskilled job* **2** having no skill; inexpert

unsling (ʌnˈslɪŋ) *vb* **unslings, unslinging, unslung** (*tr*) **1** to remove or release from a slung position **2** to remove slings from

unsnap (ʌnˈsnæp) *vb* **unsnaps, unsnapping, unsnapped** (*tr*) to unfasten (the snap or catch) of (something)

unsnarl (ʌnˈsnɑːl) *vb* (*tr*) to free from a snarl or tangle

unsociable (ʌnˈsəʊʃəbᵊl) *adj* **1** (of a person) disinclined to associate or fraternize with others **2** unconducive to social intercourse: *an unsociable neighbourhood* > **unˌsociaˈbility** *or* **unˈsociableness** *n*

unsocial (ʌnˈsəʊʃəl) *adj* **1** not social; antisocial **2** (of the hours of work of certain jobs) falling outside the normal working day

unsophisticated (ˌʌnsəˈfɪstɪˌkeɪtɪd) *adj* **1** lacking experience or worldly wisdom **2** marked by a lack of refinement or complexity: *an unsophisticated machine* **3** unadulterated or genuine > **ˌunsoˈphistiˌcatedly** *adv* > **ˌunsoˈphistiˌcatedness** *or* **ˌunsoˌphistiˈcation** *n*

unsound (ʌnˈsaʊnd) *adj* **1** diseased or unstable: *of unsound mind* **2** unreliable or fallacious: *unsound advice* **3** lacking strength or firmness: *unsound foundations* **4** of doubtful financial or commercial viability: *an unsound enterprise* > **unˈsoundly** *adv* > **unˈsoundness** *n*

unsparing (ʌnˈspɛərɪŋ) *adj* **1** not sparing or frugal; lavish **2** showing harshness or severity > **unˈsparingly** *adv* > **unˈsparingness** *n*

unspeakable (ʌnˈspiːkəbᵊl) *adj* **1** incapable of expression in words: *unspeakable ecstasy* **2** indescribably bad or evil **3** not to be uttered: *unspeakable thoughts* > **unˈspeakableness** *n* > **unˈspeakably** *adv*

unstable (ʌnˈsteɪbᵊl) *adj* **1** lacking stability, fixity, or firmness **2** disposed to temperamental or psychological variability **3** (of a chemical compound) readily decomposing **4** *physics* **4a** (of an elementary particle) having a very short lifetime **4b** spontaneously decomposing by nuclear decay: *an unstable nuclide* **5** *electronics* (of an electrical circuit, etc) having a tendency to self-oscillation > **unˈstableness** *n* > **unˈstably** *adv*

unsteady (ʌnˈstɛdɪ) *adj* **1** not securely fixed: *an unsteady foothold* **2** (of behaviour, etc) erratic **3** without regularity: *an unsteady rhythm* **4** (of a manner of walking, etc) precarious or staggering, as from intoxication > **unˈsteadily** *adv* > **unˈsteadiness** *n*

unstep (ʌnˈstɛp) *vb* **unsteps, unstepping, unstepped** (*tr*) *naut* to remove (a mast) from its step

unstick (ʌnˈstɪk) *vb* **unsticks, unsticking, unstuck** (*tr*) to free or loosen (something stuck)

unstop (ʌnˈstɒp) *vb* **unstops, unstopping, unstopped** (*tr*) **1** to remove the stop or stopper from **2** to free from any stoppage **3** to draw out the stops on (an organ)

unstoppable (ʌnˈstɒpəbᵊl) *adj* not capable of being stopped; extremely forceful > **unˈstoppably** *adv*

unstopped (ʌnˈstɒpt) *adj* **1** not obstructed or stopped up **2** *phonetics* denoting a speech sound for whose articulation the closure is not complete **3** *prosody* (of verse) having the sense of the line carried over into the next **4** (of an organ pipe or a string on a musical instrument) not stopped

unstriated (ʌnˈstraɪˌeɪtɪd) *adj* (of muscle) composed of elongated cells that do not have striations; smooth

unstring (ʌnˈstrɪŋ) *vb* **unstrings, unstringing, unstrung** (*tr*) **1** to remove the strings of **2** (of beads, etc) to remove from a string **3** to weaken emotionally (a person or his or her nerves)

unstriped (ʌnˈstraɪpt) *adj* (esp of smooth muscle) not having stripes; unstriated

unstructured (ʌnˈstrʌktʃəd) *adj* **1** without formal structure or systematic organization **2** without a preformed shape; (esp of clothes) loose; untailored

unstrung (ʌnˈstrʌŋ) *adj* **1** emotionally distressed; unnerved **2** (of a stringed instrument) with the strings detached

unstuck (ʌnˈstʌk) *adj* **1** freed from being stuck, glued, fastened, etc **2** **come unstuck** to suffer failure or disaster

unstudied (ʌnˈstʌdɪd) *adj* **1** natural **2** (foll by *in*) without knowledge or training

unsubscribe (ˌʌnsəbˈskraɪb) *vb* to cancel a subscription, for example to an emailing service: *you can unsubscribe at the following URL*

unsubstantial (ˌʌnsəbˈstænʃəl) *adj* **1** lacking weight or firmness **2** (of an argument) of doubtful validity **3** of no material existence > **ˌunsubˌstantiˈality** *n* > **ˌunsubˈstantially** *adv*

unsung (ʌnˈsʌŋ) *adj* **1** not acclaimed or honoured: *unsung deeds* **2** not yet sung

unsuspected (ˌʌnsəˈspɛktɪd) *adj* **1** not under suspicion **2** not known to exist > **ˌunsusˈpectedly** *adv* > **ˌunsusˈpectedness** *n*

unswerving (ʌnˈswɜːvɪŋ) *adj* not turning aside; constant

untangle (ʌnˈtæŋgᵊl) *vb* **untangles, untangling, untangled** (*tr*) **1** to free from a tangled condition **2** to free from confusion

untaught (ʌnˈtɔːt) *adj* **1** without training or education **2** attained or achieved without instruction

untenable (ʌnˈtɛnəbᵊl) *adj* **1** (of theories, etc) incapable of being maintained or vindicated **2** unable to be maintained against attack > **unˌtenaˈbility** *or* **unˈtenableness** *n* > **unˈtenably** *adv*

Unter den Linden (*German* ˈʊntər deːn ˈlɪndən) *n* the main street of Berlin, formerly in East Berlin, extending to the Brandenburg Gate

Unterwalden (*German* ˈʊntərˌvaldən) *n* a canton of central Switzerland, on Lake Lucerne: consists of the demicantons of **Nidwalden** (east) and **Obwalden** (west) Capitals: (Nidwalden) Stans; (Obwalden) Sarnen. Pop: (Nidwalden) 37 700 (2000 est); (Obwalden) 32 200 (2000 est). Areas: (Nidwalden) 274 sq km (107 sq miles); (Obwalden) 492 sq km (192 sq miles)

unthinkable (ʌnˈθɪŋkəbᵊl) *adj* **1** not to be contemplated; out of the question **2** unimaginable; inconceivable **3** unreasonable; improbable > **unˈthinkably** *adv*

unthinking (ʌnˈθɪŋkɪŋ) *adj* **1** lacking thoughtfulness; inconsiderate **2** heedless; inadvertent **3** not thinking or able to think > **unˈthinkingly** *adv* > **unˈthinkingness** *n*

unthread (ʌnˈθrɛd) *vb* (*tr*) **1** to draw out the thread or threads from (a needle, etc) **2** to disentangle

unthrone (ʌnˈθrəʊn) *vb* **unthrones, unthroning, unthroned** (*tr*) a less common word for **dethrone**

untidy (ʌnˈtaɪdɪ) *adj* **untidier, untidiest 1** not neat; slovenly ▷ *vb* **untidies, untidying, untidied 2** (*tr*) to make untidy > **unˈtidily** *adv* > **unˈtidiness** *n*

untie (ʌnˈtaɪ) *vb* **unties, untying, untied 1** to unfasten or free (a knot or something that is tied) or (of a knot, etc) to become unfastened **2** (*tr*) to free from constraint or restriction

until (ʌnˈtɪl) *conj* (*subordinating*) **1** up to (a time) that: *he laughed until he cried* **2** (*used with a negative*) before (a time or event): *until you change, you can't go out* ▷ *prep* **3** (often preceded by *up*) in or throughout the period before: *he waited until six* **4** (*used with a negative*) earlier than; before: *he won't come until tomorrow* [C13 *untill*; see TILL[1]]

USAGE The use of *until such time as* (as in *industrial action will continue until such time as our demands are met*) is unnecessary and should be avoided: *industrial action will continue until our demands are met*. See also at **till**

untimely (ʌnˈtaɪmlɪ) *adj* **1** occurring before the expected, normal, or proper time: *an untimely death* **2** inappropriate to the occasion, time, or season: *his joking at the funeral was most untimely* ▷ *adv* **3** prematurely or inopportunely > **unˈtimeliness** *n*

unto (ˈʌntuː) *prep arch* to [C13 from ON]

untogether (ˌʌntəˈgɛðə) *adj sl* incompetent or badly organized; mentally or emotionally unstable

untold (ʌnˈtəʊld) *adj* **1** incapable of description: *untold suffering* **2** incalculably great in number or quantity: *untold thousands* **3** not told

untouchable (ʌnˈtʌtʃəbᵊl) *adj* **1** lying beyond reach **2** above reproach, suspicion, or impeachment **3** unable to be touched ▷ *n* **4** a member of the lowest class in India, whom those of the four main castes were formerly forbidden to touch > **unˌtouchaˈbility** *n*

untoward (ˌʌntəˈwɔːd) *adj* **1** characterized by misfortune or annoyance **2** not auspicious; unfavourable **3** unseemly **4** out of the ordinary; out of the way **5** *arch* perverse **6** *obs* awkward > **ˌuntoˈwardly** *adv* > **ˌuntoˈwardness** *n*

untrue (ʌnˈtruː) *adj* **1** incorrect or false **2** disloyal **3** diverging from a rule, standard, or measure; inaccurate > **unˈtruly** *adv*

untruss (ʌnˈtrʌs) *vb* **1** (*tr*) to release from or as if from a truss; unfasten **2** *obs* to undress

untruth (ʌnˈtruːθ) *n* **1** the state or quality of being untrue **2** a statement, etc, that is not true

untruthful (ʌnˈtruːθfʊl) *adj* **1** (of a person) given to lying **2** diverging from the truth > **unˈtruthfully** *adv* > **unˈtruthfulness** *n*

untuck (ʌnˈtʌk) *vb* to become or cause to become loose or not tucked in: *to untuck the blankets*

untutored (ʌnˈtjuːtəd) *adj* **1** without formal education **2** lacking sophistication or refinement

unused *adj* **1** (ʌnˈjuːzd) not being or never having been made use of **2** (ʌnˈjuːst) (*postpositive*; foll by *to*) not accustomed or used (to something)

unusual (ʌnˈjuːʒʊəl) *adj* uncommon; extraordinary: *an unusual design* > **unˈusually** *adv*

unutterable (ʌnˈʌtərəbᵊl) *adj* incapable of being expressed in words > **unˈutterableness** *n* > **unˈutterably** *adv*

unvarnished (ʌnˈvɑːnɪʃt) *adj* not elaborated upon or glossed; plain and direct: *the unvarnished truth*

unveil (ʌnˈveɪl) *vb* **1** (*tr*) to remove the cover from, esp in the ceremonial unveiling of a monument, etc **2** to remove the veil from (one's own or another person's face) **3** (*tr*) to make (something concealed) known or public

unveiling (ʌnˈveɪlɪŋ) *n* **1** a ceremony involving the removal of a veil covering a statue, etc, for the first time **2** the presentation of something, esp for the first time

unvoice (ʌnˈvɔɪs) *vb* **unvoices, unvoicing, unvoiced** (*tr*) *phonetics* **1** to pronounce without vibration of the vocal cords **2** Also: **devoice** to make (a voiced speech sound) voiceless

unvoiced (ʌnˈvɔɪst) *adj* **1** not expressed or spoken **2** articulated without vibration of the vocal cords; voiceless

unwaged (ʌnˈweɪdʒd) *adj* of or denoting a person who is not receiving pay because of being unemployed or working in the home

unwarrantable (ʌnˈwɒrəntəbᵊl) *adj* incapable of vindication or justification > **unˈwarrantableness** *n* > **unˈwarrantably** *adv*

unwarranted (ʌnˈwɒrəntɪd) *adj* **1** lacking justification or authorization **2** another word for **unwarrantable**

unwary (ʌnˈwɛərɪ) *adj* lacking caution or prudence > **unˈwarily** *adv* > **unˈwariness** *n*

unwearied (ʌnˈwɪərɪd) *adj* **1** not abating or tiring **2** not fatigued; fresh > **unˈweariedly** *adv* > **unˈweariedness** *n*

unweighed (ʌnˈweɪd) *adj* **1** (of quantities purchased, etc) not measured for weight **2** (of statements, etc) not carefully considered

unwell (ʌnˈwɛl) *adj* (*postpositive*) not well; ill

unwept (ʌnˈwɛpt) *adj* **1** not wept for or lamented **2** *rare* (of tears) not shed

unwholesome (ʌnˈhəʊlsəm) *adj* **1** detrimental to physical or mental health: *an unwholesome climate* **2** morally harmful: *unwholesome practices* **3** indicative of illness, esp in appearance **4** (esp of food) of inferior quality > **unˈwholesomeness** *n*

unwieldy (ʌnˈwiːldɪ) *adj* **1** too heavy, large, or awkwardly shaped to be easily handled **2** ungainly; clumsy > **unˈwieldily** *adv* > **unˈwieldiness** *n*

unwilled (ʌnˈwɪld) *adj* not intentional; involuntary

unwilling (ʌnˈwɪlɪŋ) *adj* **1** reluctant **2** performed or said with reluctance > **unˈwillingly** *adv* > **unˈwillingness** *n*

unwind (ʌnˈwaɪnd) *vb* **unwinds, unwinding, unwound** **1** to slacken, undo, or unravel or cause to slacken, undo, or unravel **2** (*tr*) to disentangle **3** to make or become relaxed: *he finds it hard to unwind* > **unˈwindable** *adj*

unwise (ʌnˈwaɪz) *adj* lacking wisdom or prudence > **unˈwisely** *adv* > **unˈwiseness** *n*

unwish (ʌnˈwɪʃ) *vb* (*tr*) **1** to retract or revoke (a wish) **2** to desire (something) not to be or take place

Uu

unwitting (ʌnˈwɪtɪŋ) *adj* (*usually prenominal*) **1** not knowing or conscious **2** not intentional; inadvertent [OE *unwitende*, from UN-[1] + *witting*, present participle of *witan* to know] > **unˈwittingly** *adv* > **unˈwittingness** *n*

unwonted (ʌnˈwəʊntɪd) *adj* **1** out of the ordinary; unusual **2** (usually foll by *to*) *arch* unaccustomed; unused > **unˈwontedly** *adv*

unworldly (ʌnˈwɜːldlɪ) *adj* **1** not concerned with material values or pursuits **2** lacking sophistication; naive **3** not of this earth or world > **unˈworldliness** *n*

unworthy (ʌnˈwɜːðɪ) *adj* **1** (often foll by *of*) not deserving or worthy **2** (often foll by *of*) beneath the level considered befitting (to): *that remark is unworthy of you* **3** lacking merit or value **4** (of treatment) not warranted > **unˈworthily** *adv* > **unˈworthiness** *n*

unwound (ʌnˈwaʊnd) *vb* the past tense and past participle of **unwind**

unwrap (ʌnˈræp) *vb* **unwraps, unwrapping, unwrapped** to remove the covering or wrapping from (something) or (of something wrapped) to have the covering come off

unwritten (ʌnˈrɪtᵊn) *adj* **1** not printed or in writing **2** effective only through custom

unwritten law *n* the law based upon custom, usage, and judicial decisions, as distinguished from the enactments of a legislature, orders or decrees in writing, etc

unyoke (ʌnˈjəʊk) *vb* **unyokes, unyoking, unyoked** **1** to release (an animal, etc) from a yoke **2** (*tr*) to set free; liberate **3** (*tr*) to disconnect or separate

unzip (ʌnˈzɪp) *vb* **unzips, unzipping, unzipped** **1** to unfasten the zip of (a garment, etc) or (of a zip or garment with a zip) to become unfastened: *her skirt unzipped as she sat down* **2** (*tr*) *computing* to decompress a file that had previously been zipped

up (ʌp) *prep* **1** indicating movement from a lower to a higher position: *climbing up a mountain* **2** at a higher or further level or position in or on: *a shop up the road* ▷ *adv* **3** (*often particle*) to an upward, higher, or erect position, esp indicating readiness for an activity: *up and doing something* **4** (*particle*) indicating intensity or completion of an action: *he tore up the cheque* **5** to the place referred to or where the speaker is: *the man came up and asked the way* **6a** to a more important place: *up to London* **6b** to a more northerly place: *up to Scotland* **6c** (of a member of some British universities) to or at university **6d** in a particular part of the country: *up north* **7** above the horizon: *the sun is up* **8** appearing for trial: *up before the magistrate* **9** having gained: *ten pounds up on the deal* **10** higher in price: *coffee is up again* **11** raised (for discussion, etc): *the plan was up for consideration* **12** taught: *well up in physics* **13** (*functioning as imperative*) get, stand, etc, up: *up with you!* **14** **all up with** *inf* **14a** over; finished **14b** doomed to die **15** **up with** (*functioning as imperative*) wanting the beginning or continuation of: *up with the monarchy!* **16** **something's up** *inf* something strange is happening **17** **up against** **17a** touching **17b** having to cope with: *look what we're up against now* **18** **up for** **18a** as a candidate or applicant for: *he's up for re-election again* **18b** keen or willing to try: *she's up for anything* **19** **up for it** *inf* keen or willing to try something out or make a good effort: *it's a big challenge and I'm up for it* **20** **up to** **20a** devising or scheming: *she's up to no good* **20b** dependent or incumbent upon: *the decision is up to you* **20c** equal to (a challenge, etc) or capable of (doing, etc): *are you up to playing in the final?* **20d** as far as: *up to his waist in mud* **20e** as many as: *up to two years' waiting time* **20f** comparable with: *not up to your normal standard* **21** **up top** *inf* in the head or mind **22** **up yours** *sl* a vulgar expression of contempt or refusal **23** **what's up?** *inf* **23a** what is the matter? **23b** what is happening? ▷ *adj* **24** (*predicative*) of a high or higher position **25** (*predicative*) out of bed: *the children aren't up yet* **26** (*prenominal*) of or relating to a train or trains to a more important place or one regarded as higher: *the up platform* **27** (*predicative*) over or completed: *their time was up* **28** (*predicative*) beating one's opponent by a specified amount: *a goal up* ▷ *vb* **ups, upping, upped** **29** (*tr*) to increase or raise **30** (*intr; foll by* and *with a verb*) *inf* to do (something) suddenly, etc: *she upped and married someone else* ▷ *n* **31** a high point (esp in **ups and downs**) **32** *sl* another word (esp US) for **upper** (sense 8) **33** **on the up and up** **33a** trustworthy or honest: *you're sure these people are on the up and up?* **33b** *Brit* on the upward trend or movement: *our firm's on the up and up* [OE *upp*]

USAGE The use of *up* before *until* is redundant and should be avoided: *the talks will continue until* (not *up until*) *23rd March*

UP **1** United Press **2** Uttar Pradesh

up- *prefix* up, upper, or upwards: *uproot; upmost; upthrust; upgrade; uplift*

up-anchor *vb* (*intr*) *naut* to weigh anchor

up-and-comer *n inf* someone who shows promise in a particular field and appears likely to be successful

up-and-coming *adj* promising continued or future success; enterprising

up-and-down *adj* **1** moving or formed alternately upwards and downwards ▷ *adv, prep* **up and down** **2** backwards and forwards (along)

up-and-over *adj* (of a door, etc) opened by being lifted and moved into a horizontal position

up-and-under *n rugby league* a high kick forwards followed by a charge to the place where the ball lands

Upanishad (uːˈpʌnɪʃəd) *n Hinduism* any of a class of the Sanskrit sacred books probably composed between 400 and 200 BC and embodying the mystical and esoteric doctrines of ancient Hindu philosophy [C19 from Sansk. *upanisad* a sitting down near something]

upas (ˈjuːpəs) *n* **1** a large tree of Java having whitish bark and poisonous milky sap **2** the sap of this tree, used as an arrow poison ▷ Also called: **antiar** [C19 from Malay: poison]

upbeat (ˈʌpˌbiːt) *n* **1** *music* **1a** a usually unaccented beat, esp the last in a bar **1b** the upward gesture of a conductor's baton indicating this ▷ *adj* **2** *inf* marked by cheerfulness or optimism

upbraid (ʌpˈbreɪd) *vb* (*tr*) **1** to reprove or reproach angrily **2** to find fault with [OE *upbregdan*] > **upˈbraider** *n* > **upˈbraiding** *n*

upbringing (ˈʌpˌbrɪŋɪŋ) *n* the education of a person during his or her formative years

UPC *abbrev for* Universal Product Code: another name for **bar code**

upcast (ˈʌpˌkɑːst) *n* **1** material cast or thrown up **2** a ventilation shaft through which air leaves a mine **3** *geol* (in a fault) the section of strata that has been displaced upwards ▷ *adj* **4** directed or thrown upwards ▷ *vb* **upcasts, upcasting, upcast** **5** (*tr*) to throw or cast up

up close and personal *adv* **1** intimately: *he got to know the prime minister up close and personal* ▷ *adj* (**up-close-and-personal** when prenominal) **2** intimate: *up-close-and-personal interaction*

upcountry (ʌpˈkʌntrɪ) *adj* **1** of or coming from the interior of a country or region ▷ *n* **2** the interior part of a region or country ▷ *adv* **3** towards, in, or into the interior part of a country or region

update *vb* (ʌpˈdeɪt), **updates, updating, updated** (*tr*) **1** to bring up to date ▷ *n* (ˈʌpˌdeɪt) **2** the act of updating or something that is updated > **upˈdateable** *adj* > **upˈdater** *n*

Updike (ˈʌpˌdaɪk) *n* **John** (**Hoyer**) born 1932, US writer. His novels include *Rabbit, Run* (1960), *Couples* (1968), *Brazil* (1993), *Seek My Face* (2003), and *Rabbit is Rich* (1982) and *Rabbit at Rest* (1990), both of which won Pulitzer prizes

updraught *or US* **updraft** (ˈʌpˌdrɑːft) *n* an upward movement of air or other gas

upend (ʌpˈɛnd) *vb* **1** to turn or set or become turned or set on end **2** (*tr*) to affect or upset drastically

upfront (ˈʌpˈfrʌnt) *adj* **1** open and frank ▷ *adv, adj* **2** (of money) paid out at the beginning of a business arrangement

upgrade *vb* (ʌpˈgreɪd), **upgrades, upgrading, upgraded** (*tr*) **1** to assign or promote (a person or job) to a higher professional rank or position **2** to raise in value, importance, esteem, etc **3** to improve (a breed of livestock) by crossing with a better strain ▷ *n* (ˈʌpˌgreɪd) **4** *US & Canad* an upward slope **5** **on the upgrade** improving or progressing, as in importance, status, health, etc > **upˈgrader** *n*

upheaval (ʌpˈhiːvᵊl) *n* **1** a strong, sudden, or violent disturbance, as in politics **2** *geol* another word for **uplift** (sense 7)

upheave (ʌpˈhiːv) *vb* **upheaves, upheaving, upheaved** *or* **uphove** **1** to heave or rise upwards **2** *geol* to thrust (land) upwards or (of land) to be thrust upwards **3** (*tr*) to throw into disorder

upheld (ʌpˈhɛld) *vb* the past tense and past participle of **uphold**

uphill (ˈʌpˈhɪl) *adj* **1** inclining, sloping, or leading upwards **2** requiring protracted effort: *an uphill task* ▷ *adv* **3** up an incline or slope **4** against difficulties ▷ *n* **5** a rising incline

uphold (ʌpˈhəʊld) *vb* **upholds, upholding, upheld** (*tr*) **1** to maintain or defend against opposition **2** to give moral support to **3** *rare* to support physically **4** to lift up > **upˈholder** *n*

upholster (ʌpˈhəʊlstə) *vb* (*tr*) to fit (chairs, sofas, etc) with padding, springs, webbing, and covering

upholsterer (ʌpˈhəʊlstərə) *n* a person who upholsters furniture as a profession [C17 from *upholster* small furniture dealer]

upholstery (ʌpˈhəʊlstərɪ) *n pl* **upholsteries** **1** the padding, covering, etc, of a piece of furniture **2** the

business, work, or craft of upholstering
upkeep ('ʌpˌkiːp) *n* 1 the act or process of keeping something in good repair, esp over a long period 2 the cost of maintenance
upland ('ʌplənd) *n* 1 an area of high or relatively high ground ▷ *adj* 2 relating to or situated in an upland
uplift *vb* (ʌp'lɪft). (*tr*) 1 to raise; lift up 2 to raise morally, spiritually, etc 3 *Scot & NZ* to collect; pick up (goods, documents, etc) ▷ *n* ('ʌpˌlɪft) 4 the act, process, or result of lifting up 5 the act or process of bettering moral, social, or cultural conditions, etc 6 (*modifier*) designating a brassiere for lifting and supporting the breasts: *an uplift bra* 7 the process or result of land being raised to a higher level, as during a period of mountain building > **up'lifter** *n* > **up'lifting** *adj*
uplighter ('ʌpˌlaɪtə) *n* a lamp or wall light designed or positioned to cast its light upwards
upload (ʌp'ləʊd) *vb* to copy or transfer (data or a program) from one's own computer into the memory of another computer. Compare **download** (sense 1)
up-market *adj* relating to commercial products, services, etc, that are relatively expensive and of superior quality
upmost ('ʌpˌməʊst) *adj* another word for **uppermost**
Upolu (uː'pəʊluː) *n* an island in the SW central Pacific, in Samoa. Chief town: Apia. Pop: 116 248 (1991). Area: 1114 sq km (430 sq miles)
upon (ə'pɒn) *prep* 1 another word for **on** 2 indicating a position reached by going up: *climb upon my knee* 3 imminent for: *the weekend was upon us again* [C13 from UP + ON]
upper ('ʌpə) *adj* 1 higher or highest in relation to physical position, wealth, rank, status, etc 2 (*cap when part of a name*) lying farther upstream, inland, or farther north: *the upper valley of the Loire* 3 (*cap when part of a name*) *geol, archaeol* denoting the late part or division of a period, system, etc: *Upper Palaeolithic* 4 *maths* (of a limit or bound) greater than or equal to one or more numbers or variables ▷ *n* 5 the higher of two objects, people, etc 6 the part of a shoe above the sole, covering the upper surface of the foot 7 **on one's uppers** destitute 8 *sl* any of various drugs having a stimulant effect
upper atmosphere *n meteorol* that part of the atmosphere above the troposphere
Upper Austria *n* a state of N Austria: first divided from Lower Austria in 1251. Capital: Linz. Pop: 1 382 017 (2001). Area: 11 978 sq km (4625 sq miles). German name: **Oberösterreich**
Upper Burma *n* the inland regions of Burma, in the north of the country
Upper Canada *n* 1 *history* (from 1791–1841) the official name of the region of Canada lying southwest of the Ottawa River and north of the lower Great Lakes. Compare **Lower Canada** 2 (esp in E Canada) another name for **Ontario**
upper case *printing* ▷ *n* 1 the top half of a compositor's type case in which capital letters, reference marks, and accents are kept ▷ *adj* (**upper-case** *when prenominal*) 2 of or relating to capital letters kept in this case and used in the setting or production of printed or typed matter
upper chamber *n* another name for an **upper house**
upper class *n* 1 the class occupying the highest position in the social hierarchy, esp the aristocracy ▷ *adj* (**upper-class** *when prenominal*) 2 of or relating to the upper class
upper crust *n inf* the upper class
uppercut ('ʌpəˌkʌt) *n* 1 a short swinging upward blow with the fist delivered at an opponent's chin ▷ *vb* **uppercuts, uppercutting, uppercut** 2 to hit (an opponent) with an uppercut
Upper Egypt *n* one of the four main administrative districts of Egypt: extends south from Cairo to the Sudan
upper hand *n* **the** the position of control (esp in **have** *or* **get the upper hand**)
upper house *n* (*often cap*) one of the two houses of a bicameral legislature
uppermost ('ʌpəˌməʊst) *adj also* **upmost** 1 highest in position, power, importance, etc ▷ *adv* 2 in or into the highest position, etc
Upper Palatinate *n* See **Palatinate**
Upper Peninsula *n* a peninsula in the northern US between Lakes Superior and Michigan, constituting the N part of the state of Michigan
upper regions *pl n* **the** *chiefly literary* the sky; heavens
Upper Silesia *n* a region of SW Poland, formerly ruled by Germany: coal mining and other heavy industry
Upper Tunguska *n* See **Tunguska**
Upper Volta ('vɒltə) *n* the former name (until 1984) of **Burkina-Faso**
upper works *pl n naut* the parts of a vessel above the water line when fully laden
uppish ('ʌpɪʃ) *adj Brit inf* another word for **uppity** (sense 1) [C18 from UP + -ISH] > **'uppishly** *adv* > **'uppishness** *n*
uppity ('ʌpɪtɪ) *adj inf* 1 snobbish, arrogant, or presumptuous 2 offensively self-assertive [from UP + fanciful ending, ? infl. by -ITY]
Uppsala ('ʌpsɑːlə) *n* a city in E central Sweden: the royal headquarters in the 13th century; Gothic cathedral (the largest in Sweden) and Sweden's oldest university (1477). Pop: 188 478 (2000 est)
upraise (ʌp'reɪz) *vb* **upraises, upraising, upraised** (*tr*) *chiefly literary* to lift up; elevate > **up'raiser** *n*
uprear (ʌp'rɪə) *vb* (*tr*) to lift up; raise
upright ('ʌpˌraɪt) *adj* 1 vertical or erect 2 honest or just ▷ *adv* 3 vertically ▷ *n* 4 a vertical support, such as a stake or post 5 short for **upright piano** 6 the state of being vertical > **'upˌrightly** *adv* > **'upˌrightness** *n*
upright piano *n* a piano which has a rectangular vertical case
uprise *vb* (ʌp'raɪz), **uprises, uprising, uprose, uprisen** 1 (*tr*) to rise up ▷ *n* ('ʌpˌraɪz) 2 another word for **rise** (senses 23, 24) > **up'riser** *n*
uprising ('ʌpˌraɪzɪŋ, ʌp'raɪzɪŋ) *n* 1 a revolt or rebellion 2 *arch* an ascent
uproar ('ʌpˌrɔː) *n* a commotion or disturbance characterized by loud noise and confusion
uproarious (ʌp'rɔːrɪəs) *adj* 1 causing or characterized by an uproar 2 extremely funny 3 (of laughter, etc) loud and boisterous > **up'roariously** *adv* > **up'roariousness** *n*
uproot (ʌp'ruːt) *vb* (*tr*) 1 to pull up by or as if by the roots 2 to displace (a person or persons) from native or habitual surroundings 3 to remove or destroy utterly > **up'rooter** *n*
uprush ('ʌpˌrʌʃ) *n* an upward rush, as of consciousness
upsadaisy ('ʌpsə'deɪzɪ) *interj* a variant spelling of **upsy-daisy**
ups and downs *pl n* alternating periods of good and bad fortune, high and low spirits, etc
upscale ('ʌp'skeɪl) *adj inf* of or for the upper end of an economic or social scale; up-market
upset *vb* (ʌp'sɛt), **upsets, upsetting, upset** (*mainly tr*) 1 (*also intr*) to tip or be tipped over; overturn or spill 2 to disturb the normal state or stability of: *to upset the balance of nature* 3 to disturb mentally or emotionally 4 to defeat or overthrow, usually unexpectedly 5 to make physically ill: *seafood always upsets my stomach* 6 to thicken or spread (the end of a bar, etc) by hammering ▷ *n* ('ʌpˌsɛt) 7 an unexpected defeat or reversal, as in a contest or plans 8 a disturbance or disorder of the emotions, body, etc ▷ *adj* (ʌp'sɛt) 9 overturned or capsized 10 emotionally or physically disturbed or distressed 11 disordered; confused 12 defeated or overthrown [C14 (in the sense: to erect; C19 in the sense: to overthrow)] > **up'setter** *n* > **up'setting** *adj* > **up'settingly** *adv*

Uu

upset price *n chiefly Scot, US, & Canad* the lowest price acceptable for something that is for sale, esp a house ▷ Cf **reserve price**
upshot ('ʌpˌʃɒt) *n* **1** the final result; conclusion; outcome **2** *archery* the final shot in a match [c16 from UP + SHOT[1]]
upside ('ʌpˌsaɪd) *n* the upper surface or part
upside down *adj* **1** (*usually postpositive;* **upside-down** *when prenominal*) turned over completely; inverted **2** (**upside-down** *when prenominal*) *inf* confused; topsy-turvy: *an upside-down world* ▷ *adv* **3** in an inverted fashion **4** in a chaotic manner [c16 var., by folk etymology, of earlier *upsodown*]
upside-down cake *n* a sponge cake baked with fruit at the bottom, and inverted before serving
upsides (ˌʌp'saɪdz) *adv inf, chiefly Brit* (foll by *with*) equal or level (with), as through revenge
upsilon ('ʌpsɪˌlɒn) *n* **1** the 20th letter in the Greek alphabet (Υ or υ), a vowel transliterated as *y* or *u* **2** a heavy short-lived subatomic particle produced by bombarding beryllium nuclei with high-energy protons [c17 from Med. Gk *u psilon* simple *u*, name adopted for graphic *u* to avoid confusion with graphic *oi*, since pronunciation was the same for both in LGk]
upskill ('ʌpˌskɪl) *vb* (*tr*) NZ to improve a person's aptitude for work by additional training
upstage ('ʌp'steɪdʒ) *adv* **1** on, at, or to the rear of the stage ▷ *adj* **2** of or relating to the back half of the stage **3** *inf* haughty ▷ *vb* **upstages, upstaging, upstaged** (*tr*) **4** to move upstage of (another actor), thus forcing him or her to turn away from the audience **5** *inf* to draw attention to oneself from (someone else) **6** *inf* to treat haughtily
upstairs ('ʌp'stɛəz) *adv* **1** up the stairs; to or on an upper floor **2** *inf* to or into a higher rank or office ▷ *n* (*functioning as sing or pl*) **3a** an upper floor **3b** (*as modifier*): *an upstairs room* **4** *Brit inf, old-fashioned* the masters and mistresses of a household collectively, esp of a large house
upstanding (ʌp'stændɪŋ) *adj* **1** of good character **2** upright and vigorous in build **3 be upstanding 3a** (in a court of law) a direction to all persons present to rise to their feet before the judge enters or leaves the court **3b** (at a formal dinner) a direction to all persons present to rise to their feet for a toast
upstart ('ʌpˌstɑːt) *n* **1a** a person, group, etc, that has risen suddenly to a position of power **1b** (*as modifier*): *an upstart family* **2a** an arrogant person **2b** (*as modifier*): *his upstart ambition*
upstate ('ʌp'steɪt) US ▷ *adj, adv* **1** towards, in, or relating to the outlying or northern sections of a state ▷ *n* **2** the outlying, esp northern, sections of a state > '**up'stater** *n*
upstream ('ʌp'striːm) *adv, adj* **1** in or towards the higher part of a stream; against the current ▷ Cf **downstream** **2** (in the oil industry) of or for any of the stages prior to oil production, such as exploration or research
upstretched (ʌp'strɛtʃt) *adj* (esp of the arms) stretched or raised up
upstroke ('ʌpˌstrəʊk) *n* **1a** an upward stroke or movement, as of a pen or brush **1b** the mark produced by such a stroke **2** the upward movement of a piston in a reciprocating engine
up-sum *n* a summing-up
upsurge *vb* (ʌp'sɜːdʒ), **upsurges, upsurging, upsurged** **1** (*intr*) *chiefly literary* to surge up ▷ *n* ('ʌpˌsɜːdʒ) **2** a rapid rise or swell
upsweep *n* ('ʌpˌswiːp) **1** a curve or sweep upwards ▷ *vb* (ʌp'swiːp), **upsweeps, upsweeping, upswept** **2** to sweep, curve, or brush or be swept, curved, or brushed upwards
upswing ('ʌpˌswɪŋ) *n* **1** *econ* a recovery period in the trade cycle **2** an upward swing or movement or any increase or improvement
upsy-daisy ('ʌpsɪ'deɪzɪ) *or* **upsadaisy** *interj* an expression, usually of reassurance, uttered as when someone, esp a child, stumbles or is being lifted up [c18 *up-a-daisy*, irregularly formed from UP (adv)]
uptake ('ʌpˌteɪk) *n* **1** a pipe, shaft, etc, that is used to convey smoke or gases, esp one that connects a furnace to a chimney **2** lifting up **3** the act of accepting something on offer **4 quick** (*or* **slow**) **on the uptake** *inf* quick (or slow) to understand or learn
upthrow ('ʌpˌθrəʊ) *n geol* the upward movement of rocks on one side of a fault plane relative to rocks on the other side
upthrust ('ʌpˌθrʌst) *n* **1** an upward push or thrust **2** *geol* a violent upheaval of the earth's surface
uptight (ʌp'taɪt) *adj inf* **1** displaying tense repressed nervousness, irritability, or anger **2** unable to give expression to one's feelings
uptime ('ʌpˌtaɪm) *n commerce* time during which a machine, such as a computer, actually operates
up-to-date *adj* **a** modern or fashionable: *an up-to-date magazine* **b** (*predicative*): *the magazine is up to date* > '**up-to-'dateness** *n*
uptown ('ʌp'taʊn) *US & Canad* ▷ *adj, adv* **1** towards, in, or relating to some part of a town that is away from the centre ▷ *n* **2** such a part of a town, esp a residential part > '**up'towner** *n*
upturn *vb* (ʌp'tɜːn) **1** to turn or cause to turn over or upside down **2** (*tr*) to create disorder **3** (*tr*) to direct upwards ▷ *n* ('ʌpˌtɜːn) **4** an upward trend or improvement **5** an upheaval
UPVC *abbrev for* unplasticized polyvinyl chloride. See also **PVC**
upward ('ʌpwəd) *adj* **1** directed or moving towards a higher point or level ▷ *adv* **2** a variant of **upwards** > '**upwardly** *adv* > '**upwardness** *n*
upwardly mobile *adj* (of a person or social group) moving or aspiring to move to a higher social class or status
upward mobility *n* movement from a lower to a higher economic and social status
upwards ('ʌpwədz) *or* **upward** *adv* **1** from a lower to a higher place, level, condition, etc **2** towards a higher level, standing, etc
upwind ('ʌp'wɪnd) *adv* **1** into or against the wind **2** towards or on the side where the wind is blowing; windward ▷ *adj* **3** going against the wind: *the upwind leg of the course* **4** on the windward side
Ur (ɜː) *n* an ancient city of Sumer located on a former channel of the Euphrates
UR *text messaging abbrev for:* **1** you are **2** your
uracil ('jʊərəsɪl) *n biochem* a pyrimidine present in all living cells, usually in a combined form, as in RNA [c20 from URO- + ACETIC + -ILE]
uraemia *or US* **uremia** (jʊ'riːmɪə) *n pathol* the accumulation of waste products, normally excreted in the urine, in the blood [c19 from NL, from Gk *ouron* urine + *haima* blood] > **u'raemic** *or US* **u'remic** *adj*
uraeus (jʊ'riːəs) *n, pl* **uraeuses** the sacred serpent represented on the headdresses of ancient Egyptian kings and gods [c19 from NL, from Gk *ouraios*, from Egyptian *uro* asp]
Ural ('jʊərəl; *Russian* u'ral) *n* a river in central Russia, rising in the S Ural Mountains and flowing south to the Caspian Sea. Length: 2534 km (1575 miles)
Ural-Altaic *n* **1** a postulated group of related languages consisting of the Uralic and Altaic families of languages ▷ *adj* **2** of or relating to this group of languages, characterized by agglutination and vowel harmony
Uralic (jʊ'rælɪk) *or* **Uralian** (jʊ'reɪlɪən) *n* **1** a superfamily of languages consisting of the Finno-Ugric family together with Samoyed. See also **Ural-Altaic** ▷ *adj* **2** of or relating to these languages
Ural Mountains *or* **Urals** *pl n* a mountain system in W central Russia, extending over 2000 km (1250 miles)

from the Arctic Ocean towards the Aral Sea: forms part of the geographical boundary between Europe and Asia; one of the richest mineral areas in the world, with many associated major industrial centres. Highest peak: Mount Narodnaya, 1894 m (6214 ft)

uranalysis (ˌjʊərəˈnælɪsɪs) *n, pl* **uranalyses** (-ˌsiːz) *med* a variant spelling of **urinalysis**

uranide (ˈjʊərəˌnaɪd) *n* any element having an atomic number greater than that of protactinium

uranism (ˈjʊərænɪzəm) *n rare* homosexuality (esp male homosexuality) [c20 from G *Uranismus*, from Gk *ouranios* heavenly, i.e. spiritual]

uranium (jʊˈreɪnɪəm) *n* a radioactive silvery-white metallic element of the actinide series. It occurs in several minerals including pitchblende and is used chiefly as a source of nuclear energy by fission of the radioisotope **uranium-235** Symbol: U; atomic no.: 92; atomic wt.: 238.03; half-life of most stable isotope, ^{238}U: 4.51×10^9 years [c18 from NL, from URANUS²; from the fact that the element was discovered soon after the planet]

uranium series *n physics* a radioactive series that starts with uranium-238 and proceeds by radioactive decay to lead-206

urano- *combining form* denoting the heavens: *uranography* [from Gk *ouranos*]

uranography (ˌjʊərəˈnɒɡrəfɪ) *n* the branch of astronomy concerned with the description and mapping of the stars, galaxies, etc > ˌ**uraˈnographer** *n* > **uranographic** (ˌjʊərənəˈɡræfɪk) *adj*

Uranus¹ (jʊˈreɪnəs, ˈjʊərənəs) *n Greek myth* the personification of the sky, who, as a god, ruled the universe and fathered the Titans and Cyclopes; overthrown by his son Cronus

Uranus² (jʊˈreɪnəs, ˈjʊərənəs) *n* the seventh planet from the sun, sometimes visible to the naked eye [c19 from L *Ūranus*, from Gk *Ouranos* heaven]

▷ www.solarviews.com/eng/uranus.htm

▷ http://nssdc.gsfc.nasa.gov/planetary/planets

urate (ˈjʊəreɪt) *n* any salt or ester of uric acid > **uratic** (jʊˈrætɪk) *adj*

urban (ˈɜːbᵊn) *adj* **1** of, relating to, or constituting a city or town **2** living in a city or town ▷ Cf **rural** [c17 from L *urbānus*, from *urbs* city]

Urban II (ˈɜːbᵊn) *n* original name *Odo* or *Udo*. ?1042–99, French ecclesiastic; pope (1088–99). He inaugurated the First Crusade at the Council of Clermont (1095)

urban area *n* (in population censuses) a city area considered as the inner city plus built-up environs, irrespective of local body administrative boundaries

urban district *n* **1** (in England and Wales from 1888 to 1974 and Northern Ireland from 1898 to 1973) an urban division of an administrative county with an elected council in charge of housing and environmental services **2** (in the Republic of Ireland) any of 49 medium-sized towns with their own elected councils

urbane (ɜːˈbeɪn) *adj* characterized by elegance or sophistication [c16 from L *urbānus* of the town; see URBAN] > **urˈbanely** *adv* > **urˈbaneness** *n*

urban guerrilla *n* a guerrilla who operates in a town or city, engaging in terrorism, kidnapping, etc

urbanism (ˈɜːbəˌnɪzəm) *n chiefly US* **a** the character of city life **b** the study of this

urbanite (ˈɜːbəˌnaɪt) *n* a resident of an urban community; city dweller

urbanity (ɜːˈbænɪtɪ) *n, pl* **urbanities 1** the quality of being urbane **2** (*usually pl*) civilities or courtesies

urbanize *or* **urbanise** (ˈɜːbəˌnaɪz) *vb* **urbanizes, urbanizing, urbanized** *or* **urbanises, urbanising, urbanised** (*tr*) (*usually passive*) **a** to make (esp a predominantly rural area or country) more industrialized and urban **b** to cause the migration of an increasing proportion of (rural dwellers) into cities > ˌ**urbaniˈzation** *or* ˌ**urbaniˈsation** *n*

urban myth *or* **legend** *n* a story, esp one with a shocking or amusing ending, related as having actually happened, usually to someone vaguely connected with the teller

urban renewal *n* the process of redeveloping dilapidated or no longer functional urban areas

urbi et orbi *Latin* (ˈɜːbɪ ɛt ˈɔːbɪ) *adv RC Church.* to the city and the world: a phrase qualifying the solemn papal blessing

urceolate (ˈɜːsɪəlɪt, -ˌleɪt) *adj biol* shaped like an urn or pitcher: *an urceolate corolla* [c18 via NL from L *urceolus*, dim. of *urceus* a pitcher]

urchin (ˈɜːtʃɪn) *n* **1** a mischievous roguish child, esp one who is young, small, or raggedly dressed **2** See **sea urchin 3** *arch, dialect* a hedgehog **4** *obs* an elf or sprite [c13 *urchon*, from OF *heriçon*, from L *ēricius* hedgehog]

Urdu (ˈʊəduː, ˈɜː-) *n* an official language of Pakistan, also spoken in India. The script derives primarily from Persia. It belongs to the Indic branch of the Indo-European family of languages, being closely related to Hindi [c18 from Hindustani (*zabāni*) *urdū* (language of the) camp, from Persian *urdū* camp, from Turkish *ordū*]

-ure *suffix forming nouns* **1** indicating act, process, or result: *seizure* **2** indicating function or office: *legislature; prefecture* [from F, from L *-ūra*]

urea (ˈjʊərɪə) *n* a white water-soluble crystalline compound, produced by protein metabolism and excreted in urine. A synthetic form is used as a fertilizer and animal feed. Formula: $CO(NH_2)_2$ [c19 from NL, from F *urée*, from Gk *ouron* urine] > **uˈreal** *or* **uˈreic** *adj*

urea-formaldehyde resin *n* any one of a class of rigid odourless synthetic materials that are made from urea and formaldehyde and are used in electrical fittings, adhesives, laminates, and finishes for textiles

ureide (ˈjʊərɪˌaɪd) *n chem* **1** any of a class of organic compounds derived from urea by replacing one or more of its hydrogen atoms by organic groups **2** any of a class of derivatives of urea and carboxylic acids, in which one or more of the hydrogen atoms have been replaced by acid radical groups

-uret *suffix of nouns* formerly used to form the names of binary chemical compounds [from NL *-uretum*]

ureter (jʊˈriːtə) *n* the tube that conveys urine from the kidney to the urinary bladder or cloaca [c16 via NL from Gk *ourētēr*, from *ourein* to urinate] > **uˈreteral** *or* **ureteric** (ˌjʊərɪˈtɛrɪk) *adj*

urethane (ˈjʊərɪˌθeɪn) *or* **urethan** (ˈjʊərɪˌθæn) *n* short for **polyurethane** [c19 from URO- + ETHYL + -ANE]

urethra (jʊˈriːθrə) *n, pl* **urethrae** (-θriː) *or* **urethras** the canal that in most mammals conveys urine from the bladder out of the body. In human males it also conveys semen [c17 via LL from Gk *ourēthra*, from *ourein* to urinate] > **uˈrethral** *adj*

urethritis (ˌjʊərɪˈθraɪtɪs) *n* inflammation of the urethra [c19 from NL, from LL URETHRA] > **urethritic** (ˌjʊərɪˈθrɪtɪk) *adj*

urethroscope (jʊˈriːθrəˌskəʊp) *n* a medical instrument for examining the urethra [c20 see URETHRA, -SCOPE] > **urethroscopic** (jʊˌriːθrəˈskɒpɪk) *adj* > **urethroscopy** (ˌjʊərɪˈθrɒskəpɪ) *n*

uretic (jʊˈrɛtɪk) *adj* of or relating to the urine [c19 via LL from Gk *ourētikos*, from *ouron* urine]

Urey (ˈjʊərɪ) *n* **Harold Clayton** 1893–1981, US chemist, who discovered the heavy isotope of hydrogen, deuterium (1932), and worked on methods of separating uranium isotopes: Nobel prize for chemistry 1934

Urfa (ˈɜːfə) *n* a city in SE Turkey: market centre. Pop: 410 762 (1997). Ancient name: **Edessa**

Urga (ˈɜːɡə) *n* the former name (until 1924) of **Ulan Bator**

urge (ɜːdʒ) *vb* **urges, urging, urged** (*tr*) **1** to plead, press, or move (someone to do something): *we urged him to*

Uu

surrender **2** (*may take a clause as object*) to advocate or recommend earnestly and persistently: *to urge the need for safety* **3** to impel, drive, or hasten onwards: *he urged the horses on* ▷ *n* **4** a strong impulse, inner drive, or yearning [C16 from L *urgēre*]

urgent ('ɜːdʒənt) *adj* **1** requiring or compelling speedy action or attention: *the matter is urgent* **2** earnest and persistent [C15 via F from L *urgent-*, *urgens*, present participle of *urgēre* to URGE] > **urgency** ('ɜːdʒənsɪ) *n* > **'urgently** *adv*

-urgy *n combining form* indicating technology concerned with a specified material: *metallurgy* [from Gk *-urgia*, from *ergon* work]

Uri (*German* 'uːri) *n* one of the original three cantons of Switzerland, in the centre of the country: mainly German-speaking and Roman Catholic. Capital: Altdorf. Pop: 35 500 (2000 est). Area: 1075 sq km (415 sq miles)

-uria *n combining form* indicating a diseased or abnormal condition of the urine: *pyuria* [from Gk *-ouria*, from *ouron* urine] > **-uric** *adj combining form*

Uriah (jʊ'raɪə) *n Old Testament* a Hittite officer, who was killed in battle on instructions from David so that he could marry Uriah's wife Bathsheba (II Samuel 11)

uric ('jʊərɪk) *adj* of, concerning, or derived from urine [C18 from URO- + -IC]

uric acid *n* a white odourless tasteless crystalline product of protein metabolism, present in the blood and urine. Formula: $C_5H_4N_4O_3$

uridine ('jʊərɪˌdiːn) *n biochem* a nucleoside present in all living cells in a combined form, esp in RNA [C20 from URO- + -IDE + -INE[2]]

urinal (jʊ'raɪnᵊl, 'jʊərɪ-) *n* **1** a sanitary fitting, esp one fixed to a wall, used by men for urination **2** a room containing urinals **3** any vessel for holding urine prior to its disposal

urinalysis (ˌjʊərɪ'nælɪsɪs) *n, pl* **urinalyses** (-ˌsiːz) *med* analysis of the urine to test for the presence of disease by the presence of proteins, glucose, ketones, cells, etc

urinary ('jʊərɪnərɪ) *adj* **1** *anat* of or relating to urine or to the organs and structures that secrete and pass urine ▷ *n, pl* **urinaries** **2** a reservoir for urine
▷ www.urolog.nl

urinary bladder *n* a distensible membranous sac in which the urine excreted from the kidneys is stored

urinate ('jʊərɪˌneɪt) *vb* **urinates, urinating, urinated** (*intr*) to excrete or void urine > **ˌuri'nation** *n* > **'urinative** *adj*

urine ('jʊərɪn) *n* the pale yellow slightly acid fluid excreted by the kidneys, containing waste products removed from the blood. It is stored in the urinary bladder and discharged through the urethra [C14 via OF from L *ūrīna*]

urinogenital (ˌjʊərɪnəʊ'dʒɛnɪtᵊl) *adj* another word for **urogenital**

URL *abbrev for* uniform resource locator: a standardized address of a location on the Internet

Urmia ('ɜːmɪə) *n* **Lake** a shallow lake in NW Iran, at an altitude of 1300 m (4250 ft): the largest lake in Iran, varying in area from 4000–6000 sq km (1500–2300 sq miles) between autumn and spring

Urmston ('ɜːmstən) *n* a town in NW England, in Salford unitary authority, Greater Manchester. Pop: 41 804 (1991)

urn (ɜːn) *n* **1** a vaselike receptacle or vessel, esp a large bulbous one with a foot **2** a vase used as a receptacle for the ashes of the dead **3** a large vessel, usually of metal, with a tap, used for making and holding tea, coffee, etc [C14 from L *ūrna*] > **'urnˌlike** *adj*

urnfield ('ɜːnˌfiːld) *n* **1** a cemetery full of individual cremation urns ▷ *adj* **2** (of a number of Bronze Age cultures) characterized by cremation in urns, which began in E Europe about the second millennium BC

uro- *or before a vowel* **ur-** *combining form* indicating urine or the urinary tract: *urogenital; urology* [from Gk *ouron* urine]

urogenital (ˌjʊərəʊ'dʒɛnɪtᵊl) *or* **urinogenital** *adj* of or relating to the urinary and genital organs and their functions. Also: **genitourinary**

urogenital system *or* **tract** *n anat* the urinary tract and reproductive organs

urolith ('jʊərəʊlɪθ) *n pathol* a calculus in the urinary tract > **ˌuro'lithic** *adj*

urology (jʊ'rɒlədʒɪ) *n* the branch of medicine concerned with the study and treatment of diseases of the urogenital tract > **urologic** (ˌjʊərə'lɒdʒɪk) *adj* > **u'rologist** *n*

uropygial gland (ˌjʊərə'pɪdʒɪəl) *n* a gland, situated at the base of the tail in most birds, that secretes oil used in preening

uropygium (ˌjʊərə'pɪdʒɪəm) *n* the hindmost part of a bird's body, from which the tail feathers grow [C19 via NL from Gk *ouropugion*, from *oura* tail + *pugē* rump] > **ˌuro'pygial** *adj*

uroscopy (jʊ'rɒskəpɪ) *n med* examination of the urine. See also **urinalysis** > **uroscopic** (ˌjʊərə'skɒpɪk) *adj* > **u'roscopist** *n*

Ursa Major ('ɜːsə 'meɪdʒə) *n, Latin genitive* **Ursae Majoris** ('ɜːsiː mə'dʒɔːrɪs) an extensive conspicuous constellation in the N hemisphere. The seven brightest stars form the **Plough**. Also called: the **Great Bear**, the **Bear** [L: greater bear]

Ursa Minor ('ɜːsə 'maɪnə) *n, Latin genitive* **Ursae Minoris** ('ɜːsiː mɪ'nɔːrɪs) a small faint constellation, the brightest star of which is the Pole Star. Also called: the **Little Bear**, the **Bear** [L: lesser bear]

ursine ('ɜːsaɪn) *adj* of, relating to, or resembling a bear or bears [C16 from L *ursus* a bear]

Ursprache *German* ('uːrʃpraːxə) *n* any hypothetical extinct and unrecorded language reconstructed from groups of related recorded languages. For example, Indo-European is an Ursprache reconstructed by comparison of the Germanic group, Latin, Sanskrit, etc [from *ur-* primeval + *Sprache* language]

Ursula ('ɜːsjʊlə) *n* **Saint** a legendary British princess of the fourth or fifth century AD, said to have been martyred together with 11 000 virgins by the Huns at Cologne. Feast day: Oct 21

Ursuline ('ɜːsjʊˌlaɪn) *n* **1** a member of an order of nuns devoted to teaching in the Roman Catholic Church: founded in 1537 at Brescia ▷ *adj* **2** of or relating to this order [C16 after St URSULA, patron saint of St Angela Merici, who founded the order]

Urtext *German* ('uːrtɛkst) *n* **1** the earliest form of a text as established by linguistic scholars as a basis for variants in later texts still in existence **2** an edition of a musical score showing the composer's intentions without later editorial interpolation [from *ur-* original + TEXT]

urticaceous (ˌɜːtɪ'keɪʃəs) *adj* of or belonging to a family of plants having small flowers and, in many species, stinging hairs: includes the nettles and pellitory [C18 via NL from L *urtīca* nettle, from *ūrere* to burn]

urticaria (ˌɜːtɪ'kɛərɪə) *n* a skin condition characterized by the formation of itchy red or whitish raised patches, usually caused by an allergy. Nontechnical names: **hives, nettle rash** [C18 from NL, from L *urtīca* nettle]

urtication (ˌɜːtɪ'keɪʃən) *n* **1** a burning or itching sensation **2** another name for **urticaria**

Uru. *abbrev for* Uruguay

Uruapan (*Spanish* u'rwapan) *n* a city in SW Mexico, in Michoacán state: agricultural trading centre. Pop: 227 000 (2000 est)

Uruguay ('jʊərəˌgwaɪ) *n* a republic in South America, on the Atlantic: Spanish colonization began in 1624, followed by Portuguese settlement in 1680; revolted against Spanish rule in 1820 but was annexed by the Portuguese to Brazil; gained independence in 1825. It

consists mainly of rolling grassy plains, low hills, and plateaus. Official language: Spanish. Religion: Roman Catholic majority. Currency: peso. Capital: Montevideo. Pop: 3 303 000 (2001 est). Area: 176 215 sq km (68 037 sq miles) > ˌ**Uru'guayan** *adj, n*
▷ www.turismo.gub.uy
▷ www.visit-uruguay.com

Urumchi (uːˈruːmtʃɪ), **Urumqi**, *or* **Wu-lu-mu-ch'i** *n* a city in NW China, capital of Xinjiang Uygur Autonomous Region: trading centre on a N route between China and central Asia. Pop: 1 258 457 (1999 est). Former name: **Tihwa**

Urundi (ʊˈrʊndɪ) *n* the former name (until 1962) of **Burundi**

urus (ˈjʊərəs) *n, pl* **uruses** another name for the **aurochs** [C17 from *ūrus*, of Gmc origin]

urushiol (ˈuːrʊʃɪˌɒl, uːˈruː-) *n* a poisonous pale yellow liquid occurring in poison ivy and the lacquer tree [from Japanese *urushi* lacquer + -OL²]

us (ʌs) *pron (objective)* **1** refers to the speaker or writer and another person or other people: *don't hurt us* **2** refers to all people or people in general: *this table shows us the tides* **3** an informal word for **me**: *give us a kiss!* **4** a formal word for **me** used by editors, monarchs, etc [OE *ūs*]

USAGE See at **me**

US *or* **U.S.** *abbrev for* United States

USA *abbrev for:* **1** Also: **U.S.A.** United States of America **2** United States Army
▷ www.army.mil

usable *or* **useable** (ˈjuːzəbᵊl) *adj* able to be used > ˌ**usa'bility** *or* ˌ**usea'bility** *n*

USAF *abbrev for* United States Air Force
▷ www.airforce.com

usage (ˈjuːsɪdʒ, -zɪdʒ) *n* **1** the act or a manner of using; use; employment **2** constant use, custom, or habit **3** something permitted or established by custom or practice **4** what is actually said in a language, esp as contrasted with what is prescribed [C14 via OF from L *ūsus* USE (n)]

usance (ˈjuːzəns) *n commerce* the period of time permitted by commercial usage for the redemption of foreign bills of exchange [C14 from OF, from Med. L *ūsantia*, from *ūsāre* to USE]

USB *abbrev for* universal serial bus: a standard for connecting sockets on computers

USB key *n computing* another name for **pocket drive**

USB port *n computing* a type of serial port for connecting peripheral devices in a system

USDAW (ˈʌsdɔː) *n* (in Britain) *acronym for* Union of Shop, Distributive, and Allied Workers

use *vb* (juːz), **uses, using, used** *(tr)* **1** to put into service or action; employ for a given purpose: *to use a spoon to stir with* **2** to make a practice or habit of employing; exercise: *he uses his brain* **3** to behave towards in a particular way, esp for one's own ends: *he uses people* **4** to consume, expend, or exhaust: *the engine uses very little oil* **5** to partake of (alcoholic drink, drugs, etc) or smoke (tobacco, marijuana, etc) ▷ *n* (juːs) **6** the act of using or the state of being used: *the carpet wore out through constant use* **7** the ability or permission to use **8** the occasion to use: *I have no use for this paper* **9** an instance or manner of using **10** usefulness; advantage: *it is of no use to complain* **11** custom; habit: *long use has inured him to it* **12** the purpose for which something is used; end **13** *Christianity* a distinctive form of liturgical or ritual observance, esp one that is traditional **14** the enjoyment of property, land, etc, by occupation or by deriving revenue from it **15** *law* the beneficial enjoyment of property the legal title to which is held by another person as trustee **16 have no use for 16a** to have no need of **16b** to have a contemptuous dislike for **17 make use of 17a** to employ; use **17b** to exploit (a person) ▷ See also **use up** [C13 from OF *user*, from L *ūsus* having used, from *ūtī* to use]

use-by date *n* **1** the date by which perishable goods should be used **2** the NZ name for **sell-by date**

used (juːzd) *adj* second-hand: *used cars*

used to (juːst) *adj* **1** accustomed to: *I am used to hitchhiking* ▷ *vb (tr)* **2** *(takes an infinitive or implied infinitive)* used as an auxiliary to express habitual or accustomed actions, states, etc, taking place in the past but not continuing into the present: *I used to fish here every day.*

USAGE The most common negative forms of *used to*, according to Bank of English data, are *didn't used to* and *didn't use to*. In formal contexts *used not to* is often preferred

useful (ˈjuːsfʊl) *adj* **1** able to be used advantageously, beneficially, or for several purposes **2** *inf* commendable or capable: *a useful term's work* > ˈ**usefully** *adv* > ˈ**usefulness** *n*

useless (ˈjuːslɪs) *adj* **1** having no practical use or advantage **2** *inf* ineffectual, weak, or stupid: *he's useless at history* > ˈ**uselessly** *adv* > ˈ**uselessness** *n*

Usenet (ˈjuːzˌnɛt) *n computing* a vast collection of newsgroups that follow agreed naming, maintaining, and distribution practices

user (ˈjuːzə) *n* **1** *law* **1a** the continued exercise, use, or enjoyment of a right, esp in property **1b** a presumptive right based on long-continued use: *right of user* **2** *(often in combination)* a person or thing that uses: *a road-user* **3** *inf* a drug addict

user-friendly *adj* (**user friendly** *when postpositive*) easy to familiarize oneself with, understand, or use

username (ˈjuːzəˌneɪm) *n computing* a name that someone uses for identification purposes when logging onto a computer, using chatrooms, or as part of his or her e-mail address

use up *vb (tr, adv)* **1** to finish (a supply); consume completely **2** to exhaust; wear out

Ushant (ˈʌʃənt) *n* an island off the NW coast of France, at the tip of Brittany: scene of naval battles in 1778 and 1794 between France and Britain. Area: about 16 sq km (6 sq miles). French name: **Ouessant**

Ushas (ˈuːʃəs) *n* the Hindu goddess of the dawn

usher (ˈʌʃə) *n* **1** an official who shows people to their seats, as in a church or theatre **2** a person who acts as doorkeeper, esp in a court of law **3** (in England) a minor official charged with maintaining order in a court of law **4** an officer responsible for preceding persons of rank in a procession **5** *Brit, obs* a teacher ▷ *vb (tr)* **6** to conduct or escort, esp in a courteous or obsequious way **7** (usually foll by *in*) to be a precursor or herald (of) [C14 from OF *huissier* doorkeeper, from Vulgar L *ustiārius* (unattested), from L *ostium* door]

usherette (ˌʌʃəˈrɛt) *n* a woman assistant in a cinema, etc, who shows people to their seats

Usk (ʌsk) *n* a river in SE Wales, flowing southeast and south to the Bristol Channel. Length: 113 km (70 miles)

Üsküb (ˈʊskuːb) *n* the Turkish name (1392–1913) for **Skopje**

Üsküdar (ˌuːskuːˈdɑː) *n* a town in NW Turkey, across the Bosporus from Istanbul: formerly a terminus of caravan routes from Syria and Asia; base of the British army in the Crimean War. Pop: 261 140 (latest est). Former name: **Scutari**

USM *stock exchange abbrev for:* unlisted securities market

USN *abbrev for* United States Navy
▷ www.navy.mil

Usnach *or* **Usnech** (ˈʊʃnəx) *n* (in Irish legend) the father of Naoise

USP *abbrev for* unique selling proposition *or* point: a characteristic of a product that can be used in advertising to differentiate it from its competitors

Uspallata Pass (ˌuːspəˈlɑːtə; *Spanish* uspaˈʎata) *n* a pass over the Andes in S South America, between Mendoza (Argentina) and Santiago (Chile). Height: 3840 m (12 600 ft). Also called: **La Cumbre**

Uu

usquebaugh (ˈʌskwɪˌbɔː) *n* **1** *Irish* the former name for **whiskey** **2** *Scot* the former name for **whisky** [c16 from Irish Gaelic *uisce beathadh* or Scot. Gaelic *uisge beatha* water of life]

USS *abbrev for:* **1** United States Senate **2** United States Ship

USSR *abbrev for* (the former) Union of Soviet Socialist Republics

Ussuri (*Russian* ussuˈri) *n* a river in E central Asia, flowing north, forming part of the Chinese border with Russia, to the Amur River. Length: about 800 km (500 miles)

Ústí nad Labem (*Czech* ˈuːstjiː nad ˈlabɛm) *n* a port in the Czech Republic, on the Elbe River: textile and chemical industries. Pop: 118 000 (1993)

Ust-Kamenogorsk (*Russian* ustjkəmɪnaˈgɔrsk) *n* a city in E Kazakhstan: centre of a zinc-, lead-, and copper-mining area. Pop: 311 000 (1999)

Ustyurt *or* **Ust Urt** (*Russian* usˈtjurt) *n* an arid plateau in central Asia, between the Caspian and Aral seas in Kazakhstan and Uzbekistan. Area: about 238 000 sq km (92 000 sq miles)

usual (ˈjuːʒʊəl) *adj* **1** of the most normal, frequent, or regular type: *that's the usual sort of application to send* ▷ *n* **2** ordinary or commonplace events (esp in **out of the usual**) **3** **the usual** *inf* the habitual or usual drink, etc [c14 from LL *ūsuālis* ordinary, from L *ūsus* USE]

usually (ˈjuːʒʊəlɪ) *adv* customarily; at most times; in the ordinary course of events

usufruct (ˈjuːsjʊˌfrʌkt) *n* the right to use and derive profit from a piece of property belonging to another, provided the property itself remains undiminished and uninjured in any way [c17 from LL *ūsūfrūctus*, from L *ūsus* use + *frūctus* enjoyment] > ˌ**usuˈfructuary** *n, adj*

Usumbura (ˌuːzəmˈbʊərə) *n* the former name of **Bujumbura**

usurer (ˈjuːʒərə) *n* a person who lends funds at an exorbitant rate of interest

usurp (juːˈzɜːp) *vb* to seize or appropriate (land, a throne, etc) without authority [c14 from OF, from L *ūsūrpāre* to take into use, prob. from *ūsus* use + *rapere* to seize] > ˌ**usurˈpation** *n* > **uˈsurper** *n*

usury (ˈjuːʒərɪ) *n, pl* **usuries** **1** the practice of loaning money at an exorbitant rate of interest **2** an unlawfully high rate of interest **3** *obs* moneylending [c14 from Med. L, from L *ūsūra* usage, from *ūsus* USE] > **usurious** (juːˈʒʊərɪəs) *adj*

USW *radio abbrev for:* ultrashort wave

ut (ʌt, uːt) *n music* the syllable used in the fixed system of solmization for the note C [c14 from L *ut*; see GAMUT]

UT *abbrev for* **1** universal time **2** Utah

Utah (ˈjuːtɔː, ˈjuːtɑː) *n* a state of the western US: settled by Mormons in 1847; situated in the Great Basin and the Rockies, with the Great Salt Lake in the northwest; mainly arid and mountainous. Capital: Salt Lake City. Pop: 2 233 169 (2000). Area: 212 628 sq km (82 096 sq miles). Abbreviations: **Ut** or (with zip code) **UT** > **Utahan** (juːˈtɔːən, -ˈtɑːən) *adj, n*

Utamaro (ˌuːtəˈmɑːrəʊ) *n* **Kitagawa** (ˌkiːtəˈgɑːwə), original name *Kitagawa Nebsuyoshi*. 1753–1806, Japanese master of wood-block prints, of the ukiyo-e school; noted esp for his portraits of women

UTC *abbrev for* universal time coordinated. See **universal time**

ute (juːt) *n Austral & NZ inf* short for **utility truck**

utensil (juːˈtɛnsəl) *n* an implement, tool, or container for practical use: *writing utensils* [c14 *utensele*, via OF from L *ūtēnsilia* necessaries, from *ūtēnsilis* available for use, from *ūtī* to use]

▷ www.cookingkitchen.com/cookingutensils.html
▷ www.cookswares.com

uterine (ˈjuːtəˌraɪn) *adj* **1** of, relating to, or affecting the uterus: *uterine bleeding* **2** (of offspring) born of the same mother but not the same father

uterus (ˈjuːtərəs) *n, pl* **uteri** (ˈjuːtəˌraɪ) **1** *anat* a hollow muscular organ lying within the pelvic cavity of female mammals. It houses the developing fetus. Nontechnical name: **womb** **2** the corresponding organ in other animals [c17 from L]

Utgard (ˈʊtgɑːd, ˈuːt-) *n Norse myth* one of the divisions of Jotunheim, land of the giants, ruled by Utgard-Loki

Utgard-Loki *n Norse myth* the giant king of Utgard

Uther (ˈjuːθə) *or* **Uther Pendragon** *n* (in Arthurian legend) a king of Britain and father of Arthur

Utica (ˈjuːtɪkə) *n* an ancient city on the N coast of Africa, northwest of Carthage

utilidor (juːˈtɪlədə; *Canad* -ˌdɒr) *n Canad* above-ground insulated casing for pipes carrying water, etc, in permafrost regions

utilitarian (juːˌtɪlɪˈtɛərɪən) *adj* **1** of or relating to utilitarianism **2** designed for use rather than beauty ▷ *n* **3** a person who believes in utilitarianism

utilitarianism (juːˌtɪlɪˈtɛərɪəˌnɪzəm) *n ethics* **1** the doctrine that the morally correct course of action consists in the greatest good for the greatest number, that is, in maximizing the total benefit resulting, without regard to the distribution of benefits and burdens **2** the theory that the criterion of virtue is utility

utility (juːˈtɪlɪtɪ) *n, pl* **utilities** **1a** the quality of practical use; usefulness **1b** (*as modifier*): *a utility fabric* **2** something useful **3a** a public service, such as the bus system **3b** (*as modifier*): *utility vehicle* **4** *econ* the ability of a commodity to satisfy human wants ▷ Cf **disutility** **5** *Austral* short for **utility truck** **6** *computing* a piece of software that performs a routine task [c14 from OF *utelite*, from L *ūtilitās* usefulness, from *ūtī* to use]

utility function *n econ* a function relating specific goods and services in an economy to individual preferences

utility player *n sport* a player who is capable of playing competently in any of several positions

utility room *n* a room with equipment for domestic work like washing and ironing

utility truck *n Austral & NZ* a small truck with an open body and low sides, often with a removable tarpaulin cover; pick-up truck

utilize *or* **utilise** (ˈjuːtɪˌlaɪz) *vb* **utilizes, utilizing, utilized** *or* **utilises, utilising, utilised** (*tr*) to make practical or worthwhile use of > ˈ**utiˌlizable** *or* ˈ**utiˌlisable** *adj* > ˌ**utiliˈzation** *or* ˌ**utiliˈsation** *n* > ˈ**utiˌlizer** *or* ˈ**utiˌliser** *n*

utmost (ˈʌtˌməʊst) *or* **uttermost** *adj* (*prenominal*) **1** of the greatest possible degree or amount: *the utmost degree* **2** at the furthest limit: *the utmost town on the peninsula* ▷ *n* **3** the greatest possible degree, extent, or amount: *he tried his utmost* [OE *ūtemest*, from *ūte* out + *-mest* MOST]

utmost good faith *n* a principle used in insurance contracts, legally obliging all parties to reveal to the others any information that might influence the others' decision to enter into the contract [from L *uberrima fides*]

Utopia (juːˈtəʊpɪə) *n* (*sometimes not cap*) any real or imaginary society, place, state, etc, considered to be perfect or ideal [c16 from NL *Utopia* (coined by Sir Thomas More in 1516 as the title of his book that described an imaginary island representing the perfect society), lit.: no place, from Gk *ou* not + *topos* a place]

Utopian (juːˈtəʊpɪən) (*sometimes not cap*) ▷ *adj* **1** of or relating to a perfect or ideal existence ▷ *n* **2** an idealistic social reformer > **Uˈtopianism** *n*

Utrecht (*Dutch* ˈyːtrɛxt; *English* ˈjuːtrɛkt) *n* **1** a province of the W central Netherlands. Capital: Utrecht. Pop: 1 107 800 (2000 est). Area: 1362 sq km (526 sq miles) **2** a city in the central Netherlands, capital of Utrecht province: scene of the signing (1579) of the **Union of Utrecht** (the foundation of the later kingdom of the Netherlands) and of the **Treaty of Utrecht** (1713), ending the War of the Spanish Succession. Pop: 232 718 (1999 est)

utricle ('juːtrɪkᵊl) *n* **1** *anat* the larger of the two parts of the membranous labyrinth of the internal ear ▷ Cf **saccule** **2** *bot* the bladder-like one-seeded indehiscent fruit of certain plants, esp sedges [c18 from L *ūtriculus*, dim. of *ūter* bag] > **u'tricular** *adj*

utriculitis (juː,trɪkjʊ'laɪtɪs) *n* inflammation of the inner ear

Utrillo (*French* ytrijo) *n* **Maurice** (mɔris) 1883–1955, French painter, noted for his Parisian street scenes

Uttaranchal ('ʊtə 'ræntʃʌl) *n* a state of N India created in 2000 from the N part of Uttar Pradesh: in the Himalayas, rising to over 7500 m (25 000 ft); rice, tea, and timber. Capital: Dehra Dun. Pop: 8 479 562 (2001). Area: 51 125 sq km (19739 sq miles)

Uttar Pradesh ('ʊtə 'prɑːdɛʃ) *n* a state of N India: the most populous state; originated in 1877 with the merging of Agra and Oudh as the United Provinces; augmented by the states of Rampur, Benares, and Tehri-Garhwal in 1949; the N Himalayan region passed to the new state of Uttaranchal in 2000; now consists mostly of the Upper Ganges plain; agricultural. Capital: Lucknow. Pop: 166 052 859 (2001). Area: 243 350 sq km (93 933 sq miles)

utter[1] ('ʌtə) *vb* **1** to give audible expression to (something): *to utter a growl* **2** *criminal law* to put into circulation (counterfeit coin, forged banknotes, etc) **3** (*tr*) to make publicly known; publish: *to utter slander* [c14 prob. orig. a commercial term, from MDu. *ūteren* (modern Du. *uiteren*) to make known] > **'utterable** *adj* > **'utterableness** *n* > **'utterer** *n*

utter[2] ('ʌtə) *adj* (*prenominal*) (intensifier): *an utter fool; the utter limit* [c15 from OE *utera* outer, comp. of *ūte* out (adv)] > **'utterly** *adv*

utterance ('ʌtərəns) *n* **1** something uttered, such as a statement **2** the act or power of uttering or ability to utter

utter barrister *n law* the full title of a barrister who is not a Queen's Counsel

uttermost ('ʌtə,məʊst) *adj, n* a variant of **utmost**

U-turn *n* **1** a turn made by a vehicle in the shape of a U, resulting in a reversal of direction **2** a complete change in direction of political policy, etc

Utzon (uːtzən) *n* **Jørn** (jɜːn) born 1918, Danish architect known primarily for his unique design for the Sydney Opera House (1966)

UV *abbrev for* ultraviolet

UV-A *or* **UVA** *abbrev for* ultraviolet radiation with a range of 320–380 nanometres: *UV-A light*

uvarovite (uː'vɑːrə,vaɪt) *n* an emerald-green garnet found in chromium ores[c19 from G *Uvarovit;* after Count Sergei *Uvarov* (1785–1855), Russian author & statesman]

UV-B *or* **UVB** *abbrev for* ultraviolet radiation with a range of 280–320 nanometres

uvea ('juːvɪə) *n* the part of the eyeball consisting of the iris, ciliary body, and choroid [c16 from Med. L *ūvea*, from L *ūva* grape] > **'uveal** *adj*

UVF *abbrev for* Ulster Volunteer Force

uvula ('juːvjʊlə) *n, pl* **uvulas** *or* **uvulae** (-,liː) a small fleshy flap of tissue that hangs in the back of the throat and is an extension of the soft palate [c14 from Med. L, lit.: a little grape, from L *ūva* a grape]

uvular ('juːvjʊlə) *adj* **1** of or relating to the uvula **2** *phonetics* articulated with the uvula and the back of the tongue, such as the (r) sound of Parisian French ▷ *n* **3** a uvular consonant

UXB *abbrev for* unexploded bomb

Uxbridge ('ʌks,brɪdʒ) *n* a town in SE England, part of the Greater London borough of Hillingdon since 1965; chiefly residential; seat of Brunel University (1966)

Uxmal (*Spanish* uz'mal) *n* an ancient ruined city in SE Mexico, in Yucatán: capital of the later Maya empire

uxorial (ʌk'sɔːrɪəl) *adj* of or relating to a wife: *uxorial influence* [c19 from L *uxor* wife] > **ux'orially** *adv*

uxoricide (ʌk'sɔːrɪ,saɪd) *n* **1** the act of killing one's wife **2** a man who kills his wife [c19 from L *uxor* wife + -CIDE] > **ux,ori'cidal** *adj*

uxorious (ʌk'sɔːrɪəs) *adj* excessively attached to or dependent on one's wife [c16 from L *uxōrius* concerning a wife, from *uxor* wife] > **ux'oriously** *adv* > **ux'oriousness** *n*

Uzbek ('ʊzbɛk, 'ʌz-) *n* **1** (*pl* **Uzbeks** *or* **Uzbek**) a member of a Mongoloid people of Uzbekistan **2** the language of this people

Uzbekistan (,ʌzbɛkɪ'stɑːn) *n* a republic in central Asia: annexed by Russia in the 19th century, it became a separate Soviet Socialist republic in 1924 and gained independence in 1991; mining, textile, and chemical industries are important. Official language: Uzbek. Religion: believers are mainly Muslim. Currency: sum. Capital: Tashkent. Pop: 25 155 000 (2001 est). Area: 449 600 sq km (173 546 sq miles)
▷ www.gov.uz
▷ www.uzbekistan.org
▷ www.tashkent.org/uzland
▷ www.uzbekistanembassy.uk.net

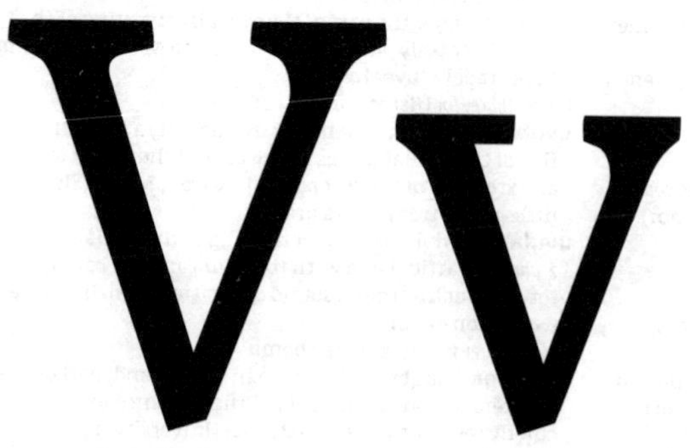

v *or* **V** (viː) *n, pl* **v's, V's,** *or* **Vs** **1** the 22nd letter of the English alphabet **2** a speech sound represented by this letter, usually a voiced fricative, as in *vote* **3a** something shaped like a V **3b** *(in combination): a V neck*

v *symbol for:* **1** *physics* velocity **2** specific volume (of a gas)

V *symbol for:* **1** *chem* vanadium **2** (in transformational grammar) verb **3** volume (capacity) **4** volt **5** victory **6** *the Roman numeral for* five

v. *abbrev for:* **1** verb **2** verse **3** verso **4** *(usually italic)* versus **5** very **6** vide [L: see] **8** volume

V. *abbrev for:* **1** Venerable **2** (in titles) Very **3** (in titles) Vice **4** Viscount

V-1 *n* a robot bomb invented by the Germans in World War II: used esp to bombard London. Also called: **doodlebug, buzz bomb, flying bomb** [from G *Vergeltungswaffe* revenge weapon]

V-2 *n* a rocket-powered ballistic missile invented by the Germans in World War II: used esp to bombard London [see V-1]

V6 *n* a car or internal-combustion engine having six cylinders arranged in the form of a V

V8 *n* a car or internal-combustion engine having eight cylinders arranged in the form of a V

VA *abbrev for:* **1** (in the US) Veterans' Administration **2** Vicar Apostolic **3** Vice Admiral **4** (Order of) Victoria and Albert **5** Virginia **6** **volt-ampere**

Va. *abbrev for:* Virginia

Vaal (vɑːl) *n* a river in South Africa, rising in the Drakensberg and flowing west to join the Orange River. Length: 1160 km (720 miles)

Vaasa (*Finnish* ˈvɑːsɑ) *n* a port in W Finland, on the Gulf of Bothnia: the provisional capital of Finland (1918); textile industries. Pop: 55 089 (1994). Former name: **Nikolainkaupunki**

vac (væk) *n Brit inf* short for **vacation**

vacancy (ˈveɪkənsɪ) *n, pl* **vacancies** **1** the state or condition of being vacant or unoccupied; emptiness **2** an unoccupied post or office: *we have a vacancy in the accounts department* **3** an unoccupied room in a hotel, etc: *the manager put up the "No Vacancies" sign* **4** lack of thought or intelligent awareness **5** *obs* idleness or a period spent in idleness

vacant (ˈveɪkənt) *adj* **1** without any contents; empty **2** *(postpositive; foll by of)* devoid (of something specified) **3** having no incumbent: *a vacant post* **4** having no tenant or occupant: *a vacant house* **5** characterized by or resulting from lack of thought or intelligent awareness **6** (of time, etc) not allocated to any activity: *it is pleasant to have a vacant hour in one's day* **7** spent in idleness or inactivity: *a vacant life* [C13 from L *vacāre* to be empty] > ˈ**vacantly** *adv*

vacant possession *n* ownership of an unoccupied house or property, any previous owner or tenant having departed

vacate (vəˈkeɪt) *vb* **vacates, vacating, vacated** *(mainly tr)* **1** to cause (something) to be empty, esp by departing from or abandoning it: *to vacate a room* **2** *(also intr)* to give up the tenure, possession, or occupancy of (a place, post, etc) **3** *law* **3a** to cancel **3b** to annul > **vaˈcatable** *adj*

vacation (vəˈkeɪʃən) *n* **1** *chiefly Brit* a period of the year when the law courts or universities are closed **2** another word (esp US and Canad.) for **holiday** (sense 1) **3** the act of departing from or abandoning property, etc ▷ *vb* **4** *(intr) US & Canad* to take a holiday [C14 from L *vacātiō* freedom, from *vacāre* to be empty] > **vaˈcationer** *or* **vaˈcationist** *n*

vaccinate (ˈvæksɪˌneɪt) *vb* **vaccinates, vaccinating, vaccinated** to inoculate (a person) with a vaccine so as to produce immunity against a specific disease > ˈ**vacciˌnator** *n*

vaccination (ˌvæksɪˈneɪʃən) *n* **1** the act of vaccinating **2** the scar left following inoculation with a vaccine

vaccine (ˈvæksiːn) *n med* **1** a suspension of dead, attenuated, or otherwise modified microorganisms for inoculation to produce immunity to a disease by stimulating the production of antibodies **2** a preparation of the virus of cowpox inoculated in humans to produce immunity to smallpox **3** (*modifier*) of or relating to vaccination or vaccinia **4** *computing* software designed to detect and remove computer viruses from a system [C18 from NL *variolae vaccīnae* cowpox, title of medical treatise (1798) by Edward Jenner, from L *vacca* a cow] > ˈ**vaccinal** *adj*

vaccinia (vækˈsɪnɪə) *n* a technical name for **cowpox** [C19 NL, from L *vaccīnus* of cows]

vacherin *French* (vaʃrɛ̃) *n* a dessert consisting of a meringue shell filled with whipped cream, ice cream, fruit, etc [also in France a kind of cheese, from *vache* cow, from L *vacca*]

vacillate (ˈvæsɪˌleɪt) *vb* **vacillates, vacillating, vacillated** (*intr*) **1** to fluctuate in one's opinions **2** to sway from side to side physically [C16 from L *vacillāre* to sway, from ?] > ˌ**vacilˈlation** *n* > ˈ**vacilˌlator** *n*

vacua (ˈvækjʊə) *n* a plural of **vacuum**

vacuity (væˈkjuːɪtɪ) *n, pl* **vacuities 1** the state or quality of being vacuous **2** an empty space or void **3** a lack or absence of something specified: *a vacuity of wind* **4** lack of normal intelligence or awareness **5** a statement, saying, etc, that is inane or pointless **6** (in customs terminology) the difference in volume between the actual contents of a container and its full capacity [C16 from L *vacuitās* empty space, from *vacuus* empty]

vacuole (ˈvækjʊˌəʊl) *n biol* a fluid-filled cavity in a cell [C19 from F, lit.: little vacuum, from L VACUUM] > **vacuolar** (ˌvækjʊˈəʊlə) *adj*

vacuous (ˈvækjʊəs) *adj* **1** empty **2** bereft of ideas or intelligence **3** characterized by or resulting from vacancy of mind: *a vacuous gaze* **4** indulging in no useful mental or physical activity [C17 from L *vacuus* empty] > ˈ**vacuously** *adv*

vacuum (ˈvækjʊəm) *n, pl* **vacuums** *or* **vacua 1** a region containing no free matter; in technical contexts now often called: **free space 2** a region in which gas is present at a low pressure **3** the degree of exhaustion of gas within an enclosed space: *a perfect vacuum* **4** a feeling of emptiness: *his death left a vacuum in her life* **5** short for **vacuum cleaner 6** (*modifier*) of, containing, producing, or operated by a low gas pressure: *a vacuum brake* ▷ *vb* **7** to clean (something) with a vacuum cleaner [C16 from L: empty space, from *vacuus* empty]

vacuum cleaner *n* an electrical household appliance used for cleaning floors, carpets, etc, by suction > **vacuum cleaning** *n*

vacuum distillation *n* distillation in which the liquid distilled is enclosed at a low pressure in order to reduce its boiling point

vacuum flask *n* an insulating flask that has double walls, usually of silvered glass, with an evacuated space between them. It is used for maintaining substances at high or low temperatures. Also called: **Thermos**

vacuum gauge *n* any of a number of instruments for measuring pressures below atmospheric pressure

vacuum-packed *adj* packed in an airtight container or packet under low pressure in order to maintain freshness, prevent corrosion, etc

vacuum pump *n* a pump for producing a low gas pressure

vacuum tube *or* **valve** *n* the US and Canad name for **valve** (sense 3)

VAD *abbrev for* **1** Voluntary Aid Detachment ▷ *n* **2** a member of this organization

vade mecum (ˈvɑːdɪ ˈmeɪkʊm) *n* a handbook or other aid carried on the person for immediate use or reference when needed [C17 from L, lit.: go with me]

Vadodara (wəˈdəʊdərə) *n* a city in W India, in SE Gujurat: textile manufacturing. Pop: 1 031 346 (1991). Former name (until 1976): **Baroda**

vadose (ˈveɪdəʊs) *adj* of, designating, or derived from water occurring above the water table: *vadose deposits* [C19 from L *vadōsus* full of shallows, from *vadum* a ford]

Vaduz (*German* faˈdʊts) *n* the capital of Liechtenstein, in the Rhine valley: an old market town, dominated by a medieval castle, residence of the prince of Liechtenstein. Pop: 5043 (2000 est)

vagabond (ˈvægəˌbɒnd) *n* **1** a person with no fixed home **2** an idle wandering beggar or thief **3** (*modifier*) of or like a vagabond [C15 from L *vagābundus* wandering, from *vagārī* to roam, from *vagus* VAGUE] > ˈ**vagaˌbondage** *n*

vagal (ˈveɪgᵊl) *adj anat* of, relating to, or affecting the vagus nerve: *vagal inhibition*

vagary (ˈveɪgərɪ, vəˈgɛərɪ) *n, pl* **vagaries** an erratic notion or action [C16 prob. from L *vagārī* to roam; cf. L *vagus* VAGUE]

vagina (vəˈdʒaɪnə) *n, pl* **vaginas** *or* **vaginae** (-niː) **1** the canal in most female mammals that extends from the cervix of the uterus to an external opening between the labia minora **2** *anat, biol* any sheath or sheathlike structure [C17 from L: sheath] > **vagˈinal** *adj*

vaginate (ˈvædʒɪnɪt, -ˌneɪt) *adj* (esp of plant parts) sheathed: *a vaginate leaf*

vaginectomy (ˌvædʒɪˈnɛktəmɪ) *n, pl* **vaginectomies 1** surgical removal of all or part of the vagina **2** surgical removal of part of the serous sheath surrounding the testis and epididymis

vaginismus (ˌvædʒɪˈnɪzməs) *n* painful spasm of the vagina [C19 from NL, from VAGINA, + *-ismus*; see -ISM]

vaginitis (ˌvædʒɪˈnaɪtɪs) *n* inflammation of the vagina

vagotomy (væˈgɒtəmɪ) *n, pl* **vagotomies** surgical division of the vagus nerve, performed to limit gastric secretion in patients with severe peptic ulcers [C19 from VAG(US) + -TOMY]

vagotonia (ˌveɪgəˈtəʊnɪə) *n* pathological overactivity of the vagus nerve, affecting various bodily functions controlled by this nerve [C19 from VAG(US) + *-tonia*, from L *tonus* tension, TONE]

vagrancy (ˈveɪgrənsɪ) *n, pl* **vagrancies 1** the state or condition of being a vagrant **2** the conduct or mode of living of a vagrant

vagrant (ˈveɪgrənt) *n* **1** a person of no settled abode, income, or job; tramp ▷ *adj* **2** wandering about **3** of or characteristic of a vagrant or vagabond **4** moving in an erratic fashion; wayward **5** (of plants) showing straggling growth [C15 prob. from OF *waucrant* (from *wancrer* to roam, of Gmc origin), but also infl. by OF *vagant* vagabond, from L *vagārī* to wander] > ˈ**vagrantly** *adv*

vague (veɪg) *adj* **1** (of statements, meaning, etc) imprecise: *vague promises* **2** not clearly perceptible or discernible: *a vague idea* **3** not clearly established or known: *a vague rumour* **4** (of a person or his or her expression) absent-minded [C16 via F from L *vagus* wandering, from ?] > ˈ**vaguely** *adv* > ˈ**vagueness** *n*

vagus *or* **vagus nerve** (ˈveɪgəs) *n, pl* **vagi** (ˈveɪdʒaɪ) *or* **vagus nerves** the tenth cranial nerve, which supplies the heart, lungs, and viscera [C19 from L *vagus* wandering] > ˈ**vagal** *adj*

vail (veɪl) *obs* ▷ *vb* (*tr*) **1** to lower (something, such as a weapon), esp as a sign of deference **2** to remove (the hat, etc) as a mark of respect ▷ *n* **3** a tip [C14 *valen*, from obs. *avalen*, from OF *avaler* to let fall, from L *ad vallem*, lit.: to the valley, i.e., down]

vain (veɪn) *adj* **1** inordinately proud of one's appearance, possessions, or achievements **2** given to ostentatious display **3** worthless **4** senseless or futile ▷ *n* **5 in vain** fruitlessly [C13 via OF from L *vānus*] > ˈ**vainly** *adv* > ˈ**vainness** *n*

vainglory (ˌveɪnˈglɔːrɪ) *n* **1** boastfulness or vanity **2** ostentation > ˌ**vainˈglorious** *adj*

vair (vɛə) *n* **1** a fur, probably Russian squirrel, used to trim robes in the Middle Ages **2** a fur used on heraldic shields, conventionally represented by white and blue skins in alternate lines [c13 from OF: of more than one colour, from L *varius* variegated]

Vaisya (ˈvaɪsjə, ˈvaɪʃjə) *n* the third of the four main Hindu castes, the traders [c18 from Sansk., lit.: settler, from *viś* settlement]

Vajpayee (ˌvædʒpaɪˈjiː) *n* **A(tal) B(ihari)** born 1926, Indian politician; prime minister of India (in 1996, and again from 1998)

Valais (*French* valɛ) *n* a canton of S Switzerland: includes the entire valley of the upper Rhône and the highest peaks in Switzerland; produces a quarter of Switzerland's hydroelectricity. Capital: Sion. Pop: 275 600 (2000 est). Area: 5231 sq km (2020 sq miles). German name: **Wallis**

valance (ˈvæləns) *n* a short piece of drapery hung along a shelf or bed to hide structural detail [c15 ? after VALENCE, noted for its textiles] > ˈ**valanced** *adj*

Valdai Hills (vɑːlˈdaɪ) *pl n* a region of hills and plateaus in NW Russia, between Moscow and St Petersburg. Greatest height: 346 m (1135 ft)

Valdemar I, II, *or* **IV** (*Danish* ˈvaldəmar) *n* a variant spelling of **Waldemar I, II** *or* **IV**

Val-de-Marne (*French* valdəmarn) *n* a department of N France, in Île-de-France region. Capital: Créteil. Pop: 1 227 250 (1999). Area: 244 sq km (95 sq miles)

Valdivia[1] (*Spanish* balˈdiβja) *n* a port in S Chile, on the **Valdivia River** about 19 km (12 miles) from the Pacific: developed chiefly by German settlers in the 1850s; university (1954). Pop: 122 166 (1999 est)

Valdivia[2] (*Spanish* balˈdiβja) *n* **Pedro de** (ˈpeðro de) ?1500–54, Spanish soldier; conqueror of Chile

Val-d'Oise (*French* valdwaz) *n* a department of N France, in Île-de-France region. Capital: Pontoise. Pop: 1 105 464 (1999). Area: 1249 sq km (487 sq miles)

vale[1] (veɪl) *n* a literary word for **valley** [c13 from OF *val*, from L *vallis* valley]

vale[2] *Latin* (ˈvɑːleɪ) *sentence substitute* farewell; goodbye

valediction (ˌvælɪˈdɪkʃən) *n* **1** the act or an instance of saying goodbye **2** any valedictory statement, etc [c17 from L *valedīcere*, from *valē* farewell + *dīcere* to say]

valedictory (ˌvælɪˈdɪktərɪ) *adj* **1** saying goodbye **2** of or relating to a farewell or an occasion of farewell ▷ *n, pl* **valedictories 3** a farewell address or speech

valence (ˈveɪləns) *n chem* **1** another name (esp US and Canad) for **valency 2** the phenomenon of forming chemical bonds

Valence (*French* valɑ̃s) *n* a town in SE France, on the River Rhône. Pop: 63 437 (1990)

Valencia (*Spanish* baˈlenθja) *n* **1** a port in E Spain, capital of Valencia province, on the Mediterranean: the third largest city in Spain; capital of the Moorish kingdom of Valencia (1021–1238); university (1501). Pop: 739 412 (1998 est). Latin name: **Valentia** (vəˈlɛntɪə) **2** a region and former kingdom of E Spain, on the Mediterranean **3** a city in N Venezuela: one of the two main industrial centres in Venezuela. Pop: 1 338 833 (2000 est)

Valenciennes[1] (ˌvælənsɪˈɛn) *n* a flat bobbin lace typically having scroll and floral designs and originally made of linen [after VALENCIENNES[2], where orig. made]

Valenciennes[2] [2] (*French* valɑ̃sjɛn) *n* a town in N France, on the River Escaut: a coal-mining and heavy industrial centre. Pop: 39 276 (1990)

valency (ˈveɪlənsɪ) *or esp US & Canad* **valence** *n, pl* **valencies** *or* **valences** *chem* a property of atoms or groups equal to the number of atoms of hydrogen that the atom or group could combine with or displace in forming compounds [c19 from L *valentia* strength, from *valēre* to be strong]

valency electron *n chem* an electron in the outer shell of an atom, responsible for forming chemical bonds

Valens (ˈveɪlɛnz) *n* ?328–378 AD, emperor of the Eastern Roman Empire (364–378); appointed by his elder brother Valentinian I, emperor of the Western Empire

valentine (ˈvælənˌtaɪn) *n* **1** a card or gift expressing love or affection, sent, often anonymously, on Saint Valentine's Day **2** a sweetheart selected for such a greeting

Valentine (ˈvælənˌtaɪn) *n* **Saint** 3rd century AD, Christian martyr, associated by historical accident with the custom of sending valentines; bishop of Terni. Feast day: Feb. 14

Valentinian I (ˌvælənˈtɪnɪən) *or* **Valentinianus I** (ˌvælənˌtɪnɪˈeɪnəs) *n* 321–375 AD, emperor of the Western Roman Empire (364–375); appointed his brother Valens to rule the Eastern Empire

Valentinian II *or* **Valentinianus II** *n* 371–392 AD, emperor of the Western Roman Empire (375–392), reigning jointly with his half brother Gratian until 383

Valentinian III *or* **Valentinianus III** *n* ?419–455 AD, emperor of the Western Roman Empire (425–455). His government lost Africa to the Vandals. With Pope Leo I he issued (444) an edict giving the bishop of Rome supremacy over the provincial churches

Valentino (ˌvælənˈtiːnəʊ) *n* **Rudolph,** original name *Rodolpho Guglielmi di Valentina d'Antonguolla*. 1895–1926, US silent-film actor, born in Italy. He is famous for his romantic roles in such films as *The Sheik* (1921)

Vale of Glamorgan (gləˈmɔːgən) *n* a county borough of S Wales, created in 1996 from parts of South Glamorgan and Mid Glamorgan. Administrative centre: Barry. Pop: 119 293 (2001). Area: 295 sq km (114 sq miles)

Valera (vəˈlɛərə, -ˈlɪərə) *n* See (Eamon) **de Valera**

valerian (vəˈlɛərɪən) *n* **1** Also called: **allheal** a Eurasian plant having small white or pinkish flowers and a medicinal root **2** a sedative drug made from the dried roots of this plant [c14 via OF from Med. L *valeriana (herba)* (herb) of *Valerius*, unexplained L personal name]

Valerian (vəˈlɛərɪən) *n* Latin name *Publius Licinius Valerianus*. died 260 AD, Roman emperor (253–260): renewed persecution of the Christians; defeated by the Persians

valeric (vəˈlɛrɪk, -ˈlɪərɪk) *adj* of, relating to, or derived from valerian

valeric acid *n* another name for **pentanoic acid**

Valéry (*French* valeri) *n* **Paul** (pɔl) 1871–1945, French poet and essayist, influenced by the symbolists, esp Mallarmé. He wrote lyric poetry, rich in imagery, as in *La Jeune Parque* (1917) and *Album de vers anciens 1890–1900* (1920)

valet (ˈvælɪt, ˈvæleɪ) *n* **1** a manservant who acts as personal attendant to his employer, looking after his clothing, serving his meals, etc **2** a manservant who attends to the requirements of patrons in a hotel, etc; steward ▷ *vb* **valets, valeting, valeted 3** to act as a valet for (a person) **4** (*tr*) to clean the bodywork and interior of (a car) as a professional service [c16 from OF *vaslet* page, from Med. L *vassus* servant]

valeta *or* **veleta** (vəˈliːtə) *n* a ballroom dance in triple time [from Sp.: weather vane]

valet de chambre *French* (valɛ də ʃɑ̃brə) *n, pl* ***valets de chambre*** (valɛ də ʃɑ̃brə) the full French term for **valet** (sense 1)

valet parking *n* a system at hotels, airports, etc, in which patrons' cars are parked by a steward

valetudinarian (ˌvælɪˌtjuːdɪˈnɛərɪən) *or* **valetudinary** (ˌvælɪˈtjuːdɪnərɪ) *n, pl* **valetudinarians** *or* **valetudinaries 1** a person who is or believes himself or herself to be chronically sick **2** a hypochondriac ▷ *adj* **3** relating to or resulting from poor health **4** being a valetudinarian [c18 from L *valētūdō* state of health, from *valēre* to be well] > ˌ**valeˌtudiˈnarianism** *n*

valgus (ˈvælgəs) *adj pathol* twisted away from the midline of the body [c19 from L: bow-legged]

Valhalla (vælˈhælə), **Walhalla, Valhall** (vælˈhæl, ˈvælhæl), *or* **Walhall** *n Norse myth* the great hall of Odin where warriors who die as heroes in battle dwell eternally [c18 from ON, from *valr* slain warriors + *höll* HALL]

valiant (ˈvæljənt) *adj* **1** courageous or intrepid **2** marked by bravery or courage: *a valiant deed* [c14 from OF, from *valoir* to be of value, from L *valēre* to be strong] > ˈ**valiantly** *adv*

valid (ˈvælɪd) *adj* **1** having some foundation; based on truth **2** legally acceptable: *a valid licence* **3a** having legal force **3b** having legal authority **4** having some force or cogency: *a valid point in a debate* **5** *logic* (of an inference or argument) having premises and a conclusion so related that if the premises are true, the conclusion must be true [c16 from L *validus* robust, from *valēre* to be strong] > **validity** (vəˈlɪdɪtɪ) *n* > ˈ**validly** *adv*

validate (ˈvælɪˌdeɪt) *vb* **validates, validating, validated** (*tr*) **1** to confirm or corroborate **2** to give legal force or official confirmation to > ˌ**valiˈdation** *n*

valine (ˈveɪliːn) *n* an essential amino acid: a component of proteins [c19 from VAL(ERIC ACID) + -INE[2]]

valise (vəˈliːz) *n* a small overnight travelling case [c17 via F from It. *valigia*, from ?]

Valium (ˈvælɪəm) *n trademark* a brand of diazepam used as a tranquillizer

Valkyrie, Walkyrie (vælˈkɪərɪ, ˈvælkɪərɪ), *or* **Valkyr** (ˈvælkɪə) *n Norse myth* any of the beautiful maidens who serve Odin and ride over battlefields to claim the dead heroes and take them to Valhalla [c18 from ON *Valkyrja*, from *valr* slain warriors + *köri* to CHOOSE] > **Valˈkyrian** *adj*

Valladolid (*Spanish* baʎaðoˈlið) *n* **1** a city in NW Spain: residence of the Spanish court in the 16th century; university (1346). Pop: 319 946 (1998 est) **2** the former name (until 1828) of **Morelia**

vallation (vəˈleɪʃən) *n* **1** the act or process of building fortifications **2** a wall or rampart [c17 from LL *vallātiō*, from L *vallum* rampart]

vallecula (vəˈlɛkjʊlə) *n, pl* **valleculae** (-ˌliː) **1** *anat* any of various natural depressions or crevices **2** *bot* a small groove or furrow in a plant stem or fruit [c19 from LL: little valley, from L *vallis* valley]

Valle d'Aosta (*Italian* ˈvalle daˈɔsta) *n* an autonomous region of NW Italy: under many different rulers until passing to the house of Savoy in the 11th century; established as an autonomous region in 1944. Capital: Aosta. Pop: 120 343 (2000 est). Area: 3263 sq km (1260 sq miles)

Valletta (vəˈlɛtə) *n* the capital of Malta, on the NE coast: founded by the Knights Hospitallers, after the victory over the Turks in 1565; became a major naval base after Malta's annexation by Britain (1814). Pop: 7100 (1999 est), with a conurbation of 102 000 (1999 est)
▷ www.visitmalta.com
▷ http://web.idirect.com/~malta/valletta.htm

valley (ˈvælɪ) *n* **1** a long depression in the land surface, usually containing a river, formed by erosion or by movements in the earth's crust **2** the broad area drained by a single river system: *the Thames valley* **3** any elongated depression resembling a valley [c13 from OF *valee*, from L *vallis*]

Valley Forge *n* an area in SE Pennsylvania, northwest of Philadelphia: winter camp (1777–78) of Washington and the American Revolutionary Army

Valley of Ten Thousand Smokes *n* a volcanic region of SW Alaska, formed by the massive eruption of Mount Katmai in 1912; jets of steam issue from vents up to 45 m (150 ft) across

Vallombrosa (*Italian* vallomˈbroːsa) *n* a village and resort in central Italy, in Tuscany region: 11th-century Benedictine monastery

vallum (ˈvæləm) *n archaeol* a Roman rampart or earthwork

Valois[1] (*French* valwa) *n* a historic region and former duchy of N France

Valois[2] (*French* valwa) *n* a royal house of France, ruling from 1328 to 1589

Valois[3] (ˈvælwɑː) *n* Dame **Ninette de** (niːˈnɛt də) original name *Edris Stannus*. 1898–2001, British ballet dancer and choreographer, born in Ireland: a founder of the Vic-Wells Ballet Company (1931), which under her direction became the Royal Ballet (1956)

Valona (vəˈləʊnə) *n* another name for **Vlorë**

valonia (vəˈləʊnɪə) *n* the acorn cups and unripe acorns of the Eurasian oak, used in tanning, dyeing, and making ink [c18 from It. *vallonia*, ult. from Gk *balanos* acorn]

valorize *or* **valorise** (ˈvæləˌraɪz) *vb* **valorizes, valorizing, valorized** *or* **valorises, valorising, valorised** (*tr*) to fix an artificial price for (a commodity) by governmental action [c20 back formation from *valorization*; see VALOUR] > ˌ**valoriˈzation** *or* ˌ**valoriˈsation** *n*

valour *or US* **valor** (ˈvælə) *n* courage or bravery, esp in battle [c15 from LL *valor*, from *valēre* to be strong] > ˈ**valorous** *adj*

Valparaíso (*Spanish* balparaˈiso) *n* a port in central Chile, on a wide bay of the Pacific: the third largest city and chief port of Chile; two universities. Pop: 283 489 (1999 est)

valse *French* (vals) *n* another word for **waltz**

valuable (ˈvæljʊəbᵊl) *adj* **1** having considerable monetary worth **2** of considerable importance or quality: *valuable information* **3** able to be valued ▷ *n* **4** (*usually pl*) a valuable article of personal property, esp jewellery > ˈ**valuably** *adv*

valuate (ˈvæljʊˌeɪt) *vb* **valuates, valuating, valuated** US another word for **value** (senses 10, 12) or **evaluate** > ˈ**valuˌator** *n*

valuation (ˌvæljʊˈeɪʃən) *n* **1** the act of valuing, esp a formal assessment of the worth of property, jewellery, etc **2** the price arrived at by the process of valuing: *I set a high valuation on technical ability* > ˌ**valuˈational** *adj*

value (ˈvæljuː) *n* **1** the desirability of a thing, often in respect of some property such as usefulness or exchangeability **2** an amount, esp a material or monetary one, considered to be a fair exchange in return for a thing: *the value of the picture is £10 000* **3** satisfaction: *value for money* **4** precise meaning or significance **5** (*pl*) the moral principles or accepted standards of a person or group **6** *maths* a particular magnitude, number, or amount: *the value of the variable was 5* **7** *music* short for **time value** **8** (in painting, drawing, etc) **8a** a gradation of tone from light to dark **8b** the relation of one of these elements to another or to the whole picture **9** *phonetics* the quality of the speech sound associated with a written character representing it: *"g" has the value* (dʒ) *in English "gem"* ▷ *vb* **values, valuing, valued** (*tr*) **10** to assess or estimate the worth, merit, or desirability of **11** to have a high regard for, esp in respect of worth, usefulness, merit, etc **12** (foll by *at*) to fix the financial or material worth of (a unit of currency, work of art, etc) [c14 from OF, from *valoir*, from L *valēre* to be worth] > ˈ**valued** *adj* > ˈ**valueless** *adj* > ˈ**valuer** *n*

value added *n* the difference between the total revenues of a firm, industry, etc, and its total purchases from other firms, industries, etc

value-added tax *n* (in Britain) the full name for **VAT**

valued policy *n* an insurance policy in which the amount payable in the event of a valid claim is agreed upon between the company and the policyholder when the policy is issued and is not related to the actual value of a loss

value judgment *n* a subjective assessment based on

one's own values or those of one's class

Valuer General *n Austral* a state official who values properties for rating purposes

valuta (və'luːtə) *n rare* the value of one currency in terms of its exchange rate with another [c20 from It., lit.: VALUE]

valvate ('vælveɪt) *adj* **1** furnished with a valve or valves **2** *bot* **2a** taking place by means of valves: *valvate dehiscence* **2b** (of petals) having the margins touching but not overlapping

valve (vælv) *n* **1** any device that shuts off, starts, regulates, or controls the flow of a fluid **2** *anat* a flaplike structure in a hollow organ, such as the heart, that controls the one-way passage of fluid through that organ **3** Also called: **tube** an evacuated electron tube containing a cathode, anode, and, usually, one or more additional control electrodes. When a positive potential is applied to the anode, it produces a one-way flow of current **4** *zool* any of the separable pieces that make up the shell of a mollusc **5** *music* a device on some brass instruments by which the effective length of the tube may be varied to enable a chromatic scale to be produced **6** *bot* any of the several parts that make up a dry dehiscent fruit, esp a capsule [c14 from L *valva* a folding door] > **'valveless** *adj* > **'valve,like** *adj*

valve-in-head engine *n* the US name for **overhead-valve engine**

valvular ('vælvjʊlə) *adj* **1** of, relating to, operated by, or having a valve or valves **2** having the shape or function of a valve

valvulitis (ˌvælvjʊ'laɪtɪs) *n* inflammation of a bodily valve, esp a heart valve [c19 from NL *valvula* dim. of VALVE + -ITIS]

vamoose (və'muːs) *vb* **vamooses, vamoosing, vamoosed** *(intr) sl, chiefly US* to leave a place hurriedly; decamp [c19 from Sp. *vamos* let us go, from L *vādere* to go, walk rapidly]

vamp¹ (væmp) *inf* ▷ *n* **1** a seductive woman who exploits men by use of her sexual charms ▷ *vb* **2** to exploit (a man) in the fashion of a vamp [c20 short for VAMPIRE]

vamp² (væmp) *n* **1** something patched up to make it look new **2** the reworking of a story, etc **3** an improvised accompaniment **4** the front part of the upper of a shoe ▷ *vb* **5** *(tr; often foll by up)* to make a renovation of **6** to improvise (an accompaniment) to (a tune) [c13 from OF *avantpié* the front part of a shoe (hence, something patched), from *avant-* fore- + *pié* foot, from L *pēs*]

vampire ('væmpaɪə) *n* **1** (in European folklore) a corpse that rises nightly from its grave to drink the blood of the living **2** See **vampire bat** **3** a person who preys mercilessly upon others [c18 from F, from G, from Magyar] > **vampiric** (væm'pɪrɪk) *adj* > **'vampirism** *n*

vampire bat *n* a bat of tropical regions of Central and South America, having sharp incisor and canine teeth and feeding on the blood of birds and mammals

van¹ (væn) *n* **1** short for **caravan** (sense 1) **2** a motor vehicle for transporting goods, etc, by road **3** *Brit* a closed railway wagon in which the guard travels, for transporting goods, etc

van² (væn) *n* short for **vanguard**

van³ (væn) *n tennis, chiefly Brit* short for **advantage** (sense 3)

van⁴ (væn) *n* **1** any device for winnowing corn **2** *arch* a wing [c17 var. of FAN¹]

Van (vɑːn) *n* **1** a city in E Turkey, on Lake Van. Pop: 226 965 (1997) **2 Lake** a salt lake in E Turkey, at an altitude of 1650 m (5400 ft): fed by melting snow and glaciers. Area: 3737 sq km (1433 sq miles)

vanadium (və'neɪdɪəm) *n* a toxic silvery-white metallic element used in steel alloys and as a catalyst. Symbol: V; atomic no.: 23; atomic wt.: 50.94 [c19 NL, from ON *Vanadis*, epithet of the goddess Freya + -IUM]

Van Allen (væn 'ælən) *n* **James Alfred** born 1914, US physicist, noted for his use of satellites to investigate cosmic radiation in the upper atmosphere

Van Allen belt *n* either of two regions of charged particles above the earth, the inner one extending from 2400 to 5600 kilometres above the earth and the outer one from 13 000 to 19 000 kilometres [c20 after its discoverer, J. A. VAN ALLEN]

Vanbrugh ('vænbrə) *n* Sir **John** 1664–1726, English dramatist and baroque architect. His best-known plays are the Restoration comedies *The Relapse* (1697) and *The Provok'd Wife* (1697). As an architect, he is noted esp for Blenheim Palace

Van Buren (væn 'bjʊərən) *n* **Martin** 1782–1862, US Democratic statesman; 8th president of the US (1837–41)

Vancouver¹ (væn'kuːvə) *n* **1** an island of SW Canada, off the SW coast of British Columbia: separated from the Canadian mainland by the Strait of Georgia and Queen Charlotte Sound, and from the US mainland by Juan de Fuca Strait; the largest island off the W coast of North America. Chief town: Victoria. Pop: 461 575 (latest est). Area: 32 137 sq km (12 408 sq miles) **2** a city in SW Canada, in SW British Columbia: Canada's chief Pacific port, named after Captain George Vancouver: university (1908). Pop: 514 008 (1996), with a conurbation of 1 826 800 (1995) **3 Mount** a mountain on the border between Canada and Alaska, in the St Elias Mountains. Height: 4785 m (15 700 ft)

Vancouver² (væn'kuːvə) *n* Captain **George** 1757–98, English navigator, noted for his exploration of the Pacific coast of North America (1792–94)

V and A (in Britain) *abbrev for* Victoria and Albert Museum

vandal ('vændᵊl) *n* a person who deliberately causes damage to personal or public property [c17 from VANDAL, from L *Vandallus*, of Gmc origin]

Vandal ('vændᵊl) *n* a member of a Germanic people that raided Roman provinces in the 3rd and 4th centuries AD before devastating Gaul, conquering Spain and N Africa, and sacking Rome > **Vandalic** (væn'dælɪk) *adj*
▷ http://campus.northpark.edu/history/WebChron/WestEurope/Vandals.html

vandalism ('vændəˌlɪzəm) *n* the deliberate destruction caused by a vandal or an instance of such destruction > ˌ**vandal'istic** *adj*

vandalize *or* **vandalise** ('vændəˌlaɪz) *vb* **vandalizes, vandalizing, vandalized** *or* **vandalises, vandalising, vandalised** *(tr)* to destroy or damage (something) by an act of vandalism

Van de Graaff generator ('væn də ˌgrɑːf) *n* a device for producing high electrostatic potentials, consisting of a hollow metal sphere on which a charge is accumulated from a continuous moving belt of insulating material: used in particle accelerators [c20 after R. J. *Van de Graaff* (1901–67), US physicist]

Vanderbilt ('vændəbɪlt) *n* **Cornelius,** known as *Commodore Vanderbilt*. 1794–1877, US steamship and railway magnate and philanthropist

Van der Post ('væn də ˌpəʊst) *n* Sir **Laurens (Jan)** 1906–96, South African writer and traveller. His works include the travel books *Venture to the Interior* (1952), *The Lost World of the Kalahari* (1958), and *Testament to the Bushmen* (1984) and the novels *The Hunter and the Whale* (1967) and *The Admiral's Baby* (1996)

van der Waals (*Dutch* vɑn dər 'waːls) *n* **Johannes Diderik** (joː'hanəs 'diːdərik) 1837–1923, Dutch physicist, noted for his research on the equations of state of gases and liquids: Nobel prize for physics in 1910

van der Weyden (*Dutch* vɑn də 'wɛjdə) *n* **Rogier** (roː'xiːr) ?1400–64, Flemish painter, esp of religious works and portraits

Van Diemen Gulf (væn 'diːmən) *n* an inlet of the Timor Sea in N Australia, in the Northern Territory

Van Diemen's Land (væn 'diːmənz) *n* the former name

(1642–1855) of **Tasmania** > ˌ**Vande'monian** *n, adj*

Van Dyck *or* **Vandyke** (væn 'daɪk) *n* Sir **Anthony** 1599–1641, Flemish painter; court painter to Charles I of England (1632–41) He is best known for his portraits of the aristocracy

Vandyke beard ('vændaɪk) *n* a short pointed beard. Often shortened to **Vandyke**

Vandyke collar *or* **cape** *n* a large white collar with several very deep points. Often shortened to **Vandyke**

vane (veɪn) *n* **1** Also called: **weather vane** a flat plate or blade of metal mounted on a vertical axis in an exposed position to indicate wind direction **2** any one of the flat blades or sails forming part of the wheel of a windmill **3** any flat or shaped plate used to direct fluid flow, esp in a turbine, etc **4** a fin or plate fitted to a projectile or missile to provide stabilization or guidance **5** *ornithol* the flat part of a feather **6** *surveying* **6a** a sight on a quadrant or compass **6b** the movable marker on a levelling staff [OE *fana*] > **vaned** *adj*

Vänern (*Swedish* 'vɛːnərn) *n* **Lake** a lake in SW Sweden: the largest lake in Sweden and W Europe; drains into the Kattegat. Area: 5585 sq km (2156 sq miles)

van Eyck (væn 'aɪk) *n* **Jan** (jɑn) died 1441, Flemish painter; founder of the Flemish school of painting. His most famous work is the altarpiece *The Adoration of the Lamb*, in Ghent, in which he may have been assisted by his brother **Hubert** ('hyːbərt), died ?1426

Van Gogh (væn 'gɒx; *Dutch* vɑn 'ɔxx) *n* **Vincent** (vɪn'sɛnt) 1853–90, Dutch postimpressionist painter, noted for his landscapes and portraits, in which colour is used essentially for its expressive and emotive value

vanguard ('vænˌgɑːd) *n* **1** the leading division or units of a military force **2** the leading position in any movement or field, or the people who occupy such a position [c15 from OF *avant-garde*, from *avant-* fore- + *garde* GUARD]

vanilla (və'nɪlə) *n* **1** any of a genus of tropical climbing orchids having spikes of large fragrant flowers and long fleshy pods containing the seeds (beans) **2** the pod or bean of certain of these plants, used to flavour food, etc **3** a flavouring extract prepared from vanilla beans and used in cooking ▹ *adj* **4** flavoured with or as with vanilla: *vanilla ice cream* **5** *sl* ordinary or conventional: *a vanilla kind of guy* [c17 from NL, from Sp. *vainilla* pod, from *vaina*, from L *vāgīna* sheath] > **va'nillic** *adj*

vanillin ('vænɪlɪn, və'nɪlɪn) *n* a white crystalline aldehyde found in vanilla and many natural balsams and resins. It is a by-product of paper manufacture and is used as a flavouring and in perfumes

Vanir ('vɑːnɪə) *pl n Norse myth.* a race of ancient gods often locked in struggle with the Aesir. The most notable of them are Njord and his children Frey and Freya [from ON *Vanr*, a fertility god]

vanish ('vænɪʃ) *vb (intr)* **1** to disappear, esp suddenly or mysteriously **2** to cease to exist **3** *maths* to become zero [c14 *vanissen*, from OF *esvanir*, from L *ēvānēscere* to evaporate, from *ē-* EX-[1] + *vānēscere*, from *vānus* empty] > '**vanisher** *n*

vanishing cream *n* a cosmetic cream that is colourless once applied, used as a foundation for powder or as a cleansing cream

vanishing point *n* **1** the point to which parallel lines appear to converge in the rendering of perspective, usually on the horizon **2** a point at which something disappears

vanity ('vænɪtɪ) *n, pl* **vanities** **1** the state or quality of being vain **2** ostentation occasioned by ambition or pride **3** an instance of being vain or something about which one is vain **4** the state or quality of being valueless or futile [c13 from OF, from L *vānitās* emptiness, from *vānus* empty]

vanity bag, case, *or* **box** *n* a woman's small bag or hand case used to carry cosmetics, etc

vanity plates *pl n inf* personalized car numberplates

vanity unit *n* a hand basin built into a wooden Formica-covered or tiled top, usually with a built-in cupboard below it. Also called (trademark): **Vanitory unit**

vanquish ('væŋkwɪʃ) *vb (tr)* **1** to defeat or overcome in a battle, contest, etc **2** to defeat in argument or debate **3** to conquer (an emotion) [c14 *vanquisshen*, from OF *venquis*, from *veintre* to overcome, from L *vincere*] > '**vanquishable** *adj* > '**vanquisher** *n*

vantage ('vɑːntɪdʒ) *n* **1** a state, position, or opportunity affording superiority or advantage **2** superiority or benefit accruing from such a position, etc **3** *tennis* short for **advantage** (sense 3) [c13 from OF *avantage* ADVANTAGE]

vantage point *n* a position or place that allows one an overall view of a scene or situation

van't Hoff (*Dutch* vɑnt 'hɔf) *n* **Jacobus Hendricus** (jaː'koːbys hɛn'driːkœs) 1852–1911, Dutch physical chemist: founded stereochemistry with his theory of the asymmetric carbon atom; the first to apply thermodynamics to chemical reactions: Nobel prize for chemistry 1901

Vanua Levu (vɑː'nuːə 'lɛvuː) *n* the second largest island of Fiji: mountainous. Area: 5535 sq km (2137 sq miles)

Vanuatu ('vænuːˌætuː) *n* a republic comprising a group of islands in the W Pacific, W of Fiji: a condominium under Anglo-French joint rule from 1906; attained partial autonomy in 1978 and full independence in 1980 as a member of the Commonwealth. Its economy is based chiefly on copra. Official languages: Bislama; French; English. Religion: Christian majority. Currency: vatu. Capital: Vila (on Efate). Pop: 195 000 (2001 est). Area: about 14 760 sq km (5700 sq miles). Official name: **Republic of Vanuatu** Former name (until 1980): **New Hebrides**

▹ www.vanuatugovernment.gov.vu
▹ www.vanuatutourism.com
▹ www.tourismvanuatu.com

vanward ('vænwəd) *adj, adv* in or towards the front

vapid ('væpɪd) *adj* **1** bereft of strength, sharpness, flavour, etc **2** boring or dull [c17 from L *vapidus*] > **va'pidity** *n* > '**vapidly** *adv*

vapor ('veɪpə) *n* the US spelling of **vapour**

vaporescence (ˌveɪpə'rɛsəns) *n* the production or formation of vapour > ˌ**vapor'escent** *adj*

vaporetto (ˌveɪpə'rɛtəʊ) *n, pl* **vaporetti** (-tɪ) *or* **vaporettos** a steam-powered passenger boat, as used on the canals in Venice [It., from *vapore* a steamboat]

vaporific (ˌveɪpə'rɪfɪk) *adj* **1** producing, causing, or tending to produce vapour **2** of, concerned with, or having the nature of vapour **3** tending to become vapour; volatile [c18 from NL *vaporificus*, from L *vapor* steam + *facere* to make]

vaporimeter (ˌveɪpə'rɪmɪtə) *n* an instrument for measuring vapour pressure, used to determine the volatility of oils

vaporize *or* **vaporise** ('veɪpəˌraɪz) *vb* **vaporizes, vaporizing, vaporized** *or* **vaporises, vaporising, vaporised** **1** to change or cause to change into vapour or into the gaseous state **2** to evaporate or disappear or cause to evaporate or disappear, esp suddenly **3** to destroy or be destroyed by turning into a gas as a result of the extreme heat generated by a nuclear explosion > ˌ**vapori'zation** *or* ˌ**vapori'sation** *n*

vaporizer *or* **vaporiser** ('veɪpəˌraɪzə) *n* **1** a substance that vaporizes or a device that causes vaporization **2** *med* a device that produces steam or atomizes medication for inhalation

vaporous ('veɪpərəs) *adj* **1** resembling or full of vapour **2** lacking permanence or substance **3** given to foolish imaginings > **vaporosity** (ˌveɪpə'rɒsɪtɪ) *n* > '**vaporously** *adv*

vapour *or US* **vapor** ('veɪpə) *n* **1** particles of moisture or other substance suspended in air and visible as clouds, smoke, etc **2** a gaseous substance at a temperature below its critical temperature **3** a substance that is in a gaseous state at a temperature below its boiling point **4 the vapours** *arch* a depressed mental condition believed originally to be the result of vaporous exhalations from the stomach ▷ *vb* **5** to evaporate or cause to evaporate **6** (*intr*) to make vain empty boasts [c14 from L *vapor*] > **'vapourer** *or US* **'vaporer** *n* > **'vapourish** *or US* **'vaporish** *adj* > **'vapour-ˌlike** *or US* **'vapor-ˌlike** *adj* > **'vapoury** *or US* **'vapory** *adj*

vapour density *n* the ratio of the density of a gas or vapour to that of hydrogen at the same temperature and pressure

vapour lock *n* a stoppage in a pipe carrying a liquid caused by a bubble of gas, esp in the pipe feeding the carburettor of an internal-combustion engine

vapour pressure *n physics* the pressure exerted by a vapour in equilibrium with its solid or liquid phase at a particular temperature

vapour trail *n* a visible trail left by an aircraft flying at high altitude or through supercold air caused by the deposition of water vapour in the engine exhaust as minute ice crystals

Var (*French* var) *n* **1** a department of SE France, in Provence-Alpes-Côte d'Azur region. Capital: Toulon. Pop: 898 441 (1999). Area: 6023 sq km (2349 sq miles) **2** a river in SE France, flowing southeast and south to the Mediterranean near Nice. Length: about 130 km (80 miles)

var. *abbrev for:* **1** variable **2** variant **3** variation **4** variety **5** various

varactor ('vɛəˌræktə) *n* a semiconductor diode that acts as a voltage-dependent capacitor, being operated with a reverse bias [c20 prob. a blend of *variable reactor*]

Varah ('værə) *n* (**Edward**) **Chad** born 1911, British Anglican clergyman, who founded (1953) the Samaritans counselling service

Varanasi (və'rɑːnəsɪ) *n* a city in NE India, in SE Uttar Pradesh on the River Ganges: probably dates from the 13th century BC; an early centre of Aryan philosophy and religion; a major place of pilgrimage for Hindus, Jains, Sikhs, and Buddhists, with many ghats along the Ganges; seat of the Banaras Hindu University (1916), India's leading university, and the Sanskrit University (1957). Pop: 929 270 (1991). Former names: **Benares, Banaras**

Vardar (*Serbo-Croat* 'vardar) *n* a river in S Europe, rising in W Macedonia and flowing northeast, then south past Skopje into Greece, where it is called the Axios and enters the Aegean at Thessaloníki. Length: about 320 km (200 miles)

varec ('værɛk) *n* **1** another name for **kelp** **2** the ash obtained from kelp [c17 from F, from ON *wrek* (unattested); see WRECK]

Varese (*Italian* va're:se) *n* a historic city in N Italy, in Lombardy near Lake Varese: manufacturing centre, esp for leather goods. Pop: 88 018 (1990)

Varèse (væ'rɛz) *n* **Edgar**(**d**) (ɛdgar) 1883–1965, US composer, born in France. His works, which combine extreme dissonance with complex rhythms and the use of electronic techniques, include *Ionisation* (1931) and *Poème électronique* (1958)

Vargas (*Portuguese* 'vargas) *n* **Getúlio Dornelles** (ʒe'tulju dur'nelәʃ) 1883–1954, Brazilian statesman; president (1930–45; 1951–54)

Vargas Llosa (*Spanish* 'baryas 'ʎosa) *n* (**Jorge**) **Mario** (**Pedro**) born 1936, Peruvian novelist, writer, and political figure. His novels include *The City and the Dogs* (1963), *Conversation in the Cathedral* (1969), *The Storyteller* (1990), and *The Notebok of Don Rigoberto* (1998). In 1990 he stood unsuccessfully for the presidency of Peru

variable ('vɛərɪəbᵊl) *adj* **1** liable to or capable of change: *variable weather* **2** (of behaviour, emotions, etc) lacking constancy **3** *maths* having a range of possible values **4** (of a species, etc) liable to deviate from the established type **5** (of a wind) varying in direction and intensity **6** (of an electrical component or device) designed so that a characteristic property, such as resistance, can be varied ▷ *n* **7** something that is subject to variation **8** *maths* **8a** an expression that can be assigned any of a set of values **8b** a symbol, esp *x*, *y*, or *z*, representing an unspecified member of a class of objects, numbers, etc **9** *logic* a symbol, esp *x*, *y*, or *z*, representing any member of a class of entities **10** *computing* a named unit of storage that can be changed to any of a set of specified values during execution of a program **11** *astron* See **variable star** **12** a variable wind **13** (*pl*) a region where variable winds occur [c14 from L *variābilis* changeable, from *variāre* to diversify] > **ˌvaria'bility** *or* **'variableness** *n* > **'variably** *adv*

variable cost *n* a cost that varies directly with output

variable-geometry *or* **variable-sweep** *adj* denoting an aircraft in which the wings are hinged to give the variable aspect ratio colloquially known as a **swing-wing**

variable star *n* any star that varies considerably in brightness, either irregularly or in regular periods. **Intrinsic variables,** in which the variation is a result of internal changes, include novae and pulsating stars

variance ('vɛərɪəns) *n* **1** the act of varying or the quality, state, or degree of being divergent **2** an instance of diverging; dissension **3 at variance** **3a** (often foll by *with*) (of facts, etc) not in accord **3b** (of persons) in a state of dissension **4** *statistics* a measure of dispersion; the square of the standard deviations **5** a difference or discrepancy between two steps in a legal proceeding, esp between a statement and the evidence given to support it **6** *chem* the number of degrees of freedom of a system, used in the phase rule

variant ('vɛərɪənt) *adj* **1** liable to or displaying variation **2** differing from a standard or type: *a variant spelling* ▷ *n* **3** something that differs from a standard or type **4** *statistics* another word for **variate** [c14 via OF from L, from *variāre* to diversify, from *varius* VARIOUS]

variant CJD *n* short for **variant Creutzfeldt-Jakob disease**: another name for **new-variant Creutzfeldt-Jakob disease**

variate ('vɛərɪɪt) *n statistics* a random variable or a numerical value taken by it [c16 from L *variāre* to VARY]

variation (ˌvɛərɪ'eɪʃən) *n* **1** the act, process, condition, or result of changing or varying **2** an instance of varying or the amount, rate, or degree of such change **3** something that differs from a standard or convention **4** *music* a repetition of a musical theme in which the rhythm, harmony, or melody is altered or embellished **5** *biol* a marked deviation from the typical form or function **6** *astron* any deviation from the mean motion or orbit of a planet, satellite, etc **7** another word for **magnetic declination** **8** *ballet* a solo dance > **ˌvari'ational** *adj*

varicella (ˌværɪ'sɛlə) *n* the technical name for **chickenpox** [c18 NL, irregular dim. of VARIOLA] > **ˌvari'cellar** *adj*

varices ('værɪˌsiːz) *n* the plural of **varix**

varico- *or before a vowel* **varic-** *combining form* indicating a varix or varicose veins: *varicotomy* [from L *varix, varic-* distended vein]

varicoloured *or US* **varicolored** ('vɛərɪˌkʌləd) *adj* having many colours

varicose ('værɪˌkəʊs) *adj* of or resulting from varicose veins: *a varicose ulcer* [c18 from L *varicōsus*, from VARIX]

varicose veins *pl n* a condition in which the superficial veins, esp of the legs, become knotted and swollen

varicosis (ˌværɪ'kəʊsɪs) *n pathol* any condition

characterized by distension of the veins [c18 from NL, from L: VARIX]
varicosity (ˌværɪˈkɒsɪtɪ) *n, pl* **varicosities** *pathol* **1** the state, condition, or quality of being varicose **2** an abnormally distended vein
varicotomy (ˌværɪˈkɒtəmɪ) *n, pl* **varicotomies** surgical excision of a varicose vein
varied (ˈvɛərɪd) *adj* **1** displaying or characterized by variety; diverse **2** modified or altered: *the amount may be varied* **3** varicoloured; variegated > ˈ**variedly** *adv*
variegate (ˈvɛərɪˌɡeɪt) *vb* **variegates, variegating, variegated** (*tr*) to alter the appearance of, esp by adding different colours [c17 from LL, from L *varius* diverse, VARIOUS + *agere* to make] > ˌ**varieˈgation** *n*
variegated (ˈvɛərɪˌɡeɪtɪd) *adj* **1** displaying differently coloured spots., streaks, etc **2** (of foliage) having pale patches
varietal (vəˈraɪɪtᵊl) *adj* **1** of, characteristic of, designating, or forming a variety, esp a biological variety ▷ *n* **2** a wine labelled with the name of the grape from which it is pressed > **vaˈrietally** *adv*
variety (vəˈraɪɪtɪ) *n, pl* **varieties 1** the quality or condition of being diversified or various **2** a collection of unlike things, esp of the same general group **3** a different form or kind within a general category: *varieties of behaviour* **4a** *Taxonomy*. a race whose distinct characters do not justify classification as a separate species **4b** *Horticulture, stockbreeding*. a strain of animal or plant produced by artificial breeding **5a** entertainment consisting of a series of short unrelated acts, such as comedy turns, songs, etc **5b** (*as modifier*): *a variety show* [c16 from L *varietās*, from VARIOUS]
varifocal (ˌvɛərɪˈfəʊkᵊl) *adj* **1** *optics* having a focus that can vary **2** relating to a lens that is gradated to permit any length of vision between near and distant
varifocals (ˌvɛərɪˈfəʊkᵊlz) *pl n* a pair of spectacles with varifocal lenses
variform (ˈvɛərɪˌfɔːm) *adj* varying in form or shape > ˈ**variˌformly** *adv*
variola (vəˈraɪələ) *n* the technical name for **smallpox** [c18 from Med. L: disease marked by little spots, from L *varius* spotted] > **vaˈriolar** *adj*
variole (ˈvɛərɪˌəʊl) *n* any of the rounded masses that make up the rock variolite [c19 from F, from Med. L; see VARIOLA]
variolite (ˈvɛərɪəˌlaɪt) *n* any basic igneous rock containing rounded bodies (varioles) [c18 from VARIOLA, referring to the pockmarked appearance of the rock] > **variolitic** (ˌvɛərɪəˈlɪtɪk) *adj*
variometer (ˌvɛərɪˈɒmɪtə) *n* **1** an instrument for measuring variations in a magnetic field **2** *electronics* a variable inductor consisting of a movable coil mounted inside and connected in series with a fixed coil
variorum (ˌvɛərɪˈɔːrəm) *adj* **1** containing notes by various scholars or various versions of the text ▷ *n* **2** an edition or text of this kind [c18 from L *ēditiō cum notīs variōrum* edition with the notes of various commentators]
various (ˈvɛərɪəs) *determiner* **1** several different: *he is an authority on various subjects* ▷ *adj* **2** of different kinds, though often within the same general category: *his disguises are many and various* **3** (*prenominal*) relating to a collection of separate persons or things: *the various members of the club* **4** displaying variety; many-sided: *his various achievements* [c16 from L *varius* changing] > ˈ**variously** *adv* > ˈ**variousness** *n*

USAGE The use of *different* after *various*, which seems to be most common in speech, is unnecessary and should be avoided in serious writing: *the disease exists in various forms* (not *in various different forms*)

varistor (vəˈrɪstə) *n* a two-electrode semiconductor device having a voltage-dependent nonlinear resistance ▷ Cf **varactor** [c20 a blend of *variable resistor*]
Varityper (ˈvɛərɪˌtaɪpə) *n trademark* a justifying typewriter used to produce copy in various type styles
varix (ˈvɛərɪks) *n, pl* **varices** *pathol* **a** a tortuous dilated vein **b** a similar condition affecting an artery or lymphatic vessel [c15 from L]
varlet (ˈvɑːlɪt) *n arch* **1** a menial servant **2** a knight's page **3** a rascal [c15 from OF, var. of *vallet* VALET] > ˈ**varletry** *n*
varmint (ˈvɑːmɪnt) *n inf* an irritating or obnoxious person or animal [c16 dialect var. of *varmin* VERMIN]
varna (ˈvɑːnə) *n* any of the four Hindu castes; Brahman, Kshatriya, Vaisya, or Sudra [from Sansk.: class]
Varna (*Bulgarian* ˈvarna) *n* a port in NE Bulgaria, on the Black Sea: founded by Greeks in the 6th century BC; under the Ottoman Turks (1391–1878). Pop: 299 801 (1999 est). Former name (1949–56): **Stalin**
varnish (ˈvɑːnɪʃ) *n* **1** a preparation consisting of a solvent, a drying oil, and usually resin, rubber, etc, for application to a surface where it yields a hard glossy, usually transparent, coating **2** a similar preparation consisting of a substance, such as shellac, dissolved in a volatile solvent, such as alcohol. It hardens to a film on evaporation of the solvent **3** the sap of certain trees used to produce such a coating **4** a smooth surface, coated with or as with varnish **5** an artificial, superficial, or deceptively pleasing manner, covering, etc **6** *chiefly Brit* another word for **nail polish** ▷ *vb* (*tr*) **7** to cover with varnish **8** to give a smooth surface to, as if by painting with varnish **9** to impart a more attractive appearance to [c14 from OF, from Med. L *veronix* sandarac, resin, from Med. Gk *berenikē*, ?from Gk *Berenikē*, city in Cyrenaica, Libya where varnishes were used] > ˈ**varnisher** *n*
varnish tree *n* any of various trees, such as the lacquer tree, yielding substances used to make varnish or lacquer

Varro (ˈværəʊ) *n* **Marcus Terentius** (ˈmɑːkəs təˈrɛntɪəs) 116–27 BC, Roman scholar and satirist
varsity (ˈvɑːsɪtɪ) *n, pl* **varsities** *Brit, S African, & NZ inf* short for **university**
Varuna (ˈværʊnə, ˈvʌ-) *n Hinduism* the ancient sky god, later the god of the waters and rain-giver. In earlier traditions he was also the all-seeing divine judge
varus (ˈvɛərəs) *adj pathol* turned inwards towards the midline of the body [c19 from L: crooked, bent]
varve (vɑːv) *n geol* a thin band of sediment deposited annually in glacial lakes, consisting of a light layer and a dark layer deposited at different seasons [c20 from Swedish *varv* layer, from *varva*, from ON *hverfa* to turn]
vary (ˈvɛərɪ) *vb* **varies, varying, varied 1** to undergo or cause to undergo change or modification in appearance, character, form, etc **2** to be different or cause to be different; be subject to change **3** (*tr*) to give variety to **4** (*intr;* foll by *from*) to differ, as from a convention, standard, etc **5** (*intr*) to change in accordance with another variable: *her mood varies with the weather* [c14 from L, from *varius* VARIOUS] > ˈ**varying** *adj*
vas (væs) *n, pl* **vasa** (ˈveɪsə) *anat, zool* a vessel or tube that carries a fluid [c17 from L: vessel]
Vasari (vəˈsɑːrɪ; *Italian* vaˈzaːri) *n* **Giorgio** (ˈdʒordʒo) 1511–74, Italian architect, painter, and art historian, noted for his *Lives of the Most Excellent Italian Architects, Painters, and Sculptors* (1550; 1568), a principal source for the history of Italian Renaissance art
Vasco da Gama (ˈvæskəʊ də ˈɡɑːmə) *n* See (Vasco da) **Gama**
vascular (ˈvæskjʊlə) *adj biol, anat* of, relating to, or having vessels that conduct and circulate liquids: *a vascular bundle* [c17 from NL *vāsculāris*, from L *vāsculum*, dim. of *vās* vessel] > **vascularity** (ˌvæskjʊˈlærɪtɪ) *n* > ˈ**vascularly** *adv*
vascular bundle *n* a longitudinal strand of vascular

tissue in the stems and leaves of higher plants

vascular tissue *n* tissue of plants occurring as a continuous system throughout the plant: it conducts water, mineral salts, and synthesized food, and provides mechanical support. Also called: **conducting tissue**

vas deferens (ˈvæs ˈdɛfəˌrɛnz) *n, pl* **vasa deferentia** (ˈveɪsə ˌdɛfəˈrɛnʃɪə) *anat* the duct that conveys spermatozoa from the epididymis to the urethra [c16 from NL, from L *vās* vessel + *deferēns*, present participle of *deferre* to bear away]

vase (vɑːz) *n* a vessel used as an ornament or for holding cut flowers [c17 via F from L *vās* vessel]

vasectomy (væˈsɛktəmɪ) *n, pl* **vasectomies** surgical removal of all or part of the vas deferens, esp as a method of contraception

Vaseline (ˈvæsɪˌliːn) *n* a trademark for **petrolatum**

Vashti (ˈvæʃtaɪ) *n Old Testament* the wife of the Persian king Ahasuerus: deposed for refusing to display her beauty before his guests (Esther 1–2). Douay spelling: **Vasthi**

vaso- *or before a vowel* **vas-** *combining form* **1** indicating a blood vessel: *vasodilator* **2** indicating the vas deferens: *vasectomy* [from L *vās* vessel]

vasoactive (ˌveɪzəʊˈæktɪv) *adj* affecting the diameter of blood vessels: *vasoactive peptides*

vasoconstrictor (ˌveɪzəʊkənˈstrɪktə) *n* a drug, agent, or nerve that causes narrowing of the walls of blood vessels

vasodilator (ˌveɪzəʊdaɪˈleɪtə) *n* a drug, agent, or nerve that can cause dilatation of the walls of blood vessels

vasoinhibitor (ˌveɪzəʊɪnˈhɪbɪtə) *n* any of a group of drugs that reduce or inhibit the action of the vasomotor nerves

vasomotor (ˌveɪzəʊˈməʊtə) *adj* (of a drug, nerve, etc) relating to or affecting the diameter of blood vessels

vasopressin (ˌveɪzəʊˈprɛsɪn) *n* a hormone secreted by the pituitary gland. It increases the reabsorption of water by the kidney tubules and increases blood pressure by constricting the arteries. Also called: **antidiuretic hormone** [from *Vasopressin*, a trademark]

vasopressor (ˈveɪzəʊˌprɛsə) *med* ▷ *adj* **1** causing an increase in blood pressure by constricting the arteries ▷ *n* **2** a substance that has such an effect

vassal (ˈvæsᵊl) *n* **1** (in feudal society) a man who entered into a relationship with a lord to whom he paid homage and fealty in return for protection and often a fief **2a** a person, nation, etc, in a subordinate or dependent position relative to another **2b** (*as modifier*): *vassal status* ▷ *adj* **3** of or relating to a vassal [c14 via OF from Med. L *vassallus*, from *vassus* servant, of Celtic origin] > **ˈvassalage** *n*

vast (vɑːst) *adj* **1** unusually large in size, degree, or number **2** (*prenominal*) (intensifier): *in vast haste* ▷ *n* **3** **the vast** *chiefly poetic* immense or boundless space [c16 from L *vastus* deserted] > **ˈvastly** *adv* > **ˈvastness** *n*

Västerås (*Swedish* vɛstərˈoːs) *n* a city in central Sweden, on Lake Mälar: Sweden's largest inland port; site of several national parliaments in the 16th century. Pop: 125 433 (2000 est)

vasty (ˈvɑːstɪ) *adj* **vastier, vastiest** an archaic or poetic word for **vast**

vat (væt) *n* **1** a large container for holding or storing liquids **2** *chem* a preparation of reduced vat dye ▷ *vb* **vats, vatting, vatted** **3** (*tr*) to place, store, or treat in a vat [OE *fæt*]

VAT (*sometimes* væt) (in Britain) *abbrev for* value-added tax: a tax levied on the difference between the cost of materials and the selling price of a commodity or service

vat dye *n* a dye, such as indigo, that is applied by first reducing it to its base, which is soluble in alkali, and then regenerating the insoluble dye by oxidation in the fibres of the material > **ˈvat-ˌdyed** *adj*

vatic (ˈvætɪk) *adj rare* of, relating to, or characteristic of a prophet; oracular [c16 from L *vātēs* prophet]

Vatican (ˈvætɪkən) *n* **1a** the palace of the popes in Rome, which includes administrative offices and is attached to the basilica of St Peter's **1b** (*as modifier*): *the Vatican Council* **2a** the authority of the Pope and the papal curia **2b** (*as modifier*): *a Vatican edict* [c16 from L *Vāticānus mons* Vatican hill, on the western bank of the Tiber, of Etruscan origin]

Vatican City *n* an independent state forming an enclave in Rome, with extraterritoriality over 12 churches and palaces in Rome: the only remaining Papal State; independence recognized by the Italian government in 1929; contains St Peter's Basilica and Square and the Vatican; the spiritual and administrative centre of the Roman Catholic Church. Languages: Italian and Latin. Currency: lira. Pop: 1000 (1997 est). Area: 44 hectares (109 acres). Italian name: **Città del Vaticano** Also called: **the Holy See**

▷ www.vatican.va

Vättern (*Swedish* ˈvɛtərn) *n* **Lake** a lake in S central Sweden: the second largest lake in Sweden; linked to Lake Vänern by the Göta Canal; drains into the Baltic. Area: 1912 sq km (738 sq miles)

Vaucluse (*French* voklyz) *n* a department of SE France, in Provence-Alpes-Côte-d'Azur region. Capital: Avignon. Pop: 499 685 (1999). Area: 3578 sq km (1395 sq miles)

Vaud (*French* vo) *n* a canton of SW Switzerland: mountainous in the southeast; chief Swiss producer of wine. Capital: Lausanne. Pop: 616 300 (2000 est). Area: 3209 sq km (1240 sq miles). German name: **Waadt**

vaudeville (ˈvəʊdəvɪl, ˈvɔː-) *n* **1** *chiefly US & Canad* variety entertainment consisting of short acts such as acrobatic turns, song-and-dance routines, etc. Brit name: **music hall** **2** a light or comic theatrical piece interspersed with songs and dances [c18 from F, from *vaudevire* satirical folk song, shortened from *chanson du vau de Vire* song of the valley of Vire, a district in Normandy] > **ˌvaudeˈvillian** *n, adj*

▷ http://memory.loc.gov/ammem/vshtml/vshome.html

▷ www.theatrelinks.com

Vaudois (ˈvəʊdwɑː) *pl n, sing* **Vaudois** **1** another name for the **Waldenses** **2** the inhabitants of Vaud

Vaughan (vɔːn) *n* **1** **Henry** 1622–95, Welsh mystic poet, best known for his *Silex Scintillans* (1650; 1655) **2** Dame **Janet** (**Maria**) 1899–1993, British physician and university official: helped set up Britain's first National Blood Transfusion Service (1939): after World War II, became Britain's expert on the effects of radiation on humans; Principal of Somerville College, Oxford (1945–67) **3** **Sarah** (**Lois**) 1924–90, US jazz vocalist and pianist, noted esp for her skill in vocal improvisation

Vaughan Williams (ˈwɪljəmz) *n* **Ralph** 1872–1958, English composer, inspired by British folk songs and music of the Tudor period. He wrote operas, symphonies, hymns, and choral music

vault¹ (vɔːlt) *n* **1** an arched structure that forms a roof or ceiling **2** a room, esp a cellar, having an arched roof down to floor level **3** a burial chamber, esp when underground **4** a strongroom for the storage of valuables **5** an underground room used for the storage of wine, food, etc **6** *anat* any arched or domed bodily cavity or space: *the cranial vault* **7** something suggestive of an arched structure, as the sky ▷ *vb* **8** (*tr*) to furnish with or as if with an arched roof **9** (*tr*) to construct in the shape of a vault **10** (*intr*) to curve in the shape of a vault [c14 *vaute*, from OF, from Vulgar L *volvita* (unattested) a turn, prob. from L *volvere* to roll]

vault² (vɔːlt) *vb* **1** to spring over (an object), esp with the aid of a long pole or with the hands resting on the object **2** (*intr*) to do, achieve, or attain something as if by a leap:

he vaulted to fame ▷ *n* **3** the act of vaulting [C16 from OF *voulter* to turn from It. *voltare*, from Vulgar L *volvitāre* (unattested) to turn, leap; see VAULT[1]] > **ˈvaulter** *n*

vaulting[1] (ˈvɔːltɪŋ) *n* one or more vaults in a building or such structures considered collectively

vaulting[2] (ˈvɔːltɪŋ) *adj* (*prenominal*) **1** excessively confident: *vaulting arrogance* **2** used to vault: *a vaulting pole*

vaunt (vɔːnt) *vb* **1** (*tr*) to describe, praise, or display (one's success, possessions, etc) boastfully **2** (*intr*) *rare or literary* to brag ▷ *n* **3** a boast [C14 from OF, from LL *vānitāre*, from L *vānus* VAIN] > **ˈvaunter** *n*

Vauxhall (ˈvɒksˌhɔːl) *n* **1** a district in London, on the south bank of the Thames **2** Also called: **Vauxhall Gardens** a public garden at Vauxhall, laid out in 1661; a fashionable meeting place and site of lavish entertainments. Closed in 1859

vavasor (ˈvævəˌsɔː) *or* **vavasour** (ˈvævəˌsʊə) *n* (in feudal society) the noble or knightly vassal of a baron or great lord who also has vassals himself [C13 from OF *vavasour*, ?from Med. L *vassus vassōrum* vassal of vassals]

vb *abbrev for* verb

VC *abbrev for:* **1** Vice-chairman **2** Vice Chancellor **3** Vice Consul **4** Victoria Cross

V-chip *n* a device within a television set that allows the set to be programmed not to receive transmissions that have been classified as containing sex, violence, or obscene language

▷ www.fcc.gov/vchip

vCJD *abbrev for* (new-)variant Creutzfeldt–Jakob disease

VCR *abbrev for* video cassette recorder

VD *abbrev for* venereal disease

V-Day *n* a day nominated to celebrate victory, as in V-E Day or V-J Day in World War II

VDQS *abbrev for* vins délimités de qualité supérieure: on a bottle of French wine, indicates that it contains high-quality wine from an approved regional vineyard: the second highest French wine classification ▷ Cf **AOC**, ***vin de pays***

VDU *computing abbrev for:* visual display unit

've *contraction of* have: *I've; you've*

veal (viːl) *n* the flesh of the calf used as food [C14 from OF *veel*, from L *vitellus*, dim. of *vitulus* calf]

vealer (ˈviːlə) *n US, Canad, & Austral* a calf bred for veal

vector (ˈvɛktə) *n* **1** *maths* a variable quantity, such as force, that has magnitude and direction and can be resolved into components that are odd functions of the coordinates **2** *maths* an element of a vector space **3** Also called: **carrier** *pathol* an organism, esp an insect, that carries a disease-producing microorganism from one host to another **4** Also called: **cloning vector** *genetics* an agent, such as a bacteriophage or a plasmid, by means of which a fragment of foreign DNA is inserted into a host cell to produce a gene clone in genetic engineering **5** the course or compass direction of an aircraft ▷ *vb* (*tr*) **6** to direct or guide (a pilot, aircraft, etc) by directions transmitted by radio **7** to alter the direction of (the thrust of a jet engine) as a means of steering an aircraft [C18 from L: carrier, from *vehere* to convey] > **vectorial** (vɛkˈtɔːrɪəl) *adj*

vector field *n* a region of space under the influence of some vector quantity, such as magnetic field strength, in which each point can be described by a vector

vector font *n computing* another name for **outline font**

vector product *n* the product of two vectors that is a pseudovector, whose magnitude is the product of the magnitudes of the given vectors and the sine of the angle between them. Its axis is perpendicular to the plane of the given vectors

vector sum *n* a vector whose length and direction are represented by the diagonal of a parallelogram whose sides represent the given vectors

Veda (ˈveɪdə) *n* any or all of the most ancient sacred writings of Hinduism, esp the Rig-Veda, Yajur-Veda, Sama-Veda, and Atharva-Veda [C18 from Sansk.: knowledge]

vedalia (vɪˈdeɪlɪə) *n* an Australian ladybird introduced elsewhere to control the scale insect, which is a pest of citrus fruits [C20 from NL]

Vedanta (vɪˈdɑːntə) *n* one of the six main philosophical schools of Hinduism, expounding the monism regarded as implicit in the Veda in accordance with the doctrines of the Upanishads [C19 from Sansk., from VEDA + *ánta* end] > **Veˈdantic** *adj* > **Veˈdantist** *n*

V-E Day *n* the day marking the Allied victory in Europe in World War II (May 8, 1945)

vedette (vɪˈdɛt) *n* **1** *naval* a small patrol vessel **2** *mil* a mounted sentry posted forward of a formation's position [C17 from F, from It. *vedetta* (infl. by *vedere* to see), from earlier *veletta*, ?from Sp., from L *vigilāre*]

Vedic (ˈveɪdɪk) *adj* **1** of or relating to the Vedas or the ancient form of Sanskrit in which they are written ▷ *n* **2** the classical form of Sanskrit; the language of the Vedas

veer (vɪə) *vb* **1** to alter direction (of) **2** (*intr*) to change from one position, opinion, etc, to another **3** (*intr*) (of the wind) to change direction clockwise in the northern hemisphere and anticlockwise in the southern ▷ *n* **4** a change of course or direction [C16 from OF *virer*, prob. of Celtic origin]

veg (vɛdʒ) *n inf* a vegetable or vegetables

Vega[1] (ˈviːgə) *n* the brightest star in the constellation Lyra and one of the most conspicuous in the N hemisphere [C17 from Med. L, from Ar. *(al nasr) al wāqi*, lit.: the falling (vulture), i.e. the constellation Lyra]

Vega[2] (ˈveɪgə; *Spanish* ˈbeɣa) *n* See **Lope de Vega**

vegan (ˈviːgən) *n* a person who uses no animal products

vegeburger *or* **veggieburger** (ˈvɛdʒɪˌbɜːgə) *n* a flat cake of chopped seasoned vegetables and pulses that is grilled or fried and often served in a bread roll

Vegemite (ˈvɛdʒɪˌmaɪt) *n Austral & NZ trademark* a yeast extract used as a spread, flavouring for stews, etc

vegetable (ˈvɛdʒtəbᵊl, ˈvɛdʒətəbᵊl) *n* **1** any of various herbaceous plants having parts that are used as food, such as peas, potatoes, cauliflower, and onions **2** *inf* a person who has lost control of his or her mental faculties, limbs, etc, as from an injury, mental disease, etc **3** a dull inactive person **4** (*modifier*) consisting of or made from edible vegetables: *a vegetable diet* **5** (*modifier*) of, characteristic of, derived from, or consisting of plants or plant material: *the vegetable kingdom* **6** *rare* any member of the plant kingdom [C14 (adj): from LL *vegetābilis*, from *vegetāre* to enliven, from L *vegēre* to excite]

▷ www.vegetablepatch.net
▷ www.vegkitchen.com
▷ www.vegetarianrecipe.com
▷ www.gardenguides.com/Vegetables/vegetabl.htm
▷ www.doityourself.com/vegetables
▷ www.cityfarmer.org
▷ http://gardening.about.com/cs/edibles

vegetable butter *n* any of a group of vegetable fats having the consistency of butter

vegetable ivory *n* the hard whitish material obtained from the endosperm of the ivory nut: used to make buttons, ornaments, etc

vegetable marrow *n* **1** a plant, probably native to America but widely cultivated for its oblong green striped fruit which is eaten as a vegetable **2** the fruit of this plant. Often shortened to **marrow**

vegetable oil *n* any of a group of oils that are obtained from plants

vegetable oyster *n* another name for **salsify** (sense 1)

vegetable silk *n* any of various silky fibres obtained from the seed pods of certain plants

vegetable wax *n* any of various waxes that occur on parts of certain plants, esp the trunks of certain palms, and prevent loss of water

vegetal ('vɛdʒɪtᵊl) *adj* **1** of or characteristic of vegetables or plant life **2** vegetative [C15 from LL *vegetāre* to quicken]

vegetarian (ˌvɛdʒɪ'tɛərɪən) *n* **1** a person who advocates or practises the exclusion of meat and fish, and sometimes eggs, milk, and cheese, from the diet ▷ *adj* **2** *cookery* strictly, consisting of vegetables and fruit only, but often including milk, cheese, eggs, etc > ˌ**vege'tarianism** *n*
▷ www.vegsoc.org
▷ www.vrg.org
▷ www.vegkitchen.com
▷ www.vegetarianrecipe.com

vegetate ('vɛdʒɪˌteɪt) *vb* **vegetates, vegetating, vegetated** (*intr*) **1** to grow like a plant **2** to lead a life characterized by monotony, passivity, or mental inactivity [C17 from LL *vegetāre* to invigorate]

vegetation (ˌvɛdʒɪ'teɪʃən) *n* **1** plant life as a whole, esp the plant life of a particular region **2** the process of vegetating > ˌ**vege'tational** *adj*

vegetative ('vɛdʒɪtətɪv) *adj* **1** of or denoting the nonreproductive parts of a plant **2** (of reproduction) characterized by asexual processes **3** of or relating to functions such as digestion and circulation rather than sexual reproduction **4** (of a style of living, etc) unthinking or passive > '**vegetatively** *adv*

veggie ('vɛdʒɪ) *n, adj* an informal word for **vegetarian**

vego ('vɛdʒəʊ) *Austral inf* ▷ *adj* **1** vegetarian ▷ *n, pl* **vegos** **2** a vegetarian

veg out *vb* **vegges, vegging, vegged** (*intr, adv*) *sl, chiefly US* to relax in an inert, passive way; vegetate: *vegging out in front of the television*

vehement ('viːɪmənt) *adj* **1** marked by intensity of feeling or conviction **2** (of actions, gestures, etc) characterized by great energy, vigour, or force [C15 from L *vehemēns* ardent] > '**vehemence** *n* > '**vehemently** *adv*

vehicle ('viːɪkᵊl) *n* **1** any conveyance in or by which people or objects are transported, esp one fitted with wheels **2** a medium for the expression or communication of ideas, power, etc **3** *pharmacol* a therapeutically inactive substance mixed with the active ingredient to give bulk to a medicine **4** Also called: **base** a painting medium, such as oil, in which pigments are suspended **5** (in the performing arts) a play, etc, that enables a particular performer to display his talents [C17 from L *vehiculum*, from *vehere* to carry] > **vehicular** (vɪ'hɪkjʊlə) *adj*

Veii ('viːjaɪ) *n* an ancient Etruscan city, northwest of Rome: destroyed by the Romans in 396 BC

veil (veɪl) *n* **1** a piece of more or less transparent material, usually attached to a hat or headdress, used to conceal or protect a woman's face and head **2** part of a nun's headdress falling round the face onto the shoulders **3** something that covers, conceals, or separates: *a veil of reticence* **4** **the veil** the life of a nun in a religious order **5** **take the veil** to become a nun **6** Also called: **velum** *bot* a membranous structure, esp the thin layer of cells covering a young mushroom ▷ *vb* **7** (*tr*) to cover, conceal, or separate with or as if with a veil **8** (*intr*) to wear or put on a veil [C13 from Norman F *veile*, from L *vēla*, pl of *vēlum* a covering] > '**veiler** *n* > '**veil-ˌlike** *adj*

veiled (veɪld) *adj* **1** disguised: *a veiled insult* **2** (of sound, tone, the voice, etc) not distinct > **veiledly** ('veɪlɪdlɪ) *adv*

veiling ('veɪlɪŋ) *n* a veil or the fabric used for veils

vein (veɪn) *n* **1** any of the tubular vessels that convey oxygen-depleted blood to the heart ▷ Cf **pulmonary vein, artery** (sense 1) **2** any of the hollow branching tubes that form the supporting framework of an insect's wing **3** any of the vascular bundles of a leaf **4** a clearly defined mass of ore, mineral, etc **5** an irregular streak of colour or alien substance in marble, wood, or other material **6** a distinctive trait or quality in speech, writing, character, etc: *a vein of humour* **7** a temporary attitude or temper: *the debate entered a frivolous vein* ▷ *vb* (*tr*) **8** to diffuse over or cause to diffuse over in streaked patterns **9** to fill, furnish, or mark with or as if with veins [C13 from OF, from L *vēna*] > '**veinless** *adj* > '**veinˌlike** *adj* > '**veiny** *adj*

veining ('veɪnɪŋ) *n* a pattern or network of veins or streaks

veinlet ('veɪnlɪt) *n* any small vein or venule

velamen (və'leɪmɛn) *n, pl* **velamina** (-'læmɪnə) **1** the thick layer of dead cells that covers the aerial roots of certain orchids **2** *anat* another word for **velum** [C19 from L: veil, from *vēlāre* to cover]

velar ('viːlə) *adj* **1** of or attached to a velum: *velar tentacles* **2** *phonetics* articulated with the soft palate and the back of the tongue, as in (k) or (ŋ) [C18 from L, from *vēlum* VEIL]

Velázquez (*Spanish* be'laθkεθ) *or* **Velásquez** (*Spanish* be'laskεθ) *n* **Diego Rodríguez de Silva y** ('djeɣo rɔ'ðriɣeθ de 'silβa i) 1599–1660, Spanish painter, remarkable for the realism of his portraits, esp those of Philip IV of Spain and the royal household

Velcro ('vɛlkrəʊ) *n trademark* a fastening consisting of two strips of nylon fabric, one having tiny hooked threads and the other a coarse surface, that form a strong bond when pressed together

veld *or* **veldt** (fɛlt, vɛlt) *n* elevated open grassland in Southern Africa. See also **bushveld, highveld** [C19 from Afrik., from earlier Du. *veldt* FIELD]

veldskoen ('fɛltˌskʊn, 'vɛlt-) *n* an ankle-length boot of soft but strong rawhide [from Afrik. *vel* skin + *skoen* shoes]

veleta (və'liːtə) *n* a variant spelling of **valeta**

veliger ('vɛlɪdʒə) *n* the free-swimming larva of many molluscs, having a rudimentary shell and a ciliated velum used for feeding and locomotion [C19 from NL, from VEL(UM) + -GER(OUS)]

Vellore (və'lɔː) *n* a town in SE India, in NE Tamil Nadu: medical centre. Pop: 175 061 (1991)

vellum ('vɛləm) *n* **1** a fine parchment prepared from the skin of a calf, kid, or lamb **2** a work printed or written on vellum **3** a creamy coloured heavy paper resembling vellum ▷ *adj* **4** made of or resembling vellum [C15 from OF, from *velin* of a calf, from *veel* VEAL]

veloce (vɪ'ləʊtʃɪ) *adj, adv music* to be played rapidly [from It., from L *vēlōx* quick]

velocipede (vɪ'lɒsɪˌpiːd) *n* an early form of bicycle, esp one propelled by pushing along the ground with the feet [C19 from F, from L *vēlōx* swift + *pēs* foot] > **ve'lociˌpedist** *n*

velocity (vɪ'lɒsɪtɪ) *n, pl* **velocities** **1** speed of motion or operation; swiftness **2** *physics* a measure of the rate of motion of a body expressed as the rate of change of its position in a particular direction with time **3** *physics* (not in technical usage) another word for **speed** (sense 3) [C16 from L *vēlōcitās*, from *vēlōx* swift]

velocity of circulation *n econ* the average number of times a unit of money is used in a given time, esp calculated as the ratio of the total money spent in that time to the total amount of money in circulation

velocity of light *n* a nontechnical name for **speed of light**

velodrome ('viːləˌdrəʊm, 'vɛl-) *n* an arena with a banked track for cycle racing [C20 from F *vélodrome*, from *vélo-* (from L *vēlōx* swift) + -DROME]

velour *or* **velours** (vɛ'lʊə) *n* any of various fabrics with a velvet-like finish, used for upholstery, clothing, etc [C18 from OF, from OProvençal *velos* velvet, from L, from *villus* shaggy hair]

velouté (və'luːteɪ) *n* a rich white sauce or soup made from stock, egg yolks, and cream [from F, lit.: velvety, from OF *velous*; see VELOUR]

Velsen (*Dutch* 'vɛlsə) *n* a port in the W Netherlands, in North Holland at the mouth of the canal connecting Amsterdam with the North Sea: fishing and heavy industrial centre. Pop: 63 617 (1994)

velum ('viːləm) *n, pl* **vela** (-lə) **1** *zool* any of various membranous structures **2** *anat* any of various veil-like bodily structures, esp the soft palate **3** *bot* another word for **veil** (sense 6) [C18 from L: veil]

velure (və'lʊə) *n* velvet or a similar fabric [C16 from OF, from *velous*; see VELOUR]

velutinous (və'luːtɪnəs) *adj* covered with short dense soft hairs [C19 from NL *velūtīnus* like velvet]

velvet ('vɛlvɪt) *n* **1a** a fabric of silk, cotton, nylon, etc, with a thick close soft pile **1b** (*as modifier*): *velvet curtains* **2** anything with a smooth soft surface **3a** smoothness **3b** (*as modifier*): *a velvet night* **4** the furry covering of the newly formed antlers of a deer **5** *sl, chiefly US* **5a** gambling winnings **5b** a gain **6** **on velvet** *sl* in a condition of ease, advantage, or wealth **7** **velvet glove** gentleness, often concealing strength or determination (esp in **an iron hand in a velvet glove**) [C14 *veluet*, from OF, from *velu* hairy, from Vulgar L *villutus* (unattested), from L *villus* shaggy hair] > **'velvet-ˌlike** *adj* > **'velvety** *adj*

velveteen (ˌvɛlvɪ'tiːn) *n* **1** a cotton fabric resembling velvet with a short thick pile, used for clothing, etc **2** (*pl*) trousers made of velveteen

Velvet Underground *n* **the** US avant-garde rock group in New York City (formed in 1965; disintegrated 1969–72; reformed for a tour in 1993). See also (Lou) **Reed**

Ven. *abbrev for* Venerable

vena ('viːnə) *n, pl* **venae** (-niː) *anat* a technical word for **vein** [C15 from L *vēna* VEIN]

vena cava ('keɪvə) *n, pl* **venae cavae** ('keɪviː) either one of two large veins that convey oxygen-depleted blood to the heart [L: hollow vein]

venal ('viːnᵊl) *adj* **1** easily bribed or corrupted: *a venal magistrate* **2** characterized by corruption or bribery [C17 from L *vēnālis*, from *vēnum* sale] > **ve'nality** *n* > **'venally** *adv*

venation (viː'neɪʃən) *n* **1** the arrangement of the veins in a leaf or in the wing of an insect **2** such veins collectively > **ve'national** *adj*

vend (vɛnd) *vb* **1** to sell or be sold **2** to sell (goods) for a living [C17 from L *vendere*, from *vēnum dare* to offer for sale]

vendace ('vɛndeɪs) *n, pl* **vendaces** *or* **vendace** either of two small whitefish occurring in lakes in Scotland and NW England [C18 from NL *vandēsius*, from OF *vandoise*, prob. of Celtic origin]

vendee (vɛn'diː) *n chiefly law* a person to whom something, esp real property, is sold

Vendée (*French* vɑ̃de) *n* a department of W France, in Pays-de-la-Loire region: scene of the **Wars of the Vendée,** a series of peasant-royalist insurrections (1793–95) against the Revolutionary government. Capital: La Roche-sur-Yon. Pop: 539 664 (1999). Area: 7016 sq km (2709 sq miles)

vendetta (vɛn'dɛtə) *n* **1** a private feud, originally between Corsican or Sicilian families, in which the relatives of a murdered person seek vengeance by killing the murderer or some member of his family **2** any prolonged feud [C19 from It., from L *vindicta*, from *vindicāre* to avenge] > **ven'dettist** *n*

vendible ('vɛndəbᵊl) *adj* **1** saleable or marketable ▷ *n* **2** (*usually pl*) *rare* a saleable object > **ˌvendi'bility** *n*

vending machine *n* a machine that automatically dispenses consumer goods such as cigarettes or food, when money is inserted

Vendôme (*French* vɑ̃dom) *n* **Louis Joseph de** (lwi ʒozɛf də) 1654–1712, French marshal, noted for his command during the War of the Spanish Succession (1701–14)

vendor ('vɛndɔː) *or* **vender** ('vɛndə) *n* **1** *chiefly law* a person who sells something, esp real property **2** another name for **vending machine**

vendor placing *n finance* a method of financing the purchase of one company by another in which the purchasing company pays for the target company in its own shares, on condition that the vendor places these shares with investors for cash payment

veneer (vɪ'nɪə) *n* **1** a thin layer of wood, plastic, etc, with a decorative or fine finish that is bonded to the surface of a less expensive material, usually wood **2** a superficial appearance: *a veneer of gentility* **3** any facing material that is applied to a different backing material ▷ *vb (tr)* **4** to cover (a surface) with a veneer **5** to conceal (something) under a superficially pleasant surface [C17 from G *furnieren* to veneer, from OF *fournir* to FURNISH] > **ve'neerer** *n*

veneering (vɪ'nɪərɪŋ) *n* material used as veneer or a veneered surface

venepuncture ('vɛnɪˌpʌŋktʃə) *n* a variant spelling of **venipuncture**

venerable ('vɛnərəbᵊl) *adj* **1** (esp of a person) worthy of reverence on account of great age, religious associations, character, etc **2** (of inanimate objects) hallowed on account of age or historical or religious association **3** *RC Church* a title bestowed on a deceased person when the first stage of his canonization has been accomplished **4** *Church of England* a title given to an archdeacon [C15 from L *venerābilis*, from *venerārī* to venerate] > **ˌvenera'bility** *or* **'venerableness** *n* > **'venerably** *adv*

venerate ('vɛnəˌreɪt) *vb* **venerates, venerating, venerated** *(tr)* **1** to hold in deep respect **2** to honour in recognition of qualities of holiness, excellence, etc [C17 from L *venerārī*, from *venus* love] > **'venerˌator** *n*

veneration (ˌvɛnə'reɪʃən) *n* **1** a feeling or expression of awe or reverence **2** the act of venerating or the state of being venerated

venereal (vɪ'nɪərɪəl) *adj* **1** of or infected with venereal disease **2** (of a disease) transmitted by sexual intercourse **3** of or involving the genitals **4** of or relating to sexual intercourse or erotic desire [C15 from L *venereus*, from *venus* sexual love, from VENUS¹]

venereal disease *n* another name for **sexually transmitted disease.** Abbrev: **VD**

venereology (vɪˌnɪərɪ'ɒlədʒɪ) *n* the branch of medicine concerned with the study and treatment of venereal disease > **veˌnere'ologist** *n*

venery¹ ('vɛnərɪ, 'viː-) *n arch* the pursuit of sexual gratification [C15 from Med. L *veneria*, from L *venus* love, VENUS¹]

venery² ('vɛnərɪ, 'viː-) *n* the art, sport, lore, or practice of hunting, esp with hounds; the chase [C14 from OF *venerie*, from *vener* to hunt, from L *vēnārī*]

venesection ('vɛnɪˌsɛkʃən) *n* surgical incision into a vein [C17 from NL *vēnae sectiō*; see VEIN, SECTION]

Venetia (vɪ'niːʃə) *n* **1** the area of ancient Italy between the lower Po valley and the Alps: later a Roman province **2** the territorial possessions of the medieval Venetian republic that were at the head of the Adriatic and correspond to the present-day region of Veneto and a large part of Friuli-Venezia Giulia

Venetian (vɪ'niːʃən) *adj* **1** of, relating to, or characteristic of Venice or its inhabitants ▷ *n* **2** a native or inhabitant of Venice **3** See **Venetian blind**

Venetian blind *n* a window blind consisting of a number of horizontal slats whose angle may be altered to let in more or less light

Venetian red *n* **1** natural or synthetic ferric oxide used as a red pigment **2a** a moderate to strong reddish-brown colour **2b** (*as adj*): *a Venetian-red coat*

Veneto (*Italian* 'vɛːneto) *n* a region of NE Italy, on the Adriatic: mountainous in the north with a fertile plain in the south, crossed by the Rivers Po, Adige, and Piave. Capital: Venice. Pop: 4 511 714 (2000 est). Area: 18 377 sq km (7095 sq miles). Also called: **Venezia-Euganea** (ve'nɛttsja eʊ'gaːnea)

Venez. *abbrev for* Venezuela

Venezia (ve'nɛttsja) *n* the Italian name for **Venice**

Venezia Giulia (*Italian* 'dʒuːlja) *n* a former region of NE

Italy at the N end of the Adriatic: divided between Yugoslavia and Italy after World War II; now divided between Italy and Slovenia

Venezia Tridentina (*Italian* triden'ti:na) *n* the former name (until 1947) of **Trentino-Alto Adige**

Venezuela (ˌvɛnɪ'zweɪlə) *n* **1** a republic in South America, on the Caribbean: colonized by the Spanish in the 16th century; independence from Spain declared in 1811 and won in 1819 after a war led by Simón Bolívar. It contains Lake Maracaibo and the northernmost chains of the Andes in the northwest, the Orinoco basin in the central part, and the Guiana Highlands in the south. Exports: petroleum, iron ore, and coffee. Official language: Spanish. Religion: Roman Catholic majority. Currency: bolívar. Capital: Caracas. Pop: 24 632 000 (2001 est). Area: 912 050 sq km (352 142 sq miles). Official name: **Bolivarian Republic of Venezuela** **2** **Gulf of** an inlet of the Caribbean in NW Venezuela: continues south as Lake Maracaibo > ˌ**Vene'zuelan** *adj, n*

▷ www.turismo-venezuela.com
▷ www.venezuelatuya.com
▷ www.embavenez-us.org
▷ www.discovervenezuela.com

vengeance ('vɛndʒəns) *n* **1** the act of or desire for taking revenge **2** **with a vengeance** (intensifier): *he's a coward with a vengeance* [C13 from OF, from *venger* to avenge, from L *vindicāre* to punish]

vengeful ('vɛndʒfʊl) *adj* **1** desiring revenge **2** characterized by or indicating a desire for revenge **3** inflicting or taking revenge: *with vengeful blows* > '**vengefully** *adv*

venial ('vi:nɪəl) *adj* easily excused or forgiven: *a venial error* [C13 via OF from LL *veniālis*, from L *venia* forgiveness] > ˌ**veni'ality** *n* > '**venially** *adv*

venial sin *n Christian theol* a sin regarded as involving only a partial loss of grace

Venice ('vɛnɪs) *n* a port in NE Italy, capital of Veneto region, built on over 100 islands and mud flats in the **Lagoon of Venice** (an inlet of the **Gulf of Venice** at the head of the Adriatic): united under the first doge in 697 AD; became an independent republic and a great commercial and maritime power, defeating Genoa, the greatest rival, in 1380; contains the Grand Canal and about 170 smaller canals, providing waterways for city transport. Pop: 277 305 (2000 est). Italian name: **Venezia** Related adj: **Venetian**

venin ('vɛnɪn) *n* any of the poisonous constituents of animal venoms [C20 from F *ven(in)* poison + -IN]

venipuncture *or* **venepuncture** ('vɛnɪˌpʌŋktʃə) *n med* the puncturing of a vein, esp to take a sample of venous blood or inject a drug

venison ('vɛnɪzᵊn, -sᵊn) *n* the flesh of a deer, used as food [C13 from OF *venaison*, from L *vēnātiō* hunting, from *vēnārī* to hunt]

Venite (vɪ'naɪtɪ) *n* **1** the opening word of the 95th psalm, an invitatory prayer at matins **2** a musical setting of this [L: come ye]

Venlo *or* **Venloo** (*Dutch* 'vɛnlo:) *n* a city in the SE Netherlands, in Limburg on the Maas River. Pop: 63 820 (latest est)

Venn diagram (vɛn) *n maths, logic* a diagram in which mathematical sets or terms of a categorial statement are represented by overlapping circles within a boundary representing the universal set, so that all possible combinations of the relevant properties are represented by the various distinct areas in the diagram [C19 after John *Venn* (1834–1923), Brit logician]

venom ('vɛnəm) *n* **1** a poisonous fluid secreted by such animals as certain snakes and scorpions and usually transmitted by a bite or sting **2** malice; spite [C13 from OF, from L *venēnum* poison, love potion] > '**venomous** *adj* > '**venomously** *adv* > '**venomousness** *n*

venose ('vi:nəʊs) *adj* **1** having veins; venous **2** (of a plant) covered with veins or similar ridges [C17 via L *vēnōsus*, from *vēna* a VEIN]

venosity (vɪ'nɒsɪtɪ) *n* **1** an excessive quantity of blood in the venous system or in an organ or part **2** an unusually large number of blood vessels in an organ or part

venous ('vi:nəs) *adj* **1** *physiol* of or relating to the blood circulating in the veins **2** of or relating to the veins [C17 see VENOSE]

vent[1] (vɛnt) *n* **1** a small opening for the escape of fumes, liquids, etc **2** the shaft of a volcano through which lava and gases erupt **3** the external opening of the urinary or genital systems of lower vertebrates **4** a small aperture at the breech of old guns through which the charge was ignited **5** **give vent to** to release (an emotion, idea, etc) in an outburst ▷ *vb (mainly tr)* **6** to release or give expression or utterance to (an emotion, etc): *he vents his anger on his wife* **7** to provide a vent for or make vents in **8** to let out (steam, etc) through a vent [C14 from OF *esventer* to blow out, from EX-[1] + *venter*, from Vulgar L *ventāre* (unattested), from L *ventus* wind]

vent[2] (vɛnt) *n* **1** a vertical slit at the back or both sides of a jacket ▷ *vb* **2** *(tr)* to make a vent or vents in (a jacket) [C15 from OF *fente* slit, from *fendre* to split, from L *findere* to cleave]

venter ('vɛntə) *n* **1** *anat, zool* **1a** the belly or abdomen of vertebrates **1b** a protuberant structure or part, such as the belly of a muscle **2** *bot* the swollen basal region of an archegonium **3** *law* the womb [C16 from L]

ventilate ('vɛntɪˌleɪt) *vb* **ventilates, ventilating, ventilated** *(tr)* **1** to drive foul air out of (an enclosed area) **2** to provide with a means of airing **3** to expose (a question, grievance, etc) to public discussion **4** *physiol* to oxygenate (the blood) [C15 from L *ventilāre* to fan, from *ventulus*, dim. of *ventus* wind] > '**ventilable** *adj*

ventilation (ˌvɛntɪ'leɪʃən) *n* **1** the act or process of ventilating or the state of being ventilated **2** an installation in a building that provides a supply of fresh air

ventilator ('vɛntɪˌleɪtə) *n* **1** an opening or device, such as a fan, used to ventilate a room, building, etc **2** *med* a machine that maintains a flow of air into and out of the lungs of a patient unable to breathe normally

ventral ('vɛntrəl) *adj* **1** relating to the front part of the body **2** of or situated on the upper or inner side of a plant organ, esp a leaf, that is facing the axis [C18 from L *ventrālis*, from *venter* abdomen] > '**ventrally** *adv*

ventral fin *n* **1** another name for **pelvic fin** **2** any unpaired median fin situated on the undersurface of fishes

ventricle ('vɛntrɪkᵊl) *n anat* **1** a chamber of the heart that receives blood from the atrium and pumps it to the arteries **2** any one of the four main cavities of the vertebrate brain **3** any of various other small cavities in the body [C14 from L *ventriculus*, dim. of *venter* belly] > **ven'tricular** *adj*

ventricose ('vɛntrɪˌkəʊs) *adj* **1** *bot, zool, anat* having a swelling on one side: *the ventricose corolla of many labiate plants* **2** another word for **corpulent** [C18 from NL, from L *venter* belly]

ventriculus (vɛn'trɪkjʊləs) *n, pl* **ventriculi** (-ˌlaɪ) **1** *zool* **1a** the midgut of an insect, where digestion takes place **1b** the gizzard of a bird **2** another word for **ventricle** [C18 from L, dim. of *venter* belly]

ventriloquism (vɛn'trɪləˌkwɪzəm) *or* **ventriloquy** *n* the art of producing vocal sounds that appear to come from another source [C18 from L *venter* belly + *loquī* to speak] > **ventriloquial** (ˌvɛntrɪ'ləʊkwɪəl) *adj* > ˌ**ventri'loquially** *adv* > **ven'triloquist** *n* > **ven'triloˌquize** *or* **ven'triloˌquise** *vb*

▷ www.bbk.ac.uk/eh/dumbstruck/archive
▷ www.axtell.com/learn.html
▷ www.comediansusa.com/vents/index.html

Ventris ('vɛntrɪs) *n* **Michael George Francis** 1922–56,

English cryptographer, who deciphered the Linear B script, identifying it as an early form of Mycenaean Greek

venture (ˈvɛntʃə) *vb* **ventures, venturing, ventured** **1** (*tr*) to expose to danger: *he ventured his life* **2** (*tr*) to brave the dangers of (something): *I'll venture the seas* **3** (*tr*) to dare (to do something): *does he venture to object?* **4** (*tr; may take a clause as object*) to express in spite of possible criticism: *I venture that he is not that honest* **5** (*intr;* often foll by *out, forth,* etc) to embark on a possibly hazardous journey, etc: *to venture forth upon the high seas* ▷ *n* **6** an undertaking that is risky or of uncertain outcome **7** a commercial undertaking characterized by risk of loss as well as opportunity for profit **8** something hazarded or risked in an adventure **9** **at a venture** at random [C15 var. of *aventure* ADVENTURE] > ˈ**venturer** *n*

venture capital *n* another name for **risk capital**

Venture Scout *or* **Venturer** *n Brit* a person aged 16–20 who is a member of the senior branch of the Scouts

venturesome (ˈvɛntʃəsəm) *or* **venturous** (ˈvɛntʃərəs) *adj* **1** willing to take risks; daring **2** hazardous

Venturi (vɛnˈtjʊərɪ) *n* **Robert** born 1925, US architect, a pioneer of the postmodernist style. His writings include *Complexity and Contradiction in Architecture* (1966)

Venturi tube (vɛnˈtjʊərɪ) *n physics* a device for measuring or controlling fluid flow, consisting of a tube so constricted that the pressure differential produced by fluid flowing through the constriction gives a measure of the rate of flow [C19 after G. B. *Venturi* (1746–1822), It. physicist]

venue (ˈvɛnjuː) *n* **1** *law* **1a** the place in which a cause of action arises **1b** the place fixed for the trial of a cause **1c** the locality from which the jurors must be summoned **2** a meeting place **3** any place where an organized gathering, such as a rock concert, is held [C14 from OF, from *venir* to come, from L *venīre*]

venule (ˈvɛnjuːl) *n* **1** *anat* any of the small branches of a vein that receives oxygen-depleted blood from the capillaries and returns it to the heart via the venous system **2** any of the branches of a vein in an insect's wing [C19 from L *vēnula,* dim. of *vēna* VEIN]

Venus[1] (ˈviːnəs) *n* the Roman goddess of love. Greek counterpart: **Aphrodite**

Venus[2] (ˈviːnəs) *n* one of the inferior planets and the second nearest to the sun, visible as a bright morning or evening star > **Venusian** (vɪˈnjuːzɪən) *n, adj*

▷ http://nssdc.gsfc.nasa.gov/planetary/planets

▷ www.solarviews.com/eng/venus.htm

Venusberg (ˈviːnəsˌbɜːg; *German* ˈveːnʊsbɛrk) *n* a mountain in central Germany: contains caverns that, according to medieval legend, housed the palace of the goddess Venus

Venus's-flytrap *or* **Venus flytrap** *n* an insectivorous plant having hinged two-lobed leaves that snap closed when the sensitive hairs on the surface are touched

Venus's looking glass *n* a purple-flowered plant of Europe, W Asia, and N Africa

veracious (vɛˈreɪʃəs) *adj* **1** habitually truthful or honest **2** accurate [C17 from L *vērax,* from *vērus* true] > **veˈraciously** *adv* > **veˈraciousness** *n*

veracity (vɛˈræsɪtɪ) *n, pl* **veracities** **1** truthfulness or honesty, esp when consistent or habitual **2** accuracy **3** a truth [C17 from Med. L *vērācitās,* from L *vērax;* see VERACIOUS]

Veracruz (ˌvɛrəˈkruːz; *Spanish* beraˈkruθ) *n* **1** a state of E Mexico, on the Gulf of Mexico: consists of a hot humid coastal strip with lagoons, rising rapidly inland to the central plateau and Sierra Madre Oriental. Capital: Jalapa. Pop: 6 901 111 (2000). Area: 72 815 sq km (28 114 sq miles) **2** the chief port of Mexico, in Veracruz state on the Gulf of Mexico. Pop: 410 000 (2000 est)

veranda *or* **verandah** (vəˈrændə) *n* **1** a porch or portico, sometimes partly enclosed, along the outside of a building **2** NZ a continuous overhead canopy that gives shelter to pedestrians [C18 from Port. *varanda* railing]

veratrine (ˈvɛrəˌtriːn) *or* **veratrin** (ˈvɛrətrɪn) *n* a white poisonous mixture obtained from sabadilla, consisting of various alkaloids: formerly used in medicine as a counterirritant [C19 from L *vērātrum* hellebore + -INE[2]]

verb (vɜːb) *n* **1** (in traditional grammar) any of a large class of words that serve to indicate the occurrence or performance of an action, the existence of a state, etc Such words as *run, make, do,* etc, are verbs **2** (in modern descriptive linguistic analysis) **2a** a word or group of words that functions as the predicate of a sentence or introduces the predicate **2b** (*as modifier*): *a verb phrase* ▷ Abbrev: **vb, v** [C14 from L *verbum* word]

verbal (ˈvɜːbᵊl) *adj* **1** of, relating to, or using words: *merely verbal concessions* **2** oral rather than written: *a verbal agreement* **3** verbatim; literal: *an almost verbal copy* **4** *grammar* of or relating to verbs or a verb ▷ See also **verbals** > ˈ**verbally** *adv*

verbalism (ˈvɜːbəˌlɪzəm) *n* **1** a verbal expression; phrase or word **2** an exaggerated emphasis on the importance of words **3** a statement lacking real content

verbalist (ˈvɜːbəlɪst) *n* **1** a person who deals with words alone, rather than facts, ideas, etc **2** a person skilled in the use of words

verbalize *or* **verbalise** (ˈvɜːbəˌlaɪz) *vb* **verbalizes, verbalizing, verbalized** *or* **verbalises, verbalising, verbalised** **1** to express (an idea, etc) in words **2** to change (any word) into a verb or derive a verb from (any word) **3** (*intr*) to be verbose > ˌ**verbaliˈzation** *or* ˌ**verbaliˈsation** *n*

verbal noun *n* a noun derived from a verb, such as *smoking* in the sentence *smoking is bad for you*

verbals (ˈvɜːbᵊlz) *pl n sl* **1** a criminal's admission of guilt on arrest **2** verbal abuse or invective

verbascum (vɜːˈbæskəm) *n* any of a genus of hairy plants, mostly biennial, having spikes of yellow, purple, or red flowers [L: mullein]

verbatim (vɜːˈbeɪtɪm) *adv, adj* using exactly the same words; word for word [C15 from Med. L: word by word, from L *verbum* word]

verbena (vɜːˈbiːnə) *n* **1** any of a genus of plants of tropical and temperate America, having red, white, or purple fragrant flowers: much cultivated as garden plants **2** any of various similar plants, esp the lemon verbena [C16 via Med. L, from L: sacred bough used by the priest in religious acts]

verbiage (ˈvɜːbɪɪdʒ) *n* the excessive and often meaningless use of words [C18 from F, from OF *verbier* to chatter, from *verbe* word, from L *verbum*]

verbose (vɜːˈbəʊs) *adj* using or containing an excess of words, so as to be pedantic or boring [C17 from L, from *verbum* word] > **verˈbosely** *adv* > **verbosity** (vɜːˈbɒsɪtɪ) *n*

verboten *German* (fɛrˈboːtən) *adj* forbidden

verb phrase *n grammar* a constituent of a sentence that contains the verb and any direct and indirect objects but not the subject

Vercelli (*Italian* verˈtʃɛlli) *n* a city in NW Italy, in Piedmont: an ancient Ligurian and later Roman city; has an outstanding library of manuscripts (notably the *Codex Vercellensis,* dating from the 10th century). Pop: 50 313 (1990)

Vercingetorix (ˌvɜːsɪnˈdʒɛtərɪks) *n* died ?45 BC, Gallic chieftain and hero, executed for leading a revolt against the Romans under Julius Caesar (52 BC)

verdant (ˈvɜːdᵊnt) *adj* **1** covered with green vegetation **2** (of plants, etc) green in colour **3** unsophisticated; green [C16 from OF, from *verdoyer* to become green, from OF *verd* green, from L *viridis*] > ˈ**verdancy** *n* > ˈ**verdantly** *adv*

verd antique (vɜːd) *n* **1** a dark green mottled impure variety of serpentine marble **2** any of various similar marbles or stones [C18 from F, from It. *verde antico* ancient green]

Verde (vɜːd) *n* **Cape** a cape in Senegal, near Dakar: the westernmost point of Africa. See also **Cape Verde**

Verdi (ˈvɛədɪ; *Italian* ˈverdi) *n* **Giuseppe** (dʒuˈzɛppe) 1813–1901, Italian composer of operas, esp *Rigoletto* (1851), *Il Trovatore* (1853), *La Traviata* (1853), and *Aïda* (1871)

verdict (ˈvɜːdɪkt) *n* **1** the findings of a jury on the issues of fact submitted to it for examination and trial **2** any decision or conclusion [C13 from Med. L *vērdictum*, from L *vērē dictum* truly spoken, from *vērus* true + *dīcere* to say]

verdigris (ˈvɜːdɪgrɪs) *n* **1** a green or bluish patina formed on copper, brass, or bronze **2** a green or blue crystalline substance obtained by the action of acetic acid on copper and used as a fungicide and pigment [C14 from OF *vert de Grice* green of Greece]

Verdun (*French* vɛrdỹ; *English* ˈvɛədʌn) *n* **1** a fortified town in NE France, on the Meuse: scene of the longest and most severe battle (1916) of World War I, in which the French repelled a powerful German offensive. Pop: 23 430 (1990). Ancient name: **Verodunum** (ˌvɛrəˈdjuːnəm) **2 Treaty of** an agreement reached in 843 AD by three grandsons of Charlemagne, dividing his empire into an E kingdom (later Germany), a W kingdom (later France), and a middle kingdom (containing what became the Low Countries, Lorraine, Burgundy, and N Italy)

verdure (ˈvɜːdʒə) *n* **1** flourishing green vegetation or its colour **2** a condition of freshness or healthy growth [C14 from OF *verd* green, from L *viridis*] > ˈ**verdured** *adj*

Vereeniging (fəˈriːnɪkɪŋ, və-) *n* a city in E South Africa: scene of the signing (1902) of the treaty ending the Boer War. Pop (urban area): 346 780 (1996)

verge[1] (vɜːdʒ) *n* **1** an edge or rim; margin **2** a limit beyond which something occurs: *on the verge of ecstasy* **3** *Brit* a grass border along a road **4** *archit* the edge of the roof tiles projecting over a gable **5** *English legal history* **5a** the area encompassing the royal court that is subject to the jurisdiction of the Lord High Steward **5b** a rod or wand carried as a symbol of office or emblem of authority, as in the Church ▷ *vb* **verges, verging, verged 6** (*intr;* foll by *on*) to be near (to): *to verge on chaos* **7** (when *intr*, sometimes foll by *on*) to serve as the edge of (something): *this narrow strip verges the road* [C15 from OF, from L *virga* rod]

verge[2] (vɜːdʒ) *vb* **verges, verging, verged** (*intr;* foll by *to* or *towards*) to move or incline in a certain direction [C17 from L *vergere*]

verger (ˈvɜːdʒə) *n chiefly Church of England* **1** a church official who acts as caretaker and attendant **2** an official who carries the verge or rod of office before a bishop or dean in ceremonies and processions [C15 from OF, from *verge*, from L *virga* rod, twig]

Vergil (ˈvɜːdʒɪl) *n* a variant spelling of **Virgil**

verglas (ˈvɛəglɑː) *n, pl* **verglases** (-glɑː, -glɑːz) a thin film of ice on rock [from OF *verre-glaz*, from *verre* glass + *glaz* ice]

veridical (vɪˈrɪdɪkᵊl) *adj* **1** truthful **2** *psychol* of revelations in dreams, etc, that appear to be confirmed by subsequent events [C17 from L, from *vērus* true + *dīcere* to say] > **veˌridiˈcality** *n* > **veˈridically** *adv*

veriest (ˈvɛrɪɪst) *adj arch* (intensifier): *the veriest coward*

verification (ˌvɛrɪfɪˈkeɪʃən) *n* **1** establishment of the correctness of a theory, fact, etc **2** evidence that provides proof of an assertion, theory, etc > ˈ**verifiˌcatory** *adj*

verify (ˈvɛrɪˌfaɪ) *vb* **verifies, verifying, verified** (*tr*) **1** to prove to be true; confirm **2** to check or determine the correctness or truth of by investigation, etc **3** *law* to substantiate or confirm (an oath) [C14 from OF, from Med. L *vērificāre*, from L *vērus* true + *facere* to make] > ˈ**veriˌfiable** *adj* > ˈ**veriˌfiably** *adv* > ˈ**veriˌfier** *n*

verily (ˈvɛrɪlɪ) *adv* (*sentence modifier*) *arch* in truth; truly: *verily, thou art a man of God* [C13 from VERY + -LY[2]]

verisimilar (ˌvɛrɪˈsɪmɪlə) *adj* probable; likely [C17 from L, from *vērus* true + *similis* like]

verisimilitude (ˌvɛrɪsɪˈmɪlɪˌtjuːd) *n* **1** the appearance or semblance of truth or reality **2** something that merely seems to be true or real, such as a doubtful statement [C17 from L, from *vērus* true + *similitūdō* SIMILITUDE]

verism (ˈvɪərɪzəm) *n* extreme naturalism in art or literature [C19 from It. *verismo*, from *vero* true, from L *vērus*] > ˈ**verist** *n, adj* > **veˈristic** *adj*

verismo (vɛˈrɪzməʊ) *n music* a school of composition that originated in Italian opera towards the end of the 19th century, drawing its themes from real life [C19 from It.; see VERISM]

veritable (ˈvɛrɪtəbᵊl) *adj* (*prenominal*) (intensifier; *usually qualifying a word used metaphorically*): *he's a veritable swine!* [C15 from OF, from *vérité* truth; see VERITY] > ˈ**veritableness** *n* > ˈ**veritably** *adv*

vérité (ˈveɪriːˌteɪ; *French* verite) *adj* involving a high degree of realism or naturalism: *a vérité look at David Bowie*. See also **cinéma vérité** [F, lit.: truth]

verity (ˈvɛrɪtɪ) *n, pl* **verities 1** the quality or state of being true, real, or correct **2** a true statement, idea, etc [C14 from OF from L *vēritās*, from *vērus* true]

verjuice (ˈvɜːˌdʒuːs) *n* **1** the acid juice of unripe grapes, apples, or crab apples, formerly much used in making sauces, etc **2** *rare* sourness or sharpness of temper, looks, etc [C14 from OF *vert jus* green (unripe) juice]

Verkhne-Udinsk (*Russian* ˈvjerxnɪuˈdjinsk) *n* the former name (until 1934) of **Ulan-Ude**

verkrampte (fəˈkramtə) *n* (in South Africa during apartheid) **a** an Afrikaner Nationalist violently opposed to the end of apartheid and to liberalism in general **b** (*as modifier*): *verkrampte politics* [C20 from Afrik. (adj), lit.: restricted]

Verlaine (*French* vɛrlɛn) *n* **Paul** (pɔl) 1844–96, French poet. His verse includes *Poèmes saturniens* (1866), *Fêtes galantes* (1869) and *Romances sans paroles* (1874). He was closely associated with Rimbaud and was a precursor of the symbolists

verligte (fəˈləxtə) *n* (in South Africa during apartheid) **a** a follower of any liberal White political party **b** (*as modifier*): *verligte politics* [C20 from Afrik. (adj), lit.: enlightened]

Vermeer (vɛəˈmɪə; *Dutch* vərˈmeːr) *n* **Jan** (jɑn) full name *Jan van der Meer van Delft*. 1632–75, Dutch genre painter, noted esp for his masterly treatment of light

vermeil (ˈvɜːmeɪl) *n* **1** gilded silver, bronze, or other metal, used esp in the 19th century **2a** vermilion **2b** (*as adj*): *vermeil shoes* [C15 from OF, from LL *vermiculus* insect (of the genus *Kermes*) or the red dye prepared from it, from L: little worm]

vermi- *combining form* worm: *vermicide; vermiform; vermifuge* [from L *vermis* worm]

vermicelli (ˌvɜːmɪˈsɛlɪ, -ˈtʃɛlɪ) *n* **1** very fine strands of pasta, used in soups **2** tiny chocolate strands used to coat cakes, etc [C17 from It.: little worms, from *verme*, from L *vermis*]

vermicide (ˈvɜːmɪˌsaɪd) *n* any substance used to kill worms > ˌ**vermiˈcidal** *adj*

vermicular (vɜːˈmɪkjʊlə) *adj* **1** resembling the form, motion, or tracks of worms **2** of worms or wormlike animals [C17 from Med. L, from L *vermiculus*, dim. of *vermis* worm] > **verˈmiculate** *adj* > **verˌmicuˈlation** *n*

vermiculite (vɜːˈmɪkjʊˌlaɪt) *n* any of a group of micaceous minerals consisting mainly of hydrated silicate of magnesium, aluminium, and iron: on heating they expand and in this form are used in heat and sound insulation [C19 from VERMICUL(AR) + -ITE[1]]

vermiform (ˈvɜːmɪˌfɔːm) *adj* resembling a worm

vermiform appendix *n* a wormlike pouch extending from the lower end of the caecum in some mammals. Also called: **appendix**

vermifuge (ˈvɜːmɪˌfjuːdʒ) *n* any drug or agent able to destroy or expel intestinal worms; an anthelmintic > **vermifugal** (ˌvɜːmɪˈfjuːgᵊl) *adj*

vermilion (vəˈmɪljən) *n* **1a** a bright red to reddish-orange colour **1b** (*as adj*): *a vermilion car* **2** mercuric sulphide, esp when used as a bright red pigment; cinnabar [c13 from OF *vermeillon*, from *vermeil*, from L *vermiculus*, dim. of *vermis* worm]

vermin (ˈvɜːmɪn) *n* **1** (*functioning as pl*) small animals collectively, esp insects and rodents, that are troublesome to man, domestic animals, etc **2** (*pl* **vermin**) an unpleasant person [c13 from OF, from L *vermis* worm] > ˈ**verminous** *adj*

vermis (ˈvɜːmɪs) *n, pl* **vermes** (-miːz) *anat* the middle lobe connecting the two halves of the cerebellum [c19 via NL from L: worm]

Vermont (vɜːˈmɒnt) *n* a state in the northeastern US: crossed from north to south by the Green Mountains; bounded on the east by the Connecticut River and by Lake Champlain in the northwest. Capital: Montpelier. Pop: 608 827 (2000). Area: 24 887 sq km (9609 sq miles). Abbreviations: **Vt** or (with zip code) **VT** > **Ver**ˈ**monter** *n*

vermouth (ˈvɜːməθ) *n* any of several wines containing aromatic herbs [c19 from F, from G *Wermut* WORMWOOD (absinthe)]

vernacular (vəˈnækjʊlə) *n* **1** **the** the commonly spoken language or dialect of a particular people or place **2** a local style of architecture, in which ordinary houses are built: *a true English vernacular* ▷ *adj* **3** relating to or in the vernacular **4** designating or relating to the common name of an animal or plant **5** built in the local style of ordinary houses [c17 from L *vernāculus* belonging to a household slave, from *verna* household slave] > **ver**ˈ**nacularly** *adv*

vernal (ˈvɜːnᵊl) *adj* **1** of or occurring in spring **2** *poetic* of or characteristic of youth [c16 from L, from *vēr* spring] > ˈ**vernally** *adv*

vernal equinox *n* See at **equinox**

vernal grass *n* any of a genus of Eurasian grasses, such as **sweet vernal grass**, having the fragrant scent of coumarin

vernalize *or* **vernalise** (ˈvɜːnəˌlaɪz) *vb* **vernalizes, vernalizing, vernalized** *or* **vernalises, vernalising, vernalised** to subject ungerminated or germinating seeds to low temperatures before planting, which is essential for many plants to ensure germination and flowering > ˌ**vernali**ˈ**zation** *or* ˌ**vernali**ˈ**sation** *n*

vernation (vɜːˈneɪʃən) *n* the way in which leaves are arranged in the bud [c18 from NL, from L *vernāre* to be springlike, from *vēr* spring]

Verne (vɜːn; *French* vɛrn) *n* **Jules** (ʒyl) 1828–1905, French writer, esp of science fiction, such as *Twenty Thousand Leagues under the Sea* (1870) and *Around the World in Eighty Days* (1873)

vernier (ˈvɜːnɪə) *n* **1** a small movable scale running parallel to the main graduated scale in certain measuring instruments, such as theodolites, used to obtain a fractional reading of one of the divisions on the main scale **2** (*modifier*) relating to or fitted with a vernier: *a vernier scale* [c18 after Paul *Vernier* (1580–1637), F mathematician, who described the scale]

vernissage (ˌvɜːnɪˈsɑːʒ) *n* a preview or the opening or the first day of an exhibition of paintings [F, from *vernis* VARNISH]

Vernoleninsk (*Russian* vɪrnəlɪˈnjiːnsk) *n* the former name of **Nikolayev**

Verny (*Russian* ˈvjɛrnɪj) *n* a former name (until 1927) of **Alma-Ata**

Verona (vəˈrəʊnə; *Italian* veˈroːna) *n* a city in N Italy, in Veneto on the Adige River: strategically situated at the junction of major routes between Italy and N Europe; became a Roman colony (89 BC); under Austrian rule (1797–1866); many Roman remains. Pop: 255 268 (2000 est) > **Veronese** (ˌvɛrəˈniːz) *adj, n*

Veronal (ˈvɛrənᵊl) *n* a trademark for **barbital**

Veronese (*Italian* veroˈneːse) *n* **Paolo** (ˈpaːolo), original name *Paolo Cagliari* or *Caliari*. 1528–88, Italian painter of the Venetian school. His works include *The Marriage at Cana* (1563) and *The Feast of the Levi* (1573)

veronica[1] (vəˈrɒnɪkə) *n* any plant of a genus, including the speedwells, of temperate and cold regions, having small blue, pink, or white flowers and flattened notched fruits [c16 from Med. L, ?from the name *Veronica*]

veronica[2] (vəˈrɒnɪkə) *n bullfighting* a pass in which the matador slowly swings the cape away from the charging bull [from Sp., from the name *Veronica*]

Verrazano *or* **Verrazzano** (*Italian* verraˈtsaːno) *n* **Giovanni da** (dʒoˈvanni da) ?1485–?1528, Florentine navigator; the first European to sight what was to become New York (1524)

Verrocchio (vəˈrəʊkɪˌəʊ; *Italian* verˈrɔkkjo) *n* **Andrea del** (anˈdrɛːa del) 1435–88, Italian sculptor, painter, and goldsmith of the Florentine school: noted esp for the equestrian statue of Bartolommeo Colleoni in Venice

verruca (vɛˈruːkə) *n, pl* **verrucae** (-siː) *or* **verrucas** **1** *pathol* a wart, esp one growing on the hand or foot **2** *biol* a wartlike outgrowth [c16 from L: wart]

verrucose (ˈvɛrʊˌkəʊs) *or* **verrucous** (ˈvɛrʊkəs, vɛˈruːkəs) *adj bot* covered with warty processes [c17 from L *verrūcōsus* full of warts, from *verrūca* a wart] > **verrucosity** (ˌvɛrʊˈkɒsɪtɪ) *n*

Versace (*Italian* verˈsatʃe) *n* **1** **Donatella** born 1955, Italian fashion designer and businesswoman; creative director of the Versace group from 1997 **2** **Gianni** (ˈdʒiani) 1946–97, Italian fashion designer

Versailles (vɛəˈsaɪ, -ˈseɪlz; *French* vɛrsaj) *n* **1** a city in N central France, near Paris: site of an elaborate royal residence built for Louis XIV; seat of the French kings (1682–1789). Pop: 87 789 (1990) **2** **Treaty of Versailles** **2a** the treaty of 1919 imposed upon Germany by the Allies (except for the US and the Soviet Union): the most important of the five peace treaties that concluded World War I **2b** another name for the (Treaty of) **Paris** of 1783

versant (ˈvɜːsᵊnt) *n* **1** *rare* the side or slope of a mountain or mountain range **2** the slope of a region [c19 from F, from *verser* to turn, from L *versāre*]

versatile (ˈvɜːsəˌtaɪl) *adj* **1** capable of or adapted for many different uses, skills, etc **2** variable **3** *bot* (of an anther) attached to the filament by a small area so that it moves freely in the wind **4** *zool* able to turn forwards and backwards [c17 from L *versātilis* moving around, from *versāre* to turn] > ˈ**versa**ˌ**tilely** *adv* > **versatility** (ˌvɜːsəˈtɪlɪtɪ) *n*

verse (vɜːs) *n* **1** (not in technical usage) a stanza of a poem **2** poetry as distinct from prose **3a** a series of metrical feet forming a rhythmic unit of one line **3b** (*as modifier*): *verse line* **4** a specified type of metre or metrical structure: *iambic verse* **5** one of the series of short subsections into which most of the writings in the Bible are divided **6** a poem ▷ *vb* **verses, versing, versed** **7** a rare word for **versify** [OE *vers*, from L *versus* furrow, lit.: a turning (of the plough), from *vertere* to turn]

versed (vɜːst) *adj* (*postpositive; foll by* in) thoroughly knowledgeable (about), acquainted (with), or skilled (in)

versed sine *n* a trigonometric function equal to one minus the cosine of the specified angle [c16 from NL, from SINE[1] + *versus*, from *vertere* to turn]

versicle (ˈvɜːsɪkᵊl) *n* **1** a short verse **2** a short sentence recited or sung by a minister and responded to by his congregation [c14 from L *versiculus* a little line, from *versus* VERSE]

versicolour *or US* **versicolor** (ˈvɜːsɪˌkʌlə) *adj* of variable or various colours [c18 from L *versicolor*, from *versāre* to turn + *color* COLOUR]

versification (ˌvɜːsɪfɪˈkeɪʃən) *n* **1** the technique or art of versifying **2** the form or metrical composition of a poem **3** a metrical version of a prose text

versify (ˈvɜːsɪˌfaɪ) *vb* **versifies, versifying, versified 1** *(tr)* to render (something) into verse **2** *(intr)* to write in verse [c14 from OF, from L, from *versus* VERSE + *facere* to make] > **ˈversiˌfier** *n*

version (ˈvɜːʃən) *n* **1** an account of a matter from a certain point of view, as contrasted with others: *his version of the accident is different from the policeman's* **2** a translation, esp of the Bible, from one language into another **3** a variant form of something **4** an adaptation, as of a book or play into a film **5** *med* manual turning of a fetus to correct an irregular position within the uterus. Also called: **cephalic version** [c16 from Med. L *versiō* a turning, from L *vertere* to turn] > **ˈversional** *adj*

vers libre *French* (vɛr librə) *n* (in French poetry) another term for **free verse**

verso (ˈvɜːsəʊ) *n, pl* **versos 1a** the back of a sheet of printed paper **1b** the left-hand pages of a book, with the even numbers ▷ Cf **recto** (sense 2) **2** the side of a coin opposite to the obverse [c19 from NL *versō foliō* the leaf having been turned, from L *vertere* to turn + *folium* leaf]

verst (vɛəst, vɜːst) *n* a unit of length, used in Russia, equal to 1.067 kilometres (0.6629 miles) [c16 from F or G, from Russian *versta* line]

versus (ˈvɜːsəs) *prep* **1** (esp in a competition or lawsuit) against. Abbrev: **v.**, (esp US) **vs 2** in contrast with [c15 from L: turned (in the direction of), opposite, from *vertere* to turn]

vertebra (ˈvɜːtɪbrə) *n, pl* **vertebrae** (-briː) *or* **vertebras** one of the bony segments of the spinal column [c17 from L: joint of the spine, from *vertere* to turn] > **ˈvertebral** *adj* > **ˈvertebrally** *adv*

vertebral column *n* another name for **spinal column**

vertebrate (ˈvɜːtɪˌbreɪt, -brɪt) *n* **1** any animal of a subphylum characterized by a bony skeleton and a well-developed brain: the group contains fishes, amphibians, reptiles, birds, and mammals ▷ *adj* **2** of or belonging to this subphylum

vertebration (ˌvɜːtɪˈbreɪʃən) *n* the formation of vertebrae or segmentation resembling vertebrae

vertex (ˈvɜːtɛks) *n, pl* **vertexes** *or* **vertices 1** the highest point **2** *maths* **2a** the point opposite the base of a figure **2b** the point of intersection of two sides of a plane figure or angle **2c** the point of intersection of a pencil of lines or three or more planes of a solid figure **3** *anat* the crown of the head [c16 from L: highest point, from *vertere* to turn]

vertical (ˈvɜːtɪkᵊl) *adj* **1** at right angles to the horizon; upright: *a vertical wall* **2** extending in a perpendicular direction **3** directly overhead **4** *econ* of or relating to associated or consecutive, though not identical, stages of industrial activity: *vertical integration* **5** of or relating to the vertex **6** *anat* of or situated at the top of the head (vertex) ▷ *n* **7** a vertical plane, position, or line **8** a vertical post, pillar, etc [c16 from LL *verticālis*, from L VERTEX] > **ˌvertiˈcality** *n* > **ˈvertically** *adv*

vertical angles *pl n geom* the pair of equal angles between a pair of intersecting lines

vertical mobility *n sociol* the movement of individuals or groups to positions in society that involve a change in class, status, and power

vertices (ˈvɜːtɪˌsiːz) *n* a plural of **vertex** (in technical and scientific senses only)

verticil (ˈvɜːtɪsɪl) *n biol* a circular arrangement of parts about an axis, esp leaves around a stem [c18 from L *verticillus* whorl (of a spindle), from VERTEX] > **verˈticillate** *adj*

vertiginous (vɜːˈtɪdʒɪnəs) *adj* **1** of, relating to, or having vertigo **2** producing dizziness **3** whirling **4** changeable; unstable [c17 from L *vertīginōsus*, from VERTIGO] > **verˈtiginously** *adv*

vertigo (ˈvɜːtɪɡəʊ) *n, pl* **vertigoes** *or* **vertigines** (vɜːˈtɪdʒɪˌniːz) *pathol* a sensation of dizziness resulting from a disorder of the sense of balance [c16 from L: a whirling round, from *vertere* to turn]

vertu (vɜːˈtuː) *n* a variant spelling of **virtu**

Vertumnus (vɜːˈtʌmnəs) *or* **Vortumnus** *n* a Roman god of gardens, orchards, and seasonal change [from L, from *vertere* to turn, change]

Verulamium (ˌvɛrʊˈleɪmɪəm) *n* the Latin name of **Saint Albans**

vervain (ˈvɜːveɪn) *n* any of several plants of the genus *Verbena*, having square stems and long slender spikes of purple, blue, or white flowers [c14 from OF *verveine*, from L *verbēna* sacred bough]

verve (vɜːv) *n* great vitality and liveliness [c17 from OF: garrulity, from L *verba* words, chatter]

vervet (ˈvɜːvɪt) *n* a variety of a South African guenon monkey having dark hair on the hands and feet and a reddish patch beneath the tail [c19 from F, from *vert* green]

Verwoerd (fəˈvʊt, fɛəˈvʊət) *n* **Hendrik Frensch** (ˈhɛndrɪk frɛns) 1901–66, South African statesman, born in the Netherlands: prime minister of South Africa (1958–66) and the principal architect of the apartheid system: assassinated

very (ˈvɛrɪ) *adv* **1** (intensifier) used to add emphasis to adjectives that are able to be graded: *very good; very tall* ▷ *adj (prenominal)* **2** (intensifier) used with nouns preceded by a definite article or possessive determiner, in order to give emphasis to the significance or relevance of a noun in a particular context, or to give exaggerated intensity to certain nouns: *the very man I want to see; the very back of the room* **3** (intensifier) used in metaphors to emphasize the applicability of the image to the situation described: *he was a very lion in the fight* **4** *arch* genuine: *the very living God* [c13 from OF *verai* true, from L *vērax*, from *vērus*]

> **USAGE** In strict usage adverbs of degree such as *very*, *too*, *quite*, *really*, and *extremely* are used only to qualify adjectives: *he is very happy; she is too sad*. By this rule, these words should not be used to qualify past participles that follow the verb *to be*, since they would then be technically qualifying verbs. With the exception of certain participles, such as *tired* or *disappointed*, that have come to be regarded as adjectives, all other past participles are qualified by adverbs such as *much*, *greatly*, *seriously*, or *excessively*: *he has been much* (not *very*) *inconvenienced; she has been excessively* (not *too*) *criticized*

very high frequency *n* a radio-frequency band or radio frequency lying between 30 and 300 megahertz. Abbrev: **VHF**

Very light (ˈvɛrɪ) *n* a coloured flare fired from a special pistol (**Very pistol**) for signalling at night, esp at sea [c19 after Edward W. *Very* (1852–1910), US naval ordnance officer]

very low frequency *n* a radio-frequency band or radio frequency lying between 3 and 30 kilohertz. Abbrev: **VLF**

Vesalius (vɪˈseɪlɪəs) *n* **Andreas** (anˈdreːas) 1514–64, Flemish anatomist, whose *De Humani Corporis fabrica* (1543) formed the basis of modern anatomical research and medicine

vesica (ˈvɛsɪkə) *n, pl* **vesicae** (-ˌsiː) *anat* a technical name for **bladder** (sense 1) [c17 from L: bladder, sac, blister] > **ˈvesical** *adj* > **vesiculate** (vɛˈsɪkjʊˌleɪt, -lɪt) *vb, adj*

vesicant (ˈvɛsɪkənt) *or* **vesicatory** (ˈvɛsɪˌkeɪtərɪ) *n, pl* **vesicants** *or* **vesicatories 1** any substance that causes blisters ▷ *adj* **2** acting as a vesicant [c19 see VESICA]

vesicate (ˈvɛsɪˌkeɪt) *vb* **vesicates, vesicating, vesicated** to blister [c17 from NL *vēsīcāre* to blister; see VESICA] > **ˌvesiˈcation** *n*

vesicle ('vɛsɪkᵊl) *n* **1** *pathol* **1a** any small sac or cavity, esp one containing serous fluid **1b** a blister **2** *geol* a rounded cavity within a rock **3** *bot* a small bladder-like cavity occurring in certain seaweeds **4** any small cavity or cell [c16 from L *vēsīcula*, dim. of VESICA] > **vesicular** (vɛ'sɪkjʊlə) *adj*

Vespasian (vɛs'peɪʒɪən) *n* Latin name *Titus Flavius Sabinus Vespasianus* 9–79 AD, Roman emperor (69–79), who consolidated Roman rule, esp in Britain and Germany. He began the building of the Colosseum

vesper ('vɛspə) *n* **1** an evening prayer, service, or hymn **2** *arch* evening **3** (*modifier*) of or relating to vespers ▷ See also **vespers** [c14 from L: evening, the evening star]

vespers ('vɛspəz) *n* (*functioning as sing*) **1** *chiefly RC Church* the sixth of the seven canonical hours of the divine office **2** another word for **evensong** (sense 1)

vespertine ('vɛspəˌtaɪn) *adj* **1** *bot, zool* appearing, opening, or active in the evening: *vespertine flowers* **2** occurring in the evening or (esp of stars) setting in the evening

vespiary ('vɛspɪərɪ) *n, pl* **vespiaries** a nest or colony of social wasps or hornets [c19 from L *vespa* a wasp, on the model of *apiary*]

vespid ('vɛspɪd) *n* **1** any of a family of hymenopterous insects, including the common wasp ▷ *adj* **2** of or belonging to this family [c19 from NL, from L *vespa* a wasp] > '**vespine** *adj*

Vespucci (vɛ'spuːtʃɪ) *n* **Amerigo** (ame'riːgo), Latin name *Americus Vespucius*. ?1454–1512, Florentine navigator in the New World (1499–1500; 1501–02), after whom the continent of America was named

vessel ('vɛsᵊl) *n* **1** any object used as a container, esp for a liquid **2** a passenger or freight-carrying ship, boat, etc **3** *anat* a tubular structure that transports such body fluids as blood and lymph **4** *bot* a tubular element of xylem tissue transporting water **5** *rare* a person regarded as a vehicle for some purpose or quality [c13 from OF, from LL *vascellum* urn, from L *vās* vessel]

vest (vɛst) *n* **1** an undergarment covering the body from the shoulders to the hips, made of cotton, nylon, etc Austral equivalent: **singlet** US and Canad equivalent: **undershirt** **2** *US, Canad, & Austral* a waistcoat **3** *obs* any form of dress ▷ *vb* **4** (*tr; foll by in*) to place or settle (power, rights, etc, in): *power was vested in the committee* **5** (*tr; foll by with*) to bestow or confer (on): *the company was vested with authority* **6** (usually foll by *in*) to confer (a right, title, etc, upon) or (of a right, title, etc) to pass (to) or devolve (upon) **7** (*tr*) to clothe **8** (*intr*) to put on clothes, ecclesiastical vestments, etc [c15 from OF *vestir* to clothe, from L *vestīre*, from *vestis* clothing]

vesta ('vɛstə) *n* a short friction match, usually of wood [c19 after VESTA]

Vesta ('vɛstə) *n* the Roman goddess of the hearth and its fire. In her temple a perpetual flame was tended by the vestal virgins. Greek counterpart: **Hestia**

vestal ('vɛstᵊl) *adj* **1** chaste or pure **2** of or relating to the Roman goddess Vesta ▷ *n* **3** a chaste woman, esp a nun

vestal virgin *n* (in ancient Rome) one of the virgin priestesses whose lives were dedicated to Vesta and to maintaining the sacred fire in her temple

vested ('vɛstɪd) *adj property law* having a present right to the immediate or future possession and enjoyment of property

vested interest *n* **1** *property law* an existing right to the immediate or future possession and enjoyment of property **2** a strong personal concern in a state of affairs, etc **3** a person or group that has such an interest

vestiary ('vɛstɪərɪ) *n, pl* **vestiaries** *obs* a room for storing clothes or dressing in, such as a vestry [c17 from LL *vestiārius*, from *vestis* clothing]

vestibule ('vɛstɪˌbjuːl) *n* **1** a small entrance hall or anteroom **2** any small bodily cavity at the entrance to a passage or canal [c17 from L *vestibulum*]

vestige ('vɛstɪdʒ) *n* **1** a small trace; hint: *a vestige of truth* **2** *biol* an organ or part of an organism that is a small nonfunctioning remnant of a functional organ in an ancestor [c17 via F from L *vestīgium* track] > **ves'tigial** *adj*

Vestmannaeyjar (ˌvɛstmæn'eɪjɑː) *n* a group of islands off the S coast of Iceland: they include the island of Surtsey (emerged 1963) and the volcano Helgafell (erupted 1974). Pop: 4888 (1994). English name: **Vestmann Islands**

vestment ('vɛstmənt) *n* **1** a garment or robe, esp one denoting office, authority, or rank **2** any of various ceremonial garments worn by the clergy at religious services, etc [c13 from OF *vestiment*, from L *vestīmentum*, from *vestīre* to clothe] > **vestmental** (vɛst'mɛntᵊl) *adj*

vest-pocket *n* (*modifier*) *chiefly US* small enough to fit into a waistcoat pocket

vestry ('vɛstrɪ) *n, pl* **vestries** **1** a room in or attached to a church in which vestments, sacred vessels, etc, are kept **2** a room in or attached to some churches, used for Sunday school, etc **3** *Church of England* **3a** a meeting of all the members of a parish or their representatives, to transact the official and administrative business of the parish **3b** the parish council [c14 prob. from OF *vestiarie*; see VEST] > '**vestral** *adj*

vestryman ('vɛstrɪmən) *n, pl* **vestrymen** a member of a church vestry

vesture ('vɛstʃə) *arch* ▷ *n* **1** a garment or something that seems like a garment: *a vesture of cloud* ▷ *vb* **vestures, vesturing, vestured** **2** (*tr*) to clothe [c14 from OF, from *vestir*, from L *vestīre*, from *vestis* clothing] > '**vestural** *adj*

Vesuvius (vɪ'suːvɪəs) *n* a volcano in SW Italy, on the Bay of Naples: first recorded eruption in 79 AD, which destroyed Pompeii, Herculaneum, and Stabiae; numerous eruptions since then. Average height: 1220 m (4003 ft). Italian name: **Vesuvio** (ve'zuːvjo)

vet[1] (vɛt) *n* **1** short for **veterinary surgeon** ▷ *vb* **vets, vetting, vetted** **2** (*tr*) *chiefly Brit* to make a prior examination and critical appraisal of (a person, document, etc): *the candidates were well vetted* **3** to examine or treat (an animal)

vet[2] (vɛt) *n US & Canad* short for **veteran** (senses 2, 3)

vet. *abbrev for:* **1** veteran **2** veterinarian **3** veterinary ▷ Also (for senses 2, 3): **veter**

vetch (vɛtʃ) *n* **1** any of various climbing plants having pinnate leaves, blue or purple flowers, and tendrils on the stems **2** any of various similar and related plants, such as the kidney vetch **3** the beanlike fruit of any of these plants [c14 *fecche*, from OF *veche*, from L *vicia*]

vetchling ('vɛtʃlɪŋ) *n* any of various tendril-climbing plants, mainly of N temperate regions, having winged or angled stems and showy flowers. See also **sweet pea**

veteran ('vɛtərən) *n* **1a** a person or thing that has given long service in some capacity **1b** (*as modifier*): *veteran firemen* **2** a soldier who has seen considerable active service **3** *US & Canad* a person who has served in the military forces [c16 from L, from *vetus* old]

veteran car *n Brit* a car constructed before 1919, esp one constructed before 1905 ▷ Cf **classic car, vintage car**

veterinary ('vɛtərɪnərɪ) *adj* of or relating to veterinary medicine [c18 from L *veterīnārius*, from *veterīnae* draught animals]

veterinary medicine *or* **science** *n* the branch of medicine concerned with the health of animals and the treatment of injuries or diseases that affect them
▷ www.merckvetmanual.com/mvm/index.jsp
▷ http://vetmedicine.about.com/

veterinary surgeon *n Brit* a person qualified to practise veterinary medicine. US and Canad term: **veterinarian**

veto ('viːtəʊ) *n, pl* **vetoes** **1** the power to prevent legislation or action proposed by others: *the presidential veto* **2** the exercise of this power ▷ *vb* **vetoes, vetoing, vetoed** (*tr*) **3** to refuse consent to (a proposal, esp a government bill) **4** to prohibit, ban, or forbid: *her parents* *vetoed her trip* [C17 from L: I forbid, from *vetāre* to forbid] > 'vetoer *n*

vex (vɛks) *vb (tr)* **1** to anger or annoy **2** to confuse; worry **3** *arch* to agitate [C15 from OF *vexer*, from L *vexāre* to jolt (in carrying), from *vehere* to convey] > **'vexer** *n* > **'vexing** *adj*

vexation (vɛk'seɪʃən) *n* **1** the act of vexing or the state of being vexed **2** something that vexes

vexatious (vɛk'seɪʃəs) *adj* **1** vexing or tending to vex **2** vexed **3** *law* (of a legal action or proceeding) instituted without sufficient grounds, esp so as to cause annoyance to the defendant > **vex'atiously** *adv*

vexed (vɛkst) *adj* **1** annoyed, confused, or agitated **2** much debated (esp in **a vexed question**) > **vexedly** ('vɛksɪdlɪ) *adv*

vexillology (ˌvɛksɪ'lɒlədʒɪ) *n* the study and collection of information about flags [C20 from L *vexillum* flag + -LOGY] > **ˌvexil'lologist** *n*

vexillum (vɛk'sɪləm) *n, pl* **vexilla** (-lə) **1** *ornithol* the vane of a feather **2** Also called: **standard** *bot* the largest petal of a papilionaceous flower [C18 from L: banner, ?from *vēlum* sail] > **'vexillate** *adj*

VF *abbrev for* video frequency

vg *abbrev for* very good

VG *abbrev for* Vicar General

VGA *abbrev for* video graphics array: a computing standard for spatial and colour resolution

VHF *or* **vhf** *radio abbrev for:* very high frequency

VHS *trademark abbrev for:* video home system: a video cassette recording system using ½″ magnetic tape

VI *abbrev for* Virgin Islands

v.i. *abbrev for* vide infra (see **vide**)

via ('vaɪə) *prep* by way of; by means of; through: *to London via Paris* [C18 from L *viā*, from *via* way]

viable ('vaɪəbᵊl) *adj* **1** capable of becoming actual, etc: *a viable proposition* **2** (of seeds, eggs, etc) capable of normal growth and development **3** (of a fetus) having reached a stage of development at which further development can occur independently of the mother [C19 from F, from *vie* life, from L *vīta*] > **ˌvia'bility** *n*

Via Dolorosa ('viːə ˌdɒlə'rəʊsə) *n* the route followed by Christ from the place of his condemnation to Calvary for his crucifixion [L, lit.: sorrowful road]

viaduct ('vaɪəˌdʌkt) *n* a bridge, esp for carrying a road or railway across a valley, etc [C19 from L *via* way + *dūcere* to bring, on the model of *aqueduct*]

Viagra (vaɪ'ægrə, viː-) *n trademark* a drug that allows increased blood flow to the penis; used to treat erectile impotence in men

vial ('vaɪəl) *n* a less common variant of **phial** [C14 *fiole*, from OF, ult. from Gk *phialē*; see PHIAL]

via media *Latin* ('vaɪə 'miːdɪə) *n* a compromise between two extremes

viand ('viːənd) *n* **1** a type of food, esp a delicacy **2** (*pl*) provisions [C14 from OF, ult. from L *vīvenda* things to be lived on, from *vīvere* to live]

Viareggio (*Italian* via'reddʒo) *n* a town and resort in W Italy, in Tuscany on the Ligurian Sea. Pop: 50 310 (latest est)

viatical (vaɪ'ætɪkᵊl) *adj* **1** of or denoting a road or a journey **2** *bot* (of a plant) growing by the side of a road [C19 from L *viāticus* belonging to a journey + -AL]

viatical settlement *n* the purchase by a charity of a life assurance policy owned by a person with only a short time to live, to enable that person to use the proceeds during his or her lifetime. See also **death futures**

viaticum (vaɪ'ætɪkəm) *n, pl* **viatica** (-kə) *or* **viaticums** **1** *Christianity* Holy Communion as administered to a person dying or in danger of death **2** *rare* provisions or a travel allowance for a journey [C16 from L, from *viāticus* belonging to a journey, from *via* way]

vibes (vaɪbz) *pl n* **1** *inf* short for **vibraphone** **2** *sl* short for **vibrations**

Viborg *n* **1** ('viːbɔrj) the Swedish name for **Vyborg** **2** (*Danish* 'vibɔr) a town in N central Denmark, in Jutland: formerly a royal town and capital of Jutland. Pop: 29 455 (1990)

vibraculum (vaɪ'brækjʊləm) *n, pl* **vibracula** (-lə) *zool* any of the specialized bristle-like polyps in certain bryozoans, the actions of which prevent parasites from settling on the colony [C19 from NL, from L *vibrāre* to brandish]

vibrant ('vaɪbrənt) *adj* **1** characterized by or exhibiting vibration **2** giving an impression of vigour and activity **3** caused by vibration; resonant **4** (of colour) strong and vivid [C16 from L *vibrāre* to agitate] > **'vibrancy** *n* > **'vibrantly** *adv*

vibraphone ('vaɪbrəˌfəʊn) *n* a percussion instrument consisting of a set of metal bars placed over tubular metal resonators, which are made to vibrate electronically > **'vibraˌphonist** *n*

vibrate (vaɪ'breɪt) *vb* **vibrates, vibrating, vibrated** **1** to move or cause to move back and forth rapidly **2** (*intr*) to oscillate **3** to resonate or cause to resonate **4** (*intr*) to waver **5** *physics* to undergo or cause to undergo an oscillatory process, as of an alternating current **6** (*intr*) *rare* to respond emotionally; thrill [C17 from L *vibrāre*] > **vibratile** ('vaɪbrəˌtaɪl) *adj* > **vi'brating** *adj* > **vibratory** ('vaɪbrətərɪ) *adj*

vibration (vaɪ'breɪʃən) *n* **1** the act or an instance of vibrating **2** *physics* **2a** a periodic motion about an equilibrium position, such as in the propagation of sound **2b** a single cycle of such a motion **3** the process or state of vibrating or being vibrated > **vi'brational** *adj*

vibrations (vaɪ'breɪʃənz) *pl n sl* **1** instinctive feelings supposedly influencing human communication **2** a characteristic atmosphere felt to be emanating from places or objects

vibration white finger *n* a condition affecting workers using vibrating machinery, which causes damage to the blood vessels and nerves of the fingers and leads to a permanent loss of feeling

vibrato (vɪ'brɑːtəʊ) *n, pl* **vibratos** *music* **1** a slight, rapid, and regular fluctuation in the pitch of a note produced on a stringed instrument by a shaking movement of the hand stopping the strings **2** an oscillatory effect produced in singing by fluctuation in breath pressure or pitch [C19 from It., from L *vibrāre* to VIBRATE]

vibrator (vaɪ'breɪtə) *n* **a** a device for producing a vibratory motion, such as one used in massage **b** such a device with a vibrating part or tip, used as a dildo

vibrissa (vaɪ'brɪsə) *n, pl* **vibrissae** (-siː) (*usually pl*) **1** any of the bristle-like sensitive hairs on the face of many mammals; a whisker **2** any of the specialized bristle-like feathers around the beak in certain insectivorous birds [C17 from L, prob. from *vibrāre* to shake] > **vi'brissal** *adj*

viburnum (vaɪ'bɜːnəm) *n* **1** any of various temperate and subtropical shrubs or trees having small white flowers and berry-like red or black fruits **2** the dried bark of several species of this tree, sometimes used in medicine [C18 from L: wayfaring tree]

vicar ('vɪkə) *n* **1** *Church of England* **1a** (in Britain) a member of the clergy appointed to act as priest of a parish **1b** a clergyman who acts as assistant to or substitute for the rector of a parish at Communion **2** *RC Church* a bishop or priest representing the pope and exercising a limited jurisdiction **3** Also called: **lay vicar, vicar choral** *Church of England* a member of a cathedral choir appointed to sing certain parts of the services [C13 from OF, from L *vicārius* (n) a deputy, from *vicārius* (adj) VICARIOUS] > **vicarial** (vɪ'kɛərɪəl) *adj* > **vi'cariate** *n* > **'vicarly** *adj*

vicarage ('vɪkərɪdʒ) *n* the residence or benefice of a vicar

vicar apostolic *n RC Church* a titular bishop having jurisdiction in missionary countries

vicar general *n, pl* **vicars general** an official, usually a layman, appointed to assist the bishop of a diocese in discharging his administrative or judicial duties

vicarious (vɪˈkɛərɪəs, vaɪ-) *adj* **1** undergone at second hand through sympathetic participation in another's experiences **2** undergone or done as the substitute for another: *vicarious punishment* **3** delegated: *vicarious authority* **4** taking the place of another [C17 from L *vicārius* substituted, from *vicis* interchange] > **viˈcariously** *adv* > **viˈcariousness** *n*

Vicar of Bray (breɪ) *n* **1** a vicar (Simon Aleyn) appointed to the parish of Bray in Berkshire during Henry VIII's reign who changed his faith to Catholic when Mary I was on the throne and back to Protestant when Elizabeth I succeeded and so retained his living **2** Also called: **In Good King Charles's Golden Days** a ballad in which the vicar's changes of faith are transposed to the Stuart period **3** a person who changes his or her views or allegiances in accordance with what is suitable at the time

Vicar of Christ *n RC Church* the pope when regarded as Christ's earthly representative

vice[1] (vaɪs) *n* **1** an immoral, wicked, or evil habit, action, or trait **2** frequent indulgence in immoral or degrading practices **3** a specific form of pernicious conduct, esp prostitution or sexual perversion **4** an imperfection in character, conduct, etc: *smoking is his only vice* **5** a bad trick or disposition, as of horses, dogs, etc [C13 via OF from L *vitium* a defect]

vice[2] *or US (often)* **vise** (vaɪs) *n* **1** an appliance for holding an object while work is done on it, usually having a pair of jaws ▷ *vb* **2** *(tr)* to grip (something) with or as if with a vice [C15 from OF *vis* a screw, from L *vītis* vine, plant with spiralling tendrils (hence the later meaning)]

vice[3] (vaɪs) *adj* **1a** *(prenominal)* serving in the place of **1b** *(in combination)*: *viceroy* ▷ *n* **2** *inf* a person who serves as a deputy to another [C18 from L, from *vicis* interchange]

vice[4] (ˈvaɪsɪ) *prep* instead of; as a substitute for [C16 from L, ablative of *vicis* change]

vice admiral *n* a commissioned officer of flag rank in certain navies, junior to an admiral and senior to a rear admiral

vice-chairman *n, pl* **vice-chairmen** a person who deputizes for a chairman and serves in his place during his absence. Also: **vice-chairperson** *or (fem)* **vice-chairwoman** > ˌ**vice-ˈchairmanship** *n*

vice chancellor *n* **1** the chief executive or administrator at some British universities **2** (in the US) a judge in courts of equity subordinate to the chancellor **3** (formerly in England) a senior judge of the court of chancery who acted as assistant to the Lord Chancellor **4** a person serving as the deputy of a chancellor > ˌ**vice-ˈchancellorship** *n*

vicegerent (ˌvaɪsˈdʒɛrənt) *n* **1** a person appointed to exercise all or some of the authority of another **2** *RC Church* the pope or any other representative of God or Christ on earth, such as a bishop ▷ *adj* **3** invested with or characterized by delegated authority [C16 from NL, from VICE[3] + L *gerere* to manage] > ˌ**viceˈgerency** *n*

vicennial (vɪˈsɛnɪəl) *adj* **1** occurring every 20 years **2** lasting for a period of 20 years [C18 from LL *vīcennium* period of twenty years, from L *vīciēs* twenty times + *-ennium*, from *annus* year]

Vicenza (*Italian* viˈtʃɛntsa) *n* a city in NE Italy, in Veneto: home of the 16th-century architect Andrea Palladio and site of some of his finest works. Pop: 109 738 (2000 est)

vice president *n* an officer ranking immediately below a president and serving as his or her deputy. A vice president takes the president's place during his or her absence or incapacity, after his or her death, and in certain other circumstances. Abbrev: **VP** > ˌ**vice-ˈpresidency** *n*

viceregal (ˌvaɪsˈriːgᵊl) *adj* **1** of or relating to a viceroy **2** *chiefly Austral & NZ* of or relating to a governor or governor general > ˌ**viceˈregally** *adv*

vicereine (ˌvaɪsˈreɪn) *n* **1** the wife of a viceroy **2** a female viceroy [C19 from F, from VICE[3] + *reine* queen, from L *rēgīna*]

viceroy (ˈvaɪsrɔɪ) *n* a governor of a colony, country, or province who acts for and rules in the name of his sovereign or government. Related adj: **viceregal** [C16 from F, from VICE[3] + *roy* king, from L *rex*] > ˈ**viceroyship** *or* ˌ**viceˈroyalty** *n*

vice squad *n* a police division to which is assigned the enforcement of gaming and prostitution laws

vice versa (ˈvaɪsɪ ˈvɜːsə) *adv* the other way around [C17 from L: relations being reversed, from *vicis* change + *vertere* to turn]

Vichy (*French* viʃi; *English* ˈviːʃiː) *n* a town and spa in central France, on the River Allier: seat of the collaborationist government under Marshal Pétain (1940–44); mineral waters bottled for export. Pop: 28 048 (1990). Latin name: **Vicus Calidus** (ˈviːkəs ˈkælɪdəs)

vichyssoise (*French* viʃiswaz) *n* a thick soup made from leeks, potatoes, chicken stock, and cream, usually served chilled [F, from *(crème) vichyssoise (glacée)* (ice-cold cream) from Vichy]

vichy water *n* **1** *(sometimes cap)* a mineral water from springs at Vichy in France, reputed to be beneficial to health **2** any sparkling mineral water resembling this

vicinage (ˈvɪsnɪdʒ) *n now rare* **1** the residents of a particular neighbourhood **2** a less common word for **vicinity** [C14 from OF *vicenage*, from *vicin* neighbouring, from L *vīcīnus*]

vicinal (ˈvɪsɪnᵊl) *adj* **1** neighbouring **2** (esp of roads) of or relating to a locality [C17 from L *vīcīnālis* nearby, from *vīcīnus*, from *vīcus* a neighbourhood]

vicinity (vɪˈsɪnɪtɪ) *n, pl* **vicinities** **1** a surrounding area; neighbourhood **2** the fact or condition of being close in space or relationship [C16 from L, from *vīcīnus* neighbouring, from *vīcus* village]

vicious (ˈvɪʃəs) *adj* **1** wicked or cruel: *a vicious thug* **2** characterized by violence or ferocity: *a vicious blow* **3** *inf* unpleasantly severe; harsh: *a vicious wind* **4** characterized by malice: *vicious lies* **5** (esp of dogs, horses, etc) ferocious **6** characterized by or leading to vice **7** invalidated by defects; unsound: *a vicious inference* [C14 from OF, from L *vitiōsus* full of faults, from *vitium* defect] > ˈ**viciously** *adv* > ˈ**viciousness** *n*

vicious circle *n* **1** Also: **vicious cycle** a situation in which an attempt to resolve one problem creates new problems that lead back to the original situation **2** *logic* **2a** a form of reasoning in which a conclusion is inferred from premises the truth of which cannot be established independently of that conclusion **2b** an explanation given in terms that cannot be understood independently of that which was to be explained

vicissitude (vɪˈsɪsɪˌtjuːd) *n* **1** variation or mutability in nature or life, esp successive alternation from one condition or thing to another **2** a variation in circumstance, fortune, etc [C16 from L *vicissitūdō*, from *vicis* change] > **viˌcissiˈtudinous** *adj*

Vicksburg (ˈvɪksˌbɜːg) *n* a city in W Mississippi, on the Mississippi River: site of one of the most decisive campaigns (1863) of the American Civil War, in which the Confederates were besieged for nearly seven weeks before capitulating. Pop: 20 908 (1990)

Vicky (ˈvɪkɪ) *n* professional name of *Victor Weisz*. 1913–66, British left-wing political cartoonist, born in Germany

Vico (ˈvɪkəʊ; *Italian* ˈviːko) *n* **Giovanni Battista** (dʒoˈvanni batˈtista) 1668–1744, Italian philosopher. In *Scienza Nuova* (1721) he postulated that civilizations rise and fall in evolutionary cycles, making use of myths, poetry, and linguistics as historical evidence

victim (ˈvɪktɪm) *n* **1** a person or thing that suffers harm, death, etc: *victims of tyranny* **2** a person who is tricked or swindled **3** a living person or animal sacrificed in a religious rite [c15 from L *victima*]

victimize *or* **victimise** ('vɪktɪˌmaɪz) *vb* **victimizes, victimizing, victimized** *or* **victimises, victimising, victimised** (*tr*) **1** to punish or discriminate against unfairly **2** to make a victim of > **ˌvictimiˈzation** *or* **ˌvictimiˈsation** *n* > **ˈvictimˌizer** *or* **ˈvictimˌiser** *n*

victimology (ˌvɪktɪˈmɒlədʒɪ) *n* the study of the psychological effects experienced by the victims of crime > **ˌvictiˈmologist** *n*

victor (ˈvɪktə) *n* **1a** a person, nation, etc, that has defeated an adversary in war, etc **1b** (*as modifier*): *the victor army* **2** the winner of any contest, conflict, or struggle [c14 from L, from *vincere* to conquer]

Victor Emmanuel II *n* 1820–78, king of Sardinia-Piedmont (1849–78) and first king of Italy from 1861

Victor Emmanuel III *n* 1869–1947, last king of Italy (1900–46): dominated after 1922 by Mussolini, whom he appointed as premier; abdicated

victoria (vɪkˈtɔːrɪə) *n* **1** a light four-wheeled horse-drawn carriage with a folding hood, two passenger seats, and a seat in front for the driver **2** Also called: **victoria plum** *Brit* a large sweet variety of plum, red and yellow in colour [c19 both after Queen VICTORIA]

Victoria[1] (vɪkˈtɔːrɪə) *n* **1** a state of SE Australia: part of New South Wales colony until 1851; semiarid in the northwest, with the Great Dividing Range in the centre and east and the Murray River along the N border. Capital: Melbourne. Pop: 4 712 170 (1999 est). Area: 227 620 sq km (87 884 sq miles) **2 Lake** Also called: **Victoria Nyanza** a lake in East Africa, in Tanzania, Uganda, and Kenya, at an altitude of 1134 m (3720 ft): the largest lake in Africa and second largest in the world; drained by the Victoria Nile. Area: 69 485 sq km (26 828 sq miles) **3** a port in SW Canada, capital of British Columbia, on Vancouver Island: founded in 1843 by the Hudson's Bay Company; made capital of British Columbia in 1868; university (1963). Pop: 287 897 (1991) **4** the capital of the Seychelles, a port on NE Mahé. Pop: 24 701 (1997) **5** an urban area in S China, part of Hong Kong, on N Hong Kong Island: financial and administrative district; university (1911). Pop: 595 000 (latest est) **6 Mount** a mountain in SE Papua New Guinea: the highest peak of the Owen Stanley Range. Height: 4073 m (13 363 ft)
▹ www.vic.gov.au
▹ www.victoria-australia.worldweb.com

Victoria[2] (vɪkˈtɔːrɪə) *n* **1** 1819–1901, queen of the United Kingdom (1837–1901) and empress of India (1876–1901). She married Prince Albert of Saxe-Coburg-Gotha (1840). Her sense of vocation did much to restore the prestige of the British monarchy **2** (*Spanish* bikˈtorja) **Tomás Luis de** ?1548–1611, Spanish composer of motets and masses in the polyphonic style

Victoria[3] (vɪkˈtɔːrɪə) *n* the Roman goddess of victory. Greek counterpart: **Nike**

Victoria and Albert Museum *n* a museum of the fine and applied arts in London, originating from 1856 and given its present name and site in 1899. Abbrev: **V and A**
▹ www.vam.ac.uk

Victoria Cross *n* the highest decoration for gallantry in the face of the enemy awarded to the British and Commonwealth armed forces: instituted in 1856 by Queen Victoria

Victoria Day *n* the Monday preceding May 24: observed in Canada as a national holiday in commemoration of the birthday of Queen Victoria

Victoria Desert *n* See **Great Victoria Desert**

Victoria Falls *pl n* a waterfall on the border between Zimbabwe and Zambia, on the Zambezi River. Height: about 108 m (355 ft). Width: about 1400 m (4500 ft)

Victoria Island *n* a large island in the Canadian Arctic, in Nunavut and the Northwest Territories. Area: about 212 000 sq km (82 000 sq miles)

Victoria Land *n* a section of Antarctica, largely in the Ross Dependency on the Ross Sea

Victorian (vɪkˈtɔːrɪən) *adj* **1** of or characteristic of Queen Victoria or the period of her reign. **2** exhibiting the characteristics popularly attributed to the Victorians, esp prudery, bigotry, or hypocrisy ▹ Cf **Victorian values** **3** of or relating to Victoria (the state or any of the cities) ▹ *n* **4** a person who lived during the reign of Queen Victoria **5** an inhabitant of Victoria (the state or any of the cities) > **Vicˈtorianˌism** *n*

Victoriana (vɪkˌtɔːrɪˈɑːnə) *pl n* objects, ornaments, etc, of the Victorian period

Victoria Nile *n* See **Nile**

Victorian values *pl n* the qualities of enterprise and initiative, the importance of the family, and the development of charitable voluntary work considered to characterize the Victorian period ▹ Cf **Victorian** (sense 2)

victorious (vɪkˈtɔːrɪəs) *adj* **1** having defeated an adversary: *the victorious nations* **2** of, indicative of, or characterized by victory: *a victorious conclusion* > **vicˈtoriously** *adv*

victory (ˈvɪktərɪ) *n, pl* **victories** **1** final and complete superiority in a war **2** a successful military engagement **3** a success attained in a contest or struggle or over an opponent, obstacle, or problem **4** the act of triumphing or state of having triumphed [c14 from OF *victorie*, from L *victōria*, from *vincere* to subdue]

Victory (ˈvɪktərɪ) *n* another name (in English) for the Roman goddess **Victoria** or the Greek **Nike**

victory roll *n* a rolling aircraft manoeuvre made by a pilot to announce or celebrate the shooting down of an enemy plane

victual (ˈvɪtᵊl) *vb* **victuals, victualling, victualled** *or US* **victuals, victualing, victualed** to supply with or obtain victuals. See also **victuals** [c14 from OF *vitaille*, from LL *victuālia* provisions, from L *victus* sustenance, from *vīvere* to live] > **ˈvictual-less** *adj*

victualler (ˈvɪtələ) *n* **1** a supplier of victuals, as to an army **2** *Brit* a licensed purveyor of spirits **3** a supply ship, esp one carrying foodstuffs

victuals (ˈvɪtᵊlz) *pl n* (*sometimes sing*) food or provisions

vicuña (vɪˈkuːnjə) *or* **vicuna** (vɪˈkjuːnə, -ˈkuːnjə) *n* **1** a tawny-coloured cud-chewing Andean mammal similar to the llama **2** the fine light cloth made from the wool obtained from this animal [c17 from Sp., from Quechuan *wikúña*]

vid (vɪd) *n inf* short for **video** (sense 4)

Vidal (viːˈdæl) *n* **Gore** born 1925, US novelist and essayist. His novels include *Julian* (1964), *Myra Breckinridge* (1968), *Burr* (1974), *Lincoln* (1984), and *The Season of Conflict* (1996)

vide (ˈvaɪdɪ) (used to direct a reader to a specified place in a text, another book, etc) refer to, see (often in **vide ante** (see before), **vide infra** (see below), **vide supra** (see above), etc) Abbrev: **v., vid.** [c16 from L]

videlicet (vɪˈdiːlɪˌsɛt) *adv* namely: used to specify items, etc Abbrev: **viz** [c15 from L]

video (ˈvɪdɪəʊ) *adj* **1** relating to or employed in the transmission or reception of a televised image **2** of, concerned with, or operating at video frequencies ▹ *n, pl* **videos** **3** the visual elements of a television broadcast **4** a film recorded on a video cassette **5** short for **video cassette, video cassette recorder** **6** *US* an informal name for **television** ▹ *vb* **videos, videoing, videoed** **7** to record (a television programme, etc) on a video cassette recorder [c20 from L *vidēre* to see, on the model of AUDIO]

video call *n* a call made via a mobile phone with a camera and a screen, allowing the participants to see each other as they talk

video cassette *n* a cassette containing video tape

video cassette recorder *n* a tape recorder for vision and sound signals using magnetic tape in closed plastic

cassettes: used for recording and playing back television programmes and films. Often shortened to **video** or **video recorder**
videodisc ('vɪdɪəʊˌdɪsk) *n* another name for **optical disk**
videofit ('vɪdɪəʊˌfɪt) *n* a computer-generated picture of a person sought by the police, created by combining facial characteristics on the basis of witnesses' descriptions [C20 from VIDEO + (PHOTO)FIT]
video frequency *n* the frequency of a signal conveying the image and synchronizing pulses in a television broadcasting system. It lies in the range from about 50 hertz to 8 megahertz
video game *n* any of various games that can be played by using an electronic control to move graphical symbols on the screen of a visual display unit
video jockey *n* a person who introduces and plays videos, esp of pop songs, on a television programme
video memory *n computing* computer memory used for the processing and displaying of images
video nasty *n, pl* **nasties** a film, usually specially made for video, that is explicitly horrific and pornographic
videophone ('vɪdɪəˌfəʊn) *n* a telephonic device through which there is both verbal and visual communication
video recorder *n* short for **video cassette recorder**
video tape *n* **1** magnetic tape used mainly for recording the sound and vision signals of a television programme or film for subsequent transmission ▷ *vb* **video-tape, video-tapes, video-taping, video-taped 2** to record (a programme, etc) on video tape
video tape recorder *n* a tape recorder for visual signals and usually accompanying sound, using magnetic tape on open spools: used in television broadcasting
Videotex ('vɪdɪəʊˌtɛks) *n trademark* an information system that displays information from a distant computer on a television screen. See also **Teletext, Viewdata**
videotext ('vɪdɪəʊˌtɛkst) *n* a means of providing a written or graphical representation of computerized information on a television screen
vidicon ('vɪdɪˌkɒn) *n* a small television camera tube, used in closed-circuit television and outside broadcasts, in which incident light forms an electric charge pattern on a photoconductive surface [C20 from VID(EO) + ICON(OSCOPE)]
vie (vaɪ) *vb* **vies, vying, vied** (*intr;* foll by *with* or *for*) to contend for superiority or victory (with) or strive in competition (for) [C15 prob. from OF *envier* to challenge, from L *invītāre* to INVITE] > '**vier** *n* > '**vying** *adj, n*
Vienna (vɪ'ɛnə) *n* the capital and the smallest state of Austria, in the northeast on the River Danube: seat of the Hapsburgs (1278–1918); residence of the Holy Roman Emperor (1558–1806); withstood sieges by Turks in 1529 and 1683; political and cultural centre in the 18th and 19th centuries, having associations with many composers; university (1365). Pop: 1 562 676 (2001). Area: 1075 sq km (415 sq miles). German name: **Wien** > **Viennese** (ˌvɪə'niːz) *adj, n*
▷ www.wien.gv.at
▷ http://info.wien.at
Vienne (*French* vjɛn) *n* **1** a department of W central France, in Poitou-Charentes region. Capital: Poitiers. Pop: 399 024 (1999). Area: 7044 sq km (2747 sq miles) **2** a town in SE France, on the River Rhône: extensive Roman remains. Ancient name: **Vienna 3** a river in SW central France, flowing west and north to the Loire below Chinon. Length: over 350 km (200 miles)
Vientiane (ˌvjɛntɪ'ɑːn) *n* the administrative capital of Laos, in the south near the border with Thailand: capital of the kingdom of Vientiane from 1707 until taken by the Thais in 1827. Pop: 534 000 (1999 est)
▷ www.visit-laos.com/where/vientiane
Vierwaldstättersee (fiːr'valtʃtɛtərˌzeː) *n* the German name for (Lake) **Lucerne**
vies (fɪs) *adj S African sl* angry, furious, or disgusted [Afrik.]
Vietnam (ˌvjɛt'næm) *or* **Viet Nam** *n* a republic in SE Asia: an ancient empire, conquered by France in the 19th century; occupied by Japan (1940–45) when the Communist-led Vietminh began resistance operations that were continued against restored French rule after 1945. In 1954 the country was divided along the 17th parallel, establishing North Vietnam (under the Vietminh) and South Vietnam (under French control), the latter becoming the independent **Republic of Vietnam** in 1955. From 1959 the country was dominated by war between the Communist Vietcong, supported by North Vietnam, and the South Vietnamese government; increasing numbers of US forces were brought to the aid of the South Vietnamese army until a peace agreement (1973) led to the withdrawal of US troops; further fighting led to the eventual defeat of the South Vietnamese government in March 1975 and in 1976 an elected National Assembly proclaimed the reunification of the country. Official language: Vietnamese. Religion: Buddhist majority. Currency: dong. Capital: Hanoi. Pop: 79 939 000 (2001 est). Area: 331 041 sq km (127 816 sq miles). Official name: **Socialist Republic of Vietnam** > ˌ**Vietna'mese** *adj, n*
▷ www.spartacus.schoolnet.co.uk/vietnam.html
▷ http://vietnam.vassar.edu
▷ www.cpv.org.vn
▷ www.vietnamtourism.com
vieux jeu *French* (vjø ʒø) *adj* old-fashioned [lit.: old game]
view (vjuː) *n* **1** the act of seeing or observing **2** vision or sight, esp range of vision: *the church is out of view* **3** a scene, esp of a fine tract of countryside: *the view from the top was superb* **4** a pictorial representation of a scene, such as a photograph **5** (*sometimes pl*) opinion: *my own view on the matter differs from yours* **6** (foll by *to*) a desired end or intention: *he has a view to securing further qualifications* **7** a general survey of a topic, subject, etc **8** visual aspect or appearance: *they look the same in outward view* **9** a sight of a hunted animal before or during the chase **10 in view of** taking into consideration **11 on view** exhibited to the public gaze **12 take a dim** *or* **poor view of** to regard (something) with disfavour **13 with a view to 13a** with the intention of **13b** in anticipation or hope of ▷ *vb* **14** (*tr*) to look at **15** (*tr*) to consider in a specified manner: *they view change with suspicion* **16** (*tr*) to examine or inspect carefully: *to view the accounts* **17** (*tr*) to contemplate: *to view the difficulties* **18** to watch (television) **19** (*tr*) to sight (a hunted animal) before or during the chase [C15 from OF, from *veoir* to see, from L *vidēre*] > '**viewable** *adj*

Viewdata ('vjuːˌdeɪtə) *n trademark* an interactive form of Videotext that sends information from a distant computer along telephone lines, enabling shopping, booking theatre and airline tickets, and banking transactions to be conducted from the home
viewer ('vjuːə) *n* **1** a person who views something, esp television **2** any optical device by means of which something is viewed, esp one used for viewing photographic transparencies
viewfinder ('vjuːˌfaɪndə) *n* a device on a camera, consisting of a lens system, enabling the user to see what will be included in his photograph
view halloo *interj* a huntsman's cry uttered when the quarry is seen breaking cover or shortly afterwards
viewing ('vjuːɪŋ) *n* **1** the act of watching television **2** television programmes collectively: *late-night viewing*
viewless ('vjuːlɪs) *adj* **1** (of windows, etc) not affording a view **2** having no opinions **3** *poetic* invisible
viewpoint ('vjuːˌpɔɪnt) *n* **1** the mental attitude that determines a person's judgments **2** a place from which something can be viewed
Vigée-Lebrun (*French* viʒeləbrỹ) *n* (**Marie Louise**) **Élisabeth** 1755–1842, French painter, noted for her

portraits of women, esp Marie Antoinette

vigesimal (vaɪˈdʒɛsɪməl) *adj* **1** relating to or based on the number 20 **2** taking place or proceeding in intervals of 20 **3** twentieth [C17 from L *vīgēsimus*, var. (infl. by *vīgintī* twenty) of *vīcēsimus* twentieth]

vigia (ˈvɪdʒɪə) *n naut* a navigational hazard marked on a chart although its existence and nature has not been confirmed [C19 from Sp. *vigía* reef, from L *vigilāre* to keep watch]

vigil (ˈvɪdʒɪl) *n* **1** a purposeful watch maintained, esp at night, to guard, observe, pray, etc **2** the period of such a watch **3** *RC Church, Church of England* the eve of certain major festivals, formerly observed as a night spent in prayer [C13 from OF, from Med. L *vigilia* watch preceding a religious festival, from L, from *vigil* alert, from *vigēre* to be lively]

vigilance (ˈvɪdʒɪləns) *n* **1** the fact, quality, or condition of being vigilant **2** the abnormal state or condition of being unable to sleep

vigilance committee *n* (in the US) a self-appointed body of citizens organized to maintain order, etc, where an efficient system of courts does not exist

vigilant (ˈvɪdʒɪlənt) *adj* keenly alert to or heedful of trouble or danger [C15 from L *vigilāns*, from *vigilāre* to be watchful; see VIGIL] > ˈ**vigilantly** *adv*

vigilante (ˌvɪdʒɪˈlæntɪ) *n* **1** a self-appointed protector of public order **2** *US* a member of a vigilance committee [C19 from Sp., from L *vigilāre* to keep watch]

vigilantism (ˌvɪdʒɪˈlæntɪzəm) *n US* the methods, conduct, attitudes, etc, associated with vigilantes, esp militancy or bigotry

Vigil Mass *n RC Church* a Mass held on Saturday evening, attendance at which fulfils one's obligation to attend Mass on Sunday

vigneron (ˈviːnjərɒn; *French* viɲrɔ̃) *n* a person who grows grapes for winemaking [F, from *vigne* vine]

vignette (vɪˈnjɛt) *n* **1** a small illustration placed at the beginning or end of a book or chapter **2** a short graceful literary essay or sketch **3** a photograph, drawing, etc, with edges that are shaded off **4** any small endearing scene, view, etc ▷ *vb* **vignettes, vignetting, vignetted** (*tr*) **5** to finish (a photograph, etc) with a fading border in the form of a vignette **6** to portray in or as in a vignette [C18 from F, lit.: little vine; with reference to the vine motif frequently used in embellishments to a text] > viˈ**gnettist** *n*

Vignola (*Italian* viɲˈɲɔːla) *n* **Giacomo Barozzi da** (ˈdʒaːkomo baˈrɔttsi da) 1507–73, Italian architect, whose cruciform design for Il Gesù, Rome, greatly influenced later Church architecture

Vigny (*French* viɲi) *n* **Alfred Victor de** (alfrɛd viktɔr də) 1797–1863, French romantic poet, novelist, and dramatist, noted for his pessimistic lyric verse *Poèmes antiques et modernes* (1826) and *Les Destinées* (1864), the novel *Cinq-Mars* (1826), and the play *Chatterton* (1835)

Vigo (ˈviːgəʊ; *Spanish* ˈbigo) *n* a port in NW Spain, in Galicia on **Vigo Bay** (an inlet of the Atlantic): site of a British and Dutch naval victory (1702) over the French and Spanish. Pop: 283 110 (1998 est)

vigoro (ˈvɪgəˌrəʊ) *n Austral* a ball game combining elements of cricket and baseball [C20 from VIGOUR]

vigorous (ˈvɪgərəs) *adj* **1** endowed with bodily or mental strength or vitality **2** displaying, characterized by, or performed with vigour: *vigorous growth* > ˈ**vigorously** *adv*

vigour *or US* **vigor** (ˈvɪgə) *n* **1** exuberant and resilient strength of body or mind **2** substantial effective energy or force: *the vigour of the tempest* **3** forcefulness: *I was surprised by the vigour of her complaints* **4** the capacity for survival or strong healthy growth in a plant or animal **5** the most active period or stage of life, manhood, etc [C14 from OF, from L *vigor*, from *vigēre* to be lively]

Viipuri (ˈviːpuri) *n* the Finnish name for **Vyborg**

Vijayawada (ˌviːdʒaɪəˈwɑːdə) *n* a town in SE India, in E central Andra Pradesh on the Krishna River: Hindu pilgrimage centre. Pop: 701 827 (1991). Former name: **Bezwada**

Viking (ˈvaɪkɪŋ) *n* (*sometimes not cap*) **1** Also called: **Norseman, Northman** any of the Danes, Norwegians, and Swedes who raided by sea most of N and W Europe from the 8th to the 11th centuries **2** (*modifier*) of, relating to, or characteristic of a Viking or Vikings: *a Viking ship* [C19 from ON *víkingr*, prob. from *vík* creek, sea inlet + *-ingr* (see -ING[3])]

▷ http://viking.no/e/

▷ www.pbs.org/wgbh/nova/vikings

vile (vaɪl) *adj* **1** abominably wicked; shameful or evil **2** morally despicable; ignoble: *vile accusations* **3** disgusting to the senses or emotions; foul: *a vile smell* **4** tending to humiliate or degrade: *only slaves would perform such vile tasks* **5** unpleasant or bad: *vile weather* [C13 from OF *vil*, from L *vīlis* cheap] > ˈ**vilely** *adv* > ˈ**vileness** *n*

vilify (ˈvɪlɪˌfaɪ) *vb* **vilifies, vilifying, vilified** (*tr*) to revile with abusive language; malign [C15 from LL, from L *vīlis* worthless + *facere* to make] > **vilification** (ˌvɪlɪfɪˈkeɪʃən) *n* > ˈ**viliˌfier** *n*

vilipend (ˈvɪlɪˌpɛnd) *vb* (*tr*) *rare* **1** to treat or regard with contempt **2** to speak slanderously of [C15 from LL, from L *vīlis* worthless + *pendere* to esteem] > ˈ**viliˌpender** *n*

villa (ˈvɪlə) *n* **1** (in ancient Rome) a country house, usually consisting of farm buildings and residential quarters around a courtyard **2** a large country residence **3** *Brit* a detached or semidetached suburban house [C17 via It. from L]

Villa (ˈviːə; *Spanish* ˈbiʎa) *n* **Francisco** (franˈsisko), called *Pancho Villa*, original name *Doroteo Arango*. ?1877–1923, Mexican revolutionary leader

Villach (*German* ˈfɪlax) *n* a city in S central Austria, on the Drava River: nearby hot mineral springs. Pop: 54 640 (1991)

village (ˈvɪlɪdʒ) *n* **1** a small group of houses in a country area, larger than a hamlet **2** the inhabitants of such a community collectively **3** an incorporated municipality smaller than a town in various parts of the US and Canada **4** (*modifier*) of or characteristic of a village: *a village green* [C15 from OF, from *ville* farm, from L: VILLA] > ˈ**villager** *n*

Villahermosa (*Spanish* biʎaɛrˈmosa) *n* a town in E Mexico, capital of Tabasco state: university (1959). Pop: 330 605 (2000 est). Former name: **San Juan Bautista**

villain (ˈvɪlən) *n* **1** a wicked or malevolent person **2** (in a novel, play, etc) the main evil character and antagonist to the hero **3** *often jocular* a rogue **4** *obs* an uncouth person; boor [C14 from OF *vilein* serf, from LL *vīllānus* worker on a country estate, from L: VILLA] > ˈ**villainess** *fem n*

villainous (ˈvɪlənəs) *adj* **1** of, like, or appropriate to a villain **2** very bad or disagreeable: *a villainous climate* > ˈ**villainously** *adv* > ˈ**villainousness** *n*

villainy (ˈvɪlənɪ) *n, pl* **villainies** **1** vicious behaviour or action **2** an evil or criminal act or deed **3** the fact or condition of being villainous

Villa-Lobos (ˈviːlɑːˈləʊbɒs, ˈvɪlə-; *Portuguese* ˈvilaˈlobus) *n* **Heitor** (ejˈtor) 1887–1959, Brazilian composer, much of whose work is based on Brazilian folk tunes

villanelle (ˌvɪləˈnɛl) *n* a verse form of French origin consisting of 19 lines arranged in five tercets and a quatrain [C16 from F, from It. *villanella*, from *villano* rustic]

-ville *n and adj combining form sl, chiefly US* (denoting) a place, condition, or quality with a character as specified: *dragsville; squaresville*

villein (ˈvɪlən) *n* (in medieval Europe) a peasant bound to his lord, to whom he paid dues and services in return for his land [C14 from OF *vilein* serf; see VILLAIN] > ˈ**villeinage** *n*

Villeneuve (*French* vilnœv) *n* **Pierre Charles Jean Baptiste Silvestre de** (pjɛr ʃarl ʒɑ̃ batist silvɛstrə də) 1763–1806,

French admiral, defeated by Nelson at the Battle of Trafalgar (1805)

Villeurbanne (*French* vijœrban) *n* a town in E France: an industrial suburb of E Lyons. Pop: 119 848 (1990)

Villiers ('vɪləz, 'vɪljəz) *n* **George** See (Dukes of) **Buckingham**

Villiers de l'Isle Adam (*French* vilje də lil adɑ̃) *n* **August, Comte de** (ogyst, kɔ̃t də) 1838–89, French poet and dramatist; pioneer of the symbolist movement. His works include *Contes cruels* (1883) and the play *Axel* (1885)

villiform ('vɪlɪˌfɔːm) *adj* having the form of a villus or a series of villi [c19 from NL *villiformis*, from L *villus* shaggy hair + -FORM]

Villon (*French* vijɔ̃) *n* **1 François** (frɑ̃swa) born 1431, French poet. His poems, such as those in *Le Petit testament* (?1456) and *Le Grand testament* (1461), are mostly ballades and rondeaux, verse forms that he revitalized. He was banished in 1463, after which nothing more was heard of him **2 Jacques** (ʒak), real name *Gaston Duchamp*. 1875–1963, French cubist painter and engraver

villus ('vɪləs) *n, pl* **villi** ('vɪlaɪ) (*usually pl*) **1** *zool, anat* any of the numerous finger-like projections of the mucous membrane lining the small intestine of many vertebrates **2** any similar membranous process **3** *bot* any of various hairlike outgrowths [c18 from L: shaggy hair] > **villosity** (vɪ'lɒsɪtɪ) *n* > '**villous** *adj*

Vilnius *or* **Vilnyus** ('vɪlnɪʊs) *n* the capital of Lithuania: passed to Russia in 1795; under Polish rule (1920–39); university (1578); an industrial and commercial centre. Pop: 577 969 (2000 est). Russian name: **Vilna** ('vilna) Polish name: **Wilno**

▷ www.vilnius.lt
▷ www.turizmas.vilnius.lt
▷ http://neris.mii.lt/homepage/lieti-1.html

vim (vɪm) *n sl* exuberant vigour and energy [c19 from L, from *vīs*; rel. to Gk *is* strength]

Viminal ('vɪmɪnᵊl) *n* one of the seven hills on which ancient Rome was built [from Latin *Vīminālis Collis* the Viminal Hill, from *vīminālis* of osiers, from *vīmen* an osier, referring to the willow grove on the hill]

vimineous (vɪ'mɪnɪəs) *adj bot, now rare* having, producing, or resembling long flexible shoots [c17 from L *vīmineus* made of osiers, from *vīmen* flexible shoot]

vina ('viːnə) *n* a stringed musical instrument, esp of India, related to the sitar [c18 from Hindi *bīnā*, from Sansk. *vīṇā*]

vinaceous (vaɪ'neɪʃəs) *adj* **1** of, relating to, or containing wine **2** having a colour suggestive of red wine [c17 from LL *vīnāceus*, from L *vīnum* wine]

Viña del Mar (*Spanish* 'biɲa ðɛl 'mar) *n* a city and resort in central Chile, just north of Valparaíso on the Pacific: the second largest city of Chile. Pop: 330 736 (1999 est)

vinaigrette (ˌvɪneɪ'grɛt) *n* **1** Also called: **vinaigrette sauce** a salad dressing made from oil and vinegar with seasonings; French dressing **2** Also called: **vinegarette** a small decorative bottle or box with a perforated top, used for holding smelling salts, etc [c17 from F, from *vinaigre* VINEGAR]

Vincennes (*French* vɛ̃sɛn; *English* vɪn'sɛnz) *n* a suburb of E Paris: 14th-century castle. Pop: 45 000 (latest est)

Vincent de Paul ('vɪnsənt də 'pɔːl; *French* vɛ̃sɑ̃ də pɔl) *n* **Saint** ?1581–1660, French Roman Catholic priest, who founded two charitable orders, the Lazarists (1625) and the Sisters of Charity (1634). Feast day: Sept. 27

Vincent's angina *or* **disease** *n* an ulcerative bacterial infection of the mouth, esp involving the throat and tonsils [c20 after J. H. *Vincent* (died 1950), F bacteriologist]

Vinci ('vɪntʃɪ) *n* See **Leonardo da Vinci**

vincible ('vɪnsɪbᵊl) *adj rare* capable of being defeated [c16 from L *vincibilis*, from *vincere* to conquer] > ˌ**vinci'bility** *n*

vincristine (vɪn'krɪstiːn) *n* an alkaloid used to treat leukaemia, derived from the tropical shrub Madagascar periwinkle [c20 from NL *Vinca* genus name of the plant + L *crista* crest + -INE²]

vinculum ('vɪŋkjʊləm) *n, pl* **vincula** (-lə) **1** a horizontal line drawn above a group of mathematical terms, used as an alternative to parentheses in mathematical expressions, as in $x+\overline{y-z}$, which is equivalent to $x+(y-z)$ **2** *anat* any bandlike structure, esp one uniting two or more parts [c17 from L: bond, from *vincīre* to bind]

vindaloo (ˌvɪndə'luː) *n, pl* **vindaloos** a type of very hot Indian curry [c20 ? from Port. *vin d'alho* wine and garlic sauce]

vin de pays *French* (vɛ̃ də pei) *n, pl* ***vins de pays*** (vɛ̃ də pei) the third highest French wine classification: indicates that the wine meets certain requirements concerning area of production, strength, etc. Also called: ***vin du pays***. Abbrev: **VDP** ▷ Cf **AOC, VDQS** [lit.: local wine]

Vindhya Pradesh ('vɪndjə) *n* a former state of central India: merged with the reorganized Madhya Pradesh in 1956

Vindhya Range *or* **Mountains** *n* a mountain range in central India: separates the Ganges basin from the Deccan, marking the limits of northern and peninsular India. Greatest height: 1113 m (3651 ft)

vindicable ('vɪndɪkəbᵊl) *adj* capable of being vindicated; justifiable > ˌ**vindica'bility** *n*

vindicate ('vɪndɪˌkeɪt) *vb* **vindicates, vindicating, vindicated** (*tr*) **1** to clear from guilt, blame, etc, as by evidence or argument **2** to provide justification for: *his promotion vindicated his unconventional attitude* **3** to uphold or defend (a cause, etc): *to vindicate a claim* [c17 from L *vindicāre*, from *vindex* claimant] > '**vindiˌcator** *n* > '**vindiˌcatory** *adj*

vindication (ˌvɪndɪ'keɪʃən) *n* **1** the act of vindicating or the condition of being vindicated **2** a fact, evidence, etc, that serves to vindicate a claim

vindictive (vɪn'dɪktɪv) *adj* **1** disposed to seek vengeance **2** characterized by spite or rancour **3** *English law* (of damages) in excess of the compensation due to the plaintiff and imposed in punishment of the defendant [c17 from L *vindicta* revenge, from *vindicāre* to VINDICATE] > **vin'dictively** *adv* > **vin'dictiveness** *n*

vin du pays *French* (vɛ̃ du pei) *n, pl* ***vins du pays*** a variant of ***vin de pays***

vine (vaɪn) *n* **1** any of various plants, esp the grapevine, having long flexible stems that creep along the ground or climb by clinging to a support by means of tendrils, leafstalks, etc **2** the stem of such a plant [c13 from OF, from L *vīnea* vineyard, from *vīnum* wine] > '**viny** *adj*

Vine (vaɪn) *n* **Barbara** See (Ruth) **Rendell**

vinedresser ('vaɪnˌdrɛsə) *n* a person who prunes, tends, or cultivates grapevines

vinegar ('vɪnɪgə) *n* **1** a sour-tasting liquid consisting of impure dilute acetic acid, made by fermentation of beer, wine, or cider. It is used as a condiment or preservative **2** sourness or peevishness of temper, speech, etc [c13 from OF, from *vin* WINE + *aigre* sour, from L *acer*] > '**vinegarish** *adj* > '**vinegary** *adj*

vinery ('vaɪnərɪ) *n, pl* **vineries 1** a hothouse for growing grapes **2** another name for a **vineyard 3** vines collectively

vineyard ('vɪnjəd) *n* a plantation of grapevines, esp where wine grapes are produced [OE *wīngeard*; see VINE, YARD²]

vingt-et-un *French* (vɛ̃teɶ̃) *n* another name for **pontoon²** [lit.: twenty-one]

Vinho Verde (ˌviːnjəʊ 'vɜːdɪ) *n* any of a variety of light sharp-tasting wines made from early-picked grapes of NW Portugal [Port., lit.: green (or young) wine]

vini- *or before a vowel* **vin-** *combining form* indicating wine: *viniculture* [from L *vīnum*]

viniculture ('vɪnɪˌkʌltʃə) *n* the process or business of growing grapes and making wine > ˌ**vini'cultural** *adj* > ˌ**vini'culturist** *n*

viniferous (vɪˈnɪfərəs) *adj* wine-producing

Vinland (ˈvɪnlənd) *n* the stretch of the E coast of North America visited by Leif Ericson and other Vikings from about 1000

Vinnitsa (*Russian* ˈvinnitsə) *n* a city in central Ukraine: passed from Polish to Russian rule in 1793. Pop: 389 100 (1998 est)

vino (ˈviːnəʊ) *n, pl* **vinos** an informal word for **wine** [jocular use of It. or Sp. *vino*]

vin ordinaire *French* (vɛ̃n ɔrdinɛr) *n, pl* ***vins ordinaires*** (vɛ̃z ɔrdinɛr) cheap table wine, esp French

vinosity (vɪˈnɒsɪtɪ) *n* the distinctive and essential quality and flavour of wine [c17 from LL *vīnōsitas*, from L *vīnōsus* VINOUS]

vinous (ˈvaɪnəs) *adj* **1** of or characteristic of wine **2** indulging in or indicative of indulgence in wine [c17 from L, from *vīnum* WINE]

vintage (ˈvɪntɪdʒ) *n* **1** the wine obtained from a harvest of grapes, esp in an outstandingly good year **2** the harvest from which such a wine is obtained **3a** the harvesting of wine grapes **3b** the season of harvesting these grapes or for making wine **4** a time of origin: *a car of Edwardian vintage* **5** *inf* a group of people or objects of the same period: *a fashion of last season's vintage* ▷ *adj* **6** (of wine) of an outstandingly good year **7** representative of the best and most typical: *vintage Shakespeare* **8** of lasting interest and importance; classic: *vintage films* **9** old-fashioned; dated [c15 from OF *vendage* (infl. by *vintener* VINTNER), from L *vindēmia*, from *vīnum* WINE, grape + *dēmere* to take away]

vintage car *n chiefly Brit* an old car, esp one constructed between 1919 and 1930 ▷ Cf **classic car, veteran car**

vintager (ˈvɪntɪdʒə) *n* a grape harvester

vintner (ˈvɪntnə) *n* a wine merchant [c15 from OF *vinetier*, from Med. L, from L *vīnētum* vineyard]

vinyl (ˈvaɪnɪl) *n* **1** (*modifier*) of or containing the monovalent group of atoms CH_2:CH–: *vinyl chloride* **2** (*modifier*) of or made of a vinyl resin: *a vinyl raincoat* **3** any vinyl resin or plastic, esp PVC **4** (collectively) conventional records made of vinyl as opposed to compact discs [c19 from VINI- + -YL]

vinyl acetate *n* a colourless volatile liquid unsaturated ester that polymerizes readily in light and is used for making polyvinyl acetate

vinyl chloride *n* a colourless flammable gaseous unsaturated compound made by the chlorination of ethylene and used as a refrigerant and in the manufacture of PVC

vinyl resin *or* **polymer** *n* any one of a class of thermoplastic materials, esp PVC and polyvinyl acetate, made by polymerizing vinyl compounds

viol (ˈvaɪəl) *n* any of a family of stringed musical instruments that preceded the violin family, consisting of a fretted fingerboard, a body like that of a violin but having a flat back and six strings, played with a curved bow [c15 from OF *viole*, from OProvençal *viola*; see VIOLA[1]]

viola[1] (vɪˈəʊlə) *n* **1** a bowed stringed instrument, the alto of the violin family; held beneath the chin when played **2** any of various instruments of the viol family, such as the viola da gamba [c18 from It., prob. from O Provençal]

viola[2] (ˈvaɪələ, vaɪˈəʊ-) *n* any of various temperate perennial herbaceous plants, the flowers of which have showy irregular petals, white, yellow, blue, or mauve in colour [c15 from L: violet]

viola clef (vɪˈəʊlə) *n* another term for **alto clef**

viola da gamba (vɪˈəʊlə də ˈgæmbə) *n* the second largest and lowest member of the viol family [c18 from It., lit.: viol for the leg]

viola d'amore (vɪˈəʊlə dæˈmɔːrɪ) *n* an instrument of the viol family having no frets, seven strings, and a set of sympathetic strings [c18 from It., lit.: viol of love]

violate (ˈvaɪəˌleɪt) *vb* **violates, violating, violated** (*tr*) **1** to break, disregard, or infringe (a law, agreement, etc) **2** to rape or otherwise sexually assault **3** to disturb rudely or improperly **4** to treat irreverently or disrespectfully: *he violated a sanctuary* [c15 from L *violāre* to do violence to, from *vīs* strength] > **ˈviolable** *adj* > **ˌvioˈlation** *n* > **ˈvioˌlator** *or* **ˈvioˌlater** *n*

violence (ˈvaɪələns) *n* **1** the exercise or an instance of physical force, usually effecting or intended to effect injuries, destruction, etc **2** powerful, untamed, or devastating force: *the violence of the sea* **3** great strength of feeling, as in language, etc **4** an unjust, unwarranted, or unlawful display of force **5** **do violence to** **5a** to inflict harm upon: *they did violence to the prisoners* **5b** to distort the sense or intention of: *the reporters did violence to my speech* [c13 via OF from L *violentia* impetuosity, from *violentus* VIOLENT]

violent (ˈvaɪələnt) *adj* **1** marked or caused by great physical force or violence: *a violent stab* **2** (of a person) tending to the use of violence, esp in order to injure or intimidate others **3** marked by intensity of any kind: *a violent clash of colours* **4** characterized by an undue use of force **5** caused by or displaying strong or undue mental or emotional force [c14 from L *violentus*, prob. from *vīs* strength] > **ˈviolently** *adv*

violent storm *n* a wind of force 11 on the Beaufort scale, reaching speeds of 64 to 72 mph

violet (ˈvaɪəlɪt) *n* **1** any of various temperate perennial herbaceous plants of the genus *Viola*, such as the **sweet** (or **garden**) **violet**, having mauve or bluish flowers with irregular showy petals **2** any other plant of the genus *Viola*, such as the wild pansy **3** any of various similar but unrelated plants, such as the African violet **4a** any of a group of colours that have a purplish-blue hue. They lie at one end of the visible spectrum **4b** (*as adj*): *a violet dress* **5** a dye or pigment of or producing these colours **6** violet clothing: *dressed in violet* [c14 from OF *violete* a little violet, from L *viola* violet]

violin (ˌvaɪəˈlɪn) *n* a bowed stringed instrument, the highest member of the violin family, consisting of a fingerboard, a hollow wooden body with waisted sides, and a sounding board connected to the back by means of a soundpost that also supports the bridge. It has two f-shaped sound holes cut in the belly [c16 from It. *violino* a little viola, from VIOLA[1]]

violinist (ˌvaɪəˈlɪnɪst) *n* a person who plays the violin

violist[1] (vɪˈəʊlɪst) *n* a person who plays the viola

violist[2] (ˈvaɪəlɪst) *n* a person who plays the viol

Viollet-le-Duc (*French* vjɔlɛlədyk) *n* **Eugène Emmanuel** (øʒɛn ɛmanɥɛl) 1814–79, French architect and leader of the Gothic Revival in France, noted for his dictionary of French architecture (1854–68) and for his restoration of medieval buildings

violoncello (ˌvaɪələnˈtʃɛləʊ) *n, pl* **violoncellos** the full name for **cello** [c18 from It., from *violone* large viol + *-cello*, dim. suffix] > **ˌviolonˈcellist** *n*

VIP *abbrev for:* **1** very important person **2** visually impaired person

viper (ˈvaɪpə) *n* **1** any of a family of venomous Old World snakes having hollow fangs in the upper jaw that are used to inject venom **2** any of various other snakes, such as the horned viper **3** a malicious or treacherous person [c16 from L *vīpera*, ?from *vīvus* living + *parere* to bear, referring to a tradition that the viper was viviparous]

viperous (ˈvaɪpərəs) *or* **viperish** *adj* **1** Also: **viperine** (ˈvaɪpəˌraɪn) of or resembling a viper **2** malicious

viper's bugloss *n* **1** Also called (US): **blueweed** a Eurasian weed, having blue flowers and pink buds **2** a related plant that has purple flowers and is naturalized in Australia and New Zealand. Also called: (Austral) **Paterson's curse, Salvation Jane**

virago (vɪˈrɑːgəʊ) *n, pl* **viragoes** *or* **viragos** **1** a loud, violent, and ill-tempered woman; scold; shrew **2** *arch* a strong, brave, or warlike woman [OE, from L: a manlike

maiden, from *vir* a man] > **vi'rago-,like** *adj*
viral ('vaɪrəl) *adj* of or caused by a virus
viral marketing *n* **1** a direct marketing technique in which a company persuades Internet users to forward its publicity material in e-mails (usually by including jokes, games, video clips, etc) **2** a marketing strategy in which conventional media are eschewed in favour of various techniques designed to generate word-of-mouth publicity, in the hope of creating a fad or craze
Virchow (*German* 'fɪrço) *n* **Rudolf Ludwig Karl** ('ru:dɔlf 'lu:tvɪç karl) 1821–1902, German pathologist, who is considered the founder of modern (cellular) pathology
virelay ('vɪrɪ,leɪ) *n* an old French verse form, rarely used in English, having stanzas of short lines with two rhymes throughout and two opening lines recurring at intervals [c14 from OF *virelai*, prob. from *vireli* (associated with *lai* LAY[4]), word used as a refrain]
Viren ('vɪərən) *n* **Lasse** ('læsɪ) born 1949, Finnish distance runner: winner of the 5000 metres and the 10 000 metres in the 1972 and 1976 Olympic Games
vireo ('vɪrɪəʊ) *n, pl* **vireos** any of a family of insectivorous American songbirds having an olive-grey back with pale underparts [c19 from L: a bird, prob. a greenfinch; cf. *virēre* to be green]
vires *Latin* ('vaɪri:z) *n* the plural of ***vis***
virescent (vɪ'rɛsᵊnt) *adj* greenish or becoming green [c19 from L *virescere*, from *virēre* to be green] > **vi'rescence** *n*
virgate[1] ('vɜ:gɪt, -geɪt) *adj* long, straight, and thin; rod-shaped: *virgate stems* [c19 from L *virgātus* made of twigs, from *virga* a rod]
virgate[2] ('vɜ:gɪt, -geɪt) *n Brit* an obsolete measure of land area, usually taken as 30 acres [c17 from Med. L *virgāta (terrae)* a rod's measurement (of land), from L *virga* rod; translation of OE *gierd landes* a yard of land]
Virgil *or* **Vergil** ('vɜ:dʒɪl) *n* Latin name *Publius Vergilius Maro*. 70–19 BC, Roman poet, patronized by Maecenas. The *Eclogues* (42–37), ten pastoral poems, and the *Georgics* (37–30), four books on the art of farming, established Virgil as the foremost poet of his age. His masterpiece is the *Aeneid* (30–19)
virgin ('vɜ:dʒɪn) *n* **1** a person, esp a woman, who has never had sexual intercourse **2** an unmarried woman who has taken a religious vow of chastity **3** any female animal that has never mated **4** a female insect that produces offspring by parthenogenesis ▷ *adj (usually prenominal)* **5** of, suitable for, or characteristic of a virgin or virgins **6** pure and natural, uncorrupted or untouched: *virgin purity* **7** not yet cultivated, explored, exploited, etc, by man: *virgin territories* **8** being the first or happening for the first time **9** (of a metal) made from an ore rather than from scrap **10** occurring naturally in a pure and uncombined form: *virgin silver* [c13 from OF *virgine*, from L *virgō* virgin]
Virgin[1] ('vɜ:dʒɪn) *n* **1** **the** See **Virgin Mary** **2** a statue or other artistic representation of the Virgin Mary
Virgin[2] ('vɜ:dʒɪn) *n* **the** the constellation Virgo, the sixth sign of the zodiac
virginal[1] ('vɜ:dʒɪnᵊl) *adj* **1** of, characterized by, or maintaining a state of virginity; chaste **2** extremely pure or fresh [c15 from L *virginālis* maidenly, from *virgō* virgin] > **'virginally** *adv*
virginal[2] ('vɜ:dʒɪnᵊl) *n (often pl)* a smaller version of the harpsichord, but oblong in shape, having one manual and no pedals [c16 prob. from L *virginālis* VIRGINAL[1], ? because it was played largely by young ladies] > **'virginalist** *n*
Virgin Birth *n* the doctrine that Jesus Christ was conceived by the intervention of the Holy Spirit so that Mary remained a virgin
virgin forest *n* a forest in its natural state, before it has been explored or exploited by man
Virginia (və'dʒɪnɪə) *n* a state of the eastern US, on the Atlantic: site of the first permanent English settlement in North America; consists of a low-lying deeply indented coast rising inland to the Piedmont plateau and the Blue Ridge Mountains. Capital: Richmond. Pop: 7 078 515 (1997 est). Area: 103 030 sq km (39 780 sq miles). Abbreviations: **Va** or (with zip code) **VA** > **Vir'ginian** *adj, n*
Virginia Beach *n* a city and resort in SE Virginia, on the Atlantic. Pop: 425 257 (2000)
Virginia creeper *n* a woody vine of North America, having tendrils with adhesive tips, bluish-black berry-like fruits, and compound leaves that turn red in autumn: widely planted for ornament
Virginia stock *n* a Mediterranean plant cultivated for its white and pink flowers
Virgin Islands *pl n* a group of about 100 small islands (14 inhabited) in the Caribbean, east of Puerto Rico: discovered by Columbus (1493); consists of the British Virgin Islands in the east and the Virgin Islands of the United States in the west and south. Pop: 141 000 (1999 est). Area: 497 sq km (192 sq miles)
Virgin Islands of the United States *pl n* a territory of the US in the Caribbean, consisting of islands west and south of the British Virgin Islands: purchased from Denmark in 1917 for their strategic importance. Capital: Charlotte Amalie. Pop: 122 000 (2001 est). Area: 344 sq km (133 sq miles). Former name: **Danish West Indies**
virginity (və'dʒɪnɪtɪ) *n* **1** the condition or fact of being a virgin **2** the condition of being untouched, unused, etc
virginium (və'dʒɪnɪəm) *n chem* a former name for **francium**
Virgin Mary *n* Mary, the mother of Christ. Also called: **the Virgin**
virgin's-bower *n* any of several American varieties of clematis
virgin soil *n* **1** soil that has not been cultivated before **2** a person or thing that is as yet undeveloped
virgin wool *n* wool that is being processed or woven for the first time

Virgo ('vɜ:gəʊ) *n, Latin genitive* **Virginis** ('vɜ:dʒɪnɪs) **1** *astron* a large constellation on the celestial equator **2** *astrol* Also called: **the Virgin** the sixth sign of the zodiac. The sun is in this sign between about Aug 23 and Sept 22 [c14 from L]
virgo intacta ('vɜ:gəʊ ɪn'tæktə) *n* a girl or woman whose hymen is unbroken [L, lit.: untouched virgin]
virgule ('vɜ:gju:l) *n printing* another name for **solidus** [c19 from F: comma, from L *virgula* dim. of *virga* rod]
viridescent (,vɪrɪ'dɛsᵊnt) *adj* greenish or tending to become green [c19 from LL *viridescere*, from L *viridis* green] > **,viri'descence** *n*
viridian (vɪ'rɪdɪən) *n* a green pigment comprising a hydrated form of chromic oxide [c19 from L *viridis* green]
viridity (vɪ'rɪdɪtɪ) *n* **1** the quality or state of being green **2** innocence, youth, or freshness [c15 from L *viriditās*, from *viridis* green]
virile ('vɪraɪl) *adj* **1** of or having the characteristics of an adult male **2** (of a male) possessing high sexual drive and capacity for sexual intercourse **3** of or capable of copulation or procreation **4** strong, forceful, or vigorous [c15 from L *virīlis* manly, from *vir* a man; rel. to OE *wer* man] > **virility** (vɪ'rɪlɪtɪ) *n*
virilism ('vɪrɪ,lɪzəm) *n med* the abnormal development in a woman of male secondary sex characteristics
virology (vaɪ'rɒlədʒɪ) *n* the branch of medicine concerned with the study of viruses > **virological** (,vaɪrə'lɒdʒɪkᵊl) *adj*
virtu *or* **vertu** (vɜ:'tu:) *n* **1** a taste or love for curios or works of fine art **2** such objects collectively **3** the quality of being appealing to a connoisseur (esp in **articles of virtu; objects of virtu**) [c18 from It. *virtù*; see VIRTUE]
virtual ('vɜ:tʃʊəl) *adj* **1** having the essence or effect but not the appearance or form of: *a virtual revolution* **2** *physics*

being or involving a virtual image: *a virtual focus* **3** *computing* of or relating to virtual storage: *virtual memory* **4** of or relating to a computer technique by which a person, wearing a headset or mask, has the experience of being in an environment created by the computer, and of interacting with and causing changes within it [C14 from Med. L *virtuālis* effective, from L *virtūs* VIRTUE]

virtual human *n* a computer-generated moving image of a human being, used esp in films as an extra in large crowd scenes

virtual image *n* an optical image formed by the apparent divergence of rays from a point, rather than their actual divergence from a point

virtuality (ˌvɜːtjʊˈælɪtɪ) *n* virtual reality

virtually (ˈvɜːtʃʊəlɪ) *adv* in effect though not in fact; practically; nearly

virtual reality *n* a computer-generated environment that, to the person experiencing it, closely resembles reality. Abbrev: **VR** See also **virtual** (sense 4)

virtual storage *or* **memory** *n* a computer system in which the size of the memory is increased by transferring sections of a program from a large capacity backing store, such as a disk, into the smaller core memory as they are required

virtue (ˈvɜːtjuː) *n* **1** the quality or practice of moral excellence or righteousness **2** a particular moral excellence: *the virtue of tolerance* **3** any of the cardinal virtues (prudence, justice, fortitude, and temperance) or theological virtues (faith, hope, and charity) **4** any admirable quality or trait **5** chastity, esp in women **6** *arch* an effective, active, or inherent power **7** **by** *or* **in virtue of** by reason of **8** **make a virtue of necessity** to acquiesce in doing something unpleasant with a show of grace because one must do it in any case [C13 *vertu*, from OF, from L *virtūs* manliness, courage]

virtuoso (ˌvɜːtjʊˈəʊzəʊ, -səʊ) *n, pl* **virtuosos** *or* **virtuosi** (-siː) **1** a consummate master of musical technique and artistry **2** a person who has a masterly or dazzling skill or technique in any field of activity **3** a connoisseur or collector of art objects **4** (*modifier*) showing masterly skill or brilliance: *a virtuoso performance* [C17 from It.: skilled, from LL *virtuōsus* good, virtuous] > **virtuosic** (ˌvɜːtjʊˈɒsɪk) *adj* > ˌ**virtuˈosity** *n*

virtuous (ˈvɜːtʃʊəs) *adj* **1** characterized by or possessing virtue or moral excellence **2** (of women) chaste > ˈ**virtuously** *adv*

virulent (ˈvɪrʊlənt) *adj* **1a** (of a microorganism) extremely infective **1b** (of a disease) having a violent effect **2** extremely poisonous, injurious, etc **3** extremely bitter, hostile, etc [C14 from L *vīrulentus* full of poison, from *vīrus* poison] > ˈ**virulence** *or* ˈ**virulency** *n* > ˈ**virulently** *adv*

virus (ˈvaɪrəs) *n, pl* **viruses** **1** any of a group of submicroscopic entities consisting of a single nucleic acid chain surrounded by a protein coat and capable of replication only within the cells of living organisms **2** *inf* a disease caused by a virus **3** any corrupting or infecting influence **4** *computing* an unauthorized program that inserts itself into a computer system, and then propagates itself to other computers via networks or disks; when activated it interferes with the operation of the computer [C16 from L: slime, poisonous liquid]
▷ www.tulane.edu/~dmsander/garryfavweb.html

vis *Latin* (vɪs) *n, pl* **vires** power, force, or strength

visa (ˈviːzə) *n, pl* **visas** **1** an endorsement in a passport or similar document, signifying that the document is in order and permitting its bearer to travel into or through the country of the government issuing it ▷ *vb* **visas, visaing, visaed** **2** (*tr*) to enter a visa into (a passport) [C19 via F from L: things seen, from *vīsus*, p.p. of *vidēre* to see]

visage (ˈvɪzɪdʒ) *n chiefly literary* **1** face or countenance **2** appearance [C13 from OF: aspect, from *vis* face, from L *vīsus* appearance]

-visaged *adj* (*in combination*) having a visage as specified: *flat-visaged*

Visakhapatnam (vɪˌsɑːkəˈpʌtnəm) *n* a variant spelling of **Vishakhapatnam**

vis-à-vis (ˌviːzɑːˈviː) *prep* **1** in relation to **2** face to face with ▷ *adv, adj* **3** face to face; opposite ▷ *n, pl* **vis-à-vis** **4** a person or thing that is situated opposite to another **5** a person who corresponds to another in office, capacity, etc [C18 F, from *vis* face]

Visayan Islands *pl n* a group of seven large and several hundred small islands in the central Philippines. Chief islands: Negros and Panay. Pop: 13 041 000 (1990). Area: about 61 000 sq km (23 535 sq miles). Spanish name: **Bisayas**

Visby (*Swedish* ˈviːsbyː) *n* a port in SE Sweden, on NW Gotland Island in the Baltic: an early member of the Hanseatic League and major N European commercial centre in the Middle Ages. Pop: 57 110 (1990)

Visc. *abbrev for* Viscount *or* Viscountess

viscacha (vɪsˈkætʃə) *n* a gregarious burrowing rodent of southern South America, similar to but larger than the chinchillas [C17 from Sp., from Quechuan *wiskácha*]

viscera (ˈvɪsərə) *pl n, sing* **viscus** **1** *anat* the large internal organs of the body collectively, esp those in the abdominal cavity **2** (less formally) the intestines; guts [C17 from L: entrails, pl of *viscus* internal organ]

visceral (ˈvɪsərəl) *adj* **1** of or affecting the viscera **2** characterized by instinct rather than intellect > ˈ**viscerally** *adv*

viscid (ˈvɪsɪd) *adj* **1** cohesive and sticky **2** (esp of a leaf) covered with a sticky substance [C17 from LL *viscidus* sticky, from L *viscum* mistletoe, birdlime] > **visˈcidity** *n*

Visconti (*Italian* visˈkonti) *n* **1** the ruling family of Milan from 1277 to 1447 **2** **Luchino,** real name *Luchino Visconti de Modrone.* 1906–76, Italian stage and film director, whose neorealist films include *Ossessione* (1942). His other films include *The Leopard* (1963), *Death in Venice* (1970), and *The Innocents* (1976)

viscose (ˈvɪskəʊs) *n* **1a** a viscous orange-brown solution obtained by dissolving cellulose in sodium hydroxide and carbon disulphide. It can be converted back to cellulose by an acid, as in the manufacture of rayon and Cellophane **1b** (*as modifier*): *viscose rayon* **2** rayon made from this material [C19 from LL *viscōsus* full of birdlime, sticky, from *viscum* birdlime]

viscosity (vɪsˈkɒsɪtɪ) *n, pl* **viscosities** **1** the state or property of being viscous **2** *physics* **2a** the extent to which a fluid resists a tendency to flow **2b** Also called: **absolute viscosity** a measure of this resistance, measured in newton seconds per metre squared. Symbol: η

viscount (ˈvaɪkaʊnt) *n* **1** (in the British Isles) a nobleman ranking below an earl and above a baron **2** (in various countries) a son or younger brother of a count **3** (in medieval Europe) the deputy of a count [C14 from OF, from Med. L, from LL *vice-* VICE[3] + *comes* COUNT[2]] > ˈ**viscountcy** *or* ˈ**viscounty** *n*

viscountess (ˈvaɪkaʊntɪs) *n* **1** the wife or widow of a viscount **2** a woman who holds the rank of viscount in her own right

viscous (ˈvɪskəs) *adj* **1** (of liquids) thick and sticky **2** having viscosity [C14 from LL *viscōsus*; see VISCOSE] > ˈ**viscously** *adv*

viscus (ˈvɪskəs) *n* the singular of **viscera**

vise (vaɪs) *n, vb* **vises, vising, vised** *US* a variant spelling of **vice**[2]

Viseu (*Portuguese* viˈzeu) *n* a city in N central Portugal: 12th-century cathedral. Pop: 20 590 (1991)

Vishakhapatnam (vɪˌʃɑːkəˈpʌtnəm) *or* **Visakhapatnam** *n* a port in E India, in NE Andhra Pradesh on the Bay of Bengal: shipbuilding and oil-refining industries. Pop: 752 037 (1991)

Vishinsky (*Russian* viˈʃinskij) *n* a variant spelling of

(Andrei Yanuaryevich) **Vyshinsky**

Vishnu ('vɪʃnuː) *n Hinduism* the Pervader or Sustainer, originally a solar deity occupying a secondary place in the Hindu pantheon, later the saviour appearing in many incarnations [C17 from Sansk. *Viṣṇu*, lit.: the one who works everywhere] > '**Vishnuism** *n*

visibility (ˌvɪzɪ'bɪlɪtɪ) *n* **1** the condition or fact of being visible **2** clarity of vision or relative possibility of seeing **3** the range of vision: *visibility is 500 yards*

visible ('vɪzɪbᵊl) *adj* **1** capable of being perceived by the eye **2** capable of being perceived by the mind: *no visible dangers* **3** available: *the visible resources* **4** of or relating to the balance of trade: *visible transactions* [C14 from L *vīsibilis*, from *vidēre* to see] > '**visibly** *adv*

visible balance *n* another name for **balance of trade**

visible radiation *n* electromagnetic radiation that causes the sensation of sight; light

vision ('vɪʒən) *n* **1** the act, faculty, or manner of perceiving with the eye; sight **2a** the image on a television screen **2b** (*as modifier*): *vision control* **3** the ability or an instance of great perception, esp of future developments: *a man of vision* **4** a mystical or religious experience of seeing some supernatural event, person, etc: *the vision of St John of the Cross* **5** that which is seen, esp in such a mystical experience **6** (*sometimes pl*) a vivid mental image produced by the imagination: *he had visions of becoming famous* **7** a person or thing of extraordinary beauty [C13 from L *vīsiō* sight, from *vidēre* to see]

visionary ('vɪʒənərɪ) *adj* **1** marked by vision or foresight: *a visionary leader* **2** incapable of being realized or effected **3** (of people) characterized by idealistic or radical ideas, esp impractical ones **4** given to having visions **5** of, of the nature of, or seen in visions ▷ *n, pl* **visionaries 6** a visionary person

vision mixer *n television* **1** the person who selects and manipulates the television signals from cameras, film, etc, to make the composite programme **2** the equipment used for vision mixing

visit ('vɪzɪt) *vb* **visits, visiting, visited 1** to go or come to see (a person, place, etc) **2** to stay with (someone) as a guest **3** to go or come to (an institution, place, etc) for the purpose of inspecting or examining **4** (*tr*) (of a disease, disaster, etc) to afflict **5** (*tr; foll by upon or on*) to inflict (punishment, etc) **6** (often foll by *with*) *US & Canad inf* to chat (with someone) ▷ *n* **7** the act or an instance of visiting **8** a stay as a guest **9** a professional or official call **10** a formal call for the purpose of inspection or examination **11** *international law* the right of an officer of a belligerent state to stop and search neutral ships in war to verify their nationality and ascertain whether they carry contraband **12** *US & Canad inf* a chat [C13 from L *vīsitāre* to go to see, from *vīsere* to examine, from *vidēre* to see] > '**visitable** *adj*

visitant ('vɪzɪtənt) *n* **1** a ghost; apparition **2** a visitor or guest, usually from far away **3** Also called: **visitor** a migratory bird that is present in a particular region only at certain times: *a summer visitant* [C16 from L *vīsitāns*, from *vīsitāre*; see VISIT]

visitation (ˌvɪzɪ'teɪʃən) *n* **1** an official call or visit for the purpose of inspecting or examining an institution **2** a visiting of punishment or reward from heaven **3** any disaster or catastrophe: *a visitation of the plague* **4** an appearance or arrival of a supernatural being **5** *inf* an unduly prolonged social call

Visitation (ˌvɪzɪ'teɪʃən) *n* **1a** the visit made by the Virgin Mary to her cousin Elizabeth (Luke 1:39–56) **1b** the Church festival commemorating this, held on July 2 **2** a religious order of nuns, the **Order of the Visitation,** founded in 1610 and dedicated to contemplation

visiting card *n Brit* a small card bearing the name and usually the address of a person, esp for giving to business or social acquaintances

visiting fireman *n US inf* a visitor whose presence is noticed because he is important, impressive, etc

visitor ('vɪzɪtə) *n* **1** a person who pays a visit **2** another name for **visitant** (sense 3)

visitor centre *n* another term for **interpretive centre**

visitor's passport *n* (formerly in Britain) a passport, valid for one year, that could be purchased from post offices. It granted entry to certain countries, usually for a restricted period of time. Also called: **British Visitor's Passport**

Vislinsky Zaliv (*Russian* vis'linski 'zaːlɪf) *n* a transliteration of the Russian name for **Vistula** (sense 2)

visor *or* **vizor** ('vaɪzə) *n* **1** a transparent flap on a helmet that can be pulled down to protect the face **2** a piece of armour fixed or hinged to the helmet to protect the face **3** another name for **peak** (on a cap) **4** a small movable screen used as protection against glare from the sun, esp one attached above the windscreen of a motor vehicle **5** *arch or literary* a mask or any other means of disguise [C14 from Anglo-F *viser*, from OF *visiere*, from *vis* face; see VISAGE] > '**visored** *or* '**vizored** *adj*

vista ('vɪstə) *n* **1** a view, esp through a long narrow avenue of trees, buildings, etc, or such a passage or avenue itself **2** a comprehensive mental view of a distant time or a lengthy series of events [C17 from It., from *vedere* to see, from L *vidēre*] > '**vistaed** *adj*

Vistula ('vɪstjʊlə) *n* **1** a river in central and N Poland, rising in the Carpathian Mountains and flowing generally north and northwest past Warsaw and Torun, then northeast to enter the Baltic via an extensive delta region. Length: 1090 km (677 miles). Polish name: **Wisla** German name: **Weichsel 2 Lagoon** a shallow lagoon on the SW coast of the Baltic Sea, between Danzig and Kaliningrad, crossed by the border between Poland and Russia. German name: **Frisches Haff** Polish name: **Wislany Zalew** Russian name: **Vislinsky Zaliv**

visual ('vɪʒʊəl, -zjʊ-) *adj* **1** of, done by, or used in seeing: *visual powers* **2** another word for **optical 3** capable of being seen; visible **4** of, occurring as, or induced by a mental image ▷ *n* **5** a sketch to show the proposed layout of an advertisement, as in a newspaper **6** (*often pl*) a photograph, film, or other display material [C15 from LL *vīsuālis*, from L *vīsus* sight, from *vidēre* to see] > '**visually** *adv*

visual aids *pl n* devices, such as films, videos, slides, models, and blackboards, that display in visual form material to be understood or remembered

visual display unit *n computing* a device that displays characters or graphics representing data in a computer memory. It usually has a keyboard for the input of information or inquiries. Abbrev: **VDU**

visual field *n* the whole extent of the image falling on the retina when the eye is fixed on a given point

visualize *or* **visualise** ('vɪʒʊəˌlaɪz) *vb* **visualizes, visualizing, visualized** *or* **visualises, visualising, visualised** to form a mental image of (something incapable of being viewed or not at that moment visible) > ˌ**visuali'zation** *or* ˌ**visuali'sation** *n*

visual magnitude *n astron* the magnitude of a star as determined by visual observation

visual purple *n* another name for **rhodopsin**

visual violet *n* another name for **iodopsin**

visual yellow *n* another name for **retinene**

vital ('vaɪtᵊl) *adj* **1** essential to maintain life: *the lungs perform a vital function* **2** forceful, energetic, or lively: *a vital person* **3** of, having, or displaying life: *a vital organism* **4** indispensable or essential: *books vital to this study* **5** of great importance: *a vital game* ▷ *n* **6** (*pl*) the bodily organs, such as the brain, liver, heart, lungs, etc, that are necessary to maintain life **7** (*pl*) the essential elements of anything [C14 via OF from L *vītālis*, from *vīta* life] > '**vitally** *adv*

vital capacity *n physiol* the volume of air that can be exhaled from the lungs after the deepest possible breath has been taken

vital force *n* (esp in early biological theory) a hypothetical force, independent of physical and chemical forces, regarded as being the causative factor of the evolution of living organisms

vitalism (ˈvaɪtəˌlɪzəm) *n* the philosophical doctrine that the phenomena of life cannot be explained in purely mechanical terms because there is something immaterial which distinguishes living from inanimate matter > ˈ**vitalist** *n, adj* > ˌ**vitalˈistic** *adj*

vitality (vaɪˈtælɪtɪ) *n, pl* **vitalities 1** physical or mental vigour, energy, etc **2** the power or ability to continue in existence, live, or grow: *the vitality of a movement*

vitalize *or* **vitalise** (ˈvaɪtəˌlaɪz) *vb* **vitalizes, vitalizing, vitalized** *or* **vitalises, vitalising, vitalised** (*tr*) to make vital, living, or alive > ˌ**vitaliˈzation** *or* ˌ**vitaliˈsation** *n*

vital staining *n* the technique of treating living cells and tissues with dyes that do not immediately kill them, facilitating observation with a microscope

vital statistics *pl n* **1** quantitative data concerning human life or the conditions affecting it, such as the death rate **2** *inf* the measurements of a woman's bust, waist, and hips

vitamin (ˈvɪtəmɪn, ˈvaɪ-) *n* any of a group of substances that are essential, in small quantities, for the normal functioning of metabolism in the body. They cannot usually be synthesized in the body but they occur naturally in certain foods [C20 *vit-* from L *vīta* life + *-amin* from AMINE; so named by Casimir FUNK, who believed the substances to be amines] > ˌ**vitaˈminic** *adj*

vitamin A *n* **1** Also called: **vitamin A_1, retinol** a fat-soluble yellow unsaturated alcohol occurring in green and yellow vegetables, butter, egg yolk, and fish-liver oil. It is essential for the prevention of night blindness and the protection of epithelial tissue **2** Also called: **vitamin A_2** a vitamin that occurs in the tissues of freshwater fish and has a function similar to that of vitamin A_1

vitamin B *n, pl* **B vitamins** any of the vitamins in the vitamin B complex

vitamin B complex *n* a large group of water-soluble vitamins occurring esp in liver and yeast: includes thiamine (**vitamin B_1**), riboflavin (**vitamin B_2**), nicotinic acid, pyridoxine (**vitamin B_6**), pantothenic acid, biotin, choline, folic acid, and cyanocobalamin (**vitamin B_{12}**) Sometimes shortened to **B complex**

vitamin C *n* another name for **ascorbic acid**

vitamin D *n, pl* **D vitamins** any of the fat-soluble vitamins, including calciferol (**vitamin D_2**) and cholecalciferol (**vitamin D_3**), occurring in fish-liver oils, milk, butter, and eggs: used in the treatment of rickets

vitamin E *n* another name for **tocopherol**

vitamin G *n* another name (esp US & Canad) for **riboflavin**

vitamin H *n* another name (esp US & Canad) for **biotin**

vitamin K *n, pl* **K vitamins** any of the fat-soluble vitamins, including phylloquinone (**vitamin K_1**) and the menaquinones (**vitamin K_2**), which are essential for the normal clotting of blood

vitamin P *n, pl* **P vitamins** any of a group of water-soluble crystalline substances occurring mainly in citrus fruits, blackcurrants, and rose-hips: they regulate the permeability of the blood capillaries

Vitebsk (*Russian* ˈvitɪpsk) *n* a city in E Belarus, a port on the Dvina river: taken by Russia in 1772. Pop: 364 000 (1998 est)

vitellin (vɪˈtɛlɪn) *n biochem* a phosphoprotein that is the major protein in egg yolk [C19 from VITELLUS + -IN]

vitelline membrane (vɪˈtɛlɪn) *n zool* a membrane that surrounds a fertilized ovum and prevents the entry of other spermatozoa

vitellus (vɪˈtɛləs) *n, pl* **vitelluses** *or* **vitelli** (-laɪ) *zool, rare* the yolk of an egg [C18 from L, lit.: little calf, later: yolk of an egg, from *vitulus* calf]

vitiate (ˈvɪʃɪˌeɪt) *vb* **vitiates, vitiating, vitiated** (*tr*) **1** to make faulty or imperfect **2** to debase or corrupt **3** to destroy the force or legal effect of (a deed, etc) [C16 from L *vitiāre* to injure, from *vitium* a fault] > ˌ**vitiˈation** *n* > ˈ**vitiˌator** *n*

viticulture (ˈvɪtɪˌkʌltʃə) *n* **1** the science, art, or process of cultivating grapevines **2** the study of grapes and the growing of grapes [C19 *viti-*, from L *vītis* vine] > ˌ**vitiˈculturist** *n*

Viti Levu (ˈviːtɪ ˈlɛvuː) *n* the largest island of Fiji: mountainous. Chief town (and capital of the state): Suva. Pop: 340 560 (latest est) Area: 10 386 sq km (4010 sq miles)

Vitoria[1] (*Spanish* biˈtorja) *n* a city in NE Spain: scene of Wellington's decisive victory (1813) over Napoleon's forces in the Peninsular War. Pop: 216 527 (1998 est)

Vitoria[2] (*Spanish* biˈtorja) *n* **Francisco de** ?1486–1546, Spanish theologian, sometimes considered the father of international law. He criticized Spanish colonial policy in the New World and argued that war was only defensible in certain strictly defined circumstances

Vitória (vɪˈtɔːrɪə; *Portuguese* viˈtɔrja) *n* a port in E Brazil, capital of Espírito Santo state, on an island in the Bay of Espírito Santo. Pop: 291 889 (2000)

vitreous (ˈvɪtrɪəs) *adj* **1** of or resembling glass **2** made of or containing glass **3** of or relating to the vitreous humour or vitreous body [C17 from L *vitreus* made of glass, from *vitrum* glass] > ˈ**vitreously** *adv*

vitreous humour *or* **body** *n* a transparent gelatinous substance that fills the interior of the eyeball between the lens and the retina

vitrescence (vɪˈtrɛsəns) *n* **1** the quality or condition of being or becoming vitreous **2** the process of producing a glass or turning a crystalline material into glass > **viˈtrescent** *adj*

vitrification (ˌvɪtrɪfɪˈkeɪʃən) *n* **1** the process or act of vitrifying or the state of being vitrified **2** something that is or has been vitrified

vitrify (ˈvɪtrɪˌfaɪ) *vb* **vitrifies, vitrifying, vitrified** to convert or be converted into glass or a glassy substance [C16 from F, from L *vitrum* glass] > ˈ**vitriˌfiable** *adj*

vitrine (ˈvɪtriːn) *n* a glass display case or cabinet for works of art, curios, etc [C19 from F, from *vitre* pane of glass, from L *vitrum* glass]

vitriol (ˈvɪtrɪˌɒl) *n* **1** another name for **sulphuric acid** **2** any one of a number of sulphate salts, such as ferrous sulphate (iron(II) sulphate; **green vitriol**), copper sulphate (**blue vitriol**), or zinc sulphate (**white vitriol**) **3** speech, writing, etc, displaying vituperation or bitterness [C14 from Med. L *vitriolum*, from LL, from L *vitrum* glass, referring to the glossy appearance of the sulphates]

vitriolic (ˌvɪtrɪˈɒlɪk) *adj* **1** (of a strong acid) highly corrosive **2** severely bitter or caustic

vitriolize *or* **vitriolise** (ˈvɪtrɪəˌlaɪz) *vb* **vitriolizes, vitriolizing, vitriolized** *or* **vitriolises, vitriolising, vitriolised** (*tr*) **1** to convert into or treat with vitriol **2** to injure with vitriol > ˌ**vitrioliˈzation** *or* ˌ**vitrioliˈsation** *n*

Vitruvius Pollio (vɪˈtruːvɪəs ˈpɒlɪˌəʊ) *n* **Marcus** (ˈmɑːkəs) 1st century BC, Roman architect, noted for his treatise *De architectura*, the only surviving Roman work on architectural theory and a major influence on Renaissance architects

vittle (ˈvɪtᵊl) *n, vb* **vittles, vittling, vittled** an obsolete or dialect spelling of **victual**

vituperate (vɪˈtjuːpəˌreɪt) *vb* **vituperates, vituperating, vituperated** to berate or rail (against) abusively; revile [C16 from L *vituperāre* to blame, from *vitium* a defect + *parāre* to make] > **viˈtuperˌator** *n*

vituperation (vɪˌtjuːpəˈreɪʃən) *n* **1** abusive language or venomous censure **2** the act of vituperating

> **vituperative** (vɪ'tjuːpərətɪv, -prətɪv) *adj*

viva¹ ('viːvə) *interj* long live; up with (a specified person or thing) [c17 from It., lit.: may (he) live! from *vivere* to live, from L *vīvere*]

viva² ('vaɪvə) *Brit* ▷ *n* **1** an oral examination ▷ *vb* **vivas, vivaing, vivaed** (*tr*) **2** to examine orally [shortened from VIVA VOCE]

vivace (vɪ'vɑːtʃɪ) *adj, adv music* to be performed in a brisk lively manner [c17 from It., from L *vīvax* vigorous, from *vīvere* to live]

vivacious (vɪ'veɪʃəs) *adj* full of high spirits and animation [c17 from L *vīvax* lively; see VIVACE] > **vi'vaciously** *adv* > **vi'vaciousness** *n*

vivacity (vɪ'væsɪtɪ) *n, pl* **vivacities** the quality or condition of being vivacious

Vivaldi (vɪ'vældɪ) *n* **Antonio** (an'tɔːnjo) ?1675–1741, Italian composer and violinist, noted esp for his development of the solo concerto. His best-known work is *The Four Seasons* (1725)

vivarium (vaɪ'vɛərɪəm) *n, pl* **vivariums** *or* **vivaria** (-ɪə) a place where live animals are kept under natural conditions for study, etc [c16 from L: enclosure where live fish or game are kept, from *vīvus* alive]

viva voce ('vaɪvə 'vəʊtʃɪ) *adv, adj* **1** by word of mouth ▷ *n, vb* **viva-voce, viva-voces, viva-voceing, viva-voced** **2** the full form of **viva²** [c16 from Med. L, lit.: with living voice]

vive (viːv) *interj* long live; up with (a specified person or thing) [from F]

Vivian ('vɪvɪən) *n* (in Arthurian legend) the mistress of Merlin, sometimes identified with the **Lady of the Lake**

vivid ('vɪvɪd) *adj* **1** (of a colour) very bright; intense **2** brilliantly coloured: *vivid plumage* **3** conveying to the mind striking realism, freshness, or trueness to life: *a vivid account* **4** (of a memory, etc) remaining distinct in the mind **5** (of the imagination, etc) prolific in the formation of lifelike images **6** uttered, operating, or acting with vigour **7** full of life or vitality: *a vivid personality* [c17 from L *vīvidus* animated, from *vīvere* to live] > **'vividly** *adv* > **'vividness** *n*

vivify ('vɪvɪ,faɪ) *vb* **vivifies, vivifying, vivified** (*tr*) **1** to bring to life; animate **2** to make more vivid or striking [c16 from LL *vīvificāre*, from L *vīvus* alive + *facere* to make] > **,vivifi'cation** *n*

viviparous (vɪ'vɪpərəs) *adj* **1** (of most animals) producing offspring that as embryos develop within and derive nourishment from the body of the female parent **2** (of plants) producing bulbils or young plants instead of flowers **3** (of seeds) germinating before separating from the parent plant [c17 from L, from *vīvus* alive + *parere* to bring forth] > **viviparity** (,vɪvɪ'pærɪtɪ) *or* **vi'viparousness** *n* > **vi'viparously** *adv*

vivisect ('vɪvɪ,sɛkt, ,vɪvɪ'sɛkt) *vb* to subject (an animal) to vivisection [c19 back formation from VIVISECTION] > **'vivi,sector** *n*

vivisection (,vɪvɪ'sɛkʃən) *n* the act or practice of performing experiments on living animals, involving cutting into or dissecting the body [c18 from *vivi-*, from L *vīvus* living + SECTION, as in DISSECTION] > **,vivi'sectional** *adj*

vivisectionist (,vɪvɪ'sɛkʃənɪst) *n* a person who practises or advocates vivisection as being useful to science

vivo ('viːvəʊ) *adj, adv music* (*in combination*) with life and vigour: *allegro vivo* [It.: lively]

vixen ('vɪksən) *n* **1** a female fox **2** a quarrelsome or spiteful woman [c15 *fixen*; rel. to OE *fyxe*, fem. of FOX] > **'vixenish** *adj* > **'vixenly** *adv, adj*

Viyella (vaɪ'ɛlə) *n trademark* a soft fabric made of wool and cotton

viz *abbrev for* videlicet

vizard ('vɪzəd) *n arch or literary* a means of disguise [c16 var. of VISOR] > **'vizarded** *adj*

vizier (vɪ'zɪə) *n* a high official in certain Muslim countries, esp in the former Ottoman Empire [c16 from Turkish *vezīr*, from Ar. *wazīr* porter, from *wazara* to bear a burden] > **vi'zierate** *n* > **vi'zierial** *adj* > **vi'ziership** *n*

vizor ('vaɪzə) *n* a variant spelling of **visor**

vizsla ('vɪʒlə) *n* a breed of Hungarian hunting dog with a smooth rusty-gold coat [c20 after *Vizsla*, town in Hungary]

VJ *abbrev for* video jockey

V-J Day *n* the day marking the Allied victory over Japan in World War II (Aug 15, 1945)

VL *abbrev for* Vulgar Latin

Vlaardingen (*Dutch* 'vlaːrdɪŋə) *n* a port in the W Netherlands, in South Holland west of Rotterdam: the third largest port in the Netherlands. Pop: 73 820 (1994)

Vladikavkaz (*Russian* vlədikaf'kas) *n* a city in S Russia, capital of the North Ossetian Republic on the N slopes of the Caucasus. Pop: 310 600 (1999 est). Former names: **Dzaudzhikau** (1944–54), **Ordzhonikidze** (1954–91)

Vladimir¹ (*Russian* vla'dimir) *n* a city in W central Russia: capital of the principality of Vladimir until the court transferred to Moscow in 1328. Pop: 339 200 (1999 est)

Vladimir² ('vlædɪ,mɪə; *Russian* vla'dimir) *n* **Saint,** called *the Great*. ?956–1015, grand prince of Kiev (980–1015); first Christian ruler of Russia. Feast day: July 15

Vladivostok (,vlædɪ'vɒstɒk; *Russian* vlədivas'tɔk) *n* a port in SE Russia, on the Sea of Japan: terminus of the Trans-Siberian Railway; the main Russian Pacific naval base since 1872 and chief commercial and civilian Russian port in the Far East; university (1956). Pop: 613 100 (1999 est)

Vlaminck (*French* vlamɛ̃k) *n* **Maurice de** (mɔris də) 1876–1958, French painter of the Fauve school

vlei (fleɪ, vleɪ) *n S African* an area of low marshy ground, esp one that feeds a stream [c19 from Afrik.]

VLF *or* **vlf** *radio abbrev for* very low frequency

Vlissingen ('vlɪsɪŋə) *n* the Dutch name for **Flushing**

Vlorë (*Albanian* 'vlorə) *or* **Vlonë** (*Albanian* 'vlonə) *n* a port in SW Albania, on the **Bay of Vlorë:** under Turkish rule from 1462 until Albanian independence was declared here in 1912. Pop: 76 000 (1991 est). Ancient name: **Avlona** Also called: **Valona**

Vltava (*Czech* 'vltava) *n* a river in the Czech Republic, rising in the Bohemian Forest and flowing generally southeast and then north to the River Elbe near Melnik. Length: 434 km (270 miles). German name: **Moldau**

V neck *n* **a** a neck on a garment that comes down to a point, resembling the shape of the letter V **b** a sweater with such a neck > **'V-,neck** *or* **'V-,necked** *adj*

voc. *or* **vocat.** *abbrev for* vocative

vocab ('vəʊkæb) *n* short for **vocabulary**

vocable ('vəʊkəbᵊl) *n* any word, either written or spoken, regarded simply as a sequence of letters or spoken sounds [c16 from L *vocābulum* a designation, from *vocāre* to call] > **'vocably** *adv*

vocabulary (və'kæbjʊlərɪ) *n, pl* **vocabularies** **1** a listing, either selective or exhaustive, containing the words and phrases of a language, with meanings or translations into another language **2** the aggregate of words in the use or comprehension of a specified person, class, etc **3** all the words contained in a language **4** a range or system of symbols or techniques constituting a means of communication or expression, as any of the arts or crafts: *a wide vocabulary of textures and colours* [c16 from Med. L *vocābulārium*, from L *vocābulum* VOCABLE]

vocal ('vəʊkᵊl) *adj* **1** of or designed for the voice: *vocal music* **2** produced or delivered by the voice: *vocal noises* **3** connected with the production of the voice: *vocal organs* **4** frequently disposed to outspoken speech, criticism, etc: *a vocal minority* **5** full of sound or voices: *a vocal assembly* **6** endowed with a voice **7** *phonetics* **7a** of or relating to a speech sound **7b** of or relating to a voiced speech sound, esp a vowel ▷ *n* **8** a piece of jazz or pop music that is sung **9** a performance of such a piece of music [c14 from L *vōcālis* possessed of a voice, from *vōx* voice] > **vocality** (vəʊ'kælɪtɪ) *n* > '**vocally** *adv*

vocal cords *pl n* either of two pairs of membranous folds in the larynx. The upper pair (**false vocal cords**) are not concerned with vocal production; the lower pair (**true vocal cords**) can be made to vibrate and produce sound when air from the lungs is forced over them

vocalic (vəʊ'kælɪk) *adj phonetics* of, relating to, or containing a vowel or vowels

vocalise (ˌvəʊkə'liːz) *n* a musical passage sung upon one vowel usually as an exercise to develop flexibility and control of pitch and tone

vocalism ('vəʊkəˌlɪzəm) *n* **1** the exercise of the voice, as in singing or speaking **2** *phonetics* **2a** a voiced speech sound, esp a vowel **2b** a system of vowels as used in a language

vocalist ('vəʊkəlɪst) *n* a singer, esp one who regularly appears with a jazz band or pop group

vocalize *or* **vocalise** ('vəʊkəˌlaɪz) *vb* **vocalizes, vocalizing, vocalized** *or* **vocalises, vocalising, vocalised** **1** to express with or use the voice **2** (*tr*) to make vocal or articulate **3** (*tr*) *phonetics* to articulate (a speech sound) with voice **4** another word for **vowelize** **5** (*intr*) to sing a melody on a vowel, etc > ˌ**vocali'zation** *or* ˌ**vocali'sation** *n* > '**vocalˌizer** *or* '**vocalˌiser** *n*

vocal score *n* a musical score with voice parts in full and orchestral parts in the form of a piano transcription

vocation (vəʊ'keɪʃən) *n* **1** a specified profession or trade **2a** a special urge or predisposition to a particular calling or career, esp a religious one **2b** such a calling or career [c15 from L *vocātiō*, from *vocāre* to call]

vocational (vəʊ'keɪʃənəl) *adj* **1** of or relating to a vocation or vocations **2** of or relating to applied educational courses concerned with skills needed for an occupation, trade, or profession

vocational guidance *n* a guidance service based on psychological tests and interviews to find out what career may best suit a person

vocative ('vɒkətɪv) *grammar* ▷ *adj* **1** denoting a case of nouns, in some inflected languages, used when the referent of the noun is being addressed ▷ *n* **2a** the vocative case **2b** a vocative noun or speech element [c15 from L *vocātīvus cāsus* the calling case, from *vocāre* to call]

voces ('vəʊsiːz) *n* the plural of **vox**

vociferate (vəʊ'sɪfəˌreɪt) *vb* **vociferates, vociferating, vociferated** to exclaim or cry out about (something) clamorously or insistently [c17 from L *vōciferārī*, from *vōx* voice + *ferre* to bear] > **voˌcifer'ation** *n*

vociferous (vəʊ'sɪfərəs) *adj* **1** characterized by vehemence or noisiness: *vociferous protests* **2** making an outcry: *a vociferous mob* > **vo'ciferously** *adv* > **vo'ciferousness** *n*

vocoder ('vəʊˌkəʊdə) *n music* a type of synthesizer that uses the human voice as an oscillator

vodka ('vɒdkə) *n* an alcoholic drink originating in Russia, made from grain, potatoes, etc, usually consisting only of rectified spirit and water [c19 from Russian, dim. of *voda* water]

▷ www.ginvodka.org
▷ www.ivodka.com
▷ www.webtender.com

voe (vəʊ) *n* (in Orkney and Shetland) a small bay or narrow creek [c17 from ON *vagr*]

voetsek ('fʊtsɛk, 'vʊt-) *interj S African sl* an expression of dismissal or rejection [c19 Afrik., from Du. *voort se ek* forward, I say, commonly applied to animals]

voetstoets *or* **voetstoots** ('fʊtstʊts, 'vʊt-) *S African* ▷ *adj* **1** denoting a sale in which the vendor is freed from all responsibility for the condition of the goods being sold ▷ *adv* **2** without responsibility for the condition of the goods sold [from Afrik. *voetstoots* as it is]

Vogel ('vəʊgəl) *n* Sir **Julius** 1835–99, New Zealand statesman; prime minister of New Zealand (1873–75; 1876)

Vogts (*German* vokts) *n* **Hans-Hubert,** known as *Berti* born 1946, German footballer and coach; played for Germany (1967–79); coach of Germany (1990–98) and Scotland (from 2002)

vogue (vəʊg) *n* **1** the popular style at a specified time (esp in **in vogue**) **2** a period of general or popular usage or favour: *the vogue for such dances is over* ▷ *adj* **3** (*usually prenominal*) fashionable: *a vogue word* [c16 from F: a rowing fashion, from OIt., from *vogare* to row, from ?] > '**voguish** *adj*

voice (vɔɪs) *n* **1** the sound made by the vibration of the vocal cords, esp when modified by the tongue and mouth **2** the natural and distinctive tone of the speech sounds characteristic of a particular person **3** the condition, quality, or tone of such sounds: *a hysterical voice* **4** the musical sound of a singing voice, with respect to its quality or tone: *she has a lovely voice* **5** the ability to speak, sing, etc: *he has lost his voice* **6** a sound resembling or suggestive of vocal utterance: *the voice of hard experience* **7** written or spoken expression, as of feeling, opinion, etc (esp in **give voice to**) **8** a stated choice, wish, or opinion: *to give someone a voice in a decision* **9** an agency through which is communicated another's purpose, etc: *such groups are the voice of our enemies* **10** *music* **10a** musical notes produced by vibrations of the vocal chords at various frequencies and in certain registers: *a tenor voice* **10b** (in harmony) an independent melodic line or part: *a fugue in five voices* **11** *phonetics* the sound characterizing the articulation of several speech sounds, including all vowels or sonants, that is produced when the vocal cords are set in vibration by the breath **12** *grammar* a category of the verb that expresses whether the relation between the subject and the verb is that of agent and action, action and recipient, or some other relation **13** **in voice** in a condition to sing or speak well **14** **with one voice** unanimously ▷ *vb* **voices, voicing, voiced** (*tr*) **15** to give expression to: *to voice a complaint* **16** to articulate (a speech sound) with voice **17** *music* to adjust (a wind instrument or organ pipe) so that it conforms to the correct standards of tone colour, pitch, etc [c13 from OF *voiz*, from L *vōx*] > '**voicer** *n*

voice box *n* another word for the **larynx**

voiced (vɔɪst) *adj* **1** declared or expressed by the voice **2** (*in combination*) having a voice as specified: *loud-voiced* **3** *phonetics* articulated with accompanying vibration of the vocal cords: *in English* (b) *is a voiced consonant*

voice input *n* the control and operation of computer systems by spoken commands

voiceless ('vɔɪslɪs) *adj* **1** without a voice **2** not articulated: *voiceless misery* **3** silent **4** *phonetics* articulated without accompanying vibration of the vocal cords: *in English* (p) *is a voiceless consonant* > '**voicelessly** *adv*

voice mail *n* an electronic system for the transfer and storage of telephone messages, which can then be dealt with by the user at his or her convenience

voice-over *n* the voice of an unseen commentator heard during a film, etc

voiceprint ('vɔɪsˌprɪnt) *n* a graphic representation of a person's voice recorded electronically, usually having time plotted along the horizontal axis and the frequency of the speech on the vertical axis

void (vɔɪd) *adj* **1** without contents **2** not legally binding: *null and void* **3** (of an office, house, etc) unoccupied **4** (*postpositive*; foll by *of*) destitute or devoid: *void of resources* **5** useless: *all his efforts were rendered void* **6** (of a card suit or player) having no cards in a particular suit: *his spades were void* ▷ *n* **7** an empty space or area: *the huge desert voids of Asia* **8** a feeling or condition of loneliness or deprivation **9** a lack of any cards in one suit: *to have a void in spades* ▷ *vb* (*mainly tr*) **10** to make ineffective or invalid **11** to empty (contents, etc) or make empty of contents **12** (*also intr*) to discharge the contents of (the bowels or urinary bladder) [c13 from OF, from Vulgar L *vocītus* (unattested), from L *vacuus*, from *vacāre* to be empty] > **'voidable** *adj* > **'voider** *n*

voidance ('vɔɪdᵊns) *n* **1** an annulment, as of a contract **2** the condition of being vacant, as an office, benefice, etc **3** the act of voiding or evacuating [c14 var. of AVOIDANCE]

voile (vɔɪl) *n* a light semitransparent fabric of silk, rayon, cotton, etc, used for dresses, scarves, shirts, etc [c19 from F: VEIL]

Voiotia (*Greek* vjɔ'ti:a) *n* a department of E central Greece: corresponds to ancient Boeotia and part of ancient Phocis. Pop: 134 108 (1991). Area: 3173 sq km (1225 sq miles). Modern Greek name: **Boeotia**

Vojvodina *or* **Voivodina** (*Serbo-Croat* 'vɔjvɔdina) *n* an autonomous region of NE Serbia and Montenegro, in N Serbia. Capital: Novi Sad. Pop: 1 954 432 (1997 est). Area: 22 489 sq km (8683 sq miles)

vol. *abbrev for:* **1** volcano **2** volume **3** volunteer

volant ('vəʊlənt) *adj* **1** (*usually postpositive*) *heraldry* in a flying position **2** *rare* flying or capable of flight [c16 from F, from *voler* to fly, from L *volāre*]

volar ('vəʊlə) *adj anat* of or relating to the palm of the hand or the sole of the foot [c19 from L *vola* hollow of the hand, palm, sole of the foot]

volatile ('vɒlə,taɪl) *adj* **1** (of a substance) capable of readily changing from a solid or liquid form to a vapour **2** (of persons) disposed to caprice or inconstancy **3** (of circumstances) liable to sudden change **4** lasting only a short time: *volatile business interests* **5** *computing* (of a memory) not retaining stored information when the power supply is cut off ▷ *n* **6** a volatile substance [c17 from L *volātilis* flying, from *volāre* to fly] > **'vola,tileness** *or* **volatility** (,vɒlə'tɪlɪtɪ) *n*

volatilize *or* **volatilise** (vɒ'lætɪ,laɪz) *vb* **vola,tilizes, volatilizing, volatilized** *or* **volatilises, volatilising, volatilised** to change or cause to change from a solid or liquid to a vapour > **vo'lati,lizable** *or* **vo'lati,lisable** *adj* > **vo,latiliz'ation** *or* **vo,latilis'ation** *n*

vol-au-vent (*French* vɔlovɑ̃) *n* a very light puff pastry case filled with a savoury mixture in a sauce [c19 from F, lit.: flight in the wind]

volcanic (vɒl'kænɪk) *adj* **1** of, produced by, or characterized by the presence of volcanoes: *a volcanic region* **2** suggestive of or resembling an erupting volcano: *a volcanic era* > **vol'canically** *adv* > **volcanicity** (,vɒlkə'nɪsɪtɪ) *n*

volcanic glass *n* any of several glassy volcanic igneous rocks, such as obsidian

volcanism ('vɒlkə,nɪzəm) *or* **vulcanism** *n* those processes collectively that result in the formation of volcanoes and their products

volcano (vɒl'keɪnəʊ) *n, pl* **volcanoes** *or* **volcanos** **1** an opening in the earth's crust from which molten lava, rock fragments, ashes, dust, and gases are ejected from below the earth's surface **2** a mountain formed from volcanic material ejected from a vent in a central crater [c17 from It., from L *Volcānus* Vulcan, Roman god of fire and metalworking, whose forges were believed to be responsible for volcanic rumblings]

Volcano Islands *pl n* a group of three volcanic islands in the W Pacific, about 1100 km (700 miles) south of Japan: the largest is Iwo Jima, taken by US forces in 1945 and returned to Japan in 1968. Area: about 28 sq km (11 sq miles). Japanese name: **Kazan Retto**

volcanology (,vɒlkə'nɒlədʒɪ) *or* **vulcanology** *n* the study of volcanoes and volcanic phenomena > **volcanological** (,vɒlkənə'lɒdʒɪkᵊl) *or* **,vulcano'logical** *adj*

vole (vəʊl) *n* any of various small rodents, mostly of Eurasia and North America, having a stocky body, short tail, and inconspicuous ears [c19 short for *volemouse*, from ON *vollr* field + *mus* MOUSE]

Volga ('vɒlgə) *n* a river in W Russia, rising in the Valdai Range and flowing through a chain of small lakes to the Rybinsk Reservoir and south to the Caspian Sea through Volgograd: the longest river in Europe. Length: 3690 km (2293 miles)

Volgograd (*Russian* vəlga'grat; *English* 'vɒlgə,græd) *n* a port in SW Russia, on the River Volga: scene of a major engagement (1918) during the civil war and again in World War II (1942–43), in which the German forces were defeated; major industrial centre. Pop: 1 000 000 (1999 est). Former names: **Tsaritsyn** (until 1925), **Stalingrad** (1925–61)

volitant ('vɒlɪtənt) *adj* **1** flying or moving about rapidly **2** capable of flying [c19 from L *volitāre* to flit, from *volāre* to fly]

volition (və'lɪʃən) *n* **1** the act of exercising the will: *of one's own volition* **2** the faculty of conscious choice, decision, and intention **3** the resulting choice or resolution [c17 from Med. L *volitiō*, from L *vol-* as in *volō* I will, present stem of *velle* to wish] > **vo'litional** *adj*

volitive ('vɒlɪtɪv) *adj* of, relating to, or emanating from the will

Volk (fɒlk) *n S African* the Afrikaner people. [from Afrik., from Du.]

Volksraad ('fɒlks,rɑ:t) *n* (formerly, in South Africa) the Legislative Assemblies of the Transvaal and Orange Free State republics [from Afrik., from Du. *volks* people's + *raad* council]

volley ('vɒlɪ) *n* **1** the simultaneous discharge of several weapons, esp firearms **2** the projectiles or missiles so discharged **3** a burst of oaths, protests, etc, occurring simultaneously or in rapid succession **4** *sport* a stroke, shot, or kick at a moving ball before it hits the ground **5** *cricket* the flight of such a ball or the ball itself ▷ *vb* **6** to discharge (weapons, etc) in or as if in a volley or (of weapons, etc) to be discharged **7** (*tr*) to utter vehemently **8** (*tr*) *sport* to strike or kick (a moving ball) before it hits the ground [c16 from F *volée* a flight, from *voler* to fly, from L *volāre*] > **'volleyer** *n*

volleyball ('vɒlɪ,bɔ:l) *n* **1** a game in which two teams hit a large ball back and forth over a high net with their hands **2** the ball used in this game

▷ www.volleyball.org/iva

Vologda (*Russian* 'vɔləgdə) *n* an industrial city in W central Russia. Pop: 304 300 (1999 est)

Vólos (*Greek* 'vɔlɔs) *n* a port in E Greece, in Thessaly on the **Gulf of Volos** (an inlet of the Aegean): the third largest port in Greece. Pop: 70 000 (latest est)

volplane ('vɒl,pleɪn) *vb* **volplanes, volplaning, volplaned** **1** (*intr*) (of an aircraft) to glide without engine power ▷ *n* **2** a glide by an aircraft [c20 from F *vol plané* a gliding flight]

vols. *abbrev for* volumes

Volsung ('vɒlsʊŋ) *n* **1** a great hero of Norse and Germanic legend and poetry who gave his name to a race of warriors; father of Sigmund and Signy **2** any member of his family

volt[1] (vəʊlt) *n* the derived SI unit of electric potential; the potential difference between two points on a conductor carrying a current of 1 ampere, when the power dissipated between these points is 1 watt. Symbol: V [c19 after Count Alessandro VOLTA]

volt[2] *or* **volte** (vɒlt) *n* **1** a circle executed in dressage **2** a leap made in fencing to avoid an opponent's thrust [c17 from F, from It. *volta*, ult. from L *volvere* to turn]

volta ('vɒltə; *Italian* 'vɔlta) *n, pl* **volte** (*Italian* -te) **1** an Italian dance popular during the 16th and 17th centuries **2** a piece of music for or in the rhythm of this dance [c17 from It.: turn; see VOLT[2]]

Volta[1] ('vɒltə) *n* **1** a river in W Africa, formed by the confluence of the **Black Volta** and the **White Volta** in N central Ghana: flows south to the Bight of Benin: the chief river of Ghana. Length: 480 km (300 miles); (including the Black Volta) 1600 km (1000 miles) **2 Lake**

an artificial lake in Ghana, extending 408 km (250 miles) upstream from the **Volta River Dam** on the Volta River: completed in 1966. Area: 8482 sq km (3275 sq miles)

Volta² ('vəʊltə; *Italian* 'vɔlta) *n* Count **Alessandro** (ales'sandro) 1745–1827, Italian physicist after whom the volt is named. He made important contributions to the theory of current electricity and invented the voltaic pile (1800), the electrophorus (1775), and an electroscope

voltage ('vəʊltɪdʒ) *n* an electromotive force or potential difference expressed in volts

voltaic (vɒl'teɪɪk) *adj* another word for **galvanic** (sense 1)

voltaic cell *n* another name for **primary cell**

voltaic couple *n physics* a pair of dissimilar metals in an electrolyte with a potential difference between the metals resulting from chemical action

voltaic pile *n* an early form of battery consisting of a pile of paired plates of dissimilar metals, such as zinc and copper, each pair being separated from the next by a pad moistened with an electrolyte

Voltaire (vɒl'tɛə, vəʊl-; *French* vɔltɛr) *n* pseudonym of *François Marie Arouet*. 1694–1778, French writer, whose outspoken belief in religious, political, and social liberty made him the embodiment of the 18th-century Enlightenment. His major works include *Lettres philosophiques* (1734) and the satire *Candide* (1759). He also wrote plays, such as *Zaïre* (1732), poems, and scientific studies. He suffered several periods of banishment for his radical views

voltameter (vɒl'tæmɪtə) *n* a device for measuring electric charge > **voltametric** (ˌvɒltə'mɛtrɪk) *adj*

voltammeter (ˌvəʊlt'æmˌmi:tə) *n* a dual-purpose instrument that can measure both potential difference and electric current, usually in volts and amperes respectively

volt-ampere ('vəʊlt'æmpɛə) *n* the product of the potential in volts across an electrical circuit and the resultant current in amperes

Volta Redonda (*Portuguese* 'vɔltə rə'dõdə) *n* a city in SE Brazil, in Rio de Janeiro state on the Paraíba River: founded in 1941; site of South America's largest steelworks. Pop: 242 773 (2000)

volte-face ('vɒlt'fɑ:s) *n, pl* **volte-face** **1** a reversal, as in opinion **2** a change of position so as to look, lie, etc, in the opposite direction [C19 from F, from It., from *volta* turn + *faccia* face]

voltmeter ('vəʊltˌmi:tə) *n* an instrument for measuring potential difference or electromotive force

Volturno (*Italian* vol'turno) *n* a river in S central Italy, flowing southeast and southwest to the Tyrrhenian Sea: scene of a battle (1860) during the wars for Italian unity, in which Garibaldi defeated the Neapolitans; German line of defence during World War II. Length: 175 km (109 miles)

voluble ('vɒljʊbᵊl) *adj* **1** talking easily and at length **2** *arch* easily turning or rotating **3** *rare* (of a plant) twining or twisting [C16 from L *volūbilis* turning readily, from *volvere* to turn] > ˌ**volu'bility** *or* '**volubleness** *n* > '**volubly** *adv*

volume ('vɒlju:m) *n* **1** the magnitude of the three-dimensional space enclosed within or occupied by an object, geometric solid, etc **2** a large mass or quantity: *the volume of protest* **3** an amount or total: *the volume of exports* **4** fullness of sound **5** the control on a radio, etc, for adjusting the intensity of sound **6** a bound collection of printed or written pages; a book **7** any of several books either bound in an identical format or part of a series **8** the complete set of issues of a periodical over a specified period, esp one year **9** *history* a roll of parchment, etc **10** **speak volumes** to convey much significant information [C14 from OF, from L *volūmen* a roll, from *volvere* to roll up]

volumetric (ˌvɒljʊ'mɛtrɪk) *adj* of, concerning, or using measurement by volume: *volumetric analysis* > ˌ**volu'metrically** *adv*

volumetric analysis *n chem* quantitative analysis of liquids or solutions by comparing the volumes that react with known volumes of standard reagents, usually by titration

voluminous (və'lu:mɪnəs) *adj* **1** of great size, quantity, or extent **2** (of writing) consisting of or sufficient to fill volumes [C17 from LL *volūminōsus* full of windings, from *volūmen* VOLUME] > **voluminosity** (vəˌlu:mɪ'nɒsɪtɪ) *n* > **vo'luminously** *adv*

Völund ('vølʊnd) *n* the Scandinavian name of **Wayland**

voluntarism ('vɒləntəˌrɪzəm) *n* **1** *philosophy* the theory that the will rather than the intellect is the ultimate principle of reality **2** a doctrine or system based on voluntary participation in a course of action **3** another name for **voluntaryism** > '**voluntarist** *n, adj*

voluntary ('vɒləntərɪ) *adj* **1** performed, undertaken, or brought about by free choice or willingly: *a voluntary donation* **2** (of persons) serving or acting in a specified function without compulsion or promise of remuneration: *a voluntary social worker* **3** done by, composed of, or functioning with the aid of volunteers: *a voluntary association* **4** exercising or having the faculty of willing: *a voluntary agent* **5** spontaneous: *voluntary laughter* **6** *law* **6a** acting or done without legal obligation, compulsion, or persuasion **6b** made without payment or recompense: *a voluntary conveyance* **7** (of the muscles of the limbs, neck, etc) having their action controlled by the will **8** maintained by the voluntary actions or contributions of individuals and not by the state: *voluntary schools* ▷ *n, pl* **voluntaries** **9** *music* a composition or improvisation, usually for organ, played at the beginning or end of a church service [C14 from L *voluntārius*, from *voluntās* will, from *velle* to wish] > '**voluntarily** *or* ˌ**volun'tarily** *adv*

voluntary arrangement *n law* a procedure enabling an insolvent company to come to an arrangement with its creditors and resolve its financial problems, often in compliance with a court order

voluntaryism ('vɒləntərɪˌɪzəm) *or* **voluntarism** *n* the principle of supporting churches, schools, and various other institutions by voluntary contributions rather than with state funds > '**voluntaryist** *or* '**voluntarist** *n*

voluntary retailer *n* another name for **symbol retailer**

volunteer (ˌvɒlən'tɪə) *n* **1a** a person who performs or offers to perform voluntary service **1b** (*as modifier*): *a volunteer system* **2** a person who freely undertakes military service **3a** a plant that grows from seed that has not been deliberately sown **3b** (*as modifier*): *a volunteer plant* ▷ *vb* **4** to offer (oneself or one's services) for an undertaking by choice and without request or obligation **5** (*tr*) to perform, give, or communicate voluntarily: *to volunteer help* **6** (*intr*) to enlist voluntarily for military service [C17 from F, from L *voluntārius*; see VOLUNTARY]

voluptuary (və'lʌptjʊərɪ) *n, pl* **voluptuaries** **1** a person devoted to luxury and sensual pleasures ▷ *adj* **2** of or furthering sensual gratification or luxury [C17 from LL *voluptuārius* delightful, from L *voluptās* pleasure]

voluptuous (və'lʌptjʊəs) *adj* **1** relating to, characterized by, or consisting of pleasures of the body or senses **2** devoted or addicted to sensual indulgence or luxurious pleasures **3** sexually alluring, esp through shapeliness or fullness: *a voluptuous woman* [C14 from L *voluptuōsus* full of gratification, from *voluptās* pleasure] > **vo'luptuously** *adv* > **vo'luptuousness** *n*

volute ('vɒlju:t, və'lu:t) *n* **1** a spiral or twisting turn, form, or object **2** Also called: **helix** a carved ornament, esp as used on an Ionic capital, that has the form of a spiral scroll **3** any of the whorls of the spirally coiled shell of a snail or similar gastropod mollusc **4** any of a family of tropical marine gastropod molluscs having a spiral shell with beautiful markings ▷ *adj also* **voluted** (və'lu:tɪd) **5** having the form of a volute; spiral [C17 from L *volūta* spiral decoration, from *volūtus*, from *volvere* to roll up] > **vo'lution** *n*

vomer ('vəʊmə) *n* the thin flat bone forming part of the separation between the nasal passages in mammals [C18 from L: ploughshare]

vomit ('vɒmɪt) *vb* **vomits, vomiting, vomited 1** to eject (the contents of the stomach) through the mouth as the result of involuntary muscular spasms of the stomach and oesophagus **2** to eject or be ejected forcefully ▷ *n* **3** the matter ejected in vomiting **4** the act of vomiting **5** an emetic [C14 from L *vomitāre* to vomit repeatedly, from *vomere* to vomit] > **'vomiter** *n*

vomit comet *n inf* an aircraft that dives suddenly in altitude, simulating freefall, in order to allow astronauts to experience the nausea that can affect people in a gravity-free environment

vomitory ('vɒmɪtərɪ) *adj* **1** Also: **vomitive** ('vɒmɪtɪv) causing vomiting; emetic ▷ *n, pl* **vomitories 2** a vomitory agent **3** Also called: **vomitorium** (ˌvɒmɪ'tɔ:rɪəm) a passage to an entrance or exit in an ancient Roman amphitheatre

von Braun (vɒn 'braʊn, fɒn) *n* **Wernher** ('vɛrnər) 1912–77, US rocket engineer, born in Germany, where he designed the V-2 missile used in World War II. In the US he worked on the Apollo project

von Euler (*German* fɔn 'ɔɪlər) *n* See (Ulf von) **Euler**

von Laue (*German* fɔn 'lauə) *n* See (Max Theodor Felix von) **Laue**

Vonnegut ('vɒnɪgʌt) *n* **Kurt** born 1922, US novelist. His works include *Cat's Cradle* (1963), *Slaughterhouse Five* (1969), *Galapagos* (1985), *Hocus Pocus* (1990), and *Timequake* (1997)

von Otter (*Swedish* fɔn 'otə) *n* **Anne Sophie** born 1955, Swedish mezzo-soprano, noted esp for her lieder recitals

von Rundstedt (*German* fɔn 'rʊntʃtɛt) *n* See (Karl Rudolf Gerd von) **Rundstedt**

von Sternberg (vɒn 'stɜ:nˌbɜ:g; *German* fɔn 'ʃtɛrnbɛrk) *n* **Joseph** ('jo:zɛf), real name *Jonas Sternberg*. 1894–1969, US film director, born in Austria, whose films include *The Blue Angel* (1930), *Blonde Venus* (1932), *The Scarlet Empress* (1934), and the unfinished *I, Claudius* (1937)

von Stroheim (vɒn 'strəʊˌhaɪm, 'ʃtrəʊ-, fɒn) *n* **Erich** ('e:rɪç), real name *Hans Erich Maria Stroheim von Nordenwall*. 1885–1957, US film director and actor, born in Austria, whose films include *Foolish Wives* (1921) and *Greed* (1923)

von Trier (fɔn 'trɪər) *n* **Lars** born 1956, Danish film director and screenwriter, a founder of the Dogme 95 movement; his films include *Europa* (1991), *Breaking the Waves* (1996), *The Idiots* (1998), and *Dancer in the Dark* (2000)

voodoo ('vu:du:) *n, pl* **voodoos 1** Also called: **voodooism** a religious belief system involving witchcraft and communication with ancestral deities, common in Haiti and other Caribbean islands **2** a person who practises voodoo **3** a charm, spell, or fetish involved in voodoo worship ▷ *adj* **4** relating to or associated with voodoo ▷ *vb* **voodoos, voodooing, voodooed 5** (*tr*) to affect by or as if by the power of voodoo [C19 from Louisiana F *voudou*, ult. of West African origin] > **'voodooist** *n*

▷ http://www.religioustolerance.org/voodoo.htm

voorkamer ('fʊəˌkɑ:mə) *n S African* the front room of a house [Afrik., from Du. *voor* fore + *kamer* chamber]

voorskot ('fʊəˌskɒt) *n S African* advance payment made to a farmer for crops ▷ Cf **agterskot** [C20 Afrik., from *voor* before + *skot* shot, payment]

Voortrekker ('fʊəˌtrɛkə) *n* (in South Africa) **1** one of the original Afrikaner settlers of the Transvaal and the Orange Free State who migrated from the Cape Colony in the 1830s **2** a member of the Afrikaner youth movement founded in 1931 [C19 from Du., from *voor-* FORE- + *trekken* to TREK]

▷ www.wikipedia.org/wiki/Voortrekkers

voracious (vɒ'reɪʃəs) *adj* **1** devouring or craving food in great quantities **2** very eager or unremitting in some activity: *voracious reading* [C17 from L *vorāx*, from *vorāre* to devour] > **voracity** (vɒ'ræsɪtɪ) *or* **vo'raciousness** *n*

Vorarlberg (*German* 'fo:rarlbɛrk) *n* a mountainous state of W Austria. Capital: Bregenz. Pop: 351 565 (2001). Area: 2601 sq km (1004 sq miles)

Voronezh (*Russian* va'rɔnɪʃ) *n* a city in W Russia: engineering, chemical, and food-processing industries; university (1918). Pop: 908 000 (1999 est)

Voroshilovgrad (*Russian* vərəʃilaw'grat) *n* the former name (1935–91) of **Lugansk**

Voroshilovsk (*Russian* vəra'ʃiləfsk) *n* the former name (1940–44) of **Stavropol**

-vorous *adj combining form* feeding on or devouring: *carnivorous* [from L *-vorus*; rel. to *vorāre* to swallow up] > **-vore** *n combining form*

Vorster ('fɔ:stə, 'vɔ:-) *n* **Balthazar Johannes,** known as *John*. 1915–83, South African statesman; Nationalist prime minister (1966–78); president (1978)

vortex ('vɔ:tɛks) *n, pl* **vortexes** *or* **vortices** (-tɪˌsi:z) **1** a whirling mass or motion of liquid, gas, flame, etc, such as the spiralling movement of water around a whirlpool **2** any activity or way of life regarded as irresistibly engulfing [C17 from L: a whirlpool] > **vortical** ('vɔ:tɪkᵊl) *adj*

vorticella (ˌvɔ:tɪ'sɛlə) *n, pl* **vorticellae** (-li:) any of a genus of protozoans consisting of a goblet-shaped ciliated cell attached to the substratum by a long contractile stalk [C18 from NL, lit.: a little eddy, from VORTEX]

vorticism ('vɔ:tɪˌsɪzəm) *n* an art movement in England in 1913 by **Wyndham Lewis**, combining the techniques of cubism with the concern for the problems of the machine age evinced in futurism [C20 referring to the "vortices" of modern life on which the movement was based] > **'vorticist** *n*

Vortumnus (vɔ:'tʌmnəs) *n* a variant spelling of **Vertumnus**

Vosges (*French* voʒ) *n* **1** a mountain range in E France, west of the Rhine valley. Highest peak: 1423 m (4672 ft) **2** a department of NE France, in Lorraine region. Capital: Épinal. Pop: 380 952 (1999). Area: 5903 sq km (2302 sq miles)

vostro account ('vɒstrəʊ) *n* a bank account held by a foreign bank with a British bank, usually in sterling ▷ Cf **nostro account**

votary ('vəʊtərɪ) *n, pl* **votaries,** *also* **votarist 1** *RC Church, Eastern Churches* a person, such as a monk or nun, who has dedicated himself or herself to religion by taking vows **2** a devoted adherent of a religion, cause, etc ▷ *adj* **3** ardently devoted to the worship of God or a saint [C16 from L *vōtum* a vow, from *vovēre* to vow] > **'votaress** *fem n*

vote (vəʊt) *n* **1** an indication of choice, opinion, or will on a question, such as the choosing of a candidate: *10 votes for Jones* **2** the opinion of a group of persons as determined by voting: *it was put to the vote* **3** a body of votes or voters collectively: *the Jewish vote* **4** the total number of votes cast **5** the ticket, ballot, etc, by which a vote is expressed **6a** the right to vote; franchise **6b** a person regarded as the embodiment of this right **7** a means of voting, such as a ballot **8** *chiefly Brit* a grant or other proposition to be voted upon ▷ *vb* **votes, voting, voted 9** (when *tr, takes a clause as object or an infinitive*) to express or signify (one's preference or will) (for or against some question, etc): *to vote by ballot* **10** (*intr*) to declare oneself as being (something or in favour of something) by exercising one's vote: *to vote socialist* **11** (*tr; foll by into or out of, etc*) to appoint or elect (a person to or from a particular post): *he was voted out of office* **12** (*tr*) to determine the condition of in a specified way by voting: *the court voted itself out of existence* **13** (*tr*) to authorize or allow by voting: *vote us a rise* **14** (*tr*) *inf* to declare by common opinion: *the party was voted a failure* [C15 from L *vōtum* a solemn promise, from *vovēre* to vow] > **'votable** *or* **'voteable** *adj*

vote down *vb (tr, adv)* to decide against or defeat in a vote: *the bill was voted down*

vote of no confidence *n parliament* a vote on a motion put by the Opposition censuring an aspect of the Government's policy; if the motion is carried the Government is obliged to resign. Also called: **vote of censure**

voter ('vəʊtə) *n* a person who can or does vote

voting machine *n* (esp in the US) a machine at a polling station that voters operate to register their votes and that mechanically or electronically counts all votes cast

votive ('vəʊtɪv) *adj* **1** given or dedicated in fulfilment of or in accordance with a vow **2** *RC Church* having the nature of a voluntary offering: *a votive Mass* [c16 from L *vōtīvus* promised by a vow, from *vōtum* a vow]

vouch (vaʊtʃ) *vb* **1** (*intr;* usually foll by *for*) to give personal assurance: *I'll vouch for his safety* **2** (when *tr, usually takes a clause as object;* when *intr*, usually foll by *for*) to furnish supporting evidence (for) or function as proof (of) **3** (*tr*) *arch* to cite (authors, principles, etc) in support of something [c14 from OF *vocher* to summon, ult. from L *vocāre* to call]

voucher ('vaʊtʃə) *n* **1** a document serving as evidence for some claimed transaction, as the receipt or expenditure of money **2** *Brit* a ticket or card serving as a substitute for cash: *a gift voucher* **3** a person or thing that vouches for the truth of some statement, etc [c16 from Anglo-F, noun use of OF *voucher* to summon; see VOUCH]

vouchsafe (ˌvaʊtʃ'seɪf) *vb* **vouchsafes, vouchsafing, vouchsafed** (*tr*) **1** to give or grant or condescend to give or grant: *she vouchsafed no reply* **2** (*may take a clause as object or an infinitive*) to agree, promise, or permit, often graciously or condescendingly: *he vouchsafed to come yesterday* [c14 *vouchen sauf;* see VOUCH, SAFE]

voussoir (vuː'swɑː) *n* a wedge-shaped stone or brick that is used with others to construct an arch or vault [c18 from F, from Vulgar L *volsōrium* (unattested), ult. from L *volvere* to turn, roll]

vow (vaʊ) *n* **1** a solemn or earnest pledge or promise binding the person making it to perform a specified act or behave in a certain way **2** a solemn promise made to a deity or saint, by which the promiser pledges himself to some future act or way of life **3** **take vows** to enter a religious order and commit oneself to its rule of life by the vows of poverty, chastity, and obedience ▷ *vb* **4** (*tr; may take a clause as object or an infinitive*) to pledge, promise, or undertake solemnly: *he vowed to return* **5** (*tr*) to dedicate or consecrate to God or a saint **6** (*tr; usually takes a clause as object*) to assert or swear emphatically **7** (*intr*) *arch* to declare solemnly [c13 from OF *vou*, from L *vōtum*; see VOTE] > **'vower** *n*

vowel ('vaʊəl) *n* **1** *phonetics* a voiced speech sound whose articulation is characterized by the absence of obstruction in the vocal tract, allowing the breath stream free passage. The timbre of a vowel is chiefly determined by the position of the tongue and the lips **2** a letter or character representing a vowel [c14 from OF, from L *vocālis littera* vowel, from *vocālis*, from *vox* voice] > **'vowel-ˌlike** *adj*

vowel gradation *n* another name for **ablaut**. See **gradation** (sense 5)

vowelize *or* **vowelise** ('vaʊəˌlaɪz) *vb* **vowelizes, vowelizing, vowelized** *or* **vowelises, vowelising, vowelised** (*tr*) to mark the vowel points in (a Hebrew word or text) > **ˌvoweli'zation** *or* **ˌvoweli'sation** *n*

vowel mutation *n* another name for **umlaut**

vowel point *n* any of several marks or points placed above or below consonants, esp those evolved for Hebrew or Arabic, in order to indicate vowel sounds

vox (vɒks) *n, pl* **voces** a voice or sound [L: voice]

vox pop *n* interviews with members of the public on a radio or television programme [c20 shortened from vox POPULI]

vox populi ('pɒpjʊˌlaɪ) *n* the voice of the people; popular or public opinion [L]

voyage ('vɔɪɪdʒ) *n* **1** a journey, travel, or passage, esp one to a distant land or by sea or air ▷ *vb* **voyages, voyaging, voyaged** **2** to travel over or traverse (something): *we will voyage to Africa* [c13 from OF *veiage*, from L *viāticum* provision for travelling, from *via* way] > **'voyager** *n*

voyage charter *n* the hire of a ship or aircraft for a specific number of voyages ▷ Cf **time charter**

voyageur (ˌvɔɪə'dʒɜː) *n* (in Canada) a woodsman, guide, trapper, boatman, or explorer, esp in the North [c19 F: traveller, from *voyager* to VOYAGE]

voyeur (vwaɪ'ɜː) *n* a person who obtains sexual pleasure from the observation of people undressing, having intercourse, etc [c20 F, lit.: one who sees, from *voir* to see, from L *vidēre*] > **vo'yeurism** *n* > **ˌvoyeur'istic** *adj*

VP *abbrev for:* **1** verb phrase **2** Vice President

VPL *jocular abbrev for:* visible panty line

VR *abbrev for:* **1** variant reading **2** Victoria Regina [L: Queen Victoria] **3** virtual reality

V. Rev. *abbrev for* Very Reverend

Vries (vriːs) *n* See (Hugo) **De Vries**

vrou (frəʊ) *n S African* an Afrikaner woman, esp a married woman [from Afrik., from Du.]

vrystater ('freɪˌstɑːtə) *n S African* a native inhabitant of the Free State, esp one who is White [from Afrik., from Du. *vrij* free + *staat* state]

vs *abbrev for* versus

VS *abbrev for* Veterinary Surgeon

v.s. *abbrev for* vide supra (see **vide**)

V-sign *n* **1** (in Britain) an offensive gesture made by sticking up the index and middle fingers with the palm of the hand inwards **2** a similar gesture with the palm outwards meaning victory or peace

VSO *abbrev for:* **1** very superior old: used to indicate that a brandy, port, etc, is between 12 and 17 years old **2** (in Britain) Voluntary Service Overseas: an organization that sends young volunteers to use and teach their skills in developing countries

VSOP *abbrev for* very special (*or* superior) old pale: used to indicate that a brandy, port, etc, is between 20 and 25 years old

Vt. *or* **VT** *abbrev for* Vermont

VTOL ('viːtɒl) *n* vertical takeoff and landing; a system in which an aircraft can take off and land vertically ▷ Cf **STOL**

VTR *abbrev for* video tape recorder

V-type engine *n* a type of internal-combustion engine having two cylinder blocks attached to a single crankcase, the angle between the two blocks forming a V

Vuelta Abajo (*Spanish* 'bwelta a'βaxo) *n* a region of W Cuba: famous for its tobacco

vug (vʌg) *n mining* a small cavity in a rock or vein, usually lined with crystals [c19 from Cornish *vooga* cave] > **'vuggy** *adj*

Vuillard (*French* vɥijar) *n* **Jean Édouard** (ʒɑ̃ edwar) 1868–1940, French painter and lithographer

Vulcan ('vʌlkən) *n* the Roman god of fire and metalworking. Greek counterpart: **Hephaestus** > **Vulcanian** (vʌl'keɪnɪən) *adj*

vulcanian (vʌl'keɪnɪən) *adj geol* of or relating to a volcanic eruption characterized by the explosive discharge of fine ash and large irregular fragments of solidified or viscous lava [c17 after VULCAN]

vulcanism ('vʌlkəˌnɪzəm) *n* a variant spelling of **volcanism**

vulcanite ('vʌlkəˌnaɪt) *n* a hard usually black rubber produced by vulcanizing natural rubber with sulphur. It is used for electrical insulators, etc. Also called: **ebonite**

vulcanize *or* **vulcanise** ('vʌlkəˌnaɪz) *vb* **vulcanizes, vulcanizing, vulcanized** *or* **vulcanises, vulcanising, vulcanised** (*tr*) **1** to treat (rubber) with sulphur under heat and pressure to improve elasticity and strength or to produce a hard substance such as vulcanite **2** to treat (substances other than rubber) by a similar process in order to improve their properties > ˌ**vulcaniˈzation** *or* ˌ**vulcaniˈsation** *n*
vulcanology (ˌvʌlkəˈnɒlədʒɪ) *n* a variant spelling of **volcanology**
Vulg. *abbrev for* Vulgate
vulgar ('vʌlgə) *adj* **1** marked by lack of taste, culture, delicacy, manners, etc: *vulgar language; vulgar behaviour* **2** (*often cap; usually prenominal*) denoting a form of a language, esp of Latin, current among common people, esp at a period when the formal language is archaic **3** *arch* of or current among the great mass of common people [c14 from L *vulgāris*, from *vulgus* the common people] > '**vulgarly** *adv*
vulgar fraction *n* another name for **simple fraction**
vulgarian (vʌl'gɛərɪən) *n* a vulgar person, esp one who is rich or has pretensions to good taste
vulgarism ('vʌlgəˌrɪzəm) *n* **1** a coarse, crude, or obscene expression **2** a word or phrase found only in the vulgar form of a language
vulgarity (vʌl'gærɪtɪ) *n, pl* **vulgarities 1** the condition of being vulgar; lack of good manners **2** a vulgar action, phrase, etc
vulgarize *or* **vulgarise** ('vʌlgəˌraɪz) *vb* **vulgarizes, vulgarizing, vulgarized** *or* **vulgarises, vulgarising, vulgarised** (*tr*) **1** to make commonplace or vulgar **2** to make (something little known or difficult to understand) widely known or popular among the public > ˌ**vulgariˈzation** *or* ˌ**vulgariˈsation** *n*
Vulgar Latin *n* any of the dialects of Latin spoken in the Roman Empire other than classical Latin
vulgate ('vʌlgeɪt, -gɪt) *n rare* **1** a commonly recognized text or version **2** the vernacular
Vulgate ('vʌlgeɪt, -gɪt) *n* **a** (from the 13th century onwards) the fourth-century Latin version of the Bible produced by Jerome **b** (*as modifier*): *the Vulgate version* [c17 from Med. L, from LL *vulgāta editiō* popular version (of the Bible), from L *vulgāre* to make common]
vulnerable ('vʌlnərəbᵊl) *adj* **1** capable of being physically or emotionally wounded or hurt **2** open to temptation, censure, etc **3** *mil* exposed to attack **4** *bridge* (of a side who have won one game towards rubber) subject to increased bonuses or penalties [c17 from LL, from L *vulnerāre* to wound, from *vulnus* a wound] > ˌ**vulneraˈbility** *n* > '**vulnerably** *adv*
vulnerary ('vʌlnərərɪ) *med* ▷ *adj* **1** of or used to heal a wound ▷ *n, pl* **vulneraries 2** a vulnerary drug or agent [c16 from L *vulnerārius* from *vulnus* wound]
vulpine ('vʌlpaɪn) *adj* **1** of, relating to, or resembling a fox **2** crafty, clever, etc [c17 from L *vulpīnus* foxlike, from *vulpēs* fox]
vulture ('vʌltʃə) *n* **1** any of various very large diurnal birds of prey of Africa, Asia, and warm parts of Europe, typically having broad wings and soaring flight and feeding on carrion **2** any similar bird of North, Central, and South America **3** a person or thing that preys greedily and ruthlessly on others, esp the helpless [c14 from OF *voltour*, from L *vultur*] > **vulturine** ('vʌltʃəˌraɪn) *or* '**vulturous** *adj*
vulva ('vʌlvə) *n, pl* **vulvae** (-viː) *or* **vulvas** the external genitals of human females, including the labia, mons veneris, clitoris, and the vaginal orifice [c16 from L: covering, womb, matrix] > '**vulvar** *adj*
vulvitis (vʌl'vaɪtɪs) *n* inflammation of the vulva
vv *abbrev for* vice versa
Vyatka (*Russian* 'vjatkə) *n* the former name (1780–1934) of **Kirov**
Vyborg (*Russian* 'vibərk) *n* a port in NW Russia, at the head of **Vyborg Bay** (an inlet of the Gulf of Finland): belonged to Finland (1918–40). Pop: 80 000 (latest est). Finnish name: **Viipuri** Swedish name: **Viborg**
Vyshinsky *or* **Vishinsky** (*Russian* vi'ʃinskij) *n* **Andrei Yanuaryevich** (an'drjej jənu'arjɪvitʃ) 1883–1954, Soviet statesman; foreign minister (1949–53). He was public prosecutor (1935–38) at the Stalin show trials.

Ww

w *or* **W** ('dʌbᵊl,juː) *n, pl* **w's, W's,** *or* **Ws** **1** the 23rd letter of the English alphabet **2** a speech sound represented by this letter, usually a bilabial semivowel, as in *web*

W *symbol for:* **1** *chem* tungsten [from NL *wolframium*, from G *Wolfram*] **2** watt **3** West **4** women's (size) **5** *physics* work

W8 *text messaging abbrev for* wait

w. *abbrev for:* **1** week **2** weight **3** *cricket* **3a** wide **3b** wicket **4** width **5** wife **6** with

W. *abbrev for:* **1** Wales **2** Welsh

WA *abbrev for:* **1** Washington (state) **2** Western Australia

WAAAF (formerly) *abbrev for* Women's Auxiliary Australian Air Force

WAAC (wæk) *n* (formerly) **1** *acronym for* Women's Army Auxiliary Corps **2** Also called: **Waac** a member of this corps

Waadt (vat) *n* the German name for **Vaud**

WAAF (wæf) *n* (formerly) **1** *acronym for* Women's Auxiliary Air Force **2** Also called: **Waaf** a member of this force

Waal (*Dutch* waːl) *n* a river in the central Netherlands: the S branch of the Lower Rhine. Length: 84 km (52 miles)

Wabash ('wɔːbæʃ) *n* a river in the E central US, rising in W Ohio and flowing west and southwest to join the Ohio River in Indiana. Length: 764 km (475 miles)

wabble ('wɒbᵊl) *vb* **wabbles, wabbling, wabbled,** *n* a variant spelling of **wobble**

Wace (weɪs) *n* **Robert** born ?1100, Anglo-Norman poet; author of the *Roman de Brut* and *Roman de Rou*

wacke ('wækə) *n obs* any of various soft earthy rocks derived from basalt [C18 from G: rock, gravel, basalt]

wacko ('wækəʊ) *inf* ▷ *adj* **1** mad or eccentric ▷ *n, pl* **wackos** **2** a mad or eccentric person [C20 back formation from WACKY]

wacky ('wækɪ) *adj* **wackier, wackiest** *sl* eccentric or unpredictable [C19 (in dialect sense: a fool): from WHACK (hence, a *whacky*, a person who behaves as if he had been whacked on the head)] > '**wackily** *adv* > '**wackiness** *n*

wad (wɒd) *n* **1** a small mass or ball of fibrous or soft material, such as cotton wool, used esp for packing or stuffing **2a** a plug of paper, cloth, leather, etc, pressed against a charge to hold it in place in a muzzle-loading cannon **2b** a disc of paper, felt, etc, used to hold in place the powder and shot in a shotgun cartridge **3** a roll or bundle of something, esp of banknotes ▷ *vb* **wads, wadding, wadded** **4** to form (something) into a wad **5** (*tr*) to roll into a wad or bundle **6** (*tr*) **6a** to hold (a charge) in place with a wad **6b** to insert a wad into (a gun) **7** (*tr*) to pack or stuff with wadding [C14 from LL *wadda*]

Wadai (wɑː'daɪ) *n* a former independent sultanate of NE central Africa: now the E part of Chad

Waddenzee (*Dutch* 'wɑdənzeː) *n* the part of the North Sea between the Dutch mainland and the West Frisian Islands

wadding ('wɒdɪŋ) *n* **1a** any fibrous or soft substance used as padding, stuffing, etc **1b** a piece of this **2** material for wads used in cartridges or guns

waddle ('wɒdᵊl) *vb* **waddles, waddling, waddled** (*intr*) **1** to walk with short steps, rocking slightly from side to side ▷ *n* **2** a swaying gait or motion [C16 prob. frequentative of WADE] > '**waddler** *n* > '**waddling** *adj*

waddy ('wɒdɪ) *n, pl* **waddies** **1** a heavy wooden club used as a weapon by native Australians ▷ *vb* **waddies, waddying, waddied** **2** (*tr*) to hit with a waddy [C19 from Abor., ? based on E WOOD]

wade (weɪd) *vb* **wades, wading, waded** **1** to walk with the feet immersed in (water, a stream, etc) **2** (*intr*; often foll by *through*) to proceed with difficulty: *to wade through a book* **3** (*intr*; foll by *in* or *into*) to attack energetically ▷ *n*

4 the act or an instance of wading [OE *wadan*] > '**wadable** *or* '**wadeable** *adj*

wader ('weɪdə) *n* **1** a person or thing that wades **2** Also called: **wading bird** any of various long-legged birds, esp herons, storks, etc, that live near water and feed on fish, etc **3** a Brit name for **shore bird**

waders ('weɪdəz) *pl n* long waterproof boots, sometimes extending to the chest like trousers, worn by anglers

wadi *or* **wady** ('wɒdɪ) *n, pl* **wadies** a watercourse in N Africa and Arabia, dry except in the rainy season [c19 from Ar.]

Wadi Halfa ('wɒdɪ 'hælfə) *n* a town in the N Sudan that was partly submerged by Lake Nasser: an important archaeological site

Wad Medani (wɑːd mɪ'dɑːniː) *n* a town in the E Sudan, on the Blue Nile: headquarters of the Gezira irrigation scheme; agricultural research centre. Pop: 218 714 (1993)

wafer ('weɪfə) *n* **1** a thin crisp sweetened biscuit, served with ice cream, etc **2** *Christianity* a thin disc of unleavened bread used in the Eucharist **3** *pharmacol* an envelope of rice paper enclosing a medicament **4** *electronics* a large single crystal of semiconductor material, such as silicon, on which numerous integrated circuits are manufactured and then separated **5** a small thin disc of adhesive material used to seal letters, etc ▷ *vb* **6** (*tr*) to seal or fasten with a wafer [c14 from OF *waufre*, from MLow G *wāfel*] > '**wafery** *adj*

waffle[1] ('wɒfᵊl) *n* **a** a crisp golden-brown pancake with deep indentations on both sides **b** (*as modifier*): *waffle iron* [c19 from Du. *wafel* (earlier *wæfel*), of Gmc origin]

waffle[2] ('wɒfᵊl) *inf, chiefly Brit* ▷ *vb* **waffles, waffling, waffled** **1** (*intr*; often foll by *on*) to speak or write in a vague and wordy manner ▷ *n* **2** vague and wordy speech or writing [c19 from ?] > '**waffling** *adj, n*

waft (wɑːft, wɒft) *vb* **1** to carry or be carried gently on or as if on the air or water ▷ *n* **2** the act or an instance of wafting **3** something, such as a scent, carried on the air **4** *naut* (formerly) a signal flag hoisted furled to signify various messages depending on where it was flown [c16 (in obs. sense: to convey by ship): back formation from c15 *wafter* a convoy vessel, from MDu. *wachter* guard]

wag[1] (wæg) *vb* **wags, wagging, wagged** **1** to move or cause to move rapidly and repeatedly from side to side or up and down **2** to move (the tongue) or (of the tongue) to be moved rapidly in talking, esp in gossip **3** to move (the finger) or (of the finger) to be moved from side to side, in or as in admonition **4** *sl* to play truant (esp in **wag it**) ▷ *n* **5** the act or an instance of wagging [c13 from OE *wagian* to shake]

wag[2] (wæg) *n* a humorous or jocular person; wit [c16 from ?] > '**waggish** *adj*

wage (weɪdʒ) *n* **1** (*often pl*) payment in return for work or services, esp that made to workers on a daily, hourly, weekly, or piecework basis ▷ Cf **salary** **2** (*pl*) *econ* the portion of the national income accruing to labour as earned income, as contrasted with the unearned income accruing to capital in the form of rent, interest, and dividends **3** (*often pl*) recompense, return, or yield ▷ *vb* **wages, waging, waged** (*tr*) **4** to engage in [c14 from OF *wagier* to pledge, from *wage*, of Gmc origin] > '**wageless** *adj*

wage differential *n* the difference in wages between workers with different skills in the same industry or between those with comparable skills in different industries or localities

wage earner *n* **1** a person who works for wages **2** the person who earns money to support a household by working

wage freeze *n* a statutory restriction on wage increases

wage indexation *n* a linking of wage rises to increases in the cost of living usually in order to maintain real wages during periods of high inflation

wager ('weɪdʒə) *n* **1** an agreement to pay an amount of money as a result of the outcome of an unsettled matter **2** an amount staked on the outcome of such an event **3** **wager of battle** (in medieval Britain) a pledge to do battle to decide guilt or innocence by single combat **4** **wager of law** *English legal history* a form of trial in which the accused offered to make oath of his innocence, supported by the oaths of 11 of his neighbours declaring their belief in his statements ▷ *vb* **5** (*when tr, may take a clause as object*) to risk or bet (something) on the outcome of an unsettled matter [c14 from Anglo-F *wageure* a pledge, from OF *wagier* to pledge; see WAGE] > '**wagerer** *n*

wage slave *n* *ironical* a person dependent on a wage or salary

wagga ('wɒgə) *n* *Austral* a blanket or bed covering of sacks stitched together [c19 after WAGGA WAGGA]

Wagga Wagga ('wɒgə 'wɒgə) *n* a city in SE Australia, in New South Wales on the Murrumbidgee River: agricultural trading centre. Pop: 50 380 (latest est)

waggle ('wægᵊl) *vb* **waggles, waggling, waggled** **1** to move or cause to move with a rapid shaking or wobbling motion ▷ *n* **2** a rapid shaking or wobbling motion [c16 from WAG[1]] > '**waggly** *adj*

waggon ('wægən) *n* a variant spelling (esp Brit) of **wagon**

wag-n-bietjie ('vɑːxᵊn,bɪkɪ) *n* *S African* any of various thorn bushes or trees [from Afrik. *wag* wait + *n* a + *bietjie* bit]

Wagner ('vɑːgnə) *n* **1** **Otto** 1841–1918, Austrian architect, whose emphasis on function and structure in such buildings as the Post Office Savings Bank, Vienna (1904–06), influenced the development of modern architecture **2** **(Wilhelm) Richard** ('rɪçart) 1813–83, German romantic composer noted chiefly for his invention of the music drama. His cycle of four such dramas *The Ring of the Nibelung* was produced at his own theatre in Bayreuth in 1876. His other operas include *Tannhäuser* (1845; revised 1861), *Tristan and Isolde* (1865), and *Parsifal* (1882)

Wagnerian (vɑːg'nɪərɪən) *adj* **1** of or suggestive of the dramatic musical compositions of Richard Wagner, their massive scale, dramatic and emotional intensity, etc ▷ *n also* **Wagnerite** ('vɑːgnə,raɪt) **2** a follower or disciple of the music or theories of Richard Wagner

Wagner-Jauregg (*German* 'vagnər'jaurɛk) *n* **Julius** 1857–1940, Austrian psychiatrist and neurologist; a pioneer of the use of fever therapy in the treatment of mental disorders. Nobel prize for physiology or medicine 1927

wagon *or* **waggon** ('wægən) *n* **1** any of various types of wheeled vehicles, ranging from carts to lorries, esp a vehicle with four wheels drawn by a horse, tractor, etc, and used for carrying heavy loads **2** *Brit* a railway freight truck, esp an open one **3** an obsolete word for **chariot** **4** **on** (*or* **off**) **the wagon** *inf* abstaining (*or* no longer abstaining) from alcohol [c16 from Du. *wagen* WAIN] > '**wagonless** *or* '**waggonless** *adj*

wagoner *or* **waggoner** ('wægənə) *n* a person who drives a wagon

wagonette *or* **waggonette** (,wægə'nɛt) *n* a light four-wheeled horse-drawn vehicle with two lengthwise seats facing each other behind a crosswise driver's seat

wagon-lit (*French* vagɔ̃li) *n, pl* **wagons-lits** (vagɔ̃li) **1** a sleeping car on a European railway **2** a compartment on such a car [c19 from F, from *wagon* railway coach + *lit* bed]

wagonload *or* **waggonload** ('wægən,ləʊd) *n* the load that is or can be carried by a wagon

wagon train *n* a supply train of horses and wagons, esp one going over rough terrain

wagon vault *n* another name for **barrel vault**

Wagram (*German* 'vaːgram) *n* a village in NE Austria: scene of the defeat of the Austrians by Napoleon in 1809

wagtail ('wæg,teɪl) *n* any of various passerine songbirds of Eurasia and Africa, having a very long tail that wags when the bird walks

Wahhabi *or* **Wahabi** (wəˈhɑːbɪ) *n, pl* **Wahhabis** *or* **Wahabis** a member of a strictly conservative Muslim sect founded in the 18th century > **Wahˈhabism** *or* **Waˈhabism** *n*

wahine (wɑːˈhiːnɪ) *n* **1** NZ a Maori woman **2** a Polynesian woman [from Maori & Hawaiian]

wahoo (wɑːˈhuː, ˈwɑːhuː) *n, pl* **wahoos** a large fast-moving food and game fish of tropical seas [from ?]

wah-wah (ˈwɑːˌwɑː) *n* **1** the sound made by a trumpet, cornet, etc, when the bell is alternately covered and uncovered **2** an electronic attachment for an electric guitar, etc, that simulates this effect [c20 imit.]

waif (weɪf) *n* **1** a person, esp a child, who is homeless, friendless, or neglected **2** anything found and not claimed, the owner being unknown [c14 from Anglo-Norman, var. of OF *gaif*, from ON] > **ˈwaif,like** *adj*

Waikaremoana (waɪˈkɒrəməʊˌɑːnə) *n* **Lake** a lake in the North Island of New Zealand in a dense bush setting. Area: about 55 sq km (21 sq miles)

Waikato (ˈwaɪˌkɑːtəʊ) *n* the longest river in New Zealand, flowing northwest across North Island to the Tasman Sea. Length: 350 km (220 miles)

▷ www.waikatodistrict.govt.nz
▷ www.waikatonz.co.nz

Waikiki (ˈwaɪkɪˌkiː, ˌwaɪkɪˈkiː) *n* a resort area in Hawaii, on SE Oahu: a suburb of Honolulu

wail (weɪl) *vb* **1** (*intr*) to utter a prolonged high-pitched cry, as of grief or misery **2** (*intr*) to make a sound resembling such a cry: *the wind wailed in the trees* **3** (*tr*) to lament, esp with mournful sounds ▷ *n* **4** a prolonged high-pitched mournful cry or sound [c14 from ON] > **ˈwailer** *n*

Wailing Wall *n* another name for **Western Wall**

wain (weɪn) *n chiefly poetic* a farm wagon or cart [OE *wægn*]

wainscot (ˈweɪnskət) *n* **1** Also called: **wainscoting** *or* **wainscotting** a lining applied to the walls of a room, esp one of wood panelling **2** the lower part of the walls of a room, esp when finished in a material different from the upper part **3** fine-quality oak used as wainscot ▷ *vb* **4** (*tr*) to line (a wall of a room) with a wainscot [c14 from MLow G *wagenschot*, ?from *wagen* WAGON + *schot* planking]

wainwright (ˈweɪnˌraɪt) *n* a person who makes wagons

waist (weɪst) *n* **1** *anat* the constricted part of the trunk between the ribs and hips **2** the part of a garment covering the waist **3** the middle part of an object that resembles the waist in narrowness or position **4** the middle part of a ship **5** the middle section of an aircraft fuselage **6** the constriction between the thorax and abdomen in wasps and similar insects [c14 from ?] > **ˈwaistless** *adj*

waistband (ˈweɪstˌbænd) *n* an encircling band of material to finish and strengthen a skirt or trousers at the waist

waistcoat (ˈweɪsˌkəʊt) *n* **1** a man's sleeveless waistlength garment worn under a suit jacket, usually buttoning up the front **2** a similar garment worn by women ▷ US and Canad name: **vest** > **ˈwaist,coated** *adj*

waistline (ˈweɪstˌlaɪn) *n* **1** a line around the body at the narrowest part of the waist **2** the intersection of the bodice and the skirt of a dress, etc, or the level of this

wait (weɪt) *vb* **1** (when *intr*, often foll by *for*, *until*, or *to*) to stay in one place or remain inactive in expectation (of something) **2** to delay temporarily or be temporarily delayed: *that work can wait* **3** (when *intr*, usually foll by *for*) (of things) to be ready or at hand; be in store (for a person): *supper was waiting for them when they got home* **4** (*intr*) to act as a waiter or waitress ▷ *n* **5** the act or an instance of waiting **6** a period of waiting **7** (*pl*) *rare* a band of musicians who go around the streets, esp at Christmas, singing and playing carols **8** **lie in wait** to prepare an ambush (for someone) ▷ See also **wait on**, **wait up** [c12 from OF *waitier*; rel. to OHG *wahtēn*]

wait-a-bit *n* any of various mainly tropical plants having sharp hooked thorns

Waitangi Day (waɪˈtʌŋiː) *n* the national day of New Zealand (Feb 6), commemorating the signing of the **Treaty of Waitangi** (1840) by Maori chiefs and a representative of the British Government. The treaty provided the basis for the British annexation of New Zealand

▷ www.archives.govt.nz/holdings/treaty_frame.html
▷ www.waitangi.com

waiter (ˈweɪtə) *n* **1** a man whose occupation is to serve at table, as in a restaurant **2** an attendant at the London stock exchange or Lloyd's who carries messages: the modern equivalent of waiters who performed these duties in the 17th-century London coffee houses in which these institutions originated **3** a person who waits **4** a tray or salver

waiting game *n* the postponement of action or decision in order to gain the advantage

waiting list *n* a list of people waiting to obtain some object, treatment, status, etc

waiting room *n* a room in which people may wait, as at a railway station, doctor's or dentist's surgery, etc

wait on *vb* (*intr, prep*) **1** to serve at the table of **2** to act as an attendant to ▷ *sentence substitute* **3** *Austral & NZ* stop! hold on! ▷ Also (for senses 1, 2): **wait upon**

waitress (ˈweɪtrɪs) *n* **1** a woman who serves at table, as in a restaurant ▷ *vb* (*intr*) **2** to act as a waitress

wait up *vb* (*intr, adv*) to delay going to bed in order to await some event

waive (weɪv) *vb* **waives, waiving, waived** (*tr*) **1** to set aside or relinquish: *to waive one's rights* **2** to refrain from enforcing or applying (a law, penalty, etc) **3** to defer [c13 from OF *weyver*, from *waif* abandoned; see WAIF]

waiver (ˈweɪvə) *n* **1** the voluntary relinquishment, expressly or by implication, of some claim or right **2** the act or an instance of relinquishing a claim or right **3** a formal statement in writing of such relinquishment [c17 from OF *weyver* to relinquish]

Wajda (*Polish* ˈvajda) *n* **Andrei** or **Andrzej** (ˈandʒɛj) born 1926, Polish film director. His films include *Ashes and Diamonds* (1958), *The Wedding* (1972), *Man of Iron* (1980), *Danton* (1982), and *Miss Nobody* (1997)

Wakayama (ˌwækəˈjɑːmə) *n* an industrial city in S Japan, on S Honshu. Pop: 393 951 (1995)

wake[1] (weɪk) *vb* **wakes, waking, woke, woken** **1** (often foll by *up*) to rouse or become roused from sleep **2** (often foll by *up*) to rouse or become roused from inactivity **3** (*intr*; often foll by *to* or *up to*) to become conscious or aware: *at last he woke up to the situation* **4** (*intr*) to be or remain awake **5** (*tr*) to arouse (feelings, etc) ▷ *n* **6** a watch or vigil held over the body of a dead person during the night before burial **7** (in Ireland) festivities held after a funeral **8** the patronal or dedication festival of English parish churches **9** a solemn or ceremonial vigil **10** (*usually pl*) an annual holiday in various towns in Northern England, when the local factories close [OE *wacian*] > **ˈwaker** *n*

> USAGE Where there is an object and the sense is the literal one *wake (up)* and *waken* are the commonest forms: *I wakened him*; *I woke him (up)*. Both verbs are also commonly used without an object: *I woke up*. *Awake* and *awaken* are preferred to other forms of *wake* where the sense is a figurative one: *he awoke to the danger*

wake[2] (weɪk) *n* **1** the waves or track left by a vessel or other object moving through water **2** the track or path left by anything that has passed: *wrecked houses in the wake of the hurricane* [c16 of Scand. origin]

wakeboarding (ˈweɪkˌbɔːdɪŋ) *n* the sport of riding over water on a short surfboard and performing stunts while

holding a rope towed by a speedboat
Wakefield ('weɪk,fiːld) *n* **1** a city in N England, in Wakefield unitary authority, West Yorkshire: important since medieval times as an agricultural and textile centre. Pop: 73 955 (1991) **2** a unitary authority in N England, in West Yorkshire. Pop: 315 173 (2001). Area: 333 sq km (129 sq miles)
wakeful ('weɪkfʊl) *adj* **1** unable or unwilling to sleep **2** sleepless **3** alert > '**wakefully** *adv* > '**wakefulness** *n*
Wake Island *n* an atoll in the N central Pacific: claimed by the US in 1899; developed as a civil and naval air station in the late 1930s. Area: 8 sq km (3 sq miles)
wakeless ('weɪklɪs) *adj* (of sleep) unbroken
waken ('weɪkən) *vb* to rouse or be roused from sleep or some other inactive state.
USAGE See at **wake**
wake-robin *n* any of a genus of North American herbaceous plants having a whorl of three leaves and three-petalled solitary flowers
wake-up *n* **a wake-up to** *Austral sl* fully alert to (a person, thing, action, etc)
wake-up call *n* **1** a telephone call that wakes a person from sleep **2** an event that alerts people to a danger or difficulty
Waksman ('wæksmən) *n* **Selman Abraham** 1888–1973, US microbiologist, born in Russia. He discovered streptomycin: Nobel prize for physiology or medicine 1952
Walachia *or* **Wallachia** (wɒ'leɪkɪə) *n* a former principality of SE Europe: a vassal state of the Ottoman Empire from the 15th century until its union with Moldavia in 1859, subsequently forming present-day Romania > **Wa'lachian** *or* **Wal'lachian** *n, adj*
Wałbrzych (*Polish* 'vaubʒix) *n* an industrial city in SW Poland. Pop: 136 923 (1999 est). German name: **Waldenburg**
Walcheren (*Dutch* 'walxərə) *n* an island in the SW Netherlands, in the Scheldt estuary: administratively part of Zeeland province; suffered severely in World War II, when the dykes were breached, and again in the floods of 1953. Area: 212 sq km (82 sq miles)
Walcott ('wɔːlkət) *n* **1 Derek (Alton)** born 1930, St Lucian poet and playwright, whose works include the poetry collections *In a Green Night* (1962) and *The Bounty* (1997), the play *The Dream on Monkey Mountain* (1967), and the long poem *Omeros* (1990): Nobel prize for literature 1992 **2 Jersey Joe,** real name *Arnold Raymond Cream*. 1914–94, US boxer: world heavyweight champion 1951–52
Waldemar I *or* **Valdemar I** ('vældɪ,mɑː) *n* known as *Waldemar the Great*. 1131–82, king of Denmark (1157–82). He conquered the Wends (1169), increased the territory of Denmark, and established the hereditary rule of his line
Waldenburg ('valdənbʊrk) *n* the German name for **Wałbrzych**
Waldenses (wɒl'dɛnsiːz) *pl n* the members of a small sect founded as a reform movement within the Roman Catholic Church by Peter Waldo, a merchant of Lyons, in the late 12th century > **Wal'densian** *n, adj*
waldo ('wɔːldəʊ) *n, pl* **waldos, waldoes** a gadget for manipulating objects by remote control [C20 after *Waldo F. Jones*, an inventor, in a science-fiction story by Robert Heinlein]
Waldorf salad ('wɔːldɔːf) *n* a salad of diced apples, celery, and walnuts mixed with mayonnaise
waldsterben ('wɔːld,stɜːbən) *n ecology* the symptoms of tree decline in central Europe from the 1970s, considered to be caused by atmospheric pollution [C20 from G *Wald* forest + *sterben* to die]
wale (weɪl) *n* **1** the raised mark left on the skin after the stroke of a rod or whip **2** the weave or texture of a fabric, such as the ribs in corduroy **3** *naut* a ridge of planking along the rail of a ship ▷ *vb* **wales, waling, waled 4** (*tr*) to raise a wale or wales on by striking **5** to weave with a wale [OE *walu* weal; rel. to ON *vala* knuckle]
Wales (weɪlz) *n* a principality that is part of the United Kingdom, in the west of Great Britain; conquered by the English in 1282; parliamentary union with England took place in 1536: a separate Welsh Assembly with limited powers was established in 1999. Wales consists mainly of moorlands and mountains and has an economy that is chiefly agricultural, with an industrial and former coal-mining area in the south. Capital: Cardiff. Pop: 2 903 085 (2001). Area: 20 768 sq km (8017 sq miles). Welsh name: **Cymru** Medieval Latin name: **Cambria**
▷ www.wales.gov.uk
▷ www.visitwales.com
Wałęsa (va'wɛnsa) *n* **Lech** (lɛx) born 1943, Polish statesman; president (1990–95); leader of the independent trade union Solidarity (1980–90); Nobel peace prize 1983
Walhalla (wæl'hælə, væl-) *or* **Walhall** (wæl'hæl, væl-) *n* variants of **Valhalla**
walk (wɔːk) *vb* **1** (*intr*) to move along or travel on foot at a moderate rate; advance in such a manner that at least one foot is always on the ground **2** (*tr*) to pass through, on, or over on foot, esp habitually **3** (*tr*) to cause, assist, or force to move along at a moderate rate: *to walk a dog* **4** (*tr*) to escort or conduct by walking: *to walk someone home* **5** (*intr*) (of ghosts, spirits, etc) to appear or move about in visible form **6** (*intr*) to follow a certain course or way of life: *to walk in misery* **7** (*tr*) to bring into a certain condition by walking: *I walked my shoes to shreds* **8** to disappear or be stolen: *Where's my pencil? It seems to have walked* **9 walk it** to win easily **10 walk on air** to be delighted or exhilarated **11 walk tall** *inf* to have self-respect or pride **12 walk the streets 12a** to be a prostitute **12b** to wander round a town, esp when looking for work or when homeless **13 walk the walk** to put theory into practice; often used in combination with the expression *talk the talk*. See also **talk** (sense 15) ▷ *n* **14** the act or an instance of walking **15** the distance or extent walked **16** a manner of walking; gait **17** a place set aside for walking; promenade **18** a chosen profession or sphere of activity (esp in **walk of life**) **19a** an arrangement of trees or shrubs in widely separated rows **19b** the space between such rows **20** an enclosed ground for the exercise or feeding of domestic animals, esp horses **21** *chiefly Brit* the route covered in the course of work, as by a tradesman or postman **22** a procession; march: *Orange walk* **23** *obs* the section of a forest controlled by a keeper ▷ See also **walk away, walk into,** etc [OE *wealcan*] > '**walkable** *adj*

walkabout ('wɔːkə,baʊt) *n* **1** a periodic nomadic excursion into the Australian bush made by a native Australian **2** an occasion when celebrities, royalty, etc, walk among and meet the public **3 go walkabout** *Austral* **3a** to wander through the bush **3b** *inf* to be lost or misplaced **3c** *inf* to lose one's concentration
walk away *vb* (*intr, adv*) **1** to leave, esp disregarding someone else's distress **2 walk away with** to achieve or win easily
walker ('wɔːkə) *n* **1** a person who walks **2** Also called: **baby walker** a tubular frame on wheels or casters to support a baby learning to walk **3** a similar support for walking, often with rubber feet, for use by disabled or infirm people
Walker ('wɔːkə) *n* **1 Alice (Malsenior)** born 1944, US writer: her works include *In Love and Trouble: Stories of Black Women* (1973) and the novels *Meridian* (1976), *The Color Purple* (1982), and *Possessing the Secret of Joy* (1992) **2 John** born 1952, New Zealand middle-distance runner, the first athlete to run one hundred sub-four-minute miles
walkie-talkie *or* **walky-talky** (,wɔːkɪ'tɔːkɪ) *n, pl* **walkie-talkies** a small combined radio transmitter and receiver that can be carried around by one person:

widely used by the police, medical services, etc

walk-in *adj* 1 (of a cupboard) large enough to allow a person to enter and move about in 2 (of a flat or house) in a suitable condition for immediate occupation

walking papers *pl n sl, chiefly US & Canad* notice of dismissal

walking stick *n* 1 a stick or cane carried in the hand to assist walking 2 the usual US name for **stick insect**

walk into *vb (intr, prep)* to meet with unwittingly: *to walk into a trap*

Walkman ('wɔːkmən) *n trademark* a small portable cassette player with headphones

walk off *vb* 1 *(intr)* to depart suddenly 2 *(tr, adv)* to get rid of by walking: *to walk off an attack of depression* 3 **walk (a person) off his** *or* **her feet** to make (a person) walk so fast or far that he or she is exhausted 4 **walk off with** 4a to steal 4b to win, esp easily

walk-on *n* a a small part in a play or theatrical entertainment, esp one without any lines b *(as modifier)*: *a walk-on part*

walk out *vb (intr, adv)* 1 to leave without explanation, esp in anger 2 to go on strike 3 **walk out on** *inf* to abandon or desert 4 **walk out with** *Brit, obs or dialect* to court or be courted by ▷ *n* **walkout** 5 a strike by workers 6 the act of leaving a meeting, conference, etc, as a protest

walkover ('wɔːkˌəʊvə) *n* 1 *inf* an easy or unopposed victory 2 *horse racing* 2a the running or walking over the course by the only contestant entered in a race at the time of starting 2b a race won in this way ▷ *vb* **walk over** *(intr, mainly prep)* 3 *(also adv)* to win a race by a walkover 4 *inf* to beat (an opponent) conclusively or easily

walk socks *pl n* NZ knee-length, usually woollen, stockings

walk through *theatre* ▷ *vb* 1 *(tr)* to act or recite (a part) in a perfunctory manner, as at a first rehearsal ▷ *n* **walk-through** 2 a rehearsal of a part

walkway ('wɔːkˌweɪ) *n* 1 a path designed and sometimes landscaped for pedestrian use 2 a passage or path, esp one for walking over machinery, connecting buildings, etc

Walkyrie (væl'kɪərɪ, 'vælkɪərɪ) *n* a variant spelling of **Valkyrie**

wall (wɔːl) *n* 1a a vertical construction made of stone, brick, wood, etc, with a length and height much greater than its thickness, used to enclose, divide, or support 1b *(as modifier)*: *wall hangings*. Related adj: **mural** 2 *(often pl)* a structure or rampart built to protect and surround a position or place for defensive purposes 3 *anat* any lining, membrane, or investing part that encloses or bounds a bodily cavity or structure: *abdominal wall*. Technical name: **paries**. Related adj: **parietal** 4 anything that suggests a wall in function or effect: *a wall of fire* 5 **drive** *(or* **push)** **to the wall** to force into an awkward situation 6 **go to the wall** *inf* to be ruined 7 **go** *(or* **drive)** **up the wall** *sl* to become *(or* cause to become) crazy or furious 8 **have one's back to the wall** to be in a difficult situation ▷ *vb (tr)* 9 to protect, provide, or confine with or as if with a wall 10 (often foll by *up*) to block (an opening) with a wall 11 (often foll by *in* or *up*) to seal by or within a wall or walls [OE *weall*, from L *vallum* palisade, from *vallus* stake] > **walled** *adj* > **'wall-less** *adj*

wallaby ('wɒləbɪ) *n, pl* **wallabies** *or* **wallaby** any of various herbivorous marsupials of Australia and New Guinea, similar to but smaller than kangaroos [c19 from Abor. *wolabā*]

Wallaby ('wɒləbɪ) *n, pl* **Wallabies** a member of the international rugby union football team of Australia

Wallace ('wɒlɪs) *n* 1 **Alfred Russel** 1823–1913, British naturalist, whose work on the theory of natural selection influenced Charles Darwin 2 **Edgar** 1875–1932, English crime novelist 3 Sir **Richard** 1818–90, English art collector and philanthropist. His bequest to the nation forms the Wallace Collection, London 4 Sir **William** ?1272–1305, Scottish patriot, who defeated the army of Edward I of England at Stirling (1297) but was routed at Falkirk (1298) and later executed

Wallace's line *n* the hypothetical boundary between the Oriental and Australasian zoogeographical regions, which runs through Indonesia and SE of the Philippines [c20 after A. R. WALLACE]

Wallachia (wɒ'leɪkɪə) *n* a variant spelling of **Walachia**

wallah *or* **walla** ('wɒlə) *n (usually in combination) inf* a person involved with or in charge of (a specified thing): *the book wallah* [c18 from Hindi *-wālā* from Sansk. *pāla* protector]

wallaroo (ˌwɒlə'ruː) *n, pl* **wallaroos** *or* **wallaroo** a large stocky Australian kangaroo of rocky or mountainous regions [c19 from Abor. *wolarū*]

Wallasey ('wɒləsɪ) *n* a town in NW England, in Wirral unitary authority, Merseyside; near the mouth of the River Mersey, opposite Liverpool. Pop: 60 895 (1991)

wall bars *pl n* a series of horizontal bars attached to a wall and used in gymnastics

wallboard ('wɔːlˌbɔːd) *n* a thin board made of materials, such as compressed wood fibres or gypsum plaster, between stiff paper, and used to cover walls, partitions, etc

wall creeper *n* a pink-and-grey woodpecker-like songbird of Eurasian mountain regions

walled plain *n* any of the largest of the lunar craters, having diameters between 50 and 300 kilometres

Wallenberg ('vɑːlənbɜːg) *n* **Raoul** (raʊᵊl) 1912–? Swedish diplomat, who helped (1944–45) thousands of Hungarian Jews to escape from the Nazis. After his arrest (1945) by the Soviets nothing is certainly known of him: despite claims that he is still alive he is presumed to have died in prison

Waller ('wɒlə) *n* 1 **Edmund** 1606–87, English poet and politician, famous for his poem "Go, Lovely Rose" 2 **Fats**, real name *Thomas Waller*. 1904–43, US jazz pianist and singer

wallet ('wɒlɪt) *n* 1 a small folding case, usually of leather, for holding paper money, documents, etc 2 *arch, chiefly Brit* a rucksack or knapsack [c14 of Gmc origin]

walleye ('wɔːlˌaɪ) *n, pl* **walleyes** *or* **walleye** 1 a divergent squint 2 opacity of the cornea 3 an eye having a white or light-coloured iris 4 Also called: **walleyed pike** a North American pikeperch valued as a food and game fish [back formation from earlier *walleyed*, from ON *vagleygr*, from *vage* ? a film over the eye + *-eygr* -eyed, from *auga* eye; infl. by WALL] > **'wallˌeyed** *adj*

wallflower ('wɔːlˌflaʊə) *n* 1 Also called: **gillyflower** a plant of S Europe, grown for its clusters of yellow, orange, brown, red, or purple fragrant flowers and naturalized on old walls, cliffs, etc 2 *inf* a person who stays on the fringes of a dance or party on account of lacking a partner or being shy

Wallis[1] ('valɪs) *n* the German name for **Valais**

Wallis[2] ('wɒlɪs) *n* Sir **Barnes (Neville)** 1887–1979, English aeronautical engineer. He designed the airship R100, the Wellesley and Wellington bombers, and the bouncing bomb (1943), which was used to destroy the Ruhr dams during World War II

Wallis and Futuna Islands ('wɒlɪs, fuː'tjuːnə) *pl n* a French overseas territory in the SW Pacific, west of Samoa. Capital: Mata-Utu. Pop: 14 400 (1993 est). Area: 367 sq km (143 sq miles)

wall of death *n* (at a fairground) a giant cylinder round the inside vertical walls of which a motorcyclist rides

Walloon (wɒ'luːn) *n* 1 a member of a French-speaking people living chiefly in S Belgium and adjacent parts of France 2 the French dialect of Belgium ▷ *adj* 3 of or characteristic of the Walloons or their dialect [c16 from OF *Wallon*, from Med. L: foreigner, of Gmc origin]

Walloon Brabant *n* a province of central Belgium, formed in 1995 from the S part of Brabant province: densely populated and intensively farmed, with large industrial centres. Pop: 349 884 (2000 est). Area: 1091 sq km (421 sq miles)

wallop ('wɒləp) *vb* **wallops, walloping, walloped** 1 (*tr*) *inf* to beat soundly; strike hard 2 (*tr*) *inf* to defeat utterly 3 (*intr*) (of liquids) to boil violently ▷ *n* 4 *inf* a hard blow 5 *inf* the ability to hit powerfully, as of a boxer 6 *inf* a forceful impression 7 *Brit sl* beer [c14 from OF *waloper* to gallop, from OF *galoper*, from ?]

walloper ('wɒləpə) *n* 1 a person or thing that wallops 2 *Austral sl* a policeman

walloping ('wɒləpɪŋ) *inf* ▷ *n* 1 a thrashing ▷ *adj* 2 (intensifier): *a walloping drop in sales*

wallow ('wɒləʊ) *vb* (*intr*) 1 (esp of certain animals) to roll about in mud, water, etc, for pleasure 2 to move about with difficulty 3 to indulge oneself in possessions, emotion, etc: *to wallow in self-pity* ▷ *n* 4 the act or an instance of wallowing 5 a muddy place where animals wallow [OE *wealwian* to roll (in mud)] > '**wallower** *n*

wallpaper ('wɔːlˌpeɪpə) *n* 1 paper usually printed or embossed with designs for pasting onto walls and ceilings 2 *computing* a picture or pattern on a computer screen between and behind program icons and windows ▷ *vb* 3 to cover (a surface) with wallpaper

wall pepper *n* a small Eurasian plant having yellow flowers and acrid-tasting leaves

wall plate *n* a horizontal timber member placed along the top of a wall to support the ends of joists, rafters, etc, and distribute the load

wallposter ('wɔːlˌpəʊstə) *n* (in China) a bulletin or political message painted in large characters on a wall

wall rocket *n* any of several yellow-flowered European cruciferous plants that grow on old walls and in waste places

wall rue *n* a delicate fern that grows in rocky crevices and walls in North America and Eurasia

Wallsend ('wɔːlzˌɛnd) *n* a town in NE England, in North Tyneside unitary authority, Tyne and Wear: situated on the River Tyne at the E end of Hadrian's Wall. Pop: 45 280 (1991)

Wall Street *n* a street in lower Manhattan, New York, where the Stock Exchange and major banks are situated, regarded as the embodiment of American finance

wall-to-wall *adj* 1 (esp of carpeting) completely covering a floor 2 *inf* nonstop; widespread: *wall-to-wall sales*

wally ('wɒlɪ) *n, pl* **wallies** *sl* a stupid person [c20 shortened from the name *Walter*]

walnut ('wɔːlˌnʌt) *n* 1 any of a genus of deciduous trees of America, SE Europe, and Asia. They have aromatic leaves and flowers in catkins and are grown for their edible nuts and for their wood 2 the nut of any of these trees, having a wrinkled two-lobed seed and a hard wrinkled shell 3 the wood of any of these trees, used in making furniture, etc 4 a light yellowish-brown colour ▷ *adj* 5 made from the wood of a walnut tree: *a walnut table* 6 of the colour walnut [OE *walh-hnutu*, lit.: foreign nut]

Walpole ('wɔːlˌpəʊl) *n* 1 **Horace,** 4th Earl of Orford. 1717–97, British writer, noted for his letters and for his delight in the Gothic, as seen in his house Strawberry Hill and his novel *The Castle of Otranto* (1764) 2 Sir **Hugh** (**Seymour**) 1884–1941, British novelist, born in New Zealand: best known for *The Herries Chronicle* (1930–33), a sequence of historical novels set in the Lake District 3 Sir **Robert,** 1st Earl of Orford, father of Horace Walpole. 1676–1745, English Whig statesman. As first lord of the Treasury and Chancellor of the Exchequer (1721–42) he was effectively Britain's first prime minister

Walpurgis Night (vælˈpʊəgɪs) *n* the eve of May 1, believed in German folklore to be the night of a witches' sabbath on the Brocken, in the Harz Mountains [c19 translation of G *Walpurgisnacht*, the eve of the feast day of St Walpurga, 8th-cent. abbess in Germany]

walrus ('wɔːlrəs, 'wɒl-) *n, pl* **walruses** *or* **walrus** a mammal of northern seas, having a tough thick skin, upper canine teeth enlarged as tusks, and coarse whiskers, and feeding mainly on shellfish [c17 prob. from Du., of Scand. origin]

walrus moustache *n* a long thick moustache drooping at the ends

Walsall ('wɔːlsɔːl) *n* 1 an industrial town in central England, in Walsall unitary authority, West Midlands: engineering, electronics. Pop: 174 739 (1991) 2 a unitary authority in central England, in the West Midlands. Pop: 253 502 (2001). Area: 106 sq km (41 sq miles)

Walsh (wɒlʃ) *n* **Courtney** (**Andrew**) born 1962, Jamaican cricketer; a fast bowler, in 2000 he became the highest wicket-taker in test match history

Walsingham[1] ('wɔːlsɪŋəm) *n* a village in E England, in Norfolk: remains of a medieval priory; site of the shrine of Our Lady of Walsingham

Walsingham[2] ('wɔːlsɪŋəm) *n* Sir **Francis** ?1530–90, English statesman. As secretary of state (1573–90) to Elizabeth I he developed a system of domestic and foreign espionage and uncovered several plots against the Queen

Walter *n* 1 (*German* 'valtər) **Bruno** ('bruːno), real name *Bruno Walter Schlesinger*. 1876–1962, US conductor, born in Germany: famous for his performances of Haydn, Mozart, and Mahler 2 ('wɔːltə) **John** 1739–1812, English publisher; founded *The Daily Universal Register* (1785), which in 1788 became *The Times*

Waltham Forest ('wɔːlθəm) *n* a borough of NE Greater London. Pop: 218 277 (2001). Area: 40 sq km (15 sq miles)

Walton ('wɔːltᵊn) *n* 1 **Ernest Thomas Sinton** 1903–95, Irish physicist. He succeeded in producing the first artificial transmutation of an atomic nucleus (1932) with Sir John Cockcroft, with whom he shared the Nobel prize for physics 1951 2 **Izaak** ('aɪzək) 1593–1683, English writer, best known for *The Compleat Angler* (1653; enlarged 1676) 3 Sir **William** (**Turner**) 1902–83, English composer. His works include *Façade* (1923), a setting of satirical verses by Edith Sitwell, the *Viola Concerto* (1929), and the oratorio *Belshazzar's Feast* (1931)

waltz (wɔːls) *n* 1 a ballroom dance in triple time in which couples spin around as they progress round the room 2 a piece of music composed for or in the rhythm of this dance ▷ *vb* 3 to dance or lead (someone) in or as in a waltz 4 (*intr*) to move in a sprightly and self-assured manner 5 (*intr*) *inf* to succeed easily 6 **waltz Matilda** *Austral* See **Matilda** [c18 from G *Walzer*, from MHG *walzen* to roll]

waltzer ('wɔːlsə) *n* 1 a person who waltzes 2 a fairground roundabout on which people are spun round and moved up and down as it revolves

Walvis Bay ('wɔːlvɪs) *n* a port in Namibia, on the Atlantic: formed an exclave of South Africa, covering an area of 1124 sq km (434 sq miles) with its hinterland, but has been administered by Namibia since 1992; formally returned to Namibia in 1994; chief port of Namibia and rich fishing centre. Pop (urban area): 23 000 (1992 est)

wampum ('wɒmpəm) *n* (formerly) money used by North American Indians, made of cylindrical shells strung or woven together. Also called: **peag, peage** [c17 of Amerind origin, short for *wampumpeag*, from *wampan* light + *api* string + *-ag* pl. suffix]

wan (wɒn) *adj* **wanner, wannest** 1 unnaturally pale, esp from sickness, grief, etc 2 suggestive of ill health, unhappiness, etc 3 (of light, stars, etc) faint or dim [OE *wann* dark] > '**wanly** *adv* > '**wanness** *n*

Wanchüan *or* **Wan-ch'uan** (ˌwæntʃʊˈɑːn) *n* a former name of **Zhangjiakou**

wand (wɒnd) *n* **1** a slender supple stick or twig **2** a thin rod carried as a symbol of authority **3** a rod used by a magician, etc **4** *inf* a conductor's baton **5** *archery* a marker used to show the distance at which the archer stands from the target [C12 from ON *vǫndr*]

wander ('wɒndə) *vb* (*mainly intr*) **1** (*also tr*) to move or travel about, in, or through (a place) without any definite purpose or destination **2** to proceed in an irregular course **3** to go astray, as from a path or course **4** (of thoughts, etc) to lose concentration **5** to think or speak incoherently or illogically ▷ *n* **6** the act or an instance of wandering [OE *wandrian*] > '**wanderer** *n* > '**wandering** *adj, n*

wandering albatross *n* a large albatross having a very wide wingspan and a white plumage with black wings

wandering Jew *n* any of several related creeping or trailing plants of tropical America, such as tradescantia

Wandering Jew *n* (in medieval legend) a character condemned to roam the world eternally because he mocked Christ on the day of the Crucifixion

wanderlust ('wɒndə,lʌst) *n* a great desire to travel and rove about [from G *Wanderlust*, lit.: wander desire]

wanderoo (,wɒndə'ruː) *n, pl* **wanderoos** a macaque monkey of India and Sri Lanka, having black fur with a ruff of long greyish fur on each side of the face [C17 from Sinhalese *vanduru* monkeys, lit.: forest-dwellers]

wandoo (wɒn'duː) *n* a eucalyptus tree of W Australia, having white bark and durable wood [from Abor.]

Wandsworth ('wɒnzwəθ) *n* a borough of S Greater London, on the River Thames. Pop: 260 383 (2001). Area: 35 sq km (13 sq miles)

wane (weɪn) *vb* **wanes, waning, waned** (*intr*) **1** (of the moon) to show a gradually decreasing portion of illuminated surface, between full moon and new moon **2** to decrease gradually in size, strength, power, etc **3** to draw to a close ▷ *n* **4** a decrease, as in size, strength, power, etc **5** the period during which the moon wanes **6** one act or an instance of drawing to a close **7** a rounded surface or defective edge of a plank, where the bark was **8 on the wane** in a state of decline [OE *wanian* (vb)] > '**waney** *or* '**wany** *adj*

Wanganui (,wɒŋə'nuːɪ) *n* a port in New Zealand, on SW North Island: centre for a dairy-farming and sheep-rearing district. Pop: 42 200 (1995 est)

wangle ('wæŋgᵊl) *inf* ▷ *vb* **wangles, wangling, wangled** **1** (*tr*) to use devious methods to get or achieve (something) for (oneself or another): *he wangled himself a salary increase* **2** to manipulate or falsify (a situation, etc) ▷ *n* **3** the act or an instance of wangling [C19 orig. printers' sl., ? a blend of WAGGLE & dialect *wankle* wavering, from OE *wancol*] > '**wangler** *n*

Wanhsien *or* **Wan-Hsien** ('wæn'ʃjɛn) *n* a variant transliteration of the Chinese name for **Wanxian**

wanigan *or* **wannigan** ('wɒnɪgən) *n Canad* **1** a lumberjack's chest or box **2** a cabin, caboose, or houseboat [C19 from Algonquian]

wank (wæŋk) *sl* ▷ *vb* **1** (*intr*) to masturbate ▷ *n* **2** an instance of wanking [from ?]

wankel engine ('wæŋkᵊl) *n* a type of rotary internal-combustion engine without reciprocating parts. It consists of a curved triangular-shaped piston rotating in an elliptical combustion chamber [C20 after Felix *Wankel* (1902–88), G engineer who invented it]

wanker ('wæŋkə) *n sl* **1** a person who wanks; masturbator **2** *derog* a worthless fellow

Wankie ('wɑːŋkɪ) *n* the former name (until 1982) of Hwange

wannabe *or* **wannabee** ('wɒnə,biː) *n inf* **a** a person who desires to be, or be like, something or someone else **b** (*as modifier*): *a wannabe film star* [C20 phonetic shortening of *want to be*]

Wanne-Eickel (*German* 'vanə'aikəl) *n* an industrial town in W Germany, in North Rhine-Westphalia on the Rhine-Herne Canal: formed in 1926 by the merging of two townships. Pop: 98 800 (latest est)

want (wɒnt) *vb* **1** (*tr*) to feel a need or longing for: *I want a new hat* **2** (when *tr, may take a clause as object or an infinitive*) to wish, need, or desire (something or to do something): *he wants to go home* **3** (*intr;* usually used with a negative and often foll by *for*) to be lacking or deficient (in something necessary or desirable): *the child wants for nothing* **4** (*tr*) to feel the absence of: *lying on the ground makes me want my bed* **5** (*tr*) to fall short by (a specified amount) **6** (*tr*) *chiefly Brit* to have need of or require (doing or being something): *your shoes want cleaning* **7** (*intr*) to be destitute **8** (*tr; often passive*) to seek or request the presence of: *you're wanted upstairs* **9** (*tr; takes an infinitive*) *inf* should or ought (to do something): *you don't want to go out so late* ▷ *n* **10** the act or an instance of wanting **11** anything that is needed, desired, or lacked: *to supply someone's wants* **12** a lack, shortage, or absence: *for want of common sense* **13** the state of being in need: *the state should help those in want* **14** a sense of lack; craving [C12 (vb, in the sense: it is lacking), C13 (n): from ON *vanta* to be deficient] > '**wanter** *n*

want ad *n inf* a classified advertisement in a newspaper, magazine, etc, for something wanted, such as property or employment

wanting ('wɒntɪŋ) *adj* (*postpositive*) **1** lacking or absent **2** not meeting requirements or expectations: *you have been found wanting*

WAN2TLK *text messaging abbrev for* want to talk?

wanton ('wɒntən) *adj* **1** dissolute, licentious, or immoral **2** without motive, provocation, or justification: *wanton destruction* **3** maliciously and unnecessarily cruel **4** unrestrained: *wanton spending* **5** *arch or poetic* playful or capricious **6** *arch* (of vegetation, etc) luxuriant ▷ *n* **7** a licentious person, esp a woman ▷ *vb* **8** (*intr*) to behave in a wanton manner [C13 *wantowen* (in the obs. sense: unruly): from *wan-* (prefix equivalent to UN-[1]) + *-towen*, from OE *togen* brought up, from *tēon* to bring up] > '**wantonly** *adv* > '**wantonness** *n*

Wanxian, Wanhsien, *or* **Wan-Hsien** ('wæn'ʃjɛn) *n* an inland port in central China, in E Sichuan province, on the Yangtze River. Pop: 156 823 (1990 est)

WAP (wɒp) *n* **a** *acronym for* Wireless Application Protocol, a global protocol for data transmission that allows mobile-phone users to access the Internet and other information services **b** (*as modifer*): *a WAP phone*

wapentake ('wɒpən,teɪk, 'wæp-) *n English legal history* a subdivision of certain shires or counties, esp in the Midlands and North of England, corresponding to the hundred in other shires [OE *wǣpen(ge)tæc*]

wapiti ('wɒpɪtɪ) *n, pl* **wapitis** a large North American deer with large much-branched antlers, now also found in New Zealand [C19 of Amerind origin, lit.: white deer, from *wap* (unattested) white; from the animal's white tail and rump]

war (wɔː) *n* **1** open armed conflict between two or more parties, nations, or states. Related adj: **belligerent** (see sense 2) **2** a particular armed conflict: *the 1999 war in Kosovo* **3** the techniques of armed conflict as a study, science, or profession **4** any conflict or contest: *the war against crime* **5** (*modifier*) of, resulting from, or characteristic of war: *war damage; a war story* **6 in the wars** *inf* (esp of a child) hurt or knocked about, esp as a result of quarrelling and fighting ▷ *vb* **wars, warring, warred** **7** (*intr*) to conduct a war [C12 from ONorthern F *werre* (var. of OF *guerre*), of Gmc origin]

War. *abbrev for* Warwickshire

Warangal ('wʌrəngəl) *n* a city in S central India, in N Andhra Pradesh: capital of a 12th-century Hindu kingdom. Pop: 447 657 (1991)

waratah ('wɒrətə) *n Austral* a shrub having dark green leaves and clusters of crimson flowers [from Abor.]

Warbeck ('wɔːbɛk) *n* **Perkin** ('pɜːkɪn) ?1474–99, Flemish impostor, pretender to the English throne. Professing to be Richard, Duke of York, he led an unsuccessful rising against Henry VII (1497) and was later executed

warble[1] ('wɔːbᵊl) *vb* **warbles, warbling, warbled 1** to sing (words, songs, etc) with trills, runs, and other embellishments **2** *(tr)* to utter in a song ▷ *n* **3** the act or an instance of warbling [c14 via OF *werbler*, of Gmc origin]

warble[2] ('wɔːbᵊl) *n vet science* **1** a small lumpy abscess under the skin of cattle caused by the larvae of the warble fly **2** a hard lump of tissue on a horse's back, caused by prolonged friction of a saddle [c16 from ?]

warble fly *n* any of a genus of hairy beelike dipterous flies, the larvae of which produce warbles in cattle

warbler ('wɔːblə) *n* **1** a person or thing that warbles **2** a small active passerine songbird of the Old World having a cryptic plumage and slender bill, that is an arboreal insectivore **3** a small bird of an American family, similar to the Old World songbird but often brightly coloured

Warburg (*German* 'varburk) *n* **Otto** (**Heinrich**) ('oto) 1883–1970, German biochemist and physiologist: Nobel prize for physiology or medicine (1931) for his work on respiratory enzymes

warchalking ('wɔːtʃɔːkɪŋ) *n* the practice of marking chalk symbols on walls and pavements at places where local wireless Internet connections may be obtained for free via a computer, usually without permission > **'warchalker** *n* [c21 from w(ireless) a(cess) r(evolution) + gerund of CHALK]

war correspondent *n* a journalist who reports on a war from the scene of action

war crime *n* a crime committed in wartime in violation of the accepted customs, such as ill-treatment of prisoners, etc > **war criminal** *n*

war cry *n* **1** a rallying cry used by combatants in battle **2** a cry, slogan, etc, used to rally support for a cause

ward (wɔːd) *n* **1** (in many countries) one of the districts into which a city, town, parish, or other area is divided for administration, election of representatives, etc **2a** a room in a hospital, esp one for patients requiring similar kinds of care: *a maternity ward* **2b** *(as modifier)*: *ward maid* **3** one of the divisions of a prison **4** an open space enclosed within the walls of a castle **5** *law* Also called: **ward of court** a person, esp a minor or one legally incapable of managing his own affairs, placed under the control or protection of a guardian or of a court **6** the state of being under guard or in custody **7** a means of protection **8a** an internal ridge or bar in a lock that prevents an incorrectly cut key from turning **8b** a corresponding groove cut in a key ▷ *vb* **9** *(tr) arch* to guard or protect ▷ See also **ward off** [OE *weard* protector] > **'wardless** *adj*

-ward *suffix* **1** *(forming adjectives)* indicating direction towards: *a backward step* **2** *(forming adverbs)* a variant and the usual US and Canad form of **-wards** [OE *-weard* towards]

Ward (wɔːd) *n* **1** Dame **Barbara** (**Mary**), Baroness Jackson. 1914–81, British economist, environmentalist, and writer. Her books include *Spaceship Earth* (1966) **2** Mrs **Humphry**, married name of *Mary Augusta Arnold*. 1851–1920, English novelist. Her novels include *Robert Elsmere* (1888) and *The Case of Richard Meynell* (1911) **3** Sir **Joseph George** 1856–1930, New Zealand statesman; prime minister of New Zealand (1906–12; 1928–30)

war dance *n* a ceremonial dance performed before going to battle or after victory, esp by certain North American Indian peoples

warden ('wɔːdᵊn) *n* **1** a person who has the charge or care of something, esp a building, or someone **2** a public official, esp one responsible for the enforcement of certain regulations: *traffic warden* **3** a person employed to patrol a national park or a safari park **4** *chiefly US & Canad* the chief officer in charge of a prison **5** *Brit* the principal of any of various universities or colleges **6** See **churchwarden** (sense 1) [c13 from OF *wardein*, from *warder* to guard, of Gmc origin]

warder ('wɔːdə) *or (fem)* **wardress** *n* **1** *chiefly Brit* an officer in charge of prisoners in a jail **2** a person who guards or has charge of something [c14 from Anglo-F *wardere*, from OF *warder* to guard, of Gmc origin]

ward heeler *n US politics, disparaging* a party worker who canvasses votes and performs chores for a political boss. Also called: **heeler**

ward off *vb (tr, adv)* to turn aside or repel

Wardour Street ('wɔːdə) *n* **1** a street in Soho where many film companies have their London offices: formerly noted for shops selling antiques and mock antiques **2** **Wardour Street English** affectedly archaic speech or writing

wardrobe ('wɔːdrəub) *n* **1** a tall closet or cupboard, with a rail or hooks on which to hang clothes **2** the total collection of articles of clothing belonging to one person **3a** the collection of costumes belonging to a theatre or theatrical company **3b** *(as modifier)*: *wardrobe mistress* [c14 from OF *warderobe*, from *warder* to guard + *robe* ROBE]

wardrobe trunk *n* a large upright rectangular travelling case, usually opening longitudinally, with one side having a hanging rail, the other having drawers or compartments

wardroom ('wɔːdˌruːm, -ˌrum) *n* **1** the quarters assigned to the officers (except the captain) of a warship **2** the officers of a warship collectively, excepting the captain

-wards *or* **-ward** *suffix forming adverbs* indicating direction towards: *a step backwards* ▷ Cf **-ward** [OE *-weardes* towards]

wardship ('wɔːdʃɪp) *n* the state of being a ward

ware[1] (wɛə) *n (often in combination)* **1** *(functioning as sing)* articles of the same kind or material: *silverware* **2** porcelain or pottery of a specified type: *jasper ware* ▷ See also **wares** [OE *waru*]

ware[2] (wɛə) *vb arch* another word for **beware** [OE *wær*. See AWARE, BEWARE]

Ww

warehouse *n* ('wɛəˌhaus) **1** a place where goods are stored prior to their use, distribution, or sale **2** See **bonded warehouse** **3** *chiefly Brit* a large commercial, esp wholesale, establishment ▷ *vb* ('wɛəˌhauz, -ˌhaus), **warehouses, warehousing, warehoused 4** *(tr)* to store or place in a warehouse, esp a bonded warehouse > **'wareˌhouseman** *n*

warehousing ('wɛəˌhauzɪŋ) *n Business.* an attempt to gain a significant stake in a company without revealing the identity of the purchaser by buying small quantities of shares in the name of nominees

wares (wɛəz) *pl n* **1** articles of manufacture considered as being for sale **2** any talent or asset regarded as a saleable commodity

warfare ('wɔːˌfɛə) *n* **1** the act, process, or an instance of waging war **2** conflict or strife

warfarin ('wɔːfərɪn) *n* a crystalline insoluble compound, used to kill rodents and, in the form of its sodium salt, as a medical anticoagulant [c20 from the patent owners *W(isconsin) A(lumni) R(esearch) F(oundation)* + (COUM)ARIN]

war game *n* **1** a notional tactical exercise for training military commanders, in which no military units are actually deployed **2** a game in which model soldiers are used to create battles, esp past battles, in order to study tactics ▷ *vb* **war-game, war-games, war-gaming, war-gamed 3** *(intr)* to prepare for battle by considering possible tactics and enemy responses

warhead ('wɔːˌhɛd) *n* the part of the fore end of a missile or projectile that contains explosives

Warhol ('wɔːhəul) *n* **Andy**, real name *Andrew Warhola*. ?1926–87, US artist and film maker; one of the foremost exponents of pop art

warhorse ('wɔːˌhɔːs) *n* **1** a horse used in battle **2** *inf* a veteran soldier or politician

Warks *abbrev for* Warwickshire

Warley ('wɔːlɪ) *n* an industrial town in W central England, in Sandwell unitary authority, West Midlands: formed in 1966 by the amalgamation of Smethwick, Oldbury, and Rowley Regis. Pop: 145 542 (1991)

warlike ('wɔːˌlaɪk) *adj* **1** of, relating to, or used in war **2** hostile or belligerent **3** fit or ready for war

warlock ('wɔːˌlɒk) *n* a man who practises black magic [OE *wǣrloga* oath breaker, from *wǣr* oath + *-loga* liar, from *lēogan* to lie]

Warlock ('wɔːˌlɒk) *n* **Peter,** real name *Philip Arnold Heseltine*. 1894–1930, British composer and scholar of early English music. His works include song cycles, such as *The Curlew* (1920–22), and the *Capriol Suite* (1926) for strings

warlord ('wɔːˌlɔːd) *n* a military leader of a nation or part of a nation: *the Chinese warlords*

Warlpiri ('walprɪ) *n* an Aboriginal language of central Australia

warm (wɔːm) *adj* **1** characterized by or having a moderate degree of heat **2** maintaining or imparting heat: *a warm coat* **3** having or showing ready affection, kindliness, etc: *a warm personality* **4** lively or passionate: *a warm debate* **5** cordial or enthusiastic: *warm support* **6** quickly or easily aroused: *a warm temper* **7** (of colours) predominantly red or yellow in tone **8** (of a scent, trail, etc) recently made **9** near to finding a hidden object or guessing facts, as in children's games **10** *inf* uncomfortable or disagreeable, esp because of the proximity of danger ▷ *vb* **11** (sometimes foll by *up*) to make or become warm or warmer **12** (when *intr*, often foll by *to*) to make or become excited, enthusiastic, etc (about): *he warmed to the idea of buying a new car* **13** (*intr*; often foll by *to*) to feel affection, kindness, etc (for someone): *I warmed to her mother from the start* ▷ *n inf* **14** a warm place or area: *come into the warm* **15** the act or an instance of warming or being warmed ▷ See also **warm up** [OE *wearm*] > '**warmer** *n* > '**warmish** *adj* > '**warmly** *adv* > '**warmness** *n*

warm-blooded *adj* **1** ardent, impetuous, or passionate **2** (of birds and mammals) having a constant body temperature, usually higher than the temperature of the surroundings. Technical term: **homoiothermic** > ˌ**warm-'bloodedness** *n*

warm-down *n* light exercises performed to aid recovery from strenuous physical activity

war memorial *n* a monument, usually an obelisk or cross, to those who die in a war, esp those from a particular locality

warm front *n meteorol* the boundary between a warm air mass and the cold air above which it is rising, at a less steep angle than at the cold front

warm-hearted *adj* kindly, generous, or readily sympathetic > ˌ**warm-'heartedly** *adv* > ˌ**warm-'heartedness** *n*

warming pan *n* a pan, often of copper and having a long handle, filled with hot coals and formerly drawn over the sheets to warm a bed

warmonger ('wɔːˌmʌŋgə) *n* a person who fosters warlike ideas or advocates war > '**warˌmongering** *n*

warmth (wɔːmθ) *n* **1** the state, quality, or sensation of being warm **2** intensity of emotion: *he denied the accusation with some warmth* **3** affection or cordiality: *he greeted me with warmth*

warm up *vb* (*adv*) **1** to make or become warm or warmer **2** (*intr*) to exercise immediately before a game, contest, or more vigorous exercise **3** (*intr*) to get ready for something important; prepare **4** to run (an engine, etc) until the working temperature is attained, or (of an engine, etc) to undergo this process **5** to make or become more animated: *the party warmed up when Tom came* **6** to reheat (already cooked food) or (of such food) to be reheated ▷ *n* **warm-up 7** the act or an instance of warming up **8** a preparatory exercise routine

warn (wɔːn) *vb* **1** to notify or make (someone) aware of danger, harm, etc **2** (*tr; often takes a negative and an infinitive*) to advise or admonish (someone) as to action, conduct, etc: *I warn you not to do that again* **3** (*takes a clause as object or an infinitive*) to inform (someone) in advance: *he warned them that he would arrive late* **4** (*tr*; usually foll by *away*, *off*, etc) to give notice to go away, be off, etc [OE *wearnian*] > '**warner** *n*

Warne (wɔːn) *n* **Shane (Keith)** born 1969, Australian cricketer, playing for Australia since 1991

warning ('wɔːnɪŋ) *n* **1** a hint, intimation, threat, etc, of harm or danger **2** advice to beware or desist **3** an archaic word for **notice** (sense 6) ▷ *adj* **4** (*prenominal*) intended or serving to warn: *a warning look* > '**warningly** *adv*

War of American Independence *n* the conflict following the revolt of the North American colonies against British rule, particularly on the issue of taxation. Hostilities began in 1775 when British and American forces clashed at Lexington and Concord. Articles of Confederation agreed in the Continental Congress in 1777 provided for a confederacy to be known as the United States of America. The war was effectively ended with the surrender of the British at Yorktown in 1781 and peace was signed at Paris in Sept 1783. Also called: **American Revolution** or **Revolutionary War**

▷ www.bbc.co.uk/history/timelines/britain/geo_america_ind.shtml

▷ www.fordham.edu/halsall/mod/modsbook12.html

warp (wɔːp) *vb* **1** to twist or cause to twist out of shape, as from heat, damp, etc **2** to turn or cause to turn from a true, correct, or proper course **3** to pervert or be perverted **4** *naut* to move (a vessel) by hauling on a rope fixed to a stationary object ashore or (of a vessel) to be moved thus **5** (*tr*) to flood (land) with water from which alluvial matter is deposited ▷ *n* **6** the state or condition of being twisted out of shape **7** a twist, distortion, or bias **8** a mental or moral deviation **9** the yarns arranged lengthways on a loom, forming the threads through which the weft yarns are woven **10** *naut* a rope used for warping a vessel **11** alluvial sediment deposited by water [OE *wearp* a throw] > '**warpage** *n* > **warped** *adj* > '**warper** *n*

war paint *n* **1** painted decoration of the face and body applied by certain North American Indians before battle **2** *inf* finery or regalia **3** *inf* cosmetics

warpath ('wɔːˌpɑːθ) *n* **1** the route taken by North American Indians on a warlike expedition **2 on the warpath 2a** preparing to engage in battle **2b** *inf* in a state of anger

warplane ('wɔːˌpleɪn) *n* any aircraft designed for and used in warfare

warrant ('wɒrənt) *n* **1** anything that gives authority for an action or decision; authorization **2** a document that certifies or guarantees, such as a receipt for goods stored in a warehouse, a licence, or a commission **3** *law* an authorization issued by a magistrate allowing a constable or other officer to search or seize property, arrest a person, or perform some other specified act **4** (in certain armed services) the official authority for the appointment of warrant officers **5** a security that functions as a stock option by giving the owner the right to buy ordinary shares in a company at a specified date, often at a specified price ▷ *vb* (*tr*) **6** to guarantee the quality, condition, etc, of (something) **7** to give authority or power to **8** to attest to the character, worthiness, etc, of **9** to guarantee (a purchaser of merchandise) against loss of, damage to, or misrepresentation concerning the merchandise **10** *law* to guarantee (the title to an estate or other property) **11** to declare confidently [c13 from Anglo-F, var. of OF *guarant*, from *guarantir* to guarantee, of Gmc origin]

> 'warrantable *adj* > ˌwarranta'bility *n* > 'warrantably *adv* > 'warranter *n*

warrantee (ˌwɒrən'tiː) *n* a person to whom a warranty is given

warrant officer *n* an officer in certain armed services who holds a rank between those of commissioned and noncommissioned officers. In the British army the rank has two classes: regimental sergeant major and company sergeant major

Warrant of Fitness *n NZ* a six-monthly certificate required for motor vehicles certifying mechanical soundness

warrantor ('wɒrənˌtɔː) *n* an individual or company that provides a warranty

warrant sale *n Scots law* a sale of someone's personal belongings or household effects that have been seized to meet unpaid debts

warranty ('wɒrəntɪ) *n, pl* **warranties** **1** *property law* a covenant, express or implied, by which the vendor of real property vouches for the security of the title conveyed **2** *contract law* an express or implied term in a contract collateral to the main purpose, such as an undertaking that goods contracted to be sold shall meet specified requirements as to quality, etc **3** *insurance law* an undertaking by the party insured that the facts given regarding the risk are as stated [C14 from Anglo-F *warantie*, from *warantir* to warrant, var. of OF *guarantir*; see WARRANT]

warren ('wɒrən) *n* **1** a series of interconnected underground tunnels in which rabbits live **2** a colony of rabbits **3** an overcrowded area or dwelling **4** *chiefly Brit* an enclosed place where small game animals or birds are kept, esp for breeding [C14 from Anglo-F *warenne*, of Gmc origin]

Warren ('wɒrən) *n* a city in the US, in SE Michigan, northeast of Detroit. Pop: 138 078 (1996 est)

warrigal ('wɒrɪgæl) *Austral* ▷ *n* **1** a dingo ▷ *adj* **2** untamed or wild [C19 from Abor.]

Warrington ('wɒrɪŋtən) *n* **1** an industrial town in NW England, in Warrington unitary authority, Cheshire on the River Mersey: dates from Roman times. Pop: 81 812 (1991 est) **2** a unitary authority in NW England, in N Cheshire. Pop: 191 084 (2001). Area: 176 sq km (68 sq miles)

warrior ('wɒrɪə) *n* **a** a person engaged in, experienced in, or devoted to war **b** (*as modifier*): *a warrior nation* [C13 from OF *werreieor*, from *werre* WAR]

Warsaw ('wɔːsɔː) *n* the capital of Poland, in the E central part on the River Vistula: became capital at the end of the 16th century; almost completely destroyed in World War II as the main centre of the Polish resistance movement; rebuilt within about six years; university (1818); situated at the junction of important trans-European routes. Pop: 1 618 468 (1999 est). Polish name: **Warszawa** (var'ʃava)

▷ www.explorewarsaw.com

Warsaw Pact *n* a military treaty and association of E European countries (1955–91)

▷ www.fordham.edu/halsall/mod/1955warsawpact.html

▷ www.nationmaster.com/encyclopedia/Warsaw-Pact

warship ('wɔːʃɪp) *n* a vessel armed, armoured, and otherwise equipped for naval warfare

▷ www.warships1.com

Wars of the Roses *pl n* the struggle for the throne in England (1455-85) between the House of York (symbolized by the white rose) and the House of Lancaster (symbolized by the red rose)

▷ www.warsoftheroses.com

▷ www.ehistory.com/middleages/warsoftheroses/overview.cfm

wart (wɔːt) *n* **1** *pathol* any firm abnormal elevation of the skin caused by a virus **2** *bot* a small rounded outgrowth **3** **warts and all** with all blemishes evident [OE *weart(e)*] > 'warty *adj*

Warta (*Polish* 'varta) *n* a river in Poland, flowing generally north and west across the whole W Polish Plain to the River Oder. Length: 808 km (502 miles)

Wartburg (*German* 'vartbʊrk) *n* a medieval castle in central Germany, in Thuringia southwest of Eisenach: residence of Luther (1521–22) when he began his German translation of the New Testament

warthog ('wɔːthɒg) *n* a wild pig of S and E Africa, having heavy tusks, wartlike protuberances on the face, and a mane of coarse hair

wartime ('wɔːˌtaɪm) *n* **a** a period or time of war **b** (*as modifier*): *wartime conditions*

war whoop *n* the yell or howl uttered, esp by North American Indians, while making an attack

Warwick[1] ('wɒrɪk) *n* a town in central England, administrative centre of Warwickshire, on the River Avon: 14th-century castle, with collections of armour and waxworks: the university of Warwick (1965) is in Coventry. Pop: 22 476 (1991)

Warwick[2] ('wɒrɪk) *n* **Earl of,** title of *Richard Neville*, known as *the Kingmaker*. 1428–71, English statesman. During the Wars of the Roses, he fought first for the Yorkists, securing the throne (1461) for Edward IV, and then for the Lancastrians, restoring Henry VI (1470). He was killed at Barnet by Edward IV

Warwickshire ('wɒrɪkʃɪə, -ʃə) *n* a county of central England: until 1974, when the West Midlands metropolitan county was created, it contained one of the most highly industrialized regions in the world, centred on Birmingham. Administrative centre: Warwick. Pop: 505 885 (2001). Area: 1981 sq km (765 sq miles)

wary ('wɛərɪ) *adj* **warier, wariest** **1** watchful, cautious, or alert **2** characterized by caution or watchfulness [C16 from WARE[2] + -Y[1]] > 'warily *adv* > 'wariness *n*

was (wɒz; *unstressed* wəz) *vb* (used with *I, he, she, it,* and with singular nouns) **1** the past tense (indicative mood) of **be** **2** *not standard* a form of the subjunctive mood used in place of *were*, esp in conditional sentences: *if the film was to be with you, would you be able to process it?* [OE *wæs*, from *wesan* to be]

wasabi (wə'sɑːbɪ) *n* **1** a Japanese plant cultivated for its thick green pungent root **2** the root of this plant, esp in paste or powder form, used as a condiment in Japanese cookery

Wasatch Range ('wɔːsætʃ) *n* a mountain range in the W central US, in N Utah and SE Idaho. Highest peak: Mount Timpanogos, 3581 m (11 750 ft)

wash (wɒʃ) *vb* **1** to apply water or other liquid, usually with soap, to (oneself, clothes, etc) in order to cleanse **2** (*tr*; often foll by *away, from, off,* etc) to remove by the application of water or other liquid and usually soap: *she washed the dirt from her clothes* **3** (*intr*) to be capable of being washed without damage or loss of colour **4** (of an animal such as a cat) to cleanse (itself or another animal) by licking **5** (*tr*) to cleanse from pollution or defilement **6** (*tr*) to make wet or moist **7** (often foll by *away*, etc) to move or be moved by water: *the flood washed away the bridge* **8** (esp of waves) to flow or sweep against or over (a surface or object), often with a lapping sound **9** to form by erosion or be eroded: *the stream washed a ravine in the hill* **10** (*tr*) to apply a thin coating of paint, metal, etc, to **11** (*tr*) to separate (ore, etc) from (gravel, etc) by immersion in water **12** (*intr; usually used with a negative*) *inf, chiefly Brit* to admit of testing or proof: *your excuses won't wash* ▷ *n* **13** the act or process of washing **14** a quantity of articles washed together **15** a preparation or thin liquid used as a coating or in washing: *a thin wash of paint* **16** *med* **16a** any medicinal lotion for application to a part of the body **16b** (*in combination*): *an eyewash* **17a** the technique of making wash drawings **17b** See **wash**

drawing 18 the erosion of soil by the action of flowing water **19** a mass of alluvial material transported and deposited by flowing water **20** land that is habitually washed by tidal or river waters **21** the disturbance in the air or water produced at the rear of an aircraft, boat, or other moving object **22** gravel, earth, etc, from which valuable minerals may be washed **23** waste liquid matter or liquid refuse, esp as fed to pigs **24** an alcoholic liquid resembling strong beer, resulting from the fermentation of wort in the production of whisky **25 come out in the wash** *inf* to become known or apparent in the course of time ▷ See also **wash down, wash out, wash up** [OE *wæscan, waxan*]

Wash (wɒʃ) *n* **the** a shallow inlet of the North Sea on the E coast of England, between Lincolnshire and Norfolk

Wash. *abbrev for* Washington

washable ('wɒʃəb^{ə}l) *adj* (esp of fabrics or clothes) capable of being washed without deteriorating > ˌ**washa'bility** *n*

wash-and-wear *adj* (of fabrics, garments, etc) requiring only light washing, short drying time, and little or no ironing

washbasin ('wɒʃˌbeɪs^{ə}n) *n* **1** Also called: **washbowl** a basin or bowl for washing the face and hands **2** Also called: **wash-hand basin** a bathroom fixture with taps, used for washing the face and hands

washboard ('wɒʃˌbɔːd) *n* **1** a board having a surface, usually of corrugated metal, on which, esp formerly, clothes were scrubbed **2** such a board used as a rhythm instrument played with the fingers in skiffle, country-and-western music, etc **3** *naut* a vertical planklike shield fastened to the gunwales of a boat to prevent water from splashing over the side

washcloth ('wɒʃˌklɒθ) *n* **1** another term for **dishcloth** **2** the US and Canad word for **face cloth**

washday ('wɒʃˌdeɪ) *n* a day on which clothes and linen are washed

wash down *vb (tr, adv)* **1** to wash completely, esp from top to bottom **2** to take drink with or after (food or another drink)

wash drawing *n* a pen-and-ink drawing that has been lightly brushed over with water to soften the lines

washed out *adj* (**washed-out** *when prenominal*) **1** faded or colourless **2** exhausted, esp when being pale in appearance

washed up *adj* (**washed-up** *when prenominal*) *inf, chiefly US, Canad, & NZ* without hope; defeated

washer ('wɒʃə) *n* **1** a person or thing that washes **2** a flat ring or drilled disc of metal used under the head of a bolt or nut **3** any flat ring of rubber, felt, metal, etc, used to provide a seal under a nut or in a tap or valve seat **4** See **washing machine** **5** *Austral* a face cloth; flannel

washerwoman ('wɒʃəˌwʊmən) *or (masc)* **washerman** *n, pl* **washerwomen** *or* **washermen** a person who washes clothes for a living

washery ('wɒʃərɪ) *n, pl* **washeries** a plant at a mine where water or other liquid is used to remove dirt from a mineral, esp coal

wash-hand basin *n* another name for **washbasin** (sense 2)

wash house *n* (formerly) an outbuilding in which clothes were washed

washing ('wɒʃɪŋ) *n* **1** articles that have been or are to be washed together on a single occasion **2** something, such as gold dust, that has been obtained by washing **3** a thin coat of something applied in liquid form

washing machine *n* a mechanical apparatus, usually powered by electricity, for washing clothing, linens, etc

washing powder *n* powdered detergent for washing fabrics

washing soda *n* crystalline sodium carbonate, esp when used as a cleansing agent

Washington[1] ('wɒʃɪŋtən) *n* **1** a state of the northwestern US, on the Pacific: consists of the Coast Range and the Olympic Mountains in the west and the Columbia Plateau in the east. Capital: Olympia. Pop: 5 894 121 (2000). Area: 172 416 sq km (66 570 sq miles). Abbreviations: **Wash** or (with zip code) **WA** **2** the capital of the US, coextensive with the District of Columbia and situated near the E coast on the Potomac River: site chosen by President Washington in 1790; contains the White House and the Capitol; a major educational and administrative centre. Pop: 572 059 (2000). Also called: **Washington, DC** **3** a town in Tyne and Wear: designated a new town in 1964. Pop: 56 848 (1991) **4 Mount** a mountain in N New Hampshire, in the White Mountains: the highest peak in the northeast US; noted for extreme weather conditions. Height: 1917 m (6288 ft) **5 Lake** a lake in W Washington, forming the E boundary of the city of Seattle: linked by canal with Puget Sound. Length: about 32 km (20 miles). Width: 6 km (4 miles) > **Washingtonian** (ˌwɒʃɪŋ'təʊnɪən) *adj, n*

▷ http://about.dc.gov
▷ www.washington.org
▷ http://dcpages.com/Tourism

Washington[2] ('wɒʃɪŋtən) *n* **1 Booker T(aliaferro)** 1856–1915, US Black educationalist and writer **2 Denzel** ('dɛnzəl) born 1954, US film actor; his films include *Glory* (1990), *Malcolm X* (1992), *The Hurricane* (1999), and *John Q.* (2002) **3 George** 1732–99, US general and statesman; first president of the US (1789–97). He was appointed commander in chief of the Continental Army (1775) at the outbreak of the War of American Independence, which ended with his defeat of Cornwallis at Yorktown (1781). He presided over the convention at Philadelphia (1787) that formulated the constitution of the US and elected him president

washing-up *n Brit* **1** the washing of dishes, cutlery, etc, after a meal **2** dishes and cutlery waiting to be washed up **3** *(as modifier): a washing-up cloth*

wash out *vb (adv)* **1** *(tr)* to wash (the inside of something) so as to remove (dirt) **2** Also: **wash off** to remove or be removed by washing: *grass stains don't wash out easily* ▷ *n* **washout** **3** *geol* **3a** erosion of the earth's surface by the action of running water **3b** a narrow channel produced by this **4** *inf* **4a** a total failure or disaster **4b** an incompetent person

wash over *vb (tr, prep)* **1** (of a feeling) to affect (a person) suddenly and profoundly: *despair washed over me* **2** to be taking place without having much of an effect on (a person): *I let these meetings wash over me*

washroom ('wɒʃˌruːm, -ˌrʊm) *n US & Canad* a euphemism for **lavatory**

washstand ('wɒʃˌstænd) *n* a piece of furniture designed to hold a basin, etc, for washing the face and hands

washtub ('wɒʃˌtʌb) *n* a tub or large container used for washing anything, esp clothes

wash up *vb (adv)* **1** *chiefly Brit* to wash (dishes, cutlery, etc) after a meal **2** *(intr) US & Canad* to wash one's face and hands ▷ *n* **washup** **3** *Austral* the end, outcome of a process: *in the washup, three were elected*

washy ('wɒʃɪ) *adj* **washier, washiest** **1** overdiluted, watery, or weak **2** lacking intensity or strength > '**washiness** *n*

Wasim Akram ('wæzɪm 'ækræm) *n* **Chaudhry** born 1966, Pakistani cricketer; captain of Pakistan 1993–94, 1995–2000

wasn't ('wɒz^{ə}nt) *contraction of* was not

wasp (wɒsp) *n* **1** a social hymenopterous insect, such as the **common wasp,** having a black-and-yellow body and an ovipositor specialized for stinging **2** any of various solitary hymenopterans, such as the digger wasp and gall wasp [OE *wæsp*] > '**wasp**ˌ**like** *adj* > '**waspy** *adj* > '**waspily** *adv* > '**waspiness** *n*

Wasp *or* **WASP** (wɒsp) *n* (in the US) *acronym for* White Anglo-Saxon Protestant: a person descended from N European, usually Protestant stock, forming a group often considered the most dominant, privileged, and influential in American society

waspish ('wɒspɪʃ) *adj* **1** relating to or suggestive of a wasp **2** easily annoyed or angered > '**waspishly** *adv*

wasp waist *n* a very slender waist, esp one that is tightly corseted > '**wasp-,waisted** *adj*

wassail ('wɒseɪl) *n* **1** (formerly) a toast or salutation made to a person at festivities **2** a festivity when much drinking takes place **3** alcoholic drink drunk at such a festivity, esp spiced beer or mulled wine ▷ *vb* **4** to drink the health of (a person) at a wassail **5** (*intr*) to go from house to house singing carols at Christmas [c13 from ON *ves heill* be in good health] > '**wassailer** *n*

Wassermann test *or* **reaction** ('wæsəmən) *n med* a diagnostic test for syphilis [c20 after August von *Wassermann* (1866–1925), G bacteriologist]

wast (wɒst; *unstressed* wəst) *vb arch or dialect* (used with the pronoun *thou* or its relative equivalent) a singular form of the past tense (indicative mood) of **be**

wastage ('weɪstɪdʒ) *n* **1** anything lost by wear or waste **2** the process of wasting **3** reduction in size of a workforce by retirement, etc (esp in **natural wastage**)

> USAGE *Waste* and *wastage* are to some extent interchangeable, but many people think that *wastage* should not be used to refer to loss resulting from human carelessness, inefficiency, etc: *a waste* (not *a wastage*) *of time, money, effort*, etc

waste (weɪst) *vb* **wastes, wasting, wasted 1** (*tr*) to use, consume, or expend thoughtlessly, carelessly, or to no avail **2** (*tr*) to fail to take advantage of: *to waste an opportunity* **3** (when *intr*, often foll by *away*) to lose or cause to lose bodily strength, health, etc **4** to exhaust or become exhausted **5** (*tr*) to ravage **6** (*tr*) *sl* to murder or kill ▷ *n* **7** the act of wasting or state of being wasted **8** a failure to take advantage of something **9** anything unused or not used to full advantage **10** anything or anyone rejected as useless, worthless, or in excess of what is required **11** garbage, rubbish, or trash **12** a land or region that is devastated or ruined **13** a land or region that is wild or uncultivated **14** *physiol* **14a** the useless products of metabolism **14b** indigestible food residue **15** *law* reduction in the value of an estate caused by act or neglect, esp by a life tenant ▷ *adj* **16** rejected as useless, unwanted, or worthless **17** produced in excess of what is required **18** not cultivated, inhabited, or productive: *waste land* **19a** of or denoting the useless products of metabolism **19b** of or denoting indigestible food residue **20** destroyed, devastated, or ruined **21 lay waste** to devastate or destroy [c13 from Anglo-F, from L *vastāre* to lay waste, from *vastus* empty]

wasted ('weɪstɪd) *adj* **1** not taken advantage of: *a wasted opportunity* **2** unprofitable: *wasted effort* **3** enfeebled and emaciated: *a thin wasted figure* **4** *sl* showing signs of habitual drug abuse

wasteful ('weɪstfʊl) *adj* **1** tending to waste or squander **2** causing waste or devastation > '**wastefully** *adv* > '**wastefulness** *n*

wasteland ('weɪst,lænd) *n* **1** a barren or desolate area of land **2** a region, period in history, etc, that is considered spiritually, intellectually, or aesthetically barren or desolate

wastepaper ('weɪst,peɪpə) *n* paper discarded after use

wastepaper basket *or* **bin** *n* an open receptacle for paper and other dry litter. Usual US and Canad word: **wastebasket**

waste pipe *n* a pipe to take excess or used water away, as from a sink to a drain

waster ('weɪstə) *n* **1** a person or thing that wastes **2** a ne'er-do-well; wastrel

wasting ('weɪstɪŋ) *adj* (*prenominal*) reducing the vitality, strength, or robustness of the body: *a wasting disease* > '**wastingly** *adv*

wasting asset *n* an unreplaceable business asset of limited life, such as an oil well

wastrel ('weɪstrəl) *n* **1** a wasteful person; spendthrift; prodigal **2** an idler or vagabond

Wast Water (wɒst) *n* a lake in NW England, in Cumbria in the Lake District. Length: 5 km (3 miles)

wat (wɑːt) *n* a Thai Buddhist monastery or temple [Thai, from Sansk. *vāta* enclosure]

watap (wæ'tɑːp, wɑː-) *n* a stringy thread made by North American Indians from the roots of various conifers and used for weaving and sewing [c18 from Canad F, from Cree *watapiy*]

watch (wɒtʃ) *vb* **1** to look at or observe closely or attentively **2** (*intr*; foll by *for*) to wait attentively **3** to guard or tend (something) closely or carefully **4** (*intr*) to keep vigil **5** (*tr*) to maintain an interest in: *to watch the progress of a child at school* **6 watch it!** be careful! ▷ *n* **7a** a small portable timepiece, usually worn strapped to the wrist (a **wristwatch**) or in a waistcoat pocket **7b** (*as modifier*): *a watch spring* **8** a watching **9** a period of vigil, esp during the night **10** (formerly) one of a set of periods into which the night was divided **11** *naut* **11a** any of the periods, usually of four hours, during which part of a ship's crew are on duty **11b** those officers and crew on duty during a specified watch **12** the period during which a guard is on duty **13** (formerly) a watchman or band of watchmen **14 on the watch** on the lookout ▷ See also **watch out** [OE *wæccan* (vb), *wæcce* (n)] > '**watcher** *n*

-watch *suffix of nouns* indicating a regular television programme or newspaper feature on the topic specified: *Crimewatch*

watchable ('wɒtʃəbᵊl) *adj* **1** capable of being watched **2** interesting, enjoyable, or entertaining: *a watchable television documentary*

watchcase ('wɒtʃ,keɪs) *n* a protective case for a watch, generally of metal such as gold or silver

watch chain *n* a chain used for fastening a pocket watch to the clothing. See also **fob**[1]

Watch Committee *n Brit history* a local government committee responsible for the efficiency of the local police force

watchdog ('wɒtʃ,dɒg) *n* **1** a dog kept to guard property **2a** a person or group that acts as a protector against inefficiency, etc **2b** (*as modifier*): *a watchdog committee*

watch fire *n* a fire kept burning at night as a signal or for warmth and light by a person keeping watch

watchful ('wɒtʃfʊl) *adj* **1** vigilant or alert **2** *arch* not sleeping > '**watchfully** *adv* > '**watchfulness** *n*

watch-glass *n* **1** a curved glass disc that covers the dial of a watch **2** a similarly shaped piece of glass used in laboratories for evaporating small samples of a solution, etc

watchmaker ('wɒtʃ,meɪkə) *n* a person who makes or mends watches > '**watch,making** *n*

watchman ('wɒtʃmən) *n, pl* **watchmen 1** a person employed to guard buildings or property **2** (formerly) a man employed to patrol or guard the streets at night

watch night *n* (in Protestant churches) **1a** the night of December 24, during which a service is held to mark the arrival of Christmas Day **1b** the night of December 31, during which a service is held to mark the passing of the old year **2** the service held on either of these nights

watch out *vb* (*intr, adv*) to be careful or on one's guard

watchstrap ('wɒtʃ,stræp) *n* a strap of leather, cloth, etc, attached to a watch for fastening it around the wrist. Also called (US and Canad): **watchband**

watchtower ('wɒtʃ,taʊə) *n* a tower on which a sentry keeps watch

watchword ('wɒtʃ,wɜːd) *n* **1** another word for **password** **2** a rallying cry or slogan

water ('wɔːtə) *n* **1** a clear colourless tasteless odourless liquid that is essential for plant and animal life and

Ww

constitutes, in impure form, rain, oceans, rivers, lakes, etc Formula: H_2O. Related adj: **aqueous** **2a** any body or area of this liquid, such as a sea, lake, river, etc **2b** (*as modifier*): *water sports; a water plant*. Related adj: **aquatic** **3** the surface of such a body or area: *fish swam below the water* **4** any form or variety of this liquid, such as rain **5** See **high water, low water** **6** any of various solutions of chemical substances in water: *ammonia water* **7** *physiol* **7a** any fluid secreted from the body, such as sweat, urine, or tears **7b** (*usually pl*) the amniotic fluid surrounding a fetus in the womb **8** a wavy lustrous finish on some fabrics, esp silk **9** *arch* the degree of brilliance in a diamond **10** excellence, quality, or degree (in **of the first water**) **11** *finance* capital stock issued without a corresponding increase in paid-up capital **12** (*modifier*) *astrol* of or relating to the three signs of the zodiac Cancer, Scorpio, and Pisces **13** **hold water** to prove credible, logical, or consistent: *the alibi did not hold water* **14** **make water** **14a** to urinate **14b** (of a boat, etc) to let in water **15** **pass water** to urinate **16** **water under the bridge** events that are past and done with ▹ *vb* **17** (*tr*) to sprinkle, moisten, or soak with water **18** (*tr; often foll by down*) to weaken by the addition of water **19** (*intr*) (of the eyes) to fill with tears **20** (*intr*) (of the mouth) to salivate, esp in anticipation of food (esp in **make one's mouth water**) **21** (*tr*) to irrigate or provide with water: *to water the land* **22** (*intr*) to drink water **23** (*intr*) (of a ship, etc) to take in a supply of water **24** (*tr*) *finance* to raise the par value of (issued capital stock) without a corresponding increase in the real value of assets **25** (*tr*) to produce a wavy lustrous finish on (fabrics, esp silk) ▹ See also **water down** [OE *wæter*] > **'waterer** *n* > **'waterless** *adj*

water bag *n* a bag, sometimes made of skin, leather, etc, but in Australia usually canvas, for carrying water

water bailiff *n* an official responsible for enforcing laws on shipping and fishing

water bear *n* another name for a **tardigrade**

water bed *n* a waterproof mattress filled with water

water beetle *n* any of various beetles that live most of the time in freshwater ponds, rivers, etc

water bird *n* any aquatic bird, including the wading and swimming birds

water biscuit *n* a thin crisp plain biscuit, usually served with butter or cheese

water blister *n* a blister containing watery or serous fluid, without any blood or pus

water boatman *n* any of various aquatic bugs having a flattened body and oarlike hind legs, adapted for swimming

water bomber *n Canad* an aircraft with special tanks for holding water that can be dropped on forest fires

waterborne ('wɔːtəˌbɔːn) *adj* **1** floating or travelling on water **2** (of a disease, etc) transported or transmitted by water

waterbuck ('wɔːtəˌbʌk) *n* any of a genus of antelopes of swampy areas of Africa, having long curved ridged horns

water buffalo *or* **ox** *n* a member of the cattle tribe of swampy regions of S Asia, having widely spreading back-curving horns. Domesticated forms are used as draught animals

water bug *n* any of various heteropterous insects adapted to living in the water or on its surface, esp any of the **giant water bugs** of North America, India, and southern Africa, which have flattened hairy legs

water butt *n* a barrel for collecting rainwater, esp from a drainpipe

water cannon *n* an apparatus for pumping water through a nozzle at high pressure, used in quelling riots

Water Carrier *or* **Bearer** *n* **the** the constellation Aquarius, the 11th sign of the zodiac

water chestnut *n* **1** a floating aquatic plant of Asia, having four-pronged edible nutlike fruits **2** **Chinese water chestnut** a Chinese plant with an edible succulent corm **3** the corm of the Chinese water chestnut, used in Oriental cookery

water clock *or* **glass** *n* any of various devices for measuring time that use the escape of water as the motive force

water closet *n* **1** a lavatory flushed by water **2** a small room that has a lavatory ▹ Usually abbreviated to **WC**

watercolour *or US* **watercolor** ('wɔːtəˌkʌlə) *n* **1** water-soluble pigment bound with gum arabic, applied in transparent washes and without the admixture of white pigment in the lighter tones **2a** a painting done in watercolours **2b** (*as modifier*): *a watercolour masterpiece* **3** the art or technique of painting with such pigments > **'waterˌcolourist** *or US* **'waterˌcolorist** *n*

water-cool *vb* (*tr*) to cool (an engine, etc) by a flow of water circulating in an enclosed jacket > **'water-ˌcooled** *adj*

water cooler *n* **1** a device for cooling and dispensing drinking water ▹ (*modifier*) **water-cooler** **2** *US inf* indicating the kind of informal conversation among office staff that takes place at such a dispenser: *water-cooler discussions*

watercourse ('wɔːtəˌkɔːs) *n* **1** a stream, river, or canal **2** the channel, bed, or route along which this flows

watercraft ('wɔːtəˌkrɑːft) *n* **1** a boat or ship or such vessels collectively **2** skill in handling boats or in water sports

watercress ('wɔːtəˌkrɛs) *n* an Old World plant of clear ponds and streams, having pungent leaves that are used in salads and as a garnish

water cure *n med* a nontechnical name for **hydropathy** or **hydrotherapy**

water cycle *n* the circulation of the earth's water, in which water evaporates from the sea into the atmosphere, where it condenses and falls as rain or snow, returning to the sea by rivers

water diviner *n Brit* a person able to locate the presence of water, esp underground, with a divining rod

water down *vb* (*tr, adv*) **1** to dilute or weaken with water **2** to modify, esp so as to omit anything unpleasant or offensive: *to water down the truth* > **ˌwatered-'down** *adj*

waterfall ('wɔːtəˌfɔːl) *n* a cascade of falling water where there is a vertical or almost vertical step in a river

water flea *n* any of numerous minute freshwater crustaceans which swim by means of hairy branched antennae. See also **daphnia**

Waterford ('wɔːtəfəd) *n* **1** a county of S Republic of Ireland, in Munster province on the Atlantic: mountainous in the centre and in the northwest. County town: Waterford. Pop: 94 680 (1996). Area: 1838 sq km (710 sq miles) **2** a port in S Republic of Ireland, county town of Co Waterford: famous glass industry; fishing. Pop: 42 540 (1996)

waterfowl ('wɔːtəˌfaʊl) *n* **1** any aquatic freshwater bird, esp any species of the family Anatidae (ducks, geese, and swans) **2** such birds collectively

waterfront ('wɔːtəˌfrʌnt) *n* the area of a town or city alongside a body of water, such as a harbour or dockyard

water gap *n* a deep valley in a ridge, containing a stream

water gas *n* a mixture of hydrogen and carbon monoxide produced by passing steam over hot carbon, used as a fuel and raw material

water gate *n* **1** a gate in a canal, etc, that can be opened or closed to control the flow of water **2** a gate through which access may be gained to a body of water

Watergate ('wɔːtəˌgeɪt) *n* **1** an incident during the 1972 US presidential campaign, when agents employed by the re-election organization of President Richard Nixon were caught breaking into the Democratic Party

headquarters in the Watergate building, Washington, DC. The political scandal was exacerbated by attempts to conceal the fact that White House officials had approved the burglary, and eventually forced the resignation of President Nixon **2** any similar public scandal, esp involving politicians or a possible cover-up
▷ http://watergate.info
▷ www.wikipedia.org/wiki/Watergate_scandal

water gauge *n* an instrument that indicates the presence or the quantity of water in a tank, reservoir, or boiler feed. Also called: **water glass**

water glass *n* **1** a viscous syrupy solution of sodium silicate in water: used as a protective coating for cement and a preservative, esp for eggs **2** another name for **water gauge**

water gum *n* any of several Australian gum trees that grow in swampy ground and beside creeks and rivers

water hammer *n* a sharp concussion produced when the flow of water in a pipe is suddenly blocked

water hen *n* another name for **gallinule**

water hole *n* **1** a depression, such as a pond or pool, containing water, esp one used by animals as a drinking place **2** a source of drinking water in a desert

Waterhouse (ˈwɔːtəˌhaʊs) *n* **1** **Alfred** 1830–1905, British architect; a leader of the Gothic Revival. His buildings include Manchester Town Hall (1868) and the Natural History Museum, London (1881) **2** **George Marsden** 1824–1906, New Zealand statesman, born in England: prime minister of New Zealand (1872–73) **3** **Keith** (**Spencer**) born 1929, British novelist, dramatist, and journalist: best known for the novel *Billy Liar* (1959) and his collaborations with the dramatist Willis Hall (born 1929)

water hyacinth *n* a floating aquatic plant of tropical America, having showy bluish-purple flowers and swollen leafstalks. It forms dense masses in rivers, ponds, etc

water ice *n* an ice cream made from a frozen sugar syrup flavoured with fruit juice or purée

watering can *n* a container with a handle and a spout with a perforated nozzle used to sprinkle water over plants

watering hole *n* **1** a pool where animals drink; water hole **2** *facetious sl* a pub

watering place *n* **1** a place where drinking water for people or animals may be obtained **2** *Brit* a spa **3** *Brit* a seaside resort

water jacket *n* a water-filled envelope surrounding a machine or part for cooling purposes, esp the casing around the cylinder block of a pump or internal-combustion engine

water jump *n* a ditch or brook over which athletes or horses must jump in a steeplechase or similar contest

water level *n* **1** the level reached by the surface of a body of water **2** the water line of a boat or ship

water lily *n* any of various aquatic plants of temperate and tropical regions, having large leaves and showy flowers that float on the surface of the water

water line *n* **1** a line marked at the level around a vessel's hull to which the vessel will be immersed when afloat **2** a line marking the level reached by a body of water

waterlogged (ˈwɔːtəˌlɒgd) *adj* **1** saturated with water **2** (of a vessel still afloat) having taken in so much water as to be unmanageable

Waterloo (ˌwɔːtəˈluː) *n* **1** a small town in central Belgium, in Walloon Brabant province south of Brussels: battle (1815) fought nearby in which British and Prussian forces under the Duke of Wellington and Blücher routed the French under Napoleon. Pop: 17 800 (latest est) **2** a total or crushing defeat (esp in **meet one's Waterloo**)

water main *n* a principal supply pipe in an arrangement of pipes for distributing water

waterman (ˈwɔːtəmən) *n, pl* **watermen** a skilled boatman > ˈ**watermanˌship** *n*

watermark (ˈwɔːtəˌmɑːk) *n* **1** a mark impressed on paper during manufacture, visible when the paper is held up to the light **2** another word for **water line** ▷ *vb* (*tr*) **3** to mark (paper) with a watermark

water meadow *n* a meadow that remains fertile by being periodically flooded by a stream

watermelon (ˈwɔːtəˌmɛlən) *n* **1** an African melon widely cultivated for its large edible fruit **2** the fruit of this plant, which has a hard green rind and sweet watery reddish flesh

water meter *n* a device for measuring the quantity or rate of water flowing through a pipe

water milfoil *n* any of various pond plants having feathery underwater leaves and inconspicuous flowers

water mill *n* a mill operated by a water wheel

water moccasin *n* a large dark grey venomous snake of swamps in the southern US. Also called: **cottonmouth**

water nymph *n* any fabled nymph of the water, such as the Naiad, Nereid, or Oceanid of Greek mythology

water of crystallization *n* water present in the crystals of certain compounds. It is chemically combined in a specific amount but can often be easily expelled

water ouzel *n* another name for **dipper** (the bird)

water paint *n* any water-based paint, such as an emulsion or an acrylic paint

water pipe *n* **1** a pipe for water **2** another name for **hookah**

water pistol *n* a toy pistol that squirts a stream of water or other liquid

water plantain *n* any of a genus of marsh plants of N temperate regions and Australia, having clusters of small white or pinkish flowers and broad pointed leaves

water polo *n* a game played in water by two teams of seven swimmers in which each side tries to throw or propel an inflated ball into the opponents' goal
▷ www.fina.org

water power *n* **1** the power latent in a dynamic or static head of water as used to drive machinery, esp for generating electricity **2** a source of such power, such as a drop in the level of a river, etc

waterproof (ˈwɔːtəˌpruːf) *adj* **1** not penetrable by water ▷ Cf **water-repellent, water-resistant** ▷ *n* **2** *chiefly Brit* a waterproof garment, esp a raincoat ▷ *vb* (*tr*) **3** to make (a fabric, etc) waterproof

water purslane *n* a marsh plant of temperate and warm regions, having reddish stems and small greenish flowers

water rail *n* a large Eurasian rail of swamps, ponds, etc, having a long red bill

water rat *n* **1** any of several small amphibious rodents, esp the water vole or the muskrat **2** any of various amphibious rats of New Guinea, the Philippines, and Australia

water rate *n* a charge made for the public supply of water

water-repellent *adj* (of fabrics, garments, etc) having a finish that resists the absorption of water

water-resistant *adj* (esp of fabrics) designed to resist but not entirely prevent the penetration of water

Waters (ˈwɔːtəz) *n* **Muddy,** real name *McKinley Morganfield*. 1915–83, US blues guitarist, singer, and songwriter. His songs include "Rollin' Stone" (1948) and "Got my Mojo Working" (1954)

water scorpion *n* a long-legged aquatic insect that breathes by means of a long spinelike tube that projects from the rear of the body and penetrates the surface of the water

watershed (ˈwɔːtəˌʃɛd) *n* **1** the dividing line between two adjacent river systems, such as a ridge **2** an

important period or factor that serves as a dividing line
waterside ('wɔːtəˌsaɪd) *n* **a** the area of land beside a body of water **b** (*as modifier*): *waterside houses*
watersider ('wɔːtəˌsaɪdə) *n Austral & NZ* a wharf labourer
water-ski *n* **1** a type of ski used for planing or gliding over water ▷ *vb* **water-skis, water-skiing, water-skied** *or* **water-ski'd** **2** (*intr*) to ride over water on water-skis while holding a rope towed by a speedboat > **'water-ˌskier** *n* > **'water-ˌskiing** *n*
water snake *n* any of various snakes that live in or near water, esp any of a genus of harmless North American snakes
water softener *n* **1** any substance that lessens the hardness of water, usually by precipitating calcium and magnesium ions **2** an apparatus that is used to remove chemicals that cause hardness
water spaniel *n* either of two large curly-coated breeds of spaniel (the Irish and the American), which are used for hunting waterfowl
water splash *n* a place where a stream runs over a road
water sports *pl n* sports, such as swimming or windsurfing, that take place in or on water
▷ www.iwsf.com
▷ www.worldwindsurfing.com
waterspout ('wɔːtəˌspaʊt) *n* **1** *meteorol* **1a** a tornado occurring over water that forms a column of water and mist **1b** a sudden downpour of heavy rain **2** a pipe or channel through which water is discharged
water table *n* **1** the level below which the ground is saturated with water **2** a string course that has a moulding designed to throw rainwater clear of the wall below
water thrush *n* either of two North American warblers having brownish backs and striped underparts and occurring near water
watertight ('wɔːtəˌtaɪt) *adj* **1** not permitting the passage of water either in or out: *a watertight boat* **2** without loopholes: *a watertight argument* **3** kept separate from other subjects or influences
water tower ('taʊə) *n* a reservoir or storage tank mounted on a tower-like structure so that water can be distributed at a uniform pressure
water vapour *n* water in the gaseous state, esp when due to evaporation at a temperature below the boiling point
water vole *n* a large amphibious vole of Eurasian river banks. Also called: **water rat**
water wagtail *n* another name for **pied wagtail**
waterway ('wɔːtəˌweɪ) *n* a river, canal, or other navigable channel used as a means of travel or transport
waterweed ('wɔːtəˌwiːd) *n* any of various weedy aquatic plants
water wheel *n* **1** a simple water-driven turbine consisting of a wheel having vanes set axially across its rim, used to drive machinery **2** a wheel with buckets attached to its rim for raising water from a stream, pond, etc
water wings *pl n* an inflatable rubber device shaped like a pair of wings, which is placed under the arms of a person learning to swim
waterworks ('wɔːtəˌwɜːks) *n* **1** (*functioning as sing*) an establishment for storing, purifying, and distributing water for community supply **2** (*functioning as pl*) a display of water in movement, as in fountains **3** (*functioning as pl*) *Brit inf, euphemistic* the urinary system **4** (*functioning as pl*) *inf* crying; tears
waterworn ('wɔːtəˌwɔːn) *adj* worn smooth by the action or passage of water
watery ('wɔːtərɪ) *adj* **1** relating to, containing, or resembling water **2** discharging or secreting water or a water-like fluid **3** tearful; weepy **4** insipid, thin, or weak
Watford ('wɒtfəd) *n* a town in SE England, in SW Hertfordshire: light industries, services. Pop: 113 080 (1991)
Watling Island ('wɒtlɪŋ) *n* another name for **San Salvador Island**
Watson ('wɒtsən) *n* **1** **James Dewey** born 1928, US biologist, whose contribution to the discovery of the helical structure of DNA won him a Nobel prize for physiology or medicine shared with Francis Crick and Maurice Wilkins in 1962 **2** **John B(roadus)** 1878–1958, US psychologist; a leading exponent of behaviourism **3** **John Christian** 1867–1941, Australian statesman, born in Chile: prime minister of Australia (1904) **4** **Russell** born 1973, British tenor, maker of the bestselling albums *The Voice* (2001) and *Encore* (2002) **5** **Tom,** full name *Thomas Sturges Watson* born 1949, US golfer: won the US Open Championship (1982), the British Open Championship (1975, 1977, 1980, 1982, 1983), and the World Series (1975, 1977, 1980)
Watson-Watt ('wɒtsən'wɒt) *n* Sir **Robert Alexander** 1892–1973, Scottish physicist, who played a leading role in the development of radar
watt (wɒt) *n* the derived SI unit of power, equal to 1 joule per second; the power dissipated by a current of 1 ampere flowing across a potential difference of 1 volt. Symbol: W [c19 after J. WATT]
Watt (wɒt) *n* **James** 1736–1819, Scottish engineer and inventor. His fundamental improvements to the steam engine led to the widespread use of steam power in industry
wattage ('wɒtɪdʒ) *n* **1** power, esp electric power, measured in watts **2** the power rating, measured in watts, of an electrical appliance
Watteau ('wɒtəʊ; *French* vato) *n* **Jean-Antoine** (ʒɑ̃ ɑ̃twan) 1684–1721, French painter, esp of *fêtes champêtres*
Wattenscheid (*German* 'vatənʃait) *n* an industrial town in NW Germany, in North Rhine-Westphalia east of Essen. Pop: 81 200 (latest est)
watt-hour *n* a unit of energy equal to a power of one watt operating for one hour
wattle ('wɒtᵊl) *n* **1** a frame of rods or stakes interwoven with twigs, branches, etc, esp when used to make fences **2** the material used in such a construction **3** a loose fold of skin, often brightly coloured, hanging from the neck or throat of certain birds, lizards, etc **4** any of various chiefly Australian acacia trees having spikes of small brightly coloured flowers and flexible branches ▷ *vb* **wattles, wattling, wattled** (*tr*) **5** to construct from wattle **6** to bind or frame with wattle **7** to weave or twist (branches, twigs, etc) into a frame ▷ *adj* **8** made of or covered with wattle [OE *watol*] > **'wattled** *adj*
wattle and daub *n* a form of wall construction consisting of interwoven twigs plastered with a mixture of clay, water, and sometimes chopped straw
wattmeter ('wɒtˌmiːtə) *n* a meter for measuring electric power in watts
Watts (wɒts) *n* **1** **George Frederick** 1817–1904, English painter and sculptor, noted esp for his painting *Hope* (1886) and his sculpture *Physical Energy* (1904) in Kensington Gardens, London **2** **Isaac** 1674–1748, English hymn-writer
Waugh (wɔː) *n* **Evelyn** (**Arthur St John**) ('iːvlɪn) 1903–66, English novelist. His early satirical novels include *Decline and Fall* (1928), *Vile Bodies* (1930), *A Handful of Dust* (1934), and *Scoop* (1938). His later novels include the more sombre *Brideshead Revisited* (1945) and the trilogy of World War II *Men at Arms* (1952), *Officers and Gentlemen* (1955), and *Unconditional Surrender* (1961) **2** **Mark** (**Edward**) born 1965, Australian cricketer **3** his twin brother **Steve,** full name *Stephen Roger Waugh*. born 1965, Australian cricketer; captain of the Australian team that won the 1999 one-day World Cup
waul *or* **wawl** (wɔːl) *vb* (*intr*) to cry or wail plaintively like a cat [c16 imit.]

wave (weɪv) *vb* **waves, waving, waved 1** to move or cause to move freely to and fro: *the banner waved in the wind* **2** (*intr*) to move the hand to and fro as a greeting **3** to signal or signify by or as if by waving something **4** (*tr*) to direct to move by or as if by waving something: *he waved me on* **5** to form or be formed into curves, undulations, etc **6** (*tr*) to set waves in (the hair) ▹ *n* **7** one of a sequence of ridges or undulations that moves across the surface of a body of a liquid, esp the sea **8 the waves** the sea **9** any undulation on or at the edge of a surface reminiscent of a wave in the sea: *a wave across the field of corn* **10** anything that suggests the movement of a wave, as by a sudden rise: *a crime wave* **11** a widespread movement that advances in a body: *a wave of settlers* **12** the act or an instance of waving **13** *physics* an energy-carrying disturbance propagated through a medium or space by a progressive local displacement of the medium or a change in its physical properties, but without any overall movement of matter **14** *physics* a graphical representation of a wave obtained by plotting the magnitude of the disturbance against time at a particular point in the medium or space **15** a prolonged spell of some particular type of weather: *a heat wave* **16** an undulating curve or series of curves or loose curls in the hair **17 make waves** to cause trouble; disturb the status quo [OE *wafian* (vb); C16 (n) changed from earlier *wāwe*, prob. from OE *wǣg* motion] > ˈ**waveless** *adj* > ˈ**wave,like** *adj*

waveband (ˈweɪv,bænd) *n* a range of wavelengths or frequencies used for a particular type of radio transmission

wave-cut platform *n* a flat surface at the base of a cliff formed by erosion by waves

wave down *vb* (*tr, adv*) to signal with a wave to (a driver or vehicle) to stop

wave energy *n* energy obtained by harnessing wave power

wave equation *n physics* a partial differential equation describing wave motion

waveform (ˈweɪv,fɔːm) *n physics* the shape of the graph of a wave or oscillation obtained by plotting the value of some changing quantity against time

wavefront (ˈweɪv,frʌnt) *n physics* a surface associated with a propagating wave and passing through all points in the wave that have the same phase

wave function *n physics* a mathematical function of position and sometimes time, used in wave mechanics to describe the state of a physical system. Symbol: ψ

waveguide (ˈweɪv,gaɪd) *n electronics* a solid rod of dielectric or a hollow metal tube, usually of rectangular cross section, used as a path to guide microwaves

wavelength (ˈweɪv,lɛŋθ) *n* **1** the distance, measured in the direction of propagation, between two points of the same phase in consecutive cycles of a wave. Symbol: λ **2** the wavelength of the carrier wave used by a particular broadcasting station **3 on someone's** (*or* **the same**) **wavelength** *inf* having similar views, feelings, or thoughts (as someone else)

wavelet (ˈweɪvlɪt) *n* a small wave

Wavell (ˈweɪvᵊl) *n* **Archibald** (**Percival**), 1st Earl. 1883–1950, British field marshal. During World War II he was commander in chief in the Middle East (1939–41), defeating the Italians in N Africa. He was commander in chief in India (1941–43) and viceroy of India (1943–47)

wave mechanics *n* (*functioning as sing*) *physics* the formulation of quantum mechanics in which the behaviour of systems, such as atoms, is described in terms of their wave functions

wave number *n physics* the reciprocal of the wavelength of a wave

waver (ˈweɪvə) *vb* (*intr*) **1** to be irresolute; hesitate between two possibilities **2** to become unsteady **3** to fluctuate **4** to move back and forth or one way and another **5** (of light) to flicker or flash ▹ *n* **6** the act or an instance of wavering [C14 from ON *vafra* to flicker] > ˈ**waverer** *n* > ˈ**wavering** *adj* > ˈ**waveringly** *adv*

wave theory *n* **1** the theory proposed by Huygens that light is transmitted by waves **2** any theory that light or other radiation is transmitted as waves ▹ Cf **corpuscular theory**

wavey (ˈweɪvɪ) *n Canad* a snow goose or other wild goose. Also called: **wawa** [via Canad F from Algonquian (Cree *wehwew*)]

wavy (ˈweɪvɪ) *adj* **wavier, waviest 1** abounding in or full of waves **2** moving or proceeding in waves **3** (of hair) set in or having waves > ˈ**wavily** *adv* > ˈ**waviness** *n*

wax[1] (wæks) *n* **1** any of various viscous or solid materials of natural origin: characteristically lustrous, insoluble in water, and having a low softening temperature, they consist largely of esters of fatty acids **2** any of various similar substances, such as paraffin wax, that have a mineral origin and consist largely of hydrocarbons **3** short for **beeswax** or **sealing wax** **4** *physiol* another name for **cerumen** **5** a resinous preparation used by shoemakers to rub on thread **6** any substance or object that is pliable or easily moulded: *he was wax in their hands* **7** (*modifier*) made of or resembling wax: *a wax figure* ▹ *vb* **8** (*tr*) to coat, polish, etc, with wax [OE *weax*] > ˈ**waxer** *n*

wax[2] (wæks) *vb* (*intr*) **1** to become larger, more powerful, etc **2** (of the moon) to show a gradually increasing portion of illuminated surface, between new moon and full moon **3** to become: *to wax eloquent* [OE *weaxan*]

wax[3] (wæks) *n Brit inf, old-fashioned* a fit of rage or temper: *he's in a wax today* [from ?]

waxberry (ˈwæksbərɪ) *n, pl* **waxberries** the waxy fruit of the wax myrtle or the snowberry

waxbill (ˈwæks,bɪl) *n* any of various chiefly African finchlike weaverbirds having a brightly coloured bill and plumage

wax cloth *n* **1** another name for **oilcloth** **2** (formerly) another name for **linoleum**

waxen (ˈwæksən) *adj* **1** made of, treated with, or covered with wax **2** resembling wax in colour or texture

waxeye (ˈwæks,aɪ) *n* a small New Zealand bird with a white circle around its eye. Also called: **silver-eye, blighty**

wax flower *n Austral* any of a genus of shrubs having waxy pink-white five-petalled flowers

wax light *n* a candle or taper of wax

wax myrtle *n* a shrub of SE North America, having evergreen leaves and a small berry-like fruit with a waxy coating. Also called: **bayberry, candleberry, waxberry**

wax palm *n* **1** a tall Andean palm tree having pinnate leaves that yield a resinous wax used in making candles **2** another name for **carnauba** (sense 1)

wax paper *n* paper treated or coated with wax or paraffin to make it waterproof

waxplant (ˈwæks,plɑːnt) *n* a climbing shrub of E Asia and Australia, having fleshy leaves and clusters of small waxy white pink-centred flowers

waxwing (ˈwæks,wɪŋ) *n* any of a genus of gregarious passerine songbirds having red waxy wing tips and crested heads

waxwork (ˈwæks,wɜːk) *n* **1** an object reproduced in wax, esp as an ornament **2** a life-size lifelike figure, esp of a famous person, reproduced in wax **3** (*pl; functioning as sing or pl*) a museum or exhibition of wax figures

waxy[1] (ˈwæksɪ) *adj* **waxier, waxiest 1** resembling wax in colour, appearance, or texture **2** made of, covered with, or abounding in wax > ˈ**waxily** *adv* > ˈ**waxiness** *n*

waxy[2] (ˈwæksɪ) *adj* **waxier, waxiest** *Brit inf, old-fashioned* bad-tempered or irritable; angry

way (weɪ) *n* **1** a manner, method, or means: *a way of life* **2** a route or direction: *the way home* **3a** a means or line of

Ww

passage, such as a path or track **3b** (*in combination*): *waterway* **4** space or room for movement or activity (esp in **make way, in the way, out of the way**) **5** distance, usually distance in general: *you've come a long way* **6** a passage or journey: *on the way* **7** characteristic style or manner: *I did it my way* **8** (*often pl*) habit: *he has some offensive ways* **9** an aspect of something; particular: *in many ways he was right* **10a** a street in or leading out of a town **10b** (*cap when part of a street name*): *Icknield Way* **11** something that one wants in a determined manner (esp in **get** *or* **have one's (own) way**) **12** the experience or sphere in which one comes into contact with things (esp in **come one's way**) **13** *inf* a state or condition, usually financial or concerning health (esp in **in a good** (*or* **bad**) **way**) **14** *inf* the area or direction of one's home: *drop in if you're ever over my way* **15** movement of a ship or other vessel **16** a guide along which something can be moved, such as the surface of a lathe along which the tailstock slides **17** (*pl*) the wooden or metal tracks down which a ship slides to be launched **18** a course of life including experiences, conduct, etc: *the way of sin* **19 by the way** incidentally **20 by way of 20a** via **20b** serving as: *by way of introduction* **20c** in the state or condition of: *by way of being an artist* **21 each way** (of a bet) laid on a horse, dog, etc, to win or gain a place **22 give way 22a** to collapse or break down **22b** to yield **23 give way to 23a** to step aside for or stop for **23b** to give full rein to (emotions, etc) **24 go out of one's way** to take considerable trouble or inconvenience oneself **25 have a way with** to have such a manner or skill as to handle successfully **26 have it both ways** to enjoy two things that would normally be mutually exclusive **27 in a way** in some respects **28 in no way** not at all **29 lead the way 29a** to go first **29b** to set an example **30 make one's way 30a** to proceed or advance **30b** to achieve success in life **31 on the way out** *inf* **31a** becoming unfashionable, etc **31b** dying **32 out of the way 32a** removed or dealt with so as to be no longer a hindrance **32b** remote **32c** unusual and sometimes improper **33 see one's way (clear)** to find it possible and be willing (to do something) **34 under way** having started moving or making progress ▷ *adv* **35** *inf* **35a** at a considerable distance or extent: *way over yonder* **35b** very far: *they're way up the mountain* **36** *inf* by far; considerably: *way better* [OE *weg*]

waybill (ˈweɪˌbɪl) *n* a document attached to goods in transit specifying their nature, point of origin, and destination as well as the route to be taken and the rate to be charged

wayfarer (ˈweɪˌfɛərə) *n* a person who goes on a journey > ˈ**way,faring** *n, adj*

wayfaring tree *n* a shrub of Europe and W Asia, having white flowers and berries that turn from red to black

Wayland *or* **Wayland Smith** (ˈweɪlənd) *n* a smith, artificer, and king of the elves in European folklore. Scandinavian name: **Völund**. German name: **Wieland**

waylay (weɪˈleɪ) *vb* **waylays, waylaying, waylaid** (*tr*) **1** to lie in wait for and attack **2** to await and intercept unexpectedly > **wayˈlayer** *n*

wayleave (ˈweɪˌliːv) *n* access to property granted by a landowner for payment, for example to allow a contractor access to a building site

waymark (ˈweɪˌmɑːk) *n* a symbol or signpost marking the route of a footpath > ˈ**way,marked** *adj*

Wayne (weɪn) *n* **John**, real name *Marion Michael Morrison*. 1907–79, US film actor, noted esp for his many Westerns, which include *Stagecoach* (1939), *The Alamo* (1960), and *True Grit* (1969), for which he won an Oscar

way-out *adj inf* **1** extremely unconventional or experimental **2** excellent or amazing

-ways *suffix forming adverbs* indicating direction or manner: *sideways* [OE *weges*, lit.: of the way, from *weg* way]

ways and means *pl n* **1** the revenues and methods of raising the revenues needed for the functioning of a state or other political unit **2** the methods and resources for accomplishing some purpose

wayside (ˈweɪˌsaɪd) *n* **1a** the side or edge of a road **1b** (*modifier*) situated by the wayside: *a wayside inn* **2 fall by the wayside** to cease or fail to continue doing something: *of the nine starters, three fell by the wayside*

wayward (ˈweɪwəd) *adj* **1** wanting to have one's own way regardless of others **2** capricious, erratic, or unpredictable [C14 changed from *awayward* turned or turning away] > ˈ**waywardly** *adv* > ˈ**waywardness** *n*

wayworn (ˈweɪˌwɔːn) *adj rare* worn or tired by travel

Waziristan (wəˌzɪərɪˈstɑːn) *n* a mountainous region of N Pakistan, on the border with Afghanistan

wazzock (ˈwæzək) *n Brit inf* a foolish or annoying person [C20 of unknown origin]

wb *abbrev for:* **1** water ballast **2** Also: **W/B, WB** waybill **3** westbound

Wb *physics symbol for* weber

WBA *abbrev for* World Boxing Association

WBC *abbrev for* World Boxing Council

WBO *abbrev for* World Boxing Organization

WBU *abbrev for* World Boxing Union

WC *abbrev for:* **1** Also: **wc** water closet **2** (in London postal code) West Central

WD *abbrev for:* **1** War Department **2** Works Department

we (wiː) *pron* (*subjective*) **1** refers to the speaker or writer and another person or other people: *we should go now* **2** refers to all people or people in general: *the planet on which we live* **3** a formal word for **I** used by editors or other writers, and formerly by monarchs **4** *inf* used instead of *you* with a tone of condescension or sarcasm: *how are we today?* [OE *wē*]

WEA (in Britain) *abbrev for* Workers' Educational Association

weak (wiːk) *adj* **1** lacking in physical or mental strength or force **2** liable to yield, break, or give way: *a weak link in a chain* **3** lacking in resolution or firmness of character **4** lacking strength, power, or intensity: *a weak voice* **5** lacking strength in a particular part: *a team weak in defence* **6a** not functioning as well as is normal: *weak eyes* **6b** easily upset: *a weak stomach* **7** lacking in conviction, persuasiveness, etc: *a weak argument* **8** lacking in political or strategic strength: *a weak state* **9** lacking the usual, full, or desirable strength of flavour: *weak tea* **10** *grammar* **10a** denoting or belonging to a class of verbs, in Germanic languages, whose conjugation relies on inflectional endings rather than internal vowel gradation, as *look, looks, looking, looked* **10b** belonging to any part-of-speech class, in any of various languages, whose inflections follow the more regular of two possible patterns ▷ Cf **strong** (sense 13) **11** (of a syllable) not accented or stressed **12** (of an industry, market, securities, etc) falling in price or characterized by falling prices [OE *wāc* soft, miserable] > ˈ**weakish** *adj*

weaken (ˈwiːkən) *vb* to become or cause to become weak or weaker > ˈ**weakener** *n*

weak interaction *n physics* an interaction between elementary particles that is responsible for certain decay processes, operates at distances less than about 10^{-15} metres, and is 10^{12} times weaker than the strong interaction. Also called: **weak nuclear interaction** *or* **force**

weak-kneed *adj inf* yielding readily to force, intimidation, etc > ˌ**weak-ˈkneedly** *adv*

weakling (ˈwiːklɪŋ) *n* a person or animal that is lacking in strength or weak in constitution or character

weakly (ˈwiːklɪ) *adj* **weaklier, weakliest 1** sickly; feeble ▷ *adv* **2** in a weak or feeble manner

weak-minded *adj* **1** lacking in stability of mind or character **2** another word for **feeble-minded** > ˌ**weak-ˈmindedly** *adv* > ˌ**weak-ˈmindedness** *n*

weakness ('wiːknɪs) *n* **1** a being weak **2** a failing, as in a person's character **3** a self-indulgent liking: *a weakness for chocolates*
weal¹ (wiːl) *n* a raised mark on the skin produced by a blow. Also called: **welt** [C19 var. of WALE, infl. in form by WHEAL]
weal² (wiːl) *n arch* prosperity or wellbeing (now esp in **the public weal, the common weal**) [OE *wela*]
weald (wiːld) *n Brit arch* open or forested country [OE]
Weald (wiːld) *n* **the** a region of SE England, in Kent, Surrey, and East and West Sussex between the North Downs and the South Downs: formerly forested
wealth (wɛlθ) *n* **1** a large amount of money and valuable material possessions **2** the state of being rich **3** a great profusion: *a wealth of gifts* **4** *econ* all goods and services with monetary or productive value [C13 *welthe*, from WEAL²]
wealth tax *n* a tax on personal property
wealthy ('wɛlθɪ) *adj* **wealthier, wealthiest 1** possessing wealth; rich **2** of or relating to wealth **3** abounding: *wealthy in friends* > '**wealthily** *adv* > '**wealthiness** *n*
wean¹ (wiːn) *vb* (*tr*) **1** to cause (a child or young mammal) to replace mother's milk by other nourishment **2** (usually foll by *from*) to cause to desert former habits, pursuits, etc [OE *wenian* to accustom]
wean² (weɪn) *n Scot & N English dialect* a child [? short form of WEANLING, or a contraction of *wee ane*]
weaner ('wiːnə) *n* **1** a person or thing that weans **2** a pig that has just been weaned and weighs less than 40 kg **3** *Austral & NZ* a lamb, pig, or calf in the year in which it is weaned
weanling ('wiːnlɪŋ) *n* a child or young animal recently weaned [C16 from WEAN¹ + -LING¹]
weapon ('wɛpən) *n* **1** an object or instrument used in fighting **2** anything that serves to get the better of an opponent: *his power of speech was his best weapon* **3** any part of an animal that is used to defend itself, to attack prey, etc, such as claws or a sting [OE *wǣpen*] > '**weaponed** *adj* > '**weaponless** *adj*
weaponize *or* **weaponise** ('wɛpəˌnaɪz) *vb* (*tr*) to adapt (a chemical, bacillus, etc) in such a way that it can be used as a weapon
weapon of mass destruction ▹ *n* a chemical, biological, or nuclear weapon. Abbrev: **WMD**
weaponry ('wɛpənrɪ) *n* weapons regarded collectively
wear¹ (wɛə) *vb* **wears, wearing, wore, worn 1** (*tr*) to carry or have (a garment, etc) on one's person as clothing, ornament, etc **2** (*tr*) to carry or have on one's person habitually: *she wears a lot of red* **3** (*tr*) to have in one's aspect: *to wear a smile* **4** (*tr*) to display, show, or fly: *a ship wears its colours* **5** to deteriorate or cause to deteriorate by constant use or action **6** to produce or be produced by constant rubbing, scraping, etc: *to wear a hole in one's trousers* **7** to bring or be brought to a specified condition by constant use or action: *to wear a tyre to shreds* **8** (*intr*) to submit to constant use or action in a specified way: *his suit wears well* **9** (*tr*) to harass or weaken **10** (when *intr*, often foll by *on*) (of time) to pass or be passed slowly **11** (*tr*) *Brit inf* to accept: *Larry won't wear that argument* ▹ *n* **12** the act of wearing or state of being worn **13a** anything designed to be worn: *leisure wear* **13b** (*in combination*): *nightwear* **14** deterioration from constant or normal use **15** the quality of resisting the effects of constant use ▹ See also **wear down, wear off, wear out** [OE *werian*] > '**wearer** *n*
wear² (wɛə) *vb* **wears, wearing, wore, worn** *naut* to tack by gybing instead of by going through stays [C17 from earlier *weare*, from ?]
Wear (wɪə) *n* a river in NE England, rising in NW Durham and flowing southeast then northeast to the North Sea at Sunderland. Length: 105 km (65 miles)
wearable ('wɛərəbᵊl) *adj* suitable for wear or able to be worn > ˌ**weara'bility** *n*
wear and tear *n* damage, depreciation, or loss resulting from ordinary use
wear down *vb* (*adv*) **1** to consume or be consumed by long or constant wearing, rubbing, etc **2** to overcome or be overcome gradually by persistent effort
wearing ('wɛərɪŋ) *adj* causing fatigue or exhaustion; tiring > '**wearingly** *adv*
wearisome ('wɪərɪsəm) *adj* causing fatigue or annoyance; tedious > '**wearisomely** *adv*
wear off *vb* (*adv*) **1** (*intr*) to decrease in intensity gradually: *the pain will wear off in an hour* **2** to disappear or cause to disappear gradually through exposure, use, etc: *the pattern has worn off*
wear out *vb* (*adv*) **1** to make or become unfit or useless through wear **2** (*tr*) to exhaust or tire
weary ('wɪərɪ) *adj* **wearier, weariest 1** tired or exhausted **2** causing fatigue or exhaustion **3** caused by or suggestive of weariness: *a weary laugh* **4** (*postpositive*; often foll by *of* or *with*) discontented or bored ▹ *vb* **wearies, wearying, wearied 5** to make or become weary **6** to make or become discontented or impatient [OE *wērig*] > '**weariless** *adj* > '**wearily** *adv* > '**weariness** *n* > '**wearying** *adj* > '**wearyingly** *adv*
weasand ('wiːzənd) *n* a former name for the **trachea** [OE *wǣsend, wāsend*]
weasel ('wiːzᵊl) *n, pl* **weasels** *or* **weasel 1** any of various small predatory mammals, such as the **European weasel**, having reddish-brown fur, an elongated body and neck, and short legs **2** *inf* a sly or treacherous person [OE *weosule, wesle*] > '**weaselly** *adj*
weasel out *vb* **weasels, weaselling, weaselled** *or US* **weasels, weaseling, weaseled** (*intr, adv*) *inf, chiefly US & Canad* **1** to go back on a commitment **2** to evade a responsibility, esp in a despicable manner
weasel words *pl n inf* intentionally evasive or misleading speech; equivocation [C20 from the weasel's supposed ability to suck an egg out of its shell without seeming to break the shell] Ww
weather ('wɛðə) *n* **1a** the day-to-day meteorological conditions, esp temperature, cloudiness, and rainfall, affecting a specific place **1b** (*modifier*) relating to the forecasting of weather: *a weather ship* **2 make heavy weather 2a** *naut* to roll and pitch in heavy seas **2b** (foll by *of*) *inf* to carry out with difficulty or unnecessarily great effort **3 under the weather** *inf* not in good health ▹ *adj* **4** (*prenominal*) on or at the side or part towards the wind: *the weather anchor* ▹ Cf **lee** (sense 2) ▹ *vb* **5** to expose or be exposed to the action of the weather **6** to undergo or cause to undergo changes, such as discoloration, due to the action of the weather **7** (*intr*) to withstand the action of the weather **8** (when *intr*, foll by *through*) to endure (a crisis, danger, etc) **9** (*tr*) to slope (a surface, such as a roof) so as to throw rainwater clear **10** (*tr*) to sail to the windward of: *to weather a point* [OE *weder*] > '**weatherer** *n*
▹ http://sciencepolicy.colorado.edu/socasp/toc_img.html
▹ www.wmo.ch
▹ www.worldweather.org
weather-beaten *adj* **1** showing signs of exposure to the weather **2** tanned or hardened by exposure to the weather
weatherboard ('wɛðəˌbɔːd) *n* a timber board, with a groove (rabbet) along the front of its top edge and along the back of its lower edge, that is fixed horizontally with others to form an exterior covering on a wall or roof > '**weatherˌboarding** *n*
weather-bound *adj* (of a vessel, aircraft, etc) delayed by bad weather
weathercock ('wɛðəˌkɒk) *n* **1** a weather vane in the form of a cock **2** a person who is fickle or changeable
weathered ('wɛðəd) *adj* **1** affected by exposure to the action of the weather **2** (of rocks and rock formations)

eroded, decomposed, or otherwise altered by the action of water, wind, frost, etc **3** (of a sill, roof, etc) having a sloped surface so as to allow rainwater to run off

weather eye *n* **1** the vision of a person trained to observe changes in the weather **2** *inf* an alert or observant gaze **3** **keep one's weather eye open** to stay on the alert

weatherglass ('wɛðə,glɑːs) *n arch* any of various instruments, esp a barometer, that measure atmospheric conditions

weather house *n* a model house, usually with two human figures, one that comes out to foretell bad weather and one that comes out to foretell good weather

weathering ('wɛðərɪŋ) *n* the mechanical and chemical breakdown of rocks by the action of rain, snow, etc

weatherly ('wɛðəlɪ) *adj* (of a sailing vessel) making very little leeway when close-hauled, even in a stiff breeze > '**weatherliness** *n*

weatherman ('wɛðə,mæn) *n, pl* **weathermen** *inf* a person who forecasts the weather, esp one who works in a meteorological office

weather map *or* **chart** *n* a chart showing weather conditions, compiled from simultaneous observations taken at various weather stations

weatherproof ('wɛðə,pruːf) *adj* **1** designed or able to withstand exposure to weather without deterioration ▷ *vb* **2** (*tr*) to render (something) weatherproof

weather station *n* one of a network of meteorological observation posts where weather data is recorded

weather strip *n* a thin strip of compressible material, such as spring metal, felt, etc, that is fitted between the frame of a door or window and the opening part to exclude wind and rain. Also called: **weatherstripping**

weather vane *n* a vane designed to indicate the direction in which the wind is blowing

weather window *n* a limited interval when weather conditions can be expected to be suitable for a particular project

weather-wise *adj* **1** skilful in predicting weather conditions **2** skilful in predicting trends in opinion, reactions, etc

weatherworn ('wɛðə,wɔːn) *adj* another word for **weather-beaten**

weave (wiːv) *vb* **weaves, weaving, wove** *or* **weaved; woven** *or* **weaved** **1** to form (a fabric) by interlacing (yarn, etc), esp on a loom **2** (*tr*) to make or construct by such a process: *to weave a shawl* **3** to construct by interlacing (cane, twigs, etc) **4** (of a spider) to make (a web) **5** (*tr*) to construct by combining separate elements into a whole **6** (*tr; often foll by in, into, through*, etc) to introduce: *to weave factual details into a fiction* **7** to create (a way, etc) by moving from side to side: *to weave through a crowd* **8** to interlace strands of artificial hair with natural hair in order to make it look more abundant **9** **get weaving** *inf* to hurry ▷ *n* **10** the method or pattern of weaving or the structure of a woven fabric: *an open weave* [OE *wefan*]

▷ www.faculty.de.gcsu.edu/~dvess/ids/fap/weav.html

weave-ons *pl n* strands of hair used to add length to natural hair

weaver ('wiːvə) *n* **1** a person who weaves, esp as a means of livelihood **2** short for **weaverbird**

Weaver ('wiːvə) *n* **Sigourney** (sɪ'gɔːnɪ) born 1949, US actress. Her films include *Alien* (1979) and its sequels, *Ghostbusters* (1984), *Gorillas in the Mist* (1988), and *The Ice Storm* (1997)

weaverbird ('wiːvə,bɜːd) *or* **weaver** *n* any of a family of small Old World passerine songbirds, having a short thick bill and a dull plumage and building covered nests: includes the house sparrow and whydahs

web (wɛb) *n* **1** any structure, fabric, etc, formed by or as if by weaving or interweaving **2** a mesh of fine tough threads built by a spider from a liquid secreted from its spinnerets and used to trap insects **3** a similar network of threads spun by certain insect larvae, such as the silkworm **4** a fabric, esp one in the process of being woven **5** a membrane connecting the toes of some aquatic birds or the digits of such aquatic mammals as the otter **6** the vane of a bird's feather **7** a thin piece of metal, esp one connecting two thicker parts as in an H-beam or an I-beam **8a** a continuous strip of paper as formed on a paper machine or fed from a reel into some printing presses **8b** (*as modifier*): *web offset* **9a** (*often cap*; preceded by *the*) short for **World Wide Web** **9b** (*as modifier*): *web pages* **10** any structure, construction, etc, that is intricately formed or complex: *a web of intrigue* ▷ *vb* **webs, webbing, webbed** **11** (*tr*) to cover with or as if with a web **12** (*tr*) to entangle or ensnare **13** (*intr*) to construct a web [OE *webb*] > '**webless** *adj*

web address *n computing* another name for **URL**

Web Address Abbreviations

NAME	USER
aero	organizations in the aerospace industry
biz	businesses
com	mainly commercial organizations
coop	cooperative organizations
ed	educational establishments
gov	reserved for US Government use
info	sites providing information
int	international organizations
mil	reserved for use by the US military
museum	museums
name	individual use
net	general use
org	any organization or company
pro	used by professionals

Webb (wɛb) *n* **1** Sir **Aston** 1849–1930, British architect. His work includes the Victoria and Albert Museum (1909), the Victoria Memorial (1911), and Admiralty Arch (1911) **2** **Mary** (**Gladys**) 1881–1927, British novelist, remembered for her novels of rustic life, notably *Precious Bane* (1924) **3** **Sidney** (**James**), Baron Passfield 1859–1947, British economist, social historian, and Fabian socialist. He and his wife (**Martha**) **Beatrice** (née *Potter*), 1858–1943, British writer on social and economic problems, collaborated in *The History of Trade Unionism* (1894) and *English Local Government* (1906–29), helped found the London School of Economics (1895), and started the *New Statesman* (1913)

webbed (wɛbd) *adj* **1** (of the feet of certain animals) having the digits connected by a thin fold of skin **2** having or resembling a web

webbing ('wɛbɪŋ) *n* **1** a strong fabric of hemp, cotton, jute, etc, woven in strips and used under springs in upholstery or for straps, etc **2** the skin that unites the digits of a webbed foot

WebBoard ('wɛb,bɔːd) *n computing* an Internet site where users can post messages, tutorials, information, and topics for discussion

webby ('wɛbɪ) *adj* **webbier, webbiest** of, relating to, resembling, or consisting of a web

webcam ('wɛb,kæm) *n* a camera that transmits still or moving images over the Internet

webcast ('wɛb,kɑːst) *n* a broadcast of an event over the World Wide Web

web design *n computing* the planning and creation of websites

web directory *n computing* a database of selected websites, ordered in such a way as to facilitate browsing

weber ('veɪbə) *n* the derived SI unit of magnetic flux; the flux that, when linking a circuit of one turn, produces in it an emf of 1 volt as it is reduced to zero at a uniform rate in one second. Symbol: Wb [c20 after W. E. WEBER]

Weber (*German* 've:bər) *n* **1** Baron **Carl Maria Friedrich Ernst von** (karl ma'ri:a 'fri:drɪç ɛrnst fɔn) 1786–1826, German composer and conductor. His three romantic operas are *Der Freischütz* (1821), *Euryanthe* (1823), and *Oberon* (1826) **2 Ernst Heinrich** (ɛrnst 'hainrɪç) 1795–1878, German physiologist and anatomist. He introduced the psychological concept of the just noticeable difference between stimuli **3 Max** (maks) 1864–1920, German economist and sociologist, best known for *The Protestant Ethic and the Spirit of Capitalism* (1904–05) **4 Wilhelm Eduard** ('vɪlhɛlm 'e:duart), brother of Ernst Heinrich Weber. 1804–91, German physicist, who conducted research into electricity and magnetism

Webern (*German* 've:bərn) *n* **Anton von** ('anto:n fɔn) 1883–1945, Austrian composer; pupil of Schoenberg, whose twelve-tone technique he adopted. His works include those for chamber ensemble, such as *Five Pieces for Orchestra* (1911–13)

web farm *n computing* a large website that uses two or more servers to handle user requests. Also called: **web server farm**

webfoot ('wɛb,fʊt) *n* **1** *zool* a foot having the toes connected by folds of skin **2** *anat* a foot having an abnormal membrane connecting adjacent toes

web-footed *or* **web-toed** *adj* (of certain animals) having webbed feet that facilitate swimming

weblish ('wɛblɪʃ) *n inf* the shorthand form of English that is used in text messaging, chat rooms, etc [c20 WEB (sense 14) + (ENG)LISH]

weblog ('wɛb,lɒg) *n* the full name for **blog** > **'web,logger** *n*

Webmail ('wɛb,meɪl) *n computing* a system of electronic mail that allows account holders to access their mail via an Internet site rather than downloading it onto their computer

webmaster ('wɛb,mɑ:stə) *n* a person responsible for the administration of a website on the World Wide Web

web pal *n inf* a person one meets and corresponds with over the Internet

website ('wɛb,saɪt) *n* a group of connected pages on the World Wide Web containing information on a particular subject

Webster ('wɛbstə) *n* **1 Daniel** 1782–1852, US politician and orator **2 John** ?1580–?1625, English dramatist, noted for his revenge tragedies *The White Devil* (?1612) and *The Duchess of Malfi* (?1613) **3 Noah** 1758–1843, US lexicographer, famous for his *American Dictionary of the English Language* (1828)

webwheel ('wɛb,wi:l) *n* **1** a wheel containing a plate or web instead of spokes **2** a wheel of which the rim, spokes, and centre are in one piece

wed (wɛd) *vb* **weds, wedding, wedded** *or* **wed 1** to take (a person of the opposite sex) as a husband or wife; marry **2** (*tr*) to join (two people) in matrimony **3** (*tr*) to unite closely [OE *weddian*] > **'wedded** *adj*

we'd (wi:d; *unstressed* wɪd) *contraction of* we had *or* we would

Wed. *abbrev for* Wednesday

Weddell Sea ('wɛdᵊl) *n* an arm of the S Atlantic in Antarctica

wedding ('wɛdɪŋ) *n* **1a** the act of marrying or the celebration of a marriage **1b** (*as modifier*): *wedding day* **2** the anniversary of a marriage (in such combinations as **silver wedding** or **diamond wedding**)

wedding breakfast *n* the meal usually served after a wedding ceremony or just before the bride and bridegroom leave for their honeymoon

wedding cake *n* a rich fruit cake, with one, two, or more tiers, covered with almond paste and decorated with royal icing, which is served at a wedding reception

wedding ring *n* a band ring with parallel sides, typically of precious metal, worn to indicate married status

▷ www.amnh.org/exhibitions/diamonds/love.html

Wedekind (*German* 've:dəkɪnt) *n* **Frank** 1864–1918, German dramatist, whose plays, such as *The Awakening of Spring* (1891) and *Pandora's Box* (1904), bitterly satirize the sexual repressiveness of society

wedge (wɛdʒ) *n* **1** a block of solid material, esp wood or metal, that is shaped like a narrow V in cross section and can be pushed or driven between two objects or parts of an object in order to split or secure them **2** any formation, structure, or substance in the shape of a wedge **3** something such as an idea, action, etc, that tends to cause division **4** a shoe with a wedge heel **5** *golf* a club, a No. 10 iron with a face angle of more than 50°, used for bunker or pitch shots **6** (formerly) a body of troops formed in a V-shape **7 thin end of the wedge** anything unimportant in itself that implies the start of something much larger ▷ *vb* **wedges, wedging, wedged 8** (*tr*) to secure with or as if with a wedge **9** to squeeze or be squeezed like a wedge into a narrow space **10** (*tr*) to force apart or divide with or as if with a wedge [OE *wecg*] > **'wedge,like** *adj* > **'wedgy** *adj*

wedge heel *n* a raised shoe heel with the heel and sole forming a solid block

wedge-tailed eagle *n* a large brown Australian eagle having a wedge-shaped tail. Also called: **eaglehawk**, *inf* **wedgie**

wedgie ('wɛdʒɪ) ▷ *n inf* the state of having one's underpants or shorts caught between one's buttocks (esp in the phrase **give someone a wedgie**) [c20 from WEDGE]

Wedgwood[1] ('wɛdʒwʊd) *n* **1** *trademark* pottery produced at the Wedgwood factories, esp such pottery having applied classical decoration in white on a blue or other coloured ground ▷ *adj* **2** relating to or characteristic of such pottery: *Wedgwood blue*

▷ www.wedgwood.com

Wedgwood[2] ('wɛdʒwʊd) *n* **Josiah** 1730–95, British potter, who founded the Wedgwood pottery works near Stoke-on-Trent in Staffordshire

▷ www.britainexpress.com/History/bio

wedlock ('wɛdlɒk) *n* **1** the state of being married **2 born** *or* **conceived out of wedlock** born or conceived when one's parents are not legally married [OE *wedlāc*, from *wedd* pledge + *-lāc*, suffix denoting activity, ?from *lāc* game]

Wednesday ('wɛnzdɪ) *n* the fourth day of the week; third day of the working week [OE *Wōdnes dæg* Woden's day, translation of L *mercurii dies* Mercury's day]

wee[1] (wi:) *adj* very small; tiny; minute [c13 from OE *wǣg* weight]

wee[2] (wi:) *inf, chiefly Brit* ▷ *n* **1a** the act or an instance of urinating **1b** urine ▷ *vb* **wees, weeing, weed 2** (*intr*) to urinate ▷ Also: **wee-wee** [from ?]

weed (wi:d) *n* **1** any plant that grows wild and profusely, esp one that grows among cultivated plants, depriving them of space, food, etc **2** *sl* **2a the weed** tobacco **2b** marijuana **3** *inf* a thin or unprepossessing person **4** an inferior horse, esp one showing signs of weakness ▷ *vb* **5** to remove (useless or troublesome plants) from (a garden, etc) [OE *weod*] > **'weeder** *n* > **'weedless** *adj*

weedkiller ('wi:d,kɪlə) *n* a substance, usually a chemical or hormone, used for killing weeds

weed out *vb* (*tr, adv*) to separate out, remove, or eliminate (anything unwanted): *to weed out troublesome students*

weeds (wi:dz) *pl n* a widow's black mourning clothes. Also called: **widow's weeds** [c16 pl of *weed* (OE *wǣd, wēd*) a band worn in mourning]

weedy ('wi:dɪ) *adj* **weedier, weediest 1** full of or containing weeds: *weedy land* **2** (of a plant) resembling a weed in straggling growth **3** *inf* thin or weakly in appearance

week (wi:k) *n* **1** a period of seven consecutive days, esp one beginning with Sunday. Related adj: **hebdomadal** **2** a period of seven consecutive days beginning from or including a specified day: *a week from Wednesday* **3** the period of time within a week devoted to work ▷ *adv* **4** *chiefly Brit* seven days before or after a specified day: *I'll visit you Wednesday week* [OE *wice, wicu*]

weekday ('wi:k,deɪ) *n* any day of the week other than Sunday and, often, Saturday

weekend *n* (,wi:k'ɛnd) **1a** the end of the week, esp the period from Friday night until the end of Sunday **1b** (*as modifier*): *a weekend party* ▷ *vb* ('wi:k,ɛnd) **2** (*intr*) *inf* to spend or pass a weekend

weekends (,wi:k'ɛndz) *adv inf* at the weekend, esp regularly or during every weekend

weekly ('wi:klɪ) *adj* **1** happening or taking place once a week or every week **2** determined or calculated by the week ▷ *adv* **3** once a week or every week ▷ *n, pl* **weeklies** **4** a newspaper or magazine issued every week

weeknight ('wi:k,naɪt) *n* the evening or night of a weekday

Weelkes (wi:lks) *n* **Thomas** ?1575–1623, English composer of madrigals

ween (wi:n) *vb arch* to think or imagine [OE *wēnan*]

weeny ('wi:nɪ) *adj* **weenier, weeniest** *inf* very small; tiny [C18 from WEE[1] with the ending -*ny* as in TINY]

weenybopper ('wi:nɪ,bɒpə) *n inf* a child of about 8 to 12 years who is a keen follower of pop music [C20 formed on the model of TEENYBOPPER, from WEENY]

weep (wi:p) *vb* **weeps, weeping, wept** **1** to shed (tears) **2** (*tr; foll by out*) to utter, shedding tears **3** (when *intr*, foll by *for*) to lament (for something) **4** to exude (drops of liquid) **5** (*intr*) (of a wound, etc) to exude a watery fluid ▷ *n* **6** a spell of weeping [OE *wēpan*]

weeper ('wi:pə) *n* **1** a person who weeps, esp a hired mourner **2** something worn as a sign of mourning

weeping ('wi:pɪŋ) *adj* (of plants) having slender hanging branches > '**weepingly** *adv*

weeping willow *n* a willow tree having long hanging branches

weepy ('wi:pɪ) *inf* ▷ *adj* **weepier, weepiest** **1** liable or tending to weep ▷ *n, pl* **weepies** **2** a sentimental film or book > '**weepily** *adv* > '**weepiness** *n*

weever ('wi:və) *n* a small marine fish having venomous spines around the gills and the dorsal fin [C17 from OF *wivre* viper, ult. from L *vīpera* VIPER]

weevil ('wi:vɪl) *n* any of numerous beetles, many having elongated snouts, that are pests, feeding on plants and plant products [OE *wifel*] > '**weevily** *adj*

wee-wee *n, vb* a variant of **wee**[2]

w.e.f. *abbrev for* with effect from

weft (wɛft) *n* the yarn woven across the width of the fabric through the lengthways warp yarn. Also called: **filling, woof** [OE]

Wegener (*German* 've:gənər) *n* **Alfred** ('alfre:t) 1880–1930, German meteorologist: regarded as the originator of the theory of continental drift

Weichsel ('vaiksəl) *n* the German name for the **Vistula** (sense 1)

weigela (waɪ'gi:lə, -'dʒi:-) *n* a shrub of an Asian genus having clusters of showy bell-shaped flowers [C19 from NL, after C. E. *Weigel* (1748–1831), G physician]

weigh[1] (weɪ) *vb* **1** (*tr*) to measure the weight of **2** (*intr*) to have weight: *she weighs more than her sister* **3** (*tr; often foll by out*) to apportion according to weight **4** (*tr*) to consider carefully: *to weigh the facts of a case* **5** (*intr*) to be influential: *his words weighed little with the jury* **6** (*intr; often foll by on*) to be oppressive (to) **7** **weigh anchor** to raise a vessel's anchor or (of a vessel) to have its anchor raised preparatory to departure ▷ See also **weigh down, weigh in,** etc [OE *wegan*] > '**weighable** *adj* > '**weigher** *n*

weigh[2] (weɪ) *n* **under weigh** a variant spelling of **under way** [C18 var. due to the infl. of phrases such as *to weigh anchor*]

weighbridge ('weɪ,brɪdʒ) *n* a machine for weighing vehicles, etc, by means of a metal plate set into a road

weigh down *vb* (*adv*) to press (a person, etc) down by or as if by weight: *his troubles weighed him down*

weigh in *vb* (*intr, adv*) **1a** (of a boxer or wrestler) to be weighed before a bout **1b** (of a jockey) to be weighed after, or sometimes before, a race **2** *inf* to contribute, as in a discussion, etc: *he weighed in with a few sharp comments* ▷ *n* **weigh-in** **3** the act of checking a competitor's weight, as in boxing, racing, etc

weight (weɪt) *n* **1** a measure of the heaviness of an object; the amount anything weighs **2** *physics* the vertical force experienced by a mass as a result of gravitation **3** a system of units used to express weight: *troy weight* **4** a unit used to measure weight: *the kilogram is the weight used in the metric system* **5** any mass or heavy object used to exert pressure or weigh down **6** an oppressive force: *the weight of cares* **7** any heavy load: *the bag was such a weight* **8** the main force; preponderance: *the weight of evidence* **9** importance; influence: *his opinion carries weight* **10** *statistics* one of a set of coefficients assigned to items of a frequency distribution that are analysed in order to represent the relative importance of the different items **11** *printing* the apparent blackness of a printed typeface **12** **pull one's weight** *inf* to do one's full or proper share of a task **13** **throw one's weight around** *inf* to act in an overauthoritarian manner ▷ *vb* (*tr*) **14** to add weight to **15** to burden or oppress **16** to add importance, value, etc, to (one side rather than another) **17** *statistics* to attach a weight or weights to [OE *wiht*] > '**weighter** *n*

weighted average *n statistics* a result produced by a technique designed to give recognition to the importance of certain factors when compiling the average of a group of values

weighting ('weɪtɪŋ) *n* **1** a factor by which some quantity is multiplied in order to make it comparable with others **2** an allowance paid to compensate for higher living costs: *a London weighting*

weightless ('weɪtləs) *adj* **1** (of a body) having no actual weight; a state in which an object has no actual weight (because it is in space and unaffected by gravitational attraction) or no apparent weight (because the gravitational attraction equals the centripetal force and the object is in free fall) **2** *business* **2a** (of economic activity) based on the supply of information and ideas rather than trade in physical goods: *the weightless economy* **2b** (of a company) having very few physical assets: *weightless dotcoms* > '**weightlessness** *n*

weightlifting ('weɪt,lɪftɪŋ) *n* the sport of lifting barbells of specified weights in a prescribed manner > '**weight,lifter** *n*

▷ www.iwf.net

weight training *n* physical exercise involving lifting weights, either heavy or light weights, as a way of improving muscle performance

weight watcher *n* a person who tries to lose weight, esp by dieting

weighty ('weɪtɪ) *adj* **weightier, weightiest** **1** having great weight **2** important **3** causing worry > '**weightily** *adv* > '**weightiness** *n*

weigh up *vb* (*tr, adv*) to make an assessment of (a person, situation, etc); judge

Weihai *or* **Wei-hai** ('weɪ'haɪ) *n* a port in NE China, in NE Shandong on the Yellow Sea: leased to Britain as a naval base (1898–1930). Pop: 287 872 (1999 est). Also called: **Weihaiwei** (,weɪ'haɪ,weɪ)

Weil (*French* vail) *n* **Simone** (simɔn) 1909–43, French philosopher and mystic, whose works include *Waiting for God* (1951), *The Need for Roots* (1952), and *Notebooks* (1956)

Tables of Weights and Measures

The Metric System

LINEAR MEASURE

1 millimetre	=	0.039 37 inch		
10 millimetre	=	1 centimetre	=	0.3937 inch
10 decimetres	=	1 metre	=	39.37 inches or 3.2808 feet
1 kilometre	=	0.621 mile or 3280.8 feet		

SQUARE MEASURE

1 square millimetre	=	0.001 55 square inch		
100 square millimetres	=	1 square centimetre	=	0.154 99 square inch
100 square decimetres	=	1 square metre	=	1549.9 square inches or 1.196 square yards
100 square hectometres	=	1 square kilometre	=	0.386 square mile or 247.1 acres

LAND MEASURE

100 centiares	=	1 are	=	119.6 square yards
100 ares	=	1 hectare	=	2.471 acres
100 hectares	=	1 square kilometre	=	0.386 square mile or 247.1 acres

VOLUME MEASURE

1000 cubic millimetres	=	1 cubic centimetre	=	0.061 02 cubic inch
1000 cubic centimetres	=	1 cubic decimetre (1 litre)	=	61.023 cubic inches or 0.0353 cubic foot
1000 cubic decimetres	=	1 cubic metre	=	35.314 cubic feet or 1.308 cubic yards

WEIGHTS

10 decigrammes	=	1 gram	=	15.432 grains or 0.035 274 ounce (avdp.)
10 hectogrammes	=	1 kilogram	=	2.2046 pounds
10 quintals	=	1 metric ton	=	2204.6 pounds

The Imperial System

LINEAR MEASURE

1 mil	=	0.001 inch	=	0.0254 mm
1 inch	=	1000 mils	=	2.54 cm
12 inches	=	1 foot	=	0.3048 metre
3 feet	=	1 yard	=	0.9144 metre
5 ½ yards or 16 ½ feet	=	1 rod (or pole or perch)	=	5.029 metres
40 rods	=	1 furlong	=	201.168 metres
8 furlongs or 1760 yards or 5280 feet	=	1 (statute) mile	=	1.6093 kilometres

SQUARE MEASURE

1 square inch	=	6.452 square centimetres		
144 square inches	=	1 square foot	=	929.03 square centimetres
9 square feet	=	1 square yard	=	0.8361 square metre
30 ¼ square yards	=	1 square rod (or square pole or square perch)	=	25.292 square metres
160 square rods or 4840 square yards or 43 560 square feet	=	1 acre	=	0.4047 hectare
640 acres	=	1 square mile	=	259.00 hectares or 2.590 square kilometres

CUBIC MEASURE

1 cubic inch	=	16.387 cubic centimetre		
1728 cubic inches	=	1 cubic foot	=	0.0283 cubic metre
27 cubic feet	=	1 cubic yard	=	0.7646 cubic metre

NAUTICAL MEASURE

6 feet	=	1 fathom	=	1.829 metres
100 fathoms	=	1 cable's length		
(in the Royal Navy, 608 feet, or 185.319 metres	=	1 cable's length)		
10 cables' length	=	1 international nautical mile	=	1.852 kilometres (exactly)
1 international nautical mile	=	1.150 779 statute miles (the length of a minute of latitude at the equator)		
60 nautical miles	=	1 degree of a great circle of the earth	=	69.047 statute miles

LIQUID AND DRY MEASURE

1 gill	=	5 fluid ounces	=	9.0235 cubic inches	=	0.1480 litre
4 gills	=	1 pint	=	34.68 cubic inches	=	0.568 litre
2 pints	=	1 quart	=	69.36 cubic inches	=	1.136 litres
4 quarts	=	1 gallon	=	277.4 cubic inches	=	4.546 litres
2 gallons	=	1 peck	=	554.8 cubic inches	=	9.092 litres
4 pecks	=	1 bushel	=	2219.2 cubic inches	=	36.37 litres
The US gallon (4 US quarts)	=	231 cubic inches	=	3.7854 litres		

APOTHECARIES' FLUID MEASURE

1 minim	=	0.0038 cubic inch	=	0.0616 millilitre		
60 minims	=	1 fluid dram	=	0.2256 cubic inch	=	3.6966 millilitres
8 fluid drams	=	1 fluid ounce	=	1.8047 cubic inches	=	0.0296 litre
20 fluid ounces	=	1 pint	=	34.68 cubic inches	=	0.568 litre
The US pint	=	16 fluid ounces				

AVOIRDUPOIS WEIGHT

(The grain, equal to 0.0648 gram, is the same in all three tables of weight.)

1 dram or 27.34 grains	=	1.772 grams		
16 drams or 437.5 grains	=	1 ounce	=	28.3495 grams
16 ounces or 7000 grains	=	1 pound	=	453.59 grams
14 pounds	=	1 stone	=	6.35 kilograms
112 pounds	=	1 hundredweight	=	50.80 kilograms
2240 pounds	=	1 (long) ton	=	1016.05 kilograms
2000 pounds	=	1 (short) ton	=	907.18 kilograms

TROY WEIGHT

(The grain, equal to 0.0648 gram, is the same in all three tables of weight.)

3.086 grains	=	1 carat	=	200.00 milligrams
24 grains	=	1 pennyweight	=	1.5552 grams
20 pennyweights or 480 grains	=	1 ounce	=	31.1035 grams
12 ounces or 5760 grains	=	1 pound	=	373.24 grams

APOTHECARIES' WEIGHT

(The grain, equal to 0.0648 gram, is the same in all three tables of weight.)

20 grains	=	1 scruple	=	1.296 grams
3 scruples	=	1 dram	=	3.888 grams
8 drams or 480 grains	=	1 ounce	=	31.1035 grams

▷ www.ex.ac.uk/cimt/dictunit/dictunit.htm
▷ www.unc.edu/~rowlett/units/metric.html
▷ www.unc.edu/~rowlett/units/usmetric.html
▷ http://scienceworld.wolfram.com/physics/AvoirdupoisSystemofUnits.html
▷ http://scienceworld.wolfram.com/physics/ApothecariesSystemofWeights.html

Weill (vaɪl) *n* **Kurt** (kʊrt) 1900–50, German composer, in the US from 1935. He wrote the music for Brecht's *The Rise and Fall of the City of Mahagonny* (1927) and *The Threepenny Opera* (1928)

Weil's disease (vaɪlz) *n* another name for **leptospirosis** [named after Adolf *Weil* (1848–1916), G physician]

Weimar (*German* 'vaimar) *n* a city in E central Germany, in Thuringia: a cultural centre in the 18th and early 19th century; scene of the adoption (1919) of the constitution of the Weimar Republic. Pop: 59 100 (1991)
▷ http://dmorgan.web.wesleyan.edu/materials/weimar.htm

Weimaraner ('vaɪməˌrɑːnə, 'waɪməˌrɑː-) *n* a breed of hunting dog, having a very short sleek grey coat and a short tail [c20 after Weimar, where the breed was developed]

Weinberg ('waɪnbɜːg) *n* **Steven** born 1933, US physicist, who shared the Nobel prize for physics (1979) with Sheldon Glashow and Abdus Salam for his role in formulating the electroweak theory

weir (wɪə) *n* **1** a low dam that is built across a river to raise the water level, divert the water, or control its flow **2** a series of traps or enclosures placed in a stream to catch fish [OE *wer*]

Weir (wɪə) *n* **1** **Judith** born 1954, Scottish composer, noted esp for her opera *A Night at the Chinese Opera* (1987) **2** **Peter** born 1944, Australian film director; his films include *Dead Poets Society* (1989), *The Truman Show* (1998), and *Master and Commander* (2003)

weird (wɪəd) *adj* **1** suggestive of or relating to the supernatural; eerie **2** strange or bizarre **3** *arch* of or relating to fate or the Fates ▷ *n* **4** *arch, chiefly Scot* **4a** fate or destiny **4b** one of the Fates [OE (*ge*)*wyrd* destiny] > '**weirdly** *adv* > '**weirdness** *n*

weirdo ('wɪədəʊ) *or* **weirdie** ('wɪədɪ) *n, pl* **weirdos** *or* **weirdies** *inf* a person who behaves in a bizarre or eccentric manner

Weismannism ('vaɪsmənˌɪzəm) *n* the theory that all inheritable characteristics are transmitted by the reproductive cells and that characteristics acquired during the lifetime of the organism are not inherited [c19 after August *Weismann* (1834–1914), G biologist]

Weisshorn ('vaɪsˌhɔːn) *n* a mountain in S Switzerland, in the Pennine Alps. Height: 4505 m (14 781 ft)

Weissmuller ('waɪsˌmʌlə) *n* **John Peter,** known as *Johnny*. 1904–84, US swimmer and film actor, who won Olympic gold medals in 1924 and 1928 and played the title role in the early Tarzan films

Weizmann ('waɪtsmən, 'waɪz-) *n* **Chaim** ('xaɪɪm) 1874–1952, Israeli statesman, born in Russia. As a leading Zionist, he was largely responsible for securing the Balfour Declaration (1917); first president of Israel (1949–52)

weka ('wɛkə) *n* a nocturnal flightless bird of New Zealand. Also called: **Maori hen, wood hen** [from Maori]

welch (wɛlʃ) *vb* a variant spelling of **welsh**

Welch (wɛlʃ) *adj, n* an archaic spelling of **Welsh**

welcome ('wɛlkəm) *adj* **1** gladly and cordially received or admitted: *a welcome guest* **2** bringing pleasure: *a welcome gift* **3** freely permitted or invited: *you are welcome to call* **4** under no obligation (only in such phrases as **you're welcome,** as conventional responses to thanks) ▷ *sentence substitute* **5** an expression of cordial greeting ▷ *n* **6** the act of greeting or receiving a person or thing; reception: *the new theory had a cool welcome* **7** **wear out** *or* **overstay one's welcome** to come more often or stay longer than is pleasing ▷ *vb* **welcomes, welcoming, welcomed** (*tr*) **8** to greet the arrival of (guests, etc) cordially **9** to receive or accept, esp gladly [c12 changed (through infl. of WELL[1]) from OE *wilcuma* (agent n referring to a welcome guest), *wilcume* (a greeting of welcome), from *wil* WILL[2] + *cuman* to come] > '**welcomely** *adv* > '**welcomer** *n*

weld[1] (wɛld) *vb* **1** (*tr*) to unite (pieces of metal or plastic), as by softening with heat and hammering or by fusion **2** to bring or admit of being brought into close union ▷ *n* **3** a joint formed by welding [c16 altered from obs. *well* to melt, weld] > '**weldable** *adj* > ˌ**welda'bility** *n* > '**welder** *or* '**weldor** *n*

weld[2] (wɛld), **wold,** *or* **woald** (wəʊld) *n* a yellow dye obtained from the plant dyer's rocket [c14 from Low G]

Weld (wɛld) *n* Sir **Frederick Aloysius** 1823–91, New Zealand statesman, born in England: prime minister of New Zealand (1864–65)

Weldon ('wɛldən) *n* **Fay** born 1931, British novelist and writer. Her novels include *Praxis* (1978), *Life and Loves of a She-Devil* (1984), and *Big Women* (1998)

welfare ('wɛlˌfɛə) *n* **1** health, happiness, prosperity, and wellbeing in general **2a** financial and other assistance given to people in need **2b** (*as modifier*): *welfare services* **3** Also called: **welfare work** plans or work to better the social or economic conditions of various underprivileged groups **4** **on welfare** *chiefly US & Canad* in receipt of financial aid from a government agency or other source [c14 from *wel fare*; see WELL[1], FARE]

welfare economics *n* (*functioning as sing*) the aspects of economic theory concerned with the welfare of society and priorities to be observed in the allocation of resources

welfare state *n* a system in which the government undertakes the chief responsibility for providing for the social and economic security of its population, usually through unemployment insurance, old age pensions, and other social-security measures

welkin ('wɛlkɪn) *n* *arch* the sky, heavens, or upper air [OE *wolcen, welcen*]

Welkom ('wɛlkəm, 'vɛl-) *n* a town in central South Africa; developed rapidly following the discovery of gold. Pop: 203 296 (1996)

well[1] (wɛl) *adv* **better, best** **1** (*often used in combination*) in a satisfactory manner: *the party went very well* **2** (*often used in combination*) in a skilful manner: *she plays the violin well; a well-chosen example* **3** in a correct or careful manner: *listen well to my words* **4** in a prosperous manner: *to live well* **5** (*usually used with auxiliaries*) suitably; fittingly: *you can't very well say that* **6** intimately: *I knew him well* **7** in a kind or favourable manner: *she speaks well of you* **8** fully: *to be well informed* **9** by a considerable margin: *let me know well in advance* **10** (preceded by *could, might,* or *may*) indeed: *you may well have to do it yourself* **11** *inf* (intensifier): *well safe* **12** **all very well** used ironically to express discontent, dissent, etc **13** **as well** **13a** in addition; too **13b** (preceded by *may* or *might*) with equal effect: *you might as well come* **14** **as well as** in addition to **15** (**just**) **as well** preferable or advisable: *it would be just as well if you paid me now* **16** **leave well** (**enough**) **alone** to refrain from interfering with something that is satisfactory **17** **well and good** used to indicate calm acceptance, as of a decision **18** **well up in** well acquainted with (a particular subject); knowledgeable about ▷ *adj* (*usually postpositive*) **19** (when *prenominal, usually used with a negative*) in good health: *I'm very well, thank you; he's not a well man* **20** satisfactory or pleasing **21** prudent; advisable: *it would be well to make no comment* **22** prosperous or comfortable **23** fortunate: *it is well that you agreed to go* ▷ *interj* **24a** an expression of surprise, indignation, or reproof **24b** an expression of anticipation in waiting for an answer or remark ▷ *sentence connector* **25** an expression used to preface a remark, gain time, etc: *well, I don't think I will come* [OE *wel*]

well[2] (wɛl) *n* **1** a hole or shaft bored into the earth to tap a supply of water, oil, gas, etc **2** a natural pool where ground water comes to the surface **3a** a cavity, space, or vessel used to contain a liquid **3b** (*in combination*): *an inkwell* **4** an open shaft through the floors of a building, such as one used for a staircase **5** a deep enclosed space in a building or between buildings that is open to the sky **6** a bulkheaded compartment built around a ship's pumps for protection and ease of access **7** (in England) the open space in the centre of a law court **8** an abundant source: *he is a well of knowledge* ▷ *vb* **9** to flow or cause to flow upwards or outwards: *tears welled from her eyes* [OE *wella*]

we'll (wiːl) *contraction of* we will *or* we shall

well-advised *adj* (**well advised** *when postpositive*) **1** acting with deliberation or reason **2** well thought out: *a well-advised plan*

well-affected *adj* (**well affected** *when postpositive*). favourably disposed (towards); steadfast or loyal

Welland Canal (ˈwɛlənd) *n* a canal in S Canada, in Ontario, linking Lake Erie to Lake Ontario: part of the St Lawrence Seaway, with eight locks. Length: 44 km (28 miles). Also called: **Welland Ship Canal**

well-appointed *adj* (**well appointed** *when postpositive*). well equipped or furnished

wellaway (ˈwɛləˈweɪ) *interj arch* woe! alas! [OE, from *wei lā wei*, var. of *wā lā wā*, lit.: woe! lo woe]

well-balanced *adj* (**well balanced** *when postpositive*) **1** having good balance or proportions **2** sane or sensible

wellbeing (ˈwɛlˈbiːɪŋ) *n* the condition of being contented, healthy, or successful; welfare

well-bred *adj* (**well bred** *when postpositive*) **1** Also: **well-born** of respected or noble lineage **2** indicating good breeding: *well-bred manners* **3** of good thoroughbred stock: *a well-bred spaniel*

well-chosen *adj* (**well chosen** *when postpositive*). carefully selected to produce a desired effect; apt: *a few well-chosen words*

well-connected *adj* (**well connected** *when postpositive*). having influential or important relatives or friends

well-disposed *adj* (**well disposed** *when postpositive*). inclined to be sympathetic, kindly, or friendly

well-done *adj* (**well done** *when postpositive*) **1** (of food, esp meat) cooked thoroughly **2** made or accomplished satisfactorily

well dressing *n* the decoration of wells with flowers, etc: a traditional annual ceremony of great antiquity in some parts of Britain, originally associated with the cult of water deities

Welles (wɛlz) *n* (**George**) **Orson** (ˈɔːsᵊn) 1915–85, US film director, actor, producer, and screenwriter. His *Citizen Kane* (1941) and *The Magnificent Ambersons* (1942) are regarded as film classics

Wellesley (ˈwɛlzlɪ) *n* **1 Arthur** See (1st Duke of) Wellington **2** his brother, **Richard Colley,** Marquis Wellesley. 1760–1842, British administrator. As governor general of Bengal (1797–1805) he consolidated British power in India

well-favoured *adj* (**well favoured** *when postpositive*). good-looking

well-formed formula *n logic* a group of logical symbols that makes sense; a logical sentence

well-found *adj* (**well found** *when postpositive*) furnished or supplied with all or most necessary things

well-founded *adj* (**well founded** *when postpositive*) having good grounds: *well-founded rumours*

well-groomed *adj* (**well groomed** *when postpositive*) having a tidy pleasing appearance

well-grounded *adj* (**well grounded** *when postpositive*) **1** well instructed in the basic elements of a subject **2** another term for **well-founded**

wellhead (ˈwɛlˌhɛd) *n* **1** the source of a well or stream **2** a source, fountainhead, or origin

well-heeled *adj* (**well heeled** *when postpositive*) *inf* rich; prosperous; wealthy

wellies (ˈwɛlɪz) *pl n Brit inf* Wellington boots

well-informed *adj* (**well informed** *when postpositive*) **1** having knowledge about a great variety of subjects: *he seems to be a well-informed person* **2** possessing reliable information on a particular subject

Wellingborough (ˈwɛlɪŋbərə, -brə) *n* a town in central England, in Northamptonshire. Pop: 41 602 (1991)

Wellington[1] (ˈwɛlɪŋtən) *n* **1** an administrative district, formerly a province, of New Zealand, on SW North Island: major livestock producer in New Zealand. Capital: Wellington. Pop: 424 461 (2001). Area: 28 153 sq km (10 870 sq miles) **2** the capital city of New Zealand. Its port, historically Port Nicholson, on **Wellington Harbour** has a car and rail ferry link between the North and South Islands; university (1899). Pop: 166 700 (1999 est)

▷ www.wellingtonnz.com
▷ www.wellingtonnewzealand.co.nz/wellington
▷ www.wrc.govt.nz
▷ www.wellingtonnz.com

Wellington[2] (ˈwɛlɪŋtən) *n* **1st Duke of,** title of *Arthur Wellesley*. 1769–1852, British soldier and statesman; prime minister (1828–30). He was given command of the British forces against the French in the Peninsular War (1808–14) and routed Napoleon at Waterloo (1815)

Wellington boots *pl n* **1** Also called: **gumboots** *Brit* knee-length or calf-length rubber boots, worn esp in wet conditions. Often shortened to **wellingtons, wellies** **2** military leather boots covering the front of the knee but cut away at the back to allow easier bending of the knee [C19 after the 1st Duke of WELLINGTON]

wellingtonia (ˌwɛlɪŋˈtəʊnɪə) *n* a giant Californian coniferous tree, often reaching 90 metres high. Also called: **big tree, sequoia** [C19 after the 1st Duke of WELLINGTON]

well-intentioned *adj* (**well intentioned** *when postpositive*). having benevolent intentions, usually with unfortunate results

well-knit *adj* (**well knit** *when postpositive*). strong, firm, or sturdy

well-known *adj* (**well known** *when postpositive*) **1** widely known; famous; celebrated **2** known fully or clearly

well-mannered *adj* (**well mannered** *when postpositive*). having good manners; polite

well-meaning *adj* (**well meaning** *when postpositive*). having or indicating good intentions, usually with unfortunate results

well-nigh *adv arch or poetic* nearly; almost: *it's well-nigh three o'clock*

well-off *adj* (**well off** *when postpositive*) **1** in a comfortable or favourable position or state **2** financially well provided for; moderately rich

well-oiled *adj* (**well oiled** *when postpositive*) *inf* drunk

well-preserved *adj* (**well preserved** *when postpositive*) **1** kept in a good condition **2** continuing to appear youthful: *she was a well-preserved old lady*

well-read (ˈwɛlˈrɛd) *adj* (**well read** *when postpositive*) having read widely and intelligently; erudite

well-rounded *adj* (**well rounded** *when postpositive*) **1** rounded in shape or well developed: *a well-rounded figure* **2** full, varied, and satisfying: *a well-rounded life*

Wells[1] (wɛlz) *n* a city in SW England, in Somerset: 12th-century cathedral. Pop: 9763 (1991)

Wells[2] (wɛlz) *n* **1 Henry** 1805–78, US businessman, who founded (1852) with William Fargo the express mail service Wells, Fargo and Company **2 H**(**erbert**) **G**(**eorge**) 1866–1946, British writer. His science-fiction stories include *The Time Machine* (1895), *War of the Worlds* (1898), and *The Shape of Things to Come* (1933). His novels on contemporary social questions, such as *Kipps* (1905), *Tono-Bungay* (1909), and *Ann Veronica* (1909), affected the opinions of his day. His nonfiction works include *The Outline of History* (1920)

well-spoken *adj* (**well spoken** *when postpositive*) **1** having a clear, articulate, and socially acceptable accent and way of speaking **2** spoken satisfactorily or pleasingly

wellspring (ˈwɛlˌsprɪŋ) *n* **1** the source of a spring or

stream **2** a source of abundant supply
well-stacked *adj* (**well stacked** *when postpositive*) *sl* (of a woman) of voluptuous proportions
well sweep *n* a device for raising buckets from and lowering them into a well, consisting of a long pivoted pole, the bucket being attached to one end by a long rope
well-tempered *adj* (**well tempered** *when postpositive*) (of a musical scale or instrument) conforming to the system of equal temperament. See **temperament** (sense 4)
well-thought-of *adj* respected
well-thumbed *adj* (**well thumbed** *when postpositive*). (of a book) having the pages marked from frequent turning
well-to-do *adj* moderately wealthy
well-turned *adj* (**well turned** *when postpositive*) **1** (of a phrase, etc) apt and pleasing **2** having a pleasing shape: *a well-turned leg*
well-upholstered *adj* (**well upholstered** *when postpositive*) *inf* (of a person) fat
well-wisher *n* a person who shows benevolence or sympathy towards a person, cause, etc > **'well-,wishing** *adj, n*
well-woman *n, pl* **well-women** *social welfare* **a** a woman who attends a health-service clinic for preventive monitoring, health education, etc **b** (*as modifier*): *well-woman clinic*
well-worn *adj* (**well worn** *when postpositive*) **1** so much used as to be affected by wear: *a well-worn coat* **2** hackneyed: *a well-worn phrase*
welly ('wɛlɪ) *n* **1** (*pl* **wellies**) *inf* Also called: **welly boot** a Wellington boot **2** *sl* energy, concentration, or commitment (esp in **give it some welly**)
Wels (*German* vɛls) *n* an industrial city in N central Austria, in Upper Austria. Pop: 52 594 (1991)
welsh *or* **welch** (wɛlʃ) *vb* (*intr; often foll by on*) **1** to fail to pay a gambling debt **2** to fail to fulfil an obligation [c19 from ?] > **'welsher** *or* **'welcher** *n*
Welsh (wɛlʃ) *adj* **1** of, relating to, or characteristic of Wales, its people, their language, or their dialect of English ▷ *n* **2** a language of Wales, belonging to the S Celtic branch of the Indo-European family **3** **the Welsh** (*functioning as pl*) the natives or inhabitants of Wales [OE *Wēlisc, Wǣlisc*]
Welsh corgi *n* another name for **corgi**
Welsh dresser *n* a sideboard with drawers and cupboards below and open shelves above
Welsh harp *n* a type of harp in which the strings are arranged in three rows
Welshman ('wɛlʃmən) *or* (*fem*) **Welshwoman** *n, pl* **Welshmen** *or* **Welshwomen** a native or inhabitant of Wales
Welsh poppy *n* a perennial W European plant with large yellow flowers
Welsh rabbit *n* a savoury dish consisting of melted cheese sometimes mixed with milk, seasonings, etc, on hot buttered toast. Also called: **Welsh rarebit, rarebit** [c18 a fanciful coinage; *rarebit* is a later folk-etymological var.]
Welsh terrier *n* a wire-haired breed of terrier with a black-and-tan coat
welt (wɛlt) *n* **1** a raised or strengthened seam in a garment **2** another word for **weal**[1] **3** (in shoemaking) a strip of leather, etc, put in between the outer sole and the inner sole and upper ▷ *vb* (*tr*) **4** to put a welt in (a garment, etc) **5** to beat soundly [c15 from ?]
welter ('wɛltə) *vb* (*intr*) **1** to roll about, writhe, or wallow **2** (esp of the sea) to surge, heave, or toss **3** to lie drenched in a liquid, esp blood ▷ *n* **4** a confused mass; jumble [c13 from MLow G, MDu. *weltern*]
welterweight ('wɛltə,weɪt) *n* **1a** a professional boxer weighing 140–147 pounds (63.5–66.5 kg) **1b** an amateur boxer weighing 63.5–67 kg (140–148 pounds) **2a** a professional wrestler weighing 155–165 pounds (71–75 kg) **2b** an amateur wrestler weighing 69–74 kg (151–161 pounds)
Welwyn Garden City ('wɛlɪn) *n* a town in SE England, in Hertfordshire: established (1920) as a planned industrial and residential community. Pop: 42 087 (1991)
Wembley ('wɛmblɪ) *n* part of the Greater London borough of Brent: site of the English national soccer stadium
wen[1] (wɛn) *n* **1** *pathol* a sebaceous cyst, esp one occurring on the scalp **2** a large overcrowded city (esp London, **the great wen**) [OE *wenn*]
wen[2] (wɛn) *n* a rune having the sound of Modern English *w* [OE *wen, wyn*]
Wenceslaus *or* **Wenceslas** ('wɛnsɪsləs) *n* **1** 1361–1419, Holy Roman Emperor (1378–1400) and, as **Wenceslaus IV**, king of Bohemia (1378–1419) **2** **Saint,** known as *Good King Wenceslaus*. ?907–929, duke of Bohemia (?925–29); patron saint of Bohemia. Feast day: Sept 28
wench (wɛntʃ) *n* **1** a girl or young woman: now used facetiously **2** *arch* a female servant **3** *arch* a prostitute ▷ *vb* (*intr*) **4** *arch* to frequent the company of prostitutes [OE *wencel* child, from *wancol* weak] > **'wencher** *n*
wend (wɛnd) *vb* to direct (one's course or way); travel [OE *wendan*]
Wend (wɛnd) *n* (esp in medieval European history) a member of the Slavonic people who inhabited the area between the Rivers Saale and Oder, in central Europe, in the early Middle Ages. Also called: **Sorb**
wendigo ('wɛndɪ,gəʊ) *n Canad* **1** (*pl* **wendigos**) (among Algonquian Indians) an evil spirit or cannibal **2** (*pl* **wendigo** *or* **wendigos**) another name for **splake** [from Algonquian: evil spirit or cannibal]
Wendy house ('wɛndɪ) *n* a small model house for children to play in [c20 after the house built for *Wendy*, the girl in J. M. Barrie's play *Peter Pan* (1904)]
wensleydale ('wɛnzlɪ,deɪl) *n* **1** a type of white cheese with a flaky texture **2** a breed of sheep with long woolly fleece [after *Wensleydale*, North Yorkshire]

Ww

went (wɛnt) *vb* the past tense of **go** [c15 p.t. of WEND used as p.t. of *go*]
wentletrap ('wɛnt°l,træp) *n* a marine gastropod mollusc having a long pointed pale-coloured longitudinally ridged shell [c18 from Du. *winteltrap* spiral shell, from *wintel*, earlier *windel*, from *wenden* to wind + *trap* a step]
Wentworth ('wɛntwəθ) *n* **1** **Thomas** See (Earl of) **Strafford** **2** **William Charles** 1790–1872, Australian explorer and statesman who was a member of the exploring party that first crossed the Blue Mountains in 1813 and was later a leader in the movement for self-government in New South Wales
Wenzhou, Wen-chou, *or* **Wenchow** ('wɛn'tʃu:) *n* a port in SE China, in Zhejiang province: noted for its historic buildings. Pop: 512 523 (1999 est)
wept (wɛpt) *vb* the past tense and past participle of **weep**
were (wɜ:; *unstressed* wə) *vb* the plural form of the past tense (indicative mood) of **be** and the singular form used with *you*. It is also used as a subjunctive, esp in conditional sentences [OE *wērun, wæron* p.t. pl of *wesan* to be]

> USAGE *Were*, as a remnant of the past subjunctive in English, is used in formal contexts to express hypotheses (*if he were to die, she would inherit everything*), suppositions contrary to fact (*if I were you, I would be careful*), and desire (*I wish he were there now*). In informal speech, however, *was* is often used instead

we're (wɪə) *contraction of* we are
weren't (wɜ:nt) *contraction of* were not
werewolf ('wɪə,wʊlf, 'wɛə-) *n, pl* **werewolves** a person fabled in folklore and superstition to have been

changed into a wolf by being bewitched or said to be able to assume wolf form at will [OE *werewulf*, from *wer* man + *wulf* wolf]

wergild, weregild ('wɜːˌgɪld, 'wɛə-), *or* **wergeld** ('wɜːˌgɛld, 'wɛə-) *n* the price set on a man's life in Anglo-Saxon and Germanic law, to be paid as compensation by his slayer [OE *wergeld*, from *wer* man + *gield* tribute]

Werner (*German* 'vɛrnər) *n* **1 Abraham Gottlieb** ('aːbraham 'gɔtloːp) 1749–1817, German geologist. He emphasized the importance of field and laboratory observation for understanding the earth **2 Alfred** ('alfreːt) 1866–1919, Swiss chemist, born in Germany. He developed a coordination theory of the valency of inorganic complexes: Nobel prize for chemistry 1913

wero ('wɜːrəʊ) *n NZ* the challenge made by an armed Maori warrior to a visitor to a marae [Maori]

wert (wɜːt; *unstressed* wət) *vb arch or dialect* (used with the pronoun *thou* or its relative equivalent) a singular form of the past tense (indicative mood) of **be**

Weser (*German* 'veːzər) *n* a river in NW Germany: flows northwest to the North Sea at Bremerhaven and is linked by the Mittelland Canal to the Ems, Rhine, and Elbe waterways. Length: 477 km (196 miles)

Wesermünde (*German* veːzər'myndə) *n* the former name (until 1947) of **Bremerhaven**

Wesker ('wɛskə) *n* **Arnold** born 1932, British dramatist, whose plays include *Roots* (1959), *Chips With Everything* (1962), *The Merchant* (1976), *Caritas* (1981), and *Break My Heart* (1997)

weskit ('wɛskɪt) *n* an informal name for **waistcoat**

Wesley ('wɛzlɪ) *n* **1 Charles** 1707–88, English Methodist preacher and writer of hymns **2** his brother, **John** 1703–91, English preacher, who founded Methodism **3 Mary**, pseudonym of *Mary Aline Siepmann*. 1912–2003, British writer: her novels include *The Camomile Lawn* (1984) and *An Imaginative Experience* (1994)

Wesleyan ('wɛzlɪən) *adj* **1** of or deriving from John Wesley **2** of or characterizing Methodism, esp in its original form ▷ *n* **3** a follower of John Wesley **4** a member of the Methodist Church > **'Wesleyan,ism** *n*

Wessex ('wɛsɪks) *n* **1** an Anglo-Saxon kingdom in S and SW England that became the most powerful English kingdom by the 10th century AD **2a** (in Thomas Hardy's works) the southwestern counties of England, esp Dorset **2b** (*as modifier*): *Wessex Poems*

west (wɛst) *n* **1** the direction along a parallel towards the sunset, at 270° clockwise from north **2 the west** (*often cap*) any area lying in or towards the west. Related adjs.: **Hesperian, Occidental 3** (*usually cap*) *cards* the player or position at the table corresponding to west on the compass ▷ *adj* **4** situated in, moving towards, or facing the west **5** (esp of the wind) from the west ▷ *adv* **6** in, to, or towards the west **7 go west** *inf* **7a** to be lost or destroyed **7b** to die [OE]

West[1] (wɛst) *n* **the 1** the western part of the world contrasted historically and culturally with the East or Orient **2** (formerly) the non-Communist countries of Europe and America contrasted with the Communist states of the East **3** (in the US) that part of the US lying approximately to the west of the Mississippi **4** (in the ancient and medieval world) the Western Roman Empire and, later, the Holy Roman Empire ▷ *adj* **5** of or denoting the western part of a specified country, area, etc

West[2] (wɛst) *n* **1 Benjamin** 1738–1820, US painter, in England from 1763 **2 Mae** 1892–1980, US film actress **3 Nathanael,** real name *Nathan Weinstein*. 1903–40, US novelist: author of *Miss Lonely-Hearts* (1933) and *The Day of the Locust* (1939) **4** Dame **Rebecca,** real name *Cicily Isabel Andrews* (née *Fairfield*). 1892–1983, British journalist, novelist, and critic

West Atlantic *n* **1** the W part of the Atlantic Ocean, esp the N Atlantic around North America **2** a branch of the Niger-Congo family of African languages, spoken in Senegal and in scattered areas eastwards, including Fulani and Wolof ▷ *adj* **3** relating to or belonging to this group of languages

West Bank *n* **the** an autonomous Palestinian region in the Middle East on the W bank of the River Jordan, comprising the hills of Judaea and Samaria and part of Jerusalem: formerly part of Palestine: became part of Jordan after the ceasefire of 1949: occupied by Israel since the 1967 Arab-Israeli War. In 1993 a peace treaty between Israel and the Palestinian Liberation Organization provided for the West Bank to become a self-governing Palestinian area; a new Palestinian National Authority assumed control of parts of the territory in 1994–95, but subsequent talks broke down and Israel reoccupied much of this in 2001–02. Pop: 1 949 000 (2000 est). Area: 5879 sq km (2270 sq miles)

West Bengal *n* a state of E India, on the Bay of Bengal: formed in 1947 from the Hindu area of Bengal; additional territories added in 1950 (Cooch Behar), 1954 (Chandernagor), and 1956 (part of Bihar); mostly low-lying and crossed by the Hooghly River. Capital: Calcutta. Pop: 80 221 171 (2001). Area: 88 752 sq km (34 260 sq miles)

West Berkshire *n* a unitary authority in S England, in Berkshire. Pop: 144 445 (2001). Area: 705 sq km (272 sq miles)

West Berlin *n* (formerly) the part of Berlin under US, British, and French control > **West Berliner** *n, adj*

westbound ('wɛstˌbaʊnd) *adj* going or leading towards the west

West Bromwich ('brɒmɪdʒ, -ɪtʃ) *n* a town in central England, in Sandwell unitary authority, West Midlands: industrial centre. Pop: 146 386 (1991)

west by north *n* one point on the compass north of west

west by south *n* one point on the compass south of west

West Country *n* **the** the southwest of England, esp Cornwall, Devon, and Somerset

West Dunbartonshire *n* a council area of W central Scotland, on Loch Lomond and the Clyde estuary: corresponds to part of the historical county of Dunbartonshire; part of Strathclyde Region from 1975 to 1996: engineering industries. Administrative centre: Dumbarton. Pop: 93 378 (2001). Area: 162 sq km (63 sq miles)

West End *n* **the** a part of W central London containing the main shopping and entertainment areas

Westenra ('wɛstənrə) *n* **Hayley Dee** born 1987, New Zealand singer, known for the purity of her voice in many musical genres

westering ('wɛstərɪŋ) *adj poetic* moving towards the west: *the westering star*

Westerlies ('wɛstəlɪz) *pl n meteorol* the prevailing winds blowing from the west on the poleward sides of the horse latitudes, often bringing depressions and anticyclones

westerly ('wɛstəlɪ) *adj* **1** of, relating to, or situated in the west ▷ *adv, adj* **2** towards or in the direction of the west **3** (esp of the wind) from the west ▷ *n, pl* **westerlies 4** a wind blowing from the west > **'westerliness** *n*

western ('wɛstən) *adj* **1** situated in or facing the west **2** going or directed to or towards the west **3** (of a wind, etc) coming from the west **4** native to the west **5** *music* See **country and western** > **'western,most** *adj*

Western ('wɛstən) *adj* **1** of or characteristic of the West as opposed to the Orient **2** of or characteristic of North America and western Europe **3** of or characteristic of the western states of the US ▷ *n* **4** (*often not cap*) a film, book, etc, concerned with life in the western states of the US, esp during the era of exploration

Western Australia *n* a state of W Australia: mostly an arid undulating plateau, with the Great Sandy Desert,

Gibson Desert, and Great Victoria Desert in the interior; settlement concentrated in the southwest; rich mineral resources. Capital: Perth. Pop: 1 861 020 (1999 est). Area: 2 527 636 sq km (975 920 sq miles)
▷ www.wa.gov.au
▷ www.westernaustralia.net

Western Cape *n* a province of W South Africa, created in 1994 from the SW part of Cape Province: agriculture (esp fruit), wine making, fishing, various industries in Cape Town. Capital: Cape Town. Pop: 4 170 970 (1999 est). Area: 129 370 sq km (49 950 sq miles). Also called: **Western Province**
▷ www.westerncape.gov/za
▷ www.capetourism.org

Western Church *n* **1** the part of Christendom that derives its liturgy, discipline, and traditions principally from the patriarchate of Rome **2** the Roman Catholic Church, sometimes together with the Anglican Communion of Churches

westerner ('wɛstənə) *n* (*sometimes cap*) a native or inhabitant of the west of any specific region

Western Ghats *pl n* a mountain range in W peninsular India, parallel to the Malabar coast of the Arabian Sea. Highest peak: Anai Mudi, 2695 m (8841 ft)

western hemisphere *n* (*often caps*) **1** that half of the globe containing the Americas, lying to the west of the Greenwich or another meridian **2** the lands contained in this, esp the Americas

Western Isles *n* (*functioning as singular or plural*) **1** an island authority in W Scotland, consisting of the Outer Hebrides; created in 1975. Administrative centre: Stornoway. Pop: 26 502 (2001). Area: 2900 sq km (1120 sq miles). Gaelic name: **Eilean Siar** **2** Also called: **Western Islands** another name for the **Hebrides**

westernize *or* **westernise** ('wɛstəˌnaɪz) *vb* **westernizes, westernizing, westernized** *or* **westernises, westernising, westernised** (*tr*) to influence or make familiar with the customs, practices, etc, of the West > **ˌwesterniˈzation** *or* **ˌwesterniˈsation** *n*

Western Ocean *n* (formerly) another name for the **Atlantic Ocean**

Western Roman Empire *n* the westernmost of the two empires created by the division of the later Roman Empire, esp after its final severance from the Eastern Roman Empire (395 AD). Also called: **Western Empire**

Western Sahara *n* a disputed region of NW Africa, on the Atlantic: mainly desert; rich phosphate deposits; a Spanish overseas province from 1958 to 1975; partitioned in 1976 between Morocco and Mauritania who faced growing resistance from the Polisario Front, an organization aiming for the independence of the region as the Democratic Saharan Arab Republic. Mauritania renounced its claim in 1979 and it was taken over by Morocco. Polisario agreed to a UN-brokered cease-fire in 1991 but attempts to settle the status of the region have failed. Pop: 288 000 (1998 est). Area: 266 000 sq km (102 680 sq miles). Former name (until 1975): **Spanish Sahara**

Western Samoa *n* See **Samoa** (sense 1)

Western Wall *n judaism* a wall in Jerusalem, the last extant part of the Temple of Herod, held sacred by Jews as a place of prayer and pilgrimage. Also called: **Wailing Wall**

Westfalen (vɛst'fa:lən) *n* the German name for **Westphalia**

West Flanders *n* a province of W Belgium: the country's chief agricultural province. Capital: Bruges. Pop: 1 128 774 (2000 est). Area: 3132 sq km (1209 sq miles)

West Germany *n* a former republic in N central Europe, on the North Sea: established in 1949 from the zones of Germany occupied by the British, Americans, and French after the defeat of Nazi Germany; a member of the European Community; reunited with East Germany in 1990. Official name: **Federal Republic of Germany**. See also **Germany** > **West German** *adj, n*

West Glamorgan *n* a former county in S Wales, formed in 1974 from part of Glamorgan and the county borough of Swansea: replaced in 1996 by the county of Swansea and the county borough of Neath Port Talbot

West Hartlepool ('hɑ:tlɪˌpu:l) *n* a former town in NE England, in Co. Durham: part of Hartlepool since 1967

West Indies ('ɪndɪz) *pl n* an archipelago off Central America, extending over 2400 km (1500 miles) in an arc from the peninsula of Florida to Venezuela, separating the Caribbean Sea from the Atlantic Ocean: consists of the Greater Antilles, the Lesser Antilles, and the Bahamas; largest island is Cuba. Area: over 235 000 sq km (91 000 sq miles). Also called: **the Caribbean**

westing ('wɛstɪŋ) *n navigation* movement, deviation, or distance covered in a westerly direction, esp as expressed in the resulting difference in longitude

West Irian *n* the English name for **Irian Jaya**

West Lothian *n* a council area and historical county of central Scotland, on the Firth of Forth: became part of Lothian region in 1975: reinstated as an independent authority (with revised boundaries) in 1996: agriculture, oil-refining. Administrative centre: Livingston. Pop: 158 714 (1996 est). Area: 425 sq km (164 sq miles)

West Lothian question *n Brit* the apparent inconsistency that members of parliament who represent Scottish constituencies are eligible to vote at Westminster on matters that relate only to England, whereas members of parliament from English constituencies are not eligible to vote on Scottish matters [c20 because the issue was first raised by the Scottish politican Tam Dalyell (born 1932) at the time when he was MP for *West Lothian*]

Westm. *abbrev for* Westminster

Westmeath (ˌwɛst'mi:ð) *n* a county of N central Republic of Ireland, in Leinster province: mostly low-lying, with many lakes and bogs. County town: Mullingar. Pop: 63 314 (1996). Area: 1764 sq km (681 sq miles)

West Midlands *n* (*functioning as singular or plural*) a metropolitan county of central England, administered since 1986 by the unitary authorities of Wolverhampton, Walsall, Dudley, Sandwell, Birmingham, Solihull, and Coventry. Area: 899 sq km (347 sq miles)

Westminster ('wɛstˌmɪnstə) *n* **1** Also called: **City of Westminster** a borough of Greater London, on the River Thames: contains the Houses of Parliament, Westminster Abbey, and Buckingham Palace. Pop: 181 279 (2001). Area: 22 sq km (8 sq miles) **2** the Houses of Parliament at Westminster

Westminster Abbey *n* a Gothic church in London: site of a Benedictine monastery (1050–65); scene of the coronations of almost all English monarchs since William I

Westmorland ('wɛstmələnd, 'wɛsmə-) *n* (until 1974) a county of NW England, now part of Cumbria

west-northwest *n* **1** the point on the compass or the direction midway between west and northwest, 292° 30′ clockwise from north ▷ *adj, adv* **2** in, from, or towards this direction

Weston standard cell ('wɛstən) *n* a primary cell used as a standard of emf: consists of a mercury anode and a cadmium amalgam cathode in an electrolyte of saturated cadmium sulphate [c20 from a trademark]

Weston-super-Mare ('wɛstənˌsu:pə'mɛə, -ˌsju:-) *n* a town and resort in SW England, in North Somerset unitary authority, Somerset, on the Bristol Channel. Pop: 69 372 (1991)

West Pakistan *n* the former name (until the end of 1971) of **Pakistan**

Ww

Westphalia (wɛstˈfeɪlɪə) *n* a historic region of NW Germany, now mostly in the state of North Rhine-Westphalia. German name: **Westfalen** > **Westˈphalian** *adj, n*

West Prussia *n* a former province of NE Prussia, on the Baltic: assigned to Poland in 1945. German name: **Westpreussen** (ˈvɛstprɔysən)

West Riding *n* (until 1974) an administrative division of Yorkshire, now part of West Yorkshire, North Yorkshire, Cumbria, and Lancashire

west-southwest *n* **1** the point on the compass or the direction midway between southwest and west, 247° 30′ clockwise from north ▷ *adj, adv* **2** in, from, or towards this direction

West Sussex *n* a county of SE England, comprising part of the former county of Sussex: mainly low-lying, with the South Downs in the S. Administrative centre: Chichester. Pop: 753 612 (2001). Area: 1989 sq km (768 sq miles)

West Virginia *n* a state of the eastern US: part of Virginia until the outbreak of the American Civil War (1861); consists chiefly of the Allegheny Plateau; bounded on the west by the Ohio River; coal-mining. Capital: Charleston. Pop: 1 808 344 (2000). Area: 62 341 sq km (24 070 sq miles). Abbreviations: **W Va.** or (with zip code) **WV** > **West Virginian** *adj, n*

westward (ˈwɛstwəd) *adj* **1** moving, facing, or situated in the west ▷ *adv* **2** Also: **westwards** towards the west ▷ *n* **3** the westward part, direction, etc > ˈ**westwardly** *adj, adv*

Westwood (ˈwɛstˌwʊd) *n* **Vivienne** (**Isabel**) born 1941, British fashion designer: noted for her punk designs of the late 1970s

West Yorkshire *n* a metropolitan county of N England, administered since 1986 by the unitary authorities of Bradford, Leeds, Calderdale, Kirklees, and Wakefield. Area: 2039 sq km (787 sq miles)

wet (wɛt) *adj* **wetter, wettest 1** moistened, covered, saturated, etc, with water or some other liquid **2** not yet dry or solid: *wet varnish* **3** rainy: *wet weather* **4** employing a liquid, usually water: *a wet method of chemical analysis* **5** *chiefly US & Canad* permitting the free sale of alcoholic beverages: *a wet state* **6** *Brit inf* feeble or foolish **7 wet behind the ears** *inf* immature or inexperienced ▷ *n* **8** wetness or moisture **9** rainy weather **10** *Brit inf* a feeble or foolish person **11** (*often cap*) *Brit inf* a Conservative politician who is not a hardliner **12** *chiefly US & Canad* a person who advocates free sale of alcoholic beverages **13 the wet** *Austral* (in northern and central Australia) the rainy season ▷ *vb* **wets, wetting, wet** *or* **wetted 14** to make or become wet **15** to urinate on (something) **16** (*tr*) *dialect* to prepare (tea) by boiling or infusing [OE *wǣt*] > ˈ**wetly** *adv* > ˈ**wetness** *n* > ˈ**wettable** *adj* > ˈ**wetter** *n* > ˈ**wettish** *adj*

wet-and-dry-bulb thermometer *n* another name for **psychrometer**

wet blanket *n inf* a person whose low spirits or lack of enthusiasm have a depressing effect on others

wet cell *n* a primary cell in which the electrolyte is a liquid

wet dream *n* an erotic dream accompanied by an emission of semen

wet fly *n angling* an artificial fly designed to float or ride below the water surface

wether (ˈwɛðə) *n* a male sheep, esp a castrated one [OE *hwæther*]

wetland (ˈwɛtlənd) *n* (*sometimes pl*) **a** an area of marshy land, esp considered as part of an ecological system **b** (*as modifier*): *wetland species*

wet look *n* a shiny finish such as that given to certain clothing and footwear materials

wet nurse *n* **1** a woman hired to suckle the child of another ▷ *vb* **wet-nurse, wet-nurses, wet-nursing, wet-nursed** (*tr*) **2** to act as a wet nurse to (a child) **3** *inf* to attend with great devotion

wet pack *n med* a hot or cold damp sheet or blanket for wrapping around a patient

wet room *n* a type of waterproofed room with shower heads and a drain in the floor

wet rot *n* **1** a state of decay in timber caused by various fungi. The hyphal strands of the fungus are seldom visible, and affected timber turns dark brown **2** any of the fungi causing this decay

wet suit *n* a close-fitting rubber suit used by skin-divers, yachtsmen, etc, to retain body heat

Wetterhorn (*German* ˈvɛtərˌhɔrn) *n* a mountain in S Switzerland, in the Bernese Alps. Height: 3701 m (12 143 ft)

wetting agent *n chem* any substance added to a liquid to lower its surface tension and thus increase its ability to spread across or penetrate a solid

wetware (ˈwɛtˌwɛə) *n* **1** *computing* the nervous system of the brain, as opposed to computer hardware or software **2** *computing* the programmers, operators, and administrators who operate a computer system, as opposed to the system's hardware or software

we've (wiːv) *contraction of* we have

Wexford (ˈwɛksfəd) *n* **1** a county of SE Republic of Ireland, in Leinster province on the Irish Sea: the first Irish county to be colonized from England; mostly low-lying and fertile. County town: Wexford. Pop: 104 371 (1996). Area: 2352 sq km (908 sq miles) **2** a port in SE Republic of Ireland, county town of Co. Wexford: sacked by Oliver Cromwell in 1649. Pop: 9540 (1991)

Weymouth (ˈweɪməθ) *n* a port and resort in S England, in Dorset on the English Channel: administratively part of the borough of **Weymouth and Melcombe** Regis. Pop (with Melcombe Regis): 53 235 (1991)

wf *printing abbrev for* wrong fount

WFF *logic abbrev for* well-formed formula

WFTU *abbrev for* World Federation of Trade Unions

whack (wæk) *vb* (*tr*) **1** to strike with a sharp resounding blow **2** (*usually passive*) *Brit inf* to exhaust completely **3** *US sl* to murder (someone): *if you were out of line you got whacked* ▷ *n* **4** a sharp resounding blow or the noise made by such a blow **5** *inf* a share or portion **6** *inf* a try or attempt (esp in **have a whack at**) **7 out of whack** *inf* out of order; unbalanced: *the whole system is out of whack* [C18 ? var. of THWACK, ult. imit.] > ˈ**whacker** *n*

whacking (ˈwækɪŋ) *inf, chiefly Brit* ▷ *adj* **1** enormous ▷ *adv* **2** (intensifier): *a whacking big lie*

whacky (ˈwækɪ) *adj* **whackier, whackiest** *US sl* a variant spelling of **wacky**

whale[1] (weɪl) *n, pl* **whales** *or* **whale 1** any of the larger cetacean mammals, excluding dolphins, porpoises, and narwhals. They have flippers, a streamlined body, and a horizontally flattened tail and breathe through a blowhole on the top of the head **2 a whale of 2a** *inf* an exceptionally large, fine, etc, example of a (person or thing) [OE *hwæl*]

whale[2] (weɪl) *vb* **whales, whaling, whaled** (*tr*) to beat or thrash soundly [C18 var. of WALE]

whaleboat (ˈweɪlˌbəʊt) *n* a narrow boat from 20 to 30 feet long having a sharp prow and stern, formerly used in whaling. Also called: **whaler**

whalebone (ˈweɪlˌbəʊn) *n* **1** Also called: **baleen** a horny elastic material forming numerous thin plates that hang from the upper jaw in the toothless (whalebone) whales and strain plankton from water entering the mouth **2** a strip of this substance, used in stiffening corsets, etc

whalebone whale *n* any whale belonging to a cetacean suborder having a double blowhole and strips of whalebone between the jaws instead of teeth: includes the rorquals, right whales, and the blue whale

whale oil *n* oil obtained either from the blubber of

whales (train oil) or the head of the sperm whale (sperm oil)

whaler (ˈweɪlə) *n* **1** Also called (US): **whaleman** a person employed in whaling **2** a vessel engaged in whaling **3** *Austral obs sl* a tramp or sundowner **4** an aggressive shark of Australian coastal waters

whaler shark *n Austral* a large voracious shark of E Australian waters

whale shark *n* a large spotted whalelike shark of warm seas, that feeds on plankton and small animals

whaling (ˈweɪlɪŋ) *n* the work or industry of hunting and processing whales for food, oil, etc

wham (wæm) *n* **1** a forceful blow or impact or the sound produced by it ▷ *vb* **whams, whamming, whammed** **2** to strike or cause to strike with great force [c20 imit.]

whammy (ˈwæmɪ) *n, pl* **whammies** *inf* **1** something which has great, often negative impact: *a double whammy of falling demand and rising prices* **2** an evil spell or curse: *she believed he had put the whammy on her* [c20 WHAM + -Y²]

whanau (ˈfɑːnaʊ) *n NZ* a family, esp an extended family [Maori]

whang (wæŋ) *vb* **1** to strike or be struck so as to cause a resounding noise ▷ *n* **2** the resounding noise produced by a heavy blow **3** a heavy blow [c19 imit.]

Whangarei (ˌwɑːŋɑːˈreɪ) *n* a port in New Zealand, the northernmost city of North Island: oil refinery. Pop: 44 800 (1994)

whangee (wæŋˈiː) *n* **1** a tall woody grass of an Asian genus, grown for its stems **2** a cane or walking stick made from the stem of this plant [c19 prob. from Chinese (Mandarin) *huangli*, from *huang* yellow + *li* bamboo cane]

whare (ˈwɔːrɪ; *Maori* ˈfɒrɛ) *n NZ* **1** a Maori hut or dwelling place **2** any simple dwelling place [from Maori]

wharepuni (ˈfɒrɛˌpʊnɪ) *n NZ* in a Maori community, a lofty carved building that is used as a guesthouse [from Maori WHARE + *puni* company]

whare wanaga (ˈfɒrɛ wəˈnɑːgə) *n NZ* a university [Maori]

wharf (wɔːf) *n, pl* **wharves** (wɔːvz) *or* **wharfs** **1** a platform built parallel to the waterfront at a harbour or navigable river for the docking, loading, and unloading of ships ▷ *vb (tr)* **2** to moor or dock at a wharf **3** to store or unload on a wharf [OE *hwearf* heap]

wharfage (ˈwɔːfɪdʒ) *n* **1** facilities for ships at wharves **2** a charge for use of a wharf **3** wharves collectively

wharfie (ˈwɔːfɪ) *n Austral & NZ* a wharf labourer; docker

wharfinger (ˈwɔːfɪndʒə) *n* an owner or manager of a wharf [c16 prob. alteration of *wharfager*]

Wharton (ˈwɔːtᵊn) *n* **Edith** (**Newbold**) 1862–1937, US novelist; author of *The House of Mirth* (1905) and *Ethan Frome* (1911)

wharve (wɔːv) *n* a wooden disc or wheel on a shaft serving as a flywheel or pulley [OE *hweorfa*, from *hweorfan* to revolve]

what (wɒt; *unstressed* wət) *determiner* **1a** used with a noun in requesting further information about the identity or categorization of something: *what job does he do?* **1b** (*as pron*): *what is her address?* **1c** (*used in indirect questions*): *tell me what he said* **2a** the (person, thing, persons, or things) that: *we photographed what animals we could see* **2b** (*as pron*): *bring me what you've written* **3** (intensifier; used in exclamations): *what a good book!* ▷ *adv* **4** in what respect? to what degree?: *what do you care?* **5** **what about** what do you think, know, etc, concerning? **6** **what for** **6a** for what purpose? why? **6b** *inf* a punishment or reprimand (esp in **give (a person) what for**) **7** **what have you** someone or something unknown or unspecified: *cars, motorcycles, or what have you* **8** **what if** **8a** what would happen if? **8b** what difference would it make if? **9** **what matter** what does it matter? **10** **what's what** *inf* the true state of affairs [OE *hwæt*]

whatever (wɒtˈɛvə, wət-) *pron* **1** everything or anything that: *do whatever he asks you to* **2** no matter what: *whatever he does, he is forgiven* **3** *inf* an unknown or unspecified thing or things: *take a hammer, chisel, or whatever* **4** an intensive form of *what*, used in questions: *whatever can he have said to upset her so much?* ▷ *determiner* **5** an intensive form of *what*: *use whatever tools you can get hold of* ▷ *adj* **6** (*postpositive*) absolutely; whatsoever: *I saw no point whatever in continuing*

whatnot (ˈwɒtˌnɒt) *n* **1** Also called: **what-d'you-call-it** *inf* a person or thing the name of which is unknown or forgotten **2** *inf* unspecified assorted material **3** a portable stand with shelves for displaying ornaments, etc

whatsit (ˈwɒtsɪt), **whatsitsname,** (*masc*) **whatshisname,** *or* (*fem*) **whatshername** *n inf* a person or thing the name of which is unknown or forgotten

whatsoever (ˌwɒtsəʊˈɛvə) *adj* **1** (*postpositive*) at all: used as an intensifier with indefinite pronouns and determiners such as *none, anybody*, etc ▷ *pron* **2** an archaic word for **whatever**

whaup (hwɔːp) *n chiefly Scot* a popular name for the **curlew** [c16 rel. to OE *huilpe*, ult. imit. of the bird's cry]

wheal (wiːl) *n* a variant spelling of **weal¹**

wheat (wiːt) *n* **1** any of a genus of grasses, native to the Mediterranean region and W Asia but widely cultivated, having erect flower spikes and light brown grains **2** the grain of any of these grasses, used in making flour, pasta, etc ▷ See also **durum** [OE *hwǣte*]

wheatbelt (ˈwiːtˌbɛlt) *n* an area in which wheat is the chief agricultural product

wheatear (ˈwiːtˌɪə) *n* a small northern songbird having a pale grey back, black wings and tail, white rump, and pale brown underparts [c16 back formation from *wheatears* (wrongly taken as pl), prob. from WHITE + ARSE]

wheaten (ˈwiːtᵊn) *adj* **1** made of the grain or flour of wheat **2** of a pale yellow colour

wheat germ *n* the vitamin-rich embryo of the wheat kernel

wheatmeal (ˈwiːtˌmiːl) *n* **a** a brown flour intermediate between white flour and wholemeal flour **b** (*as modifier*): *a wheatmeal loaf*

Wheatstone bridge (ˈwiːtstən) *n* a device for determining the value of an unknown resistance by comparison with a known standard resistance [c19 after Sir Charles *Wheatstone* (1802–75), Brit physicist and inventor]

whee (wiː) *interj* an exclamation of joy, etc

wheedle (ˈwiːdᵊl) *vb* **wheedles, wheedling, wheedled** **1** to persuade or try to persuade (someone) by coaxing words, flattery, etc **2** (*tr*) to obtain thus: *she wheedled some money out of her father* [c17 ?from G *wedeln* to wag one's tail, from OHG *wedil, wadil* tail] > ˈ**wheedler** *n* > ˈ**wheedling** *adj* > ˈ**wheedlingly** *adv*

wheel (wiːl) *n* **1** a solid disc, or a circular rim joined to a hub by spokes, that is mounted on a shaft about which it can turn, as in vehicles **2** anything like a wheel in shape or function **3** a device consisting of or resembling a wheel: *a steering wheel; a water wheel* **4** (usually preceded by *the*) a medieval torture in which the victim was tied to a wheel and then had his or her limbs struck and broken by an iron bar **5** short for **wheel of fortune** or **potter's wheel** **6** the act of turning **7** a pivoting movement of troops, ships, etc **8** a type of firework coiled to make it rotate when let off **9** a set of short rhyming lines forming the concluding part of a stanza **10** *US & Canad* an informal word for **bicycle** **11** *inf, chiefly US & Canad* a person of great influence (esp in **big wheel**) **12** **at the wheel** **12a** driving or steering a vehicle or vessel **12b** in charge ▷ *vb* **13** to turn or cause to turn on or as if on an axis **14** (when *intr*, sometimes foll by *about* or *around*) to move or cause to move on or as if on wheels;

roll **15** (*tr*) to perform with or in a circular movement **16** (*tr*) to provide with a wheel or wheels **17** (*intr; often foll by about*) to change direction **18 wheel and deal** *inf* to operate free of restraint, esp to advance one's own interests ▷ See also **wheels** [OE *hweol, hweowol*]

wheel and axle *n* a simple machine for raising weights in which a rope unwinding from a wheel is wound onto a cylindrical drum or shaft coaxial with or joined to the wheel to provide mechanical advantage

wheel animalcule *n* another name for **rotifer**

wheelbarrow ('wiːlˌbærəʊ) *n* a simple vehicle for carrying small loads, typically being an open container supported by a wheel at the front and two legs behind

wheelbase ('wiːlˌbeɪs) *n* the distance between the front and back axles of a motor vehicle

wheelchair ('wiːlˌtʃɛə) *n* special chair on large wheels, for use by invalids or others for whom walking is impossible or inadvisable

wheel clamp *n* a device fixed onto one wheel of an illegally parked car in order to immobilize it. The driver has to pay to have it removed

wheeled (wiːld) *adj* **a** having a wheel or wheels **b** (*in combination*): *four-wheeled*

wheeler ('wiːlə) *n* **1** Also called: **wheel horse** a horse or other draught animal nearest the wheel **2** (*in combination*) something equipped with a specified sort or number of wheels: *a three-wheeler* **3** a person or thing that wheels

Wheeler ('wiːlə) *n* **1 John Archibald** born 1911, US physicist, noted for his work on nuclear fission and the development (1949–51) of the hydrogen bomb, also for his work on unified field theory **2** Sir (**Robert Eric**) **Mortimer** 1890–1976, Scottish archaeologist, who did much to increase public interest in archaeology. He is noted esp for his excavations at Mohenjo-Daro and Harappa in the Indus Valley and at Maiden Castle in Dorset

wheeler-dealer *n inf* a person who wheels and deals

wheel horse *n* **1** another word for **wheeler** (sense 1) **2** *US & Canad* a person who works steadily or hard

wheelhouse ('wiːlˌhaʊs) *n* another term for **pilot house**

wheelie ('wiːlɪ) *n* a manoeuvre on a bicycle or motorbike in which the front wheel is raised off the ground

wheelie bin *or* **wheely bin** *n* a large container for rubbish, esp one used by a household, mounted on wheels so that it can be moved more easily

wheel lock *n* **1** a gunlock formerly in use in which the firing mechanism was activated by sparks produced by friction between a small steel wheel and a flint **2** a gun having such a lock

wheel of fortune *n* (in mythology and literature) a revolving device spun by a deity selecting random changes in the affairs of man

wheels (wiːlz) *pl n* **1** the main directing force behind an organization, movement, etc: *the wheels of government* **2** an informal word for **car 3 wheels within wheels** a series of intricately connected events, plots, etc

wheel trim *n* metallic decorative trim over or around the wheels of a motor vehicle

wheel window *n* another name for **rose window**

wheel wobble *n* an oscillation of the front wheels of a vehicle caused by a defect in the steering gear, unbalanced wheels, etc

wheelwright ('wiːlˌraɪt) *n* a person who makes or mends wheels as a trade

wheeze (wiːz) *vb* **wheezes, wheezing, wheezed 1** to breathe or utter (something) with a rasping or whistling sound **2** (*intr*) to make or move with a noise suggestive of wheezy breathing ▷ *n* **3** a husky, rasping, or whistling sound or breathing **4** *Brit sl* a trick, idea, or plan **5** *inf* a hackneyed joke or anecdote [C15 prob. from ON *hvǣsa* to hiss] > '**wheezer** *n* > '**wheezy** *adj* > '**wheezily** *adv* > '**wheeziness** *n*

whelk[1] (wɛlk) *n* a marine gastropod mollusc of coastal waters and intertidal regions, having a strong snail-like shell [OE *weoloc*]

whelk[2] (wɛlk) *n* a raised lesion on the skin; wheal [OE *hwylca*, from ?] > '**whelky** *adj*

whelm (wɛlm) *vb* (*tr*) *arch* to engulf entirely; overwhelm [C13 *whelmen* to turn over, from ?]

whelp (wɛlp) *n* **1** a young offspring of certain animals, esp of a wolf or dog **2** *disparaging* a youth **3** *jocular* a young child **4** *naut* any of the ridges, parallel to the axis, on the drum of a capstan to keep a rope, etc, from slipping ▷ *vb* **5** (of an animal or, disparagingly, a woman) to give birth to (young) [OE *hwelp(a)*]

when (wɛn) *adv* **1a** at what time? over what period?: *when is he due?* **1b** (*used in indirect questions*): *ask him when he's due* **2 say when** to state when an action is to be stopped or begun, as when someone is pouring a drink ▷ *conj* **3** (*subordinating*) at a time at which; just as; after: *I found it easy when I tried* **4** although: *he drives when he might walk* **5** considering the fact that: *how did you pass the exam when you hadn't worked for it?* ▷ *pron* **6** at which (time); over which (period): *an age when men were men* ▷ *n* **7** a question as to the time of some occurrence [OE *hwanne, hwænne*]

> **USAGE** *When* should not be used loosely as a substitute for *in which* after a noun which does not refer to a period of time: *paralysis is a condition in which* (not *when*) *parts of the body cannot be moved*

whenas (wɛn'æz) *conj arch* **1a** when; whenever **1b** inasmuch as; while **2** although

whence (wɛns) *arch or formal* ▷ *adv* **1** from what place, cause, or origin? ▷ *pron* **2** (*subordinating*) from what place, cause, or origin [C13 *whannes*, adv. genitive of OE *hwanon*]

> **USAGE** The expression *from whence* should be avoided, since *whence* already means 'from which place': *the tradition whence* (not *from whence*) *such ideas flowed*

whencesoever (ˌwɛnssəʊ'ɛvə) *conj* (*subordinating*), *adv arch* from whatever place, cause, or origin

whenever (wɛn'ɛvə) *conj* **1** (*subordinating*) at every or any time that; when: *I laugh whenever I see that* ▷ *adv also* **when ever 2** no matter when: *it'll be here, whenever you decide to come for it* **3** *inf* at an unknown or unspecified time: *I'll take it if it comes today, tomorrow, or whenever* **4** an intensive form of *when*, used in questions: *whenever did he escape?*

whensoever (ˌwɛnsəʊ'ɛvə) *conj, adv rare* an intensive form of **whenever**

whenua (fɛn'uə) *n NZ* land [Maori]

whenwe ('wɛ nwiː) *n S African inf* a White immigrant from Zimbabwe, caricatured as being tiresomely over-reminiscent of happier times [C20 from WHEN + WE]

where (wɛə) *adv* **1a** in, at, or to what place, point, or position?: *where are you going?* **1b** (*used in indirect questions*): *I don't know where they are* ▷ *pron* **2** in, at, or to which (place): *the hotel where we spent our honeymoon* ▷ *conj* **3** (*subordinating*) in the place at which: *where we live it's always raining* ▷ *n* **4** a question as to the position, direction, or destination of something [OE *hwǣr, hwār(a)*]

> **USAGE** It was formerly considered incorrect to use *where* as a substitute for *in which* after a noun which did not refer to a place or position, but this use has now become acceptable: *we have a situation where/in which no further action is needed*

whereabouts ('wɛərəˌbaʊts) *adv* **1** at what approximate place; where: *whereabouts are you?* ▷ *n* **2** (*functioning as sing or pl*) the place, esp the approximate place, where a person or thing is

whereas (wɛər'æz) *conj* **1** (*coordinating*) but on the other hand: *I like to go swimming whereas Sheila likes to sail* ▷ *sentence connector* **2** (in formal documents) it being the case that; since

whereat (wɛər'æt) *arch* ▷ *adv* **1** at or to which place ▷ *sentence connector* **2** upon which occasion

whereby (wɛə'baɪ) *pron* by or because of which: *the means whereby he took his life*

wherefore ('wɛə,fɔː) *n* **1** (*usually pl*) an explanation or reason (esp in **the whys and wherefores**) ▷ *adv* **2** *arch* why? ▷ *sentence connector* **3** *arch or formal* for which reason: used in legal preambles

wherefrom (wɛə'frɒm) *arch* ▷ *adv* **1** from what or where? whence? ▷ *pron* **2** from which place; whence

wherein (wɛər'ɪn) *arch or formal* ▷ *adv* **1** in what place or respect? ▷ *pron* **2** in which place, thing, etc

whereof (wɛər'ɒv) *arch or formal* ▷ *adv* **1** of what or which person or thing? ▷ *pron* **2** of which (person or thing): *the man whereof I speak is no longer alive*

whereon (wɛər'ɒn) *arch* ▷ *adv* **1** on what thing or place? ▷ *pron* **2** on which thing, place, etc

wheresoever (,wɛəsəʊ'ɛvə) *conj* (*subordinating*), *adv*, *pron rare* an intensive form of **wherever**

whereto (wɛə'tuː) *arch or formal* ▷ *adv* **1** towards what (place, end, etc)? ▷ *pron* **2** to which ▷ Also (archaic): **whereunto**

whereupon (,wɛərə'pɒn) *sentence connector* at which; at which point; upon which: *I walked off the mountain whereupon the sun came out*

wherever (wɛər'ɛvə) *pron* **1** at, in, or to every place or point which; where: *wherever she went, he would be there* ▷ *conj* **2** (*subordinating*) in, to, or at whatever place: *wherever we go the weather is always bad* ▷ *adv also* **where ever** **3** no matter where: *I'll find you, wherever you are* **4** *inf* at, in, or to an unknown or unspecified place: *I'll go anywhere to escape: London, Paris, or wherever* **5** an intensive form of *where*, used in questions: *wherever can they be?*

wherewith (wɛə'wɪθ, -'wɪð) *arch or formal* ▷ *pron* **1** (*often foll by an infinitive*) with or by which: *the pen wherewith I write* **2** something with which: *I have not wherewith to buy my bread* ▷ *adv* **3** with what? ▷ *sentence connector* **4** with or after that; whereupon

wherewithal *n* ('wɛəwɪð,ɔːl) **1** **the wherewithal** necessary funds, resources, or equipment: *these people lack the wherewithal for a decent existence* ▷ *pron* (,wɛəwɪð'ɔːl) **2** a less common word for **wherewith**

wherry ('wɛrɪ) *n*, *pl* **wherries** **1** any of certain kinds of half-decked commercial boats **2** a light rowing boat [c15 from ?] > '**wherryman** *n*

whet (wɛt) *vb* **whets, whetting, whetted** (*tr*) **1** to sharpen, as by grinding or friction **2** to increase (the appetite, desire, etc); stimulate ▷ *n* **3** the act of whetting **4** a person or thing that whets [OE *hwettan*] > '**whetter** *n*

whether ('wɛðə) *conj* **1** (*subordinating*) used to introduce an indirect question or a clause after a verb expressing or implying doubt or choice: *he doesn't know whether she's in Britain or whether she's gone to France* **2** (*coordinating*) either: *any man, whether liberal or conservative, would agree with me* **3** **whether or no** in any case: *he will be here tomorrow, whether or no* **4** **whether…or** (**whether**) if on the one hand…or even if on the other hand: *you'll eat that, whether you like it or not* [OE *hwæther, hwether*]

whetstone ('wɛt,stəʊn) *n* **1** a stone used for sharpening edged tools, knives, etc **2** something that sharpens

whew (hwjuː) *interj* an exclamation or sharply exhaled breath expressing relief, delight, etc

whey (weɪ) *n* the watery liquid that separates from the curd when milk is clotted, as in making cheese [OE *hwǣg*]

wheyface ('weɪ,feɪs) *n* **1** a pale bloodless face **2** a person with such a face > '**whey,faced** *adj*

which (wɪtʃ) *determiner* **1a** used with a noun in requesting that its referent be further specified, identified, or distinguished: *which house did you buy?* **1b** (*as pron*): *which did you find?* **1c** (*used in indirect questions*): *I wondered which apples were cheaper* **2a** whatever of a class; whichever: *bring which car you want* **2b** (*as pron*): *choose which of the cars suits you* ▷ *pron* **3** used in relative clauses with inanimate antecedents: *the house, which is old, is in poor repair* **4** as; and that: used in relative clauses with verb phrases or sentences as their antecedents: *he died of cancer, which is what I predicted* **5** **the which** an archaic form of **which** often used as a sentence connector [OE *hwelc, hwilc*]

USAGE See at **that**

whichever (wɪtʃ'ɛvə) *determiner* **1a** any (one, two, etc, out of several): *take whichever car you like* **1b** (*as pron*): *choose whichever appeals to you* **2a** no matter which (one or ones): *whichever card you pick you'll still be making a mistake* **2b** (*as pron*): *it won't make any difference, whichever comes first*

whichsoever (,wɪtʃsəʊ'ɛvə) *pron* an archaic or formal word for **whichever**

whicker ('wɪkə) *vb* (*intr*) (of a horse) to whinny or neigh; nicker [c17 imit.]

whidah ('wɪdə) *n* a variant spelling of **whydah**

whiff (wɪf) *n* **1** a passing odour **2** a brief gentle gust of air **3** a single inhalation or exhalation from the mouth or nose ▷ *vb* **4** to puff or waft **5** (*tr*) to sniff or smell **6** (*intr*) *Brit sl* to stink [c16 imit.]

whiffle ('wɪfᵊl) *vb* **whiffles, whiffling, whiffled** **1** (*intr*) to think or behave in an erratic or unpredictable way **2** to blow or be blown fitfully or in gusts **3** (*intr*) to whistle softly [c16 frequentative of WHIFF]

whiffletree ('wɪfᵊl,triː) *n chiefly US* another word for **swingletree** [c19 var. of WHIPPLETREE]

Whig (wɪg) *n* **1** a member of the English political party that opposed the succession to the throne of James, Duke of York (1679–80), on the grounds that he was a Catholic. Standing for a limited monarchy, the Whigs later represented the desires of industrialists and Dissenters for political and social reform, and provided the core of the Liberal Party **2** (in the US) a supporter of the War of American Independence ▷ Cf **Tory** **3** a member of the American political party that opposed the Democrats from about 1834 to 1855 and represented propertied and professional interests **4** *history* a 17th-century Scottish Presbyterian, esp one in rebellion against the Crown ▷ *adj* **5** of, characteristic of, or relating to Whigs [c17 prob. from *whiggamore*, one of a group of 17th-cent. Scottish rebels who joined in an attack on Edinburgh known as *the whiggamore raid*; prob. from Scot. *whig* to drive (from ?) + *more* horse] > '**Whiggery** *or* '**Whiggism** *n* > '**Whiggish** *adj*

Ww

while (waɪl) *conj also* **whilst** **1** (*subordinating*) at the same time that: *please light the fire while I'm cooking* **2** (*subordinating*) all the time that: *I stay inside while it's raining* **3** (*subordinating*) in spite of the fact that: *while I agree about his brilliance I still think he's rude* **4** (*coordinating*) whereas; and in contrast: *houses are expensive, while flats are cheap* ▷ *prep, conj* **5** *Scot & N English dialect* another word for **until**: *you'll have to wait while Monday* ▷ *n* **6** (*usually used in adverbial phrases*) a period or interval of time: *once in a long while* **7** trouble or time (esp in **worth one's while**): *it's hardly worth your while to begin work today* [OE *hwīl*]

USAGE See at **awhile**

while away *vb* (*tr, adv*) to pass (time) idly and usually pleasantly

whiles (waɪlz) *arch or dialect* ▷ *adv* **1** at times; occasionally ▷ *conj* **2** while; whilst

whilom ('waɪləm) *arch* ▷ *adv* **1** formerly; once ▷ *adj* **2** (*prenominal*) one-time; former [OE *hwīlum*, dative pl of *hwīl* while]

whilst (waɪlst) *conj chiefly Brit* another word for **while** (senses 1–4) [c13 from WHILES + -*t* as in *amidst*]

whim (wɪm) *n* **1** a sudden, passing, and often fanciful idea; impulsive or irrational thought **2** a horse-drawn winch formerly used in mining to lift ore or water [c17 from c16 *whim-wham*, from ?]

whimbrel ('wɪmbrəl) *n* a small European curlew with a

striped head [c16 from dialect *whimp* or from WHIMPER, from its cry]

whimper ('wɪmpə) *vb* 1 (*intr*) to cry, sob, or whine softly or intermittently 2 to complain or say (something) in a whining plaintive way ▷ *n* 3 a soft plaintive whine [c16 from dialect *whimp*, imit.] > '**whimperer** *n* > '**whimpering** *n, adj* > '**whimperingly** *adv*

whimsical ('wɪmzɪkᵊl) *adj* 1 spontaneously fanciful or playful 2 given to whims; capricious 3 quaint, unusual, or fantastic > **whimsicality** (ˌwɪmzɪ'kælɪtɪ) *n* > '**whimsically** *adv*

whimsy *or* **whimsey** ('wɪmzɪ) *n, pl* **whimsies** *or* **whimseys** 1 a capricious idea or notion 2 light or fanciful humour 3 something quaint or unusual ▷ *adj* **whimsier, whimsiest** 4 quaint, comical, or unusual, often in a tasteless way [c17 from WHIM]

whin (wɪn) *n* another name for **gorse** [c11 from ON]

whinchat ('wɪnˌtʃæt) *n* an Old World songbird having a mottled brown-and-white plumage with pale cream underparts [c17 from WHIN[1] + CHAT]

whine (waɪn) *n* 1 a long high-pitched plaintive cry or moan 2 a continuous high-pitched sound 3 a peevish complaint, esp one repeated ▷ *vb* **whines, whining, whined** 4 to make a whine or utter in a whine [OE *hwīnan*] > '**whiner** *n* > '**whining** *or* '**whiny** *adj*

whinge (wɪndʒ) *vb* **whinges, whingeing, whinged** (*intr*) 1 to cry in a fretful way 2 to complain ▷ *n* 3 a complaint [from Northern var. of OE *hwinsian* to whine] > '**whingeing** *n, adj* > '**whinger** *n*

whinny ('wɪnɪ) *vb* **whinnies, whinnying, whinnied** (*intr*) 1 (of a horse) to neigh softly or gently 2 to make a sound resembling a neigh, such as a laugh ▷ *n, pl* **whinnies** 3 a gentle or low-pitched neigh [c16 imit.]

whip (wɪp) *vb* **whips, whipping, whipped** 1 to strike (a person or thing) with several strokes of a strap, rod, etc 2 (*tr*) to punish by striking in this manner 3 (*tr;* foll by *out, away,* etc) to pull, remove, etc, with sudden rapid motion: *to whip out a gun* 4 (*intr;* foll by *down, into, out of,* etc) *inf* to come, go, etc, in a rapid sudden manner: *they whipped into the bar for a drink* 5 to strike or be struck as if by whipping: *the tempest whipped the surface of the sea* 6 (*tr*) to bring, train, etc, forcefully into a desired condition 7 (*tr*) *inf* to overcome or outdo 8 (*tr;* often foll by *on, out,* or *off*) to drive, urge, compel, etc, by or as if by whipping 9 (*tr*) to wrap or wind (a cord, thread, etc) around (a rope, cable, etc) to prevent chafing or fraying 10 (*tr*) (in fly-fishing) to cast the fly repeatedly onto (the water) in a whipping motion 11 (*tr*) (in sewing) to join, finish, or gather with whipstitch 12 to beat (eggs, cream, etc) with a whisk or similar utensil to incorporate air 13 (*tr*) to spin (a top) 14 (*tr*) *inf* to steal: *he whipped her purse* ▷ *n* 15 a device consisting of a lash or flexible rod attached at one end to a stiff handle and used for driving animals, inflicting corporal punishment, etc 16 a whipping stroke or motion 17 a person adept at handling a whip, as a coachman, etc 18 (in a legislative body) 18a a member of a party chosen to organize and discipline the members of his faction 18b a call issued to members of a party, insisting with varying degrees of urgency upon their presence or loyal voting behaviour 18c (in the Brit Parliament) a schedule of business sent to members of a party each week. Each item on it is underlined to indicate its importance: three lines means that the item is very important and every member must attend and vote according to the party line 19 an apparatus for hoisting, consisting of a rope, pulley, and snatch block 20 any of a variety of desserts made from egg whites or cream beaten stiff 21 See **whipper-in** 22 flexibility, as in the shaft of a golf club, etc ▷ See also **whip-round, whip up, whips** [c13 ?from MDu. *wippen* to swing] > '**whipˌlike** *adj* > '**whipper** *n*

whip bird *n Austral* any of several birds having a whistle ending in a note sounding like the crack of a whip

whipcord ('wɪpˌkɔːd) *n* 1 a strong worsted or cotton fabric with a diagonally ribbed surface 2 a closely twisted hard cord used for the lashes of whips, etc

whip graft *n horticulture* a graft made by inserting a tongue cut on the sloping base of the scion into a slit on the sloping top of the stock

whip hand *n* (usually preceded by *the*) 1 (in driving horses) the hand holding the whip 2 advantage or dominating position

whiplash ('wɪpˌlæʃ) *n* a quick lash or stroke of a whip or like that of a whip

whiplash injury *n med inf* any injury to the neck resulting from a sudden thrusting forwards and snapping back of the unsupported head. Technical name: **hyperextension-hyperflexion injury**

whipper-in *n, pl* **whippers-in** a person employed to assist the huntsman managing the hounds

whippersnapper ('wɪpəˌsnæpə) *n* an insignificant but pretentious or cheeky person, often a young one. Also called: **whipster** [c17 prob. from *whipsnapper* a person who snaps whips, infl. by earlier *snippersnapper*, from ?]

whippet ('wɪpɪt) *n* a small slender breed of dog similar to a greyhound [c16 from ?; ? based on *whip it!* move quickly!]

whipping ('wɪpɪŋ) *n* 1 a thrashing or beating with a whip or similar implement 2 cord or twine used for binding or lashing 3 the binding formed by wrapping a rope, etc, with cord or twine

whipping boy *n* a person of little importance who is blamed for the errors, incompetence, etc, of others, esp his superiors; scapegoat [c17 orig. referring to a boy who was educated with a prince and who received punishment for any faults committed by the prince]

whippletree ('wɪpᵊlˌtriː) *n* another name for **swingletree** [c18 apparently from WHIP]

whippoorwill ('wɪpʊˌwɪl) *n* a nightjar of North and Central America, having a dark plumage with white patches on the tail [c18 imit. of its cry]

whip-round *inf, chiefly Brit* ▷ *n* 1 an impromptu collection of money ▷ *vb* **whip round** 2 (*intr, adv*) to make such a collection

whips (wɪps) *pl n* (often foll by *of*) *Austral inf* a large quantity: *I've got whips of cash at the moment*

whipsaw ('wɪpˌsɔː) *n* 1 any saw with a flexible blade, such as a bandsaw ▷ *vb* **whipsaws, whipsawing, whipsawed; whipsawed** *or* **whipsawn** (*tr*) 2 to saw with a whipsaw 3 *US* to defeat in two ways at once

whip scorpion *n* any of an order of nonvenomous arachnids, typically resembling a scorpion but lacking a sting

whip snake *n* any of several long slender fast-moving nonvenomous snakes

whipstitch ('wɪpˌstɪtʃ) *n* a sewing stitch passing over an edge

whipstock ('wɪpˌstɒk) *n* a whip handle

whip up *vb* (*tr, adv*) 1 to excite; arouse: *to whip up a mob; to whip up discontent* 2 *inf* to prepare quickly: *to whip up a meal*

whir *or* **whirr** (wɜː) *n* 1 a prolonged soft swish or buzz, as of a motor working or wings flapping 2 a bustle or rush ▷ *vb* **whirs** *or* **whirrs, whirring, whirred** 3 to make or cause to make a whir [c14 prob. from ON; see WHIRL]

whirl (wɜːl) *vb* 1 to spin, turn, or revolve or cause to spin, turn, or revolve 2 (*intr*) to turn around or away rapidly 3 (*intr*) to have a spinning sensation, as from dizziness, etc 4 to move or drive or be moved or driven at high speed ▷ *n* 5 the act or an instance of whirling; swift rotation or a rapid whirling movement 6 a condition of confusion or giddiness: *her accident left me in a whirl* 7 a swift round, as of events, meetings, etc 8 a tumult; stir 9 *inf* a brief trip, dance, etc 10 **give (something) a whirl** *inf* to attempt or give a trial to (something) [c13 from ON *hvirfla* to turn about] > '**whirler** *n* > '**whirling** *adj* > '**whirlingly** *adv*

whirligig ('wɜːlɪˌɡɪɡ) *n* **1** any spinning toy, such as a top **2** another name for **merry-go-round** **3** anything that whirls about, spins, or moves in a circular or giddy way: *the whirligig of social life* [C15 *whirlegigge*, from WHIRL + GIG[1]]

whirlpool ('wɜːlˌpuːl) *n* **1** a powerful circular current or vortex of water **2** something resembling a whirlpool in motion or the power to attract into its vortex

whirlwind ('wɜːlˌwɪnd) *n* **1** a column of air whirling around and towards a more or less vertical axis of low pressure, which moves along the land or ocean surface **2a** a motion or course resembling this, esp in rapidity **2b** (*as modifier*): *a whirlwind romance* **3** an impetuously active person

whirlybird ('wɜːlɪˌbɜːd) *n* an informal word for **helicopter**

whish (wɪʃ) *n, vb* a less common word for **swish**

whisht (hwɪʃt) *or* **whist** *arch or dialect, esp Scot* ▷ *interj* **1** hush! be quiet! ▷ *adj* **2** silent or still [C14 cf. HIST]

whisk (wɪsk) *vb* **1** (*tr*; *often foll by away or off*) to brush, sweep, or wipe off lightly **2** (*tr*) to move, carry, etc, with a light or rapid sweeping motion: *the taxi whisked us to the airport* **3** (*intr*) to move, go, etc, quickly and nimbly: *to whisk downstairs for a drink* **4** (*tr*) to whip (eggs, etc) to a froth ▷ *n* **5** the act of whisking **6** a light rapid sweeping movement **7** a utensil for whipping eggs, etc **8** a small brush or broom **9** a small bunch or bundle, as of grass, straw, etc [C14 from ON *visk* wisp]

whisker ('wɪskə) *n* **1** any of the stiff sensory hairs growing on the face of a cat, rat, or other mammal. Technical name: **vibrissa** **2** any of the hairs growing on a man's face, esp on the cheeks or chin **3** (*pl*) a beard or that part of it growing on the sides of the face **4** (*pl*) *inf* a moustache **5** *chem* a very fine filamentary crystal having greater strength than the bulk material **6** a person or thing that whisks **7** a narrow margin or small distance: *he escaped death by a whisker* [see WHISK] > '**whiskered** *or* '**whiskery** *adj*

whiskey ('wɪskɪ) *n* the usual Irish and US spelling of **whisky**

whiskey sour *n US* a mixed drink of whisky and lime or lemon juice, sometimes sweetened

whisky ('wɪskɪ) *n, pl* **whiskies** a spirit made by distilling fermented cereals, which is matured and often blended [C18 shortened from *whiskybae*, from Scot. Gaelic *uisge beatha*, lit.: water of life; see USQUEBAUGH]

▷ www.scotchwhisky.net
▷ www.smws.com
▷ www.whisky-heritage.co.uk
▷ www.whiskyportal.com

whisky-jack *n Canad* another name for **Canada jay**

whisky mac *n Brit* a drink consisting of whisky and ginger wine

whisper ('wɪspə) *vb* **1** to speak or utter (something) in a soft hushed tone, esp without vibration of the vocal cords **2** (*intr*) to speak secretly or furtively, as in promoting intrigue, gossip, etc **3** (*intr*) (of leaves, trees, etc) to make a low soft rustling sound **4** (*tr*) to utter or suggest secretly or privately: *to whisper treason* ▷ *n* **5** a low soft voice: *to speak in a whisper* **6** something uttered in such a voice **7** a low soft rustling sound **8** a trace or suspicion **9** *inf* a rumour [OE *hwisprian*] > '**whisperer** *n* > '**whispery** *adj*

whispering campaign *n* the organized diffusion of defamatory rumours to discredit a person, group, etc

whispering gallery *n* a gallery or dome with acoustic characteristics such that a sound made at one point is audible at distant points

whist[1] (wɪst) *n* a card game for four in which the two sides try to win the balance of the 13 tricks: forerunner of bridge [C17 ? changed from WHISK, referring to the sweeping up or whisking up of the tricks]

whist[2] (hwɪst) *interj, adj* a variant of **whisht**

whist drive *n* a social gathering where whist is played: the winners of each hand move to different tables to play the losers of the previous hand

whistle ('wɪsᵊl) *vb* **whistles, whistling, whistled** **1** to produce (shrill or flutelike sounds), as by passing breath through a narrow constriction most easily formed by the pursed lips **2** (*tr*) to signal or command by whistling or blowing a whistle: *the referee whistled the end of the game* **3** (of a kettle, train, etc) to produce (a shrill sound) caused by the emission of steam through a small aperture **4** (*intr*) to move with a whistling sound caused by rapid passage through the air **5** (of animals, esp birds) to emit (a shrill sound) resembling human whistling **6** **whistle in the dark** to try to keep up one's confidence in spite of fear ▷ *n* **7** a device for making a shrill high-pitched sound by means of air or steam under pressure **8** a shrill sound effected by whistling or blowing a whistle **9** a whistling sound, as of a bird, bullet, the wind, etc **10** a signal, etc, transmitted by or as if by a whistle **11** the act of whistling **12** an instrument, usually made of metal, that is blown down its end to produce a tune, signal, etc **13** **blow the whistle** (*usually foll by on*) *inf* **13a** to inform (on) **13b** to bring a stop (to) **14** **clean as a whistle** perfectly clean or clear **15** **wet one's whistle** *inf* to take an alcoholic drink ▷ See also **whistle for, whistle up** [OE *hwistlian*]

whistle-blower *n inf* a person who informs on someone or puts a stop to something > '**whistle-ˌblowing** *adj, n*

whistle for *vb* (*intr, prep*) *inf* to seek or expect in vain

whistler ('wɪslə) *n* **1** a person or thing that whistles **2** *radio* an atmospheric disturbance picked up by radio receivers, caused by the electromagnetic radiation produced by lightning **3** any of various birds having a whistling call, such as certain Australian flycatchers **4** any of various North American marmots

Whistler ('wɪslə) *n* **James Abbott McNeill** 1834–1903, US painter and etcher, living in Europe. He is best known for his sequence of nocturnes and his portraits

whistle stop *n* **1** *US & Canad* **1a** a minor railway station where trains stop only on signal **1b** a small town having such a station **2a** a brief appearance in a town, esp by a political candidate **2b** (*as modifier*): *a whistle-stop tour*

whistle up *vb* (*tr, adv*) to call or summon (a person or animal) by whistling

whit (wɪt) *n* (*usually used with a negative*) the smallest particle; iota; jot: *he has changed not a whit* [C15 prob. var. of WIGHT]

Whit (wɪt) *n* **1** See **Whitsuntide** ▷ *adj* **2** of or relating to Whitsuntide

Whitaker ('wɪtəkə) *n* Sir **Frederick** 1812–91, New Zealand statesman, born in England: prime minister of New Zealand (1863–64; 1882–83)

Whitby ('wɪtbɪ) *n* a fishing port and resort in NE England, in E North Yorkshire at the mouth of the River Esk: an important ecclesiastical centre in Anglo-Saxon times; site of an abbey founded in 656. See also **Synod of Whitby**. Pop: 13 640 (1991)

white (waɪt) *adj* **1** having no hue, owing to the reflection of all or almost all incident light **2** (of light, such as sunlight) consisting of all the colours of the spectrum or produced by certain mixtures of primary colours, as red, green, and blue **3** comparatively white or whitish-grey or having parts of this colour: *white clover* **4** (of an animal) having pale-coloured or white skin, fur, or feathers **5** bloodless or pale, as from pain, emotion, etc **6** (of hair, etc) grey, usually from age **7** benevolent or without malicious intent: *white magic* **8** colourless or transparent: *white glass* **9** capped with or accompanied by snow: *a white Christmas* **10** blank, as an unprinted area of a page **11** (of coffee or tea) with milk or cream **12** (of wine) made from pale grapes or from black grapes separated from their skins **13** denoting flour, or bread made from flour, that has had part of the grain removed

14 *physics* having or characterized by a continuous distribution of energy, wavelength, or frequency: *white noise* **15** *inf* honourable or generous **16** *poetic or arch* having a fair complexion; blond **17** **bleed white** to deprive slowly of resources ▷ *n* **18** a white colour **19** the condition of being white; whiteness **20** the white or lightly coloured part of something **21** (usually preceded by *the*) the viscous fluid that surrounds the yolk of a bird's egg, esp a hen's egg; albumen **22** *anat* the white part (sclera) of the eyeball **23** any of various butterflies having white wings with scanty black markings **24** *chess, draughts* **24a** a white or light-coloured piece or square **24b** the player playing with such pieces **25** anything that has or is characterized by a white colour, such as a white paint or white clothing **26** *inf* white wine: *a bottle of white* **27** *archery* the outer ring of the target, having the lowest score ▷ *vb* **whites, whiting, whited 28** *obs* to make or become white ▷ See also **white out, whites** [OE *hwīt*] > **'whitely** *adv* > **'whiteness** *n* > **'whitish** *adj*

White[1] (waɪt) *n* **1** a member of the Caucasoid race **2** a person of European ancestry ▷ *adj* **3** denoting or relating to a White or Whites

White[2] (waɪt) *n* **1** **Gilbert** 1720–93, English clergyman and naturalist, noted for his *Natural History and Antiquities of Selborne* (1789) **2** **Marco Pierre** born 1961, British chef and restaurateur **3** **Patrick (Victor Martindale)** 1912–90, Australian novelist: his works include *Voss* (1957), *The Eye of the Storm* (1973), and *A Fringe of Leaves* (1976): Nobel prize for literature 1973 **4** **T(erence) H(anbury)** 1906–64, British novelist: author of the Arthurian sequence *The Once and Future King* (1939–58) **5** **Willard (Wentworth)** ('wɪlɑːd) born 1946, British operatic bass, born in Jamaica

white admiral *n* a butterfly of Eurasia having brown wings with white markings

white ant *n* another name for **termite**

whitebait ('waɪtˌbeɪt) *n* **1** the young of herrings, sprats, etc, cooked and eaten whole as a delicacy **2** any of various small silvery fishes [c18 from its formerly having been used as bait]

whitebeam ('waɪtˌbiːm) *n* **1** a N temperate tree having leaves with dense white hair on the undersurface and hard timber **2** any of several similar and closely related trees

white blood cell *n* a nontechnical name for **leucocyte**

whiteboard ('waɪtˌbɔːd) *n* **1** a shiny white surface that can be wiped clean after being used for writing or drawing on, used esp in teaching **2** a large screen used to project computer images to a group of people

whitecap ('waɪtˌkæp) *n* a wave with a white broken crest

white cedar *n* either of two coniferous trees of North America, having scalelike leaves

white clover *n* a Eurasian clover plant with rounded white flower heads: cultivated as a forage plant

white coal *n* water, esp when flowing and providing a potential source of usable power

white-collar *adj* of or designating nonmanual and usually salaried workers employed in professional and clerical occupations

white currant *n* a cultivated N temperate shrub having small rounded white edible berries

whitedamp ('waɪtˌdæmp) *n* a mixture of poisonous gases, mainly carbon monoxide, occurring in coal mines

whited sepulchre *n* a hypocrite [allusion to Matthew 23:27]

white dwarf *n* one of a large class of small faint stars of enormous density, thought to mark the final stage in the evolution of a sun-like star

white elephant *n* **1** a rare albino variety of the Indian elephant, regarded as sacred in parts of S Asia **2** a possession that is unwanted by its owner **3** a rare or valuable possession the upkeep of which is very expensive

White Ensign *n* the ensign of the Royal Navy and the Royal Yacht Squadron, having a red cross on a white background with the Union Jack at the upper corner of the vertical edge alongside the hoist

white-eye *n* a songbird of Africa, Australia, New Zealand, and Asia, having a greenish plumage with a white ring around each eye

white feather *n* **1** a symbol or mark of cowardice **2** **show the white feather** to act in a cowardly manner [from the belief that a white feather in a gamecock's tail was a sign of a poor fighter]

Whitefield ('wɪtˌfiːld) *n* **George** 1714–70, English Methodist preacher, who separated from the Wesleys (?1741) because of his Calvinistic views

whitefish ('waɪtˌfɪʃ) *n, pl* **whitefish** *or* **whitefishes** a food fish typically of deep cold lakes of the N hemisphere, having large silvery scales and a small head

white fish *n* (in the Brit fishing industry) any edible marine fish or invertebrate excluding herrings but including trout, salmon, and all shellfish

white flag *n* a white flag or a piece of white cloth hoisted to signify surrender or request a truce

white flour *n* flour that consists substantially of the starchy endosperm of wheat, most of the bran and the germ having been removed by the milling process

whitefly ('waɪtˌflaɪ) *n, pl* **whiteflies** any of a family of insects typically having a body covered with powdery wax. Many are pests of greenhouse crops

white friar *n* a Carmelite friar, so called because of the white cloak that forms part of the habit of this order

white gold *n* any of various white lustrous hard-wearing alloys containing gold together with platinum and palladium and sometimes smaller amounts of silver, nickel, or copper

white goods *pl n* **1** household linen such as sheets, towels, tablecloths, etc **2** large household appliances, such as refrigerators or cookers

Whitehall (ˌwaɪt'hɔːl) *n* **1** a street in London stretching from Trafalgar Square to the Houses of Parliament: site of the main government offices **2** the British Government or its central administration

white hat *n inf* **a** a computer hacker who is hired by an organization to undertake nonmalicious hacking work in order to discover computer-security flaws **b** (*as modifier*): *a white-hat hacker*. Compare **black hat**

Whitehead ('waɪtˌhɛd) *n* **Alfred North** 1861–1947, English mathematician and philosopher, who collaborated with Bertrand Russell in writing *Principia Mathematica* (1910–13), and developed a holistic philosophy of science, chiefly in *Process and Reality* (1929)

white heat *n* **1** intense heat characterized by emission of white light **2** *inf* a state of intense excitement or activity

white hope *n inf* a person who is expected to bring honour or glory to his or her group, team, etc

white horse *n* **1** the outline of a horse carved into the side of a chalk hill, usually dating to the Neolithic, Bronze, or Iron Ages **2** (*usually pl*) a wave with a white broken crest

Whitehorse ('waɪtˌhɔːs) *n* a town in NW Canada: capital of the Yukon Territory. Pop: 22 884 (1995 est)

white-hot *adj* **1** at such a high temperature that white light is emitted **2** *inf* in a state of intense emotion

White House *n* **the** **1** the official Washington residence of the president of the US **2** the US presidency

white knight *n* a champion or rescuer, esp a person or organization that rescues a company from financial difficulties, an unwelcome takeover bid, etc

white-knuckle *adj* causing or experiencing fear or anxiety: *a white-knuckle fairground ride*

Whitelaw ('waɪt,lɔː) *n* **William (Stephen Ian)**, 1st Viscount Whitelaw of Penrith. 1918–99, British Conservative politician; Home Secretary (1979–83); leader of the House of Lords (1983–88)

white lead (lɛd) *n* **1** a white solid usually regarded as a mixture of lead carbonate and lead hydroxide; basic lead carbonate: used in paint and in making putty and ointments for the treatment of burns **2** either of two similar white pigments based on lead sulphate or lead silicate

white leg *n* another name for **milk leg**

Whiteley ('waɪtlɪ) *n* **Brett** 1939–1992, Australian artist, who travelled widely in Europe and Asia; his works include landscapes, nudes, and portraits

white lie *n* a minor or unimportant lie, esp one uttered in the interests of tact or politeness

white light *n* light that contains all the wavelengths of visible light at approximately equal intensities, as in sunlight

white list *n* **1** a list of countries considered to pose an insignificant threat to human rights, from which applications for political asylum are presumed to be unfounded **2** a list of websites considered to have inoffensive and acceptable content

white-livered *adj* **1** lacking in spirit or courage **2** pallid and unhealthy in appearance

White man's burden *n* the supposed duty of the White race to bring education and Western culture to the non-White inhabitants of their colonies

white matter *n* the whitish tissue of the brain and spinal cord, consisting mainly of nerve fibres covered with a protective white fatlike substance

white meat *n* any meat that is light in colour, such as veal or the breast of turkey

white metal *n* any of various alloys, such as Babbitt metal, used for bearings

white meter *n Brit* an electricity meter used to record the consumption of off-peak electricity

White Mountains *pl n* **1** a mountain range in the US, chiefly in N New Hampshire: part of the Appalachians. Highest peak: Mount Washington, 1917 m (6288 ft) **2** a mountain range in the US, in E California and SW Nevada. Highest peak: White Mountain, 4342 m (14 246 ft)

whiten ('waɪtᵊn) *vb* to make or become white or whiter > '**whitening** *n*

whitener ('waɪtᵊnə) *n* a powdered substitute for milk or cream used in coffee or tea

White Nile *n* See **Nile**

white noise *n* sound or electrical noise that has a relatively wide continuous range of frequencies of uniform intensity

white oak *n* a large oak tree of E North America, having pale bark, leaves with rounded lobes, and heavy light-coloured wood

white out *vb (adv)* **1** *(intr)* to lose or lack daylight visibility owing to snow or fog **2** *(tr)* to create or leave white spaces in (printed or other matter) ▷ *n* **whiteout** **3** a polar atmospheric condition consisting of lack of visibility and sense of distance and direction due to a uniform whiteness of a heavy cloud cover and snow-covered ground, which reflects almost all the light it receives

white paper *n (often caps)* an official government report in any of a number of countries, which sets out the government's policy on a matter that is or will come before Parliament

white pepper *n* a condiment, less pungent than black pepper, made from the husked dried beans of the pepper plant

white pine *n* a North American coniferous tree having blue-green needle-like leaves, hanging brown cones, and rough bark

white poplar *n* **1** Also called: **abele** a Eurasian tree having leaves covered with dense silvery-white hairs **2** another name for **tulipwood** (sense 1)

white rose *n English history* an emblem of the House of York

White Russia *n* another name for **Belarus** > **White Russian** *adj, n*

whites (waɪts) *pl n* **1** household linen or cotton goods, such as sheets **2** white or off-white clothing, such as that worn for playing cricket

white sale *n* a sale of household linens at reduced prices

white sauce *n* a thick sauce made from flour, butter, seasonings, and milk or stock

White Sea *n* an almost landlocked inlet of the Barents Sea on the coast of NW Russia. Area: 90 000 sq km (34 700 sq miles)

white settler *n* a well-off incomer to a district who takes advantage of what it has to offer without regard to the local inhabitants [c20 from earlier colonial sense]

white slave *n* a girl or woman forced or sold into prostitution > **white slavery** *n* > ,**white-'slaver** *n*

white spirit *n* a colourless liquid obtained from petroleum and used as a substitute for turpentine

white spruce *n* a N North American spruce tree with grey bark

white squall *n* a violent highly localized weather disturbance at sea, in which the surface of the water is whipped to a white spray by the winds

whitethorn ('waɪt,θɔːn) *n* another name for **hawthorn**

whitethroat ('waɪt,θrəʊt) *n* either of two Old World warblers having a greyish-brown plumage with a white throat and underparts

white tie *n* **1** a white bow tie worn as part of a man's formal evening dress **2a** formal evening dress for men **2b** *(as modifier): a white-tie occasion*

white toast *n Canad* toasted white bread

white trash *n disparaging* **a** poor White people living in the US, esp the South **b** *(as modifier): white-trash culture*

White Van Man *n inf, derogatory* a male van driver, often of a white van, whose driving is selfish and aggressive

White Volta *n* a river in W Africa, rising in N Burkina-Faso flowing southwest and south to join the Black Volta in central Ghana and form the Volta River. Length: about 885 km (550 miles)

whitewall ('waɪt,wɔːl) *n* a pneumatic tyre having white sidewalls

whitewash ('waɪt,wɒʃ) *n* **1** a substance used for whitening walls and other surfaces, consisting of a suspension of lime or whiting in water **2** *inf* deceptive or specious words or actions intended to conceal defects, gloss over failings, etc **3** *inf* a defeat in a sporting contest in which the loser is beaten in every match, game, etc in a series ▷ *vb (tr)* **4** to cover with whitewash **5** *inf* to conceal, gloss over, or suppress **6** *inf* to defeat (an opponent or opposing team) by winning every match in a series > '**white,washer** *n*

white water *n* **1** a stretch of water with a broken foamy surface, as in rapids **2** light-coloured sea water, esp over shoals or shallows

whitewater rafting *n* the sport of rafting down fast-flowing rivers, esp over rapids

white whale *n* a small white toothed whale of northern waters. Also called: **beluga**

whitewood ('waɪt,wʊd) *n* **1** any of various trees with light-coloured wood, such as the tulip tree, basswood, and cottonwood **2** the wood of any of these trees

whitey *or* **whity** ('waɪtɪ) *n, pl* **whiteys** *or* **whities** *chiefly US* (used contemptuously by Black people) a White man or White men collectively

whither ('wɪðə) *arch or poetic* ▷ *adv* **1** to what place? **2** to what end or purpose? ▷ *conj* **3** to whatever place, purpose, etc [OE *hwider, hwæder;* Mod. E form infl. by HITHER]

whithersoever (ˌwɪðəsəʊˈɛvə) *adv, conj arch or poetic* to whichever place

whiting¹ (ˈwaɪtɪŋ) *n* **1** an important gadoid food fish of European seas, having a dark back with silvery sides and underparts **2** any of various similar fishes [C15 ?from OE *hwītling*]

whiting² (ˈwaɪtɪŋ) *n* white chalk that has been ground and washed, used in making whitewash, metal polish, etc. Also called: **whitening**

Whitlam (ˈwɪtləm) *n* (**Edward**) **Gough** (gɒf) born 1916, Australian Labor statesman: prime minister (1972–75)

Whitley Bay (ˈwɪtlɪ) *n* a resort in NE England, in North Tyneside unitary authority, Tyne and Wear, on the North Sea. Pop: 33 335 (1991)

whitlow (ˈwɪtləʊ) *n* any pussy inflammation of the end of a finger or toe [C14 changed from *whitflaw*, from WHITE + FLAW¹]

Whitman (ˈwɪtmən) *n* **Walt**(**er**) 1819–92, US poet, whose life's work is collected in *Leaves of Grass* (1855 and subsequent enlarged editions). His poems celebrate existence and the multiple elements that make up a democratic society

Whitney¹ (ˈwɪtnɪ) *n* **Mount** a mountain in E California: the highest peak in the Sierra Nevada Mountains and in continental US (excluding Alaska). Height: 4418 m (14 495 ft)

Whitney² (ˈwɪtnɪ) *n* **1 Eli** 1765–1825, US inventor of a mechanical cotton gin (1793) and pioneer manufacturer of interchangeable parts **2 William Dwight** 1827–94, US philologist, noted esp for his *Sanskrit Grammar* (1879)

Whitsun (ˈwɪtsᵊn) *n* **1** short for **Whitsuntide** ▷ *adj* **2** of or relating to Whit Sunday or Whitsuntide

Whitsunday (ˌhwɪtˈsʌndɪ, ˌwɪt-) *n* (in Scotland) May 15, one of the four quarter days

Whit Sunday *n* the seventh Sunday after Easter, observed as a feast in commemoration of the descent of the Holy Spirit on the apostles. Also called: **Pentecost** [OE *hwīta sunnandæg* white Sunday, prob. after the ancient custom of wearing white robes at or after baptism]

Whitsuntide (ˈwɪtsᵊnˌtaɪd) *n* the week that begins with Whit Sunday, esp the first three days

Whittier (ˈwɪtɪə) *n* **John Greenleaf** 1807–92, US poet and humanitarian: a leading campaigner in the antislavery movement. His poems include *Snow-Bound* (1866)

Whittington (ˈwɪtɪŋtən) *n* **Richard,** known as *Dick* died 1423, English merchant, three times mayor of London. According to legend, he walked to London at the age of 13 with his cat and was prevented from leaving again only by the call of the church bells

whittle (ˈwɪtᵊl) *vb* **whittles, whittling, whittled 1** to cut or shave strips or pieces from (wood, a stick, etc), esp with a knife **2** (*tr*) to make or shape by paring or shaving **3** (*tr; often foll by away, down, etc*) to reduce, destroy, or wear away gradually [C16 var. of C15 *thwittle* large knife, ult. from OE *thwītan* to cut]

Whittle (ˈwɪtᵊl) *n* Sir **Frank** 1907–96, English engineer, who invented the jet engine for aircraft; flew first British jet aircraft (1941)

whity (ˈwaɪtɪ) *n, pl* **whities 1** *inf* a variant spelling of **whitey** ▷ *adj* **2a** whitish in colour **2b** (*in combination*): *whity-brown*

whizz *or* **whiz** (wɪz) *vb* **whizzes, whizzing, whizzed 1** to make or cause to make a loud humming or buzzing sound **2** to move or cause to move with such a sound **3** (*intr*) *inf* to move or go rapidly ▷ *n, pl* **whizzes 4** a loud humming or buzzing sound **5** *inf* Also: **wizz** a person who is extremely skilful at some activity **6** a slang word for **amphetamine** [C16 imit.]

whizz-bang *or* **whiz-bang** *n* **1** a World War I shell that travelled at such high velocity that the sound of its flight was heard only an instant before the sound of its explosion **2** a type of firework that jumps around emitting a whizzing sound and occasional bangs

whizz kid, whiz kid, *or* **wiz kid** *n inf* a person who is pushing, enthusiastic, and outstandingly successful for his or her age [C20 from WHIZZ, ? infl. by WIZARD]

whizzy (ˈwɪzɪ) *adj* **whizzier, whizziest** *inf* using sophisticated technology to produce vivid effects

who (huː) *pron* **1** which person? what person? used in direct and indirect questions: *he can't remember who did it; who met you?* **2** used to introduce relative clauses with antecedents referring to human beings: *the people who lived here have left* **3** the one or ones who; whoever: *bring who you want* [OE *hwā*]

USAGE See at **whom**

Who (huː) *n* **the** British rock group (mid-1960s–1983), originally comprising Roger Daltrey (born 1944; vocals), Pete Townshend (born 1945; guitar), John Entwistle (1944–2002; bass), and Keith Moon (1947–78; drums). Their recordings include "My Generation" (1965) and *Tommy* (1969)

WHO *abbrev for* World Health Organization
▷ www.who.int/en

whoa (wəʊ) *interj* a command used esp to horses to stop or slow down [C19 var. of HO]

who-does-what *adj* (of a dispute, strike, etc) relating to the separation of kinds of work performed by different trade unions

whodunnit *or* **whodunit** (huːˈdʌnɪt) *n inf* a novel, play, etc, concerned with a crime, usually murder

whoever (huːˈɛvə) *pron* **1** any person who: *whoever wants it can have it* **2** no matter who: *I'll come round tomorrow, whoever may be here* **3** an intensive form of *who*, used in questions: *whoever could have thought that?* **4** *inf* an unspecified person: *when I get tired, Sean or Lindy or whoever will jump in the water beside me*

whole (həʊl) *adj* **1** containing all the component parts necessary to form a total; complete: *a whole apple* **2** constituting the full quantity, extent, etc **3** uninjured or undamaged **4** healthy **5** having no fractional or decimal part; integral: *a whole number* **6** designating a relationship by descent from the same parents; full: *whole brothers* **7 out of whole cloth** *US & Canad inf* entirely without a factual basis ▷ *adv* **8** in an undivided or unbroken piece: *to swallow a plum whole* ▷ *n* **9** all the parts, elements, etc, of a thing **10** an assemblage of parts viewed together as a unit **11** a thing complete in itself **12 as a whole** considered altogether; completely **13 on the whole 13a** taking all things into consideration **13b** in general [OE *hāl*, *hǣl*] > ˈ**wholeness** *n*

whole blood *n* blood for transfusion from which none of the elements has been removed

wholefood (ˈhəʊlˌfuːd) *n* (*sometimes pl*) **a** food that has been refined or processed as little as possible and is eaten in its natural state, such as brown rice, wholemeal flour, etc **b** (*as modifier*): *a wholefood restaurant*

wholehearted (ˌhəʊlˈhɑːtɪd) *adj* done, acted, given, etc, with total sincerity, enthusiasm, or commitment > ˌ**wholeˈheartedly** *adv*

whole hog *n sl* the whole or total extent (esp in **go the whole hog**)

wholemeal (ˈhəʊlˌmiːl) *adj Brit* (of flour, bread, etc) made from the entire wheat kernel. Also called (esp US and Canad): **whole-wheat**

whole milk *n* milk from which no constituent has been removed

whole note *n* the usual US and Canad name for **semibreve**

whole number *n* **1** an integer **2** a natural number

wholesale (ˈhəʊlˌseɪl) *n* **1** the business of selling goods to retailers in larger quantities than they are sold to final consumers but in smaller quantities than they are purchased from manufacturers ▷ Cf **retail** (sense 1) ▷ *adj* **2** of or engaged in such business **3** made, done, etc, on a large scale or without discrimination ▷ *adv*

4 on a large scale or without discrimination ▷ *vb* **wholesales, wholesaling, wholesaled** 5 to sell (goods) at wholesale > '**whole,saler** *n*

wholesale price index *n* an indicator of price changes in the wholesale market

wholesome ('həʊlsəm) *adj* 1 conducive to health or physical wellbeing 2 conducive to moral wellbeing 3 characteristic or suggestive of health or wellbeing, esp in appearance [C12 from WHOLE (healthy) + -SOME[1]] > '**wholesomely** *adv* > '**wholesomeness** *n*

whole tone *or US & Canad* **whole step** *n* an interval of two semitones. Often shortened to **tone**

whole-tone scale *n* either of two scales produced by commencing on one of any two notes a chromatic semitone apart and proceeding upwards or downwards in whole tones for an octave

whole-wheat *adj* another term (esp US and Canad) for **wholemeal**

who'll (hu:l) *contraction of* who will *or* who shall

wholly ('həʊllɪ) *adv* 1 completely, totally, or entirely 2 without exception; exclusively

whom (hu:m) *pron* the objective form of *who*, used when *who* is not the subject of its own clause: *whom did you say you had seen? he can't remember whom he saw* [OE *hwām*, dative of *hwā* who]

> **USAGE** It was formerly considered correct to use *whom* whenever the object form of *who* was required. This is no longer thought to be necessary and the object form *who* is now commonly used, even in formal writing: *there were several people there who he had met before*. *Who* cannot be used directly after a preposition – the preposition is usually moved, as in *the man (who) he sold his car to*. In formal writing *whom* is preferred in sentences like these: *the man to whom he sold his car*. There are some types of sentence in which *who* cannot be used: *the refugees, many of whom were old and ill, were allowed across the border*

whomever (hu:m'ɛvə) *pron* the objective form of *whoever*: *I'll hire whomever I can find*

whoop (wu:p) *vb* **whoops, whooping, whooped** 1 to utter (speech) with loud cries, as of excitement 2 (hu:p) *med* to cough convulsively with a crowing sound 3 (of certain birds) to utter (a hooting cry) 4 (*tr*) to urge on or call with or as if with whoops 5 (wʊp, wu:p) **whoop it up** *inf* 5a to indulge in a noisy celebration 5b *chiefly US* to arouse enthusiasm ▷ *n* 6 a loud cry, esp one expressing excitement 7 (hu:p) *med* the convulsive crowing sound made during whooping cough [C14 imit.]

whoopee *inf* ▷ *interj* (wʊ'pi:) 1 an exclamation of joy, excitement, etc ▷ *n* ('wʊpi:) 2 **make whoopee** 2a to engage in noisy merrymaking 2b to make love

whoopee cushion *n* a joke cushion that emits a sound like the breaking of wind when someone sits on it

whooper *or* **whooper swan** ('wu:pə) *n* a large Old World swan having a black bill with a yellow base and a noisy whooping cry

whooping cough ('hu:pɪŋ) *n* an acute infectious disease characterized by coughing spasms that end with a shrill crowing sound on inspiration. Technical name: **pertussis**

whoops (wʊps) *interj* an exclamation of surprise or of apology

whoosh *or* **woosh** (wʊʃ) *n* 1 a hissing or rushing sound ▷ *vb* 2 (*intr*) to make or move with such a sound

whop (wɒp) *inf* ▷ *vb* **whops, whopping, whopped** 1 (*tr*) to strike, beat, or thrash 2 (*tr*) to defeat utterly 3 (*intr*) to drop or fall ▷ *n* 4 a heavy blow or the sound made by such a blow [C14 var. of *wap*, ? imit.]

whopper ('wɒpə) *n inf* 1 anything uncommonly large of its kind 2 a big lie [C18 from WHOP]

whopping ('wɒpɪŋ) *adj inf* uncommonly large

whore (hɔ:) *n* 1 a prostitute or promiscuous woman: often a term of abuse ▷ *vb* **whores, whoring, whored** (*intr*) 2 to be or act as a prostitute 3 (of a man) to have promiscuous sexual relations, esp with prostitutes 4 (often foll by *after*) to seek that which is immoral, idolatrous, etc [OE *hōre*] > '**whoredom** *n* > '**whorish** *adj*

whorehouse ('hɔ:,haʊs) *n* another word for **brothel**

whoremonger ('hɔ:,mʌŋgə) *n* a person who consorts with whores; lecher. Also called: **whoremaster**

whoreson ('hɔ:sən) *arch* ▷ *n* 1 a bastard 2 a scoundrel; wretch ▷ *adj* 3 vile or hateful

whorl (wɜ:l) *n* 1 *bot* a radial arrangement of petals, stamens, leaves, etc, around a stem 2 *zool* a single turn in a spiral shell 3 anything shaped like a coil [C15 prob. var. of *wherville* whirl, infl. by Du. *worvel*] > **whorled** *adj*

whortleberry ('wɜ:tᵊl,bɛrɪ) *n, pl* **whortleberries** 1 Also called: **huckleberry** a small Eurasian ericaceous shrub with greenish-pink flowers and edible sweet blackish berries 2 the fruit of this shrub 3 **bog whortleberry** a related plant of mountain regions, having pink flowers and black fruits [C16 SW English dialect var. of *hurtleberry*, from ?]

who's (hu:z) *contraction of* who is *or* who has

whose (hu:z) *determiner* 1a of whom? belonging to whom? used in direct and indirect questions: *I told him whose fault it was; whose car is this?* 1b (*as pron*): *whose is that?* 2 of whom; of which: used as a relative pronoun: *a house whose windows are broken; a man whose reputation has suffered* [OE *hwæs*, genitive of *hwā* who & *hwæt* what]

whoso ('hu:səʊ) *pron* an archaic word for **whoever**

whosoever (,hu:səʊ'ɛvə) *pron* an archaic or formal word for **whoever**

who's who *n* a book or list containing the names and short biographies of famous people

why (waɪ) *adv* 1a for what reason?: *why are you here?* 1b (*used in indirect questions*): *tell me why you're here* ▷ *pron* 2 for or because of which: *there is no reason why he shouldn't come* ▷ *n, pl* **whys** 3 (*usually pl*) the cause of something (esp in **the whys and wherefores**) ▷ *interj* 4 an introductory expression of surprise, indignation, etc: *why, don't be silly!* [OE *hwī*]

Whyalla (waɪ'ælə) *n* a port in S South Australia, on Spencer Gulf: iron and steel and shipbuilding industries. Pop: 25 526 (1991)

whydah *or* **whidah** ('wɪdə) *n* any of various predominantly black African weaverbirds, the males of which grow very long tail feathers in the breeding season. Also called: **whydah bird, whidah bird, widow bird** [C18 after a town in Benin in W Africa]

whydunnit *or* **whydunit** ('waɪ,dʌnɪt) *n inf* a novel, film, etc, concerned with the motives of the criminal rather than his or her identity

WI *abbrev for* 1 West Indian 2 West Indies 3 Wisconsin 4 (in Britain) **Women's Institute**

Wicca ('wɪkə) *n* the cult or practice of witchcraft [C20 revival of OE *wicca* witch] > '**Wiccan** *n, adj*

▷ http://wicca.com/

▷ http://wiccanet.net/

Wichita ('wɪtʃɪ,tɔ:) *n* a city in S Kansas, on the Arkansas River: the largest city in the state; two universities. Pop: 344 284 (2000)

wick[1] (wɪk) *n* 1 a cord or band of loosely twisted or woven fibres, as in a candle, that supplies fuel to a flame by capillary action 2 **get on (someone's) wick** *Brit sl* to cause irritation to (someone) [OE *weoce*]

wick[2] (wɪk) *n arch* a village or hamlet [OE *wīc*; rel. to *-wich* in place names]

Wick (wɪk) *n* a town in N Scotland, in Highland, at the head of **Wick Bay** (an inlet of the North Sea) Pop: 7681 (1991)

wicked ('wɪkɪd) *adj* 1a morally bad 1b (*as collective n*; preceded by *the*): *the wicked* 2 mischievous or roguish in a playful way: *a charmingly wicked grin* **3** causing injury or harm **4** troublesome, unpleasant, or offensive **5** *sl* very good [C13 from dialect *wick*, from OE *wicca* sorcerer, *wicce* witch] > ˈ**wickedly** *adv* > ˈ**wickedness** *n*

wicker (ˈwɪkə) *n* **1** a slender flexible twig or shoot, esp of willow **2** short for **wickerwork** ▷ *adj* **3** made of, consisting of, or constructed from wicker [C14 from ON]

wickerwork (ˈwɪkəˌwɜːk) *n* **a** a material consisting of woven wicker **b** (*as modifier*): *a wickerwork chair*
▷ www.wickerweaver.com/bookstore/PB_wh_history.html

wicket (ˈwɪkɪt) *n* **1** a small door or gate, esp one that is near to or part of a larger one **2** *chiefly US* a small window or opening in a door, esp one fitted with a grating or glass pane **3** a small sluicegate **4a** *cricket* either of two constructions, 22 yards apart, consisting of three stumps stuck in the ground with two wooden bails resting on top, at which the batsman stands **4b** the strip of ground between these **4c** a batsman's turn at batting or the period during which two batsmen bat **4d** the act or instance of a batsman being got out: *the bowler took six wickets* **5** **keep wicket** to act as a wicketkeeper **6** **on a good, sticky,** etc, **wicket** *inf* in an advantageous, awkward, etc, situation [C18 from OF *wiket*]

wicketkeeper (ˈwɪkɪtˌkiːpə) *n* *cricket* the player on the fielding side positioned directly behind the wicket

wickiup, wikiup, *or* **wickyup** (ˈwɪkɪˌʌp) *n* *US & Canad* a crude shelter made of brushwood or grass and having an oval frame, esp of a kind used by nomadic Native Americans now in the Oklahoma area [C19 of Amerind origin]

Wickliffe *or* **Wiclif** (ˈwɪklɪf) *n* variant spellings of (John) **Wycliffe**

Wicklow (ˈwɪkləʊ) *n* **1** a county of E Republic of Ireland, in Leinster province on the Irish Sea: consists of a coastal strip rising inland to the **Wicklow Mountains;** mainly agricultural, with several resorts. County town: Wicklow. Pop: 102 683 (1996) Area: 2025 sq km (782 sq miles) **2** a port in E Republic of Ireland, county town of Co Wicklow. Pop: 5850 (1991)

widdershins (ˈwɪdəˌʃɪnz) *adv chiefly Scot* a variant spelling of **withershins**

wide (waɪd) *adj* **1** having a great extent from side to side **2** spacious or extensive **3a** (*postpositive*) having a specified extent, esp from side to side: *two yards wide* **3b** (*in combination*): extending throughout: *nationwide* **4** remote from the desired point, mark, etc: *your guess is wide of the mark* **5** (of eyes) opened fully **6** loose, full, or roomy: *wide trousers* **7** exhibiting a considerable spread: *a wide variation* **8** *phonetics* another word for **lax** (sense 4) or **open** (sense 32) ▷ *adv* **9** over an extensive area: *to travel far and wide* **10** to the full extent: *he opened the door wide* **11** far from the desired point, mark, etc ▷ *n* **12** (in cricket) a bowled ball that is outside the batsman's reach and scores a run for the batting side [OE *wīd*] > ˈ**widely** *adv* > ˈ**wideness** *n* > ˈ**widish** *adj*

wide-angle lens *n* a lens system on a camera that has a small focal length and therefore can cover an angle of view of 60° or more

wide-awake *adj* (**wide awake** *when postpositive*) **1** fully awake **2** keen, alert, or observant ▷ *n* **3** Also called: **wide-awake hat** a hat with a low crown and very wide brim

wide-body *adj* (of an aircraft) having a wide fuselage, esp wide enough to contain three rows of seats abreast

wide boy *n Brit sl* a man who is prepared to use unscrupulous methods to progress or make money

wide-eyed *adj* innocent or credulous

widen (ˈwaɪdᵊn) *vb* to make or become wide or wider

wide-open *adj* (**wide open** *when postpositive*) **1** open to the full extent **2** (*postpositive*) exposed to attack; vulnerable **3** uncertain as to outcome **4** *US inf* (of a town or city) lax in the enforcement of certain laws, esp those relating to the sale of alcohol, gambling, etc

wide receiver *n American football* a player whose function is to catch long passes from the quarterback

widespread (ˈwaɪdˌsprɛd) *adj* **1** extending over a wide area **2** accepted by or occurring among many people

widgeon (ˈwɪdʒən) *n* a variant spelling of **wigeon**

widget (ˈwɪdʒɪt) *n inf* any small mechanism or device, the name of which is unknown or temporarily forgotten [C20 changed from GADGET]

Widnes (ˈwɪdnɪs) *n* a town in NW England, in Halton unitary authority, N Cheshire, on the River Mersey: chemical industry. Pop: 57 162 (1991)

widow (ˈwɪdəʊ) *n* **1** a woman whose husband has died, esp one who has not remarried **2** (*with a modifier*) *inf* a woman whose husband frequently leaves her alone while he indulges in a sport, etc: *a golf widow* **3** *printing* a short line at the end of a paragraph, esp one that occurs as the top line of a page or column **4** (in some card games) an additional hand or set of cards exposed on the table ▷ *vb* (*tr; usually passive*) **5** to cause to become a widow **6** to deprive of something valued [OE *widuwe*] > ˈ**widowhood** *n*

widow bird *n* another name for **whydah**

widower (ˈwɪdəʊə) *n* a man whose wife has died and who has not remarried

widow's cruse *n* an endless or unfailing source of supply [allusion to I Kings 17:16]

widow's mite *n* a small contribution by a person who has very little [allusion to Mark 12:43]

widow's peak *n* a V-shaped point in the hairline in the middle of the forehead [from the belief that it presaged early widowhood]

width (wɪdθ) *n* **1** the linear extent or measurement of something from side to side **2** the state or fact of being wide **3** a piece or section of something at its full extent from side to side: *a width of cloth* **4** the distance across a rectangular swimming bath, as opposed to its length [C17 from WIDE + -TH[1], analogous to BREADTH]

Wieland[1] (ˈviːlant) *n* the German name for **Wayland**

Wieland[2] (*German* ˈviːlant) *n* **Christoph Martin** (ˈkrɪstɔf ˈmartiːn) 1733–1813, German writer, noted esp for his verse epic *Oberon* (1780)

wield (wiːld) *vb* (*tr*) **1** to handle or use (a weapon, tool, etc) **2** to exert or maintain (power or authority) [OE *wieldan, wealdan*] > ˈ**wieldable** *adj* > ˈ**wielder** *n*

wieldy (ˈwiːldɪ) *adj* **wieldier, wieldiest** easily handled, used, or managed

Wien[1] (viːn) *n* the German name for **Vienna**

Wien[2] (*German* viːn) *n* **Wilhelm** (ˈvɪlhɛlm) 1864–1928, German physicist, who studied black-body radiation: Nobel prize for physics 1911

wiener (ˈwiːnə) *or* **wienerwurst** (ˈwiːnəˌwɜːst) *n US & Canad* a kind of smoked sausage, similar to a frankfurter [C20 shortened from G *Wiener Wurst* Viennese sausage]

Wiener (ˈwiːnə) *n* **Norbert** (ˈnɔːbət) 1894–1964, US mathematician, who developed the concept of cybernetics

Wiener Neustadt (*German* ˈviːnər ˈnɔyʃtat) *n* a city in E Austria, in Lower Austria. Pop: 35 268 (1991)

Wiener schnitzel (ˈviːnə ˈʃnɪtsəl) *n* a thin escalope of veal, fried in breadcrumbs [G: Viennese cutlet]

Wiesbaden (*German* ˈviːsbaːdən) *n* a city in W Germany, capital of Hesse state: a spa resort since Roman times. Pop: 268 200 (1999 est). Latin name: **Aquae Mattiacorum** (ˈækwiː ˌmætjəˈkəʊrəm)

Wiesel (ˈviːzəl) *n* **Elie** born 1928, US human rights campaigner: noted esp for his documentaries of wartime atrocities against the Jews; Nobel peace prize 1986

Wiesenthal (ˈviːzənˌtaːl) *n* **Simon** born 1908, Austrian investigator of Nazi war crimes. A survivor of the concentration camps, he has been active since 1945 in documenting Nazi crimes against the Jews, tracking down their perpetrators, and assisting surviving victims

wife (waɪf) *n, pl* **wives** **1** a man's partner in marriage; a married woman. Related adj: **uxorial** **2** an archaic or dialect word for **woman** **3** **take to wife** to marry (a woman) [OE *wīf*] > '**wifehood** *n* > '**wifely** *adj*

wifey ('waɪfɪ) *n* an informal word for **wife**

Wi-Fi ('waɪˌfaɪ) *n computing* a system of accessing the Internet from remote machines such as laptop computers that have wireless connections [c20 from *wi(reless) fi(delity)*]

wig (wɪg) *n* **1** an artificial head of hair, either human or synthetic, worn to disguise baldness, as part of a theatrical or ceremonial dress, as a disguise, or for adornment ▷ *vb* **wigs, wigging, wigged** *(tr)* **2** *Brit sl* to berate severely [c17 shortened from PERIWIG] > **wigged** *adj* > '**wigless** *adj*

Wig. *abbrev for* Wigtownshire

Wigan ('wɪgən) *n* **1** an industrial town in NW England, in Wigan unitary authority, Greater Manchester: former coal-mining centre. Pop: 85 819 (1991) **2** a unitary authority in NW England, in Greater Manchester. Pop: 301 417 (2001). Area: 199 sq km (77 sq miles)

wigeon *or* **widgeon** ('wɪdʒən) *n* **1** a Eurasian duck of marshes, swamps, etc, the male of which has a reddish-brown head and chest and grey-and-white back and wings **2** **American wigeon** Also called: **baldpate** a similar bird of North America, the male of which has a white crown [c16 from ?]

wigging ('wɪgɪŋ) *n Brit sl* a reprimand

wiggle ('wɪgᵊl) *vb* **wiggles, wiggling, wiggled** **1** to move or cause to move with jerky movements, esp from side to side ▷ *n* **2** the act of wiggling [c13 from MLow G, MDu. *wiggelen*] > '**wiggler** *n* > '**wiggly** *adj*

wight (waɪt) *n arch* a human being [OE *wiht*; rel. to OFrisian *āwet* something]

Wight (waɪt) *n* **Isle of** an island and county of S England in the English Channel. Administrative centre: Newport. Pop: 132 719 (2001). Area: 380 sq km (147 sq miles)

Wigner ('wɪgnə) *n* **Eugene Paul** 1902–95, US physicist, born in Hungary. He is noted for his contributions to nuclear physics: shared the Nobel prize for physics 1963

Wigtownshire ('wɪgtənˌʃɪə, -ʃə) *n* (until 1975) a county of SW Scotland, now part of Dumfries and Galloway

wigwag ('wɪgˌwæg) *vb* **wigwags, wigwagging, wigwagged** **1** to move (something) back and forth **2** to communicate with (someone) by means of a flag semaphore ▷ *n* **3a** a system of communication by flag semaphore **3b** the message signalled [c16 from obs. *wig*, prob. short for WIGGLE + WAG[1]] > '**wigˌwagger** *n*

wigwam ('wɪgˌwæm) *n* **1** any dwelling of the North American Indians, esp one made of bark, rushes, or skins spread over a set of arched poles lashed together **2** a similar structure for children [from *wīkwām* (of Amerind origin), lit.: their abode]

Wilberforce ('wɪlbəˌfɔːs) *n* **1** **Samuel** 1805–73, British Anglican churchman; bishop of Oxford (1845–69) and Winchester (1869–73) **2** his father, **William** 1759–1833, British politician and philanthropist, whose efforts secured the abolition of the slave trade (1807) and of slavery (1833) in the British Empire

wilco ('wɪlkəʊ) *interj* an expression in signalling, telecommunications, etc, indicating that a message just received will be complied with [c20 abbrev for *I will comply*]

wild (waɪld) *adj* **1** (of animals) living independently of man; not domesticated or tame **2** (of plants) growing in a natural state; not cultivated **3** uninhabited; desolate: *a wild stretch of land* **4** living in a savage or uncivilized way: *wild tribes* **5** lacking restraint or control: *wild merriment* **6** of great violence: *a wild storm* **7** disorderly or chaotic: *wild talk* **8** dishevelled; untidy: *wild hair* **9** in a state of extreme emotional intensity: *wild with anger* **10** reckless: *wild speculations* **11** random: *a wild guess* **12** *(postpositive; foll by about) inf* intensely enthusiastic: *I'm wild about my new boyfriend* **13** (of a card, such as a joker in some games) able to be given any value the holder pleases **14** **wild and woolly** **14a** rough; barbarous **14b** (of theories, plans, etc) not fully thought out ▷ *adv* **15** in a wild manner **16** **run wild** **16a** to grow without cultivation or care: *the garden has run wild* **16b** to behave without restraint: *he has let his children run wild* ▷ *n* **17** *(often pl)* a desolate or uninhabited region **18** **the wild** **18a** a free natural state of living **18b** the wilderness [OE *wilde*] > '**wildish** *adj* > '**wildly** *adv* > '**wildness** *n*

wild boar *n* a wild pig of parts of Europe and central Asia, having a pale grey to black coat and prominent tusks

wild brier *n* another name for **wild rose**

wild card *n* **1** See **wild** (sense 13) **2** *sport* a player or team that has not qualified for a competition but is allowed to take part, at the organizers' discretion, after all the regular places have been taken **3** an unpredictable element in a situation **4** *computing* a symbol that can represent any character or group of characters, as in a filename

wild carrot *n* an umbelliferous plant of temperate regions, having clusters of white flowers and hooked fruits

wildcat ('waɪldˌkæt) *n, pl* **wildcats** *or* **wildcat** **1** a wild European cat that resembles the domestic tabby but is larger and has a bushy tail **2** any of various other felines, such as the lynx and the caracal **3** *US & Canad* another name for **bobcat** **4** *inf* a savage or aggressive person **5** an exploratory drilling for petroleum or natural gas **6** *(modifier) chiefly US* involving risk, esp financially or commercially unsound: *a wildcat project* ▷ *vb* **wildcats, wildcatting, wildcatted** **7** *(intr)* to drill for petroleum or natural gas in an area having no known reserves > '**wildˌcatter** *n* > '**wildˌcatting** *n, adj*

wildcat strike *n* a strike begun by workers spontaneously or without union approval

wild cherry *n* another name for **gean**

wild dog *n* another name for **dingo**

Wilde (waɪld) *n* **Oscar** (**Fingal O'Flahertie Wills**) 1854–1900, Irish writer and wit, famous for such plays as *Lady Windermere's Fan* (1892) and *The Importance of being Earnest* (1895). *The Picture of Dorian Gray* (1891) is a macabre novel about a hedonist and *The Ballad of Reading Gaol* (1898) relates to his experiences in prison while serving a two- year sentence for homosexuality

wildebeest ('wɪldɪˌbiːst, 'vɪl-) *n, pl* **wildebeests** *or* **wildebeest** another name for **gnu** [c19 from Afrik., lit.: wild beast]

wilder ('wɪldə) *vb arch* **1** to lead or be led astray **2** to bewilder or become bewildered [c17 from ?]

Wilder ('waɪldə) *n* **1** **Billy,** real name *Samuel Wilder*. 1906–2002, US film director and screenwriter, born in Austria. His films include *Double Indemnity* (1944), *The Lost Weekend* (1945), *Sunset Boulevard* (1950), *The Seven Year Itch* (1955), *Some Like it Hot* (1959), *The Apartment* (1960), and *Buddy Buddy* (1981) **2** **Thornton** 1897–1975 US novelist and dramatist. His works include the novel *The Bridge of San Luis Rey* (1927) and the play *The Skin of Our Teeth* (1942)

wilderness ('wɪldənɪs) *n* **1** a wild uninhabited uncultivated region **2** any desolate area **3** a confused mass or collection **4** **a voice (crying) in the wilderness** a person, group, etc, making a suggestion or plea that is ignored [OE *wildēornes*, from *wildēor* wild beast + -NESS]

Wilderness ('wɪldənɪs) *n* **the** the barren regions to the south and east of Palestine, esp those in which the Israelites wandered before entering the Promised Land and in which Christ fasted for 40 days and nights

wild-eyed *adj* **1** glaring in an angry, distracted, or wild

Ww

manner **2** ill-conceived or impractical

wildfire ('waɪld,faɪə) *n* **1** a highly flammable material, such as Greek fire, formerly used in warfare **2a** a raging and uncontrollable fire **2b** anything that is disseminated quickly (esp in **spread like wildfire**) **3** another name for **will-o'-the-wisp**

wild flower *n* **1** Also: **wildflower** any flowering plant that grows in an uncultivated state **2** the flower of such a plant

wildfowl ('waɪld,faʊl) *n* **1** any bird that is hunted by man, esp any duck or similar aquatic bird **2** such birds collectively > **'wild,fowler** *n* > **'wild,fowling** *adj, n*

wild-goose chase *n* an absurd or hopeless pursuit, as of something unattainable

wilding ('waɪldɪŋ) *n* **1** an uncultivated plant or a cultivated plant that has become wild **2** a wild animal ▷ Also called: **wildling**

wildlife ('waɪld,laɪf) *n* wild animals and plants collectively: a term used esp of fauna

wild pansy *n* a Eurasian plant of the violet family having purple, yellow, and pale mauve spurred flowers. Also called: **heartsease, love-in-idleness**

wild parsley *n* any of various uncultivated umbelliferous plants that resemble parsley

wild rice *n* an aquatic North American grass with dark-coloured edible grain

wild rose *n* any of numerous roses, such as the dogrose and sweetbrier, that grow wild and have flowers with only one whorl of petals

wild rubber *n* rubber obtained from uncultivated rubber trees

wild silk *n* **1** silk produced by wild silkworms **2** a fabric made from this, or from short fibres of silk designed to imitate it

wild type *n biol* the typical form of a species of organism resulting from breeding under natural conditions

Wild West *n* the western US during its settlement, esp with reference to its frontier lawlessness

wildwood ('waɪld,wʊd) *n arch* a wood or forest growing in a natural uncultivated state

wile (waɪl) *n* **1** trickery, cunning, or craftiness **2** (*usually pl*) an artful or seductive trick or ploy ▷ *vb* **wiles, wiling, wiled 3** (*tr*) to lure, beguile, or entice [c12 from ON *vel* craft]

wilful *or US* **willful** ('wɪlfʊl) *adj* **1** intent on having one's own way; headstrong or obstinate **2** intentional: *wilful murder* > **'wilfully** *or US* **'willfully** *adv* > **'wilfulness** *or US* **'willfulness** *n*

Wilhelm I ('vɪlhɛlm) *n* the German name of **William I** (sense 5)

Wilhelm II *n* the German name of **William II** (sense 4)

Wilhelmina I (,wɪlə'mi:nə; *Dutch* wɪlhɛl'mi:na:) *n* 1880–1962, queen of the Netherlands from 1890 until her abdication (1948) in favour of her daughter Juliana

Wilhelmshaven (*German* vɪlhɛlms'ha:fən) *n* a port and resort in NW Germany, in Lower Saxony: founded in 1853; was the chief German North Sea naval base until 1945; a major oil port. Pop: 91 150 (1991)

Wilhelmstrasse (*German* 'vɪlhɛlmʃtra:sə) *n* **1** a street in the centre of Berlin, where the German foreign office and other government buildings were situated until 1945 **2** Germany's ministry of foreign affairs until 1945

Wilkes (wɪlks) *n* **1 Charles** 1798–1877, US explorer of Antarctica **2 John** 1727–97, English politician, who was expelled from the House of Commons and outlawed for writing scurrilous articles about the government. He became a champion of parliamentary reform

Wilkes Land *n* a region in Antarctica south of Australia, on the Indian Ocean

Wilkins ('wɪlkɪnz) *n* **1** Sir **George Hubert** 1888–1958, Australian polar explorer and aviator **2 Maurice Hugh Frederick** born 1916, British biochemist, born in New Zealand. With Crick and Watson, he shared the Nobel prize 1962 for his work on the structure of DNA

Wilkinson ('wɪlkɪnsən) *n* **Jonny** born 1979, English Rugby Union player; he scored the last-minute drop goal that won England victory in the final of the 2003 World Cup

will¹ (wɪl) *vb past* **would** (takes an infinitive without *to* or an implied infinitive) used as an auxiliary **1** (esp with *you, he, she, it, they*, or a noun as subject) to make the future tense ▷ Cf **shall** (sense 1) **2** to express resolution on the part of the speaker: *I will buy that radio if it's the last thing I do* **3** to indicate willingness or desire: *will you help me with this problem?* **4** to express commands: *you will report your findings to me tomorrow* **5** to express ability: *this rope will support a load* **6** to express probability or expectation: *that will be Jim telephoning* **7** to express customary practice or inevitability: *boys will be boys* **8** (*with the infinitive always implied*) to express desire: usually in polite requests: *stay if you will* **9 what you will** whatever you like [OE *willan*]

USAGE See at **shall**

will² (wɪl) *n* **1** the faculty of conscious and deliberate choice of action. Related adj: **voluntary 2** the act or an instance of asserting a choice **3a** the declaration of a person's wishes regarding the disposal of his property after his death **3b** a document in which such wishes are expressed **4** desire; wish **5** determined intention: *where there's a will there's a way* **6** disposition towards others: *he bears you no ill will* **7 at will** at one's own desire or choice **8 with a will** heartily; energetically **9 with the best will in the world** even with the best of intentions ▷ *vb* (*mainly tr; often takes a clause as object or an infinitive*) **10** (*also intr*) to exercise the faculty of volition in an attempt to accomplish (something): *he willed his wife's recovery from her illness* **11** to give (property) by will to a person, society, etc: *he willed his art collection to the nation* **12** (*also intr*) to order or decree: *the king wills that you shall die* **13** to choose or prefer: *wander where you will* [OE *willa*] > **'willer** *n*

willed (wɪld) *adj* (*in combination*) having a will as specified: *weak-willed*

Willemstad (*Dutch* 'wɪləmstɑt) *n* the capital of the Netherlands Antilles, a port on the SW coast of Curaçao: important for refining Venezuelan oil. Pop: 123 000 (1999 est)

willet ('wɪlɪt) *n* a large American shore bird having a grey plumage with black-and-white wings [c19 imit. of its call]

willful ('wɪlfʊl) *adj* the US spelling of **wilful**

William ('wɪljəm) *n* **1** known as *William the Lion*. ?1143–1214, king of Scotland (1165–1214) **2 Prince** born 1982, son of Prince Charles and Diana, Princess of Wales

William I *n* **1** known as *William the Conqueror*. ?1027–1087, duke of Normandy (1035–87) and king of England (1066–87). He claimed to have been promised the English crown by Edward the Confessor, after whose death he disputed the succession of Harold II, invading England in 1066 and defeating Harold at Hastings. The conquest of England resulted in the introduction to England of many Norman customs, esp feudalism. In 1085 he ordered the Domesday Book to be compiled **2** known as *William the Bad*. 1120–66, Norman king of Sicily (1154–66) **3** known as *William the Silent*. 1533–84, prince of Orange and count of Nassau: led the revolt of the Netherlands against Spain (1568–76) and became first stadholder of the United Provinces of the Netherlands (1579–84); assassinated **4** 1772–1843, king of the Netherlands (1815–40): abdicated in favour of his son William II **5** German name *Wilhelm I*. 1797–1888, king of Prussia (1861–88) and first emperor of Germany (1871–88)

William II *n* **1** known as *William Rufus*. ?1056–1100, king of England (1087–1100); the son of William the Conqueror. He was killed by an arrow while hunting in the New Forest **2** known as *William the Good*. 1154–89, last Norman king of Sicily (1166–89) **3** 1792–1849, king of the Netherlands (1840–49); son of William I **4** German name *Kaiser Wilhelm*. 1859–1941, German emperor and king of Prussia (1888–1918): asserted Germany's claim to world leadership; forced to abdicate at the end of World War I

William III *n* known as *William of Orange*. 1650–1702, stadholder of the Netherlands (1672–1702) and king of Great Britain and Ireland (1689–1702). He was invited by opponents of James II to accept the British throne (1688) and ruled jointly with his wife Mary II (James' daughter) until her death in 1694

William IV *n* known as the *Sailor King*. 1765–1837, king of the United Kingdom and of Hanover (1830–37), succeeding his brother George IV; the third son of George III

Williams ('wɪljəmz) *n* **1 Hank,** real name *Hiram Williams*. 1923–53, US country singer and songwriter. His songs (all 1948–52) include "Jambalaya", "Your Cheatin' Heart", and "Why Don't you Love me (like you Used to Do?)" **2 John** born 1941, Australian classical guitarist, living in Britain **3 John** (**Towner**) born 1932, US composer of film music; his scores include those for *Jaws* (1975), *Star Wars* (1977), E.T. (1982), *Schindler's List* (1993), and *Harry Potter and the Philosopher's Stone* (2001) **4 Ralph Vaughan** See (Ralph) **Vaughan Williams 5 Raymond** (**Henry**) 1921–88, British literary critic and novelist, noted esp for such works as *Culture and Society* (1958) and *The Long Revolution* (1961), which offer a socialist analysis of the relationship between society and culture **6 Robbie,** full name *Robert Peter Williams* born 1974, British pop singer and songwriter. A member of Take That (1990–95), he later found success with "Angel" (1997) and the albums *Life Thru a Lens* (1997), *Swing When You're Winning* (2001), and *Escapology* (2002) **7 Robin** (**McLaurim**) born 1951, US film actor and comedian; films include *Good Morning, Vietnam* (1987), *Dead Poets' Society* (1989), *Mrs Doubtfire* (1993), and *Insomnia* (2002) **8 Rowan** (**Douglas**) born 1950, Archbishop of Canterbury from 2002; formerly Archbishop of Wales (2000–02) **9 Tennessee,** real name *Thomas Lanier Williams*. 1911–83, US dramatist. His plays include *The Glass Menagerie* (1944), *A Streetcar Named Desire* (1947), *Cat on a Hot Tin Roof* (1955), and *Night of the Iguana* (1961) **10 William Carlos** ('kɑːləs) 1883–1963, US poet, who formulated the poetic concept "no ideas but in things". His works include *Paterson* (1946–58), which explores the daily life of a man living in a modern city, and the prose work *In the American Grain* (1925)

Williamsburg ('wɪljəmz,bɜːg) *n* a city in SE Virginia: the capital of Virginia (1693–1779); the restoration of large sections of the colonial city was begun in 1926. Pop: 11 530 (1990)

Williamson ('wɪljəmsən) *n* **1 Henry** 1895–1977, British novelist, best known for *Tarka the Otter* (1927) and other animal stories **2 Malcolm** 1931–2003, Australian composer, who lived in Britain: Master of the Queen's Music (1975–2003). His works include operas and music for children

William the Conqueror *n* See **William I** (sense 1)

willies ('wɪlɪz) *pl n* **the** *sl* nervousness, jitters, or fright (esp in **give** (*or* **get**) **the willies**) [c20 from ?]

willing ('wɪlɪŋ) *adj* **1** favourably disposed or inclined; ready **2** cheerfully compliant **3** done, given, accepted, etc, freely or voluntarily > **'willingly** *adv* > **'willingness** *n*

Willis ('wɪlɪs) *n* **Ted** Baron Willis of Chislehurst. 1918–92, British author. His works include the play *Hot Summer Night* (1959) and the novel *Death May Surprise Us* (1974)

williwaw ('wɪlɪ,wɔː) *n US & Canad* **1** a sudden strong gust of cold wind blowing offshore from a mountainous coast, as in the Strait of Magellan **2** a state of great turmoil [c19 from ?]

will-o'-the-wisp (,wɪləðə'wɪsp) *n* **1** Also called: **friar's lantern, ignis fatuus, jack-o'-lantern** a pale flame or phosphorescence sometimes seen over marshy ground at night. It is believed to be due to the spontaneous combustion of methane and other hydrocarbons originating from decomposing organic matter **2** a person or thing that is elusive or allures and misleads [c17 from *Will*, short for *William* + *wisp*, in former sense of a twist of hay burning as a torch]

willow ('wɪləʊ) *n* **1** any of a large genus of trees and shrubs, such as the weeping willow and osiers of N temperate regions, which have graceful flexible branches, flowers, and catkins, and feathery seeds **2** the whitish wood of certain of these trees **3** something made of willow wood, such as a cricket bat [OE *welig*]

willowherb ('wɪləʊ,hɜːb) *n* **1** any of various temperate and arctic plants having narrow leaves, terminal clusters of pink, purplish, or white flowers, and willow-like feathery seeds **2** short for **rosebay willowherb** (see **rosebay**)

willow pattern *n* **a** a pattern incorporating a willow tree, river, bridge, and figures, typically in blue on a white ground, used on porcelain, etc **b** (*as modifier*): *a willow-pattern plate*

Willow South *n* a city in S Alaska, about 113 km (70 miles) northwest of Anchorage: chosen as the site of the projected new state capital in 1976

willowy ('wɪləʊɪ) *adj* **1** slender and graceful **2** flexible or pliant **3** covered or shaded with willows

willpower ('wɪl,paʊə) *n* **1** the ability to control oneself and determine one's actions **2** firmness of will

Wills (wɪlz) *n* **1 Helen Newington,** married name *Helen Wills Moody Roark*. 1905–98, US tennis player. She was Wimbledon singles champion eight times between 1927 and 1938. She also won the US title seven times and the French title four times **2 William John** 1834–61, English explorer: Robert Burke's deputy in an expedition on which both men died after crossing Australia from north to south for the first time

willy¹ ('wɪlɪ) *n, pl* **willies** *Brit inf* a childish or jocular term for **penis**

willy² ('wɪlɪ) *n Austral sl* a sudden loss of temper; fit: *to throw a willy*

willy-nilly ('wɪlɪ'nɪlɪ) *adv* **1** whether desired or not ▷ *adj* **2** occurring or taking place whether desired or not [OE *wile hē, nyle hē*, lit.: will he or will he not]

willy wagtail *n* a black-and-white flycatcher found in Australasia and parts of Asia, having white feathers over the brows

willy-willy ('wɪlɪ,wɪlɪ) *n, pl* **willy-willies** *Austral* a small sometimes violent upward-spiralling cyclone or dust storm [from Abor.]

Wilmington ('wɪlmɪŋtən) *n* a port in N Delaware, on the Delaware River: industrial centre. Pop: 75 838 (2000)

Wilno ('viːlnɔ) *n* the Polish name for **Vilnius**

Wilson ('wɪlsən) *n* **1 Alexander** 1766–1813, Scottish ornithologist in the US **2** Sir **Angus** (**Frank Johnstone**) 1913–91, British writer, whose works include the collection of short stories *The Wrong Set* (1949) and the novels *Anglo-Saxon Attitudes* (1956) and *No Laughing Matter* (1967) **3 Charles Thomson Rees** 1869–1959, Scottish physicist, who invented the cloud chamber: shared the Nobel prize for physics 1927 **4 Edmund** 1895–1972, US critic, noted esp for *Axel's Castle* (1931), a study of the symbolist movement **5** (**James**) **Harold,** Baron Wilson of Rievaulx. 1916–95, British Labour statesman; prime minister (1964–70; 1974–76) **6 Jacqueline** born 1945, British writer for older girls; her best-selling books include *The Story of Tracey Beaker* (1991), *The Illustrated Mum* (1998), and *Girls in Tears* (2002) **7 Richard** 1714–82, Welsh landscape painter **8** (**Thomas**) **Woodrow** ('wʊdrəʊ) 1856–1924, US Democratic statesman; 28th president of the US (1913–21). He led the US into World War I in 1917 and proposed the Fourteen Points (1918) as a basis for peace. Although he secured the formation of the League of Nations, the US Senate refused to support it: Nobel peace prize 1919

wilt[1] (wɪlt) *vb* **1** to become or cause to become limp or drooping: *insufficient water makes plants wilt* **2** (*tr*) to cook (a leafy vegetable) very briefly until it begins to collapse **3** to lose or cause to lose courage, strength, etc ▷ *n* **4** the act of wilting or state of becoming wilted **5** any of various plant diseases characterized by permanent wilting [C17 ? var. of *wilk* to wither, from MDu. *welken*]

wilt[2] (wɪlt) *vb arch or dialect* (used with the pronoun *thou* or its relative equivalent) a singular form of the present tense (indicative mood) of **will**[1]

Wilton (ˈwɪltən) *n* a kind of carpet with a close velvet pile of cut loops [after *Wilton*, town in Wiltshire, where first made]

Wilts (wɪlts) *abbrev for* Wiltshire

Wiltshire (ˈwɪltʃə, -ʃɪə) *n* a county of S England, consisting mainly of chalk uplands, with Salisbury Plain in the south and the Marlborough Downs in the north; prehistoric remains (at Stonehenge and Avebury): the geographical and ceremonial county includes Swindon unitary authority (established in 1997). Administrative centre: Trowbridge. Pop (excluding Swindon): 432 973 (2001). Area (excluding Swindon): 3481 sq km (1344 sq miles)

wily (ˈwaɪlɪ) *adj* **wilier, wiliest** sly or crafty > ˈ**wiliness** *n*

wimble (ˈwɪmbᵊl) *n* **1** any of a number of hand tools used for boring holes ▷ *vb* **wimbles, wimbling, wimbled 2** to bore (a hole) with a wimble [C13 from MDu. *wimmel* auger]

Wimbledon (ˈwɪmbᵊldən) *n* part of the Greater London borough of Merton: headquarters of the All England Lawn Tennis Club since 1877 and the site of the annual international tennis championships

wimp (wɪmp) *n inf* a feeble ineffective person [C20 from ?] > ˈ**wimpish** *or* ˈ**wimpy** *adj*

WIMP (wɪmp) *n acronym for*: **1** windows, icons, menus (*or* mice), pointers: denoting a type of user-friendly screen display used in small computing **2** *physics* weakly interacting massive particle: a hypothetical particle postulated to account for the dark matter in the universe

wimple (ˈwɪmpᵊl) *n* **1** a piece of cloth draped around the head to frame the face, worn by women in the Middle Ages and still worn by some nuns ▷ *vb* **wimples, wimpling, wimpled** *arch* **2** (*tr*) to cover with or put a wimple on **3** (esp of a veil) to lie or cause to lie in folds or pleats [OE *wimpel*]

wimp out *vb* (*intr, adv*) *sl* to fail to do or complete something through fear or lack of conviction

win (wɪn) *vb* **wins, winning, won 1** (*intr*) to achieve first place in a competition **2** (*tr*) to gain (a prize, first place, etc) in a competition **3** (*tr*) to succeed in or gain (something) with an effort: *we won recognition* **4** to gain victory or triumph in (a battle, argument, etc) **5** (*tr*) to earn (a living, etc) by work **6** (*tr*) to capture: *the Germans never won Leningrad* **7** (when *intr*, foll by *out, through*, etc) to reach with difficulty (a desired position) or become free, loose, etc, with effort: *the boat won the shore* **8** (*tr*) to gain (the sympathy, loyalty, etc) of someone **9** (*tr*) to persuade (a woman, etc) to marry one **10** (*tr*) to extract (ore, coal, etc) from a mine or (metal or other minerals) from ore **11 you can't win** *inf* an expression of resignation after an unsuccessful attempt to overcome difficulties ▷ *n* **12** *inf* a success, victory, or triumph **13** profit; winnings ▷ See also **win over** [OE *winnan*] > ˈ**winnable** *adj*

wince[1] (wɪns) *vb* **winces, wincing, winced 1** (*intr*) to start slightly, as with sudden pain; flinch ▷ *n* **2** the act of wincing [C18 (earlier (C13) meaning: to kick): via OF *wencier, guenchir* to avoid, of Gmc origin] > ˈ**wincingly** *adv*

wince[2] (wɪns) *n* a roller for transferring pieces of cloth between dyeing vats [C17 var. of WINCH[1]]

winceyette (ˌwɪnsɪˈɛt) *n Brit* a plain-weave cotton fabric with slightly raised two-sided nap [from Scot. *wincey*, prob. altered from *woolsey* in *linsey-woolsey*, a fabric made of linen & wool]

winch[1] (wɪntʃ) *n* **1** a windlass driven by a hand- or power-operated crank **2** a hand- or power-operated crank by which a machine is driven ▷ *vb* **3** (*tr*; often foll by *up* or *in*) to pull or lift using a winch [OE *wince* pulley]

winch[2] (wɪntʃ) *vb* (*intr*) an obsolete word for **wince**[1]

Winchester (ˈwɪntʃɪstə) *n* a city in S England, administrative centre of Hampshire: a Romano-British town; Saxon capital of Wessex; 11th-century cathedral; site of **Winchester College** (1382), English public school. Pop: 36 121 (1991)

Winchester rifle (ˈwɪntʃɪstə) *n trademark* a breech-loading lever-action repeating rifle. Often shortened to **Winchester** [C19 after O. F. *Winchester* (1810–80), US manufacturer]

Winckelmann (*German* ˈvɪŋkəlman) *n* **Johann Joachim** (joˈhan ˈjoːaxɪm) 1717–68, German archaeologist and art historian; one of the founders of neoclassicism

wind[1] (wɪnd) *n* **1** a current of air, sometimes of considerable force, moving generally horizontally from areas of high pressure to areas of low pressure **2** *chiefly poetic* the direction from which a wind blows, usually a cardinal point of the compass **3** air artificially moved, as by a fan, pump, etc **4** a trend, tendency, or force: *the winds of revolution* **5** *inf* a hint; suggestion: *we got wind that you were coming* **6** something deemed insubstantial: *his talk was all wind* **7** breath, as used in respiration or talk: *you're just wasting wind* **8** (often used in sports) the power to breathe normally: *his wind is weak* **9** *music* **9a** a wind instrument or wind instruments considered collectively **9b** (*often pl*) the musicians who play wind instruments in an orchestra **9c** (*modifier*) of or composed of wind instruments: *a wind ensemble* **10** an informal name for **flatus 11** the air on which the scent of an animal is carried to hounds or on which the scent of a hunter is carried to his quarry **12 between wind and water 12a** the part of a vessel's hull below the water line that is exposed by rolling or by wave action **12b** any particularly susceptible point **13 break wind** to release intestinal gas through the anus **14 get** *or* **have the wind up** *inf* to become frightened **15 how** *or* **which way the wind blows** *or* **lies** what appears probable **16 in the teeth** (*or* **eye**) **of the wind** directly into the wind **17 in the wind** about to happen **18 into the wind** against the wind or upwind **19 off the wind** *naut* away from the direction from which the wind is blowing **20 on the wind** *naut* as near as possible to the direction from which the wind is blowing **21 put the wind up** *inf* to frighten or alarm **22 raise the wind** *Brit inf* to obtain the necessary funds **23 sail close** *or* **near to the wind** to come near the limits of danger or indecency **24 take the wind out of someone's sails** to disconcert or deflate someone ▷ *vb* (*tr*) **25** to cause (someone) to be short of breath: *the blow winded him* **26a** to detect the scent of **26b** to pursue (quarry) by following its scent **27** to cause (a baby) to bring up wind after feeding **28** to expose to air, as in drying, etc [OE] > ˈ**windless** *adj*

wind[2] (waɪnd) *vb* **winds, winding, wound 1** (often foll by *around, about*, or *upon*) to turn or coil (string, cotton, etc) around some object or point or (of string, etc) to be turned, etc, around some object or point: *he wound a scarf around his head* **2** (*tr*) to cover or wreathe by or as if by coiling, wrapping, etc: *we wound the body in a shroud* **3** (*tr*; often foll by *up*) to tighten the spring of (a clockwork mechanism) **4** (*tr*; foll by *off*) to remove by uncoiling or unwinding **5** (*usually intr*) to move or cause to move in a sinuous, spiral, or circular course: *the river winds through the hills* **6** (*tr*) to introduce indirectly or deviously: *he is winding his own opinions into the report* **7** (*tr*) to cause to twist or revolve: *he wound the handle* **8** (*tr*; usually foll by *up* or *down*) to move by cranking: *please wind up the window* ▷ *n* **9** the act of winding or state of being wound **10** a single turn, bend, etc: *a wind in the river* ▷ See also **wind down, wind up** [OE *windan*] > '**windable** *adj*

wind³ (waɪnd) *vb* **winds, winding, winded** *or* **wound** (*tr*) *poetic* to blow (a note or signal) on (a horn, bugle, etc) [c16 special use of WIND¹]

windage ('wɪndɪdʒ) *n* **1a** a deflection of a projectile as a result of the effect of the wind **1b** the degree of such deflection **2** the difference between a firearm's bore and the diameter of its projectile **3** *naut* the exposed part of the hull of a vessel responsible for wind resistance

windbag ('wɪnd,bæg) *n* **1** *sl* a voluble person who has little of interest to communicate **2** the bag in a set of bagpipes, which provides a continuous flow of air to the pipes

windblown ('wɪnd,bləʊn) *adj* **1** blown by the wind **2** (of trees, shrubs, etc) growing in a shape determined by the prevailing winds

wind-borne *adj* (esp of plant seeds or pollen) transported by wind

windbound ('wɪnd,baʊnd) *adj* (of a sailing vessel) prevented from sailing by an unfavourable wind

windbreak ('wɪnd,breɪk) *n* a fence, line of trees, etc, serving as a protection from the wind by breaking its force

windburn ('wɪnd,bɜːn) *n* irritation of the skin caused by prolonged exposure to winds of high velocity

Windcheater ('wɪnd,tʃiːtə) *n Austral trademark* a warm jacket, usually with a close-fitting knitted neck, cuffs, and waistband

wind chest (wɪnd) *n* a box in an organ in which air from the bellows is stored under pressure before being supplied to the pipes or reeds

wind-chill ('wɪnd-) *n* **a** the serious chilling effect of wind and low temperature: measured on a scale that runs from hot to fatal to life **b** (*as modifier*): *wind-chill factor*

wind cone (wɪnd) *n* another name for **windsock**

wind down (waɪnd) *vb* (*adv*) **1** (*tr*) to lower or move down by cranking **2** (*intr*) (of a clock spring) to become slack **3** (*intr*) to diminish gradually in power; relax

winded ('wɪndɪd) *adj* **1** out of breath, as from strenuous exercise **2** (*in combination*) having breath or wind as specified: *broken-winded; short-winded*

winder ('waɪndə) *n* **1** a person or device that winds **2** an object, such as a bobbin, around which something is wound **3** a knob or key used to wind up a clock, watch, or similar mechanism **4** any plant that twists itself around a support **5** a step of a spiral staircase ▷ Cf **flyer** (sense 4)

Windermere ('wɪndə,mɪə) *n* **Lake** a lake in NW England, in Cumbria in the SE part of the Lake District: the largest lake in England. Length: 17 km (10.5 miles)

windfall ('wɪnd,fɔːl) *n* **1** a piece of unexpected good fortune, esp financial gain **2** something blown down by the wind, esp a piece of fruit

windfall tax *n* a tax levied on an organization considered to have made excessive profits, esp a privatized utility company that has exploited a natural monopoly

wind farm *n* a large group of wind-driven generators for electricity supply

windflower ('wɪnd,flaʊə) *n* any of various anemone plants, such as the wood anemone

wind gauge (wɪnd) *n* **1** another name for **anemometer** **2** a scale on a gun sight indicating the amount of deflection necessary to allow for windage **3** *music* a device for measuring the wind pressure in the bellows of an organ

wind harp (wɪnd) *n* a less common name for **aeolian harp**

Windhoek ('wɪnt,hʊk, 'vɪnt-) *n* the capital of Namibia, in the centre, at an altitude of 1654 m (5428 ft): formerly the capital of German South West Africa. Pop: 169 000 (1997 est)

▷ www.windhoekcc.org.na

▷ www.grnnet.gov.na/Nav_frames/Nutshell_launch.htm

windhover ('wɪndɪ,gə) *n Brit* a dialect name for a **kestrel**

windigo ('wɪnd,hɒvəʊ) *n, pl* **windigor** *or* **windigo** a variant of **wendigo**

winding ('waɪndɪŋ) *n* **1** a curving or sinuous course or movement **2** anything that has been wound or wrapped around something **3** a particular manner or style in which something has been wound **4** a curve, bend, or complete turn in wound material, a road, etc **5** (*often pl*) devious thoughts or behaviour: *the tortuous windings of political argumentation* **6** one or more turns of wire forming a continuous coil through which an electric current can pass, as used in transformers, generators, etc ▷ *adj* **7** curving; sinuous: *a winding road* > '**windingly** *adv*

winding sheet *n* a sheet in which a corpse is wrapped for burial; shroud

winding-up *n* the process of finishing or closing something, esp the process of closing down a business

wind instrument (wɪnd) *n* any musical instrument sounded by the breath, such as the woodwinds and brass instruments of an orchestra

windjammer ('wɪnd,dʒæmə) *n* a large merchant sailing ship

windlass ('wɪndləs) *n* **1** a machine for raising weights by winding a rope or chain upon a barrel or drum driven by a crank, motor, etc ▷ *vb* **2** (*tr*) to raise or haul (a weight, etc) by means of a windlass [c14 from ON *vindáss*, from *vinda* to WIND² + *ass* pole]

windlestraw ('wɪndᵊl,strɔː) *n Irish, Scot, & English dialect* the dried stalk of any of various grasses [OE *windelstrēaw*, from *windel* basket, from *windan* to wind + *strēaw* straw]

Ww

wind machine (wɪnd) *n* a machine used, esp in the theatre, to produce a wind or the sound of wind

windmill ('wɪnd,mɪl, 'wɪn,mɪl) *n* **1** a machine for grinding or pumping driven by a set of adjustable vanes or sails that are caused to turn by the force of the wind **2** the set of vanes or sails that drives such a mill **3** Also called: **whirligig** *Brit* a toy consisting of plastic or paper vanes attached to a stick in such a manner that they revolve like the sails of a windmill **4** an imaginary opponent or evil (esp in **tilt at** *or* **fight windmills**) ▷ *vb* **5** to move or cause to move like the arms of a windmill

window ('wɪndəʊ) *n* **1** a light framework, made of timber, metal, or plastic, that contains glass or glazed opening frames and is placed in a wall or roof to let in light or air or to see through. Related adj: **fenestral** **2** an opening in the wall or roof of a building that is provided to let in light or air or to see through **3** short for **windowpane** **4** the area behind a glass window in a shop used for display **5** any opening or structure resembling a window in function or appearance, such as the transparent area of an envelope revealing an address within **6** an opportunity to see or understand something usually unseen: *a window on the workings of Parliament* **7** a period of unbooked time in a diary, schedule, etc **8** short for **launch window** or **weather window** **9** *physics* a region of the spectrum in which a medium transmits electromagnetic radiation **10** an area of a VDU display that can be manipulated separately from the rest of the display area **11** (*modifier*) of or relating to a window or windows: *a window ledge* ▷ *vb* **12** (*tr*) to furnish with or as if with windows [c13 from ON *vindauga*, from *vindr* WIND¹ + *auga* eye]

window box *n* a long narrow box, placed on or outside a windowsill, in which plants are grown

window-dresser *n* a person employed to design and build up a display in a shop window
window-dressing *n* **1** the ornamentation of shop windows, designed to attract customers **2** the pleasant aspect of an idea, etc, which is stressed to conceal the real nature
windowpane ('wɪndəʊˌpeɪn) *n* a sheet of glass in a window
window sash *n* a glazed window frame, esp one that opens
window seat *n* **1** a seat below a window, esp in a bay window **2** a seat beside a window in a bus, train, etc
window-shop *vb* **window-shops, window-shopping, window-shopped** *(intr)* to look at goods in shop windows without intending to buy > '**window-ˌshopper** *n* > '**window-ˌshopping** *n*
windowsill ('wɪndəʊˌsɪl) *n* a sill below a window
windpipe ('wɪndˌpaɪp) *n* a nontechnical name for **trachea** (sense 1)
Wind River Range (wɪnd) *n* a mountain range in W Wyoming: one of the highest ranges of the central Rockies. Highest peak: Gannet Peak, 4202 m (13 785 ft)
wind rose (wɪnd) *n* a diagram with radiating lines showing the frequency and strength of winds from each direction affecting a specific place
windrow ('wɪndˌrəʊ, 'wɪnˌrəʊ) *n* **1** a long low ridge or line of hay or a similar crop, designed to achieve the best conditions for drying or curing **2** a line of leaves, snow, dust, etc, swept together by the wind
Windscale ('wɪndˌskeɪl) *n* the former name of **Sellafield**
windscreen ('wɪndˌskriːn) *n Brit* the sheet of flat or curved glass that forms a window of a motor vehicle, esp the front window. US and Canad name: **windshield**
windscreen wiper *n Brit* an electrically operated blade with a rubber edge that wipes a windscreen clear of rain, snow, etc US and Canad name: **windshield wiper**
windshield ('wɪndˌʃiːld) *n* the US and Canad name for **windscreen**
windsock ('wɪndˌsɒk) *n* a truncated cone of textile mounted on a mast so that it is free to rotate about a vertical axis: used, esp at airports, to indicate the local wind direction. Also called: **air sock, drogue, wind sleeve, wind cone**
Windsor[1] ('wɪnzə) *n* **1** a town in S England, in Windsor and Maidenhead unitary authority, Berkshire, on the River Thames, linked by bridge with Eton: site of **Windsor Castle**, residence of English monarchs since its founding by William the Conqueror; **Old Windsor**, royal residence in the time of Edward the Confessor, is 3 km (2 miles) southeast. Pop: 30 136 (1991). Official name: **New Windsor 2** a city in SE Canada, in S Ontario on the Detroit River opposite Detroit: motor-vehicle manufacturing; university (1963). Pop: 197 694 (1996)
Windsor[2] ('wɪnzə) *n* **1** the official name of the British royal family from 1917 **2 Duke of** the title of **Edward VIII** from 1937
Windsor and Maidenhead *n* a unitary authority in S England, in Berkshire. Pop: 133 606 (2001). Area: 197 sq km (76 sq miles)
Windsor chair *n* a simple wooden chair, popular in England and America from the 18th century, usually having a shaped seat, splayed legs, and a back of many spindles
Windsor knot *n* a wide triangular knot, produced by making extra turns in tying a tie
windstorm ('wɪndˌstɔːm) *n* a storm consisting of violent winds
wind-sucking *n* a harmful habit of horses in which the animal arches its neck and swallows a gulp of air
windsurfing ('wɪndˌsɜːfɪŋ) *n* the sport of riding on water using a surfboard steered and propelled by an attached sail
▷ www.worldwindsurfing.com
windswept ('wɪndˌswɛpt) *adj* open to or swept by the wind
wind tunnel (wɪnd) *n* a chamber for testing the aerodynamic properties of aircraft, aerofoils, etc, in which a current of air can be maintained at a constant velocity
wind up (waɪnd) *vb (adv)* **1** to bring to or reach a conclusion **2** *(tr)* to tighten the spring of (a clockwork mechanism) **3** *(tr; usually passive) inf* to make nervous, tense, etc: *he was all wound up before the big fight* **4** *(tr)* to roll (thread, etc) into a ball **5** an informal word for **liquidate** (sense 2) **6** *(intr) inf* to end up (in a specified state): *you'll wind up without any teeth* **7** *(tr) Brit sl* to tease (someone) ▷ *n* **wind-up 8** the act of concluding **9** the end
windward ('wɪndwəd) *chiefly naut* ▷ *adj* **1** of, in, or moving to the quarter from which the wind blows ▷ *n* **2** the windward point **3** the side towards the wind ▷ *adv* **4** towards the wind ▷ Cf **leeward**
Windward Islands *pl n* **1** a group of islands in the SE Caribbean, in the Lesser Antilles: consists of the French Overseas Department of Martinique and the independent states of Grenada, St Lucia, and St Vincent and the Grenadines **2** a group of islands in the S Pacific, in French Polynesia in the W Society Archipelago: Moorea, Maio (Tubuai Manu), and Mehetia and Tetiaoro. Pop: 162 686 (1996). French name: **Îles du Vent**
Windward Passage *n* a strait in the Caribbean, between E Cuba and NW Haiti. Width: 80 km (50 miles)
windy ('wɪndɪ) *adj* **windier, windiest 1** of, resembling, or relating to wind; stormy **2** swept by or open to powerful winds **3** marked by or given to prolonged and often boastful speech: *windy orations* **4** void of substance **5** an informal word for **flatulent 6** *sl* frightened > '**windily** *adv* > '**windiness** *n*
wine (waɪn) *n* **1a** an alcoholic drink produced by the fermenting of grapes with water and sugar **1b** *(as modifier): the wine harvest* **1c** an alcoholic drink produced in this way from other fruits, flowers, etc: *elderberry wine* **2a** a dark red colour, sometimes with a purplish tinge **2b** *(as adj): wine-coloured* **3** anything resembling wine in its intoxicating or invigorating effect **4 new wine in old bottles** something new added to or imposed upon an old or established order ▷ *vb* **wines, wining, wined 5** *(intr)* to drink wine **6 wine and dine** to entertain or be entertained with wine and fine food [OE *wīn*, from L *vīnum*] > '**wineless** *adj*
▷ www.intowine.com
▷ http://wine.about.com
▷ www.wines.com
▷ www.upenn.edu/museum/Wine/wineintro.html
wine bar *n* a bar in a restaurant, etc, or an establishment that specializes in serving wine and usually food
winebibber ('waɪnˌbɪbə) *n* a person who drinks a great deal of wine > '**wineˌbibbing** *n*
wine box *n* wine sold in a carton with a tap for pouring
wine cellar *n* **1** a place, such as a dark cool cellar, where wine is stored **2** the stock of wines stored there
wine cooler *n* **1** a bucket-like vessel containing ice in which a bottle of wine is placed to be cooled **2** the full name for **cooler** (sense 3)
wine gallon *n Brit* a former unit of capacity equal to 231 cubic inches
wineglass ('waɪnˌglɑːs) *n* **1** a glass drinking vessel, typically having a small bowl on a stem, with a flared foot **2** Also called: **wineglassful** the amount that such a glass will hold
wine grower *n* a person engaged in cultivating vines in order to make wine > **wine growing** *n*
wine palm *n* any of various palm trees, the sap of which is used, esp when fermented, as a drink. Also called: **toddy palm**
winepress ('waɪnˌprɛs) *n* any equipment used for squeezing the juice from grapes in order to make wine

winery ('waɪnərɪ) *n, pl* **wineries** *chiefly US & Canad* a place where wine is made
wineskin ('waɪn,skɪn) *n* the skin of a sheep or goat sewn up and used as a holder for wine
winey *or* **winy** ('waɪnɪ) *adj* **winier, winiest** having the taste or qualities of wine
wing (wɪŋ) *n* **1** either of the modified forelimbs of a bird that are covered with large feathers and specialized for flight in most species **2** one of the organs of flight of an insect, consisting of a membranous outgrowth from the thorax containing a network of veins **3** either of the organs of flight in certain other animals, esp the forelimb of a bat **4a** a half of the main supporting surface on an aircraft, confined to one side of it **4b** the full span of the main supporting surface on both sides of an aircraft **5** an organ, structure, or apparatus resembling a wing **6** anything suggesting a wing in form, function, or position, such as a sail of a windmill or a ship **7** *bot* **7a** either of the lateral petals of a sweetpea or related flower **7b** the outgrowth on a wind-dispersed fruit such as that of a sycamore or maple **8** a means or cause of flight or rapid motion; flight: *fear gave wings to his feet* **9** *Brit* the part of a car body that surrounds the wheels. US and Canad name: **fender** **10** *soccer, hockey, etc* **10a** either of the two sides of the pitch near the touchline **10b** a player stationed in such a position; winger **11** a faction or group within a political party or other organization. See also **left wing, right wing** **12** a part of a building that is subordinate to the main part **13** (*pl*) the space offstage to the right or left of the acting area in a theatre **14 in** *or* **on the wings** ready to step in when needed **15** either of the two pieces that project forwards from the sides of some chair backs **16** (*pl*) an insignia in the form of stylized wings worn by a qualified aircraft pilot **17** a tactical formation in some air forces, consisting of two or more squadrons **18** any of various flattened organs or extensions in lower animals, esp when used in locomotion **19 clip (someone's) wings 19a** to restrict (someone's) freedom **19b** to thwart (someone's) ambitions **20 on the wing 20a** flying **20b** travelling **21 on wings** flying or as if flying **22 spread** *or* **stretch one's wings** to make full use of one's abilities **23 take wing 23a** to lift off or fly away **23b** to depart in haste **23c** to become joyful **24 under one's wing** in one's care ▷ *vb* (*mainly tr*) **25** (*also intr*) to make (one's way) swiftly on or as if on wings **26** to shoot or wound (a bird, person, etc) superficially, in the wing or arm, etc **27** to cause to fly or move swiftly: *to wing an arrow* **28** to provide with wings [C12 from ON] > **winged** *adj* > '**wingless** *adj* > '**wing,like** *adj*
Wingate ('wɪn,geɪt) *n* **Orde (Charles)** (ɔːd) 1903–44, British soldier. During World War II he organized the Chindits in Burma (Myanmar) to disrupt Japanese communications. He died in an air crash
wing beat *or* **wing-beat** *n* a complete cycle of moving the wing by a bird when flying
wing-case *n* the nontechnical name for **elytron**
wing chair *n* an easy chair having wings on each side of the back
wing collar *n* a stiff turned-up shirt collar worn with the points turned down over the tie
wing commander *n* an officer holding commissioned rank in certain air forces, such as the Royal Air Force: junior to a group captain and senior to a squadron leader
wing covert *n* any of the covert feathers of the wing of a bird, occurring in distinct rows
wingding ('wɪŋ,dɪŋ) *n sl, chiefly US & Canad* **1** a noisy lively party or festivity **2** a real or pretended fit or seizure [C20 from ?]
winge (wɪndʒ) *vb, n Austral* a variant spelling of **whinge**
winger ('wɪŋə) *n soccer, hockey, etc* a player stationed on the wing
wing loading *n* the total weight of an aircraft divided by its wing area
wingman ('wɪŋmæn) *n pl* **wingmen** a player in the wing position in Australian Rules
wing nut *n* a threaded nut tightened by hand by means of two flat lugs or wings projecting from the central body. Also called: **butterfly nut**
wingspan ('wɪŋ,spæn) *or* **wingspread** ('wɪŋ,sprɛd) *n* the distance between the wing tips of a plane, bird, etc
wing tip *n* the outermost edge of a wing
wink (wɪŋk) *vb* **1** (*intr*) to close and open one eye quickly, deliberately, or in an exaggerated fashion to convey friendliness, etc **2** to close and open (an eye or the eyes) momentarily **3** (*tr* foll by *away, back*, etc) to force away (tears, etc) by winking **4** (*tr*) to signal with a wink **5** (*intr*) (of a light) to gleam or flash intermittently ▷ *n* **6** a winking movement, esp one conveying a signal, etc, or such a signal **7** an interrupted flashing of light **8** a brief moment of time **9** *inf* the smallest amount, esp of sleep **10 tip the wink** *Brit inf* to give a hint [OE *wincian*]
wink at *vb* (*intr, prep*) to connive at; disregard: *the authorities winked at corruption*
winker ('wɪŋkə) *n* **1** a person or thing that winks **2** *dialect or US & Canad sl* an eye **3** another name for **blinker**[1] (sense 1)
winkle ('wɪŋkᵊl) *n* **1** See **periwinkle**[1] ▷ *vb* **winkles, winkling, winkled 2** (*tr; usually foll by out, out of*, etc) *inf, chiefly Brit* to extract or prise out [C16 shortened from PERIWINKLE[1]]
winkle-pickers *pl n* shoes or boots with very pointed narrow toes
Winnebago (,wɪnɪ'beɪgəʊ) *n* **1 Lake** a lake in E Wisconsin, fed and drained by the Fox river: the largest lake in the state. Area: 557 sq km (215 sq miles) **2** (*pl* **Winnebagos** *or* **Winnebago**) a member of a North American Indian people living in Wisconsin and Nebraska **3** the language of this people, belonging to the Siouan family

winner ('wɪnə) *n* **1** a person or thing that wins **2** *inf* a person or thing that seems sure to win or succeed
winning ('wɪnɪŋ) *adj* **1** (of a person, character, etc) charming or attractive: *a winning smile* **2** gaining victory: *the winning goal* ▷ *n* **3** a shaft or seam of coal **4** (*pl*) money, prizes, or valuables won, esp in gambling > '**winningly** *adv* > '**winningness** *n*
winning gallery *n real tennis* the gallery farthest from the net on either side of the court, into which any shot played wins a point
winning opening *n real tennis* the grille or winning gallery, into which any shot played wins a point
winning post *n* the post marking the finishing line on a racecourse
Winnipeg ('wɪnɪ,pɛg) *n* **1** a city in S Canada, capital of Manitoba at the confluence of the Assiniboine and Red Rivers: University of Manitoba (1877) and University of Winnipeg (1871). Pop: 618 477 (1996) **2 Lake** a lake in S Canada, in Manitoba: drains through the Nelson River into Hudson Bay. Area: 23 553 sq km (9094 sq miles) > '**Winni,pegger** *n*
Winnipeg couch *n Canad* a couch with no arms or back, opening out into a double bed
Winnipegosis (,wɪnɪpə'gəʊsɪs) *n* **Lake** a lake in S Canada, in W Manitoba. Area: 5400 sq km (2086 sq miles)
winnow ('wɪnəʊ) *vb* **1** to separate (grain) from (chaff) by means of a wind or current of air **2** (*tr*) to examine in order to select the desirable elements **3** (*tr*) *rare* to blow upon; fan ▷ *n* **4a** a device for winnowing **4b** the act or process of winnowing [OE *windwian*] > '**winnower** *n*
wino ('waɪnəʊ) *n, pl* **winos** *inf* a down-and-out who habitually drinks cheap wine
win over *vb* (*tr, adv*) to gain the support or consent of (someone). Also: **win round**

Winslet (ˈwɪnzlət) *n* **Kate** born 1975, British film actress; her films include *Sense and Sensibility* (1995), *Titanic* (1997), and *Iris* (2001)

winsome (ˈwɪnsəm) *adj* charming; winning; engaging: *a winsome smile* [OE *wynsum*, from *wynn* joy + *-sum* -SOME[1]] > ˈ**winsomely** *adv*

Winston (ˈwɪnstən) *n* **Robert Lipson**, Baron. born 1940, British obstetrician and gynaecologist, who played a significant role in the development of in vitro fertilization; also known for his TV programmes, including *The Human Body* (1998)

Winston-Salem (ˈwɪnstənˈseɪləm) *n* a city in N central North Carolina: formed in 1913 by the uniting of Salem and Winston; a major tobacco manufacturing centre. Pop: 185 776 (2000)

winter (ˈwɪntə) *n* **1a** (*sometimes cap*) the coldest season of the year, between autumn and spring, astronomically from the December solstice to the March equinox in the N hemisphere and at the opposite time of year in the S hemisphere **1b** (*as modifier*): *winter pasture* **2** the period of cold weather associated with the winter **3** a time of decline, decay, etc **4** *chiefly poetic* a year represented by this season: *a man of 72 winters* ▷ Related adj: **hibernal** ▷ *vb* **5** (*intr*) to spend the winter in a specified place **6** to keep or feed (farm animals, etc) during the winter or (of farm animals) to be kept or fed during the winter [OE] > ˈ**winterer** *n* > ˈ**winterless** *adj*

winter aconite *n* a small Old World herbaceous plant cultivated for its yellow flowers, which appear early in spring

winter cherry *n* **1** a Eurasian plant cultivated for its ornamental inflated papery orange-red calyx **2** the calyx of this plant ▷ See also **Chinese lantern**

winter garden *n* **1** a garden of evergreen plants and plants that flower in winter **2** a conservatory in which flowers are grown in winter

wintergreen (ˈwɪntəˌgriːn) *n* **1** any of a genus of evergreen ericaceous shrubs, esp a subshrub of E North America, which has white bell-shaped flowers and edible red berries **2 oil of wintergreen** an aromatic compound, formerly made from this and various other plants but now synthesized: used medicinally and for flavouring **3** any of a genus of plants, such as **common wintergreen**, of temperate and arctic regions, having rounded leaves and small pink globose flowers **4 chickweed wintergreen** a plant of N Europe and N Asia belonging to the primrose family, having white flowers and leaves arranged in a whorl [C16 from Du. *wintergroen* or G *Wintergrün*]

winterize *or* **winterise** (ˈwɪntəˌraɪz) *vb* **winterizes, winterizing, winterized** *or* **winterises, winterising, winterised** (*tr*) *US & Canad* to prepare (a house, car, etc) to withstand winter conditions > ˌ**winteriˈzation** *or* ˌ**winteriˈsation** *n*

winter jasmine *n* a jasmine shrub widely cultivated for its winter-blooming yellow flowers

winter solstice *n* the time at which the sun is at its southernmost point in the sky (northernmost point in the S hemisphere) appearing at noon at its lowest altitude above the horizon. It occurs about December 22 (June 21 in the S hemisphere)

winter sports *pl n* sports held in the open air on snow or ice, esp skiing

Winterthur (*German* ˈvɪntərtuːr) *n* an industrial town in NE central Switzerland, in Zürich canton: has the largest technical college in the country. Pop: 88 168 (1994)

wintertime (ˈwɪntəˌtaɪm) *n* the winter season. Also (archaic): **wintertide**

winterweight (ˈwɪntəˌweɪt) *adj* (of clothes) suitably heavy and warm for wear in the winter

winter wheat *n* a type of wheat that is planted in the autumn and is harvested the following summer

wintry (ˈwɪntrɪ) *or* **wintery** (ˈwɪntərɪ) *adj* **wintrier, wintriest 1** (esp of weather) of or characteristic of winter **2** lacking cheer or warmth; bleak > ˈ**wintrily** *adv* > ˈ**wintriness** *or* ˈ**winteriness** *n*

win-win *adj* guaranteeing a favourable outcome whatever happens: *a win-win situation for NATO* [C20 modelled on NO-WIN]

winy (ˈwaɪnɪ) *adj* **winier, winiest** a variant spelling of **winey**

wipe (waɪp) *vb* **wipes, wiping, wiped** (*tr*) **1** to rub (a surface or object) lightly, esp, with a cloth, hand, etc, as in removing dust, water, etc **2** (usually foll by *off, away, from, up*, etc) to remove by or as if by rubbing lightly: *he wiped the dirt from his hands* **3** to eradicate or cancel (a thought, memory, etc) **4** to erase (a recording) from (a tape) **5** to apply (oil, etc) by wiping **6** *Austral inf* to abandon or reject (a person) **7 wipe the floor with (someone)** *inf* to defeat (someone) decisively ▷ *n* **8** the act or an instance of wiping **9** *dialect* a sweeping blow [OE *wīpian*]

wipe out *vb* (*adv*) **1** (*tr*) to destroy completely **2** (*tr*) *inf* to kill **3** (*intr*) to fall off a surfboard ▷ *n* **wipeout 4** an act or instance of wiping out **5** the interference of one radio signal by another so that reception is impossible

wiper (ˈwaɪpə) *n* **1** any piece of cloth, such as a handkerchief, etc, used for wiping **2** a cam rotated to allow a part to fall under its own weight, as used in stamping machines, etc **3** See **windscreen wiper** **4** *electrical engineering* a movable conducting arm that makes contact with a row or ring of contacts

WIPO *or* **wipo** (ˈwaɪpaʊ) *n acronym for* World Intellectual Property Organization

wire (ˈwaɪə) *n* **1** a slender flexible strand or rod of metal **2** a cable consisting of several metal strands twisted together **3** a flexible metallic conductor, esp one made of copper, usually insulated, and used to carry electric current in a circuit **4** (*modifier*) of, relating to, or made of wire: *a wire fence* **5** anything made of wire, such as wire netting **6** a long continuous wire or cable connecting points in a telephone or telegraph system **7** *old-fashioned* an informal name for **telegram** or **telegraph** **8** *US & Canad horse racing* the finishing line on a racecourse **9** a snare made of wire for rabbits and similar animals **10 (down) to the wire** *inf* right up to the last moment **11 get in under the wire** *inf, chiefly US & Canad* to accomplish something with little time to spare **12 get one's wires crossed** *inf* to misunderstand **13 pull wires** *chiefly US & Canad* to exert influence behind the scenes; pull strings ▷ *vb* **wires, wiring, wired** (*mainly tr*) **14** (*also intr*) to send a telegram to (a person or place) **15** to send (news, a message, etc) by telegraph **16** to equip (an electrical system, circuit, or component) with wires **17** to fasten or furnish with wire **18** to snare with wire **19 wire in** *inf* to set about (something, esp food) with enthusiasm [OE *wīr*] > ˈ**wireˌlike** *adj*

wire brush *n* a brush having wire bristles, used for cleaning metal, esp for removing rust, or for brushing against cymbals

wire cloth *n* a mesh or netting woven from fine wire, used in window screens, strainers, etc

wired (waɪəd) *adj sl* **1** edgy from stimulant intake **2** excited, nervous, or tense **3** using computers to send and receive information, esp via the Internet

wiredraw (ˈwaɪəˌdrɔː) *vb* **wiredraws, wiredrawing, wiredrew, wiredrawn** to convert (metal) into wire by drawing through successively smaller dies

wire-gauge *n* **1** a flat plate with slots in which standard wire sizes can be measured **2** a standard system of sizes for measuring the diameters of wires

wire gauze *n* a stiff meshed fabric woven of fine wires

wire grass *n* any of various grasses that have tough wiry roots or rhizomes

wire-guided *adj* (of a missile) able to be controlled in mid-flight by signals passed along a wire connecting the missile to the firer's control device

wire-haired *adj* (of an animal) having a rough wiry coat

wireless ('waɪəlɪs) *n, vb* **1** *chiefly Brit* another word for **radio** ▷ *adj* **2** communicating without connecting wires: *wireless communication*

wireless telegraphy *n* another name for **radiotelegraphy**

wireless telephone *n* another name for **radiotelephone** > **wireless telephony** *n*

wire netting *n* a net made of wire, often galvanized, that is used for fencing, etc

wirepuller ('waɪə,pʊlə) *n chiefly US & Canad* a person who uses private or secret influence for his or her own ends > **'wire,pulling** *n*

wire recorder *n* an early type of magnetic recorder in which sounds were recorded on a thin steel wire magnetized by an electromagnet > **wire recording** *n*

wire service *n chiefly US & Canad* an agency supplying news, etc, to newspapers, radio, and television stations, etc

wiretap ('waɪə,tæp) *vb* **wiretaps, wiretapping, wiretapped** **1** (*intr*) to make a connection to a telegraph or telephone wire in order to obtain information secretly **2** (*tr*) to tap (a telephone) or the telephone of (a person) > **'wire,tapper** *n*

wire wheel *n* a wheel in which the rim is held to the hub by wire spokes, esp one used on a sports car

wire wool *n* a mass of fine wire used for cleaning and scouring

wirework ('waɪə,wɜːk) *n* **1** functional or decorative work made of wire **2** objects made of wire, esp netting

wireworks ('waɪə,wɜːks) *n* (*functioning as sing or pl*) a factory where wire or articles of wire are made

wireworm ('waɪə,wɜːm) *n* the wormlike larva of various beetles, which feeds on the roots of many plants and is a serious pest

wiring ('waɪərɪŋ) *n* **1** the network of wires used in an electrical system, device, or circuit ▷ *adj* **2** used in wiring

Wirral ('wɪrəl) *n* **1** **the** a peninsula in NW England between the estuaries of the Rivers Mersey and Dee **2** a unitary authority in NW England, in Merseyside. Pop: 312 289 (2001). Area: 158 sq km (61 sq miles)

wiry ('waɪərɪ) *adj* **wirier, wiriest** **1** (of people or animals) slender but strong in constitution **2** made of or resembling wire, esp in stiffness: *wiry hair* **3** (of a sound) produced by or as if by a vibrating wire > **'wirily** *adv* > **'wiriness** *n*

wis (wɪs) *vb arch* to know or suppose (something) [c17 a form derived from *iwis*, (from OE *gewiss* certain), mistakenly interpreted as *I wis* I know, as if from OE *witan* to know]

Wis. *abbrev for* Wisconsin

Wisbech ('wɪzbiːtʃ) *n* a town in E England, in N Cambridgeshire: market-gardening. Pop: 24 981 (1991)

Wisconsin (wɪs'kɒnsɪn) *n* **1** a state of the N central US, on Lake Superior and Lake Michigan: consists of an undulating plain, with uplands in the north and west; over 168 m (550 ft) above sea level along the shore of Lake Michigan. Capital: Madison. Pop: 5 363 675 (2000). Area: 141 061 sq km (54 464 sq miles). Abbreviations: **Wis** or (with zip code) **WI** **2** a river in central and SW Wisconsin, flowing south and west to the Mississippi. Length: 692 km (430 miles) > **Wis'consin,ite** *n*

Wisden ('wɪzdən) *n* **John** 1826–84, English cricketer; publisher of *Wisden Cricketers' Almanack*, which first appeared in 1864

wisdom ('wɪzdəm) *n* **1** the ability or result of an ability to think and act utilizing knowledge, experience, understanding, common sense, and insight **2** accumulated knowledge, erudition, or enlightenment **3** *arch* a wise saying or wise sayings ▷ Related adj: **sagacious** [OE *wīsdōm*; see WISE[1], -DOM]

wisdom tooth *n* **1** any of the four molar teeth, one at the back of each side of the jaw, that are the last of the permanent teeth to erupt. Technical name: **third molar** **2** **cut one's wisdom teeth** to arrive at the age of discretion

wise[1] (waɪz) *adj* **1** possessing, showing, or prompted by wisdom or discernment **2** prudent; sensible **3** shrewd; crafty: *a wise plan* **4** well-informed; erudite **5** informed or knowing (esp in **none the wiser**) **6** (*postpositive; often foll by to*) *sl* in the know, esp possessing inside information (about) **7** *arch* possessing powers of magic **8** **be** *or* **get wise** (often foll by *to*) *inf* to be or become aware or informed (of something) **9** **put wise** (often foll by *to*) *sl* to inform or warn (of) ▷ *vb* **wises, wising, wised** **10** See **wise up** [OE *wīs*] > **'wisely** *adv* > **'wiseness** *n*

wise[2] (waɪz) *n arch* way, manner, fashion, or respect (esp in **any wise, in no wise**) [OE *wīse* manner]

-wise *adv combining form* **1** indicating direction or manner: *clockwise; likewise* **2** with reference to: *businesswise* [OE *-wīsan*; see WISE[2]]

wiseacre ('waɪz,eɪkə) *n* **1** a person who wishes to seem wise **2** a wise person: often used facetiously or contemptuously [c16 from MDu. *wijsseggher* soothsayer. See WISE[1], SAY]

wisecrack ('waɪz,kræk) *inf* ▷ *n* **1** a flippant gibe or sardonic remark ▷ *vb* (*intr*) **2** to make a wisecrack > **'wise,cracker** *n*

wise guy *n* **1** *inf* a person who is given to making conceited, sardonic, or insolent comments **2** *US* a member of the Mafia

Wiseman ('waɪzmən) *n* **Nicholas Patrick Stephen** 1802–65, British cardinal; first Roman Catholic archbishop of Westminster (1850–65)

wisent ('wiːzᵊnt) *n* another name for **European bison**. See **bison** (sense 2) [G, from OHG *wisunt* BISON]

wise up *vb* (*adv*) *sl, chiefly US & Canad* (often foll by *to*) to become or cause to become aware or informed (of)

wish (wɪʃ) *vb* **1** (when *tr, takes a clause as object or an infinitive*; when *intr*, often foll by *for*) to want or desire (something, often that which cannot be or is not the case): *I wish I lived in Italy* **2** (*tr*) to feel or express a desire or hope concerning the future or fortune of: *I wish you well* **3** (*tr*) to desire or prefer to be as specified **4** (*tr*) to greet as specified: *he wished us good afternoon* ▷ *n* **5** the expression of some desire or mental inclination: *to make a wish* **6** something desired or wished for: *he got his wish* **7** (*usually pl*) expressed hopes or desire, esp for someone's welfare, health, etc **8** (*often pl*) *formal* a polite order or request ▷ See also **wish on** [OE *wȳscan*] > **'wisher** *n*

wishbone ('wɪʃ,bəʊn) *n* the V-shaped bone above the breastbone in most birds consisting of the fused clavicles [c17 from the custom of two people breaking apart the bone after eating: the person with the longer part makes a wish]

wishful ('wɪʃfʊl) *adj* having wishes or characterized by wishing > **'wishfully** *adv* > **'wishfulness** *n*

wish fulfilment *n* (in Freudian psychology) any successful attempt to fulfil a wish stemming from the unconscious mind, whether in fact, in fantasy, or by disguised means

wishful thinking *n* the erroneous belief that one's wishes are in accordance with reality > **wishful thinker** *n*

wish list *n* a list of things desired by a person or organization: *the government's wish list*

wish on *vb* (*tr, prep*) to hope that (someone or something) should be imposed (on someone); foist: *I wouldn't wish my cold on anyone*

wishy-washy ('wɪʃɪ,wɒʃɪ) *adj inf* **1** lacking in substance, force, colour, etc **2** watery; thin

Wisła ('viswa) *n* the Polish name for **Vistula** (sense 1)

Wislany Zalew (*Polish* viʃ'laːni 'zaːlɛf) *n* the Polish name for the **Vistula** (sense 2)

Wismar (*German* 'vɪsmar) *n* a port in NE Germany, on an inlet of the Baltic, in Mecklenburg-West Pomerania: shipbuilding industries. Pop: 54 470 (1991)

wisp (wɪsp) *n* **1** a thin, light, delicate, or fibrous piece or strand, such as a streak of smoke or a lock of hair **2** a small bundle, as of hay or straw **3** anything slender and delicate: *a wisp of a girl* **4** a mere suggestion or hint **5** a flock of birds, esp snipe [C14 var. of *wips*, from ?] > **'wisp,like** *adj* > **'wispy** *adj*

wist (wɪst) *vb arch* the past tense and past participle of **wit²**

wisteria (wɪ'stɪərɪə) *n* any twining woody climbing plant of the genus *Wisteria*, of E Asia and North America, having blue, purple, or white flowers in large drooping clusters [C19 from NL, after Caspar *Wistar* (1761–1818), US anatomist]

wistful ('wɪstfʊl) *adj* sadly pensive, esp about something yearned for > **'wistfully** *adv* > **'wistfulness** *n*

wit¹ (wɪt) *n* **1** the talent or quality of using unexpected associations between contrasting or disparate words or ideas to make a clever humorous effect **2** speech or writing showing this quality **3** a person possessing, showing, or noted for such an ability **4** practical intelligence (esp in **have the wit to**) **5** *arch* mental capacity or a person possessing it ▷ See also **wits** [OE *witt*]

wit² (wɪt) *vb* **wits, witting, wot, wist 1** *arch* to be or become aware of (something) **2 to wit** that is to say; namely (used to introduce statements, as in legal documents) [OE *witan*]

witan ('wɪtᵊn) *n* (in Anglo-Saxon England) **1** an assembly of higher ecclesiastics and important laymen that met to counsel the king on matters such as judicial problems **2** the members of this assembly ▷ Also called: **witenagemot** [OE *witan*, pl. of *wita* wise man]

witblits ('vɪt,blɪts) *n S African* alcoholic drink illegally distilled [from Afrik. *wit* white + *blits* lightning]

witch¹ (wɪtʃ) *n* **1** a person, usually female, who practises or professes to practise magic or sorcery, esp black magic, or is believed to have dealings with the devil **2** an ugly or wicked old woman **3** a fascinating or enchanting woman ▷ *vb* (*tr*) **4** a less common word for **bewitch** [OE *wicca*] > **'witchy** *or* **'witch,like** *adj*

witch² (wɪtʃ) *n* a flatfish of N Atlantic coastal waters, having a narrow greyish-brown body marked with tiny black spots: related to the plaice, flounder, etc [C19 ?from WITCH¹, from the appearance of the fish]

witchcraft ('wɪtʃ,krɑːft) *n* **1** the art or power of bringing magical or preternatural power to bear or the act or practice of attempting to do so **2** the influence of magic or sorcery **3** fascinating or bewitching influence or charm

witch doctor *n* a man in certain societies, esp preliterate ones, who appears to possess magical powers, used esp to cure sickness but also to harm people. Also called: **shaman, medicine man**

witch-elm *n* a variant spelling of **wych-elm**

witchery ('wɪtʃərɪ) *n, pl* **witcheries 1** the practice of witchcraft **2** magical or bewitching influence or charm

witches'-broom *n* a dense abnormal growth of shoots on a tree or other woody plant, usually caused by parasitic fungi

witchetty grub ('wɪtʃɪtɪ) *n* the wood-boring edible caterpillar of an Australian moth. Also: **witchetty, witchety** [C19 *witchetty*, from Abor.]

witch hazel *or* **wych-hazel** *n* **1** any of a genus of trees and shrubs of North America, having ornamental yellow flowers and medicinal properties **2** an astringent medicinal solution containing an extract of the bark and leaves of one of these shrubs, applied to treat bruises, inflammation, etc

witch-hunt *n* a rigorous campaign to round up or expose dissenters on the pretext of safeguarding the public welfare > **'witch-,hunting** *n, adj*

witching ('wɪtʃɪŋ) *adj* **1** relating to or appropriate for witchcraft **2** *now rare* bewitching > **'witchingly** *adv*

witching hour *n* **the** the hour at which witches are supposed to appear, usually midnight

witenagemot (,wɪtɪnəgɪ'məʊt) *n* another word for **witan** [OE *witena*, genitive pl of *wita* councillor + *gemōt* meeting]

with (wɪð, wɪθ) *prep* **1** using; by means of: *he killed her with an axe* **2** accompanying; in the company of: *the lady you were with* **3** possessing; having: *a man with a red moustache* **4** concerning or regarding: *be patient with her* **5** in spite of: *with all his talents, he was still humble* **6** used to indicate a time or distance by which something is away from something else: *with three miles to go, he collapsed* **7** in a manner characterized by: *writing with abandon* **8** caused or prompted by: *shaking with rage* **9** often used with a verb indicating a reciprocal action or relation between the subject and the preposition's object: *agreeing with me* **10 with it** *inf* **10a** fashionable; in style **10b** comprehending what is happening or being said **11 with that** after that [OE]

withal (wɪ'ðɔːl) *adv* **1** *literary* as well **2** *arch* therewith ▷ *prep* **3** (*postpositive*) an archaic word for **with** [C12 from WITH + ALL]

withdraw (wɪð'drɔː) *vb* **withdraws, withdrawing, withdrew, withdrawn 1** (*tr*) to take or draw back or away; remove **2** (*tr*) to remove from deposit or investment in a bank, etc **3** (*tr*) to retract or recall (a promise, etc) **4** (*intr*) to retire or retreat: *the troops withdrew* **5** (*intr*; often foll by *from*) to depart (from): *he withdrew from public life* **6** (*intr*) to detach oneself socially, emotionally, or mentally [C13 from WITH (in the sense: away from) + DRAW] > **with'drawer** *n*

withdrawal (wɪð'drɔːəl) *n* **1** an act or process of withdrawing **2** the period a drug addict goes through following abrupt termination in the use of narcotics, usually characterized by physical and mental symptoms (**withdrawal symptoms**) **3** Also called: **withdrawal method, coitus interruptus** the deliberate withdrawing of the penis from the vagina before ejaculation, as a method of contraception

withdrawing room *n* an archaic term for **drawing room**

withdrawn (wɪð'drɔːn) *vb* **1** the past participle of **withdraw** ▷ *adj* **2** unusually reserved or shy **3** secluded or remote

withe (wɪθ, wɪð, waɪð) *n* **1** a strong flexible twig, esp of willow, suitable for binding things together; withy **2** a band or rope of twisted twigs or stems ▷ *vb* **withes, withing, withed 3** (*tr*) to bind with withes [OE *withthe*]

wither ('wɪðə) *vb* **1** (*intr*) (esp of a plant) to droop, wilt, or shrivel up **2** (*intr*; often foll by *away*) to fade or waste: *all hope withered away* **3** (*intr*) to decay or disintegrate **4** (*tr*) to cause to wilt or lose vitality **5** (*tr*) to abash, esp with a scornful look [C14 ? var. of WEATHER (vb)] > **'witherer** *n* > **'withering** *adj* > **'witheringly** *adv*

withers ('wɪðəz) *pl n* the highest part of the back of a horse, behind the neck between the shoulders [C16 short for *widersones*, from *wider* with + *-sones*, ? var. of SINEW]

withershins ('wɪðə,ʃɪnz) *or* **widdershins** *adv chiefly Scot.* in the direction contrary to the apparent course of the sun; anticlockwise [C16 from MLow G *weddersinnes*, from MHG, lit.: opposite course, from *wider* against + *sinnes*, genitive of *sin* course]

withhold (wɪð'həʊld) *vb* **withholds, withholding, withheld 1** (*tr*) to keep back: *he withheld his permission* **2** (*tr*) to hold back; restrain **3** (*intr*; usually foll by *from*) to refrain or forbear > **with'holder** *n*

within (wɪ'ðɪn) *prep* **1** in; inside; enclosed or encased by **2** before (a period of time) has elapsed: *within a week* **3** not differing by more than (a specified amount) from: *live within your means* ▷ *adv* **4** *formal* inside; internally

without (wɪ'ðaʊt) *prep* **1** not having: *a traveller without* *much money* **2** not accompanied by: *he came without his wife* **3** not making use of: *it is not easy to undo screws without a screwdriver* **4** (*foll by a verbal noun or noun phrase*) not, while not, or after not: *she can sing for two minutes without drawing breath* **5** *arch* on the outside of: *without the city walls* ▷ *adv* **6** *formal* outside

withstand (wɪðˈstænd) *vb* **withstands, withstanding, withstood** **1** (*tr*) to resist **2** (*intr*) to remain firm in endurance or opposition > **withˈstander** *n*

withy (ˈwɪðɪ) *n, pl* **withies** a variant spelling of **withe** (senses 1, 2) [OE *wīdig(e)*]

witless (ˈwɪtlɪs) *adj* lacking wit, intelligence, or sense > **ˈwitlessly** *adv* > **ˈwitlessness** *n*

witling (ˈwɪtlɪŋ) *n arch* a person who thinks himself or herself witty

witness (ˈwɪtnɪs) *n* **1** a person who has seen or can give first-hand evidence of some event **2** a person or thing giving or serving as evidence **3** a person who testifies, esp in a court of law, to events or facts within his own knowledge **4** a person who attests to the genuineness of a document, signature, etc, by adding his own signature **5** **bear witness to 5a** to give written or oral testimony to **5b** to be evidence or proof of ▷ Related adj: **testimonial** ▷ *vb* **6** (*tr*) to see, be present at, or know at first hand **7** (*tr*) to give evidence of **8** (*tr*) to be the scene or setting of: *this field has witnessed a battle* **9** (*intr*) to testify, esp in a court of law, to events within a person's own knowledge **10** (*tr*) to attest to the genuineness of (a document, etc) by adding one's own signature [OE *witnes*, from *witan* to know + -NESS] > **ˈwitnesser** *n*

witness box *or esp US* **witness stand** *n* the place in a court of law in which witnesses stand to give evidence

wits (wɪts) *pl n* **1** (*sometimes sing*) the ability to reason and act, esp quickly (esp in **have one's wits about one**) **2** (*sometimes sing*) right mind, sanity (esp in **out of one's wits**) **3** **at one's wits' end** at a loss to know how to proceed **4** **live by one's wits** to gain a livelihood by craftiness rather than by hard work

Witt (wɪt) *n* **Johan de** 1625–72, Dutch statesman; chief minister of the United Provinces of the Netherlands (1653–72)

-witted *adj* (*in combination*) having wits or intelligence as specified: *slow-witted; dim-witted*

Wittenberg (*German* ˈvɪtənbɛrk; *English* ˈwɪtᵊnˌbɜːg) *n* a city in E Germany, on the River Elbe, in Brandenburg: Martin Luther, as a philosophy teacher at Wittenberg university, began the Reformation here in 1517 by nailing his 95 theses to the doors of a church. Pop: 87 000 (1991)

witter (ˈwɪtə) *vb* (*intr; often foll by* on) *inf* to chatter or babble pointlessly or at unnecessary length [c20 ?from obs. *whitter* to warble, twitter]

Wittgenstein (ˈvɪtgənʃtaɪn, -ˌstaɪn) *n* **Ludwig Josef Johann** (ˈluːtvɪç ˈjoːzɛf joˈhan) 1889–1951, British philosopher, born in Austria. After studying with Bertrand Russell, he wrote the *Tractatus Logico-Philosophicus* (1921), which explores the relationship of language to the world. He was a major influence on logical positivism but later repudiated this, and in *Philosophical Investigations* (1953) he argues that philosophical problems arise from insufficient attention to the variety of natural language use

Wittgensteinian (vɪtgənˌʃtaɪnɪən, -ˌstaɪnɪən) *adj* (of a philosophical position or argument) derived from or related to the work of Wittgenstein and esp the later work in which he attacks essentialism and stresses the open texture and variety of the use of ordinary language

witticism (ˈwɪtɪˌsɪzəm) *n* a clever or witty remark [c17 from WITTY; coined by Dryden (1677) by analogy with *criticism*]

witting (ˈwɪtɪŋ) *adj rare* **1** deliberate; intentional **2** aware > **ˈwittingly** *adv*

witty (ˈwɪtɪ) *adj* **wittier, wittiest** **1** characterized by clever humour or wit **2** *arch or dialect* intelligent > **ˈwittily** *adv* > **ˈwittiness** *n*

Witwatersrand (wɪtˈwɔːtəzˌrænd; *Afrikaans* vətˈvɑːtərsˈrant) *n* a rocky ridge in NE South Africa: contains the richest gold deposits in the world, also coal and manganese; chief industrial centre is Johannesburg. Height: 1500–1800 m (5000–6000 ft). Also called: **the Rand, the Reef**

wive (waɪv) *vb* **wives, wiving, wived** *arch* **1** to marry (a woman) **2** (*tr*) to supply with a wife [OE *gewīfian*, from *wīf* wife]

wivern (ˈwaɪvən) *n* a less common spelling of **wyvern**

wives (waɪvz) *n* **1** the plural of **wife** **2** **old wives' tale** a superstitious tradition, occasionally one that contains an element of truth

wiz (wɪz) *n, pl* **wizzes** *inf* a variant spelling of **whizz** (sense 5)

wizard (ˈwɪzəd) *n* **1** a male witch or a man who practises or professes to practise magic or sorcery **2** a person who is outstandingly clever in some specified field **3** *computing* a program that guides a user through a complex task ▷ *adj* **4** *inf, chiefly Brit* superb; outstanding **5** of or relating to a wizard or wizardry [c15 var. of *wissard*, from WISE[1] + -ARD] > **ˈwizardly** *adj*

wizardry (ˈwɪzədrɪ) *n* the art, skills, and practices of a wizard, sorcerer, or magician

wizen (ˈwɪzᵊn) *vb* **1** to make or become shrivelled ▷ *adj* **2** a variant of **wizened** [OE *wisnian*]

wizened (ˈwɪzᵊnd) *or* **wizen** *adj* shrivelled, wrinkled, or dried up, esp with age

wk *abbrev for:* **1** (*pl* **wks**) week **2** work

WK *text messaging abbrev for* week

wkly *abbrev for* weekly

WKND *text messaging abbrev for* weekend

WMD *abbrev for* weapon(s) of mass destruction

WMO *abbrev for* World Meteorological Organization ▷ www.wmo.ch

WNW *symbol for* west-northwest

WO *abbrev for:* **1** War Office **2** Warrant Officer **3** wireless operator

woad (wəʊd) *n* **1** a European plant, formerly cultivated for its leaves, which yield a blue dye **2** the dye obtained from this plant, used esp by the ancient Britons as a body dye [OE *wād*]

wobbegong (ˈwɒbɪˌgɒŋ) *n* any of various sharks of Australian waters, having a richly patterned brown-and-white skin [from Abor.]

wobble (ˈwɒbᵊl) *vb* **wobbles, wobbling, wobbled** **1** (*intr*) to move or sway unsteadily **2** (*intr*) to shake: *her voice wobbled with emotion* **3** (*intr*) to vacillate with indecision **4** (*tr*) to cause to wobble ▷ *n* **5** a wobbling movement or sound [c17 var. of *wabble*, from Low G *wabbeln*] > **ˈwobbler** *n*

wobble board *n Austral* a piece of fibreboard used as a rhythmic musical instrument, producing a characteristic sound when flexed

wobbly (ˈwɒblɪ) *adj* **wobblier, wobbliest** **1** shaky, unstable, or unsteady ▷ *n* **2** **throw a wobbly** *sl* to become suddenly very agitated or angry > **ˈwobbliness** *n*

Wodehouse (ˈwʊdˌhaʊs) *n* Sir **P**(**elham**) **G**(**renville**) 1881–1975, US author, born in England. His humorous novels of upper-class life in England include the *Psmith* and *Jeeves* series

Woden *or* **Wodan** (ˈwəʊdᵊn) *n* the foremost Anglo-Saxon god. Norse counterpart: **Odin** [OE *Wōden*; related to ON *Ōthinn*, OHG *Wuotan*, G *Wotan*; see WEDNESDAY]

wodge (wɒdʒ) *n Brit inf* a thick lump or chunk cut or broken off something [c20 alteration of WEDGE]

woe (wəʊ) *n* **1** *literary* intense grief or misery **2** (*often pl*) affliction or misfortune **3** **woe betide** (**someone**) misfortune will befall (someone): *woe betide you if you arrive late* ▷ *interj* **4** Also: **woe is me** *arch* an exclamation of

Ww

sorrow or distress [OE *wā, wǣ*]

woebegone (ˈwəʊbɪˌɡɒn) *adj* sorrowful or sad in appearance [C14 from a phrase such as *me is wo begon* woe has beset me]

woeful (ˈwəʊfᵊl) *adj* **1** expressing or characterized by sorrow **2** bringing or causing woe **3** pitiful; miserable: *a woeful standard of work* > ˈ**woefully** *adv* > ˈ**woefulness** *n*

WOF (in New Zealand) *abbrev for* Warrant of Fitness

wog¹ (wɒɡ) *n Brit sl, derog* a person who is not White [prob. from GOLLIWOG]

wog² (wɒɡ) *n Austral sl* any ailment or disease, such as influenza, a virus infection, etc [C20 from ?]

woggle (ˈwɒɡᵊl) *n* the ring of leather through which a Scout neckerchief is threaded [C20 from ?]

Wöhler (*German* ˈvøːlər) *n* **Friedrich** (ˈfriːdrɪç) 1800–82, German chemist, who proved that organic compounds could be synthesized from inorganic compounds

wok (wɒk) *n* a large metal Chinese cooking pot having a curved base like a bowl: used esp for stir-frying [from Chinese (Cantonese)]

woke (wəʊk) *vb* the past tense of **wake¹**

woken (ˈwəʊkən) *vb* the past participle of **wake¹**

Woking (ˈwəʊkɪŋ) *n* a town in SE England, in central Surrey: mainly residential. Pop: 98 138 (1991)

Wokingham *n* a unitary authority in SE England, in Berkshire. Pop: 150 257 (2001). Area: 179 sq km (69 sq miles)

wokka board (ˈwɒkə) *n Austral* another name for **wobble board**

wold¹ (wəʊld) *n chiefly literary* a tract of open rolling country, esp upland [OE *weald* bush]

wold² (wəʊld) *n* a variant of **weld²**

Wolds (wəʊldz) *pl n* **the** a range of chalk hills in NE England: consists of the **Yorkshire Wolds** to the north, separated from the **Lincolnshire Wolds** by the Humber estuary

wolf (wʊlf) *n, pl* **wolves 1** a predatory canine mammal which hunts in packs and was formerly widespread in North America and Eurasia but is now less common. Related adj: **lupine 2** any of several similar and related canines, such as the red wolf and the coyote (**prairie wolf**) **3** the fur of any such animal **4** a voracious or fiercely cruel person or thing **5** *inf* a man who habitually tries to seduce women **6** Also called: **wolf note** *music* **6a** an unpleasant sound produced in some notes played on the violin, etc, owing to resonant vibrations of the belly **6b** an out-of-tune effect produced on keyboard instruments accommodated esp to the system of mean-tone temperament **7 cry wolf** to give a false alarm **8 have** *or* **hold a wolf by the ears** to be in a desperate situation **9 keep the wolf from the door** to ward off starvation or privation **10 lone wolf** a person or animal who prefers to be alone **11 wolf in sheep's clothing** a malicious person in a harmless or benevolent disguise ▷ *vb* **12** (*tr; often foll by down*) to gulp (down) **13** (*intr*) to hunt wolves [OE *wulf*] > ˈ**wolfish** *adj* > ˈ**wolf**ˌ**like** *adj*

Wolf (*German* vɔlf) *n* **1 Friedrich August** (ˈfriːdrɪç ˈaugʊst) 1759–1824, German classical scholar, who suggested that the Homeric poems, esp the *Iliad*, are products of an oral tradition **2 Hugo** (ˈhuːgo) 1860–1903, Austrian composer, esp of songs, including the *Italienisches Liederbuch* and the *Spanisches Liederbuch* **3** (wʊlf) **Howlin'** See **Howlin' Wolf**

Wolf Cub *n Brit* the former name for **Cub Scout**

Wolfe (wʊlf) *n* **1 James** 1727–59, English soldier, who commanded the British capture of Quebec, in which he was killed **2 Thomas** (**Clayton**) 1900–38, US novelist, noted for his autobiographical fiction, esp *Look Homeward, Angel* (1929) **3 Tom,** full name *Thomas Kennerly Wolfe.* born 1931, US author and journalist; his books include *The Right Stuff* (1979) and the novels *Bonfire of the Vanities* (1987), and *A Man in Full* (1998)

Wolfensohn (ˈwʊlfənˌsəʊn) *n* **James D,** known as *Jim.* born 1933, U.S. businessman and international official, born in Australia; president of the International Bank for Reconstruction and Development (the World Bank) from 1995

wolffish (ˈwʊlfˌfɪʃ) *n, pl* **wolffish** *or* **wolffishes** a large northern deep-sea fish. It has large sharp teeth and no pelvic fins and is used as a food fish. Also called: **catfish**

wolfhound (ˈwʊlfˌhaʊnd) *n* the largest breed of dog, used formerly to hunt wolves

Wolfit (ˈwʊlfɪt) *n* Sir **Donald** 1902–68, English stage actor and manager

wolfram (ˈwʊlfrəm) *n* another name for **tungsten** [C18 from G, orig. ?from the proper name *Wolfram*, used pejoratively of tungsten because it was thought inferior to tin]

wolframite (ˈwʊlfrəˌmaɪt) *n* a black to reddish-brown mineral, a compound of tungsten, iron, and manganese: it is the chief ore of tungsten

Wolfram von Eschenbach (*German* ˈvɔlfram fɔn ˈɛʃənbax) *n* died ?1220, German poet: author of the epic *Parzival*, incorporating the story of the Grail

wolfsbane (ˈwʊlfsˌbeɪn) *or* **wolf's bane** *n* any of several poisonous N temperate plants of the ranunculaceous genus *Aconitum* having hoodlike flowers

Wolfsburg (*German* ˈvɔlfsbʊrk) *n* a city in N central Germany, in Lower Saxony: founded in 1938; motor-vehicle industry. Pop: 122 200 (1999 est)

wolf spider *n* a spider which chases its prey to catch it. Also called: **hunting spider**

wolf whistle *n* **1** a whistle made by a man to express admiration of a woman's appearance ▷ *vb* **wolf-whistle, wolf-whistles, wolf-whistling, wolf-whistled 2** (when *intr*, sometimes foll by *at*) to make such a whistle (at someone)

Wollongong (ˈwʊlənˌɡɒŋ) *n* a city in E Australia, in E New South Wales on the Pacific: an early centre of dairy farming; now a coal-mining and heavy industrial centre. Pop: 185 397 (1998 est)

Wollstonecraft (ˈwʊlstənˌkrɑːft) *n* **Mary** 1759–97, British feminist and writer, author of *A Vindication of the Rights of Women* (1792); wife of William Godwin and mother of Mary Shelley

Wolof (ˈwɒlɒf) *n* **1** (*pl* **Wolof** *or* **Wolofs**) a member of a Negroid people of W Africa living chiefly in Senegal **2** the language of this people, belonging to the Niger-Congo family

Wolsey (ˈwʊlzɪ) *n* **Thomas** ?1475–1530, English cardinal and statesman; archbishop of York (1514–30); lord chancellor (1515–29). He dominated Henry VIII's foreign and domestic policies but his failure to obtain papal consent for the annulment of the king's marriage to Catherine of Aragon led to his arrest for high treason (1530); he died on the journey to face trial

Wolverhampton (ˌwʊlvəˈhæmptən) *n* **1** a city in W central England, in Wolverhampton unitary authority, West Midlands: iron and steel foundries; university (1992). Pop: 257 943 (1991) **2** a unitary authority in W central England, in the West Midlands. Pop: 236 573 (2001). Area: 69 sq km (27 sq miles)

wolverine (ˈwʊlvəˌriːn) *n* a large musteline mammal of northern forests of Eurasia and North America having dark very thick water-resistant fur. Also called: **glutton** [C16 *wolvering*, from WOLF + -ING³ (later altered to *-ine*)]

wolves (wʊlvz) *n* the plural of **wolf**

woman (ˈwʊmən) *n, pl* **women 1** an adult female human being **2** (*modifier*) female or feminine: *a woman politician* **3** women collectively **4** (usually preceded by *the*) feminine nature or feelings: *babies bring out the woman in him* **5** a female servant or domestic help **6** a man considered as having supposedly female characteristics, such as meekness **7** *inf* a wife or girlfriend **8 the little woman** *Brit inf, old-fashioned* one's wife **9 woman of the**

streets a prostitute ▷ *vb* (*tr*) **10** *obs* to make effeminate [OE *wīfmann, wimman*] > '**womanless** *adj* > '**woman-,like** *adj*

womanhood ('wʊmən,hʊd) *n* **1** the state or quality of being a woman or being womanly **2** women collectively

womanish ('wʊmənɪʃ) *adj* **1** having qualities regarded as unsuitable to a man **2** of or suitable for a woman > '**womanishly** *adv* > '**womanishness** *n*

womanize *or* **womanise** ('wʊmə,naɪz) *vb* **womanizes, womanizing, womanized** *or* **womanises, womanising, womanised 1** (*intr*) (of a man) to indulge in casual affairs with women **2** (*tr*) to make effeminate > '**woman,izer** *or* '**woman,iser** *n*

womankind ('wʊmən,kaɪnd) *n* the female members of the human race; women collectively

womanly ('wʊmənlɪ) *adj* **1** possessing qualities, such as warmth, attractiveness, etc, generally regarded as typical of a woman **2** of or belonging to a woman

womb (wu:m) *n* **1** the nontechnical name for **uterus 2** a hollow space enclosing something **3** a place where something is conceived: *the Near East is the womb of western civilization* **4** *obs* the belly [OE *wamb*] > **wombed** *adj* > '**womb,like** *adj*

wombat ('wɒmbæt) *n* a burrowing herbivorous Australian marsupial having short limbs, a heavy body, and coarse dense fur [C18 from Abor.]

women ('wɪmɪn) *n* the plural of **woman**

womenfolk ('wɪmɪn,fəʊk) *pl n* **1** women collectively **2** a group of women, esp the female members of one's family

Women's Institute *n* (in Britain and Commonwealth countries) a society for women interested in engaging in craft and cultural activities

Women's Liberation *n* a movement directed towards the removal of attitudes and practices that preserve inequalities based upon the assumption that men are superior to women. Also called: **women's lib**

Women's Movement *n* a grass-roots movement of women concerned with women's liberation. See **Women's Liberation**

won (wʌn) *vb* the past tense and past participle of **win**

wonder ('wʌndə) *n* **1** the feeling excited by something strange; a mixture of surprise, curiosity, and sometimes awe **2** something that causes such a feeling, such as a miracle **3** (*modifier*) exciting wonder by virtue of spectacular results achieved, feats performed, etc: *a wonder drug* **4 do** *or* **work wonders** to achieve spectacularly fine results **5 nine days' wonder** a subject that arouses general surprise or public interest for a short time **6 no wonder** (*sentence connector*) (I am) not surprised at all (that): *no wonder he couldn't come* **7 small wonder** (*sentence connector*) (I am) hardly surprised (that): *small wonder he couldn't make it tonight* ▷ *vb* (when *tr*, *may take a clause as object*) **8** (when *intr*, often foll by *about*) to indulge in speculative inquiry: *I wondered about what she said* **9** (when *intr*, often foll by *at*) to be amazed (at something): *I wonder at your impudence* [OE *wundor*] > '**wonderer** *n*

Wonder ('wʌndə) *n* **Stevie** real name *Steveland Judkins Morris* born 1950, US Motown singer, songwriter, and multi-instrumentalist. His recordings include *Up-Tight* (1966), "Superstition" (1972), *Innervisions* (1973), *Songs in the Key of Life* (1976), and "I Just Called to Say I Love You" (1985)

wonderful ('wʌndəfʊl) *adj* **1** exciting a feeling of wonder **2** extremely fine; excellent > '**wonderfully** *adv*

wonderland ('wʌndə,lænd) *n* **1** an imaginary land of marvels or wonders **2** an actual place or scene of great or strange beauty or wonder

wonderment ('wʌndəmənt) *n* **1** rapt surprise; awe **2** puzzled interest **3** something that excites wonder

wonderwork ('wʌndə,wɜ:k) *n* something done or made that excites wonder; miracle or wonder > '**wonder-,worker** *n* > '**wonder-,working** *n, adj*

wondrous ('wʌndrəs) *arch or literary* ▷ *adj* **1** exciting wonder; marvellous ▷ *adv* **2** (intensifier): *wondrous cold* > '**wondrously** *adv* > '**wondrousness** *n*

wonky ('wɒŋkɪ) *adj* **wonkier, wonkiest** *Brit sl* **1** unsteady **2** askew **3** liable to break down [C20 var. of dialect *wanky*, from OE *wancol*]

Wŏnsan ('wɒn'sæn) *n* a port in SE North Korea, on the Sea of Japan: oil refineries. Pop: 274 000 (latest est)

wont (wəʊnt) *adj* **1** (*postpositive*) accustomed (to doing something): *he was wont to come early* ▷ *n* **2** a manner or action habitually employed by or associated with someone (often in **as is my wont, as is his wont,** etc) ▷ *vb* **3** (when *tr*, *usually passive*) to become or cause to become accustomed [OE *gewunod*, p.p. of *wunian* to be accustomed to]

won't (wəʊnt) *contraction of* will not

wonted ('wəʊntɪd) *adj* **1** (*postpositive*) accustomed (to doing something) **2** (*prenominal*) usual: *she is in her wonted place*

woo (wu:) *vb* **woos, wooing, wooed 1** to seek the affection, favour, or love of (a woman) with a view to marriage **2** (*tr*) to seek after zealously: *to woo fame* **3** (*tr*) to beg or importune (someone) [OE *wōgian*, from ?] > '**wooer** *n* > '**wooing** *n*

wood (wʊd) *n* **1** the hard fibrous substance consisting of xylem tissue that occurs beneath the bark in trees, shrubs, and similar plants **2** the trunks of trees that have been cut and prepared for use as a building material **3** a collection of trees, shrubs, grasses, etc, usually dominated by one or a few species of tree: usually smaller than a forest: *an oak wood*. Related adj: **sylvan 4** fuel; firewood **5** *golf* **5a** a long-shafted club with a wooden head, used for driving **5b** (*as modifier*): *a wood shot* **6** *tennis, etc* the frame of a racket: *he hit a winning shot off the wood* **7** one of the biased wooden bowls used in the game of bowls **8** *music* short for **woodwind 9 from the wood** (of a beverage) from a wooden container rather than a metal or glass one **10 out of the wood** *or* **woods** clear of or safe from dangers or doubts: *we're not out of the wood yet* **11 see the wood for the trees** (*used with a negative*) to obtain a general view of a situation without allowing details to cloud one's analysis: *he can't see the wood for the trees* **12** (*modifier*) made of, employing, or handling wood: *a wood fire* **13** (*modifier*) dwelling in or situated in a wood: *a wood nymph* ▷ *vb* **14** (*tr*) to plant a wood upon **15** to supply or be supplied with firewood ▷ See also **woods** [OE *widu, wudu*]

Wood (wʊd) *n* **1** Mrs **Henry**, married name of *Ellen Price*. 1814–87, British novelist, noted esp for the melodramatic novel *East Lynne* (1861) **2** Sir **Henry (Joseph)** 1869–1944, English conductor, who founded the Promenade Concerts in London **3 John,** known as *the Elder*. 1707–54, British architect and town planner, working mainly in Bath, where he designed the North and South Parades (1728) and the Circus (1754) **4** his son, **John**, known as *the Younger*. 1727–82, British architect: designed the Royal Crescent (1767–71) and the Assembly Rooms (1769–71), Bath **5 Ralph** 1715–72, British potter, working in Staffordshire, who made the first toby jug (1762)

wood alcohol *n* another name for **methanol**

wood anemone *n* any of several woodland anemone plants having finely divided leaves and solitary white flowers. Also called: **windflower**

wood avens *n* another name for **herb bennet**

woodbine ('wu:d,baɪn) *n* **1** a honeysuckle of Europe, SW Asia, and N Africa, having fragrant creamy flowers **2** *US* another name for **Virginia creeper 3** *Austral sl* an Englishman

wood block *n* a small rectangular flat block of wood that is laid with others as a floor surface

woodcarving ('wʊd,kɑ:vɪŋ) *n* **1** the act of carving wood

2 a work of art produced by carving wood > **'wood,carver** *n*

woodchuck ('wʊd,tʃʌk) *n* a North American marmot having coarse reddish-brown fur. Also called: **groundhog** [C17 by folk etymology from Cree *otcheck* fisher]

woodcock ('wʊd,kɒk) *n* an Old World game bird resembling the snipe but larger and with shorter legs and neck

woodcraft ('wʊd,krɑːft) *n chiefly US & Canad* 1 ability and experience in matters concerned with living in a forest 2 ability or skill at woodwork, carving, etc

woodcut ('wʊd,kʌt) *n* 1 a block of wood with a design, illustration, etc, from which prints are made 2 a print from a woodcut

woodcutter ('wʊd,kʌtə) *n* 1 a person who fells trees or chops wood 2 a person who makes woodcuts > **'wood,cutting** *n*

wooded ('wʊdɪd) *adj* 1 covered with or abounding in woods or trees 2 (*in combination*) having wood of a specified character: *a soft-wooded tree*

wooden ('wʊdᵊn) *adj* 1 made from or consisting of wood 2 awkward or clumsy 3 bereft of spirit or animation: *a wooden expression* 4 obstinately unyielding: *a wooden attitude* 5 mentally slow or dull 6 not highly resonant: *a wooden thud* > **'woodenly** *adv*

wood engraving *n* 1 the art of engraving pictures or designs on wood by incising them with a burin 2 a block of wood so engraved or a print taken from it > **wood engraver** *n*

woodenhead ('wʊdᵊn,hɛd) *n inf* a dull, foolish, or unintelligent person > **,wooden'headed** *adj* > **,wooden'headedness** *n*

Wooden Horse *n* another name for the **Trojan Horse** (sense 1)

wooden spoon *n* a booby prize, esp in sporting contests

woodgrouse ('wʊd,graʊs) *n* another name for **capercaillie**

woodland ('wʊdlənd) *n* **a** land that is mostly covered with woods or dense growths of trees and shrubs **b** (*as modifier*): *woodland fauna* > **'woodlander** *n*

woodlark ('wʊd,lɑːk) *n* an Old World lark similar to but slightly smaller than the skylark

woodlouse ('wʊd,laʊs) *n, pl* **woodlice** (-,laɪs) any of various small terrestrial isopod crustaceans having a flattened segmented body and occurring in damp habitats

woodman ('wʊdmən) *n, pl* **woodmen** 1 a person who looks after and fells trees used for timber 2 another word for **woodsman**

woodnote ('wʊd,nəʊt) *n* a natural musical note or song, like that of a wild bird

wood nymph *n* one of a class of nymphs fabled to inhabit the woods, such as a dryad

woodpecker ('wʊd,pɛkə) *n* a climbing bird, such as the **green woodpecker**, having a brightly coloured plumage and strong chisel-like bill with which it bores into trees for insects

wood pigeon *n* a large Eurasian pigeon having white patches on the wings and neck. Also called: **ringdove**, **cushat**

woodpile ('wʊd,paɪl) *n* a pile or heap of firewood

wood preservative *n* a coating applied to timber as a protection against decay, insects, weather, etc

wood pulp *n* 1 wood that has been ground to a fine pulp for use in making newsprint and other cheap forms of paper 2 finely pulped wood that has been digested by a chemical, such as caustic soda: used in making paper

woodruff ('wʊdrʌf) *n* any of several plants, esp the sweet woodruff of Eurasia, which has small sweet-scented white flowers and whorls of narrow fragrant leaves used to flavour wine and liqueurs and in perfumery [OE *wudurofe*, from WOOD + *rōfe*]

woods (wʊdz) *pl n* 1 closely packed trees forming a forest or wood, esp a specific one 2 another word for **backwoods** (sense 2) 3 the woodwind instruments in an orchestra

Woods[1] *n* **Lake of the.** See **Lake of the Woods**

Woods[2] (wʊdz) *n* **Tiger,** real name *Eldrick Woods.* born 1975, US golfer; youngest US Masters champion (1997) and first Black golfer to win a major championship; in 2001 he became the first player to hold all four major titles at once

woodscrew ('wʊd,skruː) *n* a metal screw that tapers to a point so that it can be driven into wood by a screwdriver

woodshed ('wʊd,ʃɛd) *n* a small outbuilding where firewood, garden tools, etc, are stored

woodsman ('wʊdzmən) *n, pl* **woodsmen** a person who lives in a wood or who is skilled in woodcraft. Also called: **woodman**

wood sorrel *n* a Eurasian plant having trifoliate leaves, an underground creeping stem, and white purple-veined flowers

wood spirit *n chem* another name for **methanol**

Woodstock ('wʊdstɒk) *n* a town in New York State, the site of a large rock festival in August 1969. Pop: 1870 (1990)

wood tar *n* any tar produced by the destructive distillation of wood

wood warbler *n* 1 a European woodland warbler with a dull yellow plumage 2 another name for the **American warbler** See **warbler** (sense 3)

Woodward ('wʊdwəd) *n* 1 Sir **Clive** born 1956, English Rugby Union player and subsequently (1997–) coach of the England team that won the Rugby World Cup in 2003 2 **R(obert) B(urns)** 1917–79, US chemist. For his work on the synthesis of quinine, strychnine, cholesterol, and other organic compounds he won the Nobel prize for chemistry 1965

woodwind ('wʊd,wɪnd) *music* ▷ *adj* 1 of or denoting a type of wind instrument, formerly made of wood but now often made of metal, such as the flute ▷ *n* 2 (*functioning as pl*) woodwind instruments collectively

woodwork ('wʊd,wɜːk) *n* 1 the art or craft of making things in wood 2 components made of wood, such as doors, staircases, etc

▷ www.woodworking.com

woodworking ('wʊd,wɜːkɪŋ) *n* 1 the process of working wood ▷ *adj* 2 of, relating to, or used in woodworking > **'wood,worker** *n*

woodworm ('wʊd,wɜːm) *n* 1 any of various insect larvae that bore into wooden furniture, beams, etc, esp the larvae of the furniture beetle and the deathwatch beetle 2 the condition caused in wood by any of these larvae

woody ('wʊdɪ) *adj* **woodier, woodiest** 1 abounding in or covered with forest or woods 2 connected with, belonging to, or situated in a wood 3 consisting of or containing wood or lignin: *woody tissue; woody stems* 4 resembling wood in hardness or texture > **'woodiness** *n*

woodyard ('wʊd,jɑːd) *n* a place where timber is cut and stored

woody nightshade *n* a scrambling woody Eurasian plant, having purple flowers and producing poisonous red berry-like fruits. Also called: **bittersweet**

woof[1] (wuːf) *n* 1 the crosswise yarns that fill the warp yarns in weaving; weft 2 a woven fabric or its texture [OE *ōwef*, from *ō-*, ?from ON, + *wef* web (see WEAVE); modern form infl. by WARP]

woof[2] (wʊf) *interj* 1 an imitation of the bark or growl of a dog ▷ *vb* 2 (*intr*) (of dogs) to bark

woofer ('wuːfə) *n* a loudspeaker used in high-fidelity systems for the reproduction of low audio frequencies

woofter ('wʊftə, 'wuːf-) *n derog sl* a male homosexual [C20 altered from *poofter*; see POOF]

Wookey Hole ('wʊkɪ həʊl) *n* a village in SW England, in

Somerset, near Wells: noted for the nearby limestone cave in which prehistoric remains have been found. Pop: 1000 (latest est)

wool (wʊl) *n* **1** the outer coat of sheep, yaks, etc, which consists of short curly hairs **2** yarn spun from the coat of sheep, etc, used in weaving, knitting, etc **3a** cloth or a garment made from this yarn **3b** (*as modifier*): *a wool dress* **4** any of certain fibrous materials: *glass wool; steel wool* **5** *inf* short thick curly hair **6** a tangled mass of soft fine hairs that occurs in certain plants **7 keep one's wool on** *Brit inf* to keep one's temper **8 pull the wool over someone's eyes** to deceive or delude someone [OE *wull*] > **'wool-,like** *adj*
▷ www.kswpa.com/woolhistory.htm

wool clip *n Austral & NZ* the total amount of wool shorn from a particular flock in one year

Woolf (wʊlf) *n* **1 Leonard Sidney** 1880–1969, English publisher and political writer **2** his wife, **Virginia** 1882–1941, English novelist and critic. Her novels, which include *Mrs Dalloway* (1925), *To the Lighthouse* (1927), *The Waves* (1931), and *Between the Acts* (1941), employ such techniques as the interior monologue and stream of consciousness

wool fat *or* **grease** *n* another name for **lanolin**

woolfell ('wʊl,fɛl) *n obs* the skin of a sheep or similar animal with the fleece still attached

woolgathering ('wʊl,gæðərɪŋ) *n* idle or absent-minded daydreaming

woolgrower ('wʊl,grəʊə) *n* a person who keeps sheep for their wool > **'wool,growing** *n*

woolled (wʊld) *adj* **1** (of animals) having wool **2** (*in combination*) having wool as specified: *coarse-woolled; long-woolled*

woollen *or US* **woolen** ('wʊlən) *adj* **1** relating to or consisting partly or wholly of wool ▷ *n* **2** (*often pl*) a garment or piece of cloth made wholly or partly of wool, esp a knitted one

Woolley ('wʊlɪ) *n* Sir (**Charles**) **Leonard** 1880–1960, British archaeologist, noted for his excavations at Ur in Mesopotamia (1922–34)

woolly *or US* (*sometimes*) **wooly** ('wʊlɪ) *adj* **woollier, woolliest** *or US* (*sometimes*) **woolier, wooliest 1** consisting of, resembling, or having the nature of wool **2** covered or clothed in wool or something resembling it **3** lacking clarity or substance: *woolly thinking* **4** *bot* covered with long soft whitish hairs: *woolly stems* ▷ *n, pl* **woollies** *or US* (*sometimes*) **woolies 5** (*often pl*) a garment, such as a sweater, made of wool or something similar > **'woollily** *adv* > **'woolliness** *n*

woolly bear *n* the caterpillar of any of various tiger moths, having a dense covering of soft hairs

woolpack ('wʊl,pæk) *n* **1** the cloth wrapping used to pack a bale of wool **2** a bale of wool

woolsack ('wʊl,sæk) *n* **1** a sack containing or intended to contain wool **2** (in Britain) the seat of the Lord Chancellor in the House of Lords, formerly made of a large square sack of wool

woolshed ('wʊl,ʃɛd) *n Austral & NZ* a large building in which sheepshearing takes place

wool stapler *n* a person who sorts wool into different grades or classifications

Woolworth ('wʊlwəθ) *n* **Frank Winfield** ('wɪn,fi:ld) 1852–1919, US merchant; founder of an international chain of department stores selling inexpensive goods

woomera *or* **womera** ('wʊmərə) *n Austral* a type of notched stick used by native Australians to increase leverage and propulsion in the throwing of a spear [from Abor.]

Woomera ('wʊmərə) *n* a town in South Australia: site of the Long Range Weapons Establishment. Pop: 1660 (latest est)

Woop Woop ('wu:p ,wu:p) *n Austral sl* a jocular name for any backward or remote town or district

Wootton ('wʊtᵊn) *n* **Barbara** (**Frances**), Baroness of Abinger. 1897–1988, English economist, educationalist, social scientist, and criminologist

woozy ('wu:zɪ) *adj* **woozier, wooziest** *inf* **1** dazed or confused **2** experiencing dizziness, nausea, etc [C19 ? a blend of *woolly* + *muzzy* or *dizzy*] > **'woozily** *adv* > **'wooziness** *n*

wop (wɒp) *n sl, derog* a member of a Latin people, esp an Italian [C20 prob. from It. dialect *guappo* dandy, from Sp. *guapo*]

wop-wops ('wɒp,wɒps) *n* (*functioning as pl or sing*) **the** *NZ inf* a remote rural area; back of beyond. Sometimes shortened to **the wops**

Worcester ('wʊstə) *n* **1** a cathedral city in W central England, the administrative centre of Worcestershire on the River Severn: scene of the battle (1651) in which Charles II was defeated by Cromwell. Pop: 82 661 (1991) **2** an industrial city in the US, in central Massachusetts: Clark University (1887). Pop: 172 648 (2000) **3** a town in S South Africa; centre of a fruit-growing region. Pop: 60 324 (1990)

Worcester sauce *or* **Worcestershire sauce** *n* a commercially prepared piquant sauce, made from a basis of soy sauce, with vinegar, spices, etc

Worcestershire ('wʊstə,ʃɪə, -ʃə) *n* a county of W central England, formerly (1974–98) part of Hereford and Worcester. Administrative centre: Worcester. Pop: 542 107 (2001). Area: 1742 sq km (674 sq miles)

Worcs *abbrev for* Worcestershire

word (wɜ:d) *n* **1** one of the units of speech or writing that is the smallest isolable meaningful element of the language, although linguists would analyse these further into morphemes **2** an instance of vocal intercourse; chat, talk, or discussion: *to have a word with someone* **3** an utterance or expression, esp a brief one: *a word of greeting* **4** news or information: *he sent word that he would be late* **5** a verbal signal for action; command: *when I give the word, fire!* **6** an undertaking or promise: *he kept his word* **7** an autocratic decree; order: *his word must be obeyed* **8** a watchword or slogan, as of a political party: *the word now is "freedom"* **9** *computing* a set of bits used to store, transmit, or operate upon an item of information in a computer **10 as good as one's word** doing what one has undertaken to do **11 at a word** at once **12 by word of mouth** orally rather than by written means **13 in a word** briefly or in short **14 my word! 14a** an exclamation of surprise, annoyance, etc **14b** *Austral* an exclamation of agreement **15 of one's word** given to or noted for keeping one's promises: *I am a man of my word* **16 put in a word** *or* **good word for** to make favourable mention of (someone); recommend **17 take someone at his** *or* **her word** to assume that someone means, or will do, what he or she says: *when he told her to go, she took him at his word and left* **18 take someone's word for it** to accept or believe what someone says **19 the last word 19a** the closing remark of a conversation or argument, esp a remark that supposedly settles an issue **19b** the latest or most fashionable design, make, or model: *the last word in bikinis* **19c** the finest example (of some quality, condition, etc): *the last word in luxury* **20 the word** the proper or most fitting expression: *cold is not the word for it, it's freezing!* **21 upon my word! 21a** *arch* on my honour **21b** an exclamation of surprise, annoyance, etc **22 word for word** (of a report, etc) using exactly the same words as those employed in the situation being reported; verbatim **23 word of honour** a promise; oath **24** (*modifier*) of, relating to, or consisting of words ▷ *vb* **25** (*tr*) to state in words, usually specially selected ones; phrase ▷ See also **words** [OE] > **'wordless** *adj* > **'wordlessly** *adv*

Word (wɜ:d) *n* **the 1** *Christianity* the 2nd person of the Trinity **2** Scripture, the Bible, or the Gospels as embodying or representing divine revelation. Often called: **the Word of God** [translation of Gk *logos*, as in John 1:1]

-word *n combining form* (preceded by *the* and an initial letter) a euphemistic way of referring to a word by its first letter because it is considered unmentionable by the user: *the C-word* (meaning cancer)

wordage ('wɜːdɪdʒ) *n* words considered collectively, esp a quantity of words

word association *n* an early method of psychoanalysis in which the patient thinks of the first word that comes into consciousness on hearing a given word. In this way it was claimed that aspects of the unconscious could be revealed before defence mechanisms intervene

word blindness *n* the nontechnical name for **alexia** and **dyslexia** > 'word-ˌblind *adj*

wordbook ('wɜːdˌbʊk) *n* a book containing words, usually with their meanings

word deafness *n* loss of ability to understand spoken words, esp as the result of a cerebral lesion. Also called: **auditory aphasia**

word game *n* any game involving the formation, discovery, or alteration of a word or words

wording ('wɜːdɪŋ) *n* **1** the way in which words are used to express a statement, report, etc, esp a written one **2** the words themselves

word order *n* the arrangement of words in a phrase, clause, or sentence

word-perfect *or US* **letter-perfect** *adj* **1** correct in every detail **2** (of a speaker, actor, etc) knowing one's speech, role, etc, perfectly

wordplay ('wɜːdˌpleɪ) *n* verbal wit based on the meanings of words; puns, repartee, etc

word processing *n* the composition of documents using a computer system to input, edit, store, and print

word processor *n* **a** a computer program that performs word processing **b** a computer system designed for word processing

words (wɜːdz) *pl n* **1** the text of a part of an actor, etc **2** the text of a song, as opposed to the music **3** angry speech (esp in **have words with someone**) **4 eat** *or* **swallow one's words** to retract a statement **5 for words** (preceded by *too* and an adj or adv) indescribably; extremely: *the play was too funny for words* **6 have no words for** to be incapable of describing **7 in other words** expressing the same idea but differently **8 in so many words** explicitly or precisely **9 of many** (*or* **few**) **words** (not) talkative **10 put into words** to express in speech or writing **11 say a few words** to give a brief speech **12 take the words out of someone's mouth** to say exactly what someone else was about to say **13 words fail me** I am too happy, sad, amazed, etc, to express my thoughts

wordsearch ('wɜːdˌsɜːtʃ) *n* a puzzle made up of letters arranged in a grid that contains a number of hidden words running in various directions

word square *n* a puzzle in which the player must fill a square grid with words that read the same across as down

Wordsworth ('wɜːdzˌwəθ) *n* **1 Dorothy** 1771–1855, English writer, whose *Journals* are noted esp for their descriptions of nature **2** her brother, **William** 1770–1850, English poet, whose work, celebrating nature, was greatly inspired by the Lake District, in which he spent most of his life. *Lyrical Ballads* (1798), to which Coleridge contributed, is often taken as the first example of English romantic poetry and includes his *Lines Written above Tintern Abbey*. Among his other works are *The Prelude* (completed in 1805; revised thereafter and published posthumously) and *Poems in Two Volumes* (1807), which includes *The Solitary Reaper* and *Intimations of Immortality*

word wrapping *n computing* the automatic shifting of a word at the end of a line to a new line in order to keep within preset margins

wordy ('wɜːdɪ) *adj* **wordier, wordiest** using or containing an excess of words: *a wordy document* > '**wordily** *adv* > '**wordiness** *n*

wore (wɔː) *vb* the past tense of **wear**[1] and **wear**[2]

work (wɜːk) *n* **1** physical or mental effort directed towards doing or making something **2** paid employment at a job or a trade, occupation, or profession **3** a duty, task, or undertaking **4** something done, made, etc, as a result of effort or exertion: *a work of art* **5** another word for **workmanship** (sense 3) **6** the place, office, etc, where a person is employed **7a** decoration, esp of a specified kind **7b** (*in combination*): *wirework* **8** an engineering structure such as a bridge, building, etc **9** *physics* the transfer of energy expressed as the product of a force and the distance through which its point of application moves in the direction of the force **10** a structure, wall, etc, built or used as part of a fortification system **11 at work 11a** at one's job or place of employment **11b** in action; operating **12 make short work of** *inf* to dispose of very quickly **13** (*modifier*) of, relating to, or used for work: *work clothes; a work permit; a work song* ▷ *vb* **14** (*intr*) to exert effort in order to do, make, or perform something **15** (*intr*) to be employed **16** (*tr*) to carry on operations, activity, etc, in (a place or area): *that salesman works Yorkshire* **17** (*tr*) to cause to labour or toil: *he works his men hard* **18** to operate or cause to operate, esp properly or effectively: *to work a lathe; that clock doesn't work* **19** (*tr*) to till or cultivate (land) **20** to handle or manipulate or be handled or manipulated: *to work dough* **21** to shape or process or be shaped or processed: *to work copper* **22** to reach or cause to reach a specific condition, esp gradually: *the rope worked loose* **23** (*intr*) to move in agitation: *his face worked with anger* **24** (*tr*; often foll by *up*) to provoke or arouse: *to work someone into a frenzy* **25** (*tr*) to effect or accomplish: *to work one's revenge* **26** to make (one's way) with effort: *he worked his way through the crowd* **27** (*tr*) to make or decorate by hand in embroidery, tapestry, etc **28** (*intr*) (of liquids) to ferment, as in brewing **29** (*tr*) *inf* to manipulate or exploit to one's own advantage ▷ See also **work in, work off,** etc, **works** [OE *weorc* (n), *wircan, wyrcan* (vb)] > '**workless** *adj*

workable ('wɜːkəbᵊl) *adj* **1** practicable or feasible **2** able to be worked > ˌ**worka'bility** *or* '**workableness** *n*

workaday ('wɜːkəˌdeɪ) *adj* (*usually prenominal*) **1** being a part of general human experience; ordinary **2** suitable for working days; everyday or practical

workaholic (ˌwɜːkə'hɒlɪk) *n* **a** a person obsessively addicted to work **b** (*as modifier*): *workaholic behaviour* [C20 from WORK + -HOLIC, coined in 1971 by US author Wayne Oates]

workaround ('wɜːkəˌraʊnd) *n* a method of circumventing or overcoming a problem in a computer program or system

workbag ('wɜːkˌbæg) *n* a container for implements, tools, or materials, esp sewing equipment. Also called: **work basket, workbox**

workbench ('wɜːkˌbɛntʃ) *n* a heavy table at which work is done by a carpenter, mechanic, toolmaker, etc

workbook ('wɜːkˌbʊk) *n* **1** an exercise book used for study, esp with spaces for answers **2** a book of instructions for some process **3** a book in which is recorded all work done or planned

work camp *n* a camp set up for young people who voluntarily do manual work on a worthwhile project

workday ('wɜːkˌdeɪ) *n* **1** the usual US and Canad term for **working day** ▷ *adj* **2** another word for **workaday**

worked (wɜːkt) *adj* made or decorated with evidence of workmanship; wrought, as with embroidery or tracery

worked up *adj* excited or agitated

worker ('wɜːkə) *n* **1** a person or thing that works, usually at a specific job: *a research worker* **2** an employee, as opposed to an employer or manager **3** a manual labourer working in a manufacturing industry **4** any other member of the working class **5** a sterile female

member of a colony of bees, ants, or wasps that forages for food, cares for the larvae, etc
worker director *n* (in certain British companies) an employee of a company chosen by his or her fellow workers to represent their interests on the board of directors. Also called: **employee director**
worker-priest *n* a Roman Catholic priest who has employment in a secular job to be more in touch with the problems of the laity
work ethic *n* a belief in the moral value of work
workfare ('wɜːkˌfɛə) *n* a scheme under which the government of a country requires unemployed people to do community work or undergo job training in return for social-security payments [c20 from WORK + (WEL)FARE]
workforce ('wɜːkˌfɔːs) *n* **1** the total number of workers employed by a company on a specific job, project, etc **2** the total number of people who could be employed: *the country's workforce is growing*
work function *n physics* the minimum energy required to transfer an electron from a point within a solid to a point just outside its surface. Symbol: ϕ or Φ
work-harden *vb (tr)* to increase the strength or hardness of (a metal) by a mechanical process, such as tension, compression, or torsion
workhorse ('wɜːkˌhɔːs) *n* **1** a horse used for nonrecreational activities **2** *inf* a person who takes on the greatest amount of work in a project
workhouse ('wɜːkˌhaʊs) *n* **1** (formerly in England) an institution maintained at public expense where able-bodied paupers did unpaid work in return for food and accommodation **2** (in the US) a prison for petty offenders serving short sentences at manual labour
work in *vb (adv)* **1** to insert or become inserted: *she worked the patch in carefully* **2** *(tr)* to find space for: *I'll work this job in during the day* ▷ *n* **work-in** **3** a form of industrial action in which a factory that is to be closed down is occupied and run by its workers
working ('wɜːkɪŋ) *n* **1** the operation or mode of operation of something **2** the act or process of moulding something pliable **3** a convulsive or jerking motion, as from excitement **4** *(often pl)* a part of a mine or quarry that is being or has been worked **5** a record of the steps by which the solution of a problem, calculation, etc, is obtained: *all working is to be submitted to the examiners* ▷ *adj (prenominal)* **6** relating to or concerned with a person or thing that works: *a working man* **7** concerned with, used in, or suitable for work: *working clothes* **8** (of a meal or occasion) during which business discussions are carried on: *a working lunch* **9** capable of being operated or used: *a working model; in working order* **10** adequate for normal purposes: *a working majority; a working knowledge of German* **11** (of a theory, etc) providing a basis, usually a temporary one, on which operations or procedures may be carried out
working bee *n NZ* a voluntary group doing a job for charity
working capital *n* **1** *accounting* current assets minus current liabilities **2** current or liquid assets **3** that part of the capital of a business enterprise available for operations
working class *n* **1** Also called: **proletariat** the social stratum, usually of low status, that consists of those who earn wages, esp as manual workers ▷ *adj* **working-class** **2** of, relating to, or characteristic of the working class
working day *or esp US & Canad* **workday** *n* **1** a day on which work is done, esp for an agreed or stipulated number of hours in return for a salary or wage **2** the part of the day allocated to work **3** *(often pl) commerce* any day of the week except Sunday, public holidays, and, in some cases, Saturday
working drawing *n* a scale drawing of a part that provides a guide for manufacture
working families tax credit *n* (in Britain) a means-tested allowance paid to single parents or to families who have at least one dependent child, who work at least 16 hours per week and whose earnings are low. It replaced family credit
working girl *n* **1** a girl or woman who works, esp one who supports herself **2** *inf* a prostitute
working memory *n psychol* the current contents of consciousness
working party *n* **1** a committee established to investigate a problem, question, etc **2** a group of soldiers or prisoners assigned to perform a manual task or duty
working week *or esp US & Canad* **workweek** *n* the number of hours or days in a week allocated to work
work-in-progress *n book-keeping* the value of work begun but not completed, as shown in a profit-and-loss account
workload ('wɜːkˌləʊd) *n* the amount of work to be done, esp in a specified period
workman ('wɜːkmən) *n, pl* **workmen** **1** a man who is employed in manual labour or who works an industrial machine **2** a craftsman of skill as specified: *a bad workman*
workmanlike ('wɜːkmənˌlaɪk) *or (less commonly)* **workmanly** *adj* appropriate to or befitting a good workman
workmanship ('wɜːkmənʃɪp) *n* **1** the art or skill of a workman **2** the art or skill with which something is made or executed **3** the degree of art or skill exhibited in the finished product **4** the piece of work so produced
workmate ('wɜːkˌmeɪt) *n* a person who works with another; fellow worker
work of art *n* **1** a piece of fine art, such as a painting or sculpture **2** something that may be likened to a piece of fine art, esp in beauty, intricacy, etc
work off *vb (tr, adv)* **1** to get rid of or dissipate, as by effort: *he worked off some of his energy by digging the garden* **2** to discharge (a debt) by labour rather than payment
work on *vb (intr, prep)* to persuade or influence or attempt to persuade or influence
work out *vb (adv)* **1** *(tr)* to achieve or accomplish by effort **2** *(tr)* to solve or find out by reasoning or calculation: *to work out an answer; to work out a sum* **3** *(tr)* to devise or formulate: *to work out a plan* **4** *(intr)* to prove satisfactory: *did your plan work out?* **5** *(intr)* to happen as specified: *it all worked out well* **6** *(intr)* to take part in physical exercise, as in training **7** *(tr)* to remove all the mineral in (a mine, etc) that can be profitably exploited **8** *(intr; often foll by to or at)* to reach a total: *your bill works out at a pound* ▷ *n* **workout** **9** a session of physical exercise, esp for training or to keep oneself fit
work over *vb* **1** *(tr, adv)* to do again; repeat **2** *(intr, prep)* to examine closely and thoroughly **3** *(tr, adv) sl* to assault or thrash
workpeople ('wɜːkˌpiːpᵊl) *pl n* the working members of a population
workroom ('wɜːkˌruːm, -ˌrʊm) *n* **1** a room in which work, usually manual labour, is done **2** a room in a house set aside for a hobby
works (wɜːks) *pl n* **1** *(often functioning as sing)* a place where a number of people are employed, such as a factory **2** the sum total of a writer's or artist's achievements, esp when considered together: *the works of Shakespeare* **3** the deeds of a person, esp virtuous or moral deeds: *works of charity* **4** the interior parts of the mechanism of a machine, etc: *the works of a clock* **5** **the works** *sl* **5a** full or extreme treatment **5b** a very violent physical beating: *to give someone the works*
works council *n chiefly Brit* **1** a council composed of both employer and employees convened to discuss matters of common interest concerning a factory, plant, business

policy, etc **2** a body representing the workers of a plant, factory, etc, elected to negotiate with the management about working conditions, wages, etc ▹ Also called: **works committee**

worksheet (ˈwɜːkˌʃiːt) *n* **1** a sheet of paper used for the rough draft of a problem, design, etc **2** a piece of paper recording work in progress

workshop (ˈwɜːkˌʃɒp) *n* **1** a room or building in which manufacturing or other forms of manual work are carried on **2** a room in a private dwelling, school, etc, set aside for crafts **3** a group of people engaged in study or work on a creative project or subject: *a music workshop*

workshy (ˈwɜːkˌʃaɪ) *adj* not inclined to work

Worksop (ˈwɜːksɒp) *n* a town in N central England, in N Nottinghamshire. Pop: 37 247 (1991)

work station *n* an area in an office where one person works

work-study *n* an examination of ways of finding the most efficient method of doing a job

worktable (ˈwɜːkˌteɪbᵊl) *n* **a** any table at which writing, sewing, or other work may be done **b** (in English cabinetwork) a small elegant table fitted with sewing accessories

worktop (ˈwɜːkˌtɒp) *n* a surface in a kitchen, often of heat-resistant plastic, used for food preparation

work-to-rule *n* **1** a form of industrial action in which employees adhere strictly to all the working rules laid down by their employers, with the deliberate intention of reducing the rate of working ▹ *vb* **work to rule 2** (*intr*) to decrease the rate of working by this means

work up *vb* **1** (*tr, adv*) to arouse the feelings of; excite **2** (*tr, adv*) to cause to grow or develop: *to work up a hunger* **3** to move or cause to move gradually upwards **4** (*tr, adv*) to manipulate or mix into a specified object or shape **5** (*tr, adv*) to gain skill at (a subject) **6** (*adv*) (foll by *to*) to develop gradually or progress (towards): *working up to a climax*

world (wɜːld) *n* **1** the earth as a planet, esp including its inhabitants **2** mankind; the human race **3** people generally; the public: *in the eyes of the world* **4** social or public life: *to go out into the world* **5** the universe or cosmos; everything in existence **6** a complex united whole regarded as resembling the universe **7** any star or planet, esp one that might be inhabited **8** (*often cap*) a division or section of the earth, its history, or its inhabitants: *the Ancient World; the Third World* **9** an area, sphere, or realm considered as a complete environment: *the animal world* **10** any field of human activity or way of life or those involved in it: *the world of television* **11** a period or state of existence: *the next world* **12** the total circumstances and experience of an individual that make up his life: *you have shattered my world* **13** a large amount, number, or distance: *worlds apart* **14** worldly or secular life, ways, or people **15 bring into the world 15a** (of a midwife, doctor, etc) to deliver (a baby) **15b** to give birth to **16 come into the world** to be born **17 for all the world** in every way; exactly **18 for the world** (*used with a negative*) for any inducement, however great **19 in the world** (intensifier; *usually used with a negative*): *no-one in the world can change things* **20 man** (*or* **woman**) **of the world** a man (or woman) experienced in social or public life **21 not long for this world** nearing death **22 on top of the world** *inf* elated or very happy **23 out of this world** *inf* wonderful; excellent **24 set the world on fire** to be exceptionally or sensationally successful **25 the best of both worlds** the benefits from two different ways of life, philosophies, etc **26 think the world of** to be extremely fond of or hold in very high esteem **27 world of one's own** a state of mental detachment from other people **28 world without end** forever **29** (*modifier*) of or concerning most or all countries; worldwide: *world politics* **30** (*in combination*) throughout the world: *world-famous* [OE *w(e)orold*, from *wer* man + *ald* age, life]

World Bank *n* an international cooperative organization established in 1945 to assist economic development, esp of backward nations, by the advance of loans guaranteed by member governments. Officially called: **International Bank for Reconstruction and Development**
▹ www.worldbank.org

world-beater *n* a person or thing that surpasses all others in its category; champion

world-class *adj* of or denoting someone with a skill or attribute that puts him or her in the highest class in the world: *a world-class swimmer*

World Court *n* another name for **International Court of Justice**

World Cup *n* an international competition held between national teams in various sports, most notably association football

worldling (ˈwɜːldlɪŋ) *n* a person who is primarily concerned with worldly matters

worldly (ˈwɜːldlɪ) *adj* **worldlier, worldliest 1** not spiritual; mundane or temporal **2** Also: **worldly-minded** absorbed in material things **3** Also: **worldly-wise** versed in the ways of the world; sophisticated > **ˈworldliness** *n*

world music *n* popular music of various ethnic origins and styles
▹ http://africanmusic.org
▹ www.ceolas.org/ceolas.html
▹ www.sbgmusic.com/html/teacher/reference/cultures.html
▹ www.rootsworld.com/rw

world power *n* a state that possesses sufficient power to influence events throughout the world

world-shaking *adj* of enormous significance

World Trade Organization *n* an international body concerned with promoting and regulating trade between its member states; established in 1995 as a successor to GATT

World War I *n* the war (1914–18), fought mainly in Europe and the Middle East, in which the Allies (principally France, Russia, Britain, Italy after 1915, and the US after 1917) defeated the Central Powers (principally Germany, Austria-Hungary, and Turkey). Also called: **First World War, Great War**
▹ www.worldwar1.com
▹ www.firstworldwar.com

World War II *n* the war (1939–45) in which the Allies (principally Britain, the Soviet Union, and the US) defeated the Axis powers (principally Germany, Italy, and Japan). Britain and France declared war on Germany (Sept 3, 1939) as a result of the German invasion of Poland (Sept 1, 1939). Italy entered the war on June 10, 1940 shortly before the collapse of France (armistice signed June 22, 1940). On June 22, 1941 Germany attacked the Soviet Union and on Dec 7, 1941 the Japanese attacked the US at Pearl Harbor. On Sept 8, 1943 Italy surrendered, the war in Europe ending on May 7, 1945 with the unconditional surrender of the Germans. The Japanese capitulated on Aug 14, 1945. Also called: **Second World War**
▹ www.ibiblio.org/pha

world-weary *adj* no longer finding pleasure in living > **ˈworld-ˌweariness** *n*

worldwide (ˈwɜːldˈwaɪd) *adj* applying or extending throughout the world; universal

World Wide Web *n computing* a vast network of linked hypertext files, stored on computers throughout the world, that can provide a computer user with information on a huge variety of subjects. Abbrev: **WWW**

worm (wɜːm) *n* **1** any of various invertebrates, esp the annelids (earthworms, etc), nematodes (roundworms), and flatworms, having a slender elongated body **2** any of various insect larvae having an elongated body, such as the silkworm and wireworm **3** any of various unrelated animals that resemble annelids, nematodes, etc, such as the glow-worm and shipworm **4** a gnawing or insinuating force or agent that torments or slowly eats away **5** a wretched or spineless person **6** anything that resembles a worm in appearance or movement **7** a shaft on which a helical groove has been cut, as in a gear arrangement in which such a shaft meshes with a toothed wheel **8** a spiral pipe cooled by air or flowing water, used as a condenser in a still **9** *computing* a program that duplicates itself many times in a network and prevents its destruction. It often carries a logic bomb or virus ▷ *vb* **10** to move, act, or cause to move or act with the slow sinuous movement of a worm **11** (foll by *in, into, out of*, etc) to make (one's way) slowly and stealthily; insinuate (oneself) **12** (*tr;* often foll by *out of* or *from*) to extract (information, etc) from by persistent questioning **13** (*tr*) to free from worms ▷ See also **worms** [OE *wyrm*] > **'wormer** *n* > **'worm,like** *adj*

WORM (wɜːm) *n computing acronym for* write once read many times: an optical disk which enables users to store data but not change it

wormcast ('wɜːm,kɑːst) *n* a coil of earth or sand that has been excreted by a burrowing earthworm or lugworm

worm-eaten *adj* **1** eaten into by worms: *a worm-eaten table* **2** decayed; rotten **3** old-fashioned; antiquated

worm gear *n* **1** a device consisting of a threaded shaft (**worm**) that mates with a gear-wheel (**worm wheel**) so that rotary motion can be transferred between two shafts at right angles to each other **2** Also called: **worm wheel** a gear-wheel driven by a threaded shaft or worm

wormhole ('wɜːm,həʊl) *n* a hole made by a worm in timber, plants, etc > **'worm,holed** *adj*

worms (wɜːmz) *n* (*functioning as sing*) any disease or disorder, usually of the intestine, characterized by infestation with parasitic worms

Worms (wɜːmz; *German* vɔrms) *n* a city in SW Germany, in Rhineland-Palatinate on the Rhine: famous as the seat of imperial diets, notably that of 1521, before which Luther defended his doctrines in the presence of Charles V; river port and manufacturing centre with a large wine trade. Pop: 77 430 (1991)

worm's eye view *n* a view seen from below or from a more lowly or humble point

wormwood ('wɜːm,wʊd) *n* **1** Also called: **absinthe** any of various plants of a chiefly N temperate genus, esp a European plant yielding a bitter extract used in making absinthe **2** something that embitters, such as a painful experience [C15 changed (through infl. of WORM and WOOD) from OE *wormōd, wermōd*]

wormy ('wɜːmɪ) *adj* **wormier, wormiest** **1** worm-infested or worm-eaten **2** resembling a worm in appearance, ways, or condition **3** (of wood) having irregular small tunnels bored into it and tracked over its surface, made by worms **4** low or grovelling > **'worminess** *n*

worn (wɔːn) *vb* **1** the past participle of **wear**[1] and **wear**[2] ▷ *adj* **2** affected, esp adversely, by long use or action: *a worn suit* **3** haggard; drawn **4** exhausted; spent > **'wornness** *n*

worn-out *adj* (**worn out** *when postpositive*) **1** worn or used until threadbare, valueless, or useless **2** exhausted; very weary

worried ('wʌrɪd) *adj* feeling uneasy about a situation or thing; anxious > **'worriedly** *adv*

worried well *n* **the** *inf* the people who do not need medical treatment, but who visit the doctor for reassurance or emotional support

worriment ('wʌrɪmənt) *n inf, chiefly US* anxiety or the trouble that causes it; worry

worrisome ('wʌrɪsəm) *adj* **1** causing worry; vexing: *worrisome repercussions* **2** tending to worry: *a worrisome wife* > **'worrisomely** *adv*

worrit ('wʌrɪt) *vb* (*tr*) *dialect* to tease or worry [prob. var. of WORRY]

worry ('wʌrɪ) *vb* **worries, worrying, worried** **1** to be or cause to be anxious or uneasy, esp about something uncertain or potentially dangerous **2** (*tr*) to disturb the peace of mind of; bother: *don't worry me with trivialities* **3** (*intr;* often foll by *along* or *through*) to proceed despite difficulties **4** (*intr;* often foll by *away*) to struggle or work: *to worry away at a problem* **5** (*tr*) (of a dog, wolf, etc) to lacerate or kill by biting, shaking, etc **6** (when *intr*, foll by *at*) to bite, tear, or gnaw (at) with the teeth: *a dog worrying a bone* **7** (*tr*) to touch or poke repeatedly and idly **8** **not to worry** *inf* you need not worry ▷ *n, pl* **worries** **9** a state or feeling of anxiety **10** a person or thing that causes anxiety **11** an act of worrying **12** **no worries** an expression used to express agreement or to convey that something is proceeding or has proceeded satisfactorily; no problem [OE *wyrgan*] > **'worrying** *adj* > **'worryingly** *adv*

worry beads *pl n* a string of beads that when fingered or played with supposedly relieves nervous tension

worryguts ('wʌrɪ,gʌts) *n* (*functioning as sing*) *inf* a person who worries, esp about insignificant matters

worse (wɜːs) *adj* **1** the comparative of **bad**[1] **2** **none the worse for** not harmed by (adverse events or circumstances) **3** **the worse for wear** **3a** shabby or worn **3b** a slang term for **drunk** **4** **worse luck!** *inf* unhappily; unfortunately **5** **worse off** (*postpositive*) in a worse, esp a worse financial, condition ▷ *n* **6** something that is worse **7** **for the worse** into a less desirable or inferior state or condition: *a change for the worse* ▷ *adv* **8** in a more severe or unpleasant manner **9** in a less effective or successful manner [OE *wiersa*]

worsen ('wɜːsᵊn) *vb* to grow or cause to grow worse

worship ('wɜːʃɪp) *vb* **worships, worshipping, worshipped** *or US* **worships, worshiping, worshiped** **1** (*tr*) to show profound religious devotion and respect to; adore or venerate (God or any person or thing considered divine) **2** (*tr*) to be devoted to and full of admiration for **3** (*intr*) to have or express feelings of profound adoration **4** (*intr*) to attend services for worship ▷ *n* **5** religious adoration or devotion **6** the formal expression of religious adoration; rites, prayers, etc **7** admiring love or devotion [OE *weorthscipe*] > **'worshipper** *n*

Worship ('wɜːʃɪp) *n chiefly Brit* (preceded by *Your, His,* or *Her*) a title used to address or refer to a mayor, magistrate, etc

worshipful ('wɜːʃɪpfʊl) *adj* **1** feeling or showing reverence or adoration **2** (*often cap*) *chiefly Brit* a title used to address or refer to various people or bodies of distinguished rank > **'worshipfully** *adv*

worst (wɜːst) *adj* **1** the superlative of **bad**[1] ▷ *adv* **2** in the most extreme or bad manner or degree **3** least well, suitably, or acceptably **4** (*in combination*) in or to the smallest degree or extent; least: *worst-loved* ▷ *n* **5** **the worst** the least good or most inferior person, thing, or part in a group, narrative, etc **6** (often preceded by *at*) the most poor, unpleasant, or unskilled quality or condition: *television is at its worst these days* **7** the greatest amount of damage or wickedness of which a person or group is capable: *the invaders came and did their worst* **8** the weakest effort or poorest achievement that a person or group is capable of making: *the applicant did his worst at the test because he did not want the job* **9** **at worst** **9a** in the least favourable interpretation or view **9b** under the least favourable conditions **10** **come off worst** *or* **get the worst of it** to enjoy the least benefit from an issue or be defeated in it **11** **if the worst comes to the worst** if all the more desirable alternatives become impossible or if the worst possible thing happens ▷ *vb* **12** (*tr*) to get the advantage over; defeat or beat [OE *wierrest*]

worsted ('wʊstɪd) *n* **1** a closely twisted yarn or thread

Ww

made from combed long-staple wool **2** a fabric made from this, with a hard smooth close-textured surface and no nap **3** (*modifier*) made of this yarn or fabric: *a worsted suit* [C13 after *Worstead*, a district in Norfolk]

wort (wɜːt) *n* **1** (*in combination*) any of various unrelated plants, esp ones formerly used to cure diseases: *liverwort* **2** the sweet liquid made from warm water and ground malt, used to make a malt liquor [OE *wyrt* root]

worth (wɜːθ) *adj* (governing a noun with prepositional force) **1** worthy of; meriting or justifying: *it's not worth discussing* **2** having a value of: *the book is worth £30* **3** **for all one is worth** to the utmost **4** **worth one's weight in gold** extremely helpful, kind, etc ▷ *n* **5** high quality; excellence **6** value; price **7** the amount of something of a specified value: *five pounds' worth of petrol* [OE *weorth*]

Worthing (ˈwɜːðɪŋ) *n* a resort in S England, in West Sussex on the English Channel. Pop: 95 732 (1991)

worthless (ˈwɜːθlɪs) *adj* **1** without value or usefulness **2** without merit; good-for-nothing > ˈ**worthlessly** *adv* > ˈ**worthlessness** *n*

worthwhile (ˌwɜːθˈwaɪl) *adj* sufficiently important, rewarding, or valuable to justify time or effort spent

worthy (ˈwɜːðɪ) *adj* **worthier, worthiest** **1** (*postpositive; often foll by of or an infinitive*) having sufficient merit or value (for something or someone specified); deserving **2** having worth, value, or merit ▷ *n, pl* **worthies** **3** *often facetious* a person of merit or importance > ˈ**worthily** *adv* > ˈ**worthiness** *n*

wot (wɒt) *vb arch or dialect* (used with *I, she, he, it*, or a singular noun) a form of the present tense (indicative mood) of **wit²**

Wotan (ˈvəʊtɑːn, ˈvɔː-) *n* the supreme god in Germanic mythology. Norse counterpart: **Odin**

would (wʊd; *unstressed* wəd) *vb* (takes an infinitive without *to* or an implied infinitive) used as an auxiliary: **1** to form the past tense or subjunctive mood of **will¹** **2** (with *you, he, she, it, they*, or a noun as subject) to indicate willingness or desire in a polite manner: *would you help me, please?* **3** to describe a past action as being accustomed or habitual: *every day we would go for walks* **4** I wish: *would that he were here*

USAGE See at **should**

would-be *adj* (*prenominal*) **1** *usually derog* wanting or professing to be: *a would-be politician* **2** intended to be

wouldn't (ˈwʊdᵊnt) *contraction of* would not

wouldst (wʊdst) *vb arch or dialect* (used with the pronoun *thou* or its relative equivalent) a singular form of the past tense of **will¹**

Woulfe bottle (wʊlf) *n chem* a bottle with more than one neck, used for passing gases through liquids [C18 after Peter *Woulfe* (?1727–1803), Brit chemist]

wound¹ (wuːnd) *n* **1** any break in the skin or an organ or part as the result of violence or a surgical incision **2** any injury or slight to the feelings or reputation ▷ *vb* **3** to inflict a wound or wounds upon (someone or something) [OE *wund*] > ˈ**wounding** *adj* > ˈ**woundingly** *adv*

wound² (waʊnd) *vb* the past tense and past participle of **wind²** and **wind³**

wounded (ˈwuːndɪd) *adj* **1a** suffering from wounds; injured, esp in a battle or fight **1b** (*as collective n; preceded by the*): *the wounded* **2** (of feelings) damaged or hurt

woundwort (ˈwuːndˌwɜːt) *n* **1** any of various plants, such as field woundwort, having purple, scarlet, yellow, or white flowers and formerly used for dressing wounds **2** any of various other plants used in this way

wove (wəʊv) *vb* a past tense of **weave**

woven (ˈwəʊvᵊn) *vb* a past participle of **weave**

wove paper *n* paper with a very faint mesh impressed on it by the paper-making machine

wow¹ (waʊ) *interj* **1** an exclamation of admiration, amazement, etc ▷ *n* **2** *sl* a person or thing that is amazingly successful, attractive, etc ▷ *vb* **3** (*tr*) *sl* to arouse great enthusiasm in [C16 orig. Scot.]

wow² (waʊ, wəʊ) *n* a slow variation or distortion in pitch that occurs at very low audio frequencies in sound-reproducing systems. See also **flutter** (sense 12) [C20 imit.]

wow factor *n inf* a striking or impressive feature

wowser (ˈwaʊzə) *n Austral & NZ sl* **1** a fanatically puritanical person **2** a teetotaller [C20 from E dialect *wow* to complain]

wp *abbrev for* word processor

wpb *abbrev for* wastepaper basket

WPC (in Britain) *abbrev for* woman police constable

wpm *abbrev for* words per minute

WRAAC *abbrev for* Women's Royal Australian Army Corps

WRAAF *abbrev for* Women's Royal Australian Air Force

WRAC (in Britain) *abbrev for* Women's Royal Army Corps

wrack¹ *or* **rack** (ræk) *n* **1** collapse or destruction (esp in **wrack and ruin**) **2** something destroyed or a remnant of such [OE *wræc* persecution, misery]

USAGE The use of the spelling *wrack* rather than *rack* in sentences such as *she was wracked by grief* or *the country was wracked by civil war* is very common but is thought by many people to be incorrect

wrack² (ræk) *n* **1** seaweed or other marine vegetation that is floating in the sea or has been cast ashore **2** any of various seaweeds, such as serrated wrack [C14 (in the sense: a wrecked ship, hence later applied to marine vegetation washed ashore): ?from MDu. *wrak* wreckage; the term corresponds to OE *wræc* WRACK¹]

WRAF (in Britain) *abbrev for* Women's Royal Air Force

wraith (reɪθ) *n* **1** the apparition of a person living or thought to be alive, supposed to appear around the time of his death **2** any apparition [C16 Scot., from ?] > ˈ**wraith,like** *adj*

Wran (ræn) *n* a member of the Women's Royal Australian Naval Service

Wrangel Island (ˈræŋgᵊl) *n* an island in the Arctic Ocean, off the coast of the extreme NE of Russia: administratively part of Russia; mountainous and mostly tundra. Area: about 7300 sq km (2800 sq miles)

Wrangell (ˈræŋgᵊl) *n* **Mount** a mountain in S Alaska, in the W Wrangell Mountains. Height: 4269 m (14 005 ft)

Wrangell Mountains *pl n* a mountain range in SE Alaska, extending into the Yukon, Canada. Highest peak: Mount Blackburn, 5037 m (16 523 ft)

wrangle (ˈræŋgᵊl) *vb* **wrangles, wrangling, wrangled** **1** (*intr*) to argue, esp noisily or angrily **2** (*tr*) to encourage, persuade, or obtain by argument **3** (*tr*) *western US & Canad* to herd (cattle or horses) ▷ *n* **4** a noisy or angry argument [C14 from Low G *wrangeln*]

wrangler (ˈræŋglə) *n* **1** one who wrangles **2** *western US & Canad* a herder; cowboy **3** a person who handles or controls animals involved in the making of a film or television programme **4** *Brit* (at Cambridge University) a candidate who has obtained first-class honours in part II of the mathematics tripos. Formerly, the wrangler with the highest marks was called the **senior wrangler**

WRANS *abbrev for* Women's Royal Australian Naval Service. See also **Wran**

wrap (ræp) *vb* **wraps, wrapping, wrapped** (*mainly tr*) **1** to fold or wind (paper, cloth, etc) around (a person or thing) so as to cover **2** (often foll by *up*) to fold paper, etc, around to fasten securely **3** to surround or conceal by surrounding **4** to enclose, immerse, or absorb: *wrapped in joy* **5** to fold, wind, or roll up **6** to complete the filming of (a motion picture or television programme) **7** (*intr; often foll by about, around*, etc) to be or become wound or extended **8** (often foll by *up*) Also: **rap** *Austral inf* to praise (someone) ▷ *n* **9** a garment worn wrapped around the body, esp the shoulders, such as a shawl or cloak **10a** the end of a working day during the filming of a motion picture or television programme **10b** the completion of filming of a motion picture or television programme **11** *chiefly US* wrapping or a wrapper **12** *Brit sl* a small package of an illegal drug in powder form: *a wrap of heroin* **13 keep under wraps** to keep secret **14 take the wraps off** to reveal **15** Also: **rap** *Austral inf* a commendation [C14 from ?]

wrapover ('ræp,əʊvə) *or* **wrapround** *adj* **1** (of a garment, esp a skirt) not sewn up at one side, but worn wrapped round the body and fastened so that the open edges overlap ▷ *n* **2** such a garment

wrapped (ræpt) *vb* **1** the past tense and past participle of **wrap 2 wrapped up in** *inf* **2a** completely absorbed or engrossed in **2b** implicated or involved in ▷ *adj* **3** *Austral inf* a variant spelling of **rapt**[2]

wrapper ('ræpə) *n* **1** the cover, usually of paper or cellophane, in which something is wrapped **2** a dust jacket of a book **3** the firm tobacco leaf forming the outermost portion of a cigar **4** a loose negligee or dressing gown

wrapping ('ræpɪŋ) *n* the material used to wrap something

wrapround ('ræp,raʊnd) *or* **wraparound** *adj* **1** made so as to be wrapped round something: *a wrapround skirt* **2** surrounding, curving round, or overlapping **3** curving round in one continuous piece: *a wrapround windscreen* ▷ *n* **4** *printing* a flexible plate of plastic, metal, or rubber that is made flat but used wrapped round the plate cylinder of a rotary press **5** another name for **wrapover**

wrap up *vb* (*adv*) **1** (*tr*) to fold paper around **2** to put warm clothes on **3** (*intr; usually imperative*) *sl* to be silent **4** (*tr*) *inf* **4a** to settle the final details of **4b** to make a summary of

wrasse (ræs) *n* a marine food fish of tropical and temperate seas, having thick lips, strong teeth, and usually a bright coloration [C17 from Cornish *wrach*]

wrath (rɒθ) *n* **1** angry, violent, or stern indignation **2** divine vengeance or retribution **3** *arch* a fit of anger or an act resulting from anger [OE *wrǣththu*]

Wrath (rɒθ, rɔːθ) *n* **Cape** a promontory at the NW extremity of the Scottish mainland

wrathful ('rɒθfʊl) *adj* **1** full of wrath; raging or furious **2** resulting from or expressing wrath > '**wrathfully** *adv* > '**wrathfulness** *n*

wreak (riːk) *vb* (*tr*) **1** to inflict (vengeance, etc) or to cause (chaos, etc) **2** to express or gratify (anger, hatred, etc) **3** *arch* to take vengeance for [OE *wrecan*] > '**wreaker** *n*

wreath (riːθ) *n, pl* **wreaths** (riːðz, riːθs) **1** a band of flowers or foliage intertwined into a ring, usually placed on a grave as a memorial or worn on the head as a garland or a mark of honour **2** any circular or spiral band or formation **3** (loosely) any floral design placed on a grave as a memorial [OE *wrǣth, wrǣd*] > '**wreath,like** *adj*

wreathe (riːð) *vb* **wreathes, wreathing, wreathed 1** to form into or take the form of a wreath by intertwining or twisting together **2** (*tr*) to decorate with wreaths **3** to move or cause to move in a twisting way: *smoke wreathed up to the ceiling* [C16 ? back formation from *wrēthen*, from OE *writhen*, p.p. of *wrīthan* to writhe]

wreck (rɛk) *vb* **1** to involve in or suffer disaster or destruction **2** (*tr*) to cause the wreck of (a ship) ▷ *n* **3a** the accidental destruction of a ship at sea **3b** the ship so destroyed **4** *maritime law* goods cast ashore from a wrecked vessel **5** a person or thing that has suffered ruin or dilapidation **6** Also called: **wreckage** the remains of something that has been destroyed **7** Also called: **wreckage** the act of wrecking or the state of being wrecked [C13 from ON] > '**wrecking** *n, adj*

wrecked (rɛkt) *adj sl* in a state of intoxication, stupor, or euphoria, induced by drugs or alcohol

wrecker ('rɛkə) *n* **1** a person or thing that ruins or destroys **2** *chiefly US & Canad* a person whose job is to demolish buildings or dismantle cars **3** (formerly) a person who lures ships to destruction to plunder the wreckage **4** a US and Canad name for a breakdown van

wrecking bar *n* a short crowbar, forked at one end and slightly angled at the other to make a fulcrum

Wrekin ('riːkɪn) *n* **1 the** an isolated hill in the English Midlands in Telford and Wrekin unitary authority, Shropshire. Height: 400 m (1335 ft) **2 (all) round the Wrekin** *Midland English dialect* the long way round: *he went all round the Wrekin instead of explaining clearly*

wren (rɛn) *n* **1** any small brown passerine songbird of a chiefly American family (in Britain **wren**, in the US and Canada **winter wren**). They have a slender bill and feed on insects **2** any of various similar birds, such as the Australian warblers, New Zealand wrens, etc [OE *wrenna, werna*]

Wren[1] (rɛn) *n inf* (formerly, in Britain and certain other nations) a member of the Women's Royal Naval Service [C20 from the abbrev WRNS]

Wren[2] (rɛn) *n* Sir **Christopher** 1632–1723, English architect. He designed St Paul's Cathedral and over 50 other London churches after the Great Fire as well as many secular buildings

wrench (rɛntʃ) *vb* **1** to give (something) a sudden or violent twist or pull, esp so as to remove (something) from that to which it is attached: *to wrench a door off its hinges* **2** (*tr*) to twist suddenly so as to sprain (a limb): *to wrench one's ankle* **3** (*tr*) to give pain to **4** (*tr*) to twist from the original meaning or purpose **5** (*intr*) to make a sudden twisting motion ▷ *n* **6** a forceful twist or pull **7** an injury to a limb, caused by twisting **8** sudden pain caused esp by parting **9** a parting that is difficult or painful to make **10** a distorting of the original meaning or purpose **11** a spanner, esp one with adjustable jaws. See also **torque wrench** [OE *wrencan*]

wrest (rɛst) *vb* (*tr*) **1** to take or force away by violent pulling or twisting **2** to seize forcibly by violent or unlawful means **3** to obtain by laborious effort **4** to distort in meaning, purpose, etc ▷ *n* **5** the act or an instance of wresting **6** *arch* a small key used to tune a piano or harp [OE *wrǣstan*] > '**wrester** *n*

wrestle ('rɛsᵊl) *vb* **wrestles, wrestling, wrestled 1** to fight (another person) by holding, throwing, etc, without punching with the closed fist **2** (*intr*) to participate in wrestling **3** (when *intr*, foll by *with* or *against*) to fight with (a person, problem, or thing): *wrestle with one's conscience* **4** (*tr*) to move laboriously, as with wrestling movements ▷ *n* **5** the act of wrestling **6** a struggle or tussle [OE *wræstlian*] > '**wrestler** *n*

wrestling ('rɛslɪŋ) *n* any of certain sports in which the contestants fight each other according to various rules governing holds and usually forbidding blows with the closed fist. The principal object is to overcome the opponent either by throwing or pinning him to the ground or by causing him to submit

▷ www.fila-wrestling.com

wrest pin *n* (on a piano, harp, etc) a pin, embedded in the **wrest plank**, around which one end of a string is wound: it may be turned by means of a tuning key to alter the tension of the string

wretch (rɛtʃ) *n* **1** a despicable person **2** a person pitied for his or her misfortune [OE *wrecca*]

wretched ('rɛtʃɪd) *adj* **1** in poor or pitiful circumstances **2** characterized by or causing misery **3** despicable; base **4** poor, inferior, or paltry **5** (*prenominal*) (intensifier qualifying something undesirable): *a wretched nuisance* > '**wretchedly** *adv* > '**wretchedness** *n*

Wrexham ('rɛksəm) *n* **1** a town in N Wales, in Wrexham county borough: seat of the Roman Catholic bishopric of Wales (except the former Glamorganshire); formerly noted for coal-mining. Pop: 40 614 (1991) **2** a county borough in NE Wales, created in 1996 from part of Clwyd. Pop: 128 477 (2001). Area: 500 sq km (193 sq miles)

wrick (rɪk) *n* **1** a sprain or strain ▷ *vb* **2** (*tr*) to sprain or strain

Ww

wrier *or* **wryer** ('raɪə) *adj* the comparative of **wry**
wriest *or* **wryest** ('raɪɪst) *adj* the superlative of **wry**
wriggle ('rɪgᵊl) *vb* **wriggles, wriggling, wriggled 1** to make or cause to make twisting movements **2** (*intr*) to progress by twisting and turning **3** (*intr; foll by into or out of*) to manoeuvre oneself by clever or devious means: *wriggle out of an embarrassing situation* ▹ *n* **4** a wriggling movement or action **5** a sinuous marking or course [C15 from MLow G] > '**wriggler** *n* > '**wriggly** *adj*
wright (raɪt) *n* (*now chiefly in combination*) a person who creates, builds, or repairs something specified: *a playwright; a shipwright* [OE *wryhta, wyrhta*]
Wright (raɪt) *n* **1 Frank Lloyd** 1869–1959, US architect, whose designs include the Imperial Hotel, Tokyo (1916), the Guggenheim Museum, New York (1943), and many private houses. His "organic architecture" sought a close relationship between buildings and their natural surroundings **2 Joseph,** known as *Wright of Derby*. 1734–97, British painter, noted for his paintings of industrial and scientific subjects, esp *The Orrery* (?1765) and *The Air Pump* (1768) **3 Joseph** 1855–1930, British philologist; editor of *The English Dialect Dictionary* (1898–1905) **4 Judith** (**Arundel**) 1915–2000, Australian poet, critic, and conservationist. Her collections of poetry include *The Moving Image* (1946), *Woman to Man* (1949), and *A Human Pattern* (1990) **5 Richard** 1908–60, US Black novelist and short-story writer, best known for the novel *Native Son* (1940) **6 Wilbur** (1867–1912) and his brother, **Orville** (1871–1948), US aviation pioneers, who designed and flew the first powered aircraft (1903) **7 William,** known as *Billy*. 1924–94, English footballer: winner of 105 caps
wring (rɪŋ) *vb* **wrings, wringing, wrung 1** (often foll by *out*) to twist and compress to squeeze (a liquid) from (cloth, etc) **2** (*tr*) to twist forcibly: *wring its neck* **3** (*tr*) to clasp and twist (one's hands), esp in anguish **4** (*tr*) to distress: *wring one's heart* **5** (*tr*) to grip (someone's hand) vigorously in greeting **6** (*tr*) to obtain as by forceful means: *wring information out of* **7 wringing wet** soaking; drenched ▹ *n* **8** an act or the process of wringing [OE *wringan*]
wringer ('rɪŋə) *n* another name for **mangle²** (sense 1)
wrinkle¹ ('rɪŋkᵊl) *n* **1** a slight ridge in the smoothness of a surface, such as a crease in the skin as a result of age ▹ *vb* **wrinkles, wrinkling, wrinkled 2** to make or become wrinkled, as by crumpling, creasing, or puckering [C15 back formation from *wrinkled*, from OE *gewrinclod*, p.p. of *wrinclian* to wind around] > '**wrinkly** *adj*
wrinkle² ('rɪŋkᵊl) *n inf* a clever or useful trick, hint, or dodge [OE *wrenc* trick]
wrinklies ('rɪŋklɪz) *pl n inf, derog.* old people
wrist (rɪst) *n* **1** *anat* the joint between the forearm and the hand. Technical name: **carpus 2** the part of a sleeve or glove that covers the wrist **3** *machinery* **3a** See **wrist pin 3b** a joint in which a wrist pin forms the pivot [OE]
wristband ('rɪst,bænd) *n* **1** a band around the wrist, esp one attached to a watch or forming part of a long sleeve **2** a sweatband around the wrist
wristlet ('rɪstlɪt) *n* a band or bracelet worn around the wrist
wrist pin *n* **1** a cylindrical boss or pin attached to the side of a wheel parallel with the axis, esp one forming a bearing for a crank **2** the US and Canad name for **gudgeon pin**
wristwatch ('rɪst,wɒtʃ) *n* a watch worn strapped around the wrist
wristy ('rɪstɪ) *adj* (of a player's style of hitting the ball in cricket, tennis, etc) with much movement of the wrist
writ (rɪt) *n* **1** a document under seal, issued in the name of the Crown or a court, commanding the person to whom it is addressed to do or refrain from doing some specified act **2** *arch* a piece of writing: *Holy Writ* [OE]
write (raɪt) *vb* **writes, writing, wrote, written 1** to draw or mark (symbols, words, etc) on a surface, usually paper, with a pen, pencil, or other instrument **2** to describe or record (ideas, experiences, etc) in writing **3** to compose (a letter) to or correspond regularly with (a person, organization, etc) **4** (*tr; may take a clause as object*) to say or communicate by letter: *he wrote that he was on his way* **5** (*tr*) *inf, chiefly US & Canad* to send a letter to (a person, etc) **6** to write (words) in cursive as opposed to printed style **7** (*tr*) to be sufficiently familiar with (a specified style, language, etc) to use it in writing **8** to be the author or composer of (books, music, etc) **9** (*tr*) to fill in the details for (a document, form, etc) **10** (*tr*) to draw up or draft **11** (*tr*) to produce by writing: *he wrote ten pages* **12** (*tr*) to show clearly: *envy was written all over his face* **13** (*tr*) to spell or inscribe **14** (*tr*) to ordain or prophesy: *it is written* **15** (*intr*) to produce writing as specified **16** *computing* to record (data) in a location in a storage device **17** (*tr*) See **underwrite** (sense 3a) ▹ See also **write down, write in,** etc [OE *wrītan* (orig.: to scratch runes into bark)] > '**writable** *adj*
write down *vb* (*adv*) **1** (*tr*) to set down in writing **2** (*tr*) to harm or belittle by writing about (a person) in derogatory terms **3** (*intr; foll by to or for*) to write in a simplified way (to a supposedly less cultured readership) **4** (*tr*) *accounting* to decrease the book value of (an asset) ▹ *n* **write-down 5** *accounting* a reduction made in the book value of an asset
write in *vb* (*tr*) **1** to insert in (a document, form, etc) in writing **2** (*adv*) to write a letter to a company, institution, etc **3** (*adv*) *US* to vote for (a person not on a ballot) by inserting his or her name
write off *vb* (*tr, adv*) **1** *accounting* **1a** to cancel (a bad debt or obsolete asset) from the accounts **1b** to consider (a transaction, etc) as a loss or set off (a loss) against revenues **1c** to depreciate (an asset) by periodic charges **1d** to charge (a specified amount) against gross profits as depreciation of an asset **2** to cause or acknowledge the complete loss of **3** to dismiss from consideration **4** to send a written order (for something): *she wrote off for a brochure* **5** *inf* to damage (something, esp a car) beyond repair ▹ *n* **write-off 6** *accounting* **6a** the act of cancelling a bad debt or obsolete asset from the accounts **6b** the bad debt or obsolete asset cancelled **6c** the amount cancelled against gross profits, corresponding to the book value of the bad debt or obsolete asset **7** *inf* something damaged beyond repair, esp a car
write out *vb* (*tr, adv*) **1** to put into writing or reproduce in full form in writing **2** to exhaust (oneself or one's creativity) by excessive writing **3** to remove (a character) from a television or radio series
writer ('raɪtə) *n* **1** a person who writes books, articles, etc, esp as an occupation **2** the person who has written something specified **3** a person who is able to write or write well **4** a scribe or clerk **5** a composer of music **6 Writer to the Signet** (in Scotland) a member of an ancient society of solicitors, now having the exclusive privilege of preparing crown writs
writer's cramp *n* a muscular spasm or temporary paralysis of the muscles of the thumb and first two fingers caused by prolonged writing
write up *vb* (*tr, adv*) **1** to describe fully, complete, or bring up to date in writing: *write up a diary* **2** to praise or bring to public notice in writing **3** *accounting* **3a** to place an excessively high value on (an asset) **3b** to increase the book value of (an asset) in order to reflect more accurately its current worth in the market ▹ *n* **write-up 4** a published account of something, such as a review in a newspaper or magazine
writhe (raɪð) *vb* **writhes, writhing, writhed 1** to twist or squirm in or as if in pain **2** (*intr*) to move with such motions **3** (*intr*) to suffer acutely from embarrassment, revulsion, etc ▹ *n* **4** the act of writhing [OE *wrīthan*] > '**writher** *n*

writing (ˈraɪtɪŋ) *n* 1 a group of letters or symbols written or marked on a surface as a means of communicating 2 short for **handwriting** 3 anything expressed in letters, esp a literary composition 4 the work of a writer 5 literary style, art, or practice 6 written form: *give it to me in writing* 7 (*modifier*) related to or used in writing: *writing ink* 8 **writing on the wall** a sign or signs of approaching disaster [sense 8: allusion to Daniel 5:5]

writing desk *n* a piece of furniture with a writing surface and drawers and compartments for papers, writing materials, etc

writing paper *n* paper sized to take writing ink and used for letters and other manuscripts

writ of execution *n law* a writ ordering that a judgment be enforced

written (ˈrɪtᵊn) *vb* 1 the past participle of **write** ▷ *adj* 2 taken down in writing; transcribed: *written evidence submitted to the enquiry*

WRNS *abbrev for* (the former) Women's Royal Naval Service. See also **Wren**

Wrocław (*Polish* ˈvrɔtswaf) *n* an industrial city in SW Poland, on the River Oder: passed to Austria (1527) and to Prussia (1741); returned to Poland in 1945. Pop: 637 877 (1999 est). German name: **Breslau**

wrong (rɒŋ) *adj* 1 not correct or truthful: *the wrong answer* 2 acting or judging in error: *you are wrong to think that* 3 (*postpositive*) immoral; bad: *it is wrong to cheat* 4 deviating from or unacceptable to correct or conventional laws, usage, etc 5 not intended or wanted: *the wrong road* 6 (*postpositive*) not working properly; amiss: *something is wrong with the engine* 7 (of a side, esp of a fabric) intended to face the inside so as not to be seen 8 **get on the wrong side of** *inf* to come into disfavour with 9 **go down the wrong way** (of food) to pass into the windpipe instead of the gullet ▷ *adv* 10 in the wrong direction or manner 11 **get wrong** 11a to fail to understand properly 11b to fail to provide the correct answer to 12 **go wrong** 12a to turn out other than intended 12b to make a mistake 12c (of a machine, etc) to cease to function properly 12d to go astray morally ▷ *n* 13 a bad, immoral, or unjust thing or action 14 *law* 14a an infringement of another person's rights, rendering the offender liable to a civil action: *a private wrong* 14b a violation of public rights and duties, affecting the community as a whole and actionable at the instance of the Crown: *a public wrong* 15 **in the wrong** mistaken or guilty ▷ *vb* (*tr*) 16 to treat unjustly 17 to malign or misrepresent [OE *wrang* injustice] > ˈ**wronger** *n* > ˈ**wrongly** *adv* > ˈ**wrongness** *n*

wrongdoer (ˈrɒŋˌduːə) *n* a person who acts immorally or illegally

wrongdoing (ˈrɒŋˌduːɪŋ) *n* the act or an instance of doing something immoral or illegal

wrong-foot *vb* (*tr*) 1 *tennis, etc* to play a shot in such a way as to cause (one's opponent) to be off balance 2 to take by surprise so as to place in an embarrassing or disadvantageous situation

wrongful (ˈrɒŋfʊl) *adj* unjust or illegal > ˈ**wrongfully** *adv* > ˈ**wrongfulness** *n*

wrong-headed *adj* 1 constantly wrong in judgment 2 foolishly stubborn; obstinate > ˌ**wrong-ˈheadedly** *adv* > ˌ**wrong-ˈheadedness** *n*

wrong number *n* a telephone number wrongly connected or dialled in error, or the person so contacted

wrong 'un *n inf* 1 a dishonest or unscrupulous person 2 *cricket chiefly Austral* another term for **googly**

wrote (rəʊt) *vb* the past tense of **write**

wroth (rəʊθ, rɒθ) *adj arch or literary* angry; irate [OE *wrāth*]

wrought (rɔːt) *vb* 1 *arch* a past tense and past participle of **work** ▷ *adj* 2 *metallurgy* shaped by hammering or beating 3 (*often in combination*) formed, fashioned, or worked as specified: *well-wrought* 4 decorated or made with delicate care [C16 var. of *worht*, from OE *geworht*, p.p. of (*ge*)*wyrcan* to work]

wrought iron *n* a a pure form of iron having a low carbon content: often used for decorative work b (*as modifier*): *wrought-iron gates*

wrought-up *adj* agitated or excited

wrung (rʌŋ) *vb* the past tense and past participle of wring

WRVS *abbrev for* Women's Royal Voluntary Service

wry (raɪ) *adj* **wrier, wriest** *or* **wryer, wryest** 1 twisted, contorted, or askew 2 (of a facial expression) produced or characterized by contorting of the features 3 drily humorous; sardonic 4 warped, misdirected, or perverse ▷ *vb* **wries, wrying, wried** 5 (*tr*) to twist or contort [C16 from dialect *wry* to twist, from OE *wrīgian* to turn] > ˈ**wryly** *adv* > ˈ**wryness** *n*

wrybill (ˈraɪˌbɪl) *n* a New Zealand plover, having its bill deflected to one side enabling it to search for food beneath stones

wryneck (ˈraɪˌnɛk) *n* 1 either of two cryptically coloured Old World woodpeckers, which do not drum on trees 2 another name for **torticollis** 3 *inf* a person who has a twisted neck

WST (in Australia) *abbrev for* Western Standard Time

WSW *symbol for* west-southwest

wt. *abbrev for* weight

WTO *abbrev for* World Trade Organization
▷ www.wto.org

Wu (wuː) *n* **Harry**, real name *Wu Hongda* born 1937, Chinese dissident and human-rights campaigner, a U.S. citizen from 1994: held in labour camps (1960–79); exiled to the U.S. in 1985 but returned secretly to document forced labour in Chinese prisons

Wuchang *or* **Wu-ch'ang** (ˈwuːˈtʃæŋ) *n* a former city of E central China: now a part of Wuhan

Wuhan (ˈwuːˈhæn) *n* a city in SE China, in Hubei province, at the confluence of the Han and Yangtze Rivers: formed in 1950 by the union of the cities of Hanyang, Hankou, and Wuchang (the Han Cities); river port and industrial centre; university (1913). Pop: 3 911 824 (2000)

Ww

Wuhsien (ˈwuːˈʃjɛn) *n* another name for **Suzhou**

Wuhu (ˈwuːˈhuː) *n* a port in E China, in E Anhui province on the Yangtze River. Pop: 495 765 (1999 est)

wukkas (ˈwʌkəz) *pl n* **no wukkas** *Austral taboo sl* an expression used to express agreement or to convey that something is proceeding or has proceeded satisfactorily; no problem [C20 euphemism for *no fucking worries*]

Wu-lu-mu-ch'i (ˈwuːˈluːˈmuːˈtʃiː) *n* a variant of **Urumchi**

wunderkind (ˈwʌndəˌkɪnd; *German* ˈvʊndərˌkɪnt) *n, pl* **wunderkinds** *or* **wunderkinder** (*German* -ˌkɪndər) 1 a child prodigy 2 a person who is extremely successful in his or her field while still young [C20 from G *Wunderkind*, lit.: wonder child]

Wuppertal (*German* ˈvʊpərtaːl) *n* a city in W Germany, in North Rhine-Westphalia state on the **Wupper River** (a Rhine tributary): formed in 1929 from the amalgamation of the towns of Barmen and Elberfeld and other smaller towns; textile centre. Pop: 370 700 (1999 est)

wurst (wɜːst, wʊəst, vʊəst) *n* a sausage, esp of a type made in Germany, Austria, etc [from G *Wurst*, lit.: something rolled]

Württemberg (ˈvɜːtəmˌbɜːg; *German* ˈvyrtəmbɛrk) *n* a historic region and former state of S Germany; since 1952 part of the state of Baden-Württemberg

Würzburg (ˈvɜːtsˌbɜːg; *German* ˈvyrtsbʊrk) *n* a city in S central Germany, in NW Bavaria on the River Main: university (1582). Pop: 126 000 (1999 est)

wuss (wʊs) *or* **wussy** (ˈwʊsɪ) *n, pl* **wusses** *or* **wussies** *sl, chiefly US* a feeble or effeminate person [C20 ?from PUSSY[1] (cat)]

wuthering (ˈwʌðərɪŋ) *adj N English dialect* 1 (of a wind) blowing strongly with a roaring sound **2** (of a place) characterized by such a sound [var. of *whitherin*, from *whither* blow, from ON *hvithra*]

Wutsin (ˈwuːˈtsɪn) *n* the former name (until 1949) of **Zangzhou** (sense 1)

Wuxi, Wusih, *or* **Wu-hsi** (ˈwuːˈʃiː, -ˈsiː) *n* a city in E China, in S Jiangsu province on the Grand Canal: textile industry. Pop: 940 858 (1999 est)

WV *abbrev for* West Virginia

W. Va. *abbrev for* West Virginia

WW1 *abbrev for* World War One

WW2 *abbrev for* World War Two

WWF *abbrev for* Worldwide Fund for Nature
▷ www.wwf.org

WWW *abbrev for* World Wide Web

WY *or* **Wy.** *abbrev for* Wyoming

Wyatt (ˈwaɪət) *n* **1** **James** 1746–1813, British architect; a pioneer of the Gothic Revival **2** **Sir Thomas** ?1503–42, English poet at the court of Henry VIII

wych-elm *or* **witch-elm** (ˈwɪtʃˌɛlm) *n* **1** a Eurasian elm tree, having a rounded shape, longish pointed leaves, clusters of small flowers, and winged fruits **2** the wood of this tree [C17 from OE *wice*]

Wycherley (ˈwɪtʃəlɪ) *n* **William** ?1640–1716, English dramatist. His Restoration comedies include *The Country Wife* (1675) and *The Plain Dealer* (1676)

Wycliffe *or* **Wyclif** (ˈwɪklɪf) *n* **John** ?1330–84, English religious reformer. A precursor of the Reformation, whose writings were condemned as heretical, he attacked the doctrines and abuses of the Church. He instigated the first complete translation of the Bible into English. His followers were called Lollards. Also: **ˈWiclif, ˈWickliffe**

Wye (waɪ) *n* a river in E Wales and W England, rising in Powys and flowing southeast into Herefordshire, then south to the Severn estuary. Length: 210 km (130 miles)

Wykeham (ˈwɪkəm) *n* **William of** 1324–1404, English prelate and statesman, who founded New College, Oxford, and Winchester College: chancellor of England (1367–71; 1389–91); bishop of Winchester (1367–1404)

wynd (waɪnd) *n Scot* a narrow lane or alley [C15 from the stem of WIND²]

Wyndham (ˈwɪndəm) *n* **John,** pseudonym of *John Wyndham Parkes Lucas Beynon Harris*. 1903–69, British writer of science fiction novels and stories. His works include *The Day of the Triffids* (1951), *The Kraken Wakes* (1953), and *The Midwich Cuckoos* (1957)

Wynette (wɪˈnɛt) *n* **Tammy,** original name *Virginia Wynette Pugh*. 1942–98, US country singer; her bestselling records include "Your Good Girl's Gonna Go Bad" (1967) and "Stand By Your Man" (1969)

Wyn Jones (wɪn dʒəʊnz) *n* **Ieuan** (ˈjʊən) born 1949, Welsh politician; leader of Plaid Cymru from 2000

Wyo. *abbrev for* Wyoming

Wyoming (waɪˈəʊmɪŋ) *n* a state of the western US: consists largely of ranges of the Rockies in the west and north, with part of the Great Plains in the east and several regions of hot springs. Capital: Cheyenne. Pop: 493 782 (2000). Area: 253 597 sq km (97 914 sq miles). Abbreviations: **Wyo, Wy** or (with zip code) **WY**
> **Wyˈomingˌite** *n*

WYSIWYG (ˈwɪzɪˌwɪg) *n, adj computing acronym for* what you see is what you get: referring to what is displayed on the screen being the same as what will be printed out

wyvern *or* **wivern** (ˈwaɪvən) *n* a heraldic beast having a serpent's tail and a dragon's head and a body with wings and two legs [C17 var. of earlier *wyver*, from OF, from L *vīpera* VIPER]

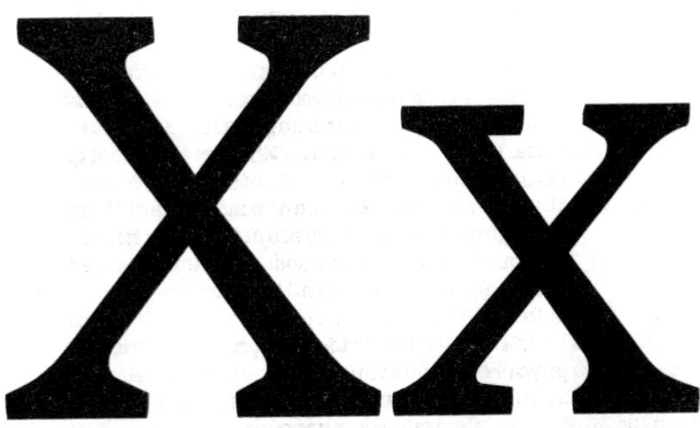

x *or* **X** (ɛks) *n, pl* **x's, X's,** *or* **Xs** **1** the 24th letter of the English alphabet **2** a speech sound sequence represented by this letter, pronounced as *ks* or *gz* or, in initial position, *z*, as in *xylophone*

x *symbol for:* **1** *commerce, finance, etc* ex **2** *maths* the *x*-axis or a coordinate measured along the *x*-axis in a Cartesian coordinate system **3** *maths* an algebraic variable **4** multiplication

X *symbol:* **1a** (in Britain, formerly) indicating a film that may not be publicly shown to anyone under 18. Since 1982 replaced by symbol 18 **1b** *(as modifier): an X film* **2** denoting any unknown, unspecified, or variable factor, number, person, or thing **3** (on letters, cards, etc) denoting a kiss **4** (on ballot papers, etc) indicating choice **5** (on examination papers, etc) indicating error **6** for Christ; Christian [from the Gk letter khi (X), first letter of *Khristos* Christ] **7** *the Roman numeral for* ten. See **Roman numerals**

xanthein (ˈzænθiːɪn) *n* the soluble part of the yellow pigment that is found in the cell sap of some flowers

xanthene (ˈzænθiːn) *n* a yellowish crystalline compound used as a fungicide

xanthic (ˈzænθɪk) *adj* **1** of, containing, or derived from xanthic acid **2** *bot, rare* having a yellow colour

xanthic acid *n* any of a class of sulphur-containing acids

xanthine (ˈzænθiːn, -θaɪn) *n* **1** a crystalline compound found in urine, blood, certain plants, and certain animal tissues. Formula: $C_5H_4N_4O_2$ **2** any of three substituted derivatives of xanthine, which act as stimulants and diuretics

Xanthippe (zænˈθɪpɪ) *or* **Xantippe** (zænˈtɪpɪ) *n* **1** the wife of Socrates, proverbial as scolding and quarrelsome **2** any nagging, peevish, or irritable woman

xantho- *or before a vowel* **xanth-** *combining form* indicating yellow: *xanthophyll* [from Gk *xanthos* yellow]

xanthochroism (zænˈθɒkrəʊˌɪzəm) *n* a condition in certain animals, esp aquarium goldfish, in which all skin pigments other than yellow and orange disappear [C19 from Gk *xanthokhro(os)* yellow-skinned + -ISM]

xanthoma (zænˈθəʊmə) *n pathol* the presence in the skin of fatty yellow or brownish plaques or nodules, esp on the eyelids, caused by a disorder of lipid metabolism

xanthophyll *or esp US* **xanthophyl** (ˈzænθəʊfɪl) *n* any of a group of yellow carotenoid pigments occurring in plant and animal tissue > ˌ**xanthoˈphyllous** *adj*

xanthous (ˈzænθəs) *adj* of, relating to, or designating races with yellowish hair and a light complexion

Xanthus (ˈzænθəs) *n* the chief city of ancient Lycia in SW Asia Minor: source of some important antiquities > ˈ**Xanthian** *adj*

Xavier (ˈzeɪvɪə, ˈzæv-; *Spanish* xaˈβjɛr) *n* **Saint Francis,** known as the *Apostle of the Indies*. 1506–52, Spanish missionary, who was a founding member of the Jesuit society (1534) and later preached in Goa, Ceylon, the East Indies, and Japan. Feast day: Dec 3

x-axis *n* a reference axis, usually horizontal, of a graph or two- or three-dimensional Cartesian coordinate system along which the *x*-coordinate is measured

X-chromosome *n* the sex chromosome that occurs in pairs in the diploid cells of the females of many animals, including humans, and as one of a pair with the Y-chromosome in those of males ▷ Cf **Y-chromosome**

Xe *the chemical symbol for* xenon

xebec, zebec, *or* **zebeck** (ˈziːbɛk) *n* a small three-masted Mediterranean vessel with both square and lateen sails, and overhanging bow and stem, formerly used by Algerian pirates and later used for commerce [C18 earlier *chebec* from F, ult. from Ar. *shabbāk;*

present spelling infl. by Catalan *xabec*, Sp. *xabeque* (now *jabeque*)]

Xenakis (zɛ'nɑːkɪs; *Greek* ksɛ'nakis) *n* **Yannis** ('janis) 1922–2001, Greek composer and musical theorist, born in Romania: later a French citizen. He was noted for his use of computers in composition: his works include *ST/10-1, 080262* (1962) and *Dox-orkh* (1991)

Xenical ('zɛnɪkᵊl) *n trademark* a drug that reduces the ability to absorb fats; used in the medical treatment of obesity

xeno- *or before a vowel* **xen-** *combining form* indicating something strange, different, or foreign: *xenogamy* [from Gk *xenos* strange]

Xenocrates (zɛ'nɒkrəˌtiːz) *n* ?396–314 BC, Greek Platonic philosopher

xenogamy (zɛ'nɒgəmɪ) *n bot* another name for **cross-fertilization** > xe'**nogamous** *adj*

xenogeneic (ˌzɛnəʊdʒɪ'neɪɪk) *adj med* derived from an individual of a different species: *a xenogeneic tissue graft*

xenoglossia (ˌzɛnə'glɒsɪə) *n* an ability claimed by some mediums, clairvoyants, etc, to speak a language with which they are unfamiliar. Also: **xenolalia** [c20 from Gk, from XENO- + *glossa* language]

xenolith ('zɛnəlɪθ) *n* a fragment of rock differing in origin, composition, structure, etc, from the igneous rock enclosing it > ˌ**xeno'lithic** *adj*

xenon ('zɛnɒn) *n* a colourless odourless gaseous element occurring in trace amounts in air; formerly considered inert, it is now known to form compounds and is used in radio valves, stroboscopic and bactericidal lamps, and bubble chambers. Symbol: Xe; atomic no.: 54; atomic wt.: 131.30 [c19 from Gk: something strange]

Xenophanes (zɛ'nɒfəˌniːz) *n* ?570–?480 BC, Greek philosopher and poet, noted for his monotheism and regarded as a founder of the Eleatic school

xenophile ('zɛnəˌfaɪl) *n* a person who likes foreigners or things foreign [c19 from Gk, from XENO- + -PHILE]

xenophobia (ˌzɛnə'fəʊbɪə) *n* hatred or fear of foreigners or strangers or of their politics or culture [c20 from Gk, from XENO- + -PHOBIA] > '**xenoˌphobe** *n* > ˌ**xeno'phobic** *adj*

Xenophon ('zɛnəfən) *n* 431–?355 BC, Greek general and historian; a disciple of Socrates. He accompanied Cyrus the Younger against Artaxerxes II and, after Cyrus' death at Cunaxa (401), he led his army of 10 000 Greek soldiers to the Black Sea, an expedition described in his *Anabasis*. His other works include *Hellenica*, a history of Greece, and the *Memorabilia*, *Apology*, and *Symposium*, which contain recollections of Socrates

Xeres (*Spanish* 'xereθ) *n* the former name of **Jerez**

xeric ('zɪərɪk) *adj ecology* of, relating to, or growing in dry conditions > '**xerically** *adv*

xero- *or before a vowel* **xer-** *combining form* indicating dryness: *xeroderma* [from Gk *xērós* dry]

xeroderma (ˌzɪərəʊ'dɜːmə) *or* **xerodermia** (ˌzɪərəʊ'dɜːmɪə) *n pathol* **1** any abnormal dryness of the skin as the result of diminished secretions from the sweat or sebaceous glands **2** another name for **ichthyosis** > **xerodermatic** (ˌzɪərəʊdə'mætɪk) *or* ˌ**xero'dermatous** *adj*

xerography (zɪ'rɒgrəfɪ) *n* a photocopying process in which an electrostatic image is formed on a selenium plate or cylinder. The plate or cylinder is dusted with a resinous powder, which adheres to the charged regions, and the image is then transferred to a sheet of paper on which it is fixed by heating > **xe'rographer** *n* > **xerographic** (ˌzɪərə'græfɪk) *adj* > ˌ**xero'graphically** *adv*

xerophilous (zɪ'rɒfɪləs) *adj* (of plants or animals) adapted for growing or living in dry surroundings > **xerophile** ('zɪərəʊˌfaɪl) *n* > **xe'rophily** *n*

xerophthalmia (ˌzɪərɒf'θælmɪə) *n pathol* excessive dryness of the cornea and conjunctiva, caused by a deficiency of vitamin A. Also called: **xeroma** (zɪ'rəʊmə) > ˌ**xeroph'thalmic** *adj*

xerophyte ('zɪərəˌfaɪt) *n* a xerophilous plant, such as a cactus > **xerophytic** (ˌzɪərə'fɪtɪk) *adj* > ˌ**xero'phytically** *adv* > '**xeroˌphytism** *n*

Xerox ('zɪərɒks) *n* **1** *trademark* **1a** a xerographic copying process **1b** a machine employing this process **1c** a copy produced by this process ▷ *vb* **2** to produce a copy of (a document, illustration, etc) by this process

Xerxes I ('zɜːksiːz) *n* ?519–465 BC, king of Persia (485–465), who led a vast army against Greece. His forces were victorious at Thermopylae but his fleet was defeated at Salamis (480) and his army at Plataea (479)

Xhosa ('kɔːsə) *n* **1** (*pl* **Xhosa** *or* **Xhosas**) a member of a cattle-rearing Negroid people of southern Africa, living chiefly in W South Africa **2** the language of this people, belonging to the Bantu group and characterized by several clicks in its sound system > '**Xhosan** *adj*

xi (zaɪ, saɪ, ksaɪ, ksiː) *n, pl* **xis** the 14th letter in the Greek alphabet (Ξ, ξ)

Xi *or* **Si** (ʃiː) *n* a river in S China, rising in Yünnan province and flowing east to the Canton delta on the South China Sea: the main river system of S China. Length: about 1900 km (1200 miles)

Xia Gui ('ʃjɑː 'kweɪ) *or* **Hsia Kuei** *n* ?1180–1230, Chinese landscape painter of the Sung dynasty; noted for his misty mountain landscapes in ink monochrome

Xiamen ('ʃjɑː'mɛn) *n* a variant transliteration of the Chinese name for **Amoy**

Xi An, Hsian, *or* **Sian** (ʃjɑːn) *n* an industrial city in central China, capital of Shaanxi province: capital of China for 970 years at various times between the 3rd century BC and the 10th century AD; seat of the Northwestern University (1937). Pop: 2 294 790 (1999 est). Former name: **Siking**

Xiang, Hsiang, *or* **Siang** (ʃjɑːŋ) *n* **1** a river in SE central China, rising in NE Guangxi Zhuang and flowing northeast and north to Dongting Lake. Length: about 1150 km (715 miles) **2** a river in S China, rising in SE Yünnan and flowing generally east to the Hongxiu (the upper course of the Xi River). Length: about 800 km (500 miles)

Xiangtan *or* **Siangtan** ('ʃjɑːŋ'tɑːn) *n* a city in S central China, in NE Hunan on the Xiang River: centre of a region noted for tea production. Pop: 518 783 (1999 est)

Ximenes *or* **Ximenez** (*Spanish* xi'menes; *English* 'zɪmɪˌniːz) *n* See (Francisco) **Jiménez de Cisneros**

Xingú (*Portuguese* ʃiŋ'gu) *n* a river in central Brazil, rising on the Mato Grosso plateau and flowing north to the Amazon delta, with over 650 km (400 miles) of rapids in its middle course. Length: 1932 km (1200 miles)

Xining, Hsining, *or* **Sining** ('ʃiː'nɪŋ) *n* a city in W China, capital of Qinghai province, at an altitude of 2300 m (7500 ft). Pop: 604 812 (1999 est)

Xinjiang Uygur ('ʃɪn'dʒjæŋ 'wiːgʊə) *or* **Sinkiang-Uighur Autonomous Region** *n* an administrative division of NW China: established in 1955 for the Uygur ethnic minority, with autonomous subdivisions for other small minorities; produces over half China's wool and contains valuable mineral resources. Capital: Urumqi. Pop: 19 250 000 (2000 est). Area: 1 646 799 sq km (635 829 sq miles)

xiphisternum (ˌzɪfɪ'stɜːnəm) *n, pl* **xiphisterna** (-nə) *anat, zool* the cartilaginous process forming the lowermost part of the breastbone (sternum). Also called: **xiphoid, xiphoid process** [c19 from Gk *xiphos* sword + STERNUM]

xiphoid ('zɪfɔɪd) *adj* **1** *biol* shaped like a sword **2** of or relating to the xiphisternum ▷ *n* **3** Also called: **xiphoid process** another name for **xiphisternum** [c18 from NL, from Gk, from *xiphos* sword + *eidos* form]

Xizang Autonomous Region ('ʃiː'zæŋ) *n* the Pinyin transliteration of the Chinese name for **Tibet**

Xmas ('ɛksməs, 'krɪsməs) *n inf* short for **Christmas** [c18 from symbol X for Christ + -MAS]

Xochimilco (ˌkɒtʃɪ'mɪlkəʊ) *n* a town in central Mexico, on Lake Xochimilco: noted for its floating gardens. Pop: 271 020 (1990)

X-rated *adj* **1** (formerly, in Britain) (of a film) considered suitable for viewing by adults only **2** *inf* involving bad language, violence, or sex: *an X-rated conversation*

X-ray *or* **x-ray** *n* **1a** electromagnetic radiation emitted when matter is bombarded with fast electrons. X-rays have wavelengths shorter than that of ultraviolet radiation, that is less than about 1×10^{-8} metres. Below about 1×10^{-11} metres they are often called gamma radiation or bremsstrahlung **1b** (*as modifier*): *X-ray astronomy* **2** a picture produced by exposing photographic film to X-rays: used in medicine as a diagnostic aid as parts of the body, such as bones, absorb X-rays and so appear as opaque areas on the picture ▷ *vb* (*tr*) **3** to photograph (part of the body, etc) using X-rays **4** to treat or examine by means of X-rays [c19 partial translation of G *X-Strahlen* (from *Strahl* ray), coined by W. K. ROENTGEN in 1895]

X-ray astronomy *n* the branch of astronomy concerned with the detection and measurement of X-rays emitted by certain celestial bodies, such as X-ray stars

X-ray binary *n* a binary star that is an intense source of X-rays and is composed of a normal star in close orbit with a white dwarf, neutron star, or black hole

X-ray crystallography *n* the study and practice of determining the structure of a crystal by passing a beam of X-rays through it and observing and analysing the diffraction pattern produced

X-ray tube *n* an evacuated tube containing a metal target onto which is directed a beam of electrons at high energy for the generation of X-rays

Xuan-tong ('ʃwɑːn'tʊŋ) *n* the Pinyin transliteration of the title as emperor of China of (Henry) **Pu-yi**

Xuthus ('zuːθəs) *n Greek myth* a son of Hellen, regarded as an ancestor of the Ionian Greeks through his son Ion

Xuzhou ('ʃuː'dʒəʊ), **Hsü-chou**, *or* **Süchow** *n* a city in N central China, in NW Jiangsu province: scene of a decisive battle (1949) in which the Communists defeated the Nationalists. Pop: 1 044 729 (1999 est)

xylem ('zaɪləm, -lɛm) *n* a plant tissue that conducts water and mineral salts from the roots to all other parts, provides mechanical support, and forms the wood of trees and shrubs [c19 from Gk *xulon* wood]

xylene ('zaɪliːn) *n* an aromatic hydrocarbon existing in three isomeric forms, all three being colourless flammable volatile liquids used as solvents and in the manufacture of synthetic resins, dyes, and insecticides. Formula: $(CH_3)_2C_6H_4$. Systematic name: **dimethyl benzene**

xylo- *or before a vowel* **xyl-** *combining form* **1** indicating wood: *xylophone* **2** indicating xylene: *xylidine* [from Gk *xulon* wood]

xylocarp ('zaɪləˌkɑːp) *n bot* a fruit, such as a coconut, having a hard woody pericarp > ˌ**xylo'carpous** *adj*

xylograph ('zaɪləˌgrɑːf) *n* **1** an engraving in wood **2** a print taken from a wood block ▷ *vb* **3** (*tr*) to print (a design, illustration, etc) from a wood engraving > **xylography** (zaɪ'lɒgrəfɪ) *n*

Xylonite ('zaɪlənaɪt) *n trademark* a thermoplastic of the cellulose nitrate type

xylophagous (zaɪ'lɒfəgəs) *adj* (of certain insects, crustaceans, etc) feeding on or living within wood

xylophone ('zaɪləˌfəʊn) *n music* a percussion instrument consisting of a set of wooden bars of graduated length. It is played with hard-headed hammers > **xylophonic** (ˌzaɪlə'fɒnɪk) *adj* > **xylophonist** (zaɪ'lɒfənɪst) *n*

xylose ('zaɪləʊz, -ləʊs) *n* a white crystalline sugar found in wood and straw. It is extracted by hydrolysis with acids and used in dyeing, tanning, and in foods for diabetics

xyster ('zɪstə) *n* a surgical instrument for scraping bone; surgical rasp or file [c17 via NL from Gk: tool for scraping, from *xuein* to scrape]

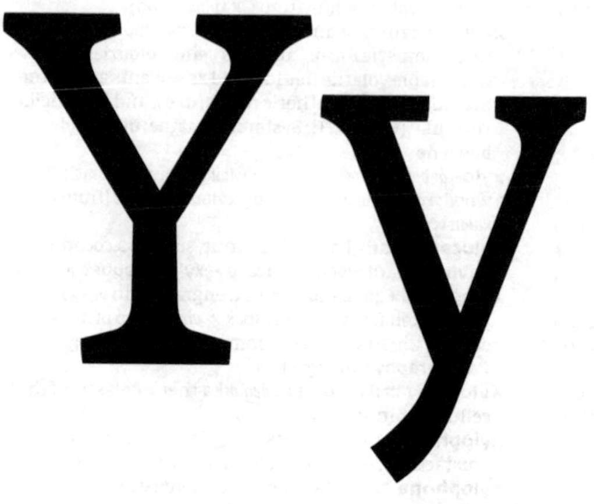

y *or* **Y** (waɪ) *n, pl* **y's, Y's,** *or* **Ys** **1** the 25th letter of the English alphabet **2** a speech sound represented by this letter, usually a semivowel, as in *yawn*, or a vowel, as in *symbol* or *shy* **3** something shaped like a Y

y *maths symbol for:* **1** the *y*-axis or a coordinate measured along the *y*-axis in a Cartesian coordinate system **2** an algebraic variable

Y *symbol for:* **1** any unknown or variable factor, number, or thing **2** *chem* yttrium

y. *abbrev for* year

-y[1] *or* **-ey** *suffix forming adjectives* **1** *(from nouns)* characterized by; consisting of; filled with; resembling: *sunny; sandy; smoky; classy* **2** *(from verbs)* tending to; acting or existing as specified: *leaky; shiny* [from OE *-ig, -ǣg*]

-y[2], **-ie,** *or* **-ey** *suffix of nouns inf* **1** denoting smallness and expressing affection and familiarity: *a doggy; Jamie* **2** a person or thing concerned with or characterized by being: *a groupie; a goalie; a fatty* [C14 from Scot *-ie, -y,* familiar suffix orig. in names]

-y[3] *suffix forming nouns* **1** *(from verbs)* indicating the act of doing what is indicated by the verbal element: *inquiry* **2** (esp with combining forms of Greek, Latin, or French origin) indicating state, condition, or quality: *geography; jealousy* [from OF *-ie,* from L *-ia*]

yabby *or* **yabbie** (ˈjæbɪ) *Austral* ▷ *n, pl* **yabbies** **1** a small edible freshwater crayfish **2** a saltwater prawn used as bait; nipper ▷ *vb* **yabbies, yabbying, yabbied** **3** *(intr)* to fish for yabbies [from Abor.]

Yablonovy Mountains (*Russian* ˈjablənəvij) *pl n* a mountain range in Siberia. Highest peak: 1680 m (5512 ft). Also called: **Yablonoi Mountains** (ˈjɑːbləˌnɔɪ)

yacca *or* **yacka** (ˈjækə) *n Austral* another word for **black boy** [from a native Australian language]

yacht (jɒt) *n* **1** a vessel propelled by sail or power, used esp for pleasure cruising, racing, etc ▷ *vb* **2** *(intr)* to sail or cruise in a yacht [C16 from obs. Du. *jaghte,* short for *jahtschip,* from *jagen* to chase + *schip* ship] > ˈ**yachting** *n, adj*

yachtie (ˈjɒtɪ) *n Austral & NZ inf* a yachtsman; sailing enthusiast

yachtsman (ˈjɒtsmən) *or (fem)* **yachtswoman** *n, pl* **yachtsmen** *or* **yachtswomen** a person who sails a yacht or yachts > ˈ**yachtsmanship** *n*

yack (jæk) *n, vb* a variant spelling of **yak**[2]

yackety-yak (ˈjækɪtɪˈjæk) *n sl* noisy, continuous, and trivial talk or conversation [imit.]

yaffle (ˈjæfᵊl) *n* another name for **green woodpecker** (see **woodpecker**) [C18 imit. of its cry]

Yafo (ˈjɑːfɔː) *n* transliteration of the Hebrew name for **Jaffa** (sense 1)

Yagi aerial (ˈjɑːgɪ, ˈjægɪ) *n* a directional aerial, used esp in television and radio astronomy, consisting of three or more elements lying parallel to each other, the principal direction of radiation being along the line of the centres [C20 after Hidetsugu *Yagi* (1886–1976), Japanese engineer]

yah (jɑː, jɛə) *sentence substitute* **1** an informal word for **yes** ▷ *interj* **2** an exclamation of derision or disgust

Yahata (ˈjɑːhɑːˌtɑː) *n* a variant of **Yawata**

yahoo (jəˈhuː) *n, pl* **yahoos** a crude, brutish, or obscenely coarse person [C18 from a race of brutish creatures resembling men in Jonathan Swift's *Gulliver's Travels* (1726)] > **yaˈhooˌism** *n*

Yahweh (ˈjɑːweɪ) *or* **Yahveh** (ˈjɑːveɪ) *n Old Testament* a vocalization of the Tetragrammaton [from Heb., from YHVH, with conjectural vowels; see also JEHOVAH]

Yahwism (ˈjɑːwɪzəm) *or* **Yahvism** (ˈjɑːvɪzəm) *n* the use of the name Yahweh, esp in parts of the Old Testament, as the personal name of God

Yahwist (ˈjɑːwɪst) *or* **Yahvist** (ˈjɑːvɪst) *n Bible* **the** the conjectured author or authors of the earliest sources of the Pentateuch in which God is called *Yahweh* throughout > **Yah'wistic** *or* **Yah'vistic** *adj*

yak[1] (jæk) *n* an ox of Tibet having long shaggy hair [c19 from Tibetan *gyag*]

yak[2] (jæk) *sl* ▹ *n* **1** noisy, continuous, and trivial talk ▹ *vb* **yaks, yakking, yakked 2** (*intr*) to chatter or talk in this way [c20 imit.]

yakka, yakker, *or* **yacker** ('jækə) *n Austral & NZ inf* work [c19 from Abor.]

Yakut Republic *n* the former name of the **Sakha Republic**

Yakutsk (*Russian* jɪ'kutsk) *n* a port in E Russia, capital of the Sakha Republic, on the Lena River. Pop: 195 500 (1999 est)

Yale lock (jeɪl) *n trademark* a type of cylinder lock using a flat serrated key [c19 after L. *Yale* (1821–68), US inventor]

Yalta (*Russian* 'jaltə) *n* a port and resort in the S Ukraine, in the Crimea on the Black Sea: scene of a conference (1945) between Churchill, Roosevelt, and Stalin, who met to plan the final defeat and occupation of Nazi Germany. Pop: 89 000 (latest est)

Yalu ('jɑː,luː) *n* a river in E Asia, rising in N North Korea and flowing southwest to Korea Bay, forming a large part of the border between North Korea and NE China. Length: 806 km (501 miles)

yam (jæm) *n* **1** any of various twining plants of tropical and subtropical regions, cultivated for their edible tubers **2** the starchy tuber of any of these plants, eaten as a vegetable **3** *Southern US* the sweet potato [c17 from Port. *inhame*, ult. of W African origin]

yammer ('jæmə) *inf* ▹ *vb* **1** to utter or whine in a complaining manner **2** to make (a complaint) loudly or persistently ▹ *n* **3** a yammering sound **4** nonsense; jabber [OE *geōmrian* to grumble] > **'yammerer** *n*

Yamoussoukro (,jæmʊ'suːkrəʊ) *n* the capital of the Côte d'Ivoire, situated in the S centre of the country. It replaced Abidjan as capital in 1983. Pop: 110 000 (1995 est)

▹ http://yamoussoukro.org

Yanan ('jæn'æn) *or* **Yenan** *n* a city in NE China, in N Shaanxi province: political and military capital of the Chinese Communists (1935–49). Pop: 133 226 (1999 est). Also called: **Fushih**

Yang (jæŋ) *n* See **Yin and Yang**

Yangon (jæŋ'gɒn) *n* the capital and chief port of Myanmar (formerly Burma): an industrial city and transport centre; dominated by the gold-covered Shwe Dagon pagoda, 112 m (368 ft) high. Pop (urban area): 3 361 700 (1993 est). Former name (until 1989): **Rangoon**

▹ www.yangoncity.com.mm

▹ www.myanmar-tourism.com/yangon.htm

Yangtze ('jæŋtsɪ, 'jæŋktsɪ) *n* the longest river in China, rising in SE Qinghai province and flowing east to the East China Sea near Shanghai: a major commercial waterway in one of the most densely populated areas of the world. Work on the **Yangtze dam** near Yichang, the world's biggest hydroelectric and flood-control project, began in 1994. Length: 5528 km (3434 miles). Also called: **Yangtze Jiang, Chang Jiang, Chang**

Yanina ('jɑːnɪnə) *n* a variant spelling of **Ioánnina**

yank (jæŋk) *vb* **1** to pull with a sharp movement; tug ▹ *n* **2** a jerk [c19 from ?]

Yank (jæŋk) *n* **1** a slang word for an **American 2** *US inf* short for **Yankee**

Yankee ('jæŋkɪ) *or* (*inf*) **Yank** *n* **1** *often disparaging* a native or inhabitant of the US; American **2** a native or inhabitant of New England **3** a native or inhabitant of the Northern US, esp a Northern soldier in the Civil War **4** *finance* a bond issued in the US by a foreign borrower ▹ *adj* **5** of, relating to, or characteristic of Yankees [c18 ?from Du. *Jan Kees* John Cheese, derisive nickname of Du. settlers for English colonists in Connecticut]

Yankee Doodle *n* **1** an American song, popularly regarded as a characteristically national melody **2** another name for **Yankee**

Yantai ('jæn'taɪ), **Yentai**, *or* **Yen-t'ai** *n* a port in E China, in NE Shandong. Pop: 452 127 (1990 est). Also called: **Chefoo**

Yaoundé *or* **Yaunde** (*French* jaunde) *n* the capital of Cameroon, in the southwest: University of Cameroon (1962). Pop: 800 000 (1992 est)

yap (jæp) *vb* **yaps, yapping, yapped** (*intr*) **1** (of a dog) to bark in quick sharp bursts; yelp **2** *inf* to talk at length in an annoying or stupid way; jabber ▹ *n* **3** a high-pitched or sharp bark; yelp **4** *sl* annoying or stupid speech; jabber **5** *sl, chiefly US* a derogatory word for **mouth** [c17 imit.] > **'yapper** *n* > **'yappy** *adj*

Yap (jɑːp, jæp) *n* a group of four main islands in the W Pacific, in the W Caroline Islands: administratively a district of the US Trust Territory of the Pacific Islands from 1947; became self-governing in 1979 as part of the Federated States of Micronesia; important Japanese naval base in World War II. Pop: 12 055 (1999 est). Area: 101 sq km (39 sq miles)

yapok (jə'pɒk) *n* an amphibious nocturnal opossum of Central and South America. Also called: **water opossum** [c19 after *Oyapok*, a river flowing between French Guiana & Brazil]

Yapurá (japu'ra) *n* the Spanish name for **Japurá**

Yaqui (*Spanish* 'jaki) *n* a river in NW Mexico, rising near the border with the US and flowing south to the Gulf of California. Length: about 676 km (420 miles)

yarborough ('jɑːbərə, -brə) *n bridge, whist* a hand of 13 cards in which no card is higher than nine [c19 supposedly after the second Earl of *Yarborough* (1809–62), said to have bet a thousand to one against its occurrence]

yard[1] (jɑːd) *n* **1** a unit of length equal to 3 feet and defined in 1963 as exactly 0.9144 metre **2** a cylindrical wooden or hollow metal spar, slung from a mast of a vessel, and used for suspending a sail [OE *gierd* rod, twig]

yard[2] (jɑːd) *n* **1** a piece of enclosed ground, often adjoining or surrounded by a building or buildings **2a** an enclosed or open area used for some commercial activity, for storage, etc: *a builder's yard* **2b** (*in combination*): *a shipyard* **3** a US and Canad word for **garden** (sense 1) **4** a dialect word for **home 5** an area having a network of railway tracks and sidings, used for storing rolling stock, making up trains, etc **6** *US & Canad* the winter pasture of deer, moose, and similar animals **7** NZ short for **stockyard** [OE *geard*]

Yard (jɑːd) *n* **the** *Brit inf* short for **Scotland Yard**

yardage[1] ('jɑːdɪdʒ) *n* a length measured in yards

yardage[2] ('jɑːdɪdʒ) *n* **1** the use of a railway yard for cattle **2** the charge for this

yardarm ('jɑːd,ɑːm) *n naut* the two tapering outer ends of a ship's yard

yard grass *n* an Old World perennial grass with prostrate leaves, growing as a troublesome weed on open ground, yards, etc

Yardie ('jɑːdɪ) *n* a member of a Black criminal syndicate originally based in Jamaica [c20 from YARD[2] (sense 4)]

yard of ale *n* **1** the beer or ale contained in a narrow horn-shaped drinking glass **2** such a drinking glass itself

yardstick ('jɑːd,stɪk) *n* **1** a measure or standard used for comparison **2** a graduated stick, one yard long, used for measurement

Yarkand (,jɑː'kænd) *n* another name for **Shache**

Yarmouth ('jɑːməθ) *n* short for **Great Yarmouth**

yarmulke ('jɑːməlkə) *n Judaism* a skullcap worn by Orthodox male Jews at all times and by others during prayer [from Yiddish, from Polish *yarmułka* cap, prob. from Turkish *yağmurluk* raincoat, from *yağmur* rain]

yarn (jɑːn) *n* **1** a continuous twisted strand of natural or

Yy

synthetic fibres, used in weaving, knitting, etc **2** *inf* a long and often involved story, usually of incredible or fantastic events **3 spin a yarn** *inf* **3a** to tell such a story **3b** to make up a series of excuses ▷ *vb* **4** *(intr)* to tell such a story or stories [OE *gearn*]

yarn-dyed *adj* (of fabric) dyed while still in yarn form, before being woven

Yaroslavl (*Russian* jıraˈslavlj) *n* a city in W Russia, on the River Volga: a major trading centre since early times and one of the first industrial centres in Russia; textile industries were established in the 18th century. Pop: 620 600 (1995 est)

yarran (ˈjærən) *n* a small hardy tree of inland Australia: useful as fodder and for firewood [from Abor.]

Yarra River (ˈjærə) *n* a river in SE Australia, rising in the Great Dividing Range and flowing west and southwest through Melbourne to Port Phillip Bay. Length: 250 km (155 miles)

yarrow (ˈjærəʊ) *n* any of several plants of the composite family of Eurasia, having finely dissected leaves and flat clusters of white flower heads. Also called: **milfoil** [OE *gearwe*]

yashmak *or* **yashmac** (ˈjæʃmæk) *n* the face veil worn by Muslim women when in public [c19 from Ar.]

yataghan (ˈjætəgən) *n* a Turkish sword with a curved blade [c19 from Turkish *yatağ an*]

Yathrib (ˈjæθrıb) *n* the ancient Arabic name for **Medina**

Yaunde (*French* jaunde) *n* a variant spelling of **Yaoundé**

yaup (jɔːp) *vb, n* a variant spelling of **yawp** > ˈ**yauper** *n*

Yavarí (jaβaˈri) *n* the Spanish name for **Javari**

yaw (jɔː) *vb* **1** *(intr)* (of an aircraft, etc) to turn about its vertical axis **2** *(intr)* (of a ship, etc) to deviate temporarily from a straight course **3** *(tr)* to cause (an aircraft, ship, etc) to yaw ▷ *n* **4** the movement of an aircraft, etc, about its vertical axis **5** the deviation of a vessel from a straight course [c16 from ?]

Yawata (ˈjɑːwɑːˌtɑː) *or* **Yahata** *n* a former city in Japan, on N Kyushu: merged with Moji, Kokura, Tobata, and Wakamatsu in 1963 to form **Kitakyushu**

yawl (jɔːl) *n* **1** a two-masted sailing vessel with a small mizzenmast aft of the rudderpost **2** a ship's small boat, usually rowed by four or six oars [c17 from Du. *jol* or MLow G *jolle*, from ?]

yawn (jɔːn) *vb* **1** *(intr)* to open the mouth wide and take in air deeply, often as in involuntary reaction to sleepiness or boredom **2** *(tr)* to express or utter while yawning **3** *(intr)* to be open wide as if threatening to engulf (someone or something): *the mine shaft yawned below* ▷ *n* **4** the act or an instance of yawning [OE *gionian*] > ˈ**yawner** *n* > ˈ**yawning** *adj* > ˈ**yawningly** *adv*

yawp (jɔːp) *dialect US & Canad inf* ▷ *vb (intr)* **1** to yawn, esp audibly **2** to shout, cry, or talk noisily **3** to bark or yowl ▷ *n* **4** a shout, bark, or cry **5** a noisy, foolish, or raucous utterance [c15 *yolpen*, prob. imit.] > ˈ**yawper** *n*

yaws (jɔːz) *n (usually functioning as sing)* an infectious disease of tropical climates characterized by red skin eruptions [c17 of Carib origin]

y-axis *n* a reference axis of a graph or two- or three-dimensional Cartesian coordinate system along which the *y*-coordinate is measured

Yazd (jɑːzd) *or* **Yezd** *n* a city in central Iran: a major centre of silk weaving. Pop: 326 776 (1996)

Yb *the chemical symbol for* ytterbium

YC (in Britain) *abbrev for* Young Conservative

Y-chromosome *n* the sex chromosome that occurs as one of a pair with the X-chromosome in the diploid cells of the males of many animals, including humans ▷ Cf **X-chromosome**

yclept (ıˈklɛpt) *adj obs* having the name of; called [OE *gecleopod*, p.p. of *cleopian* to call]

Y connection *n electrical engineering* a three-phase star connection

yd *or* **yd.** *abbrev for* yard (measure)

YDT (in Canada) *abbrev for* Yukon Daylight Time

ye[1] (jiː, *unstressed* jı) *pron* **1** *arch or dialect* refers to more than one person including the person addressed **2** Also: **ee** (iː) *dialect* refers to one person addressed: *I tell ye* [OE *gē*]

ye[2] (ðiː, *spelling pron* jiː) *determiner* a form of **the**[1], used as a supposed archaism: *ye olde oake* [from a misinterpretation of *the* as written in some ME texts. The runic letter thorn (Þ, representing *th*) was incorrectly transcribed as *y* because of a resemblance in their shapes]

yea (jeı) *sentence substitute* **1** a less common word for **aye** (yes) ▷ *adv* **2** *(sentence modifier) arch or literary* indeed; truly: *yea, though they spurn me, I shall prevail* [OE *gēa*]

yeah (jɛə) *sentence substitute* an informal word for **yes**

yean (jiːn) *vb* (of a sheep or goat) to give birth to (offspring) [OE *geēanian*]

yeanling (ˈjiːnlıŋ) *n* the young of a goat or sheep

year (jıə) *n* **1** the period of time, the **calendar year,** containing 365 days or in a **leap year** 366 days. It is divided into 12 calendar months, and reckoned from January 1 to December 31 **2** a period of twelve months from any specified date **3** a specific period of time, usually occupying a definite part or parts of a twelve-month period, used for some particular activity: *a school year* **4** Also called: **astronomical year, tropical year** the period of time, the **solar year,** during which the earth makes one revolution around the sun, measured between two successive vernal equinoxes: equal to 365.242 19 days **5** the period of time, the **sidereal year,** during which the earth makes one revolution around the sun, measured between two successive conjunctions of a particular star: equal to 365.256 36 days **6** the period of time, the **lunar year,** containing 12 lunar months and equal to 354.3671 days **7** the period of time taken by a planet to complete one revolution around the sun **8** *(pl)* age, esp old age: *a man of his years should be more careful* **9** *(pl)* time: *in years to come* **10** a group of pupils or students, who are taught or study together **11 the year dot** *inf* as long ago as can be remembered **12 year in, year out** regularly or monotonously, over a long period ▷ Related adj: **annual** [OE *gear*]

> **USAGE** In writing spans of years, it is important to choose a style that avoids ambiguity. The practice adopted in this dictionary is, in four-figure dates, to specify the last two digits of the second date if it falls within the same century as the first: *1801–08*; *1850–51*; *1899–1901*. In writing three-figure BC dates, it is advisable to give both dates in full: *159–156* BC, not *159–56* BC unless of course the span referred to consists of 103 years rather than three years. It is also advisable to specify BC or AD in years under 1000 unless the context makes this self-evident

yearbook (ˈjıəˌbʊk) *n* an almanac or other reference book published annually and containing details of events of the previous year

yearling (ˈjıəlıŋ) *n* **1** the young of any of various animals, including the antelope and buffalo, between one and two years of age **2** a thoroughbred racehorse counted as being one year old until the second January 1 following its birth **3a** a bond intended to mature after one year **3b** *(as modifier)*: *yearling bonds* ▷ *adj* **4** being a year old

yearlong (ˈjıəˈlɒŋ) *adj* throughout a whole year

yearly (ˈjıəlı) *adj* **1** occurring, done, appearing, etc, once a year or every year; annual **2** lasting or valid for a year; annual: *a yearly fee* ▷ *adv* **3** once a year; annually

yearn (jɜːn) *vb (intr)* **1** (usually foll by *for* or *after* or an infinitive) to have an intense desire or longing (for) **2** to feel tenderness or affection [OE *giernan*] > ˈ**yearner** *n* > ˈ**yearning** *n, adj* > ˈ**yearningly** *adv*

year of grace *n* any year of the Christian era, as from the presumed date of Christ's birth

year-round *adj* open, in use, operating, etc, throughout the year

yeast (jiːst) *n* **1** any of various single-celled fungi which reproduce by budding and are able to ferment sugars: a rich source of vitamins of the B complex **2** any of various similar and related fungi, esp of the genus *Candida*, which can cause thrush in parts of the body infected with it **3** a commercial preparation containing yeast cells and inert material such as meal, used in raising dough for bread or for fermenting beer, whisky, etc **4** a preparation containing yeast cells, used to treat diseases caused by vitamin B deficiency **5** froth or foam, esp on beer ▷ *vb* **6** (*intr*) to froth or foam [OE *giest*] > ˈ**yeastless** *adj* > ˈ**yeast,like** *adj*

yeasty (ˈjiːstɪ) *adj* **yeastier, yeastiest 1** of, resembling, or containing yeast **2** fermenting or causing fermentation **3** tasting of or like yeast **4** insubstantial or frivolous **5** restless, agitated, or unsettled **6** covered with or containing froth or foam > ˈ**yeastily** *adv* > ˈ**yeastiness** *n*

yebo (ˈjɛbəʊ) *sentence substitute S African inf* an expression of affirmation [Zulu *yebo* yes, I agree]

yegg (jɛg) *n sl, chiefly US* a burglar or safe-breaker [c20 ?from the surname of a burglar]

Yeisk *or* **Eisk** (*Russian* jejsk) *n* a port and resort in SW Russia, on the Sea of Azov. Pop: 86 300 (1991 est)

Yekaterinburg *or* **Ekaterinburg** (*Russian* jɪkətɪrimˈburk) *n* a city in NW Russia, in the Ural Mountains: scene of the execution (1918) of Nicholas II and his family; university (1920); one of the largest centres of heavy engineering in Russia. Pop: 1 272 900 (1999 est). Former name (1924–91): **Sverdlovsk**

Yekaterinodar *or* **Ekaterinodar** (*Russian* jɪkətɪrinaˈdar) *n* the former name (until 1920) of **Krasnodar**

Yekaterinoslav *or* **Ekaterinoslav** (*Russian* jɪkətɪrinaˈslaf) *n* the former name (1787–96, 1802–1926) of **Dnepropetrovsk**

Yelisavetgrad *or* **Elisavetgrad** (*Russian* jɪlizaˈvjɛtgrət) *n* the former name (until 1924) of **Kirovograd**

Yelisavetpol *or* **Elisavetpol** (*Russian* jɪlizaˈvjɛtpəlj) *n* the former name (until 1920) of **Kirovabad**

yell (jɛl) *vb* **1** to shout, scream, cheer, or utter in a loud or piercing way ▷ *n* **2** a loud piercing inarticulate cry, as of pain, anger, or fear **3** *US & Canad* a rhythmic cry, used in cheering in unison [OE *giellan*] > ˈ**yeller** *n*

yellow (ˈjɛləʊ) *n* **1** any of a group of colours such as that of a lemon or of gold, which vary in saturation but have the same hue. Yellow is the complementary colour of blue. Related adj: **xanthous 2** a pigment or dye of or producing these colours **3** yellow cloth or clothing: *dressed in yellow* **4** the yolk of an egg **5** a yellow ball in snooker, etc ▷ *adj* **6** of the colour yellow **7** yellowish in colour or having parts or marks that are yellowish **8** having a yellowish skin; Mongoloid **9** *inf* cowardly or afraid **10** offensively sensational, as a cheap newspaper (esp in **yellow press**) ▷ *vb* **11** to make or become yellow ▷ See also **yellows** [OE *geolu*] > ˈ**yellowish** *adj* > ˈ**yellowly** *adv* > ˈ**yellowness** *n* > ˈ**yellowy** *adj*

yellow-belly *n pl* **-lies 1** a slang word for **coward 2** *Austral* another name for **callop** > ˈ**yellow-,bellied** *adj*

yellow bile *n arch* one of the four bodily humours, choler

yellow card *n soccer* a card of a yellow colour displayed by a referee to indicate that a player has been officially cautioned for some offence

yellow fever *n* an acute infectious disease of tropical and subtropical climates, characterized by fever, haemorrhages, vomiting, and jaundice: caused by a virus transmitted by the bite of a certain mosquito. Also called: **yellow jack**

yellowhammer (ˈjɛləʊ,hæmə) *n* a European bunting, having a yellowish head and body and brown-streaked wings and tail [c16 from ?]

yellow jack *n* **1** *pathol* another name for **yellow fever 2** another name for **quarantine flag 3** any of certain large yellowish food fishes of warm and tropical Atlantic waters

yellow jacket *n US & Canad* any of several wasps with yellow markings on the body

yellow jersey *n* (in the Tour de France) a yellow jersey awarded as a trophy to the cyclist with the fastest time in each stage of the race

yellow journalism *n* the type of journalism that relies on sensationalism to attract readers [c19 ? shortened from *Yellow Kid journalism*, referring to the *Yellow Kid*, a cartoon (1895) in the *New York World*, a newspaper having a reputation for sensationalism]

Yellowknife (ˈjɛləʊ,naɪf) *n* a city in N Canada, capital of the Northwest Territories on Great Slave Lake. Pop: 15 179 (1991)

yellow line *n Brit* a yellow line painted along the edge of a road indicating vehicle waiting restrictions

yellow metal *n* **1** a type of brass having about 60 per cent copper and 40 per cent zinc **2** another name for **gold**

Yellow Pages *pl n trademark* a classified telephone directory or section of one, often on yellow paper, that lists subscribers by the business or service they provide

yellow peril *n offens* the power or alleged power of Asiatic peoples, esp the Chinese, to threaten or destroy White or Western civilization

Yellow River *n* the second longest river in China, rising in SE Qinghai and flowing east, south, and east again to the Gulf of Bohai south of Tianjin; it has changed its course several times in recorded history. Length: about 4350 km (2700 miles). Chinese name: **Hwang Ho**

yellows (ˈjɛləʊz) *n* (*functioning as sing*) **1** any of various fungal or viral diseases of plants, characterized by yellowish discoloration and stunting **2** *vet science* another name for **jaundice**

Yellow Sea *n* a shallow arm of the Pacific between Korea and NE China. Area: about 466 200 sq km (180 000 sq miles). Chinese name: **Hwang Hai**

yellow spot *n anat* another name for **macula lutea**

Yellowstone (ˈjɛləʊ,stəʊn) *n* a river rising in N Wyoming and flowing north through Yellowstone National Park, then east to the Missouri. Length: 1080 km (671 miles)

Yellowstone Falls *pl n* a waterfall in NW Wyoming, in Yellowstone National Park on the Yellowstone River

Yellowstone National Park *n* a national park in the NW central US, mostly in NW Wyoming: the oldest and largest national park in the US, containing unusual geological formations and geysers. Area: 8956 sq km (3458 sq miles)

yellow streak *n inf* a cowardly or weak trait

yellowtail kingfish *n* a large carangid game fish, *Seriola grandis*, of S Australian waters. Also called: **yellowtail**

yellow underwing *n* any of several species of noctuid moths, the hind wings of which are yellow with a black bar

yellowwood (ˈjɛləʊ,wʊd) *n* **1** any of several leguminous trees of the southeastern US, having clusters of white flowers and yellow wood yielding a yellow dye **2** Also called: **West Indian satinwood** a rutaceous tree of the West Indies, with smooth hard wood **3** any of several other trees with yellow wood, esp a conifer of southern Africa the wood of which is used for furniture and building **4** the wood of any of these trees

yelp (jɛlp) *vb* (*intr*) **1** (esp of a dog) to utter a sharp or high-pitched cry or bark, often indicating pain ▷ *n* **2** a sharp or high-pitched cry or bark [OE *gielpan* to boast] > ˈ**yelper** *n*

Yemen (ˈjɛmən) *n* a republic in SW Arabia, on the Red Sea and the Gulf of Aden: formed in 1990 from the union of North Yemen and South Yemen: consists of arid coastal lowlands, rising to fertile upland valleys and mountains in the west and to the Hadhramaut plateau in the SE: the north and east contains part of the Great Sandy Desert. Official language: Arabic. Official religion: Muslim. Currency: riyal. Capital: San'a. Pop: 18 078 000 (2001 est). Area (including territory claimed by Yemen along the undemarcated eastern border with Saudi Arabia): 472 099 sq km (182 278 sq miles). Official name: **Yemen Republic**. See also **North Yemen, South Yemen** > '**Yemeni** *adj, n*

▹ www.yementourism.com

▹ www.al-bab.com/yemen

yen[1] (jɛn) *n, pl* **yen** the standard monetary unit of Japan [c19 from Japanese *en*, from Chinese *yüan* dollar]

yen[2] (jɛn) *inf* ▹ *n* **1** a longing or desire ▹ *vb* **yens, yenning, yenned 2** (*intr*) to yearn [?from Chinese *yǎn* a craving]

Yenan ('jɛn'æn) *n* a variant transliteration of the Chinese name for **Yanan**

Yenisei *or* **Yenisey** (ˌjɛnɪ'seɪ; *Russian* jɪni'sjej) *n* a river in central Russia, in central Siberia, formed by the confluence of two headstreams in the Tuva Republic: flows west and north to the Arctic Ocean; the largest river in volume in Russia. Length: 4129 km (2566 miles)

Yentai *or* **Yen-t'ai** ('jɛn'taɪ) *n* a variant transliteration of the Chinese name for **Yantai**

yeoman ('jəʊmən) *n, pl* **yeomen 1** *history* **1a** a member of a class of small freeholders who cultivated their own land **1b** an attendant or lesser official in a royal or noble household **2** (in Britain) another name for **yeoman of the guard 3** (*modifier*) characteristic of or relating to a yeoman **4** a petty officer or noncommissioned officer in the Royal Navy or Marines in charge of signals [c15 ?from *yongman* young man]

yeomanly ('jəʊmənlɪ) *adj* **1** of, relating to, or like a yeoman **2** having the virtues attributed to yeomen, such as staunchness, loyalty, and courage ▹ *adv* **3** in a yeomanly manner

yeoman of the guard *n* a member of the ceremonial bodyguard (**Yeomen of the Guard**) of the British monarch

yeomanry ('jəʊmənrɪ) *n* **1** yeomen collectively **2** (in Britain) a volunteer cavalry force, organized in 1761 for home defence: merged into the Territorial Army in 1907

yep (jɛp) *sentence substitute* an informal word for **yes**

yerba *or* **yerba maté** ('jɜːbə) *n* another name for **maté** [from Sp. *yerba maté* herb maté]

Yerevan (*Russian* jɪrɪ'van) *n* the capital of Armenia: founded in the 8th century BC; an industrial city and a main focus of trade routes since ancient times; university. Pop: 1 248 700 (1995 est). Also called: **Erevan** *or* **Erivan**

Yerwa-Maiduguri ('jɜːwəˌmaɪdʊ'guːrɪ) *n* another name for **Maiduguri**

yes (jɛs) *sentence substitute* **1** used to express affirmation, consent, agreement, or approval or to answer when one is addressed **2** used to signal someone to speak or keep speaking, enter a room, or do something ▹ *n* **3** an answer or vote of *yes* **4** (*often pl*) a person who votes in the affirmative [OE *gēse*, from *iā sīe* may it be]

yeshiva (jə'ʃiːvə; *Hebrew* jə'ʃiːva) *n, pl* **yeshivahs** *or* **yeshivoth** (*Hebrew* -vɔt) **1** a traditional Jewish school devoted chiefly to the study of rabbinic literature and the Talmud **2** a school run by Orthodox Jews for children of primary school age, providing both religious and secular instruction [from Heb. *yĕshībhāh* a seat, hence, an academy]

Yeşil Irmak (jɛ'ʃiːl ɪə'mɑːk) *n* a river in N Turkey, flowing northwest to the Black Sea. Length: 418 km (260 miles). Ancient name: **Iris**

Yeşilköy (jɛ'ʃilˌkœi) *n* the Turkish name for **San Stefano**

yes man *n* a servile, submissive, or acquiescent subordinate, assistant, or associate

yester ('jɛstə) *adj arch* of or relating to yesterday: *yester sun* [OE *geostror*]

yester- *prefix* indicating a period of time before the present one: *yesteryear* [OE *geostran*]

yesterday ('jɛstədɪ, -ˌdeɪ) *n* **1** the day immediately preceding today **2** (*often pl*) the recent past ▹ *adv* **3** on or during the day before today **4** in the recent past

yesteryear ('jɛstəˌjɪə) *formal or literary* ▹ *n* **1** last year or the past in general ▹ *adv* **2** during last year or the past in general

yestreen (jɛ'striːn) *adv Scot* yesterday evening [c14 from YEST(E)R- + E(V)EN[2]]

yet (jɛt) *sentence connector* **1** nevertheless; still; in spite of that: *I want to and yet I haven't the courage* ▹ *adv* **2** (*usually used with a negative or interrogative*) so far; up until then or now: *they're not home yet; is it teatime yet?* **3** (often preceded by *just; usually used with a negative*) now (as contrasted with later): *we can't stop yet* **4** (*often used with a comparative*) even; still: *yet more old potatoes for sale* **5** eventually in spite of everything: *we'll convince him yet* **6 as yet** so far; up until then or now [OE *gēta*]

yeti ('jɛtɪ) *n* another term for **abominable snowman** [c20 from Tibetan]

yettie ('jɛtɪ) *n acronym for* young, entrepreneurial, and technology-based (person)

yew (juː) *n* **1** any coniferous tree of the Old World and North America having flattened needle-like leaves, fine-grained elastic wood, and solitary seeds with a red waxy aril resembling berries **2** the wood of any of these trees, used to make bows for archery **3** *archery* a bow made of yew [OE *īw*]

Yezd (jɛzd) *n* a variant of **Yazd**

Y-fronts *pl n trademark* boys' or men's underpants having a front opening within an inverted Y shape

Yggdrasil *or* **Ygdrasil** ('ɪgdrəsɪl) *n Norse myth* the ash tree that was thought to bind together earth, heaven, and hell with its roots and branches [ON (prob. meaning: Uggr's horse), from *Uggr* a name of Odin, from *yggr, uggr* frightful + *drasill* horse, from ?]

YHA *abbrev for* Youth Hostels Association

YHVH *or* **YHWH** *Bible* the letters of the **Tetragrammaton**

Yibin ('jiː'bɪn) *or* **I-pin** *n* a port in S central China, in Sichuan province: a commercial centre. Pop: 288 039 (1999 est)

Yichang ('jiː'tʃæŋ), **Ichang**, *or* **I-ch'ang** *n* a port in S central China, in Hubei province on the Yangtze River 1600 km (1000 miles) from the East China Sea: the Yangtze dam, the world's biggest hydroelectric and flood-control project, is being constructed nearby. Pop: 481 277 (1999 est)

yid (jɪd) *n sl* a derogatory word for a **Jew** [c20 prob. from *Yiddish*, from MHG *Jude* JEW]

Yiddish ('jɪdɪʃ) *n* **1** a language spoken as a vernacular by Jews in Europe and elsewhere by Jewish emigrants, usually written in the Hebrew alphabet. It is a dialect of High German with an admixture of words of Hebrew, Romance, and Slavonic origin ▹ *adj* **2** in or relating to this language [c19 from G *jüdisch*, from *Jude* JEW]

Yiddisher ('jɪdɪʃə) *adj* **1** in or relating to Yiddish **2** Jewish ▹ *n* **3** a speaker of Yiddish; Jew

yield (jiːld) *vb* **1** to give forth or supply (a product, result, etc), esp by cultivation, labour, etc; produce or bear **2** (*tr*) to furnish as a return: *the shares yielded three per cent* **3** (*tr; often foll by up*) to surrender or relinquish, esp as a result of force, persuasion, etc **4** (*intr; sometimes foll by to*) to give way, submit, or surrender, as through force or persuasion: *she yielded to his superior knowledge* **5** (*intr; often foll by to*) to agree; comply; assent: *he eventually yielded to their request for money* **6** (*tr*) to grant or allow; concede: *to yield right of way* ▹ *n* **7** the result, product, or amount yielded **8** the profit or return, as from an investment or tax **9** the annual income provided by an investment **10** the energy released by the explosion of a nuclear weapon expressed in terms of the amount of TNT necessary to produce the same energy **11** *chem* the quantity of a specified product obtained in a reaction or series of reactions [OE *gieldan*] > '**yieldable** *adj* > '**yielder** *n*

yielding ('jiːldɪŋ) *adj* **1** compliant, submissive, or flexible **2** pliable or soft: *a yielding material*

yield point *n* the stress at which an elastic material under increasing stress ceases to behave elastically; the elongation becomes greater than the increase in stress

Yin and Yang (jɪn) *n* two complementary principles of Chinese philosophy: Yin is negative, dark, and feminine, Yang is positive, bright, and masculine [from Chinese *yin* dark + *yang* bright]

Yinchuan, Yin-ch'uan, *or* **Yinchwan** ('jɪn'tʃwɑːn) *n* a city in N central China, capital of the Ningxia Hui AR, on the Yellow River. Pop: 469 180 (1999 est)

Yingkou *or* **Yingkow** ('jɪŋ'kaʊ) *n* a port in NE China, in SW Liaoning province: a major shipping centre for Manchuria. Pop: 498 300 (1999 est)

yippee (jɪ'piː) *interj* an exclamation of joy, pleasure, anticipation, etc

yips (jɪps) *pl n* **the** *inf* (in sport) nervous twitching or tension that destroys concentration [c20 from ?]

Y2K ('waɪ'tuː'keɪ) *n inf* another name for the year 2000 AD (esp referring to the millennium bug) [c20 *y(ear)* + 2 + K (in the sense: thousand)]

-yl *suffix forming nouns* (in chemistry) indicating a group or radical: *methyl* [from Gk *hulē* wood]

ylang-ylang ('iːlæŋ'iːlæŋ) *n* **1** an aromatic Asian tree with fragrant greenish-yellow flowers yielding a volatile oil **2** the oil obtained from this tree, used in perfumery [c19 from Tagalog *ilang-ilang*]

ylem ('aɪləm) *n* the original matter from which the basic elements are said to have been formed following the explosion postulated in the big-bang theory of cosmology [ME, from OF *ilem*, from L *hȳlē* stuff, from Gk *hulē* wood]

YMCA *abbrev for* Young Men's Christian Association

Ymir ('iːmɪə) *or* **Ymer** ('iːmə) *n Norse myth* the first being and forefather of the giants. He was slain by Odin and his brothers, who made the earth from his flesh, the water from his blood, and the sky from his skull

-yne *suffix forming nouns* denoting an organic chemical containing a triple bond: *alkyne* [alteration of -INE[2]]

yo (jəʊ) *sentence substitute* an expression used as a greeting, to attract someone's attention, etc [c20 of unknown origin]

yob (jɒb) *or* **yobbo** ('jɒbəʊ) *n, pl* **yobs** *or* **yobbos** *Brit sl* an aggressive and surly youth, esp a teenager [c19 ?from **boy** spelt backwards] > '**yobbery** *n* > '**yobbish** *adj*

yodel ('jəʊdᵊl) *n* **1** an effect produced in singing by an abrupt change of register from the chest voice to falsetto, esp in folk songs of the Swiss Alps ▷ *vb* **yodels, yodelling, yodelled** *or US* **yodels, yodeling, yodeled** **2** to sing (a song) in which a yodel is used [c19 from G *jodeln*, imit.] > '**yodeller** *n*

yoga ('jəʊgə) *n (often cap)* **1** a Hindu system of philosophy aiming at the mystical union of the self with the Supreme Being in a state of complete awareness and tranquillity through certain physical and mental exercises **2** any method by which such awareness and tranquillity are attained, esp a course of related exercises and postures [c19 from Sansk.: a yoking, from *yunakti* he yokes] > **yogic** ('jəʊgɪk) *adj*
▷ www.yoga.com

yogh (jɒg) *n* **1** a character (ȝ) used in Old and Middle English to represent a palatal fricative very close to the semivowel sound of Modern English *y* **2** this same character as used in Middle English for both the voiced and voiceless palatal fricatives; when final or in a closed syllable in medial position the sound approached that of German *ch* in *ich*, as in *knyȝt* (knight) [c14 ?from *yok* yoke, from the letter's shape]

yogi ('jəʊgɪ) *n, pl* **yogis** *or* **yogin** (-gɪn) a person who is a master of yoga

yogurt *or* **yoghurt** ('jəʊgət, jɒg-) *n* a thick custard-like food prepared from milk curdled by bacteria, often sweetened and flavoured with fruit [c19 from Turkish *yoğurt*]

Yogyakarta (ˌjəʊgjɑː'kɑːtɑː, 'jɒg-), **Jogjakarta**, **Jokjakarta**, *or* **Djokjakarta** *n* a city in S Indonesia, in central Java: seat of government of Indonesia (1946–49); university (1949). Pop: 419 500 (1995 est)

yo-heave-ho (ˌjəʊhiːv'həʊ) *interj* a cry formerly used by sailors while pulling or lifting together in rhythm

yohimbine (jəʊ'hɪmbiːn) *n* an alkaloid found in the bark of a West African tree and used in medicine [c19 from Bantu *yohimbé* a tropical African tree + -INE[1]]

yo-ho-ho *interj* **1** an exclamation to call attention **2** another word for **yo-heave-ho**

yoicks (haɪk; *spelling pron* jɔɪks) *interj* a cry used by fox-hunters to urge on the hounds

yoke (jəʊk) *n, pl* **yokes** *or* **yoke** **1** a wooden frame, usually consisting of a bar with an oxbow at either end, for attaching to the necks of a pair of draught animals, esp oxen, so that they can be worked as a team **2** something resembling a yoke in form or function, such as a frame fitting over a person's shoulders for carrying buckets **3** a fitted part of a garment, esp around the neck, shoulders, and chest or around the hips, to which a gathered, pleated, flared, or unfitted part is attached **4** an oppressive force or burden: *under the yoke of a tyrant* **5** a pair of oxen or other draught animals joined by a yoke **6** a part that secures two or more components so that they move together **7** (in the ancient world) a symbolic yoke, consisting of two upright spears with a third lashed across them, under which conquered enemies were compelled to march, esp in Rome **8** a mark, token, or symbol of slavery, subjection, or suffering **9** *now rare* a link, tie, or bond: *the yoke of love* ▷ *vb* **yokes, yoking, yoked** **10** *(tr)* to secure or harness (a draught animal) to (a plough, etc) by means of a yoke **11** to join or be joined by means of a yoke [OE *geoc*]

Yy

yokel ('jəʊkᵊl) *n disparaging* (used chiefly by townspeople) a person who lives in the country, esp one who appears to be simple and old-fashioned [c19 ?from dialect *yokel* green woodpecker]

Yokohama (ˌjəʊkəʊ'hɑːmə) *n* a port in central Japan, on SE Honshu on Tokyo Bay: a major port and the country's second largest city situated in the largest and most populous industrial region of Japan. Pop: 3 307 408 (1995)

Yokosuka (ˌjəʊkəʊ'suːkə) *n* a port in Japan, in SE Honshu: a major naval base with shipbuilding industries. Pop: 432 202 (1995)

yolk (jəʊk) *n* **1** the substance in an animal ovum that nourishes the developing embryo **2** a greasy substance in the fleece of sheep [OE *geoloca*, from *geolu* yellow] > '**yolky** *adj*

yolk sac *n zool* the membranous sac that is attached to the surface of the embryos of birds, reptiles, and some fishes, and contains yolk

Yom Kippur (jɒm 'kɪpə; *Hebrew* jɔm ki'pur) *n* an annual Jewish day of fasting, on which prayers of penitence are recited in the synagogue. Also called: **Day of Atonement** [from Heb., from *yōm* day + *kippūr* atonement]

yomp (jɒmp) *vb (intr)* to walk or trek laboriously, esp over difficult terrain [c20 mil. sl., from ?]

yon (jɒn) *determiner* **1** *chiefly Scot & N English* **1a** an archaic or dialect word for **that**: *yon man* **1b** *(as pronoun)*: *yon's a fool* **2** a variant of **yonder** [OE *geon*]

yond (jɒnd) *obs or dialect* ▷ *adj* **1** the farther, more distant ▷ *determiner* **2** a variant of **yon**

yonder ('jɒndə) *adv* **1** at, in, or to that relatively distant place; over there ▷ *determiner* **2** being at a distance, either within view or as if within view: *yonder valleys* [c13 from OE *geond* yond]

yoni ('jəʊnɪ) *n Hinduism* **1** the female genitalia, regarded as a divine symbol of sexual pleasure and matrix of generation **2** an image of these as an object of worship [c18 from Sansk., lit.: vulva]

Yonkers ('jɒŋkəz) *n* a city in SE New York State, near New York City on the Hudson River. Pop: 196 308 (2000)

yonks (jɒŋks) *pl n inf* a very long time; ages: *I haven't seen him for yonks* [c20 from ?]

Yonne (*French* jɔn) *n* **1** a department of N central France, in Burgundy region. Capital: Auxerre. Pop: 333 221 (1999). Area: 7461 sq km (2910 sq miles) **2** a river in N France, flowing generally northwest to the Seine at Montereau. Length: 290 km (180 miles)

yoo-hoo ('juː,huː) *interj* a call to attract a person's attention

yore (jɔː) *n* **1** time long past (now only in **of yore**) ▷ *adv* **2** *obs* in the past; long ago [OE *geāra*, genitive pl of *gēar* year]

york (jɔːk) *vb (tr) cricket* to bowl (a batsman) by pitching the ball under or just beyond the bat [c19 back formation from YORKER]

York[1] (jɔːk) *n* **1** a walled city in NE England, in York unitary authority, North Yorkshire, on the River Ouse: the military capital of Roman Britain; capital of the N archiepiscopal province of Britain since 625, with a cathedral (the Minster) begun in 1154; noted for its cycle of medieval mystery plays; university (1963). Pop: 104 100 (1994 est). Latin name: **Eboracum** **2** a unitary authority in NE England, in North Yorkshire. Pop: 181 131 (1996 est). Area: 272 sq km (105 sq miles) **3 Cape** a cape in NE Australia, in Queensland at the N tip of Cape York Peninsula, extending into Torres Strait: the northernmost point of Australia

▷ www.wikipedia.org/wiki/House_of_York

York[2] (jɔːk) *n* **1** the English royal house, a branch of the Plantagenet line, that reigned from 1461 to 1485 **2 Alvin C(ullum)** 1887–1964, US soldier and hero of World War I

Yorke Peninsula (jɔːk) *n* a peninsula in South Australia, between Spencer Gulf and St Vincent Gulf: mainly agricultural with several coastal resorts

yorker ('jɔːkə) *n cricket* a ball bowled so as to pitch just under or just beyond the bat [c19 prob. after the *Yorkshire* County Cricket Club]

yorkie ('jɔːkɪ) *n* short for **Yorkshire terrier**

Yorkist ('jɔːkɪst) *English history* ▷ *n* **1** a member or adherent of the royal House of York, esp during the Wars of the Roses ▷ *adj* **2** of, belonging to, or relating to the supporters or members of the House of York

Yorks (jɔːks) *abbrev for* Yorkshire

Yorkshire ('jɔːkʃɪə, -ʃə) *n* a historic county of N England: the largest English county, formerly divided administratively into East, West, and North Ridings. In 1974 it was much reduced in size and divided into the new counties of North, West, and South Yorkshire: in 1996 the East Riding of Yorkshire was reinstated as a unitary authority and parts of the NE were returned to North Yorkshire for geographical and ceremonial purposes

Yorkshire Dales *pl n* the valleys of the rivers flowing from the Pennines in W Yorkshire: chiefly Ribblesdale, Swaledale, Nidderdale, Wharfedale, and Wensleydale; tourist area. Also called: **the Dales**

Yorkshire pudding ('jɔːkʃɪə) *n chiefly Brit* a light puffy baked pudding made from a batter of flour, eggs, and milk, traditionally served with roast beef

Yorkshire terrier *n* a very small breed of terrier with a long straight glossy coat of steel-blue and tan. Also called: **yorkie**

Yorktown ('jɔːk,taʊn) *n* a village in SE Virginia: scene of the surrender (1781) of the British under Cornwallis to the Americans under Washington at the end of the War of American Independence

Yoruba ('jɒrʊbə) *n* **1** (*pl* **Yorubas** *or* **Yoruba**) a member of a Negroid people of W Africa, living chiefly in the coastal regions of SW Nigeria **2** the language of this people > '**Yoruban** *adj*

Yosemite Falls (jəʊ'sɛmɪtɪ) *pl n* a series of waterfalls in central California, in the Yosemite National Park, with a total drop of 770 m (2525 ft): includes the **Upper Yosemite Falls**, 436 m (1430 ft) high, and the **Lower Yosemite Falls**, 98 m (320 ft) high

Yosemite National Park *n* a national park in central California, in the Sierra Nevada Mountains: contains the **Yosemite Valley**, at an altitude of about 1200 m (4000 ft), with sheer walls rising about another 1200 m (4000 ft). Area: 3061 sq km (1182 sq miles)

Yoshkar-Ola (*Russian* jaʃ'kara'la) *n* a city in Russia, capital of the Mari El Republic. Pop: 249 800 (1999 est)

you (juː; *unstressed* jʊ) *pron (subjective or objective)* **1** refers to the person addressed or to more than one person including the person or persons addressed: *you know better; the culprit is among you* **2** refers to an unspecified person or people in general: *you can't tell the boys from the girls* ▷ *n* **3** *inf* the personality of the person being addressed: *that hat isn't really you* **4** **you know what** *or* **who** a thing or person that the speaker does not want to specify [OE *ēow*, dative & accusative of *gē* ye]

USAGE See at **me**

you'd (juːd; *unstressed* jʊd) *contraction of* you had *or* you would

you'll (juːl; *unstressed* jʊl) *contraction of* you will *or* you shall

young (jʌŋ) *adj* **younger** ('jʌŋgə), **youngest** ('jʌŋgɪst) **1a** having lived, existed, or been made or known for a relatively short time: *a young country* **1b** (*as collective n;* preceded by *the*): *the young* **2** youthful or having qualities associated with youth; vigorous or lively **3** of or relating to youth: *in my young days* **4** having been established or introduced for a relatively short time: *a young member* **5** in an early stage of progress or development; not far advanced: *the day was young* **6** (*often cap*) of or relating to a rejuvenated group or movement or one claiming to represent the younger members of the population: *Young Socialists* ▷ *n* **7** (*functioning as pl*) offspring, esp young animals: *a rabbit with her young* **8** **with young** (of animals) pregnant [OE *geong*] > '**youngish** *adj*

young blood *n* young, fresh, or vigorous new people, ideas, attitudes, etc

Young Fogey *n* a young person who adopts the conservative values of an older generation

young gun *n* an up-and-coming young man, esp one considered as being assertive and confident

young lady *n* a girlfriend; sweetheart

youngling ('jʌŋlɪŋ) *n literary* **a** a young person, animal, or plant **b** (*as modifier*): *a youngling brood* [OE *geongling*]

young man *n* a boyfriend; sweetheart

young offender institution *n* (in Britain) a place where offenders aged 15 to 21 may be detained and given training, instruction, and work. Former names: **borstal, youth custody centre**

Young's modulus *n* a modulus of elasticity, applicable to the stretching of a wire, etc, equal to the ratio of the applied load per unit area of cross section to the increase in length per unit length [after Thomas YOUNG]

youngster ('jʌŋstə) *n* **1** a young person; child or youth **2** a young animal, esp a horse

Youngstown ('jʌŋz,taʊn) *n* a city in NE Ohio: a major centre of steel production: university (1908). Pop: 82 026 (2000)

Young Turk *n* **1** a progressive, revolutionary, or rebellious member of an organization, political party, etc **2** a member of an abortive reform movement in the Ottoman Empire

younker ('jʌŋkə) *n* **1** *arch or literary* a young man; lad **2** *obs* a young gentleman or knight [c16 from Du. *jonker*, from MDu. *jonc* young]

your (jɔː, jʊə; *unstressed* jə) *determiner* **1** of, belonging to, or associated with you: *your nose; your house* **2** belonging to or associated with an unspecified person or people in general: *the path is on your left heading north* **3** *inf* used to indicate all things or people of a certain type: *your part-time worker is a problem* [OE *eower*, genitive of *gē* ye]

you're (jɔː; *unstressed* jə) *contraction of* you are

yours (jɔːz, jʊəz) *pron* **1** something or someone belonging to or associated with you **2** your family: *greetings to you and yours* **3** used in conventional closing phrases at the end of a letter: *yours sincerely; yours faithfully* **4 of yours** belonging to or associated with you

yourself (jɔːˈsɛlf, jʊə-) *pron, pl* **yourselves 1a** the reflexive form of *you* **1b** (intensifier): *you yourself control your fate* **2** (*preceded by a copula*) your usual self: *you're not yourself*

yours truly *pron* an informal term for I or *me* [from the closing phrase of letters]

youth (juːθ) *n, pl* **youths** (juːðz) **1** the quality or condition of being young, immature, or inexperienced: *his youth told against him in the contest* **2** the period between childhood and maturity **3** the freshness, vigour, or vitality characteristic of young people **4** any period of early development **5** a young person, esp a young man or boy **6** young people collectively: *youth everywhere is rising in revolt* [OE *geogoth*]

Youth (juːθ) *n* **Isle of** an island in the NW Caribbean, south of Cuba: administratively part of Cuba from 1925. Chief town: Nueva Gerona. Pop: 78 818 (1998 est). Area: 3061 sq km (1182 sq miles). Former name: **Isle of Pines** Spanish name: **Isla de la Juventud** (ˈizla ðe la xuβenˈtuð)

youth club *n* a centre providing leisure activities for young people

youthful (ˈjuːθfʊl) *adj* **1** of, relating to, possessing, or characteristic of youth **2** fresh, vigorous, or active: *he's surprisingly youthful for his age* **3** in an early stage of development: *a youthful culture* **4** Also: **young** (of a river, valley, or land surface) in the early stage of the cycle of erosion, characterized by steep slopes, lack of flood plains, and V-shaped valleys > ˈ**youthfully** *adv* > ˈ**youthfulness** *n*

youth hostel *n* one of an organization of inexpensive lodging places for people travelling cheaply. Often shortened to **hostel**

▷ www.iyhf.org

you've (juːv; *unstressed* jʊv) *contraction of* you have

yowl (jaʊl) *vb* **1** to express with or produce a loud mournful wail or cry; howl ▷ *n* **2** a wail or howl [c13 from ON *gaula*] > ˈ**yowler** *n*

yo-yo (ˈjəʊjəʊ) *n, pl* **yo-yos 1** a toy consisting of a spool attached to a string, the end of which is held while it is repeatedly spun out and reeled in **2** *sl, chiefly US* a silly or insignificant person ▷ *vb* **yo-yos, yo-yoing, yo-yoed** (*intr*) **3** to change repeatedly from one position to another; fluctuate [from Filipino *yo yo* come come, a weapon consisting of a spindle attached to a thong]

Ypres (*French* iprə) *n* a town in W Belgium, in W Flanders province near the border with France: scene of many sieges and battles, esp in World War I, when it was completely destroyed. Pop: 21 400 (1991 est). Flemish name: **Ieper**

yr *abbrev for:* **1** (*pl* **yrs**) year **2** younger **3** your

yrs *abbrev for:* **1** years **2** yours

Yser (*French* izɛr) *n* a river in NW central Europe, rising in N France and flowing through SW Belgium to the North Sea: scene of battles in World War I. Length: 77 km (48 miles)

Yseult (ɪˈsuːlt) *n* a variant spelling of **Iseult**

YST (in Canada) *abbrev for* Yukon Standard Time

YT *abbrev for* Yukon Territory

YTS (in Britain) *abbrev for* Youth Training Scheme

ytterbia (ɪˈtɜːbɪə) *n* another name for **ytterbium oxide** [c19 NL; see YTTERBIUM]

ytterbium (ɪˈtɜːbɪəm) *n* a soft malleable silvery element of the lanthanide series of metals that is used to improve the mechanical properties of steel. Symbol: Yb; atomic no.: 70; atomic wt.: 173.04 [c19 NL, after *Ytterby*, Swedish quarry where discovered]

ytterbium oxide *n* a weakly basic hygroscopic substance used in certain alloys and ceramics

yttria (ˈɪtrɪə) *n* another name for **yttrium oxide** [c19 NL; see YTTERBIUM]

yttrium (ˈɪtrɪəm) *n* a silvery metallic element used in various alloys, in lasers, and as a catalyst. Symbol: Y; atomic no.: 39; atomic wt.: 88.90 [c19 NL; see YTTERBIUM]

yttrium metal *n chem* any one of a group of elements including yttrium and the related lanthanides

yttrium oxide *n* a colourless or white insoluble solid used in incandescent mantles

yuan (ˈjuːˈæn) *n, pl* **yuan** the standard monetary unit of China [from Chinese *yüan* round object; see YEN[1]]

Yüan (ˈjuːˈæn) *or* **Yüen** (ˈjuːˈɛn) *n* a river in SE central China, rising in central Guizhou province and flowing northeast to Lake Tungting. Length: about 800 km (500 miles)

▷ www.chinaknowledge.de/History/Song-Yuan/yuan.htm

Yuan Tan (ˈjuːˈæn ˈtæn) *n* an annual Chinese festival marking the Chinese New Year. It can last over three days and includes the exchange of gifts, firework displays, and dancing

Yucatán (ˌjuːkəˈtɑːn; *Spanish* jukaˈtan) *n* **1** a state of SE Mexico, occupying the N part of the Yucatán peninsula. Capital: Mérida. Pop: 1 655 707 (2000). Area: 39 340 sq km (15 186 sq miles) **2** a peninsula of Central America between the Gulf of Mexico and the Caribbean, including the Mexican states of Campeche, Yucatán, and Quintana Roo, and part of Belize: a centre of Mayan civilization from about 100 BC to the 18th century. Area: about 181 300 sq km (70 000 sq miles)

Yucatán Channel *n* a channel between W Cuba and the Yucatán peninsula

yucca (ˈjʌkə) *n* any of a genus of plants of tropical and subtropical America, having stiff lancelike leaves and spikes of white flowers [c16 from American Sp. *yuca*, ult. from Amerind]

yuck *or* **yuk** (jʌk) *interj sl* an exclamation indicating contempt, dislike, or disgust

yucko (ˈjʌkəʊ) *Austral sl adj* **1** disgusting; unpleasant ▷ *interj* **2** an exclamation of disgust

yucky *or* **yukky** (ˈjʌkɪ) *adj* **yuckier, yuckiest** *or* **yukkier, yukkiest** *sl* disgusting; nasty

Yugo. *abbrev for* (the former) Yugoslavia

Yugoslav *or* **Jugoslav** (ˈjuːgəʊˌslɑːv) *n* **1** (formerly) a native, inhabitant, or citizen of Yugoslavia (sense 1 or 2) **2** (not in technical use) another name for **Serbo-Croat** (the language) ▷ *adj* **3** (formerly) of, relating to, or characteristic of Yugoslavia (sense 1 or 2) or its people

Yugoslavia *or* **Jugoslavia** (ˌjuːgəʊˈslɑːvɪə) *n* **1 Federal Republic of Yugoslavia** a former country of SE Europe, comprising Serbia and Montenegro, that was formed in 1991 but not internationally recognized until 2000; it was replaced by the Union of Serbia and Montenegro in 2003 **2** a former country in SE Europe, on the Adriatic: established in 1918 from the independent states of Serbia and Montenegro, and regions that until World War I had belonged to Austria-Hungary (Croatia, Slovenia, and Bosnia-Herzegovina); the name was changed from Kingdom of Serbs, Croats, and Slovenes to Yugoslavia in 1929; German invasion of 1941–44 was resisted chiefly by a Communist group led by Tito, who declared a people's republic in 1945; it became the Socialist Federal Republic of Yugoslavia in 1963; in 1991 Slovenia, Croatia, and Bosnia-Herzegovina declared independence, followed by Macedonia in 1992; Serbia and Montenegro formed the Federal Republic of Yugoslavia, subsequently (2003) replaced by the Union of Serbia and Montenegro > ,**Yugo'slavian** *or* ,**Jugo'slavian** *adj, n*

Yukon ('juːkɒn) *n* **the** a territory of NW Canada, on the Beaufort Sea, between the Northwest Territories and Alaska: arctic and mountainous, reaching 6050 m (19 850 ft) at Mount Logan, Canada's highest peak; mineral resources. Capital: Whitehorse. Pop: 29 900 (2001 est). Area: 536 327 sq km (207 076 sq miles). Abbreviation: **YT** > '**Yukoner** *n*
▷ www.gov.yk.ca
▷ www.yukonweb.com/tourism

Yukon River *n* a river in NW North America, rising in NW Canada on the border between the Yukon Territory and British Columbia: flows northwest into Alaska, US, and then southwest to the Bering Sea; navigable for about 2850 km (1775 miles) to Whitehorse. Length: 3185 km (1979 miles)

yulan ('juːlæn) *n* a Chinese magnolia that is often cultivated for its showy white flowers [C19 from Chinese, from *yu* a gem + *lan* plant]

yule (juːl) *n* (*sometimes cap*) *literary, arch, or dialect* **a** Christmas or the Christmas season **b** (*in combination*): *yuletide* [OE *geōla*, orig. a pagan feast lasting 12 days]

yule log *n* a large log of wood traditionally used as the foundation of a fire at Christmas

yummo ('jʌməʊ) *Austral sl adj* **1** tasty; delicious ▷ *interj* **2** an exclamation of delight or approval

yummy ('jʌmɪ) *sl* ▷ *interj* **1** Also: **yum-yum** an exclamation indicating pleasure or delight, as in anticipation of delicious food ▷ *adj* **yummier, yummiest** **2** delicious, delightful, or attractive: *yummy grub; he's just yummy* [C20 from *yum-yum*, imit.]

Yünnan (juː'næn) *n* a province of SW China: consists mainly of a plateau broken in the southeast by the Red and Black Rivers, with mountains in the west, rising over 5500 m (18 000 ft); large deposits of tin, lead, zinc, and coal. Capital: Kunming. Pop: 42 880 000 (2000 est). Area: 436 200 sq km (168 400 sq miles)

yuppie *or* **yuppy** ('jʌpɪ) (*sometimes cap*) ▷ *n* **1** an affluent young professional person ▷ *adj* **2** typical of or reflecting the values characteristic of yuppies [C20 from *y(oung) u(rban)* or *up(wardly mobile) p(rofessional)* + -IE] > '**yuppiedom** *n*

yuppie disease *or* **flu** *n inf, sometimes considered offens* any of a number of debilitating long-lasting viral disorders associated with stress, such as chronic fatigue syndrome, whose symptoms include muscle weakness, chronic tiredness, and depression

yuppify ('jʌpɪ,faɪ) *vb* **yuppifies, yuppifying, yuppified** (*tr*) to make yuppie in nature > ,**yuppifi'cation** *n*

Yurev (*Russian* 'jurjɪf) *n* the former name (11th century until 1918) of **Tartu**

yurt (jʊət) *n* a circular tent consisting of a framework of poles covered with felt or skins, used by Mongolian and Turkic nomads of E and central Asia [from Russian *yurta*, of Turkic origin]

Yuzovka (*Russian* 'juzəfkə) *n* a former name (1872 until after the Revolution) of **Donetsk**

Yvelines (*French* ivlin) *n* a department of N France, in Île de France region. Capital: Versailles. Pop: 1 354 304 (1999). Area: 2271 sq km (886 sq miles)

YWCA *abbrev for* Young Women's Christian Association.

Zz

z *or* **Z** (zɛd; *US* ziː) *n, pl* **z's, Z's,** *or* **Zs 1** the 26th and last letter of the English alphabet **2** a speech sound represented by this letter **3a** something shaped like a Z **3b** *(in combination): a Z-bend in a road*

z *maths symbol for:* **1** the *z*-axis or a coordinate measured along the *z*-axis in a Cartesian or cylindrical coordinate system **2** an algebraic variable

Z *symbol for:* **1** any unknown, variable, or unspecified factor, number, person, or thing **2** *chem* atomic number **3** *physics* impedance **4** zone

Zaandam (*Dutch* zaːnˈdɑm) *n* a former town in the W Netherlands, in North Holland: an important shipbuilding centre in the 17th century. It became part of Zaanstad in 1974

Zaanstad (*Dutch* zaːnˈʃtat) *n* a port in the W Netherlands, in North Holland: formed (1974) from Zaandam, Koog a/d Zaan, Zaandijk, Wormerveer, Krommenie, Westzaan, and Assendelft; food and machinery industries. Pop: 135 126 (1999 est)

zabaglione (ˌzæbəˈljəʊnɪ) *n* a light foamy dessert made of egg yolks, sugar, and marsala, whipped together and served warm in a glass [It.]

Zabrze (*Polish* ˈzabʒɛ) *n* a city in SW Poland: a Prussian and German town from 1742 until 1945, when it passed to Poland; industrial centre in a coal-mining region. Pop: 200 177 (1999 est). German name: **Hindenburg**

Zacatecas (*Spanish* θakaˈtekas) *n* **1** a state of N central Mexico, on the central plateau: rich mineral resources. Capital: Zacatecas. Pop: 1 351 207 (2000). Area: 75 040 sq km (28 973 sq miles) **2** a city in N central Mexico, capital of Zacatecas state: silver mines Pop: 113 780 (2000 est)

Zacharias (ˌzækəˈraɪəs), **Zachariah** (ˌzækəˈraɪə), *or* **Zachary** (ˈzækərɪ) *n New Testament* John the Baptist's father, who underwent a temporary period of dumbness for his lack of faith (Luke 1)

Zacynthus (zəˈsɪnθəs, -ˈkɪn-) *n* the Latin name for **Zante**

zaffer *or* **zaffre** (ˈzæfə) *n* impure cobalt oxide, used to impart a blue colour to enamels [C17 from It. *zaffera*]

Zagazig (ˈzægəˌzɪg) *or* **Zaqaziq** *n* a city in NE Egypt, in the Nile Delta: major cotton market. Pop: 267 351 (1996)

Zagreb (ˈzɑːgrɛb) *n* the capital of Croatia, on the River Sava; gothic cathedral; university (1874); industrial centre. Pop: 682 598 (2001). German name: **Agram**
▷ www.zagreb-touristinfo.hr

Zagreus (ˈzægrɪəs) *n Greek myth* a young god whose cult came from Crete to Greece, where he was identified with Dionysus. The son of Zeus by either Demeter or Persephone, he was killed by the Titans at the behest of Hera

Zagros Mountains (ˈzægrɒs) *pl n* a mountain range in S Iran: has Iran's main oilfields in its W central foothills. Highest peak: Zard Kuh, 4548 m (14 920 ft)

zaibatsu (ˈzaɪbætˈsuː) *n (functioning as sing or pl)* the group or combine comprising a few wealthy families that controls industry, business, and finance in Japan [from Japanese, from *zai* wealth + *batsu* family, person of influence]

Zaïre (zɑːˈɪə) *n* **1** the former name (1971–97) of the (Democratic Republic of) Congo (sense 2) **2** (formerly) the Zaïrian name (1971–97) for the (River) **Congo**
› **Zaˈïrean** *or* ˌ**Zaïrˈese** *adj, n*

Zákinthos (ˈzakinˌθɒs) *n* transliteration of the Modern Greek name for **Zante**

zakuski *or* **zakouski** (zæˈkʊskɪ) *pl n, sing* **zakuska** *or* **zakouska** (-kə) *Russian cookery* hors d'oeuvres, consisting of tiny open sandwiches spread with caviar, smoked sausage, etc, or a cold dish such as radishes in sour cream, all usually served with vodka [Russian, from *zakusit'* to have a snack]

Zama ('zɑːmə) *n* the name of several ancient cities in N Africa, including the one near the site of Scipio's decisive defeat of Hannibal (202 BC)

Zambezi *or* **Zambese** (zæm'biːzɪ) *n* a river in S central and E Africa, rising in NW Zambia and flowing across E Angola back into Zambia, continuing south to the Caprivi Strip of Namibia, then east forming the Zambia–Zimbabwe border, and finally crossing Mozambique to the Indian Ocean: the fourth longest river in Africa. Length: 2740 km (1700 miles) > **Zam'bezian** *adj*

Zambia ('zæmbɪə) *n* a republic in southern Africa: an early site of human settlement; controlled by the British South Africa Company by 1900 and unified as Northern Rhodesia in 1911; made a British protectorate in 1924; part of the Federation of Rhodesia and Nyasaland (1953–63), gaining independence as a member of the Commonwealth in 1964; important mineral exports, esp copper. Official language: English. Religion: Christian majority, animist minority. Currency: kwacha. Capital: Lusaka. Pop: 9 770 000 (2001 est). Area: 752 617 sq km (290 587 sq miles). Former name (until 1964): **Northern Rhodesia** > **'Zambian** *adj, n*
▷ www.state.gov.zm
▷ www.zambiatourism.com

Zamboanga (ˌzæmbəʊ'æŋgə) *n* a port in the Philippines, on SW Mindanao on Basilan Strait: founded by the Spanish in 1635; tourist centre, with fisheries. Pop: 135 000 (2000)

zambuck *or* **zambuk** ('zæmbʌk) *n Austral & NZ inf* a first-aid attendant at a sports event [from name of a proprietary ointment]

Zamenhof (*Polish* 'zamɛnɔxf) *n* **Lazarus Ludwig** (la'zarus 'ludvik) 1859–1917, Polish oculist; invented Esperanto

Zamora (*Spanish* θa'mora) *n* a city in NW central Spain, on the Douro River. Pop: 58 560 (latest est)

Zamyatin (*Russian* za'mjatjin) *n* **Yevgenii Ivanovich** (jɪv'gjenij ɪ'vanəvitʃ) 1884–1937, Russian novelist and writer, in Paris from 1931, whose works include satirical studies of provincial life in Russia and England, where he worked during World War I, and the dystopian novel *We* (1924)

Zante ('zæntɪ) *n* an island in the Ionian Sea, off the W coast of Greece: southernmost of the Ionian Islands; traditionally belonged to Ulysses, king of Ithaca. Pop: 32 557 (1991). Area: 402 sq km (155 sq miles). Latin name: **Zacynthus** Ancient Greek name: **Zakynthos** (zə'kuːnθɒs) Modern Greek name: **Zákinthos**

Zanu (PF) ('zɑːnuː) *n* the ruling political party in Zimbabwe [c20 from *Z(imbabwe) A(frican) N(ational) U(nion) + P(atriotic) F(ront)*]

zany ('zeɪnɪ) *adj* **zanier, zaniest 1** comical in an endearing way; imaginatively funny or comical, esp in behaviour ▷ *n, pl* **zanies 2** a clown or buffoon, esp one in old comedies who imitated other performers with ludicrous effect **3** a ludicrous or foolish person [c16 from It. *zanni*, from dialect *Zanni*, nickname for *Giovanni* John; one of the traditional names for a clown] > **'zanily** *adv* > **'zaniness** *n*

Zanzibar (ˌzænzɪ'bɑː) *n* an island in the Indian Ocean, off the E coast of Africa: settled by Persians and Arabs from the 7th century onwards; became a flourishing trading centre for slaves, ivory, and cloves; made a British protectorate in 1890, becoming independent within the Commonwealth in 1963 and a republic in 1964; joined with Tanganyika in 1964 to form the United Republic of Tanzania. Pop: 456 934 (1995 est) > ˌ**Zanzi'bari** *adj, n*

zap (zæp) *sl* ▷ *vb* **zaps, zapping, zapped 1** (*tr*) to attack, kill, or destroy, as with a sudden bombardment **2** (*intr*) to move quickly **3** (*tr*) *computing* **3a** to clear from the screen **3b** to erase **4** (*intr*) *television* to change channels rapidly by remote control ▷ *n* **5** energy, vigour, or pep ▷ *interj* **6** an exclamation used to express sudden or swift action [c20 imit.]

Zapata (zə'pɑːtə; *Spanish* θa'pata) *n* **Emiliano** (emi'ljano) ?1877–1919, Mexican guerrilla leader

zapateado *Spanish* (ˌθapate'aðo) *n, pl* **-dos** (-ðos) a Spanish dance with stamping and very fast footwork [from *zapatear* to tap with the shoe, from *zapato* shoe]

Zaporozhye (*Russian* zəpa'rɔʒjɛ) *n* a city in the E Ukraine on the Dnieper River: developed as a major industrial centre after the construction (1932) of the Dnieper hydroelectric station. Pop: 863 100 (1998 est). Former name (until 1921): **Aleksandrovsk**

Zappa ('zæpə) *n* **Frank** 1940–93, US rock musician, songwriter, and experimental composer: founder and only permanent member of the Mothers of Invention. His recordings include *Freak Out* (1966), *Hot Rats* (1969), and *Sheik Yerbouti* (1979)

zappy ('zæpɪ) *adj* **zappier, zappiest** *sl* full of energy; zippy; snappy

ZAPU ('zæpuː) *n acronym for* Zimbabwe African People's Union

Zaqaziq ('zækəˌzɪk) *n* a variant of **Zagazig**

Zaragoza (*Spanish* θara'ɣoθa) *n* a city in NE Spain, on the River Ebro: Roman colony established 25 BC; under Moorish rule (714–1118); capital of Aragon (12th–15th centuries); twice besieged by the French during the Peninsular War and captured (1809); university (1474). Pop: 603 367 (1998 est). Pre-Roman name: **Salduba** Latin name: **Caesaraugusta** English name: **Saragossa**

Zarathustra (ˌzærə'θuːstrə) *n* the Avestan name of **Zoroaster**

zareba *or* **zareeba** (zə'riːbə) *n* (in northern E Africa, esp formerly) **1** a stockade or enclosure of thorn bushes around a village or camp site **2** the area so protected or enclosed [c19 from Ar. *zarībah* cattlepen, from *zarb* sheepfold]

zarf (zɑːf) *n* (esp in the Middle East) a holder, usually ornamental, for a hot coffee cup [from Ar.: container]

Zaria ('zɑːrɪə) *n* a city in N central Nigeria: former capital of a Hausa state; agricultural trading centre; university (1962). Pop: 379 200 (1997 est)

Zarqa ('zɑːkə) *n* the second largest town in Jordan, northeast of Amman. Pop: 344 524 (1994)

zarzuela (zɑː'zweɪlə) *n* **1** a type of Spanish vaudeville or operetta, usually satirical in nature **2** a seafood stew [from Sp., after *La Zarzuela*, the palace near Madrid where such vaudeville was first performed (1629)]

Zátopek (*Czech* 'zaːtɔpɛk) *n* **Emil** ('emil) 1922–2000, Czech runner; winner of the 5000 and 10 000 metres and the marathon at the 1952 Olympic Games in Helsinki

z-axis *n* a reference axis of a three-dimensional Cartesian coordinate system along which the z-coordinate is measured

ZB station *n* (in New Zealand) a radio station of a commercial network

Z chart *n statistics* a chart often used in industry and constructed by plotting on it three series: monthly, weekly, or daily data, the moving annual total, and the cumulative total dating from the beginning of the current year

Zea ('tsɛːa) *n* the Italian name for **Keos**

zeal (ziːl) *n* fervent or enthusiastic devotion, often extreme or fanatical in nature, as to a religious movement, political cause, ideal, or aspiration [c14 from LL *zēlus*, from Gk *zēlos*]

Zealand ('ziːlənd) *n* the largest island of Denmark, separated from the island of Fyn by the Great Belt and from S Sweden by the Sound (both now spanned by road bridges). Chief town: Copenhagen. Pop: 2 000 254 (1988 est). Area: 7016 sq km (2709 sq miles). Danish name: **Sjælland** German name: **Seeland**

zealot ('zɛlət) *n* an immoderate, fanatical, or extremely zealous adherent to a cause, esp a religious one [c16 from LL *zēlōtēs*, from Gk, from *zēloun* to be zealous, from *zēlos* zeal] > 'zealotry *n*

Zealot ('zɛlət) *n* any of the members of an extreme Jewish sect or political party that resisted all aspects of Roman rule in Palestine in the 1st century AD

zealous ('zɛləs) *adj* filled with or inspired by intense enthusiasm or zeal; ardent; fervent > **'zealously** *adv* > **'zealousness** *n*

Zeami *or* **Seami** (si:'ɑ:mɪ) *n* **Motokiyo** (ˌməʊtəʊ'ki:əʊ) 1363–1443, Japanese dramatist, regarded as the greatest figure in the history of No drama

zebec *or* **zebeck** ('zi:bɛk) *n* variant spellings of **xebec**

Zebedee ('zɛbɪˌdi:) *n New Testament* the father of the apostles James and John (Matthew 4:21)

zebra ('zi:brə, 'zɛbrə) *n, pl* **zebras** *or* **zebra** any of several mammals of the horse family, such as the common zebra of southern and eastern Africa, having distinctive black-and-white striped hides [c16 via It. from OSp.: wild ass, prob. from Vulgar L *eciferus* (unattested) wild horse, from L *equiferus*, from *equus* horse + *ferus* wild] > **zebrine** ('zi:braɪn, 'zɛb-) *or* **'zebroid** *adj*

Zebra ('zi:brə, 'zɛbrə) *n finance* a noninterest-paying bond in which the accrued income is taxed annually rather than on redemption ▹ Cf **zero** (sense 10) [c20 from *zero-coupon bond*]

zebra crossing *n Brit* a pedestrian crossing marked on a road by broad alternate black and white stripes. Once on the crossing the pedestrian has right of way

zebra finch *n* any of various Australasian songbirds with zebra-like markings

zebrawood ('zɛbrəˌwʊd, 'zi:-) *n* **1** a tree of tropical America, Asia, and Africa, yielding striped hardwood used in cabinetwork **2** any of various other trees or shrubs having striped wood **3** the wood of any of these trees

zebu ('zi:bu:) *n* a domesticated ox having a humped back, long horns, and a large dewlap: used in India and E Asia as a draught animal [c18 from F *zébu*, ? of Tibetan origin]

Zebulun ('zɛbjʊlən, zə'bju:-) *n Old Testament* **1** the sixth son whom Leah bore to Jacob: one of the 12 patriarchs of Israel (Genesis 30:20) **2** the tribe descended from him **3** the territory of this tribe, lying in lower Galilee to the north of Mount Carmel and to the east of the coastal plain. Douay spelling: **Zabulon** ('zæbjʊlən, zə'bju:-)

Zech. *Bible abbrev for* Zechariah

Zechariah (ˌzɛkə'raɪə) *n* **1** *Old Testament* **1a** a Hebrew prophet of the late 6th century BC **1b** the book containing his oracles, which are chiefly concerned with the renewal of Israel after the exile as a national, religious, and messianic community with the restored Temple and rebuilt Jerusalem as its centre. Douay spelling: **Zacharias** **2** a variant spelling of **Zachariah.** See **Zacharias**

zed (zɛd) *n* the British and Canadian spoken form of the letter *z* [c15 from OF *zede*, via LL from Gk *zēta*]

Zedekiah (ˌzɛdə'kaɪə) *n Old Testament* the last king of Judah, who died in captivity at Babylon. Douay spelling: **Sedecias** (ˌsɛdə'kaɪəs)

zedoary ('zɛdəʊərɪ) *n* the dried rhizome of a tropical Asian plant, used as a stimulant and a condiment [c15 from Med. L *zedoaria*, from Ar. *zadwār*, of Persian origin]

zee (zi:) *n* the US word for **zed** (letter *z*)

Zeebrugge (*Flemish* 'ze:bryxə; *English* 'zi:ˌbrʊgə) *n* a port in NW Belgium, in W Flanders on the North Sea: linked by canal with Bruges; German submarine base in World War I

Zeeland (*Dutch* 'ze:lant; *English* 'zi:lənd) *n* a province of the SW Netherlands: consists of a small area on the mainland together with a number of islands in the Scheldt estuary; mostly below sea level. Capital: Middelburg. Pop: 371 900 (2000 est). Area: 1787 sq km (690 sq miles) > **'Zeelander** *n*

Zeeman effect ('zi:mən) *n* the splitting of a spectral line of a substance into several closely spaced lines when the substance is placed in a magnetic field [c20 after Pieter *Zeeman* (1865–1943), Du. physicist]

Zeffirelli (*Italian* dzeffɪ'rɛlli) *n* **Franco** ('fraŋko) born 1923, Italian stage and film director and designer, noted esp for his work in opera

zein ('zi:ɪn) *n* a protein occurring in maize and used in the manufacture of plastics, paper coatings, adhesives, etc [c19 from NL *zēa* maize, from L: a kind of grain, from Gk *zeia* barley]

Zeist (zaɪst; *Dutch* zɛjst) *n* a city in the central Netherlands, near Utrecht. Pop: 59 258 (1994)

Zeitgeist *German* ('tsaɪtˌgaɪst) *n* the spirit, attitude, or general outlook of a specific time or period, esp as it is reflected in literature, philosophy, etc [G, lit.: time spirit]

Zellweger ('zɛlˌweɪgə) *n* **Renée** (**Kathleen**) born 1969, US film actress, best known for her performances in *Nurse Betty* (2000), *Bridget Jones's Diary* (2001) and its sequel (2004), and *Chicago* (2002)

Zen (zɛn) *n Buddhism* **1** a Japanese school, of 12th-century Chinese origin, teaching that contemplation of one's essential nature to the exclusion of all else is the only way of achieving pure enlightenment **2** (*modifier*) of or relating to this school: *Zen Buddhism* [from Japanese, from Chinese *ch'an* religious meditation, from Pali *jhāna*, from Sansk. *dhyāna*] > **'Zenic** *adj* > **'Zenist** *n*

zenana (zɛ'nɑ:nə) *n* (in the East, esp in Muslim and Hindu homes) part of a house reserved for the women and girls of a household [c18 from Hindi *zanāna*, from Persian, from *zan* woman]

Zend (zɛnd) *n* **1** a former name for **Avestan** **2** short for **Zend-Avesta** **3** an exposition of the Avesta in the Middle Persian language (Pahlavi) [c18 from Persian *zand* commentary, exposition; used specifically of the MPersian commentary on the Avesta, hence of the language of the Avesta itself] > **'Zendic** *adj*

Zz

Zend-Avesta (ˌzɛndə'vɛstə) *n* the Avesta together with the traditional interpretive commentary known as the Zend, esp as preserved in the Avestan language among the Parsees [from Avestan, representing *Avesta'-va-zend* Avesta with interpretation]

Zener diode ('zi:nə) *n* a semiconductor diode that exhibits a sharp increase in reverse current at a well-defined reverse voltage: used as a voltage regulator [c20 after C. M. *Zener* (1905–93), US physicist]

zenith ('zɛnɪθ) *n* **1** *astron* the point on the celestial sphere vertically above an observer **2** the highest point; peak; acme: *the zenith of someone's achievements* [c17 from F *cenith*, from Med. L, from OSp. *zenit*, based on Ar. *samt*, as in *samt arrās* path over one's head] > **'zenithal** *adj*

zenithal projection *n* a type of map projection in which part of the earth's surface is projected onto a plane tangential to it, either at one of the poles (**polar zenithal**), at the equator (**equatorial zenithal**), or between (**oblique zenithal**)

Zenobia (zɪ'nəʊbɪə) *n* 3rd century AD, queen of Palmyra (?267–272), who was captured by the Roman emperor Aurelian

Zeno of Citium ('zi:nəʊ əv 'sɪtɪəm) *n* ?336–?264 BC, Greek philosopher, who founded the Stoic school in Athens

Zeno of Elea *n* ?490–?430 BC, Greek Eleatic philosopher; disciple of Parmenides. He defended the belief that motion and change are illusions in a series of paradoxical arguments, of which the best known is that of Achilles and the tortoise

zeolite ('zi:əˌlaɪt) *n* **1** any of a large group of glassy secondary minerals consisting of hydrated aluminium silicates of calcium, sodium, or potassium: formed in cavities in lava flows and plutonic rocks **2** any of a class of similar synthetic materials used in ion exchange and as selective absorbents [c18 *zeo-*, from Gk *zein* to boil +

-LITE; from the swelling that occurs under the blowpipe] > **zeolitic** (ˌziːəˈlɪtɪk) *adj*

Zeph. *Bible abbrev for* Zephaniah

Zephaniah (ˌzɛfəˈnaɪə) *n Old Testament* **1** a Hebrew prophet of the late 7th century BC **2** the book containing his oracles, which are chiefly concerned with the approaching judgment by God upon the sinners of Judah. Douay spelling: **Sophonias** (ˌsɒfəˈnaɪəs) **3** **Benjamin** born 1958, British poet, writer, and activist, born in Jamaica. His poetry collections include *The Dread Affair* (1985) and *Too Black, Too Strong* (2001)

zephyr (ˈzɛfə) *n* **1** a soft or gentle breeze **2** any of several delicate soft yarns, fabrics, or garments, usually of wool [C16 from L *zephyrus*, from Gk *zephuros* the west wind]

Zephyrus (ˈzɛfərəs) *n Greek myth* the god of the west wind

zeppelin (ˈzɛpəlɪn) *n* (*sometimes cap*) a large cylindrical rigid airship built from 1900 to carry passengers and used in World War I for bombing and reconnaissance [C20 after Count von ZEPPELIN]

Zeppelin (*German* ˈtsɛpəliːn) *n* Count **Ferdinand von** (ˈfɛrdinant fɔn) 1838–1917, German aeronautical pioneer, who designed and manufactured airships (zeppelins)

Zermatt (tsɛrˈmat) *n* a village and resort in S Switzerland, in Valais canton at the foot of the Matterhorn: cars are not allowed in the area. Pop: 4200 (latest est)

zero (ˈzɪərəʊ) *n, pl* **zeros** *or* **zeroes** **1** the symbol 0, indicating an absence of quantity or magnitude; nought. Former name: **cipher** **2** the integer denoted by the symbol 0; nought **3** the cardinal number between +1 and –1 **4** nothing; nil **5** a person or thing of no significance; nonentity **6** the lowest point or degree: *his prospects were put at zero* **7** the line or point on a scale of measurement from which the graduations commence **8a** the temperature, pressure, etc, that registers a reading of zero on a scale **8b** the value of a variable, such as temperature, obtained under specified conditions **9** *maths* **9a** the cardinal number of a set with no members **9b** the identity element of addition **10** *finance* Also called: **zero-coupon bond** a bond that pays no interest, the equivalent being paid in its redemption value ▷ Cf **Zebra** ▷ *adj* **11** having no measurable quantity, magnitude, etc **12** *meteorol* **12a** (of a cloud ceiling) limiting visibility to 15 metres (50 feet) or less **12b** (of horizontal visibility) limited to 50 metres (165 feet) or less ▷ *vb* **zeros** *or* **zeroes, zeroing, zeroed** **13** (*tr*) to adjust (an instrument, apparatus, etc) so as to read zero or a position taken as zero ▷ *determiner* **14** *inf, chiefly US* no (thing) at all: *this job has zero interest* ▷ See also **zero in** [C17 from It., from Med. L *zephirum*, from Ar. *sifr* empty]

zero gravity *n* the state or condition of weightlessness

zero hour *n* **1** *mil* the time set for the start of an attack or the initial stage of an operation **2** *inf* a critical time, esp at the commencement of an action

zero in *vb* (*adv*) **1** (often foll by *on*) to bring (a weapon) to bear (on a target), as while firing repeatedly **2** (*intr;* foll by *on*) *inf* to bring one's attention to bear (on a problem, etc) **3** (*intr;* foll by *on*) *inf* to converge (upon)

zero option *n* (in international nuclear arms negotiations) an offer to remove all shorter-range nuclear missiles or, in the case of the **zero-zero option** all intermediate-range nuclear missiles, if the other side will do the same

zero-rated *adj* denoting goods on which the buyer pays no value-added tax although the seller can claim back any tax he has paid

zero stage *n* a solid-propellant rocket attached to a liquid-propellant rocket to provide greater thrust at liftoff

zeroth (ˈzɪərəʊθ) *adj* denoting a term in a series that precedes the term otherwise regarded as the first term [C20 from ZERO + -TH[2]]

zero tolerance *n* **a** the policy of applying laws or penalties to even minor infringements of a code in order to reinforce its overall importance **b** (*as modifier*): *a zero-tolerance policy on drugs*

zest (zɛst) *n* **1** invigorating or keen excitement or enjoyment: *a zest for living* **2** added interest, flavour, or charm; piquancy: *her presence gave zest to the party* **3** something added to give flavour or relish **4** the peel or skin of an orange or lemon, used as flavouring in drinks, etc ▷ *vb* **5** (*tr*) to give flavour, interest, or piquancy to [C17 from F *zeste* peel of citrus fruits used as flavouring, from ?] > **ˈzestful** *adj* > **ˈzestfully** *adv* > **ˈzestfulness** *n* > **ˈzesty** *adj*

zester (ˈzɛstə) *n* a kitchen utensil used to scrape fine shreds of peel from citrus fruits

zeta (ˈziːtə) *n* the sixth letter in the Greek alphabet (Ζ, ζ) [from Gk]

ZETA (ˈziːtə) *n* a torus-shaped apparatus formerly used for research on controlled thermonuclear reactions [C20 from *z(ero-)e(nergy) t(hermonuclear) a(pparatus)*]

Zeta-Jones (zɪːtə dʒəʊnz) *n* **Catherine**, original name *Catherine Jones*. born 1969, Welsh actress, who made her name in the TV series *The Darling Buds of May* (1991) before starring in the films *Traffic* (2000), *Chicago* (2002), and *Smoke and Mirrors* (2004). She is married to the US actor Michael Douglas

Zetland (ˈzɛtlənd) *n* the official name (until 1974) of **Shetland**

zeugma (ˈzjuːgmə) *n* a figure of speech in which a word is used to modify or govern two or more words although appropriate to only one of them or making a different sense with each, as in *Mr Pickwick took his hat and his leave* (Charles Dickens) [C16 via L from Gk: a yoking, from *zeugnunai* to yoke] > **zeugmatic** (zjuːgˈmætɪk) *adj*

Zeus (zjuːs) *n* the supreme god of the ancient Greeks, who became ruler of gods and men after he dethroned his father Cronus and defeated the Titans. He was the husband of his sister Hera and father by her and others of many gods, demigods, and mortals. He wielded thunderbolts and ruled the heavens, while his brothers Poseidon and Hades ruled the sea and underworld respectively. Roman counterpart: **Jupiter**

Zeuxis (ˈzjuːksɪs) *n* late 5th century BC, Greek painter, noted for the verisimilitude of his works

Zhangjiakou (ˈdʒæŋˈdʒjækəʊ), **Changchiakow**, *or* **Changchiak'ou** *n* a city in NE China, in NW Hebei province: a military centre, controlling the route to Mongolia, under the Ming and Manchu dynasties. Pop: 660 504 (1999 est). Former names: **Wanchüan, Kalgan**

Zhangzhou (ˈdʒæŋˈdʒəʊ), **Changchow**, *or* **Ch'ang-chou** *n* **1** a city in E China, in S Jiangsu province, on the Grand Canal: also known as **Wutsin** until 1949, when the 7th-century name was officially readopted. Pop: 772 700 (1990 est) **2** a city in SE China, in S Fujian province on the Saikoe River. Pop 231 333 (1999 est). Former name: **Lungki**

Zhdanov (*Russian* ˈʒdanəf) *n* the former name (1948–91) of **Mariupol**

Zhejiang (ˈdʒɛˈdʒjæŋ) *or* **Chekiang** *n* a province of E China: mountainous and densely populated; a cultural centre since the 12th century. Capital: Hangzhou. Pop: 46 770 000 (2000 est). Area: 102 000 sq km (39 780 sq miles)

Zhengzhou (ˈdʒʌŋˈdʒəʊ), **Chengchow**, *or* **Cheng-chou** *n* a city in E central China, capital of Henan province; an administrative centre. Pop: 1 465 069 (1999 est)

Zhitomir (*Russian* ʒiˈtɔmir) *n* a city in the central Ukraine; centre of an agricultural region. Pop 297 700 (1998 est)

zho (zəʊ) *n* a variant spelling of **zo**

Zhou (dʒəʊ) *n* the Pinyin transliteration of the Chinese name for **Chou**

Zhou En Lai (ɛn laɪ) *n* the Pinyin transliteration of the Chinese name for **Chou En-lai**

Zhu De (ˈdʒuː ˈdeɪ) *n* the Pinyin transliteration of the Chinese name for **Chu Teh**

Zhu Jiang (ˈdʒuː ˈdʒjæŋ), **Chu Chiang**, *or* **Chu Kiang** *n* a river in SE China, in S Guangdong province, flowing southeast from Canton to the South China Sea. Length: about 177 km (110 miles). Also called: **Canton River, Pearl River**

Zhukov (*Russian* ˈʒukəf) *n* **Georgi Konstantinovich** (ɡɪˈɔrɡij kənstanˈtinəvitʃ) 1896–1974, Soviet marshal. In World War II, he led the offensives that broke the sieges of Stalingrad and Leningrad (1942–43) and later captured Warsaw and Berlin; minister of defence (1955–57)

Zia ul Haq (ˈzɪə ʊl ˈhak) *n* **Mohammed** (məʊˈhæmɪd) 1924–88, Pakistani general: president of Pakistan (1978–88), following the overthrow (1977) of Z. A. Bhutto by a military coup. He was killed in an air crash, possibly through sabotage

zibeline (ˈzɪbəˌlaɪn, -lɪn) *n* **1** a sable or the fur of this animal **2** a thick cloth made of wool or other animal hair, having a long nap and a dull sheen ▷ *adj* **3** of, relating to, or resembling a sable [c16 from F, from OIt. *zibellino*, ult. of Slavonic origin]

zibet (ˈzɪbɪt) *n* a large civet of S and SE Asia, having tawny fur marked with black spots and stripes [c16 from Med. L *zibethum*, from Ar. *zabād* civet]

Zibo (ˈziːˈbɔː), **Tzu-po**, *or* **Tzepo** *n* a city in NE China, in Shandong province. Pop: 1 458 000 (1999 est)

Zidane (*French* zidɑn) *n* **Zinedine** (zinedin) born 1972, French football player, known as *Zizou*; scored two goals in the 1998 World Cup final

zidovudine (zaɪˈdɒvjʊˌdiːn) *n* a drug that is used to treat AIDS. Also called: **AZT**

Ziegfeld (ˈziːɡˌfɛld) *n* **Florenz** (ˈflɒrənz) 1869–1932, US theatrical producer, noted for his series of extravagant revues (1907–31), known as the Ziegfeld Follies

ziff (zɪf) *n Austral inf* a beard [c20 from ?]

ziggurat (ˈzɪɡʊˌræt) *n* a type of rectangular temple tower or tiered mound erected by the Sumerians, Akkadians, and Babylonians in Mesopotamia [c19 from Assyrian *ziqqurati* summit]

Zigong (ˈziːˈɡʊŋ), **Tzekung**, *or* **Tzu-kung** *n* an industrial city in W central China, in Sichuan. Pop: 464 497 (1990 est)

zigzag (ˈzɪɡˌzæɡ) *n* **1** a line or course characterized by sharp turns in alternating directions **2** one of the series of such turns **3** something having the form of a zigzag ▷ *adj* **4** (*usually prenominal*) formed in or proceeding in a zigzag **5** (of a sewing machine) capable of producing stitches in a zigzag ▷ *adv* **6** in a zigzag manner ▷ *vb* **zigzags, zigzagging, zigzagged 7** to proceed or cause to proceed in a zigzag **8** (*tr*) to form into a zigzag [c18 from F, from G *zickzack*, from *Zacke* point]

zigzagger (ˈzɪɡˌzæɡə) *n* **1** a person or thing that zigzags **2** an attachment on a sewing machine for sewing zigzag stitches, as for joining two pieces of material

zilch (zɪltʃ) *n sl* **1** nothing **2** *US & Canad sport* nil [c20 from ?]

zillion (ˈzɪljən) *inf* ▷ *n, pl* **zillions** *or* **zillion 1** (*often pl*) an extremely large but unspecified number, quantity, or amount: *zillions of flies in this camp* ▷ *determiner* **2** amounting to a zillion: *a zillion different problems* [c20 coinage after MILLION]

Zilpah (ˈzɪlpə) *n Old Testament* Leah's maidservant, who bore Gad and Asher to Jacob (Genesis 30:10–13)

Zimbabwe (zɪmˈbɑːbwɪ, -weɪ) *n* **1** a country in SE Africa, formerly a self-governing British colony founded in 1890 by the British South Africa Company, which administered the country until a self-governing colony was established in 1923; joined with Northern Rhodesia (now Zambia) and Nyasaland (now Malawi) as the Federation of Rhodesia and Nyasaland from 1953 to 1963; made a unilateral declaration of independence under the leadership of Ian Smith in 1965 on the basis of White minority rule; proclaimed a republic in 1970; in 1976 the principle of Black majority rule was accepted and in 1978 a transitional government was set up; gained independence under Robert Mugabe in 1980; effectively a one-party state since 1987; a member of the Commonwealth. Official language: English. Religion: Christian majority. Currency: Zimbabwe dollar. Capital: Harare. Pop: 11 365 000 (2001 est). Area: 390 624 sq km (150 820 sq miles). Former names: **Southern Rhodesia** (until 1964), **Rhodesia** (1964–79) **2** a ruined fortified settlement in Zimbabwe, which at its height, in the 15th century, was probably the capital of an empire covering SE Africa > **Zimˈbabwean** *n, adj*
▷ www.zimbabwetourism.co.zw

Zimmer (ˈzɪmə) *n trademark* Also: **Zimmer frame** another name for **walker** (sense 3)

zinc (zɪŋk) *n* **1** a brittle bluish-white metallic element that is a constituent of several alloys, esp brass and nickel-silver, and is used in die-casting, galvanizing metals, and in battery electrodes. Symbol: Zn; atomic no.: 30; atomic wt.: 65.37 **2** *inf* corrugated galvanized iron [c17 from G *Zink*, ?from *Zinke* prong, from its jagged appearance in the furnace] > **ˈzincic, ˈzincous,** *or* **ˈzincoid** *adj* > **ˈzincky, ˈzincy,** *or* **ˈzinky** *adj*

zinc blende *n* another name for **sphalerite**

zinc chloride *n* a white soluble poisonous granular solid used in manufacturing parchment paper and vulcanized fibre and in preserving wood. It is also a soldering flux, embalming agent, and medical astringent and antiseptic

zincite (ˈzɪŋkaɪt) *n* a red or yellow mineral consisting of zinc oxide in hexagonal crystalline form. It occurs in metamorphosed limestone

zincography (zɪŋˈkɒɡrəfɪ) *n* the art or process of etching on zinc to form a printing plate > **zincograph** (ˈzɪŋkəˌɡrɑːf) *n* > **zinˈcographer** *n*

Zz

zinc ointment *n* a medicinal ointment consisting of zinc oxide, petrolatum, and paraffin, used to treat certain skin diseases

zinc oxide *n* a white insoluble powder used as a pigment in paints (**zinc white** or **Chinese white**), cosmetics, glass, and printing inks. It is an antiseptic and astringent and is used in making zinc ointment. Formula: ZnO. Also called: **flowers of zinc**

zinc sulphate *n* a colourless soluble crystalline substance used as a mordant, in preserving wood and skins, and in the electrodeposition of zinc. Also called: **zinc vitriol**

zine (ziːn) *n inf* a magazine or fanzine

zing (zɪŋ) *n inf* **1** a short high-pitched buzzing sound, as of a bullet or vibrating string **2** vitality; zest ▷ *vb* **3** (*intr*) to make or move with or as if with a high-pitched buzzing sound [c20 imit.] > **ˈzingy** *adj*

zinjanthropus (zɪnˈdʒænθrəpəs) *n* a type of australopithecine, remains of which were discovered in the Olduvai Gorge in Tanzania in 1959 [c20 NL, from Ar. *Zinj* East Africa + Gk *anthrōpos* man]

zinnia (ˈzɪnɪə) *n* any of a genus of annual or perennial plants of the composite family, of tropical and subtropical America, having solitary heads of brightly coloured flowers [c18 after J. G. *Zinn* (d. 1759), G botanist]

Zinoviev (zɪˈnəʊvɪəf; *Russian* ziˈnɔvjɪf) *n* **Grigori Yevseevich,** original name *Ovsel Gershon Aronov Radomyslsky*. 1883–1936, Soviet politician; chairman of the Comintern (1919–26) executed for supposed complicity in the murder of Kirov. He was the supposed author of the forged 'Zinoviev letter' urging British Communists to revolt, publication of which helped to defeat (1924) the first Labour Government

Zinovievsk (*Russian* ziˈnɔvjɪfsk) *n* a former name (1924–36) for **Kirovograd**

Zion ('zaɪən) *or* **Sion** *n* **1** the hill on which the city of Jerusalem stands **2** *Judaism* **2a** the ancient Israelites of the Bible **2b** the modern Jewish nation **2c** Israel as the national home of the Jewish people **3** *Christianity* heaven regarded as the city of God and the final abode of his elect

Zionism ('zaɪə,nɪzəm) *n* **1** a political movement for the establishment and support of a national homeland for Jews in Palestine, now concerned chiefly with the development of the modern state of Israel **2** a policy or movement for Jews to return to Palestine from the Diaspora > **'Zionist** *n, adj* > **,Zion'istic** *adj*

zip (zɪp) *n* **1a** Also called: **zip fastener** a fastening device operating by means of two parallel rows of metal or plastic teeth on either side of a closure that are interlocked by a sliding tab. US and Canad term: **zipper** **1b** (*modifier*) having such a device: *a zip bag* **2** a short sharp whizzing sound, as of a passing bullet **3** *inf* energy; vigour; vitality **4** *US sl* nothing **5** *sport, US & Canad sl* nil ▷ *vb* **zips, zipping, zipped** **6** (*tr;* often foll by *up*) to fasten (clothing, etc) with a zip **7** (*intr*) to move with a zip: *the bullet zipped past* **8** (*intr;* often foll by *along, through,* etc) to hurry; rush **9** (*tr*) *computing* to compress (a file) in order to reduce the amount of memory required to store it or to make sending it electronically quicker [c19 imit.]

zip code *n* the US equivalent of **postcode** [c20 from *z(one) i(mprovement) p(lan)*]

zip gun *n US & Canad sl* a crude home-made pistol, esp one powered by a spring or rubber band

zipper ('zɪpə) *n* the US & Canad word for **zip** (sense 1a)

zippy ('zɪpɪ) *adj* **zippier, zippiest** *inf* full of energy; lively

zircalloy (zɜːk'ælɔɪ) *n* an alloy of zirconium containing small amounts of tin, chromium, and nickel. It is used in pressurized-water reactors

zircon ('zɜːkɒn) *n* a reddish-brown, grey, green, blue, or colourless hard mineral consisting of zirconium silicate: it is used as a gemstone and a refractory [c18 from G *Zirkon*, from F *jargon*, via It. & Ar., from Persian *zargūn* golden]

zirconium (zɜː'kəʊnɪəm) *n* a greyish-white metallic element, occurring chiefly in zircon, that is exceptionally corrosion-resistant and has low neutron absorption. It is used as a coating in nuclear and chemical plants, as a deoxidizer in steel, and alloyed with niobium in superconductive magnets. Symbol: Zr; atomic no.: 40; atomic wt.: 91.22 [c19 from NL; see ZIRCON] > **zirconic** (zɜː'kɒnɪk) *adj*

zirconium oxide *n* a white amorphous powder that is insoluble in water and highly refractory, used as a pigment for paints, a catalyst, and an abrasive

Ziska ('zɪskə) *or* **Žižka** (*Czech* 'ʒiʃka) *n* **Jan** (jan) ?1370–1424, Bohemian soldier, who successfully led the Hussite rebellion (1420–24) against emperor Sigismund

zit (zɪt) *n sl* a pimple [from ?]

zither ('zɪðə) *n* a plucked musical instrument consisting of numerous strings stretched over a resonating box, a few of which may be stopped on a fretted fingerboard [c19 from G, from L *cithara*, from Gk *kithara*] > **'zitherist** *n*

Zlatoust (*Russian* zləta'ust) *n* a town in W Russia, on the Ay river: one of the chief metallurgical centres of the Urals since the 18th century. Pop: 198 400 (1995 est)

zloty ('zlɒtɪ) *n, pl* **zlotys** *or* **zloty** the standard monetary unit of Poland [from Polish: golden, from *zlyoto* gold]

Zn *the chemical symbol for* zinc

zo, zho, *or* **dzo** (zəʊ) *n, pl* **zos, zhos, dzos** *or* **zo, zho, dzo** a Tibetan breed of cattle, developed by crossing the yak with common cattle [c20 from Tibetan]

zo- *combining form* a variant of **zoo-** before a vowel

-zoa *suffix forming plural proper nouns* indicating groups of animal organisms: *Metazoa* [from NL, from Gk *zōia*, pl. of *zōion* animal]

Zoan ('zəʊæn) *n* the Biblical name for **Tanis**

zodiac ('zəʊdɪ,æk) *n* **1** an imaginary belt extending 8° either side of the ecliptic, which contains the 12 **zodiacal constellations** and within which the moon and planets appear to move. It is divided into 12 equal areas, called **signs of the zodiac,** each named after the constellation which once lay in it **2** *astrol* a diagram, usually circular, representing this belt and showing the symbols, illustrations, etc, associated with each of the 12 signs of the zodiac, used to predict the future [c14 from OF *zodiaque*, from L *zōdiacus*, from Gk *zōidiakos (kuklos)* (circle) of signs, from *zōidion* animal sign, from *zōion* animal] > **zodiacal** (zəʊ'daɪəkəl) *adj*

Signs of the Zodiac

Sign	Symbol		Dates
Aries	ram	♈	21 Mar–19 Apr
Taurus	bull	♉	20 Apr–20 May
Gemini	twins	♊	21 May–21 June
Cancer	crab	♋	22 June–22 July
Leo	lion	♌	23 July–22 Aug
Virgo	virgin	♍	23 Aug–22 Sept
Libra	scales	♎	23 Sept–23 Oct
Scorpio	scorpion	♏	24 Oct–21 Nov
Sagittarius	archer	♐	22 Nov–21 Dec
Capricorn	goat	♑	22 Dec–19 Jan
Aquarius	watercarrier	♒	20 Jan–18 Feb
Pisces	fish	♓	19 Feb–20 Mar

zodiacal constellation *n* any of the 12 constellations after which the signs of the zodiac are named: Aries, Taurus, Gemini, Cancer, Leo, Virgo, Libra, Scorpio, Sagittarius, Capricorn, Aquarius, or Pisces

zodiacal light *n* a very faint cone of light in the sky, visible in the east just before sunrise and in the west just after sunset

Zoffany ('zɒfənɪ) *n* **John** or **Johann** ?1733–1810, British painter, esp of portraits; born in Germany

Zog I (zɒg) *n* 1895–1961, king of Albania (1928–39), formerly prime minister (1922–24) and president (1925–28). He allowed Albania to become dominated by Fascist Italy and fled into exile when Mussolini invaded (1939)

zoic ('zəʊɪk) *adj* **1** relating to or having animal life **2** *geol* (of rocks, etc) containing fossilized animals [c19 from NL, from Gk *zōion* animal]

-zoic *adj and n combining form* indicating a geological era: *Palaeozoic* [from Gk *zōē* life + -IC]

Zola ('zəʊlə; *French* zɔla) *n* **Émile** (emil) 1840–1902, French novelist and critic; chief exponent of naturalism. In *Les Rougon-Macquart* (1871–93), a cycle of 20 novels, he explains the behaviour of his characters in terms of their heredity: it includes *L'Assommoir* (1877), *Nana* (1880), *Germinal* (1885), and *La Terre* (1887). He is also noted for his defence of Dreyfus in his pamphlet *J'accuse* (1898)

Zollverein *German* ('tsɔlfɛr,ain) *n* the customs union of German states organized in the early 1830s under Prussian auspices [c19 from *Zoll* tax + *Verein* union]

Zomba ('zɒmbə) *n* a city in S Malawi: the capital of Malawi until 1971. Pop: 62 700 (1994 est)

zombie *or* **zombi** ('zɒmbɪ) *n, pl* **zombies** *or* **zombis** **1** a person who is or appears to be lifeless, apathetic, or totally lacking in independent judgment; automaton **2** a supernatural spirit that reanimates a dead body **3** a corpse brought to life in this manner [from W African *zumbi* good-luck fetish]

zonation (zəʊ'neɪʃən) *n* arrangement in zones

zone (zəʊn) *n* **1** a region, area, or section characterized by some distinctive feature or quality **2** an area subject to a particular political, military, or government function, use, or jurisdiction: *a demilitarized zone* **3** (*often cap*) *geog* one of the divisions of the earth's surface, esp divided into latitudinal belts according to temperature. See **Torrid Zone, Frigid Zone, Temperate Zone** **4** *geol* a distinctive layer or region of rock, characterized by particular fossils (**zone fossils**), etc **5** *ecology* an area, esp a belt of land, having a particular flora and fauna determined by the prevailing environmental conditions **6** *maths* a portion of a sphere between two parallel planes intersecting the sphere **7** *sport* **7a** a state in which mind and body perform together at their optimum, as if effortlessly: *Hingis is in the zone at the moment* **7b** (*modifier*) of or relating to competitive performance that depends on the mood or state of mind of the participant: *a zone player* **8** *arch or literary* a girdle or belt **9** NZ a section on a transport route; fare stage **10** NZ a catchment area for a specific school ▷ *vb* **zones, zoning, zoned** (*tr*) **11** to divide into zones, as for different use, jurisdiction, activities, etc **12** to designate as a zone **13** to mark with or divide into zones [C15 from L *zōna* girdle, climatic zone, from Gk *zōnē*] > **'zonal** *adj* > **'zonated** *adj* > **'zoning** *n*

zone refining *n* a technique for producing solids of extreme purity, esp for use in semiconductors. The material, in the form of a bar, is melted in one small region that is passed along the solid. Impurities concentrate in the melt and are moved to the end of the bar

zonetime ('zəʊnˌtaɪm) *n* the standard time of the time zone in which a ship is located at sea, each zone extending 7½° to each side of a meridian

zonked (zɒŋkt) *adj sl* **1** incapacitated by drugs or alcohol **2** exhausted [C20 imit.]

zonk out (zɒŋk) *vb* (*intr, adv*) *sl* to fall asleep, esp from physical exhaustion or the effects of alcohol or drugs

zoo (zuː) *n, pl* **zoos** a place where live animals are kept, studied, bred, and exhibited to the public. Formal term: **zoological garden** [C19 shortened from *zoological gardens* (orig. those in London)]

zoo- *or before a vowel* **zo-** *combining form* indicating animals: *zooplankton* [from Gk *zōion* animal]

zoogeography (ˌzəʊədʒɪˈɒɡrəfɪ) *n* the branch of zoology concerned with the geographical distribution of animals > **ˌzoogeˈographer** *n* > **zoogeographic** (ˌzəʊəˌdʒɪəˈɡræfɪk) *or* **ˌzooˌgeoˈgraphical** *adj* > **ˌzooˌgeoˈgraphically** *adv*

zoography (zəʊˈɒɡrəfɪ) *n* the branch of zoology concerned with the description of animals > **zoˈographer** *n* > **zoographic** (ˌzəʊəˈɡræfɪk) *or* **ˌzooˈgraphical** *adj*

zooid ('zəʊɔɪd) *n* **1** any independent animal body, such as an individual of a coelenterate colony **2** a motile cell or body, such as a gamete, produced by an organism > **zoˈoidal** *adj*

zool. *abbrev for:* **1** zoological **2** zoology

zoolatry (zəʊˈɒlətrɪ) *n* **1** (esp in ancient or primitive religions) the worship of animals as the incarnations of certain deities, etc **2** extreme or excessive devotion to animals, particularly domestic pets > **zoˈolatrous** *adj*

zoological garden *n* the formal term for **zoo**

zoology (zəʊˈɒlədʒɪ, zuː-) *n, pl* **zoologies** **1** the study of animals, including their classification, structure, physiology, and history **2** the biological characteristics of a particular animal or animal group **3** the fauna characteristic of a particular region > **zoological** (ˌzəʊəˈlɒdʒɪkᵊl, ˌzuːə-) *adj* > **zoˈologist** *n*

▷ www.biosis.org.uk/zrdocs/zoolinfo/info_gen.htm
▷ www.academicinfo.net/zoo.html

zoom (zuːm) *vb* **1** to make or cause to make a continuous buzzing or humming sound **2** to move or cause to move with such a sound **3** (*intr*) to move very rapidly; rush: *we zoomed through town* **4** to cause (an aircraft) to climb briefly at an unusually steep angle, or (of an aircraft) to climb in this way **5** (*intr*) (of prices) to rise rapidly ▷ *n* **6** the sound or act of zooming **7** See **zoom lens** [C19 imit.]

zoom in *or* **out** *vb* (*intr, adv*) *photog, films, television* to increase or decrease rapidly the magnification of the image of a distant object by means of a zoom lens

zoom lens *n* a lens system that allows the focal length of a camera lens to be varied continuously without altering the sharpness of the image

zoomorphism (ˌzəʊəˈmɔːfɪzəm) *n* **1** the conception or representation of deities in the form of animals **2** the use of animal forms or symbols in art, etc > **ˌzooˈmorphic** *adj*

-zoon *n combining form* indicating an individual animal or an independently moving entity derived from an animal: *spermatozoon* [from Gk *zōion* animal]

zoophilism (zəʊˈɒfɪˌlɪzəm) *n* the tendency to be emotionally attached to animals > **zoophile** ('zəʊəˌfaɪl) *n*

zoophobia (ˌzəʊəˈfəʊbɪə) *n* an unusual or morbid dread of animals > **zoophobous** (zəʊˈɒfəbəs) *adj*

zoophyte ('zəʊəˌfaɪt) *n* any animal resembling a plant, such as a sea anemone > **zoophytic** (ˌzəʊəˈfɪtɪk) *or* **ˌzooˈphytical** *adj*

zooplankton (ˌzəʊəˈplæŋktən) *n* the animal constituent of plankton, which consists mainly of small crustaceans and fish larvae

zoospore ('zəʊəˌspɔː) *n* an asexual spore of some algae and fungi that moves by means of flagella > **ˌzooˈsporic** *or* **zoosporous** (zəʊˈɒspərəs, ˌzəʊəˈspɔːrəs) *adj*

zoosterol (zəʊˈɒstəˌrɒl) *n* any of a group of animal sterols, such as cholesterol

zootechnics (ˌzəʊəˈtɛknɪks) *n* (*functioning as sing*) the science concerned with the domestication and breeding of animals

zootomy (zəʊˈɒtəmɪ) *n* the branch of zoology concerned with the dissection and anatomy of animals > **zootomic** (ˌzəʊəˈtɒmɪk) *or* **ˌzooˈtomical** *adj* > **ˌzooˈtomically** *adv* > **zoˈotomist** *n*

zootoxin (ˌzəʊəˈtɒksɪn) *n* a toxin, such as snake venom, that is produced by an animal

zoot suit (zuːt) *n sl* a man's suit consisting of baggy tapered trousers and a long jacket with wide padded shoulders, popular esp in the 1940s [C20 from ?]

zorbing ('zɔːbɪŋ) ▷ *n inf* the activity of travelling downhill inside a large air-cushioned hollow ball [C20 z + ORB (sphere) + -ING[1]]

zorbonaut ('zɔːbəˌnɔːt) *n jocular* a person who engages in the activity of zorbing [C20 from ZORB(ING) + -NAUT]

zoril *or* **zorille** (zəˈrɪl) *n* a skunklike African mammal, having a long black-and-white coat [C18 from F, from Sp. *zorrillo* a little fox, from *zorro* fox]

Zoroaster (ˌzɒrəʊˈæstə) *n* Avestan name: **Zarathustra** ?628–?551 BC, Persian prophet; founder of Zoroastrianism

Zoroastrian (ˌzɒrəʊˈæstrɪən) *adj* **1** of or relating to Zoroastrianism ▷ *n* **2** an adherent of Zoroastrianism

Zoroastrianism (ˌzɒrəʊˈæstrɪənˌɪzəm) *or* **Zoroastrism** *n* the dualistic religion founded by the Persian prophet Zoroaster in the late 7th or early 6th century BC and set forth in the sacred writings of the Zend-Avesta. It is based on the concept of a continuous struggle between Ormazd (or Ahura Mazda), the god of creation, light, and goodness, and his archenemy, Ahriman, the spirit of evil and darkness

▷ http://www.avesta.org/avesta.html

Zorrilla y Moral (*Spanish* θɔˈrriʎa i moˈral) *n* **José** (xoˈse) 1817–93, Spanish poet and dramatist, noted for his romantic plays based on national legends, esp *Don Juan Tenorio* (1844)

zoster ('zɒstə) *n pathol* short for **herpes zoster** [C18 from

L: shingles, from Gk *zōster* girdle]

Zouave (zuː'ɑːv, zwɑːv) *n* **1** (formerly) a member of a body of French infantry composed of Algerian recruits noted for their dash, hardiness, and colourful uniforms **2** a member of any body of soldiers wearing a similar uniform, esp a volunteer in such a unit of the Union Army in the American Civil War [C19 from F, from *Zwāwa*, tribal name in Algeria]

Zoug *or* **zug** *n* the French name for **Zug**

zouk (zuːk) *n* a style of dance music that combines African and Latin American rhythms and uses electronic instruments and modern studio technology [C20 from West Indian Creole *zouk* to have a good time]

zounds (zaʊndz) *or* **swounds** (zwaʊndz, zaʊndz) *interj arch* a mild oath indicating surprise, indignation, etc [C16 euphemistic shortening of *God's wounds*]

Zr *the chemical symbol for* zirconium

Zsigmondy (*German* 'ʃɪgmɔndi) *n* **Richard Adolf** ('rɪçart 'aːdɔlf) 1865–1929, German chemist, born in Austria, noted for his work on colloidal particles and, with H. Siedentopf, his introduction (1903) of the ultramicroscope: Nobel prize for chemistry 1925

zucchetto (tsuː'kɛtəʊ, suː-, zuː-) *n, pl* **zucchettos** RC *Church* a small round skullcap worn by certain ecclesiastics and varying in colour according to the rank of the wearer, the Pope wearing white, cardinals red, bishops violet, and others black [C19 from It., from *zucca* a gourd, from LL *cucutia*, prob. from L *cucurbita*]

zucchini (tsuː'kiːnɪ, zuː-) *n, pl* **zucchini** *or* **zucchinis** *chiefly US, Canad, & Austral* another name for **courgette** [It., pl of *zucchino* a little gourd, from *zucca* gourd; see ZUCCHETTO]

Zug (*German* tsuːk) *n* **1** a canton of N central Switzerland: the smallest Swiss canton; mainly German-speaking and Roman Catholic; joined the Swiss Confederation in 1352. Capital: Zug. Pop: 97 800 (2000 est). Area: 239 sq km (92 sq miles) **2** a town in N central Switzerland, the capital of Zug canton, on Lake Zug. Pop: 21 467 (1990) **3 Lake** a lake in N central Switzerland, in Zug and Schwyz cantons. Area: 39 sq km (15 sq miles). French name: **Zoug**

Zugspitze ('tsʊgˌʃpɪtsə) *n* a mountain peak in S Germany in the Bavarian Alps, on the Austrian border: the highest peak in Germany. Height: 2963 m (9721 ft)

zugzwang (*German* 'tsuːktsvaŋ) *Chess* ▷ *n* **1** a position in which one player can move only with loss or severe disadvantage ▷ *vb* **2** (*tr*) to manoeuvre (one's opponent) into a zugzwang [from G, from *Zug* a pull + *Zwang* force]

Zuider Zee *or* **Zuyder Zee** ('zaɪdə 'ziː; *Dutch* 'zœidər 'zeː) *n* a former inlet of the North Sea in the N coast of the Netherlands sealed off from the sea by a dam in 1932, dividing it into the Waddenzee and the freshwater IJsselmeer, with several large areas under reclamation

Zuidholland (zœit'hɔlɑnt) *n* the Dutch name for **South Holland**

Zukerman ('zʊkəmən) *n* **Pinchas** born 1948, Israeli violinist

Zulu ('zuːlʊ, -luː) *n* **1** (*pl* **Zulus** *or* **Zulu**) a member of a tall Negroid people of SE Africa, who became dominant during the 19th century due to a warrior-clan system organized by the powerful leader, Shaka **2** the language of this people [from Zulu *amaZulu* people of the sky]

Zululand ('zuːlʊˌlænd, 'zuːluː-) *n* a region of E South Africa, on the Indian Ocean; partly corresponds to KwaZulu/Natal. Chief town: Eshowe

Zungaria (zʊŋ'gɛərɪə) *n* a variant transliteration of **Junggar Pendi**

Zuñi ('zuːnjiː, 'suː-) *n* **1** (*pl* **Zuñis** *or* **Zuñi**) a member of a North American Indian people of W New Mexico **2** the language of this people > **'Zuñian** *adj, n*

Zurbarán (*Spanish* θurβa'ran) *n* **Francisco de** (fran'θisko de) 1598–1664, Spanish Baroque painter, esp of religious subjects

Zürich ('zjʊərɪk; *German* 'tsyːrɪç) *n* **1** a canton of NE Switzerland: mainly Protestant and German-speaking. Capital: Zürich. Pop: 1 198 600 (2000 est). Area: 1729 sq km (668 sq miles) **2** a city in NE Switzerland, the capital of Zürich canton, on Lake Zürich, the largest city and industrial centre in Switzerland; centre of the Swiss Reformation; financial centre. Pop: 336 821 (1999 est) **3 Lake** a lake in N Switzerland, mostly in Zürich canton. Area: 89 sq km (34 sq miles)

Zuyder Zee ('zaɪdə 'ziː; *Dutch* 'zœidər 'zeː) *n* a variant spelling of **Zuider Zee**

Zweig (*German* tsvaik) *n* **1 Arnold** ('arnɔlt) 1887–1968, German novelist, famous for his realistic war novel *The Case of Sergeant Grischa* (1927) **2 Stefan** ('ʃtɛfan) 1881–1942, Austrian novelist, dramatist, essayist, and poet

Zwickau (*German* 'tsvɪkau) *n* a city in E Germany, in Saxony: Anabaptist movement founded here (1521); coal-mining and industrial centre. Pop: 104 900 (1999 est)

zwieback ('zwiːˌbæk; *German* 'tsviːbak) *n* a small type of rusk, which has been baked first as a loaf, then sliced and toasted [G: twice-baked]

Zwingli (*German* 'tsvɪŋli) *n* **Ulrich** ('ʊlrɪç) or **Huldreich** ('hʊltraiç) 1484–1531, Swiss leader of the Reformation, based in Zurich. He denied the Eucharistic presence, holding that the Communion was merely a commemoration of Christ's death

Zwinglian ('zwɪŋglɪən, 'tsvɪŋ-) *n* **1** an upholder of the religious doctrines or movement of Zwingli ▷ *adj* **2** of or relating to Zwingli, his religious movement, or his doctrines

zwitterion ('tsvɪtərˌaɪən) *n chem* an ion that carries both a positive and a negative charge [C20 from G *Zwitter* bisexual + ION]

Zwolle (*Dutch* 'zwɔlə) *n* a town in the central Netherlands, capital of Overijssel province. Pop: 104 431 (1999 est)

Zworykin ('zwɔːrɪkɪn) *n* **Vladimir Kosma** ('vlædɪmɪə 'kɒsmə) 1889–1982, US physicist and television pioneer, born in Russia. He developed the first practical television camera

Zyban ('zaɪˌbæn) *n trademark* a drug that acts on the brain: used to help people give up smoking

zygapophysis (ˌzɪgə'pɒfɪsɪs, ˌzaɪgə-) *n, pl* **zygapophyses** (-ˌsiːz) *anat, zool* one of several processes on a vertebra that articulates with the corresponding process on an adjacent vertebra [from Gk ZYG- + *apophusis* a sideshoot]

zygo- *or before a vowel* **zyg-** *combining form* indicating a pair or a union: *zygodactyl; zygospore* [from Gk *zugon* yoke]

zygodactyl (ˌzaɪgəʊ'dæktɪl, ˌzɪgə-) *adj also* **zygodactylous** **1** (of the feet of certain birds) having the first and fourth toes directed backwards and the second and third forwards ▷ *n* **2** a zygodactyl bird

zygoma (zaɪ'gəʊmə, zɪ-) *n, pl* **zygomata** (-mətə) another name for **zygomatic arch** [C17 via NL from Gk, from *zugon* yoke]

zygomatic (ˌzaɪgəʊ'mætɪk, ˌzɪg-) *adj* of or relating to the zygoma

zygomatic arch *n* the slender arch of bone that forms a bridge between the cheekbone and the temporal bone on each side of the skull of mammals. Also called: **zygoma**

zygomatic bone *n* either of two bones, one on each side of the skull, that form part of the side wall of the eye socket and part of the zygomatic arch; cheekbone

zygomorphic (ˌzaɪgəʊ'mɔːfɪk, ˌzɪg-) *or* **zygomorphous** *adj* (of a flower) capable of being cut in only one plane so that the two halves are mirror images

zygomycete (ˌzaɪgəʊ'maɪsiːt) *n* any of a phylum of fungi that reproduce sexually by means of zygospores. The group includes various moulds > ˌ**zygomy'cetous** *adj*

zygophyte ('zaɪgəʊˌfaɪt, 'zɪg-) *n* a plant, such as an alga, that reproduces by means of zygospores

zygospore (ˈzaɪɡəʊˌspɔː, ˈzɪɡ-) *n* a thick-walled sexual spore formed from the zygote of some fungi and algae > ˌ**zygoˈsporic** *adj*
zygote (ˈzaɪɡəʊt, ˈzɪɡ-) *n* **1** the cell resulting from the union of an ovum and a spermatozoon **2** the organism that develops from such a cell [C19 from Gk *zugōtos* yoked, from *zugoun* to yoke] > **zygotic** (zaɪˈɡɒtɪk, zɪ-) *adj* > **zyˈgotically** *adv*
zymase (ˈzaɪmeɪs) *n* a mixture of enzymes that is obtained as an extract from yeast and ferments sugars
zymo- *or before a vowel* **zym-** *combining form* indicating fermentation: *zymology* [from Gk *zumē* leaven]
zymogen (ˈzaɪməʊˌdʒɛn) *n biochem* any of a group of compounds that are inactive precursors of enzymes
zymology (zaɪˈmɒlədʒɪ) *n* the chemistry of fermentation > **zymologic** (ˌzaɪməʊˈlɒdʒɪk) *or* ˌ**zymoˈlogical** *adj* > **zyˈmologist** *n*
zymolysis (zaɪˈmɒlɪsɪs) *n* the process of fermentation. Also called: **zymosis**
zymosis (zaɪˈməʊsɪs) *n, pl* **zymoses** (-siːz) **1** *med* **1a** any infectious disease **1b** the developmental process or spread of such a disease **2** another name for **zymolysis**
zymotic (zaɪˈmɒtɪk) *adj* **1** of, relating to, or causing fermentation **2** relating to or caused by infection; denoting or relating to an infectious disease > **zyˈmotically** *adv*
zymurgy (ˈzaɪmɜːdʒɪ) *n* the branch of chemistry concerned with fermentation processes in brewing, etc

Supplement

Write on Target

Contents

Writing Essays and Dissertations

What is an essay? What is an essay for?

One of the core activities for any student, whether at school or at university, is the writing of essays. However, students often do not know either what an essay *is*, or what an essay is *for*; and if you do not know what an activity is, or what it is for, you are unlikely to do well in it. It is therefore important to begin a chapter on essay writing with some definitions of the functions and forms of essays.

Essay is defined by the *Collins Desktop Dictionary* as 'a short literary composition'. An essay is traditionally anything between 1000 and 4000 words long.

The primary function of an essay is to improve skills in argumentation, the process of reasoning methodically.

Through the writing of essays, students develop the ability to produce well-formed and persuasive arguments backed up by appropriate examples. Further, by developing these skills, they are able to appreciate whether (or not) the arguments of others are similarly well formed and persuasive. This ability is obviously a highly desirable skill: few if any organizations, and no effective participatory democracies, can function without people skilled in producing well-formed arguments and detecting ill-formed ones.

This primary function of essays determines their form.

Good essays are always focused on their readers, not their authors.

Essays are not supposed to be opportunities for showing off or expressing feelings; there are other ways of doing these things. Their organization and language must be directed to persuading readers of the case being made, through clarity of argument supported by careful choice of appropriate examples.

We are not born with the ability to write an essay; it is something we learn to do, and anyone who has to write for a living will tell you that you never stop developing your writing skills. The word *essay*, after all, is related to the French word *essayer* (to try), and this indicates that you will always need to exert effort to produce a good piece of writing.

But be encouraged: the simple ideas offered here will stand you in good stead throughout your writing career and, with practice, will soon become something you do almost (though never entirely) naturally. And, if you are ever stuck in what students all over the world call an 'essay crisis', these ideas will be something for you to fall back on.

These notes are designed to help anyone who has to produce an extended piece of writing of the kind traditionally known as an essay. Some additional notes are given at the end on two special kinds of essay: exam essays and dissertations.

SUMMARY

- **An essay is a short piece of writing which presents an argument**
- **The primary educational function of an essay is to develop skills in arguing**
- **Good essays should be so structured and expressed that they persuade their readers of the case they make**

The reader

A good essay should be seen not as an opportunity for self-expression, but as an attempt to persuade the reader of your point of view. It is therefore very important to have a clear idea of the person who is going to read your essay.

Very often you may think you know precisely who is going to read your essay – perhaps your teacher or lecturer – and you may think that this requires you to put into the essay things which will please only them. But bear in mind that your essay may not stop with your teacher or lecturer; once they have marked it, some other person may need to look at it (an external examiner, for instance, if you are a university student). You therefore need to have a rather more general idea of who your reader might be.

It is worth recalling that there is at least one other reader of your essay: you. So it makes sense to think of the reader as someone rather like you, but who happens not to know about or have thought about the topic that you are discussing. This imaginary someone very like you will, however, have the same skills as you have in determining good arguments from bad. These skills, like your own, will have been developed through hearing the arguments of others: at school or college, or at home, or through the media (TV, radio, newspapers).

The advantage of writing for an imaginary reader who is very like you is that this forces you to address issues from first principles. Just as in arithmetic, so in an essay you need to show the workings of your argument, not simply accept or assert a conclusion without arguing it out. In thinking of your imaginary reader as someone like you, it is therefore worth working out explicitly what criteria you use in distinguishing good from bad arguments.

There has been much research into what we look for in a good argument, and the following points are often identified:

Relevance A good argument is one that is relevant.

A relevant argument addresses the issue or question under discussion directly, without wandering from the point. A bad argument will introduce material irrelevant to the question, or perhaps evade the issue by attempting to distract the reader with fine-sounding language (waffle), or by discussing a question other than the one actually raised.

Coverage A good argument covers the main issues raised by the question, and offers appropriate examples.

The word *appropriate* is a very useful term, but is also rather vague; in this context, it means a well-chosen example which supports the argument being made. If there are other examples which might seem at first sight to undermine your argument, these should also be dealt with.

It is worth noting that *coverage* does not mean simply presenting all you know about a subject. The advice 'once you have dug your hole, stop digging' is relevant; simply adding examples once your point is made is not effective and may distract the reader from your argument.

Organization A good argument is an organized argument.

Each step in the argument should follow from the preceding one, and the argument should be clearly signposted, so that the reader can follow what is going on. The reader will appreciate clear, short formulations of your theme at the beginning and end of your essay.

Expression A good argument is a well-expressed argument.

The essay should be written in such a way that the reader is not distracted from your argument: to modify a well-known saying, the message is more important than the medium. Thus you should formulate your arguments using clear language. (See **Writing your essay** below.)

Critical judgment A good argument displays critical judgment.

Critical judgment is the ability to choose a plausible theme for an essay which comes as nearly as possible to the heart of the matter or to explaining the facts under consideration.

Critical judgment can only come about through developing a good knowledge of the issue being discussed, including the ability to distinguish the trivial from the important. A bad argument is one where no critical judgment is displayed, eg where the trivial outweighs the important.

It is worth using these five criteria in judging the arguments of others, in political speeches or interviews, for example. Such an exercise can be very illuminating. It is also worth seeing whether these criteria have been used by those who mark your work; although the terms are not always used explicitly, you will be surprised how often comments by markers pick up on these five categories.

SUMMARY

- ▷ **Your imaginary reader should be someone very like you**
- ▷ **Your imaginary reader is someone who is aware of the difference between good and bad arguments**
- ▷ **Your imaginary reader uses the following criteria to assess your argument: relevance, coverage, organization, expression and critical judgment**
- ▷ **Follow-up: try using these five criteria to assess the arguments of others**

Before you start

The act of writing an essay will help you formulate and sort out your ideas, but that does not mean that you should start writing your essay without considerable thought beforehand. There are a number of things you need to do before you can begin to create the work you are going to submit.

Read the question In most cases, your teacher or lecturer will ask you a specific question to focus your research. Such questions should be carefully designed to stimulate enquiry and to allow you to develop a clear argument.

Read through the question carefully, concentrating on the important little words such as *how...?* and *why...?*; these words mean different things and require different approaches.

- ▷ are you being asked to argue the case for and against something?
- ▷ is the question asking you to describe something?
- ▷ is it asking you to discuss something?

In particular, you should pay close attention to verbs used in the essay question. These give important clues to the type of answer that is required:

account for	give reasons for
analyse	break up into parts; investigate
compare	look for similarities and differences between
contrast	bring out the differences between
define	give the meaning of

describe	give a detailed account of
discuss	investigate, giving reasons for and against
distinguish	indicate the differences between
enumerate	list in order
evaluate	give a judgment based on evidence
examine	look closely into
explain	give reasons for
explore	consider from a variety of viewpoints
illustrate	make clear by using examples
interpret	show the meaning of
justify	respond to the most obvious objections concerning
outline	give only the main features of
relate	tell in order
relate to	show how one aspect is connected to another
state	present in a clear form
summarize	give a concise account of, omitting details
trace	show the development of a subject from a particular point

Remember that good questions will not expect answers which simply require you to state all you know about a subject. If you know something about the topic already – and you probably will – make a few notes on the question and formulate a rough working hypothesis. Your working hypothesis, which should be at most a couple of sentences, should ideally be very simply formulated (it could consist simply of 'yes and no'!). It will be tested at the next stage.

Research the question

Obviously the manner in which you carry out the research required for answering the question will vary from discipline to discipline, but a basic approach can be distinguished, in that you will need to study primary and secondary materials.

▷ *primary materials* include texts, data, etc

▷ *secondary materials* are studies of these texts or data by other scholars, including points made by your teachers and lecturers

You may well be able to derive some of this material from the Internet, but be aware that there is no quality guarantee; be guided by your teacher or lecturer about this material.

You may well have studied the materials before, and have notes on them, but it is worth looking through the primary materials and at least your notes on the secondary materials with the question and your working hypothesis in mind.

As you read, keep thinking about your working hypothesis. Does it still seem plausible to you in the light of your reading? Does it need modification?

Make further notes on your reading as you undertake this research, and be prepared to modify your working hypothesis. Identify a selection of examples which you may wish to use in your essay as supporting evidence for your argument, and mark them in your reading using bits of paper or stickers.

Please note: you do need to be careful about plagiarism, which is the unacknowledged use of other people's work. Plagiarism is a form of theft, and is punished very severely by examiners and teachers. It is all too easy to forget that something you have copied down is not your own work; if you are copying a quotation into your notes, put quotation marks round it to remind you that these words are not your own. It is a good idea to add a reference to these quotations; the Harvard System, which will be described further below, is useful for this purpose, and is convenient for making quick notes. Be particularly careful about plagiarism when downloading material from the Internet.

Reformulate hypothesis in the light of your research

Once you have completed your reading, it is worth spending a little time reformulating your working hypothesis in the light of your research. It is useful to keep the new working hypothesis beside you while you write, as a principal signpost. Geniuses can keep all their ideas in their heads as they write; lesser mortals find it easier to have reminders at hand.

Alongside the reformulation, you might find it useful to add a few further working notes, perhaps linked to the working hypothesis through a mental map of links and circles. These are just ways of mapping ideas before writing, and of keeping them in front of you. The notes may include some rough formulations which you could include later in the essay. If you are working on a personal computer, keep these ideas, along with your working hypothesis, in a separate file.

Plan your essay

You are now ready to move to the next stage, which is in some ways the most important part of the process of essay writing: the plan. The plan is distinct from the reformulation of the working hypothesis or the mental map discussed above. Your essay will eventually appear as a sequential argument, and your plan should as nearly as possible provide you with a linear structure for this argument.

All teachers and lecturers agree that planning is essential for a good essay, but it is a surprising fact that few teachers and lecturers agree on what a plan should look like. The following notes are based on a technique which has been fairly widely adopted. This approach seems quite mechanical at first, but it is best thought of as a kind of scaffolding; all buildings, however beautiful they may become, depend on a rather plain structure of poles and planks as an essential first stage.

We might call this method the Six-Point Plan, since it typically divides the essay into six sections, though the number of central sections (here Points 3–5) can be varied depending on the question set and how you want to develop your argument. Sometimes these sections correspond to single paragraphs, sometimes to groups of paragraphs (see **Starting to write** below).

The key is to remember that your essay should be easy for your reader to follow, and your plan should be devised with this in mind.

Here is a skeleton plan:

Point 1	**Opening section: statement of theme** This will consist of your reformulated working hypothesis
Point 2	**The roadmap: how the argument will be developed** This can appear simply as 'roadmap', but could be fleshed out a little more. See **Starting to write** below
Points 3–5	**Development of argument, with supporting examples** A single sentence should appear for each stage in the argument. Each sentence will summarize each step in the argument. Alongside each sentence should appear a note of the examples you are going to choose; you might refer to pages in your notes or in your reading
Point 6	**Conclusion: restatement of theme**

Once you have slotted your plan into this template, you are ready to write your essay.

SUMMARY

- **Read the question, and formulate a working hypothesis**
- **Research the question**
- **Reformulate your working hypothesis in the light of your research**
- **Plan your essay**

Writing your essay

Expression

As you turn your plan into the completed essay, remember the five things the reader will be looking for:

- relevance
- coverage
- organization
- critical judgment
- expression

The first four of these should have been addressed in the preliminary stages, but the last of these will not have received much attention until now.

However good your arguments are, poor expression will distract or confuse the reader (and sometimes you as well!). You may be impatient with present-day conventions of spelling and grammar and formality of expression – many creative people are – but an essay is not the place to transgress convention. There are other places where you can do this, eg in poetry, short stories etc.

An essay is a reader-centred activity, not an author-centred one, and out of courtesy to the reader you need to be as clear as possible.

Spelling punctuation, paragraphing, and grammar

In order to be as clear as possible, you should observe generally accepted conventions of spelling, punctuation, paragraphing and grammar. If you have problems with spelling, it makes sense to use resources which are available to help you:

- dictionaries and thesauruses
- books on spelling
- spellcheckers on computers, though do be careful with these; they can often confuse words or offer you wrong prompts. Remember that there are differences in spelling between (eg) American and British English, and that these differences may affect your spellchecker.

Most of us have blind spots with particular words or groups of words, so try to avoid these words if they regularly cause you problems, or write them on a note and attach them to your computer for easy reference.

Punctuation, paragraphing and grammar go together. Modern English punctuation is designed to help readers understand the structure of sentences.

Full stops mark sentences.

Semicolons link main clauses when a coordinating conjunction such as *and* or *but* is not appropriate.

Commas divide subordinate clauses from main clauses, and are used in lists. They are also used in parenthetical statements, eg *Her husband, Mr Oldwhistle, was an elderly gentleman ...*

Punctuation is a visual cue for the reader; if you use it in non-standard ways, the reader will be confused.

Like punctuation, paragraphing is designed to help the reader. Each paragraph is a step in your argument, and keeping each step distinct will help the reader follow your train of thought. Your paragraphs should be focused on a single main idea, consisting of a topic sentence (usually at the beginning) in which the main idea of the paragraph is clearly stated, followed by supporting information or evidence. If you try to cram lots of ideas into a single paragraph, the reader will find your argument hard to follow.

Similarly, if you use over-complex grammar you will confuse the reader. Vary the length of your sentences, but in general a shorter sentence is a clearer sentence.

Avoid non-standard grammar; if you use non-standard grammar you may distract the reader from what you are trying to argue. Of course, standard grammar changes over time, and in historical terms it is illogical to stigmatize forms such as *youse* (for the plural of *you*) or *ain't* (for *is not* or *are not*) while accepting forms such as *those* and *helped* (both of which are innovations in the history of English). And defining non-standard grammar in present-day English is a notorious minefield: is it right or wrong to end a sentence with a preposition? Is it right or wrong to write *I will* rather than *I shall?*

Such questions derive from prescriptive rules which have emerged in English since the Middle Ages as part of a strategy of correcting or dignifying the English language, and many of them can be safely ignored. But prescriptive rules do have a stylistic function, and you need to be aware of this.

Style

Style is a matter of choice, and style in language is a matter of choice of forms appropriate for particular situations. In some situations it is appropriate to use *Hi* or *Howdy,* or *isn't* and *won't;* in others it will be more appropriate to say *Good morning, is not* and *will not.*

In essays, you should take a generally formal approach; if you choose to use the informal style of text messaging or email rather than the more formal language appropriate for an essay – something else that could distract the reader from your argument.

Stylistic choice is particularly apparent in your choice of vocabulary. It is tempting to show off in essays, perhaps by using unusual or fine-sounding words. Avoid using such words for this purpose; far from being impressed, the reader is likely to be irritated by the use of unnecessarily complex or obscure vocabulary. On the other hand, you should avoid colloquialisms which are appropriate only for informal situations.

Referencing

In any extended piece of writing you should observe proper conventions of referencing. It is important to acknowledge the sources for your ideas, and mark quotations appropriately (eg by using inverted commas). If you fail to acknowledge particular formulations of ideas, then you are guilty of plagiarism, which is a serious academic offence. There are various conventions for referencing (eg Harvard, Modern Humanities Research Association, Modern Language Association), and there is even useful referencing software to help you. Make sure you are consistent in the pattern you decide to adopt. Most schools and universities issue standard templates for referencing in essays.

There are various ways of citing references. The Harvard System, which has been referred to already, uses the surname of the author accompanied by the date and pages referred to, thus: '(Bloggs 2002: 42-43)' or '(Doe 1999: 301-302)'. A full reference can then be given in a final bibliography at the end of your essay, eg.

Bloggs, J., 2002. *The Sky is Pink.* 2nd ed. Glasgow: Jovian Press.

Doe, J., 1999. The cerulean character of the upper atmosphere. *Journal of Odd Phenomena*, 30 (3), 299-310.

Referencing lists, etc

It can be appropriate in some essays to insert subheadings to help your reader follow your argument. Similarly, bullet points can be an effective way of presenting lists, although these can sometimes not be acceptable practice in essays unless otherwise stated. The key thing, as always, is to ask yourself: will this help my reader follow my argument? If not, do not do it.

Starting to write

As you turn your Six-Point Plan into connected prose, you need to be aware all the time of the function of the various sections you have distinguished.

Opening section

The first paragraph is in some ways the most important part of the essay, since it is designed to make the reader interested enough to want to read on. A short quotation can help, if carefully chosen, but the main point to put across in this paragraph is the theme of your essay: your working hypothesis, which you are going to develop in the rest of the essay. This paragraph is the main signpost of your essay:

- it indicates the overall direction of your argument
- it should be simply expressed
- it should not contain too much detail about your argument; detail will appear later

The roadmap

The second paragraph is the roadmap of the essay. Again brief, it should give an outline of the way in which you will proceed. Two possible approaches could be:

- presenting opposing arguments
- bringing together a number of different ideas or interpretations of facts which can be reconciled

Development of argument The third, fourth and fifth sections, in accordance with the roadmap, develop and illustrate the argument you have signposted at the beginning of the essay. Each section should treat a different stage in the argument, in a logical sequence. Typically, the third section will put one argument, the fourth another and the fifth offer some kind of resolving argument. Each argument will consist of a clear formulation of a particular position followed by one or two illustrative examples.

It may be useful to refer back to your working hypothesis from time to time; essays benefit from judicious repetition, which will remind your reader of the argument you are trying to develop.

Conclusion The sixth section consists of the concluding paragraph. Your essay should have an explicit conclusion, summing up your overall argument and restating the theme with which you began. Brevity is again a virtue; the concluding paragraph, like the opening paragraph, should be seen as a signpost pointing back to the argument that has been developed. It gathers together the argument to reassert the proposition being made.

SUMMARY

- ▷ **Remember that expression is important in essays; you must not allow your expression to distract the reader from your argument**
- ▷ **Use generally accepted conventions of punctuation, paragraphing, grammar and referencing**
- ▷ **Avoid unnecessarily complex vocabulary**
- ▷ **As you write, remember signposting. Refer regularly to your working hypothesis; this will help the reader follow your argument**

Special kinds of essays

Exam essays At some point in your career, you will probably be required to write an essay in an examination. Exams are designed to test your performance under pressure. It is worth recalling that the ability to write under pressure is a skill – journalists have to exercise such a skill all the time – and thus exams are one way of developing something which will be valuable to you in your future career.

The skills you have developed for writing an ordinary essay remain relevant when answering an exam question. Obviously, you will have carried out the research stage beforehand, and will have thought about issues which will probably come up in the exam. But many of the techniques described above can simply be transferred to the exam situation.

In particular, it is a good strategy to follow the main points outlined in **Before you start** above, and indeed the Six-Point Plan is not a bad template to adopt when writing under pressure.

You should certainly assign a fair portion of the time available in an exam for planning; for instance, in an exam where you are allowed an hour for answering each question, you should allow at least five minutes for planning. Planning is particularly important in exams, since you need to write in linear fashion; there is no cut-and-paste facility in a handwritten exam.

Dissertations

At the other end of the scale is the extended essay, or dissertation, which can be anything from 5000 to 15 000 words long. Most university courses, and some school curricula, require students to write dissertations as part of their assessed work.

Whereas exams test the ability to write under pressure, dissertations test the ability of students to research an issue and present a reasoned argument. Again, they demonstrate a particular skill, that of researching an issue in depth, which is very marketable with employers. Dissertations also offer students the chance to explore possibilities which can be developed in future study, perhaps at postgraduate level.

Dissertations frequently investigate in depth a research question which the student has identified. Thus, unlike with essays, students will frequently formulate their own questions for study, although this will usually be done in collaboration with an experienced supervisor.

It is important not to be frightened of dissertations. All the skills relevant for essays are also relevant for dissertations, and it is a good idea to split the dissertation up into a sequence of essays, each answering a particular aspect of the overall research question.
As with exam essays, the strategies outlined above for writing a standard essay are also relevant for dissertations. It can be helpful to think of the dissertation as a series of steps, each dealing with one aspect of the overall research question, and the Six-Point Plan can be adopted as a template for each step. This modular or building-block approach allows the student to develop confidence in handling a complex topic. A skilled supervisor will help students identify such stages in their research, and will help students develop realistic targets for completing each stage.

SUMMARY

- **Exam essays and dissertations help students develop valuable transferable skills**
- **The strategies described for normal essays are also relevant for exam essays and dissertations**
- **Allow an appropriate amount of time for planning when writing an exam essay (eg at least five minutes for every hour- long slot)**
- **Adopt a modular approach to dissertations**

Writing Reports

A report is a document that presents information about an investigation or a body of research. It should have a clear structure. This structure should enable specific pieces of information to be located easily by the reader. Reports are used in many areas of business, including accounting, finance, management, and marketing, as well as in scientific research work.

Initial planning

Before starting to write any report, there are a number of questions you need to be able to answer. The answers to these questions will largely define the approach you take when putting together the report.

▷ what is the purpose of the report?
Ideally, you should be able to summarize the purpose in one sentence

▷ is there an outline or remit for the report?
If there is, the purpose of the report should be clear

▷ who will read the report?
Reports can be written for internal and external office use, for professionals in a particular field, or for members of the public, for instance shareholders in a large corporation

▷ will the report be formal or informal? This largely depends on who the report is written for

▷ is there a timescale for completion of the report?

▷ is there a word limit for the report?

▷ are you the sole author of the report?

▷ how will you undertake research for the report?
Research can take a number of forms: consulting reference sources, previous reports on the subject, and the Internet; interviewing professionals in the area of research; asking colleagues for information; or undertaking new market research

▷ how will the report be presented?
The report could be for internal use only, or widely distributed inside and outside the work environment. The prospective readership will affect the design, approach, and style of the whole report

When you have answered these questions, you will be in a position to organize the subject matter for your report into sections.

Organizing the report into sections

The organization or layout of the report must make it as easy as possible for readers to get to the information they need.
By subdividing the report into sections, you should be able to accommodate all the information in a clear, straightforward fashion. The following list covers all the section headings for a major report, but smaller or less important reports may not require all of them.

Title page This page includes the report title, the author's name, and the date of completion or release. If the report has more than one author, consider putting the authors' names in alphabetical order. Alternatively, it may be more appropriate to place the main or most prestigious author first. Remember that, unless alphabetical, the order of names sends out messages about seniority or the level of contribution of each person.

Abstract A short summary of the report, including aims, methods, conclusions, and any recommendations. Scientific research abstracts generally appear in library files or journals of abstracts. As they don't appear with the main report in these instances, they need to be comprehensible in isolation.

Contents A list of the sections within the report, along with their corresponding page numbers.

Introduction or background This explains the purpose of the report and the methods used in its compilation. The introduction should be concise and explain:

- what the subject of the report is
- who commissioned the report
- what the background to the commissioning of the report is
- what the method of working in compiling the report was
- what the main sources are

Main body of the report This contains the information you have collected for the report in a number of clearly headed sections. Ensure that each section is treated in a similar way and that the most important information always comes first within a section. See **Presentation** below for more details.

Conclusions A brief, easy-to-understand section giving an overview of the results gained from the information given in the main body of the report.

Recommendations A section detailing possible action points and strategies for improvement in the light of the conclusions.

Appendices These contain additional information or samples omitted from the main body of the text but which are relevant to the report as a whole.

Notes These give details that would be too cumbersome to include in the main text. Clear cross-reference superscript numbers should appear within the text, immediately after the information to which the note refers. The notes should appear in numerical order in the Notes section.

Bibliography This is an alphabetical listing, normally by author, of all the sources used in the report. For example:

Stirling, E. Q., 2004. *Bovine Anatomy Revisited*. 2nd ed. Jersey: Hursto Press

Wilson, J., 2002. Better milking practices. *Farm and Field*, 24 (3), 36–38.

As you can see, each source should have the following information, though the order can be varied slightly but consistently, depending on the system used:

▷ the author's name
▷ the date of publication
▷ the title of the book, newspaper, or journal, or the website address
▷ the title of the newspaper or journal article, if appropriate
▷ any edition number, other than the first edition of a book
▷ the name of the publisher of the journal or magazine

Presentation All reports need to be as clear as possible. If they are not, readers will lose interest in their contents. Ways of making information easily accessible include:

▷ Organizing information into different sections (see **Organizing the report into sections**), giving each one a clear heading.
▷ Breaking up larger sections into manageable subsections, each with its own subheading. Bear in mind that the longer a section is, the less likely it is that it will be fully read. Sections and subsections should be numbered as follows:

1.	[section heading]
1.1	[subsection heading]
1.2	[subsection heading] etc
2.	[section heading]
2.1	[subsection heading] etc

▷ Maintaining consistency in the presentation of similar information.
▷ Paying attention to the numbering of sections and appendices.
▷ If appropriate, adding simple graphs, tables, and illustrations. These break up the text and often provide a quick, easy-to-understand overview of the information.
▷ Putting large and unwieldy amounts of data into appendices, so as not to interrupt the flow of the text.

▷ Using a clear typeface for all of the text in the report. The reader wants to take in the essential points of the report as quickly as possible.

SUMMARY

- ▷ **Know the subject and purpose of the report**
- ▷ **Know who is going to read the report**
- ▷ **Set out the report in clearly defined sections**
- ▷ **Make the essential points and conclusions as clear as possible**

Writing a summary

Summarizing stories, articles, and reports is a skill everyone employs from time to time, whether it is explaining to a friend what happened in the latest episode of a television serial, or condensing the findings of a long report for the benefit of others.

What are the features of a good summary?

▷ it is concise and to the point

▷ it provides an accurate overview of the information presented in the original

▷ it is objective, so does not reveal the views of the person writing the summary

▷ it is written in the summarizer's own words and does not plagiarize

▷ throughout, it contains phrases that clarify whose views are being presented, eg Murphy argues that ...; the writer claims that ...

Tips for summary writing

▷ read the text at least once, identifying the main points

▷ when you have read the whole text, note down these main points from memory

▷ go through the text again, underlining, circling, or otherwise highlighting any other key points you may have missed, and amend your notes as necessary. You may find it helpful to make notes down the side of the text

▷ unless you already have them in the correct order, number your points so that you can get the order right when writing your summary

▷ write the summary in your own words as concisely as possible, or matching any word count that has been provided

▷ reread the text, to check that you really have covered all the main points

▷ if you are writing to a prescribed number of words, make sure the summary is not too long. If it is, you will need to edit it

▷ once the summary is the right length and contains everything it should, read it again to make sure that it follows on logically and that you have not accidentally cut something vital for it to make sense

Presentation If you are working under exam conditions, you may need to leave enough time to write out a clean copy of your summary. If this is unrealistic as time is too short, be especially careful to make any alterations neatly and clearly.

Writing up experiments

The writing-up of an experiment can be divided into two parts:
▷ keeping a record of the experiment in a laboratory notebook (lab book)
▷ producing a write-up of the experiment
The most important point to remember in writing up an experiment is that your write-up should contain enough information to allow someone else to repeat the experiment in exactly the same way that you conducted it.
Experiments should be recorded in a durable lab book. It is good practice to make backup copies, either by using a duplicating book, by photocopying lab-book pages, or by scanning them into a computer. The format, layout, and information contained in both the lab book and write-up will vary considerably, depending on the scientific area in which you are working. Different institutions or companies may have different in-house rules for the format of both the lab book and the write-up. You should also note that different scientists within the same area may also use different formats.

Some general guidelines for the layout of the laboratory notebook
▷ start each experiment on a fresh, right-hand page. This will make it easier to locate experiments
▷ write the date and experiment number in the top, right-hand corner
▷ if appropriate, include literature references or references to previous experiments carried out. These can be included informally at the beginning of the experiment. For example, "Following the procedure of Smith *et al.*, [reference]...", or "This experiment follows on from experiment number 7 in this lab book"
▷ use the passive voice in the past tense, eg "the green solution was added to the red solution", not "I added the green solution ..."
▷ record enough detail to allow someone using the lab book to repeat the experiment successfully. Too much detail is better than too little
▷ a rough sketch of any non-standard apparatus may be useful
▷ pay particular attention to the accurate recording of quantities and units. If you write down 10 ml instead of 1 ml, or 1 l instead of 1 ml, it

will undoubtedly cause problems. At best, the erroneous recording of units and quantities will mean that no one will be able to repeat the experiment. At worst, it may cause an accident. Always double-check the details

As implied above, safety is of prime importance in carrying out a scientific experiment. Be sure to plan your experiment. Consider and record beforehand any safety issues that you think may arise. On completion of the experiment, make sure you record any safety issues that became apparent during the experiment.

Some general guidelines for the experimental write-up

Title This should be a concise statement, usually reflecting the aim of the experiment.

Abstract You may wish to include an abstract at the beginning of the write-up. This is a very short summary of the whole experiment, and enables the reader to decide whether the experiment is of interest. You should summarize the aim, method, results, and conclusions into one sentence each.

Introduction Set out any background to the work and what you want to learn from the experiment. State explicitly the aim of the experiment. For example, "The aim of this experiment is to investigate the relationship between the pressure and volume of a gas at a fixed temperature". You may also wish to include a justification for carrying out the experiment. Often this will include any hypothesis you wish to test. For example, "This experiment is being carried out because theory predicts that there should be a linear relationship between the pressure and volume of a gas".

Method This is perhaps the most important part of the write-up, and should contain enough detail to allow the experiment to be repeated successfully.

▷ record everything that is done in a clear and logical manner. Report any observations, expected or otherwise, eg the colour change of a solution

▷ add a list of apparatus, chemicals, solutions, etc

▷ add a diagram of any special apparatus or setup that is used. Make sure that the diagram is of an appropriate size and is labelled clearly. Any diagrams should follow the list of apparatus used

Results and discussion You should already know what sort of data you are looking for from the experiment, and have a suitable way to record it. Data may take the form of the physical properties of a new compound or material, a list of measurements taken over a time interval, etc. Presenting data

list of measurements taken over a time interval, etc. Presenting data in graph or table form may be useful when it comes to interpretation of the results.

Conclusion This is the interpretation of the data you have gathered from the experiment. Do the data help to answer the questions you posed in the experiment aim? Explain exactly how the results answer the questions posed by the experiment, and how they confirm or disprove the initial hypothesis. You should be rigorous and impartial in your interpretations and conclusions.

Even if the question has not been answered one way or the other, the knowledge gained from the experiment can be used to plan a second, more successful, experiment. This is why so-called "bad results" or "wrong answers" should always be recorded – they still provide information, help you to avoid repeating the same mistakes, and allow you to plan better experiments in the future.

To conclude, you may wish to make a general comment on the success of the experiment in achieving the stated goals and also make recommendations for future work.

References Throughout the formal experiment write-up, superscript numbers can be used to direct the reader to literature references, which themselves should be placed at the end of the write-up using standard bibliographical formats for books, journal articles, etc. References to previous experiments in your lab book could take the format:

J. Smith, unpublished results, Lab Book, ref. no. JS1/1.

Appendices Any data or methods that are not vital to the write-up, but are still of some relevance to the experiment, may be included in appendices. For example, methods used to calculate values, statistical methods used to interpret data, and graphs or tables of data, may all be included as appendices.

Putting together a Curriculum Vitae

Introduction

Curriculum vitae (CV), résumé, record of achievement, profile or biography are all terms used to describe the different ways you can market your skills and experience to a prospective employer in writing. They are all designed to summarize what you can do and persuade an employer to invite you for an interview.

Your CV is one piece of communication over which you have total control. In your CV you are free to say what you want how you want, and you have the chance to make yourself as attractive a proposition as possible.

Sadly, there is no one perfect way to write a CV nor one style that is guaranteed to be 100 per cent effective every time. What may appeal to one employer may not appeal to another and the facts that are relevant for one job may not be relevant for another. So the strategy widely adopted of producing a standard CV and then sending it speculatively to 100 different companies is actually one of the least effective methods of job hunting.

Even if your CV reaches the right person's desk in an organization, employers will typically spend no more than a minute, if you are lucky, on any one application.

So how do you market yourself on paper and improve your potential success?

How do you make sure that your presentation, whichever one you choose, will be pulled out from the 'to do' pile, elicit a 'Yes!' and get you that interview?

Imagine you are studying for a history exam. The topic is Napoleon. In preparation for the exam, you do your homework and revise all you can. You arrive at the exam hall, turn over the paper and the question asks: 'What in your view was Napoleon's greatest battle?' Now what's your strategy?

You could start immediately and write everything you know about Napoleon and hope that the examiner will sift through all the material and be impressed by the sheer volume of your knowledge.

Or:

You could think through all the information you have about Napoleon, plan out your answer so that you focus only on what the examiner is really looking for and start writing a concise, well-presented answer.

The answer is of course to opt for the second approach, and you should use a similar strategy when compiling your CV.

- ▷ do your homework, revise your topic and gather all the material about you together
- ▷ carefully think about and research what the employer is looking for
- ▷ plan your response. No employer needs or wants to know everything

about you; they want to know if you will be able to do the job

▷ think about presentation; put together a CV or résumé that is carefully tailored to show your suitability for the job in question and that looks good

This strategy is outlined in more detail below under the following headings:

Doing your homework
The writing stage
The presentation stage
Variations of the finished product

Doing your homework

Just as you might spend time revising for an exam, time spent on the preparation of your material is time well spent. Listed below are some practical things you can do to improve your chances of success.

Organize a career file Gather together all the information you might possibly need and place it in a career file. It saves time searching for that vital date or note and it has the added advantage of reminding you of all your successes. It will also be a useful confidence booster for any interviews.

Keep this career file up to date; add to it as you gain skills or experience. Think, for example, how any job you do evolves and develops and how many additional skills you have gained which perhaps were not in the original job description.

Your career file could include all or some of the following:

▷ awards and certificates
▷ past CVs or résumés
▷ job descriptions
▷ references from past employers
▷ recommendations from tutors or customers
▷ copies of thank-you letters
▷ copies of previous application forms
▷ press reports of activities

Identify your skills A period of self-assessment is a vital part of the process and not to be skipped over.

So whether you have had two or twenty jobs, have worked for twenty-five years or are searching for your first real job, this is an exercise that everyone should do first.

Skills are things that you can do. Skills come from a number of areas. These can be:

▷ paid employment

- ▷ activities
- ▷ hobbies
- ▷ education at school or college
- ▷ being a parent
- ▷ undertaking voluntary work

List all your skills and achievements up to now.

Starting with your last or current job, for example, imagine you are not allowed to use the title but have to explain as simply as you can what you did or do. To make what you write more powerful, write your achievements or skills using verbs or action words. For example, assembled an average of 70 components an hour.

The list below provides some possible prompts, but don't be restricted to those listed.

POWER LANGUAGE FOR EMPLOYMENT

▷ **administered, accelerated, advised, analysed, assembled, assessed, budgeted, built, communicated, compiled, composed, conceived, constructed, coordinated, demonstrated, decreased, designed, delivered, developed, directed, eliminated, established, evaluated, expanded, generated, implemented, increased, influenced, initiated, innovated, instructed, invented, launched, led, maintained, managed, maximized, monitored, motivated, negotiated, optimized, organized, originated, performed, persuaded, planned, proved, provided, recruited, reduced, researched, revised, saved, sold, solved, structured, supervised, taught, trained**

If you have achieved something significant, let it speak for itself. Read the following statements and see which one you remember.

▷ civil engineer. Main duties involve cost analysis, budgeting, architectural design and engineering

Or:

▷ designed the Glen Helen Dam

Use the headings below as an outline and follow a similar approach for each of your previous jobs:

- ▷ job title
- ▷ organization name, size and type
- ▷ main tasks or responsibilities

Instead of simply saying you were, for example, a bartender, itemize specific duties:

- ▷ serving customers
- ▷ keeping bar stocked

Now look again at what you have written and use numbers, time constraints, size or scope, eg the number of people reporting to you, the size of the budget you had to manage or the profit you made.

▷ led a team of four, making and serving over 70 different cocktails in a popular high street bar

Your achievements

This is the part where you need to think about what you contributed to the job. Don't be either too self-effacing or too boastful. If you were the manager and you succeeded in reducing absenteeism, say so.

Search your memory for:

▷ any changes you introduced that solved problems

▷ any events or situations that were considered successful

▷ examples of when you exceeded expectations, sales or quotas

Use a similar layout for each role in your personal life that might be relevant. For example, think about volunteer work, any hobbies or interests that have helped you develop skills or enabled you to achieve something that might be relevant for the type of job you want. Preparing budgets, public speaking or PR skills as a member of the local drama or choir group might be just as relevant as your paid skills.

Summarize your skills

When you read through everything that you have done or still do, you may have a long list. Summarize the list by looking for patterns or themes.

A fitness instructor might group together skills under the headings:

▷ sport

▷ coaching

▷ personal development

A reporter might choose the following:

▷ writing

▷ communication

▷ management

If you have not worked full time before, think about any holiday jobs, school or college activities that you could group under the main themes that employers often like to see. These are:

▷ communication

▷ problem solving

▷ IT skills

▷ personal development

Summarize your main skill areas under four or five headings.

This exercise is useful for three reasons:

▷ it will help you write a functional CV, which is a particular type of CV that will be covered later

▷ it can help prepare you for the interview question, 'Tell me about yourself'. Giving a summary of your skills is a much more effective response than relating everything you have ever done since you were twelve

▷ adding skills to your CV gives it personality. This is what can help get you an interview

Clarify your career goal

Knowing what type of employment you want is important for three reasons:

▷ you can target the right companies

▷ it can affect what you stress in your CV and letter

▷ it is an excellent preparation for the interview question, 'Why do you want this job?'

To help you start this process, try answering the following questions:

▷ what are the things I have done successfully that I have also enjoyed?

▷ which skills would I like to do use again in my next job?

▷ which skills would I like to be able to develop further?

▷ what kind of work would allow me to combine all of the above?

Writing down what you would like to do is a powerful exercise in clarifying your thoughts. It helps you take control of what you want and manage your career. This should give you the confidence you need to come across as positive and goal-orientated.

Rather than writing 'A management job in a large international company which will allow me to use my knowledge', try:

▷ to become a departmental manager responsible for leading cross-cultural teams in a multinational company with opportunities to project-manage assignments abroad

Or: Instead of 'To become a senior secretary' try:

▷ to build on my secretarial skills and become a personal assistant in

a challenging environment, preferably in a medium-sized company. I want to work exclusively for one boss, with responsibilities in all aspects of the company business

If you wish, you could start off your CV by outlining your goal, but only if it directly relates to the job for which you are applying.

You have now gathered your material, identified your important skills and clarified what you want. Next, you need to find out what your prospective employer wants.

Analyse the job advertisements

The clues about what to cover in your letter, the main thrust of your CV and the basic starting point to prepare for your interview can often be found in job advertisements. Read them carefully and you should find:

▷ the qualifications the company is looking for

▷ the personal qualities they value

▷ the general direction and tone of the company

Underline all the significant words from the advertisement and you will begin to build a picture of how to phrase your letter and what to stress in your CV:

As a family business with a 150-year reputation for reliability, we at M. Bloggs value

expertise, and offer our customers the security of knowing they are safe in our hands

This company is probably not looking for someone who has had 35 different jobs and has a reputation as a risk-taker. They want evidence of steady progression, reliable results from someone who has an expertise they need or can train, and who will value and be loyal to the company name.

We are a dynamic, young company pushing forward into new markets and seek goal-orientated team players to join our results-driven marketing department

This company wants people who can deal positively with change (*dynamic*), who work well with other people (*team players*), who are not bound by rules but can find new approaches and who will find it acceptable to be regularly assessed.

Stressing these qualities in your CV will significantly increase your chances of getting an interview.

But what should you do if you are not responding to an advertisement?

Read the employer literature or website

Most industries publish information about their activities. This could be obtainable in a variety of forms:

- ▷ annual report
- ▷ in-house journal
- ▷ newsletter
- ▷ company website

These are all accessible and should be read before you put pen to paper. If you can honestly answer 'Yes' to the following questions then you are ready to start writing your CV.

- ▷ have you read and understood the main trends and future outlook of the industry?
- ▷ can you identify which employers in this industry are likely to have the type of employment you wish to acquire?
- ▷ do you have a feel for the most appropriate way of approaching these employers?

Remember

Sending ten, well-targeted CVs to companies that you have carefully researched is much more likely to be successful than 150 speculative general applications. Save your stamps and go for quality, not quantity.

The writing stage

If possible, use a word processor, as this is one of the easiest ways to get the information in a format that you can alter. You can also play around with the presentation and typeface without significant rewrites. Expect to have at least five attempts at putting together your CV before you feel comfortable with it.

Your aim is to produce a CV that is:

- ▷ accurate. Never write anything that isn't true
- ▷ easy to read. Use bullet points and short phrases
- ▷ clear, with simple language, free of jargon
- ▷ free from typing and spelling errors
- ▷ tailored to emphasize the best in you
- ▷ relevant to the employer
- ▷ uniquely yours

Personal information

Except in Australia, you wouldn't normally write 'Curriculum Vitae' at the top of the page above your name, as this is assumed. You are the product that you are trying to market, so your name should appear first.

Add your address and contact details so that the employer can get in touch with you.

Background experience

Plan the design of your CV as a series of blocks of information divided by section headings. For most purposes you will need:

- ▷ an introduction to you
- ▷ background experience: employment and/or education
- ▷ additional information

Below are some suggestions for headings. Pick out those that appeal to you, and that which will prove most useful.

- ▷ career aim, career goal, short-term career goal, employment objective
- ▷ summary of skills and experience, summary of main areas of competency, key areas of competence, main capabilities, special areas of expertise
- ▷ employment record, career path, career summary, professional experience, work experience
- ▷ formal qualifications, educational achievements, relevant training and experience, self-development activities
- ▷ notable experience, special achievements, relevant projects
- ▷ special awards

These headings can be centred, blocked or printed in a different typeface. Add clear, simple bullet points under each heading.

Make sure you allow plenty of white space around the margins, and aim for maximum CV length of between one and two sides of A4 paper (or $8\frac{1}{2}$" x 11" paper in North America).

Previous employment

This section is important to show how closely your past experience matches the requirements of the current job. Giving clear, comprehensive information that someone reading this for the first time can understand is your goal.

- ▷ **job titles:** use job titles that are understood by most people
- ▷ **dates:** the start/finish years for each job are usually enough
- ▷ **company information:** state the name and, unless it is well known,

a short explanation of what the company does and how large it is (ie number of employees, local/national/multinational)

Don't mention your salary or reasons for leaving your previous jobs. Leave this information for the interview.

Write down your previous job titles, with your skills or achievements beneath.

A younger person on the whole needs to elaborate what they have done, whereas an older, more experienced person needs to condense their background.

Education The amount of information given here will depend on how long it is since you left school or university. As a recent graduate, for example, your education information may take up more room than that of someone who completed their studies 20 years ago.

▹ stress the most relevant qualifications first

▹ use abbreviations that are widely understood

▹ record qualifications, the institution where they were gained and then the graduating year

▹ unless recently graduated, you could leave out secondary schools

▹ if your course included a relevant research project or thesis, and it relates to your employment goal, include it

Languages It is helpful to include appropriate details if the post is with an international company or requires specific language skills, but be clear about your level of proficiency (eg beginner level, intermediate, fluent). Indicate if your skill is speaking and/or writing.

Interests This information is optional, unless you can relate the skills to the job requirements or it gives your work experience an extra dimension, for instance stressing team activities if you normally work alone.

Referees or references Except in Australia, you wouldn't normally include these on your CV or even say that they are available on request, as this is assumed. Provide them if you get to the interview.

Additional information Prospective employers do not need to know your weight, height, health, marital status, number of children, religion or if you have a clean driving licence unless this information will be directly relevant to your job.

Taking into account all the information above, now write your draft. Make sure your spelling and punctuation is correct and avoid jargon.

Once your first draft is complete, check your CV over, and over, and over again, amending it until it is perfect for you.

The presentation stage

Once you have the basic material, you can alter the emphasis depending on your situation and/or the particular job advertisement or employer requirements.

To list your name, contact details, past employers, achievements and education will satisfy most requirements. But the purpose of your CV must be to compete with other applicants and get you noticed, so the less work you make for the reader and the more you appear to fit the profile, the better your chances.

A key point to remember is that because a prospective employer will probably only spend a few moments reading your CV, you need to put the things that you want them to notice at the top.

Obvious mistakes when writing a CV include:

▷ making it either too long or too short
▷ making it hard to follow, with no clear order to the material
▷ giving a first page that consists entirely of qualifications
▷ writing long, unbroken paragraphs
▷ including too many abbreviations

You can significantly improve your chances with the design of your CV and what you choose to emphasize. But remember, whichever style you choose, you should print it on good-quality white paper.

Types of CV

The chronological CV

This is perhaps the most traditional model of presenting information. It provides the essential elements or bare bones of your work history and offers a backward look at you and your lifetime's achievements.

▷ it lists the experience (typically jobs) in reverse chronological order, starting with the most recent. If you have just left school or are a university or college graduate, you could place your educational experience first and list holiday jobs further down in reverse chronological order
▷ it should be easy to follow and show a clear pattern of development
▷ it suits those who have a solid background of work experience, with no inexplicable gaps
▷ it is understood by most recruiters, and is the safe option
▷ it is more straightforward to write but, in a competitive environment, you need to think how your CV will stand out
▷ most people writing this type of CV have to rely on stressing in their accompanying letter why their skills and experience closely match what is required. The letter becomes the narrative form of a functional CV

For examples of chronological CVs, see pages 33, 34 and 36

The functional CV

This type of CV groups the information about you around three, four or five key skills/areas of experience, and suggests or implies what you could do in the future. The themed headings come from the job identified by the jobseeker from an advertisement, a job description or from a summary of the jobseeker's main skills, for example, **communication** or **administrative skills.** The functional CV confines the listing of jobs or education to further down the page. It is designed to market you on the basis of what you can do and how closely you match the requirements rather than how many jobs you have had.

It suits those who:

▹ want to emphasize particular strengths in their career or job
▹ have a mixed employment history
▹ are trying to start or even change careers
▹ were previously self-employed
▹ have unexplained gaps in their work history

It may be more time-consuming to compile, but it is easier for the reader to see how the skills/experience can be directly related to the job. The letter accompanying this kind of CV serves to introduce the CV and your desire for an interview.

For an example of a functional CV, see page 38.

A combination CV

This approach combines elements of both the chronological and the functional CV.

▹ it could start with a brief themed approach to catch the reader's interest, followed by a reverse chronological listing of jobs/education
▹ it can give flexibility to the writer to stress certain skills, but also appeal to any employers uncomfortable with the functional approach

Care should be taken in keeping the information concise and within the limits of a maximum of two sides of A4 paper (or 81/2" x 11" paper in North America), without becoming too superficial.

For an example of a combination CV, see page 40.

In the end, the presentation is up to you and you must decide how best to market your particular skills. However, if you can access a computer, the following strategy might be worth considering:

▹ put all relevant material about you in one file
▹ write a chronological CV
▹ write a functional CV based on your key/main skills
▹ try to combine both
▹ give all three versions to several people who know you and ask which approach gives them the best and most helpful information about you
▹ having taken into account their views, you can ignore inappropriate CV approaches and amend information within specific versions

Variations of the finished product

Curriculum Vitae (CV)

This is a factual, crisp, objective presentation of working and/or education experience.

Résumé

A *résumé* is only subtly different from a CV, but can be a more variable account and sometimes includes the career or employment goal. Often the terms CV and *résumé* are used interchangeably, with the term *résumé* being preferred in the United States and Canada.

Profile/Record of Achievement

Usually a much more detailed breakdown of achievement that can be useful to remind the jobseeker of particular strengths but is perhaps too detailed to send unsolicited to an employer.

Biography

This is written in the third person and describes in a narrative form your major highlights/jobs. It can be used rather like a calling card or to avoid verbal introductions, for instance at conferences.

Variations in approach in different countries

Although it must be stressed that there is no one perfect CV or résumé, it is true that some countries tend to have slightly different preferences. If you are considering applying for jobs abroad, try to match the style. If you are unsure, then a chronological CV is probably safest, but you could add an additional skills section if you wished. Allowances are likely to be made for the fact that you are foreign but the same rule applies – as the jobseeker, you are the person who has to be flexible and able to compromise.

US Include a clear employment goal and use confident powerful language to emphasize your accomplishments.

▷ *Tip for North Americans in the UK market:* keep to objective-sounding points and a factual tone

Australia CVs often start with a summary which may include a career objective. At the very end come contact details for referees or the line 'References available on request'.

For the media or creative industries, alternatives that are acceptable include videos, audio cassettes of individuals at work, and slide narrative employment applications. This will be stipulated, not simply assumed.

▷ *Tip for Australians in the UK market*: generally, photographs are less acceptable in the UK

Mainland Europe Similar again, but, when applying in English, make sure the spelling is either all American English or all standard English. European employers are often more rigorous about documentation verifying qualifications, etc., so attach copies for additional information.
▷ *Tip for Europeans applying to the* UK: don't attach too much information with the CV

Countries other than your own ▷ *Tip for anyone applying for jobs in another country:* remember to specify a local equivalent for all your qualifications

Some final thoughts on CVs and interviews

As the sole method of job-hunting, sending out CVs speculatively has a fairly poor record of success. Even if you have produced what you consider to be the best written description of you, it may still not lead to an interview. In fact, you may have to send out many applications before you do get invited to an interview. So use carefully tailored CVs in a targeted campaign.

The great advantage of tailoring your CV to the job you want is that when you do get to the interview stage, you will already have done much of the preparation. Your CV should have given you:

▷ confidence in your experience and your ability to market yourself

▷ a clear career goal which can help you appear positive and enthusiastic, and help you answer the 'Why this job?' interview question

▷ a concise, clear answer to the interview question, 'Tell me about yourself'

▷ a thorough knowledge of the trends in the industry and the specific company goals

▷ an understanding of how well matched you are with what the job requires

▷ an appreciation of your potential training needs by clearly identifying any gaps

Example 1: Chronological CV

Recent graduate applying for trainee management position

JOHN ASHWORTH
10 Blueberry Road
Bath
BA2 6JL
Tel/Fax:01225 444444

Career goal

To work for a multinational company as a general management trainee.

Summary of key experience

Degree in Economics from Topton University, graduating summer 2003
I year full-time sandwich experience with the Personnel Department at Alfa Zip UK.
Factory Production Assistant with ABT in Germany in gap year.

Related training

▷ BA Hons in Economics from Topton University graduating in 2003
▷ Wrote thesis on 'Corporate Social Responsibility and Multinational Companies' as part of degree
▷ A levels in Maths, Further Maths and Economics from Monkton Combe Senior School, Bath (1998). All passed at Grade A

Relevant work experience

Sept 2001-2002

Project Assistant to Personnel Manager, Alfa Zip UK.
▷ Conducted a review of salary administration, produced recommendations
▷ Contributed to project team for implementation
▷ Presented case to senior management for approval
▷ This resulted in a new computerized payment system for 350 employees across four sites
▷ Assisted with the organization of the annual conference for 12 managing directors in Europe

1998-1999

Production Assistant with ABT Germany
▷ Assembled parts for use in ABT 6 series production line
▷ Awarded Employee of the Month for Speed and Accuracy, Dec 1998
▷ Improved spoken German to bilingual/completely fluent level

Additional Information

Captain of the university rugby team 2000
Keen interest in travel and meeting people from all cultural backgrounds

Example 2: Chronological CV

Showing a range of work experience, applying for a position as a career coach/trainer with a large training organization servicing multinational companies

Anita Gillespie
32, Grove Street
Wargrave
Berks BA2 7JL
01189 234 45

Professionally qualified as a Careers Adviser with 10 years' experience as a practitioner. Senior Manager of a 150-staff organization. University Lecturer and course director for a postgraduate training course. Self-employed consultant/trainer/coach for seven years.

Chronological Work Experience
1995 to date

Established Career Transitions Consultancy
▷ a consultancy training company working with multinational companies and a career coaching/training service for employees and their partners involving all aspects of change and making transitions. Clients include: Pitco (Netherlands, Oman); Ramsey University; Zeus Manufacturing (Sweden); Children's Needs; Human Relocation (Sweden).

Additional activities/interests include:
▷ speaker at international conferences on 'Managing Dual Careers'. Co-author of a publication, Together on Assignment, published in London by Career City.
▷ Initiated and obtained EU funding for a project designed to enable well-qualified foreigners to enter the Swedish labour market, 1998.
▷ Initiated funding for the EU-funded project 'The Network of Foreign Entrepreneurs', 2001.
▷ Member of international coaching and training networks, eg Global Development Network.

1990–1993

University Lecturer and Course Director at Lyme University
Main duties:
▷ the planning, organization and delivery of the one-year full-time professional training qualification for the Diploma in Careers Guidance

Additional activities initiated included:

▹ designing a distance-learning module for managers of the Careers Advisory Service to enable them to manage organizational change; initiating and developing the nationally accredited qualification for University Careers Advisers

1987–1990

Senior Assistant County Careers Adviser, Hambleshire

Main duties:

▹ responsibility for the overall management of guidance activities for a large county careers service north of London, including policy and professional development of 60 professional careers advisers and 80 employment staff via training and assessment

▹ provided in-service careers interviewing training for teachers and lecturers in education as well as coaching for professional staff working in multidisciplinary teams

1980–1987

Careers Adviser/Careers Service Manager, Dryford College

Main duties:

Guidance, information and placing of young adults into employment and training and education. Managing four specialist teams of careers advisers.

Summary of Education/Training

Postgraduate Diploma in Vocational Guidance, Distinction;
Lyme University, 1980
BA Honours in Industrial Psychology/Social Studies, First class; Mull University, 1979
Certified trainer for Jack Foot's 'Career Concepts' and 'Decision Styles'

Example 3: Chronological CV

For Australian seeking managerial work.

CURRICULUM VITAE

Sally Moran
27 Mowbray Rd
Chatswood NSW 2067
home: (02) 9410 0000
mobile: 041 489 0000
smoran@tpg.com.au

Education

1998 – 2000	Master of Business Administration (MBA) Macquarie Graduate School of Management, Sydney
1994 – 1997	Bachelor of Business Administration (B.BA) University of New South Wales, Sydney

Work experience

2003-Current.

Project Co-ordinator, Optus Communications Ltd

Organizational Profile: Optus is a leading telecommunications, billing and voice/data network solutions provider

Core accountabilities:

▹ Manage the engineering team in Sydney & Brisbane
▹ Set and calibrate shifting targets within fluid time frames
▹ Manage, coordinate and implement technical support and product training for a large client base (1000 clients)
▹ Problem-solve, crisis-manage and delegate project-related issues on a daily basis
▹ Act as Facilities Manager to premium clients

Achievements:

▹ Exceeded sales budget targets by 28.5 per cent
▹ Effectively managed a diverse portfolio of projects in the Asia Pacific Region
▹ Surpassed client satisfaction levels (based on Northern Region Management performance evaluation)
▹ Successfully coordinated all aspects of standard upgrades for client base

2001-2002

Business Consultant. Young Business Professionals of Australia (YBPA).

Organizational Profile: YBPA is a network of young business professionals that provides resources and training for recent graduates in business studies.

Core accountabilities:

▷ Advise on marketing strategies
▷ Nurture and advise young professionals in the organization
▷ Coordinate business-to-business communications
▷ Initiate, implement and oversee the organization's website

Achievements:

▷ Established a successful mentor program
▷ Secured financial support from local business to augment budget
▷ Commissioned an on-line 'Gold Pages' directory of local businesses affiliated to YBPA

Skills

▷ Computer literacy: sound knowledge of Microsoft Office, experienced in PC and Mac environments, Internet research skills.
▷ Well organised, good analysis and research skills, efficient record-keeping
▷ Excellent communication skills, spoken and written.
▷ Team player
▷ Competent managing budgets
▷ Languages: native speaker of English, fluent and literate in French and German, basic Japanese.
▷ Skilled in public speaking
▷ Sports coaching

Referees

Mr James McDonald
Managing Director
Optus Communications
278 Miller St, North Sydney.
work: 02 9657 3927
mobile: 0417 569 345

Ms Sophie Wellington
Senior Business Consultant
Young Business Professionals of Australia (YBPA)
136 Pacific Highway, Chatswood.
work: 02 9786 2560
mobile: 0415 759 324

Example 4: Functional CV

JO WALKER

Chilham Grove, West Fleet, Devon DE5 H7J

Tel: 01345 987654

Credentials for Managing a Public Relations Department in Progressive Publishing Ltd.

Management Experience

▷ Successfully managed the relocation of equipment and 90 staff to new premises

▷ Supervised all office procedures of five staff in a small publishing company

▷ Initiated and led project team of four to assess customer relations with clients

▷ Increased the sales of educational materials by 20 per cent

▷ Integrated the office systems of two departments into one

Professional Public Relations Experience

▷ Designed, edited and produced in-house magazine for five years for RWK Ltd

▷ Co-ordinated the production and sale of books and other educational materials

▷ Co-wrote customer-care manuals for 350 staff in public organization

▷ Co-ordinated sales and management seminars across the UK for over 100 staff in the organization

▷ Designed and delivered training on handling the public for a private hospital

▷ Organized fundraising activities for major charity, raising over £50,000

Personal Development

▷ Attended in-house management development seminars

▷ Enrolled on distance-learning MBA course

▷ Maintained professional development by attending courses, and gaining membership of professional association

▷ Negotiated successful office move with union representatives

▷ Created an enthusiastic, positive working environment for the team

Employment History

Current Position: Public Relations Officer

RWK Company Ltd, Exeter, Devon: 1995 to present.
RWK Company Ltd is a leading specialist in ready-to-wear safety products for the oil industry.

Main duties :
To communicate internally and externally with the public regarding RWK's products and supplies

Previous Position: Office Administrator

SPC Ltd, Taunton, Devon: 1992–95.
SPC is an educational publishing company with 15 staff providing mainly educational materials to community hospitals.

Main duties:
To manage a team of four administrators and be responsible for the smooth operation of office systems in the company.

Education/Training

- ▷ BA(Hons) 2.2 in English from Norchester University: graduated 1992
- ▷ Management courses attended include: Supervising Staff, Office Management

Additional Information

- ▷ Voluntary work at the local hospital, including Hospital Radio DJ every Thursday night and chair of the fundraising events committee
- ▷ Biggest achievements: raised funds to improve the library facilities for patients; organized the fun-run for staff

Example 5: Combination CV

Job Target: Senior Nursing Officer

Pamela D. Bart
48 Brownlow Crescent, Toronto, ON. M35 8KO
Telephone: 01443 678456416.111.2222
Cellphone: 416.111.3333
Email: pdbart@ wire.ca

Capabilities

Clinical Experience:

▷ Organizing and maintaining high standards for seven long-term patients on the ward

▷ Contributing to team meetings for the ongoing assessment of patients' home care

▷ Presenting patient procedures to other members of staff for smooth delivery of care

▷ Listening and responding effectively and appropriately to patients, doctors and relatives

Teaching

▷ Giving presentations to groups of students and junior nursing staff

▷ Writing clear plans for other staff outlining procedures for patients' needs

▷ Discussing and advising patients on the management of pain

Management

▷ Assisting in the general management of the ward and deputizing for the Senior Nursing Officer when required

▷ Maintaining a safe environment for patients, staff and visitors

▷ Responsible for the safe administration of drugs, in accordance with hospital policy

▷ Team Leader for ongoing professional development across the ten units of the hospital

Personal Development

Regularly attending courses for ongoing professional development in long-term patient care.

Training

RN, University of Toronto, B.Sc. Nursing (1992)
Graduated with Honours in Biology, Math, English Literature and French from St Michael's RC School, Toronto (1989)

Work History

Staff Nurse (Geriatrics)

St Anne's Community Hospital, Mississauga, ON. (1994– present).

St Anne's is the only community hospital in the Mississauga area and specializes in long-term care for patients.

Current responsibilities:

Admitting patients, evaluating care, prioritizing work, general assistance on seven-bed ward.

Special achievements:

▷ Received very good to excellent appraisals for management of tasks and prioritizing over the last two years

▷ Built good working relationships with colleagues, leading to appointment as Team Leader

Student Nurse

St Mark's General Hospital, Markham, ON. (1991–94)

Special achievements:

▷ Researched and produced a thesis on 'The effects of long-term care on young patients'. Awarded special merit

▷ Arranged a specialist placement in the USA to study comparative ward procedures

Giving a Presentation

As with writing, one of the keys to giving a good presentation is organizing your material. Your subject should be clearly stated, logically thought through, and explained interestingly enough to hold your audience's attention.

Notes

▷ don't learn your presentation by heart or write it down word for word. Such strategies usually result in boring delivery. Instead, make notes to refer to during the presentation so that you have something to prompt you

▷ Write the notes on numbered index cards. You can then move each card to the bottom of the pile when you have used it and will always keep your place

Content

▷ try to start with something exciting but relevant to make your audience sit up and take notice. A short, telling anecdote can be useful for this

▷ give an introductory outline of your presentation, and make sure you keep to this. Avoid introducing a completely new subject without warning halfway through, or changing the tone of your presentation

▷ use links to lead logically from one section to the next: while we're on the subject of; in view of; as for; before moving on to; in spite of

▷ provide specific examples. These give the audience something to think about, and can be a source for a later question-and-answer session

▷ if you are presenting an argument, build from the weakest point to the strongest

▷ include a few light jokes or puns, but always ensure that they are appropriate to the presentation subject and to the audience

▷ don't be afraid to express your opinions. When you are expressing opinion rather than stating facts, remember to make this clear by using expressions such as I believe that; in my opinion; to my mind. You can show how strong your beliefs are by slightly amending some of these expressions: I firmly believe that; I strongly believe that; we are absolutely certain that; we are pretty sure that

▷ consider including some aspect of audience participation. Some degree of interaction tends to make a presentation more interesting

▷ end the presentation with a brief recap of the main points and a strong, persuasive conclusion

Visual aids

▷ use visual aids to illustrate your presentation, but ensure that they are simple, useful and clearly visible from the back of the room. Well-explained, well-chosen and simple visual aids are more effective than under-explained, complicated visual aids. Avoid having too many visual aids since constant changes can be distracting. Be careful not to stand in front of any visuals

▷ if you have access to a computer, you might consider using a presentation program such as PowerPoint®. Keep the number of slides to a minimum, with no more than a few concise bullet points to each slide
▷ if you are providing handouts, ensure you have made enough copies for everyone beforehand. Remember too that you must allow some time for the handouts to be received and viewed before you continue your presentation

Practice and timing

▷ try practising your presentation on tape. This will help you get your timing and pacing right. It will also allow you to check that you sound clear and confident, that you are not mumbling or talking too fast
▷ if you can enlist the help of a supportive friend or family member, try out your presentation in front of them and ask for comments on any distracting habits you may have, such as fiddling with your hair or endlessly repeating a particular expression
▷ before the event, make sure you run through your presentation exactly as you intend to do it on the day, complete with any visuals and handouts. Time how long it takes and tailor it as necessary to fit the time allotted for it. It is very important to ensure that it does not overrun

Venue

▷ if you are using a computer or overhead projector for your presentation, ensure that you have time to find out how to work it before the presentation
▷ make sure that there are enough seats for your audience
▷ familiarize yourself with the venue and its acoustics, to ensure that you feel comfortable speaking in it and that you are able to project your voice across the whole room

You, your body and your voice

▷ if you feel nervous before giving your presentation, practise deep breathing and rehearse your opening sentences
▷ if you are very nervous, standing behind a lectern may help you feel less vulnerable, as well as giving you something to lean on and somewhere to place your notes
▷ as you give your presentation, stand straight and keep you chin up as you speak. A strong, positive posture will both improve your confidence and convince the audience that you have something interesting to say
▷ look round all the faces in the audience with sweeping glances. Look members of the audience very briefly in the eye when you can, avoiding looking at any one individual for too long
▷ speak sincerely and with warmth
▷ subtly vary your tone of voice to add interest, but make sure that you do not overdo this
▷ vary your pace, but never talk too quickly as you may well lose your audience if you do

▷ pause slightly between points to show the audience when you are about to move on to a different subject. Allow pauses for audience reaction

▷ smile from time to time where appropriate. It will make you more relaxed and it will encourage a bond with your audience

▷ do not be put off if you make a mistake during the presentation. Apologize quickly and move on

SUMMARY

- ▷ **Three helpful steps to remember when planning your presentation:**
- ▷ **Say what you are going to say.**
- ▷ **Say it.**
- ▷ **Say what you've said.**

The latest additions to the language

Defining the moment

Collins Dictionaries give you the clearest possible picture of English as it is used today. To achieve this we have had to position ourselves at the forefront of language monitoring. In addition to an extensive reading and viewing programme, our editors keep a constant watch on Collins Word Web, our unparalleled 2.5-billion-word "corpus" of lexical data. A constant flow of text is fed into it from sources around the globe – newspapers, books, websites, and even transcripts of radio and TV shows. Every month Collins Word Web grows by 35 million words, making it the biggest such resource in the world. And it's in the discovery of new words and phrases that Collins Word Web comes into its own – our "monitor corpus" automatically alerts us to new coinages at the moment of their acceptance, however fleetingly, into the language.

New words mirror their times. Even a quick look at the developments of the last decade bears this out. It's hard to imagine life without the terms Internet, home page, and text message, yet they have all achieved their prominence in the common vocabulary within the last 10 years. The following is a selection of the more interesting neologisms that our various programmes have unearthed recently. Many will undoubtedly sink back into obscurity, being bound up with today's ephemera, but others will take root and firmly establish themselves in the ever-evolving lexicon of English.

ABB syndrome *n* supposed voter antipathy towards George W Bush upon which his rivals hope to profit. ABB is short for "anybody but Bush"
Kerry supporters are hoping that ABB syndrome will get the big-money types behind him (NewYorkMetro.com)

appointocracy *n* rule by appointed, rather than elected, governors. Coined by journalist Naomi Klein to describe Iraq after the fall of Saddam Hussein

aquaceutical *n* water containing chemicals thought to promote health
The biggest buzzword in the water industry right now is "aquaceutical". This describes waters that go way beyond merely quenching thirst (The Times)

Arab street *n* Arab public opinion
Since the scandal over the American treatment of Iraqi prisoners erupted, the so-called Arab street has gone eerily quiet (The Economist)

bariatric *adj* relating to the branch of medicine concerned with obesity, eg *bariatric surgery*

bluesnarfing *n* the use of Bluetooth technology to steal personal information from other people's mobile phones

Born Free *n S African* a person born after the abolition of apartheid
It is a testament to the first decade of democracy that this era already seems like ancient history to the Born Frees (The Scotsman)

botox *vb* to inject someone with Botox™, a derivative of botulism used cosmetically. It causes short-term paralysis of the facial muscles into which it is injected, temporarily eliminating wrinkles
The fact that Sarah Ferguson hasn't been botoxed, lifted or collagen-injected should be admired, not ridiculed (The Sun)

BRICs *pl n* the economies of Brazil, Russia, India, and China viewed collectively as an area for investment

chav *n Brit inf* a lout, esp a youthful one, with a predilection for baseball caps and hooded sportswear
Football – the sport of chavs and a driver of chavery in society – has for some time been an addiction of the middle classes, but now fashion is beginning to take a distinctly chavian turn (The Times)

chugger *n* one of the legion of charity workers who stop people on the street and petition for direct debit subscriptions [a blend of "charity" and "mugger"]
The Home Office has been concerned about the "hassle factor" associated with chuggers, whose numbers have grown (The Guardian)

coasteering *n* an outdoor pursuit in which participants negotiate their way along coastlines by swimming, scrambling, rock climbing, and cliff jumping

colossal squid *n* a recently discovered species of squid, even bigger than the giant squid, with sharp hooks on its tentacles
A surface trawler caught the dead female colossal in the Antarctic Ross Sea, where it was feeding on 6ft toothfish (The Sun)

decapitation strike *n mil* an attempt to win a war quickly by killing the enemy leaders or cutting them off from communication with their troops

deep-linking *n* the practice of setting up an Internet link to another location deep within someone else's website, circumventing its home page
Legal experts say that deep-linking can violate US and European copyright and trademark laws (Wired)

desi *n* South Asian word for someone or something considered to be of genuinely South Asian origin

Dino *n* (in American politics) short for "Democrat in name only". See **Rino**

dogging *n* exhibitionist sex in parked cars, often with strangers [from the commonest excuse (walking the dog) given to police when participants or onlookers are asked to explain their presence]

downregulation *n* the body's desensitization to the effects of adrenaline, caused by over-reliance on stimulants

dysbindin *n* a protein found in the brain, linked to schizophrenia
A team from Oxford University and the University of Pennsylvania has found through post-mortem examinations that sufferers [of schizophrenia] have 40 per cent less dysbindin protein (The Times)

fat-finger *adj, n* (relating to) a keyboard error, especially in on-screen share trading
Once dealers realized that the sell-off was due to a "fat-finger" mistake – rather than breaking news of a terrorist incident – the arbitrage with the cash market was swiftly restored (The Times)

freegan *n* a person who tries to eat only food that has been, or is about to be, discarded

fundagelical *n* a fundamentalist Christian [a contraction of fundamentalist evangelical]

galactico *n* a member of a clique of supposed world-class footballers within the current Real Madrid team [from Spanish *galactico* galactic, reflecting their stellar status]
David Beckham has won his battle to be accepted by Real Madrid's galacticos. Real's superstar clique ... grumbled that

Becks was more a popstar and marketing tool than a footballer (News of The World)

generation XL *n* a collective term used to describe today's overweight youths

global dimming *n* the continuing decrease in the amount of sunlight reaching the surface of the Earth

But Farquhar had realised that the idea of global dimming could explain one of the most puzzling mysteries of climate science (The Guardian)

heartsink *n inf* a patient who makes the doctor's heart sink when he or she comes into the surgery

Heartsinks are frequent attenders who make GPs want to resign whenever we see their names on our appointment lists (The Times)

hikikomori *n* a social disorder peculiar to Japan where sufferers (typically young men) lock themselves away from society

Japan's leading hikikomori psychiatrist, Dr Tamaki Saito, believes the cause of the problem lies within Japanese history and society (BBC News)

Hinglish *n* a fusion of Hindi and English, increasingly used in Bollywood films and by Indian middle-class youth

homicide bomber *n* a new term for a suicide bomber, popularized by the Bush administration and designed to put the focus on the victim rather than the perpetrator

The homicide bomber who murdered 20 people and wounded 100 more in Jerusalem was not the usual brainwashed kid but a 29-year-old married father of two young children (The Sun)

irritable desk syndrome *n* a collection of ill effects caused at work by a combination of long hours, poor posture, and a cluttered desk

British office workers were said to be suffering from an epidemic of a new complaint called "irritable desk syndrome" resulting from longer hours spent at their desks (The Times)

kerb appeal *n* the attractiveness of a house as viewed from the road

This porch really does enhance the look of the property and adds to the "kerb appeal" immensely (Double-Glazing-Web.co.uk)

kippers *pl n* grown-up children still living with their parents, short for "kids in parents' pockets eroding retirement savings"

The kipper generation are most likely to be found slumped on their mum's sofa, flicking between MTV and the Hollyoaks omnibus (The Times)

laughter club *n* a gathering in which participants force themselves to laugh hysterically together. The practice is thought to relieve stress and is very popular in India

Members of a "laughter club" in Patna, India, described the decision to ban laughing at their local zoo as "autocratic" (The Guardian)

living bandage *n med* a plastic dressing containing a culture of the patient's own skin cells, applied to wounds or burns to facilitate speedier healing

lockstep *n* a points-based remuneration package with incremental rises every year, esp that of a partner in a law firm

... the firms are in the throes of agreeing a scheme that could see Ashurst give up its coveted pure lockstep system in favour of a merit-based scale (The Times)

marzipan layer *n inf* the stratum of managers just below board level

So we had talks about the talent available in the "marzipan layer" of management (The Sun)

mitumba *n* (in Kenya) the trade in second-hand goods (especially clothes donated to Western charity shops), a major part of the Kenyan economy

At Nairobi dinner parties, smartly dressed Kenyan women will discreetly compare their mitumba purchases in the same way that British women appraise buys from the January sales (The Guardian)

moblog *n* a weblog that can be updated via a mobile phone

And more recently, supporters of US Democratic presidential hopeful Howard Dean have started a moblog to follow their candidate (The Guardian)

NASCAR Dad *n* a stereotypical representation of a section of the American electorate: a white, male, patriotic, blue-collar worker with a family. The name comes from his supposed following of National Association Stock Car Auto Racing

Nascar Dad has inherited his mantle from the Soccer Moms whose suburban concerns scripted electoral strategy in the 1990s. He has appeared in previous incarnations as "Joe Sixpack" and the "Angry White Man" (The Times)

Ostalgie *n* nostalgia for communist East Germany, experienced by its former inhabitants

The GDR Show ... is the most high profile of a rash of Ostalgie shows; in another, Andrea Kiewel, a former East German celebrity, whips the audience into a frenzy with the old mantra: "Are you ready to fight for peace and socialism?" (The Times)

parabens *pl n* short for "para-hydroxybenzoic acids": preservatives used in some cosmetics and often found to be present in breast tumours

But this in no way proved that the preservatives ... actually caused the tumours, and most deodorants no longer contain any parabens (New Scientist)

pash rash *n Austral inf* inflammation of the skin, caused by kissing an unshaven man

Please, you may as well breeze into the office with a big love bite on your neck – or in the case of strolling in with both pash rash and a love bite, a big, flashing sign above your head that says "Hi everybody, I had Sex on the Weekend!" (The Courier-Mail)

permalancer *n* a freelancer who is virtually a permanent member of staff, but without the attendant rights and benefits

Making the "permalancer" permanent has implications for how the industry will operate (Folio)

perp walk *n inf* the parading of handcuffed suspects in front of the media. Also used of executives hauled before the courts to face charges for corporate misdeeds

Outside, the atmosphere was a cross between a perp walk and a B-movie premiere – with newsroom workers lined up and photographers jockeying for a shot of the bosses (New York Daily News)

phishing *n* an email scam in which fraudsters attempt to trick their victims into revealing credit card numbers or other banking details

Anti-spam company Brightmail, which processes about 80 billion emails a month, indicated ... phishing comprises between two and three percent of them (Computing)

Poddie *n* an iPod™ enthusiast

rainmaker *n* a proactive person with great success in winning new business

Launching property in London has been one of our key objectives. ... We needed a rainmaker to make it work ... (The Times)

R2I *n mil* a training programme undergone by soldiers to help them cope under interrogation. Short for "resistance to interrogation"

The British former officer said the dissemination of R2I techniques inside Iraq was all the more dangerous because of the general mood among American troops (The Guardian)

Rino *n* (in American politics) short for "Republican in name only". See **Dino**

spim *n* unwanted messages which attack computer IM (instant messaging) users, rather than their traditional email accounts [a blend of "spam" and "IM"]

Spim is more insidious than spam because messages pop up automatically when a user is logged in, making them harder to ignore (New Scientist)

unilateral *n* a non-embedded war correspondent, ie one not attached to a military unit

She and fellow embeds had not been happy when they discovered unilaterals broadcasting from a site from which they had been banned (News of The World)